99th ANNUAL E&P Newspaper DATABOOK

Published annually by Editor and Publisher Magazine. Since 1884,
THE authoritative voice of #NewsPublishing

EDITOR & PUBLISHER MAGAZINE
#322
23110 STATE ROAD 54
LUTZ, FL 33548

OFFICE@EDITORANDPUBLISHER.COM
EDITORANDPUBLISHER.COM

CORPORATE OFFICES	406-445-0000
PUBLISHER	*Mike Blinder* mike.blinder@editorandpublisher.com
EDITOR-IN-CHIEF	*Nu Yang* nu.yang@editorandpublisher.com
MANAGING EDITOR	*Evelyn Mateos* evelyn@editorandpublisher.com
GENERAL MANGER & ADVERTISING	*Peter Conti* peter.conti@editorandpublisher.com
BUSINESS MANAGER	*Robin Blinder* office@editorandpublisher.com
DIRECTOR OF VERTICALS	*George M. Dratelis* george@editorandpublishe.com
DESIGN AND PRODUCTION	DESIGN2PRO www.design2pro.com *Howard Barbanel* howard@design2pro.com 516-860-7440

Editor & Publisher's roots began in 1884 when The Journalist was first published to serve the U.S. newspaper industry. In 1907, a new publication Editor & Publisher was born and quickly merged with The Journalist. Editor & Publisher later acquired Newspaperdom, a trade journal for the newspaper industry that began publishing in 1892. In 1927, it merged with another trade paper, The Fourth Estate.

Editor & Publisher was purchased in 1999 by the Nielsen Company, owners of Billboard, Adweek, Mediaweek, and The Hollywood Reporter. In 2010, the Duncan McIntosh Company purchased the magazine from the Nielsen Company that was looking to cease its publication.

In September of 2019, Editor & Publisher was purchased by the Curated Experiences Group that appointed industry veteran Mike Blinder as its new publisher.

$404.75
ISBN 978-0-578-74834-4

DataBook is a registered trademark of Editor & Publisher Magazine.
Editor & Publisher is printed in the U.S.A.

Letter from the General Manager...

Welcome to *2020 Editor & Publisher Newspaper DataBook*. Inside, you will find a wealth of information concerning the daily, non-daily, community, niche, and alternative newspapers in the U.S. and Canada.

The listings in this directory are designed to give you all the important information about these newspapers.

This year, we have condensed the two books (Dailies and Weeklies) into one. One reason is that more and more users are utilizing our online DataBook. You can get all this information on our website at editorandpublisher.com. We are in the process of upgrading the online platform and you will then be able to purchase only the data that you need or purchase a one-year subscription. Plus, the data will be fresh and up to date. It also allows for any newspaper to update their information directly and securely online.

This directory is divided into three sections: section one for the dailies, section two for services and organizations, and section three for the non-daily, community, alternative, and niche publications. E&P considers a daily newspaper as one with a 90 percent paid circulation and that is published four to seven days a week. A non-daily is defined as a publication that prints one to three times a week. Community publications are defined as publications publishing once a week or less than once a week.

As always, we welcome feedback from our subscribers and listees as we continue our efforts to provide the most useful and reliable information possible. Please continue to direct your comments and suggestions to us at peter.conti@editorandpublisher.com.

Sincerely,

Peter Conti

Peter Conti
General Manager

University Libraries, University of Memphis

ONE POWERFUL BRAND, DOING ONE THING BETTER — REACHING NEWSPAPER DECISION MAKERS

Penetrating Editorial, Strategic Business Ideas and Practical Solutions

editorandpublisher.com

Section I

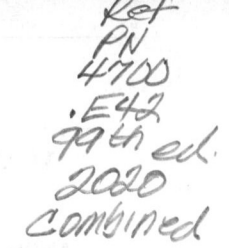

Daily Newspapers Published in the United States and Canada

United States

Alaska 2	Kentucky 47	Nevada 86
Alabama 3	Louisiana 49	Ohio 93
Arkansas 4	Massachusetts 51	Oklahoma 97
Arizona 5	Maryland 55	Oregon 99
California 6	Maine 56	Pennsylvania 100
Colorado 10	Michigan 56	Rhode Island 111
Connecticut 12	Minnesota 63	South Carolina 111
Delaware 14	Missouri 66	South Dakota 112
Florida 14	Mississippi 71	Tennessee 113
Georgia 19	Montana 73	Texas 114
Hawaii 23	North Carolina 75	Utah 123
Iowa 23	North Dakota 80	Virginia 124
Idaho 28	Nebraska 81	Vermont 126
Illinois 30	New Hampshire 83	Washington 128
Indiana 35	New Mexico 84	Wisconsin 129
Kansas 44	Nevada 85	West Virginia 134

Top 50 U.S. Newspaper Groups 138
Online Only Newspapers in the U.S. 140

Canada

Canadian Daily Newspapers 144
Canadian Newspaper Groups 147

U.S. DAILY NEWSPAPERS

ALASKA

ANCHORAGE

ALASKA DISPATCH NEWS

Corporate/Parent Company: Binkley Co.
Publication Street Address: 300 W 31st Ave
City: Anchorage
State: AK
Publication Website: www.adn.com
Postal Code: 99503-3878
Office phone: (907) 257-4200
General E-mail: website@adn.com
Publisher Name: Andy Pennington
Publisher Email: apennington@adn.com
Publisher Phone: 907-257-4210
Editor Name: David Hulen
Editor Email: dhulen@adn.com
Editor Phone: 907-257-4596
Year Established: 2014
Delivery Methods:
  Mail`Newsstand`Carrier`Racks
Own Printing Facility?: Y
Commercial printers?: Y
Mechanical specifications: Type page 11 5/8 x 20 7/8; E - 6 cols, 1 7/8, 3/16 between; A - 6 cols, 1 7/8, 3/16 between; C - 10 cols, 1 7/25, 1/8 between.
Published Days: Mon`Tues`Wed`Thur`Fri`Sat`Sun
Weekday Frequency: All day
Saturday Frequency: All day
Avg Paid Circ: 33301
Audit Company: AAM
Audit Date: 30 06 2016
Pressroom Equipment: Lines – 9-G/Headliner offset double width 1986; 4-HL/V-30 Heatset single width 1995; Press Drive – 9-GE/Motors, Fin/Controllers, 2-GE Motor/Fin/Control, 1-GE w/GE/Controllers; Folders – 2-G/3:2 (144 page);
Mailroom Equipment: Counter Stackers – 4-Hall/HT II, 3-QWI/401; Inserters & Stuffers – 1-HI/14-72, 1-GMA/S-1000, MM/227 5:1; Tying Machines – 1/Power Strap, 2-Signode/Spirit, 4-Dynamic/NP 1500, 2-Signode/LB2000, 2-QWI/Viper, PBS/Insert Management; Address Machine – Addressing machin;
Note: Semiannual Alaska job fairs (April, Sept); Best of Alaska Awards and Showcase (Jan)
Total Circulation: 33301

ANCHORAGE DAILY NEWS

Corporate/Parent Company: Anchorage Daily News LLC,
Publication Street Address: 300 W. 31st Ave.
City: Anchorage
State: AK
Publication Website: www.adn.com
Postal Code: 99503
Office phone: (907) 257-4200
General E-mail: website@adn.com
Publisher Name: Andy Pennington
Publisher Email: apennington@adn.com
Publisher Phone: 907-257-4210
Editor Name: David Hulen
Editor Email: dhulen@adn.com
Editor Phone: 907-257-4596
Year Established: 1946
Delivery Methods: Mail
Published Days: Mon`Tues`Wed`Thur`Fri`Sun
Weekday Frequency: m
Saturday Frequency: m
Avg Paid Circ: 31412
Audit Company: AAM
Audit Date: 2 09 2019
Total Circulation: 36099

FAIRBANKS

FAIRBANKS DAILY NEWS-MINER

Corporate/Parent Company: Helen E Snedded Foundation
Publication Street Address: 200 N Cushman St
City: Fairbanks
State: AK
Publication Website: www.newsminer.com
Postal Code: 99701-2832
Office phone: (907) 456-6661
General E-mail: digital@newsminer.com
Publisher Name: Richard Harris
Publisher Email: rharris@newsminer.com
Publisher Phone: (907) 459-7511
Editor Name: Rod Boyce
Editor Email: editor@newsminer.com
Editor Phone: (907) 459-7585
Advertising Executive Name: Holden Fleming
Advertising Executive Email: hfleming@newsminer.com
Advertising Executive Phone: (907) 459-7548
Year Established: 1903
Delivery Methods:
  Mail`Newsstand`Carrier`Racks
Own Printing Facility?: Y
Mechanical specifications: Type page 12 7/8 x 21; E - 6 cols, 2 1/16, 1/8 between; A - 6 cols, 2 1/16, 1/8 between; C - 10 cols, 1 1/4, 1/12 between.
Published Days: Mon`Tues`Wed`Thur`Fri`Sat`Sun
Weekday Frequency: m
Saturday Frequency: m
Avg Paid Circ: 13356
Audit Company: AAM
Audit Date: 30 09 2014
Pressroom Equipment: Lines – 11-G/Urbanite; 4-G 1965; 1-G/Urbanite 1996; 1-G/Urbanite 1997; 4-G/Urbanite 1998; Press Drive – 1-HP/75, 1-HP/100; Folders – 1-G/2:1; Reels & Stands – 6-G/Urbanite; Control System – 2;
Mailroom Equipment: Counter Stackers – QWI/108; Inserters & Stuffers – 1-MM/227, 1-MM/227; Tying Machines – 2-MLN/EE; Wrapping Singles – 1-PRM/720; Address Machine – 1-IBM/AS-400;
Buisness Equipment: 1-IBM/AS-400, 15-Gateway, Novell/LAN, Microsoft/Windows NT SQL
Buisness Software: Microsoft/Word, Microsoft/Excel, Libra, Abra Cadabra, Human Resources, Geac/Vision Shift
Classified Equipment: Hardware – 15-Pentium/PC; Printers – 3-Okidata;
Classified Software: HI/CASH, Microsoft/Windows 95.
Editorial Equipment: Hardware – 31-PC 486/1-Lf/AP Leaf Picture Desk, 1-APP/Power Mac G3; Printers – Panasonic, 1-APP/Mac LaserWriter II, Okidata
Editorial Software: HI/PEN System.
Production Equipment: Hardware – TextBridge/Pro 98, 2-Gluntz & Jensen; Cameras – 1-R/16 x 20, 1-W/20 x 24; Scanners – 1-ECR/Autokon 8400
Production Software: HI/XP-21 Images.
Total Circulation: 13356

JUNEAU

JUNEAU EMPIRE

Corporate/Parent Company: Black Press Media Ltd.
Publication Street Address: 3100 Channel Dr
City: Juneau
State: AK
Publication Website: www.juneauempire.com
Postal Code: 99801-7837
Office phone: (907) 586-3740
Publisher Name: Jeff Hayden
Editor Name: Emily Russo Miller
Editor Email: emiller@juneauempire.com
Editor Phone: (907) 523-2263
Year Established: 1980
Delivery Methods: Mail`Racks
Mechanical specifications: Tabloid size.
Published Days: Wed
Avg Free Circ: 30000
Audit Company: Sworn/Estimate/Non-Audited
Audit Date: 6 10 2019
Total Circulation: 30000

KENAI

PENINSULA CLARION

Corporate/Parent Company: Black Press Media Ltd.
Publication Street Address: 150 Trading Bay Rd
City: Kenai
State: AK
Publication Website: www.peninsulaclarion.com
Postal Code: 99611-7716
Office phone: (907) 283-7551
General E-mail: news@peninsulaclarion.com
Year Established: 1970
Delivery Methods: Mail`Newsstand`Carrier
Mechanical specifications: Type page 13 x 21 1/2; E - 6 cols, 2, 1/6 between; A - 6 cols, 2, 1/6 between; C - 8 cols, 1 1/2, 1/6 between.
Published Days: Mon`Tues`Wed`Thur`Fri`Sun
Weekday Frequency: m
Avg Paid Circ: 5710
Audit Company: Sworn/Estimate/Non-Audited
Audit Date: 7 12 2019
Pressroom Equipment: Lines – 8-G/Offset single width 1992; Press Drive – 2-Fin/60 h.p.; Reels & Stands – 3;
Mailroom Equipment: Counter Stackers – 1/BG; Inserters & Stuffers – 1-/St; Tying Machines – 3-/Bu; Wrapping Singles – 1-/St; Address Machine – 1-/St;
Buisness Equipment: Gateway/EV500
Classified Equipment: Hardware – APP/Mac.;
Editorial Equipment: Hardware – APP/Mac.
Production Equipment: Hardware – 2-Nu, XIT/Cadet, ECR/Imagesetter; Cameras – 1-R.
Total Circulation: 5710

KETCHIKAN

KETCHIKAN DAILY NEWS

Corporate/Parent Company: Pioneer Printing Co.
Publication Street Address: 501 Dock St
City: Ketchikan
State: AK
Publication Website: www.ketchikandailynews.com
Postal Code: 99901-6411
Office phone: (907) 225-3157
General E-mail: news@ketchikandailynews.com
Publisher Name: Lew Williams III
Year Established: 1934
Delivery Methods:
  Mail`Newsstand`Carrier`Racks
Mechanical specifications: Type page 13 1/2 x 21; E - 6 cols, 2 1/16, 1/8 between; A - 6 cols, 2 1/16, 1/8 between; C - 9 cols, 1 1/2, 1/16 between.
Published Days: Mon`Tues`Wed`Thur`Fri`Sat
Weekday Frequency: m
Saturday Frequency: m
Avg Paid Circ: 4117
Audit Company: Sworn/Estimate/Non-Audited
Audit Date: 7 12 2019
Pressroom Equipment: Lines – 3-G/Community; 1-G/Universal; Folders – 1-G/2:1.;
Mailroom Equipment: Address Machine – 3/Wm.;
Classified Equipment: Hardware – Point 4.;
Editorial Equipment: Hardware – APP/Mac.
Production Equipment: Hardware – 1-COM/8400, APP/Mac LaserWriter II, COM/3400 Laserprinter; Cameras – 1-R/Vertical.
Total Circulation: 4117

KODIAK

KODIAK DAILY MIRROR

Corporate/Parent Company: Helen E Snedded Foundation
Publication Street Address: 1419 Selig St
City: Kodiak
State: AK
Publication Website: www.kodiakdailymirror.com
Postal Code: 99615-6450
Office phone: (907) 486-3227
General E-mail: Info@KodiakDailyMirror.com
Publisher Name: Sara Schaefer
Publisher Email: sara@kodiakdailymirror.com
Publisher Phone: (907) 486-3227
Advertising Executive Name: Denise Davis
Advertising Executive Email: sales@kodiakdailymirror.com
Advertising Executive Phone: (907) 486-3227
Year Established: 1940
Delivery Methods: Mail`Carrier`Racks
Own Printing Facility?: Y
Commercial printers?: N
Mechanical specifications: Type page 11 1/2 x 21; E - 6 cols, 3 3/4, 3/16 between; A - 6 cols, 3 3/4, 3/16 between; C - 6 cols, 3 3/4, 3/16 between.
Published Days: Mon`Tues`Wed`Thur`Fri
Weekday Frequency: e
Avg Paid Circ: 2849
Audit Company: Sworn/Estimate/Non-Audited
Audit Date: 7 12 2019
Pressroom Equipment: Lines – 5-G/Community.;
Buisness Equipment: Compaq/586-166
Buisness Software: Synaptic
Classified Equipment: Hardware – 1-APP/Mac Mini;
Classified Software: AdManagerPro4
Editorial Equipment: Hardware – APP/iMac; Other Hardware – APP/Mac Mini; Printers – HP/LaserJet
Editorial Software: Microsoft/Word.
Production Equipment: Hardware – Nu/Flip Top FT40UP; Cameras – SCREEN/Companica 516.
Total Circulation: 2849

SITKA

DAILY SITKA SENTINEL

Corporate/Parent Company: Verstovia Corp.
Publication Street Address: 112 Barracks St
City: Sitka
State: AK
Publication Website: www.sitkasentinel.com
Postal Code: 99835-7532
Office phone: (907) 747-3219
Publisher Name: Thad & Sandy Poulson
Publisher Email: news@sitkasentinel.com
Editor Name: Thad Poulson
Editor Email: thad@sitkasentinel.com
Advertising Executive Name: Susan McFadden
Advertising Executive Email: susan@sitkasentinel.com
Year Established: 1940
Delivery Methods: Newsstand`Carrier
Own Printing Facility?: Y
Commercial printers?: Y
Mechanical specifications: Type page 13 1/2 x 21; E - 6 cols, 2 1/16, 1/8 between; A - 6 cols, 2 1/16, 1/8 between; C - 6 cols, 2 1/16, 1/8 between.
Published Days: Mon`Tues`Wed`Thur`Fri
Weekday Frequency: e
Avg Paid Circ: 2501
Audit Company: Sworn/Estimate/Non-Audited
Audit Date: 7 12 2019
Pressroom Equipment: Lines – 4-G/CommunityECRM 4x CTP
Mailroom Equipment: Tying Machines – Felins/Paktyer; Address Machine – Wm.;

Buisness Equipment: 3-Microsoft/Windows
Buisness Software: Quickbooks
Classified Equipment: Hardware – IBM; Printers – HP/Laser Jet,
Classified Software: TC 1.348. Media Span
Editorial Equipment: Hardware – 10 mac minis and two Windows computers in network. 3 laser printers, scanners, misc. modems, switches and routers
Editorial Software: Adobe InCopy, Pagemaker, Photoshop, Illustrator, Acrobat,InDesign
Production Equipment: ECRM Mako 4x CTP
Production Software: InDesign
Note: Thad
Total Circulation: 2501

ALABAMA

DECATUR

THE DECATUR DAILY

Corporate/Parent Company: Tennessee Valley Printing Co., Inc.
Publication Street Address: 201 1st Ave SE
City: Decatur
State: AL
Publication Website: http://www.decaturdaily.com
Postal Code: 35601-2333
Office phone: (256)353-4612
Editor Phone: (256)340-2430
Advertising Executive Phone: (256)340-2362
Year Established: 1912
Delivery Methods: Carrier
Own Printing Facility?: Y
Commercial printers?: Y
Mechanical specifications: Type page 11 1/2 x 21 1/2; E - 6 cols, 1 15/16, 1/8 between; A - 6 cols, 1 15/16, 1/8 between; C - 10 cols, 1 1/16, 1/16 between.
Published Days: Mon`Tues`Wed`Thur`Fri`Sat`Sun
Weekday Frequency: m
Saturday Frequency: m
Avg Paid Circ: 11823
Avg Free Circ: 823
Audit Company: AAM
Audit Date: 14 07 2020
Pressroom Equipment: Lines – 7-G/Urbanite, 1-G/3-color unit single width; Reels & Stands – 2.
Mailroom Equipment: Counter Stackers – QWI/350; Inserters & Stuffers – HI; Tying Machines – Dynaric/NP 1500; Address Machine – KR;
Buisness Equipment: IBM/AS-400
Buisness Software: INSI
Classified Equipment: Hardware – APT; Okidata;
Classified Software: APT.
Editorial Equipment: Hardware – 10-Compaq/386, 24-AST/286/2-V/XP 1000, 1-Ultre/4000 Imagesetter
Editorial Software: APT.
Production Equipment: Hardware – Adobe/Photoshop 6.0, APP/Mac G3, APP/Mac G4; Cameras – SCREEN; Scanners – Umax/Majicsan
Production Software: APT/ACT, QPS/QuarkXPress 3.2.
Total Circulation: 14132

DOTHAN

THE DOTHAN EAGLE

Corporate/Parent Company: Lee Enterprises
Publication Street Address: 227 N Oates St
City: Dothan
State: AL
Publication Website: http://www.dothaneagle.com
Postal Code: 36303-4555
Office phone: (334) 792-3141
Editor Phone: (334) 792-3141
Advertising Executive Phone: (334)702-2600 ; (334) 702-6060 (classified)
Year Established: 1903

Delivery Methods: Newsstand`Carrier
Own Printing Facility?: Y
Mechanical specifications: Type page 13 x 21 1/2; E - 6 cols, 2 1/16, 3/16 between; A - 6 cols, 2 1/16, 3/16 between; C - 9 cols, 1 3/8, 1/16 between.
Published Days: Mon`Tues`Wed`Thur`Fri`Sat`Sun
Weekday Frequency: m
Saturday Frequency: m
Avg Paid Circ: 15078
Avg Free Circ: 1585
Audit Company: AAM
Audit Date: 18 09 2018
Pressroom Equipment: Lines – 12-G/Urbanite single width (64 page capacity).;
Mailroom Equipment: Counter Stackers – 2-Id/2000-4000; Inserters & Stuffers – 8-GMA/Station, GMA/SLS 1000 (DTP); Tying Machines – 1-Dynaric/Auto Strapper; Wrapping Singles – Mailroom Control System ÃƒÂ£ÂƒÂ,Â£ GMA; Address Machine – KR/320;
Buisness Equipment: HP
Buisness Software: Oracle, PBS, ATT, CText, Microsoft/Windows
Classified Equipment: Hardware – CText; Printers – V/5300.;
Editorial Equipment: Hardware – CText; Printers – V/5300.
Production Equipment: Hardware – Caere/OmniPage, 2-Tegra/5300 Film device; Cameras – 1-LE/121-V242, 1-R/432; Scanners – 2-Umax, 1-Umax/PowerLook
Production Software: QPS/QuarkXPress 3.3.
Total Circulation: 18464

ENTERPRISE

THE ENTERPRISE LEDGER

Publication Street Address: 1110 Boll Weevil Cir
City: Enterprise
State: AL
Publication Website: http://www.eprisenow.com
Postal Code: 36330-1390
Office phone: (334) 347-9533
Editor Phone: (334) 347-9533
Advertising Executive Phone: (334) 347-9533
Year Established: 1898
Delivery Methods: Mail`Newsstand`Carrier`Racks
Mechanical specifications: Type page 13 x 21 1/2; E - 6 cols, 2 1/16, 1/8 between; A - 6 cols, 2 1/16, 1/8 between; C - 9 cols, 1 1/2, 1/8 between.
Published Days: Tues`Wed`Thur`Fri`Sun
Weekday Frequency: m
Saturday Frequency: m
Avg Paid Circ: 7100
Audit Company: Sworn/Estimate/Non-Audited
Audit Date: 7 12 2019
Total Circulation: 7100

FLORENCE

TIMES DAILY

Corporate/Parent Company: Tennessee Valley Printing Co., Inc.
Publication Street Address: 219 W Tennessee St
City: Florence
State: AL
Publication Website: http://www.timesdaily.com
Postal Code: 35630-5440
Office phone: (256) 766-3434
Editor Phone: (256) 740-4725
Advertising Executive Phone: (256) 740-5815
Year Established: 1890
Own Printing Facility?: Y
Commercial printers?: Y
Mechanical specifications: Type page 11 x 21; E - 6 cols, 1 15/16, 3/16 between; A - 6 cols, 1 5/8, 3/16 between; C - 9 cols, 11/16, 1/16 between.
Published Days: Mon`Tues`Wed`Thur`Fri`Sat`Sun
Weekday Frequency: m
Saturday Frequency: m
Avg Paid Circ: 15679
Avg Free Circ: 1126
Audit Company: AAM
Audit Date: 24 03 2020
Pressroom Equipment: Folders – 1, 1-G/Urbanite

1997
Mailroom Equipment: Counter Stackers – 5-QWI/350-400W; Inserters & Stuffers – NP1472; 632 Inserter; Tying Machines – Power Strap; Dynaric;
Buisness Software: INSI
Classified Equipment: Hardware – PC
Editorial Equipment: Hardware – PC
Editorial Software: CPU.
Production Equipment: Scanners – 1-PixelCraft/8000.
Total Circulation: 15462

FORT PAYNE

FORT PAYNE TIMES JOURNAL

Publication Street Address: 811 Greenhill Blvd. NW
City: Fort Payne
State: AL
Publication Website: times-journal.com
Postal Code: 35967
Office phone: 256-845-2550
General E-mail: news@times-journal.com
Publisher Name: Tricia Clinton
Publisher Email: tclinton@times-journal.com
Publisher Phone: 256-304-0056
Editor Name: Emily Kirby
Editor Email: kayla.beaty@times-journal.com
Editor Phone: 256-304-0053
Advertising Executive Name: Linda Stiefel
Advertising Executive Email: lstiefel@times-journal.com
Advertising Executive Phone: 256-304-0061

THE TIMES-JOURNAL

Corporate/Parent Company: Southern Newspapers, Inc.
Publication Street Address: 811 Greenhill Blvd NW
City: Fort Payne
State: AL
Publication Website: http://times-journal.com
Postal Code: 35967
Office phone: (256) 845-2550
Editor Phone: (256) 304-0053
Advertising Executive Phone: (256) 304-0061
Year Established: 1878
Delivery Methods: Mail`Newsstand`Carrier`Racks
Own Printing Facility?: N
Commercial printers?: N
Mechanical specifications: Type page 13 x 21 1/2; E - 6 cols, 2 1/16, 1/8 between; A - 6 cols, 2 1/16, 1/8 between; C - 6 cols, 2 1/16, 1/8 between.
Published Days: Tues`Wed`Thur`Fri`Sat
Weekday Frequency: m
Saturday Frequency: m
Avg Paid Circ: 2961
Avg Free Circ: 294
Audit Company: AAM
Audit Date: 8 05 2019
Pressroom Equipment: Lines – 5-G/Community;
Mailroom Equipment: Address Machine – 2-Am/1900, 2-El/3101.;
Buisness Equipment: IBM
Classified Equipment: Hardware – APP/Mac.;
Editorial Equipment: Hardware – Mk, APP/Mac.
Production Equipment: Hardware – 1-WL/30A; Cameras – AG/Repromaster/3800.
Total Circulation: 4605

GADSDEN

THE GADSDEN TIMES

Corporate/Parent Company: Gannett
Publication Street Address: 401 Locust St
City: Gadsden
State: AL
Publication Website: http://www.gadsdentimes.com
Postal Code: 35901-3737
Office phone: (256) 549-2000
Editor Phone: (256) 399-9742

Advertising Executive Phone: (256) 549-2071
Year Established: 1867
Delivery Methods: Mail`Newsstand`Carrier`Racks
Own Printing Facility?: Y
Commercial printers?: N
Mechanical specifications: Type page 13 x 21 1/2; E - 6 cols, 2 1/16, 1/8 between; A - 6 cols, 2 1/16, 1/8 between; C - 9 cols, 1 11/32, 3/32 between.
Published Days: Mon`Tues`Wed`Thur`Fri`Sat`Sun
Weekday Frequency: m
Saturday Frequency: m
Avg Paid Circ: 12597
Audit Company: AAM
Audit Date: 31 03 2016
Pressroom Equipment: Reels & Stands – 6;
Buisness Equipment: ADV/36
Classified Equipment: Hardware – APP/Mac G4; Printers – AU, AG/Accuset;
Classified Software: Baseview.
Editorial Equipment: Hardware – APP/Mac-SH; Printers – AU, AG/Accuset
Editorial Software: Baseview.
Production Equipment: Hardware – Mac Base/ AG Accuset, 1-Konica/K-280, QPS 3.31; Scanners – Mk/SilverScan, Mk/ScanMaker III, Kk, Nikon/Coolscan
Production Software: QPS 4.0.
Total Circulation: 12597

JASPER

DAILY MOUNTAIN EAGLE

Corporate/Parent Company: Daily Mountain Eagle
Publication Street Address: 1301 Viking Dr
City: Jasper
State: AL
Publication Website: http://mountaineagle.com
Postal Code: 35501-4983
Office phone: (205) 221-2840
Editor Phone: (205) 221-2840
Advertising Executive Phone: (205) 221-2840
Year Established: 1872
Mechanical specifications: Type page 13 x 21 1/2; E - 6 cols, 5/16, 1/8 between; A - 6 cols, 5/16, 1/8 between; C - 6 cols, 5/16, 1/8 between.
Published Days: Tues`Wed`Thur`Fri`Sat`Sun
Weekday Frequency: m
Saturday Frequency: m
Avg Paid Circ: 5406
Avg Free Circ: 458
Audit Company: AAM
Audit Date: 19 06 2020
Pressroom Equipment: Lines – 8-WPC/Web Leader; 3-WPC/Quadcolor; Folders – 2-WPC/2:1.;
Mailroom Equipment: Counter Stackers – 1-BG/ Count-O-Veyor; Inserters & Stuffers – 4-DG/320; Tying Machines – 1/Sa; Address Machine – 1-Ch/730.;
Editorial Equipment: Hardware – Mk/12-Mk.
Production Equipment: Hardware – 2-Mk/ Ad Touch, 2-APP/Mac LaserWriter Plus; Cameras – 1-R/Corsair, 1-DAI/5161.
Total Circulation: 4743

LANETT

THE VALLEY TIMES-NEWS

Corporate/Parent Company: The Valley Times-News
Publication Street Address: 220 N 12th St
City: Lanett
State: AL
Publication Website: http://www.valleytimes-news.com
Postal Code: 36863-6422
Office phone: (334) 644-8100
Editor Phone: (334) 644-8123
Advertising Executive Phone: (334) 644-8100
Year Established: 1950
Delivery Methods: Mail`Newsstand`Carrier`Racks
Own Printing Facility?: N
Commercial printers?: N
Mechanical specifications: Type page 13 x 21 1/2; E - 6 cols, 2 1/8, 1/4 between; A - 6 cols, 2 1/8, 1/4 between; C - 9 cols, 1 1/2,

1/8 between.
Published Days: Mon`Tues`Wed`Thur`Fri
Weekday Frequency: e
Avg Paid Circ: 4200
Audit Company: USPS
Audit Date: 10 01 2016
Pressroom Equipment: Lines – 6-G/Community; Folders – G/2:1;
Mailroom Equipment: Counter Stackers – 1/BG; Tying Machines – 1-/BG.;
Buisness Equipment: 1-RSK/Model III, 1-Bs/B96-40
Buisness Software: APP/Mac
Classified Equipment: Hardware – Mk, PC, APP/Mac; Printers – 2-COM/308 Laser;
Classified Software: Mk.
Editorial Equipment: Hardware – Mk, PC; Printers – 2-COM/308 Laser
Editorial Software: Mk, APP/Mac.
Production Equipment: Hardware – 1-LE/LD-1800A; Cameras – Roconex/1-B.
Total Circulation: 4200

MOBILE

PRESS-REGISTER

Corporate/Parent Company: Advance Newspapers
Publication Street Address: 18 S ROYAL ST
City: Mobile
State: AL
Publication Website: http://www.al.com
Postal Code: 36602
Office phone: (251) 219-5400
Editor Phone: (251) 219-5632
Advertising Executive Phone: (251) 219-5545
Mechanical specifications: Type page 11 3/5 x 20 1/2; E – 6 cols, 1 4/5, 1/8 between; A – 6 cols, 1 4/5, 1/8 between; C – 10 cols, 1 9/32, 1/32 between.
Published Days: Mon`Tues`Wed`Thur`Fri`Sat`Sun
Weekday Frequency: m
Saturday Frequency: m
Avg Paid Circ: 12928
Audit Company: AAM
Audit Date: 5 03 2020
Pressroom Equipment: Lines – 12-G/Mark I (4 half decks); Folders – 2-G/2:1; Pasters –12-G/RTP; Reels & Stands – 12;
Mailroom Equipment: Counter Stackers – 6-HL/Monitor, 4/Quipp 401; Inserters & Stuffers – 2-HI/1372P, 1-HI/1472P; Tying Machines – 8-/Dynaric; Address Machine – 2-/Ch;
Buisness Equipment: 1-HP/979
Buisness Software: Microsoft/Windows NT, Microsoft/Windows 95, Microsoft/Office 97, Platinum 4.6A, Abra Suite 5.21, MicroSystems Specialists Inc.
Classified Equipment: Hardware – SII/Sys 77; Printers – Centronics/351, HP/LaserJet 6;
Classified Software: Tandem/D20 Operating Sys, ICP.
Editorial Equipment: Hardware – 2-Sun/Ultra 2, 2-Sun/Sparc 20; Printers – HP/LaserJet 6, HP/DesignJet 1055cm
Editorial Software: HI/NME 3.31.006, HI/NMP 1.8.19, XP21 3.6.
Production Equipment: Hardware – 2-AU/APS-6-10-8C, 2-MAS, 2-Alpha RIP, 1-AII/3850, 1-AII/350 wide, 1-Graphix RIP; Cameras – 1-C/Newspager; Scanners – Sharp
Production Software: HI/XP21.
Total Circulation: 36417

MONTGOMERY

MONTGOMERY ADVERTISER

Corporate/Parent Company: Gannett
Publication Street Address: 475 Molton St
City: Montgomery
State: AL
Publication Website: http://www.montgomeryadvertiser.com
Postal Code: 36104-3523
Office phone: (334) 262-1611
Editor Phone: (334) 261-1524
Advertising Executive Phone: (334) 264-3733
Year Established: 1829
Own Printing Facility?: Y
Mechanical specifications: Type page 11 5/8 x 20 1/2; E – 6 cols, 1 5/6, 1/8 between; A – 6 cols, 1 5/6, 1/8 between; C – 10 cols, between.
Published Days: Mon`Tues`Wed`Thur`Fri`Sat`Sun
Weekday Frequency: m
Saturday Frequency: m
Avg Paid Circ: 11278
Avg Free Circ: 959
Audit Company: AAM
Audit Date: 31 03 2019
Pressroom Equipment: Folders – G/3:2 (144 page); Pasters –G/RTPReels & Stands – 8-G/3-Arm.;
Mailroom Equipment: Counter Stackers – 6-QWI/350; Inserters & Stuffers – NP/1472; Tying Machines – 5-Dynaric/NP-2; Wrapping Singles – 1-Bu/Tying Machine, 5-QWI/Viper Bottom Wraps; Address Machine – Barstrom/In-Line;
Buisness Equipment: IBM/AS-400 9406-300
Buisness Software: Microsoft/Office Pro 1997
Classified Equipment: Hardware – 20-Dell/Optiplex, Dell/Power Edge 90; Printers – HP/4si;
Classified Software: Harris/AdPower, HI/CASH 2.1.9.
Editorial Equipment: Hardware – 70-Dell/Optiplex, Sun/Enterprise 450; Printers – HP, Unity/1600 XL, HP/8150
Editorial Software: Harris/Newsmaker 2.5, HI/Newsmaker Editorial 3.5.
Production Equipment: Hardware – 2-V/Pro Panther 36, 1-V/5300-B; Cameras – 1-C; Scanners – 2-ECR, ScanView/ScanMate 5000 Drum Scanner, Kk/2035S, HP/ScanJet 4C, Nikon/LS 2000
Production Software: Solaris 2.5, HI/Newsmaker Pagination 4.0.
Total Circulation: 12237

OPELIKA

OPELIKA-AUBURN NEWS

Corporate/Parent Company: Lee Enterprises
Publication Street Address: 2901 Society Hill Rd
City: Opelika
State: AL
Publication Website: http://www.oanow.com
Postal Code: 36804-4850
Office phone: (334) 749-6271
Editor Phone: (334) 749-6271
Advertising Executive Phone: (334) 737-2488
Year Established: 1904
Delivery Methods: Mail
Mechanical specifications: Type page 11 1/2 x 21 1/2; E – 6 cols, 1 3/4, 1/6 between; A – 6 cols, 1 3/4, 1/6 between; C – 6 cols, 1 3/4, 1/6 between.
Published Days: Mon`Tues`Wed`Thur`Fri`Sat`Sun
Weekday Frequency: m
Saturday Frequency: m
Avg Paid Circ: 8281
Avg Free Circ: 737
Audit Company: AAM
Audit Date: 31 05 2019
Pressroom Equipment: Lines – 8-G/Community 1976; Folders – SC/499.;
Mailroom Equipment: Tying Machines – MLN/Sprint.;
Buisness Equipment: PBS
Buisness Software: Unix
Classified Equipment: Hardware – APP/Mac;
Classified Software: Baseview.
Editorial Equipment: Hardware – APP/Mac; Printers – V
Editorial Software: QPS/QuarkXPress, Baseview.
Production Equipment: Hardware – 1-Nu, Pre Press/Panther Plus; Cameras – Amergraph.
Total Circulation: 11154

SCOTTSBORO

SCOTTSBORO DAILY SENTINEL

Publication Street Address: 701 Veterans Drive
City: Scottsboro
State: AL
Publication Website: www.thedailysentinel.com
Postal Code: 35768
Office phone: 256-259-1020
General E-mail: support@jcsentinel.com
Editor Name: DeWayne Patterson
Editor Email: brent.miller@jcsentinel.com
Advertising Executive Name: Hannah Hulsey
Advertising Executive Email: nicole.rhoads@jcsentinel.com

TUSCALOOSA

THE TUSCALOOSA NEWS

Corporate/Parent Company: Gannett
Publication Street Address: 315 28th Ave
City: Tuscaloosa
State: AL
Publication Website: http://www.tuscaloosanews.com
Postal Code: 35401-1022
Office phone: (205) 345-0505
Editor Phone: (866)400-8477
Advertising Executive Phone: (205) 722-0148
Year Established: 1818
Delivery Methods: Carrier`Racks
Own Printing Facility?: Y
Commercial printers?: Y
Mechanical specifications: Type page 13 x 21 1/2; E – 6 cols, 2 1/16, 1/8 between; A – 6 cols, 2 1/16, 1/8 between; C – 9 cols, 1 3/8, 1/16 between.
Published Days: Mon`Tues`Wed`Thur`Fri`Sat`Sun
Weekday Frequency: m
Saturday Frequency: m
Avg Paid Circ: 17136
Audit Company: AAM
Audit Date: 31 03 2018
Pressroom Equipment: Lines – 10-G/Urbanite, 1-G/Urbanite (3 color); Pasters –8-Ebway/H535000; Control System – 2; Registration System – KFM/Pin System.
Mailroom Equipment: Counter Stackers – 3-HL/Monitor; Inserters & Stuffers – 1-S/10-48P; Tying Machines – 1-MLN/ML, 1/Power Strap, 1-MLN/MLEE, 1-Dynaric/NP-2; Address Machine – 1-/KR.;
Buisness Equipment: IBM/AS-400
Classified Equipment: Hardware – PC, Microsoft/Windows NT; Printers – HP/5000;
Classified Software: AT/IAS, Computext.
Editorial Equipment: Hardware – PC, Microsoft/Windows NT; Printers – HP/5000
Editorial Software: CompuText.
Production Equipment: Hardware – 2-COM/9600, 1-Nu/Flip Top FT52UPNS; Cameras – 1-C/Spartan III, 1-R; Scanners – 2-Kk/RFS 2035+, 2-X/11x17 Flatbed
Production Software: CompUtext.
Total Circulation: 17136

ARKANSAS

ARKADELPHIA

ARKADELPHIA SIFTINGS HERALD

Publication Street Address: 205 S 26th St
City: Arkadelphia
State: AR
Publication Website: www.siftingsherald.com
Postal Code: 71923-5423
Office phone: (870) 246-5525
General E-mail: rhaycox@siftingsherald.com

BATESVILLE

BATESVILLE DAILY GUARD

Corporate/Parent Company: Paxton Media Group, LLC
Publication Street Address: 400 Harrison St., Rm 200
City: Batesville
State: AR
Publication Website: www.guardonline.com
Postal Code: 72501-6711
Office phone: (870) 793-2383
General E-mail: webmaster@guardonline.com
Publisher Name: Teresa Harvey
Publisher Email: tharvey@guardonline.com
Publisher Phone: (870) 793-2383
Editor Name: Bruce Guthrie

BENTON

THE SALINE COURIER

Corporate/Parent Company: Horizon Publications Inc.
Publication Street Address: 321 N Market St
City: Benton
State: AR
Publication Website: www.bentoncourier.com
Postal Code: 72015-3734
Office phone: (501) 315-8228
General E-mail: news@bentoncourier.com
Publisher Name: Kelly Freudensprung
Publisher Email: kfreudensprung@bentoncourier.com
Editor Name: Josh Briggs

BLYTHEVILLE

BLYTHEVILLE COURIER NEWS

Corporate/Parent Company: Rust Communications
Publication Street Address: 900 N Broadway St
City: Blytheville
State: AR
Publication Website: www.couriernews.net
Postal Code: 72315-1714
Office phone: (870) 763-4461
General E-mail: sriley@couriernews.net
Publisher Name: Shelia Rouse
Publisher Email: srouse@stategazette.com
Publisher Phone: (731) 285-4091
Editor Name: Mark Brasfield

CAMDEN

CAMDEN NEWS

Publication Street Address: 113 Madison Ave NE
City: Camden
State: AR
Publication Website: www.camdenarknews.com
Postal Code: 71701-3514
Office phone: (870) 836-8192
General E-mail: camnews@cablelynx.com

CONWAY

LOG CABIN DEMOCRAT

Corporate/Parent Company: Paxton Media Group, LLC
Publication Street Address: 1121 Front Street
City: Conway
State: AR
Publication Website: www.thecabin.net
Postal Code: 72032
Office phone: (501) 327-6621
General E-mail: webmaster@thecabin.net
Publisher Name: Frank Leto
Publisher Email: fleto@thecabin.net
Publisher Phone: (501) 505-1213

EL DORADO

EL DORADO NEWS-TIMES / SUNDAY NEWS

Publication Street Address: 111 N Madison Ave
City: El Dorado
State: AR
Publication Website: www.eldoradonews.com
Postal Code: 71730-6124
Office phone: (870) 862-6611
General E-mail: lthompson@nwaonline.com
Editor Name: Lisa Thompson

FAYETTEVILLE

NORTHWEST ARKANSAS

U.S. Daily Newspapers

DEMOCRAT-GAZETTE
Corporate/Parent Company: WEHCO Media, Inc.
Publication Street Address: 212 N East Ave
City: Fayetteville
State: AR
Publication Website: www.nwaonline.com
Postal Code: 72701-5225
Office phone: (479) 442-1700
General E-mail: lthompson@nwaonline.com
Editor Name: Lisa Thompson

FORREST CITY

TIMES-HERALD
Corporate/Parent Company: Argent Arkansas News Media
Publication Street Address: 222 N Izard St
City: Forrest City
State: AR
Publication Website: http://thnews.com/
Postal Code: 72335-3324
Office phone: (870) 633-3130
General E-mail: addept@thnews.com

FORT SMITH

TIMES RECORD
Corporate/Parent Company: Gannett
Publication Street Address: 5111 Rogers Ave., Suite 471
City: Fort Smith
State: AR
Publication Website: www.swtimes.com
Postal Code: 72903
Office phone: (479) 785-7700
General E-mail: ahernandez@swtimes.com
Publisher Name: Ronald Benner
Publisher Email: rbenner@swtimes.com
Publisher Phone: (479) 785-7700, ext : 1300
Editor Name: John Lovett

HELENA

THE DAILY WORLD
Corporate/Parent Company: Gannett
Publication Street Address: 417 York
City: Helena
State: AR
Publication Website: www.helena-arkansas.com
Postal Code: 72342
Office phone: (870) 338-9181
Publisher Name: Teresa Hicks
Publisher Email: thicks@gatehousemedia.com
Editor Name: Rick Wright

HOPE

HOPE STAR
Publication Street Address: 522 W 3rd St
City: Hope
State: AR
Publication Website: www.hopestar.com
Postal Code: 71801-5001
Office phone: (870) 777-8841
General E-mail: hopestar71802@yahoo.com

HOT SPRINGS NATIONAL PARK

THE SENTINEL-RECORD
Corporate/Parent Company: WEHCO Media Inc. Newspaper
Publication Street Address: 300 Spring St
City: Hot Springs National Park
State: AR
Publication Website: www.hotsr.com
Postal Code: 71901-4148
Office phone: (501) 623-7711
General E-mail: debej@hotsr.com

JONESBORO

THE JONESBORO SUN
Corporate/Parent Company: Paxton Media Group, LLC
Publication Street Address: 518 Carson St
City: Jonesboro
State: AR
Publication Website: www.jonesborosun.com
Postal Code: 72401-3128
Office phone: (870) 935-5525
General E-mail: cwessel@jonesborosun.com
Publisher Name: Reece Terry
Publisher Email: rterry@jonesborosun.com
Editor Name: Randal Seyler

THE SUN
Corporate/Parent Company: Paxton Media Group
Publication Street Address: 518 Carson
City: Jonesboro
State: AR
Publication Website: jonesborosun.com
Postal Code: 72401
Office phone: 870-935-5525
General E-mail: sunweb@jonesborosun.com
Publisher Name: Reece Terry
Publisher Email: rterry@jonesborosun.com
Publisher Phone: 870-477-6067
Editor Name: Chris Wessel

LITTLE ROCK

ARKANSAS DEMOCRAT-GAZETTE
Publication Street Address: 121 E Capitol Ave
City: Little Rock
State: AR
Publication Website: www.ardemgaz.com
Postal Code: 72201-3819
Office phone: (501) 378-3400
General E-mail: dbrowning@arkansasonline.com
Publisher Name: Walter E. Hussman
Editor Name: Rex Nelson

MAGNOLIA

BANNER-NEWS
Publication Street Address: 130 S Washington
City: Magnolia
State: AR
Publication Website: www.bannernews.net
Postal Code: 71753-3523
Office phone: (870) 234-5130
General E-mail: cmartin@bannernews.net

MALVERN

MALVERN DAILY RECORD
Corporate/Parent Company: Horizon Publications Inc.
Publication Street Address: 219 Locust St
City: Malvern
State: AR
Publication Website: www.malvern-online.com
Postal Code: 72104-3721
Office phone: (501) 337-7523
General E-mail: advertising@malvern-online.com
Editor Name: Sarah Perry

MARION

THE EVENING TIMES
Corporate/Parent Company: Crittenden Publishing Co.
Publication Street Address: 1010 Hwy. 77 North
City: Marion
State: AR
Publication Website: www.theeveningtimes.com
Postal Code: 72364-9007
Office phone: (870) 735-1010
General E-mail: news@theeveningtimes.com

MOUNTAIN HOME

THE BAXTER BULLETIN
Corporate/Parent Company: Gannett
Publication Street Address: 16 W 6th St
City: Mountain Home
State: AR
Publication Website: www.baxterbulletin.com
Postal Code: 72653-3508
Office phone: (870) 508-8000
General E-mail: aramsey@localiq.com

PARAGOULD

PARAGOULD DAILY PRESS
Corporate/Parent Company: Paxton Media Group, LLC
Publication Street Address: 1401 W Hunt St
City: Paragould
State: AR
Publication Website: www.paragoulddailypress.com
Postal Code: 72450-3575
Office phone: (870) 239-8562
General E-mail: webmaster@paragoulddailypress.com
Editor Name: Steve Gillespie

PINE BLUFF

PINE BLUFF COMMERCIAL
Corporate/Parent Company: GateHouse Media
Publication Street Address: 300 S Beech St
City: Pine Bluff
State: AR
Publication Website: www.pbcommercial.com
Postal Code: 71601-4039
Office phone: (870) 534-3400
General E-mail: kbrickey@pbcommercial.com
Publisher Name: Jennifer Allen
Publisher Email: jallen@gatehousemedia.com
Publisher Phone: (870) 534-3400, ext : 1204
Editor Name: Rick Kennedy

RUSSELLVILLE

THE COURIER
Corporate/Parent Company: Gannett
Publication Street Address: 201 E 2nd St
City: Russellville
State: AR
Publication Website: www.couriernews.com
Postal Code: 72801-5102
Office phone: (479) 968-5252
General E-mail: web@couriernews.com
Publisher Name: Frank Leto
Publisher Email: fleto@couriernews.com

SEARCY

THE DAILY CITIZEN
Corporate/Parent Company: Paxton Media Group, LLC
Publication Street Address: 723 W Beebe Capps Expy
City: Searcy
State: AR
Publication Website: www.thedailycitizen.com
Postal Code: 72143-6303
Office phone: (501) 268-8621
General E-mail: classifiedads@thedailycitizen.com
Publisher Name: Teresa Harvey
Publisher Email: tharvey@thedailycitizen.com
Publisher Phone: (501) 268-8621, ext : 101
Editor Name: Steve Watts

STUTTGART

STUTTGART DAILY LEADER
Publication Street Address: 111 W 6th St
City: Stuttgart
State: AR
Publication Website: www.stuttgartdailyleader.com
Postal Code: 72160-4243
Office phone: (870) 673-8533
General E-mail: sales@stuttgartdailyleader.com
Publisher Name: Jennifer Allen
Editor Name: Eplunus Colvin

TEXARKANA

TEXARKANA GAZETTE
Corporate/Parent Company: WEHCO Media, Inc.
Publication Street Address: 101 E. Broad St.
City: Texarkana
State: AR
Publication Website: texarkanagazette.com
Postal Code: 71854
Office phone: (870) 330-7550
Editor Name: Les Minor

ARIZONA

BULLHEAD CITY

MOHAVE VALLEY DAILY NEWS
Corporate/Parent Company: Brehm Communications Inc.
Publication Street Address: 2435 Miracle Mile
City: Bullhead City
State: AZ
Publication Website: www.mohavedailynews.com
Postal Code: 86442-7311
Office phone: (928) 763-2505
General E-mail: wells@nwppub.com
Editor Name: Bill McMillen
Editor Email: bmcmillen@mohavedailynews.com
Editor Phone: (928) 763-2505 ext. 5144
Year Established: 1963
Delivery Methods: Mail`Newsstand`Carrier`Racks
Own Printing Facility?: Y
Commercial printers?: Y
Mechanical specifications: Type page 13 x 21; E - 6 cols, 1 13/16, 1/6 between; A - 6 cols, 1 13/16, 1/6 between; C - 6 cols, 1 13/16, 1/6 between.
Published Days: Mon`Tues`Wed`Thur`Fri`Sun
Weekday Frequency: m
Avg Paid Circ: 7006
Avg Free Circ: 412
Audit Company: Sworn/Estimate/Non-Audited
Audit Date: 7 12 2019
Pressroom Equipment: Lines – 3-WPC/Atlas single width, 1-WPC/Marc 25; 1-WPC/Quad stack single width, 3-WPC/Marc 25; Folders – WPC (1/4-1/2), WPC/Mark 25 1999; Reels & Stands – 4;
Mailroom Equipment: Tying Machines – MLN/2EE, OVL, I;
Buisness Equipment: Qantel
Buisness Software: Quattro/Pro
Classified Equipment: Hardware – APP/iMac; Printers – Xante/Accel-a-Writer 8300, Xante/Accel-a-Writer 3G;
Classified Software: Baseview/Ad Manager Pro.
Editorial Equipment: Hardware – APP/Mac; Printers – Xante/Accel-a-Writer 3G, Xante/Accel-a-Writer 8300
Editorial Software: Baseview/NewsEdit Pro, QPS, Aldus/Freehand, Adobe/Photoshop, Adobe/Color Access, Baseview.
Production Equipment: Hardware – GTS/OLIC, 2-Post Script/Level 3, 2-Pre Press/Panther Pro V; Cameras – B; Scanners – Lf, Microtek, Umax/Flatbed, Nikon/Coolscan LS-2000

Production Software: Baseview, Quark 4.0.
Total Circulation: 7418

FLAGSTAFF

ARIZONA DAILY SUN, FLAGSTAFF

Publication Street Address: 1751 S Thompson St
City: Flagstaff
State: AZ
Publication Website: www.azdailysun.com
Postal Code: 86001-8716
Office phone: (928) 774-4545
Editor Name: Chris Etling
Editor Email: cetling@azdailysun.com
Editor Phone: 928-556-2274
Advertising Executive Name: Lydia Smith
Advertising Executive Email: lsmith@azdailysun.com
Advertising Executive Phone: 928-556-2283
Year Established: 1883
Delivery Methods:
  Mail`Newsstand`Carrier`Racks
Own Printing Facility?: Y
Commercial printers?: Y
Mechanical specifications: Type page 9.8889 x 21 1/2; E - 6 cols, 1.5556, 1/8 between; A - 6 cols, 1.5556, 1/8 between.
Published Days: Tues`Wed`Thur`Fri`Sat`Sun
Weekday Frequency: m
Saturday Frequency: m
Avg Paid Circ: 7412
Audit Company: Sworn/Estimate/Non-Audited
Audit Date: 7 12 2019
Pressroom Equipment: Lines – 15-G/Community (3 stacked units, plus 1-4 high); Press Drive – 2-HP/75; Folders – 1-G/SSC, 1; Reels & Stands – 7 Stands;
Mailroom Equipment: Counter Stackers – 1-BG/Count-O-Veyor 109; Inserters & Stuffers – 1-Harris 848, 1-KAN/480 ; Tying Machines – Si/Spirit, 2/Oval Strapper; Address Machine – ScrippSat;
Buisness Software: PBS, Phoenix, Falcon
Classified Equipment: Hardware – PC;
Classified Software: Mactive.
Editorial Equipment: Hardware – APP/Mac; APP/Mac II Graphics; Printers – APP/Mac LaserPrinter
Editorial Software: Baseview, In Design
Production Equipment: Hardware – Amerigraph/437, LaserMaster/1200XLO, 2-AU/3850; Scanners – HP/ScanJet IIc
Production Software: In Design, QPS/QuarkXPress, Adobe/Photoshop.
Total Circulation: 7412

ORO VALLEY

ARIZONADAILYINDEPENDENT.COM

Publication Street Address: 10645 NORTH ORACLE ROAD 121-244
City: ORO VALLEY
State: AZ
Publication Website: arizonadailyindependent.com
Postal Code: 85737
Office phone: (520) 906-8081
Editor Name: Huey Freeman
Editor Email: editor@arizonadailyindependent.com
Advertising Executive Name: Greg Hall

PHOENIX

THE ARIZONA REPUBLIC

Corporate/Parent Company: Gannett Company Inc.
Publication Street Address: 200 E Van Buren St
City: Phoenix
State: AZ
Publication Website: www.azcentral.com
Postal Code: 85004-2238
Office phone: (602) 444-8000
Editor Name: Greg Burton
Editor Email: greg.burton@azcentral.com
Year Established: 1890
Delivery Methods:
  Mail`Newsstand`Carrier`Racks

Mechanical specifications: Type page 13 x 21 1/2; E - 6 cols, 1 3/4, 1/8 between; A - 6 cols, 1 3/4, 1/8 between; C - 10 cols, 1 1/8, 1/16 between.
Published Days: Mon`Tues`Wed`Thur`Fri`Sat`Sun
Weekday Frequency: m
Saturday Frequency: m
Avg Paid Circ: 161341
Audit Company: AAM
Audit Date: 29 08 2019
Pressroom Equipment: Lines – 9-G/Metroliner, 9-G/Metroliner; 9-G/Headliner offset; 9-G/Colorliner; 9-G/Colorliner; 9-G/Colorliner; 9-G/Colorliner; Folders – 7-G/3:2; Reels & Stands – Reels & Stands and Sta;
Mailroom Equipment: Counter Stackers – 36-HL/Monitor, 1-HL/HT, 4-QWI/351; Inserters & Stuffers – 6/AM Graphics/NP 2299; Tying Machines – 32-/Power Strap, 4-/Dynamics.;
Buisness Equipment: Bull/DPS-8000, Sun/2000, 4-Sun/4000
Buisness Software: Microsoft, Cyborg, Lotus Notes, Oracle:financials, In-house
Classified Equipment: Hardware – 2-Sun 4800, PCs; dat, ME-CLS, Multibox; Printers – HP/Desktops;
Classified Software: PGL, Mactive Adbase 2.24.
Editorial Equipment: Hardware – Sun/Sparc 4500, CCI; Printers – HP
Editorial Software: CCI, Microsoft/Word Office.
Production Equipment: Hardware – III/Laser Setter, 5-All/3850 Typesetter, APP/Mac; Scanners – 2-Scitex/Smart Scan
Production Software: CCI.
Total Circulation: 225405

SIERRA VISTA

HERALD/REVIEW

Publication Street Address: 102 S Fab Ave
City: Sierra Vista
State: AZ
Publication Website: www.myheraldreview.com
Postal Code: 85635
Publisher Name: Jennifer Sorenson
Publisher Email: jennifer.sorenson@myheraldreview.com
Publisher Phone: (520) 515-4605
Editor Name: Timothy J. Woods
Editor Email: tim.woods@myheraldreview.com
Editor Phone: (520) 515-4610
Advertising Executive Name: Kelsey Laggan
Advertising Executive Email: kelsey.laggan@myheraldreview.com
Advertising Executive Phone: (520) 515-4633

SUN CITY

DAILY NEWS-SUN

Corporate/Parent Company: Independent NewsMedia
Publication Street Address: 17220 N Boswell Blvd
City: Sun City
State: AZ
Publication Website: www.yourwestvalley.com
Postal Code: 85373-2065
Office phone: 623-972-6101
General E-mail: azdelivery@newszap.com
Year Established: 1956
Delivery Methods:
  Mail`Newsstand`Carrier`Racks
Own Printing Facility?: Y
Commercial printers?: Y
Mechanical specifications: Type page 11 5/8 x 21 1/2; E - 6 cols, 1 7/8, 1/8 between; A - 6 cols, 1 7/8, 1/8 between; C - 9 cols, 1 7/8, 1/8 between.
Published Days: Mon`Tues`Wed`Thur`Fri`Sat
Weekday Frequency: m
Saturday Frequency: m
Avg Paid Circ: 4079
Audit Company: CAC
Audit Date: 30 06 2016
Pressroom Equipment: Lines – 8-G/Urbanite, Folders – 1-G/Urbanite 1000; Reels & Stands – 2-G/High; Registration System – Burgess/Carlson.
Mailroom Equipment: Counter Stackers – 2-HL/Quiad; Inserters & Stuffers – GMA; Tying Machines – 2/Dynaric ND1500; Wrapping Singles – Mailroom Control System ÃƒÂ¢ÃÂÃƒÂ¢ÃÂÃƒÂ¢ÃÂ Lincs/GMA.;
Buisness Equipment: IBM/AS-400, HP/Vectra
Buisness Software: MS/Office
Classified Equipment: Hardware – Sun; 1-Umax/Scanner; Printers – 2-HP;
Classified Software: DTI.
Editorial Equipment: Hardware – SUN/2-Canon/Digital Cameras; Printers – 2-HP
Editorial Software: DTI.
Production Equipment: Hardware – NuArc; Cameras – C/Spartan III
Production Software: DTI.
Total Circulation: 4079

TUCSON

ARIZONA DAILY STAR

Corporate/Parent Company: Lee Enterprises
Publication Street Address: 4850 S Park Ave
City: Tucson
State: AZ
Publication Website: www.tucson.com
Postal Code: 85714-1637
Office phone: (520) 573-4142
General E-mail: metro@tucson.com
Publisher Name: John D'Orlando
Publisher Email: JDorlando@tucson.com
Publisher Phone: 520-573-4215
Editor Name: Debbie Kornmiller
Editor Email: dkornmiller@tucson.com
Editor Phone: 520-573-4127
Advertising Executive Name: Renee Rodriguez
Advertising Executive Email: rrodriguez@tucson.com
Advertising Executive Phone: 520-573-4408
Year Established: 1877
Delivery Methods: Mail`Newsstand`Racks
Mechanical specifications: Type page 12 x 21 1/2; E - 6 cols, 1 4/5, between; A - 6 cols, 1 4/5, between; C - 10 cols, 1 1/10, between.
Published Days: Mon`Tues`Wed`Thur`Fri`Sat`Sun
Weekday Frequency: m
Saturday Frequency: m
Avg Paid Circ: 54838
Audit Company: AAM
Audit Date: 28 06 2019
Pressroom Equipment: Lines – 8-G/Metro 3127A doublewidth (4 half decks); 8-G/Metro 3128A doublewidth (4 half decks); Folders – 4-G/3:2; Reels & Stands – G/Harmonic Drive; Registration System – WPC/Metro Color 4/4 Tower.
Mailroom Equipment: Counter Stackers – 4-GMA, 3-QWI/400, 4-QWI/500, 2-QWI/500C; Inserters & Stuffers – 1/SLS 1000 10:1, 2-/SLS 3000 22:1, GMA/PTH; Tying Machines – 6-/MLN, 3-/Power Strap, 2-HI/RS-25; Wrapping Singles – 4-QWI/Bottom Wrap, 4-QWI/Vipers w/Ink Jet Labe;
Buisness Equipment: IBM/AS-400
Classified Equipment: Hardware – Proteon/PC Network; Printers – HP/4000 Laser Jet, Tektronix/Phaser 300;
Classified Software: TECS-2 4.2.
Editorial Equipment: Hardware – MS/NT, APP/Mac Desktop; Printers – HP/LaserJet IV
Editorial Software: QPS.
Production Equipment: Hardware – 4-APP/Mac Power PC, 2-III/3810 Imagesetter, 3-3850 Sierras; Scanners – Umax/100
Production Software: HI/8900 Classified 7.6, QPS 2.08.
Note: Advertising is sold in combination with Tucson Citizen (e) for $210.20(d) & $292.10(S). Individual newspaper rates not made available. For detailed production information, see Tucson Newspapers listing.
Total Circulation: 68796

YUMA

YUMA SUN

Corporate/Parent Company: RISN Operations/Glacier Media
Publication Street Address: 2055 S Arizona Ave
City: Yuma
State: AZ
Publication Website: www.yumasun.com
Postal Code: 85364-6549
Office phone: 928-783-3333
General E-mail: newsroom@yumasun.com
Publisher Name: " Lisa Reilly"
Publisher Email: publisher@yumasun.com
Publisher Phone: (928) 539-6814
Editor Name: Roxanne Molenar
Editor Email: rmolenar@yumasun.com
Editor Phone: (928) 539-6862
Advertising Executive Name: Tim Chaulk
Advertising Executive Email: tchaulk@yumasun.com
Advertising Executive Phone: (928) 539-6832
Year Established: 1872
Delivery Methods: Mail`Carrier`Racks
Own Printing Facility?: Y
Commercial printers?: Y
Mechanical specifications: Type page 11 13/16 x 21; E - 6 cols, 1/6 between; A - 6 cols, 1/6 between; C - 6 cols, 1/6 between.
Published Days: Mon`Tues`Wed`Thur`Fri`Sat`Sun
Weekday Frequency: m
Saturday Frequency: m
Avg Paid Circ: 8840
Avg Free Circ: 244
Audit Company: AAM
Audit Date: 18 12 2019
Pressroom Equipment: Lines – 9-G/Urbanite 1970.;
Mailroom Equipment: Counter Stackers – 1-ld/2100, 1-MM/CN25; Inserters & Stuffers – 1-MM/Alphaliner 10:1; Tying Machines – 1-MLN/2EE, 1/MLN, 1-Sterling/MR40CH;
Buisness Equipment: PCs
Buisness Software: MediaSpan
Classified Equipment: Hardware – PCs; Media Span; Printers – HP/4000;
Classified Software: MediaSpan
Editorial Equipment: Hardware – 30-APP/Mac G3/1-APP/Mac Quadra 605, 1-APP/Mac Quadra 610, SMS/Stauffer Gold, Lf/AP Leaf Picture Desk, 1-Umax/Scanner, 1-Lf/Leafscan, 1-APP/Power Mac 6066, 1-Gateway/7500, 1-APP/Mac Quadra 800, Sun/Microsystems Server, Sybase/Datab
Editorial Software: MediaSpan
Production Software: MediaSpan
Note: Special Events-Boomers and Beyond, Welcome Back Winter Visitor Bash, Taste of Home
Total Circulation: 11128

CALIFORNIA

ANAHEIM

THE ORANGE COUNTY REGISTER

Corporate/Parent Company: Media News Group
Publication Street Address: 2190 S. Towne Centre Place
City: Anaheim
State: CA
Publication Website: www.ocregister.com
Postal Code: 92806
Office phone: (714) 796-7000
General E-mail: service@scng.com
Publisher Name: Ron Hasse
Publisher Email: publisher@scng.com
Publisher Phone: 818-713-3883
Editor Name: Frank Pine
Editor Email: editor@scng.com
Editor Phone: 909-483-9360
Advertising Executive Name: Kyla Rodriguez
Advertising Executive Email: krodriguez@scng.com

AUBURN

AUBURN JOURNAL

Corporate/Parent Company: Brehm Communications Inc.
Publication Street Address: 1030 High St

U.S. Daily Newspapers

City: Auburn
State: CA
Publication Website: www.auburnjournal.com
Postal Code: 95603-4707
Office phone: 530-885-5656
General E-mail: ajournal@goldcountrymedia.com
Advertising Executive Name: Beth O'Brien
Advertising Executive Email: betho@goldcountrymedia.com

BAKERSFIELD

THE BAKERSFIELD CALIFORNIAN

Corporate/Parent Company: TBC Media
Publication Street Address: 3700 Pegasus Drive
City: Bakersfield
State: CA
Publication Website: www.bakersfield.com
Postal Code: 93308
Office phone: (661) 395-7500
General E-mail: local@bakersfield.com
Publisher Name: Cliff Chandler
Publisher Email: cchandler@bakersfield.com
Publisher Phone: (661) 395-7521
Editor Name: Christine L. Peterson
Editor Email: cpeterson@bakersfield.com
Editor Phone: (661) 395-7381

BENICIA

BENICIA HERALD

Corporate/Parent Company: McNaughton Newspapers
Publication Street Address: 820 1st St
City: Benicia
State: CA
Publication Website: www.beniciaheraldonline.com
Postal Code: 94510-3216
Office phone: 707-745-6838
General E-mail: beniciaherald@gmail.com
Editor Name: Marc Ethier

CAMARILLO

VENTURA COUNTY STAR

Corporate/Parent Company: Gannett Co., Inc.
Publication Street Address: 550 Camarillo Center Dr
City: Camarillo
State: CA
Publication Website: www.vcstar.com
Postal Code: 93010-7700
Office phone: (805) 437-0000
Editor Name: Stacie N. Galang
Editor Email: stacie.galang@vcstar.com

CHICO

CHICO ENTERPRISE-RECORD

Corporate/Parent Company: Media News Group
Publication Street Address: 400 E Park Ave
City: Chico
State: CA
Publication Website: www.chicoer.com
Postal Code: 95928-7127
Office phone: (530) 891-1234
Publisher Name: Jim Gleim
Editor Name: Mike Wolcott
Editor Email: mwolcott@chicoer.com
Editor Phone: 530.896.7793
Advertising Executive Name: Fred Crosthwaite
Advertising Executive Email: fcrosthwaite@chicoer.com

CHICOSOL

Publication Street Address: P.O. Box 5026
City: Chico
State: CA
Publication Website: chicosol.org
Postal Code: 95927

Office phone: 530-433-1039
General E-mail: chicosolnews@gmail.com
Editor Name: Leslie Layton

OROVILLE MERCURY - REGISTER

Publication Street Address: 400 E. Park Ave.
City: Chico
State: CA
Publication Website: www.orovillemr.com
Postal Code: 95928
Office phone: 530.891.1234
Editor Name: Mike Wolcott
Editor Email: mwolcott@chicoer.com
Editor Phone: 530.896.7793
Advertising Executive Name: Sandra Lehman
Advertising Executive Email: slehman@orovillemr.com

COSTA MESA

DAILY PILOT

Publication Street Address: 1375 Sunflower Ave
City: Costa Mesa
State: CA
Publication Website: www.dailypilot.com
Postal Code: 92626-1665
Office phone: (714) 966-4600
Editor Name: Rob Vardon
Editor Email: robert.vardon@latimes.com
Advertising Executive Name: Ray Arroyo
Advertising Executive Email: ray.arroyo@latimes.com

DOWNIEVILLE

SIERRA COUNTY PROSPECT

Publication Street Address: 332 MAIN ST
City: DOWNIEVILLE
State: CA
Publication Website: www.sierracountyprospect.org
Postal Code: 95936
Office phone: 530 448 9092
Editor Name: Laurenc DeVita
Editor Email: editor@sierracountyprospect.org

EL CENTRO

IMPERIAL VALLEY PRESS

Corporate/Parent Company: Imperial Valley Press, Inc.
Publication Street Address: 205 N 8th St
City: El Centro
State: CA
Publication Website: www.ivpressonline.com
Postal Code: 92243-2301
Office phone: (760) 337-3418
General E-mail: webmaster@ivpressonline.com
Publisher Name: Lisa Reilly
Editor Name: Thomas Bodus
Editor Email: tbodus@ivpressonline.com
Editor Phone: 760-337-3427

EL SEGUNDO

LOS ANGELES TIMES

Corporate/Parent Company: NantMedia Holdings, LLC
Publication Street Address: 2300 E. Imperial Highway
City: El Segundo
State: CA
Publication Website: www.latimes.com
Postal Code: 90245
Office phone: (213) 283-2274
General E-mail: customerservices@latimes.com
Editor Name: Norman Pearlstine

EUREKA

TIMES-STANDARD

Publication Street Address: 930 6th St
City: Eureka
State: CA
Publication Website: www.times-standard.com
Postal Code: 95501-1112
Office phone: (707) 441-0500
Publisher Name: John Richmond
Publisher Email: jrichmond@times-standard.com
Publisher Phone: 707-441-0584
Editor Name: Marc Valles
Editor Email: mvalles@times-standard.com
Editor Phone: 707-441-0507
Advertising Executive Name: Seth Cheak
Advertising Executive Email: scheak@times-standard.com

FRESNO

GV WIRE

Publication Street Address: 1396 W. Herndon Ave., Ste. #101
City: Fresno
State: CA
Publication Website: gvwire.com
Postal Code: 93711
Office phone: (559) 492-4037
General E-mail: info@gvwire.com
Editor Name: Bill McEwen
Editor Email: bmcewen@gvwire.com
Editor Phone: 559-492-4031

GRASS VALLEY

THE UNION

Corporate/Parent Company: Swift Communications
Publication Street Address: 464 Sutton Way
City: Grass Valley
State: CA
Publication Website: www.theunion.com
Postal Code: 95945-4102
Office phone: (530) 273-9561
Publisher Name: Don Rogers
Publisher Email: drogers@theunion.com
Publisher Phone: 530-477-4299
Editor Name: Brian Hamilton
Editor Email: bhamilton@theunion.com
Editor Phone: 530-477-4249
Advertising Executive Name: Alyssa Wille
Advertising Executive Email: awille@theunion.com

HANFORD

THE HANFORD SENTINEL

Corporate/Parent Company: Santa Maria News Media
Publication Street Address: 300 W. 6th St.
City: Hanford
State: CA
Publication Website: www.hanfordsentinel.com
Postal Code: 93230
Office phone: 559-582-0471
Publisher Name: Davis Taylor
Publisher Email: publisher@hanfordsentinel.com
Publisher Phone: (559) 583-2400
Editor Name: Chris Aguirre
Editor Email: caguirre@hanfordsentinel.com
Editor Phone: (559) 583-2405
Advertising Executive Name: Mark Daniel
Advertising Executive Email: mdaniel@hanfordsentinel.com

THE SENTINEL

Corporate/Parent Company: Lee Enterprises
Publication Street Address: 300 W 6th St
City: Hanford
State: CA

Publication Website: www.hanfordsentinel.com
Postal Code: 93230-4518
Office phone: (559) 582-0471
Publisher Name: Davis Taylor
Publisher Email: publisher@hanfordsentinel.com
Publisher Phone: (559) 583-2400
Editor Name: Chris Aguirre
Editor Email: caguirre@hanfordsentinel.com
Editor Phone: (559) 583-2405
Advertising Executive Name: Mark Daniel
Advertising Executive Email: mdaniel@hanfordsentinel.com

LAKEPORT

LAKE COUNTY RECORD-BEE

Corporate/Parent Company: Media News Group
Publication Street Address: 2150 S Main St
City: Lakeport
State: CA
Publication Website: www.record-bee.com
Postal Code: 95453-5620
Office phone: (707) 263-5636
General E-mail: desk@record-bee.com
Publisher Name: Kevin McConnell
Publisher Email: udjpublisher@ukiahdj.com
Publisher Phone: (707) 900-2012
Editor Name: Ariel Carmona Jr.
Editor Email: arielcarmona@record-bee.com
Editor Phone: (707) 900-2016
Advertising Executive Name: Amy Hansmith
Advertising Executive Email: ahansmith@record-bee.com

LODI

LODI NEWS-SENTINEL

Corporate/Parent Company: Central Valley News-Sentinel, Inc.
Publication Street Address: 125 N Church St
City: Lodi
State: CA
Publication Website: www.lodinews.com
Postal Code: 95240-2102
Office phone: (209) 369-2761
General E-mail: webmaster@lodinews.com
Publisher Name: Glen Stifflemire
Publisher Email: glenns@lodinews.com
Publisher Phone: 369-2761 x208
Editor Name: Scott Howell
Editor Email: scotth@lodinews.com
Editor Phone: 369-7035 x221
Advertising Executive Name: "Dora Sieber"
Advertising Executive Email: dora@lodinews.com

LONG BEACH

LONG BEACH POST

Publication Street Address: 211 E OCEAN BLVD STE 550
City: LONG BEACH
State: CA
Publication Website: lbpost.com
Postal Code: 90802
Office phone: (562) 437-5814
General E-mail: ads@lbpost.com
Publisher Name: David Sommers
Publisher Email: david@lbpost.com
Editor Name: Melissa Evans
Editor Email: melissa@lbpost.com
Advertising Executive Name: Andrea Estrada
Advertising Executive Email: andrea@lbpost.com

LOS ANGELES

LA OPINION

Corporate/Parent Company: impreMedia LLC
Publication Street Address: 915 Wilshire Blvd
City: Los Angeles
State: CA
Publication Website: www.laopinion.com
Postal Code: 90017-3488
Office phone: (213) 896-2150
General E-mail: advertise@impremedia.com

U.S. Daily Newspapers

Editor Name: Mary Ballesteros

LOS ANGELES BULLETIN
Corporate/Parent Company: Metropolitan News Company
Publication Street Address: P.O. Box 60859
City: Los Angeles
State: CA
Publication Website: www.mnc.net/bulletin.htm
Postal Code: 90060
Office phone: (213) 346-0033
Publisher Name: Jo-Ann W. Grace, Roger M. Grace
Editor Name: Don E. Parret

NEWS-PRESS
Corporate/Parent Company: Gannett
Publication Street Address: 453 S. Spring Street, 3rd Floor
City: Los Angeles
State: CA
Publication Website: www.glendalenewspress.com
Postal Code: 90013
Office phone: (818) 637-3200
General E-mail: gnp@latimes.com
Editor Name: Carol Cormaci
Editor Phone: (818) 495-4156

MANTECA

MANTECA BULLETIN
Corporate/Parent Company: Morris Multimedia, Inc.
Publication Street Address: 531 E Yosemite Ave
City: Manteca
State: CA
Publication Website: www.mantecabulletin.com
Postal Code: 95336-5806
Office phone: (209) 249-3500
General E-mail: circulation@mantecabulletin.com
Publisher Name: Hank Vander Veen
Publisher Email: hvanderveen@mantecabulletin.com
Publisher Phone: 209-249-3503
Editor Name: Dennis Wyatt
Editor Email: dwyatt@mantecabulletin.com
Editor Phone: 209-249-3519
Advertising Executive Name: Chris Castro
Advertising Executive Email: ccastro@mantecabulletin.com

MARYSVILLE

APPEAL DEMOCRAT
Corporate/Parent Company: Vista California News Media, Inc.
Publication Street Address: 1530 Ellis Lake Dr
City: Marysville
State: CA
Publication Website: www.appealdemocrat.com
Postal Code: 95901-4258
Office phone: (530) 741-4700
General E-mail: info@appealdemocrat.com
Publisher Name: Glenn Stifflemire
Publisher Email: gstifflemire@appealdemocrat.com
Publisher Phone: (530) 749-4705
Editor Name: Steve Miller
Editor Email: smiller@appealdemocrat.com
Editor Phone: (530) 749-4767
Advertising Executive Name: Jamie Keith
Advertising Executive Email: jkeith@appealdemocrat.com

MODESTO

THE MODESTO BEE
Corporate/Parent Company: McClatchy Company
Publication Street Address: 948 11th Street, Third floor
City: Modesto
State: CA
Publication Website: www.modbee.com
Postal Code: 95354-2427
Office phone: (209) 578-2000
General E-mail: customerservice@modbee.com
Publisher Name: Tim Ritchey
Publisher Email: tritchey@modbee.com
Publisher Phone: 209-578-2040
Editor Name: Brian Clark
Editor Email: bclark@modbee.com
Editor Phone: "209-578-2362"
Advertising Executive Name: Juanita Toth
Advertising Executive Email: jtoth@modbee.com

MONROVIA

WHITTIER DAILY NEWS
Corporate/Parent Company: Media News Group
Publication Street Address: 605 E. Huntington Drive, Suite 100
City: Monrovia
State: CA
Publication Website: www.whittierdailynews.com
Postal Code: 91016
Office phone: 626-962-8811
Publisher Name: Ron Hasse
Publisher Email: publisher@scng.com
Publisher Phone: 818-713-3883
Editor Name: Frank Pine
Editor Email: editor@scng.com
Editor Phone: 909-483-9360
Advertising Executive Name: Kyla Rodriguez
Advertising Executive Email: krodriguez@scng.com

MONTEREY

MONTEREY HERALD
Publication Street Address: 2200 Garden Road
City: Monterey
State: CA
Publication Website: www.montereyherald.com
Postal Code: 93940
Office phone: 831-372-3311
General E-mail: mheditor@montereyherald.com
Publisher Name: Gary Omernick
Publisher Email: gomernick@montereyherald.com
Publisher Phone: 831-706-3228
Editor Name: David Kellogg
Editor Email: dkellogg@montereyherald.com
Editor Phone: 831-726-4351
Advertising Executive Name: Dana Arvig
Advertising Executive Email: darvig@montereyherald.com

THE MONTEREY COUNTY HERALD
Corporate/Parent Company: Media News Group
Publication Street Address: 2200 Garden Rd
City: Monterey
State: CA
Publication Website: www.montereyherald.com
Postal Code: 93940-5329
Office phone: (831) 372-3311
General E-mail: circservices@montereyherald.com
Publisher Name: Gary Omernick
Publisher Email: gomernick@montereyherald.com
Publisher Phone: 831-706-3228
Editor Name: David Kellogg
Editor Email: dkellogg@montereyherald.com
Editor Phone: 831-726-4351
Advertising Executive Name: Dana Arvig
Advertising Executive Email: darvig@santacruzsentinel.com

MT. SHASTA

SISKIYOU DAILY NEWS
Corporate/Parent Company: Gannett
Publication Street Address: 924 N. Mount Shasta Blvd
City: Mt. Shasta
State: CA
Publication Website: www.siskiyoudaily.com
Postal Code: 96067
Office phone: (530) 842-5777
Publisher Name: Amy Lanier
Publisher Email: alanier@mtshastanews.com
Editor Name: Skye Kinkade
Editor Email: skinkade@siskiyoudaily.com
Advertising Executive Name: Jim Mullins
Advertising Executive Email: jmullins@siskiyoudaily.com

NAPA

NAPA VALLEY REGISTER
Corporate/Parent Company: Lee Enterprises
Publication Street Address: 1615 Soscol Ave
City: Napa
State: CA
Publication Website: www.napavalleyregister.com
Postal Code: 94559-1901
Office phone: (707) 226-3711
Publisher Name: Davis Taylor
Publisher Email: Davis.Taylor@lee.net
Publisher Phone: 707-256-2234
Editor Name: Sean Scully
Editor Email: sscully@napanews.com
Editor Phone: 707-256-2246
Advertising Executive Name: Norma Kostecka
Advertising Executive Email: NKostecka@napanews.com

PALM SPRINGS

THE DESERT SUN
Corporate/Parent Company: Gannett
Publication Street Address: 750 N Gene Autry Trl
City: Palm Springs
State: CA
Publication Website: www.thedesertsun.com
Postal Code: 92262-5463
Office phone: (760) 322-8889
General E-mail: thedesertsun@gannett.com
Editor Name: Kat Franco
Editor Email: Kate.Franco@DesertSun.com
Editor Phone: (760) 778-4688

PALMDALE

ANTELOPE VALLEY PRESS
Corporate/Parent Company: Sound Publishing
Publication Street Address: 37404 Sierra Hwy
City: Palmdale
State: CA
Publication Website: www.avpress.com
Postal Code: 93550-9343
Office phone: (661) 273-2700
General E-mail: email@avpress.com
Publisher Name: Mike McMullin
Publisher Phone: 661-267-4252
Editor Name: Jennifer A. Garcia
Editor Phone: 661-267-4119

PORTERVILLE

THE PORTERVILLE RECORDER
Corporate/Parent Company: RISN Operations/Glacier Media
Publication Street Address: 115 E Oak Ave
City: Porterville
State: CA
Publication Website: www.portervillerecorder.com
Postal Code: 93257-3807
Office phone: (559) 784-5000
General E-mail: recorder@portervillerecorder.com
Publisher Name: Bill Parsons
Publisher Email: bwilliams@portervillerecorder.com
Publisher Phone: 559-784-5000 Ext.1040
Editor Name: Matt Sarr
Editor Email: bwilliams@portervillerecorder.com
Editor Phone: 559-784-5000 Ext.1048
Advertising Executive Name: Joann Flynn
Advertising Executive Email: aevans@portervillerecorder.com

RED BLUFF

DAILY NEWS
Corporate/Parent Company: Gannett
Publication Street Address: 728 Main St
City: Red Bluff
State: CA
Publication Website: www.redbluffdailynews.com
Postal Code: 96080-3342
Office phone: (530) 527-2151
Editor Name: Chip Thompson
Editor Email: editor@redbluffdailynews.com
Editor Phone: 530-737-5042
Advertising Executive Name: Gayla Eckels
Advertising Executive Email: geckels@redbluffdailynews.com

RED BLUFF DAILY NEWS
Corporate/Parent Company: Media News Group
Publication Street Address: 728 Main Street
City: Red Bluff
State: CA
Publication Website: www.redbluffdailynews.com
Postal Code: 96080
Office phone: 530-737-5059
Editor Name: Chip Thompson
Editor Email: editor@redbluffdailynews.com
Editor Phone: 530-737-5042
Advertising Executive Name: Gayla Eckels
Advertising Executive Email: geckels@redbluffdailynews.com

REDDING

RECORD SEARCHLIGHT
Corporate/Parent Company: Gannett Company Inc.
Publication Street Address: 1101 Twin View Blvd
City: Redding
State: CA
Publication Website: www.redding.com
Postal Code: 96003-1531
Office phone: (530) 225-8250
General E-mail: rrsedit@redding.com
Publisher Name: Steve Smith
Editor Name: Silas Lyons
Editor Email: silas.lyons@redding.com
Editor Phone: 530-225-8210

REDLANDS

REDLANDS DAILY FACTS
Corporate/Parent Company: Media News Group
Publication Street Address: 19 E. Citrus Ave. Suite 102
City: Redlands
State: CA
Publication Website: www.redlandsdailyfacts.com
Postal Code: 92373
Office phone: 909-793-3221
Publisher Name: Ron Hasse
Publisher Email: publisher@scng.com
Publisher Phone: 818-713-3883
Editor Name: Frank Pine
Editor Email: editor@scng.com
Editor Phone: 909-483-9360
Advertising Executive Name: Kyla Rodriguez
Advertising Executive Email: krodriguez@scng.com

U.S. Daily Newspapers

RIDGECREST

THE DAILY INDEPENDENT

Corporate/Parent Company: Gannett
Publication Street Address: 224 E. Ridgecrest Blvd.
City: Ridgecrest
State: CA
Publication Website: www.ridgecrestca.com
Postal Code: 93556-0007
Office phone: (760) 375-4481
Publisher Name: John Watkins
Publisher Email: jwatkins@ridgecrestca.com
Editor Name: Christopher Livingston
Editor Email: clivingston@ridgecrestca.com
Advertising Executive Name: Paula McKay
Advertising Executive Email: pmckay@ridgecrestca.com

RIVERSIDE

THE PRESS-ENTERPRISE

Publication Street Address: 1825 Chicago Ave
City: Riverside
State: CA
Publication Website: www.pe.com
Postal Code: 92507-2373
Office phone: (951) 684-1200
General E-mail: service@scng.com
Publisher Name: Ron Hasse
Publisher Email: publisher@scng.com
Publisher Phone: 818-713-3883
Editor Name: Frank Pine
Editor Email: editor@scng.com
Editor Phone: 909-483-9360
Advertising Executive Name: Kyla Rodriguez
Advertising Executive Email: krodriguez@scng.com

ROMOLAND

INTERCHURCH NEWS

Publication Street Address: P.O. Box 1724
City: Romoland
State: CA
Publication Website: www.interchurchnews.org
Postal Code: 92585
Office phone: 951.357-9953
General E-mail: costlygrace@outlook.com
Editor Name: W. Keith Sloane

SACRAMENTO

THE SACRAMENTO BEE

Corporate/Parent Company: McClatchy Company
Publication Street Address: 2100 Q St
City: Sacramento
State: CA
Publication Website: https://www.sacbee.com/
Postal Code: 95816-6816
Office phone: (916) 321-1000
Publisher Name: Gary Wortel
Editor Name: Lauren Gustus

SAN BERNARDINO

THE SAN BERNARDINO SUN

Corporate/Parent Company: Media News Group
Publication Street Address: 473 E. Carnegie Drive, Suite 250
City: San Bernardino
State: CA
Publication Website: www.sbsun.com
Postal Code: 92408
Office phone: 909-889-9666
Publisher Name: Ron Hasse
Publisher Email: publisher@scng.com
Publisher Phone: 818-713-3883
Editor Name: Frank Pine
Editor Email: editor@scng.com
Editor Phone: 909-483-9360
Advertising Executive Name: Kyla Rodriguez
Advertising Executive Email: krodriguez@scng.com

SAN DIEGO

THE SAN DIEGO UNION-TRIBUNE

Corporate/Parent Company: NantMedia Holdings, LLC
Publication Street Address: 600 B St
City: San Diego
State: CA
Publication Website: www.sandiegouniontribune.com
Postal Code: 92101-4505
Office phone: (619) 293-1211
General E-mail: customer.service@sduniontribune.com
Publisher Name: Jeff Light
Publisher Email: jeff.light@sduniontribune.com
Publisher Phone: (619) 293-1201
Editor Name: Lora Cicalo
Editor Email: lora.cicalo@sduniontribune.com
Editor Phone: (619) 293-1376
Advertising Executive Name: Paul Ingegneri
Advertising Executive Email: paul.ingegneri@sduniontribune.com

SAN FRANCISCO

SAN FRANCISCO CHRONICLE

Corporate/Parent Company: Hearst Communications Inc.
Publication Street Address: 901 Mission St
City: San Francisco
State: CA
Publication Website: www.sfchronicle.com
Postal Code: 94103-3052
Office phone: (415) 777-1111
Publisher Name: Bill Nagel
Editor Name: Audrey Cooper

SLAVIC SACRAMENTO

Publication Street Address: PO Box 16063
City: San Francisco
State: CA
Publication Website: www.slavicsac.com
Postal Code: 95608
Office phone: 916-715-2197
General E-mail: slavicsac@gmail.com
Editor Name: Ruslan Gurzhiy

SAN JOSE

THE MERCURY NEWS

Corporate/Parent Company: Media News Group
Publication Street Address: 4 N 2nd St
City: San Jose
State: CA
Publication Website: www.mercurynews.com
Postal Code: 95113-1317
Office phone: (408) 920-5000
General E-mail: local@bayareanewsgroup.com
Publisher Name: Sharon Ryan
Publisher Email: publisher@bayareanewsgroup.com
Editor Name: Frank Pine
Editor Email: editor@bayareanewsgroup.com
Editor Phone: 408-920-5456

SAN MATEO

SAN MATEO DAILY JOURNAL

Corporate/Parent Company: SMDJ LLC
Publication Street Address: 1720 S. Amphlett Blvd., Suite 123
City: San Mateo
State: CA
Publication Website: www.smdailyjournal.com
Postal Code: 94402
Office phone: (650) 344-5200
General E-mail: news@smdailyjournal.com
Publisher Name: Jerry Lee

SAN RAFAEL

MARIN INDEPENDENT JOURNAL

Corporate/Parent Company: Media News Group
Publication Street Address: 4000 Civic Center Drive; Suite 301
City: San Rafael
State: CA
Publication Website: www.marinij.com
Postal Code: 94903
Office phone: 415-883-8600
General E-mail: localnews@marinij.com
Publisher Name: Rob Devincenzi
Publisher Email: rdevincenzi@marinij.com
Publisher Phone: 415-382-7297
Editor Name: Dave Allen
Editor Email: dallen@marinij.com
Editor Phone: 415-382-7206
Advertising Executive Name: Lori Pearce
Advertising Executive Email: lpearce@marinij.com

SANTA ANA

VOICE OF OC

Publication Street Address: P.O. Box 10020
City: Santa Ana
State: CA
Publication Website: voiceofoc.org
Postal Code: 92711
Office phone: (714) 558-8642
General E-mail: admin@voiceofoc.org
Publisher Name: NORBERTO SANTANA, Jr.
Publisher Email: nsantana@voiceofoc.org
Editor Name: Tracy Wood
Editor Email: twood@voiceofoc.org

SANTA BARBARA

SANTA BARBARA NEWS-PRESS

Corporate/Parent Company: Ampersand Publishing
Publication Street Address: 715 Anacapa St
City: Santa Barbara
State: CA
Publication Website: www.newspress.com
Postal Code: 93101-2203
Office phone: (805) 564-5200
General E-mail: voices@newspress.com
Publisher Name: Wendy McCaw
Publisher Phone: 805-564-5165
Editor Name: Merrill McCarty
Editor Phone: 805-564-5278

SANTA CRUZ

SANTA CRUZ SENTINEL

Corporate/Parent Company: Media News Group
Publication Street Address: 324 Encinal St.
City: Santa Cruz
State: CA
Publication Website: www.santacruzsentinel.com
Postal Code: 95060
Office phone: (831) 423-4242
Publisher Name: Gary Omernick
Publisher Phone: 831-706-3228
Editor Name: Melissa Murphy
Editor Email: mmurphy@santacruzsentinel.com
Editor Phone: 831-429-2448
Advertising Executive Name: Steve Bennett
Advertising Executive Email: sbennett@santacruzsentinel.com

SANTA MARIA

SANTA MARIA TIMES

Corporate/Parent Company: Santa Maria News Media
Publication Street Address: 3200 Skyway Dr
City: Santa Maria
State: CA
Publication Website: www.santamariatimes.com
Postal Code: 93455-1824
Office phone: (805) 925-2691
Publisher Name: Davis Taylor
Publisher Email: publisher@leecentralcoastnews.com
Publisher Phone: (805) 739-2154
Editor Name: Marga Cooley
Editor Email: mcooley@leecentralcoastnews.com
Editor Phone: (805) 739-2143
Advertising Executive Name: Marie Schaefer
Advertising Executive Email: mschaefer@leecentralcoastnews.com

SANTA MONICA

SANTA MONICA DAILY PRESS

Publication Street Address: 1640 5th St Ste 218
City: Santa Monica
State: CA
Publication Website: www.smdp.com
Postal Code: 90401-3325
Office phone: (310) 458-7737
General E-mail: editor@smdp.com
Editor Name: Matthew Hall
Editor Email: matt@smdp.com
Editor Phone: 310-573-8350

SANTA ROSA

THE PRESS DEMOCRAT

Corporate/Parent Company: Sonoma Media Investments, LLC
Publication Street Address: 427 Mendocino Ave
City: Santa Rosa
State: CA
Publication Website: www.pressdemocrat.com
Postal Code: 95401-6313
Office phone: 707-546-2020
General E-mail: allaccess@pressdemocrat.com
Editor Name: Catherine Barnett
Editor Email: catherine.barnett@pressdemocrat.com

SONORA

THE UNION DEMOCRAT

Corporate/Parent Company: Rhode Island Suburban Newspapers
Publication Street Address: 84 S Washington St
City: Sonora
State: CA
Publication Website: www.uniondemocrat.com
Postal Code: 95370-4711
Office phone: (209) 532-7151
General E-mail: webmaster@uniondemocrat.com
Publisher Name: Peggy Pietrowicz
Publisher Email: ppietrowicz@uniondemocrat.com
Editor Name: Lyn Riddle
Editor Email: editor@uniondemocrat.com

STOCKTON

THE RECORD

Corporate/Parent Company: Media News Group
Publication Street Address: 530 E Market St
City: Stockton
State: CA
Publication Website: www.recordnet.com
Postal Code: 95202-3009
Office phone: (209) 943-6397
General E-mail: CustomerService@recordnet.com
Publisher Name: Deitra Kenoly
Publisher Email: dkenoly@recordnet.com
Publisher Phone: (209) 546-8243
Editor Name: Donald W. Blount
Editor Email: dblount@recordnet.com
Editor Phone: (209) 546-8251
Advertising Executive Name: Tammie Dimas
Advertising Executive Email: tdimas@recordnet.com

TEHACHAPI

TEHACHAPI NEWS
Corporate/Parent Company: TBC Media
Publication Street Address: 411 N Mill St
City: Tehachapi
State: CA
Publication Website: www.tehachapinews.com
Postal Code: 93561-1351
Office phone: (661) 822-6828
General E-mail: webmaster@bakersfield.com
Editor Name: Christine Peterson
Editor Email: cpeterson@bakersfield.com
Editor Phone: (661) 395-7418
Advertising Executive Name: Sandra Honea
Advertising Executive Email: shonea@tehachapinews.com

UKIAH

THE UKIAH DAILY JOURNAL
Corporate/Parent Company: Media News Group
Publication Street Address: 617 S State St
City: Ukiah
State: CA
Publication Website: www.ukiahdailyjournal.com
Postal Code: 95482-4912
Office phone: (707) 468-3500
Publisher Name: Kevin McConnell
Publisher Email: udjpublisher@ukiahdj.com
Editor Name: K.C Meadows
Editor Email: udjkcm@ukiahdj.com
Advertising Executive Name: Sarah Delk-Pritchard
Advertising Executive Email: sdelk@record-bee.com

VACAVILLE

THE REPORTER
Corporate/Parent Company: Media News Group
Publication Street Address: 401 Davis Street, Suite F
City: Vacaville
State: CA
Publication Website: www.thereporter.com
Postal Code: 95688-9338
Office phone: (707) 448-6401
Publisher Name: Jim Gleim
Publisher Email: jbungart@timesheraldonline.com
Publisher Phone: (707) 453-8189
Editor Name: Jack Bungart
Editor Email: jbungart@timesheraldonline.com
Editor Phone: (707) 553-6827
Advertising Executive Name: Kelly Spadorcio
Advertising Executive Email: kspadorcio@thereporter.com

VALLEJO

VALLEJO TIMES-HERALD
Publication Street Address: 420 Virginia St
City: Vallejo
State: CA
Publication Website: www.timesheraldonline.com
Postal Code: 94590-6018
Office phone: (707) 644-1141
Publisher Name: Jim Gleim
Publisher Email: jbungart@timesheraldonline.com
Publisher Phone: (707) 453-8189
Editor Name: Jack Bungart
Editor Email: jbungart@timesheraldonline.com
Editor Phone: (707) 553-6827

VICTORVILLE

DAILY PRESS
Corporate/Parent Company: GateHouse Media
Publication Street Address: 13891 Park Ave
City: Victorville
State: CA
Publication Website: www.vvdailypress.com
Postal Code: 92392-2435
Office phone: (760) 241-7744
Editor Name: Scott Nordhues
Editor Email: snordhues@vvdailypress.com
Editor Phone: 760-490-0052
Advertising Executive Name: Steve Nakutin
Advertising Executive Email: snakutin@vvdailypress.com

DESERT DISPATCH
Publication Street Address: 13891 Park Ave
City: Victorville
State: CA
Publication Website: www.desertdispatch.com
Postal Code: 92392-2435
Office phone: (760) 256-2257
Editor Name: Scott Nordhues
Editor Email: snordhues@vvdailypress.com
Editor Phone: 760-490-0052
Advertising Executive Name: Steve Nakutin
Advertising Executive Email: snakutin@vvdailypress.com

VISALIA

TULARE ADVANCE-REGISTER
Publication Street Address: 330 N West St
City: Visalia
State: CA
Publication Website: www.tulareadvanceregister.com
Postal Code: 93291-6010
Office phone: (559) 735-3200
General E-mail: Online@VisaliaTimesDelta.com
Editor Name: Lyons, Silas
Editor Email: sjlyons@gannett.com
Editor Phone: (530) 225-8210
Advertising Executive Name: Dean, Trey
Advertising Executive Email: tdean@gannett.com

VISALIA TIMES-DELTA
Corporate/Parent Company: Gannett Company Inc.
Publication Street Address: 330 N West St
City: Visalia
State: CA
Publication Website: www.visaliatimesdelta.com
Postal Code: 93291-6010
Office phone: (559) 735-3200
General E-mail: Online@VisaliaTimesDelta.com
Editor Name: Lyons, Silas
Editor Email: sjlyons@gannett.com
Editor Phone: (530) 225-8210
Advertising Executive Name: Dean, Trey
Advertising Executive Email: tdean@gannett.com

W HOLLYWOOD

WEHOVILLE
Corporate/Parent Company: WHMC LLC
Publication Street Address: 1138 HACIENDA PL APT 211
City: W HOLLYWOOD
State: CA
Publication Website: www.wehoville.com
Postal Code: 90069
Office phone: (323) 454-7707
General E-mail: press@WEHOville.com
Publisher Name: Henry (Hank) Scott
Publisher Email: henry@WEHOville.com
Advertising Executive Name: Douglas Stichler
Advertising Executive Email: Douglas@wehomediaco.com

WALNUT CREEK

EAST BAY TIMES
Corporate/Parent Company: Media News Group
Publication Street Address: 2850 Shadelands Dr Suite 101
City: Walnut Creek
State: CA
Publication Website: www.eastbaytimes.com
Postal Code: 94598
Office phone: (925) 935-2525
Publisher Name: Sharon Ryan
Publisher Email: publisher@bayareanewsgroup.com
Editor Name: Frank Pine
Editor Email: editor@bayareanewsgroup.com
Editor Phone: 408-920-5456

WATSONVILLE

REGISTER-PAJARONIAN
Corporate/Parent Company: New SV Media, Inc.
Publication Street Address: 21 Brennan St. | Ste: 14
City: Watsonville
State: CA
Publication Website: www.register-pajaronian.com
Postal Code: 95076
Office phone: (831) 761-7300
General E-mail: tnunez@pajaronian.com
Publisher Name: Jeanie Johnson
Publisher Email: jjohnson@pajaronian.com
Publisher Phone: (831) 761-7307
Editor Name: Tony Nunez
Editor Email: tnunez@pajaronian.com
Editor Phone: (831) 761-7353

WOODLAND

THE DAILY DEMOCRAT
Publication Street Address: 711 Main St
City: Woodland
State: CA
Publication Website: www.dailydemocrat.com
Postal Code: 95695-3406
Office phone: (530) 662-5421
Publisher Name: Jim Gleim
Publisher Email: jgleim@bayareanewsgroup.com
Publisher Phone: (707) 453-8189
Editor Name: Jim Smith
Editor Email: news@dailydemocrat.com
Editor Phone: (530) 406-6230
Advertising Executive Name: Marc Hutt
Advertising Executive Email: mhutt@dailydemocrat.com

COLORADO

ALAMOSA

VALLEY COURIER
Corporate/Parent Company: News Media Grouip
Publication Street Address: 2205 State Ave
City: Alamosa
State: CO
Publication Website: www.alamosanews.com
Postal Code: 81101-3559
Office phone: (719) 589-2553

ASPEN

ASPEN DAILY NEWS
Corporate/Parent Company: Silver News, LLC
Publication Street Address: 625 E Main St Unit 204
City: Aspen
State: CO
Publication Website: www.aspendailynews.com
Postal Code: 81611-2154
Office phone: (970) 925-2220
General E-mail: info@aspendailynews.com

THE ASPEN TIMES
Corporate/Parent Company: Swift Communications
Publication Street Address: 314 E Hyman Ave
City: Aspen
State: CO
Publication Website: www.aspentimes.com
Postal Code: 81611-1918
Office phone: (970) 925-3414
General E-mail: mail@aspentimes.com

AVON

VAIL DAILY
Corporate/Parent Company: Swift Communications
Publication Street Address: 40780 US Hwy 6 & 24
City: Avon
State: CO
Publication Website: www.vaildaily.com
Postal Code: 81620
Office phone: (970) 949-0555
General E-mail: digitalsupport@vaildaily.com

BOULDER

COLORADO DAILY
Corporate/Parent Company: Media News Group
Publication Street Address: 2500 55th St
City: Boulder
State: CO
Publication Website: www.coloradodaily.com
Postal Code: 80301
Office phone: (303) 473-1414
General E-mail: editor@coloradodaily.com

DAILY CAMERA
Publication Street Address: 2500 55th St
City: Boulder
State: CO
Publication Website: www.dailycamera.com
Postal Code: 80301-5740
Office phone: (303) 442-1202

CANON CITY

THE CANON CITY DAILY RECORD
Corporate/Parent Company: Digital First Media
Publication Street Address: Sunflower Bank, 831 Royal Gorge Blvd., Suite 325
City: Canon City
State: CO
Publication Website: www.canoncitydailyrecord.com
Postal Code: 81212-3836
Office phone: (719) 275-7565

CANON CITY DAILY RECORD
Publication Street Address: Sunflower Bank, 831 Royal Gorge Blvd., Suite 325
City: Cañon City
State: CO
Publication Website: www.canoncitydailyrecord.com
Postal Code: 81212
Office phone: (719) 275-7565

COLORADO SPRINGS

THE GAZETTE
Corporate/Parent Company: Adams Publishing Group
Publication Street Address: 30 E Pikes Peak Ave
City: Colorado Springs
State: CO

U.S. Daily Newspapers

Publication Website: www.gazette.com
Postal Code: 80903-1504
Office phone: (719) 632-5511
General E-mail: customercare@gazette.com

CRAIG

CRAIG DAILY PRESS

Publication Street Address: 466 Yampa Ave
City: Craig
State: CO
Publication Website: www.craigdailypress.com
Postal Code: 81625-2610
Office phone: (970) 824-7031
General E-mail: editor@craigdailypress.com

DENVER

COLORADO INDEPENDENT

Publication Street Address: P.O. Box 40866
City: Denver
State: CO
Publication Website: coloradoindependent.com
Postal Code: 80204
Office phone: 720-295-8006
General E-mail: tips@coloradoindependent.com

THE DENVER POST

Corporate/Parent Company: Media News Group
Publication Street Address: 5990 Washington St.
City: Denver
State: CO
Publication Website: www.denverpost.com
Postal Code: 80216
Office phone: (303) 954-1010
General E-mail: newsroom@denverpost.com

WESTWORD

Publication Street Address: 969 Broadway PO Box 5970
City: Denver
State: CO
Publication Website: www.westword.com
Postal Code: 80217
Office phone: 303-296-7744
General E-mail: editorial@westword.com

DURANGO

DURANGO HERALD

Corporate/Parent Company: Ballantine Communications, Inc.
Publication Street Address: 1275 Main Ave
City: Durango
State: CO
Publication Website: www.durangoherald.com
Postal Code: 81301-5137
Office phone: (970) 247-3504
General E-mail: herald@durangoherald.com

FORT COLLINS

FORT COLLINS COLORADOAN

Corporate/Parent Company: Gannett Company Inc.
Publication Street Address: 1300 Riverside Ave, Suite 200
City: Fort Collins
State: CO
Publication Website: www.coloradoan.com
Postal Code: 80524
Office phone: 970-493-6397

THE COLORADOAN

Corporate/Parent Company: Gannett
Publication Street Address: 1300 Riverside Ave
City: Fort Collins
State: CO
Publication Website: www.coloradoan.com
Postal Code: 80524-4353
Office phone: (970) 493-6397

FORT MORGAN

FORT MORGAN TIMES

Corporate/Parent Company: Media News Group
Publication Street Address: 230A Main Street
City: Fort Morgan
State: CO
Publication Website: www.fortmorgantimes.com
Postal Code: 80701-2108
Office phone: (970) 867-5651

FRISCO

SUMMIT DAILY NEWS

Corporate/Parent Company: Swift Communications
Publication Street Address: 331 W Main St
City: Frisco
State: CO
Publication Website: www.summitdaily.com
Postal Code: 80443
Office phone: (970) 668-3998
General E-mail: digitalsupport@summitdaily.com

GLENWOOD SPRINGS

GLENWOOD SPRINGS POST INDEPENDENT

Corporate/Parent Company: Swift Communications
Publication Street Address: 824 Grand Ave
City: Glenwood Springs
State: CO
Publication Website: www.postindependent.com
Postal Code: 81601-3557
Office phone: (970) 945-8515

GRAND JUNCTION

GRAND JUNCTION DAILY SENTINEL

Corporate/Parent Company: Cox
Publication Street Address: 734 S. 7th St.
City: Grand Junction
State: CO
Publication Website: www.gjsentinel.com
Postal Code: 81501
Office phone: 970-242-5050
General E-mail: webmaster@gjsentinel.com

THE DAILY SENTINEL

Corporate/Parent Company: Cox
Publication Street Address: 734 S 7th St
City: Grand Junction
State: CO
Publication Website: www.gjsentinel.com
Postal Code: 81501-7737
Office phone: (970) 242-5050
General E-mail: webmaster@gjsentinel.com

GREELEY

GREELEY DAILY TRIBUNE

Publication Street Address: 501 8th Ave
City: Greeley
State: CO
Publication Website: www.greeleytribune.com
Postal Code: 80631-3913
Office phone: (970) 352-0211
General E-mail: digitalsupport@greeleytribune.com

LA JUNTA

FOWLER TRIBUNE

Corporate/Parent Company: Gannett
Publication Street Address: 422 Colorado Avenue
City: La Junta
State: CO
Publication Website: www.fowlertribune.com
Postal Code: 81050
Office phone: (719) 384-4475

LA JUNTA TRIBUNE-DEMOCRAT

Publication Street Address: 422 Colorado Ave
City: La Junta
State: CO
Publication Website: www.lajuntatribunedemocrat.com
Postal Code: 81050-2336
Office phone: (719) 384-4475

LONGMONT

LONGMONT TIMES-CALL

Corporate/Parent Company: Media News Group
Publication Street Address: P.O. Box 299
City: Longmont
State: CO
Publication Website: www.timescall.com
Postal Code: 80501
Office phone: (970) 776-2244
General E-mail: opinion@times-call.com

LOVELAND

LOVELAND REPORTER-HERALD

Corporate/Parent Company: Media News Group
Publication Street Address: P.O. Box 59,
City: Loveland
State: CO
Publication Website: www.reporterherald.com
Postal Code: 80539
Office phone: (970) 669-5050

MONTROSE

MONTROSE DAILY PRESS

Corporate/Parent Company: Wick Communications
Publication Street Address: 3684 N. Townsend
City: Montrose
State: CO
Publication Website: www.montrosepress.com
Postal Code: 81401
Office phone: 970-249-3444

THE MONTROSE DAILY PRESS

Corporate/Parent Company: Wick Communications
Publication Street Address: 3684 N Townsend Ave
City: Montrose
State: CO
Publication Website: www.montrosepress.com
Postal Code: 81401-5949
Office phone: (970) 249-3444

PUEBLO

THE PUEBLO CHIEFTAIN

Corporate/Parent Company: Gannett
Publication Street Address: 825 W 6th St
City: Pueblo
State: CO
Publication Website: www.chieftain.com
Postal Code: 81003-2313
Office phone: (719) 544-3520

SALIDA

THE MOUNTAIN MAIL

Publication Street Address: 125 E 2nd St
City: Salida
State: CO
Publication Website: www.themountainmail.com
Postal Code: 81201-2114
Office phone: (719) 539-6691
General E-mail: mmweb@themountainmail.com

STEAMBOAT SPRINGS

STEAMBOAT TODAY

Publication Street Address: 32 10th St., Suite C1-C
City: Steamboat Springs
State: CO
Publication Website: www.steamboattoday.com
Postal Code: 80487-4912
Office phone: (970) 879-1502
General E-mail: news@SteamboatPilot.com

STERLING

JOURNAL-ADVOCATE

Corporate/Parent Company: Digital First Media
Publication Street Address: 100 Broadway St., Ste. 25
City: Sterling
State: CO
Publication Website: www.journal-advocate.com
Postal Code: 80751
Office phone: (970) 522-1990
General E-mail: swaite@journal-advocate.com

TELLURIDE

TELLURIDE DAILY PLANET; THE WATCH; THE NORWOOD POST

Corporate/Parent Company: Telluride Newspapers
Publication Street Address: PO Box 2315
City: Telluride
State: CO
Publication Website: www.telluridenews.com
Postal Code: 81435
Office phone: (970) 728-9788
General E-mail: publisher@telluridenews.com

TRINIDAD

THE CHRONICLE-NEWS

Corporate/Parent Company: Chronicle-News Media Group
Publication Street Address: 313 West Main Street
City: Trinidad
State: CO
Publication Website: www.thechronicle-news.com
Postal Code: 81082-2603
Office phone: (719) 846-3311
General E-mail: editor@trinidadchroniclenews.com

TRINIDAD CHRONICLE-NEWS

Publication Street Address: 313 West Main Street
City: Trinidad
State: CO
Publication Website: www.thechronicle-news.com
Postal Code: 81082

CONNECTICUT

BRISTOL

THE BRISTOL PRESS

Corporate/Parent Company: Central Connecticut Communications LLC
Publication Street Address: 188 Main St
City: Bristol
State: CT
Publication Website: www.bristolpress.com
Postal Code: 06010-6308
Office phone: (860) 584-0501
General E-mail: editor@bristolpress.com
Publisher Name: Michael E. Schroeder
Publisher Phone: (860) 801-5099
Editor Name: James Drzewiecki
Editor Phone: (860) 973-1804
Advertising Executive Name: Ben Scoville
Advertising Executive Phone: (860) 973-1813
Year Established: 1871
Own Printing Facility?: N
Commercial printers?: N
Mechanical specifications: Tabloid format. Image area 9.675" x 10.75" 5 column.
Published Days: Mon`Tues`Wed`Thur`Fri`Sat
Weekday Frequency: m
Saturday Frequency: m
Avg Paid Circ: 4019
Avg Free Circ: 496
Audit Company: AAM
Audit Date: 30 09 2015

HARTFORD

THE HARTFORD COURANT

Corporate/Parent Company: Tribune Publishing Company
Publication Street Address: 285 Broad St
City: Hartford
State: CT
Publication Website: www.courant.com
Postal Code: 06105-3785
Office phone: (860) 241-6200
Publisher Name: Andrew Julien
Publisher Email: ajulien@courant.com
Editor Name: Andrew Julien
Editor Email: ajulien@courant.com
Advertising Executive Name: Mary Lou Stoneburner
Advertising Executive Email: mstoneburner@courant.com
Advertising Executive Phone: 860-241-6241
Year Established: 1764
Delivery Methods:
    Mail`Newsstand`Carrier`Racks
Own Printing Facility?: Y
Commercial printers?: Y
Mechanical specifications: Type page 10 x 21; E - 6 cols, 1.525" , 1/8 between; A - 6 cols, 1.525" , 1/8 between; C -6 cols, 1.525", 1/8 between.
Published Days: Mon`Tues`Wed`Thur`Fri`Sat`Sun
Weekday Frequency: m
Saturday Frequency: m
Avg Paid Circ: 84023
Audit Company: AAM
Audit Date: 3 12 2019

MANCHESTER

JOURNAL INQUIRER

Corporate/Parent Company: Journal Inquirer Publishing Company
Publication Street Address: 306 Progress Dr
City: Manchester
State: CT
Publication Website: www.journalinquirer.com
Postal Code: 06042-9011
Office phone: 800-237-3606

General E-mail: service@journalinquirer.com
Editor Name: Kimberly Phillips
Editor Email: kphillips@journalinquirer.com
Year Established: 1968
Delivery Methods:
    Mail`Newsstand`Carrier`Racks
Own Printing Facility?: N
Commercial printers?: N
Mechanical specifications: Type page 10 1/2 x 11.5; E - 5 cols, 2, 1/6 between; A - 5 cols, 2, 1/6 between; C - 8 cols, 1 1/3, 1/6 between.
Published Days: Mon`Tues`Wed`Thur`Fri`Sat
Weekday Frequency: e
Saturday Frequency: m
Avg Paid Circ: 19418
Avg Free Circ: 2428
Audit Company: AAM
Audit Date: 31 03 2019

MANCHESTER

JOURNAL INQUIRER

Corporate/Parent Company: Journal Inquirer Publishing Company
Publication Street Address: 306 Progress Dr
City: Manchester
State: CT
Publication Website: www.journalinquirer.com
Postal Code: 06042-9011
Office phone: 800-237-3606
General E-mail: service@journalinquirer.com
Editor Name: Kimberly Phillips
Editor Email: kphillips@journalinquirer.com
Year Established: 1968
Delivery Methods:
    Mail`Newsstand`Carrier`Racks
Own Printing Facility?: N
Commercial printers?: N
Mechanical specifications: Type page 10 1/2 x 11.5; E - 5 cols, 2, 1/6 between; A - 5 cols, 2, 1/6 between; C - 8 cols, 1 1/3, 1/6 between.
Published Days: Mon`Tues`Wed`Thur`Fri`Sat
Weekday Frequency: e
Saturday Frequency: m
Avg Paid Circ: 19418
Avg Free Circ: 2428
Audit Company: AAM
Audit Date: 31 03 2019

MERIDEN

RECORD-JOURNAL

Corporate/Parent Company: The Record-Journal Publishing Co.
Publication Street Address: 500 S Broad St
City: Meriden
State: CT
Publication Website: www.myrecordjournal.com
Postal Code: 06450-6643
Office phone: (203) 235-1661
General E-mail: newsroom@record-journal.com
Publisher Name: Liz White Notarangelo
Publisher Email: lwhite@record-journal.com
Publisher Phone: 203-317-2226
Editor Name: Ralph Tomaselli
Editor Email: rtomaselli@record-journal.com
Editor Phone: 203-317-2220
Advertising Executive Name: Jim Mizener
Advertising Executive Email: jmizener@record-journal.com
Advertising Executive Phone: 203-317-2312
Year Established: 1867
Delivery Methods:
    Mail`Newsstand`Carrier`Racks
Own Printing Facility?: Y
Published Days: Mon`Tues`Wed`Thur`Fri`Sat`Sun
Weekday Frequency: m
Saturday Frequency: m
Audit Company: VAC
Audit Date: 31 12 2015

NEW BRITAIN

NEW BRITAIN HERALD

Corporate/Parent Company: Central Connecticut Communications LLC
Publication Street Address: One Liberty Square
City: New Britain
State: CT
Publication Website: www.newbritainherald.com
Postal Code: 6050
Office phone: (860) 225-4601
General E-mail: editor@centralctcommunications.com
Publisher Name: Michael E. Schroeder
Publisher Phone: (860) 801-5099
Editor Name: Bradford Carroll
Editor Phone: (860) 801-5071
Advertising Executive Name: Gary Curran
Advertising Executive Phone: (860) 801-5073
Year Established: 1880
Mechanical specifications: Type page 12 x 21 1/2; E - 6 cols, 1 5/6, 1/6 between; A - 6 cols, 1 5/6, 1/6 between; C - 10 cols, 1 1/4, 1/16 between.
Published Days: Mon`Tues`Wed`Thur`Fri`Sat`Sun
Weekday Frequency: m
Saturday Frequency: m
Avg Paid Circ: 4054
Avg Free Circ: 621
Audit Company: AAM
Audit Date: 31 03 2015

NEW BRITAIN HERALD

Corporate/Parent Company: Central Connecticut Communications LLC
Publication Street Address: One Liberty Square
City: New Britain
State: CT
Publication Website: www.newbritainherald.com
Postal Code: 6050
Office phone: (860) 225-4601
General E-mail: editor@centralctcommunications.com
Publisher Name: Michael E. Schroeder
Publisher Phone: (860) 801-5099
Editor Name: Bradford Carroll
Editor Phone: (860) 801-5071
Advertising Executive Name: Gary Curran
Advertising Executive Phone: (860) 801-5073
Year Established: 1880
Mechanical specifications: Type page 12 x 21 1/2; E - 6 cols, 1 5/6, 1/6 between; A - 6 cols, 1 5/6, 1/6 between; C - 10 cols, 1 1/4, 1/16 between.
Published Days: Mon`Tues`Wed`Thur`Fri`Sat`Sun
Weekday Frequency: m
Saturday Frequency: m
Avg Paid Circ: 4054
Avg Free Circ: 621
Audit Company: AAM
Audit Date: 31 03 2015

NEW HAVEN

NEW HAVEN REGISTER

Corporate/Parent Company: Hearst Communications Inc.
Publication Street Address: 100 Gando Dr
City: New Haven
State: CT
Publication Website: www.nhregister.com
Postal Code: 06513-1049
Office phone: (203) 789-5200
General E-mail: localnews@nhregister.com
Editor Name: Helen Bennett Harvey
Editor Email: helen.bennett@hearstmediact.com
Editor Phone: 203-789-5730
Year Established: 1812
Delivery Methods:
    Mail`Newsstand`Carrier`Racks
Mechanical specifications: Type page 12 x 21; E - 6 cols, 1 7/8, 1/8 between; A - 6 cols, 1 7/8, 1/8 between; C - 10 cols, 1 1/4, 1/16 between.
Published Days: Mon`Tues`Wed`Thur`Fri`Sat`Sun
Weekday Frequency: m
Saturday Frequency: m
Avg Paid Circ: 25794
Audit Company: AAM
Audit Date: 8 01 2020

NEW HAVEN REGISTER

Corporate/Parent Company: Hearst Communications Inc.
Publication Street Address: 100 Gando Dr
City: New Haven
State: CT
Publication Website: www.nhregister.com
Postal Code: 06513-1049
Office phone: (203) 789-5200
General E-mail: localnews@nhregister.com
Editor Name: Helen Bennett Harvey
Editor Email: helen.bennett@hearstmediact.com
Editor Phone: 203-789-5730
Year Established: 1812
Delivery Methods:
    Mail`Newsstand`Carrier`Racks
Mechanical specifications: Type page 12 x 21; E - 6 cols, 1 7/8, 1/8 between; A - 6 cols, 1 7/8, 1/8 between; C - 10 cols, 1 1/4, 1/16 between.
Published Days: Mon`Tues`Wed`Thur`Fri`Sat`Sun
Weekday Frequency: m
Saturday Frequency: m
Avg Paid Circ: 25794
Audit Company: AAM
Audit Date: 8 01 2020

THE MIDDLETOWN PRESS

Corporate/Parent Company: Hearst Corp.
Publication Street Address: 100 Gando Drive
City: New Haven
State: CT
Publication Website: www.middletownpress.com
Postal Code: 6513
Office phone: (860) 347-3331
General E-mail: letters@middletownpress.com
Editor Name: Cassandra Day
Editor Email: Cassandra.Day@hearstmediact.com
Editor Phone: 860-685-9125
Year Established: 1884
Mechanical specifications: Type page 13 x 22 1/2; E - 6 cols, 1 7/8, 1/8 between; A - 6 cols, 1 7/8, 1/8 between; C - 9 cols, 1 3/8, 3/16 between.
Published Days: Mon`Tues`Wed`Thur`Fri`Sat
Weekday Frequency: m
Saturday Frequency: m
Avg Paid Circ: 6114
Audit Company: Sworn/Estimate/Non-Audited
Audit Date: 7 12 2019

THE REGISTER CITIZEN

Corporate/Parent Company: Hearst Corp.
Publication Street Address: 100 Gando Drive
City: New Haven
State: CT
Publication Website: www.registercitizen.com
Postal Code: 06790-4942
Office phone: (860) 489-3121
General E-mail: editor@registercitizen.com
Editor Name: Helen Bennett
Editor Email: helen.bennett@hearstmediact.com
Editor Phone: 203-789-5730
Year Established: 1874
Delivery Methods:
    Mail`Newsstand`Carrier`Racks
Mechanical specifications: Type page 13 x 21 1/4; E - 6 cols, 1 7/8, 1/8 between; A - 6 cols, 1 7/8, 1/8 between; C - 9 cols, 1 3/8, 1/16 between.
Published Days: Mon`Tues`Wed`Thur`Fri`Sat`Sun
Weekday Frequency: m
Saturday Frequency: m
Avg Paid Circ: 2069
Audit Company: AAM
Audit Date: 30 09 2015

U.S. Daily Newspapers

NEW LONDON

THE DAY
Corporate/Parent Company: The Day
Publication Street Address: 47 Eugene Oneill Dr
City: New London
State: CT
Publication Website: www.theday.com
Postal Code: 06320-6306
Office phone: (860) 442-2200
Publisher Name: Tim Dwyer
Publisher Email: t.dwyer@theday.com
Publisher Phone: (860) 701-4379
Editor Name: Cotter, Tim
Editor Email: t.cotter@theday.com
Editor Phone: (860) 701-4372
Advertising Executive Name: Keefe, Jennifer
Advertising Executive Email: j.keefe@theday.com
Advertising Executive Phone: 860-701-4240
Year Established: 1881
Delivery Methods: Newsstand`Carrier`Racks
Own Printing Facility?: Y
Commercial printers?: Y
Mechanical specifications: Type page 12 1/4 x 21; E - 6 cols, 2 1/16, 1/8 between; A - 6 cols, 2 1/16, 1/8 between; C - 10 cols, 1 7/32, 1/16 between.
Published Days: Mon`Tues`Wed`Thur`Fri`Sat`Sun
Weekday Frequency: m
Saturday Frequency: m
Avg Paid Circ: 22471
Audit Company: AAM
Audit Date: 6 09 2018

NORWALK

CONNECTICUT POST
Corporate/Parent Company: Hearst Communications Inc.
Publication Street Address: 301 Merritt 7
City: Norwalk
State: CT
Publication Website: www.ctpost.com
Postal Code: 6851
Office phone: 203-842-2500
General E-mail: newsroom@record-journal.com
Editor Name: Keila Torres
Editor Email: ktorres@scni.com
Editor Phone: 203-330-6223
Year Established: 1883
Mechanical specifications: Type page 11 5/8 x 20 1/4; E - 6 cols, 1 5/6, 1/8 between; A - 6 cols, 1 5/6, 1/8 between; C - 10 cols, 1 2/25, 1/16 between.
Published Days: Mon`Tues`Wed`Thur`Fri`Sat`Sun
Weekday Frequency: m
Saturday Frequency: m
Avg Paid Circ: 25917
Audit Company: AAM
Audit Date: 6 01 2020

GREENWICH TIME
Corporate/Parent Company: Hearst Corp.
Publication Street Address: 301 Merritt 7 - Suite 1
City: Norwalk
State: CT
Publication Website: www.greenwichtime.com
Postal Code: 06851-1075
Office phone: 203-842-2500
General E-mail: circulation@scni.com
Editor Name: Thomas Mellana
Editor Email: tmellana@greenwichtime.com
Year Established: 1877
Delivery Methods:
  Mail`Newsstand`Carrier`Racks
Own Printing Facility?: N
Commercial printers?: N
Mechanical specifications: Type page 12 x 21 1/2; E - 6 cols, 1 7/8, 1/6 between; A - 6 cols, 1 7/8, 1/6 between; C - 10 cols, 1 7/8, 1/6 between.
Published Days: Mon`Tues`Wed`Thur`Fri`Sat`Sun
Weekday Frequency: m
Saturday Frequency: m
Avg Paid Circ: 3199

Avg Free Circ: 58
Audit Company: AAM
Audit Date: 31 03 2019

THE ADVOCATE
Corporate/Parent Company: Hearst Corp.
Publication Street Address: 301 Merritt 7 - Suite 1
City: Norwalk
State: CT
Publication Website: www.stamfordadvocate.com
Postal Code: 06851-1075
Office phone: 203-842-2500
General E-mail: circulation@scni.com
Editor Name: Thomas Mellana
Editor Email: tmellana@greenwichtime.com
Year Established: 1829
Mechanical specifications: Type page 11 5/8 x 21 1/2; E - 6 cols, 1 7/8, 1/6 between; A - 6 cols, 1 7/8, 1/6 between; C - 10 cols, 1 1/8, 1/6 between.
Published Days: Mon`Tues`Wed`Thur`Fri`Sat`Sun
Weekday Frequency: m
Saturday Frequency: m
Avg Paid Circ: 8597
Audit Company: AAM
Audit Date: 30 09 2015

THE HOUR
Corporate/Parent Company: Hearst Corp.
Publication Street Address: 301 Merritt 7
City: Norwalk
State: CT
Publication Website: www.thehour.com
Postal Code: 6851
Office phone: 203-842-2500
Editor Name: Mike Pignataro
Editor Email: mpignataro@stamfordadvocate.com
Editor Phone: 203-842-2538
Year Established: 1995
Delivery Methods: Mail`Newsstand`Carrier
Own Printing Facility?: Y
Commercial printers?: N
Mechanical specifications: Type page 13 x 21 1/4; E - 6 cols, between; A - 6 cols, between; C - 10 cols, between.
Published Days: Thur
Avg Paid Circ: 800
Avg Free Circ: 5000
Audit Company: Sworn/Estimate/Non-Audited
Audit Date: 6 10 2019

THE NEWS-TIMES
Corporate/Parent Company: Hearst Communications Inc.
Publication Street Address: 301 Merritt 7
City: Norwalk
State: CT
Publication Website: www.newstimes.com
Postal Code: 6851
Office phone: 203-842-2500
Editor Name: John Alcott
Editor Email: jalcott@ctpost.com
Editor Phone: 203-731-3361
Year Established: 1883
Delivery Methods: Newsstand`Carrier`Racks
Own Printing Facility?: Y
Commercial printers?: Y
Mechanical specifications: Type page 13 x 21; E - 6 cols, 2 1/16, 1/8 between; A - 6 cols, 2 1/16, 1/8 between; C - 9 cols, 1 3/8, 1/16 between.
Published Days: Mon`Tues`Wed`Thur`Fri`Sat`Sun
Weekday Frequency: m
Saturday Frequency: m
Avg Paid Circ: 9440
Audit Company: AAM
Audit Date: 6 01 2020

NORWICH

THE BULLETIN
Corporate/Parent Company: Gannett
Publication Street Address: 10 Railroad Place
City: Norwich
State: CT
Publication Website: www.norwichbulletin.com
Postal Code: 06360-5829
Office phone: (860) 887-9211
General E-mail: customerservice@norwichbulletin.com
Editor Name: Jim Konrad
Editor Email: jkonrad@norwichbulletin.com
Editor Phone: (860) 425-4201
Advertising Executive Name: Louvenia Brandt
Advertising Executive Email: lbrandt@norwichbulletin.com
Advertising Executive Phone: (860) 425-4329
Year Established: 1791
Delivery Methods:
  Mail`Newsstand`Carrier`Racks
Own Printing Facility?: Y
Commercial printers?: N
Mechanical specifications: Type page 11 5/8 x 21 1/2; E - 6 cols, 1 5/6, 1/8 between; A - 6 cols, 1 5/6, 1/8 between; C - 10 cols, 1 1/25, 1/12 between.
Published Days: Mon`Tues`Wed`Thur`Fri`Sat`Sun
Weekday Frequency: m
Saturday Frequency: m
Avg Paid Circ: 9087
Avg Free Circ: 93
Audit Company: AAM
Audit Date: 12 12 2018

PAWCATUCK

THE WESTERLY SUN
Corporate/Parent Company: Sun Publishing Company
Publication Street Address: 99 Mechanic St
City: Pawcatuck
State: CT
Publication Website: www.thewesterlysun.com
Postal Code: 06379-2187
Office phone: (401) 348-1000
General E-mail: news@thewesterlysun.com
Publisher Name: Jody Boucher
Publisher Email: jboucher@ricentral.com
Publisher Phone: 860-495-8277
Editor Name: Corey Fyke
Editor Email: cfyke@thewesterlysun.com
Editor Phone: 860-495-8248
Advertising Executive Name: Kathy Enders
Advertising Executive Email: kenders@thewesterlysun.com
Advertising Executive Phone: 860-495-8274
Year Established: 1856
Delivery Methods:
  Mail`Newsstand`Carrier`Racks
Own Printing Facility?: N
Commercial printers?: N
Mechanical specifications: Type page 11 5/8 x 21 1/2; E - 6 cols, 1 13/16, 1/8 between; A - 6 cols, 1 13/16, 1/8 between; C - 8 cols, 1 3/8, 1/8 between.
Published Days: Mon`Tues`Wed`Thur`Fri`Sat`Sun
Weekday Frequency: m
Saturday Frequency: m
Avg Paid Circ: 6003
Avg Free Circ: 28
Audit Company: CAC
Audit Date: 30 09 2015

THE WESTERLY SUN OF WESTERLY
Corporate/Parent Company: The Sun Media Group
Publication Street Address: 99 Mechanic Street
City: Pawcatuck
State: CT
Publication Website: www.thewesterlysun.com
Postal Code: 0 6379
Office phone: 401-348-1000

General E-mail: news@thewesterlysun.com
Publisher Name: Jody Boucher
Publisher Email: jboucher@ricentral.com
Publisher Phone: 860-495-8277
Editor Name: Corey Fyke
Editor Email: cfyke@thewesterlysun.com
Editor Phone: 860-495-8248
Advertising Executive Name: Kathy Enders
Advertising Executive Email: kenders@thewesterlysun.com
Advertising Executive Phone: 860-495-8274

WATERBURY

REPUBLICAN-AMERICAN
Corporate/Parent Company: American-Republican, Incorporated
Publication Street Address: 389 Meadow St
City: Waterbury
State: CT
Publication Website: www.rep-am.com
Postal Code: 06702-1808
Office phone: (203) 574-3636
General E-mail: webadmin@rep-am.com
Publisher Name: Linda Ploski
Publisher Email: lploski@rep-am.com
Publisher Phone: (203) 574-3636 ext.1651
Editor Name: Anne Karolyi
Editor Email: akarolyi@rep-am.com
Editor Phone: (203) 574-3636 ext.1492
Year Established: 1844
Delivery Methods:
  Mail`Newsstand`Carrier`Racks
Own Printing Facility?: Y
Commercial printers?: Y
Mechanical specifications: Full page 10 7/8 x 20, 6 cols Double truck 22-5/8 x 20, 13 cols Tabloid 9 x 10-1/2, 5 cols Tabloid Double Truck 19-1/2 x 10-1/2, 11 cols Column inch widths: 1col -15/8â€, 2col 3-1/2â€, 3col 5-11/32â€, 4col 7-3/16, 5 col 9â€, 6col 10-7/8â€.
Published Days: Mon`Tues`Wed`Thur`Fri`Sat`Sun
Weekday Frequency: m
Saturday Frequency: m
Avg Paid Circ: 33228
Avg Free Circ: 1661
Audit Company: AAM
Audit Date: 30 09 2016

REPUBLICAN-AMERICAN
Corporate/Parent Company: American-Republican, Incorporated
Publication Street Address: 389 Meadow St
City: Waterbury
State: CT
Publication Website: www.rep-am.com
Postal Code: 06702-1808
Office phone: (203) 574-3636
General E-mail: webadmin@rep-am.com
Publisher Name: Linda Ploski
Publisher Email: lploski@rep-am.com
Publisher Phone: (203) 574-3636 ext.1651
Editor Name: Anne Karolyi
Editor Email: akarolyi@rep-am.com
Editor Phone: (203) 574-3636 ext.1492
Year Established: 1844
Delivery Methods:
  Mail`Newsstand`Carrier`Racks
Own Printing Facility?: Y
Commercial printers?: Y
Mechanical specifications: Full page 10 7/8 x 20, 6 cols Double truck 22-5/8 x 20, 13 cols Tabloid 9 x 10-1/2, 5 cols Tabloid Double Truck 19-1/2 x 10-1/2, 11 cols Column inch widths: 1col -15/8â€, 2col 3-1/2â€, 3col 5-11/32â€, 4col 7-3/16, 5 col 9â€, 6col 10-7/8â€.
Published Days: Mon`Tues`Wed`Thur`Fri`Sat`Sun
Weekday Frequency: m
Saturday Frequency: m
Avg Paid Circ: 33228
Avg Free Circ: 1661
Audit Company: AAM
Audit Date: 30 09 2016

WILLIMANTIC

THE CHRONICLE

Corporate/Parent Company: Gannett
Publication Street Address: 322 Main Street, Unit 1-1B P.O. Box 229
City: Willimantic
State: CT
Publication Website: www.thechronicle.com
Postal Code: 06226-1932
Office phone: (860) 423-8466
Publisher Name: Michael Schroeder
Publisher Email: mschroeder@thechronicle.com
Editor Name: Michael Lemanski
Editor Email: news@thechronicle.com
Advertising Executive Name: Marilyn Antignani
Advertising Executive Email: marilyna@thechronicle.com
Year Established: 1877
Delivery Methods: Mail`Newsstand`Carrier`Racks
Own Printing Facility?: Y
Commercial printers?: Y
Mechanical specifications: Type page 13 x 21 1/2; E - 6 cols, 2 1/16, 1/8 between; A - 6 cols, 2 1/16, 1/8 between; C - 9 cols, 1 9/16, 1/16 between.
Published Days: Mon`Tues`Wed`Thur`Fri`Sat
Weekday Frequency: e
Saturday Frequency: m
Avg Paid Circ: 4561
Avg Free Circ: 664
Audit Company: CAC
Audit Date: 31 12 2016

DELAWARE

NEW CASTLE / WILMINGTON

THE NEWS JOURNAL

Corporate/Parent Company: Gannett
Publication Street Address: 950 W Basin Rd
City: New Castle / Wilmington
State: DE
Publication Website: www.delawareonline.com
Postal Code: 19720-1008
Office phone: 302-324-2679
General E-mail: newsdesk@delawareonline.com
Editor Name: Mike Feeley
Editor Email: mfeeley@delawareonline.com
Year Established: 1919
Delivery Methods: Mail`Newsstand
Own Printing Facility?: Y
Mechanical specifications: Type page 13 1/8 x 21 1/4; E - 6 cols, 2 1/16, 1/8 between; A - 6 cols, 2 1/16, 1/8 between; C - 10 cols, 1 1/4, 1/16 between.
Published Days: Mon`Tues`Wed`Thur`Fri`Sat`Sun
Weekday Frequency: m
Saturday Frequency: m
Avg Paid Circ: 64711
Audit Company: AAM
Audit Date: 31 12 2015
Pressroom Equipment: Lines – 8-G/Headliner Offset 1989, 1-G/Metrocolor Tower 1994; 8-G/Headliner Offset 1989, 1-G/Metro color tower 1994; Pasters –16-G/RTP CT50; Reels & Stands – Press Registration System ÃƒÂ‚Â£ 2-G/Quadtech.;
Mailroom Equipment: Counter Stackers – 3-HL/Monitor, 13/QWI; Inserters & Stuffers – 1-GE/1372, 2-HI/1472; Tying Machines – 8-/Power Strap; Wrapping Singles – 5-/Power Strap 3/4 wrap; Address Machine – 2-/Barstrom, 3-/Barstrom;
Buisness Equipment: IBM/AS-400
Buisness Software: Genesys :Circ, Adv, Lawson :Fin, Cyborg :Payroll
Classified Equipment: Hardware – IBM/Server, 35-PC;
Classified Software: Unisys 3.0.
Editorial Equipment: Hardware – IBM/Server, APP/Mac, PC/1-Colormaster/Plus, IBM, MS/NT Advanced Server, GMTI/Digital Archive; Printers – ECR/3850, ECR/Wildcat XL180 DTP
Editorial Software: QPS 2.0.10.
Production Equipment: Hardware – W/Optical Plate Bender, KFM, ECR/Wildcat XL 180, Barco; Scanners – 2-Kk/2035 Pro, Umax/1200
Production Software: QPS 2.0.10.
Total Circulation: 64711

FLORIDA

BRADENTON

BRADENTON HERALD

Corporate/Parent Company: McClatchy Company
Publication Street Address: 1111 3rd Ave W
City: Bradenton
State: FL
Publication Website: www.bradenton.com
Postal Code: 34205-7834
Office phone: (941) 748-0411
Editor Name: Marc R. Masferrer
Editor Email: mmasferrer@bradenton.com
Editor Phone: 941-745-7050
Year Established: 1922
Delivery Methods: Newsstand`Carrier
Own Printing Facility?: N
Commercial printers?: N
Mechanical specifications: Page size 11" x 21", print area 10" x 20"
Published Days: Mon`Tues`Wed`Thur`Fri`Sat`Sun
Weekday Frequency: m
Saturday Frequency: m
Avg Paid Circ: 20615
Audit Company: AAM
Audit Date: 19 03 2020
Buisness Equipment: HP4000 & Dell servers
Buisness Software: AIM Peoplesoft Kronos
Classified Equipment: HP & Dell servers
Classified Software: ATS Classified Systems
Editorial Equipment: HP & Dell
Editorial Software: Saxotech
Production Equipment: Mac & PC workstations
Production Software: Xpance, ALS, CLS (Managing Editor)
Total Circulation: 22781

CHARLOTTE HARBOR

CHARLOTTE SUN

Corporate/Parent Company: Adams Publishing Group
Publication Street Address: 23170 Harborview Road
City: Charlotte Harbor
State: FL
Publication Website: www.yoursun.com
Postal Code: 33980
Office phone: (941) 206-1000
Publisher Name: Glen Nickerson
Publisher Email: glen.nickerson@yoursun.com
Publisher Phone: (941) 207-1010
Editor Name: Garry Overbey
Editor Email: garry.overbey@yoursun.com
Editor Phone: (941) 206-1143
Advertising Executive Name: Omar Zucco
Advertising Executive Email: omar.zucco@yoursun.com
Advertising Executive Phone: (941) 205-6402

CRYSTAL RIVER

CITRUS COUNTY CHRONICLE

Corporate/Parent Company: Landmark Community Newspapers
Publication Street Address: 1624 N Meadowcrest Blvd
City: Crystal River
State: FL
Publication Website: www.chronicleonline.com
Postal Code: 34429-5760
Office phone: (352) 563-6363
General E-mail: webadmin@chronicleonline.com
Publisher Name: Gerry Mulligan
Publisher Email: gmulligan@chronicleonline.com
Publisher Phone: 352-563-3222
Editor Name: Mike Arnold
Editor Email: marnold@chronicleonline.com
Editor Phone: 352-564-2930
Advertising Executive Name: Trina Murphy
Advertising Executive Email: tmurphy@chronicleonline.com
Advertising Executive Phone: 352-563-3232
Year Established: 1890
Delivery Methods: Mail`Newsstand`Carrier`Racks
Own Printing Facility?: Y
Commercial printers?: Y
Mechanical specifications: Type page 13 x 21 1/2; E - 6 cols, 2 1/16, 1/8 between; A - 6 cols, 2 1/16, 1/8 between; C - 10 cols, 1 1/8, 1/8 between.
Published Days: Mon`Tues`Wed`Thur`Fri`Sat`Sun
Weekday Frequency: m
Saturday Frequency: m
Avg Paid Circ: 15567
Avg Free Circ: 825
Audit Company: AAM
Audit Date: 9 03 2020
Pressroom Equipment: Lines – 7-G/Community SC (1 univ offset color), 1-DGM/4-high Color; Folders – G/Community SC, DGM/1030; Pasters –7-Jardis/Splicers.
Mailroom Equipment: Counter Stackers – 1-HL/Monitor, QWI/401; Inserters & Stuffers – 1-AM/Graphics NP 1372 w/icon, 1-MM/8:1; Tying Machines – 2-MLN/Strapper; Address Machine – KR;
Buisness Equipment: IBM/Sys 36
Buisness Software: Lotus
Classified Software: APT.
Editorial Equipment: Hardware – CText; Printers – ECR/11 X 17 proof printer
Editorial Software: XYQUEST/XyWrite, QPS/QuarkXPress 3.3.
Production Equipment: Hardware – Caere/OmniPage, APP/Mac, AG/Online; Cameras – AG; Scanners – 3-Nikon, 2-AG
Production Software: Layout 8000.
Total Circulation: 20737

DAYTONA BEACH

DAYTONA BEACH NEWS-JOURNAL

Corporate/Parent Company: Gannett
Publication Street Address: 901 6th St
City: Daytona Beach
State: FL
Publication Website: www.news-journalonline.com
Postal Code: 32117-3352
Office phone: (386) 252-1511
General E-mail: letters@news-jrnl.com
Editor Name: Pat Rice
Editor Email: pat.rice@news-jrnl.com
Editor Phone: (386) 681-2222
Advertising Executive Name: James Blasco
Advertising Executive Email: james.blasco@news-jrnl.com
Advertising Executive Phone: (386) 681-2626
Year Established: 1883
Delivery Methods: Mail`Newsstand`Carrier`Racks
Own Printing Facility?: Y
Commercial printers?: Y
Mechanical specifications: Type page 11 5/8 x 20 3/4; E - 6 cols, 1 13/16, 1/8 between; A - 6 cols, 1 13/16, 1/8 between; C - 9 cols, 1 1/4, 1/16 between.
Published Days: Mon`Tues`Wed`Thur`Fri`Sat`Sun
Weekday Frequency: m
Saturday Frequency: m
Avg Paid Circ: 44833
Audit Company: AAM
Audit Date: 11 07 2019
Pressroom Equipment: Lines – 14-G/Metroliner; Folders – 2-G/3:2, 2-G/2:1;
Mailroom Equipment: Counter Stackers – 1-QWI/100, 5-QWI/200, 2-QWI/310, 3-QWI/350, 2-MM/CS70-338; Inserters & Stuffers – HI/1472, HI/1372, HI/2299, NP/120 Gripper Conveyor; Tying Machines – 8-Dynaric/NP-2, 2-Dynaric/NP-1, 4-Malow/50-S String Typer; Wrapping Singles – Wrapping Singles;
Buisness Equipment: 2-DEC/Alpha 4610
Classified Equipment: Hardware – AST/Bravo MS 5166M, 37-IBM PS/1; Printers – 2-Digital/L030W Companion, Okipage/6e;
Classified Software: Cx/Intertext, HI.
Editorial Equipment: Hardware – 2-Sun/Ultra2, 3-Sun/Sparc 10 Server, 2-Sun/Sparc Storage Arrays, 50-Dell/Dimension XPS T450, 20-Dell/Dimension V350, 10-Dell/Optiplex; Printers – QMS/1660, MON/Proofer, HP/8100N
Editorial Software: HI/Newsmaker 3.31, Microsoft/Windows NT, Microsoft/Wor
Production Equipment: Hardware – 2-MON/ExpressMaster 25, 3-MON/RIP Express, 3-Sun/Ultra Sparc 2Xs, SCREEN/Doubletruck Imagesetter, Harlequin/RIP; Cameras – 2-C, 1-Payea, 1-C/Spartan; Scanners – 3-ECR/Autokon, 1-SCREEN/608 Scanner, HP/ScanJet Plus
Production Software: HI/Newsmaker 2.0
Total Circulation: 49082

DEERFIELD BEACH

SOUTH FLORIDA SUN-SENTINEL

Corporate/Parent Company: Tribune Publishing Company
Publication Street Address: 333 S.W. 12th Ave.
City: Deerfield Beach
State: FL
Publication Website: www.sun-sentinel.com
Postal Code: 33442
Office phone: (954) 356-4000
General E-mail: letters@sunsentinel.com
Editor Name: Julie Anderson
Editor Email: janderson@sun-sentinel.com
Year Established: 1911
Own Printing Facility?: N
Commercial printers?: N
Published Days: Mon`Tues`Wed`Thur`Fri`Sat`Sun
Weekday Frequency: m
Saturday Frequency: m
Avg Paid Circ: 93173
Audit Company: AAM
Audit Date: 26 02 2019
Pressroom Equipment: Goss Color Liner
Pressroom Software: Rockwell
Mailroom Equipment: Mueller Martini
Mailroom Software: Win Lics
Total Circulation: 189421

ENGLEWOOD

ENGLEWOOD SUN

Corporate/Parent Company: Adams Publishing Group
Publication Street Address: 120 W Dearborn St
City: Englewood
State: FL
Publication Website: https://www.yoursun.com/englewood/
Postal Code: 34223-3237
Office phone: 941-206-1300
General E-mail: custserv@sun-herald.com
Publisher Name: Glen Nickerson
Publisher Email: glen.nickerson@yoursun.com
Publisher Phone: (941) 207-1010
Editor Name: Jim Gouvellis
Editor Email: jim.gorvellis@yoursun.com
Editor Phone: (941) 206-11344
Advertising Executive Name: Omar Zucco
Advertising Executive Email: omar.zucco@yoursun.com
Advertising Executive Phone: (941) 205-6402
Published Days: Mon`Tues`Wed`Thur`Fri`Sat`Sun
Weekday Frequency: m
Saturday Frequency: m
Audit Company: Sworn/Estimate/Non-Audited
Audit Date: 7 12 2019

U.S. Daily Newspapers

FORT MYERS

THE NEWS-PRESS

Corporate/Parent Company: Gannett
Publication Street Address: 2442 Dr. Martin Luther King Jr. Blvd.
City: Fort Myers
State: FL
Publication Website: www.news-press.com
Postal Code: 33901
Office phone: (239) 992-1345
General E-mail: mailbag@news-press.com
Editor Name: Cindy McCurry-Ross
Editor Email: cmcross@gannett.com
Year Established: 1884
Published Days: Mon`Tues`Wed`Thur`Fri`Sat`Sun
Weekday Frequency: m
Saturday Frequency: m
Avg Paid Circ: 37890
Audit Company: AAM
Audit Date: 11 03 2020
Total Circulation: 58866

FORT WALTON BEACH

NORTHWEST FLORIDA DAILY NEWS

Corporate/Parent Company: Gannett
Publication Street Address: 2 Eglin Pkwy NE
City: Fort Walton Beach
State: FL
Publication Website: www.nwfdailynews.com
Postal Code: 32548-4915
Office phone: (850) 863-1111
Publisher Name: Tim Thompson
Publisher Email: tthompson@nwfdailynews.com
Publisher Phone: 850-747-5001
Editor Name: Jason Blakeney
Editor Email: jblakeney@nwfdailynews.com
Editor Phone: 850-315-4404
Advertising Executive Name: Shawna Laethem
Advertising Executive Email: slaethem@nwfdailynews.com
Advertising Executive Phone: 850-315-4340
Year Established: 1946
Delivery Methods: Mail`Newsstand`Carrier`Racks
Own Printing Facility?: N
Commercial printers?: Y
Published Days: Mon`Tues`Wed`Thur`Fri`Sat`Sun
Weekday Frequency: m
Saturday Frequency: m
Avg Paid Circ: 25722
Avg Free Circ: 682
Audit Company: AAM
Audit Date: 20 11 2019
Pressroom Equipment: Goss Universal 45 with EAE control and Software
Mailroom Equipment: SOS 3000,
Mailroom Software: Window Base Software Systems
Buisness Equipment: PC
Buisness Software: Lawson
Classified Equipment: Hardware – PC;
Classified Software: APT.
Editorial Equipment: Hardware – PC
Editorial Software: APT.
Production Equipment: See press description
Production Software: Kodak Platemaker
Total Circulation: 15497

GAINESVILLE

THE GAINESVILLE SUN

Corporate/Parent Company: Gannett
Publication Street Address: 2700 SW 13th St
City: Gainesville
State: FL
Publication Website: www.gainesville.com
Postal Code: 32608-2015
Office phone: (352) 378-1411
General E-mail: news@gainesville.com
Publisher Name: Rynni Henderson
Publisher Email: rhenderson@gainesville.com
Publisher Phone: (352) 374-5001
Editor Name: Douglas Ray
Editor Email: doug.ray@gainesville.com
Editor Phone: (352) 374-5035
Advertising Executive Name: Oscar Miguel
Advertising Executive Email: omiguel@gvillesun.com
Advertising Executive Phone: 352) 374-5079
Year Established: 1876
Mechanical specifications: Type page 11 5/8 x 21; E - 6 cols, 2 1/16, 1/8 between; A - 6 cols, 2 1/16, 1/8 between; C - 10 cols, 1 3/16, 1/8 between.
Published Days: Mon`Tues`Wed`Thur`Fri`Sat`Sun
Weekday Frequency: m
Saturday Frequency: m
Avg Paid Circ: 16210
Avg Free Circ: 2551
Audit Company: AAM
Audit Date: 12 12 2018
Pressroom Equipment: Lines – 7-G/Headliner offset (5 half decks); Folders – 2-G/2:1 (with 1 motter stitch online stitching head); Reels & Stands – 7;
Mailroom Equipment: Counter Stackers – 2-Id/2200, 2-QWI/350, 1-QWI/610; Inserters & Stuffers – HI/1472P; Tying Machines – 1-MLN/2A, 2-Dynaric/NP2; Wrapping Singles – 2-QWI/Viper w/Fox Ink Jet Printers; Address Machine – 1/Ch, 1-/KR, Domino/Online, InkJet;
Buisness Equipment: 1-IBM/AS 400
Buisness Software: Microsoft/Office 97
Classified Equipment: Hardware – APP/Mac;
Classified Software: DTI/ClassSpeed 4.23.
Editorial Equipment: Hardware – AT/9000, APP/Mac; Printers – 2-HP/8000, 2-AU/APS Ace 1 3N
Editorial Software: DTI/SpeedWriter, DTI/SpeedPlanner, DTI/PageSpeed 4.2.
Production Equipment: Hardware – Caere/OmniPage, 2-AU/APS 3850 HS, 1-ECR/4550; Cameras – 1-C/Newspager; Scanners – CD/646IE Color Scanner, Kk/Pro Rfs 2035, Umax/PowerLook, Umax/Ultra Vision
Production Software: DTI/PageSpeed 4.23.
Total Circulation: 24599

JACKSONVILLE

JACKSONVILLE DAILY RECORD

Corporate/Parent Company: Observer Media Group, Inc
Publication Street Address: 10 N. Newnan St.
City: Jacksonville
State: FL
Publication Website: www.jaxdailyrecord.com
Postal Code: 32202
Office phone: 904-356-2466
General E-mail: info@jaxdailyrecord.com
Publisher Name: Matt Walsh
Editor Name: Karen Mathis
Editor Email: kmathis@jaxdailyrecord.com
Advertising Executive Name: Jay Lesowitz
Advertising Executive Email: jlesowitz@jaxdailyrecord.com

THE FLORIDA TIMES-UNION

Corporate/Parent Company: Gannett
Publication Street Address: 1 Riverside Ave
City: Jacksonville
State: FL
Publication Website: www.jacksonville.com
Postal Code: 32202-4917
Office phone: (904) 359-4111
Editor Name: Mary Kelli Palka
Editor Email: mpalka@jacksonville.com
Editor Phone: (904) 359-4107
Advertising Executive Name: Liz Borten
Advertising Executive Email: lborten@jacksonville.com
Advertising Executive Phone: (904) 359-4099
Year Established: 1864
Delivery Methods: Mail`Newsstand`Carrier`Racks
Own Printing Facility?: Y
Commercial printers?: Y
Mechanical specifications: Type page 11 5/8 x 21 1/2; E - 6 cols, 1 13/16, 1/8 between; A - 6 cols, 1 13/16, 1/16 between; C - 10 cols, 1 1/8, 1/16 between.
Published Days: Mon`Tues`Wed`Thur`Fri`Sat`Sun
Weekday Frequency: m
Saturday Frequency: m
Avg Paid Circ: 41704
Audit Company: AAM
Audit Date: 11 03 2020
Pressroom Equipment: Lines – G/Metro 3213 8Units, 4 color decks 20 print couples; G/Metro: 3076; 9 units, 5 color decks, 23 print couples; G/Metro 3019 9 units, 5 decks, 23 print couples; Folders – 6-G/3:2 4; Reels & Stands – 23;
Mailroom Equipment: Counter Stackers – 3-HI/HT, 4-QWI/501, 8-QWI/401; Inserters & Stuffers – 2-HI/MP 632; Tying Machines – 6-Dynaric/3000; Wrapping Singles – Manual.;
Buisness Equipment: SAP Accounting/Ad Order Entry PBS Circulation Management
Classified Equipment: Hardware – DTI, Sun/Server, 65-APP/Mac; Printers – Epson, HP;
Classified Software: DTI 5.01.
Editorial Equipment: Hardware – Media cloud based/Kodak CTP; Printers – HP, Xante, XIT
Editorial Software: Media Spectrum Content Watch
Production Equipment: Hardware – Lf/AP Leaf Picture Desk, 2 Kodak Trendsetter 200 CTP devices; Accutech Optical registration and Benders 10, 5-APP/Mac, 2-III/3850H, 2-III/3850H
Production Software: Media Spectrum Ad Watch and Content Wacth; DTI Pagination
Note: Advertising is sold in combination with St. Augustine Record (mS) for $243.00(d), $259.00(m-sat) and $279.00(S).
Total Circulation: 60156

KEY WEST

KEY WEST CITIZEN

Publication Street Address: 3420 Northside Dr
City: Key West
State: FL
Publication Website: www.keysnews.com
Postal Code: 33040-4254
Office phone: (305) 292-7777
Publisher Name: Richard Tamborrino
Publisher Email: rtamborrino@keysnews.com
Editor Name: Chris Seymour
Editor Email: cseymour@keysnews.com
Advertising Executive Name: Kevin Downey
Year Established: 1876
Delivery Methods: Mail`Newsstand`Carrier`Racks
Own Printing Facility?: N
Commercial printers?: N
Mechanical specifications: Type page 13 x 21 1/2; E - 6 cols, 2 1/16, 1/8 between; A - 6 cols, 2 1/16, 1/8 between; C - 9 cols, 1 5/16, 1/16 between.
Published Days: Mon`Tues`Wed`Thur`Fri`Sat
Weekday Frequency: m
Saturday Frequency: m
Avg Paid Circ: 7597
Audit Company: Sworn/Estimate/Non-Audited
Audit Date: 7 12 2019
Buisness Equipment: ATT
Classified Equipment: Hardware – APP/Mac iMac; Printers – HP/4050;
Classified Software: AdManager/Pro.
Editorial Equipment: Hardware – APP/Mac, Mk, PC; Printers – HP/5000
Editorial Software: NewsEdit Pro
Production Equipment: Hardware – Panther/Pro 62, V/5300; Cameras – SCREEN/Companica 680C; Scanners – AG/Arcus Plus
Production Software: Adobe/Illustrator, Adobe/Photoshop, QPS/QuarkXPress, QPS.
Total Circulation: 7597

LAKE CITY

LAKE CITY REPORTER

Corporate/Parent Company: Community Newspapers, Incorporated
Publication Street Address: 180 E Duval St
City: Lake City
State: FL
Publication Website: www.lakecityreporter.com
Postal Code: 32055-4085
Office phone: (386) 752-1293
Publisher Name: Todd Wilson
Publisher Phone: (386) 754-0418
Editor Name: Robert Bridges
Editor Phone: (386) 754-0428
Year Established: 1874
Delivery Methods: Mail`Newsstand`Carrier`Racks
Own Printing Facility?: Y
Commercial printers?: Y
Mechanical specifications: Type page 13 x 21 1/2; E - 6 cols, 1 5/6, 1/8 between; A - 6 cols, 1 5/6, 1/8 between; C - 6 cols, 1 5/6, 1/8 between.
Published Days: Tues`Wed`Thur`Fri`Sat`Sun
Weekday Frequency: m
Saturday Frequency: m
Avg Paid Circ: 8887
Avg Free Circ: 10000
Audit Company: Sworn/Estimate/Non-Audited
Audit Date: 7 12 2019
Buisness Equipment: IBM/AS-400
Classified Equipment: Hardware – APP/Macs; Printers – Xante/Accel-a-Writer, APP/Laserwriter;
Classified Software: Baseview.
Editorial Equipment: Hardware – APP/Macs; Printers – Panther/Imagesetter, Xante/Accel-a-Writer, APP/Laserwriter
Editorial Software: Baseview, QPS, Adobe/Photoshop.
Production Equipment: Hardware – Panther
Production Software: Baseview.
Total Circulation: 18887

LAKELAND

NEWS CHIEF

Corporate/Parent Company: GateHouse Media
Publication Street Address: 300 W. Lime St
City: Lakeland
State: FL
Publication Website: www.newschief.com
Postal Code: 33815
Office phone: 863-802-7000
Editor Name: Bob Heist
Editor Email: bheist@theledger.com
Editor Phone: 863-802-7500
Advertising Executive Name: Patricia Martin
Advertising Executive Email: pmartin@ledgermediagroup.com
Advertising Executive Phone: 863-802-7400
Year Established: 1911
Delivery Methods: Newsstand`Carrier`Racks
Own Printing Facility?: N
Commercial printers?: Y
Mechanical specifications: Type page 13 x 21 1/2; E - 6 cols, 2 1/16, 1/8 between; A - 6 cols, 2 1/16, 1/8 between; C - 6 cols, 2 1/16, 1/8 between.
Published Days: Mon`Tues`Wed`Thur`Fri`Sat`Sun
Weekday Frequency: m
Saturday Frequency: m
Avg Paid Circ: 597
Avg Free Circ: 33
Audit Company: AAM
Audit Date: 15 11 2019
Pressroom Equipment: Lines – 6-G/Urbanite (1 3-color); 8-HI/V-15A (Color deck); Folders – 1, 1.;
Mailroom Equipment: Counter Stackers – 1-MM/1231, 1-QWI/928; Inserters & Stuffers – 1-S/NP524, 1-MM/227; Tying Machines – 2-MLN/MLN; Address Machine – 1/EI, 1-KAN/Labeler.;
Buisness Equipment: ATT/6386 E-33 WGS
Classified Equipment: Hardware – APP/Mac G3 fileserver, 13-APP/Mac G3; Printers – HP/4100;
Classified Software: BaseView/AJ Manager 3.X.
Editorial Equipment: Hardware – 6-APP/G3 PowerMac fileserver, 1-APP/Mac fx fileserver, 5-APP/iMac/APP/Mac Scanner
Editorial Software: Caere/OmniPage.
Production Equipment: Hardware – 2-V/4000 RIP/5500 Typesetter, Nikon; Cameras – 1-C/Spartan II; Scanners – Howtek
Production Software: QuarkPress 4.11-.
Total Circulation: 724

I-15

THE LEDGER

Corporate/Parent Company: Gannett
Publication Street Address: 300 W Lime St
City: Lakeland
State: FL
Publication Website: www.theledger.com
Postal Code: 33815-4649
Office phone: (863) 802-7000
Editor Name: Bob Heist
Editor Email: bheist@theledger.com
Editor Phone: 863-802-7500
Advertising Executive Name: Patricia Martin
Advertising Executive Email: pmartin@ledgermediagroup.com
Advertising Executive Phone: 863-802-7400
Year Established: 1924
Delivery Methods: Mail`Newsstand`Carrier`Racks
Own Printing Facility?: Y
Commercial printers?: Y
Mechanical specifications: Type page 13 x 21 1/2; E - 6 cols, 2 1/16, 1/8 between; A - 6 cols, 2 1/16, 1/8 between; C - 9 cols, 1 3/8, between.
Published Days: Mon`Tues`Wed`Thur`Fri`Sat`Sun
Weekday Frequency: m
Saturday Frequency: m
Avg Paid Circ: 25141
Audit Company: AAM
Audit Date: 1 04 2020
Pressroom Equipment: Pasters –8-G/RIP (ea. press); Reels & Stands - 8; Control System - G/Control; Registration System - G/Pin Register.
Mailroom Equipment: Counter Stackers - 8-QWI/350; Inserters & Stuffers - 1-HI/RS25, 4-GMA/2000 14:1; Tying Machines - 8/Power Strap/News Tyers; Control System - Machine Design; Address Machine - 1-/Ch, 1-/St.;
Buisness Equipment: IBM/AS-400
Classified Equipment: Hardware - AT/SYSDECO-Classified Pagination;
Classified Software: AT/SYSDECO Classified Pagination.
Editorial Equipment: Hardware - AT/SYSDECO, APP/Mac Press-to-Go/Lf/AP Leaf Picture Desk, AP/Leafax, APP/Laserphoto; Printers - AU/Laserprinter, Okidata
Editorial Software: AT/SYSDECO.
Production Equipment: Hardware – Kk/RFS 2035, 4-Microtek/600, CD/5400; Cameras - 1-C/Spartan; Scanners - 1-Kk/RFS 2035, 2-PixelCraft/7650X, 1-Howtek/D4000
Production Software: AT/Classpage FPO, AT, Press 2go, QPS/QuarkXPress.
Total Circulation: 21997

LEESBURG

THE DAILY COMMERCIAL

Corporate/Parent Company: Gannett
Publication Street Address: 212 E Main St
City: Leesburg
State: FL
Publication Website: www.dailycommercial.com
Postal Code: 34748-5227
Office phone: (352) 787-0600
General E-mail: news@dailycommercial.com
Editor Name: Katie Sartoris
Editor Email: ksartoris@dailycommercial.com
Editor Phone: (352) 365-8257
Advertising Executive Name: Alan Hay
Advertising Executive Email: ahay@dailycommercial.com
Advertising Executive Phone: (352) 365-8276
Year Established: 1875
Published Days: Mon`Tues`Wed`Thur`Fri`Sat`Sun
Weekday Frequency: m
Saturday Frequency: m
Avg Paid Circ: 8333
Avg Free Circ: 1367
Audit Company: AAM
Audit Date: 19 11 2019
Pressroom Equipment: Lines – 10-G/Urbanite;
Mailroom Equipment: Counter Stackers – 4/QWI, 2-Id; Inserters & Stuffers – 1-HI/848; Tying Machines – 2-/MLN, 1-MLN/Spirit; Address Machine – 1-/Ch.;
Buisness Equipment: IBM/Sys 36
Classified Equipment: Hardware – 9-StarMax/4000; Printers – APP/Mac 4/600;
Classified Software: Baseview/Ad Manager Pro 1.0.4.
Editorial Equipment: Hardware – 8-StarMax/4000, 12-StarMax/3000, 10-APP/Mac G4; Printers – Teletype/MOD 40, Xante/Accel-a-Writer 8200, GCC/Elite XL 616, APP/Mac LaserWriter Pro 16
Editorial Software: Baseview/NewsEdit Pro 3.0, Baseview/IQUE, QPS/QuarkXPress.
Production Equipment: Hardware – 2-Pre Press/Panther Pro 36, 1-C/80, 1-C/80RA, 1-Konica/K-550; Cameras – 1-C, 1-LE; Scanners – Kk/RFS 2035, 2-AG/StudioScan.
Total Circulation: 10890

MARIANNA

JACKSON COUNTY FLORIDAN

Publication Street Address: 4403 Constitution Ln
City: Marianna
State: FL
Publication Website: www.jcfloridan.com
Postal Code: 32448-4472
Office phone: (850) 526-3614
General E-mail: editorial@jcfloridan.com
Editor Name: Kyle Mooty
Editor Email: kmooty@eprisenow.com
Editor Phone: (334) 393-9701
Year Established: 1928
Delivery Methods: Mail`Newsstand`Carrier`Racks
Own Printing Facility?: N
Commercial printers?: N
Mechanical specifications: Type page 12 x 21 1/2; E - 6 cols, 1 3/4, 1/6 between; A - 6 cols, 1 3/4, 1/6 between; C - 6 cols, 1 3/4, 1/6 between.
Published Days: Tues`Wed`Thur`Fri`Sun
Weekday Frequency: m
Avg Paid Circ: 3690
Audit Company: AAM
Audit Date: 31 03 2016
Total Circulation: 3690

MELBOURNE

FLORIDA TODAY

Corporate/Parent Company: Gannett
Publication Street Address: 1 Gannett Plaza
City: Melbourne
State: FL
Publication Website: www.floridatoday.com
Postal Code: 32940
Office phone: 187-74240156
General E-mail: letters@floridatoday.com
Editor Name: Mara Bellaby
Editor Email: mbellaby@floridatoday.com
Editor Phone: 321-242-3573
Year Established: 1966
Delivery Methods: Mail`Newsstand`Carrier`Racks
Own Printing Facility?: Y
Commercial printers?: Y
Mechanical specifications: Type page 10"x21". 6 cols, 1 5/6", 1/8" between
Published Days: Mon`Tues`Wed`Thur`Fri`Sat`Sun
Weekday Frequency: m
Saturday Frequency: m
Avg Paid Circ: 31998
Audit Company: AAM
Audit Date: 1 10 2018
Pressroom Equipment: Lines – 16-G/Headliner Offset double width; 8-G/C150 Community offset single width; Press Drive – Fin; Folders – r-G/3:2, 1-G/1:1, Twafolder; Pasters –16-G/45 RTP, 2-Enkel/Zero Speed Pasters; Reels & Stands – Static belt tension 3 arm Reels & Stands; Control System – Fin/Drive; Registration System – KFM
Mailroom Equipment: Counter Stackers – 1-MM, 2-HL/Dual Carrier, 2-QWI/Dual Carrier, 2-HL/Monitor, 2-QWI/401, 1-Gammerler/KL503, 1-Gammerler/STC-700; Inserters & Stuffers – 1-Mailstar, 2-HI/630, 1-HI/632; Tying Machines – 3-Dynaric/NP 1500, 3-Power Strap, Newstyer/2000; Wrapping Singles – 3-HL/Bottom Wrap, 3-HI/Bottomwrap, 2-QWI/Viper Bottomwrap; Control System – 2-Prima/Icon 300; Address Machine – 1-Ch, 1-Barstrom;
Buisness Equipment: 1-IBM/AS-400 Model F45, IBM/AS-400 500-2141
Buisness Software: Cyborg, Lawson, Gen ledger, Corporate 1997 : Adv, Circ
Classified Equipment: Hardware – Gateway; HI/Classified AdPag; Printers – Florida Data;
Classified Software: HI/AdPower, HI/AdPower.
Editorial Equipment: Hardware – 2-Sun/Enterprise 450/HI/NewsMaker Pagination; Printers – Epson
Editorial Software: HI/NewsMaker Editorial 4.5.
Production Equipment: Hardware – 2-CD/646IE, Anites/SN48 Processor, WL/Lithobender; Scanners – 2-Linotype-Hell/Topaz, 1-Kk/RFS 2035 Plus
Production Software: HI/NewsMaker.
Total Circulation: 45691

MIAMI

BROWARD DAILY BUSINESS REVIEW

Corporate/Parent Company: ALM
Publication Street Address: 1 SE 3rd Ave, Ste 1750
City: Miami
State: FL
Publication Website: www.dailybusinessreview.com
Postal Code: 33131
Office phone: 800-777-7300
General E-mail: CustomerCare@alm.com
Publisher Name: Wayne Curtis
Editor Name: Cathy Wilson
Editor Email: cwilson@alm.com

MIAMI HERALD

Corporate/Parent Company: McClatchy Company
Publication Street Address: 3511 NW 91 Ave.
City: Miami
State: FL
Publication Website: https://www.miamiherald.com/
Postal Code: 33172
Office phone: (800) 843-4372
General E-mail: customerservice@miamiherald.com
Publisher Name: Aminda 'Mindy' Marqués González
Publisher Email: amarques@MiamiHerald.com
Publisher Phone: (305) 376-3429
Editor Name: Rick Hirsch
Editor Email: rhirsch@miamiherald.com
Editor Phone: (305) 376-3504
Advertising Executive Name: Lesley DeCanio
Advertising Executive Email: ldecanio@MiamiHerald.com
Year Established: 1903
Avg Paid Circ: 80310
Audit Company: AAM
Audit Date: 26 03 2020

MIAMI-DADE DAILY BUSINESS REVIEW

Corporate/Parent Company: ALM
Publication Street Address: 1 SE 3rd Ave, Ste 1750
City: Miami
State: FL
Publication Website: www.dailybusinessreview.com
Postal Code: 33131
Office phone: 800-777-7300
General E-mail: CustomerCare@alm.com
Editor Name: Cathy Wilson
Editor Email: cwilson@alm.com

NAPLES

NAPLES DAILY NEWS

Corporate/Parent Company: Gannett
Publication Street Address: 1100 Immokalee Rd
City: Naples
State: FL
Publication Website: www.naplesnews.com
Postal Code: 34110-4810
Office phone: 239-213-6000
General E-mail: naplesdailynews@gannett.com
Editor Name: Maryann Batlle
Editor Email: maryann.batlle@naplesnews.com
Own Printing Facility?: Y
Commercial printers?: Y
Mechanical specifications: Type page 13 x 22 1/4; E - 6 cols, 2 1/16, 1/8 between; A - 6 cols, 2 1/16, 1/8 between; C - 10 cols, 1 1/5, 1/8 between.
Published Days: Mon`Tues`Wed`Thur`Fri`Sat`Sun
Weekday Frequency: m
Saturday Frequency: m
Avg Paid Circ: 49667
Audit Company: AAM
Audit Date: 17 03 2020
Pressroom Equipment: Lines – 9-G/Metro double width (5 half decks) 1994; Press Drive – 10-HP/75; Folders – 3-G/3:2 double; Reels & Stands – G/Reels & Stands.;
Mailroom Equipment: Counter Stackers – 6-HL/Monitor; Inserters & Stuffers – 1-S/1472, 1-S/1272P; Tying Machines – 1/Power Strap/PSN-2, 2/Power Strap/PSN-6, 3-Dynaric/NP 1500; Wrapping Singles – 4-/CH, 1-HL/Underwrap; Control System – 2-/PC, Image Packagi;
Buisness Equipment: Sun/Sparc
Buisness Software: PBS: Microsoft/Office
Classified Equipment: Hardware – Dell/200; Printers – Epson/DFX 5000, Konica/Laser, HP;
Classified Software: HI/AdPower.
Editorial Equipment: Hardware – HI/Newsmaker; Printers – Epson, IBM, Konica, HP
Editorial Software: HI/NME.
Production Equipment: Hardware – 2-AU/3850 Doublewidth, WL/Lith-X-Pozer III, WL/Lithobender SD 30, Automated/Optical Film Punch; Scanners – Scitex/System, Kk/2035, Graphic Enterprises/3050 Copy Dot
Production Software: QPS/QuarkXPress 3.31, HI/XP-21-DASH, HI/XP-21 NMP, HI/XP-21 NME.
Total Circulation: 32174

NORTH PORT

NORTH PORT SUN

Corporate/Parent Company: Adams Publishing Group
Publication Street Address: 13487 Tamiami Trl
City: North Port
State: FL
Publication Website: www.yoursun.com/northport/
Postal Code: 34287-1211
Office phone: (941) 429-3000
General E-mail: custserv@sun-herald.com
Publisher Name: Glen Nickerson
Publisher Email: glen.nickerson@yoursun.com
Publisher Phone: (941) 207-1010
Editor Name: Jim Gouvellis
Editor Email: jim.gorvellis@yoursun.com
Editor Phone: (941) 206-11344
Advertising Executive Name: Omar Zucco
Advertising Executive Email: omar.zucco@yoursun.com
Advertising Executive Phone: (941) 205-6402
Published Days: Mon`Tues`Wed`Thur`Fri`Sat`Sun
Weekday Frequency: m
Saturday Frequency: m
Audit Company: Sworn/Estimate/Non-Audited
Audit Date: 7 12 2019

U.S. Daily Newspapers

OCALA

OCALA STAR-BANNER
Corporate/Parent Company: GateHouse Media
Publication Street Address: 2121 SW 19th Avenue Rd
City: Ocala
State: FL
Publication Website: www.ocala.com
Postal Code: 34471-7752
Office phone: (352) 867-4010
General E-mail: news@ocala.com
Publisher Name: Rynni Henderson
Publisher Email: rhenderson@ocala.com
Publisher Phone: (352) 374-5001
Editor Name: Douglas Ray
Editor Email: doug.ray@ocala.com
Editor Phone: (352) 374-5035
Advertising Executive Name: Dennis Quinn
Advertising Executive Email: dqinn@starbanner.com
Advertising Executive Phone: (352) 867-4098
Year Established: 1866
Delivery Methods: Newsstand`Carrier`Racks
Own Printing Facility?: Y
Commercial printers?: Y
Mechanical specifications: Type page 13 x 21 1/3; E - 6 cols, 2 1/16, 1/8 between; A - 6 cols, 2 1/16, 1/8 between; C - 9 cols, 1 3/8, 1/16 between.
Published Days: Mon`Tues`Wed`Thur`Fri`Sat`Sun
Weekday Frequency: m
Saturday Frequency: m
Avg Paid Circ: 22998
Audit Company: AAM
Audit Date: 16 10 2019
Pressroom Equipment: Lines – 5-G/Headliner 1988;
Mailroom Equipment: Counter Stackers – 3/QWI; Inserters & Stuffers – 1-/HI; Tying Machines – 3-/MLN;
Buisness Equipment: 1-IBM/AS-400 36
Classified Equipment: Hardware – 15-PC, MS/NT Server;
Classified Software: AT/Advantage.
Editorial Equipment: Hardware – 2-AT/Series 60, 15-PC Power pagination editing station/46-AT; Printers – 1-QMS/860
Editorial Software: DTI/Pagespeed, DTI/SpeedPlanner, DTI/SpeedDriver.
Production Equipment: Hardware – 1-AU/APS-6 5-8, 3-Pre Press/Panther Pro 46, 1-C/80RA, 2-P/Online; Cameras – 1-C/Spartan III 1270, 1-C/Newspaper
Production Software: DTI/SpeedPlanner, DTI/SpeedDriver, MEI/Page Director.
Total Circulation: 18734

ORLANDO

ORLANDO SENTINEL
Corporate/Parent Company: Tribune Publishing
Publication Street Address: 633 N Orange Ave
City: Orlando
State: FL
Publication Website: www.orlandosentinel.com
Postal Code: 32801-1300
Office phone: (407) 420-5000
Publisher Name: Nancy A. Meyer
Publisher Email: nmeyer@tribpub.com
Editor Name: Julie Anderson
Editor Email: janderson@sun-sentinel.com
Year Established: 1876
Own Printing Facility?: Y
Commercial printers?: Y
Mechanical specifications: Type page 12 x 20 7/8; E - 6 cols, 2 1/16, 1/8 between; A - 6 cols, 2 1/16, 1/8 between; C - 10 cols, 1 1/8, 1/8 between.
Published Days: Mon`Tues`Wed`Thur`Fri`Sat`Sun
Weekday Frequency: m
Saturday Frequency: m
Avg Paid Circ: 102175
Audit Company: AAM
Audit Date: 17 08 2018
Pressroom Equipment: Lines – 27-G/Metro double width, 4-G/Imperial double width 1981; 18-G/Head double width, 3-G/Imperial double width 1985; 5-G/Newsliner 4 over 4 color towers, digital inking; Press Drive – Fin; Folders – 7-G/3:2; Pasters –45-G/RTPReels & Stands – Reel;
Mailroom Equipment: Counter Stackers – 13-QWI/351, 2-QWI/401, 6-QWI/501, 4-BG/Exactistack Count-o-veyor; Inserters & Stuffers – 2-HI/2299, 2-SLS/3000 30:22, 1-HI/1630; Tying Machines – 5-GMA/Combistack, 5-Dynaric/NP 2-3, 5-Dynaric/RLM-1, 1-Dynaric/DF-2400, 7-Signode;
Buisness Equipment: IBM/PS-2 Pentium, Dell/6x100, Dell/CPI, Dell/LS
Buisness Software: WordPerfect, Microsoft/Word, Microsoft/Excel, Microsoft/Access, Microsoft/Office 97
Classified Equipment: Hardware – 4-SII/Sys 77 S7002; Ad-Star, Fax Action, GDT/Gateway;
Classified Software: Czar I, Coyote/3 1.4, SCS/Claspag 4.44.
Editorial Equipment: Hardware – IBM/RS 6000/350-PC; Printers – HP, GEI, OSE
Editorial Software: CCI/Newsdesk 5.5.5, Microsoft/Windows NT XP 4.0.
Production Equipment: Hardware – 4-3850 SST-Wide, 9-APP/Mac, 3-Sharp/2X-610; Cameras – 1-C/Newspaper; Scanners – 2-Eskofot.
Total Circulation: 158392

PALATKA

PALATKA DAILY NEWS
Corporate/Parent Company: Community Newspapers, Incorporated
Publication Street Address: 1825 Saint Johns Ave
City: Palatka
State: FL
Publication Website: www.palatkadailynews.com
Postal Code: 32177-4442
Office phone: (386) 312-5200
Publisher Name: Michael Leonard
Publisher Email: mleonard@palatkadailynews.com
Publisher Phone: 386-312-5201
Advertising Executive Name: Mary Kaye Wells
Advertising Executive Email: mwells@palatkadailynews.com
Advertising Executive Phone: 386-312-5210
Year Established: 1885
Mechanical specifications: Type page 13 x 21 1/2; E - 6 cols, 2 1/16, 1/8 between; A - 6 cols, 2 1/16, 1/8 between; C - 9 cols, 1 3/8, 1/16 between.
Published Days: Tues`Wed`Thur`Fri`Sat
Weekday Frequency: m
Saturday Frequency: m
Avg Paid Circ: 11804
Audit Company: Sworn/Estimate/Non-Audited
Audit Date: 7 12 2019
Mailroom Equipment: Address Machine – Ch/586.;
Buisness Equipment: IBM/S-36, PC Network
Buisness Software: Microsoft/Excel, Microsoft/Word, INSI
Classified Equipment: Hardware – Computext/CompuClass; Printers – APP/Mac LaserWriter II;
Classified Software: Computext/CompuClass.
Editorial Equipment: Hardware – 8-IBM/486, 5-PC Pagination Station/APP/Mac IIcx, APP/Mac 300, Shava/Telebridge, Microcom/9600 Modem, Lf/AP Leaf Picture Desk, APP/Mac vx; Printers – 1-APP/Mac LaserWriter II NTX
Editorial Software: Computext.
Production Equipment: Hardware – TI/OmniPage, 1-Konica/K550; Scanners – 2-Microtek/II XE, 1-Kk/RFS 2035
Production Software: Computext/Comet.
Total Circulation: 11804

PALM BEACH

PALM BEACH DAILY NEWS
Corporate/Parent Company: Gannett
Publication Street Address: 400 Royal Palm Way
City: Palm Beach
State: FL
Publication Website: www.palmbeachdailynews.com
Postal Code: 33480-4117
Office phone: (561) 820-3800
Editor Name: Carol Rose
Editor Email: crose@pbdailynews.com
Editor Phone: 561-820-3871
Year Established: 1897
Delivery Methods: Mail`Racks
Published Days: Mon`Tues`Wed`Thur`Fri`Sat`Sun
Weekday Frequency: m
Saturday Frequency: m
Avg Paid Circ: 3008
Audit Company: AAM
Audit Date: 30 06 2018
Total Circulation: 3008

PANAMA CITY

PANAMA CITY NEWS HERALD (THE)
Publication Street Address: 501 W. 11th St
City: Panama City
State: FL
Publication Website: www.newsherald.com
Postal Code: 32401
Office phone: (850) 747-5000
Publisher Name: Tim Thompson
Publisher Email: tthompson@pcnh.com
Publisher Phone: (850) 747-5001
Editor Name: Katie Landeck
Editor Email: klandeck@pcnh.com
Editor Phone: (850) 522-5114
Advertising Executive Name: Michael McCabe
Advertising Executive Email: mmccabe@pcnh.com
Advertising Executive Phone: 850-747-5082

THE NEWS HERALD
Corporate/Parent Company: Gannett
Publication Street Address: 501 W 11th St
City: Panama City
State: FL
Publication Website: www.newsherald.com
Postal Code: 32401-2330
Office phone: (850) 747-5000
Publisher Name: Tim Thompson
Publisher Email: tthompson@pcnh.com
Publisher Phone: (850) 747-5001
Editor Name: Mike Cazalas
Editor Email: mmcazalas@pcnh.com
Editor Phone: (850) 747-5094
Advertising Executive Name: Michael McCabe
Advertising Executive Email: mmccabe@pcnh.com
Advertising Executive Phone: 850-747-5082
Year Established: 1937
Delivery Methods: Mail`Newsstand`Carrier`Racks
Own Printing Facility?: Y
Commercial printers?: Y
Mechanical specifications: Type page 11 2/3 x 20; E - 6 cols, 1 13/16, 1/8 between; A - 6 cols, 1 13/16, 1/8 between; C - 9 cols, 1 1/4, 1/16 between.
Published Days: Mon`Tues`Wed`Thur`Fri`Sat`Sun
Weekday Frequency: m
Saturday Frequency: m
Avg Paid Circ: 18446
Audit Company: CAC
Audit Date: 31 03 2015
Pressroom Equipment: Lines – 28 unit Goss Universal; Press Drive - Shaftless; Reels & Stands – 10; Control System – EAE; Registration System – Manual
Mailroom Equipment: Counter Stackers – 2-Gaemmeler; Inserters & Stuffers – SLS 3000 - 12 heads; Tying Machines – 3 Dynaric and 1 Sterling; Wrapping Singles – 2-/Bu; Address Machine – KAN;
Classified Equipment: Hardware – PC; Printers – HP/4000, HP/5SI;
Classified Software: APT.
Editorial Equipment: Hardware – PC; Printers – HP/5MX
Editorial Software: APT.
Production Equipment: Hardware – Kk/Newsway
Production Software: APT.
Total Circulation: 18446

PENSACOLA

PENSACOLA NEWS JOURNAL
Corporate/Parent Company: Gannett
Publication Street Address: 2 N Palafox St
City: Pensacola
State: FL
Publication Website: www.pnj.com
Postal Code: 32502-5626
Office phone: (850) 435-8500
General E-mail: news@pnj.com
Editor Name: Lisa Nellessen Savage
Editor Email: lnelless@gannett.com
Editor Phone: 850.435.8514
Mechanical specifications: Type page 11 5/8 x 20 3/4; E - 6 cols, 1 5/6, 1/8 between; A - 6 cols, 1 5/6, 1/8 between; C - 10 cols, 1, 1/8 between.
Published Days: Mon`Tues`Wed`Thur`Fri`Sat`Sun
Weekday Frequency: m
Saturday Frequency: m
Avg Paid Circ: 21426
Audit Company: AAM
Audit Date: 10 06 2019
Pressroom Equipment: Lines – 7-G/Headliner Offset double width 1997; Press Drive – 5-Fin/125 h.p. Digital; Folders – 2-G/3:2 160 PG; Control System – G/MPCS.;
Mailroom Equipment: Counter Stackers – 2-Id/2200, 1-HL/Monitor, 2/Quipp 400, 1-/Compass 180; Inserters & Stuffers – AM Graphics/630 21 hopper; Tying Machines – 2-Dynaric/NP-1, 2-Dynaric/NP-1, 2-Dynaric/NP 1500; Control System – Id/TCP Bundle Control Syste;
Buisness Equipment: IBM/AS-400E 9406-620
Buisness Software: Microsoft/Office 97 Desktop Suite
Classified Equipment: Hardware – Dell/Poweredge Server; Mobile Advertising Sales System;
Classified Software: Mactive Adbase.
Editorial Equipment: Hardware – IBM/XSeries Servers; Printers – Accel A Writer 45
Editorial Software: Harris Newsjaz 2.0.
Production Equipment: Hardware – KFM/Twin-Line Semi-auto, 2-AU/APS PIP II, 1-AU/3850; Scanners – Tecsa
Production Software: Harris/NewsJaz 2.0, M Active PGL.
Total Circulation: 28104

PORT CHARLOTTE

SUN COAST MEDIA GROUP - APG
Publication Street Address: 23170 Harborview Rd
City: Port Charlotte
State: FL
Publication Website: www.yoursun.com
Postal Code: 33980-2100
Office phone: (941) 206-1000
General E-mail: custserv@sun-herald.com
Publisher Name: Glen Nickerson
Publisher Email: glen.nickerson@yoursun.com
Publisher Phone: (941) 205-6400
Editor Name: Jim Gouvellis
Editor Email: jim.gouvellis@yoursun.com
Editor Phone: (941) 206-1134
Year Established: 1977
Delivery Methods: Mail`Newsstand`Carrier`Racks
Own Printing Facility?: Y
Commercial printers?: Y
Mechanical specifications: Type page 10 x 20.75; E - 6 cols, 21, 1/8 between; A - 6 cols, 21, 1/8 between; C Ã‚Â– 6 cols, 16, 1/8 between.
Published Days: Mon`Tues`Wed`Thur`Fri`Sat`Sun
Weekday Frequency: m
Saturday Frequency: m
Avg Paid Circ: 37544
Audit Company: AAM
Audit Date: 31 03 2018
Pressroom Equipment: Lines – 12-G/Urbanite U-5019 5 units DGM 850; Folders – 2 goss 5000 series Folders 2 goss quarter Folders; Pasters –7 JARDIS flying Pasters 1-MARTIN zero speed pasterReels & Stands – Press Control System ÃƒÂ£Ã†â€™Ã‚Â£ÃƒÂ¢Ã‚Â£ÃƒÂ¦â€™Ã‚Â£ 2-Fin/2193E-150-38D, 1-Fin/2193E-100-

38D.;
Mailroom Equipment: Counter Stackers – 1-HI/251017, 1-HL/Monitor, 1-BG/105; Inserters & Stuffers – 1-HI/848; Tying Machines – 1-MLN/ML2EE, 1-MLN/A1672A, 1/Bu.;
Buisness Equipment: Dell Workgroup Server
Buisness Software: Saxotech-Data Sciences Inc
Classified Equipment: Hardware – Dell Workgroup Server; Printers – Konica BizHub;
Classified Software: Brainworks.
Editorial Equipment: Hardware – Dell (Lattitude E6500 series and Inspiron 1500 series)/ FA/Compact, FP/230B; Printers – Konica BizHub
Editorial Software: Town News Content Publisher/Adobe InDesign & InCopy
Production Equipment: Hardware – Kodak Trendsetter 150 CTP, Kodak PDF workflow, Newsmanager/Preps. Nela Vision Bender.; Scanners – Epson Scanner
Production Software: MEI/ALS 2.0.2rl.
Total Circulation: 37544

SAINT AUGUSTINE

THE ST. AUGUSTINE RECORD

Corporate/Parent Company: Gannett
Publication Street Address: 1 News Pl
City: Saint Augustine
State: FL
Publication Website: www.staugustine.com
Postal Code: 32086-6520
Office phone: (904) 829-6562
Editor Name: Jim Sutton
Editor Email: jsutton@staugustine.com
Editor Phone: 904-819-3487
Advertising Executive Name: Bo Berezansky
Advertising Executive Email: bberezansky@staugustine.com
Advertising Executive Phone: 904-819-3421
Mechanical specifications: Type page 11 5/8 x 21 1/12; E - 6 cols, 1 5/6, 1/6 between; A - 6 cols, 1 5/6, 1/6 between; C - 9 cols, 11/72 between.
Published Days: Mon`Tues`Wed`Thur`Fri`Sat`Sun
Weekday Frequency: m
Saturday Frequency: m
Avg Paid Circ: 9836
Avg Free Circ: 1331
Audit Company: AAM
Audit Date: 2 10 2018
Pressroom Equipment: Lines – 10 1/2-G/Urbanite; Folders – G/Urbanite Half; Reels & Stands – HI/Roll Stands; Registration System – Carlson.
Mailroom Equipment: Counter Stackers – 1/MM; Inserters & Stuffers – 1-MM/227S; Tying Machines – 2-MLN/ML2EE; Address Machine – 1-Am/1900, KAN.;
Buisness Equipment: IBM
Buisness Software: PBS
Classified Equipment: Hardware – IBM, DTI; Printers – Epson;
Classified Software: DTI 5.2.
Editorial Equipment: Hardware – IBM, 40-APP/Mac/AG/1500 Imagesetter; Printers – XIT/Navigator, HP
Editorial Software: DTI 5.2.
Production Equipment: Hardware – XIT/Navigator, Ag/1500; Cameras – AG/Accuset 1500
Production Software: DTI 5.2.
Note: Advertising is sold in combination with Jacksonville Florida Times Union (mS) for $243.00(d), $259.00(m-sat) and $279.00(S).
Total Circulation: 15461

SARASOTA

SARASOTA HERALD-TRIBUNE

Corporate/Parent Company: Gannett Co., Inc.
Publication Street Address: 1777 Main St.
City: Sarasota
State: FL
Publication Website: www.heraldtribune.com
Postal Code: 34236
Office phone: (941) 953-7755
General E-mail: webmaster@heraldtribune.com
Editor Name: Brian Ries
Editor Email: brian.ries@heraldtribune.com
Editor Phone: 941-361-4814
Advertising Executive Name: Stacia King
Year Established: 1925
Delivery Methods: Mail`Newsstand`Carrier`Racks
Own Printing Facility?: Y
Commercial printers?: Y
Mechanical specifications: Type page 11 x 21; E - 6 cols, 1 4/5, 1/8 between; A - 6 cols, 1 4/5, 1/8 between
Published Days: Mon`Tues`Wed`Thur`Fri`Sat`Sun
Weekday Frequency: m
Saturday Frequency: m
Avg Paid Circ: 43489
Audit Company: AAM
Audit Date: 3 04 2020
Pressroom Equipment: Lines – G/(18 unit Lines with 1 4-color tower & 3 decks) 1994; Folders – Imperial/144-page; Pasters –G/RTP 45 DIA; Control System – G/MPCS III; Registration System – WPC/Web Control.
Mailroom Equipment: Counter Stackers – 6/QWI; Inserters & Stuffers – 3-HI/NP 1372; Tying Machines – 2-/Power Strap/PSN, 5-/Dynaric; Wrapping Singles – 8-HL/Monarch; Address Machine – 1-Ch/S42.;
Buisness Equipment: 2-IBM/4381, III/TECS 2
Buisness Software: Admarc
Classified Equipment: Hardware – AT;
Classified Software: AT.
Editorial Equipment: Hardware – AT
Editorial Software: AT.
Production Equipment: Hardware – KFM/Plate Express, 4-III/3850, WL/III; Scanners – ECR/1000, ECR/2045, ECR/8400, Nikon/Scanners.
Total Circulation: 47696

SEBRING

HIGHLANDS NEWS-SUN

Corporate/Parent Company: Sun Coast Media Group
Publication Street Address: 321 N. Ridgewood Drive
City: Sebring
State: FL
Publication Website: yoursun.com/sebring/
Postal Code: 33870
Office phone: (863) 385-6155
General E-mail: webcomments@highlandsnewssun.com
Publisher Name: Timothy D. Smolarick
Publisher Email: tim.smolarick@highlandsnewssun.com
Publisher Phone: 863-386-5624
Editor Name: Romona Washington
Editor Email: romona.washington@highlandsnewssun.com
Editor Phone: 863-386-5634
Advertising Executive Name: Cliff Yeazel
Advertising Executive Email: cliff.yeazel@highlandsnewssun.com
Advertising Executive Phone: 863-386-5844
Year Established: 1927
Delivery Methods: Mail`Newsstand`Carrier`Racks
Own Printing Facility?: Y
Commercial printers?: Y
Mechanical specifications: Type page 13 x 21 1/2, 6 col. format
Published Days: Mon`Tues`Wed`Thur`Fri`Sat`Sun
Weekday Frequency: m
Saturday Frequency: m
Avg Paid Circ: 16609
Audit Company: Sworn/Estimate/Non-Audited
Audit Date: 7 12 2019
Note: For detailed press information, see the Tampa Tribune.
Total Circulation: 16609

ST PETERSBURG

TAMPA BAY TIMES

Corporate/Parent Company: Times Publishing Company
Publication Street Address: 490 1st Ave S
City: St Petersburg
State: FL
Publication Website: www.tampabay.com
Postal Code: 33701-4204
Office phone: (727) 893-8111
General E-mail: custserv@tampabay.com
Publisher Name: Dan Autrey
Publisher Email: dautrey@tbnweekly.com
Publisher Phone: 727-397-5563
Year Established: 1884
Own Printing Facility?: Y
Commercial printers?: Y
Mechanical specifications: Type page 11 27/100 x 21 1/2; E - 6 cols, 2 1/16, 1/8 between; A - 6 cols, 2 1/16, 1/8 between; C - 10 cols, 1 5/16, 1/16 between.
Published Days: Mon`Tues`Wed`Thur`Fri`Sat`Sun
Weekday Frequency: m
Saturday Frequency: m
Avg Paid Circ: 205202
Audit Company: AAM
Audit Date: 13 08 2020
Pressroom Equipment: Lines – 21-G/Metroliner double width; 21-G/Metroliner double width; 21-G/Metroliner double width; Folders – 5-G/single, 4-G/double;
Mailroom Equipment: Counter Stackers – 5-QWI/350, 24-QWI/400; Inserters & Stuffers – 5-S/1472, 1-HI/In-Line 30 632; Tying Machines – 9-Dynaric/NP, 12-Dynaric/NP-2, 17-Dynaric/NP3, 2-Mosca/Z-5; Wrapping Singles – 10-QWI/Viper 30, 16-QWI/Viper 50; Control System – Mailroom control s;
Buisness Equipment: 1-HP/900
Buisness Software: Peoplesoft HRMS, Microsoft/Office2003, Microsoft/Windows XP XP, GEAC World Class Advertising System, WinStar
Classified Equipment: Hardware – 10-SII/K1000, SII/Tandem; 120-PCs with Coyote-3; Printers – ECR/4550 Imagesetters, 7-Ad Proof/Printers;
Classified Software: Mactive/AdBase.
Editorial Equipment: Printers – 5-HP/LaserJet.
Editorial Software: CCI/News Gate, HI/NewsMaker Pagination.
Production Equipment: Hardware – 4-KPG/85, 2-Anitec/SN48, 4-Trendsetter 200.
Production Software: CCI/New Desk.
Total Circulation: 317190

STUART

ST. LUCIE NEWS TRIBUNE

Publication Street Address: 1939 SE Federal Highway
City: Stuart
State: FL
Publication Website: www.tcpalm.com
Postal Code: 34994
Office phone: 772-287-1550
General E-mail: treasurecoastnewspapers@gannett.com
Editor Name: Adam L. Neal
Editor Email: adam.neal@tcpalm.com
Published Days: Mon`Tues`Wed`Thur`Fri`Sat`Sun
Weekday Frequency: m
Avg Paid Circ: 41540
Audit Company: AAM
Audit Date: 30 06 2018
Total Circulation: 41540

THE STUART NEWS

Corporate/Parent Company: Gannett
Publication Street Address: 1939 SE Federal Hwy
City: Stuart
State: FL
Publication Website: www.tcpalm.com
Postal Code: 34994-3915
Office phone: (772) 287-1550
Editor Name: Adam L. Neal
Editor Email: adam.neal@tcpalm.com
Published Days: Mon`Tues`Wed`Thur`Fri`Sat`Sun
Weekday Frequency: m
Avg Paid Circ: 38550
Avg Free Circ: 367
Audit Company: AAM
Audit Date: 30 06 2018
Total Circulation: 38917

TREASURE COAST NEWSPAPERS

Publication Street Address: 1939 SE Federal Highway
City: Stuart
State: FL
Publication Website: www.tcpalm.com
Postal Code: 34994
Office phone: 844-331-0264
General E-mail: treasurecoastnewspapers@gannett.com
Editor Name: Adam L. Neal
Editor Email: adam.neal@tcpalm.com

TALLAHASSEE

TALLAHASSEE DEMOCRAT

Corporate/Parent Company: Gannett
Publication Street Address: 277 N Magnolia Dr
City: Tallahassee
State: FL
Publication Website: www.tallahassee.com
Postal Code: 32301-2664
Office phone: (850) 599-2100
Editor Name: William Hatfield
Editor Email: whatfield@tallahassee.com
Editor Phone: (850) 599-2177
Advertising Executive Name: Cari Evans
Advertising Executive Email: clevans@tallahassee.com
Advertising Executive Phone: (850) 599-2189
Year Established: 1905
Delivery Methods: Mail`Newsstand`Carrier`Racks
Own Printing Facility?: Y
Commercial printers?: Y
Mechanical specifications: Type page 10 1/8 x 21 1/2; E - 6 cols, 1 9/16, 1/6 between; A - 6 cols, 1 9/16, 1/6 between; C - 9 cols, 1 3/8, 1/16 between.
Published Days: Mon`Tues`Wed`Thur`Fri`Sat`Sun
Weekday Frequency: m
Saturday Frequency: m
Avg Paid Circ: 23763
Audit Company: AAM
Audit Date: 1 04 2019
Pressroom Equipment: Lines – 7-G/Metro double width (4 decks) 1979; 6-G/Urbanite single width; Folders – 1-G/Metro, 1, 1-G/Urbanite, 2-G/Uniflow 2:1; Pasters –7-G/Automatic RTPReels & Stands – 4-G/Urbanite high roll stand.;
Mailroom Equipment: Counter Stackers – 1-MM/310-20, 2-Baldwin/108, 3-QWI/400; Inserters & Stuffers – 1-Titan G60 22 heads; Tying Machines – 2-Samuel/NT 440, 3-Samuel/Newstyer 2000; Wrapping Singles – 3-QWI/50 bottom wrap, 1-Samuel;
Buisness Software: Word Processing
Classified Equipment: Hardware – 2-Sun/Enterprise 450, 21-IBM/PC Workstation; Printers – Variety;
Classified Software: DTI/Classified 5.3.
Editorial Equipment: Hardware – 2x sunfire v440; Printers – HP5000
Editorial Software: DTI 7.3
Production Equipment: Hardware – 2-Anacoil/LX45, Anacoil/Thermal
Production Software: DTI 7.3
Total Circulation: 26170

THE VILLAGES

THE VILLAGES DAILY SUN

Corporate/Parent Company: The Villages Operating Company
Publication Street Address: 1100 Main St
City: The Villages
State: FL
Publication Website: www.thevillagesdailysun.com
Postal Code: 32159-7719
Office phone: (352) 753-1119
General E-mail: dailysun@thevillagesmedia.

U.S. Daily Newspapers

com
Editor Name: BILL BOOTZ
Editor Email: bill.bootz@thevillagesmedia.com
Editor Phone: 352-753-1119 Ext.5224
Year Established: 1997
Delivery Methods: Newsstand`Carrier`Racks
Own Printing Facility?: Y
Commercial printers?: Y
Mechanical specifications: Type page 11 5/8 x 21 7/16; E - 6 cols, 1 11/16, 3/16 between; A - 6 cols, 1 11/16, 3/16 between; C - 6 cols, 1 13/16, 1/8 between.
Published Days: Mon`Tues`Wed`Thur`Fri`Sat`Sun
Weekday Frequency: m
Saturday Frequency: m
Avg Paid Circ: 45857
Avg Free Circ: 1166
Audit Company: AAM
Audit Date: 6 05 2019
Pressroom Equipment: Lines – 7 - 8 DGM color towers/1 Goss Community color tower; 2 mono units; Press Drive – 2 Fincor 125HP drives, 4 Fincor 150 HP drives ; Folders – DGM 1035, DGM 1240; Reels & Stands – 13 Jardis Splicers; Registration System – QTI Multicam
Pressroom Software: Puzzle Flow
Mailroom Equipment: Counter Stackers – Quipp Packman, Gammerler, Inserters & Stuffers – KANSA, Muller Martini 3000; Tying Machines – Dynaric; Muller Martini Stitcher 335
Mailroom Software: Cintech BCC Mailer
Buisness Equipment: Windows PCs AS400 Mac
Buisness Software: Oracle
Classified Equipment: Hardware – Apple Servers Apple PC's; iPads; Printers – HP;
Classified Software: AdManager Pro
Editorial Equipment: Hardware – Apple Servers Apple PCs; Printers – HP
Editorial Software: WoodWing Quickwire Adobe
Production Equipment: Hardware – Pre Press/2-Kodak Trendsetter News CTP; Scanners – Nikon, Microtek. 2 Screen Platerite News 200S
Production Software: PuzzleFlow Automator Cintech
Total Circulation: 59455

VERO BEACH
INDIAN RIVER PRESS JOURNAL

Corporate/Parent Company: Gannett
Publication Street Address: 2066 14th Ave
City: Vero Beach
State: FL
Publication Website: www.tcpalm.com
Postal Code: 32960-4420
Office phone: (772) 287-1550
Editor Name: Adam L. Neal
Editor Email: adam.neal@tcpalm.com
Published Days: Mon`Tues`Wed`Thur`Fri`Sat`Sun
Weekday Frequency: m
Avg Paid Circ: 17365
Avg Free Circ: 63
Audit Company: AAM
Audit Date: 30 06 2018
Total Circulation: 17428

WEST PALM BEACH
THE PALM BEACH POST

Corporate/Parent Company: Gannett
Publication Street Address: 2751 S. Dixie Highway
City: West Palm Beach
State: FL
Publication Website: www.pbpost.com
Postal Code: 33405-1233
Office phone: (561) 820-4100
Editor Name: Nick Moschella
Editor Email: nmoschella@pbpost.com
Editor Phone: 561-820-4441
Advertising Executive Name: Andy Blizzard
Advertising Executive Email: ablizzard@pbpost.com
Advertising Executive Phone: 561-820-4696
Year Established: 1908
Mechanical specifications: Type page 11 5/8 x 22 1/2; E - 6 cols, 1 5/6, 1/8 between; A - 6 cols, 1 5/6, 1/8 between; C - 10 cols, 1 11/100, 1/16 between.
Published Days: Mon`Tues`Wed`Thur`Fri`Sat`Sun
Weekday Frequency: m
Saturday Frequency: m
Avg Paid Circ: 62179
Audit Company: AAM
Audit Date: 14 01 2020
Pressroom Equipment: Lines – 24-G/Metro (12 color decks) double width; 8-G/Suburban single width; 6-G/Colorliner double width; Reels & Stands – 32;
Mailroom Equipment: Counter Stackers – 1/HL, HI/Rima, 7-/QWI; Inserters & Stuffers – 3-GMA/SLS 1000, 1-/Stepper Solo; Tying Machines – 11-/Dynaric, 3-Dynaric/RLM-1; Wrapping Singles – 4-/Constellation, 2-/MLN; Control System – GMA; Address Machine – K;
Buisness Equipment: Unisys/2200
Buisness Software: Labrador
Classified Equipment: Hardware – Sun/OTI, 55-APP/Mac G4; Ricoh/77 Fax; Printers – HP/5000 N;
Classified Software: AT/Do Fax, DTI/Class Speed 5.5.
Editorial Equipment: Hardware – 8-Sun, 105-APP/Power Mac G4/6-Networks in Bureaus
Editorial Software: DTI/Editorial 4.3.
Production Equipment: Hardware – Harlequin/Rips 5.12, Vision Bender, Scitex/Eversmart Pro II, 2-AU/APS, 2-3850 SST, 2-AU/APS 3850 SST Wide
Production Software: DTI 4.3, Pagespeed 4.3, Speedplanner 4.3, Adspeed 5.5, Classpeed 5.5, DTI/Planbuilder 3.8.
Total Circulation: 67146

GEORGIA

AMERICUS
AMERICUS TIMES-RECORDER

Corporate/Parent Company: Boone Newspapers
Publication Street Address: 101 Hwy 27 E
City: Americus
State: GA
Publication Website: www.americustimesrecorder.com
Postal Code: 31709
Office phone: (229) 924-2751
Publisher Name: Nichole Buchanan
Publisher Email: nichole.buchanan@americustimesrecorder.com
Advertising Executive Name: Kelly Gibson
Advertising Executive Email: kelly.gibson@americustimesrecorder.com
Year Established: 1879
Delivery Methods:
  Mail`Newsstand`Carrier`Racks
Mechanical specifications: Type page 13 x 21 1/2; E - 6 cols, 2 1/16, 1/8 between; A - 6 cols, 2 1/16, 1/8 between; C - 9 cols, 1 7/8, 1/16 between.
Published Days: Tues`Wed`Thur`Fri
Weekday Frequency: m
Avg Paid Circ: 6962
Audit Company: Sworn/Estimate/Non-Audited
Audit Date: 7 12 2019
Pressroom Equipment: Lines – G/Community (upper former); Folders – G/Half, G/Quarter.;
Mailroom Equipment: Tying Machines – MLN/Auto Bundler.;
Buisness Equipment: PBS
Classified Equipment: Hardware – 1-APP/Mac Centris 610; 4-ATT.;
Editorial Equipment: Hardware – 7-APP/Mac LC III, 2-APP/Mac Centris 610/Pre Press/Panther Pro 46; Printers – HP/LaserJet 4MV
Editorial Software: QPS/QuarkXPress.
Production Equipment: Hardware – Caere/OmniPage Pro 2.12, APP/Mac 610 Centris; Cameras – B/Horizontal, SCREEN/Vertical
Production Software: QPS/QuarkXPress 3.32.
Total Circulation: 6962

ATHENS
ATHENS BANNER-HERALD

Corporate/Parent Company: GateHouse Media
Publication Street Address: 1 Press Pl
City: Athens
State: GA
Publication Website: www.onlineathens.com
Postal Code: 30601-2605
Office phone: (706) 549-0123
General E-mail: customerservice@onlineathens.com
Editor Name: Donnie Fetter
Editor Email: dfetter@onlineathens.com
Editor Phone: (706) 208-2222
Advertising Executive Name: Kevin Clark
Advertising Executive Email: kclark@onlineathens.com
Advertising Executive Phone: (706) 208-2280
Year Established: 1832
Mechanical specifications: Type page 11 5/8 x 21 1/4; E - 6 cols, 2 1/16, 1/8 between; A - 6 cols, 1 13/16, 1/8 between; C - 10 cols, 1 1/16, 5/64 between.
Published Days: Mon`Tues`Wed`Thur`Fri`Sat`Sun
Weekday Frequency: m
Saturday Frequency: m
Avg Paid Circ: 10374
Avg Free Circ: 7000
Audit Company: AAM
Audit Date: 14 11 2019
Pressroom Equipment: Lines – 12-G/Urbanite; Folders – G/2:1.;
Mailroom Equipment: Counter Stackers – 3-HL/HT II, 1/Stackpack, 2-QWI/Soin, 2-TMSI; Inserters & Stuffers – 1-/AM Graphics/048P, NP/848; Tying Machines – G-3/Titan, 3-Dynamic; Wrapping Singles – 2-/Samuels, 1-/QWI; Address Machine – 2-/Ch;
Buisness Equipment: PBS, Bay Network Hub, IBM/RISC 6000, Raid Tower, Gateway, IBM, HP/5M
Buisness Software: WordPerfect 5.0, PC file, Lotus/1-2-3, Microsoft/Windows, MPS, Microsoft/Word, Microsoft/Excel
Classified Equipment: Hardware – 8-Gateway; Printers – HP/5000 Gn;
Classified Software: DTI 5.42.
Editorial Equipment: Hardware – 21-Gateway/2000, 2-APP/Power Mac, 2-Gateway/2000, Umax/5900, APP/Mac G4; Printers – 1-HP/5M, 1-HP/5000 GN Printer
Editorial Software: Baseview 3.5.6, Adobe/Illustrator 9.0, QPS/QuarkXPress 6.5, Adobe/Acrobat 3.0, Adobe/Creative Suite 2.
Production Equipment: Hardware – Ap Windows 2000 Photo Server, 2-AG/1500, 2-APP/Mac G3; Scanners – 1-Kk/2035
Production Software: QPS/QuarkXPress 4.11, Adobe/Photoshop 7.0, Adobe/Creative Suite 2.
Total Circulation: 8215

ATLANTA
ATLANTA JOURNAL-CONSTITUTION

Corporate/Parent Company: Cox Media Group
Publication Street Address: 223 Perimeter Center Pkwy NE
City: Atlanta
State: GA
Publication Website: www.ajc.com
Postal Code: 30346-1301
Office phone: 404-522-4141
General E-mail: customercare@ajc.com
Publisher Name: Donna Hall
Publisher Email: Donna.Hall@ajc.com
Editor Name: Kevin Riley
Editor Email: kriley@ajc.com
Editor Phone: 404-526-2161
Advertising Executive Name: Beth Bowers
Advertising Executive Email: Beth.Bowers@ajc.com
Year Established: 1868
Delivery Methods:
  Mail`Newsstand`Carrier`Racks
Own Printing Facility?: Y
Commercial printers?: N
Mechanical specifications: Type page 12 5/8 x 21 1/4; E - 6 cols, 1 13/16, 1/8 between; A - 6 cols, 1 13/16, 1/8 between; C - 10 cols, 1 1/16, 1/8 between.
Published Days: Mon`Tues`Wed`Thur`Fri`Sat`Sun
Weekday Frequency: m
Saturday Frequency: m
Avg Paid Circ: 139864
Audit Company: AAM
Audit Date: 19 03 2020
Pressroom Equipment: Lines – 4-TKS/(20 half decks; 4 satellites) (Gwinnett); 2-TKS/7000CD tower units (Gwinnett); 4-TKS/(20 half decks; 4 satellites) (Fulton); Folders – 8-TKS/(Fulton), 8-TKS/(Gwinnett); Reels & Stands – 40, 40.;
Mailroom Equipment: Counter Stackers – 13-SH/257 (Fulton), 16-QWI/300-350 (Gwinnett); Inserters & Stuffers – 1-NP/1472, 3-QWI/201, 4-QWI/200 (Reach), 2-GMA/SLS 2000 30:2 (Gwinnett), 1-GMA/SLS 2000 36:2 (Gwinnett), 1-QWI/400 (Reach); Tying Machines – 11-Si/Fulton, 14;
Buisness Equipment: IBM/9672 RC4
Buisness Software: CA, Global
Classified Equipment: Hardware – 145-IBM/3192, 2-Ad Star;
Classified Software: In-house.
Editorial Equipment: Hardware – 620-APP/Mac, 175-APP/Mac Powerbook/18-Sun/Server, 2-Dell/Gu55 Server; Printers – HP, Xante, Canon
Editorial Software: DTI.
Production Equipment: Hardware – 4-KFM/Bender single width, 2-Cx/Bidco, Glunz & Jensen/K2; Cameras – 4-C/Spartan; Scanners – 1-Howtek, 2-ECR/1800, 2-ECR/Autokon 1000, 2-Pixel Craft (tab size), 1-Scitex/Smartscan, 1-Tecsa/TS2470, 1-Tecsa/TS2570
Production Software: DTI.
Total Circulation: 196911

FULTON COUNTY DAILY REPORT

Corporate/Parent Company: ALM
Publication Street Address: 190 Pryor St SW
City: Atlanta
State: GA
Publication Website: www.dailyreportonline.com
Postal Code: 30303-3607
Office phone: (404) 521-1227
General E-mail: customercare@alm.co
Editor Name: Leigh Jones
Delivery Methods:
  Mail`Newsstand`Carrier`Racks
Own Printing Facility?: N
Commercial printers?: Y
Published Days: Mon`Tues`Wed`Thur`Fri`Sat`Sun
Weekday Frequency: m
Saturday Frequency: m
Avg Paid Circ: 2805
Avg Free Circ: 225
Audit Company: VAC
Audit Date: 31 12 2016
Total Circulation: 3030

AUGUSTA
THE AUGUSTA CHRONICLE

Corporate/Parent Company: GateHouse Media
Publication Street Address: 725 Broad St
City: Augusta
State: GA
Publication Website: https://www.augustachronicle.com/
Postal Code: 30901-1336
Office phone: (706) 724-0851
General E-mail: newsroom@augustachronicle.com
Editor Name: Joe Hotchkiss
Editor Email: jhotchkiss@augustachronicle.com
Editor Phone: 706.823.3366
Advertising Executive Name: James Holmes
Advertising Executive Email: james.holmes@augustachronicle.com
Advertising Executive Phone: 706.823.3400
Year Established: 1785
Delivery Methods:

Mail`Newsstand`Carrier`Racks
Own Printing Facility?: Y
Commercial printers?: Y
Mechanical specifications: Type page 10.1667 x 21 1/4
Published Days: Mon`Tues`Wed`Thur`Fri`Sat`Sun
Weekday Frequency: m
Saturday Frequency: m
Avg Paid Circ: 41663
Audit Company: AAM
Audit Date: 16 07 2019
Pressroom Equipment: Lines – 1-G/Metro (6 color decks and 3 mono units) Folders – 2-G/3:2 Imperial folders 144 page, 8 reels & stands
Mailroom Equipment: Counter Stackers – 4/StraPack 2/Quipp 351, 2 GMA SLS 2000 inserting machines, 4 StraPack strapping machines 2Dynaric NP-2 strapping machines; 2 StraPapp bottom wrap machines and 3 Quipp bottom wrap machines
Buisness Equipment: 2-IBM/RISC6000
Buisness Software: PBS/Circ. 3.2, PBS/Adv. 2.8
Classified Equipment: Hardware – DTI, APP/Mac;
Classified Software: DTI, APP/Mac.
Editorial Equipment: Hardware – APP/Power Mac; Prinergy Evo with 2 Creo CTP devices
Editorial Software: ContentWatch
Production Equipment: 1 9 unit metro press unit with 6 color decks with 2 144 page Imperial folders Goss Metro
Production Software: QPS/Qu
Note: New Business Unit: Main Street Digital Provides full product set of digital services
Total Circulation: 22569

BRUNSWICK

THE BRUNSWICK NEWS

Publication Street Address: 3011 Altama Ave
City: Brunswick
State: GA
Publication Website: www.thebrunswicknews.com
Postal Code: 31520-4626
Office phone: (912) 265-8320
General E-mail: editor@thebrunswicknews.com
Editor Name: Buddy Hughes
Advertising Executive Name: Bill Cranford
Year Established: 1902
Delivery Methods: Newsstand`Carrier`Racks
Own Printing Facility?: Y
Commercial printers?: Y
Mechanical specifications: Type page 13 x 21; E - 6 cols, 2 1/16, 1/8 between; A - 6 cols, 2 1/16, 1/8 between; C - 8 cols, 1 1/2, 1/8 between.
Published Days: Mon`Tues`Wed`Thur`Fri`Sat
Weekday Frequency: m
Saturday Frequency: m
Avg Paid Circ: 17800
Audit Company: USPS
Audit Date: 27 09 2017
Pressroom Equipment: Lines – 8-G/Community 1974.;
Mailroom Equipment: Address Machine – Papertrack System.;
Buisness Equipment: Papertrak/System
Classified Software: Baseview, QPS/QuarkXPress.
Editorial Software: Baseview.
Production Equipment: Hardware – Nu/Flip Top, DP; Cameras – C/Spartan III
Production Software: Baseview.
Total Circulation: 17800

BRUNSWICK NEWS, INC.

Publication Street Address: 3011 Altama Ave
City: Brunswick
State: GA
Publication Website: https://thebrunswicknews.com/
Postal Code: 31520
Office phone: (912) 265-8320
General E-mail: editor@thebrunswicknews.com
Editor Name: Buddy Hughes
Year Established: 1902
Published Days: Mon`Tues`Wed`Thur`Fri`Sat
Weekday Frequency: m
Saturday Frequency: m
Audit Company: Sworn/Estimate/Non-Audited
Audit Date: 7 12 2019

CANTON

CHEROKEE TRIBUNE

Corporate/Parent Company: Times Journal Inc.
Publication Street Address: 521 E Main St
City: Canton
State: GA
Publication Website: www.cherokeetribune.com
Postal Code: 30114-2805
Office phone: (770) 479-1441
General E-mail: newsupdate@tribuneledgernews.com
Publisher Name: Otis A. Brumby III
Publisher Email: otis3@mdjonline.com
Editor Name: Gary Tanner
Editor Email: gtanner@mdjonline.com
Advertising Executive Name: Paula Milton
Advertising Executive Email: pmilton@mdjonline.com
Advertising Executive Phone: 770-479-1441
Mechanical specifications: Type page 11 5/8 x 21.
Published Days: Wed`Thur`Fri`Sat`Sun
Weekday Frequency: m
Saturday Frequency: m
Avg Paid Circ: 4238
Audit Company: AAM
Audit Date: 31 12 2014
Total Circulation: 4238

CARROLLTON

TIMES-GEORGIAN

Corporate/Parent Company: Paxton Media Group, LLC
Publication Street Address: 901 Hays Mill Rd
City: Carrollton
State: GA
Publication Website: www.times-georgian.com
Postal Code: 30117-9576
Office phone: (770) 834-6631
General E-mail: rstilley@times-georgian.com
Publisher Name: Rachael Raney
Publisher Email: publisher@times-georgian.com
Publisher Phone: 470.729.3234
Editor Name: Corey Cusick
Editor Email: corey@times-georgian.com
Editor Phone: 470.729.3249
Advertising Executive Name: Melissa Wilson
Advertising Executive Email: melissa@times-georgian.com
Advertising Executive Phone: 470.729.3237
Year Established: 1871
Delivery Methods: Mail`Newsstand`Carrier`Racks
Own Printing Facility?: Y
Commercial printers?: Y
Mechanical specifications: Type page 10 x 21; E - 6 cols, 1 9/16, 1/8 between; A - 6 cols, 1 9/16, 1/8 between; C - 1 9/16 1/8 between.
Published Days: Tues`Wed`Thur`Fri`Sun
Weekday Frequency: m
Avg Paid Circ: 5092
Avg Free Circ: 18
Audit Company: USPS
Audit Date: 28 09 2016
Pressroom Equipment: Lines – 9-G/Community.;
Mailroom Equipment: Counter Stackers – 1-BG/Count-O-Veyor; Inserters & Stuffers – 2/MM; Tying Machines – 2-/MLN; Address Machine – 1-/KR.;
Buisness Equipment: 6-APP/Mac
Buisness Software: Baseview/Ap Manager Pro
Classified Equipment: Hardware – 5-APP/Mac;
Classified Software: Baseview/Ad Manager Pro.
Editorial Equipment: Hardware – 11-APP/Mac; Printers – 1-APP/Mac LaserWriter II NTX, APP/Mac Printer
Editorial Software: Baseview, Baseview/NewsEdit Pro, QPS/QuarkXPress.

CARTERSVILLE

THE DAILY TRIBUNE NEWS

Corporate/Parent Company: Cleveland Newspapers, Inc.
Publication Street Address: 251 S Tennessee St
City: Cartersville
State: GA
Publication Website: www.daily-tribune.com
Postal Code: 30120-3605
Office phone: (770) 382-4545
Publisher Name: Alan Davis
Publisher Email: alan.davis@daily-tribune.com
Editor Name: Jason Greenberg
Editor Email: jason.greenberg@daily-tribune.com
Advertising Executive Name: Jennifer Moates
Advertising Executive Email: advertising@daily-tribune.com
Year Established: 1946
Delivery Methods: Mail`Carrier`Racks
Own Printing Facility?: Y
Commercial printers?: N
Mechanical specifications: Type page 13 x 21 1/2; E - 6 cols, 2 1/16, 1/8 between; A - 6 cols, 2 1/16, 1/8 between; C - 6 cols, 2 1/16, 1/8 between.
Published Days: Tues`Wed`Thur`Fri`Sat`Sun
Weekday Frequency: m
Saturday Frequency: m
Avg Paid Circ: 4615
Avg Free Circ: 242
Audit Company: AAM
Audit Date: 6/31/2018
Pressroom Equipment: Lines – 7-WPC/Web Leader (2-Color quad); 4-WPC/Web Leader (1-Color quad); 3-WPC/Web leader (1-Color quad);
Mailroom Equipment: Counter Stackers – 1/Mid America Graphics; Inserters & Stuffers – MM/7:1; Tying Machines – 2-/Bu, 1-Strapex/Solomat; Address Machine – 3-/Dispensa-Matic/16.;
Buisness Equipment: DEC/PC XL 466D2, 1-Mk/Digital
Classified Equipment: Hardware – 2-APP/Mac; Printers – APP/Mac LaserWriter Pro 630;
Classified Software: Baseview.
Editorial Equipment: Hardware – APP/Mac/7-APP/Mac; Printers – APP/Mac LaserWriter Pro 630
Editorial Software: Baseview 3.3.
Production Equipment: Hardware – C/Powermatic-66F, Adobe/Photoshop, V/3990; Cameras – 1-C/Spartan III; Scanners – 1-AG/Arcus II, 1-AG/Arcus Plus, 1-Polaroid/SprintScan 35
Production Software: Baseview, QPS/QuarkXPress.
Total Circulation: 4857

COLUMBUS

COLUMBUS LEDGER-ENQUIRER

Corporate/Parent Company: McClatchy
Publication Street Address: 945 Broadway Ste 102
City: Columbus
State: GA
Publication Website: www.ledger-enquirer.com
Postal Code: 31901-2772
Office phone: (706) 324-5526
Editor Name: Lauren Gorla
Editor Email: lgorla@ledger-enquirer.com
Advertising Executive Name: McDuffie, Ross
Advertising Executive Email: rmcduffie@mcclatchy.com
Advertising Executive Phone: (706) 571-8615
Year Established: 1930
Delivery Methods: Newsstand`Carrier
Mechanical specifications: Type page 9.89 x 21
Published Days: Mon`Tues`Wed`Thur`Fri`Sat`Sun
Weekday Frequency: m
Saturday Frequency: m
Production Equipment: Hardware – Caere/Omnipage Pro 6.0; Cameras – 1-C/Spartan III
Production Software: QPS/QuarkXPress 3.32.
Total Circulation: 5110

DALTON

THE DAILY CITIZEN

Corporate/Parent Company: Community Newspaper Holdings, Inc.
Publication Street Address: 308 S Thornton Ave
City: Dalton
State: GA
Publication Website: www.dailycitizen.news
Postal Code: 30720-8268
Office phone: (706) 217-6397
General E-mail: circulation@daltoncitizen.com
Publisher Name: Keith Barlow
Publisher Email: keithbarlow@dailycitizen.news
Editor Name: Jamie Jones
Editor Email: jamiejones@dailycitizen.news
Editor Phone: (706) 272-7723
Advertising Executive Name: Renee Reddix
Advertising Executive Email: reneereddix@dailycitizen.news
Advertising Executive Phone: (706) 272-7754
Mechanical specifications: Type page 11 1/2 x 21 1/2; E - 6 cols, 1 13/16, 5/32 between; A - 6 cols, 1 13/16, 5/32 between; C - 6 cols, 1 13/16, 5/32 between.
Published Days: Mon`Tues`Wed`Thur`Fri`Sat`Sun
Weekday Frequency: m
Saturday Frequency: m
Avg Paid Circ: 11040
Audit Company: Sworn/Estimate/Non-Audited
Audit Date: 7 12 2019
Pressroom Equipment: Lines – 10-G/Community.;
Mailroom Equipment: Tying Machines – 1-Bu/String Tying Machine; Address Machine – 1/KR, 1-/KAN.;
Buisness Equipment: ICanon (ATT)
Buisness Software: Microsoft/Office 97
Classified Equipment: Hardware – APP/Mac;
Classified Software: FSI.
Editorial Equipment: Hardware – APP/Mac/APP/Mac Graphics Network, APP/Mac.
Production Equipment: Hardware – Pre Press/Panther 2042; Scanners – Umax/Mirage
Production Software: QPS/QuarkXPress, Multi-Ad/Creator, Macromedia/Freehand.
Total Circulation: 11040

DUBLIN

THE COURIER HERALD

Corporate/Parent Company: Herald Newspapers, Inc.
Publication Street Address: 115 S Jefferson St
City: Dublin
State: GA
Publication Website: https://courierheraldtoday.com/
Postal Code: 31021-5146
Office phone: (478) 272-5522
General E-mail: tchnewsroom61@gmail.com
Year Established: 1876
Delivery Methods: Carrier`Racks
Own Printing Facility?: Y
Commercial printers?: Y
Mechanical specifications: Type page 13 x 21 1/2; E - 6 cols, 2 1/16, 1/8 between; A - 6 cols, 2 1/16, 1/8 between; C - 6 cols, 2 1/16, 1/8 between.
Published Days: Mon`Tues`Wed`Thur`Fri`Sat
Weekday Frequency: e
Saturday Frequency: e
Avg Paid Circ: 7141
Avg Free Circ: 29
Audit Company: AAM
Audit Date: 31 12 2018
Pressroom Equipment: 8-G/SC (with Gev-Flexicolor half deck); Folders – 1-G/SC.
Mailroom Equipment: Tying Machines – 2/AMP, 1-/MLN, 1-/Bu; Address Machine – 1-/Ch.;
Buisness Equipment: MTI/Micro-Computer
Classified Equipment: Hardware – Mk.;
Editorial Equipment: Hardware – Mk.

Avg Paid Circ: 14328
Avg Free Circ: 681
Audit Company: AAM
Audit Date: 31 03 2018
Total Circulation: 15009

U.S. Daily Newspapers

Production Equipment: Hardware – 1-APP/Mac LaserWriter NT, 1-Dataproducts/11 x 17; Cameras – 1-CL/Horizontal, 1-R/Vertical; Scanners – 1-APP/Mac, 1-Mirror/Color scanner.
Total Circulation: 7170

GAINESVILLE

THE TIMES

Publication Street Address: 345 Green St NW
City: Gainesville
State: GA
Publication Website: www.gainesvilletimes.com
Postal Code: 30501-3370
Office phone: 770-532-1234
Editor Name: Shannon Casas
Editor Email: scasas@gainesvilletimes.com
Editor Phone: 770-718-3417
Advertising Executive Name: Bernadette Mastracchio
Advertising Executive Email: bmastracchio@gainesvilletimes.com
Advertising Executive Phone: 770-535-6337
Year Established: 1947
Delivery Methods: Newsstand`Carrier`Racks
Own Printing Facility?: Y
Commercial printers?: Y
Mechanical specifications: Type page 13 x 21 1/2; E - 6 cols, 2 1/16, 1/8 between; A - 6 cols, 2 1/16, 1/8 between; C - 10 cols, 1 3/16, 1/16 between.
Published Days: Mon`Tues`Wed`Thur`Fri`Sat`Sun
Weekday Frequency: m
Saturday Frequency: m
Avg Paid Circ: 14000
Audit Company: Sworn/Estimate/Non-Audited
Audit Date: 7 12 2019
Pressroom Equipment: Lines – 4-G/Urbanite 1970, 8-G/Urbanite 1982, 2-G/Urbanite 1984, 1-G/Urbanite 1985; Press Drive – 4-Fin/100 h.p. Drive Motors; Folders – G/Urbanite U775, G/Urbanite U1362;
Mailroom Equipment: Counter Stackers – 1-QWI/300, 1/PPK, 1-QWI/351; Inserters & Stuffers – 3-/MM; Tying Machines – 2-/Bu, 2-/MLN; Address Machine – 1-Barstrom/Labeler, 1-/Ch;
Classified Equipment: Hardware – 5-PC P166, 1-Pentium/Pro 200 PC; SyQuest/Disc Reader; Printers – 1-Lexmark/Optra;
Classified Software: APT/V2.
Editorial Equipment: Hardware – 21-PC P166, 9-PC P200, 1-Pentium/PC Pro 2000; Printers – 1-Lexmark/Optra, 1-HP/LaserJet 4MV
Editorial Software: Scoop
Production Equipment: Hardware – 2-ECR/4550 Imagesetter with PC RIP, 1-ECR/Autokon 1000 DE, Pre Press/Panther Plus, Epson/Stylus ProxI Proofer, Xante/Accel-a-Writer 8900 Plain Paper, 2-ECR/4500; Scanners – ECR/Autokon 1000 DE, AG/Arcus Plus, Umax/Flat
Total Circulation: 14000

GRIFFIN

GRIFFIN DAILY NEWS

Corporate/Parent Company: Paxton Media Group, LLC
Publication Street Address: 1403 N Expressway
City: Griffin
State: GA
Publication Website: www.griffindailynews.com
Postal Code: 30223-9015
Office phone: (770) 227-3276
General E-mail: rstilley@times-georgian.com
Publisher Name: Joy Gaddy
Publisher Email: joy@griffindailynews.com
Publisher Phone: 470.771.4735
Editor Name: Tim Daly
Editor Email: tim@griffindailynews.com
Editor Phone: 470.771.4742
Advertising Executive Name: Crystal Holbert
Advertising Executive Email: cholbert@griffindailynews.com
Advertising Executive Phone: 470.771.4736

Delivery Methods: Mail`Carrier`Racks
Own Printing Facility?: N
Commercial printers?: N
Mechanical specifications: Type page 13 x 21 1/2; E - 6 cols, 2, 1/6 between; A - 6 cols, 2, 1/6 between; C - 9 cols, 1 1/3, 1/6 between.
Published Days: Tues`Wed`Thur`Fri`Sun
Weekday Frequency: m
Avg Paid Circ: 6936
Audit Company: Sworn/Estimate/Non-Audited
Audit Date: 7 12 2019
Pressroom Equipment: Lines – 8-G 1968; Folders – SC/Community.;
Mailroom Equipment: Counter Stackers – 1-BG/Count-O-Veyor; Inserters & Stuffers – 1-MM/5 pocket; Tying Machines – 1/Bu; Address Machine – KAN/Zip Code Separator, KAN/Label Applicator.;
Buisness Equipment: 1-Cumulus/GLC 1220 W
Classified Equipment: Hardware – APP/Mac; TI/Omni 800; Printers – QMS/2060.;
Editorial Equipment: Hardware – APP/Mac
Editorial Software: Baseview/NewsEdit Pro IQue, QPS/QuarkXPress 4.04.
Production Equipment: Hardware – Caere/OmniPage, QMS/2060; Cameras – 1-C/Spartan II; Scanners – 2-APP/Mac One Scanner
Production Software: QPS/QuarkXPress 4.04.
Total Circulation: 6936

LAGRANGE

LAGRANGE DAILY NEWS

Corporate/Parent Company: Boone Newspapers
Publication Street Address: 105 Ashton St
City: Lagrange
State: GA
Publication Website: www.lagrangenews.com
Postal Code: 30240-3111
Office phone: (706) 884-7311
General E-mail: news@lagrangenews.com
Editor Name: Daniel Evans
Year Established: 1843
Delivery Methods: Mail`Newsstand`Carrier`Racks
Own Printing Facility?: Y
Commercial printers?: Y
Mechanical specifications: Type page 13 3/4 x 21 1/2; E - 6 cols, 1 5/6, 1/8 between; A - 6 cols, 1 5/6, 1/8 between; C - 9 cols, 1 3/16, 1/16 between.
Published Days: Mon`Tues`Wed`Thur`Fri`Sat
Weekday Frequency: e
Saturday Frequency: m
Avg Paid Circ: 13400
Audit Company: Sworn/Estimate/Non-Audited
Audit Date: 7 12 2019
Pressroom Equipment: Lines – 7-G;
Buisness Equipment: 1-Bs/90
Editorial Equipment: Hardware – COM/One Sys.
Production Equipment: Hardware – COM/OS; Cameras – 1-B, 1-C.
Total Circulation: 13400

MACON

THE TELEGRAPH

Corporate/Parent Company: McClatchy
Publication Street Address: 1675 Montpelier Ave.
City: Macon
State: GA
Publication Website: www.macon.com
Postal Code: 31201
Office phone: (478) 744-4200
Publisher Name: Alexandra Villoch
Editor Name: Tim Regan-Porter
Advertising Executive Name: McDuffie, Ross
Advertising Executive Email: rmcduffie@mcclatchy.com
Advertising Executive Phone: (706) 571-8615
Year Established: 1826
Delivery Methods: Newsstand`Carrier`Racks
Own Printing Facility?: N
Commercial printers?: Y
Mechanical specifications: Type page 11 3/4 x 21 1/8; E - 6 cols, 1 7/8, 1/8 between; A - 6 cols, 1 7/8, 1/8 between; C - 10 cols, 1 7/100, 1/5 between.
Published Days: Mon`Tues`Wed`Thur`Fri`Sat`Sun
Weekday Frequency: m
Saturday Frequency: m
Avg Paid Circ: 21125
Audit Company: AAM
Audit Date: 30 06 2018
Buisness Equipment: 1-HP/3000 Series 957
Buisness Software: Microsoft/Excel, Microsoft/Word, Reflections, Monarc, CJ/AIM-CIS
Classified Equipment: Hardware – Sun/Ultra Enterprise Servers, APP/Macs; MON/4550, MON/1270, 2-MON/News Express; Printers – HP/Lasers
Classified Software: DTI.
Editorial Equipment: Hardware – DTI, Sun/Ultra Enterprise Servers, APP/Macs/MON/4550, MON/1270, 2-MON/News Express; Printers – HP/Lasers
Editorial Software: Saxotech
Production Equipment: Hardware – 2-MON/1200 News Express, 1-Na/FPII, 3-Glunz & Jensen
Production Software: DTI.
Total Circulation: 21125

MARIETTA

MARIETTA DAILY JOURNAL

Corporate/Parent Company: Times Journal Inc.
Publication Street Address: 47 Waddell St. SE
City: Marietta
State: GA
Publication Website: www.mdjonline.com
Postal Code: 30060
Office phone: (770) 428-9411
General E-mail: customerservice@mdjonline.com
Publisher Name: Otis Brumby
Publisher Email: otis3@mdjonline.com
Publisher Phone: (770) 428-9411 x301
Editor Name: Jon Gillooly
Editor Email: jgillooly@mdjonline.com
Editor Phone: 770-428-9411 x211
Advertising Executive Name: Travis Knight
Advertising Executive Email: tknight@mdjonline.com
Advertising Executive Phone: 770-428-9411 x510
Year Established: 1866
Mechanical specifications: Type page 11 5/8 x 21; E - 6 cols, 1 5/6, 2/5 between; A - 6 cols, 2, 2/5 between; C - 10 cols, 2/5 between.
Published Days: Mon`Tues`Wed`Thur`Fri`Sat`Sun
Weekday Frequency: m
Saturday Frequency: m
Avg Paid Circ: 12571
Avg Free Circ: 376
Audit Company: AAM
Audit Date: 31 12 2016
Pressroom Equipment: Lines – 5-MAN/4 x 2 double width 1995;
Mailroom Equipment: Counter Stackers – 3-HL/Monitor; Inserters & Stuffers – 3/KR; Tying Machines – 4-/Bu, 2-Si.;
Buisness Equipment: 1-IBM/RSC 6000, Compaq/5500
Buisness Software: APT, PBS, Quark XPress, Microsoft Word, SBS
Classified Equipment: Hardware – Ik; Printers – Panasonic;
Classified Software: Ik.
Editorial Equipment: Hardware – Ik/ECR/Scriptsetter; Printers – Okidata, Xante, QMS/6100, QMS/4032, HP/5000
Editorial Software: Ik.
Production Equipment: Hardware – 1-Konica, EV/Jetsetter, ECR/Scriptsetter; Cameras – 1-C/Spartan, 1-C/Spartan III
Production Software: ACT.
Total Circulation: 12947

MILLEDGEVILLE

THE UNION-RECORDER

Corporate/Parent Company: Community Newspaper Holdings, Inc.
Publication Street Address: 165 Garrett Way NW
City: Milledgeville
State: GA
Publication Website: www.unionrecorder.com
Postal Code: 31061-2318
Office phone: (478) 452-0567
General E-mail: nlinder@unionrecorder.com
Publisher Name: Keith Barlow
Publisher Email: kbarlow@unionrecorder.com
Publisher Phone: 478-453-1441
Editor Name: Natalie Davis Linder
Editor Email: nlinder@unionrecorder.com
Editor Phone: 478-453-1462
Mechanical specifications: Type page 11 3/4 x 21 1/2; E - 6 cols, 1 3/4, 1/8 between; A - 6 cols, 2 1/16, 1/8 between; C - 9 cols, 1, 1/16 between.
Published Days: Tues`Wed`Thur`Fri`Sat
Weekday Frequency: m
Saturday Frequency: m
Avg Paid Circ: 7416
Audit Company: Sworn/Estimate/Non-Audited
Audit Date: 7 12 2019
Pressroom Equipment: Lines – 7-G/Community.;
Mailroom Equipment: Tying Machines – Bu/Plastic and string.;
Buisness Equipment: Canyon Lake Software, Navision, Baseview/Ad Manager-Pro
Buisness Software: Microsoft/Office 4.0
Classified Equipment: Hardware – APP/Macs; Printers – Xante/8200;
Classified Software: Baseview/Ad Manage Pro.
Editorial Equipment: Hardware – APP/Mac; Printers – Xante/8200, Unity/1800 PMR
Editorial Software: Baseview/NewsEd.
Production Equipment: Hardware – Caere/OmniPage Pro 8.0, Pre Press/Panther Plus 46; Cameras – C/Spartan III; Scanners – Lf/Leafscan 35, Polaroid/Sprint ScanPlus, HP/2CX
Production Software: QPS/QuarkXPress 4.01.
Total Circulation: 7416

MOULTRIE

THE MOULTRIE OBSERVER

Corporate/Parent Company: Community Newspaper Holdings, Inc.
Publication Street Address: 25 N Main St
City: Moultrie
State: GA
Publication Website: www.moultrieobserver.com
Postal Code: 31768-3861
Office phone: (229) 985-4545
General E-mail: moultrie.observer@gaflnews.com
Publisher Name: Jeff Masters
Publisher Email: jmasters@cnhi.com
Publisher Phone: ext. 1211
Editor Name: Kevin C. Hall
Editor Email: kevin.hall@gaflnews.com
Editor Phone: ext. 1721
Advertising Executive Name: Laurie Gay
Advertising Executive Email: laurie.gay@gaflnews.com
Advertising Executive Phone: ext. 1711
Year Established: 1894
Mechanical specifications: Type page 13 x 21 1/2; E - 6 cols, 2 1/16, 1/8 between; A - 6 cols, 2 1/16, 1/8 between; C - 9 cols, 1 1/4, 1/8 between.
Published Days: Tues`Wed`Thur`Fri`Sat`Sun
Weekday Frequency: m
Saturday Frequency: m
Avg Paid Circ: 7198
Audit Company: Sworn/Estimate/Non-Audited
Audit Date: 7 12 2019
Pressroom Equipment: Lines – 8-G/Community; Folders – 1-G/2:1.;
Mailroom Equipment: Tying Machines – 2/Bu; Address Machine – 2-/Wm.;
Buisness Equipment: IBM/AS-400
Classified Equipment: Hardware – APP/Mac;
Classified Software: FSI.
Editorial Equipment: Hardware – APP/Mac
Editorial Software: FSI/Edit.
Production Equipment: Hardware – 2-Dy/Mark 4, 4-COM/4961, 1-COM/2961, 1-COM/7200; Cameras – 1-C/Spartan II, ECR/Autokon.
Total Circulation: 7198

NEWNAN
THE NEWNAN TIMES-HERALD
Publication Street Address: 16 Jefferson St
City: Newnan
State: GA
Publication Website: www.times-herald.com
Postal Code: 30263-1913
Office phone: (770) 253-1576
General E-mail: news@newnan.com
Publisher Name: Elizabeth C. Neely
Publisher Email: beth@newnan.com
Editor Name: C. Clayton Neely
Editor Email: clay@newnan.com
Advertising Executive Name: Wendy Barnes
Advertising Executive Email: wendy@newnan.com
Year Established: 1865
Delivery Methods: Newsstand`Carrier`Racks
Own Printing Facility?: N
Commercial printers?: N
Mechanical specifications: 6 columns x 20.75"
Published Days: Wed`Thur`Fri`Sun
Weekday Frequency: m
Saturday Frequency: m
Avg Paid Circ: 9300
Audit Company: USPS
Audit Date: 30 09 2016
Mailroom Equipment: PC
Buisness Equipment: PC
Classified Equipment: Hardware – APP/Mac;
Classified Software: Baseview.
Editorial Equipment: Hardware – APP/Mac
Editorial Software: InDesign
Production Equipment: Mac
Production Software: InDesign
Total Circulation: 9300

ROME
ROME NEWS-TRIBUNE
Corporate/Parent Company: Rome News-Tribune
Publication Street Address: 305 E 6th Ave
City: Rome
State: GA
Publication Website: www.romenews-tribune.com
Postal Code: 30161-6007
Office phone: 706-290-5252
General E-mail: romenewstribune@rn-t.com
Publisher Name: Doug Crow, Dir Operations
Publisher Email: dcrow@rn-t.com
Publisher Phone: 706-290-5252
Editor Name: John Bailey
Editor Email: JBailey@rn-t.com
Advertising Executive Name: Stephanie Justice
Advertising Executive Email: sjustice@rn-t.com
Year Established: 1843
Delivery Methods:
 Mail`Newsstand`Carrier`Racks
Own Printing Facility?: N
Commercial printers?: Y
Mechanical specifications: Type page 11 1/2 x 21 1/4; E - 6 cols, 1 5/6, 1/8 between; A - 6 cols, 1 5/6, 1/8 between; C - 9 cols, 1 9/50, 1/16 between.
Published Days: Mon`Tues`Wed`Thur`Fri`Sat`Sun
Weekday Frequency: m
Saturday Frequency: m
Avg Paid Circ: 14921
Audit Company: Sworn/Estimate/Non-Audited
Audit Date: 7 12 2019
Pressroom Equipment: Lines – 15 unit Dgm 430;
Mailroom Equipment: Counter Stackers – Stima/Poly Wrap Insert 12.1; Inserters & Stuffers – Newstec/SLS 1000 10:2; Tying Machines – 1-MLN/MLEE; Control System – Prism; Address Machine – KR/Inkjet, 1-Prism/InkJet Labeling System.;
Buisness Equipment: 1-IBM RS6000
Buisness Software: PBS CM 2.7, PBS/AM 2.8, SBS-GL
Classified Equipment: Hardware – Intergraph/IS 8000 Server, 7-Compaq/2000 DeskPro, Microsoft/NT Server; Printers – HP/5000;
Classified Software: ACT.
Editorial Equipment: Hardware – 1-Compaq/Proliant Server, 27-Compaq/2000 DeskPro/ACT; Printers – HP/5000
Editorial Software: Novell/Network 4.1,

Microsoft/NT 4.0.
Production Equipment: Hardware – LaserMaster/1200dpi, ECR/4550, ECR/VRL 36; Scanners – HP/ScanJet 5P, Nikon/LS-2000, Microtech/ScanMaker V6000, GEI/Tecsa 5000 Full Page
Production Software: ACT.
Total Circulation: 14921

SAVANNAH
SAVANNAH MORNING NEWS
Corporate/Parent Company: Gannett Co., Inc.
Publication Street Address: 1375 Chatham Pkwy
City: Savannah
State: GA
Publication Website: www.savannahnow.com
Postal Code: 31405-0304
Office phone: (912) 236-9511
Publisher Name: Michael Traynor
Publisher Email: michael.traynor@savannahnow.com
Publisher Phone: 912-652-0268
Editor Name: Susan Catron
Editor Email: susan.catron@savannahnow.com
Editor Phone: 912-652-0327
Advertising Executive Name: Tamara Bussie
Advertising Executive Email: tbussie@savannahnow.com
Advertising Executive Phone: 912-652-0218
Mechanical specifications: Type page 11 1/2 x 21 1/2; E - 6 cols, 1 3/4, 3/16 between; A - 6 cols, 1 3/4, 3/16 between; C - 9 cols, 1 1/16, 1/16 between.
Published Days: Mon`Tues`Wed`Thur`Fri`Sat`Sun
Weekday Frequency: m
Saturday Frequency: m
Avg Paid Circ: 19229
Avg Free Circ: 1822
Audit Company: AAM
Audit Date: 3 06 2020
Pressroom Equipment: Lines – 7-G/3176; Folders – 2-G/2:1; Reels & Stands – 7;
Mailroom Equipment: Counter Stackers – 1-HL/HT-2, 3-TMSI/Compass 180; Inserters & Stuffers – MM/227, 3-MM/6:1, Heidelberg/632 14:1; Tying Machines – 2-Dynaric/NP-2, 2-Dynaric/NP 1500; Address Machine – 2/Ch, 1-/KR, Videojet/7000;
Buisness Equipment: Gateway 2000 P5-90
Buisness Software: Microsoft/Excel, WordPerfect, Microsoft/Word
Classified Equipment: Hardware – IBM/AT; Printers – IBM/2391;
Classified Software: DTI/Classified 5.0.
Editorial Equipment: Hardware – IBM/AT, APP/Mac 8100-80, APP/Mac IIfx, APP/Mac SE, APP/Mac 8500-100/IBM/Selectric; Printers – HP/4, III/XIT, HP/5000
Editorial Software: DTI/Edit 5.2, QPS/QuarkXPress, Adobe/Illustrator, Aldus/FreeHand.
Production Equipment: Hardware – 2-Nu/Flip Top FT40UPNS, AG/Accuset 1500, Nu/Vacuum plate burner; Cameras – 1-C/Spartan III; Scanners – Polaroid/SprintScan, Nikon/ScanTouch, Epson/G36, Ag/Studio Star
Production Software: QPS/QuarkXPress, Archetype/OPI, Adobe/Illustrator, Adobe/In Des
Total Circulation: 20203

STATESBORO
STATESBORO HERALD
Corporate/Parent Company: Morris Multimedia, Inc.
Publication Street Address: 1 Proctor St
City: Statesboro
State: GA
Publication Website: www.statesboroherald.com
Postal Code: 30458-1387
Office phone: (912) 764-9031
Editor Name: Eddie Ledbetter
Editor Email: eledbetter@statesboroherald.net
Editor Phone: 912-489-9403
Advertising Executive Name: Jan Melton
Advertising Executive Email: jmelton@

statesboroherald.com
Advertising Executive Phone: 912-489-9401
Year Established: 1937
Delivery Methods:
 Mail`Newsstand`Carrier`Racks
Own Printing Facility?: Y
Commercial printers?: Y
Mechanical specifications: Type page 10 1/2 x 21; E - 6 cols, 1 16/25, 1/8 between; A - 6 cols, 1 16/25, 1/8 between; C - 6 cols, 1 16/25, 1/6 between.
Published Days: Tues`Wed`Thur`Fri`Sat`Sun
Weekday Frequency: m
Saturday Frequency: m
Avg Paid Circ: 6700
Audit Company: USPS
Audit Date: 7 10 2014
Pressroom Equipment: Lines – 12-G/Community 1993;
Mailroom Equipment: Counter Stackers – Heidelberg-Harris; Inserters & Stuffers – Alphaliner, 1997; Tying Machines – Signode;
Buisness Equipment: Dell
Classified Equipment: Hardware – Dell; Printers – HP laserjet 5000;
Classified Software: DTI
Editorial Equipment: Hardware – Dell/DTI; Printers – HP Laserjet5000
Editorial Software: InDesign Adobe Photoshop
Production Equipment: Hardware – Kodak direct to plate
Production Software: InDesign
Total Circulation: 6700

THOMASVILLE
THOMASVILLE TIMES-ENTERPRISE
Corporate/Parent Company: Community Newspaper Holdings, Inc.
Publication Street Address: 106 South St
City: Thomasville
State: GA
Publication Website: www.timesenterprise.com
Postal Code: 31792-6061
Office phone: (229) 226-2400
Editor Name: Pat Donahue
Editor Email: pat.donahue@gaflnews.com
Editor Phone: ext. 1806
Advertising Executive Name: Chris White Mohr
Advertising Executive Email: chris.mohr@gaflnews.com
Advertising Executive Phone: ext. 1810
Delivery Methods:
 Mail`Newsstand`Carrier`Racks
Own Printing Facility?: N
Commercial printers?: Y
Mechanical specifications: Type page 13 x 21 1/2; E - 6 cols, 2 1/16, 1/8 between; A - 6 cols, 2 1/16, 1/8 between; C - 9 cols, 1 5/16, 1/8 between.
Published Days: Tues`Wed`Thur`Fri`Sat`Sun
Weekday Frequency: m
Saturday Frequency: m
Avg Paid Circ: 8293
Audit Company: Sworn/Estimate/Non-Audited
Audit Date: 7 12 2019
Pressroom Equipment: Lines – 8-G, 7-G/Community (1 color unit).;
Mailroom Equipment: Tying Machines – 1-/OVL; Address Machine – 3-Wm/5.;
Buisness Equipment: 6-ATT/Business Sys
Buisness Software: WordPerfect 6.0, Lotus 4.1
Classified Equipment: Hardware – APP/Mac.;
Editorial Equipment: Hardware – FSI
Editorial Software: QPS/QuarkXPress, FSI.
Production Equipment: Hardware – 1-APP/Mac LaserWriter, Tegra/Varityper, 2-APP/Mac, 1-Mk/AdComp; Cameras – SCREEN/Vertical; Scanners – Lf/Leafscan.
Total Circulation: 8293

TIFTON
THE TIFTON GAZETTE
Corporate/Parent Company: Community Newspaper Holdings, Inc.
Publication Street Address: 211 Tift Ave N
City: Tifton

State: GA
Publication Website: www.tiftongazette.com
Postal Code: 31794-4463
Office phone: (229) 382-4321
General E-mail: stuart.taylor@gaflnews.com
Publisher Name: Jeff Masters
Publisher Email: jmasters@cnhi.com
Publisher Phone: ext. 1206
Editor Name: Stuart Taylor
Editor Email: stuart.taylor@gaflnews.com
Editor Phone: 229-382-4321 ext.1903
Advertising Executive Name: Dan Sutton
Advertising Executive Email: Dan.sutton@gaflnews.com
Advertising Executive Phone: 229-244-1880 ext.1243
Year Established: 1888
Delivery Methods: Newsstand`Carrier`Racks
Own Printing Facility?: N
Commercial printers?: Y
Mechanical specifications: Type page 13 x 21 1/2; E - 6 cols, 2 1/16, 1/8 between; A - 6 cols, 2 1/16, 1/8 between; C - 9 cols, 1 3/8, 1/16 between.
Published Days: Tues`Wed`Thur`Fri`Sun
Weekday Frequency: m
Avg Paid Circ: 9046
Audit Company: Sworn/Estimate/Non-Audited
Audit Date: 7 12 2019
Pressroom Equipment: Lines – 6-G/Community;
Mailroom Equipment: Counter Stackers – BG; Tying Machines – 1/Bu, 1-/Staplex; Address Machine – 2-/Wm.;
Buisness Equipment: ATT
Classified Equipment: Hardware – Mk/1100.;
Editorial Equipment: Hardware – Mk/1100.
Production Equipment: Hardware – 2-Mk/Laserwriter; Cameras – 1-III/Newsprint.
Total Circulation: 9046

VALDOSTA
VALDOSTA DAILY TIMES
Corporate/Parent Company: Community Newspaper Holdings, Inc.
Publication Street Address: 201 N Troup St
City: Valdosta
State: GA
Publication Website: www.valdostadailytimes.com
Postal Code: 31601-5774
Office phone: (229) 244-1880
Publisher Name: Jeff Masters
Publisher Email: jmasters@cnhi.com
Publisher Phone: ext. 1206
Editor Name: Jim Zachary
Editor Email: jim.zachary@gaflnews.com
Editor Phone: 229-269-4218 ext.1280
Year Established: 1867
Delivery Methods:
 Mail`Newsstand`Carrier`Racks
Own Printing Facility?: Y
Commercial printers?: Y
Mechanical specifications: Type page 11 1/2 x 21 1/2; E - 6 cols, 1 4/5, 1/6 between; A - 6 cols, 1 4/5, 1/6 between; C - 6 cols, 1 13/16, 1/6 between.
Published Days: Tues`Wed`Thur`Fri`Sat`Sun
Weekday Frequency: m
Saturday Frequency: m
Avg Paid Circ: 10796
Audit Company: Sworn/Estimate/Non-Audited
Audit Date: 7 12 2019
Pressroom Equipment: Lines – 16-2000; Folders – 1, 1.;
Mailroom Equipment: Counter Stackers – 2-MM/(3 station automatic inserter), 2/Sheridan, 2-/Monitors HT, 2-/Compass 100; Inserters & Stuffers – 2-GMA/SLS-1000; Tying Machines – 2-Signode, 2-/PowerStrap, 2-/Samuel; Address Machine – 1-/Kick Rudy;
Buisness Equipment: PBS, Oracle
Classified Equipment: Hardware – Baseview, APP/Mac; Pre Press/Panther Pro 62; Printers – HP/5000;
Classified Software: Baseview 2.1.1, QPS/QuarkXPress 3.32.
Editorial Equipment: Hardware – FSI, APP/Mac; Printers – Xante/Accel-A-Writer 8300, Pre Press/Panther Pro 46, Pre Press/Panther Pro 62, Canon/360 PS
Editorial Software: FSI, QPS/QuarkXPress 3.32,

U.S. Daily Newspapers

Multi-Ad/Creator 4.03, Adobe/Illustrator 7, Adobe/Photoshop 4.0.
Production Equipment: Hardware – Nu/FT40V6, Pre Press/Panther Pro 46, Pre Press/Panther Pro 62; Cameras – 1-LE/121, C, SCREEN/C 680; Scanners – Umax/Mirage, Umax/Mirage II
Production Software: FSI, Multi-Ad/Creator, QPS/QuarkXPress.
Total Circulation: 10796

WAYCROSS

WAYCROSS JOURNAL-HERALD

Publication Street Address: 400 Isabella St
City: Waycross
State: GA
Publication Website: www.wjhnews.com
Postal Code: 31501-3637
Office phone: 912.590.6268
Editor Name: Rick Head
Editor Email: sports@wjhnews.com
Advertising Executive Name: Janet Nichols
Advertising Executive Email: janetnichols@wjhnews.com
Year Established: 1875
Delivery Methods: Carrier`Racks
Own Printing Facility?: Y
Commercial printers?: Y
Mechanical specifications: type page: 12 x 20.25, display adv. 6 cols.; classified adv. 9 cols.
Published Days: Mon`Tues`Wed`Thur`Fri`Sat
Weekday Frequency: e
Saturday Frequency: e
Avg Paid Circ: 6475
Audit Company: Sworn/Estimate/Non-Audited
Audit Date: 7 12 2019
Pressroom Equipment: Lines – 10-unit Goss Community offset press;
Mailroom Equipment: Address Machine – IBM/Sys 36.;
Buisness Equipment: 1-IBM/Sys 54
Classified Equipment: Hardware – 2-Mk/Touchwriter Plus; Printers – APP/Mac LaserPrinter.;
Editorial Equipment: Hardware – APP/Mac, Mk/1100 Plus/1-COM/7200H; Printers – APP/Mac LaserPrinter
Editorial Software: QPS 3.31.
Production Equipment: Hardware – TI/OmniPage 3.1, 1-BKY; Cameras – 1-C/Spartan III
Production Software: QPS 3.31.
Total Circulation: 6475

HAWAII

HILO

HAWAII 24/7

Publication Street Address: P.O. Box 7689
City: Hilo
State: HI
Publication Website: hawaii247.com
Postal Code: 96720
Office phone: 24-02-HAWAII (240-242-9244)
General E-mail: news@hawaii247.com
Publisher Name: Baron Sekiya
Publisher Email: baron@hawaii247.com
Editor Name: Karin Stanton
Editor Email: karin@hawaii247.com

HONOLULU

HONOLULU STAR-ADVERTISER

Corporate/Parent Company: Oahu Publications Inc. / Black Press Media Ltd.
Publication Street Address: 500 Ala Moana Blvd. #7-210
City: Honolulu
State: HI
Publication Website: www.staradvertiser.com
Postal Code: 96813
Office phone: (808) 529-4747

General E-mail: letters@staradvertiser.com
Publisher Name: Dennis Francis
Publisher Phone: (808) 529-4700
Editor Name: Frank Bridgewater
Editor Email: fbridgewater@staradvertiser.com
Editor Phone: (808) 529-4791
Advertising Executive Name: Patrick Klein
Advertising Executive Email: pklein@staradvertiser.com
Advertising Executive Phone: (808) 529-4842
Year Established: 2010
Delivery Methods: Mail`Newsstand`Carrier`Racks
Own Printing Facility?: Y
Commercial printers?: Y
Mechanical specifications: Type page 11 x 21; E - 6 cols, 1 - 1/2", 1/8 between; A - 6 cols, 1 - 1/2, 1/8 between; C - 10 cols, 7/8", 3/32 between.
Published Days: Mon`Tues`Wed`Thur`Fri`Sat`Sun
Weekday Frequency: m
Saturday Frequency: m
Avg Paid Circ: 140666
Audit Company: AAM
Audit Date: 3 06 2020
Pressroom Equipment: Lines – 6 Towers Man Roland Regioman 2004; 6 Towers Man Roland Regioman 2004; Press Drive – VFD - Shaftless; Folders – KFZ 80 (2-3-3) Jaw Folder System; Pasters –CD-13Reels & Stands – CD-13; Control System – PECOM; Registration System – PECOM
Mailroom Equipment: Counter Stackers – 4 - Quipp 501 1 - Quipp 401 4 - Muller Martini Combi Stacks; Inserters & Stuffers – 2 - GMA/SLS 2000; Tying Machines – 4-Dynaric NP 3000 4-Dynaric NP 1500; Control System – SAM; News Grip Links; Address Machine – Videojet BX 6500 ink jet printer;
Buisness Equipment: Dell/Windows
Classified Equipment: Hardware – Dell/Windows; Printers – HP;
Classified Software: ATEX
Editorial Equipment: Hardware – Mac OS X
Editorial Software: Newsedit Pro
Production Equipment: Cameras – Canon

PACIFIC BUSINESS NEWS

Corporate/Parent Company: American City Business Journals
Publication Street Address: 737 Bishop St Suite 1550
City: Honolulu
State: HI
Publication Website: www.bizjournals.com/pacific
Postal Code: 96813
Office phone: 808-955-8100
General E-mail: pacific@bizjournals.com
Publisher Name: Tammy Mencel
Publisher Email: tmencel@bizjournals.com
Publisher Phone: 808-955-8052
Editor Name: A. Kam Napier
Editor Email: knapier@bizjournals.com
Editor Phone: 808-955-8030
Advertising Executive Name: Glenn Zuehls
Advertising Executive Email: gzuehls@bizjournals.com
Year Established: 1963
Published Days: Fri
Avg Free Circ: 12290
Audit Company: Sworn/Estimate/Non-Audited
Audit Date: 6 10 2019

WAILUKU

THE MAUI NEWS

Corporate/Parent Company: Ogden Newspapers, Inc.
Publication Street Address: 100 Mahalani St
City: Wailuku
State: HI
Publication Website: www.mauinews.com
Postal Code: 96793-2529
Office phone: 808-242-6363
General E-mail: opinions@mauinews.com

Publisher Name: Joe Bradley
Publisher Email: jbradley@mauinews.com
Editor Name: Lee Imada
Editor Email: leeimada@mauinews.com
Advertising Executive Name: Dawne Miguel
Advertising Executive Email: advmgr@mauinews.com
Year Established: 1900
Delivery Methods: Mail`Newsstand`Carrier`Racks
Own Printing Facility?: Y
Commercial printers?: Y
Mechanical specifications: Type page 10.25 x19.75
Published Days: Mon`Tues`Wed`Thur`Fri`Sat`Sun
Weekday Frequency: m
Saturday Frequency: m
Avg Paid Circ: 11271
Avg Free Circ: 83
Audit Company: AAM
Audit Date: 10 12 2019
Pressroom Equipment: Lines – 12 DGM Advantage II units;
Mailroom Equipment: Counter Stackers – MM/TYP 267; Inserters & Stuffers – 1 K&M 14 into 1 inserter; Tying Machines – MLN/Wilton; Address Machine – St.;
Buisness Equipment: IBM
Classified Equipment: Hardware – PC;
Classified Software: FSI.
Editorial Equipment: Hardware – Macintosh/IMACS for page layout
Editorial Software: Quark X-Press
Production Equipment: Hardware – 2 Kodak Trendsetter CTP units

IOWA

AMES

AMES TRIBUNE

Corporate/Parent Company: Gannett
Publication Street Address: 317 5th St
City: Ames
State: IA
Publication Website: www.amestrib.com
Postal Code: 50010-6101
Office phone: (515) 232-2160
Editor Name: Michael Crumb
Editor Email: mcrumb@amestrib.com
Editor Phone: 515-663-6961
Advertising Executive Name: Becky Bjork
Advertising Executive Email: RBjork@amestrib.com
Advertising Executive Phone: 515-663-6947
Year Established: 1868
Delivery Methods: Mail`Newsstand`Carrier`Racks
Own Printing Facility?: Y
Commercial printers?: N
Mechanical specifications: Type page 6 cols x 21 1/2
Published Days: Tues`Wed`Thur`Fri`Sat`Sun
Weekday Frequency: e
Saturday Frequency: e
Avg Paid Circ: 5665
Avg Free Circ: 5
Audit Company: VAC
Audit Date: 30 09 2016
Buisness Equipment: 5-Dell
Buisness Software: PBS, APT
Classified Equipment: Hardware – 2-dells; Printers – HP;
Classified Software: APT,
Editorial Equipment: Hardware – 20-Dells/Nikon cameras; Printers – HP
Editorial Software: NewsEngine; Indesign
Total Circulation: 5670

ATLANTIC

ATLANTIC NEWS TELEGRAPH

Corporate/Parent Company: Community Media Group

Publication Street Address: 410 Walnut St
City: Atlantic
State: IA
Publication Website: www.atlanticnewstelegraph.com
Postal Code: 50022-1365
Office phone: (712) 243-2624
Publisher Name: Jeff Lundquist
Publisher Email: jrlund@ant-news.com
Advertising Executive Name: Mike Ruddy
Advertising Executive Email: mjrnews53@gmail.com
Year Established: 1871
Delivery Methods: Mail`Carrier
Mechanical specifications: Type page 13 1/8 x 21 1/2; E - 6 cols, 2 1/16, 1/8 between; A - 6 cols, 2 1/16, 1/8 between; C - 6 cols, 2 1/16, 1/8 between.
Published Days: Mon`Tues`Wed`Thur`Fri`Sat`Sun
Weekday Frequency: e
Saturday Frequency: m
Avg Paid Circ: 2800
Audit Company: Sworn/Estimate/Non-Audited
Audit Date: 7 12 2019
Pressroom Equipment: Lines – 6-G; Folders – 1-G/2:1.;
Mailroom Equipment: Tying Machines – 3/Bu.;
Buisness Equipment: IBM
Classified Equipment: Hardware – 1-APP/Mac.;
Editorial Equipment: Hardware – 1-APP/Mac.
Production Equipment: Hardware – 1-Ic; Cameras – 1-Nu; Scanners – APP/Mac One, 1-APP/Mac LaserPrinter Scanner.
Total Circulation: 2800

BURLINGTON

THE HAWK EYE

Corporate/Parent Company: Gannett
Publication Street Address: 800 S Main St
City: Burlington
State: IA
Publication Website: www.thehawkeye.com
Postal Code: 52601-5870
Office phone: (319) 754-8461
Editor Name: John Gaines
Editor Email: jgaines@thehawkeye.com
Editor Phone: 319-758-8158
Advertising Executive Name: Sean Lewis
Advertising Executive Email: slewis@thehawkeye.com
Advertising Executive Phone: 319-758-8110
Year Established: 1833
Delivery Methods: Mail`Carrier`Racks
Own Printing Facility?: Y
Commercial printers?: Y
Mechanical specifications: Type page 11 63/100 x 21 1/2; E - 6 cols, 1 5/6, 1/8 between; A - 6 cols, 1 5/6, 1/8 between; C - 8 cols, 1 19/50, 4/50 between.
Published Days: Mon`Tues`Wed`Thur`Fri`Sat`Sun
Weekday Frequency: m
Saturday Frequency: m
Avg Paid Circ: 15247
Audit Company: VAC
Audit Date: 30 09 2015
Pressroom Equipment: Lines – 6-G/1008 single width (2 formers); Reels & Stands – Roll/Stands.;
Mailroom Equipment: Counter Stackers – Id/660, QWI/400; Inserters & Stuffers – MM (6 inserter, auto eject); Tying Machines – Sterling/MR50;
Buisness Equipment: Data Sciences
Classified Equipment: Hardware – 4-APP/Mac G3, APP/Mac 7350 ASIP Server; Printers – HP/6 MP;
Classified Software: Baseview.
Editorial Equipment: Hardware – APP/Mac; Printers – HP/5000, 2-HP/4000, HP/750C Plus
Editorial Software: Baseview/News Edit Pro IQue 3.1.8.
Production Equipment: Hardware – Nat/Subtractive 33-1, 1-Nu/Flip Top FT40URNS, 2-Carnfeldt/RA; Cameras – 1-R; Scanners – 1-Umax/Vista 58, 7-Umax/Flatbed
Production Software: QPS/QuarkXPress 4.11.
Total Circulation: 15247

I-23

CARROLL

CARROLL DAILY TIMES HERALD

Publication Street Address: 508 N Court St
City: Carroll
State: IA
Publication Website: www.carrollpaper.com
Postal Code: 51401-2747
Office phone: (712) 792-3573
General E-mail: newspaper@carrollpaper.com
Publisher Name: Ann Wilson
Editor Name: Larry Devine
Advertising Executive Name: Marcia Jensen
Advertising Executive Email: m.jensen@carrollpaper.com
Advertising Executive Phone: 712-792-3573
Year Established: 1868
Delivery Methods: Mail`Carrier
Mechanical specifications: Type page 12 1/2 x 21; E - 6 cols, 1 5/6, 1/6 between; A - 6 cols, 1 5/6, 1/6 between; C - 8 cols, 1 1/3, 1/6 between.
Published Days: Mon`Tues`Wed`Thur`Fri
Weekday Frequency: e
Avg Paid Circ: 6321
Audit Company: Sworn/Estimate/Non-Audited
Audit Date: 7 12 2019
Pressroom Equipment: Lines – 6-HI/Cotrell V-15A; Folders – 1-G/2:1.;
Mailroom Equipment: Tying Machines – 1-MM/Strap-Tyer.;
Buisness Equipment: Synaptic/Circulation Sys
Classified Equipment: Hardware – APP/Mac; Printers – APP/Mac LaserWriter.;
Editorial Equipment: Hardware – APP/Mac; Printers – APP/Mac LaserWriter
Editorial Software: Microsoft/Word 6.0.1.
Production Equipment: Hardware – APP/Mac LaserWriter; Cameras – 1-Nu/SST 1923.
Total Circulation: 6321

CEDAR RAPIDS

THE GAZETTE

Publication Street Address: 500 3rd Ave SE
City: Cedar Rapids
State: IA
Publication Website: www.thegazette.com
Postal Code: 52401-1303
Office phone: (319) 398-8333
General E-mail: customercare@thegazette.com
Editor Name: Zack Kucharski
Editor Email: zack.kucharski@thegazette.com
Editor Phone: 319-398-8219
Year Established: 1883
Delivery Methods: Mail`Newsstand`Carrier`Racks
Own Printing Facility?: Y
Commercial printers?: Y
Mechanical specifications: Type page 11 5/8 x 20; E - 6 cols, 2, between; A - 6 cols, 2, between; C - 6 cols, 1 1/3, 2/3 between.
Published Days: Mon`Tues`Wed`Thur`Fri`Sat`Sun
Weekday Frequency: m
Saturday Frequency: m
Avg Paid Circ: 32449
Avg Free Circ: 3127
Audit Company: AAM
Audit Date: 19 09 2018
Pressroom Equipment: Lines – 9-G/Universal 70 single width (8-four towers)(1-5 high tower) 1999; Folders – 1-G/J233 double width 1999, 3-G/J233 single width 1999; Pasters –Enkel/Universal, 14-Enkel/Autoweb; Reels & Stands – Enkel/Megtec; Control System – Honeywell/P;
Mailroom Equipment: Counter Stackers – HI/Olympian, 2-QWI/350, 2-Rima/SN 2510, 3-Rima/SL 3010, 1-Rima/105; Inserters & Stuffers – 2-GMA/SLS2000; Tying Machines – GMA/Combi Stacks; Control System – GMA/SAM; Address Machine – 2/Dm, 2-/Videojet Systems;
Buisness Equipment: 4-Sun/Sparc 1000, Alpha/2000
Buisness Software: Oracle, Microsoft/Windows, DSI
Classified Equipment: Hardware – HP; Quest/Page Pair, Mindset Live Pag; Printers – HP/LaserJet, ;
Classified Software: Atex
Editorial Equipment: Hardware – HP/Saxotech and In Design; Printers – HP
Production Equipment: Hardware – Kodak CTP
Total Circulation: 97114

CENTERVILLE

AD-EXPRESS & DAILY IOWEGIAN

Corporate/Parent Company: CNHI, LLC
Publication Street Address: 201 N 13th St
City: Centerville
State: IA
Publication Website: www.dailyiowegian.com
Postal Code: 52544-1748
Office phone: (641) 856-6336
General E-mail: newsroom@dailyiowegian.com
Publisher Name: Becky Maxwell
Publisher Email: bmaxwell@dailyiowegian.com
Publisher Phone: Extension 27
Editor Name: Kyle Ocker
Editor Email: kocker@dailyiowegian.com
Editor Phone: Extension 35
Advertising Executive Name: Jamey Foster
Advertising Executive Email: jfoster@dailyiowegian.com
Advertising Executive Phone: Extension 21
Year Established: 1864
Delivery Methods: Mail`Newsstand`Carrier
Own Printing Facility?: N
Commercial printers?: N
Mechanical specifications: Type page 12 x 21 1/2; E - 6 cols, 1 7/8, 1/8 between; A - 6 cols, 1 7/8, 1/8 between; C - 6 cols, 1 7/8, 1/8 between.
Published Days: Mon`Tues`Wed`Thur`Fri
Weekday Frequency: m
Avg Paid Circ: 2806
Audit Company: Sworn/Estimate/Non-Audited
Audit Date: 7 12 2019
Pressroom Equipment: Lines – G/Community; G/Community; G/Community; G/Community.;
Buisness Equipment: HP/2000
Classified Equipment: Hardware – APP/Mac;
Editorial Equipment: Hardware – APP/Mac; Printers – APP/Mac LaserWriter, Xante/Accel-a-Writer
Editorial Software: QPS, Baseview.
Production Equipment: Hardware – Nu; Cameras – Acti.
Total Circulation: 2806

DAILY IOWEGIAN

Corporate/Parent Company: CNHI, LLC
Publication Street Address: 201 North 13th Street
City: Centerville
State: IA
Publication Website: www.dailyiowegian.com
Postal Code: 52544
Office phone: 641-856-6336
General E-mail: newsroom@dailyiowegian.com
Publisher Name: Becky Maxwell
Publisher Email: bmaxwell@dailyiowegian.com
Publisher Phone: Extension 27
Editor Name: Kyle Ocker
Editor Email: kocker@dailyiowegian.com
Editor Phone: Extension 35
Advertising Executive Name: Emily Sivetts
Advertising Executive Email: esivetts@dailyiowegian.com
Advertising Executive Phone: Extension 26

CHARLES CITY

CHARLES CITY PRESS

Corporate/Parent Company: Enterprise Media Inc.
Publication Street Address: 801 Riverside Dr
City: Charles City
State: IA
Publication Website: www.charlescitypress.com
Postal Code: 50616-2248
Office phone: (641) 228-3211
Publisher Name: Christopher Hall
Publisher Phone: 641-228-3211
Editor Name: Bob Steenson
Editor Email: bsteenson@charlescitypress.com
Advertising Executive Name: Joel Gray
Advertising Executive Email: joel@charlescitypress.com
Year Established: 1896
Delivery Methods: Mail`Newsstand`Carrier`Racks
Own Printing Facility?: Y
Commercial printers?: Y
Mechanical specifications: Type page 11 1/2 x 21 1/2; E - 6 cols, 1 3/4, 1/6 between;
Published Days: Mon`Tues`Wed`Thur`Fri
Weekday Frequency: All day
Avg Paid Circ: 2970
Audit Company: Sworn/Estimate/Non-Audited
Audit Date: 7 12 2019
Pressroom Equipment: Lines – 13-G/Community 1984; Folders – 1-G/SC, 1-G/Community.;
Mailroom Equipment: Counter Stackers – BG/Count-O-Veyor; Tying Machines – Bu; Wrapping Singles – El.; Address Machine – VideoJet,
Classified Equipment: Hardware – APP/Mac;
Classified Software: Quark
Editorial Equipment: Hardware – APP/Mac ; Printers – APP/Mac LaserWriter Plus
Editorial Software: Quark, Baseview
Total Circulation: 2970

CLINTON

CLINTON HERALD

Corporate/Parent Company: CNHI, LLC
Publication Street Address: 221 6th Ave S
City: Clinton
State: IA
Publication Website: www.clintonherald.com
Postal Code: 52732-4305
Office phone: (563) 242-7101
General E-mail: news@clintonherald.com
Publisher Name: Ron Gutierrez
Publisher Email: rgutierrez@cnhi.com
Publisher Phone: Ext. 142
Editor Name: Charlene Bielema
Editor Email: cbielema@clintonherald.com
Editor Phone: Ext. 155
Advertising Executive Name: Kathy Huizenga
Advertising Executive Email: khuizenga@clintonherald.com
Advertising Executive Phone: Ext. 131
Year Established: 1855
Delivery Methods: Mail`Newsstand`Carrier`Racks
Own Printing Facility?: N
Commercial printers?: Y
Mechanical specifications: Type page 11 3/5 x 21 1/2; E - 6 cols, 1 4/5, 1/8 between; A - 6 cols, 1 4/5, 1/8 between; C - 9 cols, 1 1/5, 1/16 between.
Published Days: Mon`Tues`Wed`Thur`Fri`Sat
Weekday Frequency: m
Saturday Frequency: m
Avg Paid Circ: 6350
Audit Company: Sworn/Estimate/Non-Audited
Audit Date: 7 12 2019
Pressroom Equipment: Lines – 4-G/Urbanite; Folders – 1-G/2:1; Pasters –Butler/Automatic.
Total Circulation: 6350

COUNCIL BLUFFS

THE DAILY NONPAREIL

Corporate/Parent Company: Lee Enterprises
Publication Street Address: 300 W. Broadway, Ste. 108
City: Council Bluffs
State: IA
Publication Website: www.nonpareilonline.com
Postal Code: 51503-0831
Office phone: (712) 328-1811
General E-mail: cbndigital@ggl.bhminc.com
Publisher Name: Thomas Schmitt
Publisher Email: tom.schmitt@nonpareilonline.com
Publisher Phone: 712-325-5660
Editor Name: Courtney Brummer-Clark
Editor Email: courtney.brummer-clark@nonpareilonline.com
Editor Phone: 712-325-5724
Advertising Executive Name: Bob McKeon
Advertising Executive Email: robert.mckeon@nonpareilonline.com
Advertising Executive Phone: 712-325-5694
Year Established: 1849
Delivery Methods: Mail`Carrier
Own Printing Facility?: Y
Commercial printers?: Y
Mechanical specifications: Type page 12 1/2 x 21 1/2; E - 6 cols, 2 1/16, 1/8 between; A - 6 cols, 2 1/16, 1/8 between; C - 9 cols, 1 3/8, 1/16 between.
Published Days: Tues`Wed`Thur`Fri`Sat`Sun
Weekday Frequency: e
Saturday Frequency: e
Avg Paid Circ: 7094
Avg Free Circ: 726
Audit Company: AAM
Audit Date: 12 11 2018
Pressroom Equipment: Lines – 8-G/Community (3-Color Unit & 1-Stack Unit).;
Mailroom Equipment: Counter Stackers – 1-Toledo/Scale #1938; Inserters & Stuffers – 1-Mandelli/Star 100 (paper cutter); Tying Machines – 1-MLN/Spirit, 1-MLN/SP 300; Control System – MM/1511 Stitcher-Trimmer; Address Machine – 1-Ch/595.;
Buisness Equipment: 1-NCR/I9020
Buisness Software: Newzware
Classified Equipment: Hardware – 4-Cx.;
Editorial Equipment: Hardware – 15-APP/Mac 2200, 4-APP/Mac 8500/Lf/AP Leaf Picture Desk, APP/Mac Quadra; Printers – 2-Pre Press/Panther Pro 36, HP/LaserJet 4MV
Editorial Software: FSI.
Production Equipment: Hardware – Caere/OmniPage 3.0, HP/4MV, 2-Pre Press/Panther Pro 36; Cameras – 1-SCREEN; Scanners – APP/Mac Scanners
Production Software: QPS/QuarkXPress 3.3, FSI.
Total Circulation: 7529

CRESTON

CRESTON NEWS ADVERTISER

Corporate/Parent Company: Shaw Media
Publication Street Address: 503 W Adams St
City: Creston
State: IA
Publication Website: www.crestonnewsadvertiser.com
Postal Code: 50801-3112
Office phone: (641) 782-2141
General E-mail: office@crestonnews.com
Publisher Name: Rich Paulsen
Publisher Email: rpaulsen@crestonnews.com
Editor Name: "Sarah Scull
"
Editor Email: sscull@crestonnews.com
Advertising Executive Name: "Tyler Hetu
"
Advertising Executive Email: thetu@crestonnews.com
Year Established: 1879
Delivery Methods: Mail`Newsstand`Carrier`Racks
Own Printing Facility?: Y
Commercial printers?: Y
Mechanical specifications: Type page 13 x 21 1/2; E - 6 cols, 2, 1/6 between; A - 6 cols, 2, 1/6 between; C - 9 cols, 1 3/10, 3/20 between.
Published Days: Mon`Tues`Wed`Thur`Fri
Weekday Frequency: e
Avg Paid Circ: 4677
Audit Company: Sworn/Estimate/Non-Audited
Audit Date: 7 12 2019
Pressroom Equipment: Lines – G/Community single width 1965; G/Community single width 1965; G/Community single width 1965; G/Community single width 1965; G/Community single width 1976; G/Community single width 1976.;
Mailroom Equipment: Tying Machines – Bu.;
Buisness Equipment: Digital/Prioris XL 6200
Buisness Software: Vision Data
Classified Equipment: Hardware – APP/Mac; Printers – APP/Mac LaserWriter;
Classified Software: Baseview/Class Manager Pro, Claris/Hypercard.

U.S. Daily Newspapers

I-25

Editorial Equipment: Hardware – APP/Mac, APP/iMac/Polaroid/SprintScan, AG/Flatbed Scanner; Printers – APP/Mac LaserWriter
Editorial Software: Baseview/NewsEdit, Baseview/QXEdit.
Production Equipment: Hardware – Text-Bridge; Cameras – B/Caravelle; Scanners – APP/Mac Scanner, APP/Mac, AG
Production Software: Baseview 3.15.
Total Circulation: 4677

DAVENPORT
QUAD-CITY TIMES

Corporate/Parent Company: Lee Enterprises
Publication Street Address: 500 E 3rd St
City: Davenport
State: IA
Publication Website: www.qctimes.com
Postal Code: 52801-1708
Office phone: (563) 383-2200
Publisher Name: Deb Anselm
Publisher Email: danselm@qctimes.com
Publisher Phone: 563-383-2224
Editor Name: Matt Christensen
Editor Email: MChristensen@qctimes.com
Editor Phone: 563-383-2264
Advertising Executive Name: Jim Holm
Advertising Executive Email: jholm@qctimes.com
Advertising Executive Phone: 563-383-2483
Year Established: 1848
Delivery Methods: Mail`Newsstand`Carrier`Racks
Own Printing Facility?: Y
Commercial printers?: Y
Mechanical specifications: Type page 9 29/32 x 20 7/8; E - 6 cols, 1 9/16, 3/32 between; A - 6 cols, 1 9/16, 3/32 between; C - 6 cols, 1 9/16, 3/32 between.
Published Days: Mon`Tues`Wed`Thur`Fri`Sat`Sun
Weekday Frequency: m
Saturday Frequency: m
Avg Paid Circ: 21098
Audit Company: AAM
Audit Date: 29 10 2019
Pressroom Equipment: Lines – 26-G/Colorliner 1990; 10-G/Community 1976, 18-G/Community; 28-G/Colorliner; Folders – 6-G/3:2, 2-G/SSC 1995; Reels & Stands – 8;
Mailroom Equipment: Counter Stackers – 4-QWI/400; Inserters & Stuffers – 1-MM/227, 2-HI/1372 w/Icon System; Tying Machines – 1-MLN/MLN2A, 1-MLN/MLN2, 2-Dynaric/1500; Control System – HI; Address Machine – 2/CH;
Buisness Equipment: IBM/AS-400
Classified Equipment: Hardware – Gateway/P155; Printers – HP/LaserJet;
Classified Software: CText/AdVision.
Editorial Equipment: Hardware – Gateway/P155; Printers – HP/LaserJet
Editorial Software: CText/Dateline, CText/Expressline.
Production Equipment: Hardware – 2-AU/APS-800, 2-AU/APS-108; Cameras – 1-C/19, 1-Nu/19; Scanners – Howtek/2500
Production Software: CText/ALPS.
Total Circulation: 30979

DENISON
DENISON BULLETIN & REVIEW

Corporate/Parent Company: Glacier Media
Publication Street Address: 1410 Broadway
City: Denison
State: IA
Publication Website: www.dbrnews.com
Postal Code: 51442-2053
Office phone: (712) 263-2122
Publisher Name: Greg Wehle
Publisher Email: greg.wehle@bulletinreview.com
Editor Name: Gordon Wolf
Editor Email: gordon.wolf@bulletinreview.com
Advertising Executive Name: Lori Wehle
Advertising Executive Email: lori.wehle@bulletinreview.com
Year Established: 1867
Delivery Methods: Mail`Carrier
Own Printing Facility?: Y
Commercial printers?: N
Mechanical specifications: Type page 10.25x 21 1/2; E - 6 cols, 2 1/8, 1/10 between; A - 6 cols, 2 1/18, 1/10 between; C - 8 cols, 1 1/2, 1/10 between.
Published Days: Mon`Tues`Wed`Fri
Weekday Frequency: e
Avg Paid Circ: 3650
Avg Free Circ: 37500
Audit Company: Sworn/Estimate/Non-Audited
Audit Date: 7 12 2019
Total Circulation: 41150

DES MOINES
THE DES MOINES REGISTER

Corporate/Parent Company: Gannett
Publication Street Address: 400 Locust St
City: Des Moines
State: IA
Publication Website: www.desmoinesregister.com
Postal Code: 50309-2355
Office phone: (515) 284-8000
General E-mail: newsubs@dmreg.com
Editor Name: Carol Hunter
Editor Email: chunter@registermedia.com
Year Established: 1915
Delivery Methods: Newsstand`Carrier`Racks
Own Printing Facility?: Y
Commercial printers?: Y
Mechanical specifications: Type page 11 1/2 x 20 1/2; E - 6 cols, 2 1/16, 1/8 between; A - 6 cols, 2 1/16, 1/8 between; C - 10 cols, 1 3/16, 1/8 between.
Published Days: Mon`Tues`Wed`Thur`Fri`Sat`Sun
Weekday Frequency: m
Saturday Frequency: m
Avg Paid Circ: 65411
Audit Company: AAM
Audit Date: 29 04 2020
Pressroom Equipment: Folders – 3, 2;
Mailroom Equipment: Counter Stackers – 9-QWI/401, 4-QWI/351, 2-BG/STC70; Inserters & Stuffers – 2-HI/NP632-30; Tying Machines – 13-Sterling/NS50, 2-Sterling/NS45; Control System – 1-HI/PRIMA, 1-QWI/BDS; Address Machine – 1-AVY/Labeler 5209, 1-KAN/600.;
Buisness Equipment: 1-IBM AS/-400, 1-IBM AS/-400
Buisness Software: Microsoft/Office
Classified Equipment: Hardware – Sun/420; ROLM, ACD; Printers – QMS, HP/Laserjet;
Classified Software: DTI/Classpeed 5.0.1.
Editorial Equipment: Hardware – Sun/3000/APP/Mac; Printers – APP/Mac LaserWriter, HP/LaserJet, QMS
Editorial Software: DTI/Speedplanner, DTI/Pagespeed, DTI/Speedwriter.
Production Equipment: Hardware – 2-III/3850 Grafix Color Imager, 1-Aii 3850 Wide; Scanners – Horizon/Color, AGFA-T2000, PURUP-ESKOFOT 2024, Umax Mirage II, Umax Powerlook II, Kodak Pro 3570
Production Software: DTI 4.3.
Total Circulation: 85855

DUBUQUE
TELEGRAPH HERALD

Corporate/Parent Company: Woodward Communications, Inc.
Publication Street Address: 801 Bluff St
City: Dubuque
State: IA
Publication Website: https://telegraphherald.com/
Postal Code: 52001-4661
Office phone: (563) 588-5611
General E-mail: bob.woodward@wcinet.com
Publisher Name: Bob Woodward
Publisher Email: bob.woodward@wcinet.com
Editor Name: Monty Gilles
Editor Email: monty.gilles@thmedia.com
Editor Phone: (563) 588-5769
Advertising Executive Phone: (563) 588-5611
Year Established: 1836
Delivery Methods: Mail`Newsstand`Carrier`Racks

Own Printing Facility?: N
Commercial printers?: N
Mechanical specifications: Mechanical specs (Print) - type page 10 x 19.8; E - 6 cols, 1.562, 1/8 between; A - 6 cols, 1.562, 1/8 between; C-9 cols 1, 1/8 between
Published Days: Mon`Tues`Wed`Thur`Fri`Sat`Sun
Weekday Frequency: m
Saturday Frequency: m
Avg Paid Circ: 18349
Avg Free Circ: 2642
Audit Company: AAM
Audit Date: 5 09 2019
Mailroom Equipment: Counter Stackers – 2-QWI, HI/Olympian; Inserters & Stuffers – 1-SLS/1000 14:1; Tying Machines – 1-Samuel, 1/MLN, Si/LB-News 3000; Address Machine – 1-Ch/4-Up.;
Buisness Equipment: HP Desktops/Laptops, HP File Servers (Microsoft 2008 Server), Dell Equalogic SAN
Buisness Software: DTI, ATEX, Paycom, Netsuite, Microsoft Office
Classified Equipment: HP Desktops/Laptops, HP File Servers (Microsoft 2008 Server), Dell Equalogic SAN
Classified Software: Atex, Microsoft SQL Server 2008, PGL Layout, Xpance
Editorial Equipment: TownNews server cluster, HP Desktops/Laptops, MAC Laptops HP File Servers (Microsoft 2008 Server), Dell Equalogic SAN
Editorial Software: TownNews, Amendo, Intellitune, Adobe InDesign and Photoshop, Managing Editor ALS
Production Equipment: Third-party printing facility
Total Circulation: 25087

ESTHERVILLE
ESTHERVILLE NEWS

Corporate/Parent Company: Ogden Newspapers Inc.
Publication Street Address: 10 North 7th Street
City: Estherville
State: IA
Publication Website: www.esthervilledailynews.com
Postal Code: 51334
Office phone: 712-362-2622
General E-mail: editor@esthervillenews.net
Publisher Name: Glen Caron
Publisher Email: gcaron@esthervillenews.net
Editor Name: David Swartz
Editor Email: dswartz@esthervillenews.net
Advertising Executive Name: Dessa Rose
Advertising Executive Email: drose@esthervillenews.net
Delivery Methods: Mail`Carrier
Mechanical specifications: Type page 13 x 21 1/2; E - 6 cols, 2 1/16, 1/8 between; A - 6 cols, 2 1/16, 1/8 between; C - 6 cols, 2, 1/16 between.
Published Days: Sat
Saturday Frequency: m
Avg Paid Circ: 2282
Audit Company: Sworn/Estimate/Non-Audited
Audit Date: 6 10 2019
Classified Equipment: Hardware – 2-APP/Mac LC; Printers – APP/Mac LaserWriter II;
Classified Software: QPS/QuarkXPress.
Editorial Equipment: Hardware – APP/Mac Classic/7-COM/MDT 350; Printers – APP/Mac LaserWriter II
Editorial Software: WriteNow.
Production Equipment: Hardware – APP/Mac LaserWriter II.
Total Circulation: 2282

FAIRFIELD
THE FAIRFIELD LEDGER

Corporate/Parent Company: Folience
Publication Street Address: 114 E. Broadway, Box 110
City: Fairfield
State: IA
Publication Website: www.ffledger.com
Postal Code: 52556-3202
Office phone: (641) 472-4129

Publisher Name: Matt Bryant
Publisher Email: pub@southeastiowaunion.com
Editor Name: Karyn Spory
Editor Email: karyn.spory@southeastiowaunion.com
Advertising Executive Name: Leann Nolte
Advertising Executive Email: leann.nolte@southeastiowaunion.com
Year Established: 1849
Delivery Methods: Mail`Newsstand`Carrier`Racks
Own Printing Facility?: Y
Commercial printers?: Y
Mechanical specifications: Type page 13 x 21 1/2; E - 6 cols, 2 1/16, 1/8 between; A - 6 cols, 2 1/16, 1/8 between; C - 8 cols, 1 1/2, 1/8 between.
Published Days: Mon`Tues`Wed`Thur`Fri
Weekday Frequency: e
Avg Paid Circ: 2530
Audit Company: Sworn/Estimate/Non-Audited
Audit Date: 7 12 2019
Pressroom Equipment: Lines – 5-G/Community; Folders – 1-G/Community, 1-G/Gregg Plow.;
Mailroom Equipment: Tying Machines – 1/Sa; Address Machine – St/1600.;
Editorial Equipment: Hardware – Mk.
Production Equipment: Hardware – 1-Nu; Cameras – 1-K/241.
Total Circulation: 2530

FORT DODGE
THE MESSENGER

Corporate/Parent Company: Paxton Media Group
Publication Street Address: 713 Central Ave
City: Fort Dodge
State: IA
Publication Website: www.messengernews.net
Postal Code: 50501-3813
Office phone: (515) 573-2141
General E-mail: editor@messengernews.net
Publisher Name: Terry Christensen
Publisher Email: tchristensen@messengernews.net
Publisher Phone: Ext. 211
Editor Name: Bill Shea
Editor Email: bshea@messengernews.net
Editor Phone: Ext. 460
Advertising Executive Name: Cory Bargfrede
Advertising Executive Email: cbargfrede@messengernews.net
Advertising Executive Phone: Ext. 428
Year Established: 1856
Delivery Methods: Mail`Newsstand`Carrier`Racks
Own Printing Facility?: Y
Commercial printers?: N
Mechanical specifications: Type page 11 1/106 x 21 1/2; E - 6 cols, 1 3/4, 1/16 between; A - 6 cols, 1 3/4, 1/16 between; C - 9 cols, 1 1/4, 1/16 between.
Published Days: Mon`Tues`Wed`Thur`Fri`Sat`Sun
Weekday Frequency: m
Saturday Frequency: m
Avg Paid Circ: 7898
Avg Free Circ: 328
Audit Company: AAM
Audit Date: 30 01 2020
Pressroom Equipment: Lines – 14-G; Press Drive - 2-Fin/100 h.p.; Folders – 1-G/3:2, 1-G/SSC, 1-G/SSC/Quarter Folder; Pasters –8-Martin/EC Splicer.
Mailroom Equipment: Counter Stackers – 2-BG/108, HI/HT II, 1-HI/RS25; Inserters & Stuffers – HI/1372, Muller 227 6/1; Tying Machines – 3/Bu; Wrapping Singles – 1-Power Strap; Address Machine – KR/Inkjet;
Classified Equipment: Hardware – MS Windows 2003; Printers – 1-LaserJet 2035n
Editorial Equipment: Hardware – MS Windows 2003; IMAC G6; Printers – 1-HP LaserJet 5100
Editorial Software: QPS/QuarkXPress 8, Adobe/Photoshop CS6
Production Equipment: Hardware – HP 5500n Printer; HP 5550n Printer; Scanners – Epson V330 Scanner
Production Software: QPS/QuarkXPress 8; Multi-Ad/Creator 8; Adobe

Note: National advertising is sold in combination with the Webster City Daily Freeman-Journal (e) for $53.15 individual newspaper rates not made available.
Total Circulation: 10384

FORT MADISON

FORT MADISON DAILY DEMOCRAT

Publication Street Address: 1226 Avenue H
City: Fort Madison
State: IA
Publication Website: www.dailydem.com
Postal Code: 52627-4544
Office phone: (319) 372-6421
Publisher Name: Bill Helenthal
Publisher Email: bill@hancockshopper.com
Publisher Phone: (319) 372-6421
Editor Name: Robin Delaney
Editor Email: editor@dailydem.com
Editor Phone: (319) 372-6421 ext.233
Advertising Executive Name: Tony Stutzman
Advertising Executive Email: tonys@dailydem.com
Advertising Executive Phone: (319) 372-6421
Year Established: 1868
Delivery Methods:
  Mail`Newsstand`Carrier`Racks
Own Printing Facility?: Y
Commercial printers?: Y
Mechanical specifications: Type page 11 5/8 x 21 1/2; E - 6 cols, 1 5/6, 1/8 between; A - 6 cols, 1 5/6, 1/8 between; C - 6 cols, 1 5/6, 1/8 between.
Published Days: Mon`Tues`Wed`Thur`Fri
Weekday Frequency: e
Avg Paid Circ: 4847
Audit Company: Sworn/Estimate/Non-Audited
Audit Date: 7 12 2019
Pressroom Equipment: Lines – 10-G/Community; Pasters –BG/Acumeter.
Mailroom Equipment: Tying Machines – Bu, MLN/Strappers; Address Machine – Wm;
Buisness Equipment: Qantel, SBS
Buisness Software: Quatro Pro 4.0, Word Perfect 5.1, Microsoft/Windows 3.1
Classified Equipment: Hardware – APP/Mac Quadra 630; Okidata/320 Microline Printer; Printers – COM/8400;
Classified Software: Baseview/Class Manager.
Editorial Equipment: Hardware – 1-APP/Mac 7100, APP/Mac Quadra 630; Printers – 1-COM/8400, NewGen/Laser Printer, Pre Press/Panther Plus Imagesetter
Editorial Software: DragX, QPS/QuarkXPress, Baseview/Qtools, Baseview/NewsEdit Pro.
Production Equipment: Hardware – 1-Nu, Pre Press/Panther Plus, Kodak CTP; Cameras – Acti; Scanners – Lf/Leafscan 35, Umax/PowerLook, Nikon/LS1000
Production Software: QPS/QuarkXPress, Baseview/Qtools, DragX.
Note: Democrat Co. is owned by Brehm Communications Inc. Through it's subsidiaries, Democrat Co., Gull Communications, Hi-Desert Publishing Co., Inc., News West Publishing Company Inc., Penny Power Publications Inc., Placer Community Newspapers, Inc. and Princ
Total Circulation: 4847

IOWA CITY

IOWA CITY PRESS-CITIZEN

Corporate/Parent Company: Gannett
Publication Street Address: 123 N Linn St
City: Iowa City
State: IA
Publication Website: www.press-citizen.com
Postal Code: 52245-2147
Office phone: (319) 337-3181
General E-mail: customerservice@press-citizen.com
Editor Name: Tory Brecht
Editor Email: tbrecht@press-citizen.com
Year Established: 1920
Delivery Methods:
  Mail`Newsstand`Carrier`Racks
Own Printing Facility?: N
Commercial printers?: N
Mechanical specifications: Type page 11 5/8 x 21 1/2; E - 6 cols, 1 5/16, 1/8 between; A - 6 cols, 1 5/16, 1/8 between; C - 9 cols, 1 1/6, 1/8 between.
Published Days: Mon`Tues`Wed`Thur`Fri`Sat
Weekday Frequency: All day
Saturday Frequency: All day
Avg Paid Circ: 6449
Avg Free Circ: 207
Audit Company: AAM
Audit Date: 28 05 2020
Pressroom Equipment: Lines – 14-G/Urbanite 1000 Series; Control System – G.;
Mailroom Equipment: Counter Stackers – QWI/400, QWI/500, QWI/501; Inserters & Stuffers – HI/1372; Tying Machines – 1-Dynaric/1500, 1/MLN; Wrapping Singles – QWI/Underwrap;
Buisness Equipment: IBM/AS-400
Classified Equipment: Hardware – 1-APT.;
Editorial Equipment: Hardware – 1-APT.
Production Equipment: Hardware – KPG; Scanners – Diadem/200S Direct Screen
Production Software: ProImage/NewsWay.
Note: On Sundays, readers receive the Sunday state edition of the Des Moines Register wrapped in a full local news section provided by the Iowa City Press-Citizen. See the Des Moines Register listing for Sunday circulation and advertising rates.
Total Circulation: 7080

THE DAILY IOWAN

Publication Street Address: Adler Journalism Building E131
City: Iowa City
State: IA
Publication Website: www.daily-iowan.com
Postal Code: 52242
Office phone: 319-335-6030
General E-mail: daily-iowan@uiowa.edu
Publisher Name: Jason Brummond
Publisher Email: jason-brummond@uiowa.edu
Publisher Phone: 319-335-5788
Editor Name: Marissa Payne
Editor Email: mjpayne42@gmail.com
Editor Phone: 319-335-6030
Advertising Executive Name: Juli Krause
Advertising Executive Email: juli-krause@uiowa.edu
Advertising Executive Phone: 319-335-5784

KALONA

THE NEWS

Corporate/Parent Company: Paxton Media Group
Publication Street Address: 419 B Ave.
City: Kalona
State: IA
Publication Website: www.kalonanews.com
Postal Code: 52247
Office phone: 319-656-2273
Publisher Name: Jim Johnson
Publisher Email: publisher@kalonanews.com
Editor Name: James Jennings
Editor Email: News@TheNews-IA.com
Advertising Executive Name: Bridget Johnson
Advertising Executive Email: AdSales@TheNews-IA.com

KEOKUK

DAILY GATE CITY

Publication Street Address: 1016 Main St
City: Keokuk
State: IA
Publication Website: www.dailygate.com
Postal Code: 52632-4656
Office phone: (319) 524-8300
Publisher Name: Steve and Bill Helenthal
Publisher Email: steveh@dailygate.com
Editor Name: Joe Benedict
Editor Email: editordgc@dailygate.com
Year Established: 1847
Delivery Methods:
  Mail`Newsstand`Carrier`Racks
Own Printing Facility?: Y
Commercial printers?: Y
Mechanical specifications: Type page 13 1/4 x 21 1/2; E - 6 cols, 2 1/16, 1/16 between; A - 8 cols, 1 1/2, 1/8 between; C - 8 cols, 1 1/2, 1/8 between.
Published Days: Mon`Tues`Wed`Thur`Fri
Weekday Frequency: e
Avg Paid Circ: 5500
Audit Company: Sworn/Estimate/Non-Audited
Audit Date: 7 12 2019
Mailroom Equipment: Tying Machines – MLN/2EE.;
Buisness Equipment: Qantel
Classified Equipment: Hardware – APP/Mac;
Classified Software: Baseview.
Editorial Equipment: Hardware – APP/Mac
Editorial Software: Baseview.
Production Equipment: Hardware – Xante/8200, Adobe/Photoshop; Cameras – 1-R/24580
Production Software: Baseview.
Total Circulation: 5500

LE MARS

LE MARS DAILY SENTINEL

Corporate/Parent Company: Rust Communications
Publication Street Address: 41 1st Ave NE
City: Le Mars
State: IA
Publication Website: www.lemarssentinel.com
Postal Code: 51031-3535
Office phone: (712) 546-7031
Publisher Name: Monte Jost
Publisher Email: mjost70@gmail.com
Publisher Phone: 712-546-7031 ext. 14
Editor Name: Kim Fickett
Editor Email: senteditor@gmail.com
Editor Phone: 712-546-7031 ext. 15
Advertising Executive Name: Shannon Jost
Advertising Executive Email: ldsjost@gmail.com
Advertising Executive Phone: 712-546-7031 ext. 16
Year Established: 1870
Delivery Methods: Mail`Carrier`Racks
Own Printing Facility?: Y
Commercial printers?: Y
Mechanical specifications: Type page 13 x 21 1/2; E - 6 cols, 2 1/16, 1/8 between; A - 6 cols, 2 1/16, 1/8 between; C - 6 cols, 2 1/16, 1/8 between.
Published Days: Mon`Tues`Wed`Thur`Fri
Weekday Frequency: e
Avg Paid Circ: 2584
Audit Company: Sworn/Estimate/Non-Audited
Audit Date: 7 12 2019
Pressroom Equipment: Lines – 6-G/Community; Reels & Stands – 5-G/Community Stand.;
Mailroom Equipment: Tying Machines – Malow/50, Bu; Address Machine – Miller/Bevco 285.;
Buisness Equipment: 4-Gateway/2000, Compaq, Compaq
Classified Equipment: Hardware – APP/Mac, CAMS; Printers – APP/Mac LaserWriters;
Classified Software: QPS/QuarkXPress 6.0.
Editorial Equipment: Hardware – APP/Mac/Konica, Imagesetter; Printers – APP/Mac LaserWriters, QMS/860, NewGen/DesignXpress
Editorial Software: APP/Mac, QPS/QuarkXPress 6.0.
Production Equipment: Hardware – SL/GNS-28; Cameras – 1-SCREEN/C-240-D, Kyoto/Japan; Scanners – Polaroid.
Total Circulation: 2584

MARSHALLTOWN

TIMES-REPUBLICAN

Corporate/Parent Company: Ogden Newspapers, Inc.
Publication Street Address: 135 W Main St
City: Marshalltown
State: IA
Publication Website: www.timesrepublican.com
Postal Code: 50158-5843
Office phone: (641) 753-6611
General E-mail: frontdesk@timesrepublican.com
Publisher Name: Abigail Pelzer
Publisher Email: apelzer@timesrepublican.com
Editor Name: Lana Bradstream
Editor Email: lbradstream@timesrepublican.com
Advertising Executive Name: Brooke German
Advertising Executive Email: bgerman@timesrepublican.com
Year Established: 1856
Delivery Methods:
  Mail`Newsstand`Carrier`Racks
Own Printing Facility?: Y
Commercial printers?: Y
Mechanical specifications: Type page 10 x 21 1/2; E - 6 cols, 1 1/2, 1/4 between; A - 6 cols, 1 1/2, 1/4 between; C - 9 cols, 1, 1/8 between.
Published Days: Mon`Tues`Wed`Thur`Fri`Sat`Sun
Weekday Frequency: m
Saturday Frequency: m
Avg Paid Circ: 6523
Avg Free Circ: 156
Audit Company: AAM
Audit Date: 20 04 2020
Pressroom Equipment: Lines – 8-G/Community (upper former) 1988; 8-G/Community (upper former) 1988;
Mailroom Equipment: Counter Stackers – HI; Tying Machines – EAM-Mosca/Automatic, MLN; Wrapping Singles – QWI; Address Machine – Ch.;
Buisness Equipment: Dell
Classified Equipment: Hardware – Dell;
Editorial Equipment: Hardware – G-5s
Production Equipment: Hardware – ECRM - CTP
Total Circulation: 5473

MASON CITY

GLOBE GAZETTE, MASON CITY

Publication Street Address: 300 N Washington Ave
City: Mason City
State: IA
Publication Website: www.globegazette.com
Postal Code: 50401-3222
Office phone: (641) 421-0500
Editor Name: Jaci Smith
Editor Email: jaci.smith@globegazette.com
Editor Phone: 641-421-0564
Advertising Executive Name: Olivia Stalker
Advertising Executive Email: olivia.stalker@globegazette.com
Advertising Executive Phone: (641) 421-0548
Year Established: 1862
Delivery Methods:
  Mail`Newsstand`Carrier`Racks
Own Printing Facility?: Y
Commercial printers?: Y
Mechanical specifications: Type page 12 x 21; E - 6 cols, 2 1/16, 1/8 between; A - 6 cols, 2 1/16, 1/8 between; C - 9 cols, 1 3/8, 1/16 between.
Published Days: Mon`Tues`Wed`Thur`Fri`Sat`Sun
Weekday Frequency: m
Saturday Frequency: m
Avg Paid Circ: 7341
Avg Free Circ: 1101
Audit Company: AAM
Audit Date: 31 03 2019
Pressroom Equipment: Lines – 8-KBA/Mot-Colormax 5W with CIC single width; Folders – 1-G/SSC, 1.;
Mailroom Equipment: Tying Machines – 2-MLN/ML2EE; Address Machine – 1-Ch/595-596.;
Buisness Equipment: 1-IBM/AS-400
Classified Equipment: Hardware – 2-IBM/RS 6000; Printers – HP.;
Editorial Equipment: Hardware – 2-IBM/RS 6000, Compaq/Proliant Server 2500; Printers – HP
Editorial Software: MS/NT 4.0.
Production Equipment: Hardware – 2-Pre Press/Panther Pro-46, APP/Mac Preserver; Cameras – 1-R/480, 1-C/Spartan II, ECR/Autokon 1100; Scanners – AG/Argus II
Production Software: QPS/QuarkXPress 3.32.
Total Circulation: 8442

U.S. Daily Newspapers

MOUNT PLEASANT

MT. PLEASANT NEWS

Corporate/Parent Company: Folience
Publication Street Address: 119 W. Monroe St.
City: Mount Pleasant
State: IA
Publication Website: www.mpnews.net
Postal Code: 319-385-3131
Office phone: (319) 385-3131
Publisher Name: Matt Bryant
Publisher Email: pub@southeastiowaunion.com
Editor Name: Karyn Spory
Editor Email: karyn.spory@southeastiowaunion.com
Advertising Executive Name: Holly Frary
Advertising Executive Email: holly.frary@southeastiowaunion.com
Year Established: 1878
Delivery Methods:
 Mail`Newsstand`Carrier`Racks
Own Printing Facility?: N
Commercial printers?: N
Mechanical specifications: Type page 13 x 21 1/2; E - 6 cols, 2 1/16, 1/8 between; A - 6 cols, 2 1/16, 1/8 between; C - 8 cols, 1 7/16, 1/8 between.
Published Days: Mon`Tues`Wed`Thur`Fri
Weekday Frequency: e
Avg Paid Circ: 2668
Audit Company: Sworn/Estimate/Non-Audited
Audit Date: 7 12 2019
Mailroom Equipment: Tying Machines – 1/Bu; Address Machine – 2-/Wm.;
Buisness Equipment: IBM
Classified Equipment: Hardware – 1-APP/Power Mac.;
Editorial Equipment: Hardware – 1-APP/Power Mac, 1-APP/Mac G3, 1-APP/iMac.
Production Equipment: Hardware – 1-Nat/250; Cameras – 1-Nu; Scanners – APP/Mac
Production Software: QPS/QuarkXPress 4.0.
Total Circulation: 2668

MT. PLEASANT

MOUNT PLEASANT NEWS

Corporate/Parent Company: Folience
Publication Street Address: 119 W. Monroe St.
City: Mt. Pleasant
State: IA
Publication Website: www.mpnews.net
Postal Code: 52641
Office phone: 319-385-3131
General E-mail: news@southeastiowaunion.com
Publisher Name: Matt Bryant
Publisher Email: pub@southeastiowaunion.com
Editor Name: Gage Miskimen
Editor Email: gage.miskimen@southeastiowaunion.com
Advertising Executive Name: Holly Frary
Advertising Executive Email: holly.frary@southeastiowaunion.com

MUSCATINE

MUSCATINE JOURNAL

Corporate/Parent Company: Lee Enterprises
Publication Street Address: 301 E 3rd St
City: Muscatine
State: IA
Publication Website: www.muscatinejournal.com
Postal Code: 52761-4116
Office phone: 563-263-2331
Publisher Name: Debbie Anselm
Publisher Email: deb.anselm@lee.net
Publisher Phone: (563) 383-2224
Editor Name: Jim Meenan
Editor Email: Jim.Meenan@muscatinejournal.com
Editor Phone: 563-262-0545
Advertising Executive Name: Ariel Olson
Advertising Executive Email: ariel.olson@muscatinejournal.com
Advertising Executive Phone: 563-262-0557
Year Established: 1840

Delivery Methods:
 Mail`Newsstand`Carrier`Racks
Own Printing Facility?: Y
Commercial printers?: N
Mechanical specifications: Type page 11 3/5 x 20 1/2; E - 6 cols, 1 4/5, 1/8 between; A - 6 cols, 1 4/5, 1/8 between; C - 9 cols, 1 3/8, 1/16 between.
Published Days: Mon`Tues`Wed`Thur`Fri`Sat
Weekday Frequency: m
Saturday Frequency: m
Avg Paid Circ: 2097
Audit Company: AAM
Audit Date: 31 03 2016
Mailroom Equipment: Tying Machines – 1-MLN/Spirit-Strapper.;
Buisness Equipment: IBM/AS-400, Remote access via T-1, PC Workstations
Buisness Software: IBM/AS-400, Lee Business System, Microsoft/Office 2000
Classified Equipment: Hardware – APP/Mac; Printers – HP 8150;
Classified Software: Baseview.
Editorial Equipment: Hardware – APP/Mac/APP/Mac IIsi, AP/GraphicsNet, Lf/AP Leaf Picture Desk, Lf/Negative Scanner; Printers – HP 551
Editorial Software: Baseview.
Production Equipment: Hardware – Lf/AP Leaf Picture Desk, AG/Rapiline 17; Scanners – APP/Mac One Scanner, HP/ScanJet
Production Software: Baseview.
Total Circulation: 2097

NEWTON

NEWTON DAILY NEWS

Corporate/Parent Company: Shaw Media
Publication Street Address: 200 1st Ave E
City: Newton
State: IA
Publication Website: www.newtondailynews.com
Postal Code: 50208-3716
Office phone: (641) 792-3121
General E-mail: newsroom@newtondailynews.com
Publisher Name: "Rich Paulsen
"
Publisher Email: rpaulsen@shawmedia.com
Editor Name: "Pam Pratt
"
Editor Email: pampratt@newtondailynews.com
Advertising Executive Name: "Kevin Brown
"
Advertising Executive Email: kbrown@newtondailynews.com
Year Established: 1902
Delivery Methods:
 Mail`Newsstand`Carrier`Racks
Mechanical specifications: Type page 12 1/2 x 21 1/2; E - 6 cols, 1 7/8, 1/8 between; A - 6 cols, 1 7/8, 1/8 between; C - 9 cols, 1 1/4, 1/16 between.
Published Days: Mon`Tues`Wed`Thur`Fri
Weekday Frequency: e
Avg Paid Circ: 5476
Audit Company: Sworn/Estimate/Non-Audited
Audit Date: 7 12 2019
Pressroom Equipment: Lines – 6-G/Suburban 1969.;
Mailroom Equipment: Counter Stackers – 1/BG; Tying Machines – 3-Bu, 3-Strapmatic; Address Machine – KR.;
Buisness Equipment: 2-BI, ATT
Classified Equipment: Hardware – APP/iMac
Classified Software: Baseview.
Editorial Equipment: Hardware – APP/Mac; Printers – APP/Mac LaserWriter Plus
Editorial Software: QPS/QuarkXPress 4.1, Microsoft/Word.
Production Equipment: Hardware – 1-Nu, APP/Mac, Konica/5100T 5.3, Konica/3100S 5.1; Cameras – 1-Kk
Production Software: QuarkXPress 4.1.
Total Circulation: 5476

PRAIRIE CITY - PCM EXPLORER

Publication Street Address: P.O. Box 967 200 1st Ave. E.
City: Newton
State: IA
Publication Website: www.prairiecitynews.com
Postal Code: 50208
Office phone: (641) 792-3121
General E-mail: newsroom@newtondailynews.com
Publisher Name: Rich Paulsen
Publisher Email: rpaulsen@shawmedia.com
Editor Name: "Pam Pratt
"
Editor Email: pampratt@newtondailynews.com
Advertising Executive Name: "Kevin Brown
"
Advertising Executive Email: kbrown@newtondailynews.com

OELWEIN

THE OELWEIN DAILY REGISTER

Corporate/Parent Company: Community Media Group
Publication Street Address: 25 1st St SE
City: Oelwein
State: IA
Publication Website: www.oelweindailyregister.com
Postal Code: 50662-2306
Office phone: (319) 283-2144
Publisher Name: Deb Weigel
Publisher Email: debweigel@oelweindailyregister.com
Editor Name: Christopher Baldus
Editor Email: editor@oelweindailyregister.com
Advertising Executive Name: Tracy Cummings
Advertising Executive Email: tracy.cummings@oelweindailyregister.com
Year Established: 1882
Delivery Methods: Mail`Newsstand`Racks
Own Printing Facility?: Y
Commercial printers?: Y
Mechanical specifications: Type page 12 x 21 1/2; E - 6 cols, 1 7/8, 1/6 between; A - 6 cols, 1 7/8, 1/6 between; C - 9 cols, 1 1/2, 1/12 between.
Published Days: Mon`Tues`Wed`Thur`Fri`Sat
Weekday Frequency: All day
Saturday Frequency: All day
Avg Paid Circ: 2354
Avg Free Circ: 10193
Audit Company: Sworn/Estimate/Non-Audited
Audit Date: 7 12 2019
Pressroom Equipment: Lines – 7-G/C901;
Mailroom Equipment: Tying Machines – 1/Bu, 1-Sa, 1-Malow/MC-50; Address Machine – 1-SC/labeler.;
Production Equipment: Hardware – 2-COM/Unisetter, 1-COM/Area Unified Composer.
Total Circulation: 12547

OSKALOOSA

OSKALOOSA HERALD

Corporate/Parent Company: CNHI, LLC
Publication Street Address: 1901 A Ave W
City: Oskaloosa
State: IA
Publication Website: https://www.oskaloosa.com/
Postal Code: 52577-1962
Office phone: (641) 672-2581
General E-mail: oskynews@oskyherald.com
Publisher Name: Deb Van Engelenhoven
Publisher Email: debve@oskyherald.com
Publisher Phone: Ext. 413
Editor Name: Angie Holland
Editor Email: aholland@oskyherald.com
Editor Phone: Ext. 425
Year Established: 1850
Delivery Methods: Mail`Carrier
Mechanical specifications: Type page 13 x 21 1/2; E - 6 cols, 2 1/16, 1/8 between; A - 6 cols, 2 1/16, 1/8 between; C - 6 cols, 2 1/16, 1/16 between.

Published Days: Mon`Tues`Thur`Fri
Weekday Frequency: All day
Avg Paid Circ: 2174
Audit Company: Sworn/Estimate/Non-Audited
Audit Date: 7 12 2019
Pressroom Equipment: Lines – 6-WPC/Web Leader.;
Mailroom Equipment: Tying Machines – 1-Bu/182XE4, 1-Sa/SR2CTAN; Address Machine – 1-Am/1950B.;
Buisness Equipment: IBM
Classified Equipment: Hardware – APP/Mac.;
Editorial Equipment: Hardware – APP/Mac
Editorial Software: QPS.
Production Equipment: Hardware – 1-Nu/Flip Top FT40L, LE/24AQ; Cameras – Acti/S 25; Scanners – APP/Mac.
Total Circulation: 2174

OTTUMWA

THE OTTUMWA COURIER

Corporate/Parent Company: CNHI, LLC
Publication Street Address: 213 E 2nd St
City: Ottumwa
State: IA
Publication Website: www.ottumwacourier.com
Postal Code: 52501-2902
Office phone: (641) 684-4611
General E-mail: news@ottumwacourier.com
Publisher Name: Ron Gutierrez
Publisher Email: rgutierrez@cnhi.com
Publisher Phone: 563-242-7101
Editor Name: Matt Milner
Editor Email: mmilner@ottumwacourier.com
Editor Phone: 641-684-4611
Year Established: 1848
Delivery Methods: Mail`Newsstand`Carrier
Own Printing Facility?: Y
Commercial printers?: Y
Mechanical specifications: Type page 13 x 21 1/2; E - 6 cols, 2 1/16, 1/6 between; A - 6 cols, 2 1/16, 1/6 between; C - 9 cols, 1 3/8, 1/16 between.
Published Days: Tues`Wed`Thur`Fri`Sat
Weekday Frequency: m
Saturday Frequency: m
Avg Paid Circ: 9303
Audit Company: Sworn/Estimate/Non-Audited
Audit Date: 7 12 2019
Pressroom Equipment: Lines – 5-G/Urbanite 850 1971; Folders – 1-G/2:1; Reels & Stands – 1, 9.;
Mailroom Equipment: Counter Stackers – 1-HL/Monitor; Inserters & Stuffers – MM/227E 5:1; Tying Machines – 1/Cyclops, 1-/MLN, 1-Dynaric/NP1500; Wrapping Singles – 1-Id/Bottom Wrapper; Address Machine – 1-Ch/582N, 1-VideoJet/569 Labeler;
Buisness Equipment: IBM/AS-400, 4-Gateway/166, Corporate WAN
Buisness Software: Microsoft/Excel, Microsoft/Word PC Support, WordPerfect, Microsoft/Access
Classified Equipment: Hardware – 1-APP/Mac 8550 Workgroup Server, 5-APP/Mac 7200-120; Printers – HP/5MP;
Classified Software: Baseview/Class Manager Pro.
Editorial Equipment: Hardware – 2-APP/Mac 8550 Workgroup Server, 1-APP/Mac 7250 Workgroup Server, 11-Motorola/StarMax 3800-180, 6-Motorola/StarMax 4000-200; Microtek/ScanMaker, Polaroid/SprintScan, Lf/AP Leaf Picture Desk; Printers – HP/6MP
Editorial Software: News edit pro
Production Equipment: Hardware – Digi-Colour, Caere/OmniPage Direct, Adobe/Photoshop 5.0; Cameras – 1-C/Spartan II, 1-SCREEN; Scanners – HP/ScanJet Plus, HP/ScanJet IIp, 2-Microtek III, Polaroid/SprintScan
Production Software: QPS/QuarkXPress 3.32, Adobe/PageMaker 5.0.
Total Circulation: 9303

SIOUX CITY

SIOUX CITY JOURNAL

Corporate/Parent Company: Lee Enterprises
Publication Street Address: 515 Pavonia St

I-27

City: Sioux City
State: IA
Publication Website: www.siouxcityjournal.com
Postal Code: 51101-2245
Office phone: (712) 293-4250
General E-mail: SCJ-Circulation@lee.net
Publisher Name: Chad Pauling
Publisher Email: cpauling@siouxcityjournal.com
Publisher Phone: 712-293-4317
Editor Name: Bruce Miller
Editor Email: bmiller@siouxcityjournal.com
Editor Phone: 712-293-4218
Advertising Executive Name: Cynthia Donovan
Advertising Executive Email: Cynthia.Donovan@lee.net
Advertising Executive Phone: 712-293-4331
Year Established: 1864
Delivery Methods:
    Mail`Newsstand`Carrier`Racks
Own Printing Facility?: Y
Commercial printers?: N
Mechanical specifications: Type page 11 1/2 x 21 1/2; E - 6 cols, 1 3/4, 1/8 between; A - 6 cols, 1 3/4, 1/8 between; C - 9 cols, 1 1/16, 1/8 between.
Published Days: Mon`Tues`Wed`Thur`Fri`Sat`Sun
Weekday Frequency: All day
Saturday Frequency: All day
Avg Paid Circ: 15997
Avg Free Circ: 1900
Audit Company: AAM
Audit Date: 30 09 2018
Pressroom Equipment: Lines – 14-G/Urbanite (6 Stacked).;
Mailroom Equipment: Counter Stackers – 3-QWI; Inserters & Stuffers – GMA; Tying Machines – QWI; Address Machine – Kk.;
Buisness Equipment: APP/Mac G3
Buisness Software: Baseview
Classified Equipment: Hardware – COM/Intrepid 48, APP/Mac; Printers – NewGen;
Classified Software: APT.
Editorial Equipment: Hardware – COM/Intrepid 48, APP/Mac; Printers – NewGen, HP, Pre Press/Panther Imagesetter 36
Editorial Software: Lotus/Notes, QPS, QuarkXPress, News Engine.
Production Equipment: Hardware – 2-NewGen, Pre Press/Panther Pro Imagesetter 36; Scanners – Panasonic/Image Scanner 16.
Total Circulation: 17897

SPENCER

THE DAILY REPORTER

Corporate/Parent Company: Gannett
Publication Street Address: 310 E Milwaukee St
City: Spencer
State: IA
Publication Website: www.spencerdailyreporter.com
Postal Code: 51301-4569
Office phone: (712) 262-6610
General E-mail: news@spencerdailyreporter.com
Publisher Name: Paula Buenger
Publisher Email: https://www.spencerdailyreporter.com/contactus
Publisher Phone: 712-262-6610
Editor Name: Randy Cauthron
Editor Email: news@spencerdailyreporter.com
Editor Phone: 712-262-6610
Advertising Executive Name: TJ Murphy
Advertising Executive Email: tjmurphy@spencerdailyreporter.com
Advertising Executive Phone: 712-262-6610 Ext. 107
Year Established: 1959
Delivery Methods: Mail`Carrier
Mechanical specifications: Type page 13 x 21 1/2; E - 6 cols, 2 1/16, 1/8 between; A - 6 cols, 2 1/16, 1/8 between; C - 6 cols, 2 1/16, 1/8 between.
Published Days: Tues`Thur`Fri`Sat
Weekday Frequency: e
Saturday Frequency: m
Avg Paid Circ: 4004
Audit Company: Sworn/Estimate/Non-Audited

Audit Date: 7 12 2019
Pressroom Equipment: Lines – 5-G/Community.;
Mailroom Equipment: Tying Machines – Bu; Address Machine – Am.;
Buisness Equipment: APP/Mac
Classified Equipment: Hardware – Mk.;
Editorial Equipment: Hardware – Mk.
Production Equipment: Hardware – Nat/A-250; Cameras – SCREEN/Companica; Scanners – Gam.
Total Circulation: 4004

WASHINGTON

EVENING JOURNAL

Corporate/Parent Company: Folience
Publication Street Address: 111 North Marion Avenue
City: Washington
State: IA
Publication Website: www.washjrnl.com
Postal Code: 52353
Office phone: 319-653-2191
Publisher Name: Matt Bryant
Publisher Email: pub@southeastiowaunion.com
Editor Name: Gage Miskimen
Editor Email: gage.miskimen@southeastiowaunion.com
Advertising Executive Name: Julie Scott
Advertising Executive Email: Julie.Scott@southeastiowaunion.com

THE WASHINGTON EVENING JOURNAL

Corporate/Parent Company: Folience
Publication Street Address: 111 N Marion Ave
City: Washington
State: IA
Publication Website: www.washjrnl.com
Postal Code: 52353-1728
Office phone: (319) 653-2191
Publisher Name: Matt Bryant
Publisher Email: pub@southeastiowaunion.com
Editor Name: Karyn Spory
Editor Email: karyn.spory@southeastiowaunion.com
Advertising Executive Name: Julie Scott
Advertising Executive Email: Julie.Scott@southeastiowaunion.com
Delivery Methods:
    Mail`Newsstand`Carrier`Racks
Own Printing Facility?: Y
Commercial printers?: Y
Mechanical specifications: Type page 13 x 21 1/2; E - 6 cols, 2 1/16, 1/16 between; A - 6 cols, 2 1/16, 1/16 between; C - 8 cols, 1 9/16, 1/8 between.
Published Days: Mon`Tues`Wed`Thur`Fri
Weekday Frequency: e
Avg Paid Circ: 3462
Audit Company: Sworn/Estimate/Non-Audited
Audit Date: 7 12 2019
Pressroom Equipment: Lines – HI/V-15A 1972.;
Buisness Equipment: PC
Buisness Software: BMF
Classified Equipment: Hardware – APP/Mac;
Classified Software: Microsoft/Word, Aldus/PageMaker.
Editorial Equipment: Hardware – APP/Mac; Printers – APP/Mac LaserWriter II NT 630
Editorial Software: Microsoft/Word.
Production Equipment: Hardware – APP/Mac NT.
Total Circulation: 3462

WATERLOO

THE COURIER

Corporate/Parent Company: Gannett
Publication Street Address: 100 E 4th St
City: Waterloo

State: IA
Publication Website: www.wcfcourier.com
Postal Code: 50703-4714
Office phone: (800) 798-1717
Editor Name: Nancy Newhoff
Editor Email: Nancy.Newhoff@wcfcourier.com
Editor Phone: (319) 291-1445
Advertising Executive Name: Tara Seible
Advertising Executive Email: tara.seible@wcfcourier.com
Advertising Executive Phone: 319-291-1403
Year Established: 1858
Delivery Methods:
    Mail`Newsstand`Carrier`Racks
Own Printing Facility?: N
Commercial printers?: Y
Mechanical specifications: Full page: 9.889" x 20". 6 column width: 1 col: 1.556"; 2 col: 3.222"; 3 col:4.889"; 4 col: 6.556"; 5 col: 8.222"; 6 col: 9.889".
Published Days: Mon`Tues`Wed`Thur`Fri`Sun
Weekday Frequency: e
Saturday Frequency: m
Avg Paid Circ: 33427
Audit Company: AAM
Audit Date: 24 08 2018
Pressroom Equipment: Lines – Outsourced;
Buisness Equipment: 1-Sun/Sparc
Buisness Software: Vision Data
Classified Equipment: Hardware – Sun; Printers – APP/Mac LaserWriters, ECR/Pelbox;
Classified Software: Vision Data
Total Circulation: 37961

WEBSTER CITY

THE DAILY FREEMAN-JOURNAL

Corporate/Parent Company: Ogden Newspapers, Inc.
Publication Street Address: 720 2nd St
City: Webster City
State: IA
Publication Website: www.freemanjournal.net
Postal Code: 50595-1437
Office phone: (515) 832-4350
Publisher Name: Terry Christensen
Publisher Email: tchristensen@freemanjournal.net
Editor Name: Anne Blankenship
Editor Email: editor@freemanjournal.net
Advertising Executive Name: Danny Baessler
Advertising Executive Email: dbaessler@freemanjournal.net
Year Established: 1857
Delivery Methods:
    Mail`Newsstand`Carrier`Racks
Own Printing Facility?: Y
Commercial printers?: Y
Mechanical specifications: Type page 13 x 21 1/2; E - 6 cols, 2 1/16, 1/8 between; A - 6 cols, 2 1/16, 1/8 between; C - 9 cols, 1 5/16, 1/8 between.
Published Days: Mon`Tues`Wed`Thur`Fri
Weekday Frequency: e
Avg Paid Circ: 1920
Avg Free Circ: 10
Audit Company: AAM
Audit Date: 1 04 2020
Pressroom Equipment: Lines – 14-G/Suburban; Press Drive – 2-HP/100; Folders – 1-G/Urbanite, 1.;
Mailroom Equipment: Counter Stackers – 2-HI/RS 25; Inserters & Stuffers – HI; Tying Machines – 2/Bu; Address Machine – 2-/Ch;
Classified Equipment: Hardware – APP/Mac G3.;
Editorial Equipment: Hardware – 2-APP/Mac G3, APP/Power Mac, 2-APP/Mac G4; Printers – ECR/108, ECR/1500, Konica/Jetsetter.
Production Equipment: Hardware – 1-Nu, 2-Pako, APP/Mac, ECR/6200; Cameras – 1-Spartan II Flatbed Scanner
Production Software: QPS.
Note: Advertising is sold in combination with the Fort Dodge Messenger (mS) for $43.22. Individual newspaper rates not made available.
Total Circulation: 1621

IDAHO

BLACKFOOT

MORNING NEWS

Corporate/Parent Company: Lee Enterprises
Publication Street Address: 34 N Ash St
City: Blackfoot
State: ID
Publication Website: www.am-news.com
Postal Code: 83221-2101
Office phone: (208) 785-1100
General E-mail: publisher@am-news.com
Year Established: 1903
Delivery Methods:
    Mail`Newsstand`Carrier`Racks
Own Printing Facility?: Y
Commercial printers?: Y
Mechanical specifications: Image area - 10.12 x 21.5; 6 columns.
Published Days: Mon`Tues`Wed`Thur`Fri`Sat
Weekday Frequency: m
Saturday Frequency: m
Avg Paid Circ: 3450
Audit Company: Sworn/Estimate/Non-Audited
Audit Date: 7 12 2019
Pressroom Equipment: Folders – KP/KJ-6.;
Mailroom Equipment: Counter Stackers – 1-BG/Count-O-Veyor; Inserters & Stuffers – MM/227E 2:1; Tying Machines – 2/Bu; Address Machine – 1-/Sp.;
Buisness Equipment: PC's
Buisness Software: List Master Systems
Classified Equipment: Hardware – Mac Mini's;
Classified Software: Baseview/Ad Pro, Baseview/Classflow.
Editorial Equipment: Hardware – Mac Mini's; Printers – Pre Press - Two Panther 46 Imagesetters, HP/5000 Laser.
Editorial Software: InDesign
Production Equipment: Hardware – Mac Mini's - PrePress - Two Panther 46 Imagesetters
Total Circulation: 3450

BOISE

IDAHO STATESMAN

Corporate/Parent Company: McClatchy Company
Publication Street Address: 1200 N Curtis Rd
City: Boise
State: ID
Publication Website: www.idahostatesman.com
Postal Code: 83706-1239
Office phone: (208) 377-6200
Publisher Name: Rusty Dodge
Publisher Email: rdodge@mcclatchy.com
Publisher Phone: (208) 377-6301
Editor Name: Christina Lords
Editor Email: clords@idahostatesman.com
Editor Phone: (208) 377-6435
Advertising Executive Name: Kody Klenow
Advertising Executive Email: kklenow@mcclatchy.com
Advertising Executive Phone: (208) 377-6240
Year Established: 1864
Delivery Methods: Mail`Carrier`Racks
Own Printing Facility?: Y
Commercial printers?: N
Published Days: Mon`Tues`Wed`Thur`Fri`Sat`Sun
Weekday Frequency: m
Saturday Frequency: m
Avg Paid Circ: 33440
Audit Company: AAM
Audit Date: 13 12 2018
Classified Software: DTI
Editorial Software: QPS.
Production Software: DTI (classified), QPS/(news).
Total Circulation: 44767

U.S. Daily Newspapers

COEUR D ALENE

COEUR D'ALENE PRESS

Corporate/Parent Company: Hagadone Corp.
Publication Street Address: 215 N 2nd St
City: Coeur D Alene
State: ID
Publication Website: https://www.cdapress.com/
Postal Code: 83814
Office phone: (208) 664-8176
General E-mail: cschroeder@hagadone.com
Publisher Name: Clint Schroeder
Publisher Email: cschroeder@hagadone.com
Editor Name: Mike Patrick
Editor Email: mpatrick@cdapress.com
Editor Phone: (208) 664-8176, ext : 2000
Advertising Executive Name: Kari Packer
Advertising Executive Email: kpacker@cdapress.com
Advertising Executive Phone: (208) 664-8176, ext : 3025
Year Established: 1887
Delivery Methods:
   Mail`Newsstand`Carrier`Racks
Own Printing Facility?: Y
Commercial printers?: Y
Mechanical specifications: Type page 13 x 21 1/2; E - 6 cols, 2 1/16, 1/8 between; A - 6 cols, 2 1/16, 1/8 between; C - 8 cols, 1 3/8, 1/8 between.
Published Days: Mon`Tues`Wed`Thur`Fri`Sat`Sun
Weekday Frequency: m
Saturday Frequency: m
Audit Company: Sworn/Estimate/Non-Audited
Audit Date: 7 12 2019
Pressroom Equipment: Lines – Goss Magnum ;
Mailroom Equipment: Counter Stackers – Quipp; Inserters & Stuffers – 2299; Tying Machines – 1-Bu/PP8-6; Control System – OMNICON; Address Machine – 1-Ch/500PM.;
Classified Equipment: Hardware – 1-Dy/Cps 300.;
Editorial Equipment: Hardware – 1-Dy/Cps 300.
Production Equipment: Hardware – 2-Dy/Cps 300; Cameras – 1-K/Vertical 24.
Note: The North Idaho Sunday serves the five northern counties in Idaho and is a combined effort of three dailies and three weeklies: Coeur d'Alene Press (m), Sandpoint Bonner County Daily Bee (m), Kellogg Shoshone News-Press (m), Priest River Times (w), Bonner

IDAHO FALLS

POST REGISTER

Corporate/Parent Company: Adams Publishing Group
Publication Street Address: 333 Northgate Mile
City: Idaho Falls
State: ID
Publication Website: www.postregister.com
Postal Code: 83401-2529
Office phone: (208) 522-1800
General E-mail: circulation@postregister.com
Publisher Name: Travis Quast
Publisher Email: tquast@apgwest.com
Editor Name: Monte LaOrange
Editor Email: mlaorange@postregister.com
Editor Phone: (208) 542-6795
Advertising Executive Name: Donna Nims
Advertising Executive Email: dnims@postregister.com
Advertising Executive Phone: (208) 542-6701
Year Established: 1880
Delivery Methods:
   Mail`Newsstand`Carrier`Racks
Own Printing Facility?: Y
Commercial printers?: Y
Mechanical specifications: Contact us.
Published Days: Tues`Wed`Thur`Fri`Sat`Sun
Weekday Frequency: m
Saturday Frequency: m
Avg Paid Circ: 18200
Avg Free Circ: 250
Audit Company: Sworn/Estimate/Non-Audited
Audit Date: 7 12 2019
Pressroom Equipment: Lines – 16-unit Goss Magnum; Pasters –Yes
Mailroom Equipment: Control System – Goss Omnizone; Address Machine – Yes;
Buisness Software: PBS
Production Equipment: Hardware – All CTP
Note: Also own and operate three weekly newspapers and one monthly b-to-b publication with associated web sites.
Total Circulation: 18450

LEWISTON

LEWISTON MORNING TRIBUNE

Corporate/Parent Company: Verstovia Corp.
Publication Street Address: 505 Capital St
City: Lewiston
State: ID
Publication Website: www.lmtribune.com
Postal Code: 83501-1843
Office phone: 208-743-9411
General E-mail: city@lmtribune.com
Publisher Name: Nathan Alford
Publisher Email: alford@lmtribune.com
Publisher Phone: 208-848-2208
Editor Name: Craig Clohessy
Editor Email: cclohessy@lmtribune.com
Editor Phone: 208-848-2251
Advertising Executive Name: Doug Bauer
Advertising Executive Email: dbauer@lmtribune.com
Advertising Executive Phone: 208-848-2269
Year Established: 1892
Delivery Methods: Mail`Newsstand`Carrier
Own Printing Facility?: Y
Commercial printers?: Y
Mechanical specifications: Type page 12 1/2 x 21 1/2; E - 6 cols, 1 13/16, 1/8 between; A - 6 cols, 1 13/16, 1/8 between; C - 9 cols, 1 1/4, 1/8 between.
Published Days: Mon`Tues`Wed`Thur`Fri`Sat`Sun
Weekday Frequency: m
Saturday Frequency: m
Avg Paid Circ: 20626
Avg Free Circ: 2777
Audit Company: Sworn/Estimate/Non-Audited
Audit Date: 7 12 2019
Pressroom Equipment: Lines – Man Roland Uniset 75; Reels & Stands – 4-Roll/Stand; Registration System – Stoesser/Register Systems.
Mailroom Equipment: Counter Stackers – 2-BG/104; Inserters & Stuffers – 2-MM/227E; Tying Machines – 1-MLN/ML2EE; Address Machine – 1/MG.;
Buisness Equipment: Newzware
Classified Equipment: Hardware – Pentium I; Printers – HP/1200;
Classified Software: Sybase 11.5, AT/Enterprise, Microsoft/Word 6.0, Microsoft/Word 6.0, AT/Press, Windows NT 4.0.
Editorial Equipment: Hardware – AT, Compaq; Windows NT 4.0, Genic/P4 Pentium/Pentium II, Linix; Printers – HP/5SIMX, HP/8000N
Editorial Software: QPS 3.3, Microsoft/Windows 98, Dewar/DewarView, Microsoft/Word 6.0, Sybase 11.5, Novell/Netware 4.11, Windows NT 4.0.
Production Equipment: Hardware – 1-B/5KW, 2-Harlequin/RIP, ECRM/VLR, ECRM/5100; Cameras – 1-C/Spartan III; Scanners – 2-HP/Scanner
Production Software: Dewar/View 1.40, QPS/QuarkXPress 3.31, Microsoft/Word 6.0.
Total Circulation: 23403

MOSCOW

MOSCOW-PULLMAN DAILY NEWS

Corporate/Parent Company: Verstovia Corp.
Publication Street Address: 220 E 5th St Rm 218
City: Moscow
State: ID
Publication Website: www.dnews.com
Postal Code: 83843-2964
Office phone: (208) 882-5561
General E-mail: editor@dnews.com
Publisher Name: Nathan Alford
Publisher Email: alford@lmtribune.com
Publisher Phone: 208-848-2208
Editor Name: Craig Staszkow
Editor Email: cstaszkow@dnews.com
Editor Phone: 208-883-4642
Advertising Executive Name: Doug Bauer
Advertising Executive Email: dbauer@lmtribune.com
Advertising Executive Phone: 848-2269
Year Established: 1911
Delivery Methods:
   Mail`Newsstand`Carrier`Racks
Mechanical specifications: Type page 13 x 21 1/2; E - 6 cols, 2 1/16, 1/8 between; A - 6 cols, 2 1/16, 1/8 between; C - 9 cols, 1 3/8, 1/16 between.
Published Days: Mon`Tues`Wed`Thur`Fri`Sat
Weekday Frequency: m
Saturday Frequency: m
Avg Paid Circ: 6140
Audit Company: Sworn/Estimate/Non-Audited
Audit Date: 7 12 2019
Pressroom Equipment: Lines – 5-HI/Cotrell V-25; Reels & Stands – 4-HI/Cotrell.;
Mailroom Equipment: Counter Stackers – 7-KAN/480; Tying Machines – 1-MLN/ML2EE.;
Buisness Equipment: CDS
Classified Equipment: Hardware – APP/Macs;
Editorial Equipment: Hardware – APP/Macs; Printers – QMS, HP, Xante
Editorial Software: QPS.
Production Equipment: Hardware – QMS, Adobe/Photoshop; Cameras – SCREEN; Scanners – Lf, Microtek
Production Software: QPS.
Total Circulation: 6140

NAMPA

IDAHO PRESS-TRIBUNE

Publication Street Address: 1618 N Midland Blvd
City: Nampa
State: ID
Publication Website: www.idahopress.com
Postal Code: 83651-1751
Office phone: (208) 467-9251
General E-mail: newsroom@idahopress.com
Publisher Name: Matt Davison
Publisher Email: mdavison@idahopress.com
Publisher Phone: 208-465-8101
Editor Name: Holly Beech
Editor Email: hbeech@idahopress.com
Advertising Executive Name: Michelle Robinson
Advertising Executive Email: mrobinson@idahopress.com
Advertising Executive Phone: 208-465-8148
Year Established: 1883
Delivery Methods:
   Mail`Newsstand`Carrier`Racks
Own Printing Facility?: Y
Commercial printers?: Y
Mechanical specifications: Type page 12 1/2 x 20 1/2; E - 6 cols, 2 1/16, 1/8 between; A - 6 cols, 2 1/16, 1/8 between; C - 9 cols, 1 3/8, 1/16 between.
Published Days: Mon`Tues`Wed`Thur`Fri`Sat`Sun
Weekday Frequency: m
Saturday Frequency: m
Avg Paid Circ: 15404
Audit Company: CAC
Audit Date: 30 06 2017
Pressroom Equipment: Lines – 16-DGM/440.;
Mailroom Equipment: Counter Stackers – Schur; Tying Machines – 1-MLN/ML2-EE, Si/LB-News 3000;
Buisness Equipment: Sun/Ultrabox
Business Software: Media Plus, PBS, SBS
Classified Equipment: Hardware – APP/Mac Quadra 630; Printers – APP/Mac ImageWriter, Okidata/320;
Classified Software: Baseview/Class Manager 3.2.
Editorial Equipment: Hardware – APP/Power Mac 8100-80, APP/Mac G3, APP/Mac G4, APP/iMacPrinters – 2-AG/Accuset 1100
Editorial Software: Baseview/NewsEdit Pro 2.0.
Production Equipment: Hardware – 1-Nu/Flip Top FT 40LNS, AG/P-3400, PS/Laserprinter, 2-Accuset/Imagesetters; Cameras – 2-SCREEN/680C, Sony/MVC-2000 Digital, Canon/RV301-Digital, QuickTake 150; Scanners – APP/Mac, Polaroid/Neg Scanner
Production Software: QPS/QuarkXPress 4.0.
Total Circulation: 15404

OSBURN

SHOSHONE NEWS-PRESS

Corporate/Parent Company: Hagadone Corp.
Publication Street Address: 620 E Mullan
City: Osburn
State: ID
Publication Website: https://www.shoshonenewspress.com/
Postal Code: 83849
Office phone: (208) 752-1120
General E-mail: kalexander@shoshonenewspress.com
Publisher Name: Keri Alexander
Publisher Email: kalexander@shoshonenewspress.com
Publisher Phone: (208) 752-1120, ext : 301
Editor Name: Chanse Watson
Editor Email: cwatson@shoshonenewspress.com
Editor Phone: (208) 752-1120, ext : 311
Advertising Executive Name: Aafke Murdock
Advertising Executive Email: amurdock@cdapress.com
Advertising Executive Phone: (208) 664-0234
Year Established: 1897
Delivery Methods: Mail`Newsstand`Carrier
Mechanical specifications: Type page 13 x 21 1/2; E - 6 cols, 2 1/16, 1/8 between; A - 6 cols, 2 1/16, 1/8 between; C - 8 cols, 1 1/2, 1/16 between.
Published Days: Tues`Wed`Thur`Fri`Sat`Sun
Weekday Frequency: m
Saturday Frequency: m
Audit Company: Sworn/Estimate/Non-Audited
Audit Date: 7 12 2019
Pressroom Equipment: Lines – 4-G/Community; Folders – 1-G/Community.;
Mailroom Equipment: Tying Machines – 1/It; Address Machine – 2-/Am.;
Buisness Equipment: 2-DEC/UT220 B2
Classified Equipment: Hardware – 1-APP/Mac SE30.;
Editorial Equipment: Hardware – APP/Mac SE30.
Production Equipment: Hardware – 1-Nu.
Note: The North Idaho Sunday serves the five northern counties in Idaho and is a combined effort of three dailies and three weeklies: Coeur d'Alene Press (m), Sandpoint Bonner County Daily Bee (m), Shoshone News-Press (m), Priest River Times (w), Bonners Ferry

POCATELLO

IDAHO STATE JOURNAL

Corporate/Parent Company: Adams Publishing Group
Publication Street Address: 305 S Arthur Ave
City: Pocatello
State: ID
Publication Website: www.journalnet.com
Postal Code: 83204-3306
Office phone: (208) 232-4161
General E-mail: newsroom@journalnet.com
Publisher Name: Travis Quast
Publisher Email: tquast@journalnet.com
Publisher Phone: (208) 232-4275
Editor Name: Ian Fennell
Editor Email: ifennell@journalnet.com
Editor Phone: 208-239-3121
Advertising Executive Name: Taylor Smith
Advertising Executive Email: tsmith@journalnet.com
Advertising Executive Phone: (208) 604-1554
Year Established: 1890
Delivery Methods:
   Mail`Newsstand`Carrier`Racks
Own Printing Facility?: Y
Commercial printers?: Y
Mechanical specifications: Type page 13 x 21 1/2; E - 6 cols, 2 1/16, 1/8 between; A - 6 cols, 2 1/16, 1/8 between; C - 9 cols, 1 3/8, 1/16 between.
Published Days: Tues`Wed`Thur`Fri`Sun
Weekday Frequency: m
Saturday Frequency: m

Avg Paid Circ: 11691
Avg Free Circ: 1630
Audit Company: CAC
Audit Date: 30 06 2017
Pressroom Equipment: Lines – 7-G/Urbanite single width 1968; Folders – 1-G/5000; Registration System – Duarte/Punch System.
Mailroom Equipment: Counter Stackers – 1/BG; Inserters & Stuffers – 2-MM/217E; Tying Machines – 2-Si;
Buisness Equipment: Sun/Sparc fileserver
Buisness Software: PBS
Classified Equipment: Hardware – APP/Mac; Printers – APP/Mac ImageWriter II, HP/LaserJet 4M;
Classified Software: Baseview.
Editorial Equipment: Hardware – APP/Mac; Printers – HP/4M-2, HP/LaserJet 5000
Editorial Software: Baseview/NewsEdit, QPS/QuarkXPress 3.32.
Production Equipment: Hardware – AG/Accuset 1000, Graham M28; Cameras – 1-K, 1-Argile/16 x 23; Scanners – Nikon
Production Software: QPS/QuarkXPress 4.0.
Total Circulation: 13321

REXBURG

THE STANDARD-JOURNAL

Publication Street Address: 23 S 1st E
City: Rexburg
State: ID
Publication Website: www.uvsj.com
Postal Code: 83440-1901
Office phone: (208) 356-5441
General E-mail: circulation@uvsj.com
Publisher Name: Travis Quast
Publisher Email: tquast@apgwest.com
Year Established: 1881
Delivery Methods: Mail`Newsstand`Carrier
Own Printing Facility?: Y
Commercial printers?: Y
Published Days: Tues`Thur`Sat`Sun
Weekday Frequency: e
Saturday Frequency: m
Avg Paid Circ: 5000
Avg Free Circ: 7700
Audit Company: Sworn/Estimate/Non-Audited
Audit Date: 7 12 2019
Total Circulation: 12700

SANDPOINT

BONNER COUNTY DAILY BEE

Corporate/Parent Company: Hagadone Corp.
Publication Street Address: Po Box 159
City: Sandpoint
State: ID
Publication Website: https://www.bonnercountydailybee.com/
Postal Code: 83864
Office phone: (208) 263-9534
General E-mail: bdavis@bonnercountydailybee.com
Publisher Name: Bill Davis
Publisher Email: bdavis@bonnercountydailybee.com
Editor Name: Caroline Lobsinger
Editor Email: clobsinger@bonnercountydailybee.com
Advertising Executive Name: Danielle Ruhmshottel
Advertising Executive Email: drucker@bonnercountydailybee.com
Year Established: 1966
Delivery Methods: Newsstand`Carrier`Racks
Own Printing Facility?: Y
Commercial printers?: Y
Mechanical specifications: Type page 13 x 21 1/2; E - 6 cols, 2 1/16, 1/8 between; A - 6 cols, 2 1/16, 1/8 between; C - 8 cols, 1 5/8, 1/8 between.
Published Days: Tues`Wed`Thur`Fri`Sat`Sun
Weekday Frequency: m
Saturday Frequency: m
Avg Paid Circ: 5500
Audit Company: USPS

Audit Date: 10 01 2015
Mailroom Equipment: Address Machine – 1/St.;
Buisness Equipment: CIT
Classified Equipment: Hardware – APP/Mac SE.;
Editorial Equipment: Hardware – APP/Mac SE.
Production Equipment: Hardware – DP.
Note: The North Idaho Sunday serves the five northern counties in Idaho and is a combined effort of three dailies and three weeklies: Coeur d'Alene Press (m), Bonner County Daily Bee (m), Kellogg Shoshone News-Press (m), Priest River Times (w), Bonners Ferry He
Total Circulation: 5500

TWIN FALLS

THE TIMES-NEWS

Corporate/Parent Company: Gannett
Publication Street Address: 132 Fairfield St W
City: Twin Falls
State: ID
Publication Website: www.magicvalley.com
Postal Code: 83301-5492
Office phone: (208) 733-0931
Publisher Name: Matt Sandberg
Publisher Email: matt.sandberg@lee.net
Publisher Phone: 208-735-3345
Editor Name: Alison Smith
Editor Email: alison.smith@lee.net
Editor Phone: 208-735-3255
Advertising Executive Name: Debi Perkins
Advertising Executive Email: dperkins@magicvalley.com
Advertising Executive Phone: 208-735-3208
Year Established: 1904
Delivery Methods: Mail`Newsstand`Carrier`Racks
Own Printing Facility?: Y
Commercial printers?: Y
Mechanical specifications: Type page 12 1/2 x 21 1/2; E - 6 cols, 2 1/16, 1/8 between; A - 6 cols, 2 1/16, 1/8 between; C - 9 cols, 1 3/8, 1/16 between.
Published Days: Mon`Tues`Wed`Thur`Fri`Sat`Sun
Weekday Frequency: m
Saturday Frequency: m
Avg Paid Circ: 10164
Avg Free Circ: 2793
Audit Company: AAM
Audit Date: 16 03 2020
Pressroom Equipment: Lines – 7-G/Urbanite (Cole/3 Knife trimmer); 1-G/Urbanite color deck; Folders – 1, 1-G/quarter folder; Control System – 2-Fin/control, 2-DC Motors/100 h.p.;
Mailroom Equipment: Counter Stackers – 1-HL/Monitors; Inserters & Stuffers – MM/227; Tying Machines – MLN; Wrapping Singles – Id;
Buisness Equipment: Sun/Sparc, Compaq
Classified Equipment: Hardware – Sun; PC 4-286DG; Printers – APP/Mac LaserPrinters;
Classified Software: Lotus/Notes 4.6.
Editorial Equipment: Hardware – Sun, Mk; Printers – 1-Linotype-Hell/Linotronic 500, ECR/Pelbox, APP/Mac LaserPrinter
Editorial Software: Lotus/Notes 4.6.
Production Equipment: Hardware – ECR/Pelbox, Linotype-Hell/Linotronic 500, APP/Mac LaserWriter; Cameras – Canon; Scanners – Truvell, Nikon.
Total Circulation: 58017

ILLINOIS

ALTON

THE TELEGRAPH

Corporate/Parent Company: Hearst Corp.
Publication Street Address: 111 E Broadway
City: Alton
State: IL

Publication Website: www.thetelegraph.com
Postal Code: 62002-6218
Office phone: (618) 463-2500
General E-mail: obits@thetelegraph.com
Publisher Name: Denise Vonder Haar
Publisher Email: DVonderhaar@HearstNP.com
Publisher Phone: 618-208-6419
Editor Name: Ron DeBrock
Editor Email: ronald.debrock@thetelegraph.com
Editor Phone: 618-208-6456
Advertising Executive Name: Carole Fredeking
Advertising Executive Email: Carole.Fredeking@Hearst.com
Advertising Executive Phone: 618-208-6444

ARLINGTON HEIGHTS

DAILY HERALD

Corporate/Parent Company: Paddock Publications, Inc.
Publication Street Address: 95 W. Algonquin Rd.
City: Arlington Heights
State: IL
Publication Website: www.dailyherald.com
Postal Code: 60005-4617
Office phone: (847) 427-4300
General E-mail: sales@dailyherald.com
Publisher Name: Doug Ray
Publisher Email: dray@dailyherald.com
Publisher Phone: (847) 427-4510 x__
Editor Name: Baumann, Jim
Editor Email: jbaumann@dailyherald.com
Editor Phone: (847) 427-4555

DUPAGE COUNTY DAILY HERALD

Corporate/Parent Company: Paddock Publications, Inc.
Publication Street Address: P.O. Box 280
City: Arlington Heights
State: IL
Publication Website: www.dailyherald.com
Postal Code: 60006-0280
Office phone: 847.427.5500
General E-mail: news@dailyherald.com
Publisher Name: Doug Ray
Publisher Email: dray@dailyherald.com
Publisher Phone: (847) 427-4510 x__
Editor Name: Baumann, Jim
Editor Email: jbaumann@dailyherald.com
Editor Phone: (847) 427-4555
Advertising Executive Name: Bartolucci, Rob
Advertising Executive Email: rbartolucci@dailyherald.com
Advertising Executive Phone: (630) 955-3568

FOX VALLEY DAILY HERALD

Corporate/Parent Company: Paddock Publications, Inc.
Publication Street Address: P.O. Box 280
City: Arlington Heights
State: IL
Publication Website: www.dailyherald.com
Postal Code: 60006-0280
Office phone: 847.427.5500
General E-mail: news@dailyherald.com
Publisher Name: Doug Ray
Publisher Email: dray@dailyherald.com
Publisher Phone: (847) 427-4510 x__
Editor Name: Baumann, Jim
Editor Email: jbaumann@dailyherald.com
Editor Phone: (847) 427-4555
Advertising Executive Name: Bartolucci, Rob
Advertising Executive Email: rbartolucci@dailyherald.com
Advertising Executive Phone: (630) 955-3568

LAKE COUNTY DAILY HERALD

Corporate/Parent Company: Paddock

Publications, Inc.
Publication Street Address: P.O. Box 280
City: Arlington Heights
State: IL
Publication Website: www.dailyherald.com
Postal Code: 60006-0280
Office phone: 847.427.5500
General E-mail: news@dailyherald.com
Publisher Name: Doug Ray
Publisher Email: dray@dailyherald.com
Publisher Phone: (847) 427-4510 x__
Editor Name: Baumann, Jim
Editor Email: jbaumann@dailyherald.com
Editor Phone: (847) 427-4555
Advertising Executive Name: Bartolucci, Rob
Advertising Executive Email: rbartolucci@dailyherald.com
Advertising Executive Phone: (630) 955-3568

MCHENRY COUNTY DAILY HERALD

Corporate/Parent Company: Paddock Publications, Inc.
Publication Street Address: P.O. Box 280
City: Arlington Heights
State: IL
Publication Website: www.dailyherald.com
Postal Code: 60006-0280
Office phone: 847.427.5500
General E-mail: news@dailyherald.com
Publisher Name: Doug Ray
Publisher Email: dray@dailyherald.com
Publisher Phone: (847) 427-4510 x__
Editor Name: Baumann, Jim
Editor Email: jbaumann@dailyherald.com
Editor Phone: (847) 427-4555
Advertising Executive Name: Bartolucci, Rob
Advertising Executive Email: rbartolucci@dailyherald.com
Advertising Executive Phone: (630) 955-3568

NORTHWEST SUBURBS DAILY HERALD

Corporate/Parent Company: Paddock Publications, Inc.
Publication Street Address: P.O. Box 280
City: Arlington Heights
State: IL
Publication Website: www.dailyherald.com
Postal Code: 60006-0280
Office phone: 847.427.5500
General E-mail: "news@dailyherald.com
Doug Ray
dray@dailyherald.com
(847) 427-4510 x__"
Publisher Name: Doug Ray
Publisher Email: dray@dailyherald.com
Publisher Phone: (847) 427-4510 x__
Editor Name: Baumann, Jim
Editor Email: jbaumann@dailyherald.com
Editor Phone: (847) 427-4555
Advertising Executive Name: Bartolucci, Rob
Advertising Executive Email: rbartolucci@dailyherald.com
Advertising Executive Phone: (630) 955-3568

AURORA

THE COURIER-NEWS

Publication Street Address: 495 N Commons Dr
City: Aurora
State: IL
Publication Website: www.chicagotribune.com/suburbs/elgin-courier-news
Postal Code: 60504-8187
Office phone: (847) 696-6019
General E-mail: consumerservices@chicagotribune.com
Publisher Name: Par Ridder (GM)
Publisher Email: pridder@chicagotribune.com
Editor Name: Pat Reagen
Editor Email: pregan@chicagotribune.com

U.S. Daily Newspapers

BELLEVILLE

BELLEVILLE NEWS-DEMOCRAT
Corporate/Parent Company: McClatchy Company
Publication Street Address: 120 S Illinois St
City: Belleville
State: IL
Publication Website: www.bnd.com
Postal Code: 62220-2130
Office phone: (618) 234-1000
General E-mail: customerservice@bnd.com
Publisher Name: Jeff Couch
Publisher Email: jcouch@bnd.com
Publisher Phone: (618) 234-1000 x__
Editor Name: Jeffry Couch
Editor Email: jcouch@bnd.com
Editor Phone: (618) 239-2551
Advertising Executive Name: Karen Latta
Advertising Executive Email: klatta@bnd.com
Advertising Executive Phone: (618) 239-2628 x_

BELVIDERE

BELVIDERE REPUBLICAN
Corporate/Parent Company: Rock Valley Publishing LLC.
Publication Street Address: 130 S. State St., Suite 101
City: Belvidere
State: IL
Publication Website: www.belvideredailyrepublican.net
Postal Code: 61008
Office phone: 815-547-0084
General E-mail: bdroffice@rvpublishing.com
Publisher Name: Pete Cruger
Publisher Email: pete@rvpublishing.com
Publisher Phone: (815) 877-4044 x__
Editor Name: Anne Eickstadt
Editor Email: bdrnews@rvpublishing.com
Editor Phone: (815) 547-0084 x__
Advertising Executive Name: Maxine Bayer
Advertising Executive Email: mbayer@rvpublishing.com
Advertising Executive Phone: (815) 234-4821 x__

BLOOMINGTON

THE PANTAGRAPH
Corporate/Parent Company: Lee Enterprises
Publication Street Address: 205 N Main St.
City: Bloomington
State: IL
Publication Website: www.pantagraph.com
Postal Code: 61701-3827
Office phone: (309) 829-9000
General E-mail: bwinterland@pantagraph.com
Publisher Name: Barry Winterland
Publisher Email: bwinterland@pantagraph.com
Editor Name: Chris Coates
Editor Email: ccoates@herald-review.com
Editor Phone: (217) 421-8905
Advertising Executive Name: Amanda Jones
Advertising Executive Email: ajones@pantagraph.com
Advertising Executive Phone: (309) 820-3341

CANTON

DAILY LEDGER
Corporate/Parent Company: Gannett
Publication Street Address: 53 W Elm St
City: Canton
State: IL
Publication Website: www.cantondailyledger.com
Postal Code: 61520-2511
Office phone: (309) 647-5100
General E-mail: editor@cantondailyledger.com
Editor Name: Deb Robinson
Editor Email: drobinson@cantondailyledger.com
Editor Phone: 309-647-5100
Advertising Executive Name: Terri Williams
Advertising Executive Email: twilliams@cantondailyledger.com
Advertising Executive Phone: 309-647-5100

CARBONDALE

BENTON EVENING NEWS
Publication Street Address: 2015 W. Main St
City: Carbondale
State: IL
Publication Website: www.bentoneveningnews.com
Postal Code: 62812-2238
Office phone: (618) 438-5611
General E-mail: comments@localsouthernnews.com
Publisher Name: Stefanie Anderson (GM)
Publisher Email: sanderson@localsouthernnews.com
Publisher Phone: (618) 606-1208 x_
Editor Name: Geoff Ritter
Editor Email: gritter@localsouthernnews.com
Editor Phone: 618-438-5611
Advertising Executive Name: Brittany Gresham
Advertising Executive Email: bgresham@benteveningnews.com

THE SOUTHERN ILLINOISAN
Corporate/Parent Company: Lee Enterprises
Publication Street Address: 710 N. Illinois Avenue
City: Carbondale
State: IL
Publication Website: www.thesouthern.com
Postal Code: 62901
Office phone: 618-529-5454
General E-mail: news@thesouthern.com
Publisher Name: Terra Kerkemeyer
Publisher Email: terra.kerkemeyer@thesouthern.com
Publisher Phone: 618-351-5038
Editor Name: Tom English
Editor Email: tom.english@thesouthern.com
Editor Phone: 618-351-5070
Advertising Executive Name: Tina Moon
Advertising Executive Email: tina.moon@thesouthern.com
Advertising Executive Phone: 618-351-5026

CARMI

THE CARMI TIMES
Publication Street Address: 323 E Main St
City: Carmi
State: IL
Publication Website: www.carmitimes.com
Postal Code: 62821-1810
Office phone: (618) 382-4176
General E-mail: cbarche@olneydailymail.com
Publisher Name: Chip Barche
Publisher Email: cbarche@olneydailymail.com
Editor Name: Chip Barche
Editor Email: cbarche@olneydailymail.com
Editor Phone: 618-393-2931
Advertising Executive Name: Vanessa Taylor
Advertising Executive Email: vtaylor@gatehousemedia.com

CHAMPAIGN

THE NEWS-GAZETTE
Corporate/Parent Company: Community Media Group
Publication Street Address: 15 E Main St
City: Champaign
State: IL
Publication Website: www.news-gazette.com
Postal Code: 61820-3625
Office phone: (217) 351-5252
General E-mail: news@news-gazette.com
Publisher Name: Paul Barrett
Publisher Email: pmbpub@aol.com
Editor Name: Jeff D'Alessio
Editor Email: jdalessio@news-gazette.media
Editor Phone: 217-351-5363
Advertising Executive Name: Jackie Martin
Advertising Executive Email: jmartin@news-gazette.com

CHICAGO

CHICAGO SUN-TIMES
Corporate/Parent Company: ST Acquisition Holdings LLC
Publication Street Address: 30 N. Racine Ave.
City: Chicago
State: IL
Publication Website: www.suntimes.com
Postal Code: 60607
Office phone: (312) 321-3000
General E-mail: customerservice@suntimes.com
Publisher Name: Chris Fusco
Publisher Email: cfusco@suntimes.com
Publisher Phone: (312) 321-2522
Editor Name: Tom McNamee
Editor Email: tmonamee@suntimes.com
Editor Phone: 312-321-2921

CHICAGO TRIBUNE
Corporate/Parent Company: Tribune Publishing
Publication Street Address: IL
City: Chicago
State: IL
Publication Website: www.chicagotribune.com
Postal Code: 60611-4066
Office phone: (312) 222-3232
General E-mail: letters@chicagotribune.com
Publisher Name: Colin McMahon
Publisher Email: cmcmahon@chicagotribune.com
Editor Name: Christine Taylor
Editor Email: cwolfram@chicagotirbune.com

HOY
Publication Street Address: 160 N. Stetson Ave
City: Chicago
State: IL
Publication Website: www.vivelohoy.com
Postal Code: 60601
Office phone: 312-222-5555.
General E-mail: letters@chicagotribune.com
Editor Name: R. Bruce Dold
Editor Email: editor@chicagotribune.com

THE BEACON NEWS
Publication Street Address: 350 N Orleans St
City: Chicago
State: IL
Publication Website: www.chicagotribune.com/suburbs/aurora-beacon-news
Postal Code: 60654-1975
General E-mail: consumerservices@chicagotribune.com
Publisher Name: Par Ridder (GM)
Publisher Email: pridder@chicagotribune.com
Editor Name: Pat Reagen
Editor Email: pregan@chicagotribune.com

CRYSTAL LAKE

NORTHWEST HERALD
Corporate/Parent Company: Shaw Media
Publication Street Address: 7717 S Route 31
City: Crystal Lake
State: IL
Publication Website: www.nwherald.com
Postal Code: 60014
Office phone: (815) 459-4040
General E-mail: tips@nwherald.com
Publisher Name: Jim Ringness
Publisher Email: jringness@shawmedia.com
Editor Name: Jon Styf
Editor Email: jstyf@shawmedia.com
Advertising Executive Name: Norm Fossmeyer
Advertising Executive Email: nfossmeyer@shawmedia.com

DANVILLE

COMMERCIAL NEWS
Corporate/Parent Company: CNHI, LLC
Publication Street Address: 17 W. North St.
City: Danville
State: IL
Publication Website: www.commercial-news.com
Postal Code: 61832
Office phone: (217) 446-1000
General E-mail: newsroom@dancomnews.com
Publisher Name: Amy Winter
Publisher Email: awinter@dancomnews.com
Publisher Phone: 217.477.5111
Editor Name: Larry Smith
Editor Email: lsmith@dancomnews.com
Editor Phone: 217.477.5183
Advertising Executive Name: Cindy Decker
Advertising Executive Email: cdecker@dancomnews.com
Advertising Executive Phone: 217.477.5105

DAVENPORT

THE DISPATCH - THE ROCK ISLAND ARGUS
Corporate/Parent Company: Moline Dispatch & Rock Island Argus
Publication Street Address: 500 E. 3rd St.
City: Davenport
State: IL
Publication Website: www.qconline.com
Postal Code: 52801
Office phone: 309-764-4344
General E-mail: mchristensen@qctimes.com
Publisher Name: Deb Anselm
Publisher Email: danselm@qctimes.com
Publisher Phone: 563-383-2224
Editor Name: Matt Christensen
Editor Email: mchristensen@qctimes.com
Editor Phone: 563-383-2264
Advertising Executive Name: Cathy Rockwell
Advertising Executive Email: crockwell@qctimes.com
Advertising Executive Phone: 563-383-2306

DECATUR

HERALD & REVIEW
Corporate/Parent Company: Lee Enterprises
Publication Street Address: 601 E. William St.
City: Decatur
State: IL
Publication Website: www.herald-review.com
Postal Code: 62523
Office phone: 217-429-5151
General E-mail: hrnews@herald-review.com
Publisher Name: Barry Winterland
Publisher Email: bwinterland@pantagraph.com
Editor Name: Chris Coates
Editor Email: ccoates@herald-review.com
Editor Phone: (217) 421-8905
Advertising Executive Name: Jaime Reynolds
Advertising Executive Email: jreynolds@pantagraph.com
Advertising Executive Phone: (309) 820-3337

DEKALB

DAILY CHRONICLE
Corporate/Parent Company: Shaw Media
Publication Street Address: 1586 Barber Greene Rd.
City: DeKalb
State: IL
Publication Website: www.daily-chronicle.com
Postal Code: 60115
Office phone: 815-756-4841
General E-mail: news@daily-chronicle.com
Publisher Name: Laura Shaw
Publisher Email: lshaw@shawmedia.com
Publisher Phone: (815) 756-4841 x__
Editor Name: Kelsey Rettke
Editor Email: krettke@shawmedia.com
Editor Phone: (815) 756-4841 x_

I-31

DIXON

DAILY GAZETTE

Corporate/Parent Company: Shaw Media
Publication Street Address: 113 S. Peoria Ave.
City: Dixon
State: IL
Publication Website: www.saukvalley.com
Postal Code: 61021
Office phone: 815-284-2224
General E-mail: news@saukvalley.com
Editor Name: Kathleen Schultz
Editor Email: kschultz@saukvalley.com
Editor Phone: 815-632-2531
Advertising Executive Name: Jennifer Heintzelman
Advertising Executive Email: jheintzelman@saukvalley.com
Advertising Executive Phone: 815-632-2502

DIXON

SAUK VALLEY

Corporate/Parent Company: Shaw Media
Publication Street Address: 113 S Peoria Ave
City: Dixon
State: IL
Publication Website: www.saukvalley.com
Postal Code: 61021-2905
Office phone: (815) 284-2224
General E-mail: news@saukvalley.com
Publisher Name: Don T. Bricker
Publisher Email: dbricker@saukvalley.com
Editor Name: Kathleen Schultz
Editor Email: kschultz@saukvalley.com
Editor Phone: 815-632-2531
Advertising Executive Name: Jennifer Heintzelman
Advertising Executive Email: jheintzelman@saukvalley.com
Advertising Executive Phone: 815-632-2502

DU QUOIN

DU QUOIN EVENING CALL

Publication Street Address: 9 N Division St
City: Du Quoin
State: IL
Publication Website: www.duquoin.com
Postal Code: 62832-1405
Office phone: (618) 542-2133
General E-mail: comments@localsouthernnews.com
Publisher Name: Stefanie Anderson (GM)
Publisher Email: sanderson@localsouthernnews.com
Editor Name: John Homan
Editor Email: jhoman@localsouthernnews.com
Advertising Executive Name: Devan Vaughn
Advertising Executive Email: dvaughn@localsouthernnews.com

THE MARION DAILY REPUBLICAN

Publication Street Address: 18 E. Main St.
City: Du Quoin
State: IL
Publication Website: www.dailyrepublicannews.com
Postal Code: 62832
Office phone: (618) 993-2626
General E-mail: comments@localsouthernnews.com
Publisher Name: Stefanie Anderson (GM)
Publisher Email: sanderson@localsouthernnews.com
Editor Name: John Homan
Editor Email: jhoman@localsouthernnews.com
Advertising Executive Name: Kathy Metcalf

Advertising Executive Email: kmetcalf@dailyrepublicannews.com
Advertising Executive Phone: (618) 927-5735

EAST MOLINE

DISPATCH-ARGUS

Publication Street Address: 1033 7th Street, Suite 101
City: East Moline
State: IL
Publication Website: www.qconline.com
Postal Code: 61244
Office phone: (309) 764-4344
General E-mail: press@qconline.com
Publisher Name: Deb Anselm
Publisher Email: danselm@qctimes.com
Publisher Phone: 563-383-2224
Editor Name: Matt Christensen
Editor Email: mchristensen@qctimes.com
Editor Phone: 563-383-2264
Advertising Executive Name: Jaime Reyolds
Advertising Executive Email: jaime.reynolds@lee.net

EDWARDSVILLE

EDWARDSVILLE INTELLIGENCER

Corporate/Parent Company: Hearst Corp.
Publication Street Address: 116 N. Main St
City: Edwardsville
State: IL
Publication Website: www.theintelligencer.com/
Postal Code: 62025-1938
Office phone: (618) 656-4700
General E-mail: dvonderhaar@hearstnp.com
Publisher Name: Denise VonderHaar
Publisher Email: dvonderhaar@hearstnp.com
Publisher Phone: 618-659-5731
Editor Name: Brittany Johnson
Editor Email: bjohnson@edwpub.net
Editor Phone: 618-659-5734
Advertising Executive Name: Carole Fredeking
Advertising Executive Email: carole.fredeking@hearst.com

THE EDWARDSVILLE INTELLIGENCER

Corporate/Parent Company: Hearst Corp.
Publication Street Address: 116 N. Main St.
City: Edwardsville
State: IL
Publication Website: www.theintelligencer.com
Postal Code: 62025
Office phone: (618) 656-4700
General E-mail: dvonderhaar@hearstnp.com
Publisher Name: Denise VonderHaar
Publisher Email: dvonderhaar@hearstnp.com
Publisher Phone: 618-659-5731
Editor Name: Brittany Johnson
Editor Email: bjohnson@edwpub.net
Editor Phone: 618-659-5734
Advertising Executive Name: Carole Fredeking
Advertising Executive Email: carole.fredeking@hearst.com
Advertising Executive Phone: (618) 208-6444 x_

EFFINGHAM

EFFINGHAM DAILY NEWS

Corporate/Parent Company: CNHI, LLC
Publication Street Address: 201 N Banker St
City: Effingham
State: IL
Publication Website: www.effinghamdailynews.com
Postal Code: 62401-2304
Office phone: (217) 347-7151
General E-mail: advertising@effinghamdailynews.com
Publisher Name: Amy Winter

Advertising Executive Name: Maureen Ringness
Advertising Executive Email: mringness@shawsuburban.com
Advertising Executive Phone: (815) 756-4841 x_

Publisher Email: amy.winter@effinghamdailynews.com
Publisher Phone: ext. 112
Editor Name: Jeff Long
Editor Email: jeff.long@effinghamdailynews.com
Editor Phone: ext. 129
Advertising Executive Name: Jody Hardiek
Advertising Executive Email: jody.hardiek@effinghamdailynews.com
Advertising Executive Phone: ext. 141

EL PASO

EL PASO JOURNAL

Publication Street Address: 51 West Front Street
City: El Paso
State: IL
Publication Website: www.elpasojournal.org
Postal Code: 61738
Office phone: 309-527-8595
General E-mail: journal@fairpoint.net
Publisher Name: Kim Kearney
Publisher Email: journal@fairpoint.net
Publisher Phone: (309) 527-8595 x_
Editor Name: Jenny Kearney
Editor Email: journal@fairpoint.net
Editor Phone: 309-527-8595
Advertising Executive Name: Angelique Piercy
Advertising Executive Email: journal@fairpoint.net
Advertising Executive Phone: 309-527-8595

FREEPORT

THE JOURNAL-STANDARD

Corporate/Parent Company: GateHouse Media
Publication Street Address: 50 W Douglas St
City: Freeport
State: IL
Publication Website: www.journalstandard.com
Postal Code: 61032-4129
Office phone: (815) 232-1171
General E-mail: mbaldwin@rrstar.com
Editor Name: Mark Baldwin
Editor Email: mbaldwin@rrstar.com
Editor Phone: (815) 987-1358
Advertising Executive Name: Denny Lecher
Advertising Executive Email: dlecher@rrstar.com
Advertising Executive Phone: (815) 987-1320

GALESBURG

THE REGISTER-MAIL

Corporate/Parent Company: Gannett
Publication Street Address: 140 S Prairie St
City: Galesburg
State: IL
Publication Website: www.galesburg.com
Postal Code: 61401-4605
Office phone: (309) 343-7181
General E-mail: tmartin@register-mail.com
Editor Name: Tom Martin
Editor Email: tmartin@register-mail.com
Editor Phone: 309-315-6068
Advertising Executive Name: Shelly Trueblood
Advertising Executive Email: strueblood@register-mail.com
Advertising Executive Phone: 309-315-6062

GURNEE

LAKE COUNTY NEWS-SUN

Publication Street Address: 1225 Tri State Pkwy Ste 570
City: Gurnee
State: IL
Publication Website: www.newssunonline.com
Postal Code: 60031-9163
Office phone: (312) 222-2425
General E-mail: ggarvey@chicagotribune.com
Publisher Name: Par Ridder (GM)
Publisher Email: pridder@chicagotribune.com
Editor Name: Anne Halston
Editor Email: ahalston@chicagotribune.com

HARRISBURG

ELDORADO DAILY JOURNAL

Corporate/Parent Company: Paddock Publications, Inc.
Publication Street Address: 617 E. Church St.
City: Harrisburg
State: IL
Publication Website: www.dailyregister.com
Postal Code: 62946
Office phone: (618) 253-7146
Editor Name: Renee Trappe
Editor Email: rtrappe@localsouthernnews.com
Advertising Executive Name: Devan Vaughn
Advertising Executive Email: dvaughn@localsouthernnews.com

THE DAILY REGISTER

Corporate/Parent Company: News Media Corporation
Publication Street Address: 617 E. Church St.
City: Harrisburg
State: IL
Publication Website: www.dailyregister.com
Postal Code: 62946
Office phone: (618) 253-7146
General E-mail: sanderson@localsouthernnews.com
Publisher Name: Stefanie Anderson (GM)
Publisher Email: sanderson@localsouthernnews.com
Editor Name: Travis DeNeal
Editor Email: tdeneal@dailyregister.com
Advertising Executive Name: Brittany Gresham
Advertising Executive Email: bgresham@dailyregister.com

THE HARRISBURG REGISTER

Corporate/Parent Company: Paddock Publications, Inc.
Publication Street Address: 617 E. Church St.
City: Harrisburg
State: IL
Publication Website: www.dailyregister.com
Postal Code: 62946
Office phone: (618) 253-7146
General E-mail: sanderson@localsouthernnews.com
Publisher Name: Stefanie Anderson (GM)
Publisher Email: sanderson@localsouthernnews.com
Publisher Phone: (618) 606-1208 x_
Editor Name: Travis DeNeal
Editor Email: tdeneal@dailyregister.com
Advertising Executive Name: Brittany Gresham
Advertising Executive Email: bgresham@dailyregister.com

JACKSONVILLE

JACKSONVILLE JOURNAL-COURIER

Corporate/Parent Company: Hearst Corp.
Publication Street Address: 235 W State St
City: Jacksonville
State: IL
Publication Website: www.myjournalcourier.com
Postal Code: 62650-2001
Office phone: (217) 245-6121
General E-mail: news@myjournalcourier.com
Publisher Name: David C.L. Bauer
Publisher Email: dbauer@myjournalcourier.com
Publisher Phone: 217-408-2048
Editor Name: Jeff Lonergan
Editor Email: jlonergan@myjournalcourier.com
Editor Phone: 217-408-2060
Advertising Executive Name: Vicki Selby
Advertising Executive Email: vselby@myjournalcourier.com
Advertising Executive Phone: 217-408-2016

U.S. Daily Newspapers

JOURNAL-COURIER
Corporate/Parent Company: Hearst Corp.
Publication Street Address: 235 West State Street
City: Jacksonville
State: IL
Publication Website: www.myjournalcourier.com
Postal Code: 62650
Office phone: 217-245-6121
General E-mail: news@myjournalcourier.com
Publisher Name: David C.L. Bauer
Publisher Email: dbauer@myjournalcourier.com
Publisher Phone: 217-408-2048
Editor Name: David C.L. Bauer
Editor Email: dbauer@myjournalcourier.com
Editor Phone: 217-408-2048
Advertising Executive Name: Vicki Selby
Advertising Executive Email: vselby@myjournalcourier.com
Advertising Executive Phone: 217-408-2016

JOLIET
THE HERALD NEWS
Corporate/Parent Company: Gannett
Publication Street Address: 2175 Oneida Street
City: Joliet
State: IL
Publication Website: www.theherald-news.com
Postal Code: 60435
Office phone: (815) 280-4100
General E-mail: news@theherald-news.com
Publisher Name: Steve Vanisko
Publisher Email: svanisko@shawmedia.com
Publisher Phone: 815-280-4103
Editor Name: Joe Hosey
Editor Email: jhosey@shawmedia.com
Editor Phone: 815-280-4094

KANKAKEE
THE DAILY JOURNAL
Corporate/Parent Company: Gannett
Publication Street Address: 8 Dearborn Sq
City: Kankakee
State: IL
Publication Website: www.daily-journal.com
Postal Code: 60901-3909
Office phone: 815-937-3322
General E-mail: webmaster@daily-journal.com
Editor Name: Misty Knisely
Editor Email: mknisely@daily-journal.com
Editor Phone: (815) 937-1281

KEWANEE
STAR-COURIER
Corporate/Parent Company: Gannett
Publication Street Address: 105 E Central Blvd
City: Kewanee
State: IL
Publication Website: www.starcourier.com
Postal Code: 61443-2245
Office phone: 833-776-8601
General E-mail: mhelenthal@starcourier.com
Publisher Name: Shawn Fox
Publisher Email: sfox@pjstar.com
Publisher Phone: 833-776-8601
Editor Name: Mike Helenthal
Editor Email: mhelenthal@starcourier.com
Editor Phone: 833-776-8601
Advertising Executive Name: Genie Stanley
Advertising Executive Email: gstanley@starcourier.com
Advertising Executive Phone: 833-776-8601

LA SALLE
NEWSTRIBUNE
Corporate/Parent Company: Shaw Media
Publication Street Address: 426 Second Street
City: La Salle
State: IL
Publication Website: www.newstrib.com
Postal Code: 61301
Office phone: 815-223-3200
General E-mail: support@shawmedia.com
Publisher Name: Dan Goetz
Publisher Email: dgoetz@shawmedia.com
Publisher Phone: (815) 431-4014
Editor Name: Craig Sterrett
Editor Email: ntlocal@shawmedia.com
Editor Phone: (815) 220-6935
Advertising Executive Name: Jeanette Smith
Advertising Executive Email: jmsmith@shawmedia.com
Advertising Executive Phone: (815) 220-6948

LAWRENCEVILLE
DAILY RECORD
Corporate/Parent Company: Gannett
Publication Street Address: 1209 State St
City: Lawrenceville
State: IL
Publication Website: www.lawdailyrecord.com
Postal Code: 62439-2332
Office phone: (618) 943-2331
General E-mail: ads@lawdailyrecord.com
Publisher Name: Kathleen Lewis
Publisher Email: news@robdailynews.com
Editor Name: Bill Richardson
Editor Email: brichardson@lawdailyrecord.com
Advertising Executive Name: Sandie Young
Advertising Executive Email: syoung@lawdailyrecord.com

LAWRENCEVILLE DAILY RECORD
Publication Street Address: 1209 State St
City: Lawrenceville
State: IL
Publication Website: www.lawdailyrecord.com
Postal Code: 62439
Office phone: 618-943-2331
General E-mail: ads@lawdailyrecord.com
Publisher Name: Kathleen Lewis
Publisher Email: news@robdailynews.com
Publisher Phone: (618) 544-2101 x_
Editor Name: Bill Richardson
Editor Email: brichardson@lawdailyrecord.com
Editor Phone: Ex 103
Advertising Executive Name: Sandie Young
Advertising Executive Email: syoung@lawdailyrecord.com
Advertising Executive Phone: Ex 114

LINCOLN
LINCOLN COURIER
Publication Street Address: 206 S Chicago St
City: Lincoln
State: IL
Publication Website: www.lincolncourier.com
Postal Code: 62656-2701
Office phone: (217) 732-2101
General E-mail: news@lincolncourier.com
Publisher Name: Jean Ann Miller
Publisher Email: jeanann.miller@lincolncourier.com
Editor Name: Jean Ann Miller
Editor Email: jeanann.miller@lincolncourier.com
Editor Phone: (217) 732-2101 ext. 333
Advertising Executive Name: Ted Wolf
Advertising Executive Email: ted.wolf@lincolncourier.com
Advertising Executive Phone: (217) 732-2101 ext. 344

THE COURIER
Corporate/Parent Company: Gannett
Publication Street Address: 2201 Woodlawn Rd #345, P.O. Box 740
City: Lincoln
State: IL
Publication Website: www.lincolncourier.com
Postal Code: 62656
Office phone: (217) 732-2101
General E-mail: jeanann.miller@lincolncourier.com
Editor Name: Jean Ann Miller
Editor Email: jeanann.miller@lincolncourier.com
Editor Phone: (217) 732-2101
Advertising Executive Name: Ted Wolf
Advertising Executive Email: ted.wolf@lincolncourier.com
Advertising Executive Phone: (217) 732-2101

LOMBARD
DEKALB COUNTY JOURNAL
Corporate/Parent Company: Chronicle Media, LLC.
Publication Street Address: 1920 S. Highland Avenue, #333
City: Lombard
State: IL
Publication Website: www.dekalbjournal.com
Postal Code: 60148
Office phone: 866-672-1600
General E-mail: editor@chronicleillinois.com
Publisher Name: Rick Hibbert
Publisher Email: rhibbert@chronicleillinois.com
Publisher Phone: 312.690.5341
Editor Name: Judy Harvey
Editor Email: jharvey@chronicleillinois.com
Editor Phone: 866-672-1600
Advertising Executive Name: Mark Doherty
Advertising Executive Email: mdoherty@chronicleillinois.com
Advertising Executive Phone: 866.672.1600 Ext. 256

MACOMB
THE MCDONOUGH COUNTY VOICE
Corporate/Parent Company: Gannett
Publication Street Address: 26 W Side Sq
City: Macomb
State: IL
Publication Website: www.mcdonoughvoice.com
Postal Code: 61455-2219
Office phone: (309) 833-2114
General E-mail: newsroom@McDonoughVoice.com
Publisher Name: Shawn Fox
Publisher Email: sfox@pjstar.com
Editor Name: Michelle Langhout
Editor Email: editor@mcdonoughvoice.com
Editor Phone: (309) 833-2114 ext.253
Advertising Executive Name: Michelle Ringenberger
Advertising Executive Email: mringenberger@mcdonoughvoice.com
Advertising Executive Phone: (309) 833-2114 ext. 258

MONMOUTH
DAILY REVIEW ATLAS
Corporate/Parent Company: Gannett
Publication Street Address: 400 S Main St
City: Monmouth
State: IL
Publication Website: www.reviewatlas.com
Postal Code: 61462-2164
Office phone: (309) 734-3176
General E-mail: communitynews@reviewatlas.com
Publisher Name: Shawn Fox
Publisher Email: sfox@pjstar.com
Editor Name: Jeff Holt
Editor Email: sports@reviewatlas.com
Editor Phone: 309-734-3176

MOUNT CARMEL
MOUNT CARMEL REGISTER
Corporate/Parent Company: Paxton Media Group, LLC
Publication Street Address: 217 E. 9th St.
City: Mount Carmel
State: IL
Publication Website: www.mtcarmelregister.com
Postal Code: 62863-2110
Office phone: (618) 262-5144
General E-mail: news@mtcarmelregister.com
Publisher Name: Mike Weafer
Publisher Email: mweafer@messenger-inquirer.com
Editor Name: Andrea Howe
Editor Email: news@mtcarmelregister.com
Advertising Executive Name: Courtney Shuttle
Advertising Executive Email: courtney@pdclarion.com

NORTHBROOK
THE HOMER HORIZON
Corporate/Parent Company: 22nd Century Media, LLC
Publication Street Address: 60 Revere Drive Suite 888
City: Northbrook
State: IL
Publication Website: homerhorizon.com
Postal Code: 60062
Office phone: (847) 272-4565
Publisher Name: Joe Coughlin
Publisher Email: j.coughlin@22ndcenturymedia.com
Editor Name: Thomas Czaja
Editor Email: tom@homerhorizon.com

THE LOCKPORT LEGEND
Corporate/Parent Company: 22nd Century Media, LLC
Publication Street Address: 60 Revere Drive Suite 888
City: Northbrook
State: IL
Publication Website: www.lockportlegend.com
Postal Code: 60062
Office phone: (847) 272-4565
Publisher Name: Joe Coughlin
Publisher Email: j.coughlin@22ndcenturymedia.com
Editor Name: Abhinanda Datta
Editor Email: abhi@lockportlegend.com

THE MOKENA MESSENGER
Corporate/Parent Company: 22nd Century Media, LLC
Publication Street Address: 60 Revere Drive Suite 888
City: Northbrook
State: IL
Publication Website: www.mokenamessenger.com
Postal Code: 60062
Office phone: (847) 272-4565
Publisher Name: Joe Coughlin
Publisher Email: j.coughlin@22ndcenturymedia.com
Editor Name: T.J. Kremer
Editor Email: tj@mokenamessenger.com

THE NEW LENOX PATRIOT
Corporate/Parent Company: 22nd Century Media, LLC
Publication Street Address: 60 Revere Drive Suite 888
City: Northbrook
State: IL
Publication Website: newlenoxpatriot.com
Postal Code: 60062
Office phone: (847) 272-4565
Publisher Name: Joe Coughlin
Publisher Email: j.coughlin@22ndcenturymedia.com
Editor Name: Sean Hastings

U.S. Daily Newspapers

Editor Email: sean@newlenoxpatriot.com
Advertising Executive Name: Lora Healy
Advertising Executive Email: l.healy@22ndcenturymedia.com

THE NORTHBROOK TOWER

Corporate/Parent Company: 22nd Century Media, LLC
Publication Street Address: 60 Revere Drive Suite 888
City: Northbrook
State: IL
Publication Website: www.northbrooktower.com
Postal Code: 60062
Office phone: (847) 272-4565
Publisher Name: Joe Coughlin
Publisher Email: j.coughlin@22ndcenturymedia.com
Editor Name: Martin Carlino
Editor Email: martin@northbrooktower.com
Advertising Executive Name: Gail Eisenberg
Advertising Executive Email: g.eisenberg@22ndcenturymedia.com

THE ORLAND PARK PRAIRIE

Corporate/Parent Company: 22nd Century Media, LLC
Publication Street Address: 60 Revere Drive Suite 888
City: Northbrook
State: IL
Publication Website: www.opprairie.com
Postal Code: 60062
Office phone: (847) 272-4565
Publisher Name: Joe Coughlin
Publisher Email: j.coughlin@22ndcenturymedia.com
Editor Name: Jeff Vorva
Editor Email: j.vorva@22ndcm.com

THE TINLEY JUNCTION

Corporate/Parent Company: 22nd Century Media, LLC
Publication Street Address: 60 Revere Drive Suite 888
City: Northbrook
State: IL
Publication Website: www.tinleyjunction.com
Postal Code: 60062
Office phone: (847) 272-4565
Publisher Name: Joe Coughlin
Publisher Email: j.coughlin@22ndcenturymedia.com
Editor Name: Jacquelyn Schlabach
Editor Email: jacquelyn@tinleyjunction.com
Advertising Executive Name: Renee Burke
Advertising Executive Email: r.burke@22ndcenturymedia.com

THE WILMETTE BEACON

Corporate/Parent Company: 22nd Century Media, LLC
Publication Street Address: 60 Revere Drive Suite 888
City: Northbrook
State: IL
Publication Website: wilmettebeacon.com
Postal Code: 60062
Office phone: (847) 272-4565
Publisher Name: Joe Coughlin
Publisher Email: j.coughlin@22ndcenturymedia.com
Editor Name: Michael Wojtychiw
Editor Email: m.wojtychiw@22ndcenturymedia.com
Advertising Executive Name: Peter Hansen
Advertising Executive Email: p.hansen@22ndcenturymedia.com

THE WINNETKA CURRENT

Corporate/Parent Company: 22nd Century Media, LLC
Publication Street Address: 60 Revere Drive Suite 888
City: Northbrook
State: IL
Publication Website: winnetkacurrent.com
Postal Code: 60062
Office phone: (847) 272-4565
Publisher Name: Joe Coughlin
Publisher Email: j.coughlin@22ndcenturymedia.com
Editor Name: Michael Wojtychiw
Editor Email: m.wojtychiw@22ndcenturymedia.com
Advertising Executive Name: Peter Hansen
Advertising Executive Email: p.hansen@22ndcenturymedia.com

OAK PARK

VILLAGE FREE PRESS

Publication Street Address: 141 S. Oak Park Ave
City: Oak Park
State: IL
Publication Website: www.thevillagefreepress.org
Postal Code: 60302
Office phone: 708.316.8147
General E-mail: thevillagefreepress@gmail.com
Publisher Name: Michael Romain
Publisher Email: michael@vfpress.news
Publisher Phone: (708) 316-8147 x___
Editor Name: Michael Romain
Editor Email: michael@vfpress.news
Editor Phone: (708) 316-8147 x___
Advertising Executive Name: Dawn Ferrar
Advertising Executive Email: dawn@oakpark.com

OLNEY

OLNEY DAILY MAIL

Publication Street Address: 206 S Whittle Ave
City: Olney
State: IL
Publication Website: www.olneydailymail.com
Postal Code: 62450-2251
Office phone: (618) 393-2931
General E-mail: jringness@shawmedia.com
Publisher Name: Chip Barche
Publisher Email: cbarche@olneydailymail.com
Editor Name: Chip Barche
Editor Email: cbarche@olneydailymail.com
Editor Phone: 618-393-2931
Advertising Executive Name: Cathy Slunaker
Advertising Executive Email: advertising1@olneydailymail.com
Advertising Executive Phone: 618-393-2931

OTTAWA

THE TIMES

Corporate/Parent Company: Gannett
Publication Street Address: 110 W Jefferson St
City: Ottawa
State: IL
Publication Website: www.mywebtimes.com
Postal Code: 61350-5010
Office phone: (815) 433-2000
General E-mail: newsroom@mywebtimes.com
Publisher Name: Dan Goetz
Publisher Email: dgoetz@shawmedia.com
Editor Name: Tammie Sloup
Editor Email: tsloup@shawmedia.com
Advertising Executive Name: Julie Smith
Advertising Executive Email: jasmith@shawmedia.com

PEKIN

PEKIN DAILY TIMES

Corporate/Parent Company: Gannett
Publication Street Address: 306 Court St
City: Pekin
State: IL
Publication Website: www.pekintimes.com
Postal Code: 61554-3104
Office phone: (309) 346-1111
General E-mail: sales@timestoday.com
Publisher Name: Shawn Fox
Publisher Email: sfox@pjstar.com
Editor Name: Chris Kaergard
Editor Email: ckaergard@pjstar.com

PEORIA

JOURNAL STAR

Corporate/Parent Company: Gannett
City: Peoria
State: IL
Publication Website: www.pjstar.com
Postal Code: 61643
Office phone: (309) 686-3000
General E-mail: news@pjstar.com
Publisher Name: Shawn Fox
Publisher Email: sfox@pjstar.com
Publisher Phone: 309-686-3000
Editor Name: Dennis Anderson
Editor Email: danderson@pjstar.com
Editor Phone: 309-686-3159
Advertising Executive Name: Shawn Fox
Advertising Executive Email: sfox@pjstar.com
Advertising Executive Phone: 309-686-3034

PONTIAC

THE DAILY LEADER

Corporate/Parent Company: Gannett
Publication Street Address: 318 N Main St
City: Pontiac
State: IL
Publication Website: www.pontiacdailyleader.com
Postal Code: 61764-1930
Office phone: (815) 842-1153
General E-mail: ldreditor@mchsi.com
Editor Name: Erich Murphy
Editor Email: emurphy@pontiacdailyleader.com
Advertising Executive Name: Judy Sweitzer
Advertising Executive Email: jsweitzer@pontiacdailyleader.com

QUINCY

THE QUINCY HERALD-WHIG

Corporate/Parent Company: Quincy Newspapers, Inc.
Publication Street Address: 130 S 5th St
City: Quincy
State: IL
Publication Website: www.whig.com
Postal Code: 62301-3916
Office phone: (217) 223-5100
General E-mail: news@whig.com
Publisher Name: Ron Wallace
Publisher Email: rwallace@quincyinc.com
Publisher Phone: 217-221-3381
Editor Name: Jason Lewton
Editor Email: jlewton@whig.com
Editor Phone: 217-221-3321
Advertising Executive Name: Whitney Allerheiligen
Advertising Executive Email: wallerheiligen@whig.com
Advertising Executive Phone: 217-221-3305

ROBINSON

DAILY NEWS

Corporate/Parent Company: Gannett
Publication Street Address: 302 S Cross St
City: Robinson
State: IL
Publication Website: www.robdailynews.com
Postal Code: 62454-2137
Office phone: (618) 544-2101
General E-mail: ads@robdailynews.com
Publisher Name: Kathleen Lewis
Publisher Email: news@robdailynews.com
Editor Name: Tom Osborne
Editor Email: tosborne@robdailynews.com
Advertising Executive Name: Amy Teska
Advertising Executive Email: ar@robdailynews.com

ROBINSON DAILY NEWS

Corporate/Parent Company: Robinson Daily News Inc.
Publication Street Address: 113 South Court Street
City: Robinson
State: IL
Publication Website: www.robdailynews.com
Postal Code: 62454
Office phone: 618 546-1557
General E-mail: ads@robdailynews.com
Publisher Name: Kathleen Lewis
Publisher Email: news@robdailynews.com
Publisher Phone: (618) 544-2101 x___
Editor Name: Tom Osborne
Editor Email: tosborne@robdailynews.com
Advertising Executive Name: Winnie Piper
Advertising Executive Email: wpiper@robdailynews.com

ROCKFORD

ROCKFORD REGISTER STAR

Corporate/Parent Company: Gannett
Publication Street Address: 99 E. State St.
City: Rockford
State: IL
Publication Website: www.rrstar.com
Postal Code: 61104
Office phone: 815-987-1200
General E-mail: mbaldwin@rrstar.com
Publisher Name: Shawn Fox
Publisher Email: sfox@pjstar.com
Editor Name: Mark Baldwin
Editor Email: mbaldwin@rrstar.com
Editor Phone: 815-987-1358
Advertising Executive Name: Lori Gallagher
Advertising Executive Email: lgallagher@rrstar.com

SHELBYVILLE

SHELBYVILLE DAILY UNION

Corporate/Parent Company: Union Publishing Co.
Publication Street Address: 100 W. Main
City: Shelbyville
State: IL
Publication Website: www.shelbyvilledailyunion.com
Postal Code: 62565
Office phone: 217-347-7151
General E-mail: "classifieds@shelbyvilledailyunion.com
"
Publisher Name: Amy Winter
Publisher Email: amy.winter@shelbyvilledailyunion.com
Publisher Phone: 217-347-7151
Editor Name: Jeff Long
Editor Email: jeff.long@shelbyvilledailyunion.com
Editor Phone: 217-347-7151
Advertising Executive Name: Deanna Sickles
Advertising Executive Email: deanna.sickles@shelbyvilledailyunion.com
Advertising Executive Phone: 217-519-2913

SPRINGFIELD

THE STATE JOURNAL-REGISTER

Corporate/Parent Company: Gannett
Publication Street Address: P.O. Box 219
City: Springfield
State: IL
Publication Website: www.sj-r.com
Postal Code: 62701-1927
Office phone: (217) 788-1300

U.S. Daily Newspapers

General E-mail: sjr@sj-r.com
Publisher Name: Eugene Jackson
Publisher Email: ejackson@sj-r.com
Publisher Phone: 217-788-1300
Editor Name: Leisa Richardson
Editor Email: lrichardson@sj-r.com
Editor Phone: 217-788-1505

TAYLORVILLE

BREEZE COURIER

Publication Street Address: 212 S Main St
City: Taylorville
State: IL
Publication Website: www.breezecourier.com
Postal Code: 62568-2219
Office phone: (217) 824-2233
General E-mail: website@breezecourier.com
Publisher Name: Marylee Rasar
Publisher Email: mrasar@breezecourier.com
Publisher Phone: (217) 824-2233 x___
Editor Name: Owen Laswell
Editor Email: olaswell@breezecourier.com
Editor Phone: (217) 824-2233 x_

TINLEY PARK

DAILY SOUTHTOWN

Publication Street Address: 435 N Michigan Ave
City: Tinley Park
State: IL
Publication Website: www.dailysouthtown.com
Postal Code: 60611-4066
Office phone: 708-669-4017
General E-mail: southtownservice@tribpub.com
Publisher Name: Par Ridder (GM)
Publisher Email: pridder@tribpub.com
Editor Name: Anne Halston
Editor Email: ahalston@tribpub.com
Editor Phone: 312-730-6472

WATSEKA

TIMES-REPUBLIC

Publication Street Address: 1492 E Walnut St
City: Watseka
State: IL
Publication Website: www.watsekatimesrepublic.com
Postal Code: 60970-1806
Office phone: (815) 432-5227
General E-mail: watseka@intranix.com
Publisher Name: Greg Perrotto
Publisher Email: gperrotto@rensselaerrepublican.com
Editor Name: Carla Waters
Editor Email: cwaters@intranix.com
Advertising Executive Name: Roberta Kempen
Advertising Executive Email: watsekasales@intranix.com

WEST FRANKFORT

THE DAILY AMERICAN

Corporate/Parent Company: Gannett
Publication Street Address: 111 S Emma St
City: West Frankfort
State: IL
Publication Website: https://www.dailyamerican.com/
Postal Code: 62896-2729
Office phone: (618) 932-2146
General E-mail: news@dailyamerican.com
Editor Name: Brian Whipkey
Editor Email: bwhipkey@dailyamerican.com

INDIANA

ANDERSON

THE HERALD BULLETIN

Corporate/Parent Company: CNHI, LLC
Publication Street Address: 1133 Jackson St
City: Anderson
State: IN
Publication Website: www.theheraldbulletin.com
Postal Code: 46016-1433
Office phone: (765) 622-1212
General E-mail: newsroom@heraldbulletin.com
Publisher Name: Beverly Joyce
Publisher Email: beverly.joyce@heraldbulletin.com
Publisher Phone: (765) 640-2307
Editor Name: Scott Underwood
Editor Email: scott.underwood@heraldbulletin.com
Editor Phone: (765) 640-4845
Advertising Executive Name: Leslie Sadler
Advertising Executive Email: Leslie.sadler@heraldbulletin.com
Advertising Executive Phone: (765)648-4274
Year Established: 1868
Delivery Methods: Mail`Newsstand`Carrier`Racks
Own Printing Facility?: Y
Commercial printers?: Y
Mechanical specifications: Type page 13 x 21 1/2; E - 6 cols, 2 1/16, 1/8 between; A - 6 cols, 2 1/16, 1/8 between; C - 9 cols, 1 3/8, 1/16 between.
Published Days: Mon`Tues`Wed`Thur`Fri`Sat`Sun
Weekday Frequency: m
Saturday Frequency: m
Avg Paid Circ: 18691
Audit Company: Sworn/Estimate/Non-Audited
Audit Date: 7 12 2019
Pressroom Equipment: Lines - 8-G/Urbanite single width; Reels & Stands - 6-G/Stands.;
Mailroom Equipment: Counter Stackers - 1/HL, 1-/HI; Inserters & Stuffers - 1-MM/SLS 2000; Tying Machines - 1-/MLN, 1-/Bu; Address Machine - KR, FMC;
Buisness Equipment: 2-HP/9000
Buisness Software: Oracle: Financials, PBS: Circ, Adv
Classified Equipment: Hardware - 2-DEC/433 ST; 10-DEC/333C; Printers - 1-C.Itoh;
Classified Software: CText.
Editorial Equipment: Hardware - CText, 2-DEC/433 ST/23-DEC/333C, 2-DEC/420SX, 1-DEC/466LP2, 5-Compaq/DeskPro 133; Printers - V/400-5300E, 1-Pre Press/Panther Pro 46
Editorial Software: CText.
Production Equipment: Hardware - Nu/Ultra Violet burner, 1-V/Pan; Cameras - 2-SCREEN/6500C; Scanners - 1-Sharp/1200R, 1-Lf/AP Leaf 35mm, ECR/Autokon, 3-AG/Arcus
Production Software: QPS 3.312.
Total Circulation: 18691

ANGOLA

THE HERALD REPUBLICAN

Corporate/Parent Company: KPC Media Group, Inc.
Publication Street Address: 45 S Public Sq
City: Angola
State: IN
Publication Website: www.kpcnews.com
Postal Code: 46703-1926
Office phone: (260) 665-3117
General E-mail: news@kpcmedia.com
Publisher Name: Terry Housholder
Publisher Email: thousholder@kpcmedia.com
Publisher Phone: 260-347-0400 Ext. 1176
Editor Name: Mike Marturello
Editor Email: mmarturello@kpcmedia.com
Editor Phone: 260-665-3117 Ext. 2140
Advertising Executive Name: David Rigas
Advertising Executive Email: drigas@kpcmedia.com
Advertising Executive Phone: 260-347-0400 Ext. 1002
Year Established: 1857
Delivery Methods: Mail`Newsstand`Carrier`Racks
Own Printing Facility?: Y
Commercial printers?: Y
Mechanical specifications: Type page 13 x 21 1/2; E - 6 cols, 2, 1/6 between; A - 6 cols, 2 1/16, 1/6 between; C - 9 cols, 1 3/8, 1/6 between.
Published Days: Mon`Tues`Wed`Thur`Fri`Sat`Sun
Weekday Frequency: m
Saturday Frequency: m
Avg Paid Circ: 4070
Audit Company: AAM
Audit Date: 31 12 2014
Pressroom Equipment: Lines - 6-G/Community.;
Editorial Software: ACT.
Note: All production of the Herald-Republican is done at the central plant in Kendallville.
Total Circulation: 4070

AUBURN

THE STAR

Corporate/Parent Company: Gannett
Publication Street Address: 102 N Main St
City: Auburn
State: IN
Publication Website: www.kpcnews.com
Postal Code: 46706-1857
Office phone: (260) 347-0400
General E-mail: news@kpcmedia.com
Publisher Name: Terry Housholder
Publisher Email: thousholder@kpcmedia.com
Publisher Phone: 260-347-0400 Ext. 1176
Editor Name: Dave Kurtz
Editor Email: dkurtz@kpcmedia.com
Editor Phone: 260-925-2611 Ext. 2546
Advertising Executive Name: David Rigas
Advertising Executive Email: drigas@kpcmedia.com
Advertising Executive Phone: 260-347-0400 Ext. 1002
Year Established: 1871
Delivery Methods: Mail`Newsstand`Carrier`Racks
Own Printing Facility?: Y
Commercial printers?: Y
Mechanical specifications: Type page 11 1/2 x 21 1/2; E - 6 cols, 1 13/16, 1/8 between; A - 6 cols, 1 13/16, 1/8 between; C - 9 cols, 1 1/6, 1/8 between.
Published Days: Tues`Wed`Thur`Fri`Sun
Weekday Frequency: m
Saturday Frequency: m
Avg Paid Circ: 3674
Avg Free Circ: 344
Audit Company: AAM
Audit Date: 31 12 2018
Pressroom Equipment: Lines - 1-G/Floor SSC Units 1988, 1-Stalk/Pathfinder 1988; 2-G/4-High 1999; Folders - 2-G/SSC; Pasters -2-KTI/SplicerControl System - 1-Ebway/Industries Pneumatic Master Control.;
Mailroom Equipment: Counter Stackers - 1/The Stacker Machine Co/S-N 316-19, 1-BG/Count-O-Veyor; Inserters & Stuffers - 1-KAN/5 pocket, KAN/Twin Stacker, MM/Saddlebinder 4 pocket, 1-Challenge/Single Knife; Tying Machines - 1-Akebono/Strapper, IT;
Buisness Equipment: 1-Compaq/Proliant 5000
Buisness Software: Baseview/Ad Manager Pro 2.02, Dynamic Great Plains, Baseview/Circulation Pro 1.8.0
Classified Equipment: Hardware - 3-APP/Mac; Printers - 2-APP/Mac LaserWriter;
Classified Software: Baseview, QPS/QuarkXPress.
Editorial Equipment: Hardware - 12-APP/Mac/6-RSK/TRS 80 Model 100; Printers - 2-APP/Mac LaserWriter
Editorial Software: Baseview, QPS/QuarkXPress.
Production Equipment: Hardware - 2-AG/Imagesetter 1200, Luntz & Jensen, 1-Tek Color/4C Printer; Cameras - 1-B, 1-Kk/Image Maker IM600; Scanners - APP/Mac, 1-AG/Arcus, 2-AG/Arcus Plus, 1-Kk/RFS 2035
Production Software: QPS/QuarkXPress 4.0.
Note: All production of the The Star is done at the central plant in Kendallville.
Total Circulation: 4018

BLUFFTON

NEWS-BANNER

Corporate/Parent Company: News-Banner Publications, Inc.
Publication Street Address: 125 N Johnson St
City: Bluffton
State: IN
Publication Website: www.news-banner.com
Postal Code: 46714-1907
Office phone: (260) 824-0224
General E-mail: email@news-banner.com
Publisher Name: Doug Brown
Publisher Email: dougb@news-banner.com
Editor Name: David R. Schultz
Editor Email: daves@news-banner.com
Advertising Executive Name: Jean Bordner
Advertising Executive Email: jeanb@news-banner.com
Year Established: 1892
Delivery Methods: Mail`Newsstand`Carrier`Racks
Own Printing Facility?: Y
Commercial printers?: Y
Mechanical specifications: Type page 10 1/2 x 21 1/2; E - 6 cols, 1 5/8, 3/20 between; A - 6 cols, 1 5/8, 3/20 between; C - 6 cols, 1 5/8, 3/20 between.
Published Days: Mon`Tues`Wed`Thur`Fri`Sat
Weekday Frequency: e
Saturday Frequency: m
Avg Paid Circ: 3862
Audit Company: Sworn/Estimate/Non-Audited
Audit Date: 7 12 2019
Pressroom Equipment: Lines - 5-G/Community 1975.;
Mailroom Equipment: Tying Machines - 2/Bs.;
Buisness Software: Vision Data
Classified Equipment: Hardware - APP/Mac, APP/iMac;
Classified Software: Baseview/ClassAct/FP 3.
Editorial Equipment: Hardware - APP/Mac G3, APP/Power Mac, 2-APP/Mac G4; Printers - APP/Mac 8500
Editorial Software: QPS/QuarkXPress 3.32, Baseview, Adobe/Photoshop 5.0.
Production Equipment: Hardware - 1-Nu; Cameras - 1-Nu
Production Software: QPS/QuarkXPress 3.32.
Total Circulation: 3862

BRAZIL

THE BRAZIL TIMES

Corporate/Parent Company: Rust Communications
Publication Street Address: 531 E National Ave
City: Brazil
State: IN
Publication Website: www.thebraziltimes.com
Postal Code: 47834-2633
Office phone: (812) 446-2216
Publisher Name: Chris Pruett
Publisher Email: cpruett79@gmail.com
Editor Name: Frank Phillips
Editor Email: frankp.thebraziltimes@gmail.com
Advertising Executive Name: Christina Meyer
Advertising Executive Email: advertising.braziltimes@gmail.com
Year Established: 1888
Delivery Methods: Mail`Newsstand`Racks
Own Printing Facility?: Y
Commercial printers?: Y
Mechanical specifications: Type page 11 5/8 x 21 1/2; E - 6 cols, 1 13/16, 1/8 between; A - 6 cols, 1 13/16, 1/8 between; C - 9 cols, 1 3/16, 1/16 between.
Published Days: Mon`Wed`Fri`Sat
Weekday Frequency: m
Saturday Frequency: m
Avg Paid Circ: 4133
Audit Company: Sworn/Estimate/Non-Audited
Audit Date: 7 12 2019
Pressroom Equipment: Lines - 6-G/Community

CHESTERTON

CHESTERTON TRIBUNE

Corporate/Parent Company: Chesterton Tribune, Inc.
Publication Street Address: 193 S Calumet Rd
City: Chesterton
State: IN
Publication Website: www.chestertontribune.com
Postal Code: 46304-2433
Office phone: (219) 926-1131
General E-mail: news@chestertontribune.com
Publisher Name: Elizabeth Canright
Editor Name: David Canright
Year Established: 1884
Delivery Methods: Mail`Carrier`Racks
Own Printing Facility?: Y
Commercial printers?: Y
Mechanical specifications: Type page 13 x 21; E - 6 cols, 2 1/16, 1/8 between; A - 6 cols, 2 1/16, 1/8 between; C - 6 cols, 2 1/16, 1/8 between.
Published Days: Mon`Tues`Wed`Thur`Fri
Weekday Frequency: e
Avg Paid Circ: 3900
Avg Free Circ: 300
Audit Company: Sworn/Estimate/Non-Audited
Audit Date: 7 12 2019
Pressroom Equipment: Lines – 3-G/Community
Classified Equipment: Hardware – APP/Mac Quadra; Printers – HP/LaserJet 4050N;
Classified Software: Mediaspan/Classified.
Editorial Equipment: Hardware – Baseview/NewsEdit Pro; Printers – HP/LaserJet 5000N, HP/LaserJet 4050N
Editorial Software: Baseview.
Production Equipment: Hardware – HP/LaserJet 5000N; Cameras – R.
Total Circulation: 4200

COLUMBIA CITY

THE POST & MAIL

Corporate/Parent Company: Horizon Publications
Publication Street Address: 927 W Connexion Way
City: Columbia City
State: IN
Publication Website: www.thepostandmail.com
Postal Code: 46725-1031
Office phone: (260) 244-5153
General E-mail: editor@thepostandmail.com
Editor Name: Rachael Rosfeld
Editor Email: editor@thepostandmail.com
Advertising Executive Name: Jill Smith
Advertising Executive Email: jsmith@thepostandmail.com
Year Established: 2007
Delivery Methods: Mail`Newsstand`Carrier`Racks
Mechanical specifications: Type page 13 x 21 1/2; E - 6 cols, 1 3/4, 1/8 between; A - 6 cols, 1 3/4, 1/8 between; C - 9 cols, 1 1/8, 1/8 between.
Published Days: Mon`Tues`Wed`Thur`Fri`Sat
Weekday Frequency: e
Saturday Frequency: m
Avg Paid Circ: 4058
Audit Company: Sworn/Estimate/Non-Audited
Audit Date: 7 12 2019
Mailroom Equipment: Tying Machines – 2/Bu.;
Classified Equipment: Hardware – 1-Mk.;
Editorial Equipment: Hardware – Mk, APP/Mac/5-Mk; Printers – APP/Mac.
Production Equipment: Hardware – 1-Ic; Cameras – 1-SCREEN; Scanners – Microtek.

Total Circulation: 4058

COLUMBUS

THE REPUBLIC

Corporate/Parent Company: AIM Media
Publication Street Address: 2980 N. National Road, Suite A
City: Columbus
State: IN
Publication Website: www.therepublic.com
Postal Code: 47201
Office phone: (812) 372-7811
General E-mail: editorial@therepublic.com
Editor Name: Julie McClure
Editor Email: jmcclure@therepublic.com
Editor Phone: (812) 379-5631
Year Established: 1872
Delivery Methods: Mail`Newsstand`Carrier
Mechanical specifications: Type page 13 x 21 1/2; E - 6 cols, 2 1/16, 1/8 between; A - 6 cols, 2 1/16, 1/8 between; C - 9 cols, 1 3/8, 1/16 between.
Published Days: Mon`Tues`Wed`Thur`Fri`Sat`Sun
Weekday Frequency: m
Saturday Frequency: m
Avg Paid Circ: 14067
Avg Free Circ: 246
Audit Company: CAC
Audit Date: 31 03 2016
Pressroom Equipment: Lines – 12-DGM/850 single width 1998; Press Drive – 3-Fin/150 HP Drive 1998; Folders – 1, 1-1998; Reels & Stands – 2-G/Stands 1998; Control System – Smith/Spray Bars, 1998.;
Mailroom Equipment: Counter Stackers – 2-HI/Olympian, HI/Rima; Inserters & Stuffers – 1-S/1472; Tying Machines – 2-Sterling/MR45, 1-OVL/410.;
Buisness Equipment: MS/NT Server 4.0, ALR/Evolution, HP/LC2000 Exchange
Buisness Software: PBS/MediaPlus
Classified Equipment: Hardware – 9-HP/PC, 9-Gateway/Celeron 350; Printers – HP/4M Plus;
Classified Software: PPI, ACT, Classified.
Editorial Equipment: Hardware – 8-Gateway/P200, 22-IBM/486-33, 2-Novell/SFt3-ALR, 10-Gateway/PIII 500, 22-Gateway/Celerah 350, 2-HP/LC2000 NT/SQL/APP/Power Mac 7100, APP/Mac 8100-100, APP/Power Mac, 5-APP/Mac G3; Printers – 1-Panasonic/KX P1595, 1-APP/Mac LaserWr
Production Equipment: Hardware – TI/OmniPage 5.0, APP/Mac, Pre Press/Panther Pro 62, Pre Press/Panther RIP, Pre Press/Panther Imposer; Cameras – 1-C/Spartan II; Scanners – 1-ECR/1030, 3-Umax, 1-Lf/AP Leafscan 45, 3-Kk/2035
Production Software: ACT/V2, ACT/V04, ACT/V003.
Total Circulation: 14313

CONNERSVILLE

CONNERSVILLE NEWS-EXAMINER

Corporate/Parent Company: Paxton Media Group, LLC
Publication Street Address: 406 N Central Ave
City: Connersville
State: IN
Publication Website: www.newsexaminer.com
Postal Code: 47331-1926
Office phone: (765) 825-0581
General E-mail: web-support@newsexaminer.com
Editor Name: Bob Hansen
Editor Email: bhansen@newsexaminer.com
Editor Phone: 765-825-0588 x235
Advertising Executive Name: Anna Pugsley
Advertising Executive Email: apugsley@newsexaminer.com
Advertising Executive Phone: 765-825-0581 x245
Year Established: 1887
Delivery Methods: Newsstand`Carrier`Racks
Own Printing Facility?: N
Commercial printers?: N
Mechanical specifications: Type page 13 x 21; E - 6 cols, 2 1/16, 1/8 between; A - 6 cols, 2 1/16, 1/8 between; C - 9 cols, 1 5/16, 1/8 between.
Published Days: Tues`Wed`Thur`Fri`Sun
Weekday Frequency: m
Saturday Frequency: m
Avg Paid Circ: 4390
Audit Company: Sworn/Estimate/Non-Audited
Audit Date: 7 12 2019
Pressroom Equipment: Lines – none;
Total Circulation: 4390

CRAWFORDSVILLE

JOURNAL REVIEW

Corporate/Parent Company: PTS, Inc.
Publication Street Address: 119 N Green St
City: Crawfordsville
State: IN
Publication Website: www.journalreview.com
Postal Code: 47933-1708
Office phone: (765) 362-1200
Publisher Name: Shawn Storie
Publisher Email: shawn.storie@jrpress.com
Publisher Phone: 765-362-1200 Ext. 165
Editor Name: Tina McGrady
Editor Email: tmcgrady@jrpress.com
Editor Phone: 765-362-1200 Ext. 167
Advertising Executive Name: Heidi Stewart
Advertising Executive Email: hstewart@jrpress.com
Advertising Executive Phone: 765-362-1200 Ext. 173
Year Established: 1841
Delivery Methods: Mail`Newsstand`Carrier`Racks
Own Printing Facility?: N
Commercial printers?: Y
Mechanical specifications: Type page 13 x 21 1/2; E - 6 cols, 2 1/16, 1/8 between; A - 6 cols, 2 1/16, 1/8 between; C - 9 cols, 1 11/32, 1/8 between.
Published Days: Mon`Tues`Wed`Thur`Fri`Sat
Weekday Frequency: m
Saturday Frequency: m
Avg Paid Circ: 4995
Avg Free Circ: 161
Audit Company: CAC
Audit Date: 30 09 2017
Pressroom Equipment: Lines – 9-HI/V-15D 1981; Press Drive – HI/Cutler Hammer; Reels & Stands – 7;
Mailroom Equipment: Tying Machines – MLN, Bu.;
Buisness Equipment: 4-HP
Buisness Software: Great Plains, AR Works
Classified Equipment: Hardware – APP/Mac; Printers – Epson;
Classified Software: Baseview/Class Manager Plus.
Editorial Equipment: Hardware – APP/Mac; Printers – GCC/SelectPress 600, Epson
Editorial Software: Baseview 3.0.
Production Equipment: Hardware – APP/Mac, GCC/Select Press 600, QMS/860 Print System; Cameras – 1-B; Scanners – Umax/Powerlook II, Nikon/Film
Production Software: QPS/QuarkXPress 3.32.
Total Circulation: 5156

THE PAPER OF MONTGOMERY COUNTY

Corporate/Parent Company: Sagamore News Media
Publication Street Address: 201 E Jefferson St
City: Crawfordsville
State: IN
Publication Website: www.thepaper24-7.com
Postal Code: 47933-2804
Office phone: (765) 361-0100
Publisher Name: Tim Timmons
Publisher Email: ttimmons@thepaper24-7.com
Publisher Phone: ext. 22
Year Established: 2004
Delivery Methods: Mail`Newsstand`Racks
Own Printing Facility?: N
Commercial printers?: N
Published Days: Mon`Tues`Wed`Thur`Fri`Sat
Weekday Frequency: m
Saturday Frequency: m
Avg Paid Circ: 4000
Audit Company: Sworn/Estimate/Non-Audited
Audit Date: 7 12 2019
Total Circulation: 4000

CROWN POINT

POST-TRIBUNE

Publication Street Address: 2100 N Main St Ste 212
City: Crown Point
State: IN
Publication Website: www.chicagotribune.com/suburbs/post-tribune
Postal Code: 46307-1877
Office phone: (219) 663-4212
General E-mail: consumerservices@chicagotribune.com
Publisher Name: R. Bruce Dold
Publisher Email: editor@chicagotribune.com
Editor Name: Peter Kendall
Editor Email: pkendall@chicagotribune.com
Year Established: 1908
Delivery Methods: Newsstand`Carrier
Own Printing Facility?: Y
Commercial printers?: Y
Mechanical specifications: Tab format 44" web Full page 6 x 10 (10" x 9.875")
Published Days: Mon`Tues`Wed`Thur`Fri`Sat`Sun
Weekday Frequency: m
Saturday Frequency: m
Avg Paid Circ: 16000
Audit Company: AAM
Audit Date: 16 10 2013
Editorial Equipment: Hardware – APP/iMac workstations
Editorial Software: QPS.
Production Equipment: Hardware – Caere Omni Page Pro 8.0, 1-MON/Laserpress, 1-MON/News Express; Cameras – 1-C/Spartan III, 2-C/Marathon; Scanners – 1-ECR/Autokon, 2-Lf/Leafscan 35, Scanview/Scanmate 4000
Production Software: MEI/ALS 1.7.
Note: Chicago Tribune Freedom Center
Total Circulation: 16000

DECATUR

DECATUR DAILY DEMOCRAT

Corporate/Parent Company: Horizon Publications
Publication Street Address: 141 S 2nd St
City: Decatur
State: IN
Publication Website: www.decaturdailydemocrat.com
Postal Code: 46733-1664
Office phone: (260) 724-2121
Editor Name: Jannaya Andrews
Editor Email: jandrews@decaturdailydemocrat.com
Advertising Executive Name: Debbie Eichelberger
Advertising Executive Email: sales2@decaturdailydemocrat.com
Year Established: 1857
Delivery Methods: Newsstand`Carrier`Racks
Own Printing Facility?: Y
Commercial printers?: N
Mechanical specifications: Type page 10.5 x 21 1/2; E - 6 cols, 2 1/8, 1/8 between; A - 6 cols, 2 1/8, 1/8 between; C - 6 cols, 2 1/8, 1/8 between.
Published Days: Mon`Tues`Wed`Thur`Fri`Sat
Weekday Frequency: e
Saturday Frequency: m
Avg Paid Circ: 4300
Audit Company: Sworn/Estimate/Non-Audited
Audit Date: 7 12 2019
Pressroom Equipment: Lines – 8-G/Community (2 stacks);
Mailroom Equipment: Tying Machines – 1-Bu/162X;
Classified Equipment: Hardware – APP/Mac Quadra 610;
Classified Software: Claris/FileMaker Pro.
Editorial Equipment: Hardware – 4-APP/Mac Quadra 605, APP/Mac Quadra 630, 2-APP/

U.S. Daily Newspapers

I-37

Mac Quadra 610, APP/Mac Quadra 650; Printers – APP/Mac LaserWriter 630 Pro, APP/Mac LaserWriter 16-1600 PS
Editorial Software: Baseview/NewsEdit.
Production Equipment: Hardware – 2-APP/Power Mac, 1-APP/Mac Pro 630; Cameras – 1-R/400; Scanners – 3-Microtek
Production Software: QPS/QuarkXPress 3.31.
Total Circulation: 4300

ELKHART

ELKHART TRUTH

Corporate/Parent Company: Paxton Media Group, LLC
Publication Street Address: 421 S 2nd St
City: Elkhart
State: IN
Publication Website: www.elkharttruth.com
Postal Code: 46516-3230
Office phone: (574) 294-1661
General E-mail: newsroom@elkharttruth.com
Publisher Name: David Damerow
Publisher Email: ddamerow@elkharttruth.com
Publisher Phone: 574-296-5963
Editor Name: Jon Gard
Editor Email: jgard@elkharttruth.com
Editor Phone: 574-296-5939
Year Established: 1889
Delivery Methods: Mail`Newsstand`Carrier`Racks
Own Printing Facility?: N
Commercial printers?: N
Mechanical specifications: Type page 10 x 21 1/2; E – 5 cols, 1.9, 1/8 between; A – 5 cols, 1.9, 1/8 between; C – 6 cols, 1.5625, 1/8 between.
Published Days: Mon`Tues`Wed`Thur`Fri`Sat`Sun
Weekday Frequency: m
Saturday Frequency: m
Avg Paid Circ: 15250
Audit Company: Sworn/Estimate/Non-Audited
Audit Date: 7 12 2019
Buisness Equipment: Dell
Buisness Software: G/Dynamics
Classified Equipment: Hardware – APP/Mac; Printers – APP/Mac LaserWriter;
Classified Software: DTI/Class Manager Pro, QPS/QuarkXPress.
Editorial Equipment: Hardware – APP/Mac; Printers – HP/Laserjet 8100 N, NewGen
Editorial Software: Saxotech/InDesign
Total Circulation: 15250

ELWOOD

THE ELWOOD CALL-LEADER

Corporate/Parent Company: Elwood Publishing Co., Inc.
Publication Street Address: 317 S Anderson St
City: Elwood
State: IN
Publication Website: www.elwoodpublishing.com
Postal Code: 46036-2018
Office phone: (765) 552-3355
General E-mail: elpub@elwoodpublishing.com
Publisher Name: Robert Nash
Editor Name: Sandy Burton
Year Established: 1891
Delivery Methods: Mail`Newsstand`Carrier`Racks
Mechanical specifications: Type page 13 x 21 1/2; E – 6 cols, 2 1/16, 1/8 between; A – 6 cols, 2 1/16, 1/8 between; C – 8 cols, 1 1/2, 3/20 between.
Published Days: Mon`Tues`Wed`Thur`Fri`Sat
Weekday Frequency: e
Saturday Frequency: m
Avg Paid Circ: 2100
Audit Company: Sworn/Estimate/Non-Audited
Audit Date: 7 12 2019
Pressroom Equipment: Lines – 4-G/Community;
Mailroom Equipment: Tying Machines – 2/Malow; Address Machine – 2-/Am.;
Buisness Equipment: 1-BS/B-20, 1-RSK/TRS 80 model 4
Classified Equipment: Hardware – Mk/1100
Classified Software: Mk/Mycro-Comp.
Editorial Equipment: Hardware – Mk/1100
Editorial Software: Mk/Mycro-Comp.
Production Equipment: Hardware – 2-APP/Mac LaserWriter II NT/NTX; Cameras – 1-R/Commodore.
Total Circulation: 2100

EVANSVILLE

EVANSVILLE COURIER & PRESS

Corporate/Parent Company: Gannett Company Inc.
Publication Street Address: 300 E Walnut St
City: Evansville
State: IN
Publication Website: www.courierpress.com
Postal Code: 47713-1938
Office phone: 844-900-7104
Editor Name: Michael McCarter
Editor Email: mmccarter@gannett.com
Year Established: 1846
Delivery Methods: Mail`Newsstand`Carrier`Racks
Own Printing Facility?: Y
Commercial printers?: Y
Mechanical specifications: Type page 12 x 21 1/8; E – 6 cols, 2 1/16, 1/6 between; A – 6 cols, 2 1/16, 1/6 between; C – 10 cols, 1 1/4, 1/6 between.
Published Days: Mon`Tues`Wed`Thur`Fri`Sat`Sun
Weekday Frequency: m
Saturday Frequency: m
Avg Paid Circ: 32958
Audit Company: AAM
Audit Date: 24 05 2018
Pressroom Equipment: Lines – MOT/Flexo double width 1989, 12; Folders – 2-MOT/2:1, 1-MOT/3:2; Pasters –MOT/AutoReels & Stands – 12;
Mailroom Equipment: Counter Stackers – 2-HL/Monitor HT, 2-HL/Monitor HT II, 4/RIMA, QWI, 1-/QUIPP, TMSI; Inserters & Stuffers – 2-Heidelberg/2299, NP-2299; Tying Machines – Power Strap, Power Strap/PSN6E, 4-/Power Strap/PSN6, 1-/Power Strap/PSN6E, 3-/Pow;
Buisness Equipment: Wyse Thin Clients, Dell laptops
Buisness Software: Word, Excel, Access, Outlook, Mediaware, Brainworks
Classified Equipment: Hardware – Wyse Thin Clients, Dell laptops; Printers – HP/LaserJets, Ricoh MFP;
Classified Software: Brainworks
Editorial Equipment: Hardware – Wyse Thin Clients, Dell laptops; Printers – LaserJets
Editorial Software: Mediaware
Production Equipment: Hardware – Scitex/Dolev 800, Scitex/Dolev 450, Scitex/Dolev 4 Press, III/Laser; Cameras – Pager, Nu Arc SSTE-2024-C; Scanners – Scitex/Smart, Scitex/Smart 2, AG/Arcus II, 5-Kodak/RFS 2035, HP/ScanJet 40, AG Duoscan T1200
Production Software: QPS 1.12, AT/Class P
Total Circulation: 43400

FORT WAYNE

THE JOURNAL GAZETTE

Corporate/Parent Company: Fort Wayne Newspapers
Publication Street Address: 600 W MAIN ST
City: FORT WAYNE
State: IN
Publication Website: www.journalgazette.net
Postal Code: 46802-1498
Office phone: (260) 461-8773
General E-mail: jgnews@jg.net
Publisher Name: Julie Inskeep
Publisher Email: jinskeep@jg.net
Publisher Phone: 260-461-8490
Editor Name: Sherry Skufca
Editor Email: sskufca@jg.net
Editor Phone: 260-461-8201
Year Established: 1863
Delivery Methods: Mail`Newsstand`Carrier`Racks
Own Printing Facility?: Y
Commercial printers?: Y
Mechanical specifications: Type page 13 x 22; E – 6 cols, between; A – 6 cols, between; C – 10 cols, between.
Published Days: Mon`Tues`Wed`Thur`Fri`Sat`Sun
Weekday Frequency: m
Saturday Frequency: m
Avg Paid Circ: 34496
Avg Free Circ: 1608
Audit Company: AAM
Audit Date: 27 07 2020
Pressroom Equipment: TKS
Mailroom Equipment: see FWN
Buisness Equipment: HP/3000-967
Buisness Software: WordPerfect, Quattro
Classified Equipment: Hardware – Dell;
Classified Software: III/Tecs 2.
Editorial Equipment: Hardware – IBM/APP/Mac; Printers – HP/LaserJet
Editorial Software: Newscycle
Production Equipment: see FWN
Note: For detailed production and mechanical information, see Fort Wayne Newspapers Inc. listing.
Total Circulation: 52530

THE NEWS-SENTINEL

Corporate/Parent Company: Ogden Newspapers Inc.
Publication Street Address: 600 W Main St
City: Fort Wayne
State: IN
Publication Website: www.news-sentinel.com
Postal Code: 46802-1408
Office phone: (260) 461-8449
General E-mail: obits@fortwayne.com
Publisher Name: Scott Stanford
Publisher Email: sstanford@fwn.fortwayne.com
Publisher Phone: 260-461-8324
Advertising Executive Name: Lori Fritz
Advertising Executive Email: lfritz@fortwayne.com
Advertising Executive Phone: 260-461-8790
Year Established: 1833
Delivery Methods: Newsstand`Carrier`Racks
Own Printing Facility?: Y
Commercial printers?: Y
Mechanical specifications: Type page 13 x 22; E – 6 cols, 2 1/16, 1/8 between; A – 6 cols, 2 1/16, 1/8 between; C – 10 cols, 1 1/4, 1/16 between.
Published Days: Mon`Tues`Wed`Thur`Fri`Sat`Sun
Weekday Frequency: e
Saturday Frequency: e
Avg Paid Circ: 57281
Audit Company: AAM
Audit Date: 31 12 2015
Classified Equipment: Hardware – Dell; Printers – Epson, HP/LaserJet;
Classified Software: III/Tecs 2.
Editorial Equipment: Hardware – Dell; Printers – Epson, HP/LaserJet
Editorial Software: III/Tecs 2.
Note: For detailed production and mechanical information, see Fort Wayne Newspapers Inc. listing.
Total Circulation: 57281

FRANKFORT

THE TIMES - HAMILTON COUNTY

Publication Street Address: 211 N Jackson St
City: Frankfort
State: IN
Publication Website: www.ftimes.com
Postal Code: 46041-1936
Office phone: (765) 659-4622
General E-mail: web-support@ftimes.com
Publisher Name: Linda Kelsay
Publisher Email: lkelsay@ftimes.com
Publisher Phone: 765-659-4622 Ext. 111
Editor Name: Aaron Kennedy
Editor Email: akennedy@ftimes.com
Editor Phone: 765-659-4622 Ext. 111
Advertising Executive Name: Christi Kincade
Advertising Executive Email: advertising@ftimes.com
Advertising Executive Phone: 765-659-4622 Ext. 108

Year Established: 1877
Delivery Methods: Mail`Newsstand`Carrier`Racks
Own Printing Facility?: Y
Commercial printers?: Y
Mechanical specifications: Type page 10 x 21 1/2; E – 6 cols, 4.587, 1/8 between; A – 6 cols, 1.587, 1/8 between
Published Days: Tues`Wed`Thur`Fri`Sun
Weekday Frequency: m
Saturday Frequency: m
Avg Paid Circ: 4694
Audit Company: Sworn/Estimate/Non-Audited
Audit Date: 7 12 2019
Pressroom Equipment: Lines – Print at Chronicle-Tribune, Marion, IN;
Mailroom Equipment: Counter Stackers – Insert at Chronicle-Tribune, Marion, IN;
Buisness Equipment: PC
Buisness Software: MediaSpan
Classified Equipment: Hardware – PC;
Classified Software: MediaSpan
Editorial Equipment: Hardware – PC
Editorial Software: Falcon; InDesign
Production Software: InDesign
Total Circulation: 4694

GOSHEN

THE GOSHEN NEWS

Corporate/Parent Company: CNHI, LLC
Publication Street Address: 114 S Main St
City: Goshen
State: IN
Publication Website: www.goshennews.com
Postal Code: 46526-3702
Office phone: (574) 533-2151
General E-mail: webmaster@goshennews.com
Publisher Name: Tricia Johnston
Publisher Email: tricia.johnston@goshennews.com
Publisher Phone: 574-533-2151 ext. 240301
Editor Name: Sheila Selman
Editor Email: sheila.selman@goshennews.com
Editor Phone: 574-533-2151 ext. 240311
Advertising Executive Name: Sharon Hite
Advertising Executive Email: sharon.hite@goshennews.com
Advertising Executive Phone: 574-533-2151 ext. 240342
Year Established: 1837
Delivery Methods: Mail`Newsstand`Racks
Own Printing Facility?: N
Commercial printers?: N
Mechanical specifications: six column format - 10.125" x 19.75"
Published Days: Mon`Tues`Wed`Thur`Fri`Sat
Weekday Frequency: m
Saturday Frequency: m
Avg Paid Circ: 8800
Avg Free Circ: 1200
Audit Company: Sworn/Estimate/Non-Audited
Audit Date: 7 12 2019
Buisness Equipment: DEC, PC
Buisness Software: Vision Data
Editorial Equipment: Hardware – PC
Editorial Software: InCopy, InDesign
Total Circulation: 10000

GREENCASTLE

BANNER-GRAPHIC

Corporate/Parent Company: Rust Communications
Publication Street Address: 100 N Jackson St
City: Greencastle
State: IN
Publication Website: www.bannergraphic.com
Postal Code: 46135-1240
Office phone: (765) 653-5151
General E-mail: ddick@bannergraphic.com
Publisher Name: Chris Pruett
Publisher Email: cpruett79@gmail.com
Editor Name: Daryl Taylor
Editor Email: dtaylor@bannergraphic.com
Advertising Executive Name: Jeanne Burris
Advertising Executive Email: jeanne.burris.braziltimes@gmail.com
Year Established: 1843

Delivery Methods: Mail`Newsstand`Racks
Own Printing Facility?: Y
Commercial printers?: Y
Mechanical specifications: Type page 13 x 21; E - 6 cols, 2 1/16, 1/8 between; A - 6 cols, 2 1/16, 1/8 between; C - 8 cols, 1 3/4, 1/8 between.
Published Days: Mon`Wed`Fri`Sat
Weekday Frequency: m
Saturday Frequency: m
Avg Paid Circ: 10500
Audit Company: Sworn/Estimate/Non-Audited
Audit Date: 7 12 2019
Pressroom Equipment: Lines – 5-G/Community 1977; Folders – 1-G/2:1.;
Mailroom Equipment: Tying Machines – 2/BN; Address Machine – 1-/Wm.;
Classified Software: Baseview.
Editorial Software: Baseview.
Production Equipment: Hardware – Nu/Flip Top; Cameras – LE, R/500.
Total Circulation: 10500

GREENFIELD

DAILY REPORTER

Corporate/Parent Company: Gannett
Publication Street Address: 22 W New Rd
City: Greenfield
State: IN
Publication Website: www.greenfieldreporter.com
Postal Code: 46140-1090
Office phone: (317) 462-5528
General E-mail: dr-editorial@greenfieldreporter.com
Publisher Name: Bud Hunt
Publisher Email: bhunt@greenfieldreporter.com
Editor Name: David Hill
Editor Email: dhill@greenfieldreporter.com
Editor Phone: 317-477-3232
Advertising Executive Name: John Senger
Advertising Executive Email: jsenger@greenfieldreporter.com
Advertising Executive Phone: 317-477-3208
Year Established: 1908
Delivery Methods: Mail`Carrier`Racks
Own Printing Facility?: Y
Commercial printers?: Y
Mechanical specifications: Type page 11 1/2 x 21 1/2; E - 6 cols, 1 3/4, 1/8 between; A - 6 cols, 1 3/4, 1/8 between; C - 9 cols, 1 3/16, 1/16 between.
Published Days: Tues`Wed`Thur`Fri`Sat
Weekday Frequency: m
Saturday Frequency: m
Avg Paid Circ: 8729
Audit Company: Sworn/Estimate/Non-Audited
Audit Date: 7 12 2019
Pressroom Equipment: Lines – 19-G/Community; 13-G/Community; Press Drive – 4-Fin/75 h.p., 2-Fin/125 hp; Folders – 3-G/Community SSC; Pasters –6-Enkel/Zero Speed Splicer 1990Control System – Fin/Control System 1994.;
Mailroom Equipment: Counter Stackers – Rima/25 105, GMA 2000; Inserters & Stuffers – GMA; Tying Machines – 1-MLN/Spirit, 2-Bu/BT-18, 1-Bu/BT-18.;
Buisness Equipment: PC
Buisness Software: APT
Classified Equipment: Hardware – PC;
Classified Software: APT
Editorial Equipment: Hardware – PC
Editorial Software: APT
Production Equipment: Hardware – Kreo
Production Software: APT
Total Circulation: 8729

GREENSBURG

GREENSBURG DAILY NEWS

Corporate/Parent Company: CNHI, LLC
Publication Street Address: 135 S Franklin St
City: Greensburg
State: IN
Publication Website: www.greensburgdailynews.com
Postal Code: 47240-2023

Office phone: (812) 663-3111
General E-mail: news@greensburgdailynews.com
Publisher Name: Laura Welborn
Publisher Email: laura.welborn@indianamediagroup.com
Publisher Phone: 812-663-3111 x217001
Editor Name: Kevin Green
Editor Email: melissa.conrad@greensburgdailynews.com
Editor Phone: 812-663-3111 x217056
Advertising Executive Name: Jeanie York
Advertising Executive Email: jeanie.york@greensburgdailynews.com
Advertising Executive Phone: 812-663-3111 x217018
Year Established: 1894
Delivery Methods: Newsstand`Carrier`Racks
Own Printing Facility?: N
Commercial printers?: N
Mechanical specifications: Full page 10.15" x 21" - 6 cols, 1 col 1.6"' 2 col 3.31"; 3 col, 5.0"; 4 col 6.71"; 5 col 8.43"; 6 col. 10.15".
Published Days: Tues`Wed`Thur`Fri`Sat
Weekday Frequency: All day
Saturday Frequency: All day
Avg Paid Circ: 4200
Audit Company: Sworn/Estimate/Non-Audited
Audit Date: 7 12 2019
Total Circulation: 4200

HARTFORD CITY

NEWS TIMES

Publication Street Address: 100 N Jefferson St
City: Hartford City
State: IN
Publication Website: www.hartfordcitynewstimes.com
Postal Code: 47348-2201
Office phone: (765) 348-0110
General E-mail: newstimes@comcast.net
Year Established: 1885
Delivery Methods: Mail`Carrier`Racks
Own Printing Facility?: Y
Commercial printers?: Y
Mechanical specifications: Type page 13 x 21 1/2; E - 6 cols, 2, 1/8 between; A - 6 cols, 2, 1/6 between; C - 8 cols, 2, 1/6 between.
Published Days: Mon`Wed`Thur`Fri`Sat
Weekday Frequency: m
Saturday Frequency: m
Avg Paid Circ: 1500
Audit Company: USPS
Audit Date: 30 09 2011
Mailroom Equipment: Tying Machines – Bu.;
Buisness Equipment: PC
Editorial Equipment: Hardware – Macs
Editorial Software: InDesign
Total Circulation: 1500

HUNTINGTON

HUNTINGTON HERALD-PRESS

Corporate/Parent Company: Paxton Media Group, LLC
Publication Street Address: 7 N Jefferson St
City: Huntington
State: IN
Publication Website: www.h-ponline.com
Postal Code: 46750-2839
Office phone: (260) 356-6700
General E-mail: web-support@h-ponline.com
Publisher Name: Linda Kelsay
Publisher Email: lkelsay@h-ponline.com
Publisher Phone: 260-356-6700 Ext. 171
Editor Name: Andrew Maciejewski
Editor Phone: 260-356-6700 Ext. 163
Advertising Executive Name: Christi Kincade
Advertising Executive Email: ckincade@h-ponline.com
Year Established: 1848
Delivery Methods: Carrier`Racks
Commercial printers?: Y
Mechanical specifications: Type page 13 x 21; E - 6 cols, 2 1/16, 1/8 between; A - 6 cols, 2 1/16, 1/8 between; C - 8 cols, 1 3/8, 1/16 between.
Published Days: Mon`Tues`Wed`Thur`Fri`Sat`Sun

Weekday Frequency: m
Saturday Frequency: m
Avg Paid Circ: 4576
Avg Free Circ: 3000
Audit Company: USPS
Audit Date: 10 12 2012
Pressroom Equipment: Lines – 2-G/Urbanite 1967, 1-G/Urbanite (3 color) 1967.;
Mailroom Equipment: Tying Machines – Dynaric.;
Buisness Equipment: Dell PC
Buisness Software: Dynamics (Great Plains)
Classified Equipment: Hardware – APP/Power Mac; Printers – APP/Mac LaserWriter NTX;
Classified Software: AMP
Editorial Equipment: Hardware – 3-APP/Power Mac; Printers – APP/Mac LaserWriter NT, 2-APP/Mac LaserWriter NTX
Editorial Software: Baseview/NewsEdit, QPS/QuarkXPress, Adobe/Photoshop, Aldus/FreeHand, Multi-Ad.
Production Equipment: Hardware – TI/OmniPage 2.0, Mk/MSF 300, Kk/35mm Scanner; Cameras – 1-B/Caravelle; Scanners – 3-HP, HP/ScanJet, 2-Microtek/Flatbed, HP/ScanJet 5P
Production Software: QPS/QuarkXPress 3.32.
Total Circulation: 7576

INDIANAPOLIS

THE INDIANAPOLIS STAR

Corporate/Parent Company: Gannett Co., Inc.
Publication Street Address: 130 S Meridian St
City: Indianapolis
State: IN
Publication Website: www.indystar.com
Postal Code: 46225-1046
Office phone: (317) 444-4000
Editor Name: Ronnie Ramos
Editor Email: ronnie.ramos@indystar.com
Year Established: 1903
Delivery Methods:
 Mail`Newsstand`Carrier`Racks
Own Printing Facility?: Y
Commercial printers?: Y
Mechanical specifications: Type page 10 x 20 1/2; E - 6 cols, 1 1/2, 5/32 between; A - 6 cols, 1 1/2, 5/32 between; C - 10 cols, 29/32, 1/16 between.
Published Days: Mon`Tues`Wed`Thur`Fri`Sat`Sun
Weekday Frequency: m
Saturday Frequency: m
Avg Paid Circ: 99786
Audit Company: AAM
Audit Date: 19 08 2020
Pressroom Equipment: Lines – 7-MAN/Geoman 75; 7-MAN/Geoman 75; 7-MAN/Geoman 75; 3-MAN/Geoman 75; Press Drive – MAN Roland; Folders – 1-MAN/Quarterfold, 7-MAN/2:5:5 Jaw; Reels & Stands – 24-MAN/CD13 RTP; Control System – MAN/PECOM;
Mailroom Equipment: Counter Stackers – 7-HPS/Dual carrier, 5-Prim/Hail Commmercial, 3/Gammerler, 14-/QWI 401, 2-/HT, 2-QWI/501C; Inserters & Stuffers – 2-HI/1472P, 1-Na/NP2299, 1-Na/NP 630; Tying Machines – 29-/Dynaric; Wrapping Singles – Addressing machine 2-/AVY, 4-QP/Vipers 97,;
Buisness Equipment: IBM/ES9000-170, IBM/AS-400
Buisness Software: ESA, DUS/VSE
Classified Equipment: Hardware – AT/Enterprise 205-seat, Compaq, 2-Sun/E4500; AT/Classified, AT/Pagination, IBM/RISC 6000; Printers – 8-HP/LaserJet;
Classified Software: AT/Enterprise 1.7xml, AT/Classified 1.7xml, AT/Retail 1.7xml, AT/Preprints 1.7xml.
Editorial Equipment: Hardware – AT, Compaq; Printers – 25-Epson, TI, NEC, HP/LaserPrinter, HP/DeskJet
Editorial Software: CCI 6.0.
Production Equipment: Hardware – 3-Creo/Trendsetter 200, 1-ICG/3601; Scanners – 2-Creo/IQSmart2
Production Software: CCI 6.0.
Total Circulation: 110031

JASPER

THE HERALD

Corporate/Parent Company: Paxton Media Group
Publication Street Address: 216 E 4th St
City: Jasper
State: IN
Publication Website: www.duboiscountyherald.com
Postal Code: 47546-3102
Office phone: (812) 482-2424
General E-mail: news@dcherald.com
Publisher Name: Justin Rumbach
Publisher Email: justin.rumbach@dcherald.com
Publisher Phone: x129
Editor Name: Lynn Adams
Editor Email: ladams@dcherald.com
Advertising Executive Name: Brenda Adams
Advertising Executive Email: badams@dcherald.com
Advertising Executive Phone: x128
Year Established: 1895
Delivery Methods:
 Mail`Newsstand`Carrier`Racks
Own Printing Facility?: Y
Commercial printers?: Y
Mechanical specifications: Type page 10 3/16 x 16; E - 5 cols, 1 7/8, 1/8 between; A - 5 cols, 1 7/8, 1/8 between; C - 6 cols, 1 1/2, 1/8 between.
Published Days: Mon`Tues`Wed`Thur`Fri`Sat
Weekday Frequency: e
Saturday Frequency: m
Avg Paid Circ: 8191
Avg Free Circ: 95
Audit Company: Sworn/Estimate/Non-Audited
Audit Date: 7 12 2019
Pressroom Equipment: Lines – 6-G/with hump single width 1974; 1-G/Color single width.;
Mailroom Equipment: Counter Stackers – 1/Gammerler STC70; Inserters & Stuffers – KAN/480, Kan/4-Bay/Multi-Feeder; Tying Machines – 3-Bu/60-71; Address Machine – 1-Am/57;
Buisness Equipment: Novell/Network
Buisness Software: MSSI
Classified Equipment: Hardware – 2-APP/Mac;
Classified Software: Baseview.
Editorial Equipment: Hardware – 19-APP/Mac; Printers – Xerox Phaser 5500, APP/Mac HP Laserjet
Editorial Software: QPS/QuarkXPress 6.5, Baseview/NewsEdit Pro IQUE, Adobe/Photoshop CS.
Production Equipment: Hardware – Kodak CTP; Cameras – DSA; Scanners – 1-AG/Arcus 2
Production Software: InDesign, MediaSpan.
Total Circulation: 8286

JEFFERSONVILLE

NEWS AND TRIBUNE

Corporate/Parent Company: AIM Media
Publication Street Address: 221 Spring Street
City: Jeffersonville
State: IN
Publication Website: www.newsandtribune.com
Postal Code: 47130
Office phone: (812) 283-6636
General E-mail: info@newsandtribune.com
Publisher Name: Bill Hanson
Publisher Email: bill.hanson@newsandtribune.com
Publisher Phone: (812) 206-2134
Editor Name: Susan Duncan
Editor Email: susan.duncan@newsandtribune.com
Editor Phone: (812) 206-2130
Advertising Executive Name: Jeff Smith
Advertising Executive Email: jeffrey.smith@cnhimidwest.com
Advertising Executive Phone: (812) 206-2133
Year Established: 1851
Mechanical specifications: Type page 13 x 21 1/2; E - 6 cols, 2 1/16, 1/8 between; A - 6 cols, 2 1/16, 1/8 between; C - 9 cols, 1 5/16, 1/8 between.
Published Days: Mon`Tues`Wed`Thur`Fri`Sat
Weekday Frequency: e
Avg Paid Circ: 13054

U.S. Daily Newspapers

Audit Company: Sworn/Estimate/Non-Audited
Audit Date: 7 12 2019
Pressroom Equipment: Lines – 8-G; Folders – 1-G/2:1.;
Mailroom Equipment: Tying Machines – 1/Bu; Address Machine – 1-/Am.;
Buisness Equipment: 2-Auto Tape/9100
Classified Equipment: Hardware – 1-COM/One.;
Editorial Equipment: Hardware – 1-COM/One.
Production Equipment: Hardware – 1-LE; Cameras – 1-LE.
Note: The New Albany Tribune (eS) has a combination rate of $23.62 with the Jeffersonville Evening News (e). Individual newspaper rates not made available.
Total Circulation: 13054

NEWS AND TRIBUNE

Corporate/Parent Company: CNHI, LLC
Publication Street Address: 221 Spring St
City: Jeffersonville
State: IN
Publication Website: www.newsandtribune.com
Postal Code: 47130-3353
Office phone: (812) 283-6636
General E-mail: info@newsandtribune.com
Publisher Name: Bill Hanson
Publisher Email: bill.hanson@newsandtribune.com
Publisher Phone: (812) 206-2134
Editor Name: Susan Duncan
Editor Email: susan.duncan@newsandtribune.com
Editor Phone: (812) 206-2130
Advertising Executive Name: Jeff Smith
Advertising Executive Email: jeffrey.smith@cnhimidwest.com
Advertising Executive Phone: (812) 206-2133
Year Established: 1851
Delivery Methods: Mail`Newsstand`Carrier`Racks
Mechanical specifications: Type page 13 x 21 1/2; E - 6 cols, 2, 1/12 between; A - 6 cols, 2, 1/8 between; C - 9 cols, 1 1/3, 1/12 between.
Published Days: Mon`Tues`Wed`Thur`Fri`Sat
Weekday Frequency: e
Saturday Frequency: m
Avg Paid Circ: 7152
Audit Company: Sworn/Estimate/Non-Audited
Audit Date: 7 12 2019
Pressroom Equipment: Lines – 19-G/Urbanite IF 6507; 20-G/Urbanite IF 6507; 21-G/Urbanite IF 6507; 22-G/Urbanite IF 6507; 23-G/Urbanite IF 6507; Folders – G/U-1280-1D29054; Reels & Stands – 1-G/2 Tier, 1-G/3 Tier; Control System – 2;
Mailroom Equipment: Counter Stackers – BG; Inserters & Stuffers – Mc/60-40; Tying Machines – 2/Bu; Address Machine – Wm.;
Buisness Equipment: DEC/VT320
Buisness Software: Vision Data
Classified Equipment: Hardware – APP/Mac Quadra 800; Printers – LaserMaster/Unity 1200XL, APP/Mac LaserWriter IIg;
Classified Software: QPS/QuarkXPress, Baseview/NewsEdit.
Editorial Equipment: Hardware – APP/Mac Quadra 800; Printers – LaserMaster/Unity 1200XL, APP/Mac LaserWriter IIg
Editorial Software: QPS/QuarkXPress, Baseview/NewsEdit.
Production Equipment: Hardware – TI/OmniPage 2.1, LaserMaster/Unity 1200 XLO; Cameras – SCREEN/C-690-C; Scanners – Umax/840
Production Software: QPS/QuarkXPress 3.3.
Note: The Jeffersonville Evening News (e) has a combination rate of $23.62 with the New Albany Tribune (eS). Individual newspaper rates not made available.
Total Circulation: 7152

KENDALLVILLE

THE NEWS SUN

Corporate/Parent Company: KPC Media Group Inc.
Publication Street Address: 102 N Main St
City: Kendallville
State: IN
Publication Website: www.kpcnews.com
Postal Code: 46755-1714
Office phone: (260) 347-0400
General E-mail: news@kpcmedia.com
Publisher Name: Terry Housholder
Publisher Email: thousholder@kpcmedia.com
Publisher Phone: "260-347-0400 Ext. 1176"
Editor Name: Steve Garbacz
Editor Email: sgarbacz@kpcmedia.com
Editor Phone: 260-347-0400 Ext. 1136
Advertising Executive Name: David Rigas
Advertising Executive Email: drigas@kpcmedia.com
Advertising Executive Phone: 260-347-0400 Ext. 1002
Year Established: 1911
Delivery Methods: Mail`Newsstand`Carrier`Racks
Own Printing Facility?: Y
Commercial printers?: Y
Mechanical specifications: Type page 11 1/2 x 21 1/2; E - 6 cols, 1 3/4, 1/8 between; A - 6 cols, 1 3/4, 1/8 between; C - 9 cols, 1 3/4, 1/8 between.
Published Days: Mon`Tues`Wed`Thur`Fri`Sat`Sun
Weekday Frequency: m
Saturday Frequency: m
Avg Paid Circ: 6004
Audit Company: AAM
Audit Date: 19 04 2019
Pressroom Equipment: Lines – 4-G/Floor SSC Units 1988, 1-Stalk/Pathfinder 1988; 2-G/4-High 1991; 1999;
Mailroom Equipment: Counter Stackers – 1/The Stacker Machine Co/S-N 316-19; Inserters & Stuffers – 1-KAN/5 pocket, KAN/Twin Stacker, MM/Saddle Binds-5 Pocket, 1-Challenge/Single Knife; Tying Machines – It;
Buisness Equipment: 1-Covircint/580
Buisness Software: Baseview/Ad Manager Pro 2.02, Dynamics/Great Plains, Baseview/Circulation Pro 1.8.0
Classified Equipment: Hardware – 3-APP/Mac; Printers – 2-APP/Mac LaserWriter;
Classified Software: Baseview, QPS/QuarkXPress.
Editorial Equipment: Hardware – 12-APP/Mac/6-RSK/TRS 80 Model 100; Printers – 2-APP/Mac LaserWriter
Editorial Software: Baseview, QPS/QuarkXPress.
Production Equipment: Hardware – Caere/OmniPage 6.0, AG/Imagesetter 1200; Cameras – 1-B; Scanners – 1-Kk, 4-AG
Production Software: QPS/QuarkXPress 4.0.
Total Circulation: 5533

KENTLAND

THE ENTERPRISE

Corporate/Parent Company: Gannett
Publication Street Address: 305 E. Graham St.
City: Kentland
State: IN
Publication Website: www.newsbug.info/newton_county_enterprise
Postal Code: 47951
Office phone: 219-474-5532
Publisher Name: Greg Perrotto
Publisher Email: gperrotto@rensselaerrepublican.com
Editor Name: Gregory Myers
Editor Email: nceeditor@centurylink.net

KOKOMO

KOKOMO TRIBUNE

Corporate/Parent Company: CNHI, LLC
Publication Street Address: 300 N Union St
City: Kokomo
State: IN
Publication Website: www.kokomotribune.com
Postal Code: 46901-4612
Office phone: (765) 459-3121
General E-mail: webmaster@kokomotribune.com
Publisher Name: Robyn McCloskey
Publisher Email: robyn.mccloskey@indianamediagroup.com
Publisher Phone: Ext. 288563
Editor Name: Jeff Kovaleski
Editor Email: jeff.kovaleski@kokomotribune.com
Editor Phone: 765-454-8590
Advertising Executive Name: Joe Blaylock
Advertising Executive Email: Joe.blaylock@kokomotribune.com
Advertising Executive Phone: Ext. 286176
Year Established: 1850
Delivery Methods: Mail`Carrier`Racks
Own Printing Facility?: Y
Commercial printers?: Y
Mechanical specifications: Type page 13 x 21 1/2; E - 6 cols, 2 1/16, 1/8 between; A - 6 cols, 2 1/16, 1/8 between; C - 9 cols, 1 3/8, 1/16 between.
Published Days: Mon`Tues`Wed`Thur`Fri`Sat`Sun
Weekday Frequency: m
Saturday Frequency: m
Avg Paid Circ: 20100
Audit Company: Sworn/Estimate/Non-Audited
Audit Date: 7 12 2019
Mailroom Equipment: Tying Machines – 2-Signode/MLN-2A Strapper; Address Machine – Nikor Mark-Model-20.;
Buisness Equipment: 1-DEC/1170
Classified Equipment: Hardware – APP/Mac G3; Umax, Epson/Scanner; Printers – GCC;
Classified Software: AT.
Editorial Equipment: Hardware – APP/Mac 73/APP/Mac; Printers – GCC
Editorial Software: Baseview 3.1.8.
Production Equipment: Hardware – QPS/QuarkXPress 4.x, Baseview/NewsEdit Pro-Que 3.1.x.
Total Circulation: 20100

LA PORTE

HERALD-ARGUS

Corporate/Parent Company: Paxton Media Group, LLC
Publication Street Address: 701 State St
City: La Porte
State: IN
Publication Website: www.heraldargus.com
Postal Code: 46350-3328
Office phone: (219) 362-2161
General E-mail: newsroom@heraldargus.com
Publisher Name: Bill Hackney
Publisher Email: bhackney@heraldargus.com
Publisher Phone: (219) 326-3898
Editor Name: Jeff Mayes
Editor Email: aparkhouse@heraldargus.com
Editor Phone: (219) 214-4170
Advertising Executive Name: Isis Cains
Advertising Executive Email: breisig@heraldargus.com
Advertising Executive Phone: (219) 326-3881
Year Established: 1880
Delivery Methods: Mail`Newsstand`Carrier`Racks
Mechanical specifications: Type page 13 x 21 1/2; E - 6 cols, 2 1/16, 1/8 between; A - 6 cols, 2 1/16, 1/8 between; C - 9 cols, 1 3/8, 1/16 between.
Published Days: Mon`Tues`Wed`Thur`Fri`Sat
Weekday Frequency: m
Saturday Frequency: e
Avg Paid Circ: 5054
Audit Company: AAM
Audit Date: 30 09 2014
Pressroom Equipment: Lines – 6-G/Urbanite, 1-G/3-Color single width; Folders – 1-G/Universal 1963; Control System – 1995;
Mailroom Equipment: Tying Machines – 1-Bu/String Tyer, 1-MLN/EE.;
Buisness Equipment: DTK/Pentium-100
Classified Equipment: Hardware – Dewar/Sys II, 5-Dewar/Discribe;
Classified Software: Dewar/Disc Net.
Editorial Equipment: Hardware – Dewar/Sys II, DTK/16-Dewar/Discribe, 16-DTK
Editorial Software: Dewar/Disc Net, FSI.
Production Equipment: Hardware – 1-MON/PaperMaster 2, 1-MON/ImageMaster 1000, 3-MON/Image Master 1500; Cameras – 1-Nu/2024-V, 1-R/580; Scanners – Nikon/ScanTouch 8 1/2 x 14
Production Software: FSI, QPS/QuarkXPress 3.32.
Total Circulation: 5054

THE LAPORTE HERALD-ARGUS

Corporate/Parent Company: Paxton Media Group, LLC
Publication Street Address: 701 State St.
City: La Porte
State: IN
Publication Website: www.heraldargus.com
Postal Code: 46350
Office phone: 219-362-2161
General E-mail: newsroom@heraldargus.com
Publisher Name: Bill Hackney
Publisher Email: bhackney@heraldargus.com
Publisher Phone: (219) 326-3898
Editor Name: Jeff Mayes
Editor Email: jmayes@thenewsdispatch.com
Editor Phone: (219) 214-4170
Advertising Executive Name: Isis Cains
Advertising Executive Email: icains@heraldargus.com
Advertising Executive Phone: (219) 326-3881

LAFAYETTE

JOURNAL AND COURIER

Corporate/Parent Company: Gannett Company Inc.
Publication Street Address: 823 Park East Blvd
City: Lafayette
State: IN
Publication Website: www.jconline.com
Postal Code: 47905-0811
Office phone: (765) 423-5511
Editor Name: Carol Kriebel Bangert
Year Established: 1920
Delivery Methods: Mail`Newsstand`Carrier`Racks
Own Printing Facility?: Y
Commercial printers?: Y
Mechanical specifications: Type page 13 x 21 1/2; E - 6 cols, 2 1/8, 1/8 between; A - 6 cols, 2 1/8, 1/8 between; C - 9 cols, 1 3/8, 1/8 between.
Published Days: Mon`Tues`Wed`Thur`Fri`Sat`Sun
Weekday Frequency: m
Saturday Frequency: m
Avg Paid Circ: 16969
Audit Company: AAM
Audit Date: 21 08 2018
Pressroom Equipment: Lines – 6-G/Mark (2 half decks; 1 hump) 1959; Folders – G/2:1; Registration System – K&F/Pin Registration.
Mailroom Equipment: Counter Stackers – HL, 1/QWI; Inserters & Stuffers – 1-HI/1472; Tying Machines – Dynaric; Address Machine – Ch.;
Buisness Equipment: 1-IBM/AS-400 F35
Classified Equipment: Hardware – IBM/Server, Dell/Workstations; Printers – HP/8150N;
Classified Software: Mactive 2.16.50.
Editorial Equipment: Hardware – 47-APP/Mac, 32-APP/Mac Server/APP/Mac G4, APP/E-Mac; Printers – DEC/LA 180, OCE/Proof Express
Editorial Software: Baseview/NewsEdit Pro.
Production Equipment: Hardware – 1-Lf, 2-Panther/PrePress; Scanners – Kk/CoolScan
Production Software: Baseview.
Total Circulation: 20482

LEBANON

THE LEBANON REPORTER

Corporate/Parent Company: CNHI, LLC
Publication Street Address: 117 E. Washington St
City: Lebanon
State: IN
Publication Website: www.reporter.net
Postal Code: 46052
Office phone: (765) 482-4650

U.S. Daily Newspapers

General E-mail: news@reporter.net
Publisher Name: Beverly Joyce
Publisher Email: beverly.joyce@
　indianamediagroup.com
Publisher Phone: (765) 482-4650 x250121
Editor Name: Kathy Linton
Editor Email: kathy.linton@indianamediagroup.
　com
Editor Phone: (765) 482-4650 x250118
Advertising Executive Name: Mary Ball
Advertising Executive Email: mary.ball@reporter.
　net
Advertising Executive Phone: (765) 482-4650
　X250117

THE REPORTER

Corporate/Parent Company: Media News Group
Publication Street Address: 117 E Washington St
City: Lebanon
State: IN
Publication Website: www.reporter.net
Postal Code: 46052-2209
Office phone: (765) 482-4650
General E-mail: news@reporter.net
Publisher Name: Beverly Joyce
Publisher Email: beverly.joyce@
　indianamediagroup.com
Publisher Phone: (765) 482-4650 x250121
Editor Name: Kathy Linton
Editor Email: kathy.linton@indianamediagroup.
　com
Editor Phone: (765) 482-4650 x250118
Advertising Executive Name: Mary Ball
Advertising Executive Email: mary.ball@reporter.
　net
Advertising Executive Phone: (765) 482-4650
　X250117
Year Established: 1891
Delivery Methods: Mail`Racks
Own Printing Facility?: N
Mechanical specifications: Type page 13 x 21;
　E - 6 cols, 2 1/16, 1/8 between; A - 6 cols,
　2 1/16, 1/8 between; C - 6 cols, 2 1/16, 1/8
　between.
Published Days: Tues`Wed`Thur`Fri`Sat
Weekday Frequency: m
Saturday Frequency: m
Avg Paid Circ: 5264
Audit Company: Sworn/Estimate/Non-Audited
Audit Date: 7 12 2019
Pressroom Equipment: Lines – 7-G/Community;
Mailroom Equipment: Tying Machines – 1/
　Dynaric; Address Machine – Wm.;
Buisness Equipment: IBM
Total Circulation: 5264

LINTON
GREENE COUNTY DAILY WORLD

Corporate/Parent Company: Rust
　Communications
Publication Street Address: 79 S Main St
City: Linton
State: IN
Publication Website: www.gcdailyworld.com
Postal Code: 47441-1818
Office phone: (812) 847-4487
General E-mail: greenecountynewsdesk@
　gmail.com
Publisher Name: Chris Pruett
Publisher Email: cpruett79@gmail.com
Editor Name: Sabrina Stockrahm
Editor Email: sabrinagcdw@gmail.com
Advertising Executive Name: Christy Lehman
Advertising Executive Email: christy_lehman@
　hotmail.com
Year Established: 1905
Delivery Methods: Mail`Newsstand`Racks
Own Printing Facility?: Y
Commercial printers?: Y
Mechanical specifications: Type page 13 x 21
　1/2; E - 6 cols, 2 1/16, 1/8 between; A - 6
　cols, 2 1/16, 1/8 between; C - 9 cols, 1 1/2,
　1/8 between.
Published Days: Tues`Wed`Fri`Sat
Weekday Frequency: m
Saturday Frequency: m

Avg Paid Circ: 3500
Audit Company: Sworn/Estimate/Non-Audited
Audit Date: 7 12 2019
Pressroom Equipment: Lines – 7-G/Community;
　1-ABD/360; Folders – G/C.;
Editorial Equipment: Hardware – APP/Macs
Production Equipment: Cameras – 1-R
Total Circulation: 3500

LOGANSPORT
PHAROS-TRIBUNE

Corporate/Parent Company: CNHI, LLC
Publication Street Address: 517 E Broadway
City: Logansport
State: IN
Publication Website: www.pharostribune.com
Postal Code: 46947-3154
Office phone: (574) 722-5000
General E-mail: publicforum@pharostribune.
　com
Editor Name: Kevin Burkett
Editor Email: kevin.burkett@pharostribune.com
Editor Phone: 574-732-5155
Advertising Executive Name: Megan Browning
Advertising Executive Email: megan.browning@
　pharostribune.com
Advertising Executive Phone: Ext. 5154
Year Established: 1844
Delivery Methods: Mail`Newsstand`Carrier
Own Printing Facility?: Y
Commercial printers?: Y
Mechanical specifications: Type page 13 x 21
　1/2; E - 6 cols, 2 1/16, 1/8 between; A - 6
　cols, 2 1/16, 1/8 between; C - 6 cols, 2
　1/16, 1/8 between.
Published Days: Mon`Tues`Wed`Thur`Fri`Sat
Weekday Frequency: m
Saturday Frequency: m
Avg Paid Circ: 6000
Audit Company: Sworn/Estimate/Non-Audited
Audit Date: 7 12 2019
Pressroom Equipment: Lines – 19-G/SSC 1984.;
Mailroom Equipment: Tying Machines – 1-/MLN,
　OVL/415.;
Buisness Equipment: 1-Sun/4-110, 1-Sun/SLC,
　1-Compaq/Prolinca 3/25
Buisness Software: Vision Data, ADP
Classified Equipment: Hardware – Sun, NCD;
　Printers – HP/LaserJet, Copal/Dash 600;
Classified Software: Atex.
Editorial Equipment: Hardware – Sun/Lf/AP Leaf
　Picture Desk, Lf/Leafscan 35; Printers –
　2-APP/Mac LaserWriter II NTX, 2-Copal/
　Dash 600
Editorial Software: Baseview.
Production Equipment: Hardware – TI/OmniPage
　2.12, 1-AG/Focus Color Plus; Scanners –
　Horizon
Production Software: QPS/QuarkXPress 4.11.
Total Circulation: 6000

MADISON
MADISON COURIER, INC.

Publication Street Address: 310 West St
City: Madison
State: IN
Publication Website: www.madisoncourier.com
Postal Code: 47250-3711
Office phone: (812) 265-3641
General E-mail: rcull@madisoncourier.com
Publisher Name: Curt Jacobs
Publisher Email: cjacobs@madisoncourier.com
Publisher Phone: (812) 265-3641, ext. 237
Editor Name: Margaret Hillery
Editor Email: mhillery@madisoncourier.com
Editor Phone: (812) 265-3641, ext. 230
Advertising Executive Name: Robin Cull
Advertising Executive Email: rcull@
　madisoncourier.com
Advertising Executive Phone: (812) 265-3641,
　ext. 238
Year Established: 1837
Delivery Methods:
　Mail`Newsstand`Carrier`Racks
Own Printing Facility?: Y
Commercial printers?: N
Mechanical specifications: Type page 13 x 21
　1/2; E - 6 cols, 2 1/16, 1/8 between; A - 6
　cols, 2 1/16, 1/8 between; C - 8 cols, 1 1/2,
　1/8 between.
Published Days: Mon`Tues`Wed`Thur`Fri`Sat
Weekday Frequency: e
Saturday Frequency: m
Avg Paid Circ: 5400
Audit Company: USPS
Audit Date: 14 10 2017
Pressroom Equipment: Lines – 6-KP/News King;
　Reels & Stands – 6; Control System – 1;
Mailroom Equipment: Tying Machines – 2/Bu.;
Buisness Equipment: 4-TI/1505
Classified Equipment: Hardware – 3-APP/Power
　Mac G3; Printers – 1-APP/Mac ImageWriter
　II NT;
Classified Software: Baseview.
Editorial Equipment: Hardware – 9-APP/Power
　Mac 7200, 3-APP/Power Mac G3/1-RSK/
　Tandy portable Model 100, 3-APP/Power
　Mac 7200-120 for remote office; Printers –
　1-APP/Mac LaserWriter II NT
Editorial Software: Baseview, Ethernet.
Production Equipment: Hardware – 1-Nu, Pre
　Press/Panther, Pre Press/Panther 34P;
　Cameras – R/400; Scanners – 1-Nikon/LS
　1000, Epson 1600
Production Software: QPS/QuarkXPress 4.0.
Total Circulation: 5400

MARION
CHRONICLE-TRIBUNE

Corporate/Parent Company: Paxton Media
　Group, LLC
Publication Street Address: 610 S Adams St
City: Marion
State: IN
Publication Website: www.chronicle-tribune.
　com
Postal Code: 46953-2041
Office phone: (765) 664-5111
General E-mail: web-support@chronicle-
　tribune.com
Publisher Name: Linda Kelsay
Publisher Email: lkelsay@chronicle-tribune.com
Publisher Phone: 765-671-2200
Editor Name: Andrew Maciejewski
Editor Email: amaciejewski@chronicle-tribune.
　com
Editor Phone: 765-671-2250
Advertising Executive Name: Christi Kincade
Advertising Executive Email: ckincade@
　chronicle-tribune.com
Advertising Executive Phone: 765-671-2230
Year Established: 1867
Delivery Methods:
　Mail`Newsstand`Carrier`Racks
Own Printing Facility?: Y
Commercial printers?: Y
Mechanical specifications: Type page 11 5/8 x 21
　1/2; E - 7 cols, 1 2/3, between; A - 6 cols,
　2 1/16, 1/8 between; C - 9 cols, 1 3/8, 1/16
　between.
Published Days: Mon`Tues`Wed`Thur`Fri`Sat`Sun
Weekday Frequency: m
Saturday Frequency: m
Avg Paid Circ: 12536
Audit Company: AAM
Audit Date: 31 03 2014
Pressroom Equipment: Lines – 12-G/Urbanite
　845 single width 1970; 6-G/Urbanite 557
　single width 1974; Control System – Fin/
　Drive Sys.;
Mailroom Equipment: Counter Stackers – 1-HL/
　Monitor HI II, 2-HI/RS30; Inserters &
　Stuffers – 1-Mc/660-20; Tying Machines –
　1-MLN/2A, OVL/415, Bu/String; Wrapping
　Singles – Manual; Address Machine –
　Ch/596-985.;
Buisness Equipment: Time Mgt Sys, IBM/
　AS-400
Classified Equipment: Hardware – IBM;
　Accuset/1000 Imagesetters; Printers –
　HP/4MV, HP/8000;
Classified Software: APT 2.006.004.
Editorial Equipment: Hardware – IBM; Printers –
　HP/8550, HP/8000, HP/4MV
Editorial Software: APT 2.006.004.
Production Equipment: Hardware – 2-MON/1000
　Imagesetter, Nu/Flip Top FT40APRNS;
　Cameras – 1-C/Spartan III; Scanners –
Howtek/D7500, Microtek
Production Software: QPS/QuarkXPress 4.10.
Total Circulation: 12536

MICHIGAN CITY
NEWS DISPATCH

Corporate/Parent Company: Paxton Media
　Group, LLC
Publication Street Address: 422 Franklin St.,
　Suite B
City: Michigan City
State: IN
Publication Website: www.thenewsdispatch.
　com
Postal Code: 46360-3274
Office phone: (219) 874-7211
General E-mail: news@thenewsdispatch.com
Publisher Name: Bill Hackney
Publisher Email: bhackney@thenewsdispatch.
　com
Publisher Phone: (219) 214-4173
Editor Name: Jeff Mayes
Editor Email: aparkhouse@thenewsdispatch.
　com
Editor Phone: (219) 214-4170
Advertising Executive Name: Isis Cains
Advertising Executive Email: icains@
　thenewsdispatch.com
Advertising Executive Phone: (219) 214-4210
Year Established: 1938
Delivery Methods:
　Mail`Newsstand`Carrier`Racks
Own Printing Facility?: Y
Mechanical specifications: Type page 11 5/8 x
　21 1/2; E - 6 cols, 1 5/6, 1/8 between; A - 6
　cols, 1 5/6, 1/8 between; C - 9 cols, 1 1/6,
　1/8 between.
Published Days: Mon`Tues`Wed`Thur`Fri`Sat`Sun
Weekday Frequency: m
Saturday Frequency: m
Avg Paid Circ: 11004
Audit Company: AAM
Audit Date: 30 09 2014
Pressroom Equipment: Lines – 8-G/Urbanite (3
　color) 1972; Folders – G/Half & Quarter;
　Reels & Stands – 8-G/Reel Stand.;
Mailroom Equipment: Counter Stackers
　– BG/110HB; Inserters & Stuffers –
　3-KAN/320; Tying Machines – MLN.;
Buisness Equipment: Baseview
Classified Equipment: Hardware – APP/Mac;
　Printers – 2-APP/Mac LaserWriter IINTX,
　HP/4MV, QMS/860, Tektronix/300X;
Classified Software: Baseview/Class Manager
　Pro.
Editorial Equipment: Hardware – APP/Mac;
　Printers – 2-APP/Mac LaserWriter II NTX,
　HP/4MV, QMS/860, Tektronix/300X
Editorial Software: Baseview, QPS/QuarkXPress
　3.32, Baseview/NewsEdit.
Production Equipment: Hardware – Caere/
　OmniPage, AG/Rapline 17; Cameras – R;
　Scanners – Visioneer/Paperport, Nikon/
　Super Coolscan, Lf/AP Leafscan 35, AG/
　StudioScan II, Hp/ScanJet HC, AG/Studio
　Star
Production Software: QPS/QuarkXPress 3.32.
Total Circulation: 11004

MONTICELLO
HERALD JOURNAL

Corporate/Parent Company: Adams Publishing
　Group
Publication Street Address: 114 S Main St
City: Monticello
State: IN
Publication Website: www.thehj.com
Postal Code: 47960-2328
Office phone: (574) 583-5121
Publisher Name: Greg Perrotto
Publisher Email: ggperrotto@
　rensselaerrepublican.com
Editor Name: Michael Johnson
Editor Email: editor@thehj.com
Advertising Executive Name: Marty VanEe
Advertising Executive Email: martin.vanee@
　sbcglobal.net
Year Established: 1862

U.S. Daily Newspapers

Delivery Methods: Mail`Newsstand`Racks
Own Printing Facility?: Y
Commercial printers?: N
Mechanical specifications: Type page 13 x 21 1/2; E - 6 cols, 1 5/6, 1/8 between; A - 6 cols, 1 5/6, 1/8 between; C - 9 cols, 1 5/16, 1/8 between.
Published Days: Mon`Tues`Wed`Thur`Fri`Sat
Weekday Frequency: m
Saturday Frequency: m
Avg Paid Circ: 3500
Audit Company: Sworn/Estimate/Non-Audited
Audit Date: 7 12 2019
Pressroom Equipment: Lines – 5-G/Community 1963.;
Classified Equipment: Hardware – Dell/PC; Printers – APP/Mac LaserWriter II;
Classified Software: APT 4.0.
Editorial Equipment: Hardware – Dell/PC; Printers – APP/Mac LaserWriter II
Editorial Software: APT 4.0.
Production Equipment: Hardware – 1-Nu/Flip Top FT40UPNS, SCREEN; Cameras – LE, R.
Total Circulation: 3500

MUNCIE

THE STAR PRESS

Corporate/Parent Company: Gannett
Publication Street Address: 345 S High St
City: Muncie
State: IN
Publication Website: www.thestarpress.com
Postal Code: 47305-2326
Office phone: (765) 213-5701
Publisher Name: Maribel Perez Wadsworth
Editor Name: Nicole Carroll
Year Established: 1899
Delivery Methods: Mail`Newsstand`Carrier`Racks
Own Printing Facility?: Y
Commercial printers?: Y
Mechanical specifications: Type page 13 x 21 3/8; E - 6 cols, 2, 1/6 between; A - 6 cols, 2, 1/6 between; C - 9 cols, 1 3/8, 1/16 between.
Published Days: Mon`Tues`Wed`Thur`Fri`Sat`Sun
Weekday Frequency: m
Saturday Frequency: m
Avg Paid Circ: 15638
Audit Company: AAM
Audit Date: 21 02 2019
Pressroom Equipment: Lines – 6-G/double width 1964.;
Mailroom Equipment: Counter Stackers – 2/QWI; Tying Machines – 2-/Power Strap; Wrapping Singles – Manual; Address Machine – Manual, Topping.;
Buisness Equipment: 2-Sun/Ultra 10, Sun/Sparc 20
Buisness Software: PBS, SBS, Cyborg
Classified Equipment: Hardware – APP/Mac; Printers – HP/4050;
Classified Software: Baseview.
Editorial Equipment: Hardware – APP/Mac, Sun/HP/1020 Platter; Printers – APP/Mac LaserPrinter, HPM, Lexmark
Editorial Software: DTI 4.3.
Production Equipment: Hardware – 2-AG/Select 7000, 1-AG/Avantra 25; Cameras – KI
Production Software: DTI/Speed Planner 3.1.
Total Circulation: 17401

MUNSTER

THE TIMES OF NORTHWEST INDIANA

Corporate/Parent Company: Lee Enterprises
Publication Street Address: 601 45th St
City: Munster
State: IN
Publication Website: www.nwi.com
Postal Code: 46321-2875
Office phone: (219) 933-3200
Publisher Name: Chris White
Publisher Email: chris.white@nwi.com
Publisher Phone: 219-933-3330
Editor Name: Marc Chase
Editor Email: marc.chase@nwi.com

Editor Phone: 219-933-3327
Advertising Executive Name: Joseph Battistoni
Advertising Executive Email: Joe.Battistoni@nwi.com
Advertising Executive Phone: 219-933-4155
Year Established: 1906
Delivery Methods: Mail`Newsstand`Carrier`Racks
Own Printing Facility?: Y
Commercial printers?: Y
Mechanical specifications: Type page 10"x21"; E - 6 cols, 1/8 between; A - 6 cols, 1/8 between; C - 6 cols, 1/8 between
Published Days: Mon`Tues`Wed`Thur`Fri`Sat`Sun
Weekday Frequency: m
Saturday Frequency: m
Avg Paid Circ: 23826
Avg Free Circ: 1834
Audit Company: AAM
Audit Date: 5 06 2020
Pressroom Equipment: MAGNUM SINGLE WIDTH HEADLINER OFFSET HT70 DOUBLE WIDE HEADLINER OFFSET DOUBLE WIDE
Mailroom Equipment: Counter Stackers – 3/MM, 1-MM/388, 3-MM/310, 1-/HL; Inserters & Stuffers – 4-MM/308, GMA/SLS 2000; Tying Machines – 3-/MLN, 2-/OVL, 1-/Sterling, Dynaric; Wrapping Singles – 2-KP/KJ; Control System – GMA/SAM; Address Machine – 2-/Bar;
Buisness Equipment: Sun/4, COM, 10-PC
Classified Equipment: Hardware – 7-Sun/Sparc, 14-NCD, 6-Sun/Sparc, 2-NCD, 5-PC; Printers – APP/Mac Laser;
Classified Software: Vision Data.
Editorial Equipment: Hardware – 12-Sun/Sparc, 80-PC; Printers – HP/Laser, Iptech/RIP
Editorial Software: Sun/Lotus Notes.
Production Equipment: Hardware – 2-ECR/Pelbox Full-page, 2-APP/Mac Laser, Hyphen/3100, Epson/836XL; Cameras – WL/Digital Camera, Nikon/D1; Scanners – 4-Epson/836XLT, Iptech/RIP
Production Software: QPS/QuarkXPress 4.11.
Total Circulation: 58045

NEW CASTLE

THE COURIER-TIMES

Corporate/Parent Company: Paxton Media Group, LLC
Publication Street Address: 201 S 14th St
City: New Castle
State: IN
Publication Website: www.thecouriertimes.com
Postal Code: 47362-3328
Office phone: 765-575-4619
General E-mail: web-support@thecouriertimes.com
Publisher Name: Marka Sonoga
Publisher Email: msonoga@thecouriertimes.com
Publisher Phone: 765-575-4650
Editor Name: Travis Weik
Editor Email: editor@thecouriertimes.com
Editor Phone: 765-575-4651
Advertising Executive Name: Marka Sonoga
Advertising Executive Email: msonoga@thecouriertimes.com
Year Established: 1841
Delivery Methods: Mail`Newsstand`Carrier`Racks
Own Printing Facility?: N
Commercial printers?: Y
Mechanical specifications: Type page 13 x 21 1/2; E - 6 cols, 2 1/16, 1/8 between; A - 6 cols, 2 1/16, 1/8 between; C - 9 cols, 1 3/8, 1/16 between.
Published Days: Tues`Wed`Thur`Fri`Sun
Weekday Frequency: m
Avg Paid Circ: 4500
Audit Company: Sworn/Estimate/Non-Audited
Audit Date: 7 12 2019
Pressroom Equipment: Lines – 5-G/Urbanite 1990; Press Drive – Fin/120hp;
Mailroom Equipment: Counter Stackers – 1-BG/Count-O-Veyor 108; Tying Machines – 1-Bu/20, 1-Bu/String Tyer, 1-Bu/Tape Wrapper; Address Machine – 1-Am/6341B.;
Buisness Equipment: IBM/AS-400
Classified Equipment: Hardware – 4-APP/iMAC,

GCC/Elite 12/600; Printers – Okidata/3410;
Classified Software: Baseview, Ad Manager Pro.
Editorial Equipment: Hardware – 1-APP/Power Mac 9500, 1-APP/Power Mac 8150, 1-APP/Power Mac 8100, 3-APP/Power Mac 7100, 4-APP/Power Mac 6100, 5-APP/Mac Quadra 630, 1-APP/Mac Quadra 605, 2-APP/Mac PowerBook 150, 2-APP/Mac PowerBook 190, 1-APP/Mac II; Printers – Xante/Accel-A-W
Production Equipment: Hardware – Caere/OmniPage 6.0; Cameras – 1-R/580; Scanners – AG/Studio STM, Microtek/ScanMaster IIXE, Minolta/Quick Scan 35, Nikon/Coolscan 2000
Production Software: QPS/QuarkXPress 3.32.
Total Circulation: 4500

NOBLESVILLE

THE TIMES- FRANKFORT/CLINTON

Corporate/Parent Company: Sagamore News Media
Publication Street Address: 54 N 9th Street
City: Noblesville
State: IN
Publication Website: www.thetimes24-7.com
Postal Code: 46060-2261
Office phone: (317) 770-7777
General E-mail: news@thetimes24-7.com
Year Established: 1877
Delivery Methods: Mail`Newsstand`Carrier`Racks
Own Printing Facility?: Y
Commercial printers?: Y
Mechanical specifications: Type page 10 x 21 1/2; E - 6 cols, 4.587, 1/8 between; A - 6 cols, 1.587, 1/8 between
Published Days: Tues`Wed`Thur`Fri`Sun
Weekday Frequency: m
Saturday Frequency: m
Avg Paid Circ: 4694
Audit Company: Sworn/Estimate/Non-Audited
Audit Date: 7 12 2019
Pressroom Equipment: Lines – Print at Chronicle-Tribune, Marion, IN;
Mailroom Equipment: Counter Stackers – Insert at Chronicle-Tribune, Marion, IN;
Buisness Equipment: PC
Buisness Software: MediaSpan
Classified Equipment: Hardware – PC;
Classified Software: MediaSpan
Editorial Equipment: Hardware – PC
Editorial Software: Falcon; InDesign
Production Software: InDesign
Total Circulation: 4694

PERU

PERU TRIBUNE

Corporate/Parent Company: Paxton Media Group, LLC
Publication Street Address: 26 W 3rd St
City: Peru
State: IN
Publication Website: www.perutribune.com
Postal Code: 46970-2155
Office phone: (765) 473-6641
General E-mail: web-support@perutribune.com
Publisher Name: Linda Kelsay
Publisher Email: lkelsay@perutribune.com
Publisher Phone: Ext.: 132
Editor Name: Jared Keever
Editor Email: jkeever@perutribune.com
Editor Phone: Ext.: 129
Advertising Executive Name: Christi Kincade
Advertising Executive Email: ckincade@perutribune.com
Year Established: 1921
Delivery Methods: Mail`Newsstand`Carrier`Racks
Mechanical specifications: Type page 10 1/8 x 21 1/2; E - 6 cols, 1 5/8, 1/8 between; A - 6 cols, 1 5/8, 1/8 between; C - 9 cols, 1 1/16, 1/8 between.
Published Days: Tues`Wed`Thur`Fri`Sun
Weekday Frequency: m
Avg Paid Circ: 3600
Avg Free Circ: 6000
Audit Company: Sworn/Estimate/Non-Audited

Audit Date: 7 12 2019
Pressroom Equipment: Lines – 4-G/Urbanite; Folders – 1-G/2:1;
Mailroom Equipment: Tying Machines – 1/Bu, 1-/Plastic Strap; Address Machine – 1-/WM.;
Buisness Equipment: IBM/AS-400
Classified Equipment: Hardware – 2-HI/Micro-Store.;
Editorial Equipment: Hardware – APP/Mac; Printers – APP/Mac LaserWriters
Editorial Software: Baseview/NewsEdit 3.1, QPS/QuarkXPress 3.3.
Production Equipment: Hardware – Multi-Ad/Creator 3.5, 2-APP/Mac
Production Software: QPS/QuarkXPress.
Total Circulation: 9600

PLYMOUTH

PILOT NEWS

Corporate/Parent Company: Heritage Publications (2003) Inc.
Publication Street Address: 214 N Michigan St
City: Plymouth
State: IN
Publication Website: www.thepilotnews.com
Postal Code: 46563-2135
Office phone: (574) 936-3101
General E-mail: webmaster@thepilotnews.com
Publisher Name: Cindy Stockton
Publisher Email: cstockton@thepilotnews.com
Year Established: 1851
Delivery Methods: Mail`Newsstand`Carrier`Racks
Commercial printers?: Y
Mechanical specifications: Type page 13 x 21 1/2; E - 6 cols, 2 1/16, 1/8 between; A - 6 cols, 2 1/16, 1/8 between; C - 10 cols, 1 3/8, 1/16 between.
Published Days: Mon`Tues`Wed`Thur`Fri`Sat
Weekday Frequency: e
Saturday Frequency: m
Avg Paid Circ: 4100
Audit Company: Sworn/Estimate/Non-Audited
Audit Date: 7 12 2019
Mailroom Equipment: Tying Machines – 1/Bu; Address Machine – El/3101.;
Classified Equipment: Hardware – APP/Mac;
Classified Software: Baseview.
Editorial Equipment: Hardware – APP/Mac
Editorial Software: Baseview.
Production Equipment: Hardware – HP/Laserjet 4, Xante/Accel-a-Writer; Cameras – 1-B/Caravel
Production Software: QPS/QuarkXPress 3.3.
Total Circulation: 4100

PORTLAND

THE COMMERCIAL REVIEW

Corporate/Parent Company: Graphic Printing Co., Inc.
Publication Street Address: 309 W Main St
City: Portland
State: IN
Publication Website: www.thecr.com
Postal Code: 47371-1803
Office phone: (260) 726-8141
Publisher Name: Jack Ronald
Publisher Email: j.ronald@thecr.com
Editor Name: Ray Cooney
Editor Email: r.cooney@thecr.com
Year Established: 1871
Delivery Methods: Mail`Newsstand`Carrier
Own Printing Facility?: Y
Commercial printers?: Y
Mechanical specifications: Type page 13 x 21 1/4; E - 6 cols, 2 1/16, 1/8 between; A - 6 cols, 2 1/16, 1/8 between; C - 8 cols, 1 1/2, 1/16 between.
Published Days: Mon`Tues`Wed`Thur`Fri`Sat
Weekday Frequency: e
Saturday Frequency: m
Avg Paid Circ: 4000
Audit Company: Sworn/Estimate/Non-Audited
Audit Date: 7 12 2019
Pressroom Equipment: Lines – 5-G/Community (DEV Horizon Stack Unit);
Buisness Equipment: IBM/PC-AT

U.S. Daily Newspapers

Buisness Software: Great Plains
Classified Equipment: Hardware – APP/Mac; Printers – APP/Mac;
Classified Software: Baseview.
Editorial Equipment: Hardware – APP/Mac; Printers – APP/Mac
Editorial Software: Baseview, QPS/QuarkXPress.
Production Equipment: Hardware – APP/Mac LaserPrinters, 1-B/30x40; Cameras – 1-R/20x24; Scanners – HP/ScanJet.
Total Circulation: 4000

PRINCETON
PRINCETON DAILY CLARION

Corporate/Parent Company: Paxton Media Group, LLC
Publication Street Address: 100 N Gibson St
City: Princeton
State: IN
Publication Website: https://www.pdclarion.com
Postal Code: 47670-1855
Office phone: (812) 385-2525
General E-mail: news@pdclarion.com
Editor Name: Andrea Howe
Editor Email: andrea@pdclarion.com
Advertising Executive Name: Courtney Shuttle
Advertising Executive Email: courtney@pdclarion.com
Year Established: 1846
Delivery Methods: Mail`Newsstand`Carrier`Racks
Own Printing Facility?: Y
Commercial printers?: Y
Mechanical specifications: Type page 12 x 21 1/2; E – 6 cols, 1 7/10, 1/6 between; A – 6 cols, 1 7/10, 1/6 between; C – 8 cols, 1 1/4, 1/6 between.
Published Days: Mon`Tues`Wed`Thur`Fri
Weekday Frequency: m
Avg Paid Circ: 5330
Audit Company: Sworn/Estimate/Non-Audited
Audit Date: 7 12 2019
Pressroom Equipment: Lines – 8-G/Community.;
Buisness Equipment: Qantel
Classified Equipment: Hardware – APP/Macs;
Classified Software: Baseview.
Editorial Equipment: Hardware – APP/Macs; Printers – Pre Press/Panther
Production Equipment: Hardware – APP/Mac LaserWriters, Pre Press/Kodak CTP/Presteligence
Production Software: QPS/QuarkXPress.
Total Circulation: 5330

RENSSELAER
RENSSELAER REPUBLICAN

Corporate/Parent Company: Community Media Group
Publication Street Address: 117 N Van Rensselaer St
City: Rensselaer
State: IN
Publication Website: www.myrepublican.info
Postal Code: 47978-2651
Office phone: (219) 866-5111
General E-mail: misty@rensselaerrepublican.com
Publisher Name: Greg Perrotto
Publisher Email: gperrotto@rensselaerrepublican.com
Editor Name: Michael S. Johnson
Editor Email: editor@thehj.com
Year Established: 1866
Delivery Methods: Mail`Newsstand`Carrier`Racks
Mechanical specifications: Type page 13 x 21 1/2; E – 6 cols, 2, 1/4 between; A – 6 cols, 2, 1/4 between; C – 9 cols, 1/4 between.
Published Days: Mon`Tues`Wed`Thur`Fri`Sat
Weekday Frequency: m
Saturday Frequency: m
Avg Paid Circ: 2049
Audit Company: Sworn/Estimate/Non-Audited
Audit Date: 7 12 2019
Pressroom Equipment: Lines – 5-HI/V-15D single width 1994; Folders – HI/JF-25; Reels & Stands – 5;
Mailroom Equipment: Counter Stackers – BG/Count-O-Veyor 08; Tying Machines – 1-EAM-Mosca/Strapper, 1/Miller-Bevco/Strapper; Address Machine – 2-/Addressmatic.;
Buisness Equipment: 1-PC 386, 1-PC 486, APP/Mac LC III
Buisness Software: Lotus 1-2-3, Microsoft/Excel, Microsoft/Office, Listmaster
Classified Equipment: Hardware – 2-Ultra/486D-40; Printers – 2-Epson/LQ 1170;
Classified Software: Mk/Newscraft.
Editorial Equipment: Hardware – 2-APP/Mac 610, 9-APP/Mac LC II; Printers – APP/Mac LaserWriter Pro, APP/Mac LaserWriter IIg
Editorial Software: Baseview/NewsEdit 3.25, QPS/QuarkXPress 3.2.
Production Equipment: Hardware – Nu/FT40V2UP; Cameras – SCREEN/680-C; Scanners – Microtek/ScanMaker IIsp, Microtek/ScanMaker IIIxe
Production Software: QPS/QuarkXPress 3.2.
Total Circulation: 2049

RICHMOND
PALLADIUM-ITEM

Corporate/Parent Company: Gannett Co., Inc.
Publication Street Address: 1175 N A St
City: Richmond
State: IN
Publication Website: www.pal-item.com
Postal Code: 47374-3226
Office phone: (765) 962-1575
General E-mail: palitem@pal-item.com
Year Established: 1831
Delivery Methods: Mail`Newsstand`Carrier`Racks
Own Printing Facility?: Y
Commercial printers?: Y
Mechanical specifications: Type page 11 63/100 x 21; E – 6 cols, 2 1/16, 1/8 between; A – 6 cols, 1 5/6, 1/8 between; C – 9 cols, 1 6/25, 1/8 between.
Published Days: Mon`Tues`Wed`Thur`Fri`Sat`Sun
Weekday Frequency: m
Saturday Frequency: m
Avg Paid Circ: 7943
Avg Free Circ: 63
Audit Company: AAM
Audit Date: 7 04 2020
Pressroom Equipment: Lines – 18-G/Urbanite single width 1984; 4-HI/VI5A-6; Reels & Stands – G/2-Arm RTP.;
Mailroom Equipment: Counter Stackers – 1-PPK/Ministack, 2/MM, 2-QWI/350, QWI/GC610; Inserters & Stuffers – 1-MM/EM 101, 1-GMA/SLS 1000; Tying Machines – 3-/MLN, 1-Sa/Twine, Power Strap, OVL; Wrapping Singles – 1-/Sa; Address Machine – 1-/Barstrom, 1-/Ch.;
Buisness Equipment: IBM/AS-400
Classified Equipment: Hardware – APT; Printers – HP;
Classified Software: APT.
Editorial Equipment: Hardware – APT; Printers – HP
Editorial Software: Microsoft/Windows 95, Microsoft/Word, QPS/QuarkXPress.
Production Equipment: Hardware – 3-Nu/Flip Top FT4OV6UPNS, 1-Anitec; Cameras – C/Spartan III; Scanners – 2-GEI/Copydot 1000, Lf/Leafscan 35, Umax/8
Production Software: QPS/QuarkXPress.
Total Circulation: 8309

ROCHESTER
THE ROCHESTER SENTINEL

Corporate/Parent Company: Paxton Media Group, LLC
Publication Street Address: 118 E 8th St
City: Rochester
State: IN
Publication Website: www.rochsent.com
Postal Code: 46975-1508
Office phone: (574) 223-2111
General E-mail: web-support@rochsent.com
Publisher Name: Bill Hackney
Publisher Email: bhackney@rochsent.com
Publisher Phone: 574-223-2111 x331
Editor Name: Christina M. Seiler
Editor Email: christinas@rochsent.com
Editor Phone: 574-223-2111 x327
Advertising Executive Name: Jean Helt
Advertising Executive Email: jhelt@rochsent.com
Advertising Executive Phone: 574-223-2111 x321
Year Established: 1858
Delivery Methods: Mail`Newsstand`Racks
Own Printing Facility?: N
Commercial printers?: N
Mechanical specifications: 22-inch web. 6 columns wide by 21.5 inches deep. 1 column: 1.58 inches wide or 9 picas 6 points. .. 6 columns: 10.126 inches wide or 60 picas 9 points.
Published Days: Mon`Tues`Wed`Thur`Fri`Sat
Weekday Frequency: m
Saturday Frequency: m
Avg Paid Circ: 3800
Audit Company: USPS
Audit Date: 10 01 2015
Mailroom Equipment: Tying Machines – 1-Bu/169D.;
Total Circulation: 3800

SEYMOUR
THE TRIBUNE

Corporate/Parent Company: AIM Media
Publication Street Address: 100 Saint Louis Ave
City: Seymour
State: IN
Publication Website: www.tribtown.com
Postal Code: 47274-2304
Office phone: (812) 522-4871
General E-mail: readersubmit@tribtown.com
Editor Name: Aubrey Woods
Year Established: 1877
Delivery Methods: Mail`Newsstand`Carrier`Racks
Own Printing Facility?: Y
Commercial printers?: N
Published Days: Mon`Tues`Wed`Thur`Fri`Sat
Weekday Frequency: All day
Saturday Frequency: All day
Avg Paid Circ: 8951
Audit Company: Sworn/Estimate/Non-Audited
Audit Date: 7 12 2019
Pressroom Equipment: Lines – 4-G/Urbanite (retired);
Total Circulation: 8951

SHELBYVILLE
THE SHELBYVILLE NEWS

Corporate/Parent Company: Paxton Media Group, LLC
Publication Street Address: 123 E Washington St
City: Shelbyville
State: IN
Publication Website: www.shelbynews.com
Postal Code: 46176-1463
Office phone: (317) 398-6631
General E-mail: web-support@shelbynews.com
Publisher Name: Marka Sonoga
Publisher Email: msonoga@shelbynews.com
Publisher Phone: 317-398-1264
Editor Name: Jeff Brown
Editor Email: jbrown@shelbynews.com
Editor Phone: 317-395-7523
Advertising Executive Name: Rhonda Schwegman
Advertising Executive Email: rhonda@shelbynews.com
Advertising Executive Phone: 317-398-1264
Year Established: 1947
Delivery Methods: Mail`Newsstand`Carrier`Racks
Mechanical specifications: Type page 10 1/8 x 21 1/2; E – 6 cols, 1 19/32, 1/8 between; A – 6 cols, 1 5/6, 1/8 between; C – 9 cols, 1 13/32, 1/8 between.
Published Days: Tues`Wed`Thur`Fri`Sun
Weekday Frequency: e
Saturday Frequency: m
Avg Paid Circ: 8315
Audit Company: Sworn/Estimate/Non-Audited
Audit Date: 7 12 2019
Pressroom Equipment: Lines – 8-G/SC, 1-G/SSC UOP single width; 2-G/SSC single width; 1-G/SSC UOP single width; Folders – 2-G/2:1; Pasters –2-Butler/Automatic.
Mailroom Equipment: Counter Stackers – 2-BG/105; Inserters & Stuffers – 6-KAN/320, 7-KAN/760; Tying Machines – 3/Bu.;
Buisness Equipment: APP/Mac, Baseview
Buisness Software: Great Plains, Baseview
Classified Equipment: Hardware – Baseview, APP/Mac; Printers – Lexmark/Optra;
Classified Software: Baseview.
Editorial Equipment: Hardware – Baseview, APP/Mac; Printers – Lexmark/Optra RN Plus
Editorial Software: Baseview.
Production Equipment: Hardware – Caere/OmniPage Pro 6, 2-Harlequin/RIP, Pre Press/Panther Pro 46 with Ap Power Mac 8500 PC RIP, Kk/RFS; Cameras – SCREEN/C680-C; Scanners – Kk/RFS 2035, AG/Arcus, Umax/PowerBook, Nikon/LS1000
Production Software: QPS/QuarkXPress 4.1.
Total Circulation: 8315

SOUTH BEND
SOUTH BEND TRIBUNE

Corporate/Parent Company: Gannett
Publication Street Address: 225 W Colfax Ave
City: South Bend
State: IN
Publication Website: www.southbendtribune.com
Postal Code: 46626-1000
Office phone: 574-235-6161
General E-mail: sbtnews@sbtinfo.com
Publisher Name: Andrew Bruns
Editor Name: Alan Achkar
Editor Email: aachkar@sbtinfo.com
Advertising Executive Name: Shelley Chakan
Year Established: 1872
Delivery Methods: Mail`Newsstand`Carrier
Mechanical specifications: Type page 13 x 22 1/4; E – 6 cols, 2 1/16, 1/8 between; A – 6 cols, 2 1/16, 1/8 between; C – 10 cols, 1 3/16, 1/16 between.
Published Days: Mon`Tues`Wed`Thur`Fri`Sat`Sun
Weekday Frequency: m
Saturday Frequency: m
Avg Paid Circ: 32259
Avg Free Circ: 572
Audit Company: AAM
Audit Date: 11 11 2019
Pressroom Equipment: Lines – 20-KBA/Anilox Keyless Offset double width 1994; Folders – 1-KBA/gear, 2-KBA/jaw; Control System – 1994;
Mailroom Equipment: Counter Stackers – 6-S; Inserters & Stuffers – 2-Fg/Drum 6:1, HI 630 13:1; Tying Machines – 6-MVP/5000, 6-MVP/2000;
Buisness Equipment: 1-DEC/VAX 4000-300, 1-DEC/VAX 400-705
Buisness Software: GEAC, CIS 7.05, AIM 8.02H
Classified Equipment: Hardware – Compaq/Alpha-NT;
Classified Software: Compuclass.
Editorial Equipment: Hardware – Compaq/Alpha-NT
Editorial Software: Dewar.
Production Equipment: Hardware – 3-III/3850 Negative Output Devices, 2-Linotype-Hell/Lino 530; Cameras – 2-C/Marathon, 1-K/v241; Scanners – 1-III/Infoscan 3725, 1-ScanView/ScanMate 5000, Horizon/Flatbed
Production Software: Dewar.
Total Circulation: 38103

SPENCER
SPENCER EVENING WORLD

Corporate/Parent Company: Spencer Evening World Publishing, Inc.
Publication Street Address: 114 E Franklin St
City: Spencer

U.S. Daily Newspapers

State: IN
Publication Website: www.spencereveningworld.com
Postal Code: 47460-1818
Office phone: (812) 829-2255
General E-mail: editor@spencereveningworld.com
Year Established: 1927
Delivery Methods:
    Mail`Newsstand`Carrier`Racks
Own Printing Facility?: Y
Commercial printers?: Y
Mechanical specifications: Type page 15 1/8 x 21; E - 7 cols, 2 1/16, 1/8 between; A - 7 cols, 2 1/16, 1/8 between; C - 7 cols, 2 1/16, 1/8 between.
Published Days: Mon`Tues`Wed`Thur`Fri
Weekday Frequency: m
Avg Paid Circ: 3590
Audit Company: Sworn/Estimate/Non-Audited
Audit Date: 7 12 2019
Pressroom Equipment: Lines – 4-G/Community.;
Mailroom Equipment: Tying Machines – 1-Bu/29480; Address Machine – 1-El/300;
Production Equipment: Hardware – 2-APP/Mac Laser, 1-B/2500; Cameras – 1-K/240, 1-R; Scanners – Microtek.
Total Circulation: 3590

SULLIVAN

THE SULLIVAN DAILY TIMES

Corporate/Parent Company: Kelk Publishing
Publication Street Address: 110 N. Main St. Po Box 130
City: Sullivan
State: IN
Publication Website: www.sullivan-times.com
Postal Code: 47882
Office phone: (812) 268-6356
Publisher Name: Gillian Kelk
Publisher Email: publisher.sdt@gmail.com
Editor Name: Kristi Sanders
Editor Email: editor.sdt@gmail.com
Advertising Executive Name: Nikki Robinson
Advertising Executive Email: nikki.robinson.sdt@gmail.com
Year Established: 1854
Delivery Methods: Newsstand`Carrier`Racks
Mechanical specifications: Type page 13 3/8 x 21; E - 6 cols, 2 1/12, 1/6 between; A - 6 cols, 2 1/12, 1/6 between; C - 6 cols, 2 1/12, 1/6 between.
Published Days: Mon`Tues`Wed`Thur`Fri
Weekday Frequency: e
Avg Paid Circ: 4115
Audit Company: Sworn/Estimate/Non-Audited
Audit Date: 7 12 2019
Pressroom Equipment: Lines – 4-HI/V-15A 1973; Folders – HI/J-7.;
Mailroom Equipment: Tying Machines – Sa.;
Buisness Equipment: PC 386 DX, PC 286
Buisness Software: Synaptic/Micro Solutions
Classified Equipment: Hardware – 5-Pentium/PC;
Classified Software: SunType, QPS, QuarkXPress, Adobe/PhotoShop.
Editorial Equipment: Hardware – 4-APP/iMac, PC 486, PC 386 DX; Printers – Xante/11x17
Editorial Software: SunType, QPS/QuarkXPress, Adobe/Photoshop.
Production Equipment: Cameras – R/500; Scanners – APP/Mac
Production Software: QPS/QuarkXPress, Adobe/PhotoShop.
Total Circulation: 4115

TERRE HAUTE

THE TRIBUNE STAR

Corporate/Parent Company: CNHI, LLC
Publication Street Address: 222 S 7th St
City: Terre Haute
State: IN
Publication Website: www.tribstar.com
Postal Code: 47807-3601
Office phone: (812) 231-4200
General E-mail: newsalert@tribstar.com
Publisher Name: Robyn McCloskey
Publisher Email: robyn.mccloskey@indianamediagroup.com
Publisher Phone: (812) 231-4297
Editor Name: Max Jones
Editor Email: max.jones@tribstar.com
Editor Phone: (812) 231-4336
Advertising Executive Name: Director Doug Dixon
Advertising Executive Email: doug.dixon@tribstar.com
Advertising Executive Phone: (812) 231-4226
Year Established: 1983
Delivery Methods:
    Mail`Newsstand`Carrier`Racks
Own Printing Facility?: Y
Commercial printers?: Y
Mechanical specifications: Type page 11 3/4 x 21 1/2; E - 6 cols, 1 5/6, 1/8 between; A - 6 cols, 1 5/6, 1/8 between; C - 9 cols, 1 5/6, 1/16 between.
Published Days: Mon`Tues`Wed`Thur`Fri`Sat`Sun
Weekday Frequency: m
Saturday Frequency: m
Avg Paid Circ: 13827
Avg Free Circ: 1512
Audit Company: AAM
Audit Date: 31 03 2016
Pressroom Equipment: Lines – 10-G/Urbanite 1978; Reels & Stands – 4;
Mailroom Equipment: Counter Stackers – 2-Id/2000; Inserters & Stuffers – 1-GMA/SLS 1000, 1-GMA/SLS 2000 12:1; Tying Machines – 2-Dynaric/NP2; Address Machine – 1/Ch.;
Buisness Equipment: HP/9000
Buisness Software: PBS
Classified Equipment: Hardware – DEC, APP/MAC;
Classified Software: CText/Classified Advertising System, Baseview/Ad Manager Pro.
Editorial Equipment: Hardware – DEC, APP/Mac
Editorial Software: CText/AFM, Baseview, Baseview/NewsEdit Pro I Que.
Production Equipment: Hardware – X, Pre Press/Panther Pro, Pre Press/Panther Pro 46; Cameras – 1-B/1822, 1-LC/21121; Scanners – 1-Lf/Leafscan 35, 1-Sharp/JX600, 2-Nikon/Super Coolscan, 2-Polaroid/SprintScan 35
Production Software: QPS/QuarkXPress.
Total Circulation: 15339

TIPTON

TIPTON COUNTY TRIBUNE

Corporate/Parent Company: Elwood Publishing Co., Inc.
Publication Street Address: 116 S Main St
City: Tipton
State: IN
Publication Website: www.elwoodpublishing.com
Postal Code: 46072-1864
Office phone: (765) 675-2115
General E-mail: tiptoneditor@elwoodpublishing.com
Publisher Name: Robert Nash
Editor Name: Jackie Henry
Advertising Executive Name: Lori Nash
Advertising Executive Email: lorinash@elwoodpublishing.com
Year Established: 1825
Delivery Methods:
    Mail`Newsstand`Carrier`Racks
Mechanical specifications: Type page 13 x 21 1/2; E - 6 cols, 2 1/16, 1/8 between; A - 6 cols, 2 1/16, 1/8 between; C - 8 cols, 1 1/2, 1/32 between.
Published Days: Mon`Tues`Wed`Thur`Fri`Sat
Weekday Frequency: e
Saturday Frequency: m
Avg Paid Circ: 5200
Audit Company: Sworn/Estimate/Non-Audited
Audit Date: 7 12 2019
Pressroom Equipment: Lines – 4-G/Community;
Mailroom Equipment: Tying Machines – 1/Malow, 1-/Bu.;
Buisness Equipment: 1-Bs/B-20, 1-RSK/TRS 80 model 4
Classified Equipment: Hardware – Mk/1100;
Classified Software: Mk/Mycro-Comp.
Editorial Equipment: Hardware – Mk/1100
Editorial Software: Mk/Mycro-Comp.
Production Equipment: Hardware – 2-APP/Mac LaserWriter II NT/NTX; Cameras – 1-R/Commodore.
Total Circulation: 5200

VINCENNES

VINCENNES SUN-COMMERCIAL

Corporate/Parent Company: Paxton Media Group, LLC
Publication Street Address: 702 Main St
City: Vincennes
State: IN
Publication Website: www.suncommercial.com
Postal Code: 47591-2910
Office phone: (812) 886-9955
General E-mail: grobbins@suncommercial.com
Publisher Name: Gayle Robbins
Publisher Email: grobbins@suncommercial.com
Publisher Phone: ext 2449 or 812-316-5406
Editor Name: Jenny McNeece
Editor Email: jmcneece@suncommercial.com
Editor Phone: ext 2448 or 812-316-5412
Advertising Executive Name: Courtney Shuttle
Advertising Executive Email: courtney@pdclarion.com
Advertising Executive Phone: ext 1015 or (812) 220-4861
Year Established: 1804
Delivery Methods:
    Mail`Newsstand`Carrier`Racks
Own Printing Facility?: N
Commercial printers?: Y
Mechanical specifications: 6 col broadsheet format. 21.375 depth 1 col 1.6225, 2 col 3.375, 3 col 5.125, 4 col 6.875, 5 col 8.625, 6 col 10.375
Published Days: Tues`Wed`Thur`Fri`Sat`Sun
Weekday Frequency: m
Saturday Frequency: m
Avg Paid Circ: 4867
Audit Company: Sworn/Estimate/Non-Audited
Audit Date: 7 12 2019
Pressroom Equipment: Lines – 5-G/Urbanite (2 balloon formers) 1968;
Mailroom Equipment: Tying Machines – Bu.;
Buisness Equipment: 1-IBM/Sys 36
Buisness Software: In-house
Classified Equipment: Hardware – APP/Mac;PC
Classified Software: Baseview/Clas Indesign
Editorial Equipment: Hardware – APP/Mac/SCS/Linx
Editorial Software: Baseview/NewsEdit, Baseview/Wire Manager.
Production Equipment: Hardware – 1-Nat/330, Nikon, Adobe/Photoshop; Cameras – 1-R/500.
Total Circulation: 4867

WABASH

WABASH PLAIN DEALER

Corporate/Parent Company: Paxton Media Group, LLC
Publication Street Address: 99 West Canal Street
City: Wabash
State: IN
Publication Website: www.wabashplaindealer.com
Postal Code: 46992
Office phone: (260) 563-2131
General E-mail: web-support@wabashplaindealer.com
Publisher Name: Linda Kelsay
Publisher Email: lkelsay@pmginmi.com
Publisher Phone: 260-563-2131 Ext. 141
Editor Name: Mackenzi Klemann
Editor Email: mklemann@wabashplaindealer.com
Editor Phone: 260-563-2131 Ext. 142
Advertising Executive Name: Christi Kincade
Advertising Executive Email: ckincade@wabashplaindealer.com
Year Established: 1859
Delivery Methods:
    Mail`Newsstand`Carrier`Racks
Own Printing Facility?: Y
Commercial printers?: Y
Published Days: Tues`Wed`Thur`Fri`Sun
Weekday Frequency: m
Saturday Frequency: m
Avg Paid Circ: 3000
Audit Company: Sworn/Estimate/Non-Audited
Audit Date: 7 12 2019
Pressroom Equipment: Lines – 4-G/Urbanite; Folders – 1, 1-G/Quarter.;
Mailroom Equipment: Counter Stackers – 1/BG; Tying Machines – 3-/Bu.;
Classified Equipment: Hardware – APP/Mac; Printers – APP/Mac;
Classified Software: Baseview.
Editorial Equipment: Hardware – APP/Mac
Editorial Software: QPS/QuarkXPress.
Production Equipment: Hardware – 2-Nu, 1-ECR; Cameras – 1-R
Production Software: QPS/QuarkXPress.
Total Circulation: 3000

WASHINGTON

WASHINGTON TIMES-HERALD

Corporate/Parent Company: CNHI, LLC
Publication Street Address: 102 E. VanTrees St.
City: Washington
State: IN
Publication Website: www.washtimesherald.com
Postal Code: 47501
Office phone: 812-254-0480
General E-mail: newsroom@washtimesherald.com
Publisher Name: Melody Brunson
Publisher Email: mbrunson@washtimesherald.com
Publisher Phone: 812-254-0480 ext 114
Editor Name: Melody Brunson
Editor Email: mbrunson@washtimesherald.com
Editor Phone: 812-254-0480 ext 127
Advertising Executive Name: Wanita Tetreault
Advertising Executive Email: wtetreault@washtimesherald.com
Advertising Executive Phone: 812-254-0480 ext 121

WINCHESTER

THE NEWS-GAZETTE

Corporate/Parent Company: Community Media Group
Publication Street Address: 224 W Franklin St
City: Winchester
State: IN
Publication Website: www.winchesternewsgazette.com
Postal Code: 47394-1808
Office phone: (765) 584-4501
Publisher Name: Leesa Friend
Publisher Email: ngpublisher@gmail.com
Editor Name: Brian Pogue
Editor Email: newsgazettereporter@gmail.com
Advertising Executive Name: Valerie Ashley
Advertising Executive Email: cmgsales.va@gmail.com
Year Established: 1873
Delivery Methods:
    Mail`Newsstand`Carrier`Racks
Own Printing Facility?: Y
Commercial printers?: Y
Mechanical specifications: Type page 13 x 21 1/2; E - 6 cols, 2 1/14, 1/8 between; A - 6 cols, 2 1/14, 1/8 between; C - 10 cols, 1 1/5, 1/6 between.
Published Days: Mon`Tues`Wed`Thur`Fri`Sat
Weekday Frequency: e
Saturday Frequency: m
Avg Paid Circ: 3700
Audit Company: Sworn/Estimate/Non-Audited
Audit Date: 7 12 2019
Pressroom Equipment: Lines – 5-G/Community 1973;
Mailroom Equipment: Tying Machines – 2-Bu/String Tyer; Address Machine – 2/Am.;
Buisness Software: Microsoft/Office, Listmaster
Classified Equipment: Hardware – APP/Mac 605; Printers – APP/Mac LaserWriter Pro 630;
Classified Software: Baseview.
Editorial Equipment: Hardware – APP/Mac 605, APP/Mac 610, APP/Power Mac 7200; Printers – APP/Mac LaserWriter Pro 630

KANSAS

ABILENE

ABILENE REFLECTOR-CHRONICLE

Corporate/Parent Company: The White Corporation
Publication Street Address: 303 N Broadway St
City: Abilene
State: KS
Publication Website: www.abilene-rc.com
Postal Code: 67410-2616
Office phone: (785) 263-1000
General E-mail: editor@abilene-rc.com
Editor Name: Greg Doering
Year Established: 1942
Delivery Methods: Mail`Newsstand`Carrier`Racks
Own Printing Facility?: N
Commercial printers?: N
Mechanical specifications: Type page 12 1/2 x 21 1/2; E - 6 cols, 1 7/8, 1/8 between; A - 6 cols, 1 7/8, 1/8 between; C - 6 cols, 1 7/8, 1/8 between.
Published Days: Mon`Tues`Wed`Thur`Fri
Weekday Frequency: e
Saturday Frequency: m
Avg Paid Circ: 3935
Avg Free Circ: 4400
Audit Company: Sworn/Estimate/Non-Audited
Audit Date: 7 12 2019
Pressroom Equipment: Lines – 4-G; Folders – 1-G/2:1.;
Mailroom Equipment: Tying Machines – 1/Sa; Address Machine – 1-/Am.;
Classified Equipment: Hardware – 2-IBM/Typewriter;
Classified Software: Microsoft/Word, QPS/QuarkXPress.
Editorial Software: QPS/QuarkXPress.
Production Equipment: Hardware – 1-Nat/A-250; Cameras – 1-Acti.
Total Circulation: 8335

ARKANSAS CITY

THE CT COURIER TRAVELER

Publication Street Address: 200 E 5th Ave
City: Arkansas City
State: KS
Publication Website: http://www.ctnewsonline.com
Postal Code: 67005-2606
Office phone: (620) 442-4200
General E-mail: digital@ctnewsonline.com
Publisher Name: David Allen Seaton
Publisher Email: daseaton@ctnewsonline.com
Publisher Phone: 620-442-4200 ext. 122
Advertising Executive Name: Arty Hicks
Advertising Executive Email: advertising1@ctnewsonline.com
Advertising Executive Phone: 620-442-4200 ext. 103

CHANUTE

THE CHANUTE TRIBUNE

Publication Street Address: 26 W Main St
City: Chanute
State: KS
Publication Website: www.chanute.com
Postal Code: 66720-1701
Office phone: (620) 431-4100
General E-mail: amy@chanute.com
Publisher Name: Shanna L. Guiot
Publisher Email: shanna@chanute.com
Editor Name: Stu Butcher
Editor Email: stu@chanute.com
Advertising Executive Name: Alissa Meier
Advertising Executive Email: pcook@parsonssun.com
Year Established: 1892
Delivery Methods: Mail`Newsstand`Carrier`Racks
Own Printing Facility?: Y
Commercial printers?: Y
Mechanical specifications: Type page 11 5/8 x 21 1/2; E - 6 cols, 1 5/6, 1/8 between; A - 6 cols, 1 5/6, 1/8 between; C - 8 cols, 1 3/8, 1/16 between.
Published Days: Tues`Wed`Thur`Fri`Sat
Weekday Frequency: m
Saturday Frequency: m
Avg Paid Circ: 4359
Audit Company: Sworn/Estimate/Non-Audited
Audit Date: 7 12 2019
Buisness Equipment: Icanon/Newzware
Classified Equipment: Hardware – AP/Mac
Classified Software: Baseview 4.0.
Editorial Equipment: Hardware – AP/Mac; Printers – Xante
Editorial Software: InDesign
Production Equipment: Hardware – Xante/8200, Xante/G3
Production Software: InDesign
Total Circulation: 4359

CLAY CENTER

THE CLAY CENTER DISPATCH

Publication Street Address: 805 5th St
City: Clay Center
State: KS
Publication Website: www.claycenter.com
Postal Code: 67432-2502
Office phone: (785) 632-2127
General E-mail: circulation@claycenter.com
Year Established: 1871
Delivery Methods: Mail`Newsstand`Carrier
Own Printing Facility?: Y
Commercial printers?: N
Mechanical specifications: Type page 13 x 21; E - 6 cols, 2 1/16, 1/8 between; A - 6 cols, 2 1/16, 1/8 between; C - 6 cols, 2 1/16, 1/8 between.
Published Days: Mon`Tues`Wed`Thur`Fri
Weekday Frequency: e
Avg Paid Circ: 1500
Avg Free Circ: 4700
Audit Company: Sworn/Estimate/Non-Audited
Audit Date: 7 12 2019
Pressroom Equipment: Lines – G/Community; Folders – 1-G/3:1.;
Mailroom Equipment: Address Machine – 1/Ch.;
Buisness Equipment: Epson/386, Acer/486, Nobilis-Pentium
Classified Equipment: Hardware – PC; Printers – HP/LaserJet.;
Editorial Equipment: Hardware – PC; Printers – HP/LaserJet.
Production Equipment: Hardware – HP; Cameras – 1-K/240V.
Total Circulation: 6200

CONCORDIA

CONCORDIA BLADE-EMPIRE

Publication Street Address: 510 Washington St
City: Concordia
State: KS
Publication Website: www.bladeempire.com
Postal Code: 66901-2117
Office phone: (785) 243-2424
Publisher Name: Brad Lowell
Publisher Email: jbrad@nckcn.com
Editor Name: Jim Lowell
Editor Email: bladeempire@nckcn.com
Advertising Executive Name: Dixie Winter
Advertising Executive Email: dixiewinter@nckcn.com
Year Established: 1920
Delivery Methods: Mail`Newsstand`Carrier
Published Days: Mon`Tues`Wed`Thur`Fri
Weekday Frequency: e
Avg Paid Circ: 2357
Audit Company: Sworn/Estimate/Non-Audited
Audit Date: 7 12 2019
Pressroom Equipment: Lines – 4-1968.;
Mailroom Equipment: Tying Machines – Bu.;
Buisness Equipment: RSK/Tandy
Classified Equipment: Hardware – Mk;
Classified Software: Mk/Mycro-Comp AdWriter.
Editorial Equipment: Hardware – Mk
Editorial Software: Mk/Mycro-Comp AdWriter.
Production Equipment: Hardware – 1-Nu; Cameras – DAI.
Total Circulation: 2357

COUNCIL GROVE

COUNCIL GROVE REPUBLICAN

Corporate/Parent Company: Council Grove Publishing Company, Inc.
Publication Street Address: 208 W Main St
City: Council Grove
State: KS
Postal Code: 66846-1705
Office phone: (620) 767-5123
General E-mail: cgnews@cgtelco.net
Year Established: 1872
Delivery Methods: Mail`Newsstand`Carrier
Own Printing Facility?: N
Commercial printers?: N
Mechanical specifications: Type page 15 3/16 x 21 1/2; E - 7 cols, 2 1/12, 1/6 between; A - 7 cols, 2 1/12, 1/6 between; C - 7 cols, 2 1/12, 1/6 between.
Published Days: Mon`Tues`Wed`Thur`Fri
Weekday Frequency: e
Avg Paid Circ: 1400
Audit Company: Sworn/Estimate/Non-Audited
Audit Date: 7 12 2019
Mailroom Equipment: Address Machine – Ap/Mac ImageWriter II;
Classified Equipment: Hardware – 1-APP/Power Mac Performa; Printers – APP/Mac LaserWriter 16/600 PS;
Classified Software: Microsoft/Word 6.0, Aldus/PageMaker 5.0.
Editorial Equipment: Hardware – 3-APP/Mac; Printers – APP/Mac LaserWriter II NT
Editorial Software: Microsoft/Word 3.0.
Production Equipment: Hardware – 1-APP/Mac LaserWriter II NT, APP/Mac LaserWriter 16/600 PS.
Total Circulation: 1400

DODGE CITY

DODGE CITY DAILY GLOBE

Corporate/Parent Company: Gannett
Publication Street Address: 705 N 2nd Ave
City: Dodge City
State: KS
Publication Website: www.dodgeglobe.com
Postal Code: 67801-4410
Office phone: (620) 225-4151
Editor Name: Vincent Marshall
Editor Email: vmarshall@dodgeglobe.com
Editor Phone: 620-225-4151
Advertising Executive Name: Rebecca Gerber
Advertising Executive Email: rgerber@dodgeglobe.com
Advertising Executive Phone: 620-225-4151
Year Established: 1878
Delivery Methods: Mail`Newsstand`Carrier
Mechanical specifications: Type page 11 1/4 x 21 1/2; E - 6 cols, 1 7/8, 1/16 between; A - 6 cols, 1 7/8, 1/16 between; C - 6 cols, 1 7/8, 1/16 between.
Published Days: Tues`Wed`Thur`Fri`Sat
Weekday Frequency: m
Saturday Frequency: m
Avg Paid Circ: 9700
Audit Company: Sworn/Estimate/Non-Audited
Audit Date: 7 12 2019
Pressroom Equipment: Lines – 7-G/Community 1976;
Mailroom Equipment: Address Machine – Ch/705.;
Buisness Equipment: Epson/486, Unix, Wyse/terminals
Buisness Software: SMS/Business Software, Unix
Classified Equipment: Hardware – APP/Mac G3; Printers – APP/Mac LaserWriter NTX;
Classified Software: Baseview.
Editorial Equipment: Hardware – 6-APP/iMac, 3-APP/Mac SE, 4-APP/Mac Classic, 2-APP/Mac Quadra 610, APP/Mac 4400, APP/Mac 7600; Printers – APP/Mac LaserWriter NTX, MON, HP/LaserJet
Editorial Software: Baseview, QPS/QuarkXPress.
Production Equipment: Hardware – APP/Mac LaserWriter NTX, APP/Mac LaserWriter NT, MON, HP/LaserJet 4MV.
Total Circulation: 9700

FORT SCOTT

THE FORT SCOTT TRIBUNE

Corporate/Parent Company: Rust Communications
Publication Street Address: PO Box 150
City: Fort Scott
State: KS
Publication Website: www.fstribune.com
Postal Code: 66701-0150
Office phone: (620) 223-1460
General E-mail: thelm@fstribune.com
Publisher Name: Lorie Harter
Publisher Email: lharter@nevadadailymail.com
Editor Name: Tammy Helm
Editor Email: thelm@fstribune.com
Advertising Executive Name: Andrew LaSota
Advertising Executive Email: alasota@fstribune.com
Year Established: 1884
Delivery Methods: Mail`Carrier`Racks
Own Printing Facility?: Y
Commercial printers?: N
Mechanical specifications: Type page 13 x 21; E - 6 cols, 2 1/16, 1/8 between; A - 6 cols, 2 1/16, 1/8 between; C - 8 cols, 1 1/2, 1/8 between.
Published Days: Tues`Wed`Thur`Fri`Sat
Weekday Frequency: m
Saturday Frequency: m
Avg Paid Circ: 3289
Audit Company: Sworn/Estimate/Non-Audited
Audit Date: 7 12 2019
Mailroom Equipment: Tying Machines – 1-Bu/BT-17; Address Machine – Compudyne/486SX-25.;
Buisness Equipment: 1-Compudyne/386DN-25, 1-Compudyne/486DN
Buisness Software: Listmaster Systems (Omaha, NE)
Classified Equipment: Hardware – APP/Mac; 1-APP/Mac, 1-Radius/Monitor; Printers – APP/Mac LaserWriter II.;
Editorial Equipment: Hardware – APP/Mac; APP/Mac Scanner, 5-APP/Mac, 1-Radius; Printers – APP/Mac LaserWriter II.
Production Equipment: Hardware – B/Ultra-Lite 1500, LE/Line 17; Cameras – 1-Acti.
Total Circulation: 3289

GARDEN CITY

THE GARDEN CITY TELEGRAM

Corporate/Parent Company: Gannett
Publication Street Address: 310 N 7th St
City: Garden City
State: KS
Publication Website: https://www.gctelegram.com/
Postal Code: 67846
Office phone: (800) 475-8600
General E-mail: circulation@gctelegram.com
Publisher Name: Steve Wade
Publisher Email: swade@cjonline.com
Publisher Phone: (785) 295-1115
Advertising Executive Name: DJ Richmeier
Advertising Executive Email: drichmeier@gctelegram.com
Advertising Executive Phone: (620) 276-6862, ext : 210
Year Established: 1906
Delivery Methods: Mail`Newsstand`Carrier`Racks
Own Printing Facility?: Y
Commercial printers?: Y
Mechanical specifications: Type page 13 x 21 1/2; E - 6 cols, 2 1/8, 3/8 between; A - 6 cols, 2 1/8, 3/8 between; C - 8 cols, 1 1/2, 1/16 between.

U.S. Daily Newspapers

Published Days: Mon`Tues`Wed`Thur`Fri`Sat
Weekday Frequency: m
Saturday Frequency: m
Avg Paid Circ: 7432
Audit Company: Sworn/Estimate/Non-Audited
Audit Date: 7 12 2019
Pressroom Equipment: Lines – 8-G/SC 578;
Mailroom Equipment: Tying Machines – 1-Bu/66858, 1-Bu/32133; Address Machine – 1-Am/1900, 1/Ch.;
Buisness Equipment: 3-DEC/PC LPV 433 DX, 6-TI/DSI Digital Venturis
Buisness Software: Microsoft/Office, Microsoft/Windows, Informix/Smart II
Classified Equipment: Hardware – APP/Mac Centris 610s, APP/Mac Quadra 800, 2-COM; Printers – NewGen/1200B Laser Printer;
Classified Software: Multi-Ad/Creator, QPS/QuarkXPress, Baseview.
Editorial Equipment: Hardware – APP/Mac Centris 610, APP/Mac Centris 650, APP/Mac Centris 660, APP/Mac Centris 800, APP/Mac Quadra 610, APP/Mac Quadra 650, APP/Mac Quadra 660, APP/Mac Quadra 800; Printers – NewGen/1200B, ECR/Pelbox VR 36
Editorial Software: Baseview/NewsEdit IQUE, QP
Production Equipment: Hardware – Caere/OmniPage Pro, Adobe/Photoshop, APP/Power Mac 7100; Cameras – 1-R/580
Production Software: QPS/QuarkXPress 3.3.
Total Circulation: 7432

GREAT BEND

GREAT BEND TRIBUNE

Corporate/Parent Company: Morris Multimedia, Inc.
Publication Street Address: 2012 Forest Ave
City: Great Bend
State: KS
Publication Website: www.gbtribune.com
Postal Code: 67530-4014
Office phone: (620) 792-1211
Publisher Name: Mary Hoisington
Publisher Email: mhoisington@gbtribune.com
Publisher Phone: 620-792-1211
Editor Name: Dale Hogg
Editor Email: dhogg@gbtribune.com
Editor Phone: 620-792-1211, ext. 226
Advertising Executive Name: Tammy Mason
Advertising Executive Email: tmason@gbtribune.com
Advertising Executive Phone: 620-792-1211, ext. 209
Year Established: 1876
Delivery Methods: Mail`Newsstand`Carrier`Racks
Own Printing Facility?: Y
Commercial printers?: Y
Mechanical specifications: Type page 10.5 x 21 1/2; E – 6 cols, 2, 1/8 between; A – 6 cols, 1/8 between; C – 8 cols, 1 3/8, 1/8 between.
Published Days: Tues`Wed`Thur`Fri`Sun
Weekday Frequency: m
Avg Paid Circ: 5977
Audit Company: USPS
Audit Date: 30 09 2006
Pressroom Equipment: Lines – 8-G/Community.;
Mailroom Equipment: Counter Stackers – BG/Count-O-Veyor; Tying Machines – 2-Bu/Tyer; Address Machine – KR.;
Buisness Equipment: PC
Buisness Software: MAS 90
Classified Equipment: Hardware – mac Printers – HP;
Classified Software: Fake Brains
Editorial Equipment: Hardware – IBM/PC; Printers – hp
Editorial Software: adobe creative suite
Production Equipment: Hardware – pc/ Pre Press/Ctp; Cameras – 1-Op; Scanners – APP/Mac LC III
Production Software: Adobe Creative Suite
Total Circulation: 5977

HAYS

HAYS POST

Publication Street Address: 2300 Hall
City: Hays
State: KS
Publication Website: hayspost.com
Postal Code: 785-301-2211
Office phone: (785) 301-2211
General E-mail: admin@hayspost.com
Editor Name: Ron Fields
Editor Phone: (785) 301-2211, Ext. 250

THE HAYS DAILY NEWS

Corporate/Parent Company: Gannett
Publication Street Address: 507 Main St
City: Hays
State: KS
Publication Website: https://www.hdnews.net/
Postal Code: 67601
Office phone: (785) 628-1081
General E-mail: circulation@dailynews.net
Publisher Name: Mary Karst
Publisher Email: mkarst@dailynews.net
Publisher Phone: (800) 657-6017, ext : 101
Editor Name: Nick McQueen
Editor Email: nmcqueen@dailynews.net
Editor Phone: (800) 657-6017, ext : 108
Advertising Executive Name: Mary Karst
Advertising Executive Email: mkarst@dailynews.net
Advertising Executive Phone: (800) 657-6017, ext : 101
Year Established: 1929
Delivery Methods: Mail`Newsstand`Carrier`Racks
Own Printing Facility?: Y
Commercial printers?: N
Mechanical specifications: Type page 10.2917 x 21 1/2; E – 6 cols, 1.6111, 1/8 between; A – 6 cols, 1.6111, 1/8 between; C – 8 cols, 1.1892, 3/32 between.
Published Days: Tues`Wed`Thur`Fri`Sun
Weekday Frequency: e
Avg Paid Circ: 6000
Audit Company: Sworn/Estimate/Non-Audited
Audit Date: 7 12 2019
Pressroom Equipment: Lines – 8-G/SC 650 Single width 1974; Folders – 1-G/3:2.;
Mailroom Equipment: Tying Machines – Mc/40 String Tyer, Transpak/A-72 Strapper; Address Machine – Videojet/Excel inkjet printer.;
Buisness Equipment: TI/941
Buisness Software: Microsoft/Office, Newzware
Classified Equipment: Hardware – APP/Mac; Printers – Epson, Epson/LQ 1170;
Classified Software: QPS/QuarkXPress 3.3, FSI/Advance Pro.Indesign 3
Editorial Equipment: Hardware – APP/Mac
Editorial Software: FSI/Edit, QPS/QuarkXPress 3.3.
Production Equipment: Hardware – Caere/OmniPage 5.0, ECR/VR36, Elite XL 20/60; Cameras – 1-R/580; Scanners – 2-Lf/Leafscan 35, Microtek/II HR
Production Software: QPS/QuarkXPress 3.3. Indesign 3
Total Circulation: 6000

HUTCHINSON

THE HUTCHINSON NEWS

Corporate/Parent Company: Gannett
Publication Street Address: 300 W 2nd Ave
City: Hutchinson
State: KS
Publication Website: www.hutchnews.com
Postal Code: 67501-5211
Office phone: (620) 694-5700
General E-mail: newsclerk@hutchnews.com
Publisher Name: Stephen Wade
Publisher Email: swade@gatehousemedia.com
Publisher Phone: 785-295-1115
Editor Name: Cheyenne Derksen Schroeder
Editor Email: cderksen@hutchnews.com
Editor Phone: 620-694-5700 ext. 326
Advertising Executive Name: Krista Barnes
Advertising Executive Email: kbarnes@hutchnews.com
Advertising Executive Phone: 620-694-5700 ext. 212
Year Established: 1872
Delivery Methods: Mail`Newsstand`Carrier`Racks
Own Printing Facility?: Y
Commercial printers?: Y
Mechanical specifications: Type page 11 3/4 x 21 1/2; E – 6 cols, 1 4/5, 1/7 between; A – 6 cols, 1 4/5, 1/7 between; C – 9 cols, 1 1/5, 1/7 between.
Published Days: Mon`Tues`Wed`Thur`Fri`Sat`Sun
Weekday Frequency: m
Saturday Frequency: m
Avg Paid Circ: 17605
Audit Company: VAC
Audit Date: 9/31/2015
Pressroom Equipment: Lines – 8-G/1018-4-72; Press Drive – 2, 2-150 HP/Electic Motors; Folders – 1-G/1018 Folder w/upper Former; Reels & Stands – 8;
Mailroom Equipment: Counter Stackers – HL/DC, HL/Monitor; Inserters & Stuffers – 1-MM/227E, GMA/SLS 1000A; Tying Machines – 1-Sterling/MR45CH, 2-MLN/2EE; Address Machine – 1-KR/221 227.;
Buisness Equipment: 1-Dell/Poweredge 2500
Buisness Software: Microsoft/Office XP Pro, Newzware
Classified Equipment: Hardware – Dell/Pentium Server NT 4.0; Printers – HP/Laserjet 4v;
Classified Software: APT/ACT 3.05.
Editorial Equipment: Hardware – Dell/Pentium Server NT 40, 30-PC; Printers – HP/Laserjet 8000N 1999
Editorial Software: TownNews Blox
Production Equipment: Hardware – 1-Nu/FT40UPNS, Adobe/Photoshop, 2-3850 Sierra Imager, III/3850 15 Imager, HP/Laserjet 8000N
Production Software: TownNews Blox, InDesign
Total Circulation: 17605

INDEPENDENCE

INDEPENDENCE DAILY REPORTER

Publication Street Address: 320 N 6th St
City: Independence
State: KS
Publication Website: www.indydailyreporter.com
Postal Code: 67301-3129
Office phone: (620) 331-3550
Publisher Name: Josh Umholtz
Publisher Email: josh.umholtz@indydailyreporter.com
Editor Name: Taina Copeland
Editor Email: taina@indydailyreporter.com
Advertising Executive Name: Alana Justice
Advertising Executive Email: alana.g.justice@gmail.com
Delivery Methods: Mail`Newsstand
Own Printing Facility?: N
Commercial printers?: N
Mechanical specifications: Type page 13 x 21; E – 6 cols, 2 1/16, 1/8 between; A – 6 cols, 2 1/16, 1/8 between; C – 6 cols, 2 1/16, 1/8 between.
Published Days: Tues`Wed`Thur`Fri
Weekday Frequency: e
Avg Paid Circ: 6654
Audit Company: Sworn/Estimate/Non-Audited
Audit Date: 7 12 2019
Pressroom Equipment: Lines – 6-G/SC 1973.;
Mailroom Equipment: Tying Machines – 1-Malow/51; Wrapping Singles – 2-St/51OW.;
Buisness Equipment: 5-Unix/U5000-30C
Buisness Software: Unix, R&D Systems
Classified Equipment: Hardware – Mk/1100, 3-APP/Mac Quadra 630;
Classified Software: Mk/1100, FSI/Vanguard System.
Editorial Equipment: Hardware – Mk/1100, 7-APP/Mac Quadra 630
Editorial Software: Mk/1100, FSI/Vanguard System.
Production Equipment: Hardware – 2-APP/Mac LaserWriter II; Cameras – 1-Acti/183.
Total Circulation: 6654

IOLA

THE IOLA REGISTER

Corporate/Parent Company: Kansas Press Association
Publication Street Address: 302 S Washington Ave
City: Iola
State: KS
Publication Website: www.iolaregister.com
Postal Code: 66749-3255
Office phone: (620) 365-2111
Publisher Name: Susan Lynn
Publisher Email: editorial@iolaregister.com
Editor Name: Bob Johnson
Editor Email: bobjohnsonregister@yahoo.com
Advertising Executive Name: Whitney Ikehorn
Advertising Executive Email: advertise@iolaregister.com
Year Established: 1897
Delivery Methods: Mail`Newsstand`Racks
Own Printing Facility?: Y
Commercial printers?: Y
Mechanical specifications: Type page 13 x 21 1/2; E – 6 cols, 2 1/16, 3/16 between; A – 6 cols, 2 1/16, 3/16 between; C – 8 cols, 2 1/16, 3/16 between.
Published Days: Mon`Tues`Wed`Thur`Sat
Weekday Frequency: e
Saturday Frequency: m
Avg Paid Circ: 3750
Audit Company: Sworn/Estimate/Non-Audited
Audit Date: 7 12 2019
Pressroom Equipment: Lines – HI/Cotrell V-15A; Control System – 1972;
Buisness Equipment: 3-SAMTRON/SM-460
Buisness Software: Microsoft/Windows 95, Pachioli/Works
Editorial Equipment: Hardware – APP/Mac 7600, APP/Mac 9600, APP/Mac G3, APP/Mac G4; Printers – Xante, HP/4000
Editorial Software: Baseview, QPS, QuarkXPress, Microsoft/Word.
Production Equipment: Hardware – LE/LD18; Cameras – Acti/183.
Total Circulation: 3750

JUNCTION CITY

JUNCTION CITY DAILY UNION

Publication Street Address: 222 W Sixth Street
City: Junction City
State: KS
Publication Website: www.junctioncityunion.com
Postal Code: 66441
Office phone: 785-762-5000
General E-mail: info@jcdailyunion.com
Publisher Name: Ned Seaton
Editor Name: Lydia Kautz
Editor Phone: 316.323.6894

THE DAILY UNION

Corporate/Parent Company: Seaton Publishing Company Inc.
Publication Street Address: 222 W 6th St
City: Junction City
State: KS
Publication Website: www.yourdu.net
Postal Code: 66441-5500
Office phone: (785) 762-5000
General E-mail: info@jcdailyunion.com
Publisher Name: Ned Seaton
Editor Name: Lydia Kautz
Editor Phone: (785) 762-5000 ext. 112
Year Established: 1861
Delivery Methods: Mail`Newsstand`Racks
Own Printing Facility?: Y
Commercial printers?: Y
Mechanical specifications: Type page 13 x 21 1/2; E – 6 cols, 2 1/16, 1/8 between; A – 6 cols, 2 1/16, 1/8 between; C – 6 cols, 2 1/16, 1/8 between.
Published Days: Tues`Wed`Thur`Fri`Sat

Weekday Frequency: m
Saturday Frequency: m
Avg Paid Circ: 3092
Audit Company: Sworn/Estimate/Non-Audited
Audit Date: 7 12 2019
Pressroom Equipment: Lines – 6-G/Community; Folders – 1-G/Suburban.;
Mailroom Equipment: Tying Machines – 1/Bu, 2-Malow/MC Straptyer.;
Buisness Equipment: 6-APP/iMac G3, 1-Power Computing/180, 1-Power Computing/150
Buisness Software: Baseview
Classified Equipment: Hardware – 1-Power Computing/180, APP/iMac G3; Printers – 2-Tally/T-6050;
Classified Software: Baseview.
Editorial Equipment: Hardware – 14-Power Computing/180, 3-Power Computing/225, 1-APP/iMac G3
Editorial Software: Baseview.
Production Equipment: Hardware – 1-Nu, 1-QMS/2060 LaserWriter, 1-Pre Press/Panther Pro 46 Imagesetter; Cameras – 1-Acti; Scanners – 4-Microtek/Scanner, 1-Poloroid/Sprint Scan 35
Production Software: Baseview.
Total Circulation: 3092

LAWRENCE

LAWRENCE JOURNAL-WORLD

Corporate/Parent Company: Ogden Newspapers, Inc.
Publication Street Address: 1035 N. Third Street, Suite 101-B
City: Lawrence
State: KS
Publication Website: www.ljworld.com
Postal Code: 66044
Office phone: (785) 843-1000
General E-mail: subs@ljworld.com
Publisher Name: Chad Lawhorn
Publisher Email: clawhorn@ljworld.com
Publisher Phone: 785-832-6362
Editor Name: Chad Lawhorn
Editor Email: clawhorn@ljworld.com
Editor Phone: 785-832-6362
Advertising Executive Name: Kathleen Johnson
Advertising Executive Email: kjohnson@ljworld.com
Advertising Executive Phone: 785-832-7223
Year Established: 1891
Delivery Methods:
 Mail`Newsstand`Carrier`Racks
Own Printing Facility?: N
Commercial printers?: N
Mechanical specifications: Type page 10.25" x 20.833"; E – 6 cols, 1.6042, 1/8 between; A – 6 cols, 1.6042, 1/8 between; C – 8 cols, 1.222, .07" between.
Published Days: Mon`Tues`Wed`Thur`Fri`Sat`Sun
Weekday Frequency: m
Saturday Frequency: m
Avg Paid Circ: 8751
Avg Free Circ: 1807
Audit Company: AAM
Audit Date: 13 02 2019
Pressroom Equipment: Lines – Goss Urbanite, 18 units; Goss Urbanite 12 units; Press Drive – Fincor; Folders – Goss; Pasters – Enkel Autoweb
Mailroom Equipment: Counter Stackers – Quipp; Inserters & Stuffers – Muller 227, 308, and GMA SLS100A; Tying Machines – Signode, Dynaric and Oval; Address Machine – Cheshire;
Buisness Equipment: Dell, HP, IBM
Buisness Software: Great Plains
Classified Equipment: Hardware – Dell, HP, IBM;
Classified Software: Advanced Publishing Technology
Editorial Equipment: Hardware – MAC; Printers – HP 1050C
Editorial Software: Baseview/NewsEdit.
Production Equipment: Hardware – alfaQuest CTP, two lines; Cameras – 1-B
Production Software: alphaQuest Print Xpress
Total Circulation: 10841

LEAVENWORTH

THE LEAVENWORTH TIMES

Corporate/Parent Company: Gannett
Publication Street Address: 422 Seneca St
City: Leavenworth
State: KS
Publication Website: www.leavenworthtimes.com
Postal Code: 66048-1910
Office phone: (913) 682-0305
Editor Name: Mark Rountree
Editor Email: mrountree@leavenworthtimes.com
Advertising Executive Name: Sandy Hattock
Advertising Executive Email: shattock@leavenworthtimes.com
Year Established: 1857
Delivery Methods:
 Mail`Newsstand`Carrier`Racks
Own Printing Facility?: Y
Commercial printers?: N
Mechanical specifications: Type page 11 x 21 1/2; E – 6 cols, 1 13/16, 1/8 between; A – 6 cols, 1 13/16, 1/8 between; C – 9 cols, 1 3/16, 1/8 between.
Published Days: Tues`Wed`Thur`Fri`Sat
Weekday Frequency: m
Saturday Frequency: m
Avg Paid Circ: 4020
Audit Company: Sworn/Estimate/Non-Audited
Audit Date: 7 12 2019
Buisness Equipment: PC
Buisness Software: Nomads/ListMaster
Classified Equipment: Hardware – APP/iMac; Printers – APP/Mac 12-640;
Classified Software: CAMS.
Editorial Equipment: Hardware – APP/Mac/Pre Press/Panther Pro 36; Printers – HP/LaserJet 4MV
Editorial Software: Baseview.
Production Equipment: Hardware – Caere/OmniPage 7.0, 1-COM/8400, 2-APP/Mac; Cameras – 1-Nu
Production Software: QPS/QuarkXPress 4.1.
Note: Printing and mailroom outsourced
Total Circulation: 4020

LIBERAL

LIBERALFIRST

Corporate/Parent Company: Liberal Leader & Times
Publication Street Address: 16 S Kansas Ave
City: Liberal
State: KS
Publication Website: http://www.liberalfirst.com
Postal Code: 67901-3732
Office phone: (620) 626-0840
General E-mail: earl@liberalfirst.com
Publisher Name: Earl Watt
Publisher Email: earl@liberalfirst.com
Publisher Phone: 620-626-0840

MCPHERSON

MCPHERSON SENTINEL

Corporate/Parent Company: Gannett
Publication Street Address: 116 S Main St
City: McPherson
State: KS
Publication Website: www.mcphersonsentinel.com
Postal Code: 67460-4852
Office phone: (620) 241-2422
Editor Name: Chad Frey
Editor Email: news@mcphersonsentinel.com
Editor Phone: (316) 804-7728
Year Established: 1887
Delivery Methods:
 Mail`Newsstand`Carrier`Racks
Own Printing Facility?: N
Commercial printers?: Y
Mechanical specifications: Type page 11 x 21 1/2; E – 6 cols, 1 3/4, 1/6 between; A – 6 cols, 1 3/4, 1/6 between; C – 6 cols, 1 3/4, 1/6 between.
Published Days: Tues`Wed`Thur`Fri`Sat
Weekday Frequency: e
Saturday Frequency: m
Avg Paid Circ: 3600
Audit Company: Sworn/Estimate/Non-Audited
Audit Date: 7 12 2019
Pressroom Equipment: Lines – 5-G/Community 1974; 1-G/Community 1995.;
Mailroom Equipment: Tying Machines – 1/Marlo, Miller-Bevco/Strapper.;
Classified Equipment: Hardware – APP/Mac; Printers – APP/Mac LaserWriter II;
Classified Software: Baseview.
Editorial Equipment: Hardware – APP/Mac/Umax/S-6E Flatbed Scanner, Polaroid/Sprint Scan 35; Printers – Xante/Accel-A-Writer 3G
Editorial Software: Adobe/Photoshop 3.0, QPS/QuarkXPress 7.53, Baseview.
Production Equipment: Hardware – Nu/Flip Top FT4OUPNS; Cameras – Acti.
Total Circulation: 3600

NEWTON

THE NEWTON KANSAN

Corporate/Parent Company: Gannett
Publication Street Address: 121 W 6th St
City: Newton
State: KS
Publication Website: www.thekansan.com
Postal Code: 67114-2117
Office phone: (316) 283-1500
Publisher Name: Stephen Wade
Publisher Email: swade@gatehousemedia.com
Publisher Phone: (785) 295-1115
Editor Name: Chad Frey
Editor Email: cfrey@thekansan.com
Editor Phone: (316) 283-1500 x105
Advertising Executive Name: Debra Jacobsen
Advertising Executive Email: djacobsen@thekansan.com
Advertising Executive Phone: (316) 283-1500 x101
Year Established: 1872
Delivery Methods: Mail`Carrier`Racks
Mechanical specifications: Type page 13 x 21 1/2; E – 6 cols, 2 1/2, 1/6 between; A – 6 cols, 2 1/2, 1/6 between; C – 6 cols, 2 1/2, 1/6 between.
Published Days: Mon`Tues`Wed`Thur`Fri`Sat`Sun
Weekday Frequency: e
Saturday Frequency: m
Avg Paid Circ: 7513
Audit Company: Sworn/Estimate/Non-Audited
Audit Date: 7 12 2019
Pressroom Equipment: Lines – 7-G/Single Width 1972; Folders – 1-G/SC.;
Mailroom Equipment: Tying Machines – 2/Bu; Address Machine – 1-/Ch.;
Buisness Equipment: Gateway
Buisness Software: PBS
Classified Equipment: Hardware – 1-APP/iMac 333; Printers – APP/Mac Imagewriter, APP/Mac LaserWriter 16-600 PS;
Classified Software: QPS/QuarkXPress, Baseview/Classified, Adobe/Photoshop 5.0, Adobe/Acrobat 5.0.
Editorial Equipment: Hardware – 1-APP/iMac G3, APP/Mac G4, 2-APP/Mac Power PC 4400-200, 4-APP/Mac Power PC 7300-80/2-APP/Mac Quadra 650, Nikon/Film Scanner, Nikon/Scantouch Flatbed; Printers – MON/Imagesetter
Editorial Software: Adobe/Photoshop 5.5, QPS/QuarkXPress 3.32,
Production Equipment: Hardware – OmniPage, APP/Mac G3, APP/Mac G4; Cameras – DAI/DS; Scanners – Umax/Astra 4000LS, Nikon/Color Film Scanner, Nikon/Scantouch Flatbed
Production Software: QPS/QuarkXPress 4.1.
Total Circulation: 7513

PARSONS

PARSONS SUN

Corporate/Parent Company: Kansas Newspapers L.L.C
Publication Street Address: 220 S 18th St
City: Parsons
State: KS
Publication Website: www.parsonssun.com
Postal Code: 67357-4218
Office phone: (620) 421-2000
General E-mail: news@parsonssun.com
Publisher Name: Shanna Guiot
Publisher Email: shanna@chanute.com
Editor Name: Ray Nolting
Editor Email: rnolting@parsonssun.com
Advertising Executive Name: Alissa Meier
Advertising Executive Email: ameier@parsonssun.com
Year Established: 1871
Delivery Methods: Mail`Carrier`Racks
Mechanical specifications: Type page 13 x 21; E – 6 cols, 2 1/16, 1/8 between; A – 6 cols, 2 1/16, 1/8 between; C – 6 cols, 2 1/16, 1/8 between.
Published Days: Mon`Tues`Wed`Thur`Fri`Sat`Sun
Weekday Frequency: e
Saturday Frequency: m
Avg Paid Circ: 5420
Audit Company: Sworn/Estimate/Non-Audited
Audit Date: 7 12 2019
Pressroom Equipment: Lines – 7-G; Folders – 1-G/2:1.;
Mailroom Equipment: Tying Machines – 2/Bu.;
Buisness Equipment: DSI/PaperTrak
Buisness Software: Microsoft/Excel, Microsoft/Word
Classified Equipment: Hardware – APP/Mac; Printers – Okidata, Xante/3G, Xante/8200;
Classified Software: Baseview.
Editorial Equipment: Hardware – APP/Mac; Printers – Xante/3G, Xante/8200
Editorial Software: Aldus/FreeHand, QPS, Multi-Ad/Creator, Baseview, Adobe/Photoshop, QPS/QuarkXPress.
Production Equipment: Hardware – Nu, NuArc Nu; Cameras – 1-Acti; Scanners – APP/Mac One, APP/Mac, Umax/UC1260
Production Software: Baseview 2.05.
Total Circulation: 5420

PITTSBURG

PITTSBURG MORNING SUN

Publication Street Address: 701 N. Locust St
City: Pittsburg
State: KS
Publication Website: www.morningsun.net
Postal Code: 66762
Office phone: 620-231-2600
Publisher Name: Joe Leong
Publisher Email: jleong@gatehousemedia.com
Publisher Phone: 620-231-2600 ext 140

THE MORNING SUN

Corporate/Parent Company: Gannett
Publication Street Address: 701 N Locust St
City: Pittsburg
State: KS
Publication Website: www.morningsun.net
Postal Code: 66762-4038
Office phone: (620) 231-2600
Publisher Name: Joe Leong
Publisher Email: jleong@gatehousemedia.com
Publisher Phone: 620-231-2600 ext 140
Editor Name: Patrick Richardson
Editor Email: prichardson@morningsun.net
Editor Phone: 620-231-2600 ext. 140
Advertising Executive Name: Michelle Bradley
Advertising Executive Email: mbradley@morningsun.net
Advertising Executive Phone: 620-231-2600 ext. 108
Year Established: 1887
Delivery Methods:
 Mail`Newsstand`Carrier`Racks
Own Printing Facility?: Y
Commercial printers?: Y
Mechanical specifications: Type page 10 x 21 1/2; E – 6 cols, 1.55", .1389" between; A – 6 cols, 1.55, .1389 between; C – 6 cols, 1.12, 1/8 between.
Published Days: Tues`Wed`Thur`Fri`Sat`Sun
Weekday Frequency: m
Saturday Frequency: m
Avg Paid Circ: 5500

U.S. Daily Newspapers

I-47

Audit Company: Sworn/Estimate/Non-Audited
Audit Date: 7 12 2019
Pressroom Equipment: Lines – 5-G/Urbanite; Folders – 1-G/2:1.;
Mailroom Equipment: Tying Machines – 1-MLN/ML2EE; Address Machine – 1/Ch;
Buisness Equipment: MSSI
Classified Equipment: Hardware – MediaSpan Ad Pro;
Editorial Equipment: Hardware – Mac
Editorial Software: CS 3
Production Equipment: Hardware – 1-B/500-255; Cameras – 1-B/Commodore 241305.
Total Circulation: 5500

PRAIRIE VILLAGE

SHAWNEE MISSION POST

Corporate/Parent Company: Post Publishing Inc
Publication Street Address: 4121 West 74th Street
City: Prairie Village
State: KS
Publication Website: www.shawneemissionpost.com
Postal Code: 66208
Office phone: 913-626-6273
Editor Name: Jay Senter
Editor Email: jsenter@shawneemissionpost.com

PRATT

PRATT TRIBUNE

Corporate/Parent Company: Gannett
Publication Street Address: 320 S. Main, (P.O. Box 909)
City: Pratt
State: KS
Publication Website: www.pratttribune.com
Postal Code: 67124
Office phone: (620) 672-5511
Publisher Name: Stephen Wade
Publisher Email: stephen.wade@cjonline.com
Publisher Phone: (785) 295-1115
Editor Name: Jennifer Stultz
Editor Email: jstultz@pratttribune.com
Year Established: 1917
Delivery Methods: Mail`Newsstand`Carrier
Mechanical specifications: Type page 13 3/4 x 21 1/2; E - 6 cols, 2 1/16, 1/8 between; A - 6 cols, 2 1/16, 1/8 between; C - 8 cols, 2 1/16, 1/8 between.
Published Days: Tues`Thur`Sat
Weekday Frequency: e
Avg Paid Circ: 2000
Audit Company: Sworn/Estimate/Non-Audited
Audit Date: 6 10 2019
Pressroom Equipment: Lines – 4-G/Community.;
Mailroom Equipment: Tying Machines – 1/Bu; Address Machine – 1-/Am.;
Buisness Equipment: 1-Bs
Classified Equipment: Hardware – 1-Mk.;
Editorial Equipment: Hardware – 6-Mk.
Production Equipment: Hardware – 3-COM; Cameras – 1-R.
Total Circulation: 2000

SALINA

THE SALINA JOURNAL

Corporate/Parent Company: Gannett
Publication Street Address: 333 S 4th St
City: Salina
State: KS
Publication Website: https://www.salina.com
Postal Code: 67401
Office phone: (785) 823-6363
General E-mail: news@salina.com
Advertising Executive Name: Dave Gilchrist
Advertising Executive Email: dgilchrist@salina.com
Advertising Executive Phone: (785) 822-1442
Year Established: 1871
Delivery Methods: Mail`Newsstand`Carrier`Racks
Own Printing Facility?: Y
Commercial printers?: Y
Mechanical specifications: Type page 12 x 21 1/2; E - 6 cols, 1 7/8, 1/8 between; A - 6 cols, 1 7/8, 1/8 between; C - 9 cols, 1 1/4, 1/16 between.
Published Days: Mon`Tues`Wed`Thur`Fri`Sat`Sun
Weekday Frequency: m
Saturday Frequency: m
Avg Paid Circ: 18365
Audit Company: VAC
Audit Date: 31 12 2016
Pressroom Equipment: Lines – 3-G/Urbanite (color), 5-G/Urbanite (black); Folders – 1-G/2:1; Reels & Stands – 6, 2-G/Stands, 2-G/Rolls.;
Mailroom Equipment: Counter Stackers – QWI; Inserters & Stuffers – HI/1472-13 head; Tying Machines – MLN; Wrapping Singles – MLN; Address Machine – MM.;
Buisness Equipment: Data Sciences, HP
Buisness Software: PaperTrack
Classified Equipment: Hardware – APP/Mac Servers IP; Printers – Okidata/393, HP/DeskJet;
Classified Software: Baseview.
Editorial Equipment: Hardware – 12-APP/Mac G4, 3-Pentium/File Server, 3-Microsoft/Windows NT, 16-APP/iMac; Printers – HP/4MV, APP, APP/Mac 12/640 PS
Editorial Software: Citrix, 3-LiveWire.
Production Equipment: Hardware – 2-XIT, 1-Nu/Flip Top FT40APRNS; Scanners – 2-AG/Arcus Scanner
Total Circulation: 18365

TOPEKA

THE TOPEKA CAPITAL-JOURNAL

Corporate/Parent Company: Gannett
Publication Street Address: 100 S.E. 9th St., Suite 500
City: Topeka
State: KS
Publication Website: www.cjonline.com
Postal Code: 66612-1213
Office phone: (785) 295-1111
Publisher Name: Stephen Wade
Publisher Email: stephen.wade@cjonline.com
Publisher Phone: (785) 295-1115
Editor Name: Tomari Quinn
Editor Email: tomari.quinn@cjonline.com
Editor Phone: (785) 295-1212
Advertising Executive Name: Terri Benson
Advertising Executive Email: terri.benson@cjonline.com
Advertising Executive Phone: (785) 295-1175
Year Established: 1858
Delivery Methods: Mail`Newsstand`Carrier`Racks
Own Printing Facility?: N
Commercial printers?: N
Mechanical specifications: Type page 11 5/8 x 22 3/4; E - 6 cols, 2 1/16, 1/8 between; A - 6 cols, 2 1/16, 1/8 between; C - 10 cols, 1 1/16, 3/32 between.
Published Days: Mon`Tues`Wed`Thur`Fri`Sat`Sun
Weekday Frequency: m
Saturday Frequency: m
Avg Paid Circ: 20273
Avg Free Circ: 3595
Audit Company: AAM
Audit Date: 30 06 2017
Buisness Equipment: 1-IBM/RS 6000
Buisness Software: Unix, Claris Financials
Classified Equipment: Hardware – APP/Mac
Classified Software: Ad Speed
Editorial Equipment: Hardware – APP/Mac; Printers – HP
Editorial Software: Adobe/Photoshop, DTI 4.3.
Production Equipment: Hardware – 2-Nu/Flip Top; Scanners – HP/ScanJet IIcx
Production Software: QPS/QuarkXPress 3.3, DT.
Total Circulation: 23868

WICHITA

THE WICHITA EAGLE

Corporate/Parent Company: McClatchy Company
Publication Street Address: 825 E Douglas Ave
City: Wichita
State: KS
Publication Website: www.kansas.com
Postal Code: 67202-3512
Office phone: (316) 268-6000
Editor Name: Michael Roehrman
Editor Email: MRoehrman@wichitaeagle.com
Editor Phone: 316-269-6753
Year Established: 1872
Delivery Methods: Newsstand`Carrier`Racks
Own Printing Facility?: Y
Commercial printers?: Y
Mechanical specifications: Type page 12 x 21; E - 6 cols, 1 3/16, 1/6 between; A - 6 cols, 1 3/16, 1/6 between; C - 10 cols, 1 1/8, 1/12 between.
Published Days: Mon`Tues`Wed`Thur`Fri`Sat`Sun
Weekday Frequency: m
Saturday Frequency: m
Avg Paid Circ: 38968
Audit Company: AAM
Audit Date: 8 02 2019
Pressroom Equipment: Lines – 10-KBA/Colormax II 2002;
Mailroom Equipment: Counter Stackers – 4-QWI/300, 2-QWI/350, 3-QWI/400; Inserters & Stuffers – 3-S/72P; Tying Machines – 6-Dynaric/NP-2; Wrapping Singles – 2-OVL/415; Address Machine – 1/KAN;
Buisness Equipment: HP/3000-KS/969
Buisness Software: CIS 3.02:Payroll, CIS 6.05.A, GEAC/Payroll 3.02C, Mediastream/CIS 6.05B
Classified Equipment: Hardware – HP/Desktop PCs, Sun/Servers; Edgil/EdgCapture Credit Card Authorization Server; Printers – HP/LaserJet;
Classified Software: AT/Enterprise.
Editorial Equipment: Hardware – HP/Desktop PCs, MS/Windows NT/Lf/AP Leaf Picture Desk; Printers – HP/LaserJet
Editorial Software: Dewar/View.
Production Equipment: Hardware – 2-III/3850, Adobe/Photoshop 4.0; Cameras – 1-C/Marathon; Scanners – ECRM, Arcus II, Agfa/Duoscan
Production Software: Ad Manager.
Total Circulation: 57381

WICHITA EAGLE

Corporate/Parent Company: McClatchy Company
Publication Street Address: 330 N. Mead St.
City: Wichita
State: KS
Publication Website: www.kansas.com
Postal Code: 67202
Office phone: (316) 268-6000
Editor Name: Michael Roehrman
Editor Email: MRoehrman@wichitaeagle.com
Year Established: 1872
Delivery Methods: Newsstand`Carrier`Racks
Own Printing Facility?: Y
Commercial printers?: Y
Mechanical specifications: Type page 12 x 21; E - 6 cols, 1 3/16, 1/6 between; A - 6 cols, 1 3/16, 1/6 between; C - 10 cols, 1 1/8, 1/12 between.
Published Days: Mon`Tues`Wed`Thur`Fri`Sat`Sun
Weekday Frequency: m
Saturday Frequency: m
Avg Paid Circ: 38968
Audit Company: AAM
Audit Date: 8 02 2019
Pressroom Equipment: Lines – 10-KBA/Colormax II 2002;
Mailroom Equipment: Counter Stackers – 4-QWI/300, 2-QWI/350, 3-QWI/400; Inserters & Stuffers – 3-S/72P; Tying Machines – 6-Dynaric/NP-2; Wrapping Singles – 2-OVL/415; Address Machine – 1/KAN;
Buisness Equipment: HP/3000-KS/969
Buisness Software: CIS 3.02:Payroll, CIS 6.05.A, GEAC/Payroll 3.02C, Mediastream/CIS 6.05B
Classified Equipment: Hardware – HP/Desktop PCs, Sun/Servers; Edgil/EdgCapture Credit Card Authorization Server; Printers – HP/LaserJet;
Classified Software: AT/Enterprise.
Editorial Equipment: Hardware – HP/Desktop PCs, MS/Windows NT/Lf/AP Leaf Picture Desk; Printers – HP/LaserJet
Editorial Software: Dewar/View.
Production Equipment: Hardware – 2-III/3850, Adobe/Photoshop 4.0; Cameras – 1-C/Marathon; Scanners – ECRM, Arcus II, Agfa/Duoscan
Production Software: Ad Manager.
Total Circulation: 57381

KENTUCKY

ASHLAND

THE DAILY INDEPENDENT

Corporate/Parent Company: Gannett
City: Ashland
State: KY
Publication Website: www.dailyindependent.com
Postal Code: (606) 326-2600
Office phone: 41101
Publisher Name: webmaster@dailyindependent.com
Publisher Email: PATRICIA BENNETT
Publisher Phone: pbennett@dailyindependent.com
Editor Name: (606) 326-2601
Editor Email: AARON SNYDER
Editor Phone: asnyder@dailyindependent.com
Advertising Executive Name: (606)326-2664
Advertising Executive Email: KIM HARPER
Advertising Executive Phone: kharper@dailyindependent.com
Year Established: (606) 326-2622
Own Printing Facility?: 1896
Commercial printers?:
Mail`Newsstand`Carrier`Racks
Mechanical specifications: Y
Published Days: N
Published Other: Type page 13 x 21; E - 6 cols, 2 1/16, 1/8 between; A - 6 cols, 2 1/16, 1/8 between; C - 8 cols, 1 9/16, 1/16 between.
Weekday Frequency:
Mon`Tues`Wed`Thur`Fri`Sat`Sun
Avg Paid Circ: m
Avg Free Circ: m
Audit Company: 8342
Audit Date: AAM
Pressroom Software: 31 12 2017

BENTON

MARSHALL COUNTY DAILY

Publication Street Address: 1039 Eggners Ferry Rd
City: Benton
State: KY
Publication Website: www.marshallcountydaily.com
Postal Code: 42025
Office phone: 270-527-3102
General E-mail: news@marshallcountydaily.com

BOWLING GREEN

DAILY NEWS

Corporate/Parent Company: Gannett
Publication Street Address: 813 College St
City: Bowling Green
State: KY
Publication Website: www.bgdailynews.com
Postal Code: 42101-2132
Office phone: (270) 781-1700
General E-mail: webeditor@bgdailynews.com
Publisher Name: Pipes Gaines
Publisher Phone: 270-781-1700
Editor Name: Steve Gaines
Editor Email: sgaines@bgdailynews.com
Editor Phone: 270-781-1700
Year Established: 1854

CORBIN

TIMES-TRIBUNE

Corporate/Parent Company: CNHI, LLC
Publication Street Address: 201 N Kentucky Ave
City: Corbin
State: KY
Publication Website: www.thetimestribune.com
Postal Code: 40701-1529
Office phone: (606) 528-2464
General E-mail: newsroom@thetimestribune.com
Editor Name: Erin Cox
Editor Email: ecox@thetimestribune.com
Editor Phone: Ext. 37
Advertising Executive Name: Lisa Harrison
Advertising Executive Email: lharrison@thetimestribune.com
Advertising Executive Phone: Ext. 41
Year Established: 1882
Delivery Methods: Mail
Mechanical specifications: Type page 13 x 21 1/2; E - 6 cols, 2 1/16, 1/8 between; A - 6 cols, 2 1/16, 1/8 between; C - 9 cols, 1 3/8, 1/8 between.
Published Days: Mon`Tues`Wed`Thur`Fri`Sat
Weekday Frequency: e
Saturday Frequency: m
Avg Paid Circ: 6166
Audit Company: Sworn/Estimate/Non-Audited
Audit Date: 7 12 2019

DANVILLE

THE ADVOCATE-MESSENGER

Corporate/Parent Company: Boone Newspapers
Publication Street Address: 330 S 4th St
City: Danville
State: KY
Publication Website: www.amnews.com
Postal Code: 40422-2033
Office phone: (859) 236-2551
General E-mail: advocate@amnews.com
Publisher Name: Mike Caldwell
Publisher Email: mike.caldwell@winchestersun.com
Publisher Phone: 859-759-0095
Editor Name: Ben Kleppinger
Editor Email: ben.kleppinger@amnews.com
Editor Phone: 859-469-6413
Advertising Executive Name: Carrie Shields
Advertising Executive Email: carrie.shields@amnews.com
Advertising Executive Phone: 859-469-6427
Year Established: 1940
Delivery Methods: Carrier
Mechanical specifications: Type page 13 3/4 x 21 1/2; E - 6 cols, 2 1/16, 1/8 between; A - 6 cols, 2 1/16, 1/8 between; C - 9 cols, 1 3/8, 1/16 between.
Published Days: Mon`Tues`Wed`Thur`Fri`Sun
Weekday Frequency: m
Avg Paid Circ: 8214
Audit Company: Sworn/Estimate/Non-Audited
Audit Date: 7 12 2019

ELIZABETHTOWN

THE NEWS-ENTERPRISE

Corporate/Parent Company: Landmark Community Newspapers
Publication Street Address: 408 W Dixie Ave
City: Elizabethtown
State: KY
Publication Website: www.thenewsenterprise.com
Postal Code: 42701-2455
Office phone: (270) 769-1200
General E-mail: ne@thenewsenterprise.com
Publisher Name: Chris Ordway
Publisher Email: cordway@thenewsenterprise.com
Publisher Phone: 270-505-1466
Editor Name: Ben Sheroan
Editor Email: bsheroan@thenewsenterprise.com
Editor Phone: 270-505-1764
Advertising Executive Name: Erin Hahn
Advertising Executive Email: ehahn@thenewsenterprise.com
Advertising Executive Phone: 270-505-1409
Year Established: 1974
Delivery Methods: Newsstand`Carrier`Racks
Own Printing Facility?: Y
Commercial printers?: Y
Mechanical specifications: Type page 11 5/8 x 21 1/2; E - 6 cols, 1 5/6, 1/8 between; A - 6 cols, 1 5/6, 1/8 between; C - 8 cols, 1 1/2, 1/8 between.
Published Days: Mon`Tues`Wed`Thur`Fri`Sun
Weekday Frequency: m
Avg Paid Circ: 8368
Avg Free Circ: 432
Audit Company: AAM
Audit Date: 9/31/2018

FRANKFORT

THE STATE JOURNAL

Corporate/Parent Company: Boone Newspapers
Publication Street Address: 1216 Wilkinson Blvd
City: Frankfort
State: KY
Publication Website: www.state-journal.com
Postal Code: 40601-1243
Office phone: (502) 227-4556
General E-mail: news@state-journal.com
Publisher Name: Steve Stewart
Publisher Email: steve.stewart@state-journal.com
Publisher Phone: 502-209-6994
Editor Name: Chanda Veno
Editor Email: chanda.veno@state-journal.com
Editor Phone: 502-209-6299
Year Established: 1902
Delivery Methods: Mail`Newsstand`Carrier`Racks
Own Printing Facility?: Y
Mechanical specifications: Type page 13 x 21 1/2; E - 6 cols, 2, 1/9 between; A - 6 cols, 2, 1/9 between; C - 8 cols, 1 1/2, 1/9 between.
Published Days: Mon`Tues`Wed`Thur`Fri`Sun
Weekday Frequency: All day
Avg Paid Circ: 6397
Audit Company: CAC
Audit Date: 31 03 2015

GLASGOW

GLASGOW DAILY TIMES

Corporate/Parent Company: CNHI, LLC
Publication Street Address: 100 Commerce Dr
City: Glasgow
State: KY
Publication Website: www.glasgowdailytimes.com
Postal Code: 42141-1153
Office phone: (270) 678-5171
Publisher Name: Bill Hanson
Publisher Email: bhanson@cnhi.com
Publisher Phone: Ext. 294
Editor Name: Daniel Suddeath
Editor Email: dsuddeat@glasgowdailytimes.com
Editor Phone: Ext. 234
Advertising Executive Name: Allen Handley
Advertising Executive Email: ahandley@glasgowdailytimes.com
Advertising Executive Phone: Ext. 294
Year Established: 1865
Delivery Methods: Mail`Newsstand`Racks
Own Printing Facility?: N
Commercial printers?: N
Mechanical specifications: Type page 13 x 21 1/2; E - 6 cols, 2 1/16, 1/8 between; A - 6 cols, 2 1/16, 1/8 between; C - 8 cols, 1 5/16, 1/8 between.
Published Days: Tues`Wed`Thur`Fri`Sat`Sun
Weekday Frequency: m
Saturday Frequency: m
Avg Paid Circ: 5218
Audit Company: AAM
Audit Date: 30 09 2014

HENDERSON

THE GLEANER

Corporate/Parent Company: Gannett
Publication Street Address: 455 Klutey Park Plaza Dr
City: Henderson
State: KY
Publication Website: www.thegleaner.com
Postal Code: 42420-5213
Office phone: (270) 827-2000
General E-mail: thegleaner@gannett.com
Year Established: 1885
Delivery Methods: Mail`Carrier
Mechanical specifications: Type page 13 x 21 1/2; E - 6 cols, 2 1/16, 1/8 between; A - 6 cols, 1 5/6, 1/8 between; C - 9 cols, 1 1/2, 1/16 between.
Published Days: Tues`Wed`Thur`Fri`Sat`Sun
Weekday Frequency: m
Saturday Frequency: m
Avg Paid Circ: 4997
Avg Free Circ: 413
Audit Company: AAM
Audit Date: 19 04 2018

HOPKINSVILLE

KENTUCKY NEW ERA

Corporate/Parent Company: Paxton Media Group, LLC
Publication Street Address: 713 South Main Street
City: Hopkinsville
State: KY
Publication Website: https://www.kentuckynewera.com/
Postal Code: 42240-4430
Office phone: (270) 886-4444
General E-mail: webmaster@kentuckynewera.com
Publisher Name: Taylor W. Hayes
Editor Name: Eli Pace
Year Established: 1869
Delivery Methods: Newsstand`Carrier`Racks
Own Printing Facility?: Y
Mechanical specifications: Type page 11 5/8 x 21 1/2; E - 6 cols, 1/8 between; A - 6 cols, 1/8 between; C - 9 cols, 1/8 between.
Published Days: Mon`Wed`Thur`Fri`Sat
Weekday Frequency: e
Saturday Frequency: e
Avg Paid Circ: 6779
Audit Company: AAM
Audit Date: 30 09 2015

LEXINGTON

LEXINGTON HERALD-LEADER

Corporate/Parent Company: McClatchy Company
Publication Street Address: 100 Midland Ave
City: Lexington
State: KY
Publication Website: www.kentucky.com
Postal Code: 40508-1943
Office phone: (859) 231-3100
Editor Name: Baniak, Peter
Editor Email: pbaniak@herald-leader.com
Editor Phone: 859/231-3446
Advertising Executive Name: Slay, Robert
Advertising Executive Email: rslay@mcclatchy.com
Advertising Executive Phone: 859/231-3503
Delivery Methods: Mail`Newsstand`Carrier`Racks
Own Printing Facility?: N
Commercial printers?: Y
Published Days: Mon`Tues`Wed`Thur`Fri`Sat`Sun
Weekday Frequency: m
Saturday Frequency: m
Avg Paid Circ: 49012
Audit Company: AAM
Audit Date: 24 03 2020

LOUISA

THE LEVISA LAZER

Publication Street Address: 1328 Gene Wilson Blvd.
City: Louisa
State: KY
Publication Website: thelevisalazer.com
Postal Code: 41230
Office phone: 606-638-0123
Editor Name: Mark Grayson
Editor Email: markgrayson@me.com

LOUISVILLE

THE COURIER-JOURNAL

Corporate/Parent Company: Gannett Co., Inc.
Publication Street Address: 525 W Broadway
City: Louisville
State: KY
Publication Website: www.courier-journal.com
Postal Code: 40202-2206
Office phone: (502) 582-4011
Editor Name: Richard A. Green
Editor Email: rgreen@courierjournal.com
Year Established: 1868
Delivery Methods: Mail`Newsstand`Carrier`Racks
Own Printing Facility?: Y
Commercial printers?: Y
Mechanical specifications: Type page 11 x 20; E - 6 cols, 1 13/16, 1/8 between; A - 6 cols, 1 13/16, 1/8 between; C - 10 cols, 1 1/20, 1/8 between.
Published Days: Mon`Tues`Wed`Thur`Fri`Sat`Sun
Weekday Frequency: m
Saturday Frequency: m
Avg Paid Circ: 76937
Audit Company: AAM
Audit Date: 11 08 2020

MADISONVILLE

THE MESSENGER

Corporate/Parent Company: Paxton Media Group
Publication Street Address: 221 S Main St
City: Madisonville
State: KY
Publication Website: https://www.the-messenger.com/
Postal Code: 42431-2557
Office phone: (270) 824-3300
General E-mail: tdillingham@the-messenger.com
Publisher Name: Rick Welch
Publisher Email: rwelch@the-messenger.com
Publisher Phone: (270) 824-3282
Editor Name: Jon Garrett
Editor Email: jgarrett@the-messenger.com
Editor Phone: (270) 824-3300
Advertising Executive Name: Tina Dillingham
Advertising Executive Email: tdillingham@the-messenger.com
Advertising Executive Phone: (270) 824-3224
Year Established: 1917
Delivery Methods: Mail`Newsstand`Carrier`Racks
Own Printing Facility?: N
Commercial printers?: Y
Mechanical specifications: Type page ROP (6 COL) 1 COL............... 1.6225 2 CO L............... 3.375 3 COL............... .... 5.125 4 COL............... 6.875 5 COL............... 8.625 6 COL .... 10.375 Bdsheet............... 10.375x21.375; CLASSIFIED (7 COL) 1 CO L............... 1.375 2 COL............... .... 2.875 3 COL............... 4.375 4 COL............... 5.875 5 CO

Delivery Methods: Mail`Newsstand`Carrier`Racks
Own Printing Facility?: Y
Commercial printers?: N
Mechanical specifications: Type page 11 5/8 x 21; E - 6 cols, 1 4/5, 1/8 between; A - 6 cols, 1 4/5, 1/8 between; C - 9 cols, 1 1/5, 1/10 between.
Published Days: Mon`Tues`Wed`Thur`Fri`Sat`Sun
Weekday Frequency: e
Saturday Frequency: m
Avg Paid Circ: 21620
Audit Company: AAM
Audit Date: 30 09 2013

U.S. Daily Newspapers

I-49

L..............7.375 6 COL............
...............8.875 7 COL............
10.375 Bdsheet.............10.375x21.375
Published Days: Tues`Wed`Thur`Fri`Sat`Sun
Weekday Frequency: m
Saturday Frequency: m
Avg Paid Circ: 5147
Audit Company: USPS
Audit Date: 12 11 2017

MAYSVILLE

THE LEDGER INDEPENDENT

Corporate/Parent Company: Champion Media
Publication Street Address: 120 Limestone St
City: Maysville
State: KY
Publication Website: www.maysville-online.com
Postal Code: 41056-1284
Office phone: (606) 564-9091
Publisher Name: Rod Baker
Publisher Email: RBaker@cmpapers.com
Publisher Phone: Ex. 1291
Editor Name: Mary Ann Kearns
Editor Email: MKearns@cmpapers.com
Editor Phone: Ex. 1270
Advertising Executive Name: Jennifer Marshall
Advertising Executive Email: JMarshall@cmpapers.com
Advertising Executive Phone: "Ex. 1240
"
Year Established: 1968
Delivery Methods: Mail`Carrier`Racks
Own Printing Facility?: Y
Commercial printers?: Y
Mechanical specifications: Type page 13 x 21 1/2; E - 6 cols, 2 1/16, 1/8 between; A - 6 cols, 2 1/16, 1/8 between; C - 8 cols, 1 1/2, 1/8 between.
Published Days: Mon`Wed`Thur`Fri`Sat
Weekday Frequency: m
Saturday Frequency: m
Avg Paid Circ: 4581
Avg Free Circ: 315
Audit Company: AAM
Audit Date: 30 09 2016

MIDDLESBORO

MIDDLESBORO DAILY NEWS

Corporate/Parent Company: Boone Newspapers, Inc.
Publication Street Address: 1275 N 25th St
City: Middlesboro
State: KY
Publication Website: www.middlesborodailynews.com
Postal Code: 40965-1964
Office phone: (606) 248-1010
General E-mail: anthony.cloud@middlesborodailynews.com
Editor Name: Marisa Anders
Year Established: 1911
Delivery Methods: Mail`Newsstand`Carrier`Racks
Mechanical specifications: Type page 11 5/8 x 21 1/2; E - 6 cols, 1 13/16, 1/8 between; A - 6 cols, 1 13/16, 1/8 between; C - 9 cols, 1 13/16, 1/8 between.
Published Days: Tues`Wed`Thur`Fri`Sat
Weekday Frequency: e
Saturday Frequency: m
Avg Paid Circ: 5873
Audit Company: Sworn/Estimate/Non-Audited
Audit Date: 7 12 2019

MORGANTOWN

BEECH TREE NEWS

Publication Street Address: 107 West Ohio Street
City: Morgantown
State: KY
Publication Website: www.beechtreenews.com
Postal Code: 42261
Office phone: (270) 526-9527
Publisher Name: Diane Dyer
Publisher Email: diane@beechtreenews.com
Publisher Phone: 999-0822, 526-5946
Editor Name: John Embry
Editor Email: jwe@beechtreenews.com
Editor Phone: 526-7945

MURRAY

THE MURRAY LEDGER & TIMES

Corporate/Parent Company: Lancaster Management, Inc.
Publication Street Address: 1001 Whitnell Ave
City: Murray
State: KY
Publication Website: www.murrayledger.com
Postal Code: 42071-2975
Office phone: (270) 753-1916
General E-mail: circulation@murrayledger.com
Publisher Name: Mike Davis
Publisher Email: mdavis@murrayledger.com
Editor Name: Hawkins Teague
Editor Email: editor@murrayledger.com
Advertising Executive Name: Chris Woodall
Advertising Executive Email: ads@murrayledger.com
Year Established: 1879
Delivery Methods: Mail`Newsstand`Carrier`Racks
Own Printing Facility?: Y
Commercial printers?: N
Mechanical specifications: Type page 12 1/2 x 21 1/2; E - 6 cols, 1 5/6, 1/8 between; A - 6 cols, 1 5/6, 1/8 between; C - 9 cols, 1 1/4, 1/16 between.
Published Days: Mon`Tues`Wed`Thur`Fri`Sat
Weekday Frequency: m
Saturday Frequency: m
Avg Paid Circ: 7100
Avg Free Circ: 6500
Audit Company: Sworn/Estimate/Non-Audited
Audit Date: 7 12 2019

OWENSBORO

MESSENGER-INQUIRER

Corporate/Parent Company: Paxton Media Group, LLC
Publication Street Address: 1401 Frederica St
City: Owensboro
State: KY
Publication Website: https://www.messenger-inquirer.com/
Postal Code: 42301-4804
Office phone: (270) 926-0123
General E-mail: amayes@messenger-inquirer
Publisher Name: Mike Weafer
Publisher Email: mweafer@messenger-inquirer.com
Publisher Phone: (270) 691-7285
Editor Name: Jeanette Noone
Editor Email: jnoone@messenger-inquirer.com
Editor Phone: (270) 691-7309
Advertising Executive Name: Angela Mayes
Advertising Executive Email: amayes@messenger-inquirer
Advertising Executive Phone: (270) 691-7239
Year Established: 1875
Delivery Methods: Carrier
Own Printing Facility?: Y
Commercial printers?: Y
Mechanical specifications: Type page 13 x 21; E - 5 cols, 2 1/16, 1/6 between; A - 6 cols, 2 1/16, 1/6 between; C - 10 cols, 1 1/4, 1/6 between.
Published Days: Mon`Tues`Wed`Thur`Fri`Sat`Sun
Weekday Frequency: m
Saturday Frequency: m
Avg Paid Circ: 20613
Audit Company: AAM
Audit Date: 16 02 2018

PADUCAH

THE PADUCAH SUN

Corporate/Parent Company: Paxton Media Group, LLC
Publication Street Address: 408 Kentucky Ave
City: Paducah
State: KY
Publication Website: https://www.paducahsun.com/
Postal Code: 42003-1550
Office phone: (270) 575-8600
General E-mail: mjones@paducahsun.com
Publisher Name: Matt Jones
Publisher Email: mjones@paducahsun.com
Publisher Phone: (270) 575-8785
Editor Name: Carrie Dillard
Editor Email: cdillard@paducahsun.com
Editor Phone: (270) 575-8657
Year Established: 1896
Delivery Methods: Carrier
Mechanical specifications: Type page 13 1/8 x 21 1/4; E - 6 cols, 1 5/6, 1/8 between; A - 6 cols, 1 5/6, 1/8 between; C - 9 cols, 1 5/8, 1/8 between.
Published Days: Mon`Tues`Wed`Thur`Fri`Sat`Sun
Weekday Frequency: m
Saturday Frequency: m
Avg Paid Circ: 19618
Audit Company: AAM
Audit Date: 30 09 2011

RICHMOND

THE RICHMOND REGISTER

Corporate/Parent Company: CNHI, LLC
Publication Street Address: 380 Big Hill Ave
City: Richmond
State: KY
Publication Website: www.richmondregister.com
Postal Code: 40475-2012
Office phone: (859) 623-1669
General E-mail: news@richmondregister.com
Publisher Name: Bill Hanson
Editor Name: Jonathan Greene
Editor Email: editor@richmondregister.com
Editor Phone: 859-624-6690
Advertising Executive Name: Perry Stocker
Advertising Executive Email: pstocker@richmondregister.com
Advertising Executive Phone: 859-624-6685
Year Established: 1917
Delivery Methods: Carrier`Racks
Mechanical specifications: Type page 13 x 21 1/2; E - 6 cols, 2 1/16, 1/8 between; A - 6 cols, 2 1/16, 1/8 between; C - 9 cols, 1 3/8, 1/16 between.
Published Days: Tues`Wed`Thur`Fri`Sat`Sun
Weekday Frequency: e
Saturday Frequency: e
Avg Paid Circ: 4060
Audit Company: AAM
Audit Date: 31 03 2014

SOMERSET

THE COMMONWEALTH-JOURNAL

Corporate/Parent Company: CNHI, LLC
Publication Street Address: 110-112 E. Mt. Vernon Street
City: Somerset
State: KY
Publication Website: www.somerset-kentucky.com
Postal Code: 42501-1411
Office phone: (606) 678-8191
General E-mail: news@somerset-kentucky.com
Publisher Name: Michael McCleery
Publisher Email: mmcleery@somerset-kentucky.com
Publisher Phone: (606) 451-4900
Editor Name: Jeff Neal
Editor Email: jneal@somerset-kentucky.com
Editor Phone: (606) 451-4920
Advertising Executive Name: Acey Petercheff
Advertising Executive Email: apetercheff@somerset-kentucky.com
Advertising Executive Phone: (606) 451-4908
Year Established: 1895
Delivery Methods: Carrier
Mechanical specifications: Type page 13 x 21 1/2; E - 6 cols, 2 1/16, 1/8 between; A - 6 cols, 2 1/16, 1/8 between; C - 10 cols, 1 3/16, 1/12 between.
Published Days: Tues`Wed`Thur`Fri`Sat`Sun
Weekday Frequency: m
Saturday Frequency: m
Avg Paid Circ: 4200
Audit Company: Sworn/Estimate/Non-Audited
Audit Date: 7 12 2019

WINCHESTER

THE WINCHESTER SUN

Corporate/Parent Company: Boone Newspapers, Inc.
Publication Street Address: 20 Wall St
City: Winchester
State: KY
Publication Website: www.winchestersun.com
Postal Code: 40391-1900
Office phone: (859) 744-3123
General E-mail: karen.combs@winchestersun.com
Publisher Name: Mike Caldwell
Publisher Email: mike.caldwell@winchestersun.com
Publisher Phone: 859-759-0095
Editor Name: Whitney Leggett
Editor Email: whitney.leggett@winchestersun.com
Editor Phone: 859-759-0049
Advertising Executive Name: Dianna Roe
Advertising Executive Email: dianna.roe@winchestersun.com
Advertising Executive Phone: 859-759-0074
Year Established: 1878
Delivery Methods: Mail`Newsstand`Carrier`Racks
Own Printing Facility?: Y
Commercial printers?: Y
Mechanical specifications: Type page 11 x 21 1/2; E - 6 cols, 1 11/16, 1/8 between; A - 6 cols, 1 11/16, 1/8 between; C - 8 cols, 1 3/16, 1/8 between.
Published Days: Mon`Tues`Wed`Thur`Fri`Sun
Weekday Frequency: e
Saturday Frequency: e
Avg Paid Circ: 6000
Audit Company: USPS
Audit Date: 10 01 2013

LOUISIANA

BASTROP

BASTROP DAILY ENTERPRISE

Publication Street Address: 119 W Hickory Ave
City: Bastrop
State: LA
Publication Website: www.bastropenterprise.com
Postal Code: 71220-4549
Office phone: (318) 281-4421
Publisher Name: Teresa Hicks
Publisher Email: thicks@gatehousemedia.com
Publisher Phone: 870-534-3400 ext 1200
Advertising Executive Name: Monica Smith
Advertising Executive Email: msmith@bastropenterprise.com
Advertising Executive Phone: 318-281-4421
Year Established: 1898
Delivery Methods: Mail`Newsstand`Carrier`Racks
Mechanical specifications: Type page 13 x 21; E - 6 cols, 1 1/8, 1/8 between; A - 6 cols, 2 1/16, 1/8 between; C - 9 cols, 1 5/16, 1/8 between.
Published Days: Tues`Wed`Thur`Fri`Sat
Weekday Frequency: m
Saturday Frequency: m
Avg Paid Circ: 4241
Audit Company: Sworn/Estimate/Non-Audited
Audit Date: 7 12 2019

BATON ROUGE

THE ADVOCATE

Corporate/Parent Company: Capital City Press LLC
Publication Street Address: 10705 Reiger Rd
City: Baton Rouge
State: LA
Publication Website: www.theadvocate.com
Postal Code: 70809-4520
Office phone: (225) 383-1111
General E-mail: newstips@theadvocate.com
Editor Name: Peter Kovacs
Editor Email: pkovacs@theadvocate.com
Editor Phone: 225.388.0277
Advertising Executive Name: Lou Hudson
Advertising Executive Email: lhudson@theadvocate.com
Advertising Executive Phone: 225.388.0245
Year Established: 1925
Delivery Methods:
  Mail`Newsstand`Carrier`Racks
Own Printing Facility?: Y
Commercial printers?: Y
Mechanical specifications: Type page 11 1/8 x 20; E - 6 cols, 1 3/4, 1/8 between; A - 6 cols, 1 3/4, 1/8 between; C - 9 cols, 1 1/8, 1/8 between.
Published Days: Mon`Tues`Wed`Thur`Fri`Sat`Sun
Weekday Frequency: m
Saturday Frequency: m
Avg Paid Circ: 79123
Avg Free Circ: 3910
Audit Company: AAM
Audit Date: 26 09 2019

HAMMOND

THE DAILY STAR

Corporate/Parent Company: Paxton Media Group, LLC
Publication Street Address: 1010 CM Fagan Drive, Suite 105
City: Hammond
State: LA
Publication Website: www.hammondstar.com
Postal Code: 70403
Office phone: (985) 254-7827
General E-mail: editor@hammondstar.com
Publisher Name: Michelle Gallo
Publisher Email: mgallo@hammondstar.com
Publisher Phone: 985-254-7801
Editor Name: Lil Mirando
Editor Email: editor@hammondstar.com
Editor Phone: 985-254-7834
Advertising Executive Name: Myra Sharpe
Advertising Executive Email: msharpe@hammondstar.com
Advertising Executive Phone: 985-254-7818
Year Established: 1959
Delivery Methods:
  Mail`Newsstand`Carrier`Racks
Own Printing Facility?: Y
Commercial printers?: Y
Mechanical specifications: Type page 13 x 21 1/2; E - 6 cols, 2 1/6, 1/8 between; A - 6 cols, 2, 1/6 between; C - 9 cols, 1 2/5, 1/8 between.
Published Days: Tues`Wed`Thur`Fri`Sat`Sun
Weekday Frequency: m
Saturday Frequency: m
Avg Paid Circ: 9595
Audit Company: Sworn/Estimate/Non-Audited
Audit Date: 7 12 2019

HOUMA

THE COURIER

Corporate/Parent Company: Gannett
Publication Street Address: 3030 Barrow St
City: Houma
State: LA
Publication Website: www.houmatoday.com
Postal Code: 70360-7641
Office phone: (985) 850-1100
Publisher Name: Clarice Touhey
Publisher Email: ctouhey@gatehousemedia.com
Publisher Phone: (985) 850-1116
Editor Name: Keith Magill
Editor Email: keith.magill@houmatoday.com
Editor Phone: (985) 857-2201
Advertising Executive Name: Marian Long
Advertising Executive Email: marian.long@houmatoday.com
Advertising Executive Phone: (985) 857-2291
Year Established: 1878
Delivery Methods:
  Mail`Newsstand`Carrier`Racks
Own Printing Facility?: Y
Commercial printers?: Y
Mechanical specifications: Type page 11" x 22"; E - 6 cols, 1.708", 11 pts. between; A - 6 cols, 1.708", 11 pts. between; C - 9 cols, 1.126", 11 pts. between.
Published Days: Mon`Tues`Wed`Thur`Fri`Sat`Sun
Weekday Frequency: e
Saturday Frequency: m
Avg Paid Circ: 9378
Audit Company: AAM
Audit Date: 24 07 2018

JENNINGS

JENNINGS (LA) DAILY NEWS

Corporate/Parent Company: Fackelman Newspapers
Publication Street Address: 238 N Market St
City: Jennings
State: LA
Publication Website: www.jenningsdailynews.net
Postal Code: 70546-5862
Office phone: (337) 824-3011
Publisher Name: Dona H. Smith
Publisher Email: publisher@jenningsdailynews.net
Editor Name: Sheila Smith
Editor Email: editor@jenningsdailynews.net
Advertising Executive Name: Paula Bonin
Advertising Executive Email: sales@jenningsdailynews.net
Year Established: 1896
Delivery Methods:
  Mail`Newsstand`Carrier`Racks
Mechanical specifications: Type page 13 x 21 1/2; E - 6 cols, 2 1/16, 1/8 between; A - 6 cols, 2 1/16, 1/8 between; C - 8 cols, 1 1/2, 1/8 between.
Published Days: Tues`Wed`Thur`Fri`Sun
Weekday Frequency: e
Avg Paid Circ: 4816
Audit Company: Sworn/Estimate/Non-Audited
Audit Date: 7 12 2019

LAFAYETTE

THE DAILY ADVERTISER

Corporate/Parent Company: Gannett
Publication Street Address: 1100 Bertrand Dr
City: Lafayette
State: LA
Publication Website: www.theadvertiser.com
Postal Code: 70506-4110
Office phone: (337) 289-6397
Editor Name: Brett Blackledge
Editor Email: bblackledge@theadvertiser.com
Year Established: 1865
Mechanical specifications: Type page 11 1/2 x 20 1/2; E - 6 cols, 1 3/4, between; A - 6 cols, 1 5/8, between; C - 9 cols, 1 3/16, between.
Published Days: Mon`Tues`Wed`Thur`Fri`Sat`Sun
Weekday Frequency: m
Saturday Frequency: m
Avg Paid Circ: 18576
Audit Company: AAM
Audit Date: 31 03 2017

LAKE CHARLES

AMERICAN PRESS

Corporate/Parent Company: Shearman Company LLC DBA American Press
Publication Street Address: 4900 Highway 90 E
City: Lake Charles
State: LA
Publication Website: www.americanpress.com
Postal Code: 70615-4037
Office phone: (337) 433-3000
General E-mail: news@americanpress.com
Editor Name: Crystal Stevenson
Editor Email: cstevenson@americanpress.com
Editor Phone: 337-494-4083
Advertising Executive Name: Karen Cole
Advertising Executive Email: majoraccountsales@americanpress.com
Advertising Executive Phone: 337-494-4095
Year Established: 1895
Delivery Methods:
  Mail`Newsstand`Carrier`Racks
Own Printing Facility?: Y
Commercial printers?: Y
Mechanical specifications: Type page 13 x 22; E - 6 cols, 2 1/16, 1/8 between; A - 6 cols, 2 1/16, 1/8 between; C - 10 cols, 1 1/6, 1/6 between.
Published Days: Mon`Tues`Wed`Thur`Fri`Sat`Sun
Weekday Frequency: m
Saturday Frequency: m
Avg Paid Circ: 16157
Avg Free Circ: 17004
Audit Company: AAM
Audit Date: 27 08 2019

MINDEN

MINDEN PRESS HERALD

Corporate/Parent Company: Specht Newspapers Inc
Publication Street Address: 203 Gleason St
City: Minden
State: LA
Publication Website: www.press-herald.com
Postal Code: 71055-3455
Office phone: (318) 377-1866
General E-mail: newsroom@press-herald.com
Year Established: 1895
Delivery Methods:
  Mail`Newsstand`Carrier`Racks
Own Printing Facility?: Y
Commercial printers?: Y
Mechanical specifications: Type page 13 1/16 x 21; E - 6 cols, 2 1/16, 1/8 between; A - 6 cols, 2 1/16, 1/8 between; C - 9 cols, 1 3/8, 1/8 between.
Published Days: Mon`Tues`Wed`Thur`Fri
Weekday Frequency: e
Avg Paid Circ: 5150
Audit Company: Sworn/Estimate/Non-Audited
Audit Date: 7 12 2019

MONROE

THE NEWS-STAR

Corporate/Parent Company: Gannett
Publication Street Address: 411 N 4th St
City: Monroe
State: LA
Publication Website: www.thenewsstar.com
Postal Code: 71201-6743
Office phone: (318) 322-5161
Editor Name: Barbara Leader
Editor Email: barbara.leader@thenewsstar.com
Year Established: 1890
Delivery Methods:
  Mail`Newsstand`Carrier`Racks
Mechanical specifications: Type page 13 1/12 x 22 1/2; E - 6 cols, 2, 1/6 between; A - 6 cols, 2, 1/6 between; C - 9 cols, 1 7/18, 1/2 between.
Published Days: Mon`Tues`Wed`Thur`Fri`Sat`Sun
Weekday Frequency: m
Saturday Frequency: m
Avg Paid Circ: 11202
Audit Company: AAM
Audit Date: 19 04 2019

NEW IBERIA

THE DAILY IBERIAN

Corporate/Parent Company: Wick Communications
Publication Street Address: 124 E Main St
City: New Iberia
State: LA
Publication Website: www.iberianet.com
Postal Code: 70560
Office phone: (337) 365-6773
Publisher Name: Christina Pierce
Publisher Email: christina.pierce@daily-iberian.com
Publisher Phone: (337) 321-6727
Editor Name: Raymond Partsch III
Editor Email: raymond.partsch@daily-iberian.com
Editor Phone: (337) 321-6729
Advertising Executive Name: Karla Borde
Advertising Executive Email: karla.borde@daily-iberian.com
Advertising Executive Phone: (337) 321-6752
Year Established: 1893
Delivery Methods: Mail`Newsstand
Mechanical specifications: Type page 11 5/8 x 21 1/2; E - 6 cols, 1 3/4, 3/16 between; A - 6 cols, 1 3/4, 3/16 between; C - 9 cols, 1 5/16, between.
Published Days: Mon`Tues`Wed`Thur`Fri`Sun
Weekday Frequency: e
Avg Paid Circ: 7184
Audit Company: VAC
Audit Date: 30 06 2017

NEW ORLEANS

THE NEW ORLEANS ADVOCATE

Corporate/Parent Company: Georges Media
Publication Street Address: 840 St. Charles Ave.
City: New Orleans
State: LA
Publication Website: nola.com
Postal Code: 70130
Office phone: 504-636-7400
General E-mail: subscriberservices@theadvocate.com
Editor Name: Peter Kovacs
Editor Email: pkovacs@theadvocate.com
Editor Phone: 225.388.0277
Advertising Executive Name: Connie Settle
Advertising Executive Email: csettle@theadvocate.com
Advertising Executive Phone: 225.388.0250

THE TIMES PICAYUNE

Corporate/Parent Company: Georges Media
Publication Street Address: 840 St. Charles Ave.
City: New Orleans
State: LA
Publication Website: nola.com
Postal Code: 70130
Office phone: 504-636-7400
General E-mail: subscriberservices@theadvocate.com
Editor Name: Peter Kovacs
Editor Email: pkovacs@theadvocate.com
Editor Phone: 225.388.0277
Advertising Executive Name: Connie Settle
Advertising Executive Email: csettle@theadvocate.com
Advertising Executive Phone: 225.388.0250

RUSTON

RUSTON (LA) DAILY LEADER

Corporate/Parent Company: Fackelman Newspapers
Publication Street Address: 212 W Park Ave
City: Ruston
State: LA
Publication Website: www.rustonleader.com
Postal Code: 71270-4314
Office phone: (318) 255-4353
General E-mail: circulation@rustonleader.com
Year Established: 1894
Delivery Methods:
  Mail`Newsstand`Carrier`Racks
Own Printing Facility?: Y
Commercial printers?: Y
Mechanical specifications: Type page 10.5 x 21 1/2; E - 6 cols, 1.792", 1/8 between.
Published Days: Mon`Tues`Wed`Thur`Fri`Sun

U.S. Daily Newspapers

Weekday Frequency: e
Avg Paid Circ: 4834
Avg Free Circ: 6000
Audit Company: Sworn/Estimate/Non-Audited
Audit Date: 7 12 2019

SHREVEPORT

THE TIMES

Corporate/Parent Company: Gannett
Publication Street Address: 401 Market St
City: Shreveport
State: LA
Publication Website: www.shreveporttimes.com
Postal Code: 71101-6911
Office phone: (318) 459-3200
Editor Name: Scott Ferrell
Editor Email: stferrell@gannett.com
Advertising Executive Name: Bill Tice
Advertising Executive Email: btice@localiq.com
Year Established: 1872
Delivery Methods:
  Mail`Newsstand`Carrier`Racks
Own Printing Facility?: Y
Commercial printers?: Y
Mechanical specifications: Type page 10 x 17.25; E - 6 cols, 1.54", .17" between; A - 6 cols, 1.54", .17" between; C - 6 cols, 1.54", .16" between.
Published Days: Mon`Tues`Wed`Thur`Fri`Sat`Sun
Weekday Frequency: m
Saturday Frequency: m
Avg Paid Circ: 27186
Audit Company: AAM
Audit Date: 19 04 2019

THIBODAUX

DAILY COMET

Corporate/Parent Company: Gannett
Publication Street Address: 1629 St. Mary St.
City: Thibodaux
State: LA
Publication Website: www.dailycomet.com
Postal Code: 70301
Office phone: (985) 448-7600
Publisher Name: Clarice Touhey
Publisher Email: ctouhey@gatehousemedia.com
Publisher Phone: (985) 850-1123
Editor Name: Keith Magill
Editor Email: keith.magill@houmatoday.com
Editor Phone: (985) 857-2201
Advertising Executive Name: Marian Long
Advertising Executive Email: marian.long@houmatoday.com
Advertising Executive Phone: (985) 857-2291
Year Established: 1889
Delivery Methods:
  Mail`Newsstand`Carrier`Racks
Own Printing Facility?: N
Commercial printers?: Y
Mechanical specifications: Type page 11" x 22"; E - 6 cols, 1.708", 11 pts. between; A - 6 cols, 1.708", 11 pts. between; C - 9 cols, 1.126", 11 pts. between.
Published Days: Mon`Tues`Wed`Thur`Fri
Weekday Frequency: e
Saturday Frequency: e
Avg Paid Circ: 4461
Avg Free Circ: 515
Audit Company: AAM
Audit Date: 24 07 2018

MASSACHUSETTS

ATTLEBORO

THE SUN CHRONICLE

Corporate/Parent Company: Triboro Massachusetts News Media Inc.
Publication Street Address: 34 S Main St
City: Attleboro
State: MA
Publication Website: www.thesunchronicle.com
Postal Code: 02703-2920
Office phone: (508) 222-7000
General E-mail: news@thesunchronicle.com
Editor Name: Craig Borges
Editor Email: cborges@thesunchronicle.com
Editor Phone: 508-236-0337
Advertising Executive Name: Michelle Fulcher
Advertising Executive Email: mfulcher@thesunchronicle.com
Advertising Executive Phone: 508-236-0328
Year Established: 1889
Delivery Methods:
  Mail`Newsstand`Carrier`Racks
Own Printing Facility?: Y
Commercial printers?: Y
Mechanical specifications: Type page 13 x 21 1/2; E - 6 cols, 2 1/16, 1/0 between; A - 6 cols, 2 1/16, 1/8 between; C - 9 cols, 1 3/8, 1/16 between.
Published Days: Mon`Tues`Wed`Thur`Fri`Sat`Sun
Weekday Frequency: m
Saturday Frequency: m
Avg Paid Circ: 10769
Avg Free Circ: 652
Audit Company: AAM
Audit Date: 30 06 2016
Pressroom Equipment: Lines – 10-G/Urbanite;
Mailroom Equipment: Counter Stackers – 2-HL/Monitor II; Inserters & Stuffers – GMA/SLS 1000 (10 pockets); Tying Machines – 1/MLN, 2-MLN/ML2EE, Power Strap.;
Buisness Equipment: HP/3000 Model 927
Buisness Software: GEAC/Vision Shift
Classified Equipment: Hardware – Novell/Netserver; Printers – 2-Typhoon/800 dpi;
Classified Software: CText/OS-2 Advision.
Editorial Equipment: Hardware – Novell/Netserver/AU/APS 6-84 ACS, Imagesetters; Printers – Typhoon/800 dpi, Hyphen/600 dpi
Editorial Software: CText/Dateline, Microsoft/Windows NT.
Production Equipment: Hardware – 2-AU/APS 6/84 ACS, 3-APP/Mac LaserWriter NTX, Hyphen/600 dpi, 2-Typhoon/800 dpi
Production Software: QPS/QuarkXPress 3.1.
Total Circulation: 11421

BEVERLY

THE SALEM NEWS

Corporate/Parent Company: Ogden
Publication Street Address: 32 Dunham Rd
City: Beverly
State: MA
Publication Website: www.salemnews.com
Postal Code: 01915-1844
Office phone: (978) 922-1234
General E-mail: sn@salemnews.com
Publisher Name: Karen Andreas
Publisher Email: kandreas@northofboston.com
Editor Name: David Joyner
Editor Email: djoyner@northofboston.com
Editor Phone: 978.946.2189
Advertising Executive Name: Mark Zappala
Advertising Executive Email: mzappala@eagletribune.com
Advertising Executive Phone: 978-946-2174
Year Established: 1880
Delivery Methods:
  Mail`Newsstand`Carrier`Racks
Own Printing Facility?: Y
Commercial printers?: Y
Published Days: Mon`Tues`Wed`Thur`Fri`Sat
Weekday Frequency: e
Saturday Frequency: e
Avg Paid Circ: 13730
Avg Free Circ: 833
Audit Company: AAM
Audit Date: 9 12 2019
Total Circulation: 12944

BOSTON

BOSTON HERALD

Corporate/Parent Company: Media News Group
Publication Street Address: 100 Grossman Drive, 4th Floor
City: Boston
State: MA
Publication Website: www.bostonherald.com
Postal Code: 02210-2131
Office phone: (617) 426-3000
General E-mail: bhcirc@bostonherald.com
Publisher Name: Kevin Corrado
Publisher Email: kcorrado@medianewsgroup.com
Year Established: 1846
Delivery Methods:
  Mail`Newsstand`Carrier`Racks
Own Printing Facility?: N
Commercial printers?: N
Mechanical specifications: Type page 10 1/2 x 10.875; E - 6 cols, 1.5625, 1/8 between; A - 6 cols, 1.5625, 1/8 between; C - 9 cols, 1 , 1/8 between.
Published Days: Mon`Tues`Wed`Thur`Fri`Sat`Sun
Weekday Frequency: m
Saturday Frequency: m
Avg Paid Circ: 79414
Audit Company: AAM
Audit Date: 31 03 2018
Buisness Equipment: 1-Microsoft/NT CS System, 2-Unix C/S Systems, 1-Unix/SCO, 1-Unisys Advtg. System
Buisness Software: Lawson, ADP
Classified Equipment: Hardware – Sun/E450; 40-PC Clients; Printers – Panasonic/1180, 1-C.Itoh/8000, 2-HP/DeskJet 520, 1-HP/LaserJet IIP, 1-PAN/KXP-1826, 1-PAN/KXP-1624, 1-PAN/KXP-2124;
Classified Software: Unisys/Ad Manager 3.0.
Editorial Equipment: HP DL380, VMware, DTI PageSpeed, 60 Macintosh/40 Windows 7
Editorial Software: DTI PageSpeed 7.5.2
Production Equipment: Dell PowerEdge 2950
Production Software: Agfa Arkitex
Note: herald radio
Total Circulation: 79414

METRO BOSTON

Corporate/Parent Company: Metro US
Publication Street Address: 101 Arch Street
City: Boston
State: MA
Publication Website: metro.us/boston
Postal Code: 2110
Office phone: (617) 210-7905
General E-mail: letters@metro.us
Year Established: 2001
Delivery Methods: Racks
Own Printing Facility?: N
Commercial printers?: N
Published Days: Mon`Tues`Wed`Thur
Weekday Frequency: m
Avg Free Circ: 57752
Audit Company: CAC
Audit Date: 30 09 2018
Total Circulation: 57752

THE BOSTON GLOBE

Corporate/Parent Company: John W. Henry
Publication Street Address: 135 William T Morrissey Blvd
City: Boston
State: MA
Publication Website: www.bostonglobe.com
Postal Code: 02125-3310
Office phone: (617) 929-2000
Editor Name: McGrory, Brian
Editor Email: mcgrory@globe.com
Editor Phone: 617-929-3059
Year Established: 1872
Delivery Methods:
  Mail`Newsstand`Carrier`Racks
Own Printing Facility?: Y
Commercial printers?: Y
Mechanical specifications: Type page 12 1/2 x 22; E - 6 cols, 1 5/6, 1/8 between; A - 6 cols, 1 5/6, 1/8 between; C - 10 cols, 1, 1/16 between.
Published Days: Mon`Tues`Wed`Thur`Fri`Sat`Sun
Weekday Frequency: m
Saturday Frequency: m
Avg Paid Circ: 233867
Audit Company: AAM
Audit Date: 4 01 2018
Pressroom Equipment: Lines – 10-G/Metroliner, 2-G/Metro Color (4/4-color tower); 10-G/Metroliner, 2-G/Metro Color (4/4-color tower); 10-G/Metroliner, 2-G/Metro Color (4/4 color tower); 10-G/Metroliner, 2-G/Metro Color (4/4 color tower);
Mailroom Equipment: Counter Stackers – 21-QWI/301, 6-HL/Dual Carriers, 16/QWI; Inserters & Stuffers – 15-MM/6:1, 3-GMA/Alphaliner 14:1, 1-GMA/Alphaliner 6:1, 3-GMA/SLS 1000 28:2, 15-GMA/SLS 1000 6:1, 2-GMA/SLS 2000 8:1; Tying Machines – Dynaric/30, Power Strap/13;
Buisness Equipment: 1-DEC/VAX 7840, 1-DEC/VAX 7740, 2-DEC/VAX 6620, 1-DEC/VAX 6420, 3-DEC/Alpha 2000, 3-DEC/VAX 4000, 2-DEC/Alpha 4000
Classified Equipment: Hardware – PDP 11; Edgil/credit card processing, MCT/AdFax, MCT/AdFast, Ad Express, AP/AdSend, Cascade/DataFlow; Printers – HP;
Classified Software: ATEX IAS.
Editorial Equipment: Hardware – SUN 6800/Reporter System News Engin; Printers – HP
Editorial Software: CCI.
Production Equipment: Hardware – TextBridge, 5-Jensen
Production Software: AT/Ed Page 1.7, Press To Go, AT/Architect.
Total Circulation: 233867

FALL RIVER

THE HERALD NEWS

Corporate/Parent Company: Gannett
Publication Street Address: 207 Pocasset St
City: Fall River
State: MA
Publication Website: www.heraldnews.com
Postal Code: 02721-1532
Office phone: (508) 676-8211
Publisher Name: Peter Mayer
Publisher Email: publisher@heraldnews.com
Publisher Phone: 508-862-1111
Editor Name: Lynne Sullivan
Editor Email: lsullivan@heraldnews.com
Editor Phone: 508-676-2534
Advertising Executive Name: Paige Webster
Advertising Executive Email: pwebster@wickedlocal.com
Advertising Executive Phone: 508-676-2554
Year Established: 1892
Delivery Methods: Mail`Carrier
Own Printing Facility?: Y
Commercial printers?: Y
Mechanical specifications: Type page 12 x 21 1/2; E - 6 cols, 2, 1/8 between; A - 6 cols, 2, 1/8 between; C - 9 cols, 2 3/4, 1/12 between.
Published Days: Mon`Tues`Wed`Thur`Fri`Sat`Sun
Weekday Frequency: m
Saturday Frequency: m
Avg Paid Circ: 5766
Avg Free Circ: 83
Audit Company: AAM
Audit Date: 8 01 2020
Pressroom Equipment: Lines – 9-G/Urbanite single width; Folders – G/Urbanite 2:1; Pasters –8-Jardis/Automatic 4540.
Mailroom Equipment: Counter Stackers – 2-HL/Monitor, 1-MM/CN70 (388); Inserters & Stuffers – GMA/SLS 1000A 10:1; Tying Machines – 4-MLN/EE, 1-MLN/2A; Address Machine – 1-Ch/515010.;
Buisness Equipment: 1-Bs/92, IBM/AS-400
Buisness Software: INSI
Classified Equipment: Hardware – Dewar/Information System, PC Network;
Classified Software: Dewar/Sys IV.
Editorial Equipment: Hardware – Dewar/Information System, PC Network; Printers – MON
Editorial Software: Dewar/View.
Production Equipment: Hardware – 2-MON/ExpressMaster 1200, 1-MON/PaperMaster 600; Cameras – 1-C/Spartan III; Scanners – Lf/Leafscan 35
Production Software: Dewar/View, QPS.

Note: The Herald News also prints the Taunton Daily Gazette.
Total Circulation: 26812

FITCHBURG
SENTINEL & ENTERPRISE
Corporate/Parent Company: Media News Group
Publication Street Address: 808 Main St
City: Fitchburg
State: MA
Publication Website: www.sentinelandenterprise.com
Postal Code: 01420-3153
Office phone: (978) 343-6911
General E-mail: letters@sentinelandenterprise.com
Publisher Name: KEVIN CORRADO
Publisher Email: kcorrado@digitalfirstmedia.com
Publisher Phone: 978-970-4807
Editor Name: CLIFF CLARK
Editor Email: cclark@sentinelandenterprise.com
Editor Phone: (978) 516-2276
Advertising Executive Name: EDDIE R. NAJEEULLAH
Advertising Executive Email: enajeeullah@mediaonene.com
Advertising Executive Phone: 978-770-7026
Year Established: 1838
Delivery Methods: Mail`Carrier
Mechanical specifications: Type page 13 x 21 1/2; E - 6 cols, 2 1/16, 1/8 between; A - 6 cols, 2 1/16, 1/8 between; C - 9 cols, 1 3/8, 1/16 between.
Published Days: Mon`Tues`Wed`Thur`Fri`Sat`Sun
Weekday Frequency: m
Saturday Frequency: m
Avg Paid Circ: 6283
Avg Free Circ: 884
Audit Company: AAM
Audit Date: 25 04 2018
Pressroom Equipment: Lines – 8-G/Urbanite; 6-MAN; Folders – 1-G/2:1, MR/2:1; Control System – Thin Core; Registration System – Duarte.
Mailroom Equipment: Counter Stackers – S/J4109-2200-2, QWI/300-4; Inserters & Stuffers – K&M/1372-2; Tying Machines – OVL, Dynaric; Address Machine – KR;
Buisness Equipment: PBS
Buisness Software: PBS/MediaPlus
Classified Equipment: Hardware – CText, Microsoft/Windows NT; Printers – Pre Press/Panther;
Classified Software: PPI.
Editorial Equipment: Hardware – CText, APP/Mac/HP/Laser Printer; Printers – Pre Press/Panther
Editorial Software: CText, Baseview/NewsEdit Pro.
Production Equipment: Hardware – Pre Press/Panther, HP/LaserJet 4Plus, HP/LaserJet 4VMV; Cameras – LE/121; Scanners – Nikon, Polaroid
Production Software: QPS/QuarkXPress.
Total Circulation: 11982

FRAMINGHAM
METROWEST DAILY NEWS
Corporate/Parent Company: Gannett
Publication Street Address: 1 Speen St.
City: Framingham
State: MA
Publication Website: www.metrowestdailynews.com
Postal Code: 1701
Office phone: (508) 626-4412
Editor Name: Bob Tremblay
Editor Email: rtremblay@wickedlocal.com
Editor Phone: 508-626-4409
Advertising Executive Name: Mike Bentle
Advertising Executive Email: mbentle@wickedlocal.com
Advertising Executive Phone: 978-371-5757
Year Established: 1897
Delivery Methods:
  Mail`Newsstand`Carrier`Racks

Own Printing Facility?: Y
Commercial printers?: Y
Mechanical specifications: Type page 11 3/4 x 21; E - 6 cols, 2 1/16, 1/8 between; A - 6 cols, 2 1/16, 1/8 between; C - 9 cols, 1 3/8, 1/16 between.
Published Days: Mon`Tues`Wed`Thur`Fri`Sat`Sun
Weekday Frequency: m
Saturday Frequency: m
Avg Paid Circ: 6182
Avg Free Circ: 800
Audit Company: AAM
Audit Date: 8 11 2019
Pressroom Equipment: Lines – 12-G/Urbanite single width 1979; 12-G/Urbanite single width 1979; 1-G/HV single width 1979; Folders – 2-G/Urbanite 1000 Series w 1/4 Folders, 1-G/HV Signature Folder; Pasters –20-G/Automatic 2 armReels & Stands – Reels & Stands and St;
Mailroom Equipment: Counter Stackers – 4-HL/Monitor, 2/Compass, 1-/RIMA; Inserters & Stuffers – 1-GMA/Alpaliner, 1-GMA/SLS 1000; Tying Machines – 6-/MLN; Address Machine – 3-Domino/Ink Jet Printer.;
Buisness Equipment: Sun/Sparc Station 20-Unix, 2-Axiom/Netware 4.11
Buisness Software: Microsoft/Windows 95
Classified Equipment: Hardware – PC 486; Microcom/Modems; Printers – HP/LaserJet 4MV;
Classified Software: III/Classified Software.
Editorial Equipment: Hardware – Pentium/PC 586, PC 486/Microcom/Modems, US Robotics/Modems; Printers – HP/LaserJet 4MV
Editorial Software: III/Editorial System, Microsoft/Windows 95.
Production Equipment: Hardware – 3-Graham, 2-CK Optical/5; Cameras – 2-Image Maker/506A, 2-C/Newspager; Scanners – 3-Kk/2035 Film Scanner, 1-AG/Arcus Plus Color Scanner, 1-Autokon/Flatbed Scanner
Production Software: QPS/QuarkXPress 3.3.
Total Circulation: 9401

GARDNER
THE GARDNER NEWS
Corporate/Parent Company: Gannett
Publication Street Address: 330 Main St
City: Gardner
State: MA
Publication Website: www.thegardnernews.com
Postal Code: 0 1440
Office phone: (978) 632-8000
Editor Name: Matt Garay
Editor Email: mgaray@thegardnernews.com
Editor Phone: 978-669-8091
Advertising Executive Name: Debra Bilodeau
Advertising Executive Email: dbilodeau@thegardnernews.com
Advertising Executive Phone: 978-630-5416
Year Established: 1869
Delivery Methods:
  Mail`Newsstand`Carrier`Racks
Own Printing Facility?: Y
Commercial printers?: N
Mechanical specifications: Type page 12 5/8 x 21 1/4; E - 7 cols, 1 5/8, 1/6 between; A - 7 cols, 1 5/8, 1/6 between; C - 7 cols, 1 5/8, 1/6 between.
Published Days: Mon`Tues`Wed`Thur`Fri`Sat
Weekday Frequency: e
Saturday Frequency: m
Avg Paid Circ: 4099
Avg Free Circ: 158
Audit Company: AAM
Audit Date: 30 06 2016
Pressroom Equipment: Lines – Web press;
Mailroom Equipment: Counter Stackers – 6; Tying Machines – 1-Akebono/Oval Strapping.;
Buisness Equipment: Dell pc
Buisness Software: Peachtree
Classified Equipment: Hardware – Dell PC; Macs; Printers – 1-APP/Mac ImageWriter II, 1-Okidata/293, 1-NEC/90 LaserPrinter;
Classified Software: Accountsscout
Editorial Equipment: Hardware – 4-COM/Intrepid 4, COM/Power Editors-28A
Editorial Software: COM/One System.
Production Equipment: Hardware – Nu/Flip

Top FT40UNS; Cameras – Acti/Process; Scanners – Typist/3.0, Konica, ECR/Autokon 1040.
Total Circulation: 4257

GLOUCESTER
GLOUCESTER DAILY TIMES
Corporate/Parent Company: CNHI, LLC
Publication Street Address: 36 Whittemore St
City: Gloucester
State: MA
Publication Website: www.gloucestertimes.com
Postal Code: 01930-2553
Office phone: (978) 283-7000
General E-mail: gdtnews@gloucestertimes.com
Publisher Name: Karen Andreas
Publisher Email: kandreas@northofboston.com
Editor Name: David Joyner
Editor Email: djoyner@northofboston.com
Editor Phone: 978.946.2189
Advertising Executive Name: Mark Zappala
Advertising Executive Email: mzappala@eagletribune.com
Advertising Executive Phone: 978-946-2174
Year Established: 1888
Delivery Methods:
  Mail`Newsstand`Carrier`Racks
Own Printing Facility?: Y
Commercial printers?: N
Mechanical specifications: Type page 11 x 21.5; E - 6 cols
Published Days: Mon`Tues`Wed`Thur`Fri`Sat
Weekday Frequency: e
Saturday Frequency: e
Avg Paid Circ: 4506
Avg Free Circ: 463
Audit Company: AAM
Audit Date: 9 12 2019
Pressroom Equipment: Lines – 8-G/Metro (3 color decks); Folders – 1-G/Double 2:1;
Mailroom Equipment: Counter Stackers – Goss Olympian; Inserters & Stuffers – 4 wo Goss 630 inserters; Control System – Omnizone; Address Machine – Domino;
Buisness Equipment: IBM/AS-400
Classified Equipment: Hardware – APT;
Classified Software: APT
Editorial Equipment: Hardware – Mediaspan; Printers – QMS/860
Editorial Software: Mediaspan
Production Equipment: Hardware – Agfa Advantage Imagesetters; Cameras – Kodak Cannon; Scanners – ECR/100 Epson/636 Polaroid/Sprint S
Production Software: Adobe InDesign
Total Circulation: 5427

GREENFIELD
ATHOL DAILY NEWS
Corporate/Parent Company: Newspapers of New England
Publication Street Address: 14 Hope Street
City: Greenfield
State: MA
Publication Website: www.atholdailynews.com
Postal Code: 01302-1367
Office phone: (413) 772-0261
General E-mail: newsroom@atholdailynews.com
Advertising Executive Name: Michael Moses
Advertising Executive Email: mmoses@gazettenet.com
Year Established: 1934
Delivery Methods: Mail`Newsstand`Carrier
Own Printing Facility?: Y
Commercial printers?: Y
Mechanical specifications: Type page 13 x 21; E - 6 cols, 2 1/16, 1/4 between; A - 6 cols, 2 1/16, 1/4 between; C - 8 cols, 1 1/2, 1/8 between.
Published Days: Mon`Tues`Wed`Thur`Fri`Sat
Weekday Frequency: e
Saturday Frequency: m
Avg Paid Circ: 4661
Audit Company: Sworn/Estimate/Non-Audited
Audit Date: 7 12 2019
Pressroom Equipment: Lines – 4-G.;

Mailroom Equipment: Tying Machines – 1/Strapex; Address Machine – 1-RSK/TRS 80, Vision Data/Circ Sys, 1-/Ch.;
Buisness Equipment: RSK/TRS-80, Vision Data/Business Sys, APP/Mac Desktop Pub Sys
Classified Equipment: Hardware – APP/Mac;
Classified Software: Baseview.
Editorial Equipment: Hardware – APP/Mac; Printers – MON/PageScan, GCC
Editorial Software: Baseview.
Production Equipment: Hardware – 1-Nu; Cameras – 1-Nu/20 x 24.
Total Circulation: 4661

THE RECORDER
Corporate/Parent Company: Newspapers of New England
Publication Street Address: 14 Hope Street
City: Greenfield
State: MA
Publication Website: www.recorder.com
Postal Code: 01302-1367
Office phone: (413) 772-0261
General E-mail: circinfo@recorder.com
Publisher Name: Michael Moses
Publisher Email: mmoses@gazettenet.com
Publisher Phone: 413-585-3462
Editor Name: Joan Livingston
Editor Email: jlivingston@recorder.com
Editor Phone: 413-772-0261 ext. 250
Year Established: 1792
Delivery Methods: Newsstand`Carrier
Own Printing Facility?: Y
Commercial printers?: Y
Mechanical specifications: Type page 13 x 21 3/8; E - 6 cols, 2 1/2, 1/6 between; A - 6 cols, 2 1/2, 1/6 between; C - 9 cols, 1 5/16, 3/32 between.
Published Days: Mon`Tues`Wed`Thur`Fri`Sat
Weekday Frequency: m
Saturday Frequency: m
Avg Paid Circ: 9027
Avg Free Circ: 347
Audit Company: AAM
Audit Date: 30 06 2018
Pressroom Equipment: 2008 Cerrutti Flexo
Mailroom Equipment: SLS1000 12/1
Buisness Equipment: HP/3000
Classified Equipment: Hardware – 5-APP/Mac; Printers – APP/Laser Writer;
Classified Software: Baseview.
Editorial Equipment: Hardware – Pentium/Pre Press/Panther Pro 36; Printers – Epson, HP
Editorial Software: Atex/Prestige.
Production Equipment: Hardware – 2-Pre Press/Panther Pro 36, Nu; Cameras – C/Spartan I; Scanners – Nikon/LS 1000, PixelCraft/8200
Production Software: Atex Prestige.
Total Circulation: 9374

HYANNIS
CAPE COD TIMES
Corporate/Parent Company: Gannett
Publication Street Address: 319 Main St
City: Hyannis
State: MA
Publication Website: www.capecodtimes.com
Postal Code: 02601-4037
Office phone: (508) 775-1200
General E-mail: news@capecodonline.com
Editor Name: Julie Lipkin
Editor Email: jlipkin@capecodonline.com
Year Established: 1936
Delivery Methods:
  Mail`Newsstand`Carrier`Racks
Own Printing Facility?: N
Commercial printers?: Y
Mechanical specifications: Type page 13 x 21 1/2; E - 6 cols, 2, 1/3 between; A - 6 cols, 2 1/16, 1/3 between; C - 9 cols, 1 2/5, 1/6 between.
Published Days: Mon`Tues`Wed`Thur`Fri`Sat`Sun
Weekday Frequency: m
Saturday Frequency: m
Avg Paid Circ: 15376
Avg Free Circ: 527

U.S. Daily Newspapers

Audit Company: AAM
Audit Date: 31 03 2019
Buisness Equipment: HP 8000 desktops HP 7900 desktops HP 8440p laptops HP 6930 laptops
Buisness Software: Atex Adbase & ATOL (Advertising) DTI (Circulation) SAP & Lawson (Finance) Newscycle Solutions Mediaware & Saxotech Adobe Creative Suite Citrix
Classified Equipment: HP 8000 desktops HP 7900 desktops HP 8440p laptops
Classified Software: Atex AdBase
Editorial Equipment: HP 8000 desktops HP 7900 desktops HP 8440p laptops HP 6930 laptops
Editorial Software: Newscycle Solutions Mediaware & Saxotech Adobe Creative Suite Citrix
Total Circulation: 15903

LOWELL

THE SUN

Corporate/Parent Company: Paxton Media Group
Publication Street Address: 491 Dutton St Ste 2
City: Lowell
State: MA
Publication Website: www.lowellsun.com
Postal Code: 01854-4292
Office phone: (978) 458-7100
Publisher Name: KEVIN CORRADO
Publisher Email: kcorrado@digitalfirstmedia.com
Publisher Phone: 978-970-4807
Editor Name: TOM SHATTUCK
Editor Email: tshattuck@lowellsun.com
Advertising Executive Name: EDDIE R. NAJEEULLAH
Advertising Executive Email: enajeeullah@mediaonene.com
Advertising Executive Phone: 978-970-4715
Year Established: 1878
Delivery Methods: Mail`Newsstand`Carrier`Racks
Own Printing Facility?: Y
Commercial printers?: Y
Mechanical specifications: Type page 12 x 21 1/2; E - 6 cols, 1 9/10, 1/8 between; A - 6 cols, 1 9/10, 1/16 between; C - 9 cols, 1 1/5, 1/8 between.
Published Days: Mon`Tues`Wed`Thur`Fri`Sat`Sun
Weekday Frequency: e
Saturday Frequency: m
Avg Paid Circ: 25406
Audit Company: AAM
Audit Date: 30 06 2017
Pressroom Equipment: Lines – 6-MAN, H/double width; 8-G/Urbanite single width; Press Drive – GE/Tenetrol; Folders – H/2:1 1967; Control System – GE/SCR.;
Mailroom Equipment: Counter Stackers – 4-QWI/300; Tying Machines – 2-Dynaric; Address Machine – 2-KR.;
Buisness Equipment: IBM/AS-400 Advanced 36
Classified Equipment: Hardware – PPI/System; Printers – V/5100 Typesetter;
Editorial Equipment: Hardware – 1-APP/Mac LAN and WAN; Printers – HP/4MV, HP/5000N
Editorial Software: QPS/QuarkXPress, Baseview/Qtools, Baseview/QXedit, Baseview/NewsEdit, APP/Appleshare & Windows NT Network.
Production Equipment: Hardware – Mk, Caere/OmniPage Professional, Adobe/Photoshop, Cameras – AG
Production Software: QPS/QuarkXPress 4.1, Baseview/Qtools, Baseview/QXedit.
Total Circulation: 25406

LYNN

THE DAILY ITEM

Corporate/Parent Company: Essex Media Group
Publication Street Address: 38 Exchange St
City: Lynn
State: MA
Publication Website: www.itemlive.com
Postal Code: 01901-1425
Office phone: (781) 593-7700
General E-mail: contactus@itemlive.com
Editor Name: Thor Jourgensen
Editor Email: tjourgensen@itemlive.com
Year Established: 1877
Delivery Methods: Mail`Newsstand`Carrier`Racks
Own Printing Facility?: Y
Commercial printers?: N
Mechanical specifications: Type page 11 x 21; E - 6 cols, 2 1/16, 1/8 between; A - 6 cols, 2 1/16, 1/8 between; C - 9 cols, 1 5/16, 1/8 between.
Published Days: Mon`Tues`Wed`Thur`Fri`Sat`Sun
Weekday Frequency: m
Saturday Frequency: m
Avg Paid Circ: 20434
Audit Company: CAC
Audit Date: 30 06 2017
Buisness Equipment: Newzware
Buisness Software: Newzware
Classified Equipment: Hardware – AST/Bravo MS 4.66d Terminals; Icanon;
Classified Software: Newzware/Pongras
Editorial Equipment: Hardware – Gateway/Desktop/Laptops; Printers – Lexmark/Optra LXI Plus Printer
Editorial Software: Microsoft/Windows 98, Microsoft/Office 2000, QPS/QuarkXPress 4.1.
Production Equipment: Hardware – 1-Gateway/P6 NT Server on Xytron/RIP, 1-Gateway/P5, 1-ScanJet/Scanner; Cameras – Canon
Production Software: InDesign 4.0, MEI/ALS 3.0.
Note: Printed, inserted offsite
Total Circulation: 20434

MILFORD

MILFORD DAILY NEWS

Corporate/Parent Company: Gannett
Publication Street Address: 197 Main St
City: Milford
State: MA
Publication Website: www.milforddailynews.com
Postal Code: 01757-2635
Office phone: (508) 634-7522
Editor Name: Bob Tremblay
Editor Email: rtremblay@wickedlocal.com
Editor Phone: 508-626-4409
Advertising Executive Name: Mike Bentle
Advertising Executive Email: mbentle@wickedlocal.com
Advertising Executive Phone: 978-371-5757
Year Established: 1887
Delivery Methods: Mail`Carrier
Own Printing Facility?: Y
Commercial printers?: Y
Mechanical specifications: Type page 13 x 21 1/2; E - 6 cols, 2 1/16, 1/8 between; A - 6 cols, 2 1/16, 1/8 between; C - 9 cols, 1 3/8, 1/16 between.
Published Days: Mon`Tues`Wed`Thur`Fri`Sat`Sun
Weekday Frequency: m
Saturday Frequency: m
Avg Paid Circ: 2070
Avg Free Circ: 113
Audit Company: AAM
Audit Date: 29 10 2019
Buisness Equipment: TI/990-12R
Buisness Software: DSI
Classified Equipment: Hardware – 4-PC; Printers – Toshiba/P351 SX;
Classified Software: III 3.9.
Editorial Equipment: Hardware – 25-PC/18-RSK/TRS 80 Model 100, RSK/TRS 80 Model 200, Lf/Leafscan 35; Printers – Toshiba/P351 SQ, APP/Mac LaserWriter, 2-QMS/860, HP/4M Plus
Editorial Software: III 3.9.
Production Equipment: Hardware – 2-QMS/860, AG, ECR/VL 36 Imagesetter; Cameras – 1-R, 1-LE/R, AG/RPS 6100S; Scanners – Lf/Leafscan 35, Microtek, HP/Scanner
Production Software: QPS/QuarkXPress 3.3, Microsoft/Windows, APP/Mac.
Total Circulation: 2591

NEW BEDFORD

THE STANDARD-TIMES

Corporate/Parent Company: Gannett
Publication Street Address: 25 Elm St
City: New Bedford
State: MA
Publication Website: www.southcoasttoday.com
Postal Code: 02740-6228
Office phone: (508) 997-7411
General E-mail: classified@capecodonline.com
Editor Name: Boggs, Jerry
Editor Email: jboggs@s-t.com
Editor Phone: 508-979-4464
Advertising Executive Name: Rohland, Chris
Advertising Executive Email: crohland@s-t.com
Advertising Executive Phone: 508-979-4360
Year Established: 1850
Delivery Methods: Newsstand`Carrier
Own Printing Facility?: N
Commercial printers?: Y
Mechanical specifications: Type page 13 x 21 1/2; E - 6 cols, 2 1/16, 1/8 between; A - 6 cols, 2 1/16, 1/8 between; C - 9 cols, 1 3/8, 1/16 between.
Published Days: Mon`Tues`Wed`Thur`Fri`Sat`Sun
Weekday Frequency: m
Saturday Frequency: m
Avg Paid Circ: 7735
Avg Free Circ: 449
Audit Company: AAM
Audit Date: 31 03 2019
Buisness Equipment: IBM/AS-400
Buisness Software: INSI, Software Plus, Computer Associates, Lawson, ATEX
Classified Equipment: Hardware - Desktops
Classified Software: AdBase ATOL
Editorial Equipment: Hardware – 45-Dell/486 66mhz; Printers – 2-HP/4M, 1-HP/44 Color Plotter, 1-NewGen/11x17 Laser Printer
Editorial Software: Dewar/Unixaix Network.
Production Equipment: Hardware – 1-Wing Lynch/Color, 1-Lf/Leafscan 45; Cameras – 1-C/Spartan II, 1-C/Marathon; Scanners – 1-ECR/Autokon 1000DE
Production Software: QPS/QuarkXPress 3.3.
Total Circulation: 8184

NEWBURYPORT

THE DAILY NEWS

Corporate/Parent Company: Gannett
Publication Street Address: 23 Liberty St
City: Newburyport
State: MA
Publication Website: www.newburyportnews.com
Postal Code: 01950-2750
Office phone: (978) 462-6666
General E-mail: ndnnews@newburyportnews.com
Publisher Name: Karen Andreas
Publisher Email: kandreas@northofboston.com
Editor Name: David Joyner
Editor Email: djoyner@northofboston.com
Editor Phone: 978.946.2189
Advertising Executive Name: Mark Zappala
Advertising Executive Email: mzappala@eagletribune.com
Advertising Executive Phone: 978-946-2174
Year Established: 1887
Delivery Methods: Mail`Carrier
Mechanical specifications: Type page 11 1/2 x 21; E - 6 cols, 1 13/16, 5/16 between; A - 6 cols, 1 13/16, 5/16 between; C - 9 cols, 1 7/32, 3/32 between.
Published Days: Mon`Tues`Wed`Thur`Fri`Sat
Weekday Frequency: e
Saturday Frequency: e
Avg Paid Circ: 5991
Avg Free Circ: 506
Audit Company: AAM
Audit Date: 9 12 2019
Buisness Equipment: IBM/AS400
Classified Equipment: Hardware – AT.;
Editorial Equipment: Hardware – PC
Editorial Software: QPS/QuarkXPress.
Production Equipment: Hardware – Nu-Arc; Scanners – Epson
Production Software: QuarkXpress 4.0.
Total Circulation: 6900

NORTH ANDOVER

THE EAGLE-TRIBUNE

Corporate/Parent Company: CNHI, LLC
Publication Street Address: 100 Turnpike St
City: North Andover
State: MA
Publication Website: www.eagletribune.com
Postal Code: 01845-5033
Office phone: (978) 946-2000
General E-mail: news@eagletribune.com
Publisher Name: Karen Andreas
Publisher Email: kandreas@northofboston.com
Editor Name: David Joyner
Editor Email: djoyner@northofboston.com
Editor Phone: 978.946.2189
Advertising Executive Name: Mark Zappala
Advertising Executive Email: mzappala@eagletribune.com
Advertising Executive Phone: 978-946-2174
Year Established: 1868
Delivery Methods: Mail`Newsstand`Carrier`Racks
Own Printing Facility?: Y
Commercial printers?: Y
Mechanical specifications: Type page 11 1/16 x 21 1/2; E - 6 cols, 1 5/6, 1/8 between; A - 6 cols, 1 5/6, 1/8 between; C - 10 cols, 1 1/16, 1/16 between.
Published Days: Mon`Tues`Wed`Thur`Fri`Sat`Sun
Weekday Frequency: e
Saturday Frequency: e
Avg Paid Circ: 14173
Avg Free Circ: 2989
Audit Company: AAM
Audit Date: 11 12 2019
Pressroom Equipment: Lines – 8-G/Metro (3 color decks); Folders - 1-G/Double 2:1.;
Mailroom Equipment: Counter Stackers – Goss Olympian; Inserters & Stuffers – 7wo, Goss 630 inserters; Tying Machines – 4/ Power Strap; Control System – Omnizone; Address Machine – Domino;
Buisness Equipment: IBM/AS-400
Buisness Software: INSI
Classified Equipment: Hardware – APT; Printers – Epson/LaserWriter;
Classified Software: APT
Editorial Equipment: Hardware – Mediaspan; Printers – QMS/860
Editorial Software: Mediaspan
Production Equipment: Hardware – Agfa Advantage Imagesetters; Cameras – Kodak, Cannon; Scanners – ECR/1000, Epson/636, Polaroid/SprintScan
Production Software: Adobe, InDesign
Total Circulation: 18809

NORTHAMPTON

DAILY HAMPSHIRE GAZETTE

Corporate/Parent Company: Newspapers of New England
Publication Street Address: 115 Conz St
City: Northampton
State: MA
Publication Website: www.gazettenet.com
Postal Code: 01060-4445
Office phone: (413) 584-5000
General E-mail: circulation@gazettenet.com
Publisher Name: Michael Moses
Publisher Email: publisher@gazettenet.com
Editor Name: Brooke Hauser
Editor Email: bhauser@gazettenet.com
Year Established: 1786
Delivery Methods: Mail`Carrier
Own Printing Facility?: Y
Commercial printers?: Y
Mechanical specifications: Type page 11 5/8 x 21 1/2; E - 6 cols, 1 5/6, 1/8 between; A - 6 cols, 1 5/6, 1/8 between; C - 9 cols, 1 1/4, 1/8 between.
Published Days: Mon`Tues`Wed`Thur`Fri`Sat
Weekday Frequency: m
Saturday Frequency: m
Avg Paid Circ: 12043
Avg Free Circ: 719

I-53

Audit Company: AAM
Audit Date: 31 12 2018
Pressroom Equipment: Lines – 11-G/Urbanite single width (3-color satellite unit); Press Drive – 2, 100-HP/Westinghouse, 100-HP/GE; Folders – 1-G/Urbanite; Reels & Stands – 2-G/3-High Stands; Registration System – Duarte/Pin Register System.
Mailroom Equipment: Counter Stackers – 3/QWI; Inserters & Stuffers – 1-GMA/SLS 1000 12:2; Tying Machines – 2-Dynaric/SSB 70; Control System – Linc/Packaging Line Control System, Address/Linc, Stack/Line, Key/Line; Address Machine – 2-/Ch, Address/Linc I;
Buisness Equipment: 1-DEC/Prioris HX 590 System, Papertrack/2000
Buisness Software: Newzware
Classified Equipment: Hardware – 6-PC Workstation, Compaq/Proliant 1600; Printers – HP, X;
Classified Software: APT/ACT 2.06, QPS/QuarkXPress 3.32.
Editorial Equipment: Hardware – Dell/Poweredge 1300, 60-PC Workstation, 2-Compaq/Proliant 1600; Printers – X, 1-Xerox/NP32
Editorial Software: APT/ACT 2.06, Microsoft/Word 6.0.
Production Equipment: Hardware – AP Server; Scanners – Microtek/Scanmaker 3
Production Software: QPS/QuarkXPress 3.32, APT/ACT 2.06.
Total Circulation: 12762

PITTSFIELD

THE BERKSHIRE EAGLE

Corporate/Parent Company: New England Newspapers, Inc.
Publication Street Address: 75 S Church St
City: Pittsfield
State: MA
Publication Website: www.berkshireeagle.com
Postal Code: 01201-6140
Office phone: (413) 447-7311
General E-mail: news@berkshireeagle.com
Publisher Name: Fredric D. Rutberg
Publisher Email: frutberg@berkshireeagle.com
Publisher Phone: (413) 496-6380
Editor Name: Kevin Moran
Editor Email: kmoran@berkshireeagle.com
Editor Phone: (413) 496-6201
Advertising Executive Name: Jordan Brechenser
Advertising Executive Email: jbrechenser@berkshireeagle.com
Advertising Executive Phone: 413-496-6308
Year Established: 1891
Delivery Methods:
 Mail`Newsstand`Carrier`Racks
Own Printing Facility?: Y
Commercial printers?: Y
Published Days: Mon`Tues`Wed`Thur`Fri`Sat`Sun
Weekday Frequency: All day
Saturday Frequency: All day
Avg Paid Circ: 16827
Audit Company: AAM
Audit Date: 30 06 2018
Mailroom Equipment: Counter Stackers – 3-TMST/Compass; Inserters & Stuffers – GMA/SLS 1000 8:1; Tying Machines – 3-Samuel/Power Strap, Bu; Wrapping Singles – Mailroom Control System ÃƒÂ£ÃƒÂ‚Â£ÃƒÂ£ÃƒÂ‚Â£ÃƒÂ£ÃƒÂ‚Â£ÃƒÂ£ÃƒÂ‚Â£ÃƒÂ£ÃƒÂ‚Â£ÃƒÂ£ÃƒÂ‚Â£ Prism; Address Machine – Ch;
Total Circulation: 16827

QUINCY

THE PATRIOT LEDGER

Corporate/Parent Company: Gannett
Publication Street Address: 2 Adams Place
City: Quincy
State: MA
Publication Website: www.patriotledger.com
Postal Code: 2169
Office phone: (617) 786-7026
Editor Name: Gregory Mathis
Editor Email: gmathis@gatehousemedia.com

Editor Phone: 617-786-7052
Year Established: 1837
Delivery Methods: Mail`Carrier
Own Printing Facility?: N
Commercial printers?: N
Mechanical specifications: Type page 13 x 22; E - 6 cols, 2, 1/8 between; A - 6 cols, 2, 1/8 between; C - 9 cols, 1 3/8, 3/4 between.
Published Days: Mon`Tues`Wed`Thur`Fri`Sat
Weekday Frequency: e
Saturday Frequency: m
Avg Paid Circ: 18803
Audit Company: AAM
Audit Date: 8 05 2020
Mailroom Equipment: Counter Stackers – 2-HL/HT-2, 3-HL/Monitor; Inserters & Stuffers – 2-GMA/SLS 1000 8:1; Tying Machines – 4-OVL/JP-80, 1-OVL/Constellation, 1-MLN/WorldNews; Wrapping Singles – 2-HL/Bottom Wrap; Address Machine – 1-IBM/AS 400.;
Buisness Equipment: 1-IBM/AS-400 Model 9402, SCS/AdMax
Classified Equipment: Hardware – 1-Dell/6300 PowerEdge, 2-Dell/2300 PowerEdge, 27-Dell/Optiplex PC; Printers – 1-HP/4050, 1-HP/8000, 1-Citoh/SQE;
Classified Software: SCS/AdMax, SCS/ClassPag.
Editorial Equipment: Hardware – 2-Dell/6300 PowerEdge, 1-Dell/4300, 3-Dell/6400GX1, 1-AP/IBM Photo Server, 74-Dell/Optiplex PC, 16-Dell/Inspiron, 6-APP/Mac G3/G4/1-HP/Scanjet 6300C, 1-Epson/Expression 836XL, 2-Nikon/CoolScan; Printers – 1-HP/4050, 3-HP/5000, 1-HP
Production Equipment: Hardware – 2-Na/Starlite, Konica/4550 Imagesetter, Konica/6200 Imagesetter; Cameras – 1-C/Pager, 1-R/432 Mic II, 1-AG/RPS 2024 Automatic
Production Software: Tera/Good News 3.
Total Circulation: 16098

SOUTHBRIDGE

SOUTHBRIDGE EVENING NEWS

Corporate/Parent Company: Stonebridge Press, Inc.
Publication Street Address: PO Box 90
City: Southbridge
State: MA
Publication Website: www.stonebridgepress.com
Postal Code: 01550-0090
Office phone: (508) 764-4325
Year Established: 1923
Delivery Methods: Mail`Carrier
Own Printing Facility?: Y
Commercial printers?: N
Mechanical specifications: Type page 9 5/8 x 16; E - 6 cols, 1 1/2, 3/16 between; A - 6 cols, 1 1/2, 1/10 between; C - 7 cols, 1 3/8, 1/10 between.
Published Days: Mon`Tues`Wed`Thur`Fri
Weekday Frequency: All day
Avg Paid Circ: 4500
Audit Company: Sworn/Estimate/Non-Audited
Audit Date: 7 12 2019
Total Circulation: 4500

SPRINGFIELD

THE REPUBLICAN

Corporate/Parent Company: Advance Newspapers
Publication Street Address: 1860 Main St
City: Springfield
State: MA
Publication Website: www.masslive.com/republican
Postal Code: 01103-1000
Office phone: (413) 788-1000
Year Established: 1824
Delivery Methods:
 Mail`Newsstand`Carrier`Racks
Own Printing Facility?: Y
Commercial printers?: Y
Mechanical specifications: Type page 11 5/8 x 20 1/4; E - 6 cols, 1 5/6, 1/8 between; A - 6 cols, 1 5/6, 1/8 between; C - 10 cols, 1 7/100, 1/16 between.

Published Days: Mon`Tues`Wed`Thur`Fri`Sat`Sun
Weekday Frequency: m
Saturday Frequency: m
Avg Paid Circ: 50244
Audit Company: AAM
Audit Date: 25 03 2020
Pressroom Equipment: Lines – 5-MAN/Regioman (8 couples); Press Drive – Bammueller; Reels & Stands – 6-MAN/CD 13.;
Mailroom Equipment: Counter Stackers – 5-QWI/400, 2-QWI/300, 1-Gammerler/KL 503; Inserters & Stuffers – 1-SLS/3000 28:2, 2-SLS/3000 14:2; Tying Machines – 3/Strapex, 6-/Dynaric; Wrapping Singles – 6-/QWI; Address Machine – 3-Ch/525E Labeler;
Buisness Equipment: 2-Dell, IBM/AS-400, Power Edge/4200
Buisness Software: AP, GL, Platinum, Ultipro Payroll System
Classified Equipment: Hardware – Dell; Printers – Dataproducts;
Classified Software: Mactive 2.24.
Editorial Equipment: Hardware – Dell; Printers – 2-HP/Designjet 2500
Editorial Software: HI/Newsmaker Editorial.
Production Equipment: Hardware – Adobe/Photoshop, APP/Mac Desktop
Production Software: HI/Newsmaker, Mactive, PGL, Proimage/Newsway.
Total Circulation: 67083

TAUNTON

TAUNTON DAILY GAZETTE

Corporate/Parent Company: Gannett
Publication Street Address: 5 Cohannet St
City: Taunton
State: MA
Publication Website: www.tauntongazette.com
Postal Code: 02780-3903
Office phone: (508) 880-9000
Publisher Name: Peter Meyer
Publisher Email: pmeyer@heraldnews.com
Publisher Phone: 508-862-1111
Editor Name: Lynne Sullivan
Editor Email: lsullivan@heraldnews.com
Editor Phone: 508-967-3141
Advertising Executive Name: Paige Webster
Advertising Executive Email: pwebster@wickedlocal.com
Advertising Executive Phone: 508-967-3120
Year Established: 1848
Delivery Methods: Mail`Carrier
Own Printing Facility?: Y
Commercial printers?: Y
Mechanical specifications: Type page 12 x 21 1/2; E - 6 cols, 1 7/8, 3/16 between; A - 6 cols, 1 7/8, 3/16 between; C - 9 cols, 1 1/4, 1/8 between.
Published Days: Mon`Tues`Wed`Thur`Fri`Sat`Sun
Weekday Frequency: m
Saturday Frequency: m
Avg Paid Circ: 4105
Avg Free Circ: 210
Audit Company: AAM
Audit Date: 8 05 2020
Pressroom Equipment: Lines – 9-G/Urbanite single width; Pasters –8-Jardis/EbwayRegistration System – Duarte/Pin Registration System.
Mailroom Equipment: Counter Stackers – 3/Hall; Inserters & Stuffers – GMA/SLS 1000; Tying Machines – MLN/ML2E, Signode/MLN 2A; Wrapping Singles – 3-Hall/Monarch; Address Machine – CH/525.;
Buisness Equipment: CCPS
Buisness Software: Microsoft/Excel 7, Lotus 5.0, Newzware
Classified Equipment: Hardware – Mk, APP/Mac; Printers – HP;
Classified Software: AT.
Editorial Equipment: Hardware – Mk, APP/Mac; Printers – Okidata, HP/HMV
Editorial Software: Mk, APP/Mac, Baseview.
Production Equipment: Hardware – Nu; Cameras – SCREEN, R, C/Spartan 3; Scanners – Epson, Nikon/Super Coolscan
Production Software: QPS/QuarkXPress 4.0.
Total Circulation: 2703

TAUNTON

THE ENTERPRISE

Corporate/Parent Company: Gannett
Publication Street Address: 5 Cohannet St
City: Taunton
State: MA
Publication Website: www.enterprisenews.com
Postal Code: 0 2780
Office phone: 508-427-4038
General E-mail: features@enterprisenews.com
Editor Name: Rebecca Hyman
Editor Email: rhyman@gatehousemedia.com
Editor Phone: 598-967-3150
Year Established: 1880
Delivery Methods: Mail`Carrier
Own Printing Facility?: Y
Commercial printers?: Y
Mechanical specifications: Type page 13 x 21; E - 6 cols, 2 1/16, 1/8 between; A - 6 cols, 2 1/16, 1/8 between; C - 9 cols, 1 3/8, 1/16 between.
Published Days: Mon`Tues`Wed`Thur`Fri`Sat`Sun
Weekday Frequency: e
Saturday Frequency: m
Avg Paid Circ: 9284
Audit Company: AAM
Audit Date: 31 12 2018
Pressroom Equipment: Lines – G/Mark I (double width) 1960; MAN/Flexoman (double width) 1989; MAN/Flexoman (w/hump) (double width) 1989; G/Mark I (double width) 1960; G/Mark I (double width) 1960; MAN/Flexoman (double width) 1989;
Mailroom Equipment: Counter Stackers – 2-QWI/Sport; Inserters & Stuffers – 1-GMA/SLS 1000; Tying Machines – 1-OVL/JP-80, 1-OVL/JP-80, 2-OVL/Strapmaster; Wrapping Singles – Addressing machine 2-VideoJet/Series 270.;
Buisness Equipment: DEC/VAX 4100, Microsoft/Windows NT, CI/1000 Sge Printer, HP/4050, Dell/GX1 workstation, Mac/O/S, SCO/Unix
Buisness Software: CJ, Southware/Accounting Systems, Geac/Circulation Systems, SCS/ADMAX-Billing
Classified Equipment: Hardware – 1-Dell/6300 Application Server, AT/SYSDECO-Classified Pagination Server, 11-Dell/GX1 Workstation; HP/Flatbed Scanner; Printers – 1-HP/8000, HP/4050;
Classified Software: SCS/Admax-Classified, Microsoft/Office 2000, Adobe/Photoshop.
Editorial Equipment: Hardware – 2-Dell/6400 Application Server, 1-Dell/4400 Library Server, 2-Dell/GX1 AP Wire Service, 2-Dell/GX1 Primary & Secondary Domain Name Controllers, 1-Dell/GX110 Terminal Server, 45-Dell/Optiplex/GX1 workstation, 6-APP/Mac workstation, 3-APP/iMac, 3
Production Equipment: Hardware – Na/Systems Flexo Processor, 2-MON/RipExpress RIP, 2-ECR/PelBox 108C, 1-III/3850, Konica/RIP; Cameras – 1-C/Spartan III, 1-P/Pager; Scanners – 1-ECR/Autokon 1000, X/7650, Umax
Production Software: Tera/GN3-Fred.
Total Circulation: 9284

WAKEFIELD

WAKEFIELD DAILY ITEM

Corporate/Parent Company: The Wakefield Item Co.
Publication Street Address: 26 Albion St
City: Wakefield
State: MA
Publication Website: www.localheadlinenews.com
Postal Code: 01880-2803
Office phone: (781) 245-0080
General E-mail: news@wakefielditem.com
Year Established: 1894
Delivery Methods:
 Mail`Newsstand`Carrier`Racks
Mechanical specifications: Type page 13 x 21; E - 6 cols, 2 1/16, 1/8 between; A - 9 cols, 1 1/4, 1/8 between; C - 9 cols, 1 1/4, 1/8 between.
Published Days: Mon`Tues`Wed`Thur`Fri
Weekday Frequency: e

U.S. Daily Newspapers

Avg Paid Circ: 4556
Audit Company: Sworn/Estimate/Non-Audited
Audit Date: 7 12 2019
Editorial Software: Baseview/NewsEdit.
Total Circulation: 4556

WESTFIELD
THE WESTFIELD NEWS

Corporate/Parent Company: The Westfield News Group LLC
Publication Street Address: 62 School St
City: Westfield
State: MA
Publication Website: https://thewestfieldnews.com/
Postal Code: 01085-2835
Office phone: (413) 562-4181
General E-mail: floram@thewestfieldnewsgroup.com
Editor Name: Hope Tremblay
Editor Email: hope@thewestfieldnewsgroup.com
Advertising Executive Name: Flora Masciadrelli
Advertising Executive Email: floram@thewestfieldnewsgroup.com
Year Established: 1971
Delivery Methods: Mail`Newsstand`Carrier
Published Days: Mon`Tues`Wed`Thur`Fri`Sat
Weekday Frequency: m
Saturday Frequency: m
Avg Paid Circ: 4600
Audit Company: Sworn/Estimate/Non-Audited
Audit Date: 7 12 2019
Mailroom Equipment: Tying Machines – 2/Bu;
Production Equipment: Hardware – APP/Mac; Cameras – AG/1600

WOBURN
DAILY TIMES CHRONICLE

Corporate/Parent Company: Woburn Daily Times, Inc.
Publication Street Address: 1 Arrow Dr
City: Woburn
State: MA
Publication Website: www.homenewshere.com
Postal Code: 01801-2090
Office phone: (781) 933-3700
General E-mail: news@dailytimesinc.com
Editor Name: James D. Haggerty, Jr.
Editor Phone: Ext. 330
Year Established: 1901
Delivery Methods: Mail`Carrier
Mechanical specifications: Type page 11 5/8 x 21; E - 6 cols, 1 4/5, 1/8 between; A - 6 cols, 1 4/5, 1/16 between; C - 9 cols, 1 3/20, 1/8 between.
Published Days: Mon`Tues`Wed`Thur`Fri
Weekday Frequency: e
Avg Paid Circ: 10872
Audit Company: Sworn/Estimate/Non-Audited
Audit Date: 7 12 2019
Pressroom Equipment: Lines – 8-G/Community 1975.;
Mailroom Equipment: Tying Machines – 1/CYP, 2-/Sa; Wrapping Singles – Am; Address Machine – 2-Am/1800.;
Buisness Equipment: 6-Vision Data
Classified Equipment: Hardware – 6-APP/iMac;
Classified Software: Baseview.
Editorial Equipment: Hardware – 5-APP/iMac/ Okidata/Doc-IT 4000 Scanner; Printers – 2-HP/LaserJet 4
Editorial Software: Baseview.
Production Equipment: Hardware – 1-BKY, 1-Ca; Cameras – 2-DSA.
Total Circulation: 10872

WORCESTER
TELEGRAM & GAZETTE

Publication Street Address: 100 Front St Ste 500
City: Worcester
State: MA
Publication Website: www.telegram.com
Postal Code: 01608-1440
Office phone: (508) 793-9200
Editor Name: Executive Editor
Editor Email: david.nordman@telegram.com
Editor Phone: (508) 793-9375
Advertising Executive Name: Kathy Benoit
Advertising Executive Email: kbenoit@gatehousemedia.com
Advertising Executive Phone: (508) 767-9525
Year Established: 1866
Delivery Methods: Mail`Newsstand`Carrier`Racks
Own Printing Facility?: N
Commercial printers?: N
Mechanical specifications: Full broad sheet 11.625 inches x 21 inches Double truck 24.125 x 21 1 column 1.833 inches 2 column 3.792 3 column 5.750 4 column 7.708 5 Column 9.667 6 Column 11.625
Published Days: Mon`Tues`Wed`Thur`Fri`Sat`Sun
Weekday Frequency: m
Saturday Frequency: m
Avg Paid Circ: 27678
Audit Company: AAM
Audit Date: 31 12 2018
Note: In 2013, The Telegram & Gazette won 56 awards from the New England Newspaper & Press Association.
Total Circulation: 27678

MARYLAND

ANNAPOLIS
CAPITAL GAZETTE

Publication Street Address: P.O. Box 6727
City: Annapolis
State: MD
Publication Website: www.capitalgazette.com
Postal Code: 21401
Office phone: 410-268-5000
General E-mail: communitynews@capitalgazette.com
Publisher Name: Tim Thomas
Editor Name: Rick Hutzell
Editor Email: rhutzell@bladenews.com

HOMETOWN ANNAPOLIS

Publication Street Address: 888 Bestgate Road, Suite 104
City: Annapolis
State: MD
Publication Website: www.capitalonline.com
Postal Code: 21401
Office phone: tips@capgaznews.com
Publisher Name: Tim Thomas
Editor Name: Rick Hutzell
Advertising Executive Name: Marty Padden
Advertising Executive Email: mpadden@capgaznews.com
Advertising Executive Phone: 443-482-3154

THE CAPITAL

Corporate/Parent Company: Tribune Publishing Company
Publication Street Address: P.O. Box 6727
City: Annapolis
State: MD
Publication Website: www.capitalgazette.com
Postal Code: 21401
Office phone: (410) 268-5000
General E-mail: tips@capgaznews.com
Publisher Name: Tim Thomas
Editor Name: Rick Hutzell
Editor Email: rhutzell@bladenews.com

BALTIMORE
BALTIMORE CITY PAPER

Publication Street Address: 300 E. Cromwell Street
City: Baltimore
State: MD
Publication Website: www.citypaper.com
Postal Code: 21230
Office phone: (443) 692-9011
General E-mail: newstips@baltimoresun.com
Editor Name: Trif Alatzas
Editor Email: trif.alatzas@baltsun.com
Editor Phone: 410-332-6154

EDGEWOOD NEWS

Publication Street Address: 300 E. Cromwell Street
City: Baltimore
State: MD
Publication Website: www.baltimoresun.com/news/maryland/harford/abingdon
Postal Code: 21230
Office phone: (443) 692-9011
General E-mail: customersatisfaction@baltsun.com
Editor Name: Trif Alatzas
Editor Email: trif.alatzas@baltsun.com
Editor Phone: 410-332-6154

MARYLAND NEWS

Publication Street Address: 300 E. Cromwell Street
City: Baltimore
State: MD
Publication Website: www.baltimoresun.com/news/maryland
Postal Code: 21230
Office phone: (443) 692-9011
General E-mail: newstips@baltimoresun.com
Editor Name: Trif Alatzas
Editor Email: trif.alatzas@baltsun.com
Editor Phone: 410-332-6154

THE BALTIMORE SUN

Corporate/Parent Company: Tribune Publishing
Publication Street Address: 501 N Calvert St
City: Baltimore
State: MD
Publication Website: www.baltimoresun.com
Postal Code: 21278-1000
Office phone: (410) 332-6000
General E-mail: newstips@baltimoresun.com
Publisher Name: Trif Alatzas
Publisher Email: trif.alatzas@baltsun.com
Publisher Phone: 410-332-6154
Editor Name: Sam Davis
Editor Email: sam.davis@baltsun.com
Editor Phone: 410-332-6534
Advertising Executive Name: Sharon Nevins
Advertising Executive Email: snevins@baltsun.com
Advertising Executive Phone: (410) 332-6872

THE DAILY RECORD

Corporate/Parent Company: Gannett
Publication Street Address: 200 St. Paul Place, Suite 2480
City: Baltimore
State: MD
Publication Website: www.thedailyrecord.com
Postal Code: 21202
Office phone: (443) 524-8100
General E-mail: service@bridgetowermedia.com
Publisher Name: Suzanne Fischer-Huettner
Publisher Email: shuettner@thedailyrecord.com
Publisher Phone: 443-524-8103
Editor Name: Tom Baden
Editor Email: tbaden@thedailyrecord.com
Editor Phone: 443-524-8150
Advertising Executive Name: Darice Dixon
Advertising Executive Email: dmiller@thedailyrecord.com
Advertising Executive Phone: 443-524-8188

CALIFORNIA
SOUTHERN MARYLAND NEWS

Publication Street Address: P.O. Box 257
City: California
State: MD
Publication Website: smnewsnet.com
Postal Code: 20619
General E-mail: news@smnewsnet.com

COLUMBIA
MARYLANDREPORTER.COM

Publication Street Address: 6392 Shadowshape Place
City: Columbia
State: MD
Publication Website: www.marylandreporter.com
Postal Code: 21045
Publisher Name: Timothy W. Maier
Publisher Email: tim@MarylandReporter.com
Editor Name: Len Lazarick
Editor Email: len@marylandreporter.com
Editor Phone: (410) 312-9840

CUMBERLAND
THE CUMBERLAND TIMES-NEWS

Corporate/Parent Company: CNHI, LLC
Publication Street Address: 19 Baltimore St
City: Cumberland
State: MD
Publication Website: www.times-news.com
Postal Code: 21502-3023
Office phone: (301) 722-4600
General E-mail: circdept@times-news.com
Publisher Name: Robert Forcey
Publisher Phone: 301-784-2514
Editor Name: John D. Smith
Editor Email: jsmith@times-news.com
Editor Phone: 301-784-2517
Advertising Executive Name: Tiffany Eisentrout
Advertising Executive Email: teisentrout@times-news.com
Advertising Executive Phone: 301-784-2504

EASTON
THE STAR-DEMOCRAT

Publication Street Address: 29088 Airpark Dr
City: Easton
State: MD
Publication Website: www.stardem.com
Postal Code: 21601-7000
Office phone: (410) 822-1500
Publisher Name: Jim Normandin
Publisher Email: jim.normandin@adamspg.com
Editor Name: Greg Maki
Editor Email: gmaki@chespub.com
Editor Phone: 443-239-9595
Advertising Executive Name: Brandon Silverstein
Advertising Executive Email: bsilverstein@chespub.com
Advertising Executive Phone: 410-200-6469

FREDERICK
THE FREDERICK NEWS-POST

Corporate/Parent Company: Ogden Newspapers Inc.
Publication Street Address: 351 Ballenger Center Dr
City: Frederick
State: MD

Publication Website: www.fredericknewspost.com
Postal Code: 21703-7095
Office phone: (301) 662-1177
General E-mail: webmaster@fredericknewspost.com
Publisher Name: Geordie Wilson
Publisher Email: gwilson@newspost.com
Editor Name: Paul Milton
Editor Email: pmilton@newspost.com
Editor Phone: 240-215-8630
Advertising Executive Name: Jen Abrecht
Advertising Executive Email: jabrecht@newspost.com
Advertising Executive Phone: 240-215-8583

HAGERSTOWN

THE HERALD-MAIL

Corporate/Parent Company: Gannett
Publication Street Address: 100 Summit Ave
City: Hagerstown
State: MD
Publication Website: www.heraldmailmedia.com
Postal Code: 21740-5509
Office phone: (301) 733-5131
General E-mail: editor@whatsnxt.com
Publisher Name: Andy Bruns
Editor Name: Jake Womer

LA PLATA

THE SOUTHERN MARYLAND NEWSPAPERS ONLINE

Publication Street Address: 204 Washington Ave
City: La Plata
State: MD
Publication Website: www.somdnews.com
Postal Code: 20646
Office phone: 443-231-3387
General E-mail: somdcirc@somdnews.com
Publisher Name: Jim Normandin
Publisher Email: jim.normandin@adamspg.com
Advertising Executive Name: John Rives
Advertising Executive Email: jrives@chespub.com
Advertising Executive Phone: 301-848-0175

LEXINGTON PARK

THE BAY NET

Corporate/Parent Company: Logan Ventures, LLC
Publication Street Address: 22316 Three Notch Rd
City: Lexington Park
State: MD
Publication Website: www.thebaynet.com
Postal Code: 20653
Office phone: 240-309-4009
General E-mail: news@thebaynet.com

RIDGE

THE CHESAPEAKE TODAY

Publication Street Address: 10, 2019 Buzz's Marina
City: Ridge
State: MD
Publication Website: www.thechesapeaketoday.com
Postal Code: 20680
General E-mail: newsdesk.thechesapeaketoday@gmail.com

SALISBURY

THE DAILY TIMES

Corporate/Parent Company: Gannett
Publication Street Address: 115 S. Division St
City: Salisbury
State: MD
Publication Website: www.delmarvanow.com
Postal Code: 21801

Office phone: (410) 749-7171
Advertising Executive Name: Ron Pousson
Advertising Executive Email: rpousson@localiq.com
Advertising Executive Phone: 410-845-4609

WESTMINSTER

CARROLL COUNTY TIMES

Publication Street Address: 201 Railroad Ave
City: Westminster
State: MD
Publication Website: www.carrollcountytimes.com
Postal Code: 21157-4823
Office phone: (410) 848-4400
General E-mail: customersatisfaction@baltsun.com
Publisher Name: Trif Alatzas
Publisher Email: trif.alatzas@baltsun.com
Publisher Phone: 410-332-6154
Editor Name: Sam Davis
Editor Email: sam.davis@baltsun.com
Editor Phone: 410-332-6534
Advertising Executive Name: Sharon Nevins
Advertising Executive Email: snevins@baltsun.com
Advertising Executive Phone: (410) 332-6872

CARROLL STANDARD

Publication Street Address: 115 Airport Dr., Suite 170
City: Westminster
State: MD
Publication Website: www.carrollstandard.com
Postal Code: 21157
Editor Name: Marcel J. van Rossum
Editor Email: editor@carrollstandard.com

HYATTSVILLE WIRE

State: MD
Publication Website: www.hyattsvillewire.com
Editor Name: Alison Beckwith
Editor Email: news@hyattsvillewire.com

MARYLAND LEADER

Corporate/Parent Company: Midwest Radiio Network
State: MD
Publication Website: www.marylandleader.com

MAINE

AUGUSTA

KENNEBEC JOURNAL

Corporate/Parent Company: MaineToday Media
Publication Street Address: 36 Anthony Ave Ste 101
City: Augusta
State: ME
Publication Website: www.centralmaine.com
Postal Code: 04330-7891
Office phone: (207) 623-3811
General E-mail: circulation@mainetoday.com
Publisher Name: Lisa DeSisto
Publisher Email: lisa@mainetoday.com
Publisher Phone: (207) 791-6630
Editor Name: Judith Meyer
Editor Email: jmeyer@sunjournal.com
Editor Phone: (207) 689-2902
Advertising Executive Name: Jody Jalbert
Advertising Executive Email: jjalbert@sunjournal.com

Advertising Executive Phone: (207) 689-2913

BANGOR

BANGOR DAILY NEWS

Corporate/Parent Company: Bangor Publishing Company
Publication Street Address: One Merchants Plaza PO Box 1329
City: Bangor
State: ME
Publication Website: www.bangordailynews.com
Postal Code: 0 4402
Office phone: (207) 990-8000
Publisher Name: Richard Warren
Publisher Email: jluetjen@bangordailynews.com
Publisher Phone: 207.990.8220
Editor Name: Dan MacLeod
Editor Email: dmacleod@bangordailynews.com
Editor Phone: 207.990.8260
Advertising Executive Name: Todd Johnston
Advertising Executive Email: tjohnston@bangordailynews.com
Advertising Executive Phone: 207.990.8129

BIDDEFORD

JOURNAL-TRIBUNE

Corporate/Parent Company: MaineToday Media, Inc.
Publication Street Address: 457 Alfred St
City: Biddeford
State: ME
Publication Website: https://www.pressherald.com/journal-tribune/
Postal Code: 04005-9447
Office phone: (207) 282-1535
Publisher Name: Lisa DeSisto
Publisher Email: lisa@mainetoday.com
Publisher Phone: (207) 791-6630
Editor Name: Cliff Schechtman
Editor Email: cschechtman@mainetoday.com
Editor Phone: (207) 791-6693
Advertising Executive Name: Courtney Spencer
Advertising Executive Email: cspencer@pressherald.com
Advertising Executive Phone: (207) 791-6203

BOOTHBAY HARBOR

PENOBSCOT BAY PILOT

Corporate/Parent Company: Maine-OK Enterprises, Inc
Publication Street Address: 97 TOWNSEND AVE
City: BOOTHBAY HARBOR
State: ME
Publication Website: www.penbaypilot.com
Postal Code: 0 4538
Office phone: 207-633-4620
General E-mail: 87 Elm Street, Suite 215
Publisher Name: Camden
Publisher Email: ME
Publisher Phone: 4843
Advertising Executive Phone: Lynda Clancy

BRUNSWICK

THE TIMES RECORD

Corporate/Parent Company: Gannett
Publication Street Address: 3 Business Pkwy
City: Brunswick
State: ME
Publication Website: www.timesrecord.com
Postal Code: 04011-7390
Office phone: (207) 729-3311
General E-mail: circulation@mainetoday.com
Publisher Name: Lisa DeSisto
Publisher Email: lisa@mainetoday.com
Publisher Phone: (207) 791-6630
Editor Name: Cliff Schechtman
Editor Email: cschechtman@mainetoday.com
Editor Phone: (207) 791-6693
Advertising Executive Name: Courtney Spencer
Advertising Executive Email: cspencer@

pressherald.com
Advertising Executive Phone: (207) 791-6203

PORTLAND

PORTLAND PRESS HERALD / MAINE SUNDAY TELEGRAM

Corporate/Parent Company: MaineToday Media, Inc.
Publication Street Address: 1 City Ctr Stop 7
City: Portland
State: ME
Publication Website: www.pressherald.com
Postal Code: 04101-4009
Office phone: (207) 791-6650
General E-mail: circulation@mainetoday.com
Publisher Name: Lisa DeSisto
Publisher Email: lisa@mainetoday.com
Publisher Phone: (207) 791-6630
Editor Name: Cliff Schechtman
Editor Email: cschechtman@mainetoday.com
Editor Phone: (207) 791-6693
Advertising Executive Name: Courtney Spencer
Advertising Executive Email: cspencer@pressherald.com
Advertising Executive Phone: (207) 791-6203

WATERVILLE

MORNING SENTINEL

Corporate/Parent Company: MaineToday Media
Publication Street Address: 31 Front St
City: Waterville
State: ME
Publication Website: https://www.centralmaine.com
Postal Code: 04901-6626
Office phone: (207) 873-3341
General E-mail: circulation@mainetoday.com
Publisher Name: Lisa DeSisto
Publisher Email: lisa@mainetoday.com
Publisher Phone: (207) 791-6630
Editor Name: Judith Meyer
Editor Email: jmeyer@sunjournal.com
Editor Phone: (207) 689-2902
Advertising Executive Name: Jody Jalbert
Advertising Executive Email: jjalbert@sunjournal.com
Advertising Executive Phone: (207) 689-2913

MICHIGAN

ADRIAN

THE DAILY TELEGRAM

Corporate/Parent Company: Gannett
Publication Street Address: 133 N Winter St
City: Adrian
State: MI
Publication Website: www.lenconnect.com
Postal Code: 49221-2042
Office phone: (517) 265-5111
General E-mail: circulation@lenconnect.com
Editor Name: Ray Kisonas
Editor Email: rkisonas@lenconnect.com
Editor Phone: 517-417-2022
Advertising Executive Name: Ryley Schalk
Advertising Executive Email: rschalk@lenconnect.com
Advertising Executive Phone: 517-417-2019
Year Established: 1892
Delivery Methods:
Mail`Newsstand`Carrier`Racks
Own Printing Facility?: Y
Commercial printers?: Y
Mechanical specifications: Type page 13 1/16 x 21 1/2; E - 6 cols, 1 7/8, 1/8 between; A - 6 cols, 1 7/8, 1/8 between; C - 9 cols, 1/8 between.
Published Days: Mon`Tues`Wed`Thur`Fri`Sat`Sun
Weekday Frequency: e
Saturday Frequency: m

U.S. Daily Newspapers

I-57

Avg Paid Circ: 9912
Avg Free Circ: 1279
Audit Company: AAM
Audit Date: 2 07 2020
Pressroom Equipment: Lines – 1Tensor Four High 9-G/Community (3 color decks; 2 formers); Folders – 1-G/55C.;
Mailroom Equipment: Counter Stackers – 2-HL/Monitor; Inserters & Stuffers – Titan/12:1; Tying Machines – Sa; Address Machine – Prism.;
Buisness Equipment: PC
Classified Equipment: Hardware – APP/Mac; App/Mac;
Classified Software: Media Span.
Editorial Equipment: Hardware – APP/Mac
Editorial Software: QPS/QuarkXPress, Media Span IQ/NewsEdit.
Production Equipment: Hardware – ECRM/CTP
Total Circulation: 7094

ALMA

MORNING SUN

Corporate/Parent Company: Gannett
Publication Street Address: 311 E Superior St Ste A
City: Alma
State: MI
Publication Website: www.themorningsun.com
Postal Code: 48801-1832
Office phone: (989) 779-6000
Publisher Name: Greg Mazanec
Publisher Email: MiPublisher@digitalfirstmedia.com
Editor Name: Jeff Hoard
Editor Email: jeff.hoard@oakpress.com
Editor Phone: 248-284-7046
Advertising Executive Name: Tammy Fisher
Advertising Executive Email: tfisher@michigannewspapers.com
Advertising Executive Phone: 989-779-6110
Year Established: 1977
Delivery Methods: Carrier`Racks
Own Printing Facility?: Y
Commercial printers?: Y
Mechanical specifications: Type page 13 x 21; E - 6 cols, 2 1/16, 1/8 between; A - 8 cols, 3 1/5, 1/8 between; C - 8 cols, 1 1/2, 1/8 between.
Published Days: Mon`Tues`Wed`Thur`Fri`Sat`Sun
Weekday Frequency: m
Saturday Frequency: m
Avg Paid Circ: 6715
Avg Free Circ: 3309
Audit Company: AAM
Audit Date: 30 09 2014
Pressroom Equipment: Lines – 14-G/Community (2 Path finder color decks); 10-G/Community.;
Mailroom Equipment: Counter Stackers – 2/BG; Inserters & Stuffers – 1-K&M/1472, 3-MM; Tying Machines – 6-Bu;
Buisness Equipment: Compaq/PL 1500
Classified Equipment: Hardware – Compaq/PL 1500; Printers – 1-Epson/DFX-8000;
Classified Software: PBS/AdPlus.
Editorial Equipment: Printers – HP/4P, HP/5P
Editorial Software: Alfa
Production Equipment: Cameras – 1-B/4000, 1-Nu/VIC-1418, 1-TogeeMD/480, 1-Acti/253; Scanners – 1-AG/Arcus Plus, AG/Horizon Flatbed
Production Software: PBS/AdPlacer.
Total Circulation: 10024

ALPENA

THE ALPENA NEWS

Corporate/Parent Company: Ogden Newspapers, Inc.
Publication Street Address: 130 Park Pl
City: Alpena
State: MI
Publication Website: www.thealpenanews.com
Postal Code: 49707-2828
Office phone: (989) 354-3111
General E-mail: newsroom@thealpenanews.com
Publisher Name: Bill Speer
Publisher Email: bspeer@thealpenanews.com
Editor Name: Justin A. Hinkley
Editor Email: jhinkley@thealpenanews.com
Advertising Executive Name: Christie Werda
Advertising Executive Email: cwerda@thealpenanews.com
Year Established: 1899
Delivery Methods: Mail`Newsstand`Carrier`Racks
Own Printing Facility?: Y
Commercial printers?: Y
Mechanical specifications: Type page 10 x 21 1/2; E - 6 cols, 1.583, .16 between; A - 6 cols, 1.583, .16 between; C - 8 cols, 1.163, .16 between.
Published Days: Mon`Tues`Wed`Thur`Fri`Sat
Weekday Frequency: m
Saturday Frequency: m
Avg Paid Circ: 5629
Avg Free Circ: 106
Audit Company: AAM
Audit Date: 30 04 2020
Pressroom Equipment: Lines – 6-G/U 911;
Mailroom Equipment: Tying Machines – 1/Sa, 2-/MLN; Address Machine – 1-/St.;
Total Circulation: 7048

BAD AXE

HURON DAILY TRIBUNE

Corporate/Parent Company: Hearst Corp.
Publication Street Address: 211 N Heisterman St
City: Bad Axe
State: MI
Publication Website: www.michigansthumb.com
Postal Code: 48413-1239
Office phone: (989) 269-6461
Editor Name: Eric Young
Editor Email: eric.young@hearstnp.com
Editor Phone: ext, 105
Advertising Executive Name: Renee Willis
Advertising Executive Email: rgolder@hearstnp.com
Advertising Executive Phone: ext. 126
Year Established: 1876
Delivery Methods: Mail`Carrier
Own Printing Facility?: Y
Commercial printers?: Y
Mechanical specifications: Type page 13 x 21 1/2; E - 6 cols, 2 1/16, 1/8 between; A - 6 cols, 2 1/16, 1/8 between; C - 9 cols, 1 3/8, 1/16 between.
Published Days: Tues`Wed`Thur`Fri`Sat
Weekday Frequency: e
Saturday Frequency: e
Avg Paid Circ: 3800
Audit Company: Sworn/Estimate/Non-Audited
Audit Date: 7 12 2019
Pressroom Equipment: Lines – 9-KP/News King; Pasters –BG/Acumeter.
Mailroom Equipment: Tying Machines – 2/Bu; Address Machine – Ch.;
Buisness Equipment: AdMark
Buisness Software: Discus
Classified Equipment: Hardware – APP/Mac; APP/Mac Scanner; Printers – APP/Mac LaserWriter II;
Classified Software: Baseview, Mk/Class Manager 3.2.
Editorial Equipment: Hardware – APP/Mac/APP/Mac Scanner, Lf/AP Leaf Picture Desk, APP/Power Mac, APP/Power Mac/7100 Photo Desk; Printers – APP/Mac LaserWriter II, APP/Mac LaserWriter 810, AG/Imagesetter 800
Editorial Software: Baseview/NewsEdit 3.3, Baseview.
Production Equipment: Hardware – AG/800 Imagesetter, Power PC/8100; Cameras – C/Spartan III, C/Marathon; Scanners – Umax, Nikon
Production Software: AG, QPS/QuarkXPress 4.0.
Total Circulation: 3800

BATTLE CREEK

BATTLE CREEK ENQUIRER

Corporate/Parent Company: Gannett
Publication Street Address: 77 Michigan Ave E Ste 101
City: Battle Creek
State: MI
Publication Website: www.battlecreekenquirer.com
Postal Code: 49017-7033
Office phone: (269) 964-7161
General E-mail: bceeditors@battlecreekenquirer.com
Editor Name: Michael McCullough
Year Established: 1900
Delivery Methods: Mail`Newsstand`Carrier`Racks
Own Printing Facility?: N
Published Days: Mon`Tues`Wed`Thur`Fri`Sat`Sun
Weekday Frequency: m
Saturday Frequency: m
Avg Paid Circ: 7794
Avg Free Circ: 95
Audit Company: AAM
Audit Date: 27 11 2018
Production Software: Newsgate/CCI
Total Circulation: 10635

BAY CITY

THE BAY CITY TIMES

Corporate/Parent Company: Advance Newspapers
Publication Street Address: 311 5th St
City: Bay City
State: MI
Publication Website: http://www.mlive.com/bay-city
Postal Code: 48708-5802
Office phone: (989) 895-8551
General E-mail: customercare@mlive.com
Advertising Executive Name: Steve Westphal
Year Established: 1873
Delivery Methods: Mail`Newsstand`Carrier`Racks
Own Printing Facility?: Y
Commercial printers?: N
Mechanical specifications: Type page 13 x 22 1/4; E - 6 cols, 2 1/16, 1/8 between; A - 6 cols, 2 1/16, 1/8 between; C - 10 cols, 1 1/4, 1/16 between.
Published Days: Tues`Thur`Fri`Sun
Weekday Frequency: m
Avg Paid Circ: 9870
Avg Free Circ: 519
Audit Company: AAM
Audit Date: 21 03 2019
Mailroom Equipment: Counter Stackers – Flexi Roll Buffer; Inserters & Stuffers – 2/SLS 3000, 5-/AU PP 500; Tying Machines – Dyneric.;
Buisness Equipment: 1-Sun/Ultra Sparc 140, 1-Sun/Sparc 20, 1-Sun/Ultra 200 E
Buisness Software: PBS, Solaris/OS, SBS
Classified Equipment: Hardware – AT/9000;
Classified Software: AT 4.4.10.
Editorial Equipment: Hardware – Apple/APP/Mac; Printers – HP/LaserJet II
Editorial Software: Baseview.
Production Equipment: Hardware – AP; Scanners – 2-AG/Duoscan T1200
Production Software: Baseview.
Total Circulation: 17984

BIG RAPIDS

THE PIONEER - BIG RAPIDS

Corporate/Parent Company: Hearst Corp.
Publication Street Address: 115 N Michigan Ave
City: Big Rapids
State: MI
Publication Website: www.bigrapidsnews.com
Postal Code: 49307-1401
Office phone: (231) 796-4831
General E-mail: circ@pioneergroup.com
Editor Name: Tim Rath
Editor Email: trath@pioneergroup.com
Editor Phone: 231-592-8386
Advertising Executive Name: Danette Doyle
Advertising Executive Email: advertising@pioneergroup.com
Advertising Executive Phone: 231-592-8359
Year Established: 1862
Delivery Methods: Mail`Carrier
Mechanical specifications: Type page 12 x 21 1/2; E - 6 cols, 2, 1/6 between; A - 6 cols, 1 3/8, 7/16 between; C - 6 cols, 1 3/8, 7/16 between.
Published Days: Mon`Tues`Wed`Thur`Fri`Sat
Weekday Frequency: m
Saturday Frequency: m
Avg Paid Circ: 5221
Audit Company: Sworn/Estimate/Non-Audited
Audit Date: 7 12 2019
Pressroom Equipment: Lines – 2-4/HI, 2-2/HI, 2, 2-HI/JF-35 Folders; 1-4/HI, 2-2/HI, 2, HI/JF-35 Folder single width; Press Drive – 30, 100, GE/Motor Drive; Folders – 1-HI/JF7, 1-HI/JF-35; Pasters –4-Martin/EC Plus zero speedReels & Stands – 5;
Mailroom Equipment: Counter Stackers – Rima, NG/25; Inserters & Stuffers – KAN/480 6:1; Tying Machines – 2-Bu/String Tyers, 1-Mosca/Strapper; Address Machine – Wm.;
Buisness Equipment: Microsoft/Windows NT 4.0, APP/Power Mac Work Group 8550
Buisness Software: Great Plains, Baseview
Classified Equipment: Hardware – APP/Mac, Poweruser/fileserver; 2-APP/Mac, Xante, ECR/Imagesetter; Printers – ECR/Imagesetter;
Classified Software: APP/Power Mac, Baseview/Ad Manager Pro.
Editorial Equipment: Hardware – APP/Mac, Poweruser/fileserver/9-APP/Mac, 1-APP/Mac II; Printers – Xante, ECR/Imagesetter, X/Color Laser
Editorial Software: Baseview/NewsEdit Pro 2.2.2.
Production Equipment: Hardware – 2-APP/Mac LaserWriter II, 1-Nu/FT40LNS; Cameras – 1-AG/RPS 2024S, 1-LE/480; Scanners – 1-AG/Studio Star, 1-Polaroid/SprintScan Plus
Production Software: QPS/QuarkXPress 3.2.
Total Circulation: 5221

CADILLAC

CADILLAC NEWS

Publication Street Address: 130 N Mitchell St
City: Cadillac
State: MI
Publication Website: www.cadillacnews.com
Postal Code: 49601-1856
Office phone: (231) 775-6565
General E-mail: news@cadillacnews.com
Publisher Name: Christopher Huckle
Publisher Phone: 231-779-5200
Editor Name: Matthew Seward
Editor Phone: 231-779-4126
Advertising Executive Name: Josh Bailey
Advertising Executive Phone: 231-779-4138
Year Established: 1872
Delivery Methods: Mail`Carrier
Own Printing Facility?: Y
Commercial printers?: Y
Mechanical specifications: Type page 10 3/8 x 21 1/2; E - 6 cols, 2 1/16, 1/8 between; A - 6 cols, 2 1/16, 1/8 between; C - 6 cols, 2 1/16, 1/8 between.
Published Days: Mon`Tues`Wed`Thur`Fri`Sat
Weekday Frequency: m
Saturday Frequency: m
Avg Paid Circ: 7200
Audit Company: USPS
Audit Date: 10 01 2017
Pressroom Equipment: Lines – 6-HI/V-15A (Upper Former) 1969.;
Mailroom Equipment: Tying Machines – Bu; Address Machine – Domino/Ink Jet.;
Buisness Equipment: APP/Mac
Buisness Software: Baseview
Classified Equipment: Hardware – Mac; Printers – Xerox;
Classified Software: Baseview/Classified, Baseview/Ad Manager Pro.
Editorial Software: Woodwing/InDesign
Total Circulation: 7200

CHEBOYGAN

CHEBOYGAN DAILY TRIBUNE

Corporate/Parent Company: Gannett
Publication Street Address: 308 N Main St
City: Cheboygan
State: MI
Publication Website: www.cheboygannews.com
Postal Code: 49721-1545
Office phone: (231) 627-7144
Editor Name: Brenda Rigotti
Editor Email: brigotti@sooeveningnews.com
Advertising Executive Name: Jennifer Fenstermaker
Advertising Executive Email: jfenstermaker@cheboygantribune.com
Year Established: 1876
Delivery Methods: Mail`Carrier`Racks
Mechanical specifications: Type page 12 1/2 x 21; E - 6 cols, 2 1/16, 1/8 between; A - 6 cols, 2 1/16, 1/8 between; C - 6 cols, 2 1/16, 1/8 between.
Published Days: Mon`Tues`Wed`Thur`Fri`Sat
Weekday Frequency: m
Saturday Frequency: m
Avg Paid Circ: 4864
Audit Company: Sworn/Estimate/Non-Audited
Audit Date: 7 12 2019
Pressroom Equipment: Lines – 5-G/Community single width;
Mailroom Equipment: Tying Machines – Bu, Malow; Address Machine – Am.;
Buisness Equipment: PC
Classified Equipment: Hardware – APP/Mac; Printers – Xante 3G.;
Editorial Equipment: Hardware – APP/Mac; Printers – LaserWriter 16/600
Editorial Software: QPS/QuarkXPress 3.3, Macromedia/Freehand, Baseview/NewsEdit.
Production Equipment: Hardware – 1-Nu; Cameras – 2-K.
Total Circulation: 4864

CLINTON TOWNSHIP

THE MACOMB DAILY

Corporate/Parent Company: Media News Group
Publication Street Address: 19176 Hall Rd Ste 200
City: Clinton Township
State: MI
Publication Website: www.macombdaily.com
Postal Code: 48038-6914
Office phone: (586) 469-4510
General E-mail: service@macombdaily.com
Publisher Name: Greg Mazanec
Publisher Email: MiPublisher@digitalfirstmedia.com
Editor Name: Jeff Hoard
Editor Email: jeff.hoard@oakpress.com
Editor Phone: 248-284-7046
Advertising Executive Name: Noelle Klomp
Advertising Executive Email: noelle.klomp@oakpress.com
Advertising Executive Phone: 586-783-0393
Year Established: 1841
Delivery Methods: Newsstand`Carrier`Racks
Own Printing Facility?: N
Commercial printers?: Y
Mechanical specifications: Broadsheet page - 6 columns (9.89") x 20"; column gutter 8 pts.; page gutter 80 pts.; page margins 40 pts.
Published Days: Mon`Tues`Wed`Thur`Fri`Sat`Sun
Weekday Frequency: m
Saturday Frequency: m
Avg Paid Circ: 20994
Audit Company: AAM
Audit Date: 14 12 2018
Mailroom Equipment: Control System – Burt Technologies;
Total Circulation: 32112

COLDWATER

THE DAILY REPORTER

Corporate/Parent Company: Gannett
Publication Street Address: 15 W Pearl St
City: Coldwater
State: MI
Publication Website: www.thedailyreporter.com
Postal Code: 49036-1912
Office phone: (517) 278-2318
General E-mail: newsroom@thedailyreporter.com
Editor Name: Candice Phelps
Editor Email: cphelps@stugisjournal.com
Advertising Executive Name: Amy Crabtree
Advertising Executive Email: acrabtree@hillsdale.net
Advertising Executive Phone: 517-278-2318
Year Established: 1895
Delivery Methods: Mail`Carrier
Mechanical specifications: Type page 11 3/4 x 21 5/8; E - 6 cols, 1/6 between; A - 6 cols, 1/6 between; C - 9 cols, 1/6 between.
Published Days: Mon`Tues`Wed`Thur`Fri`Sat
Weekday Frequency: m
Saturday Frequency: m
Avg Paid Circ: 5316
Audit Company: Sworn/Estimate/Non-Audited
Audit Date: 7 12 2019
Buisness Equipment: Vision Data
Classified Equipment: Hardware – APP/Mac; Printers – Okidata;
Classified Software: Baseview.
Editorial Equipment: Hardware – APP/Mac; Printers – APP/Mac LaserWriter, Xante/Accel-a-Writer 8300, Epson/5200 Color
Editorial Software: Adobe/Photoshop 4.0, Macromedia/Freehand 7.0, QPS/QuarkXPress 4.04, Baseview.
Production Equipment: Hardware – Caere/OmniPage, Nikon/Scan; Scanners – Umax
Production Software: QPS/QuarkXPress 4.04.
Total Circulation: 5316

DETROIT

DETROIT FREE PRESS

Corporate/Parent Company: Gannett
Publication Street Address: 160 W. Fort St.
City: Detroit
State: MI
Publication Website: www.freep.com
Postal Code: 48226
Office phone: (313) 222-6400
Editor Name: Peter Bhatia
Editor Email: pbhatia@freepress.com
Year Established: 1831
Delivery Methods: Mail`Newsstand`Carrier`Racks
Own Printing Facility?: Y
Commercial printers?: Y
Mechanical specifications: Broadsheet Page: 11.625" x 20" Tab Page: 9.667" x 11.375"
Published Days: Mon`Tues`Wed`Thur`Fri`Sun
Weekday Frequency: m
Saturday Frequency: m
Avg Paid Circ: 124631
Audit Company: AAM
Audit Date: 4 05 2020
Pressroom Equipment: Lines – ManRoland Geoman 75 with 50 printing couples; ManRoland Geoman 75 with 50 printing couples; ManRoland Geoman 75 with 50 printing couples; ManRoland Geoman 75 with 50 printing couples; ManRoland Geoman 75 with 50 printing couples; Folders – 6 ManRoland 2:5:5; Reels & Stands – 60 ManRoland ; Control System – PPM/Pecom;
Mailroom Equipment: Counter Stackers – 10 TMSI 3 Gammler 21 Quipp 300 23 Quipp 500 ; Inserters & Stuffers – 4 Goss Heidelberg 630's 1 Goss Heidelberg 632; Tying Machines – 24 Dynaric NP 3000 28 Dynaric NP 5000 3 D 2400's; Control System – GMA Enternet BURT Cannon;
Classified Equipment: Hardware – Dell R710 running VMWare; Dell ;
Classified Software: Mactive
Editorial Equipment: Hardware – Dell 270 Optiplex PCs Macintosh Pro /Dell; Printers – HP DesignJet 1050C broadsheet proofer HP 9000 11x17 B&W proofer HP 4250 network printers
Editorial Software: CCI Newsline, Adobe, Apple
Production Equipment: Hardware – PRINTERS EPSON 9880 COLORBURST 44 HP T770 DESIGNJET HP 1050C DESIGNJET 13 MACS NEWSWAY; Scanners – EPSON EXPRESSION 1680 EPSON GT 20000
Production Software: NEWSWAY MGS CCI MACTIVE FOR CLASS ADS & PAGINATION GENESYS & FOR RETAIL ADS ADTRACKER FOR AD DATABASE ADOBE SOFTWARE: CS5 ACROBAT INDESIGN ILLUSTRATOR PHOTOSHOP OTHER: QUARK EXPRESS 8.0 PITSTOP 10 GMG INK OPTIMIZER ASSURA FILE PROCESSING SOFTWARE HARLEQUIN RIPS
Note: Effective March 30, 2009, the Detroit Fee Press will cease daily print publication, and will publish Thursdays, Fridays and Sundays. For detailed mechanical specifications, advertising, circulation, production and other business office personnel, see Detr
Total Circulation: 212246

DETROIT

THE DETROIT NEWS

Corporate/Parent Company: Media News Group
Publication Street Address: 160 W Fort St
City: Detroit
State: MI
Publication Website: www.detroitnews.com
Postal Code: 48226-3700
Office phone: (313) 222-2300
General E-mail: cserv@michigan.com
Publisher Name: Gary Miles
Publisher Email: gmiles@detroitnews.com
Publisher Phone: (313) 222-2594
Editor Name: Kelley Root
Editor Email: kroot@detroitnews.com
Editor Phone: (313) 222-2522
Year Established: 1873
Delivery Methods: Newsstand`Carrier`Racks
Own Printing Facility?: Y
Commercial printers?: Y
Published Days: Mon`Tues`Wed`Thur`Fri`Sat
Weekday Frequency: m
Saturday Frequency: m
Avg Paid Circ: 80145
Audit Company: AAM
Audit Date: 4 05 2020
Pressroom Equipment: Plateroom - AGFA Polaris CTP (6) Pressroom - MANRoland GeoMAN 75 presses (6) Siemens Demantic ASRS storage system
Pressroom Software: ProImage workflow and Man Production Management control software
Mailroom Equipment: Goss 29:1 inserter lines (5) Cannon Cart System
Mailroom Software: Burt Technologies Enternet Technology
Classified Software: Mactive Classified
Editorial Software: CCI Enterprise Newsgate System
Production Software: ProImage NewsWay
Total Circulation: 55554

ESCANABA

DAILY PRESS

Corporate/Parent Company: Ogden Newspapers, Inc.
Publication Street Address: 600 Ludington St
City: Escanaba
State: MI
Publication Website: www.dailypress.net
Postal Code: 49829-3830
Office phone: (906) 786-2021
General E-mail: news@dailypress.net
Publisher Name: Corky Deroeck
Publisher Email: cderoeck@dailypress.net
Advertising Executive Email: tbelongie@dailypress.net
Year Established: 1909
Delivery Methods: Mail`Newsstand`Carrier`Racks
Own Printing Facility?: Y
Commercial printers?: Y
Mechanical specifications: Type page 11 3/4 x 21 1/2; E - 6 cols, 1 3/4, 1/6 between; A - 6 cols, 1 3/4, 1/6 between; C - 9 cols, 1 3/8, 1/8 between.
Published Days: Mon`Tues`Wed`Thur`Fri`Sat
Weekday Frequency: e
Saturday Frequency: m
Avg Paid Circ: 5362
Avg Free Circ: 302
Audit Company: AAM
Audit Date: 18 07 2018
Pressroom Equipment: Lines – 9-G/Community (Color head);
Mailroom Equipment: Tying Machines – 2-Bu/Strapper, MLN/Spirit-Strapper; Address Machine – SAC/JR.;
Buisness Equipment: ATT
Classified Equipment: Hardware – Mk; Printers – 2-V.;
Editorial Equipment: Hardware – Mk/4-Panasonic; Printers – TI/KSR Omni Printer.
Production Equipment: Hardware – 1-LE; Cameras – 1-Nu/SST 20 x 24.
Total Circulation: 7507

FLINT

THE FLINT JOURNAL

Corporate/Parent Company: Advance Newspapers
Publication Street Address: 540 S Saginaw St Ste 101
City: Flint
State: MI
Publication Website: www.mlive.com/flint
Postal Code: 48502-1813
Office phone: (810) 766-6100
General E-mail: customercare@mlive.com
Advertising Executive Name: Steve Westphal
Year Established: 1876
Delivery Methods: Mail`Newsstand`Carrier`Racks
Mechanical specifications: Type page 11 5/8 x 20; E - 6 cols, 1 5/6, 1/8 between; A - 6 cols, 1 5/6, 1/8 between; C - 10 cols, 1 1/8, 1/8 between.
Published Days: Tues`Thur`Fri`Sun
Weekday Frequency: e
Saturday Frequency: m
Avg Paid Circ: 18812
Avg Free Circ: 2076
Audit Company: AAM
Audit Date: 4 06 2020
Pressroom Equipment: Lines – MAN/Roland Regioman; MAN/Roland Regioman; Press Drive – Baumuller; Folders – 1-MAN/Double-out 64 pg.; Reels & Stands – 4-MAN/CD13; Control System – PECOM.;
Mailroom Equipment: Counter Stackers – 4-QWI/501, 1-QWI/400, 2-HL/Dual Carrier; Inserters & Stuffers – 2-GMA/SLS3000; Tying Machines – 5-Dynaric/4.;
Buisness Equipment: Apple Xserve Dell HP Hitachi
Buisness Software: DTI CircView RouteSmart VMware 4-5
Classified Equipment: Hardware – Dell & HP PCss; Printers – HP, Canon, IKON;
Classified Software: Atex Mactive 3.0 Encompass Office 2010
Editorial Equipment: Hardware – Dell PCs/Dell & HP PCs; Printers – HP, Ikon, Canon
Editorial Software: Media Span Baseview, Adobe InDesign/InCopy
Production Equipment: Hardware – Dell & HP PC Apple Macs; Scanners – Epson Canon
Production Software: PPI AGFA IntelliTune Adobe Illustrator Adobe InDesign Adobe Flash Adobe Photoshop Xpance ATEX Mactive PageLayout ZenDesk
Total Circulation: 28178

GRAND HAVEN

GRAND HAVEN TRIBUNE

Corporate/Parent Company: Paxton Media Group
Publication Street Address: 101 N 3rd St
City: Grand Haven
State: MI
Publication Website: www.grandhaventribune.com
Postal Code: 49417-1209

U.S. Daily Newspapers

Office phone: (616) 842-6400
General E-mail: news@grandhaventribune.com
Editor Name: Matt DeYoung
Editor Email: mdeyoung@grandhaventribune.com
Editor Phone: 616-842-6400 ext. 232
Advertising Executive Name: Kim Street
Advertising Executive Phone: 616-842-6400 ext. 242
Year Established: 1885
Delivery Methods:
    Mail`Newsstand`Carrier`Racks
Own Printing Facility?: Y
Commercial printers?: Y
Mechanical specifications: Type page 13 x 21 1/2; E - 6 cols, 2 1/16, 1/8 between; A - 6 cols, 2 1/16, 1/8 between; C - 8 cols, 1 7/8, 1/8 between.
Published Days: Mon`Tues`Wed`Thur`Fri`Sat
Weekday Frequency: e
Saturday Frequency: e
Avg Paid Circ: 8813
Audit Company: AAM
Audit Date: 30 09 2011
Pressroom Equipment: Lines – 5-G/Urbanite;
Mailroom Equipment: Tying Machines – 1-Sa/BM1A.;
Buisness Equipment: 1-Unisys/5000
Classified Equipment: Hardware – 3-Sun; Printers – HP/LaserJet
Classified Software: Vision Data.
Editorial Equipment: Hardware – 2-CD/2330, 15-APP/Mac; Printers – HP/LaserJet
Editorial Software: Baseview.
Production Equipment: Hardware – 1-Nat/Super A-250; Cameras – 1-SCREEN/650C.
Total Circulation: 8813

GRAND RAPIDS

THE GRAND RAPIDS PRESS

Corporate/Parent Company: Advance Publications, Inc.
Publication Street Address: 169 Monroe Ave NW Ste 100
City: Grand Rapids
State: MI
Publication Website: www.mlive.com/grand-rapids
Postal Code: 49503-2632
Office phone: (616) 222-5400
General E-mail: customercare@mlive.com
Advertising Executive Name: Steve Westphal
Year Established: 1892
Delivery Methods:
    Mail`Newsstand`Carrier`Racks
Mechanical specifications: Type page 10 7/8 x 19 1/2; E - 6 cols, 1 23/32, 3/32 between; A - 6 cols, 1 23/32, 3/32 between; C - 10 cols, 1 1/16, 1/32 between.
Published Days: Mon`Tues`Wed`Thur`Fri`Sat`Sun
Weekday Frequency: e
Saturday Frequency: m
Avg Paid Circ: 78271
Audit Company: AAM
Audit Date: 4 06 2020
Pressroom Equipment: Lines – MAN/Geoman (64 couples); Press Drive – Baumueller; Folders – 2-MAN; Pasters –12-MAN; Reels & Stands – 12-MAN; Control System – MAN; Registration System – Graphic Control.
Mailroom Equipment: Counter Stackers – 10-QWI/500; Inserters & Stuffers – 3-GMA/SLS 3000 (30:2); Tying Machines – 13/Dynaric; Wrapping Singles – 5-Dynaric/Single tyer; Control System – GMA/SAM; Address Machine – 2-Ch/Labeler;
Buisness Equipment: Apple Xserve Dell servers HP servers Hitachi HDS
Buisness Software: DTI CircView RouteSmart VMware 4-5
Classified Equipment: Hardware – Dell & HP PCs; Dell & HP PCs; Printers – HP, Canon, IKON.
Classified Software: Atex Mactive 3.0 Encompass Office 2010
Editorial Equipment: Hardware – Dell & HP PCs; Printers – HP, Ikon, Canon
Editorial Software: Media Span Baseview, Adobe InDesign/InCopy
Production Equipment: Hardware – Epson Canon; Scanners – Epson Canon

Production Software: PPI AGFA IntelliTune Adobe Illustrator Adobe InDesign Adobe Flash Adobe Photoshop Xpance ATEX Mactive PageLayout ZenDesk.
Total Circulation: 102860

GREENVILLE

THE DAILY NEWS

Corporate/Parent Company: Gannett
Publication Street Address: 109 N Lafayette St
City: Greenville
State: MI
Publication Website: www.thedailynews.cc
Postal Code: 48838-1853
Office phone: (616) 754-9301
General E-mail: news@staffordgroup.com
Publisher Name: Julie Stafford
Publisher Email: juliestafford@thedailynews.cc
Editor Name: Darrin Clark
Editor Email: dclark@staffordgroup.com
Advertising Executive Name: Amber Rood
Advertising Executive Email: arood@staffordgroup.com
Advertising Executive Phone: (616) 548-8257
Year Established: 1855
Delivery Methods: Mail`Carrier
Mechanical specifications: Type page 13 3/4 x 21; E - 6 cols, 2 1/18, 1/8 between; A - 6 cols, 2 1/18, between; C - 6 cols, 2 1/18, between.
Published Days: Mon`Tues`Wed`Thur`Fri`Sat
Weekday Frequency: e
Saturday Frequency: m
Avg Paid Circ: 7754
Audit Company: Sworn/Estimate/Non-Audited
Audit Date: 7 12 2019
Pressroom Equipment: Lines – 8-G/Community SSC (1-4-high) 1986; Folders – 1-G/SSC; Reels & Stands – 1-FBWAY/HS-35000.;
Mailroom Equipment: Tying Machines – 1/MLN, 1-/Bu; Address Machine – 1-/KR;
Buisness Equipment: Microsoft/Windows NT, HP/133 DL Server
Buisness Software: Great Plains
Classified Equipment: Hardware – 1-APP/Mac 8150 Workgroup Server; Printers – APP/Mac LaserWriter IIg, Okidata/Line Printer;
Classified Software: Baseview/Class Flow 2.2.5, QPS/QuarkXPress 3.32, Baseview/Class Manager Pro.
Editorial Equipment: Hardware – 1-APP/Mac 8150 Workgroup Server, 4-APP/Power Mac 7100-80, 1-Power Computing/210, 7-APP/Mac Performa 638CD, APP/Mac LC III/Minolta/RP605Z microfilm reader, Kk/35 mm Film Scanner, Nikon/LS 1000 Film Scanner; Printers – APP/Mac LaserW
Production Equipment: Hardware – Caere/OmniPage Pro 7.0, 1-APP/Mac 9600-200, Tektronix/Phaser 300X Color Printer; Cameras – COM/6700; Scanners – HSD/Scan-X Pro, Kk/35mm rapid film scanner.
Total Circulation: 7754

HILLSDALE

HILLSDALE DAILY NEWS

Corporate/Parent Company: Gannett
Publication Street Address: 263 Industrial Dr.
City: Hillsdale
State: MI
Publication Website: www.hillsdale.net
Postal Code: 49242
Office phone: (517) 437-7351
Editor Name: Candice Phelps
Editor Email: cphelps@sturgisjournal.com
Editor Phone: 517-437-7351
Advertising Executive Name: Brittney Potwin
Advertising Executive Email: bgrieser@hillsdale.net
Advertising Executive Phone: 517-437-7351
Year Established: 1846
Delivery Methods: Mail`Carrier
Mechanical specifications: Type page 13 1/16 x 21 1/2; E - 6 cols, 2 1/16, 1/8 between; A - 6 cols, 2 1/16, 1/8 between; C - 8 cols, 1 7/8, 1/8 between.
Published Days: Mon`Tues`Wed`Thur`Fri`Sat
Weekday Frequency: e
Saturday Frequency: m

Avg Paid Circ: 7285
Audit Company: Sworn/Estimate/Non-Audited
Audit Date: 7 12 2019
Pressroom Equipment: Lines – 5-G/Community;
Mailroom Equipment: Tying Machines – MLN/1100, 1/MLN, 1-/Strapex; Address Machine – Ch/705, Automecha/AccuFast PL.;
Buisness Equipment: HP, 4-ATT/610
Buisness Software: Unix/SCO U-386, SMS
Classified Equipment: Hardware – APP/Mac; Printers – APP/Mac LaserWriter NTX;
Classified Software: Baseview/Classified.
Editorial Equipment: Hardware – APP/Mac; Printers – APP/Mac LaserWriter NTX
Editorial Software: Baseview/NewsEdit.
Production Equipment: Hardware – APP/Mac LaserWriter 600, Adobe/Photoshop; Cameras – SCREEN/250; Scanners – APP/Mac Scanner, Nikon/Photo, Microtek/Scanmaker II.
Total Circulation: 7285

HOLLAND

THE HOLLAND SENTINEL

Corporate/Parent Company: Gannett
Publication Street Address: 54 W 8th St
City: Holland
State: MI
Publication Website: www.hollandsentinel.com
Postal Code: 49423-3104
Office phone: (616) 546-4200
Publisher Name: Orestes Baez
Publisher Email: obaez@gatehousemedia.com
Editor Name: Sarah Leach
Editor Email: sarah.leach@hollandsentinel.com
Editor Phone: 616.546.4278
Advertising Executive Name: Haley Kelly
Advertising Executive Email: haley.kelly@hollandsentinel.com
Advertising Executive Phone: 616.355.3278
Year Established: 1896
Delivery Methods:
    Mail`Newsstand`Carrier`Racks
Own Printing Facility?: Y
Commercial printers?: Y
Mechanical specifications: Type page 10 x 21; E - 6 cols, 1 5/6, 1/8 between; A - 6 cols, 1 5/6, 1/8 between; C - 9 cols, 1 3/16, 1/8 between.
Published Days: Tues`Wed`Thur`Fri`Sat`Sun
Weekday Frequency: m
Saturday Frequency: m
Avg Paid Circ: 6476
Avg Free Circ: 746
Audit Company: AAM
Audit Date: 4 03 2020
Pressroom Equipment: Lines – 24 - Dev
Mailroom Equipment: Counter Stackers – 2/HL; Inserters & Stuffers – 1-HI/NP 848; Tying Machines – 1-Signode, 1-Sterling/MR45CH; Address Machine – 1-/Ch.;
Buisness Equipment: Pc
Buisness Software: Media Span
Classified Equipment: Hardware – APP/Power Mac 233; Printers – APP/Mac LaserWriter II NTX;
Classified Software: Media Span
Editorial Equipment: Macs and PCs
Editorial Software: Saxotech
Production Equipment: Hardware – Nat, 2-MON/1270; Cameras – R; Scanners – Epson, Microtek, HP.
Total Circulation: 13842

HOUGHTON

THE DAILY MINING GAZETTE

Corporate/Parent Company: Ogden Newspapers, Inc.
Publication Street Address: P.O. Box 368
City: Houghton
State: MI
Publication Website: www.mininggazette.com
Postal Code: 49931
Office phone: (906) 482-1500
Editor Name: Dave Karnosky
Editor Email: dkarnosky@mininggazette.com

Editor Phone: (906) 483-2215
Advertising Executive Name: Yvonne Robillard
Advertising Executive Email: yrobillard@mininggazette.com
Advertising Executive Phone: (906) 483-2220
Year Established: 1859
Delivery Methods:
    Mail`Newsstand`Carrier`Racks
Own Printing Facility?: Y
Commercial printers?: Y
Mechanical specifications: Type page 13 x 21 1/2; E - 6 cols, 2, 1/6 between; A - 6 cols, 2, 1/6 between; C - 9 cols, 1 1/3, 1/6 between.
Published Days: Mon`Tues`Wed`Thur`Fri`Sat
Weekday Frequency: e
Saturday Frequency: m
Avg Paid Circ: 5397
Avg Free Circ: 70
Audit Company: AAM
Audit Date: 12 09 2018
Pressroom Equipment: Lines – 8-G/Offset 1980.;
Mailroom Equipment: Tying Machines – 4/Bu; Address Machine – PC.;
Buisness Equipment: 6-IBM/PC network
Buisness Software: Q&A, Lotus, Microsoft/Windows
Classified Equipment: Hardware – Mk/1100 Plus; Printers – TI/810
Classified Software: Mk.
Editorial Equipment: Hardware – Mk/1100 Plus; Printers – TI/810
Editorial Software: Mk.
Production Equipment: Hardware – Lf, Lf; Cameras – COM/680C.
Total Circulation: 5430

HOWELL

THE LIVINGSTON COUNTY DAILY PRESS & ARGUS

Corporate/Parent Company: Gannett Co., Inc.
Publication Street Address: 323 E Grand River Ave
City: Howell
State: MI
Publication Website: www.livingstondaily.com
Postal Code: 48843-2322
Office phone: (517) 548-2000
General E-mail: lcp-letters@livingstondaily.com
Advertising Executive Name: Huff, Gina
Advertising Executive Email: ghuff@michigan.com
Advertising Executive Phone: 586-977-7638
Year Established: 1843
Delivery Methods: Mail`Carrier
Own Printing Facility?: Y
Commercial printers?: Y
Published Days: Mon`Tues`Wed`Thur`Fri`Sun
Weekday Frequency: m
Avg Paid Circ: 5277
Avg Free Circ: 30
Audit Company: AAM
Audit Date: 17 06 2020
Total Circulation: 7281

IONIA

IONIA SENTINEL-STANDARD

Publication Street Address: 114 N Depot St
City: Ionia
State: MI
Publication Website: www.sentinel-standard.com
Postal Code: 48846-1602
Office phone: (616) 527-2100
Publisher Name: Corky Deroeck
Publisher Email: cderoeck@ironmountaindailynews.com
Publisher Phone: (906) 774-2772 ext. 11
Year Established: 1866
Delivery Methods:
    Mail`Newsstand`Carrier`Racks
Mechanical specifications: Type page 12 x 22; E - 6 cols, 1 5/16, 1/8 between; A - 6 cols, 1 5/16, 1/8 between; C - 8 cols, 1 7/8, 1/8 between.
Published Days: Tues`Wed`Thur`Fri`Sat
Weekday Frequency: m

Saturday Frequency: m
Avg Paid Circ: 2001
Audit Company: Sworn/Estimate/Non-Audited
Audit Date: 7 12 2019
Pressroom Equipment: Lines – 4-HI/V-15A;
Mailroom Equipment: Tying Machines – 1/Sa, 1-/Bu.;
Buisness Equipment: 2-Dell, 2-Packard Bell/Legend 401CD
Classified Equipment: Hardware – APP/Mac G3; Printers – APP/Mac LaserWriter;
Classified Software: Baseview.
Editorial Equipment: Hardware – 1-APP/Mac Quadra 630, 2-APP/Power Mac 6100-60, APP/iMac, 2-APP/Mac G3; Printers – 1-APP/Mac LaserWriter 16-600 PS
Editorial Software: QPS/QuarkXPress, Baseview/NewsEdit Pro.
Production Equipment: Hardware – 1-Nat, 1-C; Cameras – 1-B
Production Software: QPS/QuarkXPress 3.3.
Total Circulation: 2001

IRONWOOD

THE DAILY GLOBE

Corporate/Parent Company: Stevenson Newspapers
Publication Street Address: 118 E McLeod Ave
City: Ironwood
State: MI
Publication Website: www.yourdailyglobe.com
Postal Code: 49938-2120
Office phone: (906) 932-2211
Advertising Executive Name: Mercedes Lynn Kessenich
Advertising Executive Email: mlcalderon@yourdailyglobe.com
Advertising Executive Phone: (906)932-2211 ext 140
Year Established: 1919
Delivery Methods: Mail`Carrier
Own Printing Facility?: Y
Commercial printers?: Y
Mechanical specifications: Type page 13 x 21 1/2; E - 6 cols, 2 1/16, 1/8 between; A - 6 cols, 2 1/16, 1/8 between; C - 9 cols, 1 3/8, 1/16 between.
Published Days: Mon`Tues`Wed`Thur`Fri`Sat
Weekday Frequency: m
Saturday Frequency: m
Avg Paid Circ: 4500
Audit Company: Sworn/Estimate/Non-Audited
Audit Date: 7 12 2019
Pressroom Equipment: Lines – 8-G/Community; Folders – 1-G/2:1.;
Mailroom Equipment: Tying Machines – 3/Bu; Address Machine – 1-Miller/Bevco 285.;
Classified Equipment: Hardware – APP/Mac; Printers – 1-QMS/Nx17;
Classified Software: 2-Baseview.
Editorial Equipment: Hardware – 9-APP/Mac/Pre Press/Panther Vorityper; Printers – 2-QMS/11x17
Editorial Software: Adobe/Photoshop, QPS/QuarkXPress.
Production Equipment: Hardware – 1-Nu; Cameras – 1-Co/Horizontal 25 CS; Scanners – Epson, Umax, Polariod/Sprintscan
Production Software: QPS/QuarkXPress 5.0, Macromedia/Freehand, Adobe/Photoshop 6.
Total Circulation: 4500

JACKSON

THE JACKSON CITIZEN PATRIOT

Corporate/Parent Company: Advance Newspapers
Publication Street Address: 100 E Michigan Ave
City: Jackson
State: MI
Publication Website: www.mlive.com/jackson
Postal Code: 49201-1403
Office phone: (517) 787-2300
General E-mail: customercare@mlive.com
Advertising Executive Name: Steve Westphal
Year Established: 1865
Delivery Methods: Mail`Newsstand`Carrier`Racks
Own Printing Facility?: Y
Commercial printers?: N
Mechanical specifications: Type page 13 x 21 3/4; E - 6 cols, 2 1/16, 1/8 between; A - 6 cols, 2 1/16, 1/8 between; C - 10 cols, 1 1/4, 1/16 between.
Published Days: Mon`Tues`Wed`Thur`Fri`Sat`Sun
Weekday Frequency: e
Saturday Frequency: e
Avg Paid Circ: 11994
Audit Company: AAM
Audit Date: 4 06 2020
Pressroom Equipment: Lines – Goss; Goss;
Buisness Equipment: Apple Xserve Dell servers HP servers Hitachi HDS
Buisness Software: DTI CircView RouteSmart VMware 4-5
Classified Equipment: Hardware – Dell & HP PCs; Printers – HP, Canon, IKON;
Classified Software: Atex Mactive 3.0 Encompass Office 2010
Editorial Equipment: Hardware – Dell & HP PCs; Printers – HP, Ikon, Canon
Editorial Software: Media Span Baseview, Adobe InDesign/InCopy
Production Equipment: Hardware – Dell & HP PC Apple Macs; Scanners – Epson Canon
Production Software: PPI AGFA IntelliTune Adobe Illustrator Adobe InDesign Adobe Flash Adobe Photoshop Xpance ATEX Mactive PageLayout ZenDesk
Total Circulation: 14989

KALAMAZOO

THE KALAMAZOO GAZETTE

Corporate/Parent Company: Advance Newspapers
Publication Street Address: 306 S Kalamazoo Mall
City: Kalamazoo
State: MI
Publication Website: www.mlive.com/kalamazoo
Postal Code: 49007-4807
Office phone: (269) 345-3511
General E-mail: customercare@mlive.com
Advertising Executive Name: Steve Westphal
Year Established: 1834
Delivery Methods: Mail`Newsstand`Carrier`Racks
Published Days: Mon`Tues`Wed`Thur`Fri`Sat`Sun
Weekday Frequency: e
Saturday Frequency: m
Avg Paid Circ: 23491
Audit Company: AAM
Audit Date: 4 06 2020
Pressroom Equipment: Lines – MAN/Roland Geoioman; MAN/Roland Geoioman; Press Drive – Baumuller; Folders – 1-MAN/Double-out 64 pg.; Reels & Stands – MAN/CD13;
Mailroom Equipment: Counter Stackers – 4-QWI/501, 1-QWI/400, 2-HL/Dual Carrier; Inserters & Stuffers - 2-GMA/SLS3000; Tying Machines – 5-Dynaric/4;
Buisness Equipment: Apple Xserve Dell servers HP servers Hitachi HDS
Buisness Software: DTI CircView RouteSmart VMware 4-5
Classified Equipment: Hardware – Dell & HP PCs; Printers – HP, Canon, IKON;
Classified Software: Atex Mactive 3.0 Encompass Office 2010
Editorial Equipment: Hardware – Dell & HP PCs; Printers – HP, Ikon, Canon
Editorial Software: Media Span Baseview, Adobe InDesign/InCopy
Production Equipment: Hardware – Dell & HP PC Apple Macs; Scanners – Epson Canon
Production Software: PPI AGFA IntelliTune Adobe Illustrator Adobe InDesign Adobe Flash Adobe Photoshop Xpance ATEX Mactive PageLayout ZenDesk
Total Circulation: 30895

LANSING

LANSING STATE JOURNAL

Corporate/Parent Company: Gannett
Publication Street Address: 300 S Washington Sq
City: Lansing
State: MI
Publication Website: www.lsj.com
Postal Code: 48933-2102
Office phone: 517-377-1000
Editor Name: Stephanie Angel
Editor Email: sangel@lsj.com
Year Established: 1856
Delivery Methods: Mail
Mechanical specifications: Type page: 10 x 10; 6 col
Published Days: Sun
Avg Paid Circ:
Avg Free Circ: 6259
Audit Company: AAM
Audit Date: 20 12 2018
Total Circulation: 34874

LUDINGTON

LUDINGTON DAILY NEWS

Corporate/Parent Company: Community Media Group
Publication Street Address: 202 N Rath Ave
City: Ludington
State: MI
Publication Website: www.ludingtondailynews.com
Postal Code: 49431-1663
Office phone: (231) 845-5181
General E-mail: ldn@ludingtondailynews.com
Publisher Name: Ray McGrew
Publisher Email: rmcgrew@cmgms.com
Publisher Phone: Ext. 305
Editor Name: David Bossick
Editor Phone: Ext. 312
Advertising Executive Name: Shelley Kovar
Advertising Executive Email: skovar@ludingtondailynews.com
Advertising Executive Phone: Ext. 322
Year Established: 1867
Delivery Methods: Mail`Newsstand`Carrier
Own Printing Facility?: Y
Commercial printers?: Y
Mechanical specifications: Type page 13 x 21 1/2; E - 6 cols, 2 1/12, 1/6 between; A - 6 cols, 2 1/12, 1/6 between; C - 6 cols, 2 1/12, 1/6 between.
Published Days: Mon`Tues`Wed`Thur`Fri`Sat
Weekday Frequency: e
Saturday Frequency: e
Avg Paid Circ: 6489
Audit Company: Sworn/Estimate/Non-Audited
Audit Date: 7 12 2019
Pressroom Equipment: Lines – 12-G/Community 1972; Folders – G/Community.;
Mailroom Equipment: Tying Machines – MLN, Bu, Malow.;
Buisness Equipment: IBM/Sys 36, IBM/PC
Buisness Software: INSI, Lotus, WordPerfect, Query
Classified Equipment: Hardware – APP/Mac; Printers – APP/Mac, NewGen/Imager, HP/LaserJet 4MV;
Classified Software: Baseview.
Editorial Equipment: Hardware – 12-APP/Mac; Printers – 2-APP/Mac, NewGen/Imager Plus 12
Editorial Software: Adobe Suite: InCopy, InDesign, Photoshop
Production Equipment: Hardware – ECR/ScriptWriter; Scanners – Umax/Mirage, HP/ScanJet
Production Software: QPS/QuarkXPress 3.31, Adobe/PageMaker 6.0.
Note: Seven time winner of Michigan Press Association, Newspaper of the Year, Dailies 10,000 circ or under.
Total Circulation: 6489

MANISTEE

MANISTEE NEWS ADVOCATE

Corporate/Parent Company: Hearst Corp.
Publication Street Address: 75 Maple St
City: Manistee
State: MI
Publication Website: www.manisteenews.com
Postal Code: 49660-1554
Office phone: (231) 723-3592
Editor Name: Michelle Graves
Editor Email: mgraves@pioneergroup.com
Editor Phone: 231-398-3106
Advertising Executive Name: Danette Doyle
Advertising Executive Email: ddoyle@pioneergroup.com
Advertising Executive Phone: 231-592-8359
Year Established: 1898
Delivery Methods: Mail`Carrier
Mechanical specifications: Type page 13 1/2 x 21 3/4; E - 6 cols, 2 1/16, 1/8 between; A - 6 cols, 2 1/16, 1/8 between; C - 9 cols, 1 3/8, 1/8 between.
Published Days: Mon`Tues`Wed`Thur`Fri`Sat
Weekday Frequency: m
Saturday Frequency: m
Avg Paid Circ: 4928
Audit Company: Sworn/Estimate/Non-Audited
Audit Date: 7 12 2019
Pressroom Equipment: Lines – 7-HI/Cotrell 15A; Folders – 1-HI/2:1.;
Mailroom Equipment: Tying Machines – Sa; Address Machine – Wm.;
Buisness Equipment: 3-IBM
Classified Equipment: Hardware – 3-APP/Mac; 2-APP/Mac; Printers – QMS;
Classified Software: Baseview.
Editorial Equipment: Hardware – 9-APP/Mac; Printers – HP, QMS
Editorial Software: Aldus/PageMaker, QPS/QuarkXPress, Baseview/NewsEdit Pro.
Production Equipment: Hardware – 1-Nu, ECR/Scriptsetter; Scanners – AG, Polaroid
Production Software: Adobe/Pagemaker 6.5, Adobe/Photoshop 4.0.
Total Circulation: 4928

MARQUETTE

THE MINING JOURNAL

Corporate/Parent Company: Ogden Newspapers, Inc.
Publication Street Address: 249 W Washington St
City: Marquette
State: MI
Publication Website: www.miningjournal.net
Postal Code: 49855-4321
Office phone: (906) 228-2500
Publisher Name: Ann Troutman
Publisher Email: atroutman@miningjournal.net
Publisher Phone: Ext. 299
Editor Name: Bud Sargent
Editor Email: bsargent@miningjournal.net
Editor Phone: Ext. 244
Advertising Executive Name: James Larsen
Advertising Executive Email: jlarsen@miningjournal.net
Advertising Executive Phone: Ext. 217
Year Established: 1846
Delivery Methods: Mail`Newsstand`Carrier`Racks
Own Printing Facility?: Y
Commercial printers?: Y
Mechanical specifications: Type page 11 x 21 1/2; E - 6 cols, 1.583
Published Days: Mon`Tues`Wed`Thur`Fri`Sat`Sun
Weekday Frequency: e
Saturday Frequency: m
Avg Paid Circ: 7464
Avg Free Circ: 40
Audit Company: AAM
Audit Date: 11 11 2019
Mailroom Equipment: Tying Machines – 2-MLN/ML1EE, 1-MLN/Spirit; Address Machine – 1/Wm.;
Buisness Equipment: Anzio
Classified Equipment: Hardware – Mac's;
Editorial Equipment: Hardware – Mac's; Printers – V/4990 LaserPrinter, Konica/2100 EV Jetsetter
Editorial Software: Mk/Mycro-Comp Touchwriter.
Production Equipment: Hardware – 1-Nu/Flip Top FT40UPNS, APP/Mac Scanner- DTP; Cameras – 1-SCREEN/Auto Companica 690C.
Total Circulation: 9167

U.S. Daily Newspapers

I-61

MIDLAND

MIDLAND DAILY NEWS

Corporate/Parent Company: Hearst Corp.
Publication Street Address: 219 E. Main St.
City: Midland
State: MI
Publication Website: www.ourmidland.com
Postal Code: 48640
Office phone: (989) 835-7171
Editor Name: Kate Hessling
Editor Email: khessling@hearstnp.com
Editor Phone: (989) 839-4240
Advertising Executive Name: Cathy Bott
Advertising Executive Email: cbott@mdn.net
Advertising Executive Phone: (989) 839-4228
Year Established: 1937
Delivery Methods: Mail`Carrier
Own Printing Facility?: Y
Commercial printers?: Y
Mechanical specifications: Type page 13 x 21 1/2; E - 6 cols, 2 1/16, 1/8 between; A - 6 cols, 2 1/16, 1/8 between; C - 9 cols, 1 1/2, 1/16 between.
Published Days: Mon`Tues`Wed`Thur`Fri`Sat`Sun
Weekday Frequency: e
Saturday Frequency: e
Avg Paid Circ: 7408
Avg Free Circ: 744
Audit Company: AAM
Audit Date: 30 09 2017
Pressroom Equipment: Lines – 8-G/Urbanite single width 1984; Reels & Stands – 2;
Mailroom Equipment: Counter Stackers – HL/Monitor; Inserters & Stuffers – S/P48; Tying Machines – OVL;
Buisness Equipment: IBM/AS-400
Classified Equipment: Hardware – 5-APP/Mac Quadra 105, 2-APP/Power Mac 7300; Printers – 1-APP/LaserJet 2100M;
Classified Software: Baseview/Class Manager 3.3.4.
Editorial Equipment: Hardware – 4-APP/Mac Quadra 650, 10-APP/Mac Quadra 605, 2-Umax/5900/2-Accuset/1500 Imagesetter; Printers – 1-APP/LaserJet 2100M, 1-APP/Mac LaserWriter Pro 630
Editorial Software: Baseview/NewsEdit 1.12, QPS/QuarkXPress 3.31.
Production Equipment: Hardware – 1-Neg, 1-APP/Mac 8500-132; Cameras – 1-C/Spartan III, AG/RPS6100S; Scanners – 1-Nikon/35mm, Epson/800C Flatbed, 1-Nikon/1000 35mm, 1-AG/Arcus II Flatbed
Production Software: QPS/QuarkXPress 3.3.2, QPS/QuarkXPress 4.04.
Total Circulation: 8152

MONROE

THE MONROE NEWS

Corporate/Parent Company: Gannett
Publication Street Address: 20 W 1st St
City: Monroe
State: MI
Publication Website: www.monroenews.com
Postal Code: 48161-2333
Office phone: (734) 242-1100
Editor Name: Ray Kisonas
Editor Email: rkisonas@monroenews.com
Editor Phone: 734-240-5778
Advertising Executive Name: Janine Nowitzke
Advertising Executive Email: janine@monroenews.com
Advertising Executive Phone: 734-240-5702
Year Established: 1825
Delivery Methods: Mail`Newsstand`Carrier`Racks
Own Printing Facility?: Y
Commercial printers?: Y
Mechanical specifications: Type page 10x19.75
Published Days: Mon`Tues`Wed`Thur`Fri`Sat`Sun
Weekday Frequency: e
Saturday Frequency: e
Avg Paid Circ: 11008
Avg Free Circ: 694
Audit Company: AAM
Audit Date: 29 03 2019
Buisness Equipment: PC Based
Buisness Software: Microsoft Dynamics DTI
Classified Equipment: Hardware – PC Based;
Classified Software: Vision Data
Editorial Equipment: Hardware – PC Based; Printers – Newscycle Solutions
Production Equipment: Hardware – PC Based; Cameras – LE; Scanners – Kk, Microtek/ScanMaker II;
Production Software: Adobe Indesign
Total Circulation: 37934

MUSKEGON

THE MUSKEGON CHRONICLE

Corporate/Parent Company: Advance Newspapers
Publication Street Address: 379 W Western Ave Ste 100
City: Muskegon
State: MI
Publication Website: www.mlive.com/muskegon
Postal Code: 49440-1265
Office phone: (231) 722-3161
General E-mail: customercare@mlive.com
Advertising Executive Name: Steve Westphal
Year Established: 1857
Delivery Methods: Mail`Newsstand`Carrier`Racks
Mechanical specifications: Type page 10 7/8 x 19 1/2; E - 6 cols, 1 23/32, 3/32 between; A - 6 cols, 1 23/32, 3/32 between; C - 10 cols, 1 1/16, 1/32 between.
Published Days: Mon`Tues`Wed`Thur`Fri`Sat`Sun
Weekday Frequency: e
Saturday Frequency: m
Avg Paid Circ: 14734
Audit Company: AAM
Audit Date: 31 12 2018
Pressroom Equipment: Lines – MAN/Geoman (64 couples); Press Drive – Baumueller; Folders – 2-MAN; Pasters –12-MAN; Reels & Stands – 12-MAN; Control System – MAN; Registration System – Graphic Control.
Mailroom Equipment: Counter Stackers – 10-QWI/500; Inserters & Stuffers – 3-GMA/SLS 3000 (30:2); Tying Machines – 13/Dynaric; Wrapping Singles – 5-Dynaric/Single tyer; Control System – GMA/SAM; Address Machine – 2-Ch/Labeler;
Buisness Equipment: Apple Xserve Dell servers HP servers Hitachi HDS
Buisness Software: DTI CircView RouteSmart VMware 4-5
Classified Equipment: Hardware – Dell & HP PCs; Dell & HP PCs; Printers – HP, Canon, IKON;
Classified Software: Atex Mactive 3.0 Encompass Office 2010
Editorial Equipment: Hardware – Dell & HP PCs; Printers – HP, Ikon, Canon
Editorial Software: Media Span Baseview, Adobe InDesign/InCopy
Production Equipment: Hardware – Epson Canon; Scanners – Epson Canon
Production Software: PPI AGFA IntelliTune Adobe Illustrator Adobe InDesign Adobe Flash Adobe Photoshop Xpance ATEX Mactive PageLayout ZenDesk.
Total Circulation: 14734

NILES

DOWAGIAC DAILY NEWS

Corporate/Parent Company: Boone Newspapers, Inc.
Publication Street Address: 217 N 4th St
City: Niles
State: MI
Publication Website: www.leaderpub.com
Postal Code: 49120-2301
Office phone: (269) 683-2100
General E-mail: news@leaderpub.com
Publisher Name: Ambrosia Neldon
Publisher Email: ambrosia.neldon@leaderpub.com
Publisher Phone: (269) 687-7701
Editor Name: Sarah Culton
Editor Email: sarah.culton@leaderpub.com
Editor Phone: (269) 687-7713
Advertising Executive Name: Phil Langer
Advertising Executive Email: phil.langer@leaderpub.com
Advertising Executive Phone: (269) 687-7726
Year Established: 1886
Delivery Methods: Mail`Newsstand`Racks
Own Printing Facility?: Y
Commercial printers?: Y
Mechanical specifications: Type page 9.75 x 14; E - 6 cols
Published Days: Mon`Tues`Wed`Thur`Fri
Weekday Frequency: m
Avg Paid Circ: 1386
Audit Company: Sworn/Estimate/Non-Audited
Audit Date: 7 12 2019
Pressroom Equipment: Lines – 10-KP/News King single width.;
Classified Equipment: Hardware – APP/Mac; Printers – HP/4MV;
Classified Software: Baseview.
Editorial Equipment: Hardware – APP/Mac; Printers – HP/4MV
Editorial Software: InDesign
Production Equipment: Hardware – QPS/QuarkXPress.
Note: For detailed production information, see the Niles Daily Star listing.
Total Circulation: 1386

NILES DAILY STAR

Corporate/Parent Company: Boone Newspapers, Inc.
Publication Street Address: 217 N 4th St
City: Niles
State: MI
Publication Website: www.leaderpub.com
Postal Code: 49120-2301
Office phone: (269) 683-2100
General E-mail: news@leaderpub.com
Publisher Name: Ambrosia Neldon
Publisher Email: ambrosia.neldon@leaderpub.com
Publisher Phone: (269) 687-7700
Editor Name: Sarah Culton
Editor Email: sarah.culton@leaderpub.com
Editor Phone: (269) 687-7712
Advertising Executive Name: Phil Langer
Advertising Executive Email: phil.langer@leaderpub.com
Advertising Executive Phone: (269) 687-7725
Year Established: 1867
Delivery Methods: Mail`Newsstand`Racks
Own Printing Facility?: Y
Commercial printers?: Y
Mechanical specifications: Tab page 9.75 x 14; E - 6 cols
Published Days: Mon`Tues`Wed`Thur`Fri
Weekday Frequency: m
Avg Paid Circ: 1531
Audit Company: Sworn/Estimate/Non-Audited
Audit Date: 7 12 2019
Pressroom Equipment: Lines – 10-KP/News King single width;
Mailroom Equipment: Counter Stackers – 1-BG/Count-O-Veyor 108; Inserters & Stuffers – MM/3 Station; Tying Machines – 3/Bu, 1-/Sa, 1-/MLN; Address Machine – Dispensa-Matic.;
Buisness Equipment: 1-IBM/5364-PC Sys 36, 2-IBM/5150, 2-RSK/1000TL2
Classified Equipment: Hardware – APP/Mac;
Classified Software: Baseview.
Editorial Equipment: Apple
Editorial Software: InDesign
Production Equipment: Apple
Production Software: InDesign
Total Circulation: 1531

OWOSSO

THE ARGUS-PRESS

Publication Street Address: 201 E Exchange St
City: Owosso
State: MI
Publication Website: www.argus-press.com
Postal Code: 48867-3009
Office phone: (989) 725-5136
General E-mail: news@argus-press.com
Publisher Name: Thomas E. Campbell
Publisher Email: tcampbell@argus-press.com
Editor Name: Dan Basso,
Editor Email: drbasso@argus-press.com
Advertising Executive Name: Cathy Campbell
Advertising Executive Email: ccampbell@argus-press.com
Year Established: 1854
Delivery Methods: Mail`Newsstand`Carrier`Racks
Own Printing Facility?: Y
Commercial printers?: Y
Mechanical specifications: Type page 13 x 21 1/2; E - 6 cols, 2 1/16, 1/8 between; A - 6 cols, 2 1/16, 1/8 between; C - 9 cols, 1 3/8, 1/16 between.
Published Days: Mon`Tues`Wed`Thur`Fri`Sat`Sun
Weekday Frequency: e
Saturday Frequency: m
Avg Paid Circ: 7150
Audit Company: Sworn/Estimate/Non-Audited
Audit Date: 7 12 2019
Pressroom Equipment: Lines – 5-G/Urbanite 1964.;
Pressroom Software: NewsXtreme
Mailroom Equipment: Tying Machines – EAM-Mosca; Inserting Machines – Kansa
Buisness Equipment: Acer/PC
Buisness Software: Quickbooks
Classified Equipment: Hardware – APP/iMac;
Classified Software: Baseview/Ad Manager Pro.
Editorial Equipment: Hardware – APP/iMac/Mac Pro/; Printers – HP/701
Editorial Software: InDesign Creative Cloud
Production Equipment: Hardware – ECRM/Mako News; Inca 70
Total Circulation: 7150

PETOSKEY

PETOSKEY NEWS-REVIEW

Publication Street Address: 319 State St
City: Petoskey
State: MI
Publication Website: www.petoskeynews.com
Postal Code: 49770-2746
Office phone: (231) 347-2544
General E-mail: petoskeynews@petoskeynews.com
Editor Name: Jeremy McBain
Editor Phone: 231-439-9316
Advertising Executive Name: Christy Lyons
Advertising Executive Phone: 231-838-9949
Year Established: 1875
Delivery Methods: Mail`Carrier
Mechanical specifications: Type page 11 5/8 x 21 1/2; E - 6 cols, 1 5/6, 1/8 between; A - 6 cols, 1 5/6, 1/8 between; C - 6 cols, 1 5/6, 1/8 between.
Published Days: Mon`Tues`Wed`Thur`Fri
Weekday Frequency: e
Avg Paid Circ: 8994
Audit Company: Sworn/Estimate/Non-Audited
Audit Date: 7 12 2019
Pressroom Equipment: Lines – 8-G/Community single width, 2-DGM/4 Highs 2000; G 2000; Folders – 1-G/SSC.;
Mailroom Equipment: Counter Stackers – BG/205; Tying Machines – 1/Bu, 2-Mosca/Strapper.;
Buisness Equipment: DEC/1000A 4-233 Alpha Server
Buisness Software: PBS
Classified Equipment: Hardware – APP/Mac; Printers – ECR/VRL 36HS;
Classified Software: Baseview/Ad Manager Pro.
Editorial Equipment: Hardware – APP/Mac; Printers – APP/Mac 8500, ECR/VRL 36HS
Editorial Software: Adobe/InDesign CSI, Baseview/NewsEdit Pro.
Production Equipment: Hardware – ECR/VRL 36HS Scriptsetter, Panther/Pro 62; Scanners – Mycro-Tek/9900XL
Production Software: Adobe/InDesign CSI.
Total Circulation: 8994

PORT HURON

TIMES HERALD

Corporate/Parent Company: Gannett
Publication Street Address: 911 Military St

U.S. Daily Newspapers

City: Port Huron
State: MI
Publication Website: www.thetimesherald.com
Postal Code: 48060-5414
Office phone: (810) 985-7171
Publisher Name: Timothy Gruber
Editor Name: Michael Eckert
Year Established: 1869
Delivery Methods: Mail`Newsstand`Carrier
Own Printing Facility?: N
Commercial printers?: Y
Mechanical specifications: Type page 10 x 21.5; E - 6 cols, 1.583, 0.069 between; A - 6 cols, 1.583, 0.069 between; C - 9 cols, 1.063, 0.069 between.
Published Days: Mon`Tues`Wed`Thur`Fri`Sat`Sun
Weekday Frequency: m
Saturday Frequency: m
Avg Paid Circ: 10407
Avg Free Circ: 95
Audit Company: AAM
Audit Date: 31 01 2019
Classified Software: APT.
Editorial Software: APT.
Total Circulation: 36998

SAGINAW

THE SAGINAW NEWS

Corporate/Parent Company: Advance Newspapers
Publication Street Address: 100 S Michigan Ave Ste 3
City: Saginaw
State: MI
Publication Website: www.mlive.com/saginaw
Postal Code: 48602-2054
Office phone: (989) 752-7171
General E-mail: customercare@mlive.com
Advertising Executive Name: Steve Westphal
Year Established: 1859
Delivery Methods: Mail`Newsstand`Carrier`Racks
Mechanical specifications: Type page 13 x 22 1/4; E - 6 cols, 2 1/16, 1/8 between; A - 6 cols, 2 1/16, 1/8 between; C - 10 cols, 1 1/4, 1/16 between.
Published Days: Mon`Tues`Wed`Thur`Fri`Sat`Sun
Weekday Frequency: m
Avg Paid Circ: 11947
Audit Company: AAM
Audit Date: 29 03 2019
Pressroom Equipment: Lines – 8-G/Mark I double width;
Mailroom Equipment: Counter Stackers – 4/QWI; Inserters & Stuffers – 2-S/9-48P single, 1-GMA/SLS 2000; Tying Machines – 2-/Sterling; Address Machine – 4-/Wm.;
Buisness Equipment: 1-PBS/Media Plus, 1-SBS/Xponet
Classified Equipment: Hardware – AT; 13-AT.;
Editorial Equipment: Hardware – 50-APP/Mac G4 400/39-AT; Printers – HP/4000, HP/5000, Xante/Accel-a-Writer 3G, ColorPass C700
Editorial Software: Baseview/NewsEdit Pro IQue 3.23, QPS/QuarkXPress 4.11.
Production Equipment: Hardware – 2-Cx/Bitsetter, 1-AU/APS-PSP2 with A156, 1-AU/APS Grafix RIP with 3850; Cameras – 1-C/NewsPager I; Scanners – AG/Desk Top
Production Software: QPS/QuarkXPress 4.11.
Total Circulation: 19608

SAINT JOSEPH

THE HERALD-PALLADIUM

Corporate/Parent Company: Paxton Media Group, LLC
Publication Street Address: 3450 Hollywood Rd
City: Saint Joseph
State: MI
Publication Website: www.the-h-p.com
Postal Code: 49085-9155
Office phone: (269) 429-2400
General E-mail: eaccounts@TheHP.com
Publisher Name: David Holgate
Publisher Email: dholgate@theh-p.com
Editor Name: Dave Brown
Editor Email: dbrown@theh-p.com
Editor Phone: 269-429-4298
Advertising Executive Name: Sara Horton
Advertising Executive Email: shorton@TheHP.com
Advertising Executive Phone: ext. 493
Year Established: 1868
Delivery Methods: Mail`Newsstand`Carrier`Racks
Own Printing Facility?: Y
Commercial printers?: Y
Mechanical specifications: Type page 13 x 21 1/2; E - 6 cols, 2 1/16, 1/8 between; A - 6 cols, 2 1/16, 1/8 between; C - 9 cols, 1 15/16, 1/8 between.
Published Days: Mon`Tues`Wed`Thur`Fri`Sat`Sun
Weekday Frequency: m
Saturday Frequency: m
Avg Paid Circ: 11659
Audit Company: AAM
Audit Date: 31 03 2014
Pressroom Equipment: Lines – 4-G/Cosmo double width 1978, 2-1990; Pasters –4-G/Automatic.
Mailroom Equipment: Counter Stackers – 1-Id/NS440, 2-Id/Marathoner; Inserters & Stuffers – 2-Mc/660; Tying Machines – 2-Dynaric/NP2.;
Buisness Equipment: 2-HP/9000
Buisness Software: Baseview
Classified Equipment: Hardware – APP/Mac;
Classified Software: Baseview/ClassFlow 2.0.
Editorial Equipment: Hardware – APP/Mac/1-APP/Mac IIci, 4-TM, 9-RSK, 5-Falcon, APP/Mac Quadra 800
Editorial Software: QPS/QuarkXPress, Baseview/NewsEdit IQUE 3.02.
Production Equipment: Hardware – 1-Nu/Flip Top FT40, 1-SCREEN/LD281Q, 1-V/1200; Cameras – 1-C/Spartan II.
Total Circulation: 11659

SAULT SAINTE MARIE

SAULT STE. MARIE EVENING NEWS

Publication Street Address: 109 Arlington St
City: Sault Sainte Marie
State: MI
Publication Website: www.sooeveningnews.com
Postal Code: 49783-1901
Office phone: (906) 632-2235
Editor Name: Brenda Rigotti
Editor Email: brigotti@sooeveningnews.com
Advertising Executive Name: Rob Roos
Advertising Executive Email: rroos@sooeveningnews.com
Year Established: 1903
Delivery Methods: Mail`Newsstand`Carrier
Own Printing Facility?: Y
Commercial printers?: Y
Mechanical specifications: Type page 13 x 21; E - 6 cols, 2 1/16, 1/8 between; A - 6 cols, 2 1/16, 1/8 between; C - 9 cols, 1 3/8, 1/16 between.
Published Days: Mon`Tues`Wed`Thur`Fri`Sat
Weekday Frequency: m
Saturday Frequency: m
Avg Paid Circ: 3772
Audit Company: Sworn/Estimate/Non-Audited
Audit Date: 7 12 2019
Pressroom Equipment: Lines – 7-HI/V-15A; Folders – HI/JF-7.;
Mailroom Equipment: Tying Machines – 2/MLN; Address Machine – 1-/Am.;
Buisness Equipment: PC Designs
Classified Equipment: Hardware – PC Designs.;
Editorial Equipment: Hardware – APP/Mac.
Production Equipment: Hardware – 5-COM; Scanners – 2-COM.
Total Circulation: 3772

STURGIS

STURGIS JOURNAL

Corporate/Parent Company: Gannett
Publication Street Address: 205 E Chicago Rd
City: Sturgis
State: MI
Publication Website: www.sturgisjournal.com
Postal Code: 49091-1753
Office phone: (269) 651-5407
Editor Name: Candice Phelps
Editor Email: phelps@sturgisjournal.com
Advertising Executive Name: Trisha Lalancette
Advertising Executive Email: tlalancette@gatewayshopper.com
Year Established: 1859
Delivery Methods: Mail`Newsstand`Carrier`Racks
Own Printing Facility?: Y
Commercial printers?: Y
Mechanical specifications: Type page 10.25 x 21 1/2; E - 6 column, 1 column=1.593"
Published Days: Mon`Tues`Wed`Thur`Fri`Sat
Weekday Frequency: m
Saturday Frequency: m
Avg Paid Circ: 5000
Audit Company: Sworn/Estimate/Non-Audited
Audit Date: 7 12 2019
Editorial Equipment: Hardware – APP/Mac.
Total Circulation: 5000

THREE RIVERS

THREE RIVERS COMMERCIAL-NEWS

Corporate/Parent Company: Surf New Media
Publication Street Address: 124 N Main St
City: Three Rivers
State: MI
Publication Website: www.threeriversnews.com
Postal Code: 49093-1522
Office phone: (269) 279-7488
General E-mail: info@threeriversnews.com
Publisher Name: Dirk Milliman
Publisher Email: publisher@threeriversnews.com
Publisher Phone: 269-279-7488, Ext. 26
Editor Name: Alek Frost
Editor Email: alek@threeriversnews.com
Editor Phone: 269-279-7488, Ext. 22
Advertising Executive Name: David Allen
Advertising Executive Email: david@threeriversnews.com
Advertising Executive Phone: 269-279-7488, Ext. 21
Year Established: 1895
Delivery Methods: Mail`Carrier`Racks
Mechanical specifications: Type page 12 3/4 x 21 1/2; E - 6 cols, 2, 1/6 between; A - 8 cols, 1 1/2, 1/9 between; C - 8 cols, 1 1/2, 1/9 between.
Published Days: Mon`Tues`Wed`Thur`Fri`Sat
Weekday Frequency: e
Saturday Frequency: m
Avg Paid Circ: 3043
Audit Company: Sworn/Estimate/Non-Audited
Audit Date: 7 12 2019
Pressroom Equipment: Lines – 5-HI/Cotrell V-15A;
Mailroom Equipment: Tying Machines – 2/Bu; Address Machine – 1-/Am.;
Buisness Equipment: Compaq/Deskpro
Classified Equipment: Hardware – 1-Mk/1100 Plus.;
Editorial Equipment: Hardware – 3-Mk/1100 Plus, 2-COM
Editorial Software: Mk/1100.
Production Equipment: Hardware – 1-COM/8400, 1-COM/Trendsetter; Cameras – 1-B/Caravelle, 1-Cl.
Total Circulation: 3043

TRAVERSE CITY

TRAVERSE CITY RECORD-EAGLE

Corporate/Parent Company: CNHI, LLC
Publication Street Address: 120 W Front St
City: Traverse City
State: MI
Publication Website: www.record-eagle.com
Postal Code: 49684-2202
Office phone: (231) 946-2000
General E-mail: webmaster@record-eagle.com
Publisher Name: Paul Heidbreder
Publisher Email: pheidbreder@record-eagle.com
Publisher Phone: 231-933-1403
Editor Name: Nathan Payne
Editor Email: npayne@record-eagle.com
Editor Phone: 231-933-1472
Year Established: 1858
Delivery Methods: Mail`Carrier
Own Printing Facility?: Y
Commercial printers?: Y
Mechanical specifications: Type page 11 3/4 x 21 1/2; E - 6 cols, 1 7/8, 1/8 between; A - 6 cols, 1 7/8, 1/8 between; C - 9 cols, 1 1/5, 1/5 between.
Published Days: Mon`Tues`Wed`Thur`Fri`Sat`Sun
Weekday Frequency: m
Saturday Frequency: m
Avg Paid Circ: 14679
Avg Free Circ: 535
Audit Company: AAM
Audit Date: 31 12 2017
Pressroom Equipment: Lines – 5-1992.;
Mailroom Equipment: Counter Stackers – 3/QWI; Inserters & Stuffers – 14-GMA/SLS 1000; Tying Machines – 3-/Power Strap;
Buisness Equipment: IBM/AS-400, APP/Mac
Classified Equipment: Hardware – Dewar/Sys II; Printers – Okidata/320;
Classified Software: Dewar/Sys II.
Editorial Equipment: Hardware – 41-PC P133, 2-IBM/RS 6000 Server; Printers – 2-Okidata/320, 3-HP/4MV, 1-HP/5SI MX
Editorial Software: Microsoft/Windows 95, Microsoft/Word 7.0, Dewar/View, Adobe/Photoshop, QPS/QuarkXPress.
Production Equipment: Hardware – Caere/OmniPage Pro, 1-Tegra/Varityper 5510, 2-MON/Imagesetter; Scanners – HP/ScanJet
Production Software: Dewar/View.
Total Circulation: 15214

TROY

THE OAKLAND PRESS

Corporate/Parent Company: Media News Group
Publication Street Address: 2125 Butterfield Dr.
City: Troy
State: MI
Publication Website: www.theoaklandpress.com
Postal Code: 48084
Office phone: (248) 332-8181
Publisher Name: Greg Mazanec
Publisher Email: MiPublisher@digitalfirstmedia.com
Editor Name: Jeff Hoard
Editor Email: jeff.hoard@oakpress.com
Editor Phone: 248-284-7046
Advertising Executive Name: Noelle Klomp
Advertising Executive Email: noelle.klomp@oakpress.com
Advertising Executive Phone: 586-783-0393
Year Established: 1844
Delivery Methods: Mail`Carrier
Own Printing Facility?: Y
Commercial printers?: Y
Mechanical specifications: Type page 13 1/4 x 21; E - 6 cols, 1 3/4, 1/8 between; A - 6 cols, 1 3/4, between; C - 10 cols, 1 3/16, 1/8 between.
Published Days: Mon`Tues`Wed`Thur`Fri`Sat`Sun
Weekday Frequency: m
Saturday Frequency: m
Avg Paid Circ: 24304
Audit Company: AAM
Audit Date: 31 03 2017
Pressroom Equipment: Lines – 10-G/Headliner Offset double width; Folders – 1-G/3:2; Reels & Stands – 10-Reels & Stands/Stands; Control System – G/MPCS.;
Mailroom Equipment: Counter Stackers – 3-QWI/300, 1-Id/2000; Inserters & Stuffers – 1/AM Graphics/NP 630, 24-/Hopper; Tying Machines – 6-/NP2, Dynarics; Control System – Burt Technologies.;
Buisness Equipment: IBM/J50 RISC 6000, 1-IBM/590 RISC 6000
Buisness Software: PBS/MediaPlus 3.0, Word Processing, PBS 3.0, SBS 3.0
Classified Equipment: Hardware – Pentium/PC-100, Pentium/II, Gateway, Compaq, Microsoft/Windows NT;
Classified Software: CompuClass/Computext.
Editorial Equipment: Hardware – 2-APP/Mac 9500, Main/Back-up Server/1-APP/Mac

U.S. Daily Newspapers

I-63

950 with Wire Manager, 1-APP/Mac 6100; Printers – 10-HP/DeskWriters
Editorial Software: Baseview/Client Server 2.2.
Production Equipment: Hardware – 2-ECR/3850, 3-XIT/Clipper Plain Paper 11 x 17, Aii/3850 Imagesetter; Cameras – C/Spartan III; Scanners – AG/Flatbed Scanner, Kk/Transparency Film Scanner
Production Software: QPS/QuarkXPress, AU, AU/OMAN OPI.
Total Circulation: 24304

MINNESOTA

ALBERT LEA

ALBERT LEA TRIBUNE
Corporate/Parent Company: Boone Newspapers, Inc.
Publication Street Address: 808 W Front St
City: Albert Lea
State: MN
Publication Website: www.albertleatribune.com
Postal Code: 56007-1947
Office phone: (507) 373-1411
Publisher Name: Crystal Miller
Publisher Email: crystal.miller@albertleatribune.com
Publisher Phone: 507-473-4396
Editor Name: Sarah Stultz
Editor Email: sarah.stultz@albertleatribune.com
Editor Phone: 507-379-3433
Advertising Executive Name: Renee Citsay
Advertising Executive Email: renee.citsay@albertleatribune.com
Advertising Executive Phone: 507-379-3430
Year Established: 1897
Delivery Methods: Mail`Newsstand`Carrier`Racks
Own Printing Facility?: Y
Commercial printers?: Y
Mechanical specifications: Type page 6 x 21 1/2; E - 6 cols, 2 1/16, 1/8 between; A - 6 cols, 2 1/16, 1/8 between; C - 10 cols, 1 3/8, 1/8 between.
Published Days: Mon`Tues`Wed`Thur`Fri`Sun
Weekday Frequency: e
Avg Paid Circ: 5456
Audit Company: Sworn/Estimate/Non-Audited
Audit Date: 7 12 2019
Buisness Equipment: Macs, Dell
Buisness Software: Quicken, PBS
Classified Equipment: Hardware – Mac; Printers – HP
Classified Software: In Design, Baseview.
Editorial Equipment: Hardware – Mac; Printers – HP Laser
Editorial Software: In Design
Production Equipment: Hardware – Mac, Dell; Cameras – All Cannon; Scanners – DTI
Total Circulation: 5456

AUSTIN

AUSTIN DAILY HERALD
Corporate/Parent Company: Boone Newspapers, Inc.
Publication Street Address: 310 2nd St NE
City: Austin
State: MN
Publication Website: www.austindailyherald.com
Postal Code: 55912-3436
Office phone: (507) 433-8851
General E-mail: newsroom@austindailyherald.com
Publisher Name: Jana Norman
Publisher Email: jana.norman@austindailyherald.com
Publisher Phone: 507-434-2220
Editor Name: Eric Johnson
Editor Email: eric.johnson@austindailyherald.com
Editor Phone: 507-434-2237

Advertising Executive Name: Heather Ryks
Advertising Executive Email: heather.ryks@austindailyherald.com
Advertising Executive Phone: 507-434-2225
Year Established: 1891
Delivery Methods: Mail`Carrier
Own Printing Facility?: Y
Commercial printers?: Y
Mechanical specifications: Type page 6 x 21 1/2; E - 6 cols, 2, 1/8 between; A - 6 cols, 2, 1/8 between; C - 9 cols, 2, 1/8 between.
Published Days: Mon`Tues`Wed`Thur`Fri`Sun
Weekday Frequency: e
Avg Paid Circ: 4200
Audit Company: Sworn/Estimate/Non-Audited
Audit Date: 7 12 2019
Pressroom Equipment: Lines – 8-G/Community 1976.;
Mailroom Equipment: Tying Machines – 2-Bu/Tyer.;
Classified Equipment: Hardware – 1-APP/Mac; Printers – HP;
Classified Software: Baseview/News Edit Pro.
Editorial Equipment: Hardware – APP/Power Mac; Printers – PrePress/Panther Pro Imagesetter
Editorial Software: QPS/QuarkXPress, Adobe/Photoshop, Baseview/News Edit Pro.
Production Equipment: Hardware – Digi-Colour; Cameras – R, LE
Production Software: QPS/QuarkXPress 4.0.
Total Circulation: 4200

BEMIDJI

THE BEMIDJI PIONEER
Corporate/Parent Company: Forum Communications
Publication Street Address: 1320 Neilson Ave SE
City: Bemidji
State: MN
Publication Website: www.bemidjipioneer.com
Postal Code: 56601-5406
Office phone: (218) 333-9200
General E-mail: news@bemidjipioneer.com
Publisher Name: Dennis Doeden
Publisher Email: ddoeden@bemidjipioneer.com
Publisher Phone: (218) 333-9771
Editor Name: Matt Cory
Editor Email: mcory@bemidjipioneer.com
Editor Phone: (218) 333-9774
Year Established: 1896
Delivery Methods: Mail`Carrier`Racks
Own Printing Facility?: N
Commercial printers?: N
Mechanical specifications: Type page 6 x 21; E - 6 cols, 1 5/6, 1/8 between; A - 6 cols, 1 5/6, 1/8 between; C - 10 cols, 1 1/4, 1/16 between.
Published Days: Tues`Wed`Thur`Fri`Sat`Sun
Weekday Frequency: m
Saturday Frequency: m
Avg Paid Circ: 5690
Avg Free Circ: 47
Audit Company: VAC
Audit Date: 30 09 2016
Buisness Equipment: Dell, Microsoft/Windows XP
Buisness Software: Microsoft/Windows XP, Citrix, Microsoft/Excel
Classified Equipment: Hardware – Microsoft/Windows XP, Dell; Printers – HP/LaserJet 4000;
Classified Software: APT/ACT.
Editorial Equipment: Hardware – Microsoft/Windows XP, Dell/Polaroid/Slide Scanner; Printers – Dataproducts/Typhoon 16
Editorial Software: APT/ACT.
Production Equipment: Hardware – 1-Nat/340; Cameras – 1-B/1822, Epson; Scanners – 2-Umax/Powerlook II, Microtek/Scanners, Polaroid/Slide Scanner
Production Software: Adobe/Photoshop 5.5, QPS/QuarkXPress 4.1.
Total Circulation: 5737

BRAINERD

BRAINERD DISPATCH
Corporate/Parent Company: Forum Communications Company
Publication Street Address: 506 James St
City: Brainerd
State: MN
Publication Website: www.brainerddispatch.com
Postal Code: 56401-2942
Office phone: (218) 829-4705
Editor Name: Matt Erickson
Editor Phone: (218) 855-5857
Advertising Executive Name: Susie Alters
Advertising Executive Phone: (218) 855-5836
Year Established: 1881
Delivery Methods: Mail`Newsstand`Carrier`Racks
Own Printing Facility?: Y
Commercial printers?: Y
Mechanical specifications: Type page 6 x 21 1/2; E - 6 cols, 1 3/4, 1/4 between; A - 6 cols, 1 3/4, 1/4 between; C - 6 cols, 1 3/4, 1/4 between.
Published Days: Mon`Tues`Wed`Thur`Fri`Sun
Weekday Frequency: m
Avg Paid Circ: 11470
Audit Company: AAM
Audit Date: 2 03 2020
Pressroom Equipment: Lines – 8-G/Community (balloon) 1978; Folders – 1-G/SSC; Registration System – Duarte.
Mailroom Equipment: Counter Stackers – BG; Inserters & Stuffers – MM/4; Tying Machines – 2/MLN; Address Machine – Ch/525E.;
Production Equipment: Cameras – D
Total Circulation: 13521

CROOKSTON

CROOKSTON-TIMES
Publication Street Address: 124 South Broadway
City: Crookston
State: MN
Publication Website: www.crookstontimes.com
Postal Code: 56716
Office phone: (218) 281-2730
Editor Name: Mike Christopherson
Editor Email: mchristopherson@crookstontimes.com
Advertising Executive Name: Janelle Berhow
Advertising Executive Email: jberhow@crookstontimes.com

DULUTH

DULUTH NEWS TRIBUNE
Corporate/Parent Company: Forum Communications
Publication Street Address: 424 W 1st St
City: Duluth
State: MN
Publication Website: www.duluthnewstribune.com
Postal Code: 55802-1596
Office phone: (218) 723-5281
General E-mail: news@duluthnews.com
Publisher Name: Neal Ronquist
Publisher Phone: (651) 301-7855
Editor Name: Rick Lubbers
Editor Email: rlubbers@duluthnews.com
Editor Phone: (218) 723-5301
Advertising Executive Name: Kathleen Pennington
Advertising Executive Phone: (218) 590-8392
Year Established: 1869
Delivery Methods: Mail`Newsstand`Carrier`Racks
Own Printing Facility?: Y
Commercial printers?: Y
Mechanical specifications: Type page 6 x 21; E - 6 cols, 1 13/16, 1/8 between; A - 6 cols, 1 13/16, 1/16 between; C - 10 cols, 1 13/16, 1/8 between.
Published Days: Mon`Tues`Wed`Thur`Fri`Sat`Sun
Weekday Frequency: m
Saturday Frequency: m

Avg Paid Circ: 22342
Avg Free Circ: 93
Audit Company: VAC
Audit Date: 30 09 2016
Pressroom Equipment: Lines – 1-MOT/Color Max (Flexo); 1-MOT/FX4 Flexo; 1-MOT/FX4 Flexo (w/half deck & 2 color tower) 1990; 2-MOT/FX4 Flexo (with half deck); Press Drive – PEC/Bond; Folders – G/2:1; Control System – PEC/James Bond, PEC/Bond.;
Mailroom Equipment: Counter Stackers – 1-Id/660, 5-QWI/200; Inserters & Stuffers – 1-MM/308-208 Biliner, 1-HI/Stuffing Machine 1372; Tying Machines – 2/Power Strap, 1-/Dynaric; Wrapping Singles – 1-/Ca, 1-/Maylo; Control System – 1-Prism/Insert Management;
Buisness Equipment: 1-HP/3000-947
Buisness Software: GEAC, CIS, AIM, Microsoft/Office Pro
Classified Equipment: Hardware – 2-Pentium/Servers, 20-Pentium/PC; Printers – 1-HP/LaserJet 5si/MX, 1-HP/LaserJet 5si/MX, 1-Epson/Dot Matrix;
Classified Software: HI/CASH.
Editorial Equipment: Hardware – Sun/Sparc 51, PCs; Printers – 1-HP/LaserJet IV, 2-Epson/LQ 550, 1-HP/LaserJet 5si/MX, 1-HP/DesignJet 755CM
Editorial Software: HI/Newsmaker Editorial 2.6.
Production Equipment: Hardware – 3-All/APS6-108c, AG/Avontra 30, Na/FP II; Scanners – Lf, X/7650, 1-Howtek/D4000, AG
Production Software: HI/PLS 2.0.
Total Circulation: 22435

FAIRMONT

SENTINEL
Corporate/Parent Company: Lee Enterprises
Publication Street Address: 64 Downtown Plz
City: Fairmont
State: MN
Publication Website: www.fairmontsentinel.com
Postal Code: 56031-1732
Office phone: (507) 235-3303
General E-mail: news@fairmontsentinel.com
Publisher Name: Gary Andersen
Publisher Email: gandersen@fairmontsentinel.com.com
Editor Name: Lee Smith
Editor Email: lsmith@fairmontsentinel.com
Year Established: 1874
Delivery Methods: Mail`Carrier
Own Printing Facility?: Y
Commercial printers?: Y
Mechanical specifications: Type page 13 x 21 1/2; E - 6 cols, 1 43/50, 1/8 between; A - 6 cols, 1 43/50, 1/8 between; C - 9 cols, 1 19/100, 1/16 between.
Published Days: Mon`Tues`Wed`Thur`Fri`Sat
Weekday Frequency: m
Saturday Frequency: m
Avg Paid Circ: 3358
Audit Company: AAM
Audit Date: 7 06 2018
Buisness Equipment: NCR
Classified Equipment: Hardware – 2-APP/PPC 7100/80.;
Editorial Equipment: Hardware – APP/Mac Pagination Network, 10-APP/Mac PPC 7100-80.
Production Equipment: Hardware – APP/Mac Laser, OCU; Cameras – 1-B; Scanners – Nikon/Coolscan 35mm
Production Software: QPS/QuarkXPress 3.31.
Total Circulation: 4182

FARIBAULT

FARIBAULT DAILY NEWS
Corporate/Parent Company: Adams Publishing Group
Publication Street Address: 514 Central Ave N
City: Faribault
State: MN
Publication Website: www.faribault.com
Postal Code: 55021-4304
Office phone: 507-333-3100
General E-mail: advertising@faribault.com

Publisher Name: Chad Hjellming
Publisher Email: chjellming@faribault.com
Publisher Phone: 507-333-3105
Editor Name: Suzanne Rook
Editor Email: srook@faribault.com
Editor Phone: 507-333-3134
Advertising Executive Name: Mark Nelson
Advertising Executive Email: mnelson@faribault.com
Advertising Executive Phone: 507-333-3109
Year Established: 1914
Delivery Methods:
  Mail`Newstand`Carrier`Racks
Own Printing Facility?: Y
Commercial printers?: Y
Mechanical specifications: Type page 11 5/8 x 21 1/2; E - 6 cols, 1 5/6, 1/8 between; A - 6 cols, 1 5/6, 1/8 between; C - 6 cols, 1 5/6, 1/8 between.
Published Days: Tues`Wed`Thur`Fri`Sat
Weekday Frequency: m
Saturday Frequency: m
Avg Paid Circ: 4065
Avg Free Circ: 9946
Audit Company: CAC
Audit Date: 12 12 2017
Pressroom Equipment: Lines – 16-G/Community Single Width; Folders – DGM/1030; Control System – Fin.;
Mailroom Equipment: Counter Stackers – 1-KAN/Newstac; Inserters & Stuffers – 1-KAN/480 Station Inserter 12:1; Tying Machines – 3-Si/LB2000, 1-Si/LB2330 Auto Strapper; Address Machine – 1-Domino/Jet-A-Ray;
Buisness Equipment: pc's
Buisness Software: DTI SBS
Classified Equipment: Hardware – macs;
Classified Software: Baseview/Ad Manager Pro
Editorial Equipment: Hardware – PC's
Editorial Software: TCMS
Production Equipment: Hardware – 1-Kk/Trendsetter 50, 1-Kk/Trendsetter 100.
Total Circulation: 14011

FERGUS FALLS

FERGUS FALLS- THE DAILY JOURNAL

Publication Street Address: 914 E. Channing Avenue
City: Fergus Falls
State: MN
Publication Website: www.fergusfallsjournal.com
Postal Code: 56537
Office phone: 218-736-7511
Publisher Name: Ken Harty
Publisher Email: kenh@fergusfallsjournal.com
Publisher Phone: 218-739-7019
Editor Name: Zach Stich
Editor Email: zach.stich@fergusfallsjournal.com
Editor Phone: 218-739-7030
Advertising Executive Name: Mary Sieling
Advertising Executive Email: mary.sieling@fergusfallsjournal.com
Advertising Executive Phone: 218-739-7021

THE FERGUS FALLS DAILY JOURNAL

Publication Street Address: 914 E Channing Ave
City: Fergus Falls
State: MN
Publication Website: www.fergusfallsjournal.com
Postal Code: 56537-3738
Office phone: (218) 736-7511
General E-mail: newsroom@fergusfallsjournal.com
Publisher Name: Ken Harty
Publisher Email: kenh@fergusfallsjournal.com
Publisher Phone: 218-739-7019
Editor Name: Zach Stich
Editor Email: zach.stich@fergusfallsjournal.com
Editor Phone: 218-739-7030
Advertising Executive Name: Deanna Forkey
Advertising Executive Email: dee.forkey@fergusfallsjournal.com
Advertising Executive Phone: 218-739-7016
Year Established: 1873
Delivery Methods: Mail`Carrier
Mechanical specifications: Type page 6 x 21; E - 6 cols, 2 1/16, 1/8 between; A - 6 cols, 2 1/16, 1/8 between; C - 9 cols, 1 1/3, 1/8 between.
Published Days: Mon`Tues`Wed`Thur`Fri`Sun
Weekday Frequency: e
Saturday Frequency: m
Avg Paid Circ: 5943
Audit Company: Sworn/Estimate/Non-Audited
Audit Date: 7 12 2019
Pressroom Equipment: Lines – 7-G/Community, 1-G/Colorliner.;
Mailroom Equipment: Tying Machines – 1/Bu, 1-/Gd; Address Machine – 1-/Ch.;
Buisness Equipment: 3-IBM/VP 486-33 SX
Buisness Software: RPG/II
Classified Equipment: Hardware – 3-APP/Mac, APP/Power Mac; Printers – APP/LaserWriter 630;
Classified Software: Baseview.
Editorial Equipment: Hardware – APP/Power Mac, APP/Mac G4, APP/iMac; Printers – HP/4MV
Editorial Software: QPS/QuarkXPress 4.1.
Production Equipment: Hardware – Nat/A-250; Cameras – SCREEN/Vertical, SCREEN/Horizontal
Production Software: QPS/QuarkXPress.
Total Circulation: 5943

HIBBING

HIBBING DAILY TRIBUNE

Corporate/Parent Company: Adams Publishing Group
Publication Street Address: 2142 1st Ave
City: Hibbing
State: MN
Publication Website: https://www.hibbingmn.com/
Postal Code: 55746
Office phone: (218) 262-1011
General E-mail: news@hibbingdailytribune.net
Publisher Name: Chris Knight
Publisher Email: cknight@mesabidailynews.net
Editor Name: Eric Killelea
Editor Email: cmanner@hibbingdailytribune.net
Advertising Executive Name: Tom Aune
Advertising Executive Email: taune@hibbingdailytribune.net
Year Established: 1893
Delivery Methods: Mail`Carrier
Own Printing Facility?: N
Commercial printers?: N
Published Days: Tues`Wed`Thur`Fri`Sat`Sun
Weekday Frequency: m
Saturday Frequency: m
Avg Paid Circ: 5523
Audit Company: Sworn/Estimate/Non-Audited
Audit Date: 7 12 2019
Mailroom Equipment: Tying Machines – 2/Bu; Wrapping Singles – 1-/Bu; Address Machine – 1-/Am.;
Buisness Equipment: Packard Bell
Buisness Software: Vision Data
Classified Equipment: Hardware – APP/Mac G3; Printers – HP/Laserjet 5000N, HP/LaserJet 8100N;
Classified Software: Baseview.
Editorial Equipment: Hardware – APP/Power Mac G3/Lf/AP Leaf Picture Desk, AP/Graphics; Printers – HP/Laserjet 5000N, HP/LaserJet 8100N
Editorial Software: Baseview.
Production Equipment: Hardware – HP/Laserjet 5000N; Cameras – B/30x 40; Scanners – Nikon/LS-2000
Production Software: Baseview/NewsEdit Pro.
Note: The Hibbing Daily Tribune is a sister paper to the Mesabi Daily News in Virginia, Minn., the Chisholm Tribune Press in Chisholm, Minn., the Grand Rapids-Herald Review in Grand Rapids, Minn., and the Walker Independent Pilot in Walker, Minn.
Total Circulation: 5523

MANKATO

THE FREE PRESS

Corporate/Parent Company: Gannett
Publication Street Address: 418 S 2nd St
City: Mankato
State: MN
Publication Website: https://www.mankatofreepress.com/
Postal Code: 56001-3727
Office phone: (507) 625-4451
General E-mail: editor@mankatofreepress.com
Publisher Name: Steve Jameson
Publisher Email: sjameson@mankatofreepress.com
Publisher Phone: 507-344-6310
Editor Name: Joe Spear
Editor Email: jspear@mankatofreepress.com
Editor Phone: 507-344-6382
Advertising Executive Name: Barb Wass
Advertising Executive Email: bwass@mankatofreepress.com
Advertising Executive Phone: 507-344-6364
Year Established: 1887
Delivery Methods: Mail`Carrier
Mechanical specifications: Type page 6 x 21 1/4; E - 6 cols, 1 7/8, 1/8 between; A - 6 cols, 1 7/8, 1/8 between; C - 9 cols, 1 3/16, 1/8 between.
Published Days: Mon`Tues`Wed`Thur`Fri`Sat`Sun
Weekday Frequency: m
Saturday Frequency: m
Avg Paid Circ: 20481
Audit Company: Sworn/Estimate/Non-Audited
Audit Date: 7 12 2019
Pressroom Equipment: Lines – 6-G/Urbanite 1969; 2-G/Urbanite 1999;
Mailroom Equipment: Counter Stackers – Id/2200, Id/Olympian, TMS I; Inserters & Stuffers – GMA/SLS 1000R; Tying Machines – 3-MLN/MLNEE, 1-MLN/2EE, 2-MLN/IEE, 1/Power Strap/Newstyer 2000, Power Strap/P-250 A; Address Machine – 1-/Ch, 1-/KR.;
Buisness Equipment: 1-IBM/AS-400
Classified Equipment: Hardware – 8-IBM/300 PL; Printers – HP/4MV;
Classified Software: AT/Enterprise.
Editorial Equipment: Hardware – 29-IBM/350/1-Lf/AP Leaf Picture Desk, 1-APP/Power Mac 7100; Printers – HP/4 MV, HP/5Si, HP/2500CP
Editorial Software: Dewar/View, QPS/QuarkXPress, Adobe/Photoshop.
Production Equipment: Hardware – 2-AG/Accuset 1500, 1-ECR/4550 JetSetter; Cameras – C/Spartan III; Scanners – 1-ECR/Autokon 1030N
Production Software: Dewar/View, QPS/QuarkXPress.
Total Circulation: 20481

MARSHALL

INDEPENDENT

Corporate/Parent Company: Gannett
Publication Street Address: PO Box 411
City: Marshall
State: MN
Publication Website: www.marshallindependent.com
Postal Code: 56258-0411
Office phone: (507) 537-1551
General E-mail: news@marshallindependent.com
Publisher Name: Greg Orear
Publisher Email: gorear@marshallindependent.com
Publisher Phone: ext. 107
Editor Name: Mike Lamb
Editor Email: mlamb@marshallindependent.com
Editor Phone: ext. 126
Advertising Executive Name: Karen Beebout
Advertising Executive Email: kbeebout@marshallindependent.com
Advertising Executive Phone: ext. 113
Year Established: 1874
Delivery Methods:
  Mail`Newsstand`Carrier`Racks
Own Printing Facility?: N
Commercial printers?: Y
Mechanical specifications: Type page 6 x 21 1/2; E - 6 cols, 1 col = 1.583" ; A - 6 cols, 1 col = 1.583"; C - 9 cols, 1 col = 1.022"
Published Days: Mon`Tues`Wed`Thur`Fri`Sat
Weekday Frequency: m
Saturday Frequency: m
Avg Paid Circ: 3761
Avg Free Circ: 191
Audit Company: AAM
Audit Date: 30 08 2019
Buisness Equipment: 1-NCR
Classified Equipment: Hardware – Power IMacs's; Printers – Canon, HP;
Classified Software: Quark
Editorial Equipment: Printers – Canon, HP
Editorial Software: Quark
Production Equipment: Hardware – CTP; Cameras – CTP
Production Software: QuarkXPress
Total Circulation: 4134

MARSHALL INDEPENDENT

Corporate/Parent Company: Ogden Newspapers Inc.
Publication Street Address: PO Box 411
City: Marshall
State: MN
Publication Website: www.marshallindependent.com
Postal Code: 56258
Office phone: (507) 537-1551
Publisher Name: Greg Orear
Publisher Email: gorear@marshallindependent.com
Publisher Phone: ext. 107
Editor Name: Mike Lamb
Editor Email: mlamb@marshallindependent.com
Editor Phone: ext. 126
Advertising Executive Name: Karen Beebout
Advertising Executive Email: kbeebout@marshallindependent.com
Advertising Executive Phone: ext. 113

MINNEAPOLIS

STAR TRIBUNE

Corporate/Parent Company: Star Tribune Media Intermediate Holdings Co. II
Publication Street Address: 650 3rd Ave. South, Suite 1300
City: Minneapolis
State: MN
Publication Website: www.startribune.com
Postal Code: 55488
Office phone: (612) 673-4000
Editor Name: Jim Anderson
Editor Email: jim.anderson@startribune.com
Editor Phone: 612-673-7199
Year Established: 1867
Delivery Methods:
  Mail`Newsstand`Carrier`Racks
Own Printing Facility?: Y
Commercial printers?: Y
Mechanical specifications: Type page 6 x 21; E - 6 cols, 1 3/4, 1/6 between; A - 6 cols, 1 3/4, 1/6 between; C - 10 cols, 1 1/16, 1/12 between.
Published Days: Mon`Tues`Wed`Thur`Fri`Sat`Sun
Weekday Frequency: m
Saturday Frequency: m
Avg Paid Circ: 261783
Audit Company: AAM
Audit Date: 7 08 2020
Pressroom Equipment: Lines – 11-G/Headliner Offset (6 half decks) 1987; 11-G/Headliner Offset (6 half decks) 1987; 11-G/Headliner Offset (6 half decks) 1987; 11-G/Headliner Offset (6 half decks) 1987; 11-G/Headliner Offset (6 half decks) 1987;
Mailroom Equipment: Counter Stackers – 14 Quipp Model 400; 1 Quipp Model 500; 9 Ferag stackers ; Inserters & Stuffers – 3 Ferag 16:1 Rollstream/Drums; 1 Ferag 6-unit disk pool; 1 Ferag 8-unit disk pool; 2 Heidelberg NP-632s ; Wrapping Singles – 2 Schur palletizer, 1 Windab shrinkwrapper; 7

U.S. Daily Newspapers

Dynaric Model 3000 strappers; 18 Dynaric Model 4000 strappers ;
Total Circulation: 414129

NEW ULM
THE JOURNAL
Corporate/Parent Company: Ogden Newspapers, Inc.
Publication Street Address: PO Box 487
City: New Ulm
State: MN
Publication Website: www.nujournal.com
Postal Code: 56073-0487
Office phone: (507) 359-2911
General E-mail: news@nujournal.com
Publisher Name: Greg Orear
Publisher Email: gorear@nujournal.com
Editor Name: Kevin Sweeney
Editor Email: ksweeney@nujournal.com
Advertising Executive Name: Tim Babel
Advertising Executive Email: tbabel@nujournal.com
Year Established: 1911
Delivery Methods: Mail`Carrier`Racks
Own Printing Facility?: Y
Commercial printers?: Y
Mechanical specifications: Type page 6x 21 1/2; E - 6 cols, 2 1/16, 1/8 between; A - 6 cols, 2 1/16, 1/8 between; C - 8 cols, 1 1/2, 1/8 between.
Published Days: Wed`Sat
Weekday Frequency: m
Saturday Frequency: m
Avg Paid Circ: 3109
Audit Company: AAM
Audit Date: 2 07 2018
Pressroom Equipment: Lines – 6-G/Community.;
Mailroom Equipment: Tying Machines – Bu; Address Machine – KR.;
Buisness Equipment: IBM/PS-2 Model 50
Buisness Software: MSSI, Quattro/Pro
Classified Equipment: Hardware – APP/Mac;
Classified Software: Baseview.
Editorial Equipment: Hardware – APP/Mac; Printers – APP/Mac
Editorial Software: NewsEdit/Pro.
Production Equipment: Hardware – APP/Mac; Cameras – SCREEN/Companica 690E; Scanners – APP/Mac, HP.
Total Circulation: 16244

OWATONNA
OWATONNA PEOPLE'S PRESS
Corporate/Parent Company: Adams Publishing Group
Publication Street Address: 135 W Pearl St
City: Owatonna
State: MN
Publication Website: https://www.southernminn.com/owatonna_peoples_press/
Postal Code: 55060
Office phone: (507) 451-2840
General E-mail: news@owatonna.com
Publisher Name: Steve Fisher
Publisher Email: sfisher@owatonna.com
Publisher Phone: (507) 444-2367
Editor Name: Jeffrey Jackson
Editor Email: jjackson@owatonna.com
Editor Phone: (507) 444-2371
Advertising Executive Name: Tom Kelling
Advertising Executive Email: tkelling@owatonna.com
Advertising Executive Phone: (507) 444-2390
Year Established: 1874
Delivery Methods: Mail`Newsstand`Carrier`Racks
Own Printing Facility?: Y
Commercial printers?: Y
Mechanical specifications: Type page 6 x 21 1/2; E - 6 cols, 1 16/25, 1/8 between; A - 6 cols, 1 16/25, 1/8 between; C - 6 cols, 1 16/25, 1/8 between.
Published Days: Tues`Wed`Thur`Fri`Sat
Weekday Frequency: m
Saturday Frequency: m
Avg Paid Circ: 4608
Avg Free Circ: 784

Audit Company: CAC
Audit Date: 31 12 2015
Pressroom Equipment: Lines – 16-G/Community single width; Folders – DGM/1030; Pasters –Jardis; Control System – Fin.;
Mailroom Equipment: Counter Stackers – KAN/Newstac; Inserters & Stuffers – KAN/480 Station Inserter12:1; Tying Machines – 3-Si/LB2000, 1-Si/LB2330 Auto Strapper; Address Machine – 1-Domino/Jet-A-Ray;
Buisness Equipment: PC's
Buisness Software: Windows 7
Editorial Equipment: Hardware – PC's
Editorial Software: TownNews TCMS, Adobe/InDesign 5.5.
Production Equipment: Hardware – 1-ECR/36 HS, 1-Kk/Trendsetter 100, 2-APP/Mac G3
Production Software: Prinergy, Integis, Pit Stop, QPS/QuarkXPress 6.1.
Total Circulation: 5392

ROCHESTER
POST-BULLETIN
Corporate/Parent Company: Forum Communications
Publication Street Address: 1700 Greenview Dr SW
City: Rochester
State: MN
Publication Website: www.postbulletin.com
Postal Code: 55902
Office phone: (507) 285-7600
General E-mail: circulation@postbulletin.com
Editor Name: Jeff Pieters
Editor Email: jpieters@postbulletin.com
Editor Phone: 507-285-7748
Year Established: 1916
Delivery Methods: Mail`Carrier
Own Printing Facility?: Y
Commercial printers?: Y
Mechanical specifications: Type page 13 x 21; E - 6 cols, 2 1/16, 1/8 between; A - 6 cols, 2 1/16, 1/8 between; C - 8 cols, 1 9/16, 1/16 between.
Published Days: Mon`Tues`Wed`Thur`Fri`Sat
Weekday Frequency: e
Saturday Frequency: e
Avg Paid Circ: 26773
Avg Free Circ: 469
Audit Company: CAC
Audit Date: 31 03 2018
Pressroom Equipment: Lines – 5-G/Headliner Offset (3 decks) double width 1988; Folders – G/2:1.;
Mailroom Equipment: Counter Stackers – 3-QWI/500, 1-QWI/401; Inserters & Stuffers – GMA/3000 20:2, GMA/10 Heads; Tying Machines – Ovalstrapping; Wrapping Singles – Mosca; Control System – GMA/SAM; Address Machine – KR, Prism;
Buisness Equipment: IBM/AS-400 720-2062, PCs, Sun/Enterprise
Buisness Software: IBM/AS-400, Microsoft/Office, Abra Suite, PBS
Classified Equipment: Hardware – APP/Mac; Printers – HP;
Classified Software: Baseview.
Editorial Equipment: Hardware – APP/Mac; Printers – HP
Editorial Software: Baseview.
Production Equipment: Hardware – 2-Polaroid/Sprintscant, 1-Devotec/DE; Scanners – Polaroid/Sprintscant, Umax, Nikon, AG
Production Software: QPS 3.11, QPS 4.0.
Total Circulation: 27242

SAINT CLOUD
ST. CLOUD TIMES
Corporate/Parent Company: Gannett Company Inc.
Publication Street Address: 3000 7th St N
City: Saint Cloud
State: MN
Publication Website: www.sctimes.com
Postal Code: 56303-3108
Office phone: (320) 255-8700
General E-mail: newsroom@stcloudtimes.com
Year Established: 1861

Delivery Methods: Mail`Newsstand`Carrier`Racks
Own Printing Facility?: Y
Commercial printers?: N
Mechanical specifications: Type page 6 x 20; E - 6 cols, 1.562, 1/8 between; A - 6 cols, 1.562, 1/8 between; C - 10 cols, 1", .02 between.
Published Days: Mon`Tues`Wed`Thur`Fri`Sat`Sun
Weekday Frequency: m
Saturday Frequency: m
Avg Paid Circ: 15107
Avg Free Circ: 193
Audit Company: AAM
Audit Date: 10 08 2018
Pressroom Equipment: MAN Uniset 70 - 6 towers; Baumueller Drives
Mailroom Equipment: 10 head GMA SLS2000 14 head GMA SLS2000 4- Dynaric in-line strappers Quipp 350 and 400 stackers In-line ink jet capabilities
Buisness Equipment: IBM/AS-400 (located in Phoenix)
Classified Equipment: 2 Mactive Servers. Both IBM 3650's; 6 classified PC's strictly classified; Another 8 PC's with Mactive in Advertising for keying
Editorial Equipment: ENG; Nothing local
Editorial Software: Newsgate
Total Circulation: 18896

SAINT PAUL
ST. PAUL PIONEER PRESS
Corporate/Parent Company: Media News Group
Publication Street Address: 10 River Park Plz
City: Saint Paul
State: MN
Publication Website: www.twincities.com
Postal Code: 55107-1223
Office phone: (651) 222-1111
General E-mail: letters@pioneerpress.com
Editor Name: Mike Burbach
Editor Email: mburbach@pioneerpress.com
Editor Phone: 651-228-5544
Year Established: 1849
Delivery Methods: Mail`Newsstand`Carrier`Racks
Own Printing Facility?: Y
Commercial printers?: Y
Mechanical specifications: Type page 6 x 21; E - 5 cols, 1 11/16, 3/16 between; A - 6 cols, 2 1/16, 3/16 between; C - 10 cols, 1 1/8, between.
Published Days: Mon`Tues`Wed`Thur`Fri`Sat`Sun
Weekday Frequency: m
Saturday Frequency: m
Avg Paid Circ: 143241
Audit Company: AAM
Audit Date: 18 03 2020
Pressroom Equipment: Lines – 6-G/Metroliner Double Width; 6-G/Metroliner Double Width; 6-G/Metroliner Double Width; Folders – 3-G/3:2 single.;
Mailroom Equipment: Counter Stackers – 7-Quipp, 5-HL/Monitor; Inserters & Stuffers – 2-Dynaric/NP;
Total Circulation: 228942

VIRGINIA
MESABI DAILY NEWS
Corporate/Parent Company: Adams Publishing Group
Publication Street Address: 704 S 7th Ave
City: Virginia
State: MN
Publication Website: https://www.virginiamn.com/
Postal Code: 55792
Office phone: (218) 741-5544
General E-mail: webmaster@mesabidailynews.net
Editor Name: Jerry Burnes
Editor Email: jburnes@mesabidailynews.net
Advertising Executive Name: Alison Stanaway
Advertising Executive Email: astanaway@mesabidailynews.net
Year Established: 1893
Delivery Methods: Mail`Carrier

Mechanical specifications: Type page 6 x 20; E - 6 cols, 1 5/6, 5/16 between; A - 6 cols, 1 5/6, 5/16 between; C - 9 cols, 1 1/6, 5/16 between.
Published Days: Tues`Wed`Thur`Fri`Sat`Sun
Weekday Frequency: m
Saturday Frequency: m
Avg Paid Circ: 9143
Audit Company: Sworn/Estimate/Non-Audited
Audit Date: 7 12 2019
Pressroom Equipment: Lines – 8-G/Urbanite; Folders – 1-G/2:1.;
Mailroom Equipment: Counter Stackers – 1/HL; Inserters & Stuffers – 6-KAN/660; Tying Machines – 1-Sterling/MR40, 1-Sterling/SSM-Mini; Wrapping Singles – 2-/Bu; Address Machine – 1-/KAN.;
Buisness Equipment: 1-IBM/Risc 6000
Classified Equipment: Printers – 1-APP/Mac LaserWriter NTX, 2-HP/8000N, 1-Ag/Accuset 1000, 1-AG/25SX;
Classified Software: Baseview.
Editorial Equipment: Hardware – 18-APP/Mac; Printers – 1-APP/Mac LaserWriter NTX, 2-HP/8000N, 1-AG/25SX, 1-AG/Accuset 1000
Editorial Software: APP/Mac, Baseview.
Production Equipment: Hardware – Caere/OmniPage, MON/1000; Cameras – 1-B; Scanners – AG/Arcus, 2-Umax 1200S
Production Software: QPS/QuarkXPress, Baseview.
Total Circulation: 9143

WILLMAR
WEST CENTRAL TRIBUNE
Corporate/Parent Company: Forum Communications
Publication Street Address: 2208 Trott Ave SW
City: Willmar
State: MN
Publication Website: www.wctrib.com
Postal Code: 56201-2723
Office phone: (320) 235-1150
General E-mail: news@wctrib.com
Publisher Name: Steve Ammermann
Publisher Email: sammermann@wctrib.com
Publisher Phone: 320-214-4307
Editor Name: Kelly Boldan
Editor Email: kboldan@wctrib.com
Editor Phone: 320-214-4331
Advertising Executive Name: Christie Steffel
Advertising Executive Email: csteffel@wctrib.com
Advertising Executive Phone: 320-214-4317
Year Established: 1895
Delivery Methods: Mail`Carrier
Own Printing Facility?: Y
Commercial printers?: Y
Mechanical specifications: Type page 6 x 20.75; E - 6 cols, 1 13/16, 1/8 between; A - 6 cols, 1 13/16, 1/8 between; C - 8 cols, 1 13/16, 1/8 between.
Published Days: Mon`Tues`Wed`Thur`Fri`Sat
Weekday Frequency: m
Saturday Frequency: m
Avg Paid Circ: 9827
Avg Free Circ: 54
Audit Company: VAC
Audit Date: 30 09 2017
Pressroom Equipment: Lines – BG/Dampening System, 8-G/Community; Folders – 1-G/SCI, G/SSC.;
Mailroom Equipment: Tying Machines – OVL; Address Machine – Ch/596.;
Buisness Equipment: DEC/VAX 6410, DEC/2100A Alpha
Buisness Software: Collier-Jackson Inc
Classified Equipment: Hardware – Dell, Micron/Workstation, Compaq; Printers – AU/APS2000, Au/Imagesetter, HP/4m;
Classified Software: APT.
Editorial Equipment: Hardware – Micron/workstation, Dell, Compaq/Server/APP/Mac G4; Printers – AU/APS2000, AU/Imagesetter, Epson/Color Proofer, HP
Editorial Software: APT.
Production Equipment: Hardware – Wordlinx 2.1, AU/108C; Cameras – 2-C/Spartan III; Scanners – 3-Umax/PowerLook
Production Software: APT.
Total Circulation: 9881

WINONA

WINONA DAILY NEWS
Corporate/Parent Company: Lee Enterprises
Publication Street Address: 902 E 2nd St
City: Winona
State: MN
Publication Website: www.winonadailynews.com
Postal Code: 55987-6512
Office phone: (507) 453-3500
Publisher Name: Sean Burke
Publisher Email: sean.burke@lee.net
Publisher Phone: 608-791-8237
Advertising Executive Name: Lisa Faulkner
Advertising Executive Email: Lisa.Faulkner@lee.net
Advertising Executive Phone: 507-453-3538
Year Established: 1855
Delivery Methods: Mail`Newsstand`Carrier
Own Printing Facility?: N
Commercial printers?: Y
Mechanical specifications: Type page 6 x 21 1/2; E - 6 cols, 1 5/6, 1/8 between; A - 6 cols, 1 5/6, 1/8 between; C - 9 cols, 1 1/5, 1/16 between.
Published Days: Mon`Tues`Wed`Thur`Fri`Sat`Sun
Weekday Frequency: m
Saturday Frequency: m
Avg Paid Circ: 5682
Avg Free Circ: 522
Audit Company: AAM
Audit Date: 2 08 2018
Pressroom Equipment: Lines – 13 - Goss Urbanite & DGM 850; 5 - Goss Urbanite; Press Drive – 2 digital drives ; Folders – 1-Goss Urbanite 2:1 1 DGM 2:1; Pasters –5 - Hurst; Reels & Stands – 1 Goss Urbanite roll stand; Registration System – Jardis
Mailroom Equipment: Counter Stackers – 1 - Hall Monitor 2 - Quipp 1 – Gammerler; Inserters & Stuffers – 1 Harris 1372 1 K&M 1372; Tying Machines – 2 – Dynaric NP-2 strappers; Address Machine – 1 - Videojet inkjet labeler ;
Buisness Equipment: IBM/AS-400
Buisness Software: Custom Software
Classified Equipment: Hardware – 3-Gateway/2000 P5-90;
Classified Software: CText/Advision OS-2 3.00.
Editorial Equipment: Hardware – 14-Gateway/2000 P5-90, 2-Gateway/2000 P5-100/1-APP/Power Mac 8500-180, 1-Nikon/Scanner, 1-APP/Mac IIci, 1-APP/Mac Classic; Printers – 2-HP/5Si, 1-HP/4Si, 1-APP/Mac LaserWriter IIf
Editorial Software: CText/Dateline OS-2 3.00.
Production Equipment: Hardware – 2-HP/5Si; Cameras – 1-B.
Total Circulation: 5824

WORTHINGTON

WORTHINGTON DAILY GLOBE
Corporate/Parent Company: Forum Communications
Publication Street Address: 300 11th St
City: Worthington
State: MN
Publication Website: www.dglobe.net
Postal Code: 56187-2451
Office phone: (507) 376-9711
Publisher Name: Joni Harms
Publisher Email: jharms@dglobe.com
Publisher Phone: (507) 376-7308
Editor Name: Ryan McGaughey
Editor Email: rmcgaughey@dglobe.com
Editor Phone: (507) 376-7320
Advertising Executive Name: Roberta Fultz
Advertising Executive Email: rfultz@dglobe.com
Advertising Executive Phone: (507) 376-7313
Year Established: 1872
Delivery Methods: Mail`Carrier
Own Printing Facility?: Y
Mechanical specifications: Type page 11 5/8 x 21; E - 6 cols, 1 7/8, 1/8 between; A - 6 cols, 1 7/8, 1/8 between; C - 9 cols, 1 1/4, 1/8 between.
Published Days: Mon`Tues`Wed`Thur`Fri`Sat
Weekday Frequency: m
Saturday Frequency: m
Avg Paid Circ: 5830
Avg Free Circ: 53
Audit Company: VAC
Audit Date: 30 09 2016
Pressroom Equipment: Lines – 11-HI/V15 SingleWidth 1999; Folders – 2, HI/JF-7, HI/JF-25.;
Mailroom Equipment: Counter Stackers – Tiger; Inserters & Stuffers – Manual; Tying Machines – 2/Akebono; Address Machine – KR;
Buisness Equipment: 10-Micron PC, 1-Dell PC
Buisness Software: Microsoft/Office, Microsoft/Windows 95, Microsoft/Windows 98, Microsoft/Excell 2000, Citrix/Great Plains Postaboft Geac
Classified Equipment: Printers – Dataproducts/Typhoon 16, HP;
Classified Software: ACT 2.06.004.
Editorial Equipment: Hardware – 4-APP/Mac; Printers – Data Products/Typhoon 16, Epson/1270
Editorial Software: ACT 2.06.004.
Production Equipment: Hardware – Nu/Flip Top FT40V6UPNS, 2-Glunz & Jensen/Online Processor; Cameras – SCREEN; Scanners – 3-Umax/Powerlook 2
Production Software: QPS/QuarkXpress 4.0.
Total Circulation: 5883

MISSOURI

CAMDENTON

LAKE SUN
Publication Street Address: 918 N. Business Route 5
City: Camdenton
State: MO
Publication Website: www.LakeNewsOnline.com
Postal Code: 65020
Office phone: 573) 346-2132
Publisher Name: Joseph Leong
Publisher Email: jleong@gatehousemedia.com
Editor Name: Amy Wilson
Editor Email: awilson@westsidestar.net
Editor Phone: 573-317-8139
Advertising Executive Name: Lisa Miller
Advertising Executive Email: lmiller@lakesunonline.com
Advertising Executive Phone: 573-317-8181

LAKE SUN LEADER
Corporate/Parent Company: Gannett
Publication Street Address: 918 N Business Route 5
City: Camdenton
State: MO
Publication Website: www.lakenewsonline.com
Postal Code: 65020-2648
Office phone: (573) 346-2132
Publisher Name: Joseph Leong
Publisher Email: jleong@gatehousemedia.com
Editor Name: Joyce L. Miller
Editor Email: jmiller@lakesunonline.com
Editor Phone: 573-346-2132
Advertising Executive Name: Michelle Bradley
Advertising Executive Email: mbradley@gatehousemedia.com
Advertising Executive Phone: 573-346-2132
Year Established: 1879
Mechanical specifications: Type page 13 x 21 1/2; E - 6 cols, 2 1/16, 1/8 between; A - 6 cols, 2 1/16, 1/8 between; C - 6 cols, 2 1/16, 1/8 between.
Published Days: Mon`Tues`Wed`Thur`Fri
Weekday Frequency: m
Avg Paid Circ: 10757
Avg Free Circ: 28855
Audit Company: Sworn/Estimate/Non-Audited
Audit Date: 7 12 2019
Mailroom Equipment: Counter Stackers – KAN/320; Tying Machines – Bu; Address Machine – Ch.;
Buisness Equipment: IBM/Sys 36, AmDek/Sys 286A
Classified Equipment: Hardware – COM/MCS.;
Editorial Equipment: Hardware – APP/Mac/IBM, HP.
Production Equipment: Hardware – HP/LaserJet; Scanners – DSA.
Total Circulation: 39612

CHILLICOTHE

CONSTITUTION-TRIBUNE
Publication Street Address: 818 Washington St
City: Chillicothe
State: MO
Publication Website: www.chillicothenews.com
Postal Code: 64601-2232
Office phone: (660) 646-2411
Editor Name: Angie Talken
Editor Email: news@chillicothenews.com
Advertising Executive Name: Connie Jones
Advertising Executive Email: advertising@chillicothenews.com
Year Established: 1860
Delivery Methods: Mail`Newsstand`Carrier`Racks
Mechanical specifications: Type page 13 1/2 x 21 1/2; E - 6 cols, 2 1/16, 1/8 between; A - 6 cols, 2 1/16, 1/8 between; C - 6 cols, 2 1/16, 1/8 between.
Published Days: Mon`Tues`Wed`Thur`Fri
Weekday Frequency: e
Avg Paid Circ: 2535
Avg Free Circ: 13220
Audit Company: Sworn/Estimate/Non-Audited
Audit Date: 7 12 2019
Pressroom Equipment: Lines – 4-G/Community.;
Mailroom Equipment: Tying Machines – 1/ Malow, 1-/Bu; Address Machine – 3-/Rp.;
Editorial Equipment: Hardware – 6-CText/CText/Fileserver, CText/AP Wire receiver.
Production Equipment: Hardware – 2-APP/Mac LaserWriter, 1-COM; Cameras – 1-Nu.
Total Circulation: 15755

CLINTON

THE CLINTON DAILY DEMOCRAT
Publication Street Address: 212 S Washington St
City: Clinton
State: MO
Publication Website: www.clintondailydemocrat.com
Postal Code: 64735-2073
Office phone: (660) 885-2281
General E-mail: dailydemocrat@embarqmail.com
Year Established: 1868
Delivery Methods: Mail`Carrier
Own Printing Facility?: Y
Mechanical specifications: Type page 13 x 21 1/2; E - 6 cols, 2 1/16, 1/8 between; A - 6 cols, 2 1/16, 1/8 between; C - 6 cols, 2 1/16, 1/8 between.
Published Days: Mon`Tues`Wed`Thur`Fri
Weekday Frequency: e
Avg Paid Circ: 3595
Avg Free Circ: 17187
Audit Company: Sworn/Estimate/Non-Audited
Audit Date: 7 12 2019
Mailroom Equipment: Tying Machines – 1/ Malow; Address Machine – 1-Am/Mail 5.;
Buisness Equipment: APP/Mac
Classified Equipment: Hardware – 1-Ro, 1-IBM.;
Editorial Equipment: Hardware – 1-IBM, 1-Ro.
Production Equipment: Hardware – 1-HA, 1-EK.
Total Circulation: 20782

COLUMBIA

COLUMBIA DAILY TRIBUNE
Corporate/Parent Company: Gannett
Publication Street Address: 101 N 4th St
City: Columbia
State: MO
Publication Website: www.columbiatribune.com
Postal Code: 65201-4416
Office phone: (573) 815-1600
Publisher Name: Terri Leifeste
Publisher Email: tleifeste@gatehousemedia.com
Publisher Phone: (573) 815-1640
Editor Name: Jim Van Nostrand
Editor Email: jimvan@gatehousemedia.com
Editor Phone: (573) 815-1707
Advertising Executive Name: Aaron Consalvi
Advertising Executive Email: aconsalvi@columbiatribune.com
Advertising Executive Phone: (573) 815-1903
Year Established: 1901
Delivery Methods: Mail`Newsstand`Carrier`Racks
Own Printing Facility?: Y
Commercial printers?: Y
Mechanical specifications: Type page 11 3/8 x 21; E - 6 cols, 1.75", 1 pica between; A - 6 cols, 1.75", 1 pica between; C - 7 cols, 1.5625", .5 pica between.
Published Days: Mon`Tues`Wed`Thur`Fri`Sat`Sun
Weekday Frequency: e
Saturday Frequency: m
Avg Paid Circ: 12665
Avg Free Circ: 699
Audit Company: AAM
Audit Date: 17 08 2018
Pressroom Equipment: Lines – 20 unit DGM 430 (22 3/4 x 35) with two Folders DGM 1030 combination folder DGM 1035 combination folder ; 48 unit Goss Universal 45 (22 x 35) 2- 1:3:3 jaw Folders with upper formers, q-fold and crosshead perf; Press Drive – Allen Bradley drives with drive shaft; Folders – DGM 1030 combination folder with q-fold and crosshead perf DGM 1035 combination folder with q-fold and crosshead perf Universal 2 1:3:3 jaw folder with uppper former; q-fold and crosshead perf; Pasters –Universal press has AMAL AR60C splicersRegistration System – Universal is equipped with I-Tech Registration System
Mailroom Equipment: Counter Stackers – Gammerler STC70 stackers on all press lines; Inserters & Stuffers – GMA SLS1000 inserter-12 into 1 Muller Martini 227 inserter-16 into 1 with CS-10 Muller stacker Muller Martini 227 inserter-4 into 1 with Rima RS counter stacker; Tying Machines – Signode LB-2330 strapper Signode LB-2000 tying machine Signode LBX-2000 tying machine; Wrapping Singles – Arpac 55G1-200 bundle shrinkwrapper; Address Machine – 3 - Domino JetArray in-line and off-line with Rima (Harris) RS12 Counter Stackers;
Production Software: Apogee Portal
Total Circulation: 15580

COLUMBIA MISSOURIAN
Corporate/Parent Company: Missouri Press Association
Publication Street Address: 221 S 8th St
City: Columbia
State: MO
Publication Website: www.columbiamissourian.com
Postal Code: 65201-4868
Office phone: (573) 882-5700
General E-mail: news@columbiamissourian.com
Editor Name: Jeanne Abbott
Editor Email: abbottjm@missouri.edu
Year Established: 1908
Delivery Methods: Mail`Newsstand`Carrier`Racks
Own Printing Facility?: N
Mechanical specifications: Broadsheet (ROP) Page Size: 11.625AÃ‚Â‚Ã‚ÂÃ‚Â" x 20.5AA 6 col = 11.625AA 5 col = 9.25AA 4 col = 7.375AAÃ‚Â" 3 col = 5.5AA 2 col = 3.625AAÃ‚Â" 1 col = 1.75AA Tab Page Size (VOX, Special Sections): Full Page = 9.75AAÃ‚Â" x 11AAÃ‚Â" 1/2 pg Hor = 9.75AAÃ‚Â" x 5.417AAÃ‚Â‚Ã‚Â" 1/2 Ver = 4.79AAÃ‚Â‚Ã‚Â" x 11AAÃ‚Â" 1/4 pg Hor = 4.79AAÃ‚Â‚Ã‚Â" x 5.417AAÃ‚Â‚Ã‚Â" Ver = 2.3125AAÃ‚Â‚Ã‚Â" x 11AAÃ‚Â‚Ã‚Â" 1/8 pg Hor = 4.79AAÃ‚Â‚Ã‚Â" x 2.625AAÃ‚Â‚Ã‚Â‚Ã‚Â"

U.S. Daily Newspapers

I-67

1/8 pg Ver = 2.3125AAÃ,Â",Ã,Â"
x 5.417AAÃ,Â",Ã,Â" 1/16 pg =
2.3125AAÃ,Â",Ã,Â" x 2.625AAÃ,Â"
Published Days: Mon`Tues`Wed`Thur`Sun
Weekday Frequency: m
Saturday Frequency: m
Avg Paid Circ: 6202
Audit Company: Sworn/Estimate/Non-Audited
Audit Date: 7 12 2019
Pressroom Equipment: Lines – N/A;
Mailroom Equipment: Counter Stackers – N/A;
Classified Equipment: Hardware – 2-HAS/Edit 8.;
Editorial Equipment: Hardware – 2-HAS/HS-55, IBM/26-IBM/PC, 7-HAS/Edit 3, 3-HAS/Edit 8, 2-HAS/Magician Layout, 2-HAS/NewsPro; Printers – Ricoh
Production Equipment: Scanners – Dest/PC Scan.
Total Circulation: 6202

DEXTER

THE DAILY STATESMAN

Corporate/Parent Company: Rust Communications
Publication Street Address: 909 Mallory St.
City: Dexter
State: MO
Publication Website: https://www.dexterstatesman.com/
Postal Code: 63841
Office phone: (573) 624-4545
General E-mail: news@dexterstatesman.com
Editor Name: Josh Ayers
Editor Email: jayers@dexterstatesman.com
Year Established: 1879
Delivery Methods: Mail`Carrier`Racks
Own Printing Facility?: Y
Mechanical specifications: Type page 13 x 22 1/2; E - 6 cols, 2 1/16, 1/8 between; A - 6 cols, 2 1/16, 1/8 between; C - 8 cols, 1 1/2, 1/8 between.
Published Days: Tues`Wed`Thur`Fri`Sun
Weekday Frequency: e
Avg Paid Circ: 2522
Audit Company: Sworn/Estimate/Non-Audited
Audit Date: 7 12 2019
Mailroom Equipment: Tying Machines – 1/Strap Tyer;
Classified Equipment: Hardware – 1-COM/MDT 350.;
Editorial Equipment: Hardware – 1-COM/MDT 350.
Production Equipment: Hardware – 1-COM/4961, 1-COM/2961; Cameras – 1-Acti/140.
Total Circulation: 2522

FULTON

THE FULTON SUN

Corporate/Parent Company: WEHCO Media, Inc.
Publication Street Address: 115 E 5th St
City: Fulton
State: MO
Publication Website: www.fultonsun.com
Postal Code: 65251-1714
Office phone: (573) 642-7272
General E-mail: news@fultonsun.com
Year Established: 1875
Delivery Methods: Mail`Newsstand`Carrier`Racks
Mechanical specifications: Type page 13 x 21; E - 6 cols, 2 1/16, 1/8 between; A - 6 cols, 2 1/16, 1/8 between; C - 9 cols, 1 3/8, 1/16 between.
Published Days: Tues`Wed`Thur`Fri`Sun
Weekday Frequency: m
Avg Paid Circ: 4300
Avg Free Circ: 9000
Audit Company: Sworn/Estimate/Non-Audited
Audit Date: 7 12 2019
Pressroom Equipment: Lines – 4-G/Community 1991;
Mailroom Equipment: Counter Stackers – 1-BG/Count-O-Veyor; Tying Machines – 1/Bu.;
Classified Equipment: Baseview.
Editorial Equipment: Printers – APP/Mac LaserWriter NTX, APP/Mac LaserWriter Pro, Xante/8300
Editorial Software: Baseview.

Production Equipment: Hardware – APP/Mac LaserWriter Pro; Cameras – R.
Total Circulation: 13300

HANNIBAL

HANNIBAL COURIER-POST

Publication Street Address: 200 N 3rd St
City: Hannibal
State: MO
Publication Website: www.hannibal.net
Postal Code: 63401-3504
Office phone: (573) 221-2800
General E-mail: newsroom@courierpost.com
Publisher Name: Ron Wallace
Publisher Email: rwallace@courierpost.com
Publisher Phone: 217-221-3381
Editor Name: Jason Lewton
Editor Email: jlewton@courierpost.com
Editor Phone: 217-221-3321
Advertising Executive Name: Shelly Bissell
Advertising Executive Email: sbissell@courierpost.com
Advertising Executive Phone: 217-221-3337
Year Established: 1838
Delivery Methods: Mail`Newsstand`Carrier
Own Printing Facility?: N
Commercial printers?: Y
Mechanical specifications: Type page 10.625 x 21.5, 6 cols
Published Days: Tues`Wed`Thur`Fri`Sat
Weekday Frequency: m
Saturday Frequency: m
Avg Paid Circ: 4060
Avg Free Circ: 70
Audit Company: Sworn/Estimate/Non-Audited
Audit Date: 7 12 2019
Pressroom Equipment: Lines – 9-G/Community single width 1968; Folders – G/Quarter.;
Mailroom Equipment: Tying Machines – MLN; Address Machine – 1/Ch.;
Buisness Software: Unix/SCO 4.2
Classified Equipment: Hardware – 2-APP/G-4; Printers – HP/4000, APP/Mac LaserWriter 630 Pro, HP/4MV, HP/Laser Jet 4050;
Classified Software: AdManager Pro
Editorial Equipment: Hardware – 6-APP/G-4, 2-PC/Power/2-APP/Mac Flatbed scanners, 1-Nikon/LS-1000 Scanner, 1-Phototherm/Automatic Film Processor; Printers – APP/Mac 16/600
Editorial Software: NewsEdit Pro
Production Equipment: Hardware – Nu/Flip Top FT40VGUPNS, Pre Press/Panther RIP, Pre Press/Set 1000/Harlequin Navigator, AG/Accuset 1000; Scanners – Epson
Production Software: InDesign CS4
Total Circulation: 4130

INDEPENDENCE

INDEPENDENCE EXAMINER

Publication Street Address: 410 S. Liberty
City: Independence
State: MO
Publication Website: www.Examiner.net
Postal Code: 64050
Office phone: 816-254-8600
Publisher Name: Julie Moreno
Publisher Email: julie.moreno@examiner.net
Publisher Phone: 816-350-6311
Editor Name: Jeff Fox
Editor Email: jeff.fox@examiner.net
Editor Phone: 816-350-6365
Advertising Executive Name: Luke Daniel
Advertising Executive Email: luke.daniel@examiner.net
Advertising Executive Phone: 816-350-6341

THE EXAMINER / EXAMINER WEEKEND

Publication Street Address: 410 S Liberty St
City: Independence
State: MO

Publication Website: www.examiner.net
Postal Code: 64050-3805
Office phone: (816) 254-8600
Publisher Name: Julie Moreno
Publisher Email: julie.moreno@examiner.net
Publisher Phone: 816-350-6311
Editor Name: Jeff Fox
Editor Email: jeff.fox@examiner.net
Editor Phone: 816-350-6365
Advertising Executive Name: Luke Daniel
Advertising Executive Email: luke.daniel@examiner.net
Advertising Executive Phone: 816-350-6341
Year Established: 1898
Delivery Methods: Mail`Carrier
Mechanical specifications: Type page 13 x 21 1/2; E - 6 cols, 2 1/16, 1/8 between; A - 6 cols, 2 1/16, 1/8 between; C - 8 cols, 1 1/2, 1/8 between.
Published Days: Mon`Tues`Wed`Fri`Sat
Weekday Frequency: m
Saturday Frequency: m
Avg Paid Circ: 5641
Audit Company: VAC
Audit Date: 30 09 2017
Pressroom Equipment: Lines – 7-G/Urbanite; Folders – 1-G/Urbanite, 1-G/Suburban.;
Mailroom Equipment: Counter Stackers – 1-Id; Inserters & Stuffers – 1-HI/NP 848; Tying Machines – 1/MLN; Address Machine – 1-/KR.;
Buisness Equipment: 1-ATT/6386E-WGS
Classified Equipment: Hardware – 8-APP/Mac Performa 630; Printers – MON/Express Master 1270;
Classified Software: Baseview.
Editorial Equipment: Hardware – 26-APP/Mac/SMS/Library System; Printers – MON/270, Pre Press/Panther 46
Editorial Software: Baseview/Editorial System.
Production Equipment: Hardware – MON/Imagesetter, Nu/40V6U, Panther 46; Cameras – 1-B
Production Software: QPS/QuarkXPress 4.0, Baseview/Editorial Systems.
Note: Advertising is sold in combination with the Blue Springs Examiner (e) for $30.55 (d). Individual newspaper rates not made available.
Total Circulation: 5641

JEFFERSON CITY

JEFFERSON CITY NEWS TRIBUNE

Publication Street Address: 210 Monroe Steet
City: Jefferson City
State: MO
Publication Website: www.NewsTribune.com
Postal Code: 65101
Office phone: 573-636-3131
General E-mail: news@newtribune.com.
Editor Name: Gary Castor
Editor Email: gary@newtribune.com
Editor Phone: 573-761-0255

NEWS TRIBUNE

Corporate/Parent Company: WEHCO Media, Inc.
Publication Street Address: 210 Monroe St
City: Jefferson City
State: MO
Publication Website: www.newstribune.com
Postal Code: 65101-3210
Office phone: (573) 636-3131
General E-mail: news@newstribune.com
Editor Name: Rick Brown
Editor Email: rbrown@newstribune.com
Editor Phone: 573-761-0267
Year Established: 1865
Delivery Methods: Mail`Newsstand`Carrier
Own Printing Facility?: Y
Commercial printers?: Y
Mechanical specifications: Type page 11 5/8 x 20 1/4; E - 6 cols, 2 1/16, 1/8 between; A - 6 cols, 2 1/16, 1/8 between; C - 6 cols, 2 1/16, 1/8 between.
Published Days: Mon`Tues`Wed`Thur`Fri`Sat`Sun
Weekday Frequency: m
Saturday Frequency: m

Avg Paid Circ: 11446
Avg Free Circ: 346
Audit Company: AAM
Audit Date: 26 11 2019
Pressroom Equipment: Lines – Man Roland Uniset 70; Reels & Stands – Megtec 70;
Mailroom Equipment: Counter Stackers – Quipp 440; Inserters & Stuffers – HI, GMA/1000; Tying Machines – Quipp; Address Machine – 1/Ch.;
Buisness Equipment: PBS-Sun
Buisness Software: PBS
Classified Equipment: Hardware – PBS-DTI; Printers – Copiers
Classified Software: PBS-DTI
Editorial Equipment: Hardware – APP/Mac; Printers – Copiers
Editorial Software: Baseview.
Production Equipment: Hardware – Trendsetter 100 Trendsetter 50; Cameras – 1-R
Production Software: InDesign
Total Circulation: 12259

JOPLIN

THE JOPLIN GLOBE

Corporate/Parent Company: CNHI, LLC
Publication Street Address: 117 E 4th St
City: Joplin
State: MO
Publication Website: www.joplinglobe.com
Postal Code: 64801-2302
Office phone: (800) 444-8514
General E-mail: news@joplinglobe.com
Publisher Name: Dale Brendel
Publisher Email: publisher@joplinglobe.com
Publisher Phone: 417-627-7291
Editor Name: Andy Ostmeyer
Editor Email: aostmeyer@joplinglobe.com
Editor Phone: 417-627-7281
Advertising Executive Name: Bob Barth
Advertising Executive Email: bbarth@joplinglobe.com
Advertising Executive Phone: 417-627-7233
Year Established: 1896
Delivery Methods: Mail`Newsstand`Carrier`Racks
Mechanical specifications: Type page 13 x 21 3/4; E - 6 cols, 2 1/16, 1/8 between; A - 6 cols, 2 1/16, 1/8 between; C - 6 cols, 2 1/16, 1/8 between.
Published Days: Mon`Tues`Wed`Thur`Fri`Sat`Sun
Weekday Frequency: m
Saturday Frequency: m
Avg Paid Circ: 13014
Avg Free Circ: 698
Audit Company: AAM
Audit Date: 31 12 2017
Pressroom Equipment: Lines – 5-G/Headliner Unit (2 color decks) 1986; Folders – 2-G/2:1; Pasters –G/Automatic 1986; Control System – PEC/Bond Drive 1985.;
Mailroom Equipment: Counter Stackers – 2/QWI, 1-/QWI; Inserters & Stuffers – MM/227 2:1; Tying Machines – 2-Si/Sni; Wrapping Singles – Bann/Tyer; Address Machine – 1-/Ch;
Buisness Equipment: IBM/AS-400
Classified Equipment: Hardware – IBM/RS 6000; Printers – HP/4;
Classified Software: AT, Enterprise.
Editorial Equipment: Hardware – IBM/RS 6000; Printers – HP/5, HP/4
Editorial Software: AT.
Production Equipment: Hardware – AmeriGraph/Magnum 453 Seds, Southern Litho/GNS 39, W/30 D; Cameras – 1-C, 1-R; Scanners – ECR/1000DE, ECR/1030C.
Total Circulation: 13712

KANSAS CITY

KANSAS CITY DAILY RECORD

Corporate/Parent Company: Missouri Lawyers Media
Publication Street Address: 920 Main St., Suite 825
City: Kansas City
State: MO
Publication Website: mlmcounties.com

Postal Code: 64105
Office phone: 816.931.2002
Publisher Name: Liz Irwin
Publisher Email: lirwin@molawyersmedia.com
Editor Name: Cindi Lash
Editor Email: clash@molawyersmedia.com
Advertising Executive Name: Johnny Aguirre
Advertising Executive Email: jaguirre@molawyersmedia.com

KANSAS CITY PULSE LEGAL PUBLICATIONS

Publication Street Address: 501 E Armour Blvd
City: Kansas City
State: MO
Publication Website: www.PulseLegal.com
Postal Code: 64109
Office phone: 816-221-2552
General E-mail: legalpubs@pulselegal.com
Publisher Name: Pamela Wingo
Publisher Email: pam@pulselegal.com
Publisher Phone: 816-221-2552

THE KANSAS CITY STAR

Corporate/Parent Company: McClatchy Company
Publication Street Address: 1601 McGee St.
City: Kansas City
State: MO
Publication Website: www.kansascity.com
Postal Code: 64108
Office phone: (816) 234-4636
Editor Name: Mike Fannin
Editor Email: mfannin@kcstar.com
Editor Phone: 816-234-4345
Year Established: 1880
Delivery Methods:
    Mail`Newsstand`Carrier`Racks
Own Printing Facility?: Y
Commercial printers?: Y
Mechanical specifications: Type page 13 x 22 1/4; E – 6 cols, 2 1/16, 1/8 between; A – 6 cols, 2 1/16, 1/8 between; C – 10 cols, 1 3/16, 1/16 between.
Published Days: Mon`Tues`Wed`Thur`Fri`Sat`Sun
Weekday Frequency: m
Saturday Frequency: m
Avg Paid Circ: 100506
Audit Company: AAM
Audit Date: 14 02 2020
Pressroom Equipment: Lines – 10-H/Colormatic converted offset 1966; 10-H/Colormatic converted offset 1967; 10-H/Colormatic converted offset 1968; 15-H/Colormatic converted offset 1969; Folders – 9-H; Reels & Stands – 45-MAN.;
Mailroom Equipment: Counter Stackers – 11-HL/Monitor II; Inserters & Stuffers – 5-HI/1372; Tying Machines – 11-Dynamic/Tying Machines NT-2; Address Machine – 2-Ch.;
Buisness Equipment: PCs, DEC/VAX
Classified Equipment: Hardware – DEC/VAX; HDS, Northern Telephones.;
Editorial Equipment: Hardware – 240-Novell/PC, 25-APP/Mac, APP/Power Mac/Lf/AP Leaf Picture Desk, APP/Mac; Printers – Epson/LaserPrinter, HP/LaserPrinter, QMS/Laser Printers
Editorial Software: Dewar/Disc System IV, QPS/QuarkXPress 3.3.
Production Equipment: Hardware – 2-WL/Lith-X-Pozer III, 2-AU/7000 Imagesetters, 2-AU/APS-108 FC Imagesetters, 1-AU/APS-3850 SST; Cameras – 2-C/Newspager; Scanners – 1-ECR/2045C, 1-Scitex/Smart 2045C, 1-Scitex/Smart 342, 2-AG/Horizon Plus, 3-Umax/PowerLook II, 2-Kk/3570, 2-Kk/
Total Circulation: 128797

KENNETT

THE DAILY DUNKLIN DEMOCRAT

Corporate/Parent Company: Rust Communications

Publication Street Address: 203 1st St
City: Kennett
State: MO
Publication Website: https://www.dddnews.com/
Postal Code: 63857
Office phone: (573) 888-4505
General E-mail: jdorris@dddnews.com
Publisher Name: Shelia Rouse
Publisher Email: srouse@stategazette.com
Publisher Phone: (731) 285-4091
Editor Name: Jeffrey Dorris
Editor Email: jdorris@dddnews.com
Advertising Executive Name: Terri Coleman
Advertising Executive Email: tcoleman@dddnews.com
Year Established: 1888
Delivery Methods:
    Mail`Newsstand`Carrier`Racks
Mechanical specifications: Type page 11 5/8 x 21; E – 6 cols, 1 5/6, 1/8 between; A – 6 cols, 1 5/6, 1/8 between; C – 9 cols, 1 1/6, 1/8 between.
Published Days: Tues`Wed`Thur`Fri`Sun
Weekday Frequency: e
Avg Paid Circ: 2500
Avg Free Circ: 5250
Audit Company: Sworn/Estimate/Non-Audited
Audit Date: 7 12 2019
Pressroom Equipment: Lines – 8-G/Community.;
Buisness Equipment: 1-IBM
Editorial Equipment: Hardware – APP/iMac; Printers – HP/8000
Editorial Software: Baseview/NewsEdit Pro.
Production Equipment: Hardware – 3M.
Total Circulation: 7750

KIRKSVILLE

KIRKSVILLE DAILY EXPRESS

Publication Street Address: 110 E McPherson St
City: Kirksville
State: MO
Publication Website: www.kirksvilledailyexpress.com
Postal Code: 63501-3506
Office phone: (660) 665-2808
Editor Name: Jason Hunsicker
Editor Email: dailyexpresseditor@gmail.com
Advertising Executive Name: Carole Murphy
Advertising Executive Email: production@kirksvilledailyexpress.com
Year Established: 1901
Delivery Methods: Mail`Newsstand`Carrier
Mechanical specifications: Type page 11 2/3 x 21; E – 6 cols, 1 15/16, 5/32 between; A – 6 cols, 1 15/16, 5/32 between; C – 6 cols, 1 15/16, 5/32 between.
Published Days: Mon`Tues`Wed`Thur`Fri`Sun
Weekday Frequency: e
Avg Paid Circ: 3035
Avg Free Circ: 14000
Audit Company: Sworn/Estimate/Non-Audited
Audit Date: 7 12 2019
Pressroom Equipment: Lines – 6-G/Community 1970;
Mailroom Equipment: Tying Machines – 2/Bu; Address Machine – 1-Miller/Bevco/LS-385.;
Buisness Equipment: RSK/12, 1-IBM/AT
Classified Equipment: Hardware – 6-APP/Mac; CD-Rom; Printers – 3-APP/Mac LaserPrinter;
Classified Software: Baseview.
Editorial Equipment: Hardware – APP/Mac
Editorial Software: APP/Mac.
Production Equipment: Hardware – 1-Nu/Double Flip Top; Cameras – 1-R/400; Scanners – 4-Scanmaker/X6EL.
Total Circulation: 17035

LEBANON

THE LEBANON DAILY RECORD

Corporate/Parent Company: Lebanon Publishing Co.
Publication Street Address: 100 E Commercial St
City: Lebanon
State: MO
Publication Website: http://www.lacledrecord.com/

Postal Code: 65536-3257
Office phone: (417) 532-9131
General E-mail: editor@lacledrecord.com
Year Established: 1934
Delivery Methods:
    Mail`Newsstand`Carrier`Racks
Own Printing Facility?: N
Commercial printers?: Y
Mechanical specifications: Type page 13 x 21 1/2; E – 6 cols, 2, 1/6 between; A – 6 cols, 2, 1/6 between; C – 6 cols, 2, 1/6 between.
Published Days: Mon`Tues`Wed`Thur`Fri`Sat
Weekday Frequency: e
Avg Paid Circ: 4300
Avg Free Circ: 2000
Audit Company: Sworn/Estimate/Non-Audited
Audit Date: 7 12 2019
Pressroom Equipment: Lines – 4-G/Community 1964; 4-G/Community 1992.;
Mailroom Equipment: Counter Stackers – BG; Tying Machines – 2/Bu; Address Machine – KR/215.;
Buisness Equipment: 3-PC 386
Buisness Software: DAC/Easy, Lotus 1-2-3, Quattro/Pro
Classified Equipment: Hardware – APP/Mac;
Classified Software: Multi-Ad/CAMS.
Editorial Equipment: Hardware – APP/Power Mac/G4/TMac, APP/Mac; Printers – HP/5000
Editorial Software: Adobe/PageMaker 6.5, Adobe/Photoshop 3.0.
Production Equipment: Hardware – APP/Mac LaserWriter 4-600, APP/Mac LaserWriter 161600, NewGen/Imager Pro; Cameras – Nu/Horizontal SSTE2024; Scanners – Umax/5-8, Polaroid/SprintScan Neg Scanners
Production Software: Adobe/PageMaker 6.5, Multi-Ad/Creator, Adobe/Photoshop, QPS/QuarkXPr
Total Circulation: 6300

MARSHALL

THE MARSHALL DEMOCRAT-NEWS

Corporate/Parent Company: Rust Communications
Publication Street Address: 121 N Lafayette Ave
City: Marshall
State: MO
Publication Website: https://www.marshallnews.com/
Postal Code: 65340
Office phone: (660) 886-2233
General E-mail: democratnews@gmail.com
Publisher Name: Sarah Gray
Publisher Email: sgray@marshallnews.com
Publisher Phone: (660) 886-2233, ext : 15
Year Established: 1879
Delivery Methods: Mail`Racks
Mechanical specifications: Type page 13 x 21 1/2; E – 6 cols, 2 1/16, 1/8 between; A – 6 cols, 2 1/16, 1/8 between; C – 6 cols, 2 1/16, 1/8 between.
Published Days: Mon`Tues`Wed`Thur`Fri
Weekday Frequency: e
Avg Paid Circ: 3007
Avg Free Circ: 8586
Audit Company: Sworn/Estimate/Non-Audited
Audit Date: 7 12 2019
Pressroom Equipment: Lines – 5-KP/News King 1976.;
Mailroom Equipment: Tying Machines – 1/Bu; Wrapping Singles – Addressing machine ÃƒÂƒÃ‚Âƒ ÃƒÂ‚Ã‚Â 1-/Ch.;
Buisness Equipment: 1-Packard Bell, 2-Acros
Classified Equipment: Hardware – 1-APP/Mac.;
Editorial Equipment: Hardware – 8-APP/Mac; Printers – 1-APP/Mac.
Production Equipment: Hardware – 1-Nu; Cameras – 1-R/500, LE; Scanners – Gam/Digital Densitometer.
Total Circulation: 11593

MARYVILLE

THE MARYVILLE DAILY FORUM

Corporate/Parent Company: Cobb Publishing, LLC

Publication Street Address: 111 E Jenkins St
City: Maryville
State: MO
Publication Website: www.maryvilledailyforum.com
Postal Code: 64468-2318
Office phone: (660) 562-2424
General E-mail: news@maryvilledailyforum.com
Publisher Name: Phil Cobb
Publisher Email: pcobb@maryvilledailyforum.com
Editor Name: Skye Pournazari
Editor Email: skyep@maryvilledailyforum.com
Advertising Executive Name: Twyla Martin
Advertising Executive Email: tmartin@maryvilledailyforum.com
Year Established: 1869
Delivery Methods: Mail`Newsstand`Racks
Own Printing Facility?: N
Commercial printers?: N
Mechanical specifications: Type page 10.25 x 20; E – 6 cols, 1.55", .1667 between;
Published Days: Mon`Tues`Wed`Thur`Fri
Weekday Frequency: m
Avg Paid Circ: 2000
Avg Free Circ: 18500
Audit Company: Sworn/Estimate/Non-Audited
Audit Date: 7 12 2019
Classified Software: Baseview.
Total Circulation: 20500

MEXICO

MEXICO LEDGER

Publication Street Address: 300 N Washington St
City: Mexico
State: MO
Publication Website: www.mexicoledger.com
Postal Code: 65265-2756
Publisher Name: Terri Leifeste
Editor Name: Allen Fennewald
Editor Email: afennewald@gatehousemedia.com
Advertising Executive Name: Kathy Dugan
Advertising Executive Email: kdugan@mexicoledger.com
Year Established: 1855
Delivery Methods: Mail`Carrier`Racks
Mechanical specifications: Type page 13 x 21 1/2; E – 6 cols, 2, 1/12 between; A – 6 cols, 2, 1/12 between; C – 7 cols, 2, 1/12 between.
Published Days: Mon`Tues`Wed`Thur`Fri`Sat
Weekday Frequency: e
Saturday Frequency: m
Avg Paid Circ: 4500
Avg Free Circ: 10820
Audit Company: Sworn/Estimate/Non-Audited
Audit Date: 7 12 2019
Pressroom Equipment: Lines – 7-G/Community;
Mailroom Equipment: Tying Machines – 1/Bu; Wrapping Singles – 1-Sa/SM; Address Machine – 1-/Ch.;
Buisness Equipment: Maxtech/ChipTex
Buisness Software: Microsoft/Windows 98, QuickBooks, Excel Microsoft/Excel, Lotus 1-2-3, Microsoft/Word
Classified Equipment: Hardware – 1-APP/Mac Performa 6300; Printers – Ap;
Classified Software: Cx.
Editorial Equipment: Hardware – 11-APP/Mac/APP/Mac; Printers – HP/4V, HP/5000
Editorial Software: QPS/QuarkXPress, Multi-Ad/Creator, Adobe/Photoshop, Adobe/PageMaker.
Production Equipment: Hardware – 1-Nu; Cameras – 1-R/580, 1-SCREEN/680C; Scanners – Lf/Leafscan, APP/Mac Scanner
Production Software: QPS/QuarkXPress.
Total Circulation: 15320

MOBERLY

MOBERLY MONITOR-INDEX

Publication Street Address: 218 N Williams
City: Moberly
State: MO
Publication Website: www.MoberlyMonitor.com
Postal Code: 65270
Office phone: 660-263-4123

U.S. Daily Newspapers

Publisher Name: Terri Leifeste
Editor Name: Allen Fennewald
Editor Email: afennewald@gatehousemedia.com
Editor Phone: 573-815-1788
Advertising Executive Name: Michaela Sawyer
Advertising Executive Email: msawyer@moberlymonitor.com
Year Established: 1869
Mechanical specifications: Type page 13 x 21 1/2; E - 6 cols, 2 1/16, 1/5 between; A - 6 cols, 2 1/16, 1/5 between; C - 8 cols, 1 1/2, 1/5 between.
Published Days: Mon`Tues`Wed`Thur`Fri
Weekday Frequency: e
Avg Paid Circ: 3360
Avg Free Circ: 700
Audit Company: Sworn/Estimate/Non-Audited
Audit Date: 7 12 2019
Pressroom Equipment: Lines - 6-Unit/Community; Folders - G/Suburban.;
Mailroom Equipment: Tying Machines - Strap-Matic 202A; Address Machine - Wm, MB-45/Labeling Machine.;
Buisness Equipment: Mk, APP/Mac
Buisness Software: QuarkXPress 7.0, Baseview, Brainworks, SSPS System
Classified Equipment: Hardware - APP/Mac; APP/Mac Scanner; Printers - NewGen/DesignXpress 17;
Classified Software: Baseview, Fox, Aldus, QPS/QuarkXPress.
Editorial Equipment: Hardware - Mk, APP/Mac/Epson/Film Scanner, APP/Mac Scanner; Printers - NewGen/Oversize, APP/Mac, APP/Mac LaserWriter Pro, NewGen/DesignXpress, Xante/Accel-A-Writer
Editorial Software: Mk, QPS/QuarkXPress, Baseview, Brainworks.
Production Equipment: Hardware - 1-Nu, APP/Power Mac 64; Cameras - Acti; Scanners - APP/Mac, Epson/Film Scanner
Production Software: Baseview.
Total Circulation: 4060

THE MOBERLY MONITOR-INDEX

Publication Street Address: 218 N Williams St
City: Moberly
State: MO
Publication Website: www.moberlymonitor.com
Postal Code: 65270-1534
Office phone: (660) 263-4123
Publisher Name: Terri Leifeste
Editor Name: Allen Fennewald
Editor Email: afennewald@gatehousemedia.com
Year Established: 1869
Mechanical specifications: Type page 13 x 21 1/2; E - 6 cols, 2 1/16, 1/5 between; A - 6 cols, 2 1/16, 1/5 between; C - 8 cols, 1 1/2, 1/5 between.
Published Days: Mon`Tues`Wed`Thur`Fri
Weekday Frequency: e
Avg Paid Circ: 3360
Avg Free Circ: 700
Audit Company: Sworn/Estimate/Non-Audited
Audit Date: 7 12 2019
Pressroom Equipment: Lines - 6-Unit/Community; Folders - G/Suburban.;
Mailroom Equipment: Tying Machines - Strap-Matic 202A; Address Machine - Wm, MB-45/Labeling Machine.;
Buisness Equipment: Mk, APP/Mac
Buisness Software: QuarkXPress 7.0, Baseview, Brainworks, SSPS System
Classified Equipment: Hardware - APP/Mac; APP/Mac Scanner; Printers - NewGen/DesignXpress 17;
Classified Software: Baseview, Fox, Aldus, QPS/QuarkXPress.
Editorial Equipment: Hardware - Mk, APP/Mac/Epson/Film Scanner, APP/Mac Scanner; Printers - NewGen/Oversize, APP/Mac, APP/Mac LaserWriter Pro, NewGen/DesignXpress, Xante/Accel-A-Writer
Editorial Software: Mk, QPS/QuarkXPress, Baseview, Brainworks.
Production Equipment: Hardware - 1-Nu, APP/Power Mac 64; Cameras - Acti; Scanners - APP/Mac, Epson/Film Scanner
Production Software: Baseview.
Total Circulation: 4060

MONETT

THE MONETT TIMES

Corporate/Parent Company: Rust Communications
Publication Street Address: 505 E Broadway St
City: Monett
State: MO
Publication Website: https://www.monett-times.com/
Postal Code: 65708
Office phone: (417) 235-3135
General E-mail: monettcommunity@gmail.com
Publisher Name: Lisa Craft
Publisher Email: community@monett-times.com
Editor Name: Kyle Troutman
Editor Email: editor@monett-times.com
Year Established: 1908
Delivery Methods: Mail`Racks
Mechanical specifications: Type page 13 x 21 1/2; E - 6 cols, 2, 1/4 between; A - 6 cols, 2, 1/4 between; C - 6 cols, 2, 1/4 between.
Published Days: Tues`Wed`Fri`Sat
Weekday Frequency: e
Saturday Frequency: e
Avg Paid Circ: 2400
Avg Free Circ: 7400
Audit Company: Sworn/Estimate/Non-Audited
Audit Date: 7 12 2019
Pressroom Equipment: Lines - 4-WPC/Quadra Color 1995;
Mailroom Equipment: Tying Machines - 2/Bu.;
Buisness Equipment: DEC/PC XL 466D2
Classified Equipment: Hardware - APP/Power Mac SE; Printers - APP/Mac LaserWriter;
Classified Software: Microsoft/Word, Aldus/PageMaker, Microsoft/Windows.
Editorial Equipment: Hardware - APP/Power Mac; Printers - APP/Mac LaserWriter
Editorial Software: Microsoft/Word, Aldus/PageMaker, Microsoft/Windows.
Production Equipment: Hardware - APP/Power Mac, Adobe/Photoshop; Cameras - CL; Scanners - 1-LaCie, Minolta.
Total Circulation: 9800

NEOSHO

NEOSHO DAILY NEWS

Corporate/Parent Company: Gannett
Publication Street Address: 1006 W. Harmony
City: Neosho
State: MO
Publication Website: www.neoshodailynews.com
Postal Code: 64850
Office phone: (417) 451-1520
Publisher Name: Joe Leong
Publisher Email: jleong@gatehousemedia.com
Editor Name: Patrick Richardson
Editor Email: prichardson@morningsun.net
Editor Phone: 620-231-2600 ext. 140
Advertising Executive Name: Shaw Banta
Advertising Executive Email: sbanta@bignickel.com
Advertising Executive Phone: 417-669-6156
Year Established: 1905
Delivery Methods: Mail`Newsstand`Carrier`Racks
Own Printing Facility?: Y
Commercial printers?: Y
Mechanical specifications: Type page 11 5/8 x 21 1/2; E - 6 cols, 2 1/16, 1/8 between; A - 6 cols, 2 1/16, 1/8 between; C - 6 cols, 2 1/16, 1/8 between.
Published Days: Tues`Wed`Thur`Fri`Sun
Weekday Frequency: m
Audit Company: Sworn/Estimate/Non-Audited
Audit Date: 7 12 2019
Pressroom Equipment: Lines - 9-G/Community 1971; Folders - 1-G/Community, 1-G/SC 1971; Registration System - 2
Mailroom Equipment: Counter Stackers - 1/BG; Tying Machines - 2/Miller-Bevco.;
Buisness Equipment: PC
Buisness Software: Nomads, QuickBooks

Classified Equipment: Hardware - APP/Mac; Printers - APP/Mac ImageWriter;
Classified Software: CAMS.
Editorial Equipment: Hardware - APP/Mac/Pre Press/Panther Pro Imagesetter
Editorial Software: Baseview.
Production Equipment: Hardware - APP/Mac LaserWriter Select, APP/Mac, HP/LaserJet 4MV, 2-Pre Press Panther Pro Imagesetter; Cameras - R; Scanners - 2-Microtek/EM6
Production Software: QPS/QuarkXPress, Pre Press/Imagesetter.

NEVADA

THE NEVADA DAILY MAIL

Corporate/Parent Company: Rust Communications
Publication Street Address: 131 S Cedar St
City: Nevada
State: MO
Publication Website: https://www.nevadadailymail.com/
Postal Code: 64772-3309
Office phone: (417) 667-3344
General E-mail: mbronson@nevadadailymail.com
Publisher Name: Lorie Harter
Publisher Email: lharter@nevadadailymail.com
Editor Name: Sarah Haney
Editor Email: shaney@nevadadailymail.com
Advertising Executive Name: Lorie Harter
Advertising Executive Email: lharter@nevadadailymail.com
Year Established: 1883
Delivery Methods: Mail`Newsstand`Racks
Own Printing Facility?: Y
Commercial printers?: Y
Mechanical specifications: Type page 13 x 21; E - 6 cols, 2 1/16, 1/8 between; A - 6 cols, 2 1/16, 1/8 between; C - 6 cols, 2 1/16, 1/8 between.
Published Days: Tues`Wed`Thur`Fri
Weekday Frequency: m
Avg Paid Circ: 1400
Avg Free Circ: 17000
Audit Company: Sworn/Estimate/Non-Audited
Audit Date: 7 12 2019
Pressroom Equipment: Lines - 5-G/Community;
Mailroom Equipment: Tying Machines - 1/Bu, 1-/St; Wrapping Singles - 2-/Sa;
Editorial Equipment: Hardware - COM/UTS, APP/Mac.
Production Equipment: Hardware - CTP
Total Circulation: 18400

OSAGE BEACH

LAKEEXPO.COM

Publication Street Address: P.O. Box 1805
City: Osage Beach
State: MO
Publication Website: www.lakeexpo.com
Postal Code: 65065
Office phone: 573-693-1990
General E-mail: Sales@LakeExpo.com
Editor Name: Nathan Bechtold
Editor Email: lakeexpo@gmail.com

PARK HILLS

DAILY JOURNAL

Corporate/Parent Company: Gannett
Publication Street Address: 1513 S Saint Joe Dr
City: Park Hills
State: MO
Publication Website: www.DailyJournalOnline.com
Postal Code: 63601
Office phone: 800-660-8166
Editor Name: Teresa Ressel
Editor Email: tressel@dailyjournalonline.com
Editor Phone: (573) 518-3613
Advertising Executive Name: Michelle Menley
Advertising Executive Email: mmenley@dailyjournalonline.com
Advertising Executive Phone: (573) 518-3603

DAILY JOURNAL, PARK HILLS

Corporate/Parent Company: Dispatch-Argus
Publication Street Address: 1513 S Saint Joe Dr
City: Park Hills
State: MO
Publication Website: www.dailyjournalonline.com
Postal Code: 63601-2402
Office phone: (573) 431-2010
Editor Name: Teresa Ressel
Editor Email: tressel@dailyjournalonline.com
Editor Phone: (573) 518-3613
Advertising Executive Name: Dale Luster
Advertising Executive Email: DLUSTER@DAILYJOURNALONLINE.COM
Advertising Executive Phone: (573) 518-3627
Year Established: 1935
Delivery Methods: Mail`Newsstand`Carrier`Racks
Own Printing Facility?: N
Commercial printers?: N
Published Days: Mon`Tues`Wed`Thur`Fri`Sat
Weekday Frequency: m
Saturday Frequency: m
Avg Paid Circ: 4491
Avg Free Circ: 165
Audit Company: AAM
Audit Date: 30 09 2014
Total Circulation: 4656

POPLAR BLUFF

DAILY AMERICAN REPUBLIC

Corporate/Parent Company: Rust Communications
Publication Street Address: PO Box 7
City: Poplar Bluff
State: MO
Publication Website: https://www.darnews.com/
Postal Code: 63902
Office phone: (573) 785-1414
General E-mail: ads@darnews.com
Publisher Name: Chris Pruett
Publisher Email: cpruett@darnews.com
Publisher Phone: (573) 772-7275
Editor Name: Donna Farley
Editor Email: dfarley@darnews.com
Editor Phone: (573) 772-7392
Advertising Executive Name: Christy Pierce
Advertising Executive Email: ads@darnews.com
Advertising Executive Phone: (573) 772-7386
Year Established: 1869
Delivery Methods: Mail`Newsstand`Carrier`Racks
Own Printing Facility?: Y
Commercial printers?: Y
Mechanical specifications: Type page 13 x 21 1/2; E - 6 cols, 2 1/16, 1/8 between; A - 6 cols, 2 1/16, 1/8 between; C - 6 cols, 2 1/16, 1/8 between.
Published Days: Mon`Tues`Wed`Thur`Fri`Sun
Weekday Frequency: e
Avg Paid Circ: 7653
Audit Company: CAC
Audit Date: 31 03 2014
Pressroom Equipment: Lines - 5-G/Urbanite; Folders - 1-G/2:1.;
Mailroom Equipment: Tying Machines - 1/Malow; Address Machine - RSK/TRS 80.;
Buisness Equipment: 1-RSK/TRS 80-16B
Classified Equipment: Hardware - 1-COM/UC.;
Editorial Equipment: Hardware - 1-COM/UTS, 1-RSK/TRS 80-100.
Production Equipment: Hardware - 1-COM/8600, 1-COM/Unisetter, 2-COM/7200; Cameras - 1-B/4000.
Total Circulation: 7653

QUINCY

QUINCY HERALD - WHIG

Corporate/Parent Company: Quincy Media Inc
Publication Street Address: 130 S. Fifth Street
City: Quincy
State: MO

U.S. Daily Newspapers

Publication Website: www.whig.com
Postal Code: 62301
Office phone: (217) 223-5100
General E-mail: news@whig.com
Editor Name: Jason Lewton
Editor Email: jlewton@whig.com
Editor Phone: 217-221-3321
Advertising Executive Name: Karen Hull
Advertising Executive Email: khull@whig.com
Advertising Executive Phone: 217-221-3380

ROLLA
ROLLA DAILY NEWS

Corporate/Parent Company: Gannett
Publication Street Address: 101 W 7th St
City: Rolla
State: MO
Publication Website: www.therolladailynews.com
Postal Code: 65401-3243
Office phone: (573) 364-2468
Publisher Name: Joseph Leong
Publisher Email: jloeng@gatehousemedia.com
Editor Name: Joyce L. Miller
Editor Email: jmiller@lakesunonline.com
Editor Phone: (573) 346-2132
Year Established: 1880
Mechanical specifications: Type page 13 3/4 x 21; E - 6 cols, 2, 1/8 between; A - 6 cols, 2, 1/8 between; C - 6 cols, 2, 1/8 between.
Published Days: Mon`Tues`Wed`Thur`Fri`Sat
Weekday Frequency: m
Saturday Frequency: m
Avg Paid Circ: 3725
Avg Free Circ: 15600
Audit Company: Sworn/Estimate/Non-Audited
Audit Date: 7 12 2019
Mailroom Equipment: Tying Machines – 1-Strapper/Transpak, S/323; Address Machine – 1/Ch.;
Buisness Equipment: 2-Amdek/268A, Nomad
Classified Equipment: Printers – Epson;
Classified Software: TC.
Editorial Equipment: Hardware – Rem; Printers – APP/Mac LaserWriter II
Editorial Software: TC.
Production Equipment: Hardware – 1-Nat/A-250; Cameras – 1-Acti/183.
Note: This publication is printed at the Waynesville Daily Guide, St. Robert.
Total Circulation: 19325

WAYNESVILLE DAILY GUIDE

Publication Street Address: 101 West 7th
City: Rolla
State: MO
Publication Website: www.WaynesvilleDailyGuide.com
Postal Code: 65401
Office phone: (573) 364-2468
Publisher Name: Joseph Leong
Publisher Email: jloeng@gatehousemedia.com
Editor Name: Joyce L. Miller
Editor Email: jmiller@lakesunonline.com
Editor Phone: (573) 346-2132
Advertising Executive Name: Michelle Bradley
Advertising Executive Email: mbradley@gatehousemedia.com

SAINT JOSEPH
ST. JOSEPH NEWS-PRESS

Corporate/Parent Company: News-Press & Gazette Co.
Publication Street Address: 825 Edmond St
City: Saint Joseph
State: MO
Publication Website: https://www.newspressnow.com
Postal Code: 64501-2737
Office phone: (816) 271-8500
General E-mail: subscribe@newspressnow.com
Editor Name: Jess DeHaven
Editor Email: jess.dehaven@newspressnow.com
Editor Phone: (816) 271-8594
Advertising Executive Phone: (816) 271-8500
Year Established: 1845
Delivery Methods: Mail`Newsstand`Carrier`Racks
Own Printing Facility?: Y
Commercial printers?: Y
Mechanical specifications: Type page 13 x 20; E - 6 cols, 2 1/16, 1/8 between; A - 6 cols, 2 1/16, 1/8 between; C - 9 cols, 1 3/8, 1/16 between.
Published Days: Mon`Tues`Wed`Thur`Fri`Sat`Sun
Weekday Frequency: m
Saturday Frequency: m
Avg Paid Circ: 18319
Avg Free Circ: 1441
Audit Company: AAM
Audit Date: 30 08 2018
Pressroom Equipment: Lines – 28-G/SSC Magnum single width 1999; Folders – 1-G/Universal 45; Reels & Stands – Enkel; Registration System – QTI.
Mailroom Equipment: Counter Stackers – 2-QWI/400; Inserters & Stuffers – MM/319 Print Roll, GMA/SLS 2000, GMA/12 Into 2; Tying Machines – 2-Dynaric/NP-3; Wrapping Singles – 2-Id/Plastic; Address Machine – 1/Videojet 4000/7000;
Buisness Equipment: Sun/Sparc Station 20, Dell/E250 Power Edge Dual 450 Mhz Processor
Buisness Software: SBS/Graphical 5.3.1, PBS/AM 3.2, PBS/CM 3.2
Classified Equipment: Hardware – 13-Dell/Dimension 260 1.8GH2; Printers – HP/Deskjet 950;
Classified Software: Brainworks.
Editorial Equipment: Hardware – 47-Nobilis/450; Printers – MON
Editorial Software: Quark, METS, Binuscan, Scitex.
Production Equipment: Hardware – Caere/OmniPage, MON/MGS, APP/Mac 8100, APP/Mac 9500 FS; Scanners – 1-ECR/Autokon 2000, PixelCraft, X/7650, Microtek/600 ZS
Production Software: FSI, Preps 3.61.
Total Circulation: 21922

SAINT LOUIS
ST. LOUIS POST-DISPATCH

Corporate/Parent Company: Lee Enterprises
Publication Street Address: 900 N Tucker Blvd
City: Saint Louis
State: MO
Publication Website: www.stltoday.com
Postal Code: 63101-1069
Office phone: (314) 340-8000
General E-mail: service@stltoday.com
Editor Name: Gilbert Bailon
Editor Email: gbailon@post-dispatch.com
Editor Phone: 314-340-8387
Year Established: 1878
Delivery Methods: Mail`Newsstand`Carrier`Racks
Own Printing Facility?: Y
Commercial printers?: Y
Mechanical specifications: Type page 9.8889" x 22"; column width: 1.5556" Modular ad sizes
Published Days: Mon`Tues`Wed`Thur`Fri`Sat`Sun
Weekday Frequency: m
Saturday Frequency: m
Avg Paid Circ: 103469
Audit Company: AAM
Audit Date: 11 06 2020
Pressroom Equipment: Lines – 8-G/Metro 3113 Double Width 1972; 8-G/Metro 3115 Double Width 1972; 8-G/Metro 3114 Double Width 1972; 8-G/Metro 3117 Double Width 1972; 8-G/Metro 3049 Double Width 1968; 8-G/Metro 3116 Double Width 197;
Mailroom Equipment: Counter Stackers – 2/Sh, 20-/QWI, 3-/Boss; Inserters & Stuffers – 3-HI/1372P, 1-HI/1472P, 1-GMA/SLS 28-2; Tying Machines – 3-/Power Strap/PSN-6, 18-Sterling/MRCH40; Wrapping Singles – 4-/Wrappers-Stretchwrap;
Buisness Equipment: 16-AT
Classified Equipment: Hardware – 2-Sun/Enterprise 4000, 79-HI/AD-Power Client Station;
Classified Software: HI/REL 2.1.
Editorial Equipment: Hardware – HI/NMP (3.5.62), HI/NME 3.5, 26-HI/NewsMaker Pagination, 185-HI/NewsMaker Editorial, 4-Sun/Enterprise 4000/100-IBM/PC
Editorial Software: 20-HI/Mac Browser.
Production Equipment: Hardware – TextBridge Pro 9.0, 3-WL/Lith-X-Pozer, 2-Eskofot/26365; Scanners – Epson/636 Scanner, ECR/Autokon 2045, 1-ECR/Autokon 1000 Scanner, 2-X, Scitex/Smartscanner, 2-X/1750, Ik/Digital
Production Software: HI, NMP (3.5.62), 3-AdPag 3.5.
Note: Other digital/print products include: Local Values Savings Guide Save Now St. Charles Suburban Journal Madison County Journal Ladue News Feast Magazine St. Louis' Best Bridal STL High School Sports ThePost-DispatchStore.com Events/Promotions/Special Programs include: Newspapers in Education Spelling Bee Scholar Athlete Program 'A' Student Program Pop & Shop Top Workplaces Great Taste (Top 100 Restaurants) Nurse's Awards Top Pours Best of St. Charles Best of Southwest Illinois Bridal Best of the Best Awards St. Louis' Best Bridal Shows Bridal Groom's Cake Dive Event Ladue News Design Awards Ladue News Charity Awards Feast 50 Old Newsboys Day Edition & Events
Total Circulation: 141015

SEDALIA
THE SEDALIA DEMOCRAT

Corporate/Parent Company: Phillips Media Group, LLC
Publication Street Address: 700 S Massachusetts Ave
City: Sedalia
State: MO
Publication Website: www.sedaliademocrat.com
Postal Code: 65301-4548
Office phone: (660) 826-1000
General E-mail: news@sedaliademocrat.com
Publisher Name: Will Weibert
Publisher Email: will@phillipsmedia.com
Publisher Phone: 660-530-0282
Editor Name: Nicole Cooke
Editor Email: ncooke@sedaliademocrat.com
Editor Phone: 660-530-0138
Advertising Executive Name: Zana Meek
Advertising Executive Email: zmeek@sedaliademocrat.com
Advertising Executive Phone: 660-530-0186
Year Established: 1868
Delivery Methods: Mail`Newsstand`Carrier`Racks
Mechanical specifications: Type page 11 1/2 x 21 1/2; E - 6 cols, 1 39/50, 1/6 between; A - 6 cols, 1 39/50, 1/6 between; C - 8 cols, 1 29/100, 1/6 between.
Published Days: Mon`Tues`Wed`Thur`Fri`Sat
Weekday Frequency: m
Saturday Frequency: m
Avg Paid Circ: 5471
Avg Free Circ: 511
Audit Company: CAC
Audit Date: 30 09 2014
Pressroom Equipment: Lines – 10-G/Urbanite single width; 12-G/Urbanite single width 1999; Folders – G/Urbanite.;
Mailroom Equipment: Counter Stackers – 1/HL; Inserters & Stuffers – 1-/MM; Tying Machines – 2-/Ovid; Address Machine – 1-/Ch.;
Buisness Equipment: Ram/486 DX66-16mb
Buisness Software: Southware, Brainworks, Vision Data
Classified Equipment: Hardware – APP/Mac; Printers – C.Itoh/On-Line, Genico/4110, Lexmark, APP/Mac II, NewGen/Imager Plus 6, GCC/Elite XL 808, Okidata/Line Printer, Pre Press/Panther Pro 46 Imagesetter;
Classified Software: Baseview, QPS/QuarkXPress.
Editorial Equipment: Hardware – APP/Mac 7200-75 PPC, APP/Mac 7200-90 PPC/Lf/AP Leaf Picture Desk; Printers – GCC/Elite XL808, New Gen/Imager Plus 6, Pre Press/Panther Pro 46
Editorial Software: Baseview.
Production Equipment: Hardware – 1-Nu, Polaroid/SprintScan, Umax/Flatbed, Epson/Flatbed; Cameras – R
Production Software: QPS/QuarkXPress 3.32.2.
Total Circulation: 5982

SIKESTON
SIKESTON STANDARD-DEMOCRAT

Publication Street Address: 205 S New Madrid St
City: Sikeston
State: MO
Publication Website: www.Standard-Democrat.com
Postal Code: 63801
Office phone: 573-471-1137
Editor Name: Leonna Heuring & David Jenkins
Editor Email: news@standard-democrat.com

STANDARD DEMOCRAT

Corporate/Parent Company: Rust Communications
Publication Street Address: 205 S New Madrid St
City: Sikeston
State: MO
Publication Website: https://standard-democrat.com/
Postal Code: 63801-2953
Office phone: (573) 471-1137
General E-mail: news@standard-democrat.com
Publisher Name: DeAnna Nelson
Publisher Email: dnelson@standard-democrat.com
Editor Name: David Jenkins
Editor Email: news@standard-democrat.com
Advertising Executive Name: DeAnna Nelson
Advertising Executive Email: dnelson@standard-democrat.com
Year Established: 1913
Delivery Methods: Mail`Newsstand`Carrier`Racks
Mechanical specifications: Type page 13 x 21 1/2; E - 6 cols, 2 1/16, 1/8 between; A - 6 cols, 2 1/16, 1/8 between; C - 9 cols, 1 3/8, 1/16 between.
Published Days: Mon`Tues`Wed`Thur`Fri`Sun
Weekday Frequency: e
Avg Paid Circ: 4387
Audit Company: CAC
Audit Date: 30 09 2014
Pressroom Equipment: Lines – 8-G/Suburban (4 + 4 side by side).;
Mailroom Equipment: Tying Machines – 2-Bu/Packaging Machine; Wrapping Singles – 7-Sa/EM; Address Machine – 1-Am/1900.;
Classified Equipment: Hardware – COM/UTS.;
Editorial Equipment: Hardware – 2-COM/UTS, Mk.
Production Equipment: Hardware – 2-COM/Universal Videosetter; Cameras – 1-R/400.
Total Circulation: 4387

SPRINGFIELD
SPRINGFIELD NEWS-LEADER

Corporate/Parent Company: Gannett
Publication Street Address: 651 N Boonville Ave
City: Springfield
State: MO
Publication Website: www.news-leader.com
Postal Code: 65806-1005
Office phone: (417) 836-1100
General E-mail: webeditor@news-leader.com
Editor Name: Matt Peterson
Editor Email: mpeterson4@gannett.com
Year Established: 1867
Delivery Methods: Mail`Newsstand`Carrier`Racks
Own Printing Facility?: Y
Commercial printers?: Y
Mechanical specifications: Type page 13 x 21 1/2; E - 6 cols, 2 1/16, 1/8 between; A - 6 cols, 2 1/16, 1/8 between; C - 9 cols, 1 3/8,

U.S. Daily Newspapers

1/16 between.
Published Days: Mon`Tues`Wed`Thur`Fri`Sat`Sun
Weekday Frequency: m
Saturday Frequency: m
Avg Paid Circ: 13940
Avg Free Circ: 140
Audit Company: AAM
Audit Date: 31 03 2019
Pressroom Equipment: Lines – 8-G/Mark II Headliner; Registration System – G/Web Control Auto Color.
Mailroom Equipment: Counter Stackers – 3-HL/Monitor, 2-HI/Dual Carrier Stackers, 2-HI/Olympian Stackers; Inserters & Stuffers – HI/72P, HI/NP 630 (26 Base/22 Head); Tying Machines – 3-MLN/News 90, 2-MLN/1-EE; Wrapping Singles – Kraft/Paper, 3-HI/Eclipse Bottomwraps;
Buisness Equipment: 1-IBM/AS-400
Buisness Software: Lotus R:5, WordPerfect, Microsoft/Windows
Classified Equipment: Hardware – SII/Synthesis 66; QPS, App/Mac System; Printers – Hyphen/Spectraset 2200, Hyphen/Spectraset 2400;
Classified Software: SII/Pongrass Czar.
Editorial Equipment: Hardware – QPS/70-APP/Power Mac 8500-7200; Printers – 2-Hyphen/Spectraset 2200, 2-Hyphen/Spectraset 2400
Editorial Software: AT, QPS/QuarkXPress.
Production Equipment: Hardware – AG/2200, Hyphen/Spectraset 2200, Hyphen/Spectraset 2400; Cameras – R/Comet 500; Scanners – 1-Microtek/MRS-600zs, 1-Pro Imager/8000 PixelCraft, 1-Pro Imager/8100 PixelCraft
Production Software: SII/Pongrass Czar.
Total Circulation: 14080

ST. LOUIS

ST. LOUIS POST-DISPATCH

Corporate/Parent Company: Lee Enterprises
Publication Street Address: 901 N. 10th St
City: St. Louis
State: MO
Publication Website: www.stltoday.com
Postal Code: 63101
Office phone: 314-340-8000
General E-mail: evydra@post-dispatch.com
Publisher Name: Ray Farris
Publisher Email: rfarris@post-dispatch.com
Publisher Phone: (314) 340-8000 x_
Editor Name: "Gilbert Bailon
"
Editor Email: gbailon@post-dispatch.com
Editor Phone: 314-340-8387

TRENTON

TRENTON REPUBLICAN-TIMES

Corporate/Parent Company: W.B. Rogers Printing Co., Inc.
Publication Street Address: 122 E 8th St
City: Trenton
State: MO
Publication Website: www.republican-times.com
Postal Code: 64683-2183
Office phone: (660) 359-2212
Editor Name: Diane Lowrey
Editor Email: rtimes@lyn.net
Year Established: 1864
Delivery Methods: Mail`Newsstand`Carrier
Own Printing Facility?: N
Commercial printers?: N
Mechanical specifications: Type page 13 x 21; E - 6 cols, 1.833 PASS, 1/8 between; A - 6 cols, 1.833 PASS, 1/8 between; C - 6 cols, 2 1/16, 1/8 between.
Published Days: Mon`Tues`Wed`Thur`Fri
Weekday Frequency: e
Avg Paid Circ: 2321
Avg Free Circ: 12226
Audit Company: Sworn/Estimate/Non-Audited
Audit Date: 7 12 2019
Mailroom Equipment: Tying Machines – Bu, Miller-Bevco/Strapper.;
Buisness Equipment: Pentium/PC
Classified Equipment: Hardware – APP/Power Mac; Printers – APP/Power Mac

LaserWriter II NTX;
Classified Software: QPS/QuarkXPress.
Editorial Equipment: Hardware – APP/Power iMac; Printers – APP/Mac LaserWriter II NTX, HP/LaserJet 4MV
Editorial Software: QPS/QuarkXPress.
Production Equipment: Hardware – APP/Mac LaserWriter II NTX, HP/LaserJet 4MR; Cameras – R/Vertical; Scanners – HP/ScanJet 3P, Polaroid/SprintScan 35, Polaroid/SprintScan 35ES
Production Software: Baseview.
Total Circulation: 14547

WARRENSBURG

THE DAILY STAR-JOURNAL

Publication Street Address: 135 E Market St
City: Warrensburg
State: MO
Publication Website: www.dailystarjournal.com
Postal Code: 64093-1817
Office phone: (660) 747-8123
Publisher Name: Sandy Nelson
Publisher Email: sandy.nelson@npgco.com
Editor Name: Derek Brizendine
Editor Email: derek.brizendine@dsjnow.com
Year Established: 1865
Delivery Methods: Mail`Racks
Own Printing Facility?: Y
Commercial printers?: N
Mechanical specifications: Full Page 10.25" x 20"
Published Days: Tues`Wed`Thur`Sat
Weekday Frequency: m
Saturday Frequency: m
Avg Paid Circ: 3300
Avg Free Circ: 18323
Audit Company: Sworn/Estimate/Non-Audited
Audit Date: 7 12 2019
Pressroom Equipment: Lines – 1-HI/Cotrell V-15D; 1-Ryobi/11x17; 1-HI/L125C(0).;
Mailroom Equipment: Tying Machines – 1-Strap Tie/50; Address Machine – Ch/582N.;
Buisness Equipment: 2-IBM/3151
Buisness Software: PBS/MediaPlus
Classified Equipment: Hardware – 1-Acer; Printers – HP/2100;
Classified Software: FSI.
Editorial Equipment: Hardware – 5-APP/iMac; Printers – 1-APP/Mac LaserWriter
Editorial Software: FSI.
Production Equipment: Hardware – 1-Nat, 1-APP/Mac G4, 1-APP/Mac; Cameras – 1-DAI
Production Software: QPS/QuarkXPress 4.1.
Note: First-place awards this year€ 2017 - Missouri Press Association Gold Cup Sweepstakes award, General Excellence, Best Editorial, Serious Column, Breaking News, Headline Writing, Feature Writing, Obituary Story, Website, Religion Story, News Photo, Sports Photo, Outdoors Story 2017 Â- Associated Press Managing Editors, Feature Writing, Photo Page, Opinion, Headline 2017 - Missouri State Teachers Association, Feature Writing and Photography.
Total Circulation: 21623

WARRENSBURG DAILY STAR-JOURNAL

Publication Street Address: 135 East Market St
City: Warrensburg
State: MO
Publication Website: www.DSJNow.com
Postal Code: 64093
Office phone: (660) 747-8123
Publisher Name: Sandy Nelson
Publisher Email: sandy.nelson@npgco.com
Editor Name: Derek Brizendine
Editor Email: derek.brizendine@dsjnow.com
Advertising Executive Name: Mendy Kenney
Advertising Executive Email: mendy.kenney@dsjnow.com
Advertising Executive Phone: (660) 747-8123

WAYNESVILLE

DAILY GUIDE

Publication Street Address: 108 Hull Dr
City: Waynesville
State: MO
Publication Website: www.waynesvilledailyguide.com
Postal Code: 65583-2364
Office phone: (573) 336-3711
Publisher Name: Joseph Leong
Publisher Email: jloeng@gatehousemedia.com
Editor Name: Joyce L. Miller
Editor Email: jmiller@lakesunonline.com
Editor Phone: (573) 346-2132
Year Established: 1967
Delivery Methods: Mail`Newsstand`Carrier`Racks
Own Printing Facility?: Y
Commercial printers?: Y
Mechanical specifications: Type page 13 x 21 1/2; E - 6 cols, 2 1/16, 1/8 between; A - 6 cols, 2 1/16, 1/8 between; C - 6 cols, 2 1/16, 1/8 between.
Published Days: Tues`Wed`Thur`Fri`Sat
Weekday Frequency: m
Saturday Frequency: m
Avg Paid Circ: 1320
Avg Free Circ: 8600
Audit Company: Sworn/Estimate/Non-Audited
Audit Date: 7 12 2019
Pressroom Equipment: Lines – 7-G/Community (balloon former) 1989; Folders – 1-G/SC, 1-G/Community.;
Mailroom Equipment: Counter Stackers – BG; Inserters & Stuffers – Mueller Martini inserter; Address Machine – 1/Am.;
Buisness Equipment: Dell
Editorial Equipment: Hardware – APP/Mac; Printers – APP/Mac LaserWriter 12-640
Editorial Software: Adobe/PageMaker.
Production Equipment: Hardware – 1-Nu, 1-AG/Rapid; Cameras – 1-Nu; Scanners – APP/Mac One.
Total Circulation: 9920

WEST PLAINS

WEST PLAINS DAILY QUILL

Corporate/Parent Company: Phillips Media Group, LLC
Publication Street Address: 205 Washington Ave
City: West Plains
State: MO
Publication Website: www.westplainsdailyquill.net
Postal Code: 65775-3439
Office phone: (417) 256-9191
General E-mail: news@wpdailyquill.net
Publisher Name: Jim Perry
Publisher Email: jimp@phillipsmedia.com
Advertising Executive Name: Vicki Johnson
Advertising Executive Email: ads@wpdailyquill.net
Year Established: 1903
Delivery Methods: Mail`Racks
Own Printing Facility?: Y
Commercial printers?: Y
Mechanical specifications: Type page 10" x 21"
Published Days: Tues`Wed`Thur`Fri`Sat
Weekday Frequency: m
Saturday Frequency: m
Avg Paid Circ: 5075
Audit Company: USPS
Audit Date: 10 01 2016
Pressroom Equipment: Goss, 8-unit; folders, pasters, inserters, labelers (inkjet); direct to plate.
Mailroom Equipment: full service including standard solo mailing
Buisness Equipment: offsite fiber optic back ups; fully integrated business system with multiple billable options.
Classified Equipment: Hardware – APP/Mac networked G6 computers with full load; APP/Mac Scanners; Digital Color Printers – APP/Mac
Editorial Equipment: Hardware – APP/iMac and G6 computers, MacBook Air and remote transmission.
Production Equipment: Full color proofing with

direct to plate technology
Total Circulation: 5075

MISSISSIPPI

BROOKHAVEN

DAILY LEADER

Corporate/Parent Company: Gannett
Publication Street Address: 128 N Railroad Ave
City: Brookhaven
State: MS
Publication Website: www.dailyleader.com
Postal Code: 39601-3043
Office phone: (601) 833-6961
General E-mail: news@dailyleader.com
Publisher Name: Luke Horton
Publisher Email: luke.horton@dailyleader.com
Publisher Phone: (601) 265-5299
Editor Name: Donna Campbell
Editor Email: (601) 265-5304
Advertising Executive Name: Kristi Carney
Advertising Executive Email: kristi.carney@dailyleader.com
Advertising Executive Phone: (601) 265-5300
Year Established: 1883
Delivery Methods: Mail`Carrier`Racks
Own Printing Facility?: Y
Commercial printers?: Y
Mechanical specifications: Type page 13 x 21 1/2; E - 6 cols, 2 1/16, 1/8 between; A - 6 cols, 2 1/16, 1/8 between; C - 6 cols, 2 1/16, 1/8 between.
Published Days: Tues`Wed`Thur`Fri`Sun
Weekday Frequency: e
Saturday Frequency: m
Avg Paid Circ: 5130
Audit Company: AAM
Audit Date: 30 09 2012
Pressroom Equipment: Lines – KP/News King 1988; KP/News King 1988; KP/News King 1988; KP/News King 1988; KP/News King 1988; KP/News King 1996; KP/News King 1994; Folders – KP/KJ-8.;
Mailroom Equipment: Tying Machines – Sivaron; Address Machine – Cheshire;
Buisness Equipment: PC
Buisness Software: Vision Data
Classified Equipment: Hardware – Imac;
Classified Software: Mk, Baseview.
Editorial Equipment: Hardware – Imac
Editorial Software: MS Word, InDesign
Production Equipment: Hardware – BaysPrint; Scanners – APP/Mac Scanner
Production Software: InDesign
Total Circulation: 5130

COLUMBUS

THE COMMERCIAL DISPATCH

Publication Street Address: 516 Main St
City: Columbus
State: MS
Publication Website: www.cdispatch.com
Postal Code: 39701-5734
Office phone: (662) 328-2424
General E-mail: news@cdispatch.com
Publisher Name: Peter Imes
Publisher Email: pimes@cdispatch.com
Editor Name: Zack Plair
Editor Email: zplair@cdispatch.com
Advertising Executive Name: Amber Dumas
Advertising Executive Email: adumas@cdispatch.com
Year Established: 1879
Delivery Methods: Mail`Carrier
Own Printing Facility?: Y
Commercial printers?: Y
Mechanical specifications: Type page 13 x 21 1/2; E - 6 cols, 2 1/16, 1/8 between; A - 6 cols, 2 1/16, 1/8 between; C - 9 cols, 1 3/8, 1/8 between.
Published Days: Mon`Tues`Wed`Thur`Fri`Sun
Weekday Frequency: e

U.S. Daily Newspapers

Saturday Frequency: m
Avg Paid Circ: 13338
Audit Company: Sworn/Estimate/Non-Audited
Audit Date: 7 12 2019
Pressroom Equipment: Lines – 7-G/501(1), G/Urbanite.;
Mailroom Equipment: Counter Stackers – HL/Monitor; Inserters & Stuffers – MM/227S 6:1; Tying Machines – 1-Sterling/GR40.;
Total Circulation: 13338

CORINTH

THE DAILY CORINTHIAN

Corporate/Parent Company: Paxton Media Group, LLC
Publication Street Address: 1607 S Harper Rd
City: Corinth
State: MS
Publication Website: www.dailycorinthian.com
Postal Code: 38834-6653
Office phone: (662) 287-6111
General E-mail: web@dailycorinthian.com
Publisher Name: Reece Terry
Publisher Email: rterry@dailycorinthian.com
Publisher Phone: 662-287-6111 ext 337
Editor Name: Mark Boehler
Editor Email: editor@dailycorinthian.com
Editor Phone: 662-287-6111 ext 340
Advertising Executive Name: Derinda Nunley
Advertising Executive Email: admanager@dailycorinthian.com
Advertising Executive Phone: 662-287-6111 ext 339
Year Established: 1895
Delivery Methods: Newsstand`Carrier`Racks
Own Printing Facility?: Y
Commercial printers?: Y
Mechanical specifications: Type page 10.125 x 21; E - 6 cols, A - 6 cols, C - 9 cols.
Published Days: Tues`Wed`Thur`Fri`Sat`Sun
Weekday Frequency: m
Saturday Frequency: m
Avg Paid Circ: 6113
Audit Company: Sworn/Estimate/Non-Audited
Audit Date: 7 12 2019
Pressroom Equipment: Lines – 9-G/Community 1982.;
Mailroom Equipment: Tying Machines – MLN/Strapper.;
Buisness Equipment: APP/Mac
Buisness Software: INSI
Classified Equipment: Hardware – APP/Mac; APP/Mac;
Classified Software: Ad Manager Pro 5.
Editorial Equipment: Hardware – APP/Mac/IQueWeb
Editorial Software: Baseview/NewsEdit Pro, QPS/QuarkXPress 3.32.
Production Equipment: Hardware – 1-Nu/Plate Burner, ECRM 6200; Cameras – 1-B/Caravel; Scanners – 2-Microtek/ScanMaker II XE Flatbed, Nikon/Coolscan-Polaroid/Sprint Scan, Microtek 9600 XL Flatbed
Production Software: InDesign
Total Circulation: 6113

GREENWOOD

THE GREENWOOD COMMONWEALTH

Corporate/Parent Company: Commonwealth Publishing, Inc.
Publication Street Address: 329 Highway 82 W
City: Greenwood
State: MS
Publication Website: www.gwcommonwealth.com
Postal Code: 38930-6538
Office phone: (662) 453-5312
General E-mail: commonwealth@gwcommonwealth.com
Publisher Name: Tim Kalich
Publisher Email: tkalich@gwcommonwealth.com
Publisher Phone: 662-581-7243
Editor Name: Ruthie Robinson
Editor Email: rrobinson@gwcommonwealth.com
Editor Phone: 662-581-7235
Advertising Executive Name: Larry Alderman
Advertising Executive Email: larry.a@gwcommonwealth.com
Advertising Executive Phone: 662-581-7230
Year Established: 1896
Delivery Methods: Mail`Newsstand`Carrier`Racks
Own Printing Facility?: Y
Commercial printers?: Y
Mechanical specifications: Type page 11 x 21 1/2; E - 6 cols, 1 3/4, 1/8 between; A - 6 cols, 1 3/4, 1/8 between; C - 8 cols, 1 1/4, 1/8 between.
Published Days: Mon`Tues`Wed`Thur`Fri`Sun
Weekday Frequency: e
Saturday Frequency: m
Avg Paid Circ: 3150
Avg Free Circ: 128
Audit Company: AAM
Audit Date: 31 03 2019
Total Circulation: 3278

GULFPORT

THE SUN HERALD

Corporate/Parent Company: McClatchy Company
Publication Street Address: 205 Debuys Rd
City: Gulfport
State: MS
Publication Website: www.sunherald.com
Postal Code: 39507-2838
Office phone: (228) 896-2100
General E-mail: mynews@sunherald.com
Editor Name: Blake Kaplan
Editor Email: bmkaplan@sunherald.com
Editor Phone: 228-896-2327
Year Established: 1884
Delivery Methods: Mail`Carrier
Mechanical specifications: Type page 13 x 21; E - 6 cols, 2 1/16, 1/8 between; A - 6 cols, 2 1/16, 1/8 between; C - 10 cols, 1 3/8, 1/16 between.
Published Days: Mon`Tues`Wed`Thur`Fri`Sat`Sun
Weekday Frequency: m
Saturday Frequency: m
Avg Paid Circ: 16082
Avg Free Circ: 225
Audit Company: AAM
Audit Date: 30 05 2019
Pressroom Equipment: Lines – 6-G/Headliner Offset double width 1987; Folders – 1-G/3:2 1987; Pasters –6/RTP; Reels & Stands – CT/50; Control System – G/MCC-MPCS.;
Mailroom Equipment: Counter Stackers – 1-QWI/400, 2-QWI/350; Inserters & Stuffers – 1-Harris 8/48, 1-HI/1572, 1-HI 8/48; Tying Machines – 3-Dynaric/1500, 1-OVL/JP-80, 1/Dynaric Q52000; Wrapping Singles – 2-/QWI, 2-Id/6113, Viper; Address Machine – 1-/Ch, 1-Ch/5;
Buisness Equipment: HP/3000-937
Buisness Software: CJ
Classified Equipment: Hardware – Cybergraphics, Cybersell; Printers – HP/LaserJet 2100TN;
Classified Software: Genera 4.6.
Editorial Equipment: Hardware – Sun; Printers – HP/LaserJet 8000N
Editorial Software: DTI/Client Software.
Production Equipment: Hardware – Visioneer, Au/3850 Imager, 1-Konica/66 RA, 2-Konica/550; Cameras – 1-C/Pager; Scanners – 1-Howtek/4000 Desktop, 1-Howtek/2500 Flatbed, AG/Arcus II Flatbed, Aii/3750
Production Software: DTI Ultra Enterprise 450.
Total Circulation: 24444

JACKSON

THE CLARION-LEDGER

Corporate/Parent Company: Gannett Co., Inc.
Publication Street Address: 201 S Congress St
City: Jackson
State: MS
Publication Website: www.clarionledger.com
Postal Code: 39201-4202
Office phone: (601) 961-7000
Editor Name: Sam R. Hall
Editor Email: srhall@gannett.com
Year Established: 1837
Delivery Methods: Mail`Carrier`Racks
Own Printing Facility?: Y
Commercial printers?: Y
Mechanical specifications: Type page 11 1/8 x 21; E - 6 cols, 1 3/4, 1/8 between; A - 6 cols, 1 3/4, 1/8 between; C - 10 cols. 1.063, .0556 between.
Published Days: Mon`Tues`Wed`Thur`Fri`Sat`Sun
Weekday Frequency: m
Saturday Frequency: m
Avg Paid Circ: 35482
Audit Company: AAM
Audit Date: 20 07 2020
Pressroom Equipment: Lines – 8-G/Metroliner (double width) 1982; 8-G/Metroliner (double width) 1995; Folders – 2-1982, 2-1995; Pasters –G/3-arm RTP.
Mailroom Equipment: Counter Stackers – 3-Id, 6/QWI; Inserters & Stuffers – 2-S/1372P, 1-NP/630; Tying Machines – 2-MLN/News 90, 4-/Sterlings, 2-/OVL;
Buisness Equipment: IBM AS/400
Classified Equipment: Hardware – DELL PC; Printers – HP, CANON;
Classified Software: DTI/ClassSpeed 4.2.2.
Editorial Equipment: Hardware – Dell PC
Editorial Software: Newsgate
Production Equipment: Hardware – APP/Server, Graham, 1-K/550; Cameras – 1-C/Spartan; Scanners – 6-Umax/UC-1260 Flatbed, 2-Tecsa/TS2470, 2-AG/Argus 2, 1-Linotype-Hell/Opal Ultra
Production Software: Newsgate
Note: The Jackson Clarion-Ledger (mS) has a combination rate of $180.35(mon to fri), $180.35(sat) and $217.66(S) with the Hattiesburg American (eS). Individual newspaper rates not made available.
Total Circulation: 26489

MERIDIAN

THE MERIDIAN STAR

Corporate/Parent Company: CNHI, LLC
Publication Street Address: 814 22nd Ave
City: Meridian
State: MS
Publication Website: www.meridianstar.com
Postal Code: 39301-5023
Office phone: (601) 693-1551
General E-mail: webmaster@themeridianstar.com
Publisher Name: Bill Atkinson
Publisher Phone: Ext. 3202
Editor Name: Dave Bohrer
Editor Phone: Ext. 3213
Advertising Executive Name: Jennifer Hammond
Advertising Executive Phone: Ext. 3211
Year Established: 1898
Delivery Methods: Carrier
Own Printing Facility?: Y
Commercial printers?: N
Mechanical specifications: Type page 11 x 21; E - 6 cols, 2, 1/6 between; A - 6 cols, 2, 1/6 between; C - 8 cols, 1 1/2, 1/6 between.
Published Days: Tues`Wed`Thur`Fri`Sat`Sun
Weekday Frequency: m
Saturday Frequency: m
Avg Paid Circ: 7295
Avg Free Circ: 398
Audit Company: AAM
Audit Date: 30 09 2014
Mailroom Equipment: Counter Stackers – 2/HL; Inserters & Stuffers – 1-/MM 4:1, 1-/KAN (6:1); Tying Machines – 4-/MLN; Address Machine – El.;
Buisness Software: Vision Data
Classified Equipment: Hardware – Vision Data; Printers – APP/Mac LaserWriter II NTX;
Classified Software: Vision Data, Baseview.
Editorial Equipment: Hardware – APP/Mac; Printers – APP/Mac LaserWriter II NTX, V
Editorial Software: APP/Mac.
Production Equipment: Cameras – C/Spartan III.
Total Circulation: 7693

NATCHEZ

THE NATCHEZ DEMOCRAT

Corporate/Parent Company: Boone Newspapers, Inc.
Publication Street Address: 503 N Canal St
City: Natchez
State: MS
Publication Website: www.natchezdemocrat.com
Postal Code: 39120-2902
Office phone: (601) 442-9101
Editor Name: Scott Hawkins
Editor Email: scott.hawkins@natchezdemocrat.com
Year Established: 1865
Delivery Methods: Newsstand`Carrier`Racks
Own Printing Facility?: Y
Commercial printers?: Y
Mechanical specifications: Type page 11 x 21 1/2; E - 6 cols, 2 1/16, 1/8 between; A - 6 cols, 2 1/16, 1/8 between; C - 9 cols, 1 3/8, 1/16 between.
Published Days: Mon`Tues`Wed`Thur`Fri`Sat`Sun
Weekday Frequency: m
Saturday Frequency: m
Avg Paid Circ: 8428
Audit Company: Sworn/Estimate/Non-Audited
Audit Date: 7 12 2019
Pressroom Equipment: Lines – 10-KP/News King; Folders – 1-KP/Balloon former; Reels & Stands – 8;
Mailroom Equipment: Counter Stackers – 1-BG/Count-O-Veyor; Tying Machines – 1/Md; Address Machine – 2-/El, 2-/Am.;
Total Circulation: 8428

OXFORD

THE OXFORD EAGLE

Corporate/Parent Company: Boone Newspapers, Inc.
Publication Street Address: 4 Private Road 2050
City: Oxford
State: MS
Publication Website: www.oxfordeagle.com
Postal Code: 38655-8887
Office phone: (662) 234-4331
General E-mail: news@oxfordeagle.com
Publisher Name: Rebecca Alexander
Publisher Email: rebecca.alexander@oxfordeagle.com
Editor Name: Anna Guizerix
Editor Email: anna.guizerix@oxfordeagle.com
Advertising Executive Name: Delia Childers
Advertising Executive Email: delia.childers@oxfordeagle.com
Year Established: 1867
Delivery Methods: Mail`Carrier
Mechanical specifications: Type page 13 1/8 x 21; E - 6 cols, 2 1/16, 1/8 between; A - 6 cols, 2 1/16, 1/8 between; C - 8 cols, 1 1/2, 1/8 between.
Published Days: Mon`Tues`Wed`Thur`Fri
Weekday Frequency: e
Avg Paid Circ: 5016
Audit Company: Sworn/Estimate/Non-Audited
Audit Date: 7 12 2019
Pressroom Equipment: Lines – 6-G/Community (upper folder).;
Mailroom Equipment: Tying Machines – 2/Felins; Address Machine – 1-/Am.;
Buisness Equipment: 1-RSK/16B, 1-RSK/DT 100, 2-RSK/100
Buisness Software: Word processing
Classified Equipment: Hardware – COM;
Classified Software: Baseview/Class Manager.
Editorial Equipment: Hardware – COM
Editorial Software: Baseview/NewsEdit.
Production Equipment: Hardware – 1-COM/CRT; Cameras – 1-R.
Total Circulation: 5016

PICAYUNE

PICAYUNE ITEM

Corporate/Parent Company: Boone Newspapers, Inc.

U.S. Daily Newspapers

Publication Street Address: 17 Richardson Ozona Rd
City: Picayune
State: MS
Publication Website: www.picayuneitem.com
Postal Code: 39466-7865
Office phone: (601) 798-4766
Publisher Name: Linda Gilmore
Publisher Email: linda.gilmore@picayuneitem.com
Editor Name: Jeremy Pittari
Editor Email: jeremy.pittari@picayuneitem.com
Year Established: 1904
Delivery Methods: Mail`Carrier
Published Days: Tues`Wed`Thur`Fri`Sun
Weekday Frequency: m
Avg Paid Circ: 6136
Audit Company: Sworn/Estimate/Non-Audited
Audit Date: 7 12 2019
Mailroom Equipment: Counter Stackers – 1/BG; Tying Machines – 1-/Bu; Address Machine – Automecha/Accufast.;
Buisness Equipment: Unisys
Classified Equipment: Hardware – 2-Mk.;
Editorial Equipment: Hardware – 5-Mk; Printers – 2-APP/Mac LaserWriter.
Production Equipment: Hardware – 2-APP/Mac LaserWriter II NTX; Cameras – Goerz/J72; Scanners – APP/Mac Scanner
Production Software: Baseview.
Total Circulation: 6136

STARKVILLE

STARKVILLE DAILY NEWS

Corporate/Parent Company: Horizon Publications Inc.
Publication Street Address: 304 E Lampkin St
City: Starkville
State: MS
Publication Website: www.starkvilledailynews.com
Postal Code: 39759-2910
Office phone: (662) 323-1642
General E-mail: joe@starkvilledailynews.com
Publisher Name: Joe Robertson
Publisher Email: joe@starkvilledailynews.com
Editor Name: Ryan Phillips
Editor Email: editor@starkvilledailynews.com
Advertising Executive Name: Wendi McMinn
Advertising Executive Email: wendi@starkvilledailynews.com
Year Established: 1875
Delivery Methods: Mail`Carrier
Mechanical specifications: Type page 10 x 21 1/2; E – 6 cols, 1 9/16, 1/8 between; A – 6 cols, 1 9/16, 1/8 between; C – 9 cols, 1 1/32, 1/8 between.
Published Days: Mon`Tues`Wed`Thur`Fri`Sat`Sun
Weekday Frequency: m
Saturday Frequency: m
Avg Paid Circ: 7071
Audit Company: Sworn/Estimate/Non-Audited
Audit Date: 7 12 2019
Buisness Equipment: PC
Classified Equipment: Hardware – APP/Mac Quadra 605;
Classified Software: Baseview.
Editorial Equipment: Hardware – APP/Power Mac, APP/Mac Quadra 605, APP/Mac G3, APP/Mac G4; Printers – APP/Mac LaserWriter II, GCC/Elite XL
Editorial Software: Baseview.
Production Equipment: Hardware – QPS/QuarkXPress 4.2.
Note: For detailed production information, see West Point Daily Times Leader.
Total Circulation: 7071

TUPELO

DAILY JOURNAL

Corporate/Parent Company: Gannett
Publication Street Address: 1242 S. Green Street
City: Tupelo
State: MS
Publication Website: djournal.com
Postal Code: 38804
Office phone: 662-842-2611
General E-mail: info@journalinc.com

Editor Name: Elizabeth Walters
Editor Email: elizabeth.walters@journalinc.com
Editor Phone: 662-678-1586

NORTHEAST MS DAILY JOURNAL

Corporate/Parent Company: Journal Inc
Publication Street Address: 1242 S Green St
City: Tupelo
State: MS
Publication Website: www.djournal.com
Postal Code: 38804-6301
Office phone: (662) 842-2611
General E-mail: info@journalinc.com
Editor Name: Elizabeth Walters
Editor Email: elizabeth.walters@journalinc.com
Editor Phone: 662-678-1586
Year Established: 1872
Delivery Methods: Mail`Newsstand`Carrier`Racks
Own Printing Facility?: Y
Commercial printers?: Y
Mechanical specifications: Type page 13 x 21 1/2; E – 6 cols, 2 1/16, 1/8 between; A – 6 cols, 2 1/16, 1/8 between; C – 8 cols, 1 1/2, 1/8 between.
Published Days: Mon`Tues`Wed`Thur`Fri`Sat`Sun
Weekday Frequency: m
Saturday Frequency: m
Avg Paid Circ: 17424
Avg Free Circ: 594
Audit Company: AAM
Audit Date: 31 03 2019
Pressroom Equipment: Lines – 12-G/Urbanite U1366 1990; Folders – 1-G/U-1366 1990, 1-G/SU-1708 1990;
Mailroom Equipment: Counter Stackers – 1 HL/Monitor; 3 TMSI-Compass; 1 TMSI4500; Inserters & Stuffers – 2 - SLS3000; Tying Machines – 4 - Dynaric NP3000; Address Machine – Scitex 120;
Buisness Equipment: Dell
Buisness Software: Brainworks (AR) Navision (GL,PR,AP) Windows XP
Classified Equipment: Hardware – Dell; Printers – HP4250 Laserjet;
Classified Software: Brainworks, AdPerks, Windows XP
Editorial Equipment: Hardware – 35-APP/Mac; Printers – HP
Editorial Software: NewsEdit; IQweb
Production Equipment: Hardware – 2 - Kodak NewsSetter TH100; Scanners – 1 - Epson 1640XL; 1 - Scanmaker 9800XL
Production Software: NewsExtremes; QPS/QuarkXpress 6.50; Photoshop
Total Circulation: 18018

VICKSBURG

THE VICKSBURG POST

Corporate/Parent Company: Boone Newspapers, Inc.
Publication Street Address: 1601F N Frontage Rd
City: Vicksburg
State: MS
Publication Website: www.vicksburgpost.com
Postal Code: 39180-5149
Office phone: (601) 636-4545
General E-mail: catherine.hadaway@vicksburgpost.com
Publisher Name: Catherine Hadaway
Publisher Email: catherine.hadaway@vicksburgpost.com
Editor Name: Tim Reeves
Editor Email: tim.reeves@vicksburgpost.com
Advertising Executive Name: Sheila Mantz
Advertising Executive Email: sheila.mantz@vicksburgpost.com
Year Established: 1883
Delivery Methods: Mail`Carrier
Mechanical specifications: Type page 13 x 21; E – 6 cols, 2 1/16, 1/8 between; A – 6 cols, 2 1/16, 1/8 between; C – 8 cols, 1 3/8, 1/16 between.
Published Days: Mon`Tues`Wed`Thur`Fri`Sat`Sun
Weekday Frequency: e
Saturday Frequency: e
Avg Paid Circ: 9811

Avg Free Circ: 7
Audit Company: VAC
Audit Date: 31 03 2013
Pressroom Equipment: Lines – 8-G/Urbanite;
Mailroom Equipment: Tying Machines – 2/MLN.;
Buisness Equipment: 1-DEC/11-21, 5-DEC/101
Classified Equipment: Hardware – 2-APP/Mac; Printers – 2-Xante;
Classified Software: FSI, QPS.
Editorial Equipment: Hardware – 30-APP/Mac; Printers – 3-Xante
Editorial Software: FSI, QPS.
Production Equipment: Hardware – 2-Nu; Cameras – 1-R; Scanners – 2-Nikon/Coolscan
Production Software: FSI.
Total Circulation: 9818

WEST POINT

DAILY TIMES LEADER

Corporate/Parent Company: Horizon Publications Inc.
Publication Street Address: 221 East Main Street
City: West Point
State: MS
Publication Website: www.dailytimesleader.com
Postal Code: 39773
Office phone: (662) 494-1422
General E-mail: editor@dailytimesleader.com
Year Established: 1867
Delivery Methods: Mail`Carrier
Mechanical specifications: Type page 11 5/8 x 21 1/2; E – 6 cols, 3 3/4, 1/8 between; A – 6 cols, 3 3/4, 1/8 between; C – 9 cols, 1 3/8, 1/8 between.
Published Days: Tues`Wed`Thur`Fri`Sun
Weekday Frequency: m
Avg Paid Circ: 2758
Audit Company: Sworn/Estimate/Non-Audited
Audit Date: 7 12 2019
Pressroom Equipment: Lines – 6-G/Community.;
Mailroom Equipment: Counter Stackers – BG; Tying Machines – Strapping.;
Buisness Equipment: PC
Classified Equipment: Hardware – IMACS;
Classified Software: Baseview.
Editorial Equipment: Hardware – IMACS; Printers – APP/Mac LaserWriter
Editorial Software: Baseview.
Production Equipment: Hardware – APP/Mac LaserWriter II; Cameras – Konica
Production Software: QPS/QuarkXPress 4.24.
Total Circulation: 2758

DAILY TIMES LEADER

Publication Street Address: 221 East Main Street
City: West Point
State: MS
Publication Website: www.dailytimesleader.com
Postal Code: 39773
Office phone: (662) 494-1422
General E-mail: editor@dailytimesleader.com

MONTANA

BILLINGS

BILLINGS GAZETTE

Corporate/Parent Company: Lee Enterprises
Publication Street Address: 401 N 28th St
City: Billings
State: MT
Publication Website: www.billingsgazette.com
Postal Code: 59101-1243
Office phone: (406) 657-1200
Publisher Name: Dave Worstell
Publisher Email: dworstell@billingsgazette.com
Publisher Phone: 406-657-1225
Editor Name: Darrell Ehrlick
Editor Email: dehrlick@billingsgazette.com

Editor Phone: 406-657-1289
Advertising Executive Name: Ryan Brosseau
Advertising Executive Email: rbrosseau@billingsgazette.com
Advertising Executive Phone: 406-657-1340
Year Established: 1885
Delivery Methods: Mail`Newsstand`Carrier
Mechanical specifications: Type page 11 5/8 x 21 1/2; E – 6 cols, 1 53/64, 3/16 between; A – 6 cols, 1 53/64, 3/16 between; C – 9 cols, 1 11/64, 3/16 between.
Published Days: Mon`Tues`Wed`Thur`Fri`Sat`Sun
Weekday Frequency: m
Saturday Frequency: m
Avg Paid Circ: 54242
Audit Company: AAM
Audit Date: 30 06 2018
Pressroom Equipment: Lines – 6-G/Metro offset double width 1967; Control System – Press Drive ÃƒÂ£Æ’Â£Ã‚Â£ÃƒÂ¢Æ’Â£ÃƒÂ£Ã‚Â£ÃƒÂ¢Æ’Â£ Harland Simon, 7-MOT; Registration System – KFM.
Mailroom Equipment: Counter Stackers – 1-QWI/350, 1-QWI/400, 1-QWI/500; Inserters & Stuffers – 1-HI/1372; Tying Machines – 2/Power Strap, Dynaric;
Buisness Equipment: IBM/Sys 38
Buisness Software: Proprietary
Classified Equipment: Hardware – PC 5-166-OS-2; Printers – HP/5Simx;
Classified Software: CText/AdVision.
Editorial Equipment: Hardware – Microsoft/Windows NT PS-166; Printers – Epson/DFX 5000, HP/75 DC, HP/5Simx
Editorial Software: APT, NT, Microsoft/Word, QPS/QuarkXPress.
Production Equipment: Hardware – AU/3850 Laser Imagers, 1-Graham, APP/Mac
Production Software: APT, QPS/QuarkXPress.
Total Circulation: 54242

BOZEMAN

BOZEMAN DAILY CHRONICLE

Corporate/Parent Company: Adams Publishing Group
Publication Street Address: 2820 W College St
City: Bozeman
State: MT
Publication Website: www.bozemandailychronicle.com
Postal Code: 59718-3925
Office phone: (406) 587-4491
General E-mail: citydesk@dailychronicle.com
Editor Name: Nick Ehli
Editor Email: nehli@dailychronicle.com
Editor Phone: 406-582-2647
Advertising Executive Name: Casey Fullem
Advertising Executive Email: cfullem@dailychronicle.com
Advertising Executive Phone: 406-582-2627
Year Established: 1883
Delivery Methods: Mail`Newsstand`Carrier`Racks
Own Printing Facility?: Y
Commercial printers?: Y
Mechanical specifications: Type page 12 1/2 x 21 1/2; E – 6 cols, 2 1/16, 1/8 between; A – 6 cols, 2 1/16, 1/8 between; C – 9 cols, 1 3/8, 1/16 between.
Published Days: Tues`Wed`Thur`Fri`Sat`Sun
Weekday Frequency: m
Saturday Frequency: m
Avg Paid Circ: 9321
Avg Free Circ: 1079
Audit Company: AAM
Audit Date: 3 03 2020
Pressroom Equipment: Lines – 16-2002, 2-G/Community 1976;
Mailroom Equipment: Counter Stackers – HI; Inserters & Stuffers – 1-MM/227; Tying Machines – MLN;
Buisness Equipment: VisionData & SBS
Classified Equipment: Hardware – 5-APP/iMac; Printers – Typhoon/20, HP/5simx, Epson/Stylus Pro XL;
Classified Software: Vision Data
Editorial Equipment: Hardware – 7-APP/iMac, 2-APP/Mac, 3-APP/Power Mac, 3-APP/Power Mac, 4-APP/Power Mac; Printers – Hyphen/RIPs, 2-AG/9800
Editorial Software: Baseview/NewsEdit, QPS/

I-74

U.S. Daily Newspapers

QuarkXPress 4.0.
Production Equipment: Hardware – Caere/OmniPage, AG/Studio Scan IIsi; Cameras – 1-K/240, 1-SCREEN; Scanners – 2-Nikon/LS-3510AF, 2-Microtek/ScanMaker E6, AG/Studio Scan IIsi
Production Software: QPS/QuarkXPress 4.0.
Total Circulation: 9961

BUTTE

THE MONTANA STANDARD

Corporate/Parent Company: Lee Enterprises
Publication Street Address: 25 W Granite St
City: Butte
State: MT
Publication Website: www.mtstandard.com
Postal Code: 59701-9213
Office phone: (406) 496-5500
Publisher Name: Anita Fasbender
Publisher Email: anita.fasbender@helenair.com
Publisher Phone: (406) 447-4012
Editor Name: David McCumber
Editor Email: david.mccumber@mtstandard.com
Editor Phone: 406-496-5513
Advertising Executive Name: Nonie Swan
Advertising Executive Email: nonie.swan@mtstandard.com
Advertising Executive Phone: 406-496-5561
Year Established: 1876
Mechanical specifications: Type page 12 x 21 1/2; E - 6 cols, 2 1/16, 1/8 between; A - 6 cols, 2 1/16, 1/8 between; C - 9 cols, 1 3/8, 1/16 between.
Published Days: Mon`Tues`Wed`Thur`Fri`Sat`Sun
Weekday Frequency: m
Saturday Frequency: m
Avg Paid Circ: 6727
Avg Free Circ: 914
Audit Company: AAM
Audit Date: 31 03 2019
Pressroom Equipment: Lines – 5-G/Urbanite U849; 6-G/Community;
Mailroom Equipment: Tying Machines – 1-Malow/50-S, 1-Malow/50, 1/MLN;
Buisness Equipment: Gateway/P5 166, IBM/AS-400
Classified Equipment: Hardware – RSK/600, Compaq, Novell/Net; Printers – HP/5Si;
Classified Software: CText/Advision.
Editorial Equipment: Hardware – RSK/600, Novell/Net, Novell/5/Pre Press/Panther Pro Imagesetter; Printers – Pre Press/Panther Pro 46
Editorial Software: CText/Dateline, CText/Expressline.
Production Equipment: Hardware – Caere/OmniPage, 1-Pre Press/VT 1200, 1-Pre Press/Panther Pro 46 Postscript; Cameras – 1-C/Spartan II, 1-Nu/2024V, 1-POS/I Daylight Camera, 1-Nu/Horizontal; Scanners – Lf/Leafscan 35, 1-HP, APP/Mac Quadra, 6-Epson/ES-1200C
Production Software: QPS/Quar
Total Circulation: 7641

GREAT FALLS

GREAT FALLS TRIBUNE

Corporate/Parent Company: Gannett
Publication Street Address: 205 River Dr S
City: Great Falls
State: MT
Publication Website: www.greatfallstribune.com
Postal Code: 59405-1854
Office phone: (406) 791-1444
General E-mail: tribcity@greatfallstribune.com
Year Established: 1884
Delivery Methods: Mail`Newsstand`Carrier`Racks
Own Printing Facility?: Y
Commercial printers?: Y
Mechanical specifications: Type page 11 5/8 x 21 1/2; E - 6 cols, 1 5/6, 1/8 between; A - 6 cols, 1 5/6, 1/8 between; C - 9 cols, 1 1/4, 1/16 between.
Published Days: Mon`Tues`Wed`Thur`Fri`Sat`Sun
Weekday Frequency: m

Saturday Frequency: m
Avg Paid Circ: 17755
Audit Company: AAM
Audit Date: 13 03 2019
Pressroom Equipment: Lines – 6-G/Metro (2 color decks) doublewidth 6; 10-Goss Community 5 roll stand; Heidelberg MO 19x25 sheet fed; Folders – 2-G/2:1; Pasters –6-G/3-Arm RTP.Registration System – N/A
Mailroom Equipment: Counter Stackers – 3-ld/440, 2-QWI/350; Inserters & Stuffers – 1472 Harris; Tying Machines – 1/OVL, 1-/MLN; Wrapping Singles – Manual; Control System – K&M; Address Machine – 3-/Wm.;
Buisness Equipment: 1-IBM/i5
Buisness Software: IBM, Gannett
Classified Equipment: Hardware – Mactive;
Classified Software: APT.
Editorial Equipment: Hardware – APT/Lf/AP Leaf Picture Desk; Printers – 2 Screen CTP
Editorial Software: APT.
Production Equipment: Hardware – 2 Screen CTP; Cameras – Nikon; Scanners – Nikon/LS 1000, Nikon/LS 2000
Production Software: APT.
Total Circulation: 16744

HAMILTON

RAVALLI REPUBLIC

Corporate/Parent Company: Lee Enterprises
Publication Street Address: 232 W Main St
City: Hamilton
State: MT
Publication Website: www.ravallirepublic.com
Postal Code: 59840-2552
Office phone: (406) 363-3300
Publisher Name: Jim Strauss
Publisher Email: jim.strauss@lee.net
Publisher Phone: 406-523-5201
Editor Name: Gwen Florio
Editor Email: gwen.florio@missoulian.com
Editor Phone: (406) 523-5268
Advertising Executive Name: Kathy Kelleher
Advertising Executive Email: kathy.kelleher@ravallirepublic.com
Advertising Executive Phone: 406-546-7410
Year Established: 1897
Delivery Methods: Carrier`Racks
Own Printing Facility?: N
Commercial printers?: N
Mechanical specifications: Type page 13 x 21 1/2; E - 6 cols, 2 1/16, 1/8 between; A - 6 cols, 2 1/16, 1/8 between; C - 9 cols, 2 1/16, 1/8 between.
Published Days: Wed`Thur`Fri`Sat`Sun
Weekday Frequency: m
Saturday Frequency: m
Avg Paid Circ: 1111
Avg Free Circ: 131
Audit Company: AAM
Audit Date: 30 09 2018
Pressroom Equipment: Lines – Folders 1
Buisness Equipment: 2-PC
Classified Software: CText.
Editorial Equipment: Printers – 1-QMS/LaserPrinter.
Production Equipment: Hardware – HP/ScanJet IIc; Cameras – 1-K/241
Total Circulation: 1242

HAVRE

THE HAVRE DAILY NEWS

Corporate/Parent Company: Stevenson Newspapers
Publication Street Address: 119 2nd St
City: Havre
State: MT
Publication Website: www.havredailynews.com
Postal Code: 59501-3507
Office phone: (406) 265-6795
General E-mail: news@havredailynews.com
Year Established: 1914
Mechanical specifications: Type page 13 x 21 1/2; E - 6 cols, 2 1/16, 1/8 between; A - 6 cols, 2 1/16, 1/8 between; C - 9 cols, 1 3/8, 1/16 between.
Published Days: Mon`Tues`Wed`Thur`Fri

Weekday Frequency: e
Avg Paid Circ: 3800
Audit Company: Sworn/Estimate/Non-Audited
Audit Date: 7 12 2019
Pressroom Equipment: Lines – 4-G/Community; Folders – 1-G/2:1.;
Mailroom Equipment: Tying Machines – 2-Bu/16.;
Buisness Equipment: 1-IBM/386 Compatible, 2-Wyse/370, 1-IBM/486-66 MHz, 1-IBM/Pentium-133 MHz, APP/Mac Performa 6400-180
Buisness Software: PBS/Media Plus 2.5B
Classified Equipment: Hardware – 1-APP/Mac LC II;
Classified Software: Baseview/Fox Base Plus 2.01.
Editorial Equipment: Hardware – 3-APP/Mac IIci, 4-APP/Mac LC II, 2-APP/Mac 7200; Printers – Dataproducts/LZR 1560, Typhoon/8
Editorial Software: APP/Mac Sys 7.1, QPS/QuarkXPress 3.31, Baseview/NewsEdit 6.0.
Production Equipment: Hardware – Polaroid/SprintScan 35, 1-Typhoon/8; Cameras – 1-K/24; Scanners – Umax/UC630 Color Scanner.
Total Circulation: 3800

HELENA

HELENA INDEPENDENT RECORD

Publication Street Address: PO Box 4249
City: Helena
State: MT
Publication Website: www.helenair.com
Postal Code: 59604
Office phone: (406) 447-4000
Publisher Name: Anita Fasbender
Publisher Email: anita.fasbender@helenair.com
Publisher Phone: (406) 447-4012
Editor Name: Jesse Chaney
Editor Email: jesse.chaney@helenair.com
Editor Phone: (406) 447-4074
Advertising Executive Name: Lisa Kuntz
Advertising Executive Email: lisa.kuntz@helenair.com
Advertising Executive Phone: (406) 447-4031
Year Established: 1867
Delivery Methods: Mail`Carrier`Racks
Own Printing Facility?: Y
Commercial printers?: Y
Mechanical specifications: Type page 11 5/8 x 21 1/2; E - 6 cols, 2 1/14, 1/6 between; A - 6 cols, 2 1/14, 1/6 between; C - 9 cols, 1 4/11, 1/6 between.
Published Days: Mon`Tues`Wed`Thur`Fri`Sat`Sun
Weekday Frequency: m
Saturday Frequency: m
Avg Paid Circ: 9065
Avg Free Circ: 1027
Audit Company: AAM
Audit Date: 30 09 2018
Pressroom Equipment: Lines – 8-G/Suburban (balloon former) 1978; Folders – G/Community SC.;
Mailroom Equipment: Counter Stackers – 1-WPC/Quarter folder; Inserters & Stuffers – 1/MM; Tying Machines – 1-/MLN, 1-/Malow; Address Machine – 1-/Ch;
Buisness Equipment: Gateway
Buisness Software: Microsoft/Windows NT, Microsoft/Office
Classified Equipment: Hardware – 6-Gateway/PIII 1 GH; Printers – Pre Press/Panther Pro, Pre Press/PantherPro 46;
Classified Software: CText/Advision.
Editorial Equipment: Hardware – 12-Gateway/P5-166, 6-Gateway/P7-450/APP/Photo Server, IBM; Printers – 1-Pre Press/Panther Pro, 1-Pre Press/Panther Pro 46
Editorial Software: CText/Dateline, QPS/QuarkXPress 3.32.
Production Equipment: Hardware – Nu/FT40UPNS; Cameras – 3-Nikon/F2, 1-Nikon/F3; Scanners – APP/Mac Scanner, APP/Mac IIci.
Total Circulation: 10092

INDEPENDENT RECORD

Corporate/Parent Company: Lee Enterprises
Publication Street Address: PO Box 4249
City: Helena
State: MT
Publication Website: www.helenair.com
Postal Code: 59604
Office phone: 406-447-4000
General E-mail: editor@helenair.com
Publisher Name: Anita Fasbender
Publisher Email: anita.fasbender@helenair.com
Publisher Phone: (406) 447-4012
Editor Name: Jesse Chaney
Editor Email: jesse.chaney@helenair.com
Editor Phone: (406) 447-4074
Advertising Executive Name: Erica Yakawich
Advertising Executive Email: erica.yakawich@lee.net
Advertising Executive Phone: (406) 447-4042

KALISPELL

DAILY INTER LAKE

Corporate/Parent Company: Hagadone Montana Publishing, LLC
Publication Street Address: 727 E Idaho St
City: Kalispell
State: MT
Publication Website: www.dailyinterlake.com
Postal Code: 59901-3202
Office phone: (406) 755-7000
Publisher Name: Rick Weaver
Publisher Email: rvweaver@dailyinterlake.com
Publisher Phone: 406-758-4444
Editor Name: Matt Baldwin
Editor Email: mbaldwin@dailyinterlake.com
Editor Phone: 406-758-4447
Advertising Executive Name: Anton Kaufer
Advertising Executive Email: akaufer@dailyinterlake.com
Advertising Executive Phone: 406-758-4410
Year Established: 1888
Delivery Methods: Mail`Newsstand`Carrier`Racks
Own Printing Facility?: Y
Commercial printers?: Y
Mechanical specifications: Type page 11 7/8 x 21; E - 6 cols, 1 7/8, 1/8 between; A - 6 cols, 1 7/8, 1/8 between; C - 9 cols, 1 1/5, 1/8 between.
Published Days: Mon`Tues`Wed`Thur`Fri`Sat`Sun
Weekday Frequency: m
Saturday Frequency: m
Avg Paid Circ: 13105
Audit Company: AAM
Audit Date: 29 08 2018
Pressroom Equipment: Lines – 8-G/Community 1995.;
Mailroom Equipment: Tying Machines – MLN/2EE; Address Machine – Ch.;
Buisness Equipment: NCS, DEC/Micro VAX, APP/Mac HP 4515
Buisness Software: Microsoft/Word, Microsoft/Excel
Classified Equipment: Hardware – APP/Mac; Printers – Brother HL2170W
Classified Software: NCS, Ethernet.
Editorial Equipment: Hardware – APP/Mac; Printers – Ricoh 6330
Editorial Software: NCS, Adobe/Photoshop, Caere/OmniPage.
Production Equipment: Hardware – Apple iMac, ECRM NewsMatic HS, Newsmatic 2 Glunz Jensen processors, Burgess bender and punch
Production Software: NCS, Indesign CS6, Adobe/Photoshop CC, Adobe/Acrobat Pro, Adobe/Illustrator CC,
Total Circulation: 13105

LIVINGSTON

THE LIVINGSTON ENTERPRISE

Corporate/Parent Company: Yellowstone Newspapers
Publication Street Address: 401 S Main St
City: Livingston

U.S. Daily Newspapers

State: MT
Publication Website: www.livingstonenterprise.com
Postal Code: 59047-3418
Office phone: (406) 222-2000
General E-mail: enterprise@livent.net
Publisher Name: John Sullivan
Publisher Email: execoffice@livent.net
Editor Name: Justin Post
Editor Email: jpost@livent.net
Year Established: 1883
Delivery Methods:
  Mail`Newsstand`Carrier`Racks
Own Printing Facility?: Y
Commercial printers?: Y
Mechanical specifications: Type page 13 x 21 1/4; E - 6 cols, 2 1/16, 1/8 between; A - 6 cols, 2 1/16, 1/8 between; C - 8 cols, 1 1/2, 1/8 between.
Published Days: Mon`Tues`Wed`Thur`Fri
Weekday Frequency: e
Avg Paid Circ: 2606
Avg Free Circ: 73
Audit Company: Sworn/Estimate/Non-Audited
Audit Date: 7 12 2019
Pressroom Equipment: Lines – 4-G/Community, 1-DEV/Color unit, 4-G/High Community; Folders – G/SSC, 1-G/Quarter Folder.;
Mailroom Equipment: Counter Stackers – BG/Count-O-Veyor; Tying Machines – 1/Bu, 2-Polychem/PC 500, Plastic Strap; Address Machine – 1/-/Ch;
Buisness Equipment: IBM
Buisness Software: SBS, BMF
Classified Equipment: Hardware – APP/Mac;
Classified Software: Fake Brains, InDesign
Editorial Equipment: Hardware – APP/Mac; Printers – APP/Mac, Pre Press/Panther Pro Imagesetter
Editorial Software: Baseview.
Production Equipment: Hardware – APP/Mac LaserWriter, APP/Mac II, APP/Mac IIx, APP/Mac SE, Pre Press/Panther Pro; Cameras – CTP AlphaQuest; Scanners – APP/Mac.
Total Circulation: 2679

MISSOULA

MISSOULIAN

Corporate/Parent Company: Lee Enterprises
Publication Street Address: 500 S Higgins Ave
City: Missoula
State: MT
Publication Website: www.missoulian.com
Postal Code: 59801-2736
Office phone: (406) 523-5200
Publisher Name: Jim Strauss
Publisher Email: jim.strauss@lee.net
Publisher Phone: 406-523-5201
Editor Name: Gwen Florio
Editor Email: gwen.florio@missoulian.com
Editor Phone: 406-523-5260
Year Established: 1905
Delivery Methods:
  Mail`Newsstand`Carrier`Racks
Mechanical specifications: Type page 13 x 21 1/2; E - 6 cols, 2 1/16, 1/8 between; A - 6 cols, 2 1/16, 1/8 between; C - 9 cols, 1 5/16, 1/8 between.
Published Days: Mon`Tues`Wed`Thur`Fri`Sat`Sun
Weekday Frequency: m
Saturday Frequency: m
Avg Paid Circ: 11158
Avg Free Circ: 5429
Audit Company: AAM
Audit Date: 30 09 2018
Pressroom Equipment: Lines – 9-G; 9-G/Urbanite; Folders – 2, 1-G/Quarter, 2-G/Urbanite 707; Reels & Stands – G/2 stands 3 high.;
Mailroom Equipment: Counter Stackers – 1-Id/Counter Stacker 660, 1-Id/Counter Stacker 2100; Inserters & Stuffers – 1-MM/227-0500 E, HI/1372; Tying Machines – 2-MLN/Automatic Power Strapping Machines; Address Machine – 1/AVY, Ch/582 M Base 721 Head;
Buisness Equipment: 2-IBM/Sys 38
Classified Equipment: Hardware – 12-Gateway/P166 Advision; 1-HP/Scanner; Printers – HP/6MP Postscript Printer;
Classified Software: CText/Advision, CText/Alps pagination system.
Editorial Equipment: Hardware – Gateway/P166 Expressline Paginator, 24-Gateway/P166 Dateline Machine, 2-APP/Mac G3, 1-APP/Mac 8500, 1-APP/Mac 7100, 11-CText, 1-DEC/VT-220, 1-APP/Mac fx, 1-APP/Mac Dash, 1-APP/Mac ci, 1-APP/Power Mac 7100/1-APP/Mac Color One Scanne
Production Equipment: Hardware – APP/iMac, 7-Umax/Astra 12200 Scanner, 1-Pre Press/Panther Pro 46, 1-Pre Press/Panther Pro Imagesetter; Cameras – 1-C/Spartan II, 1-Nu; Scanners – 1-PC 386
Production Software: CText, QPS/QuarkXPress 3.3.
Total Circulation: 16587

NORTH CAROLINA

ASHEVILLE

THE ASHEVILLE CITIZEN-TIMES

Corporate/Parent Company: Gannett
Publication Street Address: 14 Ohenry Ave
City: Asheville
State: NC
Publication Website: www.citizen-times.com
Postal Code: 28801-2604
Office phone: (828) 252-5610
Editor Name: Katie Wadington
Editor Email: KWadington@CITIZEN-TIMES.com
Editor Phone: 828-232-5829
Advertising Executive Name: Mark Koch
Advertising Executive Email: mkoch@gannett.com
Advertising Executive Phone: mkoch@gannett.com
Year Established: 1870
Delivery Methods: Carrier`Racks
Own Printing Facility?: N
Commercial printers?: N
Mechanical specifications: Type page 10 x 20; E - 6 cols, 1/6 between; A - 6 cols, 1/6 between; C - 10 cols, 1/12 between.
Published Days: Mon`Tues`Wed`Thur`Fri`Sat`Sun
Weekday Frequency: m
Saturday Frequency: m
Avg Paid Circ: 21900
Audit Company: AAM
Audit Date: 5 06 2019
Mailroom Equipment: SLS 2000
Mailroom Software: Newscom
Buisness Equipment: DELL; Canon
Buisness Software: Microsoft
Classified Equipment: Enterprise Classified Solutions
Classified Software: Adbooker
Editorial Equipment: CCI Europe
Editorial Software: NewsGate
Production Equipment: PressTeligence
Production Software: NewsXtreme
Total Circulation: 28355

BLOWING ROCK

BLOWING ROCK NEWS

Publication Street Address: PO Box 2345
City: Blowing Rock
State: NC
Publication Website: www.blowingrocknews.com
Postal Code: 28605
Office phone: 828-386-6241
Publisher Name: David Rogers
Publisher Email: editor@blowingrocknews.com

CHARLOTTE

CHARLOTTE AGENDA

Publication Street Address: 623 S Cedar, Suite B
City: Charlotte
State: NC
Publication Website: www.charlotteagenda.com
Postal Code: 28202
Publisher Name: Ted Williams
Publisher Email: ted@charlotteagenda.com
Editor Name: Michael Graff
Editor Email: michael@charlotteagenda.com

THE CHARLOTTE OBSERVER

Corporate/Parent Company: McClatchy Company
Publication Street Address: 550 S Caldwell St Ste 760
City: Charlotte
State: NC
Publication Website: www.charlotteobserver.com
Postal Code: 28202-2636
Office phone: (704) 358-5000
Publisher Phone: "
(704) 358-5000"
Editor Name: Sherry Chisenhall
Editor Email: schisenhall@charlotteobserver.com
Editor Phone: "
(704) 358-5000"
Advertising Executive Name: Dan Morgenstern
Advertising Executive Email: dmorgenstern@thestate.com
Year Established: 1886
Delivery Methods:
  Mail`Newsstand`Carrier`Racks
Own Printing Facility?: Y
Commercial printers?: Y
Mechanical specifications: Type page 10 x 21 9/16; 6 columns, 1 1/2, 1/8 to 3/16 between.
Published Days: Mon`Tues`Wed`Thur`Fri`Sat`Sun
Weekday Frequency: m
Saturday Frequency: m
Avg Paid Circ: 71352
Audit Company: AAM
Audit Date: 14 04 2020
Pressroom Equipment: 1 press line with 2 folders. 9 unit TKS/ OFFSET press, the 1 press line consists of 3 mono units 1982 these units are black only. 2, 2001 color towers, full color on ever page. And 4 2011 color towers full color on every page. 72 page capacity straight 48 pages of full color. 144 pages collect 96 pages of full color. Reels & Stands TKS as well.
Mailroom Equipment: Counter Stackers - 3 Quipp 301 stackers, 2 Quipp 400 stackers. 3 Quipp viper bottom wrap machines and 1 power strapp bottom wrap machine. 7 oval strap strapmasters single strap. 2 Dynaric single strappers and 1 Mosca single strap. 2 CCL labelers. Heidelberg Gripper, 3 ties lines, 4 boom loaders and a Harland Simon Totalizer.
Buisness Equipment: Dell OptiPlex GX270 - Windows XP Operating System Dell Optiplex GX280 - Windows XP Operating System Dell Optiplex GX620 - Windows 7 Operating System Dell Optiplex GX620 - Windows XP Operating System Dell Optiplex GX740 - Windows XP Operating System Dell Optiplex 745 - Windows 7 Operating System Dell OptiPlex 755 - Windows XP Operating System Dell Optiplex 780 - Windows 7 Operating System Dell Optiplex 790 - Windows 7 Operating System Dell Optiplex 9020 - Windows 7 Operating System HP Compaq 8000 Elite â€" Windows 7 Operating System HP Compaq 8200 Elite â€" Windows 7 Operating System HP Compaq 8300 Elite â€" Windows 7 Operating System
Buisness Software: Microsoft Office Professional 2003 Microsoft Office Standard 2008 Microsoft Office Standard 2011 Microsoft Office Standard 2013 Microsoft Office Professional 2013
Classified Equipment: Hardware – SII/Server Net; SII/ICP Pagination; Printers – Okidata, HP/Laser;
Classified Software: SII/Server Net., Microsoft Office Professional 2003 Microsoft Office Standard 2008 Microsoft Office Standard 2011 Microsoft Office Standard 2013 Microsoft Office Professional 2013
Editorial Equipment: Hardware – IBM/S-70; Printers – Okidata, HP/Laser
Editorial Software: CCI., Microsoft Office Professional 2003 Microsoft Office Standard 2008 Microsoft Office Standard 2011 Microsoft Office Standard 2013 Microsoft Office Professional 2013
Production Equipment: Hardware – Mac OS & OS X, Cannon 755 HP2025, Cameras – GoPro4; Cannon Power Shot; Scanners – Kk/RFS 3570 Scanner, Umax/PowerLook flatbed scanner, 8-LaCie/Silver Scan, 3-Topaz, Eskofot/1
Production Software: Adobe Creative Suite, Microsoft Pro, Acrobat Pro
Note: Southern Shows (4 yearly), Charlotte Observer Spelling Bee
Total Circulation: 95935

CLINTON

THE SAMPSON INDEPENDENT

Corporate/Parent Company: Champion Media
Publication Street Address: 109 W Main St
City: Clinton
State: NC
Publication Website: www.clintonnc.com
Postal Code: 28328-4046
Office phone: (910) 592-8137
Publisher Name: Sherry Matthews
Publisher Email: smatthews@clintonnc.com
Editor Name: Chris Berendt
Editor Email: cberendt@clintonnc.com
Editor Phone: (910) 592-8137 ext. 2587
Advertising Executive Name: Sherry Matthews
Advertising Executive Email: smatthews@clintonnc.com
Advertising Executive Phone: (910) 592-8137 ext. 2583
Year Established: 1924
Published Days: Tues`Wed`Thur`Fri`Sat`Sun
Weekday Frequency: e
Saturday Frequency: m
Avg Paid Circ: 7962
Audit Company: Sworn/Estimate/Non-Audited
Audit Date: 7 12 2019
Pressroom Equipment: Lines – 4-G/Community (1 folder), 8-G;
Mailroom Equipment: Tying Machines – 1/Malow, 2-/Malow.;
Buisness Software: Baseview, Baseview, Navision
Classified Equipment: Hardware – APP/Mac; Printers – APP/Mac;
Classified Software: Baseview.
Editorial Equipment: Hardware – 1-Mk/1100, 12-Mk/4100, APP/Mac; Printers – APP/Mac
Editorial Software: Baseview.
Production Equipment: Hardware – Pre Press/Panther Pro, 1-COM/7200, 2-COM/Videosetter; Cameras – 1-CL/J-76CC; Scanners – 5-Astra, Umax, Nikon/Scanner
Production Software: Pre Press/Panther Pro, QPS/QuarkXPress.
Total Circulation: 7962

DUNN

THE DAILY RECORD

Corporate/Parent Company: Gannett
Publication Street Address: 99 W Broad St
City: Dunn
State: NC
Publication Website: www.mydailyrecord.com
Postal Code: 28334-6031
Office phone: (910) 891-1234
Publisher Name: Keven Zepezauer
Publisher Email: kzepezauer@restorationnewsmedia.com
Editor Name: Emily Weaver
Editor Email: eweaver@mydailyrecord.com
Advertising Executive Name: Maria House
Advertising Executive Email: addirector@mydailyrecord.com
Year Established: 1950
Delivery Methods: Mail`Racks
Own Printing Facility?: Y
Commercial printers?: Y
Mechanical specifications: Type page 11.625"

x 21"; E - 6 cols, 1 5/6, 1/8 between; A - 6 cols, 1 5/6, 1/8 between; C - 6 cols, 1 5/6, 1/8 between.
Published Days: Mon`Tues`Wed`Thur`Fri
Weekday Frequency: m
Avg Paid Circ: 9056
Avg Free Circ: 1320
Audit Company: CAC
Audit Date: 17 10 2016
Pressroom Equipment: Lines – 6-G/Community single width 1983, 1-stacked G/community 1999; Folders – 1-G/SE.;
Mailroom Equipment: Counter Stackers – BG/Count-O-Veyor; Inserters & Stuffers – KAN/480; Tying Machines – 2/Bu; Address Machine – X.;
Buisness Equipment: Vision Data
Buisness Software: Windows
Classified Equipment: Hardware – Unix/Server; Printers – APP/HP 2300 N;
Classified Software: News Memory,Vision Data, QuarkXPress 4.04.
Editorial Equipment: Hardware – APP/Mac; Printers – HP/LaserJet 5M
Editorial Software: Baseview/NewsEdit, QPS/QuarkXPress.
Production Equipment: Hardware – Caere/OmniPage Pro 8.0, ECR/EV Jetsetter 2100, APP/Mac G3; Cameras – C/Spartan III; Scanners – Polaroid/Sprint Scan 4000, Polaroid/Sprint Scan 35, Umax/PowerLook III, HP/Scan Jet III
Production Software: QPS/QuarkXPress with Vision Data Interface.
Total Circulation: 10376

DURHAM

THE HERALD-SUN

Corporate/Parent Company: McClatchy Company
Publication Street Address: 1530 N Gregson St
City: Durham
State: NC
Publication Website: www.heraldsun.com
Postal Code: 27701-1164
Office phone: (919) 419-6500
Editor Name: Robyn Tomlin
Editor Email: rtomlin@newsobserver.com
Editor Phone: "
(919) 829-4806"
Advertising Executive Name: David Jones
Year Established: 1889
Delivery Methods:
Mail`Newsstand`Carrier`Racks
Own Printing Facility?: N
Commercial printers?: N
Published Days: Mon`Tues`Wed`Thur`Fri`Sat`Sun
Weekday Frequency: m
Saturday Frequency: m
Avg Paid Circ: 6679
Avg Free Circ: 1479
Audit Company: AAM
Audit Date: 23 03 2020
Total Circulation: 9484

ELIZABETH CITY

THE DAILY ADVANCE

Corporate/Parent Company: Cox
Publication Street Address: 1016 W Ehringhaus St
City: Elizabeth City
State: NC
Publication Website: www.dailyadvance.com
Postal Code: 27909
Office phone: 252-335-0841
Publisher Name: Sean O'Brien
Publisher Email: sobrien@dailyadvance.com
Editor Name: Julian Eure
Editor Email: jeure@dailyadvance.com
Editor Phone: (252) 329-9680
Advertising Executive Name: Sean O'Brien
Advertising Executive Email: sobrien@dailyadvance.com
Advertising Executive Phone: (252) 329-9670
Year Established: 1911
Delivery Methods:
Mail`Newsstand`Carrier`Racks
Own Printing Facility?: Y

Commercial printers?: Y
Mechanical specifications: Type page 13 1/4 x 21 1/2; E - 6 cols, 2 1/16, 1/8 between; A - 6 cols, 2 1/16, 1/8 between; C - 9 cols, 1 5/16, 1/8 between.
Published Days: Mon`Tues`Wed`Thur`Fri`Sat`Sun
Weekday Frequency: m
Saturday Frequency: m
Avg Paid Circ: 7840
Avg Free Circ: 689
Audit Company: AAM
Audit Date: 30 09 2014
Pressroom Equipment: Lines – 1-G/Urbanite; 4-G/Urbanite; Folders – 1-G/2:1, 1-G/Half, 1-G/Quarter; Registration System – Duarte/Pin Registration.
Mailroom Equipment: Counter Stackers – 1/BG; Inserters & Stuffers – 1-/MM; Tying Machines – 2-/Bu; Address Machine – Digital Label, KAN/Label;
Buisness Equipment: HP
Buisness Software: WordPerfect 6.0, Lotus 1-2-3 5.0, Microsoft/Windows 95, Microsoft/Office 97, Microsoft/Excel
Classified Equipment: Hardware – 3-APP/Mac Quadra 605; Printers – 2-ECR/VRL 36;
Classified Software: SII.
Editorial Equipment: Hardware – APP/Mac/1-APP/Power Mac 8600 Image Desk, Lf/AP Leaf Picture Desk; Printers – 2-ECR/VRL 36
Editorial Software: DTI.
Production Equipment: Hardware – Caere/OmniPage Pro 5.0, Mk, Jobo/Processor; Cameras – 1-R/500; Scanners – AG/Plus
Production Software: QPS/QuarkXPress 3.3.
Total Circulation: 8529

ELIZABETHTOWN

BLADEN ONLINE

Corporate/Parent Company: Online News & Advertising, LLC
Publication Street Address: 1110 S. Poplar Street
City: Elizabethtown
State: NC
Publication Website: bladenonline.com
Postal Code: 28337
Office phone: (910)879-1029
General E-mail: bladenonline.com@gmail.com
Publisher Name: Charlotte Smith
Publisher Email: bladenonlinesales@gmail.com
Publisher Phone: 910-876-5393

FAYETTEVILLE

THE FAYETTEVILLE OBSERVER

Corporate/Parent Company: Gannett
Publication Street Address: 458 Whitfield St
City: Fayetteville
State: NC
Publication Website: www.fayobserver.com
Postal Code: 28306-1614
Office phone: (910) 323-4848
General E-mail: news@fayobserver.com
Publisher Phone: 910-486-3501
Editor Name: Lorry Williams
Editor Email: lwilliams@fayobserver.com
Editor Phone: 910-486-3524
Advertising Executive Name: Lynnie Guzman
Advertising Executive Email: lguzman@fayobserver.com
Advertising Executive Phone: 910-486-2726
Year Established: 1816
Mechanical specifications: Type page 12 1/2 x 21; E - 6 cols, 1 17/20, 1/8 between; A - 6 cols, 1 17/20, 1/8 between; C - 10 cols, 1 3/16, 1/16 between.
Published Days: Mon`Tues`Wed`Thur`Fri`Sat`Sun
Weekday Frequency: m
Saturday Frequency: m
Avg Paid Circ: 19545
Avg Free Circ: 1531
Audit Company: AAM
Audit Date: 19 02 2019
Pressroom Equipment: Lines – 10-KB/Colora double width 1999; Pasters –7-1999, 2-1999.
Mailroom Equipment: Counter Stackers – 5-QWI/400W, 1-QWI/350, 1-Gammerler/Pathfinder 7.0; Inserters & Stuffers

– HI/1372, HI/630; Tying Machines – 2-Dynaric/NP2, 3-Dynaric/1500; Wrapping Singles – 3-Id/Bottom Wrapper, 2-QWI/Cobra 3/4 Wrap w/inkjet, 2-QWI/Viper;
Buisness Equipment: IBM/AS-400 F35
Buisness Software: PBS, Microsoft/Excel, AdMarc
Classified Equipment: Hardware – 2-Dell/6300; 30-Dell/PC; Printers – HP/5000 GN;
Classified Software: Mactive/Adbooker 2.8.18.
Editorial Equipment: Hardware – DEC, Intel, 2-Dell/4300/APP/Mac G4, HP/ScanJet IIcx, Kk/RFS 2035 Scanner, Nikon/Coolscan, 102-Dell/PC; Printers – 12-HP/5000GN
Editorial Software: Tera, 3-Good News.
Production Equipment: Hardware – WL/7AW-DW-OPB, 3-AU/Soft Pips (Window NT), 1-Au/3850 Doublewide; Scanners – 1-PixelCraft, 1-Nikon, Data/Oy-Plate Scanner
Production Software: Good News III.
Total Circulation: 25598

FOREST CITY

THE DAILY COURIER

Corporate/Parent Company: Western News & Info
Publication Street Address: 601 Oak St
City: Forest City
State: NC
Publication Website: www.thedigitalcourier.com
Postal Code: 28043-3471
Office phone: 828-202-2919
General E-mail: lspurling@thedigitalcourier.com
Publisher Name: Lori Spurling
Publisher Email: lspurling@thedigitalcourier.com
Editor Name: Jean Gordon
Editor Email: jgordon@thedigitalcourier.com
Advertising Executive Name: Erika Meyer
Advertising Executive Email: emeyer@thedigitalcourier.com
Year Established: 1969
Delivery Methods:
Mail`Newsstand`Carrier`Racks
Own Printing Facility?: Y
Commercial printers?: Y
Published Days: Tues`Wed`Thur`Fri`Sat`Sun
Weekday Frequency: m
Saturday Frequency: m
Avg Paid Circ: 7200
Audit Company: Sworn/Estimate/Non-Audited
Audit Date: 7 12 2019
Total Circulation: 7200

GASTONIA

THE GASTON GAZETTE

Corporate/Parent Company: Gannett
Publication Street Address: 1893 Remount Rd
City: Gastonia
State: NC
Publication Website: www.gastongazette.com
Postal Code: 28054-7413
Office phone: 704-869-1823
General E-mail: gastongazette@gastongazette.com
Publisher Name: Lucy Talley
Publisher Email: ltalley@gatehousemedia.com
Publisher Phone: 704-869-1702
Editor Name: Kevin Ellis
Editor Email: kellis@gastongazette.com
Editor Phone: 704-869-1823
Advertising Executive Name: Mary Pettus
Advertising Executive Email: mary.pettus@gastongazette.com
Year Established: 1880
Delivery Methods:
Mail`Newsstand`Carrier`Racks
Own Printing Facility?: N
Commercial printers?: Y
Mechanical specifications: Type page 11 5/8 x 21 1/2; E - 6 cols, 1 5/6, 1/8 between; A - 6 cols, 1 5/6, 1/8 between; C - 9 cols, 1 3/6, 1/16 between.
Published Days: Mon`Tues`Wed`Thur`Fri`Sat`Sun
Weekday Frequency: m
Saturday Frequency: m
Avg Paid Circ: 17076
Audit Company: AAM

Audit Date: 5 08 2020
Pressroom Equipment: Lines – 42-G/Magnum single width units 2001; Folders – 1-G/Universal w/ 4 formers, 1-G/Universal w/ 2 formers; Reels & Stands – 18; Control System – G/GMI.;
Mailroom Equipment: Counter Stackers – 2-QWI/401; Inserters & Stuffers – GMA/SLS 2000 12:2; Tying Machines – 2/Samuels, 2-/Dynaric; Wrapping Singles – 1-/NJP; Address Machine – 1-X/542-090.;
Buisness Equipment: MS/NT Network
Buisness Software: Vision Data, Great Plains, APT, Brainworks, Ceridian
Classified Equipment: Hardware – Compaq/Servers 300 mhz; Printers – Autologic;
Classified Software: APT.
Editorial Equipment: Hardware – APT/Paginaters (700 mhz), APT/Reporter (500 mhz); Printers – HP/Plotter, Pre Press/Panther 36, Autologic
Editorial Software: APT.
Production Equipment: Hardware – Scanview Drum Scanner, Nikon/Super Coolscan, Zip Disk Readers
Production Software: APT.
Total Circulation: 10497

GOLDSBORO

GOLDSBORO NEWS-ARGUS

Corporate/Parent Company: Paxton Media Group, LLC
Publication Street Address: 310 N Berkeley Blvd
City: Goldsboro
State: NC
Publication Website: www.newsargus.com
Postal Code: 27534-4326
Office phone: (919) 778-2211
General E-mail: news@newsargus.com
Publisher Name: John McClure
Publisher Email: jmcclure@newsargus.com
Publisher Phone: 919-739-7906
Editor Name: Duke Conover
Editor Email: dconover@newsargus.com
Editor Phone: 919-739-7840
Advertising Executive Email: John McClure
Advertising Executive Phone: jmcclure@newsargus.com
Year Established: 1885
Delivery Methods:
Mail`Newsstand`Carrier`Racks
Own Printing Facility?: Y
Commercial printers?: Y
Mechanical specifications: Type page 10 5/8 x 21 1/2; E - 6 cols, 1 4/5, 1/8 between; A - 6 cols, 1 4/5, 1/8 between; C - 8 cols, 1 1/5, 11/100 between.
Published Days: Mon`Tues`Wed`Thur`Fri`Sun
Weekday Frequency: e
Avg Paid Circ: 11888
Avg Free Circ: 441
Audit Company: AAM
Audit Date: 31 12 2016
Pressroom Equipment: Lines – 9-G/Urbanite (color deck) single width 1970; Reels & Stands – 5;
Mailroom Equipment: Counter Stackers – Quipp 500 (3); Gammerler KL-5000; Inserters & Stuffers – 1 MM SLS2000 12:1; Tying Machines – 2 - Dynaric NP3000 - Quipp Viper bottomwrap; Wrapping Singles – Mailroom Control System ÃƒÂƒÃ‚ÂƒMM/1509 Minuteman Saddle Stitcher; Address Machine – 1-Cheshire/569; 1-Barstrom Labeler (inline);
Buisness Equipment: Dell PowerEdge R410, Sun Sunfire v240
Buisness Software: DTI, BSI, Microsoft/Office
Classified Equipment: Hardware – 7-APP/iMac; Printers – HP 4250;
Classified Software: MediaSpan AMP4
Editorial Equipment: Hardware – 8-Apple iMacs, 7-Apple G5, 1-Apple MacPro; Printers – HP Laserjet 5200, HP Laserjet 2200
Editorial Software: MediaSpan 3.54
Production Equipment: Hardware – 1-Nu, 7-APP/Mac, 1-PC, ECRM/Bluefin 62, 1-Xerox Phaser 7400, ECR/Scriptsetter VRL 36HS, Xante 3G laser printer; Scanners – 6-Umax
Production Software: Baseview 3.5.4.
Total Circulation: 12329

U.S. Daily Newspapers

GREENSBORO
NEWS & RECORD
Corporate/Parent Company: Lee Enterprises
Publication Street Address: 200 E Market St
City: Greensboro
State: NC
Publication Website: www.news-record.com
Postal Code: 27401-2910
Office phone: (336) 373-7000
Publisher Name: Alton Brown
Publisher Email: abrown@wsjournal.com
Publisher Phone: (336) 727-7349
Editor Name: Cindy Loman
Editor Email: cindy.loman@greensboro.com
Editor Phone: (336) 373-7212
Advertising Executive Name: Terry Mink
Advertising Executive Email: terry.mink@Greensboro.com
Advertising Executive Phone: (336) 373-7364
Year Established: 1890
Delivery Methods: Newsstand`Carrier`Racks
Own Printing Facility?: Y
Commercial printers?: Y
Published Days: Mon`Tues`Wed`Thur`Fri`Sat`Sun
Weekday Frequency: m
Saturday Frequency: m
Avg Paid Circ: 33168
Audit Company: AAM
Audit Date: 5 04 2019
Pressroom Equipment: Lines – 13-G/Metro double width 1974;
Total Circulation: 43482

GREENVILLE
THE DAILY REFLECTOR
Corporate/Parent Company: Cox
Publication Street Address: 1150 Sugg Pkwy
City: Greenville
State: NC
Publication Website: www.reflector.com
Postal Code: 27834-9077
Office phone: (252) 329-9500
Publisher Name: Robin Quillon
Publisher Email: riquillon@apgenc.com
Editor Name: Bobby Burns
Editor Email: baburns@reflector.com
Editor Phone: (252) 329-9572
Advertising Executive Name: Craig Springer
Advertising Executive Email: cspringer@apgenc.com
Advertising Executive Phone: (252) 329-9513
Year Established: 1882
Delivery Methods:
Mail`Newsstand`Carrier`Racks
Own Printing Facility?: Y
Commercial printers?: Y
Mechanical specifications: Type page 11 5/8 x 21; E - 6 cols, 2 1/2, 1/6 between; A - 6 cols, 2 1/2, 1/6 between; C - 9 cols, 1 1/3, 1/8 between.
Published Days: Mon`Tues`Wed`Thur`Fri`Sat`Sun
Weekday Frequency: m
Saturday Frequency: m
Avg Paid Circ: 14839
Avg Free Circ: 3884
Audit Company: AAM
Audit Date: 12 12 2017
Pressroom Equipment: ColdSet – DGM 850 - 16 units/ 8 Jardis Flying Pasters DGM 1050 Folder 1 DGM 1030 Folder 1 1 Inline Quipp 9910 Stacker Coldset – DGM 430 - 18 Units / 9 Jardis 0 Speed Splicers DGM 1030 FOlder 2 1 Inline Gammerler Stacker Heatset – Harris M-110 - 4 Units / 1 Butler Splicer Goss Folder 1 2 Inline Gammerler Stackers
Pressroom Software: DTI
Mailroom Equipment: 2 SLS 1000 - 12/2 machines 4 Quipp 500 Stackers 4 Inline Dynaric Strappers 4 Moveable Dynaric Strappers 1 Inline Quipp 400 on the 850 Press 1 inline Accraply Labeler on 850 Press 1 Inline Accraply Labeler on SLS 1000
Buisness Equipment: HP/9000
Buisness Software: CJ, Geac/World Class
Classified Equipment: Hardware – APP/Macs, Unix/Server; Printers – HP, Xante;
Classified Software: DTI/ClassSpeed.
Editorial Equipment: Hardware – APP/Macs, Unix/Server; Printers – HP, Xante
Editorial Software: DTI.
Production Equipment: 4 Mac based ECRM Harlequin Rips v. 8.3.0 on Mac Pros w/ Snow Leopard 10.6.8 4 Mac Pros w/ Leopard 10.6.8. 2 Kodak Trendsetter News 100s CTP Devices 2 Glunz & Jensens Plate Processors K&F Sorta Stacker 8 Bins 2 K&F Vision Benders
Production Software: Adobe CS5, Pro PitStop 9 Arkitek Page Pairing System
Total Circulation: 18723

HENDERSON
DAILY DISPATCH
Corporate/Parent Company: Paxton Media Group, LLC
Publication Street Address: 304 S Chestnut St
City: Henderson
State: NC
Publication Website: www.hendersondispatch.com
Postal Code: 27536-4225
Office phone: 252-436-2700
General E-mail: nwykle@hendersondispatch.com
Publisher Name: Nancy Wykle
Publisher Email: nwykle@hendersondispatch.com
Publisher Phone: 252-436-2831
Editor Name: Nancy Wykle
Editor Email: nwykle@hendersondispatch.com
Editor Phone: 252-436-2850
Advertising Executive Name: Desiree Brooks
Advertising Executive Email: dbrooks@hendersondispatch.com
Advertising Executive Phone: 252-436-2821
Year Established: 1914
Delivery Methods:
Mail`Newsstand`Carrier`Racks
Own Printing Facility?: Y
Commercial printers?: Y
Mechanical specifications: Type page 10 x 21 1/2; E - 6 cols, 1 5/6, 1/6 between; A - 6 cols, 1 5/6, 1/6 between; C - 8 cols, 1 1/3, 1/6 between.
Published Days: Tues`Wed`Thur`Fri`Sat`Sun
Weekday Frequency: m
Saturday Frequency: m
Avg Paid Circ: 6250
Avg Free Circ: 19050
Audit Company: Sworn/Estimate/Non-Audited
Audit Date: 7 12 2019
Buisness Equipment: Mediaspan
Classified Software: Mediaspan
Editorial Software: Mediaspan
Total Circulation: 25300

HENDERSONVILLE
TIMES-NEWS
Corporate/Parent Company: Gannett
Publication Street Address: 106 Henderson Crossing Plz
City: Hendersonville
State: NC
Publication Website: www.blueridgenow.com
Postal Code: 28792-2879
Office phone: (828) 692-0505
Editor Name: Rich Jackson
Editor Email: rich.jackson@thetimesnews.com
Editor Phone: 828-694-7872
Advertising Executive Phone: 828-694-7845
Year Established: 1887
Delivery Methods:
Mail`Newsstand`Carrier`Racks
Own Printing Facility?: Y
Commercial printers?: Y
Mechanical specifications: Type page 11 5/8 x 21 1/2; E - 6 cols, 1 5/6, 1/8 between; A - 6 cols, 1 5/6, 1/8 between; C - 9 cols, 1 3/16, 1/8 between.
Published Days: Mon`Tues`Wed`Thur`Fri`Sat`Sun
Weekday Frequency: m
Saturday Frequency: m
Avg Paid Circ: 8785
Avg Free Circ: 436
Audit Company: AAM
Audit Date: 10 04 2019
Pressroom Equipment: Lines – 6-MAN/double width (2-half color deck) 1980; Press Drive – GE/Varitrol; Folders – 1-H/double 2:1; Reels & Stands – 5; CTP 1
Mailroom Equipment: Counter Stackers – QWI/351 QWI/501; Inserters & Stuffers – 1-GMA/SLS 2000 9:2; 1- GMA/SLS 2000 12:2 2-/Dynaric;
Buisness Equipment: Microsoft/Office, Great Plains, AR/Works, PC Netware
Classified Equipment: Hardware – PC; Printers – HP;
Classified Software: APT.
Editorial Equipment: Hardware – PC/Desk/Scanner, ; Printers – Sharp & Camera Probe 9000
Editorial Software: APT.
Total Circulation: 24257

HICKORY
THE HICKORY DAILY RECORD
Corporate/Parent Company: Lee Enterprises
Publication Street Address: 1100 11th Ave. Blvd. SE
City: Hickory
State: NC
Publication Website: www.hickoryrecord.com
Postal Code: 28602
Office phone: (828) 322-4510
General E-mail: news@hickoryrecord.com
Editor Name: Eric Millsaps
Editor Email: emillsaps@hickoryrecord.com
Editor Phone: 828-304-6909
Advertising Executive Name: Tiffany Hovis
Advertising Executive Email: thovis@hickoryrecord.com
Advertising Executive Phone: 828-304-6941
Delivery Methods: Mail`Newsstand`Racks
Mechanical specifications: Type page 13 x 21; E - 6 cols, 2 1/16, 1/8 between; A - 6 cols, 2 1/16, 1/8 between; C - 8 cols, 1 3/4, 1/16 between.
Published Days: Mon`Tues`Wed`Thur`Fri`Sat`Sun
Weekday Frequency: m
Saturday Frequency: m
Avg Paid Circ: 8330
Avg Free Circ: 303
Audit Company: AAM
Audit Date: 16 05 2017
Pressroom Equipment: Lines – 7-MAN/Uniman; Pasters –MEGReels & Stands – MEG.;
Mailroom Equipment: Counter Stackers – 2/MM; Inserters & Stuffers – 2-/MM; Tying Machines – 2-/OVL.;
Buisness Equipment: IBM/Sys 36
Classified Equipment: Hardware – 5-HP;
Classified Software: SII/Coyote XA.
Editorial Equipment: Hardware – Tandem/Server, 22-HP; Printers - Konica
Editorial Software: SII/Sys 77XR 5702A Coyote XE.
Production Equipment: Hardware – 1-Nu, 1-AU/APS-6
Production Software: Coyote/Layout.
Total Circulation: 15751

HIGH POINT
HIGH POINT ENTERPRISE
Corporate/Parent Company: Paxton Media Group, LLC
Publication Street Address: 213 Woodbine St
City: High Point
State: NC
Publication Website: www.hpenews.com/
Postal Code: 27260-8339
Office phone: (336) 888-3500
General E-mail: mward@hpenews.com
Publisher Name: Nancy Baker
Publisher Email: nbaker@hpenews.com
Publisher Phone: 336-888-3655
Editor Name: Megan Ward
Editor Email: mward@hpenews.com
Editor Phone: 336-888-3543
Advertising Executive Name: David Jones
Advertising Executive Email: djones@hpenews.com
Advertising Executive Phone: 336-888-3545
Year Established: 1883
Delivery Methods:
Mail`Newsstand`Carrier`Racks
Own Printing Facility?: Y
Commercial printers?: Y
Mechanical specifications: Type page 11 x 21; E - 6 cols, 1.4792 Image area: 9.5" X 20.0"
Published Days: Mon`Tues`Wed`Thur`Fri`Sat`Sun
Weekday Frequency: m
Saturday Frequency: m
Avg Paid Circ: 10200
Avg Free Circ: 33000
Audit Company: Sworn/Estimate/Non-Audited
Audit Date: 7 12 2019
Pressroom Equipment: Manugraph 360; 20 units; 4 color towers
Mailroom Equipment: Goss inserter (29/1. 28/2); 4 stackers; 4 strappers
Buisness Equipment: mac/pc
Buisness Software: mediaspan
Classified Equipment: mac, pc
Classified Software: mediaspan
Editorial Equipment: mac, pc
Editorial Software: mediaspan
Total Circulation: 43200

JACKSONVILLE
THE DAILY NEWS
Corporate/Parent Company: Gannett
Publication Street Address: 724 Bell Fork Rd
City: Jacksonville
State: NC
Publication Website: www.jdnews.com
Postal Code: 28540-6311
Office phone: (910) 353-1171
Publisher Name: Michael Distelhorst
Publisher Email: Mike.Distelhorst@NewBernSJ.com
Publisher Phone: 910-219-8400
Editor Name: Chris Segal
Editor Email: chris.segal@gatehousemedia.com
Editor Phone: 910-219-8467
Advertising Executive Name: Ken Warren
Advertising Executive Email: Ken.Warren@JDNews.com
Advertising Executive Phone: 910-219-8410
Mechanical specifications: Type page 13 x 21 1/2; E - 6 cols, 2 1/16, 1/8 between; A - 6 cols, 2 1/16, 1/8 between; C - 8 cols, 1 1/2, 1/8 between.
Published Days: Mon`Tues`Wed`Thur`Fri`Sat`Sun
Weekday Frequency: m
Saturday Frequency: m
Avg Paid Circ: 9736
Avg Free Circ: 582
Audit Company: AAM
Audit Date: 27 02 2020
Pressroom Equipment: Lines – 8-HI/1660 1986; 6-G/Community;
Mailroom Equipment: Counter Stackers – HL; Tying Machines – 2/MLN.;
Buisness Equipment: PC Network
Buisness Software: Great Plains/AR2000
Classified Equipment: Hardware – PC Network; Printers – HP/5000;
Classified Software: APT.
Editorial Equipment: Hardware – PC Network/APP/Mac; Printers – HP/5000
Editorial Software: APT.
Production Equipment: Hardware – 2-Nu, PrePress/Panther 46; Cameras – Spartan III; Scanners – Polaroid/Sprintscan, APP/ScanJet
Production Software: APT.
Total Circulation: 7749

KINSTON
THE KINSTON FREE PRESS
Publication Street Address: 2103 N Queen St
City: Kinston
State: NC
Publication Website: www.kinston.com
Postal Code: 28501-1622
Office phone: (252) 527-3191

Publisher Phone: 252.559.1040
Editor Name: Chris Segal
Editor Email: chris.segal@gatehousemedia.com
Advertising Executive Name: Cassie Groff
Advertising Executive Email: Cassie.Groff@Kinston.com
Advertising Executive Phone: 252.559.1055
Year Established: 1882
Mechanical specifications: Type page 13 x 21 1/2; E - 6 cols, 2 1/16, 1/8 between; A - 6 cols, 2 1/16, 1/8 between; C - 8 cols, 1 15/32, 5/32 between.
Published Days: Mon`Tues`Wed`Thur`Fri`Sat`Sun
Weekday Frequency: m
Saturday Frequency: m
Avg Paid Circ: 4031
Avg Free Circ: 208
Audit Company: AAM
Audit Date: 31 03 2019
Pressroom Equipment: Lines – 3-G/Urbanite, 1-G/Urbanite (3 color).;
Mailroom Equipment: Tying Machines – 2/MLN.;
Buisness Equipment: 2-Compaq/Pro Linea 486, Great Plains, Ceridian, Microsoft/Office 97, Intel/Pentium II Fileserver, 4-Generic/Pentium PC, 1-Epson/DFX 8000 Printer, 1-Epson/DFX 5000 Printer, 2-Compaq/386 PC, 1-Compaq/486 DX PC, 1-Generic/486 PC, 1-Genicom Printer
Classified Equipment: Hardware – APP/Mac; Printers – 2-Okidata/320;
Classified Software: Baseview.
Editorial Equipment: Hardware – APP/Mac/APP/Mac Scanner; Printers – APP/Mac Accel-a-Writer 8200
Editorial Software: QPS/QuarkXPress, Baseview.
Production Equipment: Hardware – 2-Nu, 2-Xante/8200, Pre Press/Panther Pro 36, Pre Press/Panther Plus 46; Cameras – C/Spartan III; Scanners – AG, Kk/2035 plus, Linotype-Hell
Production Software: Baseview, QPS/QuarkXPress/with FSI Extensions.
Total Circulation: 4239

LAURINBURG

THE LAURINBURG EXCHANGE

Corporate/Parent Company: Champion Media
Publication Street Address: 211 W Cronly St
City: Laurinburg
State: NC
Publication Website: www.laurinburgexchange.com
Postal Code: 28352-3637
Office phone: (910) 276-2311
Publisher Name: Brian Bloom
Publisher Email: bbloom@yourdailyjournal.com
Editor Name: W. Curt Vincent
Editor Email: cvincent@laurinburgexchange.com
Editor Phone: 910-506-3023
Advertising Executive Name: Amy Johnson
Advertising Executive Email: amyjohnson@laurinburgexchange.com
Advertising Executive Phone: 910-506-3021
Year Established: 1882
Mechanical specifications: Type page 13 x 21 1/2; E - 6 cols, 2 1/16, between; A - 6 cols, 2 1/16, between.
Published Days: Tues`Wed`Thur`Fri`Sat
Weekday Frequency: m
Saturday Frequency: m
Avg Paid Circ: 8200
Audit Company: Sworn/Estimate/Non-Audited
Audit Date: 7 12 2019
Total Circulation: 8200

LENOIR

NEWS-TOPIC

Corporate/Parent Company: Paxton Media Group, LLC
Publication Street Address: 123 Penton Ave NW
City: Lenoir
State: NC
Publication Website: www.newstopicnews.com
Postal Code: 28645-4313
Office phone: (828) 758-7381
General E-mail: news@newstopicnews.com
Publisher Name: Guy Lucas
Publisher Email: guylucas@newstopicnews.com
Publisher Phone: 828-610-8719
Editor Name: Guy Lucas
Editor Email: guylucas@newstopicnews.com
Advertising Executive Name: Jim Rash
Advertising Executive Email: jrash@newstopicnews.com
Advertising Executive Phone: 828-610-8737
Year Established: 1875
Delivery Methods: Mail`Newsstand`Carrier`Racks
Own Printing Facility?: N
Commercial printers?: N
Mechanical specifications: Type page 11 5/8 x 21 1/2; E - 6 cols, 1 5/6, 1/8 between; A - 6 cols, 1 5/6, 1/8 between; C - 9 cols, 1 19/100, 13/100 between.
Published Days: Tues`Wed`Thur`Fri`Sun
Weekday Frequency: m
Avg Paid Circ: 5135
Avg Free Circ: 75
Audit Company: Sworn/Estimate/Non-Audited
Audit Date: 7 12 2019
Pressroom Equipment: Lines – 9-G/SSC Community 1997;
Mailroom Equipment: Counter Stackers – Mid America/Exact Stack; Inserters & Stuffers – KAN/480 5:1; Tying Machines – 1/MLN;
Buisness Equipment: DPT/1800, APP/Mac
Buisness Software: Great Plains, Citrix
Classified Equipment: Hardware – 4-APP/Mac G3; APP/Laser Printer; Printers – Okidata/3410;
Classified Software: Baseview.
Editorial Equipment: Hardware – 12-APP/Mac G3/1-Microtek/Scanner; Printers – Laser Master/Unity 1200, Xante
Editorial Software: Baseview.
Production Equipment: Hardware – PRO, Konica; Cameras – 1-C; Scanners – Microtek, Kk, Microtek
Production Software: QPS/QuarkXPress 4.0.
Total Circulation: 5210

LEXINGTON

THE DISPATCH

Corporate/Parent Company: Gannett
Publication Street Address: 30 E 1st Ave
City: Lexington
State: NC
Publication Website: www.the-dispatch.com
Postal Code: 27292-3302
Office phone: (336) 249-3981
Publisher Name: Nancy Wykle
Publisher Email: nwykle@hendersondispatch.com
Publisher Phone: (336) 249-3981, ext 210
Editor Name: Nancy Wykle
Editor Email: nwykle@hendersondispatch.com
Editor Phone: (336) 249-3981, ext. 215
Advertising Executive Name: Desiree Brooks
Advertising Executive Email: dbrooks@hendersondispatch.com
Advertising Executive Phone: (336) 249-3981, ext. 208
Year Established: 1882
Delivery Methods: Mail`Newsstand`Carrier`Racks
Own Printing Facility?: Y
Commercial printers?: N
Mechanical specifications: Type page 13 x 21 1/2; E - 6 cols, 1 7/8, 1/8 between; A - 6 cols, 1 7/8, 1/8 between; C - 9 cols, 1 3/16, 1/16 between.
Published Days: Tues`Wed`Thur`Fri`Sat
Weekday Frequency: e
Saturday Frequency: m
Avg Paid Circ: 5045
Avg Free Circ: 416
Audit Company: AAM
Audit Date: 19 05 2020
Pressroom Equipment: Lines – G/Urbanite 1995; Folders – 1-Hl.;
Classified Equipment: Hardware – AT.;
Editorial Equipment: Hardware – AT.
Production Equipment: Hardware – V.
Total Circulation: 4845

LUMBERTON

THE ROBESONIAN

Corporate/Parent Company: Champion Media
Publication Street Address: 2175 N Roberts Ave
City: Lumberton
State: NC
Publication Website: www.robesonian.com
Postal Code: 28358-2867
Office phone: (910) 739-4322
Publisher Name: Denise Ward
Publisher Email: dward@robesonian.com
Publisher Phone: 910-416-5867
Editor Name: Donnie Douglas
Editor Email: ddouglas@robesonian.com
Editor Phone: 910-416-5649
Advertising Executive Name: Marty Deaver
Advertising Executive Email: mdeaver@robesonian.com
Year Established: 1889
Delivery Methods: Mail`Newsstand`Carrier`Racks
Mechanical specifications: Type page 13 x 21; E - 6 cols, 2 1/16, 1/4 between; A - 6 cols, 2 1/16, 1/4 between; C - 6 cols, 2 1/16, 1/4 between.
Published Days: Wed
Avg Paid Circ: 2300
Audit Company: Sworn/Estimate/Non-Audited
Audit Date: 6 10 2019
Total Circulation: 2300

MARION

THE MCDOWELL NEWS

Corporate/Parent Company: Lee Enterprises
Publication Street Address: 136 N Logan St
City: Marion
State: NC
Publication Website: www.mcdowellnews.com
Postal Code: 28752-3754
Office phone: (828) 652-3313
Editor Name: Scott Hollifield
Editor Email: RHollifield@mcdowellnews.com
Advertising Executive Name: Nina Linens
Advertising Executive Email: jlinens@morganton.com
Own Printing Facility?: N
Commercial printers?: N
Published Days: Tues`Wed`Thur`Fri`Sun
Weekday Frequency: m
Avg Paid Circ: 2709
Avg Free Circ: 149
Audit Company: AAM
Audit Date: 6 05 2019
Classified Equipment: Hardware – COM.;
Editorial Equipment: Hardware – COM.
Total Circulation: 3138

MORGANTON

THE NEWS HERALD

Corporate/Parent Company: Gannett
Publication Street Address: 301 Collett St
City: Morganton
State: NC
Publication Website: www.morganton.com
Postal Code: 28655-3322
Office phone: (828) 437-2161
General E-mail: news@morganton.com
Editor Name: Lisa Wall
Editor Email: lwall@morganton.com
Editor Phone: 828-432-8939
Advertising Executive Name: Nina Linens
Advertising Executive Phone: jlinens@morganton.com
Own Printing Facility?: N
Commercial printers?: N
Mechanical specifications: Type page 13 1/4 x 21 1/2; E - 6 cols, 2, 1/8 between; A - 6 cols, 2, 1/8 between; C - 10 cols, 1 3/16, 1/16 between.
Published Days: Mon`Tues`Wed`Thur`Fri`Sun
Weekday Frequency: m
Avg Paid Circ: 4368
Avg Free Circ: 391
Audit Company: AAM
Audit Date: 13 05 2019
Pressroom Equipment: Lines – 9-G 1994;
Mailroom Equipment: Tying Machines – 1/Dynaric; Address Machine – 1-X/730.;
Buisness Equipment: 3-HP/Vision Data
Classified Equipment: Hardware – 3-APP/Mac;
Classified Software: Baseview.
Editorial Equipment: Hardware – APP/Mac; Printers – ECR
Editorial Software: Baseview.
Production Equipment: Hardware – 1-3M, Adobe/Photoshop; Cameras – 1-Nu; Scanners – APP/Mac.
Total Circulation: 3138

MOUNT AIRY

MOUNT AIRY NEWS

Corporate/Parent Company: Adams Publishing Group
Publication Street Address: 319 N Renfro St
City: Mount Airy
State: NC
Publication Website: www.mtairynews.com
Postal Code: 27030-3838
Office phone: (336) 786-4141
Publisher Name: Sandra Hurley
Publisher Email: shurley@mtairynews.com
Publisher Phone: 336-415-4635
Editor Name: John Peters
Editor Email: jpeters@mtairynews.com
Editor Phone: 336-719-1931
Advertising Executive Name: Serena Bowman
Advertising Executive Email: serena.bowman@mtairynews.com
Advertising Executive Phone: 336-415-4684
Year Established: 1880
Own Printing Facility?: Y
Mechanical specifications: Type page 10 5/16 x 13; E - 4 cols, 2 1/2, 1/8 between; A - 4 cols, 2 1/2, 1/8 between; C - 4 cols, 2 1/2, 1/8 between.
Published Days: Tues`Wed`Thur`Fri`Sat`Sun
Weekday Frequency: m
Saturday Frequency: m
Avg Paid Circ: 12000
Avg Free Circ: 12000
Audit Company: Sworn/Estimate/Non-Audited
Audit Date: 7 12 2019
Pressroom Equipment: Lines – 6-G/Community 1975.;
Mailroom Equipment: Tying Machines – 2-MLN/Spirit; Wrapping Singles – KR/Quarterfolder 324; Address Machine – KR.;
Buisness Equipment: PC (IBM compatible)
Buisness Software: Business/Software
Classified Equipment: Hardware – 2-APP/Mac, 2-APP/Mac G3; Printers – Okidata;
Classified Software: Baseview.
Editorial Equipment: Hardware – 7-APP/Mac 7200-120, 6-APP/Mac 7200-90, 4-APP/iMac, 3-APP/Mac G3, 3-APP/Mac 7200-120, APP/Mac 8500-120, 1-APP/Mac G4/APP/Mac LC, Lf/AP Leaf Picture Desk, APP/Mac 8500-120, Polaroid/SprintScan, AG/Scanner, San/Disk, LF/AP Leaf Pictur
Production Equipment: Hardware – APP/Mac LaserWriter Plus, APP/Mac LaserWriter IIg, 2-APP/Mac G3, 2-APP/Mac 7200-120, 1-APP/Mac G4; Cameras – SCREEN/C-260-D; Scanners – Polaroid/SprintScan, AG/Argus II
Production Software: QPS/QuarkXPress, Multi-Ad/Creator.
Total Circulation: 24000

NAGS HEAD

OUTER BANKS VOICE

City: Nags Head
State: NC
Publication Website: www.obxvoice.com
Office phone: 252-480-2234
General E-mail: info@outerbanksvoice.com
Publisher Name: Rob Morris
Publisher Email: info@outerbanksvoice.com
Editor Name: Sam Walker
Advertising Executive Name: Mike Fulton

U.S. Daily Newspapers

NEW BERN

THE SUN JOURNAL
Corporate/Parent Company: Gannett
Publication Street Address: 3200 Wellons Blvd
City: New Bern
State: NC
Publication Website: www.newbernsj.com
Postal Code: 28562-5234
Office phone: (252) 638-8101
Publisher Phone: 252-635-5629
Editor Name: Matt Hinson
Editor Email: Matt.Hinson@GateHouseMedia.com
Editor Phone: 252-635-5663
Advertising Executive Name: Ken Warren
Advertising Executive Email: Kon.Warren@jdnews.com
Advertising Executive Phone: 910-219-8410
Year Established: 1783
Delivery Methods:
  Mail`Newsstand`Carrier`Racks
Mechanical specifications: Type page 13 x 21 1/2; E - 6 cols, 2 1/16, 1/8 between; A - 6 cols, 2 1/16, 1/8 between; C - 8 cols, 1 1/2, 1/8 between.
Published Days: Mon`Tues`Wed`Thur`Fri`Sat`Sun
Weekday Frequency: m
Saturday Frequency: m
Avg Paid Circ: 8801
Avg Free Circ: 259
Audit Company: AAM
Audit Date: 9 03 2020
Mailroom Equipment: Tying Machines – Dynaric;
Buisness Equipment: PC
Buisness Software: Vision Data, Southware
Total Circulation: 7512

NEWPORT

COASTAL REVIEW ONLINE
Corporate/Parent Company: North Carolina Coastal Federation
Publication Street Address: 3609 N.C. 24
City: Newport
State: NC
Publication Website: www.nccoast.org
Postal Code: 28570
Office phone: 252-393-8185
General E-mail: info@nccoast.org
Editor Name: Mark Hibbs
Editor Email: markh@nccoast.org
Editor Phone: 252-393-8185

NEWTON

THE OBSERVER NEWS ENTERPRISE
Corporate/Parent Company: Horizon Publications Inc.
Publication Street Address: 309 N College Ave
City: Newton
State: NC
Publication Website: www.observernewsonline.com
Postal Code: 28658-3255
Office phone: (828) 464-0221
General E-mail: onenews@observernewsonline.com
Editor Name: Seth Mabry
Editor Email: onenews@observernewsonline.com
Advertising Executive Name: Cindy Hul
Advertising Executive Email: onecirculation@observernewsonline.com
Year Established: 1879
Mechanical specifications: Type page 13 x 21; E - 6 cols, 2 1/16, 1/8 between; A - 6 cols, 2 1/16, 1/8 between; C - 10 cols, 1 3/16, 3/32 between.
Published Days: Tues`Wed`Thur`Fri`Sat
Weekday Frequency: m
Saturday Frequency: m
Avg Paid Circ: 2303
Audit Company: Sworn/Estimate/Non-Audited
Audit Date: 7 12 2019
Pressroom Equipment: Lines – 7-KP/Offset web 1976; 1-Stubbs/Stacker; Control System – TF&E/Press Room Devices;
Mailroom Equipment: Address Machine – Am.;
Buisness Equipment: L/9000
Classified Equipment: Hardware – COM.;
Editorial Equipment: Hardware – COM; Printers – COM.
Production Equipment: Hardware – COM; Cameras – LE.
Total Circulation: 2303

RALEIGH

NC POLICY WATCH
Corporate/Parent Company: North Carolina Justice Center
Publication Street Address: 224 S. Dawson Street
City: Raleigh
State: NC
Publication Website: www.ncpolicywatch.com
Postal Code: 27601
Office phone: 919-861-2065
General E-mail: info@ncpolicywatch.com
Editor Name: Billy Ball
Editor Email: illness.billy@ncpolicywatch.com
Editor Phone: 919-861-1460

REIDSVILLE

THE EDEN DAILY NEWS
Publication Street Address: 1921 Vance St
City: Reidsville
State: NC
Publication Website: www.newsadvance.com
Postal Code: 27320-3254
Office phone: (336) 349-4331
Publisher Name: Kelly E. Mirt
Publisher Email: kmirt@newsadvance.com
Publisher Phone: 434-385-5570
Editor Name: Caroline Glickman
Editor Email: cglickman@newsadvance.com
Editor Phone: 434-385-5552
Advertising Executive Name: Kevin Smith
Advertising Executive Email: Ksmith@newsadvance.com
Advertising Executive Phone: 434-385-5462
Mechanical specifications: Type page 13 x 21 1/2; E - 6 cols, 2 1/16, 1/8 between; A - 6 cols, 2 1/16, 1/8 between; C - 9 cols, 1 1/3, 1/8 between.
Published Days: Tues`Wed`Thur`Fri`Sun
Weekday Frequency: m
Avg Paid Circ: 3961
Audit Company: Sworn/Estimate/Non-Audited
Audit Date: 7 12 2019
Buisness Equipment: IBM
Buisness Software: Vision Data
Classified Equipment: Hardware – 10-Mk, APP/Mac; Printers – HP/5000;
Classified Software: Baseview.
Editorial Equipment: Hardware – APP/Mac, 10-MkPrinters – APP/Mac, HP/5000, APP/Mac LaserPrinter NT
Editorial Software: QPS 3.3, Baseview/NewsEdit.
Production Equipment: Hardware – P
Production Software: QPS 3.3.
Total Circulation: 3961

ROANOKE RAPIDS

DAILY HERALD
Corporate/Parent Company: Paxton Media Group, LLC
Publication Street Address: 916 Roanoke Ave
City: Roanoke Rapids
State: NC
Publication Website: www.rrdailyherald.com
Postal Code: 27870-2720
Office phone: (252) 537-2505
Publisher Name: Nancy Wykle
Publisher Email: nwykle@rrdailyherald.com
Publisher Phone: (252) 410-7065
Editor Name: Tia Bedwell
Editor Email: tiabedwell@rrdailyherald.com
Editor Phone: (252) 410-7056
Advertising Executive Name: Desiree Brooks
Advertising Executive Email: dbrooks@rrdailyherald.com
Advertising Executive Phone: (252) 410-7040
Year Established: 1914
Mechanical specifications: Type page 13 x 21 1/2; E - 6 cols, 2 1/16, 1/8 between; A - 6 cols, 2 1/16, 1/8 between; C - 9 cols, 1 5/16, 1/8 between.
Published Days: Tues`Wed`Thur`Fri`Sun
Weekday Frequency: e
Saturday Frequency: m
Avg Paid Circ: 6156
Audit Company: VAC
Audit Date: 30 06 2015
Pressroom Equipment: Lines – 7-WPC/Web Atlas-Leader single width 1993; Reels & Stands – 6;
Mailroom Equipment: Tying Machines – 1/Bu; Address Machine – Vision Data.;
Buisness Software: Vision Data
Classified Equipment: Hardware – APP/Mac G3;
Classified Software: Baseview 3.16.
Editorial Equipment: Hardware – Mk/3000/Nikon/Coolscan; Printers – 1-Xante/8200, 1-APP/Mac G3.
Production Equipment: Hardware – Nat; Cameras – 1-B, Acti/Prod Camera; Scanners – Konica/Scanner
Production Software: Baseview 3.16.
Total Circulation: 6156

ROCKINGHAM

RICHMOND COUNTY DAILY JOURNAL
Corporate/Parent Company: Champion Media
Publication Street Address: 607 East Broad Ave. Suite B.
City: Rockingham
State: NC
Publication Website: www.yourdailyjournal.com
Postal Code: 28379
Office phone: (910) 997-3111
General E-mail: rcdjnews@yourdailyjournal.com
Publisher Name: Brian Bloom
Publisher Email: bbloom@yourdailyjournal.com
Publisher Phone: 910-817-2667 x 2742
Editor Name: Bob Leininger
Editor Email: rleininger@yourdailyjournal.com
Advertising Executive Name: Beth Howell
Advertising Executive Email: bhowell@yourdailyjournal.com
Year Established: 1931
Delivery Methods: Newsstand`Carrier`Racks
Own Printing Facility?: Y
Commercial printers?: N
Mechanical specifications: Type page 11x 21; E - 6 cols, 1 5/6, 1/8 between; A - 6 cols, 1 5/6, 1/8 between; C - 10 cols, 1 5/6, 1/8 between.
Published Days: Tues`Wed`Thur`Fri`Sat`Sun
Weekday Frequency: m
Saturday Frequency: m
Avg Paid Circ: 6575
Avg Free Circ: 100
Audit Company: Sworn/Estimate/Non-Audited
Audit Date: 7 12 2019
Mailroom Equipment: Address Machine – 2-/El.;
Buisness Equipment: Vision Data
Classified Equipment: Hardware – Baseview.;
Editorial Equipment: Hardware – APP/Mac/Rip Mac; Printers – APP/Mac LaserWriter Pro
Editorial Software: Newsengine
Total Circulation: 6675

ROCKY MOUNT

ROCKY MOUNT TELEGRAM
Corporate/Parent Company: Cox
Publication Street Address: 1151 Falls Road Suite 2008
City: Rocky Mount
State: NC
Publication Website: www.rockymounttelegram.com
Postal Code: 27804
Office phone: 252-366-8190
Publisher Name: Kyle Stephens
Publisher Email: kstephens@rmtelegram.com
Publisher Phone: 252-366-8146
Editor Name: Gene Metrick
Editor Email: gmetrick@rmtelegram.com
Editor Phone: 252-366-8141
Advertising Executive Name: Chris Taylor
Advertising Executive Email: ctaylor@rmtelegram.com
Advertising Executive Phone: 252-366-8134
Year Established: 1910
Delivery Methods:
  Mail`Newsstand`Carrier`Racks
Own Printing Facility?: N
Commercial printers?: Y
Mechanical specifications: Type page 13 x 21; E - 6 cols, 2, 1/8 between; A - 6 cols, 2, 1/8 between; C - 6 cols, 1 1/8, 1/16 between.
Published Days: Mon`Tues`Wed`Thur`Fri`Sat`Sun
Weekday Frequency: m
Saturday Frequency: m
Avg Paid Circ: 9193
Avg Free Circ: 2095
Audit Company: AAM
Audit Date: 10 10 2017
Pressroom Software: Libercus effective 9/1/15
Mailroom Equipment: Tying Machines – 2/OVL.;
Buisness Equipment: PC
Buisness Software: Brainworks
Classified Equipment: Hardware – APP/Power Mac;
Classified Software: Brainworks
Editorial Equipment: Hardware – APP/Power Mac/APP/Mac; Printers – HP/5MP, Xante/8300
Editorial Software: DTI 4.2. Libercus
Production Equipment: Hardware/Mac – DTI.
Production Software: DTI/Libercus
Total Circulation: 11288

SALISBURY

SALISBURY POST
Corporate/Parent Company: Boone Newspapers, Inc.
Publication Street Address: 131 W Innes St
City: Salisbury
State: NC
Publication Website: www.salisburypost.com
Postal Code: 28144-4338
Office phone: (704) 633-8950
General E-mail: webmaster@salisburypost.com
Publisher Name: John Carr
Publisher Email: john.carr@salisburypost.com
Editor Name: Josh Bergeron
Editor Email: josh.bergeron@salisburypost.com
Editor Phone: 704-797-4248
Year Established: 1905
Mechanical specifications: Type page 11 1/2 x 21; E - 6 cols, 2 1/16, 1/8 between; A - 6 cols, 2 1/16, 1/8 between; C - 9 cols, 1 3/8, 1/16 between.
Published Days: Mon`Tues`Wed`Thur`Fri`Sat`Sun
Weekday Frequency: m
Saturday Frequency: m
Avg Paid Circ: 15086
Audit Company: AAM
Audit Date: 30 09 2014
Pressroom Equipment: Lines – 7-G/Metroliner 3 decks double width 1982; Folders – 4-G/2:1, Regent/2:1.;
Mailroom Equipment: Counter Stackers – 1/HL, 1-/MM, 2-QWI/SJ300, 1-QWI/J400, 2-/HL; Inserters & Stuffers – 1-/MM, 1-/1372P; Tying Machines – 1-/Dynaric, 1-/Dynaric, 1-/QWI; Address Machine – 2-/Dispensa-Matic/U-45.;
Buisness Equipment: 2-Convergent/Mighty Frame, 8-Wyse
Buisness Software: Vision Data
Classified Equipment: Hardware – Ik, Baseview, APP/Power Mac, 5-APP/Mac G3; Printers – 1-Centronics;
Classified Software: ECS 4, Ad Manager Pro, Classflow, QPS/QuarkXPress, Ad Force II.
Editorial Equipment: Hardware – Ik, QPS/QuarkXPress, APP/Mac Server, APP/iMac, APP/Mac G3, APP/Mac G4/1-APP/Mac, DTI/PageSpeed, Kk/2035 Scanner; Printers – 2-Epson, 2-C.Itoh, 1-Centronics, AU/APS 6600, APP/Mac LaserWriter, Phases/440 Color
Editorial Software: ECS 4, QPS/
Production Equipment: Hardware – Caere/OmniPage 6.0, 1-APP/Super Mac, Adobe/

SANFORD

SANFORD HERALD

Corporate/Parent Company: Paxton Media Group, LLC
Publication Street Address: 208 Saint Clair Ct
City: Sanford
State: NC
Publication Website: www.sanfordherald.com
Postal Code: 27330-3916
Office phone: (919) 708-9000
General E-mail: jayers@sanfordherald.com
Publisher Name: Jeff Ayers
Publisher Email: jayers@sanfordherald.com
Publisher Phone: (919) 718-1233
Editor Name: F.T. Norton
Editor Email: editor@sanfordherald.com
Editor Phone: (919) 718-1219
Advertising Executive Name: Laura Powers
Advertising Executive Email: laurap@sanfordherald.com
Advertising Executive Phone: (919) 718-1212

Photoshop, Kk/Scanner, Adobe/Acrobat, Macromedia/Freehand, 36-Laser Imagers, 1-Xante/Color Proofer; Cameras – 1-C/Spartan II, 1-C/Spartan III; Scanners – 1-ECR/Autokon 1000, 2-Umax/1200 dpi color scan
Total Circulation: 15086

SHELBY

THE STAR

Corporate/Parent Company: Gannett
Publication Street Address: 315 E Graham St
City: Shelby
State: NC
Publication Website: www.shelbystar.com
Postal Code: 28150-5452
Office phone: 704-669-3350
Publisher Name: Lucy Talley
Publisher Email: ltalley@gastongazette.com
Publisher Phone: 704-869-1702
Editor Name: Diane Turbyfill
Editor Email: dturbyfill@shelbystar.com
Editor Phone: 704-669-3334
Advertising Executive Name: Mary Pettus
Advertising Executive Email: mary.pettus@gastongazette.com
Advertising Executive Phone: 704-669-3305
Year Established: 1894
Delivery Methods: Carrier
Commercial printers?: Y
Mechanical specifications: Type page 11 1/3 x 21 1/2; E - 6 cols, 1 4/5, 1/8 between; A - 6 cols, 1 4/5, 1/8 between; C - 9 cols, 1 1/5, 1/8 between.
Published Days: Mon`Tues`Wed`Thur`Fri`Sat`Sun
Weekday Frequency: m
Saturday Frequency: m
Avg Paid Circ: 14164
Audit Company: Sworn/Estimate/Non-Audited
Audit Date: 7 12 2019
Pressroom Equipment: Lines – 6-G/Urbanite; Folders – G/2:1; Reels & Stands – 6;
Mailroom Equipment: Counter Stackers – 1/QWI; Tying Machines – 2-/Strapex; Wrapping Singles – 1-/QWI; Address Machine – 1-/KR;
Buisness Equipment: 1-IBM/Newzware
Buisness Software: Great Plains Dynamics, Newzware, APT, Ceridian
Classified Equipment: Hardware – 3-PC, 2-PC P166, 1-PC P100; Printers – HP/4MV;
Classified Software: APT/ACT 2.06.03.
Editorial Equipment: Hardware – 3-Compaq/Proliant Server 600/19-PC, 1-APP/Mac, 1-MS/NT Workstation, 1-SII/Workstation, 3-Compaq/Servers, 1-IBM Server, 1-Compaq/UniX Server; Printers – 1-HP/4000, 1-HP/4MV, 1-Epson/Stylus, 1-Pre Press/Panther 46, 2-HP/8150, 1-HP/5
Production Equipment: Hardware – 2-Pre Press/Panther Pro 46, AG/Duoscan, Pentium/PC II, Microtek; Cameras – 1-B, 1-SCREEN; Scanners – 1-AG/Duoscan, 1-Acer/Microtech
Production Software: APT/ACT 2.06.03, Microsoft/NT 4.0.
Total Circulation: 14164

STATESVILLE

STATESVILLE RECORD & LANDMARK

Corporate/Parent Company: Lee Enterprises
Publication Street Address: 222 E Broad St
City: Statesville
State: NC
Publication Website: www.statesville.com
Postal Code: 28677-5325
Office phone: (704) 873-1451
General E-mail: news@statesville.com
Editor Name: John Deem
Advertising Executive Name: Tiffany Hovis
Advertising Executive Email: thovis@statesville.com, advertising@statesville.com
Year Established: 1874
Delivery Methods: Mail`Newsstand`Carrier`Racks
Own Printing Facility?: Y
Commercial printers?: Y
Published Days: Mon`Tues`Wed`Thur`Fri`Sat`Sun
Weekday Frequency: m
Saturday Frequency: m
Avg Paid Circ: 5728
Avg Free Circ: 266
Audit Company: AAM
Audit Date: 15 06 2015
Mailroom Equipment: Tying Machines – Alles.;
Total Circulation: 10311

TRYON

TRYON DAILY BULLETIN

Corporate/Parent Company: Boone Newspapers, Inc.
Publication Street Address: 16 N Trade St
City: Tryon
State: NC
Publication Website: www.tryondailybulletin.com
Postal Code: 28782-6656
Office phone: (828) 859-9151
General E-mail: stacey.tully@tryondailybulletin.com
Publisher Name: Kevin Powell
Publisher Email: kevin.powell@tryondailybulletin.com
Publisher Phone: 828-859-9151
Editor Name: Kevin Powell
Editor Email: kevin.powell@tryondailybulletin.com
Advertising Executive Name: Kevin Powell
Advertising Executive Email: kevin.powell@tryondailybulletin.com
Year Established: 1928
Delivery Methods: Mail`Newsstand`Racks
Own Printing Facility?: Y
Published Days: Tues`Wed`Thur`Fri`Sun
Weekday Frequency: m
Avg Paid Circ: 4250
Audit Company: Sworn/Estimate/Non-Audited
Audit Date: 7 12 2019
Pressroom Equipment: Lines – 2-KP/News King.;
Mailroom Equipment: Address Machine – 1-Automecha/Accufast PL.;
Buisness Equipment: MAC
Classified Equipment: Hardware – PC;
Classified Software: Aldus/PageMaker, Alpha 4.
Editorial Equipment: Hardware – MAC; Printers – APP/Mac LaserPrinter, Canon/LBP4
Editorial Software: Aldus/PageMaker.
Production Equipment: Hardware – Nu/Plate Maker
Production Software: Aldus/PageMaker.
Total Circulation: 4250

WASHINGTON

WASHINGTON DAILY NEWS

Corporate/Parent Company: Boone Newspapers, Inc.
Publication Street Address: 217 N Market St
City: Washington
State: NC
Publication Website: www.wdnweb.com
Postal Code: 27889-4949
Office phone: (252) 946-2144
General E-mail: news@thewashingtondailynews.com
Publisher Name: Ashley Vansant
Publisher Email: ashley.vansant@thewashingtondailynews.com
Editor Name: Vail Rumley
Editor Email: vail.rumley@thewashingtondailynews.com
Advertising Executive Name: David Singleton
Advertising Executive Email: david.singleton@thewashingtondailynews.com
Year Established: 1909
Mechanical specifications: Type page 13 x 21 1/2; E - 6 cols, 2 1/16, 1/8 between; A - 6 cols, 2 1/16, 1/8 between; C - 6 cols, 2 1/16, 1/8 between.
Published Days: Mon`Tues`Wed`Thur`Fri`Sat`Sun
Weekday Frequency: m
Saturday Frequency: m
Avg Paid Circ: 8644
Audit Company: Sworn/Estimate/Non-Audited
Audit Date: 7 12 2019
Pressroom Equipment: Lines – 1-Zenith/Jobber 22, G/Community SC; 5-G/SC 210; Folders – 1, 1.;
Mailroom Equipment: Tying Machines – 1/Strap Tyer; Address Machine – 4-/Wm.;
Buisness Equipment: 1-Bs, 1-TI/300A, DSI/Papertrak
Buisness Software: Business/Software
Classified Equipment: Hardware – Mk.;
Editorial Equipment: Hardware – 9-Mk.
Production Equipment: Hardware – 1-Nu, 1-M; Cameras – 1-Nu, C.
Total Circulation: 8644

WILMINGTON

STARNEWS

Publication Street Address: 115 N. 3rd St., Suite 400
City: Wilmington
State: NC
Publication Website: starnewsonline.com
Postal Code: 28401
Office phone: (910) 343-2000
Publisher Phone: 910-343-2209
Editor Name: Sherry Jones
Editor Email: sherry.jones@starnewsonline.com
Editor Phone: 910-343-2378
Advertising Executive Name: Cheryl Theiss
Advertising Executive Email: cheryl.theiss@starnewsonline.com
Advertising Executive Phone: 910-343-2337
Published Days: Mon`Tues`Wed`Thur`Fri`Sat`Sun
Weekday Frequency: m
Saturday Frequency: m
Avg Paid Circ: 17738
Avg Free Circ: 1457
Audit Company: AAM
Audit Date: 31 03 2019
Total Circulation: 19195

WILSON

THE WILSON TIMES

Publication Street Address: 126 Nash St NE
City: Wilson
State: NC
Publication Website: www.wilsontimes.com
Postal Code: 27893-4013
Office phone: (252) 243-5151
General E-mail: customer@wilsontimes.com
Publisher Name: Keven Zepezauer
Publisher Email: kzepezauer@restorationnewsmedia.com
Publisher Phone: (252) 265-7812
Editor Name: Corey Friedman
Editor Email: cfriedman@wilsontimes.com
Advertising Executive Name: Shana Hoover
Advertising Executive Email: shana@wilsontimes.com
Advertising Executive Phone: (252) 265-7858
Year Established: 1896
Delivery Methods: Mail`Newsstand`Carrier`Racks
Own Printing Facility?: N
Commercial printers?: Y
Mechanical specifications: Type page 12 1/2 x 21; E - 6 cols, 1 13/16, 1/8 between; A - 6 cols, 1 13/16, 1/8 between; C - 9 cols, 1 13/16, 1/16 between.
Published Days: Mon`Tues`Wed`Thur`Fri`Sat
Weekday Frequency: m
Saturday Frequency: m
Avg Paid Circ: 10762
Audit Company: CAC
Audit Date: 31 12 2016
Buisness Equipment: Mac
Buisness Software: Quickbooks
Classified Equipment: Mac
Classified Software: Ad Manager Pro; Indesign; Creative Cloud
Editorial Equipment: Mac
Editorial Software: Folderflow; Creative Cloud
Production Equipment: Mac
Production Software: Indesign; Creative Cloud
Total Circulation: 10762

WINSTON SALEM

WINSTON-SALEM JOURNAL

Corporate/Parent Company: Lee Enterprises
Publication Street Address: 418 N Marshall St
City: Winston Salem
State: NC
Publication Website: www.journalnow.com
Postal Code: 27101-2815
Office phone: (336) 727-7211
General E-mail: contact@wsjournal.com
Publisher Name: Alton Brown
Publisher Email: abrown@wsjournal.com
Publisher Phone: 336-727-7349
Editor Name: Andy Morrissey
Editor Email: amorrissey@wsjournal.com
Editor Phone: 336-727-7389
Year Established: 1897
Delivery Methods: Newsstand`Carrier`Racks
Own Printing Facility?: Y
Commercial printers?: Y
Mechanical specifications: Type page 12 x 21; E - 6 cols, 1 7/8, 1/8 between; A - 6 cols, 1 7/8, 1/8 between; C - 9 cols, 1 3/16, 1/16 between.
Published Days: Mon`Tues`Wed`Thur`Fri`Sat`Sun
Weekday Frequency: m
Saturday Frequency: m
Avg Paid Circ: 34510
Avg Free Circ: 1357
Audit Company: AAM
Audit Date: 7 12 2018
Pressroom Equipment: Reels & Stands – 10;
Mailroom Equipment: Counter Stackers – 3-HL/Monitor, 6-QWI/300; Inserters & Stuffers – 2-GMA/SLS 1000 20:2; Tying Machines – 3/OVL, 6-/Dynaric; Address Machine – 2-/Ch, 1-/KR.;
Buisness Equipment: HP/3000 918LX
Classified Equipment: Hardware – 2-IBM/RS 6000-F40; IBM/RS6000, IBM/43P, HI/Classified Pagination; Printers – HP/LaserJet 4000;
Classified Software: AT/Enterprise.
Editorial Equipment: Hardware – 6-AT/9000/AT/Ed Page, 9-IBM/RS6000
Editorial Software: AT/Editorial 4.7.7.
Production Equipment: Hardware – 3-III/3810, 1-III/3850, 1-ECR; Scanners – 1-III/3750, 1-III/3725
Production Software: AT.
Note: Carolina Wedding Show, Scripps National Spelling Bee
Total Circulation: 43029

NORTH DAKOTA

BISMARCK

THE BISMARCK TRIBUNE

Corporate/Parent Company: Lee Enterprises
Publication Street Address: 707 E Front Ave

U.S. Daily Newspapers

City: Bismarck
State: ND
Publication Website: www.bismarcktribune.com
Postal Code: 58504-5646
Office phone: (701) 223-2500
General E-mail: news@bismarcktribune.com
Publisher Name: Gary Adkisson
Publisher Email: gary.adkisson@bismarcktribune.com
Publisher Phone: (701) 250-8299
Editor Name: Amy Dalrymple
Editor Email: amy.dalrymple@bismarcktribune.com
Editor Phone: (701) 250-8267
Advertising Executive Name: Lisa Weisz
Advertising Executive Email: lisa.weisz@bismarcktribune.com
Advertising Executive Phone: (701) 250-8232

DEVILS LAKE

DEVILS LAKE JOURNAL

Corporate/Parent Company: Gannett
Publication Street Address: 516 4th St NE
City: Devils Lake
State: ND
Publication Website: https://www.devilslakejournal.com/
Postal Code: 58301
Office phone: (701) 662-2127
General E-mail: loleson@devilslakejournal.com
Editor Name: Louise Oleson
Editor Email: loleson@devilslakejournal.com
Advertising Executive Name: Patty Schwab
Advertising Executive Email: classifieds@devilslakejournal.com

DICKINSON

THE DICKINSON PRESS

Corporate/Parent Company: Forum Communications
Publication Street Address: 1815 1st St W
City: Dickinson
State: ND
Publication Website: www.thedickinsonpress.com
Postal Code: 58601-2463
Office phone: (701) 225-8111
General E-mail: bcarruth@thedickinsonpress.com
Editor Name: James Miller
Editor Email: jmiller@thedickinsonpress.com
Editor Phone: (701) 456-1206
Advertising Executive Name: Jenn Binstock
Advertising Executive Email: jbinstock@thedickinsonpress.com
Advertising Executive Phone: (701) 456-1222

FARGO

FARGO FORUM

Corporate/Parent Company: INFORUM and Forum Communications Company
Publication Street Address: 101 5th Street North
City: Fargo
State: ND
Publication Website: www.inforum.com
Postal Code: 58102
Office phone: (701) 235-7311
General E-mail: news@forumcomm.com
Publisher Name: Bill Marcil Jr.
Editor Name: Matthew Von Pinnon
Editor Email: mvonpinnon@forumcomm.com
Editor Phone: (701) 241-5579
Advertising Executive Name: Mark Von Bank
Advertising Executive Email: mvonbank@forumcomm.com
Advertising Executive Phone: (701) 241-5561

FARGO/MOORHEAD- THE FORUM

Corporate/Parent Company: Forum Communications
Publication Street Address: 101 5th Street North
City: Fargo
State: ND
Publication Website: www.inforum.com
Postal Code: 58102
Office phone: (701) 235-7311
General E-mail: news@forumcomm.com
Editor Name: Matthew Von Pinnon
Editor Email: mvonpinnon@forumcomm.com
Editor Phone: (701) 241-5579
Advertising Executive Name: Mark VonBank
Advertising Executive Email: mvonbank@forumcomm.com
Advertising Executive Phone: (701) 241-5561

GRAND FORKS

GRAND FORKS HERALD

Corporate/Parent Company: Forum Communications
Publication Street Address: 375 2nd Ave N
City: Grand Forks
State: ND
Publication Website: www.grandforksherald.com
Postal Code: 58203
Office phone: (701) 780-1100
General E-mail: news@gfherald.com
Publisher Name: Korrie Wenzel
Publisher Email: kwenzel@gfherald.com
Publisher Phone: (701) 780-1103
Advertising Executive Name: Staci Lord
Advertising Executive Email: slord@gfherald.com
Advertising Executive Phone: (701) 780-1156

GRAND FORKS

GRAND FORKS HERALD

Corporate/Parent Company: Forum Communications
Publication Street Address: 375 2nd Ave N
City: Grand Forks
State: ND
Publication Website: https://www.grandforksherald.com/
Postal Code: 58203
Office phone: (701) 780-1100
General E-mail: letters@gfherald.com
Publisher Name: Korrie Wenzel
Publisher Email: kwenzel@gfherald.com
Publisher Phone: (701) 780-1103
Editor Name: Korrie Wenzel
Editor Email: kwenzel@gfherald.com
Editor Phone: (701) 780-1103
Advertising Executive Name: Staci Lord
Advertising Executive Email: slord@gfherald.com
Advertising Executive Phone: (701) 780-1156

MINOT

MINOT DAILY NEWS

Corporate/Parent Company: Ogden Newspapers, Inc.
Publication Street Address: 301 4th St SE
City: Minot
State: ND
Publication Website: www.minotdailynews.com
Postal Code: 58701-4066
Office phone: (701) 857-1900
General E-mail: aboyle@minotdailynews.com
Publisher Name: Robert Patchen Jr.
Editor Name: Kent Olson
Editor Email: kolson@minotdailynews.com
Advertising Executive Name: Elaine Gunderson
Advertising Executive Email: egunderson@minotdailynews.com

VALLEY CITY

VALLEY CITY TIMES-RECORD

Corporate/Parent Company: Horizon Publications Inc.
Publication Street Address: 146 3rd St NE
City: Valley City
State: ND
Publication Website: www.times-online.com
Postal Code: 58072-3047
Office phone: (701) 845-0463
General E-mail: vctr@times-online.com
Publisher Name: Tina Olson
Publisher Email: trpub@times-online.com
Editor Name: Ellie Boese
Editor Email: treditor@times-online.com
Advertising Executive Email: trads.megan@gmail.com

WAHPETON

(WAHPETON) DAILY NEWS / NEWS MONITOR

Corporate/Parent Company:
Publication Street Address: 601 Dakota Avenue
City: Wahpeton
State: ND
Publication Website: www.wahpetondailynews.com
Postal Code: 58074-0970
Office phone: (701)642-8585
General E-mail: editor@wahpetondailynews.com
Publisher Name: Tara Klostreich
Publisher Email: tarak@wahpetondailynews.com
Publisher Phone: (701) 642-8585
Editor Name: Carrie McDermott
Editor Email: editor@wahpetondailynews.com
Editor Phone: (701) 642-8585
Advertising Executive Name: Diana Hermes
Advertising Executive Email: dianah@wahpetondailynews.com
Advertising Executive Phone: (701) 642-8585

WILLISTON

WILLISTON DAILY HERALD

Publication Street Address: PO Box 1447
City: Williston
State: ND
Publication Website: www.willistonherald.com
Postal Code: 58802-1447
Office phone: (701) 572-2165
General E-mail: advertising@willistonherald.com
Publisher Name: Kelly Miller
Publisher Email: publisher@willistonherald.com
Editor Name: Jamie Kelly
Editor Email: editor@willistonherald.com
Advertising Executive Name: Michelle Yelverton
Advertising Executive Email: myelverton@willistonherald.com

NEBRASKA

ALLIANCE

ALLIANCE TIMES-HERALD

Corporate/Parent Company: Seaton Group
Publication Street Address: 114 E 4th St
City: Alliance
State: NE
Publication Website: www.alliancetimes.com
Postal Code: 69301-3402
Office phone: (308) 762-3060
General E-mail: cassie@alliancetimes.com
Advertising Executive Name: Amanda Mittan
Advertising Executive Email: athaddirector@gmail.com
Year Established: 1887
Delivery Methods:
 Mail`Newsstand`Carrier`Racks
Own Printing Facility?: Y
Commercial printers?: N
Mechanical specifications: Type page 14 x 24; E - 6 cols, 1 4/5, 1/8 between; A - 6 cols, 1 4/5, 1/8 between; C - 7 cols, 1 1/2, 1/8 between.
Published Days: Mon`Tues`Wed`Thur`Fri`Sat
Weekday Frequency: e
Saturday Frequency: m
Avg Paid Circ: 3025
Audit Company: Sworn/Estimate/Non-Audited
Audit Date: 7 12 2019
Pressroom Equipment: Lines – 5-G/Community;
Mailroom Equipment: Tying Machines – 1-/Bu.;
Buisness Equipment: PC
Buisness Software: QuickBooks Pro. 2011
Classified Equipment: Hardware – 1-APP Mac G5; Printers – HP 5000;
Classified Software: Baseview.

TIMES-HERALD

Publication Street Address: 114 East Fourth Street
City: Alliance
State: NE
Publication Website: www.alliancetimes.com
Postal Code: 69301
Office phone: 308-762-3060
General E-mail: athnewsdirector@gmail.com
Editor Name: Shaun Friedrichsen
Editor Email: athnewsdesk@gmail.com
Advertising Executive Name: Amanda Mittan
Advertising Executive Email: athaddirector@gmail.com

BEATRICE

BEATRICE DAILY SUN

Corporate/Parent Company: Lee Enterprises
Publication Street Address: 110 S 6th St
City: Beatrice
State: NE
Publication Website: www.beatricedailysun.com
Postal Code: 68310-3912
Office phone: (402) 223-5233
General E-mail: astokebrand@beatricedailysun.com
Publisher Name: Patrick Ethridge
Publisher Email: pethridge@beatricedailysun.com
Publisher Phone: (402) 223-5233
Advertising Executive Name: Amy Stokebrand
Advertising Executive Email: astokebrand@beatricedailysun.com
Year Established: 1902
Delivery Methods:
 Mail`Newsstand`Carrier`Racks
Own Printing Facility?: Y
Commercial printers?: Y
Mechanical specifications: Type page 13 x 21 1/2; E - 6 cols, 2, 1/6 between; A - 6 cols, 2, 1/6 between; C - 6 cols, 2, 1/6 between.
Published Days: Tues`Wed`Thur`Fri`Sat
Weekday Frequency: m
Saturday Frequency: m
Avg Paid Circ: 4255
Avg Free Circ: 249
Audit Company: Sworn/Estimate/Non-Audited
Audit Date: 7 12 2019
Pressroom Equipment: Lines – 7-G/Community.;
Mailroom Equipment: Tying Machines – 2/Malow.;
Classified Equipment: Hardware – 3-APP/Mac LC III;
Classified Software: Multi-Ad/CAMS.

DAILY SUN

Publication Street Address: 110 S. 6th Street
City: Beatrice
State: NE
Publication Website: beatricedailysun.com
Postal Code: 68310
Office phone: 402-223-5233
General E-mail: news@beatricedailysun.com
Editor Name: Luke Nichols
Editor Email: lukenichols@hotmail.com
Advertising Executive Name: Amy Stokebrand
Advertising Executive Email: astokebrand@beatricedailysun.com

COLUMBUS

TELEGRAM

Publication Street Address: 1254 27th Ave
City: Columbus
State: NE
Publication Website: columbustelegram.com
Postal Code: 68601
Office phone: 402-564-2741
Publisher Name: Vincent Laboy
Publisher Email: vincent.laboy@lee.net
Publisher Phone: 402-563-7501
Editor Name: Matt Lindberg
Editor Email: mlindberg@columbustelegram.com
Editor Phone: 402-563-7502
Advertising Executive Name: Kelly Muchmore
Advertising Executive Email: kmuchmore@columbustelegram.com
Advertising Executive Phone: 402-563-7554

COLUMBUS

THE COLUMBUS TELEGRAM

Corporate/Parent Company: Lee Enterprises
Publication Street Address: 1254 27th Ave
City: Columbus
State: NE
Publication Website: www.columbustelegram.com
Postal Code: 68601-5656
Office phone: (402) 564-2741
General E-mail: amy.bell@lee.net
Publisher Name: Vincent Laboy
Publisher Email: vincent.laboy@lee.net
Publisher Phone: (402) 563-7501
Editor Name: Matt Lindberg
Editor Email: mlindberg@columbustelegram.com
Editor Phone: (402) 563-7502
Advertising Executive Name: Kelly Muchmore
Advertising Executive Email: kmuchmore@columbustelegram.com
Advertising Executive Phone: (402) 563-7554
Year Established: 1875
Delivery Methods: Mail`Newsstand`Racks
Mechanical specifications: Type page 12 5/8 x 21 1/2; E - 6 cols, 2, 1/6 between; A - 6 cols, 2, 1/6 between; C - 6 cols, 2, 1/6 between.
Published Days: Thur
Avg Paid Circ: 2800
Audit Company: Sworn/Estimate/Non-Audited
Audit Date: 6 10 2019

FREMONT

FREEMONT TRIBUNE

Corporate/Parent Company: Lee Enterprises
Publication Street Address: 135 N. Main St.
City: Fremont
State: NE
Publication Website: fremonttribune.com
Postal Code: 68025
Office phone: 402-721-5000
Publisher Name: Vincent Laboy
Publisher Email: vlaboy@fremonttribune.com
Publisher Phone: 402.941.1422
Editor Name: Tony Gray
Editor Email: tgray@fremonttribune.com
Editor Phone: 402.941.1436
Advertising Executive Name: Andrew Zeplin
Advertising Executive Email: azeplin@fremonttribune.com
Advertising Executive Phone: 402-941-1403

FREMONT TRIBUNE

Corporate/Parent Company: Lee Enterprises
Publication Street Address: 135 N Main St
City: Fremont
State: NE
Publication Website: www.fremonttribune.com
Postal Code: 68025-5673
Office phone: (402) 721-5000
General E-mail: julie.veskerna@lee.net
Publisher Name: Vincent Laboy
Publisher Email: vlaboy@fremonttribune.com
Publisher Phone: (402) 941-1422
Editor Name: Tony Gray
Editor Email: tgray@fremonttribune.com
Editor Phone: (402) 941-1436
Advertising Executive Name: Andrew Zeplin
Advertising Executive Email: azeplin@fremonttribune.com
Advertising Executive Phone: (402) 941-1403
Year Established: 1868
Mechanical specifications: Type page 12 1/4 x 21 3/4; E - 6 cols, 1 7/8, 1/8 between; A - 6 cols, 1 7/8, 1/8 between; C - 9 cols, 1 1/4, 1/16 between.
Published Days: Mon`Tues`Wed`Thur`Fri`Sat
Weekday Frequency: e
Saturday Frequency: m
Avg Paid Circ: 5187
Avg Free Circ: 720
Audit Company: AAM
Audit Date: 30 09 2014
Pressroom Equipment: Lines – 4-HI/V-22-25; 6-HI/V22-25; Folders – 2-HI/2:1.;
Mailroom Equipment: Counter Stackers – 1/ PPK; Tying Machines – 1-MLN/ML2EES; Address Machine – 2-Wm/3.;
Buisness Equipment: 1-DEC/1144
Classified Equipment: Hardware – APP/Mac;
Classified Software: Baseview.

GRAND ISLAND

INDEPENDENT

Corporate/Parent Company: Gannett
Publication Street Address: 422 West First Street
City: Grand Island
State: NE
Publication Website: www.theindependent.com
Postal Code: 68801
Office phone: 308-382-1000
General E-mail: circulation@theindependent.com
Editor Name: Jim Faddis
Editor Email: jim.faddis@theindependent.com
Editor Phone: (308) 381-9413
Advertising Executive Name: Caleb Schescke
Advertising Executive Email: caleb.schescke@theindependent.com
Advertising Executive Phone: (308) 381-9445

HASTINGS

HASTINGS TRIBUNE

Corporate/Parent Company: Seaton Company, Inc.
Publication Street Address: 908 W 2nd St
City: Hastings
State: NE
Publication Website: www.hastingstribune.com
Postal Code: 68901-5063
Office phone: (402) 462-2131
General E-mail: legals@hastingstribune.com
Publisher Name: Darran Fowler
Publisher Email: dfowler@hastingstribune.com
Publisher Phone: (402) 462-2131
Editor Name: Andy Raun
Editor Email: araun@hastingstribune.com
Editor Phone: (402) 303-1419
Advertising Executive Name: Ann Blunt
Advertising Executive Email: ablunt@hastingstribune.com
Advertising Executive Phone: (402) 303-1401
Year Established: 1905
Delivery Methods: Mail`Carrier`Racks
Own Printing Facility?: Y
Commercial printers?: N
Mechanical specifications: Type page 11 1/2 x 21; E - 6 cols, 1 13/16, 1/8 between; A - 6 cols, 1 13/16, 1/8 between; C - 8 cols, 1 5/16, 1/8 between.
Published Days: Mon`Tues`Wed`Thur`Fri`Sat
Weekday Frequency: e
Saturday Frequency: m
Avg Paid Circ: 6052
Avg Free Circ: 161
Audit Company: AAM
Audit Date: 29 09 2015
Pressroom Equipment: Lines – 6-G/Urbanite 917; Folders – 1, 1-G/Cole Quarter.;
Mailroom Equipment: Counter Stackers – Newstack, Mid America Graphics, KAN; Inserters & Stuffers – KAN/480; Tying Machines – MLN/MLEE, MLN/2A; Address Machine – Kan/600 Labeler.;
Buisness Equipment: 9-IBM/RISC 6000 (9 terminals)
Buisness Software: PBS/MediaPlus
Classified Equipment: Hardware – APP/Mac; Printers – APP/Mac LaserWriter 600, ECR/Scriptsetter II VR36;
Classified Software: Baseview/Ad Manager Pro.

HOLDREGE

HOLDREGE DAILY CITIZEN

Publication Street Address: 418 Garfield St
City: Holdrege
State: NE
Publication Website: www.holdrege.org/
Postal Code: 68949-2219
Office phone: (308) 995-4441
General E-mail: holdregecitizenads@yahoo.com
Mechanical specifications: Type page 13 1/4 x 21; E - 6 cols, 2, 1/6 between; A - 6 cols, 2, 1/6 between; C - 8 cols, 1 1/2, 1/6 between.
Published Days: Mon`Tues`Wed`Thur`Fri
Weekday Frequency: e
Avg Paid Circ: 2904
Audit Company: Sworn/Estimate/Non-Audited
Audit Date: 7 12 2019
Pressroom Equipment: Lines – 4-G/Community 1973.;
Mailroom Equipment: Tying Machines – Bu; Address Machine – Am.;
Classified Equipment: Hardware – Mk.;

KEARNEY

HUB

Publication Street Address: 13 East 22 Street
City: Kearney
State: NE
Publication Website: www.kearneyhub.com
Postal Code: 68847
Office phone: (308) 237-2152
General E-mail: news@kearneyhub.com

KEARNEY HUB

Corporate/Parent Company: Lee Enterprises
Publication Street Address: 13 E 22nd St
City: Kearney
State: NE
Publication Website: https://www.kearneyhub.com/
Postal Code: 68847-5404
Office phone: (308) 237-2152
General E-mail: circulation@kearneyhub.com
Publisher Name: Shon Barenklau
Year Established: 1888
Mechanical specifications: Type page 11 5/8 x 21; E - 6 cols, 1 5/6, 1/8 between; A - 6 cols, 1 5/6, 1/8 between; C - 9 cols, 1 9/50, 1/8 between.
Published Days: Mon`Tues`Wed`Thur`Fri`Sat
Weekday Frequency: e
Saturday Frequency: m
Avg Paid Circ: 7468
Avg Free Circ: 536
Audit Company: AAM
Audit Date: 5 09 2018
Pressroom Equipment: Lines – 13-G/SSC single width (formers) 1990; Folders – 1-G/SSC; Registration System – Carlson/Ternis.
Mailroom Equipment: Counter Stackers – QWI/400W; Inserters & Stuffers – 1-KAN/480 7:1; Tying Machines – 1-MLN MLN2, 1-Dynamic/D2300; Address Machine – 1-KAN/600PS labeler.;
Buisness Equipment: DEC/VAX II
Buisness Software: Microsoft/Office
Classified Equipment: Hardware – Dell, Intergraph; Printers – Pre Press/Panther Pro Imagesetter;
Classified Software: APT.

LINCOLN

JOURNAL STAR

Corporate/Parent Company: Gannett
Publication Street Address: 926 P Street
City: Lincoln
State: NE
Publication Website: www.journalstar.com
Postal Code: 68508
Office phone: 800-742-7315
Publisher Name: Ava Thomas
Publisher Email: aThomas@journalstar.com
Publisher Phone: 402-473-7146
Editor Name: Dave Bundy
Editor Email: dbundy@journalstar.com
Editor Phone: 402-473-7334
Advertising Executive Name: Natalia Wiita
Advertising Executive Email: nwiita@journalstar.com
Advertising Executive Phone: 402-473-2643

LINCOLN JOURNAL STAR

Corporate/Parent Company: Lee Enterprises
Publication Street Address: 926 P St
City: Lincoln
State: NE
Publication Website: www.journalstar.com
Postal Code: 68508-3615
Office phone: (402) 475-4200
General E-mail: advertising@journalstar.com
Publisher Name: Ava Thomas
Publisher Email: athomas@journalstar.com
Publisher Phone: (402) 473-7146
Editor Name: Dave Bundy
Editor Email: dbundy@journalstar.com
Editor Phone: (402) 473-7334
Advertising Executive Name: Beth Corrick Loop
Advertising Executive Email: bcorrick@journalstar.com
Advertising Executive Phone: (402) 473-7421
Year Established: 1990
Delivery Methods: Newsstand`Carrier
Mechanical specifications: Type page 9 15/16 x 12; E - 5 cols, 9 15/16, 1/6 between; A - 5 cols, 9 15/16, 1/6 between.
Published Days: Sat
Avg Paid Circ: 33000
Audit Company: AAM
Audit Date: 12 11 2019

MC COOK

MCCOOK DAILY GAZETTE

Corporate/Parent Company: Rust Communications
Publication Street Address: W First & E Sts
City: Mc Cook
State: NE
Publication Website: www.mccookgazette.com
Postal Code: 69001
Office phone: (308) 345-4500
General E-mail: adsales5@mccookgazette.com
Publisher Name: Shary Skiles
Publisher Email: sskiles@ocsmccook.com
Publisher Phone: (308) 345-4500, Ext : 106
Editor Name: Bruce Crosby
Editor Email: editor@mccookgazette.com
Editor Phone: (308) 345-4500, Ext : 120
Advertising Executive Name: Jacob Warch
Advertising Executive Email: adsales1@mccookgazette.com
Advertising Executive Phone: (308) 345-4500, Ext : 124
Year Established: 1911
Delivery Methods: Mail`Newsstand`Carrier`Racks
Own Printing Facility?: Y
Mechanical specifications: Type page 13 x 21 1/2; E - 6 cols, 2, 1/8 between; A - 6 cols, 2, 1/8 between; C - 6 cols, 2, 1/8 between.
Published Days: Mon`Tues`Wed`Thur`Fri
Weekday Frequency: e
Avg Paid Circ: 5100
Audit Company: Sworn/Estimate/Non-Audited
Audit Date: 7 12 2019
Pressroom Equipment: Lines – 6-G/Suburban (2

U.S. Daily Newspapers

Stacked units).;
Mailroom Equipment: Tying Machines – 2/Bu; Wrapping Singles – 8-/Sa; Address Machine – 1-LN/25 Auto Mecha.;
Buisness Equipment: 3-IBM/PC, AT
Buisness Software: PBS
Classified Equipment: Hardware – 1-HI, 1-APP/Mac; 2-IBM;
Classified Software: PBS

NORFOLK

DAILY NEWS

Corporate/Parent Company: Gannett
Publication Street Address: 525 Norfolk Avenue
City: Norfolk
State: NE
Publication Website: norfolkdailynews.com
Postal Code: 68701
Office phone: (402)371-1020
General E-mail: webmaster@norfolkdailynews.com
Editor Name: Tim Pearson
Editor Email: tpearson@norfolkdailynews.com
Editor Phone: (402) 371-1020 ext. 232

NORFOLK DAILY NEWS

Corporate/Parent Company: Huse Publishing
Publication Street Address: 525 W Norfolk Ave
City: Norfolk
State: NE
Publication Website: www.norfolkdailynews.com
Postal Code: 68701-5236
Office phone: (402) 371-1020
General E-mail: ads@norfolkdailynews.com
Editor Name: Jerry Guenther
Editor Email: jguenther@norfolkdailynews.com
Editor Phone: (402) 371-1020, Ext : 234
Advertising Executive Name: Vickie Hrabanek
Advertising Executive Email: vhrabanek@norfolkdailynews.com
Advertising Executive Phone: (402) 371-1020, Ext : 259
Year Established: 1887
Mechanical specifications: Type page 11 3/4 x 21 1/2; E - 6 cols, 1 13/16, 1/8 between; A - 6 cols, 1 13/16, 1/8 between; C - 8 cols, 1 5/16, 1/8 between.
Published Days: Mon`Tues`Wed`Thur`Fri`Sat
Weekday Frequency: e
Saturday Frequency: e
Avg Paid Circ: 11096
Avg Free Circ: 1986
Audit Company: AAM
Audit Date: 11 05 2020
Pressroom Equipment: Lines – 8-G/Urbanite 1972; Control System – 1972;
Mailroom Equipment: Counter Stackers – 1-Id, 1/Quipp; Inserters & Stuffers – KAN/5:1, MM/4:1; Tying Machines – 2-/Bu, 1-MLN/2A, 1-/Strapack; Address Machine – 1-/KAN.;
Buisness Equipment: IBM/AS400, Gateway/Pentium, HP/Pentium
Classified Equipment: Hardware – 5-Baseview/Xante/8300 11x17; Printers – Okidata/Pacemark 3410, APP/Mac LaserWriter Pro 630;
Classified Software: Baseview/Ad Manager Pro.

OMAHA

OMAHA WORLD-HERALD

Corporate/Parent Company: Lee Enterprises
Publication Street Address: 1314 Douglas St
City: Omaha
State: NE
Publication Website: www.omaha.com
Postal Code: 68102-1848
Office phone: (402) 444-1000
General E-mail: tsears@owh.com
Publisher Name: Todd Sears
Publisher Email: todd.sears@owh.com
Publisher Phone: (402) 444-1179
Editor Name: Paul Goodsell
Editor Email: goodsell@owh.com

Editor Phone: (402) 444-1114
Advertising Executive Name: Eric Mayberry
Advertising Executive Email: eric.mayberry@owh.com
Advertising Executive Phone: (402) 444-1110
Year Established: 1885
Delivery Methods: Mail`Newsstand`Carrier`Racks
Own Printing Facility?: Y
Commercial printers?: Y
Mechanical specifications: Type page 10.0833â€ x 21.075â€; E - 6 cols, 1.54â€, .1667â€ between; A - 6 cols, 1.54â€, .1667â€ between; C - 6 cols, 1.54â€, .1667â€ between.
Published Days: Mon`Tues`Wed`Thur`Fri`Sat`Sun
Weekday Frequency: m
Saturday Frequency: m
Avg Paid Circ: 92201
Audit Company: AAM
Audit Date: 25 04 2019
Pressroom Equipment: Lines – Man/Geoman 3/8 Shaftless; 1-Line/18 Towers; 15 4/1 Towers; 3 4/4 Towers; Folders – 3, 1; Pasters –Man/AuroPrep; Reels & Stands – 18; Control System – Man/PPM-PECOM;
Mailroom Equipment: Counter Stackers – 16-Quipp; Inserters & Stuffers – 2-HI/632, 1-HI/632; Wrapping Singles – 14-Quipp/3/4 Viper; Control System – Burt, GE; Address Machine – 2-Barstrom/In-Line Labeler;
Buisness Equipment: Dell PE710.VMware
Buisness Software: Circ 2000, Mactive, Oracle Financials
Classified Equipment: Hardware – Dell PE710.VMware;
Classified Software: AdbaseE, Mactive, OPI, Xpance

WORLD-HERALD

Publication Street Address: 1314 Douglas St
City: Omaha
State: NE
Publication Website: www.omaha.com
Postal Code: 68102
Office phone: 402-444-1000
General E-mail: circulationcustomerservice@owh.com
Editor Name: Randy Essex
Editor Email: randy.essex@owh.com

SCOTTSBLUFF

STAR-HERALD

Corporate/Parent Company: Lee Enterprises
Publication Street Address: 1405 Broadway
City: Scottsbluff
State: NE
Publication Website: https://www.starherald.com/
Postal Code: 69361-3151
Office phone: (308) 632-9000
General E-mail: news@starherald.com
Publisher Name: Rich Macke
Publisher Email: rich.macke@starherald.com
Editor Name: Brad Staman
Editor Email: brad.staman@starherald.com
Advertising Executive Name: Russ Todd
Advertising Executive Email: russ.todd@starherald.com
Year Established: 1912
Mechanical specifications: Type page 10 1/4 x 21 1/2; E - 6 cols, 1 1/2, 1/12 between; A - 6 cols, 1 1/2, 1/12 between; C - 8 cols, 1 3/8, 1/12 between.
Published Days: Tues`Wed`Thur`Fri`Sat`Sun
Weekday Frequency: m
Saturday Frequency: m
Avg Paid Circ: 8287
Avg Free Circ: 404
Audit Company: CAC
Audit Date: 30 06 2018
Pressroom Equipment: Lines – 6-HI/845 1972; 4-G/Community 1968 1997; Press Drive – Haley/Control PCL; Folders – HI/Cottrell; Control System – MHI/PLC.;
Mailroom Equipment: Counter Stackers – 1-BG/107, 1-HL/Monitor, 1-BG/108;

Inserters & Stuffers – 1-HI/624P; Tying Machines – 2-MLN/ML2EE, 1/MLN Sorter-Tyer; Address Machine – 1-KR/215.;
Buisness Equipment: Gateways
Buisness Software: Archetype/Corel Draw, Microsoft/Works, Microsoft/Windows
Classified Equipment: Hardware – GraphX; Printers – Okidata;
Classified Software: GraphX/1.6 Ad taker.

SIDNEY

SUN-TELEGRAPH

Publication Street Address: 817 12th Avenue
City: Sidney
State: NE
Publication Website: www.suntelegraph.com
Postal Code: 69162
Office phone: (308) 254-2818
General E-mail: info@suntelegraph.com
Publisher Name: Forrest Hershberger
Editor Name: Jennifer Velasco
Advertising Executive Name: Roger Murphy

NEW HAMPSHIRE

CLAREMONT

EAGLE TIMES

Corporate/Parent Company: Engle Printing & Publishing Co., Inc.
Publication Street Address: 45 Crescent Street
City: Claremont
State: NH
Publication Website: www.eagletimes.com
Postal Code: 0 3743
Office phone: (603) 543-3100
Publisher Name: Mike Gonyaw
Publisher Email: publisher@eagletimes.com
Publisher Phone: 603-504-3143
Editor Name: Jordan J. Phelan
Editor Email: editor@eagletimes.com
Editor Phone: (603) 504-3101
Advertising Executive Name: Emily Deane
Advertising Executive Email: edeane@eagletimes.com
Advertising Executive Phone: (603) 504-3157

EAGLE TIMES

Corporate/Parent Company: Engle Printing & Publishing Co., Inc.
Publication Street Address: 45 Crescent St
City: Claremont
State: NH
Publication Website: www.eagletimes.com
Postal Code: 03743-2220
Office phone: (603) 543-3100
General E-mail: cheri@eagletimes.com

CONCORD

CONCORD MONITOR

Corporate/Parent Company: Newspapers of New England
Publication Street Address: 1 Monitor Dr
City: Concord
State: NH
Publication Website: www.concordmonitor.com
Postal Code: 03301-1834
Office phone: (603) 224-5301
General E-mail: ads@cmonitor.com

DOVER

FOSTER'S DAILY DEMOCRAT

Publication Street Address: 150 Venture Dr
City: Dover

State: NH
Publication Website: www.fosters.com
Postal Code: 03820-5913
Office phone: (603) 742-4455
General E-mail: news@fosters.com

KEENE

THE KEENE SENTINEL

Corporate/Parent Company: Keene Publishing Corporation
Publication Street Address: 60 West St
City: Keene
State: NH
Publication Website: www.sentinelsource.com
Postal Code: 03431-3373
Office phone: (603) 352-1234
General E-mail: adassist@keenesentinel.com

LACONIA

THE LACONIA DAILY SUN

Publication Street Address: 1127 Union Ave
City: Laconia
State: NH
Publication Website: www.laconiadailysun.com
Postal Code: 03246-2126
Office phone: (603) 737-2030
General E-mail: ads@laconiadailysun.com

MANCHESTER

NEW HAMPSHIRE UNION LEADER

Corporate/Parent Company: Union Leader Corporation
Publication Street Address: 100 William Loeb Dr
City: Manchester
State: NH
Publication Website: www.unionleader.com
Postal Code: 03109-5309
Office phone: (603) 668-4321
General E-mail: jnormandin@unionleader.com

NASHUA

THE TELEGRAPH

Corporate/Parent Company: McClatchy
Publication Street Address: 110 Main St
City: Nashua
State: NH
Publication Website: www.nashuatelegraph.com
Postal Code: 03060-2723
Office phone: (603) 882-2741
General E-mail: mgorman@nashuatelegraph.com

NORTH CONWAY

THE CONWAY DAILY SUN

Publication Street Address: 64 Seavey St
City: North Conway
State: NH
Publication Website: www.conwaydailysun.com
Postal Code: 03860-5355
Office phone: (603) 356-3456
General E-mail: joyce@conwaydailysun.com

PORTSMOUTH

PORTSMOUTH HERALD

Corporate/Parent Company: Gannett
Publication Street Address: 111 NH Ave
City: Portsmouth
State: NH
Publication Website: www.seacoastonline.com
Postal Code: 03801-2864
Office phone: (800) 439-0303
General E-mail: sales@seacoastonline.com

U.S. Daily Newspapers

WEST LEBANON

VALLEY NEWS

Corporate/Parent Company: Newspapers of New England
Publication Street Address: 24 Interchange Dr
City: West Lebanon
State: NH
Publication Website: www.vnews.com
Postal Code: 03784-2003
Office phone: (603) 298-8711
General E-mail: advertising@vnews.com

NEW MEXICO

ALAMOGORDO

ALAMOGORDO DAILY NEWS

Corporate/Parent Company: Gannett
Publication Street Address: 518 24th St
City: Alamogordo
State: NM
Publication Website: www.alamogordonews.com
Postal Code: 88310-6104
Office phone: (877) 301-0013
General E-mail: legals@alamogordonews.com
Editor Name: Duane Barbati
Year Established: 1898
Delivery Methods: Mail`Newsstand`Racks
Own Printing Facility?: N
Commercial printers?: N
Mechanical specifications: Type page 12 1/2 x 21 1/2; E - 6 cols, 2 1/16, 1/8 between; A - 6 cols, 2 1/16, 1/8 between; C - 8 cols, 1 3/8, 1/16 between.
Published Days: Tues`Wed`Thur`Fri`Sat`Sun
Weekday Frequency: m
Saturday Frequency: m
Avg Paid Circ: 2724
Avg Free Circ: 745
Audit Company: AAM
Audit Date: 19 11 2018
Total Circulation: 9046

ALBUQUERQUE

ALBUQUERQUE JOURNAL

Corporate/Parent Company: Journal Publishing Company
Publication Street Address: 7777 Jefferson St NE
City: Albuquerque
State: NM
Publication Website: www.abqjournal.com
Postal Code: 87109-4343
Office phone: (505) 823-7777
General E-mail: sfriedes@abqpubco.com
Publisher Name: Dan Herrera
Publisher Email: dherrera@abqjournal.com
Publisher Phone: (505) 823-3810
Editor Name: Helen Taylor
Editor Email: htaylor@abqjournal.com
Editor Phone: (505) 823-3927
Advertising Executive Name: Art Trujillo
Advertising Executive Email: atrujillo@abqjournal.com
Advertising Executive Phone: (505) 823-3327
Year Established: 1880
Delivery Methods: Mail`Newsstand`Carrier`Racks
Own Printing Facility?: Y
Commercial printers?: Y
Published Days: Mon`Tues`Wed`Thur`Fri`Sat`Sun
Weekday Frequency: m
Saturday Frequency: m
Avg Paid Circ: 71361
Audit Company: AAM
Audit Date: 5 05 2020
Classified Software: C-Text.
Note: For current advertising rates and detailed production and printing information please contact Albuquerque Publishing Co. at 505-823-7777
Total Circulation: 97565

ARTESIA

ARTESIA DAILY PRESS

Publication Street Address: 503 W Main St
City: Artesia
State: NM
Publication Website: www.artesianews.com
Postal Code: 88210-2067
Office phone: (575) 746-3524
General E-mail: editor@artesianews.com
Publisher Name: Danny Scott
Editor Name: Brienne Green
Editor Email: editor@artesianews.com
Year Established: 1954
Delivery Methods: Mail`Newsstand`Carrier`Racks
Own Printing Facility?: Y
Commercial printers?: N
Published Days: Tues`Wed`Thur`Fri`Sun
Weekday Frequency: e
Avg Paid Circ: 2900
Audit Company: USPS
Audit Date: 27 09 2012
Total Circulation: 2900

CARLSBAD

CURRENT-ARGUS

Publication Street Address: 620 S Main St
City: Carlsbad
State: NM
Publication Website: www.currentargus.com
Postal Code: 88220-6243
Office phone: (575) 887-5501
General E-mail: achedden@currentargus.com
Publisher Name: Rockford Hayes
Editor Name: Jessica Onsurez
Editor Email: jonsurez@currentargus.com
Editor Phone: (575) 628-5531
Year Established: 1889
Mechanical specifications: Type page 13 x 21 1/2; E - 6 cols, 2 1/16, 1/8 between; A - 6 cols, 2 1/16, 1/8 between; C - 6 cols, 2 1/16, 1/8 between.
Published Days: Tues`Wed`Thur`Fri`Sat`Sun
Weekday Frequency: m
Saturday Frequency: m
Avg Paid Circ: 3065
Avg Free Circ: 722
Audit Company: AAM
Audit Date: 30 06 2018
Pressroom Equipment: Lines – 6-G/Community 1975; Folders – G/Community Quarter.;
Mailroom Equipment: Tying Machines – Bu/Tyer.;
Buisness Equipment: IBM/5363
Classified Equipment: Hardware – CText; ECR/Imagesetter; Printers – APP/Mac LaserPrinters
Classified Software: XYQUEST/XyWrite, CText.
Editorial Equipment: Hardware – CText/ECR/Imagesetter; Printers – APP/Mac LaserPrinters
Editorial Software: XYQUEST/XyWrite, CText.
Production Equipment: Hardware – ECR/Imagesetter; Cameras – Nu/2024 M2 Camera.
Total Circulation: 3787

DEMING

DEMING HEADLIGHT

Corporate/Parent Company: Gannett
Publication Street Address: 219 E Maple St
City: Deming
State: NM
Publication Website: www.demingheadlight.com
Postal Code: 88030-4267
Office phone: (575) 546-2611
General E-mail: jngutierre@lcsun-news.com
Publisher Name: Jared Hamilton
Publisher Email: jhamilton@scsun-news.com
Publisher Phone: (575) 546-2611, Ext : 2601
Editor Name: Bill Armendariz
Editor Email: barmendariz@demingheadlight.com
Editor Phone: (575) 546-2611, Ext : 2626
Advertising Executive Name: Joseph N. Gutierrez
Advertising Executive Email: jngutierre@lcsun-news.com
Advertising Executive Phone: (575) 541-5433
Year Established: 1881
Mechanical specifications: Type page 10 3/16 x 15 3/4; E - 5 cols, 1 15/16, 1/8 between; A - 5 cols, 1 15/16, 1/8 between; C - 7 cols, 1 5/16, 1/8 between.
Published Days: Mon`Tues`Wed`Thur`Fri
Weekday Frequency: m
Avg Paid Circ: 3541
Audit Company: Sworn/Estimate/Non-Audited
Audit Date: 7 12 2019
Pressroom Equipment: Lines – G/Community; Folders – 1-G/4:1.;
Mailroom Equipment: Tying Machines – Bu; Address Machine – Dispensa-Matic.;
Buisness Equipment: 3-IBM/PC
Classified Equipment: Hardware – GraphX; 2-COM; Printers – HP/LaserJet IVsi.;
Editorial Equipment: Hardware – APP/Mac/5-COM
Editorial Software: Claris/Works, QPS/QuarkXPress.
Production Equipment: Hardware – 1-COM/Hd, 2-COM/2-Laser; Cameras – R/Horizontal.
Total Circulation: 3541

FARMINGTON

THE DAILY TIMES

Corporate/Parent Company: Gannett
Publication Street Address: 203 W Main St
City: Farmington
State: NM
Publication Website: www.daily-times.com
Postal Code: 87401-6209
Office phone: (505) 325-4545
General E-mail: chill@daily-times.com
Editor Name: John Moses
Editor Email: jmoses@daily-times.com
Editor Phone: (505) 564-4624
Advertising Executive Name: Chris Hill
Advertising Executive Email: chill@daily-times.com
Advertising Executive Phone: (505) 564-4583
Delivery Methods: Mail`Newsstand`Carrier`Racks
Own Printing Facility?: Y
Mechanical specifications: Type page 11 3/4 x 21 1/2; E - 6 cols, 1 5/6, 1/6 between; A - 6 cols, 1 5/6, 1/6 between; C - 9 cols, 1 1/12, 1/6 between.
Published Days: Mon`Tues`Wed`Thur`Fri`Sat`Sun
Weekday Frequency: m
Saturday Frequency: m
Avg Paid Circ: 5007
Avg Free Circ: 2458
Audit Company: AAM
Audit Date: 6 05 2020
Pressroom Equipment: Lines – 6-G/Urbanite 1979; Press Drive – 2-HP/100; Reels & Stands – 2;
Mailroom Equipment: Counter Stackers – 1-HL/Monitor HT II, 1/MM, 1-HL/Monitor, 1-/BG; Inserters & Stuffers – 2-MM/227; Tying Machines – 2-OVL/41E, 1-OVL/515, Samuel/NT440; Address Machine – 1-/KR;
Buisness Equipment: PC Network, 2-AT, 1-Epson/LQ2550, 2-APP/Mac Quadra 610, 1-APP/Mac Centris 660AV, 1-APP/Mac Quadra 630, APP/Power Mac 7200-75
Buisness Software: Baseview, Dynamics 4.0
Classified Equipment: Hardware – 5-APP/iMac; 1-Toshiba/Copier 2532 Turbo, 1-Toshiba/Fax TF651 Turbo, 1-Brother/Fax 1850mc, 2-Nikon/Digital; Printers – 1-APP/Mac LaserWriter 12-640 PS, 1-APP/Mac Color Stylewriter 4100, 1-Okidata/Pacemark 3410, 1-HP/Deskwriter 560C,;
Editorial Equipment: Hardware – 1-APP/Mac PowerBook 520c, 5-APP/Mac Centris 650, 1-APP/Mac Quadra 605, 2-APP/Mac Quadra 610, 4-APP/Mac Quadra 630, 1-APP/Mac Quadra 700, 1-APP/Mac Quadra 900, 2-APP/Mac PowerBook 150, 1-APP/Mac PowerBook 1400CS, 1-APP/Mac PowerBook 3400C, 1-APP
Production Equipment: Hardware – 1-Nu/FT40V6 UPNS Plate Burner, 2-APP/Mac G3, 2-APP/Mac 7300, Pre Press/Panther Pro Imagesetter; Scanners – Scitex/Eversmart
Production Software: QPS/QuarkXPress 5.0.
Total Circulation: 19629

GALLUP

GALLUP INDEPENDENT

Publication Street Address: 500 N Ninth St
City: Gallup
State: NM
Publication Website: www.gallupindependent.com
Postal Code: 87301-5379
Office phone: (505) 863-6811
General E-mail: ads1@gallupindependent.com
Publisher Name: Robert Zollinger
Publisher Email: publisher@gallupindependent.com
Editor Name: Richard Reyes
Editor Email: editor@gallupindependent.com
Editor Phone: (505) 863-6811, Ext : 213
Advertising Executive Name: Rachel Morrissette
Advertising Executive Email: ads1@gallupindependent.com
Advertising Executive Phone: (505) 863-6811, Ext : 233
Year Established: 1904
Delivery Methods: Newsstand`Carrier`Racks
Own Printing Facility?: Y
Commercial printers?: Y
Mechanical specifications: Type page 13 x 21 1/2; E - 6 cols, 2 1/16, 1/8 between; A - 6 cols, 2 1/16, 1/8 between; C - 7 cols, 1 3/4, 1/8 between.
Published Days: Mon`Tues`Wed`Thur`Fri`Sat
Weekday Frequency: e
Saturday Frequency: m
Avg Paid Circ: 11358
Avg Free Circ: 81
Audit Company: AAM
Audit Date: 31 12 2017
Pressroom Equipment: Lines – 24-G/Magnum (6 towers); Folders – Universal.;
Mailroom Equipment: Counter Stackers – 1/Exact Count; Inserters & Stuffers – 10-MM/Alphaliner; Tying Machines – 2-Wilton/Stra Pack.;
Buisness Equipment: 1-IBM/36
Classified Software: Baseview.
Editorial Equipment: Hardware – HI; Printers – MON
Editorial Software: HI.
Production Equipment: Hardware – 2-Nu, 1-Nikon/Coolscan 1000, 1-Nikon/Coolscan 2000; Cameras – R/Lens, OH, LE/500
Total Circulation: 11439

HOBBS

HOBBS NEWS-SUN

Corporate/Parent Company: Hobbs News-Sun
Publication Street Address: 201 N Thorp St
City: Hobbs
State: NM
Publication Website: www.hobbsnews.com
Postal Code: 88240-6058
Office phone: (575) 393-2123
General E-mail: hnsads@hobbsnews.com
Publisher Name: Daniel Russell
Publisher Phone: (575) 393-2123
Editor Name: Jeff Tucker
Editor Email: managingeditor@hobbsnews.com
Editor Phone: (575) 391-5438
Advertising Executive Email: advertise@hobbsnews.com
Advertising Executive Phone: (575) 391-5404
Year Established: 1928
Own Printing Facility?: Y
Commercial printers?: N
Mechanical specifications: Type page 13 x 21 1/2; E - 6 cols, 2 1/16, 1/8 between; A - 6 cols, 2 1/16, 1/8 between; C - 9 cols, 1 5/16, 1/8 between.
Published Days: Tues`Wed`Thur`Fri`Sat`Sun
Weekday Frequency: m
Saturday Frequency: m
Avg Paid Circ: 5052
Avg Free Circ: 1016
Audit Company: AAM
Audit Date: 30 05 2019
Pressroom Equipment: Lines – 6-G/Urbanite;

U.S. Daily Newspapers

Folders – G/1000.;
Mailroom Equipment: Tying Machines – Wilton/Stra Pack, 1-/OVL.;
Buisness Equipment: BFR, GAT, Standard, IBM
Buisness Software: ADP, Lotus, Zen Write & Calc, WordPerfect 5.1, BMF, Great Plains, MediaSpan
Classified Equipment: Hardware – APP/Mac; 2-OS; Printers – Okidata, Imagesetter/II, APP/Mac LaserPrinter, HP/LaserJet;
Classified Software: Baseview/Ad Manager Pro 2.06.
Editorial Equipment: Hardware – APP/Mac/2-Pre Press/Panther Pro Imagesetter; Printers – Tektronix/380, V/5300B, Pre Press/Panther Imagesetter, APP/Mac LaserPrinter Color, Tektronix/Phaser 300, Kk/Full Color
Editorial Software: Baseview/NewsEdit Pro 3.1.7.
Production Equipment: Hardware – Lf/Leafscan 35, APP/Mac LaserWriter, Imagesetter II, V/5300B, APP/Mac Color LaserWriter, Pre Press/Panther, Tektronix/Phaser 300, APP/Mac Color LaserWriter 12/600 PS; Cameras – 2-AG/NC 2000e, Nikon/D1, Nikon/Coolpix 880, 3-Olympus
Total Circulation: 10097

LAS CRUCES

LAS CRUCES SUN-NEWS

Corporate/Parent Company: Gannett
Publication Street Address: 256 W Las Cruces Ave
City: Las Cruces
State: NM
Publication Website: www.lcsun-news.com
Postal Code: 88005-1804
Office phone: (575) 541-5400
General E-mail: bmills@lcsun-news.com
Publisher Name: David McClain
Advertising Executive Name: Rynni Henderson
Advertising Executive Email: rhenderson@lcsun-news.com
Advertising Executive Phone: (575) 541-5409
Year Established: 1881
Delivery Methods:
Mail`Newsstand`Carrier`Racks
Mechanical specifications: Type page 9.89"x21.0" 6 col x 21.0"; E - 6 cols, 1 7/8, 1/5 between; A - 6 cols, 1 7/8, 1/5 between; C - 9 cols, 1 1/5, 1/5 between.
Published Days: Mon`Tues`Wed`Thur`Fri`Sat`Sun
Weekday Frequency: m
Saturday Frequency: m
Avg Paid Circ: 10334
Audit Company: AAM
Audit Date: 11 05 2020
Pressroom Equipment: Lines – 10-G/U 1187 single width; Reels & Stands – 6; Control System – 2;
Mailroom Equipment: Tying Machines – 1/Bu, 1-Ace/50, Strapack/D-52; Address Machine – 1-El/Communications.;
Buisness Equipment: PC Network, PC Wintell
Buisness Software: Geac Vision Shift
Classified Equipment: Hardware – APP/Mac; Printers – HP/LaserJet IVsi, HP/LaserJet 4MV;
Classified Software: Baseview/AdManager Pro 2.0.5.
Editorial Equipment: Hardware – APP/Mac; Printers – LaserMaster/1200 XL, HP/LaserJet IVsi, HP/LaserJet 4MV, ECR/Scriptsetter VRL 36/HS
Editorial Software: Baseview/NewsEdit Pro IQUE 2.1.3.
Production Equipment: Hardware – Caere/OmniPage 3.0, 1-Nu/Flip Top FT40; Cameras – 3-C/Spartan; Scanners – 3-AG/Arcus II, 3-Nikon/LS1000 Film Scanners
Production Software: QPS/QuarkXPress 3.32.
Total Circulation: 17431

LOS ALAMOS

LOS ALAMOS DAILY POST

Publication Street Address: 1247 Central Ave
City: Los Alamos
State: NM
Publication Website: www.ladailypost.com
Postal Code: 87544
Office phone: 505.490.0938
Editor Name: Carol A. Clark
Editor Email: caclark@ladailypost.com
Editor Phone: 505.490.0938
Advertising Executive Name: Kirsten Laskey
Advertising Executive Email: kirsten@ladailypost.com
Advertising Executive Phone: 505.695.4996

LOS ALAMOS MONITOR

Corporate/Parent Company: Landmark Community Newspapers
Publication Street Address: 256 Dp Rd
City: Los Alamos
State: NM
Publication Website: www.lamonitor.com
Postal Code: 87544-3233
Office phone: (505) 662-4185
General E-mail: laads@lamonitor.com
Publisher Name: Keven Todd
Editor Name: Jill McLaughlin
Editor Email: jill@lamonitor.com
Editor Phone: (505) 662-4185, Ext : 4
Advertising Executive Name: Jan Montoya
Advertising Executive Email: jan@lamonitor.com
Advertising Executive Phone: (505) 662-4185, Ext : 8
Year Established: 1963
Delivery Methods: Newsstand`Carrier`Racks
Own Printing Facility?: Y
Commercial printers?: Y
Mechanical specifications: Type page 13 x 21 1/2; E - 6 cols, 1 3/4, 1/8 between; A - 6 cols, 1 3/4, 1/8 between; C - 8 cols, 1 5/16, 1/8 between.
Published Days: Tues`Wed`Thur`Fri`Sun
Weekday Frequency: e
Avg Paid Circ: 4000
Audit Company: Sworn/Estimate/Non-Audited
Audit Date: 7 12 2019
Pressroom Equipment: Lines – 5-G/Community;
Mailroom Equipment: Counter Stackers – BG/104A;
Buisness Equipment: VGA PC, Dell/Hard Disc 3165X
Buisness Software: Dell/Hard Disc 3165X
Classified Equipment: Hardware – AST/Bravo 4-33;
Editorial Equipment: Hardware – APP/Mac, APP/Power Mac 7100-66; Printers – Xante/Accel-a-Writer
Editorial Software: QPS/QuarkXPress.
Production Equipment: Hardware – 1-Nu/Flip Top; Cameras – Nu/2024; Scanners – Nikon
Production Software: QPS/QuarkXPress, Multi-Ad/CAMS, Multi-Ad/Class Force.
Total Circulation: 4000

ROSWELL

ROSWELL DAILY RECORD

Corporate/Parent Company: New Mexico Press Association
Publication Street Address: 2301 N Main St
City: Roswell
State: NM
Publication Website: www.rdrnews.com
Postal Code: 88201-6452
Office phone: (575) 622-7710
General E-mail: hr@rdrnews.com
Publisher Name: Barbara Beck
Year Established: 1891
Delivery Methods:
Mail`Newsstand`Carrier`Racks
Own Printing Facility?: Y
Commercial printers?: N
Mechanical specifications: Type page 13 1/16 x 21 1/2; E - 6 cols, 2 1/16, 1/6 between; A - 6 cols, 2 1/16, 1/6 between; C - 8 cols, 1 1/2, 1/6 between.
Published Days: Tues`Wed`Thur`Fri`Sat`Sun
Weekday Frequency: m
Saturday Frequency: m
Avg Paid Circ: 9000
Audit Company: Sworn/Estimate/Non-Audited
Audit Date: 7 12 2019
Pressroom Equipment: Lines – 6-G/Urbanite (1 balloon former) single width;
Mailroom Equipment: Counter Stackers – 1/MM; Inserters & Stuffers – 1-MM/6 Pocket, 1-MM/227 6 Pocket; Tying Machines – 1-EAM-Mosca/Rom, 1-ACE/50; Address Machine – 1-Xenix/System;
Buisness Equipment: Mk/Acer-View, Epson/Printer, BMF/Newspaper System
Buisness Software: Microsoft Dynamics GP
Classified Equipment: Hardware – APP/iMacs; Printers – APP/Mac Laser Writer 16/600 PS;
Classified Software: Newscycle/AdManager Pro.
Editorial Equipment: Hardware – APP/Mac Performa 6116 CD-Roms, Polaroid/Sprintscan, AG/Arcus II Scanners/Lf/AP Leaf Picture Desk, Lf/Leafscan, Lf/AP Laserphoto, AG/Arcus II Scanners, Epson/Photo PC 600 Digital Camera; Printers – APP/Mac LaserPrinters
Production Equipment: Hardware – Caere/OmniPage 2.12, Konica EV Jetsetter 3100S, Xante/Laserprinters; Cameras – 1-C/Spartan II; Scanners – 2-APP/Mac Scanner, 2-AG/Arcus IIs
Production Software: QPS/QuarkXPress 4.00.
Total Circulation: 9000

SILVER CITY

SILVER CITY DAILY PRESS

Publication Street Address: 300 W. Market St.,
City: Silver City
State: NM
Publication Website: www.scdailypress.com
Postal Code: 88061
Office phone: (575) 388-1576
Editor Name: Nickolas Seibel
Editor Email: nick@scdailypress.com

SILVER CITY SUN-NEWS

Corporate/Parent Company: Gannett
Publication Street Address: 208 W Broadway St
City: Silver City
State: NM
Publication Website: www.scsun-news.com
Postal Code: 88061-5353
Office phone: (575) 538-5893
General E-mail: silvercitysunnews@gannett.com
Publisher Name: Jared Hamilton
Advertising Executive Name: Damarrio Mitchell
Advertising Executive Email: ddmitchell@lcsun-news.com
Advertising Executive Phone: (575) 541-5421
Delivery Methods: Mail`Racks
Published Days: Mon`Tues`Wed`Thur`Fri`Sat`Sun
Weekday Frequency: m
Saturday Frequency: m
Audit Company: Sworn/Estimate/Non-Audited
Audit Date: 7 12 2019

NEVADA

CARSON CITY

NEVADA APPEAL

Publication Street Address: 580 Mallory Way
City: Carson City
State: NV
Publication Website: www.nevadaappeal.com
Postal Code: 89701-5360
Office phone: (775) 882-2111
General E-mail: mraher@sierranevadamedia.com
Publisher Name: Peter Bernhard
Editor Name: Adam Trumble
Editor Email: atrumble@nevadaappeal.com
Editor Phone: (775) 881-1221
Advertising Executive Name: AJ Horn
Advertising Executive Email: ahorn@nevadanewsgroup.com

ELKO

ELKO DAILY FREE PRESS

Corporate/Parent Company: Lee Enterprises
Publication Street Address: 3720 E Idaho St
City: Elko
State: NV
Publication Website: www.elkodaily.com
Postal Code: 89801-4611
Office phone: (775) 738-3118
General E-mail: advertising@elkodaily.com
Publisher Name: Matt Sandberg
Publisher Email: matt.sandberg@lee.net
Publisher Phone: (208) 735-3345
Editor Name: Jeff Mullins
Editor Email: jmullins@elkodaily.com
Editor Phone: (775) 748-2707
Advertising Executive Name: Nancy Streets
Advertising Executive Email: nstreets@elkodaily.com

HENDERSON

LAS VEGAS SUN

Corporate/Parent Company: Swift Communications, Inc.
Publication Street Address: 2275 Corporate Cir
City: Henderson
State: NV
Publication Website: www.lasvegassun.com
Postal Code: 89074-7745
Office phone: (702) 385-3111
General E-mail: rebecca@lasvegassun.com
Publisher Name: Brian Greenspun
Publisher Phone: (702) 259-4003
Editor Name: Ray Brewer
Editor Phone: (702) 990-2662

LAS VEGAS

LAS VEGAS REVIEW-JOURNAL

Corporate/Parent Company: Las Vegas Review-Journal, Inc.
Publication Street Address: 1111 W Bonanza Rd
City: Las Vegas
State: NV
Publication Website: www.reviewjournal.com
Postal Code: 89106-3545
Office phone: (702) 383-0211
General E-mail: kparker@reviewjournal.com
Publisher Name: J. Keith Moyer
Publisher Email: kmoyer@reviewjournal.com
Editor Name: Anastasia Hendrix
Editor Email: ahendrix@reviewjournal.com
Editor Phone: (702) 383-0232
Advertising Executive Name: Christy Cuthbert
Advertising Executive Email: ccuthbert@reviewjournal.com

RENO

RENO GAZETTE-JOURNAL

Corporate/Parent Company: Gannett Co., Inc.
Publication Street Address: 955 Kuenzli St
City: Reno
State: NV
Publication Website: www.rgj.com
Postal Code: 89502-1160
Office phone: (775) 788-6397
General E-mail: customerservice@rgj.com
Editor Name: Brian Duggan
Editor Email: bduggan@rgj.com

NEVADA

ALBANY

TIMES UNION

Corporate/Parent Company: Hearst Communications Inc.
Publication Street Address: 645 Albany Shaker Rd
City: Albany
State: NY
Publication Website: www.timesunion.com
Postal Code: 12211-1158
Office phone: (518) 454-5694
General E-mail: schartrand@timesunion.com
Publisher Name: George R. Hearst
Publisher Email: ghearst@timesunion.com
Editor Name: Casey Seiler
Editor Email: cseiler@timesunion.com
Advertising Executive Name: Tom Eason
Advertising Executive Email: teason@timesunion.com
Year Established: 1856
Delivery Methods: Newsstand`Carrier`Racks
Own Printing Facility?: Y
Commercial printers?: Y
Mechanical specifications: Type page 11 x 21 1/2; Editorial - 6 cols, 1 7/8, 1/8 between; Advertising - 6 cols, 1 7/8, 1/8 between; Classified - 6 cols, 1 7/8, 1/8 between.
Published Days: Mon`Tues`Wed`Thur`Fri`Sat`Sun
Weekday Frequency: m
Saturday Frequency: m
Avg Paid Circ: 43297
Audit Company: AAM
Audit Date: 16 06 2020
Pressroom Equipment: Ferag conveyors 2 lines; KBA Commander GL 4 Tower - 32 couple - full color; Schur Palletizer
Pressroom Software: KBA Controls
Mailroom Equipment: Counter Stackers – 8/QWI; Inserters & Stuffers – 2-HI/2299 on-line, 1-HI/632, 1 Schur Palitzer; Tying Machines – 8-/Dynaric ; Control System – SAM, 2299; Address Machine – 1-/Ch, 2-/LSI;
Mailroom Software: SAM planning Win Lines
Classified Equipment: Hardware – Sun Cluster;
Classified Software: Mactive
Editorial Equipment: Hardware – Sun
Editorial Software: DTI
Production Equipment: AGFA Advantage NDL Platesetters - 1; VCF Chemfree Processors -2; Nela VCP Vision Benders
Production Software: Newsway Integration; Afgar Arkitek
Total Circulation: 95716

AMSTERDAM

THE RECORDER

Publication Street Address: 1 Venner Rd
City: Amsterdam
State: NY
Publication Website: www.recordernews.com
Postal Code: 12010-5617
Office phone: (518) 843-1100
General E-mail: sales@recordernews.com
Publisher Name: Kevin McClary
Publisher Email: kevin@mcclarymedia.com
Editor Name: Charlie Kraebel
Editor Email: charlie.kraebel@mcclarymedia.com
Advertising Executive Name: Brian Krohn
Advertising Executive Email: brian.krohn@mcclarymedia.com
Mechanical specifications: Type page 13 x 21 1/2; E – 6 cols, 2 1/16, 1/8 between; A – 6 cols, 2 1/16, 1/8 between; C – 8 cols, 1 9/16, 1/16 between.
Published Days: Mon`Tues`Wed`Thur`Fri`Sat
Weekday Frequency: m
Saturday Frequency: m
Avg Paid Circ: 8116
Audit Company: Sworn/Estimate/Non-Audited
Audit Date: 7 12 2019
Pressroom Equipment: Lines – 6-G/Urbanite (3- N3 in Line); Folders – G/2:1; Control System – 2-Fin/Console.;
Mailroom Equipment: Tying Machines – Bu/SA 505; Address Machine – Ch/596.;
Buisness Equipment: 1-TI/1505
Buisness Software: Papertrak
Classified Equipment: Hardware – 1-AT/7000.;
Editorial Equipment: Hardware – 1-AT/7000/1-LE/PC 13 Dry Film Processor.
Production Equipment: Hardware – 2-AU/APS U5, 1-B/MP2, 1-Amerigraph/437S-S; Cameras – 1-B/24, 1-AG/2024; Scanners – HP/Scanner
Production Software: QPS/QuarkXPress 3.3.
Total Circulation: 8116

AUBURN

THE CITIZEN, AUBURN

Publication Street Address: 25 Dill St
City: Auburn
State: NY
Publication Website: www.auburnpub.com
Postal Code: 13021-3605
Office phone: (315) 253-5311
General E-mail: jeffrey.weigand@lee.net
Publisher Name: Michelle Bowers
Publisher Email: mbowers@auburnpub.com
Publisher Phone: (315) 282-2201
Editor Name: Michael Dowd
Editor Email: michael.dowd@auburnpub.com
Editor Phone: (315) 282-2234
Advertising Executive Name: Tom Bachman
Advertising Executive Email: tom.bachman@lee.net
Advertising Executive Phone: (315) 282-2213
Year Established: 1816
Delivery Methods: Mail`Newsstand`Carrier`Racks
Own Printing Facility?: Y
Commercial printers?: Y
Mechanical specifications: Type page 11 x 21 1/2; E – 6 cols, 1.56, .167 between; A – 6 cols, 1.56, .167 between; C – 6 cols, 1.56, .167 between.
Published Days: Tues`Wed`Thur`Fri`Sat`Sun
Weekday Frequency: m
Saturday Frequency: m
Avg Paid Circ: 5391
Avg Free Circ: 1127
Audit Company: AAM
Audit Date: 30 06 2016
Pressroom Equipment: Lines – 14 G/comm, single width 2011; Folders – 1-G/2:1 1-G/4:1; Control System – Aug. 2011; Registration System – Stoesser/Register Systems.
Mailroom Equipment: Counter Stackers – 2-Id; Inserters & Stuffers – 8/MM; Tying Machines – 1-/OVL, 1-/MLN.;
Buisness Equipment: 1-Sun/Sparc Station 2, 1-Compaq/386sx
Buisness Software: Vision Data, Ciridian
Classified Equipment: Hardware – 7-Sun/Sparc IPC; Printers – 1-HP/LaserJet 4ML;
Classified Software: Vision Data/Island Write 4.0.
Editorial Equipment: Hardware – 17-Sun/3-50, 2-Sun/Sparc, 6-APP/Mac II, 2-APP/Power Mac 7100-80 CD/1-Telebit/Qblazer 9600 modem; Printers – 2-APP/Mac LaserWriter NTX
Editorial Software: Unix, Arbortext, APP/Mac OS, QPS/QuarkXPress 3.3.
Production Equipment: Hardware – 1-Graham/M-28, 1-P, 1-APP/Mac LaserWriter II NTX; Cameras – 2-SCREEN/Companion 640C; Scanners – 1-Lf/Leafscan 35, 1-Nikon/LS 3500, AG/Horizon, 1-AG
Production Software: SCS/Layout 8000, Lynx 4.0.
Total Circulation: 6518

BATAVIA

THE DAILY NEWS

Corporate/Parent Company:
Publication Street Address: 2 Apollo Dr
City: Batavia
State: NY
Publication Website: https://www.thedailynewsonline.com/
Postal Code: 14020-3002
Office phone: (585) 343-8000
General E-mail: customerservice@batavianews.com
Publisher Name: Michael Messerly
Publisher Email: mmesserly@batavianews.com
Publisher Phone: (585) 343-8000
Editor Name: Ben Beagle
Editor Email: ben@batavianews.com
Editor Phone: (585) 343-8000, ext : 1426
Advertising Executive Name: Jennifer Zambito
Advertising Executive Email: jzambito@batavianews.com
Advertising Executive Phone: (585) 343-8000, ext : 1446
Year Established: 1831
Delivery Methods: Newsstand`Carrier`Racks
Own Printing Facility?: Y
Commercial printers?: N
Mechanical specifications: Type page 10.87 x 20. 6 cols.
Published Days: Mon`Tues`Wed`Thur`Fri`Sat
Weekday Frequency: All day
Saturday Frequency: All day
Avg Paid Circ: 9937
Avg Free Circ: 141
Audit Company: AAM
Audit Date: 31 10 2019
Buisness Equipment: IBM, IBM/AS-400
Buisness Software: Microsoft/Windows 95, PBS
Classified Equipment: Hardware – 3-APP/Mac; Printers – APP/Mac LaserWriter;
Classified Software: Baseview.
Editorial Equipment: Hardware – 4-APP/Mac fileserver/2-HP/LaserJet 4MV; Printers – 1-Graphic Enterprise/Pro Setter, Graphic Enterprise/Pro Setter 1000
Editorial Software: Baseview.
Production Equipment: Hardware – Caere/OmniPage 8.0, Nu/Flip Top FT40APRNS 631, 1-Nu/FT40APRNS; Cameras – 1-R/480, 1-Eskofot/6006; Scanners – 1-AG/V20 x 24
Production Software: QPS/QuarkXPress 3.31.
Total Circulation: 397150

BINGHAMTON

PRESS & SUN-BULLETIN

Corporate/Parent Company: Gannett Company Inc.
Publication Street Address: 33 Lewis Rd
City: Binghamton
State: NY
Publication Website: www.pressconnects.com
Postal Code: 13905-1040
Office phone: (607) 798-1234
General E-mail: rscott@pressconnects.com
Editor Name: Kevin Hogan
Editor Email: khogan@gannett.com
Editor Phone: (607) 798-1338
Year Established: 1904
Own Printing Facility?: Y
Commercial printers?: Y
Published Days: Mon`Tues`Wed`Thur`Fri`Sat`Sun
Weekday Frequency: m
Saturday Frequency: m
Avg Paid Circ: 17215
Avg Free Circ: 172
Audit Company: AAM
Audit Date: 14 03 2019
Pressroom Equipment: Lines – KBA Colora; Press Drive – KBA; Control System – EAE;
Mailroom Equipment: Counter Stackers – 7; Inserters & Stuffers – 2; Tying Machines – 7; Control System – Omnizone; Address Machine – 2 Kodak;
Total Circulation: 26171

BROOKLYN

EL DIARIO LA PRENSA

Corporate/Parent Company: El Clasificado
Publication Street Address: 1 Metrotech Ctr
City: Brooklyn
State: NY
Publication Website: www.eldiariony.com
Postal Code: 11201-3948
Office phone: (212) 807-4785
General E-mail: jorge.ayala@eldiariony.com
Editor Name: Carmen Villavicencio
Advertising Executive Name: Jorge Ayala
Advertising Executive Email: advertise@impremedia.com
Year Established: 1913
Delivery Methods: Newsstand
Own Printing Facility?: N
Published Days: Mon`Tues`Wed`Thur`Fri`Sat`Sun
Weekday Frequency: m
Saturday Frequency: m
Avg Paid Circ: 25223
Avg Free Circ: 1085
Audit Company: Sworn/Estimate/Non-Audited
Audit Date: 7 12 2019
Pressroom Equipment: Folders – 1-G/Urbanite, 1-G/Community SSC.
Buisness Equipment: PBS, IBM/RISC-600 340
Buisness Software: PBS, Progress
Classified Equipment: Hardware – Dell/Power Edge 4300, Dell/PC; Printers – HP/LaserJet 4000N;
Classified Software: Admax 5.38.
Editorial Equipment: Hardware – Dell/PC; Printers – HP/LaserJet 4000N
Editorial Software: SCS/Editorial 8000, Good News 3.0.
Production Equipment: Hardware – Ofoto, 2-V/VT 5300-4000; Scanners – 4-LaCie/Silver Scan II
Production Software: QPS/QuarkXPress 3.31, Adobe/Photoshop 3.5, Adobe/Illustrator 6.0.
Total Circulation: 26308

BUFFALO

THE BUFFALO NEWS

Corporate/Parent Company: Lee Enterprises
Publication Street Address: 1 News Plz
City: Buffalo
State: NY
Publication Website: www.buffalonews.com
Postal Code: 14203-2905
Office phone: (716) 842-1111
General E-mail: adops@buffnews.com
Publisher Name: Brian Connolly
Publisher Email: bconnolly@buffnews.com
Editor Name: Margaret Kenny
Editor Email: mkenny@buffnews.com
Advertising Executive Name: Cindy Colello
Advertising Executive Email: colello@buffnews.com
Advertising Executive Phone: (716) 849-5411
Year Established: 1880
Mechanical specifications: Type page 11 5/8 x 20; E – 6 cols, 1 5/6, 1/8 between; A – 6 cols, 1 3/32, 1/8 between; C – 10 cols, 1 1/4, 1/16 between.
Published Days: Mon`Tues`Wed`Thur`Fri`Sat`Sun
Weekday Frequency: All day
Saturday Frequency: m
Avg Paid Circ: 95151
Avg Free Circ: 4942
Audit Company: AAM
Audit Date: 26 11 2019
Pressroom Equipment: Lines – 7-KBA/Color A Offset double width; 7-KBA/Color A Offset double width; 6-Wd/Metropolitan (4-color deck) double width 1958; 6-Wd/Metropolitan (4-color deck) double width 1958; 6-Wd/Metropolitan (4-color deck) dou;
Mailroom Equipment: Counter Stackers – 8-HPS/Dual Carrier, 3-HPS/Dual Carrier, 3-QWI/501; Inserters & Stuffers – 1-AM Graphics/25-head dual delivery inserter, 1-AM Graphics/29-head dual delivery inserter; Tying Machines – 9-Dynaric/NP-1, 14-Dynaric/NP-2; Wrapping Singles – Wrapping si;
Buisness Equipment: 1-HP/3000-928, 1-HP/3000-918LX, 1-HP/3000-928
Buisness Software: CJ
Classified Equipment: Hardware – SII/Servernet (2000); 80-Coyote 3; Printers – HP/LaserJet 4MV;
Classified Software: Guardian, OS/C30.9.
Editorial Equipment: Hardware – SII/Servernet

U.S. Daily Newspapers

(2000)/Lf/AP Leaf Merlin Picture System, 125-Coyote/3 PC Emulation; Printers – HP/LaserJet 4MV
Editorial Software: Guardian, OS/C30.9.
Production Equipment: Hardware – 2-AGFA/3850 CTP, 1-Horizon/Ultra, 1-Lf/Leafscan, 1-Kk/2035; Scanners – 1-AG/Horizon Plus, 1-AG/Horizon Ultra, PixelCraft 2x8100 Scanner, 1-Tecsa/TS2470
Production Software: SII/Coyote Layout.
Total Circulation: 228990

CANANDAIGUA
DAILY MESSENGER
Publication Street Address: 73 Buffalo St
City: Canandaigua
State: NY
Publication Website: www.mpnnow.com
Postal Code: 14424-1001
Office phone: (585) 394-0770
General E-mail: messenger@messengerpostmedia.com
Publisher Name: Beth Kesel
Publisher Email: bkesel@messengerpostmedia.com
Publisher Phone: (585) 337-4217
Editor Name: Jennifer Reed
Editor Email: jreed@messengerpostmedia.co
Editor Phone: (585) 337-4226
Advertising Executive Name: Beth Kesel
Advertising Executive Email: bkesel@messengerpostmedia.com
Advertising Executive Phone: (585) 337-4217
Year Established: 1776
Mechanical specifications: Type page 13 x 20 1/2; E - 6 cols, 1 13/16, 1/8 between; A - 6 cols, 1 13/16, 1/8 between; C - 8 cols, 1 3/8, 1/8 between.
Published Days: Mon`Tues`Wed`Thur`Fri`Sun
Weekday Frequency: e
Avg Paid Circ: 6700
Audit Company: Sworn/Estimate/Non-Audited
Audit Date: 7 12 2019
Pressroom Equipment: Lines – 10-G/Community 1994; Folders – 1-G/SSC-8384.;
Mailroom Equipment: Counter Stackers – Id/440; Inserters & Stuffers – Am/Sheridan I372P; Tying Machines – MLN/Spirit Auto, Bu/Semi-Auto; Address Machine – Ch/Videojet;
Buisness Equipment: 11-Intel/Pentium 188
Buisness Software: MSSI
Classified Equipment: Hardware – HP/NetServers;
Classified Software: Baseview/Ad Manager Pro.
Editorial Equipment: Hardware – APP/Mac G3, HP/NetServers; Printers – HP/5000 N
Editorial Software: APP/Appleworks, QPS/QuarkXPress, Adobe/Photoshop.
Production Equipment: Hardware – Textbridge, GRHAM, Wing-Lynch/Model 5, Glunz & Jensen/66; Cameras – Vertical; Scanners – 2-Umax/PowerLook 2000, 3-Kk/Professional 2035
Production Software: QPS/QuarkXPress 4.04.
Note: Messenger Post Newspapers also publishes the Daily Messenger in Canadaigua, New York and one monthly regional guide to arts and antiques.
Total Circulation: 6700

CORNING
THE LEADER
Corporate/Parent Company: Adams Publishing Group
Publication Street Address: 34 W Pulteney St
City: Corning
State: NY
Publication Website: www.the-leader.com
Postal Code: 14830-2211
Office phone: (607) 936-4651
General E-mail: amingos@the-leader.com
Publisher Name: Rick Emanuel
Publisher Email: remanuel@the-leader.com
Publisher Phone: (607) 936-4651, Ext : 303
Editor Name: Shawn Vargo
Editor Email: svargo@the-leader.com
Editor Phone: (607) 936-4651
Advertising Executive Name: Heather Falkey
Advertising Executive Email: hfalkey@the-leader.com
Advertising Executive Phone: (607) 936-4651, Ext : 347
Mechanical specifications: Type page 10 x 14; E - 5 cols, 2, 1/6 between; A - 5 cols, 2, 1/6 between; C - 5 cols, 2, 1/6 between.
Published Days: Wed
Avg Paid Circ: 3200
Avg Free Circ: 80
Audit Company: Sworn/Estimate/Non-Audited
Audit Date: 6 10 2019
Total Circulation: 3280

CORTLAND
CORTLAND STANDARD
Corporate/Parent Company: New York Newspaper Advertising Service, Inc.
Publication Street Address: 110 Main St
City: Cortland
State: NY
Publication Website: www.cortlandstandard.net
Postal Code: 13045-6600
Office phone: (607) 756-5665
General E-mail: office@cortlandstandard.net
Publisher Name: Evan Geibel
Publisher Email: egeibel@cortlandstandard.net
Publisher Phone: (607) 756-5665, Ext : 168
Editor Name: Todd R. McAdam
Editor Email: tmcadam@cortlandstandard.net
Editor Phone: (607) 756-5665, Ext : 166
Advertising Executive Name: Julie Lucas
Advertising Executive Email: jlucas@cortlandstandard.net
Advertising Executive Phone: (607) 756-5665, Ext : 140
Year Established: 1867
Delivery Methods: Mail`Newsstand`Carrier`Racks
Own Printing Facility?: Y
Commercial printers?: N
Mechanical specifications: Type page 11 5/8 x 21 1/2; E - 6 cols, 1 3/4, 1/8 between; A - 6 cols, 1 3/4, 1/8 between; C - 6 cols, 1 3/4, 1/8 between.
Published Days: Mon`Tues`Wed`Thur`Fri`Sat
Weekday Frequency: e
Saturday Frequency: m
Avg Paid Circ: 8240
Audit Company: Sworn/Estimate/Non-Audited
Audit Date: 7 12 2019
Pressroom Equipment: Lines – 4-G/Urbanite 1968; 1 DGM
Mailroom Equipment: Tying Machines – 1/MLN.;
Buisness Equipment: Axil/311
Buisness Software: Vision Data
Classified Equipment: Hardware – Mk/3000; Printers – TI/810;
Classified Software: Mk/NewsTouch, AT/Classified.
Editorial Equipment: Hardware – Mk/3000 System; Printers – Epson/LQ1010
Editorial Software: SCS SCOOPEdit
Production Equipment: Hardware – Read-it/Pro 3.0A, 2-LaserMaster/Unity 1800-XL Plus; Cameras – 1-Eskofot/6006, 1-B/Commodore 24; Scanners – Applescan.
Total Circulation: 8240

DUNKIRK
THE OBSERVER
Corporate/Parent Company: Ogden Newspapers Inc.
Publication Street Address: 10 E 2nd St
City: Dunkirk
State: NY
Publication Website: www.observertoday.com
Postal Code: 14048-1602
Office phone: (716) 366-3000
General E-mail: advertising@observertoday.com
Publisher Name: John D'Agostino
Publisher Email: jdagostino@observertoday.com
Editor Name: Gregory Bacon
Editor Email: gbacon@observertoday.com
Advertising Executive Name: Meredith Patton
Advertising Executive Email: mpatton@observertoday.com
Year Established: 1878
Delivery Methods: Mail`Newsstand
Own Printing Facility?: N
Commercial printers?: N
Mechanical specifications: Type page 11 x 17; E - 5 cols, 1 14/15, 1/6 between; A - 5 cols, 1 14/15, 1/6 between; C - 5 cols, 1 14/15, 1/6 between.
Published Days: Wed
Avg Paid Circ: 1400
Avg Free Circ: 300
Audit Company: Sworn/Estimate/Non-Audited
Audit Date: 6 10 2019
Total Circulation: 1700

ELMIRA
STAR-GAZETTE
Publication Street Address: 310 E Church St
City: Elmira
State: NY
Publication Website: www.stargazette.com
Postal Code: 14901-2704
Office phone: (607) 734-5151
General E-mail: sgnews@gannett.com
Publisher Name: George Troyano
Publisher Email: gtroyano@stargazette.com
Editor Name: Neill Borowski
Editor Email: nborowski@stargazette.com
Year Established: 1828
Mechanical specifications: Type page 12 1/2 x 21 1/2; E - 6 cols, 2, 1/8 between; A - 6 cols, 2, 1/8 between; C - 9 cols, 1 7/16, 1/16 between.
Published Days: Mon`Tues`Wed`Thur`Fri`Sat`Sun
Weekday Frequency: m
Saturday Frequency: m
Avg Paid Circ: 11915
Avg Free Circ: 94
Audit Company: AAM
Audit Date: 30 03 2016
Pressroom Equipment: Lines – KBA Colora 8 towers with 6 (44) & 2 (42), Two Folders, online quarter folder & stitch ; Press Drive – KBA; Folders – 2-KBA; Pasters –10 KBA; Control System – EAE; Registration System – KBAEAE
Mailroom Equipment: Counter Stackers – 6 Quipp, 2 Gamblers; Inserters & Stuffers – 2 NP630; Tying Machines – 6 Dynaric; Wrapping Singles – 2 Samual shrink Wrap; Control System – Goss; Address Machine – 2 Kodak;
Buisness Equipment: 1-IBM/AS-400
Classified Equipment: Hardware – Mac;
Classified Software: Mactive
Editorial Equipment: Hardware – APP/Mac, SII/Tandem
Editorial Software: SII.
Production Equipment: Hardware – 3 -Kodak Thermal plate processors
Production Software: Newsway
Note: Newspapers are printed at the CNY plant located in Johnson City, NY
Total Circulation: 12009

GENEVA
FINGER LAKES TIMES
Corporate/Parent Company: Community Media Group
Publication Street Address: 218 Genesee St
City: Geneva
State: NY
Publication Website: www.fltimes.com
Postal Code: 14456-2323
Office phone: (315) 789-3333
General E-mail: nneabel@fltimes.com
Publisher Name: Mark Lukas
Publisher Email: mlukas@fltimes.com
Publisher Phone: (315) 789-3333, Ext : 263
Editor Name: Michael J. Cutillo
Editor Phone: (315) 789-3333, Ext : 264
Advertising Executive Phone: (315) 789-3333, Ext : 263
Year Established: 1895
Delivery Methods: Mail`Newsstand`Carrier`Racks
Own Printing Facility?: Y
Commercial printers?: Y
Mechanical specifications: Type page 12 x 21; E - 6 cols, 1 8/9, 1/8 between; A - 6 cols, 1 2/9, 1/8 between; C - 9 cols, 1 2/9, 1/16 between.
Published Days: Mon`Tues`Wed`Thur`Fri`Sun
Weekday Frequency: e
Avg Paid Circ: 9062
Avg Free Circ: 81
Audit Company: CAC
Audit Date: 30 09 2016
Pressroom Equipment: Lines – 5-G/Urbanite;
Mailroom Equipment: Counter Stackers – 1/KAN; Inserters & Stuffers – 1-KAN/480; Tying Machines – 2-/MLN; Address Machine – 1-/El.;
Classified Software: Media Span
Editorial Software: MediaSpan, QPS/QuarkXPress 4.04.
Production Equipment: Hardware – 2-Ultra Imagesetter; Cameras – 1-AG/RPS204 Vertical; Scanners – Epson/836 XL
Production Software: QPS/QuarkXPress 4.04.
Total Circulation: 9143

GLENS FALLS
THE POST-STAR
Corporate/Parent Company: Lee Enterprises
Publication Street Address: 76 Lawrence St
City: Glens Falls
State: NY
Publication Website: www.poststar.com
Postal Code: 12801-3741
Office phone: (518) 792-3131
General E-mail: ads@poststar.com
Publisher Name: Brian Corcoran
Publisher Email: bcorcoran@poststar.com
Publisher Phone: (518) 742-3355
Editor Name: Kenneth Tingley
Editor Email: tingley@poststar.com
Editor Phone: (518) 742-3225
Advertising Executive Name: Ben Rogers
Advertising Executive Email: ben.rogers@lee.net
Year Established: 1895
Own Printing Facility?: Y
Commercial printers?: Y
Mechanical specifications: Type page 11 5/8 x 21 1/2; E - 6 cols, 1 5/6, 1/8 between; A - 6 cols, 1 5/6, 1/8 between; C - 9 cols, 1 9/50, 1/8 between.
Published Days: Mon`Tues`Wed`Thur`Fri`Sat`Sun
Weekday Frequency: m
Saturday Frequency: m
Avg Paid Circ: 13452
Avg Free Circ: 3434
Audit Company: AAM
Audit Date: 1 03 2019
Pressroom Equipment: Lines – 10-G/Urbanite single width; Reels & Stands – 8;
Mailroom Equipment: Counter Stackers – 1-MM/338, 1-Id/Marathon, 1-Compass/180; Inserters & Stuffers – 1-SLS/1000R; Tying Machines – 1-MLN/MLN2HS, 1/OVL, 1-/Dynaric; Wrapping Singles – 1-HL/Monarch;
Buisness Equipment: 10-Compaq/486, 1-Sun/Ultra
Buisness Software: Vision Data
Classified Equipment: Hardware – 3-APP/Mac G4, 1-Sun/Ultra, 10-Dell/Optiplex; Printers – HP/5000;
Classified Software: Vision Data/Island Write.
Editorial Equipment: Hardware – 2-Micron/5200, 3-IBM/327, 2-Sun/Sparc 20, 28-Dell/Optiplex G1, 15-APP/Mac G4, 2-APP/MAC G5; Printers – HP/8000
Editorial Software: QPS/QuarkXPress 4.04, NewsEngin.
Production Equipment: Hardware – 1-Nu/Flip Top FT40V6UPNS, Nu/Flip Top FT32V3UP-KR, 1-AU/3850; Scanners – Nikon/Coolscan IV, 2-Epson/164XL
Production Software: QPS/QuarkXPress 4.04.
Total Circulation: 18732

U.S. Daily Newspapers

GLOVERSVILLE

THE LEADER-HERALD

Corporate/Parent Company: Ogden Newspapers Inc.
Publication Street Address: 8 E Fulton St
City: Gloversville
State: NY
Publication Website: www.leaderherald.com
Postal Code: 12078-3227
Office phone: (518) 725-8616
General E-mail: advertising@leaderherald.com
Publisher Name: Trevor Evans
Publisher Email: tevans@leaderherald.com
Editor Name: Patricia Older
Editor Email: polder@leaderherald.com
Advertising Executive Name: Cindy Reuben
Advertising Executive Email: creuben@leaderherald.com
Year Established: 1887
Delivery Methods: Mail`Newsstand`Carrier`Racks
Own Printing Facility?: Y
Commercial printers?: Y
Mechanical specifications: Type page 13 x 21 1/4; E - 6 cols, 2 1/16, 1/8 between; A - 6 cols, 2 1/16, 1/8 between; C - 8 cols, 1 1/2, 1/8 between.
Published Days: Mon`Tues`Wed`Thur`Fri`Sat`Sun
Weekday Frequency: e
Saturday Frequency: e
Avg Paid Circ: 5603
Avg Free Circ: 361
Audit Company: AAM
Audit Date: 31 12 2017
Pressroom Equipment: Lines – 6-G/Urbanite; 6-HI/V-15A; Folders – 1-G/2, 1-HI/Combination;
Mailroom Equipment: Counter Stackers – 2-BG/Count-O-Veyor; Tying Machines – 2/MLN, 1-/Sa; Address Machine – Ch.;
Buisness Equipment: NCR/386, Unix/486 System
Classified Equipment: Hardware – 3-COM/One Sys 140.;
Editorial Equipment: Hardware – COM/One 140, 5-APP/Mac/18-COM; Printers – APP/Mac LaserWriter, MON/ExpressMaster 1270, ECR/URL 36
Editorial Software: QPS/QuarkXPress, Aldus/FreeHand, Adobe/Photoshop.
Production Equipment: Hardware – 1-WL/30C, 1-Imperial/Top Coater; Cameras – 1-R/5000H, 1-Acti; Scanners – 2-HP/ScanJet Ilcx, 1-Kk/RS-2035
Production Software: QPS/QuarkXPress 3.11.
Note: The Gloversville Leader-Herald (eS) has a combination rate of $43.00 with the Saranac Lake Adirondack Enterprise (e). Individual newspaper rates not made available.
Total Circulation: 5964

HORNELL

THE EVENING TRIBUNE

Corporate/Parent Company: Johnson Newspaper Corp.
Publication Street Address: 32 Broadway Mall
City: Hornell
State: NY
Publication Website: www.eveningtribune.com
Postal Code: 14843-1920
Office phone: (607) 324-1425
General E-mail: advertising@eveningtribune.com
Publisher Name: Rick Emanuel
Publisher Email: remanuel@the-leader.com
Publisher Phone: (607) 936-9231
Editor Name: Chris Potter
Editor Email: chrispotter@gatehousemedia.com
Editor Phone: (607) 324-1425, Ext : 205
Advertising Executive Name: Heather Falkey
Advertising Executive Email: hfalkey@gatehousemedia.com
Advertising Executive Phone: (607) 324-1425, Ext : 215
Year Established: 1872
Delivery Methods: Mail`Newsstand`Carrier`Racks
Own Printing Facility?: Y
Commercial printers?: Y
Mechanical specifications: Type page 13 x 21 1/2; E - 6 cols, 2 1/16, 1/8 between; A - 6 cols, 2 1/16, 1/8 between; C - 6 cols, 2 1/16, 1/8 between.
Published Days: Mon`Tues`Wed`Thur`Fri`Sun
Weekday Frequency: e
Avg Paid Circ: 5400
Audit Company: Sworn/Estimate/Non-Audited
Audit Date: 7 12 2019
Buisness Equipment: 3-IBM/Nomad
Classified Equipment: Hardware – APP/Macs; Printers – APP/Mac Pro 630, HP/LaserJet 4MV;
Classified Software: Baseview.
Editorial Equipment: Hardware – APP/Macs; Printers – APP/Mac 630 Pro, HP/LaserJet 4MV, Xante/8300
Editorial Software: Baseview.
Production Equipment: Hardware – APP/Mac Pro 630, HP/LaserJet 4MV, Xante/8300; Cameras – 1-C/Spartan III; Scanners – HP/ScanJet
Production Software: Baseview.
Note: The Hornell Evening Tribune (e) and the Wellsville Daily Reporter (e) share a Sunday edition.
Total Circulation: 5400

HUDSON

REGISTER-STAR

Corporate/Parent Company: Hudson-Catskill Newspapers
Publication Street Address: 1 Hudson City Ctr
City: Hudson
State: NY
Publication Website: www.hudsonvalley360.com
Postal Code: 12534-2355
Office phone: (518) 828-1616
General E-mail: advertising@registerstar.com
Editor Name: Ray Pignone
Editor Email: rpignone@registerstar.com
Editor Phone: (518) 828-1616, Ext : 2469
Advertising Executive Name: Patricia McKenna
Advertising Executive Email: pmckenna@registerstar.com
Advertising Executive Phone: (518) 828-1616, Ext : 2413
Year Established: 1785
Delivery Methods: Mail`Newsstand`Carrier`Racks
Own Printing Facility?: N
Commercial printers?: N
Mechanical specifications: Type page 10.25 x 21 1/2; E - 6 cols, 2 3/100, 1/6 between; A - 6 cols, 2 3/100, 1/6 between; C - 10 cols, 1 11/50, 1/12 between.
Published Days: Tues`Wed`Thur`Fri`Sat`Sun
Weekday Frequency: m
Saturday Frequency: m
Avg Paid Circ: 3201
Avg Free Circ: 12
Audit Company: AAM
Audit Date: 30 09 2016
Pressroom Equipment: Lines – 13-G/Community 518-943-6953; Folders – G/SC.;
Mailroom Equipment: Tying Machines – Bu/Strapper.;
Classified Equipment: Hardware – APP/Mac G3; APP/Power Mac, APP/Mac G3, AG/1500; Printers – HP/4MV;
Classified Software: QPS/QuarkXPress.
Editorial Equipment: Hardware – APP/Power Mac, APP/Mac G3/APP/Power Mac, APP/Mac G3, AG/1500; Printers – HP/4MV
Editorial Software: Baseview/NewsEdit Pro, QPS/QuarkXPress.
Production Equipment: Hardware – Caere/OmniPro, AG/1500 Imagesetter; Cameras – Ret
Production Software: QPS/QuarkXPress.
Total Circulation: 3213

THE DAILY MAIL

Publication Street Address: 1 Hudson City Ctr
City: Hudson
State: NY
Publication Website: www.hudsonvalley360.com
Postal Code: 12534-2355
Office phone: (518) 828-1616
General E-mail: editorial@thedailymail.net
Editor Name: Ray Pignone
Editor Email: rpignone@registerstar.com
Editor Phone: (518) 828-1616, Ext : 2469
Advertising Executive Name: Patricia McKenna
Advertising Executive Email: pmckenna@registerstar.com
Advertising Executive Phone: (518) 828-1616, Ext : 2413
Year Established: 1792
Delivery Methods: Mail`Newsstand`Carrier
Own Printing Facility?: N
Commercial printers?: N
Mechanical specifications: Type page 13 x 21 1/2; E - 6 cols, 2, 1/6 between; A - 6 cols, 2, 1/6 between; C - 10 cols, 1 1/5, 1/12 between.
Published Days: Tues`Wed`Thur`Fri`Sat
Weekday Frequency: m
Saturday Frequency: m
Avg Paid Circ: 1858
Avg Free Circ: 14
Audit Company: AAM
Audit Date: 30 09 2016
Pressroom Equipment: Lines – 13-G/Community; Folders – G/SC.;
Mailroom Equipment: Tying Machines – 2; Address Machine – 1/Wm, 1-/X.;
Buisness Equipment: 2-IBM
Buisness Software: PBS
Classified Equipment: Hardware – APP/mac pro IMAC 6100, APP/Power Mac 7100, APP/Mac G3; Umax/Scanner; Printers – HP;
Classified Software: Baseview.
Editorial Equipment: Hardware – APP/Mac, APP/Power Mac, APP/Mac G3/AG/1500; Printers – 3-HP
Editorial Software: Baseview/NewsEdit Pro.
Production Equipment: Hardware – 3-Laser, HP, 2-AG/Imagesetters; Cameras – Repromaster/2001
Production Software: QPS/QuarkXPress.
Total Circulation: 1872

ITHACA

THE ITHACA JOURNAL

Corporate/Parent Company: Gannett Company Inc.
Publication Street Address: 123 W State St
City: Ithaca
State: NY
Publication Website: www.ithacajournal.com
Postal Code: 14850-5427
Office phone: (607) 272-2321
General E-mail: jriesbec@ithacajournal.com
Editor Name: Neill Borowski
Own Printing Facility?: Y
Commercial printers?: Y
Published Days: Mon`Tues`Wed`Thur`Fri`Sat`Sun
Weekday Frequency: m
Saturday Frequency: m
Avg Paid Circ: 6792
Avg Free Circ: 222
Audit Company: AAM
Audit Date: 13 11 2018
Pressroom Equipment: Lines – KBA Colora; Press Drive – KBA;
Mailroom Equipment: Counter Stackers – 7; Inserters & Stuffers – 2; Tying Machines – 7; Control System – Omnizone; Address Machine – 2 Kodak;
Total Circulation: 8853

JAMESTOWN

THE POST-JOURNAL

Corporate/Parent Company: Ogden Newspapers Inc.
Publication Street Address: 15 W 2nd St
City: Jamestown
State: NY
Publication Website: www.post-journal.com
Postal Code: 14701-5215
Office phone: (716) 487-1111
General E-mail: advertising@post-journal.com
Publisher Name: Michael Bird
Publisher Email: mbird@post-journal.com
Editor Name: John Whittaker
Editor Email: jwhittaker@post-journal.com
Advertising Executive Name: Debra Brunner
Advertising Executive Email: dbrunner@post-journal.com
Year Established: 1826
Mechanical specifications: Type page 11 3/4 x 21 3/4; E - 6 cols, 1 7/8, 1/8 between; A - 6 cols, 1 7/8, 1/8 between; C - 8 cols, 1 3/8, 1/16 between.
Published Days: Mon`Tues`Wed`Thur`Fri`Sat`Sun
Weekday Frequency: m
Saturday Frequency: m
Avg Paid Circ: 10783
Audit Company: AAM
Audit Date: 30 06 2018
Pressroom Equipment: Lines – 10-G/Urbanite single width; Press Drive – 2-Fin/150 h.p.; Folders – 1-G/Urbanite, 1-G/Suburban; Pasters –6-Martin/Splicer.
Mailroom Equipment: Counter Stackers – 1-RS/25, 3-HL/Monitor, 1/FDAB; Inserters & Stuffers – HI/NP 1372; Tying Machines – 2-Mosca/P2, 1-/Power Strap/5; Address Machine – 4-Typac/Label Dispenser;
Buisness Equipment: NCR/Unix
Classified Equipment: Hardware – Pentium/III Server, 5-CEL/366; AG/Arcus II, 5-APP/Mac C500; Printers – 2-APP/Mac LaserWriter II, 1-MON/EM 1270, 2-HP/4MV, 2-HP/LJ 2100 TN;
Classified Software: Microsoft/Windows NT, Microsoft/Windows 98.
Editorial Equipment: Hardware – 2-Pentium/III Server, 22-CEL/366/3-RSK/TRS 100, 2-RSK/TRS 102, 2-RSK/TRS 200, 1-Lf/AP Leaf Picture Desk, Lf/Leafscan 35, HP/ScanJet 4C, 4-APP/Mac G3, 1-APP/Mac C500, 1-Nikon/Coolscan; Printers – 2-APP/Mac LaserWriter II, 1-MON/EM 1
Production Equipment: Hardware – Nu/Flip Top FT40UPNS, 1-Trek/25, 1-MON/EM 1270, 1-APP/Mac C500, 1-APP/Mac AWS-60 Server, 2-HP/4MV, 1-APP/Mac AWS-7250 Server, 2-HP/LT 2100 TN; Cameras – 1-C/Spartan II, 1-C/Pager; Scanners – 1-Lf/Leafscan 35, 1-Nikon/Coolscan, 1-HP/ScanJet 4C;
Note: The Jamestown Post-Journal (mS) has a combination rate of $92.08 with the Dunkirk Observer (mS). Individual newspaper rates not made available.
Total Circulation: 10783

KINGSTON

DAILY FREEMAN

Corporate/Parent Company: Media News Group
Publication Street Address: 79 Hurley Ave
City: Kingston
State: NY
Publication Website: www.dailyfreeman.com
Postal Code: 12401-2832
Office phone: (845) 331-5000
General E-mail: ttergeoglou@freemanonline.com
Publisher Name: Kevin Corrado
Publisher Email: kcorrado@medianewsgroup.com
Editor Name: Ivan Lajara
Editor Email: ilajara@21st-centurymedia.com
Editor Phone: 845-331-5000, ext. 01095
Advertising Executive Name: Timothy J. Tergeoglou
Advertising Executive Email: ttergeoglou@freemanonline.com
Advertising Executive Phone: 845-331-5000, ext. 01099
Year Established: 1871
Delivery Methods: Mail`Newsstand`Carrier`Racks
Own Printing Facility?: N
Commercial printers?: N
Published Days: Mon`Tues`Wed`Thur`Fri`Sat`Sun
Weekday Frequency: m
Saturday Frequency: m
Avg Paid Circ: 7759
Avg Free Circ: 1005
Audit Company: AAM
Audit Date: 30 06 2018
Buisness Equipment: 4 HP DC5800

U.S. Daily Newspapers

Classified Equipment: Hardware – Atex, 2-RS6000 Pagination Terminal; Printers – HP/5000 GN;
Classified Software: Enterprise/17.
Editorial Equipment: Hardware – HP 6000 (14)/6 HP 6710; Printers – HP/5000 GN
Editorial Software: Atex/Prestige Via Citrix (Cloud), Photoshop, 1 NDesign, 1N Copy
Production Equipment: Scanners – 3-HP/4c
Production Software: QPS/QuarkXPress 3.32.
Total Circulation: 8764

LOCKPORT

LOCKPORT UNION-SUN & JOURNAL

Corporate/Parent Company: CNHI, LLC
Publication Street Address: 135 Main St
City: Lockport
State: NY
Publication Website: www.lockportjournal.com
Postal Code: 14094-3728
Office phone: (716) 439-9222
General E-mail: ann.fisherbale@lockportjournal.com
Publisher Name: John Celestino
Publisher Phone: (716) 439-9222, Ext : 2280
Editor Name: Matt Winterhalter
Editor Phone: (716) 282-2311, Ext : 2259
Advertising Executive Name: Ann Fisher-Bale
Advertising Executive Phone: (716) 439-9222, Ext : 6323
Year Established: 1821
Mechanical specifications: Type page 12 1/2 x 21 1/2; E - 6 cols, 1 3/4, 1/10 between; A - 6 cols, 1 3/4, 1/10 between; C - 10 cols, 1 1/5, 1/15 between.
Published Days: Mon`Wed`Thur`Fri`Sat`Sun
Weekday Frequency: e
Saturday Frequency: m
Avg Paid Circ: 4282
Avg Free Circ: 308
Audit Company: AAM
Audit Date: 19 04 2019
Pressroom Equipment: Lines – 10-G/Community; 10-Unit/Community; Press Drive – 2-HP/60; Registration System – Duarte/Pin Registration;
Mailroom Equipment: Tying Machines – 2/Bu, 2-/Power Strappers; Wrapping Singles – 2-/Bottom Wrappers;
Buisness Equipment: Unix/E450, PBS
Buisness Software: PBS
Classified Equipment: Hardware – APP/Mac, APP/Mac; Printers – APP/Mac LaserWriter;
Classified Software: QPS/QuarkXPress, DTI.
Editorial Equipment: Hardware – APP/Mac, APP/Mac/2-HP; Printers – APP/Mac Laser
Editorial Software: QPS/QuarkXPress, Baseview/NewsEdit, DTI.
Production Equipment: Hardware – Panther Pro, APP/Mac
Production Software: DTI 4.3.
Note: This publication shares a joint Sunday edition with the Niagara Falls (NY) Niagara Gazette and the North Tonawanda (NY) Tonawanda News.
Total Circulation: 5052

MALONE

THE MALONE TELEGRAM

Corporate/Parent Company: Johnson Newpaper Corp.
Publication Street Address: 469 E Main St
City: Malone
State: NY
Publication Website: www.mymalonetelegram.com
Postal Code: 12953-2128
Office phone: (518) 483-4700
General E-mail: ads@mtelegram.com
Editor Name: EJ Conzola
Editor Email: econzola@mtelegram.com
Editor Phone: (315) 755-1521
Advertising Executive Name: Karen Carre
Advertising Executive Email: kcarre@mtelegram.com
Advertising Executive Phone: (315) 755-1527
Year Established: 1905

Delivery Methods: Mail`Newsstand`Carrier`Racks
Own Printing Facility?: N
Commercial printers?: Y
Mechanical specifications: Type page 13 x 21 1/2; E - 6 cols, 2 1/16, 1/8 between; A - 6 cols, 2 1/16, 1/8 between; C - 8 cols, 1 1/2, 1/8 between.
Published Days: Mon`Tues`Wed`Thur`Fri`Sat
Weekday Frequency: m
Saturday Frequency: m
Avg Paid Circ: 4721
Audit Company: Sworn/Estimate/Non-Audited
Audit Date: 7 12 2019
Classified Equipment: Printers – HP/LaserJet;
Editorial Equipment: Printers – HP/LaserJet
Editorial Software: Saxotech – InDesign, InCopy
Production Software: QPS/QuarkXPress 3.31.
Total Circulation: 4721

MASSENA

DAILY COURIER-OBSERVER/ ADVANCE NEWS

Publication Street Address: 1 Harrowgate Cmns
City: Massena
State: NY
Publication Website: www.mpcourier.com/
Postal Code: 13662-2201
Office phone: (315) 769-2451
General E-mail: nbellinger@ogd.com
Editor Name: John B. Johnson
Delivery Methods: Mail`Racks
Published Days: Tues`Wed`Thur`Fri`Sat
Weekday Frequency: m
Saturday Frequency: m
Avg Paid Circ: 5900
Avg Free Circ: 1900
Audit Company: Sworn/Estimate/Non-Audited
Audit Date: 7 12 2019
Total Circulation: 7800

MELVILLE

NEWSDAY

Corporate/Parent Company: Newsday Holdings LLC
Publication Street Address: 6 Corporate Center Drive
City: Melville
State: NY
Publication Website: www.newsday.com
Postal Code: 11747-4226
Office phone: (800) 639-7329
General E-mail: advertising@newsday.com
Publisher Name: Debby Krenek
Publisher Email: publisher@newsday.com
Editor Name: Deborah Henley
Editor Email: editor@newsday.com
Advertising Executive Email: advertising@newsday.com
Year Established: 1940
Own Printing Facility?: Y
Commercial printers?: N
Mechanical specifications: Type page 9 25/64 x 13; E - 6 cols, 1 1/2, 1/16 between; A - 6 cols, 1 1/2, 5/64 between; C - 8 cols, 1 3/16, 1/16 between.
Published Days: Mon`Tues`Wed`Thur`Fri`Sat`Sun
Weekday Frequency: m
Saturday Frequency: m
Avg Paid Circ: 262833
Audit Company: AAM
Audit Date: 8 05 2020
Pressroom Equipment: Lines – 2-G/Metro 144 pg., 4-G/Metro BB with half decks 1979, 4-G/Metro BB, 2-TKS/M-72; 1-G/Metro 144 pg., 4-G/Metro BB with half decks 1979, 4-G/Metro BB, 2-TKS/M-72; 1-G/Metro 144 pg., 4-G/Metro BB with half decks 1979, 4-G/Metro, 2-TKS/;
Mailroom Equipment: Counter Stackers – 15-QWI/350, 23-QWI/400; Inserters & Stuffers – 8/AM Graphics/NP 630, 2-HI/1472, 4-HI/2299; Tying Machines – 6-Dynaric/NP1, 54-Dynaric/NP2; Wrapping Singles – 6-Overhead/Spiral Wrapper; Control System – Burt/NT.;
Buisness Equipment: Dell/Laptop, Dell/PC,

1-IBM/S-390 Parallel Enterprise Server 9672-R52, IBM/Netfinity Server, IBM/Laptop, IBM/PC, Sun/Enterprise Server
Buisness Software: ATEX/Enterprise, IBM/Lotus Notes, Unisys/Hermes
Classified Equipment: Hardware – AT/IAS System 10 Series 6;
Classified Software: AT/Sysdeco 4.37.
Editorial Equipment: Hardware – Dell/PC; Printers – HP/LaserJets
Editorial Software: Unisys/Hermes 4.x.
Production Equipment: Hardware – WL, 2-Dolev/800, 2-III/3850 Sierra, 2-MON/RIP Server, NEC, Scitex; Scanners – 1-AG/XY, 2-Eskofot, 1-Scitex/EverSmart Pro
Production Software: Cascade.
Note: Circulation is combined for Nasssau, Suffolk & Long Island editions.
Total Circulation: 248221

MIDDLETOWN

THE TIMES HERALD-RECORD

Corporate/Parent Company: Gannett Company Inc.
Publication Street Address: 40 Mulberry St
City: Middletown
State: NY
Publication Website: www.recordonline.com
Postal Code: 10940-6302
Office phone: 845-341-1100
General E-mail: amcfarlane@recordonline.com
Advertising Executive Name: Anthony McFarlane
Advertising Executive Phone: (845) 346-3016
Year Established: 1960
Delivery Methods: Newsstand`Carrier`Racks
Own Printing Facility?: Y
Commercial printers?: Y
Mechanical specifications: Type page 10 1/4 x 11; E - 4 cols, 3 1/6, 1/6 between; A - 6 cols, 1 1/2, 1/6 between; C - 8 cols, 1 1/4, 1/16 between.
Published Days: Mon`Tues`Wed`Thur`Fri`Sat`Sun
Weekday Frequency: m
Saturday Frequency: m
Avg Paid Circ: 24619
Avg Free Circ: 3362
Audit Company: AAM
Audit Date: 16 04 2019
Pressroom Equipment: Lines – 7-Goss.;
Mailroom Equipment: Counter Stackers – 5-QWI/N200, 7-QWI; Inserters & Stuffers – 3-GMA/SLS 1000 8:1, 4-Newstec; Tying Machines – 5/OVL, 7-Dynaric; Control System – Newscom; Address Machine – 4-Mirajet.;
Buisness Equipment: IBM/AS-400
Buisness Software: Microsoft/Office, Lawson
Classified Equipment: Hardware – AT/Enterpriise, Dewar/View; Printers – 1-AU/APS 3850.;
Editorial Equipment: Hardware – Dell Optiplex/21-Dell/Alpha; Printers – 1-DEC/LA 120, 1-DEC/LA 75, HP/LaserJet 4V, HP/LaserJet 4MV, HP/LaserJet 5si, HP/LaserJet 5si
Editorial Software: Jazbox
Production Equipment: Hardware – Arkitex; Scanners – Agfa
Production Software: InDesign
Total Circulation: 34561

NEW YORK

AMNEW YORK

Corporate/Parent Company: Newsday Media Group
Publication Street Address: 240 W 35th St
City: New York
State: NY
Publication Website: www.amny.com
Postal Code: 10001-2506
Office phone: (646) 293-9499
General E-mail: amnymarketing@am-ny.com
Year Established: 2003
Published Days: Mon`Tues`Wed`Thur`Fri
Weekday Frequency: m
Avg Paid Circ: 167818
Avg Free Circ: 4916

Audit Company: CAC
Audit Date: 30 09 2018
Pressroom Equipment: Lines – 212-239-5555;
Total Circulation: 172734

COLLEGE PARK NEWS

Corporate/Parent Company: Patch Media
Publication Street Address: 134 W 29th Street, 11th Floor
City: New York
State: NY
Publication Website: patch.com/maryland/collegepark
Postal Code: 10010
General E-mail: CollegePark@Patch.com
Editor Name: Deb Belt
Editor Email: deb.belt@patch.com

COLUMBIA NEWS

Corporate/Parent Company: Patch Media
Publication Street Address: 134 W 29th Street, 11th Floor
City: New York
State: NY
Publication Website: patch.com/maryland/columbia
Postal Code: 10010
General E-mail: Columbia@Patch.com
Editor Name: Elizabeth Janney
Editor Email: elizabeth.janney@patch.com

ESSEX NEWS

Corporate/Parent Company: Patch Media
Publication Street Address: 134 W 29th Street, 11th Floor
City: New York
State: NY
Publication Website: patch.com/maryland/essex
Postal Code: 10010
General E-mail: Essex@Patch.com

GAITHERSBURG NEWS

Corporate/Parent Company: Patch Media
Publication Street Address: 134 W 29th Street, 11th Floor
City: New York
State: NY
Publication Website: patch.com/maryland/gaithersburg
Postal Code: 10010
General E-mail: Gaithersburg@Patch.com
Editor Name: Deb Belt
Editor Email: deb.belt@patch.com

HYATTSVILLE NEWS

Corporate/Parent Company: Patch Media
Publication Street Address: 134 W 29th Street, 11th Floor
City: New York
State: NY
Publication Website: patch.com/maryland/hyattsville
Postal Code: 10010
General E-mail: Hyattsville@Patch.com
Editor Name: Deb Belt
Editor Email: deb.belt@patch.com

LAUREL NEWS

Corporate/Parent Company: Patch Media
Publication Street Address: 134 W 29th Street,

11th Floor
City: New York
State: NY
Publication Website: patch.com/maryland/laurel
Postal Code: 10010
General E-mail: Laurel@Patch.com
Publisher Phone: Elizabeth Janney
Editor Name: elizabeth.janney@patch.com

METRO NEW YORK

Corporate/Parent Company: SB New York, Inc.
Publication Street Address: 120 Broadway
City: New York
State: NY
Publication Website: metro.us
Postal Code: 10271-0002
Office phone: (212) 457-7790
General E-mail: advertising@metro.us
Advertising Executive Email: advertising@metro.us
Year Established: 2004
Delivery Methods: Racks
Own Printing Facility?: N
Commercial printers?: N
Published Days: Mon`Tues`Wed`Thur`Fri
Weekday Frequency: m
Avg Free Circ: 186185
Audit Company: AAM
Audit Date: 21 12 2018
Total Circulation: 182472

MONTGOMERY VILLAGE NEWS

Corporate/Parent Company: Patch Media
Publication Street Address: 134 W 29th Street, 11th Floor
City: New York
State: NY
Publication Website: patch.com/maryland/montgomeryvillage
Postal Code: 10010
General E-mail: MontgomeryVillage@Patch.com
Editor Name: Deb Belt
Editor Email: deb.belt@patch.com

NEW YORK DAILY NEWS

Corporate/Parent Company: Tribune Publishing
Publication Street Address: 4 New York Plz Fl 6
City: New York
State: NY
Publication Website: www.nydailynews.com
Postal Code: 10004-2473
Office phone: (212) 210-2100
General E-mail: customerservice@nydailynews.com
Editor Name: Robert York
Editor Email: ryork@nydailynews.com
Advertising Executive: Dan Sarko
Advertising Executive Email: dsarko@nydailynews.com
Advertising Executive Phone: (212) 210-2016
Year Established: 1919
Delivery Methods: Mail`Newsstand`Carrier
Mechanical specifications: Type page 9 3/8 x 14; E - 5 cols, 1 3/4, 3/8 between; A - 6 cols, 1 1/2, 1/8 between; C - 7 cols, 1 1/4, 1/8 between.
Published Days: Mon`Tues`Wed`Thur`Fri`Sat`Sun
Weekday Frequency: m
Saturday Frequency: m
Avg Paid Circ: 149057
Audit Company: AAM
Audit Date: 31 03 2019
Pressroom Equipment: Lines – 17-G/Newsliner Units double width (3-4 over 4 units) 1996; 17-G/Newsliner Units double width (3-4 over 4 units) 1996; 17-G/Newsliner Units double width (3-4 over 4 units) 1996; Folders – 9-G/Metro 3:2 Imperial Folder;
Mailroom Equipment: Counter Stackers – 30-Id/550, 12-HL/Monitor, 9-Fg/SCC, 18-S/Olympian, 9-Fg/SCC Conveyor; Tying Machines – 40-MVP/Ultra 5000 Strappers; Control System – Fg/Integrated Bundle Management System, 2-AT/Ferag PKT Plate Conveyor;
Buisness Equipment: 1-IBM/MVS
Buisness Software: DB/Millenium
Classified Equipment: Hardware – 5-AT/9000; 25-IBM/Selectric II, 25-TM/2277, APP/Mac.;
Editorial Equipment: Hardware – AT/Series 6, IBM/RS 6000/4-APP/Mac, 2-APP/Mac Plus; Printers – HP, Canon, AG
Editorial Software: AT/J-11, AT/Ed.
Production Equipment: Hardware – 4-M/606, 3-Cx/Supersetter.
Total Circulation: 149057

NEW YORK POST

Corporate/Parent Company: News Corporation
Publication Street Address: 1211 Avenue of the Americas
City: New York
State: NY
Publication Website: www.nypost.com
Postal Code: 10036-8790
Office phone: (212) 930-8000
General E-mail: slareau@nypost.com
Editor Name: Stephen Lynch
Year Established: 1801
Mechanical specifications: Type page 9 3/4 x 12 1/2; E - 6 cols, 1 1/2, 1/8 between; A - 6 cols, 1 1/2, 1/8 between; C - 7 cols, 1 5/16, 1/8 between.
Published Days: Mon`Tues`Wed`Thur`Fri`Sat`Sun
Weekday Frequency: m
Saturday Frequency: m
Avg Paid Circ: 422662
Audit Company: AAM
Audit Date: 23 05 2019
Pressroom Equipment: Lines – 8-G/Headliner Mark II; 8-G/Headliner Mark II; 8-G/Headliner Mark II; 8-G/Headliner Mark II; Folders – 4-G/3:2, 4-G/2:1.;
Mailroom Equipment: Counter Stackers – 9/St, 1-/HL; Tying Machines – 9-/MLN; Address Machine – 1-/Am.;
Editorial Equipment: Hardware – 4-HI, 36-HI/1720, 29-HI/1740, 36-HI/1780, 55-AST.
Production Equipment: Hardware – 2-AU/APS 5, 1-Kk; Cameras – 2-C, 3-SCREEN/240; Scanners – 1-ECR/Autokon.
Total Circulation: 528017

PERRYVILLE NEWS

Corporate/Parent Company: Patch Media
Publication Street Address: 134 W 29th Street, 11th Floor
City: New York
State: NY
Publication Website: patch.com/maryland/perryville
Postal Code: 10010
General E-mail: Perryville@Patch.com
Editor Name: Elizabeth Janney
Editor Email: elizabeth.janney@patch.com

ROCKVILLE NEWS

Corporate/Parent Company: Patch Media
Publication Street Address: 134 W 29th Street, 11th Floor
City: New York
State: NY
Publication Website: patch.com/maryland/rockville
Postal Code: 10010
General E-mail: Rockville@Patch.com
Editor Name: Deb Belt
Editor Email: deb.belt@patch.com

TAKOMA PARK NEWS

Corporate/Parent Company: Patch Media
Publication Street Address: 134 W 29th Street, 11th Floor
City: New York
State: NY
Publication Website: patch.com/maryland/takomapark
Postal Code: 10010
General E-mail: TakomaPark@Patch.com

THE NEW YORK TIMES

Corporate/Parent Company: The New York Times Co.
Publication Street Address: 620 8th Ave
City: New York
State: NY
Publication Website: www.nytimes.com
Postal Code: 10018-1618
Office phone: (212) 556-1234
General E-mail: nytnews@nytimes.com
Editor Email: editorial@nytimes.com
Year Established: 1851
Mechanical specifications: Type page 13 x 21 3/8; E - 6 cols, 2, 1/8 between; A - 6 cols, 2, 1/8 between; C - 10 cols, 1 3/16, 1/16 between.
Published Days: Mon`Tues`Wed`Thur`Fri`Sat`Sun
Weekday Frequency: m
Saturday Frequency: m
Avg Paid Circ: 471456
Avg Free Circ: 54090
Audit Company: AAM
Audit Date: 30 09 2018
Pressroom Equipment: Lines – 72-PEC/Converted offset (NY) 1978; 60-G/Colorliner (Edison NJ) 1989; Press Drive - 7, 7, 1; Folders – 9, 6-G/Sovereign;
Mailroom Equipment: Counter Stackers – 20-QWI/1000, 20-Id/2000, 6-Id/3000; Inserters & Stuffers – 8-HI/1472; Tying Machines – MLN/News 90, 12-Dynaric/Strap, 29-Metaveppa/Tyer; Address Machine – KR, St.;
Buisness Equipment: 2-IBM/9121-621
Classified Equipment: Hardware – 300-IBM/327, PC Custom Front End; AU/APS Imagesetter; Printers – 1-HP/LaserJet, 3-C.Itoh;
Classified Software: IBM/CICS Custom Application.
Editorial Equipment: Hardware – 42-AT/J-11, Pentium/PC 850, APP/Mac 300/150-Think Pad, 100-RSK/Tandy 1500, 40-Panasonic; Printers – HP/LaserJet 60, HP/4M Plus
Editorial Software: AT 4.7.
Production Equipment: Hardware – 2-LE/2600 online, 3-LE/24-18-25A, 3-APP/Mac, 2-Fuji/603, 4-AU/PSPIP2, 3-AU/APS-6, 1-MON/Express Master; Cameras – Kk/Model 5068 vertical camera; Scanners – 3-ECR/Autokon 1000, 4-ECR/Autokon 2000, Scitex/Smart Scanner, AU/Information INtt3, Mon
Note: The New York Times prints a national satellite edition at eight locations around the U.S.: Chicago; Warren, OH; Austin, TX; Torrance, CA; Walnut Creek, CA; Tacoma, WA; Atlanta; Ft. Lauderdale, FL.
Total Circulation: 525546

THE WALL STREET JOURNAL

Corporate/Parent Company: News Corporation
Publication Street Address: 1211 Avenue of the Americas
City: New York
State: NY
Publication Website: www.wsj.com
Postal Code: 10036-8701
Office phone: (800) 568-7625
General E-mail: wsjcontact@wsj.com
Editor Name: Matthew J. Murray
Editor Email: editors@barrons.com
Year Established: 1889
Mechanical specifications: Type page 10 3/4 x 21 1/2.
Published Days: Mon`Tues`Wed`Thur`Fri`Sat`Sun
Weekday Frequency: m
Saturday Frequency: m
Avg Paid Circ: 1111167
Avg Free Circ: 36484
Audit Company: AAM
Audit Date: 30 09 2017
Note: The Wall Street Journal is published in three regional editions: Eastern, Central, and Western. News content is the same in all editions, but advertising can be purchased in one or all editions or a combination thereof. Eastern Edition printed in White Oa
Total Circulation: 1147651

WESTMINSTER NEWS

Corporate/Parent Company: Trib Publications
Publication Street Address: 134 W 29th Street, 11th Floor
City: New York
State: NY
Publication Website: patch.com/maryland/westminster
Postal Code: 10010
General E-mail: Westminster@Patch.com
Editor Name: Elizabeth Janney
Editor Email: elizabeth.janney@patch.com

NIAGARA FALLS

NIAGARA GAZETTE

Corporate/Parent Company: CNHI, LLC
Publication Street Address: 473 3rd St
City: Niagara Falls
State: NY
Publication Website: www.niagara-gazette.com
Postal Code: 14301-1500
Office phone: (716) 282-2311
General E-mail: ngedit@niagara-gazette.com
Publisher Name: John Celestino
Publisher Phone: (716) 282-2311, Ext : 2280
Editor Name: Matt Winterhalter
Editor Phone: (716) 282-2311, Ext : 2259
Year Established: 1854
Own Printing Facility?: Y
Commercial printers?: Y
Mechanical specifications: Type page 11 5/8 x 21 1/2; E - 6 cols, 1 13/16, 1/6 between; A - 6 cols, 1 13/16, 1/6 between; C - 8 cols, 1 7/16, 1/16 between.
Published Days: Mon`Wed`Thur`Fri`Sat`Sun
Weekday Frequency: m
Saturday Frequency: m
Avg Paid Circ: 8055
Audit Company: AAM
Audit Date: 19 04 2019
Mailroom Equipment: Counter Stackers – 2-QWI/350, 2/Rockbuilt, 1-/Count-o-Veyor; Inserters & Stuffers – 2-GMA/SLS 1000 ID:1; Tying Machines – 2-/Power Strap; Wrapping Singles – 2-QWI/Bottom Wrap.;
Buisness Equipment: IBM/AS-400
Classified Equipment: Hardware – 6-APP/iMac; Printers – APP/Mac LaserWriter Pro;
Classified Software: DTI 4.2.
Editorial Equipment: Hardware – Sun/Enterprise 450/12-APP/Mac Centris 610, 10-APP/Mac G4, 7-APP/Mac G4 Graphics Server, 2-APP/iMac, 8-APP/Mac G4
Editorial Software: DTI 4.2.
Production Equipment: Hardware – 2-Nu/Flip Top, ECR/Scriptsetter VRL36, 1-3.5gig hard drive; Cameras – Acti/125 24x36; Scanners – 2-Umax/Astra 1200, UMAX/Powerlook 2100XL, Umax/Astra 24005, Epson/Perfection 1240u
Production Software: DTI/Speedwriter 4.2, DTI/SpeedDriver, DTI/AdSpeed
Note: This publication shares a joint Sunday edition with the Lockport (NY) Union-Sun & Journal and the North Tonawanda (NY) Tonawanda News.
Total Circulation: 7949

U.S. Daily Newspapers

NORWICH

THE EVENING SUN

Corporate/Parent Company: Snyder Communications Corporation
Publication Street Address: 29 Lackawanna Ave
City: Norwich
State: NY
Publication Website: www.evesun.com
Postal Code: 13815-1404
Office phone: (607) 334-3276
General E-mail: support@evesun.com
Publisher Name: Richard Snyder
Editor Name: Tyler Murphy
Advertising Executive Name: Russ Foote
Year Established: 1891
Delivery Methods: Newsstand`Carrier`Racks
Own Printing Facility?: Y
Commercial printers?: Y
Mechanical specifications: Type page 13 x 21 1/2; E - 7 cols, 1 2/3, 1/8 between; A - 7 cols, 1 2/3, 1/8 between; C - 7 cols, 1 2/3, 1/16 between.
Published Days: Mon`Tues`Wed`Thur`Fri
Weekday Frequency: e
Avg Paid Circ: 4000
Audit Company: Sworn/Estimate/Non-Audited
Audit Date: 7 12 2019
Pressroom Equipment: G/Community single width 1970; G/Community single width 1970; G/Community single width 1974; Press Drive – Fin/100 HP; Folders – 1-G/SC, 1-G/Community SC.;
Mailroom Equipment: Counter Stackers – Baldwin/Count-O-Veyor 109; Tying Machines – MA, Bu.;
Buisness Equipment: PC, Unix
Classified Equipment: Hardware – Mk, APP/Mac;
Classified Software: Baseview/Class Pro.
Editorial Equipment: Hardware – Mk, APP/Mac
Editorial Software: Baseview/NewsEdit Pro.
Production Equipment: Hardware – Caere/OmniPage Direct; Cameras – 1-AG
Production Software: QPS/QuarkXPress 3.31.
Note: We also publish 7 Free Community Publications
Total Circulation: 4000

OLEAN

OLEAN TIMES HERALD

Corporate/Parent Company: Community Media Group
Publication Street Address: 639 W Norton Dr
City: Olean
State: NY
Publication Website: www.oleantimesherald.com
Postal Code: 14760-1402
Office phone: (716) 372-3121
General E-mail: adcomp@oleantimesherald.com
Editor Name: Jim Eckstrom
Editor Email: jeckstrom@oleantimesherald.com
Editor Phone: (716) 372-3121, Ext : 223
Advertising Executive Phone: (716) 372-3121, Ext : 208
Year Established: 2000
Mechanical specifications: Type page 13 x 21 1/2; E - 6 cols, 2 1/16, 1/8 between; A - 6 cols, 2 1/16, 1/8 between; C - 9 cols, 1 3/8, 1/16 between.
Published Days: Mon`Tues`Wed`Thur`Fri`Sat`Sun
Weekday Frequency: e
Saturday Frequency: e
Avg Paid Circ: 8113
Avg Free Circ: 61
Audit Company: AAM
Audit Date: 25 09 2018
Pressroom Equipment: Lines – 7-G/U 791 (1 balloon former).;
Mailroom Equipment: Tying Machines – 2-MLN/ML2-EE.;
Buisness Equipment: Vision Data
Classified Equipment: Hardware – 3-APP/Power Mac; Printers – Okidata/193 Line Printer, HP/LaserJet 5000N;
Classified Software: Baseview.
Editorial Equipment: Hardware – APP/Power Mac; Printers – HP/LaserJet 5000N, Pre Press/Panther Plus 36, Pre Press/Panther Plus
Editorial Software: QPS/QuarkXPress.
Production Equipment: Hardware – 1-COM/7200, 2-COM/ACM9000, 2-COM/8600, 2-Unified/Composer; Cameras – 1-B/Commodore, 1-K/187; Scanners – 3-Dewar/Disc Net 55 Terminal, 3-Dewar/Discovery Display Ad Terminal
Production Software: Baseview.
Note: This newspaper is published in tabloid format on Saturday.
Total Circulation: 9567

ONEONTA

THE DAILY STAR

Corporate/Parent Company: CNHI, LLC
Publication Street Address: 102 Chestnut St
City: Oneonta
State: NY
Publication Website: www.thedailystar.com
Postal Code: 13820-2584
Office phone: (607) 432-1000
General E-mail: mneighbour@thedailystar.com
Publisher Name: Fred Scheller
Publisher Email: fscheller@thedailystar.com
Publisher Phone: (607) 441-7214
Editor Name: Robert Cairns
Editor Email: rcairns@thedailystar.com
Editor Phone: (607) 441-7217
Advertising Executive Name: Valerie Secor
Advertising Executive Email: vsecor@thedailystar.com
Advertising Executive Phone: (607) 441-7235
Year Established: 1890
Delivery Methods: Mail`Newsstand`Carrier`Racks
Own Printing Facility?: Y
Commercial printers?: Y
Mechanical specifications: Type page 11 13/16 x 21 1/2; E - 6 cols, 1 13/16, 1/8 between; A - 6 cols, 1 13/16, 1/8 between; C - 9 cols, 1 1/4, 1/16 between.
Published Days: Mon`Tues`Wed`Thur`Fri`Sat
Weekday Frequency: m
Saturday Frequency: m
Avg Paid Circ: 7491
Avg Free Circ: 475
Audit Company: AAM
Audit Date: 14 04 2020
Pressroom Equipment: Lines – 5-G/Urbanite single width 1974, 1-G/Urbanite 3-color single width 1999; Folders – 1-G/(with balloon); Reels & Stands – 5; Control System – 2;
Mailroom Equipment: Counter Stackers – QWI; Inserters & Stuffers – MM/227E; Tying Machines – 2-Sa/SR1A, 3-Si/LB 2000; Address Machine – Ch/Quarter folder Labeler.;
Buisness Equipment: IBM/AS-400
Buisness Software: 7-Microsoft/Office XP
Classified Equipment: Hardware – 8-Dell; Printers – 1-HP;
Classified Software: Atex/Enterprise.
Editorial Equipment: Hardware – 17-Dell; Printers – 2-HP
Editorial Software: AT/Dewarview.
Production Equipment: Hardware – 2-Konica/E-V Jetsetter, Konica/K-550; Cameras – 1-C/Spartan III
Production Software: QPS/QuarkXPress 3.0.
Total Circulation: 7154

PLATTSBURGH

PRESS-REPUBLICAN

Corporate/Parent Company: CNHI, LLC
Publication Street Address: 170 Margaret St
City: Plattsburgh
State: NY
Publication Website: www.pressrepublican.com
Postal Code: 12901-1838
Office phone: (518) 561-2300
General E-mail: grock@pressrepublican.com
Publisher Name: John Celestino
Publisher Email: jcelestino@pressrepublican.com
Publisher Phone: (518) 565-4130
Editor Name: Joe LoTemplio
Editor Email: jlotemplio@pressrepublican.com
Editor Phone: (518) 565-4148
Advertising Executive Email: advertising@pressrepublican.com
Advertising Executive Phone: (518) 565-4151
Year Established: 1942
Delivery Methods: Mail`Newsstand`Carrier`Racks
Own Printing Facility?: Y
Commercial printers?: Y
Mechanical specifications: Type page 10 1/4 x 21 1/2; E - 6 cols, 1 5/8, 1/16 between; A - 6 cols, 1 5/8, 1/16 between; C - 9 cols, 1 1/32, 1/16 between.
Published Days: Mon`Tues`Wed`Thur`Fri`Sat`Sun
Weekday Frequency: m
Saturday Frequency: m
Avg Paid Circ: 11623
Avg Free Circ: 579
Audit Company: AAM
Audit Date: 7 01 2020
Pressroom Equipment: Lines – 8-G/Urbanite; Press Drive – Fincor;
Mailroom Equipment: Counter Stackers – 2/Compass 1 Canon; Inserters & Stuffers – GMA/SLS 1000; Tying Machines – 2-MLN/2EE, 1-/Power Strap; Control System – Newscom;
Classified Equipment: Hardware – Dell/HP; IBM Server Microsoft Windows 2003 Server; Printers – HP 5200;
Classified Software: VD Class Pag. and Total Ads
Editorial Equipment: Hardware – COM/ONE, IBM/300PL/AP/Photo Server, IBM/RS6000; Printers – HP 5200
Production Equipment: Hardware – 2 - ECRM CTP Violet Imagers.
Total Circulation: 21118

POUGHKEEPSIE

POUGHKEEPSIE JOURNAL

Corporate/Parent Company: Gannett Co., Inc.
Publication Street Address: 85 Civic Center Plz
City: Poughkeepsie
State: NY
Publication Website: www.poughkeepsiejournal.com
Postal Code: 12601-2498
Office phone: (845) 454-2000
General E-mail: jdewey@poughkeepsiejournal.com
Publisher Name: Jim Fogler
Publisher Email: jfogler@poughkeepsiejournal.com
Publisher Phone: (845) 437-4900
Editor Name: Stu Shinske
Editor Email: sshinske@gannett.com
Year Established: 1785
Own Printing Facility?: N
Commercial printers?: N
Mechanical specifications: Type page 11 5/8 x 21; E - 6 cols, 1 5/6, 1/8 between; A - 6 cols, 1 5/6, 1/8 between; C - 10 cols, 1, 1/16 between.
Published Days: Mon`Tues`Wed`Thur`Fri`Sat`Sun
Weekday Frequency: m
Saturday Frequency: m
Avg Paid Circ: 18844
Audit Company: AAM
Audit Date: 11 03 2020
Buisness Equipment: IBM/AS-400
Buisness Software: Microsoft/Office, Microsoft/Outlook, AdSpeed 3.0, Adobe/Photoshop, Adobe/Illustrator, Aldus/FreeHand 4.0
Note: New York State Associated Press "Newspaper of Distinction," for best print and digital report in our circulation category, in four of the last six years (including 2015)
Total Circulation: 18783

ROCHESTER

DEMOCRAT AND CHRONICLE

Corporate/Parent Company: Gannett Co., Inc.
Publication Street Address: 245 E Main St
City: Rochester
State: NY
Publication Website: www.democratandchronicle.com
Postal Code: 14604-2103
Office phone: (585) 232-7100
General E-mail: solutions@democratandchronicle.com
Publisher Name: Travis Komidar
Publisher Email: tkomidar@gannett.com
Publisher Phone: (585) 258-9900
Editor Name: Mike Kilian
Editor Email: mkilian@gannett.com
Year Established: 1833
Mechanical specifications: Type page 11 5/8 x 21; E - 6 cols, 1 5/6, 1/8 between; A - 6 cols, 1 5/6, 1/8 between; C - 10 cols, 1 5/6, 1/16 between.
Published Days: Mon`Tues`Wed`Thur`Fri`Sat`Sun
Weekday Frequency: m
Saturday Frequency: m
Avg Paid Circ: 62275
Audit Company: AAM
Audit Date: 16 07 2020
Pressroom Equipment: Lines – MAN/Geoman 80 couples in 16 Footprints (2/3 presses) 1997; Folders – 3-MAN/3.2, 3-MAN/2:3:3;
Mailroom Equipment: Counter Stackers – 5-QWI/300, 5-QWI/350; Inserters & Stuffers – 2-HI/630 Inserters (28:1 or 13:2); Tying Machines – 9/Power Strap/PSN-6, 9-Dynaric/1500, 1-Samuel/NT30; Control System – Prima, GSN, QWI/Cart Loading System; Address Machine – Addressing m;
Buisness Equipment: IBM/AS-400
Buisness Software: Microsoft/Office 97, Microsoft/Office 2000, Microsoft/Windows 95, Microsoft/Windows 98, Microsoft/Windows 2000, Microsoft/Windows NT
Classified Equipment: Hardware – SII/45 XA, SII/71 Coyote 3, 4-Tandem/K-1000 CPUS; IBM/Netfinity 5500; Printers – Lexmark/Optra LXI;
Classified Software: Mactive.
Editorial Equipment: Hardware – AT/114/60-APP/Mac, ESE, Kk/2035 Plus Negative Scanner, HP/Server, 19-APP/Mac PowerBook, 6-Wintel, 22-NC/2000, AP/Digital Cameras, MS/NT Server; Printers – 1-Okidata, Pagescan, 7-HP, 3-HP, TI/Monoprint, HP/11x17, MON/Express
Editorial Software: Softwa
Production Equipment: Hardware – AG/Advantage 3350 DL; Scanners – 2-Scitex/320, AG/Duoscan 1200T, Umax/Powerlook 2100 XL
Production Software: QPS/QuarkXPress 4.1, CCI 6.7.0.2AT, Adobe/Creative Suite 2, SCS/Linx 4.13, SCS/Layout 8000 9.1, SCS/Inlay-In Design, Mactive.
Total Circulation: 77763

THE DAILY RECORD

Corporate/Parent Company: Gannett
Publication Street Address: 16 W Main St Ste 341
City: Rochester
State: NY
Publication Website: www.nydailyrecord.com
Postal Code: 14614-1604
Office phone: (585) 232-6920
General E-mail: karla.thomas@nydailyrecord.com
Publisher Name: Kevin Momot
Publisher Email: kmomot@bridgetowermedia.com
Publisher Phone: (585) 363-7272
Editor Name: Ben Jacobs
Editor Email: bjacobs@bridgetowermedia.com
Editor Phone: (585) 232-6922
Advertising Executive Name: Jean Moorhouse
Advertising Executive Email: jmoorhouse@bridgetowermedia.com
Advertising Executive Phone: (585) 363-7273
Year Established: 1908
Published Days: Mon`Tues`Wed`Thur`Fri
Weekday Frequency: m
Audit Company: Sworn/Estimate/Non-Audited
Audit Date: 7 12 2019

ROME

ROME SENTINEL
Corporate/Parent Company: Rome Sentinel Company
Publication Street Address: 333 W Dominick St
City: Rome
State: NY
Publication Website: www.romesentinel.com
Postal Code: 13440-5701
Office phone: (315) 337-4000
General E-mail: bwaters@rny.com
Editor Name: Richard Miller
Advertising Executive Email: advertising@rnymedia.com
Year Established: 1821
Delivery Methods: Mail`Newsstand`Carrier`Racks
Own Printing Facility?: Y
Commercial printers?: N
Mechanical specifications: Type page 12 x 21 1/2; E - 6 cols, 1-11/16, 1/8 between; A - 6 cols, 1-11/16, 1/8 between; C - 8 cols, 1 1/4, 1/8 between.
Published Days: Mon`Tues`Wed`Thur`Fri`Sat
Weekday Frequency: e
Saturday Frequency: m
Avg Paid Circ: 7801
Avg Free Circ: 143
Audit Company: AAM
Audit Date: 18 05 2020
Pressroom Equipment: Lines – 6-G/Urbanite, 1-G/Urbanite (3 color); Press Drive – 1-100 HP, 1-75 HP; Folders – 1-G/Urbanite.;
Mailroom Equipment: Tying Machines – 2/Sa, 2-MLN/ML2EE, MLN.;
Buisness Equipment: Cloud
Buisness Software: Newzware
Classified Equipment: Hardware – APP/Mac ; Printers – Lexmark;
Classified Software: SCATS 1.0, Claris/Filemaker Pro 3.0.
Editorial Equipment: Hardware – APP/Mac G3, 1999-APP/iMac; Printers – Lexmark, Epson
Editorial Software: Saxotech
Production Equipment: Hardware – Adobe/Photoshop, APP/Power Mac G3; Scanners – Epson/Scanner
Production Software: Mk/Page Director, Saxotech, Adobe inDesign
Total Circulation: 8261

SARANAC LAKE

ADIRONDACK DAILY ENTERPRISE
Corporate/Parent Company: Ogden Newspapers Inc.
Publication Street Address: 54 Broadway
City: Saranac Lake
State: NY
Publication Website: www.adirondackdailyenterprise.com
Postal Code: 12983-1704
Office phone: (518) 891-2600
General E-mail: ads@adirondackdailyenterprise.com
Publisher Name: Catherine Moore
Publisher Email: cmoore@adirondackdailyenterprise.com
Editor Name: Peter Crowley
Editor Email: pcrowley@adirondackdailyenterprise.com
Advertising Executive Name: Susan Moore
Advertising Executive Email: advertising@adirondackdailyenterprise.com.
Year Established: 1894
Delivery Methods: Mail`Newsstand`Carrier`Racks
Own Printing Facility?: Y
Commercial printers?: Y
Mechanical specifications: Type page 10 x 21; E - 6 cols, 1 1/2", 1/8 between; A - 6 cols, 1 1/2", 1/8 between; C - 8 cols, 1.125", 1/8 between.
Published Days: Mon`Tues`Wed`Thur`Fri`Sat
Weekday Frequency: e
Saturday Frequency: m
Avg Paid Circ: 3600
Audit Company: USPS
Audit Date: 10 01 2016
Pressroom Equipment: Lines – 6-G/Community.;

Buisness Equipment: NCR
Editorial Equipment: Hardware – COM, APP/Mac Classic
Editorial Software: WriteNow, QPS/QuarkXPress.
Production Equipment: Hardware – X; Scanners – 4-APP/Mac
Production Software: QPS/QuarkXPress.
Note: The Saranac Lake Adirondack Daily Enterprise (e) has a combination rate of $49.25 with the Gloversville Leader-Herald (eS). Individual newspaper rates not made available.
Total Circulation: 3600

SARATOGA SPRINGS

THE RECORD
Corporate/Parent Company: Media News Group
Publication Street Address: 7 Wells St., Suite 103
City: Saratoga Springs
State: NY
Publication Website: www.troyrecord.com
Postal Code: 12866
Office phone: (518) 270-1200
General E-mail: retailmgr@troyrecord.com
Publisher Name: Kevin Corrado
Publisher Email: kcorrado@medianewsgroup.com
Editor Name: Ron Rosner
Editor Email: rrosner@21st-centurymedia.com
Advertising Executive Name: Karen Alvord
Advertising Executive Email: kalvord@adtaxi.com
Advertising Executive Phone: (315) 231-5136
Year Established: 1838
Delivery Methods: Mail`Newsstand
Mechanical specifications: Type page 10 1/4 x 13 7/8; E - 4 cols, 2 1/2, 1/4 between; A - 4 cols, 2 1/2, 1/4 between; C - 6 cols, 1 1/2, 1/6 between.
Published Days: Thur
Avg Paid Circ: 5500
Audit Company: Sworn/Estimate/Non-Audited
Audit Date: 6 10 2019
Total Circulation: 5500

THE SARATOGIAN
Corporate/Parent Company: Media News Group
Publication Street Address: 7 Wells St, Suite 103
City: Saratoga Springs
State: NY
Publication Website: www.saratogian.com
Postal Code: 12866-2314
Office phone: (518) 584-4242
General E-mail: bfignar@21st-centurymedia.com
Publisher Name: Kevin Corrado
Publisher Email: kcorrado@medianewsgroup.com
Editor Name: Ron Rosner
Editor Email: rrosner@21st-centurymedia.com
Advertising Executive Name: Karen Alvord
Advertising Executive Email: kalvord@adtaxi.com
Advertising Executive Phone: (315) 231-5136
Mechanical specifications: Type page 12 3/8 x 21; E - 6 cols, 1 7/8, 5/16 between; A - 6 cols, 1 7/8, 5/16 between; C - 9 cols, 1 1/4, 5/16 between.
Published Days: Mon`Tues`Wed`Thur`Fri`Sat`Sun
Weekday Frequency: e
Saturday Frequency: m
Avg Paid Circ: 2158
Avg Free Circ: 367
Audit Company: AAM
Audit Date: 3 07 2020
Buisness Equipment: IBM/AS-400
Buisness Software: Lotus 5.0
Classified Equipment: Hardware – Novell/Network;
Classified Software: Dewar.
Editorial Equipment: Hardware – Sun/Ultra Enterprise 2
Editorial Software: Solaris/Unix 2.5, LinoPress.
Production Equipment: Hardware – Nikon/Coolscan, APP/Mac 7200
Production Software: LinoPress/Pagination 4.0.
Total Circulation: 4910

SCHENECTADY

THE DAILY GAZETTE
Corporate/Parent Company: Shaw Media
Publication Street Address: 2345 Maxon Rd Ext
City: Schenectady
State: NY
Publication Website: www.dailygazette.com
Postal Code: 12308-1105
Office phone: (518) 374-4141
General E-mail: boleary@dailygazette.net
Publisher Name: John DeAugustine
Publisher Phone: (518) 395-3051
Editor Name: Miles Reed
Editor Phone: (518) 395-3106
Advertising Executive Name: Bob O'Leary
Advertising Executive Email: boleary@dailygazette.net
Advertising Executive Phone: (518) 395-3154
Year Established: 1894
Delivery Methods: Newsstand`Carrier`Racks
Own Printing Facility?: Y
Mechanical specifications: Type page 12 x 21 1/8; E - 6 cols, 1 7/8, 1/6 between; A - 6 cols, 1 7/8, 1/6 between; C - 9 cols, 1 1/4, 1/8 between.
Published Days: Mon`Tues`Wed`Thur`Fri`Sat`Sun
Weekday Frequency: e
Saturday Frequency: m
Avg Paid Circ: 49724
Audit Company: AAM
Audit Date: 31 12 2017
Pressroom Equipment: Lines – 4-G/PEC (1-color hump; 2-color decks); Folders – 1-G/PEC; Pasters – G/PEC Auto; Reels & Stands – 8-G/PEC.;
Mailroom Equipment: Counter Stackers – 5/QWI; Inserters & Stuffers – 2-S/NP630; Tying Machines – Power Strap, NTP 40; Wrapping Singles – 1-/QWI; Address Machine – 1-/Ch.;
Buisness Equipment: 1-IBM/AS-400, PC
Buisness Software: Brainworks
Classified Equipment: Hardware – 35-PC; LaCie/Scanner;
Classified Software: HI/Adpower-Adpag.
Editorial Equipment: Hardware – 100-PC
Editorial Software: CD/2400, HI/XP-21, Multi-Edit/Lantastic.
Production Equipment: Hardware – ISSI/Scanning System, 2-HP/Printer, 2-ECR/3850, Konica/Jetsetter; Scanners – 2-ECR
Production Software: HI/NT 3.5.15.1.
Total Circulation: 49724

STATEN ISLAND

STATEN ISLAND ADVANCE
Corporate/Parent Company: Advance Newspapers
Publication Street Address: 950 W Fingerboard Rd
City: Staten Island
State: NY
Publication Website: www.silive.com
Postal Code: 10305-1453
Office phone: (718) 981-1234
General E-mail: danryan@siadvance.com
Advertising Executive Email: advertising@siadvance.com
Year Established: 1886
Delivery Methods: Newsstand`Carrier
Own Printing Facility?: Y
Commercial printers?: Y
Mechanical specifications: Type page 11 5/8 x 21 1/4; E - 6 cols, 1 5/6, 1/8 between; A - 6 cols, 1 5/6, 1/8 between; C - 10 cols, 1 1/12, 1/12 between.
Published Days: Mon`Tues`Wed`Thur`Fri`Sat`Sun
Weekday Frequency: e
Saturday Frequency: m
Avg Paid Circ: 21486
Audit Company: AAM
Audit Date: 31 12 2017
Pressroom Equipment: Lines – MAN/Geoman 70 2002; Folders – 2-MAN; Pasters –6–MAN/AutoReels & Stands – 6-MAN; Control System – MAN/PECOM 2000 2002.; GOSS/Compact Magnum 6 unit, Single wide, 32 page broadsheet, 64 tabloid capacity, Qtr fold, in-line stitch & Trim.
Pressroom Software: Goss Compact
Mailroom Equipment: 2-18 into 1 SLS3000 Inserters, 1- 10- into 1 SLS2000, Muller Martini news-grip and buffer system. 5 Quip 500, 3 Gamuller stackers. 2 offline Muller Martini 5 signature offline stitch & trim lines.
Buisness Software: Concur
Classified Software: AdBase, AdBase-E, PGL
Editorial Equipment: MacBook
Editorial Software: Moveable Type, Merlin, HSSN, Newscycle Content
Production Equipment: 3 Krause lines CTP, NELA benders
Production Software: Proimage Newsway, PGL, Newscycle Content
Total Circulation: 21486

SYRACUSE

THE POST-STANDARD
Corporate/Parent Company: Advance Newspapers
Publication Street Address: 220 S Warren St
City: Syracuse
State: NY
Publication Website: www.syracuse.com
Postal Code: 13202-1676
Office phone: (315) 470-0011
General E-mail: kbrill@advancemediany.com
Advertising Executive Name: Marie Morelli
Advertising Executive Email: mmorelli@syracuse.com
Year Established: 1829
Delivery Methods: Newsstand`Carrier
Own Printing Facility?: Y
Commercial printers?: Y
Mechanical specifications: Type page 12 x 21 1/2; E - 6 cols, 1 7/8, 1/8 between; A - 6 cols, 1 7/8, 1/6 between; C - 10 cols, 1 5/16, 1/32 between.
Published Days: Mon`Tues`Wed`Thur`Fri`Sat`Sun
Weekday Frequency: e
Saturday Frequency: m
Avg Paid Circ: 69739
Audit Company: AAM
Audit Date: 13 07 2020
Total Circulation: 97017

UTICA

THE HERKIMER TELEGRAM
Publication Street Address: 221 Oriskany Plaza
City: Utica
State: NY
Publication Website: www.herkimertelegram.com
Postal Code: 13501
Office phone: (315) 866-2220
General E-mail: bethadv@herkimertelegram.com
Publisher Name: Terry Cascioli
Publisher Email: tcascioli@uticaod.com
Publisher Phone: (315) 792-5002
Editor Name: Rob Juteau
Editor Phone: (315) 792-5101
Advertising Executive Name: Scott Rosenburgh
Advertising Executive Email: srosenburgh@uticaod.com
Advertising Executive Phone: (315) 792-5082
Year Established: 1898
Mechanical specifications: Type page 13 1/4 x 21 1/2; E - 6 cols, 2 1/16, 1/8 between; A - 6 cols, 2 1/16, 1/8 between; C - 8 cols, 1 3/4, 1/8 between.
Published Days: Mon`Tues`Wed`Thur`Fri`Sat
Weekday Frequency: e
Avg Paid Circ: 6657
Audit Company: Sworn/Estimate/Non-Audited
Audit Date: 7 12 2019
Pressroom Equipment: Lines – 6-G/Community.;
Mailroom Equipment: Tying Machines – 1/Sa; Address Machine – 1-/El.;
Buisness Equipment: Packard Bell
Buisness Software: Microsoft/Excel
Classified Equipment: Hardware – APP/Mac; Printers – TI;
Classified Software: Baseview/AdManager Pro.
Editorial Equipment: Hardware – APP/Mac;

U.S. Daily Newspapers

Printers – APP/Mac AdWriter
Editorial Software: Baseview/News Edit.
Production Equipment: Hardware – 1-COM/4961, SCREEN; Cameras – 1-B, Olympus/Digital
Production Software: Adobe/Pagemaker, QPS/QuarkXPress.
Total Circulation: 6657

THE OBSERVER-DISPATCH

Corporate/Parent Company: Gannett Company Inc.
Publication Street Address: 221 Oriskany St E
City: Utica
State: NY
Publication Website: www.uticaod.com
Postal Code: 13501-1201
Office phone: (315) 792-5000
General E-mail: srosenburgh@uticaod.com
Publisher Name: Terry Cascioli
Publisher Email: tcascioli@uticaod.com
Publisher Phone: (315) 792-5002
Editor Name: Ron Johns
Editor Email: rjohns1@uticaod.com
Editor Phone: (315) 792-5004
Advertising Executive Name: Scott Rosenburgh
Advertising Executive Email: srosenburgh@uticaod.com
Advertising Executive Phone: (315) 792-5082
Year Established: 1817
Delivery Methods: Mail`Newsstand`Carrier`Racks
Own Printing Facility?: N
Commercial printers?: Y
Mechanical specifications: Image Area: 10" x 20.812"
Published Days: Mon`Tues`Wed`Thur`Fri`Sat`Sun
Weekday Frequency: m
Saturday Frequency: m
Avg Paid Circ: 18083
Avg Free Circ: 1294
Audit Company: AAM
Audit Date: 14 12 2018
Classified Equipment: Hardware – SII/Sys 55, 11-SII/Coyote, APP/Macs; 11-SII/Coyote; Printers – Software ÃƒÂ£Ã‚Â£ÃƒÂ£Ã‚Â£ÃƒÂ£Ã‚Â£ÃƒÂ£Ã‚Â£ÃƒÂ£Ã‚Â£ÃƒÂ£Ã‚Â£ÃƒÂ£Ã‚Â£ÃƒÂ£Ã‚Â£ÃƒÂ£Ã‚Â£ÃƒÂ£Ã‚Â£ÃƒÂ£Ã‚Â£ÃƒÂ£Ã‚Â£Ã‚Â£ SII/Ad Director, Pongrass/Classified Pagemaker.;
Production Equipment: Hardware – Caere/OmniPage 2.1, Lf/AP Leaf Picture Desk, LS/2800R; Cameras – C/Marathon; Scanners – APP/Mac Pac Interface, 3-Umax
Production Software: QPS/QuarkXPress.
Total Circulation: 24714

WATERTOWN

WATERTOWN DAILY TIMES

Corporate/Parent Company: Johnson Newspaper Corp.
Publication Street Address: 260 Washington St
City: Watertown
State: NY
Publication Website: www.watertowndailytimes.com
Postal Code: 13601-4669
Office phone: (315) 782-1000
General E-mail: relias@wdt
Publisher Name: John B. Johnson
Publisher Email: jbj@wdt.net
Publisher Phone: (315) 661-2304
Editor Name: Alec Johnson
Editor Email: aej@wdt.net
Editor Phone: (315) 661-2351
Advertising Executive Name: Cindy Aucter
Advertising Executive Email: caucter@lowville.com
Advertising Executive Phone: (315) 755-1535
Year Established: 1861
Delivery Methods: Mail`Newsstand`Carrier`Racks
Own Printing Facility?: Y
Commercial printers?: Y
Mechanical specifications: Type page 13 x 21; E - 6 cols, 2 1/16, 1/8 between; A - 6 cols, 2 1/16, 1/8 between; C - 9 cols, 1 3/8, 1/16 between.
Published Days: Mon`Tues`Wed`Thur`Fri`Sat`Sun
Weekday Frequency: m
Saturday Frequency: m
Avg Paid Circ: 14197
Audit Company: AAM
Audit Date: 31 12 2017
Pressroom Equipment: Lines – 7-MAN/Uniman 4 x 2; Pasters –7-MEG; Reels & Stands – 7-MEG.;
Mailroom Equipment: Counter Stackers – 3/HL, 1-/KAN; Inserters & Stuffers – 2-GMA/SLS 1000; Tying Machines – 1-MLN/ML2EE, 2-/Dynaric; Address Machine – 1-Ch/582N.;
Classified Software: AD PLUS
Editorial Equipment: Hardware – HP/DELL/MAC
Editorial Software: Saxotech Cloud
Total Circulation: 14197

WELLSVILLE

WELLSVILLE DAILY REPORTER

Publication Street Address: 159 N Main St
City: Wellsville
State: NY
Publication Website: www.wellsvilledaily.com
Postal Code: 14895-1149
Office phone: (607) 324-1425
General E-mail: wellsvillereader@aol.com
Publisher Name: Rick Emanuel
Publisher Email: remanuel@the-leader.com
Publisher Phone: (607) 936-9231
Editor Name: Chris Potter
Editor Email: chrispotter@gatehousemedia.com
Editor Phone: (607) 324-1425, Ext : 205
Advertising Executive Name: Bridget Roberts
Advertising Executive Email: broberts@gatehousemedia.com
Advertising Executive Phone: (585) 610-9232
Year Established: 1880
Mechanical specifications: Type page 13 x 21 1/2; E - 6 cols, 2 1/16, 1/8 between; A - 6 cols, 2 1/16, 1/8 between; C - 6 cols, 2 1/16, 1/8 between.
Published Days: Mon`Tues`Wed`Thur`Fri`Sun
Weekday Frequency: m
Avg Paid Circ: 4500
Audit Company: Sworn/Estimate/Non-Audited
Audit Date: 7 12 2019
Buisness Equipment: 1-DEC/Rainbow 100
Classified Equipment: Hardware – Mk/1100.;
Editorial Equipment: Hardware – Mk/1100/2-IBM/Selectric II.
Note: The Wellsville Daily Reporter (e) and the Hornell Evening Tribune (e) share a Sunday edition.
Total Circulation: 4500

WHITE PLAINS

THE JOURNAL NEWS

Corporate/Parent Company: Gannett Company Inc.
Publication Street Address: 1133 Westchester Ave
City: White Plains
State: NY
Publication Website: www.lohud.com
Postal Code: 10604-3511
Office phone: (914) 694-9300
General E-mail: ezaccagn@lohud.com
Editor Name: Mary Dolan
Editor Email: mdolan@lohud.com
Advertising Executive Phone: (914) 694-5158
Year Established: 1829
Mechanical specifications: Type page 13 x 21 1/2; E - 6 cols, 1 5/6, 1/8 between; A - 6 cols, 1 5/6, 1/8 between; C - 10 cols, 1 1/10, 3/50 between.
Published Days: Mon`Tues`Wed`Thur`Fri`Sat`Sun
Weekday Frequency: m
Saturday Frequency: m
Avg Paid Circ: 38226
Audit Company: AAM
Audit Date: 31 10 2019
Mailroom Equipment: Tying Machines – 2-MLN/MLM 2EE; Address Machine – 4-Barstrom/Labeler.;
Buisness Equipment: 1-IBM/AS-400 320
Buisness Software: Admarc
Editorial Equipment: Hardware – DEC/VAX Output Graphic Database; Printers – Okidata.
Production Equipment: Hardware – LE, AII/3850; Cameras – C/Spartan; Scanners – ImagiTex/940.
Total Circulation: 46721

OHIO

AKRON

AKRON BEACON JOURNAL

Corporate/Parent Company: Gannett
Publication Street Address: 388 S. Main St. Suite 720
City: Akron
State: OH
Publication Website: www.ohio.com
Postal Code: 44311
Office phone: (330) 996-3000
General E-mail: jherbert@thebeaconjournal.com
Publisher Name: Bill Albrecht
Publisher Email: balbrecht@gatehousemedia.com
Publisher Phone: (330) 996-3782
Editor Name: Darrin Werbeck
Editor Email: dwerbeck@thebeaconjournal.com

ASHLAND

ASHLAND TIMES-GAZETTE

Corporate/Parent Company: Gannett Co., Inc.
Publication Street Address: 40 E 2nd St
City: Ashland
State: OH
Publication Website: www.times-gazette.com
Postal Code: 44805-2304
Office phone: (419) 281-0581
General E-mail: classified@times-gazette.com
Publisher Name: Bill Albrecht
Publisher Email: balbrecht@gatehousemedia.com
Publisher Phone: (330) 996-3782
Editor Name: Rick Armon
Editor Email: rarmon@times-gazette.com

TIMES-GAZETTE

Corporate/Parent Company: Gannett
Publication Street Address: 40 E. Second St.
City: Ashland
State: OH
Publication Website: www.times-gazette.com
Postal Code: 44805
Office phone: 419-281-0581
General E-mail: newsroom@times-gazette.com
Publisher Name: Bill Albrecht
Publisher Email: balbrecht@gatehousemedia.com
Publisher Phone: 330-996-3782
Editor Name: Rick Armon
Editor Email: rarmon@times-gazette.com

ASHTABULA

STAR BEACON

Corporate/Parent Company: CNHI, LLC
Publication Street Address: 4626 Park Ave
City: Ashtabula
State: OH
Publication Website: www.starbeacon.com
Postal Code: 44004-6933
Office phone: (440) 998-2323
General E-mail: marketplace@starbeacon.com
Publisher Name: Sharon Sorg
Publisher Email: ssorg@starbeacon.com
Publisher Phone: (440) 998-2323, Ext : 139
Editor Name: Ed Puskas
Editor Email: epuskas@starbeacon.com

ATHENS

THE ATHENS MESSENGER

Corporate/Parent Company: Adams Publishing Group
Publication Street Address: 9300 Johnson Road
City: Athens
State: OH
Publication Website: https://www.athensmessenger.com
Postal Code: 45701
Office phone: (740) 592-6612
General E-mail: info@athensmessenger.com
Publisher Name: Mark Cohen
Publisher Email: mark.cohen@adamspg.com
Publisher Phone: (740) 592-6612, Ext : 301181

BELLEFONTAINE

BELLEFONTAINE EXAMINER

Publication Street Address: 127 E Chillicothe Ave
City: Bellefontaine
State: OH
Publication Website: www.examiner.org
Postal Code: 43311-1957
Office phone: (937) 592-3060
General E-mail: news@examiner.org
Editor Name: Miriam Baier

BOWLING GREEN

SENTINEL-TRIBUNE

Corporate/Parent Company: AIM Media Indiana
Publication Street Address: 1616 E Wooster #15
City: Bowling Green
State: OH
Publication Website: www.sent-trib.com
Postal Code: 43402
Office phone: (419) 352-4611
General E-mail: ads@sentinel-tribune.com
Publisher Name: Karmen Concannon
Editor Name: Debbie Rogers
Editor Email: drogers@aimmediamidwest.com

BROOKLYN

THE PLAIN DEALER

Corporate/Parent Company: Advance Newspapers
Publication Street Address: 4800 Tiedeman Rd
City: Brooklyn
State: OH
Publication Website: www.plaindealer.com
Postal Code: 44144-2336
Office phone: (216) 999-5000
General E-mail: circhelp@plaind.com
Editor Name: George Rodrigue
Editor Email: grodrigue@plaind.com

BRYAN

THE BRYAN TIMES

Corporate/Parent Company: Bryan Publishing Co.
Publication Street Address: 127 S Walnut St
City: Bryan
State: OH
Publication Website: www.bryantimes.com
Postal Code: 43506-1718
Office phone: (419) 636-1111
General E-mail: ads@bryantimes.com
Publisher Name: Christopher Cullis
Publisher Email: christopher@bryantimes.com
Editor Name: Don Koralewski
Editor Email: editor@bryantimes.com

CAMBRIDGE

THE DAILY JEFFERSONIAN

Corporate/Parent Company: Gannett

Publication Street Address: 831 Wheeling Ave
City: Cambridge
State: OH
Publication Website: www.daily-jeff.com
Postal Code: 43725-2316
Office phone: (740) 439-3531
General E-mail: ads@daily-jeff.com
Publisher Name: John Kridelbaugh
Publisher Email: jkridelbaugh@daily-jeff.com
Publisher Phone: (740) 439-3531, Ext : 1240
Editor Name: Beth Bailey
Editor Email: bbailey@daily-jeff.com

CANTON

THE REPOSITORY

Corporate/Parent Company: Gannett
Publication Street Address: 500 Market Ave S
City: Canton
State: OH
Publication Website: www.cantonrep.com
Postal Code: 44702-2112
Office phone: (330) 580-8500
General E-mail: sheila.casler@cantonrep.com
Publisher Name: Jim Porter
Publisher Email: jim.porter@cantonrep.com
Publisher Phone: (330) 580-8444
Editor Name: Rich Desrosiers
Editor Email: rich.desrosiers@cantonrep.com

CELINA

THE DAILY STANDARD

Publication Street Address: 123 E Market St
City: Celina
State: OH
Publication Website: www.dailystandard.com
Postal Code: 45822-1730
Office phone: (419) 586-2371
General E-mail: classad@dailystandard.com

CHILLICOTHE

CHILLICOTHE GAZETTE

Corporate/Parent Company: Gannett
Publication Street Address: 50 W Main St
City: Chillicothe
State: OH
Publication Website: www.chillicothegazette.com
Postal Code: 45601-3103
Office phone: 888-357-8728
General E-mail: gaznews@chillicothegazette.com
Editor Name: Mike Throne

CINCINNATI

THE CINCINNATI ENQUIRER

Corporate/Parent Company: Gannett Company Inc.
Publication Street Address: 312 Elm St
City: Cincinnati
State: OH
Publication Website: www.cincinnati.com; www.enquirermedia.com
Postal Code: 45202-2739
Office phone: (513) 721-2700
General E-mail: letters@enquirer.com
Editor Name: Beryl Love
Editor Email: blove@cincinnati.com

CIRCLEVILLE

THE CIRCLEVILLE HERALD

Corporate/Parent Company: Adams Publishing Group
Publication Street Address: 401 E Main St
City: Circleville
State: OH
Publication Website: www.circlevilleherald.com
Postal Code: 43113-1843
Office phone: (740) 474-3131

General E-mail: news@circlevilleherald.com
Publisher Name: Debra Tobin
Publisher Email: dtobin@circlevilleherald.com
Publisher Phone: (740) 474-3131

COLUMBUS

THE COLUMBUS DISPATCH

Corporate/Parent Company: Gannett
Publication Street Address: 62 E Broad St
City: Columbus
State: OH
Publication Website: www.dispatch.com
Postal Code: 43215-3500
Office phone: 877-734-7728
General E-mail: cpettograsso@dispatch.com
Publisher Name: Bradley M. Harmon
Publisher Email: bharmon@dispatch.com
Publisher Phone: (614) 461-5586
Editor Name: Alan D. Miller
Editor Email: amiller@dispatch.com

COSHOCTON

THE COSHOCTON TRIBUNE

Corporate/Parent Company: Gannett
Publication Street Address: 550 Main St
City: Coshocton
State: OH
Publication Website: www.coshoctontribune.com
Postal Code: 43812-1612
Office phone: (740) 622-1122
General E-mail: llhayhur@gannett.com
Editor Name: Pam James

DAYTON

DAYTON DAILY NEWS

Corporate/Parent Company: Cox Media Group
Publication Street Address: 1611 South Main Street
City: Dayton
State: OH
Publication Website: www.daytondailynews.com
Postal Code: 45409
Office phone: (937) 225-2000
General E-mail: customercare@daytondailynews.com
Publisher Name: Rob Rohr
Editor Name: Jim Bebbington

MIDDLETOWN JOURNAL

Corporate/Parent Company: Cox Media Group
Publication Street Address: 1611 S Main Street
City: Dayton
State: OH
Publication Website: www.middletownjournal.com
Postal Code: 45409
Office phone: (877) 267-0018
General E-mail: bruce.karlson@coxinc.com

DEFIANCE

THE CRESCENT-NEWS

Corporate/Parent Company: Adams Publishing Group
Publication Street Address: 624 W 2nd St
City: Defiance
State: OH
Publication Website: www.crescent-news.com
Postal Code: 43512-2105
Office phone: (419) 784-5441
General E-mail: cnads@crescent-news.com
Publisher Name: Renee Campbell
Publisher Email: rcampbell@crescent-news.com
Publisher Phone: (419) 784-5441, Ext : 700721
Editor Name: Dennis Van Scoder
Editor Email: dvanscoder@crescent-news.com

DELAWARE

THE DELAWARE GAZETTE

Corporate/Parent Company: AIM Media
Publication Street Address: 40 N Sandusky St
City: Delaware
State: OH
Publication Website: www.delgazette.com
Postal Code: 43015-1973
Office phone: (740) 363-1161
General E-mail: delnews@aimmediamidwest.com
Editor Name: Joshua Keeran
Editor Email: jkeeran@aimmediamidwest.com

EAST LIVERPOOL

THE REVIEW

Corporate/Parent Company: Shaw Media
Publication Street Address: 210 E 4th St
City: East Liverpool
State: OH
Publication Website: www.reviewonline.com
Postal Code: 43920-3144
Office phone: (330) 385-4545
General E-mail: lludovici@reviewonline.com
Publisher Name: Tammie McIntosh
Publisher Email: tmcintosh@reviewonline.com
Editor Name: J. D. Creer
Editor Email: jdcreer@reviewonline.com

ELYRIA

CHRONICLE-TELEGRAM

Corporate/Parent Company: Lorain County Printing & Publishing Company
Publication Street Address: 225 East Ave
City: Elyria
State: OH
Publication Website: www.chroniclet.com
Postal Code: 44035-5634
Office phone: (440) 329-7000
General E-mail: jpfeiffer@chroniclet.com
Editor Name: Julie Wallace
Editor Email: jwallace@chroniclet.com

FINDLAY

THE COURIER

Corporate/Parent Company: Ogden Newspapers
Publication Street Address: 701 W Sandusky St
City: Findlay
State: OH
Publication Website: www.thecourier.com
Postal Code: 45840-2325
Office phone: (419) 422-5151
General E-mail: karifaulkner@thecourier.com
Publisher Name: Jeremy Speer
Editor Name: Scott Scherf

FOSTORIA

THE REVIEW TIMES

Corporate/Parent Company: Findlay Publishing Co.
Publication Street Address: 322 North Main Street
City: Fostoria
State: OH
Publication Website: www.reviewtimes.com
Postal Code: 44830-2905
Office phone: (419) 435-6641
General E-mail: advertising@reviewtimes.com
Publisher Name: Jeremy Speer
Publisher Phone: (419) 435-6641, Ext : 230
Editor Name: Linda Woodland
Editor Email: lindawoodland@reviewtimes.com

FREMONT

NEWS HERALD

Corporate/Parent Company: Gannett

Publication Street Address: 1800 E State St
City: Fremont
State: OH
Publication Website: www.portclintonnewsherald.com
Postal Code: 43420-4083
Office phone: (419) 332-5511
General E-mail: dyonke@gannett.com
Editor Name: David Yonke
Editor Email: dyonke@gannett.com

PORT CLINTON NEWS HERALD

Publication Street Address: 1800 E. State St., Suite B
City: Fremont
State: OH
Publication Website: www.portclintonnewsherald.com
Postal Code: 43420
Office phone: 419-332-5511
Editor Name: David Yonke
Editor Email: dyonke@gannett.com

THE NEWS-MESSENGER

Corporate/Parent Company: Gannett
Publication Street Address: 1800 E State St
City: Fremont
State: OH
Publication Website: www.thenews-messenger.com
Postal Code: 43420-4083
Office phone: (419) 332-5511
General E-mail: dyonke@gannett.com
Editor Name: David Yonke
Editor Email: dyonke@gannett.com

GALLIPOLIS

GALLIPOLIS DAILY TRIBUNE

Corporate/Parent Company: AIM Media Indiana
Publication Street Address: 825 3rd Ave
City: Gallipolis
State: OH
Publication Website: www.mydailytribune.com
Postal Code: 45631-1624
Office phone: (740) 446-2342
General E-mail: jschultz@civitasmedia.com
Editor Name: Beth Sergent
Editor Email: bsergent@aimmediamidwest.com

GREENVILLE

DAILY ADVOCATE

Corporate/Parent Company: AIM Media
Publication Street Address: 100 Washington Ave
City: Greenville
State: OH
Publication Website: www.dailyadvocate.com
Postal Code: 45331-1926
Office phone: (937) 548-3151
General E-mail: advertising@dailyadvocate.com

HAMILTON

JOURNALNEWS

Corporate/Parent Company: Cox Media Group
Publication Street Address: 228 Court St
City: Hamilton
State: OH
Publication Website: www.journal-news.com
Postal Code: 45011-2820
Office phone: (513) 863-8200
General E-mail: customercare@journal-news.com
Editor Name: Kevin Aldridge

U.S. Daily Newspapers

HILLSBORO

HILLSBORO TIMES-GAZETTE

Corporate/Parent Company: AIM Media Indiana
Publication Street Address: 108 Governor Trimble Pl
City: Hillsboro
State: OH
Publication Website: www.timesgazette.com
Postal Code: 45133-1145
Office phone: (937) 393-3456
General E-mail: shughes@aimmediamidwest.com
Publisher Name: Bud Hunt
Publisher Email: bhunt@aimmediamidwest.com
Publisher Phone: (937) 382-2574
Editor Name: Jeff Gilliland
Editor Email: jgilliland@aimmediamidwest.com

IRONTON

THE IRONTON TRIBUNE

Corporate/Parent Company: Boone Newspapers, Inc.
Publication Street Address: 2903 S 5th St
City: Ironton
State: OH
Publication Website: www.irontontribune.com
Postal Code: 45638-2866
Office phone: (740) 532-1441
General E-mail: shawn.randolph@irontontribune.com
Publisher Name: Sarah Simmons
Publisher Email: sarah.simmons@irontontribune.com
Publisher Phone: (740) 532-1441, Ext : 221

KENT

RECORD-COURIER

Corporate/Parent Company: Gannett
Publication Street Address: 1050 W Main St
City: Kent
State: OH
Publication Website: www.recordpub.com
Postal Code: 44240-2006
Office phone: (330) 541-9400
General E-mail: mhersch@recordpub.com
Publisher Name: Michael Shearer
Publisher Email: mshearer@recordpub.com
Publisher Phone: (330) 298-2023
Editor Name: Heather Rainone
Editor Email: hrainone@recordpub.com

KENTON

THE KENTON TIMES

Corporate/Parent Company: Ray Barnes Newspapers, Inc.
Publication Street Address: 201 E Columbus St
City: Kenton
State: OH
Publication Website: www.kentontimes.com
Postal Code: 43326-1583
Office phone: (419) 674-4066
General E-mail: dvanbuskirk@kentontimes.com
Publisher Name: Jeff Barnes
Publisher Email: jbarnes@kentontimes.com
Editor Name: Tim Thomas
Editor Email: kteditor@kentontimes.com

LANCASTER

LANCASTER EAGLE-GAZETTE

Corporate/Parent Company: Gannett
Publication Street Address: 138 W. Chestnut St
City: Lancaster
State: OH
Publication Website: www.lancastereaglegazette.com
Postal Code: 43130-4308
Office phone: (740) 654-1321
General E-mail: laneg@gannett.com
Editor Name: Tonya Shipley
Editor Email: tshipley@gannett.com

LIMA

THE LIMA NEWS

Corporate/Parent Company: AIM Media Indiana
Publication Street Address: 3515 Elida Rd
City: Lima
State: OH
Publication Website: www.limaohio.com
Postal Code: 45807-1538
Office phone: (419) 223-1010
General E-mail: advertising@limanews.com
Publisher Name: Kirk Dougal
Publisher Email: kdougal@aimmediamidwest.com
Publisher Phone: (567) 242-0463
Editor Name: David Trinko
Editor Email: dtrinko@limanews.com

LISBON

LISBON MORNING JOURNAL

Corporate/Parent Company: Ogden Newspapers Inc.
Publication Street Address: 308 Maple Street
City: Lisbon
State: OH
Publication Website: www.morningjournalnews.com
Postal Code: 44432
Office phone: 330-424-9541
Publisher Name: Tammie McIntosh
Publisher Email: tmcintosh@mojonews.com
Editor Name: J. D. Creer
Editor Email: jdcreer@mojonews.com

MORNING JOURNAL

Corporate/Parent Company: Media News Group
Publication Street Address: 308 Maple St
City: Lisbon
State: OH
Publication Website: www.morningjournalnews.com
Postal Code: 44432-1205
Office phone: (330) 424-9541
General E-mail: lludovici@mojonews.com
Publisher Name: Tammie McIntosh
Publisher Email: tmcintosh@mojonews.com
Editor Name: J. D. Creer
Editor Email: jdcreer@mojonews.com

LOGAN

LOGAN DAILY NEWS

Corporate/Parent Company: Adams Publishing Group
Publication Street Address: 72 E Main St
City: Logan
State: OH
Publication Website: www.logandaily.com
Postal Code: 43138-1221
Office phone: (740) 385-2107
General E-mail: dtobin@logandaily.com
Editor Name: Debra Tobin
Editor Email: dtobin@logandaily.com

LONDON

THE MADISON PRESS

Corporate/Parent Company: AIM Media
Publication Street Address: 55 W High St
City: London
State: OH
Publication Website: www.madison-press.com
Postal Code: 43140-1074
Office phone: (740) 852-1616
General E-mail: editor@madison-press.com
Editor Name: Mac Cordell
Editor Email: editor@madison-press.com

LORAIN

THE MORNING JOURNAL

Corporate/Parent Company: Media News Group
Publication Street Address: 2500 West Erie Ave.
City: Lorain
State: OH
Publication Website: www.morningjournal.com
Postal Code: 44053
Office phone: (440) 245-6901
General E-mail: news@morningjournal.com
Publisher Name: Jeff Schell
Publisher Email: jschell@21st-centurymedia.com
Publisher Phone: (440) 954-7159
Editor Name: Dorma Tolson

MANSFIELD

MANSFIELD NEWS JOURNAL

Corporate/Parent Company: Gannett
Publication Street Address: 70 W. Fourth St.
City: Mansfield
State: OH
Publication Website: www.mansfieldnewsjournal.com
Postal Code: 44903
Office phone: 419-522-3311
Editor Name: David Yonke
Editor Email: dyonke@gannett.com

NEWS JOURNAL

Corporate/Parent Company: AIM Media
Publication Street Address: 70 W 4th St
City: Mansfield
State: OH
Publication Website: www.mansfieldnewsjournal.com
Postal Code: 44903
Office phone: (419) 522-3311
General E-mail: yournews@mansfieldnewsjournal.com
Editor Name: David Yonke
Editor Email: dyonke@gannett.com

TELEGRAPH-FORUM

Corporate/Parent Company: Gannett
Publication Street Address: 70 W. Fourth St.
City: Mansfield
State: OH
Publication Website: www.bucyrustelegraphforum.com
Postal Code: 44903
Office phone: (419) 562-3333
General E-mail: customerservice@nncogannett.com
Editor Name: David Yonke
Editor Email: dyonke@gannett.com

MARIETTA

THE MARIETTA TIMES

Corporate/Parent Company: Ogden Newspapers, Inc.
Publication Street Address: 700 Channel Ln
City: Marietta
State: OH
Publication Website: www.mariettatimes.com
Postal Code: 45750-2342
Office phone: (740) 373-2121
General E-mail: advertising@mariettatimes.com
Publisher Name: James T. Spanner
Publisher Email: jspanner@mariettatimes.com
Publisher Phone: (304) 485-1891, Ext : 310
Editor Name: Christina Myer
Editor Email: cmyer@mariettatimes.com

MARION

THE MARION STAR

Corporate/Parent Company: Gannett
Publication Street Address: 163 E Center St
City: Marion
State: OH
Publication Website: www.marionstar.com
Postal Code: 43302-3813
Office phone: (740) 387-0400
General E-mail: blanka@gannett.com
Publisher Name: Mike Shearer
Editor Name: Benjamin Lanka
Editor Email: blanka@gannett.com

MARTINS FERRY

THE TIMES LEADER

Corporate/Parent Company: Ogden Newspapers, Inc.
Publication Street Address: 200 S 4th St
City: Martins Ferry
State: OH
Publication Website: www.timesleaderonline.com
Postal Code: 43935-1312
Office phone: (740) 633-1131
General E-mail: abutler@timesleaderonline.com
Editor Name: Jennifer Compston-Strough
Editor Email: jcompston@timesleaderonline.com

MARYSVILLE

MARYSVILLE JOURNAL-TRIBUNE

Publication Street Address: 207 N Main St
City: Marysville
State: OH
Publication Website: www.marysvillejt.com
Postal Code: 43040-1161
Office phone: (937) 644-9111
General E-mail: mariew@marysvillejt.com
Publisher Name: Kevin Behrens
Publisher Email: kb@marysvillejt.com
Editor Name: Chad Williamson
Editor Email: chad@marysvillejt.com

MASSILLON

THE INDEPENDENT

Corporate/Parent Company: Gannett
Publication Street Address: 729 Lincoln Way E
City: Massillon
State: OH
Publication Website: www.indeonline.com
Postal Code: 44646-6829
Office phone: (330) 833-2631
General E-mail: jim.williams@cantonrep.com
Publisher Name: Jim Porter
Publisher Email: jim.porter@cantonrep.com
Publisher Phone: (330) 580-8444
Editor Name: Veronica VanDress
Editor Email: veronica.vandress@indeonline.com

MEDINA

THE MEDINA COUNTY GAZETTE

Corporate/Parent Company: Medina County Publications, Inc.
Publication Street Address: 885 W Liberty St
City: Medina
State: OH
Publication Website: www.medina-gazette.com
Postal Code: 44256-1312
Office phone: (800) 633-4623
General E-mail: jgwinnup@medina-gazette.com
Publisher Name: Bill Hudnutt
Editor Name: Lisa Roberson
Editor Email: lroberson@medina-gazette.com

MOUNT VERNON

MOUNT VERNON NEWS

Corporate/Parent Company: Ohio Newspaper Services, Inc.
Publication Street Address: 18 E Vine St
City: Mount Vernon
State: OH
Publication Website: www.mountvernonnews.com
Postal Code: 43050-3226
Office phone: (740) 397-5333
General E-mail: cwise@mountvernonnews.com
Publisher Name: Kay Culbertson
Editor Name: Fred Main
Editor Email: fmain@mountvernonnews.com

NAPOLEON

NORTHWEST SIGNAL

Corporate/Parent Company: Bryan Publishing Co.
Publication Street Address: 595 E Riverview Ave
City: Napoleon
State: OH
Publication Website: www.northwestsignal.net
Postal Code: 43545-1865
Office phone: (419) 592-5055
General E-mail: contactus@northwestsignal.net
Publisher Name: Christopher Cullis
Publisher Email: christopher@bryantimes.com
Publisher Phone: (419) 636-1111
Editor Name: Brian Koeller
Editor Email: briank@northwestsignal.net

NEW PHILADELPHIA

THE TIMES-REPORTER

Corporate/Parent Company: Gannett
Publication Street Address: 629 Wabash Ave NW
City: New Philadelphia
State: OH
Publication Website: www.timesreporter.com
Postal Code: 44663-4145
Office phone: (330) 364-5577
General E-mail: advertising@timesreporter.com
Publisher Name: John Kridelbaugh
Publisher Email: jkridelbaugh@daily-jeff.com
Publisher Phone: (330) 364-8302

NEWARK

NEWARK ADVOCATE

Corporate/Parent Company: Gannett
Publication Street Address: 22 N. First St.
City: Newark
State: OH
Publication Website: www.newarkadvocate.com
Postal Code: 43055
Office phone: 740-345-4053
Editor Name: Benjamin Lanka
Editor Email: blanka@newarkadvocate.com

THE ADVOCATE

Corporate/Parent Company: Gannett Company Inc.
Publication Street Address: 22 N 1st St
City: Newark
State: OH
Publication Website: www.newarkadvocate.com
Postal Code: 43055-5608
Office phone: (740) 345-4053
General E-mail: advocate@newarkadvocate.com
Editor Name: Benjamin Lanka
Editor Email: blanka@newarkadvocate.com

NORWALK

NORWALK REFLECTOR

Corporate/Parent Company: Ogden Newspapers Inc.
Publication Street Address: 61 E Monroe St
City: Norwalk
State: OH
Publication Website: www.norwalkreflector.com
Postal Code: 44857-1532
Office phone: (419) 668-3771
General E-mail: ashleypitts@norwalkreflector.com
Publisher Name: Ron Waite
Publisher Email: ronwaite@tandemnetwork.com
Publisher Phone: (419) 609-5830
Editor Name: Joe Centers
Editor Email: jcenters@norwalkreflector.com

POMEROY

POMEROY DAILY SENTINTEL

Corporate/Parent Company: AIM Media Midwest
Publication Street Address: 109 W. Second Street
City: Pomeroy
State: OH
Publication Website: www.mydailysentinel.com
Postal Code: 45769
Office phone: 740-992-2155
General E-mail: TDSnews@civitasmedia.com
Editor Name: Sarah Hawley
Editor Email: shawley@aimmediamidwest.com

THE DAILY SENTINEL

Corporate/Parent Company: Cox
Publication Street Address: 109 W 2nd St
City: Pomeroy
State: OH
Publication Website: www.mydailysentinel.com
Postal Code: 45769-1035
Office phone: (740) 992-2155
General E-mail: tdsnews@civitasmedia.com
Editor Name: Sarah Hawley
Editor Email: shawley@aimmediamidwest.com

PORTSMOUTH

THE DAILY TIMES

Corporate/Parent Company: Gannett
Publication Street Address: 1603 11th Street
City: Portsmouth
State: OH
Publication Website: www.portsmouth-dailytimes.com
Postal Code: 45662
Office phone: 740-353-3101
General E-mail: pdtnews@aimmediamidwest.com
Publisher Name: Hope Comer
Publisher Email: hcomer@aimmediamidwest.com
Editor Name: Chris Slone
Editor Email: cslone@aimmediamidwest.com

THE PORTSMOUTH DAILY TIMES

Corporate/Parent Company: AIM Media
Publication Street Address: 1603 11th Street
City: Portsmouth
State: OH
Publication Website: www.portsmouth-dailytimes.com
Postal Code: 45662-3924
Office phone: (740) 353-3101
General E-mail: tison@aimmediamidwest.com
Publisher Name: Hope Comer
Editor Name: Mark Richard

SAINT MARYS

THE EVENING LEADER

Corporate/Parent Company: Horizon Publications Inc.
Publication Street Address: 102 E Spring St
City: Saint Marys
State: OH
Publication Website: www.theeveningleader.com
Postal Code: 45885-2310
Office phone: (419) 394-7414
General E-mail: editor@theeveningleader.com
Publisher Name: Gayle Masonbrink
Publisher Email: publisher@theeveningleader.com
Editor Name: Jake Dowling
Editor Email: editor@theeveningleader.com

SALEM

SALEM NEWS

Corporate/Parent Company: Ogden
Publication Street Address: 161 N Lincoln Ave
City: Salem
State: OH
Publication Website: www.salemnews.net
Postal Code: 44460-2903
Office phone: (330) 332-4601
General E-mail: lludovici@salemnews.net
Publisher Name: Tammie McIntosh
Publisher Email: tmcintosh@salemnews.net
Editor Name: J.D. Creer
Editor Email: jdcreer@salemnews.net

SANDUSKY

SANDUSKY REGISTER

Corporate/Parent Company: Ogden Newspapers Inc.
Publication Street Address: 314 W Market St
City: Sandusky
State: OH
Publication Website: www.sanduskyregister.com
Postal Code: 44870-2410
Office phone: (419) 625-5500
General E-mail: advertising@sanduskyregister.com
Editor Name: Matt Westerhold

SHELBY

DAILY GLOBE

Corporate/Parent Company: Horizon Publications Inc.
Publication Street Address: 37 W Main St
City: Shelby
State: OH
Publication Website: www.sdgnewsgroup.com
Postal Code: 44875-1238
Office phone: (419) 342-4276
General E-mail: globe@sdgnewsgroup.com

SHELBY DAILY GLOBE

Corporate/Parent Company: SDGNewsgroup
Publication Street Address: 37 West Main Street
City: Shelby
State: OH
Publication Website: www.sdgnewsgroup.com
Postal Code: 44875
Office phone: 419.342.4276
General E-mail: globe@sdgnewsgroup.com
Editor Name: MINDY MCKENZIE

SIDNEY

THE SIDNEY DAILY NEWS

Corporate/Parent Company: AIM Media
Publication Street Address: 1451 N Vandemark Rd
City: Sidney
State: OH
Publication Website: www.sidneydailynews.com
Postal Code: 45365-3547
Office phone: (937) 498-8088
General E-mail: cpierce@aimmediamidwest.com
Publisher Name: Natalie Buzzard
Publisher Email: nbuzzard@aimmediamidwest.com
Publisher Phone: (937) 538-4667
Editor Name: Melanie Speicher
Editor Email: mspeicher@aimmediamidwest.com

SPRINGFIELD

SPRINGFIELD NEWS-SUN

Corporate/Parent Company: Cox Media Group
Publication Street Address: 202 N Limestone St
City: Springfield
State: OH
Publication Website: www.springfieldnewssun.com
Postal Code: 45503-4246
Office phone: (937) 328-0300
General E-mail: customercare@springfieldnewssun.com
Publisher Name: Steve Sidlo
Editor Name: Lucy Baker
Editor Email: lucy.baker@coxinc.com

STEUBENVILLE

HERALD-STAR

Corporate/Parent Company: Ogden Newspapers, Inc.
Publication Street Address: 401 Herald Sq
City: Steubenville
State: OH
Publication Website: www.heraldstaronline.com
Postal Code: 43952-2059
Office phone: (740) 283-4711
General E-mail: csteineman@heraldstaronline.com
Publisher Name: John Hale
Publisher Email: jhale@heraldstaronline.com
Editor Name: Ross Gallabrese
Editor Email: rgallabrese@heraldstaronline.com

WEIRTON DAILY TIMES

Corporate/Parent Company: Ogden Newspapers Inc.
Publication Street Address: 401 Herald Sq
City: Steubenville
State: OH
Publication Website: www.weirtondailytimes.com
Postal Code: 43952-2059
Office phone: (304) 748-0606
General E-mail: csteineman@heraldstaronline.com
Publisher Name: John Hale
Publisher Email: jhale@heraldstaronline.com
Editor Name: Craig Howell
Editor Email: chowell@weirtondailytimes.com

TIFFIN

THE ADVERTISER-TRIBUNE

Corporate/Parent Company: Ogden Newspapers, Inc.
Publication Street Address: 320 Nelson St
City: Tiffin
State: OH
Publication Website: www.advertiser-tribune.com
Postal Code: 44883-8956
Office phone: (419) 448-3200
General E-mail: advertising@advertiser-tribune.com
Publisher Name: Jeremy Speer
Publisher Email: jspeer@advertiser-tribune.com
Publisher Phone: (419) 448-3207
Editor Name: Joanna Lininger
Editor Email: jlininger@advertiser-tribune.com

TOLEDO

THE BLADE

Corporate/Parent Company: Block Communications, Inc.

U.S. Daily Newspapers

Publication Street Address: 541 N Superior St
City: Toledo
State: OH
Publication Website: www.toledoblade.com
Postal Code: 43660-1000
Office phone: (419) 724-6000
General E-mail: info@toledoblade.com
Publisher Name: Kurt G. Franck
Publisher Email: kfranck@toledoblade.com
Publisher Phone: (419) 724-6163
Editor Name: Kim Bates
Editor Email: kimbates@theblade.com

THE TOLEDO BLADE

Publication Street Address: 541 N. Superior Street
City: Toledo
State: OH
Publication Website: www.toledoblade.com
Postal Code: 43660
Office phone: 419-724-6000
Editor Name: Kurt G. Franck
Editor Email: kfranck@toledoblade.com

TROY

TROY DAILY NEWS

Corporate/Parent Company: AIM Media
Publication Street Address: 224 S Market St
City: Troy
State: OH
Publication Website: https://www.tdn-net.com/
Postal Code: 45373-3327
Office phone: (937) 335-5634
General E-mail: bsmith@aimmediamidwest.com
Publisher Name: Ron Clausen
Publisher Email: ron@aimmediamidwest.com
Publisher Phone: (937) 552-2121
Editor Name: Melody Vallieu
Editor Email: mvallieu@aimmediamidwest.com

PIQUA DAILY CALL

Corporate/Parent Company: AIM Media
Publication Street Address: 1001 N. County Road 25-A
City: Troy
State: OH
Publication Website: www.dailycall.com
Postal Code: 45373
Office phone: (937) 773-2721
General E-mail: bsmith@aimmediamidwest.com
Publisher Name: Ron Clausen
Publisher Email: ron@aimmediamidwest.com
Publisher Phone: (937) 552-2121
Editor Name: Melody Vallieu
Editor Email: mvallieu@aimmediamidwest.com

UPPER SANDUSKY

THE DAILY CHIEF-UNION

Corporate/Parent Company: Hardin County Publishing Co.
Publication Street Address: 111 W Wyandot Ave
City: Upper Sandusky
State: OH
Publication Website: www.dailychiefunion.com
Postal Code: 43351-1348
Office phone: (419) 294-2332
General E-mail: dcuads@dailychiefunion.com
Publisher Name: Jeff Barnes
Publisher Email: dcueditor@dailychiefunion.com

URBANA

DAILY CITIZEN

Corporate/Parent Company: AIM Media Midwest
Publication Street Address: 1637 E US Hwy 36
City: Urbana
State: OH

Publication Website: www.urbanacitizen.com
Postal Code: 43078
Office phone: 937-652-1331
Publisher Name: Lane Moon
Publisher Email: lmoon@aimmediamidwest.com
Editor Name: Brenda Burns
Editor Email: bburns@aimmediamidwest.com

URBANA DAILY CITIZEN

Corporate/Parent Company: AIM Media
Publication Street Address: 1637 E US Highway 36
City: Urbana
State: OH
Publication Website: www.urbanacitizen.com
Postal Code: 43078-9156
Office phone: (937) 652-1331
General E-mail: cherring@aimmediamidwest.com
Publisher Name: Lane Moon
Publisher Email: lmoon@aimmediamidwest.com
Editor Name: Brenda Burns
Editor Email: bburns@aimmediamidwest.com

WAPAKONETA

WAPAKONETA DAILY NEWS

Corporate/Parent Company: Horizon Publications Inc.
Publication Street Address: 520 Industrial Dr
City: Wapakoneta
State: OH
Publication Website: www.wapakdailynews.com
Postal Code: 45895-9200
Office phone: (419) 738-2128
General E-mail: marketingetc@wapakwdn.com
Publisher Name: Deb Zwez
Publisher Email: publisher@wapakwdn.com
Publisher Phone: (419) 739-3504

WARREN

THE TRIBUNE CHRONICLE

Corporate/Parent Company: Ogden Newspapers, Inc.
Publication Street Address: 240 Franklin St SE
City: Warren
State: OH
Publication Website: www.tribtoday.com
Postal Code: 44483-5711
Office phone: (330) 841-1600
General E-mail: hnewman@tribtoday.com
Publisher Name: Charles Jarvis
Publisher Email: charlesjarvis@tribtoday.com
Editor Name: Amy Wilson
Editor Email: awilson@tribtoday.com

WASHINGTON COURT HOUSE

RECORD HERALD

Corporate/Parent Company: Gannett
Publication Street Address: 757 W Elm St
City: Washington Court House
State: OH
Publication Website: www.recordherald.com
Postal Code: 43160-2428
Office phone: (740) 335-3611
General E-mail: admanager@recordherald.com
Editor Name: Ryan Carter

WILLOUGHBY

THE NEWS-HERALD

Corporate/Parent Company: Media News Group
Publication Street Address: 7085 Mentor Ave
City: Willoughby
State: OH
Publication Website: www.news-herald.com

Postal Code: 44094-7948
Office phone: (440) 951-0000
General E-mail: vlinhart@news-herald.com
Publisher Name: Jeff Schell
Publisher Email: publisher@news-herald.com
Editor Name: John Bertosa
Editor Email: jbertosa@news-herald.com

WILMINGTON NEWS JOURNAL

Publication Street Address: 1547 Rombach Avenue
City: Wilmington
State: OH
Publication Website: www.wnewsj.com
Postal Code: 45177-2517
Office phone: (937) 382-2574
General E-mail: emattingly@civitasmedia.com
Publisher Name: Lane Moon
Publisher Email: lmoon@aimmediamidwest.com
Publisher Phone: (937) 652-1331
Editor Name: Tom Barr
Editor Email: tbarr@wnewsj.com

WOOSTER

THE DAILY RECORD

Corporate/Parent Company: Gannett
Publication Street Address: 212 E Liberty St
City: Wooster
State: OH
Publication Website: www.the-daily-record.com
Postal Code: 44691-4348
Office phone: (330) 264-1125
General E-mail: adv@the-daily-record.com
Publisher Name: Bill Albrecht
Publisher Email: balbrecht@gatehousemedia.com
Publisher Phone: (330) 996-3782
Editor Name: Rick Armon
Editor Email: rarmon@the-daily-record.com

XENIA

FAIRBORN DAILY HERALD

Corporate/Parent Company: AIM Media
Publication Street Address: 1836 W Park Sq
City: Xenia
State: OH
Publication Website: www.fairborndailyherald.com
Postal Code: 45385-2668
Office phone: (937) 372-3993
General E-mail: bvandeventer@civitasmedia.com
Publisher Name: Barbara Vandeventer
Publisher Phone: (937) 372-4444
Editor Name: Merrilee Embs

XENIA DAILY GAZETTE

Corporate/Parent Company: AIM Media
Publication Street Address: 1836 W Park Sq
City: Xenia
State: OH
Publication Website: www.xeniagazette.com
Postal Code: 45385-2668
Office phone: (937) 372-4444
General E-mail: nlebeau@civitasmedia.com
Publisher Name: Barbara Vandeventer
Publisher Phone: (937) 372-4444
Editor Name: Darrell Wacker

YOUNGSTOWN

THE VINDICATOR

Corporate/Parent Company: Vindicator Printing Company
Publication Street Address: 107 Vindicator Sq
City: Youngstown
State: OH

Publication Website: www.vindy.com
Postal Code: 44503-1136
Office phone: (330) 747-1471
General E-mail: jsovik@vindy.com
Publisher Name: Charles Jarvis
Publisher Email: charlesjarvis@tribtoday.com
Editor Name: Amy Wilson
Editor Email: awilson@tribtoday.com

ZANESVILLE

TIMES RECORDER

Corporate/Parent Company: Gannett
Publication Street Address: 3871 Gorsky Dr
City: Zanesville
State: OH
Publication Website: www.zanesvilletimesrecorder.com
Postal Code: 43701-3449
Office phone: 740-452-4561
General E-mail: scourson@gannett.com
Editor Name: Pam James
Editor Email: psjames@gannett.com

ZANESVILLE TIMES RECORDER

Publication Street Address: 3871 Gorsky Drive, Unit G1
City: Zanesville
State: OH
Publication Website: www.zanesvilletimesrecorder.com
Postal Code: 43701
Office phone: 740-452-4561
Editor Name: Pam James
Editor Email: psjames@gannett.com

OKLAHOMA

ADA

THE ADA NEWS

Corporate/Parent Company: CNHI, LLC
Publication Street Address: 116 N Broadway Ave
City: Ada
State: OK
Publication Website: https://www.edmondsun.com/
Postal Code: 74820-5004
Office phone: (580) 332-4433
General E-mail: news@theadanews.com
Publisher Name: Maurisa Nelson
Publisher Email: mnelson@theadanews.com
Publisher Phone: (580) 310-7502
Editor Name: Carl Lewis
Editor Email: clewis@theadanews.com

ALTUS

ALTUS TIMES

Publication Street Address: 218 W Commerce St
City: Altus
State: OK
Publication Website: www.altustimes.com
Postal Code: 73521-3810
Office phone: (580) 482-1221
General E-mail: kristie@altustimes.com
Publisher Name: Rick Carpenter
Publisher Email: rick@altustimes.com
Publisher Phone: (580) 482-1221, Ext : 2071

ARDMORE

THE ARDMOREITE

Publication Street Address: 117 W Broadway St
City: Ardmore
State: OK
Publication Website: www.ardmoreite.com

Postal Code: 73401-6226
Office phone: (580) 223-2200
General E-mail: katherine.smith@ardmoreite.com
Publisher Name: Kim Benedict
Publisher Email: kim.benedict@ardmoreite.com
Publisher Phone: (580) 223-2200
Editor Name: Robby Short
Editor Email: robby.short@ardmoreite.com

BARTLESVILLE

BARTLESVILLE EXAMINER-ENTERPRISE

Publication Street Address: 4125 Nowata Rd.
City: Bartlesville
State: OK
Publication Website: www.examiner-enterprise.com
Postal Code: 74006
Office phone: (918) 335-8200
General E-mail: legals@examiner-enterprise.com

BARTLESVILLE EXAMINER-ENTERPRISE

Publication Street Address: 4125 Nowata Rd.
City: Bartlesville
State: OK
Publication Website: www.examiner-enterprise.com
Postal Code: 74006
Office phone: (918) 335-8200
General E-mail: legals@examiner-enterprise.com

EXAMINER-ENTERPRISE

Publication Street Address: 4125 Nowata Rd
City: Bartlesville
State: OK
Publication Website: www.examiner-enterprise.com
Postal Code: 74006-5120
Office phone: (918) 335-8200
General E-mail: online@examiner-enterprise.com
Publisher Name: Mathew Pearson
Publisher Email: mpearson@examiner-enterprise.com
Publisher Phone: (918) 335-8200, Ext : 271

CHICKASHA

THE EXPRESS-STAR

Corporate/Parent Company: CNHI, LLC
Publication Street Address: 411 W Chickasha Ave
City: Chickasha
State: OK
Publication Website: https://www.edmondsun.com/
Postal Code: 73018-2472
Office phone: (405) 224-2600
General E-mail: advertising@chickashanews.com
Publisher Name: Mark Millsap
Publisher Email: mark@normantranscript.com
Editor Name: Jessica Lane
Editor Email: jlane@chickashanews.com

CLAREMORE

THE CLAREMORE DAILY PROGRESS

Corporate/Parent Company: CNHI, LLC
Publication Street Address: 315 W Will Rogers Blvd
City: Claremore
State: OK

Publication Website: https://www.edmondsun.com/
Postal Code: 74018
Office phone: (918) 341-1101
General E-mail: ads@claremoreprogress.com
Publisher Name: Kristy Geisler
Publisher Email: publisher@claremoreprogress.com
Editor Name: Cydney Baron
Editor Email: cbaron@claremoreprogress.com

CLINTON

THE CLINTON DAILY NEWS

Publication Street Address: 522 Avant Ave
City: Clinton
State: OK
Publication Website: www.clintondailynews.com
Postal Code: 73601-3436
Office phone: (580) 323-5151
General E-mail: cdnews@swbell.net
Publisher Name: Rod Serfoss

DUNCAN

THE DUNCAN BANNER

Corporate/Parent Company: CNHI, LLC
Publication Street Address: 1001 Elm, PO Box 1268
City: Duncan
State: OK
Publication Website: https://www.edmondsun.com/
Postal Code: 73533-4746
Office phone: (580) 255-5354
General E-Mail: editor@duncanbanner.com
Publisher Name: Jeff Funk
Publisher Email: jfunk@enidnews.com
Editor Email: editor@duncanbanner.com

DURANT

DURANT DEMOCRAT

Corporate/Parent Company: Graystone Media Group LLC
Publication Street Address: 200 W Beech St
City: Durant
State: OK
Publication Website: www.durantdemocrat.com
Postal Code: 74701-4316
Office phone: (580) 924-4388
General E-mail: esmith@civitasmedia.com
Publisher Name: Chris Allen
Editor Name: Matt Swearengin

ELK CITY

ELK CITY DAILY NEWS

Corporate/Parent Company: The Elk City Daily News, Inc.
Publication Street Address: 109 W. Broadway
City: Elk City
State: OK
Publication Website: www.ecdailynews.com
Postal Code: 73644
Office phone: (580) 225-3000
General E-mail: ads@ecdailynews.com
Publisher Name: Elizabeth Wade
Editor Name: Jim Nicholas
Editor Email: editor@ecdailynews.com

ENID

ENID NEWS & EAGLE

Corporate/Parent Company: CNHI, LLC
Publication Street Address: 227 W Broadway Ave
City: Enid
State: OK
Publication Website: https://www.edmondsun.com/
Postal Code: 73701-4017
Office phone: (580) 233-3600
General E-mail: circ@enidnews.com
Publisher Name: Jeff Funk

Publisher Email: publisher@enidnews.com
Publisher Phone: (580) 548-8135
Editor Name: Rob Collins
Editor Email: editor@enidnews.com

GUYMON

GUYMON DAILY HERALD

Corporate/Parent Company: Horizon Publications Inc.
Publication Street Address: 515 N Ellison St
City: Guymon
State: OK
Publication Website: www.guymondailyherald.com
Postal Code: 73942-4311
Office phone: (580) 338-3355
General E-mail: dailyheraldads@gmail.com
Publisher Email: publisher@guymondailyherald.com
Editor Email: editor@guymondailyherald.com

LAWTON

THE LAWTON CONSTITUTION

Corporate/Parent Company: Southern Newspapers Inc.
Publication Street Address: 102 SW 3rd St
City: Lawton
State: OK
Publication Website: www.swoknews.com
Postal Code: 73501-4031
Office phone: (580) 353-0620
General E-mail: support@swoknews.com
Editor Name: Dee Ann Patterson

MCALESTER

MCALESTER NEWS-CAPITAL

Corporate/Parent Company: CNHI, LLC
Publication Street Address: 500 S 2nd St
City: McAlester
State: OK
Publication Website: https://www.edmondsun.com/
Postal Code: 74501-5812
Office phone: (918) 423-1700
General E-mail: web@mcalesternews.com
Publisher Name: Reina Owens
Publisher Email: rowens@mcalesternews.com
Publisher Phone: (918) 421-2010
Editor Name: James Beaty
Editor Email: jbeaty@mcalesternews.com

MIAMI

MIAMI NEWS-RECORD

Corporate/Parent Company: Gannett
Publication Street Address: 14 1st Ave NW
City: Miami
State: OK
Publication Website: www.miaminewsrecord.com
Postal Code: 74354-6224
Office phone: (918) 542-5533
General E-mail: advertising@miaminewsrecord.com
Publisher Name: Joe Leong
Publisher Email: jleong@gatehousemedia.com
Publisher Phone: (620) 231-2600, Ext : 140
Editor Name: Patrick Richardson
Editor Email: prichardson@gatehousemedia.com

MUSKOGEE

MUSKOGEE PHOENIX

Corporate/Parent Company: CNHI, LLC
Publication Street Address: 214 Wall St
City: Muskogee
State: OK
Publication Website: https://www.edmondsun.com/
Postal Code: 74401-6644

Office phone: (918) 684-2828
General E-mail: phxads@muskogeephoenix.com
Publisher Name: Ed Choate
Publisher Email: publisher@muskogeephoenix.com
Publisher Phone: (918) 684-2875
Editor Name: Elizabeth Ridenour
Editor Email: eridenour@muskogeephoenix.com

NORMAN

NORMAN TRANSCRIPT

Corporate/Parent Company: CNHI, LLC
Publication Street Address: 215 E Comanche St
City: Norman
State: OK
Publication Website: https://www.edmondsun.com/
Postal Code: 73069-6007
Office phone: (405) 321-1800
General E-mail: rebeccam@normantranscript.com
Publisher Name: Mark Millsap
Publisher Email: publisher@normantranscript.com
Publisher Phone: (405) 366-3590
Editor Name: Christie Swanson
Editor Email: cswanson@normantranscript.com

OKLAHOMA WATCH

Publication Street Address: 395 W. Lindsey St., Suite 3120-D
City: Norman
State: OK
Publication Website: oklahomawatch.org
Postal Code: 73019
Office phone: (405) 230-8450
General E-mail: editor@oklahomawatch.org
Editor Name: David Fritze
Editor Email: dfritze@oklahomawatch.org

OKLAHOMA CITY

THE OKLAHOMAN

Corporate/Parent Company: Gannett
Publication Street Address: 100 W Main St Ste 100
City: Oklahoma City
State: OK
Publication Website: www.newsok.com
Postal Code: 73102-9007
Office phone: (405) 475-3380
General E-mail: thicks@oklahoman.com
Publisher Name: Kelly Dyer Fry
Publisher Email: kfry@oklahoman.com
Publisher Phone: (405) 475-3979
Editor Name: Don Mecoy
Editor Email: dmecoy@oklahoman.com

OKMULGEE

OKMULGEE DAILY TIMES

Publication Street Address: 320 W 6th St
City: Okmulgee
State: OK
Publication Website: www.okmulgeecountynewssource.com
Postal Code: 74447-5018
Office phone: (918) 756-3600
General E-mail: carrie@bigbasinllc.com
Publisher Name: Jeff Mayo
Publisher Email: jeff@bigbasinllc.com
Editor Name: Patrick Ford
Editor Email: patrick@bigbasinllc.com

OKMULGEE TIMES

Publication Street Address: 320 W. 6th
City: Okmulgee

U.S. Daily Newspapers

I-99

State: OK
Publication Website: www.yourokmulgee.com
Postal Code: 74447
Office phone: (918) 756-3600
General E-mail: okmulgeedailytimes@yahoo.com
Publisher Name: Jeff Mayo
Publisher Email: jeff@bigbasinllc.com
Editor Name: Patrick Ford
Editor Email: patrick@bigbasinllc.com

PAWHUSKA

OSAGE NEWS

Publication Street Address: 109 E. 6th Street
City: Pawhuska
State: OK
Publication Website: www.osagenews.org
Postal Code: 74056
Office phone: (918) 287-5668
Editor Name: Shannon Shaw Duty
Editor Email: osagenews@osagenation-nsn.gov

SAPULPA

SAPULPA HERALD

Publication Street Address: 16 S Park St
City: Sapulpa
State: OK
Publication Website: www.sapulpabuzz.com
Postal Code: 74066
Office phone: 918-224-5185
Editor Name: Johnny Brock
Editor Email: editor@sapulpaheraldonline.com

OREGON

ALBANY

ALBANY DEMOCRAT-HERALD

Corporate/Parent Company: Lee Enterprises
Publication Street Address: 600 Lyon St S
City: Albany
State: OR
Publication Website: www.democratherald.com
Postal Code: 97321-2919
Office phone: (541) 926-2211
General E-mail: ads@dhonline.com
Publisher Name: Jeff Precourt
Publisher Email: jeff.precourt@lee.net
Publisher Phone: (541) 812-6125
Editor Name: Mike McInally
Advertising Executive Name: Monica Hampton
Advertising Executive Email: monica.hampton@lee.net
Advertising Executive Phone: (541) 812-6062
Year Established: 1865
Delivery Methods: Mail`Newsstand`Carrier`Racks
Own Printing Facility?: Y
Commercial printers?: Y
Mechanical specifications: Type page 11 5/8 x 21; E - 6 cols, 1 4/5, between; A - 6 cols, 1 4/5, between; C - 9 cols, 1 1/5, between.
Published Days: Mon`Tues`Wed`Thur`Fri`Sat`Sun
Weekday Frequency: e
Saturday Frequency: m
Avg Paid Circ: 6954
Avg Free Circ: 637
Audit Company: AAM
Audit Date: 27 06 2019
Pressroom Equipment: Lines – 6-G/Urbanite single width; Control System – 2; Registration System – Duarte/Pin Registration System.
Mailroom Equipment: Counter Stackers – 1/BG; Inserters & Stuffers – 2-KAN/480 6:1; Tying Machines – 1-/Strapex, 2-EAM-Mosca; Address Machine – 1-KAN/650, KR/label head.;
Total Circulation: 8398

ASTORIA

THE DAILY ASTORIAN

Corporate/Parent Company: EO Media Group
Publication Street Address: 949 Exchange St
City: Astoria
State: OR
Publication Website: www.dailyastorian.com
Postal Code: 97103-4605
Office phone: (503) 325-3211
General E-mail: editor@dailyastorian.com
Publisher Name: Kari Borgen
Publisher Email: kborgen@dailyastorian.com
Publisher Phone: (503) 325-4955
Editor Name: Derrick DePledge
Editor Email: ddepledge@dailyastorian.com
Editor Phone: (503) 791-7885
Advertising Executive Name: Sarah Silver-Tecza
Advertising Executive Email: ssilver@dailyastorian.com
Advertising Executive Phone: (971) 704-1555
Year Established: 1873
Delivery Methods: Mail`Newsstand`Carrier`Racks
Own Printing Facility?: Y
Commercial printers?: Y
Mechanical specifications: Type page 10.5 x 21.5; E - 6 cols, 2, 1/6 between; A - 6 cols, 2, 1/6 between; C - 8 cols, 1 1/2, 1/8 between.
Published Days: Mon`Tues`Wed`Thur`Fri
Weekday Frequency: e
Avg Paid Circ: 5479
Avg Free Circ: 358
Audit Company: AAM
Audit Date: 30 06 2017
Pressroom Equipment: Lines – 2 Tensor 4-hgihs and 3 Community units (installed 2010); Folders – Goss SSC;
Buisness Equipment: Vision Data
Buisness Software: Excel 5
Classified Equipment: Hardware – APP/Mac;
Classified Software: QPS/QuarkXPress, Baseview, Multi-Ad.
Editorial Equipment: Hardware – APP/Mac; Printers – APP/Mac LaserWriter NTX, APP/Mac LaserWriter IIg, APP/Mac LaserWriter Pro 630, Au/APS 6-84 Imagesetter
Editorial Software: NewsCycle Solutions, Photoshop, InCopy, InDesign
Production Equipment: Hardware – Au/APS-6-84-ACS; Cameras – K/V-241; Scanners – LaCie/Silver Scan II, Nikon/LS52000
Production Software: QPS/QuarkXPress 3.3.
Total Circulation: 5837

CORVALLIS

CORVALLIS GAZETTE-TIMES

Corporate/Parent Company: Lee Enterprises
Publication Street Address: 1835 NW Circle Blvd
City: Corvallis
State: OR
Publication Website: www.gazettetimes.com
Postal Code: 97330-1310
Office phone: (541) 753-2641
General E-mail: cyndi.sprinkel-hart@lee.net
Publisher Name: Jeff Precourt
Publisher Email: bennett.hall@lee.net
Publisher Phone: (541) 812-6125
Editor Name: Mike McInally
Advertising Executive Name: Monica Hampton
Advertising Executive Email: monica.hampton@lee.net
Advertising Executive Phone: (541) 812-6062
Year Established: 1862
Own Printing Facility?: Y
Commercial printers?: Y
Mechanical specifications: Type page 13 x 21; E - 6 cols, 2 1/16, 1/8 between; A - 6 cols, 2 1/16, 1/8 between; C - 9 cols, 1 5/16, 1/16 between.
Published Days: Mon`Tues`Wed`Thur`Fri`Sat`Sun
Weekday Frequency: m
Saturday Frequency: m
Avg Paid Circ: 6453
Avg Free Circ: 873
Audit Company: AAM
Audit Date: 18 06 2019
Pressroom Equipment: Lines – 5-G/Urbanite 1970; Control System – 2-Fin/Console.;
Mailroom Equipment: Address Machine – Bundle Tying Machines ÃƒÂƒÃ‚Â,Ã‚Â¢ÃƒÂ‚Ã‚Â¢ÃƒÂ,Ã‚Â£ 2-/MLN.;
Buisness Equipment: IBM/AS-400
Classified Equipment: Hardware – Gateway/P5-90; Printers – HP/5P;
Classified Software: CText.
Editorial Equipment: Hardware – Gateway/P5-90; Printers – Pre Press/Panther Plus, Pre Press/Panther Pro 46, LaserMaster/Unity 1800, LaserMaster/Unity 1200, LaserMaster/Unity 1000
Editorial Software: CText.
Production Equipment: Hardware – 3-Laser, Pre Press/Panther Plus, Pre Press/Panther Pro, LaserMaster/Unity 1800, LaserMaster/Unity 1200, LaserMaster/Unity 1000; Cameras – 1-C/Spartan II, 1-Nu/2024.
Total Circulation: 7924

EUGENE

THE REGISTER-GUARD

Corporate/Parent Company: Gannett
Publication Street Address: 3500 Chad Dr
City: Eugene
State: OR
Publication Website: www.registerguard.com
Postal Code: 97408-7426
Office phone: (541) 485-1234
General E-mail: kgant@registerguard.com
Publisher Name: Shanna Cannon
Publisher Email: scannon@registerguard.com
Publisher Phone: (541) 338-2525
Editor Name: Michelle Maxwell
Editor Email: mmaxwell@registerguard.com
Editor Phone: (541) 338-2272
Advertising Executive Name: Kelly Gant
Advertising Executive Email: kgant@registerguard.com
Advertising Executive Phone: (541) 338-2254
Year Established: 1867
Mechanical specifications: Type page 11 5/8 x 21; E - 6 cols, 1 5/6, 1/8 between; A - 6 cols, 2 1/16, 1/8 between; C - 9 cols, 1 1/4, 1/16 between.
Published Days: Mon`Tues`Wed`Thur`Fri`Sat`Sun
Weekday Frequency: m
Saturday Frequency: m
Avg Paid Circ: 45175
Audit Company: AAM
Audit Date: 19 05 2020
Pressroom Equipment: Lines – 10-Mitsubishi/Lithopia double width; Folders – 1-Mitsubishi/Double 3:2; Reels & Stands – 8;
Mailroom Equipment: Counter Stackers – 5/QWI; Inserters & Stuffers – 3-/AM Graphics/NP 630; Tying Machines – 5-/Dynaric; Control System – AM/Graphics/AMCS.;
Buisness Equipment: 2-DEC/4000-300, 1-DEC/3100
Classified Equipment: Hardware – Sun/Sparc 3000;
Classified Software: DTI 4.23.
Editorial Equipment: Hardware – 2-Sun/Sparc 3000, APP/Mac
Editorial Software: DTI 4.23.
Production Equipment: Hardware – 2-III/3850, 1-WL/38G
Production Software: DTI 4.2.
Total Circulation: 34292

GRANTS PASS

DAILY COURIER

Corporate/Parent Company: Western News & Info
Publication Street Address: 409 SE 7th St
City: Grants Pass
State: OR
Publication Website: www.thedailycourier.com
Postal Code: 97526-3003
Office phone: (541) 474-3700
General E-mail: display@thedailycourier.com
Publisher Name: Travis Moore
Publisher Email: tmoore@thedailycourier.com
Publisher Phone: (541) 474-3706
Editor Name: Scott Stoddard
Editor Email: sstoddard@thedailycourier.com
Editor Phone: (541) 474-3717
Advertising Executive Name: Debbie Thomas
Advertising Executive Email: dthomas@thedailycourier.com
Advertising Executive Phone: (541) 474-3807
Year Established: 1885
Delivery Methods: Mail`Newsstand`Carrier`Racks
Own Printing Facility?: Y
Mechanical specifications: Type page 13 x 21 1/2; E - 6 cols, 2 1/16, 1/8 between; A - 6 cols, 2 1/16, 1/8 between; C - 6 cols, 2 1/16, 1/8 between.
Published Days: Tues`Wed`Thur`Fri`Sun
Weekday Frequency: e
Saturday Frequency: e
Avg Paid Circ: 8979
Avg Free Circ: 551
Audit Company: AAM
Audit Date: 31 03 2019
Pressroom Equipment: Lines – 5-G/Urbanite 1240; 6-G/Community; Folders – 2, 1-G/Quarter.;
Mailroom Equipment: Counter Stackers – 2-BG/Count-O-Veyor 108; Inserters & Stuffers – 2-MM/227E; Tying Machines – 2-MLN/Strapper, 2-Bu/Tyer; Address Machine – 3-Wm/Dick Gum labeler.;
Buisness Equipment: IBM/RISC/6000
Buisness Software: CJ
Classified Equipment: Hardware – 6-APP/Mac, IBM/RS6000;
Classified Software: DTI.
Editorial Equipment: Hardware – 27-AT/Series 4/6-APP/Mac, 1-Lf/AP Leaf Picture Desk
Editorial Software: AT.
Production Equipment: Hardware – Nat/24, 2-AU/APS-6-108, 6-APP/Mac, 2-AU/APS-100; Cameras – R, AG/6100; Scanners – 2-Nikon/LS-3500
Production Software: QPS.
Total Circulation: 9530

KLAMATH FALLS

HERALD AND NEWS

Corporate/Parent Company: Adams Publishing Group
Publication Street Address: 2701 Foothills Blvd
City: Klamath Falls
State: OR
Publication Website: www.heraldandnews.com
Postal Code: 97603-3785
Office phone: (541) 885-4410
General E-mail: news@heraldandnews.com
Publisher Name: Mark Dobie
Publisher Email: mdobie@heraldandnews.com
Publisher Phone: (541) 885-4410
Editor Name: Levi Durighello
Editor Email: ldurighello@heraldandnews.com
Editor Phone: (541) 885-4452
Year Established: 1906
Delivery Methods: Mail`Racks
Mechanical specifications: Type page 12 3/8 x 21 1/2; E - 6 cols, 1 5/6, 1/6 between; A - 6 cols, 1 5/6, 1/6 between; C - 9 cols, 1 1/6, 1/8 between.
Published Days: Tues`Wed`Thur`Fri`Sat`Sun
Weekday Frequency: m
Saturday Frequency: m
Avg Paid Circ: 8651
Audit Company: AAM
Audit Date: 21 03 2019
Pressroom Equipment: Lines – 7-G/U 650;
Mailroom Equipment: Counter Stackers – 1-BG/Count-O-Veyor; Inserters & Stuffers – 2-MM/Stitcher-Trimmer; Tying Machines – MLN; Wrapping Singles – 1-Typak/#40.;
Classified Equipment: Hardware – APP/Mac;
Classified Software: Baseview/Ad Manager Pro 2.0.6.
Editorial Equipment: Hardware – APP/Mac; Printers – 2-AG, COM/Accuset
Editorial Software: QPS/QuarkXPress, Adobe/Photoshop, Baseview/NewsEdit.
Production Equipment: Hardware – 1-Nu/Flip Top; Cameras – 1-MG/Photomaster; Scanners – 4-HP/ScanJet Plus, 2-Nikon.
Total Circulation: 9009

MEDFORD

MAIL TRIBUNE
Corporate/Parent Company: Rosebud Media
Publication Street Address: 111 North Fir Street
City: Medford
State: OR
Publication Website: www.mailtribune.com
Postal Code: 97501
Office phone: (541) 776-4411
General E-mail: news@rosebudmedia.com
Publisher Name: Gail Whiting
Publisher Email: gwhiting@rosebudmedia.com
Editor Name: Justin Umberson
Editor Email: jumberson@rosebudmedia.com
Advertising Executive Name: Bill Krumpeck
Advertising Executive Email: bkrumpeck@rosebudmedia.com
Year Established: 1906
Mechanical specifications: Type page 13 x 21 1/2; E - 6 cols, 2 1/16, 1/8 between; A - 6 cols, 2 1/16, 1/8 between; C - 9 cols, 1 3/8, 1/16 between.
Published Days: Mon`Tues`Wed`Thur`Fri`Sat`Sun
Weekday Frequency: m
Saturday Frequency: m
Avg Paid Circ: 14572
Avg Free Circ: 409
Audit Company: AAM
Audit Date: 31 12 2016
Pressroom Equipment: Lines – 6-G/Metroliner double width (two half decks) 1995; Folders – 2-G/3:2; Pasters –6-G/Reel-Tension PasterReels & Stands – 6-G/Triple Reels & Stands.;
Mailroom Equipment: Counter Stackers – 2-HL/Monitor, 1-QWI/300, 1-QWI/351; Inserters & Stuffers – GMA/SLS 1000 16 pocket; Tying Machines – 2/MLN, 1-/Power Strap/PSN-6, 1-/Power Strap/PSN-6E; Wrapping Singles – 2-QWI/30; Address Machine – KR;
Buisness Equipment: IBM/AS-400, DEC/VAX-4300
Classified Equipment: Hardware – IBM/PS2, DEC/VAX 4000-200, DEC/VAX 4000-300; 12-IBM/Sys 70; Printers – DEC/LA 210, DEC/LA 75;
Classified Software: Cybergraphics 7.5.
Editorial Equipment: Hardware – DEC/VAX 4000-200, DEC/VAX 4000-300, 33-IBM/70, IBM/PS2/2-RSK/TRS 80-100, 4-RSK/TRS 80-200; Printers – DEC/LA 210, Compaq/LA-75, Printronix/LPM 600 Band Printer
Editorial Software: Cybergraphics 7.5.
Production Equipment: Hardware – 2-ECR/Autokon 12 max, 1-Anitec/D32; Cameras – 1-Spartan/III, 1-LE/17, 1-AP; Scanners – 2-Epson/ES-1200C.
Total Circulation: 14981

THE ASHLAND DAILY TIDINGS
Corporate/Parent Company: Rosebud Media
Publication Street Address: 111 N Fir St
City: Medford
State: OR
Publication Website: https://ashlandtidings.com
Postal Code: 97501-2772
Office phone: (541) 776-4411
General E-mail: ads@rosebudmedia.com
Publisher Name: Steven Saslow
Editor Name: Justin Umberson
Editor Email: jumberson@rosebudmedia.com
Year Established: 1876
Delivery Methods: Newsstand`Carrier`Racks
Own Printing Facility?: Y
Commercial printers?: Y
Mechanical specifications: Type page 13 x 21 1/2; E - 6 cols, 1 7/8, 1/8 between; A - 6 cols, 1 7/8, 1/8 between; C - 9 cols, 1 3/4, 1/16 between.
Published Days: Mon`Tues`Wed`Thur`Fri`Sat
Weekday Frequency: m
Saturday Frequency: m
Avg Paid Circ: 1297
Avg Free Circ: 137
Audit Company: AAM
Audit Date: 31 03 2015
Pressroom Equipment: Lines – 6-G/Community; Folders – 1-G/2:1.;
Mailroom Equipment: Tying Machines – MLN; Address Machine – Pressure Sensitive/Labeling.;
Buisness Equipment: NCR
Classified Equipment: Hardware – 3-APP/Mac;
Classified Software: Baseview.
Editorial Equipment: Hardware – 10-APP/Mac
Editorial Software: Baseview/NewsEdit Pro IQ 3.1.
Production Equipment: Hardware – 4-APP/Mac, 2-APP/Mac LaserPrinter, Konica/EV Jetsetter 5100S; Cameras – 1-SCREEN/650-D.
Total Circulation: 1434

ONTARIO

ARGUS OBSERVER
Corporate/Parent Company: Wick Communications
Publication Street Address: 1160 SW 4th Street
City: Ontario
State: OR
Publication Website: www.argusobserver.com
Postal Code: 97914
Office phone: 541-889-5387
Publisher Name: Stephanie Spiess
Publisher Email: stephanies@argusobserver.com
Publisher Phone: 541-823-4830
Editor Name: Leslie Thompson
Editor Email: lesliet@argusobserver.com
Editor Phone: 541-823-4818
Advertising Executive Name: Ali Thayer
Advertising Executive Email: alit@argusobserver.com
Advertising Executive Phone: 541-823-4832

ARGUS OBSERVER
Corporate/Parent Company: Wick Communications
Publication Street Address: 1160 SW 4th St
City: Ontario
State: OR
Publication Website: www.argusobserver.com
Postal Code: 97914
Office phone: (541) 889-5387
General E-mail: kellyj@argusobserver.com
Publisher Name: Stephanie Spiess
Publisher Email: stephanies@argusobserver.com
Publisher Phone: (541) 823-4830
Editor Name: Leslie Thompson
Editor Email: lesliet@argusobserver.com
Editor Phone: (541) 823-4818
Advertising Executive Name: Ali Thayer
Advertising Executive Email: alit@argusobserver.com
Advertising Executive Phone: (541) 823-4832
Year Established: 1896
Delivery Methods: Mail`Newsstand`Carrier`Racks
Own Printing Facility?: Y
Commercial printers?: Y
Mechanical specifications: Type page 13 x 21 1/2; E - 6 cols, 2 1/16, 1/8 between; A - 6 cols, 2 1/16, 1/8 between; C - 9 cols, 1 1/4, 1/8 between.
Published Days: Tues`Wed`Thur`Fri
Weekday Frequency: e
Avg Paid Circ: 4508
Avg Free Circ: 9
Audit Company: VAC
Audit Date: 30 06 2016
Pressroom Equipment: Lines – 6-G;
Buisness Equipment: DEC/Micro-VAX/3100
Buisness Software: Vision Data
Classified Equipment: Hardware – APP/Mac; CtP; Printers – 2-HP/LaserJet;
Classified Software: Baseview.
Editorial Equipment: Hardware – APP/Mac/CtP; Printers – HP/LaserJet
Production Equipment: Hardware – Nu/Ultra Plus; Cameras – SCREEN; Scanners – Umax, Polaroid/SprintScan
Production Software: Baseview.
Total Circulation: 4517

PORTLAND

THE OREGONIAN
Corporate/Parent Company: Advance Publications, Inc.
Publication Street Address: 1500 SW 1st Ave
City: Portland
State: OR
Publication Website: www.oregonlive.com
Postal Code: 97201-5870
Office phone: (503) 221-8000
General E-mail: dwalery@oregonian.com
Publisher Name: Kevin Denny
Publisher Email: kdenny@acsor.com
Editor Name: Grant Butler
Editor Email: gbutler@oregonian.com
Editor Phone: (503) 221-8566
Year Established: 1850
Delivery Methods: Carrier
Mechanical specifications: Type page 11 7/8 x 21 1/2; E - 6 cols, 1 7/8, 1/8 between; A - 6 cols, 1 7/8, 1/8 between; C - 10 cols, 1 1/8, 1/16 between.
Published Days: Mon`Tues`Wed`Thur`Fri`Sat`Sun
Weekday Frequency: All day
Saturday Frequency: All day
Avg Paid Circ: 109353
Audit Company: AAM
Audit Date: 21 07 2020
Buisness Software: Peoplesoft Analytics-Qlikview
Total Circulation: 137211

ROSEBURG

THE NEWS-REVIEW
Corporate/Parent Company: Lotus Media Group
Publication Street Address: 345 NE Winchester St
City: Roseburg
State: OR
Publication Website: www.nrtoday.com
Postal Code: 97470-3328
Office phone: (541) 672-3321
General E-mail: customerservice@nrtoday.com
Publisher Name: Rachelle Carter
Publisher Email: rachellec@nrtoday.com
Publisher Phone: (541) 733-5123
Editor Name: Ian Campbell
Editor Email: ian@nrtoday.com
Editor Phone: (541) 957-4209
Advertising Executive Name: Amber Johnson
Advertising Executive Email: amberj@nrtoday.com
Advertising Executive Phone: (541) 229-4323
Year Established: 1867
Delivery Methods: Mail`Newsstand`Carrier`Racks
Own Printing Facility?: Y
Commercial printers?: Y
Mechanical specifications: Type page 13 x 21 1/2; E - 6 cols, 2 1/16, 1/8 between; A - 6 cols, 2 1/16, 1/8 between; C - 9 cols, 1 3/8, 1/16 between.
Published Days: Mon`Tues`Wed`Thur`Fri`Sun
Weekday Frequency: e
Avg Paid Circ: 19246
Avg Free Circ: 815
Audit Company: AAM
Audit Date: 4 06 2020
Pressroom Equipment: Lines – 6-G/Urbanite; Folders – 1-G/quarter folder.;
Mailroom Equipment: Counter Stackers – 1-Quipp/500; Inserters & Stuffers – 1-MM/227E, 1-KAN/480; Tying Machines – 2-MLN/ML2EE.;
Buisness Equipment: 1-PBS/Convergent
Classified Equipment: Hardware – 4-APP/Mac SE 30.;
Editorial Equipment: Hardware – Apple Mac Minis and MacBook Airs
Editorial Software: DTI
Production Equipment: Cameras – Cannon
Production Software: DTI/Adobe
Total Circulation: 17187

SALEM

STATESMAN JOURNAL
Corporate/Parent Company: Gannett
Publication Street Address: 280 Church St NE
City: Salem
State: OR
Publication Website: www.statesmanjournal.com
Postal Code: 97301-3734
Office phone: (800) 452-2511
General E-mail: newsroom@statesmanjournal.com
Publisher Name: Ryan Kedzierski
Editor Name: Cherrill Crosby
Editor Email: crosbyc@statesmanjournal.com
Advertising Executive Name: Brian Leslie
Advertising Executive Email: bleslie@statesmanjournal.com
Advertising Executive Phone: (503) 823-9967
Year Established: 1851
Delivery Methods: Mail`Newsstand`Carrier`Racks
Mechanical specifications: Type page 10 x 21 1/2; E - 6 cols, 1 1/2, 1/6 between; A - 6 cols, 2, 1/6 between; C - 10 cols, 1, 1/12 between.
Published Days: Mon`Tues`Wed`Thur`Fri`Sat`Sun
Weekday Frequency: m
Saturday Frequency: m
Avg Paid Circ: 31518
Audit Company: AAM
Audit Date: 28 01 2020
Pressroom Equipment: Lines – 7-G/Metro double width 1975; Pasters –G/Digital Pilot & surface sensingReels & Stands – Spyder/arms.;
Mailroom Equipment: Counter Stackers – 4/Olympian; Inserters & Stuffers – HI/NP 632; Tying Machines – 4-/Dynaric; Control System – HI w/Icon System; Address Machine – Domino/InkJet.;
Classified Equipment: Hardware – IBM/Servers, Ethernet/100MB-Dell/Workstation; 2-Harlequin/Software RIP (for V/5500), 1-V/5300 Pixelburst Software RIP; Printers – V/5300 B, V/5500, HP/4000, HP/5SI, HP/8100, HP/8500;
Classified Software: APT, MEI/CLS.
Editorial Equipment: Hardware – IBM, APP/Mac G3 Workstation, Ethernet/100MP; Printers – V/5500, V/5300 B, HP/5si, HP/8100, HP/8500, HP/2500, HP/715
Editorial Software: QPS.
Production Equipment: Hardware – V/5100, V/5500, V/5300 B, QMS; Cameras - Spartan/II Page; Scanners – CD, Lf/Leafscan 35, Sharp/Flatbed, Lf/Leafscan 45, 2-Tecsa/18 x 24, 2-Tecsa/14x24
Production Software: MEI/CLS, QPS.
Total Circulation: 24416

PENNSYLVANIA

ALIQUIPPA

BEAVER COUNTY TIMES
Corporate/Parent Company: Gannett
Publication Street Address: 400 Corporation Drive, Hopewell Business Park
City: Aliquippa
State: PA
Publication Website: www.timesonline.com
Postal Code: 15001
Office phone: (724) 775-3200
General E-mail: kmccracken@timesonline.com
Publisher Name: Tina Bequeath
Publisher Email: tbequeath@timesonline.com
Publisher Phone: (724) 775-3200, Ext : 120
Editor Name: Lisa Micco
Editor Email: lmicco@timesonline.com
Editor Phone: (724) 775-3200, Ext : 157
Advertising Executive Name: Nick Hink
Advertising Executive Email: nhink@timesonline.com
Advertising Executive Phone: (724) 775-3200,

U.S. Daily Newspapers

Ext : 141
Year Established: 1851
Delivery Methods:
Mail`Newsstand`Carrier`Racks
Own Printing Facility?: N
Commercial printers?: N
Mechanical specifications: Type page 13 x 21 1/2; E - 6 cols, 2 1/16, 1/8 between; A - 6 cols, 2 1/16, 1/8 between; C - 9 cols, 1 3/8, 1/16 between.
Published Days: Mon`Tues`Wed`Thur`Fri`Sun
Weekday Frequency: m
Saturday Frequency: m
Avg Paid Circ: 21323
Audit Company: AAM
Audit Date: 5 11 2019
Pressroom Equipment: Printed at the Pittsburgh Post-Gazette facility
Mailroom Equipment: Printed at the Pittsburgh Post-Gazette facility
Buisness Equipment: IBM
Buisness Software: Microsoft/Office 97, Mactive, Open Pages
Classified Equipment: Hardware – 7-Dell/PC, 2-Dell/Server; HP/LaserJet Printer; Printers – MON/Expressmaster 1016;
Classified Software: Mactive.
Editorial Equipment: Hardware – 31-Dell/PC, 14-Compaq, 5-APP/Mac, 2-Compaq/ Servers/MON/SUN OPS System; Printers – MON/Proof Express, 2-MON/ Expressmaster 1016, 3-HP/LaserJet Printer
Editorial Software: NewsCycle; Edit UI / Saxotech
Production Equipment: Pages are designed at the Center for News & Design in Austin, Texas
Production Software: InDesign
Note: AWARDS: PNA's Newspaper of the Year, Division III (2015, 2016, 2017, 2018) PNA's News Excellence, Division III (2015, 2016, 2017, 2018) PNA's Newspaper of the Year, statewide all divisions (2015) Top honors in Keystone Press Awards, APME, and Pennsylvania Women's Press Association APSE's Triple Crown winners for three consecutive years for excellence in sports coverage (national award) National awards for digital presentation from Inland and Local News Media (national award) First place for daily design, special sections (Football Preview, Quigley at 50, Remembering Flight 427, Tornado 1985 etc.) VIDEO SHOWS: Game On (daily; preview, post-game, Beat the Experts, etc.) Week in Review (Thurs.) Notorious Beaver County (13-week video series on Beaver County serial killer) The Parajournal (explores area's unexplained, folklore, legends and hauntings) Get Out (Wed.; entertainment) Times Today (daily); You Don't Know Squat (Mon.; weight-lifting/fitness); For the Health of It (Mon.; healthy lifestyles); Cold Case (unsolved crimes); Cook This! (Tues., cooking show); Value This! With Dr. Lori (Mon.; antiques) PODCASTS: The Buzz (Mon.); From the Newsroom SPECIAL SECTIONS: Annual Football Preview (Aug.) 2-day Progress sections (Feb.) TRADE SHOWS: Bridal Fair (Jan.), Home & Garden (March), Best of the Valley (June); Job Fair (Oct.) SPECIAL EVENT: Times / Black Hawk Senior Golf Championships (Aug.)
Total Circulation: 15758

ALLENTOWN

THE MORNING CALL

Corporate/Parent Company: Tribune Publishing Company
Publication Street Address: 101 N 6th St
City: Allentown
State: PA
Publication Website: www.mcall.com
Postal Code: 18105
Office phone: (610) 820-6500
General E-mail: morningcallstore@mcall.com
Editor Name: Theresa Rang
Editor Email: terry.rang@mcall.com
Editor Phone: (610) 770-3777
Advertising Executive Name: Jim Feher
Advertising Executive Email: james.feher@mcall.com

Advertising Executive Phone: (610) 778-2212
Year Established: 1883
Published Days: Mon`Tues`Wed`Thur`Fri`Sat`Sun
Weekday Frequency: m
Saturday Frequency: m
Avg Paid Circ: 58950
Audit Company: AAM
Audit Date: 3 08 2020
Classified Software: SII.
Note: I'm only updating and verifying the Publisher's contact information.
Total Circulation: 87934

ALTOONA

ALTOONA MIRROR

Corporate/Parent Company: Ogden Newspapers, Inc.
Publication Street Address: 301 Cayuga Ave
City: Altoona
State: PA
Publication Website: www.altoonamirror.com
Postal Code: 16602-4323
Office phone: (814) 946-7411
General E-mail: tbrooks@altoonamirror.com
Publisher Name: Ed Kruger
Publisher Email: ekruger@altoonamirror.com
Editor Name: Neil Rudel
Editor Email: nrudel@altoonamirror.com
Editor Phone: (814) 946-7527
Advertising Executive Name: Tracy Brooks
Advertising Executive Email: tbrooks@altoonamirror.com
Advertising Executive Phone: (814) 949-7021
Year Established: 1876
Delivery Methods:
Mail`Newsstand`Carrier`Racks
Own Printing Facility?: Y
Commercial printers?: Y
Mechanical specifications: Type page 10 x 21.5; E - 6 cols, 2 1/16, 1/8 between; A - 6 cols, 2 1/16, 1/8 between; C - 6 cols, 2 1/16, 1/8 between.
Published Days: Mon`Tues`Wed`Thur`Fri`Sat`Sun
Weekday Frequency: m
Saturday Frequency: m
Avg Paid Circ: 19037
Avg Free Circ: 573
Audit Company: AAM
Audit Date: 20 03 2019
Pressroom Equipment: Lines – 6-G/Headliner Offset double width, 4-G/half decks double width; Reels & Stands – 5-G/Stands, 5-G/3-Arm Reels & Stands.;
Mailroom Equipment: Counter Stackers – 2/ PPK, 2-Id/2200; Inserters & Stuffers – 6-/ KAN, MC/660-20, GMA/SLS 1000; Tying Machines – 5-/Sa, 2-/MLN, Id; Control System – GMA; Address Machine – PBS/ CIS;
Buisness Software: Excel, MS Word, Microsoft/ Excel, Microsoft/Word
Classified Equipment: Printers – IBM, Konica/ Marlins.
Classified Software: Unix, CText.
Editorial Software: QPS/QuarkXPress.
Production Equipment: Hardware – KFM; Cameras – SCREEN, LD/281-Q; Scanners – ECR/Autokon, Sharp/35mm
Production Software: APP/Mac NLM 3.12, Novell/Netware 386 3.12, Microsoft/ Windows, Cheyenne/Arcserve.
Total Circulation: 25898

BEDFORD

THE BEDFORD GAZETTE

Corporate/Parent Company: Sample News Group LLC
Publication Street Address: 424 W Penn St
City: Bedford
State: PA
Publication Website: www.bedfordgazette.com
Postal Code: 15522-1230
Office phone: (814) 623-1151
General E-mail: customerservice@bedfordgazette.com
Publisher Name: Joseph A. Beegle
Publisher Email: jbeegle@bedfordgazette.com
Editor Name: Elizabeth Coyle

Editor Email: ecoyle@bedfordgazette.com
Advertising Executive Name: Kathy Arnold
Advertising Executive Email: karnold@bedfordgazette.com
Advertising Executive Phone: (814) 623-1151, Ext : 220
Year Established: 1805
Mechanical specifications: Type page 13 x 21 1/2; E - 6 cols, 2 1/16, 1/8 between; A - 6 cols, 2 1/16, 1/8 between; C - 6 cols, 2 1/16, 1/8 between.
Published Days: Mon`Tues`Wed`Thur`Fri`Sat
Weekday Frequency: m
Saturday Frequency: m
Avg Paid Circ: 10000
Audit Company: Sworn/Estimate/Non-Audited
Audit Date: 7 12 2019
Pressroom Equipment: Lines – 5-G/Community 1983; Folders – 1-G/S-C.;
Mailroom Equipment: Tying Machines – Nichiro Kogyo; Address Machine – Ch/515.;
Buisness Equipment: Real World, PC
Classified Equipment: Hardware – APP/Mac; Printers – APP/Mac Laser;
Classified Software: Baseview.
Editorial Equipment: Hardware – APP/Mac; Printers – APP/Mac Laser
Editorial Software: Baseview/NewsEdit.
Production Equipment: Hardware – APP/Mac Laser; Cameras – K.
Total Circulation: 10000

BLOOMSBURG

PRESS ENTERPRISE

Corporate/Parent Company: Press Enterprise, Inc.
Publication Street Address: 3185 Lackawanna Ave
City: Bloomsburg
State: PA
Publication Website: www.pressenterpriseonline.com
Postal Code: 17815-3329
Office phone: (570) 784-2121
General E-mail: advertising@pressenterprise.net
Publisher Name: Brandon R. Eyerly
Publisher Phone: (570) 387-1234, Ext : 1164
Editor Name: Peter Kendron
Editor Phone: (570) 387-1234, Ext : 1305
Advertising Executive Name: Donna Turner
Advertising Executive Phone: (570) 387-1234, Ext : 1399
Year Established: 1902
Own Printing Facility?: Y
Commercial printers?: Y
Mechanical specifications: Type page 12 x 21 1/2; E - 6 cols, 1 11/16', 1/10 between; A - 6 cols, 1 11/16, 1/10 between; C - 9 cols, 1 1/16, 1/10 between.
Published Days: Mon`Tues`Wed`Thur`Fri`Sat`Sun
Weekday Frequency: m
Saturday Frequency: m
Avg Paid Circ: 16678
Avg Free Circ: 428
Audit Company: AAM
Audit Date: 14 02 2020
Pressroom Equipment: Lines – 8-G/Urbanite (3 color) single width 1972; 8-HI/NC 400 single width 1985; Tensor/1400 single width 1995; Tensor/1400 single width 1999; Reels & Stands – Roll/Stands.;
Mailroom Equipment: Counter Stackers – 1-BG/108, 1-BG/107, 1/PPK, 2-HI/RS25; Inserters & Stuffers – 1-/MM, GMA/SLS 1000; Tying Machines – 2-MLN/ML2EE, 1-/Sa, 3-/BU; Address Machine – 1-KR/ Communications, 1-/KAN;
Buisness Equipment: Dell 2950
Buisness Software: DSI Software, Logic, Abra Suite, Great Plains
Classified Equipment: Hardware – Dell 2850; Printers – HP/Laserjet 4000;
Classified Software: Brainworks
Editorial Equipment: Hardware – Mac mini iMac, Xserve; Printers – Laser jet 8150
Editorial Software: Woodwing/InDesign
Production Equipment: Hardware – Nexus, Creo transetter news; Scanners – Epson
Production Software: Baseview.
Total Circulation: 17565

BRADFORD

THE BRADFORD ERA

Corporate/Parent Company: Community Media Group
Publication Street Address: 43 Main St
City: Bradford
State: PA
Publication Website: www.bradfordera.com
Postal Code: 16701-2019
Office phone: (814) 368-3173
General E-mail: news@bradfordera.com
Editor Name: Marcie Schellhammer
Editor Email: marcie@bradfordera.com
Editor Phone: (814) 362-6531
Advertising Executive Name: Jill Henry
Advertising Executive Email: jillh@bradfordera.com
Advertising Executive Phone: (814) 368-3173
Year Established: 1824
Delivery Methods:
Mail`Newsstand`Carrier`Racks
Own Printing Facility?: Y
Commercial printers?: Y
Mechanical specifications: Type page 12 x 21 1/2; E - 6 cols, 1 13/16, 1/6 between; A - 6 cols, 1 13/16, 1/6 between; C - 9 cols, 1 3/16, 1/12 between.
Published Days: Mon`Tues`Wed`Thur`Fri`Sat
Weekday Frequency: m
Saturday Frequency: m
Avg Paid Circ: 7942
Avg Free Circ: 37
Audit Company: VAC
Audit Date: 30 09 2015
Pressroom Equipment: Lines – 8-HI/V-15D; Reels & Stands – 8; Control System – 2-CH/ Responder 210.;
Mailroom Equipment: Counter Stackers – 1/ BG; Tying Machines – 2-/MLN; Address Machine – 1-/St, 1-/KR.;
Buisness Equipment: 1-Compaq/Unix Box, 5-PC
Buisness Software: Vision Data
Classified Equipment: Hardware – APP/Mac; Printers – Okidata/Microline 321 Turbo, Pre Press/Panther Pro Imagesetter;
Classified Software: Baseview.
Editorial Equipment: Hardware – APP/Power Mac/1-APP/Mac IIsi, APP/GraphicsNet, 1-Lf/AP Leaf Picture Desk (with Laser Photo); Printers – LaserWriter/Pro, Pre Press/Panther Pro Imagesetter, Pre Press/ Panther Plus Imagesetter
Editorial Software: Baseview.
Production Equipment: Hardware – Visioneer 2.0, 1-Pre Press/Panther Pro 46 (18 wide Imagesetter), 1-Pre Press/Panther Plus (13 1/3 wide Imagesetter); Cameras – R/500 Overhead; Scanners – 1-Lf/Leafscan 45, 3-Umax/Astra 12005
Production Software: QPS/QuarkXPress 4.0.
Total Circulation: 7979

CARLISLE

THE SENTINEL (CUMBERLINK)

Corporate/Parent Company: Lee Enterprises
Publication Street Address: 327 B Street
City: Carlisle
State: PA
Publication Website: www.cumberlink.com
Postal Code: 17013-2655
Office phone: (717) 243-2611
General E-mail: cvbj@cumberlink.com
Publisher Name: Kim Kamowski
Publisher Email: kkamowski@cumberlink.com
Publisher Phone: (717) 240-7114
Editor Name: Jeff Pratt
Editor Email: jpratt@cumberlink.com
Advertising Executive Name: Pam Hedrick
Advertising Executive Email: phedrick@cumberlink.com
Advertising Executive Phone: (717) 240-7124
Year Established: 1860
Delivery Methods: Mail`Newsstand`Carrier
Own Printing Facility?: N
Commercial printers?: N
Mechanical specifications: Type page 11 5/8 x 21 1/2; E - 6 cols, 2 1/16, 1/8 between; A - 6 cols, 2 1/16, 1/8 between; C - 9 cols, 1 1/4, 1/4 between.

Published Days: Mon`Tues`Wed`Thur`Fri`Sat
Weekday Frequency: m
Saturday Frequency: m
Avg Paid Circ: 8000
Audit Company: AAM
Audit Date: 5 09 2018
Buisness Equipment: Sun/Ultra 2
Buisness Software: Vision Data
Classified Equipment: Hardware – 7-Sun/Sparc II;
Classified Software: Vision Data/Classified;
Editorial Equipment: Hardware – 4-PC-NT Servers, 18-MS/NT Notes Clients/8-APP/Mac G3; Printers – 1-PT/RIP, 1-ECR/108S Pelbox
Editorial Software: Lotus/Domino Notes.
Total Circulation: 9472

CHAMBERSBURG
PUBLIC OPINION

Corporate/Parent Company: Gannett Company Inc.
Publication Street Address: 77 N 3rd St
City: Chambersburg
State: PA
Publication Website: www.publicopiniononline.com
Postal Code: 17201-1812
Office phone: (717) 264-6161
General E-mail: advertising@mediaonemarketplace.com
Advertising Executive Name: Keith Hartman
Advertising Executive Email: khartman@mediaonepa.com
Advertising Executive Phone: (717) 767-3467
Year Established: 1869
Delivery Methods:
   Mail`Newsstand`Carrier`Racks
Own Printing Facility?: Y
Commercial printers?: N
Mechanical specifications: Typed page 11 x 21 1/4
Published Days: Mon`Tues`Wed`Thur`Fri`Sat`Sun
Weekday Frequency: m
Saturday Frequency: m
Avg Paid Circ: 7899
Avg Free Circ: 3150
Audit Company: AAM
Audit Date: 19 11 2018
Pressroom Equipment: Lines – 6 units-Goss Urbanite installed 2007.;
Mailroom Equipment: Counter Stackers – 2/QWI, 1-/SH; Inserters & Stuffers – SH/1472; Tying Machines – MLN;
Buisness Equipment: PC
Buisness Software: MS Office 2003, JDE for business, Mactive for Adv, PBS for Circ
Classified Equipment: Hardware – PC; Dell;
Classified Software: Mactive
Editorial Equipment: Hardware – APP/Mac/Dell and Mac
Editorial Software: Baseview/NewsEdit Pro 3.2.3.
Production Software: Baseview/NewsEdit Pro 3.2.3.
Total Circulation: 10743

CLEARFIELD
GANTDAILY.COM

Corporate/Parent Company: GANT Media, LLC
Publication Street Address: 219 S. 2nd Street; PO Box 746
City: Clearfield
State: PA
Publication Website: www.gantdaily.com
Postal Code: 16830
Office phone: (814)765-5256
General E-mail: news@gantdaily.com
Editor Name: Jessica Shirey
Editor Email: editor@gantdaily.com
Advertising Executive Name: Amanda Rosman
Advertising Executive Email: arosman@gantdaily.com

THE PROGRESS

Publication Street Address: PO Box 952
City: Clearfield
State: PA
Publication Website: www.theprogressnews.com
Postal Code: 16830-0952
Office phone: (814) 765-5581
General E-mail: news@theprogressnews.com
Publisher Name: Pat Patterson
Editor Name: Julie Benamati
Year Established: 1913
Delivery Methods:
   Mail`Newsstand`Carrier`Racks
Own Printing Facility?: Y
Commercial printers?: N
Mechanical specifications: Type page 13 x 21 1/2; E – 6 cols, 2 1/16, 1/8 between; A – 6 cols, 2 1/16, 1/8 between; C – 8 cols, 1 5/8, 1/16 between.
Published Days: Mon`Tues`Wed`Thur`Fri`Sat
Weekday Frequency: e
Saturday Frequency: m
Avg Paid Circ: 8649
Avg Free Circ: 152
Audit Company: CAC
Audit Date: 31 03 2014
Pressroom Equipment: Lines – 9-G/Community;
Mailroom Equipment: Counter Stackers – 1-BG/Count-O-Veyor; Inserters & Stuffers – KAN/320; Tying Machines – Sa.;
Buisness Equipment: IBM
Classified Equipment: Hardware – OS; Printers – MON;
Classified Software: QPS/Q-Sales.
Editorial Equipment: Hardware – COM/One System; Printers – 4-NewGen
Editorial Software: QPS/QuarkXPress 4.1.
Production Equipment: Hardware – NewGen, Ultra 4000, Ultra/Plus; Cameras – Nipon/Screen; Scanners – HP/Scan Jet 6300C
Production Software: Quark 4.1.
Total Circulation: 8801

CLINTON
PITTSBURGH POST-GAZETTE

Corporate/Parent Company: Block Communications, Inc.
Publication Street Address: 2201 Sweeney Dr
City: Clinton
State: PA
Publication Website: www.post-gazette.com
Postal Code: 15026-1818
Office phone: (412) 263-1100
General E-mail: pgforme@post-gazette.com
Editor Name: Tom Birdsong
Editor Email: tbirdsong@post-gazette.com
Editor Phone: (412) 263-3068
Year Established: 1786
Delivery Methods:
   Mail`Newsstand`Carrier`Racks
Own Printing Facility?: Y
Commercial printers?: Y
Mechanical specifications: Type page 11 1/2 x 22; E – 6 cols, 1 13/16, 1/8 between; A – 6 cols, 1 13/16, 1/8 between; C – 10 cols, 1 2/25, 2/25 between.
Published Days: Mon`Tues`Wed`Thur`Fri`Sat`Sun
Weekday Frequency: m
Saturday Frequency: m
Avg Paid Circ: 122735
Audit Company: AAM
Audit Date: 31 03 2018
Pressroom Equipment: 2014 Goss Uniliner 6x2 Coldset Printing Press. 48 broadsheet pages, straight, all color. 96 broadsheet pages, collect, all color. Press speed 80,000 CPH straight. Two 255 jaw folders. Four Megtec Reels. Ferag Gripper Conveyor.
Pressroom Software: HarlandSimon
Mailroom Equipment: Counter Stackers – 6 Quipp 500, 4 Ferag HPS, 2-Heidelberg Olympian; Inserters & Stuffers – Goss Magnapak w/Omnizone; Heidelberg 632 w/Omnizone; Tying Machines – 4 Dynaric /NP3, 8-Dynaric/NP1500, 4 Samuel;

8-Power Strap under wrap; 3 Schur Palletizer
Mailroom Software: OmniZone
Buisness Software: Microsoft/Office
Classified Software: DTI ClassSpeed
Editorial Equipment: Hardware – 2-Sun/Enterprise 2000, 2-Sun/V880's/265-PC; Printers – Toshiba, HP/LaserJet
Editorial Software: Libercus/DTI/Indesign/InCopy.
Production Equipment: Hardware – Na, 1-Na/Starlite, 2-NA/C220
Production Software: DTI/Edit.
Total Circulation: 122735

CONNELLSVILLE
DAILY COURIER

Corporate/Parent Company: Western News & Info
Publication Street Address: 127 W Apple St
City: Connellsville
State: PA
Publication Website: www.dailycourier.com
Postal Code: 15425-3132
Office phone: (724) 628-2000
General E-mail: newsroom@dailycourier.com
Publisher Name: Joseph Beegle
Publisher Email: publisher@bedfordgazette.com
Editor Name: Cindy Ekas-Brown
Advertising Executive Name: Joanne Richey
Advertising Executive Email: jrichey@dailycourier.com
Year Established: 1879
Mechanical specifications: Type page 13 x 21 1/2; E – 6 cols, 2 1/16, 1/8 between; A – 6 cols, 2 1/16, 1/8 between; C – 9 cols, 1 3/8, 1/16 between.
Published Days: Mon`Tues`Wed`Thur`Fri`Sat`Sun
Weekday Frequency: e
Saturday Frequency: m
Avg Paid Circ: 5541
Avg Free Circ: 99
Audit Company: AAM
Audit Date: 30 09 2014
Mailroom Equipment: Tying Machines – OVL.;
Buisness Software: NCR/Software
Classified Equipment: Hardware – 3-Mk.;
Editorial Equipment: Hardware – APP/Mac
Editorial Software: QPS/QuarkXPress, Baseview, Adobe/Photoshop.
Production Equipment: Hardware – 2-XIT/Clipper; Cameras – 1-B, 2-Nu, 1-SCREEN.
Total Circulation: 5640

DU BOIS
THE COURIER EXPRESS

Corporate/Parent Company: Community Media Group
Publication Street Address: 500 Jeffers St
City: Du Bois
State: PA
Publication Website: www.thecourierexpress.com
Postal Code: 15801-2430
Office phone: (814) 371-4200
General E-mail: ads@thecourierexpress.com
Publisher Name: Pat Patterson
Publisher Email: ppatterson@thecourierexpress.com
Publisher Phone: (814) 503-8860
Editor Name: David Sullens
Editor Email: dsullens@thecourierexpress.com
Editor Phone: (814) 503-8863
Year Established: 1872
Delivery Methods:
   Mail`Newsstand`Carrier`Racks
Own Printing Facility?: Y
Commercial printers?: Y
Mechanical specifications: Type page 13 x 21 1/2; E – 6 cols, 2 1/16, 1/6 between; A – 6 cols, 2 1/16, 1/6 between; C – 8 cols, 1 1/2, 1/6 between.
Published Days: Mon`Tues`Wed`Thur`Fri`Sat`Sun
Weekday Frequency: e
Avg Paid Circ: 8420
Audit Company: AAM

Audit Date: 30 09 2012
Pressroom Equipment: Lines – 8-WPC/Atlas (with 2-Quadra-Color Unit); 8-KP/News King.;
Mailroom Equipment: Counter Stackers – 2-BG/Count-O-Veyor; Inserters & Stuffers – 1-MM/227E; Tying Machines – 2/Sa, Power Strap/250.;
Buisness Equipment: IBM/RISC 6000
Buisness Software: Solomon
Classified Equipment: Hardware – Mac;
Classified Software: MediaSpan
Editorial Equipment: Hardware – Mac OSX 10.7; Printers – HP/4MV, QMS/2060
Editorial Software: MediaSpan
Production Equipment: Hardware – Kodak Trendsetter; Cameras – SCREEN/20 x 24 Horizontal Low Bed; Scanners – Umax
Total Circulation: 8420

EASTON
LEHIGH VALLEY MEDIA GROUP/THE EXPRESS-TIMES

Corporate/Parent Company: Advance Local Media
Publication Street Address: 18 Centre Square
City: Easton
State: PA
Publication Website: www.lehighvalleylive.com
Postal Code: 18042
Office phone: 610-258-7171
General E-mail: letters@lehighvalleylive.com
Editor Name: Jim Flagg
Editor Email: jflagg@express-times.com
Advertising Executive Name: Jim Wiegers
Advertising Executive Email: JWiegers@lehighvalleylive.com
Advertising Executive Phone: (610) 553-3320

THE EXPRESS-TIMES

Corporate/Parent Company: Advance Newspapers
Publication Street Address: 18 Centre Square
City: Easton
State: PA
Publication Website: www.lehighvalleylive.com
Postal Code: 18042-3528
Office phone: (610) 258-7171
General E-mail: circulation@express-times.com
Editor Name: Jim Flagg
Editor Email: jflagg@express-times.com
Delivery Methods: Newsstand`Carrier`Racks
Mechanical specifications: Type page 13 x 21; E – 6 cols, 2 1/16, 1/8 between; A – 6 cols, 1 5/6, 1/8 between; C – 10 cols, 1 3/16, 1/16 between.
Published Days: Mon`Tues`Wed`Thur`Fri`Sat`Sun
Weekday Frequency: m
Saturday Frequency: m
Avg Paid Circ: 18368
Audit Company: AAM
Audit Date: 27 02 2019
Buisness Equipment: Dec/VAX 4000, Dec/Alpha, Addrox/50 VT 420, 20-PC WS
Buisness Software: Geac AIM/AIM, CIS, Lotus 1-2-3, WordPerfect 5.0, CJ
Classified Equipment: Hardware – 20-PPI/Advertising Management System Classified; Novell/Netware 4.11; Printers – HP/3, APP/Mac 8500;
Classified Software: PPI/Advertising Management System Classified, Class/Act Pagination.
Editorial Equipment: Hardware – Compaq/3000, Compaq/PC WS/Novell/Netware 4.11; Printers – AST/8200
Editorial Software: CNI/Database, Microsoft/Word, QPS/QuarkXPress 3.32.
Production Equipment: Hardware – Nu/Flip Top, RIP NT, 1-ECR/4500 RIP NT, G/OPI; Cameras – 1-C/Spartan II; Scanners – ECR/Autokon 1000, Umax/Mirage
Production Software: Adobe Creative Suite, CNI/Btrieve Data, MEI/CLS, ALS.
Total Circulation: 26695

U.S. Daily Newspapers

ELLWOOD CITY

ELLWOOD CITY LEDGER

Corporate/Parent Company: Gannett
Publication Street Address: 501 Lawrence Ave
City: Ellwood City
State: PA
Publication Website: www.ellwoodcityledger.com
Postal Code: 16117-1927
Office phone: (724) 758-5573
General E-mail: ads@ellwoodcityledger.com
Editor Name: Patrick O'Shea
Editor Email: poshea@timesonline.com
Advertising Executive Email: ads@ellwood.cityledger.com
Advertising Executive Phone: (724) 846-6300
Year Established: 1920
Mechanical specifications: Type page 13 x 21 1/2; E - 6 cols, 2 1/14, 1/6 between; A - 6 cols, 2 1/14, 1/6 between; C - 6 cols, 2 1/14, 1/6 between.
Published Days: Mon`Tues`Wed`Thur`Fri`Sat
Weekday Frequency: m
Saturday Frequency: m
Avg Paid Circ: 3425
Audit Company: Sworn/Estimate/Non-Audited
Audit Date: 7 12 2019
Pressroom Equipment: Lines – 5-G/Community; Folders – 1-G/SSC.;
Mailroom Equipment: Tying Machines – 2-EAM-Mosca; Address Machine – 2/Ch.;
Buisness Equipment: 3-APP/iMac
Buisness Software: Baseview
Classified Equipment: Hardware – 4-APP/iMac; Printers – HP/8000, AG/Accuset
Classified Software: Baseview, QPS/QuarkXPress 4.0.
Editorial Equipment: Hardware – 7-PC/Lf/AP Leaf Picture Desk; Printers – HP/8000, AG/Accuset
Editorial Software: Microsoft/Word, QPS/QuarkXPress 4.0.
Production Equipment: Hardware – 1-K, HP/8000 Plain Paper; Cameras – 1-B
Production Software: QPS/QuarkXPress 4.0, Microsoft/Windows, APP/Mac.
Total Circulation: 3425

ERIE

ERIE TIMES-NEWS

Corporate/Parent Company: GateHouse Media
Publication Street Address: 205 W 12th St
City: Erie
State: PA
Publication Website: www.goerie.com
Postal Code: 16534-0002
Office phone: (814) 870-1600
General E-mail: susan.schreiner@timesnews.com
Publisher Name: Terry Cascioli
Publisher Email: tcascioli@timesnews.com
Publisher Phone: (814) 870-1612
Editor Name: Pat Bywater
Editor Email: pbywater@timesnews.com
Editor Phone: (814) 870-1722
Advertising Executive Name: Jennifer Huegel
Advertising Executive Email: jennifer.huegel@timesnews.com
Advertising Executive Phone: (814) 870-1641
Year Established: 1888
Delivery Methods: Mail`Newsstand`Carrier`Racks
Own Printing Facility?: N
Commercial printers?: N
Mechanical specifications: Type page 11 1/16 x 21 1/2; E - 6 cols, 1 13/16, 1/64 between; A - 6 cols, 1 5/6, 1/8 between; C - 10 cols, 1 1/8, 7/16 between.
Published Days: Mon`Tues`Wed`Thur`Fri`Sat`Sun
Weekday Frequency: m
Saturday Frequency: m
Avg Paid Circ: 28110
Audit Company: AAM
Audit Date: 16 01 2020
Pressroom Equipment: Lines – 7-G/Metro (3 half decks) 1969; Folders – 1-G/double 2:1.;
Mailroom Equipment: Counter Stackers – 1-Id/NS550, 2-Id/NS2000, 1-Id/2100; Inserters & Stuffers – 1-GMA/SLS 1000 (17 head), 1-GMA/SLS 1000 (9 head); Tying Machines – 3-MLN/2A, 2/Sa, 3-/Power Strap.;
Buisness Equipment: 2-DEC/VAX 6510
Buisness Software: Compushare, In-house
Classified Equipment: Hardware – DEC/PDP 11-84; 12-NSSE/400, 2-Sun/Sparc II;
Classified Software: Atex.
Editorial Equipment: Hardware – DEC/PDP 11-84/30-NSSE/400, 4-APP/Mac Quadra
Editorial Software: DEC/TMS, Agile/Teambase.
Production Equipment: Hardware – Futura, Alfa-Quest, Pantera/32; Scanners – 2-AG/T-5000 Plus.
Total Circulation: 38424

EXTON

DAILY LOCAL NEWS

Corporate/Parent Company: Media News Group
Publication Street Address: 390 Eagleview Blvd.
City: Exton
State: PA
Publication Website: www.dailylocal.com
Postal Code: 19341
Office phone: 610-696-1775
Publisher Name: Edward S. Condra
Publisher Email: econdra@21st-centurymedia.com
Editor Name: Fran Maye
Editor Email: fmaye@21st-centurymedia.com
Advertising Executive Name: Beth Douglas
Advertising Executive Email: bdouglas@21st-centurymedia.com
Delivery Methods: Mail`Newsstand`Carrier`Racks
Own Printing Facility?: Y
Mechanical specifications: Type page 12 x 21 1/2; E - 6 cols, 1 7/8, 1/8 between; A - 6 cols, 1 7/8, 1/8 between; C - 10 cols, 1 3/16, 3/32 between.
Published Days: Mon`Tues`Wed`Thur`Fri`Sat`Sun
Weekday Frequency: m
Saturday Frequency: m
Avg Paid Circ: 9969
Avg Free Circ: 580
Audit Company: AAM
Audit Date: 17 10 2017
Pressroom Equipment: Lines – 10-G/Urbanite; Press Drive – 2-Fin/125H Drives; Folders – G/Urbanite 700; Pasters –7-Enkel/Autoweb 1991.
Mailroom Equipment: Counter Stackers – 2-HL/Monitor; Inserters & Stuffers – 1-GMA/SLS 1000 10:1; Tying Machines – 2/Power Strap/PSN-6; Address Machine – Ch.;
Buisness Equipment: 2-IBM/Sys 400
Buisness Software: INSI
Classified Equipment: Hardware – PPI; Printers – Bidco;
Classified Software: PPI.
Editorial Equipment: Hardware – CNI/Open, APP/Mac Network/Kodak/Scanner; Printers – Bidco/Imagesetter
Editorial Software: CNI/Open, Lf/AP Leaf Picture Desk.
Production Equipment: Hardware – Caere/OmniPage Pro 2.0, 1-Nu/Flip Top FT40APNS; Cameras – C/Spartan II; Scanners – Digi-Colour/Sys 3000, Lf/Leafscan 35, Kk/2035, Microtek/8003, Umax/Vista
Production Software: QPS/QuarkXPress 3.3, Adobe/Photoshop 4.0.
Note: The Daily Local News also prints the Phoenixville (PA) Phoenix (m), a Journal Register Newspaper.
Total Circulation: 20232

THE MERCURY

Corporate/Parent Company: Media News Group
Publication Street Address: 390 Eagleview Blvd.
City: Exton
State: PA
Publication Website: www.pottsmerc.com
Postal Code: 19341
Office phone: (610) 970-4455
General E-mail: paadvertising@medianewsgroup.com
Publisher Name: Edward S. Condra
Publisher Email: econdra@21st-centurymedia.com
Editor Name: Tony Phyrillas
Editor Email: tphyrillas@pottsmerc.com
Advertising Executive Name: Steve Batten
Advertising Executive Email: sbatten@pottsmerc.com
Year Established: 1931
Mechanical specifications: Type page 11 5/8 x 20 1/2; E - 6 cols, 1 5/6, 1/8 between; A - 6 cols, 1 5/6, 1/8 between; C - 10 cols, between.
Published Days: Mon`Tues`Wed`Thur`Fri`Sat`Sun
Weekday Frequency: m
Saturday Frequency: m
Avg Paid Circ: 6716
Avg Free Circ: 627
Audit Company: AAM
Audit Date: 26 09 2017
Pressroom Equipment: Lines – 3-MAN/double width; 3-MAN/double width; Reels & Stands – 8-MAN/CD 13; Control System – PECOM.;
Mailroom Equipment: Counter Stackers – 2/HL; Inserters & Stuffers – 1-HI/Injector 1372 w/ARS; Tying Machines – 2-Sa/Auto, 1-Sa/Man; Wrapping Singles – 1-Sa/810; Address Machine – 2-Am/1900, 1-Am/5000.;
Buisness Equipment: AS 400
Classified Equipment: Hardware – AST/Bravo LC 5133, Dell/Gx150; MEI/CLS 2.6.6; Printers – NewGen/660B;
Classified Software: Intertext/REV 12G, AT/5.7.
Editorial Equipment: Hardware – 4-Compaq/ProLiant, Microsoft/Windows NT 4.0; Printers – 1-Xante/3G
Editorial Software: CNI.
Production Equipment: Hardware – Omnipage Pro 7.0, Na, 1-R/Vertical; Cameras – 1-C/Spartan III, 1-R/Vertical; Scanners – ECR/Autokon 1030, Nikon/Scanner, HP/Scanjet 6100C
Production Software: MEI/ALS 2.5.1, MEI/CLS 2.6.6.
Total Circulation: 14914

GETTYSBURG

GETTYSBURG TIMES

Corporate/Parent Company: Gettysburg Times Publishing LLC
Publication Street Address: 1570 Fairfield Rd
City: Gettysburg
State: PA
Publication Website: www.gettysburgtimes.com
Postal Code: 17325-7252
Office phone: (717) 334-1131
General E-mail: info@gettysburgtimes.com
Publisher Name: Harry Hartman
Publisher Email: hhartman@gettysburgtimes.com
Publisher Phone: (717) 253-9403
Editor Name: Alex Hayes
Editor Email: ahayes@gettysburgtimes.com
Editor Phone: (717) 253-9413
Advertising Executive Name: Nancy Pritt
Advertising Executive Email: npritt@gettysburgtimes.com
Advertising Executive Phone: (717) 253-9402
Year Established: 1802
Delivery Methods: Mail`Newsstand`Carrier`Racks
Own Printing Facility?: Y
Commercial printers?: N
Mechanical specifications: Type page 12 1/8 x 21; E - 6 cols, 1 5/6, 1/8 between; A - 6 cols, 1 5/6, 1/16 between; C - 9 cols, 1 5/24, 1/8 between.
Published Days: Mon`Tues`Wed`Thur`Fri`Sat
Weekday Frequency: m
Saturday Frequency: m
Avg Paid Circ: 10520
Audit Company: USPS
Audit Date: 31 03 2013
Pressroom Equipment: Lines – 8-G/Community Offset 1982; 4-G 1982; Folders – 1, 2-G/2:1.;
Mailroom Equipment: Tying Machines – 2/Sa;
Buisness Equipment: Dell PC
Buisness Software: Microsoft Office
Classified Equipment: Hardware – Dell PC;
Classified Software: Newzware
Editorial Equipment: Hardware – Dell PC/Various Scanners; Printers – BizHub
Editorial Software: Newzware
Production Equipment: Hardware – Panther Pro 62 Imagesetter, ; Cameras – Nikon still Canon video; Scanners – Umax/600s, Umax/1200s, Coolscan III, Nikon
Production Software: FSI.
Total Circulation: 10520

GREENSBURG

TRIBUNE-REVIEW

Corporate/Parent Company: Trib Total Media, LLC
Publication Street Address: 622 Cabin Hill Dr
City: Greensburg
State: PA
Publication Website: www.triblive.com
Postal Code: 15601-1657
Office phone: (724) 838-5124
General E-mail: info@tribweb.com
Publisher Name: Jerry DeFlitch
Publisher Email: jdeflitch@tribweb.com
Publisher Phone: (724) 850-1273
Advertising Executive Phone: 570-348-9100 ext. 5271
Mechanical specifications: Type page 13 x 21 1/2; E - 6 cols, 2 1/16, 1/8 between; A - 6 cols, 2 1/16, 1/8 between; C - 10 cols, 1 1/4, 1/16 between.
Published Days: Mon`Tues`Wed`Thur`Fri`Sat`Sun
Weekday Frequency: m
Saturday Frequency: m
Avg Paid Circ: 62735
Audit Company: AAM
Audit Date: 31 03 2017
Pressroom Equipment: Lines – 5-G/Metro (2 color) 1978; 1-G/Metro (Color Tower) 1994; 5-G/Newsliner (31 couples) 1997; 8-G/Universal 70 1999; Folders – G/double 2:1, G/double 3:2; Reels & Stands – 7, 6, 8.;
Mailroom Equipment: Counter Stackers – 2/HL, 2-/QWI, 6-/QWI; Inserters & Stuffers – HI, GMA, 72-P/Double Out, 2-GMA/SLS 2000, 1-GMA/SLS 1000; Tying Machines – 2-/MLN, 5-/QWI; Control System – GMA/SAM; Address Machine – KR.;
Buisness Equipment: IBM
Buisness Software: Brainworks, PBS
Classified Equipment: Hardware – Intel;
Classified Software: PPI/Informatel.
Editorial Equipment: Hardware – IBM/APP/Mac Pagination
Editorial Software: Newsengin.
Production Equipment: Hardware – 3-MON/Express Master, 3-MON/Paper Express, 3-AG/Advantra 25, NewsWorks; Cameras – C, Spartan/II, Spartan/III
Production Software: QPS/QuarkXPress.
Total Circulation: 62735

TRIBUNE-REVIEW GREENSBURG

Corporate/Parent Company: Trib Total Media, LLC
Publication Street Address: 622 Cabin Hill Drive
City: Greensburg
State: PA
Publication Website: www.tribLIVE.com
Postal Code: 15601
Office phone: 724-836-6675
General E-mail: GTRCity@tribweb.com
Editor Name: Jerry DeFlitch
Editor Email: jborden@tribweb.com

HAZLETON

HAZLETON STANDARD-SPEAKER

Corporate/Parent Company: Times-Shamrock Communications
Publication Street Address: 21 N Wyoming St
City: Hazleton
State: PA
Publication Website: www.standardspeaker.com
Postal Code: 18201-6068
Office phone: (570) 455-3636

General E-mail: community@standardspeaker. com
Editor Email: editorial@standardspeaker.com
Editor Phone: (570) 455-3636, Ext : 3615
Advertising Executive Email: todisplayad@standardspeaker.com
Advertising Executive Phone: (570) 455-4244
Year Established: 1866
Delivery Methods: Newsstand`Carrier`Racks
Own Printing Facility?: Y
Mechanical specifications: Type page 13 x 21 1/2; E - 6 cols, 2 1/16, 1/8 between; A - 6 cols, 2 1/16, 1/8 between; C - 9 cols, 1 3/8, 5/64 between.
Published Days: Mon`Tues`Wed`Thur`Fri`Sun
Weekday Frequency: m
Saturday Frequency: m
Avg Paid Circ: 9681
Avg Free Circ: 1642
Audit Company: AAM
Audit Date: 31 03 2019
Pressroom Equipment: Lines – 5-G/Cosmo double width 1975; Press Drive – Fin w/2 GE 150 h.p. DC Motor; Control System – Fin/Cabinet 2.;
Mailroom Equipment: Tying Machines – 1-MLN/ML2EE, 1-EAM-Mosca.;
Buisness Equipment: IBM/C320 Power Station
Buisness Software: Vision Data 7.0, APT
Classified Equipment: Hardware – 8-HP/Vectra VE 8; APP/Mac Quadra 605, APP/Super Mac; Printers – ECR/Scriptsetter, 2-HP/LaserJet;
Classified Software: APT/Classified.
Editorial Equipment: Hardware – 18-HP/Vectra VL6/450, 3-HP/Net Server 3/2-ECR/Imagesetter; Printers – 2-HP/8000 N
Editorial Software: APT/Editorial.
Production Equipment: Hardware – LE/Maxim 26, 2-RIP with ECRM Pelbox; Cameras – C/Spartan III; Scanners – HP/Scan Jet IIC, AG/T2000XL
Production Software: QPS/QuarkXPress 4.04.
Total Circulation: 11323

HONESDALE

THE WAYNE INDEPENDENT

Publication Street Address: 220 8th St
City: Honesdale
State: PA
Publication Website: www.wayneindependent.com
Postal Code: 18431-1854
Office phone: (570) 253-3055
General E-mail: mfleece@wayneindependent.com
Publisher Name: Michelle R. Fleece
Publisher Email: mfleece@tricountyindependent.com
Publisher Phone: (570) 253-3055, Ext : 301
Editor Name: Peter Becker
Editor Email: pbecker@tricountyindependent.com
Editor Phone: (570) 253-3055, Ext : 315
Advertising Executive Name: Helen Diehl
Advertising Executive Email: hdiehl@tricountyindependent.com
Advertising Executive Phone: (570) 253-3055, Ext : 303
Year Established: 1878
Delivery Methods: Mail`Newsstand`Racks
Own Printing Facility?: N
Commercial printers?: N
Mechanical specifications: Type page 13 x 21; E - 6 cols, 2 1/6, 1/4 between; A - 6 cols, 2 1/16, 1/4 between; C - 10 cols, 1 5/16, 13/100 between.
Published Days: Tues`Wed`Thur`Fri`Sat
Weekday Frequency: m
Saturday Frequency: m
Avg Paid Circ: 2618
Audit Company: USPS
Audit Date: 10 01 2016
Buisness Software: AMP5
Classified Equipment: Hardware – Mac; Printers – APP/Mac LaserWriter II;
Classified Software: AMP5
Editorial Equipment: Hardware – Mac; Printers – APP/Mac LaserWriter II
Editorial Software: News Edit Pro/Pagemaker/Quark

Total Circulation: 2618

HUNTINGDON

DAILY NEWS

Corporate/Parent Company: Gannett
Publication Street Address: 325 Penn Street P.O. Box 384
City: Huntingdon
State: PA
Publication Website: www.huntingdondailynews.com
Postal Code: 16652
Office phone: 814-643-4040
General E-mail: circ@huntingdondailynews.com
Editor Name: Becky Weikert
Editor Email: dnews@huntingdondailynews.com

THE HUNTINGDON DAILY NEWS

Corporate/Parent Company: Sample News Group LLC
Publication Street Address: 325 Penn St
City: Huntingdon
State: PA
Publication Website: www.huntingdondailynews.com
Postal Code: 16652-1470
Office phone: (814) 643-4040
General E-mail: circ@huntingdondailynews.com
Advertising Executive Email: dnewsads@huntingdondailynews.com
Year Established: 1922
Mechanical specifications: Type page 13 x 21 1/2; E - 6 cols, 2 1/16, 1/8 between; A - 6 cols, 2 1/16, 1/8 between; C - 9 cols, 1 3/8, 1/16 between.
Published Days: Mon`Tues`Wed`Thur`Fri`Sat
Weekday Frequency: e
Saturday Frequency: m
Avg Paid Circ: 9258
Audit Company: Sworn/Estimate/Non-Audited
Audit Date: 7 12 2019
Mailroom Equipment: Tying Machines – Sa, WeldLoc; Address Machine – Wm, KR.;
Buisness Equipment: DEC/486, 6-DEC
Buisness Software: Vision Data, AR 6.2, APGL 5.0
Classified Equipment: Hardware – APP/Mac; Printers – HP;
Classified Software: Baseview/Ad Manager Pro.
Editorial Equipment: Hardware – APP; Printers – APP, HP
Editorial Software: Baseview/NewsEdit.
Production Equipment: Hardware – Caere/OmniPage; Cameras – C; Scanners – HP
Production Software: QPS/QuarkXPress 4.0.
Total Circulation: 9258

INDIANA

THE INDIANA GAZETTE

Corporate/Parent Company: Indiana Printing & Publishing Co.
Publication Street Address: 899 Water St
City: Indiana
State: PA
Publication Website: www.indianagazette.com
Postal Code: 15701-1705
Office phone: (724) 465-5555
General E-mail: webmaster@indianagazette.net
Publisher Name: Michael J. Donnelly
Publisher Email: mjd@indianagazette.net
Publisher Phone: (724) 465-5555, Ext : 202
Editor Name: Eric Ebeling
Editor Email: eebeling@indianagazette.net
Editor Phone: (724) 465-5555, Ext : 269
Advertising Executive Name: J.D. Grantz
Advertising Executive Email: jdgrantz@indianagazette.net
Advertising Executive Phone: (724) 465-5555, Ext : 206
Year Established: 1890
Delivery Methods: Mail`Carrier`Racks
Own Printing Facility?: Y
Commercial printers?: Y

Mechanical specifications: Type page 13 x 21 1/2; E - 6 cols, 2 1/16, 1/8 between; A - 6 cols, 2 1/16, 1/8 between; C - 8 cols, 1 1/2, 1/8 between.
Published Days: Mon`Tues`Wed`Thur`Fri`Sat`Sun
Weekday Frequency: e
Saturday Frequency: e
Avg Paid Circ: 8762
Avg Free Circ: 2765
Audit Company: AAM
Audit Date: 31 03 2019
Pressroom Equipment: Lines – 6-G/Urbanite (1 color unit), 1-G/Urbanite 788; 10-HI/V-15D 1990; Folders – G/2:1; Reels & Stands – 2-G/Rollstands, 4-Martin/Splicer.;
Mailroom Equipment: Counter Stackers – MM/338, Gammerler/KL 503/1; Inserters & Stuffers – MM/310; Tying Machines – MM; Address Machine – 2/Ch;
Buisness Equipment: Compaq/Proliant 3000
Buisness Software: Platinum
Classified Equipment: Hardware – Compaq/Proliant 3000; Printers – HP/4000, AU/1000;
Classified Software: APT.
Editorial Equipment: Hardware – Compaq/Proliant 3000; Printers – HP/4000, HP/4000C
Editorial Software: APT.
Production Equipment: Hardware – AU/APS-6-82 ACS, AU/1000; Cameras – 1-C/Marathon; Scanners – AG/Horizon Scanner
Production Software: APT, QPS/QuarkXPress 4.0.
Total Circulation: 11527

JOHNSTOWN

THE TRIBUNE-DEMOCRAT

Corporate/Parent Company: CNHI, LLC
Publication Street Address: 425 Locust St
City: Johnstown
State: PA
Publication Website: www.tribune-democrat.com
Postal Code: 15907-0340
Office phone: 814-532-5050
General E-mail: tpritt@tribdem.com
Publisher Name: Robert Forcey
Publisher Email: rforcey@tribdem.com
Publisher Phone: (814) 532-5111
Editor Name: Chip Minemyer
Editor Email: cminemyer@tribdem.com
Editor Phone: (814) 532-5091
Advertising Executive Name: Mary Anne Rizzo
Advertising Executive Email: marizzo@tribdem.com
Advertising Executive Phone: (814) 532-5162
Year Established: 1853
Mechanical specifications: Type page 13 x 21 1/2; E - 6 cols, 2 1/16, 1/8 between; A - 6 cols, 2 1/16, 1/8 between; C - 9 cols, 1 5/16, 1/8 between.
Published Days: Mon`Tues`Wed`Thur`Fri`Sat`Sun
Weekday Frequency: m
Saturday Frequency: m
Avg Paid Circ: 24162
Audit Company: AAM
Audit Date: 23 07 2019
Pressroom Equipment: Lines – 5-G/Metro (2 decks) 1969; Reels & Stands – 5-G/RTP.;
Mailroom Equipment: Counter Stackers – 2-QWI/SJ100A, CH/Mk II; Inserters & Stuffers – S/848; Tying Machines – 2-MVP/P-53, Sterling/MR45CH, Sterling/MR40CH; Address Machine – 1-MG/50.;
Buisness Equipment: Sun/Sparc
Buisness Software: Vision Data
Classified Equipment: Hardware – APP/Mac; 10-APP/Mac 4400; Printers – HP/6MP;
Classified Software: Baseview/Ad Manager Pro.
Editorial Equipment: Hardware – APP/Mac/APP/Mac 4400, APP/Mac 7300, APP/Mac 7200, APP/Mac G4; Printers – HP/Laser, APP/Mac
Editorial Software: Baseview.
Production Equipment: Hardware – 2-APP/Power Mac 7300 with Adobe Photoshop 4.0, Pre Press/Panther Pro 46, Konica/9449-163, Microtek/2SPX, Microtek/E6, Microtek/35T; Cameras – 1-K/Vertical 18, C/Marathon; Scanners – Microtek/2SPX, Mictrotek/E6, 1-Microtek/35T, Polaroid/SprintS

Total Circulation: 31712

KANE

THE KANE REPUBLICAN

Corporate/Parent Company: Horizon Publications Inc.
Publication Street Address: 200 N Fraley St
City: Kane
State: PA
Publication Website: www.kanerepublican.com
Postal Code: 16735-1177
Office phone: (814) 837-6000
General E-mail: krnews1@zitomedia.net
Publisher Name: Christie Gardner
Publisher Email: sales@ridgwayrecord.com
Year Established: 1894
Mechanical specifications: Type page 13 x 21 1/2; E - 6 cols, 2 1/16, 1/8 between; A - 6 cols, 2 1/16, 1/8 between; C - 8 cols, 1 1/2, 1/8 between.
Published Days: Mon`Tues`Wed`Thur`Fri`Sat`Sun
Weekday Frequency: m
Saturday Frequency: m
Avg Paid Circ: 1996
Audit Company: Sworn/Estimate/Non-Audited
Audit Date: 7 12 2019
Mailroom Equipment: Tying Machines – 1/Sa; Address Machine – 1-/Am.;
Buisness Equipment: Mk/550, APP/Mac
Editorial Equipment: Hardware – Mk/550 Sys
Editorial Software: Mk/Newswriter.
Total Circulation: 1996

KITTANNING

LEADER TIMES

Corporate/Parent Company: Sample News Group LLC
Publication Street Address: 1270 N Water St
City: Kittanning
State: PA
Publication Website: www.leadertimes.com
Postal Code: 16201-1055
Office phone: (724) 543-1303
General E-mail: newsroom@leadertimes.com
Publisher Name: Tammy Bish
Publisher Email: tbish@leadertimes.com
Editor Name: A.J. Panian
Editor Email: apanian@leadertimes.com
Advertising Executive Name: Julie McGaughey
Advertising Executive Email: jmcgaughey@leadertimes.com
Mechanical specifications: Type page 13 x 21 1/4; E - 6 cols, 2 1/16, 1/8 between; A - 6 cols, 2 1/16, 1/8 between; C - 10 cols, 1 3/8, 1/8 between.
Published Days: Mon`Tues`Wed`Thur`Fri`Sat`Sun
Weekday Frequency: e
Saturday Frequency: e
Avg Paid Circ: 6441
Avg Free Circ: 243
Audit Company: AAM
Audit Date: 30 09 2014
Mailroom Equipment: Tying Machines – 1/Sterling.;
Classified Equipment: Hardware – PPI.;
Editorial Equipment: Hardware – APP/Mac, SII.
Production Equipment: Hardware – 2-COM/Trendsetter, 2-Mk, APP/Mac, 3-Laser
Production Software: Multi-Ad/Creator.
Total Circulation: 6684

LANCASTER

LA VOZ LANCASTER

Corporate/Parent Company: LNP Media Group
Publication Street Address: 8 West King Street, PO Box 1328
City: Lancaster
State: PA
Publication Website: www.lavozlancaster.com
Postal Code: 17608
Office phone: (717) 291-8811
General E-mail: news@LNPnews.com
Editor Name: Enelly Betancourt
Editor Email: ebetancourt@lnpnews.com

U.S. Daily Newspapers

Editor Phone: (717) 481-8489
Advertising Executive Name: Chris Stahl
Advertising Executive Email: cstahl@LNPnews.com
Advertising Executive Phone: (717) 291-8722

LNP

Corporate/Parent Company: LNP Media Group
Publication Street Address: 8 W King St
City: Lancaster
State: PA
Publication Website: www.lancasteronline.com
Postal Code: 17603-3824
Office phone: (717) 291-8811
General E-mail: classexta@lnpnews.com
Editor Name: Tom Murse
Editor Email: tmurse@lnpnews.com
Editor Phone: (717) 481-6021
Advertising Executive Name: Chris Stahl
Advertising Executive Email: cstahl@lnpnews.com
Advertising Executive Phone: (717) 291-8722
Year Established: 1764
Delivery Methods: Mail`Newsstand`Carrier`Racks
Own Printing Facility?: N
Commercial printers?: N
Mechanical specifications: As per Advanced Central Services, Mechanicsburg
Published Days: Mon`Tues`Wed`Thur`Fri`Sat`Sun
Weekday Frequency: m
Saturday Frequency: m
Avg Paid Circ: 60344
Audit Company: AAM
Audit Date: 31 03 2019
Pressroom Equipment: None
Pressroom Software: None
Mailroom Equipment: None
Mailroom Software: None
Buisness Software: DTI, TMC, Document express
Classified Equipment: Hardware – Dell Server; Dell Workstations; Printers – KM300i;
Classified Software: Brainworks, Quark Xpress 8.5, Layout 8000
Editorial Equipment: Hardware – Dell Virtual servers,NetApp VMWare/ Printers – Kyocera 9520, 9130
Editorial Software: SCS/Scoop Fotoware, Photoshop, Photo mechanic
Production Equipment: Hardware – Mac Mini Scanners – Epson/a640XL, Epson/836XL, 1-X/7650C
Production Software: InDesign CS5.5,QuarkXPress 8.5, Adobe Creative Suite 5.5
Total Circulation: 60344

LANGHORNE

BUCKS COUNTY COURIER TIMES

Corporate/Parent Company: Gannett
Publication Street Address: One Oxford Valley, 2300 East Lincoln Highway, Suite 500D,
City: Langhorne
State: PA
Publication Website: www.buckscountycouriertimes.com
Postal Code: 19047
Office phone: (215) 949-4000
General E-mail: bgropper@calkins.com
Publisher Name: Brad Bailey
Publisher Email: bbailey@couriertimes.com
Editor Name: Audrey Harvin
Editor Email: aharvin@thebct.com
Editor Phone: (609) 871-8164
Advertising Executive Name: Kevin O'Malley
Advertising Executive Email: komalley@theintell.com
Advertising Executive Phone: (215) 345-3018
Year Established: 1954
Own Printing Facility?: Y
Commercial printers?: Y
Mechanical specifications: Type page 13 x 21 1/2; E - 6 cols, 2, 1/6 between; A - 6 cols, 2, 1/6 between; C - 9 cols, 1 1/3, 1/12 between.
Published Days: Mon`Tues`Wed`Thur`Fri`Sun
Weekday Frequency: m
Saturday Frequency: m
Avg Paid Circ: 15471
Avg Free Circ: 16877
Audit Company: AAM
Audit Date: 23 10 2019
Pressroom Equipment: Lines – 6-G 1960, 2-G 1972;
Mailroom Equipment: Counter Stackers – QWI; Tying Machines – 2/Power Strap.;
Buisness Equipment: IBM/9672
Buisness Software: Calkins
Classified Equipment: Hardware – IBM/9672; 17-IBM/3179; Printers – 1-IBM/3287;
Classified Software: Calkins/Adv & Acct System.
Editorial Equipment: Hardware – PCs
Editorial Software: ACI/Open Pages.
Production Equipment: Hardware – 2-Na/Starlite, 1-MON/ExpressMaster 3850
Production Software: Northwood Publishing/Class Page, QPS/QuarkXPress 3.32.
Note: There is a Greater Philadelphia Newspaper group combination of $239.00 (d) & $251.00 (S) among Levittown Bucks County Courier (mS), Doylestown Intelligencer (mS) & Willingboro (NJ Burlington County Times (mS). Individual newspaper rates not made availabl
Total Circulation: 21984

THE INTELLIGENCER

Corporate/Parent Company: Gannett
Publication Street Address: One Oxford Valley, 2300 East Lincoln Highway, Suite 500D
City: Langhorne
State: PA
Publication Website: www.theintell.com
Postal Code: 19047
Office phone: (215) 345-3000
General E-mail: customerservice@theintell.com
Publisher Name: Brad Bailey
Publisher Email: bbailey@couriertimes.com
Editor Name: Audrey Harvin
Editor Email: aharvin@thebct.com
Editor Phone: (609) 871-8164
Advertising Executive Name: Kevin O'Malley
Advertising Executive Email: komalley@theintell.com
Advertising Executive Phone: (215) 345-3018
Year Established: 1804
Mechanical specifications: Type page 13 x 21 1/2; E - 6 cols, 2 1/16, 1/8 between; A - 6 cols, 2 1/16, 1/8 between; C - 9 cols, 1 3/8, 1/16 between.
Published Days: Mon`Tues`Wed`Thur`Fri`Sun
Weekday Frequency: m
Avg Paid Circ: 14098
Avg Free Circ: 2498
Audit Company: AAM
Audit Date: 9 11 2018
Pressroom Equipment: Lines – 10-G/Urbanite 1973; Pasters –Enkel/Splicer; Reels & Stands – Press Registration System ÃƒÂ‚Â£ Duarte/Pin.;
Mailroom Equipment: Counter Stackers – 1/QWI, QWI/350B; Inserters & Stuffers – GMA/SLS 1000 8:1; Tying Machines – 1-/Power Strap, 1-/MLN; Wrapping Singles – 1-/Sa; Address Machine – 1-/KR.;
Buisness Equipment: IBM/9672
Classified Equipment: Hardware – Mac/True;
Classified Software: Cras.
Editorial Equipment: Hardware – 20-Dell/Novell/File Server, 60-PC; Printers – 1-IBM/3287, 2-EM/Imagesetter 3850
Editorial Software: ACI/Open Pages.
Production Equipment: Hardware – 1-NewGen/Laser, EM/Imagesetter 3850; Cameras – 1-C/Spartan II, 1-AG/6000; Scanners – 2-HP/Scanner
Production Software: QPS/QuarkXPress.
Note: There is a Greater Philadelphia Newspaper group combination of $239.00 (d) & $251.00 (S) among Levittown Bucks County Courier (mS), Doylestown Intelligencer (mS) & Willingboro (NJ) Burlington County Times (mS). Individual newspaper rates not made availabl
Total Circulation: 21674

LANSDALE

THE REPORTER

Corporate/Parent Company: Media News Group
Publication Street Address: 307 Derstine Ave
City: Lansdale
State: PA
Publication Website: www.thereporteronline.com
Postal Code: 19446-3532
Office phone: (215) 855-8440
General E-mail: advertising@thereporteronline.com
Publisher Name: Edward S. Condra
Publisher Email: acondra@21st-centurymedia.com
Editor Name: Nancy March
Editor Email: nmarch@thereporteronline.com
Advertising Executive Name: Beth Douglas
Advertising Executive Email: bdouglas@21st-centurymedia.com
Year Established: 1870
Mechanical specifications: Type page 11 5/8 x 20 1/2; E - 6 (& 7 columns front page) cols, 1 4/5, 1/8 between; A - 6 cols, 1 4/5, 1/8 between; C - 10 cols, 1 2/25, 1/16 between.
Published Days: Mon`Tues`Wed`Thur`Fri`Sat
Weekday Frequency: m
Saturday Frequency: m
Avg Paid Circ: 3096
Avg Free Circ: 534
Audit Company: AAM
Audit Date: 14 07 2020
Pressroom Equipment: Lines – Man Roland Offset; Pasters –8-Cary/AutomaticControl System – G/PA.;
Mailroom Equipment: Counter Stackers – HL/HT, 1/PRK, HI/RS 25, Gammerler, QWI/Sports Stacker; Inserters & Stuffers – AlphaLine; Tying Machines – 2-/MLN, 2-/Dynaric; Wrapping Singles – 1-/Power Strap, 1-/Dynaric; Control System – Linc; Address Machine – Addressing machine;
Buisness Equipment: IBM/AS-400, IBM/RISC Model 170
Buisness Software: Microsoft/Excel, Microsoft/Word 6.1
Classified Equipment: Hardware – Sun/Ultra 2, APP/Power Mac; Printers – LaserJet/5000;
Classified Software: Atex.
Editorial Equipment: Hardware – Sun/Ultra 2, APP/Power Mac/APP/Mac Quadra, AP/AdSend; Printers – HP/LaserJet 4MV
Editorial Software: Lino Press.
Production Equipment: Hardware – 2-Ultre/5400, D, Anitec/SN32; Cameras – C/Spartan II; Scanners – Hel/Sapphire, Tecsa/Copy Dot Scanner
Production Software: Lino Press 4.2.02.39, Lino Press 4.1.14.17A.
Total Circulation: 10968

LATROBE

THE LATROBE BULLETIN

Corporate/Parent Company: Sample News Group LLC
Publication Street Address: 1211 Ligonier St
City: Latrobe
State: PA
Publication Website: www.latrobebulletinnews.com/
Postal Code: 15650-1921
Office phone: (724) 537-3351
General E-mail: info@latrobebulletinnews.com
Publisher Name: Gary Siegel
Publisher Email: garysiegel1@verizon.net
Publisher Phone: (724) 537-3351, Ext : 19
Editor Name: Steve Kittey
Editor Email: lb.editor@verizon.net
Editor Phone: (724) 537-3351, Ext : 27
Advertising Executive Name: Joyce Lynn Helmetzi
Advertising Executive Email: latbull@gmail.com
Advertising Executive Phone: (724) 537-3351, Ext : 24
Delivery Methods: Newsstand`Carrier`Racks
Own Printing Facility?: Y
Commercial printers?: Y
Mechanical specifications: Type page 12 x 21 1/2; E - 6 cols, 2 1/16, 1/8 between; A - 6 cols, 2 1/16, 1/8 between; C - 8 cols, 1 1/4, 3/16 between.
Published Days: Mon`Tues`Wed`Thur`Fri`Sat`Sun
Weekday Frequency: e
Saturday Frequency: m
Avg Paid Circ: 7767
Audit Company: Sworn/Estimate/Non-Audited
Audit Date: 7 12 2019
Pressroom Equipment: Lines – 7-G/Community; Folders – 1-G/SC; Control System – FIN/3120.;
Mailroom Equipment: Counter Stackers – BG/108; Tying Machines – 1-Sa/SRIA 2460, 1-Sa/S1000 4991.;
Buisness Equipment: APP/Mac
Buisness Software: Baseview
Classified Equipment: Hardware – APP/Mac,
Classified Software: Baseview.
Editorial Equipment: Hardware – Baseview.
Production Equipment: Hardware – LE/LD-24-AQ, ECRM Stingray 63; Cameras – 24-B/Commodore, B.
Total Circulation: 7767

LEBANON

THE LEBANON DAILY NEWS

Corporate/Parent Company: Gannett
Publication Street Address: 718 Poplar St
City: Lebanon
State: PA
Publication Website: www.ldnews.com
Postal Code: 17042-6755
Office phone: (717) 272-5611
General E-mail: citydesk@ldnews.com
Publisher Name: Blake Sanderson
Year Established: 1872
Own Printing Facility?: N
Commercial printers?: N
Mechanical specifications: Broadsheet, Retail - 6 columns x 21.5 inches, 1 column = 1.556", Classified - 10 columns x 21.5 inches, 1 column = 0.889"
Published Days: Mon`Tues`Wed`Thur`Fri`Sat`Sun
Weekday Frequency: e
Saturday Frequency: e
Avg Paid Circ: 6278
Avg Free Circ: 1059
Audit Company: AAM
Audit Date: 28 05 2020
Buisness Equipment: Oracle, PBS
Classified Equipment: Hardware – PC, Microsoft/Windows NT, APP/iMac;
Editorial Equipment: Hardware – APP/Mac; Printers – 1-TI
Editorial Software: Baseview.
Production Equipment: Scanners – Polaroid
Production Software: QPS/QuarkXPress.
Total Circulation: 7762

LEHIGHTON

TIMES NEWS

Corporate/Parent Company: Pencor Services
Publication Street Address: 594 Blakeslee Boulevard Dr W
City: Lehighton
State: PA
Publication Website: www.tnonline.com
Postal Code: 18235-9818
Office phone: (610) 377-2051
General E-mail: mgouger@tnonline.com
Editor Name: Marta Gouger
Editor Email: mgouger@tnonline.com
Editor Phone: (610) 377-2051
Advertising Executive Name: Donna Hall
Advertising Executive Email: dhall@tnonline.com
Advertising Executive Phone: (610) 377-2051, Ext : 3109
Year Established: 1883
Mechanical specifications: Type page 13 x 21; E - 6 cols, 2 1/16, 1/8 between; A - 6 cols, 2 1/16, 1/8 between; C - 9 cols, 1 3/8, 1/16 between.
Published Days: Mon`Tues`Wed`Thur`Fri`Sat
Weekday Frequency: e

Saturday Frequency: m
Avg Paid Circ: 11037
Avg Free Circ: 607
Audit Company: AAM
Audit Date: 6 01 2020
Pressroom Equipment: Lines – W/Colorflex; MAN/Uniman.;
Mailroom Equipment: Counter Stackers – 1-BG/108, 1-HL/Monitor; Inserters & Stuffers – 1-MM/227E; Tying Machines – 2-MLN/ML0AE.;
Buisness Equipment: 2-IBM/AS-400
Classified Equipment: Hardware – Mk/Mycro-Comp 1100, 2-Mk/MC4001.;
Editorial Equipment: Hardware – Mk, 3-COM/MDT 350, 22-Mk/MC4003/10-APP/Mac.;
Production Equipment: Hardware – 2-Nat/250, 1-COM/Videosetter, 1-COM/7200, 1-COM/8600; Cameras – 1-R/20 x 24, 1-AG/Repromaster, 1-Eskofot, 2-Kk.
Total Circulation: 22534

LEWISTOWN

THE SENTINEL (LEWISTOWN)

Corporate/Parent Company: Lee Enterprises
Publication Street Address: 352 6th St
City: Lewistown
State: PA
Publication Website: www.lewistownsentinel.com
Postal Code: 17044-1213
Office phone: (717) 248-6741
General E-mail: mbolich@lewistownsentinel.com
Publisher Name: Ruth Eddy
Editor Name: Brian Cox
Editor Email: bcox@lewistownsentinel.com
Advertising Executive Name: Matt Bolich
Advertising Executive Email: mbolich@lewistownsentinel.com
Advertising Executive Phone: (717) 248-6741, Ext : 130
Year Established: 1860
Delivery Methods: Mail`Newsstand`Carrier
Own Printing Facility?: N
Commercial printers?: N
Mechanical specifications: Type page 11 5/8 x 21 1/2; E - 6 cols, 2 1/16, 1/8 between; A - 6 cols, 2 1/16, 1/8 between; C - 9 cols, 1 1/4, 1/4 between.
Published Days: Mon`Tues`Wed`Thur`Fri`Sat
Weekday Frequency: m
Saturday Frequency: m
Avg Paid Circ: 8000
Audit Company: AAM
Audit Date: 5 09 2018
Buisness Equipment: Sun/Ultra 2
Buisness Software: Vision Data
Classified Equipment: Hardware – 7-Sun/Sparc II;
Classified Software: Vision Data/Classified.
Editorial Equipment: Hardware – 4-PC-NT Servers, 18-MS/NT Notes Clients/8-APP/Mac G3; Printers – 1-PT/RIP, 1-ECR/108S Pelbox
Editorial Software: Lotus/Domino Notes.
Total Circulation: 9472

LOCK HAVEN

EXPRESS

Corporate/Parent Company: Ogden Newspapers, Inc.
Publication Street Address: 9-11 W. Main Street
City: Lock Haven
State: PA
Publication Website: www.lockhaven.com
Postal Code: 17745
Office phone: 570-748-6791
Publisher Name: Robert O. Rolley, Jr
Publisher Email: brolley@lockhaven.com
Publisher Phone: ext. 114
Editor Name: Lana Muthler
Editor Email: lmuthler@lockhaven.com
Editor Phone: Ext. 131
Advertising Executive Name: Jordan McCloskey
Advertising Executive Email: jmccloskey@lockhaven.com
Advertising Executive Phone: ext. 140
Audit Company: AAM
Audit Date: 22 06 2018
Total Circulation: 6866

MEADVILLE

THE MEADVILLE TRIBUNE

Corporate/Parent Company: CNHI, LLC
Publication Street Address: 947 Federal Ct
City: Meadville
State: PA
Publication Website: www.meadvilletribune.com
Postal Code: 16335-3234
Office phone: (814) 724-6370
General E-mail: tribune@meadvilletribune.com
Publisher Name: Sharon Sorg
Publisher Email: ssorg@meadvilletribune.com
Editor Name: Rick Green
Editor Email: rgreen@meadvilletribune.com
Editor Phone: (814) 724-6370, Ext : 267
Advertising Executive Name: Heidi Gebhardt
Advertising Executive Email: hgebhardt@meadvilletribune.com
Advertising Executive Phone: (814) 724-6370, Ext : 258
Delivery Methods: Mail`Newsstand`Carrier`Racks
Mechanical specifications: Type page 13 x 21 1/2; E - 6 cols, 2 1/16, 1/8 between; A - 6 cols, 2 1/16, 1/8 between; C - 9 cols, 1 5/16, 1/8 between.
Published Days: Mon`Tues`Wed`Thur`Fri`Sat`Sun
Weekday Frequency: m
Saturday Frequency: m
Avg Paid Circ: 7954
Avg Free Circ: 1092
Audit Company: AAM
Audit Date: 11 09 2018
Pressroom Equipment: Lines – 10-G/Community (color deck) 1989; Registration System – Duarte/Pin System.
Mailroom Equipment: Counter Stackers – 1/Hall Monitor; Inserters & Stuffers – GMA/Alphaliner Gintol; Tying Machines – EAM-Mosca, ROM;
Classified Equipment: Hardware – 3-APP/Mac; Printers – 1-HP/4MV;
Classified Software: Baseview/Class Manager Pro 1.7.
Editorial Equipment: Hardware – APP/Mac/APP/Mac LD; Printers – 2-HP/4MV, Pre Press/Panther Pro 36
Editorial Software: Baseview/NewsEdit Pro IQUE 1.0.
Production Equipment: Hardware – 1-SCREEN/220, 1-SCREEN/LD281Q; Cameras – 1-C/Spartan, 1-SCREEN/680C; Scanners – 2-Polaroid/SprintScan, 1-AG/Duo scan, 1-Pixelcraft
Production Software: QPS/QuarkXPress 3.32.
Total Circulation: 8726

MILTON

THE STANDARD-JOURNAL

Corporate/Parent Company: Sample News Group LLC
Publication Street Address: 21 N Arch St
City: Milton
State: PA
Publication Website: www.standard-journal.com
Postal Code: 17847-1211
Office phone: (570) 742-9671
General E-mail: advertising@standard-journal.com
Publisher Name: Amy Moyer
Publisher Email: amym@standard-journal.com
Editor Name: Chris Brady
Editor Email: chris@standard-journal.com
Advertising Executive Email: advertising@standard-journal.com
Mechanical specifications: Type page 13 x 21 1/2; E - 6 cols, 2 1/14, 1/6 between; A - 6 cols, 2 1/14, 1/6 between; C - 9 cols, 1 1/5, 1/12 between.
Published Days: Mon`Tues`Wed`Thur`Fri`Sat`Sun
Weekday Frequency: m
Saturday Frequency: m
Avg Paid Circ: 1418

Audit Company: Sworn/Estimate/Non-Audited
Audit Date: 7 12 2019
Pressroom Equipment: Lines – 6-G/Community 1973; Folders – 1-G/SC.;
Mailroom Equipment: Counter Stackers – 1-BG/Count-O-Veyor; Inserters & Stuffers – DG/320 2:1; Tying Machines – 1-Bu/SP 505, 1-MLN/MS-T; Address Machine – Dispensa-Matic/U 45.;
Buisness Equipment: 4-ATT/Unix PC 7300-3B1
Buisness Software: Vision Data
Classified Equipment: Hardware – Mk/3000, 1-Mk/NewsTouch II; Printers – APP/Mac LaserWriter Plus, Okidata/Microline 293 line printer;
Classified Software: Mk.
Editorial Equipment: Hardware – Mk/550, 3-Mk/NewsTouch; Printers – APP/Mac LaserWriter Plus
Editorial Software: Mk.
Production Equipment: Hardware – 2-APP/Mac LaserWriter Plus; Cameras – LE/Horizontal.
Total Circulation: 1418

MONESSEN

THE MON VALLEY INDEPENDENT

Publication Street Address: 996 Donner Ave
City: Monessen
State: PA
Publication Website: monvalleyindependent.com
Postal Code: 15062-1001
Office phone: (714) 314-0030
General E-mail: lbyron@yourmvi.com
Editor Name: Stacy Wolford
Editor Email: swolford@yourmvi.com
Editor Phone: (724) 314-0043
Advertising Executive Name: Lori Byron
Advertising Executive Email: lbyron@yourmvi.com
Advertising Executive Phone: (724) 314-0019
Published Days: Mon`Tues`Wed`Thur`Fri`Sat
Weekday Frequency: m
Saturday Frequency: m
Audit Company: Sworn/Estimate/Non-Audited
Audit Date: 7 12 2019

NEW CASTLE

NEW CASTLE NEWS

Corporate/Parent Company: CNHI, LLC
Publication Street Address: 27 N Mercer St
City: New Castle
State: PA
Publication Website: www.ncnewsonline.com
Postal Code: 16101-3806
Office phone: (724) 654-6651
General E-mail: advertising@ncnewsonline.com
Publisher Name: Sharon Sorg
Publisher Email: ssorg@ncnewsonline.com
Publisher Phone: (724) 654-6651, Ext : 648
Editor Name: Renee Carey
Editor Email: rcarey@ncnewsonline.com
Editor Phone: (724) 654-6551, Ext : 614
Advertising Executive Name: Laurie Doyle
Advertising Executive Email: ldoyle@ncnewsonline.com
Advertising Executive Phone: (724) 654-6651, Ext : 662
Mechanical specifications: Type page 13 x 21 1/2; E - 6 cols, 2 1/16, 1/8 between; A - 6 cols, 2 1/16, 1/8 between; C - 9 cols, 1 3/8, 1/8 between.
Published Days: Mon`Tues`Wed`Thur`Fri`Sat
Weekday Frequency: m
Saturday Frequency: e
Avg Paid Circ: 8635
Avg Free Circ: 529
Audit Company: AAM
Audit Date: 30 06 2018
Pressroom Equipment: Lines – 4-G/Metro (color deck); Pasters –G/Metro AutomaticReels & Stands – G/Reels & Stands.;
Mailroom Equipment: Tying Machines – 1-Sa/59SR1A, 1-MLN/ML2EE.;
Buisness Equipment: PBS
Buisness Software: Microsoft/Excel
Classified Equipment: Hardware – 4-PC; Printers – PAN/KXP-180;

Classified Software: III/Tecs 2.
Editorial Equipment: Hardware – APP/Mac G3, APP/Macs
Editorial Software: Baseview.
Production Equipment: Hardware – 1-LE/24AQ, 1-LE/PC13; Cameras – 1-C/Marathon, 1-B/2000, 1-K/240 Vertical
Production Software: QPS/QuarkXPress.
Total Circulation: 9164

OIL CITY

THE NEWS-HERALD/THE DERRICK

Publication Street Address: 1510 W 1st St
City: Oil City
State: PA
Publication Website: www.thederrick.com
Postal Code: 16301-3211
Office phone: (814) 676-7444
General E-mail: info.thederrick@gmail.com
Editor Name: Luka Krneta
Editor Email: lukakrneta.thederrick@gmail.com
Editor Phone: (814) 677-8367
Advertising Executive Name: Paul Hess
Advertising Executive Email: ad_man_no1958@yahoo.com
Advertising Executive Phone: (814) 677-8313
Published Days: Mon`Tues`Wed`Thur`Fri`Sat`Sun
Weekday Frequency: m
Saturday Frequency: m
Avg Paid Circ: 7373
Audit Company: Sworn/Estimate/Non-Audited
Audit Date: 7 12 2019
Pressroom Equipment: Lines – G/Community.;
Mailroom Equipment: Tying Machines – 2-MLN/SP 330; Address Machine – 2-KR/211.;
Classified Equipment: Hardware – CText; Printers – Graphic Enterprises/Pro Setter 1000;
Classified Software: CText/Adept.
Editorial Equipment: Hardware – CText; Printers – Graphic Enterprises/Pro Setter 1000.
Production Equipment: Hardware – Glensen.
Note: Advertising is sold in combination with the Oil City Derrick (m) for $62.23(d). Individual newspaper rates not made available. All business and production are handled by Venango Newspapers Inc.
Total Circulation: 7373

PHILADELPHIA

METRO PHILADELPHIA

Corporate/Parent Company: SB New York, Inc.
Publication Street Address: 1650 Market Street, 36th floor
City: Philadelphia
State: PA
Publication Website: www.metro.us/philadelphia
Postal Code: 19103
Office phone: (215) 717-2600
General E-mail: adsphilly@metro.us
Year Established: 2000
Delivery Methods: Newsstand`Racks
Own Printing Facility?: N
Commercial printers?: N
Published Days: Mon`Tues`Wed`Thur`Fri
Weekday Frequency: m
Avg Free Circ: 71165
Audit Company: AAM
Audit Date: 21 12 2018
Total Circulation: 70096

PHILADELPHIA INQUIRER, DAILY NEWS & PHILLY.COM

Corporate/Parent Company: Philadelphia Inquirer, LLC
Publication Street Address: 801 Market Street
City: Philadelphia
State: PA
Publication Website: www.philly.com
Postal Code: 19107-3126
Office phone: (215) 854-2000
General E-mail: advertising@inquirersolutions.com

U.S. Daily Newspapers

com
Publisher Name: Terrance C.Z. Egger
Editor Name:
Editor Email: jmartin@inquirer.com
Year Established: 1829
Delivery Methods: Newsstand`Carrier`Racks
Own Printing Facility?: Y
Commercial printers?: N
Mechanical specifications: Type page 13 x 21; E - 6 cols, 2 1/16, 1/8 between; A - 6 cols, 2 1/16, 1/8 between; C - 10 cols, 1 3/16, 1/16 between.
Published Days: Mon`Tues`Wed`Thur`Fri`Sat`Sun
Weekday Frequency: m
Saturday Frequency: m
Avg Paid Circ: 196285
Audit Company: AAM
Audit Date: 31 03 2018
Pressroom Equipment: Lines – 10-G/Colorliner double width (9 Lines); Folders – 9-Sovereign/160 Page 3:2; Pasters –90-G/CT-50Reels & Stands – 90-G/CT-50; Control System – G/APCS.;
Mailroom Equipment: Counter Stackers – 22-HL/HTZ, 10-QWI/400; Inserters & Stuffers – 3-GMA/SLS 1000A (23:1), 7-GMA/SLS 100 (12:1); Tying Machines – 12-Dynaric/NPI, 28-Dynaric/NP2, 4/NP3; Control System – GMA/IPCs, Map Con, Carnegie Mellon/Machine Design;
Buisness Equipment: 1-IBM/390, 2-HP/937, 2-HP/957 Processor
Buisness Software: Microsoft/Suite
Classified Equipment: Hardware – AT/IAS, 150-AT, RSK/6000; 2-Konica, 2-Bs/DEX;
Classified Software: AT 4.7.2, AT/ClassPage.
Editorial Equipment: Hardware – AT/30, 14-AT/J-11, Unisys/Hermes/AT, 27-APP/Mac
Editorial Software: AT 4.7.4, Hermes.
Production Equipment: Hardware – 3-AU/APS-6, 6-WL/Bender, 3-AU/3810; Cameras – 1-C/Pager II; Scanners – 3-AU/Page Scanners, 3-ECR/Autokon, Eskofot, 5-Kk/RS 2035, 5-Nikon/LS 2000
Production Software: Unisys/Hermes, AT/IAS.
Total Circulation: 196285

PITTSBURGH

PITTSBURGH TRIBUNE-REVIEW

Corporate/Parent Company: Trib Total Media, LLC
Publication Street Address: 503 Martindale St
City: Pittsburgh
State: PA
Publication Website: https://triblive.com/
Postal Code: 15212-5746
Office phone: (412) 321-6460
General E-mail: tribliving@tribweb.com
Publisher Name: Richard Mellon Scaife
Editor Name: LUIS FÁBREGA
Editor Email: lfabregas@tribweb.com
Editor Phone: (724) 226-4687

POTTSVILLE

THE REPUBLICAN-HERALD

Corporate/Parent Company: Times-Shamrock Communications
Publication Street Address: 111 Mahantongo St
City: Pottsville
State: PA
Publication Website: www.republicanherald.com
Postal Code: 17901-3071
Office phone: (570) 622-3456
General E-mail: mjoyce@republicanherald.com
Publisher Name: Mike Joyce
Publisher Email: mjoyce@republicanherald.com
Publisher Phone: (570) 628-6049
Editor Name: Andy Heintzelman
Editor Email: aheintzelman@republicanherald.com
Editor Phone: (570) 628-6103
Advertising Executive Name: Dawn Fisher
Advertising Executive Email: dfisher@republicanherald.com
Advertising Executive Phone: (570) 628-6053
Year Established: 1884
Delivery Methods:
Mail`Newsstand`Carrier`Racks
Own Printing Facility?: N

Commercial printers?: Y
Mechanical specifications: 1 column 1.6 inches, 9p4 picas 2 column 3.222 inches, 19p4 picas 3 column 4.889 inches, 29p4 picas 4 column 6.556 inches, 39p4 picas 5 column 8.222 inches, 49p4 picas 6 column 9.889 inches, 59p4 picas Double truck 13 column, 20.889 inches, 125p4 picas Full page broad sheet depth is 20.5 inches
Published Days: Mon`Tues`Wed`Thur`Fri`Sat`Sun
Weekday Frequency: m
Saturday Frequency: m
Avg Paid Circ: 14775
Avg Free Circ: 1584
Audit Company: AAM
Audit Date: 31 03 2019
Editorial Equipment: Hardware – Sun/Ultra 2, Dell/PII 350; Printers – AU/APS Broadsheeter, 2-AU/APS 6-84ACS 14 Imager, HP/LaserJet 5500
Editorial Software: HI/XP-21, HI/NewsMaker Pagination 3.5.15.1.
Production Equipment: Hardware – Calera/WordScan Plus, Graham/5327; Scanners – HP/Text Scanner, 1-ECR/Autokon 2045, 2-Umax/2400
Production Software: HI/NewsMaker Pagination 3.5.15.
Total Circulation: 16359

PUNXSUTAWNEY

THE PUNXSUTAWNEY SPIRIT

Corporate/Parent Company: Horizon Publications Inc.
Publication Street Address: 510 Pine St
City: Punxsutawney
State: PA
Publication Website: www.punxsutawneyspirit.com
Postal Code: 15767-1404
Office phone: (814) 938-8740
General E-mail: tlsmith@punxsutawneyspirit.com
Publisher Name: Tracy L. Smith
Publisher Email: tlsmith@punxsutawneyspirit.com
Editor Name: Zak Lantz
Editor Email: zlantz@punxsutawneyspirit.com
Advertising Executive Name: Katie Neale
Advertising Executive Email: classified@punxsutawneyspirit.com
Year Established: 1873
Delivery Methods:
Mail`Newsstand`Carrier`Racks
Own Printing Facility?: Y
Commercial printers?: Y
Mechanical specifications: Type page 11 1/16 x 21 1/2; E - 6 cols, 1 11/16, 3/8 between; A - 6 cols, 1 11/16, 3/8 between; C - 9 cols, 1 1/8, 1/8 between.
Published Days: Mon`Tues`Wed`Thur`Fri`Sat
Weekday Frequency: m
Saturday Frequency: m
Avg Paid Circ: 5545
Audit Company: Sworn/Estimate/Non-Audited
Audit Date: 7 12 2019
Pressroom Equipment: Lines – 5-G/Community single width; Folders – 1, 1.;
Mailroom Equipment: Tying Machines – Semi Ace Sk 707, Strapmatic 202A; Address Machine – Ch.;
Classified Equipment: Hardware – 9-APP/Mac;
Classified Software: Baseview.
Editorial Equipment: Hardware – 6-APP/Mac
Editorial Software: Baseview.
Production Equipment: Hardware – Graham/5-1-27.
Total Circulation: 5545

READING

READING EAGLE

Corporate/Parent Company: Media News Group
Publication Street Address: 345 Penn St
City: Reading
State: PA
Publication Website: www.readingeagle.com
Postal Code: 19601-4029

Office phone: (610) 371-5000
General E-mail: customerservice@readingeagle.com
Publisher Name: Edward S. Condra
Publisher Email: econdra@21st-centurymedia.com
Editor Name: David S. Mowery
Editor Email: dmowery@readingeagle.com
Editor Phone: (610) 371-5011
Advertising Executive Name: Denice Schaeffer
Advertising Executive Email: dschaeffer@readingeagle.com
Advertising Executive Phone: (610) 371-5125
Year Established: 1868
Delivery Methods:
Mail`Newsstand`Carrier`Racks
Own Printing Facility?: Y
Commercial printers?: Y
Mechanical specifications: 46" Web. PRINTING PROCESS: Offoot. Broadshoot Papor Dimension: 11.5" wide x 18.5" high. Full Page Image Area: 10.5" wide x 17" high. BROADSHEET MODULAR AD SIZES of Page Ad Dimension 100 10.5" x 17" 75 10.5" x 12.75" 70 8.729" x 14.28" 67 6.958" x 17" 65 10.5" x 11.05" 50 V 5.187" x 17" 50 H 10.5" x 8.5" 39 5.187" x 13.26" 33 10.5" x 5.61" 30 6.958" x 7.65" 25 5.187" x 8.5" 23 8.729" x 4.692" 20 6.958" x 5.1" 15 3.417" x 7.65" 14 10.5" x 2.38" 13 3.417" x 6.63" 12 5.187" x 4.08" 10 3.417" x 5.1" 9 5.187" x 3.06" 8 3.417" x 4.08" 6 3.417" x 3.05" 4 3.417" x 2.04" 3 1.646" x 3.06" 2 1.646" x 2.04" 1 1.646" x 1.02" Tabloid Paper Dimension: 9.25" wide x 11.5" high. Full Page Image Area: 7.708" wide x 10.5" high. WEEKEND TABLOID COLUMN-INCH AD SIZES 1 col. 1.833" 2 col. 3.792" 3 col. 5.75" 4 col. 7.708"
Published Days: Mon`Tues`Wed`Thur`Fri`Sat`Sun
Weekday Frequency: m
Saturday Frequency: m
Avg Paid Circ: 39465
Audit Company: AAM
Audit Date: 28 06 2019
Pressroom Equipment: 1 KBA Colora, 2-KF3 KBA folders, 4-KBA 4x4 printing towers, 5-KBA reel stands, inline stitcher and quarter folder, Tecnotrans dampening system, Eletta balanket wask.
Mailroom Equipment: 5-Hi/Olympia NP502, inserter - 1-Hi/NP632, Miracom control system, 2-NP-125gripper delivery, 1-NP200 online gripper conveyor, 1-NS300 belt conveyor,12-OVL/EX311, 2-OVL/415, 3-Profit packaging lable applicators.
Buisness Equipment: 2-DEC/Alpha
Buisness Software: PBS
Classified Equipment: Hardware – Dell/Poweredge 4400-NT Cluster; Printers – HP/4000;
Classified Software: Atex AdBase 3.0
Editorial Equipment: Hardware – PC Client Server/12-APP/Mac, Nikon/3510 scanners; Printers – 2-Panasonic, HP/LaserJet, APP/Mac LaserWriter
Editorial Software: Anygraaf/Doris Pagination System. NEO pagination system
Production Equipment: 2-Screen Platerite2000, 2-Protech105 processor, 1-Burgess punch bender
Note: Pretzel City Productions, LLC is a division of Reading Eagle Company created to produce and/or co-host events in the community. WEEU 830AM - news/talk
Total Circulation: 54898

READING EAGLE COMPANY

Publication Street Address: 345 Penn St.
City: Reading
State: PA
Publication Website: www.readingeagle.com
Postal Code: 19603
Office phone: 610-371-5000
General E-mail: news@readingeagle.com
Publisher Name: Edward S. Condra
Publisher Email: econdra@21st-centurymedia.com
Editor Name: David S. Mowery
Editor Email: dmowery@readingeagle.com

Editor Phone: 610-371-5011
Advertising Executive Name: Denice Schaeffer
Advertising Executive Email: dschaeffer@readingeagle.com
Advertising Executive Phone: 610-371-5125

SAYRE

MORNING TIMES

Corporate/Parent Company: Sample News Group LLC
Publication Street Address: 201 N Lehigh Ave
City: Sayre
State: PA
Publication Website: www.morning-times.com
Postal Code: 18840-2246
Office phone: (570) 888-9643
General E-mail: editor@morning-times.com
Publisher Name: Kelly Luvison
Publisher Email: kluvison@morning-times.com
Editor Name: Pat McDonald
Editor Email: editor@morning-times.com
Advertising Executive Name: Jenn Garrison
Advertising Executive Email: classifieds@morning-times.com
Year Established: 1890
Delivery Methods:
Mail`Newsstand`Carrier`Racks
Own Printing Facility?: N
Commercial printers?: Y
Mechanical specifications: Type page 11 3/4 x 21 1/2; E - 6 cols, 1 3/4, 1/6 between; A - 9 cols, 1 3/16, 1/6 between; C - 9 cols, 1 3/16, 1/6 between.
Published Days: Mon`Tues`Wed`Thur`Fri`Sat
Weekday Frequency: m
Saturday Frequency: m
Avg Paid Circ: 5200
Audit Company: Sworn/Estimate/Non-Audited
Audit Date: 7 12 2019
Buisness Equipment: Dell/PCs
Buisness Software: MSSI/Quickbooks
Classified Equipment: APP/Mac
Classified Software: Newscycle
Editorial Equipment: Hardware – APP/Mac; Printers – Xante
Editorial Software: Newscycle
Total Circulation: 5200

SCRANTON

THE TIMES TRIBUNE

Corporate/Parent Company: Times-Shamrock Communications
Publication Street Address: 149 Penn Ave.
City: Scranton
State: PA
Publication Website: https://www.thetimes-tribune.com/
Postal Code: 18503
Office phone: 855-614-5440

THE TIMES-TRIBUNE

Corporate/Parent Company: Times-Shamrock Communications
Publication Street Address: 149 Penn Ave
City: Scranton
State: PA
Publication Website: www.thetimes-tribune.com
Postal Code: 18503-2056
Office phone: (570) 348-9100
General E-mail: cdemas@timesshamrock.com
Publisher Name: Edward J. Lynett
Editor Name: Joe Butkiewicz
Editor Email: jbutkiewicz@timesshamrock.com
Editor Phone: (570) 348-9100, Ext : 3467
Year Established: 1895
Delivery Methods: Carrier
Mechanical specifications: Type page 13 x 21 1/2; E - 6 cols, 2 1/16, 1/8 between; A - 6 cols, 2 1/16, 1/8 between; C - 9 cols, 1 3/8, 1/8 between.
Published Days: Mon`Tues`Wed`Thur`Fri`Sat`Sun
Weekday Frequency: m
Saturday Frequency: m

U.S. Daily Newspapers

Avg Paid Circ: 26941
Avg Free Circ: 2431
Audit Company: AAM
Audit Date: 7 04 2020
Pressroom Equipment: 6-G/ho double width; Folders – 1-G/3:2, 1-G/Page Jaw Folder; Control System – 1-G/MPCS.
Mailroom Equipment: Counter Stackers – 3-Id/2000, 2-QWI/350; Inserters & Stuffers – 1-GMA/SLS 1000, 10/Pocket, 2-/Main Feeders; Tying Machines – 3-/Dynaric; Address Machine – 3-/WM, 1-/Ch, 1-/KR;
Buisness Equipment: IBM/AS-400
Classified Equipment: Hardware – PPI, 14-PC; Printers – HP;
Classified Software: PPI.
Editorial Equipment: Hardware – 48-PC, 2-Sun/Server; Printers – HP
Editorial Software: HI/NewsMaker.
Production Equipment: Hardware – 1-AU/APS-108C, MON/3850, Adobe/RIPs, 1-ECR/4550; Cameras – 1-C/Spartan III; Scanners – Scitex/340, VMAX
Production Software: HI/NewsMaker Pagination.
Note: The Scranton Times-Tribune (mS) has a combination rate of $132.39 (m) and $133.68 (S) with the Wilkes-Barre Citizens' Voice (mS). Individual newspaper rates not made available.
Total Circulation: 41595

SHAMOKIN

THE NEWS-ITEM

Corporate/Parent Company: Sample News Group LLC
Publication Street Address: 707 N Rock St
City: Shamokin
State: PA
Publication Website: www.newsitem.com
Postal Code: 17872-4930
Office phone: (570) 644-6397
General E-mail: jessica_w@newsitem.com
Publisher Name: Amy Moyer
Publisher Phone: (570) 644-6397, Ext : 1322
Editor Name: Tim Zyla
Editor Email: tim_z@newsitem.com
Editor Phone: (570) 644-6397, Ext : 1341
Advertising Executive Name: John Semicek
Advertising Executive Email: john_s@newsitem.com
Advertising Executive Phone: (570) 644-6397, Ext : 1338
Year Established: 1891
Delivery Methods: Mail`Newsstand`Carrier`Racks
Own Printing Facility?: N
Commercial printers?: Y
Mechanical specifications: Type page 13 x 21 1/2; E – 6 cols, 2 1/16, 1/8 between; A – 6 cols, 2 1/16, 1/8 between; C – 10 cols, 1 3/8, 1/16 between.
Published Days: Mon`Tues`Wed`Thur`Fri`Sat`Sun
Weekday Frequency: m
Saturday Frequency: m
Avg Paid Circ: 6862
Avg Free Circ: 687
Audit Company: Sworn/Estimate/Non-Audited
Audit Date: 7 12 2019
Mailroom Equipment: Tying Machines – 1-/Sa; Address Machine – 1-RSK/Printer.;
Buisness Equipment: IBM/AS-400
Classified Equipment: Hardware – APP/Mac G3/233; Printers – HP, Xante
Classified Software: Baseview/Ad Manager Pro.
Editorial Equipment: Hardware – APP/Mac G3, APP/iMac; Printers – Xante
Editorial Software: APP/Mac System 8.6, Baseview/NewsEdit 3.32, QPS/QuarkXPress 4.04.
Production Equipment: Hardware – 2-ECR/Imagesetter, HP/4MV, Xante/Accel-A-Writer 3G; Cameras – 1-C; Scanners – Epson/Expression 836 XL, Nikon LS, Nikon Coolscan III
Production Software: Baseview/News Edit 3.2.2, QPS/QuarkXPress 4.04.
Total Circulation: 7549

SHARON

THE HERALD

Corporate/Parent Company: Paxton Media Group
Publication Street Address: 52 S Dock St
City: Sharon
State: PA
Publication Website: www.sharonherald.com
Postal Code: 16146-1808
Office phone: (724) 981-6100
General E-mail: newsroom@sharonherald.com
Publisher Name: Sharon Sorg
Publisher Email: ssorg@sharonherald.com
Editor Name: Renee Carey
Editor Email: rcarey@sharonherald.com
Advertising Executive Name: Richard Work
Advertising Executive Email: rwork@sharonherald.com
Delivery Methods: Mail`Newsstand
Own Printing Facility?: Y
Commercial printers?: Y
Published Days: Thur
Avg Paid Circ: 2251
Audit Company: AAM
Audit Date: 26 03 2018
Total Circulation: 12772

SOMERSET

DAILY AMERICAN

Corporate/Parent Company: Gannett
Publication Street Address: 334 W Main St
City: Somerset
State: PA
Publication Website: www.dailyamerican.com
Postal Code: 15501-1508
Office phone: (814) 444-5900
General E-mail: news@dailyamerican.com
Advertising Executive Name: Becky Flyte
Advertising Executive Email: rflyte@dailyamerican.com
Advertising Executive Phone: (814) 444-5906
Year Established: 1929
Delivery Methods: Mail`Newsstand`Carrier`Racks
Own Printing Facility?: N
Commercial printers?: Y
Mechanical specifications: Type page 12 x 21 1/2; E – 6 cols, 1 3/4, 3/16 between; A – 6 cols, 1 3/4, 3/16 between; C – 9 cols, 1 3/16, 1/8 between.
Published Days: Mon`Tues`Wed`Thur`Fri`Sat`Sun
Weekday Frequency: m
Saturday Frequency: m
Avg Paid Circ: 11412
Audit Company: AAM
Audit Date: 30 09 2014
Pressroom Equipment: Lines – 6-G/Community 1980, 2-G/Community single width 1995;
Mailroom Equipment: Counter Stackers – 1-BG/105; Tying Machines – 2-Mosca/Rom 50-55; Address Machine – 1-KR w/Accufast.;
Buisness Equipment: Compaq/Proliant, 13-Dell/PC
Buisness Software: Brainworks, Visual Accountmate, Lotus, Microsoft/Office
Classified Equipment: Hardware – APP/Power Mac G3; Printers – HP/LaserJet 4V;
Classified Software: Baseview/Ad Manager Pro.
Editorial Equipment: Hardware – APP/Power Mac G3; Printers – HP/LaserJet 4V, Xante/Accel-a-Writer 3G
Editorial Software: Baseview.
Production Equipment: Hardware – PrePress/Panther Pro 46, 1-Nu/Flip Top FT40L; Cameras – 1-Ik/430, 1-Nu/Horizontal SST2024; Scanners – Microtek/Scanmaker IIXC, AG/Arcus 2
Production Software: QPS/QuarkXPress 4.0.
Note: The Daily American publishes a Sunday edition in partnership with the Greensburg (PA) Tribune-Review, with original content wrapped around the Tribune-Review's Sunday edition. See the Tribune-Review for more information.
Total Circulation: 11412

STATE COLLEGE

CENTRE DAILY TIMES

Corporate/Parent Company: McClatchy Company
Publication Street Address: 3400 E College Ave
City: State College
State: PA
Publication Website: www.centredaily.com
Postal Code: 16801-7528
Office phone: (814) 238-5000
General E-mail: customerservice@centredaily.com
Publisher Name: Janet Santostefano
Publisher Email: jsantostefano@centredaily.com
Publisher Phone: (814) 235-3909
Editor Name: Jessica McAllister
Advertising Executive Name: Wade Flick
Advertising Executive Email: wflick@centredaily.com
Advertising Executive Phone: (814) 231-4669
Year Established: 1898
Own Printing Facility?: Y
Commercial printers?: Y
Mechanical specifications: Type page 12 3/4 x 21 1/2; E – 6 cols, 2 1/16, 1/8 between; A – 6 cols, 2 1/16, 1/8 between; C – 10 cols, 1 1/4, 1/16 between.
Published Days: Mon`Tues`Wed`Thur`Fri`Sat`Sun
Weekday Frequency: m
Saturday Frequency: m
Avg Paid Circ: 12101
Audit Company: AAM
Audit Date: 19 09 2018
Pressroom Equipment: Lines – G/Urbanite single width 1973; Folders – 7-G/2:1.;
Mailroom Equipment: Counter Stackers – 1-Rima/RS 2517S N Compensating Stacker; Inserters & Stuffers – 2-HI/Sheridan 1372; Tying Machines – M1255, Dynaric/NP2; Control System – Prism; Address Machine – 1/Ch;
Buisness Equipment: 1-HP/3000, 8-ATT/6300, 10-PCs, 5-HP/Vectra 386
Buisness Software: Microsoft/Office 97, Reflections, Netscape
Classified Equipment: Hardware – APP/Power Mac, APP/Mac G3.;
Editorial Equipment: Hardware – APP/Power Mac 7100-66S, APP/Mac G3/Lf/AP Leaf Picture Desk; Printers – LaserMaster/Unity 1800 XLO, MON/1000
Editorial Software: Baseview, QPS, Baseview/NewsEdit, Adobe/Photoshop.
Production Equipment: Hardware – Caere/Omnipage Pro, AG/1500, MON/ImageMaster 1200; Cameras – 1-SCREEN/260D, 1-R/432 Mk II; Scanners – Kk/RFS-2035+, Sharp/JX-610, AG/Arcus+, RZ/4050
Production Software: QPS/QuarkXPress.
Total Circulation: 16034

STROUDSBURG

POCONO RECORD

Corporate/Parent Company: Gannett
Publication Street Address: 511 Lenox St
City: Stroudsburg
State: PA
Publication Website: www.poconorecord.com
Postal Code: 18360-1516
Office phone: (570) 421-3000
General E-mail: sbauer@poconorecord.com
Editor Name: Ashley Fontones
Editor Email: afontones@poconorecord.com
Editor Phone: (570) 420-4386
Advertising Executive Name: Stefanie Bauer
Advertising Executive Email: sbauer@poconorecord.com
Advertising Executive Phone: (570) 420-4378
Year Established: 1894
Delivery Methods: Newsstand`Carrier`Racks
Own Printing Facility?: N
Commercial printers?: N
Mechanical specifications: Type page 13 x 21 1/4; E – 6 cols, 2 1/16, 1/8 between; A – 6 cols, 2 1/16, 1/8 between; C – 8 cols, 1 7/16, 3/16 between.
Published Days: Mon`Tues`Wed`Thur`Fri`Sat`Sun
Weekday Frequency: m
Saturday Frequency: m

Avg Paid Circ: 6324
Avg Free Circ: 1087
Audit Company: AAM
Audit Date: 11 09 2018
Buisness Equipment: IBM/AS-400
Buisness Software: Lawson
Classified Equipment: Hardware – PC, Novell/Network, APP/Mac Quadra 800, APP/Mac II; Printers – Okidata/393 Plus;
Classified Software: Dewar/Sys IV.
Editorial Equipment: Hardware – PC, IBM/PC 350; Printers – HP/LaserJet 5si
Editorial Software: Dewar/View 1.4, Microsoft/Word 6.0, QPS/QuarkXPress 3.31.
Production Software: PC, QPS/QuarkXPress.
Total Circulation: 11408

SUNBURY

THE DAILY ITEM

Corporate/Parent Company: Community Newspaper Holdings, Inc. (CNHI)
Publication Street Address: 200 Market St
City: Sunbury
State: PA
Publication Website: www.dailyitem.com
Postal Code: 17801-3402
Office phone: (570) 286-5671
General E-mail: advertising@dailyitem.com
Publisher Name: Fred Scheller
Publisher Email: fscheller@dailyitem.com
Publisher Phone: (570) 988-5466
Editor Name: Bill Bowman
Editor Email: bbowman@dailyitem.com
Editor Phone: (570) 988-5474
Advertising Executive Name: Beth Knauer
Advertising Executive Email: eknauer@dailyitem.com
Advertising Executive Phone: (570) 863-3208
Year Established: 1937
Delivery Methods: Mail`Newsstand`Carrier`Racks
Own Printing Facility?: Y
Commercial printers?: Y
Mechanical specifications: Type page 13 1/4 x 21; E – 6 cols, 2 1/16, 1/8 between; A – 6 cols, 2 1/16, 1/8 between; C – 9 cols, 1 5/16, 1/8 between.
Published Days: Mon`Tues`Wed`Thur`Fri`Sat`Sun
Weekday Frequency: m
Saturday Frequency: m
Avg Paid Circ: 12488
Avg Free Circ: 6039
Audit Company: AAM
Audit Date: 7 03 2018
Pressroom Equipment: Lines – TKS/double width offset (1 half deck) 1979; TKS/double width (2:1 folder; 1 non-reversing 10); Folders – 2-TKS/2:1; Pasters –3-TKS/Core Tension 1979, 5-TKS/3-arm Core Tension 1979Reels & Stands – Press Control System ÃƒÆ'Ã‚Â£ÃƒÂ¢Ã‚Â£ÃƒÆ'Ã‚Â£ 1979.;
Mailroom Equipment: Counter Stackers – 2-Id, 2/PPC; Inserters & Stuffers – AM/Sheridan 630; Tying Machines – Power Strap/PSN5; Wrapping Singles – Power Strap/SP-555; Address Machine – Machtronic, Wm;
Buisness Equipment: IBM/AS-400
Classified Equipment: Hardware – IBM/PC;
Classified Software: Enterprise.
Editorial Equipment: Hardware – 2-IBM/RS-6000/Kk, Polaroid/35mm Scanner; Printers – HP/LaserJet
Editorial Software: HI/Jazbox, Adobe/Photoshop, Adobe/Illustrator.
Production Equipment: Hardware – Caere/OmniPage Pro; Cameras – 2-Konica/Spartan; Scanners – Kk, Polaroid
Production Software: HI/Jazbox.
Total Circulation: 18211

SWARTHMORE

DELAWARE CO. DAILY & SUNDAY TIMES

Publication Street Address: 639 South Chester Road
City: Swarthmore

U.S. Daily Newspapers

State: PA
Publication Website: www.delcotimes.com
Postal Code: 19081
Office phone: 610-622-8800
Publisher Name: Edward S. Condra
Publisher Email: econdra@21st-centurymedia.com
Editor Name: Phil Heron
Editor Email: editor@delcotimes.com
Advertising Executive Name: Rich Crowe
Advertising Executive Email: rcrowe@21st-centurymedia.com

DELAWARE COUNTY DAILY TIMES

Corporate/Parent Company: MediaNews Group
Publication Street Address: 639 S Chester Rd
City: Swarthmore
State: PA
Publication Website: www.delcotimes.com
Postal Code: 19081-2315
Office phone: (610) 622-8800
General E-mail: paadvertising@digitalfirstmedia.com
Publisher Name: Edward S. Condra
Publisher Email: econdra@21st-centurymedia.com
Editor Name: Phil Heron
Editor Email: editor@delcotimes.com
Advertising Executive Name: Rich Crowe
Advertising Executive Email: rcrowe@21st-centurymedia.com
Year Established: 1876
Mechanical specifications: Type page 10 1/4 x 13; E - 5 cols, 2, between; A - 6 cols, 1 9/16, 1/33 between; C - 8 cols, 1 3/16, 1/33 between.
Published Days: Mon`Tues`Wed`Thur`Fri`Sat`Sun
Weekday Frequency: m
Saturday Frequency: m
Avg Paid Circ: 10832
Avg Free Circ: 3291
Audit Company: AAM
Audit Date: 11 06 2020
Pressroom Equipment: Lines – 5-HI/1650 double width 1976; 1-HI/1650 double width 1992; Press Drive – SCR/DC 460-Volt, 3 phase, 300 h.p.; Folders – HI/1650; Pasters –4-MEGReels & Stands – 1-Rewinder/Reel Stand.;
Mailroom Equipment: Counter Stackers – 2-HL/Monitor, 2-HL/HT; Inserters & Stuffers – 2-GMA/SLS 1000 6:1, 1-KAN/480 6:1; Tying Machines – 2/Dynaric, 1-/MLN, 2-/Spirit; Wrapping Singles – 1-/Na; Control System – GMA; Address Machine – 1-/Na.;
Buisness Equipment: IBM/AS-400
Buisness Software: insi
Classified Equipment: Hardware – PC, APP/Mac, AST/Bravo LC 5133; Minolta/3700, X/7017; Printers – Okidata/2410;
Classified Software: Cx, Intertext.
Editorial Equipment: Hardware – PC/Lf/AP Leaf Picture Desk, Polaroid/SprintScan
Editorial Software: ATS with Microsoft Windows, QPS/QuarkXPress, Adobe/Photoshop, ELS.
Production Equipment: Hardware – Bidco/Imager, ECR/4550, Konica/Autokon, Sharp; Cameras – C/Spartan Vertical, BIDCO - Konica; Scanners – 1-ECR/Autokon
Production Software: MEI/ALS 1.7, MEI/CLS 1.6, MEI/ELS 1.6.
Total Circulation: 21390

THE TIMES HERALD

Corporate/Parent Company: Gannett
Publication Street Address: 639 South Chester Road
City: Swarthmore
State: PA
Publication Website: www.timesherald.com
Postal Code: 19081
Office phone: (610) 272-2500
General E-mail: classified@allaroundphilly.com
Publisher Name: Edward S. Condra
Publisher Email: econdra@21st-centurymedia.com
Editor Name: Cheryl Rodgers
Editor Email: crodgers@timesherald.com
Editor Phone: (484) 679-8475
Advertising Executive Name: Beth Douglas
Advertising Executive Email: bdouglas@21st-centurymedia.com
Year Established: 1799
Delivery Methods:
  Mail`Newsstand`Carrier`Racks
Own Printing Facility?: Y
Commercial printers?: Y
Mechanical specifications: Type page 12 x 21 1/2; E - 6 cols, 1 7/8, 1/8 between; A - 6 cols, 1 7/8, 1/8 between; C - 10 cols, 1 3/16, 1/12 between.
Published Days: Mon`Tues`Wed`Thur`Fri`Sat`Sun
Weekday Frequency: m
Saturday Frequency: m
Avg Paid Circ: 2837
Avg Free Circ: 427
Audit Company: AAM
Audit Date: 2 11 2016
Pressroom Equipment: Lines – 5-HI/1650 1993; Press Drive – GE/200 h.p. Twin; Folders – 1-HI/double 2:1; Reels & Stands – 5-G/Manual Reel.;
Mailroom Equipment: Counter Stackers – KAN, QWI/SJ101; Inserters & Stuffers – 1-KAN/480, 1-KAN/480; Tying Machines – MLN/ML2CC, 1-MLN/ML2EE; Wrapping Singles – 1-HL/Monarch, 2/Si.;
Buisness Equipment: IBM/AS-400
Buisness Software: INSI
Classified Equipment: Hardware – Dewar; Printers – Dataproducts/LB 325;
Classified Software: Dewar/Sys IV.
Editorial Equipment: Hardware – ATS; Printers – HP/5000
Editorial Software: Dewar.
Production Equipment: Hardware – LE, APP/Mac, 1-Ultra 4000, 1-Bibco; Cameras – C/Spartan III, R/Vertical; Scanners – ECR/Autokon, Ultra/4000 Full Page Imagesetter, Umax
Production Software: ATS/managing editor, Windows 2.7.
Total Circulation: 36998

TARENTUM

TRIBUNE-REVIEW VALLEY NEWS DISPATCH

Corporate/Parent Company: Trib Total Media, LLC
Publication Street Address: 210 Wood Street
City: Tarentum
State: PA
Publication Website: www.tribLIVE.com
Postal Code: 15084
Office phone: 800-909-8742
General E-mail: gateeds@tribweb.com
Editor Name: Susan K. McFarland
Editor Email: smcfarland@tribweb.com

TITUSVILLE

THE TITUSVILLE HERALD

Corporate/Parent Company: The Titusville Herald
Publication Street Address: 209 W Spring St
City: Titusville
State: PA
Publication Website: www.titusvilleherald.com
Postal Code: 16354-1687
Office phone: (814) 827-3634
General E-mail: news@titusvilleherald.com
Publisher Name: Michael Sample
Publisher Email: msample@titusvilleherald.com
Advertising Executive Name: Libby Jones
Advertising Executive Email: advertising@titusvilleherald.com
Year Established: 1865
Delivery Methods:
  Mail`Newsstand`Carrier`Racks
Own Printing Facility?: Y
Mechanical specifications: Type page 11 5/8 x 21 1/4; E - 6 cols, 1 5/6, 1/8 between; A - 6 cols, 1 5/6, 1/8 between; C - 9 cols, 1 5/6, 1/16 between.
Published Days: Mon`Tues`Wed`Thur`Fri`Sat

Weekday Frequency: m
Saturday Frequency: m
Avg Paid Circ: 4000
Audit Company: Sworn/Estimate/Non-Audited
Audit Date: 7 12 2019
Buisness Equipment: Bs/20
Classified Equipment: Hardware – APP/iMac, APP/Mac G4; Printers – HP 8150;
Classified Software: Baseview.
Editorial Equipment: Hardware – 5-APP/IMac, ; Printers – Oki Data 8800 HP 8150
Production Software: Indesign 5.0
Note: Printing contracted with Corry (PA) Journal.
Total Circulation: 4000

TOWANDA

THE DAILY REVIEW

Corporate/Parent Company: Sample News Group LLC
Publication Street Address: 116 Main St
City: Towanda
State: PA
Publication Website: www.thedailyreview.com
Postal Code: 18848-1832
Office phone: (570) 265-2151
General E-mail: reviewads@thedailyreview.com
Publisher Name: Dave Barry
Publisher Email: dbarry@thedailyreview.com
Publisher Phone: (570) 265-2151, Ext : 1601
Editor Name: Matt Hicks
Editor Email: mhicks@thedailyreview.com
Editor Phone: (570) 265-2151, Ext : 1628
Advertising Executive Email: revclass@thedailyreview.com
Advertising Executive Phone: (570) 265-2151, Ext : 1654
Year Established: 1879
Delivery Methods:
  Mail`Newsstand`Carrier`Racks
Own Printing Facility?: Y
Commercial printers?: Y
Mechanical specifications: Type page 13 x 20 3/4; E - 6 cols, 1 13/16, 1/6 between; A - 6 cols, 1 13/16, 1/6 between; C - 10 cols, 1 1/16, 1/8 between.
Published Days: Mon`Tues`Wed`Thur`Fri`Sat`Sun
Weekday Frequency: m
Saturday Frequency: m
Avg Paid Circ: 7356
Audit Company: CAC
Audit Date: 30 09 2017
Pressroom Equipment: Lines – DgM/430.;
Mailroom Equipment: Counter Stackers – 1-BG/Count-O-Veyor; Inserters & Stuffers – 9-MM/227; Tying Machines – 4-Dynaric/Strapping Machines; Address Machine – 1-CH/538-525.;
Buisness Equipment: IBM
Buisness Software: Hermes, Vision Data, Microsoft/Excel, Microsoft/Word
Classified Equipment: Hardware – CText; Printers – HP/LaserJet 4;
Classified Software: Vision Data
Editorial Equipment: Hardware – CText; Printers – HP/DeskJet 400
Editorial Software: XYQUEST/XyWrite III.
Production Equipment: Hardware – 2-ECR/VRL 36 Scriptsetter (PC level2 ECR/RIP), 1-Nu/Flip Top 40UP, Adobe/Photoshop 4.0, ECR/VRL 34 Scriptsetters; Cameras – 1-R/24-580; Scanners – Microtek/MS-II, 2-Polaroid/SprintScan 35, 2-Umax/Vista S-8, Umax/Vista S-12
Production Software: QPS/Qua
Total Circulation: 7356

TYRONE

THE DAILY HERALD

Corporate/Parent Company: Sample News Group LLC
Publication Street Address: 1067 Pennsylvania Ave
City: Tyrone
State: PA
Publication Website: www.thedailyherald.net
Postal Code: 16686-1513

Office phone: (814) 684-4000
General E-mail: ads@thedailyherald.net
Advertising Executive Email: ads@thedailyherald.net
Year Established: 1867
Delivery Methods:
  Mail`Newsstand`Carrier`Racks
Own Printing Facility?: Y
Mechanical specifications: Type page 13 x 21 1/2; E - 6 cols, 2 1/16, 1/8 between; A - 6 cols, 2 1/16, 1/8 between; C - 9 cols, 1 3/8, 1/16 between.
Published Days: Mon`Tues`Wed`Thur`Fri`Sat`Sun
Weekday Frequency: e
Saturday Frequency: m
Avg Paid Circ: 1737
Audit Company: Sworn/Estimate/Non-Audited
Audit Date: 7 12 2019
Classified Equipment: Hardware – Mk/1100 Plus;
Classified Software: Mk/1100 Plus.
Editorial Equipment: Hardware – Mk/550
Editorial Software: Mk/550.
Production Equipment: Hardware – APP/Mac LaserWriter; Scanners – APP/Mac Scanner, AG/Scanner.
Total Circulation: 1737

UNIONTOWN

HERALD-STANDARD

Corporate/Parent Company: Ogden Newspapers, Inc.
Publication Street Address: 8 E Church St
City: Uniontown
State: PA
Publication Website: www.heraldstandard.com
Postal Code: 15401-3563
Office phone: (724) 439-7500
General E-mail: hswebmaster@heraldstandard.com
Editor Name: Jennifer Garofalo
Editor Email: jgarofalo@heraldstandard.com
Editor Phone: (724) 439-7557
Advertising Executive Name: Michael Pasqua
Advertising Executive Phone: (724) 852-2251
Delivery Methods: Newsstand`Carrier`Racks
Own Printing Facility?: N
Commercial printers?: N
Mechanical specifications: Type page 11 x 21 1/2; E - 6 cols, 2 1/16, 1/8 between; A - 6 cols, 2 1/16, 1/8 between; C - 6 cols, 1 5/16, 1/8 between.
Published Days: Mon`Tues`Wed`Thur`Fri`Sun
Weekday Frequency: m
Avg Paid Circ: 10902
Avg Free Circ: 3169
Audit Company: AAM
Audit Date: 7 01 2020
Pressroom Equipment: Lines – 8-HI/845;
Mailroom Equipment: Counter Stackers – 1-HPS/Dual Carrier; Inserters & Stuffers – KAN/320 6 station; Tying Machines – 1-MLN/Sure Tyer.;
Buisness Equipment: 2-DEC/PDP 11-70, SCS/Layout 8000
Classified Equipment: Hardware – 1-DEC/PDP 11-70.;
Editorial Equipment: Hardware – 2-DEC/PDP 11-70, 8-APP/Mac IIcx/AP/GraphicsNet; Printers – 1-Compaq/LA-180
Editorial Software: TMS/CMS 5.3.
Production Equipment: Hardware – 2-COM/8600, 2-MON/1016 HS, 1-LE; Cameras – 1-Bo, 1-K/V241; Scanners – 1-HP, 1-Sharp, 1-Microtek
Production Software: QPS/QuarkXPress 3.2.
Total Circulation: 18838

WARREN

TIMES OBSERVER

Corporate/Parent Company: Ogden Newspapers, Inc.
Publication Street Address: 205 Pennsylvania Ave W
City: Warren
State: PA
Publication Website: www.timesobserver.com
Postal Code: 16365-2412
Office phone: (814) 723-8200

U.S. Daily Newspapers

General E-mail: advertising@timeobserver.com
Publisher Name: Robert Patchen
Publisher Email: bpatchen@timeobserver.com
Publisher Phone: (814) 723-8200, Ext : 606
Editor Name: Jonathan Sitler
Editor Email: jsitler@timesobserver.com
Editor Phone: (814) 723-8200, Ext : 614
Advertising Executive Name: Stacy Hathaway
Advertising Executive Email: shathaway@timesobserver.com
Advertising Executive Phone: (814) 723-8200, Ext : 612
Delivery Methods: Mail`Newsstand`Carrier`Racks
Own Printing Facility?: N
Mechanical specifications: Type page 11 37/50 x 21 1/2; E - 6 cols, 1 17/20, between; A - 6 cols, 1 17/20, between; C - 9 cols, 1 1/5, between.
Published Days: Mon`Tues`Wed`Thur`Fri`Sat
Weekday Frequency: m
Saturday Frequency: m
Avg Paid Circ: 6506
Avg Free Circ: 32
Audit Company: AAM
Audit Date: 2 10 2018
Pressroom Equipment: Lines – 5-G/Urbanite; Press Drive – Fin/100 h.p.; Folders – G/1/2.;
Mailroom Equipment: Counter Stackers – 1-BG/Count-O-Veyor; Tying Machines – 2/Sa, Gd, 1-/Nichiro Kogyo/Strapper; Wrapping Singles – Olson/Bostitcher; Address Machine – St.;
Classified Equipment: Hardware – APP/Mac Quadra; Printers – ECR/Imagesetter
Classified Software: DTI/ClassSpeed, DTI/AdSpeed, DTI, Adobe/Photoshop 2.5.
Editorial Equipment: Hardware – APP/Mac Quadra; Printers – APP/Mac LaserWriter, ECR/Imagesetter
Editorial Software: DTI/PageSpeed, DTI/Speedwriter, Adobe/Photoshop 3.0, Caere/OmniPage 2.1.
Production Equipment: Hardware – Caere/OmniPage 2.1; Cameras – 1-B/Commodore 24, 1-R/432MK II; Scanners – 1-EC
Production Software: DTI/SpeedPlanner, DTI.
Total Circulation: 6697

WASHINGTON

OBSERVER-REPORTER

Corporate/Parent Company: Ogden Newspapers, Inc.
Publication Street Address: 122 S Main St
City: Washington
State: PA
Publication Website: www.observer-reporter.com
Postal Code: 15301-4904
Office phone: (724) 222-2200
General E-mail: sales@observer-reporter.com
Publisher Name: Robert Pinarski
Publisher Email: rpinarski@observer-reporter.com
Publisher Phone: (724) 222-2200, Ext : 2626
Editor Name: Liz Rogers
Editor Email: lrogers@observer-reporter.com
Editor Phone: (724) 222-2200, Ext : 2759
Advertising Executive Name: Carole DeAngelo
Advertising Executive Email: cdeangelo@observer-reporter.com
Advertising Executive Phone: (724) 223-2622
Year Established: 1808
Delivery Methods: Mail`Newsstand`Carrier`Racks
Own Printing Facility?: Y
Commercial printers?: N
Mechanical specifications: Type page 13 x 21; E - 6 cols, 2, 3/16 between; A - 6 cols, 2, 3/16 between; C - 9 cols, 1 5/16, 1/8 between.
Published Days: Mon`Tues`Wed`Thur`Fri`Sat`Sun
Weekday Frequency: m
Saturday Frequency: m
Avg Paid Circ: 19289
Avg Free Circ: 605
Audit Company: AAM
Audit Date: 1 11 2019
Pressroom Equipment: Lines – MAN/Roland Mediaman (3 half decks) 1993; Folders – 2-MAN/2:1; Pasters –MEG/2-45; Reels & Stands – 5-G/Reel.;

Mailroom Equipment: Counter Stackers – 2/Compass, 1-/QWI; Inserters & Stuffers – 1-GMA/SLS 2000 16:2; Tying Machines – 2-EAM-Mosca, 3-/Dynaric; Address Machine – 1-/KR, 5-/Wm.;
Buisness Equipment: Axil/Unix Sun Clone, Vision Data
Buisness Software: Database, Word Processing, Microsoft/Word 6.0, Microsoft/Excel 5.0
Classified Equipment: Hardware – Axil/Unix Sun Clone; Printers – C.Itoh/1000, Dataproducts, Dataproducts/Typhoon;
Classified Software: Vision Data.
Editorial Equipment: Hardware – APP/Mac 9500/APP/Macs, APP/Mac PowerBooks
Editorial Software: Baseview IQ.
Production Equipment: Hardware – 2-MON/Lasercomp, Mk/21, 1-X/P26 LaserPrinter, XIT/Schooner-Imagesetter, ECR/Pelbox 1045, 2-ECR/4550; Cameras – 1-C/Spartan III; Scanners – 1-ECR/Autokon News Graphics
Production Software: QPS/QuarkXPress.
Total Circulation: 27026

WAYNESBORO

THE RECORD HERALD

Corporate/Parent Company: Gannett
Publication Street Address: 30 Walnut St
City: Waynesboro
State: PA
Publication Website: www.therecordherald.com
Postal Code: 17268-1644
Office phone: (717) 762-2151
General E-mail: dfriedman@therecordherald.com
Publisher Name: Ken Browall
Publisher Email: kbrowall@therecordherald.com
Editor Name: Ben Destefan
Editor Email: bdestefan@therecordherald.com
Advertising Executive Name: Dawn Friedman
Advertising Executive Email: dfriedman@therecordherald.com
Year Established: 1824
Mechanical specifications: Type page 13 x 21 1/2; E - 6 cols, 2 1/14, 1/6 between; A - 6 cols, 2 1/14, 1/6 between; C - 8 cols, 1 1/2, 1/6 between.
Published Days: Mon`Tues`Wed`Thur`Fri`Sat
Weekday Frequency: e
Saturday Frequency: m
Avg Paid Circ: 8005
Audit Company: Sworn/Estimate/Non-Audited
Audit Date: 7 12 2019
Pressroom Equipment: Lines – 4-G/Urbanite 1964; Folders – 1-G/500.;
Mailroom Equipment: Tying Machines – 2/OVL; Address Machine – 1-/Ch.;
Buisness Equipment: IBM/Sys 36
Classified Equipment: Hardware – Mk/1100 Plus; Printers – APP/Mac LaserWriter;
Classified Software: Mk/1100 Plus.
Editorial Equipment: Hardware – Mk/1100 Plus/Lf/AP Leaf Picture Desk; Printers – APP/Mac LaserWriter
Editorial Software: Mk/1100 Plus.
Production Equipment: Hardware – Nu/Flip Top FT40V3UPNS, APP/Mac LaserWriter Pro 630; Cameras – C, VG/Graphline 760, K/Vertical 24; Scanners – HP/LaserJet Plus.
Total Circulation: 8005

WHITE HAVEN

JOURNAL-HERALD

Publication Street Address: 211 Main Street
City: White Haven
State: PA
Publication Website: www.pocononewspapers.com
Postal Code: 18661
Office phone: 570-215-0204
Editor Name: Ruth Isenberg
Editor Email: journalruth@gmail.com
Year Established: 1878
Delivery Methods: Mail`Newsstand
Own Printing Facility?: N
Commercial printers?: N
Mechanical specifications: Type page 10 x 12;

E - 5 cols, 1.865", 1/8 between; A - 5 cols, 1.865", 1/8 between; C - 7 cols, 1 3/4, 1/8 between.
Published Days: Thur
Avg Paid Circ: 845
Avg Free Circ: 36
Audit Company: Sworn/Estimate/Non-Audited
Audit Date: 6 10 2019
Note: affliated with affiliated with Journal of the Pocono Plateau weekly, Journal of Penn Forest monthly, and Journal Valley Views semi-monthly
Total Circulation: 881

WILKES BARRE

THE CITIZENS' VOICE

Corporate/Parent Company: Times-Shamrock Communications
Publication Street Address: 75 N Washington St
City: Wilkes Barre
State: PA
Publication Website: www.citizensvoice.com
Postal Code: 18701-3109
Office phone: (570) 821-2000
General E-mail: maltavilla@citizensvoice.com
Publisher Name: Daniel Haggerty
Editor Name: Dave Janoski
Editor Email: djanoski@citizensvoice.com
Editor Phone: (570) 821-2178
Advertising Executive Name: Mark Altavilla
Advertising Executive Email: maltavilla@citizensvoice.com
Advertising Executive Phone: (570) 821-2037
Delivery Methods: Mail`Newsstand`Carrier`Racks
Own Printing Facility?: Y
Commercial printers?: Y
Mechanical specifications: Type page 10 1/2 x 13; E - 5 cols, 2, 1/8 between; A - 5 cols, 2, 1/8 between; C - 10 cols, 1 1/16, 1/8 between.
Published Days: Mon`Tues`Wed`Thur`Fri`Sat`Sun
Weekday Frequency: m
Saturday Frequency: m
Avg Paid Circ: 16885
Avg Free Circ: 2132
Audit Company: AAM
Audit Date: 6 04 2020
Pressroom Equipment: Lines – 8-G/Urbanite; Folders – G/1000.;
Mailroom Equipment: Counter Stackers – 3-QWI/300, 1/HL; Inserters & Stuffers – 1-Biliner/8:1; Tying Machines – 4-MLN/Spirits, 2-/Sterling;
Buisness Equipment: 1-IBM/RISC 6000
Buisness Software: Vision Data, Accts receivable 6.2, Accts payable 5.0, Gen ledger 5.0, Circ 3.9
Classified Equipment: Hardware – 1-Sun/Ultra 10, 4-GB/Tape Drives (Backup); Printers – 1-HP/5M;
Classified Software: Unisys.
Editorial Equipment: Hardware – 2-HP/Netserver LD, 20-HP/Vectra VLS Pentium 233 mhz/1-Everex/Notebook, 2-APP/Power Mac 8100, 3-APP/Mac Power Book 190, APP/Power Book G3; Printers – 1-HP
Editorial Software: Microsoft/Windows NT Server 4.0, Microsoft/SQL Server 6.5, Micros
Production Equipment: Hardware – Caere/OmniPage 3.0, Douthitt/Gemini; Scanners – 1-Epson/836L, 3-HP/ScanJet 6100C, 1-HP/ScanJet 4c, 2-HP/ScanJet G300
Production Software: QPS/QuarkXPress 4.04, Adobe/In Design.
Note: The Wilkes-Barre Citizens' Voice (mS) has a combination rate of $132.39 (m) and $133.68 (S) with the Scranton Times-Tribune (mS). Individual newspaper rates not made available.
Total Circulation: 23562

TIMES LEADER

Corporate/Parent Company: Avant Publications
Publication Street Address: 90 E. Market St.
City: Wilkes Barre

State: PA
Publication Website: www.timesleader.com
Postal Code: 18701-2604
Office phone: (570) 829-7100
General E-mail: mhoskins@timesleader.com
Publisher Name: Mike Murray
Publisher Email: mmurray@timesleader.com
Publisher Phone: (570) 704-3986
Editor Name: Joe Soprano
Editor Email: jsoprano@timesleader.com
Editor Phone: (570) 991-6393
Advertising Executive Name: Kerry Miscavage
Advertising Executive Email: kmiscavage@civitasmedia.com
Advertising Executive Phone: (570) 704-3953
Mechanical specifications: Type page 12 1/2 x 21; E - 6 cols, 2 1/16, 1/8 between; A - 6 cols, 2 1/16, 1/8 between; C - 10 cols, 1 3/8, 1/16 between.
Published Days: Mon`Tues`Wed`Thur`Fri`Sat`Sun
Weekday Frequency: m
Saturday Frequency: m
Avg Paid Circ: 12448
Avg Free Circ: 1420
Audit Company: AAM
Audit Date: 31 03 2019
Pressroom Equipment: Lines – MAN/Roland double width (20 couples, offset; 3 tower, 1996; Folders – MAN/Roland; Pasters –MEG; Reels & Stands – MEG; Control System – MAN/Rolland.;
Mailroom Equipment: Counter Stackers – 2-QWI/300, 3-QWI/350; Inserters & Stuffers – 2-GMA/SLS 1000; Tying Machines – 2/Dynaric; Wrapping Singles – 2-/QWI; Address Machine – 1-/Wm, 1-/Ch, 1-Mc/2000 PB Folder.;
Buisness Equipment: HP/3000-928, HP/3000-918, HP/MPE-IY
Buisness Software: Microsoft/Office 5.0, Boreland/Parabox 4.0
Classified Equipment: Hardware – 2-Pentium/Dual Processing Servers/266; Printers – 1-HP/III, 1-C.Itoh, 2-Dataproducts/Typhoon;
Classified Software: PPI/Microsoft Windows NT, SQL 3.11.
Editorial Equipment: Hardware – 22-PC 486-66MHz fileserver, 2-PC 286, 5-PC 386, 30-Pentium/PC 133MHZ; Printers – 2-Pre Press/Panther 46, 1-HP/III, 1-Panasonic, ECR/Pelbox 1045CS, 2-Dataproducts/Typhoon
Editorial Software: CCI 6.7.0.2AQ, Solaris/9.
Production Equipment: Hardware – Caere/OmniPage, Na/NP40; Scanners – 2-AG/1200 dpi, 6-HP/ScanJet
Production Software: CCI/Editorial Sys. 6.7.0.2AQ, MEI/CLS, QPS/QuarkXPress 4.1, MEI/ALS 4.1.7.
Total Circulation: 13868

WILLIAMSPORT

WILLIAMSPORT SUN-GAZETTE/ LOCK HAVEN EXPRESS

Corporate/Parent Company: Ogden Newspapers Inc.
Publication Street Address: 252 West Fourth Street
City: Williamsport
State: PA
Publication Website: www.sungazette.com
Postal Code: 17701-0728
Office phone: (570) 326-1551
General E-mail: news@sungazette.com
Publisher Name: Robert O. Rolley
Publisher Email: brolley@sungazette.com
Publisher Phone: (570) 326-1551, Ext : 1123
Editor Name: L. Lee Janssen
Editor Email: llee@sungazette.com
Editor Phone: (570) 326-1551, Ext : 3121
Advertising Executive Name: John Leeser
Advertising Executive Email: jleeser@sungazette.com
Advertising Executive Phone: (570) 326-1551, Ext : 2230
Year Established: 1801
Delivery Methods: Mail`Newsstand`Carrier`Racks
Own Printing Facility?: Y

U.S. Daily Newspapers

Commercial printers?: Y
Mechanical specifications: Type page 13 x 21 1/4; E - 6 cols, 2 1/16, 1/8 between; A - 6 cols, 2 1/16, 1/8 between; C - 8 cols, 1 9/16, 1/8 between.
Published Days: Mon`Tues`Wed`Thur`Fri`Sat`Sun
Weekday Frequency: m
Saturday Frequency: m
Avg Paid Circ: 13318
Avg Free Circ: 837
Audit Company: AAM
Audit Date: 31 03 2019
Pressroom Equipment: Lines – 6-G/Metro 3007;
Mailroom Equipment: Counter Stackers – HL/Monitor; Inserters & Stuffers – HI/72P;
Buisness Equipment: Motorola
Classified Equipment: Hardware – Microsoft/Winmdows NT.;
Editorial Equipment: Hardware – Microsoft/Windows NT.
Production Equipment: Hardware – Nu/Flip Top FT40UP; Cameras – C/Spartan III
Note: Advertising is sold in combination with The Lock Haven Express (e) for $76.12 (d) and $82.11 (S). Individual newspaper rates not made available.
Total Circulation: 14155

YORK

THE YORK DISPATCH

Corporate/Parent Company: Gannett Co., Inc.
Publication Street Address: 205 N George St
City: York
State: PA
Publication Website: www.yorkdispatch.com
Postal Code: 17401-1107
Office phone: (717) 854-1575
General E-mail: customerservice@ync.com
Editor Name: Jon Alexander
Editor Email: jalexander@yorkdispatch.com
Editor Phone: (717) 505-5435
Published Days: Mon`Tues`Wed`Thur`Fri
Weekday Frequency: e
Avg Paid Circ: 12724
Audit Company: AAM
Audit Date: 17 06 2020
Pressroom Equipment: Lines – 8-G/Metro 1991, 2-G/Metro CIC 1991; Pasters –8-G/RTP.
Mailroom Equipment: Counter Stackers – 4-HL/Monitor HT II; Inserters & Stuffers – 2-HI/1472; Tying Machines – 4/MLN.;
Buisness Equipment: 11-HP/928 RL
Buisness Software: CJ, DB, Vesoft
Classified Equipment: Hardware – HI; Printers – C.Itoh/CI 400;
Classified Software: HI, HI/Pagination.
Editorial Equipment: Hardware – AT, Dell/HI/Pagination; Printers – Textronix/600
Editorial Software: AT, HI.
Production Equipment: Hardware – 2-MON/3850, 2-C/R660; Cameras – 1-C/Spartan III; Scanners – ECR/1000, ECR/2045.
Note: For detailed advertising, circulation, printing and production information, see York Newspaper Company listing. Advertising in the York Dispatch automatically includes advertising in the York Daily Record (m).
Total Circulation: 9297

YORK DAILY RECORD/YORK SUNDAY NEWS

Publication Street Address: 1891 Loucks Rd
City: York
State: PA
Publication Website: www.ydr.com
Postal Code: 17408-9708
Office phone: (717) 771-2000
General E-mail: yorkdailyrecord@gannett.com
Editor Name: Randy Parker
Year Established: 1796
Delivery Methods: Mail`Newsstand`Carrier`Racks
Own Printing Facility?: N
Commercial printers?: N
Mechanical specifications: SAU
Published Days: Mon`Tues`Wed`Thur`Fri`Sat`Sun
Weekday Frequency: m
Saturday Frequency: m
Avg Paid Circ: 13656
Avg Free Circ: 215
Audit Company: AAM
Audit Date: 30 09 2018
Total Circulation: 13871

MORETHANTHECURVE.COM

State: PA
Publication Website: www.morethanthecurve.com
Office phone: (215) 962-5372
Editor Name: Kevin Tierney
Editor Email: kevin@morethanthecurve.com

RHODE ISLAND

PROVIDENCE

THE PROVIDENCE JOURNAL

Corporate/Parent Company: Gannett
Publication Street Address: 75 Fountain St.
City: Providence
State: RI
Publication Website: www.providencejournal.com
Postal Code: 0 2902
Office phone: 401-277-7000 office
General E-mail: letters@providencejournal.com
Publisher Name: Peter Meyer
Publisher Email: pmeyer@gatehousemedia.com
Publisher Phone: 401-277-7046
Editor Name: Alan Rosenberg
Editor Email: arosenberg@providencejournal.com
Editor Phone: 401-277-7409
Advertising Executive Name: Lynn Abrams
Advertising Executive Email: labrams@providencejournal.com
Advertising Executive Phone: 401-277-8226
Year Established: 1829
Delivery Methods: Mail`Newsstand`Racks
Own Printing Facility?: Y
Commercial printers?: Y
Mechanical specifications: Type page 12 x 21; E - 6 cols, 1 43/50, 1/6 between; A – 6 cols, 1 43/50, 1/6 between; C – 9 cols, 1 23/100, 1/8 between.
Published Days: Mon`Tues`Wed`Thur`Fri`Sat`Sun
Weekday Frequency: m
Saturday Frequency: m
Avg Paid Circ: 59122
Audit Company: AAM
Audit Date: 30 06 2017

WEST WARWICK

KENT COUNTY DAILY TIMES

Corporate/Parent Company: Southern Rhode Island Newspapers
Publication Street Address: 1353 Main Street
City: West Warwick
State: RI
Publication Website: www.ricentral.com
Postal Code: 2893
Office phone: 401-821-7400
General E-mail: kceditor@ricentral.com
Publisher Name: Jody A. Boucher
Publisher Email: jboucher@ricentral.com
Publisher Phone: (401) 789-9744, Ext : 105
Editor Name: Kendra Gravelle
Editor Email: kgravelle@ricentral.com
Editor Phone: (401) 821-7400, Ext : 209
Advertising Executive Name: Esther Diggins
Advertising Executive Email: ediggins@ricentral.com
Advertising Executive Phone: (401) 789-9744, Ext : 117

Year Established: 1892
Delivery Methods: Newsstand`Carrier`Racks
Own Printing Facility?: Y
Commercial printers?: N
Mechanical specifications: Call for Info
Published Days: Mon`Tues`Wed`Thur`Fri`Sat
Weekday Frequency: All day
Saturday Frequency: All day
Avg Paid Circ: 737
Avg Free Circ: 60
Audit Company: AAM
Audit Date: 25 10 2019

WOONSOCKET

THE CALL

Corporate/Parent Company: The Call Inc.
Publication Street Address: 75 Main St
City: Woonsocket
State: RI
Publication Website: www.woonsocketcall.com
Postal Code: (02895-4312
Office phone: (401) 762-3000
General E-mail: info@woonsocketcall.com
Publisher Name: Jody Boucher
Publisher Email: jboucher@ricentral.com
Publisher Phone: (401) 789-9744
Editor Name: Seth Bromley
Editor Email: sbromley@woonsocketcall.com
Advertising Executive Name: Diane Ames
Advertising Executive Email: dames@woonsocketcall.com
Advertising Executive Phone: (401) 767-8505
Year Established: 1892
Delivery Methods: Newsstand`Carrier
Own Printing Facility?: N
Commercial printers?: Y
Mechanical specifications: Type page 12 x 21 1/2; E - 6 cols, 1 7/8, 1/8 between; A - 6 cols, 1 7/8, 1/8 between; C - 9 cols, 1 5/16, 1/16 between.
Published Days: Mon`Tues`Wed`Thur`Fri`Sat`Sun
Weekday Frequency: m
Saturday Frequency: m
Avg Paid Circ: 2748
Avg Free Circ: 39
Audit Company: AAM
Audit Date: 6 11 2019

THE HAYS DAILY NEWS

Corporate/Parent Company: Gannett
Publication Street Address: 75 Main St
City: Woonsocket
State: RI
Publication Website: https://www.hdnews.net
Postal Code: 02860-2026
Office phone: 401-762-3000
General E-mail: notices@pawtuckettimes.com
Publisher Name: Jody Boucher
Publisher Email: jboucher@ricentral.com
Publisher Phone: (401) 789-9744
Editor Name: Seth Bromley
Editor Email: sbromley@woonsocketcall.com
Advertising Executive Name: Diane Ames
Advertising Executive Email: dames@woonsocketcall.com
Advertising Executive Phone: (401) 767-8505

SOUTH CAROLINA

ANDERSON

ANDERSON INDEPENDENT-MAIL

Corporate/Parent Company: Gannett
Publication Street Address: 1000 Williamston Rd
City: Anderson
State: SC
Publication Website: www.independentmail.com
Postal Code: 29621-6508
Office phone: (864) 224-4321

General E-mail: steve.bruss@independentmail.com
Publisher Name: Susan Kelly-Gilbert
Editor Name: Stephen S. Mullins
Advertising Executive Name: Lindsey Twitty
Advertising Executive Email: lindsey.twitty@independentmail.com
Year Established: 1899
Delivery Methods: Carrier

BLUFFTON

THE BEAUFORT GAZETTE

Corporate/Parent Company: McClatchy Company
Publication Street Address: 10 Buck Island Rd
City: Bluffton
State: SC
Publication Website: www.beaufortgazette.com
Postal Code: 29910-5937
Office phone: (843) 524-3183
General E-mail: bosborn@islandpack.com
Publisher Name: Brian Tolley
Publisher Email: btolley@islandpacket.com
Editor Name: Candy Hatcher
Editor Email: chatcher@islandpacket.com
Editor Phone: (843) 706-8133
Advertising Executive Name: Michelle Long
Advertising Executive Email: mblong@mcclatchy.com
Advertising Executive Phone: (843) 706-8245

THE ISLAND PACKET

Corporate/Parent Company: McClatchy Company
Publication Street Address: 10 Buck Island Rd
City: Bluffton
State: SC
Publication Website: www.islandpacket.com
Postal Code: 29910-5937
Office phone: (843) 706-8100
General E-mail: ads@islandpacket.com
Publisher Name: Brian Tolley
Publisher Email: btolley@islandpacket.com
Publisher Phone: (843) 706-8110
Editor Name: Candy Hatcher
Editor Email: chatcher@islandpacket.com
Editor Phone: (843) 706-8133
Advertising Executive Name: Michelle Long
Advertising Executive Email: mblong@mcclatchy.com
Advertising Executive Phone: (843) 706-8245
Year Established: 1970
Delivery Methods: Mail`Newsstand`Carrier`Racks
Own Printing Facility?: Y
Commercial printers?: Y

CHARLESTON

THE POST AND COURIER

Corporate/Parent Company: Evening Post Industries
Publication Street Address: 134 Columbus St
City: Charleston
State: SC
Publication Website: www.postandcourier.com
Postal Code: 29403-4809
Office phone: (843) 577-7111
General E-mail: webteam@postandcourier.com
Publisher Name: P.J. Browning
Publisher Email: pbrowning@postandcourier.com
Editor Name: Autumn Phillips
Editor Email: aphillips@postandcourier.com
Editor Phone: (843) 937-5543
Advertising Executive Name: Megan Buyer
Advertising Executive Email: mbuyer@postandcourier.com
Advertising Executive Phone: (843) 937-5470
Year Established: 1803
Delivery Methods: Mail`Newsstand`Carrier`Racks
Own Printing Facility?: Y
Commercial printers?: Y

COLUMBIA

THE STATE

Corporate/Parent Company: McClatchy Company
Publication Street Address: 1401 Shop Rd
City: Columbia
State: SC
Publication Website: www.thestate.com
Postal Code: 29201-4843
Office phone: 803-771-6161
General E-mail: customerservice@thestate.com
Publisher Name: Rodney Mahone
Publisher Email: rmahone@mcclatchy.com
Editor Name: Brian Tolley
Editor Email: btolley@thestate.com
Advertising Executive Name: Lauren Libet
Advertising Executive Email: llibet@thestate.com
Year Established: 1891
Delivery Methods: Mail`Carrier
Own Printing Facility?: Y
Commercial printers?: Y

FLORENCE

MORNING NEWS

Corporate/Parent Company: Lee Enterprises
Publication Street Address: 310 S Dargan St
City: Florence
State: SC
Publication Website: www.scnow.com
Postal Code: 29506-2537
Office phone: (843) 317-6397
General E-mail: pgray@florencenews.com
Publisher Name: Bailey Dabney
Publisher Email: bdabney@florencenews.com
Publisher Phone: (843) 317-7200
Editor Name: John Rains
Editor Email: jrains@florencenews.com
Editor Phone: (843) 317-7284
Advertising Executive Name: Carrie Lloyd
Advertising Executive Email: clloyd@florencenews.com
Advertising Executive Phone: (843) 317-7223

GREENVILLE

THE GREENVILLE NEWS

Corporate/Parent Company: Gannett
Publication Street Address: 32 E. Broad St.
City: Greenville
State: SC
Publication Website: www.greenvilleonline.com
Postal Code: 29602
Office phone: (864) 298-4100
General E-mail: dfoster3@gannett.com
Editor Name: Katrice Hardy
Editor Phone: (864) 298-4165
Advertising Executive Name: David Foster
Advertising Executive Email: dfoster3@gannett.com
Advertising Executive Phone: (864) 298-4342
Year Established: 1874

GREENWOOD

THE INDEX-JOURNAL

Corporate/Parent Company: Index Journal Co.
Publication Street Address: 610 Phoenix St
City: Greenwood
State: SC
Publication Website: www.indexjournal.com
Postal Code: 29646-3253
Office phone: (864) 223-1411
General E-mail: contactus@indexjournal.com
Publisher Name: Mundy Price
Publisher Email: mprice@indexjournal.com
Publisher Phone: (864) 943-2532, Ext : 2215
Editor Name: Richard Whiting
Editor Email: rwhiting@indexjournal.com
Editor Phone: (864) 943-2522, Ext : 3307
Advertising Executive Name: Bill Duncan
Advertising Executive Email: bduncan@indexjournal.com
Advertising Executive Phone: (864) 943-2522, Ext : 2258

Year Established: 1919
Delivery Methods: Carrier`Racks
Own Printing Facility?: Y
Commercial printers?: Y

MYRTLE BEACH

THE SUN NEWS

Corporate/Parent Company: McClatchy Company
Publication Street Address: 914 Frontage Rd E
City: Myrtle Beach
State: SC
Publication Website: www.myrtlebeachonline.com
Postal Code: 29577-6700
Office phone: (843) 626-8555
General E-mail: display@thesunnews.com
Publisher Name: Stephanie Pedersen
Year Established: 1936
Delivery Methods:
    Mail`Newsstand`Carrier`Racks

ORANGEBURG

THE TIMES AND DEMOCRAT

Corporate/Parent Company: Lee Enterprises
Publication Street Address: 1010 Broughton St
City: Orangeburg
State: SC
Publication Website: www.theTandD.com
Postal Code: 29115-5962
Office phone: (803) 533-5500
General E-mail: kfraser@timesanddemocrat.com
Publisher Name: Cathy Hughes
Publisher Email: chughes@timesanddemocrat.com
Publisher Phone: (803) 533-5535
Editor Name: Lee Harter
Editor Email: lharter@timesanddemocrat.com
Editor Phone: (803) 533-5520
Advertising Executive Name: Chanette Davis
Advertising Executive Email: cdavis@timesanddemocrat.com
Advertising Executive Phone: (803) 533-5555
Year Established: 1881
Delivery Methods:
    Mail`Newsstand`Carrier`Racks
Own Printing Facility?: Y
Commercial printers?: N

ROCK HILL

THE HERALD

Corporate/Parent Company: Paxton Media Group
Publication Street Address: 140 Main St., Suite 420
City: Rock Hill
State: SC
Publication Website: www.heraldonline.com
Postal Code: 29730-4430
Office phone: (803) 329-4000
General E-mail: dmorgenstern@mcclatchy.com
Editor Name: Cliff Harrington
Editor Email: charrington@heraldonline.com
Editor Phone: (803) 326-4303
Advertising Executive Name: Dan Morgenstern
Advertising Executive Email: dmorgenstern@mcclatchy.com
Advertising Executive Phone: (704) 358-5333
Year Established: 1872
Delivery Methods:
    Mail`Newsstand`Carrier`Racks
Own Printing Facility?: N
Commercial printers?: Y

SENECA

DAILY JOURNAL/MESSENGER

Publication Street Address: 210 W North 1st St
City: Seneca
State: SC
Publication Website: www.upstatetoday.com
Postal Code: 29678-3250
Office phone: (864) 882-2375
General E-mail: classadmgr@upstatetoday.com

Editor Name: Stephen Bradley
Delivery Methods: Newsstand`Carrier`Racks
Own Printing Facility?: Y
Commercial printers?: Y

SPARTANBURG

HERALD-JOURNAL

Corporate/Parent Company: Gannett
Publication Street Address: 189 W Main St
City: Spartanburg
State: SC
Publication Website: www.goupstate.com
Postal Code: 29306-2334
Office phone: 864-582-4511
General E-mail: caralyn.bess@shj.com
Publisher Name: Kevin Drake
Editor Name: Michael Smith
Editor Email: michael.smith@shj.com
Editor Phone: (864) 562-7200
Advertising Executive Phone: (864) 562-7435
Year Established: 1842
Delivery Methods:
    Mail`Newsstand`Carrier`Racks
Own Printing Facility?: N
Commercial printers?: N

SUMTER

THE SUMTER ITEM

Corporate/Parent Company: Osteen Publishing
Publication Street Address: 36 W Liberty St
City: Sumter
State: SC
Publication Website: www.theitem.com
Postal Code: 29150-4940
Office phone: (803) 774-1200
General E-mail: webmaster@theitem.com
Publisher Name: Vince Johnson
Publisher Email: vince@theitem.com
Publisher Phone: (803) 774-1200
Editor Name: Kayla Robins
Editor Email: kayla@theitem.com
Editor Phone: (803) 774-1235
Advertising Executive Name: Karen Cave
Advertising Executive Email: karen@theitem.com
Advertising Executive Phone: (803) 774-1242
Year Established: 1894
Delivery Methods:
    Mail`Newsstand`Carrier`Racks
Own Printing Facility?: N
Commercial printers?: Y

UNION

UNION DAILY TIMES

Corporate/Parent Company: Champion Media
Publication Street Address: 201 N Herndon St
City: Union
State: SC
Publication Website: www.uniondailytimes.com
Postal Code: 29379-2210
Office phone: (864) 427-1234
General E-mail: dmcmurray@uniondailytimes.com
Publisher Name: Donna McMurray
Publisher Email: dmcmurray@uniondailytimes.com
Publisher Phone: (864) 762-4126
Editor Name: Charles Warner
Editor Email: cwarner@uniondailytimes.com
Editor Phone: (864) 762-4090
Advertising Executive Name: Linda Johnson
Advertising Executive Email: lsims@uniondailytimes.com
Advertising Executive Phone: (864) 427-1234
Year Established: 1850
Delivery Methods: Mail
Own Printing Facility?: Y
Commercial printers?: N

SOUTH DAKOTA

ABERDEEN

AMERICAN NEWS

Corporate/Parent Company: Gannett
Publication Street Address: PO Box 4430, Aberdeen, SD 57401
City: Aberdeen
State: SD
Publication Website: www.aberdeennews.com
Office phone: 605-225-4100
General E-mail: americannews@aberdeennews.com
Editor Name: Scott Waltman
Editor Email: swaltman@aberdeennews.com
Advertising Executive Name: Christy Orwig
Advertising Executive Email: corwig@aberdeennews.com

BROOKINGS

BROOKINGS REGISTER

Corporate/Parent Company: News Media Grouip
Publication Street Address: PO Box 177, Brookings, SD 57006
City: Brookings
State: SD
Publication Website: www.brookingsregister.com
Office phone: 605-692-6271
General E-mail: news@brookingsregister.com
Publisher Name: William McMacken
Publisher Email: bmcmacken@brookingsregister.com
Editor Name: Jill Fier
Editor Email: jfier@brookingsregister.com
Advertising Executive Name: Tracy Jonas
Advertising Executive Email: tjonas@brookingsregister.com
Year Established: 1882
Mechanical specifications: Type page 13 x 21 1/2; E - 6 cols, 2, 3/16 between; A - 6 cols, 2, 3/16 between; C - 6 cols, 2, 3/16 between.
Published Days: Mon`Tues`Wed`Thur`Fri`Sat`Sun
Weekday Frequency: e
Saturday Frequency: m
Avg Paid Circ: 4263
Audit Company: Sworn/Estimate/Non-Audited
Audit Date: 7 12 2019

HURON

HURON PLAINSMAN

Corporate/Parent Company: News Media Corporation
Publication Street Address: PO Box 1278, Huron, SD 57350-1278
City: Huron
State: SD
Publication Website: www.plainsman.com
Office phone: 605-353-7414
General E-mail: mdavis@plainsman.com
Publisher Name: Mark Davis
Publisher Email: mdavis@plainsman.com
Editor Name: Curt Nettinga
Editor Email: cnettinga@plainsman.com
Advertising Executive Name: Mark Davis
Advertising Executive Email: mdavis@plainsman.com

MADISON

MADISON DAILY LEADER

Publication Street Address: PO Box 348, Madison, SD 57042-0348
City: Madison
State: SD
Publication Website: www.dailyleaderextra.com
Office phone: 605-256-4555
General E-mail: news@madisondailyleader.com
Publisher Name: Jon Hunter
Publisher Email: jon@madisondailyleader.com

U.S. Daily Newspapers

Editor Name: Marcia Schoeberl
Editor Email: marcia@madisondailyleader.com
Advertising Executive Name: Melissa Hegg
Advertising Executive Email: melissa@madisondailyleader.com
Year Established: 1880
Delivery Methods: Mail`Newsstand`Carrier`Racks
Own Printing Facility?: Y
Commercial printers?: Y
Mechanical specifications: Type page 13 1/10 x 21; E - 6 cols, 2 1/14, 1/8 between; A - 6 cols, 2 1/14, 1/8 between; C - 6 cols, 2 1/14, 1/8 between.
Published Days: Mon`Tues`Wed`Thur`Fri
Weekday Frequency: e
Avg Paid Circ: 2750
Audit Company: Sworn/Estimate/Non-Audited
Audit Date: 7 12 2019

RAPID CITY
RAPID CITY JOURNAL

Corporate/Parent Company: Lee Enterprises
Publication Street Address: PO Box 450, Rapid City, SD 57701
City: Rapid City
State: SD
Publication Website: www.rapidcityjournal.com
Office phone: 605-394-8200
General E-mail: news@rapidcityjournal.com
Publisher Name: Matthew Tranquill
Publisher Email: Matthew.Tranquill@rapidcityjournal.com
Year Established: 1878
Delivery Methods: Mail`Carrier
Commercial printers?: Y
Mechanical specifications: Type page 11 5/8 x 21; E - 6 cols, 2 1/16, 1/8 between; A - 6 cols, 2 1/16, 1/8 between; C - 9 cols, 1 3/8, 1/8 between.
Published Days: Mon`Tues`Wed`Thur`Fri`Sat`Sun
Weekday Frequency: m
Saturday Frequency: m
Avg Paid Circ: 13270
Avg Free Circ: 391
Audit Company: AAM
Audit Date: 29 08 2018

SIOUX FALLS
ARGUS LEADER

Corporate/Parent Company: Gannett
Publication Street Address: PO Box 5034, Sioux Falls, SD 57117-5034
City: Sioux Falls
State: SD
Publication Website: www.argusleader.com
Office phone: 605-331-2200
General E-mail: editor@argusleader.com
Publisher Name: Cory Myers
Publisher Email: ctmyers@argusleader.com
Editor Name: Cory Myers
Editor Email: ctmyers@argusleader.com
Year Established: 1881
Delivery Methods: Mail`Newsstand`Carrier`Racks
Mechanical specifications: Type page 12 1/2 x 21 1/2; E - 6 cols, 2 1/16, 1/8 between; A - 6 cols, 2 1/16, 1/8 between; C - 10 cols, 1 7/32, 1/16 between.
Published Days: Mon`Tues`Wed`Thur`Fri`Sat`Sun
Weekday Frequency: m
Saturday Frequency: m
Avg Paid Circ: 12641
Avg Free Circ: 615
Audit Company: AAM
Audit Date: 9 06 2020

SPEARFISH
BLACK HILLS PIONEER

Corporate/Parent Company: Seaton Publishing
Publication Street Address: 315 Seaton Circle, Spearfish, SD 57783
City: Spearfish
State: SD
Publication Website: www.bhpioneer.com

Office phone: 605-642-2761
General E-mail: news@bhpioneer.com
Publisher Name: Letitia Lister
Publisher Email: letti@bhpionner.com
Editor Name: Mark Watson
Editor Email: mwatson@bhpioneer.com
Advertising Executive Name: Sona O'Connell
Advertising Executive Email: sona@bhpioneer.com
Year Established: 1876
Mechanical specifications: Type page 10 1/4 x 13 1/2; E - 5 cols, 1, 1/12 between; A - 5 cols, 1, 1/12 between; C - 5 cols, 1, 1/12 between.
Published Days: Mon`Tues`Wed`Thur`Fri`Sat
Weekday Frequency: e
Saturday Frequency: m
Avg Paid Circ: 4300
Audit Company: Sworn/Estimate/Non-Audited
Audit Date: 7 12 2019

WATERTOWN
PUBLIC OPINION

Publication Street Address: PO Box 10, Watertown, SD 57201-0010
City: Watertown
State: SD
Publication Website: www.thepublicopinion.com
Office phone: 605-886-6901
General E-mail: news@thepublicopinion.com

YANKTON
DAILY PRESS & DAKOTAN

Publication Street Address: 319 Walnut, Yankton, SD 57078-0056
City: Yankton
State: SD
Publication Website: www.yankton.net
Office phone: 605-665-7811
General E-mail: news@yankton.net
Publisher Name: Gary Wood
Publisher Email: gary.wood@yankton.net
Editor Name: Kelly Hertz
Editor Email: kelly.hertz@yankton.net
Advertising Executive Name: Micki Schievelbein
Advertising Executive Email: micki.schievelbein@yankton.net

TENNESSEE

ATHENS
THE DAILY POST-ATHENIAN

Corporate/Parent Company: Adams Publishing Group
Publication Street Address: 320 S Jackson St
City: Athens
State: TN
Publication Website: www.dailypostathenian.com
Postal Code: 37303-4715
Office phone: (423) 745-5664

CHATTANOOGA
CHATTANOOGA TIMES FREE PRESS

Corporate/Parent Company: WEHCO Media, Inc.
Publication Street Address: 400 E 11th St
City: Chattanooga
State: TN
Publication Website: www.timesfreepress.com
Postal Code: 37403-4203
Office phone: (423) 756-6900

CLARKSVILLE
THE LEAF-CHRONICLE

Corporate/Parent Company: Gannett
Publication Street Address: 200 Commerce St
City: Clarksville
State: TN
Publication Website: www.theleafchronicle.com
Postal Code: 37040-5101
Office phone: (931) 552-1808

CLEVELAND
CLEVELAND DAILY BANNER

Corporate/Parent Company: Cleveland Newspapers, Inc.
Publication Street Address: 1505 25th St NW
City: Cleveland
State: TN
Publication Website: www.clevelandbanner.com
Postal Code: 37311-3610
Office phone: (423) 472-5041

COLUMBIA
COLUMBIA DAILY HERALD

Corporate/Parent Company: Gannett
Publication Street Address: 1115 S Main St
City: Columbia
State: TN
Publication Website: www.columbiadailyherald.com
Postal Code: 38401-3733
Office phone: (931) 388-6464

THE DAILY HERALD

Corporate/Parent Company: GateHouse Media
Publication Street Address: 1115 S. Main Street
City: Columbia
State: TN
Publication Website: www.c-dh.net
Postal Code: 38401
Office phone: 931) 388-6464

COOKEVILLE
HERALD-CITIZEN

Corporate/Parent Company: Cleveland Newspapers, Inc.
Publication Street Address: 1300 Neal St
City: Cookeville
State: TN
Publication Website: www.herald-citizen.com
Postal Code: 38501-4330
Office phone: (931) 526-9715

DYERSBURG
STATE GAZETTE

Corporate/Parent Company: Rust Communications
Publication Street Address: 294 US Highway 51 Byp N
City: Dyersburg
State: TN
Publication Website: www.stategazette.com
Postal Code: 38024-3659
Office phone: (731) 285-4091

ELIZABETHTON
ELIZABETHTON STAR

Corporate/Parent Company: Boone Newspapers, Inc.
Publication Street Address: 300 N Sycamore St
City: Elizabethton
State: TN
Publication Website: www.elizabethton.com
Postal Code: 37643-2742

Office phone: (423) 542-4151

GREENEVILLE
THE GREENEVILLE SUN

Corporate/Parent Company: Adams Publishing Group
Publication Street Address: 121 W. Summer St.
City: Greeneville
State: TN
Publication Website: https://www.greenevillesun.com/
Postal Code: 37743
Office phone: (423) 638-4181

JACKSON
THE JACKSON SUN

Corporate/Parent Company: Gannett
Publication Street Address: 245 W Lafayette St
City: Jackson
State: TN
Publication Website: www.jacksonsun.com
Postal Code: 38301-6126
Office phone: (731) 427-3333

JOHNSON CITY
JOHNSON CITY PRESS

Corporate/Parent Company: Johnson City Publishing Corp - Johnson City Press
Publication Street Address: 204 W Main St
City: Johnson City
State: TN
Publication Website: www.johnsoncitypress.com
Postal Code: 37604-6212
Office phone: (423) 929-3111

KINGSPORT
KINGSPORT TIMES-NEWS

Corporate/Parent Company: Six Rivers Media, LLC
Publication Street Address: 701 Lynn Garden Drive
City: Kingsport
State: TN
Publication Website: www.timesnews.net
Postal Code: 37660
Office phone: 423-246-8121

KNOXVILLE
KNOXVILLE NEWS SENTINEL

Corporate/Parent Company: Gannett Co., Inc.
Publication Street Address: 2332 News Sentinel Dr
City: Knoxville
State: TN
Publication Website: www.knoxnews.com
Postal Code: 37921-5766
Office phone: (865) 521-8181

NEWS SENTINEL

Publication Street Address: 2332 News Sentinel Dr
City: Knoxville
State: TN
Publication Website: www.knoxnews.com
Postal Code: 37919
Office phone: 865-342-6397

LEBANON
THE LEBANON DEMOCRAT

Corporate/Parent Company: Paxton Media Group
Publication Street Address: 402 N Cumberland St

I-113

City: Lebanon
State: TN
Publication Website: www.lebanondemocrat.com
Postal Code: 37087-2306
Office phone: (615) 444-3952

MARYVILLE

THE DAILY TIMES

Corporate/Parent Company: Gannett
Publication Street Address: 307 E Harper Ave
City: Maryville
State: TN
Publication Website: www.thedailytimes.com
Postal Code: 37804-5724
Office phone: (865) 981-1100

MEMPHIS

THE COMMERCIAL APPEAL

Corporate/Parent Company: Gannett
Publication Street Address: 119 S. Main St., Suite 300
City: Memphis
State: TN
Publication Website: www.commercialappeal.com
Postal Code: 38103-3217
Office phone: 901-529-2345

THE DAILY NEWS

Corporate/Parent Company: Gannett
Publication Street Address: 193 Jefferson Ave
City: Memphis
State: TN
Publication Website: www.memphisdailynews.com
Postal Code: 38103-2322
Office phone: (901) 523-1561

MORRISTOWN

CITIZEN TRIBUNE

Corporate/Parent Company: Lakeway Publishers, Inc.
Publication Street Address: 1609 W 1st North St
City: Morristown
State: TN
Publication Website: https://www.citizentribune.com/
Postal Code: 37815
Office phone: (423) 581-5630

MURFREESBORO

THE DAILY NEWS JOURNAL

Corporate/Parent Company: Gannett
Publication Street Address: 201 E. Main St. Suite 400
City: Murfreesboro
State: TN
Publication Website: www.dnj.com
Postal Code: 37130-3753
Office phone: (615) 893-5860

NASHVILLE

THE TENNESSEAN

Corporate/Parent Company: Gannett
Publication Street Address: 1801 West End, 17th Floor
City: Nashville
State: TN
Publication Website: www.tennessean.com
Postal Code: 37203-3116
Office phone: 615-259-8300

OAK RIDGE

THE OAK RIDGER

Corporate/Parent Company: Gannett
Publication Street Address: 575 Oak Ridge Turnpike, Suite 100
City: Oak Ridge
State: TN
Publication Website: www.oakridger.com
Postal Code: 37830-7076
Office phone: (865) 482-1021

PARIS

THE PARIS POST-INTELLIGENCER

Publication Street Address: 208 E Wood St
City: Paris
State: TN
Publication Website: www.parispi.net
Postal Code: 38242-4139
Office phone: (731) 642-1162

SEVIERVILLE

THE MOUNTAIN PRESS

Corporate/Parent Company: Paxton Media Group, LLC
Publication Street Address: 119 River Bend Drive
City: Sevierville
State: TN
Publication Website: www.themountainpress.com
Postal Code: 37876
Office phone: 865-428-0746

SHELBYVILLE

SHELBYVILLE TIMES-GAZETTE

Corporate/Parent Company: Rust Communications
Publication Street Address: 323 E Depot St
City: Shelbyville
State: TN
Publication Website: www.t-g.com
Postal Code: 37162
Office phone: (931) 684-1200

UNION CITY

THE MESSENGER

Corporate/Parent Company: Paxton Media Group
Publication Street Address: 613 E Jackson St
City: Union City
State: TN
Publication Website: www.nwtntoday.com
Postal Code: 38261-5239
Office phone: (731) 885-0744

UNION CITY DAILY MESSENGER

Corporate/Parent Company: NWTN Today
Publication Street Address: 613 E Jackson St
City: Union City
State: TN
Publication Website: www.ucmessenger.comNWTN Today
Postal Code: 38261
Office phone: 731-885-0744

TEXAS

ABILENE

ABILENE REPORTER-NEWS

Corporate/Parent Company: Gannett
Publication Street Address: 101 Cypress St
City: Abilene
State: TX
Publication Website: www.reporternews.com
Postal Code: 79601-5816
Office phone: (844) 900-7098
General E-mail: greg.jaklewicz@reporternews.com
Publisher Name: Nathan Grimm
Editor Name: Greg Jaklewicz
Editor Email: greg.jaklewicz@reporternews.com
Year Established: 1881
Delivery Methods:
 Mail`Newsstand`Carrier`Racks
Own Printing Facility?: Y
Commercial printers?: Y
Mechanical specifications: Type page 11 5/8 x 21; E - 6 cols, 1 5/6, 1/8 between; A - 6 cols, 1 5/6, 1/8 between; C - 10 cols, 1 5/64, 1/6 between.
Published Days: Mon`Tues`Wed`Thur`Fri`Sat`Sun
Weekday Frequency: m
Saturday Frequency: m
Avg Paid Circ: 8292
Avg Free Circ: 146
Audit Company: AAM
Audit Date: 9 07 2020
Pressroom Equipment: Lines – 3-G/Community single width 1984; 7-G/Headliner double width (offset, open fountain, 4 1/2 deck) 1984; 8-Didde/Web single width 1997; Press Drive – 4-GE/150LP motor; Folders – 2-Regent/2:1, 1-G/506, 1-G/Jaws; Pasters –G/Auto.
Mailroom Equipment: Counter Stackers – 1-Id, 2-QWI/350; Inserters & Stuffers – KAN/760 Inserters, 1-KAN/4-head Multifeeder; Tying Machines – 1-OVL/JP-80, 2/Dynaric; Address Machine – 1-/Scitex Ink Jet;
Buisness Equipment: HP/3000 937LX
Classified Equipment: Hardware – Compaq/Proliant 2500; Printers – 1-HP/4000N, HP/2567, 2-HP/5 si;
Classified Software: SII/Sys 25, AT/Enterprise 1.411.
Editorial Equipment: Hardware – Compaq/Proliant 3000; Printers – HP/Laser Jet 4000
Editorial Software: DPS/DBEdit.
Production Equipment: Hardware – 2-Nu/Flip Top, 3-Nat, 1-W, 1-Pre Press/Panther Pro 46 Imagesetter, 1-Pre Press/Panther Pro Imagesetter 5300W, 1-Pre Press/Panther Pro 46115; Cameras – 2-C; Scanners – APP/Mac, PixelCraft/Pro Imager 8000
Production Software: DPS DB Edit.
Total Circulation: 9196

AMARILLO

AMARILLO GLOBE-NEWS

Corporate/Parent Company: Gannett
Publication Street Address: 600 S. Tyler, Ste. 103
City: Amarillo
State: TX
Publication Website: www.amarillo.com
Postal Code: 79101-3424
Office phone: (806) 376-4488
General E-mail: bmills@amarillo.com
Publisher Name: Belinda Wheeler Mills
Publisher Email: bmills@amarillo.com
Publisher Phone: (806) 345-3373
Editor Name: Jill Nevels-Haun
Editor Email: jnevels-haun@amarillo.com
Editor Phone: (806) 345-3204
Advertising Executive Name: Belinda Wheeler Mills
Advertising Executive Email: bmills@amarillo.com
Advertising Executive Phone: (806) 345-3373
Year Established: 1909
Delivery Methods:
 Mail`Newsstand`Carrier`Racks
Mechanical specifications: Type page 13 x 21 1/2; E - 6 cols, 2 1/16, 1/8 between; A - 6 cols, 2 1/16, 1/8 between; C - 10 cols, 1 3/16, 1/8 between.
Published Days: Mon`Tues`Wed`Thur`Fri`Sat`Sun
Weekday Frequency: m
Saturday Frequency: m
Avg Paid Circ: 10127
Avg Free Circ: 2058
Audit Company: AAM
Audit Date: 11 07 2019
Pressroom Equipment: Lines – 6-G/Metro (3 half decks) 1979; Folders – G/3:1; Reels & Stands – 6;
Mailroom Equipment: Counter Stackers – 4-QWI/300; Inserters & Stuffers – 2-GMA/SLS 1000 18:1; Tying Machines – 4-Dynaric/NP-2, 2-Dynaric/Turntable; Wrapping Singles – 2-QWI/Cobra wraps; Control System – PMS; Address Machine – Wm.;
Buisness Equipment: 4-IBM/Sys II, 10-Memorex/Telex 11918
Buisness Software: Lotus 1-2-3, WordPerfect
Classified Equipment: Hardware – APP/Mac;
Classified Software: DTI.
Editorial Equipment: Hardware – 32-Gateway/2000, 13-APP/Mac; Printers – Okidata/Microline 320
Editorial Software: MPS.
Production Equipment: Hardware – AG/Accuset 1000, 1-Nu/Flip Top, AG/Accuset 1500, Xante; Cameras – 2-C/Spartan III; Scanners – AG/Horizon, 4-Microtek/Scanmaker E6
Production Software: DTI/Adobe Indesign 3.1.
Total Circulation: 18598

ATHENS

ATHENS DAILY REVIEW

Corporate/Parent Company: CNHI, LLC
Publication Street Address: 201 S Prairieville St
City: Athens
State: TX
Publication Website: www.athensreview.com
Postal Code: 75751-2541
Office phone: (903) 675-5626
General E-mail: adrretail@athensreview.com
Publisher Name: Lange Svehlak
Publisher Email: publisher@athensreview.com
Editor Name: Michael Kormos
Editor Email: editor@athensreview.com
Advertising Executive Name: Cary Reeve
Advertising Executive Email: creeve@athensreview.com
Year Established: 1901
Delivery Methods: Mail`Racks
Published Days: Tues`Wed`Thur`Fri`Sat
Weekday Frequency: e
Saturday Frequency: m
Avg Paid Circ: 4400
Audit Company: Sworn/Estimate/Non-Audited
Audit Date: 7 12 2019
Pressroom Equipment: Lines – 6-HI/V-15A (upper former);
Mailroom Equipment: Tying Machines – 2/Bu; Address Machine – 1-KR/215 (with 211).;
Classified Equipment: Hardware – Baseview/Mac;
Classified Software: Baseview.
Editorial Equipment: Hardware – APP/Mac
Editorial Software: Baseview.
Production Equipment: Cameras – 1-Acti/183
Production Software: QPS/QuarkXPress8
Total Circulation: 4400

AUSTIN

AUSTIN AMERICAN-STATESMAN

Corporate/Parent Company: Gannett
Publication Street Address: 305 S Congress Ave
City: Austin
State: TX
Publication Website: www.statesman.com
Postal Code: 78704-1200
Office phone: (512) 445-4040
General E-mail: advertising@statesmanmedia.com
Publisher Name: Patrick Dorsey
Publisher Email: publisher@statesman.com
Publisher Phone: (512) 445-3555
Editor Name: John Bridges
Editor Email: jbridges@statesman.com
Editor Phone: (512) 912-2952
Advertising Executive Name: Scott Pompe
Advertising Executive Email: spompe@statesman.com
Advertising Executive Phone: (512) 445-3715
Year Established: 1871

U.S. Daily Newspapers

I-115

Delivery Methods: Carrier`Racks
Mechanical specifications: Type page 12 1/2 x 21; E - 6 cols, 2, 1/6 between; A - 6 cols, 2, 1/6 between; C - 10 cols, 1 1/5, 1/9 between.
Published Days: Mon`Tues`Wed`Thur`Fri`Sat`Sun
Weekday Frequency: m
Saturday Frequency: m
Avg Paid Circ: 83765
Audit Company: AAM
Audit Date: 21 04 2020
Pressroom Equipment: Lines – 9-G/Metroliner double width (5 half decks) 1981; 9-G/Metroliner double width (5 half decks) 1981; 9-G/Metroliner double width (5 half decks) 1984, KBA/(2 Towers); 7-KBA/Towers (43 Couples); Folders – 4-G/3:2, 1-G/2:5:5;
Mailroom Equipment: Counter Stackers – 9-QWI/351, 3-HL/Monitor; Inserters & Stuffers – 1-S/1472, 1-S/1372, 1-GMA/SLS 2000 30:2, 1-GMA/SLS 1000 14:1; Tying Machines – 9-QWI/NS45 Strap, 2/Oval Strap; Address Machine – 2-Scitex.;
Buisness Equipment: 1-IBM/7060-H30, Sun/3500
Buisness Software: Microsoft/Windows XP, Microsoft/NT, Lawson
Classified Equipment: Hardware – AT; Ad Fast/Ad Fax (Future Tense), Ad On Time; Printers – HP;
Classified Software: AT.
Editorial Equipment: Hardware – APP/Mac, Sun/Enterprise 4000; Printers – HP
Editorial Software: DTI/PageSpeed, DTI/SpeedPlanner.
Production Equipment: Hardware – 2-BKY, 2-WL/Lith-X-Pozer III, 1-GJ/550; Cameras – 1-C/Newspager I; Scanners – 1-Nikon/Pro Imager 8000, 1-Epson/1640
Production Software: DTI/AdSpeed 5.5, DTI/ImageSpeed 4.3, DTI/PageSpeed, DTI/Speed Planner 4.3.
Total Circulation: 91705

BAYTOWN

THE BAYTOWN SUN

Corporate/Parent Company: Southern Newspapers Inc.
Publication Street Address: 1301 Memorial Dr
City: Baytown
State: TX
Publication Website: http://baytownsun.com/
Postal Code: 77520
Office phone: (281) 422-8302
General E-mail: customerservice@baytownsun.com
Publisher Name: Carol Skewes
Publisher Email: carol.skewes@baytownsun.com
Publisher Phone: (281) 425-8000
Advertising Executive Name: Dean West
Advertising Executive Email: dean.west@baytownsun.com
Advertising Executive Phone: (281) 425-8009
Year Established: 1922
Delivery Methods:
Mail`Newsstand`Carrier`Racks
Own Printing Facility?: Y
Commercial printers?: N
Mechanical specifications: Type page 12 1/2 x 21; E - 6 cols, 2 1/16, 1/8 between; A - 6 cols, 2 1/16, 1/8 between; C - 9 cols, 1 5/16, 1/8 between.
Published Days: Tues`Wed`Thur`Fri`Sun
Weekday Frequency: m
Saturday Frequency: m
Avg Paid Circ: 3460
Avg Free Circ: 2016
Audit Company: AAM
Audit Date: 23 10 2019
Classified Equipment: Printers – APP/Mac LaserWriter II NTX;
Classified Software: Mk/Proprietary.
Editorial Equipment: Hardware – Mk/4000, 13-Mk/AT/APP/Mac Quadra 700; Printers – APP/Mac LaserWriter II NTX
Editorial Software: Mk/Proprietary.
Production Equipment: Hardware – APP/Mac LaserWriter II NTX; Cameras – 1-C/Spartan III.
Total Circulation: 5804

BEAUMONT

THE BEAUMONT ENTERPRISE

Corporate/Parent Company: Hearst Communications Inc.
Publication Street Address: 380 Main St
City: Beaumont
State: TX
Publication Website: www.beaumontenterprise.com
Postal Code: 77701-2331
Office phone: (409) 880-0773
General E-mail: dvalentine@beaumontenterprise.com
Publisher Name: Clarice Touhey
Publisher Phone: (409) 838-2898
Editor Name: Ronnie Crocker
Editor Phone: (409) 838-2801
Advertising Executive Name: Jay Wilson
Advertising Executive Phone: (409) 838-2824
Year Established: 1880
Delivery Methods:
Mail`Newsstand`Carrier`Racks
Own Printing Facility?: Y
Commercial printers?: N
Mechanical specifications: Type page 11 1/2 x 21 1/2; E - 6 cols, 1 3/4, 1/8 between; A - 6 cols, 1 3/4, 1/8 between; C - 9 cols, 1 1/6, 1/8 between.
Published Days: Mon`Tues`Wed`Thur`Fri`Sat`Sun
Weekday Frequency: m
Saturday Frequency: m
Avg Paid Circ: 10417
Avg Free Circ: 169
Audit Company: AAM
Audit Date: 11 03 2019
Pressroom Equipment: Lines – 9-G/Cosmo 3502 (double balloon); Pasters –7-G/Automatic.
Mailroom Equipment: Counter Stackers – 2-QWI/300; Inserters & Stuffers – 1-S/72P, HI/12 Hopper; Tying Machines – 2-Dynaric/NPI; Wrapping Singles – 2-Id.;
Buisness Software: ADMARC, Discus
Classified Equipment: Hardware – APT, Gateway, ALR/8200; Gateway/PC E1000; Printers – IBM/Network 17 printer;
Classified Software: APT.
Editorial Equipment: Hardware – APT, Gateway, ALR/8200/Gateway/PC 3200, Gateway/PC 4200; Printers – HP/5000
Editorial Software: APT.
Production Equipment: Hardware – 2-ECR/Knockout (Harlequin RIP), 1-Nu/Flip Top FT40UPNS, 2-C/OL Conveyor System
Production Software: QPS/QuarkXPress 4.0.
Note: High School Athletic Awards SoutheastTexas.com
Total Circulation: 26424

BIG SPRING

BIG SPRING HERALD

Corporate/Parent Company: Horizon Publications Inc.
Publication Street Address: 710 Scurry Street
City: Big Spring
State: TX
Publication Website: www.bigspringherald.com
Postal Code: 79720
Office phone: (432) 263-7331
General E-mail: editor@bigspringherald.com
Publisher Name: Rick Nunez
Publisher Email: publisher@bigspringherald.com
Editor Name: Amanda Duforat
Editor Email: editor@bigspringherald.com
Advertising Executive Name: Angela Lance
Advertising Executive Email: angela@bigspringherald.com
Year Established: 1904
Delivery Methods:
Mail`Newsstand`Carrier`Racks
Own Printing Facility?: Y
Commercial printers?: Y
Mechanical specifications: Type page 12 1/2 x 21 1/2; E - 6 cols, 1 3/4, 1/16 between; A - 6 cols, 1 3/4, 1/16 between; C - 9 cols, 1 1/16 between.
Published Days: Mon`Tues`Wed`Thur`Fri`Sun
Weekday Frequency: e
Avg Paid Circ: 4337

Audit Company: Sworn/Estimate/Non-Audited
Audit Date: 7 12 2019
Pressroom Equipment: Lines – 8-G/Community 1974;
Mailroom Equipment: Tying Machines – Delta/Strapping AQ7.;
Buisness Equipment: 1-IBM/PC-XT, IBM/PC-AT, 1-IBM/PC
Buisness Software: PBS
Classified Equipment: Hardware – 2-APP/Power Mac 180-35; Printers – APP/Mac LaserWriter 16-600PS;
Classified Software: Baseview.
Editorial Equipment: Hardware – APP/Mac, 10-APP/Mac Performa 6200/1-PowerBook/190 Laptop, Umax/1200 Scanner, 1-Polaroid/SprintScan 35-LE; Printers – 1-APP/Mac 16/1600 PS, 1-Laserwriter/II
Editorial Software: QPS/QuarkXPress, Adobe/Illustrator, Aldus/FreeHand, Baseview/Ne
Production Equipment: Hardware – Roconex; Cameras – 1-R/500.
Total Circulation: 4337

BORGER

BORGER NEWS-HERALD

Corporate/Parent Company: Horizon Publications Inc.
Publication Street Address: P.O. Box 5130
City: Borger
State: TX
Publication Website: www.borgernewsherald.com
Postal Code: 79008
Office phone: (806) 273-5611
General E-mail: publisher@borgernewsherald.com
Publisher Name: Robin Dickerson
Editor Name: Courtney Marrs
Editor Email: editor@borgernewsherald.com
Advertising Executive Email: advertising@borgernewsherald.com
Year Established: 1926
Delivery Methods:
Mail`Newsstand`Carrier`Racks
Own Printing Facility?: Y
Commercial printers?: Y
Mechanical specifications: Type page 13 x 21 1/2; E - 6 cols, 2 1/16, 1/8 between; A - 6 cols, 2 1/16, 1/8 between; C - 8 cols, 1 1/2, 1/8 between.
Published Days: Mon`Tues`Wed`Thur`Fri`Sun
Weekday Frequency: m
Saturday Frequency: m
Avg Paid Circ: 2000
Audit Company: Sworn/Estimate/Non-Audited
Audit Date: 7 12 2019
Pressroom Equipment: Lines – 6-G;
Mailroom Equipment: Tying Machines – 1-Bu/77011.;
Buisness Equipment: 1-IBM/PS2 MODEL 30, 1-Unisys/5000-50
Classified Software: Baseview.
Editorial Software: Baseview.
Production Equipment: Hardware – 1-Nu; Cameras – Acti; Scanners – APP/Mac Scanner.
Total Circulation: 2000

BROWNSVILLE

THE BROWNSVILLE HERALD

Corporate/Parent Company: AIM Media
Publication Street Address: 1135 E Van Buren St
City: Brownsville
State: TX
Publication Website: https://www.brownsvilleherald.com/
Postal Code: 78520
Office phone: (956) 542-4301
General E-mail: fescobedo@brownsvilleherald.com
Publisher Name: Frank Escobedo
Publisher Email: fescobedo@brownsvilleherald.com
Publisher Phone: (956) 982-6646
Editor Name: Ryan Henry
Editor Email: rhenry@brownsvilleherald.com
Editor Phone: (956) 982-6620

Advertising Executive Name: Linda Medrano
Advertising Executive Email: lmedrano@brownsvilleherald.com
Advertising Executive Phone: (956) 982-6651
Delivery Methods: Newsstand`Carrier`Racks
Mechanical specifications: Type page 13 x 21; E - 6 cols, 2 1/16, 1/8 between; A - 6 cols, 2 1/16, 1/8 between; C - 10 cols, 1 1/4, 1/16 between.
Published Days: Mon`Tues`Wed`Thur`Fri`Sat`Sun
Weekday Frequency: m
Saturday Frequency: m
Avg Paid Circ: 16994
Audit Company: AAM
Audit Date: 23 10 2019
Pressroom Equipment: Lines – 6-HI/Cotrell 845; 4-HI/Cotrell 845; Folders – 2-HI/2:1.;
Mailroom Equipment: Tying Machines – 2-Si; Address Machine – 1/Ch.;
Buisness Equipment: 1-IBM
Classified Equipment: Hardware – APT.;
Editorial Equipment: Hardware – APT.
Production Equipment: Hardware – 2-Tegra/Varityper, Nu/Lithoplate; Cameras – 1-C.
Total Circulation: 8181

BRYAN

THE EAGLE

Corporate/Parent Company: Lee Enterprises
Publication Street Address: 1729 Briarcrest Dr
City: Bryan
State: TX
Publication Website: www.theeagle.com
Postal Code: 77802-2712
Office phone: (979) 776-4444
General E-mail: news@theeagle.com
Publisher Name: Crystal Dupre
Editor Name: Darren Benson
Editor Email: darren.benson@theeagle.com
Editor Phone: (979) 731-4653
Advertising Executive Email: advertising@theeagle.com
Advertising Executive Phone: (979) 731-4738
Year Established: 1889
Delivery Methods:
Mail`Newsstand`Carrier`Racks
Own Printing Facility?: Y
Commercial printers?: Y
Mechanical specifications: Type page 11 5/8 x 21 1/2; E - 6 cols, 2 1/16, 1/8 between; A - 6 cols, 2 1/16, 1/8 between; C - 9 cols, 1 3/8, 1/16 between.
Published Days: Mon`Tues`Wed`Thur`Fri`Sat`Sun
Weekday Frequency: m
Saturday Frequency: m
Avg Paid Circ: 10785
Avg Free Circ: 2163
Audit Company: AAM
Audit Date: 16 07 2018
Pressroom Equipment: Lines – 9-G/Urbanite single width 1979; Press Drive – Fin/125 h.p. motor.;
Mailroom Equipment: Counter Stackers – 2-Id/NS660 Counter Stacker, 1-QWI/400; Inserters & Stuffers – 1-NP/1372; Tying Machines – 1-MLN/ML2EE, MLN/SP 330, Sterling/GP30C; Address Machine – 1-KR/12.;
Buisness Equipment: HP/3000, PC Network
Buisness Software: PeopleSoft, Microsoft/Office
Classified Equipment: Hardware, APP/Mac, APP/Mac G3, APP/iMac 400SE; 1-APP/Mac Server; Printers – HP/LaserJet 4MV;
Classified Software: Baseview/Ad Manager Pro 2.2.
Editorial Equipment: Hardware – Ethernet, Printers – Dell PC, HP/LaserJet 4MV, HP/LJ 5000
Editorial Software: QPS/QuarkXPress 4.11, Adobe/Photoshop 5.5, Baseview/NewsEdit Pro 3.2, Baseview/Ique Server 3.3.
Production Equipment: Hardware – 1-Nu/FT40 APNS, 1-Douthitt/Gemini 29X40, 1-Nu/FT40 APNS; Cameras – 1-C/Spartan II; Scanners – HP/ScanJet 4c, Nikon/1000-35, Lf/Leafscan 35, AII/APS Scan 3750, Microtek/ScanMaker 9600XL, AU/Copydot
Production Software: QPS/QuarkXPress 4.11, Adobe/PageM
Total Circulation: 13901

CLEBURNE

CLEBURNE TIMES-REVIEW

Corporate/Parent Company: CNHI, LLC
Publication Street Address: 108 S Anglin St
City: Cleburne
State: TX
Publication Website: www.cleburnetimesreview.com
Postal Code: 76031-5602
Office phone: (817) 645-2441
General E-mail: editor@trcle.com
Publisher Name: Lisa Chappell
Publisher Email: lchappell@cnhi.com
Publisher Phone: (817) 645-2441, Ext : 2301
Editor Name: Monica Faram
Editor Email: editor@trcle.com
Editor Phone: (817) 645-2441, Ext : 2338
Advertising Executive Name: Renae Alexander
Advertising Executive Email: ralexander@trcle.com
Advertising Executive Phone: (817) 645-2441, Ext : 2357
Year Established: 1904
Delivery Methods: Mail`Newsstand`Racks
Own Printing Facility?: N
Commercial printers?: N
Mechanical specifications: Type page 10 1/4 x 21 1/4; E - 6 cols, 1 9/16, 1/8 between; A - 6 cols, 1 9/16, 1/8 between; C - 6 cols, 1 9/16, 1/8 between.
Published Days: Tues`Wed`Thur`Fri`Sat
Weekday Frequency: e
Saturday Frequency: e
Avg Paid Circ: 2400
Audit Company: Sworn/Estimate/Non-Audited
Audit Date: 7 12 2019
Pressroom Equipment: Lines – 6-G/Community 1976;
Mailroom Equipment: Tying Machines – 1/MLN; Address Machine – Wm.;
Buisness Equipment: PC, DOS
Buisness Software: Brainworks
Classified Equipment: Hardware – APP/Power Mac;
Classified Software: Baseview/Ad Manager Pro.
Editorial Equipment: Hardware – APP/Power Mac; Printers – Pre Press/Panthers, HP/11x17 LaserPrinter
Editorial Software: Baseview/NewsEdit Pro.
Production Equipment: Hardware – Pre Press/VT1200, Adobe/Photoshop 4.0.1, Pre Press/Panther Pro; Cameras – AG, Epson/Digital, Kk/Digital; Scanners – Umax/Vista 12
Production Software: Indesign
Total Circulation: 2400

CLUTE

THE BRAZOSPORT FACTS

Publication Street Address: 720 S Main St
City: Clute
State: TX
Publication Website: http://thefacts.com/
Postal Code: 77531
Office phone: (979) 265-7411
Year Established: 1913
Delivery Methods: Mail`Newsstand`Carrier`Racks
Own Printing Facility?: Y
Commercial printers?: Y
Mechanical specifications: Type page 13 x 21; E - 6 cols, 2 1/16, 1/8 between; A - 6 cols, 2 1/16, 1/8 between; C - 9 cols, 1 3/8, 1/16 between.
Published Days: Mon`Tues`Wed`Thur`Fri`Sat`Sun
Weekday Frequency: m
Saturday Frequency: m
Avg Paid Circ: 12457
Avg Free Circ: 1674
Audit Company: AAM
Audit Date: 30 03 2015
Pressroom Equipment: Lines – G/Urbanite 35 1993; Press Drive – A/C Drive Motors w/ Belt to Drive Shaft; Folders – G/500; Reels & Stands – Roll/Stands.
Mailroom Equipment: Counter Stackers – HL/Monitor; Inserters & Stuffers – HI; Tying Machines – MLN; Address Machine – Miller, Bevgo.;
Buisness Software: Quattro/Pro, FileMaker Pro
Classified Equipment: Hardware – 7-APP/Power Mac 7300, 1-APP/Power Mac 7100, 1-APP/Mac Quadra 650; Printers – APP/Mac LaserWriter IIq, TI/Omni 800, LaserMaster/Unity, APP/Mac LaserWriter 16/600;
Classified Software: Baseview, Adobe/Photoshop, Adobe/Illustrator.
Editorial Equipment: Hardware – 7-PC, 5-APP/Mac Centris 650, 2-APP/Mac IIc, 1-APP/Power Mac 8500, APP/Mac Quadra, 2-APP/Power Mac 7100, 1-APP/Power Mac 8600/Lf/AP Leaf Picture Desk, 2-Umax/Scanner, 1-Nikon/Coolscan 1000, 1-APP/Mac 1400 Laptop; Printers – APP/Mac
Production Equipment: Hardware – APP/Mac LaserWriter IIq, APP/Mac LaserWriter Pro 630, ECR/3850, 2-APP/Mac LaserWriter 16/600PS; Cameras – C/Spartan III with Transport; Scanners – ECR/Autokon 1000
Production Software: QPS/QuarkXPress 3.32.
Total Circulation: 14131

CONROE

THE COURIER

Corporate/Parent Company: Gannett
Publication Street Address: 100 Ave. A,
City: Conroe
State: TX
Publication Website: yourconroenews.com
Postal Code: 77301
Office phone: 281-378-1000
Editor Name: Alan Fossler
Editor Email: alan.fossler@chron.com
Editor Phone: 936-521-3400
Advertising Executive Name: Richard Davis
Advertising Executive Email: richard.davis@hcnonline.com
Advertising Executive Phone: "936-521-3451"

THE COURIER OF MONTGOMERY COUNTY

Corporate/Parent Company: Hearst Corp.
Publication Street Address: 100 Avenue A
City: Conroe
State: TX
Publication Website: www.yourconroenews.com
Postal Code: 77301-2946
Office phone: (281) 378-1950
General E-mail: bmiller-fergerson@hcnonline.com
Publisher Name: Alan Fossler
Publisher Email: alan.fossler@chron.com
Publisher Phone: (936) 521-3400
Editor Name: Catherine Dominguez
Editor Email: cdominguez@hcnonline.com
Editor Phone: (936) 521-3428
Year Established: 1892
Delivery Methods: Carrier`Racks
Own Printing Facility?: N
Commercial printers?: N
Mechanical specifications: 10.388″ x 20.5″
Published Days: Mon`Tues`Wed`Thur`Fri`Sat`Sun
Weekday Frequency: m
Saturday Frequency: m
Avg Paid Circ: 9244
Avg Free Circ: 10936
Audit Company: AAM
Audit Date: 15 03 2015
Pressroom Equipment: Lines – 10-G/C;
Mailroom Equipment: Counter Stackers – 1/BG; Inserters & Stuffers – MM/227-Z; Tying Machines – 2/Malow.;
Buisness Equipment: IBM/MS-DOS
Classified Equipment: Hardware – IBM/MS-DOS; Printers – HP;
Classified Software: Dewar.
Editorial Equipment: Hardware – IBM/MS-DOS, APP/Mac G3; Printers – APP
Editorial Software: Microsoft/Word, QPS/QuarkXPress 3.32, Adobe/Photoshop.
Production Equipment: Hardware – 1-Nu, 1-BKY; Cameras – 1-C/Spartan III; Scanners – SCREEN/1350
Production Software: Dewar.
Total Circulation: 20180

CORPUS CHRISTI

COASTAL BEND LEGAL & BUSINESS NEWS

Publication Street Address: P.O. Box 270607
City: Corpus Christi
State: TX
Publication Website: cblnews.com
Postal Code: 78427
Office phone: 361-937-4907
General E-mail: info@cblnews.com
Editor Name: Kim Gutierrez
Editor Email: cblnews@cblnews.com
Advertising Executive Name: Sam Gutierrez

CORPUS CHRISTI CALLER-TIMES

Corporate/Parent Company: Gannett
Publication Street Address: 820 N Lower Broadway St
City: Corpus Christi
State: TX
Publication Website: www.caller.com
Postal Code: 78401-2025
Office phone: (361) 884-2011
General E-mail: newstips@caller.com
Editor Name: Mary Ann Cavazos Beckett
Editor Email: maryann.beckett@caller.com
Year Established: 1883
Mechanical specifications: Type page 11 1/2 x 20 5/8; E - 6 cols, 1 5/6, 1/8 between; A - 6 cols, 1 5/6, 1/8 between; C - 10 cols, 1 1/16, 1/16 between.
Published Days: Mon`Tues`Wed`Thur`Fri`Sat`Sun
Weekday Frequency: m
Saturday Frequency: m
Avg Paid Circ: 18198
Avg Free Circ: 288
Audit Company: AAM
Audit Date: 28 09 2018
Pressroom Equipment: Lines – 9-G/Metroliner double width (offset; 5 half decks) 1994; 8-Tandemer/Narrow Web 1992; 10-HI/V15; Press Drive – Fin/Incom; Folders – 1-G/3:2; Pasters –G/AutoReels & Stands – 9; Control System – G/PCS.;
Mailroom Equipment: Counter Stackers – 3-HL/Monitor, 2-HL/Monitor; Inserters & Stuffers – 1-GMA/SLS 1000 10:2, 1-KAN/7:1; Tying Machines – 2/MLN, 2-/Dynaric; Address Machine – 3-Wm/III, 2-/BH, 1-/Ink Jet Printer,;
Buisness Equipment: HP/3000-947
Buisness Software: GEAC 7016, MCBA 2.0, GEAC/CIS 6.06, GEAC/Aim
Classified Equipment: Hardware – HP/Net Server LH4; Konica/K550 Processor; Printers – HP/LaserJet 5si;
Classified Software: CText.
Editorial Equipment: Hardware – PC P350; Printers – HP/5si
Editorial Software: Microsoft/NT, SQL/DPS Editorial.
Production Equipment: Hardware – 2-Konica/Powermatic 66f, Pre Press/Panther Pro, 1-W/Auto Unit; Cameras – 1-ECR/8400, 1-B/2000, 2-C/Spartan III; Scanners – ScanView/ScanMate 5000, Kk/RFS 2035, Umax/Mirage 16L, Umax/Super Vista S-12
Production Software: DPS/Ad Tracker.
Total Circulation: 24842

CORSICANA

CORSICANA DAILY SUN

Corporate/Parent Company: CNHI, LLC
Publication Street Address: 405 E Collin St
City: Corsicana
State: TX
Publication Website: www.corsicanadailysun.com
Postal Code: 75110-5325
Office phone: (903) 872-3931
General E-mail: dailysun@corsicanadailysun.com
Publisher Name: Jake Mienk
Publisher Email: jmienk@corsicanadailysun.com
Editor Name: Michael Kormos
Editor Email: mkormos@corsicanadailysun.com
Advertising Executive Name: Barb Vander Wyst
Advertising Executive Email: barb@corsicanadailysun.com
Year Established: 1895
Delivery Methods: Mail
Own Printing Facility?: N
Commercial printers?: Y
Mechanical specifications: Type page 13 3/4 x 21 1/2; E - 6 cols, 2 1/16, 1/8 between; A - 6 cols, 2 1/16, 1/8 between; C - 9 cols, 1 3/8, 1/16 between.
Published Days: Tues`Wed`Thur`Fri`Sat
Weekday Frequency: m
Saturday Frequency: m
Avg Paid Circ: 5690
Audit Company: Sworn/Estimate/Non-Audited
Audit Date: 7 12 2019
Pressroom Equipment: Lines – 5-G/Urbanite.;
Mailroom Equipment: Counter Stackers – 1/BG; Tying Machines – 2-/MLN; Address Machine – 1-/KR.;
Buisness Equipment: 1-MDS, 1-HP, 3-IBM/AT
Classified Equipment: Hardware – APP/Mac.;
Editorial Equipment: Hardware – 7-APP/Mac; Printers – 1-APP/Mac LaserWriter IIq, 1-APP/Mac LaserWriter IIf
Editorial Software: Baseview/NewsEdit, QPS/QuarkXPress.
Production Equipment: Hardware – 1-Nat/225; Cameras – SCREEN, 1-C.
Total Circulation: 5690

DALLAS

THE DALLAS MORNING NEWS

Corporate/Parent Company: A.H. Belo
Publication Street Address: 1954 Commerce Street
City: Dallas
State: TX
Publication Website: www.dallasnews.com
Postal Code: 75201
Office phone: (214) 745-8383
General E-mail: customercare@dallasnews.com
Editor Name: Keith Campbell
Editor Email: kcampbell@dallasnews.com
Year Established: 1885
Delivery Methods: Mail`Newsstand`Carrier`Racks
Own Printing Facility?: Y
Commercial printers?: Y
Mechanical specifications: Type page 11 5/8 x 21; E - 6 cols, 1 5/6, 1/8 between; A - 6 cols, 1 5/6, 1/8 between; C - 10 cols, 1 3/32, 1/16 between.
Published Days: Mon`Tues`Wed`Thur`Fri`Sat`Sun
Weekday Frequency: m
Saturday Frequency: m
Avg Paid Circ: 202480
Avg Free Circ: 60000
Audit Company: AAM
Audit Date: 30 07 2019
Pressroom Equipment: Lines – 1-TKS/Offset double width 1985; 1-TKS/Offset double width 1985; 1-TKS/Offset double width 1987; 1-TKS/Offset double width 1988; 1-TKS/Offset double width 1989; 1-TKS/Offset double width 1990; 1-Wifag/Offset double width 2000; Kodak Platemaking Imagers and Processors, Nela Benders and Sortation
Pressroom Software: ABB Press Controls Copytrack
Mailroom Equipment: Counter stackers – 20 Quipp 350, 3 Quipp 400, 2 Quipp 500; Inserters & Stuffers – 4-GMA/SLS 1000A 28:2, 1 GMA/SLS 2000 8:2, 1 GMA/SLS 2000 14:2, 1 GMA/SLS 2000 18:2, 1 GMA/SLS 2000 8:2; Collators - 2 Prim-Hall 80 station; Tying Machines - 28 Dynaric NP-2, 6 Dynaric 5000, 11 Dynaric 5000X
Mailroom Software: Control System - 6 Fast Technology Insert Controls, 2 Quipp Newscom Insert Controls; 1 Winlincs Insert Controls; Burt planning
Buisness Equipment: Dell Servers - Windows, Unix, ESX
Buisness Software: PeopleSoft, Hyperion,

U.S. Daily Newspapers

Essbase, Kronos, Cognos, MasterTax, Workday
Classified Equipment: Dell Servers - Linux, Windows
Classified Software: Newscycle Adbase
Editorial Equipment: Dell Servers - Windows, Unix
Editorial Software: CCI Newsgate, CCI Escenic, CNI Addesk, MerlinOne
Total Circulation: 256199

DEL RIO

DEL RIO NEWS-HERALD

Corporate/Parent Company: Southern Newspapers Inc.
Publication Street Address: 2205 N Bedell Ave
City: Del Rio
State: TX
Publication Website: www.delrionewsherald.com
Postal Code: 78840-8007
Office phone: (830) 775-1551
General E-mail: support@delrionewsherald.com
Publisher Name: David Rupkalvis
Publisher Email: david.rupkalvis@delrionewsherald.com
Publisher Phone: (830) 775-1551, Ext : 245
Editor Name: Ruben Cantu
Editor Email: ruben.cantu@delrionewsherald.com
Editor Phone: (830) 775-1551, Ext : 282
Advertising Executive Name: Xochitl Arteaga
Advertising Executive Email: xochitl.arteaga@delrionewsherald.com
Advertising Executive Phone: (830) 775-1551, Ext : 250
Year Established: 1929
Delivery Methods: Mail`Newsstand`Carrier`Racks
Own Printing Facility?: Y
Commercial printers?: Y
Mechanical specifications: Type page 13 x 21 1/2; E - 6 cols, 2 1/16, 1/8 between; A - 6 cols, 2 1/16, 1/8 between; C - 9 cols, 1 3/8, 1/16 between.
Published Days: Tues`Wed`Thur`Fri`Sun
Weekday Frequency: m
Avg Paid Circ: 2252
Avg Free Circ: 306
Audit Company: AAM
Audit Date: 23 10 2019
Pressroom Equipment: Lines – 7-G/Community; Folders – 1-G/Community.;
Mailroom Equipment: Tying Machines – MLN; Address Machine – 1/KR.;
Buisness Equipment: IBM, AT, XT, PC
Buisness Software: pbs,
Classified Equipment: Hardware – Mk.;
Classified Software: newscycle
Editorial Equipment: Hardware – Mk/1100 System.
Editorial Software: newscycle,adobe
Production Equipment: Hardware – 1-COM/Computype II, 1-COM/4961, 2-COM/8400; Cameras – 1-C/Spartan III.
Production Software: newscycle,adobe
Total Circulation: 2486

DENTON

DENTON RECORD-CHRONICLE

Corporate/Parent Company: A.H. Belo Corporation
Publication Street Address: 3555 Duchess
City: Denton
State: TX
Publication Website: www.dentonrc.com
Postal Code: 76205
Office phone: (940) 387-3811
General E-mail: feedback@dentonrc.com
Publisher Name: Bill Patterson
Publisher Email: bpatterson@dentonrc.com
Publisher Phone: (940) 566-6808
Editor Name: Sean McCrory
Editor Email: sean.mccrory@dentonrc.com
Editor Phone: (940) 566-6879
Advertising Executive Name: Shawn Reneau
Advertising Executive Email: sreneau@dentonrc.com
Advertising Executive Phone: (940) 566-6843
Year Established: 1903
Delivery Methods: Carrier
Own Printing Facility?: N
Commercial printers?: N
Mechanical specifications: Type page 13 x 21 1/2; E - 6 cols, 2 1/16, 1/6 between; A - 6 cols, 2 1/16, 1/6 between; C - 9 cols, 1 3/8, 1/8 between.
Published Days: Mon`Tues`Wed`Thur`Fri`Sat`Sun
Weekday Frequency: m
Saturday Frequency: m
Avg Paid Circ: 7521
Avg Free Circ: 2756
Audit Company: AAM
Audit Date: 31 03 2015
Buisness Equipment: Atex
Classified Equipment: Atex
Editorial Equipment: CCI Newsgate 3
Production Equipment: Apple/Indesign
Total Circulation: 10277

DESOTO

FOCUS DAILY NEWS

Publication Street Address: 1337 Marilyn Ave
City: Desoto
State: TX
Publication Website: www.focusdailynews.com
Postal Code: 75115-6414
Office phone: (972) 223-2998
General E-mail: focusnews@wans.net
Editor Email: editor@focusdailynews.com
Year Established: 1987
Delivery Methods: Newsstand`Carrier`Racks
Own Printing Facility?: Y
Commercial printers?: Y
Mechanical specifications: Type page 11 1/2 x 21; E - 6 cols, 1 3/4, between; A - 6 cols, 1 3/4, between; C - 6 cols, 1 3/4, between.
Published Days: Tues`Wed`Thur`Fri`Sun
Weekday Frequency: m
Avg Paid Circ: 37387
Audit Company: USPS
Audit Date: 12 12 2017
Pressroom Equipment: Goss Communty
Mailroom Equipment: PC
Buisness Equipment: PC
Classified Equipment: PC
Editorial Equipment: PC
Editorial Software: Quark Xpres
Production Equipment: Harlequin
Total Circulation: 37387

EL PASO

EL PASO TIMES

Corporate/Parent Company: Gannett
Publication Street Address: 500 W. Overland Ave Ste. 150
City: El Paso
State: TX
Publication Website: elpasotimes.com
Postal Code: 79901
Office phone: 915-546-6100
Editor Name: Timothy Archuleta
Editor Email: tarchuleta@elpasotimes.com
Editor Phone: (915)-546-6141
Advertising Executive Name: Sal Hernandez
Advertising Executive Email: shernandez@elpasotimes.com
Advertising Executive Phone: (915) 546-6250
Year Established: 1881
Delivery Methods: Mail`Newsstand`Carrier`Racks
Own Printing Facility?: Y
Commercial printers?: Y
Mechanical specifications: Type page 10 x 21; E - 6 cols, 1 1/3, 1/6 between; A - 6 cols, 1 1/3, 1/6 between; C - 8 cols, 1 1/6, 1/2 between.
Published Days: Mon`Tues`Wed`Thur`Fri`Sat`Sun
Weekday Frequency: m
Saturday Frequency: m
Avg Paid Circ: 17316
Audit Company: AAM
Audit Date: 11 08 2020
Pressroom Equipment: Lines – G/Metrocolor (23 couples) double width 1997; G/Metrocolor (23 couples) double width 1997; Pasters –G/Digital; Reels & Stands – CT/50; Control System – G/MPCS.;
Mailroom Equipment: Counter Stackers – 6-QWI/351; Inserters & Stuffers – GMA/5652000 24:2, GMA/562000 20:2; Tying Machines – 5-Dynaric/NP 500; Control System – GMA/SAM; Address Machine – 1-Cheshire/Labeler;
Buisness Equipment: Dell dekstops and Laptops; Canon, HP Multifunction Printers, iPad, Cisco IP Phone
Buisness Software: MS Office, JD Edwards, AdBase, Crystal, ImageNow, Outlook Soft
Classified Equipment: Dell desktops and Laptops; Canon, HP Multifunction Printers, iPads, Cisco IP Phone
Classified Software: Microsoft Office, Adbooker, Ranger Data, Crystal, Cisco Agent, Shoom, eProofs, WebToCash
Editorial Equipment: Dell desktops and Laptops; Canon, HP Multifunction Printers, iPads, Cisco IP Phone, Apple Desktop and Laptops, Microfilm Machine, Scanners, Camaras, iPhones
Editorial Software: QPS. SaxoTech, Quark, Copy Desk, Quark Express, Adobe creative suit, DC4
Production Equipment: Dell desktops and Laptops; Canon, HP Multifunction Printers, iPads, Cisco IP Phone, Apple Desktop and Laptops, Microfilm Machine, Scanners, Camaras, iPhones
Production Software: Goss, Arkitex, SAM, Cisco IP Phones, Adtrac,
Total Circulation: 21438

ENNIS

THE ENNIS DAILY NEWS

Publication Street Address: P.O. Box 100
City: Ennis
State: TX
Publication Website: www.ennisdailynews.com
Postal Code: 75120
Office phone: (972) 875-3801
General E-mail: tiffany@ennisdailynews.com
Publisher Name: Nikki Cohan
Publisher Email: nikki@ennisdailynews.com
Editor Name: Mark Warde
Editor Email: mark@ennisdailynews.com
Advertising Executive Name: Tiffany Metcalfe
Advertising Executive Email: tiffany@ennisdailynews.com
Year Established: 1891
Delivery Methods: Newsstand`Carrier`Racks
Own Printing Facility?: Y
Commercial printers?: Y
Mechanical specifications: Type page 10 x 21 1/2; E - 6 cols. .167 inch gutters.
Published Days: Tues`Wed`Thur`Fri`Sun
Weekday Frequency: e
Avg Paid Circ: 3214
Audit Company: Sworn/Estimate/Non-Audited
Audit Date: 7 12 2019
Pressroom Equipment: Lines – 6-G/Community single width; Folders – 1-G/2:1.;
Mailroom Equipment: Tying Machines – 1/Strap Tyer.;
Classified Equipment: Hardware – PC; Printers – TI/Micro Laser;
Classified Software: BMF.
Editorial Equipment: Hardware – APP/Mac; Printers – GCC/XL20/600
Editorial Software: QPS.
Production Equipment: Hardware – Reconex, 1-COM/7200; Cameras – 1-B; Scanners – AG/Snap Scan, Minolta/Quick Scan.
Total Circulation: 3214

FORT WORTH

FORT WORTH STAR-TELEGRAM

Corporate/Parent Company: McClatchy Company
Publication Street Address: 808 Throckmorton St
City: Fort Worth
State: TX
Publication Website: www.star-telegram.com
Postal Code: 76102-6315
Office phone: (800) 776-7827
General E-mail: marketguidefeedback@star-telegram.com
Publisher Name: Ryan Mote
Publisher Email: rmote@star-telegram.com
Publisher Phone: (817) 390-7454
Editor Name: Tom Johanningmeier
Editor Email: tjohanningmeier@star-telegram.com
Editor Phone: (817) 390-7383
Advertising Executive Name: Stephanie Boggins
Advertising Executive Email: sboggins@star-telegram.com
Advertising Executive Phone: (817) 390-7877
Year Established: 1906
Mechanical specifications: Type page 11 5/8 x 21 1/4; E - 6 cols, 2 1/14, 1/6 between; A - 6 cols, 2 1/14, 1/6 between; C - 6 cols, 1 1/5, 1/6 between.
Published Days: Mon`Tues`Wed`Thur`Fri`Sat`Sun
Weekday Frequency: m
Saturday Frequency: m
Avg Paid Circ: 75029
Audit Company: AAM
Audit Date: 25 09 2019
Pressroom Equipment: Lines – 11-G/Headliner (with 8 half decks) 1986, 2-G/Metro Color Tower 1999; 11-G/Headliner (with 8 half decks) 1986, 2-G/Metro Color Tower 1999; 11-G/Headliner(w/8 half decks) 1986, 2-G/Metro Color Tower 1999; 11-G/Headliner (;
Mailroom Equipment: Counter Stackers – 17-HL/Monitor, 2-QWI/351, 6-QWI/351; Inserters & Stuffers – 3-HI/72P, 2-HI/630; Tying Machines – 18-Dynaric/NP2, 3-Dynaric/Am-9000, 3/Bu; Wrapping Singles – 3-Signode/HLS; Address Machine – 2-/Ch, 1-/MM, 2-/Video jet;
Buisness Equipment: DEC, DEC/4100
Classified Equipment: Hardware – IBM/RS 6000; Printers – Lexmark;
Classified Software: CText.
Editorial Equipment: Hardware – Compaq/Pentium, Dell/Pentium; Printers – Epson, HP, Lexmark
Editorial Software: Dewar.
Production Equipment: Hardware – 4-AU/3850, 2-AU/F108, 1-AU/30 double truck, 6-Gluntz & Jensen; Cameras – 1-Acti, 1-C/New, 1-C/Marathon; Scanners – 4-Scanmate/Scanview
Production Software: QPS/QuarkXPress, Adobe/Photoshop, Adobe/Illustrator, Macromedia/Freehand.
Total Circulation: 111029

GAINESVILLE

GAINESVILLE DAILY REGISTER

Corporate/Parent Company: CNHI, LLC
Publication Street Address: 306 E California St
City: Gainesville
State: TX
Publication Website: www.gainesvilleregister.com
Postal Code: 76241
Office phone: (940) 665-5511
General E-mail: editor@gainesvilleregister.com
Publisher Name: Lisa Chappell
Publisher Phone: (940) 665-5511, Ext : 22
Editor Name: Sarah Einselen
Editor Email: editor@gainesvilleregister.com
Editor Phone: (940) 665-5511, Ext : 13
Advertising Executive Name: Barbara Martin
Advertising Executive Email: sales2@gainesvilleregister.com
Advertising Executive Phone: (940) 665-5511, Ext : 27
Year Established: 1890
Delivery Methods: Mail
Own Printing Facility?: Y
Commercial printers?: Y
Mechanical specifications: Type page 12 x 21 1/2; E - 6 cols, 1.56 inches , 1/8 between; C - 7 cols, 1.32 inches1/8 between.
Published Days: Tues`Wed`Thur`Fri`Sat
Weekday Frequency: m
Saturday Frequency: m
Avg Paid Circ: 5011
Audit Company: USPS
Audit Date: 30 09 2006
Pressroom Equipment: Lines – 24-G/

Community.;
Total Circulation: 5011

GALVESTON

THE GALVESTON COUNTY DAILY NEWS

Corporate/Parent Company: Southern Newspapers, Inc.
Publication Street Address: 8522 Teichman Rd
City: Galveston
State: TX
Publication Website: https://www.galvnews.com/
Postal Code: 77554
Office phone: (409) 683-5200
General E-mail: website.feedback@galvnews.com
Publisher Name: Leonard Woolsey
Publisher Email: leonard.woolsey@galvnews.com
Publisher Phone: (409) 683-5207
Editor Name: Michael A. Smith
Editor Email: michael.smith@galvnews.com
Editor Phone: (409) 683-5206
Advertising Executive Name: Debbie Keith
Advertising Executive Email: debbie.keith@galvnews.com
Advertising Executive Phone: (409) 683-5240
Year Established: 1842
Delivery Methods:
  Mail`Newsstand`Carrier`Racks
Own Printing Facility?: Y
Commercial printers?: Y
Mechanical specifications: Type page 13 x 21 1/2; E - 6 cols, 2 1/16, 1/8 between; A - 6 cols, 2 1/16, 1/8 between; C - 9 cols, 1 3/8, 1/16 between.
Published Days: Mon`Tues`Wed`Thur`Fri`Sat`Sun
Weekday Frequency: m
Saturday Frequency: m
Avg Paid Circ: 15007
Avg Free Circ: 932
Audit Company: AAM
Audit Date: 20 09 2017
Pressroom Equipment: Lines - 8-HI/Cotrell 845 1980; Folders - 1-HI/2:1, G/Urbanite.;
Mailroom Equipment: Counter Stackers - 1/S; Inserters & Stuffers - 1-/S; Tying Machines - 1-/MLN; Address Machine - 1-/KAN.;
Buisness Equipment: Data General
Classified Equipment: Hardware - APP/Mac, DEC; Printers - Unified/Laser;
Classified Software: DEC.
Editorial Equipment: Hardware - APP/Mac; Printers - APP/Mac LaserWriter IIg, AG/Imagesetters
Editorial Software: Microsoft/Word, QPS/QuarkXPress, Custom-Developed.
Production Equipment: Hardware - 1-Nu, AG/Star 400, 2-AG/1000 Imagesetter; Cameras - C/Spartan III; Scanners - ECR, RZ/Diadem.
Total Circulation: 20160

GREENVILLE

HERALD-BANNER

Corporate/Parent Company: CNHI, LLC
Publication Street Address: 2305 King St
City: Greenville
State: TX
Publication Website: www.heraldbanner.com
Postal Code: 75401-3257
Office phone: (903) 455-4220
General E-mail: editor@heraldbanner.com
Publisher Name: Lisa Chappell
Publisher Email: publisher@heraldbanner.com
Publisher Phone: (903) 455-4220, Ext : 345
Editor Name: Dale Gosser
Editor Email: dgosser@heraldbanner.com
Editor Phone: (903) 455-4220, Ext : 324
Advertising Executive Name: Kerri Gibbs
Advertising Executive Email: addirector@heraldbanner.com
Advertising Executive Phone: (903) 455-4220, Ext : 310
Year Established: 1869
Delivery Methods: Carrier`Racks

Mechanical specifications: Type page 13 x 21 1/2; E - 6 cols, 1 5/6, 1/8 between; A - 6 cols, 1 4/5, 1/8 between; C - 9 cols, 1 4/5, 1/16 between.
Published Days: Tues`Wed`Thur`Fri`Sat`Sun
Weekday Frequency: m
Saturday Frequency: m
Avg Paid Circ: 7945
Audit Company: Sworn/Estimate/Non-Audited
Audit Date: 7 12 2019
Pressroom Equipment: Lines - 8-G/Community 1974; Folders - 1-G/SC; Control System - VEE ARC/PWM 7000 1974.;
Mailroom Equipment: Counter Stackers - BG/108; Inserters & Stuffers - KAN; Tying Machines - 1-MLN/ML2EE, Dynaric/5580.;
Buisness Equipment: IBM, EKI/Televideo
Classified Equipment: Hardware - 3-APP/Mac LC; Printers - Okidata/Microline 320;
Classified Software: QPS/QuarkXPress 3.1.
Editorial Equipment: Hardware - APP/Mac Classic, APP/Mac LC, APP/Mac IIsi, APP/Power Mac G3/Hayes/Smart modem 9600, Express/28.8; Printers - APP/Mac LaserWriter IIg, APP/Mac LaserWriter 16-600, APP/Mac LaserWriter 8500
Editorial Software: QPS/QuarkXPress 3.32, Baseview/N
Production Equipment: Hardware - Nat/A-250, APP/Mac Quadra 700, APP/Power Mac G-3; Cameras - SCREEN/Rollmatic C-475-D, SCREEN/Companica 680C; Scanners - APP/Mac One Scanner, Mita/DC-1656 Copier, Polaroid/SprintScan 35, Umax/Vista S-12.
Total Circulation: 7945

HARLINGEN

VALLEY MORNING STAR

Corporate/Parent Company: AIM Media
Publication Street Address: 1310 S Commerce St
City: Harlingen
State: TX
Publication Website: http://www.valleymorningstar.com/
Postal Code: 78550
Office phone: (956) 430-6200
General E-mail: fescobedo@brownsvilleherald.com
Publisher Name: Frank Escobedo
Publisher Email: fescobedo@brownsvilleherald.com
Publisher Phone: (956) 982-6646
Editor Name: Ryan Henry
Editor Email: rhenry@brownsvilleherald.com
Editor Phone: (956) 982-6620
Advertising Executive Name: Chris Castillo
Advertising Executive Email: ccastillo@valleystar.com
Advertising Executive Phone: (956) 430-6235
Year Established: 1911
Delivery Methods: Newsstand`Carrier`Racks
Own Printing Facility?: Y
Commercial printers?: Y
Mechanical specifications: Type page 13 x 21; E - 6 cols, 2 1/16, 1/8 between; A - 6 cols, 2 1/16, 1/8 between; C - 10 cols, 1 1/4, 1/16 between.
Published Days: Mon`Tues`Wed`Thur`Fri`Sat`Sun
Weekday Frequency: m
Saturday Frequency: m
Avg Paid Circ: 10405
Audit Company: AAM
Audit Date: 24 10 2019
Pressroom Equipment: Lines - 6-HI/Cotrell 845; 6-HI/Cotrell 845; Folders - 2-H/2:1; Pasters -8-Jardis/FP 4540.
Mailroom Equipment: Counter Stackers - Id, QWI; Tying Machines - 2-MLN/MLN2, Dynaric.;
Buisness Equipment: Prosig, 4-PC 4DX2-66, SCSI, 7-Compaq/486
Buisness Software: Brainworks, Southware
Classified Equipment: Hardware - APT; Printers - HP/4000.;
Editorial Equipment: Hardware - APT/AP/Photo Server; Printers - HP/5000.
Production Equipment: Hardware - ECR/3850, ECR/4550; Cameras - 1-C/Spartan III; Scanners - 3-HP/Scanner
Production Software: APT.
Total Circulation: 11238

HOUSTON

HOUSTON CHRONICLE

Corporate/Parent Company: Hearst Communications Inc.
Publication Street Address: 4747 Southwest Fwy
City: Houston
State: TX
Publication Website: www.chron.com
Postal Code: 77027-6901
Office phone: (713) 220-7171
General E-mail: news@chron.com
Publisher Name: John McKeon
Editor Name: Steve Riley
Year Established: 1901
Delivery Methods:
  Mail`Newsstand`Carrier`Racks
Mechanical specifications: Type page 12 3/4 x 21 1/4; E - 6 cols, 1/6 between; A - 6 cols, 1/6 between; C - 6 cols, between.
Published Days: Mon`Tues`Wed`Thur`Fri`Sat`Sun
Weekday Frequency: m
Saturday Frequency: m
Avg Paid Circ: 161279
Audit Company: AAM
Audit Date: 3 07 2020
Pressroom Equipment: Lines - 12-G/Metro 1978; 12-G/Metro 1979; 12-G/Metroliner 1984; 12-G/Metro 1978; 12-G/Metroliner 1984; 12-G/Metroliner 1982; Press Drive - Fincor; Folders - 6G/3:2; Pasters -Simplified TensionReels & Stands - 60 reel stands; Control System - Denex; Registration System - Web/Tech.
Mailroom Equipment: Counter Stackers - Quipp 350 to 550; Inserters & Stuffers - 5-HI/1372P, 3-HI/Model 630 30 head, 1-G 22-99; Tying Machines - Dynaric; Control System - Burt/Enternet; Address Machine - 6-Sitma/Plastic Wrap w/18 head, 1/KR;
Buisness Equipment: IBM
Buisness Software: Microsoft
Classified Equipment: Hardware - SII, PC, Sun/Enterprise 3000, Sun/Enterprise 4000, Sun/450; DP/CD Merge System; Printers - HP/LaserJet
Classified Software: SII, CKP.
Editorial Equipment: Hardware - SII, Sun/Microsys/AU/APS 5, Lf/AP Leaf Picture Desk, APP/Mac, Sun/Phoenix T-1, Merlin/Photo Archive, Fox/Prodatabase, BH/Proquest Publisher; Printers - QMS/2060, HP/Laserjet
Editorial Software: DTI/Newspaper Systems Millenium Editoria
Production Equipment: Hardware - 4 AGFA Polaris CTp, 4 NELA VPB benders & sorter WL/Offset, 2-WL/Lith 7, 2-WL/Lith-X-Pozer, Scitex/342, AG/Horizon Flatbed, APP/Mac All Platform, Avanta/25 Imagers, Avanta/30 Imagers
Production Software: ProImage
Total Circulation: 249442

HUNTSVILLE

THE HUNTSVILLE ITEM

Corporate/Parent Company: CNHI, LLC
Publication Street Address: 1409 10th St
City: Huntsville
State: TX
Publication Website: www.itemonline.com
Postal Code: 77320-3805
Office phone: (936) 295-5407
General E-mail: huntsvilleitem@gmail.com
Publisher Name: Jake Mienk
Publisher Email: jmienk@itemonline.com
Editor Name: Joseph Brown
Editor Email: jbrown@itemonline.com
Advertising Executive Name: Tammy Farkas
Advertising Executive Email: tfarkas@itemonline.com
Year Established: 1850
Delivery Methods:
  Mail`Newsstand`Carrier`Racks
Own Printing Facility?: Y
Commercial printers?: Y
Mechanical specifications: Type page 13 x 21 1/2; E - 6 cols, 2 1/16, 1/8 between; A - 6 cols, 2 1/16, 1/8 between; C - 9 cols, 1 3/8, 1/16 between.

Published Days: Tues`Wed`Thur`Fri`Sun
Weekday Frequency: m
Saturday Frequency: m
Avg Paid Circ: 3800
Avg Free Circ: 20000
Audit Company: Sworn/Estimate/Non-Audited
Audit Date: 7 12 2019
Pressroom Equipment: Lines - 10-G/Community single width 1991; Folders - G/SSC (with upper and lower former) 1991.;
Mailroom Equipment: Counter Stackers - 1-BG/Count-O-Veyor 108; Inserters & Stuffers - MM/7 Station; Tying Machines - 1-MLN/MLI-EE-ML-MS;
Classified Equipment: Hardware - Mk, APP/Mac;
Classified Software: Baseview/Ad Manager Pro.
Editorial Equipment: Hardware - Mk, APP/Mac
Editorial Software: Baseview/NewsEdit, InDesign
Production Equipment: Hardware - V, Pre Press/Panther Pro 46; Cameras - 1-SCREEN/C-260; Scanners - Unimax
Production Software: QPS/QuarkXPress 4.0.
Total Circulation: 23800

KERRVILLE

KERRVILLE DAILY TIMES

Corporate/Parent Company: Southern Newspapers Inc.
Publication Street Address: 429 Jefferson St
City: Kerrville
State: TX
Publication Website: www.dailytimes.com
Postal Code: 78028-4412
Office phone: (830) 896-7000
General E-mail: advertising@dailytimes.com
Publisher Name: Carlina Villalpando
Publisher Phone: (830) 896-7000
Editor Name: Louis Amestoy
Editor Phone: (830) 257-0317
Advertising Executive Name: John Doran
Advertising Executive Phone: (830) 257-0301
Year Established: 1910
Mechanical specifications: Type page 11 5/8 x 21 1/2; E - 6 cols, 1 13/16, 1/8 between; A - 6 cols, 1 13/16, 1/8 between; C - 9 cols, 1 1/8, 1/8 between.
Published Days: Mon`Tues`Wed`Thur`Fri`Sun
Weekday Frequency: m
Avg Paid Circ: 5524
Avg Free Circ: 609
Audit Company: AAM
Audit Date: 26 03 2019
Pressroom Equipment: Lines - 6-G/Community single width; Folders - 1-G/SC.;
Mailroom Equipment: Counter Stackers - KAN; Inserters & Stuffers - KAN/380; Tying Machines - 1-Us/Q, 1-Us/TE, 1/Md.;
Buisness Software: PBC
Classified Equipment: Hardware - APP/iMac, Classified Software: Baseview/Class Pro.
Editorial Equipment: Hardware - APP/Mac G4/4-APP/Mac G4, Nikon/Coolscan; Printers - HP/4M
Editorial Software: Baseview/NewsEdit Pro.
Production Equipment: Hardware - Anitec/Imagesetter; Cameras - 1-SCREEN/Companica 680C
Total Circulation: 8773

KILLEEN

KILLEEN DAILY HERALD

Corporate/Parent Company: Frank Mayborn Enterprise, Inc.
Publication Street Address: 1809 Florence Rd
City: Killeen
State: TX
Publication Website: www.kdhnews.com
Postal Code: 76541-8977
Office phone: (254) 634-2125
General E-mail: gdominguez@kdhnews.com
Publisher Name: Terry Gandy
Publisher Email: t.gandy@kdhnews.com
Publisher Phone: (254) 501-7595
Editor Name: Rose Fitzpatrick
Editor Email: rosef@kdhnews.com
Editor Phone: (254) 501-7469

# U.S. Daily Newspapers

Advertising Executive Name: Anthony Edwards
Advertising Executive Email: aedwards@kdhnews.com
Advertising Executive Phone: (254) 501-7521
Year Established: 1890
Delivery Methods: Mail`Newsstand`Carrier`Racks
Own Printing Facility?: Y
Commercial printers?: Y
Mechanical specifications: Type page 13 x 21 1/2; E - 6 cols, 2 1/16, 1/8 between; A - 6 cols, 2 1/16, 1/8 between; C - 9 cols, 1 3/8, 1/16 between.
Published Days: Mon`Tues`Wed`Thur`Fri`Sat`Sun
Weekday Frequency: m
Saturday Frequency: m
Avg Paid Circ: 9350
Avg Free Circ: 1991
Audit Company: AAM
Audit Date: 31 08 2018
Pressroom Equipment: Lines – 7-G/Urbanite 1978, 3-G/Urbanite 1985.;
Mailroom Equipment: Counter Stackers – 1/HL; Inserters & Stuffers – 1-/S; Tying Machines – 1-/MLN, 1-/EC; Address Machine – 2-/St.;
Buisness Equipment: Dell
Buisness Software: MAS 90, AR-2000
Classified Equipment: Hardware – ALR; Printers – GCC/Elite 808;
Classified Software: APT.
Editorial Equipment: Hardware – ALR/Lf/AP Leaf Picture Desk, Lf/Leafscan 35, Linotype-Hell/L 190, Mark/40 EX, SCREEN/Katana 5055; Printers – GCC/Elite 808
Editorial Software: APT.
Production Equipment: Hardware – Textbridge/Pro, Linotronic/Mark 40EX Postscript, SCREEN/Katana 5055, SCREEN/LD-M1060; Cameras – 1-C/Spartan III; Scanners – 1-Lf, Umax, SCREEN/Cezanne, Nikon/2000
Production Software: QPS/QuarkXPress, APT.
Total Circulation: 12386

LAREDO

LAREDO MORNING TIMES

Corporate/Parent Company: Hearst Communications Inc.
Publication Street Address: 111 Esperanza Dr
City: Laredo
State: TX
Publication Website: www.lmtonline.com
Postal Code: 78041-2607
Office phone: (956) 728-2500
General E-mail: editorial@lmtonline.com
Publisher Name: Bill Green
Publisher Email: bill@lmtonline.com
Publisher Phone: (956) 728-2501
Editor Name: Zach Davis
Editor Email: zdavis@lmtonline.com
Editor Phone: (956) 728-2582
Advertising Executive Name: Angelica Salinas
Advertising Executive Phone: (956) 728-2526
Year Established: 1881
Delivery Methods: Mail`Newsstand`Carrier
Own Printing Facility?: N
Mechanical specifications: Type page 13 7/8 x 21; E - 6 cols, 2 1/16, 1/8 between; A - 6 cols, 2 1/16, 1/8 between; C - 6 cols, 2 1/16, 1/8 between.
Published Days: Mon`Tues`Wed`Thur`Fri`Sat`Sun
Weekday Frequency: m
Saturday Frequency: m
Avg Paid Circ: 9041
Avg Free Circ: 130
Audit Company: AAM
Audit Date: 10 03 2020
Pressroom Equipment: 1-Multi-Lith/1250; Folders – 1, 1.
Mailroom Equipment: Tying Machines – 2-Bu/PAT 27,744; Address Machine – 1-Am/Class 640, 1-Am/4000.;
Buisness Equipment: 1-NCR/8200
Classified Equipment: Hardware – M, 3-CRT terminal; 4-IBM/71, 1-NCR/memory unit, Dewar; Printers – 1-NCR/Lineprinter.;
Editorial Equipment: Hardware – AT, 14-IBM/71.
Production Equipment: Hardware – 1-Am/450, 2-Am/430, 1-Comp/Set 4510; Cameras – 1-C/Spartan II, 1-VG/320; Scanners – ECR/Autokon 5200.
Total Circulation: 8774

LONGVIEW

LONGVIEW NEWS-JOURNAL

Corporate/Parent Company: Cox
Publication Street Address: 320 E Methvin St
City: Longview
State: TX
Publication Website: www.news-journal.com
Postal Code: 75601-7323
Office phone: (903) 237-7744
General E-mail: advertising@news-journal.com
Publisher Name: Stephen N. McHaney
Publisher Email: snmchaney@news-journal.com
Publisher Phone: (903) 237-7700
Editor Name: Randy Ferguson
Editor Email: rferguson@news-journal.com
Editor Phone: (903) 237-7751
Advertising Executive Name: Tracy Stopani
Advertising Executive Email: tstopani@news-journal.com
Advertising Executive Phone: (903) 237-7726
Year Established: 1871
Delivery Methods: Mail`Newsstand`Carrier`Racks
Own Printing Facility?: Y
Commercial printers?: Y
Published Days: Mon`Tues`Wed`Thur`Fri`Sat`Sun
Weekday Frequency: m
Saturday Frequency: m
Avg Paid Circ: 13632
Audit Company: AAM
Audit Date: 30 01 2019
Pressroom Equipment: DGM 850 16 units with 2 folders
Mailroom Equipment: SLS 1000
Buisness Software: Brainworks
Classified Software: Brainworks
Editorial Equipment: PC and Macintosh
Editorial Software: Tera Digital Publishing GN3
Total Circulation: 16229

LUBBOCK

LUBBOCK AVALANCHE-JOURNAL

Corporate/Parent Company: Gannett
Publication Street Address: 710 Avenue J
City: Lubbock
State: TX
Publication Website: www.lubbockonline.com
Postal Code: 79401-1808
Office phone: (806) 762-8844
General E-mail: rmorse@lubbockonline.com
Editor Name: Adam Young
Editor Email: ayoung@lubbockonline.com
Editor Phone: (806) 766-8717
Advertising Executive Name: Shoni Wiseman
Advertising Executive Email: swiseman@lubbockonline.com
Advertising Executive Phone: (806) 766-8631
Year Established: 1900
Mechanical specifications: Type page 11 5/8 x 21 1/2; E - 4 cols, 1/8 between; A - 6 cols, 1 5/6, 1/8 between; C - 9 cols, between.
Published Days: Mon`Tues`Wed`Thur`Fri`Sat`Sun
Weekday Frequency: m
Saturday Frequency: m
Avg Paid Circ: 10483
Avg Free Circ: 18664
Audit Company: AAM
Audit Date: 25 06 2019
Pressroom Equipment: Lines – 12-G/Metro; Pasters –G/Automatic.
Mailroom Equipment: Counter Stackers – 4/T.M.S.I, 2-/H.T.; Inserters & Stuffers – 2-GMA/1000 18:2; Tying Machines – 4-/Dynaric; Wrapping Singles – 2-/Dynaric; Address Machine – 1-/Ch.;
Buisness Equipment: 56-IBM/PC-AT, 1-APP/Mac SE, 1-APP/Mac IIfx, Dell/Optiplex GX270
Buisness Software: MPS, DTI
Classified Equipment: Hardware – Gateway/2000 G6-233, DTI; Proteon/LAN; Printers – Toshiba/P351, 2-Xante, Konica/EV9200;
Classified Software: MPS, DTI.
Editorial Equipment: Hardware – Gateway/2000, Gateway/P5-200, Gateway/G6-233, Gateway/2000, PS-60, 1-APP/Mac SE, 5-APP/Power Mac 8100-80, 1-APP/Mac IIfx, 5-APP/Mac 9100/APP/Mac IIfx, Proteon/LAN, Asanti/Eathernet; Printers – Toshiba/P351, APP/Mac LaserWriter II,
Production Equipment: Hardware – Accuset/1000, Accuset/1500, 2-Xante, Konica/EV9200; Cameras – Epson/1640 XL; Scanners – 1-AG/T2000XL, UMAX, HP/Scanjet.
Total Circulation: 31666

LUFKIN

THE LUFKIN DAILY NEWS

Corporate/Parent Company: Cox
Publication Street Address: 300 Ellis at Herndon
City: Lufkin
State: TX
Publication Website: http://lufkindailynews.com/
Postal Code: 75904
Office phone: (936) 632-6631
General E-mail: news@lufkindailynews.com
Publisher Name: Keven Todd
Publisher Email: keven.todd@lufkindailynews.com
Publisher Phone: (936) 631-2602
Editor Name: Jeff Pownall
Editor Email: jeff.pownall@lufkindailynews.com
Editor Phone: (936) 631-2623
Advertising Executive Name: Jenna Lenderman
Advertising Executive Email: jenna.lenderman@lufkindailynews.com
Advertising Executive Phone: (936) 631-2638
Year Established: 1907
Delivery Methods: Mail`Newsstand`Carrier`Racks
Own Printing Facility?: Y
Commercial printers?: Y
Mechanical specifications: Type page 11 5/8 x 21; E - 6 cols, 1 5/6, 1/8 between; A - 6 cols, 1 5/6, 1/8 between; C - 9 cols, 1 3/16, 1/8 between.
Published Days: Mon`Tues`Wed`Thur`Fri`Sat`Sun
Weekday Frequency: m
Saturday Frequency: m
Avg Paid Circ: 7125
Avg Free Circ: 898
Audit Company: AAM
Audit Date: 8 04 2020
Pressroom Equipment: Lines – 7-G/Urbanite 1979, 1-G/Urbanite (3 color) 1979; Press Drive – 2-Fin/Digital 100 h.p. DC motor;
Mailroom Equipment: Counter Stackers – QWI/200; Inserters & Stuffers – 2-MM/227S 6:1; Tying Machines – 2-MLN/MLI-EE.;
Buisness Equipment: 1-HP/9000, HP/8175S
Buisness Software: DTI, Geac/Vision Shift
Classified Equipment: Hardware – 2-APP/Power Mac 7100-66, APP/Mac G4; Kk/DC 120 Digital Camera, APP/Mac One Scanner, HP/ScanJet 4C; Printers – HP/2100 DN;
Classified Software: MediaSpan Class Manager
Editorial Equipment: Hardware – APP/Mac G3, APP/Mac G4 700/1-Nikon/RS 3500, Howtek/ScanMaster II, Nikon/Digital Camera; Printers – HP/8150
Editorial Software: MediaSpan NewsEdit Pro
Production Equipment: Hardware – Konica/JetSetter 6100, Adobe/Photoshop; Cameras – Spartan III; Scanners – Microtek/60025, 1-Nikon/L5-3510
Production Software: MediaSpan Production Manager Pro, Puzzle Flow
Total Circulation: 7607

MARSHALL

MARSHALL NEWS MESSENGER

Corporate/Parent Company: Cox
Publication Street Address: 309 E Austin St
City: Marshall
State: TX
Publication Website: www.marshallnewsmessenger.com
Postal Code: 75670-3475
Office phone: (903) 903-7914
General E-mail: awalker@news-journal.com
Publisher Name: Jerry Pye
Publisher Email: jpye@marshallnewsmessenger.com
Publisher Phone: (903) 927-5977
Editor Name: Caleb Brabham
Editor Email: cbrabham@marshallnewsmessenger.com
Editor Phone: (903) 927-5975
Advertising Executive Name: Dianne Gray
Advertising Executive Email: dgray@marshallnewsmessenger.com
Advertising Executive Phone: (903) 927-5973
Year Established: 1877
Mechanical specifications: Type page 13 3/4 x 21 1/4; E - 6 cols, 1 5/6, 1/8 between; A - 6 cols, 1 5/6, 1/8 between; C - 9 cols, 1 9/50, 1/8 between.
Published Days: Tues`Wed`Thur`Fri`Sat`Sun
Weekday Frequency: m
Saturday Frequency: m
Avg Paid Circ: 4517
Audit Company: AAM
Audit Date: 31 03 2014
Buisness Equipment: IBM/PC-AT
Classified Equipment: Hardware – APP/iMac; Printers – TI/Omni 800 line printer;
Classified Software: DTI/ClassSpeed 1.3.2.
Editorial Equipment: Hardware – Mk/4000, APP/Mac IIcx, APP/Mac Quadra 610/APP/Mac Scanner, Lf/LeafScan 35, Lf/AP Leaf Picture Desk; Printers – TI/Omni 800 line printer, 2-Xante/8200, APP/Mac LaserWriter Plus, V/4990
Editorial Software: Mk/Ace 1.3.2, Mk/NewsTouch AT, QPS/
Production Equipment: Hardware – 2-APP/Mac Radius, 2-APP/Mac IIcx.
Total Circulation: 4517

MCALLEN

THE MONITOR

Corporate/Parent Company: AIM Media
Publication Street Address: 1400 E Nolana Ave
City: McAllen
State: TX
Publication Website: http://www.themonitor.com/
Postal Code: 78504
Office phone: (956) 683-4000
General E-mail: iservices@themonitor.com
Editor Email: news@themonitor.com
Editor Phone: (956) 683-4400
Advertising Executive Email: ads@themonitor.com
Advertising Executive Phone: (956) 683-4155
Year Established: 1974
Delivery Methods: Mail`Newsstand`Racks
Published Days: Thur`Sun
Audit Company: AAM
Audit Date: 24 10 2019
Total Circulation: 22769

MIDLAND

MIDLAND REPORTER-TELEGRAM

Corporate/Parent Company: Hearst Communications Inc.
Publication Street Address: 201 E Illinois Ave
City: Midland
State: TX
Publication Website: www.mrt.com
Postal Code: 79701-4852
Office phone: (432) 682-5311
General E-mail: jhouston@mrt.com
Publisher Name: Jeffery P Shabram
Publisher Email: jshabram@hearstnp.com
Publisher Phone: (432) 687-8880
Editor Name: Mary Dearen
Editor Email: mdearen@hearstnp.com
Editor Phone: (432) 687-8852
Advertising Executive Name: David A. Robbins
Advertising Executive Email: david.robbins@hearstnp.com
Advertising Executive Phone: (432) 687-8808
Year Established: 1929
Delivery Methods: Mail`Newsstand`Carrier`Racks
Own Printing Facility?: Y
Commercial printers?: Y
Mechanical specifications: Type page 11.00 x 21 1/2; E - 6 cols, 1.52, 0.9 between; A - 5

U.S. Daily Newspapers

cols, 1.94, 0.9 between; C - 10 cols, 0.95, 0.10 between.
Published Days: Mon`Tues`Wed`Thur`Fri`Sat`Sun
Weekday Frequency: m
Saturday Frequency: m
Avg Paid Circ: 7767
Avg Free Circ: 1534
Audit Company: AAM
Audit Date: 24 03 2020
Pressroom Equipment: Lines – 6-HI/1650 double width 1974;
Mailroom Equipment: Counter Stackers – 1-QWI/350; 1-Quipp/501 Inserters & Stuffers – S/48P (9 head); - Strappers 2-Dynaric NP 4000 - 1 Dynaric NP 1500 Computers - 1 PC (Windows 7)
Mailroom Software: MS Office Suite - 2010 Standard
Buisness Equipment: Computers - 5 -PC's (Windows 7 Professional & Windows XP) Access to IBM Mainframe & IBM AS-400 Printers - HP LaserJet P4515TN Kyocera ECO SYS FS-1128 MFP (Access to Kyocera TaskAlfa 400ci)
Buisness Software: ATEX AdBase Suite - AdBase 3.5 ATEX AdBase PGL PageLayout Applications ATEX PGL Ad Distributor Application Citrix (Web Interface for AdBase) Edgil (Tokenization for AdBase Finance Applications and Marketing G2) Affinity 4.0 (Advertising Ad Production) TownNews (BLOX CMS - mywesttexas.com) LocalEdge (Advertising Application) Microsoft Office Suites - 2003, 2007, 2010 DISCUS (IBM Mainframe) ADMARC (IBM Mainframe - Legacy system) Hyperion (IBM AS400)
Classified Equipment: Computers - 17 - PC's (Windows 7 Professional & Windows XP) Printers - Kyocera TaskAlfa 400ci
Classified Software: ATEX AdBase Suite - AdBase 3.5 Citrix (Web Interface for AdBase) Edgil (Tokenization for AdBase Finance Applications and Marketing G2) Affinity 4.0 (Advertising Ad Production) LocalEdge (Advertising Application) Microsoft Office Suites - 2003, 2007, 2010
Editorial Equipment: Computers – 28 PC's - Windows 7 & Windows XP Printers - Kyocera TASKalfa 400ci KX
Editorial Software: Baseview NewsEdit 3.2 Software Construction Company - SCC Photo Archives Microsoft Office Suite - 2010 Standard Adobe Design Premium CS5.5 (InDesign for PageLayout) AdBase PGL PageLink (to interface InDesign to AdBase PGL PageLayout) Adobe Creative Design Premium 2.0 Quark 7.3 & 7.5
Production Equipment: 2- AGFA - Advantage N-SL CTP with 2- VCF Processors Computers - 3 - PC's - Windows 7 Professional Printers - Kyocera TASKalfa 400ci KX
Production Software: ATEX AdBase Suite - AdBase 3.5 ATEX AdBase PGL PageLayout Applications Baseview NewsEdit 3.2 Software Construction Company - SCC Photo Archives Microsoft Office Suite - 2010 Standard Adobe Design Premium CS5.5 (InDesign for PageLayout) AdBase PGL PageLink (to interface InDesign to AdBase PGL PageLayout) Adobe Creative Design Premium 2.0 Quark 7.5 Microsoft Office Suite - 2010 Standard
Total Circulation: 8849

MINERAL WELLS
MINERAL WELLS INDEX
Corporate/Parent Company: CNHI, LLC
Publication Street Address: 300 SE 1st St
City: Mineral Wells
State: TX
Publication Website: www.mineralwellsindex.com
Postal Code: 76067-5331
Office phone: (940) 325-4465
General E-mail: adv@mineralwellsindex.com
Publisher Name: Lisa Chappell
Publisher Email: lchappell@cnhi.com
Publisher Phone: (817) 594-7447, Ext : 237
Editor Name: David May
Editor Email: editor@mineralwellsindex.com
Editor Phone: (940) 325-4465, Ext : 3416
Advertising Executive Name: Mary Gray
Advertising Executive Email: mgray@mineralwellsindex.com
Advertising Executive Phone: (940) 325-4465
Year Established: 1900
Mechanical specifications: Type page 13 3/4 x 21 1/2; E - 6 cols, 2, 1/8 between; A - 6 cols, 2, 1/8 between; C - 8 cols, 1 1/2, 1/8 between.
Published Days: Tues`Wed`Thur`Fri`Sun
Weekday Frequency: m
Avg Paid Circ: 3500
Audit Company: Sworn/Estimate/Non-Audited
Audit Date: 7 12 2019
Pressroom Equipment: Lines – 6-G/Community.;
Mailroom Equipment: Tying Machines – MC/Poly Strapper;
Classified Equipment: Hardware – APP/Mac G3; Printers – GCC/20-800;
Classified Software: QPS/QuarkXPress, Multi-Ad/CAMS.
Editorial Equipment: Hardware – 5-APP/Mac G3; Printers – GCC/20-800
Editorial Software: Multi-Ad/Creator, QPS/QuarkXPress.
Total Circulation: 3500

NACOGDOCHES
NACOGDOCHES DAILY SENTINEL
Corporate/Parent Company: Southern Newspapers Inc.
Publication Street Address: 4920 Colonial Dr.
City: Nacogdoches
State: TX
Publication Website: dailysentinel.com
Postal Code: 75965
Office phone: 936-564-8361
General E-mail: circulation@dailysentinel.com
Publisher Name: Rick Craig
Publisher Email: rick.craig@dailysentinel.com
Publisher Phone: 936-558-3200
Editor Name: Josh Edwards
Editor Email: josh.edwards@dailysentinel.com
Editor Phone: 936-564-8361
Advertising Executive Name: Gabrielle Dyer
Advertising Executive Email: gabrielle.dyer@dailysentinel.com
Advertising Executive Phone: 936-558-3205

THE DAILY SENTINEL
Corporate/Parent Company: Cox
Publication Street Address: 4920 Colonial Dr
City: Nacogdoches
State: TX
Publication Website: http://www.dailysentinel.com/
Postal Code: 75965
Office phone: (936) 564-8361
General E-mail: circulation@dailysentinel.com
Publisher Name: Rick Craig
Publisher Email: rick.craig@dailysentinel.com
Publisher Phone: (936) 558-3200
Editor Name: Josh Edwards
Editor Email: josh.edwards@dailysentinel.com
Editor Phone: (936) 558-3201
Advertising Executive Name: Gabrielle Dyer
Advertising Executive Email: gabrielle.dyer@dailysentinel.com
Advertising Executive Phone: (936) 558-3205
Year Established: 1899
Delivery Methods: Mail`Newsstand`Carrier`Racks
Own Printing Facility?: N
Commercial printers?: Y
Mechanical specifications: Type page 13 x 21 1/4; E - 6 cols, 2 1/16, 1/8 between; A - 6 cols, 2 1/16, 1/8 between; C - 9 cols, 1 5/16, 1/8 between.
Published Days: Mon`Tues`Wed`Thur`Fri`Sat`Sun
Weekday Frequency: m
Saturday Frequency: m
Avg Paid Circ: 4326
Avg Free Circ: 918
Audit Company: AAM
Audit Date: 3 04 2020
Classified Equipment: Hardware – Wyse/150ES; Printers – TI/880;
Classified Software: DTI/ClassSpeed.
Editorial Equipment: Hardware – APP/Mac; Printers – APP/Mac LaserWriter NTX, HP/4MV LaserJet
Editorial Software: DTI/PageSpeed.
Production Equipment: Hardware – APP/Mac NTX; Scanners – Lf/Leafscan.
Total Circulation: 27276

NEW BRAUNFELS
NEW BRAUNFELS HERALD-ZEITUNG
Corporate/Parent Company: Southern Newspapers Inc.
Publication Street Address: 549 Landa St
City: New Braunfels
State: TX
Publication Website: http://herald-zeitung.com/
Postal Code: 78130
Office phone: (830) 625-9144
General E-mail: webmaster@nbtxhz.com
Publisher Name: Neice Bell
Publisher Email: neice.bell@nbtxhz.com
Publisher Phone: (830) 358-7881
Editor Name: Chris Lykins
Editor Email: chris.lykins@nbtxhz.com
Editor Phone: (830) 358-7931
Advertising Executive Name: Brian Cartwright
Advertising Executive Email: brian.cartwright@nbtxhz.com
Advertising Executive Phone: (830) 358-7893
Year Established: 1852
Delivery Methods: Mail`Newsstand`Carrier`Racks
Own Printing Facility?: Y
Commercial printers?: Y
Published Days: Tues`Wed`Thur`Fri`Sat`Sun
Weekday Frequency: m
Saturday Frequency: m
Avg Paid Circ: 5711
Avg Free Circ: 603
Audit Company: AAM
Audit Date: 13 06 2019
Pressroom Equipment: Lines – G/Community.;
Mailroom Equipment: Tying Machines – Dynaric.;
Buisness Software: Quattro, Microsoft/Word
Classified Equipment: Hardware – Mk; Printers – TI;
Classified Software: Mk.
Editorial Equipment: Hardware – APP/Mac G3
Editorial Software: Microsoft/Word, QPS/QuarkXPress.
Production Equipment: Hardware – 1-Nu; Cameras – R
Production Software: QPS/QuarkXPress
Total Circulation: 7170

ODESSA
ODESSA AMERICAN
Corporate/Parent Company: AIM Media
Publication Street Address: 700 N. Grant Ave., Suite 800
City: Odessa
State: TX
Publication Website: https://www.oaoa.com/
Postal Code: 79761
Office phone: (432) 337-4661
General E-mail: canty@oaoa.com
Publisher Name: Pat Canty
Publisher Email: canty@oaoa.com
Publisher Phone: (432) 333-7721
Editor Name: Laura Dennis
Editor Email: ldennis@oaoa.com
Editor Phone: (432) 333-7740
Advertising Executive Name: Terry Schaub
Advertising Executive Email: tschaub@oaoa.com
Advertising Executive Phone: (432) 333-7603
Year Established: 1927
Delivery Methods: Mail`Newsstand`Carrier`Racks
Own Printing Facility?: Y
Commercial printers?: Y
Mechanical specifications: Type page 10 x 21 1/2; E - 6 cols, 1.528", 1/12 between; A - 6 cols, 1.528", 1/12 between; C - 9 cols, 1", 1/12 between.
Published Days: Mon`Tues`Wed`Thur`Fri`Sat`Sun
Weekday Frequency: m
Saturday Frequency: m
Avg Paid Circ: 10483
Audit Company: AAM
Audit Date: 23 10 2019
Pressroom Equipment: Lines – 6-HI/1650 double width 1976; Press Drive – 2-CH/150 HP; Folders – 2-HI/2:1; Pasters –MEG/Flying.
Mailroom Equipment: Counter Stackers – QWI; Inserters & Stuffers – 1-GMA/SLS 1000A 8:1; Tying Machines – 2-Dynaric/NP 1500;
Buisness Equipment: 1-Compaq/Proliant
Buisness Software: Great Plains, AR2000, Vision Data
Classified Equipment: Hardware – Compaq/Pentium 350mhz; Printers – QMS/2060;
Classified Software: Microsoft/Word 7.0, QPS/QuarkXPress 4.0, APT/ACT.
Editorial Equipment: Hardware – Compaq/Pentium 350mhz; Printers – HP/8100
Editorial Software: Microsoft/Word 7.0, QPS/QuarkXPress 4.0, APT/ACT.
Production Equipment: Hardware – ECR/VR 36, ECR/VR 36, Konica/VRL 4550; Cameras – C/Spartan II; Scanners – Umax/Powerlook
Production Software: APT/ACT.
Total Circulation: 7670

PALESTINE
PALESTINE HERALD-PRESS
Corporate/Parent Company: CNHI, LLC
Publication Street Address: 519 N Elm St
City: Palestine
State: TX
Publication Website: www.palestineherald.com
Postal Code: 75801-2927
Office phone: (903) 729-0281
General E-mail: jmienk@palestineherald.com
Publisher Name: Jake Mienk
Publisher Email: jmienk@palestineherald.com
Editor Name: Jeff Gerritt
Editor Email: jgerritt@palestineherald.com
Advertising Executive Name: Tawna Allen
Advertising Executive Email: tallen@palestineherald.com
Year Established: 1849
Delivery Methods: Mail
Own Printing Facility?: Y
Commercial printers?: Y
Mechanical specifications: Type page 13 x 21 1/2; E - 6 cols, 2 1/16, 1/8 between; A - 6 cols, 2 1/16, 1/8 between; C - 9 cols, 1 3/8, 1/8 between.
Published Days: Tues`Wed`Thur`Fri`Sun
Weekday Frequency: m
Saturday Frequency: m
Avg Paid Circ: 5013
Audit Company: Sworn/Estimate/Non-Audited
Audit Date: 7 12 2019
Pressroom Equipment: Lines – 7-HI/V-15A 1973; 8-HI/V-15A 1999; Press Drive – 75hp and 60 hp;
Mailroom Equipment: Tying Machines – Bu.;
Buisness Equipment: 1-HP/3700
Buisness Software: CJ
Classified Equipment: Hardware – 2-APP/iMac; Printers – Okidata/Microline 320;
Classified Software: Baseview.
Editorial Equipment: Hardware – 2-Ethernet/10T Hub, 6-APP/Mac Yosemite G3, 4-APP/Mac Quadra 800, APP/Mac Apple share IP Manager/LE/2100 Rapid Access Processor, Glunz & Jensen/720 Processor; Printers – 2-APP/Mac LaserWriter Pro 630
Editorial Software: Baseview, QPS/QuarkX
Production Equipment: Hardware – 1-Nu, Pre Press/Panther Plus VR Imagesetter; Cameras – B; Scanners – 2-Microtek/II XE, 2-Pre Press/Panther Plus RIP (1-VR & 1-IR), Microtek/Scanmaker 6400 XL
Production Software: Baseview/NewsEdit Pro IQue 3.2.1, QPS/QuarkXPress 4.02.
Total Circulation: 5013

PAMPA
THE PAMPA NEWS
Publication Street Address: 403 W Atchison Ave
City: Pampa
State: TX

U.S. Daily Newspapers

Publication Website: www.thepampanews.com
Postal Code: 79065-6303
Office phone: (806) 669-2525
General E-mail: rwoods@thepampanews.com
Publisher Name: Redonn Woods
Editor Name: John Lee
Year Established: 1906
Delivery Methods: Mail`Newsstand`Racks
Own Printing Facility?: Y
Commercial printers?: Y
Mechanical specifications: Type page 10 3/8 x 21; E - 6 cols, 1 5/8, 1/8 between; A - 6 cols, 1 5/8, 1/8 between; C - 9 cols, 1 1/16, 1/16 between.
Published Days: Tues`Wed`Thur`Fri`Sat
Weekday Frequency: m
Saturday Frequency: m
Avg Paid Circ: 4100
Audit Company: Sworn/Estimate/Non-Audited
Audit Date: 7 12 2019
Pressroom Equipment: Lines – 6-G/Suburban.;
Mailroom Equipment: Tying Machines – 1/Bu; Address Machine – 1-/Dispensa-Matic (computer labels).;
Production Equipment: Hardware – APP/Mac, Pre Press/Panther
Total Circulation: 4100

PLAINVIEW

PLAINVIEW HERALD

Corporate/Parent Company: Hearst Corp.
Publication Street Address: 820 Broadway St
City: Plainview
State: TX
Publication Website: www.myplainview.com
Postal Code: 79072-7316
Office phone: (806) 296-1300
General E-mail: phnews@hearstnp.com
Publisher Name: Clarice Touhey
Publisher Phone: (432) 687-8880
Editor Name: Ellysa Harris
Editor Email: ellysa.harris@hearstnp.com
Editor Phone: (806) 296-1353
Advertising Executive Name: Carmen Ortega
Advertising Executive Email: cortega@hearstnp.com
Advertising Executive Phone: (806) 296-1320
Year Established: 1889
Delivery Methods: Mail`Newsstand`Carrier`Racks
Own Printing Facility?: N
Commercial printers?: N
Published Days: Tues`Wed`Thur`Fri`Sun
Weekday Frequency: m
Avg Paid Circ: 5000
Audit Company: Sworn/Estimate/Non-Audited
Audit Date: 7 12 2019
Classified Software: FSI.
Total Circulation: 5000

PORT ARTHUR

PORT ARTHUR NEWS

Corporate/Parent Company: Cox
Publication Street Address: 2349 Memorial Blvd
City: Port Arthur
State: TX
Publication Website: www.panews.com
Postal Code: 77640-2822
Office phone: (409) 721-2417
General E-mail: panews@panews.com
Publisher Name: Stephen Hemelt
Publisher Email: stephen.hemelt@panews.com
Editor Name: Ken Stickney
Year Established: 1897
Delivery Methods: Mail`Newsstand`Carrier`Racks
Own Printing Facility?: Y
Commercial printers?: Y
Mechanical specifications: Type page 11 5/8 x 21 1/2; E - 6 cols, 1 5/8, 1/8 between; A - 6 cols, 1 5/6, 1/8 between; C - 9 cols, 1 3/16, 1/16 between.
Published Days: Tues`Wed`Thur`Fri`Sat`Sun
Weekday Frequency: m
Saturday Frequency: m
Avg Paid Circ: 8138
Audit Company: AAM
Audit Date: 31 03 2017
Pressroom Equipment: Lines – 6-G/Urbanite (3 color); 4-G/Urbanite (balloon former); Press Drive – 2-HP/100; Folders – 2-G/2:1; Reels & Stands – G.;
Mailroom Equipment: Counter Stackers – 2/BG, 1-/HL; Inserters & Stuffers – 2-MM/227; Tying Machines – 2-MLN/ML2EE, 1-MLN/2AHS; Address Machine – 1-/CH;
Buisness Equipment: PBS
Classified Equipment: Hardware – APP/Mac; Printers – APP/Mac LaserWriter;
Classified Software: Baseview.
Editorial Equipment: Hardware – APP/Mac, 1-APP/Mac; Printers – 1-APP/Mac LaserPrinter, Imagesetters/1270 Resolution
Editorial Software: Baseview.
Production Equipment: Hardware – Laser Red/460 HS Imagesetters, 1-Nu/Flip Top FT40V4UPNS, 2-Douthitt; Cameras – 1-C/Spartan II, 1-C/Spartan III; Scanners – Microtoko
Production Software: QPS/QuarkXPress.
Total Circulation: 8138

ROSENBERG

FORT BEND HERALD

Corporate/Parent Company: Hartman Newspapers LP
Publication Street Address: 1902 4th St
City: Rosenberg
State: TX
Publication Website: www.fbherald.com
Postal Code: 77471-5140
Office phone: (281) 342-4474
General E-mail: newsroom@fbherald.com
Publisher Name: Lee Hartman
Publisher Email: leehart@fbherald.com
Editor Name: Scott Reese Willey
Editor Email: swilley@fbherald.com
Advertising Executive Name: John Oliver
Advertising Executive Email: joliver@fbherald.com
Year Established: 1892
Delivery Methods: Mail`Newsstand`Carrier`Racks
Own Printing Facility?: Y
Commercial printers?: Y
Mechanical specifications: Type page 11.625 x 21, 6 cols.
Published Days: Mon`Tues`Wed`Thur`Fri`Sun
Published Other: Wednesday - Herald EXTRA, Free Shopper
Weekday Frequency: e
Avg Paid Circ: 7003
Avg Free Circ: 179
Audit Company: CVC
Audit Date: 30 06 2009
Pressroom Equipment: Lines – WPC/Atlas-Leader single width 1992; WPC/Atlas-Leader single width 1992.;
Mailroom Equipment: Tying Machines – Wilton/Strap Pack SS-80.;
Buisness Equipment: Macintosh
Buisness Software: Ad Manager Pro
Classified Equipment: Hardware – Macintosh; Printers – ECR/Scriptsetter, HP/LaserJet 4V;
Classified Software: Baseview.
Editorial Equipment: Hardware – APP/Mac/HP/Flatbed Scanner; Printers – ECR/Scriptsetter
Editorial Software: Baseview.
Total Circulation: 7182

SAN ANGELO

SAN ANGELO STANDARD-TIMES

Corporate/Parent Company: Gannett Company Inc.
Publication Street Address: 34 W Harris Ave
City: San Angelo
State: TX
Publication Website: www.gosanangelo.com
Postal Code: 76901
Office phone: (844) 331-0047
General E-mail: paul.harris@gosanangelo.com
Editor Name: Paul Harris
Year Established: 1884
Delivery Methods: Mail`Carrier`Racks
Mechanical specifications: Type page 11 5/8 x 21 1/2; E - 6 cols, 2 1/16, 1/8 between; A - 6 cols, 2 1/16, 1/8 between; C - 10 cols, 1 3/16, 4/5 between.
Published Days: Mon`Tues`Wed`Thur`Fri`Sat`Sun
Weekday Frequency: m
Saturday Frequency: m
Avg Paid Circ: 11355
Avg Free Circ: 404
Audit Company: AAM
Audit Date: 18 04 2018
Pressroom Equipment: Lines – 3-G/Cosmo double width 1980; Pasters –6, 2.
Mailroom Equipment: Counter Stackers – 1/KAN;
Buisness Equipment: HP/3000-937 RX
Buisness Software: PeopleSoft
Classified Equipment: Hardware – APP/iMac, APP/Mac G3; APP/Mac G4 Server; Printers – 1-APP/Mac LaserWriter, 1-Lexmark/Optma LX Plw;
Classified Software: Baseview/AMP 2.1.
Editorial Equipment: Hardware – Austin/APP/Power Mac G3; Printers – 1-Panasonic/KX P2411I, X/DC 220
Editorial Software: III 2.39.
Production Equipment: Hardware – APP/Mac NT Server, 2-Pre Press/Panther Pro 46; Cameras – C/Spartan II; Scanners – Kk/2035, AG/Arcus Flatbed, Nikon/Coolscan
Production Software: QPS/QuarkXPress 3.3, MEI/CLS 2.6, QPS/QuarkXPress 4.1.
Total Circulation: 12121

SAN ANTONIO

SAN ANTONIO EXPRESS-NEWS

Corporate/Parent Company: Hearst Communications Inc.
Publication Street Address: 301 Avenue E
City: San Antonio
State: TX
Publication Website: www.mySA.com
Postal Code: 78205-2006
Office phone: (210) 250-3000
General E-mail: rmccutcheon@express-news.net
Editor Name: Marc Duvoisin
Editor Email: marc.duvoisin@express-news.net
Year Established: 1865
Mechanical specifications: Type of Page: Broadsheet Full Page Ad Size: 9.94" x 21" Columns: 6 col 1 col = 1.54" Space between columns .14" Type of Page: Tab Full Page Ad Size: 9.94" x 9.75" Columns: 6 col. 1 col. = 1.54" Space between columns .14" All measures are the same for both ROP and Classified pages
Published Days: Mon`Tues`Wed`Thur`Fri`Sat`Sun
Weekday Frequency: m
Saturday Frequency: m
Avg Paid Circ: 72638
Audit Company: AAM
Audit Date: 19 05 2020
Pressroom Equipment: Lines – 3-G/Colorliner double width (8 units) 1994; 3-G/Colorliner doble width (8 units); 3-G/Colorliner double width (8 units); Folders – 4, 2-G/Sovereign 3:2 Single, 1-G/Sovereign 3:2 Double; Pasters –30-G/CT50Reels & Stands – 30;
Mailroom Equipment: Counter Stackers – 9-QWI/300, 4-QWI/SJ201A; Inserters & Stuffers – 3-HI/72P, 1-GMA/SLS 1000; Tying Machines – 8/Power Strap, 6-Sterling/Tying Machine.;
Buisness Equipment: 1-B/4955, 1-V/340, Bs, IBM/ES9000-150
Buisness Software: Admarc (7.0): Adv (input & ordering)
Classified Equipment: Hardware – SII; 100-PC Terminals, 100-NT/NT Client;
Editorial Equipment: Hardware – Unix/Enterprise 6000 Servers NT desktops/Graphic Enterprise/Page Scan; Printers – HP/LaserJet, Canon/350, HP/3500 Color, HP/4000, HP/8000, HP/5000
Editorial Software: Newsgate
Production Equipment: Hardware – 2-MON/ExpressMaster 3850, 2-MON/Lasercomp Express, Futuro; Cameras – 2-Newspagers, 1-C/Spartan III; Scanners – CD/636 Drum, CD/240 Drum, EskoFot/26365 Copydot
Production Software: QPS/QuarkXPress, CCI/Layout Champ, Newsdesk.
Total Circulation: 114428

SAN MARCOS

SAN MARCOS DAILY RECORD

Corporate/Parent Company: Moser Community Media
Publication Street Address: 1910 S Interstate 35
City: San Marcos
State: TX
Publication Website: www.sanmarcosrecord.com
Postal Code: 78666-5901
Office phone: (512) 392-2458
General E-mail: mholt@sanmarcosrecord.com
Publisher Name: Lance Winter
Publisher Email: lwinter@sanmarcosrecord.com
Editor Name: Nick Castillo
Editor Email: ncastillo@sanmarcosrecord.com
Advertising Executive Name: Marcy Holt
Advertising Executive Email: mholt@sanmarcosrecord.com
Year Established: 1912
Delivery Methods: Newsstand`Carrier`Racks
Own Printing Facility?: Y
Commercial printers?: Y
Mechanical specifications: Type page 13 x 21 1/2; E - 6 cols, 2 1/16, 1/8 between; A - 6 cols, 2 1/16, 1/8 between; C - 9 cols, 1 3/8, 1/16 between.
Published Days: Tues`Wed`Thur`Fri`Sun
Weekday Frequency: e
Avg Paid Circ: 5000
Avg Free Circ: 10000
Audit Company: USPS
Audit Date: 10 01 2017
Pressroom Equipment: Lines – 7-G/Community;
Mailroom Equipment: Tying Machines – 1/Bu; Address Machine – 1-/El.;
Buisness Equipment: DPT/1100, IBM
Editorial Equipment: Hardware – EKI/Televideo.
Production Equipment: Hardware – 1-COM/4961, 1-COM/2961, 1-COM/Unisetter; Cameras – 1-C/J75CC; Scanners – EKI/Televideo.
Total Circulation: 15000

SHERMAN

HERALD DEMOCRAT

Corporate/Parent Company: GateHouse Media
Publication Street Address: 603 S. Sam Rayburn Fwy.
City: Sherman
State: TX
Publication Website: www.heralddemocrat.com
Postal Code: 75090
Office phone: (903) 893-8181
General E-mail: advertising@heralddemocrat.com
Publisher Name: Nate Rodriguez
Publisher Email: nrodriguez@heralddemocrat.com
Publisher Phone: (903) 893-8181, Ext : 1100
Editor Name: William C. Wadsack
Editor Email: wwadsack@heralddemocrat.com
Editor Phone: (903) 893-8181, Ext : 1138
Advertising Executive Name: Kelsie Mason
Advertising Executive Email: kmason@heralddemocrat.com
Advertising Executive Phone: (903) 893-8181, Ext : 1112
Year Established: 1879
Delivery Methods: Mail`Newsstand`Carrier`Racks
Own Printing Facility?: Y
Commercial printers?: Y
Mechanical specifications: Type page 11 5/8 x 21 1/2; E - 6 cols, 1 3/4, 3/16 between; A - 6 cols, 1 3/4, 3/16 between; C - 9 cols, 1 1/4, 1/8 between.
Published Days: Mon`Tues`Wed`Thur`Fri`Sun
Weekday Frequency: m
Avg Paid Circ: 7882
Avg Free Circ: 857
Audit Company: AAM
Audit Date: 3 05 2017

U.S. Daily Newspapers

Pressroom Equipment: Lines – 7-G/Urbanite 1973, 1-G/Urbanite 1989;
Mailroom Equipment: Counter Stackers – 1-MRS/1220, 1/QWI; Inserters & Stuffers – -/1372PS; Tying Machines – 2-MLN/ML2EE.;
Buisness Equipment: 1-Unisys/5000, 1-HP/3000 927LX
Buisness Software: CJ
Classified Equipment: Hardware – APP/Mac; Printers – 1-APP/Mac LaserPrinter;
Classified Software: Baseview.
Editorial Equipment: Hardware – APP/Mac; Printers – 2-Pre Press/Panther Pro
Editorial Software: NewsEngin
Production Equipment: Hardware – 2-Pre Press/Panther Pro Imagesetter
Total Circulation: 15112

SNYDER

SNYDER DAILY NEWS

Publication Street Address: 3600 College Ave
City: Snyder
State: TX
Publication Website: www.snyderdailynews.com
Postal Code: 79550?
Office phone: (325) 573-5486
General E-mail: advertising@snyderdailynews.com
Publisher Name: Bill Crist
Publisher Email: publisher@snyderdailynews.com
Editor Name: Ben Barkley
Editor Email: barkley@snyderdailynews.com
Advertising Executive Name: Christy Rush
Advertising Executive Email: advertising@snyderdailynews.com
Year Established: 1950
Delivery Methods: Mail`Newsstand`Carrier`Racks
Own Printing Facility?: Y
Commercial printers?: Y
Mechanical specifications: Type page 14 1/2 x 21; E - 6 cols, 2 1/16, 1/8 between; A - 6 cols, 2 1/16, 1/8 between; C - 6 cols, 2 1/16, 1/8 between.
Published Days: Mon`Tues`Wed`Thur`Fri`Sat
Weekday Frequency: e
Saturday Frequency: e
Avg Paid Circ: 3400
Audit Company: Sworn/Estimate/Non-Audited
Audit Date: 7 12 2019
Pressroom Equipment: Lines – 6-G/Community; Folders – 1-G/SC.;
Buisness Equipment: TI
Classified Equipment: Hardware – FSI.;
Editorial Equipment: Hardware – FSI.
Total Circulation: 3400

STEPHENVILLE

STEPHENVILLE EMPIRE-TRIBUNE

Corporate/Parent Company: Gannett
Publication Street Address: 702 E South Loop
City: Stephenville
State: TX
Publication Website: www.yourstephenvilletx.com
Postal Code: 76401-5314
Office phone: (254) 965-3124
General E-mail: mhorton@gatehousemedia.com
Editor Name: Melissa Horton
Editor Email: mhorton@gatehousemedia.com
Editor Phone: (254) 965-3124
Advertising Executive Name: Sara Vanden Berge
Advertising Executive Email: svandenberge@empiretribune.com
Advertising Executive Phone: (254) 965-3124
Year Established: 1900
Delivery Methods: Mail`Newsstand`Carrier`Racks
Own Printing Facility?: N
Commercial printers?: N
Mechanical specifications: Type page 11 x 21 1/2; E - 6 cols, 1/8 between; A - 6 cols, 1/8 between; C - 10 cols, 1/8 between.
Published Days: Tues`Wed`Thur`Fri`Sun
Weekday Frequency: m

Avg Paid Circ: 4752
Audit Company: Sworn/Estimate/Non-Audited
Audit Date: 7 12 2019
Pressroom Equipment: Lines – 7-G/Community Offset 1972; Folders – 1-G/SC (with upper former).;
Mailroom Equipment: Tying Machines – MLN/Strapper (plastic).;
Buisness Equipment: IBM
Buisness Software: Microsoft/Word, Microsoft/Excel, Microsoft/Outlook, Microsoft/Windows 98
Classified Equipment: Hardware – APP/Mac; Printers – APP/Mac;
Classified Software: Baseview/AdManager Pro.
Editorial Equipment: Hardware – APP/Mac; Printers – APP/Mac Laser
Editorial Software: QPS/QuarkXPress 4.0.
Production Equipment: Hardware – APP/Mac Laser, Imagesetter; Cameras – C/Spartan II Roll Camera
Total Circulation: 4752

SULPHUR SPRINGS

SULPHUR SPRINGS NEWS-TELEGRAM

Corporate/Parent Company: Echo Publishing Co., Inc.
Publication Street Address: 401 Church St
City: Sulphur Springs
State: TX
Publication Website: www.myssnews.com
Postal Code: 75482-2681
Office phone: (903) 885-8663
General E-mail: dshabaz@ssnewstelegram.com
Publisher Name: Clark Smith
Publisher Email: publisher@ssnewstelegram.com
Editor Name: Jillian Smith
Editor Email: jillian.smith@ssnewstelegram.com
Advertising Executive Name: Dave Shabaz
Advertising Executive Email: dshabaz@ssnewstelegram.com
Mechanical specifications: Type page 13 x 21; E - 6 cols, 2 1/16, 1/8 between; A - 6 cols, 2 1/16, 1/8 between; C - 6 cols, 2 1/16, 1/8 between.
Published Days: Mon`Tues`Wed`Thur`Fri`Sun
Weekday Frequency: e
Avg Paid Circ: 5860
Audit Company: Sworn/Estimate/Non-Audited
Audit Date: 7 12 2019
Pressroom Equipment: Lines – 7-HI/Cotrell V-15A; 8-KP/Color King;
Mailroom Equipment: Counter Stackers – 1/BG; Inserters & Stuffers – 1-/KR; Tying Machines – 1-/Bu, 1-/Cn; Address Machine – 1-/KR.;
Buisness Equipment: 2-Northstar/Horizon, 2-IBM
Classified Equipment: Hardware – 2-APP/Mac SE.;
Editorial Equipment: Hardware – APP/Mac SE, APP/Mac SE30, APP/Mac Classic, APP/Mac fx, APP/Mac si, 2-APP/Power Mac 8100.
Production Equipment: Hardware – 3-APP/Mac LaserWriter Plus, 1-LaserMaster/1200 Laser Printer, ECR; Cameras – 1-Acti; Scanners – 4-APP/Mac SE
Production Software: QPS/QuarkXPress.
Total Circulation: 5860

SWEETWATER

SWEETWATER REPORTER

Corporate/Parent Company: Horizon Publications Inc.
Publication Street Address: 112 W 3rd St
City: Sweetwater
State: TX
Publication Website: www.sweetwaterreporter.com
Postal Code: 79556-4430
Office phone: (325) 236-6677
General E-mail: business@sweetwaterreporter.com

Publisher Name: Rick Nuñez
Publisher Email: publisher@sweetwaterreporter.com
Year Established: 1881
Delivery Methods: Mail`Carrier`Racks
Own Printing Facility?: Y
Mechanical specifications: Type page 12 x 21 1/2; E - 6 cols, 2 1/16, 1/8 between; A - 6 cols, 2 1/16, 1/8 between; C - 8 cols, 1 1/2, 1/8 between.
Published Days: Mon`Tues`Wed`Thur`Fri`Sun
Weekday Frequency: m
Saturday Frequency: m
Avg Paid Circ: 4176
Audit Company: Sworn/Estimate/Non-Audited
Audit Date: 7 12 2019
Pressroom Equipment: Lines – 5-G 1963, 1-G 1977.;
Mailroom Equipment: Tying Machines – 1/Bu; Address Machine – 1-/Wm.;
Buisness Equipment: Acer/PCs
Buisness Software: ARWorks
Classified Equipment: Hardware – APP/Mac; Printers – Okidata/320;
Classified Software: Baseview.
Editorial Equipment: Hardware – APP/Mac; Printers – NewGen/LaserWriters
Editorial Software: QPS/QuarkXPress.
Production Equipment: Hardware – 2-NewGen/Laserwriter; Cameras – 1-R/500.
Total Circulation: 4176

TEMPLE

TEMPLE DAILY TELEGRAM

Corporate/Parent Company: Frank Mayborn Enterprise, Inc.
Publication Street Address: 10 S 3rd St
City: Temple
State: TX
Publication Website: www.tdtnews.com
Postal Code: 76501-7619
Office phone: (254) 778-4444
General E-mail: tdt@tdtnews.com
Publisher Name: Don Cooper
Publisher Email: dcooper@tdtnews.com
Publisher Phone: (254) 774-5203
Editor Name: Jerry Prickett
Editor Email: jprickett@tdtnews.com
Editor Phone: (254) 774-5225
Advertising Executive Name: Lauren Ballard
Advertising Executive Email: laurenb@tdtnews.com
Advertising Executive Phone: (254) 774-5236
Year Established: 1907
Delivery Methods: Mail`Newsstand`Carrier`Racks
Own Printing Facility?: Y
Commercial printers?: Y
Mechanical specifications: Type page 11 5/8 x 21 1/2; E - 6 cols, 1 13/16, 1/8 between; A - 6 cols, 1 13/16, 1/8 between; C - 9 cols, 1 3/16, 1/16 between.
Published Days: Mon`Tues`Wed`Thur`Fri`Sat`Sun
Weekday Frequency: m
Saturday Frequency: m
Avg Paid Circ: 11431
Avg Free Circ: 1086
Audit Company: AAM
Audit Date: 24 06 2020
Pressroom Equipment: Lines – 10-G/Urbanite; Folders – 1-G/2:1;
Mailroom Equipment: Counter Stackers – 3-HL/Monitor; Inserters & Stuffers – 1-GMA/SLS 1000 8:2; Tying Machines – 1-MLN/Plastic, 1-MLN/2E.;
Buisness Equipment: 7-Dell/Pentium III
Buisness Software: Mas 90, IBM/AR 2000
Classified Equipment: Hardware – ALR/Pentium II, ALR/Fileserver; 1-Microtek/b&w Scanner with OCR, 1-Kk/40 Digital Camera, 1-QuickTake/150 Digital Camera, 1-ABS/486; Printers – Okidata/320;
Classified Software: APT.
Editorial Equipment: Hardware – ALR/Pentium II, 1-Nikon/Coolscan; Printers – Okidata/320, 1-Okidata/591, 1-Okidata/321, 1-Epson/Stylus Pro, HP/LaserJet IID
Editorial Software: APT.
Production Equipment: Hardware – 1-L/190 Postscript Imagesetter Full Page, BKY/30A, 1-Konica/EV Jetsetter, 2-Elite XL

Postscript; Cameras – 1-C/Spartan II
Production Software: APT, QPS/QuarkXPress 4.0.
Total Circulation: 11350

TYLER

TYLER MORNING TELEGRAPH

Corporate/Parent Company: Texas Community Media LLC
Publication Street Address: 410 W Erwin St
City: Tyler
State: TX
Publication Website: www.tylerpaper.com
Postal Code: 75702-7133
Office phone: (903) 597-8111
General E-mail: advertising@tylerpaper.com
Publisher Name: Justin Wilcox
Publisher Email: jwilcox@tylerpaper.com
Publisher Phone: (903) 596-6299
Editor Name: Emily Guevara
Editor Email: eguevara@tylerpaper.com
Editor Phone: (903) 596-6281
Advertising Executive Name: Alyssa Hankins
Advertising Executive Email: ahankins@tylerpaper.com
Advertising Executive Phone: (903) 596-6295
Year Established: 1929
Mechanical specifications: Type page 11 5/8 x 21 1/2; E - 6 cols, 1 5/6, 1/8 between; A - 6 cols, 1 5/6, 1/8 between; C - 9 cols, 1 3/16, 1/8 between.
Published Days: Mon`Tues`Wed`Thur`Fri`Sat`Sun
Weekday Frequency: m
Saturday Frequency: m
Avg Paid Circ: 13957
Audit Company: AAM
Audit Date: 25 02 2020
Pressroom Equipment: Lines – 12-HI/845N single width 1974; Press Drive – SECO/Warner Baldor; Folders – 2-HI/RBC-2; Control System – Entertron/PLC.;
Mailroom Equipment: Counter Stackers – 3/HL, 2-QWI/401; Inserters & Stuffers – 1-K & M/1372; Tying Machines – 3-OVL/415, 1-OVL/515; Control System – K & M/Image PC, QWI/Program 32; Address Machine – 1-KR/215;
Buisness Equipment: Advanced Publishing Technology
Buisness Software: Advanced Publishing Technology
Classified Equipment: Hardware – Novell/Network (PC Based) Client Server 4.1; Printers – Tektronix/Phaser 600;
Classified Software: Brainworks.
Editorial Equipment: Hardware – Novell/Network (PC Based) Client Server 4.1; Printers – ECR/VRL 36, Tektronix/Phaser 600
Editorial Software: Advanced Pub. Technology/Automated Complete Typesetting.
Production Equipment: Hardware – Text Bridge/Pro, Macro/JetSetter; Cameras – 3-Kk/DC50, Digital Cameras; Scanners – Lf/Leafscan, Umax/Flatbed, Epson/Flatbed, Visioneer/Single Sheet Scanner, Kk/Film Scanner, Konica/Scanner
Production Software: APT, MEI/ALS, QPS/QuarkXPress.
Total Circulation: 10965

VERNON

THE VERNON DAILY RECORD

Corporate/Parent Company: Vernon Record, Inc.
Publication Street Address: 3214 Wilbarger St
City: Vernon
State: TX
Publication Website: www.vernonrecord.com
Postal Code: 76384-7927
Office phone: (940) 552-5454
General E-mail: advertising@vernonrecord.com
Publisher Name: Bret K. McCormick
Publisher Email: publisher@vernonrecord.com
Editor Name: Daniel Walker
Editor Email: dwalker@vernonrecord.com
Advertising Executive Name: Clint McCormick
Advertising Executive Email: advertising@vernonrecord.com
Year Established: 1908

U.S. Daily Newspapers

Delivery Methods: Newsstand`Carrier`Racks
Own Printing Facility?: Y
Commercial printers?: Y
Mechanical specifications: Type page 13 x 21; E - 6 cols, 2 1/16, 1/8 between; A - 6 cols, 2 1/16, 1/8 between; C - 6 cols, 2 1/16, 1/8 between.
Published Days: Mon`Tues`Wed`Thur`Fri`Sun
Weekday Frequency: e
Avg Paid Circ: 2400
Audit Company: Sworn/Estimate/Non-Audited
Audit Date: 7 12 2019
Pressroom Equipment: Lines – 6-G/Community 1986.;
Mailroom Equipment: Tying Machines – Bu.; Address Machine – Yes;
Buisness Equipment: PC
Classified Equipment: Hardware – FSI; Printers – Xante/Accel-a-Writer;
Classified Software: FSI.
Editorial Equipment: Hardware – FSI
Editorial Software: FSI.
Production Equipment: CTP
Total Circulation: 2400

VICTORIA

VICTORIA ADVOCATE

Corporate/Parent Company: Victoria Advocate Publishing Co.
Publication Street Address: 311 E Constitution St
City: Victoria
State: TX
Publication Website: www.victoriaadvocate.com
Postal Code: 77901-8140
Office phone: (361) 575-1451
General E-mail: feedback@vicad.com
Publisher Name: Chris Cobler
Publisher Email: ccobler@vicad.com
Publisher Phone: (361) 574-1271
Editor Name: Becky Cooper
Editor Email: bcooper@vicad.com
Editor Phone: (361) 574-1285
Advertising Executive Name: Annie Andrade
Advertising Executive Email: aandrade@vicad.com
Advertising Executive Phone: (361) 574-1241
Year Established: 1846
Mechanical specifications: Type page 11 5/8 x 21 1/2; E - 6 cols, 1 5/6, 1/8 between; A - 6 cols, 1 5/6, 1/8 between; C - 9 cols, 1 3/8, 1/16 between.
Published Days: Mon`Tues`Wed`Thur`Fri`Sat`Sun
Weekday Frequency: m
Saturday Frequency: m
Avg Paid Circ: 15728
Avg Free Circ: 445
Audit Company: AAM
Audit Date: 18 04 2017
Pressroom Equipment: Lines – 6-HI/N1650 (5 Registron Reels & Stands) 1978; Press Drive – Haley/Controls/Emerson; Folders – 2-HI/2:1; Reels & Stands – 5-HI/Registron; Control System – Haley/Emerson.;
Mailroom Equipment: Counter Stackers – 1-Id/550, 1-Id/2100, 2-Id/2000; Inserters & Stuffers – 2/AM Graphics/848; Tying Machines – 1-MLN/ML2-EE, 1-OVL/JP80, 1-OVL/JP40, 1-OVL/415-A.;
Buisness Equipment: Compaq/Prosignia 300
Buisness Software: SBS Business Software, PPI Advertising Software
Classified Equipment: Hardware – Compaq; Printers – HP/5si;
Classified Software: PPI.
Editorial Equipment: Hardware – IBM; Printers – 3-HP/Laser SL, 1-Epson/Color
Editorial Software: CNI/Agile Teambase Special Edition.
Production Equipment: Hardware – Kk/XL-7700 Printer, QPS, Lf/AP Leaf Picture Desk; Scanners – Nikon/35AF, Kk/2055 Plus, 2-AG/Arcus.
Total Circulation: 24766

WACO

WACO TRIBUNE-HERALD

Corporate/Parent Company: Cox
Publication Street Address: 900 Franklin Ave
City: Waco
State: TX
Publication Website: www.wacotrib.com
Postal Code: 76701-1906
Office phone: (254) 757-5757
General E-mail: news@wacotrib.com
Publisher Name: Jim Wilson
Publisher Email: jwilson@wacotrib.com
Editor Name: Steve Boggs
Editor Email: sboggs@wacotrib.com
Advertising Executive Name: Ana Lozano-Harper
Advertising Executive Email: alharper@wacotrib.com
Year Established: 1892
Delivery Methods: Mail`Newsstand`Carrier`Racks
Own Printing Facility?: N
Commercial printers?: N
Mechanical specifications: Type page 13 x 21 1/4; E - 6 cols, 2, 1/6 between; A - 6 cols, 2, 1/6 between; C - 9 cols, 1 3/8, 1/12 between.
Published Days: Mon`Tues`Wed`Thur`Fri`Sat`Sun
Weekday Frequency: m
Saturday Frequency: m
Avg Paid Circ: 18567
Avg Free Circ: 1469
Audit Company: AAM
Audit Date: 15 04 2019
Buisness Equipment: Dell Desktops, HP Printers
Buisness Software: DSI,
Classified Equipment: Dell Desktops, Ricoh and HP Printers
Classified Software: Atex Adbase
Editorial Equipment: Dell Desktops and Laptops. Ricoh and HP Printers Canon Cameras
Editorial Software: TCMS
Production Equipment: Hardware – Dell Desktops, Ricoh and HP Printers
Production Software: TCMC, Adobe Creative Suite
Total Circulation: 22680

WAXAHACHIE

WAXAHACHIE DAILY LIGHT

Corporate/Parent Company: Gannett
Publication Street Address: 200 W Marvin Ave
City: Waxahachie
State: TX
Publication Website: www.waxahachieTX.com
Postal Code: 75165-3040
Office phone: (972) 937-3310
General E-mail: sbrooks@waxahachietx.com
Editor Name: Rebecca Jones
Editor Email: rjones1@gatehousemedia.com
Editor Phone: (469) 517-1470
Advertising Executive Name: Colten Crist
Advertising Executive Email: ccrist@waxahachietx.com
Advertising Executive Phone: (469) 517-1440
Year Established: 1867
Delivery Methods: Mail`Newsstand`Carrier`Racks
Own Printing Facility?: Y
Commercial printers?: Y
Mechanical specifications: Type page 13 x 21 1/2; E - 6 cols, 1 5/6, 1/8 between; A - 6 cols, 1 5/6, 1/8 between; C - 10 cols, 1 5/6, 1/8 between.
Published Days: Tues`Wed`Thur`Fri`Sun
Weekday Frequency: m
Avg Paid Circ: 4500
Audit Company: Sworn/Estimate/Non-Audited
Audit Date: 7 12 2019
Pressroom Equipment: Lines – 6-G/Community (upper former); Folders – 1-G/Community SC.;
Mailroom Equipment: Tying Machines – 4-/Sa, 1-/MLN; Address Machine – 1-Am/1900.;
Buisness Equipment: Gateway
Buisness Software: PBS, Accounting
Classified Equipment: Hardware – APP/Mac SE30;
Classified Software: Baseview.
Editorial Equipment: Hardware – APP/Mac SE30, APP/Mac G3, APP/Mac G4; Printers – HP/4MV
Editorial Software: QPS/InDesign, Adobe/Photoshop.
Production Equipment: Hardware – PrePress/CTP; Cameras – 1-C/Spartan III.
Total Circulation: 4500

WEATHERFORD

THE WEATHERFORD DEMOCRAT

Corporate/Parent Company: CNHI, LLC
Publication Street Address: 512 Palo Pinto St
City: Weatherford
State: TX
Publication Website: www.weatherforddemocrat.com
Postal Code: 76086-4128
Office phone: (817) 594-7447
General E-mail: editor@weatherforddemocrat.com
Publisher Name: Lisa Chappell
Publisher Email: lchappell@cnhi.com
Publisher Phone: (817) 594-7447, Ext : 237
Editor Name: Sally Sexton
Editor Email: ssexton@weatherforddemocrat.com
Editor Phone: (817) 594-7447, Ext : 236
Advertising Executive Name: Michelle Roberts
Advertising Executive Email: mroberts@weatherforddemocrat.com
Advertising Executive Phone: (817) 594-7447, Ext : 232
Year Established: 1895
Delivery Methods: Mail`Carrier
Mechanical specifications: Type page 13 x 21 1/2; E - 6 cols, 2 1/16, 1/8 between; A - 6 cols, 2 1/16, 1/8 between; C - 8 cols, 1 1/2, 1/8 between.
Published Days: Tues`Wed`Thur`Fri`Sun
Weekday Frequency: m
Avg Paid Circ: 3740
Avg Free Circ: 300
Audit Company: AAM
Audit Date: 30 09 2014
Pressroom Equipment: Lines – 8-G/Community; Folders – 6-G/2:1.;
Mailroom Equipment: Tying Machines – 1-Mk/ACE 420, 1/MLN.;
Buisness Equipment: Unisys/3105-00
Classified Equipment: Hardware – 2-APP/Mac G3; Printers – APP/Mac LaserPrinter NT;
Classified Software: Baseview/Class Manager Pro, Baseview/Class Flow.
Editorial Equipment: Hardware – 8-APP/Power Mac; Printers – GCC
Editorial Software: Baseview/NewsEdit Pro.
Production Equipment: Hardware – GCC, 6-APP/Mac G4; Cameras – Acti; Scanners – APP/Mac, 4-Umax.
Total Circulation: 4040

WICHITA FALLS

TIMES RECORD NEWS

Corporate/Parent Company: Gannett
Publication Street Address: 1301 Lamar St
City: Wichita Falls
State: TX
Publication Website: timesrecordnews.com
Postal Code: 76301-7032
Office phone: 940-767-8341
Editor Name: Deanna Watson
Editor Email: news@timesrecordnews.com
Audit Company: AAM
Audit Date: 18 04 2018
Total Circulation: 14530

WICHITA FALLS TIMES RECORD NEWS

Publication Street Address: 1301 Lamar St
City: Wichita Falls
State: TX
Publication Website: www.timesrecordnews.com
Postal Code: 76301-7032
Office phone: (940) 720-3491
General E-mail: tracyk@timesrecordnews.com
Editor Name: Deanna Watson
Year Established: 1907
Mechanical specifications: Type page 13 x 21 1/2; E - 6 cols, 2 1/16, 1/8 between; A - 6 cols, 2 1/16, 1/8 between; C - 10 cols, 1 1/10, 1/16 between.
Published Days: Mon`Tues`Wed`Thur`Fri`Sat`Sun
Weekday Frequency: m
Saturday Frequency: m
Avg Paid Circ: 13417
Avg Free Circ: 1175
Audit Company: AAM
Audit Date: 31 12 2017
Pressroom Equipment: Lines – 7-G/Cosmo 1984.;
Mailroom Equipment: Counter Stackers – 3-Id, HL; Inserters & Stuffers – 3/MM; Tying Machines – 4-/MLN; Address Machine – 1-/KR.;
Buisness Equipment: HP/3000
Classified Equipment: Hardware – Ik; Printers – NewGen;
Classified Software: Ik.
Editorial Equipment: Hardware – Ik/APP/Mac; Printers – NewGen.
Production Equipment: Hardware – Nat, Tegra; Cameras – C; Scanners – ECR, Umax
Production Software: QPS/QuarkXPress 3.3.1.
Total Circulation: 14592

UTAH

LOGAN

HERALD JOURNAL

Corporate/Parent Company: Adams Publishing Group
Publication Street Address: 1068 West 130 South
City: Logan
State: UT
Publication Website: www.hjnews.com
Postal Code: 84321
Office phone: (435) 752-2121
General E-mail: hjnews@hjnews.com
Editor Name: Charles McCollum
Editor Email: cmccollum@hjnews.com
Editor Phone: 435-752-2121 x1004
Advertising Executive Name: Mike Dayley
Advertising Executive Email: mdayley@hjnews.com
Advertising Executive Phone: 435-752-2121 x1017

THE HERALD JOURNAL

Corporate/Parent Company: Adams Publishing Group
Publication Street Address: 1068 W 130 South
City: Logan
State: UT
Publication Website: www.hjnews.com
Postal Code: 84321-3971
Office phone: (435) 752-2121
General E-mail: hjnews@hjnews.com
Publisher Name: Jeremy Colley
Publisher Email: jcooley@hjnews.com
Publisher Phone: (435) 752-2121, Ext : 1000

OGDEN

STANDARD-EXAMINER

Corporate/Parent Company: Ogden Publishing Corp.
Publication Street Address: 332 Standard Way
City: Ogden
State: UT
Publication Website: www.standard.net
Postal Code: 84404-1371
Office phone: (801) 625-4200
General E-mail: customerservice@standard.net

PROVO

DAILY HERALD

Corporate/Parent Company: Ogden Newspapers, Inc.
Publication Street Address: 86 N. University Ave. #300
City: Provo
State: UT
Publication Website: www.heraldextra.com
Postal Code: 84601-4474
Office phone: (801) 373-5050
General E-mail: cconover@heraldextra.com
Publisher Name: Scott Blonde
Publisher Email: sblonde@heraldextra.com
Publisher Phone: (801) 344-2935

SAINT GEORGE

THE SPECTRUM

Corporate/Parent Company: Gannett
Publication Street Address: 275 E Saint George Blvd
City: Saint George
State: UT
Publication Website: www.thespectrum.com
Postal Code: 84770-2954
Office phone: (435) 674-6200
General E-mail: classifieds@thespectrum.com
Publisher Name: Rhett Long
Publisher Email: rlong@thespectrum.com
Publisher Phone: (435) 674-6222

SALT LAKE CITY

DESERET NEWS

Corporate/Parent Company: Deseret News
City: Salt Lake City
State: UT
Publication Website: www.deseretnews.com
Postal Code: 84101-3502
Office phone: (801) 236-6000
General E-mail: news@deseretnews.com
Publisher Name: Jeff Simpson

THE SALT LAKE TRIBUNE

Corporate/Parent Company: The Salt Lake Tribune, Inc
Publication Street Address: 90 S 400 W
City: Salt Lake City
State: UT
Publication Website: www.sltrib.com
Postal Code: 84101-1431
Office phone: (801) 257-8742
General E-mail: webmaster@sltrib.com
Publisher Name: Paul Huntsman
Publisher Email: paul@sltrib.com

VIRGINIA

CHARLOTTESVILLE

THE DAILY PROGRESS

Corporate/Parent Company: Lee Enterprises
Publication Street Address: 685 Rio Rd W
City: Charlottesville
State: VA
Publication Website: www.dailyprogress.com
Postal Code: 22901-1213
Office phone: (434) 978-7200
General E-mail: circcontacts@dailyprogress.com
Publisher Name: Peter S. Yates
Publisher Email: pyates@dailyprogress.com
Publisher Phone: (434) 978-7203
Editor Name: Aaron Richardson
Editor Email: arichardson@dailyprogress.com
Editor Phone: (434) 978-7283
Advertising Executive Name: Dave Massey
Advertising Executive Email: dmassey@dailyprogress.com
Advertising Executive Phone: (434) 978-7237
Year Established: 1892
Delivery Methods:
  Mail`Newsstand`Carrier`Racks
Own Printing Facility?: N
Commercial printers?: N
Mechanical specifications: Type page 12 1/2 x 21; E - 6 cols, 2, 1/8 between; A - 6 cols, 2, 1/8 between; C - 9 cols, 1 1/8, 1/16 between.
Published Days: Mon`Tues`Wed`Thur`Fri`Sat`Sun
Weekday Frequency: m
Saturday Frequency: m
Avg Paid Circ: 12523
Avg Free Circ: 1092
Audit Company: AAM
Audit Date: 16 04 2019
Buisness Equipment: HP
Classified Equipment: Hardware – 5-Compaq; NewGen, Imager Plus/12; Printers – HP/LaserPrinter.
Classified Software: ACT.
Editorial Equipment: Hardware – HP/2-NewGen, Lf/Leafscan for Color Seperation; Printers – 4-APP/Mac Laser II NTX
Editorial Software: ACT.
Production Equipment: Hardware – WL/Plater, 1-NewGen, Image Plus 12; Cameras – 1-C/Spartan III L270, SCREEN; Scanners – RZ.
Total Circulation: 16737

CULPEPER

CULPEPER STAR-EXPONENT

Corporate/Parent Company: Lee Enterprises
Publication Street Address: 122 W Spencer St
City: Culpeper
State: VA
Publication Website: www.starexponent.com
Postal Code: 22701-2628
Office phone: (540) 825-0771
General E-mail: ejennings@starexponent.com
Editor Name: Marla Mckenna
Published Days: Mon`Tues`Wed`Thur`Fri`Sat`Sun
Weekday Frequency: m
Saturday Frequency: m
Avg Paid Circ: 2928
Avg Free Circ: 294
Audit Company: AAM
Audit Date: 29 08 2018
Total Circulation: 3552

DANVILLE

DANVILLE REGISTER & BEE

Corporate/Parent Company: Lee Enterprises
Publication Street Address: 700 Monument St
City: Danville
State: VA
Publication Website: www.godanriver.com
Postal Code: 24541-1512
Office phone: (434) 791-7971
General E-mail: news@registerbee.com
Publisher Name: Peter S. Yates
Publisher Email: pyates@dailyprogress.com
Publisher Phone: (434) 978-7203
Editor Name: Aaron Richardson
Editor Email: arichardson@dailyprogress.com
Editor Phone: (434) 978-7283
Advertising Executive Name: Dave Massey
Advertising Executive Email: dmassey@dailyprogress.com
Advertising Executive Phone: (434) 978-7237
Mechanical specifications: Type page 13 x 21 1/2; E - 6 cols, 2 1/16, 1/8 between; A - 6 cols, 2 1/16, 1/8 between; C - 9 cols, 1 3/8, 1/16 between.
Published Days: Mon`Tues`Wed`Thur`Fri`Sat`Sun
Weekday Frequency: m
Saturday Frequency: m
Avg Paid Circ: 9934
Avg Free Circ: 92
Audit Company: AAM
Audit Date: 22 11 2019
Pressroom Equipment: Lines – 11-G/Urbanite 1215-1244 single width 1978, 2-G/Urbanite 1214-1244 single width 1993; Registration System – Duarte/Pin Registration.
Mailroom Equipment: Counter Stackers – 1-HL/Monitor, 1-Id/2100, 1-Id/2100; Inserters & Stuffers – HI/48P; Tying Machines – 1-MLN/ML, 1-MLN/Spirit, 1-MLN/SP330; Address Machine – 1-MM/Minuteman quarter folder.;
Buisness Equipment: DEC/XL-590, Data Sciences
Classified Equipment: Hardware – 4-SII/Synthesis 66, Roadrunner/PC 486; Printers – 1-APP/Mac IIG;
Classified Software: Pongrass/Page Integrator.
Editorial Equipment: Hardware – 1-SII/Synthesis 66XR, 20-Roadrunner/PC 486, 4-APP/Mac, 1-APP/Mac fileserver/1-APP/Power Mac 8500-120 fileserver; Printers – 3-APP/Mac LaserPrinter, 2-APP/Mac LaserWriter Pro
Editorial Software: SII/Synthesis 66 XR.
Production Equipment: Hardware – 2-Accuset/Laser Imager, 1-AU/APS 6600 (Hitachi Engine), APP/Mac Quadra 840 AV, Microtek/Flatbed Scanner, Lf/Leafscan 35, Lf/Leafscan 45; Cameras – 1-C/Pager, 1-C/Spartan III
Production Software: QPS/QuarkXPress 3.1.
Total Circulation: 9165

FREDERICKSBURG

THE FREE LANCE-STAR

Corporate/Parent Company: Lee Enterprises
Publication Street Address: 1340 Central Park Blvd., Suite 100
City: Fredericksburg
State: VA
Publication Website: www.freelancestar.com
Postal Code: 22401-3887
Office phone: (540) 374-5000
General E-mail: information@freelancestar.com
Publisher Name: Dale Lachniet
Editor Name: Phil Jenkins
Editor Email: pjenkins@freelancestar.com
Editor Phone: (540) 374-5422
Advertising Executive Phone: (540) 374-5001
Year Established: 1885
Delivery Methods:
  Mail`Newsstand`Carrier`Racks
Own Printing Facility?: Y
Commercial printers?: Y
Mechanical specifications: Type page 11 5/16 x 20 1/2; E - 6 cols, 1 4/5, 1/8 between; A - 6 cols, 1 4/5, 1/8 between; C - 9 cols, 1 1/5, between.
Published Days: Mon`Tues`Wed`Thur`Fri`Sat`Sun
Weekday Frequency: m
Saturday Frequency: m
Avg Paid Circ: 22227
Avg Free Circ: 1427
Audit Company: AAM
Audit Date: 17 03 2020
Pressroom Equipment: Lines – 2 Unit 72" Triplewide Goss FPS Press-2010; 2 Unit 72" Triplewide Goss FPS Press-2010; 1 11 Meter Goss Conti Webb Dryer; Folders – 2 Goss 5:5:2 Folders and 1 Goss Quarterfold; Pasters –4 Goss Contiweb PastersControl System – Goss Omnicon; Registration System – QIPC Registration and Cut-Off
Mailroom Equipment: Counter Stackers – 4 Ferag Smart Stacks; Inserters & Stuffers – 1 32 Pocket Goss Magnapack with 2 DTP; Tying Machines – 6 Samuel Tiers; Wrapping Singles – 1 CMC JWR30; Control System – Goss Omnicon; Address Machine – Inline Domino Inkjet;
Classified Equipment: Hardware – 15-Xterms, 1-Sun/Enterprise 250; Printers – HP/4000;
Classified Software: Vision Data 6.0.
Editorial Equipment: Hardware – 2-Dell/PowerEdge 6300, 1-Dell/Poweredge 4300; Printers – 1-HP/4000, 1-HP/8100
Editorial Software: Tera/GN3 B85, Binuscan.
Production Equipment: Hardware – 2 Kodak News Generation 300 Thermal Imagers – NELA Optical Punch/Bend and Plate Sortation System
Total Circulation: 23826

HARRISONBURG

DAILY NEWS-RECORD

Corporate/Parent Company: Rockingham Publishing Co. Inc.
Publication Street Address: 231 S. Liberty St
City: Harrisonburg
State: VA
Publication Website: www.dnronline.com
Postal Code: 22803
Office phone: (540) 574-6200
General E-mail: webeditor@dnronline.com
Publisher Name: Craig Bartoldson
Publisher Email: cbartoldson@dnronline.com
Publisher Phone: (540) 574-6298
Editor Name: Jim Sacco
Editor Email: jsacco@dnronline.com
Editor Phone: (540) 574-6281
Advertising Executive Name: Rhonda Mcneal
Advertising Executive Email: rmcneal@dnronline.com
Advertising Executive Phone: (540) 574-6223
Delivery Methods: Mail`Racks
Own Printing Facility?: Y
Commercial printers?: Y
Mechanical specifications: Type page 9 13/16 x 11 1/2; E - 5 cols, 1 7/8, 1/8 between; A - 5 cols, 1 7/8, 1/8 between; C - 5 cols, 1 3/16, 1/16 between.
Published Days: Wed
Avg Free Circ: 12500
Audit Company: AAM
Audit Date: 23 08 2018
Total Circulation: 25400

LYNCHBURG

THE NEWS & ADVANCE

Corporate/Parent Company: Lee Enterprises
Publication Street Address: 101 Wyndale Dr
City: Lynchburg
State: VA
Publication Website: www.newsadvance.com
Postal Code: 24501-6710
Office phone: (434) 385-5400
General E-mail: ads@newsadvance.com
Publisher Name: Kelly E. Mirt
Publisher Email: kmirt@newsadvance.com
Publisher Phone: (434) 385-5570
Editor Name: Caroline Glickman
Editor Email: cglickman@newsadvance.com
Editor Phone: (434) 385-5552
Advertising Executive Name: Kevin Smith
Advertising Executive Email: ksmith@newsadvance.com
Advertising Executive Phone: (434) 385-5462
Year Established: 1866
Own Printing Facility?: Y
Commercial printers?: Y
Mechanical specifications: Type page 13 x 21 1/2; E - 5 cols, 2 1/2, 13/100 between; A - 6 cols, 2 1/25, 1/6 between; C - 9 cols, 1 3/8, 1/20 between.
Published Days: Mon`Tues`Wed`Thur`Fri`Sat`Sun
Weekday Frequency: m
Saturday Frequency: m
Avg Paid Circ: 12867
Avg Free Circ: 1350
Audit Company: AAM
Audit Date: 12 12 2019
Pressroom Equipment: Lines – 5-HI/1650 1974; Press Drive – 2-Fin/250 h.p.; Folders – HI/2:1.;
Mailroom Equipment: Counter Stackers – 2/QWI; Inserters & Stuffers – 1-HI/1372; Tying Machines – 1-/Dyanric, 1-Si; Address Machine – 1-/KR.;
Buisness Equipment: APT
Classified Equipment: Hardware – 10-EKI/Televideo; Printers – 1-NewGen/480;
Classified Software: EKI.
Editorial Equipment: Hardware – HP/PC/1-Lf/AP Leaf Picture Desk, 1-Lf/Leafscan 35; Printers – 1-NewGen/1200T, HP/4MV, QMS/2060
Editorial Software: APT/Editorial System, QPS/QuarkXPress, Microsoft/Word.
Production Equipment: Hardware – 1-Graham/GNS 28, 1-BKY/5000, NewGen/1200T; Cameras – 1-C/Spartan III.

U.S. Daily Newspapers

Total Circulation: 16755

MARTINSVILLE

MARTINSVILLE BULLETIN

Corporate/Parent Company: Lee Enterprises
Publication Street Address: 204 Broad St
City: Martinsville
State: VA
Publication Website: www.martinsvillebulletin.com
Postal Code: 24115
Office phone: (276) 638-8801
General E-mail: advertising@martinsvillebulletin.com
Publisher Name: Wendi Craig
Publisher Email: wcraig@martinsvillebulletin.com
Publisher Phone: (276) 638-8801, Ext : 213
Advertising Executive Email: advertising@martinsvillebulletin.com
Year Established: 1889
Delivery Methods: Mail`Newsstand`Carrier`Racks
Own Printing Facility?: N
Commercial printers?: Y
Mechanical specifications: Type page 11 2/3 x 21 1/2; E - 6 cols, 1 4/5, 1/8 between; A - 6 cols, 1 4/5, 1/8 between; C - 9 cols, 1 1/4, 1/8 between.
Published Days: Mon`Tues`Wed`Thur`Fri`Sun
Weekday Frequency: m
Avg Paid Circ: 8183
Avg Free Circ: 85
Audit Company: AAM
Audit Date: 15 04 2019
Pressroom Equipment: Lines – 5-G/Urbanite U-920; 5-DEV/2400.;
Mailroom Equipment: Counter Stackers – HI/Rima RS255; Inserters & Stuffers – KAN/480; Tying Machines – MLN, Dynaric, Interlake.;
Buisness Equipment: IBM/PCs
Buisness Software: MSSI
Classified Equipment: Hardware – APP/Mac; Printers – 2-AU/Laser Film Imager, 3-Okidata;
Classified Software: Baseview.
Editorial Equipment: Hardware – APP/Mac/Lf/Leafscan 35, AG/Flatbed Scanner; Printers – 2-AU/Laser Film Imager, 3-Okidata
Editorial Software: Baseview.
Production Equipment: Hardware – AU, W; Scanners – Lf/Leafscan 35, Leica/Flatbed, AU/Drum Scanner
Production Software: Baseview.
Total Circulation: 8834

MCLEAN

USA TODAY

Corporate/Parent Company: Gannett
Publication Street Address: 7950 Jones Branch Dr
City: McLean
State: VA
Publication`Website: www.usatoday.com
Postal Code: 22108-0003
Office phone: (703) 854-3400
General E-mail: accuracy@usatoday.com
Editor Name: Kristen Delguzzi
Editor Email: kdelguzzi@usatoday.com
Year Established: 1982
Delivery Methods: Mail`Newsstand`Carrier`Racks
Own Printing Facility?: Y
Commercial printers?: Y
Published Days: Mon`Tues`Wed`Thur`Fri`Sat`Sun
Weekday Frequency: m
Avg Paid Circ: 1794902
Audit Company: AAM
Audit Date: 31 12 2017
Note: USA TODAY does not sell advertising on an inch rate basis: advertisers can purchase the specific sizes offered by the newspaper. Classified advertising is sold at a line rate.
Total Circulation: 1794902

NEWPORT NEWS

DAILY PRESS

Corporate/Parent Company: Tribune Publishing Company
Publication Street Address: 703 Mariners Row
City: Newport News
State: VA
Publication Website: www.dailypress.com
Postal Code: 23606-4432
Office phone: (757) 247-4600
General E-mail: customerservice@dailypress.com
Publisher Name: Par Ridder
Editor Name: Ryan Gilchrest
Editor Email: rgilchrest@dailypress.com
Editor Phone: (757) 446-2385
Year Established: 1896
Delivery Methods: Mail`Newsstand`Carrier
Own Printing Facility?: N
Commercial printers?: N
Mechanical specifications: Type page 10 1/2 x 21; E - 6 cols, 1 19/32, 1/10 between; A - 6 cols, 1 19/32, 1/10 between; C - 10 cols, 1 3/32, 3/32 between.
Published Days: Mon`Tues`Wed`Thur`Fri`Sat`Sun
Weekday Frequency: m
Saturday Frequency: m
Avg Paid Circ: 32177
Audit Company: AAM
Audit Date: 16 04 2020
Pressroom Equipment: Lines – 16-G/3346-3347 (8 color half decks)
Mailroom Equipment: Counter Stackers – 6-GMA/CombiStacks, 4-QWI/401 Stackers, 2-Gammerler/Stackers; Inserters & Stuffers – 1-GMA/SLS3000 14:2, 1-GMA/SLS3000 30:2 (dual delivery); Tying Machines – 3-Dynaric/Tyer NP2, 1-Dynaric/NP3000; Control System – GMA/SA;
Buisness Equipment: Admarc, IBM/CICS, CJ, Open Pages, CCI, Advision
Buisness Software: Microsoft/Office
Classified Equipment: Hardware – Dell/Pentium, Advision/GX110, ALPS/GX110; Printers – HP/8000;
Classified Software: CText/ADV 5.1.
Editorial Equipment: Hardware – 130-Pentium/PC, 15-APP/Power Mac
Editorial Software: Open Pages.
Production Equipment: Hardware – 3-AII/3850 Typesetter, AP/Server; Scanners – 1-GEI/Tecsa Scanners, 2-Umax/2100 XL
Production Software: Open Pages, ALPS 5.1.
Total Circulation: 72568

NORFOLK

THE VIRGINIAN-PILOT

Corporate/Parent Company: Tribune Publishing
Publication Street Address: 150 W Brambleton Ave
City: Norfolk
State: VA
Publication Website: www.pilotonline.com
Postal Code: 23510-2018
Office phone: (757) 446-2983
General E-mail: kelly.till@pilotonline.com
Publisher Name: Par Ridder
Editor Name: Ryan Gilchrest
Editor Email: rgilchrest@dailypress.com
Editor Phone: (757) 446-2385
Year Established: 1866
Delivery Methods: Mail`Newsstand`Carrier`Racks
Own Printing Facility?: Y
Commercial printers?: Y
Mechanical specifications: Type page 11 1/2 x 21 1/2; E - 6 cols, 1 4/5, 1/8 between; A - 6 cols, 1 4/5, 1/8 between; C - 10 cols, 1 9/16, 1/16 between.
Published Days: Mon`Tues`Wed`Thur`Fri`Sat`Sun
Weekday Frequency: m
Saturday Frequency: m
Avg Paid Circ: 83208
Audit Company: AAM
Audit Date: 13 05 2019
Pressroom Equipment: Lines – 30-G/Metro offset double width; Press Drive – FINCOR DRIVE SHAFT; Folders – 5-G/Metro 3:2 Imperial Folder (with double delivery); Pasters –30-G/Tension SystemReels & Stands – 30; Control System – Goss PCS; Registration System – Quad-tec
Pressroom Software: Goss PCS, AGFA
Mailroom Equipment: Counter Stackers – 14 SMS Ferag; Inserters & Stuffers – 3 Goss Magna-Pak Inserters; Tying Machines – 15 Mosca Z-5 Tyers; Control System – Omnizone; Address Machine – 4 Kodak Printers;
Mailroom Software: Omnizone
Buisness Equipment: 13-IBM/4381, 1-IBM/AS-400 B60 (midrange)
Classified Equipment: Hardware – 35-AT.;
Editorial Equipment: Hardware – 200-AT, 10-APP/Mac Portable, 20-IBM/Portable, 40-IBM/Compatable, 12-AT/News Layout, 36-APP/Mac Page Design, 10-Tandem/Portable
Editorial Software: Adobe InDesign
Production Equipment: Hardware – 2-AG/Avantra 30E, 2-K&F/PlatXpress with Vision Bender
Production Software: AII/Oman.
Total Circulation: 121583

PETERSBURG

THE PROGRESS-INDEX

Corporate/Parent Company: Gannett
Publication Street Address: 15 Franklin St
City: Petersburg
State: VA
Publication Website: www.progress-index.com
Postal Code: 23803-4503
Office phone: (804) 732-3456
General E-mail: acoleman@progress-index.com
Publisher Name: Craig Richards
Publisher Email: crichards@progress-index.com
Publisher Phone: (804) 722-5103
Editor Name: Pat Sharpf
Editor Email: psharpf@progress-index.com
Editor Phone: (804) 722-5158
Commercial printers?: Y
Mechanical specifications: Type page 13 x 21 1/2; E - 6 cols, 2 1/16, 1/8 between; A - 6 cols, 2 1/16, 1/8 between; C - 9 cols, 1 5/16, 1/8 between.
Published Days: Mon`Tues`Wed`Thur`Fri`Sat`Sun
Weekday Frequency: m
Saturday Frequency: m
Avg Paid Circ: 4489
Avg Free Circ: 425
Audit Company: AAM
Audit Date: 31 03 2019
Pressroom Equipment: Lines – 8-G/Community; Folders – 1-G/SSC.;
Mailroom Equipment: Tying Machines – 1/MLN, 1-/MLN.;
Buisness Equipment: ATT
Classified Equipment: Hardware – Mk, APP/Mac; Printers – TI;
Classified Software: Mk/4000, Multi-Ad/Creator, QPS/QuarkXPress.
Editorial Equipment: Hardware – APP/Mac; Printers – TI
Editorial Software: QPS/QuarkXPress 3.11.
Production Equipment: Hardware – 2-V/5100, 1-V/5300, 1-V/Panther Plus; Cameras – SCREEN/C-690-C
Total Circulation: 4914

PULASKI

THE SOUTHWEST TIMES (PULASKI, VA)

Corporate/Parent Company: Fackelman Newspapers
Publication Street Address: 34 5th St NE
City: Pulaski
State: VA
Publication Website: www.southwesttimes.com
Postal Code: 24301-4608
Office phone: (540) 980-5220
General E-mail: brenda@southwesttimes.com
Publisher Name: Vanessa Repass
Publisher Email: vanessa.repass@southwesttimes.com
Publisher Phone: (540) 980-5220, Ext : 311
Editor Name: David Gravely
Editor Email: david@southwesttimes.com
Editor Phone: (540) 980-5220, Ext : 312
Advertising Executive Name: Cambria Dalton
Advertising Executive Email: cambria@southwesttimes.com
Advertising Executive Phone: (540) 980-5220, Ext : 316
Year Established: 1906
Delivery Methods: Mail`Newsstand`Racks
Own Printing Facility?: N
Commercial printers?: N
Published Days: Tues`Wed`Thur`Fri`Sun
Weekday Frequency: m
Avg Paid Circ: 5500
Audit Company: Sworn/Estimate/Non-Audited
Audit Date: 7 12 2019
Total Circulation: 5500

RICHMOND

RICHMOND TIMES-DISPATCH

Corporate/Parent Company: Lee Enterprises
Publication Street Address: 300 E Franklin St
City: Richmond
State: VA
Publication Website: www.timesdispatch.com
Postal Code: 23219-2214
Office phone: (804) 649-6000
General E-mail: addispatch@timesdispatch.com
Publisher Name: Thomas A. Silvestri
Editor Name: Paige Mudd
Editor Email: pmudd@timesdispatch.com
Editor Phone: (804) 649-6671
Advertising Executive Phone: (804) 649-6251
Year Established: 1850
Mechanical specifications: Type page 11 5/8 x 21; E - 6 cols, 2 1/16, 1/8 between; A - 6 cols, 2 1/16, 1/8 between; C - 10 cols, 1 1/4, 1/18 between.
Published Days: Mon`Tues`Wed`Thur`Fri`Sat`Sun
Weekday Frequency: m
Saturday Frequency: m
Avg Paid Circ: 80059
Audit Company: AAM
Audit Date: 5 09 2019
Pressroom Equipment: Lines – 36-MHI/Print couples (4 reversible half decks; 2 mono units); 36-MHI/Print couples (4 reversible half decks; 2 mono units); 36-MHI/Print couples (4 reversible half decks; 2 mono units); Folders – 2-MHI/180-page; Reels & Stands – Reels & Stands and Stands;
Mailroom Equipment: Counter Stackers – 11-Id/2100, 4/QWI, 3-HL/SH, 2-Rima/RS3100, 13-QWI/500; Inserters & Stuffers – 1-S/b-72P, 4-S/22-99, AM Graphics; Tying Machines – 13-/Dynaric; Control System – Id/Newssort, Id/Newslink; Address Machine – Ch/539, C;
Buisness Equipment: HP/917, HP/935, HP/950, HP/949, HP/947
Buisness Software: CJ, Visimage, Omnidex
Classified Equipment: Hardware – AT/Enterprise RS 6000, 1-Clarion Raid; 2-IBM/RS 6000 Workstations; Printers – 2-HP/5000TN;
Classified Software: APP/Order Entry 1.4.172, Oracle/Database 7.3.4.
Editorial Equipment: Hardware – 6-Sun/Ultra II servers, Client/200-PC 3.40/2-Dell/NAS Servers; Printers – HP/MV4, 4-HP/LaserJet 2200, X
Editorial Software: HI/NME 4.0, Microsoft/Windows XP.
Production Equipment: Hardware – 2-WL/3, AII/3850, 4-AG/Alpha Harlequin RIP; Scanners – 4-Epson
Production Software: HI/Newsmaker Pagination 2.05.12, AT/Classified Pagination 5.76.
Total Circulation: 95443

ROANOKE

THE ROANOKE TIMES

Corporate/Parent Company: Lee Enterprises
Publication Street Address: 201 Campbell Ave SW
City: Roanoke
State: VA

Publication Website: www.roanoke.com
Postal Code: 24011-1105
Office phone: (540) 981-3211
General E-mail: terry.jamerson@roanoke.com
Publisher Name: Terry Jamerson
Publisher Email: terry.jamerson@roanoke.com
Publisher Phone: (540) 981-3326
Editor Name: Dwayne Yancey
Editor Email: dwayne.yancey@roanoke.com
Editor Phone: (540) 981-3113
Advertising Executive Name: Phyllis Weber
Advertising Executive Phone: (540) 981-3398
Year Established: 1886
Delivery Methods:
    Mail`Newsstand`Carrier`Racks
Own Printing Facility?: Y
Commercial printers?: Y
Published Days: Mon`Tues`Wed`Thur`Fri`Sat`Sun
Weekday Frequency: All day
Saturday Frequency: All day
Avg Paid Circ: 39652
Audit Company: AAM
Audit Date: 27 02 2020
Total Circulation: 36403

STAUNTON

THE NEWS LEADER

Corporate/Parent Company: Gannett
Publication Street Address: 11 N Central Ave
City: Staunton
State: VA
Publication Website: www.newsleader.com
Postal Code: 24402
Office phone: (540) 885-7281
General E-mail: localnews@newsleader.com
Publisher Email: getpublished@newsleader.com
Editor Name: William Ramsey
Editor Email: wramsey@newsleader.com
Editor Phone: (540) 213-9182
Advertising Executive Name: Lindsey Twitty
Advertising Executive Email: ltwitty@localiq.com
Advertising Executive Phone: (864) 314-0377
Year Established: 1904
Mechanical specifications: Type page 13 x 21 1/4; E - 6 cols, 2 1/16, 1/8 between; A - 6 cols, 2 1/16, 1/8 between; C - 9 cols, 1 3/8, 1/16 between.
Published Days: Mon`Tues`Wed`Thur`Fri`Sat`Sun
Weekday Frequency: m
Saturday Frequency: m
Avg Paid Circ: 7934
Avg Free Circ: 172
Audit Company: AAM
Audit Date: 9 07 2020
Pressroom Equipment: Lines – 6-G/Urbanite; 1-AM/1650 MC Offset; Press Drive – 2-HP/100; Folders – 1-G/Urbanite.;
Mailroom Equipment: Counter Stackers – 1-Id/2000, 1-QWI/350; Inserters & Stuffers – GMA/Alphaliner; Tying Machines – 1/Bu, 1-MLN/MA, 1-/Akebono, 1-/Power Strap; Control System – GMA; Address Machine – 1-KR/Mailer, 1-KR/Quarter Folder;
Buisness Equipment: IBM/AS-400
Buisness Software: Lotus 3.1, Microsoft/Office
Classified Software: Baseview.
Editorial Equipment: Hardware – APP/Mac Server, APP/Mac workstation
Editorial Software: QPS/QuarkXPress.
Production Equipment: Hardware – 1-LE/LD-2600A, Harlequin, Linotronic/Ultre, ECR; Cameras – 1-C/Spartan II, 1-R/432, ECR; Scanners – 1-ECR/Autokon 1000, AG/Horizon Plus, Umax, Microtek, Nikon, Flatbed/Scanner
Production Software: QPS/QuarkXPress 3.32.
Total Circulation: 9282

STRASBURG

NORTHERN VIRGINIA DAILY

Corporate/Parent Company: Ogden Newspapers, Inc.
Publication Street Address: 152 N Holliday St
City: Strasburg
State: VA
Publication Website: www.nvdaily.com
Postal Code: 22657-2143
Office phone: (540) 465-5137
General E-mail: news@nvdaily.com
Editor Name: Linda A. Ash
Editor Email: lash@nvdaily.com
Year Established: 1932
Delivery Methods:
    Mail`Newsstand`Carrier`Racks
Own Printing Facility?: N
Commercial printers?: N
Mechanical specifications: Type page 10x 21; E - 6 cols, 2 1/16, 1/8 between; A - 6 cols, 1 5/8, 1/8 between; C - 9 cols, 1 3/8, 1/16 between.
Published Days: Mon`Tues`Wed`Thur`Fri`Sat
Weekday Frequency: m
Saturday Frequency: m
Avg Paid Circ: 7002
Avg Free Circ: 372
Audit Company: AAM
Audit Date: 18 03 2020
Pressroom Equipment: Lines – 6-G/Urbanite 1978; 2-DEV/Horizon 1985; Reels & Stands – 6;
Mailroom Equipment: Counter Stackers – BG/Count-O-Veyor; Inserters & Stuffers – KAN; Tying Machines – Dynaric/Strapper; Address Machine – 2/St.;
Classified Equipment: Hardware – SUN/Server, APP/eMac Workstation, ON X11; Printers – HP/4 Plus;
Classified Software: Vison Data/Classified Pagination System.
Editorial Equipment: Hardware – APP/Mac G4 400 MHZ Towers, APP/Mac G4 933 Mhz, APP/Mac 800Mhz/LiMax/Scanner, Nikon/Scanner; Printers – HP/4000
Editorial Software: Baseview/Newsedit Pro IQUE, QPS/QuarkXPress 4.11, Adobe/Photoshop.
Production Equipment: Hardware – Nu/Flip Top FT40V6 UPNS, ECR, HP/1700D, ECRM/EVJet 6200, ECRM/EVJet 3100; Cameras – 1-B/18 x 24; Scanners – Nikon/CoolScan, Umax/UTA 11 8 1/2 x 14 Page Scanner
Production Software: Baseview/Managing Editor, ALS/Page Director 40.4, Adobe/Quark 4.11
Total Circulation: 8967

SUFFOLK

SUFFOLK NEWS-HERALD

Corporate/Parent Company: Boone Newspapers, Inc.
Publication Street Address: 130 S Saratoga St
City: Suffolk
State: VA
Publication Website: www.suffolknewsherald.com
Postal Code: 23434-5323
Office phone: (757) 539-3437
General E-mail: dana.snow@suffolknewsherald.com
Publisher Name: John Carr
Publisher Email: john.carr@suffolknewsherald.com
Editor Name: Tracy Agnew
Editor Email: tracy.agnew@suffolknewsherald.com
Advertising Executive Name: Hope Rose
Advertising Executive Email: hope.rose@suffolknewsherald.com
Year Established: 1873
Delivery Methods:
    Mail`Newsstand`Carrier`Racks
Own Printing Facility?: N
Commercial printers?: N
Mechanical specifications: Type page 11.25 x 21.5, 6 cols.
Published Days: Tues`Wed`Thur`Fri`Sat`Sun
Weekday Frequency: m
Saturday Frequency: m
Avg Paid Circ: 80
Avg Free Circ: 12119
Audit Company: Sworn/Estimate/Non-Audited
Audit Date: 7 12 2019
Pressroom Equipment: Lines – 6-G/Community (24 pg b/w capacity).;
Mailroom Equipment: Tying Machines – 1/Us.;
Buisness Equipment: 2-EKI/Televideo 950
Classified Equipment: Hardware – APP/iMac; Printers – HP/5000;
Classified Software: Baseview.
Editorial Equipment: Hardware – HP; Printers – HP/5000
Editorial Software: QPS/QuarkXPress.
Production Equipment: Hardware – APP/Mac LaserPrinter
Production Software: QPS/QuarkXPress.
Total Circulation: 12199

WARRENTON

FAUQUIER NOW

Publication Street Address: 50 Culpeper Street, Suite 3
City: Warrenton
State: VA
Publication Website: www.fauquiernow.com
Postal Code: 20187
Office phone: 540.359.6574
Publisher Name: Ellen Fox Emerson
Publisher Email: Ellen@FauquierNow.com
Publisher Phone: 540-270-8339
Editor Name: Lawrence Emerson
Editor Email: LKE@FauquierNow.com
Editor Phone: 540-270-1845

WAYNESBORO

THE NEWS VIRGINIAN

Corporate/Parent Company: Lee Enterprises
Publication Street Address: 201 C Rosser Avenue
City: Waynesboro
State: VA
Publication Website: www.newsvirginian.com
Postal Code: 22980-2414
Office phone: (540) 949-8213
General E-mail: stwitty@newsvirginian.com
Publisher Name: Peter S. Yates
Publisher Email: pyates@dailyprogress.com
Publisher Phone: (540) 978-7203
Editor Name: Derek M. Armstrong
Editor Email: darmstrong@newsvirginian.com
Editor Phone: (540) 932-3556
Advertising Executive Name: Stephanie Twitty
Advertising Executive Email: stwitty@newsvirginian.com
Advertising Executive Phone: (540) 932-3545
Mechanical specifications: Type page 10 7/8 x 20 3/4; E - 6 cols, 1 73/100, 1/10 between; A - 6 cols, 1 73/100, 1/10 between; C - 10 cols, 1 2/25, 1/8 between.
Published Days: Mon`Tues`Wed`Thur`Fri`Sat`Sun
Weekday Frequency: m
Saturday Frequency: m
Avg Paid Circ: 3362
Avg Free Circ: 317
Audit Company: AAM
Audit Date: 19 04 2019
Pressroom Equipment: Lines – 4-G/Urbanite;
Mailroom Equipment: Tying Machines – 1-Bu/42409, 1/MLN.;
Buisness Software: Vision Data
Classified Equipment: Hardware – Mk/3000, 7-PC Microsystem;
Classified Software: HI/AdPower, Microsoft/Word 6.0, QPS/QuarkXPress 4.1.
Editorial Equipment: Hardware – Mk/3000, 10-PC Microsystem; Printers – HP/4MV Postscript, HP/4 Plus
Editorial Software: Microsoft/Word 6.0, QPS/QuarkXPress 4.1, ACT.
Production Equipment: Hardware – Visioneer/Paper Port, Caere/OmniPage; Cameras – 1-B/24 x 24, COM/M, 1-LE/R 20 x 24
Production Software: QPS/QuarkXPress, Adobe/Photoshop, Caere/OmniPage.
Total Circulation: 4152

WINCHESTER

THE WINCHESTER STAR

Corporate/Parent Company: Gannett
Publication Street Address: 100 N. Loudoun StreetSuite 110
City: Winchester
State: VA
Publication Website: www.winchesterstar.com
Postal Code: 22601-5038
Office phone: (540) 667-3200
General E-mail: citydesk@winchesterstar.com
Publisher Name: Mike Gochenour
Publisher Email: mgochenour@winchesterstar.com
Publisher Phone: (540) 665-4941
Editor Name: Cynthia Burton
Editor Email: cburton@winchesterstar.com
Editor Phone: (540) 665-4951
Advertising Executive Name: Chrissy Hill
Advertising Executive Email: chill@winchesterstar.com
Advertising Executive Phone: (540) 667-3200, Ext : 5230
Year Established: 1896
Delivery Methods:
    Mail`Newsstand`Carrier`Racks
Own Printing Facility?: Y
Mechanical specifications: Type page 13 x 21 1/2; E - 6 cols, 2, 1/5 between; A - 6 cols, 2, 1/5 between; C - 9 cols, 1 5/16, 1/5 between.
Published Days: Mon`Tues`Wed`Thur`Fri`Sat
Weekday Frequency: m
Saturday Frequency: m
Avg Paid Circ: 15911
Avg Free Circ: 873
Audit Company: AAM
Audit Date: 7 11 2017
Pressroom Equipment: Lines – 8-G/Urbanite U-1327 single width 1981; Folders – 1-G/Double former; Control System – 1-Ebway/SU 300.;
Mailroom Equipment: Counter Stackers – 1-HL/Dual Carrier, 2-QWI/501; Inserters & Stuffers – GMA/Alphaliner; Tying Machines – 2-EAM-Mosca, 1-Samuel/Automatic; Address Machine – 2-Am/1900;
Buisness Equipment: IBM/Sys 3600
Classified Equipment: Hardware – Dell/2300; Printers – CText/ALPS ALQ324E, NewGen/Turbo PS-400, HP/Laserjet 5000;
Classified Software: SCS/Admax, SCS/Classpag.
Editorial Equipment: Hardware – COM, Dell/Optiplex-GS, Dell/2100, Dell/200, 2-Dell/PowerEdge 4200 Server/1-APP/Mac Quadra 700, 1-APP/Mac SE; Printers – HP/LaserJet 4000N, NewGen/Design Express 6
Editorial Software: Falcon/Indesign
Production Equipment: Hardware – 4-Xante/8200, Konica, 2-ECR; Cameras – C/Spartan III, SCREEN; Scanners – Microtek/ScanMaker III, HP ScanJet II cx
Production Software: Good News.
Total Circulation: 18802

VERMONT

BARRE

THE TIMES ARGUS

Corporate/Parent Company: Brunswick Publishing
Publication Street Address: 47 N Main St
City: Barre
State: VT
Publication Website: www.timesargus.com
Postal Code: 05641-4168
Office phone: (802) 479-0191
General E-mail: customerservices@timesargus.com
Publisher Name: R. John Mitchell
Editor Name: Steven Pappas
Year Established: 1806
Mechanical specifications: Type page 11 5/8 x 21 1/4; E - 6 cols, 2, 3/8 between; A - 6 cols, 1 13/16, 3/16 between; C - 9 cols, 1 1/8, 1/8 between.
Published Days: Thur`Fri`Sat`Sun
Weekday Frequency: m
Saturday Frequency: m
Avg Paid Circ: 5796
Audit Company: AAM
Audit Date: 30 09 2013
Pressroom Equipment: Lines – 4-G/Urbanite;
Mailroom Equipment: Counter Stackers – BG/Count-O-Veyor 108, 1-S/Olympian,

U.S. Daily Newspapers

1-MM/310-14; Inserters & Stuffers – 1-S/1472, Heidelberg; Tying Machines – MLN/2A, Signode/Tyer, Alaebond Tyer; Wrapping Singles – 2-S/Eclipse; Control System – Icon; Address Machine – Addressing m;
Buisness Equipment: Sun
Buisness Software: Vision Data
Classified Equipment: Hardware – Vision Data; 5-APP/Mac G3.;
Editorial Equipment: Hardware – ACI; Printers – HP, Xante
Editorial Software: Open Pages.
Production Equipment: Hardware – 2-Nu/Flip Top FT40UPNS; Cameras – 1-C/Spartan III; Scanners – Nikon/Coolscan, 2-Umax
Production Software: American Computer Innovators, QPS/QuarkXPress.

BENNINGTON
BENNINGTON BANNER
Corporate/Parent Company: New England Newspapers, Inc.
Publication Street Address: 425 Main St
City: Bennington
State: VT
Publication Website: www.benningtonbanner.com
Postal Code: 05201-2141
Office phone: (802) 442-7567
General E-mail: news@benningtonbanner.com
Publisher Name: Fredric D. Rutberg
Publisher Email: frutberg@berkshireeagle.com
Publisher Phone: (413) 496-6380
Editor Name: Dave Lachance
Editor Email: dlachance@benningtonbanner.com
Editor Phone: (802) 447-7567, Ext : 115
Advertising Executive Name: Susan Plaisance
Advertising Executive Email: splaisance@manchesterjournal.com
Advertising Executive Phone: (802) 733-8827
Year Established: 1905
Own Printing Facility?: Y
Commercial printers?: Y
Mechanical specifications: Type page 13 x 21 1/4; E - 6 cols, 2 1/16, 1/8 between; A - 6 cols, 2 1/16, 1/8 between; C - 9 cols, 1 3/8, 1/16 between.
Published Days: Mon`Tues`Wed`Thur`Fri`Sat
Weekday Frequency: m
Saturday Frequency: m
Avg Paid Circ: 3423
Avg Free Circ: 540
Audit Company: AAM
Audit Date: 30 06 2017
Buisness Equipment: DEC/PDP 11-73
Buisness Software: GEAR
Classified Equipment: Printers – 1-TI/810 Printer;
Classified Software: PPI.
Editorial Equipment: Hardware – APP/Power Mac/2-AST/PC 286 Premium, 1-Leading Edge/286, 2-PC 386SX
Editorial Software: QPS/QuarkXPress.
Production Equipment: Hardware – 2-APP/Power Mac, Konica/Imagesetter.
Total Circulation: 3963

BRATTLEBORO
BRATTLEBORO REFORMER
Corporate/Parent Company: New England Newspapers, Inc.
Publication Street Address: 62 Black Mountain Rd
City: Brattleboro
State: VT
Publication Website: www.reformer.com
Postal Code: 05301-9281
Office phone: (802) 254-2311
General E-mail: news@reformer.com
Publisher Name: Fredric D. Rutberg
Publisher Email: frutberg@berkshireeagle.com
Publisher Phone: (413) 496-6380
Editor Name: Kevin Moran
Editor Email: kmoran@reformer.com
Editor Phone: (413) 496-6201
Advertising Executive Name: Jonathan Stafford
Advertising Executive Email: jstafford@reformer.com
Advertising Executive Phone: (802) 254-2311, Ext : 200
Year Established: 1913
Delivery Methods: Mail`Newsstand`Carrier`Racks
Own Printing Facility?: Y
Commercial printers?: Y
Mechanical specifications: Type page 13 x 21 1/4; E - 6 cols, 2 1/16, 1/8 between; A - 6 cols, 2 1/16, 1/8 between; C - 9 cols, 1 3/8, 1/16 between.
Published Days: Mon`Tues`Wed`Thur`Fri`Sat`Sun
Weekday Frequency: m
Saturday Frequency: m
Avg Paid Circ: 3722
Avg Free Circ: 591
Audit Company: AAM
Audit Date: 31 03 2018
Pressroom Equipment: Lines – 8-G/Community; Folders – 2-G/SSC.;
Mailroom Equipment: Counter Stackers – 1/Fg; Tying Machines – 1-/MLN, 1-/OVL; Address Machine – Wm.;
Buisness Equipment: DEC/PDP 11-73
Buisness Software: Vision Data
Classified Equipment: Hardware – 2-Dewar/Sys II;
Classified Software: Dewar.
Editorial Equipment: Hardware – 2-Dewar/Sys II
Editorial Software: Dewar.
Production Equipment: Hardware – C; Cameras – C/Marathon; Scanners – Panasonic/505.
Total Circulation: 4313

BURLINGTON
THE BURLINGTON FREE PRESS
Corporate/Parent Company: Gannett
Publication Street Address: 100 Bank St Ste 700
City: Burlington
State: VT
Publication Website: www.burlingtonfreepress.com
Postal Code: 05401-4946
Office phone: (802) 863-3441
General E-mail: gannettmediaeducation@gannett.com
Publisher Name: Trevor Chase
Publisher Email: tchase2@freepressmedia.com
Publisher Phone: (802) 660-1805
Editor Name: Emilie Stigliani
Editor Email: estigliani@freepressmedia.com
Editor Phone: (802) 660-1897
Advertising Executive Name: Steph Levesque
Advertising Executive Email: smoran@freepressmedia.com
Advertising Executive Phone: (802) 660-1834
Year Established: 1827
Delivery Methods: Newsstand`Carrier`Racks
Own Printing Facility?: Y
Commercial printers?: Y
Mechanical specifications: Type page 6 col x 13.58"
Published Days: Mon`Tues`Wed`Thur`Fri`Sat`Sun
Weekday Frequency: m
Saturday Frequency: m
Avg Paid Circ: 10266
Avg Free Circ: 143
Audit Company: AAM
Audit Date: 25 03 2020
Pressroom Equipment: Lines – 5-G/Metro (2 color decks) double width 1967; Press Drive – 6-Fin/3260 1989; Pasters –G/Automatic.
Mailroom Equipment: Counter Stackers – 2-QWI/SJ20X, 1-HI/Rima RS-30, 2-QW/501; Inserters & Stuffers – 1-HI/1472A, 2-Dynaric/NP-3; Tying Machines – 1-MLN/2A, 1-MLN/2EE, 2/Power Strap; Address Machine – KR;
Buisness Equipment: 1-IBM/AS-400
Buisness Software: Microsoft/Windows 95, Microsoft/Windows NT, Microsoft/Office 97, Microsoft/Windows 2000
Classified Equipment: Hardware – 17-PC P111; Printers – HP/LaserJet;
Classified Software: HI/Ad Power.
Editorial Equipment: Hardware – 13-PC P300, 37-PC P100
Editorial Software: HI/NMP Newsmaker HI/NME Newsmaker Edit.
Production Equipment: Hardware – 2-MON/Express Master 6000, 1-OCE/Thermal Proofer 9000G, 1-Alfa Quest/Proof Xpress II
Production Software: HI/NMP Newsmaker, HI/CPAG Classified Pagination.
Total Circulation: 19134

NEWPORT
THE NEWPORT DAILY EXPRESS
Corporate/Parent Company: Horizon Publications Inc.
Publication Street Address: 178 Hill St
City: Newport
State: VT
Publication Website: www.newportvermontdailyexpress.com
Postal Code: 05855-9430
Office phone: (802) 334-6568
General E-mail: advertising@newportvermontdailyexpress.com
Editor Name: Laura Carpenter
Year Established: 1936
Delivery Methods: Mail`Newsstand`Carrier`Racks
Own Printing Facility?: Y
Commercial printers?: Y
Mechanical specifications: Type page 13 1/8 x 21 1/2; E - 6 cols, 2 1/5, 1/12 between; A - 6 cols, 2 1/8, 1/12 between; C - 6 cols, 2 1/8, 1/12 between.
Published Days: Mon`Tues`Wed`Thur`Fri
Weekday Frequency: m
Avg Paid Circ: 5000
Audit Company: Sworn/Estimate/Non-Audited
Audit Date: 7 12 2019
Pressroom Equipment: Lines – 4-G/Community;
Mailroom Equipment: Counter Stackers – Bundle Tying Machines ÃƒÂƒÃ‚Â£ÃƒÂ‚Â 1/Saxmyer; Address Machine – Wm.;
Buisness Equipment: Synaptic/Micro Solutions, Acct/100, Okidata/393 Plus, Sun/Suntype
Classified Equipment: Hardware – APP/Mac; Printers – Okidata/320 Turbo;
Classified Software: QPS/Class Flo 4.0.
Editorial Equipment: Hardware – APP/Mac/Adobe/Photoshop, Sprint/ScanMaker E6; Printers – APP/Mac Laser 8500
Editorial Software: QPS/QuarkXPress 4.0.
Production Equipment: Hardware – Paper Port/Strobe Scanner; Cameras - 1-K/241; Scanners – HP/ScanJet
Production Software: QPS/QuarkXPress 4.0.
Total Circulation: 5000

RUTLAND
RUTLAND HERALD
Corporate/Parent Company: Sample News Group LLC
Publication Street Address: 77 Grove Street, Suite 102
City: Rutland
State: VT
Publication Website: www.rutlandherald.com
Postal Code: 05702-0668
Office phone: (802) 747-6121
General E-mail: customerservices@rutlandherald.com
Publisher Name: R. John Mitchell
Editor Name: Randal Smathers
Year Established: 1794
Delivery Methods: Mail`Newsstand`Carrier`Racks
Own Printing Facility?: Y
Mechanical specifications: Image 10 x 21 1/4; SAU for 22" Web
Published Days: Thur`Fri`Sat`Sun
Weekday Frequency: m
Saturday Frequency: m
Avg Paid Circ: 11200
Audit Company: AAM
Audit Date: 30 09 2013
Buisness Equipment: Vision Data, SUN. HP PC Workstations
Buisness Software: Vision Data
Classified Equipment: Hardware – Vision Data SUN, HP PC Workstations; Vision Data; Printers – HP;
Classified Software: Vision Data.
Editorial Equipment: Hardware – HP PC; Printers – HP
Editorial Software: Saxotech Media ware Center
Production Equipment: Cameras – Nikon Digital; Scanners – Nikon
Production Software: Adobe Indesign Saxotech
Total Circulation: 11200

SAINT ALBANS
ST. ALBANS MESSENGER
Corporate/Parent Company: Jim O'Rourke
Publication Street Address: 281 N Main St
City: Saint Albans
State: VT
Publication Website: www.samessenger.com
Postal Code: 05478-2503
Office phone: (802) 524-9771
General E-mail: news@samessenger.com
Publisher Name: Suzanne Lynn
Editor Name: Emerson Lynn
Year Established: 1861
Mechanical specifications: Type page 13 1/2 x 21; E - 6 cols, 2 1/16, 1/8 between; A - 6 cols, 2 1/16, 1/8 between; C - 6 cols, 2 1/16, 1/8 between.
Published Days: Mon`Tues`Wed`Thur`Fri`Sat
Weekday Frequency: e
Saturday Frequency: m
Avg Paid Circ: 5695
Audit Company: Sworn/Estimate/Non-Audited
Audit Date: 7 12 2019
Pressroom Equipment: Lines – 6-Wd/240; Folders – 1-Wd/2:1.;
Mailroom Equipment: Counter Stackers – 1/BG; Wrapping Singles – 2-/Us; Address Machine – 1-/Am.;
Buisness Equipment: RSK/TRS 80
Classified Equipment: Hardware – APP/Mac Plus.;
Editorial Equipment: Hardware – 17-APP/Mac Plus; Printers – 4-APP/Mac LaserWriter Plus.
Production Equipment: Hardware – 1-B/3200, 1-Nat/250; Cameras – 1-Nu/20-24, 1-K/18-20 V241; Scanners – AG/FJF74/2200, Densitometer, Entre/Scanner.
Total Circulation: 5695

SAINT JOHNSBURY
THE CALEDONIAN-RECORD
Publication Street Address: 190 Federal St
City: Saint Johnsbury
State: VT
Publication Website: www.caledonianrecord.com
Postal Code: 05819-5616
Office phone: (802) 748-8121
General E-mail: news@caledonian-record.com
Publisher Name: Todd M. Smith
Editor Name: Dana Gray
Advertising Executive Email: adv@caledonian-record.com
Year Established: 1837
Delivery Methods: Mail`Newsstand`Carrier`Racks
Own Printing Facility?: N
Commercial printers?: Y
Mechanical specifications: Type page 10 7/8 x 21; E - 6 cols per page, each col. 1.708" with 1/8" between columns
Published Days: Mon`Tues`Wed`Thur`Fri`Sat
Weekday Frequency: m
Saturday Frequency: m
Avg Paid Circ: 6694
Avg Free Circ: 1840
Audit Company: Sworn/Estimate/Non-Audited
Audit Date: 7 12 2019
Buisness Equipment: Various HP
Buisness Software: Quickbooks, Vision Data
Classified Equipment: Hardware – Various HP; Printers – Various HP;
Classified Software: Vision Data
Editorial Equipment: Hardware – Various HP'S Mac G3/Nikon/CoolScan III, AG/Arcus II Scanner; Printers – Various HP
Editorial Software: GPS
Production Equipment: Scanners – AG/Arcus II, Epson/636 Pro, Nikon/CoolScan III

Production Software: FAlcon
Total Circulation: 8534

WASHINGTON

BELLINGHAM

THE BELLINGHAM HERALD

Corporate/Parent Company: McClatchy Company
Publication Street Address: 1155 N State St
City: Bellingham
State: WA
Publication Website: www.bellinghamherald.com
Postal Code: 98225-5024
Office phone: (360) 676-2600
General E-mail: classifieds@bellinghamherald.com
Editor Name: Julie Shirley
Editor Email: julie.shirley@bellinghamherald.com
Editor Phone: (360) 715-2261
Advertising Executive Name: Travis Kane
Advertising Executive Email: travis.kane@bellinghamherald.com
Advertising Executive Phone: (360) 715-2202
Year Established: 1890
Delivery Methods:
    Mail`Newsstand`Carrier`Racks
Own Printing Facility?: N
Commercial printers?: N
Mechanical specifications: 1 col: 1.5278" wide 6 col: 10" wide Full pg height: 20.125"
Published Days: Mon`Tues`Wed`Thur`Fri`Sat`Sun
Weekday Frequency: m
Saturday Frequency: m
Avg Paid Circ: 12146
Audit Company: AAM
Audit Date: 29 05 2020

BREMERTON

KITSAP SUN

Corporate/Parent Company: Gannett
Publication Street Address: PO Box 259
City: Bremerton
State: WA
Publication Website: www.kitsapsun.com/
Postal Code: 98337-1413
Office phone: (360) 377-3711
General E-mail: ad-support@kitsapsun.com
Editor Name: David Nelson
Editor Email: david.nelson@kitsapsun.com
Advertising Executive Email: ad-support@kitsapsun.com
Year Established: 1935
Mechanical specifications: Type page 10 1/2 x 21 1/2; E - 6 cols, 1 14/25, 1/8 between; A - 6 cols, 1 14/25, 1/8 between; C - 9 cols, 1 7/100, 1/8 between.
Published Days: Mon`Tues`Wed`Thur`Fri`Sat`Sun
Weekday Frequency: m
Saturday Frequency: m
Avg Paid Circ: 8270
Avg Free Circ: 105
Audit Company: AAM
Audit Date: 21 02 2020

ELLENSBURG

DAILY RECORD

Corporate/Parent Company: Gannett
Publication Street Address: 401 N Main St
City: Ellensburg
State: WA
Publication Website: www.kvnews.com
Postal Code: 98926-3107
Office phone: (509) 925-1414
General E-mail: webmaster@kvnews.com
Editor Name: Michael Gallagher
Editor Email: mgallagher@kvnews.com
Editor Phone: (509) 925-1414, Ext : 240
Advertising Executive Name: Amy Kaiser
Advertising Executive Email: akaiser@kvnews.com
Advertising Executive Phone: (509) 925-1414, Ext : 231
Year Established: 1883
Delivery Methods:
    Mail`Newsstand`Carrier`Racks
Own Printing Facility?: N
Commercial printers?: N
Mechanical specifications: Type page 12 15/16 x 21; E - 6 cols, 2, 1/6 between; A - 6 cols, 2, 1/6 between; C - 9 cols, 1 1/2, 1/12 between.
Published Days: Mon`Tues`Wed`Thur`Fri`Sat`Sun
Weekday Frequency: e
Saturday Frequency: m
Avg Paid Circ: 5523
Audit Company: Sworn/Estimate/Non-Audited
Audit Date: 7 12 2019

KENNEWICK

TRI-CITY HERALD

Corporate/Parent Company: McClatchy Company
Publication Street Address: 333 W Canal Dr
City: Kennewick
State: WA
Publication Website: www.tricityherald.com
Postal Code: 99336-3811
Office phone: (509) 582-1500
General E-mail: ads@tricityherald.com
Publisher Name: Jerry Hug
Editor Name: Laurie Williams
Year Established: 1947
Delivery Methods:
    Mail`Newsstand`Carrier`Racks
Own Printing Facility?: N
Commercial printers?: N
Mechanical specifications: Type page 11 1/2 x 21; E - 6 cols, 1 3/4, 3/16 between; A - 6 cols, 1 3/4, 3/16 between; C - 9 cols, 1 3/16, 1/8 between.
Published Days: Mon`Tues`Wed`Thur`Fri`Sat`Sun
Weekday Frequency: m
Saturday Frequency: m
Avg Paid Circ: 19919
Audit Company: AAM
Audit Date: 9 04 2020

LONGVIEW

THE DAILY NEWS

Corporate/Parent Company: Gannett
Publication Street Address: 770 11th Ave
City: Longview
State: WA
Publication Website: www.tdn.com
Postal Code: 98632-2412
Office phone: (360) 577-2500
General E-mail: lexy.smart@tdn.com
Publisher Name: David Thornberry
Publisher Email: david.thornberry@lee.net
Publisher Phone: (360) 577-2505
Advertising Executive Name: Lexy Smart
Advertising Executive Email: lexy.smart@tdn.com
Advertising Executive Phone: (360) 577-2508
Year Established: 1923
Mechanical specifications: Type page 11 1/8 x 21 1/2; E - 6 cols, 1 11/16, 1/8 between; A - 6 cols, 1 11/16, 1/8 between; C - 9 cols, 1 1/8, 1/16 between.
Published Days: Mon`Tues`Wed`Thur`Fri`Sat`Sun
Weekday Frequency: m
Saturday Frequency: m
Avg Paid Circ: 8544
Avg Free Circ: 5205
Audit Company: AAM
Audit Date: 31 03 2019

MOSES LAKE

COLUMBIA BASIN HERALD

Corporate/Parent Company: Hagadone Corp.
Publication Street Address: 813 W 3rd Ave
City: Moses Lake
State: WA
Publication Website: www.columbiabasinherald.com
Postal Code: 98837-2008
Office phone: (509) 765-4561
General E-mail: chogan@columbiabasinherald.com
Publisher Name: Caralyn Bess
Publisher Email: cbess@columbiabasinherald.com
Editor Name: Dave Burgess
Editor Email: dburgess@columbiabasinherald.com
Advertising Executive Name: Courtney Hogan
Advertising Executive Email: chogan@columbiabasinherald.com
Year Established: 1941
Delivery Methods:
    Mail`Newsstand`Carrier`Racks
Own Printing Facility?: Y
Commercial printers?: Y
Mechanical specifications: Type page 13 x 21 1/2; E - 6 cols, 1 5/6, 1/8 between; A - 6 cols, 1 5/6, 1/8 between; C - 8 cols, 1 1/3, 1/8 between.
Published Days: Mon`Tues`Wed`Thur`Fri
Weekday Frequency: e
Avg Paid Circ: 4406
Avg Free Circ: 25000
Audit Company: Sworn/Estimate/Non-Audited
Audit Date: 7 12 2019

MOUNT VERNON

SKAGIT VALLEY HERALD

Corporate/Parent Company: Adams Publishing Group
Publication Street Address: 1215 Anderson Rd
City: Mount Vernon
State: WA
Publication Website: www.goskagit.com
Postal Code: 98274-7615
Office phone: (360) 424-3251
General E-mail: news@skagitpublishing.com
Publisher Name: Heather Hernandez
Advertising Executive Name: Duby Petit
Advertising Executive Email: dpetit@skagitpublishing.com
Advertising Executive Phone: (360) 416-2128
Year Established: 1884
Delivery Methods:
    Mail`Newsstand`Carrier`Racks
Own Printing Facility?: Y
Commercial printers?: Y
Mechanical specifications: Type page 10 x 20 1/2; E - 6 cols, 1 19/32, 3/32 between; A - 6 cols, 1 19/32, 3/32 between; C - 6 cols, 1 19/32, 3/32 between.
Published Days: Mon`Tues`Wed`Thur`Fri`Sat`Sun
Weekday Frequency: m
Saturday Frequency: m
Avg Paid Circ: 9311
Avg Free Circ: 383
Audit Company: AAM
Audit Date: 12 07 2019

OLYMPIA

THE OLYMPIAN

Corporate/Parent Company: McClatchy Company
Publication Street Address: 522 Franklin Street SE
City: Olympia
State: WA
Publication Website: www.theolympian.com
Postal Code: 98501
Office phone: (360) 754-5400
General E-mail: news@theolympian.com
Editor Name: Dusti Demarest
Year Established: 1889
Delivery Methods:
    Mail`Newsstand`Carrier`Racks
Own Printing Facility?: N
Commercial printers?: N
Mechanical specifications: Type page 11 5/8 x 21 1/2; E - 6 cols, 1 3/4, 1/6 between; A - 6 cols, 1 3/4, 1/6 between; C - 9 cols, 1 3/4, 1/8 between.
Published Days: Mon`Tues`Wed`Thur`Fri`Sat`Sun
Weekday Frequency: m
Saturday Frequency: m
Avg Paid Circ: 12746
Audit Company: AAM
Audit Date: 9 04 2019

PORT ANGELES

PENINSULA DAILY NEWS

Corporate/Parent Company: Sound Publishing, Inc.
Publication Street Address: 305 W 1st St
City: Port Angeles
State: WA
Publication Website: www.peninsuladailynews.com
Postal Code: 98362-2205
Office phone: (360) 452-2345
General E-mail: adinfo@peninsuladailynews.com
Publisher Name: Terry Ward
Publisher Email: tward@soundpublishing.com
Editor Name: Leah Leach
Editor Email: lleach@soundpublishing.com
Advertising Executive Email: adinfo@peninsuladailynews.com
Year Established: 1916
Delivery Methods: Mail`Carrier`Racks
Own Printing Facility?: N
Commercial printers?: N
Mechanical specifications: 22-inch web; 6-col ROP
Published Days: Mon`Tues`Wed`Thur`Fri`Sun
Weekday Frequency: m
Avg Paid Circ: 9976
Avg Free Circ: 134
Audit Company: AAM
Audit Date: 21 06 2019

SEATTLE

SEATTLE DAILY JOURNAL OF COMMERCE

Publication Street Address: 83 Columbia St
City: Seattle
State: WA
Publication Website: www.djc.com
Postal Code: 98104-1432
Office phone: (206) 622-8272
General E-mail: editor@djc.com
Publisher Name: Phil Brown
Publisher Email: phil.brown@djc.com
Editor Name: Jon Silver
Editor Email: jon.silver@djc.com
Advertising Executive Name: Jeff Mosely
Advertising Executive Email: jeff.mosely@djc.com
Year Established: 1893
Delivery Methods: Mail`Newsstand
Own Printing Facility?: Y
Commercial printers?: N
Mechanical specifications: Type page 15 x 21 1/2; E - 7 cols, 2, 1/6 between; A - 7 cols, 2, 1/6 between; C - 8 cols, 1 2/3, 1/4 between.
Published Days: Mon`Tues`Wed`Thur`Fri`Sat
Weekday Frequency: m
Saturday Frequency: m
Avg Paid Circ: 4500
Audit Company: Sworn/Estimate/Non-Audited
Audit Date: 7 12 2019

SEATTLE

THE SEATTLE TIMES

Corporate/Parent Company: Seattle Times Company
Publication Street Address: 1000 Denny Way
City: Seattle
State: WA
Publication Website: www.seattletimes.com
Postal Code: 98109-5323
Office phone: (206) 464-2988
General E-mail: advertising@seattletimes.com
Publisher Name: Frank A. Blethen
Publisher Email: publisherfeedback@seattletimes.com
Editor Name: Michele Matassa Flores
Editor Email: mflores@seattletimes.com
Editor Phone: (206) 464-2292

U.S. Daily Newspapers

I-129

Year Established: 1896
Delivery Methods:
 Mail`Newsstand`Carrier`Racks
Own Printing Facility?: Y
Commercial printers?: Y
Published Days: Mon`Tues`Wed`Thur`Fri`Sat`Sun
Weekday Frequency: m
Saturday Frequency: m
Avg Paid Circ: 200805
Audit Company: AAM
Audit Date: 27 09 2019

SPOKANE
THE SPOKESMAN-REVIEW

Corporate/Parent Company: Cowles Publishing Co.
Publication Street Address: 999 W Riverside Ave
City: Spokane
State: WA
Publication Website: www.spokesman.com
Postal Code: 99201-1005
Office phone: (509) 459-5400
General E-mail: miked@spokesman.com
Publisher Name: William Stacey Cowles
Editor Name: Paul Smith
Editor Email: pauls@spokesman.com
Editor Phone: (509) 459-5528
Year Established: 1883
Delivery Methods: Newsstand`Carrier`Racks
Own Printing Facility?: Y
Commercial printers?: N
Mechanical specifications: Type page 9 5/8" x 21 1/2; E - 6 cols, 1 7/8, 1/8 between; , A & C - 6 cols, 1 9/16, 1/10 between.
Published Days: Mon`Tues`Wed`Thur`Fri`Sat`Sun
Weekday Frequency: m
Saturday Frequency: m
Avg Paid Circ: 59489
Audit Company: AAM
Audit Date: 15 10 2019

SUNNYSIDE
DAILY SUN NEWS

Corporate/Parent Company: Eagle Newspapers, Inc.
Publication Street Address: 600 S 6th St
City: Sunnyside
State: WA
Publication Website: www.sunnyside.net
Postal Code: 98944-2111
Office phone: (509) 837-4500
General E-mail: news@sunnysidesun.com
Year Established: 1901
Mechanical specifications: Type page 10 1/3 x 16 1/2; E - 5 cols, 1 93/100, 1/6 between; A - 5 cols, 1 93/100, 1/6 between; C - 5 cols, 1 93/100, 1/6 between.
Published Days: Mon`Tues`Wed`Thur`Fri
Weekday Frequency: e
Avg Paid Circ: 3818
Audit Company: Sworn/Estimate/Non-Audited
Audit Date: 7 12 2019

TACOMA
THE NEWS TRIBUNE

Corporate/Parent Company: WEHCO Media, Inc.
Publication Street Address: 1950 S State St
City: Tacoma
State: WA
Publication Website: www.thenewstribune.com
Postal Code: 98405-2817
Office phone: (253) 597-8742
General E-mail: john.dzaran@thenewstribune.com
Publisher Name: Rebecca Poynter
Editor Name: Dale Phelps
Year Established: 1880
Delivery Methods:
 Mail`Newsstand`Carrier`Racks
Own Printing Facility?: Y
Commercial printers?: N
Mechanical specifications: Type page 10 x 21.5"; E - 6 cols, 1.562", .125"between; A - 6 cols, 1.562", .125"between; C - 6 cols, 1.562", .125"between.
Published Days: Mon`Tues`Wed`Thur`Fri`Sat`Sun
Weekday Frequency: m
Saturday Frequency: m
Avg Paid Circ: 38192
Audit Company: AAM
Audit Date: 24 01 2019

VANCOUVER
THE COLUMBIAN

Corporate/Parent Company: Columbian Publishing Co.
Publication Street Address: 701 W 8th St
City: Vancouver
State: WA
Publication Website: www.columbian.com
Postal Code: 98660-3008
Office phone: (360) 694-3391
General E-mail: circulation@columbian.com
Publisher Name: Scott Campbell
Publisher Email: scott.campbell@columbian.com
Publisher Phone: (360) 735-4500
Editor Name: Craig Brown
Editor Email: craig.brown@columbian.com
Year Established: 1890
Delivery Methods:
 Mail`Newsstand`Carrier`Racks
Own Printing Facility?: Y
Commercial printers?: Y
Mechanical specifications: 6 units; 4 half decks; Open Fountain ink system; 2 Uniflow 2:1 folders; 4 former boards. Max. 44" web width.
Published Days: Mon`Tues`Wed`Thur`Fri`Sat`Sun
Weekday Frequency: m
Saturday Frequency: m
Avg Paid Circ: 24347
Audit Company: AAM
Audit Date: 1 10 2018

WALLA WALLA
WALLA WALLA UNION-BULLETIN

Corporate/Parent Company: The Seattle Times
Publication Street Address: 112 S 1st Ave
City: Walla Walla
State: WA
Publication Website: www.union-bulletin.com
Postal Code: 99362-3011
Office phone: (509) 525-3301
General E-mail: advertising@wwub.com
Publisher Name: Brian Hunt
Publisher Email: brianhunt@wwub.com
Publisher Phone: (509) 526-8331
Editor Name: Dian Ver Valen
Editor Email: dianvervalen@wwub.com
Editor Phone: (509) 526-8320
Advertising Executive Name: Matt Lohrmann
Advertising Executive Email: mattlohrmann@wwub.com
Advertising Executive Phone: (509) 526-8314
Year Established: 1869
Delivery Methods:
 Mail`Newsstand`Carrier`Racks
Own Printing Facility?: Y
Commercial printers?: N
Mechanical specifications: Type page 11 1/2 x 21 1/2; E - 6 cols, 1 5/6, 1/8 between; A - 6 cols, 1 5/6, 1/16 between; C - 9 cols, 1 9/50, 1/8 between.
Published Days: Mon`Tues`Wed`Thur`Fri`Sun
Weekday Frequency: e
Avg Paid Circ: 9104
Avg Free Circ: 2627
Audit Company: AAM
Audit Date: 30 09 2015

WENATCHEE
THE WENATCHEE WORLD

Corporate/Parent Company: Wick Communications
Publication Street Address: 14 N Mission St
City: Wenatchee
State: WA
Publication Website: www.wenatcheeworld.com
Postal Code: 98801-2250
Office phone: (509) 663-5161
General E-mail: newsroom@wenatcheeworld.com
Publisher Name: Sean Flaherty
Publisher Email: flaherty@wenatcheeworld.com
Publisher Phone: (509) 664-7136
Editor Name: Russ Hemphill
Editor Email: hemphill@wenatcheeworld.com
Editor Phone: (509) 665-5161
Advertising Executive Name: David Anderson
Advertising Executive Email: anderson@wenatcheeworld.com
Advertising Executive Phone: (509) 664-7141
Year Established: 1905
Delivery Methods: Mail`Newsstand`Carrier
Own Printing Facility?: Y
Commercial printers?: Y
Mechanical specifications: Type page 11 5/6 x 20 7/20; E - 6 cols, 1 5/6, 1/6 between; A - 6 cols, 1 5/6, 1/6 between; C - 8 cols, 1 19/50, 1/9 between.
Published Days: Tues`Wed`Thur`Fri`Sun
Weekday Frequency: e
Avg Paid Circ: 15001
Audit Company: CAC
Audit Date: 30 09 2014

WISCONSIN

ANTIGO
ANTIGO DAILY JOURNAL

Corporate/Parent Company: Adams Publishing Group
Publication Street Address: 612 Superior St
City: Antigo
State: WI
Publication Website: www.antigodailyjournal.com
Postal Code: 54409-2049
Office phone: (715) 623-4191
General E-mail: adj@dwave.net
Publisher Name: Fred Berner
Year Established: 1905
Delivery Methods:
 Mail`Newsstand`Carrier`Racks
Own Printing Facility?: Y
Commercial printers?: N
Mechanical specifications: Type page 11.625 x 21; E - 6 cols, 1 13/16, 1/8 between; A - 6 cols, 1 13/16, 1/8 between; C - 6 cols, 1 3/8, 1/16 between.
Published Days: Mon`Tues`Wed`Thur`Fri`Sat
Weekday Frequency: e
Saturday Frequency: m
Avg Paid Circ: 5660
Audit Company: Sworn/Estimate/Non-Audited
Audit Date: 7 12 2019
Pressroom Equipment: Lines – 5-G/Community.;
Mailroom Equipment: Tying Machines – 1/Bu; Address Machine – Stepper;
Buisness Equipment: PC/Business Mac/Production
Classified Equipment: Hardware – Mac; Printers – HP;
Classified Software: Baseview.
Editorial Equipment: Hardware – Mac; Printers – HP
Editorial Software: Baseview.
Production Equipment: Hardware – Mac; Scanners – HP, Epson
Production Software: QuarkXpress, Adobe Photoshop
Total Circulation: 5660

APPLETON
DAILY TRIBUNE

Corporate/Parent Company: Media News Group
Publication Street Address: PO Box 59
City: Appleton
State: WI
Publication Website: www.wisconsinrapidstribune.com
Postal Code: 54912
Office phone: (715) 423-7200
General E-mail: wisconsincoe@gannett.com
Mechanical specifications: Type page 11 5/8 x 21 1/2; E - 6 cols, 1 5/6, 1/6 between; A - 6 cols, 1 5/16, 1/6 between; C - 9 cols, 1 1/5, 2/25 between.
Published Days: Mon`Tues`Wed`Thur`Fri`Sat`Sun
Weekday Frequency: e
Saturday Frequency: m
Avg Paid Circ: 4549
Avg Free Circ: 50
Audit Company: AAM
Audit Date: 29 04 2020
Pressroom Equipment: Lines – 10-G/Community 1989.;
Mailroom Equipment: Tying Machines – 1/MLN.;
Classified Equipment: Hardware – APP/Mac G3; Printers – HP/5000;
Classified Software: Baseview.
Editorial Equipment: Hardware – APP/Mac G3, APP/iMacPrinters – HP/5000
Editorial Software: QPS/QuarkXPress, Baseview/IQUE.
Production Equipment: Hardware – Caere/OmniPage Pro, AP; Scanners – Epson
Production Software: QPS/QuarkXPress.
Total Circulation: 4793

MARSHFIELD NEWS-HERALD MEDIA

Publication Street Address: P.O. Box 59
City: Appleton
State: WI
Publication Website: www.marshfieldnewsherald.com
Postal Code: 54912
Office phone: (715) 384-3131
General E-mail: taramondloch@marshfieldnewsherald.com
Year Established: 1927
Delivery Methods: Carrier`Racks
Own Printing Facility?: N
Commercial printers?: N
Mechanical specifications: Type page 13 1/2 x 22 1/2; E - 6 cols, 2 1/16, 1/8 between; A - 6 cols, 2 1/16, 1/8 between; C - 8 cols, 1 1/2, 1/8 between.
Published Days: Mon`Tues`Wed`Thur`Fri`Sat`Sun
Weekday Frequency: e
Saturday Frequency: e
Avg Paid Circ: 4041
Avg Free Circ: 96
Audit Company: AAM
Audit Date: 31 03 2019
Pressroom Equipment: Lines – 6-G/Urbanite
Mailroom Equipment: Counter Stackers – 1-BG/108; Tying Machines – 2/Bu; Address Machine – 2-Am/4000, St/labeler.;
Buisness Equipment: NCR/Tower
Classified Equipment: Hardware – 4-COM.;
Editorial Equipment: Hardware – 1-COM.
Production Equipment: Hardware – 2-APP/Mac LaserWriter II; Cameras – 1-B.
Total Circulation: 4137

POST-CRESCENT

Corporate/Parent Company: Gannett
Publication Street Address: 306 W Washington St
City: Appleton
State: WI
Publication Website: www.postcrescent.com
Postal Code: 54911-5452
Office phone: (920) 993-1000
General E-mail: mtreinen@gannett.com
Year Established: 1853
Delivery Methods: Newsstand`Carrier`Racks
Own Printing Facility?: Y
Commercial printers?: Y
Mechanical specifications: Type page 11 1/8 x 20 5/8; E - 6 cols, 1 3/4, 1/8 between; A - 6 cols, 1 3/4, 1/8 between; C - 10 cols, 1 1/20, 1/8 between.
Published Days: Mon`Tues`Wed`Thur`Fri`Sat`Sun

U.S. Daily Newspapers

I-130

Weekday Frequency: m
Saturday Frequency: m
Avg Paid Circ: 30444
Audit Company: AAM
Audit Date: 4 10 2018
Pressroom Equipment: 8 (32 Couples)-2000; 8 (32 Couples)-2000; Registration System - Prazision/Comet EP.
Mailroom Equipment: Counter Stackers - 8-Compass/180; Inserters & Stuffers - 3-Printroll/GMA; Tying Machines - 7/Strapmaster; Wrapping Singles - 3-Dynaric/D2100; Control System - GMA;
Buisness Equipment: iSeries
Buisness Software: Gannett Genesys
Classified Equipment: Hardware - Sun Unix;
Classified Software: Mediaspan Ad Power
Editorial Software: CCI Europe NewsGate
Production Equipment: Hardware - AGFA
Total Circulation: 37070

THE SHEBOYGAN PRESS

Corporate/Parent Company: Gannett
Publication Street Address: P.O. Box 59
City: Appleton
State: WI
Publication Website: www.sheboyganpress.com
Postal Code: 54912
Office phone: (920) 457-7711
General E-mail: wisconsincoe@gannett.com
Publisher Name: Kevin Corrado
Editor Name: Matthew Piper
Editor Email: mpiper@gannett.com
Editor Phone: (920) 810-7164
Year Established: 1907
Delivery Methods: Mail`Newsstand`Carrier`Racks
Own Printing Facility?: N
Commercial printers?: Y
Mechanical specifications: Type page 12 x 22 3/4; E - 6 cols, 1 5/6, 1/6 between; A - 6 cols, 1 5/6, 1/6 between; C - 9 cols, 1 1/20, 1/8 between.
Published Days: Mon`Tues`Wed`Thur`Fri`Sat`Sun
Weekday Frequency: m
Saturday Frequency: m
Avg Paid Circ: 10488
Avg Free Circ: 481
Audit Company: AAM
Audit Date: 30 07 2018
Pressroom Equipment: Lines - 5-G/Headliner Anti-Friction double width Letterpress 1954; Folders - 2-G/2:1.;
Mailroom Equipment: Tying Machines - 1/ Bu, 2-Wilton Pro/Standard 80; Address Machine - KAN/550 2.;
Buisness Equipment: CTS, IBM/36
Classified Equipment: Hardware - AText; Printers - Pre Press/Panther;
Classified Software: AText.
Editorial Equipment: Hardware - AText/APP/Mac IIci, APP/Mac SE 30; Printers - Pre Press/ Panther
Editorial Software: Prestige.
Production Equipment: Hardware - AG
Production Software: QPS/QuarkXPress 4.0.
Total Circulation: 12140

ASHLAND

THE ASHLAND DAILY PRESS

Corporate/Parent Company: Adams Publishing Group
Publication Street Address: 122 3rd St W
City: Ashland
State: WI
Publication Website: www.apg-wi.com
Postal Code: 54806-1661
Office phone: (715) 682-2313
General E-mail: ar@adamspg.com
Publisher Name: Jim Moran
Publisher Email: jmoran@ashlanddailypress.net
Publisher Phone: (715) 718-6401
Editor Name: Pete Wasson
Editor Email: pwasson@ashlanddailypress.net
Editor Phone: (715) 718-6241
Advertising Executive Name: Bill Schneeberger

Advertising Executive Email: pressclass@ashlanddailypress.net
Advertising Executive Phone: (715) 718-6427
Delivery Methods: Mail`Newsstand`Carrier`Racks
Own Printing Facility?: Y
Mechanical specifications: Type page 11 5/8 x 21 1/2; E - 6 cols, 1 5/6, 1/8 between; A - 6 cols, 1 5/6, 1/8 between; C - 6 cols, 1 5/6, 1/8 between.
Published Days: Mon`Wed`Thur`Fri`Sat
Weekday Frequency: m
Saturday Frequency: m
Avg Paid Circ: 6153
Audit Company: Sworn/Estimate/Non-Audited
Audit Date: 7 12 2019
Pressroom Equipment: Lines - 8 (single width)-G/Community; Press Drive - HP/60 Motor; Folders - SC/Folder.;
Mailroom Equipment: Tying Machines - 3/Bu.;
Buisness Equipment: 2-RSK/12, 2-RSK/3000 HD, APP/Power Mac
Buisness Software: Quickbooks 5.0
Classified Equipment: Hardware - APP/Mac.;
Editorial Equipment: Hardware - APP/Mac.
Production Equipment: Hardware - 1-NuArc/Flip Top; Cameras - AG/2200II, 1-B; Scanners - Microtek/E6
Production Software: Baseview.
Total Circulation: 6153

BEAVER DAM

DAILY CITIZEN, BEAVER DAM

Publication Street Address: 805 Park Ave
City: Beaver Dam
State: WI
Publication Website: www.wiscnews.com
Postal Code: 53916-2205
Office phone: (920) 887-0321
General E-mail: dc-circulation@wiscnews.com
Editor Name: Aaron Holbrook
Editor Email: aholbrook@wiscnews.com
Editor Phone: (920) 356-6752
Advertising Executive Name: Scott Zeinemann
Advertising Executive Email: szeinemann@madison.com
Advertising Executive Phone: (608) 252-6092
Mechanical specifications: Type page 15 1/4 x 21 3/8; E - 6 cols, 2 1/16, 1/8 between; A - 8 cols, 1 9/16, 1/8 between; C - 8 cols, 1 3/8, 1/16 between.
Published Days: Mon`Tues`Wed`Thur`Fri`Sat
Weekday Frequency: e
Saturday Frequency: m
Avg Paid Circ: 3832
Avg Free Circ: 296
Audit Company: AAM
Audit Date: 31 03 2019
Pressroom Equipment: Lines - 12-G/Community; 20-G/Community; Folders - 5-G/Community; Pasters -7-MEG.
Mailroom Equipment: Counter Stackers - 5-BG/Count-O-Veyor 104-108; Inserters & Stuffers - 4-MM/227E, 6-MM/227; Tying Machines - 4/Bu, 1-/CYP; Address Machine - 2-/Am, 1-/Kk.;
Buisness Equipment: 10-IBM/PS2, 6-APP/Mac II
Classified Equipment: Hardware - 3-APP/Mac II.;
Editorial Equipment: Hardware - 2-APP/Mac Plus, 8-APP/Mac II
Editorial Software: Concept.
Production Equipment: Hardware - 1-Nu/Flip Top FT40LNS, 1-Nu/Flip Top FT40UPNS; Cameras - 1-B/Commodore
Production Software: Concept.
Total Circulation: 4128

BELOIT

BELOIT DAILY NEWS

Corporate/Parent Company: Adams Publishing Group
Publication Street Address: 149 State St
City: Beloit
State: WI
Publication Website: www.beloitdailynews.com
Postal Code: 53511-6251

Office phone: (608) 365-8811
General E-mail: advertising@beloitdailynews.com
Publisher Name: Todd Colling
Publisher Email: tcolling@beloitdailynews.com
Publisher Phone: (608) 364-9236
Editor Name: Bill Barth
Editor Email: bbarth@beloitdailynews.com
Editor Phone: (608) 364-9221
Advertising Executive Name: Kimberly Muller
Advertising Executive Email: kmuller@beloitdailynews.com
Advertising Executive Phone: (608) 364-9203
Year Established: 1848
Delivery Methods: Mail`Newsstand`Carrier`Racks
Own Printing Facility?: Y
Commercial printers?: Y
Mechanical specifications: Type page 11 5/8 x 21 1/2; E - 6 cols, 1 5/6, 1/8 between; A - 6 cols, 1 5/6, 1/8 between; C - 8 cols, 1 9/25, 1/8 between.
Published Days: Mon`Tues`Wed`Thur`Fri`Sat
Weekday Frequency: m
Saturday Frequency: m
Avg Paid Circ: 9309
Avg Free Circ: 20
Audit Company: Sworn/Estimate/Non-Audited
Audit Date: 7 12 2019
Pressroom Equipment: Lines - 6-G/Urbanite; Folders - 1-G/2:1.;
Mailroom Equipment: Tying Machines - 1-MLN/ Plastic Strap.;
Buisness Equipment: 1-DEC/TC 3800
Buisness Software: Micro/VMS 5.1
Classified Equipment: Hardware - Mac; Mac; Printers - OTC/850X2;
Classified Software: NCS
Editorial Equipment: Hardware - Mac/Mac; Printers - HP
Editorial Software: NCS
Production Equipment: Hardware - Mac computers, ECRM CTP plate setter.; Cameras - None; Scanners - Dest top
Production Software: NCS
Total Circulation: 9329

CHIPPEWA FALLS

THE CHIPPEWA HERALD

Corporate/Parent Company: Lee Enterprises
Publication Street Address: 321 Frenette Dr
City: Chippewa Falls
State: WI
Publication Website: www.chippewavalleynewspapers.com
Postal Code: 54729-3372
Office phone: (715) 723-5515
General E-mail: sean.burke@lee.net
Publisher Name: Sean Burke
Publisher Email: sean.burke@lee.net
Publisher Phone: (608) 791-8237
Advertising Executive Name: Erin Brunke
Advertising Executive Email: erin.brunke@lee.net
Advertising Executive Phone: (715) 738-1615
Year Established: 1870
Mechanical specifications: Type page 12 1/2 x 21 1/2; E - 6 cols, 2 1/16, 1/8 between; A - 6 cols, 2 1/16, 1/8 between; C - 6 cols, 2 1/16, 1/8 between.
Published Days: Mon`Tues`Wed`Thur`Sat`Sun
Weekday Frequency: m
Saturday Frequency: m
Avg Paid Circ: 3578
Avg Free Circ: 570
Audit Company: AAM
Audit Date: 31 03 2016
Pressroom Equipment: Lines - G/4-hi, 2-DEV/ Flexicolor; Folders - 4-G/2:1.;
Mailroom Equipment: Counter Stackers - 2/BG; Inserters & Stuffers - USA/Leader; Tying Machines - 2-/Bu, 1-/It; Address Machine - KR.;
Classified Equipment: Hardware - Gateway;
Classified Software: APT.
Editorial Equipment: Hardware - APP/Power Macs/Nikon/Coolscan; Printers - APP/Mac LaserPrinter
Editorial Software: Baseview.
Production Equipment: Hardware - 2-COM/ Laserwriter, Pre Press/Panther Pro; Cameras - SCREEN; Scanners - HP/

ScanJet Plus, 2-Nikon/Coolscan
Production Software: QPS/QuarkXPress.
Total Circulation: 4148

EAU CLAIRE

LEADER-TELEGRAM

Corporate/Parent Company: Adams Publishing Group
Publication Street Address: 701 S Farwell St
City: Eau Claire
State: WI
Publication Website: www.leadertelegram.com
Postal Code: 54701-3831
Office phone: (715) 833-9200
General E-mail: dan.graaskamp@ecpc.com
Publisher Name: Randy Rickman
Publisher Email: randy.rickman@ecpc.com
Publisher Phone: (715) 833-7429
Editor Name: Gary Johnson
Editor Email: gary.johnson@ecpc.com
Editor Phone: (715) 833-9211
Advertising Executive Name: Brian Maki
Advertising Executive Email: brian.maki@ecpc.com
Advertising Executive Phone: (715) 830-5821
Year Established: 1912
Mechanical specifications: Type page 12 1/2 x 21; E - 6 cols, 1 13/16, 1/8 between; A - 6 cols, 1 13/16, 1/8 between; C - 9 cols, 1 3/16, 1/8 between.
Published Days: Mon`Tues`Wed`Thur`Fri`Sat`Sun
Weekday Frequency: m
Saturday Frequency: m
Avg Paid Circ: 18260
Audit Company: AAM
Audit Date: 31 03 2017
Pressroom Equipment: Lines - 14-DGM/850 single width 1998; Folders - 1-G/Half, 1-G/Quarter.;
Mailroom Equipment: Counter Stackers - 2-QWI/350; Inserters & Stuffers - 1-GMA/10:1; Tying Machines - 2/MLN; Wrapping Singles - Mailroom Control System ÃƒÂƒÃ‚Â£ GMA; Address Machine - 2-/KR;
Buisness Equipment: 1-HP, 2-Dell Poweredge 6300, 1-Dell Poweredge 6400
Buisness Software: Mactive
Classified Equipment: Hardware - 10-PC, Microsoft/Windows NT 4.0; Printers - Canon/BX-II, HP/LJ 4ML;
Classified Software: Mactive.
Editorial Equipment: Hardware - 35-PC; Printers - Canon/BXII, HP/LS9700
Editorial Software: Microsoft/Word, QPS/ QuarkXPress 4.11rl, ATS/Mediadesk.
Production Equipment: Hardware - 1-AG/5000 Recorder, 1-AG/Phoenix 2250, 1-AG/Avatru 44; Cameras - 1-Liberator; Scanners - 2-Nikon, 2-Epson/Expressions 800XL
Production Software: QPS/QuarkXPress 4.11rl, Adobe/Illustrator 5.5,6.5.
Total Circulation: 18260

FOND DU LAC

THE FOND DU LAC REPORTER

Publication Street Address: N6637 Rolling Meadows Dr
City: Fond Du Lac
State: WI
Publication Website: www.fdlreporter.com
Postal Code: 54936
Office phone: (920) 922-4600
General E-mail: mtreinen@gannett.com
Publisher Name: Pamala Henson
Editor Name: Taima Kern
Editor Email: taima.kern@gannettwisconsin.com
Editor Phone: (920) 907-7819
Year Established: 1856
Delivery Methods: Mail`Newsstand`Carrier
Own Printing Facility?: N
Commercial printers?: Y
Mechanical specifications: Type page 11 5/8 x 21 1/2; E - 6 cols, 1 5/6, 1/8 between; A - 6 cols, 1 5/6, 1/8 between; C - 9 cols, 1 1/4, 1/16 between.
Published Days: Mon`Tues`Wed`Thur`Fri`Sat`Sun

U.S. Daily Newspapers

Weekday Frequency: e
Avg Paid Circ: 8529
Avg Free Circ: 178
Audit Company: AAM
Audit Date: 31 03 2016
Pressroom Equipment: Lines – 7-G/Urbanite single width 1977; 1-Ik/Sheet Fed Press 1992; 12-G/Urbanite; 7-G/Urbanite; Folders – 1-G/Half, 1-G/Quarter, 2-G/Folders-Half Width, 2-1998; Pasters –8-Enkel/Auto Splicers
Mailroom Equipment: Counter Stackers – HL/Monitor HT, 2/HL, 2-/MRS; Inserters & Stuffers – 2-GMA/SLS 1000 2:12; Tying Machines – OVL, 2-/Samuel, 1-/Dynaric, 2-OVL/415; Wrapping Singles – 2-/Samuel, 2-Id; Address Machine – Video Jet/Ink Jet, Ch.;
Buisness Equipment: ATT, Oracle
Buisness Software: IBM
Classified Equipment: Hardware – 1-HI;
Classified Software: Ad Power.
Editorial Equipment: Hardware – Atex/Pagination System; Printers – HP/P1180.
Production Equipment: Hardware – LaserJet 4mv, Digital Darkroom, Adobe/Photoshop, V/Film Recorder; Cameras – Auto/Companica 690D; Scanners – AG/StudioScan
Production Software: CText.
Total Circulation: 8707

FOND DU LAC

THE REPORTER

Corporate/Parent Company: Media News Group
Publication Street Address: N6637 Rolling Meadows Drive
City: Fond Du Lac
State: WI
Publication Website: www.fdlreporter.com
Postal Code: 54936
Office phone: 920-922-4600
Editor Name: Kern, Taima
Editor Email: Taima.Kern@gannettwisconsin.com target
Editor Phone: 920-907-7819
Audit Company: AAM
Audit Date: 11 09 2018
Total Circulation: 10968

FORT ATKINSON

DAILY JEFFERSON COUNTY UNION

Corporate/Parent Company: Adams Publishing Group
Publication Street Address: 28 Milwaukee Ave W
City: Fort Atkinson
State: WI
Publication Website: www.dailyunion.com
Postal Code: 53538-2018
Office phone: (920) 563-5553
General E-mail: advertising@dailyunion.com
Publisher Name: Robb Grindstaff
Publisher Email: rgrindstaff@dailyunion.com
Publisher Phone: (920) 691-3624
Editor Name: Christine Spangler
Editor Email: cspangler@dailyunion.com
Editor Phone: (920) 691-3631
Advertising Executive Name: Megan Vergenz
Advertising Executive Email: advertising@dailyunion.com
Advertising Executive Phone: (920) 691-3637
Year Established: 1870
Delivery Methods: Mail`Newsstand`Carrier`Racks
Own Printing Facility?: N
Commercial printers?: Y
Mechanical specifications: Type page 11.125 X 19.5; E - 6 cols, 1.75" per col, 0.125" between; C - 8 cols, 1.281", 0.125" between.
Published Days: Mon`Tues`Wed`Thur`Fri
Weekday Frequency: e
Avg Paid Circ: 7325
Audit Company: USPS
Audit Date: 28 09 2018
Buisness Software: Pre1 SmartPublisher
Classified Software: Pre1 SmartPublisher
Editorial Software: Town News Blox TCMS
Production Software: Creative Cloud

Total Circulation: 7325

GREEN BAY

GREEN BAY PRESS-GAZETTE

Corporate/Parent Company: Gannett
Publication Street Address: 435 E Walnut St
City: Green Bay
State: WI
Publication Website: www.greenbaypressgazette.com
Postal Code: 54305-3430
Office phone: (920) 431-8400
General E-mail: circulation@greenbaypressgazette.com
Publisher Name: Scott Johnson
Editor Name: Robert Zizzo
Year Established: 1915
Delivery Methods: Mail`Carrier`Racks
Own Printing Facility?: Y
Mechanical specifications: Type page 11 5/8 x 20 3/4; E - 6 cols, 1 5/6, 1/8 between; A - 6 cols, 1 5/6, 1/8 between; C - 9 cols, 1 6/25, 1/16 between.
Published Days: Mon`Tues`Wed`Thur`Fri`Sat`Sun
Weekday Frequency: m
Saturday Frequency: m
Avg Paid Circ: 33485
Audit Company: AAM
Audit Date: 18 10 2018
Pressroom Equipment: Lines – 6-G/Mark II double width, 2-G/Mark I double width 1969; Press Drive – CH/60 h.p.; Folders – 2-G/2:1; Reels & Stands – G/3-Arm.;
Mailroom Equipment: Counter Stackers – 4/HL, QWI/Hall; Inserters & Stuffers – HI/1472, S/NP630; Tying Machines – 2-MLN/2A, 2-/Dynaric, 1-/Power Strap; Wrapping Singles – QWI/Hall; Control System – Ic, HL/Spec 09; Address Machine – Dispensa-Matic-V4.;
Buisness Equipment: IBM/AS-400
Buisness Software: Microsoft/Office 97
Classified Equipment: Hardware – Sun; Printers – AU/APS;
Classified Software: HI/AdPower 1.2.
Editorial Equipment: Hardware – 28-AT/7000, 60-AT/Prestige 4.2.1/4-APP/Mac
Editorial Software: AT, Aldus/Freehand, QPS/QuarkXPress, Adobe/Photoshop.
Production Equipment: Hardware – 3-AU/Software RIP & Imagesetter, 5-LE; Cameras – 1-C/Marathon, 1-B/Admiral; Scanners – 1-Hel/Sapphire, 1-ECR/Autokon 1000, 1-X/1200 dpi, 3-Umax/Color 1200 DPI, 2-Epson, 2-Nikon/Slide Scanner
Production Software: QPS/QuarkXPress 3.5, AT.
Total Circulation: 44572

JANESVILLE

THE JANESVILLE GAZETTE - GAZETTEXTRA

Publication Street Address: 1 S Parker Dr
City: Janesville
State: WI
Publication Website: www.gazetteextra.com
Postal Code: 53545-3928
Office phone: (800) 362-6712
General E-mail: newsroom@gazettextra.com
Advertising Executive Email: advertising@gazettextra.com
Advertising Executive Phone: (608) 755-8344
Year Established: 1845
Delivery Methods: Newsstand`Carrier`Racks
Own Printing Facility?: Y
Mechanical specifications: Type page 13 x 21 1/2; E - 6 cols, 2 1/16, 1/8 between; A - 6 cols, 2 1/16, 1/8 between; C - 9 cols, 1 3/8, 1/16 between.
Published Days: Mon`Tues`Wed`Thur`Fri`Sat`Sun
Weekday Frequency: m
Saturday Frequency: m
Avg Paid Circ: 13713
Avg Free Circ: 335
Audit Company: AAM
Audit Date: 31 03 2019
Pressroom Equipment: Lines – 4-G/Metro; Folders – 1-G/2:1.;
Mailroom Equipment: Counter Stackers –

1-Id/2000, 1-Id/2200; Inserters & Stuffers – GMA/SLS 1000 8 x 1; Tying Machines – MLN/Spirit; Address Machine – BH/1530;
Buisness Equipment: 1-HP/3000
Buisness Software: CJ
Classified Equipment: Hardware – Tandem/CLX;
Classified Software: SII.
Editorial Equipment: Hardware – Tandem/CLX/1-APP/Mac IIci, APP/Power Mac 8100 Color Darkroom, Epson/Color Dye Subprinter
Editorial Software: SII.
Production Equipment: Hardware – 2-Pre Press/Panther Pm 36 with Mac RIP, APP/Mac Quadra 950; Cameras – 1-B/Commodore; Scanners – 4-Epson/Flatbed, 1-HP/Flatbed, Kk/Neg Scanner.
Total Circulation: 14048

KENOSHA

KENOSHA NEWS

Corporate/Parent Company: Lee Enterprises
Publication Street Address: 6535 Green Bay Rd.
City: Kenosha
State: WI
Publication Website: www.kenoshanews.com
Postal Code: 53142
Office phone: (262) 657-1000
General E-mail: faune@kenoshanews.com
Editor Name: Bob Heisse
Editor Email: bheisse@kenoshanews.com
Editor Phone: (262) 656-6337
Advertising Executive Name: Sarah Sukus
Advertising Executive Email: ssukus@kenoshanews.com
Advertising Executive Phone: (262) 656-6212
Year Established: 1894
Delivery Methods: Newsstand`Carrier`Racks
Own Printing Facility?: N
Commercial printers?: Y
Mechanical specifications: Type page 10.875 inches x 20 inches
Published Days: Mon`Tues`Wed`Thur`Fri`Sat`Sun
Weekday Frequency: m
Saturday Frequency: m
Avg Paid Circ: 15810
Avg Free Circ: 1281
Audit Company: AAM
Audit Date: 2 04 2019
Pressroom Equipment: Lines – production off-site.;
Mailroom Equipment: – production off-site;
Classified Equipment: Hardware – SIA/NT 4.0; Printers – HP/6MP;
Classified Software: Unysis/Ad Management Systems 3.
Editorial Equipment: Hardware – SIA; Printers – Kyocera/Royal, 4P5si
Editorial Software: CTEXT/Dateline Expressline, HP/5Si.
Production Equipment: Hardware – production off site
Production Software: In-Design Suite
Total Circulation: 17954

LA CROSSE

JACKSON COUNTY CHRONICLE

Publication Street Address: 401 N. Third Street
City: La Crosse
State: WI
Publication Website: www.jacksoncountychronicle.com
Postal Code: 54601
Office phone: 608-782-9710
General E-mail: news@lacrossetribune.com
Publisher Name: Sean Burke
Publisher Email: sean.burke@lee.net
Publisher Phone: 608-791-8237
Advertising Executive Name: Paul Pehler
Advertising Executive Email: paul.pehler@lee.net
Advertising Executive Phone: 608-791-8300

LA CROSSE TRIBUNE

Corporate/Parent Company: Lee Enterprises

Publication Street Address: 401 3rd St N
City: La Crosse
State: WI
Publication Website: www.lacrossetribune.com
Postal Code: 54601-3267
Office phone: (608) 782-9710
General E-mail: rusty.cunningham@lee.net
Publisher Name: Sean Burke
Publisher Email: sean.burke@lee.net
Publisher Phone: (608) 791-8237
Editor Name: Rusty Cunningham
Editor Email: rusty.cunningham@lee.net
Editor Phone: (608) 791-8285
Advertising Executive Name: Paul Pehler
Advertising Executive Email: paul.pehler@lee.net
Advertising Executive Phone: (608) 791-8300
Published Days: Wed
Audit Company: AAM
Audit Date: 1 10 2018
Total Circulation: 22140

MADISON

PORTAGE DAILY REGISTER

Corporate/Parent Company: Lee Enterprises, Incorporated
Publication Street Address: 1901 Fish Hatchery Rd
City: Madison
State: WI
Publication Website: www.portagedailyregister.com
Postal Code: 53901
Office phone: (608) 745-3500
General E-mail: pdr-news@wiscnews.com
Audit Company: AAM
Audit Date: 13 03 2020
Total Circulation: 2425

WISCONSIN STATE JOURNAL, MADISON

Publication Street Address: 1901 Fish Hatchery Rd
City: Madison
State: WI
Publication Website: https://madison.com/wsj/
Postal Code: 53713-1248
Office phone: (608) 252-6100
General E-mail: jschroeter@madison.com
Publisher Name: John Humenik
Editor Name: John Smalley
Editor Email: jsmalley@madison.com
Editor Phone: (608) 252-6104
Year Established: 1839
Delivery Methods: Mail`Newsstand`Carrier`Racks
Own Printing Facility?: Y
Mechanical specifications: Type page 11 5/8 x 21 1/2; E - 6 cols, 1 5/6, 1/8 between; A - 6 cols, 2 1/16, 1/8 between; C - 10 cols, 1 1/6, between.
Published Days: Mon`Tues`Wed`Thur`Fri`Sat`Sun
Weekday Frequency: m
Saturday Frequency: m
Avg Paid Circ: 57857
Audit Company: AAM
Audit Date: 31 03 2018
Pressroom Equipment: Lines – 17-G/Metro double width 1975; 5-G/Community (2-Four H16A; 4-single width) 1994; Folders – 3-G/Imperial 3:2, 2-G/Community SSE; Reels & Stands – 15-G/Metro; Registration System – Web Tech/Auto Registration.
Mailroom Equipment: Counter Stackers – 7-Id/N5550, BG/Count-O-Veyor; Inserters & Stuffers – 2-HI/1372, GMA/SLS 2000; Tying Machines – 5-Dynaric/NP2; Wrapping Singles – 4-Bu/Strapper; Control System – GMA; Address Machine – 2-Ch/545, 5/CH, 4-/Ideal;
Buisness Equipment: IBM/AS-400
Buisness Software: Microsoft/Office
Classified Equipment: Hardware – 56-Pentium/PC; Printers – HP/LaserJet;
Classified Software: Insiight 5.0.
Editorial Equipment: Hardware – Sun/fileservers, Dell/Workstations/Dell/Latitude Laptops,

Nikon/Digital Camera; Printers – HP/LaserJet
Editorial Software: HI/Newsmaker 2.6.
Production Equipment: Hardware – AU/APS-108-S, 3-AU/3850; Cameras – 1-C/Newspaper, 2-DSA; Scanners – 3-AG/Horizon Plus, AG/XL 2000, AG/Scanner, Tecsa/Scanner
Production Software: HI 2.0.
Total Circulation: 57857

MANITOWOC

HERALD TIMES REPORTER

Corporate/Parent Company: Gannett
Publication Street Address: 902 Franklin St
City: Manitowoc
State: WI
Publication Website: www.htrnews.com
Postal Code: 54220-4514
Office phone: (920) 684-4433
General E-mail: legals@htrnews.com
Editor Name: Brandon Reid
Editor Email: brandon.reid@gannettwisconsin.com
Editor Phone: (920) 686-2984
Year Established: 1898
Delivery Methods: Carrier
Own Printing Facility?: N
Mechanical specifications: Type page 11 5/8 x 20 1/4; E – 6 cols, 1 13/16, 1/8 between; A – 6 cols, 1 13/16, 1/8 between; C – 9 cols, 1 3/16, 1/16 between.
Published Days: Mon`Tues`Wed`Thur`Fri`Sat`Sun
Weekday Frequency: e
Saturday Frequency: e
Avg Paid Circ: 7284
Avg Free Circ: 164
Audit Company: AAM
Audit Date: 27 07 2018
Mailroom Equipment: Tying Machines – 1/Bu, 1-/MLN.;
Buisness Equipment: Oracle, PBS
Classified Equipment: Hardware – AT.;
Editorial Equipment: Hardware – AT, DEC/Nikon/Scanners; Printers – Pre Press/Panther, AGFA/CTP AG
Editorial Software: QPS/QuarkXPress 3.32, Dewar/Dewarview.
Production Software: Lf/AP Leaf Picture Desk, Adobe/Photoshop.
Total Circulation: 8046

MARINETTE

EAGLEHERALD - EHEXTRA.COM

Publication Street Address: 1809 Dunlap Ave
City: Marinette
State: WI
Publication Website: www.ehextra.com
Postal Code: 54143-1706
Office phone: (715) 735-6611
General E-mail: addesign@eagleherald.com
Publisher Name: Kathy Springberg
Publisher Email: kspringberg@eagleherald.com
Publisher Phone: (715) 735-6611, Ext : 101
Editor Name: Dan Kitkowski
Editor Email: dkitkowski@eagleherald.com
Editor Phone: (715) 735-6611, Ext : 155
Advertising Executive Name: Becki Minton
Advertising Executive Email: bminton@eagleherald.com
Advertising Executive Phone: (715) 735-6562, Ext : 119
Year Established: 1867
Own Printing Facility?: Y
Mechanical specifications: Type page 10 x 21 1/2; E – 6 cols, 1 5/6, 1/8 between; A – 6 cols, 1 5/6, 1/8 between; C – 6 cols, 1 5/6, 1/8 between.
Published Days: Mon`Tues`Wed`Thur`Fri`Sat
Weekday Frequency: m
Saturday Frequency: m
Avg Paid Circ: 7589
Audit Company: Sworn/Estimate/Non-Audited
Audit Date: 7 12 2019
Pressroom Equipment: Lines – 6-G/Urbanite Single Width; 4-G/Community Single Width; Folders – 1-G/2:1, 1-G/4:1.;
Mailroom Equipment: Tying Machines – 2/Bu, 1-Sa/SR1A.;
Buisness Equipment: IBM
Buisness Software: Vision Data
Classified Software: Baseview.
Editorial Equipment: Hardware – 1-APP/Mac
Editorial Software: Baseview.
Production Equipment: Hardware – 1-3M/Deadliner, 3M/Pyrofax.
Total Circulation: 7589

MILWAUKEE

MILWAUKEE JOURNAL SENTINEL

Corporate/Parent Company: Gannett
Publication Street Address: P.O. Box 371
City: Milwaukee
State: WI
Publication Website: www.jsonline.com
Postal Code: 53201
Office phone: (414) 224-2000
General E-mail: milwaukeejournalsentinel@gannett.com
Editor Name: George Stanley
Editor Email: george.stanley@jrn.com
Editor Phone: (414) 224-2248
Advertising Executive Email: class@journalsentinel.com
Year Established: 1882
Delivery Methods: Mail`Newsstand`Carrier`Racks
Mechanical specifications: Type page 13 x 21 7/16; A – 6 cols, 2 1/16, 1/8 between; C – 10 cols, 1 1/4, 1/16 between.
Published Days: Mon`Tues`Wed`Thur`Fri`Sat`Sun
Weekday Frequency: m
Saturday Frequency: m
Avg Paid Circ: 116537
Audit Company: AAM
Audit Date: 11 03 2020
Pressroom Equipment: Lines – 9-H/Colormatic double width 1962; 9-H/Colormatic double width 1962; 9-H/Colormatic double width 1967; 9-H/Colormatic double width 1967; Folders – 8-H/2:1; Reels & Stands – 36-H; Control System – H/Reflex drive (;
Mailroom Equipment: Counter Stackers – 12-HL/Dual Carrier, 2-HL/Monitor, 5-TMSI/Compass 180; Inserters & Stuffers – 1-HI/1372P, 1-HI/1472P, 1-GMA/SLS 1000, 1-HI/1472, 1-GMA/SLS 2000; Tying Machines – 28/Dynaric; Wrapping Singles – 5-HL/3/4 wrap, 5-ld/3-4 wrap, 2-5/;
Buisness Software: Ross, CJ, Discus
Classified Equipment: Hardware – 2-Sun/Enterprisr 4500, 3-Dell/1300; Printers – HP/Laser Jet 4000, HP/Laser Jet 5000, HP/Laser Jet 6000;
Classified Software: Mactive/Ad Base 2.10.17.
Editorial Equipment: Hardware – SII/Tandem, 6-Tandem/K1000 Himalaya; Printers – HP/Laser Jet 4000, HP/Laser Jet 5000, HP/Laser Jet 6000
Editorial Software: SII/Coyote, Coyote/3.
Production Equipment: Hardware – 5-MON/Express, MAS/1000, 5-Konica/Processor, 1-MON/Futuro, 1-Carnfelot/Processor; Cameras – 1-C/Marathon, 1-C/Olympia, 2-C/Newspager; Scanners – 2-Pro/Imager 8000, Linotype-Hell/Linocolor Opal, 1-Scitex/Eversmart Supreme
Production Software: HI/CPAG
Total Circulation: 155797

MONROE

THE MONROE TIMES

Publication Street Address: 1065 4th Ave W
City: Monroe
State: WI
Publication Website: www.themonroetimes.com
Postal Code: 53566-1318
Office phone: (608) 328-4202
General E-mail: circulation@themonroetimes.com
Publisher Name: Matt Johnson
Publisher Email: mjohnson@themonroetimes.net
Publisher Phone: (608) 328-4202, Ext : 15
Editor Name: Emily Massingill
Editor Email: editor@themonroetimes.com
Editor Phone: (608) 328-4202, Ext : 22
Advertising Executive Name: Laura Hughes
Advertising Executive Email: lhughes@themonroetimes.com
Advertising Executive Phone: (608) 328-4202, Ext : 24
Year Established: 1898
Delivery Methods: Mail
Own Printing Facility?: N
Commercial printers?: N
Mechanical specifications: Type page 11 x 20; E – 6 cols, 1 3/4, 1/8 between; A – 6 cols, 1 3/4, 1/8 between; C – 9 cols, 1 1/8, 1/16 between.
Published Days: Mon`Tues`Wed`Thur`Fri`Sat
Weekday Frequency: All day
Saturday Frequency: All day
Avg Paid Circ: 3100
Audit Company: CVC
Audit Date: 30 09 2018
Buisness Software: Vision Data
Total Circulation: 3100

OSHKOSH

OSHKOSH NORTHWESTERN

Publication Street Address: 224 State St
City: Oshkosh
State: WI
Publication Website: www.thenorthwestern.com
Postal Code: 54901-4839
Office phone: (920) 235-7700
General E-mail: nathaniel.shuda@gannettwisconsin.com
Editor Name: Nathaniel Shuda
Editor Email: nathaniel.shuda@gannettwisconsin.com
Editor Phone: (920) 426-6632
Mechanical specifications: Type page 13 x 22; E – 6 cols, 1 5/6, 1/8 between; A – 6 cols, 1 5/6, 1/8 between; C – 9 cols, 1 3/16, 1/8 between.
Published Days: Mon`Tues`Wed`Thur`Fri`Sat`Sun
Weekday Frequency: m
Saturday Frequency: m
Avg Paid Circ: 10218
Avg Free Circ: 359
Audit Company: AAM
Audit Date: 31 03 2016
Pressroom Equipment: Lines – 5-HI/1660 1979; Pasters –5-MEG/D500.
Mailroom Equipment: Tying Machines – 1/Dynaric.;
Buisness Equipment: 1-Sun/Sparcstation 20
Buisness Software: PBS, Media Plus, SBS
Classified Equipment: Hardware – 6-Pentium/PC, 2-Compaq/fileserver Pentium 150; Printers – 1-HP/4MP;
Classified Software: Harris/Classified, Informatel/Classified Pagination, Novell/Network 4.1, Novell/SFT III.
Editorial Equipment: Hardware – 1-APP/Power Mac 6100, 10-Pentium/200, 4-Pentium/100, 13-Pentium/166, 6-Compaq/fileserver Pentium 200 dual processors/Lf/Leafscan 35, APP/Mac 8100-100, APP/Mac IIfx, APP/Mac 8500-180; Printers – 1-HP/5000, AU/6600
Editorial Software: ATEX/D
Production Equipment: Hardware – Caere/OmniPage; Scanners – Umax/PowerLook
Production Software: ATEX/Dewarview.
Total Circulation: 10577

PORTAGE

BARABOO NEWS REPUBLIC

Corporate/Parent Company: Lee Enterprises, Incorporated
Publication Street Address: 1640 LaDawn Drive, P.O. Box 470
City: Portage
State: WI
Publication Website: https://www.wiscnews.com/baraboonewsrepublic/
Postal Code: 53913-3152
Office phone: (800) 236-2110
General E-mail: szeinemann@madison.com
Editor Name: Aaron Holbrook
Editor Email: aholbrook@wiscnews.com
Editor Phone: (920) 356-6752
Advertising Executive Name: Scott Zeinemann
Advertising Executive Email: szeinemann@madison.com
Advertising Executive Phone: (608) 252-6092
Delivery Methods: Mail`Newsstand`Racks
Own Printing Facility?: Y
Commercial printers?: N
Mechanical specifications: Type page 13 x 21 1/2; E – 6 cols, 1 7/8, 1/8 between; A – 6 cols, 1 7/8, 1/8 between; C – 9 cols, 1 3/16, 1/8 between.
Published Days: Mon`Tues`Wed`Thur`Fri`Sat
Weekday Frequency: m
Saturday Frequency: m
Avg Paid Circ: 2522
Avg Free Circ: 181
Audit Company: AAM
Audit Date: 12 03 2020
Pressroom Equipment: Lines – 12-G/Community 1998.;
Mailroom Equipment: Counter Stackers – 1/MM; Inserters & Stuffers – 2-KAN/8; Tying Machines – 1-/Bu; Address Machine – VideoJet.;
Buisness Software: SMS
Classified Software: Baseview.
Editorial Software: Baseview.
Production Equipment: Hardware – 2-Nu; Cameras – B/Vertical; Scanners – 3-COM/2961HS, 1-COM/7200, 1-COM/4
Production Software: QPS/QuarkXPress 4.0.
Total Circulation: 2055

PORTAGE

DAILY REGISTER

Publication Street Address: 1640 La Dawn Dr
City: Portage
State: WI
Publication Website: www.portagedailyregister.com
Postal Code: 53901-8822
Office phone: (608) 745-3500
General E-mail: pdr-news@capitalnewspapers.com
Year Established: 1886
Delivery Methods: Mail`Newsstand`Carrier`Racks
Own Printing Facility?: Y
Commercial printers?: Y
Mechanical specifications: Type page 12 1/8 x 21 1/2; E – 6 cols, 1 7/8, 1/8 between; A – 6 cols, 1 7/8, 1/8 between; C – 9 cols, 1 3/16, 1/16 between.
Published Days: Mon`Tues`Wed`Thur`Fri`Sat
Weekday Frequency: m
Saturday Frequency: m
Avg Paid Circ: 2879
Avg Free Circ: 292
Audit Company: AAM
Audit Date: 30 06 2017
Total Circulation: 3171

RACINE

THE JOURNAL TIMES

Corporate/Parent Company: Lee Enterprises, Incorporated
Publication Street Address: 212 4th St
City: Racine
State: WI
Publication Website: www.journaltimes.com
Postal Code: 53403-1005
Office phone: (262) 634-3322
General E-mail: david.habrat@journaltimes.com
Publisher Name: Stephanie Jones
Publisher Email: stephanie.jones@journaltimes.com
Publisher Phone: (262) 631-1717
Editor Name: David Habrat
Editor Email: david.habrat@journaltimes.com
Editor Phone: (262) 631-1709
Advertising Executive Name: Mark Lewis
Advertising Executive Email: mark.lewis@journaltimes.com
Advertising Executive Phone: (262) 631-1778
Mechanical specifications: Type page 13 x 21 1/2; E – 6 cols, 2 1/16, 1/8 between; A – 6

U.S. Daily Newspapers

cols, 2 1/16, 1/8 between; C - 10 cols, 1 1/4, 1/16 between.
Published Days: Mon`Tues`Wed`Thur`Fri`Sat`Sun
Weekday Frequency: m
Saturday Frequency: m
Avg Paid Circ: 14744
Avg Free Circ: 820
Audit Company: AAM
Audit Date: 22 03 2019
Pressroom Equipment: Lines – 1-MOT/Colormax double width (Flexo 1-5 Impression Unit) 1994; 1-MOT/Colormax double width (Flexo 1-5 Impression Unit) 1995; 1-MOT/Colormax double width (Flexo 1-3 Impression Unit) 1995; Folders – 2-G/2:1; Reels & Stands – G/Re;
Mailroom Equipment: Counter Stackers – 3-Compass/180, HL/Monitor HT; Inserters & Stuffers – 1372 HI/Inserter; Tying Machines – 1/Power Strap/PNS6, 1-/Power Strap/PNS5, 2-Dynaric/NP2; Wrapping Singles – 2-QWI/Viper, Powerstrap w/ siderollers, Bottom wrapppers;
Buisness Equipment: IBM/AS-400
Buisness Software: WordPerfect, Microsoft/ Excel, Microsoft/Word, XYQUEST/XyWrite, Paradox
Classified Equipment: Hardware – Compaq/ Proliant; Printers – HP/2000C, OCE/9400;
Classified Software: HI 3.6, CText/advision, Sybase.
Editorial Equipment: Hardware – APP/Mac G3/2-AG/Avantra Select set 25, 2-APP/ OSX Servers, Harlequin/NT RIPs; Printers – OCC/9400, HP/2000C, HP/8500C
Editorial Software: HI 8.0, Baseview/IQue.
Production Equipment: Hardware – 2-AG/ Avantra 25, 1-Na/FX VIII; Cameras – C/ Spartan III; Scanners – Epson/836XL, Lf/ Leafscan 35, Polaroid/SprintScan
Production Software: QPS/QuarkXPress 4.0.
Total Circulation: 17447

RHINELANDER
THE NORTHWOODS RIVER NEWS

Corporate/Parent Company: Walker Communications LLC
Publication Street Address: 232 S Courtney St
City: Rhinelander
State: WI
Publication Website: www.rivernewsonline.com
Postal Code: 54501-3319
Office phone: (715) 365-6397
General E-mail: advertising@rivernewsonline.com
Publisher Name: Gregg Walker
Publisher Email: gwalker@lakelandtimes.com
Publisher Phone: (715) 356-5236
Editor Name: Heather Schaefer
Editor Email: heather@rivernewsonline.com
Editor Phone: (715) 365-6397, Ext : 383
Advertising Executive Email: advertising@rivernewsonline.com
Year Established: 1882
Delivery Methods: Mail`Newsstand`Carrier
Own Printing Facility?: N
Commercial printers?: N
Mechanical specifications: Type page 11 5/8 x 21 1/2; E - 6 cols, 1 5/6, 1/8 between; A - 6 cols, 1 5/6, 1/8 between; C - 6 cols, 1 5/6, 1/8 between.
Published Days: Mon`Tues`Wed`Thur`Fri`Sun
Weekday Frequency: e
Avg Paid Circ: 5302
Audit Company: Sworn/Estimate/Non-Audited
Audit Date: 7 12 2019
Pressroom Equipment: Lines – 4-G/Community;
Mailroom Equipment: Tying Machines – 1-Bu/69175.;
Buisness Equipment: 4-Mk/Acer
Classified Equipment: Hardware – PC; Printers – QMS/810;
Classified Software: Suntype.
Editorial Equipment: Hardware – APP/ MacPrinters – 2-QMS/810
Editorial Software: Baseview.
Production Equipment: Hardware – 2-QMS/ Laserprinter; Cameras – 1-K/241, 1-K/V2 41; Scanners – HP/ScanJet 3C.
Total Circulation: 5302

STEVENS POINT
STEVENS POINT JOURNAL

Corporate/Parent Company: Gannett
Publication Street Address: 1200 3rd St
City: Stevens Point
State: WI
Publication Website: www.stevenspointjournal.com
Postal Code: 54481-2855
Office phone: (715) 344-6100
General E-mail: lbolle@gannett.com
Editor Name: Mark Treinen
Mechanical specifications: Type page 12 1/2 x 21; E - 6 cols, 2 1/16, 1/8 between; A - 6 cols, 2 1/16, 1/8 between; C - 9 cols, 1 2/3, 1/8 between.
Published Days: Mon`Tues`Wed`Thur`Fri`Sat`Sun
Weekday Frequency: e
Saturday Frequency: e
Avg Paid Circ: 5224
Avg Free Circ: 192
Audit Company: AAM
Audit Date: 19 11 2018
Pressroom Equipment: Lines – 12-G/Community;
Mailroom Equipment: Counter Stackers – 1/ BG; Inserters & Stuffers – 1-/KAN; Tying Machines – 4-/Bu; Address Machine – 2-/Ch;
Buisness Equipment: PC LAN
Buisness Software: Synaptic, Gyma
Classified Equipment: Hardware – Baseview; Printers – 2-HP/5M;
Classified Software: I-Que Server 3.16.
Editorial Equipment: Hardware – Baseview; Printers – 2-HP/5M
Editorial Software: Baseview/Ad Manager Pro 2.06.
Production Equipment: Hardware – Caere/Omni Page Pro 6.0, 2-Caere/Panther Pro 46; Cameras – 2-R
Production Software: QPS/QuarkXPress 4.1.
Total Circulation: 5036

WATERTOWN
WATERTOWN DAILY TIMES

Corporate/Parent Company: Adams Publishing Group
Publication Street Address: 218 S. First St.
City: Watertown
State: WI
Publication Website: www.wdtimes.com
Postal Code: 53094-7623
Office phone: (920) 261-4949
General E-mail: news1@wdtimes.com
Publisher Name: Robb Grindstaff
Publisher Email: rgrindstaff@dailyunion.com
Publisher Phone: (920) 261-4949
Editor Name: Scott Peterson
Editor Email: scottp@wdtimes.com
Editor Phone: (920) 261-5161
Advertising Executive Name: Will Wiley
Advertising Executive Email: willw@wdtimes.com
Advertising Executive Phone: (920) 261-4102
Year Established: 1895
Delivery Methods: Mail`Newsstand`Carrier`Racks
Own Printing Facility?: N
Commercial printers?: Y
Mechanical specifications: Type page 11 5/8 x 21 1/2; E - 6 cols, 1 5/6, 1/8 between; A - 6 cols, 1 5/6, 1/8 between; C - 8 cols, 1 1/3, 1/8 between.
Published Days: Mon`Tues`Wed`Thur`Fri`Sat`Sun
Weekday Frequency: e
Saturday Frequency: m
Avg Paid Circ: 9287
Audit Company: Sworn/Estimate/Non-Audited
Audit Date: 7 12 2019
Pressroom Equipment: Lines – 5-G/ Community 1971; 1-G/Community 1984; 1-G/Community 1989; Folders – 1-G/Community.;
Mailroom Equipment: Tying Machines – 2-Ty-Tech/TM45; Address Machine – St/1600-2344.;
Buisness Equipment: ATT/382-500
Classified Equipment: Hardware – APP/Mac; Printers – Okidata;
Classified Software: Baseview.
Editorial Equipment: Hardware – APP/Mac; Printers – Okidata, 3-APP/Mac LaserWriter, Xante/3G
Editorial Software: Baseview 2.0.6.
Production Equipment: Hardware – 30-Nu/ Flip Top FT40APRNS, APP/Power Mac G3, Nikon/Coolscan, APP/Power Mac 7200, APP/Power Mac 200; Cameras – B/ Horizontal; Scanners – APP/Mac One Scanner, Microtek/ScanMaker, Nikon/ Coolscan
Production Software: QPS/QuarkXPress 6.1, Adobe/Photoshop.
Total Circulation: 9287

WAUKESHA
THE FREEMAN

Corporate/Parent Company: Conley Media LLC
Publication Street Address: PO Box 7
City: Waukesha
State: WI
Publication Website: www.gmtoday.com
Postal Code: 53187-0007
Office phone: (262) 542-2500
General E-mail: webmaster@conleynet.com
Publisher Name: Bill Yorth
Publisher Email: byorth@conleynet.com
Publisher Phone: (262) 513-2671
Editor Name: Katherine Beck
Editor Email: kbeck@conleynet.com
Editor Phone: (262) 513-2644
Advertising Executive Name: Jim Baumgart
Advertising Executive Email: jbaumgart@conleynet.com
Advertising Executive Phone: (262) 513-2621
Year Established: 1858
Delivery Methods: Mail`Newsstand`Carrier`Racks
Own Printing Facility?: Y
Commercial printers?: Y
Mechanical specifications: Type page 13 x 21 1/2; E - 6 cols, 2, 3/16 between; A - 6 cols, 2, 3/16 between; C - 9 cols, 1 3/8, 1/16 between.
Published Days: Tues`Wed`Thur`Fri`Sat
Weekday Frequency: e
Saturday Frequency: m
Avg Paid Circ: 9386
Avg Free Circ: 256
Audit Company: CVC
Audit Date: 31 03 2017
Pressroom Equipment: Lines – 8-G/Urbanite.;
Mailroom Equipment: Counter Stackers – 2/ MM, Id; Inserters & Stuffers – 2-/MM; Tying Machines – 2-/Dynaric; Address Machine – KR.;
Buisness Equipment: APP/iMac
Buisness Software: Microsoft/Office 97, Microsoft/Office 2000, Oracle, PBS
Classified Equipment: Hardware – APP/iMac; Printers – HP/Laserjet 4000N;
Classified Software: Concept/Classworks.
Editorial Equipment: Hardware – APP/Mac G3; Printers – GCC/Elite 1208, HP/Laserjet 5M
Editorial Software: Adobe/Illustrator, Adobe/ Photoshop, Concept/Adworks, Concept/ Copy Works.
Production Equipment: Hardware – NU/FT 40V6UPNS, 2-Violet Laser/VSP85-S.
Total Circulation: 9642

WAUSAU
THE WAUSAU DAILY HERALD

Corporate/Parent Company: Gannett
Publication Street Address: 800 Scott St
City: Wausau
State: WI
Publication Website: www.wausaudailyherald.com
Postal Code: 54403-4951
Office phone: (715) 842-2101
General E-mail: wisconsinco@gannett.com
Year Established: 1907
Delivery Methods: Mail`Newsstand`Carrier`Racks
Own Printing Facility?: Y
Commercial printers?: N
Mechanical specifications: Type page 11 13/100 x 21 1/2; E - 6 cols, 1 3/4, 1/8 between; A - 6 cols, 1 3/4, 1/8 between; C - 10 cols, 1 1/20, 7/100 between.
Published Days: Mon`Tues`Wed`Thur`Fri`Sat`Sun
Weekday Frequency: e
Saturday Frequency: e
Avg Paid Circ: 9619
Avg Free Circ: 213
Audit Company: AAM
Audit Date: 21 11 2018
Pressroom Equipment: Lines – 4-G/Metro double width (Hump on 3-10 side) 1968; 2-G/Metro double width 5-10; Folders – 1-G/2:1; Pasters –G/Flying Paster.
Mailroom Equipment: Counter Stackers – 3-QWI/401 Narrow; Inserters & Stuffers – HI/1372, HI/Alphaliner; Tying Machines – 2/ Power Strap; Address Machine – Ch.;
Buisness Equipment: 1-IBM/AS-400
Classified Equipment: Hardware – APP/Mac G3; Printers – TI/810, HP/LaserJet 5M, HP/ LaserJet 400N;
Classified Software: Baseview.
Editorial Equipment: Hardware – Mk/6000/Mk; Printers – APP/Mac LaserPrinter
Editorial Software: Mk/ACE II, Caere/OmniPage.
Production Equipment: Hardware – Nu, Ultra/ Plus; Cameras – 2-Tesca Copydot; Scanners – 1-AG/Duoscan, 1-AG/Duoscan T1200
Production Software: QPS/QuarkXPress, Baseview/Newsedit Pro.
Total Circulation: 22437

WEST BEND
THE DAILY NEWS

Corporate/Parent Company: Gannett
Publication Street Address: 100 S 6th Ave
City: West Bend
State: WI
Publication Website: www.gmtoday.com
Postal Code: 53095-3309
Office phone: (262) 306-5000
General E-mail: dailynews@conleynet.com
Editor Name: Ashley Haynes
Editor Email: ahaynes@conleynet.com
Editor Phone: (262) 513-2681
Advertising Executive Name: Jim Baumgart
Advertising Executive Email: jbaumgart@conleynet.com
Advertising Executive Phone: (262) 513-2621
Year Established: 1856
Delivery Methods: Mail`Newsstand
Own Printing Facility?: Y
Commercial printers?: Y
Mechanical specifications: Full page 10.6" x 21" 1 column 1.7" wide
Published Days: Tues`Wed`Thur`Fri`Sat
Weekday Frequency: All day
Saturday Frequency: All day
Avg Paid Circ: 7454
Audit Company: CVC
Audit Date: 31 03 2017
Pressroom Equipment: Lines – 8-G/Community, 10-G/Community; Folders – G/SC.;
Total Circulation: 7454

WOODVILLE
THE WOODVILLE LEADER

Publication Street Address: 102 Trient Dr
City: Woodville
State: WI
Publication Website: www.mygatewaynews.com
Postal Code: 54028
Office phone: 715-698-2401
General E-mail: editor@mygateway.news

WEST VIRGINIA

BECKLEY

THE REGISTER HERALD

Corporate/Parent Company: CNHI, LLC
Publication Street Address: 801 N Kanawha St
City: Beckley
State: WV
Publication Website: www.register-herald.com
Postal Code: 25802
Office phone: (304) 255-4400
General E-mail: rhnews@register-herald.com
Publisher Name: Randy Mooney
Publisher Email: rmooney@register-herald.com
Editor Name: J. Damon Cain
Editor Email: dcain@register-herald.com
Advertising Executive Name: Lisa Stadelman
Advertising Executive Email: lstadelman@register-herald.com
Year Established: 1981
Mechanical specifications: Type page 13 x 21 3/4; E - 6 cols, 2 1/16, 1/8 between; A - 6 cols, 2 1/16, 1/8 between; C - 9 cols, 1 11/32, 1/16 between.
Published Days: Mon`Tues`Wed`Thur`Fri`Sat`Sun
Weekday Frequency: m
Saturday Frequency: m
Avg Paid Circ: 15414
Avg Free Circ: 1421
Audit Company: AAM
Audit Date: 30 09 2014
Pressroom Equipment: Lines – 10-G/Urbanite 1981; Press Drive – 2-Fin/150 h.p.;
Mailroom Equipment: Counter Stackers – 1-Id, 1/Olympian; Inserters & Stuffers – GMA/9 pockets, MM/7 pockets; Tying Machines – 2-Dynaric/NP 30; Wrapping Singles – St; Address Machine – Chegier.;
Buisness Equipment: IBM/AS-400
Buisness Software: Oracle, NewzWare
Classified Equipment: Hardware – CText, DEC/486; Printers – 2-Tegra/Varityper 5100e, 1-Tegra/Varityper 6990, 2-Pre Press/Panther Pro 36;
Classified Software: CText, CText/ALPS Pagination.
Editorial Equipment: Hardware – CText, DEC, APP/Power Mac 8100-00/1-Tegra/Varityper 6990, 2-Pre Press/Panther Pro 36; Printers – 2-Tegra/Varityper 5100e
Editorial Software: CText, QPS/QuarkXPress 3.31r5.
Production Equipment: Hardware – 2-Tegra/Varityper 5100e Laserprinter, 1-Tegra/Varityper 6990 Laser, APP/Power Mac 8100-100; Cameras – C/Spartan III, C/Newspager; Scanners – 2-Lf/Leafscan 35, 2-Flatbed, Microtek/Scanmaker III
Production Software: CText, QPS/QuarkXPress 7.0.
Total Circulation: 16835

BLUEFIELD

BLUEFIELD DAILY TELEGRAPH

Corporate/Parent Company: CNHI, LLC
Publication Street Address: 928 Bluefield Ave
City: Bluefield
State: WV
Publication Website: www.bdtonline.com
Postal Code: 24701-2744
Office phone: (304) 327-2800
General E-mail: editor@bdtonline.com
Publisher Name: Randy Mooney
Publisher Email: rmooney@bdtonline.com
Publisher Phone: (304) 327-2840
Editor Name: Samantha Perry
Editor Email: sperry@bdtonline.com
Advertising Executive Name: Terri Hale
Advertising Executive Email: thale@bdtonline.com
Advertising Executive Phone: (304) 327-2817
Year Established: 1896
Delivery Methods:
 Mail`Newsstand`Carrier`Racks
Own Printing Facility?: Y
Commercial printers?: Y
Mechanical specifications: Type page 13 x 21 1/2; E - 6 cols, 2 1/16, 1/8 between; A - 6 cols, 2 1/16, 1/8 between; C - 9 cols, 1 3/8, 1/11 between.
Published Days: Mon`Tues`Wed`Thur`Fri`Sat`Sun
Weekday Frequency: m
Saturday Frequency: m
Avg Paid Circ: 6818
Avg Free Circ: 701
Audit Company: AAM
Audit Date: 30 06 2018
Pressroom Equipment: Lines – 6-G/Cosmo double width; Reels & Stands – 5;
Mailroom Equipment: Counter Stackers – HL/2; Inserters & Stuffers – MM/2; Tying Machines – 1/Power Strap, 1-/Power Strap.;
Buisness Equipment: 7-ATT/3B25100, Newsware 5.1
Buisness Software: Microsoft/Office 97, Microsoft/Office 98, Microsoft/Office 2000, Oracle/Version 1.0, Newsware 5.1
Classified Equipment: Hardware – 3-EKI/Televideo;
Classified Software: CText.
Editorial Equipment: Hardware – 25-EKI/Televideo, Baseview; Printers – Pre Press/Panthers
Editorial Software: Baseview/NewsEdit Pro.
Production Equipment: Hardware – Nu, Graham/Sub., Xante/Accel-A-Writer; Cameras – C/Spartan III, SCREEN/C-680C; Scanners – Nikon, MK, Umax
Production Software: QPS/QuarkXPress 4.0.
Total Circulation: 7519

CHARLESTON

THE CHARLESTON GAZETTE-MAIL

Corporate/Parent Company: HD Media
Publication Street Address: 1001 Virginia St E
City: Charleston
State: WV
Publication Website: https://www.wvgazettemail.com/
Postal Code: 25301-2816
Office phone: (304) 348-5140
General E-mail: support@wvgazettemail.com
Publisher Name: Jim Heady
Editor Name: Greg Moore
Editor Email: gmoore@wvgazettemail.com
Year Established: 1873
Delivery Methods:
 Mail`Newsstand`Carrier`Racks
Own Printing Facility?: Y
Commercial printers?: N
Mechanical specifications: Type page 12 1/4 x 21 3/4; E - 6 cols, 1 7/8, 1/9 between; A - 6 cols, 1 7/8, 1/9 between; C - 9 cols, between.
Published Days: Mon`Tues`Wed`Thur`Fri`Sat`Sun
Weekday Frequency: m
Saturday Frequency: m
Avg Paid Circ: 36935
Audit Company: AAM
Audit Date: 8 06 2018
Pressroom Equipment: Lines – 11-G/Metro offset (double width) 1973;
Mailroom Equipment: Counter Stackers – 7/QWI; Inserters & Stuffers – HI; Tying Machines – 4-/Dynaric; Wrapping Singles – PM; Control System – Icon; Address Machine – 2-/KR, AVY.;
Buisness Equipment: IBM/AS 400
Buisness Software: JD Edwards GL, APP/Neasi-Weber Admarc 6.4
Classified Equipment: Hardware – Dell/PC, 14-Dell/PC;
Classified Software: TECS-2.
Editorial Equipment: Hardware – IBM/Netfinity, 2-IBM/Netfinity/Dell/PC; Printers – HP/8100
Editorial Software: Microsoft/Word.
Production Equipment: Hardware – AP Leafdesk, 3-Prepress Panther 4600 Imagesetters, 2-Ap Leafdesk; Scanners – 1-Graphic Enterprise TESCA
Production Software: QPS/QuarkXPress 4.0, 50-IBM PC.
Note: For detailed general management, business personnel & production information, see Charleston Newspapers listing. The Saturday Gazette-Mail and the Sunday Gazette-Mail are published jointly by the Daily Mail Publishing Co. and the Daily Gazette Co.
Total Circulation: 43917

CLARKSBURG

THE EXPONENT TELEGRAM

Publication Street Address: 324 Hewes Ave
City: Clarksburg
State: WV
Publication Website: https://www.wvnews.com/theet/
Postal Code: 26301-2744
Office phone: (304) 626-1400
General E-mail: advertising@theet.com
Publisher Name: Andrew B. Kniceley
Editor Name: John Miller
Advertising Executive Email: advertising@therepublicannews.com
Year Established: 1927
Delivery Methods:
 Mail`Newsstand`Carrier`Racks
Own Printing Facility?: Y
Commercial printers?: Y
Mechanical specifications: Type page 13 5/8 x 20; E - 6 cols, 2 1/8, 1/6 between; A - 6 cols, 2 1/8, 1/6 between; C - 10 cols, 1 1/4, 1/12 between.
Published Days: Tues`Wed`Thur`Fri`Sat`Sun
Weekday Frequency: m
Saturday Frequency: m
Avg Paid Circ: 12966
Avg Free Circ: 1202
Audit Company: Sworn/Estimate/Non-Audited
Audit Date: 7 12 2019
Pressroom Equipment: Lines – 1-G/High Speed Straight Line; H/Right Angle; Folders – 1, 1.;
Mailroom Equipment: Counter Stackers – KAN/MSI; Inserters & Stuffers – MM; Tying Machines – 1/Bu, 1-/Power Strap.;
Buisness Equipment: IBM/Sys 36
Buisness Software: IBM/Sys 36
Classified Equipment: Hardware – CD/2330; Printers – Okidata;
Classified Software: CD/TOPS.
Editorial Equipment: Hardware – CD/2330/5-Leading Edge/D-2
Editorial Software: CD/TOPS.
Production Equipment: Hardware – 1-LE/Verter, APP/Mac Sys 7.5, Multi-Ad/Creator, Adobe/Photoshop; Cameras – 1-C/Spartan III; Scanners – Microtek/Flatbed, Microtek/35mm, Adobe/Photoshop
Production Software: CD, Magician Plus, APP/Mac Quadra 950, APP/Mac Quadra 800, APP/Mac Sys 7.5.
Total Circulation: 14168

ELKINS

THE INTER-MOUNTAIN

Corporate/Parent Company: Ogden Newspapers, Inc.
Publication Street Address: 520 Railroad Ave
City: Elkins
State: WV
Publication Website: http://www.theintermountain.com/
Postal Code: 26241-3861
Office phone: (304) 636-2121
General E-mail: mmorris@theintermountain.com
Publisher Name: Steve Herron
Publisher Email: sherron@theintermountain.com
Publisher Phone: (304) 636-2127, ext : 104
Editor Name: Brad Johnson
Editor Email: bjohnson@theintermountain.com
Editor Phone: (304) 636-2127, ext : 120
Advertising Executive Name: Michelle Hammonds
Advertising Executive Email: mhammonds@theintermountain.com
Advertising Executive Phone: (304) 636-2127, ext : 126
Year Established: 1892
Delivery Methods:
 Mail`Newsstand`Carrier`Racks
Own Printing Facility?: Y
Commercial printers?: Y
Mechanical specifications: Type page 13 x 22; E - 6 cols, 2 1/16, 1/8 between; C - 6 cols, 2 1/16, 1/8 between.
Published Days: Mon`Tues`Wed`Thur`Fri`Sat
Weekday Frequency: e
Saturday Frequency: m
Avg Paid Circ: 4281
Avg Free Circ: 358
Audit Company: AAM
Audit Date: 11 12 2019
Pressroom Equipment: Lines – 8-HI/Cotrell V-15A;
Mailroom Equipment: Counter Stackers – 1-BG/108;
Buisness Equipment: 1-NCR
Classified Equipment: Hardware – 1-COM/350.;
Editorial Equipment: Hardware – 8-COM/350.
Production Equipment: Hardware – 1-COM/2961, 1-COM/Trendsetter; Cameras – 1-Nu.
Note: The Inter-Mountain was named the 2014 Newspaper of the Year through the West Virginia Press Association's Better Newspaper Contest. It also has garnered more than 30 awards per year for each of the past three consecutive years, often winning recognition as a paper of General Excellence.
Total Circulation: 5196

FAIRMONT

TIMES WEST VIRGINIAN

Corporate/Parent Company: CNHI, LLC
Publication Street Address: 300 Quincy St
City: Fairmont
State: WV
Publication Website: www.timeswv.com
Postal Code: 26554-3136
Office phone: (304) 367-2500
General E-mail: timeswv@timeswv.com
Publisher Name: Titus Workman
Publisher Email: tworkman@timeswv.com
Publisher Phone: (304) 367-2503
Editor Name: Eric Cravey
Editor Email: ecravey@timeswv.com
Editor Phone: (304) 367-2523
Advertising Executive Name: Cathy Morrison
Advertising Executive Email: cmorrison@timeswv.com
Advertising Executive Phone: (304) 367-2560
Year Established: 1976
Delivery Methods: Carrier
Own Printing Facility?: Y
Commercial printers?: Y
Mechanical specifications: Type page 11 63/100 x 21 1/2; E - 6 cols, 1 5/6, 1/8 between; A - 6 cols, 1 5/6, 1/8 between; C - 9 cols, 1 5/6, 1/16 between.
Published Days: Mon`Tues`Wed`Thur`Fri`Sat`Sun
Weekday Frequency: m
Saturday Frequency: m
Avg Paid Circ: 6590
Avg Free Circ: 730
Audit Company: AAM
Audit Date: 31 03 2016
Pressroom Equipment: Lines – 7-G/Urbanite;
Mailroom Equipment: Counter Stackers – 1-BG/Count-O-Veyor 109; Inserters & Stuffers – 1-KAN/480; Tying Machines – 1-SP/330, 1/Gd.;
Buisness Equipment: Pentium/PC
Buisness Software: Lotus, WordPerfect
Classified Equipment: Hardware – APP/Mac G3, APP/Mac Pagination System; Printers – TI/Lineprinter, HP/405N;
Classified Software: QPS/QuarkXPress, Baseview/Ad Manager Pro.
Editorial Equipment: Hardware – APP/Mac Pagination System, APP/MAC G3/APP/Mac Quadra 950, Lf/Leafscan 35, APP/Mac G3, APP/Server NT, Nikon/Cool Scan; Printers – TI/Lineprinter, HP/4050
Editorial Software: Baseview/News Edit Pro, QPS/QuarkXPress, Baseview, Adobe/Photoshop
Production Equipment: Hardware – 1-COM/IV, Lf/AP Leaf Picture Desk, ApServer NT, APP/Mac G3, Pre Press/Panther Pro 36, 3-HP/4050N, PrePress/Panther Plus 46; Cameras – 1-R/500, C, SCREEN/

U.S. Daily Newspapers

Companica 680; Scanners – Lf/Leafscan 35, Nikon/Cool Scan, UMAX/PowerLook III
Production Software: Equipment ÃƒÂƒÂ£
Total Circulation: 7320

HUNTINGTON
THE HERALD-DISPATCH
Corporate/Parent Company: HD Media
Publication Street Address: 946 5th Ave
City: Huntington
State: WV
Publication Website: https://www.herald-dispatch.com/
Postal Code: 25701-2004
Office phone: (304) 526-4002
General E-mail: hdnews@hdmediallc.com
Publisher Name: NA
Editor Name: Les Smith
Editor Email: lessmith@hdmediallc.com
Editor Phone: (304) 526-2779
Advertising Executive Name: Jerry Briggs
Advertising Executive Email: jwbriggs@hdmediallc.com
Advertising Executive Phone: (304) 526-2820
Year Established: 1909
Delivery Methods:
  Mail`Newsstand`Carrier`Racks
Own Printing Facility?: Y
Commercial printers?: Y
Mechanical specifications: Type page 13 x 21 1/2; E - 6 cols, 2, 1/6 between; A - 6 cols, 2, 1/6 between; C - 10 cols, 1 1/5, 1/10 between.
Published Days: Mon`Tues`Wed`Thur`Fri`Sat`Sun
Weekday Frequency: m
Saturday Frequency: m
Avg Paid Circ: 16619
Audit Company: AAM
Audit Date: 7 06 2019
Pressroom Equipment: Lines – 6-Wd/Metropolitan double width (3 half decks) 1957; Press Drive – 5-GE/Motors 1994; Folders – 1-SC/3:2, 1-SC/Folder 2:1.;
Mailroom Equipment: Counter Stackers – HL/HT, HL/Monitor; Inserters & Stuffers – HI/1472 (13 Heads); Tying Machines – 2/Power Strap/PSD 5;
Buisness Equipment: Dell, Linux Red Hat server
Buisness Software: Newzware
Classified Equipment: Hardware – Subsystem, Dell/Workstations; Printers – HP/4000;
Classified Software: AdPower
Editorial Equipment: Hardware – Apple Server X version 10.5; Printers – HP/4000
Editorial Software: Newsedit pro
Production Equipment: Hardware – 1-EV-jetsetter 7100 1-EV-jetsetter 6200 2 Harlequin Rips, version 7.2; Scanners – 1-11X17 flatbed scanner 1- 8.5X11 flatbed scanner
Total Circulation: 20786

KEYSER
MINERAL DAILY NEWS-TRIBUNE
Publication Street Address: 21 Shamrock Dr
City: Keyser
State: WV
Publication Website: www.newstribune.info
Postal Code: 26726-6012
Office phone: (304) 788-3333
General E-mail: advertising@newstribune.info
Publisher Name: Kenneth Browall
Publisher Email: kbrowall@therecordherald.com
Editor Name: Liz Beavers
Editor Email: lbeavers@newstribune.info
Advertising Executive Name: Carla Braithwaite
Advertising Executive Email: cbraithwaite@newstribune.info
Advertising Executive Phone: (304) 788-3333, Ext : 116
Year Established: 1885
Delivery Methods:
  Mail`Newsstand`Carrier`Racks
Own Printing Facility?: N
Commercial printers?: N
Published Days: Tues`Thur`Fri`Sat
Weekday Frequency: m
Saturday Frequency: m
Avg Paid Circ: 3935
Audit Company: Sworn/Estimate/Non-Audited
Audit Date: 7 12 2019
Total Circulation: 3935

LEWISBURG
WEST VIRGINIA DAILY NEWS
Corporate/Parent Company: Moffitt Newspapers
Publication Street Address: 188 Foster St
City: Lewisburg
State: WV
Publication Website: www.wvdailynews.net
Postal Code: 24901-2099
Office phone: (304) 645-1206
General E-mail: editor@wvdailynews.net
Publisher Name: Judy K. Steele
Editor Name: Theresa Flerx
Editor Email: editor@wvdailynews.net
Advertising Executive Name: Susan Smith-Linton
Advertising Executive Phone: (304) 645-1206
Year Established: 1969
Delivery Methods:
  Mail`Newsstand`Carrier`Racks
Own Printing Facility?: Y
Commercial printers?: Y
Mechanical specifications: Type page 13 x 21 1/2; E - 6 cols, 2 1/16, 1/8 between; A - 6 cols, 2 1/16, 1/8 between; C - 6 cols, 2 1/16, 1/8 between.
Published Days: Mon`Tues`Wed`Thur`Fri
Weekday Frequency: e
Avg Paid Circ: 4100
Audit Company: Sworn/Estimate/Non-Audited
Audit Date: 7 12 2019
Pressroom Equipment: Lines – 5-G/Community.;
Mailroom Equipment: Tying Machines – 1-/CE, 1-/Signode.;
Buisness Equipment: 2-Leading Edge/MOD 2
Editorial Equipment: Hardware – 3-APP/Mac; Printers – X/N 2025
Editorial Software: Aldus/PageMaker 5.0.
Production Equipment: Hardware – 1-P; Cameras – 1-R.
Total Circulation: 4100

MARTINSBURG
THE JOURNAL
Corporate/Parent Company: Ogden Newspapers, Inc.
Publication Street Address: 207 W King St
City: Martinsburg
State: WV
Publication Website: http://www.journal-news.net/
Postal Code: 25401-3211
Office phone: (304) 263-8931
General E-mail: webmaster@journal-news.net
Publisher Name: Christopher Kinsler
Publisher Email: ckinsler@journal-news.net
Publisher Phone: (304) 596-6447, ext : 111
Editor Name: Christopher Kinsler
Editor Email: ckinsler@journal-news.net
Editor Phone: (304) 596-6447, ext : 111
Advertising Executive Name: Judy Gelestor
Advertising Executive Email: jgelestor@journal-news.net
Advertising Executive Phone: (304) 596-6447, ext : 110
Year Established: 1907
Delivery Methods: Newsstand`Carrier`Racks
Own Printing Facility?: Y
Commercial printers?: Y
Mechanical specifications: Type page 11 4/5 x 21 1/2; E - 6 cols, 1 7/8, 1/8 between; A - 6 cols, 1 7/8, 1/8 between; C - 8 cols, 1 5/16, 1/16 between.
Published Days: Mon`Tues`Wed`Thur`Fri`Sat`Sun
Weekday Frequency: m
Saturday Frequency: m
Avg Paid Circ: 10279
Avg Free Circ: 411
Audit Company: AAM
Audit Date: 12 11 2019
Buisness Equipment: NCR, Unix
Classified Equipment: Hardware – Umax/C500-240; NCR/UNIX, 2-Sun; Printers – HP/8150 DN;
Classified Software: ONI/Class 0.5.4.
Editorial Equipment: Hardware – APP/Mac G4, 6-Umax/C500/APP/Mac Centris 610, APP/Mac Centris 650, APP/Mac PC 6100-66, APP/Mac G-3 Workgroup Server; Printers – HP/8000 N
Editorial Software: ONI/Class 0.5.4.
Total Circulation: 16244

MORGANTOWN
THE DOMINION POST
Corporate/Parent Company: WV Newspaper Publishing Company, Inc.
Publication Street Address: 1251 Earl L Core Rd
City: Morgantown
State: WV
Publication Website: www.dominionpost.com
Postal Code: 26505-6298
Office phone: (304) 292-6301
General E-mail: classads@dominionpost.com
Publisher Name: David Raese
Editor Name: Pam Queen
Editor Email: pqueen@dominionpost.com
Editor Phone: (304) 291-9433
Advertising Executive Name: Melissa Rancjik
Advertising Executive Email: billing@dominionpost.com
Advertising Executive Phone: (304) 284-0301
Year Established: 1923
Delivery Methods:
  Mail`Newsstand`Carrier`Racks
Own Printing Facility?: Y
Commercial printers?: Y
Mechanical specifications: Type page 13 1/4 x 21 1/2; E - 6 cols, 2 1/16, 1/8 between; A - 6 cols, 2 1/16, 1/8 between; C - 9 cols, 1 3/8, 1/16 between.
Published Days: Mon`Tues`Wed`Thur`Fri`Sat`Sun
Weekday Frequency: m
Saturday Frequency: m
Avg Paid Circ: 10855
Avg Free Circ: 1788
Audit Company: AAM
Audit Date: 23 05 2019
Pressroom Equipment: Lines – 12-G/Urbanite;
Mailroom Equipment: Counter Stackers – 1/QWI, 1-QWI/400 1-QWI/500; Inserters & Stuffers – SLS1000; Tying Machines – 1-/MLN; Address Machine – KAN.;
Buisness Equipment: Oracle
Buisness Software: Vision Data, DSI
Classified Equipment: Hardware – Miles 33; Printers – QMS/860 Laser;
Classified Software: Miles 33
Editorial Equipment: Hardware – Miles 33 31 PC, 10-APP/Mac; Printers – QMS/860 Laser
Editorial Software: Miles 33
Production Equipment: Hardware – 2-Newsmatic ECRM/CTP
Production Software: Adobe CS5
Total Circulation: 14459

MOUNDSVILLE
MOUNDSVILLE DAILY ECHO
Publication Street Address: 713 Lafayette Ave
City: Moundsville
State: WV
Publication Website: http://echo-media.com/medias/details/8550/moundsville+daily+echo
Postal Code: 26041-2143
Office phone: (304) 845-2660
General E-mail: mdsvecho@gmail.com
Publisher Name: Marion Walto
Year Established: 1891
Delivery Methods:
  Mail`Newsstand`Carrier`Racks
Own Printing Facility?: Y
Commercial printers?: N
Mechanical specifications: Type page 13 x 21 1/2; E - 6 cols, 2 inch, 1/8 between.
Published Days: Mon`Tues`Wed`Thur`Fri
Weekday Frequency: e
Avg Paid Circ: 2100
Audit Company: Sworn/Estimate/Non-Audited
Audit Date: 7 12 2019
Pressroom Equipment: Control System – GE/SCR.
Mailroom Equipment: Address Machine – 2-Am/Dispensa-Matic.;
Buisness Equipment: 1-PC 586
Editorial Equipment: Hardware – PC; Printers – APP/Mac LaserWriter
Editorial Software: Aldus/PageMaker 3.01, Microsoft/Windows 3.1.
Production Equipment: Hardware – APP/Mac Laser Plus; Cameras – R.
Total Circulation: 2100

PARKERSBURG
PARKERSBURG NEWS & SENTINEL
Corporate/Parent Company: Ogden Newspapers Inc.
Publication Street Address: 519 Juliana St
City: Parkersburg
State: WV
Publication Website: http://www.newsandsentinel.com/
Postal Code: 26101-5135
Office phone: (304) 485-1891
General E-mail: advertising@newsandsentinel.com
Publisher Name: James Spanner
Publisher Email: jspanner@newsandsentinel.com
Publisher Phone: (304) 485-1891, ext : 310
Editor Name: Paul LaPann
Editor Email: plapann@newsandsentinel.com
Editor Phone: (304) 485-1891, ext : 221
Advertising Executive Name: Lisa Northcraft
Advertising Executive Email: lnorthcraft@newsandsentinel.com
Advertising Executive Phone: (304) 485-1891, ext : 360
Delivery Methods:
  Mail`Newsstand`Carrier`Racks
Own Printing Facility?: Y
Mechanical specifications: Type page 12 1/2 x 21 3/4; E - 6 cols, 2 1/16, 1/8 between; A - 6 cols, 2 1/16, 1/8 between; C - 8 cols, 1 9/16, 1/16 between.
Published Days: Mon`Tues`Wed`Thur`Fri`Sat`Sun
Weekday Frequency: e
Avg Paid Circ: 14259
Avg Free Circ: 120
Audit Company: AAM
Audit Date: 31 12 2018
Pressroom Equipment: Lines – 12-Urbinite; Folders – 2-Urbinite.;
Mailroom Equipment: Counter Stackers – 2-Quipp/401; Inserters & Stuffers – 1-HI/NP 1372; Tying Machines – MLN/ML2EE, 1/Power Strap/TS2504.;
Classified Equipment: Hardware – PC;
Classified Software: Microsoft/Windows NT 4.0.
Editorial Equipment: Hardware – PC; Printers – HP/6M
Editorial Software: Microsoft/Windows NT 4.0.
Production Equipment: Hardware – 1-WL/30B, ECR/VRL 36; Cameras – 1-K/N243, 1-C/Newspager.
Total Circulation: 14379

POINT PLEASANT
POINT PLEASANT REGISTER
Corporate/Parent Company: AIM Media
Publication Street Address: 200 Main St
City: Point Pleasant
State: WV
Publication Website: www.mydailyregister.com
Postal Code: 25550-1030
Office phone: (304) 675-1333
General E-mail: jschultz@civitasmedia.com
Publisher Name: Beth Sergent
Publisher Email: bsergent@aimmediamidwest.com
Publisher Phone: (304) 675-1333, Ext : 1992
Editor Name: Matt Rodgers
Editor Email: mrodgers@aimmediamidwest.com
Editor Phone: (740) 578-4828
Delivery Methods:
  Mail`Newsstand`Carrier`Racks
Own Printing Facility?: Y
Mechanical specifications: Type page 13 x 21

I-136   U.S. Daily Newspapers

1/4; E - 6 cols, 2 1/16, 1/8 between; A - 6 cols, 2 1/16, 1/8 between; C - 8 cols, 1 1/2, 1/8 between.
Published Days: Mon`Tues`Wed`Thur`Fri`Sat
Weekday Frequency: e
Saturday Frequency: m
Avg Paid Circ: 3918
Audit Company: Sworn/Estimate/Non-Audited
Audit Date: 7 12 2019
Buisness Equipment: IBM, IBM/AS-400
Classified Equipment: Hardware – APP/Mac;
Classified Software: Baseview.
Editorial Equipment: Hardware – APP/Mac Quadra 650, APP/Mac Quadra 610; Printers – APP/Mac LaserWriter Pro
Editorial Software: Baseview.
Production Equipment: Hardware – Caere/OmniPage; Scanners – HP/ScanJet Plus.
Note: Printed at the Gallipolis (OH) Daily Tribune. For pressroom information, see the Gallipolis Daily Tribune listing.
Total Circulation: 3918

WHEELING
THE INTELLIGENCER
Corporate/Parent Company: Gannett
Publication Street Address: 1500 Main St
City: Wheeling
State: WV
Publication Website: www.theintelligencer.net
Postal Code: 26003-2826
Office phone: (304) 233-0100
General E-mail: pbennett@theintelligencer.net
Publisher Name: Perry Nardo
Publisher Email: pnardo@theintelligencer.net
Editor Name: John Mccabe
Editor Email: jmccabe@theintelligencer.net
Advertising Executive Name: Pam Bennett
Advertising Executive Email: pbennett@news-register.net

THE INTELLIGENCER
Corporate/Parent Company: Ogden Newspapers, Inc.
Publication Street Address: 1500 Main St
City: Wheeling
State: WV
Publication Website: www.theintelligencer.net
Postal Code: 26003-2826
Office phone: (304) 233-0100
General E-mail: pbennett@theintelligencer.net
Publisher Name: Perry Nardo
Publisher Email: pnardo@theintelligencer.net
Editor Name: John Mccabe
Editor Email: jmccabe@theintelligencer.net
Advertising Executive Name: Pam Bennett
Advertising Executive Email: pbennett@news-register.net
Year Established: 1852
Delivery Methods: Newsstand`Carrier`Racks
Own Printing Facility?: Y
Commercial printers?: Y
Mechanical specifications: Print Area 10" x 21 6 col format
Published Days: Mon`Tues`Wed`Thur`Fri`Sat
Weekday Frequency: m
Saturday Frequency: m
Avg Paid Circ: 8630
Avg Free Circ: 389
Audit Company: AAM
Audit Date: 31 03 2019
Pressroom Equipment: Lines – DGM; DGM;
Mailroom Equipment: Counter Stackers – 2-HL/Monitor, 1-HL/HI II; Inserters & Stuffers – S/1372; Tying Machines – 2-MLN/2EE, 1-MLN/2, 1-MLN/2A; Wrapping Singles – Sa; Address Machine – Ch.;
Buisness Equipment: NCR S20
Buisness Software: In house
Classified Equipment: Hardware – PC;
Classified Software: Microsoft/Windows NT.
Editorial Equipment: Hardware – PC
Editorial Software: Microsoft/Windows NT.
Production Equipment: Hardware – 2-APP/Mac LaserWriter NTX, 2-MON/1270 Imagesetter, 2-Konica/4550 Imagesetters; Cameras – 1-C/Pager, 1-AG/2024; Scanners – HP IIci, Kk/RFS-2035, Nikon/Coolscan, Umax
Production Software: QPS/QuarkXPress 3.31.
Total Circulation: 9019

WILLIAMSON
WILLIAMSON DAILY NEWS
Corporate/Parent Company: HD Media
Publication Street Address: 48 West Second Avenue
City: Williamson
State: WV
Publication Website: https://www.williamsondailynews.com/
Postal Code: 25661-3500
Office phone: (304) 235-4242
General E-mail: jmccormick@hdmediallc.com
Publisher Name: NA
Editor Name: NA
Advertising Executive Name: Melissa Blair
Advertising Executive Email: mblair@hdmediallc.com
Advertising Executive Phone: (304) 236-3543
Year Established: 1912
Mechanical specifications: Type page 13 x 21 3/4; E - 6 cols, 1 5/6, 1/8 between; A - 6 cols, 1 5/6, 1/8 between; C - 9 cols, between.
Published Days: Mon`Tues`Wed`Thur`Fri`Sat`Sun
Weekday Frequency: m
Saturday Frequency: m
Avg Paid Circ: 8028
Audit Company: Sworn/Estimate/Non-Audited
Audit Date: 7 12 2019
Pressroom Equipment: Lines – 6-KP/Daily King.;
Mailroom Equipment: Counter Stackers – 1/BG; Inserters & Stuffers – 4-DG/320; Tying Machines – 1-Bu/42409; Address Machine – 1-/Am, 1-/KR.;
Buisness Equipment: Solomon/PC
Classified Equipment: Hardware – Server; Printers – APP/Mac LaserWriter 16-600PS
Classified Software: APP/Mac Pro, APP/Mac Class Pro.
Editorial Equipment: Hardware – Server; Printers – 3-APP/Mac LaserWriter 16-600 PS
Editorial Software: Baseview.
Production Equipment: Hardware – 2-COM/Unisetters, AG/Accuset, Star/400 RIP; Cameras – 1-B/24x24, 1-DAI/24x24; Scanners – Nikon/Coolscan, AG/Arcus Flatbed
Production Software: QPS/QuarkXPress 3.32.

CASPER
CASPER STAR-TRIBUNE
Corporate/Parent Company: Lee Enterprises
Publication Street Address: 170 Star Ln
City: Casper
State: WY
Publication Website: www.trib.com
Postal Code: 82604-2883
Office phone: (307) 266-0500
General E-mail: sean.johnson@trib.com
Publisher Name: Dale Bohren
Publisher Email: dale.bohren@trib.com
Publisher Phone: (307) 266-0516
Editor Name: Brandon Foster
Editor Email: brandon.foster@trib.com
Editor Phone: (314) 922-3744
Advertising Executive Name: Sean Johnson
Advertising Executive Email: sean.johnson@trib.com
Advertising Executive Phone: (307) 266-0569
Mechanical specifications: Type page 12 x 21 1/2; E - 6 cols, 1 13/16, 1/8 between; A - 6 cols, 1 13/16, 1/8 between; C - 9 cols, 1 7/32, 1/16 between.
Published Days: Mon`Tues`Wed`Thur`Fri`Sat`Sun
Weekday Frequency: m
Saturday Frequency: m
Avg Paid Circ: 16329
Audit Company: AAM
Audit Date: 12 02 2019
Pressroom Equipment: Lines – 9-G/Cosmo offset double width; Reels & Stands – 5;
Mailroom Equipment: Counter Stackers – 3/HL; Inserters & Stuffers – 2-/MM; Tying Machines – 2-/MLN.;
Buisness Equipment: 2-Sun, 1-Unix/PC
Classified Equipment: Hardware – 1-Sun/Sparc.;
Editorial Equipment: Hardware – 1-Sun/Sparc.
Production Equipment: Hardware – 1-Nu, 2-COM/8600, LaCie; Cameras – 2-SCREEN/Companica; Scanners – 2-Data Copy/730GS.
Total Circulation: 20030

CHEYENNE
WYOMING TRIBUNE-EAGLE
Corporate/Parent Company: Adams Publishing Group
Publication Street Address: 702 W Lincolnway
City: Cheyenne
State: WY
Publication Website: www.wyomingnews.com
Postal Code: 82001-4359
Office phone: (307) 634-3361
General E-mail: aeres@wyomingnews.com
Publisher Name: Jeff Robertson
Editor Name: Brian Martin
Editor Email: bmartin@wyomingnews.com
Editor Phone: (307) 633-3120
Advertising Executive Name: Aubrie Eres
Advertising Executive Email: aeres@wyomingnews.com
Advertising Executive Phone: (307) 633-3192
Year Established: 1894
Delivery Methods: Mail`Newsstand`Carrier`Racks
Own Printing Facility?: Y
Commercial printers?: Y
Mechanical specifications: Type page 11 5/8 x 21 1/2; E - 6 cols, 2 1/16, 1/8 between; A - 6 cols, 1 13/16, 1/8 between; C - 9 cols, 1 1/4, 1/16 between.
Published Days: Mon`Tues`Wed`Thur`Fri`Sat`Sun
Weekday Frequency: m
Saturday Frequency: m
Avg Paid Circ: 13864
Audit Company: AAM
Audit Date: 30 09 2012
Pressroom Equipment: Lines – 8-G/Urbanite 1010 (1 color unit) 1972; Folders – 1-G/Urbanite SU.;
Mailroom Equipment: Counter Stackers – S; Inserters & Stuffers – GMA/SLS 1000; Tying Machines – MLN; Address Machine – Mg;
Buisness Equipment: Sun/Ultra 10
Buisness Software: PBS, SBS
Classified Equipment: Hardware – 6-Dell;
Classified Software: Automated Complete Typesetting System.
Editorial Equipment: Hardware – 25-Dell
Editorial Software: Automated Complete Typesetting System.
Production Equipment: Hardware – P, 1-Nu, QPS, Photoshop; Cameras – C/Spartan III; Scanners – Microtek/Flatbed, HP/ScanJet II, Nikon/4000
Production Software: QPS/QuarkXPress 4.01, Automated Complete Typesetting System, Konica/9100.
Total Circulation: 13864

GILLETTE
THE NEWS-RECORD
Publication Street Address: 1201 W. Second Street
City: Gillette
State: WY
Publication Website: www.gillettenewsrecord.com
Postal Code: 82718
Office phone: (307) 682-9306
General E-mail: webadmin@gillettenewsrecord.com
Publisher Name: Ann Turner
Publisher Email: aturner@gillettenewsrecord.net
Publisher Phone: (307) 682-9306, Ext : 203
Editor Name: Greg Johnson
Editor Email: gjohnson@gillettenewsrecord.net
Editor Phone: (307) 682-9306, Ext : 202
Advertising Executive Name: Jade Stevenson
Advertising Executive Email: newsad@vcn.com
Advertising Executive Phone: (307) 682-9306, Ext : 217
Year Established: 1904
Delivery Methods: Mail
Own Printing Facility?: Y
Commercial printers?: Y
Mechanical specifications: Type page 13 x 21; E - 6 cols, 2 1/16, 1/8 between; A - 6 cols, 2 1/16, 1/8 between; C - 8 cols, 1 1/2, 1/8 between.
Published Days: Mon`Tues`Wed`Thur`Fri`Sun
Weekday Frequency: e
Avg Paid Circ: 6479
Audit Company: Sworn/Estimate/Non-Audited
Audit Date: 7 12 2019
Pressroom Equipment: Lines – 6-G; Folders – 1-G/2:1.;
Mailroom Equipment: Tying Machines – 1/Bu, Felins/F16, Allpack/351.610.001; Address Machine – 1-/El.;
Classified Equipment: Hardware – 3-APP/Power Mac G3, 1-APP/iMac; 1-Nikon/ScanTouch 210; Printers – 1-Epson/Stylus Color 850 Ne;
Classified Software: Baseview/AdManagerPro 2.0.5, QPS/QuarkXPress 4.0, Caere/OmniPage Pro 8.0.
Editorial Equipment: Hardware – 1-Mk, 9-APP/Power Mac G3, 1-APP/Mac Blue G3, 1-APP/Mac Server Blue G3, 1-APP/Power Mac 7100/80/1-Polaroid/SprintScan 35 Plus, 1-HP/ScanJet 3c, 1-Iomega/Jaz Drive; Printers – 1-HP/LaserJet 4MV, 1-ECR/Scriptsetter VRL 36
Production Equipment: Hardware – 1-LE; Cameras – 1-SCREEN/Companica
Production Software: QPS/QuarkXPress 3.31.
Total Circulation: 6479

LARAMIE
LARAMIE BOOMERANG
Corporate/Parent Company: Adams Publishing Group
Publication Street Address: 320 E Grand Ave
City: Laramie
State: WY
Publication Website: www.laramieboomerang.com
Postal Code: 82070-3712
Office phone: (307) 742-2176
General E-mail: online@laramieboomerang.com
Publisher Name: Jeff Robertson
Editor Name: Peter Baumann
Advertising Executive Email: gloftus@laramieboomerang.com
Year Established: 1881
Delivery Methods: Mail`Newsstand`Carrier`Racks
Own Printing Facility?: Y
Commercial printers?: Y
Mechanical specifications: Type page 13 x 21 1/2; E - 6 cols, 2 1/16, 1/4 between; A - 6 cols, 2 1/16, 1/4 between; C - 6 cols, 2 1/16, 1/4 between.
Published Days: Tues`Wed`Thur`Fri`Sat`Sun
Weekday Frequency: m
Saturday Frequency: m
Avg Paid Circ: 5233
Avg Free Circ: 7000
Audit Company: Sworn/Estimate/Non-Audited
Audit Date: 7 12 2019
Pressroom Equipment: Lines – 6-G/Community.;
Buisness Equipment: PC
Buisness Software: Cyma
Classified Equipment: Hardware – PC; Printers – Okidata/320;
Classified Software: QPS/QuarkXPress.
Editorial Equipment: Hardware – PC
Editorial Software: QPS/QuarkXPress. Creative Suite
Production Equipment: Hardware – 2-ECR/VRL36
Production Software: QPS/QuarkXPress. Creative Suite
Total Circulation: 12233

U.S. Daily Newspapers

I-137

RIVERTON

THE RIVERTON RANGER

Publication Street Address: 421 E Main St
City: Riverton
State: WY
Publication Website: www.dailyranger.com
Postal Code: 82501-4438
Office phone: (307) 856-2244
General E-mail: fremontnews@wyoming.com
Publisher Name: Steve Peck
Advertising Executive Name: Cathleen Cline
Year Established: 1953
Delivery Methods:
  Mail`Newsstand`Carrier`Racks
Own Printing Facility?: Y
Commercial printers?: Y
Mechanical specifications: Type page 13 x 21 1/2; E - 6 cols, 2 1/16, 1/8 between; A - 6 cols, 2 1/16, 1/8 between; C - 6 cols, 2 1/16, 1/8 between.
Published Days: Tues`Wed`Thur`Fri`Sun
Weekday Frequency: e
Avg Paid Circ: 7200
Audit Company: USPS
Audit Date: 10 01 2017
Pressroom Equipment: Lines – 6-G/Community offset 1973; 2-G/Community offset 1983; 2-G/Community offset 1999; Folders – 1-G/Suburban.;
Mailroom Equipment: Tying Machines – 2;
Buisness Equipment: 3-IBM/PC, Pentium
Buisness Software: Quick Books
Classified Equipment: Hardware – PC, Mac;
Classified Software: account scout
Editorial Equipment: Hardware – 6-Scoop Editorial/3-APP/Mac G4; Printers – 2-APP/Mac 8500, LaserMaster/1800, APP/Mac LaserPro
Editorial Software: Scoop/Editorial.
Production Equipment: Hardware – Caere/OmniPage, Magic/Separator; Cameras – 1-Nu
Production Software: QPS/QuarkXPress 8.5.
Total Circulation: 7200

ROCK SPRINGS

ROCKET-MINER

Publication Street Address: 215 D St
City: Rock Springs
State: WY
Publication Website: www.rocketminer.com
Postal Code: 82901-6234
Office phone: (307) 362-3736
General E-mail: reporter1@rocketminer.com
Publisher Name: Kellie Nicholson
Publisher Email: knicholson@rocketminer.com
Editor Name: Caleb Michael Smith
Editor Email: editor@rocketminer.com
Advertising Executive Name: Chelsey Mcmicheal
Advertising Executive Email: cmcmicheal@rocketminer.com
Year Established: 1883
Delivery Methods:
  Mail`Newsstand`Carrier`Racks
Own Printing Facility?: Y
Commercial printers?: Y
Mechanical specifications: Type page 10.955 x 19.75
Published Days: Tues`Wed`Thur`Fri`Sat`Sun
Weekday Frequency: m
Saturday Frequency: m
Avg Paid Circ: 6000
Audit Company: USPS
Audit Date: 30 09 2011
Pressroom Equipment: Lines – 5-G/Community 1974;
Mailroom Equipment: Tying Machines – 1-It/MS-AF, 1-Us/TE; Address Machine – 2-Am/4000.;
Buisness Equipment: IBM
Buisness Software: Advanced Publishing Technologies
Classified Equipment: Hardware – HP, IBM; Printers – HP;
Classified Software: Microsoft/Windows 98 APT
Editorial Equipment: Hardware – HP, IBM/HP; Printers – HP
Editorial Software: Quark, apt
Production Equipment: Hardware – CTP Thermal; Cameras – Kodak DH; Scanners – none
Production Software: CREO
Total Circulation: 6000

SHERIDAN

THE SHERIDAN PRESS

Corporate/Parent Company: Seaton Group
Publication Street Address: 144 E Grinnell Plz
City: Sheridan
State: WY
Publication Website: www.thesheridanpress.com
Postal Code: 82801-3933
Office phone: (307) 672-2431
General E-mail: beth@thesheridanpress.com
Publisher Name: Kristen Czaban
Editor Name: Ashleigh Snoozy

THE SHERIDAN PRESS

Corporate/Parent Company: Sheridan Newspapers
Publication Street Address: 144 E Grinnell Plz
City: Sheridan
State: WY
Publication Website: www.thesheridanpress.com
Postal Code: 82801-3933
Office phone: (307) 672-2431
General E-mail: beth@thesheridanpress.com
Publisher Name: Kristen Czaban
Editor Name: Ashleigh Snoozy
Year Established: 1887
Mechanical specifications: Type page 12 3/4 x 21 1/2; E - 6 cols, 2 1/16, 1/8 between; A - 6 cols, 2 1/16, 1/8 between; C - 7 cols, 1 3/4, 1/8 between.
Published Days: Mon`Tues`Wed`Thur`Fri`Sat
Weekday Frequency: m
Saturday Frequency: m
Avg Paid Circ: 3523
Avg Free Circ: 28
Audit Company: VAC
Audit Date: 30 06 2014
Pressroom Equipment: Lines – 9-G/Community 1975, 2; Folders – 1-G/SC.;
Mailroom Equipment: Tying Machines – 1-Samuel/SA 625 Strapping, MLN, Signode.;
Buisness Equipment: Pentium
Buisness Software: Baseview
Classified Equipment: Hardware – 4-APP/Power Mac, 4-APP/G4; Printers – Xante/Accel-a-Writer 39
Classified Software: Baseview 4.0.
Editorial Equipment: Hardware – 3-APP/G4, 5-APP/Power Mac/2-APP/Mac 30SE, APP/Power Mac fileserver; Printers – Xante/Accel-a-Writer 39
Editorial Software: Baseview 1.1, QPS/QuarkXPress 3.32r5, APP/Mac Appleshare 5.0.2.
Production Equipment: Hardware – ECR/VRL 36; Cameras – Acti; Scanners – 1-Epson/836XL, Epson/1680, Nikon/4000
Production Software: QPS/QuarkXPress 3.32r5.
Total Circulation: 3551

WORLAND

NORTHERN WYOMING DAILY NEWS

Corporate/Parent Company: Stevenson Newspapers
Publication Street Address: 201 N 8th St
City: Worland
State: WY
Publication Website: www.wyodaily.com
Postal Code: 82401-2614
Office phone: (307) 347-3241
General E-mail: webmaster@wyodaily.com
Editor Name: Karla Pomeroy
Advertising Executive Name: Amanda Owens
Year Established: 1905
Delivery Methods: Mail
Own Printing Facility?: Y
Mechanical specifications: Type page 13 x 21 1/2; E - 6 cols, 2 1/16, 1/8 between; A - 6 cols, 2 1/16, 1/8 between; C - 6 cols, 2 1/16, 1/8 between.
Published Days: Tues`Wed`Thur`Fri`Sat
Weekday Frequency: m
Saturday Frequency: m
Avg Paid Circ: 3468
Audit Company: Sworn/Estimate/Non-Audited
Audit Date: 7 12 2019
Pressroom Equipment: Lines – 4-G/Community;
Mailroom Equipment: Tying Machines – 1-Bu/BT 16 String Tyer; Address Machine – 2/Wm.;
Buisness Equipment: 2-IBM/OS 2
Classified Equipment: Hardware – DP/Imaging 2355.;
Editorial Equipment: Hardware – DP/Imaging 2355.
Production Equipment: Hardware – 1-Nu/Flip Top FT40; Cameras – 1-SCREEN.
Total Circulation: 3468

CATSKILL DAILY MAIL

Corporate/Parent Company: Register Star
Publication Website: www.hudsonvalley360.com

HUDSON REGISTER-STAR

Publication Website: www.hudsonvalley360.com

NEW YORK DAILY RECORD

Corporate/Parent Company: BridgeTower Media
Publication Website: nydailyrecord.com

THE CITIZEN

Corporate/Parent Company: Lee Enterprises
Publication Website: auburnpub.com

THE TIMES HERALD

Corporate/Parent Company: Gannett
Publication Website: www.oleantimesherald.com

TOP 50 U.S. NEWSPAPER GROUPS

BROOKLYN
SCHNEPS MEDIA
Mailing Address: One MetroTech Center
State: NY
ZIP Code: 11201
Main Phone: 718-224-5863
Dailies: 2
Non-Dailies: 33

CAPE GIRARDEAU
RUST COMMUICATIONS
Mailing Address: 301 Broadway
State: MO
ZIP Code: 63701
Main Phone: 573-335-6611
Dailies: 16
Non-Dailies: 21

CHARLOTTE
AMERICAN CITY BUSINESS JOURNALS
Mailing Address: 120 West Morehead Street
State: NC
ZIP Code: 28202
Main Phone: 800-433-4565
Dailies: 0
Non-Dailies: 42

CHATHAM
WOMACK PUBLISHING
Mailing Address: 30 N Main St
State: VA
ZIP Code: 24531
Main Phone: 434-432-1654
Dailies: 0
Non-Dailies: 17

CHERRY HILL
NEWSPAPER MEDIA GROUP
Mailing Address: Two Executive Campus, Suite 400
State: NJ
ZIP Code: 08002
Main Phone: 215-354-3000
Dailies: 0
Non-Dailies: 47

CHESTER
STRAUS NEWS
Mailing Address: 20 West Avenue
State: NY
ZIP Code: 10918-1053
Main Phone: 845-469-9000
Dailies: 0
Non-Dailies: 17

CHICAGO
TRIBUNE PUBLISHING
Mailing Address: 435 N Michigan Ave
State: IL
ZIP Code: 60611
Main Phone: 312-222-9100
Dailies: 10
Non-Dailies: 13

COEUR D'ALENE
HAGADONE CORP.
Mailing Address: 111 S 1st Street
State: ID
ZIP Code: 83814
Main Phone: 208-667-3431
Dailies: 3
Non-Dailies: 14

CRYSTAL LAKE
SHAW MEDIA (UNITED STATES)
Mailing Address: 7717 South Illinois Route 31
State: IL
ZIP Code: 60014
Main Phone: 815-459-4040
Dailies: 9
Non-Dailies: 27

DAVENPORT
LEE ENTERPRISES
Mailing Address: 4600 E 53rd St.
State: IA
ZIP Code: 52801
Main Phone: 563-383-2100
Dailies: 62
Non-Dailies: 25

DENVER
DIGITAL FIRST MEDIA
Mailing Address: 101 W. Colfax Ave.,
State: CO
ZIP Code: 80202-5177
Main Phone: 303-954-6360
Dailies: 68
Non-Dailies: 27

DOVER
INDEPENDENT NEWSMEDIA USA
Mailing Address: 110 Galaxy Dr.
State: DE
ZIP Code: 19901
Main Phone: 302-674-3600
Dailies: 1
Non-Dailies: 18

ENGLEWOOD
COLORADO COMMUNITY MEDIA
Mailing Address: 750 W Hampden Ave Ste 225
State: CO
ZIP Code: 80110
Main Phone: 303-566-4100
Dailies: 0
Non-Dailies: 19

EVERETT
SOUND PUBLISHING
Mailing Address: PO Box 930
State: WA
ZIP Code: 98206-0930
Main Phone: 360-394-5800
Dailies: 9
Non-Dailies: 43

FARGO
FORUM COMMUNICATIONS
Mailing Address: 101 5th ST N
State: ND
ZIP Code: 58102
Main Phone: 701-235-7311
Dailies: 9
Non-Dailies: 25

FORT WAYNE
KPC MEDIA GROUP
Mailing Address: 3306 Independence Dr.
State: IN
ZIP Code: 46808
Main Phone: 260-426-2640
Dailies: 3
Non-Dailies: 12

GARDEN CITY
RICHNER COMMUNICATIONS
Mailing Address: 2 Endo Blvd
State: NY
ZIP Code: 11530
Main Phone: 516-569-4000
Dailies: 0
Non-Dailies: 25

HAMPTON
MID-AMERICA PUBLISHING
Mailing Address: 9 Second Street NW
State: IA
ZIP Code: 50441
Main Phone: 641-456-2585
Dailies: 0
Non-Dailies: 23

JACKSON
EMMERICH NEWSPAPERS
Mailing Address: 246 Briarwood Dr., Ste. 110
State: MS
ZIP Code: 39236
Main Phone: 601-957-1122
Dailies: 3
Non-Dailies: 22

LAFAYETTE
LSN PUBLISHING COMPANY
Mailing Address: 600 Jefferson St., Ste. 913
State: LA
ZIP Code: 70508
Main Phone: 337-266-2152
Dailies: 0
Non-Dailies: 19

LAPEER
VIEW NEWSPAPER GROUP
Mailing Address: P.O. Box 220
State: MI
ZIP Code: 48446
Main Phone: 810-664-0811
Dailies: 0
Non-Dailies: 17

LIVINGSTON
YELLOWSTONE NEWSPAPERS
Mailing Address: PO Box 2000
State: MT
ZIP Code: 59047
Main Phone: 406-222-2000
Dailies: 0
Non-Dailies: 14

MCALLEN
AIM MEDIA USA
Mailing Address: 1400 E. Nola Loop
State: TX
ZIP Code: 78504-6111
Main Phone: 956-683-4060
Dailies: 32
Non-Dailies: 11

MCLEAN
GANNETT
Mailing Address: 7950 Jones Branch Drive
State: VA
ZIP Code: 22107
Main Phone: 703-854-6000
Dailies: 250
Non-Dailies: 242

MINEOLA
ANTON MEDIA GROUP
Mailing Address: 132 East 2nd Street
State: NY
ZIP Code: 11501
Main Phone: 516-747-8282
Dailies: 0
Non-Dailies: 18

MINNEAPOLIS
ADAMS PUBLISHING GROUP
Mailing Address: 4095 Coon Rapids Blvd.
State: MN
ZIP Code: 55433
Main Phone: 423-359-3113
Dailies: 37
Non-Dailies: 158

MONROVIA
HLR MEDIA, LLC
Mailing Address: 121 E. Chestnut Ave.
State: CA
ZIP Code: 91016
Main Phone: 626-301-1010
Dailies: 0
Non-Dailies: 18

MONTGOMERY
CNHI
Mailing Address: 201 Monroe Street, Ste. 450
State: AL
ZIP Code: 36104
Main Phone: 334-293-5800
Dailies: 40
Non-Dailies: 28

Top 50 U.S. Newspaper Groups

MORRISTOWN
LAKEWAY PUBLISHERS

Mailing Address: 1609 W 1st North St
State: TN
ZIP Code: 37814
Main Phone: 423-581-5630
Dailies: 0
Non-Dailies: 22

NATCHEZ
BOONE NEWSPAPERS

Mailing Address: 503 North Canal St.
State: MS
ZIP Code: 39121-1447
Main Phone: 601-442-9101
Dailies: 0
Non-Dailies: 83

NEW YORK
ADVANCE PUBLICATIONS

Mailing Address: 1 World Trade Ctr FL 43
State: NY
ZIP Code: 10007-0090
Main Phone: 718-981-1234
Dailies: 15
Non-Dailies: 24

NEW YORK
HEARST COMMUNICATIONS

Mailing Address: 300 West 57th Street
State: NY
ZIP Code: 10019
Main Phone: 212-649-2000
Dailies: 48
Non-Dailies: 27

PADUCAH
PAXTON MEDIA GROUP

Mailing Address: 100 Television Lane
State: KY
ZIP Code: 4203-7905
Main Phone: 270-575-8630
Dailies: 32
Non-Dailies: 26

PFLUGERVILLE
COMMUNITY IMPACT NEWSPAPERS

Mailing Address: 16225 Impact Way
State: TX
ZIP Code: 78660
Main Phone: 512-989-1000
Dailies: 0
Non-Dailies: 32

PLANO
STAR LOCAL MEDIA

Mailing Address: 3501 E. Plano Parkway Suite 200
State: TX
ZIP Code: 75074
Main Phone: 972-398-4200
Dailies: 0
Non-Dailies: 14

PORTLAND
PAMPLIN MEDIA GROUP

Mailing Address: 6605 SE Lake Rd
State: OR
ZIP Code: 09722
Main Phone: 503-684-0360
Dailies: 1
Non-Dailies: 23

PRESCOTT VALLEY
WESTERN NEWS & INFO

Mailing Address: 8303 E State Route 69
State: AZ
ZIP Code: 86314
Main Phone: 928-759-7630
Dailies: 2
Non-Dailies: 32

RUSSELL
MAIN STREET MEDIA

Mailing Address: 958 E Wichita Ave
State: KS
ZIP Code: 67665
Main Phone: 785-483-2116
Dailies: 0
Non-Dailies: 33

SACRAMENTO
MCCLATCHY

Mailing Address: 2100 Q Street
State: CA
ZIP Code: 95816-6899
Main Phone: 916-321-1855
Dailies: 23
Non-Dailies: 0

SAN DIEGO
BREHM COMMUNICATIONS

Mailing Address: PO Box 28429
State: CA
ZIP Code: 92198
Main Phone: 858-451-6200
Dailies: 2
Non-Dailies: 26

SAVANNAH
MORRIS MULTIMEDIA

Mailing Address: 27 Abercorn Street
State: GA
ZIP Code: 31401
Main Phone: 912-233-1281
Dailies: 0
Non-Dailies: 43

SHELBYVILLE
LANDMARK COMMUNITY NEWSPAPERS

Mailing Address: 601 Taylorsville Road
State: KY
ZIP Code: 40065
Main Phone: 502-633-4334
Dailies: 3
Non-Dailies: 40

SIERRA VISTA
WICK COMMUNICATIONS

Mailing Address: 333 W Wilcox Dr Ste 302
State: AZ
ZIP Code: 85635
Main Phone: 520-458-0200
Dailies: 6
Non-Dailies: 17

STATE COLLEGE
SAMPLE NEWS GROUP

Mailing Address: 1001 University Drive
State: PA
ZIP Code: 16801
Main Phone: 814-278-1325
Dailies: 18
Non-Dailies: 52

TARENTUM
TRIB TOTAL MEDIA

Mailing Address: 210 Wood St.
State: PA
ZIP Code: 15084
Main Phone: 800-909-8742
Dailies: 1
Non-Dailies: 14

WARREN
C&G NEWSPAPERS

Mailing Address: 13650 E 11 Mile Rd
State: MI
ZIP Code: 48089
Main Phone: 586-498-8100
Dailies: 0
Non-Dailies: 19

WEST FRANKFORT
COMMUNITY MEDIA GROUP

Mailing Address: PO Box 10
State: IL
ZIP Code: 62896
Main Phone: 618-937-6412
Dailies: 10
Non-Dailies: 40

WHEELING
OGDEN NEWSPAPERS

Mailing Address: 1500 Main St
State: WV
ZIP Code: 26003-2826
Main Phone: 304-233-0100
Dailies: 39
Non-Dailies: 48

WHIPPANY
NEW JERSEY HILLS MEDIA GROUP

Mailing Address: Suite 104 100 South Jefferson Rd.
State: NJ
ZIP Code: 07981
Main Phone: 908-766-3900
Dailies: 0
Non-Dailies: 14

ONLINE ONLY NEWSPAPERS IN THE U.S.

ALAMEDA

THE BERKELEY DAILY PLANET

Street address 1: 3023 Shattuck Ave
Street address city: Berkeley
Street address state: CA
Street Zip Code: 94705

BURNET

DAILYTRIB.COM

Street address 1: 1007 AVENUE K
Street address city: MARBLE FALLS
Street address state: TX
Street Zip Code: 78654-5039
Country: USA
General Phone: (479) 966-4860
Advertising Phone: (479) 387-1002
Display Advertising e-mail: contact@fayettevilleflyer.com
Website: www.fayettevilleflyer.com
Mthly Avg Views: 200000
Mthly Avg Unique Visitors: 75000
Days Published: Other
Personnel: Dustin Bartholomew (Co-Owner); Todd Gill (Co-Owner)
Parent Company/Group: Wonderstate Media, LLC
Main (survey) contact: Dustin Bartholomew

BUTLER

BEECH TREE NEWS

Street address 1: PO Box 140
Street address city: Aberdeen
Street address state: KY
Street Zip Code: 42201-0140
Country: USA
General Phone: (520) 302-5989
Display Advertising e-mail: ads@tucsonsentinel.com
Editorial e-mail: news@tucsonsentinel.com
Website: tucsonsentinel.com
Year newspaper established: 2009
Days Published: Mon`Tues`Wed`Thur`Fri`Sat`Sun
Other Type of Frequency: Online Only
Personnel: Dylan Smith (Pub./Ed.); Maria Coxon-Smith (News/Engagement Ed.)
Main (survey) contact: Dylan Smith

CA

SACRAMENTO PRESS

Street address 1: PO Box 7981
Street address city: Citrus Heights
Street address state: CA
Street Zip Code: 95621
Country: USA
Mailing address 1: PO Box 5534
Mailing city: Berkeley
Mailing state or province: CA
Mailing Zip Code: 94705-0534
General Phone: (510) 845-8440
Editorial e-mail: news@berkeleydailyplanet.com
Website: berkeleydailyplanet.com
Days Published: Other
Other Type of Frequency: Online Only
Personnel: Mike O'Malley (Pub.); Becky O'Malley (Ed.)
Main (survey) contact: Mike O'Malley

CABELL

HUNTINGTONNEWS.NET

Street address 1: 528 Ridgewood Rd
Street address city: Huntington

Street address state: WV
Street Zip Code: 25701-4852
Country: USA
Mailing address 1: PO Box 7981
Mailing city: Citrus Heights
Mailing state or province: CA
Mailing Zip Code: 95621
General Phone: (916) 572-7609
Display Advertising e-mail: advertising@sacramentopress.com
Editorial e-mail: newstip@sacramentopress.com
Website: sacramentopress.com
Year newspaper established: 2008
Digital Platforms - Mobile: Apple`Android`Windows`Blackberry
Digital Platforms - Tablet: Apple iOS`Android`Windows 7`Blackberry Tablet OS`Kindle`Kindle Fire
Days Published: Mon`Tues`Wed`Thur`Fri
Other Type of Frequency: Online Only
Personnel: Bethany Harris (Editor); Cesar Alexander (Editorial Assistant)
Main (survey) contact: Bethany Harris

CLEARFIELD

GANT DAILY

Street address 1: 219 S 2nd St
Street address city: Clearfield
Street address state: PA
Street Zip Code: 16830-2205
Country: USA
General Phone: (949) 287-8330
Display Advertising e-mail: editor@southcoasteditorcom
Website: www.southcoasteditor.com
Days Published: Other
Other Type of Frequency: Online Only
Personnel: Saboohi Currim (Ed.)
Main (survey) contact: Saboohi Currim

COOK

PEOPLE'S WORLD

Street address 1: 3339 S Halsted St
Street address city: Chicago
Street address state: IL
Street Zip Code: 60608-6882
Country: USA
Mailing address 1: 398 Wildbriar Lane
Mailing city: Loveland
Mailing state or province: CO
Mailing Zip Code: 80537
General Phone: (970) 532-3715
Advertising Phone: (970) 235-3715
Editorial Phone: (970) 532-3715
Display Advertising e-mail: editor@berthoudrecorder.com
Classified Advertising e-mail: editor@berthoudrecorder.com
Editorial e-mail: editor@berthoudrecorder.com
Website: www.berthoudrecorder.com
Mthly Avg Views: 2000
Days Published: Other
Other Type of Frequency: Online Only
Personnel: Gary Wamsley (Pub/Ed/Rep/Photo)
Main (survey) contact: Gary Wamsley

COOK

THE ONION

Street address 1: 212 W Superior St.
Street address 2: Suite 200
Street address city: Chicago
Street address state: IL
Street Zip Code: 60654-3562
Country: USA
Mailing address 1: 36 Russ Street
Mailing city: Hartford

Mailing state or province: CT
Mailing Zip Code: 06106
General Phone: (860) 218-6380
Advertising Phone: (860) 218-6380
Editorial Phone: 860-218-6380
Display Advertising e-mail: bputterman@ctmirror.org
Classified Advertising e-mail: bputterman@ctmirror.org
Editorial e-mail: ehamilton@ctmirror.org
Website: www.ctmirror.org
Mthly Avg Views: 500000
Mthly Avg Unique Visitors: 190000
Year newspaper established: 2009
Advertising: 2013
Digital Platforms - Mobile: Apple`Android`Windows
Digital Platforms - Tablet: Apple iOS`Android`Windows 7
Days Published: Mon`Tues`Wed`Thur`Fri`Sun
Personnel: Mark Pazniokas (Capital Bur. Chief); Bruce Putterman (CEO / Publisher); Elizabeth Hamilton (Executive Editor)
Parent Company/Group: The Connecticut News Project, Inc.
Main (survey) contact: Bruce Putterman

DAUPHIN

LINGLESTOWN GAZETTE

Street address 1: 6204 Elmer Ave.
Street address city: Linglestown
Street address state: PA
Street Zip Code: 17112
Country: USA
General Phone: (203) 624-8007
Editorial e-mail: editor@newhavenindependent.org
Website: newhavenindependent.org
Days Published: Other
Other Type of Frequency: Online Only
Personnel: Paul Bass (Ed.); Melissa Bailey (Managing Editor)
Main (survey) contact: Paul Bass

FAUQUIER

FAUQUIER NOW

Street address 1: 50 Culpeper St
Street address 2: Suite 3
Street address city: Warrenton
Street address state: VA
Street Zip Code: 20188
Country: USA
Mailing address 1: PO BOX 500158
Mailing city: MARATHON
Mailing state or province: FL
Mailing Zip Code: 33050-0158
General Phone: (305) 376-4636
Display Advertising e-mail: jpulis@flkeysnews.com
Classified Advertising e-mail: jpulis@flkeysnews.com
Editorial e-mail: dgoodhue@flkeysnews.com
Website: flkeysnews.com
Mthly Avg Views: 550000
Mthly Avg Unique Visitors: 175000
Year newspaper established: 1953
Advertising: Open inch rate $19.30
Digital Platforms - Mobile: Apple`Android
Days Published: Wed`Sat
Personnel: David Goodhue (Ed./ Reporter); Glenn Brandt (Adv. Consult.); Omar Mercado (Local Adv. Mgr.); Gwen Filosa (Reporter)
Parent Company/Group: The McClatchy Company
Main (survey) contact: David Goodhue
Advertising: SRDS (11/19/2014)

HAMILTON

CHATTANOOGAN.COM

Street address 1: 100 Cherokee Boulevard
Street address 2: #109
Street address city: Chattanooga
Street address state: TN
Street Zip Code: 37405
Country: USA
Mailing address 1: 3339 S Halsted St
Mailing city: Chicago
Mailing state or province: IL
Mailing Zip Code: 60608-6882
General Phone: (773) 446-9920
General Fax: (773) 446-9928
Display Advertising e-mail: contact@peoplesworld.org
Website: www.peoplesworld.org
Days Published: Other
Other Type of Frequency: Online Only
Personnel: John Wojcik (Ed.-in-Chief); Mariya Strauss (Mng. Ed.)
Main (survey) contact: John Wojcik

HARRIS

THE PAPER

Street address 1: 23503 Briarcreek Blvd.
Street address city: Spring
Street address state: TX
Street Zip Code: 77373
Country: USA
General Phone: (312) 751-0503
General Fax: (312) 751-4137
Display Advertising e-mail: advertising@theonion.com
Website: theonion.com
Days Published: Other
Other Type of Frequency: Online Only
Personnel: Joe Randazzo
Main (survey) contact: Mike McAvoy

HARTFORD

THE CONNECTICUT MIRROR

Street address 1: 36 Russ Street
Street address city: Hartford
Street address state: CT
Street Zip Code: 06106
Country: USA
Mailing address 1: 600 W Main St
Mailing city: Fort Wayne
Mailing state or province: IN
Mailing Zip Code: 46801-0088
General Phone: (260) 461-8773
General Fax: (260) 461-8648
Advertising Phone: (260) 461-8350
Advertising Fax: (260) 461-8489
Editorial Phone: (260) 461-8773
Editorial Fax: (260) 461-8648
Display Advertising e-mail: advertising@fwn.fortwayne.com
Classified Advertising e-mail: advertising@fwn.fortwayne.com
Editorial e-mail: jgnews@jg.net
Website: www.journalgazette.net
Year newspaper established: 1863
Advertising: Open inch rate $81.65 (Mon-Thur); $95.90 (Fri-Sat)
Digital Platforms - Mobile: Apple`Android
Digital Platforms - Tablet: Apple iOS`Android
Days Published: Mon`Tues`Wed`Thur`Fri`Sat`Sun
Note: For detailed production and mechanical information, see Fort Wayne Newspapers Inc. listing.
Personnel: Julie Inskeep (Pres./Pub.); Jim Chapman (Assistant Metro Ed./day city Ed.); Jim Touvell (Managing Ed.); Terri Richardson (Features Ed.); Tom Pellegrene Jr. (News Technology Mgr.); Sherry Skufca (Ed.)
Parent Company/Group: Ogden Newspapers Inc.

Online Only Newspapers in the U.S.

Main (survey) contact: Julie Inskeep

HENNEPIN

MINNPOST

Street address 1: 900 6th Avenue SE, Suite 220
Street address city: Minneapolis
Street address state: MN
Street Zip Code: 55414
Country: USA
General Phone: (270) 526-9527
General Fax: (270) 526-2178
Display Advertising e-mail: diane@beechtreenews.com
Website: www.beechtreenews.com
Year newspaper established: 2009
Advertising: Strip Ad-1mth run/$125, 6mth/$112, 12mth/$93.75. Block Ad-1mth/$250, 6mth/$225, 12mth/$187.50
Days Published: Other
Other Type of Frequency: Online Only
Personnel: Diane Dyer; John Embry
Main (survey) contact: Diane Dyer

HOWARD

BALTIMORE POST-EXAMINER

Street address 1: PO Box 2094
Street address city: Columbia
Street address state: MD
Street Zip Code: 21045-2094
Country: USA
General Phone: (606) 638-0123
Website: www.thelevisalazer.com
Year newspaper established: 2008
Days Published: Other
Other Type of Frequency: Online Only
Personnel: Mark Grayson (Ed.)
Main (survey) contact: Mark Grayson

IN

THE JOURNAL GAZETTE

Street address 1: 600 W MAIN ST
Street address city: FORT WAYNE
Street address state: IN
Street Zip Code: 46802-1498
Country: USA
General Phone: (270) 772-1544
Display Advertising e-mail: jimturner@loganjournal.com
Website: www.loganjournal.com
Days Published: Other
Other Type of Frequency: Online Only
Personnel: Jim Turner
Main (survey) contact: Jim Turner

KENT

RHODY BEAT

Street address 1: 1944 Warwick Avenue
Street address city: Warwick
Street address state: RI
Street Zip Code: 02889
Country: USA
General Phone: (443) 745-4363
Display Advertising e-mail: BaltimorePostExaminer@gmail.com
Website: baltimorepostexaminer.com
Mthly Avg Unique Visitors: 100000
Year newspaper established: 2012
Days Published: Mon`Tues`Wed`Thur`Fri`Sat`Sun`Other
Other Type of Frequency: Online Only
Note: Sister site is Los Angeles Post-Examiner
Personnel: Timothy Maier (Pub)
Main (survey) contact: Tim Maier

KING

CROSSCUT

Street address 1: 401 Mercer St
Street address city: Seattle
Street address state: WA
Street Zip Code: 98109
Country: USA
Mailing address 1: 6930 Carroll Avenue, Suite 625
Mailing city: Takoma Park
Mailing state or province: MD
Mailing Zip Code: 20912
General Phone: (301) 270-7240
General Fax: (301) 270-7241
Advertising Phone: (301) 270-7240
Editorial Phone: (301) 270-7240
Display Advertising e-mail: advertising@current.org
Classified Advertising e-mail: publicmediajobs@current.org
Editorial e-mail: news@current.org
Website: current.org
Mthly Avg Views: 115835
Mthly Avg Unique Visitors: 53235
Year newspaper established: 1980
Digital Platforms - Mobile: Apple`Android
Digital Platforms - Tablet: Apple iOS`Android
Days Published: Mon`Tues`Wed`Thur`Fri
Other Type of Frequency: Print edition of curated content and special coverage published 8 times per year
Note: Current started as a biweekly print trade newspaper in 1980. In 2019, we will publish all 8 print editions plus two digital only editions through ISSUU.
Personnel: Julie Drizin (Exec. Dir.); Karen Everhart (Mng. Ed.); Mike Janssen (Dig. Ed.); Dru Sefton (Sr. Ed.); Tyler Falk (Asst. Ed.); Laura Rogers (Business Manager)
Main (survey) contact: Julie Drizin

KING

SEATTLE POST-INTELLIGENCER

Street address 1: 2901 3rd Ave
Street address 2: Suite 120
Street address city: Seattle
Street address state: WA
Street Zip Code: 98121
Country: USA
General Phone: (612) 455-6950
General Fax: (612) 455-6960
Advertising Phone: (612) 455-6953
Display Advertising e-mail: info@minnpost.com
Website: minnpost.com
Mthly Avg Views: 1000000
Mthly Avg Unique Visitors: 450000
Year newspaper established: 2007
Days Published: Mon`Tues`Wed`Thur`Fri`Sat
Other Type of Frequency: Online Only
Note: MinnPost is a 501(c)3 nonprofit corporation.
Personnel: Andrew Wallmeyer (Publisher & CEO); Corey Anderson (Web Editor); Sally Waterman (Ad. Director); Andrew Putz (Editor)
Main (survey) contact: Susan Albright; Andrew Wallmeyer

LARIMER

BERTHOUD RECORDER ONLINE

Street address 1: 398 Wildbriar Lane
Street address city: Loveland
Street address state: CO
Street Zip Code: 80537
Country: USA
General Phone: (877) 343-5207
Display Advertising e-mail: advertise@newwest.net
Editorial e-mail: info@newwest.net
Website: newwest.net
Days Published: Other
Other Type of Frequency: Online Only
Main (survey) contact: Survey Contact

LAWRENCE

LEVISA LAZER

Street address 1: 1328 Gene Wilson Blvd
Street address city: Louisa
Street address state: KY
Street Zip Code: 41230-9581

Country: USA
Mailing address 1: 1000 NC MUSIC FACTORY BLVD APT C2
Mailing city: CHARLOTTE
Mailing state or province: NC
Mailing Zip Code: 28206-6010
General Phone: (704) 522-8334
General Fax: (704) 522-8088
Display Advertising e-mail: Publisher@yesweekly.com
Website: http://clclt.com/
Year newspaper established: 1987
Advertising: 25
Days Published: Wed
Parent Company/Group: Womack Newspapers, inc
Main (survey) contact: Charles Womack

LOGAN

THE LOGAN JOURNAL

Street address 1: 2575 Bowling Green Rd
Street address city: Russellville
Street address state: KY
Street Zip Code: 42276-9617
Country: USA
Display Advertising e-mail: allan@ahherald.com
Website: ahherald.com
Mthly Avg Views: 30000
Mthly Avg Unique Visitors: 15000
Year newspaper established: 1999
Digital Platforms - Mobile: Apple`Android`Windows`Blackberry
Digital Platforms - Tablet: Apple iOS`Android`Windows 7`Blackberry Tablet OS`Kindle`Nook`Kindle Fire
Days Published: Other
Other Type of Frequency: Online Only
Note: We exclude many foreign visitors and bots.
Personnel: Allan Dean (Pub. & Ed.)
Main (survey) contact: Allan Dean

MANHATTAN

GOTHAM GAZETTE

Street address 1: 299 Broadway
Street address 2: Suite 700
Street address city: New York
Street address state: NY
Street Zip Code: 10007
Country: USA
Mailing address 1: PO Box 3639
Mailing city: Union
Mailing state or province: NJ
Mailing Zip Code: 07083-1596
General Phone: (908) 686-7700
General Fax: (908) 686-4169
Display Advertising e-mail: ads@thelocalsource.com
Classified Advertising e-mail: class@thelocalsource.com
Editorial e-mail: editorial@thelocalsource.com
Website: www.essexnewsdaily.com
Year newspaper established: 1949
Days Published: Thur
Note: E-Edition Only
Personnel: David Worrall (Pub.); Raymond Worrall (Gen. Mgr.); Peter Worrall (Adv. Mgr.); Nancy Worrall
Parent Company/Group: Worrall Community Newspapers, Inc.
Main (survey) contact: Survey Contact

MANHATTAN

THE FISCAL TIMES

Street address 1: 712 5th Ave
Street address 2: Fl 17
Street address city: New York
Street address state: NY
Street Zip Code: 10019-4108
Country: USA
Mailing address 1: 200 E. Main St. #5
Mailing city: Batavia
Mailing state or province: NY
Mailing Zip Code: 14020
General Phone: (585) 250-4118

Display Advertising e-mail: lisa@thebatavian.com
Classified Advertising e-mail: lisa@thebatavian.com
Editorial e-mail: billie@thebatavian.com
Website: thebatavian.com
Mthly Avg Views: 1500000
Mthly Avg Unique Visitors: 120000
Year newspaper established: 2008
Digital Platforms - Mobile: Apple`Android
Digital Platforms - Tablet: Apple iOS`Android
Days Published: Other
Other Type of Frequency: Online Only
Personnel: Howard Owens (Pub); Billie Owens (Ed.); Lisa Ace (Sales/Mktg. Coord.)
Main (survey) contact: Howard Owens

MANHATTAN

THE HUFFINGTON POST

Street address 1: 770 Broadway
Street address city: New York
Street address state: NY
Street Zip Code: 10012
Country: USA
General Phone: (212) 227-0342
General Fax: (212) 227-0345
Display Advertising e-mail: advertise@gothamgazette.com
Editorial e-mail: info@gothamgazette.com
Website: gothamgazette.com
Year newspaper established: 1999
Days Published: Other
Other Type of Frequency: Online Only
Personnel: Ben Max (Exec. Ed.)
Parent Company/Group: Citizens Union Foundation
Main (survey) contact: Ben Max

MANHATTAN

THE NEW YORK SUN

Street address 1: 105 Chambers St.
Street address 2: 2nd Floor
Street address city: New York
Street address state: NY
Street Zip Code: 10007-3516
Country: USA
General Phone: (212) 313-9680
General Fax: (877) 291-7606
Display Advertising e-mail: info@thefiscaltimes.com
Website: www.thefiscaltimes.com
Days Published: Other
Other Type of Frequency: Online Only
Personnel: Jacqueline Leo (Ed.-in-Chief); Jeff Czaplicki (Acct. Mgr.)
Main (survey) contact: Jacqueline Leo

MECKLENBURG

CREATIVE LOAFING CHARLOTTE

Street address 1: 1000 NC Music Factory Blvd
Street address 2: Apt C2
Street address city: Charlotte
Street address state: NC
Street Zip Code: 28206-6010
Country: USA
General Phone: (212) 652-6400
Display Advertising e-mail: blogteam@huffingtonpost.com
Website: huffingtonpost.com
Days Published: Other
Other Type of Frequency: Online Only
Personnel: Karen Mahabir (Managing Editor); Arianna Huffington (Pres.); Lydia polgreen (Ed.-in-Chief)
Main (survey) contact: Survey Contact

MISSOULA

NEW WEST

Street address 1: 415 N Higgins Ave
Street address 2: Suite 103
Street address city: Missoula
Street address state: MT

Street Zip Code: 59802
Country: USA
Mailing address 1: 105 Chambers St Fl 2
Mailing city: New York
Mailing state or province: NY
Mailing Zip Code: 10007-3516
General Phone: (212) 406-2000
General Fax: (212) 571-9836
Advertising Phone: (212) 901-2700
Display Advertising e-mail: inquiries@nysun.com
Classified Advertising e-mail: advertising@nysun.com; classified@nysun.com
Editorial e-mail: editor@nysun.com
Website: www.nysun.com
Days Published: Other
Other Type of Frequency: Online Only
Personnel: John Garrett (Dir., Classified); Linda Seto (Circ. Dir.); Seth Lipsky (Ed.); Ira Stoll (Mng. Ed.); Dave Propson (Art Ed.); Richard Thomson (Bus. Ed.); Emily Gitter (Features Ed.); Michael Woodsworth (Sports Ed.)
Main (survey) contact: Seth Lipsky

MONMOUTH

ATLANTIC HIGHLANDS HERALD

Street address 1: 25 Second Avenue
Street address city: Atlantic Highlands
Street address state: NJ
Street Zip Code: 07716
Country: USA
General Phone: (914) 738-8717
Display Advertising e-mail: maggieklein@pelhamwplus.com
Website: www.pelhamwplus.com
Year newspaper established: 1992
Advertising: $80-$100 per month
Digital Platforms - Mobile: Apple`Android`Windows`Blackberry
Digital Platforms - Tablet: Apple iOS`Android
Days Published: Other
Other Type of Frequency: Online Only
Personnel: Margaret A. Klein (Ed.)
Parent Company/Group: Klein Information Resources, Inc.
Main (survey) contact: Margaret A. Klein

MONROE

FLORIDA KEYS KEYNOTER

Street address 1: 3015 Overseas Hwy
Street address city: Marathon
Street address state: FL
Street Zip Code: 33050-2236
Country: USA
General Phone: (610) 649-1454
General Fax: (610) 649-0255
Advertising Phone: (215) 849-2312
Editorial Phone: (610) 649-0998
Display Advertising e-mail: ads@pjvoice.org
Classified Advertising e-mail: ads@pjvoice.org
Editorial e-mail: editor@pjvoice.com
Website: pjvoice.org
Mthly Avg Views: 10000
Mthly Avg Unique Visitors: 9000
Year newspaper established: 2005
Advertising: Ronit Treatman
Digital Platforms - Mobile: Apple`Android`Windows`Blackberry`Other
Digital Platforms - Tablet: Apple iOS`Android`Windows 7`Blackberry Tablet OS`Kindle`Nook`Kindle Fire`Other
Days Published: Other
Other Type of Frequency: Online Only
Personnel: Daniel Loeb (Pub); Ronit Tretman (Food Editor); Bonnie Squires (President); Ken Myers (VP)
Main (survey) contact: Daniel Loeb

MONTGOMERY

CURRENT

Street address 1: 6930 Carroll Avenue
Street address 2: Suite 625
Street address city: Takoma Park
Street address state: MD
Street Zip Code: 20912
Country: USA
Mailing address 1: PO Box 746
Mailing city: Clearfield
Mailing state or province: PA
Mailing Zip Code: 16830-0746
General Phone: (814) 765-5256
General Fax: (814) 765-5631
Display Advertising e-mail: dkilmer@gantdaily.com
Classified Advertising e-mail: sales@gantdaily.com
Editorial e-mail: jshirey@gantdaily.com
Website: www.gantdaily.com
Mthly Avg Unique Visitors: 300000
Year newspaper established: 2006
Digital Platforms - Mobile: Apple`Android`Windows`Blackberry
Digital Platforms - Tablet: Apple iOS`Android`Windows 7`Blackberry Tablet OS`Kindle`Nook`Kindle Fire
Days Published: Other
Other Type of Frequency: Online Only
Personnel: Christene Dahlem (Pres.); Jessica Shirey (Ed.); Ray Serafini (Adv./Digital Media Sales); Morgan Dubensky (Bus. Dev't. Mgr.)
Parent Company/Group: Gant Media LLC
Main (survey) contact: Christene Dahlem

MONTGOMERY

PHILADELPHIA JEWISH VOICE

Street address 1: 327 Pembroke Road
Street address city: Bala Cynwyd
Street address state: PA
Street Zip Code: 19004
Country: USA
General Phone: (717) 512-0722
Display Advertising e-mail: linglestowngazette@gmail.com
Website: linglestowngazette.com
Mthly Avg Views: 300
Mthly Avg Unique Visitors: 2000
Days Published: Other
Other Type of Frequency: Online Only
Personnel: Bill Bostic (Ed./Pub.)
Main (survey) contact: Bill Bostic

NEW HAVEN

THE NEW HAVEN INDEPENDENT

Street address 1: 51 Elm St.
Street address 2: Suite 307
Street address city: New Haven
Street address state: CT
Street Zip Code: 06510
Country: USA
General Phone: (26) 519-4500
Display Advertising e-mail: Sales@PhillyVoice.com
Website: PhillyVoice.com
Days Published: Other
Other Type of Frequency: Online Only
Personnel: Lexie Norcross (Exec. Dir); Matt Romanoski (Exe. Ed.); Bob McGovern (Exec. Ed.); Hal Donnelly (VP of Sales/Mktg.)
Parent Company/Group: WWB Holdings, LLC
Main (survey) contact: Lexie Norcross

NUECES

COASTAL BEND LEGAL & BUSINESS NEWS

Street address 1: 526 Mediterranean Drive
Street address city: Corpus Christi
Street address state: TX
Street Zip Code: 78418-3967
Country: USA
Mailing address 1: 1944 Warwick Avenue
Mailing city: Warwick
Mailing state or province: RI
Mailing Zip Code: 02889
General Phone: (401) 732-3100
General Fax: (401) 732-3110
Display Advertising e-mail: suzannew@rhodybeat.com
Classified Advertising e-mail: sueh@rhodybeat.com
Website: rhodybeat.com
Days Published: Other
Other Type of Frequency: Online Only
Personnel: Richard G. Fleischer (Gen. Mgr.); John Howell (Pub./Beacon Ed.)
Parent Company/Group: Beacon Communications, Inc
Main (survey) contact: John Howell

NY

THE BATAVIAN

Street address 1: 200 E. Main St.
Street address 2: Suite 5
Street address city: Batavia
Street address state: NY
Street Zip Code: 14020
Country: USA
Mailing address 1: PO Box 2331
Mailing city: Chattanooga
Mailing state or province: TN
Mailing Zip Code: 37409-0331
General Phone: (423) 266-2325
Display Advertising e-mail: news@chattanoogan.com
Website: www.chattanoogan.com
Days Published: Other
Other Type of Frequency: Online Only
Personnel: John Wilson (Pub.)
Main (survey) contact: John Wilson

ORANGE

SOUTH COAST EDITOR

Street address 1: 5319 University Drive
Street address 2: Suite 227
Street address city: Irvine
Street address state: CA
Street Zip Code: 92612
Country: USA
General Phone: (512) 716-8600
General Fax: (512) 716-8601
Advertising Phone: (512) 716-8634
Display Advertising e-mail: ahinkle@texastribune.org
Website: texastribune.org
Mthly Avg Views: 3632933
Mthly Avg Unique Visitors: 617068
Days Published: Other
Other Type of Frequency: Online Only
Personnel: Emily Ramshaw (Ed.-in-Chief); Ross Ramsey (Exec. Editor); Maggie Gilburg (Development Director); April Hinkle (CRO & Advertising)
Main (survey) contact: Emily Ramshaw

PHILADELPHIA

PHILLYVOICE.COM

Street address 1: 1430 Walnut St
Street address city: Philadelphia
Street address state: PA
Street Zip Code: 19102
Country: USA
Mailing address 1: PO Box 270607
Mailing city: Corpus Christi
Mailing state or province: TX
Mailing Zip Code: 78427-0607
General Phone: 361-937-4907
General Fax: 361-937-1849
Display Advertising e-mail: info@cblnews.com
Classified Advertising e-mail: info@cblnews.com
Editorial e-mail: cblnews@cblnews.com
Website: www.cblnews.com
Year newspaper established: 1981
Advertising: 1/8 Pg $75.00
Days Published: Mon`Tues`Wed`Thur`Fri
Personnel: Kim Gutierrez (Pub./Ed./Adv. Dir.)
Main (survey) contact: Kim Gutierrez
Display Advertising e-mail: SRDS (11/3/2014); Classified Advertising e-mail: SRDS (11/3/2014)

PIMA

TUCSONSENTINEL.COM

Street address 1: 1960 N. Painted Hills
Street address city: Tuscon
Street address state: AZ
Street Zip Code: 85745
Country: USA
Mailing address 1: PO BOX 10
Mailing city: MARBLE FALLS
Mailing state or province: TX
Mailing Zip Code: 78654-0010
General Phone: (830) 693-7152
General Fax: (830) 693-3085
Display Advertising e-mail: advertising@thepicayune.com
Classified Advertising e-mail: advertising@thepicayune.com
Editorial e-mail: editor@thepicayune.com
Website: www.dailytrib.com
Mthly Avg Views: 89000
Mthly Avg Unique Visitors: 21500
Year newspaper established: 1991
Days Published: Wed
Personnel: Mandy Wyatt (Associate Publisher); Amber Weems (Pres./Pub./Adv. Sales)
Parent Company/Group: Victory Publishing Co., Ltd.
Main (survey) contact: Daniel Clifton

SHEBOYGAN

MYSHEBOYGAN.COM

Street address 1: P.O. Box 33
Street address city: Kohler
Street address state: WI
Street Zip Code: 53044
Country: USA
Mailing address 1: 23503 Briarcreek Blvd.
Mailing city: Spring
Mailing state or province: TX
Mailing Zip Code: 77373
General Phone: (832) 296-6887
Advertising Phone: (832) 296-6887
Editorial Phone: 8322966887
Display Advertising e-mail: bobgunner@gmail.com
Classified Advertising e-mail: bobgunner@gmail.com
Editorial e-mail: bobgunner@gmail.com
Website: thepapermagazine.com
Year newspaper established: 2008
Advertising: 2008
Digital Platforms - Mobile: Other
If other, please specify: Responsive
If other, please specify: Should work on all
Days Published: Other
Other Type of Frequency: Online Only Daily
Personnel: Bob Gunner (Pub./Ed.)
Main (survey) contact: Bob Gunner

TRAVIS

THE TEXAS TRIBUNE

Street address 1: 823 Congress Ave.
Street address 2: Suite 1400
Street address city: Austin
Street address state: TX
Street Zip Code: 78701
Country: USA
Mailing state or province: VA
General Phone: (888) 678-6008
General Fax: (540) 635-4374
Advertising Phone: (888) 678-6008 ext 928
Display Advertising e-mail: cmaagad@lifesitenews.com
Classified Advertising e-mail: cmaagad@lifesitenews.com
Editorial e-mail: editor@lifesitenews.com
Website: www.lifesitenews.com
Mthly Avg Views: 4000000
Mthly Avg Unique Visitors: 2200000
Year newspaper established: 1997
Digital Platforms - Mobile: Apple`Android`Windows`Blackberry
Digital Platforms - Tablet: Apple iOS`Android`Windows 7`Blackberry Tablet OS`Kindle`Nook`Kindle Fire

Online Only Newspapers in the U.S.

I-143

Days Published: Other
Other Type of Frequency: Online Only
Personnel: Clare Maagad (Adv. Mgr.); Patrick Craine (Editor / Journalist); John Jalsevac (Managing Ed.); John-Henry Westen (Ed. & Chief); Steve Jalsevac (Managing Director); Lisa Bourne (Journalist / Photographer); Claire Chretien (Journalist); Doug Bean (Journalist); Doug Mainwaring (Journlaist); Diane Montagna (Rome Correspondent); Lianne Laurence (Journalist); Diane Montagna (Rome Correspondent); Martin Barillas (Journalist); Calvin Freiberger (Journalist); Rebecca Fidero (Business Manager)
Main (survey) contact: Clare Maagad

UNION

VAILSBURG LEADER

Street address 1: 1291 Stuyvesant Ave
Street address city: Union
Street address state: NJ
Street Zip Code: 07083-3823
Country: USA
Mailing address 1: PO BOX 3090
Mailing city: Warrenton
Mailing state or province: VA
Mailing Zip Code: 20188
General Phone: (540) 359-6574
Display Advertising e-mail: Ellen@FauquierNow.com

Days Published: Other
Other Type of Frequency: Online Only
Personnel: Ellen Emerson (Pub.); Lawrence Emerson (Ed.)
Main (survey) contact: Ellen Emerson

WARREN

LIFESITENEWS.COM, INC

Street address 1: 4 Family Life Lane
Street address city: Front Royal
Street address state: VA
Street Zip Code: 22630
Country: USA
General Phone: (206) 382-6137
General Fax: (206) 443-6691
Display Advertising e-mail: advertising@crosscut.com
Website: www.crosscut.com
Days Published: Other
Other Type of Frequency: Online Only
Personnel: Greg Hascom (Ed.-in-Chief); Tamara Power-Drutis (Exec. Dir.); Jonah Fruchter (Acc. Mgr.); Joe Copeland (Ed.)
Main (survey) contact: Tamara Power-Drutis

WASHINGTON

THE FAYETTEVILLE FLYER

Street address 1: 205 N College Ave
Street address city: Fayetteville
Street address state: AR
Street Zip Code: 72701-4238
Country: USA
General Phone: (206) 448-8030
General Fax: (206) 515-5577
Advertising Phone: (206) 448-8036
Advertising Fax: (206) 493-0993
Editorial Phone: (206) 464-2496
Editorial Fax: (206) 382-6760
Display Advertising e-mail: advertising@seattlepi.com
Editorial e-mail: citydesk@seattlepi.com
Website: WWW.seattlepi.com
Year newspaper established: 2009
Digital Platforms - Mobile: Apple`Android
Digital Platforms - Tablet: Apple iOS`Android
Days Published: Other
Other Type of Frequency: Online Only
Personnel: Ryan Blethen (Assoc. Pub./Editorial Ed.); Suki Dardarian (Mng. Ed.); Sarah Rupp (Exec. Prod.); Denise Clifton (Dir. of Visuals); Leon Espinoza (Exec. News Ed.); Michael Shepard (Sr. VP, Bus. Ops.); Buster Brown (Sr. VP, Finance); Jill Mackie (VP, Public Affairs); Eileen Takeuchi (VP/CFO); Chris Biencourt (Dir., Labor Rel./Safety); Anna Bertrand (Mktg. Dir., New Media); Dominic Gates (Aerospace/Boeing Reporter)
Parent Company/Group: Metro Newspaper Advertising Services, Inc.-OOB
Main (survey) contact: Sarah Rupp

WESTCHESTER

THE PELHAMS-PLUS

Street address 1: P.O. Box 8605
Street address city: Pelham
Street address state: NY
Street Zip Code: 10803
Country: USA
General Phone: (920) 917-6311
Display Advertising e-mail: ads@mysheboygan.com
Editorial e-mail: news@mysheboygan.com
Website: mysheboygan.com
Mthly Avg Views: 100000
Year newspaper established: 2012
Digital Platforms - Mobile: Apple`Android
Digital Platforms - Tablet: Apple iOS`Android`Kindle
Days Published: Other
Other Type of Frequency: Online Only
Personnel: Jane Van Treeck (News Dir.)
Main (survey) contact: Jane Van Treeck

CANADIAN DAILY NEWSPAPERS

BELLEVILLE

THE INTELLIGENCER

Publication Website: www.intelligencer.ca
Parent Company: Postmedia Network Inc.
Corporate Website: www.postmedia.com
Publication Street Address: 199 Front St. Ste 535
Province: AB
Postal Code: T2E 7P5
Office Phone: (403) 235-7100
Publisher Name: Lorne Motley
Editor Name: Monica Zurowski
Advertising Executive Name: Dean Jager

BRANDON

BRANDON SUN

Publication Website: www.brandonsun.com
Parent Company: F.P. Canadian Newspapers Limited Partnership
Corporate Website: www.fpnewspapers.com
Publication Street Address: 501 Rosser Ave.
Province: AB
Postal Code: T2E 7W9
Office Phone: (403) 410-1010
Publisher Name: Lorne Motley
Editor Name: Monica Zurowski
Advertising Executive Name: Lisa Bateman

BRANTFORD

THE EXPOSITOR

Publication Website: www.brantfordexpositor.ca
Parent Company: Postmedia Network Inc.
Corporate Website: www.postmedia.com
Publication Street Address: 195 Henry St., Bldg 4, Unit 1
Province: AB
Postal Code: T5J 0S1
Office Phone: (780) 429-5100
Editor Name: Colin McGarrigle
Advertising Executive Name: Anthony Gallace

BROCKVILLE

THE BROCKVILLE RECORDER AND TIMES

Publication Website: www.recorder.ca
Parent Company: Postmedia Network Inc.
Corporate Website: www.postmedia.com
Publication Street Address: 2479 Parkedale Ave.
Province: AB
Postal Code: T5J 0S1
Office Phone: (780) 468-0100
Editor Name: Dave Breakenridge
Advertising Executive Name: Anthony Gallace

CALGARY

CALGARY HERALD

Publication Website: www.calgaryherald.com
Parent Company: Postmedia Network Inc.
Corporate Website: www.postmedia.com
Publication Street Address: 215 16 St. SE
Province: AB
Postal Code: T8V 6V4
Office Phone: (780) 532-1110
Editor Name: Peter Shokeie

CALGARY

THE CALGARY SUN

Publication Website: www.calgarysun.com
Parent Company: Postmedia Network Inc.
Corporate Website: www.postmedia.com
Publication Street Address: 2615 12th St. NE
Province: AB
Postal Code: T1J 2H1
Office Phone: (403) 328-4411
Publisher Name: Brian Hancock
Editor Name: Randy Jensen
Advertising Executive Name: Brian Hancock

CARAQUET

L'ACADIE NOUVELLE

Publication Website: www.acadienouvelle.com
Parent Company: Les Editions de l'Acadie Nouvelle (1984) Ltée.
Publication Street Address: 476 St-Pierre Blvd. West
Province: AB
Postal Code: T1A 7E6
Office Phone: (403) 527-1101
Publisher Name: Kerri Sandford
Editor Name: Scott Schmidt
Advertising Executive Name: Kerri Sandford

CHARLOTTETOWN

THE GUARDIAN

Publication Website: www.theguardian.pe.ca
Parent Company: SaltWire Network Inc.
Corporate Website: www.saltwire.com
Publication Street Address: 165 Prince St.
Province: AB
Postal Code: T4R 1M9
Office Phone: (403) 343-2400
Publisher Name: Mary Kemmis
Editor Name: David Marsden
Advertising Executive Name: Wendy Moore

CHATHAM

THE CHATHAM DAILY NEWS

Publication Website: www.chathamdailynews.ca
Parent Company: Postmedia Network Inc.
Corporate Website: www.postmedia.com
Publication Street Address: 138 King St. West
Province: BC
Postal Code: V1Y 7V1
Office Phone: (250) 762-4445
Publisher Name: Stephanie Goodban
Editor Name: Pat Bulmer
Advertising Executive Name: Stephanie Goodban

CORNWALL

CORNWALL STANDARD-FREEHOLDER

Publication Website: www.standard-freeholder.com
Parent Company: Postmedia Network Inc.
Corporate Website: www.postmedia.com
Publication Street Address: 1150 Montreal Rd.
Province: BC
Postal Code: V2A 1N4
Office Phone: (250) 492-4002
Publisher Name: Shannon Huggard
Editor Name: James Miller
Advertising Executive Name: Shannon Huggard

EDMONTON

EDMONTON JOURNAL

Publication Website: www.edmontonjournal.com
Parent Company: Postmedia Network Inc.
Corporate Website: www.postmedia.com
Publication Street Address: 10006 - 101 St.
Province: BC
Postal Code: V1R 4B8
Office Phone: (250) 368-8551
Publisher Name: Eric Lawson
Editor Name: Guy Bertrand
Advertising Executive Name: Dave Dykstra

EDMONTON

THE EDMONTON SUN

Publication Website: www.edmontonsun.com
Parent Company: Postmedia Network Inc.
Corporate Website: www.postmedia.com
Publication Street Address: 10006 - 101 St
Province: BC
Postal Code: V5M 4X7
Office Phone: (604) 605-2000
Editor Name: Harold Munro
Advertising Executive Name: Mark Dowell

FREDERICTON

THE DAILY GLEANER

Publication Website: www.tj.news/dailygleaner.ca
Parent Company: Brunswick News, Inc.
Publication Street Address: 984 Prospect St
Province: BC
Postal Code: V5M 4X7
Office Phone: (604) 605-2000
Editor Name: Harold Munro
Advertising Executive Name: Mark Dowell

GRANBY

LA VOIX DE L'EST

Publication Website: www.lavoixdelest.ca
Parent Company: Coopérative nationale de l'information indépendante (CN2i)
Publication Street Address: 76 Dufferin St.
Province: BC
Postal Code: V8T 4M2
Office Phone: (250) 380-5211
Publisher Name: Dave Obee
Editor Name: Dave Obee
Advertising Executive Name: Peter Baillie

GRANDE PRAIRIE

DAILY HERALD-TRIBUNE

Publication Website: www.dailyheraldtribune.com
Parent Company: Postmedia Network Inc.
Corporate Website: www.postmedia.com
Publication Street Address: 10604 100 St.
Province: MB
Postal Code: R7A 0K4
Office Phone: (204) 727-2451
Publisher Name: Jim Mihaly
Editor Name: Matt Goerzen
Advertising Executive Name: Jim Mihaly

HALIFAX

THE CHRONICLE HERALD

Publication Website: www.thechronicleherald.ca
Parent Company: Halifax Herald Ltd.; SaltWire Network Inc.
Corporate Website: www.saltwire.com
Publication Street Address: 2717 Joseph Howe Dr
Province: MB
Postal Code: R2X 3A2
Office Phone: (204) 694-2022
Editor Name: Mark Hamm
Advertising Executive Name: Jennifer Bilsky

HAMILTON

THE HAMILTON SPECTATOR

Publication Website: www.thespec.com
Parent Company: Metroland Media Group Ltd.; Torstar Corporation
Corporate Website: www.metroland.com
Publication Street Address: 44 Frid St.
Province: MB
Postal Code: R2X 3B6
Office Phone: (204) 697-7122
Publisher Name: Bob Cox
Editor Name: Paul Samyn
Advertising Executive Name: Karen Buss

KELOWNA

THE DAILY COURIER

Publication Website: www.kelownadailycourier.ca
Parent Company: Continental Newspapers Canada Ltd.; Okanagan Valley Newspaper Group
Publication Street Address: 550 Doyle Ave.
Province: NB
Postal Code: E1W 1B7
Office Phone: (506) 727-4444
Publisher Name: Francis Sonier
Editor Name: Gaetan Chiasson
Advertising Executive Name: Carole Shabot Roy

KINGSTON

THE KINGSTON WHIG-STANDARD

Publication Website: www.thewhig.com
Parent Company: Postmedia Network Inc.
Corporate Website: www.postmedia.com
Publication Street Address: 6 Cataraqui St.
Province: NB
Postal Code: E3B 2T5
Office Phone: (506) 458-6435
Publisher Name: Jamie Irving
Editor Name: Richard Foot
Advertising Executive Name: Paul MacIntosh

KITCHENER

THE RECORD

Publication Website: www.therecord.com
Parent Company: Metroland Media Group Ltd.; Torstar Corporation
Corporate Website: www.metroland.com
Publication Street Address: 160 King St. East
Province: NB
Postal Code: E1C 8P3
Office Phone: (506) 859-4945
Publisher Name: Jamie Irving
Editor Name: Erica Bajer
Advertising Executive Name: Andrew Bishop

LETHBRIDGE

THE LETHBRIDGE HERALD

Publication Website: www.lethbridgeherald.com
Parent Company: ALTA Newspaper Group; Glacier Media
Corporate Website: www.glaciermedia.ca
Publication Street Address: 504 7th St. S.
Province: NB
Postal Code: E2L 3V8
Office Phone: (506) 632-8888
Publisher Name: Jamie Irving
Editor Name: Jackson Doughart
Advertising Executive Name: Michele Horncastle

Canadian Daily Newspapers

LONDON
THE LONDON FREE PRESS
Publication Website: www.lfpress.com
Parent Company: Postmedia Network Inc.
Corporate Website: www.postmedia.com
Publication Street Address: 210 Dundas Street, Suite 201
Province: NL
Postal Code: A1E 4N1
Office Phone: (709) 364-6300
Editor Name: Steve Bartlett

MEDICINE HAT
MEDICINE HAT NEWS
Publication Website: www.medicinehatnews.com
Parent Company: ALTA Newspaper Group; Glacier Media
Corporate Website: www.glaciermedia.ca
Publication Street Address: 3257 Dunmore Rd SE
Province: NS
Postal Code: B3J 2T2
Office Phone: (902) 426-2811
Publisher Name: Sarah Dennis
Editor Name: Paul O'Connell
Advertising Executive Name: Shelly Phillips

MONCTON
TIMES & TRANSCRIPT
Publication Website: www.tj.news/timesandtranscript.ca
Parent Company: Brunswick News, Inc.
Publication Street Address: 939 Main St.
Province: NS
Postal Code: B1P 6K6
Office Phone: (902) 564-5451
Editor Name: Carl Fleming
Advertising Executive Name: Scott MacQuarrie

MONTREAL
LE DEVOIR
Publication Website: www.ledevoir.com
Parent Company: Le Devoir Inc.
Publication Street Address: 1265 Berri, 8th Floor
Province: ON
Postal Code: K8N 5H5
Office Phone: (613) 962-9171
Editor Name: Dave Vachon
Advertising Executive Name: Joe Southwell

MONTREAL
LE JOURNAL DE MONTREAL
Publication Website: www.journaldemontreal.com
Parent Company: Quebecor Inc.
Corporate Website: www.quebecor.com
Publication Street Address: 4545 Frontenac St.
Province: ON
Postal Code: N3S 5C9
Office Phone: (519) 756-2020
Editor Name: Kim Novak

MONTREAL
MONTREAL GAZETTE
Publication Website: www.montrealgazette.com
Parent Company: Postmedia Network Inc.
Corporate Website: www.postmedia.com
Publication Street Address: 1010 Sainte-Catherine St. W.
Province: ON
Postal Code: K6V 3H2
Office Phone: (613) 342-4441
Editor Name: Ron Zajac
Advertising Executive Name: Kerry Sammon

NIAGARA FALLS
NIAGARA FALLS REVIEW
Publication Website: www.niagarafallsreview.ca
Parent Company: Metroland Media Group Ltd.; Torstar Corporation
Corporate Website: www.metroland.com
Publication Street Address: 4424 Queen St
Province: ON
Postal Code: N7M 1E3
Office Phone: (519) 354-2000
Editor Name: Andy Cornell

NORTH BAY
NORTH BAY NUGGET
Publication Website: www.nugget.ca
Parent Company: Postmedia Network Inc.
Corporate Website: www.postmedia.com
Publication Street Address: 259 Worthington St. W.
Province: ON
Postal Code: K6H 1E2
Office Phone: (613) 933-3160
Editor Name: Hugo Rodriques
Advertising Executive Name: Kerry Sammon

OTTAWA
LE DROIT
Publication Website: www.ledroit.com
Parent Company: Coopérative nationale de l'information indépendante (CN2i)
Publication Street Address: 47 Rue Clarence, Bureau 222
Province: ON
Postal Code: L8N 3G3
Office Phone: (905) 526-3333
Publisher Name: Neil Oliver
Editor Name: Paul Berton
Advertising Executive Name: Len Offless

OTTAWA
OTTAWA CITIZEN
Publication Website: www.ottawacitizen.com
Parent Company: Postmedia Network Inc.
Corporate Website: www.postmedia.com
Publication Street Address: 1101 Baxter Rd.
Province: ON
Postal Code: K7L 4Z7
Office Phone: (613) 544-5000
Editor Name: Steve Serviss
Advertising Executive Name: Kerry Sammon

OTTAWA
THE OTTAWA SUN
Publication Website: www.ottawasun.com
Parent Company: Postmedia Network Inc.
Corporate Website: www.postmedia.com
Publication Street Address: 1101 Baxter Rd.
Province: ON
Postal Code: N2G 4E5
Office Phone: (519) 894-2231
Publisher Name: Donna Luelo
Editor Name: Jim Poling
Advertising Executive Name: Tamara Gostlin

OWEN SOUND
THE SUN TIMES
Publication Website: www.owensountimes.com
Parent Company: Postmedia Network Inc.
Corporate Website: www.postmedia.com
Publication Street Address: 290 9th St., East
Province: ON
Postal Code: N6A 5J3
Office Phone: (519) 679-1111
Editor Name: Joe Ruscitti
Advertising Executive Name: Lisa Catania

PEMBROKE
THE DAILY OBSERVER
Publication Website: www.thedailyobserver.ca
Parent Company: Postmedia Network Inc.
Corporate Website: www.postmedia.com
Publication Street Address: 100 Crandall St.
Province: ON
Postal Code: L2E 2L3
Office Phone: (905) 358-5711
Publisher Name: Neil Oliver
Editor Name: Angus Scott
Advertising Executive Name: Mike Thomson

PENTICTON
PENTICTON HERALD
Publication Website: www.pentictonherald.ca
Parent Company: Continental Newspapers Canada Ltd.; Okanagan Valley Newspaper Group
Publication Street Address: 101 - 186 Nanaimo Ave W
Province: ON
Postal Code: P1B 3B5
Office Phone: (705) 472-3200
Editor Name: Mark Sanford
Advertising Executive Name: Steve Page

PETERBOROUGH
THE PETERBOROUGH EXAMINER
Publication Website: www.thepeterboroughexaminer.com
Parent Company: Metroland Media Group Ltd.; Torstar Corporation
Corporate Website: www.metroland.com
Publication Street Address: 60 Hunter St. East
Province: ON
Postal Code: K1N 9K1
Office Phone: (613) 562-0111
Publisher Name: Éric Brousseau
Editor Name: Patrice Gaudreault
Advertising Executive Name: Sylvie Charrette

PRINCE ALBERT
PRINCE ALBERT DAILY HERALD
Publication Website: www.paherald.sk.ca
Parent Company: FolioJumpline Publishing Inc.
Publication Street Address: 30 10th St E
Province: ON
Postal Code: K2C 3M4
Office Phone: (613) 829-9100
Editor Name: Nicole MacAdam
Advertising Executive Name: Jon Stewart

QUEBEC
LE SOLEIL
Publication Website: www.lesoleil.com
Parent Company: Coopérative nationale de l'information indépendante (CN2i)
Publication Street Address: 410 Charest Blvd. East
Province: ON
Postal Code: K2H 5B1
Office Phone: (613) 829-9100
Editor Name: Nicole MacAdam
Advertising Executive Name: Jon Stewart

RED DEER
RED DEER ADVOCATE
Publication Website: www.reddeeradvocate.com
Parent Company: Black Press Group Ltd.
Corporate Website: www.blackpress.ca
Publication Street Address: 2950 Bremner Ave.
Province: ON
Postal Code: N4K 5P2
Office Phone: (519) 376-2250
Editor Name: Doug Edgar

REGINA
REGINA LEADERPOST
Publication Website: www.leaderpost.com
Parent Company: Postmedia Network Inc.
Corporate Website: www.postmedia.com
Publication Street Address: 1964 Park St.
Province: ON
Postal Code: K8A 0B1
Office Phone: (613) 732-3691
Editor Name: Anthony Dixon

SAGUENAY
LE QUOTIDIEN
Publication Website: www.lequotidien.com
Parent Company: Coopérative nationale de l'information indépendante (CN2i)
Publication Street Address: 1051 Talbot Blvd.
Province: ON
Postal Code: K9H 1G5
Office Phone: (705) 745-4641
Publisher Name: Neil Oliver
Editor Name: Kennedy Gordon
Advertising Executive Name: Michael Everson

SAINT CATHARINES
ST. CATHARINES STANDARD
Publication Website: www.stcatharinesstandard.ca
Parent Company: Metroland Media Group Ltd.; Torstar Corporation
Corporate Website: www.metroland.com
Publication Street Address: 55 King Street, Suite 600
Province: ON
Postal Code: L2R 7L4
Office Phone: (905) 684-7251
Publisher Name: Neil Oliver
Editor Name: Angus Scott
Advertising Executive Name: Mike Thomson

SAINT CATHARINES
WELLAND TRIBUNE
Publication Website: www.wellandtribune.ca
Parent Company: Metroland Media Group Ltd.; Torstar Corporation
Corporate Website: www.metroland.com
Publication Street Address: 55 King Street, Suite 600
Province: ON
Postal Code: L2R 7L4
Office Phone: (905) 732-2411
Publisher Name: Neil Oliver
Editor Name: Angus Scott
Advertising Executive Name: Mike Thomson

SAINT JOHN
THE TELEGRAPH-JOURNAL
Publication Website: www.telegraphjournal.com
Parent Company: Brunswick News, Inc.
Publication Street Address: 210 Crown St.
Province: ON
Postal Code: N5R 5Z2
Office Phone: (519) 631-2790
Editor Name: Don Biggs
Advertising Executive Name: Ian Dowding

SAINT THOMAS
ST. THOMAS TIMES-JOURNAL
Publication Website: www.stthomastimesjournal.com
Parent Company: Postmedia Network Inc.
Corporate Website: www.postmedia.com
Publication Street Address: 16 Hincks St.
Province: ON
Postal Code: N7T 7M8
Office Phone: (519) 344-3641
Editor Name: Peter Epp

Advertising Executive Name: Greg Holmes

SARNIA
THE OBSERVER (SARNIA)
Publication Website: www.theobserver.ca
Parent Company: Postmedia Network Inc.
Corporate Website: www.postmedia.com
Publication Street Address: 140 South Front St.
Province: ON
Postal Code: P6A 5M5
Office Phone: (705) 759-3030
Editor Name: Frank Rupnik
Advertising Executive Name: Maureen Montanini

SASKATOON
SASKATOON STARPHOENIX
Publication Website: www.thestarphoenix.com
Parent Company: Postmedia Network Inc.
Corporate Website: www.postmedia.com
Publication Street Address: 204 5th Ave. N.
Province: ON
Postal Code: N3Y 4L2
Office Phone: (519) 426-5710
Editor Name: Kimberly Novak
Advertising Executive Name: Sue Downs

SAULT SAINTE MARIE
THE SAULT STAR
Publication Website: www.saultstar.com
Parent Company: Postmedia Network Inc.
Corporate Website: www.postmedia.com
Publication Street Address: 145 Old Garden River Rd.
Province: ON
Postal Code: N5A 6S4
Office Phone: (519) 271-2222
Editor Name: Bruce Urquhart
Advertising Executive Name: Ian Dowding

SHERBROOKE
LA TRIBUNE
Publication Website: www.latribune.ca
Parent Company: Coopérative nationale de l'information indépendante (CN2i)
Publication Street Address: 1950 Roy St.
Province: ON
Postal Code: P3C 1X3
Office Phone: (705) 674-5271
Editor Name: Don MacDonald

SHERBROOKE
THE RECORD
Publication Website: www.sherbrookerecord.com
Parent Company: ALTA Newspaper Group; Glacier Media
Corporate Website: www.glaciermedia.ca
Publication Street Address: 6 Mallory
Province: ON
Postal Code: P7B 1A3
Office Phone: (807) 343-6200
Publisher Name: Clint Harris
Editor Name: Greg Giddens
Advertising Executive Name: Frank Augruso

SIMCOE
SIMCOE REFORMER
Publication Website: www.simcoereformer.ca
Parent Company: Postmedia Network Inc.
Corporate Website: www.postmedia.com
Publication Street Address: 50 Gilbertson Dr.
Province: ON
Postal Code: P4N 7G1
Office Phone: (705) 268-5050
Editor Name: Ron Grech
Advertising Executive Name: Lisa Wilson

ST. JOHN'S
THE TELEGRAM
Publication Website: www.thetelegram.com
Parent Company: SaltWire Network Inc.
Corporate Website: www.saltwire.com
Publication Street Address: 430 Topsail Rd
Province: ON
Postal Code: M4W3L4
Office Phone: (416) 383-2300
Editor Name: Rob Roberts
Advertising Executive Name: Darren Murphy

ST-LAURENT
JOURNAL MÉTRO
Publication Website: www.journalmetro.com
Parent Company: Métro Média
Corporate Website: www.metromedia.ca
Publication Street Address: 101 Marcel-Laurin Blvd., Suite 320
Province: ON
Postal Code: M2J 1P8
Office Phone: (416) 298-1933
Publisher Name: Cindy Gu
Editor Name: Jason Loftus
Advertising Executive Name: Henry Guo

STRATFORD
THE STRATFORD BEACON HERALD
Publication Website: www.stratfordbeaconherald.com
Parent Company: Postmedia Network Inc.
Corporate Website: www.postmedia.com
Publication Street Address: 59 Lorne Ave. E., Unit C
Province: ON
Postal Code: M5A 0N1
Office Phone: (416) 585-5000
Publisher Name: Phillip Crawley
Editor Name: David Walmsley
Advertising Executive Name: Mike Iker

SUDBURY
THE SUDBURY STAR
Publication Website: www.thesudburystar.com
Parent Company: Postmedia Network Inc.
Corporate Website: www.postmedia.com
Publication Street Address: 128 Pine Street Suite 201
Province: ON
Postal Code: M5E 1E6
Office Phone: (416) 367-2000
Publisher Name: John Boynton
Editor Name: Irene Gentle

SYDNEY
THE CAPE BRETON POST
Publication Website: www.capebretonpost.com
Parent Company: SaltWire Network Inc.
Corporate Website: www.saltwire.com
Publication Street Address: 255 George St.
Province: ON
Postal Code: M4W 3L4
Office Phone: (416) 947-2222
Editor Name: Adrienne Batra
Advertising Executive Name: Darren Murphy

THUNDER BAY
THE CHRONICLE-JOURNAL
Publication Website: www.chroniclejournal.com
Parent Company: Continental Newspapers Canada Ltd.
Publication Street Address: 75 S. Cumberland St.
Province: ON
Postal Code: N9A 7B4
Office Phone: (519) 255-5768
Editor Name: Craig Pearson
Advertising Executive Name: Amanda Reid

TIMMINS
THE TIMMINS DAILY PRESS
Publication Website: www.timminspress.com
Parent Company: Postmedia Network Inc.
Corporate Website: www.postmedia.com
Publication Street Address: 187 Cedar St. South
Province: ON
Postal Code: N4V 0A2
Office Phone: (519) 537-2341
Editor Name: Bruce Urquhart
Advertising Executive Name: Ian Dowding

TORONTO
NATIONAL POST
Publication Website: www.nationalpost.com
Parent Company: Postmedia Network Inc.
Corporate Website: www.postmedia.com
Publication Street Address: 365 Bloor St. East
Province: PE
Postal Code: C1A 4R7
Office Phone: (902) 629-6000
Editor Name: Jocelyne Lloyd
Advertising Executive Name: Colin Sly

TORONTO
THE EPOCH TIMES
Publication Website: www.theepochtimes.ca
Parent Company: Epoch Times Media Inc.
Publication Street Address: 344 Consumers Rd
Province: QC
Postal Code: J2G 9L4
Office Phone: (450) 375-4555
Publisher Name: Alain Turcotte
Editor Name: Isabelle Gaboriault
Advertising Executive Name: Sylvain Denault

TORONTO
THE GLOBE AND MAIL
Publication Website: www.theglobeandmail.com
Parent Company: The Globe and Mail Inc.
Publication Street Address: 351 King St. E., Suite 1600
Province: QC
Postal Code: H2K 4X4
Office Phone: (514) 985-3333
Publisher Name: Brian Myles
Editor Name: Marie-Andrée Chouinard
Advertising Executive Name: Richard Nguyen

TORONTO
TORONTO STAR
Publication Website: www.thestar.ca
Parent Company: Torstar Corporation
Corporate Website: www.torstar.com
Publication Street Address: 1 Yonge St.
Province: QC
Postal Code: H2H 2R7
Office Phone: (514) 521-4545
Publisher Name: Lyne Robitaille
Editor Name: Dany Doucet

TORONTO
TORONTO SUN
Publication Website: www.torontosun.com
Parent Company: Postmedia Network Inc.
Corporate Website: www.postmedia.com
Publication Street Address: 365 Bloor St. East, 6th Floor
Province: QC
Postal Code: H3B 5L1
Office Phone: (514) 987-2222
Editor Name: Lucinda Chodan
Advertising Executive Name: Angleo Pacitto

TRAIL
THE TRAIL TIMES
Publication Website: www.trailtimes.ca
Parent Company: Black Press Group Ltd.
Corporate Website: www.blackpress.ca
Publication Street Address: 1136 Cedar Ave
Province: QC
Postal Code: G1K 7J6
Office Phone: (418) 686-3233
Publisher Name: Gilles Carignan
Editor Name: Valérie Gaudreau
Advertising Executive Name: Réal Marcotte

TROIS-RIVIÈRES
LE NOUVELLISTE
Publication Website: www.lenouvelliste.ca
Parent Company: Coopérative nationale de l'information indépendante (CN2i)
Publication Street Address: 1920 Bellefeuille St.
Province: QC
Postal Code: G7H 5C1
Office Phone: (418) 545-4474
Publisher Name: Michel Simard
Editor Name: Denis Bouchard
Advertising Executive Name: Catherine Morency

VANCOUVER
THE PROVINCE
Publication Website: www.theprovince.com
Parent Company: Postmedia Network Inc.
Corporate Website: www.postmedia.com
Publication Street Address: 400 - 2985 Virtual Way
Province: QC
Postal Code: J1K 2X8
Office Phone: (819) 564-5450
Publisher Name: Alain Turcotte
Editor Name: Maurice Cloutier
Advertising Executive Name: Sylvain Denault

VANCOUVER
THE VANCOUVER SUN
Publication Website: www.vancouversun.com
Parent Company: Postmedia Network Inc.
Corporate Website: www.postmedia.com
Publication Street Address: 400 - 2985 Virtual Way
Province: QC
Postal Code: J1M 2E2
Office Phone: (819) 569-9525
Publisher Name: Sharon McCully
Editor Name: Gordon Lambie
Advertising Executive Name: Jerry Bryant

VANIER
LE JOURNAL DE QUEBEC
Publication Website: www.journaldequebec.com
Parent Company: Quebecor Inc.
Corporate Website: www.quebecor.com
Publication Street Address: 450 Béchard Ave.
Province: QC
Postal Code: H4N 2M3
Office Phone: (514) 286-1066
Publisher Name: Andrew Mulé
Editor Name: Sylviane Lussier
Advertising Executive Name: Patrick Marsan

VICTORIA
VICTORIA TIMES COLONIST
Publication Website: www.timescolonist.com
Parent Company: Glacier Media
Corporate Website: www.glaciermedia.ca
Publication Street Address: 2621 Douglas St.
Province: QC
Postal Code: G9A 3Y2
Office Phone: (819) 376-2501
Publisher Name: Alain Turcotte

Canadian Daily Newspapers

I-147

Editor Name: Stephan Frappier
Advertising Executive Name: Yves Neault

WINDSOR

THE WINDSOR STAR

Publication Website: www.windsorstar.com
Parent Company: Postmedia Network Inc.
Corporate Website: www.postmedia.com
Publication Street Address: 300 Ouellette Ave
Province: QC
Postal Code: G1M 2E9
Office Phone: (418) 683-1573
Editor Name: Sebastien Menard
Advertising Executive Name: Nathalie Langevin

WINNIPEG

THE WINNIPEG SUN

Publication Website: www.winnipegsun.com
Parent Company: Postmedia Network Inc.
Corporate Website: www.postmedia.com
Publication Street Address: 1700 Church Ave.
Province: SK
Postal Code: S6V 0Y5
Office Phone: (306) 764-4276
Publisher Name: Donna Pfeil
Editor Name: Peter Lozinski
Advertising Executive Name: Mitzi Munro

WINNIPEG

WINNIPEG FREE PRESS

Publication Website: www.winnipegfreepress.com
Parent Company: F.P. Canadian Newspapers Limited Partnership
Corporate Website: www.fpnewspapers.com
Publication Street Address: 1355 Mountain Ave.
Province: SK
Postal Code: S4P 3G4
Office Phone: (306) 781-5211
Editor Name: Heather Persson
Advertising Executive Name: Randy Bryden

WOODSTOCK

WOODSTOCK SENTINEL-REVIEW

Publication Website: www.woodstocksentinelreview.com
Parent Company: Postmedia Network Inc.
Corporate Website: www.postmedia.com
Publication Street Address: 1269 Commerce Way
Province: SK
Postal Code: S7K 2P1
Office Phone: (306) 657-6397
Editor Name: Heather Persson
Advertising Executive Name: Heath Mulligan

CANADIAN NEWSPAPER GROUPS

HALIFAX

THE CHRONICLE HERALD

Street Address: 2717 Joseph Howe Dr
Province: NS
Postal Code: B3J 2T2
Country: Canada
General Phone: (902) 426-2811
General Fax: (902) 426-1170
Website: http://www.thechronicleherald.ca
Year Founded: 1875
Personnel: G.W. Dennis (Pub.); Sarah Dennis (Pub./CEO/Vice Pres.); Mary Lou Croft (Dir., Cor. Admin.); Theresa Williams (HR Mgr.); Ken Jennex (Purchasing); Paul Jacquart (Adv. Mgr., Retail Sales); Pam Nauss-Redden (Mktg. Mgr.); Tracey King (Research Analyst/ROP Specialist); Jim LaPierre (Dir., Dist. and Log.); Terry O'Neil (Dir., News Admin.); Dan Leger (Dir., News Content); John Howitt (Asst. Dir., Design); Frank De Palma (Asst. Dir., Newsroom); Brian Ward (Assignment Ed., Day); Eva Hoare (Assignment Ed., Night); Christine Soucie (Books Ed.); Robert Howse (Editorial Page Ed.); Greg Guy (Entertainment Ed.); Margaret MacKay (Lifestyle Ed.); Barry Saunders (Director of Sales); Bruce MacCormack (Vice Pres., Bus. Devel.); Nancy Cook (Sales Dir.); Alex Liot (Mgr., Bus. Devel.); Claire McIlveen (Ed.); Jennifer Punch (Senior Mktg. Mgr.); Ian Scott (VP Operations); Shawn Woodford (Dir., Mktg. and Prod. Devel.)
Advertising (Open Inch Rate) Weekday/Saturday: CARDonline; Mechanical specifications: CARDonline

KELOWNA

OKANAGAN VALLEY NEWSPAPER GROUP

Street Address: 550 Doyle Ave
Province: BC
Postal Code: V1Y 7V1
Country: Canada
General Phone: (250) 762-4445
Website: http://www.kelownadailycourier.ca
Year Founded: 1904
Personnel: James Miller (Editor and Dir. of Content)
Newspapers: The Daily Courier, Kelowna; Penticton Herald, Penticton; Okanagan Advertiser, Armstrong

MISSISSAUGA

METROLAND MEDIA GROUP LTD.

Street Address: 3715 Laird Road, Unit 6
Province: ON
Postal Code: L5L 0A3
Country: Canada
General Phone: (866) 838-8960
General Fax: (905) 279-5103
Website: http://www.metroland.com
Personnel: Ian Oliver (Pres.); Kathie Bride (Vice Pres.); Tim Whittaker (Sr. Vice Pres.); Ian McLeod (Sr. Vice Pres.); Ian Proudfoot (Vice Pres.); Brenda Biller (Vice Pres., HR); Joe Anderson (Vice Pres.); Bruce Danford (Vice Pres.); Ron Lenyk (Vice Pres.); Ken Nugent (Vice Pres.); Carol Peddie (Vice Pres.); Gordon Paolucci; Kukle Terry (Vice President); Lois Tuffin (Ed-In-Chief); John Willems; Scott Miller Cressman; Tracy Magee-Graham; Haggert Peter (Editor-In-Chief); Terry Kukle (VP, Business Development & Acquisitions)
Newspapers: The Wasaga Sun, Wasaga Beach; Banner Post, Grimshaw; Belleville News, Belleville; Fort Erie Post, Thorold; Independent & Free Press, Georgetown; Ajax-pickering News Advertiser, Oshawa; The Alliston Herald, Alliston; Almaguin News, Burks Falls; Ancaster News, Stoney Creek; Arnprior Chronicle-Guide, Arnprior; Arthur Enterprise News, Mount Forest; The Aurora Banner, Aurora; The Barrie Advance, Barrie; Beach-Riverdale Mirror, Toronto; Belleville News Emc, Belleville; Bloor West Villager, Toronto; Bracebridge Examiner, Bracebridge; Bradford & West Gwillimbury Topic, Newmarket; Brampton Guardian, Mississauga; Brant News, Brantford; The Brighton Independent, Brighton; Brock Citizen, Cannington; The Burlington Post, Burlington; Caledon Enterprise, Bolton; Cambridge Times, Cambridge; The Carleton Place-almonte Canadian Gazette Emc, Smith Falls; City Centre Mirror, Toronto; Clarington This Week, Oshawa; Dundas Star News, Stoney Creek; Express, Meaford; The East York Mirror, Willowdale; The Elmira Independent, Elmira; The Erin Advocate, Erin; Etobicoke Guardian, Etobicoke; Times Advocate, Exeter; The Fergus-elora News Express, Fergus; The Flamborough Review, Waterdown; The Frontenac Gazette, Kingston; The Georgina Advocate, Keswick; Glanbrook Gazette, Caledonia; The Gravenhurst Banner, Gravenhurst; The Grimsby Lincoln News, Grimsby; The Guelph Mercury Tribune, Guelph; Guelph Tribune, Guelph; Hamilton Mountain News, Stoney Creek; The Hamilton Spectator, Hamilton; Huntsville Forester, Huntsville; Innisfil Journal, Barrie; Kanata Kourier-standard Emc, Ottawa; Kawartha Lakes This Week, Lindsay; Kemptville Advance Emc, Smiths Falls; Kingston Heritage Emc, Kingston; Kitchener Post, Kitchener; The Listowel Banner, Listowel; Manotick News Emc, Ottawa; Markham Economist & Sun, Markham; The Mirror, Midland; The Milton Canadian Champion, Milton; Minto Express, Palmerston; Mississauga News, Mississauga; The Mount Forest Confederate, Mount Forest; The Muskokan, Bracebridge; Nepean-barrhaven News Emc, Ottawa; New Hamburg Independent, New Hamburg; The Newmarket Era-banner, Newmarket; North York Mirror, Toronto; Northumberland News, Cobourg; Niagara This Week, Thorold; Oakville Beaver, Oakville; The Orangeville Banner, Orangeville; Orillia Today, Orillia; Orleans News Emc, Ottawa; Oshawa-whitby This Week, Oshawa; Ottawa East Emc, Ottawa; Ottawa South Emc, Ottawa; Ottawa West Emc, Ottawa; The Parkdale Villager, Toronto; Parry Sound Beacon Star, Parry Sound; Parry Sound North Star, Parry Sound; The Perth Courier Emc, Smith Falls; Peterborough This Week, Peterborough; The Port Perry Star, Port Perry; Quinte West Emc, Belleville; The Renfrew Mercury Emc, Renfrew; The Richmond Hill Liberal, Markham; The Grand River Sachem, Caledonia; The Scarborough Mirror, Toronto; Smiths Falls Record News Emc, Smiths Falls; South Asian Focus, Brampton; St. Lawrence News, Brockville; St. Mary's Journal Argus, St Marys; St. Thomas/elgin Weekly News, Saint Thomas; The Stayner Sun, Wasaga Beach; The Stittsville News, Ottawa; Stoney Creek News, Stoney Creek; Stratford Gazette, Stratford; Collingwood Connection, Collingwood; Uxbridge Times-journal, Uxbridge; Vaughan Citizen, Vaughan; Walkerton Herald-times, Walkerton; Waterloo Chronicle, Waterloo; The Record, Kitchener; West Carleton Review, Arnprior; The Wingham Advance-times, Wingham; The York Guardian, Toronto

MONTREAL

QUEBECOR COMMUNICATIONS, INC.

Street Address: 612 Saint-Jacques Street
Province: QC
Postal Code: H3C 4M8
Country: Canada
General Phone: (514) 380-1999
Website: http://www.quebecor.com
Notes: Pierre Karl Peladeau (Pres., CEO); Jean-Francois Pruneau (Sr. VP, CFO)

MONTREAL

TRANSCONTINENTAL MEDIA

Street Address: 1 Place Ville Marie, Ste. 3315
Province: ON
Postal Code: H3B 3N2
Country: Canada
General Phone: (514) 954-4000
General Fax: (514) 954-4016
Website: http://www.transcontinental.com
Year Founded: 1976
Personnel: Remi Marcoux (Exec. Chrmn. of the Bd.); Francois Olivier (Pres./CEO); Benoit Huard (CFO); Natalie Larivi (Pres., Transcontinental Media Inc.); Christine Desaulniers (Vice Pres./Chief Legal Officer/Cor. Sec.); Isabelle Marcoux (Vice Pres. Corp. Devel.); Marc N. Ouellette (Sr. Vice Pres., Transcontinental Media Inc./Newspapaper Grp.); Nessa Brendergast (Media Relations Dir.)
Newspapers: Amherst Daily News, Amherst; Broadview Express, Grenfell; Charlesbourg Express, Quebec; Cites Nouvelles, Dorval; Courrier-ahuntsic, Saint Laurent; Courrier-laval, Laval; Courrier-sud, Nicolet; Grenfell Sun, Grenfell; Hants Journal, Windsor; Harbour Breton Coaster, Harbour Breton; Hebdo Rive Nord, Repentigny; Hebdo Du St. Maurice, Shawinigan; Journal L'actuel, Quebec; L'action, Joliette; L'artisan, Repentigny; L'avenir De L'erable, Plessisville; L'echo De La Tuque, La Tuque; L'echo De Maskinonge, Louiseville; L'express, Drummondville; L'hebdo Journal, Trois-Rivieres; L'hebdo Mekinac/des Chenaux, Shawinigan; La Nouvelle, Victoriaville; La Petite Nation, Saint Andre-Avellin; La Revue De Gatineau, Gatineau; La Voix Populaire, Lasalle; La Voix Du Sud, Lac Etchemin; Le Courrier Bordeaux/cartierville, Saint Laurent; Le Lac St. Jean, Alma; Northern Pen, Saint Anthony; Prince Albert Daily Herald, Prince Albert; Progres Saint-leonard, Saint Leonard; Radville Deep South Star, Radville; Register, Kentville; Saint-laurent News, Saint Laurent; The Advance, Liverpool; The Advertiser, Kentville; The Advertiser, Grand Falls; The Aurora, Labrador City; The Citizen-record, Amherst; The Coast Guard, Shelburne; The Compass, Carbonear; The Daily News, Dartmouth; The Daily News, Truro; The Gander Beacon, Gander; The Gulf News, Port aux Basques; The Labradorian, Happy Valley; The Moose Jaw Times-Herald - OOB, Moose Jaw; The News, New Glasgow; The Nor'wester, Springdale; The Packet, Clarenville; The Pilot, Lewisporte; The Sackville Tribune-post, Sackville; The Southern Gazette, Marystown; The Southwest Booster, Swift Current; The Spectator, Middleton; The Star, Ottawa; The Telegram, Saint John's; The Vanguard, Yarmouth; The Westmount Examiner, Westmount; Transcontinental Medias, Montreal; The Digby County Courier, Digby; The Chronicle, Dorval; L'etoile Du Lac, Roberval; The Oxbow Herald, Oxbow; The Georgian, Stephenville; Seaway News, Cornwall

SURREY

BLACK PRESS GROUP LTD.

Street Address: Unit 210 - 15288 54A Ave
Province: BC
Postal Code: V3S 6T4
Country: Canada
General Phone: (604) 575-2744
General Fax: (604) 575-5329
Website: http://www.blackpress.ca
Year Founded: 1975
Notes: In the U.S., Black Press owns Sound Publishing Inc. and Oahu Publications, publishers of the Honolulu Star Advertiser as well as the Akron Beacon Journal and San Francisco Examiner and SF Weekly newspapers.
Personnel: David Black (Chair/Founder); Rick

O'Connor (Pres. and CEO); Sue Borthwick; Rebecca Contrell (EA); Oliver Sommer (Nat'l Acct. Mgr.)

Newspapers: Kelowna Capital News, Kelowna; Juneau Empire, Juneau; Peninsula Clarion, Kenai; 100 Mile House Free Press, 100 Mile House; Alberni Valley News, Port Alberni; Shuswap Market News, Salmon Arm; The Abbotsford News, Abbotsford; The Agassiz-harrison Observer, Agassiz; Alberni Valley Times, Port Alberni; The Aldergrove Star, Aldergrove; Arrow Lakes News, Nakusp; The Ashcroft-Cache Creek Journal, Ashcroft; Barriere Star Journal, Barriere; The Boundary Creek Times, Greenwood; Burns Lakes District News, Burns Lake; Caledonia Courier, Fort St. James; The Campbell River Mirror, Campbell River; The Castlegar News, Castlegar; The Chilliwack Progress, Chilliwack; North Thompson Times, Clearwater; Cloverdale Reporter, Surrey; Comox Valley Record, Courtenay; Cranbrook Daily Townsman, Cranbrook; Eagle Valley News, Salmon Arm; Golden Star, Golden; Goldstream Gazette, Sidney; The Grand Forks Gazette, Grand Forks; The Kimberley Daily Bulletin, Kimberley; Northern Sentinel - Kitimat, Kitimat; Kootenay Advertiser - OOB, Cranbrook; The Ladysmith Chronicle, Ladysmith; The Lake Cowichan Gazette, Duncan; Lakeshore News, Salmon Arm; Langley Advance, Langley; Langley Times, Langley; The Maple Ridge News, Maple Ridge; Maple Ridge & Pitt Meadow Times - OOB, Langley; Mission City Record, Mission; Monday Magazine, Victoria; Nanaimo News Bulletin, Nanaimo; Nelson Star, Nelson; North Island Gazette, Port Hardy; North Island Midweek, Courtenay; Oak Bay News, Victoria; Parksville Qualicum Beach News, Parksville; The Peace Arch News, Surrey; The Peninsula News Review, Sidney; Penticton Western News, Penticton; Quesnel Cariboo Observer, Quesnel; Revelstoke Review, Revelstoke; Rossland News, Castlegar; Saanich News, Victoria; Salmon Arm Observer, Salmon Arm; Princeton Similkameen Spotlight, Princeton; The Smithers Interior News, Smithers; The Sooke News Mirror, Sooke; Summerland Review, Summerland; Surrey Now-leader, Surrey; The Terrace Standard, Terrace; The Free Press, Fernie; Tri-City News, Port Coquitlam; Westerly News, Ucluelet; Trail Daily Times, Trail; Vanderhoof Omineca Express, Vanderhoof; Victoria News, Victoria; The Williams Lake Tribune, Williams Lake; The Yukon Review, Yukon; The Bashaw Star, Ponoka; Castor Advance, Castor; Eckville Echo, Sylvan Lake; Ponoka News, Ponoka; Red Deer Advocate, Red Deer; Red Deer Express, Red Deer; Rimbey Review, Rimbey; Stettler Independent, Stettler; Sylvan Lake News, Sylvan Lake; Leduc-wetaskiwin Pipestone Flyer, Millet; The Arlington Times, Marysville; Bainbridge Island Review, Poulsbo; Bellevue Reporter, Bellevue; Bellingham Business Journal, Bellingham; Bothell/Kenmore Reporter, Kirkland; Bremerton Patriot-OOB, POULSBO; Central Kitsap Reporter, Poulsbo; Federal Way Mirror, Federal Way; Forks Forum, Forks; The Islands' Sounder, Eastsound; The Islands' Weekly, Lopez Island; Issaquah/ Sammamish Reporter, Bellevue; The Journal of the San Juan Islands, Friday Harbor; Kirkland Reporter, Kirkland; The Marysville Globe, Marysville; Mercer Island Reporter, Kirkland; Okanogan Valley Gazette-Tribune, Oroville; Port Orchard Independent, Port Orchard; Redmond Reporter, Kirkland; Renton Reporter, Kent; The Sequim Gazette, Sequim; Snoqualmie Valley Record, Snoqualmie; South Whidbey Record, Coupeville; Tacoma Daily Index, Tacoma; Tukwila Reporter, Kent; Vashon-Maury Island Beachcomber, Vashon; Veterans' Life-OOB, Silverdale; The Whidbey Examiner, Coupeville; Whidbey News Times, Coupeville; Friday Forward, Red Deer; Oahu Publications Inc., Honolulu; The Daily World, Aberdeen; BOnny Lake Sumner Courier, Sumner; Boulevard Chinese, Victoria; Chemainus Valley, Chemainus; Clearwater Times, Clearwater; Coast Mountian News, Bella Coola; Cowichan Valley News, Duncan; Creston Valley Advance, Creston; Haida Gwaii Observer, Queen Charlotte; Hawaii Tribune-Herald, Hilo; Hope Standard, Hope; Houston Today, Houston; Kaua'i Midweek, Kaua'i; Keremeos Review, Keremeos; Kingston Community, Kingston; Lacombe Express, Lacombe; Lake Country Calendar, Winfield; Metro HNL, Honolulu; Midweek, Honolulu; North Delta Reporter, North Delta; North Kitsap Herald, Kitsap; SF Weekly, San Francisco; Street Pulse, Honolulu; Garden ISland, Lihue; The Northern View, Prince Rupert; San Francisco Examiner, San Francisco; Vernon Morning Star, Vernon; West Hawaii Today, Kilua-Kona

TORONTO

POSTMEDIA NETWORK INC.

Street Address: 365 Bloor Street East
Province: ON
Postal Code: M4W 3L4
Country: Canada
General Phone: (416) 383-2300
Website: http://www.postmedia.com
Year Founded: 2010
Newspapers: National Post, Toronto; The Peace River Record-gazette, Peace River; The Calgary Sun, Calgary; Calgary Herald, Calgary; Daily Herald-Tribune, Grande Prairie; The Edmonton Sun, Edmonton; Edmonton Journal, Edmonton; The Province, Vancouver; The Vancouver Sun, Vancouver; The Winnipeg Sun, Winnipeg; The Stratford Beacon Herald, Stratford; The Chatham Daily News, Chatham; Observer & News (Pembroke), Pembroke; The Timmins Daily Press, Timmins; Brandtford Expositor, Brantford; Belleville Intelligencer, Belleville; Kenora Daily Miner & News, Kenora; The Kingston Whig-Standard, Kingston; The London Free Press, London; North Bay Nugget, North Bay; The Ottawa Citizen, Ottawa; The Ottawa Sun, Ottawa; The Observer (Sarnia), Sarnia; The Brockville Recorder and Times, Brockville; The Sault Star, Sault Sainte Marie; Woodstock Sentinel-Review, Woodstock; Simcoe Reformer, Simcoe; St. Thomas Times-Journal, Saint Thomas; Cornwall Standard-Freeholder, Cornwall; The Sudbury Star, Sudbury; Owensound Sun Times, Owen Sound; Toronto Sun, Toronto; The Windsor Star, Windsor; Montreal Gazette, Montreal; Regina LeaderPost, Regina; Saskatoon StarPhoenix, Saskatoon; Airdrie Echo, Airdrie; Bow Valley Crag & Canyon, Banff; Cochrane Times, Cochrane; Cold Lake Sun, Cold Lake; Devon Dispatch News, Devon; Drayton Valley Western Review, Drayton Valley; Edmonton Examiner, Edmonton; Edson Leader, Edson; Fairview Post, Fairview; Fort McMurray Today, Fort McMurray; The Fort Saskatchewan Record, Fort Saskatchewan; The Grove Examiner, Spruce Grove; Hanna Herald, Hanna; The High River Times, High River; The Hinton Parklander, Hinton; Lacombe Globe, Lacombe; Leduc Representative, Leduc; The Nanton News, Nanton; Pincher Creek Echo, Pincher Creek; Sherwood Park/ strathcona County News, Sherwood Park; The Stony Plain Reporter, Spruce Grove; Vulcan Advocate, Vulcan; Wetaskiwin Times, Wetaskiwin; The Whitecourt Star, Whitecourt; Vermilion Standard, Vermilion; Melfort Journal, Melfort; Nipawin Journal, Nipawin; Northeast Sun, Los Angeles; The Interlake Spectator, Stonewall; Morden Times, Winkler; The Red River Valley Echo, Altona; Selkirk Journal, Selkirk; The Stonewall Argus & Teulon Times, Stonewall; The Valley Leader, Carman; Winkler Times, Winkler; Chatham-Kent This Week, Chatham; Clinton News-record, Clinton; Cochrane Times-post, Cochrane; The County Weekly News, Picton; Wallaceburg Courier Press, Chatham; Delhi News-record, Delhi; The Elgin County Market (St. Thomas)-OOB, Saint Thomas; Strathroy Age Dispatch, Strathroy; Goderich Signal-star, Goderich; The Kincardine News, Kincardine; The Kingsville Reporter, Kingsville; Lake Of The Woods Enterprise, Kenora; Lake Shore Shopper (Tillsonburg), Tillsonburg; Londoner, London; The Lakeshore News, Tecumseh; The Lucknow Sentinel, Lucknow; The Mid-north Monitor, Elliot Lake; The Mitchell Advocate, Mitchell; Napanee Guide, Napanee; Northern News This Week (Kirkland Lake), Kirkland Lake; Paris Star, Brantford; The Post (Hanover), Hanover; Oxford Review (Woodstock)-OOB, Woodstock; Sarnia & Lambton County This Week, Sarnia; Sault Ste. Marie This Week, Sault Sainte Marie; Seaforth Huron Expositor, Seaforth; Shoreline Beacon, Port Elgin; Tecumseh Shoreline Week, Tecumseh; The Standard (Elliot Lake), Elliot Lake; The Strathroy Age Dispatch, Strathroy; The Tillsonburg News, Tillsonburg; The Tilbury Times, Tilbury; Timmins Times, Timmins; Trentonian, Trenton; The Wiarton Echo, Wiarton; The Chatham Daily News; La Nouvelle Beaumont News (Beaumont); Community Press (Belleville); Brockville This Week/Extra; The Complimentary (Cornwall); Edson Town & Country; The Standard Extra (Elliot Lake); Exeter Lakeshore Times-Advance; Weekender Times-Advance (Exeter); Fort McMurray This Week; Gananoque Reporter; Focus Magazine (Goderich); Goderich Super-Saver; The Peace Country Sun (Grande Prairie); Frontenac This Week; The Leduc-Wetaskiwin County Market; The Mayerthorpe Freelancer; The Nugget Extra (North Bay); Grey Bruce This Week (Owen Sound); The Graphic-Leader (Portage La Prairie); Prescott This Week; QC (Regina); Bridges (Saskatoon); Stratford Marketplace; Simcoe Reformer (TMC); Focus (Strathroy); West Elgin Chronicle; Kingsville Extra; LaSalle Post; Windsor Star Review; The Barrie Examiner - OOB, Barrie; Northumberland Today - OOB, Cobourg; Orillia Packet - OOB, Orillia; The Peterborough Examiner, Peterborough; St. Catharines Standard, Saint Catharine's; Welland Tribune, Welland; The Camrose Canadian, Camrose; Lloydminster Meridian Booster, Lloydminster; Strathmore Standard, Strathmore; The Daily Graphic, Portage la Prairie; Central Plains Herald Leader, Portage La Prairie; The Enterprise-bulletin, Collingwood; Fort Erie Shopping Times, Thorold; The Fort Erie Times, Fort Erie; The Reporter-OOB, Gananoque; In Port News, Port Colborne; The Ingersoll Times, Woodstock; The News (Lakeshore), Pembroke; The Niagara Advance, Virgil; The Northern Times, Kapuskasing; The Norwich Gazette, Woodstock; Pennysaver-OOB, Chatham; The Petrolia Topic, Sarnia; Thorold Niagara News, Saint Catharine's; Times-reformer, Simcoe; The Weekender, Kapuskasing; What's Up Muskoka, Bracebridge

TORONTO

TORSTAR

Street Address: One Yonge St.
Province: ON
Postal Code: M5E 1P9
Country: Canada
General Phone: (416) 869-4010
General Fax: (416) 869-4183
Website: http://torstar.ca
Notes: Torstar owns Metroland Media Group, which owns three daily newspapers.
Personnel: John Boynton (Pres., CEO); Lorenzo DeMarchi (VP, CFO)
Newspapers: Ajax-pickering News Advertiser, Oshawa; Cowichan Valley Citizen, Duncan; Creston Valley Advance, Creston; Hope Standard, Hope; Houston Today, Houston; Invermere Valley Echo, Invermere; Keremeos Review, Keremeos; Lake Country Calendar, Kelowna; The Morning Star, Vernon; Ancaster News, Stoney Creek; Annex Guardian, Toronto; Arthur Enterprise News, Mount Forest; Beach-Riverdale Mirror, Toronto; Bloor West Villager, Toronto; Bracebridge Examiner, Bracebridge; Brock Citizen, Cannington; Caledon Enterprise, Bolton; Cambridge Times, Cambridge; Clarington This Week, Oshawa; Collingwood Connection, Collingwood; Dresden-Bothwell Leader-Spirit (OOB), Dresden; Dundas Star News, Stoney Creek; Etobicoke Guardian, Etobicoke; Guelph Tribune, Guelph; Huntsville Forester, Huntsville; Independent & Free Press, Georgetown; Kawartha Lakes This Week, Lindsay; Markham Economist & Sun, Markham; Minto Express, Palmerston; New Hamburg Independent, New Hamburg; Niagara This Week, Thorold; North York Mirror, Toronto; Northumberland News, Cobourg; Oakville Beaver, Oakville; Orillia Today, Orillia; Oshawa-whitby This Week, Oshawa; Peterborough This Week, Peterborough; Shopping News, Oakville; St. Mary's Journal Argus, St Marys; The Burlington Post, Burlington; The East York Mirror, Willowdale; The Elmira Independent, Elmira; The Erin Advocate, Erin; The Fergus-elora News Express, Fergus; The Flamborough Review, Waterdown; The Gravenhurst Banner, Gravenhurst; The Grimsby Lincoln News, Grimsby; The Listowel Banner, Listowel; The Milton Canadian Champion, Milton; The Mirror, Midland; The Muskokan, Bracebridge; The Newmarket Era-banner, Newmarket; The Orangeville Banner, Orangeville; The Richmond Hill Liberal, Markham; The Scarborough Mirror, Toronto; The Stayner Sun, Wasaga Beach; The Wingham Advance-times, Wingham; The York Guardian, Toronto; Times Advocate, Exeter; Toronto Star, Toronto; Uxbridge Times-journal, Uxbridge; Walkerton Herald-times, Walkerton; Waterloo Chronicle, Waterloo

VANCOUVER

GLACIER MEDIA GROUP

Street Address: 2188 Yukon Street
Province: BC
Postal Code: V5Y 3P1
Country: Canada
General Phone: (604) 872-8565
General Fax: (604) 638-2453
Website: http://www.glaciermedia.ca
Year Founded: 1999
Personnel: Sam Grippo (Chairman); Jonathan J.L. Kennedy (Pres./CEO); Bruce W. Aunger (Dir.); Peter Kvarnstrom (Pres., Comm. Media); Orest Smysnuik (CFO)
Newspapers: New Westminster Record, New Westminster; The Northern Horizon, Dawson Creek; The Westender, Vancouver; Alaska Highway News, Fort Saint John; Assiniboia Times, Assiniboia; Barrhead Leader, Barrhead; Bonnyville Nouvelle, Bonnyville; Bowen Island Undercurrent, Bowen Island; Bridge River Lillooet News, Lillooet; Burnaby Now, Burnaby; Canora Courier, Canora; Carlyle Observer, Carlyle; Carstairs Courier, Olds; Coast Reporter, Sechelt; The Deloraine Times And Star, Deloraine; Delta Optimist, Delta; The Didsbury Review (OOB), Didsbury; Elk Point Review, Elk Point; Southeast Lifestyles, Estevan; Estevan Mercury, Estevan; Flin Flon Reminder, Flin Flon; The Humboldt Journal, Humboldt; Innisfail Province, Innisfail; The Kamsack Times, Canora; Lac La Biche Post, Lac La Biche; Melita New Era, Melita; North Shore News, North Vancouver; Okotoks Western Wheel, Okotoks; Olds Albertan, Olds; Pique Newsmagazine, Whistler; Powell River Peak, Powell River; Preeceville Progress, Canora; The Prince George Citizen, Prince George; Redvers Optimist (OOB), Redvers; The Reston Recorder, Reston; Richmond News, Richmond; Rocky Mountain Outlook, Canmore; Rocky View Weekly, Airdrie; Souris Plaindealer, Souris; Squamish Chief, Squamish; St. Albert Gazette, St. Albert; St. Paul Journal, Saint Paul; Sundre Round-up, Sundre; Battlefords News-optimist, North Battleford; Kipling Citizen, Kipling; Dawson Creek Mirror, Dawson Creek; Yorkton News Review, Yorkton; The Outlook, Outlook; The Tisdale Recorder, Tisdale; Parkland Review, Tisdale; Thompson Citizen/ nickel Belt News, Thompson; Victoria Times Colonist, Victoria; Tri-City News, Port Coquitlam; The Vancouver Courier, Vancouver; Virden Empire-advance, Virden; The Westlock News, Westlock; Westman Journal, Brandon; Weyburn Review, Weyburn; Weyburn This Week, WEYBURN; The Whistler Question, Whistler; Yorkton This Week, YORKTON

Section II

Services & Organizations in the U.S. & Canada

Professional, Business and Special Services 2
News, Picture and Syndicate Services 16
Newspaper Comics Section Groups and Networks 37
Equipment, Supplies and Services 37
Interactive Products and Services Companies 86
Advertising/Circulation Newspaper Promotion Services 103
Associations, Clubs and Press Clubs - City, State and Regional 104
Associations, Clubs and Press Clubs - National and International 113
U.S. State Newspaper Associations 124
Canadian Newspaper Associations 128
Circulation Audit Services 129
Clip Art Services 130
Clipping Bureaus 131
Electronic Clipping Bureaus 133
Newspaper Representatives - Foreign 134
Newspaper Representatives - National 135
Newspaper Representatives - State 137
Trade Unions in the Newspaper Field 141

PROFESSIONAL, BUSINESS AND SPECIAL SERVICES

AGRICULTURAL

AGWEEK

Street address 1: 375 2nd Ave N
Street address city: Grand Forks
Street address state: ND
Postal code: 58203-3707
County: Grand Forks
Country: USA
Mailing address 1: 375 2nd Ave North
Mailing city: Grand Forks
Mailing state: ND
Mailing zip: 58201
Office phone: (800) 477-6572 ext. 1236
Web address: www.agweek.com

THE DELMARVA FARMER

Street address 1: 7913 Industrial Park Rd
Street address city: Easton
Street address state: MD
Postal code: 21601-8603
County: Talbot
Country: USA
Mailing address 1: 7913 Industrial Park Rd
Mailing city: Easton
Mailing state: MD
Mailing zip: 21601-8603
Office phone: 410-822-3965
Office fax: 410-822-5068
Web address: www.americanfarm.com
General e-mail: editorial@americanfarm.com
Year established: 1978

URNER BARRY'S PRICE-CURRENT

Frequency: mon to fri
Street address 1: 182 Queens Blvd
Street address city: Bayville
Street address state: NJ
Postal code: 08721-2741
County: Ocean
Country: USA
Mailing address 1: PO Box 389
Mailing city: Toms River
Mailing state: NJ
Mailing zip: 08754-0389
Office phone: (732) 240-5330
Office fax: (732) 341-0891
Web address: www.urnerbarry.com
General e-mail: help@urnerbarry.com
Advertising (Open inch rate) Weekday/Saturday:
    Open inch rate $17.00

APPAREL

WOMEN'S WEAR DAILY

Frequency: mon to fri
Street address 1: 11175 Santa Monica Blvd
Street address city: Los Angeles
Street address state: CA
Postal code: 90025
County: New York
Country: USA
Mailing address 1: 11175 Santa Monica Blvd
Mailing city: Los Angeles
Mailing state: CA
Mailing zip: 90025
Office phone: (310) 484-2536
Web address: www.wwd.com
Year established: 1910
Advertising (Open inch rate) Weekday/Saturday:
    Open inch rate $322.00
Circulation Paid: 56562
Audited By: ABC

ARCHITECTURE

DAILY JOURNAL OF COMMERCE

Frequency: mon to fri
Street address 1: 921 SW Washington St
    Ste 210
Street address city: Portland
Street address state: OR
Postal code: 97205-2810
County: Multnomah
Country: USA
Mailing address 1: 921 SW Washington St Ste
    210
Mailing city: Portland
Mailing state: OR
Mailing zip: 97205-2810
Office phone: (503) 226-1311
Office fax: (503) 226-1315
Advertising phone: (503) 226-1311
Advertising fax: (503) 802-7219
Editorial fax: (503) 802-7239
Web address: www.djcoregon.com
General e-mail: newsroom@djcoregon.com
Advertising e-mail: rynni.henderson@djcoregon.com
Editorial e-mail: stephanie.basalyga@djcoregon.com
Year established: 1872
News services: AP, RN, TMS
Advertising (Open inch rate) Weekday/Saturday:
    Open inch rate $25.00
Digital Platform - Mobile: Apple`Android

DAILY JOURNAL OF COMMERCE

Frequency: mon to fri
Street address 1: 3445 N Causeway Blvd
    Ste 901
Street address city: Metairie
Street address state: LA
Postal code: 70002-3768
County: Jefferson
Country: USA
Mailing address 1: 3445 N. Causeway Blvd.
    Suite 901
Mailing city: Metairie
Mailing state: LA
Mailing zip: 70002
Office phone: (504) 834-9292
Office fax: (504) 832-3534
Web address: www.djcgulfcoast.com
General e-mail: mail@nopg.com
Advertising e-mail: anne.lovas@nopg.com
Editorial e-mail: greg.larose@nopg.com
Year established: 1922
Advertising (Open inch rate) Weekday/Saturday:
    Email or call for rates

DODGE CONSTRUCTION NEWS CHICAGO

Frequency: mon to fri
Street address 1: 130 E Randolph St
    Fl 14
Street address city: Chicago
Street address state: IL
Postal code: 60601-6207
County: Cook
Country: USA
Mailing address 1: 130 E Randolph St Fl 14
Mailing city: Chicago
Mailing state: IL
Mailing zip: 60601-6207
Office phone: (312) 233-7499
Office fax: (312) 233-7486
Web address: www.mediacourier.net
Year established: 1946
Advertising (Open inch rate) Weekday/Saturday:
    Open inch rate $34.00

THE DAILY NEWS

Frequency: mon to fri
Street address 1: 193 Jefferson Ave
Street address city: Memphis
Street address state: TN
Postal code: 38103-2322
County: Shelby
Country: USA
Mailing address 1: 193 JEFFERSON AVE
Mailing city: MEMPHIS
Mailing state: TN
Mailing zip: 38103-2339
Office phone: (901) 523-1561
Office fax: (901) 526-5813
Advertising phone: (901) 528-5283
Advertising fax: (901) 526-5813
Editorial phone: (901) 523-8501
Editorial fax: (901) 526-5813
Web address: www.memphisdailynews.com
General e-mail: jjenkins@memphisdailynews.com
Advertising e-mail: jjenkins@memphisdailynews.com
Editorial e-mail: releases@memphisdailynews.com
Year established: 1886
News services: CNS
Advertising (Open inch rate) Weekday/Saturday:
    Open inch rate $13.50 (legal)
Circulation Paid: 1000
Circulation Free: 2000
Audited By: USPS

THE DAILY REPORTER

Frequency: mon to fri
Street address 1: 225 E Michigan St
    Ste 300
Street address city: Milwaukee
Street address state: WI
Postal code: 53202-4900
County: Milwaukee
Country: USA
Mailing address 1: 225 E. Michigan St.
    Suite 300
Mailing city: Milwaukee
Mailing state: WI
Mailing zip: 53202
Office phone: (414) 276-0273
Office fax: (414) 276-4416
Editorial phone: (414) 225-1807
Web address: www.dailyreporter.com
General e-mail: news@dailyreporter.com
Advertising e-mail: squinn@dailyreporter.com
Editorial e-mail: dshaw@dailyreporter.com
Year established: 1897
News services: AP
Digital Platform - Mobile:
    Apple`Android`Windows
Digital Platform - Tablet: Apple
    iOS`Android`Windows 7
Circulation Paid: 3105

BANKING

AMERICAN BANKER

Frequency: mon to fri
Street address 1: 1 State St
    Fl 27
Street address city: New York
Street address state: NY
Postal code: 10004-1561
County: New York
Country: USA
Mailing address 1: 1 State St Fl 26
Mailing city: New York
Mailing state: NY
Mailing zip: 10004-1483
Office phone: (212) 803-8200
Office fax: (212) 843-9600
Advertising phone: (212) 803-8691
Editorial phone: (212) 803-8399
Web address: www.americanbanker.com
General e-mail: Liesbeth.Severiens@sourcemedia.com
Advertising e-mail: Liesbeth.Severiens@sourcemedia.com
Editorial e-mail: Dean.Anason@sourcemedia.com
Year established: 1835
News services: AP, RN, UPI
Advertising (Open inch rate) Weekday/Saturday:
    $6,280 (1/2P); $3,735 (1/4P); $3,370 (1/8P)
Digital Platform - Mobile:
    Apple`Android`Windows`Blackberry
Digital Platform - Tablet: Apple iOS
Circulation Paid: 2373
Audited By: AAM

BROOKLYN DAILY EAGLE & DAILY BULLETIN

Frequency: mon to fri
Street address 1: 16 Court St
    Ste 1208
Street address city: Brooklyn
Street address state: NY
Postal code: 11241-1012
County: Kings
Country: USA
Mailing address 1: 16 Court St Ste 1208
Mailing city: Brooklyn
Mailing state: NY
Mailing zip: 11241-1012
Office phone: (718) 858-2300
Office fax: (718) 858-8281
Web address: www.brooklyneagle.net
General e-mail: publisher@brooklyneagle.net
Advertising (Open inch rate) Weekday/Saturday:
    Open inch rate $24.00

DAILY RECORD

Frequency: mon to fri
Street address 1: 3323 Leavenworth St
Street address city: Omaha
Street address state: NE
Postal code: 68105-1915
County: Douglas
Country: USA
Mailing address 1: 3323 Leavenworth St
Mailing city: Omaha
Mailing state: NE
Mailing zip: 68105-1900
Office phone: (402) 345-1303
Office fax: (402) 345-2351
Web address: www.omahadailyrecord.com
General e-mail: lhenningsen@omahadailyrecord.com
Advertising e-mail: diane@omahadailyrecord.com
Editorial e-mail: lorraine@omahadailyrecord.com
Year established: 1886
News services: Associated Press, Creators Syndicate, U.S. News Syndicate
Advertising (Open inch rate) Weekday/Saturday:
    Open inch rate $7.25

INVESTOR'S BUSINESS DAILY

Frequency: m-mon to fri
Street address 1: 12655 Beatrice St
Street address city: Los Angeles
Street address state: CA
Postal code: 90066-7300
County: Los Angeles
Country: USA
Mailing address 1: 12655 Beatrice St
Mailing city: Los Angeles
Mailing state: CA
Mailing zip: 90066-7303
Office phone: (310) 448-6700
Office fax: (310) 577-7301
Advertising phone: (310) 448-6700
Advertising fax: (310) 577-7301
Editorial phone: (310) 448-6373
Editorial fax: (310) 577-7350
Web address: www.investors.com
Editorial e-mail: IBDnews@investors.com
Year established: 1984
News services: AP
Circulation Paid: 113547

PROFESSIONAL, BUSINESS AND SPECIAL SERVICES

II-3

Circulation Free: 5572
Audited By: AAM

MIAMI DAILY BUSINESS REVIEW

Frequency: mon to fri
Street address 1: 1 SE 3rd Ave
Ste 900
Street address city: Miami
Street address state: FL
Postal code: 33131-1706
County: Miami-Dade
Country: USA
Mailing address 1: PO Box 10589
Mailing city: Miami
Mailing state: FL
Mailing zip: 33101-0589
Office phone: (305) 377-3721
Office fax: (305) 374-0474
Advertising phone: (305) 347-6623
Advertising fax: (305) 347-6644
Editorial phone: (305) 347-6694
Editorial fax: (305) 347-6626
Web address: www.dailybusinessreview.com
General e-mail: DailyBusinessReview@alm.com
Advertising e-mail: ccurbelo@alm.com
Editorial e-mail: dlyons@alm.com
Year established: 1926
News services: AP, Bloomberg, Florida News Service
Advertising (Open inch rate) Weekday/Saturday:
Varies; http://www.dailybusinessreview.com/advertising.jsp
Advertising (Open inch rate) Sunday: N/A

PALM BEACH DAILY BUSINESS REVIEW

Frequency: mon to fri
Street address 1: 1 SE 3rd Ave
Ste 900
Street address city: Miami
Street address state: FL
Postal code: 33131-1706
County: Miami-Dade
Country: USA
Mailing address 1: 1 SE 3rd Ave
Suite 900
Mailing city: Miami
Mailing state: FL
Mailing zip: 33131-1700
Office phone: (305) 377-3721
Office fax: (561) 820-2077
Advertising phone: (305) 347-6623
Advertising fax: (305) 347-6644
Editorial phone: (305) 347-6694
Editorial fax: (305) 347-6626
Web address: www.dailybusinessreview.com
General e-mail: DailyBusinessReview@alm.com
Advertising e-mail: ccurbelo@alm.com
Editorial e-mail: dlyons@alm.com
Year established: 1979
News services: AP, Bloomberg, Florida News Service
Advertising (Open inch rate) Weekday/Saturday:
http://www.dailybusinessreview.com/advertising.jsp
Advertising (Open inch rate) Sunday: N/A

THE DAILY NEWS

Frequency: mon to fri
Street address 1: 193 Jefferson Ave
Street address city: Memphis
Street address state: TN
Postal code: 38103-2322
County: Shelby
Country: USA
Mailing address 1: 193 JEFFERSON AVE
Mailing city: MEMPHIS
Mailing state: TN
Mailing zip: 38103-2339
Office phone: (901) 523-1561
Office fax: (901) 526-5813
Advertising phone: (901) 528-5283
Advertising fax: (901) 526-5813
Editorial phone: (901) 523-8501
Editorial fax: (901) 526-5813
Web address: www.memphisdailynews.com
General e-mail: jjenkins@memphisdailynews.com

Advertising e-mail: jjenkins@memphisdailynews.com
Editorial e-mail: releases@memphisdailynews.com
Year established: 1886
News services: CNS
Advertising (Open inch rate) Weekday/Saturday:
Open inch rate $13.50 (legal)
Circulation Paid: 1000
Circulation Free: 2000
Audited By: USPS

THE DAILY RECORD

Frequency: mon to fri
Street address 1: 300 S Izard St
Street address city: Little Rock
Street address state: AR
Postal code: 72201-2114
County: Pulaski
Country: USA
Mailing address 1: PO Box 3595
Mailing city: Little Rock
Mailing state: AR
Mailing zip: 72203-3595
Office phone: (501) 374-5103
Office fax: (501) 372-3048
Web address: www.dailyrecord.us
General e-mail: bobby@dailydata.com
Advertising e-mail: jedwards@dailydata.com
Editorial e-mail: editor@dailydata.com
Year established: 1925
News services: NNS, TMS, DRNW, INS
Advertising (Open inch rate) Weekday/Saturday:
Column Inch Rate - $20.00
Circulation Paid: 3210
Circulation Free: 25
Audited By: USPS

THE DAILY RECORD

Frequency: mon to fri
Street address 1: 11 E Saratoga St
Street address city: Baltimore
Street address state: MD
Postal code: 21202-2115
County: Baltimore City
Country: USA
Mailing address 1: 11 E SARATOGA ST STE 1
Mailing city: BALTIMORE
Mailing state: MD
Mailing zip: 21202-2199
Office phone: (443) 524-8100
Office fax: (410) 752-2894
Advertising phone: (443) 524-8100
Advertising fax: (410) 752-2894
Editorial phone: (443) 524-8150
Editorial fax: (410) 752-2894
Web address: www.thedailyrecord.com
General e-mail: suzanne.huettner@thedailyrecord.com
Advertising e-mail: advertising@thedailyrecord.com
Editorial e-mail: tbaden@thedailyrecord.com
Year established: 1888
Advertising (Open inch rate) Weekday/Saturday:
Open inch rate $510.00/Day
Circulation Paid: 2572
Circulation Free: 384
Audited By: Sworn/Estimate/Non-Audited

THE LEGAL INTELLIGENCER

Frequency: mon to fri
Street address 1: 1617 John F Kennedy Blvd
Ste 1750
Street address city: Philadelphia
Street address state: PA
Postal code: 19103-1854
County: Philadelphia
Country: USA
Mailing address 1: 1617 John F Kennedy Blvd
Ste 1750
Mailing city: Philadelphia
Mailing state: PA
Mailing zip: 19103-1854
Office phone: (215) 557-2300
Office fax: (215) 557-2301
Advertising phone: (215) 557-2359
Advertising fax: (215) 557-2301
Editorial phone: (215) 557-2489
Editorial fax: (215) 557-2301

Web address: www.thelegalintelligencer.com
General e-mail: HGREZLAK@ALM.COM
Advertising e-mail: dchalphin@alm.com
Editorial e-mail: hgrezlak@alm.com
Year established: 1843
News services: AP

THE RECORD REPORTER

Frequency: Mon`Wed`Fri
Street address 1: 2025 N 3rd St
Ste 155
Street address city: Phoenix
Street address state: AZ
Postal code: 85004-1425
County: Maricopa
Country: USA

Office phone: (602) 417-9900
Office fax: (602) 417-9910
Web address: www.recordreporter.com
General e-mail: Diane_Heuel@dailyjournal.com
Advertising e-mail: record_reporter@dailyjournal.com
Editorial e-mail: diane_heuel@dailyjournal.com
Year established: 1914
Digital Platform - Mobile:
Apple`Android`Blackberry
Digital Platform - Tablet: Apple
iOS`Android`Windows 7`Blackberry Tablet OS

DAILY JOURNAL OF COMMERCE

Frequency: mon to fri
Street address 1: 3445 N Causeway Blvd
Ste 901
Street address city: Metairie
Street address state: LA
Postal code: 70002-3768
County: Jefferson
Country: USA
Mailing address 1: 3445 N. Causeway Blvd. Suite 901
Mailing city: Metairie
Mailing state: LA
Mailing zip: 70002
Office phone: (504) 834-9292
Office fax: (504) 832-3534
Web address: www.djcgulfcoast.com
General e-mail: mail@nopg.com
Advertising e-mail: anne.lovas@nopg.com
Editorial e-mail: greg.larose@nopg.com
Year established: 1922
Advertising (Open inch rate) Weekday/Saturday:
Email or call for rates

DAILY RECORD

Frequency: mon to fri
Street address 1: 3323 Leavenworth St
Street address city: Omaha
Street address state: NE
Postal code: 68105-1915
County: Douglas
Country: USA
Mailing address 1: 3323 Leavenworth St
Mailing city: Omaha
Mailing state: NE
Mailing zip: 68105-1900
Office phone: (402) 345-1303
Office fax: (402) 345-2351
Web address: www.omahadailyrecord.com
General e-mail: lhenningsen@omahadailyrecord.com
Advertising e-mail: diane@omahadailyrecord.com
Editorial e-mail: lorraine@omahadailyrecord.com
Year established: 1886
News services: Associated Press, Creators Syndicate, U.S. News Syndicate
Advertising (Open inch rate) Weekday/Saturday:
Open inch rate $7.25

TACOMA DAILY INDEX

Frequency: mon to fri
Street address 1: 402 Tacoma Ave S
Ste 200
Street address city: Tacoma
Street address state: WA
Postal code: 98402-5400

County: Pierce
Country: USA
Mailing address 1: 402 Tacoma Ave S Ste 200
Mailing city: Tacoma
Mailing state: WA
Mailing zip: 98402-5400
Office phone: (253) 627-4853
Office fax: (253) 627-2253
Advertising phone: (253) 627-4853
Advertising fax: (253) 627-2253
Editorial phone: (253) 627-4853
Editorial fax: (253) 627-2253
Other phone: (253) 627-4853
Web address: www.tacomadailyindex.com
General e-mail: legals@tacomadailyindex.com
Advertising e-mail: publisher@tacomadailyindex.com
Editorial e-mail: editor@tacomadailyindex.com
Year established: 1890
News services: American Court & Commercial Printing
Advertising (Open inch rate) Weekday/Saturday:
Open inch rate $9.65

THE DAILY NEWS

Frequency: mon to fri
Street address 1: 193 Jefferson Ave
Street address city: Memphis
Street address state: TN
Postal code: 38103-2322
County: Shelby
Country: USA
Mailing address 1: 193 JEFFERSON AVE
Mailing city: MEMPHIS
Mailing state: TN
Mailing zip: 38103-2339
Office phone: (901) 523-1561
Office fax: (901) 526-5813
Advertising phone: (901) 528-5283
Advertising fax: (901) 526-5813
Editorial phone: (901) 523-8501
Editorial fax: (901) 526-5813
Web address: www.memphisdailynews.com
General e-mail: jjenkins@memphisdailynews.com
Advertising e-mail: jjenkins@memphisdailynews.com
Editorial e-mail: releases@memphisdailynews.com
Year established: 1886
News services: CNS
Advertising (Open inch rate) Weekday/Saturday:
Open inch rate $13.50 (legal)
Circulation Paid: 1000
Circulation Free: 2000
Audited By: USPS

THE DAILY REPORTER

Frequency: mon to fri
Street address 1: 225 E Michigan St
Ste 300
Street address city: Milwaukee
Street address state: WI
Postal code: 53202-4900
County: Milwaukee
Country: USA
Mailing address 1: 225 E. Michigan St.
Suite 300
Mailing city: Milwaukee
Mailing state: WI
Mailing zip: 53202
Office phone: (414) 276-0273
Office fax: (414) 276-4416
Editorial phone: (414) 225-1807
Web address: www.dailyreporter.com
General e-mail: news@dailyreporter.com
Advertising e-mail: squinn@dailyreporter.com
Editorial e-mail: dshaw@dailyreporter.com
Year established: 1897
News services: AP
Digital Platform - Mobile:
Apple`Android`Windows
Digital Platform - Tablet: Apple
iOS`Android`Windows 7
Circulation Paid: 3105

THE RECORD REPORTER

Frequency: Mon`Wed`Fri
Street address 1: 2025 N 3rd St

Ste 155
Street address city: Phoenix
Street address state: AZ
Postal code: 85004-1425
County: Maricopa
Country: USA

Office phone: (602) 417-9900
Office fax: (602) 417-9910
Web address: www.recordreporter.com
General e-mail: Diane_Heuel@dailyjournal.com
Advertising e-mail: record_reporter@dailyjournal.com
Editorial e-mail: diane_heuel@dailyjournal.com
Year established: 1914
Digital Platform - Mobile: Apple`Android`Blackberry
Digital Platform - Tablet: Apple iOS`Android`Windows 7`Blackberry Tablet OS

BUSINESS

GREATER BATON ROUGE BUSINESS REPORT

Frequency: Bi-Weekly
Street address 1: 9029 Jefferson Hwy
Ste 300
Street address city: Baton Rouge
Street address state: LA
Postal code: 70809-2417
County: East Baton Rouge
Country: USA
Mailing address 1: 9029 Jefferson Hwy Ste 300
Mailing city: Baton Rouge
Mailing state: LA
Mailing zip: 70809-2417
Office phone: (225) 928-1700
Office fax: (225) 928-5019
Other phone: (225) 928-8899
Web address: businessreport.com
Editorial e-mail: editor@businessreport.com
Year established: 1982
Circulation Paid: 1585
Circulation Free: 8640
Audited By: CVC

DAILY COMMERCIAL RECORD

Frequency: mon to fri
Street address 1: 706 Main St Bsmt
Street address city: Dallas
Street address state: TX
Postal code: 75202-3620
County: Dallas
Country: USA
Mailing address 1: 706 Main St Bsmt
Mailing city: Dallas
Mailing state: TX
Mailing zip: 75202-3699
Office phone: (214) 741-6366
Office fax: (214) 741-6373
Web address: www.dailycommercialrecord.com
General e-mail: dcr@dailycommercialrecord.com
Advertising (Open inch rate) Weekday/Saturday: Open inch rate $14.76

DAILY COURT REVIEW

Frequency: mon to fri
Street address 1: 8 Greenway Plz
Ste 101
Street address city: Houston
Street address state: TX
Postal code: 77046-0830
County: Harris
Country: USA
Mailing address 1: PO Box 1889
Mailing city: Houston
Mailing state: TX
Mailing zip: 77251-1889
Office phone: (713) 869-5434
Office fax: (713) 869-8887
Editorial phone: (713) 869-5434
Web address: www.dailycourtreview.com
Editorial e-mail: editor@dailycourtreview.com
Year established: 1889
News services: RN, National Newspaper Association, Texas Press Association
Advertising (Open inch rate) Weekday/Saturday: Open inch rate $16.80

DAILY JOURNAL OF COMMERCE

Frequency: mon to fri
Street address 1: 921 SW Washington St
Ste 210
Street address city: Portland
Street address state: OR
Postal code: 97205-2810
County: Multnomah
Country: USA
Mailing address 1: 921 SW Washington St Ste 210
Mailing city: Portland
Mailing state: OR
Mailing zip: 97205-2810
Office phone: (503) 226-1311
Office fax: (503) 226-1315
Advertising phone: (503) 226-1311
Advertising fax: (503) 802-7219
Editorial fax: (503) 802-7239
Web address: www.djcoregon.com
General e-mail: newsroom@djcoregon.com
Advertising e-mail: rynni.henderson@djcoregon.com
Editorial e-mail: stephanie.basalyga@djcoregon.com
Year established: 1872
News services: AP, RN, TMS
Advertising (Open inch rate) Weekday/Saturday: Open inch rate $25.00
Digital Platform - Mobile: Apple`Android

DAILY RECORD

Frequency: mon to fri
Street address 1: 3323 Leavenworth St
Street address city: Omaha
Street address state: NE
Postal code: 68105-1915
County: Douglas
Country: USA
Mailing address 1: 3323 Leavenworth St
Mailing city: Omaha
Mailing state: NE
Mailing zip: 68105-1900
Office phone: (402) 345-1303
Office fax: (402) 345-2351
Web address: www.omahadailyrecord.com
General e-mail: lhenningsen@omahadailyrecord.com
Advertising e-mail: diane@omahadailyrecord.com
Editorial e-mail: lorraine@omahadailyrecord.com
Year established: 1886
News services: Associated Press, Creators Syndicate, U.S. News Syndicate
Advertising (Open inch rate) Weekday/Saturday: Open inch rate $7.25

DAILY REPORT

Frequency: mon to fri
Street address 1: 190 Pryor St SW
Street address city: Atlanta
Street address state: GA
Postal code: 30303-3607
County: Fulton
Country: USA
Mailing address 1: 190 Pryor St SW
Mailing city: Atlanta
Mailing state: GA
Mailing zip: 30303-3607
Office phone: (404) 521-1227
Office fax: (404) 523-5924
Web address: www.dailyreportonline.com
General e-mail: fcdr@amlaw.com
Year established: 1890
Advertising (Open inch rate) Weekday/Saturday: Open inch rate $1,800.00 (page)

FINANCE AND COMMERCE

Frequency: tues to sat
Street address 1: 222 South Ninth Street
Suite 900, Campbell Mithun Tower
Street address city: Minneapolis
Street address state: MN
Postal code: 55402
County: Hennepin
Country: USA
Mailing address 1: 222 South Ninth Street, Suite 900, Campbell Mithun Tower
Mailing city: Minneapolis
Mailing state: MN
Mailing zip: 55402
Office phone: (612) 333-4244
Office fax: (612) 333-3243
Advertising phone: (612) 584-1534
Editorial phone: (612) 584-1556
Other phone: (877) 615-9536
Web address: www.finance-commerce.com
General e-mail: service@bridgetowermedia.com
Year established: 1887
News services: AP
Advertising (Open inch rate) Weekday/Saturday: Open inch rate $12.00

METROPOLITAN NEWS-ENTERPRISE

Frequency: mon to fri
Street address 1: 210 S Spring St
Street address city: Los Angeles
Street address state: CA
Postal code: 90012-3710
County: Los Angeles
Country: USA
Mailing address 1: 210 S Spring St
Mailing city: Los Angeles
Mailing state: CA
Mailing zip: 90012-3710
Office phone: (213) 346-0033
Office fax: (213) 687-3886
Web address: www.metnews.com
General e-mail: news@metnews.com
Year established: 90012
News services: AP
Advertising (Open inch rate) Weekday/Saturday: Open inch rate $6.00

SAN FERNANDO VALLEY BUSINESS JOURNAL

Frequency: Bi-Weekly, Mondays
Street address 1: 21550 Oxnard St
Ste 540
Street address city: Woodland Hills
Street address state: CA
Postal code: 91367
County: Los Angeles
Country: USA
Mailing address 1: 21550 Oxnard St
Ste 540
Mailing city: Woodland Hills
Mailing state: CA
Mailing zip: 91367
Office phone: 818-676-1750
Office fax: 818-676-1747
Web address: sfvbj.com
General e-mail: circulation@labusinessjournal.com
Advertising e-mail: dglezerman@sfvbj.com
Editorial e-mail: ccrumpley@sfvbj.com
Year established: 2001
Circulation Paid: 2673
Circulation Free: 2060
Audited By: CVC

THE DAILY COMMERCIAL RECORDER

Frequency: mon to fri
Street address 1: 301 Avenue E
Street address city: San Antonio
Street address state: TX
Postal code: 78205-2006
County: Bexar
Country: USA
Mailing address 1: P.O. Box 2171
Mailing city: San Antonio
Mailing state: TX
Mailing zip: 78297
Office phone: (210) 250-2438
Office fax: (210) 250-2360
Web address: www.primetimenewspapers.com
General e-mail: dcr@primetimenewspapers.com
News services: ACCN, Creator Syndicates, LAT-WP, National American Press Syndicate, NYT.
Advertising (Open inch rate) Weekday/Saturday: Open inch rate $25.00

THE DAILY DEAL

Frequency: mon to fri
Street address 1: 14 Wall St
Fl 15
Street address city: New York
Street address state: NY
Postal code: 10005-2139
County: New York
Country: USA
Mailing address 1: 14 Wall St Fl 15
Mailing city: New York
Mailing state: NY
Mailing zip: 10005-2139
Office phone: (212) 313-9200
Office fax: (212) 545-8442
Advertising phone: (212) 313-9264
Editorial phone: (212) 313-9293
Web address: www.thedeal.com
General e-mail: advertising@thedeal.com
Editorial e-mail: epaisley@thedeal.com; rteitelman@thedeal.com

THE DAILY JOURNAL

Frequency: mon to fri
Street address 1: 1114 W 7th Ave
Ste 100
Street address city: Denver
Street address state: CO
Postal code: 80204-4455
County: Denver
Country: USA
Mailing address 1: 1114 W 7th Ave Ste 100
Mailing city: Denver
Mailing state: CO
Mailing zip: 80204-4455
Office phone: (303) 756-9995
Office fax: (303) 756-4465
Advertising phone: (303) 584-6737
Advertising fax: (303) 584-6717
Editorial phone: (303) 584-6724
Editorial fax: (303) 756-4465
Web address: www.colorado.construction.com
Year established: 1897
Advertising (Open inch rate) Weekday/Saturday: Open inch rate $25.20

THE DAILY LEGAL NEWS AND CLEVELAND RECORDER

Frequency: tues to sat
Street address 1: 2935 Prospect Ave E
Street address city: Cleveland
Street address state: OH
Postal code: 44115-2607
County: Cuyahoga
Country: USA
Mailing address 1: 2935 Prospect Ave E
Mailing city: Cleveland
Mailing state: OH
Mailing zip: 44115-2688
Office phone: (216) 696-3322
Office fax: (216) 696-6329
Web address: www.dln.com
General e-mail: dln@dln.com
Advertising e-mail: ads@dln.com
Editorial e-mail: editor@dln.com
Year established: 1885
News services: AP, National Newspaper Association, Ohio Newspaper Association
Advertising (Open inch rate) Weekday/Saturday: Open inch rate $16.00

THE DAILY NEWS

Frequency: mon to fri
Street address 1: 193 Jefferson Ave
Street address city: Memphis
Street address state: TN

PROFESSIONAL, BUSINESS AND SPECIAL SERVICES

Postal code: 38103-2322
County: Shelby
Country: USA
Mailing address 1: 193 JEFFERSON AVE
Mailing city: MEMPHIS
Mailing state: TN
Mailing zip: 38103-2339
Office phone: (901) 523-1561
Office fax: (901) 526-5813
Advertising phone: (901) 528-5283
Advertising fax: (901) 526-5813
Editorial phone: (901) 523-8501
Editorial fax: (901) 526-5813
Web address: www.memphisdailynews.com
General e-mail: jjenkins@memphisdailynews.com
Advertising e-mail: jjenkins@memphisdailynews.com
Editorial e-mail: releases@memphisdailynews.com
Year established: 1886
News services: CNS
Advertising (Open inch rate) Weekday/Saturday:
 Open inch rate $13.50 (legal)
Circulation Paid: 1000
Circulation Free: 2000
Audited By: USPS

THE DAILY RECORD

Frequency: mon to fri
Street address 1: 300 S Izard St
Street address city: Little Rock
Street address state: AR
Postal code: 72201-2114
County: Pulaski
Country: USA
Mailing address 1: PO Box 3595
Mailing city: Little Rock
Mailing state: AR
Mailing zip: 72203-3595
Office phone: (501) 374-5103
Office fax: (501) 372-3048
Web address: www.dailyrecord.us
General e-mail: bobby@dailydata.com
Advertising e-mail: jedwards@dailydata.com
Editorial e-mail: editor@dailydata.com
Year established: 1925
News services: NNS, TMS, DRNW, INS
Advertising (Open inch rate) Weekday/Saturday:
 Column Inch Rate - $20.00
Circulation Paid: 3210
Circulation Free: 25
Audited By: USPS

THE DAILY RECORD

Frequency: mon to fri
Street address 1: 16 W Main St
Street address city: Rochester
Street address state: NY
Postal code: 14614-1602
County: Monroe
Country: USA
Mailing address 1: PO Box 30006
Mailing city: Rochester
Mailing state: NY
Mailing zip: 14603-3006
Office phone: (585) 232-6920
Office fax: (585) 232-2740
Web address: www.nydailyrecord.com
General e-mail: kevin.momot@nydailyrecord.com
Year established: 14603-3006
News services: American Court & Commercial Newspapers, National Newspaper Association
Advertising (Open inch rate) Weekday/Saturday:
 Open inch rate $.90 (agency line), $.75 (retail line)

THE DAILY RECORD

Frequency: mon to fri
Street address 1: 436 S 7th St
Ste 300
Street address city: Louisville
Street address state: KY
Postal code: 40203-1980
County: Jefferson
Country: USA
Mailing address 1: PO Box 1062
Mailing city: Louisville
Mailing state: KY
Mailing zip: 40201-1062
Office phone: (502) 583-4471
Office fax: (502) 585-5453
General e-mail: janicep@nacms-c.com
Year established: 40201
News services: National Association of Credit Management
Advertising (Open inch rate) Weekday/Saturday:
 Open inch rate $1.20 (legal line)

THE DAILY RECORDER

Frequency: mon to fri
Street address 1: 901 H St
Ste 312
Street address city: Sacramento
Street address state: CA
Postal code: 95814-1808
County: Sacramento
Country: USA
Mailing address 1: PO Box 1048
Mailing city: Sacramento
Mailing state: CA
Mailing zip: 95812-1048
Office phone: (916) 444-2355
Office fax: (916) 444-0636
Advertising phone: (800) 652-1700
Web address: www.dailyjournal.com
General e-mail: daily_recorder@dailyjournal.com
Editorial e-mail: jt_long@dailyjournal.com
Year established: 1901
News services: AP, dj
Advertising (Open inch rate) Weekday/Saturday:
 Open inch rate $26.00

THE DAILY REPORTER

Frequency: mon to fri
Street address 1: 225 E Michigan St
Ste 300
Street address city: Milwaukee
Street address state: WI
Postal code: 53202-4900
County: Milwaukee
Country: USA
Mailing address 1: 225 E. Michigan St. Suite 300
Mailing city: Milwaukee
Mailing state: WI
Mailing zip: 53202
Office phone: (414) 276-0273
Office fax: (414) 276-4416
Editorial phone: (414) 225-1807
Web address: www.dailyreporter.com
General e-mail: news@dailyreporter.com
Advertising e-mail: squinn@dailyreporter.com
Editorial e-mail: dshaw@dailyreporter.com
Year established: 1897
News services: AP
Digital Platform - Mobile:
 Apple`Android`Windows
Digital Platform - Tablet: Apple iOS`Android`Windows 7
Circulation Paid: 3105

THE DAILY TRANSCRIPT

Frequency: m-mon to fri
Street address 1: 2131 3rd Ave
Street address city: San Diego
Street address state: CA
Postal code: 92101-2021
County: San Diego
Country: USA
Mailing address 1: PO Box 85469
Mailing city: San Diego
Mailing state: CA
Mailing zip: 92186-5469
Office phone: (619) 232-4381
Office fax: (619) 239-5716
Advertising phone: (619) 232-4381
Advertising fax: (619) 239-4312
Editorial phone: (619) 232-4381
Editorial fax: (619) 236-8126
Web address: www.sddt.com
General e-mail: editor@sddt.com
Advertising e-mail: sales@sddt.com
Editorial e-mail: editor@sddt.com
Year established: 1886

News services: AP, Bloomberg.
Advertising (Open inch rate) Weekday/Saturday:
 Open inch rate $100.00
Circulation Paid: 6404
Audited By: Sworn/Estimate/Non-Audited

THE JOURNAL RECORD

Frequency: mon to fri
Street address 1: 101 N Robinson Ave
Ste 101
Street address city: Oklahoma City
Street address state: OK
Postal code: 73102-5500
County: Oklahoma
Country: USA
Mailing address 1: PO Box 26370
Mailing city: Oklahoma City
Mailing state: OK
Mailing zip: 73126 0370
Office phone: (405) 235-3100
Office fax: (405) 278-6907
Advertising phone: (405) 278-2830
Editorial phone: (405) 278-2850
Editorial fax: (405) 278-2890
Other phone: (877) 615-9536
Web address: www.journalrecord.com
Editorial e-mail: news@journalrecord.com
Year established: 1903
News services: AP
Advertising (Open inch rate) Weekday/Saturday:
 Open inch rate $18.62
Circulation Paid: 2800
Circulation Free: 69
Audited By: VAC

THE LEGAL INTELLIGENCER

Frequency: mon to fri
Street address 1: 1617 John F Kennedy Blvd
Ste 1750
Street address city: Philadelphia
Street address state: PA
Postal code: 19103-1854
County: Philadelphia
Country: USA
Mailing address 1: 1617 John F Kennedy Blvd Ste 1750
Mailing city: Philadelphia
Mailing state: PA
Mailing zip: 19103-1854
Office phone: (215) 557-2300
Office fax: (215) 557-2301
Advertising phone: (215) 557-2359
Advertising fax: (215) 557-2301
Editorial phone: (215) 557-2489
Editorial fax: (215) 557-2301
Web address: www.thelegalintelligencer.com
General e-mail: HGREZLAK@ALM.COM
Advertising e-mail: dchalphin@alm.com
Editorial e-mail: hgrezlak@alm.com
Year established: 1843
News services: AP

THE LOS ANGELES DAILY JOURNAL

Frequency: mon to fri
Street address 1: 915 E 1st St
Street address city: Los Angeles
Street address state: CA
Postal code: 90012-4050
County: Los Angeles
Country: USA
Mailing address 1: 915 E 1st St
Mailing city: Los Angeles
Mailing state: CA
Mailing zip: 90012-4042
Office phone: (213) 229-5300
Office fax: (213) 229-5481
Editorial fax: (213) 229-5462
Web address: www.dailyjournal.com
News services: AP, NYT, CNS, McClatchy
Advertising (Open inch rate) Weekday/Saturday:
 Open inch rate $69.16 (page)

THE RECORD REPORTER

Frequency: Mon`Wed`Fri
Street address 1: 2025 N 3rd St
Ste 155
Street address city: Phoenix

Street address state: AZ
Postal code: 85004-1425
County: Maricopa
Country: USA
Office phone: (602) 417-9900
Office fax: (602) 417-9910
Web address: www.recordreporter.com
General e-mail: Diane_Heuel@dailyjournal.com
Advertising e-mail: record_reporter@dailyjournal.com
Editorial e-mail: diane_heuel@dailyjournal.com
Year established: 1914
Digital Platform - Mobile:
 Apple`Android`Blackberry
Digital Platform - Tablet: Apple iOS`Android`Windows 7`Blackberry Tablet OS

THE ST. LOUIS COUNTIAN

Frequency: mon to sat; S
Street address 1: 319 N 4th St
Street address city: Saint Louis
Street address state: MO
Postal code: 63102-1910
County: Saint Louis City
Country: USA
Mailing address 1: 319 N 4th St
Mailing city: Saint Louis
Mailing state: MO
Mailing zip: 63102-1906
Office phone: (314) 421-1880
Office fax: (314) 421-0436
Advertising phone: (314) 421-1880
Advertising fax: (314) 421-0436
Editorial phone: (314) 421-1880
Editorial fax: (314) 421-0436
Web address: www.thedailyrecord.com
Advertising e-mail: carol.prycma@thedailyrecord.com
Editorial e-mail: willc@thedailyrecord.com
News services: RN
Advertising (Open inch rate) Weekday/Saturday:
 Open inch rate $6.56

WYOMING BUSINESS REPORT

Street address 1: 702 W Lincolnway
Street address city: Cheyenne
Street address state: WY
Postal code: 82001-4359
County: Laramie
Country: USA
Office phone: (307) 633-3193
Office fax: (307) 633-3191
Web address: www.wyomingbusinessreport.com
Advertising e-mail: bnelson@wyomingbusinessreport.com

COMMERCE

COMMERCIAL RECORDER

Frequency: mon to fri
Street address 1: 3032 S Jones St
Street address city: Fort Worth
Street address state: TX
Postal code: 76104-6747
County: Tarrant
Country: USA
Mailing address 1: PO Box 11038
Mailing city: Fort Worth
Mailing state: TX
Mailing zip: 76134
Office phone: (817) 255-0779
Office fax: (817) 926-5377
Advertising phone: (817) 255-0779
Editorial phone: (817) 255-0779
Other phone: (817) 255-0779
Web address: www.commercialrecorder.com
General e-mail: johnybska@gmail.com
Advertising e-mail: johnybska@gmail.com
Editorial e-mail: johnybska@gmail.com
Year established: 1903
Advertising (Open inch rate) Weekday/Saturday:
 Open inch rate $9.00

PROFESSIONAL, BUSINESS AND SPECIAL SERVICES

DAILY RECORD
Frequency: mon to fri
Street address 1: 3323 Leavenworth St
Street address city: Omaha
Street address state: NE
Postal code: 68105-1915
County: Douglas
Country: USA
Mailing address 1: 3323 Leavenworth St
Mailing city: Omaha
Mailing state: NE
Mailing zip: 68105-1900
Office phone: (402) 345-1303
Office fax: (402) 345-2351
Web address: www.omahadailyrecord.com
General e-mail: lhenningsen@omahadailyrecord.com
Advertising e-mail: diane@omahadailyrecord.com
Editorial e-mail: lorraine@omahadailyrecord.com
Year established: 1886
News services: Associated Press, Creators Syndicate, U.S. News Syndicate
Advertising (Open inch rate) Weekday/Saturday:
  Open inch rate $7.25

DAILY SHIPPING NEWS
Frequency: mon to fri
Street address 1: 13715 SE Eastridge Dr Apt 12
Street address city: Vancouver
Street address state: WA
Postal code: 98683-4717
County: Clark
Country: USA
Mailing address 1: 4106 SE Llewellyn St
Mailing city: Portland
Mailing state: OR
Mailing zip: 97222-5870
Office phone: (360) 254-5504
Office fax: (360) 254-7145
Web address: www.wwshipper.com
General e-mail: dsnews@europa.com
Year established: 98607
Advertising (Open inch rate) Weekday/Saturday:
  Open inch rate $10.00

DETROIT LEGAL NEWS
Frequency: mon to fri
Street address 1: 1409 Allen Dr Ste B
Street address city: Troy
Street address state: MI
Postal code: 48083-4003
County: Oakland
Country: USA
Mailing address 1: 1409 Allen Dr Ste B
Mailing city: Troy
Mailing state: MI
Mailing zip: 48083-4003
Office phone: (248) 577-6100
Office fax: (248) 577-6111
Advertising phone: (248) 577-6100
Advertising fax: (248) 577-6111
Editorial phone: (248) 577-6100
Editorial fax: (248) 967-5532
Other phone: (800) 875-5275
Web address: www.legalnews.com
General e-mail: editor@legalnews.com
Advertising e-mail: paul@legalnews.com
Editorial e-mail: editor@legalnews.com
News services: AP
Advertising (Open inch rate) Weekday/Saturday:
  Open inch rate $23.00

THE DAILY NEWS
Frequency: mon to fri
Street address 1: 193 Jefferson Ave
Street address city: Memphis
Street address state: TN
Postal code: 38103-2322
County: Shelby
Country: USA
Mailing address 1: 193 JEFFERSON AVE
Mailing city: MEMPHIS
Mailing state: TN
Mailing zip: 38103-2339

Office phone: (901) 523-1561
Office fax: (901) 526-5813
Advertising phone: (901) 528-5283
Advertising fax: (901) 526-5813
Editorial phone: (901) 523-8501
Editorial fax: (901) 526-5813
Web address: www.memphisdailynews.com
General e-mail: jjenkins@memphisdailynews.com
Advertising e-mail: jjenkins@memphisdailynews.com
Editorial e-mail: releases@memphisdailynews.com
Year established: 1886
News services: CNS
Advertising (Open inch rate) Weekday/Saturday:
  Open inch rate $13.50 (legal)
Circulation Paid: 1000
Circulation Free: 2000
Audited By: USPS

THE DAILY RECORD
Frequency: mon to fri
Street address 1: 11 E Saratoga St
Street address city: Baltimore
Street address state: MD
Postal code: 21202-2115
County: Baltimore City
Country: USA
Mailing address 1: 11 E SARATOGA ST STE 1
Mailing city: BALTIMORE
Mailing state: MD
Mailing zip: 21202-2199
Office phone: (443) 524-8100
Office fax: (410) 752-2894
Advertising phone: (443) 524-8100
Advertising fax: (410) 752-2894
Editorial phone: (443) 524-8150
Editorial fax: (410) 752-2894
Web address: www.thedailyrecord.com
General e-mail: suzanne.huettner@thedailyrecord.com
Advertising e-mail: advertising@thedailyrecord.com
Editorial e-mail: tbaden@thedailyrecord.com
Year established: 1888
Advertising (Open inch rate) Weekday/Saturday:
  Open inch rate $510.00/Day
Circulation Paid: 2572
Circulation Free: 384
Audited By: Sworn/Estimate/Non-Audited

THE DAILY REPORTER
Frequency: mon to fri
Street address 1: 580 S High St Ste 316
Street address city: Columbus
Street address state: OH
Postal code: 43215-5659
County: Franklin
Country: USA
Mailing address 1: 580 S High St Ste 316
Mailing city: Columbus
Mailing state: OH
Mailing zip: 43215-5659
Office phone: (614) 224-4835
Office fax: (614) 224-8649
Web address: www.thedailyreporteronline.com
General e-mail: editor@sourcenews.com
Editorial e-mail: editor@thedailyreporteronline.com
Year established: 1896
News services: AP
Advertising (Open inch rate) Weekday/Saturday:
  Open inch rate $3,880.00 (Page)

THE JOURNAL RECORD
Frequency: mon to fri
Street address 1: 101 N Robinson Ave Ste 101
Street address city: Oklahoma City
Street address state: OK
Postal code: 73102-5500
County: Oklahoma
Country: USA
Mailing address 1: PO Box 26370
Mailing city: Oklahoma City
Mailing state: OK
Mailing zip: 73126-0370

Office phone: (405) 235-3100
Office fax: (405) 278-6907
Advertising phone: (405) 278-2830
Advertising fax: (405) 526-5813
Editorial phone: (405) 278-2850
Editorial fax: (405) 278-2890
Other phone: (877) 615-9536
Web address: www.journalrecord.com
Editorial e-mail: news@journalrecord.com
Year established: 1903
News services: AP
Advertising (Open inch rate) Weekday/Saturday:
  Open inch rate $18.62
Circulation Paid: 2800
Circulation Free: 69
Audited By: VAC

THE RECORD REPORTER
Frequency: Mon`Wed`Fri
Street address 1: 2025 N 3rd St Ste 155
Street address city: Phoenix
Street address state: AZ
Postal code: 85004-1425
County: Maricopa
Country: USA

Office phone: (602) 417-9900
Office fax: (602) 417-9910
Web address: www.recordreporter.com
General e-mail: Diane_Heuel@dailyjournal.com
Advertising e-mail: record_reporter@dailyjournal.com
Editorial e-mail: diane_heuel@dailyjournal.com
Year established: 1914
Digital Platform - Mobile:
  Apple`Android`Blackberry
Digital Platform - Tablet: Apple iOS`Android`Windows 7`Blackberry Tablet OS

CONSTRUCTION

AMERICAN METAL MARKET
Frequency: mon to fri
Street address 1: 225 Park Ave S Fl 6
Street address city: New York
Street address state: NY
Postal code: 10003-1604
County: New York
Country: USA
Mailing address 1: 225 Park Ave S Fl 6
Mailing city: New York
Mailing state: NY
Mailing zip: 10003-1604
Office phone: (212) 213-6202
Office fax: (212) 213-1804
Advertising phone: (646) 274-6213
Advertising fax: (412) 471-7203
Editorial phone: (212) 213-6202
Editorial fax: (212) 213-6202
Web address: www.amm.com
General e-mail: ammnews@amm.com
Advertising e-mail: kross@amm.com
Editorial e-mail: jisenberg@amm.com
Year established: 1882
News services: RN, AP, PRN, Bridge News, Business Wire.
Advertising (Open inch rate) Weekday/Saturday:
  Open inch rate $36.48 (page)

DAILY COMMERCIAL NEWS AND CONSTRUCTION RECORD
Frequency: mon to fri
Street address 1: 500 Hood Rd., 4th Fl.
Street address city: Markham
Street address state: ON
Postal code: L3R 9Z3
Country: Canada
Mailing address 1: 500 Hood Rd., 4th Fl.
Mailing city: Markham
Mailing state: ON
Mailing zip: L3R 9Z3
Office phone: (905) 752-9292

Office fax: (905) 752-5450
Web address: www.dcnonl.com
General e-mail: bev.akerfeldt@cmdg.com
Advertising e-mail: cindy.littler@cmdg.com
Editorial e-mail: john.leckie@cmdg.com
Advertising (Open inch rate) Weekday/Saturday:
  Open inch rate $63.00 (Canadian)

DAILY JOURNAL OF COMMERCE
Frequency: mon to fri
Street address 1: 3445 N Causeway Blvd Ste 901
Street address city: Metairie
Street address state: LA
Postal code: 70002-3768
County: Jefferson
Country: USA
Mailing address 1: 3445 N. Causeway Blvd. Suite 901
Mailing city: Metairie
Mailing state: LA
Mailing zip: 70002
Office phone: (504) 834-9292
Office fax: (504) 832-3534
Web address: www.djgulfcoast.com
General e-mail: mail@nopg.com
Advertising e-mail: anne.lovas@nopg.com
Editorial e-mail: greg.larose@nopg.com
Year established: 1922
Advertising (Open inch rate) Weekday/Saturday:
  Email or call for rates

DAILY JOURNAL OF COMMERCE
Frequency: mon to fri
Street address 1: 921 SW Washington St Ste 210
Street address city: Portland
Street address state: OR
Postal code: 97205-2810
County: Multnomah
Country: USA
Mailing address 1: 921 SW Washington St Ste 210
Mailing city: Portland
Mailing state: OR
Mailing zip: 97205-2810
Office phone: (503) 226-1311
Office fax: (503) 226-1315
Advertising phone: (503) 226-1311
Advertising fax: (503) 802-7219
Editorial fax: (503) 802-7239
Web address: www.djcoregon.com
General e-mail: newsroom@djcoregon.com
Advertising e-mail: rynni.henderson@djcoregon.com
Editorial e-mail: stephanie.basalyga@djcoregon.com
Year established: 1872
News services: AP, RN, TMS
Advertising (Open inch rate) Weekday/Saturday:
  Open inch rate $25.00
Digital Platform - Mobile: Apple`Android

DAILY RECORD
Frequency: mon to fri
Street address 1: 3323 Leavenworth St
Street address city: Omaha
Street address state: NE
Postal code: 68105-1915
County: Douglas
Country: USA
Mailing address 1: 3323 Leavenworth St
Mailing city: Omaha
Mailing state: NE
Mailing zip: 68105-1900
Office phone: (402) 345-1303
Office fax: (402) 345-2351
Web address: www.omahadailyrecord.com
General e-mail: lhenningsen@omahadailyrecord.com
Advertising e-mail: diane@omahadailyrecord.com
Editorial e-mail: lorraine@omahadailyrecord.com
Year established: 1886
News services: Associated Press, Creators Syndicate, U.S. News Syndicate
Advertising (Open inch rate) Weekday/Saturday:
  Open inch rate $7.25

PROFESSIONAL, BUSINESS AND SPECIAL SERVICES

DODGE CONSTRUCTION NEWS
CHICAGO
Frequency: mon to fri
Street address 1: 130 E Randolph St Fl 14
Street address city: Chicago
Street address state: IL
Postal code: 60601-6207
County: Cook
Country: USA
Mailing address 1: 130 E Randolph St Fl 14
Mailing city: Chicago
Mailing state: IL
Mailing zip: 60601-6207
Office phone: (312) 233-7499
Office fax: (312) 233-7486
Web address: www.mediacourier.net
Year established: 1946
Advertising (Open inch rate) Weekday/Saturday: Open inch rate $34.00

DODGE CONSTRUCTION NEWS
GREENSHEET
Frequency: mon to fri
Street address 1: 1333 S Mayflower Ave Fl 3
Street address city: Monrovia
Street address state: CA
Postal code: 91016-4066
County: Los Angeles
Country: USA
Mailing address 1: 1333 S Mayflower Ave Fl 3
Mailing city: Monrovia
Mailing state: CA
Mailing zip: 91016-4066
Office phone: (626) 932-6161
Office fax: (626) 932-6163
Editorial phone: (626) 932-6175
Editorial fax: (626) 932-6163
Web address: www.construction.com
Year established: 91016
Advertising (Open inch rate) Weekday/Saturday: Open inch rate $36.90 (display); $25.00 (classified)

THE DAILY JOURNAL
Frequency: mon to fri
Street address 1: 1114 W 7th Ave Ste 100
Street address city: Denver
Street address state: CO
Postal code: 80204-4455
County: Denver
Country: USA
Mailing address 1: 1114 W 7th Ave Ste 100
Mailing city: Denver
Mailing state: CO
Mailing zip: 80204-4455
Office phone: (303) 756-9995
Office fax: (303) 756-4465
Advertising phone: (303) 584-6737
Advertising fax: (303) 584-6717
Editorial phone: (303) 584-6724
Editorial fax: (303) 756-4465
Web address: www.colorado.construction.com
Year established: 1897
Advertising (Open inch rate) Weekday/Saturday: Open inch rate $25.20

THE DAILY NEWS
Frequency: mon to fri
Street address 1: 193 Jefferson Ave
Street address city: Memphis
Street address state: TN
Postal code: 38103-2322
County: Shelby
Country: USA
Mailing address 1: 193 JEFFERSON AVE
Mailing city: MEMPHIS
Mailing state: TN
Mailing zip: 38103-2339
Office phone: (901) 523-1561
Office fax: (901) 526-5813
Advertising phone: (901) 528-5283
Advertising fax: (901) 526-5813
Editorial phone: (901) 523-8501
Editorial fax: (901) 526-5813

Web address: www.memphisdailynews.com
General e-mail: jjenkins@memphisdailynews.com
Advertising e-mail: jjenkins@memphisdailynews.com
Editorial e-mail: releases@memphisdailynews.com
Year established: 1886
News services: CNS
Advertising (Open inch rate) Weekday/Saturday: Open inch rate $13.50 (legal)
Circulation Paid: 1000
Circulation Free: 2000
Audited By: USPS

THE DAILY REPORTER
Frequency: mon to fri
Street address 1: 225 E Michigan St Ste 300
Street address city: Milwaukee
Street address state: WI
Postal code: 53202-4900
County: Milwaukee
Country: USA
Mailing address 1: 225 E. Michigan St. Suite 300
Mailing city: Milwaukee
Mailing state: WI
Mailing zip: 53202
Office phone: (414) 276-0273
Office fax: (414) 276-4416
Editorial phone: (414) 225-1807
Web address: www.dailyreporter.com
General e-mail: news@dailyreporter.com
Advertising e-mail: squinn@dailyreporter.com
Editorial e-mail: dshaw@dailyreporter.com
Year established: 1897
News services: AP
Digital Platform - Mobile: Apple`Android`Windows
Digital Platform - Tablet: Apple iOS`Android`Windows 7
Circulation Paid: 3105

COURT

COMMERCIAL RECORDER
Frequency: mon to fri
Street address 1: 3032 S Jones St
Street address city: Fort Worth
Street address state: TX
Postal code: 76104-6747
County: Tarrant
Country: USA
Mailing address 1: PO Box 11038
Mailing city: Fort Worth
Mailing state: TX
Mailing zip: 76134
Office phone: (817) 255-0779
Office fax: (817) 926-5377
Advertising phone: (817) 255-0779
Editorial phone: (817) 255-0779
Other phone: (817) 255-0779
Web address: www.commercialrecorder.com
General e-mail: johnybska@gmail.com
Advertising e-mail: johnybska@gmail.com
Editorial e-mail: johnybska@gmail.com
Year established: 1903
Advertising (Open inch rate) Weekday/Saturday: Open inch rate $9.00

COURT & COMMERCIAL RECORD
Street address 1: 41 E Washington St Ste 200
Street address city: Indianapolis
Street address state: IN
Postal code: 46204-3517
County: Marion
Country: USA
Mailing address 1: 41 E Washington St Ste 200
Mailing city: Indianapolis
Mailing state: IN
Mailing zip: 46204-3517
Office phone: (317) 363-5408

Advertising fax: (317) 263-5259
Web address: www.courtcommercialrecord.com
General e-mail: judy.smith@ibj.com
Advertising e-mail: karuta@ibj.com
Year established: 1895
Advertising (Open inch rate) Weekday/Saturday: Notice of Administration: $82.00, Adoptions: $132.00, Car Sales: $44.00, Determine Heirship: $132.00, Dissolution of Corporation: $52.00, Foundation Report: $72.00, Guardianship Notice: $132.00, Final Account or Intermediate Account: $68.00, Name Change: $132.00, Summons Notice of Suit: $132.00

DAILY RECORD
Frequency: mon to fri
Street address 1: 3323 Leavenworth St
Street address city: Omaha
Street address state: NE
Postal code: 68105-1915
County: Douglas
Country: USA
Mailing address 1: 3323 Leavenworth St
Mailing city: Omaha
Mailing state: NE
Mailing zip: 68105-1900
Office phone: (402) 345-1303
Office fax: (402) 345-2351
Web address: www.omahadailyrecord.com
General e-mail: lhenningsen@omahadailyrecord.com
Advertising e-mail: diane@omahadailyrecord.com
Editorial e-mail: lorraine@omahadailyrecord.com
Year established: 1886
News services: Associated Press, Creators Syndicate, U.S. News Syndicate
Advertising (Open inch rate) Weekday/Saturday: Open inch rate $7.25

DETROIT LEGAL NEWS
Frequency: mon to fri
Street address 1: 1409 Allen Dr Ste B
Street address city: Troy
Street address state: MI
Postal code: 48083-4003
County: Oakland
Country: USA
Mailing address 1: 1409 Allen Dr Ste B
Mailing city: Troy
Mailing state: MI
Mailing zip: 48083-4003
Office phone: (248) 577-6100
Office fax: (248) 577-6111
Advertising phone: (248) 577-6100
Advertising fax: (248) 577-6111
Editorial phone: (248) 577-6100
Editorial fax: (248) 967-5532
Other phone: (800) 875-5275
Web address: www.legalnews.com
General e-mail: editor@legalnews.com
Advertising e-mail: paul@legalnews.com
Editorial e-mail: editor@legalnews.com
News services: AP
Advertising (Open inch rate) Weekday/Saturday: Open inch rate $23.00

MISSOURI LAWYERS MEDIA
Street address 1: 319 N 4th St Fl 5 5th Floor
Street address city: Saint Louis
Street address state: MO
Postal code: 63102-1907
County: Saint Louis City
Country: USA
Mailing address 1: 319 N 4th St Fl 5 5th Floor
Mailing city: Saint Louis
Mailing state: MO
Mailing zip: 63102-1907
Office phone: (314) 421-1880
Office fax: (314) 621-1913
Advertising phone: (314) 558-3260
Advertising fax: (314) 421-7080
Editorial phone: (314) 558-3220
Editorial fax: (314) 621-1913
Web address: www.molawyersmedia.com

General e-mail: service@bridgetowermedia.com
Year established: 1890
Advertising (Open inch rate) Weekday/Saturday: Full Page $2,360.00
Digital Platform - Mobile: Apple`Android`Windows
Digital Platform - Tablet: Apple iOS`Android`Windows 7
Circulation Paid: 4500
Circulation Free: 10820
Audited By: Sworn/Estimate/Non-Audited

TACOMA DAILY INDEX
Frequency: mon to fri
Street address 1: 402 Tacoma Ave S Ste 200
Street address city: Tacoma
Street address state: WA
Postal code: 98402-5400
County: Pierce
Country: USA
Mailing address 1: 402 Tacoma Ave S Ste 200
Mailing city: Tacoma
Mailing state: WA
Mailing zip: 98402-5400
Office phone: (253) 627-4853
Office fax: (253) 627-2253
Advertising phone: (253) 627-4853
Advertising fax: (253) 627-2253
Editorial phone: (253) 627-4853
Editorial fax: (253) 627-2253
Other phone: (253) 627-4853
Web address: www.tacomadailyindex.com
General e-mail: legals@tacomadailyindex.com
Advertising e-mail: publisher@tacomadailyindex.com
Editorial e-mail: editor@tacomadailyindex.com
Year established: 1890
News services: American Court & Commercial Printing
Advertising (Open inch rate) Weekday/Saturday: Open inch rate $9.65

THE DAILY COMMERCIAL RECORDER
Frequency: mon to fri
Street address 1: 301 Avenue E
Street address city: San Antonio
Street address state: TX
Postal code: 78205-2006
County: Bexar
Country: USA
Mailing address 1: P.O. Box 2171
Mailing city: San Antonio
Mailing state: TX
Mailing zip: 78297
Office phone: (210) 250-2438
Office fax: (210) 250-2360
Web address: www.primetimenewspapers.com
General e-mail: dcr@primetimenewspapers.com
News services: ACCN, Creator Syndicates, LAT-WP, National American Press Syndicate, NYT.
Advertising (Open inch rate) Weekday/Saturday: Open inch rate $25.00

THE DAILY EVENTS
Frequency: mon to fri
Street address 1: 310 W Walnut St
Street address city: Springfield
Street address state: MO
Postal code: 65806-2118
County: Greene
Country: USA
Mailing address 1: PO Box 1
Mailing city: Springfield
Mailing state: MO
Mailing zip: 65801-0001
Office phone: (417) 866-1401
Office fax: (417) 866-1491
Web address: www.thedailyevents.com
General e-mail: info@dailyevents.com
Year established: 1881
News services: American Court & Commercial Newspapers

PROFESSIONAL, BUSINESS AND SPECIAL SERVICES

THE DAILY NEWS
Frequency: mon to fri
Street address 1: 193 Jefferson Ave
Street address city: Memphis
Street address state: TN
Postal code: 38103-2322
County: Shelby
Country: USA
Mailing address 1: 193 JEFFERSON AVE
Mailing city: MEMPHIS
Mailing state: TN
Mailing zip: 38103-2339
Office phone: (901) 523-1561
Office fax: (901) 526-5813
Advertising phone: (901) 528-5283
Advertising fax: (901) 526-5813
Editorial phone: (901) 523-8501
Editorial fax: (901) 526-5813
Web address: www.memphisdailynews.com
General e-mail: jjenkins@memphisdailynews.com
Advertising e-mail: jjenkins@memphisdailynews.com
Editorial e-mail: releases@memphisdailynews.com
Year established: 1886
News services: CNS
Advertising (Open inch rate) Weekday/Saturday:
    Open inch rate $13.50 (legal)
Circulation Paid: 1000
Circulation Free: 2000
Audited By: USPS

THE DAILY RECORD
Frequency: mon to fri
Street address 1: 436 S 7th St
Ste 300
Street address city: Louisville
Street address state: KY
Postal code: 40203-1980
County: Jefferson
Country: USA
Mailing address 1: PO Box 1062
Mailing city: Louisville
Mailing state: KY
Mailing zip: 40201-1062
Office phone: (502) 583-4471
Office fax: (502) 585-5453
General e-mail: janicep@nacms-c.com
Year established: 40201
News services: National Association of Credit Management
Advertising (Open inch rate) Weekday/Saturday:
    Open inch rate $1.20 (legal line)

THE DAILY RECORD
Frequency: mon to fri
Street address 1: 11 E Saratoga St
Street address city: Baltimore
Street address state: MD
Postal code: 21202-2115
County: Baltimore City
Country: USA
Mailing address 1: 11 E SARATOGA ST STE 1
Mailing city: BALTIMORE
Mailing state: MD
Mailing zip: 21202-2199
Office phone: (443) 524-8100
Office fax: (410) 752-2894
Advertising phone: (443) 524-8100
Advertising fax: (410) 752-2894
Editorial phone: (443) 524-8150
Editorial fax: (410) 752-2894
Web address: www.thedailyrecord.com
General e-mail: suzanne.huettner@thedailyrecord.com
Advertising e-mail: advertising@thedailyrecord.com
Editorial e-mail: tbaden@thedailyrecord.com
Year established: 1888
Advertising (Open inch rate) Weekday/Saturday:
    Open inch rate $510.00/Day
Circulation Paid: 2572
Circulation Free: 384
Audited By: Sworn/Estimate/Non-Audited

THE DAILY RECORD
Frequency: mon to fri

Street address 1: 300 S Izard St
Street address city: Little Rock
Street address state: AR
Postal code: 72201-2114
County: Pulaski
Country: USA
Mailing address 1: PO Box 3595
Mailing city: Little Rock
Mailing state: AR
Mailing zip: 72203-3595
Office phone: (501) 374-5103
Office fax: (501) 372-3048
Web address: www.dailyrecord.us
General e-mail: bobby@dailydata.com
Advertising e-mail: jedwards@dailydata.com
Editorial e-mail: editor@dailydata.com
Year established: 1925
News services: NNS, TMS, DRNW, INS
Advertising (Open inch rate) Weekday/Saturday:
    Column Inch Rate - $20.00
Circulation Paid: 3210
Circulation Free: 25
Audited By: USPS

THE DAILY REPORTER
Frequency: mon to fri
Street address 1: 580 S High St
Ste 316
Street address city: Columbus
Street address state: OH
Postal code: 43215-5659
County: Franklin
Country: USA
Mailing address 1: 580 S High St Ste 316
Mailing city: Columbus
Mailing state: OH
Mailing zip: 43215-5659
Office phone: (614) 224-4835
Office fax: (614) 224-8649
Web address: www.thedailyreporteronline.com
General e-mail: editor@sourcenews.com
Editorial e-mail: editor@thedailyreporteronline.com
Year established: 1896
News services: AP
Advertising (Open inch rate) Weekday/Saturday:
    Open inch rate $3,880.00 (Page)

THE DAILY REPORTER
Frequency: mon to fri
Street address 1: 225 E Michigan St
Ste 300
Street address city: Milwaukee
Street address state: WI
Postal code: 53202-4900
County: Milwaukee
Country: USA
Mailing address 1: 225 E. Michigan St. Suite 300
Mailing city: Milwaukee
Mailing state: WI
Mailing zip: 53202
Office phone: (414) 276-0273
Office fax: (414) 276-4416
Editorial phone: (414) 225-1807
Web address: www.dailyreporter.com
General e-mail: news@dailyreporter.com
Advertising e-mail: squinn@dailyreporter.com
Editorial e-mail: dshaw@dailyreporter.com
Year established: 1897
News services: AP
Digital Platform - Mobile:
    Apple`Android`Windows
Digital Platform - Tablet: Apple
    iOS`Android`Windows 7
Circulation Paid: 3105

THE DAILY TERRITORIAL
Frequency: m-mon to fri
Street address 1: 7225 N. Mona Lisa Rd. #125
Street address city: Tucson
Street address state: AZ
Postal code: 85741
County: Pima
Country: USA
Mailing address 1: 7225 N. Mona Lisa Rd., #125
Mailing city: Tucson
Mailing state: AZ

Mailing zip: 85741
Office phone: (520) 797-4384
Office fax: (520) 575-8891
Advertising phone: (520) 294-1200
Editorial phone: (520) 294-1200
Web address: www.azbiz.com
General e-mail: tucsoneditor@tucsonlocalmedia.com
Advertising e-mail: classifieds@tucsonlocalmedia.com
Editorial e-mail: tucsoneditor@tucsonlocalmedia.com
Year established: 1966
News services: American Newspaper Representatives Inc..
Advertising (Open inch rate) Weekday/Saturday:
    Open inch rate $5.45
Circulation Paid: 753
Audited By: Sworn/Estimate/Non-Audited

THE LOS ANGELES DAILY JOURNAL
Frequency: mon to fri
Street address 1: 915 E 1st St
Street address city: Los Angeles
Street address state: CA
Postal code: 90012-4050
County: Los Angeles
Country: USA
Mailing address 1: 915 E 1st St
Mailing city: Los Angeles
Mailing state: CA
Mailing zip: 90012-4042
Office phone: (213) 229-5300
Office fax: (213) 229-5481
Editorial fax: (213) 229-5462
Web address: www.dailyjournal.com
News services: AP, NYT, CNS, McClatchy
Advertising (Open inch rate) Weekday/Saturday:
    Open inch rate $69.16 (page)

THE RECORD REPORTER
Frequency: Mon`Wed`Fri
Street address 1: 2025 N 3rd St
Ste 155
Street address city: Phoenix
Street address state: AZ
Postal code: 85004-1425
County: Maricopa
Country: USA
Office phone: (602) 417-9900
Office fax: (602) 417-9910
Web address: www.recordreporter.com
General e-mail: Diane_Heuel@dailyjournal.com
Advertising e-mail: record_reporter@dailyjournal.com
Editorial e-mail: diane_heuel@dailyjournal.com
Year established: 1914
Digital Platform - Mobile:
    Apple`Android`Blackberry
Digital Platform - Tablet: Apple
    iOS`Android`Windows 7`Blackberry Tablet OS

THE RECORDER
Frequency: mon to fri
Street address 1: 1035 Market St
Ste 500
Street address city: San Francisco
Street address state: CA
Postal code: 94103-1650
County: San Francisco
Country: USA
Mailing address 1: 1035 Market St Ste 500
Mailing city: San Francisco
Mailing state: CA
Mailing zip: 94103-1650
Office phone: (415) 749-5400
Office fax: (415) 749-5449
Advertising phone: (415) 749-5444
Advertising fax: (415) 749-5566
Editorial fax: (415) 749-5549
Other phone: (415) 749-5500
Web address: www.therecorder.com
General e-mail: recorder_editor@alm.com
Year established: 1877
News services: AP
Advertising (Open inch rate) Weekday/Saturday:
    Open inch rate $3,200.00 (Full Page Display)

THE ST. LOUIS COUNTIAN
Frequency: mon to sat; S
Street address 1: 319 N 4th St
Street address city: Saint Louis
Street address state: MO
Postal code: 63102-1910
County: Saint Louis City
Country: USA
Mailing address 1: 319 N 4th St
Mailing city: Saint Louis
Mailing state: MO
Mailing zip: 63102-1906
Office phone: (314) 421-1880
Office fax: (314) 421-0436
Advertising phone: (314) 421-1880
Advertising fax: (314) 421-0436
Editorial phone: (314) 421-1880
Editorial fax: (314) 421-0436
Web address: www.thedailyrecord.com
Advertising e-mail: carol.prycma@thedailyrecord.com
Editorial e-mail: willc@thedailyrecord.com
News services: RN
Advertising (Open inch rate) Weekday/Saturday:
    Open inch rate $6.56

TOLEDO LEGAL NEWS
Frequency: mon to fri
Street address 1: 247 Gradolph St
Street address city: Toledo
Street address state: OH
Postal code: 43612-1421
County: Lucas
Country: USA
Mailing address 1: PO Box 6816
Mailing city: Toledo
Mailing state: OH
Mailing zip: 43612-0816
Office phone: (419) 470-8600
Office fax: (419) 470-8602
Web address: www.toledolegalnews.com
General e-mail: tlnmain@bex.net
Year established: 1894
Advertising (Open inch rate) Weekday/Saturday:
    Open inch rate $12.00
Audited By: Sworn/Estimate/Non-Audited

CREDIT

CHICAGO DAILY LAW BULLETIN
Frequency: mon to fri
Street address 1: 415 N State St
Street address city: Chicago
Street address state: IL
Postal code: 60654-4607
County: Cook
Country: USA
Mailing address 1: 415 N State St
Mailing city: Chicago
Mailing state: IL
Mailing zip: 60654-4674
Office phone: (312) 644-7800
Office fax: (312) 644-4255
Web address: www.lawbulletin.com
General e-mail: displayads@lbpc.com
News services: AP, NYT
Advertising (Open inch rate) Weekday/Saturday:
    Open inch rate $26.40 (Classified), $2,588.00 (Full Page Display)

DAILY RECORD
Frequency: mon to fri
Street address 1: 3323 Leavenworth St
Street address city: Omaha
Street address state: NE
Postal code: 68105-1915
County: Douglas
Country: USA
Mailing address 1: 3323 Leavenworth St
Mailing city: Omaha
Mailing state: NE
Mailing zip: 68105-1900
Office phone: (402) 345-1303

PROFESSIONAL, BUSINESS AND SPECIAL SERVICES

II-9

Office fax: (402) 345-2351
Web address: www.omahadailyrecord.com
General e-mail: lhenningsen@
  omahadailyrecord.com
Advertising e-mail: diane@omahadailyrecord.com
Editorial e-mail: lorraine@omahadailyrecord.com
Year established: 1886
News services: Associated Press, Creators Syndicate, U.S. News Syndicate
Advertising (Open inch rate) Weekday/Saturday:
  Open inch rate $7.25

THE RECORD REPORTER

Frequency: Mon`Wed`Fri
Street address 1: 2025 N 3rd St
Ste 155
Street address city: Phoenix
Street address state: AZ
Postal code: 85004-1425
County: Maricopa
Country: USA

Office phone: (602) 417-9900
Office fax: (602) 417-9910
Web address: www.recordreporter.com
General e-mail: Diane_Heuel@dailyjournal.com
Advertising e-mail: record_reporter@
  dailyjournal.com
Editorial e-mail: diane_heuel@dailyjournal.com
Year established: 1914
Digital Platform - Mobile:
  Apple`Android`Blackberry
Digital Platform - Tablet: Apple
  iOS`Android`Windows 7`Blackberry Tablet OS

ENTERTAINMENT

DAILY VARIETY

Frequency: mon to fri
Street address 1: 5900 Wilshire Blvd
Ste 3100
Street address city: Los Angeles
Street address state: CA
Postal code: 90036-5030
County: Los Angeles
Country: USA
Mailing address 1: 5900 Wilshire Blvd Ste 3100
Mailing city: Los Angeles
Mailing state: CA
Mailing zip: 90036-5805
Office phone: (323) 617-9100
Advertising phone: (323) 857-6600
Advertising fax: (323) 932-0393
Editorial phone: (323) 965-4476
Web address: www.variety.com
Advertising e-mail: advertising@variety.com
News services: DJ, AP
Advertising (Open inch rate) Weekday/Saturday:
  Open inch rate $216.00
Audited By: Sworn/Estimate/Non-Audited

THE HOLLYWOOD REPORTER

Frequency: mon to fri
Street address 1: 5700 Wilshire Blvd
Ste 500
Street address city: Los Angeles
Street address state: CA
Postal code: 90036-3767
County: Los Angeles
Country: USA
Mailing address 1: 5700 Wilshire Blvd, Suite 500
Mailing city: Los Angeles
Mailing state: CA
Mailing zip: 90036-3767
Office phone: (323) 525-2000
Advertising phone: (323) 525-2013
Advertising fax: (323) 525-2372
Editorial phone: (323) 525-2130
Editorial fax: (323) 525-2377
Other phone: (866) 525-2150
Web address: www.hollywoodreporter.com
General e-mail: subscriptions@thr.com

Editorial e-mail: thrnews@thr.com
Year established: 1930
News services: AP
Advertising (Open inch rate) Weekday/Saturday:
  Open inch rate $100.00(fri)(classified)
Digital Platform - Mobile:
  Apple`Android`Windows`Blackberry
Digital Platform - Tablet: Apple
  iOS`Android`Windows 7`Blackberry Tablet OS`Kindle`Nook`Kindle Fire

FINANCE

AMERICAN BANKER

Frequency: mon to fri
Street address 1: 1 State St
Fl 27
Street address city: New York
Street address state: NY
Postal code: 10004-1561
County: New York
Country: USA
Mailing address 1: 1 State St Fl 26
Mailing city: New York
Mailing state: NY
Mailing zip: 10004-1483
Office phone: (212) 803-8200
Office fax: (212) 843-9600
Advertising phone: (212) 803-8691
Editorial phone: (212) 803-8399
Web address: www.americanbanker.com
General e-mail: Liesbeth.Severiens@
  sourcemedia.com
Advertising e-mail: Liesbeth.Severiens@
  sourcemedia.com
Editorial e-mail: Dean.Anason@sourcemedia.com
Year established: 1835
News services: AP, RN, UPI
Advertising (Open inch rate) Weekday/Saturday:
  $6,280 (1/2P); $3,735 (1/4P); $3,370 (1/8P)
Digital Platform - Mobile:
  Apple`Android`Windows`Blackberry
Digital Platform - Tablet: Apple iOS
Circulation Paid: 2373
Audited By: AAM

DAILY RECORD

Frequency: mon to fri
Street address 1: 3323 Leavenworth St
Street address city: Omaha
Street address state: NE
Postal code: 68105-1915
County: Douglas
Country: USA
Mailing address 1: 3323 Leavenworth St
Mailing city: Omaha
Mailing state: NE
Mailing zip: 68105-1900
Office phone: (402) 345-1303
Office fax: (402) 345-2351
Web address: www.omahadailyrecord.com
General e-mail: lhenningsen@
  omahadailyrecord.com
Advertising e-mail: diane@omahadailyrecord.com
Editorial e-mail: lorraine@omahadailyrecord.com
Year established: 1886
News services: Associated Press, Creators Syndicate, U.S. News Syndicate
Advertising (Open inch rate) Weekday/Saturday:
  Open inch rate $7.25

INVESTOR'S BUSINESS DAILY

Frequency: m-mon to fri
Street address 1: 12655 Beatrice St
Street address city: Los Angeles
Street address state: CA
Postal code: 90066-7300
County: Los Angeles
Country: USA
Mailing address 1: 12655 Beatrice St
Mailing city: Los Angeles
Mailing state: CA

Mailing zip: 90066-7303
Office phone: (310) 448-6700
Office fax: (310) 577-7301
Advertising phone: (310) 448-6700
Advertising fax: (310) 577-7301
Editorial phone: (310) 448-6373
Editorial fax: (310) 577-7350
Web address: www.investors.com
Editorial e-mail: IBDnews@investors.com
Year established: 1984
News services: AP
Circulation Paid: 113547
Circulation Free: 5572
Audited By: AAM

THE DAILY NEWS

Frequency: mon to fri
Street address 1: 193 Jefferson Ave
Street address city: Memphis
Street address state: TN
Postal code: 38103-2322
County: Shelby
Country: USA
Mailing address 1: 193 JEFFERSON AVE
Mailing city: MEMPHIS
Mailing state: TN
Mailing zip: 38103-2339
Office phone: (901) 523-1561
Office fax: (901) 526-5813
Advertising phone: (901) 528-5283
Advertising fax: (901) 526-5813
Editorial phone: (901) 523-8501
Editorial fax: (901) 526-5813
Web address: www.memphisdailynews.com
General e-mail: jjenkins@memphisdailynews.com
Advertising e-mail: jjenkins@
  memphisdailynews.com
Editorial e-mail: releases@memphisdailynews.com
Year established: 1886
News services: CNS
Advertising (Open inch rate) Weekday/Saturday:
  Open inch rate $13.50 (legal)
Circulation Paid: 1000
Circulation Free: 2000
Audited By: USPS

THE DAILY RECORD

Frequency: mon to fri
Street address 1: 436 S 7th St
Ste 300
Street address city: Louisville
Street address state: KY
Postal code: 40203-1980
County: Jefferson
Country: USA
Mailing address 1: PO Box 1062
Mailing city: Louisville
Mailing state: KY
Mailing zip: 40201-1062
Office phone: (502) 583-4471
Office fax: (502) 585-5453
General e-mail: janicep@nacms-c.com
Year established: 1886
News services: National Association of Credit Management
Advertising (Open inch rate) Weekday/Saturday:
  Open inch rate $1.20 (legal line)

THE DAILY RECORD

Frequency: mon to fri
Street address 1: 300 S Izard St
Street address city: Little Rock
Street address state: AR
Postal code: 72201-2114
County: Pulaski
Country: USA
Mailing address 1: PO Box 3595
Mailing city: Little Rock
Mailing state: AR
Mailing zip: 72203-3595
Office phone: (501) 374-5103
Office fax: (501) 372-3048
Web address: www.dailyrecord.us
General e-mail: bobby@dailydata.com
Advertising e-mail: jedwards@dailydata.com
Editorial e-mail: editor@dailydata.com
Year established: 1925
News services: NNS, TMS, DRNW, INS

Advertising (Open inch rate) Weekday/Saturday:
  Column Inch Rate - $20.00
Circulation Paid: 3210
Circulation Free: 25
Audited By: USPS

THE LOS ANGELES DAILY JOURNAL

Frequency: mon to fri
Street address 1: 915 E 1st St
Street address city: Los Angeles
Street address state: CA
Postal code: 90012-4050
County: Los Angeles
Country: USA
Mailing address 1: 915 E 1st St
Mailing city: Los Angeles
Mailing state: CA
Mailing zip: 90012-4042
Office phone: (213) 229-5000
Office fax: (213) 229-5481
Editorial fax: (213) 229-5462
Web address: www.dailyjournal.com
News services: AP, NYT, CNS, McClatchy
Advertising (Open inch rate) Weekday/Saturday:
  Open inch rate $69.16 (page)

THE ST. LOUIS COUNTIAN

Frequency: mon to sat; S
Street address 1: 319 N 4th St
Street address city: Saint Louis
Street address state: MO
Postal code: 63102-1910
County: Saint Louis City
Country: USA
Mailing address 1: 319 N 4th St
Mailing city: Saint Louis
Mailing state: MO
Mailing zip: 63102-1906
Office phone: (314) 421-1880
Office fax: (314) 421-0436
Advertising phone: (314) 421-1880
Advertising fax: (314) 421-0436
Editorial phone: (314) 421-1880
Editorial fax: (314) 421-0436
Web address: www.thedailyrecord.com
Advertising e-mail: carol.prycma@
  thedailyrecord.com
Editorial e-mail: willc@thedailyrecord.com
News services: RN
Advertising (Open inch rate) Weekday/Saturday:
  Open inch rate $6.56

GOVERNMENT

DAILY JOURNAL OF COMMERCE

Frequency: mon to fri
Street address 1: 3445 N Causeway Blvd
Ste 901
Street address city: Metairie
Street address state: LA
Postal code: 70002-3768
County: Jefferson
Country: USA
Mailing address 1: 3445 N. Causeway Blvd. Suite 901
Mailing city: Metairie
Mailing state: LA
Mailing zip: 70002
Office phone: (504) 834-9292
Office fax: (504) 832-3534
Web address: www.djcgulfcoast.com
General e-mail: mail@nopg.com
Advertising e-mail: anne.lovas@nopg.com
Editorial e-mail: greg.larose@nopg.com
Year established: 1922
Advertising (Open inch rate) Weekday/Saturday:
  Email or call for rates

DAILY RECORD

Frequency: mon to fri
Street address 1: 3323 Leavenworth St
Street address city: Omaha
Street address state: NE

PROFESSIONAL, BUSINESS AND SPECIAL SERVICES

Postal code: 68105-1915
County: Douglas
Country: USA
Mailing address 1: 3323 Leavenworth St
Mailing city: Omaha
Mailing state: NE
Mailing zip: 68105-1900
Office phone: (402) 345-1303
Office fax: (402) 345-2351
Web address: www.omahadailyrecord.com
General e-mail: lhenningsen@omahadailyrecord.com
Advertising e-mail: diane@omahadailyrecord.com
Editorial e-mail: lorraine@omahadailyrecord.com
Year established: 1886
News services: Associated Press, Creators Syndicate, U.S. News Syndicate
Advertising (Open inch rate) Weekday/Saturday: Open inch rate $7.25

METROPOLITAN NEWS-ENTERPRISE

Frequency: mon to fri
Street address 1: 210 S Spring St
Street address city: Los Angeles
Street address state: CA
Postal code: 90012-3710
County: Los Angeles
Country: USA
Mailing address 1: 210 S Spring St
Mailing city: Los Angeles
Mailing state: CA
Mailing zip: 90012-3710
Office phone: (213) 346-0033
Office fax: (213) 687-3886
Web address: www.metnews.com
General e-mail: news@metnews.com
Year established: 90012
News services: AP
Advertising (Open inch rate) Weekday/Saturday: Open inch rate $6.00

ROLLCALL

Frequency: Daily
Street address 1: 1201 Pennsylvania Ave, NW Suite 600
Street address city: Washington
Street address state: DC
Postal code: 20004
County: District Of Columbia
Country: USA
Mailing address 1: 1201 Pennsylvania Ave, NW, Suite 600
Mailing city: Washington
Mailing state: DC
Mailing zip: 20004
Office phone: (202) 650-6500
Office fax: (202) 824-0902
Other phone: (800) 432-2250
Web address: www.rollcall.com
General e-mail: customerservice@cqrollcall.com
Advertising e-mail: advertisedept@cqrollcall.com
Editorial e-mail: tips@rollcall.com
Year established: 1945

SAN FRANCISCO DAILY JOURNAL

Frequency: mon to fri
Street address 1: 44 Montgomery St Ste 500
Street address city: San Francisco
Street address state: CA
Postal code: 94104-4607
County: San Francisco
Country: USA
Mailing address 1: 44 Montgomery St Ste 500
Mailing city: San Francisco
Mailing state: CA
Mailing zip: 94104-4607
Office phone: (415) 296-2400
Office fax: (415) 296-2440
Web address: www.dailyjournal.com
News services: AP
Advertising (Open inch rate) Weekday/Saturday: Open inch rate $754.00 (quarter page)

THE DAILY COMMERCIAL

RECORDER

Frequency: mon to fri
Street address 1: 301 Avenue E
Street address city: San Antonio
Street address state: TX
Postal code: 78205-2006
County: Bexar
Country: USA
Mailing address 1: P.O. Box 2171
Mailing city: San Antonio
Mailing state: TX
Mailing zip: 78297
Office phone: (210) 250-2438
Office fax: (210) 250-2360
Web address: www.primetimenewspapers.com
General e-mail: dcr@primetimenewspapers.com
News services: ACCN, Creator Syndicates, LAT-WP, National American Press Syndicate, NYT.
Advertising (Open inch rate) Weekday/Saturday: Open inch rate $25.00

THE DAILY NEWS

Frequency: mon to fri
Street address 1: 193 Jefferson Ave
Street address city: Memphis
Street address state: TN
Postal code: 38103-2322
County: Shelby
Country: USA
Mailing address 1: 193 JEFFERSON AVE
Mailing city: MEMPHIS
Mailing state: TN
Mailing zip: 38103-2339
Office phone: (901) 523-1561
Office fax: (901) 526-5813
Advertising phone: (901) 528-5283
Advertising fax: (901) 526-5813
Editorial phone: (901) 523-8501
Editorial fax: (901) 526-5813
Web address: www.memphisdailynews.com
General e-mail: jjenkins@memphisdailynews.com
Advertising e-mail: jjenkins@memphisdailynews.com
Editorial e-mail: releases@memphisdailynews.com
Year established: 1886
News services: CNS
Advertising (Open inch rate) Weekday/Saturday: Open inch rate $13.50 (legal)
Circulation Paid: 1000
Circulation Free: 2000
Audited By: USPS

THE DAILY RECORD

Frequency: mon to fri
Street address 1: 11 E Saratoga St
Street address city: Baltimore
Street address state: MD
Postal code: 21202-2115
County: Baltimore City
Country: USA
Mailing address 1: 11 E SARATOGA ST STE 1
Mailing city: BALTIMORE
Mailing state: MD
Mailing zip: 21202-2199
Office phone: (443) 524-8100
Office fax: (410) 752-2894
Advertising phone: (443) 524-8100
Advertising fax: (410) 752-2894
Editorial phone: (443) 524-8150
Editorial fax: (410) 752-2894
Web address: www.thedailyrecord.com
General e-mail: suzanne.huettner@thedailyrecord.com
Advertising e-mail: advertising@thedailyrecord.com
Editorial e-mail: tbaden@thedailyrecord.com
Year established: 1888
Advertising (Open inch rate) Weekday/Saturday: Open inch rate $510.00/Day
Circulation Paid: 2572
Circulation Free: 384
Audited By: Sworn/Estimate/Non-Audited

THE DAILY RECORDER

Frequency: mon to fri
Street address 1: 901 H St Ste 312
Street address city: Sacramento
Street address state: CA
Postal code: 95814-1808
County: Sacramento
Country: USA
Mailing address 1: PO Box 1048
Mailing city: Sacramento
Mailing state: CA
Mailing zip: 95812-1048
Office phone: (916) 444-2355
Office fax: (916) 444-0636
Advertising phone: (800) 652-1700
Web address: www.dailyjournal.com
General e-mail: daily_recorder@dailyjournal.com
Editorial e-mail: jt_long@dailyjournal.com
Year established: 1901
News services: AP, dj
Advertising (Open inch rate) Weekday/Saturday: Open inch rate $26.00

THE DAILY REPORTER

Frequency: mon to fri
Street address 1: 225 E Michigan St Ste 300
Street address city: Milwaukee
Street address state: WI
Postal code: 53202-4900
County: Milwaukee
Country: USA
Mailing address 1: 225 E. Michigan St. Suite 300
Mailing city: Milwaukee
Mailing state: WI
Mailing zip: 53202
Office phone: (414) 276-0273
Office fax: (414) 276-4416
Editorial phone: (414) 225-1807
Web address: www.dailyreporter.com
General e-mail: news@dailyreporter.com
Advertising e-mail: squinn@dailyreporter.com
Editorial e-mail: dshaw@dailyreporter.com
Year established: 1897
News services: AP
Digital Platform - Mobile: Apple˙Android˙Windows
Digital Platform - Tablet: Apple iOS˙Android˙Windows 7
Circulation Paid: 3105

THE JOURNAL RECORD

Frequency: mon to fri
Street address 1: 101 N Robinson Ave Ste 101
Street address city: Oklahoma City
Street address state: OK
Postal code: 73102-5500
County: Oklahoma
Country: USA
Mailing address 1: PO Box 26370
Mailing city: Oklahoma City
Mailing state: OK
Mailing zip: 73126-0370
Office phone: (405) 235-3100
Office fax: (405) 278-6907
Advertising phone: (405) 278-2830
Editorial phone: (405) 278-2850
Editorial fax: (405) 278-2890
Other phone: (877) 615-9536
Web address: www.journalrecord.com
Editorial e-mail: news@journalrecord.com
Year established: 1903
News services: AP
Advertising (Open inch rate) Weekday/Saturday: Open inch rate $18.62
Circulation Paid: 2800
Circulation Free: 69
Audited By: VAC

LAW

AKRON LEGAL NEWS

Frequency: mon to fri
Street address 1: 60 S Summit St
Street address city: Akron
Street address state: OH
Postal code: 44308-1719
County: Summit
Country: USA
Mailing address 1: 60 S Summit St
Mailing city: Akron
Mailing state: OH
Mailing zip: 44308-1775
Office phone: (330) 376-0917
Office fax: (330) 376-7001
Advertising phone: (330) 376-0917
Web address: www.akronlegalnews.com
General e-mail: aln97@apk.net
News services: AP
Advertising (Open inch rate) Weekday/Saturday: Open inch rate $11.00

BROOKLYN DAILY EAGLE & DAILY BULLETIN

Frequency: mon to fri
Street address 1: 16 Court St Ste 1208
Street address city: Brooklyn
Street address state: NY
Postal code: 11241-1012
County: Kings
Country: USA
Mailing address 1: 16 Court St Ste 1208
Mailing city: Brooklyn
Mailing state: NY
Mailing zip: 11241-1012
Office phone: (718) 858-2300
Office fax: (718) 858-8281
Web address: www.brooklyneagle.net
General e-mail: publisher@brooklyneagle.net
Advertising (Open inch rate) Weekday/Saturday: Open inch rate $24.00

CHICAGO DAILY LAW BULLETIN

Frequency: mon to fri
Street address 1: 415 N State St
Street address city: Chicago
Street address state: IL
Postal code: 60654-4607
County: Cook
Country: USA
Mailing address 1: 415 N State St
Mailing city: Chicago
Mailing state: IL
Mailing zip: 60654-4674
Office phone: (312) 644-7800
Office fax: (312) 644-4255
Web address: www.lawbulletin.com
General e-mail: displayads@lbpc.com
News services: AP, NYT
Advertising (Open inch rate) Weekday/Saturday: Open inch rate $26.40 (Classified), $2,588.00 (Full Page Display)

CINCINNATI COURT INDEX

Frequency: mon to fri
Street address 1: 119 W Central Pkwy Fl 2
Street address city: Cincinnati
Street address state: OH
Postal code: 45202-1075
County: Hamilton
Country: USA
Mailing address 1: 119 W Central Pkwy Fl 2
Mailing city: Cincinnati
Mailing state: OH
Mailing zip: 45202-1075
Office phone: (513) 241-1450
Office fax: (513) 684-7821
Web address: www.courtindex.com
General e-mail: support@courtindex.com
News services: AP
Advertising (Open inch rate) Weekday/Saturday: Open inch rate $9.00

PROFESSIONAL, BUSINESS AND SPECIAL SERVICES

DAILY COMMERCE
Frequency: e-mon to fri
Street address 1: 915 E 1st St
Street address city: Los Angeles
Street address state: CA
Postal code: 90012-4050
County: Los Angeles
Country: USA
Mailing address 1: PO Box 54026
Mailing city: Los Angeles
Mailing state: CA
Mailing zip: 90054-0026
Office phone: (213) 229-5300
Office fax: (213) 229 5481
Advertising phone: (213) 229-5511
Advertising fax: (213) 229 5481
Editorial phone: (213) 229-5558
Editorial fax: (213) 229 6462
Web address: www.dailyjournal.com
General e-mail: audreymiller@dailyjournal.com
Year established: 1888
News services: AP, LAT-WP, NYT.
Advertising (Open inch rate) Weekday/Saturday:
  Open inch rate $12.00
Circulation Paid: 1254
Audited By: Sworn/Estimate/Non-Audited

DAILY COMMERCIAL RECORD
Frequency: mon to fri
Street address 1: 706 Main St
Bsmt
Street address city: Dallas
Street address state: TX
Postal code: 75202-3620
County: Dallas
Country: USA
Mailing address 1: 706 Main St Bsmt
Mailing city: Dallas
Mailing state: TX
Mailing zip: 75202-3699
Office phone: (214) 741-6366
Office fax: (214) 741-6373
Web address: www.dailycommercialrecord.com
General e-mail: dcr@dailycommercialrecord.com
Advertising (Open inch rate) Weekday/Saturday:
  Open inch rate $14.76

DAILY COURT REPORTER
Frequency: mon to fri
Street address 1: 120 W 2nd St
Ste 418
Street address city: Dayton
Street address state: OH
Postal code: 45402-1602
County: Montgomery
Country: USA
Mailing address 1: 120 W 2nd St Ste 418
Mailing city: Dayton
Mailing state: OH
Mailing zip: 45402-1602
Office phone: (419) 470-8602
Office fax: (937) 341-5020
Web address: www.dailycourt.com
General e-mail: info@thedailycourt.com
News services: American Court & Commercial Newspapers
Advertising (Open inch rate) Weekday/Saturday:
  Open inch rate $12.00
Audited By: Sworn/Estimate/Non-Audited

DAILY COURT REVIEW
Frequency: mon to fri
Street address 1: 8 Greenway Plz
Ste 101
Street address city: Houston
Street address state: TX
Postal code: 77046-0830
County: Harris
Country: USA
Mailing address 1: PO Box 1889
Mailing city: Houston
Mailing state: TX
Mailing zip: 77251-1889
Office phone: (713) 869-5434
Office fax: (713) 869-8887
Editorial phone: (713) 869-5434
Web address: www.dailycourtreview.com
Editorial e-mail: editor@dailycourtreview.com

Year established: 1889
News services: RN, National Newspaper Association, Texas Press Association
Advertising (Open inch rate) Weekday/Saturday:
  Open inch rate $16.80

DAILY JOURNAL OF COMMERCE
Frequency: mon to fri
Street address 1: 921 SW Washington St
Ste 210
Street address city: Portland
Street address state: OR
Postal code: 97205-2810
County: Multnomah
Country: USA
Mailing address 1: 921 SW Washington St Ste 210
Mailing city: Portland
Mailing state: OR
Mailing zip: 97205-2810
Office phone: (503) 226-1311
Office fax: (503) 226-1315
Advertising phone: (503) 226-1311
Advertising fax: (503) 802-7219
Editorial fax: (503) 802-7239
Web address: www.djcoregon.com
General e-mail: newsroom@djcoregon.com
Advertising e-mail: rynni.henderson@djcoregon.com
Editorial e-mail: stephanie.basalyga@djcoregon.com
Year established: 1872
News services: AP, RN, TMS
Advertising (Open inch rate) Weekday/Saturday:
  Open inch rate $25.00
Digital Platform - Mobile: Apple`Android

DAILY LEGAL NEWS
Frequency: mon to fri
Street address 1: 100 E Federal St
Ste 126
Street address city: Youngstown
Street address state: OH
Postal code: 44503-1834
County: Mahoning
Country: USA
Mailing address 1: 100 E Federal St Ste 126
Mailing city: Youngstown
Mailing state: OH
Mailing zip: 44503-1834
Office phone: (330) 747-7777
Office fax: (330) 747-3977
Web address: www.dlnnews.com
General e-mail: john@akronlegalnews.com
Advertising (Open inch rate) Weekday/Saturday:
  Open inch rate $5.00

DAILY RECORD
Frequency: mon to fri
Street address 1: 3323 Leavenworth St
Street address city: Omaha
Street address state: NE
Postal code: 68105-1915
County: Douglas
Country: USA
Mailing address 1: 3323 Leavenworth St
Mailing city: Omaha
Mailing state: NE
Mailing zip: 68105-1900
Office phone: (402) 345-1303
Office fax: (402) 345-2351
Web address: www.omahadailyrecord.com
General e-mail: lhenningsen@omahadailyrecord.com
Advertising e-mail: diane@omahadailyrecord.com
Editorial e-mail: lorraine@omahadailyrecord.com
Year established: 1886
News services: Associated Press, Creators Syndicate, U.S. News Syndicate
Advertising (Open inch rate) Weekday/Saturday:
  Open inch rate $7.25

DAILY REPORT
Frequency: mon to fri
Street address 1: 190 Pryor St SW
Street address city: Atlanta
Street address state: GA

Postal code: 30303-3607
County: Fulton
Country: USA
Mailing address 1: 190 Pryor St SW
Mailing city: Atlanta
Mailing state: GA
Mailing zip: 30303-3607
Office phone: (404) 521-1227
Office fax: (404) 523-5924
Web address: www.dailyreportonline.com
General e-mail: fcdr@amlaw.com
Year established: 1890
Advertising (Open inch rate) Weekday/Saturday:
  Open inch rate $1,800.00 (page)

FINANCE AND COMMERCE
Frequency: tues to sat
Street address 1: 222 South Ninth Street
Suite 000, Campbell Mithun Tower
Street address city: Minneapolis
Street address state: MN
Postal code: 55402
County: Hennepin
Country: USA
Mailing address 1: 222 South Ninth Street, Suite 900, Campbell Mithun Tower
Mailing city: Minneapolis
Mailing state: MN
Mailing zip: 55402
Office phone: (612) 333-4244
Office fax: (612) 333-3243
Advertising phone: (612) 584-1534
Editorial phone: (612) 584-1556
Other phone: (877) 615-9536
Web address: www.finance-commerce.com
General e-mail: service@bridgetowermedia.com
Year established: 1887
News services: AP
Advertising (Open inch rate) Weekday/Saturday:
  Open inch rate $12.00

FULTON COUNTY DAILY REPORT
Street address 1: 190 Pryor St SW
Street address city: Atlanta
Street address state: GA
Postal code: 30303-3607
County: Fulton
Country: USA
Mailing address 1: 190 PRYOR ST SW
Mailing city: ATLANTA
Mailing state: GA
Mailing zip: 30303-3685
Office phone: (404) 521-1227
Advertising phone: (404) 419-2870
Advertising fax: (404) 419 - 2819
Web address: www.dailyreportonline.com
General e-mail: lsimcoe@alm.com
Digital Platform - Mobile:
  Apple`Android`Windows`Blackberry
Circulation Paid: 2805
Circulation Free: 225
Audited By: VAC

GARFIELD COUNTY LEGAL NEWS
Street address 1: 302 E Maine Ave
Street address city: Enid
Street address state: OK
Postal code: 73701-5746
County: Garfield
Country: USA
Mailing address 1: 302 E Maine Ave
Mailing city: Enid
Mailing state: OK
Mailing zip: 73701-5746
Office phone: (580) 234-7739
Office fax: (580) 237-3237
Advertising phone: (580) 234-7739
Advertising fax: (580) 237-3237
Editorial phone: (580) 234-7739
Editorial fax: (580) 237-3237
Web address: www.garfieldcountylegalnews.com
General e-mail: info@garfieldcountylegalnews.com
Editorial e-mail: publisher@garfieldcountylegalnews.com
Year established: 1913
Advertising (Open inch rate) Weekday/Saturday:

$50.00 ($0.15 per word) (Notice to Creditors)

MIAMI DAILY BUSINESS REVIEW
Frequency: mon to fri
Street address 1: 1 SE 3rd Ave
Ste 900
Street address city: Miami
Street address state: FL
Postal code: 33131-1706
County: Miami-Dade
Country: USA
Mailing address 1: PO Box 10589
Mailing city: Miami
Mailing state: FL
Mailing zip: 33101-0589
Office phone: (305) 377-3721
Office fax: (305) 374-8474
Advertising phone: (305) 347-6623
Advertising fax: (305) 347-6644
Editorial phone: (305) 347-6694
Editorial fax: (305) 347-6626
Web address: www.dailybusinessreview.com
General e-mail: DailyBusinessReview@alm.com
Advertising e-mail: ccurbelo@alm.com
Editorial e-mail: dlyons@alm.com
Year established: 1926
News services: AP, Bloomberg, Florida News Service
Advertising (Open inch rate) Weekday/Saturday:
  Varies: http://www.dailybusinessreview.com/advertising.jsp
Advertising (Open inch rate) Sunday: N/A

MISSOURI LAWYERS MEDIA
Street address 1: 319 N 4th St Fl 5
5th Floor
Street address city: Saint Louis
Street address state: MO
Postal code: 63102-1907
County: Saint Louis City
Country: USA
Mailing address 1: 319 N 4th St Fl 5
5th Floor
Mailing city: Saint Louis
Mailing state: MO
Mailing zip: 63102-1907
Office phone: (314) 421-1880
Office fax: (314) 621-1913
Advertising phone: (314) 558-3260
Advertising fax: (314) 421-7080
Editorial phone: (314) 558-3220
Editorial fax: (314) 621-1913
Web address: www.molawyersmedia.com
General e-mail: service@bridgetowermedia.com
Year established: 1890
Advertising (Open inch rate) Weekday/Saturday: Full Page $2,360.00
Digital Platform - Mobile:
  Apple`Android`Windows
Digital Platform - Tablet: Apple
  iOS`Android`Windows 7
Circulation Paid: 4500
Circulation Free: 10820
Audited By: Sworn/Estimate/Non-Audited

NEW YORK LAW JOURNAL
Frequency: mon to fri
Street address 1: 150 East 42nd Street
Mezzanine Level
Street address city: New York
Street address state: NY
Postal code: 10017
County: New York
Country: USA
Mailing address 1: 150 East 42nd Street, Mezzanine Level
Mailing city: New York
Mailing state: NY
Mailing zip: 10017
Office phone: (720) 895-4985
Web address: www.nylj.com
General e-mail: customercare@alm.com
Year established: 10271
News services: AP
Advertising (Open inch rate) Weekday/Saturday:
  Open inch rate $99.40

PROFESSIONAL, BUSINESS AND SPECIAL SERVICES

PALM BEACH DAILY BUSINESS REVIEW

Frequency: mon to fri
Street address 1: 1 SE 3rd Ave
Ste 900
Street address city: Miami
Street address state: FL
Postal code: 33131-1706
County: Miami-Dade
Country: USA
Mailing address 1: 1 SE 3rd Ave
Suite 900
Mailing city: Miami
Mailing state: FL
Mailing zip: 33131-1700
Office phone: (305) 377-3721
Office fax: (561) 820-2077
Advertising phone: (305) 347-6623
Advertising fax: (305) 347-6644
Editorial phone: (305) 347-6694
Editorial fax: (305) 347-6626
Web address: www.dailybusinessreview.com
General e-mail: DailyBusinessReview@alm.com
Advertising e-mail: ccurbelo@alm.com
Editorial e-mail: dlyons@alm.com
Year established: 1979
News services: AP, Bloomberg, Florida News Service
Advertising (Open inch rate) Weekday/Saturday: http://www.dailybusinessreview.com/advertising.jsp
Advertising (Open inch rate) Sunday: N/A

PITTSBURGH LEGAL JOURNAL

Frequency: mon to fri
Street address 1: 436 7th Ave
Street address city: Pittsburgh
Street address state: PA
Postal code: 15219-1826
County: Allegheny
Country: USA
Mailing address 1: 436 7th Ave Ste 4
Mailing city: Pittsburgh
Mailing state: PA
Mailing zip: 15219-1827
Office phone: (412) 402-6623
Office fax: (412) 320-7965
Web address: www.pittsburghlegaljournal.com
General e-mail: JPULICE@SCBA.ORG
Year established: 1853
Advertising (Open inch rate) Weekday/Saturday: Open inch rate $8.75

SAINT PAUL LEGAL LEDGER

Frequency: mon to thur
Street address 1: 332 Minnesota St
Ste E1432
Street address city: Saint Paul
Street address state: MN
Postal code: 55101-1309
County: Ramsey
Country: USA
Mailing address 1: 332 Minnesota St Ste E1432
Mailing city: Saint Paul
Mailing state: MN
Mailing zip: 55101-1309
Office phone: (612) 333-4244
Office fax: (651) 222-2640
Editorial phone: (651) 602-0575
Web address: www.legal-ledger.com
General e-mail: steve.jahn@finance-commerce.com
Year established: 55101-1163
News services: AP
Advertising (Open inch rate) Weekday/Saturday: Open inch rate $12.00 (legal)

SAN FRANCISCO DAILY JOURNAL

Frequency: mon to fri
Street address 1: 44 Montgomery St
Ste 500
Street address city: San Francisco
Street address state: CA
Postal code: 94104-4607
County: San Francisco
Country: USA
Mailing address 1: 44 Montgomery St Ste 500
Mailing city: San Francisco
Mailing state: CA
Mailing zip: 94104-4607
Office phone: (415) 296-2400
Office fax: (415) 296-2440
Web address: www.dailyjournal.com
News services: AP
Advertising (Open inch rate) Weekday/Saturday: Open inch rate $754.00 (quarter page)

ST. JOSEPH DAILY COURIER

Frequency: mon to fri
Street address 1: 1020 S 10th St
Street address city: Saint Joseph
Street address state: MO
Postal code: 64503-2407
County: Buchanan
Country: USA
Mailing address 1: 1020 S 10th St
Mailing city: Saint Joseph
Mailing state: MO
Mailing zip: 64503-2407
Office phone: (816) 279-3441
Office fax: (816) 279-2091
General e-mail: sjdailycourier@sbcglobal.net

ST. LOUIS DAILY RECORD

Frequency: mon to sat; S
Street address 1: 319 N 4th St
Fl 5
Street address city: Saint Louis
Street address state: MO
Postal code: 63102-1907
County: Saint Louis City
Country: USA
Mailing address 1: PO Box 88910
Mailing city: Saint Louis
Mailing state: MO
Mailing zip: 63188-1910
Office phone: (314) 421-1880
Office fax: (314) 421-0436
Advertising phone: (314) 421-1880
Advertising fax: (314) 421-7080
Editorial phone: (314) 421-1880
Editorial fax: (314) 421-0436
Web address: www.molawyers.com
General e-mail: editcopy@thedailyrecord.com
Advertising e-mail: johnny.aguirre@molawyersmedia.com
Editorial e-mail: fred.ehrlich@molawyersmedia.com
News services: RN
Advertising (Open inch rate) Weekday/Saturday: Open inch rate $6.56
Digital Platform - Mobile: Apple Android Windows
Digital Platform - Tablet: Apple iOS Android Windows 7

THE DAILY COMMERCIAL RECORDER

Frequency: mon to fri
Street address 1: 301 Avenue E
Street address city: San Antonio
Street address state: TX
Postal code: 78205-2006
County: Bexar
Country: USA
Mailing address 1: P.O. Box 2171
Mailing city: San Antonio
Mailing state: TX
Mailing zip: 78297
Office phone: (210) 250-2438
Office fax: (210) 250-2360
Web address: www.primetimenewspapers.com
General e-mail: dcr@primetimenewspapers.com
News services: ACCN, Creator Syndicates, LAT-WP, National American Press Syndicate, NYT.
Advertising (Open inch rate) Weekday/Saturday: Open inch rate $25.00

THE DAILY EVENTS

Frequency: mon to fri
Street address 1: 310 W Walnut St
Street address city: Springfield
Street address state: MO
Postal code: 65806-2118
County: Greene
Country: USA
Mailing address 1: PO Box 1
Mailing city: Springfield
Mailing state: MO
Mailing zip: 65801-0001
Office phone: (417) 866-1401
Office fax: (417) 866-1491
Web address: www.thedailyevents.com
General e-mail: info@dailyevents.com
Year established: 1881
News services: American Court & Commercial Newspapers

THE DAILY JOURNAL

Frequency: mon to fri
Street address 1: 1114 W 7th Ave
Ste 100
Street address city: Denver
Street address state: CO
Postal code: 80204-4455
County: Denver
Country: USA
Mailing address 1: 1114 W 7th Ave Ste 100
Mailing city: Denver
Mailing state: CO
Mailing zip: 80204-4455
Office phone: (303) 756-9995
Office fax: (303) 756-4465
Advertising phone: (303) 584-6737
Advertising fax: (303) 584-6717
Editorial phone: (303) 584-6724
Editorial fax: (303) 756-4465
Web address: www.colorado.construction.com
Year established: 1897
Advertising (Open inch rate) Weekday/Saturday: Open inch rate $25.20

THE DAILY LEGAL NEWS AND CLEVELAND RECORDER

Frequency: tues to sat
Street address 1: 2935 Prospect Ave E
Street address city: Cleveland
Street address state: OH
Postal code: 44115-2607
County: Cuyahoga
Country: USA
Mailing address 1: 2935 Prospect Ave E
Mailing city: Cleveland
Mailing state: OH
Mailing zip: 44115-2688
Office phone: (216) 696-3322
Office fax: (216) 696-6329
Web address: www.dln.com
General e-mail: dln@dln.com
Advertising e-mail: ads@dln.com
Editorial e-mail: editor@dln.com
Year established: 1885
News services: AP, National Newspaper Association, Ohio Newspaper Association
Advertising (Open inch rate) Weekday/Saturday: Open inch rate $16.00

THE DAILY NEWS

Frequency: mon to fri
Street address 1: 193 Jefferson Ave
Street address city: Memphis
Street address state: TN
Postal code: 38103-2322
County: Shelby
Country: USA
Mailing address 1: 193 JEFFERSON AVE
Mailing city: MEMPHIS
Mailing state: TN
Mailing zip: 38103-2339
Office phone: (901) 523-1561
Office fax: (901) 526-5813
Advertising phone: (901) 528-5283
Advertising fax: (901) 526-5813
Editorial phone: (901) 523-8501
Editorial fax: (901) 526-5813
Web address: www.memphisdailynews.com
General e-mail: jjenkins@memphisdailynews.com
Advertising e-mail: jjenkins@memphisdailynews.com
Editorial e-mail: releases@memphisdailynews.com
Year established: 1886
News services: CNS
Advertising (Open inch rate) Weekday/Saturday: Open inch rate $13.50 (legal)
Circulation Paid: 1000
Circulation Free: 2000
Audited By: USPS

THE DAILY RECORD

Frequency: mon to fri
Street address 1: 300 S Izard St
Street address city: Little Rock
Street address state: AR
Postal code: 72201-2114
County: Pulaski
Country: USA
Mailing address 1: PO Box 3595
Mailing city: Little Rock
Mailing state: AR
Mailing zip: 72203-3595
Office phone: (501) 374-5103
Office fax: (501) 372-3048
Web address: www.dailyrecord.us
General e-mail: bobby@dailydata.com
Advertising e-mail: jedwards@dailydata.com
Editorial e-mail: editor@dailydata.com
Year established: 1925
News services: NNS, TMS, DRNW, INS
Advertising (Open inch rate) Weekday/Saturday: Column Inch Rate - $20.00
Circulation Paid: 3210
Circulation Free: 25
Audited By: USPS

THE DAILY RECORD

Frequency: mon to fri
Street address 1: 16 W Main St
Street address city: Rochester
Street address state: NY
Postal code: 14614-1602
County: Monroe
Country: USA
Mailing address 1: PO Box 30006
Mailing city: Rochester
Mailing state: NY
Mailing zip: 14603-3006
Office phone: (585) 232-6920
Office fax: (585) 232-2740
Web address: www.nydailyrecord.com
General e-mail: kevin.momot@nydailyrecord.com
Year established: 14603-3006
News services: American Court & Commercial Newspapers, National Newspaper Association
Advertising (Open inch rate) Weekday/Saturday: Open inch rate $.90 (agency line), $.75 (retail line)

THE DAILY RECORD

Frequency: mon to fri
Street address 1: 436 S 7th St
Ste 300
Street address city: Louisville
Street address state: KY
Postal code: 40203-1980
County: Jefferson
Country: USA
Mailing address 1: PO Box 1062
Mailing city: Louisville
Mailing state: KY
Mailing zip: 40201-1062
Office phone: (502) 583-4471
Office fax: (502) 585-5453
General e-mail: janicep@nacms-c.com
Year established: 40201
News services: National Association of Credit Management
Advertising (Open inch rate) Weekday/Saturday: Open inch rate $1.20 (legal line)

THE DAILY RECORDER

Frequency: mon to fri
Street address 1: 901 H St
Ste 312
Street address city: Sacramento
Street address state: CA
Postal code: 95814-1808

PROFESSIONAL, BUSINESS AND SPECIAL SERVICES

II-13

County: Sacramento
Country: USA
Mailing address 1: PO Box 1048
Mailing city: Sacramento
Mailing state: CA
Mailing zip: 95812-1048
Office phone: (916) 444-2355
Office fax: (916) 444-0636
Advertising phone: (800) 652-1700
Web address: www.dailyjournal.com
General e-mail: daily_recorder@dailyjournal.com
Editorial e-mail: jt_long@dailyjournal.com
Year established: 1901
News services: AP, dj
Advertising (Open inch rate) Weekday/Saturday:
 Open inch rate $26.00

THE DAILY REPORTER

Frequency: mon to fri
Street address 1: 225 E Michigan St
Ste 300
Street address city: Milwaukee
Street address state: WI
Postal code: 53202-4900
County: Milwaukee
Country: USA
Mailing address 1: 225 E. Michigan St.
Suite 300
Mailing city: Milwaukee
Mailing state: WI
Mailing zip: 53202
Office phone: (414) 276-0273
Office fax: (414) 276-4416
Editorial phone: (414) 225-1807
Web address: www.dailyreporter.com
General e-mail: news@dailyreporter.com
Advertising e-mail: squinn@dailyreporter.com
Editorial e-mail: dshaw@dailyreporter.com
Year established: 1897
News services: AP
Digital Platform - Mobile:
 Apple`Android`Windows
Digital Platform - Tablet: Apple
 iOS`Android`Windows 7
Circulation Paid: 3105

THE DAILY TERRITORIAL

Frequency: m-mon to fri
Street address 1: 7225 N. Mona Lisa Rd.
#125
Street address city: Tucson
Street address state: AZ
Postal code: 85741
County: Pima
Country: USA
Mailing address 1: 7225 N. Mona Lisa Rd., #125
Mailing city: Tucson
Mailing state: AZ
Mailing zip: 85741
Office phone: (520) 797-4384
Office fax: (520) 575-8891
Advertising phone: (520) 294-1200
Editorial phone: (520) 294-1200
Web address: www.azbiz.com
General e-mail: tucsoneditor@
 tucsonlocalmedia.com
Advertising e-mail: classifieds@
 tucsonlocalmedia.com
Editorial e-mail: tucsoneditor@
 tucsonlocalmedia.com
Year established: 1966
News services: American Newspaper
 Representatives Inc..
Advertising (Open inch rate) Weekday/Saturday:
 Open inch rate $5.45
Circulation Paid: 753
Audited By: Sworn/Estimate/Non-Audited

THE INTER-CITY EXPRESS

Frequency: mon to fri
Street address 1: 1109 Oak St
Street address city: Oakland
Street address state: CA
Postal code: 94607-4904
County: Alameda
Country: USA
Mailing address 1: 1109 Oak St Ste 103
Mailing city: Oakland

Mailing state: CA
Mailing zip: 94607-4917
Office phone: (510) 272-4747
Office fax: (510) 465-1576
Web address: www.intercityexpress.news/
 home.cfm

THE JOURNAL RECORD

Frequency: mon to fri
Street address 1: 101 N Robinson Ave
Ste 101
Street address city: Oklahoma City
Street address state: OK
Postal code: 73102-5500
County: Oklahoma
Country: USA
Mailing address 1: PO Box 26370
Mailing city: Oklahoma City
Mailing state: OK
Mailing zip: 73126-0370
Office phone: (405) 235-3100
Office fax: (405) 278-6907
Advertising phone: (405) 278-2830
Editorial phone: (405) 278-2850
Editorial fax: (405) 278-2890
Other phone: (877) 615-9536
Web address: www.journalrecord.com
Editorial e-mail: news@journalrecord.com
Year established: 1903
News services: AP
Advertising (Open inch rate) Weekday/Saturday:
 Open inch rate $18.62
Circulation Paid: 2800
Circulation Free: 69
Audited By: VAC

THE LEGAL INTELLIGENCER

Frequency: mon to fri
Street address 1: 1617 John F Kennedy Blvd
Ste 1750
Street address city: Philadelphia
Street address state: PA
Postal code: 19103-1854
County: Philadelphia
Country: USA
Mailing address 1: 1617 John F Kennedy Blvd
 Ste 1750
Mailing city: Philadelphia
Mailing state: PA
Mailing zip: 19103-1854
Office phone: (215) 557-2300
Office fax: (215) 557-2301
Advertising phone: (215) 557-2359
Advertising fax: (215) 557-2301
Editorial phone: (215) 557-2489
Editorial fax: (215) 557-2301
Web address: www.thelegalintelligencer.com
General e-mail: HGREZLAK@ALM.COM
Advertising e-mail: dchalphin@alm.com
Editorial e-mail: hgrezlak@alm.com
Year established: 1843
News services: AP

THE LOS ANGELES DAILY JOURNAL

Frequency: mon to fri
Street address 1: 915 E 1st St
Street address city: Los Angeles
Street address state: CA
Postal code: 90012-4050
County: Los Angeles
Country: USA
Mailing address 1: 915 E 1st St
Mailing city: Los Angeles
Mailing state: CA
Mailing zip: 90012-4042
Office phone: (213) 229-5300
Office fax: (213) 229-5481
Editorial fax: (213) 229-5462
Web address: www.dailyjournal.com
News services: AP, NYT, CNS, McClatchy
Advertising (Open inch rate) Weekday/Saturday:
 Open inch rate $69.16 (page)

THE RECORD REPORTER

Frequency: Mon`Wed`Fri
Street address 1: 2025 N 3rd St
Ste 155
Street address city: Phoenix

Street address state: AZ
Postal code: 85004-1425
County: Maricopa
Country: USA
Office phone: (602) 417-9900
Office fax: (602) 417-9910
Web address: www.recordreporter.com
General e-mail: Diane_Heuel@dailyjournal.com
Advertising e-mail: record_reporter@
 dailyjournal.com
Editorial e-mail: diane_heuel@dailyjournal.com
Year established: 1914
Digital Platform - Mobile:
 Apple`Android`Blackberry
Digital Platform - Tablet: Apple
 iOS`Android`Windows 7`Blackberry Tablet
 OS

THE RECORDER

Frequency: mon to fri
Street address 1: 1035 Market St
Ste 500
Street address city: San Francisco
Street address state: CA
Postal code: 94103-1650
County: San Francisco
Country: USA
Mailing address 1: 1035 Market St Ste 500
Mailing city: San Francisco
Mailing state: CA
Mailing zip: 94103-1650
Office phone: (415) 749-5400
Office fax: (415) 749-5449
Advertising phone: (415) 749-5444
Advertising fax: (415) 749-5566
Editorial fax: (415) 749-5549
Other phone: (415) 749-5500
Web address: www.therecorder.com
General e-mail: recorder_editor@alm.com
Year established: 1877
News services: AP
Advertising (Open inch rate) Weekday/Saturday:
 Open inch rate $3,200.00 (Full Page
 Display)

THE ST. LOUIS COUNTIAN

Frequency: mon to sat; S
Street address 1: 319 N 4th St
Street address city: Saint Louis
Street address state: MO
Postal code: 63102-1910
County: Saint Louis City
Country: USA
Mailing address 1: 319 N 4th St
Mailing city: Saint Louis
Mailing state: MO
Mailing zip: 63102-1906
Office phone: (314) 421-1880
Office fax: (314) 421-0436
Advertising phone: (314) 421-1880
Advertising fax: (314) 421-0436
Editorial phone: (314) 421-1880
Editorial fax: (314) 421-0436
Web address: www.thedailyrecord.com
Advertising e-mail: carol.prycma@
 thedailyrecord.com
Editorial e-mail: willc@thedailyrecord.com
News services: RN
Advertising (Open inch rate) Weekday/Saturday:
 Open inch rate $6.56

MEDICAL

LOUISIANA MEDICAL NEWS

Frequency: Monthly
Street address 1: 600 Guilbeau Rd
Ste A
Street address city: Lafayette
Street address state: LA
Postal code: 70506-8405
County: Lafayette
Country: USA
Mailing address 1: PO Box 60010
Mailing city: Lafayette

Mailing state: LA
Mailing zip: 70596-0010
Office phone: (337) 235-5455
Office fax: (337) 232-2959
Web address: www.louisianamedicalnews.com
Advertising e-mail: brandycav@gmail.com
Editorial e-mail: editor@medicalnewsinc.com

MUNICIPAL BONDS

DAILY JOURNAL OF COMMERCE

Frequency: mon to fri
Street address 1: 3445 N Causeway Blvd
Ste 901
Street address city: Metairie
Street address state: LA
Postal code: 70002-3768
County: Jefferson
Country: USA
Mailing address 1: 3445 N. Causeway Blvd.
 Suite 901
Mailing city: Metairie
Mailing state: LA
Mailing zip: 70002
Office phone: (504) 834-9292
Office fax: (504) 832-3534
Web address: www.djcgulfcoast.com
General e-mail: mail@nopg.com
Advertising e-mail: anne.lovas@nopg.com
Editorial e-mail: greg.larose@nopg.com
Year established: 1922
Advertising (Open inch rate) Weekday/Saturday:
 Email or call for rates

DAILY RECORD

Frequency: mon to fri
Street address 1: 3323 Leavenworth St
Street address city: Omaha
Street address state: NE
Postal code: 68105-1915
County: Douglas
Country: USA
Mailing address 1: 3323 Leavenworth St
Mailing city: Omaha
Mailing state: NE
Mailing zip: 68105-1900
Office phone: (402) 345-1303
Office fax: (402) 345-2351
Web address: www.omahadailyrecord.com
General e-mail: lhenningsen@
 omahadailyrecord.com
Advertising e-mail: diane@omahadailyrecord.
 com
Editorial e-mail: lorraine@omahadailyrecord.
 com
Year established: 1886
News services: Associated Press, Creators
 Syndicate, U.S. News Syndicate
Advertising (Open inch rate) Weekday/Saturday:
 Open inch rate $7.25

MUNICIPAL FINANCE

DAILY RECORD

Frequency: mon to fri
Street address 1: 3323 Leavenworth St
Street address city: Omaha
Street address state: NE
Postal code: 68105-1915
County: Douglas
Country: USA
Mailing address 1: 3323 Leavenworth St
Mailing city: Omaha
Mailing state: NE
Mailing zip: 68105-1900
Office phone: (402) 345-1303
Office fax: (402) 345-2351
Web address: www.omahadailyrecord.com
General e-mail: lhenningsen@
 omahadailyrecord.com

PROFESSIONAL, BUSINESS AND SPECIAL SERVICES

Advertising e-mail: diane@omahadailyrecord.com
Editorial e-mail: lorraine@omahadailyrecord.com
Year established: 1886
News services: Associated Press, Creators Syndicate, U.S. News Syndicate
Advertising (Open inch rate) Weekday/Saturday: Open inch rate $7.25

THE BOND BUYER

Frequency: mon to fri
Street address 1: 1 State St
Street address city: New York
Street address state: NY
Postal code: 10004-1561
County: New York
Country: USA
Mailing address 1: 1 State St Fl 26
Mailing city: New York
Mailing state: NY
Mailing zip: 10004-1483
Office phone: (212) 803-8200
Office fax: (212) 803-1592
Advertising phone: (212) 843-9617
Advertising fax: (212) 843-9617
Editorial fax: (212) 843-9614
Web address: www.bondbuyer.com
General e-mail: michael.stanton@sourcemedia.com
Advertising (Open inch rate) Weekday/Saturday: Open inch rate $168.00

PUBLIC NOTICE

DAILY JOURNAL OF COMMERCE

Frequency: mon to fri
Street address 1: 3445 N Causeway Blvd Ste 901
Street address city: Metairie
Street address state: LA
Postal code: 70002-3768
County: Jefferson
Country: USA
Mailing address 1: 3445 N. Causeway Blvd. Suite 901
Mailing city: Metairie
Mailing state: LA
Mailing zip: 70002
Office phone: (504) 834-9292
Office fax: (504) 832-3534
Web address: www.djcgulfcoast.com
General e-mail: mail@nopg.com
Advertising e-mail: anne.lovas@nopg.com
Editorial e-mail: greg.larose@nopg.com
Year established: 1922
Advertising (Open inch rate) Weekday/Saturday: Email or call for rates

DAILY JOURNAL OF COMMERCE

Frequency: mon to fri
Street address 1: 921 SW Washington St Ste 210
Street address city: Portland
Street address state: OR
Postal code: 97205-2810
County: Multnomah
Country: USA
Mailing address 1: 921 SW Washington St Ste 210
Mailing city: Portland
Mailing state: OR
Mailing zip: 97205-2810
Office phone: (503) 226-1311
Office fax: (503) 226-1315
Advertising phone: (503) 226-1311
Advertising fax: (503) 802-7219
Editorial fax: (503) 802-7239
Web address: www.djcoregon.com
General e-mail: newsroom@djcoregon.com
Advertising e-mail: rynni.henderson@djcoregon.com
Editorial e-mail: stephanie.basalyga@djcoregon.com

Year established: 1872
News services: AP, RN, TMS
Advertising (Open inch rate) Weekday/Saturday: Open inch rate $25.00
Digital Platform - Mobile: Apple`Android

DAILY RECORD

Frequency: mon to fri
Street address 1: 3323 Leavenworth St
Street address city: Omaha
Street address state: NE
Postal code: 68105-1915
County: Douglas
Country: USA
Mailing address 1: 3323 Leavenworth St
Mailing city: Omaha
Mailing state: NE
Mailing zip: 68105-1900
Office phone: (402) 345-1303
Office fax: (402) 345-2351
Web address: www.omahadailyrecord.com
General e-mail: lhenningsen@omahadailyrecord.com
Advertising e-mail: diane@omahadailyrecord.com
Editorial e-mail: lorraine@omahadailyrecord.com
Year established: 1886
News services: Associated Press, Creators Syndicate, U.S. News Syndicate
Advertising (Open inch rate) Weekday/Saturday: Open inch rate $7.25

MISSOURI LAWYERS MEDIA

Street address 1: 319 N 4th St Fl 5 5th Floor
Street address city: Saint Louis
Street address state: MO
Postal code: 63102-1907
County: Saint Louis City
Country: USA
Mailing address 1: 319 N 4th St Fl 5 5th Floor
Mailing city: Saint Louis
Mailing state: MO
Mailing zip: 63102-1907
Office phone: (314) 421-1880
Office fax: (314) 621-1913
Advertising phone: (314) 558-3260
Advertising fax: (314) 421-7080
Editorial phone: (314) 558-3220
Editorial fax: (314) 621-1913
Web address: www.molawyersmedia.com
General e-mail: service@bridgetowermedia.com
Year established: 1890
Advertising (Open inch rate) Weekday/Saturday: Full Page $2,360.00
Digital Platform - Mobile: Apple`Android`Windows
Digital Platform - Tablet: Apple iOS`Android`Windows 7
Circulation Paid: 4500
Circulation Free: 10820
Audited By: Sworn/Estimate/Non-Audited

THE DAILY COMMERCIAL RECORDER

Frequency: mon to fri
Street address 1: 301 Avenue E
Street address city: San Antonio
Street address state: TX
Postal code: 78205-2006
County: Bexar
Country: USA
Mailing address 1: P.O. Box 2171
Mailing city: San Antonio
Mailing state: TX
Mailing zip: 78297
Office phone: (210) 250-2438
Office fax: (210) 250-2360
Web address: www.primetimenewspapers.com
General e-mail: dcr@primetimenewspapers.com
News services: ACCN, Creator Syndicates, LAT-WP, National American Press Syndicate, NYT.
Advertising (Open inch rate) Weekday/Saturday: Open inch rate $25.00

THE DAILY NEWS

Frequency: mon to fri
Street address 1: 193 Jefferson Ave
Street address city: Memphis
Street address state: TN
Postal code: 38103-2322
County: Shelby
Country: USA
Mailing address 1: 193 JEFFERSON AVE
Mailing city: MEMPHIS
Mailing state: TN
Mailing zip: 38103-2339
Office phone: (901) 523-1561
Office fax: (901) 526-5813
Advertising phone: (901) 528-5283
Advertising fax: (901) 526-5813
Editorial phone: (901) 523-8501
Editorial fax: (901) 526-5813
Web address: www.memphisdailynews.com
General e-mail: jjenkins@memphisdailynews.com
Advertising e-mail: jjenkins@memphisdailynews.com
Editorial e-mail: releases@memphisdailynews.com
Year established: 1886
News services: CNS
Advertising (Open inch rate) Weekday/Saturday: Open inch rate $13.50 (legal)
Circulation Paid: 1000
Circulation Free: 2000
Audited By: USPS

THE DAILY RECORD

Frequency: mon to fri
Street address 1: 300 S Izard St
Street address city: Little Rock
Street address state: AR
Postal code: 72201-2114
County: Pulaski
Country: USA
Mailing address 1: PO Box 3595
Mailing city: Little Rock
Mailing state: AR
Mailing zip: 72203-3595
Office phone: (501) 374-5103
Office fax: (501) 372-3048
Web address: www.dailyrecord.us
General e-mail: bobby@dailydata.com
Advertising e-mail: jedwards@dailydata.com
Editorial e-mail: editor@dailydata.com
Year established: 1925
News services: NNS, TMS, DRNW, INS
Advertising (Open inch rate) Weekday/Saturday: Column Inch Rate - $20.00
Circulation Paid: 3210
Circulation Free: 25
Audited By: USPS

THE DAILY RECORD

Frequency: mon to fri
Street address 1: 11 E Saratoga St
Street address city: Baltimore
Street address state: MD
Postal code: 21202-2115
County: Baltimore City
Country: USA
Mailing address 1: 11 E SARATOGA ST STE 1
Mailing city: BALTIMORE
Mailing state: MD
Mailing zip: 21202-2199
Office phone: (443) 524-8100
Office fax: (410) 752-2894
Advertising phone: (443) 524-8100
Advertising fax: (410) 752-2894
Editorial phone: (443) 524-8150
Editorial fax: (410) 752-2894
Web address: www.thedailyrecord.com
General e-mail: suzanne.huettner@thedailyrecord.com
Advertising e-mail: advertising@thedailyrecord.com
Editorial e-mail: tbaden@thedailyrecord.com
Year established: 1888
Advertising (Open inch rate) Weekday/Saturday: Open inch rate $510.00/Day
Circulation Paid: 2572
Circulation Free: 384
Audited By: Sworn/Estimate/Non-Audited

THE DAILY REPORTER

Frequency: mon to fri
Street address 1: 225 E Michigan St Ste 300
Street address city: Milwaukee
Street address state: WI
Postal code: 53202-4900
County: Milwaukee
Country: USA
Mailing address 1: 225 E. Michigan St. Suite 300
Mailing city: Milwaukee
Mailing state: WI
Mailing zip: 53202
Office phone: (414) 276-0273
Office fax: (414) 276-4416
Editorial phone: (414) 225-1807
Web address: www.dailyreporter.com
General e-mail: news@dailyreporter.com
Advertising e-mail: squinn@dailyreporter.com
Editorial e-mail: dshaw@dailyreporter.com
Year established: 1897
News services: AP
Digital Platform - Mobile: Apple`Android`Windows
Digital Platform - Tablet: Apple iOS`Android`Windows 7
Circulation Paid: 3105

THE JOURNAL RECORD

Frequency: mon to fri
Street address 1: 101 N Robinson Ave Ste 101
Street address city: Oklahoma City
Street address state: OK
Postal code: 73102-5500
County: Oklahoma
Country: USA
Mailing address 1: PO Box 26370
Mailing city: Oklahoma City
Mailing state: OK
Mailing zip: 73126-0370
Office phone: (405) 235-3100
Office fax: (405) 278-6907
Advertising phone: (405) 278-2830
Editorial phone: (405) 278-2850
Editorial fax: (405) 278-2890
Other phone: (877) 615-9536
Web address: www.journalrecord.com
Editorial e-mail: news@journalrecord.com
Year established: 1903
News services: AP
Advertising (Open inch rate) Weekday/Saturday: Open inch rate $18.62
Circulation Paid: 2800
Circulation Free: 69
Audited By: VAC

THE LEGAL INTELLIGENCER

Frequency: mon to fri
Street address 1: 1617 John F Kennedy Blvd Ste 1750
Street address city: Philadelphia
Street address state: PA
Postal code: 19103-1854
County: Philadelphia
Country: USA
Mailing address 1: 1617 John F Kennedy Blvd Ste 1750
Mailing city: Philadelphia
Mailing state: PA
Mailing zip: 19103-1854
Office phone: (215) 557-2300
Office fax: (215) 557-2301
Advertising phone: (215) 557-2359
Advertising fax: (215) 557-2301
Editorial phone: (215) 557-2489
Editorial fax: (215) 557-2301
Web address: www.thelegalintelligencer.com
General e-mail: HGREZLAK@ALM.COM
Advertising e-mail: dchalphin@alm.com
Editorial e-mail: hgrezlak@alm.com
Year established: 1843
News services: AP

THE RECORD REPORTER

Frequency: Mon`Wed`Fri

PROFESSIONAL, BUSINESS AND SPECIAL SERVICES

Street address 1: 2025 N 3rd St
Ste 155
Street address city: Phoenix
Street address state: AZ
Postal code: 85004-1425
County: Maricopa
Country: USA

Office phone: (602) 417-9900
Office fax: (602) 417-9910
Web address: www.recordreporter.com
General e-mail: Diane_Heuel@dailyjournal.com
Advertising e-mail: record_reporter@dailyjournal.com
Editorial e-mail: diane_heuel@dailyjournal.com
Year established: 1914
Digital Platform - Mobile: Apple`Android`Blackberry
Digital Platform - Tablet: Apple iOS`Android`Windows 7`Blackberry Tablet OS

REAL ESTATE

BROOKLYN DAILY EAGLE & DAILY BULLETIN

Frequency: mon to fri
Street address 1: 16 Court St
Ste 1208
Street address city: Brooklyn
Street address state: NY
Postal code: 11241-1012
County: Kings
Country: USA
Mailing address 1: 16 Court St Ste 1208
Mailing city: Brooklyn
Mailing state: NY
Mailing zip: 11241-1012
Office phone: (718) 858-2300
Office fax: (718) 858-8281
Web address: www.brooklyneagle.net
General e-mail: publisher@brooklyneagle.net
Advertising (Open inch rate) Weekday/Saturday:
    Open inch rate $24.00

DAILY JOURNAL OF COMMERCE

Frequency: mon to fri
Street address 1: 921 SW Washington St
Ste 210
Street address city: Portland
Street address state: OR
Postal code: 97205-2810
County: Multnomah
Country: USA
Mailing address 1: 921 SW Washington St Ste 210
Mailing city: Portland
Mailing state: OR
Mailing zip: 97205-2810
Office phone: (503) 226-1311
Office fax: (503) 226-1315
Advertising phone: (503) 226-1311
Advertising fax: (503) 802-7219
Editorial fax: (503) 802-7239
Web address: www.djcoregon.com
General e-mail: newsroom@djcoregon.com
Advertising e-mail: rynni.henderson@djcoregon.com
Editorial e-mail: stephanie.basalyga@djcoregon.com
Year established: 1872
News services: AP, RN, TMS
Advertising (Open inch rate) Weekday/Saturday:
    Open inch rate $25.00
Digital Platform - Mobile: Apple`Android

DAILY RECORD

Frequency: mon to fri
Street address 1: 3323 Leavenworth St
Street address city: Omaha
Street address state: NE
Postal code: 68105-1915
County: Douglas
Country: USA

Mailing address 1: 3323 Leavenworth St
Mailing city: Omaha
Mailing state: NE
Mailing zip: 68105-1900
Office phone: (402) 345-1303
Office fax: (402) 345-2351
Web address: www.omahadailyrecord.com
General e-mail: lhenningsen@omahadailyrecord.com
Advertising e-mail: diane@omahadailyrecord.com
Editorial e-mail: lorraine@omahadailyrecord.com
Year established: 1886
News services: Associated Press, Creators Syndicate, U.S. News Syndicate
Advertising (Open inch rate) Weekday/Saturday:
    Open inch rate $7.25

MIAMI DAILY BUSINESS REVIEW

Frequency: mon to fri
Street address 1: 1 SE 3rd Ave
Ste 900
Street address city: Miami
Street address state: FL
Postal code: 33131-1706
County: Miami-Dade
Country: USA
Mailing address 1: PO Box 10589
Mailing city: Miami
Mailing state: FL
Mailing zip: 33101-0589
Office phone: (305) 377-3721
Office fax: (305) 374-8474
Advertising phone: (305) 347-6623
Advertising fax: (305) 347-6644
Editorial phone: (305) 347-6694
Editorial fax: (305) 347-6626
Web address: www.dailybusinessreview.com
General e-mail: DailyBusinessReview@alm.com
Advertising e-mail: ccurbelo@alm.com
Editorial e-mail: dlyons@alm.com
Year established: 1926
News services: AP, Bloomberg, Florida News Service
Advertising (Open inch rate) Weekday/Saturday:
    Varies: http://www.dailybusinessreview.com/advertising.jsp
Advertising (Open inch rate) Sunday: N/A

PALM BEACH DAILY BUSINESS REVIEW

Frequency: mon to fri
Street address 1: 1 SE 3rd Ave
Ste 900
Street address city: Miami
Street address state: FL
Postal code: 33131-1706
County: Miami-Dade
Country: USA
Mailing address 1: 1 SE 3rd Ave
Suite 900
Mailing city: Miami
Mailing state: FL
Mailing zip: 33131-1700
Office phone: (305) 377-3721
Office fax: (561) 820-2077
Advertising phone: (305) 347-6623
Advertising fax: (305) 347-6644
Editorial phone: (305) 347-6694
Editorial fax: (305) 347-6626
Web address: www.dailybusinessreview.com
General e-mail: DailyBusinessReview@alm.com
Advertising e-mail: ccurbelo@alm.com
Editorial e-mail: dlyons@alm.com
Year established: 1979
News services: AP, Bloomberg, Florida News Service
Advertising (Open inch rate) Weekday/Saturday:
    http://www.dailybusinessreview.com/advertising.jsp
Advertising (Open inch rate) Sunday: N/A

THE DAILY NEWS

Frequency: mon to fri
Street address 1: 193 Jefferson Ave
Street address city: Memphis
Street address state: TN

Postal code: 38103-2322
County: Shelby
Country: USA
Mailing address 1: 193 JEFFERSON AVE
Mailing city: MEMPHIS
Mailing state: TN
Mailing zip: 38103-2339
Office phone: (901) 523-1561
Office fax: (901) 526-5813
Advertising phone: (901) 528-5283
Advertising fax: (901) 526-5813
Editorial phone: (901) 523-8501
Editorial fax: (901) 526-5813
Web address: www.memphisdailynews.com
General e-mail: jjenkins@memphisdailynews.com
Advertising e-mail: jjenkins@memphisdailynews.com
Editorial e-mail: releases@memphisdailynews.com
Year established: 1886
News services: CNS
Advertising (Open inch rate) Weekday/Saturday:
    Open inch rate $13.50 (legal)
Circulation Paid: 1000
Circulation Free: 2000
Audited By: USPS

THE DAILY RECORD

Frequency: mon to fri
Street address 1: 11 E Saratoga St
Street address city: Baltimore
Street address state: MD
Postal code: 21202-2115
County: Baltimore City
Country: USA
Mailing address 1: 11 E SARATOGA ST STE 1
Mailing city: BALTIMORE
Mailing state: MD
Mailing zip: 21202-2199
Office phone: (443) 524-8100
Office fax: (410) 752-2894
Advertising phone: (443) 524-8100
Advertising fax: (410) 752-2894
Editorial phone: (443) 524-8150
Editorial fax: (410) 752-2894
Web address: www.thedailyrecord.com
General e-mail: suzanne.huettner@thedailyrecord.com
Advertising e-mail: advertising@thedailyrecord.com
Editorial e-mail: tbaden@thedailyrecord.com
Year established: 1888
Advertising (Open inch rate) Weekday/Saturday:
    Open inch rate $510.00/Day
Circulation Paid: 2572
Circulation Free: 384
Audited By: Sworn/Estimate/Non-Audited

THE DAILY RECORD

Frequency: mon to fri
Street address 1: 300 S Izard St
Street address city: Little Rock
Street address state: AR
Postal code: 72201-2114
County: Pulaski
Country: USA
Mailing address 1: PO Box 3595
Mailing city: Little Rock
Mailing state: AR
Mailing zip: 72203-3595
Office phone: (501) 374-5103
Office fax: (501) 372-3048
Web address: www.dailyrecord.us
General e-mail: bobby@dailydata.com
Advertising e-mail: jedwards@dailydata.com
Editorial e-mail: editor@dailydata.com
Year established: 1925
News services: NNS, TMS, DRNW, INS
Advertising (Open inch rate) Weekday/Saturday:
    Column Inch Rate - $20.00
Circulation Paid: 3210
Circulation Free: 25
Audited By: USPS

THE DAILY REPORTER

Frequency: mon to fri
Street address 1: 225 E Michigan St
Ste 300

Street address city: Milwaukee
Street address state: WI
Postal code: 53202-4900
County: Milwaukee
Country: USA
Mailing address 1: 225 E. Michigan St.
Suite 300
Mailing city: Milwaukee
Mailing state: WI
Mailing zip: 53202
Office phone: (414) 276-0273
Office fax: (414) 276-4416
Editorial phone: (414) 225-1807
Web address: www.dailyreporter.com
General e-mail: news@dailyreporter.com
Advertising e-mail: squinn@dailyreporter.com
Editorial e-mail: dshaw@dailyreporter.com
Year established: 1897
News services: AP
Digital Platform - Mobile: Apple`Android`Windows
Digital Platform - Tablet: Apple iOS`Android`Windows 7
Circulation Paid: 3105

THE JOURNAL RECORD

Frequency: mon to fri
Street address 1: 101 N Robinson Ave
Ste 101
Street address city: Oklahoma City
Street address state: OK
Postal code: 73102-5500
County: Oklahoma
Country: USA
Mailing address 1: PO Box 26370
Mailing city: Oklahoma City
Mailing state: OK
Mailing zip: 73126-0370
Office phone: (405) 235-3100
Office fax: (405) 278-6907
Advertising phone: (405) 278-2830
Advertising fax: (405) 278-2850
Editorial fax: (405) 278-2890
Other phone: (877) 615-9536
Web address: www.journalrecord.com
Editorial e-mail: news@journalrecord.com
Year established: 1903
News services: AP
Advertising (Open inch rate) Weekday/Saturday:
    Open inch rate $18.62
Circulation Paid: 2800
Circulation Free: 69
Audited By: VAC

THE LEGAL INTELLIGENCER

Frequency: mon to fri
Street address 1: 1617 John F Kennedy Blvd
Ste 1750
Street address city: Philadelphia
Street address state: PA
Postal code: 19103-1854
County: Philadelphia
Country: USA
Mailing address 1: 1617 John F Kennedy Blvd
Ste 1750
Mailing city: Philadelphia
Mailing state: PA
Mailing zip: 19103-1854
Office phone: (215) 557-2300
Office fax: (215) 557-2301
Advertising phone: (215) 557-2359
Advertising fax: (215) 557-2301
Editorial phone: (215) 557-2489
Editorial fax: (215) 557-2301
Web address: www.thelegalintelligencer.com
General e-mail: HGREZLAK@ALM.COM
Advertising e-mail: dchalphin@alm.com
Editorial e-mail: hgrezlak@alm.com
Year established: 1843
News services: AP

THE RECORD REPORTER

Frequency: Mon`Wed`Fri
Street address 1: 2025 N 3rd St
Ste 155
Street address city: Phoenix
Street address state: AZ
Postal code: 85004-1425
County: Maricopa

II-16 — News, Picture and Syndicate Services

Country: USA
Office phone: (602) 417-9900
Office fax: (602) 417-9910
Web address: www.recordreporter.com
General e-mail: Diane_Heuel@dailyjournal.com
Advertising e-mail: record_reporter@dailyjournal.com
Editorial e-mail: diane_heuel@dailyjournal.com
Year established: 1914
Digital Platform - Mobile: Apple`Android`Blackberry
Digital Platform - Tablet: Apple iOS`Android`Windows 7`Blackberry Tablet OS

SPORTS

DAILY RACING FORM

Frequency: mon to sat; S
Street address 1: 708 3rd Ave Fl 12
Street address city: New York
Street address state: NY
Postal code: 10017-4129
County: New York
Country: USA
Mailing address 1: 708 3rd Ave Fl 12
Mailing city: New York
Mailing state: NY
Mailing zip: 10017-4129
Office phone: (212) 366-7600
Advertising phone: (212) 366-7607
Editorial fax: (212) 366-7718
Web address: www.drf.com
General e-mail: Daily Racing Form publishes several editions nationwide.
Advertising e-mail: advert@drf.com
Editorial e-mail: editor@drf.com
News services: RN, UPI
Advertising (Open inch rate) Weekday/Saturday: Open inch rate $21.75 (national)

THE DAILY NEWS

Frequency: mon to fri
Street address 1: 193 Jefferson Ave
Street address city: Memphis
Street address state: TN
Postal code: 38103-2322
County: Shelby
Country: USA
Mailing address 1: 193 JEFFERSON AVE
Mailing city: MEMPHIS
Mailing state: TN
Mailing zip: 38103-2339
Office phone: (901) 523-1561
Office fax: (901) 526-5813
Advertising phone: (901) 528-5283
Advertising fax: (901) 526-5813
Editorial phone: (901) 523-8501
Editorial fax: (901) 526-5813
Web address: www.memphisdailynews.com
General e-mail: jjenkins@memphisdailynews.com
Advertising e-mail: jjenkins@memphisdailynews.com
Editorial e-mail: releases@memphisdailynews.com
Year established: 1886
News services: CNS
Advertising (Open inch rate) Weekday/Saturday: Open inch rate $13.50 (legal)
Circulation Paid: 1000
Circulation Free: 2000
Audited By: USPS

NEWS, PICTURE AND SYNDICATE SERVICES

ALBANY

GANNETT NEWS SERVICE - ALBANY, NY

Street address 1: 150 State St
Street address state: MD
Postal code: 20814-4582
Country: USA
Mailing address: 4350 E West Hwy Ste 555
Mailing city: Bethesda
Mailing state: MD
Mailing zip: 20814-4582
Office phone: (202) 364-4401
Office fax: (202) 364-4098
General e-mail: info@aim.org
Web address: www.aim.org
Personnel: Donald K. Irvine (Chrmn.); Deborah Lambert (Special Projects Dir.); Roger Aronoff (Exec. Secretary)
Main contact: Spencer Irvine

ALGIERS

EFE NEWS SERVICES - ALGIERS, ALGERIA

Street address 1: 4 Ave. Pasteur, 1st Fl.
Street address state: PA
Postal code: 16803-2215
Country: USA
Mailing address: 385 Science Park Rd.
Mailing city: State College
Mailing state: PA
Mailing zip: 16803
Office phone: (814) 237-0309
Office fax: (814) 235-8609
General e-mail: support@accuweather.com
Web address: www.accuweather.com
Personnel: Dr. Joel N. Myers (Founder & President); Evan Myers (CEO); Steven Smith (Pres., Digital Media); Jonathan Porter (Vice Pres. of Business Services and General Mgr. of Enterprise Solutions); John Dokes (Chief Content Officer); James Candor (Chief Strategy Officer); John Dokes (Chief Marketing Officer)
Main contact: Survey Contact

ALLENTOWN

GOLF PUBLISHING SYNDICATE

Street address 1: 2743 Saxon St
Postal code: WC1H 0AF
Country: United Kingdom
Mailing address: 16 Upper Woburn Street
Mailing city: London
Mailing zip: WC1H 0AF
Telephone country code: 44
Telephone city code:
Office phone: 330 606 1438
Office fax: 330 606 1468
General e-mail: info@adlinkinternational.com
Web address: www.adlinkinternational.com
Note/Syndicate Information: Publishers Representatives, Advertising services in Africa, Middle East, Far East, Caribbean, Europe, Press Freedom in Africa, Editorial services, Special Supplements.
Personnel: Shamlal Puri (Mng. Dir.)
Main contact: Shamlal Puri

ALLSTON

JONATHON ALSOP (BOSTON WINE SCHOOL)

Street address 1: 1354 Commonwealth Ave
Street address state: OK
Postal code: 73019-0001
Country: USA
Mailing city: Norman
Mailing state: OK
Mailing zip: 73019-0001
Office phone: (405) 325-5209
Office fax: (405) 325-7565
General e-mail: javery@ou.edu
Web address: www.ou.edu/gaylord
Note/Syndicate Information: University of Oklahoma-Gaylord/AMC, Herbert School of Journalism & Mass Communication
Personnel: Jim Avery (Self-Syndicator); Kelly Storm (Staff Asst.)
Main contact: Jim Avery

ANN ARBOR

SCHWADRON CARTOON & ILLUSTRATION SERVICE

Street address 1: PO Box 1347
Street address state: D.C.
Postal code: 20005-1200
Country: USA
Mailing address: 1500 K St NW Ste 600
Mailing city: Washington
Mailing state: DC
Mailing zip: 20005-1200
Office phone: (202) 289-0700
Office fax: (202) 414-0634
General e-mail: afp-us@afp.com
Web address: www.afp.com
Personnel: Gilles Tarot (Mktg & Sales Dir., North America); Sue Lisk (Senior Account Manager)
Main contact: Gilles Tarot

ARDMORE

CRICKET COMMUNICATIONS, INC.

Street address 1: PO Box 527
Street address state: CA
Postal code: 90015-1529
Country: USA
Mailing address: 112 W 9th Street Suite 518
Mailing city: Los Angeles
Mailing state: CA
Mailing zip: 90015
Office phone: 213-800-9896
Office fax: (213) 388-0563
General e-mail: prensa@agenciapi.com
Web address: agenciapi.com
Personnel: Javier Rojas (Media Mgr.); Antonio Nava (Ed.)
Main contact: Javier Rojas

ARLINGTON

YELLOWBRIX

Street address 1: 200 North Glebe Road, Ste. 1025
Street address 2: Ste 1025
Street address state: FL
Postal code: 32073-5619
Country: USA
Mailing address: 2199 Astor Street, Suite 503
Mailing city: Orange Park
Mailing state: FL
Mailing zip: 32073
Office phone: (904) 629-6020
General e-mail: demko@AgeVentureNewsService.com
Web address: www.demko.com
Note/Syndicate Information: See print and broadcast news placements at: www.demko.com/circulation.html
Personnel: David J. Demko (Editor, Clinical Gerontologist)
Main contact: David Demko

BATON ROUGE

GANNETT NEWS SERVICE - BATON ROUGE, LA

Street address 1: 900 N 3rd St
Street address state: FL
Postal code: 33410-5141
Country: USA
Mailing address: 10199 Willow Ln
Mailing city: Palm Beach Gardens
Mailing state: FL
Mailing zip: 33410-5141
Office phone: (561) 630-7112
General e-mail: mwliblav@aol.com
Personnel: Alan Lavine (Chrmn./Pres.); Gail Liberman (Mktg. Mgr.)
Main contact: Alan Lavine

BEIJING

EFE NEWS SERVICES - BEIJING, CHINA

Street address 1: Julong Garden, 7-14 L. Xinzhongjie, 68 Dongcheng
Street address state: NY
Postal code: 10271-1100
Country: USA
Mailing address: 120 Broadway Fl 5
Mailing city: New York
Mailing state: NY
Mailing zip: 10271-1100
Office phone: (212) 457-9400
Web address: www.alm.com
Personnel: William L. Pollak (Pres./CEO); Jack Berkowitz (Sr. Vice Pres.); Ellen Sigel (Vice Pres., Licensing/Bus. Devel.); Aric Press (Editorial Dir.); Jeffrey Litvack (Chief Digital Officer)
Main contact: Ellen Sigel

BERLIN

EFE NEWS SERVICES - BERLIN, GERMANY

Street address 1: Reinhardtstrasse 58
Street address state: CA
Postal code: 94107-1414
Country: USA
Mailing address: 1881 Harmon St
Mailing city: Berkeley

News, Picture and Syndicate Services

Mailing state: CA
Mailing zip: 94703-2415
Office phone: (415) 284-1420
Office fax: (415) 284-1414
General e-mail: info@alternet.org
Web address: www.alternet.org
Personnel: Don Hazen (Pub./Exec. Ed.); Leigh Johnson (Bus. Mgr.); Tai Moses (Sr. Ed.); Davina Baum (Mng. Ed.)
Main contact: Leigh Johnson

BETHESDA

ACCURACY IN MEDIA

Street address 1: 4350 E West Hwy
Street address 2: Ste 555
Street address state: NY
Postal code: 11762-0069
Country: USA
Mailing address: PO Box 69
Mailing city: Massapequa Park
Mailing state: NY
Mailing zip: 11762
Office phone: (561) 989-0550
General e-mail: snpuzz@aol.com
Web address: www.stanxwords.com
Personnel: Stanley Newman (Pres./Ed. in Chief); Joseph Vallely (Vice Pres./Sales Dir.)
Main contact: Stanley Newman

BIRMINGHAM

CAREER SOURCE/COLUMN

Street address 1: PO Box 94
Street address state: D.C.
Postal code: 20001-2029
Country: USA
Mailing address: 555 New Jersey Ave NW Ste A
Mailing city: Washington
Mailing state: DC
Mailing zip: 20001-2029
Office phone: (202) 879-4400
Office fax: (202) 879-4545
General e-mail: aftpres@aol.com; online@aft.org
Web address: www.aft.org
Personnel: Randi Weingarten (Pres.); Antonia Portese (Sec./Treasurer); Lorretta Johnson (Exec. Vice Pres.)
Main contact: Randi Weingart'en

BOCA RATON

UNITED PRESS INTERNATIONAL

Street address 1: 1200 N Federal Hwy
Street address 2: Ste 200
Street address state: FL
Postal code: 33133-4728
Country: USA
Mailing address: 2311 S Bayshore Dr
Mailing city: Miami
Mailing state: FL
Mailing zip: 33133-4728
Office phone: (305) 285-2200
General e-mail: amprsnd@aol.com
Web address: www.ampersandcom.com
Personnel: George Leposky (Ed.); Rosalie E. Leposky (Mng. Partner)
Main contact: Rosalie E. Leposky

BOGOTA

DOW JONES NEWSWIRES - BOGOTA, COLOMBIA

Street address 1: Calle 93B No. 13-30 Oficina 301
Street address state: MO
Postal code: 64106-2109
Country: USA
Mailing address: 1130 Walnut Street
Mailing city: Kansas City
Mailing state: MO
Mailing zip: 64106-2109
Office phone: (816) 581-7500
General e-mail: press@amuniversal.com

Web address: http://syndication.andrewsmcmeel.com/
Personnel: John Vivona (Vice Pres. of Sales); Jan Flemington (Office Manager)
Main contact: Julie Bunge

EFE NEWS SERVICES - BOGOTA, COLOMBIA

Street address 1: Calle 67 No 7-35
Street address state: FL
Postal code: 33437-4264
Country: USA
Mailing address: 5808 Royal Club Dr
Mailing city: Boynton Beach
Mailing state: FL
Mailing zip: 33437-4264
Office phone: (561) 364-5798
General e-mail: antique2@bellsouth.net
Personnel: Anne Gilbert (Pres./Writer)
Main contact: Anne Gilbert

BOONE

WATAUGA CONSULTING, INC.

Street address 1: 192 Abbey Rd
Street address state: IL
Postal code: 60659-7401
Country: USA
Mailing address: PO Box 597401
Mailing city: Chicago
Mailing state: IL
Mailing zip: 60659-7401
Office phone: (773) 267-9773
General e-mail: thecapecod@aol.com
Web address: www.anitagold.com
Personnel: Anita Gold (Author/Creator/Owner)
Main contact: Anita Gold

BOSTON

BUSINESS WIRE - BOSTON, MA

Street address 1: 2 Center Plz
Street address 2: Ste 500
Street address state: NY
Postal code: 10001-2603
Country: USA
Mailing address: 450 W 33rd St
Mailing city: New York
Mailing state: NY
Mailing zip: 10001-2603
Office phone: (212) 621-1997
Office fax: (212) 621-1955
Web address: www.apimages.com
Personnel: Ian Cameron (Vice Pres.)
Main contact: Ian Cameron

THE CHRISTIAN SCIENCE MONITOR NEWS SERVICE

Street address 1: 210 Massachusetts Ave
Street address state: CA
Postal code: 94930-1413
Country: USA
Mailing address: PO Box 1030
Mailing city: Fairfax
Mailing state: CA
Mailing zip: 94978-1030
Office phone: (415) 456-2697
Office fax: (415) 456-2697
General e-mail: patarrigoni@comcast.net
Web address: www.travelpublishers.com
Note/Syndicate Information: Creeators Syndicate freelancer
Personnel: Patricia Arrigoni (Pres.)
Main contact: Patricia Arrigoni

BOYNTON BEACH

ANTIQUE DETECTIVE SYNDICATE

Street address 1: 5808 Royal Club Dr
Street address state: MI
Postal code: 48331-2044
Country: USA
Mailing address: 35336 Spring Hill Rd
Mailing city: Farmington Hills

Mailing state: MI
Mailing zip: 48331-2044
Office phone: (248) 661-8585
Office fax: (248) 788-1022
General e-mail: info@artistmarket.com
Web address: www.artistmarket.com
Personnel: A. David Kahn (CEO/Ed.)
Main contact: A. David Kahn

BRENTWOOD

ON THE HOUSE SYNDICATION, INC.

Street address 1: 2420 Sand Creek Rd
Street address 2: C-1318
Street address state: AB
Postal code: T5B 2C5
Country: Canada
Mailing address: 11136 - 75 A St. NW
Mailing city: Edmonton
Mailing state: AB
Mailing zip: T5B 2C5
Office phone: (780) 471-6112
Office fax: (877) 642-8666
General e-mail: sales@artizans.com; support@artizans.com
Web address: www.artizans.com; www.dialanartist.com
Personnel: Malcolm Mayes (Pres.)
Main contact: Malcolm Mayes

BROCKTON

TV TIMES/NEW ENGLAND MOTORSPORTS SYNDICATION

Street address 1: 1324 Belmont St
Street address 2: Ste 102
Street address state: CA
Postal code: 93101-2927
Country: USA
Mailing address: 117 W Valerio St
Mailing city: Santa Barbara
Mailing state: CA
Mailing zip: 93101-2927
Office phone: (805) 682-0531
General e-mail: ashleigh@ashleighbrilliant.com
Web address: www.ashleighbrilliant.com
Personnel: Ashleigh Brilliant (Pres.); Dorothy Brilliant (Vice Pres.)
Main contact: Dorothy Brilliant

BRONXVILLE

MARION JOYCE

Street address 1: 52 Sagamore Rd
Street address state: NY
Postal code: 10281
Country: USA
Mailing address: 200 Liberty St.
Mailing city: New York
Mailing state: NY
Mailing zip: 10281
Office phone: (877) 836-9477
General e-mail: info@ap.org
Web address: www.ap.org
Note/Syndicate Information: U.S. States and Territories: ALABAMA Birmingham: (205) 251-4221 Montgomery: (334) 262-5947 ALASKA Anchorage: (907) 272-7549 Juneau: (907) 586-1515 ARIZONA Phoenix: (602) 258-8934 ARKANSAS Little Rock: (501) 225-3668 CALIFORNIA Sacramento: (916) 448-9555 Los Angeles: (213) 626-1200 San Diego: (619) 231-9365 San Francisco: (415) 495-1708 COLORADO Denver: (303) 825-0123 CONNECTICUT Hartford: (860) 246-6876 New Haven: (203) 964-9270 DISTRICT OF COLUMBIA Washington: (202) 641-9000 FLORIDA Cape Canaveral: (212) 621-1699 Orlando: (407) 425-4547 Tallahassee: (850) 224-1211 West Palm Beach: (305) 594-5825 Miami: (305) 594-5825 GEORGIA Atlanta: (404) 653-8460 HAWAII Honolulu: (808) 536-5510 IDAHO Boise: (208) 343-1894 ILLINOIS Springfield: (217) 789-2700 Chicago: (312) 781-0500 INDIANA Indianapolis: (317) 639-5501 IOWA Des Moines: (515) 243-3281 Iowa City: (319) 337-5615 KANSAS

Topeka: (785) 234-5654 Wichita: (316) 263-4601 KENTUCKY Frankfort: (502) 227-2410 Louisville: (502) 583-7718 LOUISIANA Baton Rouge: (225) 343-1325 New Orleans: (504) 523-3931 MAINE Augusta: (207) 622-3018 Portland: (207) 772-4157 MARYLAND Baltimore: (410) 837-8315 MASSACHUSETTS Boston: (617) 357-8100 MICHIGAN Lansing: (517) 482-8011 Traverse City: (231) 929-4180 Detroit: (313) 259-0650 MINNESOTA Minneapolis: (612) 332-2727 St. Paul: (651) 222-4821 MISSISSIPPI Jackson: (601) 948-5897 MISSOURI Columbia: (573) 884-9934 Jefferson City: (573) 636-9415 St. Louis: (314) 241-2496 Kansas City: (816) 421 4844 MONTANA Billings: (406) 896-1528 Helena: (406) 442-7440 NEBRASKA Lincoln: (402) 476-2525 Omaha: (402) 391-0031 NEVADA Carson City: (775) 322-3639 Las Vegas: (702) 382-7440 Reno: (775) 322-3639 NEW HAMPSHIRE Concord: (603) 224-3327 NEW JERSEY Newark: (973) 642-0151 Atlantic City: (609) 645-2063 Trenton: (609) 392-3622 NEW MEXICO Albuquerque: (505) 822-9022 NEW YORK New York: (212) 621-1500 Albany: (518) 458-7821 Buffalo: (716) 852-1051 NORTH CAROLINA Charlotte: (704) 334-4624 Raleigh: (919) 510-8937 NORTH DAKOTA Bismarck: (701) 223-8450 Fargo: (701) 235-1908 OHIO Cincinnati: (513) 241-2386 Cleveland: (216) 771-2172 Columbus: (614) 885-2727 Toledo: (419) 255-7113 OKLAHOMA Oklahoma City: (405) 525-2121 Tulsa: (918) 584-4346 OREGON Portland: (503) 228-2169 PENNSYLVANIA Allentown: (610) 207-9297 Harrisburg: (717) 238-9413 Philadelphia: (215) 561-1133 Pittsburgh: (412) 281-3747 State College: (814) 238-3649 PUERTO RICO San Juan: (717) 793-5833 or (305) 594-1845 RHODE ISLAND Providence: (401) 274-2270 SOUTH CAROLINA Charleston: (843) 722-1660 Columbia: (803) 799-5510 SOUTH DAKOTA Pierre: (605) 224-7811 TENNESSEE Memphis: (901) 525-1972 Nashville: (615) 373-9988 TEXAS Austin: (512) 472-4004 Dallas: (972) 991-2100 Fort Worth: (817) 348-0367 Lubbock: (806) 765-0394 San Antonio: (210) 222-2713 Houston: (281) 872-8900 UTAH Salt Lake City: (801) 322-3405 VERMONT Montpelier: (802) 229-0577 VIRGINIA Richmond: (804) 643-6646 McLean: (703) 761-0187 WASHINGTON Olympia: (360) 753-7222 Seattle: (206) 682-1812 Spokane: (800) 300-8340 Yakima: (509) 453-1951 WEST VIRGINIA Charleston: (304) 346-0897 WISCONSIN Milwaukee: (414) 225-3580 Madison: (608) 255-3679 WYOMING Cheyenne: (307) 632-9351
Personnel: Gary Pruitt (Pres./CEO); Jessica Bruce (Sen. V.P./HR); Sally Buzbee (Senior V.P./Exec. Ed.); Ken Dale (Senior V.P./CFO); Gianluca D'Aniello (Senior V.P./CTO); Dave Gwizdowski (Senior V.P./ Revenue, Americas); Karen Kaiser (Senior V.P./Gen. Counsel, Corp. Sec.); Jim Kennedy (Senior V.P./Strategic Planning); Daisy Veerasingham (Senior V.P. Revenue, Int.'l)
Main contact: Main Corporate

BROOKLYN

THIS MODERN WORLD

Street address 1: PO Box 150673
Street address state: NY
Postal code: 10001-2603
Country: USA
Mailing address: 450 W 33rd St Fl 15
Mailing city: New York
Mailing state: NY
Mailing zip: 10001-2647
Office phone: (212) 621-1500
Office fax: (212) 621-7520
General e-mail: info@ap.org
Web address: www.ap.org
Personnel: Ted Mendelsohn (Dir. Sales)
Main contact: Ted Mendelsohn

BRUSSELS

DOW JONES NEWSWIRES -

BRUSSELS, BELGIUM

Street address 1: Blvd. Brand Whitlock 30
Street address state: NY
Postal code: 10001-2603
Country: USA
Mailing address: 450 W 33rd St
Mailing city: New York
Mailing state: NY
Mailing zip: 10001-2603
Office phone: (212) 621-1838
Office fax: (212) 506-6102
General e-mail: apme@ap.org
Web address: www.apme.com
Note/Syndicate Information: Elections held in Oct
Personnel: Sally Jacobsen (Gen. Mgr.)
Main contact: Sally Jacobsen

EFE NEWS SERVICES - BRUSSELS, BELGIUM

Street address 1: Residence Palace, Rue de la Loi, 155
Street address state: MA
Postal code: 02176-4222
Country: USA
Mailing address: 16 Slayton Rd
Mailing city: Melrose
Mailing state: MA
Mailing zip: 02176-4222
Office phone: (781) 665-4442
General e-mail: lynn@offthemarkcartoons.com
Web address: www.offthemark.com
Personnel: Mark Parisi (Pres.); Lynn Reznick (Mktg. Dir.)
Main contact: Lynn Reznick

BRYN MAWR

HOLLISTER KIDS

Street address 1: 763 W Lancaster Ave
Street address 2: Ste 250
Street address state: CA
Postal code: 94019-2212
Country: USA
Mailing address: 186 CYPRESS POINT ROAD
Mailing city: HALF MOON BAY
Mailing state: CA
Mailing zip: 94019-2212
Telephone country code: United States
Telephone city code: HALF MOON BAY
Office phone: (650) 726-2386
Office fax: (650) 726-2386
General e-mail: brian@autoeditor.com
Web address: 186 CYPRESS POINT ROAD
Note/Syndicate Information: Automotive editorial website
Personnel: Brian Douglas (Ed./Pub.)
Main contact: Brian Douglas

BUENOS AIRES

CLARIN CONTENIDOS

Street address 1: Tacuari 1840
Street address state: DE
Postal code: 19804-4305
Country: USA
Mailing address: PO Box 3305
Mailing city: Wilmington
Mailing state: DE
Mailing zip: 19804-4305
Office phone: (302) 998-1650
General e-mail: info@motormatters.biz
Web address: www.motormatters.biz
Note/Syndicate Information: Motor Matters helps publications drive revenue growth across print/digital platforms, and build marketing partnerships with advertisers, the business community, and readers. Revenue-driven content assets to build advertising dollars include high-value article titles and photography: Truck Talk, Get Off the Road, Green Wheeling, New on Wheels, Ask the Auto Doctor, Down the Road, Tech Out My New Car, Automotive Female, Classic Classics, Rolling Homes and 2-Wheeling Today. Motor Matters supports publications in maximizing advertising to in-market new car buyers and recapture buyers in the used-car market with the annual Buyers Guides. Strengths we promise to deliver are are rooted in accuracy, credibility, and clarity in messaging. Plus, we are eagle-eyed editors and fierce under deadlines. (www.motormatters.biz).
Personnel: Connie Keane (Owner); Julienne Crane (Contributor, Rolling Homes); Junior Damato (Contributor, Ask the Auto Doctor); Evelyn Kanter (Contributor, FreeWheeling); Dan Lyons (Contributor, Get Off the Road); Sue Mead (Contributor, Bonus Wheels, New on Wheels); Kate McLeod (Contributor, FreeWheeling); Vern Parker (Contributor, Classic Classics); Tim Spell (Contributor, Truck Talk); Arv Voss (Contributor, 2-Wheeling Today, New On Wheels, Bonus Wheels); Brandy Schaffels (Editor, Contributor, Women Auto Know); Frank Aukofer (Contributor, New On Wheels, Get Off the Road, Bonus Wheels); Steve Wheeler (Contributor, Classic Classics, New on Wheels, Bonus Wheels); Lyndon Conrad Bell (Contributor, New On Wheels, Down the Road, Bonus Wheels); Joe Michaud; Lynn Walford
Main contact: Connie Keane

DOW JONES NEWSWIRES - BUENOS AIRES, ARGENTINA

Street address 1: Leandro N. Alem 712, Piso 4
Street address state: FL
Postal code: 33408-3003
Country: USA
Mailing address: 11760 US Highway 1 Ste 200
Mailing city: North Palm Beach
Mailing state: FL
Mailing zip: 33408-3003
Office phone: (561) 630-2400
Office fax: (561) 625-4540
Web address: www.bankrate.com
Personnel: Tom Evans (President & CEO (Former)); Donald M. Ross (Sr. Vice Pres./Chief Revenue Officer); Robert J. DeFranco (Sr. Vice Pres., Finance/CFO); Bruce Zanca (Sr. Vice Pres./Chief Mktg./Commun. Officer); Beth Planakis (Mktg. Dir.)
Main contact: Tom Evans

EFE NEWS SERVICES - BUENOS AIRES, ARGENTINA

Street address 1: Av. Alicia Moreau de Justo 1720
Street address state: NY
Postal code: 13865-3304
Country: USA
Mailing address: 102 Blatchley Rd
Mailing city: Windsor
Mailing state: NY
Mailing zip: 13865-3304
Office phone: (607) 775-0587
General e-mail: slyman@tds.net
Personnel: Shelby Lyman (Pres.)
Main contact: Shelby Lyman

CAIRO

EFE NEWS SERVICES - CAIRO, EGYPT

Street address 1: 4 Mohamed Mazhar, 3 - apt. 5. Zamalek
Street address state: OH
Postal code: 44111-2105
Country: USA
Mailing address: 3508 W 151st St
Mailing city: Cleveland
Mailing state: OH
Mailing zip: 44111-2105
Office phone: (216) 251-1389
General e-mail: dnorman@bge.net
Web address: www.sites.google.com/site/wallyswoods
Personnel: Dean Norman (Artist/Owner)
Main contact: Dean Norman

CALGARY

CANADIAN PRESS, THE - CALGARY, AB

Street address 1: 131 9 Avenue SW, Suite 310
Street address state: ID
Postal code: 47250-0231
Country: USA
Mailing address: PO Box 231
Mailing city: Madison
Mailing state: IN
Mailing zip: 47250-0231
Office phone: (812) 265-6313
Office fax: (812) 418-3368
General e-mail: info@bigringwriting.com
Web address: www.bigringwriting.com
Personnel: Richard Ries (Dir.); Julie Ries (Admin. Asst.)
Main contact: Julie Ries

CAMERON

THE WILD SIDE

Street address 1: 2222 Fish Ridge Rd
Street address state: NJ
Postal code: 07666-4543
Country: USA
Mailing address: 995 Teaneck Rd Apt 3N
Mailing city: Teaneck
Mailing state: NJ
Mailing zip: 07666-4543
Office phone: (201) 833-2350
Office fax: (201) 833-2350
General e-mail: mrbiofile@aol.com
Web address: www.thebiofile.com
Personnel: Mark (Scoop) Malinowski (Ed.)
Main contact: Mark (Scoop) Malinowski

CANANDAIGUA

TRADE NEWS SERVICE (FATS AND OILS)

Street address 1: 3701 State Route 21
Street address state: NY
Postal code: 10016-3323
Country: USA
Mailing address: 375 5th Ave Fl 3
Mailing city: New York
Mailing state: NY
Mailing zip: 10016-3323
Telephone country code: 001
Telephone city code: 212
Office phone: (212) 686-6850
Office fax: (212) 686-7308
General e-mail: news@blackradionetwork.com
Web address: www.blackradionetwork.com
Personnel: Jay R. Levy (Pres.); Peter Knight (Sales Mgr.); Roy Thompson (Ed.); Bill Baldwin (Assoc. Ed.)
Main contact: Jay R. Levy

CARMEL

DR. BEE EPSTEIN-SHEPHERD

Street address 1: PO Box 221383
Street address state: NY
Postal code: 10605-1440
Country: USA
Mailing address: 333 Mamaroneck Ave # 175
Mailing city: White Plains
Mailing state: NY
Mailing zip: 10605-1440
Office phone: (212) 679-3288
General e-mail: sales@blackstar.com
Web address: www.blackstar.com
Personnel: Ben Chapnick (Pres.); John P. Chapnick (Vice Pres.)
Main contact: Ben Chapnick; John P. Chapnick

CARY

THE ROMANTIC SYNDICATED

COLUMN

Street address 1: PO Box 1567
Postal code: 75009
Country: France
Mailing address: 7 Rue Scribe
Mailing city: Paris
Mailing zip: 75009
Web address: https://www.bloomberg.com
Main contact: Stacey Kennedy

CENTREVILLE

MILITARY UPDATE

Street address 1: PO Box 231111
Street address state: CA
Postal code: 94111
Country: USA
Mailing address: Pierre 3., Ste., 101
Mailing city: San Francisco
Mailing state: CA
Mailing zip: 94111
Web address: https://www.bloomberg.com
Main contact: Stacey Kennedy

WORLD IMAGES NEWS SERVICE

Street address 1: 14745 Green Park Way
Postal code: 49481
Country: Singapore
Mailing address: Capital Square, 23 Church St., 12th Fl.
Mailing city: Singapore
Mailing zip: 49481
Web address: https://www.bloomberg.com
Main contact: Stacey Kennedy

CHANTILLY

DISABILITY NEWS SERVICE

Street address 1: 13703 Southernwood Ct
Postal code: 2000
Country: Australia
Mailing address: 1 Macquarie Pl., Level 36, Gtwy. 36
Mailing city: Sydney
Mailing zip: 2000
Web address: https://www.bloomberg.com
Main contact: Stacey Kennedy

CHAPPAQUA

WERNER RENBERG

Street address 1: PO Box 496
Street address state: NY
Postal code: 10022-1331
Country: USA
Mailing address: 731 Lexington Ave Frnt 6
Mailing city: New York
Mailing state: NY
Mailing zip: 10022-1343
Web address: https://www.bloomberg.com
Main contact: Stacey Kennedy

CHARLOTTE

INTERNATIONAL PUZZLE FEATURES

Street address 1: 4507 Panther Pl
Street address state: NJ
Postal code: 08558-2601
Country: USA
Mailing address: 100 Business Park Dr
Mailing city: Skillman
Mailing state: NJ
Mailing zip: 08558-2693
Web address: https://www.bloomberg.com
Main contact: Stacey Kennedy

CHARLOTTESVILLE

KEISTER WILLIAMS NEWSPAPER SERVICES, INC.

Street address 1: 1807 Emmet St N

News, Picture and Syndicate Services

Street address 2: Ste 6B
Street address state: D.C.
Postal code: 20005-4749
Country: USA
Mailing address: 1399 New York Ave NW Fl 11
Mailing city: Washington
Mailing state: DC
Mailing zip: 20005-4749
Web address: https://www.bloomberg.com
Main contact: Stacey Kennedy

CHICAGO

ANTIQUES & COLLECTIBLE SELF-SYNDICATED COLUMN

Street address 1: PO Box 597401
Country: Hong Kong
Mailing address: 27 Fl., Cheung Kong Ctr., 2 Queens Rd. Central
Mailing city: Hong Kong
Web address: https://www.bloomberg.com
Main contact: Stacey Kennedy

BLOOMBERG NEWS

Street address 1: 111 S Wacker Dr
Street address 2: Ste 4950
Street address state: ON
Postal code: M5J 2S1
Country: Canada
Mailing address: 161 Bay St., Ste. 4300
Mailing city: Toronto
Mailing state: ON
Mailing zip: M5J 2S1
Web address: https://www.bloomberg.com
Main contact: Stacey Kennedy

CONTENT THAT WORKS

Street address 1: 4410 N Ravenswood Ave
Street address 2: Ste 101
Postal code: 100
Country: Japan
Mailing address: Yusen Bldg., 1st Fl., 2-3-2 Marunouchi
Mailing city: Tokyo
Mailing zip: 100
General e-mail: https://www.bloomberg.com
Main contact: Stacey Kennedy

HURST SPORTS MEDIA

Street address 1: 2740 N Pine Grove Ave
Street address 2: Apt 4C
Street address state: IL
Postal code: 60606-4418
Country: USA
Mailing address: 111 S Wacker Dr Ste 4950
Mailing city: Chicago
Mailing state: IL
Mailing zip: 60606-4418
Web address: https://www.bloomberg.com
Main contact: Stacey Kennedy

REUTERS

Street address 1: 311 S Wacker Dr
Street address 2: Ste 1200
Postal code: 60311
Country: Germany
Mailing address: Neue Mainzer Strasse 75
Mailing city: Frankfurt
Mailing zip: 60311
Web address: https://www.bloomberg.com
Main contact: Stacey Kennedy

STRAIGHT DOPE - WRAPPORTS/ SUN-TIMES MEDIA, INC.

Street address 1: 350 N Orleans St
Street address state: MB
Postal code: R3C 3R6
Country: Canada
Mailing address: 386 Broadway Ave., Ste. 101
Mailing city: Winnipeg
Mailing state: MB
Mailing zip: R3C 3R6
Office phone: (204) 988-1781
Office fax: (204) 942-4788
Personnel: Steve Lambert (Manitoba Correspondent)
Main contact: Steve Lambert

TAIPEI ECONOMIC AND CULTURAL OFFICE IN CHICAGO

Street address 1: 55 W Wacker Dr
Street address 2: Ste 1200
Street address state: ON
Postal code: M5C 2L9
Country: Canada
Mailing address: 36 King St. E.
Mailing city: Toronto
Mailing state: ON
Mailing zip: M5C 2L9
Office phone: (416) 364-0321
Office fax: (416) 364-8896
Web address: www.thecanadianpress.com
Personnel: Ellen Huebert (News Editor); David Ross (CFO); Terry Scott (Gen. Exec./Client Liaison); Charles Messina (Sales/Mktg. Dir.); Sandra Clarke
Main contact: Ellen Huebert; Charles Messina

TMS SPECIALTY PRODUCTS

Street address 1: 435 N Michigan Ave
Street address 2: Ste 1400
Street address state: QC
Postal code: G1R 5A4
Country: Canada
Mailing address: 1050 rue Des Parlementaires, Bureau 207
Mailing city: Quebec City
Mailing state: QC
Mailing zip: G1R 5A4
Office phone: (418) 646-5377
Office fax: (418) 523-9686
Personnel: Martin Ouellett (Correspondent)
Main contact: Martin Ouellett

TRIBUNE CONTENT AGENCY

Street address 1: 160 N. Stetson Ave
Street address 2: 4th floor
Street address state: ON
Postal code: K1P 5B9
Country: Canada
Mailing address: P.O. Box 595, Station B
Mailing city: Ottawa
Mailing state: ON
Mailing zip: K1P 5P7
Office phone: (613) 238-4142
Office fax: (613) 232-5163
Web address: www.thecanadianpress.com
Personnel: Robert Russo (Bureau Chief)
Main contact: Robert Russo

TRIBUNE NEWS SERVICE

Street address 1: 160 N. Stetson Ave
Street address 2: 4th floor
Street address state: SK
Postal code: S4S 0B3
Country: Canada
Mailing address: Rm. 335, Press Gallery
Mailing city: Regina
Mailing state: SK
Mailing zip: S4S 0B3
Office phone: (306) 585-1024
Office fax: (306) 585-1027
Personnel: Jay Branch (Saskatchewan Correspondent)
Main contact: Jay Branch

CINCINNATI

STARCOTT MEDIA SERVICES, INC.

Street address 1: 6906 Royalgreen Dr
Street address state: NB
Postal code: E3B 5H1
Country: Canada
Mailing address: The Press Gallery, Box 6000, Queen St.
Mailing city: Fredericton
Mailing state: NB
Mailing zip: E3B 5H1
Office phone: (506) 457-0746
Office fax: (506) 457-9708
Personnel: Kevin Bissett (New Brunswick Correspondent)
Main contact: Kevin Bissett

UNITED MEDIA/EW SCRIPPS

Street address 1: 312 Walnut St
Street address 2: Ste 2800
Street address state: ON
Postal code: M5C 2L9
Country: Canada
Mailing address: 36 King St. E.
Mailing city: Toronto
Mailing state: ON
Mailing zip: M5C 2L9
Office phone: (416) 507-2099
General e-mail: support@thecanadianpress.com
Web address: www.thecanadianpress.com
Note/Syndicate Information: Elections held in April
Personnel: John Honderich (Chrmn.); Ellen Huebert (News Editor); Keith Leslie (Legislature Correspondent); Eric Morrison (Pres.); David Ross (CFO); Wendy McCann (Chief, Ontario Servs.); Terry Scott (Vice Pres., Broadcasting); Jean Roy (Vice Pres., French Servs.); Paul Woods (Dir., HR); Sharon Hockin (Office Mgr.); Philipe Mercure (Exec. Dir.)
Main contact: ()

CLEVELAND

BEAVER CREEK FEATURES

Street address 1: 3508 W 151st St
Street address state: NS
Postal code: B3J 3J8
Country: Canada
Mailing address: 1888 Brunswick St., Ste. 100
Mailing city: Halifax
Mailing state: NS
Mailing zip: B3J 3J8
Office phone: (902) 422-9284
Office fax: (902) 565-7588
Personnel: Dean Beeby (Bureau Chief); Murray Brewster (Legislative Reporter)
Main contact: Dean Beeby; Murray Brewster

BUSINESS WIRE - CLEVELAND, OH

Street address 1: 1001 Lakeside Ave E
Street address 2: Ste 1525
Street address state: QC
Postal code: H2Y 1M6
Country: Canada
Mailing address: 215 St. Jacques W., Ste. 100
Mailing city: Montreal
Mailing state: QC
Mailing zip: H2Y 1M6
Office phone: (514) 849-8008
Office fax: (514) 282-6915
Personnel: Peter Ray (Quebec Correspondent)
Main contact: Rina Steuerman

COHASSET

J FEATURES

Street address 1: 10 Wood Way
Street address state: BC
Postal code: V6Z 2L2
Country: Canada
Mailing address: 840 Howe St., Ste. 250
Mailing city: Vancouver
Mailing state: BC
Mailing zip: V6Z 2L2
Office phone: (604) 687-1662
Office fax: (604) 687-5040
Personnel: Jill St. Louis (Bureau Chief)
Main contact: Jill St. Louis

CONCORD

SERVICEQUALITY.US

Street address 1: 2401 Stanwell Dr.
Street address 2: Ste 340
Street address state: AB
Postal code: T5J 3L7
Country: Canada
Mailing address: PO Box 10109, 106th St.,
Ste. 504
Mailing city: Edmonton
Mailing state: AB
Mailing zip: T5J 3L7
Office phone: (780) 428-6490
Office fax: (780) 428-0663
Personnel: Kathy Bell (Bureau Chief)
Main contact: Kathy Bell

DANBURY

THE CLASSIFIED GUYS

Street address 1: 12 Bates Pl
Street address state: AB
Postal code: T2P 1K1
Country: Canada
Mailing address: 131 9 Avenue SW, Suite 310
Mailing city: Calgary
Mailing state: AB
Mailing zip: T2P 1K1
Office phone: (403) 543-7238
Office fax: (403) 262-7520
General e-mail: calgary@thecanadianpress.com
Web address: www.thecanadianpress.com
Personnel: Bill Graveland (National Correspondent); Lauren Krugel (National Business Correspondent); Dan Healing (Business reporter)
Main contact: Bill Graveland

DENVER

BUSINESS WIRE - DENVER, CO

Street address 1: 1725 Blake St
Street address 2: Ste 100
Street address state: MI
Postal code: 48236-2820
Country: USA
Mailing address: 417 Lexington Rd
Mailing city: Grosse Pointe Farms
Mailing state: MI
Mailing zip: 48236-2820
Office phone: (313) 929 - 0800
General e-mail: cmeyering@ameritech.net
Personnel: Robert H. Meyering (Writer, Computer Columns); Carl E. Meyering (Ed.)
Main contact: Carl E. Meyering

INDEPENDENCE FEATURE SYNDICATE

Street address 1: 727 E 16th Ave
Street address state: MA
Postal code: 02108-1921
Country: USA
Mailing address: 1 Boston Pl Ste 2330
Mailing city: Boston
Mailing state: MA
Mailing zip: 02108-4473
Office phone: (617) 742-2760
Office fax: (617) 742-2782
General e-mail: news@businesswire.com
Web address: Business Wire - Boston, MA
Personnel: Cathy Baron Tamraz (Pres./COO)
Main contact: Neil Hershberg

SENIOR WIRE NEWS SERVICE

Street address 1: 2377 Elm St
Street address state: OH
Postal code: 44114-1193
Country: USA
Mailing address: 1001 Lakeside Ave E Ste 1525
Mailing city: Cleveland
Mailing state: OH
Mailing zip: 44114-1193
Office phone: (800) 769-0220
Office fax: (800) 827-0237
Web address: www.businesswire.com
Personnel: Jill Connor (Midwest Reg. Mgr.)
Main contact: Neil Hershberg

DETROIT

CRAINÂ‚¬Â„¢S DETROIT BUSINESS

Street address 1: 1155 Gratiot Ave

Street address state: CO
Postal code: 80202-5917
Country: USA
Mailing address: 1725 Blake St Ste 100
Mailing city: Denver
Mailing state: CO
Mailing zip: 80202-5917
Office phone: (800) 308-0166
Office fax: (303) 830-2442
Web address: www.businesswire.com
Personnel: Dylan Frusciano (Vice Pres.)
Main contact: Neil Hershberg

DUBLIN

CRITICS, INC.

Street address state: CA
Postal code: 90025-1281
Country: USA
Mailing address: 12100 Wilshire Blvd Ste 780
Mailing city: Los Angeles
Mailing state: CA
Mailing zip: 90025-1281
Office phone: (800) 237-8212
Office fax: (310) 820-7363
Web address: www.businesswire.com
Personnel: Mike Iannuzzi (Mgr., Southwest Reg.); Tom Becktold (Nat'l Dir., Mktg. Programs)
Main contact: Mike Iannuzzi

EAST PROVIDENCE

CREATIVE CIRCLE MEDIA SYNDICATION

Street address 1: 945 Waterman Ave
Street address state: NY
Postal code: 10022-5911
Country: USA
Mailing address: 40 E 52nd St Fl 14
Mailing city: New York
Mailing state: NY
Mailing zip: 10022-5911
Office phone: (212) 752-9600
Web address: www.businesswire.com
Personnel: Geff Scott (CEO); Richard DeLeo (COO)
Main contact: Neil Hershberg

EAST SYRACUSE

GARY JAMES

Street address 1: 111 Shearin Ave
Street address state: CA
Postal code: 94104-4602
Country: USA
Mailing address: 44 Montgomery St Fl 39
Mailing city: San Francisco
Mailing state: CA
Mailing zip: 94104-4812
Office phone: (415) 986-4422
Office fax: (415) 788-5335
General e-mail: news@businesswire.com
Web address: www.businesswire.com
Personnel: Cathy Baron Tamraz; Gregg Castano (Co-Chief Opns.); news@businesswire.com Neil (Vice Pres., Global Media)
Main contact: Neil Hershberg

EDMONTON

ARTIZANS.COM SYNDICATE

Street address 1: 11136 - 75 A St. NW
Street address state: CA
Postal code: 93121-2342
Country: USA
Mailing address: PO Box 22342
Mailing city: Santa Barbara
Mailing state: CA
Mailing zip: 93121-2342
Office phone: (805) 969-2829
General e-mail: cari@cagle.com
Web address: www.caglecartoons.com
Note/Syndicate Information: Cagle Cartoons, Inc.

does not accept unsolicited submissions.
Personnel: Daryl Cagle (Pres./CEO); Cari Dawson Bartley (Exec. Ed./Mktg. Dir.)
Main contact: ()

BROADCAST NEWS LIMITED

Street address 1: PO Box 10109, 106th St., Ste. 504
Street address state: NS
Postal code: B3P 2S6
Country: Canada
Mailing address: 5 Ramsgate Lane, Suite 116
Mailing city: Halifax
Mailing state: NS
Mailing zip: B3P 2S6
Telephone city code: 902
Office phone: (902) 407-3440
General e-mail: rvroom@artistsyndicate.ca
Web address: www.artistsyndicate.ca
Personnel: Richard Vroom (President)
Main contact: Richard Vroom

CANADIAN PRESS, THE - EDMONTON, AB

Street address 1: Cornerpoint, 10109 106th St., Ste. 504
Street address state: AB
Postal code: T5J 3L7
Country: Canada
Mailing address: Cornerpoint, 10109 106th St., Ste. 504
Mailing city: Edmonton
Mailing state: AB
Mailing zip: T5J 3L7
Office phone: (780) 428-6490
Office fax: (780) 428-0663
Web address: www.thecanadianpress.com
Personnel: Heather Boyd (Bureau Chief)
Main contact: Heather Boyd

EMERYVILLE

INMAN NEWS

Street address 1: 4225 Hollis St
Street address state: NB
Postal code: E3B 1C5
Country: Canada
Mailing address: PO Box 6000
Mailing city: Fredericton
Mailing state: NB
Mailing zip: E3B 5H1
Office phone: (506) 457-0746
Office fax: (506) 457-9708
Web address: www.thecanadianpress.com
Personnel: Kevin Bissett (Correspondent)
Main contact: Kevin Bissett

ENCINITAS

SUN FEATURES

Street address 1: 1100 Garden View Rd
Street address 2: Apt 122
Street address state: NS
Postal code: B3J 3J8
Country: Canada
Mailing address: PO Box 37, Sta. M
Mailing city: Halifax
Mailing state: NS
Mailing zip: B3J 2L4
Office phone: (902) 422-8496
Office fax: (902) 425-2675
Web address: www.thecanadianpress.com
Personnel: Dean Beeby (Bureau Chief)
Main contact: Dean Beeby

FAIR LAWN

COLLINS COMMUNICATIONS

Street address 1: 21-07 Maple Ave
Street address state: QC
Postal code: H2Y 1M6
Country: Canada
Mailing address: 215 St. Jacques St., Ste. 100
Mailing city: Montreal
Mailing state: QC

Mailing zip: H2Y 1M6
Office phone: (514) 849-3212
Office fax: (514) 282-6915
General e-mail: info@thecanadianpress.com
Web address: www.thecanadianpress.com
Personnel: Eric Morrison (Pres.); Claude Papineau (Vice Pres.-French Serv.)
Main contact: Claude Papineau

FAIRFAX

ARRIGONI TRAVEL SYNDICATION

Street address 1: 15 Rock Ridge Rd
Street address state: ON
Postal code: K1P 5P7
Country: Canada
Mailing address: PO Box 595, Sta. B (Letters)
Mailing city: Ottawa
Mailing state: ON
Mailing zip: K1P 5P7
Office phone: (613) 238-4142
Office fax: (613) 238-4452
General e-mail: ottowa@thecanadianpress.com
Web address: www.thecanadianpress.com
Personnel: Robert Russo (Bureau Chief)
Main contact: Dean Beeby

FAIRHOPE

J.D. CROWE

Street address 1: 212 Fig Ave
Street address state: QC
Postal code: G1R 5J1
Country: Canada
Mailing address: 1050 Des Parlementaires, Ste. 2
Mailing city: Quebec City
Mailing state: QC
Mailing zip: G1R 5J1
Office phone: (418) 646-5377
Office fax: (418) 523-9686
General e-mail: info@thecanadianpress.com
Web address: www.thecanadianpress.com
Personnel: Jean Roy (Director)
Main contact: Jean Roy

FALLS CHURCH

NEWSUSA, INC.

Street address 1: 1069 W Broad St
Street address 2: Ste 205
Street address state: SK
Postal code: S4S 0B3
Country: Canada
Mailing address: Legislative Bldg., Press Gallery, Rm. 335
Mailing city: Regina
Mailing state: SK
Mailing zip: S4S 0B3
Office phone: (306) 585-1024
Office fax: (306) 585-1027
General e-mail: info@thecanadianpress.com
Web address: www.thecanadianpress.com
Personnel: Stephanie Graham (Correspondent)
Main contact: Stephanie Graham

FARMINGTON HILLS

ARTISTMARKET.COM

Street address 1: 35336 Spring Hill Rd
Street address state: NL
Postal code: A1C 1B2
Country: Canada
Mailing address: PO Box 5951
Mailing city: Saint John's
Mailing state: NL
Mailing zip: A1C 5X4
Office phone: (709) 576-0687
Office fax: (709) 576-0049
Web address: www.thecanadianpress.com
Personnel: Michelle MacAfee (Correspondent)
Main contact: Michelle MacAfee

FRANKFURT

BLOOMBERG NEWS

Street address 1: Neue Mainzer Strasse 75
Street address state: BC
Postal code: V6Z 2L2
Country: Canada
Mailing address: 840 Howe St., Ste. 250
Mailing city: Vancouver
Mailing state: BC
Mailing zip: V6Z 2L2
Office phone: (604) 687-1662
Office fax: (604) 687-5040
Web address: www.thecanadianpress.com
Personnel: Wendy Cox (Bureau Chief)
Main contact: Wendy Cox

DOW JONES NEWSWIRES - FRANKFURT, GERMANY

Street address 1: Wilhem Leuschner Strasse 78
Street address state: BC
Postal code: V8V 1X4
Country: Canada
Mailing address: Press Gallery
Mailing city: Victoria
Mailing state: BC
Mailing zip: V8V 1X4
Office phone: (250) 384-4912
Office fax: (250) 356-9597
General e-mail: dirk.meissner@thecanadianpress.com
Web address: www.thecanadianpress.com
Personnel: Dirk Meissner (Correspondent)
Main contact: Dirk Meissner

FREDERICTON

BROADCAST NEWS LIMITED

Street address 1: The Press Gallery, Box 6000, Queen St.
Street address state: D.C.
Postal code: 20005-4051
Country: USA
Mailing address: 1100 13th St NW
Mailing city: Washington
Mailing state: DC
Mailing zip: 20005-4051
Office phone: (202) 638-3367
Office fax: (202) 638-3369
Web address: www.thecanadianpress.com
Personnel: Robert Russo (Bureau Chief)
Main contact: Rob Russo

CANADIAN PRESS, THE - FREDERICTON, NB

Street address 1: Press Gallery, 96 Saint John St
Street address state: MB
Postal code: R3C 3R6
Country: Canada
Mailing address: 386 Broadway Ave., Ste. 101
Mailing city: Winnipeg
Mailing state: MB
Mailing zip: R3C 3R6
Office phone: (204) 988-1781
Office fax: (204) 942-4788
General e-mail: info@thecanadianpress.com
Web address: www.thecanadianpress.com
Personnel: Steve Lambert (Manitoba Correspondent)
Main contact: Steve Lambert

GAINESVILLE

COMMUNITY FEATURES

Street address 1: 1733 Dawsonville Hwy
Street address state: D.C.
Postal code: 20007-2969
Country: USA
Mailing address: 304 E 65th St Apt 26C
Mailing city: New York
Mailing state: NY
Mailing zip: 10065-6785
Office phone: (202) 337-2044
Office fax: (202) 338-4750

News, Picture and Syndicate Services

General e-mail: karen@karenfeld.com
Web address: www.karenfeld.com
Personnel: Karen Feld (Owner/Editor)
Main contact: Karen Feld

GENEVA

EFE NEWS SERVICES - GENEVA, SWITZERLAND

Street address 1: Bureau 49, Palas des Nations B, Ave. Paix
Street address state: CA
Postal code: 95811-0101
Country: USA
Mailing address: 530 Bercut Dr Ste E
Mailing city: Sacramento
Mailing state: CA
Mailing zip: 95811-0101
Office phone: (916) 445-6336
Office fax: (916) 443-5871
General e-mail: editor@senior-spectrum.com
Web address: www.senior-spectrum.com
Personnel: Susan Carlson
Main contact: Vahn Babigian

GLEN

PAPPOCOM

Street address 1: 3 Birch Ledge Rd
Street address state: MI
Postal code: 48012-0094
Country: USA
Mailing address: PO Box 94
Mailing city: Birmingham
Mailing state: MI
Mailing zip: 48012-0094
Office phone: (248) 647-3662
General e-mail: sgsilver2002@yahoo.com; sheryl.silver@yahoo.com
Personnel: Sheryl Silver (Owner/Author)
Main contact: Sheryl Silver

GLENCOE

THINK GLINK INC.

Street address 1: 361 Park Ave
Street address 2: Ste 200
Street address state: MI
Postal code: 49546-2141
Country: USA
Mailing address: 3568 Cascade Rd SE
Mailing city: Grand Rapids
Mailing state: MI
Mailing zip: 49546-2141
Office phone: (616) 551-2238
General e-mail: andrew@cartoonresource.com
Web address: www.cartoonresource.com
Note/Syndicate Information: Cartoon Resource delivers customized editorial art with rapid turn-around.
Personnel: Andrew Grossman (Creative Dir.); Nancy Terrell (Mktg. Dir.)
Main contact: Andrew Grossman

GOLETA

JACKSON MEDICAL GROUP, INC.

Street address 1: 220 Pacific Oaks Rd.
Street address state: NY
Postal code: 10023-7708
Country: USA
Mailing address: 15 Central Park W
Mailing city: New York
Mailing state: NY
Mailing zip: 10023-7708
Office phone: (212) 980-0855
Office fax: (212) 980-1664
General e-mail: cartoonews@aol.com; luriestudios@aol.com
Web address: www.luriecartoon.com
Personnel: T.R. Fletcher (Pres.); L. Raymond (Vice Pres., Sales); Lisa Duval (Admin. Dir.); John Schmitt (Accountant/CPA)
Main contact: L. Raymond

GRAND RAPIDS

CARTOON RESOURCE

Street address 1: 3568 Cascade Rd SE
Street address state: NY
Postal code: 10024-6136
Country: USA
Mailing address: 67 Riverside Dr Apt 7A
Mailing city: New York
Mailing state: NY
Mailing zip: 10024-6136
Office phone: (212) CARTOON (277-8666)
General e-mail: cwss@cartoonweb.com
Web address: www.nytsyn.com/cartoons
Personnel: Jerry Robinson (Pres.)
Main contact: Roddy Salazar

GRASS VALLEY

CLEAR CREEK FEATURES

Street address 1: PO Box 3289
Street address state: CA
Postal code: 90275-3132
Country: USA
Mailing address: 28028 Lobrook Dr
Mailing city: Rancho Palos Verdes
Mailing state: CA
Mailing zip: 90275-3132
Office phone: (212) 227-8666
Office fax: (310) 541-9017
General e-mail: cwsmedia@cartoonweb.com
Web address: www.nytsyn.com/cartoons
Personnel: Jerry Robinson (Pres.); Jens Robinson (Vice Pres./Ed.); Bojan Jovanovic (Assoc. Ed.)
Main contact: Jens Robinson

GRIMES

MOTOR NEWS MEDIA CORP.

Street address 1: 3710 SE Capitol Cir
Street address 2: Ste F
Street address state: D.C.
Postal code: 20017-1104
Country: USA
Office phone: (202) 541-3250
General e-mail: cns@catholicnews.com
Web address: www.catholicnews.com
Note/Syndicate Information: Catholic news since 1920.
Personnel: Tony Spence (Director/Editor in Chief); Julie Asher (General News Editor); Edmond Brosnan (Features Editor); Katherine M. Nuss (Library/Information Services/Archives); James Lackey (Web Editor)
Main contact: Tony Spence

GROSSE POINTE FARMS

BUSINESS NEWSFEATURES

Street address 1: 417 Lexington Rd
Street address state: CA
Postal code: 90064-1553
Country: USA
Mailing address: 11400 W Olympic Blvd Ste 780
Mailing city: Los Angeles
Mailing state: CA
Mailing zip: 90064-1553
Office phone: (310) 481-0407
Office fax: (310) 481-0416
General e-mail: citynews@pacbell.net; info@socalnews.com
Web address: www.socalnews.com
Personnel: Doug Faigin (Pres.); Lori Streifler (Ed.); Marty Sauerzopf (City Ed.)
Main contact: Doug Faigin

GUATEMALA CITY

EFE NEWS SERVICES - GUATEMALA CITY, GUATEMALA

Street address 1: 8 Ave. 8-56 Zone 1, Edif. 10-24, Segundo Nivel, Oficina 203
Street address state: CA
Postal code: 92101-4806
Country: USA
Mailing address: 202 C St Rm 13A
Mailing city: San Diego
Mailing state: CA
Mailing zip: 92101-4806
Office phone: (619) 231-9097
Office fax: (619) 231-9633
General e-mail: fdrim@fdcglobal.net
Personnel: Kelly Wheeler (Bureau Chief); Lori Streifler (Ed.)
Main contact: Kelly Wheeler

HALF MOON BAY

AUTOEDITOR SYNDICATION

Street address 1: 186 Cypress Point Rd
Street address state: CA
Postal code: 1139
Country: Argentina
Mailing address: abeltrame@clarin.com
Mailing city: Buenos Aires
Mailing zip: 1139
Telephone country code: 54
Telephone city code: 11
Office phone: 4309-7216
Office fax: 4309-7635
General e-mail: contenidos@clarin.com
Web address: www.clarin.com
Personnel: Matilde Sanchez (Ed.); Agustin Beltrame (Photo Editor); Hernan DiMenna (Ed.)
Main contact: ()

HALIFAX

BROADCAST NEWS LIMITED

Street address 1: 1888 Brunswick St., Ste. 100
Street address state: PA
Postal code: 19104-5228
Country: USA
Mailing address: 4203 Locust St
Mailing city: Philadelphia
Mailing state: PA
Mailing zip: 19104-5290
Office phone: (215) 386-6300
Office fax: (215) 386-3521
General e-mail: robertag@classicstock.com
Web address: www.classicstock.com
Personnel: H. Armstrong Roberts (Pres., ClassicStock); Roberta Groves (Vice Pres., Creative)
Main contact: Roberta Groves

CANADIAN ARTISTS SYNDICATE INCORPORATED

Street address 1: 5 Ramsgate Lane, Suite 116
Street address state: CA
Postal code: 95945-3289
Country: USA
Mailing address: PO Box 3289
Mailing city: Grass Valley
Mailing state: CA
Mailing zip: 95945-3289
Office phone: (530) 272-7176
General e-mail: clearcreekrancher@yahoo.com
Personnel: Mike Drummond (Author/Self-Syndicator/Pub.)
Main contact: Tom Fildey

CANADIAN PRESS, THE - HALIFAX, NS

Street address 1: 1888 Brunswick St., Ste. 701
Street address state: NJ
Postal code: 07410-1524
Country: USA
Mailing address: 21-07 Maple Ave
Mailing city: Fair Lawn
Mailing state: NJ
Mailing zip: 07410-1524
Office phone: (201) 703-0911
Office fax: (201) 703-0211
General e-mail: stepoutmag@aol.com
Web address: www.so-mag.com

Personnel: Lawrence Collins (Publisher); Dan Lorenzo (Editor)
Main contact: Lawrence Collins

HAMILTON

WOMBANIA

Street address 1: 249 Kensington Ave. N.
Street address state: GA
Postal code: 30501-1531
Country: USA
Mailing address: 1733 Dawsonville Hwy
Mailing city: Gainesville
Mailing state: GA
Mailing zip: 30501-1531
Office phone: (770) 287-3798
Office fax: (770) 287-0112
General e-mail: commfeat@charter.net
Web address: www.communityfeatures.com
Note/Syndicate Information: Community Features sells and maintains church and Bible verse pages, and offers features for religious pages.
Personnel: Christina Smith (Co-Owner); Bill Johnson (Co-Owner)
Main contact: Christina Smith

HERMOSA BEACH

CREATORS

Street address 1: 737 3rd St
Street address state: MN
Postal code: 55402-4501
Country: USA
Mailing address: 220 S 6th St Ste 500
Mailing city: Minneapolis
Mailing state: MN
Mailing zip: 55402-4501
Office phone: (612) 339-7571
General e-mail: info@computeruser.com
Web address: www.computeruser.com
Personnel: Dan Heilman (Ed.); Nathaniel Opperman (Vice Pres., Publishing)
Main contact: Nathaniel Opperman

HOBART

LISTENING, INC.

Street address 1: 105 E 3rd St
Street address state: NY
Postal code: 10017
Country: USA
Mailing address: 885 Second Avenue, 40th floor
Mailing city: New York
Mailing state: NY
Mailing zip: 10017
Office phone: (212) 583-2560
Office fax: (212) 583-2585
General e-mail: generalkonsulat.new-york@gov.se
Web address: www.swedenabroad.se
Main contact: Consulate Guide

HONG KONG

BLOOMBERG NEWS

Street address 1: 27 Fl., Cheung Kong Ctr., 2 Queens Rd. Central
Street address state: IL
Postal code: 60640-5873
Country: USA
Mailing address: 4410 N Ravenswood Ave Ste 101
Mailing city: Chicago
Mailing state: IL
Mailing zip: 60640-5873
Office phone: (773) 728-8351
Office fax: (773) 728-8326
General e-mail: info@contentthatworks.com
Web address: www.contentthatworks.com
Personnel: Paul A. Camp (CEO); Jenn Goebel (COO); Dan Dalton (Vice Pres., Sales); Mary Connors (Editorial Director)
Main contact: Mary Connors

HONG KONG

DOW JONES NEWSWIRES - HONG KONG, HONG KONG

Street address 1: 25F Central Plz., 18 Harbour Rd., Wanchai
Street address state: CA
Postal code: 92101-3562
Country: USA
Mailing address: 501 W Broadway Ste A PMB 265
Mailing city: San Diego
Mailing state: CA
Mailing zip: 92101-3562
Office phone: (858) 492-8696
General e-mail: continentalnewsservice@yahoo.com
Web address: www.continentalnewsservice.com
Note/Syndicate Information: CF/CNS publishes (1) Continental Newstime general-interest newsmagazine as an available newspaper insert, with its individual newspaper features also marketed separately; (2) the children's newspaper, Kids' Newstime approximately 154-158 times a year; (3) a Northern California community newspaper regularly and a San Diego News Edition intermittently; (4) CF/CNS has launched special, periodic, on-line Washington D.C., Chicago, Atlanta, Honolulu, Miami, Anchorage, Minneapolis, Rochester (N.Y.), Houston, Seattle, and Boston News Editions; and (5) CF/CNS now offers a Country Neighbor Edition of Continental Newstime for our rural friends in the West and East.
Personnel: Gary P. Salamone (Ed. in-Chief)
Main contact: Gary P. Salamone

HURLEYVILLE

RON BERNTHAL

Street address 1: PO Box 259
Street address state: MI
Postal code: 48207-2732
Country: USA
Mailing address: 1155 Gratiot Ave
Mailing city: Detroit
Mailing state: MI
Mailing zip: 48207-2732
Office phone: (313) 446-6000
Office fax: (313) 446-8030
General e-mail: info@crain.com
Web address: www.crain.com
Personnel: Keith Crain (Chairman); KC Crain (President, Chief Operating Officer); Bob Recchia (CFO); Mary Kramer (Vice President, Group Publisher)
Main contact: Dan Jones

INDIAN WELLS

RAFFERTY CONSULTING GROUP

Street address 1: 45775 Indian Wells Ln
Street address state: RI
Postal code: 02914-1342
Country: USA
Mailing address: 945 Waterman Ave
Mailing city: East Providence
Mailing state: RI
Mailing zip: 02914-1342
Telephone country code: 01
Office phone: (401) 455-1555
Office fax: (401) 272-1150
General e-mail: info@creativecirclemedia.com
Web address: www.creativecirclemedia.com
Personnel: Bill Ostendorf (Pres.)
Main contact: Bill Ostendorf

INVERNESS

GOT INFLUENCE? PUBLISHING

Street address 1: 190 Dundee Rd
Street address state: SD
Postal code: 57105-1819
Country: USA
Mailing address: 1608 S Dakota Ave
Mailing city: Sioux Falls
Mailing state: SD
Mailing zip: 57105-1819
Office phone: (605) 336-9434
General e-mail: smoments7@aol.com
Web address: www.creativecomics.net
Personnel: Ken Alvine (Owner/Mgr.)
Main contact: Ken Alvine

IOWA CITY

SHARPNACK, JOE

Street address 1: PO Box 3325
Street address state: CA
Postal code: 90254-4714
Country: USA
Mailing address: 737 3rd St
Mailing city: Hermosa Beach
Mailing state: CA
Mailing zip: 90254-4714
Office phone: (310) 337-7003
Office fax: (310) 337-7625
General e-mail: sales@creators.com; info@creators.com
Web address: www.creators.com
Personnel: Rick Newcombe (CEO); Margo Sugrue (National Sales Director); Mary Ann Veldman (Sales Director); Marianne Sugawara (Vice President of Operations); Sheila Telle (Sales Administrator); Jessica Burtch (Editor); Anthony Zurcher (Editor); Anica Wong (Associate, Business Development, Operations & Sales); Brandon Telle (Head of development, programming and technology); David Yontz (Managing Editor); Gunner Coil (Associate, Business Development, Operations & Sales); Mikaela Conley (Editor); Simone Slykhous (Editor); Sarah Follette (Head of accounting); Pete Kaminski (Production; Animator); Katie Ransom (Accounting/finance analyst); Jack Newcombe (President & COO)
Main contact: Margo Sugrue; Anica Wong

JAMAICA

WORLDWATCH/FOREIGN AFFAIRS SYNDICATE

Street address 1: 14421 Charter Rd
Street address 2: Apt 5C
Street address state: PA
Postal code: 19003-0527
Country: USA
Mailing address: PO Box 527
Mailing city: Ardmore
Mailing state: PA
Mailing zip: 19003-0527
Office phone: (610) 924-9158
Office fax: (610) 924-9159
General e-mail: crcktinc@aol.com
Personnel: Edwin Marks (Pres./Pub.); Mark E. Battersby (Vice Pres./Ed.); E. Arthur Stern (Mng. Ed.)
Main contact: Mark E. Battersby

JERSEY CITY

JOE HARKINS

Street address 1: 2595 John F Kennedy Blvd
Street address state: OH
Postal code: 43017
Country: USA
Mailing city: Dublin
Mailing state: OH
Mailing zip: 43017-3202
Office phone: (614) 408-3865
General e-mail: info@criticsinc.com
Web address: www.criticsinc.com
Personnel: Aris T. Christofides (Pub./Ed.); Lori Pearson (Commun. Dir.); Teressa L. Elliott (Contributing Ed.); Wade R. Gossett (Contributing Ed.); Ethan Cuhulinn (Bus. Mgr.)
Main contact: Lori Pearson

JERUSALEM

THE JERUSALEM POST FOREIGN SERVICE

Street address 1: The Jerusalem Post Bldg.
Street address state: NJ
Postal code: 07675-6034
Country: USA
Mailing address: 646 Jones Rd
Mailing city: Rivervale
Mailing state: NJ
Mailing zip: 07675-6034
Office phone: (201) 391-7135
General e-mail: writa1@me.com
Personnel: Curt Schleier (Pres./Ed.)
Main contact: Curt Schleier

KANSAS CITY

ANDREWS MCMEEL SYNDICATION

Street address 1: 1130 Walnut St
Street address state: FL
Postal code: 33141-1115
Country: USA
Mailing address: 721 86th St.
Mailing city: Miami Beach
Mailing state: FL
Mailing zip: 33141
Telephone city code: 305
Office phone: (305) 865-0158
General e-mail: davegoodwi@aol.com
Web address: www.davegoodwin.weebly.com
Personnel: Dave Goodwin (Author/Owner); Ari Goodwin (Writer)
Main contact: Dave Goodwin

UNIVERSAL UCLICK INTERNATIONAL DIVISON

Street address 1: 1130 Walnut St
Street address state: NY
Postal code: 10019-1107
Country: USA
Mailing address: 25 Columbus Cir # 55E
Mailing city: New York
Mailing state: NY
Mailing zip: 10019-1107
Office phone: (212) 2090847
Office fax:
General e-mail: expert@deg.com
Web address: www.deg.com
Personnel: Marisa D'Vari (Pres./Writer)
Main contact: Marisa D'Vari

KENT

MARKS & FREDERICK ASSOC., LLC

Street address 1: 11 Green Hill Rd
Street address state: VA
Postal code: 20151-3345
Country: USA
Mailing address: 13703 Southernwood Ct
Mailing city: Chantilly
Mailing state: VA
Mailing zip: 20151-3345
Office phone: (703) 437-6635
Main contact: John Pring

KINNELON

MIC INSURANCE SERVICES

Street address 1: 170 Kinnelon Rd
Street address 2: Rm 11
Street address state: GA
Postal code: 30076-5114
Country: USA
Mailing address: 1865 River Falls Dr
Mailing city: Roswell
Mailing state: GA
Mailing zip: 30076-5114
Office phone: (770) 998-9911
General e-mail: info@thewritepublicist.com
Web address: www.thewritepublicist.com
Personnel: Regina Lynch-Hudson (Creator/Writer)
Main contact: Regina Lynch-Hudson

KUALA LUMPUR

DOW JONES NEWSWIRES - KUALA LUMPUR, MALAYSIA

Street address 1: Ste. 21A-8-2, 8th Floor, Faber Imperial Ct., Jalan Sultan Ismail
Street address state: WI
Postal code: 53744-5063
Country: USA
Mailing address: PO Box 45063
Mailing city: Madison
Mailing state: WI
Mailing zip: 53744-5063
Office phone: (608) 222-5522
Office fax: (608) 222-5585
General e-mail: john@kovalic.com
Web address: www.kovalic.com
Personnel: Alexander Schiller (Office Mgr.); Eleanor Williams (Ed.); Alex Aulisi (Business Manager)
Main contact: Robert Kovalic

LA JOLLA

WORLD FEATURES SYNDICATE

Street address 1: 5842 Sagebrush Rd
Country: Colombia
Mailing address: Calle 93B No. 13-30 Oficina 301
Mailing city: Bogota
Telephone country code: 57
Office phone: 481-1785
Office fax: 483-5623
General e-mail: datanewsdj@hotmail.com
Web address: www.dowjones.com/djnewswires.asp
Personnel: Richard Sanders (Correspondent); Martha De Rengifo (Sales Exec.)
Main contact: Martha de Rengifo

LA PAZ

EFE NEWS SERVICES - LA PAZ, BOLIVIA

Street address 1: Avda. Sanchez Lima, 2520. Edificio Anibal - MZ 01
Postal code: 1200
Country: Belgium
Mailing address: Blvd. Brand Whitlock 87
Mailing city: Brussels
Mailing zip: 1200
Telephone country code: 32
Telephone city code: 2
Office phone: 285-0130
Office fax: 741 1429
General e-mail: dirk.geeraerts@dowjones.com; vanessa.stolk@dowjones.com
Web address: www.dowjones.com/djnewswires.asp
Personnel: Vanessa Stolk (Rep.); Peter Greiff (Correspondent); Dirk Geeraerts (Acct. Mgr.)
Main contact: Dirk Geeraerts

LILBURN

W.D. FARMER RESIDENCE DESIGNER, INC.

Street address 1: 5238 Rocky Hill Dr SW
Postal code: 1001
Country: Argentina
Mailing address: Leandro N. Alem 712, Piso 4
Mailing city: Buenos Aires
Mailing zip: 1001
Telephone country code: 54
Telephone city code: 1
Office phone: 4314-8788
Office fax: 4311-0083
General e-mail: ana.del-riccio@dowjones.com
Web address: www.dowjones.com/djnewswires.asp

News, Picture and Syndicate Services

II-23

Personnel: Michelle Wallin (Correspondent); Ana Del-Riccio (Sales Exec.)
Main contact: Ana Del-Riccio

LIMA

EFE NEWS SERVICES - LIMA, PERU

Street address 1: Mauel Gonzalez Olaechea, 207
Postal code: D-60329
Country: Germany
Mailing address: Wilhem Leuschner Strasse 78
Mailing city: Frankfurt
Mailing zip: D-60329
Telephone country code: 49
Telephone city code: 69
Office phone: 29 725 200
Office fax: 29 725 222
Web address: www.dowjones.com/djnewswires.asp
Personnel: Fridrich Geiger (Ed.)
Main contact: Friedrich Geiger

LISBON

EFE NEWS SERVICES - LISBON, PORTUGAL

Street address 1: Rua Castilho, 13 D, 5A
Country: Hong Kong
Mailing address: 25F Central Plz., 18 Harbour Rd., Wanchai
Mailing city: Hong Kong
Telephone country code: 852
Office phone: 2573 7121
General e-mail: djnews.hk@dowjones.com
Web address: www.dowjones.com
Personnel: Jeffrey Ng (Correspondent)
Main contact: Jeffrey Ng

LIVONIA

Q SYNDICATE

Street address 1: 20222 Farmington Rd
Postal code: 50250
Country: Malaysia
Mailing address: Ste. 21A-8-2, 8th Floor, Faber Imperial Ct., Jalan Sultan Ismail
Mailing city: Kuala Lumpur
Mailing zip: 50250
Telephone country code: 60
Telephone city code: 3
Office phone: (65) 6415-4200
Office fax: (65) 6225-8959
General e-mail: janet.leau@dowjones.com
Personnel: Matthew Geiger (Correspondent); Janet Leau (Acct. Mgr.)
Main contact: Janet Leau

LONDON

ADLINK-INTERNATIONAL LTD

Street address 1: Global Advertising Services
Street address 2: 16 Upper Woburn Street
Postal code: E1W 1AZ
Country: United Kingdom
Mailing address: Commodity Quay, E. Smithfield
Mailing city: London
Mailing zip: E1W 1AZ
Telephone country code: 44
Telephone city code: 20
Office phone: 726-7903
Office fax: 726-7855
General e-mail: adam.howes@dowjones.com
Web address: www.dowjones.com
Personnel: Adam Howes (Regl. Sales Mgr.)
Main contact: Adam Howes

DOW JONES NEWSWIRES - LONDON, UNITED KINGDOM

Street address 1: Commodity Quay, E. Smithfield
Postal code: EC4A 1QN
Country: United Kingdom
Mailing address: 12 Norwich St.
Mailing city: London
Mailing zip: EC4A 1QN
Telephone country code: 44
Telephone city code: 227
Office phone: 842-9550
Office fax: 842-9551
Personnel: Bhushan Bahree (Correspondent); Sarah Money (Sales Mgr.)
Main contact: Sarah Money

DOW JONES NEWSWIRES - LONDON, UNITED KINGDOM

Street address 1: 12 Norwich St.
Postal code: 28003
Country: Spain
Mailing address: Espronceda 32 1st Planta
Mailing city: Madrid
Mailing zip: 28003
Telephone country code: 34
Telephone city code: 91
Office phone: 395-8120
Office fax: 399-1930
Personnel: Santiago Perez (Bureau Chief)
Main contact: Santiago Perez

EFE NEWS SERVICES - LONDON, UNITED KINGDOM

Street address 1: 299 Oxford St. 6th Fl.
Country: Philippines
Mailing address: 12/F Tower One & Exchange Plaza Ayala Triangle, Ayala Ave, Makati City
Mailing city: Manila
Telephone country code: 63
Telephone city code: 2
Office phone: 574-616
Office fax: 885-0293
General e-mail: Lilian.Karununean@dowjones.com
Web address: www.djnewswires.com
Personnel: Lilian Karununean (Correspondent)
Main contact: Lilian Karununean

FINANCIAL TIMES

Street address 1: 1 Southwark Bridge
Postal code: 11560
Country: Mexico
Mailing address: Av. Issac Newton No. 286, Piso 9, Col. Chapultepec Morales
Mailing city: Mexico City
Mailing zip: 11560
Telephone country code: 55
Office phone: (525) 254-5581
Office fax: (525) 254-7510
Personnel: Peter R. Fritsch (Correspondent)
Main contact: Peter R. Fritsch

NEWS LICENSING

Street address 1: The News Building, 13th Floor,
Street address 2: 1 London Bridge
Postal code: 20122
Country: Italy
Mailing address: Via Burigozzo 5
Mailing city: Milano
Mailing zip: 20122
Telephone country code: 39
Telephone city code: 02
Office phone: 7601-5386
Office fax: 5821 9752
Personnel: Susan Peiffer (Correspondent)
Main contact: Jennifer Clark

TELEGRAPH MEDIA GROUP

Street address 1: 111 Buckingham Palace Road
Street address state: NY
Postal code: 10036-2758
Country: USA
Mailing address: 1155 Avenue of the Americas Fl 7
Mailing city: New York
Mailing state: NY
Mailing zip: 10036-2711
Office phone: (609) 520-4000
General e-mail: SpotNews@dowjones.com
Web address: www.djnewswires.com

Personnel: Gregory White (Correspondent)
Main contact: Gregory White

LOS ANGELES

AGENCIA PRENSA INTERNACIONAL INC.

Street address 1: 112 W 9th St
Street address 2: Ste 518
Street address state: NY
Postal code: 10036-8701
Country: USA
Mailing address: 1211 Avenue of the Americas Lowr C3
Mailing city: New York
Mailing state: NY
Mailing zip: 10030-0711
Office phone: (212) 416-2400
Office fax: (212) 416-2410
General e-mail: spotnews@priority.dowjones.com
Web address: www.djnewswires.com
Personnel: Tim Turner (Vice Pres./Gen. Mgr.); James Donoghue (Vice Pres., Sales/Mktg.); Neal Lipschutz (Mng. Ed., Dow Jones Newswire Americas)
Main contact: James Donoghue

BUSINESS WIRE - LOS ANGELES, CA

Street address 1: 12100 Wilshire Blvd
Street address 2: Ste 780
Postal code: 75009
Country: France
Mailing address: 6-8 Boulevard Haussmann
Mailing city: Paris
Mailing zip: 75009
Telephone country code: 33
Telephone city code: 1
Office phone: 7036 5502
Office fax: 4017-1781
General e-mail: thierry.cadin@dowjones.com
Personnel: Thierry Cadi (Reg'l Sales Mgr.); David Pearson (Correspondent)
Main contact: Thierry Cadi

CITY NEWS SERVICE, INC. - LOS ANGELES, CA

Street address 1: 11400 W Olympic Blvd
Street address 2: Ste 780
Postal code: 04534 002
Country: Brazil
Mailing address: Rua Joaquim Floriano 488. 6 andar
Mailing city: Sao Paulo
Mailing zip: 04534 002
Telephone country code: 55
Telephone city code: 11
Office phone: 256-0520
Office fax: 3044-2813
General e-mail: ana.gresenberg@dowjones.com
Personnel: John Wright (Correspondent); Ana Gresenberg (Sales Exec.)
Main contact: Ana Gresenberg

EXHIBITOR RELATIONS CO.

Street address 1: 1262 Westwood Blvd
Postal code: 079903
Country: Singapore
Mailing address: 10 Anson Rd., Ste. 32-09/10 Int'l Plz.
Mailing city: Singapore
Mailing zip: 079903
Telephone country code: 65
Office phone: 6415-4200
Office fax: 6225-8959
General e-mail: hweekun.ho@dowjones.com
Personnel: Lim Mui Khi (Correspondent); Hwee-Kun Ho (Regl. Sales Mgr.)
Main contact: Hwee-Kun Ho

LUMBERTON

HEART TONES

Street address 1: PO Box 304
Street address 2: P. O. Box 304
Postal code: 2000
Country: Australia
Mailing address: Level 10 56 Titt St.
Mailing city: Sydney
Mailing zip: 2000
Telephone country code: 61
Telephone city code: 2
Office phone: 8272 4600
Office fax: 8272 4601
Web address: www.dowjones.com
Personnel: Ian McDonald (Correspondent); Tom Rustowski (Regl. Sales Mgr.)
Main contact: Tom Rustowski

MADISON

BIG RING MEDIA TEAM, INC.

Street address 1: PO Box 231
Postal code: 100 0004
Country: Japan
Mailing address: Marunouchi Mitsui Bldg. 1F, 2-2-2, Marunouchi Chiyoda-ku
Mailing city: Tokyo
Mailing zip: 100 0004
Telephone country code: 81
Telephone city code: 3
Office phone: 5220 2730
Office fax: 5220-2746
General e-mail: masashi.takeuchi@dowjones.com
Personnel: Masashi Takeuchi (Sales Mgr.)
Main contact: Masashi Takeuchi

MADISON

DORK STORM PRESS/SHETLAND PRODUCTIONS

Street address 1: PO Box 45063
Street address state: D.C.
Postal code: 20036-5419
Country: USA
Mailing address: 1025 Connecticut Ave NW Ste 800
Mailing city: Washington
Mailing state: DC
Mailing zip: 20036-5419
Office phone: (202) 862-9272
Office fax: (202) 862-6621
Personnel: Rob Wells (Bureau Chief)
Main contact: Rob Wells

MADISON

MIDWEST FEATURES SYNDICATE

Street address 1: PO Box 259623
Postal code: 8031
Country: Switzerland
Mailing address: Sihlquai 253, Postfach 1128
Mailing city: Zurich
Mailing zip: 8031
Telephone country code: 41
Telephone city code: 43
Office phone: 960 5870
Office fax: 960 5701
General e-mail: sarah.money@dowjones.com; penny.greenwood@awp.ch
Personnel: Penny Greenwood (Sr. Acct. Mgr.)
Main contact: Penny Greenwood

MADRID

DOW JONES NEWSWIRES - MADRID, SPAIN

Street address 1: Espronceda 32 1st Planta
Street address state: FL
Postal code: 34145-2310
Country: USA
Mailing address: 836 Buttonwood Ct.

Mailing city: Marco Island
Mailing state: FL
Mailing zip: 34145
Telephone country code: 1
Telephone city code: 9782702590
Office phone: 9782702590
General e-mail: andy.singer@singerexecutivedevelopment.com
Web address: www.singerexecutivedevelopment.com
Note/Syndicate Information: Weekly and well liked business column sent out every Tuesday. Discusses any and all aspects of business.
Main contact: Andy Singer

EUROPA PRESS NEWS SERVICE

Street address 1: Paseo de la Castellana, 210
Street address state: CA
Postal code: 93922-1383
Country: USA
Mailing address: PO Box 221383
Mailing city: Carmel
Mailing state: CA
Mailing zip: 93922-1383
Office phone: (831) 625-3188
Office fax: (831) 625-0611
General e-mail: drbeemm@aol.com
Web address: www.drbee.com
Personnel: Dr. Bee Epstein-Shepherd (Mental Skills Coach/Writer)
Main contact: Dr. Bee Epstein-Shepherd

MAMARONECK

MALE CALL

Street address 1: 721 Shore Acres Dr
Street address state: OH
Postal code: 44089-0318
Country: USA
Mailing address: PO Box 318
Mailing city: Vermilion
Mailing state: OH
Mailing zip: 44089-0318
Office phone: (440) 967-0293
Office fax: (440) 967-0293
General e-mail: dave@northshorepublishing.com; dave@thecomedybook.com
Web address: www.thecomedybook.com; www.davelaughs.com; www.beatlesincleveland.com; www.northshorepublishing.com
Personnel: Dave Schwensen (Author/Award-Winning Humor Columnist)
Main contact: Dave Schwensen

MANAGUA

EFE NEWS SERVICES - MANAGUA, NICARAGUA

Street address 1: Garden City S-22
Street address state: VA
Postal code: 22121-0133
Country: USA
Mailing address: PO Box 133
Mailing city: Mount Vernon
Mailing state: VA
Mailing zip: 22121-0133
Office phone: (202) 253-3899
General e-mail: dunkelratings@msn.com
Web address: www.dunkelindex.com
Personnel: Richard H. Dunkel Jr. (Co-Ed./Co-Owner); Bob Dunkel (Co-Ed./Co-Owner)
Main contact: Bob Dunkel

MANCHESTER

PLAIN LABEL PRESS

Street address 1: 1690 Carman Mill Dr
Street address state: CT
Postal code: 06851-4719
Country: USA
Mailing address: PO Box 5098
Mailing city: Westport
Mailing state: CT
Mailing zip: 06881-5098

Office phone: (203) 854-5559/x106
Office fax: (203) 866-0602
General e-mail: earthtalkcolumn@emagazine.com
Web address: www.earthtalk.org
Personnel: Doug Moss (Pub./Exec. Ed.)
Main contact: Doug Moss

MANILA

DOW JONES NEWSWIRES - MANILA, PHILIPPINES

Street address 1: 12/F Tower One & Exchange Plaza Ayala Triangle
Street address 2: Ayala Ave, Makati City
Street address state: MN
Postal code: 55901-2497
Country: USA
Mailing address: 215 Elton Hills Number 56
Mailing city: Rochester
Mailing state: MN
Mailing zip: 55906-4019
Office phone: (651) 491-3613
General e-mail: ed.fischer.toons@gmail.com
Web address: www.edfischer.com
Note/Syndicate Information: 75 newspapers pay to receive 9 Ed Fischer cartoons a week plus Cartoonstock. Com sells my cartoons world-wide plus selling 500,000 books
Personnel: Ed Fischer (Self-Syndicator plus 3,500 cartoons on a variety of subjects for papers, books, advertising, newsletters,magazines. 28 awards)
Main contact: Ed Fischer

EFE NEWS SERVICES - MANILA, PHILIPPINES

Street address 1: Unit 1006, 88 Corporate Center, 141 Sedeno corner
Postal code: 16000
Country: Algeria
Mailing address: 4 Ave. Pasteur, 1st Fl.
Mailing city: Algiers
Mailing zip: 16000
Telephone country code: 213
Telephone city code: 2
Office phone: 173 5680
Office fax: 174 0456
General e-mail: javiergarcia@efe.com
Personnel: Javier Garcia (Rep.)
Main contact: Javier Garcia

MARCO ISLAND

DOWN TO BUSINESS - COLUMN

Street address 1: 836 Buttonwood Ct
Postal code: 100027
Country: China
Mailing address: Julong Garden, 7-14 L. Xinzhongjie, 68 Dongcheng
Mailing city: Beijing
Mailing zip: 100027
Telephone country code: 86
Telephone city code: 10
Office phone: 6553 1198
Office fax: 6552 7861
Web address: www.efe.es
Personnel: Paloma Caballero (Rep.)
Main contact: Paloma Caballero

MASSAPEQUA PARK

AMERICAN CROSSWORD FEDERATION

Street address 1: PO Box 69
Street address state: NY
Postal code: 10117
Country: Germany
Mailing address: Reinhardtstrasse 58
Mailing city: Berlin
Mailing zip: 10117
Telephone country code: 49
Telephone city code: 30

Office phone: (206) 039-860
Office fax: (206) 039-840
General e-mail: berlin@efe.com
Personnel: Noelia LÃƒÂ³pez
Main contact: Noelia LÃƒÂ³pez

MC LEAN

GANNETT NEWS SERVICE - MCLEAN, VA

Street address 1: 7950 Jones Branch Dr
Country: Colombia
Mailing address: Calle 67 No 7-35
Mailing city: Bogota
Telephone country code: 57
Telephone city code: 1
Office phone: 321 48 55
Office fax: 321 47 51
General e-mail: efecol@efebogota.com.co
Personnel: Esther Rebollo (Rep.)
Main contact: Esther Rebollo

MELROSE

ATLANTIC FEATURE SYNDICATE

Street address 1: 16 Slayton Rd
Postal code: 1040
Country: Belgium
Mailing address: Residence Palace, Rue de la Loi, 155
Mailing city: Brussels
Mailing zip: 1040
Telephone country code: 32
Telephone city code: 2
Office phone: 285-4831
Office fax: 230-9319
General e-mail: bruselas@efe.com
Personnel: Jose Manuel Sanz (Rep.)
Main contact: Jose Manuel Sanz

MEXICO CITY

DOW JONES NEWSWIRES - MEXICO CITY, MEXICO

Street address 1: Av. Issac Newton No. 286, Piso 9, Col. Chapultepec Morales
Postal code: 1107
Country: Argentina
Mailing address: Av. Alicia Moreau de Justo 1720
Mailing city: Buenos Aires
Mailing zip: 1107
Telephone country code: 54
Telephone city code: 11
Office phone: 43 11 12 11
Office fax: 43 12 75 18
General e-mail: redaccion@efe.com.ar
Personnel: Mar Marin (Rep.)
Main contact: Mar Marin

EFE NEWS SERVICES - MEXICO CITY, MEXICO

Street address 1: Lafayette, 69, Colonia Ave.
Country: Egypt
Mailing address: 4 Mohamed Mazhar, 3 - apt. 5. Zamalek
Mailing city: Cairo
Telephone country code: 20
Telephone city code: 2
Office phone: 738-0792
Office fax: 361-2198
Personnel: Grace Augustine (Rep.)
Main contact: Grace Augustine

MIAMI

AMPERSAND COMMUNICATIONS

Street address 1: 2311 S Bayshore Dr
Postal code: 1211
Country: Switzerland
Mailing address: Bureau 49, Palas des Nations B, Ave. Paix

Mailing city: Geneva
Mailing zip: 1211
Telephone country code: 41
Telephone city code: 22
Office phone: 7336273
General e-mail: ginebra@efe.com
Web address: www.efe.com
Personnel: Celine Aemisegger (Bureau Chief)
Main contact: Celine Aemisegger

MIAMI BEACH

DAVE GOODWIN & ASSOCIATES

Street address 1: 721 86th St
Country: Guatemala
Mailing address: 8 Ave. 8-56 Zone 1, Edif. 10-24, Segundo Nivel, Oficina 203
Mailing city: Guatemala City
Telephone country code: 502
Telephone city code: 2
Office phone: 51 94 84
Office fax: 51 84 59
General e-mail: guatemala@acan-efe.com
Personnel: Carlos Arrazola (Rep.)
Main contact: Carlos Arrazola

MIDDLETOWN

OASIS NEWSFEATURES, INC.

Street address 1: PO Box 2144
Postal code: 7403
Country: Bolivia
Mailing address: Avda. Sanchez Lima, 2520. Edificio Anibal - MZ 01
Mailing city: La Paz
Mailing zip: 7403
Telephone country code: 591
Telephone city code: 2
Office phone: 235-9837
Office fax: 239-1441
General e-mail: efebol@entelnet.bo
Web address: www.efe
Personnel: Soledad Alvarez (Rep.)
Main contact: Agustin de Gracia; Soledad Alvarez

MILANO

DOW JONES NEWSWIRES - MILANO, ITALY

Street address 1: Via Burigozzo 5
Postal code: 27
Country: Peru
Mailing address: Mauel Gonzalez Olaechea, 207
Mailing city: Lima
Mailing zip: 27
Telephone country code: 51
Telephone city code: 1
Office phone: 441 24 22
Office fax: 421 13 72
General e-mail: lima@efe.com
Personnel: Javier Otazu (Rep.)
Main contact: Javier Otazu

MILWAUKEE

REEL TO REAL CELEBRITY PROFILES

Street address 1: 8643 N Fielding Rd
Street address state: DC
Postal code: 1250 066
Country: Portugal
Mailing address: Rua Castilho, 13 D, 5A
Mailing city: Lisbon
Mailing zip: 1250 066
Telephone country code: 351
Telephone city code: 21
Office phone: 351 39 30
Office fax: 351 39 38
General e-mail: lisboa@efe.com
Personnel: Emilio Crespo (Rep.)
Main contact: Emilio Crespo

News, Picture and Syndicate Services

MINNEAPOLIS

COMPUTERUSER
Street address 1: 220 S 6th St
Street address 2: Ste 500
Postal code: W1C 2DZ
Country: United Kingdom
Mailing address: 299 Oxford St. 6th Fl.
Mailing city: London
Mailing zip: W1C 2DZ
Telephone country code: 44
Telephone city code: 20
Office phone: 7493 7313
Office fax: 7493-7114
Personnel: Joaquin Rabago (Rep.)
Main contact: Joaquin Rabago

MISSION

FAMILY FEATURES EDITORIAL SYNDICATE, INC.
Street address 1: 5825 Dearborn St
Country: Nicaragua
Mailing address: Garden City S-22
Mailing city: Managua
Telephone country code: 505
Telephone city code: 2
Office phone: 49 11 66
Office fax: 49 59 28
General e-mail: nicaragua@acan-efe.com
Personnel: Philadelphius Martinez (Rep.)
Main contact: Philadelphius Martinez

MONTEVIDEO

EFE NEWS SERVICES - MONTEVIDEO, URUGUAY
Street address 1: Wilson Ferreira Aldunate 1294
Postal code: 1227
Country: Philippines
Mailing address: Unit 1006, 88 Corporate Center, 141 Sedeno corner
Mailing city: Manila
Mailing zip: 1227
Telephone country code: 63
Telephone city code: 2
Office phone: 843 1986
Office fax: 843 1973
General e-mail: manila@efe.com
Web address: www.efe.es
Personnel: Miguel Frau Rovira (Bureau Chief); Marco Zabaleta (Ed.)
Main contact: Marco Zabaleta

MONTOURSVILLE

WILD BILL'S CARTOON SHOW!
Street address 1: 179 Old Cement Rd
Street address 2: Lot B40
Postal code: 011590
Country: Mexico
Mailing address: Lafayette, 69, Colonia Ave.
Mailing city: Mexico City
Mailing zip: 011590
Telephone country code: 52
Telephone city code: 55
Office phone: 5545 8256
Office fax: 5254 1412
Personnel: Alejandro Amezcua (Sales Mgr.); Manuel Fuentes (Rep.)
Main contact: Alejandro Amezcua

MONTREAL

BROADCAST NEWS LIMITED
Street address 1: 215 St. Jacques W., Ste. 100
Postal code: 11100
Country: Uruguay
Mailing address: Wilson Ferreira Aldunate 1294
Mailing city: Montevideo
Mailing zip: 11100
Telephone country code: 598
Telephone city code: 2

Office phone: 902 03 38
Office fax: 902 67 26
General e-mail: montevideo@efe.com
Personnel: Raul Cortes (Rep.)
Main contact: Raul Cortes

CANADIAN PRESS, THE - MONTREAL, QC
Street address 1: 215 St. Jacques St., Ste. 100
Postal code: 119021
Country: Russia
Mailing address: Ria Novosti International Press Center, Zubovski blvd. 4
Mailing city: Moscow
Mailing zip: 119021
Telephone country code: 7
Telephone city code: 495
Office phone: 637 5137
Office fax: 637 5137
General e-mail: efemos@gmail.com
Personnel: Miguel Bas (Rep.)
Main contact: Miguel Bas

MOSCOW

EFE NEWS SERVICES - MOSCOW, RUSSIA
Street address 1: Ria Novosti International Press Center, Zubovski blvd. 4
Postal code: 110001
Country: India
Mailing address: 48, Hanuman Road. Instituto Cervantes building. Connaught Palce
Mailing city: New Delhi
Mailing zip: 110001
Telephone country code: 91
Telephone city code: 11
Office phone: 41501999
General e-mail: india@efe.com
Web address: www.efe.com
Personnel: Moncho Torres (Correspondent)
Main contact: office staff

MOUNT VERNON

DUNKEL SPORTS RESEARCH SERVICE
Street address 1: PO Box 133
Postal code: 0834 00749
Country: Panama
Mailing address: Avda. Samuel Lewis y Manuel Icaza. Edif. Comosa 22
Mailing city: Panama City
Mailing zip: 0834 00749
Telephone country code: 507
Telephone city code: 2
Office phone: 23 90 14
Office fax: 64 84 42
General e-mail: panama@acan-efe.com
Personnel: Hernan Martin (Rep.)
Main contact: Hernan Martin

MOUNTAIN BROOK

HEALTHY MINDS
Street address 1: 3709 Crestbrook Rd
Postal code: 75002
Country: France
Mailing address: 10 rue St. Marc, Buro. 165
Mailing city: Paris
Mailing zip: 75002
Telephone country code: 33
Telephone city code: 1
Office phone: 44 82 65 40
Office fax: 40 39 91 78
General e-mail: paris@efe.com
Web address: www.efe.com
Personnel: Javier Alonso (Rep.)
Main contact: Javier Alonso

MUNCIE

TRAVELIN' LIGHT
Street address 1: 4001 W Kings Row St
Postal code: 4043
Country: Ecuador
Mailing address: Edificio Platinum Oficinas, piso 8 C. Carlos Padilla s/n
Mailing city: Quito
Mailing zip: 4043
Telephone country code: 593
Telephone city code: 2
Office phone: 251-9466
Office fax: 225-5769
General e-mail: redacquito@efe.com
Personnel: Enrique Ibanez (Rep.)
Main contact: Enrique Ibanez

NEW DELHI

EFE NEWS SERVICES - NEW DELHI, INDIA
Street address 1: 48, Hanuman Road. Instituto Cervantes building
Street address 2: Connaught Place
Country: Morocco
Mailing address: 14, rue de Kairoajne, Apt. 13, 5 ME (Angle rue d'Alger)
Mailing city: Rabat
Telephone country code: 212
Telephone city code: 537
Office phone: 723 218
Office fax: 732 195
General e-mail: efe@menara.ma
Personnel: Javier Otazu (Director); Enrique Rubio (Rep.)
Main contact: Enrique Rubio

NEW YORK

ALM
Street address 1: 120 Broadway
Street address 2: Fl 5
Street address state: AL
Postal code: 22359-900
Country: Brazil
Mailing address: Praia de Botafogo, 228 Rm. 605 B
Mailing city: Rio de Janeiro
Mailing state: AL
Mailing zip: 22359-900
Telephone country code: 55
Telephone city code: 212
Office phone: 553-6355
Office fax: 553-8823
General e-mail: rio@efebrasil.com.br
Web address: www.efe.com
Personnel: Jaime Ortega (Rep.)
Main contact: Jaime Ortega

AP DIGITAL AND COMMERCIAL SERVICES
Street address 1: 450 W 33rd St
Postal code: 00186
Country: Italy
Mailing address: Via dei Canestrari, 5-2
Mailing city: Rome
Mailing zip: 00186
Telephone country code: 39
Telephone city code: 06
Office phone: 683-4087
Office fax: 687-4918
General e-mail: roma@efe.com
Personnel: Javier Alonso (Director)
Main contact: Javier Alonso

ASSOCIATED PRESS
Street address 1: 200 Liberty St.
Postal code: 1000
Country: Costa Rica
Mailing address: Avda., 10 Calles 19/21 n. 1912, Apanado 8.4930
Mailing city: San Jose
Mailing zip: 1000
Telephone country code: 506

Office phone: 2222-6785
Office fax: 2233-7681
General e-mail: costarica@acan-efe.com
Web address: Curridabat
Personnel: Nancy De Lemos (Director)
Main contact: Nancy De Lemos

ASSOCIATED PRESS INFORMATION SERVICES
Street address 1: 450 W 33rd St
Country: El Salvador
Mailing address: Condominio Balam Quitze, Local 17. 2. P. General Sta.
Mailing city: San Salvador
Telephone country code: 503
Office phone: 263 7063
Office fax: 263 5281
General e-mail: elsalvador@acan-efe.com
Personnel: Laura Barros (Rep.)
Main contact: Laura Barros

ASSOCIATED PRESS MANAGING EDITORS ASSOCIATION
Street address 1: 450 W 33rd St
Country: Chile
Mailing address: Almirante Pastene, 333 - office 502
Mailing city: Santiago
Telephone country code: 56
Telephone city code: 2
Office phone: 632-4946
Office fax: 519-3912
General e-mail: redaccion@agenciaefe.tie.cl
Personnel: Manuel Fuentes (Rep.)
Main contact: Manuel Fuentes

BLACK PRESS SERVICE, INC.
Street address 1: 375 5th Ave
Street address state: PR
Postal code: 00909
Country: Puerto Rico
Mailing address: Edificio Cobian's Plz., Of. 214 Av Ponce de León 1607
Mailing city: San Juan
Mailing state: PR
Mailing zip: 00909
Office phone: (787) 721-8821
General e-mail: redacpr@efe.com
Personnel: Cristina Ozaeta (Head of Puerto Ricos Bureau)
Main contact: Cristina Ozaeta

BLOOMBERG NEWS
Street address 1: 731 Lexington Ave
Country: Honduras
Mailing address: Col. Elvel, Segunda Calle, Apt. 2012
Mailing city: Tegucigalpa
Telephone country code: 504
Office phone: 231 1730
Office fax: 231 1772
General e-mail: honduras@acan-efe.com
Personnel: German Reyes (Rep.)
Main contact: German Reyes

BUSINESS WIRE - NEW YORK, NY
Street address 1: 40 E 52nd St
Street address 2: Fl 14
Postal code: 1050
Country: Austria
Mailing address: Rechte Wienzeile 51/16
Mailing city: Vienna
Mailing zip: 1050
Telephone country code: 43
Telephone city code: 1
Office phone: 368 4174
Office fax: 369 8842
General e-mail: viena@efe.com
Personnel: Ramon Santaularia (Rep.)
Main contact: Ramon Santaularia

CARTOONEWS, INC.
Street address 1: 15 Central Park W
Street address state: D.C.
Postal code: 20045
Country: USA

News, Picture and Syndicate Services

Mailing address: 1252 National Press Building. 529, 14 street, NW
Mailing city: Washington D.C.
Mailing state: DC
Mailing zip: 20045
Telephone country code: -202
Office phone: (202) 745 76 92
Office fax: (202) 393 41 18 / 19
General e-mail: info@efeamerica.com
Web address: www.efe.com
Personnel: Manuel Ortega (Business Development Director)
Main contact: Elena Montero

CARTOONISTS & WRITERS SYNDICATE/CARTOON ARTS INTERNATIONAL - NEW YORK, NY

Street address 1: 67 Riverside Dr
Street address 2: Apt 7A
Street address state: D.C.
Postal code: 20045-1217
Country: USA
Mailing address: 529 14th St NW Ste 1252
Mailing city: Washington
Mailing state: DC
Mailing zip: 20045-2202
Office phone: (202) 745-7692
Office fax: (305) 262-7557
General e-mail: info@efeamerica.com
Web address: www.efe.com
Note/Syndicate Information: EFE is the leading Spanish-language news agency and the fourth largest in the world.
Personnel: Jose Antonio Vera (Pres.); Maria Luisa Azpiazu (Vice Pres.); Rafael Carranza (Sales and Business Dev. Dir.); Mar Gonzalo (Bureau Chief-Miami); Elena Moreno (Bureau Chief- New York); Marcela Romero (Marketing Coordinator)
Main contact: Rafael Carranza

CONSULATE GENERAL OF SWEDEN IN NEW YORK

Street address 1: 885 Second Avenue
Street address 2: 40th Floor
Street address state: WA
Postal code: 98105-5511
Country: USA
Mailing address: 5735 27th Ave NE
Mailing city: Seattle
Mailing state: WA
Mailing zip: 98105-5511
General e-mail: doctor@practicalprevention.com
Web address: www.practicalprevention.com
Personnel: Elizabeth S. Smoots MD (Self-Syndicator)
Main contact: Elizabeth S. Smoots, M.D.

DEG SYNDICATION

Street address 1: 25 Columbus Cir
Street address 2: # 55E
Postal code: 28046
Country: Spain
Mailing address: Paseo de la Castellana, 210
Mailing city: Madrid
Mailing zip: 28046
Telephone country code: 91
Office phone: 359-2600
Office fax: 350-3251
General e-mail: noticias@europapress.es
Web address: www.europapress.es

DOW JONES NEWSWIRES - NEW YORK, NY

Street address 1: 1155 Avenue of the Americas
Street address 2: Fl 7
Street address state: CA
Postal code: 90024-4801
Country: USA
Mailing address: 550 N Larchmont Blvd Ste 102
Mailing city: Los Angeles
Mailing state: CA
Mailing zip: 90004-1318
Office phone: (310) 441-7400
Office fax: (310) 475-0316

General e-mail: info@ercboxoffice.com
Web address: www.ercboxoffice.com
Personnel: Robert Bucksbaum (Pres.); Jeff Bock (Box Office Analyst)
Main contact: Robert Bucksbaum

DOW JONES NEWSWIRES - NEW YORK, NY

Street address 1: 1211 Avenue of the Americas
Street address state: D.C.
Postal code: 20002-5924
Country: USA
Mailing address: 420 Constitution Ave NE
Mailing city: Washington
Mailing state: DC
Mailing zip: 20002-5924
Office phone: (202) 544-5698
Office fax: (202) 544-5699
General e-mail: marguerite.kelly@gmail.com
Web address: www.margueritekelly.com
Note/Syndicate Information: retired free-lance columnist of Family Almanac which ran in the Washington Post for 35 years and was syndicated in other papers for nearly that long.
Personnel: Marguerite Kelly (Columnist of Family Almanac, WA Post and other papers)
Main contact: Marguerite Kelly

FEATURE PHOTO SERVICE, INC.

Street address 1: 450 7th Ave
Street address 2: Ste 1700
Street address state: KS
Postal code: 66202-2745
Country: USA
Mailing address: 5825 Dearborn St
Mailing city: Mission
Mailing state: KS
Mailing zip: 66202-2745
Office phone: (913) 563-4752
Office fax: (913) 789-9228
General e-mail: clong@familyfeatures.com
Web address: www.familyfeatures.com
Personnel: Dianne Hogerty (Owner); Clarke Smith (President); Cindy Long (Media Relations Manager)
Main contact: Cindy Long

FEATUREWELL.COM

Street address 1: 238 W 4th St
Street address state: VT
Postal code: 05091-0727
Country: USA
Mailing address: PO Box 727
Mailing city: Woodstock
Mailing state: VT
Mailing zip: 05091-0727
Office phone: (917) 749-8421
Office fax: (212) 202-4604
General e-mail: fashionshowroom@yahoo.com
Web address: www.fashionsyndicatepress.com
Note/Syndicate Information: Films, video and photos syndication.
Personnel: Andres Aquino (Owner); Elaine Hallgren (Ed.); Justin Alexander (Prodn. Art Dir.)
Main contact: Andres Aquino

FOCUS ON STYLE

Street address 1: PO Box 532
Street address state: NY
Postal code: 10123-0096
Country: USA
Mailing address: 450 7th Avenue, Suite 1700
Mailing city: New Yiork
Mailing zip: 10123
Office phone: (212) 944-1060
Office fax: (212) 944-7801
General e-mail: editor@featurephoto.com
Web address: https://www.featurephoto.com
Note/Syndicate Information: Photo distribution via: AP, FeaturePhoto.com, NewsCom and 25+ worldwide media partners
Personnel: Oren Hellner (Pres./CEO); Marla Edwards (Office Mgr.)
Main contact: Oren Hellner

GLOBAL INFORMATION NETWORK

Street address 1: 220 5th Ave
Street address 2: Fl 8
Street address state: NY
Postal code: 10014-2610
Country: USA
Mailing address: 238 W 4th St
Mailing city: New York
Mailing state: NY
Mailing zip: 10014-2610
Office phone: (212) 924-2283
General e-mail: featurewell@featurewell.com; sales@featurewell.com; contactus@featurewell.com
Web address: www.featurewell.com
Personnel: David Wallis (Founder/CEO); Marc Deveaux (CTO)
Main contact: David Wallis

JEWISH TELEGRAPHIC AGENCY, INC.

Street address 1: 24 W 30th St
Street address 2: Fl 4
Postal code: SE1 9HL
Country: United Kingdom
Mailing address: 1 Southwark Bridge
Mailing city: London
Mailing zip: SE1 9HL
Telephone country code: 44
Telephone city code: 20
Office phone: 7775 6248
Office fax: 873-3070
General e-mail: synd.admin@ft.com
Web address: www.ft.com
Personnel: Sophie DeBrito (Synd. Mgr.); Richard Pigden (Picture Synd.)
Main contact: Sophie deBrito

JIJI PRESS AMERICA LTD.

Street address 1: 120 W 45th St
Street address 2: Ste 1401
Street address state: DC
Postal code: 20004
Country: USA
Mailing address: 1201 Pennsylvania Ave NW
Mailing city: Washington
Mailing state: DC
Mailing zip: 20004
Office phone: (202) 793-5300
General e-mail: contact@fiscalnote.com
Web address: www.fiscalnote.com
Personnel: Tim Hwang (CEO); Richard Kim (CFO); Mike Stubbs (Vice President, Operations)
Main contact: ()

JOURNAL PRESS SYNDICATE

Street address 1: 545 W End Ave
Street address 2: Apt 2C
Street address state: NY
Postal code: 10276-0532
Country: USA
Mailing address: PO Box 1476
Mailing city: New York
Mailing state: NY
Mailing zip: 10276-1476
Office phone: (212) 473-8353
General e-mail: information@focusonstyle.com
Web address: www.sharonhaver.com; www.focusonstyle.com
Personnel: Sharon Haver (Syndicated Columnist, Newspaper/Online)
Main contact: Sharon Haver

KING FEATURES SYNDICATE

Street address 1: 300 W 57th St
Street address 2: Fl 41
Street address state: D.C.
Postal code: 20011-5313
Country: USA
Telephone country code: 1
Telephone city code: 202
Office phone: (202) 723-2477
General e-mail: goody.solomon@verizon.net
Web address: www.fnhnews.com
Personnel: Goody L. Solomon (Owner/Exec. Ed./Author)
Main contact: Goody L. Solomon

KYODO NEWS INTERNATIONAL, INC.

Street address 1: 780 3rd Ave
Street address 2: Rm 1103
Street address state: ON
Postal code: K9J 2V4
Country: Canada
Mailing address: 266 Charlotte St., Ste. 297
Mailing city: Peterborough
Mailing state: ON
Mailing zip: K9J 2V4
Office phone: (705) 745-5770
Office fax: (705) 745-9459
General e-mail: kubikjohn@fotopressnews.org
Web address: www.fotopressnews.org
Personnel: John M. Kubik (Opns. Dir.); Steven Brown (Accts. Administrator); Hugo Fernandez (South America Journalist); Vincent Delgado (Central America Photo Journalist); Elizabeth McKinney Bennett (North America Journalist); Frederick Brown (North America Journalist); Irene Clark (North America Journalist); Jarrett Dubois (North America Journalist); Barbara Jividen (North America Journalist); Jacquelyn Johnson (North America Journalist); Kevin G. Marty (North America Journalist); Lauren McFaul (North America Photographer); Peter Kozak (Australia Artist); Mulenga Chola (Africa Journalist); Luis Managonde (Africa Journalist); Nariz Bhugaloo (Africa Photographer); Gordon Irving (United Kingdom Journalist); Robert O'Connor (United Kingdom Journalist); Edward Neilam (Japan Journalist); Naohiro Kimura (Japan Photo Journalist)
Main contact: John M. Kubik

MAGNUM PHOTOS, INC.

Street address 1: 12 W 31st St
Street address 2: Fl 11
Street address state: NY
Postal code: 12207-1646
Country: USA
Mailing address: 150 State St
Mailing city: Albany
Mailing state: NY
Mailing zip: 12207-1626
Office phone: (518) 436-9781
Office fax: (518) 436-0130
Personnel: Joe Spector (Bureau Chief); Robert Hauptman (Account Executive); Keith Zurenda (Account Executive); Mary Murcko (President of Sales); Howard Griffin (VP, Gannett National Sales, USCP)
Main contact: Joe Spector

MARKET NEWS INTERNATIONAL

Street address 1: 40 Fulton St
Street address 2: Fl 5
Street address state: LA
Postal code: 70802-5236
Country: USA
Mailing address: 900 N 3rd St
Mailing city: Baton Rouge
Mailing state: LA
Mailing zip: 70802
Office phone: (225) 342-7333
Personnel: Mike Hasten (Bureau Chief)
Main contact: Mike Hasten

MEGALO MEDIA

Street address 1: PO Box 1503
Street address state: VA
Postal code: 22108-0003
Country: USA
Mailing address: 7950 Jones Branch Dr
Mailing city: Mc Lean
Mailing state: VA
Mailing zip: 22102-3302
Office phone: (703) 854-6000
Office fax: (703) 854-2152
General e-mail: candrews@gns.gannett.com
Web address: www.gannett.com
Personnel: Marie Marino (Office Mgr.); Jeannette Barrett-Stokes (Mng. Ed., Features/Graphics/Photography); Phil Pruitt (Mng. Ed., News); Bev Winston (Copy Desk Chief); Michelle Washington (Asst. Copy Desk Chief); Laura Rehrmann (Regl. Ed.); Val Ellicott (Regl. Ed.); Theresa

News, Picture and Syndicate Services

Harrah (Regl. Ed.); Robert Benincasa (Regl./Database Ed.); Craig Schwed (News/Sports/Technology Ed.); Jeff Franko (Photo Ed.); Linda Dono (Special Projects Ed.); John Yaukey (Nat'l Correspondent, Defense/Security); Chuck Raasch (Nat'l Ed./Correspondent, Politics); Mike Lopresti (Sports Correspondent); Doug Abrahms (Regl. Correspondent, California/Nevada); Faith Bremner (Regl. Correspondent, Colorado/Montana/Idaho); Erin Kelly (Regl. Correspondent, Delaware/Maryland/Vermont); Larry Wheeler (Regl. Correspondent, Florida/Georgia); Maureen Groppe (Regl. Correspondent, Indiana/Illinois)
Main contact: Bob Dickey

METRO EDITORIAL SERVICES

Street address 1: 519 8th Ave
Street address 2: Fl 18
Street address state: NY
Postal code: 13057-1847
Country: USA
Mailing address: 111 Shearin Ave.
Mailing city: East Syracuse
Mailing state: NY
Mailing zip: 13057
General e-mail: garyjames111@hotmail.com
Web address: www.famousinterview.com
Note/Syndicate Information: I am a Celebrity Interviewer for 2 websites: www.classicbands.com Click: Rock And Roll Interviews And: www.famousinterview.com Click: Interviews
Personnel: Gary James (Feature Interviewer/Investigative Journalist)
Main contact: Gary James

NEW YORK PRESS PHOTOGRAPHERS ASSOCIATION

Street address 1: 225 W 36th St
Street address 2: Ste 1-P
Country: USA
Mailing state: CA
General e-mail: george@georgewaters.net
Web address: www.georgewaters.net
Personnel: George Waters (Humor Columnist)
Main contact: George Waters

NORTH AMERICA SYNDICATE

Street address 1: 300 W 57th St
Street address 2: Fl 41
Street address state: CA
Postal code: 92103-6269
Country: USA
Mailing address: 2707 3rd Ave
Mailing city: San Diego
Mailing state: CA
Mailing zip: 92103-6269
Office phone: (858) 375-6150
General e-mail: info@gutcheckfitness.com
Web address: www.gutcheckfitness.com
Personnel: Joe Decker (Pres./Author)
Main contact: Joe Decker

NORTH AMERICAN PRECIS SYNDICATE, INC.

Street address 1: 415 Madison Ave
Street address 2: Fl 12
Street address state: WA
Postal code: 98104
Country: USA
Mailing address: 605 5th Avenue South, Suite 400
Mailing city: Seattle
Mailing state: WA
Mailing zip: 98104
Office phone: (206) 925-5000
Office fax: (206) 925-562
General e-mail: service.na@gettyimages.com
Web address: www.gettyimages.com
Personnel: Craig Peters (CEO); Jonathan D. Klein (Co-Founder & Chairman); Mark H. Getty (Co-Founder and Director)
Main contact: ()

PR NEWSWIRE

Street address 1: 350 Hudson St
Street address 2: Ste 300
Street address state: CA
Postal code: 95490-3107
Country: USA
Mailing address: 75 N Main St No 203
Mailing city: Willits
Mailing state: CA
Mailing zip: 95490-3107
Office phone: (707) 367-4608
Office fax: (707) 459-6106
General e-mail: glenmoorent@yahoo.com
Personnel: Ron C. Moorhead (Gen. Mgr.)
Main contact: Ron C. Moorhead

PUNCH IN TRAVEL, FOOD, WINE & ENTERTAINMENT NEWS SYNDICATE

Street address 1: 400 E 59th St
Street address 2: Apt 9F
Street address state: D.C.
Postal code: 20036-6311
Country: USA
Mailing address: 1330 New Hampshire Ave NW Apt 609
Mailing city: Washington
Mailing state: DC
Mailing zip: G20036-6311
Office phone: (202) 363-1270
General e-mail: edflattau@msn.com
Web address: www.edflattau.com
Personnel: Edward Flattau (Pres.); Pam Ebert (Ed.)
Main contact: Edward Flattau

REUTERS

Street address 1: 3 Times Sq
Street address 2: Fl 17
Street address state: NY
Postal code: 10001-7708
Country: USA
Telephone country code: 1
Telephone city code: 212
Office phone: (212) 244-3123
General e-mail: ipsgin@igc.org
Personnel: Lisa Vives (Exec. Dir.)
Main contact: Lisa Vives

REUTERS MEDIA

Street address 1: 3 Times Sq
Street address state: NY
Postal code: 11795-4016
Country: USA
Mailing address: 24 Edmore Ln S
Mailing city: West Islip
Mailing state: NY
Mailing zip: 11795-4016
Office phone: (631) 661-3131
Office fax: (631) 321-4063
General e-mail: requests@globephotos.com
Web address: www.globephotos.com
Personnel: Mary Beth Whelan (Pres.); Raymond D. Whelan (Vice Pres.)
Main contact: Mary Beth Whelan

SIPA NEWS SERVICE

Street address 1: 59 E 54th St
Street address state: VA
Postal code: 22657-5236
Country: USA
Mailing address: 499 Richardson Rd
Mailing city: Strasburg
Mailing state: VA
Mailing zip: 22657-5236
Office phone: (540) 635-3229
General e-mail: publisher@globesyndicate.com
Web address: www.globesyndicate.com
Personnel: Gavin Bourjaily (Ed./Pub.); M.F. Bourjaily, III (Asst. Pub/Assoc. Ed.)
Main contact: Gavin Bourjaily

SOVFOTO/EASTFOTO

Street address 1: 263 W 20th St
Street address 2: Apt 3
Street address state: PA
Postal code: 18103-2825
Country: USA

Mailing address: 2743 Saxon St
Mailing city: Allentown
Mailing state: PA
Mailing zip: 18103-2825
Office phone: (610) 437-4982
General e-mail: info@galvgolf.com
Web address: www.galvgolf.com
Personnel: Karl D. Gilbert (Pres.)
Main contact: Karl D. Gilbert

SPRINGER FOREIGN NEWS SERVICE

Street address 1: 500 5th Ave
Street address 2: Ste 2800
Street address state: IL
Postal code: 60010-5254
Country: USA
Mailing address: 190 Dundee Rd
Mailing city: Inverness
Mailing state: IL
Mailing zip: 60010-5254
Office phone: (847) 359-7860
General e-mail: info@GotInfluenceInc.com
Web address: www.GotInfluenceInc.com
Personnel: Dan Seidman (Founder/Self-Syndicator/Columnist)
Main contact: Dan Seidman

STADIUM CIRCLE FEATURES

Street address 1: 82 Nassau St
Street address 2: Ste 521
Street address state: AL
Postal code: 35223-1512
Country: USA
Mailing address: 3709 Crestbrook Rd
Mailing city: Mountain Brk
Mailing state: AL
Mailing zip: 35223-1512
Office phone: (205) 969-2963
Office fax: (205) 969-1972
General e-mail: wfleisig@hotmail.com
Personnel: Dr. Wayne Fleisig (Writer/Self-Syndicator)
Main contact: Wayne Fleisig

SYLVIA DI PIETRO

Street address 1: 55 W 14th St
Street address 2: Apt 4H
Street address state: D.C.
Postal code: 20005-3994
Country: USA
Mailing address: 700 12th St NW Ste 1000
Mailing city: Washington
Mailing state: DC
Mailing zip: 20005-3994
Office phone: (202) 263-6400
Office fax: (202) 263-6441
General e-mail: chuck@hearstdc.com
Web address: www.hearst.com
Personnel: David McCumber (Bureau Chief)
Main contact: Charles Lewis

TAIPEI ECONOMIC & CULTURAL OFFICE, PRESS DIVISION - NEW YORK, NY

Street address 1: 1E E 42nd St
Street address 2: Fl 11
Street address state: NC
Postal code: 28359-0304
Country: USA
Mailing address: P. O. Box 304
Mailing city: Lumberton
Mailing state: NC
Mailing zip: 28359
Office phone: (913) 433-3877
General e-mail: info@hearttones.com
Web address: www.hearttones.com
Personnel: Gloria Thomas-Anderson (Pres./Founder); Tracee Jackson (Public Relations Director); Tammy Iroku (Webmaster and Graphics Specialist)
Main contact: Gloria Anderson

THE NEW YORK TIMES NEWS SERVICE & SYNDICATE

Street address 1: 620 8th Ave
Street address state: CO

Postal code: 81428-9905
Country: USA
Mailing address: PO Box 1090
Mailing city: Paonia
Mailing state: CO
Mailing zip: 81428-1090
Office phone: (970) 527-4898
Office fax: (970) 527-4897
General e-mail: hcnsyndicate@hcnsyndicate.org
Web address: www.hcn.org
Personnel: Jonathan Thompson (Ed. in Chief); JoeAnn Kalenak (Syndicate Representative); Paul Larmer (Exec. Dir.)
Main contact: Paul Larmer

THE NYT NEWS SERVICE/SYNDICATE - PHOTOS & GRAPHICS

Street address 1: 620 8th Ave
Street address 2: Fl 9
Street address state: D.C.
Postal code: 20005-2843
Country: USA
Mailing address: 1420 N St NW Ste 101
Mailing city: Washington
Mailing state: DC
Mailing zip: 20005-2895
Office phone: (202) 234-0280
Office fax: (202) 234-4090
General e-mail: editor@hispaniclink.org
Web address: www.hispaniclink.org
Personnel: Carlos Ericksen-Mendoza (Pub.); Patricia Guadalupe (Capitol Hill Ed.)
Main contact: Carlos Ericksen-Mendoza

THE WALL STREET JOURNAL SUNDAY

Street address 1: 1211 Avenue of the Americas
Street address state: PA
Postal code: 19010-3401
Country: USA
Mailing address: 763 W Lancaster Ave Ste 250
Mailing city: Bryn Mawr
Mailing state: PA
Mailing zip: 19010-3401
Office phone: (484) 829-0024
Office fax: (484) 829-0027
General e-mail: contactus@hollisterkids.com
Web address: www.hollisterkids.com
Personnel: Kim Landry (Pres.); Peter Landry (Vice Pres.); Heidi Karl (Art Dir.)
Main contact: Peter Landry

UNITED FEATURE SYNDICATE (DIV. OF UNITED MEDIA)

Street address 1: 200 Madison Ave
Street address state: CA
Postal code: 91423-3700
Country: USA
Mailing address: Same
Office phone: (818) 986-8168
Office fax: (818) 789-8047
General e-mail: editor@newscalendar.com
Web address: www.newscalendar.com
Note/Syndicate Information: Hollywood News Service is an entertainment wire service and does not accept solicitations for new features.
Personnel: Carolyn Fox (Ed. in Chief); Susan Fox (Mng. Ed.); Fujita Greg; Margaret Miller; John Carlin; John Fox; Sindy Saito (Editor)
Main contact: Carolyn Fox

WAGNER INTERNATIONAL PHOTOS, INC.

Street address 1: 62 W 45th St
Street address 2: Fl 6
Street address state: PA
Postal code: 15071-9311
Country: USA
Mailing address: PO Box 247
Mailing city: Oakdale
Mailing state: PA
Mailing zip: 15071-0247
Office phone: (412) 787-2881
Office fax: (412) 787-3233

General e-mail: info@homeimprovementtime.com
Web address: www.homeimprovementtime.com
Personnel: Carole C. Stewart (President); Jeff Stewart (Website Marketing Manager)
Main contact: Carole C. Stewart

NEWBURYPORT

PEDIATRIC POINTS

Street address 1: 5 Chain Bridge Dr
Street address state: PA
Postal code: 19095-0183
Country: USA
Mailing address: PO Box 183
Mailing city: Wyncote
Mailing state: PA
Mailing zip: 19095-0183
Office phone: (215) 635-1120
General e-mail: nie@hottopicshotserials.com
Web address: www.hottopicshotserials.com
Personnel: Deborah Carroll (Pres.); Ned Carroll (Vice Pres.)
Main contact: Deborah Carroll

NEWTON

NEW ENGLAND NEWS SERVICE, INC.

Street address 1: 66 Alexander Rd
Street address state: IL
Postal code: 60614-6101
Country: USA
Mailing address: 2740 N Pine Grove Ave Apt 4C
Mailing city: Chicago
Mailing state: IL
Mailing zip: 60614-6101
Office phone: (773) 871-3918
General e-mail: hurstsportsmedia@yahoo.com
Web address: www.hurstsportsmedia.blogspot.com
Personnel: Bob Hurst (Owner/Editor/Columnist)
Main contact: Bob Hurst

NORMAN

ADVERTISING WORKSHOP

Street address 1: University of Oklahoma-Gaylord/Amc, Herbert School of Journalism & Mass Co
Street address 2: 395 W Lindsey St
Street address state: AZ
Postal code: 85261-5795
Country: USA
Mailing address: PO Box 5795
Mailing city: Scottsdale
Mailing state: AZ
Mailing zip: 85261-5795
Office phone: (480) 905-8000
Office fax: (480) 905-8190
General e-mail: info@imortgageguide.com
Web address: www.imortgageguide.com
Note/Syndicate Information: Revenue-sharing content for real estate/print and online
Main contact: iMortgage.com Info

NORTH GRAFTON

LITERARY FEATURES SYNDICATE

Street address 1: 92 East St
Street address state: CO
Postal code: 80203-2048
Country: USA
Mailing address: 727 E 16th Ave
Mailing city: Denver
Mailing state: CO
Mailing zip: 80203-2048
Office phone: (303) 279-6536
Office fax: (303) 279-4176
General e-mail: mike@i2i.org
Web address: www.independenceinstitute.org
Personnel: Jon Caldara (Pres.); David Kopel (Research Dir.); Mike Krause (Media/Publications Mgr.)
Main contact: David Kopel

NORTH NEWTON

THIS SIDE OF 60

Street address 1: PO Box 332
Street address state: CA
Postal code: 94608-3507
Country: USA
Mailing address: 4225 Hollis St
Mailing city: Emeryville
Mailing state: CA
Mailing zip: 94608
Telephone country code: 1
Telephone city code: 720
Office phone: (720)635-9065
General e-mail: amber@inman.com
Web address: www.inman.com
Personnel: Andrea Brambila (Assoc. Ed.); Amber Taufen (Ed. In Chief); Caroline Feeney (Assoc. Ed.)
Main contact: Amber Taufen

NORTH PALM BEACH

BANKRATE.COM

Street address 1: 11760 US Highway 1
Street address 2: Ste 200
Street address state: FL
Postal code: 33407-6742
Country: USA
Mailing address: 2902 29th Way
Mailing city: West Palm Beach
Mailing state: FL
Mailing zip: 33407-6742
Office phone: (561) 683-9090
Office fax: (561) 683-9090
General e-mail: jay@jaykravetz.com
Web address: www.jaykravetz.com
Personnel: Jay N. Kravetz (Ed.); Cheryl Dupree (Ed.)
Main contact: Jay N. Kravetz

NORWALK

EARTH TALK: QUESTIONS & ANSWERS ABOUT OUR ENVIRONMENT

Street address 1: 28 Knight St
Street address state: NC
Postal code: 28269-3189
Country: USA
Mailing address: 4507 Panther Pl
Mailing city: Charlotte
Mailing state: NC
Mailing zip: 28269-3189
Office phone: (704) 921-1818
Office fax: (704) 597-1331
General e-mail: publisher@cleverpuzzles.com
Web address: www.cleverpuzzles.com
Personnel: Pat Battaglia (Owner)
Main contact: Pat Battaglia

OAKDALE

HOME IMPROVEMENT TIME, INC.

Street address 1: 7425 Steubenville Pike
Street address state: MA
Postal code: 02025-2127
Country: USA
Mailing address: 10 Wood Way
Mailing city: Cohasset
Mailing state: MA
Mailing zip: 02025-2127
Office phone: (781) 383-6688
General e-mail: jfeatures@aol.com
Personnel: Chuck Jaffe (Columnist)
Main contact: Chuck A. Jaffe

OCEANSIDE

U-BILD NEWSPAPER FEATURES

Street address 1: 821 S Tremont St
Street address 2: Ste B
Street address state: AL

Postal code: 36532-1415
Country: USA
Mailing address: 212 Fig Avenue
Mailing city: Fairhope
Mailing state: AL
Mailing zip: 36532
Office phone: (251) 219-5676
Office fax: (251) 219-5799
General e-mail: jdcrowe@AL.com
Web address: http://connect.al.com/user/jcrowe/posts.html
Note/Syndicate Information: Artizans.com
Personnel: J.D. Crowe (Statewide Editorial Cartoonist, AL.com & Alabama Media Group)
Main contact: J.D. Crowe

OMAHA

JANDON FEATURES

Street address 1: 2319 S 105th Ave
Street address state: CA
Postal code: 93117
Country: USA
Mailing address: 220 Pacific Oaks Rd.
Mailing city: Goleta
Mailing state: CA
Mailing zip: 93117
Office phone: (805) 979-4646
Office fax: (805) 685-2800
Web address: www.jacksonmedicalgroup.com
Personnel: Karen M. Engberg, M.D. (Self-Syndicator)
Main contact: Karen M. Engberg M.D.

ORANGE PARK

AGEVENTURE NEWS SERVICE

Street address 1: 2199 Astor St
Street address 2: Suite 503
Street address state: CA
Postal code: 95819-2102
Country: USA
Mailing address: 122 43rr Street
Mailing city: Sacramento
Mailing state: CA
Office phone: (916) 508-5122
General e-mail: james@jamesraia.com
Web address: www.jamesraia.com
Note/Syndicate Information: The Weekly Driver is a automotive column featuring new and vintage car reviews and automotive news, www.theweeklydriver.com. It appears on Sunday in two newspapers in the Bay Area News Group as well as monthly in Gulfshore Business, a monthly business magazine in Naples, Florida.
Personnel: James Raia (Self-Syndicator)
Main contact: James Raia

OTTAWA

BROADCAST NEWS LIMITED

Street address 1: 165 Sparks St., Ste. 800
Street address state: NE
Postal code: 68124-1821
Country: USA
Mailing address: 2319 S 105th Ave
Mailing city: Omaha
Mailing state: NE
Mailing zip: 68124-1821
Office phone: (402) 502-4367
General e-mail: jan@riggenbach.info
Web address: www.midwestgardening.com
Note/Syndicate Information: Garden columns and features for Midwestern U.S. newspapers only. Midwest Gardening, 1tw illus. 450 words; Garden Variety, 1tw illus. 200 words.
Personnel: Jan Riggenbach (Columnist)
Main contact: Jan Riggenbach

CANADIAN PRESS, THE - OTTAWA, ON

Street address 1: 165 Sparks St., Ste. 800
Street address state: CA

Postal code: 93041-3061
Country: USA
Mailing address: 165 N 5th St Apt 208
Mailing city: Port Hueneme
Mailing state: CA
Mailing zip: 93041-3061
Office phone: (805) 271-9560
General e-mail: mail@jasonlove.com
Web address: www.jasonlove.com
Personnel: Jason Love (Sole Proprietor); Yahaira Quintero (Office Mgr.); Philippe Marquis (Agent); Rima Rudner (Writer); Vladimir Stankovski (Illustrator); Jose Angel (Gogue) Rodriguez (Illustrator); Thaum Blumel (Illustrator)
Main contact: Jason Love

PALM BEACH GARDENS

ALAN LAVINE, INC.

Street address 1: 10199 Willow Ln
Street address state: NY
Postal code: 10001-4443
Country: USA
Mailing address: 24 W 30th St Fl 4
Mailing city: New York
Mailing state: NY
Mailing zip: 10001-4443
Office phone: (212) 643-1890
Office fax: (212) 643-8498
General e-mail: newsdesk@jta.org
Web address: www.jta.org
Personnel: Andrew Sillow-Carrol (Ed.); Marc Brodsky (Copy Ed.); Gabe Friedman (Assoc. Dig. Ed.); Ami Eden (CEO & Exec. Ed.); Deborah Kolben (COO)
Main contact: Andrew Silow-Carroll

PANAMA CITY

EFE NEWS SERVICES - PANAMA CITY, PANAMA

Street address 1: Avda. Samuel Lewis y Manuel Icaza. Edif. Comosa 22
Street address state: NY
Postal code: 10036-4062
Country: USA
Mailing address: 70 E 55th St Ste 4L
Mailing city: New York
Mailing state: NY
Mailing zip: 10022-3395
Office phone: (212) 575-5830
Office fax: (212) 764-3950
General e-mail: edit@jijiusa.com
Web address: www.jiji.com
Personnel: Hiroshi Masuda (Pres.)
Main contact: Hiroshi Masuda

PAONIA

HIGH COUNTRY NEWS

Street address 1: 119 Grand Ave
Street address 2: PO Box 1090
Street address state: NJ
Postal code: 07306-6014
Country: USA
Mailing address: 2595 John F Kennedy Blvd
Mailing city: Jersey City
Mailing state: NJ
Mailing zip: 07306-6014
Office phone: (201) 985-2105
General e-mail: joe@travelthenet.com
Web address: www.travelthenet.com
Personnel: Joe Harkins (Self-Syndicator)
Main contact: Joe Harkins

PARIS

BLOOMBERG NEWS

Street address 1: 7 Rue Scribe
Street address state: MA
Postal code: 02134-3809
Country: USA
Mailing address: 1354 Commonwealth Ave
Mailing city: Allston

News, Picture and Syndicate Services

Mailing state: MA
Mailing zip: 02134-3809
Office phone: (617) 784-7150
Office fax: (888) 833-9528
General e-mail: jalsop@BostonWineSchool.com
Web address: www.bostonwineschool.com
Personnel: Jonathon Alsop (Wine Writer/Self-Syndicator)
Main contact: Jonathon Alsop

PARIS

DOW JONES NEWSWIRES - PARIS, FRANCE

Street address 1: 6-8 Boulevard Haussmann
Street address state: NY
Postal code: 10024-2723
Country: USA
Mailing address: 545 W End Ave Apt 2C
Mailing city: New York
Mailing state: NY
Mailing zip: 10024-2723
Office phone: (212) 580-8559
General e-mail: ijbnyc@aol.com
Personnel: Irwin J. Breslauer (Ed.); John Lynker (Mng. Ed.); Todd Lewis (Automotive Ed.); William Kresse (Comics Ed.)
Main contact: Irwin J. Breslauer

EFE NEWS SERVICES - PARIS, FRANCE

Street address 1: 10 rue St. Marc, Buro. 165
Street address state: VA
Postal code: 22901-3616
Country: USA
Mailing address: PO Box 8187
Mailing city: Charlottesville
Mailing state: VA
Mailing zip: 22906-8187
Office phone: (434) 293-4709
Office fax: (434) 293-4884
General e-mail: ky@kwnews.com
Web address: www.kwnews.com
Personnel: Walton C. (Ky) Lindsay (Pres./Treasurer); Meta L. Nay (Vice Pres., Mktg.); Carol Lindsay (Admin.); Walton Lindsay (Pres.)
Main contact: Meta L. Nay; Walton Lindsay

PATCHOGUE

NEW LIVING SYNDICATE

Street address 1: 99 Waverly Ave
Street address 2: Apt 6D
Street address state: CA
Postal code: 92672-4717
Country: USA
Mailing address: 408 N El Camino Real
Mailing city: San Clemente
Mailing state: CA
Mailing zip: 92672-4717
Office phone: (949) 481-3747
Office fax: (949) 481-3941
General e-mail: info@zumapress.com
Web address: www.zumapress.com
Personnel: Scott McKiernan (Dir.)
Main contact: Scott McKiernan

PENSACOLA

THE FUNNY PAGES

Street address 1: 4185 Bonway Dr
Street address state: CA
Postal code: 95476-1802
Country: USA
Mailing address: PO Box 1802
Mailing city: Sonoma
Mailing state: CA
Mailing zip: 95476-1802
Office phone: (707) 996-6077
Office fax: (707) 938-8718
General e-mail: thescoop@kidscoop.com
Web address: www.kidscoop.com
Personnel: Vicki Whiting (Pres./CEO)
Main contact: Vicki Whiting

PETERBOROUGH

FOTOPRESS INDEPENDENT NEWS SERVICE INTERNATIONAL

Street address 1: 266 Charlotte St., Ste. 297
Street address state: CA
Postal code: 94590
Country: USA
Mailing address: PO Box 7914
Mailing city: Vallejo
Mailing state: CA
Mailing zip: 94590-1914
Office phone: (707) 704-2086
General e-mail: Tuckyart@att.net
Web address: www.tuckyart.com
Personnel: Tucky McKey (Pub.)
Main contact: Tucky McKey

PHILADELPHIA

CLASSICSTOCK / ROBERTSTOCK

Street address 1: 4203 Locust St
Street address state: NY
Postal code: 10019-3741
Country: USA
Mailing address: 300 W 57th St
Mailing city: New York
Mailing state: NY
Mailing zip: 10019-5238
Office phone: (212) 969-7550
Office fax: (646) 280-1550
General e-mail: kfs-cartoonists@hearst.com
Web address: www.kingfeatures.com
Personnel: Keith McCloat (VP, Gen. Mgr.); David Cohea (Gen. Mgr., King Feat. Weekly Service Inside Sales); Claudia Smith (Dir., PR); Jack Walsh (Sr. Sales Consultant/Printing & New England Newspaper Sales); Dennis Danko (Inside Sales Mgr.); Michael Mancino (Sales Mgr., New Media Inside Sales); John Killian (VP, Syndication Sales); Jim Clarke (Editorial Dir., King Feat. Weekly Service); Brendan Burford (Gen. Mgr., Syndication); Randy Noble (SE Sales); Diana Smith (Executive Editor); Evelyn Smith (Senior Comics Editor); Chris Richcreek (Senior Features Editor); Curtis Trammell (Western Region Sales); Robin Graham (International Sales Consultant); Monique Prioleau (Sales Coordinator); C.J. Kettler (President)
Main contact: ()

NATIONAL NEWS BUREAU

Street address 1: PO Box 43039
Street address state: NY
Postal code: 10017-2158
Country: USA
Mailing address: 780 3rd Ave Ste. 1103
Mailing city: New York
Mailing state: NY
Mailing zip: 10017-2024
Office phone: (212) 508-5440
Office fax: (212) 508-5441
General e-mail: kni@kyodonews.com
Web address: www.kyodo.co.jp; www.kyodonews.com
Personnel: Toshi Mitsudome (Vice President)
Main contact: Daisuke Ota

PLAINFIELD

SLIGHTLY OFF!

Street address 1: 24730 Illini Dr
Street address state: CA
Postal code: 90405-3664
Country: USA
Mailing address: 2402 4th St Apt 6
Mailing city: Santa Monica
Mailing state: CA
Mailing zip: 90405-3664
Office phone: (310) 392-5146
Office fax: (310) 392-3856
General e-mail: deblevin@aol.com
Web address: www.callahanonline.com
Personnel: Deborah Levin (Pres.)
Main contact: Deborah Levin

PLANO

THE WITZZLE CO.

Street address 1: PO Box 866933
Street address state: ID
Postal code: 46342-4308
Country: USA
Mailing address: PO Box 187
Mailing city: Hobart
Mailing state: IN
Mailing zip: 46342-0187
Office phone: (219) 947-5478
General e-mail: info@familiesbesafe.com
Web address: www.listeninginc.com
Personnel: Patricia Work Bennett (Pres.); Richard Bennett (Vice Pres.)
Main contact: Richard Bennett

PLANTATION

THE NAME GAME INTERNATIONAL, INC.

Street address 1: 401 SW 54th Ave
Street address state: MA
Postal code: 01536-1806
Country: USA
Mailing address: 92 East St
Mailing city: North Grafton
Mailing state: MA
Mailing zip: 01536-1806
Office phone: (508) 839-4404
General e-mail: nick@gentlymad.com
Personnel: Constance V. Basbanes (Pres.); Nicholas A. Basbanes (Mng. Ed./Columnist)
Main contact: Nicholas A. Basbanes

PORT HUENEME

JASON LOVE (HUMOR FEATURES)

Street address 1: 165 N 5th St
Street address 2: Apt 208
Street address state: FL
Postal code: 33405-1233
Country: USA
Mailing address: 2751 S Dixie Hwy
Mailing city: West Palm Beach
Mailing state: FL
Mailing zip: 33405-1233
Office phone: (561) 820-4100
General e-mail: lona_oconnor@pbpost.com
Web address: www.palmbeachpost.com
Personnel: Lona O'Connor (Author, journalist)
Main contact: Lona O'Connor; Rick Christie

PROVIDENCE

WHITEGATE FEATURES SYNDICATE

Street address 1: 71 Faunce Dr
Street address 2: Ste 1
Street address state: NY
Postal code: 10001-4415
Country: USA
Mailing address: 12 W 31st St Fl 11
Mailing city: New York
Mailing state: NY
Mailing zip: 10001-4415
Office phone: (212) 929-6000
Office fax: (212) 929-9325
General e-mail: photography@magnumphotos.com
Web address: www.magnumphotos.com
Main contact: Diane Raimondo

QUEBEC CITY

BROADCAST NEWS LIMITED

Street address 1: 1050 rue Des Parlementaires, Bureau 207
Street address state: NY
Postal code: 10543-4214
Country: USA
Mailing address: 721 Shore Acres Dr
Mailing city: Mamaroneck
Mailing state: NY
Mailing zip: 10543-4214
Office phone: (914) 698-0721
General e-mail: lois.fenton@prodigy.net
Note/Syndicate Information: Columnist/Advice, Men's Business & Social Dress Consultant/Men's Personal Shopper, Blogger
Personnel: Lois Fenton (Columnist/Advice, Men's Business & Social Dress Consultant/Men's Personal Shopper, Blogger)
Main contact: Lois Fenton

CANADIAN PRESS, THE - QUEBEC CITY, QC

Street address 1: 1050 Des Parlementaires, Ste. 2
Street address state: NY
Postal code: 10708-1544
Country: USA
Mailing address: 52 Sagamore Rd
Mailing city: Bronxville
Mailing state: NY
Mailing zip: 10708-1544
Office phone: (914) 961-2020
Office fax: (914) 793-3434
Personnel: Marion Joyce (Pres.)
Main contact: Marion Joyce

QUEENSBURY

TRIBUNE MEDIA SERVICES ENTERTAINMENT PRODUCTS

Street address 1: 40 Media Dr
Street address state: NY
Postal code: 10038-5092
Country: USA
Mailing address: 40 Fulton St Fl 5
Mailing city: New York
Mailing state: NY
Mailing zip: 10038-5065
Office phone: (212) 669-6400
Office fax: (212) 608-3024
General e-mail: tony@marketnews.com
Web address: www.marketnews.com
Note/Syndicate Information: Market News Service has bureaus in New York, Chicago, Washington DC, London, Frankfurt, Berlin, Paris, Brussels, Beijing, Tokyo, Singapore and Sydney.
Personnel: Tony Mace (Mng. Ed.); Denis Gulino (Washington Bureau Chief); Kevin Woodfield (London Bureau Chief/European Ed.); John Carter (managing editor); Clive Tillbrook
Main contact: Tony Mace

QUITO

EFE NEWS SERVICES - QUITO, ECUADOR

Street address 1: Edificio Platinum Oficinas, piso 8 C. Carlos Padilla s/n
Street address state: CT
Postal code: 06757-1246
Country: USA
Mailing address: 11 Green Hill Rd
Mailing city: Kent
Mailing state: CT
Mailing zip: 06757-1246
Office phone: (860) 927-3948
Office fax: (860) 927-3062
General e-mail: info@mfamedia.com
Web address: www.mfamedia.com
Note/Syndicate Information: Marks & Frederick Associates represents various publishing interests in Europe and Asia.
Personnel: Ted Marks (Pres.)
Main contact: Ted Marks

RABAT

EFE NEWS SERVICES - RABAT, MOROCCO

Street address 1: 14, rue de Kairoajne, Apt. 13,

News, Picture and Syndicate Services

5 ME (Angle rue d'Alger)
Street address state: CA
Postal code: 92109-6130
Country: USA
Mailing address: PO Box 9720
Mailing city: San Diego
Mailing state: CA
Mailing zip: 92169-0720
Office phone: (858) 483-3412
General e-mail: cecilscag@aol.com
Web address: www.maturelifefeatures.com
Personnel: Cecil F. Scaglione (Ed. in Chief/Financial Ed.); Beverly Rahn Scaglione (Book Ed.); James B. Gaffney (Nat'l Affairs/Health Ed.); Igor Lobanov (Travel Ed.)
Main contact: Cecil F. Scaglione

RANCHO PALOS VERDES

CARTOONISTS & WRITERS SYNDICATE/CARTOON ARTS INTERNATIONAL - RANCHO PALOS VERDES, CA

Street address 1: 28028 Lobrook Dr
Street address state: NJ
Postal code: 07070-2819
Country: USA
Mailing address: 20 Nevins St
Mailing city: Rutherford
Mailing state: NJ
Mailing zip: 07070-2819
Office phone: (201) 939-7875
Office fax: (201) 896-8619
General e-mail: salfino@comcast.net
Web address: www.rotoaction.com
Personnel: Catherine Salfino (Pres.); Michael Salfino (Columnist); David Ferris (Columnist)
Main contact: Michael Salfino

REGINA

BROADCAST NEWS LIMITED

Street address 1: Rm. 335, Press Gallery
Street address state: NC
Postal code: 27101-2815
Country: USA
Mailing address: 418 N Marshall St
Mailing city: Winston Salem
Mailing state: NC
Mailing zip: 27101-2815
Office phone: (800) 457-1156
Office fax: (336) 727-7461
General e-mail: jsarver@wsjournal.com
Personnel: Jodi Stephenson Sarver (Rep.)
Main contact: Jodi Stephenson Sarver

REGINA

CANADIAN PRESS, THE - REGINA, SK

Street address 1: Legislative Bldg., Press Gallery, Rm. 335
Street address state: NY
Postal code: 10021-0042
Country: USA
Mailing address: PO Box 1503
Mailing city: New York
Mailing state: NY
Mailing zip: 10021-0042
Office phone: (212) 861-8048
General e-mail: megalomedia@lawtv.com
Web address: www.megalomedia.biz; www.crossword.org
Personnel: J. Baxter Newgate (Pres.); Sandy Applegreen (Ed./Vice Pres.); Paul Merenbloom (Assoc. Ed.); Arthur Wynne (Puzzle Ed.)
Main contact: J. Baxter Newgate

RICHARDSON

WIECK

Street address 1: 1651 N Collins Blvd
Street address 2: Ste 100
Street address state: NY
Postal code: 10018-4577
Country: USA
Mailing address: 519 8th Ave Fl 18
Mailing city: New York
Mailing state: NY
Mailing zip: 10018-4577
Office phone: (212) 947-5100
Office fax: (212) 714-9139
General e-mail: mes@metro-email.com
Web address: www.mcg.metrocreativeconnection.com
Note/Syndicate Information: Metro is a leading provider of advertising, creative and editorial resources designed to help media companies make money with their print, online, and mobile products. We provide ready-to-use images, ads, stock-quality photos, logos/trademarks, auto photos, marketing/sales materials, copyright-free features, print templated sections, online e-Sections, and groundbreaking digital ad development tools, plus custom image, ad design and editorial services.
Personnel: Robert Zimmerman (Publisher); Debra Weiss (Exec. Vice Pres./Mktg. Dir.); Lauren Lekoski (Mktg. Mgr.); Jo Ann Shapiro (VP, Sales); Lou Ann Sornson (Regional Sales Mgr.); Tina Dentner (Regional Sales Mgr.); Cathy Agee (Regional Sales Mgr.); Gwen Tomaselli (Regional Sales Mgr.); Jennifer Steiner (Regional Sales Mgr.); Joann Johnson
Main contact: Lauren Lekoski; Debra Weiss

RICHMOND

PEARY PERRY ENTERPRISES

Street address 1: 2002 N Greens Blvd
Street address state: NJ
Postal code: 07405-2324
Country: USA
Mailing address: 170 Kinnelon Rd Rm 11
Mailing city: Kinnelon
Mailing state: NJ
Mailing zip: 07405-2324
Office phone: (973) 492-2828
Office fax: 973-492-9068
Web address: www.micinsurance.com
Note/Syndicate Information: Medical Insurance Claims, Inc. changed name to MIC Insurance Services
Personnel: Irene C. Card (Pres./Author); Betsy Chandler (Sec./Treasurer/Author)
Main contact: Irene C. Card

RIO DE JANEIRO

EFE NEWS SERVICES - RIO DE JANEIRO, BRAZIL

Street address 1: Praia de Botafogo, 228 Rm. 605 B
Street address state: WI
Postal code: 53725-9623
Country: USA
Mailing address: PO Box 259623
Mailing city: Madison
Mailing state: WI
Mailing zip: 53725-9623
Office phone: (608) 274-8925
General e-mail: info@roadstraveled.com
Web address: www.roadstraveled.com; www.marybergin.com
Note/Syndicate Information: Producing since 2002 weekly travel columns, with art, usually about America's Heartland, especially the Upper Midwest.
Personnel: Mary Bergin (Columnist)
Main contact: Mary Bergin

RIVER VALE

CURT SCHLEIER REVIEWS

Street address 1: 646 Jones Rd
Street address state: OH
Postal code: 44139-4433
Country: USA
Mailing address: 33289 East Nimrod St
Mailing city: Solon
Mailing state: OH
Mailing zip: 44139
Office phone: (203) 378 2893
General e-mail: bmiko@pacificdialogue.com
Web address: www.pacificdialogue.com
Personnel: Robert J. Miko (Ed.)
Main contact: Robert J. Miko

ROCHESTER

ED FISCHER PRODUCTION

Street address 1: 215 Elton Hills Dr NW
Street address 2: Apt 56
Street address state: VA
Postal code: 20120-7111
Country: USA
Mailing address: PO Box 231111
Mailing city: Centreville
Mailing state: VA
Mailing zip: 20120-7111
Office phone: (703) 830-6863
General e-mail: tomphilpott@militaryupdate.com
Web address: www.militaryupdate.com
Note/Syndicate Information: For daily newspapers near military bases across the country, Military Update has for 20 years covered breaking news affecting service members – active, reserve, retirees and family members.
Personnel: Tom Philpott (Self-Syndicator)
Main contact: Tom Philpott

ROME

EFE NEWS SERVICES - ROME, ITALY

Street address 1: Via dei Canestrari, 5-2
Street address state: IA
Postal code: 50111-5046
Country: USA
Mailing address: 3710 SE Capitol Cir Ste F
Mailing city: Grimes
Mailing state: IA
Mailing zip: 50111-5046
Office phone: (515) 986-1155
General e-mail: motornewsmedia@live.com
Web address: www.motornewsmedia.com
Note/Syndicate Information: automotive news and photography service.
Personnel: Kenneth J. Chester (Pres./CEO)
Main contact: Kenneth J. Chester, Jr.

ROSCOE

THE GELMAN FEATURE SYNDICATE

Street address 1: PO Box 399
Street address state: CA
Postal code: 91362-9500
Country: USA
Mailing address: 30700 Russell Ranch Rd Ste 100
Mailing city: Westlake Village
Mailing state: CA
Mailing zip: 91362-9501
Office phone: (805) 557-2300
Office fax: (805) 557-2680
General e-mail: corporateinfo@move.com
Web address: www.move.com
Personnel: Joe F. Hanauer (Chrmn.); W. Michael Long (CEO)
Main contact: Joe F. Hanauer

ROSWELL

DOING BIZ IN

Street address 1: 1865 River Falls Dr
Street address state: PA
Postal code: 19129-3039
Country: USA
Telephone country code: 1
Telephone city code: 215
Office phone: (215) 849-9016
Office fax: 215-754-4488
General e-mail: nnbfeature@aol.com; fashionnnb@aol.com; travelnnb@aol.com; foodandwinennb@aol.com; booksnnb@aol.com
Web address: www.nationalnewsbureau.com
Note/Syndicate Information: We specialize in fashion, food, wine, theater, movie reviews, celebrity interviews, Our "BEST" series from kitchen appliances to household items, travel to exotic, romantic destinations, men and women's apparel.
Personnel: Harry Jay Katz (Pub./Ed. in Chief); Debra Renee Cruz (Fashion/Beauty/Lifestyles Ed.); Andy Edelman (Features Ed.)
Main contact: Harry Jay Katz

RUTHERFORD

MEADOWLANDS MEDIA GROUP

Street address 1: 20 Nevins St
Street address state: MA
Postal code: 02461-1831
Country: USA
Mailing address: 66 Alexander Rd
Mailing city: Newton
Mailing state: MA
Mailing zip: 02461-1831
Office phone: 617-244-3075
General e-mail: nenewsnow@rcn.com
Web address: www.rcn.com
Personnel: Milton J. Gun (Bureau Chief); Lee Ann Jacob (Staff); Eleanor Margolis (Staff); Howard Neal (Staff); Kate Tattlebaum (Staff); Steve Richards (Corresp.)
Main contact: Milton J. Gun

SACRAMENTO

CAPITOL NEWS SERVICE

Street address 1: 530 Bercut Dr
Street address 2: Ste E
Street address state: NY
Postal code: 11772-1922
Country: USA
Mailing address: PO Box 1001
Mailing city: Patchogue
Mailing state: NY
Mailing zip: 11772-0800
Office phone: (631) 751-8819
General e-mail: charvey@newliving.com
Web address: www.newliving.com
Personnel: Christine Lynn Harvey (Pub./Ed. in Chief)
Main contact: Christine Lynn Harvey

JAMES RAIA

Street address 1: 122 43rd St
Street address state: NY
Postal code: 10018-7525
Country: USA
Mailing address: 225 W 36th St Ste 1P
Mailing city: New York
Mailing state: NY
Mailing zip: 10018-7525
Telephone country code: (212) 889-6633
Telephone city code: (212) 889-6634
General e-mail: office@nyppa.org
Web address: www.nyppa.org

SPECTRUM FEATURES SYNDICATE

Street address 1: 2351 Wyda Way
Street address 2: Apt 1113
Postal code: SE1 9GF
Country: United Kingdom
Mailing address: The News Building, 13th Floor,
Mailing city: London
Mailing zip: SE1 9GF
Telephone country code: 44
Telephone city code: 207
Office phone: 711 7888

News, Picture and Syndicate Services

Office fax: n/a
General e-mail: enquiries@newslicensing.co.uk
Web address: www.newslicensing.co.uk
Personnel: Darren Hendry (Licensing Sales Mngr.)
Main contact: Darren Hendry

STATE NET

Street address 1: 2101 K St
Street address state: UT
Postal code: 84108-1261
Country: USA
Mailing address: 375 S Chipeta Way Ste B
Mailing city: Salt Lake City
Mailing state: UT
Mailing zip: 84108-1261
Office phone: (801) 584-3900
Office fax: (202) 383-6190
General e-mail: sales@newscom.com
Web address: www.newscom.com
Personnel: Bill Creighton (Gen. Mgr.); Tom Bannon (Sales Mgr.); Lily Cheung (IP Rel. Mgr.); Ericka Calvert (Mktg. Dir.)
Main contact: Ericka Calvert

SAINT JOHN'S

CANADIAN PRESS, THE - SAINT JOHN'S, NL

Street address 1: 139 Water St., Ste. 901
Street address 2: The Fortis Bldg.
Street address state: WI
Postal code: 53186-6934
Country: USA
Mailing address: 1700 E Racine Ave
Mailing city: Waukesha
Mailing state: WI
Mailing zip: 53186-6934
Office phone: (262) 544-5252
General e-mail: nf-support@newsfinder.com
Web address: www.newsfinder.com
Note/Syndicate Information: Full AP wire of stories and photos for non-daily publications.
Personnel: Sandy Hamm (Gen. Mgr.); Linda Kalinowski (Acct. Mgr.); Colleen Hamm (Account Manager)
Main contact: Sandy Hamm

SALT LAKE CITY

NEWSCOM

Street address 1: 375 S Chipeta Way
Street address 2: Ste B
Street address state: VA
Postal code: 22046-4610
Country: USA
Mailing address: 1069 W Broad St Ste 205
Mailing city: Falls Church
Mailing state: VA
Mailing zip: 22046
Office phone: (703) 462-2700
Web address: www.newsusa.com
Personnel: Richard Rothstein (Vice Pres., Sales); Rick Smith (Pub.)
Main contact: Rick Smith

SAN CLEMENTE

KEYSTONE PICTURES

Street address 1: 408 N El Camino Real
Street address state: NY
Postal code: 10019-3741
Country: USA
Mailing address: 300 W 57th St Fl 41
Mailing city: New York
Mailing state: NY
Mailing zip: 10019-3741
Office phone: (212) 969-7550
Office fax: (646) 280-1550
General e-mail: kfs-public-relations@hearst.com
Web address: www.kingfeatures.com
Note/Syndicate Information: North America Syndicate is an affiliated company of King Features Syndicate.

Personnel: T.R. Shepard III (Pres.); Keith McCloat (Vice Pres./Gen. Mgr.); John Killian (VP, Syndication Sales); David Cohea (Gen. Mgr., King Feat. Weekly Service); Jack Walsh (Sr. Sales Consultant/Printing & New England Newspaper Sales); Claudia Smith (PR Dir.); Dennis Danko (Inside Sales Mgr.); Michael Mancino (Sales Mgr., New Media Inside Sales Rep); Brendan Burford (Gen. Mgr., Syndication); Jim Clarke (Editorial Dir., King Feat. Weekly Service); Randy Noble (SE Sales); Curtis Trammell (West Coast Sales); Robin Graham (International Sales Consultant); Diana Smith (Executive Editor); Chris Richcreek (Senior Features Editor); Evelyn Smith (Senior Comics Editor); Monique Prioleau (Sales Coordinator)
Main contact: Claudia Smith

ZUMA PRESS, INC.

Street address 1: 408 N El Camino Real
Street address state: NY
Postal code: 10017-7947
Country: USA
Mailing address: 415 Madison Ave Fl 12
Mailing city: New York
Mailing state: NY
Mailing zip: 10017-7956
Office phone: (212) 867-9000
Office fax: (800) 990-4329
General e-mail: service@napsnet.com; info@napsnet.com
Web address: www.napsnet.com
Personnel: Dorothy York (Pres.); Gary Lipton (Vice Pres., Media Rel.); Candace Leiberman (Ed. in Chief); Yauling Wagner (Serv. Mgr.)
Main contact: Gary Lipton

SAN DIEGO

CITY NEWS SERVICE, INC. - SAN DIEGO, CA

Street address 1: 202 C St
Street address 2: Rm 13A
Street address state: OH
Postal code: 45042
Country: USA
Mailing address: PO Box 2144
Mailing city: Middletown
Mailing state: OH
Mailing zip: 45042
Office phone: (800) 245-7515
General e-mail: kwilliams@oasisnewsfeatures.com
Web address: www.oasisnewsfeatures.com
Personnel: Kevin Williams (Exec. Ed.)
Main contact: Kevin Williams

CONTINENTAL FEATURES/ CONTINENTAL NEWS SERVICE

Street address 1: 501 W Broadway
Street address 2: Ste A PMB 265
Street address state: CA
Postal code: 94513-2707
Country: USA
Mailing address: 2420 Sand Creek Rd
Mailing city: Brentwood
Mailing state: CA
Mailing zip: 94513-2707
Office phone: (925) 432-7246 x24
Office fax: (925) 420-5690
General e-mail: info@onthehouse.com
Web address: www.onthehouse.com
Personnel: James Carey (Pres./Co-Host); Morris Carey (Vice Pres./Co-Host); Sylvie Castaniada (Affiliate Rel. Dir.)
Main contact: James Carey

GET FIT WITH THE WORLD'S FITTEST MAN

Street address 1: 2707 3rd Ave
Street address state: CA
Postal code: 94103-6500
Country: USA
Mailing address: 209 9th St Ste 200
Mailing city: San Francisco

Mailing state: CA
Mailing zip: 94103-6800
Telephone country code: (415) 503-4170
Telephone city code: (415) 503-0970
General e-mail: eshore@newamericamedia.org
Web address: www.newamericamedia.org

MATURE LIFE FEATURES

Street address 1: 3911 Kendall St
Street address state: NH
Postal code: 03838-6453
Country: USA
Mailing address: PO Box 1253
Mailing city: Glen
Mailing state: NH
Mailing zip: 03838-1253
Office phone: (603) 383-6729
General e-mail: info@waynegouldpuzzles.com
Web address: www.waynegouldpuzzles.com
Personnel: Wayne Gould (Dir.); Scott Gould (Mgr.)
Main contact: Scott Gould

WIRELESS FLASH NEWS, INC.

Street address 1: PO Box 633030
Street address state: MO
Postal code: 63040-1222
Country: USA
Mailing address: 2464 Taylor Rd Ste 131
Mailing city: Wildwood
Mailing state: MO
Mailing zip: 63040-1222
Office phone: (636) 236-6236
Office fax: (636) 458-7688
General e-mail: editor@parenttoparent.com
Web address: www.parenttoparent.com
Note/Syndicate Information: Self syndicated
Personnel: Jodie Lynn (Owner); Kyle Johnson (Personal Assistant Assistant Editor)
Main contact: Jodie Lynn

SAN FRANCISCO

ALTERNET

Street address 1: 77 Federal St
Street address state: TX
Postal code: 77406-6673
Country: USA
Mailing address: 2002 N. Greens Blvd
Mailing city: Richmond
Mailing state: TX
Mailing zip: 77406
Telephone country code: 001
Telephone city code: 512
Office phone: (512) 653-8545
Office fax: 832-201-9818
General e-mail: pperry@pearyperry.com
Web address: www.pearyperry.com
Note/Syndicate Information: Political column - 'A Nation of Fools' General commentary on life (satire) - 'Letters From North America' Trivia column - 'Ponder Points'
Personnel: Peary Perry (Self-Synd/Columnist)
Main contact: Peary Perry

BLOOMBERG NEWS

Street address 1: Pierre 3., Ste, 101
Street address state: MA
Postal code: 01950-1723
Country: USA
Mailing address: 5 Chain Bridge Dr
Mailing city: Newburyport
Mailing state: MA
Mailing zip: 01950-1723
Office phone: (978) 476-9121
Office fax: (978) 521-8372
General e-mail: carolynroybornstein@gmail.com
Web address: www.carolynroybornstein.com
Personnel: Carolyn Roy-Bornstein (MD)
Main contact: Carolyn Roy-Bornstein

BUSINESS WIRE - SAN FRANCISCO, CA

Street address 1: 44 Montgomery St
Street address 2: Fl 39
Street address state: MO

Postal code: 63021-7107
Country: USA
Mailing address: PO Box 240331
Mailing city: Ballwin
Mailing state: MO
Mailing zip: 63024-0331
Office phone: (636) 207-9880
Office fax: (636) 207-9880
General e-mail: mail@plainlabelpress.com
Web address: www.creativeon-line.com/syndicate
Personnel: Ed Chermoore (Vice Pres./Mng. Ed.); Laura Meyer (Submissions Ed.)
Main contact: Ed Chermoore

PACIFIC NEWS SERVICE

Street address 1: 209 9th St
Street address 2: Ste 200
Street address state: NY
Postal code: 10014-4504
Country: USA
Mailing address: 350 Hudson St Ste 300
Mailing city: New York
Mailing state: NY
Mailing zip: 10014-5827
Office phone: 1.888-776-0942
General e-mail: MediaInquiries@prnewswire.com
Web address: www.prnewswire.com
Personnel: Christine Cube (Audience Relations Manager); Dave Haapaoja (SVP, Global Operations); Victoria Harres (VP, Strategic Communications & Content)
Main contact: Victoria Harres

THE WEATHER UNDERGROUND, INC.

Street address 1: 185 Berry St
Street address 2: Ste 5501
Street address state: MI
Postal code: 49684-3610
Country: USA
Mailing address: 125 S. Park Street, Suite 430
Mailing city: Traverse City
Mailing state: MI
Mailing zip: 49684
Office phone: (231) 946-0606
General e-mail: kmurdock@practicalecommerce.com
Web address: http://www.practicalecommerce.com
Personnel: Kerry Murdock (Pub and Ed); Armando Roggio (Senior Contributing Editor)
Main contact: Kerry Murdock

WEATHER UNDERGROUND, INC., THE

Street address 1: 185 Berry St
Street address 2: Ste 5501
Street address state: D.C.
Postal code: 20007-5029
Country: USA
Mailing address: 2605 P St NW Ste A
Mailing city: Washington
Mailing state: DC
Mailing zip: 20007-5029
Office phone: (202) 898-4825
General e-mail: press_associates@yahoo.com
Personnel: Mark J. Gruenberg (Ed. in Chief); Janet Brown (Ed.); Dick Belland (Cartoonist); Martha Turner (Accounting)
Main contact: Mark J. Gruenberg

SAN JOSE

EFE NEWS SERVICES - SAN JOSE, COSTA RICA

Street address 1: Avda., 10 Calles 19/21 n. 1912, Apanado 8.4930
Street address state: MN
Postal code: 55102
Country: USA
Mailing address: 626 Armstrong
Mailing city: St Paul
Mailing state: MN
Mailing zip: 55102
Office phone: (651) 224-2856

News, Picture and Syndicate Services

General e-mail: getajob@prototypecareerservice.com
Web address: www.prototypecareerservice.com
Note/Syndicate Information: Award-winning 800- word weekly column on careers topics such as job search strategies, salary negotiations, career transition, business start-up, etc. Special content for millennials, older workers, others. Reliable, clean, engaging content has appeared in 100+ publications since 1995. Weekly rates start at $20 depending on publication size and/or contract. Careers expert, Amy Lindgren also appears frequently on public radio call-in shows.
Personnel: Amy Lindgren (Columnist/Career Expert)
Main contact: Amy Lindgren; Sheila Simon

SAN JUAN

EFE NEWS SERVICES - SANTURCE, PUERTO RICO

Street address 1: Edificio Cobian's Plz., Of. 214
Street address 2: Av Ponce de 1607
Street address state: NY
Postal code: 10022-2344
Country: USA
Mailing address: 400 E 59th St Apt 9F
Mailing city: New York
Mailing state: NY
Mailing zip: 10022-2344
Office phone: (212) 755-4363
General e-mail: info@punchin.com
Web address: www.punchin.com
Personnel: Nancy Preiser (Pres./Mng. Ed.); Betty Andrews (Contributing Writer); Bob Andrews (Contributing Writer); John Edwards (Contributing Writer); Bette Johns (Contributing Writer); Nina Lindt (Contributing Writer); Tom Weston (Contributing Writer)
Main contact: John Edwards

SAN SALVADOR

EFE NEWS SERVICES - SAN SALVADOR, EL SALVADOR

Street address 1: Condominio Balam Quitze, Local 17. 2. P. General Sta.
Street address state: MI
Postal code: 48152-1412
Country: USA
Mailing address: 20222 Farmington Rd
Mailing city: Livonia
Mailing state: MI
Mailing zip: 48152-1412
Office phone: (734) 293-7200
Office fax: (734) 293-7201
General e-mail: qsyndicate@pridesource.com
Web address: www.qsyndicate.com
Note/Syndicate Information: Q Syndicate provides content and community to the gay and lesbian press.
Personnel: Susan Horowitz (Pres.); Jan Stevenson (CFO); Christopher Azzopardi (Ed.)
Main contact: Jan Stevenson

SANTA BARBARA

ASHLEIGH BRILLIANT

Street address 1: 117 W Valerio St
Street address state: CA
Postal code: 92210-8835
Country: USA
Mailing address: 20960 Hilliard Blvd
Mailing city: Rocky River
Mailing state: OH
Mailing zip: 44116-3311
Office phone: (760) 776-9606
Office fax: (760) 776-9608
General e-mail: rrafferty@raffertyconsulting.com
Web address: www.raffertyconsulting.com

Personnel: Renata J. Rafferty (Pres.)
Main contact: Renata J. Rafferty

CAGLE CARTOONS, INC.

Street address 1: PO Box 22342
Street address state: WI
Postal code: 53217-2427
Country: USA
Mailing address: 8643 N Fielding Rd
Mailing city: Milwaukee
Mailing state: WI
Mailing zip: 53217-2427
General e-mail: david.fantle@gmail.com
Web address: www.reeltoreal.com
Note/Syndicate Information: We specialize in interviews with stars that have a track record and appeal to 50 plus readers. We do not need to be pitched reality stars or young "flavor of the month" stars who desperately need some press.
Personnel: David Fantle (Creator/Writer); Tom Johnson (Creator/Writer)
Main contact: David Fantle

SANTA MONICA

LEVIN REPRESENTS

Street address 1: 2402 4th St
Street address 2: Apt 6
Street address state: D.C.
Postal code: 20045-2001
Country: USA
Mailing address: 529 14th St NW Ste 1009
Mailing city: Washington
Mailing state: DC
Mailing zip: 20045-2001
Office phone: (202) 463-8777
Office fax: (202) 662-7154
General e-mail: info@religionnews.com
Web address: www.religionnews.com
Personnel: David E. Anderson (Senior Editor); Kevin Eckstrom (Editor-in-Chief); Tracy Gordon (Editorial/Publishing Consultant); Adelle Banks (Production Editor); Daniel Burke (Associate Editor); Lauren Markoe (National Correspondent); Claudia M. Sans Werner (Bus./Sales Mgr.); David Shaw (Bus. Coord.)
Main contact: Kevin Eckstrom

THE SCIENCE ADVICE GODDESS-AMY ALKON

Street address 1: 171 Pier Ave
Street address 2: Ste 280
Street address state: IL
Postal code: 60606-6623
Country: USA
Mailing address: 311 S Wacker Dr Ste 1200
Mailing city: Chicago
Mailing state: IL
Mailing zip: 60606-6623

SANTIAGO

EFE NEWS SERVICES - SANTIAGO, CHILE

Street address 1: Almirante Pastene, 333 - office 502
Street address state: NY
Postal code: 10036-6564
Country: USA
Mailing address: 3 Times Sq Lbby F
Mailing city: New York
Mailing state: NY
Mailing zip: 10036-6567

SAO PAULO

DOW JONES NEWSWIRES - SAO PAULO, BRAZIL

Street address 1: Rua Joaquim Floriano 488. 6 andar
Street address state: NY

Postal code: 10036-6564
Country: USA
Mailing address: 3 Times Sq
Mailing city: New York
Mailing state: NY
Mailing zip: 10036-6564
Office phone: (646) 223-4000
Office fax: (646) 223-4393
General e-mail: rosalina.thomas@thomsonreuters.com
Web address: www.reuters.com/newsagency
Personnel: Ms. Rosalina Thomas (Vice Pres./Head of Sales - The Americas, Reuters News Agency, Thomson Reuters); Melissa Metzger (Publishing Solutions Specialist); Bipasha Ghosh (Global Director of Marketing)
Main contact: Bipasha Ghosh; James C. Smith

SCOTTSDALE

IMORTGAGEGUIDE.COM LLC

Street address 1: PO Box 5795
Street address state: WI
Postal code: 53211-1844
Country: USA
Mailing address: 4014 N Morris Blvd
Mailing city: Shorewood
Mailing state: WI
Mailing zip: 53211-1844
Office phone: (414) 963-9333
General e-mail: rickhoro@execpc.com
Web address: www.huffingtonpost.com/rick-horowitz/
Personnel: Rick Horowitz (Self-Syndicator); Charlie White (Webmaster)
Main contact: Rick Horowitz

SEATTLE

ELIZABETH S. SMOOTS

Street address 1: 5735 27th Ave NE
Street address state: NY
Postal code: 12747-0259
Country: USA
Mailing address: PO Box 259
Mailing city: Hurleyville
Mailing state: NY
Mailing zip: 12747-0259
Telephone country code: 1
Office phone: (845) 292-3071
Office fax: (845) 434-4806
General e-mail: ronbernthal@wjffradio.org
Personnel: Ron Bernthal (Self-Syndicator, Travel/Historic Preservation Audio Programs)
Main contact: Ron Bernthal

SEATTLE

GETTY IMAGES

Street address 1: 605 5th Avenue South
Street address 2: Suite 400
Street address state: FL
Postal code: 32963-1514
Country: USA
Mailing address: 3650 Mockingbird Dr
Mailing city: Vero Beach
Mailing state: FL
Mailing zip: 32963-1514
Office phone: (772) 492-9032
Office fax: (772) 492-9032
General e-mail: jancook@myvocabulary.com
Web address: www.syndicate.com; myvocabulary.com; www.rootonym.com
Note/Syndicate Information: We syndicate vocabulary word puzzles, word games and educational activities (K-12+.)
Personnel: Carey Orr Cook (Pres./Cartoon Ed.); Jan Cook (Bus. Devel.); Keith Cook (Sr. Vice Pres., Mktg./Sales); Kylie Cook (Internet/Web Ed.); Brad Cook (Prodn. Mgr., Opns.); Corry Cook (Senior Ed.)
Main contact: Carey Orr Cook

SHAMOKIN

THE NEWS ITEM

Street address 1: 707 N Rock St
Street address state: MI
Postal code: 48106-1347
Country: USA
Mailing address: P.O. Box 1347
Mailing city: Ann Arbor
Mailing state: MI
Mailing zip: 48106
Office phone: (734) 665-8272
Office fax: (734) 665-8272
General e-mail: schwaboo@comcast.net
Web address: www.schwadroncartoons.com
Personnel: Harley Schwadron (Ed.); Sally Booth (Sec.)
Main contact: Harley Schwadron

SHERMAN OAKS

HOLLYWOOD NEWS SERVICE

Street address 1: 13636 Ventura Blvd
Street address 2: Ste 303
Street address state: D.C.
Postal code: 20005-4965
Country: USA
Mailing address: 1090 Vermont Ave NW Ste 1000
Mailing city: Washington
Mailing state: DC
Mailing zip: 20005-4906
Office phone: (202) 408-1484
Office fax: (202) 408-5950
Web address: www.shns.com
Personnel: Peter Copeland (Ed./Gen. Mgr.); David Johnson (Chief Tech. Officer/Webmaster); Lisa Klem Wilson (Sales & Mktg. Contact/Sr. Vice Pres. & Gen. Mgr., United Media); Bob Jones (Desk Ed.); John Lindsay (Sports Ed.)
Main contact: Peter Copeland

SHOREWOOD

RICK HOROWITZ

Street address 1: 4014 N Morris Blvd
Street address state: D.C.
Postal code: 20005-4965
Country: USA
Mailing address: 1090 Vermont Ave NW Ste 1000
Mailing city: Washington
Mailing state: DC
Mailing zip: 20005-4965
Office phone: (202) 408-1484
Office fax: (202) 408-5950

SINGAPORE

BLOOMBERG NEWS

Street address 1: Capital Square, 23 Church St., 12th Fl.
Street address state: CO
Postal code: 80207-3206
Country: USA
Mailing address: 2377 Elm St
Mailing city: Denver
Mailing state: CO
Mailing zip: 80207-3206
Office phone: (303) 355-3882
General e-mail: clearmountain@tde.com
Web address: www.seniorwire.com
Note/Syndicate Information: Contact through website or email. Use submission or query and subject of article in subject line for editorial matter. Paste stories into email rather than as an attachment.
Personnel: Allison St. Claire (Pub./Ed.)
Main contact: Allison St. Claire

DOW JONES NEWSWIRES - SINGAPORE, SINGAPORE

Street address 1: 10 Anson Rd., Ste. 32-09/10 Int'l Plz.

News, Picture and Syndicate Services

Street address state: CA
Postal code: 94520
Country: USA
Mailing address: 2401 Stanwell Dr., Ste 340
Mailing city: Concord
Mailing state: CA
Mailing zip: 94520
Office phone: (925) 798-0896
Office fax: (925) 215-2320
General e-mail: support@servicequality.us
Web address: www.service-quality.com
Personnel: Dr. Jeffrey S. Kasper (Pres.)
Main contact: Jeffrey S. Kasper

SIOUX FALLS

CREATIVE COMIC PRODUCTIONS

Street address 1: 1608 S Dakota Ave
Street address state: IA
Postal code: 52244-3325
Country: USA
Mailing city: Iowa City
Mailing state: IA
Mailing zip: 52240-5755
Office phone: (319) 512 9705
General e-mail: sharptoons@yahoo.com
Web address: www.sharptoons.com
Personnel: Joe Sharpnack (Self-Syndicator)
Main contact: Joe Sharpnack

SKILLMAN

BLOOMBERG NEWS

Street address 1: 100 Business Park Dr
Street address state: NY
Postal code: 10022-4211
Country: USA
Mailing address: 59 E 54th St
Mailing city: New York
Mailing state: NY
Mailing zip: 10022-4211
Office phone: (212) 758-0740
Office fax: (212) 593-5194
General e-mail: info@leadersmag.com
Web address: www.leadersmag.com
Personnel: Henry O. Dormann (Chrmn./Ed. in Chief); Darrell Brown (Vice Pres./Exec. Ed.)
Main contact: Darrell Brown

SOLON

MIKO'S PACIFIC NEWS SERVICE

Street address 1: 33280 E Nimrod St
Street address state: IL
Postal code: 60544-2435
Country: USA
Mailing address: 24730 Illini Dr
Mailing city: Plainfield
Mailing state: IL
Mailing zip: 60544-2435
Office phone: (815) 954-5817
General e-mail: deb@slightlyoff.com
Web address: www.slightlyoff.com
Personnel: Deb DiSandro (Author/Owner)
Main contact: Deb DiSandro

SONOMA

KID SCOOP

Street address 1: PO Box 1802
Street address state: NY
Postal code: 10011-3542
Country: USA
Mailing address: 263 W 20th St Apt 3
Mailing city: New York
Mailing state: NY
Mailing zip: 10011-3542
Office phone: (212) 727-8170
Office fax: (212) 727-8228
General e-mail: info@sovfoto.com
Web address: www.sovfoto.com
Personnel: Vanya Edwards (President)
Main contact: Vanya Edwards

SPARTA

THE BOOKWORM SEZ, LLC

Street address 1: 18857 Icestorm Road
Street address state: CA
Postal code: 95825-1609
Country: USA
Mailing address: 2460 2nd St
Mailing city: Bloomsburg
Mailing state: PA
Mailing zip: 17815-3113
Office phone: (916)417-1688
General e-mail: editor@greeleyandstone.com
Web address: www.greeleyandstone.com
Personnel: Walter Brasch (Ed. in Chief); Rose Renn (Exec. Ed.); Matt Gerber (Assoc. Ed.); Mary Jayne Reibsome (Art/Prodn. Dir.); Diana Saavedra (Dir. of Mktg.)
Main contact: Walter Brasch

ST PAUL

PROTOTYPE CAREER SERVICES

Street address 1: 626 Armstrong Ave
Street address state: NY
Postal code: 10110-0002
Country: USA
Mailing address: 500 5th Ave Ste 2800
Mailing city: New York
Mailing state: NY
Mailing zip: 10110-0002
Office phone: (212) 983-1983

STATE COLLEGE

ACCUWEATHER, INC.

Street address 1: 385 Science Park Rd
Street address state: NY
Postal code: 10038-3703
Country: USA
Mailing address: 82 Nassau St., Ste. 521
Mailing city: New York
Mailing state: NY
Mailing zip: 10038
Office phone: (917) 267-2493
General e-mail: info@paperpc.net
Web address: www.paperpc.com
Note/Syndicate Information: Home of The Paper PC blog: www.paperpc.com Twitter: @newyorkbob Pinterest: Top 250 worldwide with 1.2 million followers: www.paperpcpicks.com
Personnel: Robert Anthony (Ed./Columnist)
Main contact: Robert Anthony

STRASBURG

GLOBE SYNDICATE

Street address 1: 499 Richardson Rd
Street address state: OH
Postal code: 45244-4004
Country: USA
Mailing address: 6906 Royalgreen Dr
Mailing city: Cincinnati
Mailing state: OH
Mailing zip: 45244-4004
Office phone: (513) 231-6034
General e-mail: dulley@dulley.com; contact@dulley.com
Web address: www.dulley.com
Personnel: James T. Dulley (Pres.)
Main contact: James T. Dulley

SYDNEY

BLOOMBERG NEWS

Street address 1: 1 Macquarie Pl., Level 36, Gtwy. 36
Street address state: CA
Postal code: 95816-4920
Country: USA
Mailing address: 2101 K St
Mailing city: Sacramento
Mailing state: CA
Mailing zip: 95816-4920

Office phone: (916) 444-0840
Office fax: (916) 446-5369
General e-mail: info@statenet.com
Web address: www.statenet.com
Personnel: Laurie Stinson (Pres.); Jud Clark (Pres.)
Main contact: Laurie Stinson; Jud Clark

SYDNEY

DOW JONES NEWSWIRES - SYDNEY, AUSTRALIA

Street address 1: Level 10 56 Titt St.
Street address state: IL
Postal code: 60654-1975
Country: USA
Mailing address: 350 N Orleans St
Mailing city: Chicago
Mailing state: IL
Mailing zip: 60654-1975
General e-mail: cecil@straightdope.com
Web address: www.straightdope.com
Note/Syndicate Information: Direct business inquiries to: webmaster@straightdope.com
Personnel: Cecil Adams (Creator/Writer); Ed Zotti (Editor/General Mgr)
Main contact: Ed Zotti

TEANECK

BIOFILE

Street address 1: 995 Teaneck Rd
Street address 2: Apt 3N
Street address state: CA
Postal code: 92024-1360
Country: USA
Mailing address: above
Mailing city: Encinitas
Mailing state: CA
Mailing zip: 92024
Office phone: (760) 652-5302
General e-mail: jlk@sunfeatures.com
Web address: www.sunfeatures.com
Personnel: Joyce Lain Kennedy (Pres.); Tim K. Horrell (Vice Pres.)
Main contact: Joyce Lain Kennedy

TEGUCIGALPA

EFE NEWS SERVICES - TEGUCIGALPA, HONDURAS

Street address 1: Col. Elvel, Segunda Calle, Apt. 2012
Street address state: NY
Postal code: 10011-7409
Country: USA
Mailing address: 55 W 14th St Apt 4H
Mailing city: New York
Mailing state: NY
Mailing zip: 10011-7409
Office phone: (212) 242-8800
Office fax: (212) 633-6298
General e-mail: info@sylviadipietro.com
Web address: www.sylviadipietro.com
Personnel: Sylvia Di Pietro (Self-Syndicator)
Main contact: Sylvia Di Pietro

TOKYO

BLOOMBERG NEWS

Street address 1: Yusen Bldg., 1st Fl., 2-3-2 Marunouchi
Street address state: NY
Postal code: 10017-6904
Country: USA
Mailing address: 1 E 42nd St Fl 11
Mailing city: New York
Mailing state: NY
Mailing zip: 10017-6904
Telephone country code: 002
Telephone city code: 212
Office phone: (212) 557-5122
Office fax: (212) 557-3043

General e-mail: roctaiwan@taipei.org
Web address: www.taiwanembassy.org
Personnel: Ching Yi Ting (Contact)
Main contact: Ching Yi Ting

TOKYO

DOW JONES NEWSWIRES - TOKYO, JAPAN

Street address 1: Marunouchi Mitsui Bldg. 1F, 2-2-2, Marunouchi Chiyoda-ku
Street address state: D.C.
Postal code: 20016-2146
Country: USA
Mailing address: 4201 Wisconsin Ave. NW
Mailing state: DC
Mailing zip: 20016
Office phone: (202) 895-1800
Office fax: (202) 362-6144
General e-mail: tecroinfodc@tecro.us
Web address: http://www.roc-taiwan.org/US
Personnel: Frank Wang (Dir. Press)
Main contact: Frank Wang

TORONTO

BLOOMBERG NEWS

Street address 1: 161 Bay St., Ste. 4300
Street address state: IL
Postal code: 60601-1797
Country: USA
Mailing address: 55 West Wacker Drive, Suite 1200
Mailing city: Chicago
Mailing state: IL
Mailing zip: 60601
Telephone country code: 1
Office phone: (312) 616-0100
Office fax: (312) 616-1486
General e-mail: teco@tecochicago.org
Web address: www.taiwanembassy.org
Personnel: Justin Lee (Deputy Director)

BROADCAST NEWS LIMITED

Street address 1: 36 King St. E.
Postal code: SW1W 0DT
Country: United Kingdom
Mailing address: 111 Buckingham Palace Rd.
Mailing city: London
Mailing zip: SW1W 0DT
Telephone country code: 44
Telephone city code: 20
Office phone: 020 7931 1010
General e-mail: syndication@telegraph.co.uk
Web address: www.telegraph.co.uk/syndication
Note/Syndicate Information: Syndication manages all commercial licensing and content partnerships for all print publications and digital platforms for The Telegraph Media Group.
Personnel: Sophie Hanbury (Content Partnerships Director)
Main contact: Sophie Hanbury

CANADIAN PRESS, THE - TORONTO, ON

Street address 1: 36 King St. E.
Street address state: WI
Postal code: 54656
Country: USA
Mailing address: 18857 Icestorm Road
Mailing city: Sparta
Mailing state: WI
Mailing zip: 54656
Office phone: (608) 782-2665
Office fax: (608) 787-8222
General e-mail: bookwormsez@yahoo.com; bookwormsez@gmail.com
Web address: www.bookwormsez.com
Note/Syndicate Information: Book reviewer ONLY; work with more than 250 publications in print and online.
Personnel: Terri Schlichenmeyer (Book Reviewer)
Main contact: Terri Schlichenmeyer

TORSTAR SYNDICATION SERVICES
Street address 1: One Yonge St.
Street address state: MA
Postal code: 02115-3012
Country: USA
Mailing address: 210 Massachusetts Ave
Mailing city: Boston
Mailing state: MA
Mailing zip: 02115-3195
Office phone: (617) 450-2123
General e-mail: syndication@csmonitor.com
Web address: www.csmonitor.com
Personnel: Andy Bickerton
Main contact: John Yemma

TRAVERSE CITY

PRACTICAL ECOMMERCE
Street address 1: 125 S Park St
Street address 2: Ste 430
Street address state: CT
Postal code: 06810-6803
Country: USA
Mailing address: 12 Bates Pl
Mailing city: Danbury
Mailing state: CT
Mailing zip: 06810-6803
Office phone: (203) 798-0462
General e-mail: comments@classifiedguys.com
Web address: www.classifiedguys.com
Personnel: Duane Holze (Co-Pres.); Todd Holze (Co-Pres.)
Main contact: Todd Holze

VALLEJO

KING & KANGO KOMIX & ILLUSTRATIONS
Street address 1: PO Box 7914
Street address state: FL
Postal code: 32504-7701
Country: USA
Mailing address: 4185 Bonway Dr
Mailing city: Pensacola
Mailing state: FL
Mailing zip: 32504-7701
Office phone: (850) 484-8622
Office fax: (850) 484-8622
General e-mail: thejoker@thefunnypages.com
Web address: www.thefunnypages.com
Personnel: Phillip A. Ryder (Creator)
Main contact: Phillip A. Ryder

VANCOUVER

BROADCAST NEWS LIMITED
Street address 1: 840 Howe St., Ste. 250
Street address state: NY
Postal code: 12776-0399
Country: USA
Mailing address: PO Box 399
Mailing city: Roscoe
Mailing state: NY
Mailing zip: 12776-0399
Office phone: (607) 498-4700
Personnel: Bernard Gelman (Owner/Ed.)
Main contact: Bernard Gelman

VANCOUVER

CANADIAN PRESS, THE - VANCOUVER, BC
Street address 1: 840 Howe St., Ste. 250
Postal code: 91000
Country: Israel
Mailing address: PO Box 81
Mailing city: Jerusalem
Mailing zip: 91000
Telephone country code: 972
Telephone city code: 2
Office phone: 5315666
Office fax: 5389527
General e-mail: ads@jpost.co.il

Web address: www.jpost.com
Personnel: Steve Linde (Editor in Chief); David Brinn (Managing Ed.)
Main contact: Steve Linde

VERMILION

DSENTERTAINMENT/NORTH SHORE PUBLISHING
Street address 1: PO Box 318
Street address state: FL
Postal code: 33317-3628
Country: USA
Mailing address: 401 SW 54th Ave
Mailing city: Plantation
Mailing state: FL
Mailing zip: 33317-3628
Office phone: (954) 321-0032
Office fax: (954) 321-8617
General e-mail: namegameco@aol.com
Personnel: Melodye Hecht Icart (Pres.); Mitchell J. Free (Vice Pres., Sales/Dev.)
Main contact: Melodye Hecht Icart

VERO BEACH

SAM MANTICS ENTERPRISES
Street address 1: 3650 Mockingbird Dr
Street address state: NY
Postal code: 10018-1618
Country: USA
Mailing address: 620 8th Ave
Mailing city: New York
Mailing state: NY
Mailing zip: 10018
Telephone country code: 1
Telephone city code: 212
Office phone: 212-556-1927
General e-mail: nytsyn-sales@nytimes.com
Web address: www.nytsyn.com
Personnel: Andrea Mariano (Mkt Mgr.); Aidan McNulty (Regional Director, US & Canada); Christopher Lalime (Regional Director, Latin America, Mexico & the Caribbean); Patti Sonntag (Managing Editor, Syndicate); Whye-Ko Tan (Regional Director, Asia Pacific); Michael Greenspon (General Manager, News Services & Print Innovation); Nancy Lee (Vice President and Executive Editor, News Service & Syndicate); Alice Ting (Vice President, Licensing & Syndication); Cass Adamson (Regional Director, Europe, Middle East & Africa); Anita Patil (Editorial Director, News Service & Syndicate); Sergio Florez (Managing Editor, Images); Ray Krueger (Managing Editor, News Service)
Main contact: Nancy Lee; Dessy Germosen; Andrea Mariano

VICTORIA

CANADIAN PRESS, THE - VICTORIA, BC
Street address 1: Press Gallery, Rm. 360
Street address state: PA
Postal code: 17872-4930
Country: USA
Mailing address: 707 N Rock St
Mailing city: Shamokin
Mailing state: PA
Mailing zip: 17872-4956
Office phone: (570) 644-6397
Office fax: (570) 648-7581
General e-mail: publisher@newsitem.com
Web address: www.newsitem.com
Personnel: Andy Hentzelman (Ed.); Greg Zyla (Pub.)
Main contact: Andy Heintzelman

VIENNA

EFE NEWS SERVICES - VIENNA,

AUSTRIA
Street address 1: Rechte Wienzeile 51/16
Street address state: NY
Postal code: 10018-1618
Country: USA
Mailing address: 620 8th Ave
Mailing city: New York
Mailing state: NY
Mailing zip: 10018-1618
Office phone: (212) 556-4204
Office fax: (212) 556-3535
Web address: www.nytsyn.com
Personnel: Sergio Florez (Managing Editor/Images)
Main contact: Sergio Florez

WASHINGTON

AGENCE FRANCE-PRESSE - WASHINGTON, DC
Street address 1: 1500 K St NW
Street address 2: Ste 600
Street address state: NC
Postal code: 27512-1567
Country: USA
Mailing address: PO Box 1567
Mailing city: Cary
Mailing state: NC
Mailing zip: 27512-1567
Office phone: (919) 701-9818
General e-mail: column@theromantic.com
Web address: www.theromantic.com
Personnel: Michael Webb (Writer)
Main contact: Michael Webb

AMERICAN FEDERATION OF TEACHERS
Street address 1: 555 New Jersey Ave NW
Street address state: CA
Postal code: 90405-5311
Country: USA
Mailing address: 171 Pier Ave Ste 280
Mailing city: Santa Monica
Mailing state: CA
Mailing zip: 90405-5311
General e-mail: adviceamy@aol.com
Web address: http://www.advicegoddess.com
Note/Syndicate Information: Award-winning science-based nationally-syndicated advice columnist. Author of science-based books including "Good Manners For Nice People Who Sometimes Say Fck" (St. Martin's Press, 2014). Next book, "Unfckology," "science-help" on how to live with guts and confidence (Jan 2018). Weekly science podcast featuring the luminaries of behavioral science talking about their books. Speaking engagements through Macmillan.
Personnel: Amy Alkon (Syndicated science-based advice columnist on love, dating, sex, relationships. Science-based manners expert. Upcoming book, "Unfckology" - a "science-help" book on how to transform to live with guts and confidence. @amyalkon on Twitter.); Lucy Furry (Vice Pres., Syndication)
Main contact: Amy Alkon

BLOOMBERG NEWS
Street address 1: 1399 New York Ave NW
Street address 2: Fl 11
Street address state: NY
Postal code: 10036-8701
Country: USA
Mailing address: 1211 Avenue of the Americas Lowr C3
Mailing city: New York
Mailing state: NY
Mailing zip: 10036-0003
Office phone: (212) 597-5733
Office fax: (212) 597-5633
General e-mail: wsj.ltrs@wsj.com
Web address: www.wsj.com
Personnel: Paul Bell (Vice Pres., Partner Businesses); Steven Townsley (Dir., Sales); David Crook (Ed.)

Main contact: Steven Townsley

CANADIAN PRESS, THE - WASHINGTON, DC
Street address 1: 1100 13th St NW
Street address state: DC
Postal code: 20071-0004
Country: USA
Mailing address: 1301 K Street, NW
Mailing city: Washington
Mailing state: DC
Mailing zip: 20071
Office phone: (202) 334-5375
Office fax: (202) 334-5669
General e-mail: syndication@washpost.com
Web address: https://syndication.washingtonpost.com/
Personnel: Karen H. Greene (Ops. Mgr.); Maria Gatti (Dir., Sales & Mktg.); Amy Lago (Comics Ed.); Richard Aldacushion (CEO/General Manager); Rob Cleland (Sr. Systems Admin.); Sophie Yarborough (Mgr., Editorial Prod.); Gabriella Ferrufino (Marketing Rep.); Josh Alvarez (Manager/Editorial Production); Jim Toler (Marketing Rep.); Claudia Mendez (Customer Service Coordinator)
Main contact: Karen H. Greene

CAPITAL CONNECTIONS
Street address 1: 1698 32nd St NW
Street address state: CA
Postal code: 94107-1761
Country: USA
Mailing address: 185 Berry St Ste 5501
Mailing city: San Francisco
Mailing state: CA
Mailing zip: 94107-1761
Office phone: (415) 983-2602
Office fax: (415) 543-5044
General e-mail: chuck@wunderground.com
Web address: www.wunderground.com
Personnel: Alan Steremberg (Pres.); Brian Read (Office Mgr.); Andria Stark (Vice Pres. Sales/Mktg.)
Main contact: Andria Stark

CATHOLIC NEWS SERVICE
Street address 1: 3211 4th St NE
Street address state: WV
Postal code: 26033-1367
Country: USA
Mailing address: 2222 Fish Ridge Rd
Mailing city: Cameron
Mailing state: WV
Mailing zip: 26033-1367
Office phone: (304) 686-2630
General e-mail: sshalaway@aol.com
Web address: http://scottshalaway.googlepages.com
Note/Syndicate Information: Provide a 700-word weekly column about nature, wild birds, and conservation to newspapers
Personnel: Scott Shalaway (Nature Writer, Wildlife Biologist)
Main contact: Scott Shalaway

DOW JONES NEWSWIRES - WASHINGTON, DC
Street address 1: 1025 Connecticut Ave NW
Street address 2: Ste 800
Street address state: TX
Postal code: 75086-6933
Country: USA
Mailing address: PO Box 866933
Mailing city: Plano
Mailing state: TX
Mailing zip: 75086-6933
Office phone: (972) 398-3897
Office fax: (972) 398-8154
General e-mail: care@kaidy.com
Web address: www.mathfun.com
Personnel: Louis Y. Sher (Owner/Pres.)
Main contact: Louis Y. Sher

EFE NEWS SERVICES -

News, Picture and Syndicate Services

WASHINGTON, D.C

Street address 1: 1252 National Press Building. 529, 14 Street, NW
Street address 2: Washington D.C. 20045Â
Street address state: IL
Postal code: 60022-1585
Country: USA
Mailing address: 361 Park Avenue
Mailing city: Glencoe
Mailing state: IL
Mailing zip: 60022
Office phone: 847-242-0550
General e-mail: ilyce@ThinkGlink.com
Web address: www.thinkglink.com; www.lawproblems.com; www.expertrealestatetips.net
Note/Syndicate Information: We offer a thrice weekly written column, called "Real Estate Matters," and a daily (M-F) video minute called "The Real Estate Minute." Samples are available at http://thinkglinkpublishing.com/real-estate-minutes/. The REMs are available via a simple widget and can be customized. If you are looking to design a deep, content-rich online real estate section, we can help with that, too. Contact Sam Tamkin (sam@thinkglink.com) for details.
Personnel: Ilyce R. Glink (Pub.); Samuel J. Tamkin (Ed.)
Main contact: Ilyce R. Glink

EFE NEWS SERVICES - WASHINGTON, DC

Street address 1: 529 14th St NW
Street address state: NY
Postal code: 11215-0673
Country: USA
Mailing address: PO Box 150673
Mailing city: Brooklyn
Mailing state: NY
Mailing zip: 11215-0673
Office phone: (718) 768-2522
General e-mail: tom.tomorrow@gmail.com
Web address: www.thismodernworld.com
Note/Syndicate Information: Please do not send submissions for syndication.
Personnel: Dan Perkins (Creator)
Main contact: Dan Perkins

FAMILY ALMANAC

Street address 1: 420 Constitution Ave NE
Street address state: KS
Postal code: 67117-0332
Country: USA
Mailing address: PO Box 332
Mailing city: North Newton
Mailing state: KS
Mailing zip: 67117-0332
Office phone: (316) 283-5231
General e-mail: vsnider@southwind.net
Web address: www.thisside60.com
Note/Syndicate Information: Motivational column about empowerment in mature years
Personnel: Snider Vada
Main contact: Vada Snider

FISCALNOTE

Street address 1: 1201 Pennsylvania Ave NW
Street address 2: 6th Floor
Street address state: IL
Postal code: 60611-7551
Country: USA
Mailing address: 435 N Michigan Ave Ste 1400
Mailing city: Chicago
Mailing state: IL
Mailing zip: 60611-7551
Office phone: (800) 637-4082
Office fax: (312) 527-8256
General e-mail: ctrammell@tribune.com
Web address: www.tmsspecialtyproducts.com
Note/Syndicate Information: TMS Specialty Products provides articles and images suitable for use in advertorial sections, niche publications and other targeted media, as well as custom ordered content, including local and paginated products.
Personnel: Marco Buscaglia (Gen. Mgr.); Curtis Trammell (Sales manager); Mary Elson

(Mng. Ed.); Todd Rector (Art Dir.)
Main contact: Marco Buscaglia

FOOD NUTRITION HEALTH NEWS SERVICE

Street address 1: 1712 Taylor St NW
Street address state: ON
Postal code: M5E 1E6
Country: Canada
Mailing address: One Yonge St.
Mailing city: Toronto
Mailing state: ON
Mailing zip: M5E 1E6
Office phone: (416) 869-4994 (Sales)
Office fax: (416) 869-4587
General e-mail: syndicate@torstar.com
Web address: www.torstarsyndicate.com; www.tsscontent.ca; www.getstock.com
Personnel: Robin Graham (Managing Director); Ted Cowan (Sales Representative Torstar Syndication Services GetStock.com); Evi Docherty (Account Information); Joanne MacDonald (Sales Asst.); Julie Murtha (Associate Director, Business Development)
Main contact: Ted Cowan

GLOBAL HORIZONS

Street address 1: 1330 New Hampshire Ave NW
Street address 2: Apt 609
Street address state: NY
Postal code: 14424-9020
Country: USA
Mailing address: 3701 State Route 21
Mailing city: Canandaigua
Mailing state: NY
Mailing zip: 14424-9020
Office phone: (585) 396-0027
General e-mail: tns@rochester.rr.com
Web address: www.fats-and-oils.com
Note/Syndicate Information: Serving the fats and oils industry exclusively, since 1914.
Personnel: Dennis C Maxfield (Sr. Ed.)
Main contact: Dennis C Maxfield

HEARST NEWS SERVICE

Street address 1: 700 12th St NW
Street address 2: Ste 1000
Street address state: ID
Postal code: 47304-2431
Country: USA
Mailing address: 4001 W Kings Row St
Mailing city: Muncie
Mailing state: IN
Mailing zip: 47304-2431
Office phone: (937) 423-3517
General e-mail: kelsey@travelin-light.com
Web address: www.travelin-light.com
Personnel: Kelsey Timmerman (Writer/ Photographer); Geoff Hassing (Cartoonist)
Main contact: Geoff Hassing

HISPANIC LINK NEWS SERVICE

Street address 1: 1420 N St NW
Street address state: IL
Postal code: 60601
Country: USA
Mailing address: 160 N. Stetson ave
Mailing city: Chicago
Mailing state: IL
Mailing zip: 60601
Office phone: (800) 637-4082
General e-mail: tcasales@tribuneinteractive.com
Web address: www.tribunecontentagency.com
Personnel: Scott Cameron (Sales Dir. New Mkts.); Rick DeChantal (Sales Dir.); Jack Barry (VP Opertns & Acqs Ed.); Wayne Lown (Gen. Mgr.); Matt Maldre (Mktg. Mgr.); Karyn Esken (VP/Bus. Dvp.); Andres Lombana (VP/Intl Bus. Dev.)
Main contact: Matt Maldre

PRESS ASSOCIATES, INC.

Street address 1: 2605 P St NW
Street address 2: Ste A
Street address state: NY
Postal code: 12804-4086
Country: USA

Mailing address: 40 Media Dr
Mailing city: Queensbury
Mailing state: NY
Mailing zip: 12804-4086
Office phone: (800) 833-9581
Office fax: (518) 792-4414
General e-mail: cyung@tribune.com
Web address: www.tribunemediaentertainment.com
Personnel: Cameron Yung (Exec. Dir., Newspapers); Kathleen Tolstrup (Gen. Mgr., Sales/Mktg.); Ken Hyatt (Account Executive)
Main contact: Cameron Yung

RELIGION NEWS SERVICE

Street address 1: 529 14th St NW
Street address 2: Ste 1009
Street address state: IL
Postal code: 60601
Country: USA
Mailing address: 160 N. Stetson Ave
Mailing city: Chicago
Mailing state: IL
Mailing zip: 60601
Office phone: (800) 637-4082
General e-mail: tcasales@tribuneinteractive.com
Web address: www.tribunenewsservice.com
Personnel: Rick DeChantal (Sales Dir.); Wayne Lown (Gen. Mgr.); Zach Finken (Assoc. Ed.)
Main contact: Rick DeChantal; Matt Maldre

SCRIPPS HOWARD NEWS SERVICE

Street address 1: 1090 Vermont Ave NW
Street address 2: Ste 1000
Street address state: MA
Postal code: 02301-4435
Country: USA
Mailing address: 1324 Belmont St Unit 2
Mailing city: Brockton
Mailing state: MA
Mailing zip: 02301-4435
Office phone: (781) 784-7857
Office fax: (781) 784-7857
General e-mail: lmodestino@hotmail.com
Web address: www.enterprisenews.com/tracktalk
Note/Syndicate Information: My webpage changed for 2012 and beyond
Personnel: Lou Modestino (Author)
Main contact: Lou Modestino

SCRIPPS-MCCLATCHY WESTERN SERVICES

Street address 1: 1090 Vermont Ave NW
Street address 2: Ste 1000
Street address state: CA
Postal code: 92054-4158
Country: USA
Mailing address: 821 S Tremont St Ste B
Mailing city: Oceanside
Mailing state: CA
Mailing zip: 92054-4158
Office phone: (800) 828-2453
Office fax: (760) 754-2356
General e-mail: ktaylor@u-bild.com
Web address: www.u-bild.com
Personnel: Kevin Taylor (Pres.); Jeffrey Reeves (Features Ed.)
Main contact: Kevin Taylor

TAIPEI ECONOMIC & CULTURAL REPRESENTATIVE OFFICE, PRESS DIVISION - WASHINGTON, DC

Street address 1: 4201 Wisconsin Ave NW
Street address state: NY
Postal code: 10016-3903
Country: USA
Mailing address: 200 Madison Ave Fl 4
Mailing city: New York
Mailing state: NY
Mailing zip: 10016-3905
Office phone: (800) 221-4816
Office fax: (212) 293-8600
Web address: www.unitedfeatures.com; www.comics.com

Personnel: Douglas R. Stern (Pres./CEO); Lisa Klem Wilson (Sr. Vice Pres./Gen. Mgr.); Mary Anne Grimes (Exec. Dir., Pub. Rel.); Suma CM (Exec. Ed.); Carmen Puello (Sales/Admin. Mgr.); Colette Cogley (Regl. Sales Mgr.); Ron O'Neal (Regl. Sales Mgr.); Jim Toler (Regl. Sales Mgr.); Dawn Gregory (Customer Serv. Rep); Emily Stephens (Sales Mgr., Int'l/E-rights); Reprint Rights Coord. (Reprint Rights Sales); Vincent Marciano
Main contact: Carmen Puello; Jan Flemington

THE WASHINGTON POST NEWS SERIVICE & SYNDICATE

Street address 1: 1301 K St NW
Street address state: OH
Postal code: 45202-4019
Country: USA
Mailing address: 312 Walnut St
Mailing city: Cincinnati
Mailing state: OH
Mailing zip: 45202-4024
Office phone: (513) 977-3000
Office fax: (513) 977-3024
Web address: www.scripps.com
Note/Syndicate Information: United Media's operations were outsourced to Universal Uclick in Kansas City, Mo., June 1, 2011. Please direct all inquiries to Universal Uclick.
Personnel: Vincent Marciano (General Manager, United Media); Donald Murray (Senior Analyst/ Systems Engineer)
Main contact: Vince Marciano

VOTERAMA IN CONGRESS - THOMAS VOTING REPORTS

Street address 1: PO Box 363
Street address state: FL
Postal code: 33432-2813
Country: USA
Mailing address: 1200 N. Federal Hwy., Suite 200
Mailing city: Boca Raton
Mailing state: FL
Mailing zip: 33432
Office phone: 202-898-8000
General e-mail: media@upi.com
Web address: www.upi.com
Note/Syndicate Information: United Press International is a leading provider of news, photos and information to millions of readers around the globe via UPI.com and its licensing services. With a history of reliable reporting dating back to 1907, today's UPI is a credible source for the most important stories of the day, continually updated - a one-stop site for U.S. and world news, as well as entertainment, trends, science, health and stunning photography. UPI also provides insightful reports on key topics of geopolitical importance, including energy and security. UPI is based in Washington, D.C., and Boca Raton, Fla.
Personnel: Nicholas Chiaia (President); Charlene Pacenti (Chief Content Officer); Franco Fernandez (Business Manager)
Main contact: Nicholas Chiaia

WASHINGTON MONTHLY LLC

Street address 1: 1200 18th St NW
Street address 2: Ste 330
Street address state: MO
Postal code: 64106-2109
Country: USA
Mailing address: 1130 Walnut St
Mailing city: Kansas City
Mailing state: MO
Mailing zip: 64106-2109
Office phone: (816) 581-7500
General e-mail: sales@amuniversal.com
Web address: www.amuniversal.com
Personnel: Kerry Slagle (Pres.); Milka Pratt (Mng. Dir., Latin America)
Main contact: Kerry Slagle

WASHINGTON POST NEWS SERVICE

News, Picture and Syndicate Services

WITH BLOOMBERG NEWS
Street address 1: 1301 K St NW
Street address state: D.C.
Postal code: 22747-0363
Country: USA
Mailing address: PO Box 363
Mailing city: Washington
Mailing state: VA
Mailing zip: 22747-0363
Office phone: (202) 332-0857
General e-mail: info@voterama.info
Web address: www.voterama.info
Note/Syndicate Information: Covers House and Senate legislative actions and members' voting records and campaign-finance data for U.S. news media – a finished editorial product transmitted daily and weekly in text, graphic and online formats.
Personnel: Mr. Richard G. Thomas (Pub./Ed.)
Main contact: Richard G. Thomas

WAUKESHA

NEWSFINDER
Street address 1: 1700 E Racine Ave
Street address state: GA
Postal code: 30047-6631
Country: USA
Mailing address: PO Box 450025
Mailing city: Atlanta
Mailing state: GA
Mailing zip: 31145-0025
Office phone: (770) 934-7380
Office fax: (770) 934-1700
General e-mail: wdfarmer@wdfarmerplans.com; vstarkey@wdfarmerplans.com
Web address: www.wdfarmer.com; www.wdfarmerplans.com/featurehomes; www.wdfplans.com
Personnel: W.D. Farmer (Designer); Vickie Starkey (Pres.)
Main contact: Vickie Starkey

WELLINGTON

WINGO, LLC
Street address 1: 12161 Ken Adams Way
Street address 2: Ste 110J
Street address state: NY
Postal code: 10036-4208
Country: USA
Mailing address: 62 W 45th St Fl 6
Mailing city: New York
Mailing state: NY
Mailing zip: 10036-4208
Office phone: (212) 827-0500
Office fax: (212) 944-9536
General e-mail: larry@nycphoto.com; info@nycphoto.com
Web address: www.nycphoto.com
Personnel: Larry Lettera (Adv. Mgr.); Jeff Connell (Chief Photographer)
Main contact: Larry Lettera

WEST ISLIP

GLOBE PHOTOS, INC.
Street address 1: 24 Edmore Ln S
Street address state: D.C.
Postal code: 20036-2556
Country: USA
Mailing address: 1200 18th St NW Ste 330
Mailing city: Washington
Mailing state: DC
Mailing zip: 20036-2556
Office phone: (202) 955-9010
Office fax: (202) 955-9011
General e-mail: editors@washingtonmonthly.com
Web address: www.washingtonmonthly.com
Personnel: Diane Straus Tucker (Publisher); Carl Iseli (VP, Operations & Marketing); Claire Iseli (VP Cir.); Charles Peters (Founding Ed.); Paul Glastris (Ed. in Chief); Ambi Ambachew (Adv. Mgr.)
Main contact: Claire Iseli

WEST PALM BEACH

INTERNATIONAL PHOTO NEWS
Street address 1: 2902 29th Way
Street address state: D.C.
Postal code: 20071-0004
Country: USA
Mailing address: 1301 K Street NW
Mailing city: Washington
Mailing state: DC
Mailing zip: 20071-0002
Telephone country code: 1
Office phone: (800) 879-9794 ext. 1
General e-mail: syndication@washpost.com
Web address: syndication.washingtonpost.com
Personnel: Brian Patten (Sales Mgr./North America); Maria Gatti (Dir., Int. Sales & Marketing); Jim Toler (Marketing Representative/Northeast & South); Robert Cleland (Senior Systems Administrator); Gabriella Ferrufino (Marketing Representative/Midwest & West); Richard Aldacushion (General Manager/Editorial Director); Sally Ragsdale (Marketing Representative/Midwest)
Main contact: Robert S. Cleland

LONA O'CONNOR
Street address 1: 2751 S Dixie Hwy
Street address state: NC
Postal code: 28607-8606
Country: USA
Mailing address: 192 Abbey Rd
Mailing city: Boone
Mailing state: NC
Mailing zip: 28607-8606
Office phone: (828) 773-3481
General e-mail: info@supin.com
Web address: www.supin.com
Note/Syndicate Information: Helping you make changes that matter.
Personnel: Jeanne Supin
Main contact: Jeanne Supin

WESTLAKE VILLAGE

MOVE, INC.
Street address 1: 30700 Russell Ranch Rd
Street address state: CA
Postal code: 94107-1761
Country: USA
Mailing address: 550 Kearny St Ste 600
Mailing city: San Francisco
Mailing state: CA
Mailing zip: 94108-2599
Office phone: (415) 983-2602
Office fax: (415) 543-5044
General e-mail: press@wunderground.com
Web address: www.wunderground.com
Personnel: Andria Stark (Press & Media)
Main contact: Chuck Prewitt

WHITE PLAINS

BLACK STAR PUBLISHING CO., INC.
Street address 1: 333 Mamaroneck Ave
Street address 2: # 175
Street address state: NY
Postal code: 10514-0496
Country: USA
Mailing address: PO Box 496
Mailing city: Chappaqua
Mailing state: NY
Mailing zip: 10514-0496
Office phone: (914) 241-2038
Office fax: (914) 242-0470
General e-mail: werren@att.net
Personnel: Werner Renberg (Self-Syndicator)
Main contact: Werner Renberg

WILDWOOD

PARENT TO PARENT
Street address 1: 2464 Taylor Rd
Street address 2: Ste 131
Street address state: RI
Postal code: 02906-4805
Country: USA
Mailing address: 71 Faunce Dr Ste 1
Mailing city: Providence
Mailing state: RI
Mailing zip: 02906-4805
Office phone: (401) 274-2149
General e-mail: webmaster@whitegatefeatures.com; staff@whitegatefeatures.com
Web address: www.whitegatefeatures.com
Personnel: Ed Isaac (Pres./CEO); Steve Corey (Vice Pres./Gen. Mgr.); Mari Howard (Office Mgr.); Eve Green (Talent Dir./Special Projects Mgr.)
Main contact: Mari Howard

WILLITS

GLENMOOR ENTERPRISE MEDIA GROUP
Street address 1: 75 N Main St
Street address 2: No 203
Street address state: TX
Postal code: 75080-3604
Country: USA
Mailing address: 1651 N. Collins Blvd., Suite 100
Mailing city: Richardson
Mailing state: TX
Mailing zip: 75080
Office phone: (972) 392-0888
Office fax: (972) 934-8848
General e-mail: info@wieck.com
Web address: www.wieck.com
Personnel: James Wieck (Chrmn.); Tim Roberts (Pres.); Marc Newman (Sr. VP)
Main contact: Tim Roberts

WILMINGTON

AUTOWRITERS ASSOCIATES, INC. (MOTOR MATTERS)
Street address 1: PO Box 3305
Street address state: PA
Postal code: 17754-8252
Country: USA
Mailing address: 179 Old Cement Rd
Mailing city: Montoursville
Mailing state: PA
Mailing zip: 17754-8248
Office phone: (570) 494-6789
Office fax: 866 923 0401
General e-mail: wildbill@wildbillsartshow.net
Web address: www.wildbillsartshow.net
Personnel: Bill Stanford (Creator)
Main contact: Bill Stanford

WINDSOR

BASIC CHESS FEATURES
Street address 1: 102 Blatchley Rd
Street address state: FL
Postal code: 33414-3194
Country: USA
Mailing address: 12161 Ken Adams Way Suite 110J
Mailing city: Wellngton
Mailing state: FL
Mailing zip: 33414
Office phone: (561) 379-2635
General e-mail: sat@amerimarketing.com
Web address: www.wingopromo.com; www.amerimarketing.com
Personnel: Scott Thompson (Pres.)
Main contact: Scott Thompson

WINNIPEG

BROADCAST NEWS LIMITED
Street address 1: 386 Broadway Ave., Ste. 101
Street address state: CA
Postal code: 92163-3030
Country: USA
Mailing address: PO Box 633030
Mailing city: San Diego
Mailing state: CA
Mailing zip: 92163-3030
Office phone: (619) 220-7191
Office fax: (619) 220-8590
General e-mail: newsdesk2@flashnews.com
Web address: www.flashnews.com
Personnel: Patrick Glynn (Mng. Ed.); Monica Garske (Sr. Ed.); David Louie (Sales/Mktg. Mgr.)
Main contact: Monica Garske

CANADIAN PRESS, THE - WINNIPEG, MB
Street address 1: 386 Broadway Ave., Ste. 101
Street address state: ON
Postal code: L8L 7N8
Country: Canada
Mailing address: 249 Kensington Ave. N.
Mailing city: Hamilton
Mailing state: ON
Mailing zip: L8L 7N8
Office phone: (905) 544-6174
General e-mail: wombania@wombania.com
Web address: www.wombania.com; www.comics.wombania.com
Note/Syndicate Information: Color and B&W weekly comic strip since 2003
Personnel: Peter Marinacci (Owner/Cartoonist); R.L.B. Hartmann (Ed.)
Main contact: Peter Marinacci

WINSTON SALEM

MEDIA GENERAL SYNDICATION SERVICES
Street address 1: 418 N Marshall St
Street address state: CA
Postal code: 92037-7037
Country: USA
Mailing address: 5842 Sagebrush Rd
Mailing city: La Jolla
Mailing state: CA
Mailing zip: 92037-7037
Office phone: (858) 456-6215
General e-mail: info@worldfeaturessyndicate.com
Web address: www.worldfeaturessyndicate.com
Personnel: Tom Robbins (Sales Dir.); Ronald A. Sataloff (Ed.); Karl A. Van Asselt (Sr. Assoc. Ed./Columnist); Ernie A. Gomez (Assoc. Ed.)
Main contact: Ronald A. Sataloff

WOODSTOCK

FASHION SYNDICATE PRESS
Street address 1: PO Box 727
Street address state: VA
Postal code: 20120-3126
Country: USA
Mailing address: 14745 Green Park Way
Mailing city: Centreville
Mailing state: VA
Mailing zip: 20120
Telephone country code: USA
Telephone city code: Centreville
Office phone: (703) 380-2808
General e-mail: jack@winsphoto.com
Web address: http://www.winsphoto.com
Note/Syndicate Information: International photo agency
Personnel: Jack Sykes (CEO/Chief Photographer)
Main contact: Jack W. Sykes

WYNCOTE

HOT TOPICS PUBLICATIONS, INC.
Street address 1: PO Box 183
Street address state: NY
Postal code: 11435-1292
Country: USA
Mailing address: 14421 Charter Rd Apt 5C

News, Picture and Syndicate Services

Mailing city: Jamaica
Mailing state: NY
Mailing zip: 11435-1292
Office phone: (718) 591-7246
General e-mail: jjmcolumn@earthlink.net
Personnel: John J. Metzler (Editor)
Main contact: John J. Metzler

ZURICH

DOW JONES NEWSWIRES - ZURICH, SWITZERLAND

Street address 1: Sihlquai 253, Postfach 1128
Street address state: VA
Postal code: 22203
Country: USA
Mailing address: PO Box 1509
Mailing city: Centreville
Mailing state: VA
Mailing zip: 20122-8509
Office phone: (703) 548-3300
Office fax: (703) 548-9151

General e-mail: info@yellowbrix.com
Web address: www.yellowbrix.com
Personnel: Jeffrey P. Massa (Founder/Pres./CEO); Tom Hargis (Adv. Mgr.)
Main contact: Jeffrey P. Massa

GEORGE WATERS

Street address state: CA
Postal code: 92672-4717
Country: USA
Mailing address: 408 N El Camino Real

Mailing city: San Clemente
Mailing state: CA
Mailing zip: 92672
Telephone country code: United States
Telephone city code: San Clemente
General e-mail: zinfo@zumapress.com
Web address: 408 N El Camino Real
Personnel: Scott McKiernan (CEO/Founder); Ruaridh Stewart (News Dir./Picture Desk Mgr.); Patrick Johnson (CTO); Julie Mason (CFO)
Main contact: Ruaridh Stewart

NEWSPAPER COMICS SECTION GROUPS AND NETWORKS

KANSAS CITY

GOCOMICS

Street address 1: 1130 Walnut St.
Street address state: MO
Postal code: 64109-2109
Country: USA
Mailing address 1: 1130 Walnut St.
Mailing state: MO
Mailing zip: 64106-2109

Office phone: 844-426-1256
General e-mail: ComicArtPrints@AMUniversal.com
Web address: GoComics.com
Personnel: Go Comics; Go Comics Art
Main contact: Go Comics

NEW YORK

KING FEATURES SYNDCATE

Street address 1: 300 West 57th Street
Street address state: NY
Postal code: 10019-5238
Country: USA
Mailing address 1: 300 West 57th Street
Mailing state: NY
Mailing zip: 10019-5238

Office phone: 212-969-7550
Office fax: 646-280-1550
Web address: kingfeatures.com
Personnel: CJ Kettler; Keith McCloat (VP, GM)
Main contact: Keith McCloat

THE DAILY CARTOONIST

Web address: dailycartoonist.com
Personnel: D.D. Degg (Ed.); John Glynn (Ed.)
Parent company: Andrews McMeel Universal
Main contact: D.D. Degg; John Glynn

EQUIPMENT, SUPPLIES AND SERVICES

ACWORTH

PACESETTER GRAPHIC SERVICE CORP.

Street address 1: 2672 Hickory Grove Rd NW
Street address state: GA
Zip/Postal code: 30101-3643
Country: USA
Mailing address: 2672 Hickory Grove Rd NW
Mailing city: Acworth
Mailing state: GA
Mailing zip: 30101-3643
General Phone: (800) 241-7970
General Fax: 770-974-2980
Primary Website: www.pacesetterusa.com
Year Established: 1977
Product/Services: Blankets; Rollers; Rollers: Dampening;
Personnel: Robert Allen (Pres.)
Personnel: Jeri Hammond (Exec. Vice Pres.)

ADA

NATIONAL MEDIA ASSOCIATES

Street address 1: 1412 Kerr Research Dr
Street address state: OK
Zip/Postal code: 74820
Country: USA
Mailing address: PO Box 849
Mailing city: Ada
Mailing state: OK
Mailing zip: 74821-0849
General Phone: (580) 421-9590
General Fax: (580) 421-9960
Email: bolitho@bolitho.com
Primary Website: www.nationalmediasales.com
Year Established: 1966
Product/Services: Brokers & Appraisers; Consulting Services: Financial;
Personnel: Thomas C. Bolitho (Broker)

AGAWAM

KIDDER, INC.

Street address 1: 270 Main St
Street address state: MA
Zip/Postal code: 01001-1838
Country: USA
Mailing address: 270 Main St
Mailing city: Agawam
Mailing state: MA
Mailing zip: 01001-1838
General Phone: (413) 786-8692
General Fax: (413) 786-8785
Email: kidderpress@worldnet.att.net
Year Established: 1876
Product/Services: Dryers: Film and Papers; Ink Fountains & Accessories; Presses: Flexographic; Rewinders;
Personnel: Charles Rae (Pres.)
Personnel: Thomas K. Trant (CFO)
Personnel: John Rico (Vice Pres.-HR)
Harris Barnard (Vice Pres.-Engineering)
Cheryl N. Smith (Mktg. Mgr.)

ALBERTSON

DAIGE PRODUCTS, INC.

Street address 1: 1 Albertson Ave
Street address 2: Ste 5
Street address state: NY
Zip/Postal code: 11507-1444
Country: USA
Mailing address: 1 Albertson Ave Ste 5
Mailing city: Albertson
Mailing state: NY
Mailing zip: 11507-1444
General Phone: (800) 645-3323
Email: info@daige.com
Primary Website: www.daige.com
Year Established: 1965

Product/Services: Adhesive Wax Coaters; Adhesives;
Personnel: Ike Harris (Pres.)

ALBUQUERQUE

G.T. SPECIALTIES

Street address 1: 2901A Edith Blvd NE
Street address state: NM
Zip/Postal code: 87107-1517
Country: USA
Mailing address: PO Box 6383
Mailing city: Albuquerque
Mailing state: NM
Mailing zip: 87197-6383
General Phone: (505) 343-0600
General Fax: (505) 343-0606
Email: Sales@gt-specialties.com
Primary Website: www.gt-specialties.com
Year Established: 1980
Product/Services: Offset Press, New made in USA grippers, Recondition grippers with a Diamond Coating
Personnel: Louis Nunez (Owner)

ALLENDALE

FUJIFILM HUNT CHEMICALS U.S.A., INC.

Street address 1: 40 Boroline Rd
Street address state: NJ
Zip/Postal code: 07401-1616
Country: USA
Mailing address: 40 Boroline Rd
Mailing city: Allendale
Mailing state: NJ
Mailing zip: 07401-1616
General Phone: (201) 236-8633
General Fax: (201) 995-2299

Primary Website: www.fujihuntusa.com
Year Established: 1989
Product/Services: Chemicals: Photographic; Chemicals: Pressroom;
Personnel: Scott Clouston (Vice Pres.)
Personnel: Albert Adrts (Pres.)

LONZA GROUP LTD.

Street address 1: 90 Boroline Road
Street address state: NJ
Zip/Postal code: 07401
Country: USA
Mailing address: 90 Boroline Road
Mailing city: Allendale
Mailing state: NJ
Mailing zip: 07401
General Phone: (201) 316-9200
General Fax: (201) 785-9973
Email: allendale@lonza.com
Primary Website: www.lonza.com
Year Established: 1986
Product/Services: Acid Dispensing Systems; Chemicals: Plate Processing; Chemicals: Pressroom;
Personnel: Albert M. Baehny (Chairman)
Personnel: Richard Ridinger (CEO)

ALPHARETTA

DEAN MACHINERY INTERNATIONAL, INC.

Street address 1: 6855 Shiloh Rd E
Street address state: GA
Zip/Postal code: 30005-8372
Country: USA
Mailing address: 6855 Shiloh Rd E
Mailing city: Alpharetta
Mailing state: GA
Mailing zip: 30005-8372
General Phone: (678) 947-8550

Equipment, Supplies and Services

General Fax: (678) 947-8554
Email: sales@deanmachinery.com
Primary Website: www.deanmachinery.com
Year Established: 1991
Product/Services: Adhesive Wax Coaters; Brokers & Appraisers; Equipment Dealers (Used); Label Printing Machines; Presses: Flexographic; Presses: Offset; Presses: Rotogravure;
Personnel: Walter Dean (Pres.)

THE SOFTWARE CONSTRUCTION CO. (SCC)

Street address 1: 3810 Hamby Rd
Street address state: GA
Zip/Postal code: 30004-3953
Country: USA
Mailing address: 3810 Hamby Rd
Mailing city: Alpharetta
Mailing state: GA
Mailing zip: 30004-3953
General Phone: (770) 751-8500
General Fax: (770) 772-6800
Email: sales@sccmediaserver.com
Primary Website: www.sccmediaserver.com
Year Established: 1995
Product/Services: Software: Digital Asset Management; Software: Multimedia Photo Story Archiving; Software: News Budgeting; Software: Workflow Management; Software: Assignment Tracking; Software: Syndicated Data Delivery
Personnel: Rick Marucci (CEO)
Personnel: Lee Funnell (Vice Pres.)

ALTAMONTE SPRINGS

ADVANCED INTERACTIVE MEDIA GROUP, LLC

Street address 1: 402 Spring Valley Rd
Street address state: FL
Zip/Postal code: 32714-5845
Country: USA
Mailing address: 402 Spring Valley Rd
Mailing city: Altamonte Springs
Mailing state: FL
Mailing zip: 32714
General Phone: (407) 788-2780
General Fax: (866) 611-6551
Email: pzollman@aimgroup.com
Primary Website: www.aimgroup.com
Year Established: 1997
Product/Services: Consulting Services Industry Trade Publication Conferences — Automotive advertising, recruitment advertising and technology
Product or Service: Consultants Publisher/Media
Note: The AIM Group is a global team of consulting experts in classified advertising, marketplaces and interactive media. We help publishers grow their businesses through strategic and tactical support. We publish Classified Intelligence Report, the international continuous advisory service that is often called "the bible of the classified advertising industry." We work with news media publishers, dot-coms, print classified publishers, yellow page publishers, broadcasters and technology vendors worldwide to help develop, launch and grow revenue-generating services. We are first and foremost "consultants who publish," not "publishers who do a little consulting on the side." Most of our consulting work is performed on a proprietary basis, so our clients often see only a small fraction of our work-product. We offer solutions for companies planning their strategies, increasing revenue, market share, and in developing products and packing strategies to grow their business. We help build interactive products and services; we don't just talk about them based on flimsy research. We support investors and analysts trying to determine the health of a company, or to find companies ripe for investment or acquisition. Our team includes long-time senior executives, so we work with senior executives to help them understand where their interactive-media and classified services need to evolve. We've been sales reps and sales managers, so we can help sales teams grow and develop traditional and interactive media services. Our writer/analysts get to the heart of the matter, and understand the business inside and out. We work with clients globally. Our worldwide team of almost 40 people follows the evolution in interactive media and classified advertising more closely than anyone else.
Personnel: Peter M. Zollman (Founding Principal)
Personnel: Jim Townsend (Editorial Director)
Personnel: Katja Riefler (Europe Director)
Rob Paterson (Principal, director of consulting)
Diana Bogdan

AMHERST

INTERNATIONAL IMAGING MATERIALS, INC.

Street address 1: 310 Commerce Drive
Street address state: NY
Zip/Postal code: 14228
Country: USA
Mailing address: 310 Commerce Drive
Mailing city: Amherst
Mailing state: NY
Mailing zip: 14228
General Phone: (716) 691-6333
General Fax: (888) 329-0260
Email: salesinfo@iimak.com
Primary Website: www.iimak.com
Year Established: 1983
Product/Services: Inks
Personnel: Douglas C. Wagner (Pres./CEO)
Personnel: Joseph G. Perna (CFO)
Personnel: Susan Stamp (Sr. VP, HR and Admin.)
Jose Morlin (VP, Sales and Marketing)

ANCHORAGE

UNICOM, INC.

Street address 1: 5450 A St
Street address state: AK
Zip/Postal code: 99518-1278
Country: USA
Mailing address: PO Box 92730
Mailing city: Anchorage
Mailing state: AK
Mailing zip: 99509-2730
General Phone: (907) 561-1674
General Fax: (907) 563-3185
Email: unicom@unicom-alaska.com
Primary Website: www.unicom-alaska.com
Year Established: 1977
Product/Services: Telecommunications
Personnel: Rob Taylor (Vice Pres./Gen. Mgr.)

ANDOVER

MONACO SYSTEMS, INC.

Street address 1: 100 Burtt Rd
Street address 2: Ste 203
Street address state: MA
Zip/Postal code: 01810-5920
Country: USA
Mailing address: 100 Burtt Rd Ste 203
Mailing city: Andover
Mailing state: MA
Mailing zip: 01810-5920
General Phone: (978) 749-9944
General Fax: (978) 749-9977
Email: corporateemail@xrite.com
Primary Website: www.monacosys.com
Year Established: 1993
Product/Services: Color Management Software; Software: Workflow Management/Tracking;
Personnel: Bonnie Fladung (Dir.-Mktg.)

ANN ARBOR

PROQUEST LLC

Street address 1: 789 E Eisenhower Pkwy
Street address state: MI
Zip/Postal code: 48108-3218
Country: USA
Mailing address: PO Box 1346
Mailing city: Ann Arbor
Mailing state: MI
Mailing zip: 48106-1346
General Phone: (734) 761-4700
Email: info@proquest.com
Primary Website: www.proquest.com
Product/Services: Archiving Systems
Personnel: Marty Kahn (CEO)
Personnel: Simon Beale (Sr. Vice Pres., Global Sales)
Personnel: Lynda James-Gilboe (Sr. Vice Pres., Mktg.)
Chris Cowan

XITRON

Street address 1: 4750 Venture Drive
Street address 2: Suite 200A
Street address state: MI
Zip/Postal code: 48108
Country: USA
Mailing address: 4750 Venture Drive, Suite 200A
Mailing city: Ann Arbor
Mailing state: MI
Mailing zip: 48108
General Phone: (734) 913-8080
General Fax: (734) 913-8088
Email: xitronsales@xitron.com
Primary Website: www.xitron.com
Year Established: 1977
Product/Services: CtP RIPs and Workflows, High-Speed Digital and Inkjet RIPs and workflows, Ink Key Presetting software, Ctp Interfaces, CtP TIFF Catchers, Prepress Software Development
Personnel: Bret Farrah (Executive Vice President)
Personnel: Jennifer Graustein (Marketing Coordinator)

APOPKA

DAN-BAR, INC.

Street address 1: 2502 Jmt Industrial Dr
Street address 2: Unit 104
Street address state: FL
Zip/Postal code: 32703-2138
Country: USA
Mailing address: 2502 JMT Industrial Dr. Suite 104
Mailing city: Apopka
Mailing state: FL
Mailing zip: 32703-6542
General Phone: (407) 292-0600
General Fax: (407) 292-0602
Email: dcmdanbar@aol.com; contact@danbarinc.com
Primary Website: www.danbarinc.com
Year Established: 1998
Product/Services: Automatic Plastic Bagging Equipment; Baling Machines; Collating Equipment; System Installations;
Personnel: Dan Baratta (Pres.)

ARLINGTON

FUJIFILM GRAPHIC SYSTEMS USA, INC.

Street address 1: 330 Westway Pl
Street address 2: Ste 446
Street address state: TX
Zip/Postal code: 76018-1025
Country: USA
Mailing address: 330 Westway Pl Ste 446
Mailing city: Arlington
Mailing state: TX
Mailing zip: 76018-1025
General Phone: (800) 404.3228
General Fax: (817) 467-7351
Primary Website: www.fujifilmusa.com/products/graphic_arts_printing/index.html
Product/Services: Blankets; Chemicals: Pressroom; Color Management Software; Imagesetters; Inks; Offset Chemicals & Supplies; Platemakers: Flexographic (Computer to Plate); Plates: Offset (Conventional); Proofing Systems; Software: Press/Post Press;
Personnel: Bob O'Shea (Reg'l Sales Mgr.)

ARLINGTON HEIGHTS

AAA PRESS INTERNATIONAL

Street address 1: 3160 N Kennicott Ave
Street address state: IL
Zip/Postal code: 60004-1426
Country: USA
Mailing address: 3160 N Kennicott Ave
Mailing city: Arlington Heights
Mailing state: IL
Mailing zip: 60004-1426
General Phone: (847) 818-1100
General Fax: (800) 678-7983
Email: info@aaapress.com
Primary Website: www.aaapress.com
Product/Services: Cameras & Accessories; Circulation Equipment & Supplies; Equipment Dealers (New); Equipment Dealers (Used); Imagesetters; Plate Mounting & Register Systems; Press Accessories, Parts & Supplies; Presses: Flexographic; Proofing Systems; Rewinders
Personnel: Jack Ludwig (Pres.)
Personnel: Mark Hahn (Vice Pres., Sales/Mktg.)

BALDWIN AMERICAS

Street address 1: 3350 W Salt Creek Ln
Street address 2: Ste 110
Street address state: IL
Zip/Postal code: 60005-1089
Country: USA
Mailing address: 3350 West Salt Creek
Mailing city: Arlington Heights
Mailing state: IL
Mailing zip: 60005
General Phone: 913-888-9800
Email: csrteam@baldwintech.com
Primary Website: www.baldwintech.com/home
Year Established: 1918
Product/Services: Sales, Service, and Parts; Sheetfed and Web, Blanket Cleaner/Washer (Automatic); UV/IR/LED Drying Systems; Web Printing Controls (WPC) systems; Press Accessories, Parts & Supplies, Cleaning Cloth;
Personnel: Denise Jabotte (Sales Contact)

WEB PRINTING CONTROLS, A BALDWIN COMPANY

Street address 1: 3350 W Salt Creek Ln
Street address 2: Ste 110
Street address state: IL
Zip/Postal code: 60005-1089
Country: USA
Mailing address: 3350 West Salt Creek Ln., Ste 110
Mailing city: Arlington Heights
Mailing state: IL
Mailing zip: 60005
General Phone: 847-477-6323
Email: mark.krueger@baldwintech.com
Primary Website: www.wpcteam.com
Year Established: 1971
Product/Services: Controls: Color Register; Color Density: Cut-off, Press controls, ribbon controls: Web Break Detector systems: Web Guides
Personnel: Herman Gnuechtel (Product Line Leader WPC)
Personnel: Mark Krueger (Director Of Sales
Personnel: WPC)

Equipment, Supplies and Services

ASHBURN

MCI
Street address 1: 22001 Loudoun County Pkwy
Street address state: VA
Zip/Postal code: 20147-6105
Country: USA
Mailing address: 22001 Loudoun County Pkwy
Mailing city: Ashburn
Mailing state: VA
Mailing zip: 20147-6122
General Phone: (703) 206-5600
General Fax: (703) 206-5601
Email: info@mci.com
Primary Website: www.mci.com
Year Established: 1968
Product/Services: Data Communication
Product or Service: Online Service Provider and Internet Hosts`Telecommunications/Service Bureaus
Personnel: Ivan Siedenberg (Chrmn./CEO)
Personnel: Fred Briggs (Pres., Opns./Tech.)
Personnel: Robert Blakely (Exec. Vice Pres./CFO)
Daniel Casaccia (Exec. Vice Pres., HR)
Jonathan Crane (Exec. Vice Pres., Strategy/Cor. Devel.)
Grace Chentent (Sr. Vice Pres., Commun.)
Nancy B. Gofus (Sr. Vice Pres., Mktg./CMO)
Shane King

ASHLAND

KIDDE FIRE SYSTEMS
Street address 1: 400 Main Street
Street address state: MA
Zip/Postal code: 01721
Country: USA
Mailing address: 400 Main Street
Mailing city: Ashland
Mailing state: MA
Mailing zip: 01721
General Phone: (508) 881-2000
General Fax: (708) 748-2847
Primary Website: www.kidde-fenwal.com/Public/Kidde
Year Established: 1917
Product/Services: Architects/Engineers (Includes Design/Construction Firms); Fire Protection; System Installations; System Integration Services; Telecommunications;
Personnel: Kelly Sanderson (West Coast Sales Director)
Personnel: Greg Lindsey (Northwest Sales)
Personnel: Ron Parker (Southwest Sales)

SCHLENK-BOTH INDUSTRIES
Street address 1: 40 Nickerson Rd
Street address state: MA
Zip/Postal code: 01721-1912
Country: USA
Mailing address: 40 Nickerson Rd
Mailing city: Ashland
Mailing state: MA
Mailing zip: 01721-1912
General Phone: (508) 881-4100
General Fax: (508) 881-1278
Email: customerservice@schlenkusa.com
Primary Website: www.schlenk.com/about-us/global/usa-global/
Product/Services: Inks
Personnel: Carl-Joachim von Schlenk-Barnsdorf (CEO)
Personnel: Alois Seidl (Pres.)

STEEL CITY CORP.
Street address 1: 1000 Hedstrom Dr
Street address state: OH
Zip/Postal code: 44805-3587
Country: USA
Mailing address: 1000 Hedstrom Dr
Mailing city: Ashland
Mailing state: OH
Mailing zip: 44805
General Phone: (800) 321-0350
General Fax: (330) 797-2947
Email: jsmith@scity.com
Primary Website: 1000 Hedstrom Drive
Year Established: 1939
Product/Services: In addition to offering traditional circulation and distribution supplies (Home Delivery/Single Copy), Steel City Corp. now offers a digital in-store display; providing publishers an opportunity to increase circulation and advertising revenue .The company also provides circulation marketing ideas via their Gaining Readers and Subscribers Program (G.R.A.S.P).
Note: Circulation Supplies: Home Delivery/Distribution/Single Copy
Personnel: Jim Smith (National Sales Mgr.)
Personnel: Deb Walker (Customer Service)
Personnel: Heather Beasley (Operations Manager)

ASSONET

BARRY FRENCH
Street address 1: 3 Ashlawn Rd
Street address state: MA
Zip/Postal code: 02702-1105
Country: USA
Mailing address: 3 Ashlawn Rd
Mailing city: Assonet
Mailing state: MA
Mailing zip: 02702-1105
General Phone: (508) 644-5772
Email: barryfrench@yahoo.com
Year Established: 1986
Product/Services: Brokers & Appraisers; Consulting Services: Financial;
Note: Brokerage, consulting & appraisals"
Personnel: Barry French (Owner)

ATLANTA

GEORGIA-PACIFIC CORP.
Street address 1: 133 Peachtree St NE
Street address state: GA
Zip/Postal code: 30303-1804
Country: USA
Mailing address: 133 Peachtree St NE Ste 3700
Mailing city: Atlanta
Mailing state: GA
Mailing zip: 30303-1862
General Phone: (404) 652-4000
General Fax: (404) 230-1674
Email: gpfinance@gapac.com
Primary Website: www.gp.com
Year Established: 1927
Product/Services: Photostat: Paper
Personnel: Dave Robertson (Chrmn.)
Personnel: Jim Hannan (Pres./CEO)
Personnel: Simon H. Davies (Pres., Recycled Fibers)
John P. O'Donnell (Pres., N. American Retail Bus.)
Richard G. Urschel (Pres., Chemicals)
Sean R. Fallmann (Pres., Dixie)
Kathleen A. Walters (Exec. Vice Pres., Global Consumer Pdcts.)
Ronald L. Paul (Exec. Vice Pres., Wood Pdcts.)
Sheila M. Weidman (Sr. Vice Pres., Commun. government and Pub. Aff.)
Rob Lorys (Vice Pres., Mktg. Commun.)
Chris Beyer (Dir., Mktg. Servs.)
Gino Biondi (Brand Mktg. Dir., Brawny)
H. James Dallas (Vice Pres., Information Resources/CIO)

MACDERMID GRAPHICS SOLUTIONS
Street address 1: 5210 Phillip Lee Dr SW
Street address state: GA
Zip/Postal code: 30336-2217
Country: USA
Mailing address: 245 Freight St
Mailing city: Atlanta
Mailing state: GA
Mailing zip: 30336
General Phone: (404) 696-4565
General Fax: (404) 699-3354
Email: mpsproductinfo@macdermid.com
Primary Website: www.macdermid.com/companies/macdermid-graphics-solutions
Year Established: 1922
Product/Services: Blanket Mounting and Bars; Blankets; Platemakers: Direct; Platemakers: Flexographic (Computer to Plate); Platemakers: Flexographic (Traditional); Platemakers: Letterpress; Plates: Flexographic (Conventional); Plates: Letterpress; Plates: Offset (Computer to Plate);
Personnel: Scot Benson (Pres.)
Personnel: Steve Racca (V. P. and Gen. Mgr.)

MEDIA AMERICA BROKERS
Street address 1: 1130 Piedmont Ave NE
Street address 2: Apt 912
Street address state: GA
Zip/Postal code: 30309-3783
Country: USA
Mailing address: 1130 Piedmont Ave NE Ste. 912
Mailing city: Atlanta
Mailing state: GA
Mailing zip: 30309-3783
General Phone: (404) 875-8787
Email: lonwwilliams@aol.com
Year Established: 1989
Product/Services: Brokers & Appraisers
Personnel: Lon W Williams (Owner)

NOBLE SYSTEM CORPORATION
Street address 1: 1200 Ashwood Pkwy
Street address 2: Ste 300
Street address state: GA
Zip/Postal code: 30338-4747
Country: USA
Mailing address: 1200 Ashwood Pkwy Ste 300
Mailing city: Atlanta
Mailing state: GA
Mailing zip: 30338-4747
General Phone: (404) 851 1331
General Fax: (404) 851 1421
Email: info@noblesystems.com
Primary Website: www.noblesystems.com
Year Established: 1985
Product/Services: Omnichannel Contact Management Call Center Software Telecommunications
Personnel: Jim Noble Jr (Pres./CEO)
Personnel: Rita Dearing (COO)
Personnel: Jay S. Mayne (CFO)
Mark M. Moore (CTO)
Christopher Saulkner (Vice Pres., Sales/Mktg.)

ONE CORP.
Street address 1: 455 E Paces Ferry Rd NE
Street address 2: Ste 350
Street address state: GA
Zip/Postal code: 30305-3315
Country: USA
Mailing address: 455 E Paces Ferry Rd NE Ste 350
Mailing city: Atlanta
Mailing state: GA
Mailing zip: 30305-3315
General Phone: (404) 842-0111
General Fax: (404) 848-0525
Email: dboles@onecorp.com
Primary Website: www.onecorp.com; www.webpresses.com
Year Established: 1971
Product/Services: Equipment Dealers (New); Equipment Dealers (Used); Web Offset Presses; Flying Pasters; Presses: Offset; Remanufactures Equipment; Splicers, Automatic;
Personnel: Durelle Boles (Pres.)
Personnel: Jennifer Boles (CFO)

PERMA-FIX ENVIRONMENTAL SERVICES
Street address 1: 8302 Dunwoody Pl
Street address 2: Ste 250
Street address state: GA
Zip/Postal code: 30350-3390
Country: USA
Mailing address: 8302 Dunwoody Pl Ste 250
Mailing city: Atlanta
Mailing state: GA
Mailing zip: 30350-3390
General Phone: (770) 587-9898
General Fax: (770) 587-9937
Email: corporate@perma-fix.com
Primary Website: www.perma-fix.com
Year Established: 1989
Product/Services: Environmental Control Systems
Personnel: Lou Centofanti (Pres./CEO)
Personnel: Pam Ittah (Mgr.)

TRANSPORTATION CONSULTANTS, INC.
Street address 1: 8302 Dunwoody Pl
Street address 2: Ste 352
Street address state: GA
Zip/Postal code: 30350-3351
Country: USA
Mailing address: 8302 Dunwoody Pl Ste 352
Mailing city: Atlanta
Mailing state: GA
Mailing zip: 30350-3351
General Phone: (404) 250-0100
General Fax: (404) 250-0253
Email: tci@transpconsult.com
Primary Website: www.transpconsult.com
Year Established: 1981
Product/Services: Consulting Services: Fleet Operations
Personnel: Paul Gold (Pres.)

VERITIV CORPORATION
Street address 1: 400 Northpark Town Center, 1000 Abernathy Road
Street address 2: Suite 1700
Street address state: GA
Zip/Postal code: 30328
Country: USA
Mailing address: 400 Northpark Town Center, 1000 Abernathy Road NE, Building 400, Suite 1700
Mailing city: Atlanta
Mailing state: GA
Mailing zip: 30328
General Phone: (770) 391-8200
Primary Website: www.veritivcorp.com
Year Established: 2014
Product/Services: Cutters & Trimmers; Paper Handling Equipment; Presses: Offset;
Personnel: Mary A. Laschinger (Chairman & CEO)
Personnel: Stephen J. Smith (Sr. V. P. & CFO)
Personnel: John Biscanti (V. P. of Publishing & Print Management)
Thomas S. Lazzaro (Sr. V. P. Field Sales & Operations)

AUBURN

CIRCULATION SOLUTIONS, INC.
Street address 1: 633 Lee Road 51
Street address state: AL
Zip/Postal code: 36832-8318
Country: USA
Mailing address: PO Box 1575
Mailing city: Auburn
Mailing state: AL
Mailing zip: 36831-1575
General Phone: (334) 826-6847
Email: van@circulationsolutions.com
Year Established: 1985
Product/Services: Circulation Equipment & Supplies; Consulting Services: Circulation; Newspaper Marketing;
Note: Marketing Company Dedicated to Newspaper Subscription Sales
Personnel: Van Dozier (Pres.)
Personnel: Wyndol Smith (Sec.)

FOX BAY INDUSTRIES, INC.
Street address 1: 4150 B Pl NW
Street address 2: Ste 101
Street address state: WA
Zip/Postal code: 98001-2449
Country: USA
Mailing address: 4150 B Pl NW Ste 101
Mailing city: Auburn
Mailing state: WA
Mailing zip: 98001-2449
General Phone: (253) 941-9155
General Fax: (253) 941-9197

Equipment, Supplies and Services

Email: info@foxbay.com; sales@foxbay.com
Primary Website: www.foxbay.com
Year Established: 1989
Product/Services: Consulting Services: Ergonomics
Personnel: Ladele Walker (Pres.)
Personnel: Wayne Walker (Sales Mgr.)

FUJIFILM GRAPHIC SYSTEMS USA, INC.

Street address 1: 5103 "D" Street NW
Street address 2: Suite 102
Street address state: WA
Zip/Postal code: 98001
Mailing address: 5103 "D" Street NW, Suite 102
Mailing city: Auburn
Mailing state: WA
Mailing zip: 98001
General Phone: (800) 628-0317
General Fax: (253) 852-4701
Primary Website: www.fujifilmusa.com/products/graphic_arts_printing/index.html
Product/Services: Blankets; Chemicals: Pressroom; Color Management Software; Imagesetters; Inks; Offset Chemicals & Supplies; Platemakers: Flexographic (Computer to Plate); Plates: Offset (Conventional); Proofing Systems; Software: Press/Post Press;
Personnel: Jeffrey Buchman (Reg'l Sales Mgr.)

AURORA

SUNSHINE PAPER CO.

Street address 1: 12601 E 33rd Ave
Street address 2: Ste 109
Street address state: CO
Zip/Postal code: 80011-1839
Country: USA
Mailing address: 12601 E 33rd Ave Ste 109
Mailing city: Aurora
Mailing state: CO
Mailing zip: 80011-1839
General Phone: (303) 341-2990
General Fax: (303) 341-2995
Email: mgallagher@sunshinepaper.com
Primary Website: www.sunshinepaper.com
Year Established: 1983
Product/Services: Calibrated Under-Packing made from Fiber Based, Synthetic, Compressible and Hybrid materials, ParaTex compressible under lay, Plate and Blanket Under-Packing, Offset Blanket Thickness Gauge; Offset Supplies; Ink Jet Papers and Substrates,
Personnel: Michael S. Gallagher (Vice Pres., Sales/Mktg.)
Personnel: Geri Hancock (Adv. Customer Info Serv.)

AUSTIN

BUFFALO TECHNOLOGY INC.

Street address 1: 11100 Metric Blvd
Street address 2: Ste 750
Street address state: TX
Zip/Postal code: 78758-4072
Country: USA
Mailing address: 11100 Metric Blvd Ste 750
Mailing city: Austin
Mailing state: TX
Mailing zip: 78758-4072
General Phone: (512) 349-1580
General Fax: (512) 339-7272
Email: sales@buffalotech.com
Primary Website: www.buffalotech.com
Year Established: 1986
Product/Services: Computers: Hardware & Software Integrators; Computers: Local Area Network (LANS); Computers: Storage Devices;
Personnel: Jay Pechek (PR)

XEROX CORP.

Street address 1: 6336 Austin Center Blvd, Ste.300
Street address state: TX
Zip/Postal code: 78712
Country: USA
Mailing address: 6336 Austin Center Blvd., Ste.300
Mailing city: Austin
Mailing state: TX
Mailing zip: 78729
General Phone: (512) 343-5600
General Fax: (512) 343-5635
Email: marketing@omnifax.xerox.com
Primary Website: www.omnifax.com
Year Established: 1993
Product/Services: Facsimilie/Fax Transmission Systems
Personnel: Erin Hunt (Mgr.)

AVON LAKE

HALL CONTRACTING SERVICES, INC.

Street address 1: 33530 Pin Oak Pkwy.
Street address state: OH
Zip/Postal code: 44012
Country: Avon Lake
Mailing address: 33530 Pin Oak Pkwy.
Mailing city: Avon Lake
Mailing state: OH
Mailing zip: 44012
General Phone: (440) 930-0050
General Fax: (440) 930-0025
Email: hcs@hallcontractingservices.com
Primary Website: www.hallcontractingservices.com
Year Established: 1956
Product/Services: New Press controls;Equipment Dealer (Used); Erectors & Riggers; Press Engineers; Press Rebuilding; Press Repairs; Remanufactures Equipment; Web Width Change mods;
Personnel: Robert Bowers (CEO)
Personnel: Tom Julius (Vice President of Operations)
Personnel: Larry Wojcik (Director of Sales)

BALDWIN

SKO BRENNER AMERICAN

Street address 1: 841 Merrick Rd
Street address 2: # CS9320
Street address state: NY
Zip/Postal code: 11510-3331
Country: USA
Mailing address: 841 Merrick Rd # CS9320
Mailing city: Baldwin
Mailing state: NY
Mailing zip: 11510-3331
General Phone: (516) 771-4400
General Fax: (516) 771-7810
Email: stu@skobrenner.com
Primary Website: www.skobrenner.com
Year Established: 1939
Product/Services: Credit & Collections
Personnel: Stuart Brenner (CEO)
Personnel: Jon R. Lunn (COO)
Personnel: Jim Graziano (Sr. Vice Pres.)

BASINGSTOKE

DEVLIN ELECTRONICS LTD.

Street address 1: Unit A1, Davy Close
Street address 2: Hampshire
Zip/Postal code: RG22 6PW
Country: England
Mailing address: Unit A1, Davy Close, Hampshire
Mailing city: Basingstoke
Mailing zip: RG22 6PW
General Phone: +44 1256 467 367
General Fax: +44 1256 840 048
Email: sales@devlin.co.uk
Primary Website: www.devlin.co.uk
Product/Services: Composing Room Equipment & Supplies; Interfaces;
Personnel: Martin Baker (Mng. Dir.)

BATON ROUGE

LOUISIANA SHERIFF'S ASSOCIATION

Street address 1: 1175 Nicholson Drive
Street address state: LA
Zip/Postal code: 70802
Country: USA
Mailing address: 1175 Nicholson Drive
Mailing city: Baton Rouge
Mailing state: LA
Mailing zip: 70802
General Phone: (225) 343-8402
General Fax: (225) 336-0343
Primary Website: www.lsa.org
Year Established: 1945
Product/Services: Art & Layout Equipment and Services; Consulting Services; Advertising; Editorial; Software: Design/Graphics; Software: Editorial: mobile
Product or Service: Consultants`Editorial`Graphic/Design Firm`Marketing`Other Services`Trade Association
Personnel: Michael Ranatza (Executive Director)
Personnel: Cynthia Butler (Office Manager)
Personnel: Lauren Labbe' Meher (Dir. of Comm. and Pub. Affairs)
Darlene Petty (Accounting)

BEACHWOOD

WEBER SYSTEMS, INC.

Street address 1: 23850 Commerce Park Rd, Ste 108
Street address state: OH
Zip/Postal code: 44122-5829
Country: USA
Mailing address: 23850 Commerce Park Rd., Ste. 108
Mailing city: Beachwood
Mailing state: OH
Mailing zip: 44122-5829
General Phone: (432) 687-5445
General Fax: (432) 687-5445
Primary Website: www.jeffweber.net
Year Established: 1981
Product/Services: Prepress Color Proofing Systems; Storage Retrieval Systems; Computers: Hardware & Software Integrators; Equipment Dealers (New); Equipment Dealers (Used); Software: Pagination/Layout;
Personnel: Jeff Weber (Pres.)

BEAVER DAM

CONLEY PUBLISHING SYSTEMS

Street address 1: 555 Beichl Ave
Street address state: WI
Zip/Postal code: 53916-3110
Country: USA
Mailing address: PO Box 478
Mailing city: Beaver Dam
Mailing state: WI
Mailing zip: 53916-0478
General Phone: (920) 887-3731
General Fax: (920) 887-0439
Email: concept@conleynet.com
Primary Website: www.conleynet.com
Year Established: 1984
Product/Services: Input & Editing Systems; Pagination Systems; Phototypesetting Fonts; Publishing Systems; Software: Advertising (Includes Display; Classified); Software: Design/Graphics; Software: Editorial; Software: Pagination/Layout; Typesetting Programs;
Personnel: James E. Conley (Pres.)

BEDFORD

INTERACTIVE DATA REAL-TIME SERVICES, INC.

Street address 1: 32 Crosby Dr
Street address state: MA
Zip/Postal code: 01730-1448
Country: USA
Mailing address: 32 Crosby Dr
Mailing city: Bedford
Mailing state: MA
Mailing zip: 01730-1448
General Phone: 781-687-8500
General Fax: 781-687-8005
Email: sales.us@interactivedata.com
Primary Website: www.interactivedata-rts.com
Product/Services: Consulting Services: Financial
Personnel: Mark Hopsworth (Pres.)
Personnel: Azriane Carnan (Mktg. Mgr.)

SAXOTECH

Street address 1: 360 Route 101
Street address 2: Ste 1302C
Street address state: NH
Zip/Postal code: 03110-5030
Country: USA
Mailing address: 302 Knights Run Ave Ste 1150
Mailing city: Tampa
Mailing state: FL
Mailing zip: 33602-5974
General Phone: (603) 472-5825
General Fax: (603) 472-3082
Email: ussales@saxotech.com
Primary Website: www.ckp.com; www.saxotech.com
Product/Services: Pagination Systems; Software: Advertising (Includes Display; Classified); Software: Editorial; Software: Pagination/Layout;
Personnel: Pat Stewart (Pres.)
Personnel: Dick Mooney (Mng. Partner/CFO)
Personnel: James Mooney (Vice Pres., Opns.)
Jeff Rapson (Dir., Sales)

BEECHER

HAMILTON CIRCULATION SUPPLIES CO.

Street address 1: 522 Gould St
Street address state: IL
Zip/Postal code: 60401-6662
Country: USA
Mailing address: PO Box 398
Mailing city: Beecher
Mailing state: IL
Mailing zip: 60401-0398
General Phone: 708-946-2208
General Fax: (708) 946-3733
Email: info@hamiltoncirculation.com
Primary Website: www.theservicechamps.com
Year Established: 1965
Product/Services: Adhesives; Circulation Equipment & Supplies; Delivery Equipment; Material Handling Equipment: Pallets & Palletizers; Newspaper Bags; Newspaper Dispensers (Mechanical/Electronic); Newspaper Marketing; Rack Display Cards; Software: Circulation; Tubes, Racks (Includes Racks: Motor Route Tubes); Strapping and Twine. Rubber Bands
Note: Main Products: Rubber Bands, Plastic Bags, Motor Route Tubes & Posts, Hot Dots, Single Copy & POP items. Plus Mailroom Supplies."
Personnel: Joseph M. Beaudry (Pres.)
Personnel: Thomas P. Hamilton (Vice Pres.)
Personnel: Susan Beaudry (Vice Pres.)
Carrie Dolan (Administration)

BELCAMP

BOTTCHER AMERICA CORP.

Street address 1: 4600 Mercedes Dr
Street address state: MD
Zip/Postal code: 21017-1223
Country: USA
Mailing address: 4600 Mercedes Dr
Mailing city: Belcamp
Mailing state: MD

Equipment, Supplies and Services

Mailing zip: 21017-1225
General Phone: (800) 637-8120
General Fax: (410) 273-7174
Email: support@boettcher-systems.com
Primary Website: www.bottcher.com
Product/Services: Rollers
Personnel: Jeff Hoover

BELLEVUE

SMARTFOCUS INC.

Street address 1: 13810 SE Eastgate Way
Street address 2: Suite 550
Street address state: WA
Zip/Postal code: 98005
Country: USA
Mailing address: 13810 SE Eastgate Way, Suite 550
Mailing city: Bellevue
Mailing state: WA
Mailing zip: 98005
General Phone: (425) 460-1000
Primary Website: www.smartfocus.com
Year Established: 1998
Product/Services: Consulting Services: Advertising; Consulting Services: Circulation; Consulting Services: Computer; Consulting Services: Marketing; Marketing Database Design and Implementation; Software: Circulation; Training: Sales & Marketing
Product or Service: Online Service Provider and Internet Hosts
Personnel: Chris Allan (CEO)
Personnel: Jamie Gunn (COO)

BELVIDERE

BOB RAY & ASSOCIATES, INC.

Street address 1: 3575 Morreim Dr
Street address state: IL
Zip/Postal code: 61008-6307
Country: USA
Mailing address: 3575 Morreim Dr
Mailing city: Belvidere
Mailing state: IL
Mailing zip: 61008-6307
General Phone: (815) 547-9393
General Fax: (815) 547-5572
Email: chuck@bobray.com
Primary Website: www.bobray.com
Year Established: 1988
Personnel: Chuck Britton (Pres.)
Personnel: Nolen G. Lee (Vice Pres., Admin.)
Personnel: John R. Steker (Vice Pres., Sales)
John F. Nicoli (Technical Sales Mgr.)

FRANKLIN WIRE WORKS, INC.

Street address 1: 910 E Lincoln Ave
Street address state: IL
Zip/Postal code: 61008-2928
Country: USA
Mailing address: 910 E Lincoln Ave
Mailing city: Belvidere
Mailing state: IL
Mailing zip: 61008-2928
General Phone: (815) 544-6676
General Fax: (815) 547-5536
Primary Website: www.franklindisplay.com
Year Established: 1978
Product/Services: Circulation Equipment & Supplies
Personnel: Dick Boyett (Sales Mgr.)

BEND

BELLATRIX SYSTEMS, INC.

Street address 1: 1015 SW Emkay Dive
Street address state: OR
Zip/Postal code: 97702
Country: USA
Mailing address: 1015 SW Emkay Dr
Mailing city: Bend
Mailing state: OR
Mailing zip: 97702-1010
General Phone: (541) 382-2208

General Fax: (541) 385-3277
Email: frontoffice@bellatrix.net
Primary Website: www.bellatrix.com
Year Established: 1987
Product/Services: Circulation Equipment & Supplies; Electronic Coin Totalizers for Newspaper Vending machines, Credit Card Systems for newspaper vending machines
Personnel: Steve Morris (President and CEO)
Personnel: William Raven (Sr. Vice Pres., Sales/Mktg.)

WESTERN ROLLER CORP.

Street address 1: 63393 Nels Anderson Rd
Street address state: OR
Zip/Postal code: 97701-5743
Country: USA
Mailing address: 63393 Nels Anderson Rd
Mailing city: Bend
Mailing state: OR
Mailing zip: 97701-5743
General Phone: (541) 382-5643
General Fax: (541) 382-0159
Primary Website: www.westernroller.com
Year Established: 1972
Product/Services: Delivery Equipment; Mailroom Systems & Equipment; Web Press - Special Equipment;
Personnel: Doug Collver (Owner)

BERRIEN SPRINGS

INTERLINK

Street address 1: 9046 US Highway 31
Street address 2: Ste 7
Street address state: MI
Zip/Postal code: 49103-1698
Country: USA
Mailing address: PO Box 207
Mailing city: Berrien Springs
Mailing state: MI
Mailing zip: 49103-0207
General Phone: (269) 473-3103
General Fax: (206) 984-2240
Email: info@ilsw.com
Primary Website: www.ilsw.com
Year Established: 1980
Product/Services: Software: Circulation Management. Software: Advertising Billing (Includes Display; Classified)
Note: Circulation-management software provider for community newspapers.
Personnel: William E. Garber (Founder)
Personnel: Bradley Hill (President)

BIRMINGHAM

WOLK ADVERTISING, INC. (RETAIL CARPET AD SERVICE)

Street address 1: 920 E Lincoln St
Street address state: MI
Zip/Postal code: 48009-3608
Country: USA
Mailing address: 920 E Lincoln St
Mailing city: Birmingham
Mailing state: MI
Mailing zip: 48009-3608
General Phone: (248) 540-5980
Email: wolkadv@earthlink.net
Primary Website: www.flooringads.com
Year Established: 1954
Product/Services: Art & Layout Equipment and Services; Consulting Services: Advertising; Training: Design & Layout;
Personnel: Erv Wolk (Pres.)

BIXBY

DUNNING PHOTO EQUIPMENT, INC.

Street address 1: 605 W Needles Ave
Street address state: OK
Zip/Postal code: 74008-4131
Country: USA
Mailing address: 605 W Needles Ave
Mailing city: Bixby
Mailing state: OK

Mailing zip: 74008-4131
General Phone: (918) 366-4917
General Fax: (918) 366-4918
Email: ernie@dunningphoto.com
Primary Website: www.dunningphoto.com
Year Established: 1955
Product/Services: Dark Room Equipment; Processors: Film & Paper;
Personnel: Ernie Dunning (Pres.)

BLISSFIELD

SAXMAYER CORP.

Street address 1: 318 W Adrian St
Street address state: MI
Zip/Postal code: 49228-1205
Country: USA
Mailing address: PO Box 10
Mailing city: Blissfield
Mailing state: MI
Mailing zip: 49228-0010
General Phone: (517) 486-2164
General Fax: (517) 486-2055
Email: info@saxmayercorp.com
Primary Website: www.erichbaumeister.com
Year Established: 1912
Product/Services: Newsprint Handling Equipment; Strapping Machines;
Personnel: Michael Vennekotter (Pres., Mktg./Sales)
Personnel: James Fischer (Vice Pres., Engineering/Mfg.)
Personnel: Jeremy Sell (Process Supvr., Information Technology)

BLOOMINGTON

NEWSCYCLE SOLUTIONS

Street address 1: 7900 International Dr
Street address 2: Ste 800
Street address state: MN
Zip/Postal code: 55425-1581
Country: USA
Mailing address: 7900 International Drive Suite 800
Mailing city: Bloomington
Mailing state: MN
Mailing zip: 55425
General Phone: 651-639-0662
Email: info@newscycle.com
Primary Website: www.newscycle.com
Product/Services: Software: Advertising (Includes Display; Classified); Software: Circulation; Software: Design/Graphics; Software: Editorial; Software: Pagination/Layout;
Product or Service: Circulation`Consultants`Editorial`Hardware/Software Supplier`Multimedia/Interactive Products`Online Service Provider and Internet Hosts`Publisher/Media
Note: Newscycle Solutions, which was formed by the combination of DTI, SAXOTECH, Atex AdBase and MediaSpan, delivers the most complete range of software solutions for the global news media industry, including news content management, advertising, circulation, audience, and analytics. Newscycle is a trusted technology partner serving more than 1,200 media companies with 8,000 properties across more than 30 countries on six continents. The company is headquartered in Bloomington, MN and has U.S. offices in Florida, Michigan and Utah; with international offices in Australia, Canada, Denmark, Germany, Malaysia, Norway, Sweden, and the United Kingdom. For more information, go to: http://www.newscycle.com.
Personnel: Paul Mrozinski (Sales Director)
Personnel: John Pukas (VP., Business Relations)
Personnel: Steve Moon (Rgl. Sales Dir.)
Marc Thompson (Rgl. Sales Dir.)
Lisa Speth (Marketing Communications Mgr.)
Bryan Hooley (Asia-Pacific Bus. Mgr.)
Ken Freedman (Vice President of Market Development)
Pete Marsh (Vice President of Marketing)

Julie Maas (Sales Director)
Chris McKee (Sales Director)
Mike McLaughlin (Sales Director)
Geoff Kehrer (Sales Engineer)
Robert Bohlin (Executive Sales Director, EMEA)

NEWSCYCLE SOLUTIONS

Street address 1: 7900 International Drive
Street address 2: Suite 800
Street address state: MN
Zip/Postal code: 55425-1581
Country: USA
Mailing address: 7900 International Dr Ste 800
Mailing city: Minneapolis
Mailing state: MN
Mailing zip: 55425-1581
General Phone: (651) 639-0662
General Fax: (651) 639-0306
Email: Info@newscycle.com
Primary Website: www.newscycle.com
Year Established: 2013
Product/Services: Software: Advertising (Includes Display; Classified); Software: Business (Includes Administration/Accounting); Software: Circulation;
Personnel: Scott Roessler (CEO)
Personnel: Dan Paulus (Chief Revenue Officer)
Personnel: Jeff Neunsinger (CFO)
Bill Mercer (Executive VP of Services and Support)
Patrick Glennon (Executive VP Subscriber Platform)

BLOOMSBURG

PRESS-ENTERPRISE, INC. (COLOR GRAPHICS DEPT.)

Street address 1: 3185 Lackawanna Ave
Street address state: PA
Zip/Postal code: 17815-3329
Country: USA
Mailing address: 3185 Lackawanna Ave
Mailing city: Bloomsburg
Mailing state: PA
Mailing zip: 17815-3398
General Phone: (570) 784-2121
General Fax: (570) 784-9226
Primary Website: www.pressenterpriseonline.com
Year Established: 1902
Product/Services: Color Proofing; Color Seperations, Positives; Electronic Pre-Scan Systems; Input & Editing Systems;
Personnel: Bill Bason (Prodn. Mgr., Color Graphics)

BLUE BELL

UNISYS CORP.

Street address 1: 801 Lakeview Drive
Street address 2: Ste 100
Street address state: PA
Zip/Postal code: 19422
Country: USA
Mailing address: 801 Lakeview Drive, Ste 100
Mailing city: Blue Bell
Mailing state: PA
Mailing zip: 19422
General Phone: (215) 274-2742
Primary Website: www.unisys.com
Year Established: 1986
Product/Services: Archiving Systems; Computers: Hardware & Software Integrators; Electronic Ad Delivery; Software: Advertising (Includes Display; Classified); Software: Business (Includes Administration/Accounting); Software: Editorial; Software: Pagination/Layout; Software: Workflow Management/Tracking; System Integration Services;
Product or Service: Hardware/Software Supplier
Personnel: Maria Allen (Vice Pres. and Global Head of Financial Services)
Personnel: Lakshmi Ashok (CTO)
Personnel: Mark Cohn (CTO)

BOCA RATON

DUNHILL INTERNATIONAL LIST CO.,

Equipment, Supplies and Services

INC.
Street address 1: 6400 Congress Ave
Street address 2: Ste 1750
Street address state: FL
Zip/Postal code: 33487-2898
Country: USA
Mailing address: 6400 Congress Ave Ste 1750
Mailing city: Boca Raton
Mailing state: FL
Mailing zip: 33487-2898
General Phone: (561) 998-7800
General Fax: (561) 998-7880
Email: dunhill@dunhillintl.com
Primary Website: www.dunhills.com
Year Established: 1938
Product/Services: Mailing List Compiler Mailing List Broker Email List Broker
Personnel: Robert Dunhill (Pres.)
Personnel: Candy Dunhill (Vice Pres.)
Personnel: Cindy Dunhill (Vice Pres.)

SALES TRAINING CONSULTANTS, INC.
Street address 1: 5550 Glades Rd
Street address 2: Ste 515
Street address state: FL
Zip/Postal code: 33431-7205
Country: USA
Mailing address: 5550 Glades Rd Ste 515
Mailing city: Boca Raton
Mailing state: FL
Mailing zip: 33431
General Phone: (561) 482-8801
Email: akemper@salestrainingconsultants.com
Primary Website: www.newspapertraining.com
Year Established: 1983
Product/Services: Training: Sales, Leadership, Subscription Retention (Stopbusters), Customer Service
Note: Newspaper Training Experts Since 1983
Personnel: Alice Kemper (Pres.)
Personnel: Diane Rossi (Consultant/Trainer)
Personnel: Denise Zagnoli (Consultant/Trainer)
Margo Berman (Consultant/Trainer)
Ed Baron (Consultant/Trainer)
Anne Stein (Consultant/Trainer)

BOHEMIA

FLEXOGRAPHIC TECHNICAL ASSOCIATION
Street address 1: 3920 Veterans Memorial Hwy
Street address 2: Ste 9
Street address state: NY
Zip/Postal code: 11716-1074
Country: USA
Mailing address: 3920 Veterans Memorial Hwy Ste 9
Mailing city: Bohemia
Mailing state: NY
Mailing zip: 11716-1074
General Phone: (631) 737-6020
General Fax: (631) 737-6813
Email: membership@flexography.org
Primary Website: www.flexography.org
Year Established: 1958
Product/Services: Trade Publications; Training: Post Press; Training: Pre Press; Training: Press Operation & Maintenance;
Note: Technical association for the flexographic printing industry
Personnel: Mark Cisternino (Pres.)
Personnel: Robert Moran (Pub., FLEXO Mag.)
Personnel: Jay Kaible (Membership & Buss. Dev. Dir.)
Joe Tuccitto (Education Director)
Eileen Cosma (Marketing Manager)

BOLTON

MARATEK ENVIRONMENTAL TECHNOLOGIES, INC.
Street address 1: 60 Healey Rd
Street address 2: Unit 8-10
Street address state: ON
Zip/Postal code: L7E 5A6
Country: Canada
Mailing address: 60 Healey Rd., Unit 8-10
Mailing city: Bolton
Mailing state: ON
Mailing zip: L7E 5A5
General Phone: (905) 857-2738
Email: sales@maratek.com
Primary Website: www.maratek.com
Year Established: 1968
Product/Services: Environmental Control Systems; Equipment Dealers (New); Fluid Handeling: Pressroom; Ink Recovery Systems; Silver Recovery; Wastewater Treatment; Solvent Recovery Systems;
Personnel: Colin Darcel (Owner/Pres.)

SAPPI FINE PAPER NORTH AMERICA
Street address 1: 255 State St
Street address 2: Fl 4
Street address state: MA
Zip/Postal code: 02109-2618
Country: USA
Mailing address: 255 State St Fl 4
Mailing city: Boston
Mailing state: MA
Mailing zip: 02109-2618
General Phone: (617) 423-7300
General Fax: (617) 423-5494
Email: info@sappi.com
Primary Website: www.sappi.com
Product/Services: Paper: Coated Groundwood Offset; Paper: Groundwood Specialties; Paper: Specialty Printing Paper; Photostat: Paper;
Personnel: Mark Gardner (Pres./CEO)
Personnel: Annette Luchene (Vice Pres., Finance/CFO)
Personnel: Bob Forsberg (Vice Pres., Sales)

TELETYPE CO.
Street address 1: 20 Park Plz
Street address state: MA
Zip/Postal code: 02116-4303
Country: USA
Mailing address: 20 Park Plz
Mailing city: Boston
Mailing state: MA
Mailing zip: 02116-4303
General Phone: (617) 542-6220
General Fax: (617) 542-6289
Email: info@teletype.com
Primary Website: www.teletype.com
Year Established: 1981
Product/Services: Publishing Systems
Personnel: Marlene Winer (Mktg. Mgr.)
Personnel: Edward Freeman (Mktg. Mgr.)

BOULDER

SPECTRA LOGIC
Street address 1: 1700 55th St
Street address state: CO
Zip/Postal code: 80301-2974
Country: USA
Mailing address: 6285 Lookout Rd # 100
Mailing city: Boulder
Mailing state: CO
Mailing zip: 80301-3318
General Phone: (303) 449-6400
General Fax: (303) 939-8844
Email: sales@spectralogic.com
Primary Website: www.spectralogic.com
Year Established: 1979
Product/Services: Computers: Hardware & Software Integrators; Library Retrieval Systems;
Personnel: Molly Rector (Dir., Cor. Mktg.)

BOYNTON BEACH

EPUBLISH4ME
Street address 1: 1375 Gateway Blvd
Street address state: FL
Zip/Postal code: 33426-8304
Country: USA
Mailing address: 1375 Gateway Blvd
Mailing city: Boynton Beach
Mailing state: FL
Mailing zip: 33426-8304
General Phone: (561) 370-3336
Email: sales@epublish4me.com
Primary Website: www.epublish4me.com
Product/Services: Advertising
Product or Service: Advertising/Marketing Agency`Graphic/Design Firm`Multimedia/Interactive Products`Online Service Provider and Internet Hosts`Publisher/Media
Note: Digitize your pubs at http://www.epublish4me.com/?r=403. It automatically posts them on TitleStand where you can sell them by getting local and worldwide distribution (see http://titlestand.com/t). Your PDFs are converted into digital 3-D page flipping revenue generator books, newspapers or magazines with video, audio, hyperlinks and extensive tracking where they can be read on Tablet, PC, Mac, iPad, iPhone, iTouch, iOS, Android and Kindle Fire. Kind regards, Nick.Koriakin@ ePublish4me.com 561-370-3336
Personnel: Nicholas Koriakin (Senior Account Executive)

BRADENTON

IPC
Street address 1: 618 148th Ct NE
Street address state: FL
Zip/Postal code: 34212-5596
Country: USA
Mailing address: 618 148TH CT. N.E.
Mailing city: BRADENTON
Mailing state: FL
Mailing zip: 34212
General Phone: (941) 484-3622
General Fax: 877-290-7176
Email: charlie@ipcpoly.com
Primary Website: www.ipcpoly.com
Year Established: 1995
Product/Services: Newspaper Poly Bags, RACKS & Supplies, Single Copy Items, PROMOTIONAL ITEMS, Twine, Rubber Bands, Business Cards
Note: GREAT PROMOTIONAL TUMBLERS FOR FUNDRAISING AND GIFTS
Personnel: Charlie Hencye (Pres.)
Personnel: Cheryl Hencye (Asst. Mgr.)

BRANSON

NATIONAL MEDIA ASSOCIATES
Street address 1: PO Box 2001
Street address state: MO
Zip/Postal code: 65615-2001
Country: USA
Mailing address: PO Box 2001
Mailing city: Branson
Mailing state: MO
Mailing zip: 65615-2001
General Phone: (417) 338-6397
General Fax: (417) 338-6510
Email: Brokered1@gmail.com
Primary Website: www.nationalmediasales.com
Year Established: 1997
Product/Services: Brokers & Appraisers; Consulting Services: Financial;
Personnel: Edward M. Anderson (Owner)

BRONX

INDUSTRIAL ACOUSTICS CO.
Street address 1: 1160 Commerce Ave
Street address state: NY
Zip/Postal code: 10462-5537
Country: USA
Mailing address: 1160 Commerce Ave
Mailing city: Bronx
Mailing state: NY
Mailing zip: 10462-5537
General Phone: (718) 931-8000
General Fax: (718) 863-1138
Email: newyork@iac-acoustics.com
Primary Website: www.industrialacoustics.com
Year Established: 1949
Product/Services: Environmental Control Systems
Personnel: Kenneth Delasho (Pres.)

BRONXVILLE

LISSOM CORP. INC.
Street address 1: Pondfield Rd W
Street address state: NY
Zip/Postal code: 10708
Country: USA
Mailing address: PO Box 441
Mailing city: Bronxville
Mailing state: NY
Mailing zip: 10708
General Phone: (914) 761-6360
Email: hank@weboffsetpress.com
Primary Website: www.weboffsetpress.com
Year Established: 1981
Product/Services: Presses: Web Offset
Note: Web Offset Presses & Auxiliary Equipment
Personnel: Hank Damhuis

BROOKLYN

HERMAN H. STICHT CO., INC.
Street address 1: 45 Main St
Street address 2: Ste 701
Street address state: NY
Zip/Postal code: 11201-1075
Country: USA
Mailing address: 45 Main St Ste 401
Mailing city: Brooklyn
Mailing state: NY
Mailing zip: 11201-1084
General Phone: (718) 852-7602
General Fax: (718) 852-7915
Email: stichtco@aol.com
Primary Website: www.stichtco.com
Year Established: 1917
Product/Services: Static Eliminators
Personnel: Paul H. Plotkin (Pres.)

BROOKLYN CENTER

FUJIFILM GRAPHIC SYSTEMS USA, INC.
Street address 1: 4001 Lakebreeze Avenue N.
Street address 2: Ste 400
Street address state: MN
Zip/Postal code: 554429-3844
Country: USA
Mailing address: 4001 Lakebreeze Avenue N., Ste 400
Mailing city: Brooklyn Center
Mailing state: MN
Mailing zip: 554429-3844
General Phone: (651) 855-6000
General Fax: (651) 855-6025
Primary Website: www.fujifilmusa.com/products/graphic_arts_printing/index.html
Product/Services: Blankets; Chemicals: Pressroom; Color Management Software; Imagesetters; Inks; Offset Chemicals & Supplies; Platemakers: Flexographic (Computer to Plate); Plates: Offset (Conventional); Proofing Systems; Software: Press/Post Press;
Personnel: Jamie Walsh (Reg'l Sales Mgr.)

BROOKLYN PARK

BURGESS INDUSTRIES, INC.
Street address 1: 7500 Boone Ave N
Street address 2: Ste 111
Street address state: MN
Zip/Postal code: 55428-1026
Country: USA
Mailing address: 7500 Boone Ave N Ste 111
Mailing city: Brooklyn Park
Mailing state: MN

Mailing zip: 55428-1026
General Phone: (763) 553-7800
General Fax: (763) 553-9289
Email: djburgess@burgessind.com
Primary Website: www.burgessind.com
Year Established: 1977
Product/Services: Color Proofing; Color Registration; Controls: Exposure; Controls: Register; Light Integrators; Plate Bending Systems; Plate Mounting & Register Systems; Proofing Systems; Static Eliminators; Vacuum Frames
Personnel: Dennis Burgess (Pres./CEO)
Personnel: Joe Stein (Nat'l Pdct. Mgr.)
Personnel: Richard Fream (Nat'l Sales Dir.)

BRYAN

INGERSOLL-RAND-ARO FLUID PRODUCT DIV.

Street address 1: 1 Aro Ctr
Street address state: OH
Zip/Postal code: 43506-1100
Country: USA
Mailing address: PO Box 151
Mailing city: Bryan
Mailing state: OH
Mailing zip: 43506-0151
General Phone: (419) 636-4242
General Fax: (419) 633-1674
Email: arowebleads@irco.com
Primary Website: www.ingersollrandproducts.com
Year Established: 1930
Product/Services: Ink Bleeding Equipment; Ink Pumping Systems; Pumps (Air, Ink, Vacuum);
Personnel: Herbert L. Henkel (Chrmn./Pres.)

BUFFALO

HFW INDUSTRIES

Street address 1: 196 Philadelphia St
Street address state: NY
Zip/Postal code: 14207-1734
Country: USA
Mailing address: PO Box 8
Mailing city: Buffalo
Mailing state: NY
Mailing zip: 14207-0008
General Phone: (716) 875-3380
General Fax: (716) 875-3385
Primary Website: www.hfwindustries.com
Year Established: 1940
Product/Services: Cylinder reconditioning
Personnel: John Watson (Pres.)
Personnel: Ron Jurewicz (Manufacturing Manager)

BURBANK

COMMODITY RESOURCE & ENVIRONMENT

Street address 1: 116 E Prospect Ave
Street address state: CA
Zip/Postal code: 91502-2035
Country: USA
Mailing address: 116 E Prospect Ave
Mailing city: Burbank
Mailing state: CA
Mailing zip: 91502-2035
General Phone: (818) 843-2811
General Fax: (818) 843-2862
Email: info@creweb.com
Primary Website: www.creweb.com
Year Established: 1980
Product/Services: Hazardous Waste Disposal Services; Silver Recovery
Personnel: Larry Dewitt (Pres.)

BURLINGTON

NUANCE COMMUNICATIONS INC.

Street address 1: 1 Wayside Rd
Street address state: MA
Zip/Postal code: 01803-4609
Country: USA
Mailing address: 1 Wayside Rd
Mailing city: Burlington
Mailing state: MA
Mailing zip: 01803-4609
General Phone: (781) 565-5000
General Fax: (781) 565-5001
Email: info@dragonsys.com
Primary Website: www.nuance.com
Year Established: 1982
Product/Services: Speech Recognition
Personnel: Renee Blodgett (Mgr., Cor. Commun.)
Personnel: Paul Ricci (Chrmn./CEO)
Personnel: Thomas Beaudoin (Exec. Vice Pres./CFO)
Richard Palmer (Sr. Vice Pres., Cor. Devel.)
Robert Weideman (Sr. Vice Pres., Mktg.)
Rick Broyles (Vice Pres., Opns.)
Steve Chambers (Sr. Vice Pres., Worldwide Sales)
Dawn Howarth (Vice Pres., HR)

SAMUEL, SON & CO.

Street address 1: 735 Oval Crt
Street address state: ON
Zip/Postal code: L7L 6A9
Country: Canada
Mailing address: 735 Oval Ct.
Mailing city: Burlington
Mailing state: ON
Mailing zip: L7L 6A9
General Phone: (905) 279-9580
General Fax: (905) 639-2290
Email: packaging@samuel.com
Primary Website: www.goval.com
Year Established: 1855
Product/Services: Baling Machines; Bundling and Tying Machines; Conveyors; Counting, Stacking, Bundling Machines; Flooring; Mailroom Systems & Equipment; Roll Handling Equipment; Strapping Machines;
Personnel: Kevin McEldowney (U.S. Manager of Inside Sales and Administration)

CAMAS

AMERICAN CONSULTING SERVICES

Street address 1: 440 NE 4th Ave
Street address state: WA
Zip/Postal code: 98607-2173
Country: USA
Mailing address: 440 NE 4th Ave
Mailing city: Camas
Mailing state: WA
Mailing zip: 98607-2173
General Phone: (800) 597-9798
General Fax: (360) 833-4620
Email: info@toma.com
Primary Website: www.toma.com
Year Established: 1985
Product/Services: Consulting Services: Advertising
Personnel: Mark Rood (Pres.)
Personnel: Kate Rood (Office Manager)
Personnel: Shirley Jones (Research Manager)

CAMP HILL

WILSON GREGORY AGENCY, INC.

Street address 1: 2309 Market St
Street address state: PA
Zip/Postal code: 17011-4627
Country: USA
Mailing address: PO Box 8
Mailing city: Camp Hill
Mailing state: PA
Mailing zip: 17001-0008
General Phone: (717) 730-9777
General Fax: (717) 730-9328
Email: info@wilsongregory.com
Primary Website: www.wilsongregory.com
Year Established: 1923
Product/Services: Consulting Services: Circulation; Insurance;
Personnel: Ted Gregory (Chrmn./CEO)
Personnel: Richard Hively (Pres.)
Personnel: Todd Gregory (Vice Pres.)
Mark Gregory (Vice Pres., Opns.)

CANTON

GO PLASTICS/STREETSMART LLC

Street address 1: 515 Brown Industrial Pkwy
Street address state: GA
Zip/Postal code: 30114-8013
Country: USA
Mailing address: 515 Brown Industrial Pkwy
Mailing city: Canton
Mailing state: GA
Mailing zip: 30114-8013
General Phone: 866-366-6166
General Fax: 877-894-9966
Email: brianb@goplastics.com
Primary Website: www.goplastics.com
Year Established: 1987
Product/Services: Circulation Equipment & Supplies; Newspaper Dispensers (Mechanical/Electronic);
Personnel: Brian Bauman (Dir.-Sales/Mktg.)
Personnel: Michelle Gollob (Adv. Customer Info Serv.)

CARLSBAD

SCHUR PACKAGING SYSTEMS, INC.

Street address 1: 3200 Lionshead Ave
Street address 2: Suite 110
Street address state: CA
Zip/Postal code: 92010
Country: USA
Mailing address: 3200 Lionshead Ave, Suite 110
Mailing city: Carlsbad
Mailing state: CA
Mailing zip: 92010
General Phone: (760) 421-6404
Email: schurstarusa@schur.com
Primary Website: www.schur.com
Year Established: 2003
Product/Services: Mailroom Systems & Equipment;
Personnel: Magnus Wall (Parts/Serv. Dir.)
Personnel: Dan Kemper (President)
Personnel: Gert Jensen (Technical Sales Dir.)

CARLSTADT

BETA SCREEN CORP.

Street address 1: 707 Commercial Ave
Street address state: NJ
Zip/Postal code: 07072-2602
Country: USA
Mailing address: 707 Commercial Ave
Mailing city: Carlstadt
Mailing state: NJ
Mailing zip: 07072-2602
General Phone: (201) 939-2400
General Fax: (201) 939-7656
Email: info@betascreen.com
Primary Website: www.betascreen.com
Year Established: 1958
Product/Services: Calibration Software/Hardware; Color Proofing; Color Viewing Equipment; Dark Room Equipment; Densitometers; Gauges, Measuring; Layout Tables, Light Tables & Workstations; Optical Products; Static Eliminators; Tables (Dot, Etch, Opaquing, Register, Retouching, Stripping)
Personnel: Arnold Serchuk (Pres.)
Personnel: Larry Goldberg (Contact)

PANTONE, INC.

Street address 1: 590 Commerce Blvd
Street address state: NJ
Zip/Postal code: 07072-3013
Country: USA
Mailing address: 590 Commerce Blvd
Mailing city: Carlstadt
Mailing state: NJ
Mailing zip: 07072-3098
General Phone: (201) 935-5500
General Fax: (201) 935-3338
Email: support@pantone.com
Primary Website: www.pantone.com
Year Established: 1962
Product/Services: Color Management Software; Software: Design/Graphics;
Personnel: Ron Potesky (Pres.)

CAROLINA

MOTTERSTITCH COMPANY, INC.

Street address 1: 220 Richmond Townhouse Rd
Street address state: RI
Zip/Postal code: 02812-1106
Country: USA
Mailing address: P.O. Box 97
Mailing city: Carolina
Mailing state: RI
Mailing zip: 02812
General Phone: (401)364-6061
General Fax: (401)364-6063
Email: tom@motterstitch.com
Primary Website: www.motterstitch.com
Year Established: 1985
Product/Services: In-Line Stapling/Stitching Machine for Newspaper and Commercial Press, Stitching Wire Sales
Note: Custom In-Line High Speed Stapling/Stitching Machines for Newspaper and Commercial Press and Stitching Wire Sales
Personnel: Thomas Northup (President)
Personnel: Linda Northup (Office Admin.)
Personnel: Roland Reuterfors (Consultant)
Bengt Magnusson (Consultant Engineer)
David Mr. Gilman (Chief Engineer)
Adam Mr. Northup (Office Assist.)
Cheryl Mrs. Bernat (Secretary)
David Northup (Sales VP)

CARY

LORENTZEN & WETTRE

Street address 1: 305 Gregson Drive
Street address state: NC
Zip/Postal code: 27511
Country: USA
Mailing address: 305 Gregson Drive
Mailing city: Cary
Mailing state: NC
Mailing zip: 27511
General Phone: 919 653 0840
Email: contact.center@us.abb.com
Primary Website: www.lorentzen-wettre.com
Year Established: 1980
Product/Services: Consulting Services: Production; Maintenance, Plant & Equipment; Paper Testing Instruments;
Personnel: Phillip Westmoreland (Pres.)

CEDAR RAPIDS

DECISIONMARK CORP.

Street address 1: 818 Dows Rd
Street address state: IA
Zip/Postal code: 52403-7000
Country: USA
Mailing address: 818 Dows Rd Ste 100
Mailing city: Cedar Rapids
Mailing state: IA
Mailing zip: 52403-7000
General Phone: (319) 365-5597
General Fax: (319) 365-5694
Email: sales@decisionmark.com
Primary Website: www.decisionmark.com
Year Established: 1993
Product/Services: Software: Advertising (Includes Display; Classified); Software: Circulation; Software: Editorial;
Personnel: Jack Perry (Pres./CEO)
Personnel: Mick Rinehart (Vice Pres., Pdct. Devel.)
Personnel: Herb Skoog (Vice Pres., Opns.)

THE GAZETTE COMPANY

Street address 1: 501 2nd Ave SE
Street address state: IA
Zip/Postal code: 52401-1303
Country: USA
Mailing address: 501 2nd Ave SE

Mailing city: Cedar Rapids
Mailing state: IA
Mailing zip: 52401-1303
General Phone: (319) 398-8422
General Fax: (319) 368-8505
Email: customercare@thegazettecompany.com
Primary Website: www.thegazettecompany.com
Year Established: 1981
Product or Service: Multimedia/Interactive Products'Publisher/Media
Personnel: Joe Hadky (Chrmn.)
Personnel: Chuck Peters (President and CEO)
Personnel: Chris Edwards (VP Sales & Marketing)

CEDARTOWN

THE NEWARK GROUP

Street address 1: 312 E Ellawood Ave
Street address state: GA
Zip/Postal code: 30125-3902
Country: USA
Mailing address: 312 E Ellawood Ave
Mailing city: Cedartown
Mailing state: GA
Mailing zip: 30125-3902
General Phone: (770) 748-3715
General Fax: (770) 748-7414
Product/Services: Newsprint Handeling Equipment
Personnel: Mickey Thompson (Vice Pres.)
Personnel: Randy Tillery (Sales Mgr.)

CENTER VALLEY

OLYMPUS AMERICA, INC.

Street address 1: 3500 Corporate Pkwy
Street address state: PA
Zip/Postal code: 18034-8229
Country: USA
Mailing address: 3500 Corporate Pkwy
Mailing city: Center Valley
Mailing state: PA
Mailing zip: 18034-8229
General Phone: (888) 553-4448
General Fax: (484) 896-7115
Primary Website: www.olympusamerica.com
Year Established: 1977
Product/Services: Cameras & Audio; Medical & Surgical Components; Industrial Microscopes; Aerospace; Automotive; Oil & Gas;
Personnel: Michael C. Woodford (CEO & Pres.)
Personnel: Karl Watanabe (Pres. & CFO)
Personnel: Stephanie Sherry (Executive Director)

CENTERBROOK

ESSEX PRODUCTS GROUP

Street address 1: 30 Industrial Park Rd
Street address state: CT
Zip/Postal code: 06409-1019
Country: USA
Mailing address: 30 Industrial Park Rd
Mailing city: Centerbrook
Mailing state: CT
Mailing zip: 06409-1019
General Phone: (800) 394-7130
General Fax: (860) 767-9137
Email: sales@epg-inc.com
Primary Website: www.epg-inc.com
Year Established: 1951
Product/Services: Ink Controls, Computerized
Personnel: Peter Griffin (Pres.)
Personnel: Matt Strand (Operations Mgr.)

CHALFONT

JBT CORPORATION (FORMERLY FMC TECHNOLOGIES)

Street address 1: 400 Highpoint Dr
Street address state: PA
Zip/Postal code: 18914-3924
Country: USA
Mailing address: 400 Highpoint Dr
Mailing city: Chalfont
Mailing state: PA
Mailing zip: 18914-3924
General Phone: (215) 822-4600
General Fax: (215) 822-4553
Email: sgv.sales@jbtc.com
Primary Website: www.jbtc-agv.com
Year Established: 1920
Product/Services: Material Handling Equipment: Automatic Guided Vehicles; Newsprint Handling Equipment; Paper Handling Equipment; Roll Handling Equipment; Roll Preparation Equipment; Software: Workflow Management/Tracking; System Integration Services;
Personnel: Mark Longacre (Mktg. Mgr.)

CHARLOTTE

ARC INTERNATIONAL

Street address 1: 10955 Withers Cove Park Dr
Street address state: NC
Zip/Postal code: 28278-0020
Country: USA
Mailing address: 10955 Withers Cove Park Dr
Mailing city: Charlotte
Mailing state: NC
Mailing zip: 28278-0020
General Phone: (704) 588-1809
General Fax: (704) 588-9921
Primary Website: www.arcinternational.com
Year Established: 1984
Product/Services: Cleaners & Solvents; Platemakers: Flexographic (Computer to Plate); Platemakers: Laser; Roll Coverings; Rollers
Personnel: Mike Foran (Pres.)
Personnel: Steven Wilkinson (Gen. Mgr.)
Personnel: Steve Woodard (Vice Pres., Cor. Sales)

HARPER CORPORATION OF AMERICA

Street address 1: 11625 Steele Creek Rd
Street address state: NC
Zip/Postal code: 28273-3731
Country: USA
Mailing address: PO Box 38490
Mailing city: Charlotte
Mailing state: NC
Mailing zip: 28278-1008
General Phone: 800-438-3111
General Fax: (704) 588-3819
Email: customer@harperimage.com
Primary Website: www.harperimage.com
Year Established: 1971
Product/Services: Anilox manufacturer
Personnel: Margaret Harper Kluttz (President)
Personnel: Lee Kluttz (VP of Operations)
Personnel: Alan Rogers (VP of Sales)

MCGRANN PAPER CORP.

Street address 1: 2101 Westinghouse Blvd
Street address state: NC
Zip/Postal code: 28273-6310
Country: USA
Mailing address: 2101 Westinghouse Blvd # A
Mailing city: Charlotte
Mailing state: NC
Mailing zip: 28273-6310
General Phone: (704) 583-2101
General Fax: (704) 369-2229
Primary Website: www.mcgrann.com
Year Established: 1996
Product/Services: Newsprint; Paper: Coated Groundwood Offset; Paper: Groundwood Specialties; Paper: Specialty Printing Paper;
Personnel: Karl McGrann (Owner/Pres.)
Personnel: Bob Marko (Sales Rep.)
Personnel: Kirk Castle (Sr. VP, Sales)

CHARLOTTESVILLE

BADGER FIRE PROTECTION

Street address 1: 944 Glenwood Station Ln
Street address 2: Ste 303
Street address state: VA
Zip/Postal code: 22901-1480
Country: USA
Mailing address: 944 Glenwood Station Ln Ste 303
Mailing city: Charlottesville
Mailing state: VA
Mailing zip: 22901-1480
General Phone: (800) 446-3857
General Fax: (800) 248-7809
Email: vmodic@badgerfire.com
Primary Website: www.badgerfire.com
Year Established: 1960
Product/Services: Fire Protection
Personnel: Alan Owens (Sales/Mktg. Dir.)

KEISTER WILLIAMS NEWSPAPER SERVICES, INC.

Street address 1: 1807 Emmet St N
Street address 2: Ste 6B
Street address state: VA
Zip/Postal code: 22901-3616
Country: USA
Mailing address: PO Box 8187
Mailing city: Charlottesville
Mailing state: VA
Mailing zip: 22906-8187
General Phone: (434) 293-4709
General Fax: (434) 293-4884
Email: ky@kwnews.com
Primary Website: www.kwnews.com
Year Established: 1973
Product/Services: Consulting Services: Advertising; Consulting Services: Marketing;
Personnel: Walton C. (Ky) Lindsay (Pres./Treasurer)
Personnel: Meta L. Nay (Vice Pres., Mktg.)
Personnel: Carol Lindsay (Admin.)
Walton Lindsay (Pres.)

CHESTERFIELD

NEWSENGIN, INC.

Street address 1: 15560 Golden Ridge Ct
Street address state: MO
Zip/Postal code: 63017-5124
Country: USA
Mailing address: 15560 Golden Ridge Ct
Mailing city: Chesterfield
Mailing state: MO
Mailing zip: 63017-5124
General Phone: (636) 537-8548
General Fax: (636) 532-9408
Primary Website: www.newsengin.com
Product/Services: Archiving Systems; News Wire Capture Systems; Software: Editorial; Software: Pagination/Layout;
Personnel: Jim Mosley (CEO)
Personnel: George Landau (Pres.)
Personnel: Virgil Tipton (CTO)

PRESSTEK, INC.

Street address 1: 18081 Chesterfield Airport Road
Street address state: MO
Zip/Postal code: 63005
Country: USA
Mailing address: 18081 Chesterfield Airport Road
Mailing city: Chesterfield
Mailing state: MO
Mailing zip: 63005
General Phone: (800) 225-4835
Primary Website: www.presstek.com
Year Established: 1987
Product/Services: Presstek DI Digital Offset Presses; ABDick Conventional Offset Presses Platemakers: Offset (Computer to Plate); Plates: Offset (Computer to Plate); Press Accessories, Parts & Supplies; Press Repairs; Presses: Offset; Processors: Film & Paper; Proofing Systems; Punching Equipment; Post Press
Personnel: Eric Vandenberg (Equipment Sales)
Personnel: Chris Yanko (Digital Sales Director)
Personnel: Steve Schulte (Vice President Sales & Marketing)
Mike Russell (International Sales Director)

CHICAGO

AECOM

Street address 1: 303 E Wacker Dr
Street address 2: Ste 1400
Street address state: IL
Zip/Postal code: 60601-5214
Country: USA
Mailing address: 303 E Wacker Dr Ste 1400
Mailing city: Chicago
Mailing state: IL
Mailing zip: 60601-5214
General Phone: (312) 373-7700
General Fax: (312) 373-7710
Primary Website: www.aecom.com
Year Established: 1989
Product/Services: Architects/Engineers (Includes Design/Construction Firms); Consulting Services: Equipment; Consulting Services: Production;
Personnel: Betty Hendricks (Office Mgr.)

A-KORN ROLLER, INC.

Street address 1: 3545 S Morgan St
Street address state: IL
Zip/Postal code: 60609-1525
Country: USA
Mailing address: 3545 S Morgan St
Mailing city: Chicago
Mailing state: IL
Mailing zip: 60609-1590
General Phone: (773) 254-5700
General Fax: (773) 650-7355
Email: a-kornroller@a-kornroller.com
Primary Website: www.a-kornroller.com
Year Established: 1970
Product/Services: Roll Cleaning Equipment; Roll Coverings; Roller Grinders; Roller Grinding Services; Rollers; Rollers: Dampening;
Personnel: Michael Koren (Pres.)

BODINE ELECTRIC

Street address 1: 2500 W Bradley Pl
Street address state: IL
Zip/Postal code: 60618-4716
Country: USA
Mailing address: 201 Northfield Rd
Mailing city: Northfield
Mailing state: IL
Mailing zip: 60093-3311
General Phone: (773) 478-3515
General Fax: (773) 478-3232
Primary Website: www.bodine-electric.com
Year Established: 1905
Product/Services: Motors
Personnel: John Bodine (Pres.)

H.R. SLATER CO., INC.

Street address 1: 2050 W 18th St
Street address state: IL
Zip/Postal code: 60608-1816
Country: USA
Mailing address: 2050 W 18th St
Mailing city: Chicago
Mailing state: IL
Mailing zip: 60608-1816
General Phone: (312) 666-1855
General Fax: (312) 666-1856
Email: hrslatercompany@aol.com
Year Established: 1965
Product/Services: Delivery Equipment; Gauges, Measuring; Mailroom Systems & Equipment; Newsprint Handeling Equipment; Paper Handeling Equipment;
Personnel: Robert Kurzka (Pres.)
Personnel: William C. St. Hilaire (Office Mgr.)

LITHO RESEARCH, INC.

Street address 1: 1621 W Carroll Ave

Equipment, Supplies and Services

Street address state: IL
Zip/Postal code: 60612-2501
Country: USA
Mailing address: 1621 W Carroll Ave
Mailing city: Chicago
Mailing state: IL
Mailing zip: 60612-2501
General Phone: (312) 738-0292
General Fax: (312) 738-2386
Year Established: 1985
Product/Services: Environmental Control Systems; Offset Blankets, Blanket Wash; Offset Chemicals & Supplies; Plate Cleaners; Roll Cleaning Equipment; Static Eliminators;
Personnel: Michael T. Miske (Pres.)

NORTH SHORE CONSULTANTS, INC.

Street address 1: 4910 N Monitor Ave
Street address state: IL
Zip/Postal code: 60630-2025
Country: USA
Mailing address: 613 Thorndale Ave
Mailing city: Elk Grove Village
Mailing state: IL
Mailing zip: 60007-4334
General Phone: (773) 286-7245
General Fax: (773) 286-1974
Email: nsc@enescee.com
Primary Website: www.enescee.com
Product/Services: Adhesives; Flying Pasters; Splicers, Automatic; Tape Splicing Equipment;
Personnel: Audrey Mysliwiec (Pres.)
Personnel: Dennis B. Wojtecki (Mgr.)

NORWOOD PAPER

Street address 1: 7001 W 60th St
Street address state: IL
Zip/Postal code: 60638-3101
Country: USA
Mailing address: 7001 W 60th St
Mailing city: Chicago
Mailing state: IL
Mailing zip: 60638-3101
General Phone: (773) 788-1508
General Fax: (773) 788-1528
Email: sales@norwoodpaper.com
Primary Website: www.norwoodpaper.com
Year Established: 1972
Product/Services: Newsprint; Paper: Coated Groundwood Offset; Paper: Groundwood Specialties; Paper: Specialty Printing Paper; Rewinders;
Personnel: Laura Martin (President)
Personnel: Robert Zeman (Vice President)
Personnel: Kathleen Zemen (COO)

PRINTSOFT AMERICAS, INC.

Street address 1: 70 West Madison St Three First National Plaza
Street address 2: Suite 1400
Street address state: IL
Zip/Postal code: 60602
Country: USA
Mailing address: 70 West Madison St. Three First National Plaza Suite 1400
Mailing city: Chicago
Mailing state: IL
Mailing zip: 60602
General Phone: (630) 625-5400
General Fax: (630) 625-5401
Email: sales@printsoftamericas.com
Primary Website: www.printsoft.com
Year Established: 1995
Product/Services: Laser Printers; Software: Circulation;
Personnel: Daniel Sheedy (Nat'l Sales Mgr.)

R.R. DONNELLEY & SONS CO.

Street address 1: 35 West Wacker Drive
Street address 2: Suite 1
Street address state: IL
Zip/Postal code: 60601
Country: USA
Mailing address: 35 West Wacker Drive, Suite 1
Mailing city: Chicago
Mailing state: IL
Mailing zip: 60606-4300
General Phone: 312-326-8000

General Fax: 312-326-8001
Email: info@rrd.com
Primary Website: www.rrdonnelley.com
Year Established: 1985
Product/Services: Marketing & Business Communications; Commercial Printing & Related Services;
Personnel: Daniel L. Knotts (CEO)
Personnel: Ken O'Brien (Executive Vice President, Chief Information Officer)
Personnel: John Pecaric (President, Business Services)
Terry D. Peterson (Exec. V. Pres., CFO)
Sheila Rutt (Exec. V. Pres., C.H.R.O.)
Doug Ryan (Pres., Marketing Solutions)

RESEARCH USA, INC.

Street address 1: 180 N Wacker Dr
Street address 2: Ste 202
Street address state: IL
Zip/Postal code: 60606-1600
Country: USA
Mailing address: 180 N Wacker Dr Ste 202
Mailing city: Chicago
Mailing state: IL
Mailing zip: 60606-1600
General Phone: (800) 863-4800
General Fax: (312) 658-0085
Email: info@researchusainc.com; hr@researchusainc.com
Primary Website: www.researchusainc.com
Year Established: 1972
Product/Services: Market Research

SCHAWK

Street address 1: 225 W Superior St
Street address state: IL
Zip/Postal code: 60654-3507
Country: USA
Mailing address: 1 N Dearborn St Ste 700
Mailing city: Chicago
Mailing state: IL
Mailing zip: 60602-4340
General Phone: (312) 943-0400
General Fax: (312) 943-2450
Primary Website: www.schawk.com
Product/Services: Color Management Software; Library Retrieval Systems; Preprint Service & Production; Storage Retrieval Systems;
Personnel: Jamie Mandarion (Sales Mgr.)

UV PROCESS SUPPLY, INC.

Street address 1: 1229 W Cortland St
Street address state: IL
Zip/Postal code: 60614-4805
Country: USA
Mailing address: 1229 W Cortland St
Mailing city: Chicago
Mailing state: IL
Mailing zip: 60614-4805
General Phone: (773) 248-0099
General Fax: (773) 880-6647
Email: info@uvps.com
Primary Website: www.uvprocess.com
Year Established: 1979
Product/Services: Color Analyzers; Drying Systems; Ink Bleeding Equipment; Ink Fountains & Accessories; Ink Pumping Systems; Ink Storage Tanks; Lubricants; Offset Chemicals & Supplies; Pumps (Air, Ink, Vacuum); Static Eliminators;
Personnel: Stephen Siegel (Pres.)

VEGRA USA

Street address 1: 1621 W Carroll Ave
Street address state: IL
Zip/Postal code: 60612-2501
Country: USA
Mailing address: 1621 W Carroll Ave
Mailing city: Chicago
Mailing state: IL
Mailing zip: 60612-2501
General Phone: (312) 733-3400
General Fax: (312) 738-2386
Email: info@vegra.de
Primary Website: www.vegra.de
Year Established: 1997
Product/Services: Chemicals: Pressroom; Core Strippers & Seperators; Dies (Perforating and Slitting); Offset Blankets, Blanket Wash; Offset Chemicals & Supplies; Offset Fountain Solutions; Static Eliminators;
Personnel: Michael Miske (Vice Pres., Sales)

WINTON ENGINEERING CO.

Street address 1: 2303 W 18th St
Street address state: IL
Zip/Postal code: 60608-1808
Country: USA
Mailing address: 2303 W 18th St
Mailing city: Chicago
Mailing state: IL
Mailing zip: 60608-1808
General Phone: (312) 733-5200
General Fax: (312) 733-0446
Email: d.allison@w-rindustries.com
Primary Website: ^www.w-rindustries.com
Year Established: 1896
Product/Services: Chemicals: Pressroom; Chemicals: Roller Cleaning; Cleaners & Solvents; Offset Chemicals & Supplies; Press Accessories, Parts & Supplies;
Personnel: David Allison (Vice Pres.)

CHINO

KYE SYSTEMS CORP

Street address 1: 12675 Colony Ct
Street address state: CA
Zip/Postal code: 91710-2975
Country: USA
Mailing address: 12675 Colony Ct
Mailing city: Chino
Mailing state: CA
Mailing zip: 91710-2975
General Phone: 909) 628-8836
Email: webmaster@geniusnet.com.tw
Primary Website: www.geniusnet.com
Year Established: 1986
Product/Services: PC products, mobile phone and Tablet PC, including mice, keyboards, graphics tablets, touch pen, power banks, webcams, speakers, headphones, microphones, sleeves, backpacks, and professional gaming gear, digital cameras, camcorders, vehicle recorders, and projectors.
Personnel: Geoffrey Lin (Pres.)
Personnel: Ken Chao

CIBOLO

TECH-ENERGY CO.

Street address 1: 1111 Schneider
Street address state: TX
Zip/Postal code: 78108-3101
Country: USA
Mailing address: 1111 Schneider
Mailing city: Cibolo
Mailing state: TX
Mailing zip: 78108-3101
General Phone: (210) 658-0614
General Fax: (210) 658-0653
Email: techenergy@techenergy.com
Primary Website: www.techenergy.com
Year Established: 1977
Product/Services: Blanket Mounting and Bars; Blankets; Ink Fountains & Accessories; Press Accessories, Parts & Supplies; Press Engineers; Press Rebuilding; Press Repairs; Presses: Letterpress; Presses: Offset; Rollers;
Personnel: John E. Pickard (Pres.)
Personnel: Beth Benke (Vice Pres.)
Personnel: Phyllis Pickard (Sec.)
Teresa Moeller (Treasurer)
Louis Benke (Serv. Mgr.)
Rachel Bell (Int'l Sales Mgr.)
David N. Moeller (Nat'l Sales Mgr.)

MAH MACHINE CO., INC.

Street address 1: 3301 S Central Ave
Street address state: IL
Zip/Postal code: 60804-3941
Country: USA
Mailing address: 3301 S Central Ave
Mailing city: Cicero
Mailing state: IL

Mailing zip: 60804-3986
General Phone: (708) 656-1826
General Fax: (708) 656-4152
Email: info@mahmachine.com
Primary Website: www.mahmachine.com
Year Established: 1977
Product/Services: Cylinder Repair; Equipment Dealers (New); Equipment Dealers (Used); Feeding, Folding, Delivery Equipment; Presses: Offset; Roller Grinding Services; Rollers; Rollers: Dampening;
Personnel: Martin Hozjan (Pres.)

CINCINNATI

CELEBRO

Street address 1: 312 Elm St
Street address 2: Fl 20
Street address state: OH
Zip/Postal code: 45202-2739
Country: USA
Mailing address: 151 W 4th St Ste 201
Mailing city: Cincinnati
Mailing state: OH
Mailing zip: 45202-2746
General Phone: (513) 665-3777
General Fax: (513) 768-8958
Email: info@celebro.com
Primary Website: www.gmti.com
Year Established: 1994
Product/Services: Computers: Hardware & Software Integrators; Electronic Ad Delivery; Software: Advertising (Includes Display; Classified); Software: Electronic Data Interchange
Product or Service: Hardware/Software Supplier
Personnel: Steve Fuschetti (Pres./CEO)
Personnel: Tom Foster (Vice Pres., Celebro Opns.)
Personnel: Michael Hibert (Dir., Implementation Servs.)

FUJIFILM GRAPHIC SYSTEMS USA, INC.

Street address 1: 1650 Magnolia Dr
Street address state: OH
Zip/Postal code: 45215-1976
Country: USA
Mailing address: 1650 Magnolia Dr
Mailing city: Cincinnati
Mailing state: OH
Mailing zip: 45215-1976
General Phone: (800) 582-7406
General Fax: (513) 563-0377
Primary Website: www.fujifilmusa.com/products/graphic_arts_printing/index.html
Product/Services: Blankets; Chemicals: Pressroom; Color Management Software; Imagesetters; Inks; Offset Chemicals & Supplies; Platemakers; Plates: Flexographic (Computer to Plate); Plates: Offset (Conventional); Proofing Systems; Software: Press/Post Press;
Personnel: Kurt Paskert (Reg'l Sales Mgr.)

GANNETT MEDIA TECHNOLOGIES INTERNATIONAL (GMTI)

Street address 1: 312 Elm St
Street address 2: Fl 20
Street address state: OH
Zip/Postal code: 45202-2739
Country: USA
Mailing address: 312 Elm St Ste 2G
Mailing city: Cincinnati
Mailing state: OH
Mailing zip: 45202-2763
General Phone: (513) 665-3777
General Fax: (513) 768-8958
Email: gmti-info@gmti.gannett.com
Primary Website: www.gmti.com
Year Established: 1994
Product/Services: Archiving Systems; Computers: Hardware & Software Integrators; Library Retrieval Systems; Marketing Database Design and Implementation; Photo Archiving; Software: Advertising (Includes Display; Classified); Storage Retrieval Systems;

Equipment, Supplies and Services

Product or Service: Multimedia/Interactive Products
Personnel: Steve Fuschetti (Pres./CEO)

GMTI (DIGITAL COLLECTIONS)

Street address 1: 312 Elm St
Street address 2: Fl 20
Street address state: OH
Zip/Postal code: 45202-2739
Country: USA
Mailing address: 312 Elm St Fl 20
Mailing city: Cincinnati
Mailing state: OH
Mailing zip: 45202-2739
General Phone: (513) 665-3777
General Fax: (513) 768-8958
Email: contentfeedback@gannett.com
Primary Website: www.gannett.com
Year Established: 1995
Product/Services: Digital Asset Management Systems: Full service contractor; Hardware & Software Integrators; Content Aggregation and Distribution; Semantic Engine Services; Archive Content Management software.
Product or Service: Consultants`Hardware/Software Supplier`Online Service Provider and Internet Hosts
Personnel: Steve Fuschetti (Pres./CEO)
Personnel: Bill Mahlock (Vice Pres., Installations/Support)
Personnel: Michael Tucker (Dir., Sales & Marketing)

HADRONICS

Street address 1: 4570 Steel Pl
Street address state: OH
Zip/Postal code: 45209-1133
Country: USA
Mailing address: 4570 Steel Pl.
Mailing city: Cincinnati
Mailing state: OH
Mailing zip: 45209
General Phone: (513) 321-9350
General Fax: (513) 321-9377
Email: sales@hadronics.com
Primary Website: www.hadronics.com
Year Established: 1969
Product/Services: Copper Plating Drums; Cylinder Repair; Dampening Systems; Ink Fountains & Accessories; Roller Grinding Services; Rollers; Rollers: Dampening;
Personnel: Jeff McCarty (VP., Sales)

WHITWORTH KNIFE COMPANY

Street address 1: 825 Delta Ave
Street address 2: Ste C
Street address state: OH
Zip/Postal code: 45226-1220
Country: USA
Mailing address: 508 Missouri Ave
Mailing city: Cincinnati
Mailing state: OH
Mailing zip: 45226-1121
General Phone: (513) 321-9177
General Fax: (513) 321-9938
Email: sales@whitworthknifecompany.com
Primary Website: www.whitworthknifecompany.com
Year Established: 1995
Product/Services: Consulting Services: Production; Core Cutters, Restorers, Rounders; Core Strippers & Seperators; Cutters & Trimmers; Cutting Tools; Dies (Perforating and Slitting); Folder Knives; In-Line Trimming Systems; Ink Fountains & Accessories; Roller Grinders;
Personnel: Ray Whitworth (Owner)

AG INDUSTRIES, INC.

Street address 1: 1 American Rd
Street address state: OH
Zip/Postal code: 44144-2301
Country: USA
Mailing address: 1 American Rd
Mailing city: Cleveland
Mailing state: OH
Mailing zip: 44144-2398
General Phone: (216) 252-6737
General Fax: (216) 252-6773

Primary Website: www.agifixtures.com
Year Established: 1960
Product/Services: Newspaper Dispensers (Mechanical/Electronic)
Personnel: Sandy Saunders (Mktg./Adv. Coord.)

BOB WEBER, INC.

Street address 1: 23850 Commerce Park Rd
Street address state: OH
Zip/Postal code: 44122
Country: USA
Mailing address: 23850 Commerce Park Rd.
Mailing city: Cleveland
Mailing state: OH
Mailing zip: 44122
General Phone: (800) 399-4294
General Fax: (800) 837-8973
Email: info@bob-weber.com
Primary Website: www.bob-weber.com
Year Established: 1982
Product/Services: Equipment Dealers (New) - BWI Series CTP; Printing Consumables - Plates and Chemistry; Used PrePress Equipment; Platesetters; CTP; Computer-to-plate; Plate Processors; Raster Image Processors; Workflow RIPS; Xitron RIPs, Plate Readers
Note: Equipment Dealer selling new and reconditioned computer-to-plate machines (CTP), along with Paragon Plates and Chemistries - for the newspaper industry. Individual components sold as well as complete systems. We sell new RIP solutions such as the Xitron Navigator GPS, Elite and Sierra RIPs. All equipment is warranted and supported by the BWI network of service people. Sales and service.
Personnel: Leslie DiVincenzo (Director of Marketing)
Personnel: Steve Fondriest (Senior Technician)
Personnel: Bill Weber (Business Development Director)

CRYOGENESIS (A DIV. OF WM & C SERVICES, INC.)

Street address 1: 2140 Scranton Rd
Street address state: OH
Zip/Postal code: 44113-3544
Country: USA
Mailing address: 2140 Scranton Rd
Mailing city: Cleveland
Mailing state: OH
Mailing zip: 44113-3544
General Phone: (216) 696-8797
General Fax: (216) 696-8794
Email: cryogen@cryogenesis-usa.com
Primary Website: www.cryogenesis-usa.com
Product/Services: Cleaners & Solvents; Roll Cleaning Equipment;
Personnel: James Becker (Pres.)
Personnel: John R. Whalen (Vice Pres., Sales)

DAY-GLO COLOR CORP.

Street address 1: 4515 Saint Clair Ave
Street address state: OH
Zip/Postal code: 44103-1203
Country: USA
Mailing address: 4515 Saint Clair Ave
Mailing city: Cleveland
Mailing state: OH
Mailing zip: 44103-1268
General Phone: (216) 391-7070
General Fax: (216) 391-7751
Email: dayglo@dayglo.com
Primary Website: www.dayglo.com
Year Established: 1946
Product/Services: Inks
Personnel: Mark Wright (Vice Pres., Sales)

HORIZONS, INC.

Street address 1: 18531 S Miles Rd
Street address state: OH
Zip/Postal code: 44128-4237
Country: USA
Mailing address: 18531 S Miles Rd
Mailing city: Cleveland
Mailing state: OH

Mailing zip: 44128-4237
General Phone: 1.800.482.7758
Email: info@horizonsisg.com
Primary Website: www.horizonsisg.com
Year Established: 1960
Product/Services: Adhesives; Chemicals: Photographic; Input & Editing Systems; Label Printing Machines;
Personnel: Herb Wainer (Pres.)
Personnel: Wayne Duignan (Vice Pres., Mktg.)

KOLBUS AMERICA, INC.

Street address 1: 812 Huron Rd E
Street address 2: Ste 750
Street address state: OH
Zip/Postal code: 44115-1126
Country: USA
Mailing address: 812 Huron Rd E Ste 750
Mailing city: Cleveland
Mailing state: OH
Mailing zip: 44115-1126
General Phone: (216) 931-4940
General Fax: (216) 931-5101
Email: robert.shafer@kolbus.com
Primary Website: www.kolbus.com
Year Established: 1960
Product/Services: Counting, Stacking, Bundling Machines; Cutters & Trimmers; Material Handling Equipment: Palletizing Machines;
Personnel: Ruth Wilson (Office Mgr.)
Personnel: Robert Shafer (Pres./Dir., Sales/Distr. Americas)

NETWORK NEWSPAPER ADVERTISING, INC.

Street address 1: 23811 Chagrin Blvd
Street address 2: Ste LL25
Street address state: OH
Zip/Postal code: 44122-5525
Country: USA
Mailing address: 23811 Chagrin Blvd Ste LL25
Mailing city: Cleveland
Mailing state: OH
Mailing zip: 44122-5525
General Phone: (216) 595-3990
General Fax: (216) 595-3992
Email: cccamh@aol.com
Year Established: 1907
Product/Services: Consulting Services: Advertising
Personnel: Charles Hickman (Pres.)

THE AUSTIN COMPANY

Street address 1: 6095 Parkland Blvd
Street address state: OH
Zip/Postal code: 44124-6139
Country: USA
Mailing address: 6095 Parkland Blvd Ste 100
Mailing city: Cleveland
Mailing state: OH
Mailing zip: 44124-6140
General Phone: (440) 544-2600
General Fax: (440) 544-2690
Email: austin.info@theaustin.com; ne@theaustin.com
Primary Website: www.theaustin.com
Year Established: 1878
Product/Services: Architects/Engineers (Includes Design/Construction Firms); Consulting Services: Equipment; Consulting Services: Financial; Consulting Services: Marketing; Consulting Services: Production; Mailroom Systems & Equipment; Maintenance, Plant & Equipment; Newsprint Handling Equipment; Roll Handling Equipment; System Integration Services
Note: The Austin Company's Newspaper Group offers in-house business, process and facility consulting, architectural, engineering, construction services that address the unique requirements of the printing and publishing industry. Our mission is to assist Newspa"
Personnel: Curt Miller (Gen. Mgr.)
Personnel: Duane Lofdahl (Vice Pres., Planning/Design)
Personnel: Michael G. Pierce (Sr. Vice Pres., Sales/Mktg. Gen. Mgr.)
Michael Craft (Sr. Newspaper Consultant)

CLINTON

WALTERRY INSURANCE BROKERS

Street address 1: 7411 Old Branch Ave
Street address state: MD
Zip/Postal code: 20735-1323
Country: USA
Mailing address: 7411 Old Branch Ave
Mailing city: Clinton
Mailing state: MD
Mailing zip: 20735-1323
General Phone: (301) 868-7200
General Fax: (301) 868-2611
Email: insurance@walterry.com
Primary Website: www.walterry.com
Year Established: 1968
Product/Services: Insurance
Personnel: Walter J. Coady (Dir., Mktg.)

COLUMBIA

MISSOURI PRESS SERVICE, INC.

Street address 1: 802 Locust St
Street address state: MO
Zip/Postal code: 65201-4888
Country: USA
Mailing address: 802 Locust St
Mailing city: Columbia
Mailing state: MO
Mailing zip: 65201-7799
General Phone: (573) 449-4167
General Fax: (573) 874-5894
Email: mmaassen@socket.net
Primary Website: www.mopress.com
Year Established: 1940
Product/Services: Newspapers. Consulting Services: Advertising; Consulting Services: Editorial;
Note: Represents daily and weekly newspapers in Missouri
Personnel: Mark Maassen (Exec. Dir.)

COLUMBUS

METALS RECOVERY SERVICE

Street address 1: 1660 Georgesville Rd
Street address state: OH
Zip/Postal code: 43228-3613
Country: USA
Mailing address: 1660 Georgesville Rd.
Mailing city: Columbus
Mailing state: OH
Mailing zip: 43228
General Phone: (614) 870-9444
General Fax: (614) 878-6000
Email: sales@msitarget.com
Primary Website: www.msitarget.com
Year Established: 2001
Product/Services: Silver Recovery
Personnel: Steven P. Dahms (Vice Pres.)

CONCORD

NORTH ATLANTIC PUBLISHING SYSTEMS, INC.

Street address 1: 66 Commonwealth Ave
Street address state: MA
Zip/Postal code: 01742-2974
Country: USA
Mailing address: 66 Commonwealth Ave
Mailing city: Concord
Mailing state: MA
Mailing zip: 01742-2974
General Phone: (978) 371-8989
General Fax: (978) 371-5678
Email: naps@napsys.com; xthelp@napsys.com
Primary Website: www.napsys.com
Year Established: 1989
Product/Services: Consulting Services: Editorial; Software: Asset Management; Software: Editorial; Software: Pagination/Layout; Software: Workflow Management/Tracking;
Personnel: Andrew W. Koppel (Retail Sales Mgr.)

Equipment, Supplies and Services

POLAROID HOLDING CO.
Street address 1: 300 Baker Ave
Street address state: MA
Zip/Postal code: 01742-2131
Country: USA
Mailing address: 300 Baker Ave Ste 330
Mailing city: Concord
Mailing state: MA
Mailing zip: 01742-2131
General Phone: (781) 386-2000
General Fax: (781) 386-6243
Email: marketing@polaroid.com
Primary Website: www.polaroid.com
Personnel: Mary L. Jeffries (CEO)
Personnel: Jim Koestler (Vice Pres., Product Mgmt.)
Personnel: Jon Pollock (Vice Pres./Gen. Mgr., Digital Imaging)
Cheryl Mau (Vice Pres., Mktg.)
Lorrie Parent (Media Rel.)

COSTA MESA

CONTROL ENGINEERING CO.
Street address 1: 2306 Newport Blvd
Street address state: CA
Zip/Postal code: 92627-1548
Country: USA
Mailing address: 2306 Newport Blvd
Mailing city: Costa Mesa
Mailing state: CA
Mailing zip: 92627-1548
General Phone: (949) 722-7821
Email: ccarrillo@controlengineering.com
Primary Website: www.controlengineering.com
Product/Services: Cabinets; Conveyors; Material Handling Equipment: Automatic Guided Vehicles; Material Handling Equipment: Truck Loaders; Newsprint Handeling Equipment; Paper Handeling Equipment;
Personnel: Carlos Carrillo (Engineering Mgr.)

COVINGTON

ROTADYNE
Street address 1: 15151 Prater Dr
Street address 2: Ste L
Street address state: GA
Zip/Postal code: 30014-4961
Country: USA
Mailing address: 15151 Prater Dr Ste L
Mailing city: Covington
Mailing state: GA
Mailing zip: 30014-4961
General Phone: (630) 769-9700
General Fax: (770) 787-4589
Primary Website: www.rotadyne.com
Year Established: 1917
Product/Services: Blanket Mounting and Bars
Personnel: Rita Harper (Mgr., Customer Serv.)

CROWN POINT

BALEMASTER
Street address 1: 980 Crown Ct
Street address state: IN
Zip/Postal code: 46307-2732
Country: USA
Mailing address: 980 Crown Ct
Mailing city: Crown Point
Mailing state: IN
Mailing zip: 46307-2732
General Phone: (219) 663-4525
General Fax: (219) 663-4591
Email: sales@balemaster.com
Primary Website: www.balemaster.com
Year Established: 1949
Product/Services: Baling Machines
Personnel: Mike Connell (Sales Mgr.)

CULVER CITY

LITHCO INC.
Street address 1: 9449 Jefferson Blvd
Street address state: CA
Zip/Postal code: 90232-2915
Country: USA
Mailing address: 9449 Jefferson Blvd
Mailing city: Culver City
Mailing state: CA
Mailing zip: 90232-2913
General Phone: (310) 559-7770
Email: lithco@lithcoinc.com
Primary Website: www.lithcoinc.com
Year Established: 1946
Product/Services: Gauges, Measuring; Layout Tables, Light Tables & Workstations; Optical Products; Prepress Color Proofing Systems; Rules;
Personnel: Gerald Gaebel (Pres.)
Personnel: Sheila Martin (Office Mgr.)
Personnel: Jeff Simon (President)

CUMMING

BELT CORPORATION OF AMERICA
Street address 1: 253 Castleberry Industrial Dr
Street address state: GA
Zip/Postal code: 30040-9051
Country: USA
Mailing address: 253 Castleberry Industrial Dr
Mailing city: Cumming
Mailing state: GA
Mailing zip: 30040-9051
General Phone: (800) 235-0947
General Fax: (770) 887-4138
Email: sales@beltcorp.com
Primary Website: www.beltcorp.com
Year Established: 1985
Product/Services: Belts, Belting, V-Belts
Personnel: William C. Levensalor (Pres.)
Personnel: Rich Blais (Sales Mgr.)
Personnel: Mike Bridges (Inside Sales Supvr.)

CUPERTINO

APPLE, INC.
Street address 1: 1 Infinite Loop
Street address state: CA
Zip/Postal code: 95014-2083
Country: USA
Mailing address: 1 Infinite Loop
Mailing city: Cupertino
Mailing state: CA
Mailing zip: 95014-2084
General Phone: (408) 996â€"1010
General Fax: (408) 996-0275
Email: media.help@apple.com
Primary Website: www.apple.com
Year Established: 1976
Product/Services: Consumer Electronics; Computer Software; Online Services;
Product or Service: Hardware/Software Supplier
Personnel: Timothy Cook (CEO)
Personnel: Philip W. Schiller (Sr. V. P. Worldwide Marketing)
Personnel: Jonathan Ive (Chief Design Officer)
Craig Federighi (Senior Vice President, Software Engineering)

CUSHING

ELECTRONIC SYSTEMS ENGINEERING CO.
Street address 1: 1 E Eseco Rd
Street address state: OK
Zip/Postal code: 74023-5531
Country: USA
Mailing address: 1 E Eseco Rd
Mailing city: Cushing
Mailing state: OK
Mailing zip: 74023-5531
General Phone: (918) 225-1266
General Fax: (918) 225-1284
Email: wallace@eseco-speedmaster.com
Primary Website: www.eseco-speedmaster.com
Year Established: 1956
Product/Services: Color Analyzers; Dark Room Equipment; Densitometers; Enlargers (Photographic); Film & Paper: Film Processing Machines;
Personnel: Ed Handlin (CFO)
Personnel: Wallace Hallman (Pres.)

CYPRESS

FUJIFILM GRAPHIC SYSTEMS USA, INC.
Street address 1: 6200 Phyllis Drive
Street address state: CA
Zip/Postal code: 90630
Country: USA
Mailing address: 6200 Phyllis Drive
Mailing city: Cypress
Mailing state: CA
Mailing zip: 90630
General Phone: (714) 933-3300
General Fax: (714) 899-4707
Primary Website: www.fujifilmusa.com/products/graphic_arts_printing/index.html
Product/Services: Blankets; Chemicals: Pressroom; Color Management Software; Imagesetters; Inks; Offset Chemicals & Supplies; Platemakers: Flexographic (Computer to Plate); Plates: Offset (Conventional); Proofing Systems; Software: Press/Post Press;
Personnel: Jeffrey Buchman (Reg'l Sales Mgr.)

DALLAS

ABB INC.
Street address 1: 9011 Bretshire Dr
Street address state: TX
Zip/Postal code: 75228-5105
Country: USA
Mailing address: 9011 Bretshire Dr
Mailing city: Dallas
Mailing state: TX
Mailing zip: 75228-5105
General Phone: (214) 328-1202
Primary Website: www.abb.com/printing
Product/Services: Drives & Controls; Press Control Systems; Plate workflow, System Integration Services;
Personnel: Jeff Gelfand (Nat'l Sales/Mktg. Dir.)

AUTOMATED MAILING SYSTEMS CORP.
Street address 1: 10730 Spangler Rd
Street address state: TX
Zip/Postal code: 75220-7102
Country: USA
Mailing address: PO Box 541326
Mailing city: Dallas
Mailing state: TX
Mailing zip: 75354-1326
General Phone: (972) 869-2844
General Fax: (972) 869-2735
Email: amsco@amscodallas.com
Primary Website: www.amscodallas.com
Year Established: 1946
Product/Services: Addressing Machines; Bundling and Tying Machines; Inserting Equipment (Includes Stuffing Machines); Mailroom Systems & Equipment; Strapping Machines
Personnel: Scott Helsley (Vice Pres.)
Personnel: Thomas Helsley (Mktg. Mgr)

KBA NORTH AMERICA, INC. (KOENIG & BAUER AG)
Street address 1: 2555 Regent Blvd
Street address state: TX
Zip/Postal code: 75261
Country: USA
Mailing address: 2555 Regent Blvd
Mailing city: Dallas
Mailing state: TX
Mailing zip: 75261
General Phone: 469-532-8040
General Fax: 469-532-8190
Email: na-marketing@kba.com
Primary Website: www.kba.com
Year Established: 1814
Product/Services: Flexogrpahic Press Conversion; Flying Pasters; Pasters; Presses: Flexographic; Presses: Offset; Reels & Tensions; Reels (Inlcudes Paper Reels); Tension & Web Controls;
Personnel: Mark Hischar (Pres./CEO)
Personnel: Eric Frank (Vice Pres., Mktg.)
Personnel: Ulrich Wicke (Vice-President of Sales & Service)
Pernice Samuel (Executive Sales)
Bruce Richardson (National Sales Manager)
Schenker Winfried (Sales Director Web Presses)
Denise Prewitt (Digital Sales and Marketing Specialist)
Alex Stepanian (Regional Sales Dir.)

OUTSOURCING USA
Street address 1: 1200 Twin Stacks Dr
Street address state: PA
Zip/Postal code: 18612-8507
Country: USA
Mailing address: 1200 Twin Stacks Dr
Mailing city: Dallas
Mailing state: PA
Mailing zip: 18612
General Phone: (570) 674-5600
Email: info@outsourcingusa.net
Primary Website: www.outsourcingusa.net
Year Established: 2009
Product/Services: Pre-press ad production services for both print and web
Personnel: Lynn Banta (CEO)
Personnel: Maureen Missal (VP Business Development)
Personnel: Tony Banta (VP of Information Systems)

RICKENBACHER MEDIA
Street address 1: 6731 Desco Dr
Street address state: TX
Zip/Postal code: 75225-2704
Country: USA
Mailing address: 6731 Desco Dr
Mailing city: Dallas
Mailing state: TX
Mailing zip: 75225-2704
General Phone: (214) 384 2779
Email: rmedia@msn.com
Primary Website: www.rickenbachermedia.com
Year Established: 1985
Product/Services: Brokers & Appraisers
Personnel: Ted Rickenbacher (Pres./Exec. Dir.)
Personnel: Jim Afinowich (Western States Dir.)

SCA PROMOTIONS, INC.
Street address 1: 3030 Lbj Fwy
Street address 2: Ste 300
Street address state: TX
Zip/Postal code: 75234-2753
Country: USA
Mailing address: 3030 Lbj Fwy Ste 300
Mailing city: Dallas
Mailing state: TX
Mailing zip: 75234-2753
General Phone: (214) 860-3700
General Fax: (214) 860-3480
Email: info@scapromo.com
Primary Website: www.scapromotions.com
Year Established: 1986
Product/Services: Insurance; Newspaper Marketing; Promotion Services;
Personnel: Robert D. Hamman (Pres.)
Personnel: Shiela Bryan (Vice Pres., Sales)

TEK-TOOLS, INC.
Street address 1: 4040 McEwen Rd
Street address 2: Ste 240
Street address state: TX
Zip/Postal code: 75244-5032
Country: USA
Mailing address: 4040 McEwen Rd Ste 240
Mailing city: Dallas
Mailing state: TX
Mailing zip: 75244-5032
General Phone: (972) 980-2890
General Fax: (972) 866-0714
Email: contact@tek-tools.com
Primary Website: www.tek-tools.com
Year Established: 1993
Product/Services: Software: Advertising (Includes Display; Classified); Software:

Editorial; Software: Electronic Data Interchange; Software: Workflow Management/Tracking;
Personnel: Ken Barth (Pres./CEO)
Personnel: Cindy Whitley (Dir., Sales)
Personnel: Stephen Harding (Dir., Mktg.)

UMAX TECHNOLOGIES, INC.

Street address 1: 10460 Brockwood Rd
Street address state: TX
Zip/Postal code: 75238-1640
Country: USA
Mailing address: 10460 Brockwood Rd
Mailing city: Dallas
Mailing state: TX
Mailing zip: 75238-1640
General Phone: (214) 342-9799
General Fax: (214) 342-9046
Email: sales@umax.com
Primary Website: www.umax.com
Product/Services: Color Seperation Scanners; Scanners: Color B & W, Plates, Web;
Personnel: Tenny Sin (Vice Pres., Mktg.)
Personnel: Linn Lin (Sr. Line Mgr.)

DANBURY

PRAXAIR, INC.

Street address 1: 10 Riverview Dr.
Street address state: CT
Zip/Postal code: 06810
Country: USA
Mailing address: 10 Riverview Dr.
Mailing city: Danbury
Mailing state: CT
Mailing zip: 06810
General Phone: (800) 772-9247
General Fax: (800) 772-9985
Email: info@praxair.com
Primary Website: www.praxair.com
Year Established: 1992
Product/Services: Rollers
Personnel: Stephen F. Angel (Chrmn./Pres./CEO)
Personnel: Matthew J. White (Sr. V. P. & CFO)
Personnel: Eduardo Menezes (Exec. Vice Pres.)
Kelcey E. Hoyt (V. P. & Controller)
Lisa A. Esneault (Vice Pres., Global Commun./Pub. Rel.)

DANVERS

EDGIL ASSOCIATES, INC.

Street address 1: 222 Rosewood Dr
Street address 2: Ste 210
Street address state: MA
Zip/Postal code: 01923-4520
Country: USA
Mailing address: 222 Rosewood Dr Ste 210
Mailing city: Danvers
Mailing state: MA
Mailing zip: 01923-4520
General Phone: (800) 457-9932
General Fax: (978) 667-6050
Email: sales@edgil.com
Primary Website: www.edgil.com
Product/Services: Payment Processing
Product or Service: Hardware/Software Supplier
Personnel: Sean Callahan (Dir., Sales)

DANVILLE

M.W. BURKE & ASSOCIATES, INC.

Street address 1: 185 Front St
Street address 2: Ste 207
Street address state: CA
Zip/Postal code: 94526-3340
Country: USA
Mailing address: 185 Front St Ste 207
Mailing city: Danville
Mailing state: CA
Mailing zip: 94526-3340
General Phone: (925) 838-9070
General Fax: (925) 838-4695
Email: mwburke@aol.com
Year Established: 1976

Product/Services: Consulting Services: Advertising; Consulting Services: Circulation; Consulting Services: Production; Prepress Color Proofing Systems;
Personnel: M.W. (Maury) Burke (Pres./Chrmn.)

MCCAIN PRINTING CO.

Street address 1: 525 Wilson St
Street address state: VA
Zip/Postal code: 24541-1437
Country: USA
Mailing address: 525 Wilson St
Mailing city: Danville
Mailing state: VA
Mailing zip: 24541-1490
General Phone: (434) 792-1331
General Fax: (434) 793-5473
Email: efsounders@mccainprint.com
Primary Website: www.mccainprint.com
Personnel: Eugene Sounders (Owner)

DARIEN

ROTADYNE CORP.

Street address 1: 8140 Cass Ave
Street address state: IL
Zip/Postal code: 60561-5013
Country: USA
Mailing address: 8140 S Cass Ave
Mailing city: Darien
Mailing state: IL
Mailing zip: 60561-5013
General Phone: (630) 769-9700
General Fax: (630) 769-9255
Email: rotadynecorp@rotadyne.com
Primary Website: www.rotadyne.com
Year Established: 1982
Product/Services: Blankets; Roll Coverings; Rollers; Rollers; Dampening;
Personnel: John A. Costello (Vice Pres., OEM Sales)
Personnel: John Kaminski (Vice Pres. Industrial Sales)
Personnel: John Breau (Vice Pres. Graphic Sales)

DE PERE

MEGTEC SYSTEMS

Street address 1: 830 Prosper St
Street address state: WI
Zip/Postal code: 54115-3104
Country: USA
Mailing address: PO Box 5030
Mailing city: De Pere
Mailing state: WI
Mailing zip: 54115-5030
General Phone: (920) 337-1410
General Fax: (920) 558-5535
Email: info@megtec.com
Primary Website: www.megtec.com
Year Established: 1969
Product/Services: Dryers: Film and Papers; Drying Systems; Environmental Control Systems; Flying Pasters; Roll Handling Equipment;
Personnel: Mary Van Vonderen (Mktg. Mgr.)

DECATUR

JOHN JULIANO COMPUTER SERVICES CO.

Street address 1: 2152 Willivee Pl
Street address state: GA
Zip/Postal code: 30033-4114
Country: USA
Mailing address: 2152 Willive Pl.
Mailing city: Decatur
Mailing state: GA
Mailing zip: 30033
General Phone: (404) 327-6010
General Fax: (815) 301-8581
Email: info@jjcs.com
Primary Website: www.jjcs.com
Year Established: 1982

Product/Services: Consulting Services: Computer; Consulting Services: Marketing;
Personnel: John Juliano (Pres.)
Personnel: L. Carol Christopher (Principal Analyst)

DEEP RIVER

SCHAEFER MACHINE CO., INC.

Street address 1: 200 Commercial Dr
Street address state: CT
Zip/Postal code: 06417-1682
Country: USA
Mailing address: 200 Commercial Dr
Mailing city: Deep River
Mailing state: CT
Mailing zip: 06417-1682
General Phone: (860) 526-4000
General Fax: (860) 526-4654
Email: schaefer01@snet.net
Primary Website: www.schaeferco.com
Year Established: 1945
Product/Services: Adhesives; Gluing Systems;
Personnel: Bob Gammons (Pres.)
Personnel: Virginia Gammons (Vice Pres.)

DENVER

QUARK, INC.

Street address 1: 1225 17th St
Street address 2: Ste 1200
Street address state: CO
Zip/Postal code: 80202-5503
Country: USA
Mailing address: 1225 17th St Ste 1200
Mailing city: Denver
Mailing state: CO
Mailing zip: 80202-5503
General Phone: (303) 894-8888
General Fax: (303) 894-3399
Email: quarkxpress@quark.com
Primary Website: www.quark.com
Year Established: 1981
Product/Services: Software: Asset Management; Software: Design/Graphics; Software: Editorial; Software: Pagination/Layout;
Personnel: Kamar Aulakh (Pres./CEO)

SPECTRUM HUMAN RESOURCE SYSTEMS CORP.

Street address 1: 707 17th St
Street address 2: Ste 3800
Street address state: CO
Zip/Postal code: 80202-3438
Country: USA
Mailing address: 999 18th St Ste 200
Mailing city: Denver
Mailing state: CO
Mailing zip: 80202-2424
General Phone: (303) 592-3200
General Fax: (303) 595-9970
Email: info@spectrumhr.com
Primary Website: www.spectrumhr.com
Year Established: 1984
Product/Services: Software: Asset Management; Software: Business (Includes Administration/Accounting);
Personnel: Sybll Romley (Pres.)
Personnel: Matthew Keitlen (Exec. Vice Pres.)

THOUGHT EQUITY MANAGEMENT, INC.

Street address 1: 1530 16th St
Street address 2: Fl 6
Street address state: CO
Zip/Postal code: 80202-1447
Country: USA
Mailing address: 1530 16th St Ste 600
Mailing city: Denver
Mailing state: CO
Mailing zip: 80202-1447
General Phone: (720) 382-2869
General Fax: (720) 382-2719
Email: sales@thoughtequity.com
Primary Website: www.thoughtequity.com

Year Established: 2003
Product/Services: Electronic Ad Delivery
Note: Thought Equity Libraries: Supplier of motion content to newspaper, cable and broadcast companies. Thousands of affordable, top-quality ads and commercials are searchable and accessible online."
Personnel: Kevin Schaff (Founder/CEO)
Personnel: Mark Lemmons (CTO)
Personnel: Mike Emerson (Vice Pres., Mktg.)
Frank Cardello (Vice Pres., Bus. Devel.)

DENVILLE

FULCO, INC.

Street address 1: 30 Broad St
Street address state: NJ
Zip/Postal code: 07834-1236
Country: USA
Mailing address: 30 Broad St.
Mailing city: Denville
Mailing state: NJ
Mailing zip: 07834
General Phone: (973) 627-2427
General Fax: 973-627-5872
Email: support@fulcoinc.com
Primary Website: www.fulcoinc.com
Year Established: 1981
Product/Services: Subscription Fulfillment
Note: Subscription Fulfillment Company
Personnel: Jim Duffy (Owner/Pres.)
Personnel: Dave Ross (Client Services Director)

DES PLAINES

SRDS, A KANTAR MEDIA COMPANY

Street address 1: 1700 E Higgins Rd
Street address 2: Fl 5
Street address state: IL
Zip/Postal code: 60018-5621
Country: USA
Mailing address: 1700 E Higgins Rd Ste 500
Mailing city: Des Plaines
Mailing state: IL
Mailing zip: 60018-5610
General Phone: (847) 375-5000
General Fax: (847) 375-5001
Email: contact@srds.com
Primary Website: www.srds.com
Year Established: 1919
Product/Services: Trade Publications
Note: Media buyers today develop integrated plans from a media landscape that is more complex than ever. They use the SRDS multimedia planning platform daily to navigate that landscape and effectively identify their best options from 125,000+ media brands.
Personnel: Kevin McNally (CFO)
Personnel: Stephen Davis (President)
Personnel: Valerie LaMorte (Vice Pres., HR)
Trish DeLaurier (VP, Information Sales & Client Service)
Gayle Paprocki (Vice Pres., Pdct. Opns.)
Dave Kostolansky (Vice Pres., Mktg./Bus. Devel.)
Lindsay Morrison (VP Marketing Communications)
Ronald Speechley (Publisher)
June Levy (Director, Data Services)
John Cronan (Sales Director, Southwest Region)

DETROIT

DOUTHITT CORP.

Street address 1: 245 Adair St
Street address state: MI
Zip/Postal code: 48207-4214
Country: USA
Mailing address: 245 Adair St
Mailing city: Detroit
Mailing state: MI
Mailing zip: 48207-4287
General Phone: (313) 259-1565
General Fax: (313) 259-6806
Email: em@douthittcorp.com
Primary Website: www.douthittcorp.com

Equipment, Supplies and Services

Year Established: 1919
Product/Services: Controls: Exposure; Exposure Lamps; Layout Tables, Light Tables & Workstations; Light Integrators; Offset Plate-Making Service & Equipment; Pin Register Systems; Plate Exposure Units; Platemakers: Flexographic (Traditional); Platemakers: Offset (Computer to Plate); Vacuum Frames;
Personnel: Mark W. Diehl (Int'l Sales)

DEXTER

PHOTO SYSTEMS, INC.

Street address 1: 7200 Huron River Dr
Street address state: MI
Zip/Postal code: 48130-1099
Country: USA
Mailing address: 7200 Huron River Dr
Mailing city: Dexter
Mailing state: MI
Mailing zip: 48130-1099
General Phone: (734) 424-9625
Email: lori@photosys.com
Primary Website: www.photosys.com
Year Established: 1968
Product/Services: Chemicals: Photographic; Chemicals: Plate Processing; Chemicals: Pressroom; Chemicals: Roller Cleaning; Film & Paper: Film Processing Machines;
Personnel: Alan Fischer (Pres.)

DK-8700 HORSENS

SCHUR INTERNATIONAL A/S

Street address 1: DK-8700 Horsens
Country: Denmark
Mailing address: J.W. Schurs Vej 1
Mailing city: Dk-8700 Horsens
General Phone: +45 7627 2727
General Fax: +45 7627 2700
Email: sin@schur.com
Primary Website: www.schur.com
Personnel: Hans Schur (Owner)

DOWNERS GROVE

BALDWIN TECHNOLOGY COMPANY, INC.

Street address 1: 3041 Woodcreek Dr
Street address 2: Ste 102
Street address state: IL
Zip/Postal code: 60515-5418
Country: USA
Mailing address: 3041 Woodcreek Dr Ste 102
Mailing city: Downers Grove
Mailing state: IL
Mailing zip: 60515-5418
General Phone: 630-595-3651
General Fax: 630-595-5433
Email: info@baldwintech.com
Primary Website: www.baldwintech.com
Product/Services: UV & LED Curing and IR Drying Systems; Automatic Blanket Cleaners; Circulation Equipment & Supplies; Dampening Systems; Environmental Control Systems; Fluid Management Systems: Pressroom; Ink Controls, Computerized; Press Accessories, Parts & Supplies; Recirculators; Solvent Recovery Systems; Powder Applicators; Gluing Systems; Anti-Offset Powder; Blanket Cleaning Cloth Consumables; UV Lamps
Note: Baldwin Technology Company, Inc. is a leading international supplier of process automation equipment and related consumables for the graphic arts industry. Newspaper, sheetfed, commercial web, flexographic and digital pressrooms are enhanced and transformed with Baldwin's extensive product lines and systems. Baldwin's cutting edge systems include UV and LED curing, IR drying, spray dampening, blanket, plate and web cleaning, fluid management, ink control, web press protection, and press consumables. New product development and marketing are key initiatives for Baldwin as response to constantly changing market demands is critical in a rapidly evolving marketplace.
Personnel: Donald Gustafson (Vice President, Baldwin Americas Sales & Marketing)

CLIPPER BELT LACER CO.

Street address 1: 2525 Wisconsin Ave
Street address state: IL
Zip/Postal code: 60515-4241
Country: USA
Mailing address: 2525 Wisconsin Ave
Mailing city: Downers Grove
Mailing state: IL
Mailing zip: 60515-4241
General Phone: 800-323-3444
General Fax: 630-971-1180
Email: info@flexco.com
Primary Website: www.flexco.com
Year Established: 1908
Product/Services: Belts, Belting, V-Belts; Cutting Tools;
Personnel: Nancy Ayres (Gen. Mgr.)
Personnel: Bro Ballentine (Treasurer)
Personnel: Dick Reynolds (Sales Mgr.)
John H. Meulenberg (Mktg. Mgr.)
Beth Miller (Pdct. Mgr.)

NSA MEDIA

Street address 1: 3025 Highland Pkwy,
Street address 2: Suite 700
Street address state: IL
Zip/Postal code: 60515
Country: USA
Mailing address: 3025 Highland Pkwy Ste 700
Mailing city: Downers Grove
Mailing state: IL
Mailing zip: 60515-5553
General Phone: (630) 729-7500
Email: info@nsamedia.com
Primary Website: www.nsamedia.com
Year Established: 1991
Product/Services: Consulting Services: Advertising
Personnel: Randy Novak (VP, Bus. Dev.)

DRESDEN

NET-LINX AG

Street address 1: Kathe-Kollwitz-Ufer 76-79
Country: Germany
Mailing address: Kathe-Kollwitz-Ufer 76-79
Mailing city: Dresden
Mailing zip: 01309
General Phone: +49 351 3187 5888
General Fax: +49 351 3187 5550
Email: nxinfo@net-linx.com
Primary Website: www.net-linx.com
Personnel: Holm Hallbauer (Pres.)

DUPO

PRESSLINE SERVICES, INC.

Street address 1: 731 Prairie Dupont Dr
Street address state: IL
Zip/Postal code: 62239-1819
Country: USA
Mailing address: 731 Prairie Dupont Dr
Mailing city: Dupo
Mailing state: IL
Mailing zip: 62239
General Phone: (314) 682-3800
General Fax: (314) 487-3150
Primary Website: www.pressline.info; www.presslineservices.com
Year Established: 1995
Product/Services: Consulting Services: Equipment; Cylinder Repair; Press Rebuilding; Press Repairs; Web Width Changer;
Personnel: Jim Gore (Pres.)

DURHAM

BELL & HOWELL SCANNERS

Street address 1: 3791 South Alston Ave
Street address state: NC
Zip/Postal code: 27713
Country: USA
Mailing address: 3791 South Alston Ave
Mailing city: Durham
Mailing state: NC
Mailing zip: 27713
General Phone: 800-961-7282
Email: info@bhemail.com
Primary Website: www.bellhowell.net
Year Established: 1907
Product/Services: Mailroom Systems & Equipment; Publishing Systems
Personnel: Ramesh Ratan (Vice-Chairman)
Personnel: Larry Blue (Pres.)
Personnel: Arthur Bergens (CFO)

GOSS INTERNATIONAL CORPORATION

Street address 1: 121 Technology Dr
Street address state: NH
Zip/Postal code: 03824-4721
Country: USA
Mailing address: 121 Technology Dr
Mailing city: Durham
Mailing state: NH
Mailing zip: 03824-4716
General Phone: 603-749-6600
General Fax: 603-750-6860
Email: info@gossinternational.com
Primary Website: www.gossinternational.com
Year Established: 1885
Product/Services: Press Accessories, Parts & Supplies; Press Rebuilding; Press Repairs; Presses: Offset;
Personnel: Ed Padilla (Chrmn.)
Personnel: Jochen Meissner (CEO)
Personnel: Joseph Gaynor (CFO)
Richard Schultz (Sr. Vice Pres., Global Sales)
Cecilia Chou (Mktg. Mgr.)
Greg Norris

EAST HAVEN

HART INDUSTRIES

Street address 1: 43 Doran St
Street address state: CT
Zip/Postal code: 06512-2212
Country: USA
Mailing address: 43 Doran St
Mailing city: East Haven
Mailing state: CT
Mailing zip: 06512-2212
General Phone: (203) 469-6344
General Fax: (203) 469-6592
Email: steve@hartindus.com
Primary Website: www.hartindus.com
Year Established: 1984
Product/Services: Dark Room Equipment; Environmental Control Systems; Silver Recovery; Wastewater Treatment;
Personnel: Steve Mancuso (Pres.)

EAST MONTPELIER

PRINTMARK

Street address 1: 432 Johnson Rd
Street address state: VT
Zip/Postal code: 05651-4250
Country: USA
Mailing address: 432 Johnson Rd
Mailing city: East Montpelier
Mailing state: VT
Mailing zip: 05651-4250
General Phone: (802) 229-9743
Email: alex@printmark.net
Primary Website: www.printmark.net
Year Established: 1983
Product/Services: Consulting Services: Computer; Consulting Services: Editorial; Consulting Services: Production;
Note: Consultants to publishers on manufacturing, distribution, and technology."
Personnel: Alex Brown (Dir., Prodn.)

EAST PROVIDENCE

CREATIVE CIRCLE MEDIA SOLUTIONS

Street address 1: 945 Waterman Ave
Street address state: RI
Zip/Postal code: 02914-1342
Country: USA
Mailing address: 945 Waterman Ave.
Mailing city: East Providence
Mailing state: RI
Mailing zip: 02914
General Phone: (401) 272-1122
Email: info@creativecirclemedia.com
Primary Website: www.creativecirclemedia.com
Year Established: 1984
Product/Services: Software: web CMS, advertising, native content; Consulting; Outsourcing; Training; Web and print redesigns; print editorial production platform.
Product or Service: Advertising/Marketing

Agency`Circulation`Consultants`Editorial`Graphic/Design Firm`Hardware/Software Supplier`Marketing`Multimedia; Interactive Products`Other Services`Online Service Provider and Internet Hosts

Note: Full service and custom software provider with a dynamic web CMS, user-contributed content, classifieds, hosting, pay wall, native content, QuickAds and print editorial production systems. We also provide strategic consulting, newsroom training, ad design training, new revenue ideas, high-end outsourcing services and extensive print and web redesigns.

Personnel: Bill Ostendorf (Pres & Founder)
Personnel: Lynn Rognsvoog (Design director)
Personnel: Tim Benson (IT director)

EASTCHESTER

MIRACOM COMPUTER CORP.

Street address 1: PO Box 44
Street address state: NY
Zip/Postal code: 10709-0044
Country: USA
Mailing address: PO Box 44
Mailing city: Eastchester
Mailing state: NY
Mailing zip: 10709
General Phone: (888) 309-0639
Email: info@miracomcomputer.com
Primary Website: www.miracomcomputer.com
Year Established: 1995
Product/Services: Inserter Control Systems Production Control Systems Planning Systems Inventory Systems Inkjet Labeling Systems
Note: Miracom is the Newspaper Post-Press control and software leader. Producers of MiraSert for inserter control, MiraLabel for in-line address labeling, MiraPkg for planning and inventory, and other software systems for managing your production facility from start to finish.
Personnel: Judah Holstein (CEO)
Personnel: Bill Harley (Vice President)
Personnel: Tom Whelan (Director, Customer Service)
Ralph Valero (Field Application Engineer)
Michael Dodds (Project Engineer)
Alex Gray (Application Developer)
Amy Arkawy (Inside Sales)
Tina Dalton (Finance Representative)

EASTON

PARAGON TECHNOLOGIES INC.

Street address 1: 600 Kuebler Rd
Street address state: PA
Zip/Postal code: 18040-9201
Country: USA
Mailing address: 101 Larry Holmes Dr Ste 500
Mailing city: Easton
Mailing state: PA
Mailing zip: 18042-7723
General Phone: (610) 252-7321
General Fax: (610) 252-3102
Email: info@sihs.com; sales@sihs.com
Primary Website: www.sihs.com
Year Established: 1958
Product/Services: Conveyors; Mailroom Systems & Equipment; Material Handling Equipment: Automatic Guided Vehicles;
Personnel: Theodore W. Myers (Chrmn.)

TOWER PRODUCTS, INC.

Street address 1: 2703 Freemansburg Ave
Street address state: PA
Zip/Postal code: 18045-6090
Country: USA
Mailing address: PO Box 3070
Mailing city: Palmer
Mailing state: PA
Mailing zip: 18043-3070
General Phone: (610) 253-6206
General Fax: (610) 258-9695
Email: info@towerproducts.com
Primary Website: www.towerproducts.com
Year Established: 1964
Product/Services: Chemicals: Pressroom; Chemicals: Roller Cleaning; Cleaners & Solvents; Fountain Solutions, Low VOC Cleaners
Note: Tower Products is a manufacturer of pressroom chemical products including fountain solutions, low voc washes and specialty chemicals."
Personnel: Richard Principato (Pres./CEO)

EDINA

SOFTWARE BUSINESS SYSTEMS

Street address 1: 7401 Metro Blvd
Street address 2: Ste 550
Street address state: MN
Zip/Postal code: 55435
Country: USA
Mailing address: 7401 Metro Blvd Ste 550
Mailing city: Edina
Mailing state: MN
Mailing zip: 55435
General Phone: (952) 835-0100
Email: marketing@sbsweb.com
Primary Website: www.sbsweb.com
Year Established: 1980
Product/Services: Software: Business (Includes Administration/ Accounting); Payroll/HR; Procurement; System Installations; System Integration Services;
Personnel: Curtis Cerf (Pres.)
Personnel: Katherine Gladney (Office Manager)

EDISON

FUJIFILM GRAPHIC SYSTEMS USA, INC.

Street address 1: 1100 King Georges Post Road
Street address state: NJ
Zip/Postal code: 08837
Country: USA
Mailing address: 1100 King Georges Post Road
Mailing city: Edison
Mailing state: NJ
Mailing zip: 08837
General Phone: (732) 857-3280
General Fax: (732) 857-3470
Primary Website: www.fujifilmusa.com/products/graphic_arts_ printing/index.html
Product/Services: Blankets; Chemicals: Pressroom; Color Management Software; Imagesetters; Inks; Offset Chemicals & Supplies; Platemakers: Flexographic (Computer to Plate); Plates: Offset (Conventional); Proofing Systems; Software: Press/Post Press;
Personnel: Michael Sharpe (Regional Sales Manager)

EFFINGHAM

B & L MACHINE & DESIGN

Street address 1: 1 Legend Park
Street address state: IL
Zip/Postal code: 62401-9442
Country: USA
Mailing address: PO Box 743
Mailing city: Effingham
Mailing state: IL
Mailing zip: 62401-0743
General Phone: (217) 342-3918
General Fax: (217) 342-2081
Email: info@blmachinedesign.com
Primary Website: www.blmachinedesign.com
Year Established: 1981
Product/Services: Presses: Offset; Training: Press Operation & Maintenance
Personnel: Larry Hines (Pres.)
Personnel: Lara Westjohn (Mktg. Mgr.)
Personnel: Jim Strange (Prodn. Mgr., Mfg.)

SUPPORT PRODUCTS, INC.

Street address 1: 309 Professional Park Ave
Street address state: IL
Zip/Postal code: 62401-2940
Country: USA
Mailing address: PO Box 1185
Mailing city: Effingham
Mailing state: IL
Mailing zip: 62401-1185
General Phone: (217) 536-6171
General Fax: (217) 536-6828
Email: supprot@supportproducts.com; custserv@ supportproducts.com; sales@supportproducts.com
Primary Website: www.supportproducts.com
Year Established: 1984
Product/Services: Adhesives; Chemicals: Roller Cleaning; Composing Room Equipment & Supplies; Ink Fountains & Accessories; Layout Tables, Light Tables & Workstations; Masking Materials; Offset Blanket Thickness Gauge; Plate Cleaners; Rules; Static Eliminators;

Personnel: Jim Calhoon (CEO)
Personnel: Rob Bradshaw (Dir., Sales)

TECHNOLOGY INTEGRATORS

Street address 1: 2 Legend Park
Street address state: IL
Zip/Postal code: 62401-9442
Country: USA
Mailing address: PO Box 334
Mailing city: Effingham
Mailing state: IL
Mailing zip: 62401-0334
General Phone: 217-342-3981
General Fax: 217-3421286
Primary Website: www.technologyintegrators.net; www. airstamping.com
Year Established: 1992
Product/Services: Press Accessories, Parts & Supplies; Vacuum Frames;
Personnel: Gene Williams (Sales Engineer)
Personnel: Troy Ramey (Sales Engineer)
Personnel: Kim Schmidt (Acct. Exec.)

EL SEGUNDO

LEARNING TREE INTERNATIONAL

Street address 1: 400 Continental Blvd
Street address 2: Ste 150
Street address state: CA
Zip/Postal code: 90245-5059
Country: USA
Mailing address: 400 Continental Blvd Ste 150
Mailing city: El Segundo
Mailing state: CA
Mailing zip: 90245-5059
General Phone: (310) 417-9700
General Fax: (310) 410-2952
Email: uscourses@learningtree.com
Primary Website: www.learningtree.com
Year Established: 1974
Product/Services: Training: Keyboard Operation
Personnel: David Collins (Chrmn.)
Personnel: Nicholas Schacht (Pres./CEO)

ELIZABETH

AMERICAN GRAPHIC ARTS, INC.

Street address 1: 150 Broadway
Street address state: NJ
Zip/Postal code: 07206-1856
Country: USA
Mailing address: PO Box 240
Mailing city: Elizabeth
Mailing state: NJ
Mailing zip: 07206-0240
General Phone: (908) 351-6906
General Fax: (908) 351-7156
Primary Website: www.agamachinery.com
Year Established: 1927
Product/Services: Equipment Dealers (Used); Gluing Systems
Personnel: John Jacobson (Pres.)

ELK GROVE VILLAGE

KIMOTO TECH

Street address 1: 1701 Howard St
Street address 2: Ste G
Street address state: IL
Zip/Postal code: 60007-2479
Country: USA
Mailing address: 1701 Howard St Ste G
Mailing city: Elk Grove Village
Mailing state: IL
Mailing zip: 60007-2479
General Phone: (847) 640-8022
General Fax: (847) 640-7942
Email: info@kimototech.com
Primary Website: www.kimototech.com
Year Established: 1980
Product/Services: Film & Paper: Filters (Photographic); Film & Paper: Phototypesetting;
Personnel: Alex Jasinowski (Sales Supvr.)
Personnel: Serina Vartanian (Kimosetter Support)

SIIX USA CORP.

Street address 1: 651 Bonnie Ln

Equipment, Supplies and Services

Street address state: IL
Zip/Postal code: 60007-1911
Country: USA
Mailing address: 651 Bonnie Ln
Mailing city: Elk Grove Village
Mailing state: IL
Mailing zip: 60007-1911
General Phone: (847) 593-3211
General Fax: (847) 364-5290
Email: bpusczan@siix-usa.com
Primary Website: www.siix.co.jp
Year Established: 1972
Product/Services: Scanners: Color B & W, Plates, Web
Personnel: Steve Swanson (Mgr., Sales/Engineering)

ELKRIDGE

FUJIFILM GRAPHIC SYSTEMS USA, INC.

Street address 1: 6810 Deerpath Road
Street address 2: Suite 405
Street address state: MD
Zip/Postal code: 21075
Country: USA
Mailing address: 6810 Deerpath Road, Suite 405
Mailing city: Elkridge
Mailing state: MD
Mailing zip: 21075
General Phone: (301) 317-7480
General Fax: (301) 317-7480
Primary Website: www.fujifilmusa.com/products/graphic_arts_printing/index.html
Product/Services: Blankets; Chemicals: Pressroom; Color Management Software; Imagesetters; Inks; Offset Chemicals & Supplies; Platemakers: Flexographic (Computer to Plate); Plates: Offset (Conventional); Proofing Systems; Software: Press/Post Press;
Personnel: Tony Aquino (Reg'l Sales Mgr.)

ELMHURST

BST PRO MARK

Street address 1: 650 W Grand Ave
Street address 2: Ste 301
Street address state: IL
Zip/Postal code: 60126-1026
Country: USA
Mailing address: 650 W Grand Ave Ste 301
Mailing city: Elmhurst
Mailing state: IL
Mailing zip: 60126-1026
General Phone: (630) 833-9900
General Fax: (630) 833-9909
Email: sales@bstpromark.com
Primary Website: www.bstpromark.com
Year Established: 1987
Product/Services: Color Management Software; Color Registration; Color Viewing Equipment; Press Accessories, Parts & Supplies; Produciton Control Systems; Web Cleaners; Web Guides
Personnel: John Thome (Vice Pres., Mktg.)

G&K-VIJUK INTERNATIONAL

Street address 1: 715 N Church Rd
Street address state: IL
Zip/Postal code: 60126-1415
Country: USA
Mailing address: 715 N Church Rd
Mailing city: Elmhurst
Mailing state: IL
Mailing zip: 60126-1415
General Phone: (630) 530-2203
General Fax: (630) 530-2245
Email: info@guk-vijuk.com
Primary Website: www.guk-vijuk.com
Year Established: 1967
Product/Services: Folding Machines
Personnel: Rick Jasnica (Op. Mgr.)
Personnel: Kevin Boivin (Sales Mgr.)

ELMWOOD PARK

AGFA GRAPHICS

Street address 1: 611 River Drive
Street address 2: Center 3
Street address state: NJ
Zip/Postal code: 07407
Country: USA
Mailing address: 611 River Drive, Center 3
Mailing city: Elmwood Park
Mailing state: NJ
Mailing zip: 07407
General Phone: (201) 440-2500
Primary Website: www.agfagraphics.com
Year Established: 1867
Product/Services: Commercial Printing; Sign & Display; Newspapers; Packaging & Labels; Industrial Printing; Security Printing;
Personnel: Julien De Wilde (Chairman)
Personnel: Christian Reinaudo (CEO)
Personnel: Deborah Hutcheson (Director Marketing)
Lois Catala

EMPORIA

KANSA TECHNOLOGY, LLC

Street address 1: 3700 Oakes Dr
Street address state: KS
Zip/Postal code: 66801-5132
Country: USA
Mailing address: 3700 Oakes Dr
Mailing city: Emporia
Mailing state: KS
Mailing zip: 66801-5136
General Phone: (620) 343-6700
General Fax: (620) 343-2108
Email: marketing@kansa.com
Primary Website: www.kansa.com
Year Established: 1977
Product/Services: Addressing Machines; Collating Equipment; Conveyors; Counting, Stacking, Bundling Machines; Feeding, Folding, Delivery Equipment; Folding Machines; Infeed Stackers; Inserting Equipment (Includes Stuffing Machines); Mailroom Systems & Equipment; Remanufactures Equipment;
Personnel: Jerry Waddell (CEO)
Personnel: Lonnie Worthington (Chief Operating Officer)
Personnel: Megan Kropff

ERLANGER

TKM UNITED STATES, INC.

Street address 1: 1845 Airport Exchange Blvd
Street address 2: Ste 150
Street address state: KY
Zip/Postal code: 41018-3503
Country: USA
Mailing address: PO Box 75015
Mailing city: Cincinnati
Mailing state: OH
Mailing zip: 45275-0015
General Phone: (859) 689-7094
General Fax: (859) 689-7565
Email: sales@tkmus.com
Primary Website: www.tkmus.com
Year Established: 2002
Product/Services: Cutters & Trimmers
Personnel: Michael Clark (Market Mgr.)

EVERGREEN

BURT TECHNOLOGIES, INC.

Street address 1: 32156 Castle Ct
Street address 2: Ste 206
Street address state: CO
Zip/Postal code: 80439-9500
Country: USA
Mailing address: 32156 Castle Ct Ste 206
Mailing city: Evergreen
Mailing state: CO
Mailing zip: 80439-9500
General Phone: (303) 674-3232
General Fax: (303) 670-0978
Email: info@burtmountain.com; sales@burtmountain.com; support@burtmountain.com
Primary Website: www.burtmountain.com
Year Established: 1985
Product/Services: Computers: Hardware & Software Integrators; Inserting Equipment (Includes Stuffing Machines); Interfaces; Mailroom Systems & Equipment; Software: Press/Post Press; Training: Post Press
Personnel: Jim Burt (Founder/Pres.)
Personnel: Rich Burt (CEO)
Personnel: Billy Calva (Burt Response Center Manager)

FAIR LAWN

WRUBEL COMMUNICATIONS

Street address 1: 12-32 River Rd
Street address state: NJ
Zip/Postal code: 07410-1802
Country: USA
Mailing address: 12-32 River Rd
Mailing city: Fair Lawn
Mailing state: NJ
Mailing zip: 07410-1802
General Phone: (201) 796-3331
General Fax: (201) 796-5083
Email: Chasnews@aol.com
Year Established: 1988
Product/Services: Consulting Services: Advertising; Consulting Services: Circulation; Consulting Services: Editorial; Consulting Services: Financial; Consulting Services: Marketing;
Personnel: Charles Wrubel (Pres.)

FAIRFIELD

UNIQUE PHOTO

Street address 1: 123 US Highway 46
Street address state: NJ
Zip/Postal code: 07004-3225
Country: USA
Mailing address: 123 US Highway 46
Mailing city: Fairfield
Mailing state: NJ
Mailing zip: 07004-3225
General Phone: (973) 377-5555
General Fax: (973) 377-8800
Primary Website: www.uniquephoto.com
Year Established: 1947
Product/Services: Cameras & Accessories; Chemicals: Photographic; Cutters & Trimmers; Dark Room Equipment; Developing and Processing; Film & Paper: Film Roll Dispensers; Film & Paper: Filters (Photographic); Lenses (Camera); Photography: Digital/Electronic Cameras; Photostat: Chemicals;
Personnel: Matthew Sweetwood (COO)
Personnel: Jonathon Sweetwood (CFO)

FAIRVIEW

CASCADE CORP.

Street address 1: 2201 NE 201st Ave
Street address state: OR
Zip/Postal code: 97024-9718
Country: USA
Mailing address: PO Box 20187
Mailing city: Portland
Mailing state: OR
Mailing zip: 97294-0187
General Phone: (503) 669-6300
General Fax: (800) 693-3768
Email: sales@cascorp.com
Primary Website: www.cascorp.com
Year Established: 1943
Product/Services: Material Handling Equipment: Truck Loaders; Paper Handling Equipment;
Personnel: Pete Drake (Sr. V. P.)
Personnel: Keith Miller (Dir. of Sales)
Personnel: Jim Farance (Corporate Manager)

FALLS CHURCH

LOGETRONICS CORP.

Street address 1: 6521 Arlington Blvd
Street address 2: Ste 210
Street address state: VA
Zip/Postal code: 22042-3009
Country: USA
Mailing address: 6521 Arlington Blvd Ste 210
Mailing city: Falls Church
Mailing state: VA
Mailing zip: 22042-3009
General Phone: (703) 536-9841
General Fax: (703) 912-7745
Email: loge@starpower.net
Year Established: 1955
Product/Services: Film & Paper: Film Processing Machines; Film & Paper: Film Roll Dispensers; Plate Coating Machines; Plate Exposure Units; Plate Processors; Plate Scanning Systems; Processors: Diffusion Transfer; Processors: Film & Paper; Remanufactures Equipment;
Personnel: Raymond Luca (Pres.)

FARMINGDALE

BULBTRONICS

Street address 1: 45 Banfi Plz
Street address state: NY
Zip/Postal code: 11753
Country: USA
Mailing address: 45 Banfi Plz N
Mailing city: Farmingdale
Mailing state: NY
Mailing zip: 11735-1539
General Phone: (631) 249-2272
General Fax: (631) 249-6066
Email: bulbs@bulbtronics.com
Primary Website: www.bulbtronics.com
Year Established: 1976
Product/Services: Lighting Equipment
Personnel: Lee Vestrich (Vice Pres., Sales)
Personnel: Beckie Mullin (Mgr., Mktg.)

PUBLISHERS CIRCULATION FULFILLMENT INC.

Street address 1: 303 Smith St
Street address 2: Ste 1
Street address state: NY
Zip/Postal code: 11735-1110
Country: USA
Mailing address: 303 Smith Street, Suite One
Mailing city: Farmingdale
Mailing state: NY
Mailing zip: 11735
General Phone: (631) 2703133
Email: sales@pcfcorp.com
Primary Website: www.pcfcorp.com
Product/Services: Newspaper Distribution Technology Services
Personnel: Jerry Giordana (Pres./CEO)
Personnel: Tom Dressler (VP of Growth and Development)
Personnel: James Cunningham

FARMINGTON HILLS

JERVIS B. WEBB CO.

Street address 1: 34375 W 12 Mile Rd
Street address state: MI
Zip/Postal code: 48331-3375
Country: USA
Mailing address: 34375 W 12 Mile Rd
Mailing city: Farmington Hills
Mailing state: MI
Mailing zip: 48331-5624
General Phone: (248) 553-1000
Email: info@jerviswebb.com
Primary Website: www.daifukuna.com
Year Established: 1919
Product/Services: Computers: Hardware & Software Integrators; Consulting Services: Equipment; Conveyors; Mailroom Systems & Equipment; Material Handling Equipment: Automatic Guided Vehicles; Material Handling Equipment: Vehicle Loading;

Newsprint Handling Equipment; Paper Handling Equipment; Roll Handling Equipment; Storage Retrieval Systems;
Personnel: John S. Doychich (Sr. Vice Pres./CFO)
Personnel: Aki Nishimura (Daifuku North America Holding Company President and CEO)

FISHERS

J. THOMAS MCHUGH CO., INC.

Street address 1: 12931 Ford Dr
Street address state: IN
Zip/Postal code: 46038-2899
Country: USA
Mailing address: 12931 Ford Dr
Mailing city: Fishers
Mailing state: IN
Mailing zip: 46038-2899
General Phone: (317) 577-2121
General Fax: (317) 577-2125
Email: tbryant@jtmchugh.com
Primary Website: www.jtmchugh.com
Year Established: 1933
Product/Services: Blanket Mounting and Bars; Blankets; Offset Blanket Thickness Gauge; Offset Blankets, Blanket Wash;
Personnel: Thomas J. Bryant (Owner/CEO)

FLORHAM PARK

BASF CORPORATION

Street address 1: 100 Park Ave
Street address state: NJ
Zip/Postal code: 07932-1049
Country: USA
Mailing address: 100 Park Ave
Mailing city: Florham Park
Mailing state: NJ
Mailing zip: 07932-1089
General Phone: (973) 245-6000
Email: Procurement-Resource-Center@basf.com
Primary Website: www.basf.us
Year Established: 1865
Product/Services: Chemicals; Plastics; Catalysts; Coatings; Crop Technology; Crude Oil & Natural Gas Exploration and Production;
Personnel: Wayne T. Smith (Chairman and CEO)
Personnel: Andre Becker (CFO)

FOLSOM

GOLD COUNTY ADVISORS, INC.

Street address 1: 604 Sutter St
Street address 2: Ste 394
Street address state: CA
Zip/Postal code: 95630-2698
Country: USA
Mailing address: 604 Sutter St Ste 394
Mailing city: Folsom
Mailing state: CA
Mailing zip: 95630-2698
General Phone: (916) 673-9778
General Fax: (888) 933-0807
Email: jeff@goldcountryadvisors.com
Primary Website: www.goldcountryadvisors.com
Year Established: 2003
Product/Services: Brokers & Appraisers, Merger & Acquisition Advisors for the newspaper business.
Personnel: Jeffrey Potts (Principal)

FOREST HILLS

MANASSY SALES INC.

Street address 1: 6861 Yellowstone Blvd
Street address state: NY
Zip/Postal code: 11375-9403
Country: USA
Mailing address: 6861 Yellowstone Blvd Ste 106
Mailing city: Forest Hills
Mailing state: NY
Mailing zip: 11375-9404
General Phone: (718) 544-4739
General Fax: (347) 642 8060
Email: manassyparts@yahoo.com
Year Established: 1961
Product/Services: Press Accessories, Parts & Supplies; Rollers;
Note: Replacement Parts for Newspaper folders Primarily gain rings for TKS & Man Rolland
Personnel: Joel Marcus (Pres.)

FORT SMITH

BALDOR ELECTRIC CO.

Street address 1: 5711 Rs Boreham Jr St
Street address state: AR
Zip/Postal code: 72901-8301
Country: USA
Mailing address: PO Box 2400
Mailing city: Fort Smith
Mailing state: AR
Mailing zip: 72902-2400
General Phone: (479) 646-4711
General Fax: (479) 648-5752
Primary Website: www.baldor.com
Year Established: 1920
Product/Services: Drives & ControlsMotors
Personnel: Peter Voser (Chrmn.)
Personnel: Ulrich Spiesshofer (CEO)

FORT WAYNE

MCCRRORY PUBLISHING

Street address 1: 2530 Deerwood Dr.
Street address state: IN
Zip/Postal code: 46825
Country: USA
Mailing address: 2530 Deerwood Dr.
Mailing city: Fort Wayne
Mailing state: IN
Mailing zip: 46825
General Phone: (260) 485-1812
Email: info@mccpub.com
Primary Website: www.mccpub.com
Year Established: 2001
Product/Services: Computers: Hardware & Software Integrators; Consulting Services: Computer; Consulting Services: Editorial; Software: Advertising (Includes Display; Classified); Software: Editorial; Software: Electronic Data Interchange; Software: Pagination/Layout; System Integration Services;
Note: Digital Graphics and Printing

FORT WORTH

FLEMING ENTERPRISES

Street address 1: 928 S Blue Mound Rd
Street address state: TX
Zip/Postal code: 76131-1402
Country: USA
Mailing address: 928 S Blue Mound Rd
Mailing city: Fort Worth
Mailing state: TX
Mailing zip: 76131-1402
General Phone: (817) 232-9575
General Fax: (817) 847-6705
Primary Website: www.flemingenterprises.net
Year Established: 1982
Product/Services: Drives & Controls; Drying Systems; Equipment Dealers (Used); Erectors & Riggers; Feeder Press; Feeding, Folding, Delivery Equipment; Produciton Control Systems; Roll Handling Equipment; Roller Grinders; Tension & Web Controls;
Note: We specialize in (but not limited to) web offset services
Personnel: Jeff M. Fleming (Owner)
Personnel: Patrick Fleming (Office Manager)

FOUNTAIN VALLEY

CACHET FINE ART PHOTOGRAPHIC PAPER

Street address 1: 11661 Martens River Cir
Street address 2: Ste D
Street address state: CA
Zip/Postal code: 92708-4212
Country: USA
Mailing address: 11661 Martens River Cir Ste D
Mailing city: Fountain Valley
Mailing state: CA
Mailing zip: 92708-4212
General Phone: (714) 432-6331
General Fax: (714) 432-7102
Email: onecachet@aol.com
Primary Website: www.onecachet.com
Year Established: 1979
Product/Services: Chemicals: Photographic; Dark Room Equipment; Film & Paper; Filters (Photographic);
Personnel: Ike Royer (Pres.)

EDITOR & PUBLISHER MAGAZINE

Street address 1: 18475 Bandilier Cir
Street address state: CA
Zip/Postal code: 92708-7000
Country: USA
Mailing address: 18475 Bandilier Circle
Mailing city: Fountain Valley
Mailing state: CA
Mailing zip: 92708
General Phone: 949-660-6150
General Fax: 949-660-6172
Email: circulation@editorandpublisher.com
Primary Website: www.editorandpublisher.com
Year Established: 1884
Product/Services: Trade Publications
Personnel: Duncan McIntosh (Pres./ Pub.)
Personnel: Jeff Fleming (V.P./ Editor-in-Chief)
Personnel: Nu Yang (Mng. Ed.)
Wendy MacDonald (Sales/Mktg. Consult.)
Evelyn Mateos (Asst. Ed.)

FRAMINGHAM

CRAFTSMEN MACHINERY CO., INC.

Street address 1: 1257 Worcester Rd
Street address 2: Unit 167
Street address state: MA
Zip/Postal code: 01701-5217
Country: USA
Mailing address: PO Box 2006
Mailing city: Framingham
Mailing state: MA
Mailing zip: 01703-2006
General Phone: (508) 376-2001
General Fax: (508) 376-2003
Email: sales@craftsnmenmachinery.com
Primary Website: www.craftsmenmachinery.com
Year Established: 1925
Product/Services: Corner Rounders; Drilling Equipment; Densitometers; Folders, Creasers, Gauges, Measuring; Presses: Offset;
Personnel: Sherwin Marks (Pres./Chief Exec. Officer)

FRANKLIN

AIRLOC LLC

Street address 1: 5 Fisher St
Street address state: MA
Zip/Postal code: 02038-2114
Country: USA
Mailing address: PO Box 260
Mailing city: Franklin
Mailing state: MA
Mailing zip: 02038-0260
General Phone: (508) 528-0022
General Fax: (508) 528-7555
Email: info@airloc.com
Primary Website: www.airloc.com
Year Established: 1954
Product/Services: Vibration Isolation & Machine Leveling Mounts
Personnel: Philip Littlewood (Engineering Mgr.)

FRANKLIN PARK

SEMLER INDUSTRIES, INC. (PRESSROOM FLUIDS EQUIPMENT DIV.)

Street address 1: 3800 Carnation St
Street address state: IL
Zip/Postal code: 60131-1202
Country: USA
Mailing address: 3800 Carnation St
Mailing city: Franklin Park
Mailing state: IL
Mailing zip: 60131-1202
General Phone: (847) 671-5650
General Fax: (847) 671-7686
Email: semler@semlerindustries.com
Primary Website: www.semlerindustries.com
Year Established: 1905
Product/Services: Circulation Equipment & Supplies; Fluid Handling: Pressroom; Ink Recovery Systems; Ink Storage Tanks; Wastewater Treatment;
Personnel: Loren H. Semler (Pres.)
Personnel: William E. Schulz (Dir. Sales)

FRIBOURG

WIFAG

Street address 1: 26, route de la GlâÃ¢ne,
Street address state: NJ
Zip/Postal code: 1701
Country: Switzerland
Mailing address: 26, route de la GlâÃ¢ne
Mailing city: Fribourg
Mailing zip: 1701
General Phone: +41 26 426 11 11
General Fax: +41 26 426 11 12
Email: info@wifag-polytype.com
Primary Website: www.wifag-polytype.com
Year Established: 1904
Product/Services: Printing Presses: Offset & Digital, New & Preowned, Automation & Press Controls, Upgrades, Rertrofits and Service
Personnel: Noel McEvoy (Director of Sales & Marketing)

GARDEN GROVE

BATON LOCK & HARDWARE CO., INC.

Street address 1: 11521 Salinaz Ave
Street address state: CA
Zip/Postal code: 92843-3702
Country: USA
Mailing address: 11521 Salinaz Ave
Mailing city: Garden Grove
Mailing state: CA
Mailing zip: 92843-3702
General Phone: (714) 590-6969
General Fax: (714) 590-6960
Email: info@batonlockusa.com
Primary Website: www.batonlockusa.com
Product/Services: Calibration Software/Hardware
Personnel: Hwei Ying Chen (Pres.)

GARDENA

K-JACK ENGINEERING CO., INC.

Street address 1: 1522 W 134th St
Street address state: CA
Zip/Postal code: 90249-2216
Country: USA
Mailing address: PO Box 2320
Mailing city: Gardena
Mailing state: CA
Mailing zip: 90247-0320
General Phone: (310) 327-8389
General Fax: (310) 769-6997
Email: info@kjack.com
Primary Website: www.kjack.com
Year Established: 1963
Product/Services: Cart Distribution Systems;

Equipment, Supplies and Services

Circulation Equipment & Supplies; Delivery Equipment; Newspaper Dispensers (Mechanical/Electronic); Software: Circulation; Tubes, Racks (Includes Racks: Motor Route Tubes);
Personnel: Jack S. Chalabian (Pres.)
Personnel: Jacqueline Chalabian-Jernigan (Vice Pres.)
Personnel: Steven H. Chalabian (Vice Pres., Sales)
Steve Rultenschild (Engineer)

GENOA

ENGINEERING PRODUCTS CO., INC.

Street address 1: 3278 Pleasant Hill Rd
Street address state: IL
Zip/Postal code: 60135
Country: USA
Mailing address: 3278 Pleasant Hill Rd
Mailing city: Genoa
Mailing state: IL
Mailing zip: 60135
General Phone: (815) 784-4020
General Fax: (815) 784-4020
Primary Website: www.engineeringproductco.com
Year Established: 1963
Product/Services: Conveyors
Personnel: Jamie Courtney (Owner)

GERETSRIED-GELTING

GAMMERLER AG

Street address 1: Lietenstr. 26
Zip/Postal code: D-82538
Country: Germany
Mailing address: Lietenstr. 26
Mailing city: Geretsried-Gelting
Mailing zip: D-82538
General Phone: +49 8171 404-326
General Fax: +49 8171 404-244
Email: dietrich.lauber@gammerler.de
Primary Website: www.gammerler.com
Personnel: Dietrich Lauber (Sales Mgr.)

GERMANTOWN

BLOWER APPLICATION CO., INC.

Street address 1: N1114 W19125 Clinton Dr
Street address state: WI
Zip/Postal code: 53022
Country: USA
Mailing address: PO Box 279
Mailing city: Germantown
Mailing state: WI
Mailing zip: 53022-0279
General Phone: (800) 959-0880
General Fax: (262) 255-3446
Email: info@bloapco.com
Primary Website: www.bloapco.com
Year Established: 1933
Product/Services: Cutters & Trimmers; In-Line Trimming Systems; Paper Shredders; System Installations;
Personnel: John Stanislowski (Pres.)
Personnel: Michael J. Young (CEO)
Personnel: Ric Johnson (Mgr., Sales)

GILBERTSVILLE

THE JOSS GROUP

Street address 1: PO Box 544
Street address state: PA
Zip/Postal code: 19525
Country: USA
Mailing address: PO Box 544
Mailing city: Gilbertsville
Mailing state: PA
Mailing zip: 19525
General Phone: (610) 427-1512
Email: contact@thejossgroup.com
Primary Website: www.thejossgroup.wildapricot.org
Year Established: 1971
Product/Services: Trade Publications

Note: The first rule of any technology used in business is automation applied to an efficient operation will magnify the efficiency. The second is automation applied to an inefficient operation will magnify the inefficiency. Bill Gates said that, and we agree but from what we have seen there is a ten-fold increase in magnification of all inefficiencies!
Personnel: Molly Joss (Publisher, Editor, Owner)

GLASTONBURY

PORTAGE NEWSPAPER SUPPLY CO.

Street address 1: 655 Winding Brook Dr
Street address 2: Ste 205
Street address state: CT
Zip/Postal code: 06033-4364
Country: USA
Mailing address: 655 Winding Brook Dr Ste 205
Mailing city: Glastonbury
Mailing state: CT
Mailing zip: 06033-4364
General Phone: (877) 659-8318
General Fax: (877) 806-6397
Email: info@portagegraphic.com
Primary Website: www.portagenotebooks.com
Year Established: 1955
Product/Services: Cutters & Trimmers
Personnel: Robert Belter (Pres.)

GLEN ELLYN

FORREST CONSULTING

Street address 1: 725 Kenilworth Ave
Street address state: IL
Zip/Postal code: 60137-3805
Country: USA
Mailing address: 725 Kenilworth Ave
Mailing city: Glen Ellyn
Mailing state: IL
Mailing zip: 60137-3805
General Phone: (630) 730-9619
Email: fasttrackhelp@strategicbusinessleader.com
Primary Website: www.strategicbusinessleader.com
Year Established: 1988
Product/Services: Consulting Services: Advertising; Consulting Services: Circulation; Consulting Services: Financial; Consulting Services: Marketing;
Personnel: Lee Crumbaugh (Pres.)

GLEN ROCK

ADHESIVES RESEARCH, INC.

Street address 1: 400 Seaks Run Rd
Street address state: PA
Zip/Postal code: 17327-9500
Country: USA
Mailing address: PO Box 100
Mailing city: Glen Rock
Mailing state: PA
Mailing zip: 17327-0100
General Phone: (717) 235-7979
General Fax: (717) 235-8320
Primary Website: www.adhesivesresearch.com
Year Established: 1961
Product/Services: Adhesives
Personnel: George Cramer (Vice Pres., Commercial Devel.)

GLENVIEW

ILLINOIS TOOL WORKS INC.

Street address 1: 155 Harlem Avenue
Street address state: IL
Zip/Postal code: 60025
Country: USA
Mailing address: 155 Harlem Avenue
Mailing city: Glenview
Mailing state: IL
Mailing zip: 60025
General Phone: (224) 661-8870
Primary Website: www.itw.com

Year Established: 1912
Product/Services: Strapping Machines
Personnel: E. Scott Santi (Chairman & CEO)
Personnel: Michael M. Larsen (Vice Pres. & CFO)
Personnel: Norman D. Finch Jr. (Senior Vice President, General Counsel & Secretary)

GOODLETTSVILLE

ROWLETT ADVERTISING SERVICE, INC.

Street address 1: 2003 Crencor Dr
Street address state: TN
Zip/Postal code: 37072-4314
Country: USA
Mailing address: PO Box 50
Mailing city: Goodlettsville
Mailing state: TN
Mailing zip: 37070-0050
General Phone: (615) 859-6609
General Fax: (615) 851-7187
Email: rowlettadvertising@att.net
Primary Website: www.rowlettadv.com
Year Established: 1978
Product/Services: Church Page Advertising Sales
Personnel: Richard Rowlett (Pres.)
Personnel: Mary Belcher (Sec./Treasurer)

GRAND ISLAND

NRD LLC

Street address 1: 2937 Alt Blvd
Street address state: NY
Zip/Postal code: 14072-1285
Country: USA
Mailing address: PO Box 310
Mailing city: Grand Island
Mailing state: NY
Mailing zip: 14072-0310
General Phone: (716) 773-7634
General Fax: (716) 773-7744
Email: sales@nrdinc.com
Primary Website: www.nrdinc.com
Year Established: 1970
Product/Services: Static Eliminators
Personnel: John Glynn (Director of Sales and Marketing)

GRAND RAPIDS

DEMATICS

Street address 1: 507 Plymouth Ave NE
Street address state: MI
Zip/Postal code: 49505-6029
Country: USA
Mailing address: 507 Plymouth Ave NE
Mailing city: Grand Rapids
Mailing state: MI
Mailing zip: 49505-6029
General Phone: (877) 725-7500
General Fax: (616) 913-7701
Email: usinfo@dematic.com
Primary Website: www.dematic.us
Year Established: 1939
Product/Services: Conveyors; Material Handling Equipment: Automatic Guided Vehicles; Material Handling Equipment: Truck Loaders;
Personnel: John Baysore (Pres.)
Personnel: S. Buccella (Vice Pres., Field Sales)
Personnel: R. Klaasen (Mgr., Purchasing)

X-RITE INC.

Street address 1: 4300 44th St SE
Street address state: MI
Zip/Postal code: 49512-4009
Country: USA
Mailing address: 4300 44th St SE
Mailing city: Grand Rapids
Mailing state: MI
Mailing zip: 49512-4009
General Phone: (616) 803-2100
General Fax: (888) 826-3061
Email: info@xrite.com; investor@xrite.com;

customerservice@xrite.com
Primary Website: www.xrite.com
Year Established: 1958
Product/Services: Color Analyzers; Color Proofing; Color Viewing Equipment; Densitometers; Ink Controls, Computerized; Lighting Equipment; Photo Proofing Systems; Proofing Systems; Testing Instruments;
Personnel: Thomas J. Vacchiano (Pres./CEO/COO)
Personnel: Mary E Chowning (CFO)
Personnel: Raj Shah (Exec. Vice Pres./CFO)
Francis Lamy (CTO)

GREEN BAY

ADVANCE SYSTEMS, INC.

Street address 1: PO Box 9428
Street address state: WI
Zip/Postal code: 54308-9428
Country: USA
Mailing address: PO Box 9428
Mailing city: Green Bay
Mailing state: WI
Mailing zip: 54308-9428
General Phone: (920) 468-5477
General Fax: (920) 468-0931
Email: asi_sales@advancesystems.com
Primary Website: www.advancesystems.com
Year Established: 1987
Product/Services: Dryers: Film and Papers; Drying Systems
Personnel: Mike Conway (Pres.)
Personnel: Chelly Pierquet (Office Mgr.)
Personnel: Mike Sellers (Sales/Mktg. Mgr.)

HUDSON-SHARP

Street address 1: 975 Lombardi Ave
Street address state: WI
Zip/Postal code: 54304-3735
Country: USA
Mailing address: 975 Lombardi Ave
Mailing city: Green Bay
Mailing state: WI
Mailing zip: 54304-3735
General Phone: (920) 494-4571
Email: sales@hudsonsharp.com
Primary Website: www.hudsonsharp.com
Year Established: 1978
Product/Services: Automatic Plastic Bagging Equipment
Personnel: Rod Drummond (CEO)

GREENE

RANDOM ACCESS

Street address 1: 62 Birdsall St
Street address state: NY
Zip/Postal code: 13778-1049
Country: USA
Mailing address: 62 Birdsall St
Mailing city: Greene
Mailing state: NY
Mailing zip: 13778-1049
General Phone: (607) 656-7584
Email: marsland@aol.com
Year Established: 1986
Product/Services: Consulting Services: Computer; System Integration Services;
Personnel: William Marsland (Pres.)

GREENVILLE

B E & K BUILDING GROUP

Street address 1: 201 East McBee Avenue, Suite 400
Street address state: SC
Zip/Postal code: 29601
Country: USA
Mailing address: 201 East McBee Avenue, Suite 400
Mailing city: Greenville
Mailing state: SC
Mailing zip: 29601
General Phone: (864) 250-5000
General Fax: (864) 250-5099

Primary Website: www.bekbg.com
Year Established: 1972
Product/Services: Architects/Engineers (Includes Design/Construction Firms)
Note: RESEARCH TRIANGLE PARK 100 Capitola Drive, Suite 301 Durham, North Carolina 27713 Phone: 919. 781. 0054 Fax: 919. 326. 2999 Business Development: Courtney Skunda 919.326.2947 Frank Holley 919.326.2948 CHARLOTTE 1031 South Caldwell Street, Suite 100 Charlotte, North Carolina 28203 Phone: 704. 412. 9300 Fax: 704. 659. 4161 Business Development: Jeff Thompson 704.351.0007 CHICAGO 205 West Wacker Drive, Suite 615 Chicago, Illinois 60606 Phone: 312. 638. 5680 Fax: 864. 250. 5099 Business Development: Hope Alexander 312.543.8094 HOUSTON 4545 Post Oak Place, Suite 110 Houston, Texas 77027 Phone: 281. 245. 3940 Fax: 713. 583. 7903 Business Development: Steve Olson 972.532.2420 DALLAS 13727 Noel Road, Tower II, Suite 200 Dallas, Texas 75240 Phone: 972. 532. 2420 Fax: 864. 250. 5099 Business Development: Steve Olson 972.532.2420
Personnel: Tim Parker (Business Development)
Personnel: Grant McCullagh (Chairman)
Personnel: Mac Carpenter (Vice President HR)

PENCO PRODUCTS

Street address 1: 1820 Stonehenge Dr
Street address state: NC
Zip/Postal code: 27858-5965
Country: USA
Mailing address: 1820 Stonehenge Drive
Mailing city: Greenville
Mailing state: PA
Mailing zip: 27585
General Phone: 800-562-1000
Email: general@pencoproducts.com
Primary Website: www.pencoproducts.com
Year Established: 1869
Product/Services: Cabinets; Storage Retrieval Systems;
Personnel: Greg Grogan (Pres.)
Personnel: Philip H. Krugler (Mktg. Mgr.)

YALE MATERIALS HANDLING CORP.

Street address 1: 1400 Sullivan Dr
Street address state: NC
Zip/Postal code: 27834-9007
Country: USA
Mailing address: 1400 Sullivan Dr
Mailing city: Greenville
Mailing state: NC
Mailing zip: 27834-9007
General Phone: (800) 233-9253
General Fax: (252) 931-7873
Email: ayinfo@yale.com
Primary Website: www.yale.com
Year Established: 1920
Product/Services: Lift Trucks
Personnel: Don Chance (Pres.)
Personnel: Tina Goodwin (Dir., Financial Servs.)
Personnel: Jay Costello (Vice Pres., Aftermarket Sales)
Walt Nawicki (Dir., Dealer Devel.)

GREENWICH

WHITE BIRCH PAPER

Street address 1: 80 Field Point Rd
Street address state: CT
Zip/Postal code: 06830-6416
Country: USA
Mailing address: 80 Field Point Rd Ste 1
Mailing city: Greenwich
Mailing state: CT
Mailing zip: 06830-6416
General Phone: (203) 661-3344
General Fax: (203) 661-3349
Primary Website: www.whitebirchpaper.com
Year Established: 1941
Product/Services: Newsprint; Paper: Groundwood Specialties;
Note: Mfg. of Pulpa paper.. Newsprint, specialties & directory. "
Personnel: Peter M. Brant (Chrmn./CEO)

Personnel: Edward D. Sherrick (Sr. Vice Pres./CFO)
Personnel: Christopher M. Brant (President & COO)
Russel Lowder (Sr. Vice Pres., Sales)

GURNEE

DOMINO NORTH AMERICA

Street address 1: 1290 Lakeside Dr
Street address state: IL
Zip/Postal code: 60031-2400
Country: USA
Mailing address: 1290 Lakeside Dr
Mailing city: Gurnee
Mailing state: IL
Mailing zip: 60031-2499
General Phone: (800) 444-4512
General Fax: (847) 244-1421
Email: solutions@domino-na.com
Primary Website: www.domino-printing.com/en-us/home.aspx
Year Established: 1987
Product/Services: Addressing Machines; Label Printing Machines; Laser Printers; Numbering Machines

GURNEE

PC INDUSTRIES

Street address 1: 176 Ambrogio Dr
Street address state: IL
Zip/Postal code: 60031-3373
Country: USA
Mailing address: 176 Ambrogio Dr.
Mailing city: Gurnee
Mailing state: IL
Mailing zip: 60031
General Phone: (847) 336-3300
General Fax: (847) 336-3232
Email: sales@pcindustries.com
Primary Website: www.pcindustries.com
Year Established: 1975
Product/Services: Cameras & Accessories; Color Registration; Controls: Register; Optical Character Recognition (OCR); Press Control Systems; Proofing Systems;
Personnel: John Woolley (Pres./Sales Mgr.)

HAMBURG

PPI MEDIA GMBH

Street address 1: Hindenburgstrasse 49
Zip/Postal code: D-22297
Country: Germany
Mailing address: Hindenburgstrasse 49
Mailing city: Hamburg
Mailing zip: D-22297
General Phone: +49 40 227433-60
General Fax: +49 40 227433-666
Email: ppimedia.de
Primary Website: www.ppimedia.de
Year Established: 1984
Product/Services: Mailroom Systems & Equipment; Output Management and Preflight Software; Pagination Systems; Produciton Control Systems; Software: Advertising (Includes Display; Classified); Software: Pagination/Layout; Software: Workflow Management/Tracking; System Integration Services;
Personnel: Hauke Berndt (COO)
Personnel: Jan Kasten (CTO)
Personnel: Thomas Reinacher (CEO ppi Media US Inc.)
Annika Schulz (Marketing Manager)
Heiko Bichel (PR Manager)
Jan Kasten (Managing Director (R&D) I CTO)
Sven ClauÄŸen (IT Infrastructure Manager)
Manuel Scheyda (SVP Business Innovation)
Cindy Eggers (Senior Product Designer)
Steffen Landsberg (VP Sales (Europe))
Claus Harders (Head of Key Account Mgmt)

HAMDEN

EARMARK

Street address 1: 1125 Dixwell Ave
Street address state: CT
Zip/Postal code: 06514-4735
Country: USA
Mailing address: 1125 Dixwell Ave
Mailing city: Hamden
Mailing state: CT
Mailing zip: 06514-4788
General Phone: (203) 777-2130
General Fax: (203) 777-2886
Email: staff@earmark.com
Primary Website: www.earmark.com
Year Established: 1973
Product/Services: Wireless Radio Communication Headsets
Note: â€¢ EARMARK has manufactured durable wireless communication systems for over 30 years to support professionals operating in high noise environments. EARMARK is renowned for its rugged, reliable, yet easy to use products. Our commitment to understanding the challenges facing production teams have allowed us to develop products that have the range, flexibility and performance needed to increase efficiency and safety on the job.

HAMPTON

MAXX MATERIAL HANDLING LLC

Street address 1: 315 E St
Street address state: VA
Zip/Postal code: 23661-1209
Country: USA
Mailing address: 315 E St
Mailing city: Hampton
Mailing state: VA
Mailing zip: 23661-1209
General Phone: (757) 825-8100
General Fax: (757) 825-8800
Email: mhogan@maxxmh.com
Primary Website: www.maxxmh.com
Product/Services: Material Handling Equipment: Truck Loaders; Material Handling Equipment: Vehicle Loading;
Personnel: Randy Gilliland (Pres.)
Personnel: Mark Hogan (Vice Pres.)

HANOVER PARK

FUJI PHOTO FILM USA/GRAPHIC SYSTEMS DIV.

Street address 1: 850 Central Ave
Street address state: IL
Zip/Postal code: 60133-5422
Country: USA
Mailing address: 850 Central Ave
Mailing city: Hanover Park
Mailing state: IL
Mailing zip: 60133-5422
General Phone: (630) 259-7200
General Fax: (630) 259-7078
Email: contact@fujifilmgs.com
Primary Website: www.fujifilm.com
Year Established: 1934
Product/Services: Chemicals: Plate Processing; Color Proofing; Film & Paper: Contact; Film & Paper: Duplicating; Film & Paper: Filters (Photographic); Imagesetters; Plates: Offset (Computer to Plate); Proofing Systems; Plates: Offset (Conventional); Scanners: Color B & W, Plates, Web;
Personnel: Tim Combs (Pres., Industrial Imaging Markets Grp.)
Personnel: Bill Diminno (Sr. Vice Pres./Gen. Mgr., PhotoImaging Grp.)

FUJIFILM GRAPHIC SYSTEMS USA, INC.

Street address 1: 850 Central Ave
Street address state: IL
Zip/Postal code: 60133-5422

Country: USA
Mailing address: 850 Central Ave
Mailing city: Hanover Park
Mailing state: IL
Mailing zip: 60133-5422
General Phone: (630) 259-7200
General Fax: (630) 259-7078
Primary Website: www.fujifilmusa.com/products/graphic_arts_printing/index.html
Product/Services: Blankets; Chemicals: Pressroom; Color Management Software; Imagesetters; Inks; Offset Chemicals & Supplies; Platemakers: Flexographic (Computer to Plate); Plates: Offset (Conventional); Proofing Systems; Software: Press/Post Press;
Personnel: John Briar (Reg'l Sales Mgr.)

FUJIFILM NORTH AMERICA CORPORATION

Street address 1: 850 Central Ave
Street address state: IL
Zip/Postal code: 60133-5422
Country: USA
Mailing address: 850 Central Ave.
Mailing city: Hanover Park
Mailing state: IL
Mailing zip: 60133
General Phone: (866) 378-1429
General Fax: (765) 482-0288
Primary Website: www.fujifilmus.com
Product/Services: Plates Chemistry Films Pressroom products CTP equipment Processors Workflow Proofing supplies Safety equipment Service Color management
Personnel: Lane Palmer (VP, Corp. Accounts & Newspapers)
Personnel: Lorna Borghese (Newspaper Acct. Mgr., SE Region)
Personnel: Bob Veyera (Newspaper Acct. Mgr., NW Reg.)
Michael Mossman (Newspaper Support Specialist)
Brian Moser (Newspaper Acct. Mgr., SW Reg.)
J. Faulkner (Newspaper Acct. Mgr., NE Reg.)

HARAHAN

INTRALOX, LLC

Street address 1: 301 Plantation Rd
Street address state: LA
Zip/Postal code: 70123-5326
Country: USA
Mailing address: 301 Plantation Rd
Mailing city: Harahan
Mailing state: LA
Mailing zip: 70123-5326
General Phone: (504) 733-0463
General Fax: (504) 734-0063
Primary Website: www.intralox.com
Year Established: 1971
Product/Services: Conveyors
Personnel: Edel Blanks (Sales Mgr.)

HARLINGEN

CARIWEB PRODUCTS

Street address 1: PO Box 1349
Street address state: TX
Zip/Postal code: 78551-1349
Country: USA
Mailing address: PO Box 1349
Mailing city: Harlingen
Mailing state: TX
Mailing zip: 78551-1349
General Phone: (956) 423-5766
General Fax: (956) 748-3417
Email: cariwebproducts@aol.com
Year Established: 1978
Product/Services: Tape Splicing Equipment
Personnel: Jose Henderson (Pres.)

HARRISBURG

THE SIEBOLD COMPANY, INC. (TSC)

Street address 1: 808 S 26th Street

Equipment, Supplies and Services

Street address state: PA
Zip/Postal code: 66061-6859
Country: USA
Mailing address: 4201 NW 124TH Avenue
Mailing city: Coral Springs
Mailing state: FL
Mailing zip: 33065
Email: Sales@siebold.com
Primary Website: www.sieboldgraphicarts.com
Year Established: 1989
Product/Services: Single and Double-Width Press Parts; Service; Web Offset Press Equipment Brokers & Appraisers; Consulting Services: Equipment; Equipment Dealers (New); Equipment Dealers (Used); Press Rebuilding; Press Reconditioning; Press Repairs; Presses: Offset.
Note: TSC has completed over 5,000 successful equipment installation projects since 1989 throughout North America and the English-speaking Caribbean Islands, and specializes in the Graphic Arts and Material Handling industries. TSC is the parent company of: DR Press Equipment, Inc. (Single & Double-Width Press Parts); DGM; and Smith Pressroom Products. TSC also offers press equipment brokering services and is the exclusive distributor for GWS Printing Systems. For additional TSC information, please visit our website: www.sieboldgraphicarts.com or call 800-452-9481.
Personnel: Bruce Barna (VP Sales & Marketing)

HARRISONVILLE

MID-AMERICA GRAPHICS, INC.

Street address 1: 1501 W Vine St
Street address state: MO
Zip/Postal code: 64701-4017
Country: USA
Mailing address: PO Box 466
Mailing city: Harrisonville
Mailing state: MO
Mailing zip: 64701-0466
General Phone: (816) 887-2414
General Fax: (816) 887-2762
Email: sales@midamericagraphics.com
Primary Website: www.midamericagraphics.com
Year Established: 1983
Product/Services: Conveyors; In-Line Trimming Systems; Infeed Stackers; Inserting Equipment (Includes Stuffing Machines); Newsprint Handling Equipment;
Personnel: Charles George (Pres.)
Personnel: William David George (Exec. Vice Pres.)
Personnel: Dan George (Gen. Mgr.)
Terri Widdle (Sec.)

HARTSVILLE

SONOCO PRODUCTS CO.

Street address 1: 1 N 2nd St
Street address state: SC
Zip/Postal code: 29550-3300
Country: USA
Mailing address: PO Box 160
Mailing city: Hartsville
Mailing state: SC
Mailing zip: 29551-0160
General Phone: (843) 383-7000
General Fax: (843) 383-7008
Primary Website: www.sonoco.com
Year Established: 1899
Product/Services: Newspaper Bags; Recycling Newsprint; Tubes, Racks (Includes Racks: Motor Route Tubes);
Personnel: Harris Deloach (Pres.)
Personnel: Don Gore (Division Vice Pres., Sales)

HARWOOD HEIGHTS

MIDWEST PUBLISHERS SUPPLY CO.

Street address 1: 4640 N Olcott Ave
Street address state: IL
Zip/Postal code: 60706-4604
Country: USA
Mailing address: 4640 N. Olcott Ave.
Mailing city: Harwood Heights
Mailing state: IL
Mailing zip: 60706
General Phone: (708) 867-4646
General Fax: (708) 867-6954
Email: info@mps-co.com
Year Established: 1947
Product/Services: Art & Layout Equipment and Services; Blankets; Blue Line Grids; Chemicals: Pressroom; Composing Room Equipment & Supplies; Lift Trucks; Mailroom Systems & Equipment; Offset Chemicals & Supplies; Press Accessories, Parts & Supplies;
Personnel: James Rezabek (Pres.)

HATFIELD

ICANON ASSOCIATES, INC.

Street address 1: 2321 N Penn Rd
Street address 2: Suite C
Street address state: PA
Zip/Postal code: 19440-1972
Country: USA
Mailing address: 2321 N Penn Rd Ste C
Mailing city: Hatfield
Mailing state: PA
Mailing zip: 19440-1972
General Phone: (800) 544-4450
Email: sales@icanon.com
Primary Website: www.newzware.com
Year Established: 1990
Product/Services: Computers: Hardware & Software Integrator; Consulting Services: Computer; Consulting Services: Financial; Software: Advertising (Includes Display; Classified); Software: Business (Includes Administration/Accounting); Software: Circulation; Software: Editorial; Software: Pagination/Layout;
Personnel: Joe Lewinski (Pres.)
Personnel: Gary Markle (Dir., Mktg.)
Personnel: Mike Hanson (Engineering)

SIMCO INDUSTRIAL STATIC CONTROL PRODUCTS

Street address 1: 2257 N Penn Rd
Street address state: PA
Zip/Postal code: 19440-1906
Country: USA
Mailing address: 2257 N Penn Rd
Mailing city: Hatfield
Mailing state: PA
Mailing zip: 19440-1998
General Phone: (215) 822-6401
Email: customerservice@simco-ion.com
Primary Website: www.simco-ion.com
Year Established: 1936
Product/Services: Inserting Equipment (Includes Stuffing Machines); Paper Cleaners; Press Accessories, Parts & Supplies; Static Eliminators; Testing Instruments;
Personnel: Ed Huber (Customer Serv. Mgr.)
Personnel: Brian Mininger (Technical Rep.)

HAUPPAUGE

MULLER MARTINI CORP.

Street address 1: 456 Wheeler Rd
Street address state: NY
Zip/Postal code: 11788-4343
Country: USA
Mailing address: 456 Wheeler Rd
Mailing city: Hauppauge
Mailing state: NY
Mailing zip: 11788-4343
General Phone: (631) 582-4343
General Fax: (631) 582-1961
Email: info@mullermartiniusa.com
Primary Website: www.mullermartiniusa.com
Year Established: 1946
Product/Services: Bundling and Tying Machines; Counting, Stacking, Bundling Machines; Cutters & Trimmers; Inserting Equipment (Includes Stuffing Machines); Mailroom Systems & Equipment; Material Handling Equipment: Palletizing Machines; Newsprint Handeling Equipment; Paper Handeling Equipment; Shrink Wrapping Equipment; Storage Retrieval Systems;
Personnel: Weiner Naegeli (Vice-President)
Personnel: Anthony Quaranta
Personnel: Herbert Carrington

HAWKESBURY

MASTER FLO TECHNOLOGY

Street address 1: 1233 Tessier St
Street address state: ON
Zip/Postal code: K6A 3R1
Country: Canada
Mailing address: 1233 Tessier St.
Mailing city: Hawkesbury
Mailing state: ON
Mailing zip: K6A 3R1
General Phone: (613) 636-0539
General Fax: (613) 636-0762
Email: info@mflo.com
Primary Website: www.mflo.com
Year Established: 1984
Product/Services: Circulation Equipment & Supplies; Dampening Systems; Delivery Equipment; Feeding, Folding, Delivery Equipment; Ink Fountains & Accessories; Inserting Equipment (Includes Stuffing Machines); Material Handling Equipment: Pallets & Palletizers; Offset Fountain Controls; Press Accessories, Parts & Supplies; Recirculators;
Personnel: Edward Desaulniers (President)
Personnel: Tim Duffy (Vice Pres., Opns)

HAWTHORNE

D & R ENGINEERING

Street address 1: 12629 Prairie Ave
Street address state: CA
Zip/Postal code: 90250-4611
Country: USA
Mailing address: 12629 Prairie Ave
Mailing city: Hawthorne
Mailing state: CA
Mailing zip: 90250-4611
General Phone: (310) 676-4896
General Fax: (310) 676-3420
Year Established: 1976
Product/Services: Counting, Stacking, Bundling Machines; Gluing Systems; Web Cleaners; Web Offset Remoisturizers; Web Press - Special Equipment;
Personnel: Daws Waffer (Owner)

HAYWARD

FUJIFILM GRAPHIC SYSTEMS USA, INC.

Street address 1: 30962 San Benito St
Street address state: CA
Zip/Postal code: 94544-7935
Country: USA
Mailing address: 30962 San Benito St
Mailing city: Hayward
Mailing state: CA
Mailing zip: 94544-7935
General Phone: (800) 734.8745
General Fax: (510) 266.0707
Primary Website: www.fujifilmusa.com/products/graphic_arts_printing/index.html
Product/Services: Blankets; Chemicals: Pressroom; Color Management Software; Imagesetters; Inks; Offset Chemicals & Supplies; Platemakers: Flexographic (Computer to Plate); Plates: Offset (Conventional); Proofing Systems; Software: Press/Post Press;
Personnel: Richard Cay (Reg'l Sales Mgr.)

HEAT AND CONTROL, INC.

Street address 1: 21121 Cabot Blvd
Street address state: CA
Zip/Postal code: 94545-1132
Country: USA
Mailing address: 21121 Cabot Blvd
Mailing city: Hayward
Mailing state: CA
Mailing zip: 94545-1177
General Phone: 800-227-5980
General Fax: (510) 259-0600
Email: info@heatandcontrol.com
Primary Website: www.heatandcontrol.com
Year Established: 1950
Product/Services: Counting, Stacking, Bundling Machines
Personnel: Andy Caridis (Chrmn./CEO)
Personnel: Tony Caridis (Pres.)
Personnel: Audrey Waidelich (Dir., Mktg.)

HAZLE TOWNSHIP

EAM-MOSCA CORP.

Street address 1: 675 Jaycee Dr
Street address state: PA
Zip/Postal code: 18202-1155
Country: USA
Mailing address: 675 Jaycee Dr., Valmont Industrial Pk.
Mailing city: Hazle Township
Mailing state: PA
Mailing zip: 18202-1155
General Phone: (570) 459-3426
General Fax: (570) 455-2442
Email: info@eammosca.com
Primary Website: www.eammosca.com
Year Established: 1982
Product/Services: Bundling and Tying Machines; Strapping Machines;
Personnel: Pam Kuzmak (Sales Admin.)
Personnel: Edward Martin (VP, Sales)
Personnel: Dan Dreher (Pres.)

HELENA

CRIBB, GREENE & COPE

Street address 1: 825 Great Northern Blvd
Street address 2: Ste 202
Street address state: MT
Zip/Postal code: 59601-3340
Country: USA
Mailing address: 825 Great Northern Blvd
Mailing city: Helena
Mailing state: MT
Mailing zip: 59601
General Phone: (406) 579-2925
General Fax: (866) 776-8010
Email: jcribb@cribb.com
Primary Website: www.cribb.com
Year Established: 1923
Product/Services: Brokers, Consultants & Appraisers
Personnel: John Cribb (Director)
Personnel: Gary Greene (Director)
Personnel: Randy Cope (Managing Director)
John Thomas Cribb (Associate)
Jeffrey Potts (Senior Associate)

HEMPSTEAD

ROLLEM CORP. OF AMERICA

Street address 1: 43 Polk Ave
Street address state: NY
Zip/Postal code: 11550-5434
Country: USA
Mailing address: 95 Hoffman Ln Ste T
Mailing city: Islandia
Mailing state: NY
Mailing zip: 11749-5020
General Phone: (516) 485-6655
General Fax: (516) 485-5936
Email: info@rollemusa.com
Primary Website: www.rollemusa.com
Year Established: 1963
Product/Services: Numbering Machines
Personnel: Richard Nigro (Vice Pres., Sales)

HERNDON

VIDAR SYSTEMS CORP.

Street address 1: 365 Herndon Pkwy
Street address state: VA
Zip/Postal code: 20170-5613
Country: USA
Mailing address: 365 Herndon Pkwy Ste 105
Mailing city: Herndon
Mailing state: VA
Mailing zip: 20170-6236
General Phone: (703) 471-7070
General Fax: (703) 471-1165
Email: order@3dsystems.com
Primary Website: www.vidar.com
Year Established: 1984
Product/Services: Scanners: Color B & W, Plates, Web
Personnel: Greg Elfering (V. P.)
Personnel: Joe Barden (Global Sales Mgr.)
Personnel: Bob May (Global Customer Support)

HIGH POINT

ADI/PDM TRADE GROUP

Street address 1: 1509 Bethel Dr
Street address state: NC
Zip/Postal code: 27260-8348
Country: USA
Mailing address: PO Box 220
Mailing city: Sylvania
Mailing state: GA
Mailing zip: 30467-0220
General Phone: (912) 564-2400
General Fax: (912) 564-2402
Email: jlmcd1492@aol.com
Primary Website: www.arcdoyle.com
Year Established: 1983
Product/Services: Computers: Storage Devices; Counting, Stacking, Bundling Machines; Feeding, Folding, Delivery Equipment; Folding Machines; Material Handling Equipment: Automatic Guided Vehicles; Material Handling Equipment: Palletizing Machines; Material Handling Equipment: Pallets & Palletizers; Presses: Flexographic; Solvent Recovery Systems
Personnel: Jim McDonald (Pres.)

HOBART

EMT INTERNATIONAL, INC.

Street address 1: 780 Centerline Drive
Street address state: WI
Zip/Postal code: 54155
Country: USA
Mailing address: 780 Centerline Drive
Mailing city: Hobart
Mailing state: WI
Mailing zip: 54155
General Phone: (920) 468-5475
General Fax: (920) 468-7991
Email: info@emtinternational.com
Primary Website: www.emtinternational.com
Year Established: 1990
Product/Services: Slitting systems; Printing machinery; Equipment and Consumables for Web Processing Applications; Air-Actuated Lug, Leaf, and Multi-Bladder Shafts and Chucks; and Pneumatic-Mechanical Chucks and Mechanical Shafts;
Personnel: Bron Tamulion (Engineering Manager)
Personnel: Chad Winkka (Production Manager)
Personnel: Carl Castelic (Director of Finance and Cost Accounting)
Jim Driscoll (VP)

HODGKINS

WRANGLER TECH, LLC

Street address 1: 9000 67th St
Street address state: IL
Zip/Postal code: 60525-7606
Country: USA
Mailing address: 9000 67th St
Mailing city: Hodgkins
Mailing state: IL
Mailing zip: 60525-7606
General Phone: (312) 301-7254
Primary Website: www.wranglertech.net
Year Established: 2016
Product/Services: IT; Telecomm; Data Center; Security;
Personnel: Susie Cassidy (Sales)
Personnel: Danene McMahon (Co-Owner/Manager)

HOFFMAN ESTATES

BOSCH REXROTH

Street address 1: 5150 Prairie Stone Pkwy
Street address state: IL
Zip/Postal code: 60192-3707
Country: USA
Mailing address: 5150 Prairie Stone Pkwy
Mailing city: Hoffman Estates
Mailing state: IL
Mailing zip: 60192-3707
General Phone: (847) 645-3600
General Fax: (847) 645-6201
Primary Website: www.boschrexroth-us.com
Product/Services: Press Control Systems
Personnel: Berend Bracht (Pres./CEO)

HOLMEN

LASER PRODUCTS TECHNOLOGIES

Street address 1: 3936 Circle Dr
Street address state: WI
Zip/Postal code: 54636-9187
Country: USA
Mailing address: 3936 Circle Dr
Mailing city: Holmen
Mailing state: WI
Mailing zip: 54636-9187
General Phone: 800-999-9749
Email: info@lptnow.com
Primary Website: www.lptnow.com
Product/Services: Laser Printers
Personnel: Michael Marty (Pres.)
Personnel: Bob King (Vice Pres.)

HOMER GLEN

NAMA GRAPHICS E, LLC

Street address 1: 15751 Annico Dr
Street address state: IL
Zip/Postal code: 60491-8449
Country: USA
Mailing address: 15751 Annico Dr Ste 2
Mailing city: Homer Glen
Mailing state: IL
Mailing zip: 60491-4739
General Phone: (630) 668-6262
General Fax: (262) 966-3852
Email: rsnama@wi.rr.com
Primary Website: www.namagraphicse.com
Year Established: 1991
Product/Services: Environmental Control Systems; Flying Pasters; Ink Fountains & Accessories; Rollers; Dampening;
Personnel: John Griffin (Owner)
Personnel: Rick Smith (Owner)

HOT SPRINGS

ALLIANCE RUBBER CO.

Street address 1: 210 Carpenter Dam Rd
Street address state: AR
Zip/Postal code: 71901-8219
Country: USA
Mailing address: PO Box 20950
Mailing city: Hot Springs
Mailing state: AR
Mailing zip: 71903-0950
General Phone: (501) 262-2700
General Fax: (501) 262-3948
Email: sales@alliance-rubber.com
Primary Website: www.rubberband.com
Year Established: 1923
Product/Services: Rubber Band Manufacturer
Personnel: Joan Dennis (Director Sales & Marketing)
Personnel: Sheryl Koller

HOUSTON

KANALY TRUST CO.

Street address 1: 5555 San Felipe St
Street address 2: Ste 200
Street address state: TX
Zip/Postal code: 77056-2760
Country: USA
Mailing address: 5555 San Felipe St Ste 200
Mailing city: Houston
Mailing state: TX
Mailing zip: 77056-2760
General Phone: (713)561-9300
General Fax: (713) 877-8744
Email: kanaly@kanaly.com
Primary Website: www.kanaly.com
Product/Services: Consulting Services: Financial
Personnel: Drew Kanaly (Chairman/CEO)

TSA

Street address 1: 2050 W Sam Houston Pkwy N
Street address state: TX
Zip/Postal code: 77043-2422
Country: USA
Mailing address: 2050 W Sam Houston Pkwy N
Mailing city: Houston
Mailing state: TX
Mailing zip: 77043-2422
General Phone: (713) 935-1500
General Fax: (713) 935-1555
Email: info@tsa.com
Primary Website: www.tsa.com
Year Established: 1985
Product/Services: Computers: Hardware & Software Integrators; Equipment Dealers (New); Equipment Dealers (Used);
Personnel: William C. Smith (Pres.)
Personnel: Steven Perry (Sales Mgr.)
Personnel: Rick Valanta (Servs. Devel. Mgr.)

HSINCHU

MICROTEK

Street address 1: No.6 Industry East Road 3
Street address 2: Science-based Industrial Park
Zip/Postal code: 30075
Country: Taiwan
Mailing address: No.6 Industry East Road 3, Science-based Industrial Park
Mailing city: Hsinchu
Mailing zip: 30075
General Phone: +886-3-577-2155 Ext.551
General Fax: +886-3-577-2598 Ext.551
Email: sales@microtek.com
Primary Website: www.microtek.com
Year Established: 1980
Product/Services: Color Seperation Scanners; Scanners: Color B & W, Plates, Web;
Personnel: Jerry Su (Sales OEM projects)
Personnel: Jerry Tsai (Sales (USA))

HUNTINGTON

SHUTTLEWORTH, LLC

Street address 1: 10 Commercial Rd
Street address state: IN
Zip/Postal code: 46750-8805
Country: USA
Mailing address: 10 Commercial Rd
Mailing city: Huntington
Mailing state: IN
Mailing zip: 46750-9044
General Phone: (260) 356-8500
General Fax: (260) 359-7810
Email: inc@shuttleworth.com
Primary Website: www.shuttleworth.com
Year Established: 1962
Product/Services: Conveyors; Masking Materials; Paper Handling Equipment; Roll Handling Equipment;

INCINO

SHOOM, INC.

Street address 1: 6345 Balbow Blvd, Ste 247
Street address state: CA
Zip/Postal code: 91316
Country: USA
Mailing address: 6345 Balboa Blvd Ste 247
Mailing city: Encino
Mailing state: CA
Mailing zip: 91316-1580
General Phone: (408) 702-2167
General Fax: (408) 824-1543
Primary Website: www.inpixon.com/solutions/shoom/
Product/Services: Software: Electronic Data Interchange
Personnel: Nadir Ali (Chairman & CEO)
Personnel: Soumya Das (COO)

INDIANAPOLIS

BERTING COMMUNICATIONS

Street address 1: 6330 Woburn Dr
Street address state: IN
Zip/Postal code: 46250-2710
Country: USA
Mailing address: 6330 Woburn Dr
Mailing city: Indianapolis
Mailing state: IN
Mailing zip: 46250
General Phone: (317) 849-5408
General Fax: (317) 849-5408
Email: bob@bobberting.com
Primary Website: 6330 Woburn Drive
Year Established: 1990
Product/Services: Publisher Consultant Services:Merchant Advertising Seminars; Marketing; Training: Sales & Marketing-webinars,tele-seminars
Personnel: Bob Berting (Pres.)
Personnel: Barbara Berting (Vice Pres.)
Personnel: Dan Cooper (Graphic Artist)

EGENOLF MACHINE, INC. (EGENOLF CONTRACTING & RIGGING)

Street address 1: 350 Wisconsin St
Street address state: IN
Zip/Postal code: 46225-1536
Country: USA
Mailing address: 350 Wisconsin St
Mailing city: Indianapolis
Mailing state: IN
Mailing zip: 46225-1536
General Phone: (317) 637-9891
General Fax: (317) 631-8153
Email: egenolfma@gmail.com
Year Established: 1927
Product/Services: Press Rebuilding; Press Repairs;
Personnel: James Egenolf (Pres.)

PRINTING TECHNOLOGIES, INC.

Street address 1: 6266 Morenci Trail
Street address state: IN
Zip/Postal code: 46268
Country: USA
Mailing address: 6266 Morenci Trail
Mailing city: Indianapolis
Mailing state: IN
Mailing zip: 46268
General Phone: (800) 428-3786
Email: info@ptionaroll.com
Primary Website: www.ptionaroll.com
Year Established: 1994
Product/Services: Cylinder Repair; Equipment Dealers (Used); Folder Knives; Ink Fountains & Accessories; Press Accessories, Parts & Supplies; Press Rebuilding; Press Repairs; Presses: Offset; Rollers; Rollers; Dampening;
Personnel: Walt Alfred (Pres.)

STERLING TYPE FOUNDRY

Street address 1: 7830 Ridgeland Dr
Street address state: IN
Zip/Postal code: 46250-2269

Equipment, Supplies and Services

Country: USA
Mailing address: PO Box 50234
Mailing city: Indianapolis
Mailing state: IN
Mailing zip: 46250-0234
General Phone: (317) 849-5665
General Fax: (317) 849-1616
Primary Website: www.sterlingtype.com
Year Established: 1922
Product/Services: Platemakers: Letterpress; Presses: Letterpress; Type, Fonts;
Personnel: David C. Churchman (Works Mgr.)

INGLEWOOD

N/S CORPORATION

Street address 1: 235 W Florence Ave
Street address state: CA
Zip/Postal code: 90301-1212
Country: USA
Mailing address: 235 W Florence Ave
Mailing city: Inglewood
Mailing state: CA
Mailing zip: 90301-1293
General Phone: (800) 782-1582
Email: info@nswash.com
Primary Website: www.nswash.com
Year Established: 1961
Product/Services: Conveyors; Drying Systems; Environmental Control Systems;
Personnel: Thomas Ennis (CEO)
Personnel: Thomas G. Ennis (Pres.)
Personnel: Gary Avrech (Mktg. Mgr.)

IRVINE

CAPITA TECHNOLOGIES

Street address 1: 17600 Gillette Ave
Street address state: CA
Zip/Postal code: 92614-5715
Country: USA
Mailing address: 17600 Gillette Ave
Mailing city: Irvine
Mailing state: CA
Mailing zip: 92614-5715
General Phone: (949) 260-3000
General Fax: (949) 851-9875
Email: sales@capita.com
Primary Website: www.capita.com
Product/Services: Software: Pagination/Layout; System Integration Services;
Personnel: Charles Granville (CEO)
Personnel: Imelda Ford (Exec. Vice Pres., Techn./Opns.)

CARLSON DESIGN CONSTRUCT

Street address 1: 34 Executive Park
Street address 2: Ste 250
Street address state: CA
Zip/Postal code: 92614-4707
Country: USA
Mailing address: 34 Executive Park Ste 250
Mailing city: Irvine
Mailing state: CA
Mailing zip: 92614-4707
General Phone: (949) 251-0455
General Fax: (949) 251-0465
Email: carlson@carlson-dc.com
Primary Website: www.carlson-dc.com
Year Established: 1945
Product/Services: Architects/Engineers (Includes Design/Construction Firms)
Personnel: Tom Ryan (Vice Pres., Mktg)

PRINTRONIX, INC.

Street address 1: 6440 Oak Canyon Dr. Ste. 200
Street address state: CA
Zip/Postal code: 92618
Country: USA
Mailing address: 6440 Oak Canyon Dr. Ste. 200
Mailing city: Irvine
Mailing state: CA
Mailing zip: 92618
General Phone: (714) 368-2300
General Fax: (714) 368-2600
Primary Website: www.printronix.com
Year Established: 1974
Product/Services: Computers: Hardware & Software Integrators
Personnel: Werner Heid (CEO)
Personnel: Mark Tobin (CFO)
Personnel: Ron Gillies (V. Pres. of Sales and Marketing)

SAP AMERICA, INC.

Street address 1: 18101 Von Karman Ave
Street address 2: Ste 900
Street address state: CA
Zip/Postal code: 92612-0151
Country: USA
Mailing address: 18101 Von Karman Ave Ste 900
Mailing city: Irvine
Mailing state: CA
Mailing zip: 92612-0151
General Phone: (949) 622-2200
Email: press@sap.com
Primary Website: www.sap.com
Product/Services: Software: Advertising (Includes Display; Classified); Software: Circulation;
Product or Service: Hardware/Software Supplier
Personnel: Mark White (CFO)
Personnel: Costanza Tedesco (Vice Pres., Global Adv./Branding)
Personnel: Brian Ellefritz (Sr. Dir., Social Media Mktg.)

STM NETWORKS

Street address 1: 2 Faraday
Street address state: CA
Zip/Postal code: 92618-2737
Country: USA
Mailing address: 2 Faraday
Mailing city: Irvine
Mailing state: CA
Mailing zip: 92618-2737
General Phone: (949) 753-7864
General Fax: (949) 273-6020
Email: info@stmi.com
Primary Website: www.stmi.com
Year Established: 1982
Product/Services: Facsimilie/Fax Transmission Systems; Interfaces;
Personnel: Emil Youssefzadeh (Chrmn.)
Personnel: Faramarz Youssefzadeh (COB)
Personnel: Umar Javed (Vice Pres., Sales)
Rick Forberg (Vice Pres., Mktg.)

TALLY GENICOM

Street address 1: 15345 Barranca Parkway
Street address state: CA
Zip/Postal code: 92618
Country: USA
Mailing address: 15345 Barranca Parkway
Mailing city: Irvine
Mailing state: CA
Mailing zip: 92618
General Phone: (714) 368-2300
Primary Website: www.tallygenicom.com
Product/Services: Laser Printers
Personnel: Randy Eisenbach (CEO)

BROCK SOLUTIONS U.S. INC.

Street address 1: 8080 Tristar Dr
Street address 2: Ste 126
Street address state: TX
Zip/Postal code: 75063-2823
Country: USA
Mailing address: 8080 Tristar Dr Ste 126
Mailing city: Irving
Mailing state: TX
Mailing zip: 75063-2823
General Phone: (972) 373-2500
General Fax: (972) 444-0352
Email: info@brocksolutions.com ; hr@brocksolutions.com
Primary Website: www.brocksolutions.com
Product/Services: Addressing Machines; Consulting Services: Production;
Personnel: Bill Mctuire (Project Mgr.)

NEXSTAR-TRIBUNE MEDIA

Street address 1: 545 E. John Carpenter Freeway
Street address 2: Suite 700
Street address state: TX
Zip/Postal code: 75062
Country: USA
Mailing address: 545 E. John Carpenter Freeway
Mailing city: Irving
Mailing state: TX
Mailing zip: 75062
General Phone: (972) 373-8800
General Fax: (972) 373-8888
Primary Website: www.nexstar.tv
Year Established: 1965
Product/Services: Software: Pagination/Layout; Training: Design & Layout;
Note: As one of the nation's largest independent broadcasters, Tribune Media combines distinctive content with nationwide broadcast distribution and cutting-edge digital properties. WGN America, the company's widely distributed general entertainment cable channel, is home to a number of high quality exclusives and original series. In every aspect of the company, whether in producing critical local news, riveting programming, or premier sporting events, Tribune Media engages and connects viewers with must-have content across every distribution platform.
Personnel: Perry A. Sook (Chairman, Pres. and CEO)
Personnel: Thomas E. Carter (CFO)

TEL-AIRE PUBLICATIONS, INC.

Street address 1: 3105 E John Carpenter Fwy
Street address state: TX
Zip/Postal code: 75062-4933
Country: USA
Mailing address: 3105 E John Carpenter Fwy
Mailing city: Irving
Mailing state: TX
Mailing zip: 75062-4933
General Phone: (972) 438-4111
General Fax: (972) 579-7483
Email: sales@tel-aire.com
Primary Website: www.tel-aire.com
Year Established: 1969
Product/Services: Trade Publications
Note: WE NO LONGER SELL FEATURES.
Personnel: David McGee (Pres.)

ISLANDIA

VAN SON HOLLAND INK CORP. OF AMERICA

Street address 1: 185 Oval Dr
Street address state: NY
Zip/Postal code: 11749-1402
Country: USA
Mailing address: 185 Oval Dr
Mailing city: Islandia
Mailing state: NY
Mailing zip: 11749-1402
General Phone: (800) 645-4182
General Fax: (800) 442-8744
Email: info@vansonink.com
Primary Website: www.vansonink.com
Product/Services: Inks
Personnel: Joseph Bendowski (Pres.)

ITASCA

JARDIS INDUSTRIES INC.

Street address 1: 1201 Ardmore Ave
Street address state: IL
Zip/Postal code: 60143-1187
Country: USA
Mailing address: 1201 Ardmore Ave
Mailing city: Itasca
Mailing state: IL
Mailing zip: 60143-1187
General Phone: (630) 860-5959
General Fax: (630) 860-6515
Email: info@jardis
Primary Website: www.jardis.com
Year Established: 1986
Product/Services: Architects/Engineers (Includes Design/Construction Firms); Consulting Services: Equipment; Ink Pumping Systems; Pasters; Press Accessories, Parts & Supplies; Pumps (Air, Ink, Vacuum); Remanufactures Equipment; Splicers, Automatic; Tension & Web Controls; Web Press - Special Equipment;
Personnel: Allan Jardis (Pres.)
Personnel: Gary Klawinski (Mgr.)

ITASCA

JARDIS INDUSTRIES, INC.

Street address 1: 1201 Ardmore Ave
Street address state: IL
Zip/Postal code: 60143-1187
Country: USA
Mailing address: 1201 Ardmore Ave
Mailing city: Itasca
Mailing state: IL
Mailing zip: 60143-1187
General Phone: (630) 860-5959
General Fax: (630) 860-6515
Email: info@jardis
Primary Website: www.jardis.com
Year Established: 1986
Product/Services: Film and Papers; Drying Systems; Festoon Splicers; Flying Pasters; Constant tension Infeeds; Web guides;Plow folders; Angle Bar arrangemdnts ; Custom designed web handling Equipment;Offset and Flexographic printing press for newspaper, commercial , book and packaging applications
Personnel: Alan W. Jardis (Pres.)
Personnel: Adam Jardis (Gen. Mgr.)

IVYLAND

TOBIAS ASSOCIATES, INC.

Street address 1: 50 Industrial Dr
Street address state: PA
Zip/Postal code: 18974-1433
Country: USA
Mailing address: PO Box 2699
Mailing city: Ivyland
Mailing state: PA
Mailing zip: 18974-0347
General Phone: (800) 877-3367
General Fax: (215) 322-1504
Email: sales@tobiasinc.com
Primary Website: www.densitometer.com
Year Established: 1960
Product/Services: Calibration Software/Hardware; Color Analyzers; Dark Room Equipment; Densitometers; Electronic Pre-Scan Systems; Press Accessories, Parts & Supplies; Testing Instruments;
Personnel: Eric M. Tobias (Vice Pres.)
Personnel: William D. Bender (Sales Mgr.)

JACKSONVILLE

RAYONIER ADVANCED MATERIALS

Street address 1: 1301 Riverplace Blvd.
Street address 2: Suite 2300
Street address state: FL
Zip/Postal code: 32207
Country: Canada
Mailing address: 1301 Riverplace Blvd.
Mailing city: Jacksonville
Mailing state: FL
Mailing zip: 32207
General Phone: (904) 357-4600
Primary Website: www.rayonieram.com
Year Established: 1926
Product/Services: Newsprint
Personnel: Paul G. Boynton (Chairman, Pres. and CEO)
Personnel: Chris Black (Senior VP)
Personnel: James L. Posze (Senior Vice President HR)
Frank A. Ruperto (CFO and Senior VP)

THE HASKELL CO.

Street address 1: 111 Riverside Ave
Street address state: FL
Zip/Postal code: 32202-4905
Country: USA

Equipment, Supplies and Services

Mailing address: PO Box 44100
Mailing city: Jacksonville
Mailing state: FL
Mailing zip: 32231-4100
General Phone: (904) 791-4500
General Fax: (904) 791-4699
Primary Website: www.thehaskellco.com
Year Established: 1965
Product/Services: Architects/Engineers (Includes Design/Construction Firms); Consulting Services: Equipment;
Personnel: Steve Halverson (Pres.)
Personnel: Sara Guthrie (Resource Center Administrator)

JENKINTOWN

MANAGING EDITOR, INC.

Street address 1: 610 York Rd
Street address 2: Ste 400
Street address state: PA
Zip/Postal code: 19046-2866
Country: USA
Mailing address: 610 York Rd., Ste. 400
Mailing city: Jenkintown
Mailing state: PA
Mailing zip: 19046
General Phone: (215) 886-5662
General Fax: (215) 886-5681
Email: info@maned.com
Primary Website: www.maned.com
Year Established: 1989
Product/Services: Pagination Systems; Preprint Service & Production; Software: Advertising (Includes Display; Classified); Software: Editorial; Software: Pagination/Layout; Software: Workflow Management/Tracking; Digital Publishing;
Personnel: Mark Leister (Managing Director)
Personnel: Mark Wasserman (Head of Global Sales and Marketing)

JERSEY CITY

DESKNET, INC.

Street address 1: 30 Montgomery St.
Street address 2: Suite 650
Street address state: NJ
Zip/Postal code: 07302
Country: USA
Mailing address: 30 Montgomery St., Suite 650
Mailing city: Jersey City
Mailing state: NJ
Mailing zip: 07302
General Phone: (201) 946-7080
Primary Website: www.desknetinc.com
Year Established: 1992
Product/Services: Software: Asset Management; Software: Design/Graphics; Software: Editorial; Software: Electronic Data Interchange; Software: Pagination/Layout; Software: Workflow Management/Tracking; System Integration Services;
Personnel: Mike Fitzsimons (CEO)

GLOBIX CORP.

Street address 1: 95 Christopher Columbus Dr
Street address 2: Fl 16
Street address state: NJ
Zip/Postal code: 07302-2927
Country: USA
Mailing address: 95 Christopher Columbus Dr Fl 16
Mailing city: Jersey City
Mailing state: NJ
Mailing zip: 07302-2927
General Phone: (212) 334-8500
General Fax: (212) 625-8650
Email: support@qualitytech.com
Primary Website: www.qualitytech.com
Year Established: 1989
Product/Services: Computers: Hardware & Software Integrators; Computers: Laptop & Portable; Computers: Local Area Network (LANS); Computers: Storage Devices;
Personnel: Kurt Van Wagenen (Pres./CEO/COO)
Personnel: Shelagh Montgomery (Gen. Mgr.)

JOPLIN

ROBERTSON EQUIPMENTS

Street address 1: 1301 S Maiden Ln
Street address state: MO
Zip/Postal code: 64801-3844
Country: USA
Mailing address: 1301 S Maiden Ln
Mailing city: Joplin
Mailing state: MO
Mailing zip: 64801-3844
General Phone: (800) 288-1929
General Fax: (417) 781-3704
Email: sales@robertsonpress.com
Primary Website: www.robertsonpress.com
Year Established: 1991
Product/Services: Consulting Services: Computer; System Integration Services; Conveyors; Material Handling Equipment: Automatic Guided Vehicles; Material Handling Equipment: Truck Loaders;
Personnel: Bob Robertson (Owner)
Personnel: Charles J. Robertson (Pres.)
Personnel: Jason Bard (Dir., Mktg.)
Dave Reddick (Parts Mgr.)

ROBERTSON PRESS MACHINERY CO., INC.

Street address 1: 1301 S Maiden Ln
Street address state: MO
Zip/Postal code: 64801-3844
Country: USA
Mailing address: 1301 S Maiden Ln
Mailing city: Joplin
Mailing state: MO
Mailing zip: 64801-3844
General Phone: (417) 673-1929
General Fax: (417) 781-3704
Email: sales@robertsonpress.com
Primary Website: www.robertsonpress.com
Year Established: 1991
Product/Services: Color Registration; Dampening Systems; Equipment Dealers (New); Equipment Dealers (Used); Press Accessories, Parts & Supplies; Press Rebuilding; Presses: Offset; Remanufactures Equipment; Tension & Web Controls; Web Press - Special Equipment;
Personnel: Charles Robertson (Pres.)

KANSAS CITY

AXIS INSURANCE

Street address 1: 1201 Walnut St
Street address 2: Ste 1800
Street address state: MO
Zip/Postal code: 64106-2247
Country: USA
Mailing address: 1201 Walnut St Ste 1800
Mailing city: Kansas City
Mailing state: MO
Mailing zip: 64106-2247
General Phone: (816) 471-6118
General Fax: (816) 471-6119
Primary Website: www.axiscapital.com/insurance
Year Established: 1979
Product/Services: Insurance
Personnel: Peter Wilson (CEO)
Personnel: Eric Gesick (Chief Underwriting Officer)
Personnel: Noreen McMullan (Chief Human Resource Officer)

KENILWORTH

BELTING INDUSTRIES CO., INC.

Street address 1: 20 Boright Ave
Street address state: NJ
Zip/Postal code: 07033-1015
Country: USA
Mailing address: PO Box 310
Mailing city: Kenilworth
Mailing state: NJ
Mailing zip: 07033-0310
General Phone: (908) 272-8591
General Fax: (908) 272-3825
Email: info@beltingindustries.com
Primary Website: www.beltingindustries.com
Year Established: 1958
Product/Services: Belts, Belting, V-Belts
Personnel: Webb A. Cooper (Chrmn.)
Personnel: Scott Cooper (Pres.)
Personnel: Gene Hobson (COO)
Paul West (Controller)
Jeff Smith (Sales Mgr.)

KENNESAW

CCI EUROPE, INC.-GEORGIA BRANCH

Street address 1: 3550 George Busbee Pkwy NW
Street address 2: Ste 300
Street address state: GA
Zip/Postal code: 30144-5433
Country: USA
Mailing address: 600 Townpark Ln NW Ste 350
Mailing city: Kennesaw
Mailing state: GA
Mailing zip: 30144-3758
General Phone: (770) 420-1100
General Fax: (770) 420-5588
Email: info@ccieurope.com
Primary Website: www.ccieurope.com
Year Established: 1979
Product/Services: Content Management Systems
Personnel: Dan Korsgaard (CEO)
Personnel: Tor Lillegraven (Business Development Director)
Personnel: Thea Schmidt Borgholm (Vice President of Digital Services)

HEIDELBERG USA

Street address 1: 1000 Gutenberg Dr NW
Street address state: GA
Zip/Postal code: 30144-7028
Country: USA
Mailing address: 1000 Gutenberg Dr
Mailing city: Kennesaw
Mailing state: GA
Mailing zip: 30144
General Phone: (800) 437-7388
Email: info@heidelberg.com
Primary Website: www.heidelberg.com/us
Year Established: 1895
Product/Services: Manufacturing
Personnel: Felix Mueller (President, Heidelberg Americas)

HEIDELBERG USA, INC.

Street address 1: 1000 Gutenberg Dr NW
Street address state: GA
Zip/Postal code: 30144-7028
Country: USA
Mailing address: 1000 Gutenberg Dr NW
Mailing city: Kennesaw
Mailing state: GA
Mailing zip: 30144-7028
General Phone: (888) 472-9655
Email: info@heidelberg.com
Primary Website: www.us.heidelberg.com
Year Established: 1850
Product/Services: Sheetfed offset presses; digital production presses; wide format inkjet; prepress software and CtP output systems; inkjet proofing systems; color managment; business and production managment software; cutters, stitchers, folders, binders, and other postpress package producing systems; all consumables including plates, inks, coating solutions, blanket washes, and much more.
Personnel: Susan Nofi (Sr. Vice Pres., HR/Gen. Counsel)
Personnel: Thomas Topp (Sr. Vice Pres., Finance)
Personnel: Harald Weimer (President)
Andrew Rae (Sr. V.P. Equipment Marketing)
Ulrich Koehler (Sr. V.P. Service)

MARKEM-IMAJE

Street address 1: 100 Chastain Center Blvd NW
Street address 2: Ste 165
Street address state: GA
Zip/Postal code: 30144-5561
Country: USA
Mailing address: 100 Chastain Center Blvd NW Ste 165
Mailing city: Kennesaw
Mailing state: GA
Mailing zip: 30144-5561
General Phone: (770) 421-7700
General Fax: (770) 421-7702
Primary Website: www.markem-imaje.com
Year Established: 1987
Product/Services: Addressing Machines; Inks; Label Printing Machines; Mailroom Systems & Equipment;
Personnel: Omar Kerbage (President)
Personnel: Jacques Desroches (Gen. Mgr.)
Personnel: Alisha Howard (Mgr., Mktg.)

KENOSHA

BECKART ENVIRONMENTAL, INC.

Street address 1: 6900 46th St
Street address state: WI
Zip/Postal code: 53144-1749
Country: USA
Mailing address: 6900 46th St
Mailing city: Kenosha
Mailing state: WI
Mailing zip: 53144-1779
General Phone: (262) 656-7680
General Fax: (262) 656-7699
Email: information@beckart.com
Primary Website: www.beckart.com
Year Established: 1978
Product/Services: Wastewater Treatment
Personnel: Thomas M. Fedrigon (Pres.)
Personnel: Dan Fedrigon (Mgr., Mktg./Sales)

KENOSHA

KEPES, INC.

Street address 1: 9016 58th Pl
Street address state: WI
Zip/Postal code: 53144-7818
Country: USA
Mailing address: 9016 58th Pl Ste 600
Mailing city: Kenosha
Mailing state: WI
Mailing zip: 53144-7819
General Phone: (262) 652-7889
General Fax: (262) 652-7787
Email: inquire@kepes.com
Primary Website: www.kepes.com
Product/Services: Equipment Dealers (Used); Feeding, Folding, Delivery Equipment; Gluing Systems; Remanufactures Equipment; Roll Handeling Equipment; Rollers;
Personnel: Wayne Pagel (Pres./Sales Mgr.)
Personnel: John Slanchik (Mktg. Mgr.)

KERNERSVILLE

COMPUTER TREE PROFESSIONAL TRAINING

Street address 1: 121 Peddycord Park Dr
Street address state: NC
Zip/Postal code: 27284-0030
Country: USA
Mailing address: 121 Peddycord Park Dr.
Mailing city: Kernersville
Mailing state: NC
Mailing zip: 27284
General Phone: (336) 768-9820
Email: sales@computertree.com
Primary Website: www.computertree.com
Product/Services: As an Apple Authorized Training Center (AATC), ComputerTree Professional Training provides skills training, certification training, and testing at our own facilities in North Carolina and

Equipment, Supplies and Services

Georgia or on-site anywhere.
Note: http://www.computertree.com/aboutus.html
Personnel: Bob Young (Pres.)
Personnel: Joe Young (Vice President)

KEY LARGO

AMERICAN INTERNATIONAL COMMUNICATIONS, INC.

Street address 1: 101425 Overseas Hwy
Street address 2: 922
Street address state: FL
Zip/Postal code: 33037-4505
Country: USA
Mailing address: 101425 Overseas Hwy #922
Mailing city: Key Largo
Mailing state: FL
Mailing zip: 33037-4505
General Phone: (305) 453-5456
General Fax: (305) 453-5455
Email: pkaic@aol.com
Year Established: 1985
Product/Services: Telephone Automated Inbound Programs, Product information, Answering Services, Voice & video Conferencing, Voice Mail, Games, Horoscope, Health info; Voice Over IP; System Programming; Internet; Web site building; Consulting Services; 30 years in business.
Note: Connections World Wide
Personnel: Paul Keever (Pres./CEO)

KING OF PRUSSIA

PAGE

Street address 1: 700 American Ave
Street address 2: Ste 101
Street address state: PA
Zip/Postal code: 19406-4031
Country: USA
Mailing address: 700 American Ave Ste 101
Mailing city: King Of Prussia
Mailing state: PA
Mailing zip: 19406-4031
General Phone: (610) 592-0646
General Fax: (610) 592-0647
Primary Website: www.pagecooperative.com
Year Established: 1984
Product/Services: Composing Room Equipment & Supplies; Inks; Newsprint; Paper: Groundwood Specialties; Plates: Offset (Conventional);
Personnel: John Snyder (CEO)
Personnel: Evelyn Jayne (Office Mgr.)

KIRKLAND

R.B. INTERMARK, INC.

Street address 1: 15 Kirkland Blvd
Street address 2: Suite 108
Street address state: QC
Zip/Postal code: H9J 1N2
Country: Canada
Mailing address: 15 Kirkland Blvd., Ste. 108
Mailing city: Kirkland
Mailing state: QC
Mailing zip: H9J 1N2
General Phone: (514) 695-7172
General Fax: (514) 695-2108
Email: social@theloop.ca
Year Established: 1996
Product/Services: Silver Recovery; Solvent Recovery Systems; Wastewater Treatment; Water Management Systems;
Personnel: Rene J. Brimo (Pres.)

KRUM

DRAKE COMMUNICATIONS, INC.

Street address 1: 202 W McCart St
Street address 2: Ste 200
Street address state: TX
Zip/Postal code: 76249-5580
Country: USA
Mailing address: 202 W McCart St. Ste 200
Mailing city: Krum
Mailing state: TX
Mailing zip: 76249-5580
General Phone: (214) 206-3333
Year Established: 1979
Product/Services: Elections Interactive Voice Response (IVR) Information systems
Personnel: Cecil Drake (Pres.)
Personnel: L.G. Drake (Vice Pres.)

LA GRANGE

WHITING TECHNOLOGIES

Street address 1: PO 222
Street address state: IL
Zip/Postal code: 60525
Country: USA
Mailing state: IL
General Phone: (630) 850-9680
Email: fred@whitingtech.com
Primary Website: www.whitingtech.com
Product/Services: Press Equipment
Note: Press Design, Custom Engineering Products, Engineering Analysis"
Personnel: Fred Whiting (Pres.)

LACHINE

METAFIX, INC.

Street address 1: 1925 46e Ave
Street address state: QC
Zip/Postal code: H8T 2P1
Country: Canada
Mailing address: 1925 46th Ave.
Mailing city: Montreal
Mailing state: QC
Mailing zip: H8T 2P1
General Phone: (514) 633-8663
General Fax: (514) 633-1678
Email: sales@metafix.com
Primary Website: www.metafix.com
Year Established: 1988
Product/Services: Environmental Control Systems; Silver Recovery;

LAKE FOREST

PETCO ROLLER CO.

Street address 1: 28041 N Bradley Rd
Street address state: IL
Zip/Postal code: 60045-1163
Country: USA
Mailing address: 28041 N Bradley Rd
Mailing city: Lake Forest
Mailing state: IL
Mailing zip: 60045-1163
General Phone: (847) 362-1820
General Fax: (847) 362-1833
Email: mail@petcorolls.com
Primary Website: www.petcorolls.com
Year Established: 1964
Product/Services: Roll Coverings; Rollers; Rollers: Dampening;
Personnel: Dale Glen (Sales Mgr.)

LAKE VILLA

BURNISHINE PRODUCTS

Street address 1: 25392 W Park Ct
Street address state: IL
Zip/Postal code: 60046-9710
Country: USA
Mailing address: 25392 W Park Ct
Mailing city: Lake Villa
Mailing state: IL
Mailing zip: 60046-9710
General Phone: 847-356-0222
General Fax: 847-306-3550
Email: rgiza@burnishine.com
Primary Website: www.burnishine.com
Year Established: 1887
Product/Services: Offset Fountain Solutions; Plate Cleaners; Miscellaneous Pressroom Chemicals
Personnel: Patty Vick (Graphic Arts Customer Service)
Personnel: Roger Giza (President)

LAKE WORTH

QUICKSET USA INC

Street address 1: PO Box 542707
Street address state: FL
Zip/Postal code: 33454
Country: USA
Mailing address: PO Box 542707
Mailing city: Lake Worth
Mailing state: FL
Mailing zip: 33454
General Phone: (206) 849-7770
General Fax: (561) 721-0959
Email: info@quicksetcorporation.com
Primary Website: www.quicksetcorporation.com
Year Established: 1981
Product/Services: Ink Pre-setting Systems
Note: QuickSet has installed its proprietary ink presetting system on hundreds of press lines and has over 250,000 retrofit levers installed worldwide. With a 100 track record of providing users with an ROI in one year, QuickSet's ink presets use unique technology that has never been duplicated. QuickSet provides great value to the customer since the ink density accuracy rivals closed-loop ink control. QuickSet's new streamlined press-mapping process allows capture of complete press unit behavior at every inking position. Installations range from the smallest community printers to top 100 commercial printers.
Personnel: Steve Surbrook (Pres.)

LAKE ZURICH

ALFAQUEST TECHNOLOGIES

Street address 1: 1150 Rose Rd
Street address state: IL
Zip/Postal code: 60047-1567
Country: USA
Mailing address: 1150 Rose Rd
Mailing city: Lake Zurich
Mailing state: IL
Mailing zip: 60047-1567
General Phone: (847) 427-8800
General Fax: (847) 427-8860
Email: keith.roeske@alfactp.com
Primary Website: www.alfactp.com
Year Established: 1982
Product/Services: Computers: Hardware & Software Integrators; Imagesetters; Interfaces; Laser Printers; Multiplexers/Routers; Output Management and Preflight Software; Photo Archiving; Platemakers: Laser; Raster Image Processors;
Note: Developers and Manufacturers of Newspaper production workflow and CTP.
Personnel: Keith Roeske (Vice President Of Operations)

GENERAL BINDING CORP.

Street address 1: 4 Corporate Dr
Street address state: IL
Zip/Postal code: 60047-8924
Country: USA
Mailing address: 4 Corporate Dr
Mailing city: Lake Zurich
Mailing state: IL
Mailing zip: 60047-8924
General Phone: (800) 723-4000
General Fax: (800) 914-8178
Email: info@acco.com
Primary Website: www.gbcconnect.com
Year Established: 1947
Product/Services: Paper Shredders

LAKELAND

B.H. BUNN CO.

Street address 1: 2730 Drane Field Rd
Street address state: FL
Zip/Postal code: 33811-1325
Country: USA
Mailing address: 2730 Drane Field Rd
Mailing city: Lakeland
Mailing state: FL
Mailing zip: 33811-1325
General Phone: (863) 647-1555
General Fax: (863) 686-2866
Email: info@bunntyco.com
Primary Website: www.bunntyco.com
Year Established: 1907
Product/Services: Bundling and Tying Machines; Strapping Machines;
Note: Did you know that Bunn introduced to the world the First Automatic Package Tying Machine? You can say that Bunn ushered in Automatic Packaging. Did you also know that your fathers father used a Bunn Tying Machine and they liked it! As a matter of fact they liked it so much that they purchased many more over the years! It's not an old way of bundling, its the best way of bundling. Why not try it again? Why not buy American? Bunn Always has been American Made since 1907. Call Bunn Today! We are here to help! 800-222-BUNN
Personnel: John R. Bunn (Pres.)

LANGHORNE

JUST NORMLICHT, INC.

Street address 1: 2000 Cabot Blvd W
Street address 2: Ste 120
Street address state: PA
Zip/Postal code: 19047-2408
Country: USA
Mailing address: 2000 Cabot Blvd W Ste 120
Mailing city: Langhorne
Mailing state: PA
Mailing zip: 19047-2408
General Phone: (267) 852-2200
General Fax: (267) 852-2207
Email: sales@justnormlicht.com
Primary Website: www.justnormlicht.com
Year Established: 1985
Product/Services: Color Proofing; Color Viewing Equipment;
Personnel: Eric Dalton (Vice President)

LASALLE

POLKADOTS SOFTWARE INC.

Street address 1: 216-2555 Av Dollard
Street address state: QC
Zip/Postal code: H8N 3A9
Country: Canada
Mailing state: QC
General Phone: (514) 595-6866
Email: info@polkadots.ca
Primary Website: www.polkadots.ca
Year Established: 1998
Product/Services: Newspaper prepress automation, page pairing, ink optimizing, RIP, web growth compensation, internet proofing, internet job definition
Note: PrePress Software
Personnel: Gilles Duhamel (Pres.)
Personnel: Sylvain Audet (VP)

LAWRENCEVILLE

COLORVISION, INC.

Street address 1: 5 Princess Rd
Street address state: NJ
Zip/Postal code: 08648-2301
Country: USA
Mailing address: 5 Princess Rd
Mailing city: Lawrenceville
Mailing state: NJ
Mailing zip: 08648-2301
General Phone: (609) 895-7430
General Fax: (609) 895-8110
Email: info@colovision.com
Primary Website: www.datacolor.com
Year Established: 2000
Product/Services: Software: Electronic Data Interchange

Personnel: Brian Levey (Vice Pres. Mktg./Sales)

LEBANON

AMERICAN ULTRAVIOLET CO., INC.

Street address 1: 212 S Mount Zion Rd
Street address state: IN
Zip/Postal code: 46052-9479
Country: USA
Mailing address: 212 S Mount Zion Rd
Mailing city: Lebanon
Mailing state: IN
Mailing zip: 46052-9479
General Phone: (765) 483-9514
General Fax: (765) 483-9525
Primary Website: www.auvco.com
Product/Services: Press Accessories, Parts & Supplies
Personnel: David Snyder (Sales Rep.)

LENEXA

PERFORMANCE CONTRACTING GROUP

Street address 1: 16400 College Blvd
Street address state: KS
Zip/Postal code: 66219-1389
Country: USA
Mailing address: 16400 College Blvd
Mailing city: Lenexa
Mailing state: KS
Mailing zip: 66219-1389
General Phone: 1-800-255-6886
Email: info@pcg.com
Primary Website: www.pcg.com

SOLNA WEB USA, INC.

Street address 1: 14500 W 105th St
Street address state: KS
Zip/Postal code: 66215-2014
Country: USA
Mailing address: PO Box 15066
Mailing city: Lenexa
Mailing state: KS
Mailing zip: 66285-5066
General Phone: (913) 492-9925
General Fax: (913) 492-0170
Email: rkerns@solnaweb.com
Primary Website: www.solnaweb.com
Year Established: 1992
Product/Services: Presses: Offset
Personnel: Richard Kerns (Pres.)

LEXINGTON

CLARK MATERIAL HANDLING CO.

Street address 1: 700 Enterprise Dr
Street address state: KY
Zip/Postal code: 40510-1028
Country: USA
Mailing address: 700 Enterprise Dr
Mailing city: Lexington
Mailing state: KY
Mailing zip: 40510-1028
General Phone: (859) 422-6400
General Fax: (859) 422-7408
Primary Website: www.clarkmhc.com
Year Established: 1917
Product/Services: Equipment Dealers (New); Equipment Dealers (Used); Lift Trucks; Material Handling Equipment: Palletizing Machines; Material Handling Equipment: Pallets & Palletizers; Material Handling Equipment: Truck Loaders; Material Handling Equipment: Vehicle Loading;
Personnel: Dennis Lawrence (Pres.)
Personnel: Sherry Myers (Dir., HR)

LINCOLN

MESA CORP.

Street address 1: 4546 S 86th St
Street address 2: Ste B
Street address state: NE
Zip/Postal code: 68526-9252
Country: USA
Mailing address: 4546 S 86th St Ste B
Mailing city: Lincoln
Mailing state: NE
Mailing zip: 68526-9252
General Phone: (402) 489-9303
General Fax: (402) 489-7524
Email: info@mesacorp.com; sales@mesacorp.com
Primary Website: www.mesacorp.com
Product/Services: Storage Retrieval Systems
Personnel: Thomas Manning (Vice Pres.-Sales/Mktg.)

WINDMOELLER AND HOELSCHER CORP.

Street address 1: 23 New England Way
Street address state: RI
Zip/Postal code: 02865-4252
Country: USA
Mailing address: 23 New England Way
Mailing city: Lincoln
Mailing state: RI
Mailing zip: 02865-4200
General Phone: (401) 333-2770
General Fax: (401) 333-6491
Email: info@whcorp.com
Primary Website: www.whcorp.com
Year Established: 1977
Product/Services: Presses: Flexographic; Presses: Rotogravure;
Personnel: Andrew Wheeler (President)
Personnel: Klaus Kleeman (Vice President of Sales)
Personnel: Buch Javeed (Sr. VP)

LINDEN

BRODIE SYSTEM, INC.

Street address 1: 1539 W Elizabeth Ave
Street address state: NJ
Zip/Postal code: 07036-6322
Country: USA
Mailing address: 1539 W. Elizabeth Ave.
Mailing city: Linden
Mailing state: NJ
Mailing zip: 07036
General Phone: (908) 862-8620
General Fax: (908) 862-8632
Email: customerservice@brodiesystem.com
Primary Website: www.brodiesystem.com
Year Established: 1929
Product/Services: Cylinder Repair; Ink Fountains & Accessories; Press Accessories, Parts & Supplies; Roller Grinding Services; Rollers; Rollers: Dampening;
Personnel: Thomas W. Nielsen (Pres.)
Personnel: Nicholas Lloyd (Eng.)
Personnel: John Farrell (Prodn. Mgr., Opns.)

LISLE

MANROLAND WEB SYSTEMS INC.

Street address 1: 2150 Western Ct
Street address 2: Ste 420
Street address state: IL
Zip/Postal code: 60532-1973
Country: USA
Mailing address: 2150 Western Ct Ste 420
Mailing city: Lisle
Mailing state: IL
Mailing zip: 60532-1973
General Phone: (630) 920-5850
General Fax: (630) 920-5851
Primary Website: www.manroland-web.com
Year Established: 2012
Product/Services: Material Handling Equipment: Automatic Guided Vehicles; Newsprint Handling Equipment; Press Accessories, Parts & Supplies; Press Control Systems; Presses: Flexographic; Presses: Offset; Reels (Includes Paper Reels); Roll Cleaning Equipment; Ink Jet & Digital Press Equipment; Folding & Finishing Equipment
Note: Leading with the broadest and freshest product portfolio in web offset printing, manroland web systems Inc., based in Augsburg, Germany, and operating in North America out of Westmont, Illinois, Toronto, Ontario, and Ansonia, Connecticut, is part of the Lubeck, Germany-based Possehl Group, as their 10th business division. Their clear strategy £ stability, investment security, groundbreaking technology, and a strong service offerings £ gives the principles that guide manroland web systems. Web offset presses from Augsburg provide tailor-made solutions for newspaper, publishing, and commercial printing. A worldwide sales and service network also markets ancillary printing equipment and pressroom products as well as software products and workflow management systems. The company£s partnership with Oc£ Printing Systems features the first innovations in industrial digital four-color printing, including graphics networking and finishing equipment, developed by manroland web systems.
Personnel: Denise Lease (Marketing Manager)
Personnel: Greg Blue (CEO)
Personnel: Ron Sams (VP of Sales)

LITTLETON

FAKE BRAINS, INC.

Street address 1: 791 Southpark Dr Ste 300
Street address 2: Fake Brains Software
Street address state: CO
Zip/Postal code: 80120-6401
Country: USA
Mailing address: 791 Southpark Dr Ste 300
Mailing city: Littleton
Mailing state: CO
Mailing zip: 80120-6401
General Phone: (303) 791-3301
General Fax: (303) 470-5218
Email: sales@fakebrains.com
Primary Website: www.fakebrains.com
Year Established: 1991
Product/Services: Software: Advertising (Includes Display; Classified; Digital Media); Software: Business (Includes Administration/Accounting); Software: CRM (Customer Relations); Software: Cloud; Software: OnPremise
Personnel: Pat Pfeifer (Pres.)
Personnel: Lisa Pfeifer (VP/Sales Dir.)

LIVONIA

COMTEL INSTRUMENTS CO.

Street address 1: 37000 Plymouth Rd
Street address state: MI
Zip/Postal code: 48150-1132
Country: USA
Mailing address: 37000 Plymouth Rd
Mailing city: Livonia
Mailing state: MI
Mailing zip: 48150-1132
General Phone: (800) 335-2505
General Fax: (734) 542-1353
Email: comtelcorp@comtel.com
Primary Website: www.comtel.com
Product/Services: Software: Electronic Data Interchange
Personnel: Gregg Montgomery (Sales Engineer- Kentucky)
Personnel: Eric Hubbard (Sales Engineer- OH, PA, W. VA)
Personnel: Brian Carr (Sales Engineer- Michigan)
Jim Bull (Sales Engineer-IN, SW MI, W. KY)
Dr. Barbara J. Boroughf PhD. (Government Contract Officer-North America)
Lynne Williams (Administrative Assistant)
Paul Williams (Inside Sales)
Jenny Seaks (Accounting Mgr., Inside Sales)
Jenny Boroughf (Controller)

LODI

KAIM & ASSOCIATES

INTERNATIONAL MARKETING, INC.

Street address 1: 102 Industrial Park Rd
Street address state: WI
Zip/Postal code: 53555-1374
Country: USA
Mailing address: 102 Industrial Park Rd
Mailing city: Lodi
Mailing state: WI
Mailing zip: 53555-1374
General Phone: (608) 592-7404
General Fax: (608) 592-7404
Year Established: 1988
Product/Services: Color Registration; Controls: Register; Paper Shredders; Pasters; Reels & Tensions; Roll Cleaning Equipment; Rollers; Tension & Web Controls; Web Break Detector; Web Cleaners;
Personnel: Wayne Kaim (Pres.)

LOMBARD

SCHERMERHORN BROS. CO.

Street address 1: 340 Eisenhower Ln N
Street address state: IL
Zip/Postal code: 60148-5405
Country: USA
Mailing address: 340 Eisenhower Ln N
Mailing city: Lombard
Mailing state: IL
Mailing zip: 60148-5470
General Phone: (630) 627-9860
General Fax: (630) 627-1178
Primary Website: www.schermerhornbrosco.com
Year Established: 1893
Product/Services: Circulation Equipment & Supplies
Note: Circulation Supplies
Personnel: Dennis Jenkins (Sales Contact)

LONDON

MIDSYSTEMS TECHNOLOGY LTD.

Street address 1: One Kingdom Street
Zip/Postal code: W8 5SF
Country: United Kingdom
Mailing address: One Kingdom Street
Mailing city: London
Mailing zip: W8 5SF
General Phone: (0)20 3320 5000
General Fax: (0)20 3320 1771
Email: sales@midsys.co.uk
Primary Website: www.misys.co.uk
Product/Services: Produciton Control Systems
Personnel: John Sussens (Mng. Dir.)

LONG BEACH

DESIGN SCIENCE, INC.

Street address 1: 140 Pine Ave
Street address 2: Fl 4
Street address state: CA
Zip/Postal code: 90802-9440
Country: USA
Mailing address: 140 Pine Ave Fl 4
Mailing city: Long Beach
Mailing state: CA
Mailing zip: 90802-9440
General Phone: (562) 432-2920
General Fax: (562) 432-2857
Email: sales@dessci.com
Primary Website: www.dessci.com
Product/Services: Input & Editing Systems; Type, Fonts;
Personnel: Paul Topping (Pres.)

LOS ANGELES

LEXISNEXIS

Street address 1: 555 W 5th St
Street address 2: Ste 4500
Street address state: CA
Zip/Postal code: 90013-3003
Country: USA
Mailing address: 555 W 5th St Ste 4500

Equipment, Supplies and Services

Mailing city: Los Angeles
Mailing state: CA
Mailing zip: 90013-3003
General Phone: (213) 627-1130
Email: lexisnexiscommunities@lexisnexis.com
Primary Website: www.lexisnexis.com
Product or Service: Consultants
Personnel: Andrew Prozes (CEO, Lexis-Nexis Grp.)
Personnel: Kurt Sanford (Pres./CEO, Cor. & Fed. Mkts.)
Personnel: Michael Walsh (Pres./CEO, U.S. Legal Mkts.)
James M. Peck (CEO, Risk Mgmt.)
Richard Sobelsohn

LOUISVILLE

ARCO ENGINEERING, INC. (NEWSPAPER DIV.)

Street address 1: 3317 Gilmore Industrial Blvd
Street address state: KY
Zip/Postal code: 40213-2174
Country: USA
Mailing address: 3317 Gilmore Industrial Blvd
Mailing city: Louisville
Mailing state: KY
Mailing zip: 40213-2174
General Phone: (502) 966-3134
General Fax: (502) 966-3135
Email: sales@arcoengineering.com
Primary Website: www.arcoengineering.com
Year Established: 1954
Product/Services: Belts, Belting, V-Belts; Equipment Dealers (New); Equipment Dealers (Used); Gauges, Measuring; Noise Control; Pasters; Reels & Tensions; Reels (Inlcudes Paper Reels); Scanners: Color B & W, Plates, Web; Tension & Web Controls
Personnel: James Gunn (Pres.)

KINETIC CORPORATION

Street address 1: 200 Distillery Cmns
Street address 2: Ste 200
Street address state: KY
Zip/Postal code: 40206-1987
Country: USA
Mailing address: 200 Distillery Commons Ste 200
Mailing city: Louisville
Mailing state: KY
Mailing zip: 40206-1987
General Phone: (502) 719-9500
General Fax: (502) 719-9569
Email: info@theTechnologyAgency.com
Primary Website: www.theTechnologyAgency.com
Year Established: 1979
Product/Services: Consulting Services: Production; Photo Archiving; Preprint Service & Production; Software: Asset Management; Software: Design/Graphics; Software: Pagination/Layout; Software: Workflow Management/Tracking;
Product or Service: Graphic/Design Firm
Personnel: G. Raymond Schuhmann (Pres.)
Personnel: Cindi Ramm (Chief Brand Strategist)

LYNNE MEENA CO.

Street address 1: 130 Saint Matthews Ave Ste 302
Street address 2: Advertising Federation
Street address state: KY
Zip/Postal code: 40207-3142
Country: USA
Mailing address: 130 St. Matthews Avenue, Suite 303
Mailing city: Louisville
Mailing state: KY
Mailing zip: 40207
General Phone: (800) 818-1181
Year Established: 1992
Product/Services: Advertising headlines. Rewrite your advertising headlines for more effective results.
Note: Former Creative VP of Newspaper Association of America,

MEENA COPY & LAYOUT

Street address 1: 130 Saint Matthews Ave
Street address state: KY
Zip/Postal code: 40207-3148
Country: USA
Mailing address: 130 Saint Matthews Ave
Mailing city: Louisville
Mailing state: KY
Mailing zip: 40207-3105
General Phone: (800) 818-1181
General Fax: (800) 818-8329
Email: lynnemeena@aol.com
Year Established: 1990
Product/Services: Consulting Services: Advertising: How to make a good ad better. Advertising: Design & Layout;
Personnel: Lynne Meena (Pres.)

LOVELAND

COLD JET, INC.

Street address 1: 455 Wards Corner Rd
Street address state: OH
Zip/Postal code: 45140-9062
Country: USA
Mailing address: 455 Wards Corner Rd Ste 100
Mailing city: Loveland
Mailing state: OH
Mailing zip: 45140-9033
General Phone: (513) 831-3211
Email: info@coldjet.com
Primary Website: www.coldjet.com; www.dryiceblasting.com
Product/Services: Cleaners & Solvents
Personnel: Gene Cooke (Pres./CEO)

LYONS

SIEBERT, INC.

Street address 1: 8134 47th St
Street address state: IL
Zip/Postal code: 60534-1836
Country: USA
Mailing address: 8134 47th St
Mailing city: Lyons
Mailing state: IL
Mailing zip: 60534-1836
General Phone: (708) 442-2010
General Fax: (708) 447-9353
Email: customerservice@siebertinc.com
Primary Website: www.siebertinc.com
Year Established: 1969
Product/Services: Chemicals: Roller Cleaning; Cleaners & Solvents;
Personnel: J.P. Mulcahy (Pres.)

MALVERN

RICOH CORP.

Street address 1: 70 Valley Stream Parkway
Street address state: PA
Zip/Postal code: 19355
Country: USA
Mailing address: 5 Dedrick Pl
Mailing city: West Caldwell
Mailing state: NJ
Mailing zip: 07006-6398
General Phone: (973) 882-2000
General Fax: (973) 808-7555
Primary Website: www.ricoh-usa.com
Year Established: 1936
Product/Services: Digital Copiers; Facsimiles; Multi-functional Systems; Scanners; Printers; Digital Cameras; Projectors;
Personnel: Joji Tokunaga (President and CEO)
Personnel: Jeff Paterra (Executive Vice President)
Personnel: Peter H. Stuart (Executive Vice President, Office Solutions Business Group)
Donna Venable (Exec. V. Pres., HR & Dep. Gen. Mgr.)
Dennis Dispenziere (Sr. V. P. & CFO of Ricoh Americas)
Glenn Laverty (Sr. V.P., Marketing, Shared Services)

MAPLE GROVE

INNOTEK CORPORATION

Street address 1: 9140 Zachary Ln N
Street address state: MN
Zip/Postal code: 55369-4003
Country: USA
Mailing address: 9140 Zachary Ln N
Mailing city: Maple Grove
Mailing state: MN
Mailing zip: 55369-4003
General Phone: (763) 488 9902
General Fax: (763)488 9904
Email: sales@innotek-ep.com
Primary Website: www.innotek-ep.com
Year Established: 1960
Product/Services: Hydraulic & Pneumatic components and systems. Electronic systems / UL panel shop. Power Units / Test cells. contract manufacturing / machine shop/ hydraulic service and repair. Hydraulic hose assemblies.
Personnel: Dennis Burns (CEO President)
Personnel: David Kalina (Vice Pres., Finance)
Personnel: Tom Wiese (Vice President of Sales & Engineering)

MARIETTA

EWERT AMERICA ELECTRONICS LTD.

Street address 1: 869 Pickens Industrial Dr
Street address 2: Ste 12
Street address state: GA
Zip/Postal code: 30062-3164
Country: USA
Mailing address: 869 Pickens Industrial Dr Ste 12
Mailing city: Marietta
Mailing state: GA
Mailing zip: 30062-3164
General Phone: 678-996-2411
General Fax: 770-421-0731
Email: ceickhoff@eaeusa.com
Primary Website: www.eaeusa.com
Year Established: 1962
Product/Services: Computers: Hardware & Software Integrators; Drives & Controls; Press Control Systems; Software: Workflow Management/Tracking; Closed loop ink density controls System Installations; System Integration Services; Training: Press Operation & Maintenance;
Personnel: Chris Eickhoff (CM, COO)

MARIETTA

PAMARCO GLOBAL GRAPHICS

Street address 1: 150 Marr Ave NW
Street address state: GA
Zip/Postal code: 30060-1050
Country: USA
Mailing address: 150 Marr Ave NW
Mailing city: Marietta
Mailing state: GA
Mailing zip: 30060-1050
General Phone: (770) 795-8556
General Fax: (770) 795-8943
Email: info@pamarcoglobal.com
Primary Website: www.pamarcoglobal.com
Year Established: 1970
Product/Services: Press Accessories, Parts & Supplies; Presses: Offset; Rollers; Rollers: Dampening;
Personnel: James Miller (Vice Pres., Mfg.)
Personnel: Greg Anderson (Vice Pres., Sales/Mktg.)

MARKHAM

ADVANTEX MARKETING INTERNATIONAL, INC.

Street address 1: 600 Alden Rd
Street address 2: Suite 606
Street address state: ON
Zip/Postal code: L3R 0E7
Country: Canada
Mailing address: 600 Alden Road, Suite 606
Mailing city: Markham
Mailing state: ON
Mailing zip: L3R 0E7
General Phone: (416) 481-5657
General Fax: (416) 481-5692
Email: info@advantex.com
Primary Website: www.advantex.com
Year Established: 1983
Product/Services: Consulting Services: Circulation; Consulting Services: Marketing; Promotion Services
Personnel: Kelly Ambrose (Pres.)

COMPUTER TALK TECHNOLOGY, INC.

Street address 1: 150 Commerce Valley Drive West
Street address 2: Suite 800
Street address state: ON
Zip/Postal code: L3T 7Z3
Country: Canada
Mailing address: 150 Commerce Valley Drive West, Suite 800
Mailing city: Markham
Mailing state: ON
Mailing zip: L3T 7Z3
General Phone: (905) 882-5000
General Fax: (905) 882-5501
Primary Website: www.computer-talk.com
Year Established: 1987
Product/Services: Software: Electronic Data Interchange; System Integration Services;
Product or Service: Hardware/Software Supplier
Personnel: Mandle Cheung (Pres./CEO)
Personnel: Donald Mcdonald (V. P.)

MAYNARD

ADVANCED TECHNICAL SOLUTIONS, INC.

Street address 1: 36 Nason St
Street address state: MA
Zip/Postal code: 01754-2502
Country: USA
Mailing address: PO Box 386
Mailing city: Maynard
Mailing state: MA
Mailing zip: 01754-0386
General Phone: (978) 849-0533
General Fax: (978) 849-0544
Email: support@atsusa.com
Primary Website: www.atsusa.com
Year Established: 1987
Product/Services: Computers: Hardware & Software Integrators; Input & Editing Systems; Publishing Systems; Software: Advertising (Includes Display; Classified); Software: Circulation; Software: Editorial; Software: Press/Post Press
Personnel: Bill Page (Exec. Vice Pres.)

MECHANICSBURG

FRY COMMUNICATIONS, INC.

Street address 1: 800 W Church Rd
Street address state: PA
Zip/Postal code: 17055-3179
Country: USA
Mailing address: 800 W. Church Rd.
Mailing city: Mechanicsburg
Mailing state: PA
Mailing zip: 17055
General Phone: (800) 334-1429
Email: info@frycomm.com
Primary Website: www.frycomm.com
Year Established: 1934
Product/Services: Publishing Systems; Trade Publications; Commercial Printer
Note: Fry consultants develop solutions from traditional print and distribution to progressive digital device delivery and custom web publishing.
Personnel: Henry Fry (Chairman of the Board)
Personnel: Kevin Quinn (VP Sales)

Personnel: Mike Lukas (CEO)
Mike Weber (VP Manufacturing)

IMPACT RACKS, INC.

Street address 1: 12 Wheatland Dr
Street address state: PA
Zip/Postal code: 17050-1600
Country: USA
Mailing address: 12 Wheatland Dr.
Mailing city: Mechanicsburg
Mailing state: PA
Mailing zip: 17050
General Phone: (717) 200-1213
Email: impactracks@aol.com
Year Established: 1995
Product/Services: Circulation Equipment & Supplies; Newspaper Dispensers (Mechanical/Electronic); Remanufactures Equipment; Strapping Machines; Tubes, Racks (Includes Racks: Motor Route Tubes);
Personnel: John Knowles (Pres.)
Personnel: Stefan Knowles (VP)

MEDLEY

RYDER SYSTEM, INC.

Street address 1: 11690 NW 105th St
Street address state: FL
Zip/Postal code: 33178-1103
Country: USA
Mailing address: 11690 NW 105th St
Mailing city: Medley
Mailing state: FL
Mailing zip: 33178-1103
General Phone: (305) 500-3726
General Fax: (305) 500-4339
Primary Website: www.ryder.com
Year Established: 1933
Product/Services: Lift Trucks
Personnel: Robert E. Sanchez (Chrmn./CEO)
Personnel: Dennis C. Cooke (Pres. Global Fleet Management Solutions)
Personnel: Art A. Garcia (Executive VP and CFO)
Todd Skiles (SVP, Global Supply Chain Solutions Sales)

MELBOURNE

ATEX NORTH AMERICA

Street address 1: 410 N Wickham Rd
Street address state: FL
Zip/Postal code: 32935-8648
Country: USA
Mailing address: 410 N Wickham Rd
Mailing city: Melbourne
Mailing state: FL
Mailing zip: 32935-8648
General Phone: (321) 254-5559
General Fax: (321) 254-4392
Email: adbase.support-services.us@atex.com
Primary Website: www.atex.com
Year Established: 1996
Product/Services: Consulting Services: Advertising; Software: Advertising (Includes Display; Classified); Software: Business (Includes Administration/Accounting);
Personnel: Scott Roessler (CEO of North America)
Personnel: Lars Jiborn (Vice Pres., Product Mgmt.)
Personnel: Steve Roessler (Vice Pres., Mktg.)

HARRIS CORP.

Street address 1: 1025 W Nasa Blvd
Street address state: FL
Zip/Postal code: 32919-0002
Country: USA
Mailing address: 1025 W Nasa Blvd # A11-0
Mailing city: Melbourne
Mailing state: FL
Mailing zip: 32919-0001
General Phone: (321) 727-9100
Primary Website: www.harris.com
Year Established: 1895
Product/Services: Business Computers; Data Communication; Facsimilie/Fax Transmission Systems; Pagination Systems; Input & Editing Systems; Press Control Systems; Publishing Systems; Visual Display Terminals;
Personnel: Howard L. Lance (Pres./CEO/Chrmn.)
Personnel: Robert K. Henry (COO)
Personnel: Gary L. McArthur (Sr. Vice Pres./CFO)
Pamela Padgett (Vice Pres., Investor Rel.)
Charles J. Greene (Treasurer)

MELVILLE

NIKON, INC.

Street address 1: 1300 Walt Whitman Rd
Street address state: NY
Zip/Postal code: 11747-3001
Country: USA
Mailing address: 1300 Walt Whitman Rd Fl 2
Mailing city: Melville
Mailing state: NY
Mailing zip: 11747-3064
General Phone: (631) 547-4200
General Fax: (631) 547-0299
Primary Website: www.nikonusa.com
Product/Services: Consumer Electronics
Personnel: Nobuyoshi Gokyu (Pres./CEO)
Personnel: David Lee (Sr. Vice Pres.)
Personnel: Steve Heiner (Gen. Mgr., Mktg. Pro Pdcts./Digital SLR Systems/Speedlights)
William Giordano (Nat'l Mktg. Mgr., Nikon USA)
Kristina Kurtzke (Communications Coordinator)

MEMPHIS

FUJIFILM GRAPHIC SYSTEMS USA, INC.

Street address 1: 3926 Willow Lake Blvd
Street address state: TN
Zip/Postal code: 38118-7040
Country: USA
Mailing address: 3926 Willow Lake Blvd
Mailing city: Memphis
Mailing state: TN
Mailing zip: 38118-7040
General Phone: (800) 365-2457
General Fax: (901) 795-1251
Primary Website: www.fujifilmusa.com/products/graphic_arts_printing/index.html
Product/Services: Blankets; Chemicals: Pressroom; Color Management Software; Imagesetters; Inks; Offset Chemicals & Supplies; Platemakers; Flexographic (Computer to Plate); Plates: Offset (Conventional); Proofing Systems; Software: Press/Post Press;
Personnel: Tommy Aquino (Reg'l Sales Mgr.)

MEMPHIS

GREAT SOUTHERN CORP. (SIRCO DIV.)

Street address 1: PO Box 18710
Street address state: TN
Zip/Postal code: 38181-0710
Country: USA
Mailing address: PO Box 18710
Mailing city: Memphis
Mailing state: TN
Mailing zip: 38181-0710
General Phone: (901) 365-1611
General Fax: (901) 365-4498
Email: sales@gsmemphis.com
Primary Website: www.gsmemphis.com
Year Established: 1961
Product/Services: Circulation Equipment & Supplies; Newspaper Bags;
Personnel: Scott Vaught (Pres.)

MENTOR

STERLING PACKAGING SYSTEMS

Street address 1: 6275 Heisley Rd
Street address state: OH
Zip/Postal code: 44060-1858
Country: USA
Mailing address: 6275 Heisley Rd
Mailing city: Mentor
Mailing state: OH
Mailing zip: 44060-1858
General Phone: (440) 358-7060
General Fax: (440) 358-7061
Primary Website: www.polychem.com
Year Established: 1992
Product/Services: Bundling and Tying Machines; Consulting Services: Equipment; Conveyors; Mailroom Systems & Equipment; Remanufactures Equipment;
Personnel: Mihia Cojocaru (Gen. Mgr.)

MEXICO

BROWN'S WEB PRESS SERVICE & MACHINE SHOP

Street address 1: 21386 Hwy Ff
Street address state: MO
Zip/Postal code: 65265
Country: USA
Mailing address: PO Box 326
Mailing city: Mexico
Mailing state: MO
Mailing zip: 65265-0326
General Phone: (573) 581-6275
General Fax: (573) 581-7278
Email: lgbrown59@gmail.com
Year Established: 1983
Product/Services: Cylinder Repair; Drives & Controls; Equipment Dealers (Used); Erectors & Riggers; Press Rebuilding; Press Repairs; Presses: Offset; Roller Grinding Services;
Note: Machine Shop , Printing Press Sales and Servive "
Personnel: L.G. Brown (Pres.)
Personnel: Gena Brown (Vice President)

CONTINENTAL PRODUCTS

Street address 1: 2000 W Boulevard St
Street address state: MO
Zip/Postal code: 65265-1209
Country: USA
Mailing address: PO Box 760
Mailing city: Mexico
Mailing state: MO
Mailing zip: 65265-0760
General Phone: (800) 325-0216
Email: mail@continentalproducts.com
Primary Website: www.continentalproducts.com
Year Established: 1927
Product/Services: Circulation Equipment & Supplies; Newspaper Bags; Tubes, Racks (Includes Racks: Motor Route Tubes);
Personnel: Thad Fisher (Vice Pres., Sales/Mktg.)
Personnel: Loyd Smith (Cust. Serv. Supervisor)

MIAMI

LATIN AMERICAN DIV./FLINT INK

Street address 1: 9100 S Dadeland Blvd
Street address 2: Ste 1800
Street address state: FL
Zip/Postal code: 33156-7817
Country: USA
Mailing address: 9100 S Dadeland Blvd Ste 1800
Mailing city: Miami
Mailing state: FL
Mailing zip: 33156-7817
General Phone: (305) 670-0066
General Fax: (305) 670-0060
Primary Website: www.flintink.com
Year Established: 1983
Product/Services: Blankets; Chemicals: Plate Processing; Chemicals: Pressroom; Chemicals: Roller Cleaning; Ink Pumping Systems; Ink Recovery Systems; Inks; Plates: Offset (Conventional); Presses: Offset;
Personnel: Jerko E. Rendic (Pres.)
Personnel: Claudia Anderson (Bus. Mgr.)
Personnel: Paul Chmielewicz (Regl. Sales Mgr., Brazil)
Fernando Tavara (Regl. Sales Mgr., South America)
Nestor Porto (Regl. Sales Mgr., Central America/Caribbean)
Al Miller (Technical Serv. Mgr.)

NEWSTECH CO. (DIV. OF ROVINTER, INC.)

Street address 1: 675 NW 97th St
Street address state: FL
Zip/Postal code: 33150-1652
Country: USA
Mailing address: 675 NW 97th St
Mailing city: Miami
Mailing state: FL
Mailing zip: 33150-1652
General Phone: (305) 757-5577
General Fax: (305) 757-2255
Email: e-mail@newstech.com
Primary Website: www.newstech.com
Year Established: 1979
Product/Services: Blankets; Film & Paper: Phototypesetting; Inks; Offset Chemicals & Supplies; Plate Mounting & Register Systems; Plate Processors; Plates: Offset (Computer to Plate); Plates: Offset (Conventional); Press Parts; Rollers;
Personnel: Oscar Rovito (Pres.)
Personnel: Diego A. Rovito (Vice Pres.)

PAN AMERICAN PAPERS, INC.

Street address 1: 5101 NW 37th Ave
Street address state: FL
Zip/Postal code: 33142-3232
Country: USA
Mailing address: 5101 NW 37th Ave
Mailing city: Miami
Mailing state: FL
Mailing zip: 33142-3232
General Phone: (305) 635-2534
General Fax: (305) 635-2538
Primary Website: www.panampap.com
Year Established: 1967
Product/Services: Newsprint; Paper: Specialty Printing Paper;
Personnel: Jesus A. Roca (Sr. Vice Pres.)

PITMAN PHOTO SUPPLY

Street address 1: 13911 S Dixie Hwy
Street address state: FL
Zip/Postal code: 33176-7234
Country: USA
Mailing address: 13911 S Dixie Hwy
Mailing city: Miami
Mailing state: FL
Mailing zip: 33176-7234
General Phone: 800-252-3008
Email: pitmanphoto@att.net
Primary Website: www.pitmanphotosupply.com
Year Established: 1928
Product/Services: Cameras & Accessories; Chemicals: Photographic; Dark Room Equipment; Dryers: Film and Papers; Enlargers (Photographic); Film & Paper: Film Roll Dispensers; Film & Paper: Filters (Photographic); Fixing & Stop Baths; Lenses (Camera); Photography: Digital/Electronic Cameras;
Personnel: Michael Werner (Pres.)
Personnel: Lowell H. Elsea (Sales Mgr.)

MIAMI LAKES

QUIPP SYSTEM, INC.

Street address 1: 5881 NW 151 St
Street address 2: Suite 102
Street address state: FL
Zip/Postal code: 33014
Country: USA
Mailing address: 5881 NW 151 St, Suite 102
Mailing city: Miami Lakes
Mailing state: FL
Mailing zip: 33014
General Phone: (800) 258-1390
General Fax: (305) 623-0980
Primary Website: www.quipp.com

Equipment, Supplies and Services

II-63

Year Established: 1983
Product/Services: Conveyors; Material Handling Equipment; Pallets & Palletizers; Material Handling Equipment: Truck Loaders; Software: Press/Post Press; System Installations; System Integration Services; Training: Post Press;
Personnel: Angel Arrabal (Vice Pres., Sales.)
Personnel: Leticia Gostisa (Mktg. Mgr.)
Personnel: David Switalski (Vice Pres., Opns.)

MIDDLEBORO

BUTLER AUTOMATIC

Street address 1: 41 Leona Dr
Street address state: MA
Zip/Postal code: 02346-1404
Country: USA
Mailing address: 41 Leona Dr
Mailing city: Middleboro
Mailing state: MA
Mailing zip: 02346-1404
General Phone: (508) 923-0544
General Fax: (508) 923-0886
Email: butler@butlerautomatic.com
Primary Website: www.butlerautomatic.com
Year Established: 1956
Product/Services: Conveyors; Counting, Stacking, Bundling Machines; Cutters & Trimmers; Flying Pasters; Material Handling Equipment: Palletizing Machines; Pasters; Roll Handling Equipment; Splicers, Automatic; Tension & Web Controls;
Personnel: John Clifford (Vice Pres., Engineering)

MIDDLETON

NEWSCURRENTS

Street address 1: 2320 Pleasant View Rd
Street address state: WI
Zip/Postal code: 53562-5521
Country: USA
Mailing address: PO Box 52
Mailing city: Madison
Mailing state: WI
Mailing zip: 53701-0052
General Phone: 608 836-6660
General Fax: 608 836-6684
Email: csis@newscurrents.com
Primary Website: www.newscurrents.com
Year Established: 1983
Product/Services: NIE Print & Website Weekly Content
Personnel: Matt Cibula (Marketing Mgr.)

MIDLAND

THE DOW CHEMICAL CO.

Street address 1: 2030 Dow Ctr
Street address state: MI
Zip/Postal code: 48674-1500
Country: USA
Mailing address: 2030 Dow Ctr
Mailing city: Midland
Mailing state: MI
Mailing zip: 48674-2030
General Phone: (989) 636-1000
General Fax: (989) 636-3518
Email: dowmedia.relations@dow.com
Primary Website: www.dow.com
Product/Services: Adhesives; Cleaners & Solvents;
Personnel: Andrew Liveris (Chrmn./Pres./CEO)
Personnel: Matt Davis (Vice Pres., Global Pub. Aff.)
Personnel: Fernando Ruiz (Vice Pres./Treasurer)

MILFORD

CNI CORP.

Street address 1: 394 Elm St
Street address state: NH
Zip/Postal code: 03055-4305
Country: USA
Mailing address: 468 Route 13 S Ste A
Mailing city: Milford
Mailing state: NH
Mailing zip: 03055-3488
General Phone: (603) 673-6600
Email: info@breezeadops.com
Primary Website: www.breezeadworkflow.com
Year Established: 1988
Product/Services: Consulting Services: Production; Data Communication; Input & Editing Systems; Optical Character Recognition (OCR); Pagination Systems; Prepress Color Proofing Systems; Publishing Systems; Training: Keyboard Operation; Typesetters: Laser; Word Processing System;
Note: CNI Corporation is a software development company with over 20 years of publishing industry experience specializing in workflow automation. Our solutions have 3 key components; AdDesk the advertisers' facing web portal, Breeze, the sales reps' component and Breeze Creative Suite, the production/creative component. Breeze is a browser-based solution that allows reps to work remotely with tablets and smart phones and manage their accounts more efficiently. The time saved through our centralized automation tools provide sales reps more selling time which results in increased sales totals overall. CNI continues to provide innovation with an online credit card payment solution, Google DFP integration, E-signature capture and electronic insertion order management. Our software solutions streamline and simplify the advertising and production workflows. Through automation and elimination of duplicated manual tasks, CNI provides significant business benefits for media companies.
Personnel: Jon Dickinson (Pres.)
Personnel: Chris Prinos (EVP Business Dev.)

MILLBROOK

MICRO SYSTEMS SPECIALISTS, INC. (MSSI)

Street address 1: 3272 Franklin Ave
Street address state: NY
Zip/Postal code: 12545-5975
Country: USA
Mailing address: PO Box 347
Mailing city: Millbrook
Mailing state: NY
Mailing zip: 12545-0347
General Phone: (845) 677-6150
General Fax: (845) 677-6620
Email: mssisoftware@cs.com
Year Established: 1988
Product/Services: Software: Advertising Billing; Software: Business (Includes Administration/Accounting); Software: Circulation
Note: Newspaper Business, Advertising & Circulation Software
Personnel: Dawn Blackburn (Pres.)

MILWAUKEE

DANFOSS GRAHAM

Street address 1: 8800 W Bradley Rd
Street address state: WI
Zip/Postal code: 53224-2820
Country: USA
Mailing address: 8800 W Bradley Rd
Mailing city: Milwaukee
Mailing state: WI
Mailing zip: 53224-2820
General Phone: (414) 355-8800
General Fax: (414) 355-6117
Primary Website: www.danfoss.com
Year Established: 1936
Product/Services: Drives & Controls; Motors;
Personnel: Niels B. Christiansen (Pres./CEO)

FELINS, INC.

Street address 1: 8306 W Parkland Ct
Street address state: WI
Zip/Postal code: 53223-3832
Country: USA
Mailing address: 8306 W Parkland Ct
Mailing city: Milwaukee
Mailing state: WI
Mailing zip: 53223-3832
General Phone: (800) 843-5667
General Fax: (414) 355-7759
Email: sales@felins.com
Primary Website: www.felins.com
Year Established: 1921
Product/Services: Bundling and Tying Machines; Mailroom Systems & Equipment; Strapping Machines;

FORTEC, INC.

Street address 1: 3831 W Wells St
Street address state: WI
Zip/Postal code: 53208-3167
Country: USA
Mailing address: 613 N 36th St
Mailing city: Milwaukee
Mailing state: WI
Mailing zip: 53208-3826
General Phone: (414) 344-1900
General Fax: (414) 935-3309
Email: email@fortec.com
Primary Website: www.fortec.com
Year Established: 1979
Product/Services: Newspaper Dispensers (Mechanical/Electronic); Tubes, Racks (Includes Racks: Motor Route Tubes);
Personnel: Jack Olson (Pres.)

ROCKWELL AUTOMATION

Street address 1: 1201 S 2nd St
Street address state: WI
Zip/Postal code: 53204-2410
Country: USA
Mailing address: PO Box 760
Mailing city: Milwaukee
Mailing state: WI
Mailing zip: 53201-0760
General Phone: (262) 512-8200
General Fax: (262) 512-8579
Primary Website: www.rockwellautomation.com
Product/Services: Controllers: Press; Drives & Controls; Press Control Systems;
Personnel: Michael Faase (Mktg. Commun. Specialist)

MINNEAPOLIS

ACCRAPLY, INC.

Street address 1: 3580 Holly Ln N
Street address state: MN
Zip/Postal code: 55447-1366
Country: USA
Mailing address: 3580 Holly Ln N Ste 60
Mailing city: Plymouth
Mailing state: MN
Mailing zip: 55447-1367
General Phone: (763) 557-1313
General Fax: (763) 519-9656
Primary Website: www.accraply.com
Product/Services: Label Printing Machines
Personnel: Dave Hansen (Vice Pres., Sales)

MINNESOTA OPINION RESEARCH, INC. (MORI)

Street address 1: 8500 Normandale Lake Blvd
Street address 2: Ste 630
Street address state: MN
Zip/Postal code: 55437-3809
Country: USA
Mailing address: 8500 Normandale Lake Blvd Ste 630
Mailing city: Minneapolis
Mailing state: MN
Mailing zip: 55437-3809
General Phone: (952) 835-3050
General Fax: (952) 835-3385
Email: minneapolis@magid.com
Primary Website: www.moriresearch.com
Year Established: 1982
Product/Services: Consulting Services: Advertising; Consulting Services: Circulation; Consulting Services: Editorial; Consulting Services: Marketing; Market Research; Newspaper Marketing; Research Studies;
Personnel: Ron Mulder (Pres.)
Personnel: Brent Stahl (Vice Pres., Research)

MSP COMMUNICATIONS

Street address 1: 220 S 6th St
Street address 2: Ste 500
Street address state: MN
Zip/Postal code: 55402-4501
Country: USA
Mailing address: 220 S 6th St Ste 500
Mailing city: Minneapolis
Mailing state: MN
Mailing zip: 55402-4507
General Phone: (612) 339-7571
General Fax: (612) 339-5806
Email: edit@mspmag.com
Primary Website: www.mspmag.com
Year Established: 1982
Product/Services: Trade Publications
Personnel: Gary Johnson (Pres.)
Personnel: Brian Anderson (Ed. in Chief)

MISSISSAUGA

EDIWISE

Street address 1: 2227 S. Millway
Street address 2: Suite 200
Street address state: ON
Zip/Postal code: L5L 3R6
Country: Canada
Mailing address: 2227 S. Millway, Ste. 200
Mailing city: Mississauga
Mailing state: ON
Mailing zip: L5L 3R6
General Phone: (905) 820-3084
General Fax: (905) 820-1498
Email: info@ediwise.com
Primary Website: www.ediwise.com
Year Established: 1986
Product/Services: Computers: Hardware & Software Integrators; Newsprint; Newsprint Handling Equipment; Paper Handling Equipment; Software: Asset Management; Software: Business (Includes Administration/Accounting); Software: Electronic Data Interchange
Personnel: Eric Wee

KUBRA

Street address 1: 5050 Tomken Rd
Street address state: ON
Zip/Postal code: L4W 5B1
Country: Canada
Mailing address: 5050 Tomken Rd.
Mailing city: Mississauga
Mailing state: ON
Mailing zip: L4W 5B1
General Phone: (905) 624-2220
General Fax: (905) 624-2886
Primary Website: www.kubra.com
Personnel: Rick Watkin (Pres./CEO)
Personnel: Robert Iantorno (Vice Pres., Opns.)
Personnel: Rick Huff (Vice Pres., Sales/Mktg.)
Mark Visic (Sr. Vice Pres., Bus. Devel.)

METROLAND PRINTING/PUBLISHING & DISTRIBUTING LTD.

Street address 1: 3125 Wolfedale Rd
Street address state: ON
Zip/Postal code: L5C 1V8
Country: Canada
Mailing address: 3125 Wolfedale Rd.
Mailing city: Mississauga
Mailing state: ON
Mailing zip: L5C 1W1
General Phone: 905-281-5656
General Fax: 905-279-5103
Primary Website: www.metroland.com
Year Established: 1981
Product/Services: Presses: Offset; Publishing Systems;
Personnel: Brenda Biller (Vice Pres., HR)

MOBILE COMPUTING CORPORATION

USA

Street address 1: 2600 Skymark Ave
Street address 2: Bldg # 8 Suite 202
Street address state: ON
Zip/Postal code: L4W 5B2
Country: Canada
Mailing address: 2600 Skymark Ave, Bldg # 8 Suite 202
Mailing city: Mississauga
Mailing state: ON
Mailing zip: L4W 5B2
General Phone: (800) 392-8651
General Fax: (905) 676-9191
Email: MCCMarketing@mobilecom.com
Primary Website: www.mobilecom.com
Year Established: 1977
Product/Services: Business Computers; Computers: Hardware & Software Integrators; Consulting Services: Circulation; Consulting Services: Computer; Software: Circulation;
Personnel: Les Feasey (Sales Rep.)

ROTOFLEX MARK ANDY CANADA, INC.

Street address 1: 420 Ambassador Dr.
Street address state: ON
Zip/Postal code: L5T 2J3
Country: Canada
Mailing address: 420 Ambassador Dr.
Mailing city: Mississauga
Mailing state: ON
Mailing zip: L5T 2R5
General Phone: (905) 670-8700
General Fax: (905) 670-3402
Email: sales@rotoflex.com
Primary Website: www.rotoflex.com
Year Established: 1974
Product/Services: Conversion Equipment; Dies (Perforating and Slitting); Rewinders;
Personnel: Rod Allen (Vice Pres., Finance)
Personnel: Brian Nicoll (Dir., Mfg.)
Personnel: Val Rimas (Gen. Mgr./Vice Pres., Sales/Mktg.)

MOKENA

ALAR ENGINEERING CORPORATION

Street address 1: 9651 196th St
Street address state: IL
Zip/Postal code: 60448-9305
Country: USA
Mailing address: 9651 196th St
Mailing city: Mokena
Mailing state: IL
Mailing zip: 60448-9305
General Phone: (708) 479-6100
Email: info@alarcorp.com
Primary Website: www.alarcorp.com
Year Established: 1970
Product/Services: Waste Water Treatment Systems
Personnel: Paula Jackfert (President)
Personnel: Vickey Gorski (Vice Pres., Int'l Sales)
Personnel: Steve Gorski (Sales Mgr.)

MONROE

K & M NEWSPAPER SERVICES, INC.

Street address 1: 45 Gilbert St Ext
Street address state: NY
Zip/Postal code: 10950-2815
Country: USA
Mailing address: 45 Gilbert St Ext
Mailing city: Monroe
Mailing state: NY
Mailing zip: 10950-2815
General Phone: (845) 782-3817
General Fax: (845) 783-2972
Email: info@kmnewspaper.com
Primary Website: www.kmnewspaper.com
Product/Services: Belts, Belting, V-Belts; Controls: Photo Electric; Conveyors; Mailroom Systems & Equipment; Motors; Remanufactures Equipment;
Personnel: Mark Jacobs (Pres.)
Personnel: Micki Jacobs (Controller)
Personnel: Karla Hahan (Office Mgr.)
Personnel: Rick Walter (Vice Pres., Sales)

MONTERREY

INFORMATICA DALAI SA DE CV

Street address 1: Prolongacion A. Reyes 4508, Col. Villa del Rio
Country: Mexico
Mailing address: Prolongacion A. Reyes 4508, Col. Villa del Rio
Mailing city: Monterrey
Mailing zip: 64850
General Phone: +52 81 365-4077
General Fax: +52 81 365-5990
Primary Website: www.dalai.com
Year Established: 1990
Product/Services: Pagination Systems; Software: Advertising (Includes Display; Classified); Software: Asset Management; Software: Editorial;
Personnel: Gerardo Trevino (Devel. Mgr.)
Personnel: Juan Lauro Aguirre (Mng. Dir.)
Personnel: David Valdez (Adv. Mgr.)

MONTGOMERYVILLE

FOSTER MFG. CO.

Street address 1: 204B Progress Dr
Street address state: PA
Zip/Postal code: 18936-9616
Country: USA
Mailing address: 204B Progress Dr
Mailing city: Montgomeryville
Mailing state: PA
Mailing zip: 18936-9616
General Phone: 267-413-6220
General Fax: 267-413-6227
Email: information@fostermfg.com
Primary Website: www.fostermfg.com
Year Established: 1947
Product/Services: Archiving Systems; Art & Layout Equipment and Services; Cabinets; Color Viewing Equipment; Composing Room Equipment & Supplies; Cutters & Trimmers; Cutting Tools; Dark Room Equipment; Files, Storage; Layout Tables, Light Tables & Workstations; Offset Plate Files; Photo Archiving; Plastic Folders; Prepress Color Proofing Systems; Proofing Systems; Storage Retrieval Systems; Tables (Dot, Etch, Opaquing, Register, Retouching, Stripping)
Personnel: Ted Borowsky (Pres.)

MONTREAL

DOMTAR, INC.

Street address 1: 395 de Maisonneuve Blvd W
Street address state: QC
Zip/Postal code: H3A 1L6
Country: Canada
Mailing address: 395 de Maisonneuve Blvd. W.
Mailing city: Montreal
Mailing state: QC
Mailing zip: H3A 1L6
General Phone: (514) 848-5400
General Fax: (514) 848-6878
Primary Website: www.domtar.com
Year Established: 1929
Product/Services: Paper: Specialty Printing Paper
Personnel: Brian Levitt (Chrmn.)
Personnel: Raymond Royer (Pres./CEO)

QUEBECOR WORLD

Street address 1: 612 Rue Saint-Jacques
Street address state: QC
Zip/Postal code: H3C 4M8
Country: Canada
Mailing address: 612 Rue Saint-Jacques
Mailing city: Montréal
Mailing state: QC
Mailing zip: H3C 4M8
General Phone: (514) 380-1999
Primary Website: www.quebecor.com
Year Established: 1990
Product/Services: Consulting Services: Production; Input & Editing Systems; Preprint Service & Production; Presses: Rotogravure;
Personnel: Charles Cavell (Pres./CEO)
Personnel: Brian Freschi (Exec. Vice Pres., Sales)
Personnel: Jeremy Roberts (Dir. Cor. Commun.)

RESOLUTE FOREST PRODUCTS

Street address 1: 111 Duke St
Street address 2: Suite 5000
Street address state: QC
Zip/Postal code: H3C 2M1
Country: Canada
Mailing address: 111 Duke Street, Suite 5000
Mailing city: Montréal
Mailing state: QC
Mailing zip: H3C 2M1
General Phone: (514) 875-2160
General Fax: (423) 336-7950
Email: info@resolutefp.com
Primary Website: www.resolutefp.com
Year Established: 1954
Product/Services: Pulp & Paper
Personnel: Devon Mike (VP, Sales-Southern Market)
Personnel: Garry Grissom (Rgl. Mgr.)

MORRIS PLAINS

CAPROCK DEVELOPMENTS, INC.

Street address 1: 475 Speedwell Ave
Street address 2: PO Box 95
Street address state: NJ
Zip/Postal code: 07950-2149
Country: USA
Mailing address: PO Box 95
Mailing city: Morris Plains
Mailing state: NJ
Mailing zip: 07950-0095
General Phone: (973) 267-9292
General Fax: (973) 292-0614
Email: info@caprockdev.com
Primary Website: www.caprockdev.com
Year Established: 1953
Product/Services: Densitometers; Exposure Lamps; Gauges, Measuring; Lighting Equipment; Offset Blanket Thickness Gauge; Optical Products; Paper Testing Instruments; Testing Instruments;
Personnel: Alan Schwartz (President)

MORRISTOWN

HONEYWELL, INC.

Street address 1: 101 Columbia Rd
Street address state: NJ
Zip/Postal code: 07960-4640
Country: USA
Mailing address: 101 Columbia Rd
Mailing city: Morristown
Mailing state: NJ
Mailing zip: 07960-4658
General Phone: (973) 455-2000
General Fax: (973) 455-4002
Email: lois.sills@honeywell.com
Primary Website: www.honeywell.com
Product/Services: Fire Protection; Humidifiers; Press Control Systems;
Personnel: Dave Cote (CEO)

MOUNT LAUREL

ROOSEVELT PAPER

Street address 1: 1 Roosevelt Dr
Street address state: NJ
Zip/Postal code: 08054-6307
Country: USA
Mailing address: 1 Roosevelt Dr
Mailing city: Mount Laurel
Mailing state: NJ
Mailing zip: 08054-6312
General Phone: (856) 303-4100
General Fax: (856) 642-1949
Primary Website: www.rooseveltpaper.com
Year Established: 1932
Product/Services: Newsprint; Paper: Coated Groundwood Offset; Paper: Specialty Printing Paper;
Personnel: David Kosloff (President)
Personnel: Ted Kosloff (CEO)
Personnel: Lynn Perce (Mktg. Dir.)

MOUNT PROSPECT

TECHNOTRANS AMERICA, INC.

Street address 1: 1441 E Business Center Dr
Street address state: IL
Zip/Postal code: 60056-2182
Country: USA
Mailing address: 1050 E Business Center Dr
Mailing city: Mount Prospect
Mailing state: IL
Mailing zip: 60056-2180
General Phone: (847) 227-9200
General Fax: (847) 227-9400
Email: ttasales@technotrans.com; info@technotrans.com
Primary Website: www.technotrans.com
Year Established: 1967
Product/Services: Blanket Cleaner/Washer (Automatic); Dampening Systems; Dies (Perforating and Slitting); Water Management Systems; Web Offset Remoisturizers;
Personnel: Thomas Carbery (Vice Pres.)
Personnel: Victoria Moore (Sales Admin.)

MOUNT VERNON

DIRECT REPRODUCTION CORP.

Street address 1: 34 S Macquesten Pkwy
Street address state: NY
Zip/Postal code: 10550-1704
Country: USA
Mailing address: 34 S Macquesten Pkwy
Mailing city: Mount Vernon
Mailing state: NY
Mailing zip: 10550-1704
General Phone: (914) 665-6515
General Fax: (914) 665-6518
Email: Technical@LRADX.com
Primary Website: www.lradx.com/site/
Year Established: 1941
Product/Services: Color Proofing; Color Registration; Masking Materials; Offset Negative Masking Paper; Prepress Color Proofing Systems;
Personnel: Ronald L. Russo (Pres.)

MT PROSPECT

GAMMERLER (US) CORP.

Street address 1: 431 Lakeview Ct
Street address 2: Ste B
Street address state: IL
Zip/Postal code: 60056-6048
Country: Canada
Mailing address: 431 Lakeview Ct Ste B
Mailing city: Mt Prospect
Mailing state: IL
Mailing zip: 60103
General Phone: 224 361-8300
General Fax: (224) 361-8301
Email: joe.jastrzebski@gammerler.com
Primary Website: www.gammerler.com
Year Established: 1985
Product/Services: Conveyors; Counting, Stacking, Bundling Machines; Cutters & Trimmers; Feeding, Folding, Delivery Equipment; Gluing Systems; In-Line Trimming Systems; Mailroom Systems & Equipment; Material Handling Equipment: Palletizing Machines; Material Handling Equipment: Pallets & Palletizers;
Personnel: Joe Jastrzebski (Managing Director)

Equipment, Supplies and Services

MT PROSPECT

MALOW CORP.
Street address 1: 1835 S Nordic Rd
Street address state: IL
Zip/Postal code: 60056-5715
Country: USA
Mailing address: 1835 S Nordic Rd
Mailing city: Mt Prospect
Mailing state: IL
Mailing zip: 60056-5715
General Phone: (847) 956-0200
General Fax: (847) 956-0935
Primary Website: www.malow.com
Year Established: 1947
Product/Services: Automatic Plastic Bagging Equipment; Bundling and Tying Machines; Strapping Machines;
Personnel: Terry Luzader (Sales Mgr.)

MYRTLE BEACH

MARKETING STRATEGIES INCORPORATED
Street address 1: 4603 OLEANDER DRIVE, SUITE 4
Street address state: SC
Zip/Postal code: 29577
Country: USA
Mailing address: 4603 OLEANDER DRIVE, SUITE 4
Mailing city: Myrtle Beach
Mailing state: SC
Mailing zip: 29577
General Phone: (843)692-9662
General Fax: (843) 692-0558
Email: info@marketingstrategiesinc.com
Primary Website: www.marketingstrategies.org
Year Established: 1980
Product/Services: Consulting Services: Advertising; Consulting Services: Marketing;
Personnel: Denise Blackburn-Gay (Pres., CEO)
Personnel: Samantha Bower (Mktg. Dir.)
Personnel: Lauren Davis (Graphic Designer)
Pablo Marin (Creative Dir.)

MYRTLE CREEK

ARTBEATSEXPRESS
Street address 1: 1405 N Myrtle Rd
Street address state: OR
Zip/Postal code: 97457-9615
Country: USA
Mailing address: PO Box 709
Mailing city: Myrtle Creek
Mailing state: OR
Mailing zip: 97457-0110
General Phone: (541)863-4429
General Fax: (541)863-4547
Email: info@artbeats.com
Primary Website: www.artbeatsEXPRESS.com
Year Established: 1989
Product/Services: Royalty Free Stock Media
Personnel: Phil Bates (Pres.)
Personnel: Laura Hollifield (COO)
Personnel: Julie Hill (Adv./Mktg. Mgr.)
Peggy Nichols (Global Dist. Mgr.)
Bob Hayes (Dir., Tech.)

NANUET

MICROFILM PRODUCTS CO.
Street address 1: 157 Avalon Gardens Dr
Street address state: NY
Zip/Postal code: 10954-7417
Country: USA
Mailing address: 266 Germonds Rd
Mailing city: West Nyack
Mailing state: NY
Mailing zip: 10994-1320
General Phone: (845) 371-3700
General Fax: (845) 371-3780
Email: info@microfilmproducts.com
Primary Website: www.microfilmproducts.com

Product/Services: Addressing Machines; Bundling and Tying Machines; Equipment Dealers (New); Equipment Dealers (Used); Folding Machines;
Personnel: Gary Moelis (Pres.)

NAPLES

CHUCK BLEVINS & ASSOC.
Street address 1: 8396 Northhampton Ct
Street address state: FL
Zip/Postal code: 34120-1687
Country: USA
Mailing address: 8396 Northhampton Ct
Mailing city: Naple
Mailing state: FL
Mailing zip: 34120
General Phone: (239) 595-3840
Email: chuckblevins@aol.com
Primary Website: www.chuckblevins.com
Year Established: 1989
Product/Services: Consulting Services: Equipment; Consulting Services: Ergonomics; Consulting Services: Production; Mailroom Systems & Equipment; Press Systems and equipment

NASHUA

HOWTEK
Street address 1: 98 Spit Brook Rd
Street address 2: Ste 100
Street address state: NH
Zip/Postal code: 03062-5737
Country: USA
Mailing address: 98 Spit Brook Rd Ste 100
Mailing city: Nashua
Mailing state: NH
Mailing zip: 03062-5737
General Phone: 866-280-2239
General Fax: 937-431-1465
Email: sales@icadmed.com
Primary Website: www.icadmed.com
Year Established: 1984
Product/Services: Color Seperation Scanners
Personnel: Ken Ferry (Pres.)

NASHVILLE

NOVATECH, INC.
Street address 1: 4106 Charlotte Ave
Street address state: TN
Zip/Postal code: 37209
Country: USA
Mailing address: 4106 Charlotte Ave
Mailing city: Nashville
Mailing state: TN
Mailing zip: 37209
General Phone: (615) 577-7677
Email: novatechusa@novatech.net
Primary Website: www.novatech.net
Year Established: 1987
Product/Services: Facsimilie/Fax Transmission Systems; Laser Printers;
Personnel: Darren Metz (CEO)
Personnel: Joe White (Pres.)
Personnel: Jeff Hoctor (CPA, CFO)
Jason Levkulich (Dir. of Marketing)
John Sutton (Dir. of Sales)

NAZARETH

SOFTWARE CONSULTING SERVICES, LLC
Street address 1: 630 Municipal Dr
Street address 2: Ste 420
Street address state: PA
Zip/Postal code: 18064-8990
Country: USA
Mailing address: 630 Municipal Dr Ste 420
Mailing city: Nazareth
Mailing state: PA
Mailing zip: 18064-8990
General Phone: (610) 746-7700
General Fax: (610) 746-7900

Email: sales@newspapersystems.com
Primary Website: www.newspapersystems.com
Year Established: 1975
Product/Services: Software: Advertising (Includes Display; Classified); Page Design (dummying); Editorial; Digital Asset Management; Ad Tracking; Managed Services
Personnel: Richard J. Cichelli (Pres.)
Personnel: Curtis Jackson (Vice Pres., Opns.)
Personnel: Martha J. Cichelli (Mktg. Dir.)

NEEDHAM

CREO
Street address 1: 140 Kendrick Street
Street address state: MA
Zip/Postal code: 02494
Country: USA
Mailing address: 140 Kendrick Street
Mailing city: Needham
Mailing state: MA
Mailing zip: 02494
General Phone: (781) 370-5000
General Fax: (781) 370-6000
Primary Website: www.ptc.com/en/products/cad
Year Established: 1985
Product/Services: Color Proofing; Color Seperation Scanners; Computers: Hardware & Software Integrators;
Personnel: James E. Heppelmann (Pres., CEO)
Personnel: Andrew Miller (Exec VP, CFO)
Personnel: Barry F. Cohen (Exec V.P., Chief Strategy Officer)
Kathleen Mitford (Executive V. P., Products)

NEW ALBANY

TECHNIDYNE CORP.
Street address 1: 100 Quality Ave
Street address state: IN
Zip/Postal code: 47150-2272
Country: USA
Mailing address: 100 Quality Ave
Mailing city: New Albany
Mailing state: IN
Mailing zip: 47150-7222
General Phone: (812) 948-2884
General Fax: (812) 945-6847
Email: spectrum@technidyne.com
Primary Website: www.technidyne.com
Year Established: 1974
Product/Services: Color Analyzers; Color Management Software; Equipment Dealers (New); Equipment Dealers (Used); Paper Testing Instruments;
Personnel: M. Todd Popson (Pres./CEO)
Personnel: Paul M. Crawford (Bus. Dir.)
Personnel: Thomas Crawford (Vice Pres., Sales/Mktg.)
Patrick Robertson (Mgr., Technical Servs.)

NEW BERLIN

ABB, INC. (PRINTING SYSTEMS)
Street address 1: 16250 W Glendale Dr
Street address state: WI
Zip/Postal code: 53151-2840
Country: USA
Mailing address: 16250 W Glendale Dr
Mailing city: New Berlin
Mailing state: WI
Mailing zip: 53151-2858
General Phone: (262) 785-3206
General Fax: (262) 785-6295
Primary Website: www.abb.com/printing
Product/Services: Drives & Controls; Press Control Systems; System Integration Services
Personnel: Rick Hepperla (Vice Pres.-Paper Drives Systems/Printing)
Personnel: Jeffrey Gelfand (Nat'l Sales/Mktg. Dir.-Printing Systems)
Personnel: Hans Wirth (Mgr.-Sales Applications/Printing Drives Systems)

NEW BRITAIN

INSURANCE SPECIALTIES SERVICES, INC.
Street address 1: 946 Town Ctr
Street address state: PA
Zip/Postal code: 18901-5182
Country: USA
Mailing address: 946 Town Ctr
Mailing city: New Britain
Mailing state: PA
Mailing zip: 18901-5182
General Phone: 800-533-4579
General Fax: 215-918-0507
Email: info@issisvs.com
Primary Website: www.issisvs.com
Year Established: 1987
Product/Services: Insurance
Note: An Insurance Brokerage Firm Specializing In Liability Insurance Coverage For All Types of Media
Personnel: Kenneth P. Smith (Pres.)
Personnel: Kathy Liney (Sales)

WILLIAM DUNKERLEY PUBLISHING CONSULTANT
Street address 1: 275 Batterson Dr
Street address state: CT
Zip/Postal code: 06053-1005
Country: USA
Mailing address: 275 Batterson Dr.
Mailing city: New Britain
Mailing state: CT
Mailing zip: 06053
General Phone: (860) 827-8896
General Fax: (508) 507-3021
Email: wdpc@publishinghelp.com
Primary Website: www.publishinghelp.com
Year Established: 1981
Product/Services: Consulting Services: Business Analysis; Consulting Services: Advertising; Consulting Services: Editorial; Consulting Services: Financial; Consulting Services: Marketing; Market Research
Personnel: William Dunkerley (Principal)

NEW DELHI

PRINTERS HOUSE AMERICAS LLC
Street address 1: 10, Scindia House, Connaught Place
Country: India
Mailing address: 10, Scindia House, Connaught Place
Mailing city: New Delhi
General Phone: 91-11-23313071
General Fax: 91-11-23356637
Email: tphindia@bol.net.in
Primary Website: www.phaorient.com
Note: Printers House Americas, LLC is the distributor of Orient Web Presses. Orient models are single width presses with production"

NEW HYDE PARK

CANON USA, INC.
Street address 1: 1 Dakota Dr
Street address state: NY
Zip/Postal code: 11042-1135
Country: USA
Mailing address: 1 Canon Park
Mailing city: Melville
Mailing state: NY
Mailing zip: 11747-3036
General Phone: (632) 330-5000
Email: mediacontact@cusa.canon.com
Primary Website: www.usa.canon.com
Year Established: 1937
Personnel: Yoroku Adachi (Pres./CEO, Canon U.S.A., Inc.)
Personnel: Seymour Liebman (Exec. Vice Pres./Gen. Counsel Admin./Reg'l Opns.)
Personnel: Tod D. Pike (Sr. Vice Pres./Gen Mgr., Sales Mktg./Admin.)
Rick Booth (Adv. Dir., Cameras/Camcorders, Dir.,

Mktg. Serv./Adv.)

NEW LENOX

MCCAIN BINDERY SYSTEMS

Street address 1: 14545 W Edison Dr
Street address state: IL
Zip/Postal code: 60451-3672
Country: USA
Mailing address: 14545 W Edison Dr
Mailing city: New Lenox
Mailing state: IL
Mailing zip: 60451-3672
General Phone: 800-225-9363
General Fax: 815-462-1471
Email: mccainbind@earthlink.net
Primary Website: www.mccainbindery.com
Year Established: 1926
Product/Services: Saddle Stitching, Side Sewers, Sheeters, Inserting Equipment (Includes Stuffing Machines); Bindery and Mailroom Systems & Equipment;
Personnel: Nancy Jones (Pres.)
Personnel: Bill Whitehead (Sales Manager)
Personnel: Chester Zurek (National Service/Product Manager)
Dennis Keem (Vice Pres./Gen. Mgr.)

NEW PROVIDENCE

ALCATEL-LUCENT

Street address 1: 600 Mountain Ave
Street address 2: # 700
Street address state: NJ
Zip/Postal code: 07974-2008
Country: USA
Mailing address: 600 Mountain Ave # 2F-147
Mailing city: New Providence
Mailing state: NJ
Mailing zip: 07974-2008
General Phone: (908) 582-3000
General Fax: (908) 582-2576
Email: execoffice@alcatel-lucent.com
Primary Website: www.alcatel-lucent.com
Personnel: Ben Verwaayen (CEO)
Personnel: Jeong H. Kim (Pres., Bell Labs)

NEW ROCHELLE

FLYNN BURNER CORP.

Street address 1: 425 5th Ave
Street address state: NY
Zip/Postal code: 10801-2203
Country: USA
Mailing address: PO Box 431
Mailing city: New Rochelle
Mailing state: NY
Mailing zip: 10802-0431
General Phone: (914) 636-1320
General Fax: (914) 636-3751
Primary Website: www.flynnburner.com
Year Established: 1942
Product/Services: Web Press - Special Equipment
Personnel: Julian Modzeleski (Pres.)
Personnel: Dom Medina (Vice Pres.)

NEW YORK

ADVERTISING CHECKING BUREAU, INC.

Street address 1: 675 3rd Ave
Street address 2: Fl 29
Street address state: NY
Zip/Postal code: 10017-5704
Country: USA
Mailing address: 675 Third Ave. Suite 2905
Mailing city: New York
Mailing state: NY
Mailing zip: 10017
General Phone: (212) 684-3377
General Fax: (212) 684-3381
Email: sales@acbcoop.com
Primary Website: www.acbcoop.com
Year Established: 1917

Product/Services: Library Retrieval Systems; Market Research; Research Studies;Co-op advertising management
Personnel: Brian T. McShane (Pres./CEO)
Personnel: John Portelli (VP., Nat'l Sales)

DENNIS STORCH CO.

Street address 1: 175 W 72nd St
Street address 2: Apt 8G
Street address state: NY
Zip/Postal code: 10023-3208
Country: USA
Mailing address: 175 W 72nd St Apt 8G
Mailing city: New York
Mailing state: NY
Mailing zip: 10023-3208
General Phone: (212) 877-2622
Email: dstorch@aol.com
Primary Website: www.dennis-storch.com
Year Established: 1979
Product/Services: Printing Equipment Dealer. Used Presses and Offset Presses.
Personnel: Dennis Storch (President)

GRIMES, MCGOVERN & ASSOCIATES

Street address 1: 10 W 15th St
Street address 2: Ste 903
Street address state: NY
Zip/Postal code: 10011-6823
Country: USA
Mailing address: 10 West 15th Street
Mailing city: New York City
Mailing state: NY
Mailing zip: 10011
General Phone: (917) 881-6563
Email: lgrimes@mediamergers.com
Primary Website: www.mediamergers.com
Year Established: 1959
Product/Services: Brokers & Appraisers; Consulting Services: Advertising; Consulting Services: Financial; Consulting Services: Human Resources; Consulting Services: Marketing;
Note: Over 1,600 newspapers sold. Thousands Appraised. Regional Offices nationwide.
Personnel: Julie Bergman (V.P., Head of Newspaper Division)
Personnel: John Szefc (Senior Associate-Northeast/New England)
Personnel: David Slavin (Senior Associate-Southeast/South)
John McGovern (Owner, CEO)
Lewis Floyd (Senior Associate-Southern States)
Gary Borders (Sr. Assoc.-SW/Plains)
Gord Carley (Sr. Assoc.-CANADA-Mag. & Newspapers)
Joe Bella (Sr. Advisor-Newspapers)
Ken Amundson (Sr. Assoc.-Western/Mtn. States)
Ken Blum (Senior Associate-Sales Nationwide)

INTERNATIONAL TRADEMARK ASSOCIATION

Street address 1: 655 3rd Ave
Street address 2: Fl 10
Street address state: NY
Zip/Postal code: 10017-5646
Country: USA
Mailing address: 655 3rd Ave Fl 10
Mailing city: New York
Mailing state: NY
Mailing zip: 10017-5646
General Phone: (212) 642-1700
General Fax: (212) 768-7796
Email: info@inta.org
Primary Website: www.inta.org
Year Established: 1878
Personnel: Alan Drewsen (Exec. Dir.)
Personnel: Devin Toporek

MACDONALD MEDIA

Street address 1: 141 West 36th Street
Street address 2: 16th floor
Street address state: NY
Zip/Postal code: 10018
Country: USA
Mailing address: 141 West 36th Street, 16th floor
Mailing city: New York
Mailing state: NY
Mailing zip: 10018
General Phone: (212) 578-8735
Email: Hello@macdonaldmedia.com
Primary Website: www.macdonaldmedia.com
Product/Services: Art & Layout Equipment and Services; Consulting Services: Advertising; Software: Design/Graphics; Trade Publications;
Personnel: Andrea MacDonald (Pres./CEO)

METRO EDITORIAL SERVICES

Street address 1: 519 8th Ave
Street address 2: Fl 18
Street address state: NY
Zip/Postal code: 10018-4577
Country: USA
Mailing address: 519 8th Ave Fl 18
Mailing city: New York
Mailing state: NY
Mailing zip: 10018-4577
General Phone: (212) 947-5100
General Fax: (212) 714-9139
Email: mes@metro-email.com
Primary Website: www.mcg.metrocreativeconnection.com
Year Established: 1910
Product/Services: Art & Layout Equipment and Services; Consulting Services: Advertising; Consulting Services: Editorial; Software: Design/Graphics; Software: Editorial;
Note: Metro is a leading provider of advertising, creative and editorial resources designed to help media companies make money with their print, online, and mobile products. We provide ready-to-use images, ads, stock-quality photos, logos/trademarks, auto photos, marketing/sales materials, copyright-free features, print templated sections, online e-Sections, and groundbreaking digital ad development tools, plus custom image, ad design and editorial services.
Personnel: Robert Zimmerman (Publisher)
Personnel: Debra Weiss (Exec. Vice Pres./Mktg. Dir.)
Personnel: Lauren Lekoski (Mktg. Mgr.)
Jo Ann Shapiro (VP, Sales)
Lou Ann Sornson (Regional Sales Mgr.)
Tina Dentner (Regional Sales Mgr.)
Cathy Agee (Regional Sales Mgr.)
Gwen Tomaselli (Regional Sales Mgr.)
Jennifer Steiner (Regional Sales Mgr.)
Joann Johnson

MITCHELL'S

Street address 1: PO Box 2431
Street address state: NY
Zip/Postal code: 11106
Country: USA
Mailing address: PO Box 2431
Mailing city: New York
Mailing state: NY
Mailing zip: 10116-2431
General Phone: 800-662-2275
General Fax: (212) 594-7254
Email: papers@mitchellsny.com
Primary Website: www.mitchellsny.com
Year Established: 1946
Product/Services: Delivery Equipment
Personnel: Mitchell Newman (Owner)
Personnel: Roy Newman (Owner)

POYRY MANAGEMENT CONSULTING (USA) INC.

Street address 1: 52 Vanderbilt Ave
Street address 2: Rm 1405
Street address state: NY
Zip/Postal code: 10017-0080
Country: USA
Mailing address: 52 Vanderbilt Ave Rm 1405
Mailing city: New York
Mailing state: NY
Mailing zip: 10017-0080
General Phone: (646) 651-1547
General Fax: (212) 661-3830
Primary Website: www.poyry.us
Product/Services: Consulting Services;

Management Consulting; Market Research; Market Strategy; paper; media
Personnel: Soile Kilpi (Director)

SCARBOROUGH RESEARCH

Street address 1: 85 Broad St
Street address state: NY
Zip/Postal code: 10004
Country: USA
Mailing address: 85 Broad St
Mailing city: New York
Mailing state: NY
Mailing zip: 10004
General Phone: (800) 864-1224
Email: corporatepressinquiries@nielsen.com
Primary Website: www.nielsen.com/us/en/solutions/capabilities/scarborough-local.html
Year Established: 1974
Product/Services: Consulting Services: Advertising; Consulting Services: Marketing; Market Research; Newspaper Marketing; Research Studies; Software: Advertising (Includes Display; Classified); Training: Keyboard Operation;
Personnel: David Kenny (CEO)
Personnel: Dave Anderson (CFO)
Personnel: Nancy Phillips (Chief Human Resources Officer)
Eric Dale (Chief Legal Officer)
John Burbank (Corporate Development & Strategy)

TNS GLOBAL

Street address 1: 11 Madison Ave
Street address 2: Ste 1201
Street address state: NY
Zip/Postal code: 10010-3624
Country: USA
Mailing address: 11 Madison Ave Ste 1201
Mailing city: New York
Mailing state: NY
Mailing zip: 10010-3624
General Phone: (212) 991-6000
Email: enquiries@tnsglobal.com
Primary Website: www.tnsglobal.com
Year Established: 1946
Product/Services: Consulting Services: Advertising; Consulting Services: Marketing; Market Research;
Product or Service: Advertising/Marketing Agency
Personnel: Leendert De Voogd (Sales Rep.)
Personnel: Mark Francas (Sales Rep.)

UNITED PAPER MILLS KYMMENE, INC.

Street address 1: 1270 Avenue of the Americas
Street address 2: Ste 203
Street address state: NY
Zip/Postal code: 10020-1700
Country: USA
Mailing address: 1270 Avenue of the Americas Ste 203
Mailing city: New York
Mailing state: NY
Mailing zip: 10020-1700
General Phone: (212) 218-8232
General Fax: (212) 218-8240
Primary Website: www.upm.com
Year Established: 1930
Product/Services: Newsprint
Personnel: Tapio Korpeinen (Pres.)
Personnel: Jyrki Salo (Exec. Vice Pres./CFO)

NEWARK

PRINTERS' SERVICE/PRISCO/PRISCODIGITAL

Street address 1: 26 Blanchard St
Street address state: NJ
Zip/Postal code: 07105-4702
Country: USA
Mailing address: 26 Blanchard St.
Mailing city: Newark
Mailing state: NJ
Mailing zip: 07105-4784
General Phone: (973) 589-7800

Equipment, Supplies and Services

General Fax: (973) 589-3225
Email: inquiries@prisco.com
Primary Website: www.prisco.com
Year Established: 1903
Product/Services: Chemicals: Pressroom; Circulation Equipment & Supplies; Cleaners & Solvents; Lubricants; Offset Blankets, Blanket Wash; Offset Chemicals & Supplies; Offset Fountain Solutions; Plate Cleaners; Press Accessories, Parts & Supplies; Solvent Recovery Systems; Wide Format Inkjet systems, Wide Format Inkjet supplies, Automated Cutting Systems, Software
Personnel: Richard B. Liroff (Chrmn.)
Personnel: Bruce Liroff (Pres.)
Personnel: Russ Mantione (CFO)
David Gerson (Vice Pres., Research/Technology)
Eric A. Gutwillig (Vice Pres., Mktg.)
Steve Zunde (President, PriscoDigital LLC)
Joe Schleck (Vice Pres., Prodn./Mfg.)
Michael White (Senior VP)

NEWBURGH

GRAPHIC TECHNOLOGY, INC. (GTI)

Street address 1: 211 Dupont Ave
Street address state: NY
Zip/Postal code: 12550-4019
Country: USA
Mailing address: PO Box 3138
Mailing city: Newburgh
Mailing state: NY
Mailing zip: 12550-0651
General Phone: (845) 562-7066
General Fax: (845) 562-2543
Email: sales@gtilite.com
Primary Website: www.gtilite.com
Year Established: 1975
Product/Services: Art & Layout Equipment and Services; Color Viewing Equipment; Layout Tables, Light Tables & Workstations; Lighting Equipment; Press Accessories, Parts & Supplies;
Personnel: Frederic McCurdy (Pres.)
Personnel: Robert McCurdy (Vice Pres., Sales/Mktg.)
Personnel: Linda Sutherland (Sales/Mktg Coord.)

NEWBURYPORT

BRADY & PAUL COMMUNICATIONS

Street address 1: 7 Orange St
Street address state: MA
Zip/Postal code: 01950-2805
Country: USA
Mailing address: 7 Orange St
Mailing city: Newburyport
Mailing state: MA
Mailing zip: 01950-2805
General Phone: (978) 463-2255
Email: bradybrady@aol.com; contact@johnbrady.info
Primary Website: www.bradyandpaul.com; www.johnbrady.info
Year Established: 1984
Product/Services: Art & Layout Equipment and Services; Consulting Services: Editorial;
Personnel: John Brady (Pres.)
Personnel: Greg Paul (Designer)

NILES

AWS, A THERMAL CARE DIVISION

Street address 1: 5680 W Jarvis Ave
Street address state: IL
Zip/Postal code: 60714-4016
Country: USA
Mailing address: 5680 W. Jarvis Ave.
Mailing city: Niles
Mailing state: IL
Mailing zip: 60714
General Phone: (630) 595-3651
General Fax: (630) 595-5433
Email: info@thermalcare.com
Primary Website: www.thermalcare.com
Product/Services: Circulation Equipment & Supplies; Ink Fountains & Accessories; Ink Pumping Systems; Press Accessories, Parts & Supplies
Personnel: Audrey Guidarelli (Mktg. Servs. Mgr.)

NORCROSS

BAUMUELLER-NUERMONT CORP.

Street address 1: 1555 Oakbrook Dr. Ste. 120
Street address state: GA
Zip/Postal code: 30093
Country: USA
Mailing address: 1555 Oakbrook Dr. Ste. 120
Mailing city: Norcross
Mailing state: GA
Mailing zip: 30093
General Phone: (678) 291-0535
General Fax: (678) 291-0537
Email: info@baumuller.com
Primary Website: www.bnc-america.com
Product/Services: Motors
Note: Chicago Office: Baumueller-Nuermont Corp. 1858 S. Elmhurst Road Mount Prospect, IL 60056 T: (847) 439-5363 F: (847) 890-6632 Mexico Location: Baumueller-Nuermont S.A. de C.V. Carretera Estatal 431 km 2+200, Lote 95 Módulo 11 Parque Industrial Tecnológico Innovación El Marqués, Querétaro, Mexico 76246. T: +52 (442) 221 6670 Canada Location: Baumueller Canada 6581 Kitimat Road Unit 8 Mississauga, ON. L5N3T5 T: (905) 228-1095 F: (905) 247-0609

NORTH AURORA

IAC ACOUSTICS

Street address 1: 401 Airport Rd
Street address state: IL
Zip/Postal code: 60542-1818
Country: USA
Mailing address: 401 Airport Rd
Mailing city: North Aurora
Mailing state: IL
Mailing zip: 60542-1818
General Phone: (800) 954-1998
General Fax: (630) 966-9710
Email: sales@industrialnoisecontrol.com
Primary Website: www.industrialnoisecontrol.com
Year Established: 1971
Product/Services: Architects/Engineers (Includes Design/Construction Firms); Noise Control;
Personnel: Dana Cullum (Pres.)

NORTH CANTON

PRESTELIGENCE

Street address 1: 8328 Cleveland Ave NW
Street address state: OH
Zip/Postal code: 44720-4820
Country: USA
Mailing address: 8328 Cleveland Ave NW
Mailing city: North Canton
Mailing state: OH
Mailing zip: 44720-4820
General Phone: (330) 305-6960
General Fax: (330) 497-5562
Email: info@presteligence.com
Primary Website: www.presteligence.com
Year Established: 1990
Product/Services: Calibration Software/Hardware; Color Proofing; Multiplexers/Routers; Ink Controls, Computerized; Output Management and Preflight Software; Prepress Color Proofing Systems; Software: Advertising (Includes Display; Classified); Software: Press/Post Press; Software: Workflow Management/Tracking; System Integration Services; eTearsheets & eInvoices, e-Editions, Mobile Apps, High School Sports Platform and Web CMS
Note: With more than 1500 installations, Presteligence offers a suite of solutions including online ad proofing, e-tearsheets & invoice delivery + payment, color calibrated hard and soft proofing systems, prepress production workflow, ink optimization, print production consolidation projects, web cms, digital replicas, high school sports management platform, and mobile apps. These cost-effective and time efficient solutions, combined with the responsive support team make Presteligence a best-in-class partner for media companies.
Personnel: Bob Behringer (Pres. & CEO)
Personnel: Melissa McBride (Controller)
Personnel: Denise Franken (Dir. of Mktg.)
Randy Plant (VP, Ops.)
Jeff Bernhardt (Major Accnt. Mgr.)

NORTH CHARLESTON

MBM CORP.

Street address 1: 3134 Industry Dr
Street address state: SC
Zip/Postal code: 29418-8450
Country: USA
Mailing address: PO Box 40249
Mailing city: North Charleston
Mailing state: SC
Mailing zip: 29423-0249
General Phone: (843) 552-2700
General Fax: (843) 552-2974
Primary Website: www.mbmcorp.com
Year Established: 1936
Product/Services: Cutters & Trimmers; Cutting Tools; Feeding, Folding, Delivery Equipment; Folding Machines; In-Line Trimming Systems;
Personnel: Ned Ginsburg (Pres. and CFO)
Personnel: Michael Venittelli (Senior VP of Sales and Marketing)
Personnel: Wanda Ford (VP of National Sales)
Lisa Hutchinson (Product Manager)
Jeffery Chase (Service Manager)
Sandra Robinson (Parts Representative)

NORTH CHESTERFIELD

H & M PASTER SALES & SERVICE, INC.

Street address 1: 21828 87th Ave SE
Street address state: VA
Zip/Postal code: 23236
Country: USA
Mailing address: 21828 87th Ave SE
Mailing city: North Chesterfield
Mailing state: VA
Mailing zip: 23236
General Phone: 804-276-4668
Primary Website: www.hmrva.com
Year Established: 1991
Product/Services: Adhesives; Gluing Systems; Pasters; Web Press - Special Equipment;

NORTH EGREMONT

ROGGEN MANAGEMENT CONSULTANTS, INC.

Street address 1: 223 Egremont Plain Rd
Street address 2: # 603
Street address state: MA
Zip/Postal code: 01230-2284
Country: USA
Mailing address: 223 Egremont Plain Rd #603
Mailing city: North Egremont
Mailing state: MA
Mailing zip: 01230
General Phone: (413) 528-2300
General Fax: (413) 528-2300
Email: mark.roggen@roggenconsultants.com; mnroggen@aol.com
Primary Website: www.roggenconsultants.com
Year Established: 1975
Product/Services: Newspaper Distribution & Logistics Consultant
Note: Operations & Distribution Consultant
Personnel: Mark N. Roggen (Pres.)

NORTH KINGSTOWN

HEXAGON METROLOGY, INC.

Street address 1: 250 Circuit Dr
Street address state: RI
Zip/Postal code: 02852-7441
Country: USA
Mailing address: 250 Circuit Dr
Mailing city: North Kingstown
Mailing state: RI
Mailing zip: 02852-7441
General Phone: (401) 886-2000
General Fax: (401) 886-2727
Primary Website: www.hexagonmetrology.com
Year Established: 1833
Product/Services: Gauges, Measuring
Personnel: William Fetter (Adv. Mgr.)

NORTHBOROUGH

DARIO DESIGNS, INC.

Street address 1: 318 Main St
Street address 2: Ste 120
Street address state: MA
Zip/Postal code: 01532-3611
Country: USA
Mailing address: 318 Main St. Ste 120
Mailing city: Northborough
Mailing state: MA
Mailing zip: 01532
General Phone: (508) 877-4444
General Fax: (508) 877-4474
Email: dario@dariodesigns.com
Primary Website: www.dariodesigns.com
Year Established: 1994
Product/Services: Architects/Engineers (Includes Design/Construction Firms)
Note: www.dariodesigns.com
Personnel: Dario Dimare (Pres.)
Personnel: David Ehrhardt (VP)

NORWALK

KODAK GCG

Street address 1: 401 Merritt 7
Street address state: CT
Zip/Postal code: 06851-1000
Country: USA
Mailing address: 401 Merritt 7 Ste 22
Mailing city: Norwalk
Mailing state: CT
Mailing zip: 06851-1068
General Phone: (203) 845-7115
General Fax: (203) 845-7173
Primary Website: www.kodak.com
Year Established: 1935
Product/Services: Chemicals: Photographic; Chemicals: Plate Processing; Color Management Software; Color Proofing; Film & Paper: Contact; Film & Paper: Duplicating; Film & Paper: Filters (Photographic); Offset Plate-Making Service & Equipment; Plates: Offset (Computer to Plate); Plates: Offset (Conventional);
Personnel: Andrew Copley (Sr. Cor. Vice Pres.)

MILES 33

Street address 1: 40 Richards Ave
Street address 2: Pendegast Street, 5170
Street address state: CT
Zip/Postal code: 06854-2319
Country: USA
Mailing address: 40 Richards Ave Ste 29
Mailing city: Norwalk
Mailing state: CA
Mailing zip: 06854-2322
General Phone: (203) 838-2333
General Fax: (203) 838-4473
Email: info@miles33.com
Primary Website: www.miles33.com
Year Established: 1976
Product/Services: Computers: Hardware & Software Integrators; Consulting Services: Advertising; Consulting Services: Editorial; Software: Advertising (Includes Display; Classified; Digital and Print); Software: Digital Asset Management; Software:

Content Management Systems for newsroom and Web; Software: Pagination/Layout; Software: Ad Tracking; Software: Self Service Advertising; Software: Digital Video Ad Production; Software: Ipad and Android Apps; Software: Business Analytics/Datamining
Product or Service: Hardware/Software Supplier`Multimedia/Interactive Products
Personnel: Chris Habasinski (Pres.)
Personnel: Albert De Bruijn (VP Marketing and Western USA Sales)
Personnel: Edward Hubbard (VP, Business Development)

TERA DIGITAL PUBLISHING

Street address 1: 40 Richards Ave
Street address 2: Ste 29
Street address state: CT
Zip/Postal code: 06854-2289
Country: USA
Mailing address: 40 Richards Ave Ste 29
Mailing city: Norwalk
Mailing state: CT
Mailing zip: 06854-2322
General Phone: (203) 838-2333
General Fax: (203) 838-4473
Email: info@miles33.com
Primary Website: www.teradp.com
Product/Services: Consulting Services: Editorial; Software: Editorial Content Management Systems; Software: Web Publishing; Software: Digital Asset Management/Archiving
Personnel: Don Sullivan (Sr. VP Sales)
Personnel: Albert De Bruijn (VP Marketing and Sales for Western USA)

XEROX CORP.

Street address 1: 201 Merritt 7
Street address state: CT
Zip/Postal code: 06851-1056
Country: USA
Mailing address: 201 Merritt 7
Mailing city: Norwalk
Mailing state: CT
Mailing zip: 06851-1056
General Phone: (203) 968-3000
Primary Website: www.xerox.com
Year Established: 1906
Product/Services: Xerox provides business process services, printing equipment, hardware and software technology for managing information – from data to documents. Learn more at www.xerox.com.
Note: Xerox Corporation provides business process and document management solutions worldwide. Its Services segment offers business process outsourcing services, such as customer care, transaction processing, finance and accounting, human resources, communication and marketing, and consulting and analytics services, as well as services in the areas of healthcare, transportation, financial services, retail, and telecommunications areas. This segment also provides document outsourcing services comprising managed print services, including workflow automation and centralized print services. The companyÂ's Document Technology segment offers desktop monochrome and color printers, multifunction printers, copiers, digital printing presses, and light production devices; and production printing and publishing systems for the graphic communications marketplace and large enterprises. Its Other segment sells paper, wide-format systems, global imaging systems network integration solutions, and electronic presentation systems. The company sells its products and services directly to its customers; and through its sales force, as well as through a network of independent agents, dealers, value-added resellers, systems integrators, and the Web. Xerox Corporation was founded in 1906 and is headquartered in Norwalk, Connecticut.
Personnel: Keith Cozza (Chairman)
Personnel: John Visentin (Vice Chairman & CEO)
Personnel: Steve Bandrowczak (Exec. V. P. & Pres. & COO)
William F. Osbourn (Exec. V. Pres. & CFO)
Farooq Muzaffar (Sr. V. P. & Chief Strategy and Marketing Officer)

NOVATO

IMSI

Street address 1: 25 Leveroni Ct
Street address state: CA
Zip/Postal code: 94949-5726
Country: USA
Mailing address: 25 Leveroni Ct Ste B
Mailing city: Novato
Mailing state: CA
Mailing zip: 94949-5726
General Phone: 415-483-8000
General Fax: 415-884-9023
Email: sales@imsisoft.com
Primary Website: www.imsidesign.com
Year Established: 1985
Product/Services: Software: Design/Graphics; Software: Electronic Data Interchange; Software: Pagination/Layout;
Personnel: Royal Farros (Chrmn./CEO)
Personnel: Robert Mayer (COO)

OAK BROOK

GRAPHIC ARTS BLUE BOOK ONLINE

Street address 1: 2000 Clearwater Dr
Street address state: IL
Zip/Postal code: 60523-8809
Country: USA
Mailing address: 2000 Clearwater Dr
Mailing city: Oak Brook
Mailing state: IL
Mailing zip: 60523-8809
General Phone: 800/323-4958, x8333
General Fax: 678/680-1667
Email: info@gabb.com
Primary Website: www.gabb.com
Year Established: 1929
Product/Services: Trade Publications
Personnel: Mary Miller (Global Marketing Director)

HARLAND SIMON

Street address 1: 210 W 22nd St
Street address 2: Ste 138
Street address state: IL
Zip/Postal code: 60523-4061
Country: USA
Mailing address: 210 W 22nd St Ste 138
Mailing city: Oak Brook
Mailing state: IL
Mailing zip: 60523-4061
General Phone: (630) 572-7650
General Fax: (630) 572-7653
Email: sales@harlandsimon.com
Primary Website: www.harlandsimon.com
Product/Services: Color Proofing; Drives & Controls; Ink Controls, Computerized; Mailroom Systems & Equipment; Inserting Equipment (Includes Stuffing Machines); Press Control Systems; Press Data Accumulators; Produciton Control Systems; Software: Pagination/Layout; Software: Press/Post Press; Software: Workflow Management/Tracking;
Personnel: John Staiano (Managing Director - Americas)

OAKTON

ED BARON & ASSOCIATES, INC.

Street address 1: PO Box 3203
Street address state: VA
Zip/Postal code: 22124-9203
Country: USA
Mailing address: PO Box 3203
Mailing city: Oakton
Mailing state: VA
Mailing zip: 22124-9203
General Phone: (703) 620-1725
General Fax: (703) 620-9037
Email: edbaron@edbaron.com
Primary Website: www.edbaron.com
Year Established: 1995
Product/Services: Consulting Services: Advertising; Consulting Services: Circulation; Consulting Services: Financial; Consulting Services: Marketing; Training: Sales & Marketing
Personnel: Ed Baron (Pres.)

OGDENSBURG

CONDAIR LTD.

Street address 1: 835 Commerce Park Drive
Street address state: NY
Zip/Postal code: 13669
Country: USA
Mailing address: 835 Commerce Park Drive
Mailing city: Ogdensburg
Mailing state: NY
Mailing zip: 13669
General Phone: 1.866.667.8321
Email: na.info@condair.com
Primary Website: www.humidity.com
Year Established: 1974
Product/Services: Humidifiers
Personnel: Urs Schenk (Pres.)
Personnel: Gary Berlin (Vice Pres., Sales)
Personnel: Mike Hurley (Vice Pres., Mktg.)
Naomi Cassidy (Mktg. Coord.)

OKLAHOMA CITY

AMERICAN FIDELITY ASSURANCE CO.

Street address 1: 2000 N Classen Blvd
Street address state: OK
Zip/Postal code: 73106-6016
Country: USA
Mailing address: PO Box 25523
Mailing city: Oklahoma City
Mailing state: OK
Mailing zip: 73125-0523
General Phone: (405) 523-2000
Primary Website: www.americanfidelity.com
Year Established: 1960
Product/Services: Insurance
Personnel: William B. Cameron (CEO and Chairman)
Personnel: Dave Carpenter (President and COO)
Personnel: Jeanette Rice (AVP of Communications)

APPLIED INDUSTRIAL MACHINERY

Street address 1: 1930 SE 29th St
Street address state: OK
Zip/Postal code: 73129-7626
Country: USA
Mailing address: 1930 SE 29th St
Mailing city: Oklahoma City
Mailing state: OK
Mailing zip: 73129-7626
General Phone: (405) 672-2222
General Fax: (405) 672-2272
Year Established: 1981
Product/Services: Equipment Dealers (New); Feeding, Folding, Delivery Equipment; Folding Machines; In-Line Trimming Systems; Three Knife Trimmer; Web Press - Special Equipment
Personnel: Robert Gilson (Pres.)

FIFE CORPORATION

Street address 1: 222 W Memorial Rd
Street address state: OK
Zip/Postal code: 73114-2300
Country: USA
Mailing address: PO Box 26508
Mailing city: Oklahoma City
Mailing state: OK
Mailing zip: 73126-0508
General Phone: (405) 755-1600
General Fax: (405) 755-8425
Email: fife@fife.com
Primary Website: www.fife.com
Product/Services: Visual Display Terminals; Web Break Detector; Web Guides; Web Press - Special Equipment;
Personnel: Marcel Hage (Mgr.)

MAXCESS

Street address 1: 222 W Memorial Rd
Street address state: OK
Zip/Postal code: 73114-2300
Country: USA
Mailing address: PO Box 26508
Mailing city: Oklahoma City
Mailing state: OK
Mailing zip: 73126-0508
General Phone: (405) 755-1600
General Fax: (405) 755-8425
Email: sales@maxcessintl.com
Primary Website: www.maxcessintl.com
Product/Services: Chemicals: Chuck (Paper Roll); Cutters & Trimmers; Cutting Tools; Drives & Controls; Reels & Tensions; Tension & Web Controls; Visual Display Terminals; Web Break Detector; Web Guides; Web Press - Special Equipment;
Personnel: Greg Jehlik (CEO, Pres.)
Personnel: Doug Knudtson (COO, VP)
Personnel: Robert Sweet (CFO)
Andy Wissenback (Sales Rep)
Pat Johnson (Sales Rep)

THE WELLMARK COMPANY

Street address 1: 1903 SE 29th St
Street address state: OK
Zip/Postal code: 73129-7625
Country: USA
Mailing address: 1903 SE 29th St
Mailing city: Oklahoma City
Mailing state: OK
Mailing zip: 73129-7625
General Phone: (405) 672-6660
General Fax: (405) 672-6661
Email: twc@wellmarkco.com
Primary Website: www.wellmarkco.com
Year Established: 1963
Product/Services: Gauges, Measuring; Ink Storage Tanks;
Personnel: Dick Pfieffer (Pres.)
Personnel: Steve Lawson (VP Sales/Mktg.)

OLYMPIA

NOTEADS.COM, INC./POST-IT NOTE ADVERTISING

Street address 1: 6906 Martin Way E
Street address state: WA
Zip/Postal code: 98516-5567
Country: USA
Mailing address: 6906 Martin Way E
Mailing city: Olympia
Mailing state: WA
Mailing zip: 98516-5567
General Phone: 800-309-7502
General Fax: (800) 309-7503
Email: john@noteads.com
Primary Website: www.noteads.com
Year Established: 1997
Product/Services: Consulting Services: Advertising
Note: Hand and Machine Applied Front Page Sticky Note Ads
Personnel: John Grantham (President)
Personnel: Kristin Gustin (Sales)

OMAHA

PRESSROOM CLEANERS, INC.

Street address 1: 5709 S 60th St
Street address 2: Ste 100B
Street address state: NE
Zip/Postal code: 68117-2204
Country: USA
Mailing address: 5709 SOUTH 60TH STREET, SUITE 100B
Mailing city: OMAHA
Mailing state: NE
Mailing zip: 68117-2204
General Phone: (402) 597-3199
General Fax: (402) 597-8765
Email: theresa@pressroomcleaners.com

Equipment, Supplies and Services

Primary Website: www.pressroomcleaners.com
Year Established: 1956
Product/Services: Industrial Cleaning Services
Personnel: Theresa Frangoulis (Pres.)
Personnel: Angie Clarke (Office Mgr.)

OMAHA

U.S. PETROLON INDUSTRIAL

Street address 1: 11442 Queens Dr
Street address state: NE
Zip/Postal code: 68164-2229
Country: USA
Mailing address: 11442 Queens Dr
Mailing city: Omaha
Mailing state: NE
Mailing zip: 68164-2229
General Phone: (402) 727-1577
General Fax: (402) 445-8608
Email: al@uspetrolon.com
Primary Website: www.uspetrolon.com
Year Established: 1979
Product/Services: Fluid Handeling: Pressroom
Personnel: Al Harrell (Regl. Distributor)

ONTARIO

BISHAMON INDUSTRIES CORP.

Street address 1: 5651 E Francis St
Street address state: CA
Zip/Postal code: 91761-3601
Country: USA
Mailing address: 5651 E Francis St
Mailing city: Ontario
Mailing state: CA
Mailing zip: 91761-3601
General Phone: (909) 390-0055
General Fax: (909) 390-0060
Email: info@bishamon.com
Primary Website: www.bishamon.com
Year Established: 1949
Product/Services: Mailroom Systems & Equipment; Material Handling Equipment: Vehicle Loading; Newsprint Handling Equipment; Paper Handeling Equipment;
Personnel: Wataru Sugiura (Pres.)
Personnel: Bob Clark (Vice Pres., Sales/Mktg.)

ONTARIO

RFC WIRE FORMS

Street address 1: 525 Brooks St
Street address state: CA
Zip/Postal code: 91762-3702
Country: USA
Mailing address: 525 Brooks St
Mailing city: Ontario
Mailing state: CA
Mailing zip: 91762-3702
General Phone: (909) 984-5500
General Fax: (909) 984-2322
Email: rfccompany@aol.com
Primary Website: www.rfcwireforms.com
Year Established: 1946
Product/Services: Rack Display Cards
Personnel: Don Kemby (Pres.)
Personnel: Greg Lunsmann (Gen. Mgr.)

ORELAND

CHAPEL HILL MANUFACTURING CO.

Street address 1: 1807 Walnut Ave
Street address state: PA
Zip/Postal code: 19075-1528
Country: USA
Mailing address: PO Box 208
Mailing city: Oreland
Mailing state: PA
Mailing zip: 19075-0208
General Phone: (215) 884-3614
General Fax: (215) 884-3617
Email: sales@chapelhillmfg.com
Primary Website: www.chapelhillmfg.com
Year Established: 1962
Product/Services: Dampening Systems
Personnel: John Seeburger (Pres./Vice Pres., Mktg.)
Personnel: J. Robert Seeburger (Vice Pres., Sales)

ORLANDO

REED BRENNAN MEDIA ASSOCIATES, INC.

Street address 1: 628 Virginia Dr
Street address state: FL
Zip/Postal code: 32803-1858
Country: USA
Mailing address: 628 Virginia Dr
Mailing city: Orlando
Mailing state: FL
Mailing zip: 32803-1858
General Phone: (407) 894-7300
General Fax: (407) 894-7900
Email: rbma@rbma.com
Primary Website: www.rbma.com
Year Established: 1993
Product/Services: Input & Editing Systems; Pagination Systems;
Personnel: Jeff Talbert (VP)
Personnel: Timothy Brennan (Mgr., Mktg.)
Personnel: David Cohea (King Features Weekly Service)

ORMOND BEACH

SUPERIOR HANDLING EQUIPMENT, INC.

Street address 1: 8 Aviator Way
Street address state: FL
Zip/Postal code: 32174-2983
Country: USA
Mailing address: 8 Aviator Way
Mailing city: Ormond Beach
Mailing state: FL
Mailing zip: 32174-2983
General Phone: (386) 677-0004
Email: info@superiorlifts.com
Primary Website: www.superiorlifts.com
Year Established: 1977
Product/Services: Material Handling Equipment: Truck Loaders; Material Handling Equipment: Vehicle Loading; Paper Handeling Equipment;
Personnel: Mike Vollmar (CEO)
Personnel: Beth Vollmar (Pres.)
Personnel: Gary Clark (Operations Dir.)
Carle Davis (Sales Dir.)

OVERLAND PARK

EURO-KNIVES USA

Street address 1: 11516 W 90th St
Street address state: KS
Zip/Postal code: 66214-1710
Country: USA
Mailing address: 11516 W 90th St
Mailing city: Overland Park
Mailing state: KS
Mailing zip: 66214-1710
General Phone: (913) 648-7860
General Fax: (913) 859-0334
Email: al@euro-knivesusa.com; rob@euro-knivesusa.com
Primary Website: www.euro-knivesusa.com/index.php
Year Established: 1984
Product/Services: Cut-off knives, slitters, Tucker's, grippers, pin screws, cutting sticks, cheekwoods
Personnel: Al Elton (Owner)
Personnel: Rob Elton (Sales Mgr.)

OVERLAND PARK

SMITH PRESSROOM PRODUCTS, INC.

Street address 1: 9215 Bond St
Street address state: KS
Zip/Postal code: 66214-1728
Country: USA
Mailing address: 9215 Bond St.
Mailing city: Overland Park
Mailing state: KS
Mailing zip: 66214
General Phone: (913) 888-0695
General Fax: (913) 888-0699
Email: info@smithpressroomproducts.com
Primary Website: www.smithpressroomproducts.com
Year Established: 1968
Product/Services: Blanket Cleaner/Washer (Automatic); Dampening Systems; Offset Fountain Controls; Offset Fountain Solutions; Pumps (Air, Ink, Vacuum); Recirculators; Solvent Recovery Systems; Wastewater Treatment; Water Management Systems; Web Offset Remoisturizers;
Personnel: Dennis Schupp (Pres.)
Personnel: Ross Hart (VP)

OWINGS MILLS

ANYGRAAF USA

Street address 1: 10451 Mill Run Cir
Street address 2: Ste 400
Street address state: MD
Zip/Postal code: 21117-5594
Country: USA
Mailing address: 10451 Mill Run Cir Ste 400
Mailing city: Owings Mills
Mailing state: MD
Mailing zip: 21117-5594
General Phone: (240) 379-6620
Email: anyinc@anygraaf.com
Primary Website: www.anygraaf.com
Product/Services: Proofing Systems
Personnel: Andy Hunn (Managing Dir.)
Personnel: Bill Ryker (SALES DIR.)

OXFORD

GENERAL DATACOMM, LLC

Street address 1: 353 Christian Street
Street address state: CT
Zip/Postal code: 06478
Country: USA
Mailing address: 353 Christian Street
Mailing city: Oxford
Mailing state: CT
Mailing zip: 06478
General Phone: (203) 729-0271
General Fax: (203) 266-2133
Primary Website: www.gdc.com
Year Established: 1969
Product/Services: Computers: Hardware & Software Integrators; Telecommunications;
Personnel: Mike Conway (Pres. & CEO)
Personnel: Mark Johns (COO)
Personnel: Joe Autem (CFO)

PALO ALTO

HP INC.

Street address 1: 1501 Page Mill Road
Street address state: CA
Zip/Postal code: 94304-1112
Country: USA
Mailing address: 1501 Page Mill Road
Mailing city: Palo Alto
Mailing state: CA
Mailing zip: 94304-1112
General Phone: (650) 857-1501
Email: hp-leads@hp.com
Primary Website: www8.hp.com
Year Established: 1939
Product/Services: Personal computers; Printers; 3D Printers; Inks; Scanners; Copiers; Displays;
Personnel: Dion Weisler (Pres./CEO)
Personnel: Steve Fieler (CFO)
Personnel: Alex Cho (Pres., Personal Systems)
Enrique Lores (Pres., Imaging & Printing)
Christoph Schell (Pres., 3D Printing & Digital Manufacturing)
Tracy Keogh (CHRO)
Vikrant Batra (Chief Marketing Officer)

PARK RIDGE

NUS CONSULTING GROUP

Street address 1: 1 Maynard Dr
Street address state: NJ
Zip/Postal code: 07656-1878
Country: USA
Mailing address: PO Box 712
Mailing city: Park Ridge
Mailing state: NJ
Mailing zip: 07656-0712
General Phone: (201) 391-4300
General Fax: (201) 391-8158
Email: contact@nusconsulting.com
Primary Website: www.nusconsulting.com
Year Established: 1933
Product/Services: Telecommunications
Personnel: Gary Soultanian (Co-Pres.)
Personnel: Richard Soultanian (Co-Pres.)

PARKESBURG

JOHNSTONE ENGINEERING & MACHINE CO.

Street address 1: PO Box 66
Street address state: PA
Zip/Postal code: 19365-0066
Country: USA
Mailing address: PO Box 66
Mailing city: Parkesburg
Mailing state: PA
Mailing zip: 19365-0066
General Phone: 610-593-6350
General Fax: 610-593-2172
Email: jemco2@comcast.net
Year Established: 1940
Product/Services: Reels & Tensions; Reels (Inlcudes Paper Reels); Rewinders; Roll Handeling Equipment;
Personnel: Raymond E. Sullivan (Sales Mgr.)
Personnel: Bill Haag (President)

PARSIPPANY

GLOBAL TURNKEY SYSTEMS, INC.

Street address 1: 2001 US Highway 46
Street address 2: Ste 203
Street address state: NJ
Zip/Postal code: 07054-1315
Country: USA
Mailing address: 2001 US Highway 46 Ste 203
Mailing city: Parsippany
Mailing state: NJ
Mailing zip: 07054-1315
General Phone: (973) 331-1010
General Fax: (973) 331-0042
Email: sales@gtsystems.com
Primary Website: www.gtsystems.com
Year Established: 1969
Product/Services: Computers: Hardware & Software Integrators; Computers: Local Area Network (LANS); Consulting Services: Circulation; Consulting Services: Computer; Software: Circulation; Software: Electronic Data Interchange; Subscription Fulfillment Software; System Installations; System Integration Services
Personnel: Al Alteslane (Pres./CEO)

SUN CHEMICAL CORPORATION

Street address 1: 35 Waterview Boulevard
Street address state: NJ
Zip/Postal code: 07054-1285
Country: USA
Mailing address: 35 Waterview Boulevard
Mailing city: Parsippany
Mailing state: NJ
Mailing zip: 07054-1285
General Phone: (973) 404-6000
General Fax: (973) 404-6001
Primary Website: www.sunchemical.com
Year Established: 1945
Product/Services: Blankets; Chemicals: Plate Processing; Chemicals: Pressroom; Circulation Equipment & Supplies; Cleaners & Solvents; Offset Blanket Thickness Gauge; Offset Blankets, Blanket Wash;

Offset Chemicals & Supplies; Offset Fountain Solutions;
Personnel: Rudi Lenz (Pres. & CEO)
Personnel: Kevin Michaelson (VP & CFO)
Personnel: Felipe Mellado (Chief Marketing Officer and Board Member)

PASADENA

PARSONS CORPORATION

Street address 1: 100 W Walnut St
Street address state: CA
Zip/Postal code: 91124-0001
Country: USA
Mailing address: 100 W Walnut St
Mailing city: Pasadena
Mailing state: CA
Mailing zip: 91124-0001
General Phone: (626) 440-2000
General Fax: (626) 440-2630
Primary Website: www.parsons.com
Year Established: 1944
Product/Services: Engineering, construction, technical, and professional services
Personnel: Charles Harrington (Chairman and CEO)
Personnel: Erin Kuhlman (Corporate Vice President, Marketing & Communications)

PASO ROBLES

WESTERN QUARTZ PRODUCTS, INC.

Street address 1: 2432 Spring St
Street address state: CA
Zip/Postal code: 93446-1226
Country: USA
Mailing address: 2432 Spring St
Mailing city: Paso Robles
Mailing state: CA
Mailing zip: 93446-1296
General Phone: (805) 238-3524
General Fax: (805) 238-6811
Email: info@westernquartz.com
Primary Website: www.westernquartz.com
Year Established: 1931
Product/Services: UV Exposure Lamps
Personnel: Jon Dallons (President/CEO)
Personnel: Katy Wetterstrand (Director/CFO)

PATERSON

COLTER PETERSON

Street address 1: 414 E 16th St
Street address state: NJ
Zip/Postal code: 07514-2638
Country: USA
Mailing address: 414 E 16th St
Mailing city: Paterson
Mailing state: NJ
Mailing zip: 07514-2638
General Phone: (515) 276-4528
General Fax: (515) 276-8324
Email: sales@colterpeterson.com
Primary Website: www.colterpeterson.com
Year Established: 1932
Product/Services: Paper Cutters, Material Handling, Perfect Binders and & Three Knife Trimmers
Personnel: Vince Payne (Vice President)

PENNSAUKEN

INSERT EAST, INC.

Street address 1: 7045 Central Hwy
Street address state: NJ
Zip/Postal code: 08109-4312
Country: USA
Mailing address: 7045 Central Hwy
Mailing city: Pennsauken
Mailing state: NJ
Mailing zip: 08109-4312
General Phone: (856) 663-8181
General Fax: (856) 663-3288
Primary Website: www.insertseast.com
Year Established: 1996
Product/Services: Circulation Equipment & Supplies
Personnel: Gino Maiale (Owner)
Personnel: Nick Maiale (Pres.)
Personnel: Frank Oliveti (Plant Mgr.)

PENSACOLA

GE INSTRUMENT CONTROL SYSTEMS, INC.

Street address 1: PO Box 7126
Street address state: FL
Zip/Postal code: 32503
Country: USA
Mailing address: PO Box 7126
Mailing city: Pensacola
Mailing state: FL
Mailing zip: 32534-0126
General Phone: 800-433-2682
General Fax: 780-420-2010
Email: customercare.ip@ge.com
Primary Website: www.geautomation.com
Product/Services: Architects/Engineers (Includes Design/Construction Firms); Controls: Exposure; Controls: Photo Electric; Controls: Register;
Personnel: Sharon Stall (Sales)

MO-MONEY ASSOCIATES, INC.

Street address 1: 3838 N Palafox St
Street address state: FL
Zip/Postal code: 32505-5239
Country: USA
Mailing address: 3838 N Palafox St
Mailing city: Pensacola
Mailing state: FL
Mailing zip: 32505-5222
General Phone: (850) 432-6301
General Fax: (850) 434-5645
Email: momoney@momoney.com
Primary Website: www.momoney.com
Year Established: 1979
Personnel: Cliff Mowe (Pres.)
Personnel: Tom McVoy (Mktg. Mgr.)

PEORIA

JUPITER IMAGES CORP.

Street address 1: 6000 N Forest Park Dr
Street address state: IL
Zip/Postal code: 61614-3556
Country: USA
Mailing address: 6000 N Forest Park Dr
Mailing city: Peoria
Mailing state: IL
Mailing zip: 61614-3556
General Phone: (309) 688-8800
General Fax: (309) 688-3075
Email: sales@jupiterimages.com
Primary Website: www.jupiterimages.com
Year Established: 1964
Product/Services: Software: Design/Graphics; Trade Publications;
Product or Service: Hardware/Software Supplier
Note: All-purpose art and idea service.
Personnel: Mark Nickerson (Vice Pres., Opns.)

PHILADELPHIA

I-MANY, INC.

Street address 1: 1735 Market St
Street address state: PA
Zip/Postal code: 19103-7501
Country: USA
Mailing address: 1735 Market St Ste 3700
Mailing city: Philadelphia
Mailing state: PA
Mailing zip: 19103-7527
General Phone: (800) 832-0228
Email: info@imany.com
Primary Website: www.imany.com
Product/Services: Consulting Services: Financial
Personnel: John A. Rade (Pres./CEO)

SIMON MILLER SALES CO.

Street address 1: 1218 Chestnut St
Street address state: PA
Zip/Postal code: 19107-4848
Country: USA
Mailing address: 3409 W Chester Pike Ste 204
Mailing city: Newtown Square
Mailing state: PA
Mailing zip: 19073-4290
General Phone: (215) 923-3600
General Fax: (215) 923-1173
Email: info@simonmiller.com
Primary Website: www.simonmiller.com
Year Established: 1920
Product/Services: Newspaper Couter; Newspaper Marketing; Newsprint; Paper: Coated Groundwood Offset; Paper: Groundwood Specialties; Paper: Specialty Printing Paper; Roll Converters;
Personnel: Joseph Levit (Pres.)
Personnel: Henri C. Levit (COO)
Personnel: David Donde (Vice Pres., Mktg.)

TRAUNER CONSULTING SERVICES, INC.

Street address 1: 1617 John F Kennedy Blvd
Street address 2: Ste 600
Street address state: PA
Zip/Postal code: 19103-1807
Country: USA
Mailing address: 1617 John F Kennedy Blvd Frnt
Mailing city: Philadelphia
Mailing state: PA
Mailing zip: 19103-1856
General Phone: (215) 814-6400
General Fax: (215) 814-6440
Email: philadelphia@traunerconsulting.com
Primary Website: www.traunerconsulting.com
Year Established: 1988
Product/Services: Architects/Engineers (Includes Design/Construction Firms); Training: Keyboard Operation;
Personnel: Russ Thomas (Mgr., New Bus.)

PHILLIPS

BW PAPERSYSTEMS

Street address 1: 1300 N. Airport Road
Street address state: WI
Zip/Postal code: 54555
Country: USA
Mailing address: 1300 N. Airport Road
Mailing city: Phillips
Mailing state: WI
Mailing zip: 54555
General Phone: (715) 339-2191
General Fax: (715) 339â4469
Email: sales@bwpapersystems.com
Primary Website: www.bwpapersystems.com
Year Established: 1982
Product/Services: Conversion Equipment; Conveyors; Cutters & Trimmers; Photostat: Paper; Reels & Tensions; Reels (Inlcudes Paper Reels); Roll Handling Equipment; Splicers, Automatic; Tension & Web Controls; Web Guides;
Personnel: Neal McConnellogue (Pres.)

PHOENIX

MASTHEAD INTERNATIONAL, INC.

Street address 1: 3602 S 16th St
Street address state: AZ
Zip/Postal code: 85040-1311
Country: USA
Mailing address: 3602 S 16th St
Mailing city: Phoenix
Mailing state: AZ
Mailing zip: 85040-1311
General Phone: 602-276-5373
General Fax: 602-276-8116
Email: steve.stone@masthead.net
Primary Website: www.masthead.net
Year Established: 1971
Product/Services: Controllers: Press; Drives & Controls; Erectors & Riggers; Pasters; Press Parts; Press Rebuilding; Press Repairs; Presses: Flexographic; Presses: Letterpress; Presses: Offset; Tension & Web Controls; Training: Press Operation & Maintenance; Web Width Changer;
Personnel: Steve Stone (Branch Mgr.)
Personnel: Kent Kraft (Bus. Devel. Mgr.)

MIRACHEM CORP.

Street address 1: PO Box 14059
Street address state: AZ
Zip/Postal code: 85063-4059
Country: USA
Mailing address: PO Box 14059
Mailing city: Phoenix
Mailing state: AZ
Mailing zip: 85063-4059
General Phone: 808-847-3527
General Fax: (602) 353-1411
Email: cservice@mirachem.com
Primary Website: www.mirachem.com
Year Established: 1978
Product/Services: Chemicals: Pressroom; Chemicals: Roller Cleaning; Cleaners & Solvents;
Personnel: Pat Doughty (COO)
Personnel: Bob Boyle (Sales Mgr.)

SYNTELLECT, INC.

Street address 1: 2095 W Pinnacle Peak Rd
Street address 2: Ste 110
Street address state: AZ
Zip/Postal code: 85027-1262
Country: USA
Mailing address: 2095 W Pinnacle Peak Rd Ste 110
Mailing city: Phoenix
Mailing state: AZ
Mailing zip: 85027-1262
General Phone: (602) 789-2800
General Fax: (602) 789-2768
Email: info.ie@enghouse.com
Primary Website: www.syntellect.com
Year Established: 1984
Product/Services: Computers: Hardware & Software Integrators; Computers: Local Area Network (LANS); Consulting Services: Advertising; Consulting Services: Circulation; Consulting Services: Equipment; Consulting Services: Marketing; Speech Recognition; Subscription Fulfillment Software; System Integration Services; Telecommunications;
Product or Service: Telecommunications/ Service Bureaus
Personnel: Steve Dodenhoff (Pres.)
Personnel: Peter Pamplin (CFO)
Personnel: Keith Gyssler (Vice Pres., Sales Americas)
Tricia Lester (Vice Pres., Pdct. Mktg.)
Jackie Dasta (Contact)

PITTSBURGH

AD-A-NOTE

Street address 1: 1000 Rockpointe Blvd
Street address state: PA
Zip/Postal code: 15084
Country: USA
Mailing address: 1000 RockPointe Blvd
Mailing city: Pittsburgh
Mailing state: PA
Mailing zip: 15084-2806
General Phone: (724) 889-7707
Email: Bruce@ad-a-note.com
Primary Website: www.ad-a-note.com
Year Established: 2009
Product/Services: Sticky Notes
Note: Front page sticky note advertising application equipment and printed note system. FREE AD-A-NOTE EQUIPMENT FOR QUALIFIED NEWSPAPERS!
Personnel: Bruce Barna (Executive Vice President)

MATTHEWS INTERNATIONAL CORP.

Street address 1: 6515 Penn Ave
Street address state: PA
Zip/Postal code: 15206-4407

Equipment, Supplies and Services

Country: USA
Mailing address: 6515 Penn Ave
Mailing city: Pittsburgh
Mailing state: PA
Mailing zip: 15206-4482
General Phone: (412) 665-2550
General Fax: (412) 365-2055
Email: info@matw.com
Primary Website: www.matthewsmarking.com; www.matw.com
Year Established: 1850
Product/Services: Laser Printers
Personnel: Joseph C. Bartolacci (Pres./CEO)

PLANO

TKS (USA), INC.

Street address 1: 101 E Park Blvd
Street address 2: Ste 600
Street address state: TX
Zip/Postal code: 75074-8818
Country: USA
Mailing address: 3001 E Plano Pkwy Ste 200
Mailing city: Plano
Mailing state: TX
Mailing zip: 75074-7480
General Phone: (972) 983 0600
General Fax: (972) 870-5857
Email: sales@tkspress.com
Primary Website: www.tksusa.com
Year Established: 1980
Product/Services: Presses: Offset and digital ink jet and gripper conveyor
Personnel: Mike Shafer (Vice President of Sales and Marketing)

PLATTSBURGH

PRIM HALL ENTERPRISES, INC.

Street address 1: 11 Spellman Rd
Street address state: NY
Zip/Postal code: 12901-5326
Country: USA
Mailing address: 11 Spellman Rd
Mailing city: Plattsburgh
Mailing state: NY
Mailing zip: 12901-5326
General Phone: (518) 561-7408
General Fax: (518) 563-1472
Email: sales@primhall.com; primhall@primhall.com
Primary Website: www.primhall.com
Year Established: 1988
Product/Services: Collating Equipment; Conveyors; Mailroom Systems & Equipment; Paper Handling Equipment; Three Knife Trimmer;
Personnel: John E. Prim (Pres.)
Personnel: David E. Hall (Vice Pres.)
Personnel: Matt Demers (Mktg. Coord.)

PLEASANT VIEW

THE KEENAN GROUP, INC.

Street address 1: 155 Keenan Ct
Street address state: TN
Zip/Postal code: 37146-3706
Country: USA
Mailing address: PO Box 458
Mailing city: Pleasant View
Mailing state: TN
Mailing zip: 37146-0458
General Phone: (615) 746-2443
General Fax: (615) 746-2270
Email: info@keenangroup.com
Primary Website: www.keenangroup.com
Year Established: 1984
Product/Services: Consulting Services: Advertising; Consulting Services: Circulation; Consulting Services: Equipment; Consulting Services: Marketing; Consulting Services: Production; Newspaper Bags; Newspaper Dispensers (Mechanical/Electronic); Newspaper Marketing;
Personnel: Robert P. Keenan (Pres.)
Personnel: Debra B. Keenan (Vice Pres., Sales/Mktg.)

PLYMOUTH

FLINT GROUP

Street address 1: 14909 N Beck Rd
Street address state: MI
Zip/Postal code: 48170-2411
Country: USA
Mailing address: 14909 N Beck Rd
Mailing city: Plymouth
Mailing state: MI
Mailing zip: 48170-2411
General Phone: (734) 781-4600
General Fax: (734) 781-4699
Email: info@na.flintgrp.com
Primary Website: www.flintgrp.com
Year Established: 1920
Product/Services: Ink Pumping Systems; Ink Storage Tanks; Inks;
Personnel: Bill Miller (Pres., North Amer.)
Personnel: Mike Green (Vice Pres./Gen. Mgr., News Ink/Pub. Div.)
Personnel: Norm Harbin (Vice Pres., Bus./Technical Devel.)

FLINT GROUP.

Street address 1: 14909 N Beck Rd
Street address state: MI
Zip/Postal code: 48170-2411
Country: USA
Mailing address: 14909 North Beck
Mailing city: Plymouth
Mailing state: MI
Mailing zip: 48170
General Phone: (734) 781-4600
General Fax: (734) 781-4699
Email: info@flintgrp.com
Primary Website: www.flintgrp.com
Product/Services: Printing inks (including coldset UV; black and color; and soy-based options); Offset fabric and Metalback Blankets; Blanket Mounting and Bars; Pressroom Chemicals including Washes Fountain Solutions, Cleaners and more; Pressroom Supplies; Digital inks; and more.
Note: The only company to develop and manufacture inks, chemistry and blankets, making printers' jobs easier and pressroom performance stronger.

POINTE-CLAIRE

INNOVATIVE SYSTEMS DESIGN, INC.

Street address 1: 222 Brunswick Blvd
Street address state: QC
Zip/Postal code: H9R 1A6
Country: Canada
Mailing address: 222 Brunswick Blvd.
Mailing city: Pointe-Claire
Mailing state: QC
Mailing zip: H9R 1A6
General Phone: (514) 459-0200
General Fax: (514) 459-0300
Email: sales@isd.ca
Primary Website: www.isd.ca
Year Established: 1983
Product/Services: Telecommunications
Product or Service: Telecommunications/Service Bureaus
Personnel: Jeff Tierney (Pres.)
Personnel: Rob Dumas (Director of Sales and Marketing)
Personnel: Monica Steibelt (Sales Coord.)

PORTLAND

PULSE RESEARCH, INC.

Street address 1: PO Box 2884
Street address state: OR
Zip/Postal code: 97208-2884
Country: USA
Mailing address: PO Box 2884
Mailing city: Portland
Mailing state: OR
Mailing zip: 97208-2884
General Phone: (503) 626-5224
General Fax: (503) 277-2184
Email: info@pulseresearch.com; support@pulseresearch.com
Primary Website: www.pulseresearch.com
Year Established: 1985
Product/Services: Consulting Services: Advertising; Consulting Services: Circulation; Consulting Services: Marketing;
Personnel: John W. Marling (PRESIDENT)
Personnel: John Bertoglio (CIO)
Personnel: Denice Nichols (Vice Pres., Sales)
Andrew Dove (Vice Pres.)
Brian Knapp (Vice Pres.)

POUGHKEEPSIE

PERRETTA GRAPHICS CORP.

Street address 1: 46 Violet Ave
Street address state: NY
Zip/Postal code: 12601-1521
Country: USA
Mailing address: 46 Violet Ave
Mailing city: Poughkeepsie
Mailing state: NY
Mailing zip: 12601-1521
General Phone: (845) 473-0550
General Fax: (845) 454-7507
Email: mailbox@perretta.com; service@perretta.com
Primary Website: www.perretta.com
Year Established: 1981
Product/Services: Controls: Register; Ink Controls, Computerized; Keyless Inking Conversion & Add-ons; Web Press - Special Equipment;
Personnel: Christopher Perretta (Pres.)
Personnel: Bruce Quilliam (Bus. Mgr., Int'l Sales)
Personnel: Bruce L. Quilliam (Vice Pres., Sales/Mktg.)
Jean Laird (Sales Mgr.)
Paul Jorde (Serv. Mgr.)
Jordan Terziyski (Asst. Serv. Mgr.)

PRAIRIE VILLAGE

NEWMAN INTERNATIONAL, LLC

Street address 1: 4121 W 83rd St
Street address 2: Ste 155
Street address state: KS
Zip/Postal code: 66208-5323
Country: USA
Mailing address: 5405 W 97th Cir
Mailing city: Overland Park
Mailing state: KS
Mailing zip: 66207-3271
General Phone: (913) 648-2000
General Fax: (913) 648-7750
Email: j.newman@att.net
Primary Website: www.timsonsusedprintingpresses.com
Year Established: 1977
Product/Services: Presses: Offset; Web Press - Special Equipment;
Personnel: John T. Newman (Pres.)
Personnel: Mary C. Newman (Vice Pres.)

PRESCOTT

NORTHEAST INDUSTRIES, INC.

Street address 1: 2965 Tolemac Way
Street address state: AZ
Zip/Postal code: 86305-2179
Country: USA
Mailing address: 2965 Tolemac Way
Mailing city: Prescott
Mailing state: AZ
Mailing zip: 86305-2179
General Phone: 800-821-6257
General Fax: (928) 443-0851
Email: sam@neiinc.com
Primary Website: www.neiinc.com
Year Established: 1978
Product/Services: Consulting Services: Equipment; Presses: DiLitho; Presses: Flexographic; Presses: Letterpress; Presses: Offset;
Personnel: Sam W. Boyles (Pres.)

PRESTON LANCS

PRINTING PRESS SERVICES, INC.

Street address 1: Sellers St. Works
Zip/Postal code: PR1 5EU
Country: United Kingdom
Mailing address: Sellers St. Works
Mailing city: Preston Lancs
Mailing zip: PR1 5EU
General Phone: +44 1772 797 050
General Fax: +44 1772 705 761
Email: stephenm@ppsi.co.uk
Primary Website: www.ppsi.co.uk
Year Established: 1976
Product/Services: Conversion Equipment; Drives & Controls; Equipment Dealers (New); Equipment Dealers (Used); Erectors & Riggers; Ink Controls, Computerized; Ink Fountains & Accessories; Presses: Offset; Splicers, Automatic;
Personnel: Joe McManamon (Pres.)
Personnel: Stephen McManamon (Mng. Dir.-Press Division)
Personnel: David McManamon (Mng. Dir.-Inking Systems Division)
Marilyn Lloyd (Office Mgr.)

PRINCETON

AMERICAN OPINION RESEARCH

Street address 1: 279 Wall St
Street address state: NJ
Zip/Postal code: 08540-1519
Country: USA
Mailing address: 279 Wall St., Research Pk.
Mailing city: Princeton
Mailing state: NJ
Mailing zip: 8540
General Phone: (609) 683-4035
General Fax: (609) 683-8398
Email: acasale@imsworld.com
Primary Website: www.imsworld.com
Product/Services: Consulting Services: Advertising; Consulting Services: Circulation; Consulting Services: Editorial; Consulting Services: Marketing
Personnel: Tony Casale (Chrmn./CEO)
Personnel: Lois Kaufman (Pres.)

PROIMAGE AMERICA, INC.

Street address 1: 103 Carnegie Ctr
Street address 2: Ste 300
Street address state: NJ
Zip/Postal code: 08540-6235
Country: USA
Mailing address: 103 Carnegie Ctr Ste 300
Mailing city: Princeton
Mailing state: NJ
Mailing zip: 08540-6235
General Phone: (609) 844-7576
General Fax: (609) 895-2666
Email: sales.us@new-proimage.com
Primary Website: www.new-proimage.com
Year Established: 1995
Product/Services: Calibration Software/Hardware; Color Management; Consulting Services: Production; Software: Electronic Data Interchange; Software: Pagination/Layout; Software: Workflow Management/Tracking, Ripping, Imposition; Training: Automated Pre Press workflow; Ink Optimization; Press Registration; Content Management Systems; Tablet & Mobile Solutions
Note: ProImage America, Inc. is a solutions provider specializing in digital workflow management and production tracking systems and is dedicated to newspaper and magazine workflow systems. Our NewsWay solution uses a standard browsers to manage imposition, job planning, network workflow management, output management, resource scheduling, and plateroom management. The system also performs load balancing on all resources under its control such as RIPs & output devices and is ideal for centralized workflows. ProImage has standalone Modules for Ink Optimization, Press Registration, Color Management, and Remote Softproofing systems. In

Equipment, Supplies and Services

addition, MediaWay is an integrated CMS publishing system that combines content creation and management with layout and editorial workflows for output to print and web. Designed for use in a production environment where content creators can collaborate with each other, sharing assets, re-using content, and exchanging messages. This collaborative workspace allows multiple users to work simultaneously on different areas of the same project, thereby increasing the efficiencies. TabellaNews is an innovative Cloud-based solution for the creation of digital publications for tablets and other mobile devices. The content is analyzed and automatically processed through ProImageÃ¢Â€Â™s intelligent content mapping and template technology to produce a HTML 5 edition that is ready to preview and, if necessary, edit.
Personnel: John J. Ialacci (President/CEO)
Personnel: Mike Monter (Vice President, Operations)
Personnel: Rick Shafranek (Vice President, Sales and Marketing)

PROVIDENCE

GILBANE BUILDING CO.

Street address 1: 7 Jackson Walkway
Street address state: RI
Zip/Postal code: 02903-3638
Country: USA
Mailing address: 7 Jackson Walkway
Mailing city: Providence
Mailing state: RI
Mailing zip: 02903-3694
General Phone: (401) 456-5800
General Fax: (401) 456-5930
Primary Website: www.gilbaneco.com
Year Established: 1873
Product/Services: Architects/Engineers (Includes Design/Construction Firms)
Personnel: Paul J. Choquette (Chrmn./CEO)
Personnel: Thomas F. Gilbane (Pres./COO)
Personnel: William Gilbane (Exec. Vice Pres.)
Alfred K. Potter (Sr. Vice Pres.-Mktg./Sales)
Walter Mckelvey (Sr. Vice Pres./Mgr.-Central Reg.)
Wandell Holmes (Sr. Vice Pres./Mgr., Southwest)
Bruce Hoffman (Sr. Vice Pres./Mgr., Mid Atlantic)
George Cavallo (Sr. Vice Pres./Mgr.-North East Reg.)

QUAKERTOWN

GLUNZ & JENSEN, INC.

Street address 1: 500 Commerce Dr
Street address state: PA
Zip/Postal code: 18951-3730
Country: USA
Mailing address: 500 Commerce Drive
Mailing city: Quakertown
Mailing state: PA
Mailing zip: 18951
General Phone: (267) 405-4000
General Fax: (267) 227-3615
Email: gj-americas@glunz-jensen.com
Primary Website: www.glunz-jensen.com
Year Established: 1973
Product/Services: Offset Platemaking: processors for thermal, UV and violet plates Offset Plate; plate stackers and conveyors Flexo Platemaking: exposure units, processors, dryers, light finishers, automated plate making plate mounting, sleeve trimming and plate cleaning equipment CtP: inkjet computer to plate system
Personnel: Michael Bugge' (VP Sales)

QUINCY

MERLINONE, INC.

Street address 1: 17 Whitney Rd
Street address state: MA
Zip/Postal code: 02169-4309
Country: USA
Mailing address: 17 Whitney Rd.
Mailing city: Quincy
Mailing state: MA
Mailing zip: 02169
General Phone: (617) 328-6645
General Fax: (617) 328-9845
Email: info@merlinone.com
Primary Website: www.merlinone.com
Year Established: 1988
Product/Services: publishing, print, online, broadcast media, marketing departments across all industries-Picture Desks, Assignment systems, Archiving and Digital Asset Management systems for all your data types including audio, video, PDF's, electronic tearsheets
Personnel: David M. Tenenbaum (Pres./CEO)
Personnel: Rande Simpson (Merlin Sales Manager)
Personnel: Jeff Seidensticker (VP of IT & Managed Services)
David Breslauer (Inside sales rep)

RAMSEY

KONICA MINOLTA BUSINESS SOLUTIONS USA INC.

Street address 1: 100 Williams Dr
Street address state: NJ
Zip/Postal code: 07446-2907
Country: USA
Mailing address: 100 Williams Dr
Mailing city: Ramsey
Mailing state: NJ
Mailing zip: 07446-2907
General Phone: (201) 825-4000
Email: PR@kmbs.konicaminolta.us
Primary Website: 100 Williams Drive
Year Established: 1899
Product/Services: IT Services and Solutions and Technology
Personnel: Rick Taylor (Pres., CEO)
Personnel: Sam Errigo (Exec. VP, Sales and Business Development)
Personnel: Kay Du Fernandez (Senior VP, Marketing)

RANCHO CUCAMONGA

MCGRANN PAPER CORPORATION

Street address 1: 10865 Jersey Blvd
Street address state: CA
Zip/Postal code: 91730-5113
Country: USA
Mailing address: 2101 Westinghouse Blvd
Mailing city: Charlotte
Mailing state: NC
Mailing zip: 28273-6310
General Phone: 909-595-2727
General Fax: 704-369-2227
Primary Website: www.mcgrann.com
Year Established: 1974
Product/Services: Paper - Marchant - Converter- Distributor
Personnel: Anthony V. Nanna (Partner)

READING

ATEX

Street address 1: 87 Castle Street
Zip/Postal code: RG1 7SN
Country: United Kingdom
Mailing address: 87 Castle Street
Mailing city: Reading
Mailing zip: RG1 7SN
General Phone: 118 958 7537
General Fax: 118 958 7537
Email: info@atex.com
Primary Website: www.atex.com
Year Established: 1973
Product/Services: Software: Advertising (Includes Display; Classified); Software: Asset Management; Software: Circulation; Software: Editorial; Software: Pagination/Layout;
Product or Service: Hardware/Software Supplier
Personnel: Peter Marsh (Sr. Vice Pres./Chief Integration Officer)
Personnel: Malcolm McGrory (Sr. Vice Pres., Sales Americas)

RED LION

IGS KNIVES, INC.

Street address 1: 760 W Wallick Ln
Street address state: PA
Zip/Postal code: 17356-8859
Country: USA
Mailing address: 760 W Wallick Ln
Mailing city: Red Lion
Mailing state: PA
Mailing zip: 17356-8859
General Phone: (888) 295-3747
General Fax: (717) 244-6529
Email: info@igsknives.com
Primary Website: www.igsknives.com
Year Established: 1992
Product/Services: Web Press - Special Equipment
Personnel: Katie Howard (Corporate Sec)

RENSSELAER

VISION DATA EQUIPMENT CORP.

Street address 1: 1377 3rd St
Street address state: NY
Zip/Postal code: 12144-1815
Country: USA
Mailing address: 1377 3rd St
Mailing city: Rensselaer
Mailing state: NY
Mailing zip: 12144-1899
General Phone: (518) 434-2193
General Fax: (518) 434-3457
Email: sales@vdata.com
Primary Website: www.vdata.com
Year Established: 1973
Product/Services: Print & Digital Media Software: Total Advertising & sales management for print & web pubs. (Includes CRM, Sales, A/R/Accounting, VisionWeb customer ad entry); Software: Total Circulation Management for print & web pubs; Software: Electronic Data Interchange; Software: Pagination/Layout; Software: Ad tracking, production management; Software: Remote Workflow Management.
Personnel: Dempsey Tom (President)
Personnel: Timothy Donnelly (Sales Mgr)
Personnel: Amy Weaver (Southwest U.S. Sales manager)

RICHFIELD

SNAP-ON BUSINESS SOLUTIONS

Street address 1: 3900 Kinross Lakes Pkwy
Street address state: OH
Zip/Postal code: 44286-9381
Country: USA
Mailing address: 4025 Kinross Lakes Pkwy
Mailing city: Richfield
Mailing state: OH
Mailing zip: 44286-9371
General Phone: (330) 659-1600
General Fax: (330) 659-1601
Email: info@snaponbusinesssolutions.com
Primary Website: www.snaponbusinesssolutions.com
Product/Services: Computers: Storage Devices; Developing and Processing
Personnel: Mary Beth Siddons (Pres.)

RICHMOND

CATALYST PAPER CORP.

Street address 1: 3600 Lysander Ln. 2nd Fl.
Street address state: BC
Zip/Postal code: V7B 1C3
Country: Canada
Mailing address: 3600 Lysander Ln., 2nd Fl.
Mailing city: Richmond
Mailing state: BC
Mailing zip: V7B 1C3
General Phone: (604) 247-4400
General Fax: (604) 247-0512
Email: contactus@catalystpaper.com
Primary Website: www.catalystpaper.com
Year Established: 1950
Product/Services: Manufacturing
Note: Pulp and paper manufacturing
Personnel: Jim Bayles (Vice-President and General Manager Newsprint and International)

SUPPORT SYSTEMS INTERNATIONAL CORP.

Street address 1: 136 S 2nd St
Street address 2: Fiber Optic Cable Shop
Street address state: CA
Zip/Postal code: 94804-2110
Country: USA
Mailing address: 136 S 2nd St
Mailing city: Richmond
Mailing state: CA
Mailing zip: 94804-2110
General Phone: (510) 234-9090
General Fax: (510) 233-8888
Email: sales@FiberMailbox.com
Primary Website: www.FiberOpticCableShop.com
Year Established: 1976
Product/Services: fiber optic cable assembly manufacturing; fiber optic related products.
Personnel: Ben Parsons (Pres.)

RICHMOND HILL

GRAPHIC ROLL COVERINGS

Street address 1: 300B Newkirk Road
Street address state: ON
Zip/Postal code: L4C 3G7
Country: Canada
Mailing address: 300-B, Newkirk Road
Mailing city: Richmond Hill
Mailing state: ON
Mailing zip: L4C 3G7
General Phone: (905) 475-2357
General Fax: (905) 475-3421
Email: info@graphicroller.com
Primary Website: www.graphicroller.com
Year Established: 1972
Product/Services: Ink Rollers; Rollers; Dampening; Rollers; UV; Nylon Roller Coating; Chrome Roller Coating; Split Nip Folder Rolls; Infeed Nip Rolls; Grater Wrap-Roller Covering; Ink Fountains & Accessories; Press Accessories, Parts & Supplies; Roller Grinding Services;
Personnel: Brian Venis (Pres.)

RIO RANCHO

MASTHEAD INTERNATIONAL, INC.

Street address 1: 700 Quantum Rd NE
Street address state: NM
Zip/Postal code: 87124-4500
Country: USA
Mailing address: 700 Quantum Rd NE
Mailing city: Rio Rancho
Mailing state: NM
Mailing zip: 87124-4500
General Phone: 505-890-7103
General Fax: 505-890-7104
Email: info@masthead.net
Primary Website: www.masthead.net
Personnel: Joel Birket (Proj. Mgr./Estimator)

RIVER FALLS

NELA

Street address 1: 610 Whitetail Blvd
Street address state: WI
Zip/Postal code: 54022-5209
Country: USA
Mailing address: 610 Whitetail Blvd
Mailing city: River Falls
Mailing state: WI
Mailing zip: 54022-5209
General Phone: (715) 425-1900

Equipment, Supplies and Services

General Fax: (751) 425-1901
Email: info@nela-usa.com
Primary Website: www.nela-usa.com
Year Established: 2000
Product/Services: Color Registration; Controls: Register; Offset Plate-Making Service & Equipment; Pin Register Systems; Plate Bending Systems; Plate Mounting & Register Systems; Press Accessories, Parts & Supplies; Punching Equipment; Web Press - Special Equipment;
Personnel: David Klein (Pres.)
Personnel: Bob Deis (Mgr., Engineering)
Personnel: Taag Erickson (Pdct. Mgr., Web & Sheetfed)
Jurgen Gruber (Sales Dir.)
Katharina Gruber (Mktg. Mgr.)

ROANOKE

CAPCO MACHINERY SYSTEMS, INC.

Street address 1: 307 Eastpark Dr
Street address state: VA
Zip/Postal code: 24019-8227
Country: USA
Mailing address: PO Box 11945
Mailing city: Roanoke
Mailing state: VA
Mailing zip: 24022-1945
General Phone: (540) 977-0404
General Fax: (540) 977-2781
Primary Website: www.capcomachinery.com
Year Established: 1940
Product/Services: Roller Grinders
Personnel: Edward E. West (Pres.)
Personnel: Amy S. West (Vice Pres., Finance)

ROCHESTER

EASTMAN KODAK CO.

Street address 1: 343 State St
Street address state: NY
Zip/Postal code: 14650-0001
Country: USA
Mailing address: 343 State St
Mailing city: Rochester
Mailing state: NY
Mailing zip: 14650-0002
General Phone: (800) 698-3324
General Fax: (585) 724-1089
Primary Website: www.kodak.com
Year Established: 1888
Product/Services: Cameras & Accessories; Film & Paper: Contact; Film & Paper: Filters (Photographic); Film & Paper: Phototypesetting; Microfilming; Offset Plate-Making Service & Equipment; Photo Proofing Papers; Plate Processors; Plates: Offset (Conventional); Processors: Film & Paper;
Personnel: Jeffrey J. Clarke (CEO)
Personnel: David Bullwinkle (Pres./COO)
Personnel: Christopher Payne (Vice Pres.)

MERCER, LLC

Street address 1: 70 Linden Oaks
Street address 2: Ste 310
Street address state: NY
Zip/Postal code: 14625-2804
Country: USA
Mailing address: 70 Linden Oaks
Mailing city: Rochester
Mailing state: NY
Mailing zip: 14625-2804
General Phone: (585) 389-8700
General Fax: (585) 389-8801
Primary Website: www.mercer.com
Year Established: 1937
Product/Services: Human Resources Consulting;
Personnel: Micaela McPadden (Press Contact)
Personnel: Julio Portalatin (Pres. & CEO)
Personnel: RenÃ© Beaudoin (COO)
Jackie Marks (CFO)

ROCHESTER INSTITUTE OF TECHNOLOGY

Street address 1: 69 Lomb Memorial Dr
Street address state: NY
Zip/Postal code: 14623-5602
Country: USA
Mailing address: 69 Lomb Memorial Dr
Mailing city: Rochester
Mailing state: NY
Mailing zip: 14623-5602
General Phone: (585) 475-2728
General Fax: (585) 475-7029
Email: spmofc@rit.edu
Primary Website: www.rit.edu
Year Established: 1829
Product/Services: Abrasives; Cameras & Accessories; Consulting Services: Computer; Consulting Services: Equipment; Consulting Services: Production;
Personnel: Patricia Sores (Admin. Chair)

ROCHESTER HILLS

FANUC ROBOTICS AMERICA, INC.

Street address 1: 3900 W Hamlin Rd
Street address state: MI
Zip/Postal code: 48309-3253
Country: USA
Mailing address: 3900 W Hamlin Rd
Mailing city: Rochester Hills
Mailing state: MI
Mailing zip: 48309-3253
General Phone: 888-326-8287
General Fax: 847-898-5001
Email: marketing@fanucrobotics.com
Primary Website: www.fanucrobotics.com
Year Established: 1982
Product/Services: Conveyors; Material Handling Equipment: Palletizing Machines; Newsprint Handling Equipment; Paper Handling Equipment; Roll Handling Equipment;
Personnel: Cathy Powell (Sr. Mktg. Analyst)

ROCKCLIFFE

IMAPRO CORP.

Street address 1: 85 Pond St
Street address state: ON
Zip/Postal code: K1L 8J1
Country: Canada
Mailing address: 400 St. Laurent Blvd
Mailing city: Ottawa
Mailing state: ON
Mailing zip: K1G 6C4
General Phone: (613) 738-3000
General Fax: (613) 738-5038
Email: sales@imapro.com
Primary Website: www.imapro.com
Year Established: 1976
Product/Services: Computers: Hardware & Software Integrators; Computers: Local Area Network (LANS); Disk Drive Sales/Repair; Dryers: Film and Papers; Software: Pagination/Layout;
Personnel: Fred Andreone (Pres.)

ROCKFORD

A-AMERICAN MACHINE & ASSEMBLY (PRESS PARTS DIV.)

Street address 1: 2620 Auburn St
Street address state: IL
Zip/Postal code: 61101-4222
Country: USA
Mailing address: 2620 Auburn St
Mailing city: Rockford
Mailing state: IL
Mailing zip: 61101-4222
General Phone: (815) 965-0884
General Fax: (815) 965-1049
Email: sales@a-americanpressparts.com
Primary Website: www.a-americanpressparts.com
Year Established: 1986
Product/Services: Complete line of repair / replacement parts for printing presses, folders and RTP's Large inventories of mechanical consumable parts including, Knives, Slitters, Knife Box Components, Nip (Gain) Rings, Folding Blades, spindles, gears and much, much more. Also stocking many pneumatic and electrical components. In house manufacturing allows for shortened lead time and the quality you expect.
Personnel: Mark Keller (Pres.)
Personnel: Tom Sweeney (Vice Pres., Opns.)

MARTIN AUTOMATIC, INC.

Street address 1: 1661 Northrock Ct
Street address state: IL
Zip/Postal code: 61103-1202
Country: USA
Mailing address: 1661 Northrock Ct
Mailing city: Rockford
Mailing state: IL
Mailing zip: 61103-1296
General Phone: (815) 654-4800
General Fax: (815) 654-4810
Email: info@martinauto.com
Primary Website: www.martinauto.com
Year Established: 1968
Product/Services: Conversion Equipment; Flying Pasters; Newsprint Handling Equipment; Pasters; Press Accessories, Parts & Supplies; Rewinders; Web Guides;
Personnel: David A. Wright (Vice Pres., Sales)
Personnel: Bob Sanderson (Contract Admin.)
Personnel: Tim Delhotal (Contract Admin.)
Tim Ward (Mktg. Mgr.)

ROCKVILLE

EXTRATEC CORP.

Street address 1: 5930 Muncaster Mill Rd
Street address state: MD
Zip/Postal code: 20855-1734
Country: USA
Mailing address: 5930 Muncaster Mill Rd
Mailing city: Rockville
Mailing state: MD
Mailing zip: 20855-1734
General Phone: (301) 924-5150
General Fax: (301) 924-5151
Email: sales@extratek.com
Year Established: 1979
Product/Services: Environmental Control Systems
Personnel: Regis E. Finn (Pres.)

MEDIA CYBERNETICS LP

Street address 1: 401 N Washington St
Street address 2: Ste 350
Street address state: MD
Zip/Postal code: 20850-0707
Country: USA
Mailing address: 401 N Washington St Ste 350
Mailing city: Rockville
Mailing state: MD
Mailing zip: 20850-0707
General Phone: (301) 495-3305
General Fax: 240-328-6193
Email: info@mediacy.com
Primary Website: www.mediacy.com
Year Established: 1981
Product/Services: Optical Character Recognition (OCR)
Personnel: Doug Paxson (Pres.)

SUPERIOR LITHOPLATE OF INDIANA, INC.

Street address 1: Strawberry Rd
Street address state: IN
Zip/Postal code: 47872
Country: USA
Mailing address: PO Box 192
Mailing city: Rockville
Mailing state: IN
Mailing zip: 47872-0192
General Phone: (765) 569-2094
General Fax: (765) 569-2096
Primary Website: www.superiorlithoplate.com
Year Established: 1984
Product/Services: Chemicals: Plate Processing;
Chemicals: Pressroom; Offset Chemicals & Supplies; Plate Cleaners; Platemakers: Offset (Conventional);
Personnel: Robert T. Blane (Pres.)
Personnel: Steven C. Blane (Vice Pres.)
Personnel: Miriam Blane (Office Mgr.)
Thomas J. Casson (Nat'l Sales Mgr.)

ROCKWALL

GRAPHICS MICROSYSTEMS, INC.

Street address 1: 1655 Science Pl
Street address state: TX
Zip/Postal code: 75032-6202
Country: USA
Mailing address: 1655 Science Pl
Mailing city: Rockwall
Mailing state: TX
Mailing zip: 75032-6202
General Phone: (972) 290-3120
General Fax: (972) 722-1128
Email: avt@avt-inc.com
Primary Website: www.avt-inc.com
Year Established: 1983
Product/Services: Color Registration; Controls: Register; Densitometers; Ink Controls, Computerized; Press Control Systems;
Personnel: Bill Fleck (Southern Regional Sales Mgr.)

ROCKY RIVER

VER-A-FAST CORPORATION

Street address 1: 20545 Center Ridge Rd
Street address 2: Ste 300
Street address state: OH
Zip/Postal code: 44116-3423
Country: USA
Mailing address: 20545 Center Ridge Rd Ste 300
Mailing city: Rocky River
Mailing state: OH
Mailing zip: 44116-3423
General Phone: (800) 327-8463
Email: info@verafast.com
Primary Website: www.verafast.com
Year Established: 1976
Product/Services: Consulting Services: Circulation; Market Research; Research Studies; Telecommunications; Complete Data Services; Sunday Select; Complete Telemarketing Services Outbound
Personnel: Robert Bensman (President)
Personnel: Cathy Soprano (Exec. Vice Pres.)
Personnel: James Tanner (Mktg./Research Specialist)

ROLLING MEADOWS

KOMORI AMERICA CORP.

Street address 1: 5520 Meadowbrook Industrial Ct
Street address state: IL
Zip/Postal code: 60008-3800
Country: USA
Mailing address: 5520 Meadowbrook Industrial Ct
Mailing city: Rolling Meadows
Mailing state: IL
Mailing zip: 60008-3898
General Phone: 847-806-9000
Email: contact@komori-america.us
Primary Website: www.komori-america.us
Year Established: 1983
Product/Services: Presses: Offset; Proofing Systems;
Personnel: Kosh Miyao (Pres./COO, Komori America Cor.)
Personnel: Angelo Possemato (Director of National Accounts)
Personnel: Susan Baines (Director of Marketing)
Clark Scherer (District Sales Manager)

SCREEN (USA)

Street address 1: 5110 Tollview Dr
Street address state: IL

Equipment, Supplies and Services

Zip/Postal code: 60008-3715
Country: USA
Mailing address: 5110 Tollview Dr
Mailing city: Rolling Meadows
Mailing state: IL
Mailing zip: 60008-3715
General Phone: (847) 870-7400
General Fax: (847) 870-0149
Email: rsiwicki@screenusa.com
Primary Website: www.screenusa.com
Year Established: 1943
Product/Services: Color Proofing; Color Seperation Scanners; Imagesetters; Proofing Systems; Raster Image Processors; Software: Pagination/Layout; Tables (Dot, Etch, Opaquing, Register, Retouching, Stripping);
Personnel: Mike Fox (Pres)
Personnel: Robert Bernstein (CFO)
Personnel: Richard Siwicki (Application Support Mgr.)
Edvardo Navarro (Opns. Mgr.)

SPARTANICS

Street address 1: 3605 Edison Pl
Street address state: IL
Zip/Postal code: 60008-1012
Country: USA
Mailing address: 3605 Edison Pl
Mailing city: Rolling Meadows
Mailing state: IL
Mailing zip: 60008-1077
General Phone: (847) 394-5700
General Fax: (847) 394-0409
Email: sales@spartanico.com
Primary Website: www.spartanics.com
Year Established: 1963
Product/Services: Laser Cutting Machines, Die Cutting Machines, Screen Printing Lanes, Plastic Card Counting, Plastic Card Inspection, Registration Shears
Personnel: Mike Bacon (VP., Sales/Mktg.)

ROME

XYONICZ

Street address 1: 6754 Martin St
Street address state: NY
Zip/Postal code: 13440-7119
Country: USA
Mailing address: 6754 Martin St
Mailing city: Rome
Mailing state: NY
Mailing zip: 13440-7119
General Phone: (315) 334-4214
General Fax: (315) 336-3177
Year Established: 1994
Product/Services: Equipment Dealers (New); Feeding, Folding, Delivery Equipment; Mailroom Systems & Equipment; Material Handling Equipment: Truck Loaders; Newsprint Handling Equipment;
Personnel: Ed Zionc (Pres./Mgr., Mktg.)

ROMEOVILLE

CENTRAL GRAPHICS

Street address 1: 1302 Enterprise Dr
Street address state: IL
Zip/Postal code: 60446-1016
Country: USA
Mailing address: 1302 Enterprise Dr
Mailing city: Romeoville
Mailing state: IL
Mailing zip: 60446-1016
General Phone: (630) 759-1696
General Fax: (630) 759-1792
Email: cgi@cgipressparts.com
Primary Website: www.cgipressparts.com
Year Established: 1984
Product/Services: Belts, Belting, V-Belts; Copper Plating Drums; Cylinder Repair; Equipment Dealers (Used); Folder Knives; Pin Register Systems; Press Accessories, Parts & Supplies; Presses: Offset; Roller Grinding Services; Rollers: Dampening;
Personnel: Jim Crivellone (Pres.)
Personnel: Pat Murphy (Sales/Opns. Mgr.)

ROSELLE

NOVUS IMAGING, INC.

Street address 1: 440 Medinah Rd.
Street address state: IL
Zip/Postal code: 60172
Country: USA
Mailing address: 440 Medinah Rd.
Mailing city: Roselle
Mailing state: IL
Mailing zip: 60172
General Phone: 630-858-6101
Email: info@mrprint.com
Primary Website: www.mrprint.com
Year Established: 1948
Product/Services: Cameras & Accessories; Color Printing Frames; Controls: Exposure; Dark Room Equipment; Diffusion Transfer Processors; Offset Plate-Making Service & Equipment; Plate Exposure Units; Platemakers: Offset (Conventional); Processors: Diffusion Transfer; Proofing Systems;

ROSELLE

PAMARCO GLOBAL GRAPHICS

Street address 1: 235 E 11th Ave
Street address state: NJ
Zip/Postal code: 07203-2015
Country: USA
Mailing address: 235 E 11th Ave
Mailing city: Roselle
Mailing state: NJ
Mailing zip: 07203-2015
General Phone: (908) 241-1200
General Fax: (908) 241-4009
Primary Website: www.pamarcoglobal.com
Year Established: 1944
Product/Services: Rollers
Personnel: Terry Ford (Pres./CEO)

ROSEMOUNT

CANNON EQUIPMENT

Street address 1: 15100 Business Pkwy
Street address state: MN
Zip/Postal code: 55068-1793
Country: USA
Mailing address: 324 Washington St W
Mailing city: Cannon Falls
Mailing state: MN
Mailing zip: 55009-1142
General Phone: (800) 533-2071
General Fax: (651) 322-1583
Email: info@cannonequipment.com
Primary Website: www.cannonequipment.com
Year Established: 1973
Product/Services: Cart Distribution Systems; Circulation Equipment & Supplies; Conveyors; Mailroom Systems & Equipment;
Personnel: Chuck Gruber (Pres.)
Personnel: Pat Geraghty (Nat'l Sales Mgr./ Newspaper Handling Systems)

SAINT JOSEPH

BROWN MANNSCHRECK BUSINESS SYSTEM

Street address 1: 5901 NE Woodbine Rd
Street address state: MO
Zip/Postal code: 64505-9353
Country: USA
Mailing address: 5901 NE Woodbine Rd
Mailing city: Saint Joseph
Mailing state: MO
Mailing zip: 64505-9353
General Phone: 816-387-8180
General Fax: 816-364-7925
Email: customerservice@browncompanies.net
Primary Website: www.browncompanies.net
Year Established: 1867
Product/Services: Sales and design Office Furniture
Personnel: Steven Pitluck (CEO)

Personnel: Craig Greer (Vice Pres.)
Personnel: Cathie Wayman (Vice Pres., Sales)

ROSBACK CO.

Street address 1: 125 Hawthorne Ave
Street address state: MI
Zip/Postal code: 49085-2636
Country: USA
Mailing address: 125 Hawthorne Ave
Mailing city: Saint Joseph
Mailing state: MI
Mailing zip: 49085-2636
General Phone: (269) 983-2582
General Fax: (269) 983-2516
Email: Sales@RosbackCompany.com
Primary Website: www.rosbackcompany.com
Year Established: 1881
Product/Services: Adhesives; Collating Equipment; Equipment Dealers (New); Folding Machines;
Personnel: Larry R. Bowman (Pres.)
Personnel: Ron F. Bowman (Vice Pres., Sales/Mktg.)

SAINT LOUIS

FKI LOGISTEX

Street address 1: 9301 Olive Blvd
Street address state: MO
Zip/Postal code: 63132-3207
Country: USA
Mailing address: 9301 Olive Blvd
Mailing city: Saint Louis
Mailing state: MO
Mailing zip: 63132-3207
General Phone: (314) 993-4700
General Fax: (314) 995-2400
Primary Website: www.fkilogistex.com
Product/Services: Material Handling Equipment: Palletizing Machines; Remanufactures Equipment

GATEWAY JOURNALISM REVIEW

Street address 1: 8380 Olive Blvd
Street address state: MO
Zip/Postal code: 63132-2814
Country: USA
Mailing address: PO Box 12474
Mailing city: Saint Louis
Mailing state: MO
Mailing zip: 63132-0174
General Phone: (314) 991-1699
General Fax: (314) 963-6104
Email: gatewayjr@siu.edu
Primary Website: www.gatewayjr.org
Year Established: 1970
Product/Services: Consulting Services: Editorial
Personnel: Bill Freivogel (Pub.)
Personnel: Jackie Spinner (Ed.)

LINCOLN INDUSTRIAL

Street address 1: 5148 N. Hanley Road
Street address state: MO
Zip/Postal code: 63134
Country: USA
Mailing address: 5148 N. Hanley Road
Mailing city: Saint Louis
Mailing state: MO
Mailing zip: 63134
General Phone: (314) 679-4200
General Fax: (314) 679-4359
Primary Website: www.lincolnindustrial.com
Year Established: 1910
Product/Services: Lubricants; Pumps (Air, Ink, Vacuum);
Personnel: Bart Aitken (Pres.)

TALX CORP.

Street address 1: 11432 Lackland Rd
Street address state: MO
Zip/Postal code: 63146-3516
Country: USA
Mailing address: 11432 Lackland Rd
Mailing city: Saint Louis
Mailing state: MO
Mailing zip: 63146-3516
General Phone: (314) 214-7000
General Fax: (314) 214-7588

Email: moreinfo@talx.com
Primary Website: www.talx.com
Year Established: 1973
Product/Services: Speech Recognition
Product or Service: Telecommunications/ Service Bureaus
Personnel: William Canfield (CEO)
Personnel: Michael Smith (Vice Pres., Market Devel.)

WEATHERLINE, INC.

Street address 1: 12119 St Charles Rock Rd
Street address state: MO
Zip/Postal code: 63103
Country: USA
Mailing address: 12119 St. Charles Rock Rd.
Mailing city: Saint Louis
Mailing state: MO
Mailing zip: 63044
General Phone: (314) 291-1000
General Fax: (314) 291-3226
Email: info@weatherline.com
Primary Website: www.weatherline.com
Year Established: 1968
Product/Services: Consulting Services: Advertising; Consulting Services: Marketing; Promotion Services;
Personnel: Richard H. Friedman (Pres.)
Personnel: Michelle Parent (Exec. Vice Pres.)
Personnel: Nancy J. Friedman (Sr. Vice Pres.)
Martha Murphy (Sr. Vice Pres.)
Stephen L. Smith (Sr. Vice Pres.)

SAINT MICHAEL

TILT-LOCK

Street address 1: 12070 43rd St NE
Street address state: MN
Zip/Postal code: 55376-8427
Country: USA
Mailing address: 12070 43rd St NE
Mailing city: Saint Michael
Mailing state: MN
Mailing zip: 55376-8427
General Phone: (800) 999-8458
General Fax: (763) 497-7046
Email: sales@tiltlock.com
Primary Website: www.tiltlock.com
Year Established: 1963
Product/Services: Chemicals: Chuck (Paper Roll); Roll Handeling Equipment;
Personnel: Jerry Morton (Sales Mgr.)

SAINT PAUL

ERGOTRON, INC.

Street address 1: 1181 Trapp Rd
Street address state: MN
Zip/Postal code: 55121-1325
Country: USA
Mailing address: 1181 Trapp Rd Ste 100
Mailing city: Saint Paul
Mailing state: MN
Mailing zip: 55121-1266
General Phone: (651) 681-7600
General Fax: (651) 681-7715
Email: sales@ergotron.com
Primary Website: www.ergotron.com
Year Established: 1982
Product/Services: Cabinets; Computers: Local Area Network (LANS); Computers: Storage Devices; Consulting Services: Ergonomics;
Personnel: Pete Segar (Pres.)

PRINTWARE

Street address 1: 2935 Waters Rd
Street address 2: Ste 160
Street address state: MN
Zip/Postal code: 55121-1688
Country: USA
Mailing address: 2935 Waters Rd Ste 160
Mailing city: Saint Paul
Mailing state: MN
Mailing zip: 55121-1688
General Phone: (651) 456-1400
General Fax: (651) 454-3684
Email: sales@printwarellc.com
Primary Website: www.printwarellc.com

Equipment, Supplies and Services

Year Established: 1985
Product/Services: Offset Plate-Making Service & Equipment; Plate Processors; Platemakers: Offset (Conventional); Plates: Offset (Conventional);
Personnel: Stan Goldberg (Pres.)
Personnel: Tim Murphy (Vice Pres.-Sales/Mktg.)

SITMA USA, INC.

Street address 1: 45 Empire Dr
Street address state: MN
Zip/Postal code: 55103-1856
Country: USA
Mailing address: 45 Empire Dr
Mailing city: Saint Paul
Mailing state: MN
Mailing zip: 55103-1856
General Phone: (651) 222-2324
General Fax: (651) 222-4652
Email: sitma@sitma.com
Primary Website: www.sitma.com
Year Established: 1980
Product/Services: Automatic Plastic Bagging Equipment; Collating Equipment; Conveyors; Counting, Stacking, Bundling Machines; Feeding, Folding, Delivery Equipment; Folding Machines; Inserting Equipment (Includes Stuffing Machines); Mailroom Systems & Equipment; Remanufactures Equipment; Shrink Wrapping Equipment;
Personnel: Ann Butzer (Mktg. Mgr.)

WHITNEY WORLDWIDE, INC.

Street address 1: 553 Hayward Ave N
Street address 2: Ste 250
Street address state: MN
Zip/Postal code: 55128-9006
Country: USA
Mailing address: 553 Hayward Ave N Ste 250
Mailing city: Saint Paul
Mailing state: MN
Mailing zip: 55128-9006
General Phone: (800) 597-0227
General Fax: (651) 748-4000
Email: whitney@whitneyworld.com
Primary Website: www.whitneyworld.com
Year Established: 1983
Product/Services: Consulting Services: Circulation; Consulting Services: Marketing; Mailing List Compiler; Market Research; Newspaper Marketing;
Personnel: Les Layton (CEO)

SAINT-LAURENT

ELCORSY TECHNOLOGY, INC.

Street address 1: 4405 Poirier Blvd
Street address state: QC
Zip/Postal code: H4R 2A4
Country: Canada
Mailing address: 4405 Poirier Blvd.
Mailing city: Saint Laurent
Mailing state: QC
Mailing zip: H4R 2A4
General Phone: (888) 352-6779
General Fax: (514) 337-0042
Email: marketing@elcorsy.com
Primary Website: www.elcorsy.com
Year Established: 1981
Product/Services: Inks; Presses: DiLitho;
Personnel: Pierre Castegnier (Vice Pres., Mktg.)
Personnel: Robert Jollet (Sales Rep.)

SALEM

STANFORD PRODUCTS

Street address 1: 1139 S Broadway Ave
Street address state: IL
Zip/Postal code: 62881-2404
Country: USA
Mailing address: 1139 S Broadway Ave
Mailing city: Salem
Mailing state: IL
Mailing zip: 62881-2404
General Phone: (618) 548-2600
General Fax: (618) 548-6782
Primary Website: www.stanfordproductsllc.com
Year Established: 1940
Product/Services: Rewinders
Personnel: Deann Sager (Customer Serv. Mgr.)
Personnel: Tim Andrews (Sales Mgr.)
Personnel: Larry Boyles (Sales Mgr.)

SALINA

ARROW PRINTING CO.

Street address 1: 115 W Woodland Ave
Street address state: KS
Zip/Postal code: 67401-2935
Country: USA
Mailing address: PO Box 2898
Mailing city: Salina
Mailing state: KS
Mailing zip: 67402-2898
General Phone: (785) 825-8124
General Fax: (785) 825-0784
Email: arrow@arrowprintco.com
Primary Website: www.arrowprintco.com
Year Established: 1946
Product/Services: Consulting Services: Advertising; Offset Camera, Darkroom Equipment; Offset Plate Files; Photo Proofing Systems; Platemakers: Offset (Conventional); Plates: Offset (Conventional); Prepress Color Proofing Systems; Presses: Offset; Processors: Film & Paper; Scanners: Color B & W, Plates, Web
Personnel: Kent Fellers (Pres.)
Personnel: Dennis Suelter (Adv. Mgr.)

SALT LAKE CITY

DATAFEST TECHNOLOGIES, INC.

Street address 1: 5961 S Redwood Rd
Street address state: UT
Zip/Postal code: 84123-5261
Country: USA
Mailing address: 5961 S Redwood Rd
Mailing city: Salt Lake City
Mailing state: UT
Mailing zip: 84123-5261
General Phone: (801) 261-4608
Email: sales@datafest.com
Primary Website: www.datafest.com
Year Established: 1986
Product/Services: Software: Advertising (Includes Display; Classified); Software: Business (Includes Administration/Accounting);
Note: Datafest's AdSystem is an industry-leading ad management / CRM package designed for magazines and newspapers.
Personnel: Scott A. Clawson (Pres.)

FUJIFILM GRAPHIC SYSTEMS USA, INC.

Street address 1: 1795 Fremont Drive
Street address state: UT
Zip/Postal code: 84104
Mailing address: 1795 Fremont Drive
Mailing city: Salt Lake City
Mailing state: UT
Mailing zip: 84104
General Phone: (801) 975-1234
General Fax: (801) 972-3981
Product/Services: Blankets; Chemicals: Pressroom; Color Management Software; Imagesetters; Inks; Offset Chemicals & Supplies; Platemakers: Flexographic (Computer to Plate); Plates: Offset (Conventional); Proofing Systems; Software: Press/Post Press;
Personnel: Matt Miller (Regional Sales Manager)

SAN BERNARDINO

SYSTEMS TECHNOLOGY, INC.

Street address 1: 1351 Riverview Dr
Street address state: CA
Zip/Postal code: 92408-2945
Country: USA
Mailing address: 1351 E. Riverview Dr.
Mailing city: San Bernardino
Mailing state: CA
Mailing zip: 92408
General Phone: (909) 799-9950
General Fax: (909) 796-8297
Email: info@systems-technology-inc.com
Primary Website: www.systems-technology-inc.com
Year Established: 2000
Product/Services: Bundling and Tying Machines; Counting, Stacking, Compensating Stackers, Count-O-Veyors, Bundling Machines; Cutters & Trimmers; In-Line Trimming Systems; Material Handling Equipment: Palletizing Machines; Strapping Machines; Conveyors
Personnel: John St. John (Pres.)
Personnel: Brad Siegel (Sales. Dir.)

SAN DIEGO

OVERLAND STORAGE, INC.

Street address 1: 9112 Spectrum Center Blvd
Street address state: CA
Zip/Postal code: 92123-1439
Country: USA
Mailing address: 9112 Spectrum Center Blvd
Mailing city: San Diego
Mailing state: CA
Mailing zip: 92123-1599
General Phone: (858) 571-5555
General Fax: (858) 571-3664
Email: sales@overlandstorage.com
Primary Website: www.overlandstorage.com
Year Established: 1980
Product/Services: Computers: Storage Devices
Personnel: Eric Kelly (Pres)
Personnel: Veritta Wells (Vice Pres., HR)
Personnel: Mike Gawarecki (Vice Pres., Opns.)
Ravi Pendekanti (Vice Pres., Sales)

PALOS SOFTWARE

Street address 1: 520 Kearny Villa Way, Ste 108
Street address state: CA
Zip/Postal code: 92123
Country: USA
Mailing address: 520 Kearny Villa Way, Ste. 108
Mailing city: San Diego
Mailing state: CA
Mailing zip: 92123-1869
General Phone: (858) 836-4400
Email: marketing@palos.com
Primary Website: www.palos.com
Year Established: 1988
Product/Services: Software: Pagination/Layout
Personnel: David Altomare (Pres.)

SAN JOSE

ACER AMERICA

Street address 1: 333 W San Carlos St
Street address 2: Ste 1500
Street address state: CA
Zip/Postal code: 95110-2738
Country: USA
Mailing address: 333 W San Carlos St Ste 1500
Mailing city: San Jose
Mailing state: CA
Mailing zip: 95110-2738
General Phone: (408) 533-7700
General Fax: (408) 533-4555
Primary Website: www.acer.com
Year Established: 1976
Product/Services: Computers: Laptop & Portable
Personnel: George Huang (Chairman)
Personnel: Jason Chen (Chairman and CEO)

ADOBE SYSTEMS, INC.

Street address 1: 345 Park Ave
Street address state: CA
Zip/Postal code: 95110-2704
Country: USA
Mailing address: 345 Park Ave
Mailing city: San Jose
Mailing state: CA
Mailing zip: 95110-2704
General Phone: (408) 536-6000
General Fax: (408) 537-6000
Primary Website: www.adobe.com
Product or Service: Hardware/Software Supplier
Personnel: Ann Lewnes (Sr. Vice Pres., Global Mktg.)
Personnel: Jennifer Reynolds (Dir., Worldwide Adv.)

AIRSYSTEMS, INC.

Street address 1: 940 Remillard Ct.
Street address state: CA
Zip/Postal code: 95122
Country: USA
Mailing address: 940 Remillard Ct.
Mailing city: San Jose
Mailing state: CA
Mailing zip: 95122
General Phone: (408) 280-1666
General Fax: (408) 280-1020
Email: emcor_info@emcorgroup.com
Primary Website: www.airsystemsinc.com
Year Established: 1982
Product/Services: Inks; Controllers: Press
Personnel: Art Williams (Pres.)

TAPCLICKS

Street address 1: 3101 Tisch Way
Street address 2: Ste 1002
Street address state: CA
Zip/Postal code: 95128
Country: USA
Mailing address: 3101 Tisch Way, Suite 1002
Mailing city: San Jose
Mailing state: CA
Mailing zip: 95128-2533
General Phone: 408-725-2942
Email: sales@tapclicks.com
Primary Website: www.tapclicks.com
Year Established: 2009
Product/Services: Marketing Technology Big Data Marketing Analytics

SAN LUIS OBISPO

CYGNET STORAGE SOLUTIONS, INC.

Street address 1: 1880 Santa Barbara Ave
Street address 2: Ste 220
Street address state: CA
Zip/Postal code: 93401-4482
Country: USA
Mailing address: 1880 Santa Barbara Ave Ste 220
Mailing city: San Luis Obispo
Mailing state: CA
Mailing zip: 93401-4482
General Phone: 805-781-3580
General Fax: 805-781-3583
Email: waynea@cygnet.
Product/Services: Archiving Systems; Disk Drive Sales/Repair; Files, Storage; Library Retrieval Systems; Software: Asset Management; Storage Retrieval Systems;
Personnel: Wayne Augsburger (Vice Pres., Mktg.)

SANTA ANA

MARKZWARE SOFTWARE, INC.

Street address 1: 1805 E Dyer Rd
Street address 2: Ste 101
Street address state: CA
Zip/Postal code: 92705-5742
Country: USA
Mailing address: 1805 E Dyer Rd Ste 101
Mailing city: Santa Ana
Mailing state: CA
Mailing zip: 92705-5742
General Phone: (949) 756-5100
Email: info@markzware.com
Primary Website: www.markzware.com
Year Established: 1985
Product/Services: Software: Editorial; Software: Electronic Data Interchange;
Personnel: Patrick Marchese (Pres./CEO)

Personnel: Mary Gay Marchese (Public Relations)
Personnel: Patty Talley

OLEC

Street address 1: 1850 E Saint Andrew Pl
Street address state: CA
Zip/Postal code: 92705-5043
Country: USA
Mailing address: 1850 E Saint Andrew Pl
Mailing city: Santa Ana
Mailing state: CA
Mailing zip: 92705-5043
General Phone: (714) 881-2000
General Fax: (714) 881-2001
Email: sales@olec.com
Primary Website: www.olec.com
Product/Services: Produciton Control Systems
Personnel: Don Ohlig (Mng. Dir.)
Personnel: Al Mora (Sales Mgr.)
Personnel: Gordon Quinn (Vice Pres.,Electronics Sales)

SANTA FE

DIRKS, VAN ESSEN, MURRAY & APRIL

Street address 1: 119 E Marcy St
Street address 2: Ste 100
Street address state: NM
Zip/Postal code: 87501-2092
Country: USA
Mailing address: 119 E Marcy St Ste 100
Mailing city: Santa Fe
Mailing state: NM
Mailing zip: 87501-2092
General Phone: (505) 820-2700
General Fax: (505) 820-2900
Primary Website: www.dirksvanessen.com
Year Established: 1980
Product/Services: Brokers & Appraisers; Consulting Services: Financial;
Personnel: Owen D. Van Essen (Pres.)
Personnel: Philip W. Murray (Exec. Vice Pres.)
Personnel: Sara April (Vice Pres.)
Holly Myers (Analyst)

LYON ENTERPRISES

Street address 1: 4305 Cloud Dance
Street address state: NM
Zip/Postal code: 87507-2591
Country: USA
Mailing address: 4305 Cloud Dance
Mailing city: Santa Fe
Mailing state: NM
Mailing zip: 87507
General Phone: (800) 243-1144
General Fax: (505) 471-1665
Email: ray@lyonenterprises.com
Primary Website: www.lyonenterprises.com
Year Established: 1992
Product/Services: Circulation Equipment & Supplies; Tubes, Racks (Includes Racks: Motor Route Tubes); Carrier Bags; Point of Purchase; Imprinted Merchandise
Personnel: Ray Lyon (Pres.)

SAUSALITO

CHANNELNET

Street address 1: 3 Harbor Dr
Street address 2: Ste 206
Street address state: CA
Zip/Postal code: 94965-1491
Country: USA
Mailing address: 3 Harbor Dr Ste 206
Mailing city: Sausalito
Mailing state: CA
Mailing zip: 94965-1491
General Phone: (415) 332-4704
General Fax: (415) 332-1635
Email: info@channelnet.com
Primary Website: www.softad.com; www.channelnet.com
Product/Services: Consulting Services;

Advertising; Software: Advertising (Includes Display; Classified);
Product or Service: Consultants`Hardware/Software Supplier
Personnel: Paula George Tompkins (Founder/CEO)
Personnel: Kevin Kelly (CFO)
Personnel: Mike Behr (Sr. Dir., Professional Servs.)

SAVANNAH

PHELPS, CUTLER & ASSOCIATES

Street address 1: 35 Barnard St
Street address 2: Ste 300
Street address state: GA
Zip/Postal code: 31401-2515
Country: USA
Mailing address: 35 Barnard St Ste 300
Mailing city: Savannah
Mailing state: GA
Mailing zip: 31401
General Phone: (912) 388-4692
General Fax: (678) 826-4708
Email: sales@coastalempirenews.com
Primary Website: www.phelpscutler.com
Year Established: 1991
Product/Services: M&A Broker; Expert Witness on Valuation; General Operational Consulting: Print and Digital Revenue Strategies; Niche (print and digital websites) specialist; Circulation Consulting Services: Editorial; Consulting Services: Financial; Consulting Services: Human Resources; Consulting Services: Marketing;
Note: PC&A is a diverse media consulting and Mergers & Acquisition firm. Proven core competencies in new revenue strategies for print and digital. Turnaround specialist. Recent clients include some of the largest media companies in the U.S. Qualified Expert Witness in Valuation. Owner of Coastal Empire News, Savannah, GA. with eight online-only news and content sites. www.CoastalEmpireNews.com.
Personnel: Louise Phelps (Managing Partner)

PLUMTREE CO.

Street address 1: PO Box 14216
Street address state: GA
Zip/Postal code: 31416-1216
Country: USA
Mailing address: PO Box 14216
Mailing city: Savannah
Mailing state: GA
Mailing zip: 31416-1216
General Phone: (912) 354-5155
General Fax: (912) 354-1375
Email: email@plumtreecompany.com
Primary Website: www.plumtreecompany.com
Year Established: 1985
Product/Services: Consulting Services: Production; Mailroom Systems & Equipment; Newspaper Couter; Newspaper Marketing; Newsprint Handling Equipment; Promotion Services; Software: Press/Post Press; Software: Workflow Management/Tracking; Totalizing Systems;
Personnel: Tim Cooper (Pres.)
Personnel: Julian Cooper (Vice Pres., Sales)

SAYVILLE

BRAINWORKS SOFTWARE

Street address 1: 100 South Main Street
Street address state: NY
Zip/Postal code: 11782
Mailing address: 100 South Main Street
Mailing city: Sayville
Mailing state: NY
Mailing zip: 11782
General Phone: (631) 563-5000
General Fax: (631) 563-6320
Email: info@brainworks.com
Primary Website: www.brainworks.com
Year Established: 1996
Product/Services: Software: Asset Management; Software: Workflow Management/Tracking; Training: Design

& Layout; Training: Keyboard Operation; Training: Pre Press;
Note: We design, develop and deploy advertising solutions to the newspaper industry. With over 350 customers, we make your current and future workflows more efficient.
Personnel: Rick Sanders (President and CEO)

BRAINWORKS SOFTWARE DEVELOPMENT CORP.

Street address 1: 100 S Main St
Street address state: NY
Zip/Postal code: 11782-3100
Country: USA
Mailing address: 100 S Main St Ste 102
Mailing city: Sayville
Mailing state: NY
Mailing zip: 11782-3148
General Phone: (631) 563-5000
General Fax: (631) 563-6320
Email: info@brainworks.com
Primary Website: www.brainworks.com
Year Established: 1988
Product/Services: Pagination Systems; Software: Advertising (Includes Display; Classified, Preprints and Digital); Software: Business (Includes Administration/Accounting); Software: Design/Graphics; Software: Pagination/Layout; System Integration Services; Software: Circulation Software; Digital Subscriptions, CRM; Digital Advertising; Software: Customer Relationship Management (CRM); iPad Application
Note: Brainworks is the leading provider of Advertising, CRM, Circulation, Production and Web solutions for the Newspaper Media industry.
Personnel: John Barry (President)
Personnel: Rick Sanders (Director of Sales)
Personnel: Frank Collinsworth (Business Development Manager)
Matt Griffith (Business Development Manager)

SCHAUMBURG

AEC, INC.

Street address 1: 1100 E Woodfield Rd
Street address 2: Ste 588
Street address state: IL
Zip/Postal code: 60173-5135
Country: USA
Mailing address: 1100 E Woodfield Rd Ste 550
Mailing city: Schaumburg
Mailing state: IL
Mailing zip: 60173-5135
General Phone: (847) 273-7700
General Fax: (847) 273-7804
Email: dazzarello@corpemail.com
Primary Website: www.aecinternet.com
Year Established: 1964
Product/Services: Architects/Engineers (Includes Design/Construction Firms); Press Accessories, Parts & Supplies
Personnel: Tom Breslin (Pres.)

INX INTERNATIONAL INK CO.

Street address 1: 150 N Martingale Rd
Street address 2: Ste 700
Street address state: IL
Zip/Postal code: 60173-2009
Country: USA
Mailing address: 150 N Martingale Rd Ste 700
Mailing city: Schaumburg
Mailing state: IL
Mailing zip: 60173-2009
General Phone: (630) 682-1800
General Fax: (847) 969-9758
Email: general@inxinternational.com; info@inxintl.com
Primary Website: www.inxinternational.com
Year Established: 1990
Product/Services: Chemicals: Pressroom; Cleaners & Solvents; Consulting Services: Marketing; Ink Bleeding Equipment; Ink Fountains & Accessories; Ink Pumping Systems; Ink Storage Tanks; Inks;
Personnel: M. Matsuzawa (Chrmn.)

Personnel: Richard Clendenning (Pres./CEO)
Personnel: Joe Cichon (Sr. Vice Pres., Product/Mfg. Technology)
John Carlson (Sr. Vice Pres.-Gen. Affairs/Admin.)
Charles Weinholzer (Sr. Vice Pres.-Liquid Div.)
Kenneth O'Callaghan (Sr. Vice Pres.-Metal Div.)
George Polasik (Sr. Vice Pres.-Offset Div./COO)
Betty Leavitt (Dir., PR)

NB FINISHING, INC.

Street address 1: 1075 Morse Ave
Street address state: IL
Zip/Postal code: 60193-4503
Country: USA
Mailing address: 1075 Morse Ave
Mailing city: Schaumburg
Mailing state: IL
Mailing zip: 60193-4503
General Phone: (847) 895-0900
General Fax: (847) 895-0999
Email: info@nbfinishing.com
Primary Website: www.nbfinishing.com
Year Established: 1983
Product/Services: Plate Processors; Roller Grinding Services;
Personnel: Bruce Nichols (Pres.)
Personnel: Dave Nichols (Mgr., Opns.)

SAKURAI USA

Street address 1: 1700 Basswood Rd
Street address state: IL
Zip/Postal code: 60173-5318
Country: USA
Mailing address: 1700 Basswood Rd
Mailing city: Schaumburg
Mailing state: IL
Mailing zip: 60173-5318
General Phone: (847) 490-9400
General Fax: (847) 490-4200
Email: sales@sakurai.com; info@sakurai.com; inquiry@sakurai.com
Primary Website: www.sakurai.com
Year Established: 1928
Product/Services: Presses: Offset
Personnel: Don Bence (Vice Pres., Sales)

USSPI MEDIA

Street address 1: 424 E State Pkwy
Street address 2: Ste 228
Street address state: IL
Zip/Postal code: 60173-6406
Country: USA
Mailing address: 424 E. State Pkwy., Ste. 228
Mailing city: Schaumburg
Mailing state: IL
Mailing zip: 60173
General Phone: (847) 490-6000
General Fax: (847) 843-9058
Email: info@usspi.com
Primary Website: www.usspi.com
Year Established: 1989
Product/Services: Newspaper, email, digital solutions.
Personnel: Phil Miller (CEO)
Personnel: Rick Baranski (VP Media Relations)
Personnel: Michelle Hammons (Executive VP)
Barbara Ancona (VP Sales)

SCHILLER PARK

ARPAC GROUP

Street address 1: 9511 River St
Street address state: IL
Zip/Postal code: 60176-1019
Country: USA
Mailing address: 9511 River St
Mailing city: Schiller Park
Mailing state: IL
Mailing zip: 60176-1019
General Phone: (847) 678-9034
General Fax: (847) 671-7006
Email: info@arpacgroup.com
Primary Website: www.arpacgroup.com
Year Established: 1971
Product/Services: Bundling and Tying Machines; Conveyors; Shrink Wrapping Equipment
Personnel: Michael Levy (Pres.)

Equipment, Supplies and Services

WESTERN PRINTING MACHINERY

Street address 1: 9228 Ivanhoe St
Street address state: IL
Zip/Postal code: 60176-2305
Country: USA
Mailing address: 9228 Ivanhoe St
Mailing city: Schiller Park
Mailing state: IL
Mailing zip: 60176-2348
General Phone: (847) 678-1740
General Fax: (847) 678-6176
Email: Info@wpm.com
Primary Website: www.wpm.com
Year Established: 1933
Product/Services: Counting, Stacking, Bundling Machines; Cutters & Trimmers; Dies (Perforating and Slitting); Web Press - Special Equipment;

SCHONBERG

ELAPLAN BUCHHOLZ GMBH & CO.

Street address 1: D-24217
Country: Germany
Mailing address: D-24217
Mailing city: Schonberg
General Phone: +49 4344 309 158
General Fax: +49 4344 309 172
Email: info@uniton.de
Primary Website: www.elaplan.de
Product/Services: Facsimilie/Fax Transmission Systems; Press Control Systems;
Personnel: Hans-Herbert Buchholz (Mng. Dir.)

SEATTLE

CATALYST PAPER (USA), INC.

Street address 1: 2200 6th Ave
Street address 2: Ste 800
Street address state: WA
Zip/Postal code: 98121-1827
Country: USA
Mailing address: 2200 6th Avenue, Suite 800
Mailing city: Seattle
Mailing state: WA
Mailing zip: 98121-2312
General Phone: (206) 838-2070
General Fax: (206) 838-2071
Primary Website: www.catalystpaper.com
Year Established: 1993
Product/Services: Newsprint; Paper: Coated Groundwood Offset; Paper: Groundwood Specialties; Paper: Specialty Printing Paper;
Personnel: James Hardt (Sales Director)
Personnel: Mark Petersen (VP International Sales)
Personnel: Sean Curran (SVP Sales & Marketing)

SHELDON

CREATIVE HOUSE PRINT MEDIA CONSULTANTS

Street address 1: 227 9th St
Street address state: IA
Zip/Postal code: 51201-1419
Country: USA
Mailing address: PO Box 160
Mailing city: Sheldon
Mailing state: IA
Mailing zip: 51201-0160
General Phone: (712) 324-5347
General Fax: (712) 324-2345
Email: pww@iowainformation.com
Year Established: 1962
Product/Services: Consulting Services: Advertising; Circulation; Design; Promotion Ideas; Advertising Design
Note: Author of month GET REAL column to press associations, free PAPER MONEY column to publishers and monthly column in Publisher's Auxiliary. Conference and publisher seminars
Personnel: Peter W. Wagner (Pres.)
Personnel: Jeff Wagner (Sec./Treasurer)

SHELTON

DAC SYSTEMS

Street address 1: 4 Armstrong Park Rd, Bldg II
Street address state: CT
Zip/Postal code: 6484
Country: USA
Mailing address: 4 Armstrong Park Rd., Bldg II
Mailing city: Shelton
Mailing state: CT
Mailing zip: 6484
General Phone: (203) 924-7000
General Fax: (203) 944-1618
Email: sales@dacsystems.com
Primary Website: www.dacsystems.com
Year Established: 1988
Product/Services: Audiotex Systems & Software; Facsimilie/Fax Transmission Systems; Integrated Fax Servers; Optical Character Recognition (OCR); Speech Recognition; Telecommunications;
Personnel: Mark Nickson (Pres.)

SHINER

KASPAR MANUFACTURING

Street address 1: 959 State Hwy 95 N
Street address state: TX
Zip/Postal code: 77984
Country: USA
Mailing address: 959 State Hwy 95 N
Mailing city: Shiner
Mailing state: TX
Mailing zip: 77984
General Phone: (361) 594.3327
General Fax: (361) 594.3311
Email: info@kasparmfg.com
Primary Website: www.kasparmfg.com
Year Established: 1898
Product/Services: Circulation Equipment & Supplies; Cleaners & Solvents; Newspaper Dispensers (Mechanical/Electronic); Software: Circulation;
Personnel: Stephen Bindus (Director of Operations)
Personnel: Lori Hamilton (Director of Business & Brand Development)
Personnel: Ronnie Kresta (Supervisor of Quality Assurance)
Dan Jalufka (Wire Forming Supervisor)

SHOAL LAKE

NESBITT PUBLISHING LTD.

Street address 1: 353 Station Road
Street address state: MB
Zip/Postal code: R0J 1Z0
Country: Canada
Mailing address: PO Box 160
Mailing city: Shoal Lake
Mailing state: MB
Mailing zip: R0J 1Z0
General Phone: 204-759-2644
General Fax: 204-759-2521
Email: smpnews@mymts.net
Year Established: 2007
Product/Services: South Mountain Press community newspaper
Product or Service: Publisher/Media
Personnel: Ryan Nesbitt (Publisher)
Personnel: Marcie Harrison (Editor)
Personnel: Connie Kay (Advertising)
Ryan Nesbitt (Publisher)

SHREVEPORT

SHREVE SYSTEMS

Street address 1: 1200 Marshall St
Street address state: LA
Zip/Postal code: 71101-3936
Country: USA
Mailing address: 3080 Knolin Dr Ste 2
Mailing city: Bossier City
Mailing state: LA
Mailing zip: 71112-2465
General Phone: (318) 424-9791
General Fax: (318) 424-9771
Email: ssystems@bellsouth.net
Primary Website: www.shrevesystems.com
Year Established: 1981
Product/Services: Computers: Hardware & Software Integrators
Personnel: Rich Harold (Pres.)

SIDNEY

BAUMFOLDER CORP.

Street address 1: 1660 Campbell Rd
Street address state: OH
Zip/Postal code: 45365-2480
Country: USA
Mailing address: 1660 Campbell Rd
Mailing city: Sidney
Mailing state: OH
Mailing zip: 45365-2480
General Phone: (937) 492-1281
General Fax: (937) 492-7280
Email: baumfolder@baumfolder.com
Primary Website: www.baumfolder.com
Year Established: 1917
Product/Services: Belts, Belting, V-Belts; Collating Equipment; Counting, Stacking, Bundling Machines; Cutters & TrimmersCutters & Trimmers; Delivery Equipment; Feeding, Folding, Delivery Equipment; Folding Machines; Inserting Equipment (Includes Stuffing Machines); Pumps (Air, Ink, Vacuum)
Personnel: Janice A. Benanzer (Pres.)
Personnel: Mark Pellman (Dir., Sales/Mktg.)

SILVERTON

NEWSCOLOR, LLC

Street address 1: PO Box 802
Street address state: OR
Zip/Postal code: 97381-0802
Country: USA
Mailing address: PO Box 802
Mailing city: Silverton
Mailing state: OR
Mailing zip: 97381-0802
General Phone: (503) 873-2414
Email: sales@newscolor.com
Primary Website: www.newscolor.com
Year Established: 2004
Product/Services: Color Proofing
Note: NEWSCOLOR proofing software (formerly SeeColor) is the standard for inkjet newsprint proofing, used by customers including USA TODAY, The Washington Post, Houston Chronicle, Investors Business Daily, Dallas Morning News, & Seattle Times.
Personnel: Ron LaForge (Mng. Dir.)
Personnel: Karen Barr (Sales Dir.)

SIMPSONVILLE

FIBERWEB

Street address 1: 842 SE Main St
Street address state: SC
Zip/Postal code: 29681-7118
Country: USA
Mailing address: 842 SE Main St
Mailing city: Simpsonville
Mailing state: SC
Mailing zip: 29681-7118
General Phone: (864) 963-2106
Email: sdavis@fiberweb.com
Primary Website: www.fiberwebgraphics.com
Product/Services: Cleaners & Solvents; Plate Cleaners; Press Accessories, Parts & Supplies;
Personnel: Shawn Davis (Area Mgr.)

SLATON

THE SLATONITE

Street address 1: 139 S 9th St
Street address state: TX
Zip/Postal code: 79364-4121
Country: USA
Mailing address: PO Box 667
Mailing city: Slaton
Mailing state: TX
Mailing zip: 79364-0667
General Phone: 806-828-6201
General Fax: 806-828-6202
Email: slatonite@sbcglobal.net
Primary Website: www.slatonitenews.com
Year Established: 1911
Product/Services: newspaper, advertising
Personnel: Ken Richardson (Ed./Pub.)
Personnel: James Villanueva (Managing Editor)
Personnel: D'Etta Brown (Production Editor / advertising director)
Malva Richardson (Business Manager)
Gloria Olivares (Copy Editor)

SMITHFIELD

RICHMOND/GRAPHIC PRODUCTS, INC.

Street address 1: 20 Industrial Dr
Street address state: RI
Zip/Postal code: 02917-1502
Country: USA
Mailing address: 20 Industrial Dr
Mailing city: Smithfield
Mailing state: RI
Mailing zip: 02917-1502
General Phone: (401) 233-2700
General Fax: (401) 233-0179
Email: info@richmond-graphic.com
Primary Website: www.richmond-graphic.com
Year Established: 1984
Product/Services: Art & Layout Equipment and Services; Exposure Lamps; Film & Paper: Film Processing Machines; Layout Tables, Light Tables & Workstations; Offset Plate-Making Service & Equipment; Plate Processors; Processors: Diffusion Transfer; Processors: Film & Paper; Tables (Dot, Etch, Opaquing, Register, Retouching, Stripping); Vacuum Frames;
Personnel: Hugh C. Neville (CEO)
Personnel: P.J. Griffee (Controller)
Personnel: Frank Ragazzo (Vice Pres., Sales/Mktg.)

SOLANA BEACH

NISUS SOFTWARE, INC.

Street address 1: 107 S Cedros Ave
Street address state: CA
Zip/Postal code: 92075-1994
Country: USA
Mailing address: PO Box 1302
Mailing city: Solana Beach
Mailing state: CA
Mailing zip: 92075-7302
General Phone: (858) 481-1477
General Fax: (858) 764-0573
Email: info@nisus.com
Primary Website: www.nisus.com
Year Established: 1984
Product/Services: Word Processing System

SOMERSET

ROYAL CONSUMER INFORMATION PRODUCTS, INC.

Street address 1: 2 Riverview Dr
Street address 2: Ste 3
Street address state: NJ
Zip/Postal code: 08873-1150
Country: USA
Mailing address: 2 Riverview Dr Ste 1
Mailing city: Somerset
Mailing state: NJ
Mailing zip: 08873-1150
General Phone: (732) 627-9977
General Fax: (800) 232-9769
Email: info@royalsupplies.com
Primary Website: www.royal.com
Product/Services: Facsimilie/Fax Transmission Systems; Laser Printers;

II-77

Personnel: Salomon Suwalsky (Pres.)
Personnel: Terry Setar (Vice Pres., Sales (Royal))
Personnel: Wendy Donnelly (Mgr., Sales/Supplies)

SOMERSET

WRH GLOBAL AMERICAS

Street address 1: 24 Worlds Fair Dr
Street address 2: Ste G
Street address state: NJ
Zip/Postal code: 08873-1349
Country: USA
Mailing address: 24 World's Fair Dr. Unit G
Mailing city: Somerset
Mailing state: NJ
Mailing zip: 08873
General Phone: (856) 842-0600
General Fax: (732) 356-1637
Email: info@wrh-global-americas.com
Primary Website: www.wrh-global-americas.com
Year Established: 1969
Product/Services: Provider of Ferag Systems, Service and Spare Parts
Personnel: Barry Evans (VP)
Personnel: Rene Luchsinger (CEO)

SOUTH BELOIT

KEENE TECHNOLOGY, INC. (KTI)

Street address 1: 14357 Commercial Pkwy
Street address state: IL
Zip/Postal code: 61080-2621
Country: USA
Mailing address: 14357 Commercial Pkwy
Mailing city: South Beloit
Mailing state: IL
Mailing zip: 61080-2621
General Phone: (815) 624-8989
General Fax: (815) 624-4223
Email: info@keenetech.com
Primary Website: www.keenetech.com
Year Established: 1985
Product/Services: Rewinders; Splicers, Automatic;
Personnel: Kery Wallace (Office Mgr.)

SOUTH BEND

ACUTECH LLC

Street address 1: 3702 W Sample St
Street address 2: Unit 1128
Street address state: IN
Zip/Postal code: 46619-2947
Country: USA
Mailing address: PO Box 543
Mailing city: Granger
Mailing state: IN
Mailing zip: 46530
General Phone: (574) 262-8228
Primary Website: www.acu-tech.net
Year Established: 2004
Product/Services: Plate Cylinder Lock Ups Web Register Systems Used Plate Benders Legacy Press and Pre Press equipment Repair and Services Used Presses Used Auxiliary Equipment Installation
Note: Plate Cylinder Lock Ups Web Register Systems Used Plate Benders Legacy Press and Pre Press equipment Repair and Services Used Presses Used Auxiliary Equipment Installation
Personnel: Joe Bella (Managing Director)

SOUTH BEND LATHE CORP.

Street address 1: 1735 N Bendix Dr
Street address state: IN
Zip/Postal code: 46628-1601
Country: USA
Mailing address: 1735 N Bendix Dr
Mailing city: South Bend
Mailing state: IN
Mailing zip: 46628-1601
General Phone: (574) 289-7771
General Fax: (574) 236-1210

Email: sales@southbendlathe.com
Primary Website: www.southbendlathe.com
Year Established: 1906
Product/Services: Roller Grinders
Personnel: Carmine Martino (Pres.)
Personnel: Joseph Mittiga (Vice Pres.)

SOUTH HADLEY

MEDIA DATA TECHNOLOGY, INC. (MDTI)

Street address 1: 20 Roundelay Rd
Street address state: MA
Zip/Postal code: 01075-1614
Country: USA
Mailing address: 20 Roundelay Rd
Mailing city: South Hadley
Mailing state: MA
Mailing zip: 01075-1614
General Phone: (413) 534-3307
Email: jpeters@mediadatatech.com
Product/Services: Software: Advertising (Includes Display; Classified)
Personnel: John Peters (Pres.)

SOUTH TAMWORTH

MERRIMAC SOFTWARE ASSOCIATES

Street address 1: 9 Mason Hill Rd
Street address state: NH
Zip/Postal code: 3883
Country: USA
Mailing address: PO Box 28
Mailing city: South Tamworth
Mailing state: NH
Mailing zip: 03883-0028
General Phone: 603-323-5077
General Fax: (603) 218-2140
Email: sales@merrsoft.com
Primary Website: www.merrsoft.com
Year Established: 1987
Product/Services: Publishing Software: Advertising (includes Display and Classified); Pagination/Layout; Circulation and Distribution; Commercial Sales; Management (includes Administration and Accounting);
Note: Merrimac Software Associates
Personnel: Tom Vachon (Owner)
Personnel: Sabrina Fobes (Support Manager)
Personnel: Jim Loughner (Programmer)

SOUTHERN PINES

DENEX, INC.

Street address 1: 135 W Illinois Ave
Street address state: NC
Zip/Postal code: 28387-5808
Country: USA
Mailing address: 135 W Illinois Ave
Mailing city: Southern Pines
Mailing state: NC
Mailing zip: 28387-5808
General Phone: (910) 692-5463
General Fax: (910) 222-3100
Email: gcarroll@denexinc.com
Primary Website: www.denex.se; www.denex.com
Year Established: 1992
Product/Services: Laser Printers
Personnel: Gary J. Carroll (Pres.)

SOUTHINGTON

BAUMER ELECTRIC LTD.

Street address 1: 122 Spring Street
Street address 2: Unit C-6
Street address state: CT
Zip/Postal code: 06489-1534
Country: USA
Mailing address: 122 Spring Street, Unit C-6
Mailing city: Southington
Mailing state: CT

Mailing zip: 06489-1534
General Phone: (800) 937 9336
Email: sales.us@baumer.com
Primary Website: www.baumer.com
Year Established: 1952
Product/Services: Controls: Photo Electric; Newspaper Couter; Totalizing Systems; Web Break Detector
Personnel: Jeremy Jones (Pdct. Mgr.)
Personnel: Kristian Santamaria (Mrkt.)

SPARKS

NORTHERN GRAPHIC SUPPLY

Street address 1: 64 Hardy Dr
Street address state: NV
Zip/Postal code: 89431-6307
Country: USA
Mailing address: 64 Hardy Dr
Mailing city: Sparks
Mailing state: NV
Mailing zip: 89431-6307
General Phone: (775) 359-6466
General Fax: (775) 359-6966
Email: 4ngs@sbcglobal.net
Year Established: 1965
Product/Services: Newspaper Marketing
Personnel: Barbara Gouldstone (Pres.)

SPARTA

AMERGRAPH CORPORATION

Street address 1: 520 Lafayette Rd
Street address state: NJ
Zip/Postal code: 07871-3447
Country: USA
Mailing address: 520 Lafayette Rd
Mailing city: Sparta
Mailing state: NJ
Mailing zip: 07871-3447
General Phone: (973) 383-8700
General Fax: (973) 383-9225
Email: sales@amergraph.com
Primary Website: www.amergraph.com
Year Established: 1975
Product/Services: Exposure Lamps; Film & Paper: Film Processing Machines; Ink Bleeding Equipment; Ink Pumping Systems; Offset Plate-Making Service & Equipment; Plate Exposure Units; Plate Processors; Platemakers: Offset (Computer to Plate); Processors: Film & Paper; Vacuum Frames
Personnel: Robert Lesko (Pres.)

SPARTANBURG

REEVES BROTHERS, INC.

Street address 1: 790 Reeves St
Street address state: SC
Zip/Postal code: 29301-5078
Country: USA
Mailing address: PO Box 1531
Mailing city: Spartanburg
Mailing state: SC
Mailing zip: 29304-1531
General Phone: (864) 576-1210
General Fax: (864) 595-2270
Primary Website: www.trelleborg.com
Product/Services: Blanket Mounting and Bars; Blankets;
Personnel: Keith Dye (CEO)

SPRINGBORO

GRAPHIC SYSTEMS SERVICES

Street address 1: 400 South Pioneer Blvd.
Street address state: OH
Zip/Postal code: 45066
Country: USA
Mailing address: 400 South Pioneer Blvd.
Mailing city: Springboro
Mailing state: OH
Mailing zip: 45066
General Phone: (937) 746-0708
General Fax: (937) 746-0783

Email: john.sillies@gsspress.com
Primary Website: www.gsspress.com
Year Established: 1954
Product/Services: Printing Presses & Color Inkjet Web Presses
Personnel: John Sillies (Support)
Personnel: Mark Pellman (Engineering & Product Development)
Personnel: Lynn Dahm
Mike Deno (Service Support)

SPRINGFIELD

NATIONAL NEWSPAPER ASSOCIATION PUBLISHERS' AUXILIARY

Street address 1: 900 Community Dr
Street address state: IL
Zip/Postal code: 62703-5180
Country: USA
Mailing address: 900 Community Drive
Mailing city: Springfield
Mailing state: IL
Mailing zip: 62703
General Phone: (217) 241-1400
Email: pubaux@nna.org
Primary Website: www.nnaweb.org
Year Established: 1865
Product/Services: Trade Publications
Personnel: Stan Schwartz (Comm. Dir.)
Personnel: Lynne Lance (Chief Operating Officer)
Personnel: Sam Fisher (Publisher)

VERSAR INC.

Street address 1: 6850 Versar Ctr
Street address 2: Suite 201
Street address state: VA
Zip/Postal code: 22151-4175
Country: USA
Mailing address: 6850 Versar Ctr, Suite 201
Mailing city: Springfield
Mailing state: VA
Mailing zip: 22151-4196
General Phone: 703-750-3000
General Fax: 703-642-6825
Primary Website: www.versar.com
Year Established: 1988
Product/Services: Architects/Engineers (Includes Design/Construction Firms); System Installations.
Personnel: Dwane Stone (CEO)
Personnel: Christine Tarrago (CFO)
Personnel: Nayna Diehl (V.P. Corporate Counsel & Director for Contracts)
Alessandria Albers (V. P. of H.R.)
Travis C. Cooper (Corporate Vice President Engineering & Construction Management)

ST CATHARINES

DIENAMIC MICROPRINT

Street address 1: 71 King St
Street address 2: Suite 3024
Street address state: ON
Zip/Postal code: L2R 3H6
Country: Canada
Mailing address: 71 King St., Ste.3024
Mailing city: Saint Catharine's
Mailing state: ON
Mailing zip: L2R 3H7
General Phone: (905) 688-5593
General Fax: (905) 688-6132
Email: microprint@vaxxine.com
Primary Website: www.dienamicmis.com
Year Established: 1986
Product/Services: Mailroom Systems & Equipment
Personnel: Mark Porter (Pres.)
Personnel: Lori Walsh (Vice Pres.-Finance)

STAMFORD

PASSUR AEROSPACE, INC.

Street address 1: 1 Landmark Sq

Equipment, Supplies and Services

Street address 2: Ste 1900
Street address state: CT
Zip/Postal code: 06901-2671
Country: USA
Mailing address: 1 Landmark Sq Ste 1900
Mailing city: Stamford
Mailing state: CT
Mailing zip: 06901-2671
General Phone: (888) 340-3712
Email: sales@passur.com
Primary Website: www.passur.com
Year Established: 1974
Product/Services: Data Communication; Input & Editing Systems;
Personnel: Ron Dunsky (Media)
Personnel: G.S. Beckwith Gilbert (Chairman)
Personnel: James T. Barry (Pres. & CEO)
 Tim Campbell (COO)
 Louis J. Petrucelly (Sr. V. P. & CFO)

STORAENSO

Street address 1: 6 Landmark Sq
Street address 2: Fl 4
Street address state: CT
Zip/Postal code: 06901-2704
Country: USA
Mailing address: 201 Broad St
Mailing city: Stamford
Mailing state: CT
Mailing zip: 06901-2004
General Phone: (203) 359-5707
General Fax: (203) 359-5858
Primary Website: www.storaenso.com
Year Established: 1996
Product/Services: Paper: Coated Groundwood Offset
Personnel: Paul Lukaszewski (Mgr., Mktg.)

XEROX (CORP. HEADQUARTERS)

Street address 1: 800 Long Ridge Rd
Street address state: CT
Zip/Postal code: 06902-1227
Country: USA
Mailing address: PO Box 1600
Mailing city: Stamford
Mailing state: CT
Mailing zip: 06904-1600
General Phone: (800) ASK-XEROX (275-9376)
Year Established: 1906
Product/Services: Scanners: Color B & W, Plates, Web
Personnel: Paul Allaire (Chrmn. of the Bd./ Chrmn.-Exec. Committee)
Personnel: Anne Mulcahy (Pres./CEO)

STOCKHOLM

TOLERANS AB SWEDEN

Street address 1: Vindkraftsvagen 6
Street address 2: Vindkraftsvagen 6
Zip/Postal code: 135 70
Country: Sweden
Mailing address: P.O Box 669
Mailing city: Tyreso
Mailing zip: 135 26
General Phone: +46 8 4487030
General Fax: +46 8 4487040
Email: info@tolerans.com
Primary Website: www.tolerans.com
Product/Services: Printing
Personnel: Jan Melin (CEO)

STOCKTON

WEST COAST COMPUTER SYSTEMS

Street address 1: 2010 N Wilson Way
Street address state: CA
Zip/Postal code: 95205-3126
Country: USA
Mailing address: 2010 N Wilson Way
Mailing city: Stockton
Mailing state: CA
Mailing zip: 95205-3126
General Phone: (209) 948-5499
Email: sales@wccsys.com
Primary Website: www.wccsys.com
Year Established: 1976
Product/Services: Ink Storage Tanks;

Lubricants; Offset Chemicals & Supplies; Pumps (Air, Ink, Vacuum); Static Eliminators; Consulting Services: Marketing; Market Research;
Personnel: Ed Kobrin (Sales/Mktg. Mgr.)
Personnel: Simon Young (Application Software Mgr.)
Personnel: Jim Ponder (System Software Mgr.)

SUMMERVILLE

LINDE LIFT TRUCK CORP.

Street address 1: 2450 W 5th North St
Street address state: SC
Zip/Postal code: 29483-9621
Country: USA
Mailing address: 2450 W 5th North St
Mailing city: Summerville
Mailing state: SC
Mailing zip: 29483-9621
General Phone: (843) 875-8000
General Fax: (843) 875-8362
Primary Website: www.linde-mh.com
Year Established: 1853
Product/Services: Material Handling Equipment: Automatic Guided Vehicles; Material Handling Equipment: Truck Loaders; Material Handling Equipment: Vehicle Loading;
Personnel: Andreas Krinninger (CEO)
Personnel: Christophe Lautray (Chief Sales Officer)

SUSSEX

LAUTERBACH GROUP

Street address 1: W222 N5710 Miller Way
Street address state: WI
Zip/Postal code: 53089
Country: USA
Mailing address: W222 N5710 Miller Way
Mailing city: Sussex
Mailing state: WI
Mailing zip: 53089
General Phone: (262) 820-8130
General Fax: (262) 820-1806
Email: info@lauterbachgroup.com
Primary Website: www.masclabels.com
Year Established: 1970
Product/Services: Label Printing Machines
Personnel: Shane Lauterbach (Chief Executive Officer, President and Director)
Personnel: Rebecca Kerschinske (Vice President of Sales)
Personnel: Derek Wilcox (Director of Marketing)

QUAD GRAPHICS

Street address 1: N61 W23044 Harry's Way
Street address state: WI
Zip/Postal code: 53089
Country: USA
Mailing address: N61 W23044 Harry's Way
Mailing city: Sussex
Mailing state: WI
Mailing zip: 53089
General Phone: (888) 782.3226
Email: info@qg.com
Primary Website: www.qg.com
Product/Services: Software: Advertising (Includes Display; Classified)
Personnel: Joel Quadracci (Pres., CEO)
Personnel: Bill Blackmer (Global Procurement)
Personnel: Chris Grond (Paper Serv.)

QUAD TECH

Street address 1: N64W23110 Main St
Street address state: WI
Zip/Postal code: 53089-3230
Country: USA
Mailing address: N64W23110 Main St
Mailing city: Sussex
Mailing state: WI
Mailing zip: 53089-5301
General Phone: (414) 566-7500
General Fax: (414) 566-9670
Email: info@qtiworld.com
Primary Website: www.quadtechworld.com

Year Established: 1979
Product/Services: Color Registration; Controls: Register; Ink Controls, Computerized; Press Control Systems; Web Break Detector;
Personnel: Karl Fritchen (Pres.)
Personnel: Randy Freeman (Vice Pres.,Sales)

QUADTECH

Street address 1: N64W23110 Main St
Street address state: WI
Zip/Postal code: 53089-3230
Country: USA
Mailing address: N64W23110 Main St
Mailing city: Sussex
Mailing state: WI
Mailing zip: 53089-3230
General Phone: (414) 566-7500
General Fax: (414) 566-9670
Email: sales@quadtechworld.com
Primary Website: www.quadtechworld.com
Year Established: 1979
Product/Services: Color Registration; Controls: Register; Ink Controls, Computerized; Press Control Systems; Web Break Detector;
Personnel: Karl Fritchen (Pres.)
Personnel: Randy Freeman (Vice Pres., Bus. Devel.)
Personnel: Vince Balistrieri (Dir., Engineering Gen. Mgr.,Commercial/Newspaper)
 Greg Kallman (Regional Sales Manager)

TACOMA

INTERSTATE DISTRIBUTOR CO.

Street address 1: 11707 21st Avenue Ct S
Street address state: WA
Zip/Postal code: 98444-1236
Country: USA
Mailing address: 11707 21st Avenue Ct S
Mailing city: Tacoma
Mailing state: WA
Mailing zip: 98444-1236
General Phone: (253) 537-9455
Email: web_info@intd.com
Primary Website: www.intd.com
Year Established: 1933
Personnel: George Payne (President & CEO)
Personnel: Gary McLean (Pres.)
Personnel: Dolores Fitzerald (Sec.)
 Peter M. Carlander (Sr. Vice Pres., Sales/Mktg.)

WEBPRESS, LLC

Street address 1: 701 E D St
Street address state: WA
Zip/Postal code: 98421-1811
Country: USA
Mailing address: PO Box 2274
Mailing city: Tacoma
Mailing state: WA
Mailing zip: 98401-2274
General Phone: 253-620-4747
General Fax: 253-722-0378
Email: info@webpressllc.com
Primary Website: www.webpressllc.com
Year Established: 1965
Product/Services: Folding Machines; Presses: Offset; Remanufactures Equipment; Roll Handling Equipment; Web Press - Special Equipment;
Note: WebPress LLC is the proud manufacturer of the Quad-Stack 4 over 4 color printing unit and the UPM perfector system. Units combine with WPC folders to make an efficient, cost saving press line with low waste, tight registration, and single level operation."
Personnel: Rick Guinn (Operations Manager)
Personnel: Brian Haun (President)
Personnel: Brian Hilsendager (Customer Service/Parts)
 Jim Merek (Sales)

TAMPA

ATEX NORTH AMERICA

Street address 1: 5405 Cypress Center Dr

Street address 2: Ste 200
Street address state: FL
Zip/Postal code: 33609-1025
Country: USA
Mailing address: 6767 N Wickham Rd Ste 111
Mailing city: Melbourne
Mailing state: FL
Mailing zip: 32940-2024
General Phone: (813) 739-1700
General Fax: (813) 739-1710
Email: info@atex.com
Primary Website: www.atex.com
Year Established: 2001
Product/Services: Software: Advertising (Includes Display; Classified); Software: Business (Includes Administration/ Accounting); Software: Circulation; Software: Editorial; Software: Pagination/ Layout;
Personnel: John Hawkins (CEO)
Personnel: Scott Rossler (CEO, Atex North America)
Personnel: Malcom McGregory (Sales Mgr.)

ATLAS SPECIALTY LIGHTING

Street address 1: 7304 N Florida Ave
Street address state: FL
Zip/Postal code: 33604-4838
Country: USA
Mailing address: 7304 N Florida Ave
Mailing city: Tampa
Mailing state: FL
Mailing zip: 33604-4889
General Phone: (813) 238-6481
General Fax: (813) 238-6656
Primary Website: www.asltg2.com
Product/Services: Lighting Equipment
Personnel: Ralph Felten (Mgr.)

SAXOTECH, INC.

Street address 1: 302 Knights Run Ave Ste 1150
Street address 2: Suite 1150
Street address state: FL
Zip/Postal code: 33602-5974
Country: USA
Mailing address: 302 Knights Run Ave Ste 1150
Mailing city: Tampa
Mailing state: FL
Mailing zip: 33602-5974
General Phone: (813) 221-1600
General Fax: (813) 221-1604
Email: info@saxotechonline.com
Primary Website: www.saxotechonline.com
Year Established: 1991
Product/Services: Archiving Systems; News Wire Capture Systems; Pagination Systems; Photo Archiving; Publishing Systems; Software: Asset Management; Software: Editorial; Software: Pagination/ Layout; Software: Workflow Management/ Tracking;
Personnel: Anders Christiansen (CEO)
Personnel: Bill Gilmour (Exec. V. P. & CFO)
Personnel: Jesper Frank (Sr. V. P.)
 Ed Ross (V. P. Sales)
 Mette Kvistgaard (Director of Global HR)

TATAMY

CONSOLIDATED STORAGE COS.

Street address 1: 225 Main St
Street address state: PA
Zip/Postal code: 18085-7059
Country: USA
Mailing address: 225 Main St
Mailing city: Tatamy
Mailing state: PA
Mailing zip: 18085-7059
General Phone: (610) 253.2775
General Fax: (610) 675.2869
Email: sales@equipto.com
Primary Website: www.equipto.com
Year Established: 1907
Product/Services: Material handling and storage equipment including modular drawer cabinets, other storage cabinets, shelving, shelving with drawers, bulk storage racks, workcenters and work benches, mezzanine and deckover units, stairways, carts and small parts storage

units, pallet rack, mobile aisle systems
Note: Manufacturer of Material Handling and Storage Systems for Industrial, Comercial and Distribution Applications
Personnel: Collin Straus (Vice President of Sales and Installations)

TAYLOR

INTERCONTINENTAL ENGINEERING CO.

Street address 1: 25944 Northline Rd
Street address state: MI
Zip/Postal code: 48180-4413
Country: USA
Mailing address: 25944 Northline Rd
Mailing city: Taylor
Mailing state: MI
Mailing zip: 48180-4413
General Phone: (734) 946-9931
General Fax: (734) 946-9992
Product/Services: Presses: Offset
Personnel: Michael Schwartz (Pres.)
Personnel: Somendra Khosla (Dir.)

TEMPE

FUJIFILM GRAPHIC SYSTEMS USA, INC.

Street address 1: 2507 W Erie Dr
Street address 2: Ste 103
Street address state: AZ
Zip/Postal code: 85282-3117
Country: USA
Mailing address: 2507 W Erie Dr Ste 103
Mailing city: Tempe
Mailing state: AZ
Mailing zip: 85282-3117
General Phone: (800) 279-1673
General Fax: (602) 437-8483
Primary Website: www.fujifilmusa.com/products/graphic_arts_printing/index.html
Product/Services: Blankets; Chemicals: Pressroom; Color Management Software; Imagesetters; Inks; Offset Chemicals & Supplies; Platemakers: Flexographic (Computer to Plate); Plates: Offset (Conventional); Proofing Systems; Software: Press/Post Press;
Personnel: Richard Pyane (Reg'l Sales Mgr.)

TEMPLE CITY

PASTE-UP SUPPLY

Street address 1: 10930 1/2 Grand Ave
Street address state: CA
Zip/Postal code: 91780-3551
Country: USA
Mailing address: 10930 1/2 Grand Ave
Mailing city: Temple City
Mailing state: CA
Mailing zip: 91780-3551
General Phone: (626) 448-4543
Year Established: 1965
Product/Services: Adhesive Wax Coaters
Personnel: Pat Treanor (Owner)

TEWKSBURY

ALFA CTP SYSTEMS INC.

Street address 1: 554 Clark Rd
Street address 2: Ste 2
Street address state: MA
Zip/Postal code: 01876-1631
Country: USA
Mailing address: 554 Clark Rd Ste 2
Mailing city: Tewksbury
Mailing state: MA
Mailing zip: 01876-1631
General Phone: (603) 689-1101
General Fax: 978-429-0870
Email: info@alfactp.com
Primary Website: www.alfactp.com
Year Established: 2007
Product/Services: Imagesetters; Plates: Offset (Computer to Plate); Proofing Systems; Software: Pagination/Layout; Typesetters: Laser;
Personnel: Tony Ford (President)
Personnel: Keith Roeske (VP Operations)
Personnel: Paul Norton

TEWKSBURY

ECRM

Street address 1: 554 Clark Rd
Street address state: MA
Zip/Postal code: 01876-1631
Country: USA
Mailing address: 554 Clark Rd
Mailing city: Tewksbury
Mailing state: MA
Mailing zip: 01876-1631
General Phone: (978) 851-0207
General Fax: (978) 851-7016
Email: sales@ecrm.com
Primary Website: www.ecrm.com
Year Established: 1968
Product/Services: Imagesetters; Platemakers: Offset (Computer to Plate); Prepress Color Proofing Systems; Processors: Film & Paper; Proofing Systems;
Personnel: Richard Black (President&CEO)

THOUSAND OAKS

APLUSA BELL FALLA

Street address 1: 199 West Hillcrest Drive
Street address state: CA
Zip/Postal code: 91320
Country: USA
Mailing address: 199 West Hillcrest Drive
Mailing city: Thousand Oaks
Mailing state: CA
Mailing zip: 91320
General Phone: (203) 520 9491
Year Established: 1978
Product/Services: Market Research; Research Studies;
Personnel: Steve Bell (Senior Partner)
Personnel: Juan Falla (Senior Partner)

AUTOLOGIC INFORMATION INTERNATIONAL

Street address 1: 1050 Rancho Conejo Blvd
Street address state: CA
Zip/Postal code: 91320-1717
Country: USA
Mailing address: 1050 Rancho Conejo Blvd
Mailing city: Thousand Oaks
Mailing state: CA
Mailing zip: 91320-1717
General Phone: (805) 498-9611
General Fax: (805) 499-1167
Email: abrunner@autologic.com
Primary Website: www.autologic.com
Year Established: 1964
Product/Services: Archiving Systems; Computers: Hardware & Software Integrators; Facsimilie/Fax Transmission Systems; Multiplexers/Routers; Platemakers: Direct; Platemakers: Flexographic (Computer to Plate); Publishing Systems; Scanners: Color B & W, Plates, Web; Software: Advertising (Includes Display, Classified); Software: Electronic Data Interchange; Typesetters: Laser
Personnel: Al Brunner (Pres.)
Personnel: Ratan Bhaunani (Vice Pres., Software Engineering)
Personnel: Doug Arlt (Vice Pres., Mfg.)
Jack Embree (Dir., Americas Opns.)
Tom LeJeune (Mktg. Mgr.)

THREE RIVERS

REPUBLIC ROLLER CORP.

Street address 1: 1233 Millard St
Street address state: MI
Zip/Postal code: 49093
Country: USA
Mailing address: PO Box 330
Mailing city: Three Rivers
Mailing state: MI
Mailing zip: 49093-0330
General Phone: (800) 765-5377
General Fax: (269) 273-7655
Email: bestroll@aol.com
Primary Website: www.republicroller.com
Year Established: 1981
Product/Services: Roll Coverings; Roller Grinding Services; Rollers; Rollers: Dampening;
Personnel: G.L. Umphrey (Pres.)
Personnel: Bill Gross (Sales Mgr.)

TOKYO

TKS LTD.

Street address 1: 26-24 Shiba 5-Chome Minato-Ku
Zip/Postal code: 108-8375
Country: Japan
Mailing address: 26-24 Shiba 5-Chome Minato-Ku
Mailing city: Tokyo
Mailing zip: 108-8375
General Phone: +81 3 3451-8141
General Fax: +81 3 3451-7425
Email: sales@tkspress.com
Primary Website: www.tks-net.co.jp
Year Established: 1874
Product/Services: Newspaper Web Offset Presses & Digital Presses; Automated and Manpower Saving Equipment for Newspaper Presses; Commercial Web Offset Presses; Automated and Manpower Saving Equipment for Commercial Presses;
Personnel: Noriyuki Shiba (Pres.)
Personnel: Osamu Kurata (Sales Chief Officer)

TOLLAND

MEGASYS INTERNATIONAL, INC.

Street address 1: 45 Industrial Park Rd W
Street address 2: Ste H
Street address state: CT
Zip/Postal code: 06084-2839
Country: USA
Mailing address: 45 Industrial Park Rd W Ste H
Mailing city: Tolland
Mailing state: CT
Mailing zip: 06084-2839
General Phone: (860) 871-8713
General Fax: (860) 871-8710
Email: megasysint@aol.com
Primary Website: megasysinternational.com
Year Established: 1990
Product/Services: Bundling and Tying Machines; Composing Room Equipment & Supplies; Equipment Dealers (New); Equipment Dealers (Used); Folding Machines; Label Printing Machines; Paper Shredders; Photostat: Machines;
Note: "HP Designjet and Wide Format Equipment Sales, Service and Supplies"
Personnel: Fred McNutt (Pres.)

TORRANCE

SOLAR SYSTEMS

Street address 1: 605 Hawaii Ave.
Street address state: CA
Zip/Postal code: 90503
Country: USA
Mailing address: 605 Hawaii Ave.
Mailing city: Torrance
Mailing state: CA
Mailing zip: 90503
General Phone: (425) 270-6100
General Fax: (425) 270-6150
Primary Website: www.solarsystems.com
Year Established: 1990
Product/Services: Computers: Hardware & Software Integrators; Remanufactures Equipment; Storage Retrieval Systems;
Personnel: Jean McCall (CFO)

TRACY

WESCO GRAPHICS

Street address 1: 410 E Grant Line Rd
Street address 2: Ste B
Street address state: CA
Zip/Postal code: 95376-2838
Country: USA
Mailing address: 410 E Grant Line Rd Ste B
Mailing city: Tracy
Mailing state: CA
Mailing zip: 95376-2838
General Phone: (209) 832-1000
General Fax: (209) 832-7800
Email: jim@wescographics.com
Primary Website: www.wescographics.com
Year Established: 1977
Product/Services: Consulting Services: Equipment; Equipment Dealers (Used); Erectors & Riggers; Inserting Equipment (Includes Stuffing Machines); Press Rebuilding; Press Repairs; Presses: Offset; Reels & Tensions; Roll Handeling Equipment; Web Press - Special Equipment;
Personnel: Jim Estes (Pres.)
Personnel: Betty Estes (Vice Pres.)

TROY

ACCUFAST PACKAGE PRINTING SYSTEMS

Street address 1: 120 Defreest Dr
Street address state: NY
Zip/Postal code: 12180-7608
Country: USA
Mailing address: 125 Wolf Rd Ste 318
Mailing city: Albany
Mailing state: NY
Mailing zip: 12205-1221
General Phone: (518) 283-0988
General Fax: (518) 283-0977
Email: sales@accufastpps.com
Primary Website: www.accufastpps.com
Product/Services: Label Printing Machines; Mailroom Systems & Equipment;
Personnel: Ken St. John (Pres.)
Personnel: Meg Flanigan (Mgr.)

AMERICAN NEWSPAPER REPRESENTATIVES

Street address 1: 2075 W Big Beaver Rd
Street address 2: Ste 310
Street address state: MI
Zip/Postal code: 48084-3439
Country: USA
Mailing address: 2075 W Big Beaver Rd Ste 310
Mailing city: Troy
Mailing state: MI
Mailing zip: 48084-3439
General Phone: (248) 643-9910
General Fax: (248) 643-9914
Email: accountsales@gotoanr.com
Primary Website: www.anrinc.net
Year Established: 1943
Product/Services: Consulting Services: Advertising
Personnel: John Jepsen (Pres.)
Personnel: Robert Sontag (Exec. Vice Pres./COO)
Personnel: Melanie Cox (Regl. Sales Mgr., Minneapolis)
Hilary Howe

ITW HOBART BROTHERS CO.

Street address 1: 400 Trade Sq E
Street address state: OH
Zip/Postal code: 45373-2463
Country: USA
Mailing address: 400 Trade Sq E
Mailing city: Troy
Mailing state: OH
Mailing zip: 45373-2463
General Phone: (937) 332-4000
General Fax: (937) 332-5224
Primary Website: www.hobartbrothers.com
Year Established: 1917

Equipment, Supplies and Services

Product/Services: Motors
Personnel: Dean Phillips (Welding Equip. Mgr.)
Personnel: Debbie Doench (Adv./Commun. Mgr.)

RANGER DATA TECHNOLOGIES INC.

Street address 1: 360 E Maple Rd
Street address 2: Ste X
Street address state: MI
Zip/Postal code: 48083-2707
Country: USA
Mailing address: 360 E Maple Rd Ste X
Mailing city: Troy
Mailing state: MI
Mailing zip: 48083-2707
General Phone: (248) 336-7300
General Fax: (248) 336-8775
Email: info@rangerdata.com
Primary Website: www.rangerdata.com
Year Established: 2001
Product/Services: Software: Advertising (Includes Display; Classified)
Product or Service: Hardware/Software Supplier
Personnel: George Willard (Sr. VP of Operations)
Personnel: Grace Shields (Director of Marketing & Customer Service)
Personnel: Dolores Gauthier (National Dir. of Sales & Marketing)

ROCONEX CORP.

Street address 1: 20 Marybill Dr S
Street address state: OH
Zip/Postal code: 45373-1034
Country: USA
Mailing address: 20 Marybill Dr S
Mailing city: Troy
Mailing state: OH
Mailing zip: 45373-1034
General Phone: (937) 339-2616
General Fax: (937) 339-1470
Email: info@roconex.com
Primary Website: www.roconex.com
Year Established: 1954
Product/Services: Art & Layout Equipment and Services; Cabinets; Files, Storage, Layout Tables, Light Tables & Workstations; Offset Plate Holders; Plate Exposure Units; Platemakers: Offset (Conventional); Storage Retrieval Systems; Tables (Dot, Etch, Opaquing, Register, Retouching, Stripping)
Personnel: Tyrone Spear (Pres.)

TRUMBULL

COMMUNICATIONS MANAGEMENT SERVICE, INC.

Street address 1: 30 Nutmeg Dr
Street address state: CT
Zip/Postal code: 06611-5453
Country: USA
Mailing address: 30 Nutmeg Dr
Mailing city: Trumbull
Mailing state: CT
Mailing zip: 06611-5453
General Phone: (203) 377-3000
General Fax: (203) 377-2632
Email: dan@bargainnews.com
Primary Website: www.bargainnews.com
Year Established: 1971
Product/Services: Consulting Services: Circulation; Consulting Services: Marketing; Newspaper Marketing;
Personnel: John F. Roy (Pres.)
Personnel: Daniel F. Rindos (Vice Pres.)
Personnel: Daniel Firoa (New Media Sales Dir.)

UNION

ERNEST SCHAEFER, INC.

Street address 1: 731 Lehigh Ave
Street address state: NJ
Zip/Postal code: 07083-7626
Country: USA
Mailing address: 731 Lehigh Ave
Mailing city: Union
Mailing state: NJ
Mailing zip: 07083-7626
General Phone: (908) 964-1280
General Fax: (908) 964-6787
Email: eschaefe@aol.com
Primary Website: www.ernestschaeferinc.com
Year Established: 1922
Product/Services: Type, Fonts, Letters, Cover Board, Book Glue.
Note: Hot Stamping Type & Bookbinding Supplies
Personnel: Ernest Schaefer (Pres.)

PSC FLO-TURN, INC.

Street address 1: 1050 Commerce Ave
Street address state: NJ
Zip/Postal code: 07083-5087
Country: USA
Mailing address: 1050 Commerce Ave Ste 1
Mailing city: Union
Mailing state: NJ
Mailing zip: 07083-5080
General Phone: (908) 687-3225
General Fax: (908) 687-1715
Email: sales@flow-turn.com
Primary Website: www.flow-turn.com
Year Established: 1981
Product/Services: Conveyors
Personnel: Rod Chrysler (Pres.)

UNION GROVE

AMERICAN ROLLER CO.

Street address 1: 1440 13th Ave
Street address state: WI
Zip/Postal code: 53182-1515
Country: USA
Mailing address: 1440 13th Ave.
Mailing city: Union Grove
Mailing state: WI
Mailing zip: 53182
General Phone: (262) 878-2445
General Fax: (262) 878-2241
Primary Website: www.americanroller.com
Year Established: 1938
Product/Services: Roll Coverings; Rollers; Rollers: Dampening;

UNIONDALE

KAMEN & CO. GROUP SERVICES

Street address 1: 626 Rxr Plz
Street address state: NY
Zip/Postal code: 11556-0626
Country: USA
Mailing address: 626 RXR Plz
Mailing city: Uniondale
Mailing state: NY
Mailing zip: 11556-0626
General Phone: (516) 379-2797
General Fax: (516) 379-3812
Email: info@kamengroup.com
Primary Website: www.kamengroup.com
Year Established: 1981
Product/Services: Architects/Engineers (Includes Design/Construction Firms); Brokers & Appraisers; Circulation Equipment & Supplies; Consulting Services: Advertising; Consulting Services: Circulation; Consulting Services: Financial; Consulting Services: Human Resources; Consulting Services: Marketing; Training: Sales & Marketing; Tubes, Racks (Includes Racks: Motor Route Tubes);
Note: Media Appraisers, Accountants, Advisors & Brokers
Personnel: Kevin Brian Kamen (Pres./CEO)
Personnel: Celeste Myers (Vice Pres.)

UPLAND

UVP, LLC

Street address 1: 2066 W 11th St
Street address state: CA
Zip/Postal code: 91786-3509
Country: USA
Mailing address: 2066 W 11th St
Mailing city: Upland
Mailing state: CA
Mailing zip: 91786-3509
General Phone: (909) 946-3197
General Fax: (909) 946-3597
Email: uvp@uvp.com
Primary Website: www.uvp.com
Year Established: 1932
Product/Services: Exposure Lamps; Inks;
Personnel: Leighton Smith (Pres.)
Personnel: Alex Waluszko (Vice Pres., Mktg./Sales)
Personnel: Kathy Buckman (Commun. Mktg. Serv.)

VALENCIA

NEASI-WEBER INTERNATIONAL

Street address 1: 25115 Avenue Stanford
Street address 2: Ste A300
Street address state: CA
Zip/Postal code: 91355-1290
Country: USA
Mailing address: 25115 Avenue Stanford Ste 300
Mailing city: Valencia
Mailing state: CA
Mailing zip: 91355-4806
General Phone: (818) 895-6900
General Fax: (818) 830-0889
Email: info@nwintl.com
Primary Website: www.nwintl.com
Year Established: 1977
Product/Services: Mailroom Systems & Equipment; Software: Advertising (Includes Display; Classified); Software: Circulation;
Personnel: Jim S. Weber (Pres.)
Personnel: Dennis J. Neasi (CEO)

VANCOUVER

IDEAFISHER SYSTEMS, INC.

Street address 1: 5640 SE Riverside Way
Street address state: WA
Zip/Postal code: 98661-7175
Country: USA
Mailing address: 5640 SE Riverside Way
Mailing city: Vancouver
Mailing state: WA
Mailing zip: 98661-7175
General Phone: 360-450-6888
Email: info@ideafisher.com
Primary Website: www.ideafisher.com
Year Established: 1988
Product/Services: Software: Advertising (Includes Display; Classified)
Personnel: Marsh Fisher (CEO)
Personnel: Mark Effinger (CEO)

VANDALIA

ESKO-GRAPHICS

Street address 1: 721 Crossroads Ct
Street address state: OH
Zip/Postal code: 45377-9676
Country: USA
Mailing address: 8535 Gander Creek Dr
Mailing city: Miamisburg
Mailing state: OH
Mailing zip: 45342-5436
General Phone: (937) 454-1721
General Fax: (937) 454-1522
Primary Website: www.esko.com
Year Established: 1989
Product/Services: Software: Design/Graphics
Personnel: Tony Wiley (Division Mgr., Printers Systems)
Personnel: Carrie Woryk (Mktg. Commun. Mgr.)

VENTURA

COAST GRAPHIC SUPPLY

Street address 1: 1363 Donlon St
Street address 2: Ste 16
Street address state: CA
Zip/Postal code: 93003-5638
Country: USA
Mailing address: 1112 Casitas ct.
Mailing city: Ventura
Mailing state: CA
Mailing zip: 93004
General Phone: (805) 642-5585
Email: coastgraphic@earthlink.net
Primary Website: www.coastgraphicsupply.com
Year Established: 1978
Product/Services: Digital printing & proofing: Supplies & equipment Ink & Bulk Ink Systems Sublimation Ink Paper & Blanks Chemicals: Plate Processing; Chemicals: Pressroom; Composing Room Equipment & Supplies; Densitometers; Film & Paper: Contact; Film & Paper: Phototypesetting;
Note: Digital Ptng Supplies & Equip Pre & Press
Personnel: James Cagnina (Pres.)

VERNON

BENDER MACHINE, INC.

Street address 1: 2150 E 37th St
Street address state: CA
Zip/Postal code: 90058-1417
Country: USA
Mailing address: 2150 E 37th St
Mailing city: Vernon
Mailing state: CA
Mailing zip: 90058-1491
General Phone: (323) 232-1790
General Fax: (323) 232-6456
Email: info@bendermachine.com
Primary Website: www.bendermachine.com
Year Established: 1946
Product/Services: Newsprint; Newsprint Handling Equipment; Roller Grinders; Roller Grinding Services;
Personnel: Bruce Perry (Mktg. Mgr.)
Personnel: Doug Martin (Acct. Mgr.)

VERNON ROCKVILLE

ANOCOIL CORPORATION

Street address 1: 60 E Main St
Street address state: CT
Zip/Postal code: 06066-3245
Country: USA
Mailing address: PO Box 1318
Mailing city: Vernon Rockville
Mailing state: CT
Mailing zip: 06066-1318
General Phone: (860) 871-1200
General Fax: (860) 872-0534
Primary Website: www.anocoil.com
Year Established: 1958
Product/Services: Chemicals: Plate Processing; Plates: Offset (Computer to Plate); Plates: Offset (Conventional)
Personnel: H.A. Fromson (CEO)
Personnel: David Bujese (Pres.)
Personnel: Timothy A. Fromson (Vice Pres., Anocoil)
Bud Knorr (Vice President- Sales)

VIENNA

LITCO INTERNATIONAL, INC.

Street address 1: 1 Litco Dr
Street address state: OH
Zip/Postal code: 44473-9600
Country: USA
Mailing address: PO Box 150
Mailing city: Vienna
Mailing state: OH
Mailing zip: 44473
General Phone: 330-539-5433
General Fax: (330) 539-5388
Email: info@litco.com
Primary Website: www.litco.com/molded-wood-pallets
Year Established: 1962
Product/Services: Material Handling Equipment: Pallets & Palletizers

NOTE: LITCO OFFERS ENGINEERED

MOLDED WOOD PALLETS. PALLETS ARE CLEAN AND DRY AT 8 MC AT THE TIME OF MANUFACTURE. CERTIFIED SUSTAINABLE AND USDA BIOPREFERRED, MEETS ALL EXPORT REQUIREMENTS OF IPPC-ISPM15.
Personnel: Gary L. Trebilcock (President)
Personnel: Lionel F. Trebilcock (CEO)
Personnel: Gary A. Sharon (Executive Vice President)

VIRGINIA BEACH

BUSCH, INC.

Street address 1: 516 Viking Dr
Street address state: VA
Zip/Postal code: 23452-7316
Country: USA
Mailing address: 516 Viking Dr
Mailing city: Virginia Beach
Mailing state: VA
Mailing zip: 23452-7316
General Phone: (757) 463-7800
General Fax: (757) 463-7407
Email: marketing@buschusa.com
Primary Website: www.buschpump.com
Year Established: 1975
Product/Services: Pumps (Air, Ink, Vacuum)
Personnel: Charles Kane (Pres.)
Personnel: Linda Katz (Mktg. Specialist)

DYC SUPPLY CO.

Street address 1: 5740 Bayside Rd
Street address state: VA
Zip/Postal code: 23455-3004
Country: USA
Mailing address: 5740 Bayside Rd
Mailing city: Virginia Beach
Mailing state: VA
Mailing zip: 23455-3004
General Phone: (800) 446-8240
General Fax: (757) 486-5689
Email: kevink@d-y-c.com
Primary Website: www.dyc.com
Product/Services: Blankets; Offset Blankets, Blanket Wash;
Personnel: Joseph Martinez (Pres.)
Personnel: Marc Banks (Asst. Mktg. Mgr.)

DYNARIC, INC.

Street address 1: 5740 Bayside Rd
Street address state: VA
Zip/Postal code: 23455-3004
Country: USA
Mailing address: 5740 Bayside Rd
Mailing city: Virginia Beach
Mailing state: VA
Mailing zip: 23455-3004
General Phone: (800) 526-0827
General Fax: (757) 363-8016
Email: gd@dynaric.com
Primary Website: www.dynaric.com
Year Established: 1973
Product/Services: PLASTIC STRAPPING AND STRAPPING EQUIPMENT
Personnel: Joseph Martinez (Pres.)
Personnel: Marc Banks (Asst. Mktg. Mgr.)

WABASH

MARTIN YALE, INC.

Street address 1: 251 Wedcor Ave
Street address state: IN
Zip/Postal code: 46992-4201
Country: USA
Mailing address: 251 Wedcor Ave
Mailing city: Wabash
Mailing state: IN
Mailing zip: 46992-4201
General Phone: (260) 563-0641
General Fax: (260) 563-4575
Email: info@martinyale.com
Primary Website: www.martinyale.com
Year Established: 1934
Product/Services: Cutters & Trimmers; Folding Machines; Label Printing Machines; Paper Handeling Equipment; Paper Shredders;
Personnel: Greg German (Pres.)

WAKARUSA

UTILIMASTER

Street address 1: 100 State Road 19 N
Street address state: IN
Zip/Postal code: 46573-9312
Country: USA
Mailing address: 603 Earthway Blvd
Mailing city: Bristol
Mailing state: IN
Mailing zip: 46507-9182
General Phone: (574) 862-4561
General Fax: (574) 862-4517
Email: info@utilimaster.com
Primary Website: www.utilimaster.com
Year Established: 1973
Product/Services: Delivery Equipment
Personnel: John Marshall (Sr. Vice Pres., Sales/Mktg.)

WASHINGTON

SIEMENS COMMUNICATIONS GROUP

Street address 1: 300 New Jersey Avenue
Street address 2: Suite 1000
Street address state: DC
Zip/Postal code: 20001
Country: USA
Mailing address: 300 New Jersey Avenue, Suite 1000
Mailing city: Washington
Mailing state: DC
Mailing zip: 20001
General Phone: (800) 743-6367
General Fax: (678) 297-8316
Email: email.us@siemens.com
Primary Website: www.siemens.com
Product/Services: Telecommunications
Personnel: Lisa Davis (Chairman)
Personnel: Barbara Humpton (CEO)
Personnel: Heribert Stumpf (CFO)

WASHINGTON

UNITED STATES POSTAL SERVICE

Street address 1: 475 Lenfant Plz SW
Street address state: DC
Zip/Postal code: 20260-0004
Country: USA
Mailing address: 475 Lenfant Plz SW
Mailing city: Washington
Mailing state: DC
Mailing zip: 20260-0004
General Phone: (202) 268-2500
General Fax: (202) 268-5211
Primary Website: www.usps.gov; www.usps.com; www.usps.com/mailingonline
Product/Services: Mailroom Systems & Equipment
Personnel: Megan Brennan (CEO & Postmaster General)
Personnel: Guy Cottrell (Chief Postal Inspector)
Personnel: Janice Walker (Corporate Communications VP)
Ronald Stroman (Deputy Postmaster Gen. & Chief Govt. Relations Officer)
David Williams (COO and Exec. VP)
Kristin Seaver (Chief Information Officer & Exec. VP)
Joseph Corbett (CFO & Exec. VP)
Jeffrey Williamson (CHRO and Exec. VP)
Jacqueline Krage Strako (Chief Customer & Marketing Officer and Exec. VP)
Thomas Marshall (General Counsel and Exec. VP)
Kevin McAdams (Delivery Operations VP)

WATER MILL

STOCK, FUND, OR ETF

Street address 1: PO Box 488
Street address 2: 122 Mill Pond Lane,
Street address state: NY
Zip/Postal code: 11976-0488
Country: USA
Mailing address: 122 Mill Pond Lane, PO Box 488
Mailing city: Water Mill
Mailing state: NY
Mailing zip: 11976
General Phone: (631) 204-9100
General Fax: (631) 204-0002
Email: stevea@hamptons.com
Primary Website: www.VATinfo.org
Year Established: 1990
Product/Services: Process Color Reference Guides
Note: 4-color printing guides; 4-color system in Adobe, Corel, Quark
Personnel: Steve Abramson (Pres.)
Personnel: Jane E. Nichols (Vice Pres.)
Personnel: Joan Dalessandro (Office Mgr.)

WATERBURY

MAC DERMID AUTOTYPE INC.

Street address 1: 245 Freight Street
Street address state: CT
Zip/Postal code: 06702
Country: USA
Mailing address: 245 Freight Street
Mailing city: Waterbury
Mailing state: CT
Mailing zip: 06702
General Phone: (800) 323-0632
General Fax: (800) 933-2345
Email: autotypeusinfo@macdermid.com
Primary Website: www.autotype.macdermid.com
Year Established: 1981
Product/Services: Chemicals: Photographic; Masking Materials; Plates: Offset (Computer to Plate)
Personnel: Terry Watson (Lead Operator)

WATERLOO

DESCARTES SYSTEMS GROUP

Street address 1: 120 Randall Dr
Street address state: ON
Zip/Postal code: N2V 1C6
Country: Canada
Mailing address: 120 Randall Dr.
Mailing city: Waterloo
Mailing state: ON
Mailing zip: N2V 1C6
General Phone: (519) 746-8110
General Fax: (519) 747-0082
Email: info@descartes.com
Primary Website: www.descartes.com
Year Established: 1985
Product/Services: Computers: Hardware & Software Integrators
Personnel: Arthur Mesher (CEO)
Personnel: Stephanie Ratza (CFO)
Personnel: Chris Jones (Exec. Vice Pres., Solutions/Servs.)
Scott J. Pagan (Exec. Vice Pres., Cor. Devel./Gen. Counsel)
Edward J. Ryan (Exec. Vice Pres., Global Field Opns.)
Raimond Diederik (Exec. Vice Pres., Information Servs.)

WAUCONDA

HERCO GRAPHIC PRODUCTS

Street address 1: PO Box 369
Street address state: IL
Zip/Postal code: 60084-0369
Country: USA
Mailing address: PO Box 369
Mailing city: Wauconda
Mailing state: IL
Mailing zip: 60084-0369
General Phone: (800) 235-5541
General Fax: (815) 578-9593
Email: hercographics@aol.com
Primary Website: www.hercographics.com
Year Established: 1979
Product/Services: Roll Coverings; Rollers;
Personnel: Christine Polanzi (Dir. Sales)

WAUKESHA

ELECTRONIC TELE-COMMUNICATIONS, INC.

Street address 1: 1915 Mac Arthur Rd
Street address state: WI
Zip/Postal code: 53188-5702
Country: USA
Mailing address: 1915 Mac Arthur Rd
Mailing city: Waukesha
Mailing state: WI
Mailing zip: 53188-5702
General Phone: (262) 542-5600
General Fax: (262) 542-1524
Email: etc_mkt@etcia.com
Primary Website: www.etcia.com
Year Established: 1980
Product/Services: Telecommunications
Product or Service: Telecommunications/Service Bureaus
Personnel: Dean W. Danner (Pres./CEO)
Personnel: Joseph A. Voight (Vice Pres., Sales)

WELS

TEUFELBERGER GMBH

Street address 1: Vogelweiderstrasse 50
Zip/Postal code: 4600
Country: Austria
Mailing address: Vogelweiderstrasse 50
Mailing city: Wels
Mailing zip: 4600
General Phone: 43 7242 4130
General Fax: 43 7242 413100
Email: fibersplastics@teufelberger.com; mailbox@teufelberger.com
Primary Website: www.teufelberger.com
Year Established: 1890
Product/Services: Bundling and Tying Machines; Counting, Stacking, Bundling Machines; Strapping Machines;
Personnel: Teufel Berger (Owner)
Personnel: Harald Katzinger (Mgr., Mktg./Sales Agriculture)

WENTZVILLE

CIRCULATION DEVELOPMENT, INC.

Street address 1: PO Box 6
Street address state: MO
Zip/Postal code: 63385-0006
Country: USA
Mailing address: PO Box 6
Mailing city: Wentzville
Mailing state: MO
Mailing zip: 63385-0006
General Phone: (800) 247-2338
General Fax: (800) 400-4453
Email: increase@circulation.net
Primary Website: www.circulation.net
Year Established: 1986
Product/Services: Consulting Services: Circulation; Consulting Services: Marketing;
Note: newspaper circulation telemarketing
Personnel: Bill Wesa (Chrmn.)
Personnel: Jim Oden (Pres.)
Personnel: Rob Oden (Vice Pres.)
Carmen Salvati (Mktg. Dir.)
David Wesa (Dir., Info. Servs.)

WEST CARROLLTON

FCI DIGITAL

Street address 1: 2032 S Alex Rd

Equipment, Supplies and Services

Street address 2: Ste A
Street address state: OH
Zip/Postal code: 45449-4023
Country: USA
Mailing address: 2032 S Alex Rd Ste A
Mailing city: West Carrollton
Mailing state: OH
Mailing zip: 45449-4023
General Phone: (937) 859-9701
General Fax: (937) 859-9709
Email: service@fcidigital.com
Primary Website: www.fcidigital.com
Year Established: 1989
Product/Services: Color Proofing; Color Seperation Scanners; Color Seperations, Positives; Prepress Color Proofing Systems
Personnel: George Dick (CEO)

WEST CHICAGO

WPC MACHINERY CORP.

Street address 1: 1600 Downs Dr
Street address 2: Ste 4
Street address state: IL
Zip/Postal code: 60185-1888
Country: USA
Mailing address: 23872 N Kelsey Rd
Mailing city: Lake Barrington
Mailing state: IL
Mailing zip: 60010-1563
General Phone: (630) 231-7721
General Fax: (630) 231-7827
Year Established: 1989
Product/Services: Consulting Services: Production; Cylinder Repair; Drives & Controls; Erectors & Riggers; Ink Fountains & Accessories; Paper Handeling Equipment; Press Rebuilding; Press Repairs; Rollers;
Personnel: Mark Krueger (Prodn. Mgr., Press Servs.)

WESTCHESTER

CHURCH RICKARDS, WHITLOCK & CO., INC.

Street address 1: 10001 W Roosevelt Rd
Street address state: IL
Zip/Postal code: 60154-2664
Country: USA
Mailing address: 10001 W Roosevelt Rd
Mailing city: Westchester
Mailing state: IL
Mailing zip: 60154-2664
General Phone: (708) 345-7500
General Fax: (708) 345-1166
Email: crwfred@aol.com
Year Established: 1945
Product/Services: Consulting Services: Circulation; Consulting Services: Human Resources; Insurance;
Personnel: Fred C. Hohnke (Pres.)
Personnel: Daniel Demjanik (Regl. Mgr.)
Personnel: Tim Solt (Reg. Mgr.)

WESTERLY

GSP, INC.

Street address 1: 78 Airport Rd
Street address state: RI
Zip/Postal code: 02891-3402
Country: USA
Mailing address: PO Box 2358
Mailing city: Westerly
Mailing state: RI
Mailing zip: 02891-0922
General Phone: (401) 348-0210
General Fax: (401) 348-0689
Email: gspmystic@gsptoday.com
Primary Website: www.gsptoday.com
Year Established: 1987
Product/Services: Presses: Offset; Web Press - Special Equipment; Labeling Equipment
Personnel: Jens E. Ljungberg (Pres.)
Personnel: Maurice Blanchet (Vice Pres.)
Personnel: Mary Ponte (Controller)

WESTERVILLE

PDI PLASTICS

Street address 1: 5037 Pine Creek Dr
Street address state: OH
Zip/Postal code: 43081-4849
Country: USA
Mailing address: 5037 Pine Creek Dr
Mailing city: Westerville
Mailing state: OH
Mailing zip: 43081-4849
General Phone: (800)634-0017
General Fax: (614) 890-0467
Email: sales@pdisaneck.com
Primary Website: www.newsbags.com
Year Established: 1984
Product/Services: Circulation Equipment & Supplies
Personnel: Frank Cannon (Pres.)
Personnel: Todd Wilson (Exec. VP)

SALESFUEL, INC.

Street address 1: 600 N Cleveland Ave
Street address 2: Ste 260
Street address state: OH
Zip/Postal code: 43082-7265
Country: USA
Mailing address: 600 N Cleveland Ave Ste 260
Mailing city: Westerville
Mailing state: OH
Mailing zip: 43082-7265
General Phone: (614) 794-0500
General Fax: (614) 961-3268
Email: info@salesdevelopment.com
Primary Website: www.salesfuel.com
Year Established: 1989
Product/Services: Consulting Services: Advertising; Consulting Services: Computer; Consulting Services: Marketing; Facsimilie/Fax Transmission Systems; Integrated Fax Servers; Market Research; Marketing Database Design and Implementation; Software: Advertising (Includes Display; Classified); Trade Publications;
Personnel: Audrey Strong (VP of Communications)
Personnel: C. Lee Smith (President/CEO)

THE CANNON GROUP, INC.

Street address 1: 5037 Pine Creek Dr
Street address state: OH
Zip/Postal code: 43081-4849
Country: USA
Mailing address: 5037 Pine Creek Dr
Mailing city: Westerville
Mailing state: OH
Mailing zip: 43081-4849
General Phone: (614) 890-0343
General Fax: (614) 890-0467
Email: sales@pdisaneck.com
Primary Website: www.newsbags.com
Product/Services: Circulation Supplies and Equipment
Personnel: Frank Cannon (Pres.)

WHITE PLAINS

MEDIA MONITORS, INC.

Street address 1: 445 Hamilton Ave
Street address 2: Fl 7
Street address state: NY
Zip/Postal code: 10601-1807
Country: USA
Mailing address: 445 Hamilton Ave Ste 700
Mailing city: White Plains
Mailing state: NY
Mailing zip: 10601-1828
General Phone: (914) 428-5971
General Fax: (914) 259-4541
Email: jselig@mediamonitors.com
Primary Website: www.mediamonitors.com
Year Established: 1982
Product/Services: Consulting Services: Advertising
Personnel: Philippe Generali (Pres.)
Personnel: John L. Selig (Sales Executive)
Personnel: Cheryl Lohr (National Account Manager)

Frank Cammarata (VP, Sales)

WILLIAMSVILLE

MEDIA SALES PLUS, INC.

Street address 1: 6400 Main St
Street address 2: Ste 201
Street address state: NY
Zip/Postal code: 14221-5858
Country: USA
Mailing address: 6400 Main Street, Suite 201
Mailing city: Williamsville
Mailing state: NY
Mailing zip: 14221-5858
General Phone: (716) 250-6884
General Fax: (716) 634-0574
Primary Website: www.mediasalesplus.com
Year Established: 2001
Product/Services: A preeminent provider of multi-media advertising sales and support services.
Note: Strategic Outsourcing Advertising Sales
Personnel: Dominick Bordonaro (Chief Executive Officer)
Personnel: Debra Chase (Client Partnerships)

WILMINGTON

E.I. DU PONT DE NEMOURS & CO.

Street address 1: 1007 Market St
Street address state: DE
Zip/Postal code: 19898-1100
Country: USA
Mailing address: 1007 Market St
Mailing city: Wilmington
Mailing state: DE
Mailing zip: 19898-1100
General Phone: (302) 774-1000
General Fax: (302) 355-4013
Email: contact@dupont.com
Primary Website: www2.dupont.com
Product/Services: Color Analyzers; Color Proofing; Color Registration; Color Seperation Scanners; Color Viewing Equipment; Controls: Register; Phototypesetting Interface Equipment; Prepress Color Proofing Systems; Press Control Systems;
Personnel: Ellen J. Kullman (Chrmn./Pres./CEO)
Personnel: Jeffrey L. Keefer (Exec., Vice Pres./CFO)
Personnel: Thomas M. Connelly (Exec. Vice Pres./Chief Innovation Officer)
Richard R. Goodmanson (Exec. Vice Pres./COO)
W. Donald Johnson (Exec. Vice Pres./Human Resources)
Diane H. Gulyas (Grp. Vice Pres., Chief Mktg./Sales Officer)
Barry J. Niziolek (Vice Pres./Controller)
Harry Parker (Vice Pres., DuPont Sales Effectiveness)
Susan M. Stalnecker (Vice Pres./Treasurer)
Cynthia C. Green (Vice Pres./CMO/Chief Sales Officer)

WILMINGTON

TELESONIC PACKAGING CORP., AMES ENGINEERING DIV.

Street address 1: 805 E 13th St
Street address state: DE
Zip/Postal code: 19802-5000
Country: USA
Mailing address: 805 E 13th St
Mailing city: Wilmington
Mailing state: DE
Mailing zip: 19802-5000
General Phone: (302) 658-6945
General Fax: (302) 658-6946
Email: telesonics@aol.com
Primary Website: www.telesoniconline.com
Year Established: 1958
Product/Services: Automatic Plastic Bagging Equipment; Shrink Wrapping Equipment; Packaging machinery
Personnel: Bernard Katz (Pres.)

WINCHESTER

ASHWORTH BROTHERS, INC.

Street address 1: 450 Armour Dl
Street address state: VA
Zip/Postal code: 22601-3459
Country: USA
Mailing address: 450 Armour Dl
Mailing city: Winchester
Mailing state: VA
Mailing zip: 22601-3459
General Phone: (540) 662-3494
General Fax: (540) 662-3150
Primary Website: www.ashworth.com
Product/Services: Belts, Belting, V-Belts; Conveyors;
Personnel: Joe Lackner (Vice Pres. Mktg)
Personnel: Tim Jones (Mktg. Mgr.)

WINNIPEG

LAZER-FARE MEDIA SERVICES

Street address 1: PO Box 48114 RPO Lakewood
Street address state: MB
Zip/Postal code: R2J 4A3
Country: Canada
Mailing address: PO Box 48114 RPO Lakewood
Mailing city: Winnipeg
Mailing state: MB
Mailing zip: R2J 4A3
General Phone: (204) 452-5023
General Fax: (204) 272-3499
Email: sales@lazerfare.com
Primary Website: www.lazerfare.com
Year Established: 1985
Product/Services: Archiving Systems; Consulting Services: Advertising; Consulting Services: Computer; Consulting Services: Editorial; Content and Digital Asset Management systems
Product or Service: Consultants'Hardware/ Software Supplier
Personnel: Kelly Armstrong (Pres.)

WINNIPEG

QUICKWIRE LABS

Street address 1: 300 Carlton St.
Street address state: MB
Zip/Postal code: R3B 2K6
Country: Canada
Mailing address: 300 Carlton St.
Mailing city: Winnipeg
Mailing state: MB
Mailing zip: R3B 2K6
General Phone: (905) 785-0748
General Fax: (204) 926-4686
Email: bmiller@quickwire.com
Primary Website: www.quickwire.com
Year Established: 1993
Product/Services: Software: Advertising (Includes Display; Classified); Software: Editorial; Software: Pagination/Layout;
Personnel: Bill Miller (Gen. Mgr.)
Personnel: Paul Medland (Quicktrac Developer)
Personnel: Richard Bliss (Integrator)

WINSTED

MIRACLE INDUSTRIES, INC.

Street address 1: 118 Colebrook River Rd
Street address state: CT
Zip/Postal code: 06098-2241
Country: USA
Mailing address: 118 Colebrook River Rd Ste 1
Mailing city: Winsted
Mailing state: CT
Mailing zip: 06098-2241
General Phone: (203) 723-0928
General Fax: (203) 723-0394
Product/Services: Motors; Press Accessories, Parts & Supplies; Press Control Systems; Press Engineers; Presses: Offset; Roller Grinding Services; Web Break Detector; Web Press - Special Equipment;

Personnel: John Chabot (Pres.)
Personnel: Phyllis Fennlly (Vice Pres., Sales/Mktg.)

WOBURN

ALL SYSTEMS GO

Street address 1: 2 Cedar St
Street address state: MA
Zip/Postal code: 01801-7248
Country: USA
Mailing address: 2 Cedar St Ste 1
Mailing city: Woburn
Mailing state: MA
Mailing zip: 01801-6352
General Phone: (781) 932-6700
General Fax: (781) 932-6711
Email: info@allsysgo.com
Primary Website: www.allsysgo.com
Year Established: 1993
Product/Services: Computers: Hardware & Software Integrators; Computers: Laptop & Portable; Computers: Storage Devices; Consulting Services: Advertising; Consulting Services: Circulation; Consulting Services: Computer; Consulting Services: Equipment; Consulting Services: Marketing; Imagesetters; Software: Design/Graphics
Personnel: Richard Pape (Pres.)

WONDER LAKE

GRAPHIC MACHINE SALES, INC.

Street address 1: 8917 Hickory Ln
Street address state: IL
Zip/Postal code: 60097-9179
Country: USA
Mailing address: 8917 Hickory Ln
Mailing city: Wonder Lake
Mailing state: IL
Mailing zip: 60097-9179
General Phone: (815) 382-1914
Email: graphic@stans.net
Primary Website: www.graphicmachinesales.com
Year Established: 1986
Product/Services: Used web presses and auxiliaries
Note: Markets used and reconditioned web presses and auxiliary equipment worldwide
Personnel: James Anzelmo (Pres.)

WOOD DALE

VIDEOJET TECHNOLOGIES INC.

Street address 1: 1500 N Mittel Blvd
Street address state: IL
Zip/Postal code: 60191-1072
Country: USA
Mailing address: 1500 Mittel Blvd.
Mailing city: Wood Dale
Mailing state: IL
Mailing zip: 60191
General Phone: (630) 860-7300
General Fax: (630) 582-1343
Email: info@videojet.com
Primary Website: www.videojet.com
Year Established: 1980
Product/Services: Addressing Machines; Inks; Label Printing Machines; Mailroom Systems & Equipment;

WOODBRIDGE

MARKETING PLUS, INC.

Street address 1: 135 Green St
Street address state: NJ
Zip/Postal code: 07095-2961
Country: USA
Mailing address: 135 Green St
Mailing city: Woodbridge
Mailing state: NJ
Mailing zip: 07095-2961
General Phone: (732) 694-1020
Email: mpi@marketingplusinc.com
Primary Website: www.marketingplusinc.com
Product/Services: Consulting Services: Marketing; Market Research;
Personnel: Monty Cerasani (Pres./CEO)
Personnel: Susan Taylor (Gen. Mgr.)
Personnel: John Saparito (Office Mgr.)
Karen Marov (HR Mgr.)
John Lederer (Vice Pres., Bus. Devel.)
Phil Lyman (IT Mgr.)

NORMAN X GUTTMAN, INC.

Street address 1: 135 Green St
Street address state: NJ
Zip/Postal code: 07095-2961
Country: USA
Mailing address: 135 Green St
Mailing city: Woodbridge
Mailing state: NJ
Mailing zip: 07095-2961
General Phone: (732) 636-8671
General Fax: (732) 636-8673
Primary Website: www.advertoon.com
Year Established: 1975
Product/Services: Inks; Roll Converters; Roller Grinding Services; Rollers; Rollers: Dampening; Tension & Web Controls;
Personnel: Daniel Guttman (Pres.)

WOODRIDGE

SAMUEL PACKAGING SYSTEMS GROUP

Street address 1: 1401 Davey Road
Street address state: IL
Zip/Postal code: 60517
Country: USA
Mailing address: 1401 Davey Road
Mailing city: Woodridge
Mailing state: IL
Mailing zip: 60517
General Phone: (630) 783-8900
Email: packaging@samuel.com
Primary Website: www.samuelpsg.com
Year Established: 1855
Product/Services: Strapping Machines
Personnel: Dean Campbell (Director Sales and Marketing, Admin)
Personnel: Morris Gant (Service Manager)

SAMUEL STRAPPING SYSTEM

Street address 1: 1401 Davey Rd
Street address 2: Ste 300
Street address state: IL
Zip/Postal code: 60517-4963
Country: USA
Mailing address: 1401 Davey Rd Ste 300
Mailing city: Woodridge
Mailing state: IL
Mailing zip: 60517-4991
General Phone: (800) 667-1264
General Fax: (630) 783-8901
Email: info@samuelsystem.com
Primary Website: www.samuelsystems.com
Year Established: 1857
Product/Services: Bundling and Tying Machines; Strapping Machines;

TENSOR INTERNATIONAL LLC

Street address 1: 10330 Argonne Woods Dr
Street address 2: Ste 300
Street address state: IL
Zip/Postal code: 60517-5088
Country: USA
Mailing address: 10330 Argonne Woods Dr Ste 300
Mailing city: Woodridge
Mailing state: IL
Mailing zip: 60517-5088
General Phone: (630) 739-9600
General Fax: (630) 739-9339
Email: info@ustensor.com
Primary Website: www.ustensor.com
Product/Services: Presses: Offset
Personnel: Michael Pavone (COO)
Personnel: Scott Ahlberg (Director of Eng.)
Personnel: John Bonk (VP of Projects & Service Operations)
Christopher Dalu (V.P. Production & Purchasing)

Rick R. (Accounting)

WOODSTOCK

KIRK-RUDY, INC.

Street address 1: 125 Lorraine Pkwy
Street address state: GA
Zip/Postal code: 30188-2487
Country: USA
Mailing address: 125 Lorraine Pkwy
Mailing city: Woodstock
Mailing state: GA
Mailing zip: 30188-2487
General Phone: (770) 427-4203
General Fax: (770) 427-4036
Primary Website: www.kirkrudy.com
Year Established: 1967
Product/Services: Addressing Machines; Inserting Equipment (Includes Stuffing Machines); Mailroom Systems & Equipment;
Personnel: Rick Marshal (Pres.)

WUERZBURG

KOENIG & BAUER AKTIENGESELLSCHAFT (KBA)

Street address 1: Friedrich-Koenig-Str. 4
Zip/Postal code: D 97080
Country: Germany
Mailing address: Postfach 6060
Mailing city: Wuerzburg
Mailing zip: D 97010
General Phone: +49 931 909 4336
General Fax: +49 931 909 6015
Email: kba-wuerzburg@kba-print.de
Primary Website: www.kba-print.de
Year Established: 1817
Product/Services: Flexogrpahic Press Conversion; Flying Pasters; Press Control Systems; Presses: Flexographic; Presses: Offset; Presses: Rotogravure; Reels & Tensions; Roll Handling Equipment; Roll Preparation Equipment; Web Press - Special Equipment;
Personnel: Helge Hansen (Pres.)
Personnel: Klaus Schmidt (Dir., Mktg.)

WYCKOFF

MIDLANTIC EQUIPMENT CO., INC.

Street address 1: 567 Wyckoff Ave
Street address state: NJ
Zip/Postal code: 07481-1336
Country: USA
Mailing address: 567 Wyckoff Ave
Mailing city: Wyckoff
Mailing state: NJ
Mailing zip: 07481-1336
General Phone: (201) 891-1448
General Fax: (201) 891-2664
Email: midequip@yahoo.com
Primary Website: www.agfa-imagesetters.com
Year Established: 1985
Product/Services: Imagesetters
Personnel: Arlene Vanderweert (Mktg. Mgr.)

WYNDMOOR

ECLIPSE SERVICES (DIV. OF QUADRIVIUM, INC.)

Street address 1: 7721 Beech Ln
Street address state: PA
Zip/Postal code: 19038-7615
Country: USA
Mailing address: 7721 Beech Lane
Mailing city: Wyndmoor
Mailing state: PA
Mailing zip: 19038-7615
General Phone: (484) 462-4300
General Fax: 207-373-0723
Email: sales@eclipseservices.com
Primary Website: www.eclipseservices.com
Year Established: 1984

Product/Services: Software: Advertising (Includes Display; Classified, Online); Software: Business (Includes Administration/Accounting). New: Available on iPhone, iPad for sales reps.
Note: Business software for print and online publications.
Personnel: Jeanette MacNeille (President)

YORK

GRAFIKAMERICA

Street address 1: 1285 W King St
Street address state: PA
Zip/Postal code: 17404-3409
Country: USA
Mailing address: 1285 W King St
Mailing city: York
Mailing state: PA
Mailing zip: 17404-3409
General Phone: (717) 843-3183
General Fax: (717) 845-8828
Email: sales@grafikam.com
Year Established: 1993
Product/Services: Color Registration; Controls: Register; Ink Controls, Computerized; Tension & Web Controls; Web Offset Remoisturizers;
Personnel: Ward Walsh (Pres.)

IMC AMERICA

Street address 1: 1285 W King St
Street address state: PA
Zip/Postal code: 17404-3409
Country: USA
Mailing address: PO Box 2771
Mailing city: York
Mailing state: PA
Mailing zip: 17405-2771
General Phone: (717) 845-4807
General Fax: (717) 845-8828
Email: sales@imcamerica.com
Primary Website: www.imcamerica.com
Year Established: 1983
Product/Services: Newsprint Handling Equipment; Paper Handling Equipment; Roll Handling Equipment;
Personnel: Ward Walsh (Pres.)
Personnel: Ric Mayle (Vice Pres., Sales./Mktg.)

IMC AMERICA

Street address 1: 1285 W King St
Street address state: PA
Zip/Postal code: 17404-3409
Country: USA
Mailing address: 1285 W King St
Mailing city: York
Mailing state: PA
Mailing zip: 17404-3409
General Phone: (717) 845-4807
General Fax: (717) 845-8828
Email: imcsales@imcamerica.com
Primary Website: www.imcamerica.com
Year Established: 1981
Product/Services: Blanket Cleaner/Washer (Automatic); Conveyors; Counting, Stacking, Bundling Machines; Cutters & Trimmers; In-Line Trimming Systems; Material Handling Equipment: Automatic Guided Vehicles; Material Handling Equipment: Palletizing Machines; Paper Handling Equipment; Roll Handling Equipment;
Personnel: Ward Walsh (Pres.)
Personnel: Ric Mayle (Vice Pres., Mktg./Sales)

YOUNGSVILLE

SOUTHERN LITHOPLATE, INC.

Street address 1: 105 Jeffrey Way
Street address state: NC
Zip/Postal code: 27596-9759
Country: USA
Mailing address: PO Box 9400
Mailing city: Wake Forest
Mailing state: NC
Mailing zip: 27588-6400
General Phone: (800) 638-7990
General Fax: (919) 556-1977

Equipment, Supplies and Services

Email: info@slp.com
Primary Website: www.slp.com
Year Established: 1934
Product/Services: Chemicals: Plate Processing; Chemicals: Pressroom; Film & Paper: Film Processing Machines; Film & Paper: Filters (Photographic); Offset Chemicals & Supplies; Offset Film; Offset Fountain Solutions; Plate Processors; Plates: Offset (Computer to Plate); Plates: Offset (Conventional);
Personnel: Edward A. Casson (Chrmn./CEO)
Personnel: Steve Mattingly (Sr. VP)
Personnel: Ted McGrew (VP Sales)
Gary Blakeley (Dir. Global Technical Solutions)

XERIUM TECHNOLOGIES INC.

Street address 1: 14101 Capital Blvd
Street address state: NC
Zip/Postal code: 27596-0166
Country: USA
Mailing address: 14101 Capital Blvd
Mailing city: Youngsville
Mailing state: NC
Mailing zip: 27596
General Phone: 919-556-7235
General Fax: 919-556-1063
Year Established: 1886
Product/Services: Roll Coverings; Roller Grinding Services; Rollers;
Personnel: Kevin Frank (Vice Pres., Sales)

ZANESVILLE

STEWART GLAPAT CORP.

Street address 1: 1639 Moxahala Ave
Street address state: OH
Zip/Postal code: 43701-5950
Country: USA
Mailing address: PO Box 3030
Mailing city: Zanesville
Mailing state: OH
Mailing zip: 43702-3030
General Phone: (740) 452-3601
General Fax: (740) 452-9140
Email: sglapat@adjustoveyor.com
Primary Website: www.adjustoveyor.com
Year Established: 1939
Product/Services: Material Handling Equipment: Telescopic Conveyors, Truck Loaders & Unloaders
Personnel: Charles T. Stewart (C.E.O and Chairman)
Personnel: David T. Stewart (Sales Manager)
Personnel: Amy Stewart (Executive Vice President)
William T. Stewart (President & C.O.O)
Mike Hinton (Director of Engineering)
Russ Lindamood (Production Manager)
Jerry Funk (Purchasing Manager)
Ron Bachelor (Spare Parts Sales Mgr.)

PUBLICATION DESIGN, INC.

Street address 1: 6449 Meadowview Ter S
Street address state: PA
Zip/Postal code: 18092-2091
Country: USA
Mailing address: 6449 Meadowview Ter S
Mailing city: Zionsville
Mailing state: PA
Mailing zip: 18092-2091
General Phone: (610) 928-1111
Email: ayers@publicationdesign.com
Primary Website: www.publicationdesign.com
Year Established: 1987
Product/Services: Media Kit Design Support; Newsletter Design; Etc.;
Personnel: Robert Ayers (Owner)

PUBLICATION DESIGN, INC.

Street address 1: 6449 Meadowview Ter S
Street address state: PA
Zip/Postal code: 18092-2091
Country: USA
Mailing address: 6449 Meadowview Ter S
Mailing city: Zionsville
Mailing state: PA
Mailing zip: 18092-2091
General Phone: (610) 928-1111
General Fax: (610) 928-1110
Email: ayers@publicationdesign.com
Primary Website: www.publicationdesign.com
Year Established: 1987
Product/Services: Publication Design & Layout Services
Personnel: Robert Ayers (Pres., V.P., Sec. Tres.)

ZURICH

ABB LTD.

Street address 1: Affolternstr. 44, PO Box 8131
Zip/Postal code: CH-8050
Country: Switzerland
Mailing address: Affolternstr. 44, PO Box 8131
Mailing city: Zurich
Mailing zip: CH-8050
General Phone: 41 43 317-7111
General Fax: 41 43 317-4420
Email: engage.abb@ch.abb.com
Primary Website: www.abb.com
Personnel: Joseph Hogan (CEO)
Personnel: Michel Demare (CFO)

BUHRS BV

Street address 1: Vredeweg 7
Street address 2: 1505 HH Zaandam
Zip/Postal code: 1505
Country: Netherlands
Mailing address: Vredeweg 7, 1505 HH Zaandam
Mailing zip: 1505
General Phone: +31 (0)75 7990600
General Fax: +31 (0)75 7990610
Email: info@buhrs.com
Primary Website: www.buhrs.com
Year Established: 1908
Product/Services: Automatic Plastic Bagging Equipment; Feeding, Folding, Delivery Equipment; Folding Machines; Inserting Equipment (Includes Stuffing Machines); Mailroom Systems & Equipment; Newspaper Couter; Software: Press/Post Press;
Personnel: Dick Verheij (Managing Director)
Personnel: Koos Buis (Sales Support)
Personnel: Ton Warger (Service Manager)
Arjan de Vries (Manager Engineering)

IKS KLINGELNBERG GMBH

Street address 1: In der Fleute 18
Street address 2: 42897 Remscheid
Country: Germany
Mailing address: In der Fleute 18
Mailing city: 42897 Remscheid
General Phone: 2191 969-0
General Fax: 2191 969-111
Email: info@interknife.com
Primary Website: www.interknife.com
Year Established: 1863
Personnel: Thomas Meyer (Pres./CEO)

INTERACTIVE PRODUCTS AND SERVICES COMPANIES

AKRON

HITCHCOCK FLEMING AND ASSOCIATES, INC.
Product or Service: Advertising/Marketing Agency
Street address 1: 500 Wolf Ledges Pkwy
Street address state: OH
Postal code: 44311-1022
County: Summit
Country: USA
Mailing address 1: 500 Wolf Ledges Pkwy
Mailing city: Akron
Mailing state: OH
Mailing zip: 44311-1080
Office phone: (330) 376-2111
Office fax: (330) 376-2808
Other fax: www.teamhfa.com
Web address: jdeleo@teamhfa.com

ALAMEDA

ELFWORKS 3D CONSTRUCTION CO.
Product or Service: Graphic/Design Firm
Street address 1: 1421 Page St
Street address state: CA
Postal code: 94501-3822
County: Alameda
Country: USA
Mailing address 1: 1421 Page St
Mailing city: Alameda
Mailing state: CA
Mailing zip: 94501-3822
Office phone: (510) 769-9391
Other fax: www.elfworks.com
Web address: first_contact@elfworks.com
Note: Erik Flom (Owner)
Employee Associations: Erik Flom

ALBANY

AUDIO SERVICE AMERICA PRODUCTIONS / FREEHOLD DIVISION
Product or Service: Advertising/Marketing Agency`Consultants`Multimedia/Interactive Products
Street address 1: 28 Ten Eyck Ave
Street address state: NY
Postal code: 12209-1518
County: Albany
Country: USA
Mailing address 1: 28 Ten Eyck Ave
Mailing city: Albany
Mailing state: NY
Mailing zip: 12209-1518
Office phone: (800) 723-4272
Other fax: www.4asap.com
Web address: holdit@4asap.com
General e-mail: Production Division: FreeHold Business Marketing Solutions
Note: Kevin Childs (Consultant); T. Raymond Gruno (Mktg. Dir.)
Employee Associations: Kevin Childs

MEDIA LOGIC USA, LLC
Product or Service: Advertising/Marketing Agency`Graphic/Design Firm`Marketing`Multimedia/Interactive Products
Street address 1: 59 Wolf Rd
Street address state: NY
Postal code: 12205-2612
County: Albany
Country: USA
Mailing address 1: 59 Wolf Road
Mailing city: Albany
Mailing state: NY
Mailing zip: 12205
Office phone: (518) 456-3015
Office fax: (518) 456-4279
Other fax: www.medialogic.com
Web address: jmcdonald@medialogic.com
Note: Jim McDonald (New Business); David Schultz (Press Mgr.)
Employee Associations: Jim McDonald

ALBUQUERQUE

D & H INFORMATION SERVICES, INC.
Street address 1: 5720 Osuna Rd NE
Street address state: NM
Postal code: 87109-2527
County: Bernalillo
Country: USA
Mailing address 1: 5720 Osuna Rd NE
Mailing city: Albuquerque
Mailing state: NM
Mailing zip: 87109-2527
Office phone: (505) 888-3620
Office fax: (505) 888-3722
Other fax: www.dhinfo.com
Web address: dhinfo@dhinfo.com

ALPHARETTA

CONVERGENT MEDIA SYSTEMS
Product or Service: Multimedia/Interactive Products
Street address 1: 190 Bluegrass Valley Pkwy
Street address state: GA
Postal code: 30005-2204
County: Forsyth
Country: USA
Mailing address 1: 190 Bluegrass Valley Pkwy
Mailing city: Alpharetta
Mailing state: GA
Mailing zip: 30005-2204
Office phone: (770) 369-9000
Office fax: (770) 369-9100
Other fax: www.convergent.com
Web address: convergent@convergent.com
Note: Bryan Allen (CEO); Rick Hutcheson (Vice Pres., Mktg.)
Employee Associations: Rick Hutcheson

EASE CT SOLUTIONS
Product or Service: Hardware/Software Supplier
Street address 1: 5995 Windward Pkwy
Street address state: GA
Postal code: 30005-4184
County: Fulton
Country: USA
Mailing address 1: 5995 Windward Pkwy
Mailing city: Alpharetta
Mailing state: GA
Mailing zip: 30005-4184
Office phone: (404) 338-2241
Office fax: (404) 338-6101

ALTAMONTE SPRINGS

ADVANCED INTERACTIVE MEDIA GROUP, LLC
Product or Service: Consultants`Publisher/Media
Street address 1: 402 Spring Valley Rd
Street address state: FL
Postal code: 32714-5845
County: Seminole
Country: USA
Mailing address 1: 402 Spring Valley Rd
Mailing city: Altamonte Springs
Mailing state: FL
Mailing zip: 32714
Office phone: (407) 788-2780
Office fax: (866) 611-6551
Other phone: (321) 356-3182
Other fax: www.aimgroup.com
Web address: pzollman@aimgroup.com
General e-mail: The AIM Group is a global team of consulting experts in classified advertising, marketplaces and interactive media. We help publishers grow their businesses through strategic and tactical support. We publish Classified Intelligence Report, the international continuous advisory service that is often called "the bible of the classified advertising industry." We work with news media publishers, dot-coms, print classified publishers, yellow page publishers, broadcasters and technology vendors worldwide to help develop, launch and grow revenue-generating services. We are first and foremost "consultants who publish," not "publishers who do a little consulting on the side." Most of our consulting work is performed on a proprietary basis, so our clients often see only a small fraction of our work-product. We offer solutions for companies planning their strategies, increasing revenue, market share, and in developing products and packing strategies to grow their business. We help build interactive products and services; we don't just talk about them based on flimsy research. We support investors and analysts trying to determine the health of a company, or to find companies ripe for investment or acquisition. Our team includes long-time senior executives, so we work with senior executives to help them understand where their interactive-media and classified services need to evolve. We've been sales reps and sales managers, so we can help sales teams grow and develop traditional and interactive media services. Our writer / analysts get to the heart of the matter, and understand the business inside and out. We work with clients globally. Our worldwide team of almost 40 people follows the evolution in interactive media and classified advertising more closely than anyone else.
Note: Peter M. Zollman (Founding Principal); Jim Townsend (Editorial Director); Katja Riefler (Europe Director); Rob Paterson (Principal, director of consulting); Diana Bogdan
Employee Associations: Peter M. Zollman; Luke Smith

DANIEL LAMPERT COMMUNICATIONS CORP.
Product or Service: Multimedia/Interactive Products`Online Service Provider and Internet Hosts
Street address 1: PO Box 151719
Street address state: FL
Postal code: 32715-1719
County: Seminole
Country: USA
Mailing address 1: PO Box 151719
Mailing city: Altamonte Springs
Mailing state: FL
Mailing zip: 32715-1719
Office phone: (407) 327-7000
Office fax: (407) 695-9014
Other fax: www.dlc2.com
Web address: service@dlc2.com
Note: Dan Lampert (Pres.)
Employee Associations: Dan Lampert

ARLINGTON HEIGHTS

ALLIANCE FOR AUDITED MEDIA
Product or Service: Consultants`Trade Association`Web Site Auditor
Street address 1: 48 W Seegers Rd
Street address state: IL
Postal code: 60005-3900
County: Cook
Country: USA
Mailing address 1: 48 W Seegers Rd
Mailing city: Arlington Heights
Mailing state: IL
Mailing zip: 60005-3900
Office phone: (224) 366-6939
Office fax: (224) 366-6949
Other fax: www.auditedmedia.com/services/digital-services.aspx
Note: Steve Guenther (VP, Digital Auditing Services); Tom Drouillard (CEO, President and Managing Director)
Employee Associations: Susan Kantor

COMMUNITECH SERVICES INC.
Product or Service: Telecommunications/Service Bureaus
Street address 1: 2340 S Arlington Heights Rd
Street address 2: Ste 360
Street address state: IL
Postal code: 60005-4517
County: Cook
Country: USA
Mailing address 1: 2340 S Arlington Heights Rd Ste 360
Mailing city: Arlington Heights
Mailing state: IL
Mailing zip: 60005-4517
Office phone: (847) 981-1200
Office fax: (847) 981-9085
Other fax: www.communitechservices.com
Web address: info@communitechservices.com
Note: Barb Gendes Shact (Vice Pres.)
Employee Associations: Barb Gendes Shact

ARMONK

IBM CORP.
Product or Service: Hardware/Software Supplier
Street address 1: 1 New Orchard Rd
Street address state: NY
Postal code: 10504-1722
County: Westchester
Country: USA
Mailing address 1: 6303 Barfield Rd
Mailing city: Atlanta
Mailing state: GA
Mailing zip: 30328-4233
Office phone: (404) 236-2600
Office fax: (404) 236-2626
Other fax: www.ibm.com
Note: Virginia Rometty (Chrmn./Pres./CEO); Michelle Browdy (Sr. Vice Pres./Legal & Reg. Affairs & Gen. Counsel); James J. Kavanaugh (Sr. Vice Pres., CFO); Michelle Peluso (Sr. Vice Pres., Chief Marketing Officer); John E. Kelly III (Sr. Vice Pres., Dir. of Research)
Employee Associations: Lennart Malm

ASHBURN

MCI
Product or Service: Online Service Provider and Internet Hosts`Telecommunications/Service Bureaus
Street address 1: 22001 Loudoun County Pkwy
Street address state: VA
Postal code: 20147-6105
County: Loudoun

Interactive Products and Services Companies

Country: USA
Mailing address 1: 22001 Loudoun County Pkwy
Mailing city: Ashburn
Mailing state: VA
Mailing zip: 20147-6122
Office phone: (703) 206-5600
Office fax: (703) 206-5601
Other fax: www.mci.com
Web address: info@mci.com
Note: Ivan Siedenberg (Chrmn./CEO); Fred Briggs (Pres., Opns./Tech.); Robert Blakely (Exec. Vice Pres./CFO); Daniel Casaccia (Exec. Vice Pres., HR); Jonathan Crane (Exec. Vice Pres., Strategy/Cor. Devel.); Grace Chentent (Sr. Vice Pres., Commun.); Nancy B. Gofus (Sr. Vice Pres., Mktg./CMO); Shane King
Employee Associations: Nancy B. Gofus

AUSTIN

IGNITE OLIVE SOFTWARE SOLUTIONS

Product or Service: Multimedia/Interactive Products`Online Service Provider and Internet Hosts
Street address 1: 401 Congress Ave.
Street address 2: Suite 2650
Street address state: TX
Postal code: 78701
County: Travis
Country: USA
Mailing address 1: 401 Congress Ave., Suite 2650
Mailing city: Austin
Mailing state: TX
Mailing zip: 78701
Office phone: 855-453-8174
Other fax: www.ignitetech.com
Web address: success@ignitetech.com
Note: Davin Cushman (CEO); Eric Vaughan (COO)
Employee Associations: Survey Contact

BATH

M2 COMMUNICATIONS LTD.

Product or Service: Publisher/Media
Street address 1: PO Box 4030
Street address state: ENG
Postal code: BA1 0EE
Country: United Kingdom
Mailing address 1: PO Box 4030
Mailing city: Bath
Mailing state: ENG
Mailing zip: BA1 0EE
Office phone: 7047 0200
Office fax: 7057 0200
Other fax: www.m2.com
Web address: info@m2.com
Note: Jamie Ayres (Ed. in Cheif)
Employee Associations: Jamie Ayres

BATON ROUGE

LOUISIANA SHERIFF'S ASSOCIATION

Product or Service: Consultants`Editorial`Graphic/Design Firm`Marketing`Other Services`Trade Association
Street address 1: 1175 Nicholson Drive
Street address state: LA
Postal code: 70802
Country: USA
Mailing address 1: 1175 Nicholson Drive
Mailing city: Baton Rouge
Mailing state: LA
Mailing zip: 70802
Office phone: (225) 343-8402
Office fax: (225) 336-0343
Other fax: www.lsa.org
Note: Michael Ranatza (Executive Director); Cynthia Butler (Office Manager); Lauren Labbe' Meher (Dir. of Comm. and Pub. Affairs); Darlene Petty (Accounting)
Employee Associations: Cynthia Butler

BERKELEY

AARON MARCUS AND ASSOCIATES.

Product or Service: CD-ROM Designer/Manufacturer`Consultants`Graphic/Design Firm`POP/Kiosk Designer`Research
Street address 1: 1196 Euclid Ave
Street address state: CA
Postal code: 94708-1640
County: Alameda
Country: USA
Mailing address 1: 1196 Euclid Avenue
Mailing city: Berkeley
Mailing state: CA
Mailing zip: 94708-1640
Office phone: (510)599-3195
Other fax: www.bamanda.com
Web address: aaron.marcus@bamanda.com
General e-mail: Available to author research and other publications, to be interviewed, or to give lectures/workshops
Note: Aaron Marcus (Principal)
Employee Associations: Aaron Marcus

BERNARDSVILLE

CYBERSMART

Product or Service: Multimedia/Interactive Products
Street address 1: 201 Lloyd Rd
Street address state: NJ
Postal code: 07924-1711
County: Somerset
Country: USA
Mailing address 1: 201 Lloyd Rd
Mailing city: Bernardsville
Mailing state: NJ
Mailing zip: 07924-1711
Office phone: (908) 221-1516
Office fax: (908) 221-0617
Other phone: (800) 615-9806
Other fax: www.cybersmart.org
Web address: information@cybersmart.org
Note: Jim Teicher (Exec. Dir.); Mala Bawer (Exec. Dir.)
Employee Associations: Jim Teicher

BETHESDA

ARLEN COMMUNICATIONS LLC

Product or Service: Consultants
Street address 1: 6407 Landon Ln
Street address state: MD
Postal code: 20817-5603
County: Montgomery
Country: USA
Mailing address 1: 6407 Landon Lane
Mailing city: Bethesda
Mailing state: MD
Mailing zip: 20817
Office phone: (301) 229 2199
Other fax: www.arlencom.com
Web address: garlen@arlencom.com
Note: Gary Arlen (Pres.)
Employee Associations: Gary Arlen

L-SOFT INTERNATIONAL, INC.

Product or Service: Hardware/Software Supplier
Street address 1: 7550 Wisconsin Ave # 400
Street address state: MD
Postal code: 20814-3573
Country: USA
Mailing address 1: 7550 Wisconsin Ave # 400
Mailing city: Bethesda
Mailing state: MD
Mailing zip: 20814-3573
Office phone: (301) 731-0440
Office fax: (301) 731-6302
Other fax: www.lsoft.com
Web address: sales@lsoft.com
Note: Eric Thomas (CEO); Outi Tuomaala (Vice Pres., Marketing)
Employee Associations: Eric Thomas

BETHLEHEM

ACTIVE DATA EXCHANGE

Product or Service: Publisher/Media
Street address 1: 190 Brodhead Rd Ste 300
Street address 2: Lehigh Valley Industrial Pk. IV
Street address state: PA
Postal code: 18017-8617
County: Northampton
Country: USA
Mailing address 1: 190 Brodhead Rd Ste 300 Lehigh Valley Industrial Pk. IV
Mailing city: Bethlehem
Mailing state: PA
Mailing zip: 18017-8617
Office phone: (610) 997-8100
Office fax: (610) 866-7899
Other fax: www.activedatax.com
Web address: info@activedatax.com
Note: Susan C. Yee (Pres./CEO); Kendra Hollinger (COO)
Employee Associations: Kendra Hollinger

BETHPAGE

CABLEVISION SYSTEMS CORPORATION

Product or Service: Telecommunications/Service Bureaus
Street address 1: 1111 Stewart Ave
Street address state: NY
Postal code: 11714-3533
County: Nassau
Country: USA
Mailing address 1: 1111 Stewart Ave
Mailing city: Bethpage
Mailing state: NY
Mailing zip: 11714-3581
Office phone: (516) 803-2300
Other fax: www.cablevision.com
Note: Charles F. Dolan (Chairman); James L. Dolan (President and CEO); Hank Ratner (Vice Chairman); David Ellen (Executive Vice President & General Counsel); Gregg Seibert (Vice Chairman & CFO); Tad Smith (President, Local Media); Wilt Hildenbrand (Sr. Advisor, Customer Care, Technology and Networks); Kristin Dolan (President, Optimum Services)
Employee Associations: Lisa Anselmo

BIRMINGHAM

DTN/THE PROGRESSIVE FARMER

Product or Service: Online Service Provider and Internet Hosts`Publisher/Media
Street address 1: 2204 Lakeshore Dr
Street address 2: Ste 415
Street address state: AL
Postal code: 35209-8856
County: Jefferson
Country: USA
Mailing address 1: PO Box 62400
Mailing city: Tampa
Mailing state: FL
Mailing zip: 33662-2400
Office phone: (800) 292-2340
Other fax: www.dtn.com
Web address: onlinehelp@dtn.com
Note: Gregg Hillyer (Ed.-in-Chief)
Employee Associations: Gregg Hillyer

BLOOMINGTON

CONVERGEONE

Product or Service: Telecommunications/Service Bureaus
Street address 1: 10900 Nesbitt Avenue South
Street address state: MN
Postal code: 55437
County: Hennepin
Country: USA
Mailing address 1: 10900 Nesbitt Avenue South
Mailing city: Bloomington
Mailing state: MN
Mailing zip: 55437
Office phone: (888) 321-6227
Other fax: www.convergeone.com
Web address: Econtactus@convergeone.com
Note: John A. Mckenna (Chairman & CEO); Jeffrey E. Nachbor (CFO); Scott Clark (Vice Pres., Mrkt.)
Employee Associations: Scott Clark

BOCA RATON

INTERACTIVE PUBLISHING CORP.

Product or Service: CD-ROM Designer/Manufacturer
Street address 1: 7639 Edarwood Cir
Street address state: FL
Postal code: 33434-
County: Palm Beach
Country: USA
Mailing address 1: 7639 Cedarwood Cir
Mailing city: Boca Raton
Mailing state: FL
Mailing zip: 33434-4248
Office phone: (561) 483-7734
Other fax: www.victormilt.com
Web address: vicmilt@victormilt.com
Note: Kim Milt (CEO); Victor Milt (Creative Dir.); Martin Ross (Exec. Producer)
Employee Associations: Victor Milt

BOONTON

INTERACTIVE MEDIA ASSOCIATES

Product or Service: Consultants
Street address 1: 612 Main St
Street address state: NJ
Postal code: 07005-1761
County: Morris
Country: USA
Mailing address 1: 612 Main St
Mailing city: Boonton
Mailing state: NJ
Mailing zip: 07005-1761
Office phone: (973) 539-5255
Office fax: (973) 917-4730
Other fax: www.imediainc.com
Web address: info@imediainc.com
Note: Len Muscarella (Founder); Sally Muscarella (Pres.); Michelle Camaron (Vice Pres./Creative Dir.); Anthony Zarro (Vice Pres., Bus. Devel.); Brian McGovern (Dir., Devel.); Geri Ricciani (Dir., Pjct. Mgmt.)
Employee Associations: Joel Macaluso

BOSTON

COLLEGE PUBLISHER, INC.

Product or Service: Hardware/Software Supplier
Street address 1: 31 Saint James Ave
Street address 2: Ste 920
Street address state: MA
Postal code: 02116-4155
County: Suffolk
Country: USA
Mailing address 1: 31 Saint James Ave Ste 920
Mailing city: Boston
Mailing state: MA
Mailing zip: 02116-4155
Office phone: (888) 735-5578
Other fax: www.collegepublisher.com
Web address: support@collegemedianetwork.com
Note: Chris Gillon (Contact)
Employee Associations: Chris Gillon

BOYNTON BEACH

EPUBLISH4ME

Product or Service: Advertising/Marketing Agency`Graphic/Design Firm`Multimedia/Interactive Products`Online Service Provider and Internet Hosts`Publisher/Media
Street address 1: 1375 Gateway Blvd
Street address state: FL
Postal code: 33426-8304
County: Palm Beach

Country: USA
Mailing address 1: 1375 Gateway Blvd
Mailing city: Boynton Beach
Mailing state: FL
Mailing zip: 33426-8304
Office phone: (561) 370-3336
Other fax: www.epublish4me.com
Web address: sales@epublish4me.com
General e-mail: Digitize your pubs at http://www.epublish4me.com/?r=403. It automatically posts them on TitleStand where you can sell them by getting local and worldwide distribution (see http://titlestand.com/t). Your PDFs are converted into digital 3-D page flipping revenue generator books, newspapers or magazines with video, audio, hyperlinks and extensive tracking where they can be read on Tablet, PC, Mac, iPad, iPhone, iTouch, iOS, Android and Kindle Fire. Kind regards, Nick.Koriakin@ePublish4me.com 561-370-3336
Note: Nicholas Koriakin (Senior Account Executive)
Employee Associations: Nicholas Koriakin

BRONXVILLE

CYBER SALES ONE, INC.

Product or Service: Advertising/Marketing Agency
Street address 1: PO Box 84
Street address state: NY
Postal code: 10708-0084
County: Westchester
Country: USA
Mailing address 1: PO Box 84
Mailing city: Bronxville
Mailing state: NY
Mailing zip: 10708-0084
Office phone: (917) 250-6074
Web address: albertcran@aol.com
Note: Albert H. Crane (Pres./CEO)
Employee Associations: Albert H. Crane

BROOKHAVEN

GREAT!

Product or Service: Telecommunications/Service Bureaus
Street address 1: 3527 Knollhaven Dr NE
Street address state: GA
Postal code: 30319-1908
County: Dekalb
Country: USA
Mailing address 1: 3527 Knollhaven Dr NE
Mailing city: Atlanta
Mailing state: GA
Mailing zip: 30319-1908
Office phone: (404) 303-7311
Office fax: (404) 252-0697
Other fax: www.greattv.com
Web address: dan@greattv.com
Note: Dan Smigrod (CEO/Chief Creative Officer)
Employee Associations: Dan Smigrod

BROOKLYN

AMPLIFY EDUCATION, INC.

Product or Service: Multimedia/Interactive Products
Street address 1: 5 Washington St.
Street address 2: #800
Street address state: NY
Postal code: 11201
County: Fulton
Country: USA
Mailing address 1: 5 Washington St., #800
Mailing city: Brooklyn
Mailing state: NY
Mailing zip: 11201
Office phone: (800) 823-1969
Other fax: www.amplify.com
Web address: help@amplify.com
Note: Larry Berger (CEO)
Employee Associations: Survey Contact

BROOMFIELD

ESOFT

Product or Service: Hardware/Software Supplier
Street address 1: 295 Interlocken Blvd
Street address 2: Ste 500
Street address state: CO
Postal code: 80021-8002
County: Broomfield
Country: USA
Mailing address 1: 1490 W 121st Ave Ste 205
Mailing city: Denver
Mailing state: CO
Mailing zip: 80234-3497
Office phone: (866) 233-2296
Other fax: www.esoft.com
Web address: info@esoft.com
Note: Jeff Finn (CEO/Pres.); Patrick Walsh (CTO); Tim Olson (Dir., Finance); Jason Rollings (Vice Pres., Opns.)
Employee Associations: Jeff Finn

BURBANK

ADVANCED PUBLISHING TECHNOLOGY

Product or Service: Circulation`Editorial`Hardware/Software Supplier`Online Service Provider and Internet Hosts
Street address 1: 123 S Victory Blvd
Street address state: CA
Postal code: 91502-2347
County: Los Angeles
Country: USA
Mailing address 1: 123 S Victory Blvd
Mailing city: Burbank
Mailing state: CA
Mailing zip: 91502-2347
Office phone: (818) 557-3035
Office fax: (818) 557-1281
Other fax: www.advpubtech.com
Web address: aptsales@advpubtech.com
Note: David Kraai (Pres.); Ken Barber (COO); Diane Duren (Online Product Mgr.); Shellie Sommersen (Adv. Prod. Mgr.); Sid Kendrick (Cir. Prod. Mgr.); Joe Kennedy (Ed. Prod. Mgr.)
Employee Associations: Ken Barber

CALVERTON

MICRO PERFECT CORP.

Product or Service: Hardware/Software Supplier
Street address 1: PO Box 285
Street address state: NY
Postal code: 11933-0285
County: Suffolk
Country: USA
Mailing address 1: PO Box 285
Mailing city: Calverton
Mailing state: NY
Mailing zip: 11933-0285
Office phone: (631) 727-9639
Office fax: (631) 727-9638
Other fax: www.microperfect.com
Web address: info@microperfect.com; perfect@microperfect.com
Note: Gregory Fischer (Mgr.)
Employee Associations: Gregory Fischer

CAMERON PARK

CBS MAXPREPS, INC.

Product or Service: Multimedia/Interactive Products`Publisher/Media
Street address 1: 4080 Plaza Goldorado Cir
Street address 2: Ste A
Street address state: CA
Postal code: 95682-7455
County: El Dorado
Country: USA
Mailing address 1: 4080 Plaza Goldorado Cir Ste A
Mailing city: Cameron Park
Mailing state: CA
Mailing zip: 95682-7455
Office phone: (800) 329-7324
Office fax: (530) 672-8559
Other fax: www.maxpreps.com
Web address: sales@maxpreps.com
Note: Andy Beal (Pres.)
Employee Associations: Andy Beal

CARLSBAD

ANIMATED SOFTWARE CO.

Product or Service: Multimedia/Interactive Products
Street address 1: PO Box 1936
Street address state: CA
Postal code: 92018-1936
County: San Diego
Country: USA
Mailing address 1: PO Box 1936
Mailing city: Carlsbad
Mailing state: CA
Mailing zip: 92018-1936
Office phone: (760) 720-7261
Other fax: www.animatedsoftware.com
Web address: rhoffman@animatedsoftware.com
Note: Ace Hoffman (Owner/Chief Programmer)
Employee Associations: Ace Hoffman

CSTV ONLINE, INC.

Product or Service: Multimedia/Interactive Products
Street address 1: 2035 Corte Del Nogal
Street address 2: Ste 250
Street address state: CA
Postal code: 92011-1465
County: San Diego
Country: USA
Mailing address 1: 2035 Corte Del Nogal Ste 250
Mailing city: Carlsbad
Mailing state: CA
Mailing zip: 92011-1465
Office phone: (760) 431-8221
Office fax: (760) 431-8108
Other fax: www.cstv.com
Web address: customersupport@cstv.com
Note: Tim Rivere (Vice Pres., Sales); George Scott (Dir., Finance); Tom Keyes (Exec. Producer)
Employee Associations: George Scott

CARMEL

JUDSON ROSEBUSH CO.

Product or Service: Multimedia/Interactive Products
Street address 1: 15 China Circle Ct
Street address state: NY
Postal code: 10512-4452
County: Putnam
Country: USA
Mailing address 1: 15 China Circle Court
Mailing city: Carmel
Mailing state: NY
Mailing zip: 10512
Office phone: (212) 581-3000
Other fax: www.rosebush.com
Web address: info@rosebush.com
Note: Judson Rosebush (Pres.)
Employee Associations: Judson Rosebush

CARROLLTON

LAUNCH AGENCY

Product or Service: Advertising/Marketing Agency
Street address 1: 4100 Midway Rd
Street address 2: Ste 2110
Street address state: TX
Postal code: 75007-1965
County: Denton
Country: USA
Mailing address 1: 4100 Midway Rd Ste 2110
Mailing city: Carrollton
Mailing state: TX
Mailing zip: 75007-1965
Office phone: (972) 818-4100
Office fax: (972) 818-4101
Other fax: www.launchagency.com
Web address: mboone@launchagency.com

CARSON CITY

COBBEY & ASSOCIATES FULL SERVICE MARKETING RESEARCH

Product or Service: Consultants
Street address 1: PO Box 12
Street address state: NV
Postal code: 89702-0012
County: Carson City
Country: USA
Mailing address 1: PO Box 12
Mailing city: Carson City
Mailing state: NV
Mailing zip: 89702-0012
Office phone: (877) 433-3242
Office fax: (775) 847-0327
Other phone: (775) 847-0321
Other fax: www.cobbey.com
Web address: cobbey@cobbey.com

CHAMPAIGN

DREAMSCAPE DESIGN, INC.

Product or Service: Advertising/Marketing Agency`CD-ROM Designer/Manufacturer`Consultants`Graphic/Design Firm`Multimedia/Interactive Products`POP/Kiosk Designer`Web Site Auditor
Street address 1: 10 Henson Pl
Street address 2: Ste A
Street address state: IL
Postal code: 61820-7836
County: Champaign
Country: USA
Mailing address 1: 10 Henson Pl Ste A
Mailing city: Champaign
Mailing state: IL
Mailing zip: 61820-7836
Office phone: (217) 359-8484
Office fax: (217) 239-5858
Other fax: www.dreamscapedesign.com
Web address: info@dreamscapedesign.com
Note: Amy Moushon (Bus. Devel. Mgr.)
Employee Associations: Amy Moushon

CHANTILLY

BIAKELSEY

Product or Service: Publisher/Media
Street address 1: 15120 Enterprise Ct
Street address state: VA
Postal code: 20151-1274
County: Fairfax
Country: USA
Mailing address 1: 15120 Enterprise Ct Ste 100
Mailing city: Chantilly
Mailing state: VA
Mailing zip: 20151-1275
Office phone: (800) 331-5086
Other fax: www.kelseygroup.com
Web address: info@biakelsey.com
Note: Neal Polachek (CEO)
Employee Associations: Neal Polachek

CHAPEL HILL

B-LINKED, INC.

Product or Service: Online Service Provider and Internet Hosts
Street address 1: PO Box 3721
Street address state: NC
Postal code: 27515-3721
County: Orange
Country: USA
Mailing address 1: PO Box 3721
Mailing city: Chapel Hill
Mailing state: NC
Mailing zip: 27515-3721
Office phone: (919) 883-5362

Interactive Products and Services Companies

Other fax: www.adtransit.com
Web address: tmelet@b-linked.com
Note: Todd Melet (President); Michael-Anne Ashman (VP of Technology)
Employee Associations: Todd Melet

CHICAGO

AMASIS
Product or Service: Graphic/Design Firm
Street address 1: 1538 W Cullerton St
Street address state: IL
Postal code: 60608-2918
County: Cook
Country: USA
Mailing address 1: 1538 W Cullerton St
Mailing city: Chicago
Mailing state: IL
Mailing zip: 60608-2918
Office phone: (312) 850-9459
Office fax: (312) 850-9459
Other fax: www.amasis.com
Web address: amasis@amasis.com
Note: Tamara Manning (Head Designer)
Employee Associations: Tamara Manning

ANSWERS MEDIA INC.
Product or Service: Multimedia/Interactive Products
Street address 1: 30 N Racine Ave
Street address 2: Ste 300
Street address state: IL
Postal code: 60607-2184
County: Cook
Country: USA
Mailing address 1: 30 N Racine Ave Ste 300
Mailing city: Chicago
Mailing state: IL
Mailing zip: 60607-2184
Office phone: (312) 421-0113
Office fax: (312) 421-1457
Other fax: www.answersmediainc.com
Web address: info@answersmediainc.com
Note: Jeff Bohnson (Pres.)
Employee Associations: Jeff Bohnson

ATOMIC IMAGING, INC.
Product or Service: Graphic/Design Firm
Street address 1: 1501 N Magnolia Ave
Street address state: IL
Postal code: 60642-2427
County: Cook
Country: USA
Mailing address 1: 1501 N Magnolia Ave
Mailing city: Chicago
Mailing state: IL
Mailing zip: 60642-2427
Office phone: (312) 649-1800
Office fax: (312) 642-7441
Other fax: www.atomicimaging.com
Web address: info@atomicimaging.com
Note: Ari Golan (Pres.); Nick Brown (Commun. Consultant); Aigar Dombrouskis (Producer); Jim Abreu (Interactive Design)
Employee Associations: Candice Gerber

DESIGNORY.COM
Product or Service: Advertising/Marketing Agency
Street address 1: 200 E Randolph St
Street address 2: Ste 3620
Street address state: IL
Postal code: 60601-6512
County: Cook
Country: USA
Mailing address 1: 200 E Randolph St Suite 3620
Mailing city: Chicago
Mailing state: IL
Mailing zip: 60601-6436
Office phone: (312) 729-4500
Other fax: www.designory.com

MOTOROLA MOBILITY, LLC.
Product or Service: Telecommunications/Service Bureaus
Street address 1: 500 W Monroe Street
Street address 2: Ste 4400
Street address state: IL
Postal code: 60661-3781
Country: USA
Mailing address 1: 500 W Monroe Street, Ste 4400
Mailing city: Chicago
Mailing state: IL
Mailing zip: 60661-3781
Office phone: (847) 523-5000
Office fax: (847) 523-8770
Other fax: htwww.motorola.com
Note: Sergio Buniac (Pres.); Grant Hoffman (Vice Pres. Bus. Op.); Terry Vega (Vice Pres. & Gen. Mgr.); Sanjay Vanjani (CFO)
Employee Associations: Derek Wimmer

CINCINNATI

CELEBRO
Product or Service: Hardware/Software Supplier
Street address 1: 312 Elm St
Street address 2: Fl 20
Street address state: OH
Postal code: 45202-2739
County: Hamilton
Country: USA
Mailing address 1: 151 W 4th St Ste 201
Mailing city: Cincinnati
Mailing state: OH
Mailing zip: 45202-2746
Office phone: (513) 665-3777
Office fax: (513) 768-8958
Other fax: www.gmti.com
Web address: info@celebro.com
Note: Steve Fuschetti (Pres./CEO); Tom Foster (Vice Pres., Celebro Opns.); Michael Hibert (Dir., Implementation Servs.)
Employee Associations: Steve Fuschetti

CONVERGYS
Product or Service: Multimedia/Interactive Products
Street address 1: 201 E 4th St
Street address state: OH
Postal code: 45202-4248
County: Hamilton
Country: USA
Mailing address 1: 201 E 4th St Bsmt
Mailing city: Cincinnati
Mailing state: OH
Mailing zip: 45202-4206
Office phone: (513) 723-7000
Other fax: www.convergys.com
Web address: marketing@convergys.com
Note: Keith Wolters (Sr. Dir., Mktg.)
Employee Associations: Keith Wolters

GANNETT MEDIA TECHNOLOGIES INTERNATIONAL (GMTI)
Product or Service: Multimedia/Interactive Products
Street address 1: 312 Elm St
Street address 2: Fl 20
Street address state: OH
Postal code: 45202-2739
County: Hamilton
Country: USA
Mailing address 1: 312 Elm St Ste 2G
Mailing city: Cincinnati
Mailing state: OH
Mailing zip: 45202-2763
Office phone: (513) 665-3777
Office fax: (513) 768-8958
Other fax: www.gmti.com
Web address: gmti-info@gmti.gannett.com
Note: Steve Fuschetti (Pres./CEO)
Employee Associations: Steve Fuschetti

GMTI (DIGITAL COLLECTIONS)
Product or Service: Consultants`Hardware/Software Supplier`Online Service Provider and Internet Hosts
Street address 1: 312 Elm St
Street address 2: Fl 20
Street address state: OH
Postal code: 45202-2739
County: Hamilton
Country: USA
Mailing address 1: 312 Elm St Fl 20
Mailing city: Cincinnati
Mailing state: OH
Mailing zip: 45202-2739
Office phone: (513) 665-3777
Office fax: (513) 768-8958
Other phone: (513) 768-8938
Other fax: www.gannett.com
Web address: contentfeedback@gannett.com
Note: Steve Fuschetti (Pres./CEO); Bill Mahlock (Vice Pres., Installations/Support); Michael Tucker (Dir., Sales & Marketing)
Employee Associations: ()

COHOES

INTERACTIVE PICTURES CORPORATION (IPIX)
Product or Service: Multimedia/Interactive Products
Street address 1: 48 Western Ave
Street address state: NY
Postal code: 12047-3903
County: Albany
Country: USA
Mailing address 1: 48 Western Avenue
Mailing city: Cohoes
Mailing state: NY
Mailing zip: 12047
Office phone: (518) 235-3455
Other phone: (518) 235-3455
Other fax: https://www.ipix.com
Web address: support@ipix.com
Note: Mary Pam Claiborne (Contact)
Employee Associations: Mary Pam Claiborne

CUPERTINO

APPLE, INC.
Product or Service: Hardware/Software Supplier
Street address 1: 1 Infinite Loop
Street address state: CA
Postal code: 95014-2083
County: Santa Clara
Country: USA
Mailing address 1: 1 Infinite Loop
Mailing city: Cupertino
Mailing state: CA
Mailing zip: 95014-2084
Office phone: (408) 996â€"1010
Office fax: (408) 996-0275
Other fax: www.apple.com
Web address: media.help@apple.com
Note: Timothy Cook (CEO); Philip W. Schiller (Sr. V. P. Worldwide Marketing); Jonathan Ive (Chief Design Officer); Craig Federighi (Senior Vice President, Software Engineering)
Employee Associations: Semonti Stephens

DALLAS

AT&T, INC.
Product or Service: Telecommunications/Service Bureaus
Street address 1: 208 S. Akard Street
Street address 2: Suite 2954
Street address state: TX
Postal code: 75202
County: Bexar
Country: USA
Mailing address 1: 208 S. Akard Street
Mailing city: Dallas
Mailing state: TX
Mailing zip: 75202
Office phone: (210) 821-4105
Office fax: (210) 351-2071
Other fax: www.att.com
Note: Randall L. Stephenson (Chrmn./CEO); Dennis M. Payne (Pres./CEO, AT&T Directory Opns.); Lea Ann Champion (Sr. Exec. Vice Pres./CMO); Cathy Coughlin (SVP/Global Mktg. Officer); Linda Hanacek
Employee Associations: Lea Ann Champion

CENTURYTEL INTERACTIVE
Product or Service: Telecommunications/Service Bureaus
Street address 1: 8750 N Central Expy
Street address 2: Ste 720
Street address state: TX
Postal code: 75231-6462
County: Dallas
Country: USA
Mailing address 1: 8750 N Central Expy Ste 720
Mailing city: Dallas
Mailing state: TX
Mailing zip: 75231-6462
Office phone: (214) 360-6280
Office fax: (972) 996-0868
Other fax: www.centuryinteractive.com
Web address: jd@centuryinteractive.com
Note: Jack Doege (COO)
Employee Associations: Jack Doege

DEX MEDIA
Product or Service: Advertising/Marketing Agency`Marketing
Street address 1: 2200 W Airfield Dr
Street address state: TX
Postal code: 75261-4008
County: Dallas
Country: USA
Mailing address 1: 2200 W. Airfield Dr.
Mailing city: Grapevine
Mailing state: TX
Mailing zip: 75261
Office phone: (919) 297-1600
Other fax: www.dexmedia.com
Note: Richard C. Notebaert (Chrmn./CEO, Qwest); Oren G. Shaffer (Vice Chrmn./CFO); George Burnett (Pres./CEO, Qwest Dex); Robin R. Szeliga (Exec. Vice Pres., Finance); Joan H. Walker (Sr. Vice Pres., Cor. Commun.)
Employee Associations: Cindi Barrington

DEX ONE CORP.
Product or Service: Publisher/Media
Street address 1: 2200 W Airfield Dr
Street address state: TX
Postal code: 75261-4008
County: Dallas
Country: USA
Mailing address 1: 1001 Winstead Dr
Mailing city: Cary
Mailing state: NC
Mailing zip: 27513-2117
Office phone: (919) 297-1600
Office fax: (919) 297-1285
Other fax: www.dexone.com
Web address: info@dexone.com
Note: Steven M. Blondy (Exec. Vice Pres./CFO); Maggie LeBeau (Sr. Vice Pres./CMO)
Employee Associations: Maggie LeBeau

D-SQUARED STUDIOS, INC.
Product or Service: Multimedia/Interactive Products
Street address 1: 4312 Elm St
Street address state: TX
Postal code: 75226-1133
County: Dallas
Country: USA
Mailing address 1: 4312 Elm St
Mailing city: Dallas
Mailing state: TX
Mailing zip: 75226-1133
Office phone: (214) 746-6336
Office fax: (214) 746-6338
Other fax: www.d2studios.net

Web address: doug.davis@d2studios.net
Note: Doug Davis (Pres.)
Employee Associations: Doug Davis

IMAGEN, INC.

Product or Service: Graphic/Design Firm
Street address 1: PO Box 814270
Street address state: TX
Postal code: 75381-4270
County: Dallas
Country: USA
Mailing address 1: PO Box 814270
Mailing city: Dallas
Mailing state: TX
Mailing zip: 75381-4270
Office phone: (214) 232-3385
Office fax: (419) 821-2047
Other fax: www.imageninc.com
Web address: al@imageninc.com
Note: Al Schmidt (Pres.)
Employee Associations: Claudia Espinosa

M/C/C

Product or Service: Advertising/Marketing Agency
Street address 1: 12377 Merit Dr.
Street address 2: Suite 800
Street address state: TX
Postal code: 75251
County: Dallas
Country: USA
Mailing address 1: 12377 Merit Dr., Suite 800
Mailing city: Dallas
Mailing state: TX
Mailing zip: 75251
Office phone: (972) 480-8383
Office fax: (972) 669-8447
Other fax: www.mccom.com
Web address: pam_watkins@mccom.com
Note: Mike Crawford (Pres.); Pam Watkins (SVP, Business and Media Strategy); Jim Terry (SVP, Account Service); Shannon Sullivan (Vice President, Account Supervisor); Todd Brashear (Vice President, Creative Director)
Employee Associations: Elizabeth Byrd

DANBURY

AL BREDENBERG CREATIVE SERVICES

Product or Service: Advertising/Marketing Agency
Street address 1: 71 Franklin St
Street address state: CT
Postal code: 06810-5483
County: Fairfield
Country: USA
Mailing address 1: 71 Franklin St
Mailing city: Danbury
Mailing state: CT
Mailing zip: 06810-5483
Office phone: (203) 791-8204
Other fax: www.copywriter.com
Web address: ab@copywriter.com
Note: Al Bredenberg (Contact)
Employee Associations: Al Bredenberg

DANVERS

EDGIL ASSOCIATES, INC.

Product or Service: Hardware/Software Supplier
Street address 1: 222 Rosewood Dr
Street address 2: Ste 210
Street address state: MA
Postal code: 01923-4520
County: Essex
Country: USA
Mailing address 1: 222 Rosewood Dr Ste 210
Mailing city: Danvers
Mailing state: MA
Mailing zip: 01923-4520
Office phone: (800) 457-9782
Office fax: (978) 667-6050
Other fax: www.edgil.com
Web address: sales@edgil.com
Note: Sean Callahan (Dir., Sales)
Employee Associations: Sean Callahan

DENVER

LIQUID LUCK PRODUCTIONS

Product or Service: Multimedia/Interactive Products
Street address 1: 1221 Auraria Pkwy
Street address state: CO
Postal code: 80204-1836
County: Denver
Country: USA
Mailing address 1: 1221 Auraria Pkwy
Mailing city: Denver
Mailing state: CO
Mailing zip: 80204-1836
Office phone: (303) 518-8909
Other fax: www.liquidluckproductions.com
Web address: info@LiquidLuckProductions.com
Note: Lena Telep (Marketing Manager)
Employee Associations: Lena Telep

DES MOINES

APPLIED ART & TECHNOLOGY

Product or Service: Multimedia/Interactive Products
Street address 1: 2430 106th St
Street address state: IA
Postal code: 50322-3763
County: Polk
Country: USA
Mailing address 1: 2430 106th St
Mailing city: Des Moines
Mailing state: IA
Mailing zip: 50322-3763
Office phone: (515) 331-7400
Office fax: (515) 331-7401
Other fax: www.appliedart.com
Web address: mail@appliedart.com; info@appliedart.com
Note: Jeanie Jorgensen (Media Mgr.)
Employee Associations: Jeanie Jorgensen

DOVE CREEK

COMPETENCE SOFTWARE

Product or Service: Multimedia/Interactive Products
Street address 1: PO Box 353
Street address state: CO
Postal code: 81324-0353
County: Dolores
Country: USA
Mailing address 1: PO Box 353
Mailing city: Dove Creek
Mailing state: CO
Mailing zip: 81324-0353
Office phone: (727) 459-0531
Other fax: www.competencesoftware.net
Note: Larry Byrnes (Founder); Mary Lou Dewyngaert (Vice Pres., Devel.); Shannon Byrnes (Vice Pres., Mkt. Devel.); Jessica Byrnes (Asst. to CEO)
Employee Associations: Jessica Byrnes

DUESSELDORF

MPS MEDIA PHONE SERVICE KG

Product or Service: Telecommunications/Service Bureaus
Street address 1: Markenstrasse 21
Postal code: D-40014
Country: Germany
Mailing address 1: PO Box 10 23 43
Mailing city: Duesseldorf
Mailing zip: D-40014
Office phone: 777 3237
Office fax: 167 5994
Other fax: www.mediaphone.de
Web address: hjkruse@mediaphone.de
Note: Hans-Joachim Kruse (Mng. Dir.)
Employee Associations: Hans-Joachim Kruse

DULLES

AOL INC.

Product or Service: Publisher/Media
Street address 1: 22000 Aol Way
Street address state: VA
Postal code: 20166-9302
County: Loudoun
Country: USA
Mailing address 1: 22000 Aol Way
Mailing city: Dulles
Mailing state: VA
Mailing zip: 20166-9302
Office phone: (703) 265-2100
Other fax: www.aol.com
Note: Guru Gowrappan (CEO); Sowmyanarayan Sampath (CFO)
Employee Associations: ()

DULUTH

MOVIUS INTERACTIVE CORPORATION

Product or Service: Telecommunications/Service Bureaus
Street address 1: 11360 Lakefield Dr
Street address state: GA
Postal code: 30097-1569
County: Fulton
Country: USA
Mailing address 1: 11360 Lakefield Dr
Mailing city: Duluth
Mailing state: GA
Mailing zip: 30097-1569
Office phone: (770) 283-1000
Office fax: (770) 497-3990
Other fax: www.moviuscorp.com
Note: Oscar Rodriguez (CEO)
Employee Associations: Dominic Gomez

EAST PROVIDENCE

CREATIVE CIRCLE MEDIA SOLUTIONS

Product or Service: Advertising/Marketing Agency`Circulation`Consultants`Editorial`Graphic/Design Firm`Hardware/Software Supplier`Marketing`Multimedia/Interactive Products`Other Services`Online Service Provider and Internet Hosts
Street address 1: 945 Waterman Ave
Street address state: RI
Postal code: 02914-1342
County: Providence
Country: USA
Mailing address 1: 945 Waterman Ave.
Mailing city: East Providence
Mailing state: RI
Mailing zip: 02914
Office phone: (401) 272-1122
Other fax: www.creativecirclemedia.com
Web address: info@creativecirclemedia.com
General e-mail: Full service and custom software provider with a dynamic web CMS, user-contributed content, classifieds, hosting, pay wall, native content, QuickAds and print editorial production systems. We also provide strategic consulting, newsroom training, ad design training, new revenue ideas, high-end outsourcing services and extensive print and web redesigns.
Note: Bill Ostendorf (Pres & Founder); Lynn Rognsvoog (Design director); Tim Benson (IT director)
Employee Associations: Bill Ostendorf

EMERYVILLE

GRACENOTE

Product or Service: Multimedia/Interactive Products
Street address 1: 2000 Powell Street
Street address 2: Suite 1500
Street address state: CA
Postal code: 94608
County: Warren
Country: USA
Mailing address 1: 2000 Powell Street, Suite 1500
Mailing city: Emeryville
Mailing state: CA
Mailing zip: 94608
Office phone: (510) 428-7200
Other fax: www.gracenote.com
Web address: support@gracenote.com
Note: Karthik Rao (Pres.); Amilcar Perez (Chief Revenue Officer); Shannon Buggy (Senior Vice President, Human Resources)
Employee Associations: Graham McKenna

ERIE

LARSON TEXTS, INC.

Product or Service: Multimedia/Interactive Products`Publisher/

Interactive Products and Services Companies

Media
Street address 1: 1762 Norcross Rd
Street address state: PA
Postal code: 16510-3838
County: Erie
Country: USA
Mailing address 1: 1762 Norcross Rd
Mailing city: Erie
Mailing state: PA
Mailing zip: 16510-3838
Office phone: (814) 824-6365
Office fax: (814) 824-6377
Other phone: (800) 530-2355
Other fax: www.larsontexts.com
Web address: eforish@larsontexts.com
Employee Associations: Emily Forish

EXTON

MEDIA SUPPLY, INC.

Product or Service: CD-ROM Designer/Manufacturer
Street address 1: 611 Jeffers Cir
Street address state: PA
Postal code: 19341-2525
County: Chester
Country: USA
Mailing address 1: 611 Jeffers Cir
Mailing city: Exton
Mailing state: PA
Mailing zip: 19341-2525
Office phone: (610) 884-4400
Office fax: (610) 884-4500
Other fax: www.mediasupply.com
Web address: info@mediasupply.com
Note: Steven P. Derstine (Sales Mgr.)
Employee Associations: Steven P. Derstine

FARMINGTON HILLS

ADITYA BIRLA MINACS

Product or Service: Telecommunications/Service Bureaus
Street address 1: 34115 W 12 Mile Rd
Street address state: MI
Postal code: 48331-3368
County: Oakland
Country: USA
Mailing address 1: 34115 W 12 Mile Rd
Mailing city: Farmington Hills
Mailing state: MI
Mailing zip: 48331-3368
Office phone: (248) 553-8255
Other fax: www.minacs.adityabirla.com
Web address: info@minacs.adityabirla.com
Note: Anil Bhalia (COO); Deepak Patel (CEO)
Employee Associations: Anil Bhalia

MORPACE INTERNATIONAL

Product or Service: Consultants
Street address 1: 31700 Middlebelt Rd
Street address 2: Ste 200
Street address state: MI
Postal code: 48334-2375
County: Oakland
Country: USA
Mailing address 1: 31700 Middlebelt Rd Ste 200
Mailing city: Farmington Hills
Mailing state: MI
Mailing zip: 48334-2375
Office phone: (248) 737-5300
Office fax: (248) 737-5326
Other fax: www.morpace.com
Web address: information@morpace.com
Note: Jack McDonald (Pres.); Francis Ward (CEO)
Employee Associations: Jack McDonald

FLORHAM PARK

LOGICAL DESIGN SOLUTIONS, INC.

Product or Service: Multimedia/Interactive Products
Street address 1: 200 Park Ave
Street address 2: Ste 210
Street address state: NJ
Postal code: 07932-1026
County: Morris
Country: USA
Mailing address 1: 200 Park Ave Ste 210
Mailing city: Florham Park
Mailing state: NJ
Mailing zip: 07932-1026
Office phone: (973) 210-6300
Office fax: (973) 971-0103
Other fax: www.lds.com
Web address: info@lds.com
Note: Mimi Brooks (Pres./CEO); E. Bruce Lovenberg (CFO); Mauricio Barberi (Sr. Vice Pres., Bus. Devel.); Ken Kuhl (Vice Pres., Pjct. Mgmt.); Marty Burns (Vice Pres., Techn.); John Fee (Vice Pres., Sales); Kevin Casey (Vice Pres., Mktg.); Eric Dalessio (Vice Pres., Client Servs.); Gary Sikorski (Vice Pres., Opns.)
Employee Associations: John Fee

FRANKLIN

DIALOGIC COMMUNICATIONS CORP.

Product or Service: Telecommunications/Service Bureaus
Street address 1: 730 Cool Springs Blvd
Street address 2: Ste 300
Street address state: TN
Postal code: 37067-7290
County: Williamson
Country: USA
Mailing address 1: 117 Seaboard Ln Ste D100
Mailing city: Franklin
Mailing state: TN
Mailing zip: 37067-2871
Office phone: (615) 790-2882
Office fax: (615) 790-1329
Other fax: www.dccusa.com
Web address: sales@dccusa.com; bcarman@dccusa.com
Note: Bill Carman (Sales Rep.)
Employee Associations: Bill Carman

GAITHERSBURG

MICROLOG CORP.

Product or Service: Hardware/Software Supplier
Street address 1: 401 Professional Dr
Street address 2: Ste 125
Street address state: MD
Postal code: 20879-3468
County: Montgomery
Country: USA
Mailing address 1: 401 Professional Dr Ste 125
Mailing city: Gaithersburg
Mailing state: MD
Mailing zip: 20879-3468
Office phone: (301) 540-5500
Office fax: (301) 330-2450
Other fax: www.mlog.com
Web address: sales@mlog.com
Note: W. Joseph Brookman (Pres./CEO/Dir.); John C. Mears (CTO); Steve Feldman (Exec. Vice Pres., Worldwide Sales)
Employee Associations: Steve Feldman

GLEN HEAD

FILESTREAM, INC.

Product or Service: Hardware/Software Supplier
Street address 1: PO Box 93
Street address state: NY
Postal code: 11545-0093
County: Nassau
Country: USA
Mailing address 1: PO Box 93
Mailing city: Glen Head
Mailing state: NY
Mailing zip: 11545-0093
Office phone: (516) 759-4100
Office fax: (516) 759-3011
Other fax: www.filestream.com
Web address: info@filestream.com ; support@filestream.com; server@filestream.com; reseller@filestream.com
Note: Yao Chu (Chrmn./CEO)
Employee Associations: Yao Chu

GLEN ROCK

HOLDCOM

Product or Service: Advertising/Marketing Agency
Street address 1: 955 Lincoln Ave
Street address state: NJ
Postal code: 07452-3226
County: Bergen
Country: USA
Mailing address 1: 955 Lincoln Ave
Mailing city: Glen Rock
Mailing state: NJ
Mailing zip: 07452-3226
Office phone: (201) 444-6488
Office fax: (201) 445-4653
Other fax: www.holdcom.com
Web address: info@holdcom.com
Note: Neil Fishman (Pres.); Harvey Edelman (CEO)
Employee Associations: Neil Fishman

HAGERSTOWN

CONSERVIT, INC.

Product or Service: Telecommunications/Service Bureaus
Street address 1: 18656 Leslie Dr
Street address state: MD
Postal code: 21740
County: Lake
Country: USA
Mailing address 1: P.O. Box 1517
Mailing city: Hagerstown
Mailing state: MD
Mailing zip: 21741-1517
Office phone: (301) 791-0100
Office fax: (301) 739-8548
Other phone: (301) 416-7395
Other fax: www.conservit.net
Web address: sales@conservit.com
Note: Peter F. Theis (Pres.)
Employee Associations: Peter F. Theis

HOLLYWOOD

LAURA SMITH ILLUSTRATION

Product or Service: Editorial`Graphic/Design Firm`Marketing
Street address 1: 6545 Cahuenga Ter
Street address state: CA
Postal code: 90068-2744
County: Los Angeles
Country: USA
Mailing address 1: 6545 Cahuenga Ter
Mailing city: Hollywood
Mailing state: CA
Mailing zip: 90068-2744
Office phone: (323) 467-1700
Office fax: (323) 467-1700
Other phone: (323) 467-1700
Other fax: www.laurasmithart.com
Web address: Laura@LauraSmithArt.com
Employee Associations: Laura Smith

HOPEWELL

DANA COMMUNICATIONS

Product or Service: Advertising/Marketing Agency
Street address 1: 2 E Broad St
Street address state: NJ
Postal code: 08525-1810
County: Mercer
Country: USA
Mailing address 1: 2 E Broad St
Mailing city: Hopewell
Mailing state: NJ
Mailing zip: 08525-1899
Office phone: (609) 466-9187
Office fax: (609) 466-0285
Other fax: www.danacommunications.com
Web address: bprewitt@danacommunications.com

HORSHAM

CYBERTECH, INC.

Product or Service: Hardware/Software Supplier`POP/Kiosk Designer
Street address 1: 935 Horsham Rd
Street address state: PA
Postal code: 19044-1230
County: Montgomery
Country: USA
Mailing address 1: 935 Horsham Rd Ste I
Mailing city: Horsham
Mailing state: PA
Mailing zip: 19044-1270

Office phone: (215) 957-6220
Office fax: (215) 674-8515
Other fax: www.cbrtech.com
Web address: sales@cbrtech.com
Note: Ronald Schmidt (Pres.); Lloyd Barnett (Sec./Treasurer)
Employee Associations: Ronald Schmidt

HOUSTON

AGILITY

Product or Service: Telecommunications/Service Bureaus
Street address 1: 15900 Morales Rd
Street address state: TX
Postal code: 77032-2126
County: Harris
Country: USA
Mailing address 1: 15900 Morales Rd
Mailing city: Houston
Mailing state: TX
Mailing zip: 77032-2126
Office phone: (714) 617-6300
Other fax: www.agilitylogistics.com
Web address: americas@logistics.com
Note: Pam Holdrup (Sales)
Employee Associations: Pam Holdrup

INTERNATIONAL DEMOGRAPHICS/THE MEDIA AUDIT

Product or Service: Advertising/Marketing Agency
Street address 1: 10333 Richmond Ave
Street address 2: Ste 200
Street address state: TX
Postal code: 77042-4142
County: Harris
Country: USA
Mailing address 1: 10333 Richmond Ave Ste 200
Mailing city: Houston
Mailing state: TX
Mailing zip: 77042-4142
Office phone: (713) 626-0333
Office fax: (713) 626-0418
Other fax: www.themediaaudit.com
Web address: tma@themediaaudit.com
Note: James B. Higginbotham (Chrmn.); Robert A. Jordan (Pres.); J. Phillip Beswick (Exec. Vice Pres., Sales); Michael W. Bustell (Exec. Vice Pres./Sales Mgr.)
Employee Associations: Robert A. Jordan

HUNTSVILLE

ADTRAN

Product or Service: Hardware/Software Supplier
Street address 1: 901 Explorer Blvd NW
Street address state: AL
Postal code: 35806-2807
County: Madison
Country: USA
Mailing address 1: 901 Explorer Blvd NW
Mailing city: Huntsville
Mailing state: AL
Mailing zip: 35806-2807
Office phone: (800) 923-8726
Other fax: www.adtran.com
Web address: info@adtran.com
Note: Tammie Dodson (PR Dir.)
Employee Associations: Tammie Dodson

MAGNACOM, INC.

Product or Service: Telecommunications/Service Bureaus
Street address 1: 615 Discovery Dr NW
Street address 2: Ste B
Street address state: AL
Postal code: 35806-2801
County: Madison
Country: USA
Mailing address 1: 310 Voyager Way NW
Mailing city: Huntsville
Mailing state: AL
Mailing zip: 35806-3200

Office phone: (256) 327-8900
Office fax: (256) 327-8998
Other fax: www.magnacom-inc.com
Web address: info@magnacom-inc.com
Note: John Trainor (Pres.)
Employee Associations: John Trainor

IRVINE

EDITOR & PUBLISHER INTERACTIVE

Product or Service: Publisher/Media
Street address 1: 17782 Cowan
Street address 2: Ste C
Street address state: CA
Postal code: 92614-6042
County: Orange
Country: USA
Mailing address 1: 17782 Cowan Ste C
Mailing city: Irvine
Mailing state: CA
Mailing zip: 92614-6042
Office phone: (949) 660-6150
Office fax: (949) 660-6172
Other fax: www.editorandpublisher.com

AUTHORLINK

Product or Service: Multimedia/Interactive Products Publisher/Media
Street address 1: 103 Guadalupe Dr
Street address state: TX
Postal code: 75039-3334
County: Dallas
Country: USA
Mailing address 1: 103 Guadalupe Dr
Mailing city: Irving
Mailing state: TX
Mailing zip: 75039-3334
Office phone: (972) 402-0101
Office fax: (866) 381-1587
Other fax: www.authorlink.com
Web address: dbooth@authorlink.com
General e-mail: Authorlink specializes in e-book conversion and distribution. We also provide news and informatin for editors, agents, writers and readers.
Note: Doris Booth (Ed. in Chief)
Employee Associations: Doris Booth

ITHACA

IRON DESIGN

Product or Service: Graphic/Design Firm
Street address 1: 120 N Aurora St
Street address 2: Ste 5A
Street address state: NY
Postal code: 14850-4337
County: Tompkins
Country: USA
Mailing address 1: 120 N Aurora St Ste 5A
Mailing city: Ithaca
Mailing state: NY
Mailing zip: 14850-4337
Office phone: (607) 275-9544
Office fax: (607) 275-0370
Other fax: www.irondesign.com
Web address: todd@irondesign.com

JERSEY CITY

DESKNET, INC.

Product or Service: Consultants
Street address 1: 10 Exchange Pl
Street address 2: Fl 20
Street address state: NJ
Postal code: 07302-3918
County: Hudson
Country: USA
Mailing address 1: 10 Exchange Pl Ste 2040
Mailing city: Jersey City
Mailing state: NJ
Mailing zip: 07302-3935
Office phone: (201) 946-7080
Other fax: www.desknetinc.com
Web address: sales@desknetinc.com
Note: Michael Fitzsimons (Co-CEO)
Employee Associations: Michael Fitzsimons

KING OF PRUSSIA

ADVANCED TELECOM SERVICES, INC. (CANADA)

Product or Service: Telecommunications/Service Bureaus
Street address 1: 1150 1st Ave
Street address 2: Ste 105
Street address state: PA
Postal code: 19406-1350
County: Montgomery
Country: USA
Mailing address 1: 1150 First Ave. Ste. 105
Mailing city: King of Prussia
Mailing state: PA
Mailing zip: 19406
Office phone: (416) 800-2490
Office fax: (610) 964-9117
Other fax: www.advancedtele.com
Web address: sales@advancedtele.com
Note: Bob Bentz (Dir. of Marketing)
Employee Associations: Bob Bentz

LAGUNA NIGUEL

GRIFFIN CHASE OLIVER, INC.

Product or Service: POP/Kiosk Designer
Street address 1: 25262 Monte Verde Dr
Street address state: CA
Postal code: 92677-1535
County: Orange
Country: USA
Mailing address 1: 25262 Monte Verde Dr
Mailing city: Laguna Niguel
Mailing state: CA
Mailing zip: 92677-1535
Office phone: (949) 495-1144
Office fax: (815) 366-3885
Other fax: www.griffinchaseoliver.com
Web address: sales@GriffinChaseOliver.com
Note: Jim Redfield (CEO)
Employee Associations: Jim Redfield

LAKEVILLE

BUZZ360 LLC

Product or Service: Marketing
Street address 1: 17728 Kingsway Path
Street address 2: # 120
Street address state: MN
Postal code: 55044-5208
County: Dakota
Country: USA
Mailing address 1: 17728 Kingsway Path #120
Mailing city: Lakeville
Mailing state: MN
Mailing zip: 55044
Office phone: (612) 567 0396
Other fax: www.buzz360.co
Web address: info@buzz360.co
General e-mail: A new world of Partner Marketing
Employee Associations: Klaus Schneegans

LAKEWOOD

CUSTOMER COMMUNICATIONS GROUP

Product or Service: Advertising/Marketing Agency
Street address 1: 165 S Union Blvd
Street address 2: Ste 260
Street address state: CO
Postal code: 80228-2241
County: Jefferson
Country: USA
Mailing address 1: 165 S Union Blvd Ste 260
Mailing city: Lakewood
Mailing state: CO
Mailing zip: 80228-2241
Office phone: (303) 986-3000
Office fax: (303) 989-4805
Other fax: www.customer.com
Web address: info@customer.com
Note: Sandra Gudat (Pres.)

Employee Associations: Sandra Gudat

LANCASTER

GODFREY

Product or Service: Advertising/Marketing Agency
Street address 1: 40 N Christian St
Street address state: PA
Postal code: 17602-2828
County: Lancaster
Country: USA
Mailing address 1: 40 N Christian St
Mailing city: Lancaster
Mailing state: PA
Mailing zip: 17602-2828
Office phone: (717) 393-3831
Office fax: (717) 393-1403
Other fax: www.godfrey.com
Web address: curt@godfrey.com

LINCOLN

COMMGRAPHICS INTERACTIVE, INC.

Product or Service: Multimedia/Interactive Products
Street address 1: 9259 Pioneer Ct
Street address state: NE
Postal code: 68520-9307
County: Lancaster
Country: USA
Mailing address 1: 9259 Pioneer Ct
Mailing city: Lincoln
Mailing state: NE
Mailing zip: 68520-9307
Office phone: (402) 432-1450
Web address: nwineman@commgraphics.com
Note: Neil Wineman (New Bus. Dir.)
Employee Associations: Neil Wineman

LITTLETON

INFORONICS, INC.

Product or Service: Multimedia/Interactive Products
Street address 1: 25 Porter Rd
Street address state: MA
Postal code: 01460-1434
County: Middlesex
Country: USA
Mailing address 1: 25 Porter Rd Ste 4
Mailing city: Littleton
Mailing state: MA
Mailing zip: 01460-1434
Office phone: (978) 698-7400
Office fax: (978) 698-7500
Other fax: www.inforonics.com
Note: Bruce Mills (Pres.); Andy Kramer (Vice Pres., Sales); Tom Pellegriti (Vice Pres., Opns.)
Employee Associations: Andy Kramer

LONDON

ADVANCED TELECOM SERVICES, INC. (U.K.)

Product or Service: Telecommunications/Service Bureaus
Street address 1: 12-16 Clerkenwell Rd.
Postal code: EC1M 5PQ
Country: United Kingdom
Mailing address 1: 12-16 Clerkwell Rd.
Mailing city: London
Mailing zip: EC1M 5PQ
Office phone: 7608 7787
Office fax: 7608 7788
Other fax: www.advancedtele.com
Web address: uksales@advancedtele.co.uk
Note: Ian Scott (Mng. Dir./Gen. Mgr.); Cindy Aspland (Dir., Sales)
Employee Associations: Ian Scott

Interactive Products and Services Companies

LONG BEACH

DESIGNORY.COM
Product or Service: Advertising/Marketing Agency
Street address 1: 211 E Ocean Blvd
Street address 2: Ste 100
Street address state: CA
Postal code: 90802-4850
County: Los Angeles
Country: USA
Mailing address 1: 211 E Ocean Blvd
Mailing city: Long Beach
Mailing state: CA
Mailing zip: 90802-4809
Office phone: (562) 624-0200
Other fax: www.designory.com

LONG ISLAND CITY

COSMOS COMMUNICATIONS, INC.
Product or Service: Graphic/Design Firm
Street address 1: 1105 44th Dr
Street address state: NY
Postal code: 11101-5107
County: Queens
Country: USA
Mailing address 1: 1105 44th Dr
Mailing city: Long Island City
Mailing state: NY
Mailing zip: 11101-7027
Office phone: (718) 482-1800
Office fax: (718) 482-1968
Other fax: www.cosmoscommunications.com
Note: Arnold Weiss (Pres.)
Employee Associations: Arnold Weiss

LONGWOOD

INETUSA
Product or Service: Multimedia/Interactive Products`Online Service Provider and Internet Hosts
Street address 1: PO Box 917208
Street address state: FL
Postal code: 32791-7208
County: Seminole
Country: USA
Mailing address 1: 3935 Fenner Rd
Mailing city: Cocoa
Mailing state: FL
Mailing zip: 32926-4205
Office phone: (321) 733-5391
Office fax: (321) 723-4552
Other fax: www.inetusa.com
Web address: info@inetusa.com
Note: Tim Yandell (Pres.)
Employee Associations: Tim Yandell

LOS ANGELES

B/HI
Product or Service: Advertising/Marketing Agency
Street address 1: 11500 W Olympic Blvd
Street address 2: Ste 399
Street address state: CA
Postal code: 90064-1530
County: Los Angeles
Country: USA
Mailing address 1: 11500 W Olympic Blvd Ste 399
Mailing city: Los Angeles
Mailing state: CA
Mailing zip: 90064-1530
Office phone: (310) 473-4147
Office fax: (310) 478-4727
Other fax: www.bhimpact.com
Web address: info@bhimpact.com
Note: Dean Bender (Partner); Shawna Lynch (Sr. Vice Pres.); Jerry Griffin (Managing Partner)
Employee Associations: Dean Bender

EUR/ELECTRONIC URBAN REPORT
Product or Service: Publisher/Media
Street address 1: PO Box 412081
Street address state: CA
Postal code: 90041-9081
County: Los Angeles
Country: USA
Mailing address 1: PO Box 412081
Mailing city: Los Angeles
Mailing state: CA
Mailing zip: 90041-9081
Office phone: (323) 254-9599
Office fax: (323)-421-9383
Other fax: www.eurweb.com
Web address: editorial@eurweb.com
Note: Lee Bailey (Pub.)
Employee Associations: Lee Bailey

L@IT2'D (LATITUDE)
Product or Service: Graphic/Design Firm
Street address 1: 714 N Laurel Ave
Street address state: CA
Postal code: 90046-7008
County: Los Angeles
Country: USA
Mailing address 1: 714 N Laurel Ave
Mailing city: Los Angeles
Mailing state: CA
Mailing zip: 90046-7008
Office phone: (323) 852-1425
Office fax: (323) 856-0704
Other fax: www.lati2d.com
Web address: info@lati2d.com
Note: Water Kerner (CCO)
Employee Associations: Water Kerner

LEXISNEXIS
Product or Service: Consultants
Street address 1: 555 W 5th St
Street address 2: Ste 4500
Street address state: CA
Postal code: 90013-3003
County: Los Angeles
Country: USA
Mailing address 1: 555 W 5th St Ste 4500
Mailing city: Los Angeles
Mailing state: CA
Mailing zip: 90013-3003
Office phone: (213) 627-1130
Other phone: (800) 253-4182
Other fax: www.lexisnexis.com
Web address: lexisnexiscommunities@lexisnexis.com
Note: Andrew Prozes (CEO, Lexis-Nexis Grp.); Kurt Sanford (Pres./CEO, Cor. & Fed. Mkts.); Michael Walsh (Pres./CEO, U.S. Legal Mkts.); James M. Peck (CEO, Risk Mgmt.); Richard Sobelsohn
Employee Associations: James M. Peck

LIEBERMAN RESEARCH WORLDWIDE
Product or Service: Advertising/Marketing Agency
Street address 1: 1900 Avenue of the Stars
Street address 2: Ste 1600
Street address state: CA
Postal code: 90067-4412
County: Los Angeles
Country: USA
Mailing address 1: 1900 Avenue of the Stars Ste 1600
Mailing city: Los Angeles
Mailing state: CA
Mailing zip: 90067-4483
Office phone: (310) 553-0550
Office fax: (310) 553-4607
Other fax: www.lrwonline.com
Web address: info@lrwonline.com
Note: Dave Sackman (Chairman and CEO)
Employee Associations: Joan Cassidy

LOUISVILLE

C-T INNOVATIONS
Product or Service: Telecommunications/Service Bureaus
Street address 1: 11509 Commonwealth Dr
Street address state: KY
Postal code: 40299-2379
County: Jefferson
Country: USA
Mailing address 1: 11509 Commonwealth Dr Ste 101
Mailing city: Louisville
Mailing state: KY
Mailing zip: 40299-2379
Office phone: (502) 814-5100
Office fax: (502) 814-5110
Other fax: www.ct-innovations.com
Note: Robert Flynn (Pres.)
Employee Associations: Robert Flynn

KINETIC CORPORATION
Product or Service: Graphic/Design Firm
Street address 1: 200 Distillery Cmns
Street address 2: Ste 200
Street address state: KY
Postal code: 40206-1987
County: Jefferson
Country: USA
Mailing address 1: 200 Distillery Commons Ste 200
Mailing city: Louisville
Mailing state: KY
Mailing zip: 40206-1987
Office phone: (502) 719-9500
Office fax: (502) 719-9569
Other fax: www.theTechnologyAgency.com
Web address: info@theTechnologyAgency.com
Note: G. Raymond Schuhmann (Pres.); Cindi Ramm (Chief Brand Strategist)
Employee Associations: G. Raymond Schuhmann

KIOSK INFORMATION SYSTEMS
Product or Service: POP/Kiosk Designer
Street address 1: 346 S Arthur Ave
Street address state: CO
Postal code: 80027-3010
County: Boulder
Country: USA
Mailing address 1: 346 S Arthur Ave
Mailing city: Louisville
Mailing state: CO
Mailing zip: 80027-3010
Office phone: (303) 466-5471
Office fax: (303) 466-6730
Other phone: (888) 661-1697
Other fax: www.kiosk.com
Web address: sales@kiosk.com
Note: Rick Malone (Pres.); Tom Weaver (Vice Pres., Sales/Mktg.)
Employee Associations: Tom Weaver

MADISON

MIDWEST DIGITAL COMMUNICATIONS
Product or Service: Advertising/Marketing Agency
Street address 1: 701 Walsh Rd
Street address state: WI
Postal code: 53714-1372
County: Dane
Country: USA
Mailing address 1: PO Box 8431
Mailing city: Madison
Mailing state: WI
Mailing zip: 53708-8431
Office phone: (608) 257-5673
Office fax: (608) 257-5669
Other fax: www.midwestdigital.com
Web address: info@midwestdigital.com
Note: Jay Jurado (CEO)
Employee Associations: Jay Jurado

MANHATTAN BEACH

ADSTREAM AMERICA
Product or Service: Hardware/Software Supplier
Street address 1: 1240 Rosecrans Avenue
Street address 2: Suite 120
Street address state: CA
Postal code: 90266
County: New York
Country: USA
Mailing address 1: 1240 Rosecrans Avenue, Suite 120
Mailing city: Manhattan Beach
Mailing state: CA
Mailing zip: 90266
Office phone: (818) 860-0420
Other fax: www.adstream.com
Web address: hello@adstream.com
Note: Bruce Akhurst (Executive Chairman); Daniel Mark (CEO)
Employee Associations: ()

MARION

FRANK N MAGID ASSOCIATES
Product or Service: Consultants`Research
Street address 1: 1 Research Ctr
Street address state: IA
Postal code: 52302-5868
County: Linn
Country: USA
Mailing address 1: 1 Research Ctr
Mailing city: Marion
Mailing state: IA
Mailing zip: 52302-5868
Office phone: (319) 377-7345
Office fax: (319) 377-5861
Other phone: (847) 922-0418
Other fax: www.magid.com
Web address: Bhague@magid.com
Note: Bill Hague (Exec. Vice Pres.); Bill Day
Employee Associations: Bill Hague; Bill Day

MARKHAM

COMPUTER TALK TECHNOLOGY, INC.
Product or Service: Hardware/Software Supplier
Street address 1: 150 Commerce Valley Drive West
Street address 2: Suite 800
Street address state: ON
Postal code: L3T 7Z3
Country: Canada
Mailing address 1: 150 Commerce Valley Drive West, Suite 800
Mailing city: Markham
Mailing state: ON
Mailing zip: L3T 7Z3
Office phone: (905) 882-5000
Office fax: (905) 882-5501
Other fax: www.computer-talk.com
Note: Mandle Cheung (Pres./CEO); Donald Mcdonald (V. P.)

MAYWOOD

KEN PETRETTI PRODUCTIONS, LLC
Product or Service: Advertising/Marketing Agency`CD-ROM Designer/Manufacturer`Consultants`Graphic/Design Firm`Multimedia/Interactive Products`Online Service Provider and Internet Hosts`POP/Kiosk Designer`Publisher/Media`Web Site Auditor
Street address 1: 33 Parkway
Street address state: NJ
Postal code: 07607-1556
County: Bergen
Country: USA
Mailing address 1: 33 Parkway
Mailing city: Maywood
Mailing state: NJ
Mailing zip: 07607-1556
Office phone: (201) 368-2296
Office fax: (201) 368-1489

MCHENRY

CORPORATE DISK COMPANY

Product or Service: CD-ROM Designer/Manufacturer
Street address 1: 4610 Prime Pkwy
Street address state: IL
Postal code: 60050-7005
County: McHenry
Country: USA
Mailing address 1: 4610 Prime Pkwy
Mailing city: McHenry
Mailing state: IL
Mailing zip: 60050-7005
Office phone: (815) 331-6000
Office fax: (815) 331-6030
Other phone: 800-634-3475
Other fax: www.disk.com
Web address: info@disk.com
General e-mail: Specializing in CD and DVD Manufacturing along with all the related printing, packaging, technical, and fulfillment services. Providing complete start to finish solutions.
Note: William Mahoney (Pres.)
Employee Associations: Joe Foley

MELROSE

BKJ PRODUCTIONS

Product or Service: Multimedia/Interactive Products
Street address 1: 99 Washington St
Street address state: MA
Postal code: 02176-6024
County: Middlesex
Country: USA
Mailing address 1: 99 Washington St Ste 21A
Mailing city: Melrose
Mailing state: MA
Mailing zip: 02176-6026
Office phone: (781) 662-8800
Other fax: www.bkjproductions.com
Web address: info@bkjproductions.com
Note: Brian K. Johnson (Pres.)
Employee Associations: Brian K. Johnson

METHUEN

3M TOUCH SYSTEMS, INC.

Product or Service: Hardware/Software Supplier
Street address 1: 501 Griffin Brook Dr
Street address state: MA
Postal code: 01844
County: Essex
Country: USA
Mailing address 1: 501 Griffin Brook Dr
Mailing city: Methuen
Mailing state: MA
Mailing zip: 01844
Office phone: (978) 659-9000
Other fax: www.3mtouch.com
Note: Chris Tsourides (Bus. Unit Mgr.)
Employee Associations: Jodi Huber

MIAMI

EMPHASYS SOFTWARE

Product or Service: Hardware/Software Supplier
Street address 1: 9675 NW 117 Avenue
Street address 2: Suite 305
Street address state: FL
Postal code: 33178
County: San Diego
Country: USA
Mailing address 1: 9675 NW 117 Avenue, Suite 305
Mailing city: Miami
Mailing state: FL
Mailing zip: 33178
Office phone: (800) 968-6884
Other fax: www.emphasys-software.com
Web address: info@emphasys-software.com
Note: Mike Byrne (CEO)
Employee Associations: ()

MILAN

ET SRL ELETTRONICA TELECOMUNICAZIONI

Product or Service: Hardware/Software Supplier
Street address 1: Viale Veneto 4, Cinisello Balsamo
Postal code: 20092
Country: Italy
Mailing address 1: Viale Veneto 4, Cinisello Balsamo
Mailing city: Milan
Mailing zip: 20092
Office phone: 39 02 66033
Office fax: 39 02 66033270
Other fax: www.et_spa.com
Web address: info@et_spa.com
Note: Marco Prandi (Mgr., Projects/Devel.); Massimo Fiocchi (Commercial Mgr.)
Employee Associations: Marco Prandi

MILWAUKEE

CATALYST INTERNATIONAL, INC.

Product or Service: Hardware/Software Supplier
Street address 1: 8989 N Deerwood Dr
Street address state: WI
Postal code: 53223-2446
County: Milwaukee
Country: USA
Mailing address 1: 8989 N Deerwood Dr
Mailing city: Milwaukee
Mailing state: WI
Mailing zip: 53223-2446
Office phone: (414) 362-6800
Office fax: (414) 362-6794
Other fax: www.ctcsoftware.com
Web address: info@ctcsoftware.com
Note: Mark Shupac (Contact)
Employee Associations: Mark Shupac

MINNEAPOLIS

INTERALIA COMMUNICATIONS

Product or Service: Telecommunications/Service Bureaus
Street address 1: 701 24th Ave SE
Street address state: MN
Postal code: 55414-2691
County: Hennepin
Country: USA
Mailing address 1: 701 24th Ave SE
Mailing city: Minneapolis
Mailing state: MN
Mailing zip: 55414-2691
Office phone: (952) 942-6088
Office fax: (952) 942-6172
Other fax: www.interalia.com
Web address: info@interalia.com
Note: Mary Mcracken (Bus. Admin. Assoc.)
Employee Associations: Mary Mcracken

MISSION

FAMILY FEATURES EDITORIAL SYNDICATE, INC.

Product or Service: Multimedia/Interactive Products
Street address 1: 5825 Dearborn St
Street address state: KS
Postal code: 66202-2745
County: Johnson
Country: USA
Mailing address 1: 5825 Dearborn St
Mailing city: Mission
Mailing state: KS
Mailing zip: 66202-2745
Office phone: (913) 563-4752
Office fax: (913) 789-9228
Other fax: www.familyfeatures.com
Web address: clong@familyfeatures.com
Note: Dianne Hogerty (Owner); Clarke Smith (President); Cindy Long (Media Relations Manager)
Employee Associations: Cindy Long

MONMOUTH JUNCTION

DOW JONES INTERACTIVE PUBLISHING

Product or Service: Multimedia/Interactive Products
Street address 1: RR 1 Box 4300
Street address state: NJ
Postal code: 08852-9801
County: Middlesex
Country: USA
Mailing address 1: PO Box 300
Mailing city: Princeton
Mailing state: NJ
Mailing zip: 08543-0300
Office phone: (609) 520-4000
Office fax: (609) 520-4662
Other fax: www.dowjones.com
Web address: marianne.krafinski@dowjones.com
Note: Les Hinton (CEO)
Employee Associations: ()

MONROVIA

MCMONIGLE & ASSOCIATES

Product or Service: Advertising/Marketing Agency
Street address 1: 818 E Foothill Blvd
Street address state: CA
Postal code: 91016-2408
County: Los Angeles
Country: USA
Mailing address 1: 818 E Foothill Blvd
Mailing city: Monrovia
Mailing state: CA
Mailing zip: 91016-2408
Office phone: (626) 303-1090
Office fax: (626) 303-5431
Other fax: www.mcmonigle.com
Web address: jamie@mcmonigle.com

MONTEREY

COMMUNICATION DESIGN

Product or Service: Multimedia/Interactive Products
Street address 1: 24 Caribou Ct
Street address state: CA
Postal code: 93940-6303
County: Monterey
Country: USA
Mailing address 1: 24 Caribou Court
Mailing city: Monterey
Mailing state: CA
Mailing zip: 93940
Office phone: (831) 373-3925
Other phone: (888) 980-2797
Web address: www.ittelson.com
Note: John C. Ittelson (Prof); Bobbi Kamil (Project Mgr.); Brendan Ittelson (Webmaster)
Employee Associations: John C. Ittelson

MOUNT KISCO

LOGOPREMIUMS.COM

Product or Service: Advertising/Marketing Agency
Street address 1: PO Box 295
Street address state: NY
Postal code: 10549-0295
County: Westchester
Country: USA
Mailing address 1: PO Box 295
Mailing city: Mount Kisco
Mailing state: NY
Mailing zip: 10549-0295
Office phone: (914) 244-0735
Office fax: (914) 244-1995
Other phone: (800) 477-0138
Other fax: www.logopremiums.com
Web address: manager@logopremiums.com
Note: Jeff Levine (Project Mgr.)
Employee Associations: Jeff Levine

MOUNT PLEASANT

ASSIGNMENT DESK

Product or Service: Multimedia/Interactive Products`Telecommunications/Service Bureaus
Street address 1: 665 Johnnie Dodds Blvd.
Street address 2: Suite 201
Street address state: SC
Postal code: 29464
County: Cook
Country: USA
Mailing address 1: 665 Johnnie Dodds Blvd., Suite 201
Mailing city: Mount Pleasant
Mailing state: SC
Mailing zip: 29464
Office phone: (312) 464-8600
Other fax: www.assignmentdesk.com
Web address: cya@assignmentdesk.com
Note: Evelyn Beldam (Bus. Mgr.)
Employee Associations: Bill Scheer

NASHVILLE

DESIGNORY.COM

Product or Service: Advertising/Marketing Agency
Street address 1: 209 10th Ave S
Street address 2: Ste 409
Street address state: TN
Postal code: 37203-0767
County: Davidson
Country: USA
Mailing address 1: 209 10th Ave S Suite 209
Mailing city: Nashville
Mailing state: TN
Mailing zip: 37203-4144
Office phone: (615) 514-7514
Other fax: www.designory.com

NASHVILLE

HEALTHSTREAM

Product or Service: Multimedia/Interactive Products
Street address 1: 209 10th Ave S
Street address 2: Ste 450
Street address state: TN
Postal code: 37203-0788
County: Davidson
Country: USA
Mailing address 1: 209 10th Ave S Ste 450
Mailing city: Nashville
Mailing state: TN
Mailing zip: 37203-0788
Office phone: (615) 301-3100
Office fax: (615) 301-3200
Other fax: www.healthstream.com
Web address: contact@healthstream.com
Note: Robert A. Frist (CEO); Arthur E. Newman (Sr. Vice Pres., Finance)
Employee Associations: Arthur E. Newman

NEPTUNE

ASBURY PARK PRESS

Product or Service: Multimedia/Interactive Products`Publisher/Media
Street address 1: 3601 Hwy 66
Street address state: NJ
Postal code: 7754-
County: Monmouth
Country: USA
Mailing address 1: PO Box 1550
Mailing city: Neptune
Mailing state: NJ

Interactive Products and Services Companies

Mailing zip: 07754-1550
Office phone: (732) 922-6000
Office fax: (732) 922-0783
Other fax: www.app.com
Web address: htowns@njpressmedia.com
Employee Associations: Hollis R Town

NEW YORK

24/7 REAL MEDIA, INC.
Product or Service: Advertising/Marketing Agency
Street address 1: 132 W 31st St
Street address 2: Fl 9
Street address state: NY
Postal code: 10001-3406
County: New York
Country: USA
Mailing address 1: 132 W 31st St Fl 9
Mailing city: New York
Mailing state: NY
Mailing zip: 10001-3406
Office phone: (212) 231-7100
Office fax: (646) 259-4200
Other fax: www.247realmedia.com
Web address: info@xaxis.com

ADVANCE LOCAL
Product or Service: Publisher/Media
Street address 1: 1 World Trade Center
Street address 2: 40th Floor
Street address state: NY
Postal code: 10007
County: Hudson
Country: USA
Mailing address 1: 1 World Trade Center
Mailing city: New York
Mailing state: NY
Mailing zip: 10007
Other fax: www.advancelocal.com
Web address: advancelocalinfo@advance.net
Note: Randy Siegel (CEO); Caroline Harrison (Pres.)
Employee Associations: ()

ADVERTISING AGE
Product or Service: Publisher/Media
Street address 1: 711 3rd Ave
Street address state: NY
Postal code: 10017-4014
County: New York
Country: USA
Mailing address 1: 711 3rd Ave Fl 3
Mailing city: New York
Mailing state: NY
Mailing zip: 10017-9214
Office phone: (212) 210-0100
Office fax: (212) 210-0200
Other fax: www.adage.com
Web address: editor@adage.com
Note: Allison Price Arden (Pub.)
Employee Associations: Allison Price Arden

AMERIKIDS USA
Product or Service: Multimedia/Interactive Products
Street address 1: 10 Leonard St
Street address 2: Apt 3SW
Street address state: NY
Postal code: 10013-2961
County: New York
Country: USA
Mailing address 1: 10 Leonard St Apt 3SW Ste. 3SW
Mailing city: New York
Mailing state: NY
Mailing zip: 10013-2961
Office phone: (212) 941-8461
Other fax: www.amerikids.com
Web address: developer@amerikids.com
General e-mail: We just launched Green Kids Media's Endanger Games http:// www.amerikids.com
Note: Lynn Rogoff (CEO); Mark Tabashnick (Media Producer)

Employee Associations: Lynn Rogoff

ASSOCIATED PRESS INFORMATION SERVICES
Product or Service: Publisher/Media
Street address 1: 450 W 33rd St
Street address state: NY
Postal code: 10001-2603
County: New York
Country: USA
Mailing address 1: 450 W 33rd St Fl 15
Mailing city: New York
Mailing state: NY
Mailing zip: 10001-2647
Office phone: (212) 621-1500
Office fax: (212) 621-7520
Other fax: www.ap.org
Web address: info@ap.org
Note: Ted Mendelsohn (Dir. Sales)
Employee Associations: Ted Mendelsohn

BMC GROUP, INC.
Product or Service: Hardware/Software Supplier
Street address 1: 477 Madison Ave
Street address 2: Fl 6
Street address state: NY
Postal code: 10022-5827
County: New York
Country: USA
Mailing address 1: 12 W 31st St Fl 2
Mailing city: New York
Mailing state: NY
Mailing zip: 10001-4415
Office phone: (212) 310-5900
Office fax: (212) 644-4552
Other fax: www.bmcgroup.com
Note: Matt Morris (Sales Contact)
Employee Associations: Sean Allen

BUSINESS WIRE - NEW YORK, NY
Product or Service: Online Service Provider and Internet Hosts
Street address 1: 40 E 52nd St
Street address 2: Fl 14
Street address state: NY
Postal code: 10022-5911
County: New York
Country: USA
Mailing address 1: 40 E 52nd St Fl 14
Mailing city: New York
Mailing state: NY
Mailing zip: 10022-5911
Office phone: (212) 752-9600
Other fax: www.businesswire.com
Note: Geff Scott (CEO); Richard DeLeo (COO)
Employee Associations: Neil Hershberg

CARL WALTZER DIGITAL SERVICES, INC.
Product or Service: Telecommunications/ Service Bureaus
Street address 1: 873 Broadway
Street address 2: Ste 412
Street address state: NY
Postal code: 10003-1234
County: New York
Country: USA
Mailing address 1: 873 Broadway Ste 412
Mailing city: New York
Mailing state: NY
Mailing zip: 10003-1234
Office phone: (212) 475-8748
Office fax: (212) 475-9559
Other fax: www.waltzer.com
Web address: wdigital@nyc.rr.com
Note: Carl Waltzer (Pres.); Bill Waltzer (Photographer)
Employee Associations: Carl Waltzer

COMTEX NEWS NETWORK
Product or Service: Online Service Provider and Internet Hosts
Street address 1: 295 Madison Avenue
Street address 2: 12th Floor
Street address state: NY
Postal code: 10017â€‹
County: Alexandria City
Country: USA
Mailing address 1: 295 Madison Avenue, 12th Floor
Mailing city: New York
Mailing state: NY
Mailing zip: 10017â€‹
Office phone: (703) 797-8135
Office fax: (212) 688-6241
Other fax: www.comtex.com
Web address: sales@comtex.com
Note: Kan Devnani (Pres. & CEO); Chip Brian (Chairman); Robert J. Lynch (Dir.)
Employee Associations: ()

DLS DESIGN
Product or Service: Graphic/Design Firm
Street address 1: 232 Madison Ave
Street address 2: Rm 800
Street address state: NY
Postal code: 10016-2940
County: New York
Country: USA
Mailing address 1: 232 Madison Ave Rm 800
Mailing city: New York
Mailing state: NY
Mailing zip: 10016-2901
Office phone: (212) 255-3464
Other fax: www.dlsdesign.com
Web address: info@dlsdesign.com
Note: David Schiffer (Pres.)
Employee Associations: David Schiffer

DOUBLECLICK
Product or Service: Advertising/Marketing Agency
Street address 1: 111 8th Ave
Street address 2: Fl 10
Street address state: NY
Postal code: 10011-5210
County: New York
Country: USA
Mailing address 1: 111 8th Ave Fl 10
Mailing city: New York
Mailing state: NY
Mailing zip: 10011-5210
Office phone: (212) 271-2542
Office fax: (212) 287-1203
Other fax: www.doubleclick.com
Web address: publicrelations@doubleclick.net

ENIGMA
Product or Service: Hardware/Software Supplier
Street address 1: 245 Fifth Avenue
Street address 2: Floor 17
Street address state: NY
Postal code: 10016
County: Norfolk
Country: USA
Mailing address 1: 245 Fifth Avenue, Floor 17
Mailing city: New York
Mailing state: NY
Mailing zip: 10016
Office phone: (800) 510-2856
Other fax: www.enigma.com
Web address: press@enigma.com
Note: Hicham Oudghiri (CEO); Craig Danton (Vice Pres., Product)
Employee Associations: ()

EPSILON INTERACTIVE
Product or Service: Advertising/Marketing Agency
Street address 1: 11 W 19th St
Street address 2: Fl 9
Street address state: NY
Postal code: 10011-4275

County: New York
Country: USA
Mailing address 1: 11 W 19th St Fl 9
Mailing city: New York
Mailing state: NY
Mailing zip: 10011-4275
Office phone: (212) 457-7000
Office fax: (212) 457-7040
Other fax: www.epsilon.com
Web address: info@epsilon.com

FUSEBOX, INC.
Product or Service: Graphic/Design Firm
Street address 1: 36 W 20th St
Street address 2: Fl 11
Street address state: NY
Postal code: 10011-4241
County: New York
Country: USA
Mailing address 1: 36 W 20th St Fl 11
Mailing city: New York
Mailing state: NY
Mailing zip: 10011-4241
Office phone: (212) 929-7644
Office fax: (212) 929-7947
Other fax: www.fusebox.com
Web address: info@fusebox.com

G2 DIRECT & DIGITAL
Product or Service: Advertising/Marketing Agency
Street address 1: 636 11th Ave
Street address state: NY
Postal code: 10036-2005
County: New York
Country: USA
Mailing address 1: 636 11th Ave
Mailing city: New York
Mailing state: NY
Mailing zip: 10036-2005
Office phone: (212) 537-3700
Office fax: (212) 537-3737
Other fax: www.g2.com
Web address: steve.harding@geometry.com

ICONNICHOLSON
Product or Service: Multimedia/Interactive Products
Street address 1: 11 W 19th St
Street address 2: Fl 3
Street address state: NY
Postal code: 10011-4280
County: New York
Country: USA
Mailing address 1: 295 Lafayette St
Mailing city: New York
Mailing state: NY
Mailing zip: 10012-2701
Office phone: (212) 274-0470
Office fax: (888) 847-5321
Other fax: www.iconnicholson.com
Note: Tom Nicholson (CEO)
Employee Associations: Tom Nicholson

IMAGE ZONE, INC.
Product or Service: Multimedia/Interactive Products
Street address 1: 11 W 69th St
Street address 2: # 10
Street address state: NY
Postal code: 10023-4720
County: New York
Country: USA
Mailing address 1: 11 W 69th St # 10
Mailing city: New York
Mailing state: NY
Mailing zip: 10023-4720
Office phone: (212) 924-8804
Other phone: (201) 741-8901
Other fax: www.imagezone.com
Web address: mail@imagezone.com
Note: Doug Ehrlich (MD); Peter Smallman (Creative Dir.)
Employee Associations: Doug Ehrlich

INTERACTIVE EDUCATIONAL SYSTEMS DESIGN, INC.

Product or Service: Consultants
Street address 1: 33 W 87th St
Street address state: NY
Postal code: 10024-3082
County: New York
Country: USA
Mailing address 1: 33 W 87th St
Mailing city: New York
Mailing state: NY
Mailing zip: 10024-3082
Office phone: (631) 691-2606
Other fax: www.iesdinc.com
Web address: iesdinc@aol.com
Note: Ellen Bialo (Pres.); Jay Sivin Kachala (Vice Pres.)
Employee Associations: Ellen Bialo

INTERACTIVE INTERNATIONAL, INC.

Product or Service: Hardware/Software Supplier
Street address 1: 290 W End Ave
Street address state: NY
Postal code: 10023-8106
County: New York
Country: USA
Mailing address 1: 290 W End Ave
Mailing city: New York
Mailing state: NY
Mailing zip: 10023-8106
Office phone: (212) 580-5015
Office fax: (212) 580-5017
Other phone: (212) 580-5015
Other fax: www.erols.com
Web address: ivie@erols.com
Note: George M. Bulow (Pres.)
Employee Associations: George M. Bulow

KING FEATURES SYNDICATE

Product or Service: Publisher/Media
Street address 1: 300 W 57th St
Street address 2: Fl 41
Street address state: NY
Postal code: 10019-3741
County: New York
Country: USA
Mailing address 1: 300 W 57th St 41st Floor
Mailing city: New York
Mailing state: NY
Mailing zip: 10019-5238
Office phone: (212) 969-7550
Office fax: (646) 280-1550
Other phone: (800) 526-5464
Other fax: www.kingfeatures.com
Web address: kfs-cartoonists@hearst.com
Note: Keith McCloat (VP, Gen. Mgr.); David Cohea (Gen. Mgr., King Feat. Weekly Service Inside Sales); Claudia Smith (Dir., PR); Jack Walsh (Sr. Sales Consultant/ Printing & New England Newspaper Sales); Dennis Danko (Inside Sales Mgr.); Michael Mancino (Sales Mgr., New Media Inside Sales); John Killian (VP, Syndication Sales); Jim Clarke (Editorial Dir., King Feat. Weekly Service); Brendan Burford (Gen. Mgr., Syndication); Randy Noble (SE Sales); Diana Smith (Executive Editor); Evelyn Smith (Senior Comics Editor); Chris Richreek (Senior Features Editor); Curtis Trammell (Western Region Sales); Robin Graham (International Sales Consultant); Monique Prioleau (Sales Coordinator); C.J. Kettler (President)
Employee Associations: ()

MARKE COMMUNICATIONS, INC.

Product or Service: Advertising/Marketing Agency
Street address 1: 45 W 45th St
Street address 2: Fl 16
Street address state: NY
Postal code: 10036-4602
County: New York
Country: USA
Mailing address 1: 45 W 45th St Fl 16
Mailing city: New York
Mailing state: NY
Mailing zip: 10036-4602
Office phone: (212) 201-0600
Office fax: (212) 213-0785
Other fax: www.marke.com

NEWBURY PARK

CAPTURED DIGITAL, INC.

Product or Service: Telecommunications/ Service Bureaus
Street address 1: 2520 Turquoise Cir
Street address 2: Ste B
Street address state: CA
Postal code: 91320-1218
County: Ventura
Country: USA
Mailing address 1: 2520 Turquoise Cir Ste B
Mailing city: Newbury Park
Mailing state: CA
Mailing zip: 91320-1218
Office phone: (805) 499-7333
Office fax: (805) 499-4590
Other fax: www.capturedimages.com
Web address: jobs@captureddigital.com
Note: John Chater
Employee Associations: John Chater

NEWPORT

EN TECHNOLOGY CORP.

Product or Service: Telecommunications/ Service Bureaus
Street address 1: 322 N Main St
Street address state: NH
Postal code: 03773-1496
County: Sullivan
Country: USA
Mailing address 1: PO Box 505
Mailing city: Marlow
Mailing state: NH
Mailing zip: 03456-0505
Office phone: (603) 863-8102
Office fax: (603) 863-7316
Other fax: www.entechnology.com
Web address: sales@entechnology.com
Note: David Hall (Chrmn. of the Bd.); Patricia Gallup (Pres.); Matt Cookson (Opns. Mgr.)
Employee Associations: Matt Cookson

NEWTON

CYWAYS, INC.

Product or Service: Online Service Provider and Internet Hosts
Street address 1: 19 Westchester Rd
Street address state: MA
Postal code: 02458-2519
County: Middlesex
Country: USA
Mailing address 1: 19 Westchester Rd
Mailing city: Newton
Mailing state: MA
Mailing zip: 02458-2519
Office phone: (617) 965-9465
Office fax: (617) 796-8997
Web address: support@cyways.com
Note: Peter H. Lemieux (Pres.)
Employee Associations: Peter H. Lemieux

NORTH BALDWIN

LIGHT FANTASTIC STUDIOS, INC.

Product or Service: Multimedia/Interactive Products
Street address 1: 618 Portland Ave
Street address state: NY
Postal code: 11510-2642
County: Nassau
Country: USA
Mailing address 1: 618 Portland Ave
Mailing city: North Baldwin
Mailing state: NY
Mailing zip: 11510-2642
Office phone: (212) 604-0666
Office fax: (212) 604-0666
Other fax: www.lightfantasticstudios.com
Web address: info@lightfantasticstudios.com
Note: Paul Hollett (Pres./Creative Dir.); Ray Rue (Art Dir.); Ranee Chong (Designer)
Employee Associations: Paul Hollett

NORWALK

GCN PUBLISHING

Product or Service: Multimedia/Interactive Products
Street address 1: 194 Main St
Street address 2: Ste 2NW
Street address state: CT
Postal code: 06851-3502
County: Fairfield
Country: USA
Mailing address 1: 194 Main St Ste 2NW
Mailing city: Norwalk
Mailing state: CT
Mailing zip: 06851-3502
Office phone: (203) 665-6211
Office fax: (203) 665-6212
Other fax: www.one-count.com
Web address: info@one-count.com
Note: Joanne Persico (President/Co-founder); Sean Fulton (Vice President of Technology/ Co-founder)
Employee Associations: Peter Cianfaglione

MILES 33

Product or Service: Hardware/Software Supplier`Multimedia/Interactive Products
Street address 1: 40 Richards Ave
Street address 2: Pendegast Street, 5170
Street address state: CT
Postal code: 06854-2319
County: Fairfield
Country: USA
Mailing address 1: 40 Richards Ave Ste 29
Mailing city: Norwalk
Mailing state: CA
Mailing zip: 06854-2322
Office phone: (203) 838-2333
Office fax: (203) 838-4473
Other fax: www.miles33.com
Web address: info@miles33.com
Note: Chris Habasinski (Pres.); Albert De Bruijn (VP Marketing and Western USA Sales); Edward Hubbard (VP, Business Development)
Employee Associations: Diana Fox; Albert de Bruijn

NORWICH

ICENI TECHNOLOGY

Product or Service: Multimedia/Interactive Products
Street address 1: Sackville Place 44-48 Magdalen St.
Postal code: NR3 1JV
Country: United Kingdom
Mailing address 1: Sackville Place 44-48 Magdalen St.
Mailing city: Norwich
Mailing zip: NR3 1JV
Office phone: 603-628-289
Office fax: 603-627-415
Other fax: www.iceni.com
Web address: sales@iceni.com
Note: Simon Crowfoot (Dir.)
Employee Associations: Simon Crowfoot

NOVI

DENSO TEN AMERICA LIMITED

Product or Service: Multimedia/Interactive Products
Street address 1: 30155 Hudson Dr.
Street address state: MI
Postal code: 48377
Country: USA
Mailing address 1: 30155 Hudson Dr.
Mailing city: Novi
Mailing state: MI
Mailing zip: 48377
Office phone: (734) 414-6620
Office fax: (734) 414-6660
Other fax: www.denso-ten.com
Web address: info@lao.ten.fujitsu.com
Note: Satoshi Iwata (President and Representative Director)
Employee Associations: ()

OAK PARK

HUTCHINSON ASSOCIATES, INC.

Product or Service: Advertising/Marketing Agency`Consultants`Graphic/Design Firm`Marketing`Other Services`Web Site Auditor
Street address 1: 822 Linden Ave
Street address 2: Ste 200
Street address state: IL
Postal code: 60302-1562
County: Cook
Country: USA
Mailing address 1: 822 Linden Ave Ste 200
Mailing city: Oak Park
Mailing state: IL
Mailing zip: 60302-1562
Office phone: (312) 455-9191
Other fax: www.thisishutchinson.com
Web address: hutch@thisishutchinson.com
Note: Jerry Hutchinson (Pres.); Doug White (Prod.)
Employee Associations: Jerry Hutchinson

OCEANSIDE

BRANFMAN LAW GROUP, P.C.

Product or Service: Consultants
Street address 1: 708 Civic Center Dr
Street address state: CA
Postal code: 92054-2504
County: San Diego
Country: USA
Mailing address 1: 708 Civic Center Dr
Mailing city: Oceanside
Mailing state: CA
Mailing zip: 92054-2504
Office phone: (760) 637-2400
Office fax: (760) 687-7421
Other fax: www.branfman.com
Web address: info@branfman.com
Note: David Branfman (Owner); Mark Reichenthal (Assoc.)
Employee Associations: David Branfman

OLD CHATHAM

BLASS COMMUNICATIONS

Product or Service: Advertising/Marketing Agency
Street address 1: 17 Drowne Rd
Street address state: NY
Postal code: 12136-3006
County: Columbia
Country: USA
Mailing address 1: 17 Drowne Rd
Mailing city: Old Chatham
Mailing state: NY
Mailing zip: 12136-3006
Office phone: (518) 766-2222
Office fax: (518) 766-2445
Other fax: www.blasscommunications.com
Web address: info@blasscommunications.com

OMAHA

FIRST DATA VOICE SERVICES

Product or Service: Telecommunications/ Service Bureaus
Street address 1: 10910 Mill Valley Rd
Street address state: NE
Postal code: 68154-3930
County: Douglas
Country: USA

Interactive Products and Services Companies

Mailing address 1: 10910 Mill Valley Rd
Mailing city: Omaha
Mailing state: NE
Mailing zip: 68154-3930
Office phone: (402) 777-2100
Office fax: (402) 222-7910
Other fax: www.callit.com/FDVSSite/contact.aspx
Web address: fdvsinfo@firstdata.com
Note: James Harvey (Vice Pres., Devel.); Bob Van Stry (Vice Pres., Sales)
Employee Associations: James Harvey

ORLAND PARK

MPI MEDIA GROUP

Product or Service: Publisher/Media
Street address 1: 16101 108th Ave
Street address state: IL
Postal code: 60467-5305
County: Cook
Country: USA
Mailing address 1: 16101 108th Ave
Mailing city: Orland Park
Mailing state: IL
Mailing zip: 60467-5305
Office phone: (708) 460-0555
Office fax: (708) 873-3177
Other phone: (800) 323-0442
Other fax: www.mpimedia.com
Web address: info@mpimedia.com
Note: Nicola Goelzhaeufer (Contact)
Employee Associations: Nicola Goelzhaeufer

OTTAWA

COREL

Product or Service: Hardware/Software Supplier
Street address 1: 1600 Carling Ave.
Street address state: ON
Postal code: K1Z 8R7
Country: Canada
Mailing address 1: 1600 Carling Ave.
Mailing city: Ottawa
Mailing state: ON
Mailing zip: K1Z 8R7
Office phone: (613) 728-8200
Office fax: (613) 728-9790
Other fax: www.corel.com
Note: Patrick Nichols (CEO); Brad Jewett (CFO); Jason Wesbecher (Exec. Vice Pres. of Sales and Marketing)
Employee Associations: Jason Wesbecher

PARAMUS

JABLONSKI DESIGN, INC.

Product or Service: Graphic/Design Firm
Street address 1: 8 Daisy Way
Street address 2: Ste B
Street address state: NJ
Postal code: 07652-4305
County: Bergen
Country: USA
Mailing address 1: 8 Daisy Way Ste B
Mailing city: Paramus
Mailing state: NJ
Mailing zip: 07652-4305
Office phone: (201) 843-0228
Other fax: www.jablonskidesign.com
Web address: info@jablonskidesign.com
Note: Carl Jablonski (Pres.)
Employee Associations: Carl Jablonski

PARSIPPANY

DIALOGIC CORP.

Product or Service: Telecommunications/Service Bureaus
Street address 1: 1515 State Rt 10
Street address state: NJ
Postal code: 07054-4538
County: Morris
Country: USA
Mailing address 1: 1515 State Rt 10 Ste 1
Mailing city: Parsippany

Mailing state: NJ
Mailing zip: 07054-4538
Office phone: (973) 967-6000
Office fax: (973) 967-6006
Other fax: www.dialogic.com
Web address: sales@dialogic.com
Note: Howard Bubb (Pres./CEO); Athena Mandros (Contact)
Employee Associations: Athena Mandros

PEMBROKE

MRW COMMUNICATIONS, LLC.

Product or Service: Hardware/Software Supplier
Street address 1: 6 Barker Square Dr
Street address state: MA
Postal code: 02359-2225
County: Plymouth
Country: USA
Mailing address 1: 6 Barker Square Dr
Mailing city: Pembroke
Mailing state: MA
Mailing zip: 02359-2225
Office phone: (781) 924-5282
Office fax: (781) 926-0371
Other fax: www.mrwinc.com
Web address: jim@mrwinc.com
Note: Jim Watts (Account Services Dir.); Tom Matzell (Creative Dir., Copy); Kristen Balunas (Creative Dir., Art)
Employee Associations: Jim Watts

PEORIA

JUPITER IMAGES CORP.

Product or Service: Hardware/Software Supplier
Street address 1: 6000 N Forest Park Dr
Street address state: IL
Postal code: 61614-3556
County: Peoria
Country: USA
Mailing address 1: 6000 N Forest Park Dr
Mailing city: Peoria
Mailing state: IL
Mailing zip: 61614-3556
Office phone: (309) 688-8800
Office fax: (309) 688-3075
Other fax: www.jupiterimages.com
Web address: sales@jupiterimages.com
General e-mail: All-purpose art and idea service.
Note: Mark Nickerson (Vice Pres., Opns.)
Employee Associations: Mark Nickerson

PHILADELPHIA

CRAMP + TATE, INC.

Product or Service: Advertising/Marketing Agency
Street address 1: 230 S 15th St
Street address 2: Fl 2
Street address state: PA
Postal code: 19102-3806
County: Philadelphia
Country: USA
Mailing address 1: 230 S. 15th St., 2nd Floor
Mailing city: Philadelphia
Mailing state: PA
Mailing zip: 19102-3837
Office phone: (215) 893-0500
Office fax: (215) 893-0543
Other fax: www.cramp.com
Web address: jeff.cramp@cramp.com

PHOENIX

ARIZONA REPUBLIC DIGITAL MEDIA

Product or Service: Publisher/Media
Street address 1: 200 E Van Buren St
Street address state: AZ
Postal code: 85004-2238
County: Maricopa
Country: USA
Mailing address 1: PO Box 1950
Mailing city: Phoenix
Mailing state: AZ

Mailing zip: 85001-1950
Office phone: (602) 444-8000
Office fax: (602) 444-8044
Other fax: www.azcentral.com
Note: Nicole Carroll (VP News Executive Editor)
Employee Associations: Nicole Carroll

ASPECT COMMUNICATIONS

Product or Service: Hardware/Software Supplier
Street address 1: 2325 East Camelback Road
Street address 2: Suite 700
Street address state: AZ
Postal code: 85016
Country: USA
Mailing address 1: 2325 East Camelback Road, Suite 700
Mailing city: Phoenix
Mailing state: CA
Mailing zip: 85016
Office phone: (978) 250 7900
Office fax: (602) 954 2294
Other fax: www.aspect.com
Web address: contact@aspect.com
Note: Patrick Dennis (Pres./CEO); Chris DeBiase (CFO); Michael Harris (Chief Marketing Officer)
Employee Associations: Justin Braden

PITTSBURGH

DIGITAL DESIGN GROUP LIMITED

Product or Service: Multimedia/Interactive Products
Street address 1: 955 Milton St
Street address state: PA
Postal code: 15218-1031
County: Allegheny
Country: USA
Mailing address 1: 955 Milton St
Mailing city: Pittsburgh
Mailing state: PA
Mailing zip: 15218-1031
Office phone: (412) 243-9119
Office fax: (412) 243-2285
Other fax: www.ddg-designs.com
Web address: rob@ddg-designs.com

PLAINSBORO

CREATIVE DIRECT

Product or Service: Advertising/Marketing Agency
Street address 1: 10 Schalks Crossing Rd
Street address 2: Ste 501
Street address state: NJ
Postal code: 08536-1612
County: Middlesex
Country: USA
Mailing address 1: 10 Schalks Crossing Rd Ste 501
Mailing city: Plainsboro
Mailing state: NJ
Mailing zip: 08536-1612
Office phone: (908) 239-8965

POINTE-CLAIRE

INNOVATIVE SYSTEMS DESIGN, INC.

Product or Service: Telecommunications/Service Bureaus
Street address 1: 222 Brunswick Blvd
Street address state: QC
Postal code: H9R 1A6
Country: Canada
Mailing address 1: 222 Brunswick Blvd.
Mailing city: Pointe-Claire
Mailing state: QC
Mailing zip: H9R 1A6
Office phone: (514) 459-0200
Office fax: (514) 459-0300
Other fax: www.isd.ca
Web address: sales@isd.ca
Note: Jeff Tierney (Pres.); Rob Dumas (Director of Sales and Marketing); Monica Steibelt (Sales Coord.)

Employee Associations: Monica Steibelt

PORTLAND

HTS INTERACTIVE HEALTH CARE

Product or Service: Multimedia/Interactive Products
Street address 1: 434 NW 6th Ave
Street address 2: Ste 202
Street address state: OR
Postal code: 97209-3651
County: Multnomah
Country: USA
Mailing address 1: 434 NW 6th Ave Ste 202
Mailing city: Portland
Mailing state: OR
Mailing zip: 97209-3651
Office phone: (503) 241-9315
Office fax: (503) 241-8466
Other fax: www.interactivehealthinc.com
Web address: sales@interactivehealthinc.com
Note: Bill Goldberg (Pres & CEO); Christine Solberg (CFO)
Employee Associations: ()

INFOCUS CORP.

Product or Service: Hardware/Software Supplier
Street address 1: 13190 SW 68th Pkwy
Street address 2: Ste 200
Street address state: OR
Postal code: 97223-8368
County: Washington
Country: USA
Mailing address 1: 13190 SW 68th Pkwy Ste 200
Mailing city: Portland
Mailing state: OR
Mailing zip: 97223-8368
Office phone: (503) 207-4700
Office fax: (503) 207-4707
Other fax: www.infocus.com
Note: Randy Arnold (Pres.); Loren Shaw (Vice Pres., Marketing); Surendra Arora (Vice Pres., Strategic Relationships & Business Development)

RADNOR

BACKE DIFITAL BRAND MARKETING

Product or Service: Advertising/Marketing Agency
Street address 1: 100 W Matsonford Rd
Street address 2: Bldg 101
Street address state: PA
Postal code: 19087-4558
County: Delaware
Country: USA
Mailing address 1: 100 Matsonford Rd Ste 101
Mailing city: Radnor
Mailing state: PA
Mailing zip: 19087-4566
Office phone: (610) 947-6900
Office fax: (610) 896-9242
Other fax: www.backemarketing.com
Web address: info@backemarketing.com
Note: John E. Backe (Pres./CEO); Malcolm Brown (Sr. Vice Pres.)
Employee Associations: Malcolm Brown

RALEIGH

MCCLATCHY INTERACTIVE

Product or Service: Publisher/Media
Street address 1: 1100 Situs Ct
Street address state: NC
Postal code: 27606-5446
County: Wake
Country: USA
Mailing address 1: 1100 Situs Ct Ste 100
Mailing city: Raleigh
Mailing state: NC
Mailing zip: 27606-4295
Office phone: (919) 861-1200
Office fax: (919) 861-1300
Other fax: www.mcclatchyinteractive.com
Web address: jcalloway@mcclatchyinteractive.

RAMSEY

HOTWAX MULTIMEDIA, INC.

Product or Service: Multimedia/Interactive Products
Street address 1: 16 Stoney Brook Ct
Street address state: NJ
Postal code: 07446-1456
County: Bergen
Country: USA
Mailing address 1: 16 Stoney Brook Ct
Mailing city: Ramsey
Mailing state: NJ
Mailing zip: 07446-1456
Office phone: (201) 818-0001
Other fax: www.hotwax.com
Web address: info@hotwax.com
Note: David R. Huber (Owner)
Employee Associations: David R. Huber

READING

ATEX

Product or Service: Hardware/Software Supplier
Street address 1: 87 Castle Street
Postal code: RG1 7SN
Country: United Kingdom
Mailing address 1: 87 Castle Street
Mailing city: Reading
Mailing zip: RG1 7SN
Office phone: 118 958 7537
Office fax: 118 958 7537
Other fax: www.atex.com
Web address: info@atex.com
Note: Peter Marsh (Sr. Vice Pres./Chief Integration Officer); Malcolm McGrory (Sr. Vice Pres., Sales Americas)
Employee Associations: Malcolm McGrory

REDMOND

MICROSOFT CORP.

Product or Service: Hardware/Software Supplier
Street address 1: 1 Microsoft Way
Street address state: WA
Postal code: 98052-8300
County: King
Country: USA
Mailing address 1: 1 Microsoft Way # 41-375
Mailing city: Redmond
Mailing state: WA
Mailing zip: 98052-8300
Office phone: (425) 882-8080
Office fax: (425) 936-7329
Other fax: www.microsoft.com
Web address: storesoc@microsoft.com
Note: John W. Thompson (Chrmn.); Satya Nadella (CEO); Judson Althoff (Exec. Vice Pres.); Chris Capossela (Chief Marketing Officer); Jean-Philippe Courtois (Pres., Global Sales, Marketing and Operations); Amy Hood (Exec. Vice Pres. & CFO); Kevin Scott (CTO and Exec. Vice Pres.)
Employee Associations: ()

REDWOOD CITY

BROADVISION

Product or Service: Hardware/Software Supplier
Street address 1: 1700 Seaport Blvd
Street address 2: Ste 210
Street address state: CA
Postal code: 94063-5579
County: San Mateo
Country: USA
Mailing address 1: 1700 Seaport Blvd Ste 210
Mailing city: Redwood City
Mailing state: CA
Mailing zip: 94063-5579
Office phone: (650) 295-0716
Office fax: (650) 364-3425
Other fax: www.broadvision.com
Web address: info@broadvision.com
Note: Jean Mc Corthy (Dir.)
Employee Associations: Jean Mc Corthy

RESTON

FOUR PALMS, INC.

Product or Service: Multimedia/Interactive Products
Street address 1: 11260 Roger Bacon Dr
Street address 2: Fl 4
Street address state: VA
Postal code: 20190-5227
County: Fairfax
Country: USA
Mailing address 1: 11260 Roger Bacon Dr Fl 4
Mailing city: Reston
Mailing state: VA
Mailing zip: 20190-5227
Office phone: (703) 834-0200
Office fax: (703) 834-0219
Other fax: www.fourpalms.com
Web address: info@fourpalms.com
Note: Pat Buteux (Pres.)
Employee Associations: Pat Buteux

RICHMOND

BIG, (BEATLEY GRAVITT, INC.)

Product or Service: Graphic/Design Firm
Street address 1: One East Cary Street
Street address state: VA
Postal code: 23219
County: Richmond City
Country: USA
Mailing address 1: One East Cary Street
Mailing city: Richmond
Mailing state: VA
Mailing zip: 23219
Office phone: (804) 355-9151
Other fax: www.bigaddress.com
Web address: hello@bigaddress.com
Note: Ed Lacy (Pres./Dir., Mktg.)
Employee Associations: Ed Lacy

ROCHESTER

BBS COMPUTING

Product or Service: Online Service Provider and Internet Hosts
Street address 1: 3400 W Ridge Rd
Street address state: NY
Postal code: 14626
County: Monroe
Country: USA
Mailing address 1: 3400 W Ridge Rd
Mailing city: Rochester
Mailing state: NY
Mailing zip: 14626
Office phone: (585) 544-3669
Other phone: (585) 723-3360
Other fax: www.bbscomputing.com
Note: Russell Frey (Pres.)

ROCKVILLE

CABLEFAX DAILY LLC

Product or Service: Online Service Provider and Internet Hosts
Street address 1: 4 Choke Cherry Rd
Street address 2: Fl 2
Street address state: MD
Postal code: 20850-4024
County: Montgomery
Country: USA
Mailing address 1: 4 Choke Cherry Rd Fl 2
Mailing city: Rockville
Mailing state: MD
Mailing zip: 20850-4024
Office phone: (301) 354-2000
Office fax: (301) 738-8453
Other fax: www.cablefax.com
Web address: sarenstein@accessintel.com
Note: Seth Arenstein (Editorial Dir.)
Employee Associations: Michael Grebb

MICRO FOCUS

Product or Service: Multimedia/Interactive Products
Street address 1: One Irvington Center
Street address 2: 700 King Farm Boulevard, Suite 400
Street address state: MD
Postal code: 20850-5736
Country: USA
Mailing address 1: One Irvington Center 700 King Farm Boulevard, Suite 400
Mailing city: Rockville
Mailing state: MD
Mailing zip: 20850-5736
Office phone: (301) 838-5000
Office fax: (301) 838-5025
Other fax: www.microfocus.com
Note: Kevin Loosemore (Exec. Chrmn.); Stephen Murdoch (CEO)
Employee Associations: Adam Lee

ROGERS

DIGICONNECT

Product or Service: Telecommunications/Service Bureaus
Street address 1: 8004 Cedar Dr
Street address state: AR
Postal code: 72756-7729
County: Benton
Country: USA
Mailing address 1: 8004 Cedar Dr
Mailing city: Rogers
Mailing state: AR
Mailing zip: 72756
Office phone: (877) 235-7714
Office fax: (479) 595-8748
Other fax: www.digiconow.com
Web address: info@digiconow.com
Note: Kim Gustafson (CEO)
Employee Associations: Kim Gustafson

ROSELLE

COPIA INTERNATIONAL LTD.

Product or Service: Hardware/Software Supplier`Other Services
Street address 1: 52 Salt Creek Rd
Street address state: IL
Postal code: 60172-1420
County: Dupage
Country: USA
Mailing address 1: 52 Salt Creek Road
Mailing city: Roselle
Mailing state: IL
Mailing zip: 60172
Office phone: (630) 388-6900
Office fax: (630) 778-8848
Other fax: www.copia.com
Web address: sales@copia.com
Note: Steve Hersee (Pres.); Dorothy Gaden-Flanagan (Vice Pres., Mktg.); Terry Flanagan (VP, Eng.)
Employee Associations: Dorothy Gaden-Flanagan

ROY

MALL MARKETING MEDIA

Product or Service: Advertising/Marketing Agency
Street address 1: 1877 W 4000 S
Street address state: UT
Postal code: 84067-3500
County: Weber
Country: USA
Mailing address 1: 1877 W 4000 S
Mailing city: Roy
Mailing state: UT
Mailing zip: 84067-3500
Office phone: (801) 927-2600
Other fax: www.thecpsgroup.com
Web address: michael@mallmarketingmedia.com
Note: Michael O'Connell (Pres. & CEO); Jazz Mann (Dir., Business Development); Maria Bell (Vice Pres.)
Employee Associations: Michael O'Connell

SAINT LOUIS

ARCH COMMUNICATIONS, INC.

Product or Service: Telecommunications/Service Bureaus
Street address 1: 1327 Hampton Ave
Street address state: MO
Postal code: 63139-3113
County: Saint Louis City
Country: USA
Mailing address 1: 1327 Hampton Ave
Mailing city: Saint Louis
Mailing state: MO
Mailing zip: 63139-3113
Office phone: (314) 645-8000
Office fax: (314) 645-8100
Other fax: www.archcom.net
Web address: info@archcom.net
Note: David Brandstetter (Pres.)
Employee Associations: David Brandstetter

CYBERCON.COM

Product or Service: Online Service Provider and Internet Hosts
Street address 1: 210 N Tucker Blvd
Street address 2: Fl 7
Street address state: MO
Postal code: 63101-1941
County: Saint Louis City
Country: USA
Mailing address 1: 210 N Tucker Blvd Fl 7
Mailing city: Saint Louis
Mailing state: MO
Mailing zip: 63101-1978
Office phone: (314) 621-9991
Office fax: (314) 241-1777
Other fax: www.cybercon.com
Web address: staff@cybercon.com
Note: Joshua Chen (Pres.)
Employee Associations: Joshua Chen

SAINT PETERSBURG

KOBIE MARKETING, INC.

Product or Service: Advertising/Marketing Agency
Street address 1: 100 2nd Ave S
Street address 2: Ste 1000
Street address state: FL
Postal code: 33701-4360
County: Pinellas
Country: USA
Mailing address 1: 100 2nd Ave S Ste 1000
Mailing city: Saint Petersburg
Mailing state: FL
Mailing zip: 33701-6307
Office phone: (727) 822-5353
Office fax: (727) 822-5265
Other fax: www.kobie.com
Web address: info@kobie.com
Note: Don Hughes (CIO); Robert Gilley (Project Mgr.)
Employee Associations: Don Hughes

SAN DIEGO

CLARITAS

Product or Service: Consultants`Research
Street address 1: 9444 Waples St
Street address 2: Ste 280
Street address state: CA
Postal code: 92121-2985
County: San Diego
Country: USA
Mailing address 1: 9444 Waples Street SUite 280
Mailing city: San Diego
Mailing state: CA

---

com
Note: Christian A. Hendricks (Vice Pres.); Fraser Van Asch (Exec. Vice Pres./Gen. Mgr.); James Calloway (Vice President Strategic Development); Kathy Lehmen (Product Management Director); Damon Kiesow (Senior Manager Mobile Initiatives)
Employee Associations: Jim Puryear

Interactive Products and Services Companies

Mailing zip: 92121
Office phone: (800) 234-5973
Office fax: (858) 500-5800
Other fax: www.claritas.com
Web address: Marketing@Claritas.com
Note: Dave Miller (Sr. VP)
Employee Associations: Sandi Settle

SAN FRANCISCO

DESIGN MEDIA, INC.

Product or Service: Multimedia/Interactive Products
Street address 1: 650 Alabama St
Street address state: CA
Postal code: 94110-2039
County: San Francisco
Country: USA
Mailing address 1: 650 Alabama St Ste 203
Mailing city: San Francisco
Mailing state: CA
Mailing zip: 94110-2038
Office phone: (415) 641-4848
Office fax: (415) 641-5245
Other fax: www.designmedia.com
Web address: info@designmedia.com
Note: Pamela May (Pres./CEO); Marlita Kahn (Sr. Project Mgr.); Barbara Berry (Sr. Project Mgr.); Wallace Murray (Project Mgr.); Alison DeGrassi (Project Mgr.); Cori Freeland (Office Mgr.); Rylan North (Sr. Web Developer)
Employee Associations: Pamela May

LUMINARE

Product or Service: CD-ROM Designer/Manufacturer
Street address 1: 65 Norfolk St
Street address 2: Unit 4
Street address state: CA
Postal code: 94103-4357
County: San Francisco
Country: USA
Mailing address 1: 65 Norfolk St Unit 4
Mailing city: San Francisco
Mailing state: CA
Mailing zip: 94103-4357
Office phone: (415) 661-1436
Other fax: www.luminare.com
Web address: info@luminare.com
Note: Caitlin Curtin (Pres.)
Employee Associations: Caitlin Curtin

SAN JOSE

ADOBE SYSTEMS, INC.

Product or Service: Hardware/Software Supplier
Street address 1: 345 Park Ave
Street address state: CA
Postal code: 95110-2704
County: Santa Clara
Country: USA
Mailing address 1: 345 Park Ave
Mailing city: San Jose
Mailing state: CA
Mailing zip: 95110-2704
Office phone: (408) 536-6000
Office fax: (408) 537-6000
Other fax: www.adobe.com
Note: Ann Lewnes (Sr. Vice Pres., Global Mktg.); Jennifer Reynolds (Dir., Worldwide Adv.)
Employee Associations: Jennifer Reynolds

LUMINA NETWORKS

Product or Service: Hardware/Software Supplier
Street address 1: 2077 Gateway Pl
Street address 2: Ste 500
Street address state: CA
Postal code: 95110-1085
County: Santa Clara
Country: USA
Mailing address 1: 2077 Gateway Pl
Mailing city: San Jose
Mailing state: CA
Mailing zip: 95110-1085

Office phone: (669) 231-3838
Other fax: www.luminanetworks.com
Note: Andrew Coward (CEO); Nitin Serro (COO); Kevin Woods (V. P. Marketing)

MERCURY CENTER

Product or Service: Online Service Provider and Internet Hosts
Street address 1: 750 Ridder Park Dr
Street address state: CA
Postal code: 95131-2432
County: Santa Clara
Country: USA
Mailing address 1: 750 Ridder Park Dr
Mailing city: San Jose
Mailing state: CA
Mailing zip: 95190-0001
Office phone: (408) 920-5000
Office fax: (408) 288-8060
Other fax: www.mercurycenter.com
Web address: tmooreland@sjmercury.com
Note: Tom Mooreland (Dir., Mercury Center)
Employee Associations: Tom Mooreland

METRO NEWSPAPER

Product or Service: Online Service Provider and Internet Hosts
Street address 1: 550 S 1st St
Street address state: CA
Postal code: 95113-2806
County: Santa Clara
Country: USA
Mailing address 1: 550 S 1st St
Mailing city: San Jose
Mailing state: CA
Mailing zip: 95113-2806
Office phone: (408) 298-8000
Office fax: (408) 279-5813
Other fax: www.metroactive.com; www.metronews.com
Web address: press@metronews.com
Note: Dan Pulcrano (Pres.)
Employee Associations: Dan Pulcrano

SAN LEANDRO

DIRECT IMAGES INTERACTIVE, INC.

Product or Service: Multimedia/Interactive Products
Street address 1: 1933 Davis St
Street address 2: Ste 314
Street address state: CA
Postal code: 94577-1259
County: Alameda
Country: USA
Mailing address 1: 1933 Davis St Ste 314
Mailing city: San Leandro
Mailing state: CA
Mailing zip: 94577-1259
Office phone: (510) 613-8299
Other fax: www.directimages.com
Web address: info@directimages.com
Note: Bill Knowland (Producer/Dir.); Beverly Knowland (Art Dir.)
Employee Associations: Bill Knowland

SAN LUIS OBISPO

INFORMATION PRESENTATION TECH.

Product or Service: Multimedia/Interactive Products
Street address 1: 825 Buckley Rd
Street address 2: Ste 200
Street address state: CA
Postal code: 93401-8193
County: San Luis Obispo
Country: USA
Mailing address 1: 4072 Campbellsville Pike
Mailing city: Columbia
Mailing state: TN
Mailing zip: 38401-8632
Office phone: (805) 541-3000
Office fax: (805) 541-3037
Other fax: www.iptech.com

Web address: info@iptech.com
Note: Olivia Favela (Vice Pres., Sales/Mktg.)
Employee Associations: Olivia Favela

SANTA BARBARA

MAPS.COM

Product or Service: Online Service Provider and Internet Hosts
Street address 1: 120 Cremona Dr
Street address 2: Ste 260
Street address state: CA
Postal code: 93117-5564
County: Santa Barbara
Country: USA
Mailing address 1: 120 Cremona Dr Ste 260
Mailing city: Santa Barbara
Mailing state: CA
Mailing zip: 93117-5564
Office phone: (805) 685-3100
Office fax: (805) 685-3330
Other fax: www.maps.com
Web address: info@maps.com
Note: John Serpa (Pres.); Robert H. Temkin (Founder/Chrmn./CEO); Charles Regan (Exec. Vice Pres.); Anne Messner (Vice Pres., Finance/Admin.); Bruce Kurtz (Dir., Mktg.); Bill Spicer (Dir., Online Commerce); Ed Easton (Dir., Mapping Servs.); Mitch McCoy (Dir., Tech./Project Devel.); Erik Davis (Dir., Education Mktg.)
Employee Associations: ()

SANTA CLARA

CD TECHNOLOGY

Product or Service: CD-ROM Designer/Manufacturer
Street address 1: 1112 Walsh Ave
Street address state: CA
Postal code: 95050-2646
County: Santa Clara
Country: USA
Mailing address 1: 1112 Walsh Ave
Mailing city: Santa Clara
Mailing state: CA
Mailing zip: 95050-2646
Office phone: (408) 982-0990
Office fax: (408) 982-0991
Other fax: www.cdtechnology.com
Note: William W. Liu (Pres.)
Employee Associations: William W. Liu

SANTA MONICA

FLI, INCORPORATED

Product or Service: Consultants
Street address 1: 400 Palisades Ave
Street address state: CA
Postal code: 90402-2720
County: Los Angeles
Country: USA
Mailing address 1: 400 Palisades Ave
Mailing city: Santa Monica
Mailing state: CA
Mailing zip: 90402-2720
Office phone: (310) 451-3307
Office fax: (310) 451-4207
Other fax: www.fliinc.com
Web address: jcwills@fliinc.com
Note: John Wills (President/CEO); Jane Wills (Vice President)
Employee Associations: John Wills

MEDIA DESIGN GROUP

Product or Service: CD-ROM Designer/Manufacturer
Street address 1: 3250 Ocean Park Blvd
Street address 2: Ste 200
Street address state: CA
Postal code: 90405-3250
County: Los Angeles
Country: USA
Mailing address 1: 3250 Ocean Park Blvd Ste 200

Mailing city: Santa Monica
Mailing state: CA
Mailing zip: 90405-3250
Office phone: (310) 584-9200
Office fax: (310) 584-9725
Other fax: www.mediadesigngroup.com
Web address: info@mediadesigngroup.com
Note: John D. Slack (CEO)
Employee Associations: John D. Slack

MOTION CITY FILMS

Product or Service: Multimedia/Interactive Products
Street address 1: 1424 4th St
Street address 2: Ste 604
Street address state: CA
Postal code: 90401-3447
County: Los Angeles
Country: USA
Mailing address 1: 1424 4th St Ste 604
Mailing city: Santa Monica
Mailing state: CA
Mailing zip: 90401-3447
Office phone: (310) 434-1272
Other fax: www.motioncity.com
Web address: editor@motioncity.com
Note: G. Michael Witt (Producing Dir.); Marty Blasick (Composer/Audio Engineer)
Employee Associations: G. Michael Witt

SAUSALITO

CHANNELNET

Product or Service: Consultants`Hardware/Software Supplier
Street address 1: 3 Harbor Dr
Street address 2: Ste 206
Street address state: CA
Postal code: 94965-1491
County: Marin
Country: USA
Mailing address 1: 3 Harbor Dr Ste 206
Mailing city: Sausalito
Mailing state: CA
Mailing zip: 94965-1491
Office phone: (415) 332-4704
Office fax: (415) 332-1635
Other fax: www.softad.com; www.channelnet.com
Web address: info@channelnet.com
Note: Paula George Tompkins (Founder/CEO); Kevin Kelly (CFO); Mike Behr (Sr. Dir., Professional Servs.)
Employee Associations: Alexis Elley

SCHAUMBURG

MOTOROLA SOLUTIONS, INC.

Product or Service: Telecommunications/Service Bureaus
Street address 1: 1303 E Algonquin Rd
Street address state: IL
Postal code: 60196-4041
County: Cook
Country: USA
Mailing address 1: 1303 E Algonquin Rd
Mailing city: Schaumburg
Mailing state: IL
Mailing zip: 60196-1079
Office phone: (847) 576-5000
Office fax: (561) 739-2341
Other phone: (855) 619-9714
Other fax: www.motorolasolutions.com
Web address: Training.NA@motorolasolutions.com
Note: Gregory Brown (Pres./CEO); David Dorman (Lead Independent Dir. of the Board)
Employee Associations: Gregory Brown

SCOTTSDALE

INTACTIX

Product or Service: Hardware/Software Supplier
Street address 1: 15059 N Scottsdale Rd
Street address 2: Ste 400

Street address state: AZ
Postal code: 85254-2666
Country: USA
Mailing address 1: 15059 N Scottsdale Rd Ste 400
Mailing city: Scottsdale
Mailing state: AZ
Mailing zip: 85254-2666
Office phone: (888) 441-1532
Other fax: www.jda.com
Web address: support.jda.com
Note: Girish Rishi (CEO)
Employee Associations: Sharon Mills

JDA SOFTWARE GROUP, INC.

Product or Service: Hardware/Software Supplier
Street address 1: 14400 N 87th St
Street address state: AZ
Postal code: 85260-3649
County: Maricopa
Country: USA
Mailing address 1: 14400 N 87th St
Mailing city: Scottsdale
Mailing state: AZ
Mailing zip: 85260-3657
Office phone: (480) 308-3000
Office fax: (480) 308-3001
Other fax: www.jda.com
Web address: info@jda.com
Note: Hamish Brewer (CEO)
Employee Associations: Hamish Brewer

SEATTLE

CHASE BOBKO, INC.

Product or Service: Multimedia/Interactive Products
Street address 1: 750 N 34th St
Street address state: WA
Postal code: 98103-8801
County: King
Country: USA
Mailing address 1: 750 N 34th St
Mailing city: Seattle
Mailing state: WA
Mailing zip: 98103-8801
Office phone: (206) 547-4310
Office fax: (206) 548-0749
Web address: information@chasebobko.com
Note: Bob Boiko (Pres.); Jayson Antonoff (CEO); Patricia Chase (Vice Pres.)
Employee Associations: Bob Boiko

ENVISION INTERACTIVE

Product or Service: Multimedia/Interactive Products
Street address 1: 901 5th Ave
Street address 2: Ste 3300
Street address state: WA
Postal code: 98164-2024
County: King
Country: USA
Mailing address 1: 901 5th Ave Ste 3300
Mailing city: Seattle
Mailing state: WA
Mailing zip: 98164-2024
Office phone: (206) 225-0800
Office fax: (206) 225-0801
Other fax: www.envisioninc.com
Web address: info@envisioninc.com

METHODOLOGIE, INC.

Product or Service: CD-ROM Designer/ Manufacturer`Graphic/Design Firm`Multimedia/Interactive Products
Street address 1: 720 3rd Ave
Street address 2: Ste 800
Street address state: WA
Postal code: 98104-1870
County: King
Country: USA
Mailing address 1: 720 3rd Ave Ste 800
Mailing city: Seattle
Mailing state: WA
Mailing zip: 98104-1870
Office phone: (206) 623-1044
Office fax: (206) 625-0154
Other fax: www.methodologie.com
Web address: info@methodologie.com

SHELTON

DAC SYSTEMS

Product or Service: Telecommunications/ Service Bureaus
Street address 1: 4 Armstrong Park Rd
Street address state: CT
Postal code: 6484-
County: Fairfield
Country: USA
Mailing address 1: 4 Armstrong Park Rd.
Mailing city: Shelton
Mailing state: CT
Mailing zip: 6484
Office phone: (203) 924-7000
Office fax: (203) 944-1618
Other fax: www.dacsystems.com
Web address: sales@dacsystems.com
Note: Mark Nickson (Pres.)
Employee Associations: Mark Nickson

SKOKIE

DUNN SOLUTIONS GROUP

Product or Service: Multimedia/Interactive Products
Street address 1: 5550 Touhy Ave
Street address state: IL
Postal code: 60077-3253
County: Cook
Country: USA
Mailing address 1: 5550 Touhy Ave Ste 400A
Mailing city: Skokie
Mailing state: IL
Mailing zip: 60077-3254
Office phone: (847) 673-0900
Office fax: (847) 673-0904
Other fax: www.dunnsolutions.com
Note: David Skwarczek (Pres.)
Employee Associations: David Skwarczek

SMYRNA

BLUECIELO ECM SOLUTIONS

Product or Service: Hardware/Software Supplier
Street address 1: 2400 Lake Park Dr SE
Street address 2: Ste 450
Street address state: GA
Postal code: 30080-7644
County: Cobb
Country: USA
Mailing address 1: 2400 Lake Park Dr SE Ste 450
Mailing city: Smyrna
Mailing state: GA
Mailing zip: 30080-7644
Office phone: (404) 634-3302
Office fax: (404) 633-4604
Other fax: www.bluecieloecm.com
Web address: info@bluecieloecm.com
Note: Karen Rhymer (Contact)
Employee Associations: Karen Rhymer

SOMERSET

CASCADE TECHNOLOGIES, INC.

Product or Service: Telecommunications/ Service Bureaus
Street address 1: 1075 Eastern Ave
Street address state: NJ
Postal code: 8873-
County: Somerset
Country: USA
Mailing address 1: 1075 Eastern Ave.
Mailing city: Somerset
Mailing state: NJ
Mailing zip: 08873-2220
Office phone: (732) 560-9908
Office fax: (908) 626-1209
Other fax: www.cascadetechnologies.com
Web address: info@cascadetechnologies.com
Note: Vigdis Austad (Pres.); Frank Joicy (Vice Pres.-Technology); Barbara Bishop (Sales); Janice Harrison (Mktg. Assoc.)
Employee Associations: Barbara Bishop

SOUTH BEND

BKR STUDIO, INC.

Product or Service: Multimedia/Interactive Products
Street address 1: 110 East Madison Street
Street address state: IN
Postal code: 46601
County: St Joseph
Country: USA
Mailing address 1: 110 East Madison Street
Mailing city: South Bend
Mailing state: IN
Mailing zip: 46601
Office phone: (574) 245-9576
Office fax: (574) 245-9577
Other fax: www.bkrstudio.com
Web address: info@bkrstudio.com
Note: Brian Rideout (Pres.); Tina Merrill (Studio Mgr.)
Employee Associations: Tina Merrill

SOUTH ST PAUL

GOLDEN GATE ENTERPRISES, LLC

Product or Service: Multimedia/Interactive Products
Street address 1: 490 Villaume Ave
Street address state: MN
Postal code: 55075-2443
Country: USA
Mailing address 1: 490 Villaume Ave
Mailing city: South Saint Paul
Mailing state: MN
Mailing zip: 55075-2443
Office phone: (651) 450-1000
Office fax: (651) 493-0372
Other fax: http://www.ggedigital.com
Web address: info@ggedigital.com
Note: Marco Scibora (Pres./CEO)
Employee Associations: Marco Scibora

STATE COLLEGE

ACCUWEATHER, INC.

Product or Service: Multimedia/Interactive Products`Other Services`Online Service Provider and Internet Hosts
Street address 1: 385 Science Park Rd
Street address state: PA
Postal code: 16803-2215
County: Centre
Country: USA
Mailing address 1: 385 Science Park Rd.
Mailing city: State College
Mailing state: PA
Mailing zip: 16803
Office phone: (814) 237-0309
Office fax: (814) 235-8609
Other fax: www.accuweather.com
Web address: support@accuweather.com
Note: Dr. Joel N. Myers (Founder & President); Evan Myers (CEO); Steven Smith (Pres., Digital Media); Jonathan Porter (Vice Pres. of Business Services and General Mgr. of Enterprise Solutions); John Dokes (Chief Content Officer); James Candor (Chief Strategy Officer); John Dokes (Chief Marketing Officer)
Employee Associations: Survey Contact

THE VILLAGES

ISRAEL FAXX

Product or Service: CD-ROM Designer/ Manufacturer`Publisher/Media
Street address 1: 611 Saint Andrews Blvd
Street address state: FL
Postal code: 32159-2280
County: Lake
Country: USA
Mailing address 1: 611 Saint Andrews Blvd
Mailing city: The Villages
Mailing state: FL
Mailing zip: 32159-2280
Office phone: (352) 750-9420
Other fax: www.israelfaxx.com
Web address: dcanaan@israelfaxx.com
Note: Don Canaan (Contact)
Employee Associations: ()

THE WOODLANDS

EPIC SOFTWARE GROUP, INC.

Product or Service: Multimedia/Interactive Products
Street address 1: 701 Sawdust Rd
Street address state: TX
Postal code: 77380-2943
County: Montgomery
Country: USA
Mailing address 1: 701 Sawdust Rd
Mailing city: The Woodlands
Mailing state: TX
Mailing zip: 77380-2943
Office phone: (281) 363-3742
Office fax: (281) 419-4509
Other fax: www.epicsoftware.com
Web address: epic@epicsoftware.com
Note: Vic Cherubini (Pres.)
Employee Associations: Vic Cherubini

INTERCOM

Product or Service: Multimedia/Interactive Products
Street address 1: 3 Grogans Park Dr
Street address 2: Ste 200
Street address state: TX
Postal code: 77380-2922
County: Montgomery
Country: USA
Mailing address 1: 3 Grogans Park Dr Ste 200
Mailing city: The Woodlands
Mailing state: TX
Mailing zip: 77380-2922
Office phone: (800) 298-7070
Office fax: (281) 364-7032
Other fax: www.intercom-interactive.com
Web address: intercom@intercom-interactive.com
Note: Bob Yeager (Pres.); Margo Pearson (Gen. Mgr.)
Employee Associations: Margo Pearson

THOUSAND OAKS

FLIP YOUR LID

Product or Service: Graphic/Design Firm`Multimedia/Interactive Products
Street address 1: 1288 Paseo Rancho Serrano
Street address 2: Ste 200
Street address state: CA
Postal code: 91356-6082
County: Los Angeles
Country: USA
Mailing address 1: 1288 Paseo Rancho Serrano
Mailing city: Thousand Oaks
Mailing state: CA
Mailing zip: 91362
Office phone: (818) 307-4165
Other fax: www.flipyourlid.com
Web address: jay@flipyourlid.com
General e-mail: Design, character design. Flash, 3d, and logo graphic design and traditional animation.
Note: Jay Jacoby (CEO)
Employee Associations: Jay Jacoby

TROY

CIBER, INC.

Product or Service: Consultants
Street address 1: 3270 West Big Beaver Road
Street address state: MI
Postal code: 48084
Country: USA
Mailing address 1: 3270 West Big Beaver Road
Mailing city: Troy

Interactive Products and Services Companies

Mailing state: MI
Mailing zip: 48084
Office phone: (303) 220-0100
Other phone: (833) 609-4950
Other fax: www.ciber.com
Note: Madhava Reddy (Pres./CEO); Vicki Hickman (Sr. Vice Pres., Reg. Sales)
Employee Associations: Bonnie Bird

TUCKAHOE

CAMPUS GROUP COMPANIES

Product or Service: Telecommunications/Service Bureaus
Street address 1: 42 Oak Ave
Street address state: NY
Postal code: 10707-4025
County: Westchester
Country: USA
Mailing address 1: 42 Oak Ave
Mailing city: Tuckahoe
Mailing state: NY
Mailing zip: 10707-4025
Office phone: (914) 395-1010
Other fax: www.campusgroup.com
Web address: sales@campusgroup.com
Note: Steve Campus (Owner)
Employee Associations: Steve Campus

TUCKER

EMERGENCE LABS, INC.

Product or Service: Advertising/Marketing Agency
Street address 1: 5150 N Royal Atlanta Dr
Street address state: GA
Postal code: 30084-3047
County: Dekalb
Country: USA
Mailing address 1: 5150 N Royal Atlanta Dr
Mailing city: Tucker
Mailing state: GA
Mailing zip: 30084-3047
Office phone: (770) 908-5650
Office fax: (770) 908-5673
Other fax: www.emergencelabs.com

TUSTIN

MEDIA ENTERPRISES

Product or Service: Advertising/Marketing Agency`Consultants`Editorial`Graphic/Design Firm`Marketing`Multimedia/Interactive Products`Research`Trade Association
Street address 1: 360 E 1st St
Street address 2: # 605
Street address state: CA
Postal code: 92780-3211
County: Orange
Country: USA
Mailing address 1: 360 E. 1st Street #605
Mailing city: Tustin
Mailing state: CA
Mailing zip: 92806
Office phone: (714) 778-5336
Other fax: www.media-enterprises.com
Web address: john@media-enterprises.com
Note: John Lemieux Rose (Principal)
Employee Associations: John Lemieux Rose

VESTAVIA HILLS

INFOMEDIA, INC.

Product or Service: Advertising/Marketing Agency`Consultants`Graphic/Design Firm`Marketing`Online Service Provider and Internet Hosts`Publisher/Media`Web Site Auditor
Street address 1: 2081 Columbiana Rd
Street address state: AL
Postal code: 35216-2139
County: Jefferson
Country: USA
Mailing address 1: 2081 Columbiana Rd

Mailing city: Birmingham
Mailing state: AL
Mailing zip: 35216-2139
Office phone: (205) 823-4440
Other fax: www.infomedia.com
Web address: jason@infomedia.com
Note: Jason Lovoy (President)
Employee Associations: Jason Lovoy

WAKEFIELD

EPSILON

Product or Service: Advertising/Marketing Agency
Street address 1: 601 Edgewater Dr
Street address state: MA
Postal code: 01880-6237
County: Middlesex
Country: USA
Mailing address 1: 601 Edgewater Dr Ste 250
Mailing city: Wakefield
Mailing state: MA
Mailing zip: 01880-6238
Office phone: (781) 685-6000
Office fax: (781) 685-0830
Other fax: www.epsilon.com

WALDORF

APDI-APPLICATION PROGRAMMING & DEVELOPMENT, INC.

Product or Service: Online Service Provider and Internet Hosts
Street address 1: 1282 Smallwood Dr W
Street address 2: Ste 276
Street address state: MD
Postal code: 20603-4732
County: Charles
Country: USA
Mailing address 1: 1282 Smallwood Dr W Ste 276
Mailing city: Waldorf
Mailing state: MD
Mailing zip: 20603-4732
Office phone: (301) 893-9115
Office fax: (301) 645-5035
Other fax: www.apdi.net
Web address: mburnett@apdi.net
Note: Mark Burnett (Pres./CEO)
Employee Associations: Mark Burnett

WALNUT CREEK

MARCOLE ENTERPRISES, INC.

Product or Service: Hardware/Software Supplier`Multimedia/Interactive Products`Online Service Provider and Internet Hosts`POP/Kiosk Designer
Street address 1: 2920 Camino Diablo
Street address 2: Ste 200
Street address state: CA
Postal code: 94597-3966
County: Contra Costa
Country: USA
Mailing address 1: 2920 Camino Diablo Ste 200
Mailing city: Walnut Creek
Mailing state: CA
Mailing zip: 94597-3966
Office phone: (888) 885-3939
Other fax: www.marcole.com
Web address: salesteam@marcole.com
Note: David Pava (Vice Pres., Sales & Marketing)
Employee Associations: David Pava

WALTHAM

CGI GROUP, INC.

Product or Service: Consultants
Street address 1: 460 Totten Pond Rd
Street address 2: Ste 530
Street address state: MA
Postal code: 02451-1944
County: Middlesex
Country: USA

Mailing address 1: 460 Totten Pond Rd Ste 530
Mailing city: Waltham
Mailing state: MA
Mailing zip: 02451-1944
Office phone: (781) 810-4022
Office fax: (781) 890-4361
Other fax: www.cgi.com
Web address: web@cgi.com
Note: Jennifer Peters (Global Mktg. Mgr.)
Employee Associations: Jennifer Peters

WASHINGTON

APCO WORLDWIDE

Product or Service: Advertising/Marketing Agency`Consultants
Street address 1: 700 12th St NW
Street address 2: Ste 800
Street address state: DC
Postal code: 20005-3949
County: District Of Columbia
Country: USA
Mailing address 1: 700 12th St NW Ste 800
Mailing city: Washington
Mailing state: DC
Mailing zip: 20005-3949
Office phone: (202) 778-1000
Office fax: (202) 466-6002
Other fax: www.apcoworldwide.com
Web address: information@apcoworldwide.com

COGENT COMMUNICATIONS, INC.

Product or Service: Online Service Provider and Internet Hosts
Street address 1: 1015 31st St NW
Street address state: DC
Postal code: 20007-4406
County: District Of Columbia
Country: USA
Mailing address 1: 1015 31st St NW
Mailing city: Washington
Mailing state: DC
Mailing zip: 20007-4406
Office phone: (202) 295-4200
Office fax: (202) 338-8798
Other fax: www.cogentco.com
Web address: info@cogentco.com
Note: Dave Schaeffer (Founder/CEO); Reed Harrison (Pres./COO); Tad Weed (CFO)
Employee Associations: Dave Schaeffer

FISCALNOTE

Product or Service: Publisher/Media
Street address 1: 1201 Pennsylvania Ave NW
Street address 2: 6th Floor
Street address state: DC
Postal code: 20004
County: District Of Columbia
Country: USA
Mailing address 1: 1201 Pennsylvania Ave NW
Mailing city: Washington
Mailing state: DC
Mailing zip: 20004
Office phone: (202) 793-5300
Other fax: www.fiscalnote.com
Web address: contact@fiscalnote.com
Note: Tim Hwang (CEO); Richard Kim (CFO); Mike Stubbs (Vice President, Operations)
Employee Associations: ()

FISHER PHOTOGRAPHY

Product or Service: Graphic/Design Firm
Street address 1: 2234 Cathedral Ave NW
Street address state: DC
Postal code: 20008-1504
County: District Of Columbia
Country: USA
Mailing address 1: 2234 Cathedral Ave NW
Mailing city: Washington
Mailing state: DC
Mailing zip: 20008-1504
Office phone: (202) 232-3781
Other fax: www.fisherphoto.com
Web address: info@fisherphoto.com
Note: Patricia Fisher (Owner); Wayne W. Fisher

(Contact)
Employee Associations: Wayne W. Fisher

WAUKESHA

ELECTRONIC TELE-COMMUNICATIONS, INC.

Product or Service: Telecommunications/Service Bureaus
Street address 1: 1915 Mac Arthur Rd
Street address state: WI
Postal code: 53188-5702
County: Waukesha
Country: USA
Mailing address 1: 1915 Mac Arthur Rd
Mailing city: Waukesha
Mailing state: WI
Mailing zip: 53188-5702
Office phone: (262) 542-5600
Office fax: (262) 542-1524
Other fax: www.etcia.com
Web address: etc_mkt@etcia.com
Note: Dean W. Danner (Pres./CEO); Joseph A. Voight (Vice Pres., Sales)
Employee Associations: Dean W. Danner; Joseph A. Voight

WEST HOLLYWOOD

CITYSEARCH.COM

Product or Service: Multimedia/Interactive Products
Street address 1: 8833 W Sunset Blvd
Street address state: CA
Postal code: 90069-2110
County: Los Angeles
Country: USA
Mailing address 1: 8833 W Sunset Blvd
Mailing city: West Hollywood
Mailing state: CA
Mailing zip: 90069-2110
Office phone: (310) 360-4500
Other phone: (800) 611-4827
Other fax: www.citysearch.com
Web address: customerservice@citygrid.com
Note: Jay Herratti (CEO)
Employee Associations: Jay Herratti

WESTLAKE VILLAGE

ILIO ENTERTAINMENT

Product or Service: Hardware/Software Supplier
Street address 1: 5356 Sterling Center Dr
Street address state: CA
Postal code: 91361-4612
County: Los Angeles
Country: USA
Mailing address 1: 5356 Sterling Center Dr
Mailing city: Westlake Village
Mailing state: CA
Mailing zip: 91361-4612
Office phone: (818) 707-7222
Office fax: (818) 707-8552
Other fax: www.ilio.com
Web address: info@ilio.com
Note: Shelly Williams (Co-Owner); Mark Hiskey (Co-Owner)
Employee Associations: Shelly Williams

MACTECH MAGAZINE

Product or Service: Publisher/Media
Street address 1: PO Box 5200
Street address state: CA
Postal code: 91359-5200
County: Ventura
Country: USA
Mailing address 1: PO Box 5200
Mailing city: Westlake Village
Mailing state: CA
Mailing zip: 91359-5200
Office phone: (805) 494-9797
Office fax: (805) 494-9798
Other fax: www.mactech.com
Web address: press_releases@mactech.com

Note: Neil Ticktin (Pub.); Dave Mark (Ed. in Chief); Michael R. Harvey (Reviews/KoolTools Ed.)
Employee Associations: Neil Ticktin

WHITE PLAINS

AUTOMATED GRAPHIC SYSTEMS

Product or Service: CD-ROM Designer/Manufacturer
Street address 1: 4590 Graphics Dr
Street address state: MD
Postal code: 20695-3122
County: Charles
Country: USA
Mailing address 1: 4590 Graphics Dr
Mailing city: White Plains
Mailing state: MD
Mailing zip: 20695-3122
Office phone: (301) 843-1800
Office fax: (301) 843-6339
Other fax: www.ags.com
Web address: mike.donohue@rrd.com
Note: Mike Donohue (Pres.); Mike Akers (Sr. Acct. Exec.)
Employee Associations: Mike Donohue

WHITE PLAINS

BLACK STAR PUBLISHING CO., INC.

Product or Service: Advertising/Marketing Agency
Street address 1: 333 Mamaroneck Ave
Street address 2: # 175
Street address state: NY
Postal code: 10605-1440
County: Westchester
Country: USA
Mailing address 1: 333 Mamaroneck Ave # 175
Mailing city: White Plains
Mailing state: NY
Mailing zip: 10605-1440
Office phone: (212) 679-3288
Other fax: www.blackstar.com
Web address: sales@blackstar.com
Note: Ben Chapnick (Pres.); John P. Chapnick (Vice Pres.)
Employee Associations: Ben Chapnick; John P. Chapnick

WINNIPEG

LAZER-FARE MEDIA SERVICES

Product or Service: Consultants`Hardware/Software Supplier
Street address 1: PO Box 48114 RPO Lakewood
Street address state: MB
Postal code: R2J 4A3
Country: Canada
Mailing address 1: PO Box 48114 RPO Lakewood
Mailing city: Winnipeg
Mailing state: MB
Mailing zip: R2J 4A3
Office phone: (204) 452-5023
Office fax: (204) 272-3499
Other fax: www.lazerfare.com
Web address: sales@lazerfare.com
Note: Kelly Armstrong (Pres.)
Employee Associations: Kelly Armstrong

WINSTED

MEDIABIDS, INC.

Product or Service: Advertising/Marketing Agency`Multimedia/Interactive Products
Street address 1: 448 Main St
Street address state: CT
Postal code: 06098-1528
County: Litchfield
Country: USA
Mailing address 1: 448 Main St
Mailing city: Winsted
Mailing state: CT
Mailing zip: 06098-1528
Office phone: (860) 379-9602
Office fax: (860) 379-9617
Other phone: 800-545-1135
Other fax: www.mediabids.com
Web address: info@mediabids.com
General e-mail: MediaBids connects publications with thousands of advertisers nationwide. Additionally, MediaBids offers a unique performance-based print advertising program that provides publications with high-quality ads from national advertisers and a way to monetize unused inventory.
Note: Jedd Gould (President); June Peterson (Director, Media Relations)
Employee Associations: Jedd Gould; June Peterson

WOODLAND HILLS

FILM ARTISTS ASSOCIATES

Product or Service: Advertising/Marketing Agency
Street address 1: 21044 Ventura Blvd
Street address 2: Ste 215
Street address state: CA
Postal code: 91364-6501
County: Los Angeles
Country: USA
Mailing address 1: 21044 Ventura Blvd Ste 215
Mailing city: Woodland Hills
Mailing state: CA
Mailing zip: 91364-6501
Office phone: (818) 883-5008
Office fax: (818) 386-9363
Note: Chris Dennis (Contact)
Employee Associations: Chris Dennis

ADVERTISING /CIRCULATION NEWSPAPER PROMOTION SERVICES

DEERFIELD BEACH

SIMMONS RESEARCH, LLC

Street address 1: 800 Fairway Drive
Street address 2: Suite 295
Street address state: FL
Postal code: 33441
County: Broward
Country: USA
Mailing address 1: 800 Fairway Drive, Suite 295
Mailing city: Deerfield Beach
Mailing state: FL
Mailing zip: 33441
Office phone: (866) 256-4468
Other phone: (800) 551-6425
Web address: www.simmonsresearch.com

GARDEN CITY

MARDEN-KANE, INC

Street address 1: 1055 Franklin Ave
Street address 2: Ste 300
Street address state: NY
Postal code: 11530-2903
County: Nassau
Country: USA
Mailing address 1: 1055 Franklin Ave Ste 300
Mailing city: Garden City
Mailing state: NY
Mailing zip: 11530-2903
Office phone: 516-365-3999
Office fax: 516-365-5520
General e-mail: expert@mardenkane.com
Web address: www.mardenkane.com
Personnel: Fary Rosenthal (President); Robert Rosenthal (Vice-President/Sales Mgr.)
Main (survey) contact: Fary Rosenthal

HOLLYWOOD

EYE CATCHER PRODUCTIONS

Street address 1: 2718 Wilshire Dr
Street address state: CA
Postal code: 90068
County: Los Angeles
Country: USA
Mailing address 1: 2718 Wilshire Dr.
Mailing city: Hollywood
Mailing state: CA
Mailing zip: 90068
Office phone: 323-467-7011

General e-mail: frankpierson@gmail.com

Personnel: Maynard Small (Pres.)
Main (survey) contact: Maynard Small

KANSAS CITY

CREATIVE MARKETING ASSOCIATES, INC.

Street address 1: 4741 Central Street
Street address 2: STE 300
Street address state: MO
Postal code: 64112
County: Jackson
Country: USA
Mailing address 1: 4741 Central Street, STE 300
Mailing city: Kansas City
Mailing state: MO
Mailing zip: 64112
Office phone: (816) 474-1400
Office fax: (816) 931-3000

Advertising e-mail: maynard@creativemarketingkc.com
Web address: www.creativemarketingkc.com
Main (survey) contact: Frank Pierson

LIVONIA

VALASSIS COMMUNICATIONS, INC.

Street address 1: 19975 Victor Parkway
Street address state: MI
Postal code: 48152
County: Fairfield
Country: USA
Mailing address 1: 19975 Victor Parkway
Mailing city: Livonia
Mailing state: MI
Mailing zip: 48152
Office phone: 734-591-3000
Other phone: 800-437-0479
Web address: www.valassis.com
Personnel: Peter Farago (President); Scott Drewiecki (Prod. Mngr.)
Main (survey) contact: Peter Farago

MIDDLETON

KNOWLEDGE UNLIMITED, INC

Street address 1: 2320 Pleasant View Rd
Street address state: WI
Postal code: 53562-5521
County: Dane
Country: USA
Mailing address 1: PO Box 52
Mailing city: Madison
Mailing state: WI
Mailing zip: 53701-0052
Office phone: (800) 356-2303
Office fax: (800) 618-1570
General e-mail: csis@newscurrents.com
Web address: www.knowledgeunlimited.com
Personnel: Harry Campbell (President); Patricia Campbell (Vice-President)
Main (survey) contact: Harry Campbell

NEW SMYRNA BEACH

HOT OFF THE PRESS PROMOTIONS, INC.

Street address 1: 480 Luna Bella Ln
Street address state: FL
Postal code: 32168-5346
County: Volusia
Country: USA
Mailing address 1: 480 Luna Bella Ln
Mailing city: New Smyrna Beach
Mailing state: FL
Mailing zip: 32168-5346
Office phone: 386-423-8156

General e-mail: info@hot-promos.com
Web address: www.hotoffthepress.com
Personnel: Judith Laitman (President)
Main (survey) contact: Judith Laitman

NEW YORK

NEWS AMERICA FSI

Street address 1: 1185 Avenue of the Americas
Street address 2: 27th Floor
Street address state: NY
Postal code: 10036
County: Manhattan
Country: USA
Mailing address 1: 1185 Avenue of the Americas
Mailing address 2: 27th Floor
Mailing city: New York
Mailing state: NY
Mailing zip: 10036
Office phone: 612-395-7340
Office fax: 612-376-0990
Advertising phone: (212) 782-8000
Advertising fax: (212) 575-5845
Other phone: (800) 462-0852
Web address: www.newsamerica.com

Personnel: Ray Lyon (Pres.)
Main (survey) contact: Ray Lyon

NEW YORK

NEWS AMERICA MARKETING

Street address 1: 1185 Avenue of the Americas
Street address 2: 27th Floor
Street address state: NY
Postal code: 10036
County: New York
Country: USA
Mailing address 1: 1185 Avenue of the Americas, 27th Floor
Mailing city: New York
Mailing state: NY
Mailing zip: 10036
Office phone: (212) 782-8000

Web address: www.newsamerica.com
Personnel: Alan Richter (CFO); Leonard Bierman (Exec. Vice Pres.); Paul Goldman (Exec. Vice Pres.); Marc Wortsman (Exec. Vice Pres.); Fae Savignano (Vice-Pres); Jessie Auletti (Vice-Pres.); Richard Facianella (Acct. Exec.)
Main (survey) contact: Alan Richter

SANTA FE

LYON ENTERPRISES

Street address 1: 4305 Cloud Dance
Street address state: NM
Postal code: 87507-2591
County: Santa Fe
Country: USA
Mailing address 1: 4305 Cloud Dance
Mailing city: Santa Fe
Mailing state: NM
Mailing zip: 87507
Office phone: (800) 243-1144
Office fax: (505) 471-1665
General e-mail: ray@lyonenterprises.com
Web address: www.lyonenterprises.com
Year established: 1992
Personnel: Anne Crassweller (Exec. Dir.); MeLing Johnston (Client Services Dir)
Main (survey) contact: Anne Crassweller

SOUTHFIELD

FARAGO & ASSOCIATES

Street address 1: 29200 Northwestern Hwy
Street address 2: Ste 114
Street address state: MI
Postal code: 48034-1055
County: Oakland
Country: USA
Mailing address 1: 29200 Northwestern Hwy Ste 114
Mailing city: Southfield
Mailing state: MI
Mailing zip: 48034-1055
Office phone: (248) 546-7070

Web address: www.faragoassoc.com
Personnel: Marty Garofalo (CEO); Ajay Singh (COO & CFO); Heidi Gray (Chief Human Resources Officer); Robert Spitz (Chief Revenue Officer)
Main (survey) contact: Stacy Drosatou

TORONTO

NADBANK-NEWSPAPER AUDIENCE DATABANK

Street address 1: 890 Yonge St
Street address 2: Suite 200
Street address state: ON
Postal code: M4W 3P4
County: York
Country: Canada
Mailing address 1: 890 Yonge St., Ste. 200
Mailing city: Toronto
Mailing state: ON
Mailing zip: M4W 3P4
Office phone: 416-923-3569
Office fax: 416-923-4002
General e-mail: acrassweller@nadbank.com
Web address: www.nadbank.com
Personnel: Marty Garofalo (CEO); Heidi Gray (COO & CFO); Robert Spitz (Chief Revenue Officer)
Main (survey) contact: Stacy Drosatou

TUCKER

ATLAS FLAGS, INC.

Street address 1: 2010 Weems Rd
Street address state: GA
Postal code: 30084-5207
County: Dekalb
Country: USA
Mailing address 1: 2010 Weems Rd
Mailing city: Tucker
Mailing state: GA
Mailing zip: 30084-5283
Office phone: 770-938-0003
Office fax: 770-493-4083
General e-mail: cs@atlasflags.com
Web address: www.atlasflags.com
Personnel: Andrew Feigenson (CEO); Gerry Dirksz (SVP, COO); Kalyan Lanka (Chief Strategy Officer); Dana Sergenian (Vice President, Brand Sales); Alan Resneck (CFO); Matt Cumello (Sr. Director, Marketing)
Main (survey) contact: Matt Cumello

WELLINGTON

WINGO, LLC

Street address 1: 12161 Ken Adams Way
Street address 2: Ste 110J
Street address state: FL
Postal code: 33414-3194
County: Palm Beach
Country: USA
Mailing address 1: 12161 Ken Adams Way Suite 110J
Mailing city: Wellngton
Mailing state: FL
Mailing zip: 33414
Office phone: (561) 379-2635

General e-mail: sat@amerimarketing.com
Advertising e-mail: info@amerimarketing.com
Web address: www.wingopromo.com; www.amerimarketing.com
Year established: 1980
Company Profile: Advertising print inserts
Personnel: Dan Singleton (CEO); Cali Tran (President); Greg Green; Grant Fritz (CFO); Laura Lofthouse (SVP)
Main (survey) contact: Mary Broaddus
Personnel: Scott Thompson (Pres.)
Main (survey) contact: Scott Thompson

ASSOCIATIONS, CLUBS AND PRESS CLUBS - CITY, STATE AND REGIONAL

ALBANY

LEGISLATIVE CORRESPONDENTS ASSOCIATION OF NYS

Street address 1: 25 Eagle St.
Street address 2: NYS Capital
Street address state: NY
Street address state: 12224
Postal code: USA
Country: PO Box 7269
Mailing address 1: Albany
Mailing city: NY
Mailing state: 12224-0269
Mailing zip: (518) 455-2388
Web address: www.lcapressroom.com
Year established: 1885
Personnel: Matthew Hamilton (President)
Main contact: Kyle Hughes

NEW YORK NEWS PUBLISHERS ASSOCIATION

Street address 1: 252 Hudson Ave
Street address state: NY
Street address state: 12210
Postal code: USA
Country: 252 Hudson Ave
Mailing address 1: Albany
Mailing city: NY
Mailing state: 12210-1802
Mailing zip: (518) 449-1667
Web address: www.nynpa.com
Year established: 1927
Personnel: Diane Kennedy (Pres.)
Main contact: Diane Kennedy

NEW YORK STATE ASSOCIATED PRESS ASSOCIATION

Street address 1: 450 W. 33rd St.
Street address state: NY
Street address state: 10001
Postal code: USA
Country: 450 W 33rd St
Mailing address 1: New York
Mailing city: NY
Mailing state: 10001-2603
Mailing zip: 212-621-1670
Office phone: 212-621-1679
Web address: www.ap.org
General e-mail: info@ap.org
Year established: 1848
Note: Elections held in Sept
Personnel: Howard Goldberg (Bureau Chief)
Main contact: Howard Goldberg

AMERICUS

KANSAS PROFESSIONAL COMMUNICATORS

Street address 1: 2369 Road J5
Street address state: KS
Street address state: 66835
Postal code: USA
Country: 2369 Road J5
Mailing address 1: Americus
Mailing city: KS
Mailing state: 66835-9540
Mailing zip: 620-227-1807
Office phone: 620 227-1806
Office fax: (620) 340-7544
Advertising fax: 620 227-1806
Editorial phone: 620 227-1806
Editorial fax: 620 227-1806
Other phone: 620 227-1806
Web address: www.
   kansasprofessionalcommunicators.org
General e-mail: kansasprocom@gmail.com
Advertising e-mail: jlatzke@hpj.com
Editorial e-mail: jlatzke@hpj.com
Year established: 1941
Note: We are the Kansas affiliate of the National Federation of Press Women.
Personnel: Jennifer Latzke (Pres.); Les Anderson (Professor, WSU Elliott School of Communication); Becky Funke; Wilma Moore-Black; Miller Jill
Main contact: Jennifer Latzke

ANNAPOLIS

MARYLAND-DELAWARE-DC PRESS ASSOCIATION

Street address 1: 60 West St.
Street address 2: Ste. 107
Street address state: MD
Street address state: 21401-2479
Postal code: USA
Country: 60 West St.
Mailing address 1: Annapolis
Mailing city: MD
Mailing state: 21401-2479
Mailing zip: (855) 721-6332
Office phone: (855) 721-6332
Office fax: 410-212-0616
Advertising fax: 855-721-6332
Web address: www.mddcpress.com
General e-mail: rsnyder@mddc.com
Advertising e-mail: wsmith@mddcpress.com
Editorial e-mail: rsnyder@mddcpress.com
Year established: 1908
Profile : Press Association representing news media organizations in Maryland, Delaware and DC.
Personnel: Rebecca Snyder (Exec. Dir.)
Main contact: Rebecca Snyder

ATLANTA

SOUTHERN NEWSPAPER PUBLISHERS ASSOCIATION

Street address 1: 3680 N. Peachtree Rd., Ste. 300
Street address state: GA
Street address state: 30341
Postal code: USA
Country: 3680 N Peachtree Rd Ste 300
Mailing address 1: Atlanta
Mailing city: GA
Mailing state: 30341-2346
Mailing zip: (404) 256-0444
Office phone: (404) 252-9135
Web address: www.snpa.org
General e-mail: edward@snpa.org
Year established: 1903
Note: Elections held at the annual convention in Oct.
Personnel: Cindy Durham (Asst ED); Edward VanHorn (Exec. Dir.); Paulette Sheffield (Office Mgr.); Charles H. Morris; Thomas A. Silvestri; David Dunn-Rankin
Main contact: Edward VanHorn

AUSTIN

FREEDOM OF INFORMATION FOUNDATION OF TEXAS

Street address 1: 3001 N Lamar Blvd., Ste. 302
Street address state: TX
Street address state: 78705
Postal code: USA
Country: 3001 N Lamar Blvd Ste 302
Mailing address 1: Austin
Mailing city: TX
Mailing state: 78705-2024
Mailing zip: (512) 377 1575
Office phone: (512) 377 1578
Web address: www.foift.org
General e-mail: kelley.shannon@foift.org
Year established: 1978
Note: Elections held in Dec
Personnel: Kelley Shannon (Executive Director)

BATON ROUGE

LOUISIANA PRESS WOMEN, INC.

Street address 1: The Advocate, 7290 Blue Bonnet Rd.
Street address state: LA
Street address state: 70810
Postal code: USA
Country: PO Box 588
Mailing address 1: Baton Rouge
Mailing city: LA
Mailing state: 70821-0588
Mailing zip: (225) 383-1111
Office phone: (225) 388-0323
Web address: www.theadvocate.com
General e-mail: mshuler@theadvocate.com
Note: Elections held even years
Personnel: David Manship (Pres.)
Main contact: David Manship

BISMARCK

NORTH DAKOTA ASSOCIATED PRESS

Street address 1: PO Box 1018
Street address state: ND
Street address state: 58502-5646
Postal code: USA
Country: PO Box 1018
Mailing address 1: Bismarck
Mailing city: ND
Mailing state: 58502-1018
Mailing zip: (701) 223-8450
Office phone: (701) 224-0158
General e-mail: apbismarck@ap.org
Personnel: Blake Nicholson
Main contact: Blake Nicholson

BOISE

IDAHO PRESS CLUB

Street address 1: PO Box 2221
Street address state: ID
Street address state: 83701-2221
Postal code: USA
Country: PO Box 2221
Mailing address 1: Boise
Mailing city: ID
Mailing state: 83701-2221
Mailing zip: (208) 389-2879
Web address: www.idahopressclub.org
General e-mail: email@idahopressclub.org
Note: IPC accepts individual memberships for reporters and public information officers in several areas. Elections and awards ceremony held in the spring. One annual seminars held in spring and fall
Personnel: Martha Borchers (Exec. Dir.)
Main contact: Martha Borchers

BOSTON

ASSOCIATED PRESS

Street address 1: 184 High St #3
Street address state: MA
Street address state: 02110
Postal code: USA
Country: 184 High St Fl 3
Mailing address 1: Boston
Mailing city: MA
Mailing state: 02110-3029
Mailing zip: (617) 357-8100
Office phone: (617) 338-8125
Web address: www.ap.org/boston
General e-mail: apboston@ap.org
Personnel: William Kole (News Ed.); Dwayne Desaulniers (Dir., Local Media); Gary Pruitt (Pres. & CEO)
Main contact: William J. Kole

THE AD CLUB

Street address 1: 9 Hamilton Pl.
Street address state: MA
Street address state: 02108-3210
Postal code: USA
Country: 9 Hamilton Pl Ste 200
Mailing address 1: Boston
Mailing city: MA
Mailing state: 02108-4715
Mailing zip: (617) 262-1100
Office phone: (617) 456-1772
Web address: www.adclub.org
General e-mail: newsfeed@adclub.org
Year established: 1904
Profile : The trade association for marketing & communications industries of New England.

THE AD CLUB

Street address 1: 22 Batterymarch Street
Street address 2: 1st Floor
Street address state: MA
Street address state: 02109
Postal code: USA
Country: 22 Batterymarch St
Mailing address 1: Boston
Mailing city: MA
Mailing state: 02109-4812
Mailing zip: 617-262-1100
Web address: www.adclub.org
Personnel: Kathy Kiely (Pres.)
Main contact: Kathy Kiely

BURLINGTON

ONTARIO COMMUNITY NEWSPAPERS ASSOCIATION

Street address 1: 3228 South Service Rd. Ste 116
Street address state: ON
Street address state: L7N 3H8
Postal code: Canada
Country: 3228 South Service Rd. Ste 116
Mailing address 1: Burlington
Mailing city: ON
Mailing state: L7N 3H8
Mailing zip: (905) 639-8720
Office phone: (905) 639-6962
Web address: www.ocna.org
General e-mail: info@ocna.org
Year established: 1950
Profile : Provides Advertising and Editorial Services for more than 300 community newspapers in Ontario.
Personnel: Anne Lannan (Executive Director)
Main contact: Anne Lannan

CAMDEN

THE MAINE PRESS ASSOCIATION

Street address 1: P.O. Box 336
Street address state: ME
Street address state: 04843
Postal code: USA
Country: P.O. Box 336
Mailing address 1: Camden
Mailing city: ME
Mailing state: 04843
Mailing zip: (207) 691-0131
Web address: www.mainepressassociation.org
General e-mail: scostello@sunjournal.com
Note: Elections held in June

Associations, Clubs and Press Clubs - City, State and Regional

Personnel: Gary Gagne
Main contact: ()

CHELMSFORD

NEW ENGLAND ASSOCIATION OF CIRCULATION EXECUTIVES

Street address 1: 4 Trotting Rd.
Street address state: MA
Street address state: 1824
Postal code: USA
Country: 4 Trotting Rd
Mailing address 1: Chelmsford
Mailing city: MA
Mailing state: 01824-1928
Mailing zip: (978) 256-0691
Office phone: (978) 256-4873
Web address: www.neace.com
General e-mail: neace@neace.com
Note: Elections held in May
Personnel: William H. Hoar (Sec.)
Main contact: Lou Brambilla

CHEYENNE

WYOMING ASSOCIATED PRESS

Street address 1: 320 W. 25th St., Ste. 310
Street address state: WY
Street address state: 82001
Postal code: USA
Country: 2121 Evans Ave
Mailing address 1: Cheyenne
Mailing city: WY
Mailing state: 82001-3733
Mailing zip: (307) 632-9351
Office phone: (307) 637-8538
Web address: www.ap.org
Personnel: Jim Clark (Bureau Chief)
Main contact: Jim Clark

CHICAGO

ILLINOIS ASSOCIATED PRESS MANAGING EDITORS

Street address 1: 10 S. Wacker Drive
Street address 2: Suite 2500
Street address state: IL
Street address state: 60606
Postal code: USA
Country: 10 S Wacker Dr
Mailing address 1: Chicago
Mailing city: IL
Mailing state: 60606-7453
Mailing zip: (312) 781-0500
Web address: www.ap.org
General e-mail: chifax@ap.org
Note: Elections held in Sept

ILLINOIS WOMAN'S PRESS ASSOCIATION, INC.

Street address 1: PO Box 180150
Street address state: IL
Street address state: 60618-9997
Postal code: USA
Country: PO Box 180150
Mailing address 1: Chicago
Mailing city: IL
Mailing state: 60618-9997
Mailing zip: (708) 296-8669
Web address: www.iwpa.org
General e-mail: iwpa@gmail.com
Advertising e-mail: iwpa1885@gmail.com
Editorial e-mail: iwpa1885@gmail.com
Year established: 1885
Profile : The IWPA (since 1885) is an organization of professionals whose objective is to maintain and improve the standards of members in mass communications in Illinois, to promote their interests, and to provide for the sharing of ideas and information. IWPA is an affiliate of the National Federation of Press Women. Celebrating 130 years in 2015, IWPA continues to hold a firm place in the history of women communicators. Today, IWPA embraces members of all gender and generations. A record of IWPA's legacy can be found on Wikipedia.
Personnel: Cora Weisenberger (Pres.)
Main contact: Cora Weisenberger

CHURUBUSCO

FREE LANCE JOURNALIST/BLOGGER

Street address 1: 121 South Street
Street address 2: 121 South Street
Street address state: IN
Street address state: 46723
Postal code: USA
Country: 121 South Street
Mailing address 1: Churubusco
Mailing city: IN
Mailing state: 46801-0088
Mailing zip: (260) 241-7737
General e-mail: vsade8@gmail.com
Advertising e-mail: vsade8@gmail.com
Profile : 27 years experience with weekly and daily newspapers in northeast Indiana, including the Auburn Evening Star, KPC Media, Churubusco News, Northwest News, Albion New Era and the Journal Gazette. Current president of the Woman's Press Club of Indiana, an affiliate of the National Federation of Press Women.
Personnel: Vivian Sade (Freelance writer/blogger 2017-18 WPCI President; WPCI Communications Contest co-chair)
Main contact: Vivian Sade

CLEVELAND

THE PRESS CLUB OF CLEVELAND

Street address 1: 28022 Osborn Road
Street address state: OH
Street address state: 44140
Postal code: USA
Country: 28022 Osborn Rd
Mailing address 1: Cleveland
Mailing city: OH
Mailing state: 44140-2011
Mailing zip: 440-899-1222
Office fax: 440-899-1222
Advertising fax: 440-899-1222
Web address: pressclubcleveland.com
General e-mail: pressclubcleveland@oh.rr.com
Advertising e-mail: same
Editorial e-mail: same
Year established: 1887
Profile : Founded in 1887, The Press Club of Cleveland is an organization for journalists, communications professionals, aspiring communications professionals in Ohio and anyone who works with them. Now in its 125th year, The Press Club of Cleveland is the premier organization, which media and communications professionals rely on for information, education, inspiration and celebration. The Club serves it members by providing social and educational opportunities, promoting excellence in journalism, and honoring and maintaining the rich history of journalism in Greater Cleveland and the state of Ohio.
Personnel: Amy McGahan (Managing Director); Carol Kovach (Editor)
Main contact: Amy McGahan

COLOMBUS

GREAT LAKES/MIDSTATES NEWSPAPER CONFERENCE, INC.

Street address 1: 1335 Dublin Rd., Suite 216-B
Street address state: OH
Street address state: 43215
Postal code: USA
Country: 1335 Dublin Rd Ste 216B
Mailing address 1: Columbus
Mailing city: OH
Mailing state: 43215-1000
Mailing zip: (614) 486-6677
Office phone: (614) 486-4940
Web address: www.ohionews.org
General e-mail: glmsconf@comcast.net
Year established: 1945
Note: Elections held in Feb
Personnel: Jack Gahagan (Bus. Mgr./Sec./Treasurer)
Main contact: Jack Gahagan

COLUMBIA

SOUTH CAROLINA ASSOCIATED PRESS

Street address 1: 1401 Shop Road, Suite B
Street address state: SC
Street address state: 29201
Postal code: USA
Country: 1401 Shop Rd Ste B
Mailing address 1: Columbia
Mailing city: SC
Mailing state: 29201-4843
Mailing zip: (803) 799-5510
Office phone: (803) 252-2913
General e-mail: apcolumbia@ap.org
Personnel: Maryann Mrowca (Bureau Chief)
Main contact: Tim Rogers

SOUTHEASTERN ADVERTISING PUBLISHERS ASSOCIATION

Street address 1: 104 Westland Dr
Street address state: TN
Street address state: 38401-6522
Postal code: USA
Country: 104 Westland Dr
Mailing address 1: Columbia
Mailing city: TN
Mailing state: 38401-6522
Mailing zip: (931) 223-5708
Office phone: (888) 450-8329
Web address: www.sapatoday.com
General e-mail: info@sapatoday.com
Year established: 1979
Note: Classified advertising for 75 publications in 10 Southeastern states. Display Network also available.
Personnel: Douglas Fry (Exec. Dir.)
Main contact: Douglas Fry

COLUMBUS

OHIO CIRCULATION MANAGERS ASSOCIATION

Street address 1: 1335 Dublin Rd., Suite 216-B
Street address state: OH
Street address state: 43215
Postal code: USA
Country: 1335 Dublin Rd Ste 216B
Mailing address 1: Columbus
Mailing city: OH
Mailing state: 43215-1000
Mailing zip: (614) 486-6677
Office phone: (614) 486-4940
Web address: www.ohiocirculation.com
General e-mail: bbarker@plaind.com
Note: Elections held in Oct
Personnel: Kim Wilhelm (Committee Chair)
Main contact: Kim Wilhelm

OHIO NEWSPAPER ADVERTISING EXECUTIVES

Street address 1: 1335 Dublin Rd. S., Ste. 216-B
Street address state: OH
Street address state: 43215
Postal code: USA
Country: 1335 Dublin Rd Ste 216B
Mailing address 1: Columbus
Mailing city: OH
Mailing state: 43215-1000
Mailing zip: (614) 486-6677
Office phone: (614) 486-6373
Web address: www.adohio.net
General e-mail: mhenry@adohio.net
Note: Elections held in Feb.
Personnel: Mark Henry (Mgr.)
Main contact: Walt Dozier

CONCORD

FREE COMMUNITY PAPERS OF NEW ENGLAND

Street address 1: 100-1 Domino Drive
Street address state: CT
Street address state: 01742
Postal code: USA
Country: 100 Domino Dr # 1
Mailing address 1: Concord
Mailing city: MA
Mailing state: 01742-2817
Mailing zip: 877-423-6399
Web address: www.communitypapersne.com
General e-mail: bne@fcpne.com
Personnel: Lynn Duval (Admin.)
Main contact: Steven Silver

COSTA MESA

ORANGE COUNTY PRESS CLUB

Street address 1: 1835 Newport Blvd., #A-109-538
Street address state: CA
Street address state: 92627
Postal code: USA
Country: 1835 Newport Blvd # A-109-538
Mailing address 1: Costa Mesa
Mailing city: CA
Mailing state: 92627-5031
Mailing zip: (714) 564-1052
Office phone: (714) 564-1047
Web address: www.ocpressclub.org
General e-mail: OCPressClub@orangecountypressclub.com
Note: Elections held in July
Personnel: Jean O. Pasco (Sec./Treasurer)
Main contact: Jean O. Pasco

CROWN POINT

COMMUNITY PAPERS OF INDIANA

Street address 1: PO Box 1004
Street address state: IN
Street address state: 46308
Postal code: USA
Country: PO Box 1004
Mailing address 1: Crown Point
Mailing city: IN
Mailing state: 46308-1004
Mailing zip: (219) 689-6262
Office phone: (219) 374-7558
Note: Elections held in April
Personnel: Shari Foreman (Pub./Owner)
Main contact: Shari Foreman

DALLAS

SOUTHWEST CLASSIFIED ADVERTISING MANAGERS ASSOCIATION

Street address 1: Dallas Morning News
Street address 2: 508 Young St.
Street address state: TX
Street address state: 75265-5237
Postal code: USA
Country: Dallas Morning News
Mailing address 1: Dallas
Mailing city: TX
Mailing state: 75265-5237
Mailing zip: 214-977-8222
Web address: www.dallasnews.com
General e-mail: jmckeon@dallasnews.com
Year established: 1885
Personnel: John Mckeon (President and General Manager); Michael Mayer (General Manager, Recruitment, Real Estate, General Classifieds)
Main contact: Sandra Carcamo

Associations, Clubs and Press Clubs - City, State and Regional

TEXAS ASSOCIATED PRESS MANAGING EDITORS

Street address 1: The Dallas Morning News, 508 Young St.
Street address state: TX
Street address state: 75202
Postal code: USA
Country: 508 Young St
Mailing address 1: Dallas
Mailing city: TX
Mailing state: 75202-4808
Mailing zip: (214) 977-8222
Web address: www.txapme.org
Note: Elections held in March
Personnel: Leona Allen (Deputy Mng. Ed.)
Main contact: Kelly Brown

DEDHAM

NEW ENGLAND SOCIETY OF NEWSPAPER EDITORS

Street address 1: 370 Common Street, 3rd Floor Ste 319
Street address 2: Barletta Hall
Street address state: MA
Street address state: 02026
Postal code: USA
Country: 370 Common St
Mailing address 1: Dedham
Mailing city: MA
Mailing state: 02026-4097
Mailing zip: 781-320-8050
Office phone: 781-320-8055
Web address: www.nesne.org
General e-mail: info@nenpa.com
Note: Elections held in Nov
Personnel: George Geers (Ed.)
Main contact: Dr. Brett M. Rhyne

DEKALB

NORTHERN ILLINOIS NEWSPAPER ASSOCIATION

Street address 1: Campus Life Building, Suite 130
Street address state: IL
Street address state: 60115
Postal code: USA
Country: Campus Life Building, Suite 130
Mailing address 1: Dekalb
Mailing city: IL
Mailing state: 60115
Mailing zip: (815) 753-4239
Office phone: (815) 753-0708
Web address: www.ninaonline.org
Year established: 1961
Personnel: Shelley Hendricks (Communications Coordinator)
Main contact: Shelley Hendricks

DENVER

COLORADO ASSOCIATED PRESS EDITORS AND REPORTERS

Street address 1: 1444 Wazee St., Ste. 130
Street address state: CO
Street address state: 80202-1395
Postal code: USA
Country: 1444 Wazee St Ste 130
Mailing address 1: Denver
Mailing city: CO
Mailing state: 80202-1326
Mailing zip: (303) 825-0123
Office phone: (303) 892-5927
Web address: www.ap.org/colorado
General e-mail: apdenver@ap.org
Note: Elections held in Feb
Personnel: Jim Clarke (Bureau Chief)
Main contact: Jim Clarke

DES MOINES

CUSTOMIZED NEWSPAPER ADVERTISING (IOWA)

Street address 1: 319 E 5th St
Street address state: IA
Street address state: 50309-1927
Postal code: USA
Country: 319 E 5th St
Mailing address 1: Des Moines
Mailing city: IA
Mailing state: 50309-1927
Mailing zip: (515) 244-2145
Office phone: (515) 244-4855
Web address: www.cnaads.com; www.inanews.com
Note: Represents 302 daily and weekly newspapers in Iowa and can place advertising in any newspaper in the country.
Personnel: Chris Mudge (Exec. Dir.); Bryan Rohe (Acct. Exec.); Ron Bode (Sales Dir.); Bruce Adams (Sales Rep.)
Main contact: Chris Mudge

IOWA ASSOCIATED PRESS MEDIA EDITORS ASSOCIATION

Street address 1: 505 Fifth Ave., Ste. 1000
Street address state: IA
Street address state: 50309
Postal code: USA
Country: 505 5th Ave Ste 1000
Mailing address 1: Des Moines
Mailing city: IA
Mailing state: 50309-2335
Mailing zip: (515) 243-3281
Office phone: (515) 243-3884
Web address: www.apiowa.org
General e-mail: apdesmoines@ap.org
Note: Elections held in June
Personnel: Kia Breaux (Reg. Dir.)
Main contact: Kia Breaux

IOWA NEWSPAPER ASSOCIATION, INC.

Street address 1: 319 E 5th St
Street address 2: Fl 2
Street address state: IA
Street address state: 50309-1927
Postal code: USA
Country: 319 E 5th St Fl 2nd
Mailing address 1: Des Moines
Mailing city: IA
Mailing state: 50309-1931
Mailing zip: (515) 244-2145
Office phone: (515) 244-4855
Web address: www.inanews.com
General e-mail: ina@inanews.com
Year established: 1931
Note: Elections held in May
Personnel: Susan Patterson Plank (Exec. Dir.); Brent Steemken (Business Mgr.); Jodi Hulbert (Comm. Dir.); Geof Fischer (Dev. Dir); Samantha Fett (Inside Sales Mgr.); Heidi Geisler (Media Dir.); Jana Shepherd (Program Dir.); Susan James (Tech. & Digital Dev. Mgr.); Ryan Harvey (Pres.); Kaitlyn Van Patten (Sales & Mktg. Assist.)
Main contact: Susan Patterson Plank

INLAND PRESS ASSOCIATION

Street address 1: 701 Lee St., Ste. 925
Street address state: IL
Street address state: 60016
Postal code: USA
Country: 701 Lee Street, Suite 925
Mailing address 1: Des Plaines
Mailing city: IL
Mailing state: 60016
Mailing zip: (847) 795-0380
Office phone: (847) 795-0385
Web address: www.inlandpress.org
General e-mail: inland@inlandpress.org
Year established: 1885
Note: Elections held in Oct
Personnel: Karla Zander (Mgr. of Research & Member Services); Patty Slusher (Dir. of Membership and Programming); Tom Slaughter (Exec. Dir.); Mark Fitzgerald (Ed.); Steve Hoffman (Accounting Mgr.)
Main contact: Tom Slaughter; Mark Fitzgerald

DETROIT

MICHIGAN ASSOCIATED PRESS EDITORIAL ASSOCIATION

Street address 1: 300 River Pl., Ste. 2400
Street address state: MI
Street address state: 48207
Postal code: USA
Country: 300 River Place Dr Ste 2400
Mailing address 1: Detroit
Mailing city: MI
Mailing state: 48207-4260
Mailing zip: (313) 259-0650
Office phone: (313) 259-4966
Web address: www.ap.org
General e-mail: apmichigan@ap.org
Personnel: Eva Parziale (Regional Director - East)
Main contact: Janet Talbott

EAST LANSING

COMMUNITY PAPERS OF MICHIGAN

Street address 1: 5000 Northwind Dr., Ste. 240
Street address state: MI
Street address state: 48823
Postal code: USA
Country: 5000 Northwind Dr Ste 240
Mailing address 1: East Lansing
Mailing city: MI
Mailing state: 48823-5032
Mailing zip: (517) 333-3355
Office phone: (517) 333-3322
Editorial fax: 800-783-0267
Web address: www.communitypapersofmichigan.com
General e-mail: jackguza@cpapersmi.com;slkotecki@cpapersmi.com
Year established: 1969
Profile : Trade association representing 100 community publications across Michigan. Our association specializes in advertising placement within select member publications, which can be singular buys, DMA buys or our entire membership. These publications can be reached easily through our association which offers streamlined ad placement and singular billing.
Personnel: Jack Guza (Exec. Dir.)
Main contact: Jack Guza

EDMONTON

ALBERTA WEEKLY NEWSPAPERS ASSOCIATION

Street address 1: 3228 Parsons Rd
Street address state: AB
Street address state: T6N 1M2
Postal code: Canada
Country: 3228 Parsons Rd
Mailing address 1: Edmonton
Mailing city: AB
Mailing state: T6N 1M2
Mailing zip: (780) 434-8746
Office phone: (780) 438-8356
Web address: www.awna.com
General e-mail: info@awna.com
Personnel: Dennis Merrell (Exec. Dir.)
Main contact: Dennis Merrell

FOND DU LAC

WISCONSIN FREE COMMUNITY PAPERS

Street address 1: 101 S. Main St.
Street address state: WI
Street address state: 54935
Postal code: USA
Country: 101 S Main St
Mailing address 1: Fond Du Lac
Mailing city: WI
Mailing state: 54935-4228
Mailing zip: 800-727-8745
Office phone: 920-922-0861
Web address: wisad.com
General e-mail: wcp@wisad.com
Personnel: Jeanne Scmal; Janelle Anderson (Exec. Dir.)
Main contact: Jeanne Schmal; Janelle Anderson

GATINEAU

QUEBEC COMMUNITY NEWSPAPERS ASSOCIATION

Street address 1: 400 Maloney Blvd
Street address 2: Suite 205
Street address state: QC
Street address state: J8P 1E6
Postal code: Canada
Country: 400 Maloney Blvd
Mailing address 1: Gatineau
Mailing city: QC
Mailing state: J8P 1E6
Mailing zip: (514) 697-6330
Office phone: (514) 697-6331
Web address: www.qcna.org
General e-mail: execdir@qcna.qc.ca
Personnel: Sylvie Goneau (Exec. Dir.); Info Email (Info Email)
Main contact: Sylvie Goneau; Info Email

GRAND RAPIDS

NORTHERN STATES CIRCULATION MANAGERS ASSOCIATION

Street address 1: PO Box 220
Street address state: MN
Street address state: 55744
Postal code: USA
Country: PO Box 220
Mailing address 1: Grand Rapids
Mailing city: MN
Mailing state: 55744-0220
Mailing zip: (218) 326-6623
Office phone: (218) 326-6627
Web address: www.grandrapidsmn.com
General e-mail: ron.oleheiser@grandrapidsmn.com
Note: Elections held in Sept
Personnel: Ron Oleheiser (Pub.)
Main contact: Ron Oleheiser

HALIFAX

ATLANTIC COMMUNITY NEWSPAPERS ASSOCIATION

Street address 1: 7075 Bayers Rd., Ste. 216
Street address state: NS
Street address state: B3L 2C2
Postal code: Canada
Country: 7075 Bayers Rd., Ste. 216
Mailing address 1: Halifax
Mailing city: NS
Mailing state: B3L 2C2
Mailing zip: (902) 832-4480
Office phone: (902) 832-4484
Web address: www.acna.com
General e-mail: info@newspapersatlantic.ca
Personnel: Mike Kierstead (Exec. Dir.)
Main contact: Mike Kierstead

HAMBURG

MID-ATLANTIC COMMUNITY PAPERS ASSOCIATION

Street address 1: 375 Jalappa Road
Street address state: PA
Street address state: 19526
Postal code: USA

Associations, Clubs and Press Clubs - City, State and Regional

Country: PO Box 408
Mailing address 1: Hamburg
Mailing city: PA
Mailing state: 19526-0408
Mailing zip: 800-450-7227
Web address: www.macpa.net
General e-mail: info@macpa.net
Advertising e-mail: Info@macnetonline.com
Year established: 1955
Profile : MACPA is the association for independently owned community papers in the mid-atlantic region. We represent Pennsylvania, Ohio, New York (partial), New Jersey, Delaware, Maryland, and West Virginia. Through our network programs we provide advertisers with
Note: Elections Held in April for both Boards
Personnel: Alyse Mitten (Exec. Dir.)
Main contact: Alyse Mitten

HARMONY

NORTH CAROLINA PRESS CLUB

Street address 1: 200 Countryside Rd
Street address state: NC
Street address state: 28634-9420
Postal code: USA
Country: 200 Countryside Rd
Mailing address 1: Harmony
Mailing city: NC
Mailing state: 28634-9420
Mailing zip: (704)546-7900
Web address: www.nfpw.org
General e-mail: suzyb3@gmail.com
Profile : NC affiliate of National Federation of Press Women
Note: Elections held in March
Personnel: Suzy Barile (Past President)
Main contact: Clara Cartrette

HARRISBURG

PENNSYLVANIA SOCIETY OF NEWS EDITORS

Street address 1: 3899 N. Front St.
Street address state: PA
Street address state: 17110
Postal code: USA
Country: 3899 N Front St
Mailing address 1: Harrisburg
Mailing city: PA
Mailing state: 17110-1583
Mailing zip: (717) 703-3000
Office phone: (717) 703-3001
Web address: www.panewsmedia.org
General e-mail: teresas@pa-news.org
Note: Elections held in May
Personnel: Teri Henning (President, PA Newspaper Association)
Main contact: Teresa Shaak

HARTFORD

CONNECTICUT ASSOCIATED PRESS MANAGING EDITORS ASSOCIATION

Street address 1: 10 Columbus Blvd.
Street address state: CT
Street address state: 06106
Postal code: USA
Country: 10 Columbus Blvd
Mailing address 1: Hartford
Mailing city: CT
Mailing state: 06106-1976
Mailing zip: (860) 246-6876
Office phone: (860) 727-4003
Web address: www.ap.org
General e-mail: aphartford@ap.org
Personnel: William Kole (Bureau Chief)
Main contact: William Kole

HELENA

MONTANA ASSOCIATED PRESS ASSOCIATION

Street address 1: 321 Fuller Ave. #2
Street address state: MT
Street address state: 59601
Postal code: USA
Country: 825 Great Northern Blvd Ste 203
Mailing address 1: Helena
Mailing city: MT
Mailing state: 59601-3340
Mailing zip: (406) 442-7440
Office phone: (406) 442-5162
Web address: www.ap.org/montana
General e-mail: apmontana@ap.org
Note: Elections held in June every two years
Personnel: Jim Clark (Bureau Chief)
Main contact: Jim Clark

INDIANAPOLIS

HOOSIER STATE PRESS ASSOCIATION

Street address 1: 41 E Washington St
Street address 2: Ste 101
Street address state: IN
Street address state: 46204-3560
Postal code: USA
Mailing zip: (317) 803-4772
Office phone: (317) 624-4428
Web address: www.hspa.com
Advertising e-mail: map@hspa.com
Year established: 1933
Note: Represents daily and weekly newspapers in Indiana
Personnel: Stephen Key (Exec. Dir./Gen. Counsel); Pamela Lego (Adv. Dir.); Milissa Tuley (Communications Specialist); Karen Braeckel (HSPA Foundation Dir.); Yvonne Yeadon (Office Mgr.); Shawn Goldsby (Adv. Coord.)
Main contact: Stephen Key

INDIANA ASSOCIATED PRESS MANAGING EDITORS

Street address 1: 251 N. Illinois St., Ste. 1600
Street address state: IN
Street address state: 46204
Postal code: USA
Country: 251 N Illinois St Ste 1600
Mailing address 1: Indianapolis
Mailing city: IN
Mailing state: 46204-4309
Mailing zip: (317) 639-5501
General e-mail: indy@ap.org

INDIANAPOLIS PRESS CLUB FOUNDATION

Street address 1: PO Box 40923
Street address state: IN
Street address state: 46240
Postal code: USA
Country: PO Box 40923
Mailing address 1: Indianapolis
Mailing city: IN
Mailing state: 46240-0923
Mailing zip: (317) 701-1130
Web address: www.indypressfoundation.org
General e-mail: jlabalme@indypress.att.net
Note: Elections held in January
Personnel: Jenny Labalme (Executive Director)
Main contact: Jenny Labalme

IOWA CITY

MIDWEST FREE COMMUNITY PAPERS

Street address 1: PO Box 1350
Street address state: IA
Street address state: 52244-1350
Postal code: USA
Country: PO Box 1350
Mailing address 1: Iowa City
Mailing city: IA
Mailing state: 52244-1350
Mailing zip: (319) 341-4352
Office phone: (319) 341-4358
Web address: www.mfcp.org
General e-mail: mfcp@mchsi.com
Year established: 1955
Note: Classified advertising for 124 publications
Personnel: Jori Hendon (Office Mgr.)
Main contact: Jori Hendon

JACKSON

LOUISIANA-MISSISSIPPI ASSOCIATED PRESS MANAGING EDITORS ASSOCIATION

Street address 1: 125 south congress st. suite 1330
Street address state: MS
Street address state: 39201
Postal code: USA
Country: 125 S Congress St Ste 1330
Mailing address 1: Jackson
Mailing city: MS
Mailing state: 39201-3310
Mailing zip: 601-948-5897
Office phone: 601-948-7975
Web address: www.ap.org
General e-mail: jkme@ap.org
Personnel: Brian Schwaner (News Ed.)
Main contact: Brian Schwaner

KANSAS CITY

KANSAS ASSOCIATED PRESS MANAGING EDITORS ASSOCIATION

Street address 1: Associated Press, 215 W. Pershing St., Ste. 221
Street address state: MO
Street address state: 64108
Postal code: USA
Country: 215 W Pershing Rd Ste 221
Mailing address 1: Kansas City
Mailing city: MO
Mailing state: 64108-4300
Mailing zip: (816) 421-4844
Office phone: (816) 421-3590
Web address: www.ap.org/kansas
General e-mail: apkansascity@ap.org
Note: Elections held in Oct
Personnel: Randy Picht (Bureau Chief)
Main contact: Randy Picht

KANSAS ASSOCIATED PRESS PUBLISHERS AND EDITORS

Street address 1: Associated Press, 215 W. Pershing, Ste. 221
Street address state: MO
Street address state: 64108
Postal code: USA
Country: 215 W Pershing Rd Ste 221
Mailing address 1: Kansas City
Mailing city: MO
Mailing state: 64108-4300
Mailing zip: (816) 421-4844
Office phone: (816) 421-3590
Note: Elections held in Dec
Personnel: Paul Stevens (Bureau Chief); Tom Bell (Bd. Chrmn.)
Main contact: Susan Lynn; Paul Stevens

MISSOURI ASSOCIATED PRESS MANAGING EDITORS

Street address 1: Associated Press, 215 W. Pershing, Ste. 221
Street address state: MO
Street address state: 64108
Postal code: USA
Country: 215 W Pershing Rd Ste 221
Mailing address 1: Kansas City
Mailing city: MO
Mailing state: 64108-4300
Mailing zip: (816) 421-4844
Office phone: (816) 421-3590
Web address: www.ap.org
General e-mail: apkansascity@ap.org
Note: Elections held in April
Personnel: Randy Picht (Bureau Chief)
Main contact: Randy Picht

KINGSPORT

SOUTHERN CIRCULATION MANAGERS ASSOCIATION

Street address 1: P.O. Box 1163
Street address state: TN
Street address state: 37662
Postal code: USA
Country: PO Box 1163
Mailing address 1: Kingsport
Mailing city: TN
Mailing state: 37662-1163
Web address: www.southerncma.com
General e-mail: info@scmaonline.net
Note: Elections held in April. Organization accepts shoppers as Associate Members
Personnel: Debra Casciano (Sec.); Glen Tabor (Treasurer)
Main contact: Debra Casciano

KIRKWOOD

MISSOURI PRESS WOMEN

Street address 1: 528 Pamela Ln.
Street address state: MO
Street address state: 63122-1138
Postal code: USA
Country: 528 Pamela Ln
Mailing address 1: Kirkwood
Mailing city: MO
Mailing state: 63122-1138
Editorial fax: (314) 965-1079
Web address: www.mpc-nfpw.org
General e-mail: MPCNFPW@gmail.com
Year established: 1937
Profile : Professional organization for women and men in communications fields. Missouri affiliate of the National Federation of Press Women.
Personnel: Janice Denham (treasurer); Deborah Reinhardt
Main contact: Janice Denham

KNOXVILLE

TENNESSEE PRESS ASSOCIATION

Street address 1: 412 N. Cedar Bluff Road
Street address 2: Suite 403
Street address state: TN
Street address state: 37923
Postal code: USA
Country: 412 N. Cedar Bluff Road
Mailing address 1: Knoxville
Mailing city: TN
Mailing state: 37923
Mailing zip: 865-584-5761
Office phone: 865-558-8687
Web address: www.tnpress.com
General e-mail: info@tnpress.com
Year established: 1947
Note: Elections held in June
Personnel: Carol Daniels (Exec. V. P.); Shelley Davis (Sales and Marketing); Robyn Gentile (Member Services Manager); Earl Goodman (Senior Media Buyer); Becky Moats (Networks Coordinator); Jason Davidson (National Sales Rep.)
Main contact: Carol Daniels

LA CONNER

NORTHWEST INTERNATIONAL CIRCULATION EXECUTIVES

Street address 1: PO Box 778
Street address state: WA
Street address state: 98257
Postal code: USA
Country: PO Box 778

Mailing address 1: La Conner
Mailing city: WA
Mailing state: 98257-0778
Mailing zip: (360) 466-2006
Office phone: (360) 466-2006
Web address: www.nicex.org
General e-mail: nice@galaxynet.com
Note: Management seminars sponsored in Oct. (non-dailies welcome). Elections held at annual conference in May
Personnel: Dale Irvine (Sec./Treasurer)
Main contact: Dale Irvine

LAKE MARY

FLORIDA NEWSPAPER ADVERTISING & MARKETING EXECUTIVES

Street address 1: 610 Crescent Executive Court
Street address 2: Suite 112
Street address state: FL
Street address state: 32746
Postal code: USA
Country: 610 Crescent Executive Court
Mailing address 1: Lake Mary
Mailing city: FL
Mailing state: 32746
Mailing zip: (321) 283-5273
Web address: www.fname.org
General e-mail: hello@fname.org
Year established: 1929
Profile : FNAME provides a network to exchange creative ideas understand customer's needs, learn new selling techniques and implement innovative sales programs.
Personnel: Sandy Osteen (Exec. Dir.)
Main contact: Sandy Osteen

LANSING

MICHIGAN PRESS ASSOCIATION

Street address 1: 827 N Washington Ave
Street address state: MI
Street address state: 48906-5135
Postal code: USA
Country: 827 N Washington Ave
Mailing address 1: Lansing
Mailing city: MI
Mailing state: 48906-5199
Mailing zip: (517) 372-2424
Office phone: (517) 372-2429
Web address: www.michiganpress.org
General e-mail: mpa@michiganpress.org
Year established: 1868
Note: Elections held in Jan
Personnel: Roselie Lucus (Growth & Operations Manager); Lisa McGraw (Public Affairs Manager); Sean Wickham (Design & Communications Specialist); Janet Mendler (Mgr.); James Tarrant (Exec. Dir.); Paul Biondi (Adv. Dir.)
Main contact: ()

LATHAM

NASJA EAST

Street address 1: 22 Cavalier Way
Street address state: NY
Street address state: 12110
Postal code: USA
Country: 22 Cavalier Way
Mailing address 1: Latham
Mailing city: NY
Mailing state: 12110
Mailing zip: 518 339-5334
Web address: http://www.nasja.org/east/index.cfm
General e-mail: nasjaeast@nasja.org
Advertising e-mail: nasjaeast@nasja.org
Editorial e-mail: nasjaeast@nasja.org
Year established: 1963
Profile : Founded in 1963, as the Eastern Ski Writers Association (ESWA) is the Eastern regional chapter of the North American Snow Sports Journalists Association, known as NASJA. In March of 2014 ESWA was renamed to NASJA-East to better conform to the other NASJA Regional chapters, i.e., NASJA Midwest and NASJA West. Membership includes press, corporate, honorary press and retired press. Press members include writers, photographers, artists, videographers and broadcasters.
Personnel: Peter Hines (Pres.)
Main contact: Peter Hines

LEXINGTON

UNIVERSITY PRESS OF KENTUCKY

Street address 1: 663 S. Limestone St.
Street address state: KY
Street address state: 40508-4008
Postal code: USA
Country: 663 S Limestone
Mailing address 1: Lexington
Mailing city: KY
Mailing state: 40508-4008
Mailing zip: (859) 257-8419
Office phone: (859) 323-1873
Web address: www.kentuckypress.com
General e-mail: smwrin2@uky.edu
Note: Elections held in spring/fall of odd numbered years
Personnel: John Hussey (Mktg. Dir.); Stephen Wrinn (Dir.)
Main contact: Stephen Wrinn

LINCOLN

NEBRASKA ASSOCIATED PRESS ASSOCIATION

Street address 1: 845 €œS⊠ Street
Street address state: NE
Street address state: 68508
Postal code: USA
Country: 845 ?Ç£S?Ç¥ Street
Mailing address 1: Lincoln
Mailing city: NE
Mailing state: 68508
Mailing zip: (402)476-2851
Office phone: (402)476-2942
Web address: www.ap.org/nebraska
General e-mail: nebpress@nebpress.com
Note: Elections held in Sept
Personnel: Tina Heraldson (Bureau Chief)
Main contact: Tina Heraldson

LITTLE FALLS

MINNESOTA FREE PAPER ASSOCIATION

Street address 1: 21998 Hwy. 27
Street address state: MN
Street address state: 56345
Postal code: USA
Country: 21998 Highway 27
Mailing address 1: Little Falls
Mailing city: MN
Mailing state: 56345-6279
Mailing zip: 320-630-5312
Office phone: (320) 632-2348
Web address: www.mfpa.com
General e-mail: terry@littlefalls.net
Note: Elections held in Feb
Personnel: Terry Lehrke (Asst. Sec./Treasurer); Trevor Slette (Pres.)
Main contact: Terry Lehrke

LITTLE ROCK

ARKANSAS PRESS WOMEN ASSOCIATION, INC.

Street address 1: 1301 Golden Pond Rd
Street address state: AR
Street address state: 72223-9549
Postal code: USA
Country: 1301 Golden Pond Rd
Mailing address 1: Little Rock
Mailing city: AR
Mailing state: 72223-9549
Mailing zip: 501-671-2126
Office phone: 501-671-2121
Web address: www.arkpresswomen.wordpress.com
General e-mail: arkpresswomen@yahoo.com
Year established: 1949
Profile : Arkansas Press Women, established in 1949, is an organization dedicated to helping all communicators improve their skills.
Note: Elections held in the fall of spring odd numbered years
Personnel: Mary Hightower (President); Terry Hawkins (Treasurer)
Main contact: Mary Hightower

LONGVIEW

M. ROBERTS MEDIA

Street address 1: 320 E. Methvin St.
Street address state: TX
Street address state: 75601
Postal code: USA
Country: 320 E. Methvin St.
Mailing address 1: Longview
Mailing city: TX
Mailing state: 75601
Mailing zip: (903) 757-3311
Web address: www.mrobertsmedia.com
Year established: 1942
Personnel: Stephen McHaney (Publisher); Justin Wilcox (Chief Revenue Officer)
Main contact: Stephen McHaney

LOS ALAMOS

NEW MEXICO PRESS WOMEN

Street address 1: 256 DP Rd.
Street address state: NM
Street address state: 87544
Postal code: USA
Country: 256 Dp Rd
Mailing address 1: Los Alamos
Mailing city: NM
Mailing state: 87544-3233
Mailing zip: (505) 662-4185
Office phone: (505) 827-6496
Web address: www.newmexicopresswomen.org
General e-mail: lanews@lamonitor.com
Note: Elections held May 1st of even numbered years
Personnel: Carol Clark (Pres.)
Main contact: Carol Clark

LOS ANGELES

ASSOCIATED PRESS/CALIFORNIA-NEVADA NEWS EXECUTIVES

Street address 1: 221 S. Figueroa St., Ste. 300
Street address state: CA
Street address state: 90012
Postal code: USA
Country: 221 S Figueroa St Ste 300
Mailing address 1: Los Angeles
Mailing city: CA
Mailing state: 90012-2553
Mailing zip: (213) 626-5833
Editorial fax: (213) 626-1200
Web address: www.ap.org/losangeles
General e-mail: losangeles@ap.org
Year established: 1848
Note: Elections held in May
Personnel: Anthony Marquez (Bureau Chief, Los Angeles); John Raess (Bureau Chief, San Francisco); Sue Cross (Reg'l Vice Pres. Newyork)
Main contact: Anthony Marquez

LOS ANGELES PRESS CLUB

Street address 1: 4773 Hollywood Blvd.
Street address state: CA
Street address state: 90027
Postal code: USA
Country: 4773 Hollywood Blvd
Mailing address 1: Los Angeles
Mailing city: CA
Mailing state: 90027-5333
Mailing zip: (323) 669-8081
Office phone: (323) 669-8069
Web address: www.lapressclub.org
General e-mail: info@lapressclub.org
Year established: 1913
Note: Elections held in Nov
Personnel: Diana Ljungaeus (Exec. Dir.)
Main contact: Diana Ljungaeus

LOUISVILLE

KENTUCKY ASSOCIATED PRESS EDITORS ASSOCIATION

Street address 1: 525 W. Broadway
Street address state: KY
Street address state: 40202
Postal code: USA
Country: 525 W Broadway
Mailing address 1: Louisville
Mailing city: KY
Mailing state: 40202-2206
Mailing zip: (502) 583-7718
Office phone: (502) 589-4831
Web address: www.ap.org/kentucky
General e-mail: ayeomans@ap.org
Note: Elections held in Nov

MADISON

STATE HISTORICAL SOCIETY OF WISCONSIN

Street address 1: 816 State St.
Street address state: WI
Street address state: 53706-1482
Postal code: USA
Country: 816 State St
Mailing address 1: Madison
Mailing city: WI
Mailing state: 53706-1482
Mailing zip: (608) 264-6534
Office phone: (608) 264-6520
Web address: www.wisconsinhistory.org
Personnel: Anna Altschwager (Assistant Director, Guest Experience)
Main contact: Anna Altschwager

MILWAUKEE

WISCONSIN ASSOCIATED PRESS ASSOCIATION

Street address 1: 111 E. Wisconsin Ave., Ste.1925
Street address state: WI
Street address state: 53202
Postal code: USA
Country: 111 E Wisconsin Ave Ste 1925
Mailing address 1: Milwaukee
Mailing city: WI
Mailing state: 53202-4825
Mailing zip: (414) 225-3580
Web address: www.ap.org
General e-mail: apmlw@ap.org
Note: Elections held in May
Personnel: Roger Schneider (News Ed.)
Main contact: Roger Schneider

MINNEAPOLIS

ASSOCIATED COLLEGIATE PRESS

Street address 1: 2221 University Ave. SE, Ste. 121
Street address state: MN
Street address state: 55414
Postal code: USA
Country: 2221 University Ave SE Ste 121
Mailing address 1: Minneapolis
Mailing city: MN
Mailing state: 55414-3074
Mailing zip: (612) 625-8335
Office phone: (612) 626-0720

Associations, Clubs and Press Clubs - City, State and Regional

Web address: www.studentpress.org
General e-mail: info@studentpress.org
Year established: 1921
Personnel: Logan Aimone (Exec. Dir.)
Main contact: Logan Aimone

MINNESOTA ASSOCIATED PRESS ASSOCIATION

Street address 1: 425 Portland Ave
Street address 2: Third Floor
Street address state: MN
Street address state: 55488
Postal code: USA
Mailing zip: (612) 332-2727
Office phone: (612) 342-5299
Web address: www.ap.org
General e-mail: apminneapolis@ap.org
Personnel: Doug Glass (News Ed.)
Main contact: Doug Glass

MONTREAL

CONSEIL DE PRESSE DU QUEBEC

Street address 1: 1000, rue Fullum, Ste. A.208
Street address state: QC
Street address state: H2K 3L7
Postal code: Canada
Country: 1000, rue Fullum, Ste. A.208
Mailing address 1: Montreal
Mailing city: QC
Mailing state: H2K 3L7
Mailing zip: (514) 529-2818
Office phone: (514) 873-4434
Web address: www.conseildepresse.qc.ca
General e-mail: info@conseildepresse.qc.ca
Year established: 1973
Personnel: Guy Amyot (Contact); Julien Acosta (Director of communication)
Main contact: Julien Acosta

MOUNTAIN BROOK

SOCIETY OF CLASSIFIED ADVERTISING MANAGERS OF AMERICA, INC.

Street address 1: PO Box 531335
Street address state: AL
Street address state: 352530-1335
Postal code: USA
Country: PO Box 531335
Mailing address 1: Mountain Brook
Mailing city: AL
Mailing state: 35253-1335
Mailing zip: (205) 592-0389
Office phone: (205)599-5598
Web address: www.scama.com
General e-mail: hrushing@usit.net
Year established: 1947
Profile : Trade association for paper and digital advertising.
Note: Elections held in Feb
Personnel: Hugh J. Rushing (Exec. Officer)
Main contact: Hugh J. Rushing

MT. PLEASANT

MID-ATLANTIC NEWSPAPER ADVERTISING & MARKETING EXECUTIVES

Street address 1: 359-C Wando Place Drive
Street address state: SC
Street address state: 29464
Postal code: USA
Country: 359 Wando Place Dr Ste C
Mailing address 1: Mt Pleasant
Mailing city: SC
Mailing state: 29464-7926
Mailing zip: (509)540-1534
Web address: www.midatlanticname.com
General e-mail: edwardrbryant@yahoo.com
Note: Elections held in March
Personnel: Terri Saylor (Exec. Dir.)
Main contact: Terri Saylor

NASHVILLE

TENNESSEE ASSOCIATED PRESS MANAGING EDITORS

Street address 1: John Siegenthaler Center
Street address 2: 1207 18th Avenue South, Suite 261-A
Street address state: TN
Street address state: 37212
Postal code: USA
Country: John Seigenthaler Center
Mailing address 1: Nashville
Mailing city: TN
Mailing state: 37212
Mailing zip: (615) 373-9988
Office phone: (615) 376-0947
Web address: www.ap.org/states/tennessee
General e-mail: apnashville@ap.org
Personnel: Adam Yeomans (Bureau Chief)
Main contact: Adam Yeomans

NEW ORLEANS

NEW ORLEANS PRESS CLUB

Street address 1: 846 Howard Avenue
Street address state: LA
Street address state: 70113
Postal code: USA
Country: 846 Howard Ave
Mailing address 1: New Orleans
Mailing city: LA
Mailing state: 70113-1134
Mailing zip: 504-259-4687
Web address: www.pressclubneworleans.org
General e-mail: info@pressclubneworleans.org
Note: Elections held in July
Personnel: Bill Langkopp (Exec. Dir.)
Main contact: Bill Langkopp

NEW YORK

ADVERTISING CLUB OF GREATER NEW YORK

Street address 1: 989 Avenue of the Americas
Street address 2: 7th floor
Street address state: NY
Street address state: 10018
Postal code: USA
Country: 989 Avenue of the Americas Fl 7
Mailing address 1: New York
Mailing city: NY
Mailing state: 10018-0872
Mailing zip: (212) 533-8080
Office phone: (212) 533-1929
Web address: www.theadvertisingclub.org
General e-mail: memberships@theadvertisingclub.org
Note: Elections held in July
Personnel: Gina Grillo (Exec. Dir.)
Main contact: Gina Grillo

NEW YORK PRESS PHOTOGRAPHERS ASSOCIATION, INC.

Street address 1: PO Box 3346
Street address state: NY
Street address state: 10008-3346
Postal code: USA
Country: Box 3346 Church Street Station
Mailing address 1: New York
Mailing city: NY
Mailing state: 10008-3346
Mailing zip: (212) 889-6533
Web address: www.nyppa.org
General e-mail: office@nyppa.org
Year established: 1915
Profile : The New York Press Photographers Association was established in 1915 as the News Photographers Association of New York, and since that time has served as a fraternal and professional organization, representing the interests of working photographers and visual journalists in the New York metro area.
Note: Elections held every other year
Personnel: Ray Stubblebine (Trustee); Marc Hermann (Secretary - Historian); Bruce Cotler (President); Todd Maisel (Vice President)
Main contact: Marc Hermann

OVERSEAS PRESS CLUB OF AMERICA

Street address 1: 40 West 45 Street
Street address state: NY
Street address state: 10036
Postal code: USA
Mailing zip: (212) 626-9220
Office phone: (212) 626-9210
Web address: www.opcofamerica.org
General e-mail: info@opcofamerica.org
Year established: 1939
Profile : The Overseas Press Club of America is the nation's oldest and largest association of journalists engaged in international news. Every April, it awards the most prestigious prizes devoted exclusively to international news coverage. It was founded in 1939 by nine foreign correspondents in New York City, and has grown to 450 members world-wide. The club's mission is to uphold the highest standards in news reporting, advance press freedom and promote good fellowship among colleagues. It also aims to help educate a new generation of journalists and to contribute to the freedom and independence of the press throughout the world.
Note: Elections held in late summer
Personnel: Patricia Kranz (Exec. Dir.)
Main contact: Patricia Kranz

NOVATO

CAL WESTERN CIRCULATION MANAGERS' ASSOCIATION

Street address 1: 123 Sequoia Glen Ln
Street address state: CA
Street address state: 94947
Postal code: USA
Country: 123 Sequoia Glen Ln
Mailing address 1: Novato
Mailing city: CA
Mailing state: 94947-5181
Mailing zip: (415) 297-8836
Office fax: (415) 297-8836
Web address: www.cwcma.org
General e-mail: cwcma@imblake.com
Advertising e-mail: cwcma@imblake.com
Year established: 1919
Profile : CWCMA currently boasts a membership over 175. An excerpt from the By-Laws states: The object of the Association shall be the mutual enlightenment of members and the furtherance of the best interests of the circulation departments of the newspapers with which they are connected.
Note: Election of officers is held during the annual meeting. Annual meeting is in June every year.
Personnel: Blake Webber (Executive Director); Aaron Kotarek (Pres.)
Main contact: Blake Webber

OKLAHOMA CITY

ASSOCIATED PRESS/OKLAHOMA NEWS EXECUTIVES

Street address 1: 525 Central Park Dr., Ste. 202
Street address state: OK
Street address state: 73105
Postal code: USA
Country: 525 Central Park Dr Ste 202
Mailing address 1: Oklahoma City
Mailing city: OK
Mailing state: 73105-1799
Mailing zip: (405) 525-2121
Office phone: (405) 524-7465
Web address: www.ap.org/oklahoma
General e-mail: apoklahoma@ap.org
Personnel: Dale Leach (Bureau Chief)
Main contact: Ken Miller

OLYMPIA

ALLIED DAILY NEWSPAPERS OF WASHINGTON

Street address 1: 1110 Capitol Way S
Street address state: WA
Street address state: 98501-2251
Postal code: USA
Country: 1110 Capitol Way S
Mailing address 1: Olympia
Mailing city: WA
Mailing state: 98501-2251
Mailing zip: (360) 943-9960
Office phone: (360) 943-9962
General e-mail: anewspaper@aol.com
Personnel: Rowland Thompson (Exec. Dir.)
Main contact: Rowland Thompson

PERRYTON

WEST TEXAS PRESS ASSOCIATION

Street address 1: 706 SW 10th St.
Street address state: TX
Street address state: 79070
Postal code: USA
Country: 706 SW 10th Ave
Mailing address 1: Perryton
Mailing city: TX
Mailing state: 79070-3802
Mailing zip: (806) 435-3631
Office phone: (806) 435-2420
Web address: www.wtpa.org
General e-mail: secretary@wtpa.org
Note: Elections held at annual convention in July
Personnel: Mary Dudley (Secretary-Treasurer)
Main contact: Mary Dudley

PHOENIX

ARIZONA ASSOCIATED PRESS MANAGING EDITORS ASSOCIATION

Street address 1: 1850 N. Central Ave., Ste. 640
Street address state: AZ
Street address state: 85004
Postal code: USA
Country: 1850 N Central Ave Ste 640
Mailing address 1: Phoenix
Mailing city: AZ
Mailing state: 85004-4573
Mailing zip: (602) 258-8934
Office phone: (602) 254-9573
Web address: www.ap.org/arizona
General e-mail: aparizona@ap.org
Note: Elections held in the summer
Personnel: Michelle Williams (Bureau Chief)
Main contact: Michelle Williams

POUGHKEEPSIE

NEW YORK STATE CIRCULATION MANAGERS ASSOCIATION

Street address 1: 85 Civic Center Plz.
Street address state: NY
Street address state: 12601
Postal code: USA
Country: 85 Civic Center Plz
Mailing address 1: Poughkeepsie
Mailing city: NY
Mailing state: 12601-2498
Mailing zip: (845) 437-4738
Office phone: (845) 437-4902
Web address: www.poughkeepsiejournal.com
General e-mail: farrellb@poughkee.gannett.com
Note: Elections held in May

Personnel: Bill Farrell (Board Member)
Main contact: Bill Farrell

QUINCY

CENTRAL STATES CIRCULATION MANAGERS ASSOCIATION

Street address 1: 130 S. 5th St.
Street address state: IL
Street address state: 62301
Postal code: USA
Country: Central States Circulation Managers Association
Mailing address 1: Munster
Mailing city: IL
Mailing state: 46321
Mailing zip: (217) 221-3327
Web address: 130 S. 5th St.
General e-mail: rrobertson@whig.com
Advertising e-mail: rrobertson@whig.com
Editorial e-mail: rrobertson@whig.com
Year established: 1935
Profile : Central States Circulation Managers' Association is a professional organization comprised of circulation managers and circulation management personnel of daily and weekly newspapers in Illinois, Indiana, Iowa, Kentucky, Michigan, Minnesota, North Dakota, South Dakota, and Wisconsin. Associate members include CSCMA advertisers, authorized salespersons, exhibitors not eligible for regular membership, and circulation managers outside the CSCMA nine state area.
Note: Elections held in April
Personnel: Scott Kinter (Chairman); Robert Robertson (President); Erin Gallagher (Secretary Treasurer); Paul Hart (Vice President); Scott Daily (Web Chair)
Main contact: Robert Robertson; Erin Gallagher

RALEIGH

CAPITOL PRESS ASSOCIATION

Street address 1: PO Box 191
Street address state: NC
Street address state: 27602
Postal code: USA
Country: PO Box 191
Mailing address 1: Raleigh
Mailing city: NC
Mailing state: 27602-9150
Mailing zip: (919) 836-2858
Web address: www.ncinsider.com
General e-mail: smooneyh@ncinsider.com
Note: Elections held in Jan
Personnel: Scott Mooneyham (Mgr.)
Main contact: Megan Dew

RENTON

WASHINGTON PRESS ASSOCIATION

Street address 1: c/o 15642 129th Court SE
Street address state: WA
Street address state: 98058
Postal code: USA
Country: c/o 15642 129th Court SE
Mailing address 1: Renton
Mailing city: WA
Mailing state: 98058
Web address: www.washingtonpressassociation.com
Year established: 1946
Profile : Washington Press Association is a professional development and networking organization for working and student journalists and communicators in the state of Washington. It operates an annual communications contest.
Personnel: Bill Virgin (President); Mike Maltais (Vice President); Sarah Smith (Secretary)
Main contact: Bill Virgin

RIDGEWOOD

NEW YORK FINANCIAL WRITERS ASSOCIATION, INC.

Street address 1: PO Box 338
Street address state: NJ
Street address state: 07451-0338
Postal code: USA
Country: PO Box 338
Mailing address 1: Ridgewood
Mailing city: NJ
Mailing state: 07451-0338
Mailing zip: (201) 612-0100
Office phone: (201) 612-9915
Web address: www.nyfwa.org
General e-mail: nyfwa@aol.com
Year established: 1938
Note: Elections held on fourth Wed. of Jan. Members are journalists in the business or financial media
Personnel: Jane Reilly (Exec. Mgr.)
Main contact: Jane Reilly

ROANOKE RAPIDS

MID-ATLANTIC CIRCULATION MANAGERS ASSOCIATION

Street address 1: Daily Herald, PO Box 520
Street address state: NC
Street address state: 27870-0520
Postal code: USA
Country: PO Box 520
Mailing address 1: Roanoke Rapids
Mailing city: NC
Mailing state: 27870-0520
Mailing zip: (252) 537-2505
Office phone: (252) 537-1887
Web address: www.midatlanticcma.org
Note: Elections held in May
Personnel: Carol Moseley (Sec./Treasurer); Robyn Ashley (President); Keven Zepezauer (First Vice President); David Adams (Second Vice President); Kevin Craig (Representative); Patricia Speziale Edwards (Representative); Sean Torain (Representative); Clayton Hall (Representative)
Main contact: Carol Moseley

ROCKPORT

MASSACHUSETTS NEWSPAPER PUBLISHERS ASSOCIATION

Street address 1: 7 S Street Ct.
Street address state: MA
Street address state: 01966
Postal code: USA
Country: 7 S Street Ct
Mailing address 1: Rockport
Mailing city: MA
Mailing state: 01966-2135
Mailing zip: (978) 546-3400
Office phone: (978) 418-9161
Web address: www.masspublishers.org
General e-mail: info@masspublishers.org
Profile : The MNPA is an association that represents daily, weekly and monthly newspapers in Massachusetts.
Personnel: Robert J. Ambrogi (Exec. Dir.)
Main contact: Robert J. Ambrogi

ROSELAND

METROPOLITAN NEW YORK FOOTBALL WRITERS ASSOCIATION

Street address 1: American Football Networks, Inc.
Street address 2: P.O. Box 477
Street address state: NJ
Street address state: 07068-0477
Postal code: USA
Country: PO Box 477
Mailing address 1: Roseland
Mailing city: NJ
Mailing state: 07068-0477
Mailing zip: (973) 364-0605
Office phone: (973) 364-0425
Web address: www.mnyfwa.com
General e-mail: americanfootballnetworks@gmail.com
Year established: 1935
Profile : Nation's oldest and largest regional football writers association
Personnel: Dennis Wilson (Pres.)
Main contact: Dennis Wilson

SACRAMENTO

CALIFORNIA PRESS ASSOCIATION

Street address 1: Cal. Newspr. Publs. Assoc., 2000 O St., Suite 120
Street address state: CA
Street address state: 95811
Postal code: USA
Country: 2000 O St Ste 120
Mailing address 1: Sacramento
Mailing city: CA
Mailing state: 95811-5299
Mailing zip: (916) 288-6000
Web address: www.cnpa.com
Year established: 1878
Note: Elections held in Dec
Personnel: Thomas Newton (Exec. Dir.)
Main contact: Tom Newton

PACIFIC NORTHWEST NEWSPAPER ASSOCIATION

Street address 1: 708 Tenth St.
Street address state: CA
Street address state: 95814
Postal code: USA
Country: 708 10th St
Mailing address 1: Sacramento
Mailing city: CA
Mailing state: 95814-1803
Mailing zip: (888) 344-7662
Office phone: (916) 288-6002
Web address: www.pnna.com
General e-mail: tom@cnpa.com
Note: Elections held in the July
Personnel: Jack Bates (Exec. Dir.)
Main contact: Tom Newton

SALT LAKE CITY

UTAH-IDAHO-SPOKANE ASSOCIATED PRESS ASSOCIATION

Street address 1: 30 E. 100 South St., Ste. 200
Street address state: UT
Street address state: 84111
Postal code: USA
Country: 30 E. 100 South St., Ste. 200
Mailing address 1: Salt Lake City
Mailing city: UT
Mailing state: 84111
Mailing zip: (801) 322-3405
Office phone: (801) 322-0051
General e-mail: apsaltlake@ap.org
Note: Elections held in June
Personnel: Jim Clarke (Bureau Chief)
Main contact: Jim Clarke

SAN JUAN

OVERSEAS PRESS CLUB OF PUERTO RICO (ESTABLISHED 1968)

Street address 1: 1399 Ave. Ana G. M?ndez
Street address state: PR
Street address state: 00928-1345
Postal code: Puerto Rico
Country: P.O Box 12326, Loiza St. Station, Santurce
Mailing address 1: San Juan
Mailing city: PR
Mailing state: 00914-0326
Mailing zip: (787) 525-8901
Office phone: N/A

Office fax: N/A
Advertising phone: N/A
Advertising fax: 787-810-3377
Editorial phone: N/A
Editorial fax: 787-408-3033
Other phone: N/A
Web address: www.opcpr.wordpress.com
General e-mail: opcpr@yahoo.com
Advertising e-mail: opcpr@yahoo.com
Editorial e-mail: opcpr@yahoo.com
Year established: 1968
Profile : NON-PROFIT Journalist/Communications Association
Note: Martha Alonso - 787-408-3033
Personnel: Ãngel RodrÃguez (Pres.)
Main contact: Mariazell VÃ©lez

SANTA MONICA

CCNMA: LATINO JOURNALISTS OF CALIFORNIA

Street address 1: ASU Walter Cronkite School of Journalism
Street address 2: 725 Arizona Ave. Ste. 404
Street address state: CA
Street address state: 90401-1723
Postal code: USA
Country: ASU Walter Cronkite School of Journalism
Mailing address 1: Santa Monica
Mailing city: CA
Mailing state: 90401-1723
Mailing zip: (424) 229-9482
Office phone: (424) 238-0271
Web address: www.ccnma.org
General e-mail: ccnmainfo@ccnma.org
Year established: 1972
Profile : CCNMA: Latino Journalists of California is the oldest organization of journalists of color in the country, incorporating in 1972. Its mission is to develop and support Latino journalists through scholarships, training and job placement, and to foster an accurate and fair portrayal of Latinos in the news media.
Personnel: Julio Moran (Executive Director)
Main contact: Julio Moran

SASKATOON

SASKATCHEWAN WEEKLY NEWSPAPERS ASSOCIATION

Street address 1: 14-401 45th St. W.
Street address state: SK
Street address state: S7L 5Z9
Postal code: Canada
Country: 14-401 45th St. W.
Mailing address 1: Saskatoon
Mailing city: SK
Mailing state: S7L 5Z9
Mailing zip: (306) 382-9683
Office phone: (306) 382-9421
Editorial fax: 800-661-7962
Web address: www.swna.ca
General e-mail: swna@swna.com
Personnel: Cameron Just (Tech. Officer); Julie Schau (Commun.Coord.); Louise Simpson (Office Mgr.); Nicole Nater (Adv. Coord., Classified); Steve Nixon (Exec. Dir.)
Main contact: Steve Nixon

SEATTLE

WASHINGTON ASSOCIATED PRESS NEWSPAPER EXECUTIVES ASSOCIATION

Street address 1: 3131 Elliott Ave., Ste. 750
Street address state: WA
Street address state: 98121
Postal code: USA
Country: 3131 Elliott Ave Ste 750
Mailing address 1: Seattle
Mailing city: WA
Mailing state: 98121-1095

Associations, Clubs and Press Clubs - City, State and Regional

Mailing zip: (206) 682-1812
Office phone: (206) 621-1948
Web address: www.ap.org
General e-mail: apseattle@ap.org
Note: Elections held in Oct./Nov
Personnel: Nancy Trott (Bureau Chief)
Main contact: Nancy Trott

SPOKANE

PACIFIC NORTHWEST ASSOCIATION OF WANT AD NEWSPAPERS (PNAWAN) & WESTERN REGIONAL ADVERTISING PROGRAM (WRAP)

Street address 1: 304 W 3rd Ave
Street address 2: C/O Exchange Publishing
Street address state: WA
Street address state: 99201-4314
Postal code: USA
Country: PO Box 427
Mailing address 1: Spokane
Mailing city: WA
Mailing state: 99210
Mailing zip: (509) 922-3456
Office phone: (509) 455-7940
Office fax: 509-922-3456
Advertising phone: 509-455-7940
Editorial fax: (800) 326-2223
Web address: www.RegionalAds.org
General e-mail: Ads@PNAWAN.org
Advertising e-mail: Kylah@ExchangePublishing.com
Year established: 1977
Profile : Reach a bigger audience & Advertise in local community papers throughout the Pacific Northwest region! PNAWAN (Pacific NW Assoc. of Want Ad Newspapers) makes advertising on a regional scale easy and affordable. Prices start at just $50 per Regional Ad! Place both classified & display ads in up to 30 different publications throughout Washington, Oregon, Idaho, Montana, Alberta & British Columbia in just 1 easy phone call. Our publications believe in high standards of quality and ethics in advertising. PNAWAN publications are well-known in their communities and have very loyal readerships.   Total weekly distribution: 537,006 We are audited and verified by the Circulation Verification Council annually.   Classified Ad Rates: $6.25 per edition, minimum 8 editions required (Note: Editions are calculated as number of weeks x number of running publications) Examples: 8 publications x 1 week = $50 4 publications x 2 weeks = $50 12 publications x 1 week = $75 6 publications x 2 weeks = $75 16 publications x 1 week = $100 8 publications x 2 weeks = $100 ....etc. Maximum USA coverage: 23 pubs x 1 week = $143.75 Maximum coverage incl. Canada: 30 pubs x 1 week = $187.50   25 word max. Extra words = 10 cents per word per edition Call today to place your Pacific Northwest Regional Ads! 509-922-3456 or 1-800-326-2223 (toll-free). Note: PNAWAN is hosted by member company, Exchange Publishing, so be sure to ask for PNAWAN Regional Ads when calling. You may also email ads@pnawan.org for any inquiries, or contact the Executive Director of PNAWAN, Kylah Strohte, directly at Kylah@ExchangePublishing.com   More information about the Pacific Northwest Association of Want Ad Newspapers (PNAWAN) online at www.RegionalAds.org Mission: To unite, promote, and facilitate advertising between the free community newspaper publications of the Pacific Northwest so that our advertisers can easily reach a bigger audience.
Note: We are audited and verified by the Circulation Verification Council annually. PNAWAN headquarters are located at the offices of hosting member publication, Exchange Publishing, in Spokane, WA.
Personnel: Kylah Strohte (Executive Director of the Pacific Northwest Association of Want Ad Newspapers (PNAWAN) & Western Regional Advertising Program (WRAP)); PNAWAN Office
Main contact: Kylah Strohte

SPRINGFIELD

NATIONAL NEWSPAPER ASSOCIATION

Street address 1: 900 Community Drive
Street address state: IL
Street address state: 62703
Postal code: USA
Country: 900 Community Drive
Mailing address 1: Springfield
Mailing city: IL
Mailing state: 62703
Mailing zip: (217)241-1400
Office phone: (217) 241-1301
Web address: www.nna.org
General e-mail: lynne@nna.org
Advertising e-mail: wendy@nna.org
Year established: 1835
Note: Officer elections held in Sept/Oct during Annual Convention; annual Leadership Conference in March; annual Better Newspaper Contest entry deadline Spring
Personnel: Stan Schwartz (Comm. Dir.); Lynne Lance (Chief Operating Officer); Sam Fisher (CEO)
Main contact: Lynne Lance

VALLEY PRESS CLUB, INC.

Street address 1: PO Box 5475
Street address state: MA
Street address state: 01101-5475
Postal code: USA
Country: PO Box 5475
Mailing address 1: Springfield
Mailing city: MA
Mailing state: 01101-5475
Mailing zip: (413) 682-0007
Editorial fax: (413) 796-2261
Web address: www.valleypressclub.com
General e-mail: info@valleypressclub.com
Note: Elections held in March
Personnel: Charlie Bennett (Pres.)
Main contact: Charlie Bennett

ST. CHARLES

MIDWEST TRAVEL WRITERS ASSOCIATION

Street address 1: 902 S. Randall Road, Suite C311
Street address state: IL
Street address state: 60174
Postal code: USA
Country: 902 S Randall Rd Ste C311
Mailing address 1: Saint Charles
Mailing city: IL
Mailing state: 60174-1554
Mailing zip: 888-551-8184
Web address: www.mtwa.org
General e-mail: sylvia@forbesfreelance.com
Year established: 1951
Profile : Association for Professional Travel Writers. Members are from 13 Midwest states, but write about travel everywhere in the world.
Note: Elections held in Mar or April
Personnel: Carla Waldemar (Active Dir.); Rich Warren (Treasurer); Susan Pollack (Active Dir.); Sylvia Forbes (Administrative Assistant)
Main contact: Sylvia Forbes

STROUDSBURG

PENNSYLVANIA WOMEN'S PRESS ASSOCIATION

Street address 1: 511 Lenox St.
Street address state: PA
Street address state: 18360
Postal code: USA
Country: 511 Lenox St
Mailing address 1: Stroudsburg
Mailing city: PA
Mailing state: 18360-1516
Mailing zip: (717) 295-7869
Web address: www.pwpa.us
General e-mail: pwpa@lancasteronline.com
Note: Elections held in May. Organization accepts freelancers
Main contact: Linda Espenshade

SYRACUSE

FREE COMMUNITY PAPERS OF NEW YORK

Street address 1: 750 W. Genesee St.
Street address state: NY
Street address state: 13204
Postal code: USA
Country: PO Box 11279
Mailing address 1: Syracuse
Mailing city: NY
Mailing state: 13218-1279
Mailing zip: (315) 472-6007
Office phone: (315) 472-5919
Editorial fax: 877-275-2726
Web address: www.fcpny.org
General e-mail: ads@fcpny.com
Personnel: Dan Holmes (Executive Director); Tom Cuskey (Sales & Training)
Main contact: Dan Holmes

SYRACUSE

NEW YORK SOCIETY OF NEWSPAPER EDITORS

Street address 1: 222 Waverly Avenue
Street address state: NY
Street address state: 13244
Postal code: USA
Country: 222 Waverly Ave
Mailing address 1: Syracuse
Mailing city: NY
Mailing state: 13210-2412
Mailing zip: (315) 443-2305
Office phone: (315) 443-3946
Web address: https://library.syr.edu/about/
Personnel: Joann M. Crupi (Pres.)
Main contact: Susan Beitz; Steve Davis

TALLAHASSEE

FLORIDA SOCIETY OF NEWSPAPER EDITORS

Street address 1: 336 E. College Ave. Suite 203
Street address state: FL
Street address state: 32301
Postal code: USA
Country: 336 E College Ave Ste 203
Mailing address 1: Tallahassee
Mailing city: FL
Mailing state: 32301-1559
Mailing zip: (850) 222-5790
Office phone: 850-224-6012
Web address: www.fsne.org
General e-mail: fpa-info@flpress.com
Note: Elections held at June convention
Personnel: Marcia Cyr (Membership Coordinator)
Main contact: Marcia Cyr

THE WOODLANDS

TEXAS CIRCULATION MANAGEMENT ASSOCIATION

Street address 1: c/o PO Box 9577
Street address state: TX
Street address state: 77387
Postal code: USA
Country: c/o TCMA, PO Box 9577
Mailing address 1: The Woodlands
Mailing city: TX
Mailing state: 77387
Web address: www.texascma.org
General e-mail: tcma@texascma.org
Year established: 1913
Profile : The purpose of this organization is to contribute to the growth and development of circulation executives, to disseminate the most effective methods of marketing daily newspapers, and to promote the well being of our publishers, the circulation profession and the reading public.
Note: America's First Circulation Sectional Founded September 18, 1913
Personnel: J W Smith (Secretary/Treasurer)
Main contact: J W Smith

TRENTON

NEW JERSEY ASSOCIATED PRESS MANAGING EDITORS ASSOCIATION

Street address 1: 50 W. State St., Ste. 1114
Street address state: NJ
Street address state: 8608
Postal code: USA
Country: 50 W State St Ste 1114
Mailing address 1: Trenton
Mailing city: NJ
Mailing state: 08608-1220
Mailing zip: (609) 392-3622
Office phone: (609) 392-3525
Web address: www.ap.org/nj
General e-mail: aptrenton@ap.org
Personnel: Sally Hale (BC)
Main contact: Sally Hale

NEW JERSEY LEGISLATIVE CORRESPONDENTS CLUB

Street address 1: Hackensack Record
Street address state: NJ
Street address state: 8625
Postal code: USA
Country: PO Box 21
Mailing address 1: Trenton
Mailing city: NJ
Mailing state: 08625-0021
Mailing zip: (609) 292-5159
Office phone: (609) 984-1888
Note: This group accepts news organizations with correspondents based in Trenton, N.J
Personnel: Jim Hooker (Pres.)
Main contact: Jim Hooker

VANCOUVER

BRITISH COLUMBIA/YUKON COMMUNITY NEWSPAPERS ASSOCIATION

Street address 1: #9 West Broadway
Street address state: BC
Street address state: V5Y 1P1
Postal code: Canada
Country: #9 West Broadway
Mailing address 1: Vancouver
Mailing city: BC
Mailing state: V5Y 1P1
Mailing zip: (604) 669-9222
Office phone: (604) 684-4713
Web address: www.bccommunitynews.com
General e-mail: info@bccommunitynews.com
Note: Elections held in May
Personnel: George Affleck (Gen. Mgr.)
Main contact: George Affleck

WASHINGTON

WHITE HOUSE CORRESPONDENTS ASSOCIATION

Street address 1: 600 New Hampshire Ave., Ste. 800
Street address state: DC
Street address state: 20037
Postal code: USA

Country: 600 New Hampshire Ave NW Ste 800
Mailing address 1: Washington
Mailing city: DC
Mailing state: 20037
Mailing zip: 202-266-7453
Office phone: (202) 266-7454
Web address: www.whca.net
General e-mail: director@whca.net
Editorial e-mail: director@whca.net
Year established: 1914
Note: Elections held in July
Personnel: Steven Thomma (Executive Director)
Main contact: Steven Thomma

WHITE HOUSE NEWS PHOTOGRAPHERS ASSOCIATION, INC.

Street address 1: PO Box 7119
Street address state: DC
Street address state: 20044-7119
Postal code: USA
Country: PO Box 7119
Mailing address 1: Washington
Mailing city: DC
Mailing state: 20044-7119
Mailing zip: (202) 785-5230
Web address: www.whnpa.org
General e-mail: info@whnpa.org
Year established: 1921

Note: Elections held in Mar.
Personnel: Jon Elswick (Treasurer); Whitney Shefte (President); Jim Bourg (Vice President)
Main contact: Jon Elswick

WEST HOLLYWOOD

HOLLYWOOD FOREIGN PRESS ASSOCIATION

Street address 1: 646 N. Robertson Blvd.
Street address state: CA
Street address state: 90069-5078
Postal code: USA
Country: 646 N Robertson Blvd
Mailing address 1: West Hollywood
Mailing city: CA
Mailing state: 90069-5022
Mailing zip: (310) 657-1731
Office phone: (310) 657-5576
Web address: www.hfpa.org
General e-mail: info@hfpa.org
Year established: 1943
Personnel: Michael Russell (Head, Mktg.); Philip Berk (Pres.)
Main contact: Michael Russell

WINNIPEG

MANITOBA COMMUNITY NEWSPAPER ASSOCIATION

Street address 1: 943 McPhillips Street
Street address state: MB
Street address state: R2X 2J9
Postal code: Canada
Country: 943 McPhillips Street
Mailing address 1: Winnipeg
Mailing city: MB
Mailing state: R2X 2J9
Mailing zip: (204) 947-1691
Office phone: (204) 947-1919
Web address: www.mcna.com
Note: Elections held at annual April convention

WOBURN

NEW ENGLAND NEWSPAPER & PRESS ASSOCIATION

Street address 1: 1 Arrow Drive, Suite 6
Street address state: MA
Street address state: 01801
Postal code: USA
Country: 1 Arrow Drive, Suite 6
Mailing address 1: Woburn

Mailing city: MA
Mailing state: 01801
Mailing zip: (781) 281-2053
Office phone: (339) 999-2174
Web address: www.nenpa.com
General e-mail: info@nenpa.com
Year established: 1930
Note: Elections held in March
Main contact: Linda Conway

NEW ENGLAND NEWSPAPER & PRESS ASSOCIATION

Street address 1: 1 Arrow Drive
Street address 2: Suite 6
Street address state: MA
Street address state: 01801
Postal code: USA
Country: 1 Arrow Drive, Suite 6
Mailing address 1: Woburn
Mailing city: MA
Mailing state: 01801
Mailing zip: (781) 281-2053
Office phone: (339) 999-2174
Web address: www.nenpa.com
General e-mail: info@nenpa.com
Note: Elections held in Oct
Personnel: Dan Cotter (Exec. Dir. NENPA)
Main contact: Dan Cotter

ASSOCIATIONS, CLUBS AND PRESS CLUBS - NATIONAL AND INTERNATIONAL

1050 BRUXELLES

EUROPEAN NEWSPAPER PUBLISHERS' ASSOCIATION

Street address 1: Square du Bastion 1A, Bte 3
Mailing address 1: Square du Bastion 1A, Bte 3
Mailing city: 1050 Bruxelles
Telephone country code: 32
Telephone city code: 2
Office phone: 551 0190
Office fax: 551 0199
Other phone: enpa@enpa.be
General e-mail: www.enpa.be
Year established: The ENPA is an association of European daily newspaper publishers organizations
Company Profile: Valtteri Niiranen (Dir.); Viviane Garceau (Office Mgr.)
Special Notes: Valtteri Niiranen

ALEXANDRIA

ASSOCIATION FOR WOMEN IN COMMUNICATIONS

Street address 1: 3337 Duke St
Street address state: VA
Postal code: 22314-5219
County: Alexandria City
Country: USA
Mailing address 1: 3337 Duke St
Mailing city: Alexandria
Mailing state: VA
Mailing zip: 22314-5219
Office phone: (703) 370-7436
Office fax: (703) 342-4311
Other phone: info@womcom.org
General e-mail: www.womcom.org
Advertising e-mail: 1909
Web address: The Association for Women in Communications is a professional organization that champions the advancement of women across all communications disciplines by recognizing excellence, promoting leadership and positioning its members at the forefront of the evolving communications era.
Year established: Group and individual memberships only from all communications disciplines
Company Profile: Pamela Valenzuela (Exec. Dir.)
Special Notes: Pamela Valenzuela

EPICOMM

Street address 1: 1800 Diagonal Rd
Street address 2: Ste 320
Street address state: VA
Postal code: 22314-2862
County: Alexandria City
Country: USA
Mailing address 1: 1800 Diagonal Road, Ste. 320
Mailing city: Alexandria
Mailing state: VA
Mailing zip: 22314
Office phone: 703-836-9200
Office fax: 703-548-8204
Other phone: info@epicomm.org
General e-mail: www.epicomm.org
Advertising e-mail: 1933
Web address: Epicomm is a not-for-profit business management association representing companies in the $100+ billion commercial printing and graphic communications industry in North America.
Company Profile: J. Ken Garner (President & CEO)

IDEALLIANCE

Street address 1: 1600 Duke St
Street address 2: Ste 420
Street address state: VA
Postal code: 22314-3421
County: Alexandria City
Country: USA
Mailing address 1: 1600 Duke St Ste 420
Mailing city: Alexandria
Mailing state: VA
Mailing zip: 22314-3421
Office phone: (703)837-1070
Other phone: http://idealliance.org
General e-mail: www.ipa.org
Year established: Elections held in Oct.
Company Profile: Donna McDevitt (Exec. Asst.); Steven Bonoff (Pres.)
Special Notes: David Steinhardt

MEDIA HUMAN RESOURCES ASSOCIATION

Street address 1: 1800 Duke St
Street address state: VA
Postal code: 22314-3494
County: Alexandria City
Country: USA
Mailing address 1: 1800 Duke St
Mailing city: Alexandria
Mailing state: VA
Mailing zip: 22314-3494
Office phone: (800) 283-7476
Office fax: (703) 535-6490
Other phone: shrm@shrm.org
General e-mail: www.shrm.org
Year established: Elections held in June
Company Profile: Laurence O'Neil (Pres.)
Special Notes: Laurence O'Neil

SPECIAL LIBRARIES ASSOCIATION, NEWS DIVISION

Street address 1: 331 S Patrick St
Street address state: VA
Postal code: 22314-3501
County: Alexandria City
Country: USA
Mailing address 1: 331 S Patrick St
Mailing city: Alexandria
Mailing state: VA
Mailing zip: 22314-3501
Office phone: (703) 647-4900
Office fax: (703) 647-4901
Other phone: sla@sla.org
General e-mail: www.sla.org
Year established: Elections held in May
Company Profile: Janice R. Lachance (CEO); Nancy A. Sansalone (COO/CFO); Natasha Kenner (Dir., Exec. Office Relations)
Special Notes: Natasha Kenner

ARLINGTON

AMERICAN PRESS INSTITUTE

Street address 1: 4401 N. Fairfax Drive
Street address 2: Suite 300
Street address state: VA
Postal code: 22203
County: Arlington
Country: USA
Mailing address 1: 4401 N. Fairfax Drive
Mailing address 2: Suite 300
Mailing city: Arlington
Mailing state: VA
Mailing zip: 22203
Office phone: (571) 366-1200
Other phone: hello@pressinstitute.org
General e-mail: www.americanpressinstitute.org
Advertising e-mail: 1946
Company Profile: Tom Rosenstiel (Exec. Dir.); Jeff Sonderman (Deputy Executive Director and Executive Vice President); Susan Benkelman (Director, Accountability Journalism Program); Stephanie Castellano (Editorial Manager); Katherine Ellis (Program Associate); Amy Kovac-Ashley (Editorial Coordinator); Katie Kutsko (Partner Development Manager, Metrics for News); Kevin Loker (Director of Program Operations and Partnerships); Shirley Qiu (Audience Engagement Strategist); Gwen Vargo (Director of Reader Revenue); David Chavern (President and Chief Executive Officer, News Media Alliance and API)
Special Notes: Tom Rosenstiel

NEWS MEDIA ALLIANCE

Street address 1: 4401 Wilson Blvd
Street address 2: Ste 900
Street address state: VA
Postal code: 22203-4195
County: Arlington
Country: USA
Mailing address 1: 4401 Wilson Blvd Ste 900
Mailing city: Arlington
Mailing state: VA
Mailing zip: 22203-4195
Office phone: (571) 366-1000
Office fax: (571) 366-1195
Other phone: sheila.owens@naa.org
General e-mail: www.naa.org
Advertising e-mail: 1979
Web address: NMA is a nonprofit organization representing the newspaper industry and more than 2,000 newspapers in the U.S. and Canada. Most NMA members are daily newspapers accounting for 87 of the U.S. daily circulation
Year established: Elections held in April/May
Company Profile: David Chavern (Pres. & CEO); Robert Walden (CFO); Sarah Burkman (VP of HRO); Rich Schiekofer (SVP Bus. Dev.); John Murray (VP of Audience Dev.); Lindsey Loving (Comm. Mgr.); Paul Boyle (SVP of Public Policy); Danielle Coffey (VP of Strategic Initiatives and Counsel); Jim Conaghan (VP, Research & Industry Analysis); Kristina Zaumseil (Public Policy Mgr.)
Special Notes: David Chavern

REPORTERS COMMITTEE FOR FREEDOM OF THE PRESS

Street address 1: 1101 Wilson Blvd
Street address 2: Ste 1100
Street address state: VA
Postal code: 22209-2275
County: Arlington
Country: USA
Mailing address 1: 1101 Wilson Blvd Ste 1100
Mailing city: Arlington
Mailing state: VA
Mailing zip: 22209-2275
Office phone: (703) 807-2100
Office fax: (703) 807-2109
Other phone: rcfp@rcfp.org
General e-mail: www.rcfp.org
Advertising e-mail: 1908
Company Profile: Dahlia Lithwick (Exec. Committee); Lucy A. Dalglish (Exec. Dir.); Neil Lewis (Exec. Committee); Tony Mauro (Exec. Committee)
Special Notes: Lucy A. Dalglish

ARLINGTON HEIGHTS

ALLIANCE FOR AUDITED MEDIA (AAM)

Street address 1: 48 W Seegers Rd
Street address state: IL
Postal code: 60005-3900
County: Cook
Country: USA
Mailing address 1: 48 W Seegers Rd
Mailing city: Arlington Heights
Mailing state: IL
Mailing zip: 60005
Office phone: (224) 366-6939
Office fax: (224) 366-6949
General e-mail: www.auditedmedia.com
Advertising e-mail: 1914
Web address: The Alliance for Audited Media powers transparency and collaboration between North America's leading media professionals. AAM is the industry's recognized leader in cross-media verification with unparalleled expertise across all brand platforms including web, mobile, email and print. More than 4,000 publishers, advertisers, agencies and technology vendors depend on AAM's data-driven insights, certification audits and information services to transact with trust. An AAM audit differentiates your premium news media brand in today's competitive market. By partnering with AAM, you gain confidence in your newspaper circulation and cross-media metrics, credibility with local and national advertisers, and visibility for your vibrant brand story with a custom Brand View profile in AAM's Media Intelligence Center. Learn more at auditedmedia.com.
Company Profile: Joe Hardin (VP, Product Leadership); Brian Condon (EVP, Com. Dev.); Kevin Rehberg (Dir., Client Dev.)
Special Notes: Susan Kantor

BAYSIDE

BASEBALL WRITERS ASSOCIATION OF AMERICA

Street address 1: PO Box 610611
Street address state: NY
Postal code: 11361-0611
County: Queens
Country: USA
Mailing address 1: PO Box 610611
Mailing city: Bayside
Mailing state: NY
Mailing zip: 11361-0611
Office phone: (718) 767-2582
Office fax: (718) 767-2583
Other phone: bbwaa@aol.com
General e-mail: http://bbwaa.com
Advertising e-mail: 1908
Year established: Elections held in Oct
Company Profile: Jack O'Connell (Secretary-Treasurer)
Special Notes: Jack O'Connell

BERKELEY

NATIONAL ASSOCIATION OF SCIENCE WRITERS

Street address 1: PO Box 7905
Street address state: CA

Postal code: 94707-0905
County: Alameda
Country: USA
Mailing address 1: PO Box 7905
Mailing city: Berkeley
Mailing state: CA
Mailing zip: 94707-0905
Office phone: 510-647-9500
Other phone: director@nasw.org
General e-mail: www.nasw.org
Advertising e-mail: 1934
Special Notes: Tinsley Davis

BOCA RATON

NATIONAL ASSOCIATION OF REAL ESTATE EDITORS (NAREE)

Street address 1: 1003 NW 6th Ter
Street address state: FL
Postal code: 33486-3455
County: Palm Beach
Country: USA
Mailing address 1: 1003 NW 6th Ter
Mailing city: Boca Raton
Mailing state: FL
Mailing zip: 33486-3455
Office phone: (561) 391-3599
Office fax: (561) 391-0099
Other phone: madkimba@aol.com
General e-mail: www.naree.org
Advertising e-mail: 1929
Web address: Professional association of writers, editors, columnists, bloggers and editors covering residential, commercial and financial real estate founded in 1929. Members meet three times per year in different cities. Writer workshops, editor exchange and freelancer forum at 47th annual conference - June 2013 in Atlanta. Plus panels on all aspects of real estate and home and urban design. Details on www.naree.org.
Year established: 63rd Annual Journalism Competition - Entry Deadline March 1, 2013 for work published in 2012. Platinum, Gold, Silver and Bronze Awards, plus awards for Best Freelance Collection and Best Young Journalist. 25 categories for journalists specializing in residential and commercial real estate, mortgage finance, green building, home design and urban planning. New category this year: "Best Breaking News Report."
Company Profile: Mary Doyle-Kimball (Executive Director)
Special Notes: Mary Doyle-Kimball

BRYAN

NORTH AMERICAN AGRICULTURAL JOURNALISTS

Street address 1: 6434 Hurta Ln
Street address state: TX
Postal code: 77808-9283
County: Brazos
Country: USA
Mailing address 1: 6434 Hurta Ln
Mailing city: Bryan
Mailing state: TX
Mailing zip: 77808-9283
Office phone: (979) 845-2872
Office fax: (979) 862-1202
Other phone: ka-phillips@tamu.edu
General e-mail: www.naaj.net
Year established: Elections held in April
Company Profile: Kathleen Phillips (Exec. Sec./ Treasurer)
Special Notes: Kathleen Phillips

BUFFALO

NEW YORK MEDIA CREDIT GROUP

Street address 1: 1100 Main St
Street address state: NY
Postal code: 14209-2308
County: Erie
Country: USA
Mailing address 1: 1100 Main St
Mailing city: Buffalo
Mailing state: NY
Mailing zip: 14209-2308
Office phone: 716-887-9547
Office fax: 716-878-0479
Other phone: robert.gagliardi@abc-amega.com
Year established: Elections held in March
Company Profile: Robert Gagliardi (Regional Account Manager); Nina Link (Pres.); Vaughn P. Benjamin (Dir.)
Special Notes: Robert Gagliardi; Vaughn P. Benjamin

CAMDENTON

NORTH AMERICAN MATURE PUBLISHERS ASSOCIATION

Street address 1: 1140 Jupiter Rd
Street address state: MO
Postal code: 65020-4403
County: Camden
Country: USA
Mailing address 1: PO Box 19510
Mailing city: Shreveport
Mailing state: LA
Mailing zip: 71149-0510
Office phone: (877) 466-2672
Office fax: (573) 873-9993
Other phone: kzarky@maturepublishers.com
General e-mail: www.maturepublishers.com
Year established: Election held in Nov
Company Profile: Karen Zarky (Exec. Dir.)
Special Notes: Karen Zarky

CHICAGO

AMERICAN MARKETING ASSOCIATION

Street address 1: 311 S Wacker Dr
Street address 2: Ste 5800
Street address state: IL
Postal code: 60606-6629
County: Cook
Country: USA
Mailing address 1: 311 S Wacker Dr Ste 5800
Mailing city: Chicago
Mailing state: IL
Mailing zip: 60606-6629
Office phone: (312) 542-9000
Office fax: (312) 542-9001
Other phone: info@ama.org
General e-mail: www.marketingpower.com
Advertising e-mail: 1937
Year established: Elections held in spring

CATHOLIC PRESS ASSOCIATION

Street address 1: 205 W Monroe St
Street address 2: Ste 470
Street address state: IL
Postal code: 60606-5011
County: Cook
Country: USA
Mailing address 1: 205 W Monroe St Ste 470
Mailing city: Chicago
Mailing state: IL
Mailing zip: 60606-5011
Office phone: (312) 380-6789
Office fax: (312) 361-0256
Other phone: cathjourn@catholicpress.org
General e-mail: www.catholicpress.org
Web address: An association of 230 Catholic publications and 620 additional individual members with a combined circulation of 10 million households. Provides education, networking and an annual conference for members primarily in North America.
Year established: Elections held in Feb
Company Profile: Timothy Walter (Exec. Dir)
Special Notes: Timothy Walter

INTERNATIONAL PRESS CLUB OF CHICAGO (IPCC)

Street address 1: PO Box 2498
Street address state: IL
Postal code: 60690-2498
County: Cook
Country: USA
Mailing address 1: PO Box 2498
Mailing city: Chicago
Mailing state: IL
Mailing zip: 60690-2498
Telephone country code: 312-834-7728
Telephone city code: Chicago
Office phone: 312-834-7228
Other phone: info@ipcc.org
General e-mail: www.internationalpressclubofchicago.org
Advertising e-mail: 1992
Web address: One of the oldest press club of Chicago. Publishers, editors, writers, television, newspapers, magazines, radio, educators
Year established: Lunch meetings every Thursday monthly at Union League Club Chicago
Company Profile: Wayne Toberman (President)
Special Notes: Wayne Toberman

NATIONAL PAPER TRADE ASSOCIATION, INC.

Street address 1: 330 N Wabash Ave
Street address 2: Ste 2000
Street address state: IL
Postal code: 60611-7621
County: Cook
Country: USA
Mailing address 1: 330 N Wabash Ave Ste 2000
Mailing city: Chicago
Mailing state: IL
Mailing zip: 60611-7621
Office phone: (312) 321-4092
Office fax: (312) 673-6736
Other phone: npta@gonpta.com
General e-mail: www.gonpta.com
Advertising e-mail: 1903
Year established: Elections held in Oct
Company Profile: Newell Holt (Pres.)
Special Notes: Newell Holt

COATESVILLE

DOG WRITERS' ASSOCIATION OF AMERICA

Street address 1: 173 Union Rd
Street address state: PA
Postal code: 19320-1326
County: Chester
Country: USA
Mailing address 1: 173 Union Rd
Mailing city: Coatesville
Mailing state: PA
Mailing zip: 19320-1326
Office phone: (610) 384-2436
Office fax: (610) 384-2471
Other phone: dwaa@dwaa.org
General e-mail: www.dwaa.org
Advertising e-mail: 1935
Year established: Elections held in Feb. Writers contest closes Sept. 1 each year
Company Profile: Pat Santi (Sec.); Dr. Carmen Battaglia (Pres.); Carmen Battaglia (Pres.)
Special Notes: Pat Santi

COLLEGE PARK

NATIONAL ASSOCIATION OF BLACK JOURNALISTS

Street address 1: 1100 Knight Hall
Street address 2: Suite 3100
Street address state: MD
Postal code: 20742-0001
County: Prince Georges
Country: USA
Mailing address 1: 1100 Knight Hall
Mailing address 2: Suite 3100
Mailing city: College Park
Mailing state: MD
Mailing zip: 20742-0001
Office phone: (301) 405-0248
Office fax: (301) 314-1714
Other phone: nabj@nabj.org
General e-mail: www.nabj.org
Year established: Elections held every two years
Company Profile: Drew Berry (Exec. Dir.); Kathy Times (Pres.)
Special Notes: Drew Berry

COLLEGE PARK

SOCIETY FOR FEATURES JOURNALISM

Street address 1: 1100 Knight Hall
Street address state: MD
Postal code: 20742-0001
County: Prince Georges
Country: USA
Mailing address 1: 1100 Knight Hall
Mailing city: College Park
Mailing state: MD
Mailing zip: 20742-0001
Office phone: (301) 314-2631
Office fax: (301) 314-9166
Other phone: aasfe@jmail.umd.edu
General e-mail: www.aasfe.org
Advertising e-mail: 19473
Year established: Elections held in Sept./Oct
Company Profile: Denise Joyce (Pres.); Kalyani Chadda (Exec. Dir.)
Special Notes: Merrilee Cox

COLUMBIA

AMERICAN SOCIETY OF NEWS EDITORS

Street address 1: 209 Reynolds Journalism Institute
Street address 2: Missouri School of Journalism
Street address state: MO
Postal code: 65211-0001
County: Boone
Country: USA
Mailing address 1: 209 Reynolds Journalism Institute
Mailing address 2: Missouri School of Journalism
Mailing city: Columbia
Mailing state: MO
Mailing zip: 65211-0001
Office phone: (573)884-2405
Office fax: (573)884-3824
Other phone: asne@asne.org
General e-mail: www.asne.org
Advertising e-mail: 1922
Web address: The American Society of News Editors focuses on leadership development and journalism-related issues. Founded in 1922 as a nonprofit professional organization, ASNE promotes fair, principled journalism, defends and protects First Amendment rights, and fights for freedom of information and open government. Leadership, innovation, diversity and inclusion in coverage and the journalism work force, opinion journalism, news literacy and the sharing of ideas are also key ASNE initiatives.
Year established: Elections held in June
Company Profile: Teri Hayt (Exec. Dir.); Jiyoung Won (Comm. Mgr.); Megan Schumacher (Sr. Info. Specialist)
Special Notes: Teri Hayt

ASSOCIATION FOR EDUCATION IN JOURNALISM AND MASS COMMUNICATION

Street address 1: 234 Outlet Pointe Blvd
Street address 2: Ste A

Associations, Clubs and Press Clubs - National and International

Street address state: SC
Postal code: 29210-5667
County: Lexington
Country: USA
Mailing address 1: 234 Outlet Pointe Blvd Ste A
Mailing city: Columbia
Mailing state: SC
Mailing zip: 29210-5667
Office phone: (803) 798-0271
Office fax: (803) 772-3509
Other phone: aejmchq@aol.com
General e-mail: www.aejmc.org
Advertising e-mail: 1912
Web address: AEJMC is an international association of more than 3,400 journalism and mass communication faculty, students, and administrators as well as a few professionals.
Year established: Elections held in March; conventions in early August.
Company Profile: Jennifer McGill (Exec. Dir.)
Special Notes: Jennifer McGill

ASSOCIATION OF SCHOOLS OF JOURNALISM AND MASS COMMUNICATION

Street address 1: 234 Outlet Pointe Blvd
Street address 2: Ste A
Street address state: SC
Postal code: 29210-5667
County: Lexington
Country: USA
Mailing address 1: 234 Outlet Pointe Blvd Ste A
Mailing city: Columbia
Mailing state: SC
Mailing zip: 29210-5667
Office phone: (803) 798-0271
Office fax: (803) 772-3509
Other phone: aejmchq@aol.com
Other fax: aejmcwebsite@aol.com
General e-mail: www.asjmc.org
Advertising e-mail: 1912
Year established: Elections held in April
Company Profile: Jennifer McGill (Exec. Dir.)
Special Notes: Jennifer McGill

INVESTIGATIVE REPORTERS AND EDITORS (IRE)

Street address 1: 141 Neff Annex
Street address state: MO
Postal code: 65211-0001
County: Boone
Country: USA
Mailing address 1: 141 Neff Anx
Mailing city: Columbia
Mailing state: MO
Mailing zip: 65211-0001
Office phone: (573) 882-2042
Office fax: (573) 882-5431
Other phone: info@ire.org
General e-mail: www.ire.org
Advertising e-mail: 1975
Year established: Elections held in June
Company Profile: Mark Horvit (Exec. Dir.)
Special Notes: Mark Horvit

KAPPA ALPHA MU HONORARY SOCIETY IN PHOTO JOURNALISM

Street address 1: 316F Lee Hills Hall
Street address state: MO
Postal code: 65211-1370
County: Boone
Country: USA
Mailing address 1: 316F Lee Hills Hall
Mailing city: Columbia
Mailing state: MO
Mailing zip: 65211-1370
Office phone: 573-882-4821
Office fax: 573-884-5400
Other phone: kratzerb@missouri.edu
General e-mail: www.photojournalism.missouri.edu

Year established: An affiliate of the National Press Photographers Association. Elections held in the fall.
Company Profile: David Rees (Chrmn.); Brian Kratzer (Director of Photography, Assistant Professor)
Special Notes: David Rees; Brian Kratzer

KAPPA TAU ALPHA NATIONAL HONOR SOCIETY FOR JOURNALISM & MASS COMMUNICATION

Street address 1: University of Missouri
Street address 2: 76 Gannett Hall
Street address state: MO
Postal code: 65211-0001
County: Boone
Country: USA
Mailing address 1: University of Missouri
Mailing address 2: 76 Gannett Hall
Mailing city: Columbia
Mailing state: MO
Mailing zip: 65211-1200
Office phone: (573) 882-7685
Office fax: (573) 884-1720
Other phone: umcjourkta@missouri.edu
General e-mail: www.kappataualpha.org
Advertising e-mail: 1910
Year established: Elections held every two years
Company Profile: Jeff Fruit (P, Kent State University); Holly Hunt (VP, Arkansas State); Beverly Horvit (Exec. Dir./Treasurer)
Special Notes: Beverly Horvit

NATIONAL ASSOCIATION OF CREDIT MANAGEMENT

Street address 1: 8840 Columbia 100 Pkwy
Street address state: MD
Postal code: 21045-2100
County: Howard
Country: USA
Mailing address 1: 8840 Columbia 100 Pkwy
Mailing city: Columbia
Mailing state: MD
Mailing zip: 21045-2100
Office phone: (410) 740-5560
Office fax: (410) 740-5574
Other phone: info@nacm.org
General e-mail: www.nacm.org
Year established: Elections held in May
Company Profile: Caroline Zimmerman (Dir., Commun.); James E. Vanghel (Treasurer); Robin D. Schauseil (Pres.)
Special Notes: Robin D. Schauseil

RELIGION NEWS ASSOCIATION

Street address 1: University of Missouri
Street address 2: 30 Neff Annex
Street address state: MO
Postal code: 65211-0001
County: Boone
Country: USA
Mailing address 1: 30 Neff Annex
Mailing city: Columbia
Mailing state: MO
Mailing zip: 65211-0001
Office phone: (740)263-7875
Advertising fax: (740) 263-7875
Other phone: McCallen@RNA.org
Other fax: wendy@rrna.org
General e-mail: www.RNA.org
Advertising e-mail: 1949
Web address: RNA encourages excellence in reporting religion in the mainstream media.
Company Profile: Tiffany McCallen (Chief Ops. Officer); Amy Schiska (Business Mgr.)
Special Notes: Tiffany McCallen

DALLAS

INTERNATIONAL NEWS MEDIA

ASSOCIATION (INMA)
Street address 1: PO Box 740186
Street address state: TX
Postal code: 75374-0186
County: Dallas
Country: USA
Mailing address 1: PO Box 740186
Mailing city: Dallas
Mailing state: TX
Mailing zip: 75374-0186
Office phone: (214) 373-9111
Office fax: (214) 373-9112
Other phone: inma@inma.org
General e-mail: www.inma.org
Year established: Elections held in May
Company Profile: Earl J. Wilkinson (Exec. Dir.); Kris Williams (Membership Director); Dawn McMullan (Senior Editor); Shelley Seale (Editor); Raquel Melkle (Business Development Manager)
Special Notes: Earl J. Wilkinson

DENVER

GRAVURE ASSOCIATION OF AMERICA

Street address 1: 8281 Pine Lake Rd
Street address state: NC
Postal code: 28037-8812
County: Lincoln
Country: USA
Mailing address 1: 8281 Pine Lake Rd
Mailing city: Denver
Mailing state: NC
Mailing zip: 28037-8812
Office phone: (201) 523-6042
Office fax: (201) 523-6048
Other phone: gaa@gaa.org
General e-mail: www.gaa.org
Year established: Elections held in April
Company Profile: Bill Martin (Pres./CEO); Bernadette Carlson (Exec. Dir.); Michelle Jones Aronowitz (Dir.); Roger Ynosroza (Ed.)
Special Notes: Philip Pimlott

DURHAM

NATIONAL PRESS PHOTOGRAPHERS ASSOCIATION, INC.

Street address 1: 3200 Croasdaile Dr
Street address 2: Ste 306
Street address state: NC
Postal code: 27705-2588
County: Durham
Country: USA
Mailing address 1: 3200 Croasdaile Dr Ste 306
Mailing city: Durham
Mailing state: NC
Mailing zip: 27705-2588
Office phone: (919) 383-7246
Office fax: (919) 383-7261
Other phone: info@nppa.org
General e-mail: www.nppa.org
Advertising e-mail: 1946
Year established: Elections held in June
Company Profile: Jim Straight (Exec. Dir.); Mindy Hutchison (Membership Dir.)
Special Notes: Mindy Hutchison

FALLS CHURCH

NATIONAL FEDERATION OF PRESS WOMEN

Street address 1: 200 Little Falls St
Street address 2: Ste 405
Street address state: VA
Postal code: 22046-4302
County: Falls Church City
Country: USA
Mailing address 1: PO Box 5556
Mailing city: Arlington
Mailing state: VA
Mailing zip: 22205-0056

Office phone: 800-780-2715
Office fax: (703) 237-9808
Other phone: presswomen@aol.com
General e-mail: www.nfpw.org
Advertising e-mail: 1937
Year established: Elections held odd years in June
Company Profile: Carol Pierce (Executive Director)
Special Notes: Carol Pierce

FLORENCE

NATIONAL ASSOCIATION OF REAL ESTATE PUBLISHERS

Street address 1: PO Box 5292
Street address state: SC
Postal code: 29502-5292
County: Florence
Country: USA
Other phone: narep2014@gmail.com
General e-mail: www.narep.org
Year established: Elections held in May
Company Profile: Sheila Stepp (Secretary/Treasurer)
Special Notes: Sheila Stepp

FRANKFURT

WORLD ASSOCIATION OF NEWSPAPERS AND NEWS PUBLISHERS (WAN-IFRA)

Street address 1: Rotfeder-Ring 11
Postal code: 60327
Country: Germany
Mailing address 1: Rotfeder-Ring 11
Mailing city: Frankfurt
Mailing zip: 60327
Telephone country code: 49
Telephone city code: 69
Office phone: 240063-0
Office fax: 240063-300
Other phone: info@wan-ifra.org
General e-mail: www.wan-ifra.org
Company Profile: Vincent PeyrÃ`gne (CEO)
Special Notes: Yvonne Zimmermann; Vincent Peyregne

FRANKFURT AM MAIN

WORLD ASSOCIATION OF NEWSPAPERS AND NEWS PUBLISHERS (WAN-IFRA)

Street address 1: Rotfeder-Ring 11
Postal code: 60327
Country: Germany
Mailing address 1: Rotfeder-Ring 11
Mailing city: Frankfurt am Main
Mailing zip: 60327
Telephone country code: 49
Telephone city code: 69
Office phone: 240063-0
Office fax: 240063-300
Advertising phone: 240063-289
Other phone: info@wan-ifra.org
Other fax: maria.belem@wan-ifra.org
General e-mail: www.wan-ifra.org
Advertising e-mail: WAN: 1948 / IFRA: 1961 / WAN-IFRA: 2009
Web address: The World Association of Newspapers and News Publishers, or WAN-IFRA, is the global organisation of the world€™s press. It derives its authority from its global network of 3,000 news publishing companies and technology entrepreneurs, and its legitimacy from its 80 member publisher associations representing 18,000 publications in 120 countries. Our mission is to defend and promote press freedom, clear the way to innovation and help independent news publishing companies to succeed in their transformation process, increase their

HALES CORNERS

INTERMARKET AGENCY NETWORK

Street address 1: 5307 S 92nd St
Street address state: WI
Postal code: 53130-1681
County: Milwaukee
Country: USA
Mailing address 1: 5307 S 92nd St
Mailing city: Hales Corners
Mailing state: WI
Mailing zip: 53130-1677
Office phone: (414) 425-8800
Office fax: (414) 425-0021
General e-mail: www.intermarketnetwork.com
Company Profile: Bill Eisner (Exec. Dir.)
Special Notes: Bill Eisner

HARRISBURG

ASSOCIATION OF AMERICAN EDITORIAL CARTOONISTS

Street address 1: 3899 N Front St
Street address state: PA
Postal code: 17110-1583
County: Dauphin
Country: USA
Mailing address 1: 3899 N Front St
Mailing city: Harrisburg
Mailing state: PA
Mailing zip: 17110-1583
Office phone: (717) 703-3003
Office fax: (717) 703-3008
Other phone: info@pa-news.org; aaec@pa-news.org
General e-mail: www.editorialcartoonists.com
Web address: The Association of American Editorial Cartoonists is a professional association concerned with promoting the interests of staff, freelance and student editorial cartoonists in the United States. The AAEC sponsors a Cartoons for the Classroom program designed to aid educators at all levels in teaching history, economics, social studies and current events. We have an annual convention, typically in June, to give member cartoonists an opportunity to meet and consider issues through panel discussions and guest speakers.
Year established: Elections held each year at the annual convention.
Company Profile: Teresa Shaak (Manager)
Special Notes: Teresa Shaak

INDIANAPOLIS

SOCIETY OF PROFESSIONAL JOURNALISTS

Street address 1: 3909 N Meridian St
Street address 2: Ste 200
Street address state: IN
Postal code: 46208-4011
County: Marion
Country: USA
Mailing address 1: 3909 N Meridian St
Mailing address 2: Suite 200
Mailing city: Indianapolis
Mailing state: IN
Mailing zip: 46208-4011
Office phone: (317) 927-8000
Office fax: (317) 920-4789
Other phone: spj@spj.org
General e-mail: www.spj.org
Advertising e-mail: 1909
Company Profile: Alison McKenzie (Executive Director)
Special Notes: Alison McKenzie

IOWA CITY

QUILL AND SCROLL SOCIETY

Street address 1: 100 Adler Journalism Bldg Ste W111
Street address 2: Univ. of Iowa School of Journalism and Mass Comm.
Street address state: IA
Postal code: 52242-2004
County: Johnson
Country: USA
Office phone: (319) 335-3457
Office fax: (319) 335-3989
Other phone: quill-scroll@uiowa.edu
General e-mail: www.uiowa.edu
Advertising e-mail: 1926
Special Notes: JUDY HAUGE

IRVING

PROMOTIONAL PRODUCTS ASSOCIATION INTERNATIONAL

Street address 1: 3125 Skyway Cir N
Street address state: TX
Postal code: 75038-3526
County: Dallas
Country: USA
Mailing address 1: 3125 Skyway Cir N
Mailing city: Irving
Mailing state: TX
Mailing zip: 75038-3539
Office phone: 972-252-0404
Office fax: (972) 258-3004
Other phone: pr@ppai.org
General e-mail: www.ppai.org
Advertising e-mail: 1903
Company Profile: Paul Bellantone (Vice Pres., Mktg./Commun.); Steve Slagle (Pres./CEO)
Special Notes: Paul Bellantone

JACKSON

NEWSPAPER ASSOCIATION MANAGERS, INC.

Street address 1: 371 Edgewood Terrace
Street address state: MS
Postal code: 39206
County: Hinds
Country: USA
Mailing address 1: 371 Edgewood Terrace
Mailing city: Jackson
Mailing state: MS
Mailing zip: 39206
Office phone: (601) 981-3060
Office fax: (601) 981-3676
Other phone: mlp52@comcast.net
General e-mail: www.nammembers.com
Advertising e-mail: 1923
Web address: Trade association for managers of press associations in US and Canada.
Year established: Elections held in Aug
Company Profile: Michelle Rea (President); Steve Nixon (Vice President)
Special Notes: ()

JENKINTOWN

SOCIETY OF ENVIRONMENTAL JOURNALISTS (SEJ)

Street address 1: PO Box 2492
Street address 2: Suite 301
Street address state: PA
Postal code: 19046-8492
County: Montgomery
Country: USA
Mailing address 1: PO Box 2492
Mailing city: Jenkintown
Mailing state: PA
Mailing zip: 19046-8492
Office phone: (215) 884-8174
Office fax: (215) 884-8175
Other phone: sej@sej.org
General e-mail: www.sej.org
Advertising e-mail: 1990
Web address: SEJ is a 501(c)3 Educational Membership Association of Journalists in Print, Broadcast and Online News Media, dedicated to strengthening the quality, reach and viability of journalism across all media to advance public understanding of environmental issues. Programs include comprehensive website, annual conference
Year established: Board elections held each fall
Company Profile: Beth Parke (Exec. Dir.)
Special Notes: Beth Parke

JOPLIN

INTERNATIONAL SOCIETY OF WEEKLY NEWSPAPER EDITORS

Street address 1: 3950 Newman Rd
Street address state: MO
Postal code: 64801-1512
County: Jasper
Country: USA
Mailing address 1: 3950 Newman Rd
Mailing city: Joplin
Mailing state: MO
Mailing zip: 64801-1512
Office phone: (417) 625-9736
Office fax: (417) 659-4445
Other phone: stebbins-c@mssu.edu
General e-mail: www.iswne.org
Advertising e-mail: 1955
Web address: ISWNE was founded in 1955 to encourage and promote high standards of editorial writing, to facilitate the exchange of ideas, and to foster freedom of the press in all nations. We publish a monthly newsletter and Grassroots Editor, a quarterly journal.
Year established: Elections held in June or July at the annual conference.
Company Profile: Chad Stebbins (Exec. Dir.); Jan Haupt (Webmaster)
Special Notes: Chad Stebbins

KANKAKEE

HUBERGROUP USA, INC.

Street address 1: 2850 Festival Drive
Street address state: IL
Postal code: 60901
County: Kankakee
Country: USA
Mailing address 1: 2850 Festival Drive
Mailing city: Kankakee
Mailing state: IL
Mailing zip: 60901
Office phone: (815) 929-9293
Office fax: (815) 929-0412
Other phone: info.us@hubergroup.com
General e-mail: www.cpima.org
Advertising e-mail: 1934
Year established: Elections held in Aug. for a two year term
Company Profile: Dorothea Nace (Exec. Dir./Sec./Treasurer); Neil Marshall (Pres.); Vivy da Costa (Vice Pres.)
Special Notes: Michelle Connolly

LAKE CITY

LOCAL MEDIA ASSOCIATION

Street address 1: PO Box 450
Street address state: MI
Postal code: 49651-0450
County: Missaukee
Country: USA
Mailing address 1: P.O. Box 450
Mailing city: Lake City
Mailing state: MI
Mailing zip: 49651-0450
Office phone: (888) 486-2466
Office fax: (888) 317-0856
Other phone: hq@localmedia.org
General e-mail: www.localmedia.org
Advertising e-mail: 1971
Year established: Elections held in the fall
Company Profile: Nancy Lane (CEO); Lindsey Estes (Sales & Marketing Manager); Janice Norman (Accounting & Finance Director); Jack Zavoral (Director of Sales)
Special Notes: Lindsey Estes

LAVAL

HEBDOS QUEBEC

Street address 1: 2550 Daniel-Johnson,
Street address 2: Bureau 345
Street address state: QC
Postal code: H7T 2L1
County: QC
Country: Canada
Mailing address 1: 2550 Daniel-Johnson
Mailing address 2: Bureau 345
Mailing city: Laval
Mailing state: QC
Mailing zip: H7T 2L1
Telephone city code: 514
Office phone: (514) 861-2088
Office fax: (514) 861-1966
Other phone: communications@hebdos.com
General e-mail: hebdos.com
Advertising e-mail: 1932
Web address: Hebdos Québec is a not-for-profit organization created in 1932. The association promotes the local independent press in Québec, supports its development and takes concerted action on its behalf. Hebdos Québec represents 31 independent French-language weeklies that together reach some 1.5 million readers every week.
Company Profile: Gilber Paquette (Exec. Dir.)
Special Notes: Gilber Paquette

LAWRENCE

ACCREDITING COUNCIL ON EDUCATION IN JOURNALISM AND MASS COMMUNICATIONS

Street address 1: University of Kansas
Street address 2: 1435 Jayhawk Blvd.
Street address state: KS
Postal code: 66045-0001
County: Douglas
Country: USA
Mailing address 1: Stauffer-Flint Hall
Mailing address 2: 1435 Jayhawk Blvd
Mailing city: Lawrence
Mailing state: KS
Mailing zip: 66045-7575
Office phone: (785) 864-3973
Office fax: (785)864-5225
Other phone: sshaw@ku.edu
General e-mail: www.acejmc.org
Advertising e-mail: 1947
Company Profile: Peter Bhatia (Pres); Susanne Shaw (Exec. Dir.); Paul Parsons (Vice President)
Special Notes: Cheryl Klug

LIVERPOOL

ASSOCIATION OF FREE COMMUNITY PAPERS

Street address 1: 7445 Morgan Rd
Street address 2: Ste 203
Street address state: NY
Postal code: 13090-3990
County: Onondaga
Country: USA
Mailing address 1: 7445 Morgan Rd Ste 5
Mailing address 2: Suite 103
Mailing city: Liverpool
Mailing state: NY
Mailing zip: 13090-3990
Office phone: 877-203-2327
Office fax: 781-859-7770
Other phone: loren@afcp.org
General e-mail: www.afcp.org

---

business and perform their crucial role in open societies. (See: http://www.wan-ifra.org/who-we-are)
Year established: Elections held every two years in June.
Company Profile: Michael Golden (WAN-IFRA President); Vincent Peyrègne (WAN-IFRA CEO)
Special Notes: Cherilyn Ireton

Associations, Clubs and Press Clubs - National and International

Web address: The Association of Free Community Papers represents publishers of community papers from coast to coast, reaching millions of homes on a weekly, biweekly or monthly basis. These papers are united in providing the best advertising coverage to their clients and valuable advertising information to their strong and loyal readership base.
Company Profile: Loren Colburn (Executive Director); Alix Browne (Administrative Assistant); Cassey Recore (Administrative Assistant); Dave Neuharth (Editor); Barbara Holmes (Production Manager); Wendy MacDonald (Marketing Representative)
Special Notes: Loren Colburn

LOUISVILLE

ADVERTISING MEDIA CREDIT EXECUTIVES ASSOCIATION INTERNATIONAL

Street address 1: PO Box 43514
Street address state: KY
Postal code: 40253-0514
County: Jefferson
Country: USA
Mailing address 1: PO Box 40253
Mailing city: Louisville
Mailing state: KY
Mailing zip: 40253
General e-mail: www.amcea.org
Advertising e-mail: 1953
Year established: Elections held in May
Company Profile: Norman Taylor (President)
Special Notes: ()

MAITLAND

NATIONAL CARTOONISTS SOCIETY

Street address 1: 341 N Maitland Ave
Street address 2: Ste 130
Street address state: FL
Postal code: 32751-4761
County: Orange
Country: USA
Mailing address 1: 341 N Maitland Ave Ste 260
Mailing city: Maitland
Mailing state: FL
Mailing zip: 32751-4782
Office phone: (407) 647-8839
Office fax: (407) 629-2502
Other phone: crowsegal@crowsegal.com
General e-mail: www.reuben.org
Advertising e-mail: 1946
Year established: Elections held annually
Company Profile: Jeff Keane (Pres.)
Special Notes: Jeff Keane

MARKHAM

RTDNA - CANADA (RADIO TELEVISION DIGITAL NEWS ASSOCIATION)

Street address 1: 2800 - 14th Ave.
Street address 2: Ste. 210
Street address state: ON
Postal code: L3R 0E4
Country: Canada
Office phone: (416) 756 2213
Office fax: (416) 491-1670
Other phone: sherry@associationconcepts.ca; info@rtdnacanada.com
General e-mail: www.rtdnacanada.com
Advertising e-mail: 1962
Web address: RTDNA Canada is a progressive organization offering a forum for open discussion and action in the broadcast news industry. The Association speaks for the leaders of Canada's radio and television news operations on the issues that impact the newsroom. RTDNA fosters education, career development, national and regional awards recognition, and active dialogue with the membership. Benefits of Membership Â•RTDNA Online Job Bank Â•Weekly RTDNA Update report on all relevant industry news Â•Representation to the CRTC and government on policy changes Â•National and regional conventions with strong educational and instructional components Â•Prestigious national and regional awards program recognizing excellence in broadcast journalism Â•Annual RTDNF Scholarships awarded to broadcast journalism students Â•Representation on RTDNA International Board of Directors Â•Opportunities to network with news directors, news managers, producers, internet journalists, educators, students and industry-related associates Â•Professional Development Seminars Â•Annual Lifetime Achievement Awards, honouring those who have served with excellence and distinction in Broadcast Journalism
Year established: Elections held in June
Company Profile: Sherry Denesha (Operations Manager)
Special Notes: Sherry Denesha

MARYLAND HEIGHTS

PROFESSIONAL FOOTBALL WRITERS OF AMERICA (PFWA)

Street address 1: 11345 Frontage Ave
Street address state: MO
Postal code: 63043-5000
County: Saint Louis
Country: USA
Mailing address 1: 11345 Frontage Ave
Mailing city: Maryland Heights
Mailing state: MO
Mailing zip: 63043-5000
Office phone: (314) 298-2681
Other phone: hbalzer@aol.com
General e-mail: www.pfwa.org
Advertising e-mail: 1966
Year established: Elections held in Jan
Company Profile: Howard Balzer (Secretary)
Special Notes: Howard Balzer

MIAMI

INTER AMERICAN PRESS ASSOCIATION

Street address 1: 1801 SW 3rd Ave
Street address 2: Fl 7
Street address state: FL
Postal code: 33129-1500
County: Miami-Dade
Country: USA
Mailing address 1: 1801 SW 3rd Ave Fl 7
Mailing city: Miami
Mailing state: FL
Mailing zip: 33129-1487
Office phone: (305) 634-2465
Office fax: (305)635-2272
Other phone: info@sipiapa.org
General e-mail: www.sipiapa.org
Year established: Elections held in Nov
Company Profile: Alfonso Juarez (Librarian); Julio Munoz (Exec. Dir.); Horacio Ruiz (Editor)
Special Notes: Alfonso Juarez

MILTON

THE NATIONAL SOCIETY OF NEWSPAPER COLUMNISTS, INC.

Street address 1: 205 Gun Hill St
Street address state: MA
Postal code: 02186-4026
County: Norfolk
Country: USA
Mailing address 1: 205 Gun Hill Street
Mailing city: Milton
Mailing state: CA
Mailing zip: 02186
Office phone: 617 322-1420
Other phone: director@columnists.com
General e-mail: www.columnists.com
Advertising e-mail: 1972
Web address: A professional organization of newspaper and on-line columnists and bloggers dedicated to education and the improvement of our craft.
Year established: Annual conference held in June.
Company Profile: Suzette Standring (Executive Director (as of January 2017))
Special Notes: Suzette Standring

MINNEAPOLIS

NATIONAL SCHOLASTIC PRESS ASSOCIATION

Street address 1: 2221 University Ave SE
Street address 2: Ste 121
Street address state: MN
Postal code: 55414-3074
County: Hennepin
Country: USA
Mailing address 1: 2221 University Ave SE Ste 121
Mailing city: Minneapolis
Mailing state: MN
Mailing zip: 55414-3074
Office phone: (612) 625-8335
Office fax: 612-605-0072
Other phone: info@studentpress.org
General e-mail: www.studentpress.org
Advertising e-mail: 1921
Company Profile: Logan Aimone (Exec. Dir.)
Special Notes: Logan Aimone

MISSOULA

OUTDOOR WRITERS ASSOCIATION OF AMERICA, INC.

Street address 1: 615 Oak St
Street address 2: Ste 201
Street address state: MT
Postal code: 59801-2469
County: Missoula
Country: USA
Office phone: (406) 728-7434
Office fax: (406) 728-7445
Other phone: info@owaa.org
General e-mail: www.owaa.org
Advertising e-mail: 1927
Web address: The mission of Outdoor Writers Association of America is to improve the professional skills of our members, set the highest ethical and communications standards, encourage public enjoyment and conservation of natural resources, and be mentors for the next generation of professional outdoor communicators. http://owaa.org/about/
Year established: Elections held in Spring
Company Profile: Brandon Shuler (Executive Director)
Special Notes: Jessica Seitz

NEW YORK

AIGA, THE PROFESSIONAL ASSOCIATION FOR DESIGN

Street address 1: 233 Broadway
Street address 2: Suite 1740
Street address state: NY
Postal code: 10279-1803
County: New York
Country: USA
Mailing address 1: 233 Broadway
Mailing address 2: Suite 1740
Mailing city: New York
Mailing state: NY
Mailing zip: 10279-1803
Office phone: (212) 807-1990
General e-mail: www.aiga.org
Advertising e-mail: 1914
Web address: http://aiga.org/about
Year established: AIGA is the professional association for design, a nonprofit organization dedicated to advancing design as a professional craft, strategic tool and vital cultural force. Founded in 1914, AIGA today serves more than 22,000 members through 66 chapters and 200 student groups across the United States. AIGA stimulates thinking about design, demonstrates the value of design and empowers the success of designers at each stage of their careers.
Company Profile: Julie Anixter (Exec. Dir.); Hezron Gurley (CEO/CFO); Amy Chapman (Chief of Staff)
Special Notes: ()

AMERICAN BUSINESS MEDIA

Street address 1: 201 E 42nd St Fl 7
Street address 2: Suite 2200
Street address state: NY
Postal code: 10017-5704
County: New York
Country: USA
Mailing address 1: 201 E 42nd St Rm 2200
Mailing address 2: Suite 2200
Mailing city: New York
Mailing state: NY
Mailing zip: 10017-5714
Office phone: (212) 661-6360
Office fax: (212) 370-0736
Other phone: info@abmmail.com
General e-mail: www.abmassociation.com
Advertising e-mail: 1906
Web address: ABM, the association of business information and media companies, is the center of the global b-to-b ecosystem. As the only association focused on the integrated b-to-b media model Ã¢Â€Â" which includes business information, digital, print and events Ã¢Â€Â" ABM delivers intelligence to industry professionals worldwide, including Madison Avenue, Wall Street and the Beltway. With more than $20 billion in annual revenues, ABM's 200-plus member companies reach an audience of more than 100 million professionals, publish nearly 4,000 print and online titles, and host over 1,000 trade shows.
Year established: Elections held in May
Special Notes: Clark Pettit

AMERICAN BUSINESS MEDIA AGRICULTURAL COUNCIL

Street address 1: 201 E 42nd St
Street address 2: Rm 2200
Street address state: NY
Postal code: 10017-5714
County: New York
Country: USA
Mailing address 1: 201 E 42nd St Rm 2200
Mailing address 2: Suite 2200
Mailing city: New York
Mailing state: NY
Mailing zip: 10017-5714
Office phone: (212) 661-6360
Office fax: (212) 370-0736
Other phone: info@abmmail.com
General e-mail: www.americanbusinessmedia.com
Company Profile: Todd Hittle (Exec. Dir.)
Special Notes: Todd Hittle

AMERICAN SOCIETY OF JOURNALISTS AND AUTHORS

Street address 1: 1501 Broadway
Street address 2: Ste 302
Street address state: NY
Postal code: 10036-5501
County: New York
Country: USA
Mailing address 1: 1501 Broadway Ste 403
Mailing city: New York
Mailing state: NY
Mailing zip: 10036-5507
Office phone: (212) 997-0947

Office fax: (212) 937-2315
Other phone: staff@asja.org
General e-mail: www.asja.org
Advertising e-mail: 1948
Company Profile: Alexandra Owens (Exec. Dir.); Salley Shannon (Pres.)
Special Notes: Alexandra Owens

ANA BUSINESS MARKETING

Street address 1: 708 Third Avenue
Street address 2: 33rd Floor
Street address state: NY
Postal code: 10017
County: Manhattan
Country: USA
Mailing address 1: 708 Third Avenue, 33rd Floor
Mailing city: New York
Mailing state: NY
Mailing zip: 10017
Office phone: (212) 697-5950
Office fax: (212) 687-7310
Other phone: info@ana.net
General e-mail: www.marketing.org
Year established: Elections held in June
Company Profile: Kelly Staley (Membership Mgr.); Patrick Farrey (Exec. Dir.)
Special Notes: Patrick Farrey

ASSOCIATED PRESS MANAGING EDITORS ASSOCIATION

Street address 1: 450 W 33rd St
Street address state: NY
Postal code: 10001-2603
County: New York
Country: USA
Mailing address 1: 450 W 33rd St
Mailing city: New York
Mailing state: NY
Mailing zip: 10001-2603
Office phone: (212) 621-1838
Office fax: (212) 506-6102
Other phone: apme@ap.org
General e-mail: www.apme.com
Advertising e-mail: 1933
Year established: Elections held in Oct
Company Profile: Sally Jacobsen (Gen. Mgr.)
Special Notes: Sally Jacobsen

ASSOCIATION OF NATIONAL ADVERTISERS, INC.

Street address 1: 708 3rd Ave
Street address 2: 33rd Flr.
Street address state: NY
Postal code: 10017-4201
County: New York
Country: USA
Mailing address 1: 708 3rd Ave
Mailing address 2: 33rd Flr.
Mailing city: New York
Mailing state: NY
Mailing zip: 10017-4201
Office phone: (212) 697-5950
Office fax: (212) 687-7310
General e-mail: www.ana.net
Special Notes: Robert D. Liodice

COLLEGE MEDIA ASSOCIATION

Street address 1: 355 Lexington Ave
Street address 2: Fl 15
Street address state: NY
Postal code: 10017-6603
County: New York
Country: USA
Mailing address 1: 355 Lexington Avenue, 15
Mailing city: New York
Mailing state: NY
Mailing zip: 10017
Office phone: 212-297-2195
Other phone: info@collegemedia.org
General e-mail: www.collegemedia.org
Advertising e-mail: 1954
Year established: Elections held in Oct every two years.
Company Profile: Meredith Taylor (Executive Director)
Special Notes: Meredith Taylor

DIGITAL CONTENT NEXT

Street address 1: 1350 Broadway
Street address 2: Rm 606
Street address state: NY
Postal code: 10018-7205
County: New York
Country: USA
Mailing address 1: 1350 Broadway Rm 606
Mailing address 2: Suite 606
Mailing city: New York
Mailing state: NY
Mailing zip: 10018-7205
Office phone: (646) 473-1000
Office fax: (646) 473-0200
Other phone: info@online-publishers.org
General e-mail: www.online-publishers.org
Advertising e-mail: 2001

FOREIGN PRESS ASSOCIATION

Street address 1: 1501 Broadway
Street address 2: 12th Floor
Street address state: NY
Postal code: 10036
County: New York
Country: USA
Mailing address 1: 1501 Broadway, 12th Floor
Mailing city: New York
Mailing state: NY
Mailing zip: 10036
Office phone: (212) 370-1054
Other phone: fpa@foreignpressassociation.org
General e-mail: www.foreignpressassociation.org
Advertising e-mail: 1918
Year established: Elections held in Dec
Company Profile: â€‹David P. Michaels (President); Ian Williams (Vice President); Jeffery P. Laner (Treasurerâ€‹â€‹)
Special Notes: ()

INTERNATIONAL ADVERTISING ASSOCIATION, INC.

Street address 1: 747 3rd Ave
Street address 2: Fl 2
Street address state: NY
Postal code: 10017-2878
County: New York
Country: USA
Mailing address 1: 747 3rd Ave Rm 200
Mailing city: New York
Mailing state: NY
Mailing zip: 10017-2878
Office phone: 646-722-2612
Office fax: 646 722 2501
Other phone: iaa@iaaglobal.org; membership@iaaglobal.org
General e-mail: www.iaaglobal.org
Advertising e-mail: 1938
Year established: Elections held every two years at the IAA World-Advertising Congress. The IAA is a global partnership of advertisers, agencies, and media. The Association has 3,700 members in 95 countries, 105 corporate members, 65 organizational members and 61 chapters
Company Profile: Karl Kam (Mgr. IT.); Michael Lee (Exec. Dir.)
Special Notes: Alison Burns

LEAGUE OF ADVERTISING AGENCIES, INC.

Street address 1: 65 Reade St
Street address 2: Apt 3A
Street address state: NY
Postal code: 10007-1841
County: New York
Country: USA
Mailing address 1: 65 Reade St Apt 3A
Mailing city: New York
Mailing state: NY
Mailing zip: 10007-1841
Office phone: (212) 528-0364
Office fax: (212) 766-1181
General e-mail: www.adagencies.com
Year established: Elections held in May
Company Profile: Deana Boles (Exec. Dir.); Lori Fabisiak (Pres.); Mark Levit (Treasurer); Mindy Gale (Sec.); Richard Harrow (Vice Pres.)
Special Notes: Deana Boles

OVERSEAS PRESS CLUB OF AMERICA

Street address 1: 40 West 45 Street
Street address state: NY
Postal code: 10036
County: New York
Country: USA
Office phone: (212) 626-9220
Office fax: (212) 626-9210
Other phone: info@opcofamerica.org
General e-mail: www.opcofamerica.org
Advertising e-mail: 1939
Web address: The Overseas Press Club of America is the nationâ€™s oldest and largest association of journalists engaged in international news. Every April, it awards the most prestigious prizes devoted exclusively to international news coverage. It was founded in 1939 by nine foreign correspondents in New York City, and has grown to 450 members worldwide. The clubâ€™s mission is to uphold the highest standards in news reporting, advance press freedom and promote good fellowship among colleagues. It also aims to help educate a new generation of journalists and to contribute to the freedom and independence of the press throughout the world.
Year established: Elections held in late summer
Company Profile: Patricia Kranz (Exec. Dir.)
Special Notes: Patricia Kranz

PROMOTION MARKETING ASSOCIATION, INC.

Street address 1: 650 1st Ave
Street address 2: Ste 2-SW
Street address state: NY
Postal code: 10016-3240
County: New York
Country: USA
Mailing address 1: 650 1st Ave Fl 2
Mailing city: New York
Mailing state: NY
Mailing zip: 10016-3207
Office phone: (212) 420-1100
Office fax: (212) 533-7622
Other phone: pma@pmalink.org
General e-mail: www.pmalink.org
Advertising e-mail: 1911
Year established: Elections held in June

PUBLIC RELATIONS SOCIETY OF AMERICA, INC.

Street address 1: 33 Maiden Ln
Street address 2: Fl 11
Street address state: NY
Postal code: 10038-5149
County: New York
Country: USA
Mailing address 1: 33 Maiden Ln Fl 11
Mailing city: New York
Mailing state: NY
Mailing zip: 10038-5150
Office phone: (212) 460-1400
Office fax: (212) 995-0757
Other phone: hq@prsa.org
General e-mail: www.prsa.org
Advertising e-mail: 1947
Year established: Elections held in October
Company Profile: Willam Murray (Pres.)
Special Notes: Willam Murray

SOCIETY OF THE SILURIANS

Street address 1: PO Box 1195
Street address 2: Madison Square Station
Street address state: NY
Postal code: 10159-1195
County: New York
Country: USA
Mailing address 1: PO Box 1195
Mailing address 2: Madison Square Station
Mailing city: New York
Mailing state: NY
Mailing zip: 10159-1195
Office phone: (212) 532-0887
Other phone: silurians@aol.org
General e-mail: www.silurians.org
Advertising e-mail: 1924
Web address: We are an organization of journalists either currently or formerly employed by print, broadcast and digital news organizations in the New York metropolitan area. We conduct two awards dinners each year honoring fellow journalists for outstanding accomplishments; we also host monthly lunches for our members and their guests, featuring speakers from journalism or government. In addition, the Society of the Silurians offers a scholarship award in the name of the late columnist Dennis Duggan to an outstanding student at the CUNY Graduate School of Journalism. We also offer scholarships to journalism schools in the New York metropolitan area.
Year established: Elections of officers and board members held in May
Company Profile: Mort Sheinman (Membership Chairman); David Andelman (President)
Special Notes: Mort Sheinman

THE 4 A'S

Street address 1: 1065 Avenue of the Americas
Street address 2: Fl 16
Street address state: NY
Postal code: 10018-0174
County: New York
Country: USA
Mailing address 1: 1065 Avenue of the Americas Fl 16
Mailing city: New York
Mailing state: NY
Mailing zip: 10018-0174
Office phone: (212) 682-2500
Office fax: (212) 682-8391
Other phone: info@aaaa.com
General e-mail: www.aaaa.org
Advertising e-mail: 1917
Year established: Election held in April
Company Profile: Marla Kaplowitz (Pres. & CEO)
Special Notes: Media Contact

THE ADVERTISING COUNCIL, INC.

Street address 1: 815 2nd Ave
Street address 2: Fl 9
Street address state: NY
Postal code: 10017-4500
County: New York
Country: USA
Mailing address 1: 815 2nd Ave Fl 9
Mailing city: New York
Mailing state: NY
Mailing zip: 10017-4500
Office phone: (212) 922-1500
Office fax: (212) 922-1676
Other phone: info@adcouncil.org
General e-mail: www.adcouncil.org
Advertising e-mail: 1942
Company Profile: Lisa Sherman (Pres. & Chief Exec. Officer)
Special Notes: Laurie Leith

THE ADVERTISING RESEARCH

… **FOUNDATION (ARF)**
Street address 1: 432 Park Ave S
Street address 2: Fl 6
Street address state: NY
Postal code: 10016-8013
County: New York
Country: USA
Mailing address 1: 432 Park Ave S Fl 6
Mailing city: New York
Mailing state: NY
Mailing zip: 10016-8013
Office phone: (212) 751-5656
Office fax: (212) 689-1859
Other phone: help@thearf.org
General e-mail: www.thearf.org
Advertising e-mail: 1936
Year established: Elections held in March
Company Profile: Gayle Fuguitt (CEO & Pres.)
Special Notes: Leslie Hutchings

THE DIRECT MARKETING ASSOCIATION, INC.
Street address 1: 1120 Avenue of the Americas
Street address state: NY
Postal code: 10036-6700
County: New York
Country: USA
Mailing address 1: 1120 Avenue of the Americas Fl 14
Mailing city: New York
Mailing state: NY
Mailing zip: 10036-6713
Office phone: (212) 768-7277
Office fax: (212) 302-6714
General e-mail: www.the-dma.org
Advertising e-mail: 1917
Year established: Elections held in Oct
Company Profile: Lawrence M. Kimmel (CEO)
Special Notes: Joanne L Gamel

UNITED NATIONS CORRESPONDENTS ASSOCIATION
Street address 1: United Nations, Room S-308
Street address state: NY
Postal code: 10017
County: New York
Country: USA
Mailing address 1: United Nations, Rm. S-308
Mailing city: New York
Mailing state: NY
Mailing zip: 10017
Office phone: (212) 963-7137
Other phone: contactus@unca.com
General e-mail: www.unca.com
Year established: Elections held in Dec
Company Profile: Giam Paolo Pioli (Pres.); Louis Charbonneau (1st Vice Pres.); Masood Haider (2nd Vice Pres.)
Special Notes: Office Manager

NORMAN

NATIVE AMERICAN JOURNALISTS ASSOCIATION
Street address 1: 395 W Lindsey St
Street address state: OK
Postal code: 73019-4201
County: Cleveland
Country: USA
Mailing address 1: 395 W Lindsey St
Mailing city: Norman
Mailing state: OK
Mailing zip: 73019-4201
Office phone: (405) 325-1649
Office fax: (405) 325-6945
Other phone: info@naja.com
General e-mail: www.naja.com
Year established: Elections held in August
Company Profile: Cristina Azocar (Pres.); Jeff Harjo (Interim. Dir.)
Special Notes: Jeff Harjo

NORTHFIELD

MEDIA FINANCIAL MANAGEMENT ASSOCIATION
Street address 1: 550 W Frontage Rd
Street address 2: Ste 3600
Street address state: IL
Postal code: 60093-1243
County: Cook
Country: USA
Mailing address 1: 550 W Frontage Rd Ste 3600
Mailing city: Northfield
Mailing state: IL
Mailing zip: 60093-1243
Office phone: 847-716-7000
Office fax: 847-716-7004
Other phone: info@mediafinance.org
Other fax: info@mediafinance.org
General e-mail: www.mediafinance.org
Advertising e-mail: 1961
Web address: The Media Financial Management Association (MFM) is a not-for profit professional association dedicated to the interests and needs of business and finance executives in the media industry. Founded in 1961, MFM (formerly BCFM) membership is open to all industry business professionals. MFM also welcomes associate members from allied fields including: accounting; auditing; brokerage; law; tax; and other related disciplines. The Association£s more than 1,200 active members represent the top financial, general management, IT, internal audit, human resource, and other media management positions from all five major television networks, more than 60 of all network affiliates, 4,000 radio stations, nearly 300 newspaper publishers, in excess of 50 cable programming networks, and cable MSOs throughout the U.S. and Canada.
Company Profile: Mary Collins (President & CEO); Jamie Smith (Director of Operations)
Special Notes: Mary Collins

OAK CREEK

SOCIETY OF AMERICAN TRAVEL WRITERS, INC.
Street address 1: 7044 S 13th St
Street address state: WI
Postal code: 53154-1429
County: Milwaukee
Country: USA
Mailing address 1: 11950 W Lake Park Dr Ste 320
Mailing city: Milwaukee
Mailing state: WI
Mailing zip: 53224-3049
Office phone: (414) 908-4949
Office fax: (414) 768-8001
Other phone: satw@satw.org
General e-mail: www.satw.org
Company Profile: Nancy Short (Exec. Dir.)
Special Notes: Nancy Short

OAKVILLE

CANADIAN BUSINESS PRESS
Street address 1: 2100 Banbury Cresent
Street address state: ON
Postal code: L6H 5P6
Country: Canada
Mailing address 1: 2100 Banbury Crescent
Mailing city: Oakville
Mailing state: ON
Mailing zip: L6H 5P6
Office phone: 905-844-6822
Other phone: torrance@cbp.ca
General e-mail: www.cbp.ca
Company Profile: Trish Torrance (Executive Director)
Special Notes: Trish Torrance

OKLAHOMA CITY

ASSOCIATION OF ALTERNATE POSTAL SYSTEMS
Street address 1: 1725 Oaks Way
Street address state: OK
Postal code: 73131-1220
County: Oklahoma
Country: USA
Mailing address 1: 1725 Oaks Way
Mailing city: Oklahoma City
Mailing state: OK
Mailing zip: 73131-1220
Office phone: (405) 478-0006
Other phone: aaps@cox.net
General e-mail: www.aapsinc.org
Year established: Elections held at annual conference
Company Profile: John White (Exec. Dir.); Michael Lynch (Pres.)
Special Notes: Michael Lynch

ORLANDO

SOCIETY FOR NEWS DESIGN, INC.
Street address 1: 424 E Central Blvd
Street address 2: Ste 406
Street address state: FL
Postal code: 32801-1923
County: Orange
Country: USA
Mailing address 1: 424 E Central Blvd Ste 406
Mailing city: Orlando
Mailing state: FL
Mailing zip: 32801-1923
Office phone: (407) 420-7748
Office fax: (407) 420-7697
Other phone: snd@snd.org
General e-mail: www.snd.org
Advertising e-mail: 1979
Year established: Annual competition deadline is mid-January. Officer elections held in fall prior to annual workshop exhibition.
Company Profile: Stephen Komives (Exec. Dir.)
Special Notes: Stephen Komives

PARIS

ANGLO-AMERICAN PRESS ASSOCIATION OF PARIS
Street address 1: 67 Rue Halle
Postal code: 75014
Country: France
Mailing address 1: 67 Rue Halle
Mailing city: Paris
Mailing zip: 75014
Telephone country code: 33
Telephone city code: 1
Office phone: 4545 7400
Other phone: axelkrause@wanadoo.fr
General e-mail: www.aapafrance.com
Advertising e-mail: 1907
Company Profile: Axel Krause (Sec. Gen.); Georgina Oliver (British Co-Pres.); Gregory Viscusi (American Co-Pres.)
Special Notes: Axel Krause

PARIS

INTERNATIONAL ASSOCIATION OF SPORTS NEWSPAPERS (IASN)
Street address 1: 7 rue Geoffroy Saint Hilaire
Postal code: 75005
Country: France
Mailing address 1: 7 rue Geoffroy Saint Hilaire
Mailing city: Paris
Mailing zip: 75005
Telephone country code: 33
Telephone city code: 1
Office phone: 47 42 85 29
Office fax: 47 42 49 48
Other phone: rcuccoli@press-iasn.org
General e-mail: www.press-iasn.org
Advertising e-mail: 2008
Company Profile: Rosarita Cuccoli (Sec. Gen.)
Special Notes: Rosarita Cuccoli

PARKER

NATIONAL WRITERS ASSOCIATION
Street address 1: 10940 S Parker Rd
Street address 2: Ste 508
Street address state: CO
Postal code: 80134-7440
County: Douglas
Country: USA
Mailing address 1: 10940 S Parker Rd Ste 508
Mailing city: Parker
Mailing state: CO
Mailing zip: 80134-7440
Office phone: (303) 841-0246
Other phone: natlwritersassn@hotmail.com
General e-mail: www.nationalwriters.com
Advertising e-mail: 1937
Web address: This 75-year-old writer's service organization assists writers at all levels with everything from formatting manuscripts to marketing assistance.
Company Profile: Sandy Whelchel (Exec. Dir.)
Special Notes: Sandy Whelchel

PHOENIX

SOCIETY OF AMERICAN BUSINESS EDITORS AND WRITERS, INC.
Street address 1: 555 N Central Ave
Street address 2: Ste 302
Street address state: AZ
Postal code: 85004-1248
County: Maricopa
Country: USA
Office phone: (602) 496-7862
Office fax: (602) 496-7041
Other phone: sabew@sabew.org
General e-mail: www.sabew.org
Advertising e-mail: 1964
Web address: SABEW is an organization of business and economic journalists with 3,500 members
Year established: Elections held in April
Special Notes: Kathleen Graham

PITTSBURGH

MARKETING ADVERTISING GLOBAL NETWORK
Street address 1: 1017 Perry Hwy
Street address 2: Ste 5
Street address state: PA
Postal code: 15237-2173
County: Allegheny
Country: USA
Mailing address 1: 1017 Perry Hwy Ste 5
Mailing city: Pittsburgh
Mailing state: PA
Mailing zip: 15237-2173
Office phone: (412) 366-6850
Office fax: (412) 366-6840
Other phone: cheri@magnetglobal.org
General e-mail: www.magnetglobal.org
Advertising e-mail: 1944
Web address: Independent Advertising Network
Year established: Elections held in Oct
Company Profile: Cheri Gmiter (Executive Director)
Special Notes: Cheri Gmiter

RESTON

GRAPHIC COMMUNICATIONS COUNCIL
Street address 1: 1899 Preston White Dr
Street address state: VA
Postal code: 20191-5458
County: Fairfax
Country: USA

Mailing address 1: 1899 Preston White Dr
Mailing city: Reston
Mailing state: VA
Mailing zip: 20191-5435
Office phone: (703) 264-7200
Office fax: (703) 620-0994
Other phone: npes@npes.org
General e-mail: www.npes.org
Advertising e-mail: 1950
Company Profile: Carol J. Hurlburt (Administrator); Carol Lee Hawkins (Asst. Dir., Membership)
Special Notes: Ralph J. Nappi

RESTON

NPES

Street address 1: 1899 Preston White Dr
Street address state: VA
Postal code: 20191-5458
County: Fairfax
Country: USA
Mailing address 1: 1899 Preston White Dr Ste A
Mailing city: Reston
Mailing state: VA
Mailing zip: 20191-5435
Office phone: (703) 264-7200
Office fax: (703) 620-0994
Other phone: npes@npes.org
General e-mail: www.npes.org
Advertising e-mail: 1933
Year established: NPES is the association for suppliers of printing, publishing and converting technologies. Elections held at fall meeting
Company Profile: Judy Durham (Dir., Commun.); Ralph Nappi (Pres.); Tom Saggiomo (Chrmn.)
Special Notes: Judy Durham

RIO GRANDE

INDEPENDENT FREE PAPERS OF AMERICA

Street address 1: 107 Hemlock Dr
Street address state: NJ
Postal code: 08242-1731
County: Cape May
Country: USA
Mailing address 1: 107 Hemlock Dr
Mailing city: Rio Grande
Mailing state: NJ
Mailing zip: 08242-1731
Office phone: (609) 408-8000
Office fax: (609) 889-0141
General e-mail: www.ifpa.com
Year established: Elections held in Sept
Company Profile: Douglas Fry
Special Notes: Douglas Fry

SAINT PAUL

WORLD PRESS INSTITUTE

Street address 1: 3415 University Ave W
Street address state: MN
Postal code: 55114-1019
County: Ramsey
Country: USA
Mailing address 1: 3415 University Ave W
Mailing city: Saint Paul
Mailing state: MN
Mailing zip: 55114-1019
Office phone: 612-205-7582
Other phone: info@worldpressinstitute.org
General e-mail: www.worldpressinstitute.org
Advertising e-mail: 1961
Web address: The World Press Institute fosters understanding among international journalists about the role and responsibilities of a free press in a democracy and promotes excellence in journalism. Through its fellowship program, WPI brings 10 international journalists to the United States each year to experience the complexities of U.S. life through the prism of a reporter working under First Amendment conditions. The fellowship provides immersion into the governance, politics, business, media, journalistic ethics and culture of the U.S. through a demanding schedule of study, travel and interviews throughout the country.
Company Profile: David McDonald (Exec. Dir.)
Special Notes: David McDonald

SAINT PETERSBURG

ASSOCIATION OF OPINION JOURNALISTS (FORMERLY THE NATIONAL CONFERENCE OF EDITORIAL WRITERS)

Street address 1: 801 3rd St S
Street address state: FL
Postal code: 33701-4920
County: Pinellas
Country: USA
Mailing address 1: 3899 N Front St
Mailing city: Harrisburg
Mailing state: PA
Mailing zip: 33701
Office phone: 727-821-9494
Other phone: david.haynes@jrn.com
General e-mail: aoj.wildapricot.org
Advertising e-mail: 1947
Web address: Founded in 1947 as the National Conference of Editorial Writers, AOJ is a non-profit professional organization that exists to improve the quality of opinion writing across all platforms and to promote high standards among opinion writers and editors. The AOJ Foundation is a 501(c)3 corporation dedicated to promoting the craft of opinion writing in all its forms and supporting the work of the Association of Opinion Journalists.
Special Notes: David Haynes

SAN FRANCISCO

ASIAN AMERICAN JOURNALISTS ASSOCIATION

Street address 1: 5 3rd St
Street address 2: Ste 1108
Street address state: CA
Postal code: 94103-3212
County: San Francisco
Country: USA
Mailing address 1: 5 3rd St Ste 1108
Mailing city: San Francisco
Mailing state: CA
Mailing zip: 94103-3212
Office phone: (415) 346-2051
Office fax: (415) 346-6343
Other phone: national@aaja.org
General e-mail: www.aaja.org
Advertising e-mail: 1981
Company Profile: Annabelle Udo-O'Malley (Contact)
Special Notes: Annabelle Udo-O'Malley

INTERNATIONAL ASSOCIATION OF BUSINESS COMMUNICATORS (IABC)

Street address 1: 601 Montgomery St
Street address 2: Ste 1900
Street address state: CA
Postal code: 94111-2690
County: San Francisco
Country: USA
Mailing address 1: 601 Montgomery St Ste 1900
Mailing city: San Francisco
Mailing state: CA
Mailing zip: 94111-2623
Office phone: (415) 544-4700
Office fax: (415) 544-4747
Other phone: service_centre@iabc.com
General e-mail: www.iabc.com
Year established: Elections held at international conference
Company Profile: Julie Freeman (Pres./CEO)
Special Notes: Kerby Meyers

MEDIA ALLIANCE

Street address 1: 2830 20th St Ste 102
Street address 2: Pacific Felt Factory
Street address state: CA
Postal code: 94110-2825
County: San Francisco
Country: USA
Mailing address 1: Pacific Felt Factory
Mailing address 2: 2830 20th Street, Suite 102
Mailing city: San Francisco
Mailing state: CA
Mailing zip: 94110
Telephone country code: 01
Telephone city code: 415
Office phone: 746-9475
Office fax: N/A
Advertising fax: 510-684-6853
Other phone: tracy@media-alliance.org
General e-mail: www.media-alliance.org
Advertising e-mail: 1976
Web address: Media Alliance is a democratic communications advocate. Our mission is excellence, ethics, diversity, and accountability in all aspects of the media in the interests of peace, justice, and social responsibility. Media Alliance is a leader in building coalitions for press freedom and media access, accountability and alternatives. Our members and allies throughout California are working to ensure that local radio, TV and newspaper outlets are meeting the needs of diverse communities. Tactics include conducting media monitoring, convening town hall forums and meetings with media representatives, and when appropriate, organizing for changes at outlets that are not fulfilling their public interest obligations. Internet freedom is under heavy attack by telecom giants who are spending billions to consolidate. These mega-corporations also exacerbate the digital divide with discriminatory redlining practices. We work actively to bridge the digital divide, create competition, and make sure the Internet stays open for us all. Initially founded as a legal defense committee for journalists under fire, MA actively supports media workers in organizing for better working conditions, freedom from government and law enforcement surveillance, and increased resources for rigorous, investigative, community-based reporting.Media Alliance offers workshops for nonprofit staffers and activists - in three ways. Our regular calender of "Communication Skills for Social Justice Workshops" features working professionals and affordable fees. Customized workshops are available in any of the subjects we teach for groups of five or more. We try to provide capacity building training to under-represented groups to reframe media myths and deliver authentic first-voice expression on important social justice issues.
Company Profile: Tracy Rosenberg (Exec. Dir.)
Special Notes: Tracy Rosenberg

SANTA FE

ASSOCIATION OF FOOD JOURNALISTS, INC.

Street address 1: 7 Avenida Vista Grande
Street address 2: Ste B7 # 467
Street address state: NM
Postal code: 87508-9207
County: Santa Fe
Country: USA
Mailing address 1: 7 Avenida Vista Grande
Mailing address 2: Ste B7 #467
Mailing city: Santa Fe
Mailing state: NM
Mailing zip: 87508-9198
Office phone: 505-466-4742
Other phone: caroldemasters@yahoo.com
General e-mail: www.afjonline.com
Advertising e-mail: 1974
Year established: Election held in summer of even years
Company Profile: Carol DeMasters (Exec. Dir.)
Special Notes: Carol DeMasters

SEATTLE

COUNCIL FOR THE ADVANCEMENT OF SCIENCE WRITING, INC.

Street address 1: PO Box 17337
Street address state: WA
Postal code: 98127
County: King
Country: USA
Mailing address 1: PO Box 17337
Mailing city: SEATTLE
Mailing state: WA
Mailing zip: 98127
Office phone: (206) 880-0177
Other phone: info@casw.org
General e-mail: www.casw.org
Advertising e-mail: 1959
Web address: CASW's core mission is to improve public understanding, appreciation and enjoyment of science by enhancing the quantity and quality of science news reaching the public. CASW's core program activities and fundraising advance this mission by educating science writers, encouraging talented individuals to pursue careers in science writing, promoting good science communication, and supporting and recognizing independent journalism. The Council is made up of senior science journalists and others committed to supporting and improving science writing and public understanding of science.
Year established: Elections held in April. Not a membership organization.
Company Profile: Alan Boyle (Pres.); Rosalind Reid (Exec. Dir.); Sylvia Kantor (Admin. / Comm.Mgr.)
Special Notes: Rosalind Reid

SEWICKLEY

PRINTING INDUSTRIES OF AMERICA

Street address 1: 200 Deer Run Rd
Street address state: PA
Postal code: 15143-2324
County: Allegheny
Country: USA
Mailing address 1: 200 Deer Run Rd
Mailing city: Sewickley
Mailing state: PA
Mailing zip: 15143-2600
Office phone: (412) 741-6860
Office fax: (412) 741-2311
Other phone: printing@printing.org
General e-mail: www.printing.org
Advertising e-mail: 1924
Company Profile: Lisa Erdner (Mktg. Mgr.); Gary Jones (VP)
Special Notes: Joe Deemer

TECHNICAL ASSOCIATION OF THE GRAPHIC ARTS

Street address 1: 200 Deer Run Rd
Street address state: PA
Postal code: 15143-2324
County: Allegheny
Country: USA
Mailing address 1: 200 Deer Run Rd
Mailing city: Sewickley
Mailing state: PA
Mailing zip: 15143-2324
Office phone: (412) 259-1706
Office fax: (412) 741-2311
Other phone: taga@printing.org
General e-mail: www.taga.org
Advertising e-mail: 1948
Year established: Elections held in February
Company Profile: Mark Bohan (Managing Director)
Special Notes: Mark Bohan

Associations, Clubs and Press Clubs - National and International

SHELTON

BPA WORLDWIDE

Street address 1: 100 Beard Sawmill Rd
Street address 2: Fl 6
Street address state: CT
Postal code: 06484-6156
County: Fairfield
Country: USA
Mailing address 1: 100 Beard Sawmill Rd Fl 6
Mailing city: Shelton
Mailing state: CT
Mailing zip: 06484-6151
Office phone: (203) 447-2800
Office fax: (203) 447-2900
General e-mail: www.bpaww.com
Advertising e-mail: 1931
Web address: BPA International is the world's leading auditor of media, including circulations of consumer magazines, business publications, and newspapers; tradeshows; databases; and electronic media.
Year established: Elections held in May
Company Profile: Carole A. Walker (Chairman); Glenn Hansen (Pres./CEO); Karlene Lukeovitz (Vice Pres., Commun.); Richard Murphy (Sr. Vice Pres., Auditing); Peter Black (Sr. Vice Pres., Mktg. Servs.)
Special Notes: Larry Clayman

SPRINGFIELD

NATIONAL NEWSPAPER ASSOCIATION

Street address 1: 900 Community Drive
Street address state: IL
Postal code: 62703
County: Sangamon
Country: USA
Mailing address 1: 900 Community Drive
Mailing city: Springfield
Mailing state: IL
Mailing zip: 62703
Office phone: (217)241-1400
Office fax: (217) 241-1301
Other phone: lynne@nna.org
Other fax: wendy@nna.org
General e-mail: www.nna.org
Advertising e-mail: 1835
Year established: Officer elections held in Sept/Oct during Annual Convention; annual Leadership Conference in March; annual Better Newspaper Contest entry deadline Spring
Company Profile: Stan Schwartz (Comm. Dir.); Lynne Lance (Chief Operating Officer); Sam Fisher (CEO)
Special Notes: Lynne Lance

SUMAS

SALES AND MARKETING EXECUTIVES INTERNATIONAL

Street address 1: PO Box 1390
Street address state: WA
Postal code: 98295-1390
County: Whatcom
Country: USA
Mailing address 1: PO Box 1390
Mailing city: Sumas
Mailing state: WA
Mailing zip: 98295-1390
Office phone: (312) 893-0751
Office fax: (604) 855-0165
Other phone: willis.turner@smei.org
Other fax: marketing.times@smei.org
General e-mail: www.smei.org
Advertising e-mail: 1935
Year established: Elections held on a rolling basis
Company Profile: Willis Turner (Pres./CEO)
Special Notes: Willis Turner

TORONTO

ASSOCIATION OF CANADIAN ADVERTISERS

Street address 1: 95 St Clair Ave. W., Ste. 1103
Street address state: ON
Postal code: M4V 1N6
Country: Canada
Mailing address 1: 95 St Clair Ave. W., Ste. 1103
Mailing city: Toronto
Mailing state: ON
Mailing zip: M4V 1N6
Office phone: (416) 964-3805
Office fax: (416) 964-0771
General e-mail: www.acaweb.ca
Advertising e-mail: 1914
Special Notes: Ron Lund

CANADIAN CIRCULATIONS AUDIT BOARD (CCAB, INC.)

Street address 1: 1 Concorde Gate Suite 800
Street address 2: SUITE 800
Street address state: ON
Postal code: M3C 3N6
County: Ontario
Country: Canada
Mailing address 1: 1 Concorde Gate Ste. 800
Mailing city: Toronto
Mailing state: ON
Mailing zip: M3C 3N6
Office phone: (416) 487-2418
Office fax: (416) 487-6405
Other phone: info@bpaww.com
General e-mail: www.bpaww.com
Advertising e-mail: 1937
Year established: Elections held in April
Company Profile: Neil Ta (Mktg. Mgr.)
Special Notes: Zia Hasan

CANADIAN NEWS MEDIA ASSOCITION

Street address 1: 37 Front Street East Suite 200
Street address state: ON
Postal code: M5E 1B3
Country: Canada
Mailing address 1: 37 Front Street East, Suite 200
Mailing city: Toronto
Mailing state: ON
Mailing zip: M5E 1B3
Telephone country code: 1
Telephone city code: 416
Office phone: (416) 923-3567
Office fax: (416) 923-7206
Other phone: info@newsmediacanada.ca
General e-mail: https://nmc-mic.ca
Advertising e-mail: 2017
Year established: News Media Canada was formed by the merger of the Canadian Newspaper Association and the Canadian Community Newspapers Association in 2017
Company Profile: John Hinds (Pres./CEO); Kelly Levson (Vice-Chairmain)
Special Notes: John Hinds

CANADIAN PRESS, THE - TORONTO, ON

Street address 1: 36 King St. E.
Street address state: ON
Postal code: M5C 2L9
County: York
Country: Canada
Mailing address 1: 36 King St. E.
Mailing city: Toronto
Mailing state: ON
Mailing zip: M5C 2L9
Office phone: (416) 507-2099
Advertising phone: (416) 507-2074
Other phone: support@thecanadianpress.com
Other fax: sales@thecanadianpress.com
General e-mail: www.thecanadianpress.com
Year established: Elections held in April
Company Profile: John Honderich (Chrmn.); Ellen Huebert (News Editor); Keith Leslie (Legislature Correspondent); Eric Morrison (Pres.); David Ross (CFO); Wendy McCann (Chief, Ontario Servs.); Terry Scott (Vice Pres., Broadcasting); Jean Roy (Vice Pres., French Servs.); Paul Woods (Dir., HR); Sharon Hockin (Office Mgr.); Philipe Mercure (Exec. Dir.)
Special Notes: ()

NEWS MEDIA CANADA

Street address 1: 37 Front Street East Suite 200
Street address state: ON
Postal code: M5E 1B3
Country: Canada
Mailing address 1: 37 Front Street East, Suite 200
Mailing city: Toronto
Mailing state: ON
Mailing zip: M5E 1B3
Office phone: (416) 923-3567
Office fax: (416) 923-7206
Other phone: info@newspaperscanada.ca
General e-mail: www.ccna.org
Company Profile: John Hinds (Pres.)
Special Notes: John Hinds

NEWSPAPER CANADA

Street address 1: 890 Yonge Street Ste 200
Street address state: ON
Postal code: M4W 3P4
Country: Canada
Office phone: (416) 923-3567
Office fax: (416) 923-7206
Advertising fax: (877) 305-2262
Other phone: info@newspapercanada.ca
General e-mail: www.newspapercanada.ca

NUMERIS

Street address 1: 1500 Don Mills Rd.
Street address 2: 3rd Fl.
Street address state: ON
Postal code: M3B 3L7
County: York
Country: Canada
Mailing address 1: 1500 Don Mills Rd., 3rd Fl.
Mailing city: Toronto
Mailing state: ON
Mailing zip: M3B 3L7
Office phone: (416) 445-9800
Office fax: (416) 445-8644
General e-mail: en.numeris.ca
Advertising e-mail: 1944
Company Profile: Anita Boyle Evans (Director, Member Engagement, TV); Irina Kharakh (Accounting Supervisor); Derrick Gray (Director, Research Sample Design & Control); Gabriella Fabik (Business Systems Analyst); Fred DeHaan (Director, Respondent Contact Centres); Serge Plante (National Manager, PPM Panel Administration)

TRANS-CANADA ADVERTISING AGENCY NETWORK

Street address 1: 25 Sheppard Ave. West, Suite 300
Street address state: ON
Postal code: M2N 6S6
Country: Canada
Mailing address 1: 25 Sheppard Ave. West, Suite 300
Mailing city: Toronto
Mailing state: ON
Mailing zip: M2N 6S6
Office phone: 416-221-8883
Other phone: bill@waginc.ca
General e-mail: www.tcaan.ca
Advertising e-mail: 1963
Company Profile: Alice Zaharchuk (Exec. Dir.); Bill Whitehead (Mng. Dir./Treasurer)
Special Notes: ()

VANCOUVER

ORGANIZATION OF NEWS OMBUDSMEN

Street address 1: 6336 Hawthorn Lane
Street address state: BC
Postal code: V6T 2J6
County: British Columbia
Country: Canada
Mailing address 1: 6336 Hawthorn Lane
Mailing city: Vancouver
Mailing state: BC
Mailing zip: V6T 2J6
Office phone: (604) 353-6228
Other phone: klapointe@newsombudsmen.org
Other fax: kirklapointe@gmail.com
General e-mail: www.newsombudsmen.org
Advertising e-mail: 1980
Company Profile: Kirk LaPointe (Executive Director)
Special Notes: Kirk LaPointe

VIENNA

INTERNATIONAL PRESS INSTITUTE

Street address 1: Spiegelgasse 2
Postal code: A-1010
Country: Austria
Mailing address 1: Spiegelgasse 2
Mailing city: Vienna
Mailing zip: A-1010
Telephone country code: 43
Telephone city code: 1
Office phone: 512 9011
Office fax: 512 9014
Other phone: ipi@freemedia.at
General e-mail: www.freemedia.at
Year established: Elections held annually on a rotation basis
Company Profile: David Dadge (Dir.)
Special Notes: David Dadge

WASHINGTON

AAF COLLEGE CHAPTERS

Street address 1: 1101 Vermont Ave NW
Street address 2: Ste 500
Street address state: DC
Postal code: 20005-3521
County: District Of Columbia
Country: USA
Mailing address 1: 1101 Vermont Ave NW Ste 500
Mailing city: Washington
Mailing state: DC
Mailing zip: 20005-3521
Office phone: (202) 898-0089
Office fax: (202) 898-0159
Other phone: education@aaf.org
General e-mail: www.aaf.org
Year established: Elections held in June
Company Profile: James Datri (Pres./CEO); Joanne Schecter (Sr. Vice Pres.)
Special Notes: Lisa Rubin

AMERICAN ADVERTISING FEDERATION

Street address 1: 1101 Vermont Ave NW
Street address 2: Ste 500
Street address state: DC
Postal code: 20005-3521
County: District Of Columbia
Country: USA
Mailing address 1: 1101 Vermont Ave NW Ste 500
Mailing city: Washington
Mailing state: DC
Mailing zip: 20005-6306
Office phone: (202) 898-0089
Office fax: (202) 898-0159
Other phone: aaf@aaf.org
General e-mail: www.aaf.org
Advertising e-mail: 1905
Web address: The AAF, headquarted in Washington, D.C., is the trade association

that represents 50,000 professionals in the advertising industry. AAF's 130 corporate members are advertisers, agencies and media companies that comprise the nation's leading brands and cor
Special Notes: James Datri

AMERICAN ASSOCIATION OF INDEPENDENT NEWS DISTRIBUTORS

Street address 1: PO Box 70244
Street address state: DC
Postal code: 20024-0244
County: District Of Columbia
Country: USA
Mailing address 1: PO Box 70244
Mailing city: Washington
Mailing state: DC
Mailing zip: 20024-0244
Office phone: (202)678-8350
Office fax: (202)889-9209
Other phone: cnnorthrop@southwestdistribution.com
General e-mail: www.aaind.org
Company Profile: Cary Northrop (Pres.)
Special Notes: Cary Northrop

AMERICAN FOREST & PAPER ASSOCIATION, INC.

Street address 1: 1101 K Street, NW
Street address 2: Suite 700
Street address state: DC
Postal code: 20005
County: District Of Columbia
Country: USA
Mailing address 1: 1101 K Street, NW, Suite 700
Mailing city: Washington
Mailing state: DC
Mailing zip: 20005
Office phone: (202) 463-2700
Other phone: info@afandpa.org
General e-mail: www.afandpa.org
Company Profile: Donna Harman (Pres./CEO)
Special Notes: Barbara Riley

AMERICAN JEWISH PRESS ASSOCIATION

Street address 1: C/O Kca Association Management
Street address 2: 107 S. Southgate Dr.
Street address state: DC
Postal code: 20036
County: District Of Columbia
Country: USA
Mailing address 1: c/o KCA Association Management
Mailing address 2: 107 S Southgate Dr
Mailing city: Chandler
Mailing state: AZ
Mailing zip: 85226-3222
Office phone: 480-403-4602
Office fax: 480-893-7775
Other phone: info@aipa.org
General e-mail: www.ajpa.org
Year established: Elections held in June
Company Profile: Craig Burke (Publisher & CEO); Alan Smason (Editor); Alan Abbey (Director of Media Relations and Internet Services)
Special Notes: Craig Burke

AMERICAN NEWS WOMEN'S CLUB, INC.

Street address 1: 1607 22nd St NW
Street address state: DC
Postal code: 20008-1921
County: District Of Columbia
Country: USA
Mailing address 1: 1607 22nd St NW
Mailing city: Washington
Mailing state: DC

Mailing zip: 20008-1921
Office phone: (202) 332-6770
Office fax: (202) 265-6092
Other phone: anwclub@comcast.net
General e-mail: www.anwc.org
Advertising e-mail: 1932
Year established: Elections held in May.
Company Profile: Pam Ginsbach (Pres.)
Special Notes: Natalie Diblasio

ASSOCIATION OF ALTERNATIVE NEWSMEDIA

Street address 1: 1156 15th St NW
Street address 2: Ste 1005
Street address state: DC
Postal code: 20005-1722
County: District Of Columbia
Country: USA
Mailing address 1: 1156 15th St NW Ste 1005
Mailing city: Washington
Mailing state: DC
Mailing zip: 20005-1722
Office phone: 289-8484
Office fax: (202) 289-2004
Other phone: web@aan.org
Other fax: jason@aan.org
General e-mail: www.altweeklies.com
Advertising e-mail: 1978
Year established: Annual convention held in summer.
Company Profile: Debra Silvestrin (Dir. of Meetings); Jason Zaragoza (Int. Exec. Dir.)
Special Notes: Jason Zaragoza

ASSOCIATION OF NATIONAL ADVERTISERS, INC.

Street address 1: 2020 K St NW
Street address 2: Ste 660
Street address state: DC
Postal code: 20006-1900
County: District Of Columbia
Country: USA
Mailing address 1: 2020 K St NW
Mailing address 2: Ste 660
Mailing city: Washington
Mailing state: DC
Mailing zip: 20006-1806
Office phone: (202) 296-1883
Office fax: (202) 296-1430
General e-mail: www.ana.net
Special Notes: Bob Liodice

COUNCIL FOR ADVANCEMENT AND SUPPORT OF EDUCATION

Street address 1: 1307 New York Ave NW
Street address 2: Ste 1000
Street address state: DC
Postal code: 20005-4726
County: District Of Columbia
Country: USA
Mailing address 1: 1307 New York Ave NW Ste 1000
Mailing city: Washington
Mailing state: DC
Mailing zip: 20005-4726
Office phone: (202) 328-2273
Office fax: (202) 387-4973
Other phone: memberservicecenter@case.org
General e-mail: www.case.org
Year established: Elections held in July.
Company Profile: Ben Patrusky (Exec. Dir.); Cristine Russell (Pres.); Diane McGurgan (Admin.); John Lippincott (Pres.)
Special Notes: ()

FREEDOM FORUM

Street address 1: 555 Pennsylvania Ave NW
Street address state: DC
Postal code: 20001-2114
County: District Of Columbia
Country: USA
Mailing address 1: 555 Pennsylvania Ave NW

Mailing city: Washington
Mailing state: DC
Mailing zip: 20001-2114
Office phone: (202) 292-6100
Other phone: firstamendmentcenter@newseum.org
General e-mail: www.freedomforuminstitute.org
Year established: Not a membership organization
Company Profile: Gene Policinski; Ken Paulson (Sr. Vice Pres., Int'l Programs); David L. Hudson Jr.
Special Notes: Gene Policinski

GRAPHIC COMMUNICATIONS CONFERENCE/INTERNATIONAL BROTHERHOOD OF TEAMSTERS

Street address 1: 25 Louisiana Ave NW
Street address state: DC
Postal code: 20001-2130
County: District Of Columbia
Country: USA
Mailing address 1: 25 Louisiana Ave NW
Mailing city: Washington
Mailing state: DC
Mailing zip: 20001-2130
Office phone: (202) 508-6800
Office fax: (202) 508-6661
General e-mail: www.gciu.org
Year established: Elections held quadrennially.
Company Profile: Robert Lacey (Secretary-Treasurer/Vice President)
Special Notes: Lorraine Ferrell

INTERNATIONAL CENTER FOR JOURNALISTS

Street address 1: 1616 H St NW
Street address 2: Fl 3
Street address state: DC
Postal code: 20006-4903
County: District Of Columbia
Country: USA
Mailing address 1: 1616 H St NW Fl 3
Mailing city: Washington
Mailing state: DC
Mailing zip: 20006-4903
Office phone: (202) 737-3700
Office fax: (202) 737-0530
Other phone: editor@icfj.org
General e-mail: www.icfj.org
Advertising e-mail: 1984
Web address: The International Center for Journalists, a non-profit organization, promotes quality journalism worldwide in the belief that independent, vigorous media are crucial in improving the human condition. For 27 years, ICFJ has worked directly with more than 70,000 journalists from 180 countries.
Year established: International Center for Journalists is not a membership organization.
Company Profile: Joyce Barnathan (Pres.); Nancy Frye (Vice Pres., Finance); Patrick Butler (Vice Pres., Programs); Vjollca Shtylla (Vice Pres., Development); Sharon Moshavi (Vice Pres., New Initiatives)
Special Notes: Sonja Matanovic

INTERNATIONAL LABOR COMMUNICATIONS ASSOCIATION AFL/CIO/CLC

Street address 1: 815 16th St NW
Street address state: DC
Postal code: 20006-4101
County: District Of Columbia
Country: USA
Mailing address 1: 815 16th St NW
Mailing city: Washington
Mailing state: DC
Mailing zip: 20006-4101
Office phone: (202) 637-5068
Office fax: (202) 637-5069

Other phone: info@ilcaonline.org
General e-mail: www.ilcaonline.org
Advertising e-mail: 1995
Year established: Elections held biennially.
Company Profile: Lisa Martin (Pres.)
Special Notes: ()

NATIONAL ASSOCIATION OF BROADCASTERS

Street address 1: 1771 N St NW
Street address state: DC
Postal code: 20036-2800
County: District Of Columbia
Country: USA
Mailing address 1: 1771 N St NW
Mailing city: Washington
Mailing state: DC
Mailing zip: 20036-2800
Office phone: (202) 429-5300
Office fax: (202) 429-4199
Other phone: nab@nab.org
General e-mail: www.nab.org
Year established: Elections held once in two years.
Company Profile: Bruce T. Reese (Joint Board Chrmn.); Janet McGregor (COO/CFO)
Special Notes: Janet McGregor

NATIONAL ASSOCIATION OF HISPANIC JOURNALISTS

Street address 1: 1050 Connecticut Ave NW
Street address 2: Fl 10
Street address state: DC
Postal code: 20036-5334
County: District Of Columbia
Country: USA
Mailing address 1: 1050 Connecticut Ave NW Fl 10
Mailing city: Washington
Mailing state: DC
Mailing zip: 20036-5334
Office phone: (202) 662-7145
Office fax: (202) 662-7144
Other phone: nahj@nahj.org
General e-mail: www.nahj.org
Company Profile: Anna M. Lopez Buck (Interim Executive Director)
Special Notes: Anna M. Lopez Buck

NATIONAL ASSOCIATION OF HISPANIC PUBLICATIONS

Street address 1: 529 14th St NW
Street address 2: Ste 1126
Street address state: DC
Postal code: 20045-2120
County: District Of Columbia
Country: USA
Mailing address 1: 529 14th St NW Ste 923
Mailing city: Washington
Mailing state: DC
Mailing zip: 20045-1930
Office phone: (202) 662-7250
Other phone: directory@nahp.org
General e-mail: www.nahp.org
Year established: Elections held every two years
Company Profile: Kerry Stackpole (Exec. Dir.)
Special Notes: Kerry Stackpole

NATIONAL LESBIAN AND GAY JOURNALISTS ASSOCIATION

Street address 1: 2120 L St NW
Street address 2: Ste 850
Street address state: DC
Postal code: 20037-1550
County: District Of Columbia
Country: USA
Mailing address 1: 2120 L St NW Ste 850
Mailing city: Washington
Mailing state: DC
Mailing zip: 20037-1550

Associations, Clubs and Press Clubs - National and International

Office phone: (202) 588-9888
Office fax: (202) 588-1818
Other phone: info@nlgja.org
General e-mail: www.nlgja.org
Advertising e-mail: 1990
Year established: Elections held annually
Company Profile: David Barrie (Pres.)
Special Notes: David Barrie

NATIONAL NEWSPAPER PUBLISHERS ASSOCIATION BLACK PRESS OF AMERICA

Street address 1: 1816 12th St NW
Street address state: DC
Postal code: 20009-4422
County: District Of Columbia
Country: USA
Mailing address 1: 1816 12th St NW
Mailing city: Washington
Mailing state: DC
Mailing zip: 20009-4422
Office phone: 202-588-8764
Office fax: 202-588-8960
Other phone: nnpadc@nnpa.org
General e-mail: www.nnpa.org
Advertising e-mail: 1939
Year established: Elections held every two years in June.
Company Profile: Hazel Trice Edney (Interim Exec. Ed.)
Special Notes: Cloves Campbell, Jr.

NATIONAL PRESS CLUB

Street address 1: 529 14th St NW
Street address 2: 13th Floor
Street address state: DC
Postal code: 20045-1217
County: District Of Columbia
Country: USA
Mailing address 1: 529 14th St NW, 13th floor
Mailing city: Washington
Mailing state: DC
Mailing zip: 20045-1217
Office phone: (202) 662-7500
Office fax: (202) 662-7569
General e-mail: www.press.org
Year established: Elections held in Nov
Company Profile: William McCarren (Exec. Dir.)

NATIONAL PRESS FOUNDATION

Street address 1: 1211 Connecticut Ave NW
Street address 2: Ste 310
Street address state: DC

Postal code: 20036-2709
County: District Of Columbia
Country: USA
Mailing address 1: 1211 Connecticut Ave NW Ste 310
Mailing city: Washington
Mailing state: DC
Mailing zip: 20036-2709
Office phone: (202) 663-7280
Office fax: (202) 530-2855
Other phone: npf@nationalpress.org
General e-mail: www.nationalpress.org
Web address: The primary mission of the National Press Foundation is to increase journalists' knowledge of complex issues in order to improve public understanding. The foundation recognizes and encourages excellence in journalism through its awards and programs.
Company Profile: Sandy Johnson (President and COO)
Special Notes: Sandy Johnson

NATIONAL RETAIL FEDERATION

Street address 1: 325 7th St Nw, Liberty Pl, Ste 1100
Street address state: DC
Postal code: 20004
County: District Of Columbia
Country: USA
Mailing address 1: 325 7th St. NW, Liberty Pl., Ste. 1100
Mailing city: Washington
Mailing state: DC
Mailing zip: 20004
Office phone: (202) 783-7971
Office fax: (202) 737-2849
Advertising fax: 800-673-4692
General e-mail: www.nrf.com
Year established: Elections held in Jan
Company Profile: Carleen C. Kohut (CFO); Tracy Mullin (Pres.)
Special Notes: Carleen C. Kohut

OUTDOOR ADVERTISING ASSOCIATION OF AMERICA (OAAA)

Street address 1: 1850 M St NW
Street address 2: Ste 1040
Street address state: DC
Postal code: 20036-5821
County: District Of Columbia
Country: USA
Mailing address 1: 1850 M St NW Ste 1040
Mailing city: Washington
Mailing state: DC
Mailing zip: 20036-5821

Office phone: (202) 833-5566
Office fax: (202) 833-1522
Other phone: info@oaaa.org
General e-mail: www.oaaa.org
Advertising e-mail: 1891
Company Profile: Marla Kaplowitz (Pres. & CEO)

PRINTING, PUBLISHING & MEDIA WORKERS SECTOR-CWA

Street address 1: 501 3rd St NW
Street address 2: Ste 950
Street address state: DC
Postal code: 20001-2760
County: District Of Columbia
Country: USA
Mailing address 1: 501 3rd St NW Ste 950
Mailing city: Washington
Mailing state: DC
Mailing zip: 20001-2760
Office phone: (202) 434-1106
Office fax: (202) 434-1482
Other phone: bshippe@cwa-union.org
General e-mail: www.cwa-union.org
Year established: Elections to be held at CWA convention in August 2008.
Company Profile: Larry Cohen (Pres.)
Special Notes: Larry Cohen

RADIO TELEVISION DIGITAL NEWS ASSOCIATION

Street address 1: 529 14th St NW
Street address 2: Ste 1240
Street address state: DC
Postal code: 20045-2520
County: District Of Columbia
Country: USA
Mailing address 1: 529 14th Street, NW Ste 1240
Mailing city: Washington
Mailing state: DC
Mailing zip: 20045
Office phone: (770) 622-7011
Office fax: (202) 223-4007
Other phone: mikec@rtdna.org
General e-mail: www.rtdna.org
Advertising e-mail: 1945
Web address: Professional association serving electronic journalists in radio, television and digital media.
Company Profile: Mike Cavender (Exec. Dir.); Katie Switchenko (Awards, Membership and Programs Manager); Derrick Hinds (Digital, Communications and Marketing Manager); Karen Hansen (Manager of Membership and Programs); Noukla Ruble (Meetings and Events Manager)
Special Notes: Mike Cavender

REGIONAL REPORTERS ASSOCIATION

Street address 1: 1575 Eye St NW Suite 350
Street address state: DC
Postal code: 20008
County: District Of Columbia
Country: USA
Mailing address 1: 1575 I St NW Ste 350
Mailing city: Washington
Mailing state: DC
Mailing zip: 20005-1114
Office phone: (202) 408-2705
Other phone: president@rra.org
General e-mail: www.rra.org
Company Profile: Adrianne Flynn (Sec.); Suzanne Struglinski (Pres.)
Special Notes: Todd Gillman

THE NEWSGUILD-CWA

Street address 1: 501 3rd St NW
Street address 2: Fl 6
Street address state: DC
Postal code: 20001-2797
County: District Of Columbia
Country: USA
Mailing address 1: 501 3rd St NW, Fl 6
Mailing city: Washington
Mailing state: DC
Mailing zip: 20001-2797
Office phone: (202) 434-7177
Office fax: (202) 434-1472
Advertising fax: (202) 434-7177
Other phone: guild@cwa-union.org
General e-mail: www.newsguild.org
Advertising e-mail: 1933
Web address: The NewsGuild-CWA, previously known as The Newspaper Guild-CWA, represents 25,000 digital and print journalists and other media workers in the United States, Canada and Puerto Rico. In addition to fair wages and working conditions, TNG-CWA is a voice for the rights and safety of journalists worldwide, for freedom of information, transparency in government and First Amendment issues.
Company Profile: Bernard Lunzer (President); Martha Waggoner (International Chairperson); Marian Needham (Exec. VP)
Special Notes: Bernard Lunzer

U.S. STATE NEWSPAPER ASSOCIATIONS

ALBUQUERQUE
NEW MEXICO PRESS ASSOCIATION
Street address 1: 700 Silver Ave SW
Street address state: NM
Postal code: 87102-3019
Country: USA
Mailing address 1: PO Box 95198
Mailing city: Albuquerque
Mailing state: NM
Mailing zip: 87199-5198
Office phone: (505) 275-1241
Office fax: (505) 275-1449
Advertising phone: (505) 275-1377
Web address: www.nmpress.org
General e-mail: info@nmpress.org
Advertising e-mail: Ads@NMPress.org
Note: Elections held in Oct
Personnel: Holly Aguilar (Office Mgr.)

ATLANTA
GEORGIA PRESS ASSOCIATION
Street address 1: 3066 Mercer University Dr
Street address 2: Ste 200
Street address state: GA
Postal code: 30341-4137
Country: USA
Mailing address 1: 3066 Mercer University Dr Ste 200
Mailing city: Atlanta
Mailing state: GA
Mailing zip: 30341-4137
Office phone: (770) 454-6776
Office fax: (770) 454-6778
Web address: www.gapress.org
General e-mail: mail@gapress.org
Year established: 1887
Note: Elections held at annual convention in June
Personnel: Robin Rhodes (Exec. Dir. & Pub); Mary Pat Hodges (Member Services Director); Rick Hammell (Sales & Marketing Director); Sean Ireland (Publications Editor); Michelle Pearson (Business Development Manager); Mesha Wind (President)
Main Contatct: Robin Rhodes

AUSTIN
TEXAS PRESS ASSOCIATION
Street address 1: 8800 Business Park Dr
Street address 2: Ste 100
Street address state: TX
Postal code: 78759-7403
Country: USA
Mailing address 1: 8800 Business Park Drive
Mailing city: Austin
Mailing state: TX
Mailing zip: 78759-7403
Office phone: (512) 477-6755
Office fax: (512) 477-6759
Web address: www.texaspress.com
General e-mail: mhodges@texaspress.com
Advertising e-mail: jweatherall@texaspress.com
Year established: 1880
Personnel: Micheal Hodges (Exec. Dir.); Donnis Baggett (Exec. VP); Ed Sterling (Member Serv. Dir.); Stephanie Hearne (Controller)
Main Contatct: Micheal Hodges

BATON ROUGE
LOUISIANA PRESS ASSOCIATION
Street address 1: 404 Europe St
Street address state: LA
Postal code: 70802-6403
Country: USA
Office phone: (225) 344-9309
Office fax: (225) 344-9344
Advertising phone: (225) 344-9309 x 111
Advertising fax: (225) 336-9921
Editorial fax: (225) 346-5060
Other phone: (800) 701-8753
Web address: www.lapress.com
General e-mail: pam@lapress.com
Advertising e-mail: erin@LaPress.com
Year established: 1880
Personnel: Mike Rood (Communications Dir.); Pamela Mitchell (Exec. Dir.); Mitchell-Ann Droge (Dir. of Ops.); Erin Palmintier (Adv. Dir.)
Main Contatct: Pamela Mitchell

BIRMINGHAM
ALABAMA PRESS ASSOCIATION
Street address 1: 3324 Independence Dr
Street address 2: Ste 200
Street address state: AL
Postal code: 35209-5602
Country: USA
Mailing address 1: 3324 Independence Dr Ste 200
Mailing city: Birmingham
Mailing state: AL
Mailing zip: 35209-5602
Office phone: (205) 871-7737
Office fax: (205) 871-7740
Other phone: (800) 264-7043
Web address: www.alabamapress.org
General e-mail: felicia@alabamapress.org
Year established: 1871
Note: Elections held in Feb
Personnel: Felicia Mason (Exec. Dir.); Brad English (Adv. Mgr.); Leigh Tortorici (Senior Marketing Rep.); Amy Metzler (Sales/Mktg Exec); Chris McDaniel (Member Services/Network Coordinator)
Main Contatct: Felicia Mason

BISMARCK
NORTH DAKOTA NEWSPAPER ASSOCIATION
Street address 1: 1435 Interstate Loop
Street address state: ND
Postal code: 58503-0567
Country: USA
Mailing address 1: 1435 Interstate Loop
Mailing city: Bismarck
Mailing state: ND
Mailing zip: 58503-0567
Office phone: (701) 223-6397
Office fax: (701) 223-8185
Other phone: (800) 685-8889
Web address: www.ndna.com
General e-mail: info@ndna.com
Year established: 1885
Profile: Advertising placed in 89 North Dakota newspapers and related publications. Statewide classified advertising and small space advertising programs.
Note: Represents daily and weekly newspapers in North Dakota
Personnel: Kelli Richey (Mktg. Dir.); Steve Andrist (Exec. Dir.); Mike Casey (Adv. Dir.); Colleen Park (Adv./Public Notice Coord.); Shari Peterson (Office Coord./Adv. Assist.); Paul Erdelt (NDNA President)
Main Contatct: Steve Andrist

BOISE
NEWSPAPER ASSOCIATION OF IDAHO
Street address 1: 407 W Jefferson St
Street address state: ID
Postal code: 83702-6049
Country: USA
Office phone: (208) 345-9929
Office fax: (208) 345-9928
Web address: www.newspaperassociationofidaho.com
General e-mail: amber@rischpisca.com
Year established: 2011
Profile: An association of Idaho's daily and weekly newspapers, combining the former Idaho Allied Dailies and Idaho Newspaper Association.
Personnel: Amber Hauge (Dir.)
Main Contatct: Amber Hauge

BROOKINGS
SOUTH DAKOTA NEWSPAPER ASSOCIATION
Street address 1: 1125 32nd Ave
Street address state: SD
Postal code: 57006-4707
Country: USA
Mailing address 1: 1125 32nd Ave
Mailing city: Brookings
Mailing state: SD
Mailing zip: 57006-4707
Office phone: (605) 692-4300
Office fax: (605) 692-6388
Other phone: (800) 658-3697
Web address: www.sdna.com
General e-mail: sdna@sdna.com
Year established: 1882
Note: Elections held in May
Personnel: David Bordewyk (Exec. Dir.); John Brooks (Advertising Sales Director); Nicole Herrig (Business Manager); Sandy DeBeer (Advertising Placement Coordinator)
Main Contatct: David Bordewyk; David Bordewyk

CAPE ELIZABETH
MAINE PRESS ASSOCIATION
Street address 1: 26 Elmwood Rd
Street address state: ME
Postal code: 04107-1337
Country: USA
Mailing address 1: 26 Elmwood Rd
Mailing city: Cape Elizabeth
Mailing state: ME
Mailing zip: 04107-1337
Office phone: 207-799-2996
Office fax: (800) 799-6008
Web address: www.mainepressassociation.org
General e-mail: mainepressmail@gmail.com
Year established: 1864
Note: Elections held in Sept
Personnel: Jeff Ham (Exec. Dir.); Diane Norton (Exec. Dir.)
Main Contatct: Diane Norton

CARSON CITY
NEVADA PRESS ASSOCIATION, INC.
Street address 1: 102 N Curry St
Street address state: NV
Postal code: 89703-4934
Country: USA
Mailing address 1: 102 N Curry St
Mailing city: Carson City
Mailing state: NV
Mailing zip: 89703-4934
Office phone: (775) 885-0866
Office fax: (775) 885-8233
Web address: www.nevadapress.com
General e-mail: nevadapress@att.net
Advertising e-mail: nevadapress@att.net
Year established: 1924
Note: Elections held in Sept
Personnel: Barry Smith (Exec. Dir.); Scott Sibley (Pres.)
Main Contatct: Barry Smith

CHARLESTON
WEST VIRGINIA PRESS ASSOCIATION, INC.
Street address 1: 3422 Pennsylvania Ave
Street address state: WV
Postal code: 25302-4633
Country: USA
Mailing address 1: 3422 Pennsylvania Ave
Mailing city: Charleston
Mailing state: WV
Mailing zip: 25302-4633
Office phone: (800) 235-6881
Office fax: (800) 526-6939
Advertising phone: (304)342-1011
Editorial phone: (304)342-1011
Other phone: (304) 342-1011
Web address: www.wvpress.org
General e-mail: wvpress@wvpress.org
Advertising e-mail: theady@wvpress.org
Year established: 1868
Note: The WVPA Annual Convention is held in August.
Personnel: Don Smith (Exec. Dir.); Toni Heady (Adv. Dir.); Dalton Walker (Adv. Staff)
Main Contatct: Don Smith

CHEYENNE
WYOMING PRESS ASSOCIATION
Street address 1: 2121 Evans Ave
Street address state: WY
Postal code: 82001-3733
Country: USA
Mailing address 1: 2121 Evans Ave
Mailing city: Cheyenne
Mailing state: WY
Mailing zip: 82001-3733
Office phone: (307) 635-3905
Office fax: (307) 635-3912
Web address: www.wyopress.org
General e-mail: wyopress@wyopress.org
Year established: 1899
Note: Elections held in Jan
Personnel: Jim Angell (Exec. Dir.); Cecilia Moats (Deputy Dir.)
Main Contatct: Jim Angell

COHOES
FREE COMMUNITY PAPERS OF NEW YORK
Street address 1: 621 Columbia Street Ext
Street address 2: Ste 100
Street address state: NY
Postal code: 12047-3876
Country: USA
Mailing address 1: 621 Columbia Street Extension
Mailing city: Cohoes
Mailing state: NY
Mailing zip: 12047
Office phone: (518) 464-6483
Office fax: (518) 464-6489
Web address: fcpny.org
General e-mail: nypa@nynewspapers.com
Advertising e-mail: ads@fcpny.com
Year established: 1950
Profile: Trade association for more than 800 newspapers in New York including daily, weekly, religious, alternative, senior, family and ethnic newspapers. Own and operate statewide newspaper advertising agency specializing in production of high-impact newspaper advertising including campaign planning and placement, space

U.S. State Newspaper Associations

reservations, ad copy trafficking, proof of publication, billing, and payment to newspapers.
Note: Election of officers held in Sept; largest newspaper industry training convention and trade show in the country held in March or April
Personnel: Richard Hotaling (Member Services Mgr.); Dave Worden (VP Adv.); Doug Rea (VP Adv.); Jill Van Dusen (Assist. Gen. Mgr. for Membership Systems); Michelle Rea (Exec. Dir.); Scott Lavigne (Controller)
Main Contatct: Dan Holmes

COLCHESTER

VERMONT PRESS ASSOCIATION

Street address 1: Journalism Dept / 169D Jeanmarie Hall
Street address 2: St. Michael's College
Street address state: VT
Postal code: 05439-0284
Country: USA
Mailing address 1: c/o Journalism Dept
Mailing city: Colchester
Mailing state: VT
Mailing zip: 05439-0284
Office phone: (802) 654-2442
Web address: www.vtpress.org
General e-mail: mdonoghue@smcvt.edu
Year established: 1867
Profile: The VPA represents the interests of the 11 daily and roughly four dozen non-daily print newspapers circulating in Vermont. The primary focus is monitoring legislative issues that impact the First Amendment, newsgathering and the operation of newspapers, including advertising and circulation. Various kinds of professional training sessions are offered, along with an annual writing and photography contest.
Note: Elections held in the Fall
Personnel: Mike Donoghue (Executive Director)
Main Contatct: Mike Donoghue

COLUMBIA

MISSOURI PRESS ASSOCIATION

Street address 1: 802 Locust St
Street address state: MO
Postal code: 65201-4888
Country: USA
Mailing address 1: 802 Locust St
Mailing city: Columbia
Mailing state: MO
Mailing zip: 65201
Office phone: (573) 449-4167
Office fax: (573) 874-5894
Web address: www.mopress.com
Advertising e-mail: mopressads@socket.net
Year established: 1867
Profile: Missouri Press Association is the statewide trade association for newspapers, some 275 titles, in Missouri.
Note: Elections held in Sep.
Personnel: Ted Lawrence (Missouri Press Service); Kristie Williams (Membership Services Director); Mark Maassen
Main Contatct: Mark Maassen

SOUTH CAROLINA PRESS ASSOCIATION

Street address 1: 106 Outlet Pointe Blvd
Street address state: SC
Postal code: 29210-5669
Country: USA
Mailing address 1: PO Box 11429
Mailing city: Columbia
Mailing state: SC
Mailing zip: 29211-1429
Office phone: (803) 750-9561
Office fax: (803) 551-0903
Web address: www.scpress.org
General e-mail: scpress@scpress.org
Advertising e-mail: aritchie@scpress.org
Year established: 1852
Profile: Representing 108 S.C. Newspapers
Note: Elections held in March.
Personnel: Alanna Ritchie (Adv. Dir.); Randall Savely (Director of Operations); Bill Rogers (Executive Director); Jen Madden (Assistant Director)
Main Contatct: Bill Rogers

COLUMBUS

OHIO NEWSPAPER ASSOCIATION

Street address 1: 1335 Dublin Rd
Street address 2: Ste 216B
Street address state: OH
Postal code: 43215-1000
Country: USA
Office phone: (614) 486-6677
Office fax: (614) 486-6373
Advertising phone: (614) 485-6677 x1020
Advertising fax: (614) 486-6373
Web address: www.ohionews.org
General e-mail: dhetzel@ohionews.org
Advertising e-mail: wdozier@adohio.net
Year established: 1933
Note: Elections held in Feb
Personnel: Dennis Hetzel (Exec. Dir.); Sue Bazzoli (Mgr. Admin. Services); Jason Sanford (Comm. Mgr.); Walt Dozier (Adv. Dir.); Ann Riggs (Admin. Asst.); Mitch Colton (Network Acct. Exec. & Digital Specialist); Josh Park (Program Support Asst.); Patricia Conkle (Operations Manager)
Main Contatct: Dennis Hetzel

DENVER

COLORADO PRESS ASSOCIATION

Street address 1: 1120 N Lincoln St
Street address 2: Ste 912
Street address state: CO
Postal code: 80203-2138
Country: USA
Office phone: (303) 571-5117
Office fax: (303) 571-1803
Web address: www.coloradopressassociation.com
General e-mail: colopress@colopress.net
Advertising e-mail: ads@sync2media.com
Year established: 1878
Personnel: Jerry Raehal (CEO); Jean Creel (Office Man.); Russell Bassett (Membership and Projects); Judy Quelch (Advertising)
Main Contatct: Jerry Raehal

DES MOINES

IOWA NEWSPAPER ASSOCIATION, INC.

Street address 1: 319 E 5th St
Street address 2: Fl 2
Street address state: IA
Postal code: 50309-1927
Country: USA
Mailing address 1: 319 E 5th St Fl 2nd
Mailing city: Des Moines
Mailing state: IA
Mailing zip: 50309-1931
Office phone: (515) 244-2145
Office fax: (515) 244-4855
Web address: www.inanews.com
General e-mail: ina@inanews.com
Year established: 1931
Note: Elections held in May
Personnel: Susan Patterson Plank (Exec. Dir.); Brent Steemken (Business Mgr.); Jodi Hulbert (Comm. Dir.); Geof Fischer (Dev. Dir.); Samantha Fett (Inside Sales Mgr.); Heidi Geisler (Media Dir.); Jana Shepherd (Program Dir.); Susan James (Tech. & Digital Dev. Mgr.); Ryan Harvey (Pres.); Kaitlyn Van Patten (Sales & Mktg. Assist.)
Main Contatct: Susan Patterson Plank

EWING

NEW JERSEY PRESS ASSOCIATION

Street address 1: 810 Bear Tavern Rd
Street address 2: Ste 307
Street address state: NJ
Postal code: 08628-1022
Country: USA
Mailing address 1: 810 Bear Tavern Rd Ste 307
Mailing city: Ewing
Mailing state: NJ
Mailing zip: 08628-1022
Office phone: (609) 406-0600
Office fax: (609) 406-0300
Advertising fax: (609) 406-0399
Web address: www.njpa.org
General e-mail: njpress@njpa.org
Advertising e-mail: aclear@njpa.org
Year established: 1857
Personnel: John J. O'Brien (Foundation Director); George H. White (Executive Director); Amy C. Lear (NJNN Director); Scott Kutcher (Business Manager); Catherine Langley (Communications Manager); Peggy Stephan Arbitell (Member Services Manager); Jane Hartsough (Accounting Coordinator); Julianne Mangano (Marketing Specialist)
Main Contatct: Peggy Stephan Arbitell

FRANKFORT

KENTUCKY PRESS ASSOCIATION, INC.

Street address 1: 101 Consumer Ln
Street address state: KY
Postal code: 40601-8489
Country: USA
Mailing address 1: 101 Consumer
Mailing city: Frankfort
Mailing state: KY
Mailing zip: 40601
Office phone: (502) 223-8821
Office fax: (502) 226-3867
Advertising phone: (502) 227-7992
Advertising fax: (502) 875-2624
Web address: www.kypress.com
General e-mail: dthompson@kypress.com
Advertising e-mail: trevlett@kypress.com
Year established: 1869
Profile: Membership organization representing all Kentucky newspapers
Note: Elections held in Jan
Personnel: David T. Thompson (Exec. Dir.); Bonnie Howard (Controller)
Main Contatct: David T. Thompson

GLEN ALLEN

VIRGINIA PRESS ASSOCIATION, INC.

Street address 1: 11529 Nuckols Rd
Street address state: VA
Postal code: 23059-5508
Country: USA
Mailing address 1: 11529 Nuckols Rd
Mailing city: Glen Allen
Mailing state: VA
Mailing zip: 23059-5508
Office phone: (804) 521-7570
Office fax: (804) 521-7590
Advertising phone: (804) 521-7580
Other fax: (800) 849-8717
Web address: www.vpa.net
Advertising e-mail: susanw@vpa.net
Year established: 1881
Note: Elections held in April
Personnel: Betsy Edwards (Executive Director); Janet Madison (Member Services Manager); Diana Shaban (Advertising Director); Jeremy Slayton (Communications Manager); Kim Woodward (Assistant Executive Director)
Main Contatct: Betsy Edwards

HARRISBURG

MANSI MEDIA

Street address 1: 3899 N Front St
Street address state: PA
Postal code: 17110-1583
Country: USA
Office phone: (717) 703-3030
Office fax: (717) 703-3033
Web address: www.mansimedia.com
General e-mail: sales@mansimedia.com
Note: Represents daily and weekly newspapers and their digital products anywhere in the U.S. and beyond.
Personnel: Lisa Knight (VP/Adv.); Chris Kazlauskas; Wes Snider (Dir. Client Solutions); Ronaldo Davis (Sr. Media Buyer); Matthew Caylor (Dir., Interactive Media); Lindsey Artz (Account Manager); Shannon Mohar (Account Manager); Brian Hitchings (Director, Client Solutions)
Main Contatct: Lisa Knight

PENNSYLVANIA NEWSMEDIA ASSOCIATION

Street address 1: 3899 N Front St
Street address state: PA
Postal code: 17110-1583
Country: USA
Mailing address 1: 3899 N Front Street
Mailing city: Harrisburg
Mailing state: PA
Mailing zip: 17110-1583
Office phone: (717) 703-3000
Office fax: (717) 703-3001
Advertising phone: (717) 703-3071
Web address: www.panewsmedia.org
General e-mail: info@pa-news.org
Advertising e-mail: communications@pa-news.org
Year established: 1925
Note: Represents daily, weekly, collegiate and online newspapers in Pennsylvania & the U.S.
Personnel: Tricia Greyshock (Vice President, Association Services); Lisa Knight (Vice President, Advertising); Amanda Shafer; Bob Schnarrs; Chris Hagan; David Rhoads; Deborah Musselman; Diane Brinser; Kristin Bleiler; Lauren Fox; Lisa Strohl (Communications Manager); Melissa Melewsky; Paula Knudsen; Rae Elise Williard; Sherid Virnig; Mark Cohen (Pres.)
Main Contatct: Tricia Greyshock

HARTFORD

CONNECTICUT DAILY NEWSPAPERS ASSOCIATION

Street address 1: 330 Main St
Street address 2: Fl 3
Street address state: CT
Postal code: 06106-1851
Country: USA
Mailing address 1: 330 Main St Fl 3
Mailing city: Hartford
Mailing state: CT
Mailing zip: 06106-1851
Office phone: (860) 716-4461
Office fax: (860) 541-6484
Web address: www.ctdailynews.com
Year established: 1904
Note: Elections held in April/May
Personnel: Chris VanDeHoef (Executive Director)
Main Contatct: Jim Leahy; Chris VanDeHoef

HELENA

MONTANA NEWSPAPER ASSOCIATION

Street address 1: 825 Great Northern Blvd

Street address 2: Ste 202
Street address state: MT
Postal code: 59601-3340
Country: USA
Mailing address 1: 825 Great Northern Blvd., Ste. 202
Mailing city: Helena
Mailing state: MT
Mailing zip: 59601-3358
Office phone: (406) 443-2850
Office fax: (406) 443-2860
Web address: www.mtnewspapers.com
General e-mail: jim@mtnewspapers.com
Advertising e-mail: campbell@mtnewspapers.com
Year established: 1885
Personnel: Jim Rickman (Executive Director); Kev Campbell (Business Development Manager); Pamela Chriske (Accounting Specialist)
Main Contatct: Jim Rickman

HONOLULU

HAWAII PUBLISHERS ASSOCIATION

Street address 1: 500 Ala Moana Blvd
Street address 2: Ste 7-500
Street address state: HI
Postal code: 96813-4930
Country: USA
Mailing address 1: 500 Ala Moana Blvd Ste 7500
Mailing city: Honolulu
Mailing state: HI
Mailing zip: 96813-4930
Office phone: (808) 738-4992
Office fax: (808) 664-8892
Web address: www.hawaiipublishersassociation.com
General e-mail: info@hawaiipublishersassociation.com
Personnel: Rick Asbach (Executive Director)
Main Contatct: ()

INDIANAPOLIS

HOOSIER STATE PRESS ASSOCIATION

Street address 1: 41 E Washington St
Street address 2: Ste 101
Street address state: IN
Postal code: 46204-3560
Country: USA
Office phone: (317) 803-4772
Office fax: (317) 624-4428
Web address: www.hspa.com
Advertising e-mail: map@hspa.com
Year established: 1933
Note: Represents daily and weekly newspapers in Indiana
Personnel: Stephen Key (Exec. Dir./Gen. Counsel); Pamela Lego (Adv. Dir.); Milissa Tuley (Communications Specialist); Karen Braeckel (HSPA Foundation Dir.); Yvonne Yeadon (Office Mgr.); Shawn Goldsby (Adv. Coord.)
Main Contatct: Stephen Key

JACKSON

MISSISSIPPI PRESS ASSOCIATION

Street address 1: 371 Edgewood Terrace Dr
Street address state: MS
Postal code: 39206-6217
Country: USA
Mailing address 1: 371 Edgewood Terrace Dr
Mailing city: Jackson
Mailing state: MS
Mailing zip: 39206-6217
Office phone: (601) 981-3060
Office fax: (601) 981-3676
Web address: www.mspress.org
General e-mail: mspress@mspress.org
Advertising e-mail: mps@mspress.org
Year established: 1866
Note: Elections held in June
Personnel: Layne Bruce (Exec. Dir.); Andrea Ross (Media Dir.); Monica Gilmer (Member Services Mgr.)
Main Contatct: Layne Bruce

KINGSTON

RHODE ISLAND PRESS ASSOCIATION

Street address 1: University of Rhode Island
Street address 2: Journalism Dept.
Street address state: RI
Postal code: 2881
Country: USA
Mailing address 1: 282 Doyle Avenue
Mailing city: Providence
Mailing state: RI
Mailing zip: 02906
Office phone: (401) 874-4287
Office fax: (401) 874-4450
Web address: www.ripress.org
General e-mail: lllevin@uri.edu
Year established: 1886
Note: Elections held in Jan
Personnel: Linda Levin (Secretary); Fran Ostendorf (Treasurer)
Main Contatct: Linda Levin; Linda Levin

KNOXVILLE

TENNESSEE PRESS ASSOCIATION, INC.

Street address 1: 625 Market St
Street address 2: Ste 1100
Street address state: TN
Postal code: 37902-2219
Country: USA
Mailing address 1: 625 Market Street Suite 1100
Mailing city: Knoxville
Mailing state: TN
Mailing zip: 37902
Office phone: (865) 584-5761
Office fax: (865) 558-8687
Other phone: (800) 565-7377
Web address: www.tnpress.com
General e-mail: info@tnpress.com
Advertising e-mail: knoxads@tnpress.com
Year established: 1870-71
Note: Elections held in June
Personnel: Carol Daniels (Exec. Dir.); Shelley Davis (Sales and Marketing Director); Robyn Gentile (Member Services Manager)
Main Contatct: Carol Daniels

LAKE MARY

FLORIDA PRESS ASSOCIATION

Street address 1: 1025 Greenwood Blvd
Street address 2: Ste 191
Street address state: FL
Postal code: 32746-5410
Country: USA
Mailing address 1: 1025 Greenwood Blvd., Suite 191
Mailing city: Lake Mary
Mailing state: FL
Mailing zip: 32746-5410
Office phone: (321) 283-5255
Advertising phone: (800) 742-1373
Web address: www.flpress.com
General e-mail: fpa-info@flpress.com
Advertising e-mail: info@intersectmediasolutions.com
Year established: 1879
Profile: FPA is the trade association for Florida's newspapers.
Note: Association accepts free newsapers if they meet the requirements. FPA is the parent company of Intersect Media Solutions
Personnel: Dean Ridings (Pres. & CEO); Carolyn Klinger (VP, Strategy); Sam Morley (Gen. Counsel)
Main Contatct: Dean Ridings

LAKE OSWEGO

OREGON NEWSPAPER PUBLISHERS ASSOCIATION

Street address 1: 4000 Kruse Way Pl
Street address 2: Bldg 160
Street address state: OR
Postal code: 97035-5545
Country: USA
Mailing address 1: 4000 Kruse Way Pl, Bldg 2 Ste 160
Mailing city: Lake Oswego
Mailing state: OR
Mailing zip: 97223-8365
Office phone: (503) 624-6397
Office fax: (503) 639-9009
Advertising phone: (503) 624-6397 x22
Advertising fax: (503) 639-9009
Web address: www.orenews.com
General e-mail: onpa@orenews.com
Advertising e-mail: linda@orenews.com
Year established: 1887
Note: Elections held in June
Personnel: Laurie Hieb (Exec. Dir.); Linda Hutcheson (Advertising Services Manager); Laurie Sterkowicz (Accounting Assistant); Patricia Murphy; Edward Wistos; Jackie Thomas
Main Contatct: Jackie Thomas

LANSING

MICHIGAN PRESS ASSOCIATION

Street address 1: 827 N Washington Ave
Street address state: MI
Postal code: 48906-5135
Country: USA
Mailing address 1: 827 N Washington Ave
Mailing city: Lansing
Mailing state: MI
Mailing zip: 48906-5199
Office phone: (517) 372-2424
Office fax: (517) 372-2429
Web address: www.michiganpress.org
General e-mail: mpa@michiganpress.org
Year established: 1868
Note: Elections held in Jan
Personnel: Roselie Lucus (Growth & Operations Manager); Lisa McGraw (Public Affairs Manager); Sean Wickham (Design & Communications Specialist); Janet Mendler (Mgr.); James Tarrant (Exec. Dir.); Paul Biondi (Adv. Dir.)
Main Contatct: ()

LINCOLN

NEBRASKA PRESS ASSOCIATION/NEBRASKA PRESS ADVERTISING SERVICE

Street address 1: 845 'S' Street
Street address state: NE
Postal code: 68508-1226
Country: USA
Mailing address 1: 845 "S" Street
Mailing city: Lincoln
Mailing state: NE
Mailing zip: 68508-1226
Office phone: (402) 476-2851
Office fax: (402) 476-2942
Web address: www.nebpress.com
General e-mail: nebpress@nebpress.com
Advertising e-mail: vk@nebpress.com
Year established: 1872
Profile: Trade association representing the Nebraska daily and weekly newspapers in the state
Note: Annual convention and election of officers held in April
Personnel: Allen Beermann (Exec. Dir.); Carolyn Bowman (Adv. Mgr., Nebr Press Adv. Service); Jenelle Plachy (Office Mgr.); Susan Watson (Admin. Asst./Press Release Coord.); Violet Kirk (Adv. Sales Asst., Nebr. Press Adv. Service)
Main Contatct: Susan Watson

MADISON

WISCONSIN NEWSPAPER ASSOCIATION

Street address 1: 34 Schroeder Ct
Street address 2: Ste 220
Street address state: WI
Postal code: 53711-2528
Country: USA
Office phone: (608) 283-7620
Office fax: (608) 283-7631
Other phone: (800) 261-4242
Web address: www.wnanews.com
General e-mail: wna@wnanews.com
Year established: 1853
Note: Represents 34 daily and over 225 weekly and specialty newspapers
Personnel: Beth Bennett (Exec. Dir.); Denise Guttery (Media Services Dir.); James Debilzen (Communications Dir.); Julia Hunter (Member Services Dir.)
Main Contatct: Beth Bennett

MINNEAPOLIS

MINNESOTA NEWSPAPER ASSOCIATION

Street address 1: 12 S 6th St
Street address 2: Ste 1120
Street address state: MN
Postal code: 55402-1501
Country: USA
Mailing address 1: 10 S 5th St Ste 1105
Mailing city: Minneapolis
Mailing state: MN
Mailing zip: 55402-1036
Office phone: (612) 332-8844
Office fax: (612) 342-2958
Other phone: (800) 279-2979
Web address: www.mna.org
General e-mail: info@mna.org
Advertising e-mail: advertising@mna.org
Year established: 1867
Profile: MNA is the trade association for the newspapers in Minnesota with 345 daily and weekly newspaper members.
Note: Convention, trade show and elections in January.
Personnel: Lisa Hills (Executive Director); Dan Lind (Managing Director); Barbara Trebisovsky (Asst. Exec. Dir.); Phil Morin (Advertising Account Manager)
Main Contatct: Lisa Hills

NEW YORK

NEW YORK PRESS PHOTOGRAPHERS ASSOCIATION, INC.

Street address 1: PO Box 3346
Street address state: NY
Postal code: 10008-3346
Country: USA
Mailing address 1: Box 3346 Church Street Station
Mailing city: New York
Mailing state: NY
Mailing zip: 10008-3346
Office phone: (212) 889-6633
Web address: www.nyppa.org
General e-mail: office@nyppa.org
Year established: 1915
Profile: The New York Press Photographers Association was established in 1915 as the News Photographers Association of New York, and since that time has served as a fraternal and professional organization, representing the interests of working photographers and visual journalists in the New York metro area.
Note: Elections held every other year
Personnel: Ray Stubblebine (Trustee); Marc Hermann (Secretary - Historian); Bruce Cotler (President); Todd Maisel (Vice President)
Main Contatct: Marc Hermann

U.S. State Newspaper Associations

OKLAHOMA CITY
OKLAHOMA PRESS ASSOCIATION

Street address 1: 3601 N Lincoln Blvd
Street address state: OK
Postal code: 73105-5411
Country: USA
Mailing address 1: 3601 N Lincoln Blvd
Mailing city: Oklahoma City
Mailing state: OK
Mailing zip: 73105-5499
Office phone: (405) 499-0020
Office fax: (405) 499-0048
Advertising phone: (405) 499-0022
Other phone: (888) 815-2672
Web address: www.okpress.com
General e-mail: swilkerson@okpress.com
Advertising e-mail: lcobb@okpress.com
Year established: 1906
Note: Elections held in June
Personnel: Mark Thomas (Exec. VP); Scott Wilkerson (Office Mgr.); Landon Cobb (Sales Dir.); Lisa Sutliff (Mbr. Serv. Dir.); Jennifer Gilliland (Creat. Serv. Dir.); Keith Burgin (Dig. Clip Serv. Mgr.); Cindy Shea (Adv. Mgr.)
Main Contatct: Mark Thomas; Mark Thomas

PHOENIX
ARIZONA NEWSPAPERS ASSOCIATION

Street address 1: 1001 N Central Ave
Street address 2: Ste 670
Street address state: AZ
Postal code: 85004-1947
Country: USA
Office phone: (602) 261-7655
Office fax: (602) 261-7525
Advertising phone: (602) 261-7655 x112
Web address: www.ananews.com
General e-mail: p.casey@ananews.com
Advertising e-mail: p.casey@ananews.com
Year established: 1929
Note: Elections held in Sept. Statewide and national one order/one bill advertising placement service
Personnel: Paula Casey (Exec. Dir.); Julie O'Keefe (Communications Manager); Cindy London (Ad Placement Manager)
Main Contatct: Paula Casey

PORT TOWNSEND
WASHINGTON NEWSPAPER PUBLISHERS ASSOCIATION, INC.

Street address 1: PO Box 389
Street address state: WA
Postal code: 98368-0389
Country: USA
Mailing address 1: PO Box 389
Mailing city: Port Townsend
Mailing state: WA
Mailing zip: 98368
Office phone: 360-344-2938
Web address: www.wnpa.com
General e-mail: fredobee@wnpa.com
Advertising e-mail: ads@wnpa.com
Year established: 1887
Note: Elections held in Oct; officers installed in Oct
Personnel: Fred Obee (Exec. Dir.); Janay Collins (Member Services Director)
Main Contatct: Fred Obee

RALEIGH
NORTH CAROLINA PRESS ASSOCIATION

Street address 1: 5171 Glenwood Ave
Street address 2: Ste 364
Street address state: NC
Postal code: 27612-3266
Country: USA
Mailing address 1: 5171 Glenwood Ave Ste 364
Mailing city: Raleigh
Mailing state: NC
Mailing zip: 27612-3266
Office phone: (919) 787-7443
Office fax: (919) 787-5302
Advertising phone: (919) 789-2083
Web address: www.ncpress.com
General e-mail: laurie@ncpress.com
Advertising e-mail: cindy@ncpress.com
Year established: 1873
Note: Elections held in July
Personnel: Beth Grace (Publisher); Laura Nakoneczny (Editor); Megan Dew (Media Director); Phil Lucey (Exec. Dir.); Mark Wilson (President); Bart Adams (Vice President); Regina Howard-Glaspie (President); Pat Taylor (Vice President); Tammy Dunn (NCPA Secretary/Treasurer); Bill Moss (NCPS Secretary/Treasurer); Les High (Immediate Past President); Paul Mauney (President)
Main Contatct: Phil Lucey

SACRAMENTO
CALIFORNIA NEWS PUBLISHERS ASSOCIATION

Street address 1: 2701 K St
Street address state: CA
Postal code: 95816-5131
Country: USA
Mailing address 1: 2701 K St.
Mailing city: Sacramento
Mailing state: CA
Mailing zip: 95816-5131
Office phone: (916) 288-6000
Office fax: (916) 288-6002
Web address: www.cnpa.com
Year established: 1889
Personnel: William Johnson (President); Paulette Brown-Hinds (VP, Sec/Trea); Thomas Newton (Exec. Dir.); Jim Ewert (Gen. Counsel); Simon Birch (Dir. of Membership); Cecelia Drake (Director of Advertising); Joe Wirt (Director of Affiliate Relations); Renee Smith (Director of Meetings)
Main Contatct: Joe Wirt

SANDY
UTAH PRESS ASSOCIATION, INC.

Street address 1: 9716 S 500 W
Street address state: UT
Postal code: 84070-2565
Country: USA
Mailing address 1: 9716 S 500 W
Mailing city: Sandy
Mailing state: UT
Mailing zip: 84070-2565
Office phone: 801-237-2376
Advertising phone: (801) 237-2376
Web address: www.utahpress.com
General e-mail: upa@utahpress.com
Advertising e-mail: denice@utahpress.com
Year established: 1893
Profile: The mission of the Utah Press Association is to serve the common interests of its members by promoting, improving and protecting the welfare of the newspaper business and the news media industry in Utah, which includes printing, publishing and distributing news and information on paper, the Internet and other digital media; fostering the highest ideals, ethics and traditions of journalism, a free press and the newspaper profession; and acquiring, providing and disseminating among its membership, information, services and material relating to the best policies and practices for the general improvement of members' businesses.
Note: Elections held in March
Personnel: Brian Allfrey (Exec. Dir.); Denice Page (Advertising Coordinator); Michael Wolsey (Accounting)
Main Contatct: Brian Allfrey

SPRINGFIELD
ILLINOIS PRESS ASSOCIATION

Street address 1: 900 Community Dr
Street address state: IL
Postal code: 62703-5180
Country: USA
Office phone: (217) 241-1300
Office fax: (217) 241-1301
Advertising phone: (217) 241-1700
Advertising fax: (217) 241-1701
Web address: www.illinoispress.org
General e-mail: ipa@illinoispress.org
Year established: 1865
Profile: The Illinois Press Association represents the business and journalistic interests of more than 480 member newspapers in Illinois.
Note: The Illinois Press Advertising Service can place any newspaper product available in Illinois and has several well-established, low-cost networks.
Personnel: Sam Fisher (Pres./CEO); Tracy Spoonmore (CFO); Jeff Holman (Advertising Director); Cindy Bedolli (Administrative Assistant & Member Relations); Ron Kline (Tech & Online Coord.); Melissa Calloway (Dig. Adv. Mgr.); Cindy Bedolli (Admin Assist & Member Rel.)
Main Contatct: Cindy Bedolli

TOPEKA
KANSAS PRESS ASSOCIATION

Street address 1: 5423 SW 7th St
Street address state: KS
Postal code: 66606-2330
Country: USA
Mailing address 1: 5423 SW 7th St.
Mailing city: Topeka
Mailing state: KS
Mailing zip: 66606
Office phone: (785) 271-5304
Office fax: (785) 271-7341
Other phone: (855) 572-1863
Web address: www.kspress.com
General e-mail: info@kspress.com
Advertising e-mail: KSAds@kspress.com
Year established: 1863
Profile: Association of daily and non-daily newspapers in the state of Kansas.
Note: Represents 28 daily and 185 weekly newspapers in Kansas
Personnel: Emily Bradbury (Director of Member Services); Lori Jackson (Admin. Assist./Adv.); Doug Anstaett (Exec. Dir.); Amber Jackson (Adv. Dir.); Judy Beach (Accountant)
Main Contatct: Doug Anstaett

CANADIAN NEWSPAPER ASSOCIATIONS

BURLINGTON

ONTARIO COMMUNITY NEWSPAPERS ASSOCIATION

Street address 1: 3228 South Service Rd. Ste 116
Province: ON
Postal Code: L7N 3H8
Country: Canada
Mailing address: 3228 South Service Rd. Ste 116
Mailing city: Burlington
Province: ON
Postal code: L7N 3H8
General Phone: (905) 639-8720
General Fax: (905) 639-6962
General/National Adv. E-mail: info@ocna.org
Primary Website: www.ocna.org
Year Established: 1950
Personnel: Anne Lannan (Executive Director)

EDMONTON

ALBERTA WEEKLY NEWSPAPERS ASSOCIATION

Street address 1: 3228 Parsons Rd
Province: AB
Postal Code: T6N 1M2
Country: Canada
Mailing address: 3228 Parsons Rd
Mailing city: Edmonton
Province: AB
Postal code: T6N 1M2
General Phone: (780) 434-8746
General Fax: (780) 438-8356
General/National Adv. E-mail: info@awna.com
Primary Website: www.awna.com
Personnel: Dennis Merrell (Exec. Dir.)

GATINEAU

QUEBEC COMMUNITY NEWSPAPERS ASSOCIATION

Street address 1: 400 Maloney Blvd
Street address 2: Suite 205
Province: QC
Postal Code: J8P 1E6
Country: Canada
Mailing address: 400 Maloney Blvd
Mailing city: Gatineau
Province: QC
Postal code: J8P 1E6
General Phone: (514) 697-6330
General Fax: (514) 697-6331
General/National Adv. E-mail: execdir@qcna.qc.ca
Primary Website: www.qcna.org
Personnel: Sylvie Goneau (Exec. Dir.); Info Email (Info Email)

HALIFAX

ATLANTIC COMMUNITY NEWSPAPERS ASSOCIATION

Street address 1: 7075 Bayers Rd., Ste. 216
Province: NS
Postal Code: B3L 2C2
Country: Canada
Mailing address: 7075 Bayers Rd., Ste. 216
Mailing city: Halifax
Province: NS
Postal code: B3L 2C2
General Phone: (902) 832-4480
General Fax: (902) 832-4484
General/National Adv. E-mail: info@newspapersatlantic.ca

Primary Website: www.acna.com
Personnel: Mike Kierstead (Exec. Dir.)

KANKAKEE

HUBERGROUP USA, INC.

Street address 1: 2850 Festival Drive
Province: IL
Postal Code: 60901
County: Kankakee
Country: USA
Mailing address: 2850 Festival Drive
Mailing city: Kankakee
Province: IL
Postal code: 60901
General Phone: (815) 929-9293
General Fax: (815) 929-0412
General/National Adv. E-mail: info.us@hubergroup.com
Primary Website: www.cpima.org
Year Established: 1934
Note: Elections held in Aug. for a two year term
Personnel: Dorothea Nace (Exec. Dir./Sec./Treasurer); Neil Marshall (Pres.); Vivy da Costa (Vice Pres.)

LAVAL

HEBDOS QUEBEC

Street address 1: 2550 Daniel-Johnson,
Street address 2: Bureau 345
Province: QC
Postal Code: H7T 2L1
County: QC
Country: Canada
Mailing address: 2550 Daniel-Johnson
Mailing city: Laval
Province: QC
Postal code: H7T 2L1
General Phone: (514) 861-2088
General Fax: (514) 861-1966
General/National Adv. E-mail: communications@hebdos.com
Primary Website: hebdos.com
Year Established: 1932
Personnel: Gilber Paquette (Exec. Dir.)

MARKHAM

RTDNA - CANADA (RADIO TELEVISION DIGITAL NEWS ASSOCIATION)

Street address 1: 2800 - 14th Ave.
Street address 2: Ste. 210
Province: ON
Postal Code: L3R 0E4
Country: Canada
General Phone: (416) 756 2213
General Fax: (416) 491-1670
General/National Adv. E-mail: sherry@associationconcepts.ca; info@rtdnacanada.ca
Primary Website: www.rtdnacanada.com
Year Established: 1962
Note: Elections held in June
Personnel: Sherry Denesha (Operations Manager)

MONTREAL

CONSEIL DE PRESSE DU QUEBEC

Street address 1: 1000, rue Fullum, Ste. A.208
Province: QC
Postal Code: H2K 3L7
Country: Canada
Mailing address: 1000, rue Fullum, Ste. A.208
Mailing city: Montreal

Province: QC
Postal code: H2K 3L7
General Phone: (514) 529-2818
General Fax: (514) 873-4434
General/National Adv. E-mail: info@conseildepresse.qc.ca
Primary Website: www.conseildepresse.qc.ca
Year Established: 1973
Personnel: Guy Amyot (Contact); Julien Acosta (Director of communication)

NEW YORK

FOREIGN PRESS ASSOCIATION

Street address 1: 1501 Broadway
Street address 2: 12th Floor
Province: NY
Postal Code: 10036
County: New York
Country: USA
Mailing address: 1501 Broadway, 12th Floor
Mailing city: New York
Province: NY
Postal code: 10036
General Phone: (212) 370-1054
General/National Adv. E-mail: fpa@foreignpressassociation.org
Primary Website: www.foreignpressassociation.org
Year Established: 1918
Note: Elections held in Dec
Personnel: â€‹David P. Michaels (President); Ian Williams (Vice President); Jeffery P. Lanerâ€‹â€‹

OAKVILLE

CANADIAN BUSINESS PRESS

Street address 1: 2100 Banbury Cresent
Province: ON
Postal Code: L6H 5P6
Country: Canada
Mailing address: 2100 Banbury Crescent
Mailing city: Oakville
Province: ON
Postal code: L6H 5P6
General Phone: 905-844-6822
General/National Adv. E-mail: torrance@cbp.ca
Primary Website: www.cbp.ca
Personnel: Trish Torrance (Executive Director)

SASKATOON

SASKATCHEWAN WEEKLY NEWSPAPERS ASSOCIATION

Street address 1: 14-401 45th St. W.
Province: SK
Postal Code: S7L 5Z9
Country: Canada
Mailing address: 14-401 45th St. W.
Mailing city: Saskatoon
Province: SK
Postal code: S7L 5Z9
General Phone: (306) 382-9683
General Fax: (306) 382-9421
General/National Adv. E-mail: swna@swna.com
Primary Website: www.swna.com
Personnel: Cameron Just (Tech. Officer); Julie Schau (Commun.Coord.); Louise Simpson (Office Mgr.); Nicole Nater (Adv. Coord., Classified); Steve Nixon (Exec. Dir.)

TORONTO

ASSOCIATION OF CANADIAN ADVERTISERS

Street address 1: 95 St Clair Ave. W., Ste. 1103
Province: ON

Postal Code: M4V 1N6
Country: Canada
Mailing address: 95 St Clair Ave. W., Ste. 1103
Mailing city: Toronto
Province: ON
Postal code: M4V 1N6
General Phone: (416) 964-3805
General Fax: (416) 964-0771
Primary Website: www.acaweb.ca
Year Established: 1914

CANADIAN CIRCULATIONS AUDIT BOARD (CCAB, INC.)

Street address 1: 1 Concorde Gate Suite 800
Street address 2: SUITE 800
Province: ON
Postal Code: M3C 3N6
County: Ontario
Country: Canada
Mailing address: 1 Concorde Gate Ste. 800
Mailing city: Toronto
Province: ON
Postal code: M3C 3N6
General Phone: (416) 487-2418
General Fax: (416) 487-6405
General/National Adv. E-mail: info@bpaww.com
Primary Website: www.bpaww.com
Year Established: 1937
Note: Elections held in April
Personnel: Neil Ta (Mktg. Mgr.)

CANADIAN NEWS MEDIA ASSOCITION

Street address 1: 37 Front Street East Suite 200
Province: ON
Postal Code: M5E 1B3
Country: Canada
Mailing address: 37 Front Street East, Suite 200
Mailing city: Toronto
Province: ON
Postal code: M5E 1B3
General Phone: (416) 923-3567
General Fax: (416) 923-7206
General/National Adv. E-mail: info@newsmediacanada.ca
Primary Website: https://nmc-mic.ca
Year Established: 2017
Note: News Media Canada was formed by the merger of the Canadian Newspaper Association and the Canadian Community Newspapers Association in 2017
Personnel: John Hinds (Pres./CEO); Kelly Levson (Vice-Chairmain)

CANADIAN PRESS, THE - TORONTO, ON

Street address 1: 36 King St. E.
Province: ON
Postal Code: M5C 2L9
County: York
Country: Canada
Mailing address: 36 King St. E.
Mailing city: Toronto
Province: ON
Postal code: M5C 2L9
General Phone: (416) 507-2099
General/National Adv. E-mail: support@thecanadianpress.com
Primary Website: www.thecanadianpress.com
Note: Elections held in April
Personnel: John Honderich (Chrmn.); Ellen Huebert (News Editor); Keith Leslie (Legislature Correspondent); Eric Morrison (Pres.); David Ross (CFO); Wendy McCann (Chief, Ontario Servs.); Terry Scott (Vice Pres., Broadcasting); Jean Roy (Vice Pres., French Servs.); Paul Woods (Dir., HR); Sharon Hockin (Office Mgr.); Philipe Mercure (Exec. Dir.)

Canadian Newspaper Associations

NEWS MEDIA CANADA

Street address 1: 37 Front Street East Suite 200
Province: ON
Postal Code: M5E 1B3
Country: Canada
Mailing address: 37 Front Street East, Suite 200
Mailing city: Toronto
Province: ON
Postal code: M5E 1B3
General Phone: (416) 923-3567
General Fax: (416) 923-7206
General/National Adv. E-mail: info@newspaperscanada.ca
Primary Website: www.ccna.ca
Personnel: John Hinds (Pres.)

NEWSPAPER CANADA

Street address 1: 890 Yonge Street Ste 200
Province: ON
Postal Code: M4W 3P4
Country: Canada
General Phone: (416) 923-3567
General Fax: (416) 923-7206
General/National Adv. E-mail: info@newspapercanada,ca
Primary Website: www.newspapercanada.ca

NUMERIS

Street address 1: 1500 Don Mills Rd.
Street address 2: 3rd Fl.
Province: ON
Postal Code: M3B 3L7
County: York
Country: Canada
Mailing address: 1500 Don Mills Rd., 3rd Fl.
Mailing city: Toronto
Province: ON
Postal code: M3B 3L7
General Phone: (416) 445-9800
General Fax: (416) 445-8644
Primary Website: en.numeris.ca
Year Established: 1944
Personnel: Anita Boyle Evans (Director, Member Engagement, TV); Irina Kharakh (Accounting Supervisor); Derrick Gray (Director, Research Sample Design & Control); Gabriella Fabik (Business Systems Analyst); Fred DeHaan (Director, Respondent Contact Centres); Serge Plante (National Manager, PPM Panel Administration)

TRANS-CANADA ADVERTISING AGENCY NETWORK

Street address 1: 25 Sheppard Ave. West, Suite 300
Province: ON
Postal Code: M2N 6S6
Country: Canada
Mailing address: 25 Sheppard Ave. West, Suite 300
Mailing city: Toronto
Province: ON
Postal code: M2N 6S6
General Phone: 416-221-8883
General/National Adv. E-mail: bill@waginc.ca
Primary Website: www.tcaan.ca
Year Established: 1963
Personnel: Alice Zaharchuk (Exec. Dir.); Bill Whitehead (Mng. Dir./Treasurer)

VANCOUVER

BRITISH COLUMBIA/YUKON COMMUNITY NEWSPAPERS ASSOCIATION

Street address 1: #9 West Broadway
Province: BC
Postal Code: V5Y 1P1
Country: Canada
Mailing address: #9 West Broadway
Mailing city: Vancouver
Province: BC
Postal code: V5Y 1P1
General Phone: (604) 669-9222
General Fax: (604) 684-4713
General/National Adv. E-mail: info@bccommunitynews.com
Primary Website: www.bccommunitynews.com
Note: Elections held in May
Personnel: George Affleck (Gen. Mgr.)

ORGANIZATION OF NEWS OMBUDSMEN

Street address 1: 6336 Hawthorn Lane
Province: BC
Postal Code: V6T 2J6
County: British Columbia
Country: Canada
Mailing address: 6336 Hawthorn Lane
Mailing city: Vancouver
Province: BC
Postal code: V6T 2J6
General Phone: (604) 353-6228
General/National Adv. E-mail: klapointe@newsombudsmen.org
Primary Website: www.newsombudsmen.org
Year Established: 1980
Personnel: Kirk LaPointe (Executive Director)

WINNIPEG

MANITOBA COMMUNITY NEWSPAPER ASSOCIATION

Street address 1: 943 McPhillips Street
Province: MB
Postal Code: R2X 2J9
Country: Canada
Mailing address: 943 McPhillips Street
Mailing city: Winnipeg
Province: MB
Postal code: R2X 2J9
General Phone: (204) 947-1691
General Fax: (204) 947-1919
Primary Website: www.mcna.com
Note: Elections held at annual April convention

CIRCULATION AUDIT SERVICES

ARLINGTON HEIGHTS

ALLIANCE FOR AUDITED MEDIA (AAM)

Street Address: 48 W Seegers Rd.
State/Province: IL
ZIP/Postal Code: 60005-3900
Country: USA
Mailing Address: 48 W Seegers Rd
Mailing City: Arlington Heights
Mailing State/Provience: IL
Mailing ZIP/Postal: 60005
General Phone: (224) 366-6939
General Fax: (224) 366-6949
Website: http://www.auditedmedia.com
Year Established: 1914
Personnel: Joe Hardin (VP, Product Leadership); Brian Condon (EVP, Com. Dev.); Kevin Rehberg (Dir., Client Dev.)

SAINT LOUIS

CIRCULATION VERIFICATION COUNCIL

Street Address: 338 S Kirkwood Rd, Unit 102
State/Province: MO
ZIP/Postal Code: 63122-6166
Country: USA
Mailing Address: 338 South Kirkwood Road, Suite 102
Mailing City: Saint Louis
Mailing State/Provience: MO
Mailing ZIP/Postal: 63122
General Phone: (314) 966-7711
General Fax: (314) 822-0666
General/National Adv. E-mail: tbingaman@cvcaudit.com
Website: http://www.cvcaudit.com
Year Established: 1992
Personnel: Jim Kennedy (VP Audit Services); Tim Bingaman (Pres./CEO); Sarah Black (Receptionist); Hannah Stevens (Audit Coord.); Darlene Lucy (Buss. Mgr.); Denise Baur (Audit Coord.)

SAN RAFAEL

VERIFIED AUDIT CIRCULATION (VAC)

Street Address: 1001 5th Ave., Ste 270
State/Province: CA
ZIP/Postal Code: 94901-2904
Country: USA
Mailing Address: 1001 Fifth Ave.
Mailing City: San Rafael
Mailing State/Provience: CA
Mailing ZIP/Postal: 94901
General Phone: (415) 461-6006
General Fax: (415) 461-6007
General/National Adv. E-mail: info@verifiedaudit.com
Website: http://www.verifiedaudit.com
Year Established: 1951
Personnel: Tim Prouty (CEO); Alan Levy (VP Marketing and Sales); Jennifer Armor (Audit Mgr.); Josh Luck (Field Verification Mgr.); Tara Taylor (Audit Mgr.); Wren Tracy (Audit Mgr.); Julie Vega (Accountant); Julie Ghezzi (Account Coord.)

SHELTON

BPA WORLDWIDE

Street Address: 100 Beard Sawmill Rd.
State/Province: CT
ZIP/Postal Code: 06484-6150
Country: USA
Mailing Address: 100 Beard Sawmill Rd.
Mailing City: Shelton
Mailing State/Provience: CT
Mailing ZIP/Postal: 06484
General Phone: (203) 447-2800
General Fax: (203) 447-2900
Website: http://www.bpaww.com
Year Established: 1930
Personnel: Glenn Hansen (Pres./CEO); Richard J. Murphy (Sr. Vice Pres., Auditing)

TORONTO

CANADIAN CIRCULATIONS AUDIT BOARD (CCAB, INC.)

Street Address: 1 Concorde Gate Suite 800, Suite 800
State/Province: ON
ZIP/Postal Code: M3C 3N6
Country: Canada
Mailing Address: 1 Concorde Gate Ste. 800
Mailing City: Toronto
Mailing State/Provience: ON
Mailing ZIP/Postal: M3C 3N6
General Phone: (416) 487-2418
General Fax: (416) 487-6405
General/National Adv. E-mail: info@bpaww.com
Website: http://www.bpaww.com
Year Established: 1937
Personnel: Neil Ta (Mktg. Mgr.)

CANADIAN MEDIA CIRCULATION AUDIT

Street Address: 37 Front Street East Suite
State/Province: ON
ZIP/Postal Code: M5E 1B3
Country: Canada
Mailing Address: 37 Front Street East, Suite 200
Mailing City: Toronto
Mailing State/Provience: ON
Mailing ZIP/Postal: M5E 1B3
General Phone: (416) 923-3567
General Fax: (416) 923-7206
General/National Adv. E-mail: audit@newspaperscanada.ca
Website: http://www.newspaperscanada.ca
Year Established: 1919
Personnel: John Hinds (Pres.); Tina Ongkeko (MD); Winnie Legaspi (CMCA Manager)

WAYNE

CERTIFIED AUDIT OF CIRCULATIONS, INC.

Street Address: 155 Willowbrook Blvd, Fl 4
State/Province: NJ
ZIP/Postal Code: 07470-7032
Country: USA
Mailing Address: 155 Willowbrook Blvd Ste 400
Mailing City: Wayne
Mailing State/Provience: NJ
Mailing ZIP/Postal: 07470-7033
General Phone: (973) 785-3000
General Fax: (973) 785-8341
General/National Adv. E-mail: esodt@certifiedaudit.com
Website: http://www.certifiedaudit.com
Year Established: 1956
Personnel: David Roe (Dir., Opns.); Debbie Maragoudakis (Audit Mgr.); Evelina Sodt (Dir., Mktg.); Mark Stoecklin (CEO)

CLIP ART SERVICES

CHARLOTTESVILLE

KEISTER-WILLIAMS NEWSPAPER SERVICES, INC.
Street Address 1: 1807 Emmet St N
Street Address 2: # 6
State: VA
ZIP Code: 22901-3616
County: Charlottesville City
Country: USA
Mailing Address: P.O. Box 8187
Mailing City: Charlottesville
Mailing State: VA
Mailing ZIP Code: 22906
General Phone: (800) 293-4709
General Fax: (434) 293-4884
General/National Adv. E-mail: kw@kwnews.com
Website: https://www.kwnews.com
Year Established: 1939
Personnel: Walton C. Lindsay (Pres.)

DENVER

THOUGHT EQUITY MANAGEMENT, INC.
Street Address 1: 1530 16th St
Street Address 2: Fl 6
State: CO
ZIP Code: 80202-1447
County: Denver
Country: USA
Mailing Address: 1530 16th St Ste 600
Mailing City: Denver
Mailing State: CO
Mailing ZIP Code: 80202-1447
General Phone: (720) 382-2869
General Fax: (720) 382-2719
General/National Adv. E-mail: sales@thoughtequity.com
Website: https://www.thoughtequity.com
Year Established: 2003
Industry: Electronic Ad Delivery
Note: Thought Equity Libraries: Supplier of motion content to newspaper, cable and broadcast companies. Thousands of affordable, top-quality ads and commercials are searchable and accessible online."
Personnel: Kevin Schaff (Founder/CEO); Mark Lemmons (CTO); Mike Emerson (Vice Pres., Mktg.); Frank Cardello (Vice Pres., Bus. Devel.)

FALLS CHURCH

NEWS USA, INC.
Street Address 1: 1069 W Broad St
Street Address 2: Ste 205
State: VA
ZIP Code: 22046-4610
County: Falls Church City
Country: USA
Mailing Address: 1069 West Broad Street, Suite 105
Mailing City: Falls Church
Mailing ZIP Code: 22046
General Phone: (800) 355-9500
General/National Adv. E-mail: office@newsusa.com

LAFAYETTE

EZADSPRO
Street Address 1: 302 Ferry St
Street Address 2: Fl 2
State: IN
ZIP Code: 47901-1185
County: Tippecanoe
Country: USA
Mailing Address: 302 Ferry St Fl 2
Mailing City: Lafayette
Mailing State: IN
Mailing ZIP Code: 47901-1185
General Phone: (765) 742-9012
General Fax: (765) 742-2843
General/National Adv. E-mail: info@ezadspro.com
Website: https://www.ezadspro.com
Personnel: Perry Rice (Managing Partner)

NEW YORK

METRO EDITORIAL SERVICES
Street Address 1: 519 8th Ave
Street Address 2: Fl 18
State: NY
ZIP Code: 10018-4577
County: New York
Country: USA
Mailing Address: 519 8th Ave Fl 18
Mailing City: New York
Mailing State: NY
Mailing ZIP Code: 10018-4577
General Phone: (212) 947-5100
General Fax: (212) 714-9139
General/National Adv. E-mail: mes@metro-email.com
Website: https://www.mcg.metrocreativeconnection.com
Year Established: 1910
Industry: Art & Layout Equipment and Services; Consulting Services: Advertising; Consulting Services: Editorial; Software: Design/Graphics; Software: Editorial;
Note: Metro is a leading provider of advertising, creative and editorial resources designed to help media companies make money with their print, online, and mobile products. We provide ready-to-use images, ads, stock-quality photos, logos/trademarks, auto photos, marketing/sales materials, copyright-free features, print templated sections, online e-Sections, and groundbreaking digital ad development tools, plus custom image, ad design and editorial services.
Personnel: Robert Zimmerman (Publisher); Debra Weiss (Exec. Vice Pres./Mktg. Dir.); Lauren Lekoski (Mktg. Mgr.); Jo Ann Shapiro (VP, Sales); Lou Ann Sornson (Regional Sales Mgr.); Tina Dentner (Regional Sales Mgr.); Cathy Agee (Regional Sales Mgr.); Gwen Tomaselli (Regional Sales Mgr.); Jennifer Steiner (Regional Sales Mgr.); Joann Johnson

NEW YORK

NORTH AMERICAN PRECIS SYNDICATE, INC.
Street Address 1: 415 Madison Ave
Street Address 2: Fl 12
State: NY
ZIP Code: 10017-7947
County: New York
Country: USA
Mailing Address: 415 Madison Ave Fl 12
Mailing City: New York
Mailing State: NY
Mailing ZIP Code: 10017-7956
General Phone: (212) 867-9000
General Fax: (800) 990-4329
General/National Adv. E-mail: service@napsnet.com; info@napsnet.com
Website: https://www.napsnet.com
Year Established: 1958
Personnel: Dorothy York (Pres.); Gary Lipton (Vice Pres., Media Rel.); Candace Leiberman (Ed. in Chief); Yauling Wagner (Serv. Mgr.)

PEORIA

JUPITER IMAGES CORP.
Street Address 1: 6000 N Forest Park Dr
State: IL
ZIP Code: 61614-3556
County: Peoria
Country: USA
Mailing Address: 6000 N Forest Park Dr
Mailing City: Peoria
Mailing State: IL
Mailing ZIP Code: 61614-3556
General Phone: (309) 688-8800
General Fax: (309) 688-3075
General/National Adv. E-mail: sales@jupiterimages.com
Website: https://www.jupiterimages.com
Year Established: 1964
Industry: Software: Design/Graphics; Trade Publications;
Product or Service: Hardware/Software Supplier
Note: All-purpose art and idea service.
Personnel: Mark Nickerson (Vice Pres., Opns.)

PITTSBURGH

CENTURY FEATURES, INC.
Street Address 1: 1420 Centre Ave
Street Address 2: Apt 2213
State: PA
ZIP Code: 15219-3535
County: Allegheny
Country: USA
Mailing Address: 1420 Centre Ave Apt 2213
Mailing City: Pittsburgh
Mailing State: PA
Mailing ZIP Code: 15219-3535
General Phone: (412) 471-6533
General Fax: (412) 765-3672
Website:
Personnel: Charles Reichblum (Contact)

TROY

B&B - BANKER & BRISEBOIS ADVERTISING
Street Address 1: 901 Tower Dr
Street Address 2: Ste 315
State: MI
ZIP Code: 48098-2817
County: Oakland
Country: USA
Mailing Address: 901 Tower Dr Ste 315
Mailing City: Troy
Mailing State: MI
Mailing ZIP Code: 48098-2817
General Phone: (248) 519-9200
General Fax: (248) 519-9206
General/National Adv. E-mail: bbinfo@bbfurnitureadvertising.com
Website: https://www.bbfurnitureadvertising.com
Year Established: 1912
Personnel: Lee Gilmore (Pres.)

TUCSON

JUPITERIMAGES
Street Address 1: 232 E Pima St Ste 200-C
State: AZ
ZIP Code: 85712
County: Pima
Country: USA
Mailing Address: 5232 E Pima St Ste 200C
Mailing City: Tucson
Mailing State: AZ
Mailing ZIP Code: 85712-3659
General Phone: (520) 811-8101
General Fax: (520) 881-1841
Website: https://www.jupiterimages.com
Personnel: Peter Gariepy (Pres.); Dan Burk (Dir., Mktg.)

WALPOLE

SYNDICATED AD FEATURES, INC.
Street Address 1: 1 Foxhill Dr
Street Address 2: Ste 110
State: MA
ZIP Code: 02081-4418
County: Norfolk
Country: USA
Mailing Address: 1 Foxhill Drive, Suite 110
Mailing City: Walpole
Mailing State: MA
Mailing ZIP Code: 02081
General Phone: (800) 783-5600
General Fax: (508) 668-2168
General/National Adv. E-mail: info@synadinc.com
Website: https://www.synadinc.com
Year Established: 1967
Personnel: David G. Margolis (Pres.); Bill Blumsack (Vice Pres./Eastern Regl. Sales Dir.); Tim Wydro (Mid-Atlantic Regl. Sales Mgr.); Susan Gundersen (Office Mgr.); Jodi Rutkowski (Controller)

CLIPPING BUREAUS

ASHLAND

VIRGINIA CLIPPING SERVICE
Street address 1: 10195 Maple Leaf Ct
Postal code: 23005-8136
County: Hanover
Country: USA
Mailing address 1: 10195 Maple Leaf Ct
Mailing city: Ashland
Mailing state: VA
Mailing zip: 23005-8136
Office phone: (804) 550-5114
Office fax: (804) 550-5116
General e-mail: virginiaclipping@burrellesluce.com
Web address: www.vaclippingservice.com
Personnel: Duska Adams (Client Servs. Mgr.)
Main (survey) contact: Duska Adams

BROOKINGS

SOUTH DAKOTA NEWSPAPER ASSOCIATION
Street address 1: 1125 32nd Ave
Street address state: SD
Postal code: 57006-4707
County: Brookings
Country: USA
Mailing address 1: 1125 32nd Ave
Mailing city: Brookings
Mailing state: SD
Mailing zip: 57006-4707
Office phone: (605) 692-4300
Office fax: (605) 692-6388
Other phone: (800) 658-3697
General e-mail: sdna@sdna.com
Web address: www.sdna.com
Year established: 1882
Special Notes: Elections held in May
Personnel: David Bordewyk (Exec. Dir.); John Brooks (Advertising Sales Director); Nicole Herrig (Business Manager); Sandy DeBeer (Advertising Placement Coordinator)
Main (survey) contact: David Bordewyk; David Bordewyk

CHICAGO

CISION
Street address 1: 130 E Randolph St, 7th Floor
Street address state: IL
Postal code: 60601
Country: USA
Mailing address 1: 130 E Randolph St, 7th Floor
Mailing city: Chicago
Mailing state: IL
Mailing zip: 60601
Office phone: 866-639-5087
General e-mail: CisionPR@cision.com
Web address: www.cision.com
Year established: 1867
Personnel: Kevin Akeroyd (CEO); Jack Pearlstein (Exec. VP And CFO); Whitney Benner (Chief HR Officer)
Main (survey) contact: ()

CISION US, INC.
Street address 1: 332 S Michigan Ave
Street address state: IL
Postal code: 60604-4434
County: Cook
Country: USA
Mailing address 1: 332 S Michigan Ave Ste 900
Mailing city: Chicago
Mailing state: IL
Mailing zip: 60604-4393
Office phone: (866) 639-5087
Office fax: (312) 922-3127
General e-mail: info.us@cision.com
Web address: www.cision.com
Personnel: Michael Renderman (Vice Pres., Bus. Devel.); Diana Eagen (Exec.Dir.)
Main (survey) contact: Dawn Conway

COLUMBIA

KENTUCKY PRESS CLIPPING SERVICE - NEWZ GROUP
Street address 1: 409 W. Vandiver, Bldg #3, Ste. 100
Street address 2: Bldg 3 # STE 100
Street address state: MO
Postal code: 65202
County: Boone
Country: USA
Mailing address 1: PO Box 873
Mailing city: Columbia
Mailing state: MO
Mailing zip: 65205-0873
Office phone: (573) 474-1000
Office fax: (573) 474-1001
Other phone: (800) 474-1111
General e-mail: info@newzgroup.com
Web address: www.newzgroup.com
Year established: 1995
Association Description: Newz Group provides publisher solutions including digital archiving, archive monetization, e-edition publishing, public notice website hosting and online tear sheets.
Parent company: Geotel
Main (survey) contact: Sierra Rudloff

MISSOURI PRESS CLIPPING BUREAU - NEWZ GROUP
Street address 1: 409 W. Vandiver, Bldg #3, Ste. 100
Street address 2: Bldg 3 # STE 100
Street address state: MO
Postal code: 65202
County: Boone
Country: USA
Mailing address 1: PO Box 873
Mailing city: Columbia
Mailing state: MO
Mailing zip: 65205-0873
Office phone: (573) 474-1000
Office fax: (573) 474-1001
Other phone: (800) 474-1111
General e-mail: info@newzgroup.com
Web address: www.newzgroup.com
Year established: 1995
Association Description: Newz Group provides publisher solutions including digital archiving, archive monetization, e-edition publishing, public notice website hosting and online tear sheets.
Personnel: Brad Buchanan (President/CEO); Lee Brooks (Mgr.)
Parent company: Geotel
Main (survey) contact: Sierra Rudloff

NEW MEXICO PRESS CLIPPING BUREAU - NEWZ GROUP
Street address 1: 409 W. Vandiver, Bldg #3, Ste. 100
Street address 2: Bldg 3 # STE 100
Street address state: MO
Postal code: 65202
County: Boone
Country: USA
Mailing address 1: PO Box 873
Mailing city: Columbia
Mailing state: MO
Mailing zip: 65205-0873
Office phone: (573) 474-1000
Office fax: (573) 474-1001
Other phone: (800) 474-1111
General e-mail: info@newzgroup.com
Web address: www.newzgroup.com
Year established: 1995
Association Description: Newz Group provides publisher solutions including digital archiving, archive monetization, e-edition publishing, public notice website hosting and online tear sheets.
Parent company: Geotel
Main (survey) contact: Sierra Rudloff

NEWZ GROUP
Street address 1: 409 Vandiver Dr
Street address 2: Bldg 3
Street address state: MO
Postal code: 65202-3754
County: Boone
Country: USA
Mailing address 1: PO Box 873
Mailing city: Columbia
Mailing state: MO
Mailing zip: 65205-0873
Office phone: (573) 474-1000
Office fax: (573) 474-1001
General e-mail: info@newzgroup.com
Web address: www.newzgroup.com
Year established: 1991
Company Profile: Newz Group´s mission is to identify, extract and deliver media information to news consumers in a high quality, timely and easy-to-use fashion, along with tools to help them parse and analyze data in meaningful ways.
Personnel: Brad Buchanan (Pres.); Scott Buchanan (Vice Pres.); Ian Buchanan (Vice President)
Main (survey) contact: Ian Buchanan

SOUTH CAROLINA PRESS CLIPPING BUREAU
Street address 1: 106 Outlet Pointe Blvd
Street address state: SC
Postal code: 29210-5669
County: Lexington
Country: USA
Mailing address 1: PO Box 873
Mailing city: Columbia
Mailing state: MO
Mailing zip: 65205
Office phone: (573) 474-1000
Other phone: (800) 474-1111
General e-mail: service@newzgroup.com
Web address: www.newzgroup.com
Year established: 1999
Company Profile: Newz Group monitors print, online and broadcast media, offering the most comprehensive monitoring service available.
Personnel: Sarah Frieling (Director of Customer Service)
Parent company: Newz Group
Main (survey) contact: Sarah Frieling

WEST VIRGINIA PRESS CLIPPING BUREAU - NEWZ GROUP
Street address 1: 409 W. Vandiver, Bldg #3, Ste. 100
Street address 2: Bldg 3 # STE 100
Street address state: MO
Postal code: 65202
County: Boone
Country: USA
Mailing address 1: PO Box 873
Mailing city: Columbia
Mailing state: MO
Mailing zip: 65205-0873
Office phone: (573) 474-1000
Office fax: (573) 474-1001
Other phone: (800) 474-1111
General e-mail: info@newzgroup.com
Web address: www.newzgroup.com
Year established: 1995
Association Description: Newz Group provides publisher solutions including digital archiving, archive monetization, e-edition publishing, public notice website hosting and online tear sheets.
Parent company: Geotel
Main (survey) contact: Sierra Rudloff

WYOMING NEWSPAPER CLIPPING SERVICE
Street address 1: 409 Vandiver Dr
Street address 2: Bldg 3 # STE 100
Street address state: MO
Postal code: 65202-3754
County: Boone
Country: USA
Mailing address 1: PO Box 873
Mailing city: Columbia
Mailing state: MO
Mailing zip: 65205-0873
Office phone: (573) 474-1000
Office fax: (573) 474-1001
Other phone: (800) 474-1111
General e-mail: info@newzgroup.com
Web address: www.newzgroup.com
Year established: 1995
Parent company: Geotel
Main (survey) contact: Matthew Davis

DENVER

COLORADO PRESS CLIPPING SERVICE
Street address 1: 1120 N Lincoln St
Street address 2: Ste 912
Street address state: CO
Postal code: 80203-2138
County: Denver
Country: USA
Mailing address 1: 1120 Lincoln St., Ste 912
Mailing city: Denver
Mailing state: CO
Mailing zip: 80203
Office phone: (303) 571-5117
Office fax: (303) 571-1803
General e-mail: coloradopress@colopress.net
Web address: www.coloradopressassociation.com
Association Description: We are the trade association dedicated to the preservation, progression and modernization of Colorado's newspaper and related industries. It is organized to represent the common interests of Colorado's news organizations.
Personnel: Jerry Raehal (CEO)
Main (survey) contact: Jean Creel

DES MOINES

IOWA PRESS CLIPPING BUREAU
Street address 1: 319 E. 5th St., Ste. 6
Street address 2: Ste 6
Street address state: IA
Postal code: 50309
County: Polk
Country: USA
Mailing address 1: PO Box 873
Mailing city: Columbia
Mailing state: MO
Mailing zip: 65205
Office phone: (573) 474-1000
Other phone: (800) 474-1111
General e-mail: service@newzgroup.com
Web address: www.newzgroup.com/

Clipping Bureaus

Year established: 1996
Company Profile: Newz Group monitors print, online and broadcast media, offering the most comprehensive monitoring service available.
Personnel: Sarah Frieling (Director of Customer Service)
Parent company: Newz Group
Main (survey) contact: Sarah Frieling

FLORHAM PARK

BURRELLESLUCE

Street address 1: 30 B Vreeland Road
Street address 2: # B
Street address state: NJ
Postal code: 7932
County: Morris
Country: USA
Mailing address 1: PO Box 674
Mailing city: Florham Park
Mailing state: NJ
Mailing zip: 07932
Office phone: (973) 992-6600
Office fax: (973) 992-7675
Other phone: (800) 631-1160
General e-mail: inquiry@burrellesluce.com
Web address: www.burrellesluce.com
Year established: 1888
Personnel: Robert C. Waggoner (Chrmn./CEO); John P. French (Pres./COO); Rick Melchers (VP, Director of National Sales); Steven Townsley (Director of Publisher Services); Daniel Schaible (Senior VP, Content Management); Michael Lillis (Content Acquisition Specialist)
Main (survey) contact: Johna Burke; Rick Melchers; Robert C. Waggoner

NEW ENGLAND NEWSCLIP AGENCY, INC.

Street address 1: 30 Vreeland Rd
Street address 2: # B
Street address state: NJ
Postal code: 07932-1901
County: Morris
Country: USA
Mailing address 1: PO Box 674
Mailing city: Florham Park
Mailing state: NJ
Mailing zip: 07932-0674
Office phone: (800) 631-1160
Office fax: (973) 992-7675
General e-mail: mmckenna@burrellesluce.com
Web address: www.burrellesluce.com
Company Profile: media monitoring
Personnel: Michael McKenna (National Sales Manager)
Parent company: BurrellesLuce
Main (survey) contact: Michael McKenna

KNOXVILLE

TENNESSEE PRESS ASSOCIATION

Street address 1: 412 N. Cedar Bluff Road
Street address 2: Suite 403
Street address state: TN
Postal code: 37923
County: Knox

Country: USA
Mailing address 1: 412 N. Cedar Bluff Road
Mailing address 2: Suite 403
Mailing city: Knoxville
Mailing state: TN
Mailing zip: 37923
Office phone: 865-584-5761
Office fax: 865-558-8687
General e-mail: info@tnpress.com
Web address: www.tnpress.com
Year established: 1947
Special Notes: Elections held in June
Personnel: Carol Daniels (Exec. V. P.); Shelley Davis (Sales and Marketing); Robyn Gentile (Member Services Manager); Earl Goodman (Senior Media Buyer); Becky Moats (Networks Coordinator); Jason Davidson (National Sales Rep.)
Main (survey) contact: Carol Daniels

LITTLE ROCK

ARKANSAS NEWSPAPER CLIPPING SERVICE

Street address 1: 411 S Victory St
Street address 2: Ste 201
Street address state: AR
Postal code: 72201-2935
County: Pulaski
Country: USA
Mailing address 1: 411 S Victory St Ste 201
Mailing city: Little Rock
Mailing state: AR
Mailing zip: 72201-2935
Office phone: (573) 474-1000
Office fax: (573) 474-1001
General e-mail: sfrieling@newsgroup.com
Web address: www.newzgroup.com
Year established: 1995
Personnel: Shirley Anderson (Mgr.)
Main (survey) contact: Ian Buchanan

LONDON

INTERNATIONAL PRESS CUTTING BUREAU

Street address 1: 224/236 Walworth Rd.
Street address state: ENG
Postal code: SE17 1JE
Country: UK
Mailing address 1: 224/236 Walworth Rd.
Mailing city: London
Mailing state: ENG
Mailing zip: SE17 1JE
Office phone: 7708 2113
Office fax: 7701 4489
General e-mail: info@ipcb.co.uk
Web address: www.ipcb.co.uk
Personnel: Robert Podro (Sr. Partner/Gen. Mgr.)
Main (survey) contact: Robert Podro

LONDON

ROMEIKE LTD.

Street address 1: Romeike House, 290-296 Green Lanes, Palmers Green
Postal code: N13 5TP

Country: UK
Mailing address 1: Romeike House, 290-296 Green Lanes
Mailing address 2: Palmers Green
Mailing city: London
Mailing zip: N13 5TP
Office phone: 882 0155
Office fax: 882 6716
Web address: www.romeike.com
Personnel: Giselle Bodie (Mng. Dir.); Michael Higgins (Mng. Dir.)
Main (survey) contact: Michael Higgins

LOS ANGELES

ALLEN'S PRESS CLIPPING BUREAU

Street address 1: 215 W 6th St
Street address 2: Apt 1100
Street address state: CA
Postal code: 90014-1931
County: Los Angeles
Country: USA
Mailing address 1: 215 W 6th St Apt 1100
Mailing city: Los Angeles
Mailing state: CA
Mailing zip: 90014-1931
Office phone: (213) 628-4214
Office fax: (213) 627-0889
General e-mail: la@allenspcb.com
Web address: www.allenspress.4t.com
Personnel: Linda Wiser (Office Mgr)
Main (survey) contact: Whit Draper

PORTLAND

ALLEN'S PRESS CLIPPING BUREAU

Street address 1: 621 SW Alder St
Street address 2: Ste 540
Street address state: OR
Postal code: 97205-3620
County: Multnomah
Country: USA
Mailing address 1: 621 SW Alder St Ste 540
Mailing city: Portland
Mailing state: OR
Mailing zip: 97205-3691
Office phone: (503) 223-7824
Office fax: (503) 223-3819
General e-mail: portland@allenspcb.com
Web address: www.allenspress.4t.com
Personnel: Whit Draper (Office Mgr.)
Main (survey) contact: Whit Draper

SAN FRANCISCO

ALLEN'S PRESS CLIPPING BUREAU

Street address 1: 657 Mission St
Street address 2: Ste 602
Street address state: CA
Postal code: 94105-4120
County: San Francisco
Country: USA
Mailing address 1: 657 Mission St Ste 602
Mailing city: San Francisco
Mailing state: CA
Mailing zip: 94105-4197
Office phone: (415) 392-2353
Office fax: (415) 362-6208
Web address: www.allenspress.4t.com
Personnel: John N. McCombs (Gen. Mgr.)

Main (survey) contact: Whit Draper

SEATTLE

ALLEN'S PRESS CLIPPING BUREAU

Street address 1: 1218 3rd Ave
Street address 2: Ste 1010
Street address state: WA
Postal code: 98101-3290
County: King
Country: USA
Mailing address 1: 1218 3rd Ave # 1010
Mailing city: Seattle
Mailing state: WA
Mailing zip: 98101-3097
Office phone: (206) 622-8312
Office fax: (206) 622-5748
General e-mail: seattle@allenspcb.com
Web address: www.allenspress.4t.com
Year established: 1888
Association Description: Complete News Media Monitoring Servcie
Personnel: Grace Chrystie (Regional Manager)
Main (survey) contact: Whit Draper

SPRINGFIELD

ILLINOIS PRESS CLIPPING BUREAU

Street address 1: 900 Community Dr
Street address state: IL
Postal code: 62703-5180
County: Sangamon
Country: USA
Mailing address 1: 900 Community Dr
Mailing city: Springfield
Mailing state: IL
Mailing zip: 62703-5180
Office phone: (217) 241-1300
Office fax: (217) 241-1301
General e-mail: rkline@illinoispress.org
Web address: www.IllinoisPress.org
Personnel: Sam Fisher (Executive Director)
Main (survey) contact: Jeff Holman

TOPEKA

KANSAS PRESS CLIPPING SERVICE

Street address 1: 5423 SW 7th St
Street address state: KS
Postal code: 66606-2330
County: Shawnee
Country: USA
Mailing address 1: PO Box 873
Mailing city: Columbia
Mailing state: MO
Mailing zip: 65205
Office phone: (573) 474-1000
Other phone: (800) 474-1111
General e-mail: service@newzgroup.com
Web address: www.newzgroup.com
Year established: 2005
Company Profile: Newz Group monitors print, online and broadcast media, offering the most comprehensive monitoring service available.
Personnel: Sarah Frieling (Director of Customer Service)
Parent company: Newz Group
Main (survey) contact: Sarah Frieling

ELECTRONIC CLIPPING BUREAUS

ANN ARBOR

PROQUEST DIALOG

Street address 1: 789 E Eisenhower Pkwy
Street address state: MI
Postal code: 48108-3218
Country: USA
Mailing state: MI
General e-mail: customer@dialog.com
Web address: proquest.com/go/pqd
Main Contact: Alison Roth

ARLINGTON

YELLOWBRIX

Street address 1: 200 North Glebe Road, Ste. 1025
Street address 2: Ste 1025
Street address state: VA
Postal code: 22203
Country: USA
Mailing address 1: PO Box 1509
Mailing city: Centreville
Mailing state: VA
Mailing zip: 20122-8509
Office phone: (703) 548-3300
Office fax: (703) 548-9151
General e-mail: info@yellowbrix.com
Web address: www.yellowbrix.com
Personnel: Jeffrey P. Massa (Founder/Pres./CEO); Tom Hargis (Adv. Mgr.)
Main Contact: Jeffrey P. Massa

COLUMBIA

KENTUCKY PRESS CLIPPING SERVICE - NEWZ GROUP

Street address 1: 409 W. Vandiver, Bldg #3, Ste. 100
Street address 2: Bldg 3 # STE 100
Street address state: MO
Postal code: 65202
Country: USA
Mailing address 1: PO Box 873
Mailing city: Columbia
Mailing state: MO
Mailing zip: 65205-0873
Office phone: (573) 474-1000
Office fax: (573) 474-1001
Other phone: (800) 474-1111
General e-mail: info@newzgroup.com
Web address: www.newzgroup.com
Year established: 1995
Association Description: Newz Group provides publisher solutions including digital archiving, archive monetization, e-edition publishing, public notice website hosting and online tear sheets.
Parent company: Geotel
Main Contact: Sierra Rudloff

MISSOURI PRESS CLIPPING BUREAU - NEWZ GROUP

Street address 1: 409 W. Vandiver, Bldg #3, Ste. 100
Street address 2: Bldg 3 # STE 100
Street address state: MO
Postal code: 65202
Country: USA
Mailing address 1: PO Box 873
Mailing city: Columbia
Mailing state: MO
Mailing zip: 65205-0873
Office phone: (573) 474-1000
Office fax: (573) 474-1001
Other phone: (800) 474-1111
General e-mail: info@newzgroup.com
Web address: www.newzgroup.com
Year established: 1995
Association Description: Newz Group provides publisher solutions including digital archiving, archive monetization, e-edition publishing, public notice website hosting and online tear sheets.
Personnel: Brad Buchanan (President/CEO); Lee Brooks (Mgr.)
Parent company: Geotel
Main Contact: Sierra Rudloff

NEW MEXICO PRESS CLIPPING BUREAU - NEWZ GROUP

Street address 1: 409 W. Vandiver, Bldg #3, Ste. 100
Street address 2: Bldg 3 # STE 100
Street address state: MO
Postal code: 65202
Country: USA
Mailing address 1: PO Box 873
Mailing city: Columbia
Mailing state: MO
Mailing zip: 65205-0873
Office phone: (573) 474-1000
Office fax: (573) 474-1001
Other phone: (800) 474-1111
General e-mail: info@newzgroup.com
Web address: www.newzgroup.com

WEST VIRGINIA PRESS CLIPPING BUREAU - NEWZ GROUP

Street address 1: 409 W. Vandiver, Bldg #3, Ste. 100
Street address 2: Bldg 3 # STE 100
Street address state: MO
Postal code: 65202
Country: USA
Mailing address 1: PO Box 873
Mailing city: Columbia
Mailing state: MO
Mailing zip: 65205-0873
Office phone: (573) 474-1000
Office fax: (573) 474-1001
Other phone: (800) 474-1111
General e-mail: info@newzgroup.com
Web address: www.newzgroup.com
Year established: 1995
Association Description: Newz Group provides publisher solutions including digital archiving, archive monetization, e-edition publishing, public notice website hosting and online tear sheets.
Parent company: Geotel
Main Contact: Sierra Rudloff

DES MOINES

IOWA PRESS CLIPPING BUREAU

Street address 1: 319 E. 5th St., Ste. 6
Street address 2: Ste 6
Street address state: IA
Postal code: 50309
Country: USA
Mailing address 1: PO Box 873
Mailing city: Columbia
Mailing state: MO
Mailing zip: 65205
Office phone: (573) 474-1000
Other phone: (800) 474-1111
General e-mail: service@newzgroup.com
Web address: www.newzgroup.com/
Year established: 1996
Company Profile: Newz Group monitors print, online and broadcast media, offering the most comprehensive monitoring service available.
Personnel: Sarah Frieling (Director of Customer Service)
Parent company: Newz Group
Main Contact: Sarah Frieling

FLORHAM PARK

BURRELLESLUCE

Street address 1: 30 B Vreeland Road
Street address 2: # B
Street address state: NJ
Postal code: 7932
Country: USA
Mailing address 1: PO Box 674
Mailing city: Florham Park
Mailing state: NJ
Mailing zip: 07932
Office phone: (973) 992-6600
Office fax: (973) 992-7675
Other phone: (800) 631-1160
General e-mail: inquiry@burrellesluce.com
Web address: www.burrellesluce.com
Year established: 1888
Personnel: Robert C. Waggoner (Chrmn./CEO); John P. French (Pres./COO); Rick Melchers (VP, Director of National Sales); Steven Townsley (Director of Publisher Services); Daniel Schaible (Senior VP, Content Management); Michael Lillis (Content Acquisition Specialist)
Main Contact: Johna Burke; Rick Melchers; Robert C. Waggoner

NEW YORK

ASSOCIATED PRESS INFORMATION SERVICES

Street address 1: 450 W 33rd St
Street address state: NY
Postal code: 10001-2603
Country: USA
Mailing address 1: 450 W 33rd St Fl 15
Mailing city: New York
Mailing state: NY
Mailing zip: 10001-2647
Office phone: (212) 621-1500
Office fax: (212) 621-7520
General e-mail: info@ap.org
Web address: www.ap.org
Association Description: News Desk Software.
Personnel: Ted Mendelsohn (Dir. Sales)
Main Contact: Ted Mendelsohn

NEWSPAPER REPRESENTATIVES - FOREIGN

EASTON

LEE & STEEL LLC
Street address 1: 25 Burroughs Rd
Street address state: CT
Postal code: 06612-1409
County: Fairfield
Country: USA
Mailing address 1: PO Box 2007
Mailing city: Darien
Mailing state: CT
Mailing zip: 06820-0007
Office phone: (203) 445-8900
Office fax: (203) 445-1885
General e-mail: michael.lee@leeandsteel.com
Year established: 1991
Employee Associations: Michael Lee (CEO)
Main (survey) contact: Michael Lee

FAYETTEVILLE

ADVANTAGE NEWSPAPER CONSULTANTS
Street address 1: 2850 Village Dr
Street address 2: Ste 102
Street address state: NC
Postal code: 28304-3864
County: Cumberland
Country: USA
Mailing address 1: 2850 Village Dr
Mailing address 2: Suite 102
Mailing city: Fayetteville
Mailing state: NC
Mailing zip: 28304
Office phone: (910) 323-0349
Office fax: (910) 323-9280
General e-mail: info@newspaperconsultants.com
Web address: newspaperconsultants.com
Year established: 1996
Note: Advantage Newspaper Consultants (ANC) is recognized as the leader in TV Magazine advertising sales in the United States. ANC works with both independent publishers and major newspaper chains to increase their core product ad revenue using innovative campaigns and creative, seasoned sales professionals that produce quantifiable results. Our sales manager's work with newspaper management to set goals and create an incentive plan which accelerates a TV Magazine sales campaign targeted towards finding key hidden revenue in their market in two weeks or less. Using the same proven formula of enthusiastic joint sales calls and dedicated management support that has lead to thousands of successful TV magazine sales campaigns, ANC also offers a cross-platform advertising sales program - Total Market Reach (TMR) - which includes print, mobile and digital ad combo sales.
Employee Associations: Timothy O. Dellinger (President); Susan M. Jolley (General Mgr.); Marie Smith (Exec. Dir. of Sales)
Main (survey) contact: Shelby Adams

HAMBURG

AXEL SPRINGER VERLAG AG
Street address 1: Axel Springer Platz 1
Postal code: D-203
Country: Germany
Mailing address 1: Axel Springer Platz 1
Mailing city: Hamburg
Mailing zip: D-20350
Telephone country code: 49
Telephone city code: 40
Office phone: 34700
Office fax: 3472 5540
Web address: www.asv.de
Employee Associations: Mathias Dopfner (Chrmn.)
Main (survey) contact: Barbara Krist

LAWTON

LAWTON MEDIA INC.
Street address 1: 102 SW 3rd St
Street address state: OK
Postal code: 73501-4031
County: Comanche
Country: USA
Mailing address 1: P.O. Box 2069
Mailing city: Lawton
Mailing state: OK
Mailing zip: 73502
Telephone country code: 1
Office phone: (580) 353-0620
Office fax: (580) 585-5140
General e-mail: srobertson@swoknews.com
Web address: www.swoknews.com
Year established: 1901
Employee Associations: David Hale (Pres.)
Main (survey) contact: David Hale

MIAMI

CHARNEY/PALACIOS & CO.
Street address 1: 5201 Blue Lagoon Dr
Street address 2: Ste 200
Street address state: FL
Postal code: 33126-2065
County: Miami-Dade
Country: USA
Mailing address 1: 5201 Blue Lagoon Dr Ste 200
Mailing city: Miami
Mailing state: FL
Mailing zip: 33126-2065
Office phone: (786) 388-6340
Office fax: (786) 388-9113
General e-mail: miami@publicitas.com
Web address: www.publicitas.com
Note: Charney/Palacios is a subsidiary of Publicitas
Employee Associations: Grace Palacios (CEO); Maria Jose Torres (Sales Mktg. Mgr.)
Main (survey) contact: Grace Palacios

NEW YORK

DICOMM MEDIA
Street address 1: 350 5th Ave
Street address 2: Fl 59
Street address state: NY
Postal code: 10118-5999
County: New York
Country: USA
Mailing address 1: 350 Fifth Ave. 59th Floor
Mailing city: New York
Mailing state: NY
Mailing zip: 10118
Office phone: (646) 536-7206
Office fax: (973) 335-1038
General e-mail: info@dicommintl.com
Web address: www.dicommintl.com
Year established: 1995
Note: A unique media sales firm which represents numerous different Canadian media companies and publishers. We also work with many clients on assisting with their planning and buying efforts in Canada across all media types including print, digital/mobile, broadcast, radio, out of home and any other medium available.
Employee Associations: Thibaud Wallaert (Gen. Mgr.)
Main (survey) contact: Thibaud Wallaert

DOW JONES INTERNATIONAL MARKETING SERVICES
Street address 1: 1211 Avenue of the Americas
Street address state: NY
Postal code: 10036
County: New York
Country: USA
Mailing address 1: 1211 Avenue of the Americas
Mailing city: New York
Mailing state: NY
Mailing zip: 10036
Office phone: (800) 369-0166
General e-mail: service@dowjones.com
Web address: www.dowjones.com
Year established: 1882
Employee Associations: William Lewis (CEO); Almar Latour (Pub. Exec. V. P.); Christina Tassell (CFO); Matthew Murray (Editor In Chief)
Main (survey) contact: Toby Doman

MARSTON WEBB INTERNATIONAL
Street address 1: 60 Madison Ave
Street address 2: Ste 1212
Street address state: NY
Postal code: 10010-1636
County: New York
Country: USA
Mailing address 1: 270 Madison Ave Rm 1203
Mailing city: New York
Mailing state: NY
Mailing zip: 10016-0601
Office phone: (212) 684-6601
Office fax: (212) 725-4709
General e-mail: marwebint@cs.com
Web address: www.marstonwebb.com
Year established: 1981
Note: MWI also represents South African and Middle Eastern papers
Employee Associations: Victor Webb (Pres.); Madlene Olson (Vice Pres.)
Main (survey) contact: Victor Webb

ORLANDO

MULTIMEDIA, INC.
Street address 1: 7061 Grand National Dr
Street address 2: Ste 127
Street address state: FL
Postal code: 32819-8992
County: Orange
Country: USA
Mailing address 1: 7061 Grand National Dr Ste 127
Mailing city: Orlando
Mailing state: FL
Mailing zip: 32819-8992
Office phone: (407) 903-5000
Office fax: (407) 363-9809
General e-mail: info@multimediausa.com
Web address: www.multimediausa.com
Employee Associations: Fernando Mariano (Pres.)
Main (survey) contact: Fernando Mariano

SOUTHPORT

ADMARKET INTERNATIONAL (DIV. OF MARCOM INTERNATIONAL, INC.)
Street address 1: 105 Woodrow Ave
Street address state: CT
Postal code: 06890-1121
County: Fairfield
Country: USA
Mailing address 1: 105 Woodrow Ave
Mailing city: Southport
Mailing state: CT
Mailing zip: 06890-1121
Office phone: (203) 319-1000
Office fax: (203) 319-1004
Year established: 1986
Note: AdMarket International plans and places advertising in 15,000 media newspapers in over 200 countries worldwide
Employee Associations: Nabil E. Fares (Pres./CEO); Kristina Kalman (Acct. Exec.)

TORONTO

MEMBER SERVICES COORDINATOR
Street address 1: 37 Front St E
Street address 2: Suite 200
Street address state: ON
Postal code: M5E 1B3
County: York
Country: Canada
Mailing address 1: 37 Front Street E
Mailing address 2: Suite 200
Mailing city: Toronto
Mailing state: ON
Mailing zip: M5E 1B3
Office phone: (416) 923-7724
General e-mail: adreach@ocna.org
Web address: www.adreach.ca
Employee Associations: Kelly Gorven (Member Services Coordinator); Caroline Medwell (Executive Director)
Parent company: Ontario Community Newspapers Association
Main (survey) contact: Kelly Gorven

NEWBASE
Street address 1: 468 Queen Str. E
Street address 2: Suite 500
Street address state: ON
Postal code: M5A 1T7
Country: USA
Mailing address 1: 468 Queen Str. E, Suite 500
Mailing city: Toronto
Mailing state: ON
Mailing zip: M5A 1T7
Office phone: (416) 363 1388
Office fax: (416) 363 2889
Web address: www.thenewbase.com
Employee Associations: Lesley Conway (Pres.); Doug St. John (Digital Director)
Main (survey) contact: Wayne St. John

WEST HILLS

ADMAX INTERNATIONAL MEDIA
Street address 1: 7326 McLaren Ave
Street address state: CA
Postal code: 91307-2123
County: Los Angeles
Country: USA
Mailing address 1: 7326 McLaren Ave
Mailing city: West Hills
Mailing state: CA
Mailing zip: 91307-2123
Office phone: (818) 715-9931
Office fax: (253) 648-4574
General e-mail: admax@sbcglobal.net
Web address: www.admaxinternational.com
Year established: 1992
Employee Associations: Maria de los Angeles (Pres.); Edward G. Wilson (Pres.); Maria Teresa Perez (Media Dir.); Brad Brigg (Acct. Exec.); Simon English (Acct. Exec.); Larry Redd (Acct. Exec.); Julio Vender (Acct. Exec.)
Main (survey) contact: Maria de los Angeles

NEWSPAPER REPRESENTATIVES - NATIONAL

BLOOMINGTON

CAMPUS MEDIA GROUP

Street address 2: 7760 France Ave S
Street address city: Ste 800
Street address state: MN
Postal code: 55435-5929
County: Hennepin
Country: USA
Mailing address 1: 7760 France Ave South, Suite 800
Mailing address 2: Suite 800
Mailing city: Bloomington
Mailing state: MN
Mailing zip: 55435
Office phone: (952) 854-3100
General e-mail: sales@campusmediagroup.com
Web address: www.campusmediagroup.com
Year established: 2002
Note: College marketing agency.
Personnel: Jason Bakker (COO); Tom Borgerding (Pres./CEO)
Main Contact: Jason Bakker

BOSTON

AD REPS

Street address 2: 51 Church St
Postal code: 02116-5417
County: Suffolk
Country: USA
Mailing address 1: 51 Church St
Mailing city: Boston
Mailing state: MA
Mailing zip: 02116-5417
Office phone: (617) 542-6913
Office fax: (617) 542-7227
General e-mail: adreps1@yahoo.com
Personnel: Steve Ganak (Pres.)
Main Contact: Steve Ganak

CARLSBAD

LATINO 247 MEDIA GROUP

Street address 2: 3445 Catalina Dr
Street address state: CA
Postal code: 92010-2856
County: San Diego
Country: USA
Mailing address 1: 3445 Catalina Dr.
Mailing city: Carlsbad
Mailing state: CA
Mailing zip: 92010-2856
Office phone: (760) 579-1696
Office fax: (760) 434-7476
General e-mail: kirk@whisler.com
Web address: www.latinos247.com
Year established: 1996
Personnel: Kirk Whisler (Pres.); Ana PatiÃ±o (General Manager); Ericka Benitez (Accounting Manager)
Main Contact: Kirk Whisler; Laura Najera

CHARLOTTESVILLE

C-VILLE HOLDINGS LLC

Street address 2: 308 E Main St
Street address state: VA
Postal code: 22902-5234
County: Charlottesville City
Country: USA
Mailing address 1: P.O. Box 119
Mailing city: Charlottesville
Mailing state: VA
Mailing zip: 22902
Office phone: 434/817-2749
Office fax: 434/817-2758
Other phone: (916) 551-1776

General e-mail: aimee@c-ville.com
Web address: www.c-ville.com
Year established: 1995
Personnel: Jessica Luck (Ed)
Main Contact: Jessica Luck

CHICAGO

CENTRO INC.

Street address 2: 11 E Madison St
Street address city: 6th Fl.
Street address state: IL
Postal code: 60602-4574
County: Cook
Country: USA
Mailing address 1: 11 E. Madison St.
Mailing address 2: 6th Fl.
Mailing city: Chicago
Mailing state: IL
Mailing zip: 60602
Office phone: (312) 423-1565
General e-mail: socialmedia@centro.net
Web address: www.centro.net
Year established: 2001
Personnel: Katie Risch (EVP, Customer Experience); John Hyland (VP, Pub. Solutions)
Main Contact: Anthony Loredo

COLUMBIA

ADVERTISING MEDIA PLUS, INC.

Street address 2: 5397 Twin Knolls Rd
Street address city: Ste 17
Street address state: MD
Postal code: 21045-3256
County: Howard
Country: USA
Mailing address 1: PO Box 1529
Mailing city: Ellicott City
Mailing state: MD
Mailing zip: 21041-1529
Office phone: (410) 740-5009
Office fax: (410) 740-5888
General e-mail: info@ampsinc.net
Web address: www.ampsinc.net
Year established: 2001
Personnel: Daniel Medinger (Owner and President)
Parent company: Medinger Media LLC
Main Contact: Daniel Medinger

DALLAS

TRIBUNE MEDIA NETWORK

Street address 2: 12900 Preston Rd
Street address city: Ste 615
Street address state: TX
Postal code: 75230-1322
County: Dallas
Country: USA
Mailing address 1: 12900 Preston Rd Ste 615
Mailing city: Dallas
Mailing state: TX
Mailing zip: 75230-1322
Office phone: (972) 789-6920
Office fax: (972) 239-2737
Web address: www.tribunemediagroup.com
Personnel: Grant Moise (Southwestern Regl. Sales Dir.)
Main Contact: Gary Weitman

DENVER

VOICE MEDIA GROUP

Street address 2: 969 N Broadway
Street address state: CO
Postal code: 80203-2705
County: Denver

Country: USA
Mailing address 1: 969 Broadway
Mailing city: Denver
Mailing state: CO
Mailing zip: 80203-2705
Office phone: (602) 271-0040
General e-mail: joe.larkin@voicemediagroup.com
Web address: www.voicemediagroup.com
Note: Newspaper represents for 50 alternative newsweeklies
Personnel: Joe Larkin (Sr. Vice Pres. Sales); Susan Belair (Vice Pres., Sales)
Main Contact: Susan Belair; Joe Larkin

FAYETTEVILLE

ADVANTAGE NEWSPAPER CONSULTANTS

Street address 2: 2850 Village Dr
Street address city: Ste 102
Street address state: NC
Postal code: 28304-3864
County: Cumberland
Country: USA
Mailing address 1: 2850 Village Dr
Mailing address 2: Suite 102
Mailing city: Fayetteville
Mailing state: NC
Mailing zip: 28304
Office phone: (910) 323-0349
Office fax: (910) 323-9280
General e-mail: info@newspaperconsultants.com
Web address: newspaperconsultants.com
Year established: 1996
Note: Advantage Newspaper Consultants (ANC) is recognized as the leader in TV Magazine advertising sales in the United States. ANC works with both independent publishers and major newspaper chains to increase their core product ad revenue using innovative campaigns and creative, seasoned sales professionals that produce quantifiable results. Our sales managerâ€™s work with newspaper management to set goals and create an incentive plan which accelerates a TV Magazine sales campaign targeted towards finding key hidden revenue in their market in two weeks or less. Using the same proven formula of enthusiastic joint sales calls and dedicated management support that has lead to thousands of successful TV magazine sales campaigns, ANC also offers a cross-platform advertising sales program - Total Market Reach (TMR) - which includes print, mobile and digital ad combo sales.
Personnel: Timothy O. Dellinger (President); Susan M. Jolley (General Mgr.); Marie Smith (Exec. Dir. of Sales)
Main Contact: Shelby Adams

GAINESVILLE

SHELBY PUBLISHING CO. INC.

Street address 2: 517 Green St NW
Street address state: GA
Postal code: 30501-3313
County: Hall
Country: USA
Office phone: (770) 534-8380
Office fax: (678) 343-2197
Web address: www.theshelbyreport.com
Year established: 1967
Personnel: Geoffrey Welch (VP/Sales Mgr. Midwest); C. Ronald Johnston
Main Contact: Geoffrey Welch

LAKE MARY

INTERSECT MEDIA SOLUTIONS

Street address 2: 1025 Greenwood Blvd.
Street address city: Suite 191
Street address state: FL
Postal code: 32746-5410
County: Seminole
Country: USA
Mailing address 1: 1025 Greenwood Blvd., Suite 191
Mailing city: Lake Mary
Mailing state: FL
Mailing zip: 32746-5410
Office phone: (866) 404-5913
General e-mail: info@mediagenius.com
Web address: www.intersectmediasolutions.com
Year established: 1959
Personnel: Dean Ridings (Pres./CEO); Mark Burger (VP, Finance & CFO); Carolyn Nolte (VP, Strategy); Jessica Pitts (VP, Operations)
Parent company: Florida Press Association
Main Contact: Carolyn Nolte

LOS ANGELES

CALIFORNIA NEWSPAPER SERVICE BUREAU (CNSB)

Street address 2: 915 E 1st St
Street address state: CA
Postal code: 90012-4050
County: Los Angeles
Country: USA
Mailing address 1: 915 E 1st St
Mailing city: Los Angeles
Mailing state: CA
Mailing zip: 90012-4000
Office phone: (213) 229-5500
Office fax: (213) 229-5481
Other phone: 800-7887540
Other fax: 800-474-9444
General e-mail: bulksales@dailyjournal.com
Web address: www.legaladstore.com
Year established: 1888
Note: The Daily Journal Corporation is a publisher of legal and business publications, including the Los Angeles and San Francisco Daily Journals, distributed in major California cities. Additionally, its in-house clearinghouse service provides ad placement services to government agencies, attorney's and other advertisers for legally mandated and outreach advertising including class action notices in any daily, community and/or ethnic publication and/or websites.
Personnel: Noemi Mendoza (Bulk Sale of Business Assets)
Main Contact: Noemi Mendoza

LOS ANGELES

TRIBUNE MEDIA NETWORK

Street address 2: 202 W 1st St
Street address state: CA
Postal code: 90012-4299
County: Los Angeles
Country: USA
Mailing address 1: 202 W 1st St
Mailing city: Los Angeles
Mailing state: CA
Mailing zip: 90012-4299
Office phone: (213) 237-2135
Office fax: (213) 237-2007
Personnel: Peter Liguori (Pres./CEO); Richard Jones (Dir., Western Reg.)
Main Contact: Gary Weitman

MEXICO CITY

TOWMAR REPRESENTACIONES S.A.

Street address 2: Presa Endho # 11
Street address city: Col. Irrigacion, M.H.
Street address state: FL
Postal code: 11500
County: Distrito Federal
Country: Mexico
Mailing address 1: Presa Endho # 11
Mailing address 2: Col. Irrigacion, D.F.
Mailing city: Mexico City
Mailing zip: 11500
Office phone: (55) 5395-5888
Office fax: (55) 5395-4985
General e-mail: INFO@towmar.net
Web address: www.towmar.net
Year established: 1967
Note: New address
Personnel: Juan Martinez Dugay (Pres.); Juan Martinez Dugay (Pres.); Cesar Quijas (VP, Sales)
Main Contact: Juan Martinez Dugay; Juan Martinez Dugay

MINNETONKA

MEDIASPACE SOLUTIONS

Street address 2: 5600 Rowland Rd
Street address city: Suite 170
Street address state: MN
Postal code: 55343
County: Hennepin
Country: USA
Mailing address 1: 5600 Rowland Rd, Suite 170
Mailing city: Minnetonka
Mailing state: MN
Mailing zip: 55343
Office phone: (612) 253-3900
Office fax: (612) 454-2848
Other phone: (888) 672-2100
General e-mail: bstcyr@mediaspace.com
Web address: www.mediaspacesolutions.com
Year established: 1999
Personnel: Randy Grunow (Chief Operating Officer); Brian St. Cyr (VP of Business Development & Marketing); Tony Buesing (Dir., Account Development); Brian Kieser (Sr. Med. Supervisor); Colin May (Director of Media Development); Carol Wagner (Buying Manager); Jason Armstrong (Buying Supervisor); Tom Johnson (Director Media Planning)
Main Contact: Brian St. Cyr

MISSISSAUGA

METROLAND MEDIA GROUP LTD.

Street address 2: 3715 Laird Road
Street address city: Unit 6
Street address state: ON
Postal code: L5L 0A3
Country: Canada
Mailing address 1: 3715 Laird Road, Unit 6
Mailing city: Mississauga
Mailing state: ON
Mailing zip: L5L 0A3
Office phone: (866) 838-8960
Office fax: (905) 279-5103
General e-mail: result@metroland.com
Web address: www.metroland.com
Personnel: Ian Oliver (Pres.); Kathie Bride (Vice Pres.); Tim Whittaker (Sr. Vice Pres.); Ian McLeod (Sr. Vice Pres.); Ian Proudfoot (Vice Pres.); Brenda Biller (Vice Pres., HR); Joe Anderson (Vice Pres.); Bruce Danford (Vice Pres.); Ron Lenyk (Vice Pres.); Ken Nugent (Vice Pres.); Carol Peddie (Vice Pres.); Gordon Paolucci; Kukle Terry (Vice President); Lois Tuffin (Ed-In-Chief); John Willems; Scott Miller Cressman; Tracy Magee-Graham; Haggert Peter (Editor-In-Chief); Terry Kukle (VP, Business Development & Acquisitions)
Main Contact: Kathie Bride; Ian Oliver

MOUNTAINSIDE

RIVENDELL MEDIA, INC.

Street address 2: 1248 US Highway 22
Street address state: NJ
Postal code: 07092-2692
County: Union
Country: USA
Mailing address 1: 1248 US Highway 22 Ste 2
Mailing city: Mountainside
Mailing state: NJ
Mailing zip: 07092-2692
Office phone: (908) 232-2021 EXT 200
Office fax: (908) 232-0521
General e-mail: info@rivendellmedia.com; sales@rivendellmedia.com
Web address: www.rivendellmedia.com
Year established: 1979
Note: Represents LGBT publications and digital properties.
Personnel: Todd Evans (Pres.)
Main Contact: Todd Evans

NEW ULM

WIDE AREA CLASSIFIED

Street address 2: 113 N Minnesota St
Street address state: MN
Postal code: 56073-1729
County: Brown
Country: USA
Mailing address 1: PO Box 9
Mailing city: New Ulm
Mailing state: MN
Mailing zip: 56073-0009
Office phone: 800-324-8236
Office fax: 866-822-5487
General e-mail: info@wideareaclassifieds.com
Web address: www.wideareaclassifieds.com
Year established: 1986
Note: Represents shopper publications in 50 states
Personnel: Shannon Reinhart (Exec. Dir.)
Main Contact: Shannon Reinhart

NEW YORK

JOSEPH JACOBS ORGANIZATION

Street address 2: 349 W 87th St
Street address city: Ste 1
Street address state: NY
Postal code: 10024-2662
County: New York
Country: USA
Mailing address 1: 349 W 87th St Ste 1
Mailing city: New York
Mailing state: NY
Mailing zip: 10024-2662
Office phone: (212) 787-9400
Office fax: (212) 787-8080
General e-mail: erosenfeld@josephjacobs.org
Web address: www.josephjacobs.org
Year established: 1919
Note: Represents Jewish publications
Personnel: David Koch (Pres.)
Main Contact: David Koch

METRO SUBURBIA, INC./NEWHOUSE NEWSPAPERS

Street address 2: 711 3rd Ave
Street address city: Fl 6
Street address state: NY
Postal code: 10017-4029
County: New York
Country: USA
Mailing address 1: 711 3rd Ave Rm 1500
Mailing city: New York
Mailing state: NY
Mailing zip: 10017-9201
Office phone: (212) 697-8020
Office fax: (212) 972-3146
General e-mail: johnt@metrosuburbia.com
Web address: www.metrosuburbia.com
Personnel: Kevin Drolet (Adv. Sales Mgr.); John Tingwall (Adv. Sales Mgr.); Chad Johnson (Adv. Sales Mgr.); Robert N. Schoenbacher (Pres.); John A. Colombo (New York Sales Mgr.); Jon Gold (Adv. Sales Mgr.); Brenda Goodwin-Garcia (Adv. Sales Mgr.)
Main Contact: Kevin Drolet; John Tingwall; Chad Johnson; Robert N. Schoenbacher; Jon Gold; Brenda Goodwin-Garcia

REFUEL AGENCY, INC

Street address 2: 1350 Broadway
Street address city: Suite 830
Street address state: NY
Postal code: 10018
County: New York
Country: USA
Mailing address 1: 1350 Broadway, Suite 830
Mailing city: New York
Mailing state: NY
Mailing zip: 10018
Office phone: (866) 360-9688
General e-mail: info@refuelagency.com
Web address: www.refuelagency.com
Year established: 1968
Note: Refuel Agency, Inc specializes in the military, college, Hispanic, African-American, ethnic and senior markets.
Personnel: Derik S. White (President/CEO); David Silver (Chief Revenue Officer); Chris Cassino (COO)
Main Contact: ()

NORTHVILLE

NEWSPAPER NATIONAL NETWORK

Street address 2: 41899 Waterfall Rd
Street address state: MI
Postal code: 48168-3267
County: Wayne
Country: USA
Mailing address 1: 41899 Waterfall Rd
Mailing city: Northville
Mailing state: MI
Mailing zip: 48168-3267
Office phone: (248) 680-4676
Office fax: (248) 680-4667
Personnel: Larry Doyle (Sales Exec.)
Main Contact: Ray Chelstowski

PHOENIX

RUXTON GROUP/VMG ADVERTISING

Street address 2: 1201 E Jefferson St
Street address state: AZ
Postal code: 85034-2300
County: Maricopa
Country: USA
Mailing address 1: 1201 E. Jefferson Street
Mailing city: Phoenix
Mailing state: AZ
Mailing zip: 85034
Office phone: 1800-278-9866
Office fax: 602.238-4805
Other phone: 1.602.229.8452
General e-mail: ads@voicemediagroup.com
Web address: www.vmgadvertising.com
Year established: 1983
Personnel: Joe Larkin (SVP Sale & Operations); Susan Belair (SVP Sales); Veronica Villela (Business Manager)
Parent company: Voice Media Group
Main Contact: Joe Larkin

SAN ANTONIO

HARTE-HANKS COMMUNICATIONS, INC.

Street address 2: 9601 McAllister Fwy
Street address city: Ste 610
Street address state: TX
Postal code: 78216-4632
County: Bexar
Country: USA
Mailing address 1: 9601 McAllister Fwy Ste 610
Mailing city: San Antonio
Mailing state: TX
Mailing zip: 78216-4632
Office phone: (210) 829-9000
Office fax: (210) 829-9101
General e-mail: media@hartehanks.com
Web address: www.hartehanks.com
Note: Represents shopper publications
Personnel: Jon Biro (CFO)
Main Contact: ()

SAN DIEGO

MOTIVATE, INC.

Street address 2: 4141 Jutland Dr Ste 300
Street address city: Suite 300
Street address state: CA
Postal code: 92117-3658
County: San Diego
Country: USA
Mailing address 1: 4141 Jutland Dr
Mailing address 2: Suite 300
Mailing city: San Diego
Mailing state: CA
Mailing zip: 92117
Office phone: (866) 664-4432
General e-mail: marcia@MotivateROI.com
Web address: www.motivateROI.com
Year established: 1977
Note: Motivate, Inc. represents the following target markets: Multicultural (Hispanic, African American, Asian); Youth, LGBTQ, Senior, Military.
Personnel: Marcia A. Hansen (Prtnr.); Trevor Hansen (CEO)
Main Contact: Marcia A. Hansen

SAN FRANCISCO

TRIBUNE MEDIA NETWORK

Street address 2: 100 Bush St
Street address city: Ste 925
Street address state: CA
Postal code: 94104-3920
County: San Francisco
Country: USA
Mailing address 1: 100 Bush St Ste 925
Mailing city: San Francisco
Mailing state: CA
Mailing zip: 94104-3920
Office phone: (415) 693-5600
Office fax: (415) 391-4992
Web address: www.tribunemediagroup.com
Personnel: Neal Zimmerman (Mgr.)
Main Contact: Gary Weitman

SCHAUMBURG

MCNAUGHTON NEWSPAPERS

Street address 2: 424 E State Pkwy
Street address city: Ste 228
Street address state: IL
Postal code: 60173-6406
County: Cook
Country: USA
Mailing address 1: 424 E State Pkwy Ste 228
Mailing city: Schaumburg
Mailing state: IL
Mailing zip: 60173-6408
Office phone: (847) 490-6000
Office fax: (847) 843-9058
General e-mail: rickb@usspi.com
Web address: www.usspi.com
Note: Designs cost effective print and digital solutions for national/regional/local advertisers.
Personnel: Rick Baranski (Vice President Media Relations); Philip Miller (CEO); Barbara Ancona (Vice President Sales); Michelle Hammons (Executive Vice President)
Main Contact: Rick Baranski

TORONTO

NEWBASE

Street address 2: 468 Queen Str. E
Street address city: Suite 500
Street address state: ON
Postal code: M5A 1T7

Newspaper Representatives - National

Country: USA
Mailing address 1: 468 Queen Str. E, Suite 500
Mailing city: Toronto
Mailing state: ON
Mailing zip: M5A 1T7
Office phone: (416) 363 1388
Office fax: (416) 363 2889
Web address: www.thenewbase.com
Personnel: Lesley Conway (Pres.); Doug St. John (Digital Director)
Main Contact: Wayne St. John

NEWBASE

Street address 2: 468 Queen Str. E
Street address city: Suite 500
Street address state: ON
Postal code: M5A 1T7
Country: Canada
Mailing address 1: 468 Queen Str. E, Suite 500
Mailing city: Toronto
Mailing state: ON
Mailing zip: M5A 1T7
Office phone: (416) 363 1388
Office fax: (416) 363 2889
Web address: http://www.thenewbase.com
Personnel: Lesley Conway (Pres.); Doug St. John (Digital Director, Americas); Cyndy Fleming (Account Dir.); Sheila Cohen (Programmatic Manager)
Main Contact: Dana Francoz

TROY

AMERICAN NEWSPAPER REPRESENTATIVES, INC.

Street address 2: 2075 W Big Beaver Rd
Street address city: Ste 310
Street address state: MI
Postal code: 48084-3439
County: Oakland
Country: USA
Mailing address 1: 2075 W Big Beaver Rd Ste 310
Mailing city: Troy
Mailing state: MI
Mailing zip: 48084-3439
Office phone: (248) 643-9910
Office fax: (248) 643-9914
General e-mail: accountsales@gotoanr.com
Web address: www.gotoanr.com
Year established: 1943
Note: ANR represents over 9,000 daily and weekly community newspapers nationwide
Personnel: Melanie Cox (Sales Mgr.); John Jepsen (Pres.); Robert Sontag (Exec. Vice Pres./COO)
Main Contact: Melanie Cox; John Jepsen

NEWSPAPER REPRESENTATIVES - STATE

ALBANY

NEW YORK NEWS PUBLISHERS ASSOCIATION

Street address 1: 252 Hudson Ave
Street address state: NY
Postal code: 12210-1802
County: Albany
Country: USA
Office phone: (518) 449-1667
Office fax: (518) 449-1667
Web address: www.nynpa.com
Year established: 1927
Association Description: NYNPA is the non-profit trade association representing the daily, weekly, and online newspapers of New York State. NYNPA monitors the New York State Legislature on behalf of the newspaper industry, opposing unfavorable legislation and working to craft new laws to open up government activities to public scrutiny. The Association also provides training and professional networking opportunities to its member publishers, advertising and marketing, and circulation staff. It organizes an annual contest to recognize excellence in journalism, provides curriculum guides and support to Newspaper in Education programs, and assists advertisers in placing advertising in member newspapers. Additionally, the association manages the New York Newspapers Foundation, which provides grants to literacy-oriented community organizations.
Company Profile: Represents daily newspapers in New York State. Offers statewide and regional newspaper advertising solutions to general public at discounted rates.
Personnel: Diane Kennedy (Pres.); Mary H. Miller (Education Services Dir.); Don Ferlazzo (Dir. of Adv. & Event Mgmt.)
Main (survey) contact: Don Ferlazzo

NEW YORK PRESS SERVICE

Street address 1: 1681 Western Ave
Street address state: NY
Postal code: 12203-4305
County: Albany
Country: USA
Mailing address 1: 1681 Western Ave
Mailing city: Albany
Mailing state: NY
Mailing zip: 12203-4340
Office phone: (518) 464-6483
Office fax: (518) 464-6489
Web address: www.nynewspapers.com
General e-mail: nypa@nynewspapers.com
Year established: 1853
Company Profile: New York Press Service is a nationwide newspaper advertising, buying and placement service. Market analysis, rate/coverage spreadsheets. Nine publications, ethnic, senior family, alternative and mainstream community newspapers. Target marketing solutions
Special Notes: Represents weekly newspapers in New York
Personnel: Phil Anthony (Adv. Rep., Classified Sales); Jill Van Dusen (Mktg. Dir.)
Main (survey) contact: Phil Anthony

ALBUQUERQUE

NEW MEXICO PRESS ASSOCIATION

Street address 1: 700 Silver Ave SW
Street address state: NM
Postal code: 87102-3019
County: Bernalillo
Country: USA
Mailing address 1: PO Box 95198
Mailing city: Albuquerque
Mailing state: NM
Mailing zip: 87199-5198
Office phone: (505) 275-1241
Office fax: (505) 275-1449
Web address: www.nmpress.org
General e-mail: info@nmpress.org
Special Notes: Elections held in Oct
Personnel: Holly Aguilar (Office Mgr.)

ALLEN

TEXCAP

Street address 1: 1226 Newberry Dr
Street address state: TX
Postal code: 75013-3669
County: Collin
Country: USA
Mailing address 1: 570 Dula St
Mailing city: Alvin
Mailing state: TX
Mailing zip: 77511-2942
Office phone: (972) 741-6258
Office fax: (866) 822-4920
Web address: www.tcnatoday.com
General e-mail: jack@tcnatoday.com
Year established: 1964
Special Notes: Classified advertising for 109 publications. In cooperation with Texas Community Newspapers Assoc
Personnel: Dick Colvin (Exec. Dir.)
Main (survey) contact: Dick Colvin

ATLANTA

GEORGIA NEWSPAPER SERVICE, INC.

Street address 1: 3066 Mercer University Dr
Street address 2: Ste 200
Street address state: GA
Postal code: 30341-4137
County: Dekalb
Country: USA
Mailing address 1: 3066 Mercer University Dr Ste 200
Mailing city: Atlanta
Mailing state: GA
Mailing zip: 30341-4137
Office phone: (770) 454-6776
Office fax: (770) 454-6778
Web address: www.gapress.org
General e-mail: mail@gapress.org
Special Notes: Represents daily and weekly newspapers in Georgia
Personnel: Robin Rhodes (Exec. Dir.)
Main (survey) contact: Robin Rhodes

BATON ROUGE

LOUISIANA PRESS ASSOCIATION

Street address 1: 404 Europe St
Street address state: LA
Postal code: 70802-6403
County: East Baton Rouge
Country: USA
Office phone: (225) 344-9309
Office fax: (225) 344-9344
Other phone: (800) 701-8753
Web address: www.lapress.com
General e-mail: pam@lapress.com
Year established: 1880
Association Description: State Newspaper Trade Association
Personnel: Mike Rood (Communications Dir.); Pamela Mitchell (Exec. Dir.); Mitchell-Ann Droge (Dir. of Ops.); Erin Palmintier (Adv. Dir.)
Main (survey) contact: Pamela Mitchell

BELLEVIEW

COMMUNITY PAPERS OF FLORIDA

Street address 1: 12601 SE 53rd Terrace Rd
Street address state: FL
Postal code: 34420-5106
County: Marion
Country: USA
Mailing address 1: PO Box 1149
Mailing city: Summerfield
Mailing state: FL
Mailing zip: 34492-1149
Office phone: (352) 237-3409
Office fax: (352) 347-3384
Other phone: (352) 362-7350
Web address: www.communitypapersofflorida.com
General e-mail: djneuharth@aol.com
Year established: 1960
Association Description: Florida statewide association for free papers
Special Notes: Classified advertising in 82 community news and shopper publications in Florida.
Personnel: Dave Neuharth (Exec. Dir.); Barbara Holmes (Admin. Asst.)
Main (survey) contact: Barbara Holmes

BIRMINGHAM

ALABAMA NEWSPAPER ADVERTISING SERVICE, INC.

Street address 1: 3324 Independence Dr
Street address 2: Ste 200
Street address state: AL
Postal code: 35209-5602
County: Jefferson
Country: USA
Mailing address 1: 3324 Independence Dr Ste 200
Mailing city: Birmingham
Mailing state: AL
Mailing zip: 35209-5602
Office phone: (205) 871-7737
Office fax: (205) 871-7740
Web address: www.alabamapress.org
General e-mail: mail@alabamapress.org
Personnel: Felicia Mason (Exec. Dir.); Brad English (Adv. Mgr.)
Main (survey) contact: Felicia Mason

BISMARCK

NORTH DAKOTA NEWSPAPER ASSOCIATION

Street address 1: 1435 Interstate Loop
Street address state: ND
Postal code: 58503-0567
County: Burleigh
Country: USA
Mailing address 1: 1435 Interstate Loop
Mailing city: Bismarck
Mailing state: ND
Mailing zip: 58503-0567
Office phone: (701) 223-6397
Office fax: (701) 223-8185
Other phone: (800) 685-8889
Web address: www.ndna.com
General e-mail: info@ndna.com
Year established: 1885
Company Profile: Advertising placed in 89 North Dakota newspapers and related publications. Statewide classified advertising and small space advertising programs.
Special Notes: Represents daily and weekly newspapers in North Dakota
Personnel: Kelli Richey (Mktg. Dir.); Steve Andrist (Exec. Dir.); Mike Casey (Adv. Dir.); Colleen Park (Adv./Public Notice Coord.); Shari Peterson (Office Coord./Adv. Assist.); Paul Erdelt (NDNA President)

Main (survey) contact: Steve Andrist

COLUMBIA

SOUTH CAROLINA PRESS SERVICES, INC.

Street address 1: 106 Outlet Pointe Blvd
Street address state: SC
Postal code: 29210-5669
County: Lexington
Country: USA
Mailing address 1: PO Box 11429
Mailing city: Columbia
Mailing state: SC
Mailing zip: 29211-1429
Office phone: (803) 750-9561
Office fax: (803) 551-0903
Web address: http://www.scnewspapernetwork.com/
General e-mail: rsavely@scpress.org
Year established: 1985
Special Notes: Represents all South Carolina newspapers in placement of classified and display advertising
Personnel: Randall Savely (Director of Opertions)
Parent company: S.C. Press Association
Main (survey) contact: William C. Rogers

SOUTHEASTERN ADVERTISING PUBLISHERS ASSOCIATION

Street address 1: 104 Westland Dr
Street address state: TN
Postal code: 38401-6522
County: Maury
Country: USA
Mailing address 1: 104 Westland Dr
Mailing city: Columbia
Mailing state: TN
Mailing zip: 38401-6522
Office phone: (931) 223-5708
Office fax: (888) 450-8329
Web address: www.sapatoday.com
General e-mail: info@sapatoday.com
Year established: 1979
Special Notes: Classified advertising for 75 publications in 10 Southeastern states. Display Network also available.
Personnel: Douglas Fry (Exec. Dir.)
Main (survey) contact: Douglas Fry

OHIO NEWSPAPER SERVICES, INC.

Street address 1: 1335 Dublin Rd
Street address 2: Ste 216B
Street address state: OH
Postal code: 43215-1000
County: Franklin
Country: USA
Mailing address 1: 1335 Dublin Rd Ste 216B
Mailing city: Columbus
Mailing state: OH
Mailing zip: 43215-1000
Office phone: (614) 486-6677
Office fax: (614) 486-4940
Other fax: (614) 486-6373
Web address: www.ohionews.org; www.adohio.net
Year established: 1933
Special Notes: Represents all 81 daily and 154 weekly Ohio newspaper and affiliated websites.
Personnel: Dennis Hetzel (Executive Director Ohio Newspaper Association); Walt Dozier (Acting Director of Advertising); Sue Bazzoli (Manager, Administrative Services); Jason Sanford (Manager of Communications & Content); Ann Riggs (Receptionist and Secretary); Patricia Conkle (Advertising Coordinator); Kathy McCutcheon (Network Account Executive); Casey Null (Advertising Account Executive)
Main (survey) contact: Dennis Hetzel

COVINGTON

OHIAD

Street address 1: PO Box 69
Street address state: OH
Postal code: 45318-0069
County: Miami
Country: USA
Mailing address 1: PO Box 69
Mailing city: Covington
Mailing state: OH
Mailing zip: 45318-0069
Office phone: (937) 473-2028
Office fax: (937) 473-2500
Web address: www.arenspub.com
General e-mail: dselanders@woh.rr.com
Special Notes: Classified advertising for 16 publications. In cooperation with Community Papers of Ohio.
Personnel: Gary Godfrey (Secreatary/Treasurer)
Main (survey) contact: Don Selanders

DENVER

SYNC2 MEDIA

Street address 1: 1120 N Lincoln St
Street address 2: Ste 912
Street address state: CO
Postal code: 80203-2138
County: Denver
Country: USA
Office phone: (303) 571-5117
Office fax: (303) 571-1803
Web address: www.sync2media.com
General e-mail: info@sync2media.com
Special Notes: Represents daily and weekly newspapers in Colorado
Personnel: Jerry Raehal (CEO); Judy Quelch (Account Executive); Peyton Jacobson (Account Executive)
Parent company: Colorado Press Association
Main (survey) contact: Jerry Raehal

DES MOINES

CUSTOMIZED NEWSPAPER ADVERTISING (IOWA)

Street address 1: 319 E 5th St
Street address state: IA
Postal code: 50309-1927
County: Polk
Country: USA
Mailing address 1: 319 E 5th St
Mailing city: Des Moines
Mailing state: IA
Mailing zip: 50309-1927
Office phone: (515) 244-2145
Office fax: (515) 244-4855
Web address: www.cnaads.com; www.inanews.com
Special Notes: Represents 302 daily and weekly newspapers in Iowa and can place advertising in any newspaper in the country.
Personnel: Chris Mudge (Exec. Dir.); Bryan Rohe (Acct. Exec.); Ron Bode (Sales Dir.); Bruce Adams (Sales Rep.)
Main (survey) contact: Chris Mudge

EAST LANSING

COMMUNITY PAPERS OF MICHIGAN, INC.

Street address 1: 5000 Northwind Dr
Street address 2: Ste 240
Street address state: MI
Postal code: 48823-5032
County: Ingham
Country: USA
Mailing address 1: 5000 Northwind Dr Ste 240
Mailing city: East Lansing
Mailing state: MI
Mailing zip: 48823-5032
Office phone: (800) 783-0267
Office fax: (517) 333-3322
Web address: www.communitypapersofmichigan.com
General e-mail: jackguza@cpapersmi.com
Special Notes: Display advertising for 90 publications in Michigan that in cooperation with Community Papers of Michigan reaches more than 2.5 million Michigan households. Classifed advertising reaches 1.7 million Michigan households
Personnel: Terry Roby (Pres.); Jack Guza (Exec.Dir.); Stacy Kotecki (Office Mgr.)
Main (survey) contact: Stacy Kotecki

EWING

NEW JERSEY NEWSMEDIA NETWORK (NJNN)

Street address 1: 810 Bear Tavern Rd
Street address 2: Ste 307
Street address state: NJ
Postal code: 08628-1022
County: Mercer
Country: USA
Mailing address 1: 810 Bear Tavern Rd Ste 307
Mailing city: Ewing
Mailing state: NJ
Mailing zip: 08628-1022
Office phone: (609) 406-0600
Office fax: (609) 406-0399
Web address: www.njpa.org/njnn
General e-mail: njnn@njpa.org
Year established: 1991
Special Notes: Media planning and placement service for print and digital campaigns. Specializing in daily, weekly, ethnic and specialty pubs reaching New Jersey.
Personnel: Amy Lear (Adv. Dir.); George White (NJPA Exec Dir); Diane Trent (NJNN Networks Mgr)
Parent company: New Jersey Press Association
Main (survey) contact: Amy Lear

FOND DU LAC

PUBLISHERS DEVELOPMENT SERVICE

Street address 1: PO Box 1256
Street address state: WI
Postal code: 54936-1256
County: Fond Du Lac
Country: USA
Mailing address 1: PO Box 1256
Mailing city: Fond Du Lac
Mailing state: WI
Mailing zip: 54936-1256
Office phone: (920) 922-4864
Office fax: (920) 922-0861
Web address: www.pdsadnet.com
General e-mail: janelle@pdsadnet.com
Year established: 1978
Company Profile: Media placement firm specializing in print media in particular community papers.
Special Notes: Display advertising for 122 publications. In cooperation with Wisconsin Free Community Papers
Personnel: Janelle Anderson (CEO); Jeanne Schmal (Gen. Mgr.); Kathy Braun (Classified Sales Mgr.)
Main (survey) contact: Janelle Anderson

FRANKFORT

KENTUCKY PRESS SERVICE, INC.

Street address 1: 101 Consumer Ln
Street address state: KY
Postal code: 40601-8489
County: Franklin
Country: USA
Mailing address 1: 101 Consumer Ln
Mailing city: Frankfort
Mailing state: KY
Mailing zip: 40601-8489
Office phone: (502) 223-8821
Office fax: (502) 875-2624
Web address: www.kypress.com
General e-mail: dthompson@kypress.com
Year established: 1959
Association Description: Membership organization of all Kentucky newspapers
Special Notes: Represents daily and weekly newspapers in Kentucky
Personnel: David Thompson (Exec. Dir.); Bonnie Howard (Controller)
Main (survey) contact: David Thompson

HAMBURG

MACNET

Street address 1: PO Box 408
Street address state: PA
Postal code: 19526-0408
County: Berks
Country: USA
Mailing address 1: PO Box 408
Mailing city: Hamburg
Mailing state: PA
Mailing zip: 19526-0408
Office phone: (800) 450-7227
Office fax: (610) 743-8500
Web address: www.macpa.net; www.macnetonline.com
General e-mail: info@macpa.net
Special Notes: Classified advertising for 360 publications in PA, OH, NY, NJ, DE, MD, WV, VA, Washington DC.
Personnel: Alyse Mitten (Exec. Dir.)
Main (survey) contact: Alyse Mitten

HARRISBURG

MANSI MEDIA

Street address 1: 3899 N Front St
Street address state: PA
Postal code: 17110-1583
County: Dauphin
Country: USA
Office phone: (717) 703-3030
Office fax: (717) 703-3033
Web address: www.mansimedia.com
General e-mail: sales@mansimedia.com
Special Notes: Represents daily and weekly newspapers and their digital products anywhere in the U.S. and beyond.
Personnel: Lisa Knight (VP/Adv.); Chris Kazlauskas; Wes Snider (Dir. Client Solutions); Ronaldo Davis (Sr. Media Buyer); Matthew Caylor (Dir., Interactive Media); Lindsey Artz (Account Manager); Shannon Mohar (Account Manager); Brian Hitchings (Director, Client Solutions)
Main (survey) contact: Lisa Knight

HELENA

MONTANA NEWSPAPER ADVERTISING SERVICE, INC.

Street address 1: 825 Great Northern Blvd
Street address 2: Ste 202
Street address state: MT
Postal code: 59601-3340
County: Lewis And Clark
Country: USA
Mailing address 1: 825 Great Northern Blvd Ste 202
Mailing city: Helena
Mailing state: MT
Mailing zip: 59601-3358
Office phone: (406) 443-2850
Office fax: (406) 443-2860
Web address: www.mtnewspapers.com
General e-mail: randy@mtnewspapers.com
Year established: 1955
Special Notes: Represents daily and weekly newspapers in Montana.
Personnel: Randy Schmoldt (Accounting Specialist)
Main (survey) contact: Randy Schmoldt

Newspaper Representatives - State

IOWA CITY

MIDWEST FREE COMMUNITY PAPERS

Street address 1: PO Box 1350
Street address state: IA
Postal code: 52244-1350
County: Johnson
Country: USA
Mailing address 1: PO Box 1350
Mailing city: Iowa City
Mailing state: IA
Mailing zip: 52244-1350
Office phone: (319) 341-4352
Office fax: (319) 341-4358
Web address: www.mfcp.org
General e-mail: mfcp@mchsi.com
Year established: 1955
Special Notes: Classified advertising for 124 publications
Personnel: Jori Hendon (Office Mgr.)
Main (survey) contact: Jori Hendon

JACKSON

MISSISSIPPI PRESS SERVICES, INC.

Street address 1: 371 Edgewood Terrace Dr
Street address state: MS
Postal code: 39206-6217
County: Hinds
Country: USA
Mailing address 1: 371 Edgewood Terrace Dr.
Mailing city: Jackson
Mailing state: MS
Mailing zip: 39206-6217
Office phone: (601) 981-3060
Office fax: (601) 981-3676
Web address: www.mspress.org
General e-mail: mspress@mspress.org
Year established: 1866
Special Notes: Represents daily and weekly newspapers in Mississippi
Personnel: Layne Bruce (Exec. Dir.); Monica Gilmer (Member Services Manager); Sue Hicks (Business Development Manager); Andrea Ross (Media Director)
Main (survey) contact: Layne Bruce

LAKE MARY

INTERSECT MEDIA SOLUTIONS

Street address 1: 1025 Greenwood Blvd.
Street address 2: Suite 191
Street address state: FL
Postal code: 32746-5410
County: Seminole
Country: USA
Mailing address 1: 1025 Greenwood Blvd., Suite 191
Mailing city: Lake Mary
Mailing state: FL
Mailing zip: 32746-5410
Office phone: (866) 404-5913
Web address: www.intersectmediasolutions.com
General e-mail: info@mediagenius.com
Year established: 1959
Association Description: Intersect Media Solutions is the advertising agency of the Florida Press Association.
Company Profile: Our mission is to provide outstanding client services with innovative media solutions that reach relevant and prospective audiences, to promote our relationships with our media partners, and to be profitable in the pursuit.
Personnel: Dean Ridings (Pres./CEO); Mark Burger (VP, Finance & CFO); Carolyn Nolte (VP, Strategy); Jessica Pitts (VP, Operations)
Parent company: Florida Press Association
Main (survey) contact: Carolyn Nolte

LANSING

MNI

Street address 1: 827 N Washington Ave
Street address state: MI
Postal code: 48906-5135
County: Ingham
Country: USA
Mailing address 1: 827 N Washington Ave
Mailing city: Lansing
Mailing state: MI
Mailing zip: 48906-5135
Office phone: (517) 372-2424
Office fax: (517) 372-2429
Web address: www.michiganpress.org
General e-mail: mpa@michiganpress.org
Year established: 1868
Special Notes: Represents print and digital media in Michigan
Personnel: Mike MacLaren (Executive Director); Rose Lucas (Growth & Operations Manager); Lisa McGraw (Public Affairs Manager)
Parent company: Michigan Press Association
Main (survey) contact: Michael MacLaren

LENA

GREAT NORTHERN CONNECTION

Street address 1: 8703 Midway Rd
Street address state: WI
Postal code: 54139-9769
County: Oconto
Country: USA
Mailing address 1: 8703 Midway Rd
Mailing city: Lena
Mailing state: WI
Mailing zip: 54139-9769
Office phone: (920) 829-5145
Web address: www.greatnorthernconn.com
General e-mail: classifieds@greatnorthernconn.com
Year established: 1985
Special Notes: Represents 35 publications in northeastern Wisconsin and upper peninsula Michigan
Personnel: Char Meier (Adv. Contact)
Main (survey) contact: Char Meier

LINCOLN

NEBRASKA PRESS ADVERTISING SERVICE

Street address 1: 845 S St
Street address state: NE
Postal code: 68508-1226
County: Lancaster
Country: USA
Office phone: (402) 476-2851
Office fax: (402) 476-2942
Web address: www.nebpress.com
General e-mail: nebpress@nebpress.com
Year established: 1879
Association Description: Professional trade association that represents the daily and weekly newspapers in Nebraska.
Personnel: Rob James (Adv. Sales Dir.); Allen Beermann (Exec. Dir., Nebraska Press Assoc.)
Main (survey) contact: Rob James

LITTLE ROCK

ARKANSAS PRESS SERVICES

Street address 1: 411 S Victory St
Street address state: AR
Postal code: 72201-2933
County: Pulaski
Country: USA
Mailing address 1: 411 S Victory St Ste 100
Mailing city: Little Rock
Mailing state: AR
Mailing zip: 72201-2934
Office phone: (501) 374-1500
Office fax: (501) 374-7509
Web address: www.arkansaspress.org
General e-mail: info@arkansaspress.org
Year established: 1873
Association Description: The Arkansas Press Association is the trade association for the newspapers of Arkansas. We represent Arkansas newspapers will national advertisers and hand advertising placement for a broad spectrum of advertisers, including political and advocacy advertisers.
Special Notes: Represents daily and weekly newspapers in Arkansas
Personnel: Tom Larimer (Exec. Dir.); Ashley Wimberley (Adv. & Mktg. Dir.)
Main (survey) contact: Tom Larimer

MADISON

WISCONSIN NEWSPAPER ASSOCIATION

Street address 1: 34 Schroeder Ct
Street address 2: Ste 220
Street address state: WI
Postal code: 53711-2528
County: Dane
Country: USA
Office phone: (608) 283-7620
Office fax: (608) 283-7631
Other phone: (800) 261-4242
Web address: www.wnanews.com
General e-mail: wna@wnanews.com
Year established: 1853
Special Notes: Represents 34 daily and over 225 weekly and specialty newspapers
Personnel: Beth Bennett (Exec. Dir.); Denise Guttery (Media Services Dir.); James Debilzen (Communications Dir.); Julia Hunter (Member Services Dir.)
Main (survey) contact: Beth Bennett

MONTREAL

RESEAU SELECT/SELECT NETWORK

Street address 1: 8000 Av Blaise-Pascal
Street address state: QC
Postal code: H1E 2S7
County: Quebec
Country: Canada
Mailing address 1: 8000 Ave. Blaise-Pascal
Mailing city: Montreal
Mailing state: QC
Mailing zip: H1E 2S7
Office phone: (514) 643-2300
Office fax: (514) 866-3030
Web address: www.reseauselect.com
General e-mail: inforeseauselect@tc.tc
Year established: 1976
Special Notes: Represents more than 148 weekly French-language newspapers in Quebec, Ontario, Manitoba and New Brunswick
Personnel: François Laferrière (General Manager)
Main (survey) contact: Francois Laferriere

OKLAHOMA CITY

OKLAHOMA PRESS SERVICE

Street address 1: 3601 N Lincoln Blvd
Street address state: OK
Postal code: 73105-5411
County: Oklahoma
Country: USA
Mailing address 1: 3601 N Lincoln Blvd
Mailing city: Oklahoma City
Mailing state: OK
Mailing zip: 73105-5499
Office phone: (405) 524-4421
Office fax: (405) 499-0048
Web address: www.okpress.com
General e-mail: sysop@okpress.com
Special Notes: Represents daily and weekly newspapers in Oklahoma
Personnel: Mark Thomas (Exec. Vice Pres.)
Main (survey) contact: Jennifer Gilliland

OLYMPIA

ALLIED DAILY NEWSPAPERS OF WASHINGTON

Street address 1: 1110 Capitol Way S
Street address state: WA
Postal code: 98501-2251
County: Thurston
Country: USA
Mailing address 1: 1110 Capitol Way S
Mailing city: Olympia
Mailing state: WA
Mailing zip: 98501-2251
Office phone: (360) 943-9960
Office fax: (360) 943-9962
General e-mail: anewspaper@aol.com
Personnel: Rowland Thompson (Exec. Dir.)
Main (survey) contact: Rowland Thompson

PHOENIX

ANA ADVERTISING SERVICES, INC. (ARIZONA NEWSPAPER ASSOCIATION)

Street address 1: 1001 N Central Ave
Street address 2: Ste 670
Street address state: AZ
Postal code: 85004-1947
County: Maricopa
Country: USA
Office phone: (602) 261-7655
Office fax: (602) 261-7525
Web address: www.ananews.com
General e-mail: office@ananews.com
Year established: 1931
Special Notes: Represents daily and weekly newspapers in Arizona
Personnel: Paula Casey (Exec. Dir.); Cindy London (Media Buyer); Julie O'Keefe (Communications Manager)
Parent company: Arizona Newspapers Association
Main (survey) contact: Paula Casey

PLYMOUTH MEETING

HITCHINGS & CO.

Street address 1: 580 W Germantown Pike
Street address 2: Ste 108
Street address state: PA
Postal code: 19462-1370
County: Montgomery
Country: USA
Mailing address 1: Plymouth Plz., 580 W. Germantown Pk., Ste. 108
Mailing city: Plymouth Meeting
Mailing state: PA
Mailing zip: 19462
Office phone: (610) 941-3555
Office fax: (610) 941-1289
Web address: www.phillyareapapers.com
General e-mail: brian@phillyareapapers.com
Personnel: Brian Hitchings (Pres.); Donna DeFrangesco (Acct. Supvr.)
Main (survey) contact: Brian Hitchings

RALEIGH

NORTH CAROLINA PRESS SERVICE, INC.

Street address 1: 5171 Glenwood Ave
Street address 2: Ste 364
Street address state: NC
Postal code: 27612-3266
County: Wake
Country: USA
Mailing address 1: 5171 Glenwood Ave Ste 364
Mailing city: Raleigh
Mailing state: NC
Mailing zip: 27612-3266
Office phone: (919) 787-7443
Office fax: (919) 787-5302
Web address: www.ncpress.com
Year established: 1985
Special Notes: Represents all daily and weekly newspapers in North Carolina
Personnel: Beth Grace (Exec. Dir.); Laura

Nakoneczny (Member Services Director); Mark Holmes (Director of Sales)
Main (survey) contact: Beth Grace

SACRAMENTO

CNPA ADVERTISING SERVICES

Street address 1: 2000 O St
Street address 2: Ste 120
Street address state: CA
Postal code: 95811-5299
County: Sacramento
Country: USA
Mailing address 1: 2000 O St Ste 120
Mailing city: Sacramento
Mailing state: CA
Mailing zip: 95811-5299
Office phone: (916) 288-6000
Office fax: (916) 288-6003
Web address: www.cnpa.com
General e-mail: bryan@cnpa.com
Personnel: Jack Bates (Exec. Dir.); Sharla Trillo (Dir.); Patrice Bayard-Miller (Client Rel./Sales Mgr.)
Main (survey) contact: Tom Newton

SPOKANE

PACIFIC NORTHWEST ASSOCIATION OF WANT AD NEWSPAPERS (PNAWAN) & WESTERN REGIONAL ADVERTISING PROGRAM (WRAP)

Street address 1: 304 W 3rd Ave
Street address 2: C/O Exchange Publishing
Street address state: WA
Postal code: 99201-4314
County: Spokane
Country: USA
Mailing address 1: PO Box 427
Mailing city: Spokane
Mailing state: WA
Mailing zip: 99210
Office phone: (509) 922-3456
Office fax: (509) 455-7940
Other phone: (800) 326-2223
Web address: www.RegionalAds.org
General e-mail: Ads@PNAWAN.org
Year established: 1977
Association Description: PNAWAN is an association of 30 different publications throughout the greater Pacific Northwest region: Washington, Oregon, Idaho, Montana, Alberta & British Columbia. The combined total distribution is approximately 600,000 per week.

Company Profile: Reach a bigger audience & Advertise in local community papers throughout the Pacific Northwest region! PNAWAN (Pacific NW Assoc. of Want Ad Newspapers) makes advertising on a regional scale easy and affordable. Prices start at just $50 per Regional Ad! Place both classified & display ads in up to 30 different publications throughout Washington, Oregon, Idaho, Montana, Alberta & British Columbia in just 1 easy phone call. Our publications believe in high standards of quality and ethics in advertising. PNAWAN publications are well-known in their communities and have very loyal readerships. Total weekly distribution: 537,006 We are audited and verified by the Circulation Verification Council annually. Classified Ad Rates: $6.25 per edition, minimum 8 editions required (Note: Editions are calculated as number of weeks x number of running publications) Examples: 8 publications x 1 week = $50 4 publications x 2 weeks = $50 12 publications x 1 week = $75 6 publications x 2 weeks = $75 16 publications x 1 week = $100 8 publications x 2 weeks = $100 .....etc. Maximum USA coverage: 23 pubs x 1 week = $143.75 Maximum coverage incl. Canada: 30 pubs x 1 week = $187.50   25 word max. Extra words = 10 cents per word per edition   Call today to place your Pacific Northwest Regional Ads! 509-922-3456 or 1-800-326-2223 (toll-free). Note: PNAWAN is hosted by member company, Exchange Publishing, so be sure to ask for PNAWAN Regional Ads when calling.   You may also email ads@pnawan.org for any inquiries, or contact the Executive Director of PNAWAN, Kylah Strohte, directly at Kylah@ExchangePublishing.com   More information about the Pacific Northwest Association of Want Ad Newspapers (PNAWAN) online at www.RegionalAds.org Mission: To unite, promote, and facilitate advertising between the free community newspaper publications of the Pacific Northwest so that our advertisers can easily reach a bigger audience.
Special Notes: We are audited and verified by the Circulation Verification Council annually.   PNAWAN headquarters are located at the offices of hosting member publication, Exchange Publishing, in Spokane, WA.
Personnel: Kylah Strohte (Executive Director of the Pacific Northwest Association of Want Ad Newspapers (PNAWAN) & Western Regional Advertising Program (WRAP)); PNAWAN Office
Parent company: Exchange Publishing, LLC
Main (survey) contact: Kylah Strohte

SYRACUSE

ADNETWORKNY

Street address 1: 109 Twin Oaks Dr
Street address 2: Ste D
Street address state: NY
Postal code: 13206-1204
County: Onondaga
Country: USA
Mailing address 1: 109 Twin Oaks Dr
Mailing address 2: Suite D
Mailing city: Syracuse
Mailing state: NY
Mailing zip: 13206
Office phone: (315) 472-6007
Office fax: (877) 790-1976
Other phone: (877) 275-2726
Web address: www.fcpny.com
General e-mail: ads@fcpny.com
Year established: 1950
Association Description: AdNetworkNY is the advertising arm of Free Community Papers of NY (FCPNY), an association of free distribution publishers delivering to more than 3.2 million homes across the Empire State.
Company Profile: AdNetworkNY enables advertisers to reach all or parts of New York through classified, display and insert advertising. Low CPM's and high readership brings great value for your ad dollar.
Special Notes: Classified and display advertising
Personnel: Dan Holmes (Exec. Dir.); Tom Cuskey (Sales & Training Director)
Parent company: Free Community Papers of NY
Main (survey) contact: Dan Holmes

TALLAHASSEE

FLORIDA PRESS SERVICE, INC.

Street address 1: 336 E College Ave
Street address 2: Ste 203
Street address state: FL
Postal code: 32301-1559
County: Leon
Country: USA
Mailing address 1: 336 E College Ave Ste 203
Mailing city: Tallahassee
Mailing state: FL
Mailing zip: 32301-1559
Office phone: (850) 222-5790
Office fax: (850) 222-4498
Web address: www.flpress.com
General e-mail: fps-info@flpress.com
Company Profile: Florida Press is an intergrated, full service placement, research invoicing and verification firm owned and operated by all of Florida's newspapers. Our mission is to help our client advertisors coordinate multi-market newspaper campaigns quickly, effecie
Special Notes: Represents 42 daily and 135 weekly newspapers in Florida
Personnel: Dean Riddings (Pres./CEO)
Main (survey) contact: Dean Riddings

TORONTO

RESEAU SELECT/SELECT NETWORK

Street address 1: 25 Sheppard Ave W
Street address 2: Suite 500
Street address state: ON
Postal code: M2N 6S7
County: York
Country: Canada
Mailing address 1: 25 Sheppard Ave. West Suite 500
Mailing city: Toronto
Mailing state: ON
Mailing zip: M2N 6S7
Office phone: (416) 733-7600
Office fax: (416) 726-8519
Web address: www.reseauselect.com
General e-mail: inforeseauselect@tc.tc

WOBURN

NENPA AD NETWORK (NEW ENGLAND NEWSPAPER AND PRESS ASSOCIATION)

Street address 1: 1 Arrow Dr
Street address 2: Ste 6
Street address state: MA
Postal code: 01801-2039
County: Middlesex
Country: USA
Mailing address 1: 1 Arrow Drive, Suite 6
Mailing city: Woburn
Mailing state: MA
Mailing zip: 01801
Office phone: (781) 281-2053
Office fax: (339) 999-2174
Web address: www.nenpa.com
General e-mail: info@nenpa.com
Year established: 1930
Special Notes: Represents daily, weekly and specialty newspapers in the six New England states
Personnel: Linda Conway (Executive Director)
Main (survey) contact: Linda Conway

TRADE UNIONS IN THE NEWSPAPER FIELD

WASHINGTON

COMMUNICATIONS WORKERS OF AMERICA

Street address 1: 501 3rd St NW
Street address state: DC
Postal code: 20001-2760
County: District Of Columbia
Country: USA
Mailing address: 501 3rd St NW
Mailing city: Washington
Mailing state: DC
Mailing zip: 20001-2760
Office phone: (202) 434-1100
Office fax: (202) 434-1279
Web address: www.cwa-union.org
Personnel: Larry Cohen (Pres.); Jeffrey Rechenbach (Sec./Treasure)
Larry Cohen

GRAPHIC COMMUNICATIONS INTERNATIONAL

Street address 1: 1900 L St NW
Street address state: DC
Postal code: 20036-5002
County: District Of Columbia
Country: USA
Mailing address: 1900 L St NW Fl 8
Mailing city: Washington
Mailing state: DC
Mailing zip: 20036-5007
Office phone: (202) 721-0537
Office fax: (202) 721-0641
Web address: gtedeschi@gciu.org
General e-mail: webmessenger@gciu.org
Personnel: George Tedeschi (Pres.); Robert Lacey (Vice Pres.); Richard Whitworth (Executive Assistant to the President)
George Tedeschi

INTERNATIONAL UNION OF OPERATING ENGINEERS

Street address 1: 1125 17th St NW
Street address state: DC
Postal code: 20036-4709
County: District Of Columbia
Country: USA
Mailing address: 1125 17th St NW
Mailing city: Washington
Mailing state: DC
Mailing zip: 20036-4709
Office phone: (202) 429-9100
Office fax: (202) 778-2688
Web address: www.iuoe.org
Personnel: Vincent J. Giblin (Gen. Pres.); Christopher Hanley (Gen. Sec./Treasurer)
Vincent J. Giblin

SERVICE EMPLOYEES INTERNATIONAL UNION, CLC

Street address 1: 1800 Massachusetts Ave NW
Street address state: DC
Postal code: 20036-1806
County: District Of Columbia
Country: USA
Mailing address: 1800 Massachusetts Ave NW
Mailing city: Washington
Mailing state: DC
Mailing zip: 20036-1806
Office phone: (202) 730-7000
Office fax: (202) 429-5660
Web address: www.seiu.org
Personnel: Andrew L. Stern (Int'l Pres.); Anna Burger (Sec./Treasurer); Mary Kay Henry (Int'l Exec. Vice Pres.); Gerald Hudson (Int'l Vice Pres.); Eliseo Medina (Int'l Exec. Vice Pres.); Tom Woodruff (Int'l Exec. Vice Pres.)
Andrew L. Stern

THE LABORERS' INTERNATIONAL UNION OF NORTH AMERICA

Street address 1: 905 16th St NW
Street address state: DC
Postal code: 20006-1703
County: District Of Columbia
Country: USA
Mailing address: 905 16th St NW
Mailing city: Washington
Mailing state: DC
Mailing zip: 20006-1703
Office phone: (202) 737-8320
Office fax: (202) 737-2754
Web address: www.liuna.org
General e-mail: communications@liuna.org
Year established: 1903
Personnel: Greg Davis (Director)
Greg Davis

THE NEWSGUILD-CWA

Street address 1: 501 3rd St NW
Street address 2: Fl 6
Street address state: DC
Postal code: 20001-2797
County: District Of Columbia
Country: USA
Mailing address: 501 3rd St NW, Fl 6
Mailing city: Washington
Mailing state: DC
Mailing zip: 20001-2797
Office phone: (202) 434-7177
Office fax: (202) 434-1472
Other phone: (202) 434-7177
Web address: www.newsguild.org
General e-mail: guild@cwa-union.org
Year established: 1933
Company Profile: The NewsGuild-CWA, previously known as The Newspaper Guild-CWA, represents 25,000 digital and print journalists and other media workers in the United States, Canada and Puerto Rico. In addition to fair wages and working conditions, TNG-CWA is a voice for the rights and safety of journalists worldwide, for freedom of information, transparency in government and First Amendment issues.
Personnel: Bernard Lunzer (President); Martha Waggoner (International Chairperson); Marian Needham (Exec. VP)
Bernard Lunzer

Section III

Non-Daily, Community & Niche Newspapers in the U.S. & Canada

Non-Daily Newspapers in the U.S. 2
Community Newspapers in the U.S. 157
Non-Daily Newspapers in Canada 432
Community Newspapers in Canada 513
Shopper Publications in Canada 596
Shopper Publications in the U.S. 602
Alternative Newspapers in Canada 627
Alternative Newspapers in the U.S. 628
Black Newspapers in the U.S. 631
College and University Newspapers 644
Ethnic Newspapers in Canada 733
Ethnic Newspapers in the U.S. 735
Gay & Lesbian Newspapers in the U.S. 736
Hispanic Newspapers in the U.S. 738
Jewish Newspapers in the U.S. 753
Military Newspapers in the U.S. 762
Parenting Publications in the U.S. 769
Real Estate Publications in the U.S. 777
Religious Newspapers in the U.S. 781
Schools and Departments of Journalism 793
Senior Publications in the U.S. 815
Alternate Delivery Services 819
Newspaper Brokers and Appraisers 824
Newspaper Distributed Magazines and TMC Publications 826

NON-DAILY NEWSPAPERS IN THE U.S.

ALASKA

ANCHORAGE

ALASKA JOURNAL OF COMMERCE
Corporate/Parent Company: Binkley Co.
Street Address: 300 W. 31st Avenue
City: Anchorage
State: AK
Postal Code: 99503
Office phone: 907-257-4200
Publication Website: www.alaskajournal.com
Editor Name: Andrew Jensen
Editor Email: andrew.jensen@alaskajournal.com
Editor Phone: 907-257-4271
Advertising Executive Name: Jada Nowling
Advertising Executive Email: jada.nowling@alaskajournal.com
Advertising Executive Phone: 907-257-4268

ANCHORAGE PRESS
Corporate/Parent Company: Wick Communications
Street Address: 731 I St, Suite 102
City: Anchorage
State: AK
Postal Code: 99501
Office phone: (907) 561-7737
Publication Website: https://www.anchoragepress.com/
General E-mail: tawni.davis@frontiersman.com
Publisher Name: Matt Hickman
Publisher Email: matt.hickman@frontiersman.com
Publisher Phone: (907) 352-2268
Editor Name: Matt Hickman
Editor Email: matt.hickman@frontiersman.com
Editor Phone: (907) 352-2268
Advertising Executive Name: Tawni Davis
Advertising Executive Email: tawni.davis@frontiersman.com
Advertising Executive Phone: (907) 982-6969

HOMER TRIBUNE
Corporate/Parent Company: Anchorage Daily News
Street Address: 300 W. 31st Ave.
City: Anchorage
State: AK
Postal Code: 99503
Office phone: 907-257-4251
Publication Website: www.homertribune.com
Publisher Name: Ryan Binkley, Andy Pennington, David Hulen
Editor Name: Tommy Wells
Editor Email: twells@reportalaska.com
Editor Phone: 940-329-1540
Advertising Executive Name: Terri Dale
Advertising Executive Email: terri@homertribune.com
Advertising Executive Phone: (678)558-5197

BETHEL

THE DELTA DISCOVERY
Corporate/Parent Company: The Delta Discovery, Inc.
Street Address: P.O. Box 1028 401 Ridgecrest Drive
City: Bethel
State: AK
Postal Code: 99559
Office phone: (907) 543-4113
Publication Website: www.deltadiscovery.com
General E-mail: realnews@deltadiscovery.com
Editor Name: Greg Lincoln

DELTA JUNCTION

DELTA WIND
Corporate/Parent Company: TriDelta, Inc. Publishing
Street Address: PO Box 986
City: Delta Junction
State: AK
Postal Code: 99737
Office phone: 907-895-5115
Publication Website: www.deltawindonline.com
General E-mail: webeditor@deltawindonline.com
Publisher Name: Michael Paschall

THE SEWARD JOURNAL
Corporate/Parent Company: TriDelta, Inc. Publishing
Street Address: P.O. Box 986
City: Delta Junction
State: AK
Postal Code: 99737
Office phone: (907) 460-8629
Publication Website: www.sewardjournal.com
General E-mail: news@sewardjournal.com
Publisher Name: Michael Paschall
Editor Name: Vanta Shafer

HOMER

HOMER NEWS
Corporate/Parent Company: Black Press Media Ltd.
Street Address: 3482 Landings St.
City: Homer
State: AK
Postal Code: 99603
Office phone: 907-235-7767
Publication Website: www.homernews.com
General E-mail: news@homernews.com
Editor Name: Michael Armstrong
Editor Email: letters@homernews.com
Year Established: 1964
Delivery Methods: Mail`Newsstand`Racks
Published Days: Thur
Audit Company: Sworn/Estimate/Non-Audited
Audit Date: 6 10 2019

JUNEAU

CAPITAL CITY WEEKLY
Corporate/Parent Company: Black Press Media Ltd.
Street Address: 3100 Channel Drive
City: Juneau
State: AK
Postal Code: 99801
Office phone: 907-586-3740
Publication Website: www.juneauempire.com/tag/ccw/
General E-mail: editor@juneauempire.com
Publisher Name: Terry Ward
Publisher Email: tward@soundpublishing.com
Publisher Phone: (360) 417-3500
Editor Name: Emily Russo Miller
Editor Email: emiller@juneauempire.com
Editor Phone: (907) 523-2263

WASILLA

FRONTIERSMAN
Street Address: 5751 E Mayflower Ct
City: Wasilla
State: AK
Postal Code: 99654-7880
Office phone: (907) 352-2250
Publication Website: https://www.frontiersman.com/
General E-mail: petra.albecker@frontiersman.com
Publisher Name: Dennis Anderson
Publisher Email: dennis.anderson@frontiersman.com
Publisher Phone: (970) 252-7099
Editor Name: Jeremiah Bartz
Editor Email: editor@frontiersman.com
Editor Phone: (907) 352-2273
Advertising Executive Name: Petra Albecker
Advertising Executive Email: petra.albecker@frontiersman.com
Advertising Executive Phone: (907) 352-2262

MAT-SU VALLEY FRONTIERSMAN
Corporate/Parent Company: Wick Communications
Street Address: 5751 E. Mayflower Ct.
City: Wasilla
State: AK
Postal Code: 99654
Office phone: 907-352-2250
Publication Website: www.frontiersman.com
General E-mail: contact@frontiersman.com
Publisher Name: Dennis Anderson
Publisher Email: dennis.anderson@frontiersman.com
Publisher Phone: 970-252-7099
Editor Name: Jeremiah Bartz
Editor Email: editor@frontiersman.com
Editor Phone: 907-352-2273
Advertising Executive Name: Petra Albecker
Advertising Executive Email: petra.albecker@frontiersman.com
Advertising Executive Phone: 907-352-2262

ALABAMA

ALEXANDER CITY

ALEXANDER CITY OUTLOOK
Corporate/Parent Company: Boone Newspapers, Inc.
Street Address: 548 Cherokee Road
City: Alexander City
State: AL
Postal Code: 35010
Office phone: (256) 234-4281
Publication Website: https://www.alexcityoutlook.com/
General E-mail: editor@alexcityoutlook.com
Publisher Name: Steve Baker
Publisher Email: steve.baker@alexcityoutlook.com
Publisher Phone: (256) 414-3190
Editor Name: Santana Wood
Editor Email: santana.wood@alexcityoutlook.com
Editor Phone: (256) 234-3412
Advertising Executive Name: Tippy Hunter
Advertising Executive Email: tippy.hunter@alexcityoutlook.com
Advertising Executive Phone: (256) 414-3177
Year Established: 1892
Delivery Methods: Mail`Newsstand`Carrier`Racks
Own Printing Facility?: Y
Commercial printers?: Y
Mechanical specifications: Type page 13 x 21 1/2; E - 6 cols, 2 1/16, 1/8 between; A - 6 cols, 2 1/16, 1/8 between; C - 9 cols, 2 1/16, 1/8 between.
Published Days: Tues`Wed`Thur`Fri`Sat
Weekday Frequency: m
Saturday Frequency: m
Avg Paid Circ: 5300
Audit Company: Sworn/Estimate/Non-Audited
Audit Date: 7 12 2019
Pressroom Equipment: Lines – 5-KP/News King.;

DADEVILLE RECORD
Corporate/Parent Company: Tallapoosa Publishers, Inc
Street Address: 548 Cherokee Rd
City: Alexander City
State: AL
Postal Code: 35010
Office phone: (256) 234-4281
Publication Website: https://www.alexcityoutlook.com/news/dadeville/
General E-mail: editor@alexcityoutlook.com
Publisher Name: Steve Baker
Publisher Email: steve.baker@alexcityoutlook.com
Publisher Phone: (256) 414-3190
Editor Name: Santana Wood
Editor Email: santana.wood@alexcityoutlook.com
Editor Phone: (256) 234-3412
Advertising Executive Name: Tippy Hunter
Advertising Executive Email: tippy.hunter@alexcityoutlook.com
Advertising Executive Phone: (256) 414-3177
Delivery Methods: Mail`Racks
Published Days: Thur
Avg Paid Circ: 1600
Audit Company: Sworn/Estimate/Non-Audited
Audit Date: 6 10 2019
Total Circulation: 1575

ANDALUSIA

ANDALUSIA STAR-NEWS
Corporate/Parent Company: Boone Newspapers, Inc.
Street Address: 207 Dunson St
City: Andalusia
State: AL
Postal Code: 36420
Office phone: (334) 222-2402
Publication Website: https://www.andalusiastarnews.com/
General E-mail: lisa.eisenberger@andalusiastarnews.com
Publisher Name: Kendra Majors
Publisher Email: kendra.majors@andalusiastarnews.com
Editor Name: Christopher Smith
Editor Email: christopher.smith@andalusiastarnews.com
Advertising Executive Name: Ruck Ashworth
Advertising Executive Email: ruck.ashworth@andalusiastarnews.com
Year Established: 1939
Delivery Methods: Mail`Newsstand`Carrier`Racks
Mechanical specifications: Type page 10 x 21 1/2; E - 6 cols
Published Days: Tues`Wed`Thur`Fri`Sat
Weekday Frequency: m

Non-Daily Newspapers in the U.S.

Saturday Frequency: m
Avg Paid Circ: 3395
Audit Company: Sworn/Estimate/Non-Audited
Audit Date: 7 12 2019
Pressroom Equipment: Lines – 10-KP/News King single width 1994; Folders – KP/KJ 6; Reels & Stands – 6;
Total Circulation: 32497

ANNISTON

PIEDMONT JOURNAL

Street Address: 4305 McClellan Blvd
City: Anniston
State: AL
Postal Code: 36206
Office phone: (256) 235-3563
Publication Website: https://www.annistonstar.com/piedmont_journal/piedmont_eedition/
General E-mail: jalred@jaxnews.com
Publisher Name: John Alred
Publisher Email: jalred@jaxnews.com
Publisher Phone: (256) 235-3531
Editor Name: Anita Kilgore
Editor Email: akilgore@jaxnews.com
Editor Phone: (256) 235-3538
Advertising Executive Name: Shannon Martin
Advertising Executive Email: smartin@annistonstar.com
Advertising Executive Phone: (256) 235-9234
Year Established: 1907
Published Days: Tues
Avg Paid Circ: 3300
Audit Company: Sworn/Estimate/Non-Audited
Audit Date: 6 10 2019
Mailroom Equipment: Counter Stackers – BG/Count-O-Veyor 104A; Tying Machines – 1/Ca.;
Classified Equipment: Hardware – 2-APP/Mac.;
Editorial Equipment: Hardware – 7-APP/Mac/3-APP/Mac, 2-APP/Mac LaserWriter.
Production Equipment: Hardware – Nu; Cameras – CL.

THE ANNISTON STAR

Corporate/Parent Company: Consolidated Publishing Co.
Street Address: 4305 McClellan Blvd
City: Anniston
State: AL
Postal Code: 36206
Office phone: (256) 236-1551
Publication Website: https://www.annistonstar.com/
General E-mail: jpayne@annistonstar.com
Publisher Name: Josephine Ayers
Editor Name: Ben Cunningham
Editor Email: bcunningham@annistonstar.com
Editor Phone: (256) 235-3541
Advertising Executive Name: Kim Kirk
Advertising Executive Email: kkirk@annistonstar.com
Advertising Executive Phone: (256) 235-9218
Year Established: 1883
Delivery Methods: Mail`Newsstand`Carrier`Racks
Own Printing Facility?: Y
Commercial printers?: Y
Mechanical specifications: Type page 9.88 x 21
Published Days: Tues`Wed`Thur`Fri`Sat`Sun
Weekday Frequency: m
Saturday Frequency: m
Avg Paid Circ: 9983
Avg Free Circ: 613
Audit Company: AAM
Audit Date: 31 03 2019
Pressroom Equipment: Lines – 12 DGM 850; Pasters –6 Jardis Pasters
Mailroom Equipment: Counter Stackers – BG/Count-O-Veyor; Inserters & Stuffers – KAN/480; Tying Machines – Wilton; Address Machine – 2/Dispensa-Matic/16.;
Buisness Equipment: Dell/PC
Buisness Software: Microsoft/Excel
Classified Equipment: Hardware – APP/Mac G3; Printers – APP/Mac LaserWriter 810 Pro, Xante/Accel-a-Writer 8200;
Classified Software: Baseview/Class Manager Plus.
Editorial Equipment: Hardware – 6-APP/Mac Quadra 610, 2-APP/Power Mac 8100, 1-APP/Power Mac 8500, 10-APP/Mac G3, 2-APP/Mac 8500/2-V/Panther 3990 Imagesetter, XYQUEST/270 Mb drive, XYQUEST/28.8 modem, Polaroid/SprintScan 35; Printers – 2-APP/Mac LaserWriter 810 Pr
Production Equipment: Hardware – Nat/Universal 33 Subtractive; Cameras – Horizontal/Clyesdale; Scanners – 2-HP/ScanJet IIcx, 1-Lf/Leafscan 35, 1-Polaroid/Sprintscan 35ES
Production Software: QPS/QuarkXPress 4.0.
Total Circulation: 3395

THE JACKSONVILLE NEWS

Street Address: 4305 McClellan Blvd
City: Anniston
State: AL
Postal Code: 36206
Office phone: (256) 435-5021
Publication Website: https://www.annistonstar.com/news/jacksonville/
General E-mail: jpayne@annistonstar.com
Publisher Name: Josephine Ayers
Editor Name: Ben Cunningham
Editor Email: bcunningham@annistonstar.com
Editor Phone: (256) 235-3541
Advertising Executive Name: Kim Kirk
Advertising Executive Email: kkirk@annistonstar.com
Advertising Executive Phone: (256) 235-9218
Year Established: 1936
Mechanical specifications: Type page 11 9/16 x 21 1/4; E - 6 cols, 1 13/16, between; A - 6 cols, 1 13/16, between; C - 10 cols, 1 2/25, between.
Published Days: Tues
Avg Paid Circ: 3300
Audit Company: Sworn/Estimate/Non-Audited
Audit Date: 6 10 2019
Total Circulation: 9100

THE NEWS JOURNAL

Corporate/Parent Company: AIM Media
Street Address: 4305 McClellan Blvd
City: Anniston
State: AL
Postal Code: 36206
Office phone: (256) 435-5021
Publication Website: www.annistonstar.com/newsjournal
General E-mail: jpayne@annistonstar.com
Publisher Name: John Alred
Publisher Email: jalred@jaxnews.com
Publisher Phone: (256) 235-3531
Advertising Executive Name: Shannon Martin
Advertising Executive Email: smartin@annistonstar.com
Advertising Executive Phone: (256) 235-9234

ATHENS

THE NEWS-COURIER

Corporate/Parent Company: CNHI, LLC
Street Address: 410 W Green St
City: Athens
State: AL
Postal Code: 35611
Office phone: (256) 232-2720
Publication Website: https://www.enewscourier.com/
General E-mail: assist@athensnews-courier.com
Publisher Name: Katherine Miller
Publisher Email: Katherine@athensnews-courier.com
Editor Name: Adam Smith
Editor Email: adam@athensnews-courier.com
Advertising Executive Name: Heather Casillas
Advertising Executive Email: heather@athensnews-courier.com
Year Established: 1880
Delivery Methods: Mail`Newsstand`Racks
Own Printing Facility?: N
Commercial printers?: N
Mechanical specifications: Type page 13 x 21 1/2; E - 6 cols, 2 1/16, 1/8 between; A - 6 cols, 2 1/16, 1/8 between; C - 8 cols, 1 3/4, 1/8 between.
Published Days: Tues`Wed`Thur`Fri`Sat
Weekday Frequency: m
Saturday Frequency: m
Avg Paid Circ: 3841
Avg Free Circ: 0,5
Audit Company: Sworn/Estimate/Non-Audited
Audit Date: 7 12 2019

ATMORE

ATMORE ADVANCE

Corporate/Parent Company: Boone Newspapers, Inc.
Street Address: 301 S Main St
City: Atmore
State: AL
Postal Code: 36504
Office phone: (251) 368-2123
Publication Website: https://www.atmoreadvance.com/
General E-mail: advertising@atmoreadvance.com
Publisher Name: Andrew Garner
Publisher Email: andrew.garner@atmoreadvance.com
Publisher Phone: (251) 368-2123
Mechanical specifications: Type page 13 x 21 1/2; E - 6 cols, 2, 3/25 between; A - 6 cols, 2, 3/25 between; C - 10 cols, 1 1/5, 1/10 between.
Published Days: Wed
Avg Paid Circ: 3100
Avg Free Circ: 6000
Audit Company: Sworn/Estimate/Non-Audited
Audit Date: 6 10 2019

BIRMINGHAM

ALABAMA MESSENGER

Street Address: 2100 1st Avenue North, Suite 240
City: Birmingham
State: AL
Postal Code: 35203
Office phone: (205) 252-3672
Publication Website: www.alabamamessenger.com
General E-mail: alamsgr@bellsouth.net
Editor Name: Traci Smeraglia
Year Established: 1918
Published Days: Wed`Sat
Avg Paid Circ: 1500
Avg Free Circ: 75
Audit Company: Sworn/Estimate/Non-Audited
Audit Date: 6 10 2019
Total Circulation: 8466

BIRMINGHAM BUSINESS JOURNAL

Corporate/Parent Company: American City Business Journals
Street Address: 2140 11th Avenue South Suite 205
City: Birmingham
State: AL
Postal Code: 35205
Office phone: 205-443-5600
Publication Website: bbj.com
General E-mail: birmingham@bizjournals.com
Publisher Name: Joel Welker
Publisher Email: jwelker@bizjournals.com
Editor Name: Ty West
Editor Email: twest@bizjournals.com
Advertising Executive Name: Ginger Gardner Aarons
Advertising Executive Email: gaarons@bizjournals.com
Delivery Methods: Mail
Published Days: Fri
Audit Company: Sworn/Estimate/Non-Audited
Audit Date: 6 10 2019

BREWTON

THE BREWTON STANDARD

Corporate/Parent Company: Boone Newspapers, Inc.
Street Address: 407 Saint Nicholas Ave
City: Brewton
State: AL
Postal Code: 36426
Office phone: (251) 867-4876
Publication Website: http://www.brewtonstandard.com/
General E-mail: jennifer.lazzaro@brewtonstandard.com
Year Established: 1906
Mechanical specifications: Type page 12 x 21 1/2; E - 6 cols, 1 13/16, 1/8 between; A - 6 cols, 1 13/16, 1/8 between; C - 10 cols, 1 1/4, 1/8 between.
Published Days: Wed`Sat
Avg Paid Circ: 3180
Avg Free Circ: 150
Audit Company: Sworn/Estimate/Non-Audited
Audit Date: 6 10 2019
Total Circulation: 2850

CENTRE

CHEROKEE COUNTY HERALD

Corporate/Parent Company: Rome News-Tribune
Street Address: 1460 W Main St E
City: Centre
State: AL
Postal Code: 35960
Office phone: 256-927-5037
Publication Website: www.cherokeeherald.com
General E-mail: office@cherokeeherald.com
Editor Name: Terry Dean
Editor Email: tdean@npco.com
Advertising Executive Name: Vickie Robinson
Advertising Executive Email: vrobinson@npco.com
Year Established: 1938
Delivery Methods: Mail`Racks
Own Printing Facility?: Y
Commercial printers?: Y
Mechanical specifications: 10.625 x 21.25; A - 6 cols, 1.6667, 1/8 between; C - 8 cols, 1.181, 6pts between
Published Days: Wed
Avg Paid Circ: 2594
Avg Free Circ: 5872
Audit Company: Sworn/Estimate/Non-Audited
Audit Date: 6 10 2019

CLANTON

THE CLANTON ADVERTISER

Corporate/Parent Company: Boone Newspapers, Inc.
Street Address: 1109 7th St N
City: Clanton
State: AL
Postal Code: 35045
Office phone: (205) 755-5747
Publication Website: https://www.clantonadvertiser.com/
General E-mail: classifieds@clantonadvertiser.com
Publisher Name: Tim Prince
Publisher Email: tim.prince@shelbycountyreporter.com
Editor Name: J.R. Tidwell
Editor Email: joseph.tidwell@clantonadvertiser.com
Advertising Executive Email: classifieds@clantonadvertiser.com
Mechanical specifications: Type page 11 5/8 x 21 1/2; E - 6 cols, 1 5/6, 1/8 between; A - 6

cols, 1 5/6, 1/8 between; C - 10 cols, 1 1/16, 7/64 between.
Published Days: Tues`Wed`Thur`Fri`Sat
Weekday Frequency: m
Saturday Frequency: m
Avg Paid Circ: 5000
Audit Company: Sworn/Estimate/Non-Audited
Audit Date: 7 12 2019
Pressroom Equipment: Lines – G/Community.;
Total Circulation: 3800

COLUMBIANA

ALABASTER REPORTER

Corporate/Parent Company: Boone Newspapers
Street Address: 115 N Main St
City: Columbiana
State: AL
Postal Code: 35051
Office phone: (205) 669-3131
Publication Website: https://www.shelbycountyreporter.com/category/alabaster-news/
General E-mail: daniel.holmes@shelbycountyreporter.com
Publisher Name: Tim Prince
Publisher Email: tim.prince@shelbycountyreporter.com
Publisher Phone: (205) 669-3131
Editor Name: Alec Etheredge
Editor Email: alec.etheredge@shelbycountyreporter.com
Editor Phone: (205) 669-3131
Advertising Executive Phone: (205) 280-5667
Year Established: 1843
Mechanical specifications: Type page 11 5/8 x 21 1/2; E - 6 cols, 1 13/16, 1 between; A - 6 cols, 1 13/16, 1 between; C - 10 cols, 1 1/2, between.
Published Days: Wed
Avg Paid Circ: 7997
Avg Free Circ: 24500
Audit Company: Sworn/Estimate/Non-Audited
Audit Date: 6 10 2019
Total Circulation: 1737

PELHAM REPORTER

Corporate/Parent Company: Boone Newspapers, Inc.
Street Address: 115 N Main St
City: Columbiana
State: AL
Postal Code: 35051
Office phone: (205) 669-3131
Publication Website: https://www.shelbycountyreporter.com/category/pelham-news/
General E-mail: daniel.holmes@shelbycountyreporter.com
Publisher Name: Tim Prince
Publisher Email: tim.prince@shelbycountyreporter.com
Publisher Phone: (205) 669-3131
Editor Name: Alec Etheredge
Editor Email: alec.etheredge@shelbycountyreporter.com
Editor Phone: (205) 669-3131
Advertising Executive Phone: (205) 280-5667
Year Established: 1843
Mechanical specifications: Type page 11 5/8 x 21 1/2; E - 6 cols, 1 13/16, 1 between; A - 6 cols, 1 13/16, 1 between; C - 10 cols, 1 1/2, between.
Published Days: Wed
Avg Paid Circ: 7997
Avg Free Circ: 24500
Audit Company: Sworn/Estimate/Non-Audited
Audit Date: 6 10 2019
Total Circulation: 6600

SHELBY COUNTY REPORTER

Corporate/Parent Company: Boone Newspapers, Inc.
Street Address: 115 N Main St
City: Columbiana
State: AL
Postal Code: 35051
Office phone: (205) 669-3131
Publication Website: https://www.shelbycountyreporter.com/
General E-mail: daniel.holmes@shelbycountyreporter.com
Publisher Name: Tim Prince
Publisher Email: tim.prince@shelbycountyreporter.com
Publisher Phone: (205) 669-3131
Editor Name: Alec Etheredge
Editor Email: alec.etheredge@shelbycountyreporter.com
Editor Phone: (205) 669-3131
Advertising Executive Phone: (205) 280-5667
Year Established: 1843
Mechanical specifications: Type page 11 5/8 x 21 1/2; E - 6 cols, 1 13/16, 1 between; A - 6 cols, 1 13/16, 1 between; C - 10 cols, 1 1/2, between.
Published Days: Wed
Avg Paid Circ: 7997
Avg Free Circ: 24500
Audit Company: Sworn/Estimate/Non-Audited
Audit Date: 6 10 2019
Total Circulation: 1900

CULLMAN

THE CULLMAN TIMES

Corporate/Parent Company: CNHI, LLC
Street Address: 300 4th Ave SE
City: Cullman
State: AL
Postal Code: 35055
Office phone: (256) 734-2131
Publication Website: https://www.cullmantimes.com/
General E-mail: editorial@cullmantimes.com
Publisher Name: Katherine Miller
Publisher Email: kimiller@cullmantimes.com
Publisher Phone: (256) 734-2131, ext : 111
Editor Name: Amy Henderson
Editor Email: ahenderson@cullmantimes.com
Editor Phone: (256) 734-2131, ext : 116
Advertising Executive Name: Debbie Miller
Advertising Executive Email: dmiller@cullmantimes.com
Advertising Executive Phone: (256) 734-2131, ext : 113
Year Established: 1901
Mechanical specifications: Type page 12 x 21 1/2; E - 6 cols, 1 7/8, 1/8 between; A - 6 cols, 1 7/8, 1/8 between; C - 8 cols, 1 1/3, 1/8 between.
Published Days: Mon`Tues`Wed`Thur`Fri`Sat`Sun
Weekday Frequency: m
Saturday Frequency: m
Avg Paid Circ: 10000
Audit Company: Sworn/Estimate/Non-Audited
Audit Date: 7 12 2019
Pressroom Equipment: Lines – 10-HI/Cotrell V-30 1993; Folders – HI/JF-25C (Main), HI/JF-25B (Aux).;

THE CULLMAN TRIBUNE

Corporate/Parent Company: Humble Roots LLC
Street Address: 219 Second Ave.
City: Cullman
State: AL
Postal Code: 35055
Office phone: 256-739-1351
Publication Website: cullmansense.com
General E-mail: dustin@cullmantribune.com
Editor Name: Wendy Milligan Sack
Editor Email: news@cullmantribune.com
Mechanical specifications: Type page 13 x 21; E - 6 cols, 2 1/16, between; A - 6 cols, 2 1/16, between.
Published Days: Thur
Avg Paid Circ: 13400
Audit Company: Sworn/Estimate/Non-Audited
Audit Date: 6 10 2019
Total Circulation: 2310

DEMOPOLIS

BLACKBELT GAZETTE

Corporate/Parent Company: Tallapoosa Publishers, Inc
Street Address: 315 East Jefferson Street
City: Demopolis
State: AL
Postal Code: 36732
Office phone: (334) 289-4017
Publication Website: https://www.demopolistimes.com/category/blackbelt-gazette/
General E-mail: news@demopolistimes.com
Publisher Name: Robert Blankenship
Publisher Email: robert.blankenship@demopolistimes.com
Editor Name: Robert Blankenship
Editor Email: robert.blankenship@demopolistimes.com
Advertising Executive Name: Jeanne Glass
Advertising Executive Email: jeanne.glass@demopolistimes.com
Published Days: Wed
Audit Company: Sworn/Estimate/Non-Audited
Audit Date: 6 10 2019

DEMOPOLIS TIMES

Corporate/Parent Company: Boone Newspapers, Inc.
Street Address: 315 E Jefferson St
City: Demopolis
State: AL
Postal Code: 36732
Office phone: (334) 289-4017
Publication Website: https://www.demopolistimes.com/
General E-mail: news@demopolistimes.com
Publisher Name: Robert Blankenship
Publisher Email: robert.blankenship@demopolistimes.com
Editor Name: Robert Blankenship
Editor Email: robert.blankenship@demopolistimes.com
Advertising Executive Name: Jeanne Glass
Advertising Executive Email: jeanne.glass@demopolistimes.com
Year Established: 1887
Delivery Methods: Mail
Mechanical specifications: Type page 13 1/3 x 21 1/2; E - 6 cols, 1/6 between; A - 6 cols, 1/6 between; C - 10 cols, between.
Published Days: Wed`Sat
Weekday Frequency: m
Avg Paid Circ: 2850
Audit Company: Sworn/Estimate/Non-Audited
Audit Date: 6 10 2019
Total Circulation: 32497

EAST RAINSVILLE

SOUTHERN TORCH

Street Address: 203 Main Street
City: East Rainsville
State: AL
Postal Code: 35986
Office phone: 256.638.4040
Publication Website: southerntorch.com
General E-mail: sales@southerntorch.com
Editor Name: Marla Jones
Editor Email: marla@southerntorch.com
Advertising Executive Name: Jenna Payne
Advertising Executive Phone: 256.259.2341
Total Circulation: 3300

FOLEY

GULF COAST NEWS

Corporate/Parent Company: Gulf Coast Media
Street Address: 901 N. McKenzie St
City: Foley
State: AL
Postal Code: 36535
Office phone: 251.943.2151
Publication Website: www.gulfcoastnewstoday.com
Publisher Name: Parks Rogers
Publisher Email: parks@gulfcoastmedia.com
Publisher Phone: 251.923.3930
Editor Name: Melanie LeCroy
Editor Email: melanie@gulfcoastmedia.com
Editor Phone: 251.923.3934
Advertising Executive Name: April Wallace
Advertising Executive Email: april@gulfcoastmedia.com
Advertising Executive Phone: 251.345.6805
Year Established: 1977
Published Days: Wed`Fri
Avg Paid Circ: 1737
Audit Company: Sworn/Estimate/Non-Audited
Audit Date: 6 10 2019
Total Circulation: 32497

THE BALDWIN TIMES INDEPENDENT

Corporate/Parent Company: Gulf Coast Media
Street Address: 901 N McKenzie St
City: Foley
State: AL
Postal Code: 36535
Office phone: (251) 943-2151
Publication Website: http://www.gulfcoastnewstoday.com/baldwin-times/
General E-mail: classifieds@gulfcoastmedia.com
Publisher Name: Parks Rogers
Publisher Email: parks@gulfcoastmedia.com
Publisher Phone: (251) 923-3930
Editor Name: Allison Marlow
Editor Email: allisonm@gulfcoastmedia.com
Editor Phone: (251) 923-3937
Advertising Executive Name: April Wallace
Advertising Executive Email: april@gulfcoastmedia.com
Advertising Executive Phone: (251) 345-6805
Year Established: 1890
Own Printing Facility?: Y
Commercial printers?: Y
Mechanical specifications: Type page 13 x 21 1/2; E - 6 cols, 2 1/16, 1/8 between; A - 6 cols, 2 1/16, 1/8 between; C - 9 cols, between.
Published Days: Thur
Avg Paid Circ: 3200
Avg Free Circ: 4500
Audit Company: Sworn/Estimate/Non-Audited
Audit Date: 6 10 2019

THE FAIRHOPE COURIER

Corporate/Parent Company: Gulf Coast Media
Street Address: 901 N McKenzie St
City: Foley
State: AL
Postal Code: 36535
Office phone: (251) 943-2151
Publication Website: http://www.gulfcoastnewstoday.com/the-courier/
General E-mail: classifieds@gulfcoastmedia.com
Publisher Name: Parks Rogers
Publisher Email: parks@gulfcoastmedia.com
Publisher Phone: (251) 923-3930
Editor Name: Guy Busby
Editor Email: guy@gulfcoastmedia.com
Editor Phone: (251) 923-3931
Advertising Executive Name: April Wallace
Advertising Executive Email: april@gulfcoastmedia.com
Advertising Executive Phone: (251) 345-6805
Year Established: 1894
Own Printing Facility?: Y
Commercial printers?: Y
Mechanical specifications: Type page 13 x 21 1/2; E - 6 cols, 1 7/8, 1/8 between; A - 6

Non-Daily Newspapers in the U.S.

cols, 1 7/8, 1/6 between; C - 9 cols, 1 1/4, between.
Published Days: Wed`Fri
Avg Paid Circ: 1752
Audit Company: Sworn/Estimate/Non-Audited
Audit Date: 6 10 2019
Total Circulation: 5500

THE FOLEY ONLOOKER
Corporate/Parent Company: Gulf Coast Media
Street Address: 901 N. McKenzie St
City: Foley
State: AL
Postal Code: 36535
Office phone: 251.943.2151
Publication Website: www.gulfcoastnewstoday.com
Publisher Name: Parks Rogers
Publisher Email: parks@gulfcoastmedia.com
Publisher Phone: 251.923.3930
Editor Name: John Underwood
Editor Email: john@gulfcoastmedia.com
Editor Phone: 251.923.3933
Advertising Executive Name: April Wallace
Advertising Executive Email: april@gulfcoastmedia.com
Advertising Executive Phone: 251.345.6805

THE ISLANDER
Corporate/Parent Company: Gulf Coast Media
Street Address: 901 N McKenzie St
City: Foley
State: AL
Postal Code: 36535
Office phone: (251) 943-2151
Publication Website: http://www.gulfcoastnewstoday.com/the-islander/
General E-mail: classifieds@gulfcoastmedia.com
Publisher Name: Parks Rogers
Publisher Email: parks@gulfcoastmedia.com
Publisher Phone: (251) 923-3930
Editor Name: Melanie LeCroy
Editor Email: melanie@gulfcoastmedia.com
Editor Phone: (251) 923-3934
Advertising Executive Name: April Wallace
Advertising Executive Email: april@gulfcoastmedia.com
Advertising Executive Phone: (251) 345-6805
Year Established: 1977
Published Days: Wed`Fri
Avg Paid Circ: 1737
Audit Company: Sworn/Estimate/Non-Audited
Audit Date: 6 10 2019
Mailroom Equipment: Counter Stackers – Quipp 400; Inserters & Stuffers – 1-Mueller/227 GMA SLS 1000; Tying Machines – Dynaric ;
Buisness Equipment: IBM/AS-200
Classified Equipment: Hardware – Microsoft/Windows NT Server 4.0; Printers – HP/LaserWriter;
Classified Software: Baseview/Classified.
Editorial Equipment: Hardware – PC LAN, Microsoft/Windows NT Server 4.0; Printers – HP/LaserJet 4MV
Editorial Software: Microsoft/Windows, Microsoft/Word.
Production Equipment: Hardware – SCREEN PlateRite News 2000 Thermal Platesetter
Production Software: InDesign
Total Circulation: 10596

THE ONLOOKER
Corporate/Parent Company: Gulf Coast Media
Street Address: 901 N McKenzie St
City: Foley
State: AL
Postal Code: 36535
Office phone: (251) 943-2151
Publication Website: http://www.gulfcoastnewstoday.com/the-onlooker/
General E-mail: classifieds@gulfcoastmedia.com
Publisher Name: Parks Rogers
Publisher Email: parks@gulfcoastmedia.com
Publisher Phone: (251) 923-3930
Editor Name: John Underwood
Editor Email: john@gulfcoastmedia.com
Editor Phone: (251) 923-3933
Advertising Executive Name: April Wallace
Advertising Executive Email: april@gulfcoastmedia.com
Advertising Executive Phone: (251) 345-6805
Year Established: 1907
Own Printing Facility?: Y
Commercial printers?: Y
Mechanical specifications: Type page 13 x 21 1/2; E - 6 cols, 2 1/16, between; A - 6 cols, 2 1/16, between; C - 6 cols, 2 1/16, between.
Published Days: Wed`Sat
Avg Paid Circ: 4600
Audit Company: Sworn/Estimate/Non-Audited
Audit Date: 6 10 2019
Total Circulation: 7700

FORT DEPOSIT
LOWNDES SIGNAL
Corporate/Parent Company: Boone Newspapers, Inc.
Street Address: 118 Ellis Street
City: Fort Deposit
State: AL
Postal Code: 36032
Office phone: (334) 382-3111
Publication Website: http://www.lowndessignal.com/
General E-mail: dianne.mathews@lowndessignal.com
Publisher Name: Adam Prestridge
Publisher Email: adam.prestridge@lowndessignal.com
Editor Name: Mark Rogers
Editor Email: mark.rogers@lowndessignal.com
Published Days: Thur
Avg Paid Circ: 1900
Audit Company: Sworn/Estimate/Non-Audited
Audit Date: 6 10 2019
Total Circulation: 3330

GADSDEN
THE MESSENGER (GADSDEN)
Street Address: 1957 Rainbow Drive
City: Gadsden
State: AL
Postal Code: 35901
Office phone: (256) 547-1049
Publication Website: www.gadsdenmessenger.com
General E-mail: info@gadsdenmessenger.com
Editor Name: Chris McCarthy
Editor Email: cmccarthy@gadsdenmessenger.com
Advertising Executive Name: Valerie White
Advertising Executive Email: vwhite@gadsdenmessenger.com
Advertising Executive Phone: 256-547-1049
Total Circulation: 5000

GARDENDALE
NORTH JEFFERSON NEWS
Corporate/Parent Company: CNHI, LLC
Street Address: 1110 Main St.
City: Gardendale
State: AL
Postal Code: 35071
Office phone: (205) 631-8716
Publication Website: https://www.njeffersonnews.com/
General E-mail: editor@njeffersonnews.com
Editor Email: editor@njeffersonnews.com
Year Established: 1970
Delivery Methods: Mail`Racks
Published Days: Wed

Avg Paid Circ: 2310
Audit Company: Sworn/Estimate/Non-Audited
Audit Date: 6 10 2019
Total Circulation: 3000

GREENVILLE
BUTLER COUNTY NEWS-OOB
Corporate/Parent Company: Boone Newspapers
Street Address: P.O. Box 620
City: Greenville
State: AL
Postal Code: 36033
Office phone: (334) 382-3111
Publication Website: http://www.boonenewspapers.com/community/butler/
General E-mail: dennis.palmer@greenvilleadvocate.com
Mailroom Equipment: Tying Machines – 1/Bu, 1-/Power Strapper; Wrapping Singles – 1-/St; Address Machine – 1-/Am, 1-/KR, 1-KR/4-up head, Prism/Ink Jet.;
Buisness Equipment: SUN, E-450
Buisness Software: PBS, AM 3.0, CMS 3.0
Classified Equipment: Hardware – 4-APP/Mac; Printers – Xante/Accel-a-Writer 8200;
Classified Software: 5-Baseview/Ad Manager Pro, 2-Baseview/Class Flow.
Editorial Equipment: Hardware – 7-COM/Intrepid, 6-APP/Mac, 8-APP/Mac; Printers – APP/Mac Laser Writer 560, Xante/Accel-a-Writer 8200
Editorial Software: Microsoft/Word 6.1, APP/Mac Write Now 4.0, QPS/QuarkXPress.
Production Equipment: Hardware – Pre Press/Panther Plus Imagesetter, Gluntz & Jensen/Multi-Line 21; Cameras – 1-R, 1-Cl, Kk/Image Maker; Scanners – APP/Mac II.
Total Circulation: 10000

THE GREENVILLE ADVOCATE
Corporate/Parent Company: Boone Newspapers, Inc.
Street Address: 103 Hickory St
City: Greenville
State: AL
Postal Code: 36037
Office phone: (334) 382-3111
Publication Website: https://www.greenvilleadvocate.com/
General E-mail: adam.prestridge@greenvilleadvocate.com
Publisher Name: Adam Prestridge
Publisher Email: adam.prestridge@greenvilleadvocate.com
Editor Name: Mark Rogers
Editor Email: mark.rogers@greenvilleadvocate.com
Advertising Executive Name: Chloe Langston
Advertising Executive Email: chloe.langston@greenvilleadvocate.com
Year Established: 1865
Published Days: Wed`Sat
Avg Paid Circ: 3000
Avg Free Circ: 9700
Audit Company: Sworn/Estimate/Non-Audited
Audit Date: 6 10 2019
Total Circulation: 13400

THE GREENVILLE STANDARD
Street Address: 113 West Commerce Street P.O. Box 186
City: Greenville
State: AL
Postal Code: 36037
Office phone: 334-371-9900
Publication Website: www.thegreenvillestandard.com
General E-mail: publisher@thegreenvillestandard.com
Buisness Equipment: IBM
Classified Equipment: Hardware – APP/Mac;
Printers – APP/Mac LaserWriter I;
Classified Software: Baseview.
Editorial Equipment: Hardware – APP/Mac/HP/Flatbed Scanner, Polaroid/Film Scanner; Printers – APP/Mac LaserWriter I
Editorial Software: Aldus/PageMaker, Microsoft/Word, QPS/QuarkXPress.
Total Circulation: 9872

HARTSELLE
HARTSELLE ENQUIRER
Corporate/Parent Company: Boone Newspapers, Inc.
Street Address: 407 Chestnut St NW
City: Hartselle
State: AL
Postal Code: 35640
Office phone: (256) 773-6566
Publication Website: https://m.hartselleenquirer.com/
General E-mail: classifieds@hartselleenquirer.com
Editor Name: Rebekah Martin
Editor Email: rebekah.martin@hartselleenquirer.com
Editor Phone: (256) 773-6566
Advertising Executive Name: Baretta Taylor
Advertising Executive Email: baretta.taylor@tnvalleymedia.com
Advertising Executive Phone: (256) 340-2370
Year Established: 1933
Delivery Methods: Mail`Newsstand`Racks
Published Days: Thur
Avg Paid Circ: 3100
Avg Free Circ: 3500
Audit Company: Sworn/Estimate/Non-Audited
Audit Date: 6 10 2019
Total Circulation: 1752

HEFLIN
THE CLEBURNE NEWS
Corporate/Parent Company: Consolidated Publishing Co.
Street Address: 926 Ross St
City: Heflin
State: AL
Postal Code: 36264
Office phone: (256) 463-2872
Publication Website: https://www.annistonstar.com/cleburne_news/
General E-mail: news@cleburnenews.com
Publisher Name: John Alred
Publisher Email: jalred@jaxnews.com
Publisher Phone: (256) 235-3531
Editor Name: Bill Wilson
Editor Email: news@cleburnenews.com
Editor Phone: (256) 463-2872
Year Established: 1906
Published Days: Mon`Thur
Avg Paid Circ: 3000
Audit Company: Sworn/Estimate/Non-Audited
Audit Date: 6 10 2019

LUVERNE
THE LUVERNE JOURNAL
Corporate/Parent Company: Boone Newspapers, Inc.
Street Address: 506 S Forest Ave
City: Luverne
State: AL
Postal Code: 36049
Office phone: (334) 335-3541
Publication Website: https://www.greenvilleadvocate.com/
General E-mail: adam.prestridge@greenvilleadvocate.com
Publisher Name: Adam Prestridge
Publisher Email: adam.prestridge@greenvilleadvocate.com
Editor Name: Mark Rogers
Editor Email: mark.rogers@greenvilleadvocate.com
Advertising Executive Name: Chloe Langston

Advertising Executive Email: chloe.langston@greenvilleadvocate.com
Year Established: 1890
Own Printing Facility?: Y
Commercial printers?: Y
Mechanical specifications: Type page 13 1/2 x 23 1/3; E - 6 cols, 2 1/4, 1/4 between; A - 6 cols, 2 1/4, 1/4 between; C - 6 cols, 2 1/4, 1/4 between.
Published Days: Thur
Avg Paid Circ: 2400
Audit Company: Sworn/Estimate/Non-Audited
Audit Date: 6 10 2019
Total Circulation: 12700

MONTGOMERY

THE MONTGOMERY INDEPENDENT

Street Address: 141 Market Place
City: Montgomery
State: AL
Postal Code: 36117
Office phone: 334-265-7323
Publication Website: www.montgomeryindependent.com
General E-mail: webmaster@montgomeryindependent.com
Publisher Name: Jeff Martin
Editor Name: Art Parker
Advertising Executive Name: Jim Turner
Advertising Executive Email: jim@montgomeryindependent.com

OPELIKA

OPELIKA OBSERVER

Street Address: 216 S. 8th Street
City: Opelika
State: AL
Postal Code: 36801
Office phone: (334) 749-8003
Publication Website: www.opelikaobserver.com
General E-mail: editor@opelikaobserver.com
Editor Name: Michelle Key
Editor Email: Michelle@opelikaobserver.com
Advertising Executive Name: Doug Horn
Advertising Executive Email: sales@opelikaobserver.com
Total Circulation: 1737

PELL CITY

ST. CLAIR NEWS-AEGIS

Corporate/Parent Company: CNHI, LLC
Street Address: 1820 2nd Ave N
City: Pell City
State: AL
Postal Code: 35125
Office phone: (205) 884-2310
Publication Website: https://www.newsaegis.com/
General E-mail: ads@newsaegis.com
Editor Email: editor@newsaegis.com
Advertising Executive Email: ads@newsaegis.com
Published Days: Thur
Avg Paid Circ: 5500
Audit Company: Sworn/Estimate/Non-Audited
Audit Date: 6 10 2019
Total Circulation: 3300

THE SAINT CLAIR TIMES

Street Address: 1911 Martin St S
City: Pell City
State: AL
Postal Code: 35128
Office phone: (205) 884-3400
Publication Website: https://www.annistonstar.com/the_st_clair_times/
General E-mail: news@dailyhome.com
Publisher Name: Robert Jackson
Publisher Email: rjackson@annistonstar.com
Publisher Phone: (256) 235-9220
Editor Name: Anthony Cook
Editor Email: acook@dailyhome.com
Editor Phone: (256) 299-2110
Advertising Executive Name: Pam Isbell
Advertising Executive Email: pisbell@dailyhome.com
Advertising Executive Phone: (256) 299-2140
Year Established: 2000
Delivery Methods: Mail`Carrier
Published Days: Thur
Avg Paid Circ: 34000
Avg Free Circ: 34000
Audit Company: Sworn/Estimate/Non-Audited
Audit Date: 6 10 2019

RAINSVILLE

MOUNTAIN VALLEY NEWS

Street Address: 450 Main St E
City: Rainsville
State: AL
Postal Code: 35986
Office phone: (256) 638-6397
Publication Website: mountainvalleynewspaper.com
General E-mail: mtnvalley@farmerstel.com
Total Circulation: 2400

RUSSELLVILLE

FRANKLIN COUNTY TIMES

Corporate/Parent Company: Boone Newspapers, Inc.
Street Address: 14131 Highway 43
City: Russellville
State: AL
Postal Code: 35653
Office phone: (256) 332-1881
Publication Website: https://franklincountytimes.com/
General E-mail: betty.newton@franklincountytimes.com
Editor Name: Alison James
Editor Email: alison.james@franklincountytimes.com
Editor Phone: (256) 332-1881
Advertising Executive Name: Tori Waits
Advertising Executive Email: tori.waits@franklincountytimes.com
Advertising Executive Phone: (256) 766-3440
Year Established: 1879
Delivery Methods: Mail`Racks
Own Printing Facility?: Y
Commercial printers?: Y
Published Days: Wed
Avg Paid Circ: 3800
Audit Company: Sworn/Estimate/Non-Audited
Audit Date: 6 10 2019

SELMA

THE SELMA TIMES-JOURNAL

Corporate/Parent Company: Boone Newspapers, Inc.
Street Address: 1018 Water Ave
City: Selma
State: AL
Postal Code: 36701
Office phone: (334) 875-2110
Publication Website: https://www.selmatimesjournal.com
General E-mail: clara.gary@selmatimesjournal.com
Publisher Name: Dennis Palmer
Publisher Email: dennis.palmer@selmatimesjournal.com
Editor Name: Adam Powell
Editor Email: adam.powell@selmatimesjournal.com
Advertising Executive Name: Tina Yelverton
Advertising Executive Email: tina.yelverton@selmatimesjournal.com
Year Established: 1827
Delivery Methods: Mail`Newsstand`Carrier`Racks
Own Printing Facility?: Y
Commercial printers?: Y
Mechanical specifications: Type page 13 x 21 1/2; E - 6 cols, 2 1/16, 1/8 between; A - 6 cols, 2 1/16, 1/8 between; C - 10 cols, 1 3/8, 1/16 between.
Published Days: Tues`Wed`Thur`Fri`Sat`Sun
Weekday Frequency: m
Saturday Frequency: m
Avg Paid Circ: 8500
Avg Free Circ: 8000
Audit Company: Sworn/Estimate/Non-Audited
Audit Date: 7 12 2019
Pressroom Equipment: Lines – 10-KP/News King.;

TALLADEGA

THE DAILY HOME

Corporate/Parent Company: Consolidated Publishing Co.
Street Address: 6 Fort Lashley Ave
City: Talladega
State: AL
Postal Code: 35160
Office phone: (256) 362-1000
Publication Website: https://www.annistonstar.com/the_daily_home/
General E-mail: news@dailyhome.com
Editor Name: Anthony Cook
Editor Email: acook@dailyhome.com
Editor Phone: (256) 299-2110
Advertising Executive Name: Pam Isbell
Advertising Executive Email: pisbell@dailyhome.com
Advertising Executive Phone: (256) 299-2140
Year Established: 1867
Delivery Methods: Mail`Newsstand`Carrier`Racks
Own Printing Facility?: N
Commercial printers?: N
Mechanical specifications: Type page 13 x 21 1/2; E - 6 cols, 2 1/16, 1/8 between; A - 6 cols, 2 1/16, 1/8 between; C - 9 cols, 1 3/8, 1/16 between.
Published Days: Tues`Wed`Thur`Fri`Sat`Sun
Weekday Frequency: m
Saturday Frequency: m
Avg Paid Circ: 9872
Audit Company: Sworn/Estimate/Non-Audited
Audit Date: 7 12 2019

TALLASSEE

TALLASSEE TRIBUNE

Corporate/Parent Company: Boone Newspapers, Inc.
Street Address: 211 Barnette Blvd
City: Tallassee
State: AL
Postal Code: 36078
Office phone: (334) 283-6568
Publication Website: https://www.tallasseetribune.com/
General E-mail: editorelmore@tallasseetribune.com
Publisher Name: Steve Baker
Publisher Email: steve.baker@alexcityoutlook.com
Publisher Phone: (256) 414-3190
Editor Name: Betsy Iler
Editor Email: betsy.iler@alexcityoutlook.com
Editor Phone: (256) 234-4282
Advertising Executive Name: Tippy Hunter
Advertising Executive Email: tippy.hunter@alexcityoutlook.com
Advertising Executive Phone: (256) 414-3177
Year Established: 1899
Delivery Methods: Mail`Newsstand`Racks
Mechanical specifications: Type page 13 x 21 1/2.
Published Days: Wed
Avg Paid Circ: 4200
Audit Company: Sworn/Estimate/Non-Audited
Audit Date: 6 10 2019
Classified Equipment: Hardware – APP/Mac; COM/4961, COM/2414; Printers – APP/Mac 810;
Classified Software: Baseview.
Editorial Equipment: Hardware – APP/Mac/6-ECR/Autokon; Printers – 1-HP/4MV, 1-APP/Mac 810
Editorial Software: QPS/QuarkXPress 4.0, Adobe/Photoshop 5.0.
Production Equipment: Hardware – Caere/OmniPage 6.0.
Total Circulation: 3841,5

THE TALLASSEE TRIBUNE

Corporate/Parent Company: Boone Newspapers, Inc.
Street Address: 211 Barnette Blvd
City: Tallassee
State: AL
Postal Code: 36078
Office phone: (334) 283-6568
Publication Website: https://www.tallasseetribune.com
General E-mail: editorelmore@tallasseetribune.com
Publisher Name: Steve Baker
Publisher Email: steve.baker@alexcityoutlook.com
Publisher Phone: (256) 414-3190
Editor Name: Betsy Iler
Editor Email: betsy.iler@alexcityoutlook.com
Editor Phone: (256) 234-4282
Advertising Executive Name: Tippy Hunter
Advertising Executive Email: tippy.hunter@alexcityoutlook.com
Advertising Executive Phone: (256) 414-3177
Year Established: 1899
Delivery Methods: Mail`Newsstand`Racks
Mechanical specifications: Type page 13 x 21 1/2.
Published Days: Wed
Avg Paid Circ: 4200
Audit Company: Sworn/Estimate/Non-Audited
Audit Date: 6 10 2019
Total Circulation: 4600

TROY

THE TROY MESSENGER

Corporate/Parent Company: Boone Newspapers
Street Address: 918 S Brundidge St
City: Troy
State: AL
Postal Code: 36081
Office phone: (334) 566-4270
Publication Website: https://www.troymessenger.com/
Publisher Name: Stacy Graning
Publisher Email: stacy.graning@troymessenger.com
Publisher Phone: 334-670-6308
Advertising Executive Name: Stephanie Gurba
Advertising Executive Email: stephanie.gurba@troymessenger.com
Advertising Executive Phone: 334-670-6318
Year Established: 1866
Mechanical specifications: Type page 13 1/2 x 21 1/2; E - 6 cols, 2, 1/4 between; A - 6 cols, 2, 1/4 between; C - 9 cols, 1 5/16, 1/4 between.
Published Days: Tues`Wed`Thur`Fri`Sun
Weekday Frequency: m
Avg Paid Circ: 2814
Audit Company: Sworn/Estimate/Non-Audited
Audit Date: 7 12 2019
Total Circulation: 68000

UNION SPRINGS

UNION SPRINGS HERALD

Street Address: 324 Ellis Street
City: Union Springs
State: AL
Postal Code: 36089
Office phone: 334-738-2360
Publication Website: unionspringsherald.com
General E-mail: webeditor@unionspringsherald.com
Publisher Name: Kim Graham

Non-Daily Newspapers in the U.S.

III-7

Publisher Email: kim@unionspringsherald.com
Publisher Phone: 334-738-2360
Editor Name: Johnny Adams
Editor Email: johnny@unionspringsherald.com
Editor Phone: 334-738-2360
Mailroom Equipment: Counter Stackers – 1/BG; Inserters & Stuffers – By hand; Tying Machines – 1-/Bu; Address Machine – 1-/KR.;
Buisness Equipment: PC
Classified Equipment: Hardware – APP/Mac; APP/Mac;
Classified Software: Baseview 1.
Editorial Equipment: Hardware – APP/Mac.
Production Equipment: Hardware – Kodak, Trendsetter direct to plate
Total Circulation: 16500

VERNON

THE LAMAR DEMOCRAT

Street Address: P.O. Box 587
City: Vernon
State: AL
Postal Code: 35592
Office phone: 205.695.7029
Publication Website: lamardemocratnews.com
General E-mail: lamardemocrat@gmail.com
Editor Name: Howard Reeves

WETUMPKA

ECLECTIC OBSERVER

Corporate/Parent Company: Tallapoosa Publishers, Inc
Street Address: 127 Company Street
City: Wetumpka
State: AL
Postal Code: 36092
Office phone: (334) 567-7811
Publication Website: https://www.thewetumpkaherald.com/news/eclectic/
General E-mail: editorelmore@thewetumpkaherald.com
Publisher Name: Steve Baker
Publisher Email: steve.baker@alexcityoutlook.com
Publisher Phone: (256) 414-3190
Editor Name: Santana Wood
Editor Email: santana.wood@alexcityoutlook.com
Editor Phone: (256) 234-3412
Advertising Executive Name: Tippy Hunter
Advertising Executive Email: tippy.hunter@alexcityoutlook.com
Advertising Executive Phone: (256) 414-3177
Published Days: Thur
Avg Paid Circ: 1200
Avg Free Circ: 100
Audit Company: Sworn/Estimate/Non-Audited
Audit Date: 6 10 2019
Classified Equipment: Hardware – Mk.;
Editorial Equipment: Hardware – Mk/Newswriter.
Production Equipment: Hardware – Mk/LaserWriter.
Note: For printing information see Andalusia Star News.
Total Circulation: 2814

THE WETUMPKA HERALD

Corporate/Parent Company: Boone Newspapers, Inc.
Street Address: 127 Company Street
City: Wetumpka
State: AL
Postal Code: 36092
Office phone: (334) 567-7811
Publication Website: https://www.thewetumpkaherald.com/
General E-mail: editorelmore@thewetumpkaherald.com
Publisher Name: Steve Baker
Publisher Email: steve.baker@alexcityoutlook.com
Publisher Phone: (256) 414-3190
Editor Name: Betsy Iler
Editor Email: betsy.iler@alexcityoutlook.com
Editor Phone: (256) 234-4282

Advertising Executive Name: Tippy Hunter
Advertising Executive Email: marketing@alexcityoutlook.com
Advertising Executive Phone: (256) 414-3177
Year Established: 1898
Delivery Methods: Mail`Newsstand
Mechanical specifications: Type page 13 x 21 1/2; E – 6 cols, 2, 3/16 between; A – 6 cols, 2, 3/16 between; C – 6 cols, 2, 3/16 between.
Published Days: Wed
Avg Paid Circ: 5700
Avg Free Circ: 100
Audit Company: Sworn/Estimate/Non-Audited
Audit Date: 6 10 2019

ARKANSAS

BATESVILLE

ARKANSAS WEEKLY

Street Address: 920 Harrison St
City: Batesville
State: AR
Postal Code: 72501-6949
Office phone: 870-793-4196
Publication Website: arkansasweekly.com
Editor Name: Rob Grace

BOLIVAR

COMMUNITY PUBLISHERS, INC./ NEIGHBOR NEWS

Street Address: 335 S. Springfield Ave.
City: Bolivar
State: AR
Postal Code: 65613
Office phone: (417) 326-7636
Publication Website: https://bolivarmonews.com/neighbors/
General E-mail: news@bolivarmonews.com
Publisher Name: Jamey Honeycutt
Publisher Email: jameyh@phillipsmedia.com
Editor Name: Jessica Franklin Maul

BRINKLEY

CENTRAL DELTA ARGUS-SUN

Street Address: PO Box 711
City: Brinkley
State: AR
Postal Code: 72021-0711
Office phone: 870-734-1056
Publication Website: argussunonline.com
Editor Name: Katie Jacques

DANVILLE

YELL COUNTY RECORD

Street Address: 602 Main St
City: Danville
State: AR
Postal Code: 72833
Office phone: 479-495-2354
Publication Website: theyellcountyrecord.com
General E-mail: ycrecord@arkwest.com
Editor Name: David Fisher

DARDANELLE

POST DISPATCH

Street Address: 218 N Front Street, PO Box 270
City: Dardanelle
State: AR
Postal Code: 72834
Office phone: 479 229-2250
Publication Website: dardanellepostdispatch.com

General E-mail: news@dardanellepostdispatch.com
Editor Name: Mary Fisher

FORT SMITH

PRESS ARGUS-COURIER

Street Address: P.O. Box 1359
City: Fort Smith
State: AR
Postal Code: 72902
Office phone: 479.474.5215
Publication Website: pressargus.com
General E-mail: info@pressargus.com
Publisher Name: Ronald Benner
Publisher Email: rbenner@swtimes.com
Publisher Phone: (479) 785-7700 ext. 1300

HAMPTON

SOUTH ARKANSAS SUN

Street Address: PO Box 1183
City: Hampton
State: AR
Postal Code: 71744
Office phone: (870)798-3786
Publication Website: southarkansassun.net
General E-mail: calhouncountynews@gmail.com

HARRISON

HARRISON DAILY TIMES

Corporate/Parent Company: Phillips Media Group, LLC
Street Address: 111 W Rush Ave
City: Harrison
State: AR
Postal Code: 72601
Office phone: (870) 741-2325
Publication Website: https://harrisondaily.com/
General E-mail: news@harrisondaily.com
Publisher Name: Jim Perry
Publisher Email: jimp@phillipsmedia.com
Editor Name: Lynn Blevins

HAZEN

GRAND PRAIRIE HERALD

Street Address: 111 Hwy. 70 East
City: Hazen
State: AR
Postal Code: 72064
Office phone: 870-255-4538
Publication Website: herald-publishing.com
General E-mail: heraldpublishing@gmail.com
Editor Name: Roxanne Bradow

JASPER

THE NEWTON COUNTY TIMES

Corporate/Parent Company: Phillips Media Group, LLC
Street Address: PO Box 453
City: Jasper
State: AR
Postal Code: 72641
Office phone: (870) 446-2645
Publication Website: https://newtoncountytimes.com/
General E-mail: news@newtoncountytimes.com
Publisher Name: Jim Perry
Publisher Email: jimp@phillipsmedia.com
Editor Name: Lynn Blevins

LITTLE ROCK

ARKANSAS BUSINESS

Corporate/Parent Company: Five Legged Stool LLC
Street Address: 114 Scott St
City: Little Rock

State: AR
Postal Code: 72201
Office phone: 501-372-1443
Publication Website: arkansasbusiness.com
General E-mail: info@abpg.com
Publisher Name: Mitch Bettis
Publisher Email: MBettis@ABPG.com
Editor Name: Gwen Moritz

OZARK

OZARK SPECTATOR

Street Address: 207 West Main
City: Ozark
State: AR
Postal Code: 72949
Office phone: (479) 667-2136
Publication Website: ozarkspectator.net
General E-mail: spectator@centurytel.net
Editor Name: Joselyn Eveld

PEA RIDGE

PEA RIDGE TIMES

Corporate/Parent Company: WEHCO Media, Inc.
Street Address: P.O. Box 25
City: Pea Ridge
State: AR
Postal Code: 72751
Office phone: 800-641-6882
Publication Website: tnebc.nwaonline.com
General E-mail: prtnews@nwadg.com
Editor Name: Annette Beard
Total Circulation: 21100

PINE BLUFF

WHITE HALL JOURNAL

Street Address: 300 Beech St.
City: Pine Bluff
State: AR
Postal Code: 71601
Office phone: (870) 534-3400
Publication Website: whitehalljournal.com
Publisher Name: Jennifer Allen
Publisher Email: jallen@gatehousemedia.com
Publisher Phone: 870-534-3400 ext. 1204
Editor Name: Rick Kennedy

SALEM

SOUTH MISSOURIAN-NEWS

Corporate/Parent Company: Rust Communications
Street Address: P.O. Box 248
City: Salem
State: AR
Postal Code: 72576
Office phone: (870) 895-3207
Publication Website: https://www.areawidenews.com/
General E-mail: news@areawidenews.com
Publisher Name: Patti Sanders
Editor Name: Kim Break
Advertising Executive Name: Stephanie Pierce
Advertising Executive Phone: (870) 895-3207
Mechanical specifications: Type page 13 x 21; E – 6 cols, 2, 1/6 between; A – 6 cols, 2, 1/6 between; C – 6 cols, 2, 1/6 between.
Published Days: Thur
Avg Paid Circ: 1500
Avg Free Circ: 19600
Audit Company: Sworn/Estimate/Non-Audited
Audit Date: 30 09 2017

SILOAM SPRINGS

THE HERALD-LEADER

Corporate/Parent Company: NWA Media
Street Address: 151 HWY 412 E. Suite B
City: Siloam Springs
State: AR
Postal Code: 72761
Office phone: 479-202-9255

Publication Website: hl.nwaonline.com
General E-mail: hleditor@nwadg.com
Editor Name: Graham Thomas

ARIZONA

BENSON

SAN PEDRO VALLEY NEWS-SUN

Corporate/Parent Company: Wick Communications
Street Address: 200 S. Ocotillo Ave., PO Box 1000
City: Benson
State: AZ
Postal Code: 85602-6407
Office phone: (520) 586-3382
Publication Website: https://www.bensonnews-sun.com/
General E-mail: advertising@bensonnews-sun.com
Publisher Name: Ian Kirkwood
Publisher Email: publisher@bensonnews-sun.com
Editor Name: Chris Dabovich
Editor Email: managingeditor@bensonnews-sun.com
Advertising Executive Name: Tammy Dalton
Advertising Executive Email: advertising@bensonnews-sun.com
Year Established: 1900
Mechanical specifications: Type page 11 1/2 x 21 1/2; E - 6 cols, 1 5/6, 3/16 between; A - 6 cols, 1 5/6, 3/16 between; C - 6 cols, 1 5/6, 3/16 between.
Published Days: Wed
Avg Paid Circ: 1466
Audit Company: VAC
Audit Date: 31 05 2017

BULLHEAD CITY

LAUGHLIN NEVADA TIMES

Corporate/Parent Company: Brehm Communications, Inc.
Street Address: 2435 Miracle Mile
City: Bullhead City
State: AZ
Postal Code: 86442
Office phone: (928) 296-8455
Publication Website: http://mohavedailynews.com
General E-mail: wells@nwppub.com
Editor Name: Bill McMillen
Editor Email: bmcmillen@mohavedailynews.com
Editor Phone: Ext 5144
Advertising Executive Name: Wells Andrews
Advertising Executive Email: wells@nwppub.com

CAMP VERDE

CAMP VERDE BUGLE

Corporate/Parent Company: Western News & Info
Street Address: 283 3rd St
City: Camp Verde
State: AZ
Postal Code: 86322
Office phone: (928) 634-2241
Publication Website: https://www.verdenews.com/news/camp-verde-bugle/
General E-mail: editorial@verdevalleynews.com
Publisher Name: Babette Cubitt
Editor Name: Dan Engler
Editor Email: editorial@verdevalleynews.com
Editor Phone: (928) 635-4426, ext : 6032
Advertising Executive Name: Jessica Ryan
Advertising Executive Email: jryan@verdenews.com
Advertising Executive Phone: (928) 635-4426, ext : 6021
Year Established: 1947
Delivery Methods: Mail`Newsstand

Published Days: Wed`Fri`Sun
Avg Paid Circ: 824
Audit Company: Sworn/Estimate/Non-Audited
Audit Date: 6 10 2019

CASA GRANDE

ARIZONA CITY INDEPENDENT/ EDITION

Corporate/Parent Company: Kramer Media
Street Address: 200 W. 2nd St.
City: Casa Grande
State: AZ
Postal Code: 85122
Office phone: 520-836-7461
Publication Website: www.pinalcentral.com/arizona_city_independent
General E-mail: web@pinalcentral.com
Editor Name: Donovan Kramer Jr.
Editor Email: dkramerjr@pinalcentral.com
Editor Phone: (520) 423-8611
Advertising Executive Name: Kara K. Cooper
Advertising Executive Email: kcooper@pinalcentral.com
Advertising Executive Phone: (520) 423-8654

ARIZONA JACKPOT

Street Address: 6031 Lakeshore Drive
City: Casa Grande
State: AZ
Postal Code: 85122
Office phone: 520-723-9530
Publication Website: www.thearizonajackpot.com
General E-mail: ropin@thearizonajackpot.com
Publisher Name: Bob Tuley

CASA GRANDE DISPATCH

Corporate/Parent Company: Kramer Media
Street Address: 200 W 2nd St
City: Casa Grande
State: AZ
Postal Code: 85122-4409
Office phone: (520) 836-7461
Publication Website: https://www.pinalcentral.com/
General E-mail: kcooper@pinalcentral.com
Publisher Name: Donovan Kramer
Publisher Email: dkramerjr@pinalcentral.com
Publisher Phone: (520) 423-8611
Editor Name: Donovan Kramer
Editor Email: dkramerjr@pinalcentral.com
Editor Phone: (520) 423-8611
Advertising Executive Name: Kara K. Cooper
Advertising Executive Email: kcooper@pinalcentral.com
Advertising Executive Phone: (520) 423-8654
Year Established: 1912
Delivery Methods: Newsstand`Carrier
Own Printing Facility?: Y
Commercial printers?: Y
Mechanical specifications: Type page 13 x 21 1/2; E - 6 cols, 2 1/16, 1/8 between; A - 6 cols, 2 1/16, 1/8 between; C - 8 cols, 1 9/16, 1/8 between.
Published Days: Tues`Wed`Thur`Fri`Sat`Sun
Weekday Frequency: m
Saturday Frequency: m
Avg Paid Circ: 6252
Avg Free Circ: 1032
Audit Company: AAM
Audit Date: 31 12 2016
Pressroom Equipment: Lines – 13-G/Community; 2, 3; Folders – 2-G/Suburban (with balloon), G/SSC;

CHINO VALLEY

CHINO VALLEY REVIEW

Corporate/Parent Company: Western News & Info

Street Address: 8307 E. State Route 69
City: Chino Valley
State: AZ
Postal Code: 86323-0370
Office phone: (928) 445-3333
Publication Website: https://www.dcourier.com/news/chino-valley-review/
General E-mail: msmith@prescottaz.com
Publisher Name: Kit K. Atwell
Publisher Email: katwell@prescottaz.com
Publisher Phone: (928) 445-3333, ext : 1070
Editor Name: Tim Wiederaenders
Editor Email: twieds@prescottaz.com
Editor Phone: (928) 445-3333, ext : 2032
Advertising Executive Name: Megan Smith
Advertising Executive Email: msmith@prescottaz.com
Advertising Executive Phone: (928) 445-3333, ext : 2023
Delivery Methods: Newsstand`Carrier
Own Printing Facility?: Y
Commercial printers?: Y
Mechanical specifications: Type page 11 5/8 x 21 1/2; E - 6 cols, 2 1/16, 1/4 between; A - 6 cols, 2 1/16, 1/4 between; C - 6 cols, 2 1/16, 1/4 between.
Published Days: Wed
Avg Paid Circ: 51
Avg Free Circ: 6691
Audit Company: Sworn/Estimate/Non-Audited
Audit Date: 6 10 2019

PRESCOTT VALLEY TRIBUNE

Corporate/Parent Company: Western News & Info
Street Address: 8307 E. State Route 69
City: Chino Valley
State: AZ
Postal Code: 86323-0370
Office phone: (928) 445-3333
Publication Website: https://www.dcourier.com/news/prescott-valley-tribune/
General E-mail: msmith@prescottaz.com
Publisher Name: Kit K. Atwell
Publisher Email: katwell@prescottaz.com
Publisher Phone: (928) 445-3333, ext : 1070
Editor Name: Tim Wiederaenders
Editor Email: twieds@prescottaz.com
Editor Phone: (928) 445-3333, ext : 2032
Advertising Executive Name: Megan Smith
Advertising Executive Email: msmith@prescottaz.com
Advertising Executive Phone: (928) 445-3333, ext : 2023
Published Days: Wed
Avg Paid Circ: 131
Avg Free Circ: 15389
Audit Company: Sworn/Estimate/Non-Audited
Audit Date: 6 10 2019

CLIFTON

COPPER ERA

Corporate/Parent Company: Wick Communications
Street Address: 1 Wards Canyon • P.O. Box 1357
City: Clifton
State: AZ
Postal Code: 85533
Office phone: 928.865.3162
Publication Website: www.eacourier.com/copper_era
Publisher Name: Sarah Keith
Publisher Email: sarah@eacourier.com
Publisher Phone: (928) 428-2560 ext. 225
Editor Name: David Bell
Editor Email: editor@eacourier.com
Editor Phone: (928) 428-2560 ext. 236
Advertising Executive Name: Sarah Keith
Advertising Executive Email: sarah@eacourier.com
Advertising Executive Phone: (928) 428-2560
Year Established: 1899
Delivery Methods: Mail`Newsstand`Carrier`Racks
Mechanical specifications: Type page 9.88 x 21 1/2; E - 6 cols, 1 13/16, 1/8 between; A - 6

cols, 1 13/16, 1/8 between; C - 6 cols, 1 13/16, 1/8 between.
Published Days: Wed
Avg Paid Circ: 871
Audit Company: VAC
Audit Date: 31 05 2017
Mailroom Equipment: Counter Stackers – 2-BG/105; Inserters & Stuffers – 1-KAN/480 Inserter; Tying Machines – 2-MLN/ML2EE; Address Machine – 1/Wm.;
Buisness Equipment: GEAC/Vision Shift, Covalent
Classified Equipment: Hardware – APP/Mac Quadra 630; Printers – Okidata;
Classified Software: Baseview/Class Manager 3.0.6.
Editorial Equipment: Hardware – APP/ Power Mac, APP/Mac Quadra/Phrasea/ Archive (photo/text); Printers – APP/Mac LaserWriter IIq
Editorial Software: Baseview/NewsEdit Pro IQUE, Baseview/Wire Manager IQ Pro, QPS/QuarkXPress 3.32.
Production Equipment: Hardware – Caere/ OmniPage Direct, AG/Accuset 1500, AG/ Viper RIP, Vista/88; Cameras – 1-DAI/C-260-D
Production Software: QPS/QuarkXPress 3.32.
Total Circulation: 7284

COOLIDGE

COOLIDGE EXAMINER

Corporate/Parent Company: Kramer Media
Street Address: 353 W Central Ave
City: Coolidge
State: AZ
Postal Code: 85128-4706
Office phone: (520) 723-5441
Publication Website: https://www.pinalcentral.com/coolidge_examiner/
General E-mail: coolidgeexaminer@yahoo.com
Publisher Name: Donovan Kramer
Publisher Email: dkramerjr@pinalcentral.com
Publisher Phone: (520) 423-8611
Editor Name: Donovan Kramer
Editor Email: dkramerjr@pinalcentral.com
Editor Phone: (520) 423-8611
Advertising Executive Name: Song Ja Haas
Advertising Executive Email: coolidgeexaminer@yahoo.com
Advertising Executive Phone: (520) 723-5441
Own Printing Facility?: Y
Commercial printers?: Y
Mechanical specifications: Type page 13 x 21 1/2; E - 6 cols, 2 1/16, 1/8 between; A - 6 cols, 2 1/16, 1/8 between; C - 6 cols, 2 1/16, 1/8 between.
Published Days: Wed
Avg Paid Circ: 1943
Audit Company: Sworn/Estimate/Non-Audited
Audit Date: 6 10 2019

THE COOLIDGE EXAMINER

Corporate/Parent Company: Kramer Media
Street Address: 353 W. Central Ave.
City: Coolidge
State: AZ
Postal Code: 85128
Office phone: 520-836-7461
Publication Website: www.pinalcentral.com/coolidge_examiner
General E-mail: web@pinalcentral.com
Editor Name: Donovan Kramer Jr.
Editor Email: dkramerjr@pinalcentral.com
Editor Phone: (520) 423-8611
Advertising Executive Name: Kara K. Cooper
Advertising Executive Email: kcooper@pinalcentral.com
Advertising Executive Phone: (520) 423-8654
Total Circulation: 1943

COTTONWOOD

KUDOS

Corporate/Parent Company: Western News &

Non-Daily Newspapers in the U.S.

Info, Inc.
Street Address: 116 S Main St
City: Cottonwood
State: AZ
Postal Code: 86326-3909
Office phone: (928) 634-2241
Publication Website: https://www.verdenews.com/news/kudos/
General E-mail: editorial@verdevalleynews.com
Publisher Name: Babette Cubitt
Editor Name: Dan Engler
Editor Email: editorial@verdevalleynews.com
Editor Phone: (928) 635-4426, ext : 6032
Advertising Executive Name: Jessica Ryan
Advertising Executive Email: jryan@verdenews.com
Advertising Executive Phone: (928) 635-4426, ext : 6021

SMART SHOPPER

Corporate/Parent Company: Western News & Info, Inc.
Street Address: 116 S Main St
City: Cottonwood
State: AZ
Postal Code: 86326-3909
Office phone: (928) 634-2241
Publication Website: https://www.verdenews.com/
General E-mail: editorial@verdevalleynews.com
Publisher Name: Babette Cubitt
Editor Name: Dan Engler
Editor Email: editorial@verdevalleynews.com
Editor Phone: (928) 635-4426, ext : 6032
Advertising Executive Name: Jessica Ryan
Advertising Executive Email: jryan@verdenews.com
Advertising Executive Phone: (928) 635-4426, ext : 6021

THE VERDE INDEPENDENT

Corporate/Parent Company: Western News & Info
Street Address: 116 S Main St
City: Cottonwood
State: AZ
Postal Code: 86326-3998
Office phone: (928) 634-2241
Publication Website: http://www.verdenews.com/
General E-mail: msmith@prescottaz.com
Publisher Name: Kit K. Atwell
Publisher Email: katwell@prescottaz.com
Publisher Phone: (928) 445-3333, ext : 1070
Editor Name: Tim Wiederaenders
Editor Email: twieds@prescottaz.com
Editor Phone: (928) 445-3333, ext : 2032
Advertising Executive Name: Megan Smith
Advertising Executive Email: msmith@prescottaz.com
Advertising Executive Phone: (928) 445-3333, ext : 2023
Year Established: 1947
Delivery Methods: Mail`Newsstand`Racks
Published Days: Wed`Fri`Sun
Avg Paid Circ: 2522
Audit Company: Sworn/Estimate/Non-Audited
Audit Date: 6 10 2019
Buisness Equipment: APP/Mac
Classified Equipment: Hardware – APP/Mac Centris 610; Printers – QMS/860;
Classified Software: Baseview.
Editorial Equipment: Hardware – APP/iMac, APP/Mac G3/APP/Mac
Editorial Software: Adobe/Photoshop 7.0, Microsoft/Word 5.1, QPS/QuarkXPress 6.5.
Production Equipment: Hardware – APP/Mac Performa 6400; Cameras – 1-LE/4 Vertical; Scanners – Umax/S-6E.

DOUGLAS

DOUGLAS DISPATCH

Corporate/Parent Company: Wick Communications
Street Address: 530 E 11th Street
City: Douglas
State: AZ
Postal Code: 85607
Office phone: (520) 364-3424
Publication Website: www.douglasdispatch.com
Publisher Name: Manuel Coppola
Publisher Email: manuel.coppola@wickcommunications.com
Publisher Phone: (520) 415-1836
Editor Name: Bruce Whetten
Editor Email: editor@douglasdispatch.com
Editor Phone: (520) 234-0145
Advertising Executive Name: David Dominguez
Advertising Executive Email: advertising@douglasdispatch.com
Advertising Executive Phone: (520) 220-8775
Year Established: 1902
Mechanical specifications: Type page 13 x 21; E - 6 cols, 2 1/16, 1/8 between; A - 6 cols, 2 1/16, 1/8 between; C - 6 cols, 2 1/16, 1/8 between.
Published Days: Wed
Weekday Frequency: e
Avg Paid Circ: 1435
Audit Company: Sworn/Estimate/Non-Audited
Audit Date: 6 10 2019
Pressroom Equipment: Lines – 3-G/Community.
Production Software: DTI/PageSpeed 4.1, DTI/AdSpeed 4.1.

THE DOUGLAS DISPATCH

Corporate/Parent Company: Wick Communications
Street Address: 530 E 11th St
City: Douglas
State: AZ
Postal Code: 85607-2014
Office phone: (520) 364-3424
Publication Website: https://www.douglasdispatch.com/
General E-mail: advertising@douglasdispatch.com
Publisher Name: Manuel Coppola
Publisher Email: manuel.coppola@wickcommunications.com
Publisher Phone: (520) 415-1836
Editor Name: Bruce Whetten
Editor Email: editor@douglasdispatch.com
Editor Phone: (520) 234-0145
Advertising Executive Name: David Dominguez
Advertising Executive Email: advertising@douglasdispatch.com
Advertising Executive Phone: (520) 220-8775
Year Established: 1902
Mechanical specifications: Type page 13 x 21; E - 6 cols, 2 1/16, 1/8 between; A - 6 cols, 2 1/16, 1/8 between; C - 6 cols, 2 1/16, 1/8 between.
Published Days: Wed
Weekday Frequency: e
Avg Paid Circ: 1435
Audit Company: Sworn/Estimate/Non-Audited
Audit Date: 6 10 2019
Pressroom Equipment: Lines – 3-G/Community.

ELOY

ELOY ENTERPRISE

Corporate/Parent Company: Kramer Media
Street Address: 710 N. Main St.
City: Eloy
State: AZ
Postal Code: 85131
Office phone: (520) 466-7333
Publication Website: https://www.pinalcentral.com/eloy_enterprise/
General E-mail: lmetz@pinalcentral.com
Publisher Name: Donovan Kramer
Publisher Email: dkramerjr@pinalcentral.com
Publisher Phone: (520) 423-8611
Editor Name: Donovan Kramer
Editor Email: dkramerjr@pinalcentral.com
Editor Phone: (520) 423-8611
Advertising Executive Name: Linda Metz
Advertising Executive Email: lmetz@pinalcentral.com
Advertising Executive Phone: (520) 723-5441
Year Established: 1947
Own Printing Facility?: Y
Commercial printers?: Y
Mechanical specifications: Type page 13 x 21 1/2; E - 6 cols, 2 1/16, 1/8 between; A - 6 cols, 2 1/16, 1/8 between; C - 6 cols, 2 1/16, 1/8 between.
Published Days: Thur
Avg Paid Circ: 1623
Avg Free Circ: 8
Audit Company: Sworn/Estimate/Non-Audited
Audit Date: 6 10 2019

FLAGSTAFF

NAVAJO-HOPI OBSERVER

Corporate/Parent Company: Western News & Info
Street Address: 2717 N. Fourth St., Ste. 110
City: Flagstaff
State: AZ
Postal Code: 86004-1813
Office phone: (928) 635-4426
Publication Website: https://www.nhonews.com/
General E-mail: rsmart@nhonews.com
Publisher Name: Blake DeWitt
Publisher Email: bdewitt@westernnews.com
Editor Name: Loretta McKenney
Editor Email: lmckenney@williamsnews.com
Advertising Executive Name: Robb Smart
Advertising Executive Email: rsmart@nhonews.com
Total Circulation: 1631

FLORENCE

FLORENCE REMINDER & BLADE-TRIBUNE

Corporate/Parent Company: Kramer Media
Street Address: 190 N Main St
City: Florence
State: AZ
Postal Code: 85132
Office phone: (520) 868-5897
Publication Website: https://www.pinalcentral.com/florence_reminder_blade_tribune/
General E-mail: info@florencereminder.com
Publisher Name: Donovan Kramer
Publisher Email: dkramerjr@pinalcentral.com
Publisher Phone: (520) 423-8611
Editor Name: Donovan Kramer
Editor Email: dkramerjr@pinalcentral.com
Editor Phone: (520) 423-8611
Advertising Executive Name: Jotina McCann
Advertising Executive Email: info@florencereminder.com
Advertising Executive Phone: (480) 819-8393
Delivery Methods: Mail`Newsstand
Own Printing Facility?: Y
Commercial printers?: Y
Mechanical specifications: Type page 13 x 21 1/2; E - 6 cols, 2 1/16, 1/8 between; A - 6 cols, 2 1/16, 1/8 between; C - 6 cols, 2 1/16, 1/8 between.
Published Days: Thur
Avg Paid Circ: 1623
Avg Free Circ: 8
Audit Company: Sworn/Estimate/Non-Audited
Audit Date: 6 10 2019

GLOBE

ARIZONA SILVER BELT

Corporate/Parent Company: Newspaper Media Group
Street Address: 298 N. Pine St
City: Globe
State: AZ
Postal Code: 85501
Office phone: 928-425-7121
Publication Website: silverbelt.com
General E-mail: news@silverbelt.com
Publisher Name: Richard Taylor
Publisher Email: rtaylor@silverbelt.com
Publisher Phone: 928-425-7121
Editor Name: Cassie Tafoya
Editor Email: ctafoya@silverbelt.com
Editor Phone: 928-425-7121
Advertising Executive Name: Justin Justice
Advertising Executive Email: jjustice@silverbelt.com
Advertising Executive Phone: 9282006807
Year Established: 1878
Own Printing Facility?: Y
Commercial printers?: Y
Published Days: Wed
Avg Paid Circ: 1800
Audit Company: Sworn/Estimate/Non-Audited
Audit Date: 6 10 2019

COPPER COUNTRY NEWS

Corporate/Parent Company: News Media Gorup
Street Address: 298 N. Pine St
City: Globe
State: AZ
Postal Code: 85501
Office phone: 928-425-0355
Publication Website: coppercountrynews.com
Publisher Name: Richard Taylor
Publisher Email: rtaylor@silverbelt.com
Publisher Phone: 928-425-7121
Editor Name: Cassie Tafoya
Editor Email: ctafoya@silverbelt.com
Editor Phone: 928-425-7121
Advertising Executive Name: Kathy Riley
Advertising Executive Email: kriley@silverbelt.com
Advertising Executive Phone: 928-425-7121
Year Established: 1984
Mechanical specifications: Type page 10 x 16; E - 5 cols, 1 5/6, 1/6 between; A - 5 cols, 1 5/6, 1/6 between; C - 5 cols, 1 5/6, 1/6 between.
Published Days: Wed
Avg Free Circ: 19000
Audit Company: Sworn/Estimate/Non-Audited
Audit Date: 6 10 2019

GOODYEAR

PEORIA TIMES

Corporate/Parent Company: Times Media Group
Street Address: 250 N. Litchfield Rd #100
City: Goodyear
State: AZ
Postal Code: 85338
Office phone: 623-847-4600
Publication Website: www.peoriatimes.com
General E-mail: dacosta@star-times.com
Publisher Name: Steve Strickbine
Editor Name: Christina Fuoco-Karasinski
Editor Email: christina@star-times.com
Editor Phone: 623-777-1492
Advertising Executive Name: Laura Meehan
Advertising Executive Email: lmeehan@star-times.com
Advertising Executive Phone: 623-777-1042
Year Established: 1952
Delivery Methods: Mail`Newsstand
Own Printing Facility?: Y
Commercial printers?: Y
Mechanical specifications: Type page 10 5/16 x 16; E - 6 cols, 1 9/16, 1/6 between; A - 6 cols, 1 9/16, 1/6 between; C - 6 cols, 1 9/16, 1/6 between.
Published Days: Fri
Avg Paid Circ: 4200
Avg Free Circ: 800
Audit Company: Sworn/Estimate/Non-Audited
Audit Date: 6 10 2019
Mailroom Equipment: Counter Stackers – 2-HL/Monitor; Inserters & Stuffers – SH/1372 (12 pocket); Tying Machines – 2-MLN/2A; Address Machine – KR;
Classified Software: CAMS.
Editorial Software: QPS/QuarkXPress.
Production Equipment: Hardware – Caere/OmniPage; Cameras – SCREEN/C-240-D; Scanners – Umax, Polaroid/SprintScan 35
Production Software: QPS/QuarkXPress.

WEST VALLEY VIEW

Corporate/Parent Company: Times Media Group
Street Address: 250 Litchfield Rd #130
City: Goodyear
State: AZ
Postal Code: 85338
Office phone: 623-535-8439
Publication Website: www.westvalleyview.com
General E-mail: dacosta@westvalleyview.com
Publisher Name: Steve Strickbine
Editor Name: Christina Fuoco-Karasinski
Editor Email: christina@westvalleyview.com
Editor Phone: 623-777-1492
Advertising Executive Name: Laura Meehan
Advertising Executive Email: lmeehan@westvalleyview.com
Advertising Executive Phone: 623-777-1042
Year Established: 1986
Delivery Methods: Mail`Newsstand`Carrier`Racks
Mechanical specifications: Type page 10" x 16"; Editorial - 4 cols, 2 1/4, 1/6 between; Advertising - 6 cols, 1 1/2, 1/6 between; Classified - 6 cols, 1 1/2, 1/6 between.
Published Days: Wed
Avg Free Circ: 72800
Audit Company: Sworn/Estimate/Non-Audited
Audit Date: 6 10 2019

GREEN VALLEY

GREEN VALLEY NEWS

Street Address: 18705 S I 19 Frontage Rd
City: Green Valley
State: AZ
Postal Code: 85614-5014
Office phone: (520) 625-5511
Publication Website: https://www.gvnews.com/
General E-mail: skeith@gvnews.com
Publisher Name: Dru Sanchez
Publisher Email: dsanchez@gvnews.com
Editor Name: Dan Shearer
Editor Email: dshearer@gvnews.com
Editor Phone: (520) 547-9770
Advertising Executive Name: Sarah Keith
Advertising Executive Email: skeith@gvnews.com
Advertising Executive Phone: (520) 547-9729
Delivery Methods: Carrier`Racks
Mechanical specifications: Type page 11 5/8 x 21; E - 6 cols, 1 5/6, 1/8 between; A - 6 cols, 1 5/6, 1/8 between; C - 6 cols, 1 5/6, 1/8 between.
Published Days: Wed`Sun
Avg Paid Circ: 7126
Avg Free Circ: 162
Audit Company: Sworn/Estimate/Non-Audited
Audit Date: 6 10 2019

SAHUARITA SUN

Corporate/Parent Company: Wick Communications
Street Address: 18705 S. I-19 Frontage Road, Ste. 125
City: Green Valley
State: AZ
Postal Code: 85614-5014
Office phone: (520) 625-5511
Publication Website: https://www.sahuaritasun.com/
General E-mail: asaenz@sahuaritasun.com
Publisher Name: Rebecca Bradner
Publisher Email: publisher@sahuaritasun.com
Publisher Phone: (520) 547-9722
Editor Name: Dan Shearer
Editor Email: dshearer@sahuaritasun.com
Editor Phone: (520) 547-9770
Advertising Executive Name: Andrew Saenz
Advertising Executive Email: asaenz@sahuaritasun.com
Advertising Executive Phone: (520) 547-9757
Year Established: 2005
Published Days: Wed
Avg Paid Circ: 813
Avg Free Circ: 8141

Audit Company: Sworn/Estimate/Non-Audited
Audit Date: 6 10 2019

KINGMAN

KINGMAN DAILY MINER

Corporate/Parent Company: Western News & Info
Street Address: 3015 N Stockton Hill Rd
City: Kingman
State: AZ
Postal Code: 86401-4162
Office phone: (928) 753-6397
Publication Website: https://kdminer.com/
General E-mail: advertising@kdminer.com
Publisher Name: Debbie White-Hoel
Editor Name: Casey Jones
Editor Email: cjones@kdminer.com
Editor Phone: (928) 753-6397, ext : 5226
Advertising Executive Email: advertising@kdminer.com
Year Established: 1882
Mechanical specifications: Type page 12 1/2 x 21 1/2; E - 6 cols, 1 27/32, 1/8 between; A - 6 cols, 1 27/32, 1/8 between; C - 6 cols, 1 27/32, 1/8 between.
Published Days: Mon`Tues`Wed`Thur`Fri`Sun
Weekday Frequency: m
Avg Paid Circ: 7969
Audit Company: Sworn/Estimate/Non-Audited
Audit Date: 7 12 2019
Pressroom Equipment: Lines – 8-G/Suburban, 8; Folders – G/SC, G/Suburban; Reels & Stands – 2;

LAKE HAVASU CITY

RIVER EXTRA

Street Address: 2225 Acoma Blvd W
City: Lake Havasu City
State: AZ
Postal Code: 86403-2907
Office phone: (928) 453-4237
Publication Website: https://www.havasunews.com/
General E-mail: sales@havasunews.com
Publisher Name: Michael Quinn
Publisher Email: quinn@havasunews.com
Publisher Phone: (928) 453-4237
Editor Name: Brandon Bowers
Editor Email: bbowers@havasunews.com
Editor Phone: (928) 453-4237, ext : 206
Advertising Executive Name: Christine Hammers
Advertising Executive Email: sales@havasunews.com

SMART BUYER

Corporate/Parent Company: Western News & Info, Inc.
Street Address: 2225 Acoma Blvd W
City: Lake Havasu City
State: AZ
Postal Code: 86403-2907
Office phone: (928) 453-4237
Publication Website: https://www.havasunews.com/smart-buyer/html_33f301a6-a2e5-11e3-a998-001a4bcf887a.html
General E-mail: sales@havasunews.com
Publisher Name: Michael Quinn
Publisher Email: quinn@havasunews.com
Publisher Phone: (928) 453-4237
Editor Name: Brandon Bowers
Editor Email: bbowers@havasunews.com
Editor Phone: (928) 453-4237
Advertising Executive Name: Michael Evans
Advertising Executive Email: sales@havasunews.com
Advertising Executive Phone: (928) 453-4237

TODAY'S NEWS-HERALD

Street Address: 2225 Acoma Blvd W
City: Lake Havasu City
State: AZ

Postal Code: 86403-2907
Office phone: (928) 453-4237
Publication Website: https://www.havasunews.com/
General E-mail: sales@havasunews.com
Publisher Name: Michael Quinn
Publisher Email: quinn@havasunews.com
Publisher Phone: (928) 453-4237
Editor Name: Brandon Bowers
Editor Email: bbowers@havasunews.com
Editor Phone: (928) 453-4237x206
Advertising Executive Name: Michael Evans
Advertising Executive Email: sales@havasunews.com
Advertising Executive Phone: (928) 453-4237, ext : x201
Delivery Methods: Mail`Newsstand`Carrier`Racks
Own Printing Facility?: N
Commercial printers?: N
Mechanical specifications: Type page 13 x 21; E - 6 cols, 2 1/16, 1/4 between; A - 6 cols, 2 1/16, 1/4 between; C - 6 cols, 2 1/16, 1/4 between.
Published Days: Mon`Tues`Wed`Thur`Fri`Sun
Weekday Frequency: m
Saturday Frequency: m
Avg Paid Circ: 8635
Avg Free Circ: 120
Audit Company: VAC
Audit Date: 30 06 2017
Pressroom Equipment: Lines – Press Control System 1993.;

MARICOPA

MARICOPA MONITOR

Corporate/Parent Company: Kramer Media
Street Address: 19428 N. Maricopa Rd., Suite 103
City: Maricopa
State: AZ
Postal Code: 85139-8964
Office phone: (520) 568-4198
Publication Website: https://www.pinalcentral.com/maricopa_monitor/
General E-mail: kdodge@pinalcentral.com
Publisher Name: Donovan Kramer
Publisher Email: dkramerjr@pinalcentral.com
Publisher Phone: (520) 423-8611
Editor Name: Donovan Kramer
Editor Email: dkramerjr@pinalcentral.com
Editor Phone: (520) 423-8611
Advertising Executive Name: Kathy Dodge
Advertising Executive Email: kdodge@pinalcentral.com
Advertising Executive Phone: (520) 227-9128
Year Established: 2003
Published Days: Tues`Fri
Audit Company: Sworn/Estimate/Non-Audited
Audit Date: 6 10 2019
Total Circulation: 16346

NOGALES

NOGALES INTERNATIONAL

Corporate/Parent Company: Wick Communications
Street Address: 268 W View Point Dr
City: Nogales
State: AZ
Postal Code: 85621
Office phone: (520) 375-5760
Publication Website: www.nogalesinternational.com/news
Publisher Name: Manuel Coppola
Publisher Email: publisher@nogalesinternational.com
Publisher Phone: (520) 415-1836
Editor Name: Jonathan Clark
Editor Email: editorial@nogalesinternational.com
Editor Phone: (520) 415-1837
Advertising Executive Name: Maria Castillo
Advertising Executive Email: maria.castillo@nogalesinternational.com
Advertising Executive Phone: (520) 415-1832
Year Established: 1925
Published Days: Tues`Fri

Avg Paid Circ: 1736
Avg Free Circ: 68
Audit Company: CVC
Audit Date: 31 05 2017

PAGE

LAKE POWELL CHRONICLE

Corporate/Parent Company: News Media Grouip
Street Address: 635 Elm St. Suite 7, P.O. Box 1716
City: Page
State: AZ
Postal Code: 86040
Office phone: 928-645-8888
Publication Website: lakepowellchronicle.com
Publisher Name: Mike Caywood
Publisher Email: mcaywood@lakepowellchronicle.com
Publisher Phone: 928-645-8888
Editor Name: Krista Allen
Editor Email: kallen@lakepowellchronicle.com
Editor Phone: 928-645-8888
Advertising Executive Name: Norma Tsinnijinnie
Advertising Executive Email: ntsinnijinnie@lakepowellchronicle.com
Advertising Executive Phone: 928-645-8888

PARKER

THE PARKER PIONEER

Street Address: 1317 Joshua Ave., Suite L
City: Parker
State: AZ
Postal Code: 85344-5768
Office phone: (928) 669-2275
Publication Website: https://www.parkerpioneer.net/
General E-mail: sales@havasunews.com
Publisher Name: Michael Quinn
Publisher Email: quinn@havasunews.com
Publisher Phone: (928) 453-4237
Editor Name: Brandon Bowers
Editor Email: bbowers@havasunews.com
Editor Phone: (928) 453-4237
Advertising Executive Name: Michael Evans
Advertising Executive Email: sales@havasunews.com
Advertising Executive Phone: (928) 453-4237
Published Days: Wed
Avg Paid Circ: 2075
Avg Free Circ: 32
Audit Company: Sworn/Estimate/Non-Audited
Audit Date: 6 10 2019

PHOENIX

ARIZONA INFORMANT

Street Address: 1301 E. Washington St. Ste 101
City: Phoenix
State: AZ
Postal Code: 85034
Office phone: 602-257-9300
Publication Website: www.azinformant.com
General E-mail: ainewspaper@qwestoffice.net
Publisher Name: Cloves Campbell, Jr.
Editor Name: Roland Campbell
Year Established: 1971
Published Days: Wed
Avg Paid Circ: 15000
Audit Company: Sworn/Estimate/Non-Audited
Audit Date: 6 10 2019

PHOENIX BUSINESS JOURNAL

Corporate/Parent Company: American City Business Journals
Street Address: 101 N. First Avenue Suite 2300
City: Phoenix
State: AZ
Postal Code: 85003
Office phone: 602-230-8400
Publication Website: www.bizjournals.com/phoenix

Non-Daily Newspapers in the U.S.

General E-mail: phoenix@bizjournals.com
Publisher Name: Ray Schey
Publisher Email: rschey@bizjournals.com
Editor Name: Greg Barr
Editor Email: gbarr@bizjournals.com
Advertising Executive Name: Amy Lindsey
Advertising Executive Email: alindsey@bizjournals.com

RECORD REPORTER

Street Address: 2025 N Third St, #155
City: Phoenix
State: AZ
Postal Code: 85004
Office phone: (602) 417-9900
Publication Website: www.recordreporter.com/rrhome.cfm
Publisher Name: Diane Heuel
Publisher Email: diane_heuel@dailyjournal.com
Editor Name: Ben Armistead
Editor Email: Ben_Armistead@dailyjournal.com
Advertising Executive Name: Leona Gibson
Advertising Executive Email: record_reporter@dailyjournal.com

TOWN OF PARADISE VALLEY INDEPENDENT

Corporate/Parent Company: Independent NewsMedia
Street Address: 23043 N. 16th Ln.
City: Phoenix
State: AZ
Postal Code: 85027
Office phone: (623) 445-2777
Publication Website: paradisevalleyindependent.com/about
Publisher Name: Bret McKeand
Publisher Email: bmckeand@newszap.com
Publisher Phone: (623) 445-2867
Editor Name: Terrance Thronton
Editor Email: tthornton@newszap.com
Editor Phone: (623) 445-2744
Year Established: 1984
Delivery Methods: Mail
Own Printing Facility?: Y
Commercial printers?: Y
Mechanical specifications: Full page: 10" wide by 10.625" high
Published Days: Wed
Avg Free Circ: 8500
Audit Company: Sworn/Estimate/Non-Audited
Audit Date: 6 10 2019

PRESCOTT

SMART SHOPPER ASH FORK

Corporate/Parent Company: Western News & Info, Inc.
Street Address: 1958 Commerce Center Cir
City: Prescott
State: AZ
Postal Code: 86301-4454
Office phone: (928) 445-3333
Publication Website: http://smartshopperaz.com/
General E-mail: ncolwell@prescottaz.com
Advertising Executive Name: Nora Colwell
Advertising Executive Email: ncolwell@prescottaz.com

PRESCOTT VALLEY

THE DAILY COURIER

Corporate/Parent Company: Western News & Info
Street Address: 8307 E. State Route 69
City: Prescott Valley
State: AZ
Postal Code: 86314
Office phone: (928) 445-3333
Publication Website: https://www.dcourier.com/
General E-mail: msmith@prescottaz.com
Publisher Name: Kit K. Atwell
Publisher Email: katwell@prescottaz.com
Publisher Phone: (928) 445-3333, ext : 1070
Editor Name: Tim Wiederaenders
Editor Email: twieds@prescottaz.com
Editor Phone: (928) 445-3333, ext : 2032
Advertising Executive Name: Megan Smith
Advertising Executive Email: msmith@prescottaz.com
Advertising Executive Phone: (928) 445-3333, ext : 2023
Year Established: 1882
Delivery Methods: Mail`Newsstand`Carrier`Racks
Own Printing Facility?: Y
Commercial printers?: Y
Mechanical specifications: Type page 11 3/4 x 21 1/2; E - 6 cols, between; A - 6 cols, between; C - 6 cols, between.
Published Days: Mon`Tues`Wed`Thur`Fri`Sat`Sun
Weekday Frequency: m
Saturday Frequency: m
Avg Paid Circ: 12534
Avg Free Circ: 246
Audit Company: VAC
Audit Date: 30 09 2015
Pressroom Equipment: Lines – 1-G/Community; 1-DIDDE/UV; Press Drive – 2, 1, 150, 100, 75; Folders – 1-G/Universal 45, 1-G/SSC; Reels & Stands – 6-Enkel/Splicer.;

SAFFORD

EASTERN ARIZONA COURIER

Corporate/Parent Company: Wick Communications
Street Address: 301 East Highway 70, Suite A
City: Safford
State: AZ
Postal Code: 85546
Office phone: (928) 428-2560
Publication Website: www.eacourier.com
Publisher Name: Sarah Keith
Publisher Email: sarah@eacourier.com
Publisher Phone: (928) 428-2560 ext. 225
Editor Name: David Bell
Editor Email: editor@eacourier.com
Editor Phone: (928) 428-2560 ext. 236
Advertising Executive Name: Sarah Keith
Advertising Executive Email: sarah@eacourier.com
Advertising Executive Phone: (928) 428-2560
Year Established: 1889
Delivery Methods: Mail`Newsstand`Carrier`Racks
Mechanical specifications: Type page 11 5/8 x 21 1/2; E - 6 cols, 1 13/16, 1/8 between; A - 6 cols, 1 13/16, 1/8 between; C - 6 cols, 1 13/16, 1/8 between.
Published Days: Wed`Sat
Avg Paid Circ: 4094
Avg Free Circ: 25
Audit Company: VAC
Audit Date: 31 05 2017

THE COPPER ERA

Corporate/Parent Company: Wick Communications
Street Address: 301 East Highway 70, Suite A
City: Safford
State: AZ
Postal Code: 85546
Office phone: (928) 428-2560
Publication Website: https://www.eacourier.com/
General E-mail: sarah@eacourier.com
Publisher Name: Sarah Keith
Publisher Email: sarah@eacourier.com
Publisher Phone: (928) 428-2560, ext : 225
Editor Name: David Bell
Editor Email: editor@eacourier.com
Editor Phone: (928) 428-2560, ext : 236
Advertising Executive Name: Sarah Keith
Advertising Executive Email: sarah@eacourier.com
Advertising Executive Phone: (928) 428-2560
Year Established: 1899

Delivery Methods: Mail`Newsstand`Carrier`Racks
Mechanical specifications: Type page 9.88 x 21 1/2; E - 6 cols, 1 13/16, 1/8 between; A - 6 cols, 1 13/16, 1/8 between; C - 6 cols, 1 13/16, 1/8 between.
Published Days: Wed
Avg Paid Circ: 871
Audit Company: VAC
Audit Date: 31 05 2017

SIERRA VISTA

SIERRA VISTA HERALD - SUNDAY BRAVO SHOPPER

Street Address: 102 Fab Ave
City: Sierra Vista
State: AZ
Postal Code: 85635-1741
Office phone: (520) 458-9440
Publication Website: https://www.myheraldreview.com
General E-mail: mike.summerville@myheraldreview.com
Publisher Name: Jennifer Sorenson
Publisher Email: jennifer.sorenson@myheraldreview.com
Publisher Phone: (520) 515-4605
Editor Name: Timothy J. Woods
Editor Email: tim.woods@myheraldreview.com
Editor Phone: (520) 515-4610
Advertising Executive Name: Mike Summerville
Advertising Executive Email: mike.summerville@myheraldreview.com
Advertising Executive Phone: (520) 515-4634

WICK COMMUNICATIONS - HERALD/REVIEW

Street Address: 102 Fab Ave
City: Sierra Vista
State: AZ
Postal Code: 85635-1741
Office phone: (520) 458-9440
Publication Website: https://www.myheraldreview.com/s
General E-mail: mike.summerville@myheraldreview.com
Publisher Name: Jennifer Sorenson
Publisher Email: jennifer.sorenson@myheraldreview.com
Publisher Phone: (520) 515-4605
Editor Name: Timothy J. Woods
Editor Email: tim.woods@myheraldreview.com
Editor Phone: (520) 515-4610
Advertising Executive Name: Mike Summerville
Advertising Executive Email: mike.summerville@myheraldreview.com
Advertising Executive Phone: (520) 515-4634
Year Established: 1955
Delivery Methods: Mail`Newsstand`Carrier`Racks
Own Printing Facility?: Y
Commercial printers?: Y
Mechanical specifications: Type page 9 89/100 x 21; E - 6 cols, 1 56/100, 5/6 between; A - 6 cols, 1 56/100, 5/6 between; C - 9 cols, 1, 58/100 between.
Published Days: Tues`Wed`Thur`Fri`Sun
Weekday Frequency: m
Saturday Frequency: m
Avg Paid Circ: 5228
Avg Free Circ: 130
Audit Company: VAC
Audit Date: 30 09 2017
Pressroom Equipment: Lines – 15-G/Community; Control System – Perretta;
Total Circulation: 12776

SUN CITY

SURPRISE INDEPENDENT

Corporate/Parent Company: Independent NewsMedia

Street Address: 17220 N Boswell Blvd
City: Sun City
State: AZ
Postal Code: 85373-2065
Office phone: (623) 972-6101
Publication Website: https://www.yourvalley.net/surprise-independent/
General E-mail: azads@newszap.com
Advertising Executive Email: iniclassads@newszap.com
Advertising Executive Phone: (623) 972-6101
Year Established: 1997
Delivery Methods: Carrier
Mechanical specifications: Full page: 11 inches by 12.4 inches
Published Days: Wed
Avg Free Circ: 32000
Audit Company: CAC
Audit Date: 7 01 2017

GLENDALE INDEPENDENT

Corporate/Parent Company: Independent NewsMedia
Street Address: 17220 N Boswell Blvd Suite 101
City: Sun City
State: AZ
Postal Code: 85373
Office phone: 623-972-6101
Publication Website: yourvalley.net/glendale-independent
General E-mail: wvnews@newszap.com
Publisher Name: Charlene Bisson
Publisher Email: cbisson@newszap.com
Publisher Phone: (623) 445-2823
Editor Name: Philip Haldiman
Editor Email: phaldiman@newszap.com
Editor Phone: (623) 876-3697
Total Circulation: 32000

PEORIA INDEPENDENT

Corporate/Parent Company: Independent NewsMedia
Street Address: 17220 N Boswell Blvd Suite 101
City: Sun City
State: AZ
Postal Code: 85373
Office phone: 623-972-6101
Publication Website: yourvalley.net
General E-mail: wvnews@newszap.com
Publisher Name: Charlene Patti-Bisson
Publisher Email: cbisson@newszap.com
Publisher Phone: (623) 445-2823
Editor Name: Celia Chan
Editor Phone: (623) 972-6101
Year Established: 1999
Delivery Methods: Carrier`Racks
Mechanical specifications: Special ROP ad prices discounts for NON contract of 1X-6X runs: 2-4 markets we can offer the 26 week rate Plus 50% off each additional market (Discount applies to less-expensive markets) with $25 for color per market. Five market buy: (receive 20,000 impressions for a month, per run Full pg $500 per market + $50 color = $2,500 B/W + $250 = $2,750 for a 5 market buy per run ½ pg $325 per market + $25 color = $1,625 B/W + $125 = $1,750 for a 5 market buy per run ¼ pg $200 per market + $25 color = $1,000 B/W + $125 = $1,125 for a 5 market buy per run
Published Days: Wed
Avg Paid Circ: 6
Avg Free Circ: 16340
Audit Company: Sworn/Estimate/Non-Audited
Audit Date: 6 10 2019

SUN CITY WEST INDEPENDENT

Corporate/Parent Company: Independent NewsMedia
Street Address: 17220 N Boswell Blvd Suite 101
City: Sun City

State: AZ
Postal Code: 85373
Office phone: 623-972-6101
Publication Website: www.yourvalley.net/sun-city-west-independent
General E-mail: wvnews@newszap.com
Publisher Name: Charlene Bisson
Publisher Email: cbisson@newszap.com
Publisher Phone: (623) 445-2823
Editor Name: Philip Haldiman
Editor Email: phaldiman@newszap.com
Editor Phone: (623) 876-3697
Year Established: 1978
Delivery Methods: Carrier`Racks
Mechanical specifications: Special ROP ad prices discounts for NON contract of 1X-6X runs: 2-4 markets we can offer the 26 week rate Plus 50% off each additional market (Discount applies to less-expensive markets) with $25 for color per market. Five market buy: (receive 20,000 impressions for a month, per run Full pg $500 per market + $50 color = $2,500 B/W + $250 = $2,750 for a 5 market buy per run ½ pg $325 per market + $25 color = $1,625 B/W + $125 = $1,750 for a 5 market buy per run ¼ pg $200 per market + $25 color = $1,000 B/W + $125 = $1,125 for a 5 market buy per run
Published Days: Wed
Avg Paid Circ: 9
Avg Free Circ: 12767
Audit Company: CAC
Audit Date: 31 03 2019

SUPERIOR

SUPERIOR SUN

Corporate/Parent Company: Copper Area News Publishers
Street Address: 467 Main Street
City: Superior
State: AZ
Postal Code: 85173
Office phone: (520) 363-5554
Publication Website: www.copperarea.com/pages/category/publications/superior-sun
General E-mail: cbnsun@minersunbasin.com
Publisher Name: James Carnes
Editor Name: Jennifer Carnes
Editor Email: jenniferc@minersunbasin.com
Mailroom Equipment: Counter Stackers – 1-HL/Monitor, 1-QWI; Inserters & Stuffers – HI/Sheridan 1372, MM/227; Tying Machines – Strap-Pack/Strapper 35-80 AKN, MLN/ML2-EE, Si/LB 2000, Si/LB 2330; Address Machine – 3/Dispensa-matic;
Buisness Equipment: DEC/200, APP/Mac PowerBook 160, APP/Mac PowerBook 550, Mk/ScanMaker IIG Scanner, APP/Mac LaserWriter II NTX, 2-DEC/server, 6-DEC/VT-420 monitor, 2-DEC/VT-220 monitor, DEC/LA-424 Desktop printer, C.Itoh/Dot Matrix Printer, AST/PC, APP/Mac Plus,
Classified Equipment: Hardware – 6-APP/Mac Beige G3, 1-APP/Mac 7200/120, 1-APP/Mac Powerbook G3, 1-APP/Apple Design Keyboard, 1-Kensington/Keyboard, 1-APP/Mac Pro Plus Keyboard, 1-APP/Apple 14 Monitor, 1-APP/Apple 17 Monitor, 5-Sony/Monitors; 1-Umax/Astra 2200S S;
Editorial Equipment: Hardware – APP/Mac 19 color monitor/AG/Focus Scanner; Printers – APP/Mac LaserWriter 16-1600 PS
Editorial Software: Adobe/Photoshop, QPS/QuarkXPress 4.0, Microsoft/Word, Aldus/Freehand.
Production Equipment: Hardware – 2-Pre Press/Panther Fast Track CTP, 3-Sony/Monitors, 3-APP/USB Extended Keyboards, 3-APP/USB Optical Mouse
Production Software: Adobe/Acrobat 4.0, MultiAd/Creator2, Flightcheck 4.5r22, Adobe/Illustrator 9.0, Adobe/Indesign 2.0, Insposition 2.5.4, Adob

TEMPE

AHWATUKEE FOOTHILLS NEWS

Corporate/Parent Company: Times Media Group
Street Address: 1620 W Fountainhead PkwySuite 219
City: Tempe
State: AZ
Postal Code: 85282
Office phone: 480-898-7900
Publication Website: www.ahwatukee.com
General E-mail: ldionisio@ahwatukee.com
Publisher Name: Steve Strickbine
Editor Name: Paul Maryniak
Editor Email: pmaryniak@ahwatukee.com
Editor Phone: 480-898-5647
Advertising Executive Name: Karen Mays
Advertising Executive Email: kmays@ahwatukee.com
Advertising Executive Phone: 480-898-7909
Year Established: 1978
Delivery Methods: Mail`Carrier`Racks
Mechanical specifications: Type page 10" x 13.75"; 6 cols
Published Days: Wed
Avg Free Circ: 27750
Audit Company: Sworn/Estimate/Non-Audited
Audit Date: 6 10 2019
Mailroom Equipment: Counter Stackers – BG/Count-O-Veyor; Tying Machines – 2-Ace/Tyer; Address Machine – 1-Ch/612.;
Buisness Equipment: NCR/LAN Sys
Classified Equipment: Hardware – Mk/3000, 1-PC.;
Editorial Equipment: Hardware – 1-Mk/3000, 10-PC/Mk.
Production Equipment: Hardware – Microtek/Scanmaker Plus, HP/Laserwriter 4MV (11x17), Pre Press/Panther Plus 46; Cameras – 1-SCREEN/Companica-6500D, 1-AG/20 x 24; Scanners – Umax/Powerlook II
Production Software: Adobe/PageMaker 6.5.

EAST VALLEY TRIBUNE

Corporate/Parent Company: Times Media Group
Street Address: 1620 W. Fountainhead Parkway, Ste. 219
City: Tempe
State: AZ
Postal Code: 85282
Office phone: 480-898-6500
Publication Website: www.eastvalleytribune.com
General E-mail: ldionisio@evtrib.com
Publisher Name: Steve Strickbine
Editor Name: Paul Maryniak
Editor Email: pmaryniak@timespublications.com
Editor Phone: 480-898-5647
Advertising Executive Name: Zac Reynolds
Advertising Executive Email: national@evtrib.com
Advertising Executive Phone: 480-898-5603
Year Established: 1891
Delivery Methods: Carrier`Racks
Mechanical specifications: Type page 10 x 13.75; 6 cols
Published Days: Sun
Weekday Frequency: m
Avg Free Circ: 139800
Audit Company: AAM
Audit Date: 30 06 2018
Buisness Equipment: APP/Mac
Classified Equipment: Hardware – APP/Mac Centris 610; Printers – QMS/860;
Classified Software: Baseview.
Editorial Equipment: Hardware – APP/iMac, APP/Mac G3/APP/Mac
Editorial Software: Adobe/Photoshop 7.0, Microsoft/Word 5.1, QPS/QuarkXPress 6.5.
Production Equipment: Hardware – APP/Mac Performa 6400; Cameras – 1-LE/4 Vertical; Scanners – Umax/S-6E.

SANTAN SUN NEWS

Corporate/Parent Company: Times Media Group
Street Address: 1620 W. Fountainhead Parkway, Ste. 219
City: Tempe
State: AZ
Postal Code: 85282
Office phone: (480) 898-6500
Publication Website: santansun.com
General E-mail: News@SANTANSUN.COM
Publisher Name: Steve Strickbine
Publisher Email: Steve@TimesPublications.com
Editor Name: Lee Shappell
Editor Email: Lshappell@timespublications.com
Advertising Executive Name: Jane Meyer
Advertising Executive Email: jane@timespublications.com
Advertising Executive Phone: 602.672.1447

TUCSON

INSIDE TUCSON BUSINESS

Corporate/Parent Company: TucsonLocalMedia.com
Street Address: 7225 N. Mona Lisa Road, Ste. 125
City: Tucson
State: AZ
Postal Code: 85741
Office phone: (520) 797-4384
Publication Website: www.insidetucsonbusiness.com
General E-mail: tucsoneditor@tucsonlocalmedia.com
Publisher Name: Jason Joseph
Publisher Email: jjoseph@azlocalmedia.com
Editor Name: Logan Burtch-Buus
Editor Email: logan@tucsonlocalmedia.com
Editor Phone: Ext. 36
Advertising Executive Name: Kristin Chester
Advertising Executive Email: Kristin@tucsonlocalmedia.com
Advertising Executive Phone: Ext. 25
Own Printing Facility?: Y
Commercial printers?: Y
Mechanical specifications: Type page 10 1/4 x 16; A - 4 cols, 2 1/2, 1/6 between; C - 6 cols, 1 3/5, 1/6 between.
Published Days: Fri
Avg Paid Circ: 1845
Avg Free Circ: 3047
Audit Company: Sworn/Estimate/Non-Audited
Audit Date: 6 10 2019

MARANA NEWS

Corporate/Parent Company: TucsonLocalMedia.com
Street Address: 7225 N. Mona Lisa Road, Ste. 125
City: Tucson
State: AZ
Postal Code: 85741
Office phone: (520) 797-4384
Publication Website: www.tucsonlocalmedia.com/marana
General E-mail: tucsoneditor@tucsonlocalmedia.com
Publisher Name: Jason Joseph
Publisher Email: jjoseph@azlocalmedia.com
Editor Name: Logan Burtch-Buus
Editor Email: logan@tucsonlocalmedia.com
Editor Phone: Ext. 36
Advertising Executive Name: Kristin Chester
Advertising Executive Email: Kristin@tucsonlocalmedia.com
Advertising Executive Phone: Ext. 25
Year Established: 2007
Delivery Methods: Mail`Racks
Published Days: Thur`Mthly
Audit Company: Sworn/Estimate/Non-Audited
Audit Date: 6 10 2019
Buisness Equipment: ATT/Unix PC
Buisness Software: Vision Data
Classified Equipment: Hardware – 2-APP/Power Mac;
Classified Software: Multi-Ad/CAMS.
Editorial Equipment: Hardware – 12-APP/Mac
Editorial Software: Microsoft/Word, Aldus/PageMaker, QPS/QuarkXPress.
Production Equipment: Hardware – Microtek; Scanners – Microtek/II SI, Microtek
Production Software: QPS/QuarkXPress 3.3.
Note: This paper is equally owned by Western Newspapers Inc. and Wick Communications.

THE DAILY TERRITORIAL

Corporate/Parent Company: Wick Communications
Street Address: 7225 N. Mona Lisa Road, Ste. 125
City: Tucson
State: AZ
Postal Code: 85741
Office phone: (520) 797-4384
Publication Website: https://www.tucsonweekly.com/
General E-mail: casey@tucsonlocalmedia.com
Publisher Name: Jason Joseph
Publisher Email: jjoseph@azlocalmedia.com
Publisher Phone: (520) 797-4384, ext : 11
Editor Name: Jim Nintzel
Editor Email: jimnintzel@gmail.com
Editor Phone: (520) 797-4384, ext : 38
Advertising Executive Name: Casey Anderson
Advertising Executive Email: casey@tucsonlocalmedia.com
Advertising Executive Phone: (520) 797-4384, ext : 22
Year Established: 1966
Mechanical specifications: Type page 10 1/4 x 13; E - 4 cols, 2 3/8, 1/8 between; A - 4 cols, 2 3/8, 1/8 between; C - 6 cols, 1 1/2, 3/16 between.
Published Days: Mon`Tues`Wed`Thur`Fri
Weekday Frequency: m
Avg Paid Circ: 753
Audit Company: Sworn/Estimate/Non-Audited
Audit Date: 7 12 2019
Pressroom Equipment: Lines – 6-HI/V-15A; Atlas/Web Leader 2000;
Note: Town of Paradise Valley Independent is mailed every week to every home in the town.
Total Circulation: 8500

WILLCOX

ARIZONA RANGE NEWS

Corporate/Parent Company: Wick Communications
Street Address: 122 S. Haskell Ave
City: Willcox
State: AZ
Postal Code: 85635-1791
Office phone: (520) 384-3571
Publication Website: https://www.willcoxrangenews.com/
General E-mail: steve.reno@willcoxrangenews.com
Publisher Name: Sarah Keith
Publisher Email: sarah@eacourier.com
Publisher Phone: (928) 428-2560, ext : 225
Editor Name: David Bell
Editor Email: editor@eacourier.com
Editor Phone: (928) 428-2560, ext : 236
Advertising Executive Name: Steve Reno
Advertising Executive Email: steve.reno@willcoxrangenews.com
Advertising Executive Phone: (520) 384-3571, ext : 22
Year Established: 1884
Delivery Methods: Mail`Newsstand`Racks
Mechanical specifications: Type page 9.88 x 21.5 inches 6 column - 1.55; 3.22; 4.88; 6.55; 8.22; 9.88 inches
Published Days: Wed
Avg Paid Circ: 1514
Audit Company: Sworn/Estimate/Non-Audited
Audit Date: 6 10 2019

WILLIAMS

WILLIAMS-GRAND CANYON NEWS

Corporate/Parent Company: Western News & Info
Street Address: 118 S 3rd St
City: Williams
State: AZ
Postal Code: 86046-2404
Office phone: (928) 635-4426

Non-Daily Newspapers in the U.S.

III-13

Publication Website: https://www.williamsnews.com/
General E-mail: chiemenz@williamsnews.com
Publisher Name: Blake DeWitt
Publisher Email: bdewitt@westernnews.com
Editor Name: Loretta McKenney
Editor Email: lmckenney@williamsnews.com
Advertising Executive Name: Connie Hiemenz
Advertising Executive Email: chiemenz@williamsnews.com
Year Established: 1889
Delivery Methods: Mail Racks
Own Printing Facility?: Y
Commercial printers?: Y
Mechanical specifications: Type page 12 1/2 x 22 3/4; E - 6 cols, 1 5/6, 1/6 between; A - 6 cols, 1 5/6, 1/6 between; C - 6 cols, 1 5/6, 1/6 between.
Published Days: Wed
Avg Paid Circ: 3000
Audit Company: Sworn/Estimate/Non-Audited
Audit Date: 6 10 2019
Mailroom Equipment: Counter Stackers – BG/Count-O-Veyor 106; Inserters & Stuffers – 1-HI/Sheridan; Tying Machines – 2-Wilton/Strap Pack 55-80; Control System – Prism.;
Buisness Equipment: DEC
Buisness Software: Vision Data
Classified Equipment: Hardware – APP/Mac; Printers – APP/Mac;
Classified Software: Baseview.
Editorial Equipment: Hardware – APP/Mac; Printers – APP/Mac
Editorial Software: Baseview. Adobe Creative Suite
Production Equipment: Hardware – Southern Lithoplate MX33
Production Software: Adobe/Creative Suite.

CALIFORNIA

ACTON

ROSAMOND NEWS

Corporate/Parent Company: Joyce Media Inc.
Street Address: 3413 Soledad Cyn. Rd. P.O. Box 57
City: Acton
State: CA
Postal Code: 93510-0057
Office phone: (661) 269-1169
Publication Website: joycemediainc.com/papers/rosamondmall.html
General E-mail: rosamondnews@joycemediainc.com
Publisher Name: John Joyce

ALAMEDA

ALAMEDA SUN

Street Address: 3215J Encinal Ave
City: Alameda
State: CA
Postal Code: 94501
Office phone: (510) 263-1470
Publication Website: www.alamedasun.com
General E-mail: ekos@alamedasun.com
Publisher Name: Eric J. Kos
Publisher Email: ekos@alamedasun.com
Editor Name: Ekene Ikeme
Editor Email: eikeme@alamedasun.com
Advertising Executive Name: Jamie DaSilva
Advertising Executive Email: sales@alamedasun.com

ALAMEDA

THE PIEDMONTER

Street Address: 1516 OAK ST STE 105
City: ALAMEDA
State: CA
Postal Code: 94501
Office phone: 925-935-2525

Publication Website: www.eastbaytimes.com/location/piedmont
Publisher Name: Sharon Ryan
Publisher Email: publisher@bayareanewsgroup.com
Editor Name: Frank Pine
Editor Email: editor@bayareanewsgroup.com
Editor Phone: 408-920-5456

ANAHEIM

COASTAL CURRENT — NORTH

Corporate/Parent Company: Southern California News Group
Street Address: 2190 S. Towne Centre Place
City: Anaheim
State: CA
Postal Code: 92806
Office phone: 714-796-7000
Publication Website: www.ocregister.com/news/local-news
Publisher Name: Ron Hasse
Publisher Email: publisher@scng.com
Publisher Phone: 818-713-3883
Editor Name: Frank Pine
Editor Email: editor@scng.com
Editor Phone: 909-483-9360
Advertising Executive Name: Kyla Rodriguez
Advertising Executive Email: krodriguez@scng.com

COASTAL CURRENT — SOUTH

Corporate/Parent Company: Southern California News Group
Street Address: 2190 S. Towne Centre Place
City: Anaheim
State: CA
Postal Code: 92806
Office phone: 714-796-7000
Publication Website: www.ocregister.com/location/california/orange-county/newport-beach
Publisher Name: Ron Hasse
Publisher Email: publisher@scng.com
Publisher Phone: 818-713-3883
Editor Name: Frank Pine
Editor Email: editor@scng.com
Editor Phone: 909-483-9360
Advertising Executive Name: Kyla Rodriguez
Advertising Executive Email: krodriguez@scng.com

BAKERSFIELD

DELANO RECORD

Corporate/Parent Company: Sound Publishing
Street Address: 3700 Pegasus Drive
City: Bakersfield
State: CA
Postal Code: 93308
Office phone: (661) 395-7500
Publication Website: www.bakersfield.com/delano-record
General E-mail: news@thedelanorecord.com
Editor Name: Mark Nessia
Editor Email: mnessia@bakersfield.com
Editor Phone: (661) 395-7583

BANNING

RECORD GAZETTE

Corporate/Parent Company: Century Group Newspapers
Street Address: 218 N Murray St
City: Banning
State: CA
Postal Code: 92220-5512
Office phone: (951) 849-4586
Publication Website: https://www.recordgazette.net/
General E-mail: classifieds@recordgazette.net
Publisher Name: Tim Shoffeitt
Publisher Email: tshoffeitt@recordgazette.net
Editor Name: Rachael Garcia

Editor Email: editor@recordgazette.net
Advertising Executive Name: Ana Rivera
Advertising Executive Email: classifieds@recordgazette.net

BIG BEAR LAKE

BIG BEAR GRIZZLY

Corporate/Parent Company: Brehm Communications Inc.
Street Address: 42007 Fox Farm Road, Suite 3B
City: Big Bear Lake
State: CA
Postal Code: 92315
Office phone: (909) 866-3456
Publication Website: http://www.bigbeargrizzly.net/
General E-mail: kbowers.grizzly@gmail.com
Publisher Name: Judi Bowers
Publisher Email: jbowers.grizzly@gmail.com
Publisher Phone: (909) 866-3456, ext : 6033
Editor Name: Kathy Portie
Editor Email: kportie.grizzly@gmail.com
Editor Phone: (909) 866-3456, ext : 6037
Advertising Executive Name: Kelsey Bowers
Advertising Executive Email: kbowers.grizzly@gmail.com

BIG BEAR SHOPPER

Corporate/Parent Company: Brehm Communications, Inc.
Street Address: PO Box 1789
City: Big Bear Lake
State: CA
Postal Code: 92315-1789
Office phone: (909) 866-3456
Publication Website: http://www.bigbeargrizzly.net/
General E-mail: kbowers.grizzly@gmail.com
Publisher Name: Judi Bowers
Publisher Email: jbowers.grizzly@gmail.com
Publisher Phone: (909) 866-3456, ext : 6033
Editor Name: Kathy Portie
Editor Email: kportie.grizzly@gmail.com
Editor Phone: (909) 866-3456, ext : 6037
Advertising Executive Name: Kelsey Bowers
Advertising Executive Email: kbowers.grizzly@gmail.com

GRIZZLY WEEKENDER

Corporate/Parent Company: Brehm Communications, Inc.
Street Address: 42007 Fox Farm Road, Suite 3B
City: Big Bear Lake
State: CA
Postal Code: 92315-1789
Office phone: (909) 866-3456
Publication Website: http://www.bigbeargrizzly.net/home/grizzly_weekender/
General E-mail: kbowers.grizzly@gmail.com
Publisher Name: Judi Bowers
Publisher Email: jbowers.grizzly@gmail.com
Publisher Phone: (909) 866-3456, ext : 6033
Editor Name: Kathy Portie
Editor Email: kportie.grizzly@gmail.com
Editor Phone: (909) 866-3456, ext : 6037
Advertising Executive Name: Kelsey Bowers
Advertising Executive Email: kbowers.grizzly@gmail.com

BRAWLEY

THE DESERT REVIEW

Street Address: 110 South Plaza
City: Brawley
State: CA
Postal Code: 92227
Office phone: 760-351-0100
Publication Website: www.thedesertreview.com
General E-mail: editor@thedesertreview.com
Publisher Name: Lloyd Miller
Publisher Email: lmiller@thedesertreview.com

Publisher Phone: (760) 996 – 2800
Editor Name: Betty Miller
Editor Email: bmiller@thedesertreview.com
Editor Phone: (760) 996 – 3070

BRENTWOOD

ANTIOCH PRESS

Corporate/Parent Company: Brentwood Press & Publishing Corporation
Street Address: 248 Oak St.
City: Brentwood
State: CA
Postal Code: 94513
Office phone: (925) 634-1441
Publication Website: www.thepress.net/news/antioch
Publisher Name: Greg Robinson
Publisher Email: greg@brentwoodpress.com
Editor Name: Ruth Roberts
Editor Email: rroberts@brentwoodpress.com
Editor Phone: (925) 634-1441 ext. 110
Advertising Executive Name: Sharon Finerty
Advertising Executive Email: ads@brentwoodpress.com

BRENTWOOD PRESS

Corporate/Parent Company: Brentwood Press & Publishing Corporation
Street Address: 248 Oak St
City: Brentwood
State: CA
Postal Code: 94513
Office phone: (925) 634-1441
Publication Website: www.thepress.net
Publisher Name: Greg Robinson
Publisher Email: greg@brentwoodpress.com
Editor Name: Ruth Roberts
Editor Email: rroberts@brentwoodpress.com
Editor Phone: (925) 634-1441 ext. 110
Advertising Executive Name: Sharon Finerty
Advertising Executive Email: ads@brentwoodpress.com

DISCOVERY BAY PRESS

Corporate/Parent Company: Brentwood Press & Publishing Corporation
Street Address: 248 Oak Street
City: Brentwood
State: CA
Postal Code: 94513
Office phone: 925-634-1441
Publication Website: www.discoverybaypress.com
General E-mail: web@brentwoodpress.com
Publisher Name: Greg Robinson
Publisher Email: greg@brentwoodpress.com
Editor Name: Ruth Roberts
Editor Email: rroberts@brentwoodpress.com
Advertising Executive Name: Sharon Finerty
Advertising Executive Email: ads@brentwoodpress.com

OAKLEY PRESS

Corporate/Parent Company: Brentwood Press & Publishing Corporation
Street Address: 248 Oak Street
City: Brentwood
State: CA
Postal Code: 94513
Office phone: 925-634-1441
Publication Website: www.thepress.net
Publisher Name: Greg Robinson
Publisher Email: greg@brentwoodpress.com
Editor Name: Ruth Roberts
Editor Email: rroberts@brentwoodpress.com
Advertising Executive Name: Rebecca Porterfield
Advertising Executive Email: rporterfield@brentwoodpress.com

CALISTOGA

CALISTOGA TRIBUNE

Street Address: 1007 Washington Street #3
City: Calistoga
State: CA
Postal Code: 94515
Office phone: (707) 942-5181
Publication Website: www.calistogatribune.com
General E-mail: editor@calistogatribune.com
Publisher Name: Pat Hampton
Publisher Email: pat@calistogatribune.com
Editor Name: Kim Beltran
Advertising Executive Name: Christy Webb
Advertising Executive Email: editor@calistogatribune.com

CARMICHAEL

AMERICAN RIVER MESSENGER

Corporate/Parent Company: Messenger Publishing Group
Street Address: 7144 Fair Oaks Blvd
City: Carmichael
State: CA
Postal Code: 95608
Office phone: 916-773-1111
Publication Website: www.americanrivermessenger.com
Publisher Name: Paul V. Scholl
Publisher Email: publisher@mpg8.com
Publisher Phone: 916-773-1111

GOLD RIVER MESSENGER

Corporate/Parent Company: Messenger Publishing Group
Street Address: 7144 Fair Oaks Blvd Suite #5
City: Carmichael
State: CA
Postal Code: 95608
Office phone: 916-773-1111
Publication Website: goldrivermessenger.com
Publisher Name: Paul V. Scholl
Publisher Email: publisher@mpg8.com

WEST SACRAMENTO SUN

Corporate/Parent Company: Messenger Publishing Group
Street Address: 7144 Fair Oaks Blvd Suite #5
City: Carmichael
State: CA
Postal Code: 95608
Office phone: 916-773-1111
Publication Website: westsacramentosun.com
Publisher Name: Paul V. Scholl
Publisher Email: publisher@mpg8.com

CHESTER

CHESTER PROGRESSIVE

Corporate/Parent Company: Feather Publishing Co., Inc.
Street Address: 135 MAIN ST
City: Chester
State: CA
Postal Code: 96020
Office phone: (530) 283-0800
Publication Website: https://www.plumasnews.com/category/public-notices/chester-progressive-public-notices/
General E-mail: info@plumasnews.com
Publisher Name: Mike Taborski
Editor Name: Debra Moore

CLOVERDALE

CLOVERDALE REVEILLE

Street Address: 207 N. Cloverdale Blvd.
City: Cloverdale
State: CA
Postal Code: 95425
Office phone: 707-894-3339
Publication Website: www.sonomawest.com/cloverdale_reveille
General E-mail: zoe@sonomawest.com
Publisher Name: Rollie Atkinson
Publisher Email: rollie@sonomawest.com
Editor Name: Zoë Strickland
Editor Email: zoe@sonomawest.com
Advertising Executive Name: Brad Schmaltz
Advertising Executive Email: brad@sonomawest.com

CLOVIS

CLOVIS ROUNDUP

Street Address: 55 Shaw Avenue Suite 106
City: Clovis
State: CA
Postal Code: 93612
Office phone: (559) 324-8757
Publication Website: www.clovisroundup.com
General E-mail: info@clovisroundup.com
Publisher Name: Donna Melchor
Publisher Email: dmelchor@clovisroundup.com

COALINGA

COALINGA PRESS

Street Address: 194 East Elm Avenue Suite 102
City: Coalinga
State: CA
Postal Code: 93210
Office phone: 559-362-9668
Publication Website: coalingapress.org
General E-mail: coalingapress@gmail.com

COLFAX

COLFAX RECORD

Corporate/Parent Company: Brehm Communications Inc.
Street Address: 233 S Auburn St
City: Colfax
State: CA
Postal Code: 95713-9753
Office phone: (916) 346-2232
Publication Website: http://www.colfaxrecord.com/
General E-mail: bills@goldcountrymedia.com
Publisher Name: Bill Sullivan
Publisher Email: bills@goldcountrymedia.com
Publisher Phone: (916) 351-3750
Advertising Executive Name: Bill Sullivan
Advertising Executive Email: bills@goldcountrymedia.com

COLUSA

WILLIAMS PIONEER REVIEW

Street Address: 310 5th Street
City: Colusa
State: CA
Postal Code: 95932
Office phone: (530) 458-4141
Publication Website: williamspioneer.com
General E-mail: news@colusacountynews.com
Publisher Name: Lloyd Green
Publisher Email: lloyd@colusacountynews.com
Editor Name: Susan Meeker
Editor Email: susan@colusacountynews.com
Advertising Executive Name: Lloyd Green
Advertising Executive Email: lloyd@colusacountynews.com

CULVER CITY

BLUE PACIFIC NEWS

Corporate/Parent Company: CommunityMedia Corp.
Street Address: 4351 Sepulveda Blvd
City: Culver City
State: CA
Postal Code: 90230
Office phone: 310.437.4401
Publication Website: www.bluepacificnews.com
General E-mail: info@bluepacificnews.com
Editor Name: Alan Moskal
Editor Email: publisher@bluepacificnews.com
Advertising Executive Name: Gary Kohatsu
Advertising Executive Email: editor@bluepacificnews.com

CULVER CITY NEWS

Corporate/Parent Company: CommunityMedia Corp.
Street Address: 4351 Sepulveda Blvd.
City: Culver City
State: CA
Postal Code: 90230
Office phone: 310-437-4401
Publication Website: www.culvercitynews.org
General E-mail: info@culvercitynews.org
Publisher Name: Alan Moskal
Publisher Email: publisher@culvercitynews.org
Publisher Phone: (310) 437-4401 x 301
Editor Name: Gary Kohatsu
Editor Email: editor@culvercitynews.org
Editor Phone: (310) 437-4401 x 303
Advertising Executive Name: Alan Moskal

CYPRESS

BUENA PARK/ANAHEIM INDEPENDENT

Street Address: 5119 Ball Road
City: Cypress
State: CA
Postal Code: 90630
Office phone: 714-952-8505
Publication Website: mybuenapark.com
General E-mail: info@mybuenapark.com
Publisher Name: Steven Remery
Publisher Email: publisher@localnewspapers.org
Advertising Executive Name: Carlos Munoz
Advertising Executive Email: carlos@sunnews.org

DAVIS

THE DAVIS ENTERPRISE

Corporate/Parent Company: McNaughton Newspapers, Inc.
Street Address: 315 G ST
City: DAVIS
State: CA
Postal Code: 95616-4119
Office phone: (530) 756-0800
Publication Website: http://www.davisenterprise.com/
General E-mail: nhannell@davisenterprise.net
Publisher Name: R. Burt McNaughton
Publisher Email: bmcnaughton@davisenterprise.net
Publisher Phone: (530) 747-8030
Editor Name: Sebastian Onate
Editor Email: sonate@davisenterprise.net
Editor Phone: (530) 747-8034
Advertising Executive Name: Nancy Hannell
Advertising Executive Email: nhannell@davisenterprise.net

DOWNEY

THE DOWNEY PATRIOT

Street Address: 8301 E. Florence Avenue, Suite 100
City: Downey
State: CA
Postal Code: 90240
Office phone: 562-904-3668
Publication Website: www.thedowneypatriot.com
General E-mail: news@thedowneypatriot.com
Publisher Name: Jennifer DeKay
Publisher Email: jennifer@thedowneypatriot.com
Editor Name: Eric Pierce
Editor Email: eric@thedowneypatriot.com
Advertising Executive Name: Julie Ledesma
Advertising Executive Email: julie@thedowneypatriot.com

DOWNIEVILLE

MOUNTAIN MESSENGER

Corporate/Parent Company: Sierra County Prospect
Street Address: 313 MAIN ST
City: DOWNIEVILLE
State: CA
Postal Code: 95936
Office phone: (530) 289 3262
Publication Website: www.sierracountyprospect.com/Mountain_Messenger.html
General E-mail: mtnmess@cwo.com
Editor Name: L. DeVita
Editor Email: meditor@sierracountyprospect.com

EL CENTRO

CALEXICO CHRONICLE

Street Address: 1239 W Main St
City: El Centro
State: CA
Postal Code: 92243
Office phone: 760.339.4899
Publication Website: www.tribwekchron.com
General E-mail: holtvillenews@aol.com
Editor Name: Gary Redfern

IMPERIAL VALLEY WEEKLY

Street Address: 1239 W Main St
City: El Centro
State: CA
Postal Code: 92243
Office phone: 760.339.4899
Publication Website: tribwekchron.com
General E-mail: info@calexicochronicle.com

EL SEGUNDO

GLENDALE NEWS-PRESS

Corporate/Parent Company: Los Angeles Times Communications LLC
Street Address: 2300 E. Imperial Highway
City: El Segundo
State: CA
Postal Code: 90245
Office phone: (213) 283-2274
Publication Website: www.latimes.com/socal/glendale-news-press
General E-mail: gnp@latimes.com
Editor Name: Scott Kraft

ELK GROVE

ELK GROVE CITIZEN

Corporate/Parent Company: Herburger Publications, Inc.
Street Address: PO Box 1777
City: Elk Grove
State: CA
Postal Code: 95624-1971
Office phone: (209) 685-3945
Publication Website: http://www.egcitizen.com/
General E-mail: advertising@herburger.net
Publisher Name: David Herburger
Publisher Email: dherburger@herburger.net
Editor Name: Cameron Macdonald
Editor Email: cameronjmacdonald@gmail.com
Advertising Executive Name: Jim O'Donnell
Advertising Executive Email: advertising@herburger.net

Non-Daily Newspapers in the U.S.

EXETER

THE SUN-GAZETTE

Street Address: P.O. Box 7
City: Exeter
State: CA
Postal Code: 93221
Office phone: 559-592-3171.
Publication Website: www.thesungazette.com
Publisher Name: Reggie Ellis
Publisher Email: publisher@thesungazette.com
Editor Name: Paul Myers
Editor Email: editor@thesungazette.com

FAIRFIELD

DAILY REPUBLIC

Corporate/Parent Company: McNaughton Newspapers, Inc.
Street Address: 1250 Texas St
City: Fairfield
State: CA
Postal Code: 94533-5748
Office phone: (707) 425-4646
Publication Website: https://www.dailyrepublic.com/
General E-mail: bbarno@dailyrepublic.net
Publisher Name: Foy McNaughton
Publisher Email: fmcnaughton@dailyrepublic.net
Publisher Phone: (707) 427-6962
Editor Name: Glen Faison
Editor Email: gfaison@dailyrepublic.net
Editor Phone: (707) 427-6925
Advertising Executive Name: Bill Barno
Advertising Executive Email: bbarno@dailyrepublic.net

FOLSOM

FOLSOM TELEGRAPH

Corporate/Parent Company: Brehm Communications Inc.
Street Address: 921 Sutter St, Suite 100
City: Folsom
State: CA
Postal Code: 95630
Office phone: (916) 985-2581
Publication Website: https://goldcountrymedia.com/
General E-mail: bills@goldcountrymedia.com
Publisher Name: Bill Sullivan
Publisher Email: bills@goldcountrymedia.com
Publisher Phone: (916) 351-3750
Advertising Executive Name: Bill Sullivan
Advertising Executive Email: bills@goldcountrymedia.com

THE FOLSOM TELEGRAPH

Corporate/Parent Company: Brehm Communications Inc.
Street Address: 921 Sutter St Suite 100
City: Folsom
State: CA
Postal Code: 95630
Office phone: (916) 985-2581
Publication Website: www.folsomtelegraph.com
Publisher Name: Bill Sullivan
Publisher Email: bills@goldcountrymedia.com
Publisher Phone: 916-351-3750

FONTANA

FONTANA HERALD NEWS

Corporate/Parent Company: Century Group Newspapers
Street Address: 16981 Foothill Blvd
City: Fontana
State: CA
Postal Code: 92335-3566
Office phone: (909) 822-2231
Publication Website: http://www.fontanaheraldnews.com/
General E-mail: sdawkins@fontanaheraldnews.com
Publisher Name: Tim Shoffeitt
Publisher Email: tshoffeitt@fontanaheraldnews.com
Editor Name: Russ Ingold
Editor Email: ringold@fontanaheraldnews.com
Advertising Executive Name: Sonja Dawkins
Advertising Executive Email: sdawkins@fontanaheraldnews.com

FORESTVILLE

SONOMA COUNTY GAZETTE

Corporate/Parent Company: Vesta Publishing, LLC
Street Address: 6490 Front Street #300
City: Forestville
State: CA
Postal Code: 95436
Office phone: (707) 887-0253
Publication Website: sonomacountygazette.com
General E-mail: vesta@sonic.net

FRAZIER PARK

THE MOUNTAIN ENTERPRISE

Street Address: P.O. Box 610
City: Frazier Park
State: CA
Postal Code: 93225
Office phone: 661-245-3794
Publication Website: www.mountainenterprise.com
Editor Name: Patric Hedlund

FRESNO

THE FRESNO BEE

Street Address: 1626 E St
City: Fresno
State: CA
Postal Code: 93786-0001
Office phone: (559) 441-6111
Publication Website: http://www.fresnobee.com/
General E-mail: darreguin@modbee.com
Publisher Name: Tim Ritchey
Publisher Email: tritchey@fresnobee.com
Publisher Phone: (559) 441-6060
Editor Name: Joe Kieta
Editor Email: jkieta@fresnobee.com
Editor Phone: (559) 441-6307
Advertising Executive Name: Daniel Arreguin
Advertising Executive Email: darreguin@modbee.com

FRESNO

VIDA EN EL VALLE

Street Address: 1626 E St
City: Fresno
State: CA
Postal Code: 93786
Office phone: (559) 441-6780
Publication Website: https://www.vidaenelvalle.com/
General E-mail: pvillarreal@mcclatchy.com
Publisher Name: Tim Ritchey
Publisher Email: tritchey@fresnobee.com
Publisher Phone: (559) 441-6060
Editor Name: Juan Esparza Loera
Advertising Executive Name: Paco Villarreal
Advertising Executive Email: pvillarreal@mcclatchy.com

GALT

GALT SHOPPER

Corporate/Parent Company: Herburger Publications, Inc.
Street Address: 604 N Lincoln Way
City: Galt
State: CA
Postal Code: 95632-8601
Office phone: (209) 745-1551
Publication Website: http://www.herburger.net/
General E-mail: advertising@herburger.net
Publisher Name: David Herburger
Publisher Email: dherburger@herburger.net
Editor Name: Cameron Macdonald
Editor Email: cameronjmacdonald@gmail.com
Advertising Executive Name: Jim O'Donnell
Advertising Executive Email: advertising@herburger.net

LAGUNA CITIZEN

Corporate/Parent Company: Herburger Publications, Inc.
Street Address: 604 N Lincoln Way
City: Galt
State: CA
Postal Code: 95632-8601
Office phone: (209) 745-1551
Publication Website: http://www.herburger.net/
General E-mail: advertising@herburger.net
Publisher Name: David Herburger
Publisher Email: dherburger@herburger.net
Editor Name: Cameron Macdonald
Editor Email: cameronjmacdonald@gmail.com
Advertising Executive Name: Jim O'Donnell
Advertising Executive Email: advertising@herburger.net

RIVER VALLEY TIMES

Corporate/Parent Company: Herburger Publications, Inc.
Street Address: 604 N Lincoln Way
City: Galt
State: CA
Postal Code: 95632-8601
Office phone: (209) 745-1551
Publication Website: http://www.herburger.net/
General E-mail: advertising@herburger.net
Publisher Name: David Herburger
Publisher Email: dherburger@herburger.net
Editor Name: Cameron Macdonald
Editor Email: cameronjmacdonald@gmail.com
Advertising Executive Name: Jim O'Donnell
Advertising Executive Email: advertising@herburger.net

THE GALT HERALD

Corporate/Parent Company: Herburger Publications, Inc.
Street Address: 604 N Lincoln Way
City: Galt
State: CA
Postal Code: 95632-8601
Office phone: (209) 745-1551
Publication Website: http://www.galtheraldonline.com/
General E-mail: advertising@herburger.net
Publisher Name: David Herburger
Publisher Email: dherburger@herburger.net
Editor Name: Bonnie Rodriguez
Editor Email: editor@galtherald.com
Advertising Executive Name: Jim O'Donnell
Advertising Executive Email: advertising@herburger.net

GARDEN GROVE

ORANGE COUNTY NEWS

Corporate/Parent Company: CommunityMedia Corp.
Street Address: 7441 Garden Grove Blvd., Suite G
City: Garden Grove
State: CA
Postal Code: 92841
Office phone: 714-894-2575
Publication Website: www.localocn.com
General E-mail: info@localocn.com
Publisher Name: Steven Remery
Publisher Email: publisher@localnewspapers.org
Publisher Phone: 714-894-2575 ext 510
Editor Name: Brady Rhoades
Editor Email: brhoades@localnewspapers.org
Editor Phone: 657-233-2550
Advertising Executive Name: Carlos Munoz
Advertising Executive Email: carlos@sunnews.org

GILROY

THE GILROY DISPATCH

Corporate/Parent Company: New SV Media, Inc.
Street Address: 64 W 6th St
City: Gilroy
State: CA
Postal Code: 95020-6102
Office phone: (408) 842-6400
Publication Website: https://gilroydispatch.com/
General E-mail: jclose@newsvmedia.com
Publisher Name: Jeanette Close
Publisher Email: jclose@newsvmedia.com
Publisher Phone: (408) 842-8313
Editor Name: Michael Moore
Editor Email: mmoore@newsvmedia.com
Editor Phone: (408) 963-0121

GOLETA

SANTA BARBARA FAMILY AND LIFE MAGAZINE

Street Address: 3000 ALISAL RD
City: GOLETA
State: CA
Postal Code: 93117
Office phone: 805-350-8786
Publication Website: www.santabarbarafamilylife.com
Publisher Name: Raiza Giorgi
Publisher Email: publisher@santabarbarafamilylife.com
Publisher Phone: 805-350-8786
Editor Name: Dave Bemis
Editor Email: news@santaynezvalleystar.com
Advertising Executive Name: Jen Trupiano
Advertising Executive Email: ads@santabarbarafamilylife.com

GREENVILLE

INDIAN VALLEY RECORD

Corporate/Parent Company: Feather Publishing Co., Inc.
Street Address: PO Box 469
City: Greenville
State: CA
Postal Code: 95947-0469
Office phone: (530) 283-0800
Publication Website: https://www.plumasnews.com/
General E-mail: info@plumasnews.com
Publisher Name: Mike Taborski
Editor Name: Debra Moore

HANFORD

THE LEMOORE NAVY NEWS

Street Address: 300 West 6th Street
City: Hanford
State: CA
Postal Code: 93230
Office phone: 559-582-0471
Publication Website: hanfordsentinel.com/lemoorenavynews
Publisher Name: Davis Taylor
Publisher Email: publisher@hanfordsentinel.com
Publisher Phone: (559) 583-2400
Editor Name: Chris Aguirre
Editor Email: caguirre@hanfordsentinel.com
Editor Phone: (559) 583-2405
Advertising Executive Name: Mark Daniel
Advertising Executive Email: mdaniel@hanfordsentinel.com

HAWTHORNE

CALIFORNIA CRUSADER NEWS
Street Address: 12519 CRENSHAW BLVD
City: HAWTHORNE
State: CA
Postal Code: 90250
Office phone: 424-269-1359
Publication Website: calcrusnews.com
General E-mail: calcrus@pacbell.net

HEALDSBURG

THE HEALDSBURG TRIBUNE
Corporate/Parent Company: Sonoma West Publishers
Street Address: 230 Center Street
City: Healdsburg
State: CA
Postal Code: 95448
Office phone: 707-823-7845
Publication Website: www.sonomawest.com/the_healdsburg_tribune
Publisher Name: Rollie Atkinson
Publisher Email: rollie@sonomawest.com
Editor Name: Laura Hagar Rush
Editor Email: laura@sonomawest.com
Advertising Executive Name: Jim Schaefer
Advertising Executive Email: jim@sonomawest.com

HEMET

THE HEMET & SAN JACINTO CHRONICLE
Street Address: 555 E Florida Ave.
City: Hemet
State: CA
Postal Code: 92543
Office phone: (951) 262-7611
Publication Website: hsjchronicle.com
General E-mail: contact@hsjchronicle.com
Publisher Name: Pati Galarza
Publisher Email: pgalarza@hsjchronicle.com
Advertising Executive Name: Michael Peterson
Advertising Executive Email: mpeterson@hsjchronicle.com

HERMOSA BEACH

THE BEACH REPORTER
Corporate/Parent Company: Media News Group
Street Address: 2615 Paci?c Coast Highway, Suite 329
City: Hermosa Beach
State: CA
Postal Code: 90254
Office phone: (310) 372-0388
Publication Website: www.tbrnews.com
General E-mail: editor@tbrnews.com
Publisher Name: Simon Grieve
Publisher Email: sgrieve@tbrnews.com
Publisher Phone: (310) 904-6046
Editor Name: Lisa Jacobs
Editor Email: lisa.jacobs@tbrnews.com
Editor Phone: (310) 904-6038

HIGHLAND

HIGHLAND COMMUNITY NEWS
Corporate/Parent Company: Century Group Newspapers
Street Address: 27000 Baseline St
City: Highland
State: CA
Postal Code: 92346-3169
Office phone: (909) 862-1771
Publication Website: https://www.highlandnews.net/
General E-mail: pdavis@highlandnews.net
Publisher Name: Tim Shoffeitt
Publisher Email: tshoffiett@highlandnews.net
Editor Name: Hector Hernandez
Editor Email: editor@highlandnews.net
Advertising Executive Name: Pam Davis
Advertising Executive Email: pdavis@highlandnews.net

HILMAR

HILMAR TIMES
Corporate/Parent Company: Mid-Valley Publications
Street Address: 19920 1st St
City: Hilmar
State: CA
Postal Code: 95324-9096
Office phone: (209) 669-0109
Publication Website: https://hilmartimes.weebly.com
General E-mail: info@midvalleypub.com
Publisher Name: John Derby
Editor Name: Wendy Krier
Editor Email: wendyk@midvalleypub.com
Editor Phone: (209) 669-0109
Advertising Executive Name: Wendy Krier
Advertising Executive Email: wendyk@midvalleypub.com

HOLLISTER

FREE LANCE
Corporate/Parent Company: New SV Media, Inc.
Street Address: 615 San Benito Street
City: Hollister
State: CA
Postal Code: 95021
Office phone: 831-847-7037
Publication Website: sanbenito.com
General E-mail: bholtzclaw@newsvmedia.com

HUGHSON

HUGHSON CHRONICLE & DENAIR DISPATCH
Corporate/Parent Company: Mid-Valley Publications
Street Address: 7012 Pine St. Suite 1
City: Hughson
State: CA
Postal Code: 95326
Office phone: 209-883-9215
Publication Website: hughsonchronicle-denairdispatch.weebly.com
Editor Name: Wendy Krier
Editor Email: info@midvalleypub.com

HUNTINGTON BEACH

HUNTINGTON BEACH INDEPENDENT (OOB)
Corporate/Parent Company: Los Angeles Times Communications LLC
Street Address: 10540 Talbert Ave Ste 300
City: Huntington Beach
State: CA
Postal Code: 92708-6027
Office phone: (714) 966-4600
Publication Website: https://www.latimes.com/socal/daily-pilot/
General E-mail: robert.vardon@latimes.com
Editor Name: Rob Vardon
Editor Email: robert.vardon@latimes.com
Advertising Executive Name: Ray Arroyo
Advertising Executive Email: ray.arroyo@latimes.com

IVANHOE

VALLEY VOICE
Street Address: PO Box 325
City: Ivanhoe
State: CA
Postal Code: 93235
Publication Website: www.ourvalleyvoice.com
Editor Name: Joseph Oldenbourg
Editor Email: joseph@ourvalleyvoice.com
Editor Phone: 559-731-8687

JACKSON

AMADOR LEDGER-DISPATCH
Corporate/Parent Company: Amador Hometown Media, LLC; Mainstreet Media Group, LLC
Street Address: PO Box 1240
City: Jackson
State: CA
Postal Code: 95642
Office phone: (209) 223-8761
Publication Website: http://www.ledger.news/
General E-mail: bbarnard@ledger.news
Publisher Name: Jack Mitchell
Publisher Email: jmitchell@ledger.news
Publisher Phone: (209) 223-8761
Editor Name: Jeremy Malamed
Editor Email: jmalamed@ledger.news
Editor Phone: (209) 223-8761
Advertising Executive Name: Beth Barnard
Advertising Executive Email: bbarnard@ledger.news

KENWOOD

KENWOOD PRESS
Street Address: 8910 Sonoma Highway P.O. Box 277
City: Kenwood
State: CA
Postal Code: 95452
Office phone: (707) 833-5155
Publication Website: www.kenwoodpress.com
General E-mail: info@kenwoodpress.com
Publisher Name: Alec & Ann Quenon Peters
Publisher Email: Alec@kenwoodpress.com
Editor Name: Sarah Campbell Phelps
Editor Email: Sarah@kenwoodpress.com

KERMAN

FIREBAUGH-MENDOTA JOURNAL
Street Address: 14693 W WHITESBRIDGE AVE
City: KERMAN
State: CA
Postal Code: 93630
Office phone: (559) 659-3057
Publication Website: www.kerwestnewspapers.com
General E-mail: kerwest@msn.com
Editor Name: Mark O. Kilen

WEST SIDE ADVANCE
Corporate/Parent Company: Kerwest Newspapers
Street Address: 14693 W WHITESBRIDGE AVE
City: KERMAN
State: CA
Postal Code: 93630
Office phone: (559) 846-6689
Publication Website: kerwestnewspapers.com
General E-mail: kerwest@msn.com
Editor Name: Mark O. Kilen

KING CITY

KING CITY RUSTLER
Corporate/Parent Company: New SV Media, Inc.
Street Address: 522-B Broadway
City: King City
State: CA
Postal Code: 93930
Office phone: 831-385-4880
Publication Website: www.kingcityrustler.com
General E-mail: rcronk@newsvmedia.com
Publisher Name: Jeanie Johnson
Publisher Email: jjohnson@newsvmedia.com
Publisher Phone: 831.385.4880
Editor Name: Ryan Cronk
Editor Email: rcronk@newsvmedia.com
Editor Phone: 831.385.4880 ext 15
Advertising Executive Name: Sheryl Bailey
Advertising Executive Email: sbailey@newsvmedia.com

LA CANADA FLINTRIDGE

LA CANADA FLINTRIDGE OUTLOOK
Corporate/Parent Company: Outlook Newspapers
Street Address: 800 Foothill Blvd
City: La Canada Flintridge
State: CA
Postal Code: 91011
Office phone: (818) 790-7500
Publication Website: outlooknewspapers.com/category/la-canada-flintridge
Publisher Name: Charlie Plowman

PASADENA OUTLOOK
Corporate/Parent Company: Outlook Newspapers
Street Address: 800 Foothill Blvd
City: La Canada Flintridge
State: CA
Postal Code: 91011
Office phone: (818) 790-7500
Publication Website: outlooknewspapers.com/category/pasadena/
Publisher Name: Charlie Plowman

SAN MARINO OUTLOOK
Corporate/Parent Company: Outlook Newspapers
Street Address: 800 Foothill Blvd
City: La Canada Flintridge
State: CA
Postal Code: 91011
Office phone: (818) 790-7500
Publication Website: outlooknewspapers.comcategory/san-marino
Publisher Name: Charlie Plowman

LAKE ARROWHEAD

MOUNTAIN NEWS & CRESTLINE COURIER-NEWS
Corporate/Parent Company: Brehm Communications, Inc.
Street Address: PO Box 2410
City: Lake Arrowhead
State: CA
Postal Code: 92352-2410
Office phone: (909) 336-3555
Publication Website: http://www.mountain-news.com/
General E-mail: ayap@mountain-news.com
Publisher Name: Harry Bradley
Publisher Email: hbradley@mountain-news.com
Publisher Phone: (909) 337-6145, ext : 215
Editor Email: editor@mountain-news.com
Editor Phone: (909) 337-6145, ext : 229
Advertising Executive Name: Angela Yap
Advertising Executive Email: ayap@mountain-news.com

LINCOLN

LINCOLN NEWS MESSENGER
Corporate/Parent Company: Brehm Communications Inc.
Street Address: 553 F St
City: Lincoln
State: CA
Postal Code: 95648-1849
Office phone: (916) 645-7733
Publication Website: https://goldcountrymedia.com/live-content/lincoln-news-messenger/
General E-mail: bills@goldcountrymedia.com
Publisher Name: Bill Sullivan
Publisher Email: bills@goldcountrymedia.com
Publisher Phone: (916) 351-3750

Non-Daily Newspapers in the U.S.

Advertising Executive Name: Bill Sullivan
Advertising Executive Email: bills@goldcountrymedia.com

LONG BEACH

PRESS-TELEGRAM

Street Address: 5225 E. Second St., Suite 400
City: Long Beach
State: CA
Postal Code: 90813-4321
Office phone: (562) 435-1161
Publication Website: https://www.presstelegram.com/
General E-mail: krodriguez@scng.com
Publisher Name: Ron Hasse
Publisher Email: publisher@scng.com
Publisher Phone: (818) 713-3883
Editor Name: Carlos Aviles
Editor Email: caviles@scng.com
Editor Phone: (951) 368-9330
Advertising Executive Name: Kyla Rodriguez
Advertising Executive Email: krodriguez@scng.com

LOOMIS

LOOMIS NEWS

Corporate/Parent Company: Brehm Communications Inc.
Street Address: 3550 Taylor Rd
City: Loomis
State: CA
Postal Code: 95650-9501
Office phone: (916) 786-8746
Publication Website: https://goldcountrymedia.com/live-content/the-loomis-news/
General E-mail: bills@goldcountrymedia.com
Publisher Name: Bill Sullivan
Publisher Email: bills@goldcountrymedia.com
Publisher Phone: (916) 351-3750
Advertising Executive Name: Bill Sullivan
Advertising Executive Email: bills@goldcountrymedia.com

LOS ANGELES

BURBANK LEADER

Corporate/Parent Company: Los Angeles Times Communications LLC
Street Address: 202 W 1st St
City: Los Angeles
State: CA
Postal Code: 90012-4299
Office phone: (818) 637-3200
Publication Website: https://www.latimes.com/socal/burbank-leader/
General E-mail: robert.vardon@latimes.com
Editor Name: Rob Vardon
Editor Email: robert.vardon@latimes.com
Advertising Executive Name: Ray Arroyo
Advertising Executive Email: ray.arroyo@latimes.com

LOS ANGELES

HERALD-AMERICAN

Corporate/Parent Company: Los Angeles Wave Newspapers
Street Address: 3731 Wilshire Blvd Suite 840
City: LOS ANGELES
State: CA
Postal Code: 90010
Office phone: (323)-602-5720
Publication Website: wavenewspapers.com/category/news/local/herald_american
General E-mail: newsroom@wavepublication.com
Editor Name: Don Wanlass
Advertising Executive Name: Linda Lodder
Advertising Executive Email: llodder@wavepublication.com

LOS ANGELES

LA CANADA VALLEY SUN

Corporate/Parent Company: Los Angeles Times Communications LLC
Street Address: 453 S. Spring Street, 3rd Floor
City: Los Angeles
State: CA
Postal Code: 90012-4299
Office phone: (818) 495-4440
Publication Website: https://www.latimes.com/socal/la-canada-valley-sun/
General E-mail: lcnews@valleysun.net
Editor Name: Carol Cormaci
Editor Email: carol.cormaci@latimes.com
Editor Phone: (818) 495-4156

LOS ANGELES INDEPENDENT

Corporate/Parent Company: Los Angeles Wave Newspapers
Street Address: 3731 wilshire blvd Suite 840
City: Los Angeles
State: CA
Postal Code: 90010
Office phone: (310)-602-5720
Publication Website: laindependent.com
General E-mail: newsroom@wavepublication.com
Advertising Executive Name: Linda Lodder
Advertising Executive Email: llodder@wavepublication.com

LOS FELIZ LEDGER

Street Address: 1933 Hillhurst Ave.
City: Los Angeles
State: CA
Postal Code: 90027
Office phone: (323) 741-0019
Publication Website: www.losfelizledger.com
Publisher Name: Allison Cohen
Publisher Email: acohen@losfelizledger.com
Publisher Phone: (323) 741-0019

LYNWOOD PRESS

Corporate/Parent Company: Los Angeles Wave Newspapers
Street Address: 3731 Wilshire Blvd Suite 840
City: Los Angeles
State: CA
Postal Code: 90010
Office phone: (323)-602-5720
Publication Website: wavenewspapers.com/category/news/local/lynwood_press
General E-mail: newsroom@wavepublication.com
Advertising Executive Name: Linda Lodder
Advertising Executive Email: llodder@wavepublication.com

PARK LABREA NEWS & BEVERLY PRESS

Corporate/Parent Company: Times Community News (TCN)
Street Address: 5150 Wilshire Blvd, #330
City: Los Angeles
State: CA
Postal Code: 90036-4480
Office phone: (323) 933-5518
Publication Website: https://beverlypress.com/
General E-mail: michael@beverlypress.com
Publisher Name: Michael Villalpando
Publisher Email: michael@beverlypress.com
Editor Email: editor@beverlypress.com
Advertising Executive Name: Michael Villalpando
Advertising Executive Email: michael@beverlypress.com

LOS BANOS

LOS BANOS ENTERPRISE

Street Address: 907 6th St
City: Los Banos
State: CA
Postal Code: 93635-4215
Office phone: (800) 540-4200
Publication Website: https://www.losbanosenterprise.com
General E-mail: glieb@losbanosenterprise.com
Publisher Name: Gene Lieb
Publisher Email: glieb@losbanosenterprise.com
Publisher Phone: (209) 826-3831, ext : 6551

MOUNT SHASTA

WEED PRESS

Corporate/Parent Company: Gannett
Street Address: 924 N. Mount Shasta Blvd. (P.O. Box 127)
City: Mount Shasta
State: CA
Postal Code: 96067
Office phone: (530) 926-5214
Publication Website: www.mtshastanews.com
Editor Name: Skye Kinkade
Editor Email: news@mtshastanews.com
Advertising Executive Name: Haley Brown
Advertising Executive Email: hbrown@mtshastanews.com

MARYSVILLE

GLENN COUNTY TRANSCRIPT

Corporate/Parent Company: Appeal Democrat
Street Address: 1530 Ellis Lake Drive
City: Marysville
State: CA
Postal Code: 95901
Office phone: 530- 749-4700
Publication Website: www.appeal-democrat.com/glenn_county_transcript
General E-mail: info@appealdemocrat.com
Publisher Name: Glenn Stifflemire
Publisher Email: gstifflemire@appealdemocrat.com
Publisher Phone: (530) 749-4705
Editor Name: Steve Miller
Editor Email: smiller@appealdemocrat.com
Editor Phone: (530) 749-4767
Advertising Executive Name: Jamie Keith
Advertising Executive Email: lnash@appealdemocrat.com

MERCED

ATWATER SIGNAL

Street Address: 1190 W. Olive Avenue, Suite F
City: Merced
State: CA
Postal Code: 95348
Office phone: (209) 722-1511
Publication Website: www.mercedsunstar.com/news/local/community/atwater
Publisher Name: Tim Ritchey
Publisher Email: tritchey@fresnobee.com
Publisher Phone: (559) 441-6060
Editor Name: Joe Kieta
Editor Email: jkieta@fresnobee.com
Editor Phone: (559) 441-6307

MERCED

CHOWCHILLA NEWS

Street Address: 1190 W OLIVE AVE STE F
City: MERCED
State: CA
Postal Code: 95348
Office phone: (209) 722-1511
Publication Website: www.mercedsunstar.com/news/local/community/chowchilla
Publisher Name: Tim Ritchey
Publisher Email: tritchey@fresnobee.com
Publisher Phone: (559) 441-6060
Editor Name: Joe Kieta
Editor Email: jkieta@fresnobee.com
Editor Phone: (559) 441-6307

LIVINGSTON CHRONICLE

Street Address: 3033 North G St
City: Merced
State: CA
Postal Code: 95340-2108
Office phone: (209) 722-1511
Publication Website: https://www.mercedsunstar.com/news/local/community/livingston/
General E-mail: atombelaine@mcclatchy.com
Publisher Name: Tim Ritchey
Publisher Email: tritchey@fresnobee.com
Publisher Phone: (559) 441-6060
Editor Name: Joe Kieta
Editor Email: jkieta@fresnobee.com
Editor Phone: (559) 441-6307
Advertising Executive Name: Angela Tombelaine
Advertising Executive Email: atombelaine@mcclatchy.com

MERCED COUNTY TIMES

Corporate/Parent Company: Mid-Valley Publications
Street Address: 2221 K St
City: Merced
State: CA
Postal Code: 95340-3868
Office phone: (209) 383-0433
Publication Website: https://mercedcountytimes.com/
General E-mail: mallori@midvalleypub.com
Publisher Name: John Derby
Editor Name: Jonathan Whitaker
Editor Email: johnwhitaker@midvalleypub.com
Editor Phone: (209) 383-0433
Advertising Executive Name: Mallori Resendez
Advertising Executive Email: mallori@midvalleypub.com

MERCED SUN-STAR

Street Address: 1190 W. Olive Avenue, Suite F
City: Merced
State: CA
Postal Code: 95340-2108
Office phone: (209) 722-1511
Publication Website: https://mcciservices.newscyclecloud.com
General E-mail: atombelaine@mcclatchy.com
Publisher Name: Tim Ritchey
Publisher Email: tritchey@fresnobee.com
Publisher Phone: (559) 441-6060
Editor Name: Joe Kieta
Editor Email: jkieta@fresnobee.com
Editor Phone: (559) 441-6307
Advertising Executive Name: Angela Tombelaine
Advertising Executive Email: atombelaine@mcclatchy.com

THE CHOWCHILLA NEWS

Street Address: 3033 G St
City: Merced
State: CA
Postal Code: 95340-2108
Office phone: (559) 665-5751
Publication Website: http://www.thechowchillanews.com/
General E-mail: atombelaine@mcclatchy.com
Publisher Name: Tim Ritchey
Publisher Email: tritchey@fresnobee.com
Publisher Phone: (559) 441-6060
Editor Name: Joe Kieta
Editor Email: jkieta@fresnobee.com
Editor Phone: (559) 441-6307
Advertising Executive Name: Angela Tombelaine

MILPITAS

MILPITAS POST
Street Address: 59 MARYLINN DR
City: MILPITAS
State: CA
Postal Code: 95035
Office phone: 408-262-2454
Publication Website: www.mercurynews.com/location/milpitas
Publisher Name: Sharon Ryan
Publisher Email: publisher@bayareanewsgroup.com
Editor Name: Frank Pine
Editor Email: editor@bayareanewsgroup.com
Editor Phone: 408-920-5456

MILPITAS

THE ARGUS
Corporate/Parent Company: Adams Publishing Group
Street Address: 59 MARYLINN DR
City: MILPITAS
State: CA
Postal Code: 95035
Office phone: 925-935-2525
Publication Website: www.eastbaytimes.com/location/fremont
Publisher Name: Sharon Ryan
Publisher Email: publisher@bayareanewsgroup.com
Editor Name: Frank Pine
Editor Email: editor@bayareanewsgroup.com
Editor Phone: 408-920-5456

MONROVIA

ALHAMBRA PRESS
Corporate/Parent Company: HLR Media, LLC
Street Address: 121 E CHESTNUT AVE
City: MONROVIA
State: CA
Postal Code: 91016
Office phone: (626) 301-1010
Publication Website: www.alhambra-press.com
Editor Name: Amelia Lucero
Editor Email: editor@HLRmedia.com
Advertising Executive Name: Fred Bankston

ANAHEIM PRESS
Corporate/Parent Company: HLR Media, LLC
Street Address: 125 E. Chestnut Ave.
City: Monrovia
State: CA
Postal Code: 91016
Office phone: (626) 301-1010
Publication Website: www.anaheimpress.com
Publisher Name: Von Raees
Editor Name: Amelia Lucero
Editor Email: editor@HLRmedia.com
Advertising Executive Name: Fred Bankston

ARCADIA WEEKLY
Corporate/Parent Company: Beacon Media News
Street Address: 125 E. Chestnut Ave.
City: Monrovia
State: CA
Postal Code: 91016
Office phone: 626.301.1010
Publication Website: www.arcadiaweekly.com
General E-mail: info@beaconmedianews.com
Editor Name: Terry MILLER
Editor Email: editorial@beaconmedianews.com
Advertising Executive Name: Alejandra BECERRIL
Advertising Executive Email: advertising@beaconmedianews.com

AZUSA BEACON
Corporate/Parent Company: HLR Media, LLC
Street Address: 125 E. Chestnut Ave.
City: Monrovia
State: CA
Postal Code: 91016
Office phone: (626) 301-1010
Publication Website: www.azusabeacon.com
General E-mail: editor@HLRmedia.com

BALDWIN PARK PRESS
Corporate/Parent Company: HLR Media, LLC
Street Address: 121 E CHESTNUT AVE
City: MONROVIA
State: CA
Postal Code: 91016
Office phone: (626) 386-3457
Publication Website: www.bppress.com
General E-mail: hlrmediallc@gmail.com
Editor Name: Terry Miller
Advertising Executive Name: Annette Reyes
Advertising Executive Email: advertising@beaconmedianews.com

BELMONT BEACON
Corporate/Parent Company: HLR Media, LLC
Street Address: 125 E CHESTNUT AVE
City: MONROVIA
State: CA
Postal Code: 91016
Office phone: (626) 301-1010
Publication Website: www.belmontbeacon.com
General E-mail: advertising@HLRmedia.com
Publisher Name: Von Raees
Editor Name: Amelia Lucero
Editor Email: editor@HLRmedia.com
Advertising Executive Name: Annette Reyes

BURBANK INDEPENDENT
Corporate/Parent Company: HLR Media, LLC
Street Address: 121 E CHESTNUT AVE
City: MONROVIA
State: CA
Postal Code: 91016
Office phone: (626) 386-3457
Publication Website: www.burbankindependent.com
General E-mail: hlrmediallc@gmail.com
Publisher Name: Von Raees
Editor Name: Terry Miller

CORONA NEWS PRESS
Corporate/Parent Company: HLR Media, LLC
Street Address: 121 E CHESTNUT AVE
City: MONROVIA
State: CA
Postal Code: 91016
Office phone: (626) 301-1010
Publication Website: coronanewspress.com
Publisher Name: Von Raees
Editor Name: Amelia Lucero
Editor Email: editor@HLRmedia.com
Advertising Executive Name: Annette Reyes

EL MONTE EXAMINER
Corporate/Parent Company: HLR Media, LLC
Street Address: 125 E CHESTNUT AVE
City: MONROVIA
State: CA
Postal Code: 91016
Office phone: (626) 301-1010
Publication Website: www.elmonteexaminer.com
Publisher Name: Von Raees
Editor Name: Amelia Lucero
Editor Email: editor@HLRmedia.com
Advertising Executive Name: Annette Reyes

EXCELSIOR ORANGE COUNTY
Street Address: 605 East Huntington Drive, Suite # 100
City: Monrovia
State: CA
Postal Code: 91016
Office phone: (714) 796-7000
Publication Website: https://www.excelsiorcalifornia.com/
General E-mail: jkrup@scng.com
Publisher Name: James Krup
Publisher Email: jkrup@scng.com
Publisher Phone: (714) 796-7000
Editor Name: Carlos Aviles
Editor Email: caviles@scng.com
Editor Phone: (951) 368-9330
Advertising Executive Name: James Krup
Advertising Executive Email: jkrup@scng.com

GLENDALE INDEPENDENT
Corporate/Parent Company: HLR Media, LLC
Street Address: 121 E CHESTNUT AVE
City: MONROVIA
State: CA
Postal Code: 91016
Office phone: (626) 301-1010
Publication Website: www.glendaleindependent.com
Publisher Name: Von Raees
Editor Name: Amelia Lucero
Editor Email: editor@HLRmedia.com
Advertising Executive Name: Annette Reyes

MONROVIA WEEKLY
Street Address: 125 E. Chestnut Ave.
City: Monrovia
State: CA
Postal Code: 91016
Office phone: 626.301.1010
Publication Website: www.monroviaweekly.com
General E-mail: info@beaconmedianews.com
Editor Name: Terry Miller
Editor Email: editorial@beaconmedianews.com

MONTEREY PARK PRESS
Corporate/Parent Company: HLR Media, LLC
Street Address: 121 E CHESTNUT AVE
City: MONROVIA
State: CA
Postal Code: 91016
Office phone: (626) 386-3457
Publication Website: www.montereyparkpress.com
General E-mail: hlrmediallc@gmail.com
Publisher Name: Von Raees
Editor Name: Terry Miller

ONTARIO NEWS PRESS
Corporate/Parent Company: HLR Media, LLC
Street Address: 121 E CHESTNUT AVE
City: MONROVIA
State: CA
Postal Code: 91016
Office phone: (626) 301-1010
Publication Website: ontarionewspress.com
Publisher Name: Von Raees
Editor Name: Amelia Lucero
Editor Email: editor@HLRmedia.com
Advertising Executive Name: Annette Reyes

PASADENA INDEPENDENT
Corporate/Parent Company: Beacon Media News
Street Address: 125 E. Chestnut Ave.
City: Monrovia
State: CA
Postal Code: 91016
Office phone: 626.301.1010
Publication Website: www.pasadenaindependent.com
General E-mail: info@beaconmedianews.com
Editor Name: Terry MILLER
Editor Email: editorial@beaconmedianews.com
Advertising Executive Name: Alejandra BECERRIL
Advertising Executive Email: advertising@beaconmedianews.com

PASADENA PRESS
Corporate/Parent Company: HLR Media, LLC
Street Address: 121 E CHESTNUT AVE
City: MONROVIA
State: CA
Postal Code: 91016
Office phone: (626) 301-1010
Publication Website: www.pasadenapress.com
Publisher Name: Von Raees
Editor Name: Amelia Lucero
Editor Email: editor@HLRmedia.com
Advertising Executive Name: Annette Reyes

RIVERSIDE INDEPENDENT
Corporate/Parent Company: HLR Media, LLC
Street Address: 121 E CHESTNUT AVE
City: MONROVIA
State: CA
Postal Code: 91016
Office phone: (626) 301-1010
Publication Website: www.riversideindependent.com
Publisher Name: Von Raees
Editor Name: Amelia Lucero
Editor Email: editor@HLRmedia.com
Advertising Executive Name: Annette Reyes

ROSEMEAD READER
Corporate/Parent Company: HLR Media, LLC
Street Address: 125 E CHESTNUT AVE
City: MONROVIA
State: CA
Postal Code: 91016
Office phone: (626) 301-1010
Publication Website: www.rosemeadreader.com
Publisher Name: Von Raees
Editor Name: Amelia Lucero
Editor Email: editor@HLRmedia.com
Advertising Executive Name: Annette Reyes

SAN BERNARDINO PRESS
Corporate/Parent Company: HLR Media, LLC
Street Address: 121 E CHESTNUT AVE
City: MONROVIA
State: CA
Postal Code: 91016
Office phone: (626) 301-1010
Publication Website: www.sanbernardinopress.com
Publisher Name: Von Raees
Editor Name: Amelia Lucero

Advertising Executive Email: atombelaine@mcclatchy.com

Non-Daily Newspapers in the U.S.

Editor Email: editor@HLRmedia.com
Advertising Executive Name: Annette Reyes

SAN GABRIEL SUN
Corporate/Parent Company: HLR Media, LLC
Street Address: 125 E CHESTNUT AVE
City: MONROVIA
State: CA
Postal Code: 91016
Office phone: (626) 301-1010
Publication Website: www.sangabrielsun.com
Publisher Name: Von Raees
Editor Name: Amelia Lucero
Editor Email: editor@HLRmedia.com
Advertising Executive Name: Annette Reyes

SAN GABRIEL VALLEY TRIBUNE
Corporate/Parent Company: Media News Group
Street Address: 605 E. Huntington Drive, Suite 100
City: Monrovia
State: CA
Postal Code: 91016-6353
Office phone: (626) 962-8811
Publication Website: http://www.sgvtribune.com/
General E-mail: krodriguez@scng.com
Publisher Name: Ron Hasse
Publisher Email: publisher@scng.com
Publisher Phone: (818) 713-3883
Editor Name: Carlos Aviles
Editor Email: caviles@scng.com
Editor Phone: (951) 368-9330
Advertising Executive Name: Kyla Rodriguez
Advertising Executive Email: krodriguez@scng.com

TEMPLE CITY TRIBUNE
Corporate/Parent Company: HLR Media, LLC
Street Address: 125 E CHESTNUT AVE
City: MONROVIA
State: CA
Postal Code: 91016
Office phone: (626) 301-1010
Publication Website: www.templecitytribune.com
Publisher Name: Von Raees
Editor Name: Amelia Lucero
Editor Email: editor@HLRmedia.com
Advertising Executive Name: Annette Reyes

THE WHITTIER DAILY NEWS
Corporate/Parent Company: Media News Group
Street Address: 605 E. Huntington Drive, Suite 100
City: Monrovia
State: CA
Postal Code: 91016-6353
Office phone: (626) 962-8811
Publication Website: https://www.whittierdailynews.com/
General E-mail: krodriguez@scng.com
Publisher Name: Ron Hasse
Publisher Email: publisher@scng.com
Publisher Phone: (818) 713-3883
Editor Name: Carlos Aviles
Editor Email: caviles@scng.com
Editor Phone: (951) 368-9330
Advertising Executive Name: Kyla Rodriguez
Advertising Executive Email: krodriguez@scng.com

DUARTE DISPATCH
Corporate/Parent Company: HLR Media, LLC
Street Address: 125 E CHESTNUT AVE
City: "MONROVIA "
State: CA
Postal Code: 91016
Office phone: (626) 301-1010
Publication Website: www.duartedispatch.com
Publisher Name: Von Raees
Editor Name: Amelia Lucero
Editor Email: editor@HLRmedia.com
Advertising Executive Name: Annette Reyes

MONTEREY
SALINAS VALLEY WEEKLY
Street Address: 8 Upper Ragsdale Dr
City: Monterey
State: CA
Postal Code: 93940-5730
Office phone: (831) 646-4301
Publication Website: https://www.montereyherald.com/tag/salinas-valley/
General E-mail: dkrolczyk@montereyherald.com
Publisher Name: Gary Omernick
Publisher Email: gomernick@montereyherald.com
Publisher Phone: (831) 648-1192
Editor Name: Don Miller
Editor Email: dmiller@montereyherald.com
Editor Phone: (831) 646-4416
Advertising Executive Name: Dan Krolczyk
Advertising Executive Email: dkrolczyk@montereyherald.com

MORAGA
LAMORINDA WEEKLY
Street Address: P.O. Box 6133
City: Moraga
State: CA
Postal Code: 94570-6133
Office phone: (925)377 0977
Publication Website: www.lamorindaweekly.com
General E-mail: info@lamorindaweekly.com
Publisher Name: Andy Scheck
Publisher Email: andy@lamorindaweekly.com
Publisher Phone: (925)330 7916
Editor Name: Jennifer Wake
Editor Email: jennifer@lamorindaweekly.com
Advertising Executive Name: Wendy Wuerth-Scheck
Advertising Executive Email: wendy@lamorindaweekly.com

MOUNT SHASTA
MOUNT SHASTA HERALD
Street Address: 924 N. Mount Shasta Blvd. (P.O. Box 127)
City: Mount Shasta
State: CA
Postal Code: 96067
Office phone: (530) 926-5214
Publication Website: www.mtshastanews.com
Publisher Name: Amy Lanier
Publisher Email: alanier@mtshastanews.com
Editor Name: Skye Kinkade
Editor Email: news@mtshastanews.com
Advertising Executive Name: Haley Brown
Advertising Executive Email: hbrown@mtshastanews.com

NEEDLES
NEEDLES DESERT STAR
Corporate/Parent Company: Brehm Communications Inc.
Street Address: 800 W Broadway St
City: Needles
State: CA
Postal Code: 92363-2755
Office phone: (760) 326-2222
Publication Website: http://www.mohavedailynews.com/needles_desert_star/
General E-mail: needlesdesertstar@nwppub.com
Publisher Name: Larry Kendrick
Publisher Email: larry@nwppub.com
Editor Name: Robin Richards
Editor Email: needlesdesertstar@nwppub.com

NEWMAN
GUSTINE PRESS-STANDARD
Corporate/Parent Company: Mattos Newspapers
Street Address: 1021 Fresno St.
City: Newman
State: CA
Postal Code: 95360
Office phone: 209-862-2222
Publication Website: www.westsideconnect.com
General E-mail: webeditor@mattosnews.com
Publisher Name: Susan Mattos
Publisher Email: smattos@mattosnews.com
Publisher Phone: 209-862-2222
Editor Name: Dean Harris
Editor Email: dharris@mattosnews.com
Editor Phone: 209-862-2222
Advertising Executive Name: Kyle Souza
Advertising Executive Email: advertising@mattosnews.com

THE WEST SIDE INDEX
Corporate/Parent Company: Mattos Newspapers
Street Address: 1021 Fresno St.
City: Newman
State: CA
Postal Code: 95360
Office phone: 209-862-2222
Publication Website: www.westsideconnect.com
General E-mail: webeditor@mattosnews.com
Publisher Name: Susan Mattos
Publisher Email: smattos@mattosnews.com
Publisher Phone: 209-862-2222
Editor Name: Dean Harris
Editor Email: dharris@mattosnews.com
Editor Phone: 209-862-2222
Advertising Executive Name: Kyle Souza
Advertising Executive Email: advertising@mattosnews.com

NORTH HOLLYWOOD
THE TOLUCAN TIMES
Street Address: 10701 Riverside Dr #A
City: North Hollywood
State: CA
Postal Code: 91602
Office phone: 818-762-2171
Publication Website: www.tolucantimes.com
General E-mail: info@tolucantimes.com
Editor Name: Jon Konjoyan
Editor Email: editorial@tolucantimes.com
Advertising Executive Name: Alicia Apaghian
Advertising Executive Email: alicia@tolucantimes.com

NOVATO
ROSS VALLEY REPORTER
Street Address: 1301-B Grant Avenue
City: Novato
State: CA
Postal Code: 94948
Office phone: 415-892-1516
Publication Website: www.marinscope.com/ross_valley_reporter
General E-mail: mmckellips@marinscope.com
Editor Name: Sherman Frederick

OAKHURST
SIERRA STAR
Street Address: 1626 E Street, PO BOX 305
City: Oakhurst
State: CA
Postal Code: 93644-0305
Office phone: (800) 877-9886
Publication Website: https://www.sierrastar.com/
General E-mail: ads@sierrastar.com
Advertising Executive Email: ads@sierrastar.com

OXNARD
TRI COUNTY SENTRY
Street Address: 451 West Fifth Street
City: Oxnard
State: CA
Postal Code: 93030
Office phone: 805-983-0015
Publication Website: www.tricountysentry.com
General E-mail: news@tricountysentry.com
Publisher Name: Peggy Hunt

PALM DESERT
DESERT ENTERTAINER
Corporate/Parent Company: Brehm Communications, Inc.
Street Address: 41995 Boardwalk
City: Palm Desert
State: CA
Postal Code: 92211-9065
Office phone: (760) 365-3315
Publication Website: http://www.desertentertainer.com/
Publisher Name: Deb Geissler
Advertising Executive Name: Kimberly Brucks

PIEDMONT
PIEDMONT POST
Street Address: 1139 Oakland Avenue
City: Piedmont
State: CA
Postal Code: 94611
Office phone: (510) 922-8711
Publication Website: www.piedmontpost.org
Editor Name: Gray Cathrall
Editor Email: news@piedmontpost.org
Advertising Executive Name: Nancy Kurkjian
Advertising Executive Email: nancy@cmc-ads.com

PLACERVILLE
CAMERON PARK LIFE
Corporate/Parent Company: McNaughton Newspapers, Inc.
Street Address: 2889 RAY LAWYER DR
City: PLACERVILLE
State: CA
Postal Code: 95667
Publication Website: www.villagelife.com/cameron-park-life
Publisher Name: Richard B. Esposito
Publisher Email: resposito@mtdemocrat.net
Publisher Phone: (530) 344-5055
Editor Name: Noel Stack
Editor Email: editor@villagelife.com
Editor Phone: (530) 344-5073
Advertising Executive Name: Kristi Massey
Advertising Executive Email: kmassey@mtdemocrat.net

PLACERVILLE
VILLAGE LIFE
Corporate/Parent Company: McNaughton Newspapers, Inc.
Street Address: 2889 Ray Lawyer Dr
City: Placerville
State: CA
Postal Code: 95667-3914
Office phone: (530) 622-1255
Publication Website: https://www.villagelife.com/

General E-mail: ibalentine@mtdemocrat.net
Publisher Name: Richard B. Esposito
Publisher Email: resposito@mtdemocrat.net
Publisher Phone: (530) 344-5055
Editor Name: Noel Stack
Editor Email: editor@villagelife.com
Editor Phone: (530) 344-5073
Advertising Executive Name: Ian Balentine
Advertising Executive Email: ibalentine@mtdemocrat.net

PORTOLA

PORTOLA REPORTER

Corporate/Parent Company: Feather Publishing Co., Inc.
Street Address: 96 E Sierra St
City: Portola
State: CA
Postal Code: 96122-8436
Office phone: (530) 832-4646
Publication Website: https://www.plumasnews.com/
General E-mail: info@plumasnews.com
Publisher Name: Mike Taborski
Editor Name: Debra Moore

QUINCY

FEATHER RIVER BULLETIN

Corporate/Parent Company: Feather Publishing Co., Inc.
Street Address: 287 Lawrence St
City: Quincy
State: CA
Postal Code: 95971-9477
Office phone: (530) 283-0800
Publication Website: https://www.plumasnews.com/category/public-notices/feather-river-bulletin-public-notices/
General E-mail: info@plumasnews.com
Publisher Name: Mike Taborski
Editor Name: Debra Moore

RANCHO CUCAMONGA

INLAND VALLEY DAILY BULLETIN

Corporate/Parent Company: Media News Group
Street Address: 9616 Archibald Ave
City: Rancho Cucamonga
State: CA
Postal Code: 91730-7940
Office phone: (909) 987-6397
Publication Website: https://www.dailybulletin.com/
General E-mail: krodriguez@scng.com
Publisher Name: Ron Hasse
Publisher Email: publisher@scng.com
Publisher Phone: (818) 713-3883
Editor Name: Carlos Aviles
Editor Email: caviles@scng.com
Editor Phone: (951) 368-9330
Advertising Executive Name: Kyla Rodriguez
Advertising Executive Email: krodriguez@scng.com

REDDING

AFTER FIVE: THE NORTH STATE MAGAZINE

Street Address: PO Box 492905
City: Redding
State: CA
Postal Code: 96049
Office phone: 530-275-1716
Publication Website: www.after5online.com
General E-mail: editorial@after5online.com

REDLANDS

REDLANDS COMMUNITY NEWS

Street Address: 296 Tennessee Street
City: Redlands
State: CA
Postal Code: 92373
Office phone: 909-335-6100
Publication Website: www.redlandscommunitynews.com
General E-mail: news@redlandscommunitynews.com
Publisher Name: Jerry Bean
Publisher Email: jbean@redlandscommunitynews.com
Editor Name: James Folmer
Editor Email: jfolmer@redlandscommunitynews.com
Advertising Executive Name: Jack Galloway
Advertising Executive Email: jgalloway@redlandscommunitynews.com

THE FACTS (REDLANDS)

Street Address: 19 E. Citrus Ave. Suite 102
City: Redlands
State: CA
Postal Code: 92373-4763
Office phone: (909) 793-3221
Publication Website: https://www.redlandsdailyfacts.com/
General E-mail: tparadis@scng.com
Publisher Name: Ron Hasse
Publisher Email: publisher@scng.com
Publisher Phone: (818) 713-3883
Editor Name: Jerry Rice
Editor Email: jrice@scng.com
Editor Phone: (951) 541-1825
Advertising Executive Name: Tom Paradis
Advertising Executive Email: tparadis@scng.com

RICHMOND

JOURNAL (EL CERRITO)

Street Address: 1050 MARINA WAY S
City: RICHMOND
State: CA
Postal Code: 94804
Office phone: 925-935-2525
Publication Website: https://www.eastbaytimes.com/location/el-cerrito
Publisher Name: Sharon Ryan
Publisher Email: publisher@bayareanewsgroup.com
Editor Name: Frank Pine
Editor Email: editor@bayareanewsgroup.com
Editor Phone: 408-920-5456

RIVERSIDE

LA PRENSA

Street Address: 1825 Chicago Avenue
City: Riverside
State: CA
Postal Code: 92507
Office phone: (951) 684-1200
Publication Website: https://www.pe.com/
General E-mail: krodriguez@scng.com
Publisher Name: Ron Hasse
Publisher Email: publisher@scng.com
Publisher Phone: (818) 713-3883
Editor Name: Carlos Aviles
Editor Email: caviles@scng.com
Editor Phone: (951) 368-9330
Advertising Executive Name: Kyla Rodriguez
Advertising Executive Email: krodriguez@scng.com

ROCKLIN

PLACER HERALD

Corporate/Parent Company: Brehm Communications Inc.
Street Address: 901 Sunrise Ave. Suite A-12
City: Rocklin
State: CA
Postal Code: 95677-2707
Office phone: (916) 624-9713
Publication Website: https://goldcountrymedia.com/live-content/placer-herald/
General E-mail: bills@goldcountrymedia.com
Publisher Name: Bill Sullivan
Publisher Email: bills@goldcountrymedia.com
Publisher Phone: (916) 351-3750
Advertising Executive Name: Bill Sullivan
Advertising Executive Email: bills@goldcountrymedia.com

ROSEVILLE

EL DORADO HILLS TELEGRAPH

Corporate/Parent Company: Brehm Communications, Inc.
Street Address: 188 Cirby Way
City: Roseville
State: CA
Postal Code: 95678-6481
Office phone: (916) 774-7910
Publication Website: https://goldcountrymedia.com/live-content/lincoln-news-messenger/
General E-mail: bills@goldcountrymedia.com
Publisher Name: Bill Sullivan
Publisher Email: bills@goldcountrymedia.com
Publisher Phone: (916) 351-3750
Advertising Executive Name: Bill Sullivan
Advertising Executive Email: bills@goldcountrymedia.com

THE ROSEVILLE PRESS TRIBUNE

Corporate/Parent Company: Gold Country Media
Street Address: 901 Sunrise Ave. Suite A-12
City: Roseville
State: CA
Postal Code: 95661
Office phone: 916-624-9713
Publication Website: www.thepresstribune.com
Publisher Name: Bill Sullivan
Publisher Email: bills@goldcountrymedia.com
Publisher Phone: 916-351-3750
Advertising Executive Name: John Love
Advertising Executive Email: johnl@goldcountrymedia.com

SACRAMENTO

ARDEN CARMICHAEL NEWS

Corporate/Parent Company: Valley Community Newspapers, Inc.
Street Address: 1109 Markham Way
City: Sacramento
State: CA
Postal Code: 95818
Office phone: (916) 429-9901
Publication Website: www.valcomnews.com/category/archives/ardencarmichaelnews
General E-mail: vcnnews@valcomnews.com
Editor Name: Monica Stark
Editor Email: editor@valcomnews.com
Advertising Executive Name: Melissa Andrews
Advertising Executive Email: melissa@valcomnews.com

EAST SACRAMENTO NEWS

Corporate/Parent Company: Valley Community Newspapers, Inc.
Street Address: 1109 MARKHAM WAY
City: SACRAMENTO
State: CA
Postal Code: 95818
Office phone: (916) 429-9901
Publication Website: www.valcomnews.com/category/archives/eastsacnews
General E-mail: vcnnews@valcomnews.com
Editor Name: Monica Stark
Editor Email: editor@valcomnews.com
Advertising Executive Name: Melissa Andrews
Advertising Executive Email: melissa@valcomnews.com

LAND PARK NEWS

Corporate/Parent Company: Valley Community Newspapers, Inc.
Street Address: 1109 Markham Way
City: Sacramento
State: CA
Postal Code: 95818
Office phone: (916) 429-9901
Publication Website: www.valcomnews.com
General E-mail: vcnnews@valcomnews.com
Editor Name: Monica Stark
Editor Email: editor@valcomnews.com
Advertising Executive Name: Melissa Andrews
Advertising Executive Email: melissa@valcomnews.com

POCKET NEWS

Corporate/Parent Company: Valley Community Newspapers, Inc.
Street Address: 1109 Markham Way
City: Sacramento
State: CA
Postal Code: 95818
Office phone: (916) 429-9901
Publication Website: www.valcomnews.com/category/archives/pocketnews
General E-mail: vcnnews@valcomnews.com
Editor Name: Monica Stark
Editor Email: editor@valcomnews.com
Advertising Executive Name: Melissa Andrews
Advertising Executive Email: melissa@valcomnews.com

SAN ANDREAS

SIERRA LODESTAR

Street Address: 15 N. Main St
City: San Andreas
State: CA
Postal Code: 95249
Office phone: 209.754.3861
Publication Website: www.calaverasenterprise.com/sierra_lodestar
Publisher Name: Ralph Alldredge
Publisher Email: publisher@calaverasenterprise.com
Publisher Phone: 209.754.3861
Editor Name: Marc Lutz
Editor Email: editor@calaverasenterprise.com
Editor Phone: 209.500.6182
Advertising Executive Name: Jason Currier
Advertising Executive Email: jcurrier@calaverasenterprise.com

SAN BERNARDINO

SAN BERNARDINO BULLETIN

Street Address: PO Box 13111
City: San Bernardino
State: CA
Postal Code: 92423-3111
Office phone: (909) 889-6477
Publication Website: www.mnc.net/sbbulletin.htm
Publisher Name: Roger M. Grace

THE SUN

Corporate/Parent Company: Paxton Media Group
Street Address: 473 E. Carnegie Drive, Suite 250
City: San Bernardino
State: CA
Postal Code: 92401-1711
Office phone: (909) 889-9666
Publication Website: https://www.sbsun.com/
General E-mail: krodriguez@scng.com
Publisher Name: Ron Hasse
Publisher Email: publisher@scng.com
Publisher Phone: (818) 713-3883

Non-Daily Newspapers in the U.S.

Editor Name: Carlos Aviles
Editor Email: caviles@scng.com
Editor Phone: (951) 368-9330
Advertising Executive Name: Kyla Rodriguez
Advertising Executive Email: krodriguez@scng.com

SAN FERNANDO

SAN FERNANDO VALLEY SUN

Street Address: 1150 San Fernando Road Suite 100
City: San Fernando
State: CA
Postal Code: 91340
Office phone: (818) 365-3111
Publication Website: www.sanfernandosun.com
General E-mail: production@sanfernandosun.com
Publisher Name: Martha Diaz Aszkenazy
Editor Name: Diana Martinez
Editor Email: editor@sanfernandosun.com

SAN FRANCISCO

SAN FRANCISCO BUSINESS TIMES

Corporate/Parent Company: American City Business Journals
Street Address: 275 Battery St. Suite 600
City: San Francisco
State: CA
Postal Code: 94111
Office phone: 415-989-2522
Publication Website: www.bizjournals.com/sanfrancisco
General E-mail: sanfrancisco@bizjournals.com
Publisher Name: Mary Huss
Publisher Email: mhuss@bizjournals.com
Publisher Phone: 415-288-4934
Editor Name: Douglas Fruehling
Editor Email: dfruehling@bizjournals.com
Editor Phone: 415-288-4910
Advertising Executive Name: Michael S. Fernald
Advertising Executive Email: mfernald@bizjournals.com

SAN JOSE

CAMBRIAN RESIDENT

Street Address: 4 N. Second Street Suite 800
City: San Jose
State: CA
Postal Code: 95113
Office phone: 408-920-5000
Publication Website: www.mercurynews.com/location/cambrian
Publisher Name: Sharon Ryan
Publisher Email: publisher@bayareanewsgroup.com
Editor Name: Frank Pine
Editor Email: editor@bayareanewsgroup.com
Editor Phone: 408-920-5456

LOS GATOS WEEKLY-TIMES

Street Address: 4 N 2ND ST STE 800
City: SAN JOSE
State: CA
Postal Code: 95113
Office phone: 408-920-5000
Publication Website: www.mercurynews.com/location/los-gatos
Publisher Name: Sharon Ryan
Publisher Email: publisher@bayareanewsgroup.com
Editor Name: Frank Pine
Editor Email: editor@bayareanewsgroup.com
Editor Phone: 408-920-5456

METRO SILICON VALLEY

Corporate/Parent Company: Metro Newspapers
Street Address: 380 S 1ST ST
City: SAN JOSE
State: CA
Postal Code: 95113
Office phone: 408-298-8000
Publication Website: www.metrosiliconvalley.com
Editor Name: Dan Pulcrano
Editor Email: editor@metronews.com

OAKLAND TRIBUNE

Corporate/Parent Company: Media News Group
Street Address: 1095 THE ALAMEDA
City: SAN JOSE
State: CA
Postal Code: 95126
Office phone: 510-208-6450
Publication Website: www.eastbaytimes.com/location/oakland
Publisher Name: Sharon Ryan
Publisher Email: publisher@bayareanewsgroup.com
Editor Name: Frank Pine
Editor Email: editor@bayareanewsgroup.com
Editor Phone: 408-920-5456

SILICON VALLEY BUSINESS JOURNAL

Corporate/Parent Company: American City Business Journals
Street Address: 50 West San Fernando St Suite 425
City: San Jose
State: CA
Postal Code: 95113
Office phone: 408-295-3800
Publication Website: www.bizjournals.com/sanjose
General E-mail: sanjose@bizjournals.com
Publisher Name: Mary Huss
Publisher Email: mhuss@bizjournals.com
Editor Name: J. Jennings Moss
Editor Email: jmoss@bizjournals.com
Editor Phone: 408-299-1828
Advertising Executive Name: Jay Jensky
Advertising Executive Email: jjensky@bizjournals.com

THE DAILY REVIEW

Street Address: 1095 THE ALAMEDA
City: SAN JOSE
State: CA
Postal Code: 95126
Office phone: 925-935-2525
Publication Website: www.eastbaytimes.com/location/hayward
Publisher Name: Sharon Ryan
Publisher Email: publisher@bayareanewsgroup.com
Editor Name: Frank Pine
Editor Email: editor@bayareanewsgroup.com
Editor Phone: 408-920-5456

THE SUNNYVALE SUN

Street Address: 4 North 2nd Street, 8th Floor
City: San Jose
State: CA
Postal Code: 95126-3142
Office phone: (408) 200-1053
Publication Website: https://www.mercurynews.com/location/sunnyvale
General E-mail: local@bayareanewsgroup.com
Publisher Name: Sharon Ryan
Publisher Email: publisher@bayareanewsgroup.com
Editor Name: Randall Keith
Editor Email: rkeith@bayareanewsgroup.com
Editor Phone: (408) 271-3747
Advertising Executive Name: Michael Turpin
Advertising Executive Email: mturpin@bayareanewsgroup.com

WILLOW GLEN RESIDENT

Street Address: 4 N. Second Street Suite 800
City: San Jose
State: CA
Postal Code: 95113
Office phone: 408-920-5000
Publication Website: www.mercurynews.com/location/willow-glen
Publisher Name: Sharon Ryan
Publisher Email: publisher@bayareanewsgroup.com
Editor Name: Frank Pine
Editor Email: editor@bayareanewsgroup.com
Editor Phone: 408-920-5456

SAN LEANDRO

CASTRO VALLEY FORUM

Corporate/Parent Company: East Bay Publishing
Street Address: 2060 Washington Avenue
City: San Leandro
State: CA
Postal Code: 94577
Office phone: 510-614-1555
Publication Website: www.castrovalleyforum.com
Publisher Name: Fred Zehnder
Publisher Email: fredz@ebpublishing.com
Advertising Executive Name: Claudette Morrison
Advertising Executive Email: claudettem@ebpublishing.com

SAN LEANDRO TIMES

Corporate/Parent Company: East Bay Publishing
Street Address: 2060 Washington Avenue
City: San Leandro
State: CA
Postal Code: 94577
Office phone: 510-614-1555
Publication Website: www.sanleandrotimes.com
Editor Name: Jim Knowles
Editor Email: jimk@ebpublishing.com
Editor Phone: 510-614-1557

SAN LUIS OBISPO

THE TRIBUNE

Corporate/Parent Company: AIM Media
Street Address: 735 Tank Farm Road Suite 220
City: San Luis Obispo
State: CA
Postal Code: 93401-7438
Office phone: (805) 781-7800
Publication Website: https://www.sanluisobispo.com/
General E-mail: newsroom@thetribunenews.com
Publisher Name: Tim Ritchey
Publisher Email: tritchey@fresnobee.com
Editor Name: Joe Tarica
Editor Email: jtarica@thetribunenews.com
Editor Phone: (805) 781-7911
Advertising Executive Name: Jane Durand
Advertising Executive Email: ttlegals@thetribunenews.com

SAN MARINO

SAN MARINO TRIBUNE

Street Address: 2650 Mission Street, Suite 208
City: San Marino
State: CA
Postal Code: 91108
Office phone: (626) 792-NEWS
Publication Website: www.sanmarinotribune.com
General E-mail: events@sanmarinotribune.com
Publisher Name: Chuck Champion
Editor Name: Mitch Lehman
Editor Email: mrenn@sanmarinotribune.com
Editor Phone: (626) 792-6397 x1008
Advertising Executive Name: Joelle Conzonire Grossi
Advertising Executive Email: jgrossi@sanmarinotribune.com

SAN QUENTIN

SAN QUENTIN NEWS

Street Address: 1 MAIN ST
City: SAN QUENTIN
State: CA
Postal Code: 94964
Office phone: (415) 454-1460
Publication Website: sanquentinnews.com
Editor Name: Marcus Henderson

SANTA BARBARA

VOICE MAGAZINE

Street Address: 924 ANACAPA ST STE B1F
City: SANTA BARBARA
State: CA
Postal Code: 93101
Office phone: 805-965-6448
Publication Website: www.casasb.com
General E-mail: news@voicesb.com
Publisher Name: Mark Whitehurst
Publisher Email: publisher@voicesb.com
Editor Name: Kerry Methner
Editor Email: editor@voicesb.com

SANTA CLARA

SANTA CLARA WEEKLY

Street Address: 3000 Scott Blvd, Suite 105
City: Santa Clara
State: CA
Postal Code: 95054
Office phone: 408-243-2000
Publication Website: www.svvoice.com
General E-mail: info@svvoice.com
Editor Name: Alissa Soroten

SANTA CRUZ

GOOD TIMES

Street Address: 107 Dakota Avenue
City: Santa Cruz
State: CA
Postal Code: 95060
Office phone: 831.458.1100
Publication Website: goodtimes.sc
General E-mail: Letters@GoodTimes.SC
Publisher Name: Dan Pulcrano
Editor Name: Steve Palopoli
Editor Email: steve@goodtimes.sc
Advertising Executive Name: Debra Whizin

SANTA CRUZ GOOD TIMES

Corporate/Parent Company: Nuz, Inc
Street Address: 107 Dakota Avenue
City: Santa Cruz
State: CA
Postal Code: 95060-3936
Office phone: (831) 458-1100
Publication Website: http://goodtimes.sc/contact-good-times-santacruz-com/
General E-mail: debra@goodtimes.sc
Publisher Name: Dan Pulcrano
Editor Name: Alisha Green
Editor Email: alisha@goodtimes.sc
Advertising Executive Name: Debra Whizin
Advertising Executive Email: debra@goodtimes.sc

SANTA ROSA

BOHEMIAN

Corporate/Parent Company: Metro News
Street Address: 847 Fifth St
City: Santa Rosa
State: CA
Postal Code: 95404
Office phone: 707.527.1200
Publication Website: www.bohemian.com
Publisher Name: Rosemary Olson
Publisher Phone: ext. 201
Editor Name: Gary Brandt
Editor Email: editor@bohemian.com
Editor Phone: ext. 250
Advertising Executive Name: Lisa Santos

SEAL BEACH

EVENT-NEWS ENTERPRISE

Street Address: 216 Main Street
City: Seal Beach
State: CA
Postal Code: 90740
Office phone: 562-431-1397
Publication Website: event-newsenterprise.com
General E-mail: info@event-newsenterprise.com
Publisher Name: Steven Remery
Publisher Email: publisher@localnewspapers.org
Publisher Phone: (562) 431-1397
Editor Name: David Young
Editor Email: editor@event-newsenterprise.com
Editor Phone: (562) 251-6628

SUN NEWSPAPERS

Corporate/Parent Company: Advance Newspapers
Street Address: 216 Main Street
City: Seal Beach
State: CA
Postal Code: 90740
Office phone: 562-430-7555
Publication Website: www.sunnews.org
General E-mail: info@sunnews.org
Publisher Name: Steven Remery
Publisher Email: publisher@localnewspapers.org
Publisher Phone: (562) 430-7555 ext. 510
Editor Name: Ted Apodaca
Editor Email: editor@sunnews.org
Editor Phone: (562) 317-1100
Advertising Executive Name: Carlos Munoz
Advertising Executive Email: carlos@sunnews.org

SHAFTER

WASCO TRIBUNE

Corporate/Parent Company: Shafter-Wasco Publishing LLC
Street Address: P.O. Box 789
City: Shafter
State: CA
Postal Code: 93263
Office phone: (661) 292-5100
Publication Website: www.wascotrib.com
General E-mail: info@WascoTrib.com
Editor Name: Toni DeRosa

SHASTA LAKE

SHASTA LAKE BULLETIN

Street Address: PO Box 8025 4138 Ashby Court
City: Shasta Lake
State: CA
Postal Code: 96019
Office phone: 530-275-1716
Publication Website: northstate.news
General E-mail: slb@shasta.com
Editor Name: Ron Harrington

SHINGLETOWN

THE RIDGE RIDER NEWS

Street Address: PO Box 210
City: Shingletown
State: CA
Postal Code: 96088-0210
Office phone: 530-474-3434
Publication Website: shingletownridgeridernews.com
Editor Name: Diana Robanske
Editor Email: editor@shingletownridgerider.com

SIGNAL HILL

SIGNAL TRIBUNE

Street Address: 1399 E. 28th Street
City: Signal Hill
State: CA
Postal Code: 90755
Office phone: (562) 595-7900
Publication Website: www.signaltribune.com
General E-mail: newspaper@signaltribune.com
Editor Name: Sebastian Echeverry

SOLVANG

SANTA YNEZ VALLEY STAR

Street Address: 423 2ND ST
City: SOLVANG
State: CA
Postal Code: 93463
Office phone: 805-350-8786
Publication Website: www.santaynezvalleystar.com
Publisher Name: Raiza Giorgi
Publisher Email: news@santaynezvalleystar.com
Editor Name: Dave Bemis
Editor Email: news@santaynezvalleystar.com
Advertising Executive Name: Jen Trupiano
Advertising Executive Email: ads@santaynezvalleystar.com

SONOMA

WINE COUNTRY THIS WEEK

Corporate/Parent Company: Brehm Communications, Inc.
Street Address: 669 Broadway, Suite B
City: Sonoma
State: CA
Postal Code: 95476-7085
Office phone: (707) 938-3494
Publication Website: http://www.winecountrythisweek.com/
General E-mail: chandra@winecountrythisweek.com
Publisher Name: Chandra Grant
Publisher Email: chandra@winecountrythisweek.com
Publisher Phone: (707) 938-1783

SUSANVILLE

LASSEN COUNTY TIMES

Corporate/Parent Company: Feather Publishing Co., Inc.
Street Address: 100 Grand Ave
City: Susanville
State: CA
Postal Code: 96130-4451
Office phone: (530) 257-5321
Publication Website: http://www.lassennews.com/
General E-mail: info@lassennews.com
Publisher Name: Mike Taborski
Editor Name: Debra Moore

WESTWOOD PINEPRESS

Corporate/Parent Company: Feather Publishing Co., Inc.
Street Address: 100 Grand Ave
City: Susanville
State: CA
Postal Code: 96130-4451
Office phone: (530) 257-5321
Publication Website: http://www.lassennews.com/
General E-mail: info@lassennews.com
Publisher Name: Mike Taborski
Editor Name: Debra Moore

TAFT

TAFT MIDWAY DRILLER

Street Address: 800 Center St.
City: Taft
State: CA
Postal Code: 93268
Office phone: (661) 763-3171
Publication Website: www.taftmidwaydriller.com
Publisher Name: John Watkins
Publisher Email: jwatkins@ridgecrestca.com
Publisher Phone: (760) 375-4481
Editor Name: Doug Keeler
Editor Email: dkeeler@taftmidwaydriller.com
Advertising Executive Name: Christine Thompson
Advertising Executive Email: cthompson@taftmidwaydriller.com

THREE RIVERS

THE KAWEAH COMMONWEALTH

Street Address: 41841 Sierra Dr
City: Three Rivers
State: CA
Postal Code: 93271
Office phone: 559-561-3627
Publication Website: www.kaweahcommonwealth.com
General E-mail: info@3riversnews.com
Editor Name: Sarah Elliott
Editor Email: sarah@3riversnews.com

TORRANCE

DAILY BREEZE

Corporate/Parent Company: Media News Group
Street Address: 21250 Hawthorne Blvd
City: Torrance
State: CA
Postal Code: 90503-5514
Office phone: (310) 540-5511
Publication Website: https://www.dailybreeze.com/
General E-mail: krodriguez@scng.com
Publisher Name: Ron Hasse
Publisher Email: publisher@scng.com
Publisher Phone: (818) 713-3883
Editor Name: Carlos Aviles
Editor Email: caviles@scng.com
Editor Phone: (951) 368-9330
Advertising Executive Name: Kyla Rodriguez
Advertising Executive Email: krodriguez@scng.com

PASADENA STAR-NEWS

Corporate/Parent Company: Media News Group
Street Address: 21250 Hawthorne Blvd
City: Torrance
State: CA
Postal Code: 90503-5514
Office phone: (310) 543-6110
Publication Website: https://www.pasadenastarnews.com/
General E-mail: krodriguez@scng.com
Publisher Name: Ron Hasse
Publisher Email: publisher@scng.com
Publisher Phone: (818) 713-3883
Editor Name: Carlos Aviles
Editor Email: caviles@scng.com
Editor Phone: (951) 368-9330
Advertising Executive Name: Kyla Rodriguez
Advertising Executive Email: krodriguez@scng.com

TWENTYNINE PALMS

DESERT TRAIL

Corporate/Parent Company: Brehm Communications Inc.
Street Address: 6396 Adobe Rd
City: Twentynine Palms
State: CA
Postal Code: 92277-2648
Office phone: (760) 367-3577
Publication Website: http://www.hidesertstar.com/the_desert_trail/
General E-mail: news@deserttrail.com
Publisher Name: Cindy Melland
Publisher Email: cmelland@hidesertstar.com
Publisher Phone: (760) 365-3315
Editor Name: Kurt Schauppner
Editor Email: kurts@thedeserttrail.com
Editor Phone: (760) 257-2751, ext : 25

VALLEJO

TIMES-HERALD

Street Address: 420 Virginia St., Ste. 2A
City: Vallejo
State: CA
Postal Code: 94590
Office phone: (707) 644-1141
Publication Website: www.timesheraldonline.com
Publisher Name: Jim Gleim
Publisher Email: jgleim@bayareanewsgroup.com
Publisher Phone: (707) 453-8189
Editor Name: Jack Bungart
Editor Email: jbungart@timesheraldonline.com
Editor Phone: (707) 553-6827
Advertising Executive Name: Shawna Gilroy
Advertising Executive Email: sgilroy@timesheraldonline.com

WALNUT CREEK

ANTIOCH NEWS

Street Address: 2850 Shadelands Dr Suite 101
City: Walnut Creek
State: CA
Postal Code: 94598
Office phone: 510-208-6450
Publication Website: www.eastbaytimes.com/locationtioch
Publisher Name: Sharon Ryan
Publisher Email: publisher@bayareanewsgroup.com
Editor Name: Frank Pine
Editor Email: editor@bayareanewsgroup.com
Editor Phone: 408-920-5456

CONCORD TRANSCRIPT

Street Address: 2850 Shadelands Dr Suite 101
City: Walnut Creek
State: CA
Postal Code: 94598
Office phone: 510-208-6450
Publication Website: www.contracostatimes.com
Publisher Name: Sharon Ryan
Publisher Email: publisher@bayareanewsgroup.com
Editor Name: Frank Pine
Editor Email: editor@bayareanewsgroup.com
Editor Phone: 408-920-5456

OAKLEY NEWS

Street Address: 175 LENNON LN STE 100
City: WALNUT CREEK
State: CA
Postal Code: 94598

Non-Daily Newspapers in the U.S.

Office phone: 510-208-6450
Publication Website: www.eastbaytimes.com/location/oakley
Publisher Name: Sharon Ryan
Publisher Email: publisher@bayareanewsgroup.com
Editor Name: Frank Pine
Editor Email: editor@bayareanewsgroup.com
Editor Phone: 408-920-5456

PITTSBURG NEWS

Street Address: 175 LENNON LN STE 100
City: WALNUT CREEK
State: CA
Postal Code: 94598
Office phone: 925-935-2525
Publication Website: www.eastbaytimes.com/location/pittsburg
Publisher Name: Sharon Ryan
Publisher Email: publisher@bayareanewsgroup.com
Editor Name: Frank Pine
Editor Email: editor@bayareanewsgroup.com
Editor Phone: 408-920-5456

PLEASANT HILL-MARTINEZ RECORD

Street Address: 175 LENNON LN STE 100
City: WALNUT CREEK
State: CA
Postal Code: 94598
Office phone: 925-935-2525
Publication Website: www.contracostatimes.com
Publisher Name: Sharon Ryan
Publisher Email: publisher@bayareanewsgroup.com
Editor Name: Frank Pine
Editor Email: editor@bayareanewsgroup.com
Editor Phone: 408-920-5456

VALLEY JOURNAL

Street Address: 175 LENNON LN STE 100
City: "WALNUT CREEK "
State: CA
Postal Code: 94598
Office phone: 925-935-2525
Publication Website: www.eastbaytimes.com/location/san-ramon
Publisher Name: Sharon Ryan
Publisher Email: publisher@bayareanewsgroup.com
Editor Name: Frank Pine
Editor Email: editor@bayareanewsgroup.com
Editor Phone: 408-920-5456

WALNUT CREEK JOURNAL

Street Address: 175 LENNON LN STE 100
City: "WALNUT CREEK "
State: CA
Postal Code: 94598
Office phone: 925-935-2525
Publication Website: www.contracostatimes.com
Publisher Name: Sharon Ryan
Publisher Email: publisher@bayareanewsgroup.com
Editor Name: Frank Pine
Editor Email: editor@bayareanewsgroup.com
Editor Phone: 408-920-5456

WATERFORD

WATERFORD NEWS

Corporate/Parent Company: Mid-Valley Publications
Street Address: 12717 Bentley St
City: Waterford
State: CA
Postal Code: 95386-9012
Office phone: (209) 874-1927
Publication Website: https://waterfordnews.weebly.com/
General E-mail: info@midvalleypub.com
Publisher Name: John Derby
Editor Name: Wendy Krier
Editor Email: wendyk@midvalleypub.com
Editor Phone: (209) 874-1927
Advertising Executive Name: Wendy Krier
Advertising Executive Email: wendyk@midvalleypub.com

WEST SACRAMENTO

WEST SACRAMENTO NEWS-LEDGER

Corporate/Parent Company: The News-Ledger, LLC
Street Address: 1040 W. Capitol Avenue, Suite B
City: West Sacramento
State: CA
Postal Code: 95691
Office phone: (916) 371-8030
Publication Website: www.news-ledger.com
Editor Name: Monica Stark
Editor Email: editor@news-ledger.com

WINTERS

WINTERS EXPRESS

Corporate/Parent Company: McNaughton Newspapers, Inc.
Street Address: 203 1st Street
City: Winters
State: CA
Postal Code: 95694-1730
Office phone: (530) 795-4551
Publication Website: https://www.wintersexpress.com/
General E-mail: ads@wintersexpress.com
Publisher Name: Taylor Buley
Publisher Email: taylor@wintersexpress.com
Editor Name: Crystal Apilado
Editor Email: crystal@wintersexpress.com
Advertising Executive Email: ads@wintersexpress.com

WINTON

ATWATER-WINTON TIMES

Corporate/Parent Company: Mid-Valley Publications
Street Address: 6950 Gerard Ave. • P. O. Box 65
City: Winton
State: CA
Postal Code: 95388
Office phone: 209 358 5311
Publication Website: www.mercedcountytimes.net
General E-mail: Info@MidValleyPub.com
Editor Name: John Whitaker
Editor Email: JohnWhitaker@MidValleyPub.com
Editor Phone: 209 383 0433
Advertising Executive Name: Gwen Emens
Advertising Executive Email: GwenE@MidValleyPub.com

WINTON TIMES

Corporate/Parent Company: Mid-Valley Publications
Street Address: 6950 Gerard Ave
City: Winton

State: CA
Postal Code: 95388
Office phone: (209) 358-5311
Publication Website: http://www.mercedcountytimes.net/
General E-mail: info@midvalleypub.com
Publisher Name: John Whitaker
Publisher Email: johnwhitaker@midvalleypub.com
Editor Name: Wendy Krier
Editor Email: wendyk@midvalleypub.com

WOODLAND HILLS

LOS ANGELES DAILY NEWS

Corporate/Parent Company: Media News Group
Street Address: 21860 Burbank Blvd
City: Woodland Hills
State: CA
Postal Code: 91367-7439
Office phone: (818) 713-3000
Publication Website: https://www.dailynews.com/
General E-mail: krodriguez@scng.com
Publisher Name: Ron Hasse
Publisher Email: publisher@scng.com
Publisher Phone: (818) 713-3883
Editor Name: Carlos Aviles
Editor Email: caviles@scng.com
Editor Phone: (951) 368-9330
Advertising Executive Name: Kyla Rodriguez
Advertising Executive Email: krodriguez@scng.com

YUCAIPA

YUCAIPA / CALIMESA NEWS MIRROR

Corporate/Parent Company: Century Group Newspapers
Street Address: 35154 Yucaipa Blvd
City: Yucaipa
State: CA
Postal Code: 92399-4339
Office phone: (909) 797-9101
Publication Website: https://www.newsmirror.net/
General E-mail: pbunker@newsmirror.net
Publisher Name: Tim Shoffeitt
Publisher Email: tshoffiett@newsmirror.net
Editor Name: Rachael Gustuson
Editor Email: rgustuson@newsmirror.net
Advertising Executive Name: Pamela Bunker
Advertising Executive Email: pbunker@newsmirror.net

YUCCA VALLEY

DESERT MOBILE HOME NEWS

Corporate/Parent Company: Brehm Communications, Inc.
Street Address: 56445 29 PALMS HWY
City: YUCCA VALLEY
State: CA
Postal Code: 92284
Office phone: 760-820-2610
Publication Website: www.desertmobilehomenews.com
General E-mail: news@desertmobilehomenews.com

HI-DESERT STAR

Corporate/Parent Company: Brehm Communications Inc.
Street Address: 56445 29 Palms Hwy
City: Yucca Valley
State: CA
Postal Code: 92284-2861
Office phone: (760) 365-3315
Publication Website: http://www.hidesertstar.com/site/contact_the_hi-desert_star.html
General E-mail: advertising@hidesertstar.com
Publisher Name: Cindy Melland

Publisher Email: cmelland@hidesertstar.com
Publisher Phone: (760) 257-5582
Editor Name: Stacy Moore
Editor Email: editor@hidesertstar.com
Editor Phone: (760) 820-2385
Advertising Executive Name: Kim Brucks
Advertising Executive Email: advertising@hidesertstar.com

OBSERVATION POST

Corporate/Parent Company: Brehm Communications, Inc.
Street Address: 56445 29 Palms Hwy
City: Yucca Valley
State: CA
Postal Code: 92284-2861
Office phone: (760) 365-3315
Publication Website: http://www.hidesertstar.com/observation_post/
General E-mail: editor@hidesertstar.com
Publisher Name: Cindy Melland
Publisher Email: cmelland@hidesertstar.com
Publisher Phone: (760) 257-5582
Editor Name: Stacy Moore
Editor Email: editor@hidesertstar.com
Editor Phone: (760) 820-2385
Advertising Executive Name: Kim Brucks
Advertising Executive Email: advertising@hidesertstar.com

COLORADO

ASPEN

ASPEN JOURNALISM

Street Address: P.O. Box 10101
City: Aspen
State: CO
Postal Code: 81612-7313
Office phone: 970 948 1930
Publication Website: www.aspenjournalism.org
General E-mail: info@aspenjournalism.org

ASPEN TIMES-WEEKLY

Street Address: 314 E. Hyman Avenue
City: Aspen
State: CO
Postal Code: 81611
Office phone: 970-925-3414
Publication Website: www.aspentimes.com

BAILEY

PARK COUNTY REPUBLICAN & FAIRPLAY FLUME

Street Address: 5138 CO RD 64 / P.O. Box 460
City: Bailey
State: CO
Postal Code: 80421
Office phone: 303-838-4423
Publication Website: www.theflume.com
General E-mail: info@theflume.com

BERTHOUD

BERTHOUD WEEKLY SURVEYOR

Street Address: 440 Mountain Avenue
City: Berthoud
State: CO
Postal Code: 80513
Office phone: 970-532-2252
Publication Website: www.berthoudsurveyor.com

BLACK HAWK

WEEKLY REGISTER-CALL
Street Address: PO Box 93
City: Black Hawk
State: CO
Postal Code: 80422
Office phone: 303-582-0133
Publication Website: www.weeklyregistercall.com

BOULDER

BIZWEST
Corporate/Parent Company: BizWest Media LLC
Street Address: 1600 Range St.
City: Boulder
State: CO
Postal Code: 80308
Office phone: (303) 440-4950
Publication Website: http://bizwest.com/
General E-mail: jnuttall@bizwest.com

CASTLE PINES

CASTLE PINES CONNECTION
Street Address: 7437 Village Square Drive, Suite 220
City: Castle Pines
State: CO
Postal Code: 80108
Office phone: 303-785-6520
Publication Website: www.castlepinesconnection.com

COLORADO CITY

GREENHORN VALLEY VIEW NEWSPAPER
Street Address: 4491 Bent Brothers Blvd
City: Colorado City
State: CO
Postal Code: 81019
Office phone: 719-676-3401
Publication Website: www.greenhornvalleyview.com

COLORADO SPRINGS

PIKES PEAK BULLETIN
Street Address: P.O. Box 50125
City: Colorado Springs
State: CO
Postal Code: 80949
Office phone: (719) 418-2717
Publication Website: www.pikespeakpublishing.com

CORTEZ

THE JOURNAL
Corporate/Parent Company: Ballantine Communications, Inc.
Street Address: 8 W Main St
City: Cortez
State: CO
Postal Code: 81321
Office phone: 970-565-8527
Publication Website: the-journal.com
General E-mail: news@the-journal.com

DELTA

DELTA COUNTY INDEPENDENT
Corporate/Parent Company: Wick Communications
Street Address: 401 Meeker Street
City: Delta
State: CO
Postal Code: 81416
Office phone: (970) 874-4421
Publication Website: www.deltacountyindependent.com
General E-mail: editor@deltacountyindependent.com

DENVER

COLORADO POLITICS
Street Address: 555 17th St
City: Denver
State: CO
Postal Code: 80202
Office phone: 303-837-8600
Publication Website: coloradopolitics.com
General E-mail: news@coloradopolitics.com

GLENDALE CHERRY CREEK CHRONICLE
Street Address: 945 S Birch St
City: Denver
State: CO
Postal Code: 80246
Office phone: 303-312-1808
Publication Website: www.glendalecherrycreek.com

GREATER PARK HILL NEWS
Street Address: 2823 Fairfax St
City: Denver
State: CO
Postal Code: 80207
Office phone: 303-388-0918
Publication Website: greaterparkhill.org/newspaper
General E-mail: newspaper@greaterparkhill.org

DOVE CREEK

DOVE CREEK PRESS
Street Address: PO Box 598 321 Main St.
City: Dove Creek
State: CO
Postal Code: 81324
Office phone: 970-677-2214
Publication Website: www.dovecreekpress.com

ENGLEWOOD

ARVADA PRESS
Corporate/Parent Company: Colorado Community Media
Street Address: 750 W. Hampden Ave., Suite 225
City: Englewood
State: CO
Postal Code: 80110
Office phone: (303) 566-4100
Publication Website: http://arvadapress.com/
General E-mail: circulation@coloradocommunitymedia.com

CASTLE ROCK NEWS-PRESS
Corporate/Parent Company: Colorado Community Media
Street Address: 750 W. Hampden Avenue Suite #225
City: Englewood
State: CO
Postal Code: 80110
Office phone: 1-303-566-4100
Publication Website: castlerocknewspress.net
General E-mail: letters@coloradocommunitymedia.com

CENTENNIAL CITIZEN
Corporate/Parent Company: Colorado Community Media
Street Address: 750 W. Hampden Ave., Suite 225
City: Englewood
State: CO
Postal Code: 80110
Office phone: (303) 566-4100
Publication Website: http://centennialcitizen.net/
General E-mail: circulation@coloradocommunitymedia.com

DENVER HERALD-DISPATCH
Corporate/Parent Company: Colorado Community Media
Street Address: 750 W. Hampden Avenue Suite #225
City: Englewood
State: CO
Postal Code: 80110
Office phone: 303.566.4100
Publication Website: denverherald.net
General E-mail: letters@coloradocommunitymedia.com

DOUGLAS COUNTY NEWS PRESS
Corporate/Parent Company: Colorado Community Media
Street Address: 750 W. Hampden Ave., Suite 225
City: Englewood
State: CO
Postal Code: 80110
Office phone: (303) 566-4100
Publication Website: http://douglascountynewspress.net/
General E-mail: circulation@coloradocommunitymedia.com

ENGLEWOOD HERALD
Corporate/Parent Company: Colorado Community Media
Street Address: 750 W. Hampden Avenue Suite #225
City: Englewood
State: CO
Postal Code: 80110
Office phone: 303.566.4100
Publication Website: englewoodherald.net
General E-mail: letters@coloradocommunitymedia.com

HIGHLANDS RANCH HERALD
Corporate/Parent Company: Colorado Community Media
Street Address: 750 W. Hampden Ave., Suite 225
City: Englewood
State: CO
Postal Code: 80110
Office phone: (303) 566-4100
Publication Website: https://highlandsranchherald.net/
General E-mail: circulation@coloradocommunitymedia.com

LAKEWOOD SENTINEL
Corporate/Parent Company: Colorado Community Media
Street Address: 750 W. Hampden Avenue, Suite #225
City: Englewood
State: CO
Postal Code: 80110
Office phone: (303) 566-4100
Publication Website: http://lakewoodsentinel.com/
General E-mail: circulation@coloradocommunitymedia.com

LIFE ON CAPITOL HILL
Corporate/Parent Company: Colorado Community Media
Street Address: 750 W. Hampden Avenue Suite #225
City: Englewood
State: CO
Postal Code: 80110
Office phone: 303.566.4100
Publication Website: lifeoncaphill.com
General E-mail: letters@coloradocommunitymedia.com

LITTLETON INDEPENDENT
Corporate/Parent Company: Colorado Community Media
Street Address: 750 W. Hampden Avenue Suite #225
City: Englewood
State: CO
Postal Code: 80110
Office phone: 303.566.4100
Publication Website: littletonindependent.net
General E-mail: letters@coloradocommunitymedia.com

LONE TREE VOICE
Corporate/Parent Company: Colorado Community Media
Street Address: 750 W. Hampden Ave., Suite 225
City: Englewood
State: CO
Postal Code: 80110
Office phone: (303) 566-4100
Publication Website: http://lonetreevoice.net/
General E-mail: circulation@coloradocommunitymedia.com

NORTHGLENN-THORNTON SENTINEL
Corporate/Parent Company: Colorado Community Media
Street Address: 750 W. Hampden Avenue, Suite #225
City: Englewood
State: CO
Postal Code: 80110
Office phone: (303) 566-4100
Publication Website: http://northglenn-thorntonsentinel.com/
General E-mail: circulation@coloradocommunitymedia.com

PARKER CHRONICLE
Corporate/Parent Company: Colorado Community Media
Street Address: 750 W. Hampden Ave., Suite 225
City: Englewood
State: CO
Postal Code: 80110

Non-Daily Newspapers in the U.S.

Office phone: (303) 566-4100
Publication Website: http://parkerchronicle.net/
General E-mail: circulation@coloradocommunitymedia.com

SOUTH PLATTE INDEPENDENT
Corporate/Parent Company: Colorado Community Media
Street Address: 750 W. Hampden Ave., Suite 225
City: Englewood
State: CO
Postal Code: 80110
Office phone: (303) 566-4100
Publication Website: http://southplatteindependent.net/
General E-mail: circulation@coloradocommunitymedia.com

THE ENGLEWOOD HERALD
Corporate/Parent Company: Colorado Community Media
Street Address: 750 W. Hampden Avenue, Suite #225
City: Englewood
State: CO
Postal Code: 80110
Office phone: (303) 566-4100
Publication Website: http://englewoodherald.net/
General E-mail: circulation@coloradocommunitymedia.com

WASHINGTON PARK PROFILE
Corporate/Parent Company: Colorado Community Media
Street Address: 750 W. Hampden Avenue Suite #225
City: Englewood
State: CO
Postal Code: 80110
Office phone: 303.566.4100
Publication Website: washparkprofile.com
General E-mail: letters@coloradocommunitymedia.com

WESTMINSTER WINDOW
Corporate/Parent Company: Colorado Community Media
Street Address: 750 W. Hampden Ave., Suite 225
City: Englewood
State: CO
Postal Code: 80110
Office phone: (303) 566-4100
Publication Website: https://westminsterwindow.com/
General E-mail: circulation@coloradocommunitymedia.com

WHEAT RIDGE TRANSCRIPT
Corporate/Parent Company: Colorado Community Media
Street Address: 750 W. Hampden Avenue Suite #225
City: Englewood
State: CO
Postal Code: 80110
Office phone: 303.566.4100
Publication Website: wheatridgetranscript.com
General E-mail: letters@coloradocommunitymedia.com

EVERGREEN

CANYON COURIER
Corporate/Parent Company: Landmark Community Newspapers
Street Address: 27972 Meadow Drive, Suite 320
City: Evergreen
State: CO
Postal Code: 80439
Office phone: 303-674-5534
Publication Website: www.canyoncourier.com

FORT COLLINS

NORTH FORTY NEWS
Street Address: 2601 Lemay, Ste 7, PMB 227
City: Fort Collins
State: CO
Postal Code: 80525
Office phone: 970-221-0213
Publication Website: northforty.news
General E-mail: info@northfortynews.com

GOLDEN

GOLDEN TRANSCRIPT
Corporate/Parent Company: Milehigh Newspapers
Street Address: 1000 10th St.
City: Golden
State: CO
Postal Code: 80401
Office phone: (303) 279-5541
Publication Website: http://www.goldentranscript.com/
General E-mail: newsroom@jeffconews.com

GREELEY

FENCE POST
Corporate/Parent Company: Swift Communications
Street Address: 501 8th Avenue / PO Box 1690
City: Greeley
State: CO
Postal Code: 80631
Office phone: 970-686-5691
Publication Website: www.thefencepost.com

GREENWOOD VILLAGE

THE VILLAGER
Street Address: 8933 E Union Ave, Ste 230
City: Greenwood Village
State: CO
Postal Code: 80111
Office phone: 303-773-8313
Publication Website: www.villagerpublishing.com
General E-mail: editorial@villagerpublishing.com

IGNACIO

SOUTHERN UTE DRUM
Corporate/Parent Company: Southern Ute Indian Tribe
Street Address: 356 Ouray Drive PO Box 737 #96
City: Ignacio
State: CO
Postal Code: 81137
Office phone: 970-563-0118
Publication Website: www.sudrum.com

KEENESBURG

CARBON VALLEY INDEPENDENT
Street Address: 105 Woodward Avenue
City: Keenesburg
State: CO
Postal Code: 80643
Office phone: 303-833-5997
Publication Website: carbonvinews.com

LOST CREEK GUIDE
Street Address: 105 Woodward Ave.
City: Keenesburg
State: CO
Postal Code: 80643
Office phone: 303-732-4080
Publication Website: lcgnews.com

KREMMLING

GRAND GAZETTE
Street Address: 116 North 3rd St
City: Kremmling
State: CO
Postal Code: 80459
Office phone: (970) 724-8977
Publication Website: grandgazette.net
General E-mail: gazetteeditor@outlook.com

LAKE CITY

LAKE CITY SILVER WORLD
Street Address: Post Office Box 100
City: Lake City
State: CO
Postal Code: 81235
Office phone: 970-944-2515
Publication Website: www.lakecitysilverworld.com

LYONS

REDSTONE REVIEW
Street Address: P.O. BOX 68
City: LYONS
State: CO
Postal Code: 80540
Publication Website: issuu.com/sdcmc
General E-mail: redstonereviewads@gmail.com

MONUMENT

THE TRIBUNE
Corporate/Parent Company: AIM Media
Street Address: 153 Washington St
City: Monument
State: CO
Postal Code: 80132-9181
Office phone: (719) 476-1618
Publication Website: https://gazette.com/thetribune/
General E-mail: michelle.karas@pikespeaknewspapers.com

NEDERLAND

MOUNTAIN-EAR
Street Address: P.O. Box 99
City: Nederland
State: CO
Postal Code: 80466
Office phone: 303-810-5409
Publication Website: www.themtnear.com

NIWOT

LEFT HAND VALLEY COURIER
Street Address: P.O. Box 652
City: Niwot
State: CO
Postal Code: 80544
Office phone: (303) 845-3077
Publication Website: www.lhvc.com
General E-mail: editorial@lhvc.com

OTIS

OTIS TELEGRAPH
Street Address: P.O. Box 12
City: Otis
State: CO
Postal Code: 80743
Office phone: (970) 246-3355
Publication Website: www.otistelegraph.com
General E-mail: telegraph@centurytel.net

RIDGWAY

OURAY COUNTY PLAINDEALER
Street Address: 1075 Sherman St., #210 PO Box 529
City: Ridgway
State: CO
Postal Code: 81432
Office phone: 970-325-4412
Publication Website: www.ouraynews.com

RIFLE

CITIZEN TELEGRAM
Corporate/Parent Company: Swift Communications
Street Address: 111 E. Third St., Ste. 219
City: Rifle
State: CO
Postal Code: 81650
Office phone: 970-625-3245
Publication Website: www.citizentelegram.com
General E-mail: editorial@citizentelegram.com

STERLING

SOUTH PLATTE SENTINEL
Corporate/Parent Company: Digital First Media
Street Address: 100 Broadway, Ste. 25
City: Sterling
State: CO
Postal Code: 80751
Office phone: 970-526-9297
Publication Website: www.southplattesentinel.com
General E-mail: cjones@journal-advocate.com

STRASBURG

I-70 SCOUT
Street Address: P.O. Box 829
City: Strasburg
State: CO
Postal Code: 80136
Office phone: (303) 622-9796
Publication Website: www.i-70scout.com

WALSENBURG

WORLD JOURNAL
Street Address: 508 Main Street
City: Walsenburg
State: CO
Postal Code: 81089
Office phone: 719-738-1415
Publication Website: www.huerfanoworldjournal.com
General E-mail: editor.worldjournal@gmail.com

WHEAT RIDGE

NEIGHBORHOOD GAZETTE
Street Address: 4385 WADSWORTH BLVD
City: Wheat Ridge
State: CO
Postal Code: 80033
Office phone: 303-995-2806
Publication Website: ngazette.com
General E-mail: editor@ngazette.com

WOODLAND PARK

THE PIKES PEAK COURIER

Corporate/Parent Company: Pikes Peak Newspapers, Inc.
Street Address: P.O. Box 340
City: Woodland Park
State: CO
Postal Code: 80866
Office phone: (719) 687-3006
Publication Website: https://gazette.com/pikespeakcourier
General E-mail: michelle.karas@pikespeaknewspapers.com

CONNECTICUT

BRIDGEPORT

SHELTON HERALD

Corporate/Parent Company: HAN Network
Street Address: 1057 Broad St.
City: Bridgeport
State: CT
Postal Code: 6604
Office phone: 203-402-2332
Publication Website: www.sheltonherald.com
Editor Name: Brian Gioiele
Editor Email: editor@sheltonherald.com
Editor Phone: 203-402-2332
Advertising Executive Name: Donna Cosenza
Advertising Executive Email: dcosenza@hersamacorn.com
Advertising Executive Phone: 203-402-2327
Year Established: 1981
Delivery Methods: Mail`Newsstand
Own Printing Facility?: Y
Commercial printers?: Y
Mechanical specifications: Type page 10.75 x 21; E - 6 cols, 1 7/8, between; A - 6 cols, 1 7/8, between; C - 9 cols, 1 1/8, between.
Published Days: Wed
Avg Paid Circ: 3306
Avg Free Circ: 125
Audit Company: Sworn/Estimate/Non-Audited
Audit Date: 6 10 2019

TRUMBULL TIMES

Corporate/Parent Company: HAN Network
Street Address: 1057 Broad Street
City: Bridgeport
State: CT
Postal Code: 6604
Office phone: 203-330-6222
Publication Website: www.trumbulltimes.com
Editor Name: Donald Eng
Editor Email: deng@trumbulltimes.com
Editor Phone: 203-330-6222
Advertising Executive Name: Donna Cosenza
Advertising Executive Email: donna.cosenza@hearstmediact.com
Advertising Executive Phone: 203-842-2747
Year Established: 1959
Delivery Methods: Mail`Newsstand
Own Printing Facility?: Y
Commercial printers?: Y
Mechanical specifications: Type page 10.75 x 21; E - 6 cols, 1 7/8, between; A - 6 cols, 1 7/8, between; C - 9 cols, 1 1/8, between.
Published Days: Thur
Avg Paid Circ: 3760
Avg Free Circ: 136
Audit Company: Sworn/Estimate/Non-Audited
Audit Date: 6 10 2019

DANBURY

WILTON BULLETIN

Corporate/Parent Company: HAN Network
Street Address: 345 Main Street
City: Danbury
State: CT
Postal Code: 6877
Office phone: (203) 894-3330
Publication Website: www.wiltonbulletin.com
Editor Name: Jeannette Ross
Editor Email: editor@wiltonbulletin.com
Editor Phone: 203-731-3319
Advertising Executive Name: Charlie Howe
Advertising Executive Email: chowe@hersamacorn.com
Advertising Executive Phone: 203-966-9541, ext. 130
Year Established: 1937
Delivery Methods: Mail`Newsstand`Racks
Mechanical specifications: Type page 10.75 x 21; E - 6 cols, 1 7/8, between; A - 6 cols, 1 7/8, between; C - 9 cols, 1 1/8, between.
Published Days: Thur
Avg Paid Circ: 2527
Audit Company: Sworn/Estimate/Non-Audited
Audit Date: 6 10 2019

DARIEN

DARIEN TIMES

Corporate/Parent Company: HAN Network
Street Address: 10 Corbin Dr
City: Darien
State: CT
Postal Code: 06820-5403
Office phone: (203) 656-4230
Publication Website: www.darientimes.com
General E-mail: sports@darientimes.com
Editor Name: Susan Shultz
Editor Phone: 203-912-4564
Advertising Executive Name: Lauren Spicehandler
Advertising Executive Phone: 203-842-2734
Year Established: 1993
Delivery Methods: Mail`Newsstand
Commercial printers?: Y
Mechanical specifications: Type page 10.75 x 21; E - 6 cols, 1 7/8, between; A - 6 cols, 1 7/8, between; C - 9 cols, 1 1/8, between.
Published Days: Thur
Avg Paid Circ: 6015
Audit Company: Sworn/Estimate/Non-Audited
Audit Date: 6 10 2019

MERIDEN

BERLIN CITIZEN

Corporate/Parent Company: The Record-Journal Publishing Co.
Street Address: 500 S Broad St
City: Meriden
State: CT
Postal Code: 06450-6643
Office phone: (203) 235-1661
Publication Website: www.myrecordjournal.com/news/berlin-citizen/berlin-citizen-epaper
General E-mail: newsroom@record-journal.com
Publisher Name: Liz White Notarangelo
Publisher Email: lwhite@record-journal.com
Publisher Phone: 203-317-2226
Editor Name: Ralph Tomaselli
Editor Email: rtomaselli@record-journal.com
Editor Phone: 203-317-2220
Advertising Executive Name: Jim Mizener
Advertising Executive Email: jmizener@record-journal.com
Advertising Executive Phone: 203-317-2312
Year Established: 1997
Published Days: Thur
Avg Free Circ: 9200
Audit Company: Sworn/Estimate/Non-Audited
Audit Date: 6 10 2019

THE CHESHIRE CITIZEN

Corporate/Parent Company: The Record-Journal Publishing Co.
Street Address: 500 S Broad St
City: Meriden
State: CT
Postal Code: 06450-6643
Office phone: (203) 235-1661
Publication Website: www.myrecordjournal.com/news/cheshire-citizen/cheshire-citizen-epaper
General E-mail: newsroom@record-journal.com
Publisher Name: Liz White Notarangelo
Publisher Email: lwhite@record-journal.com
Publisher Phone: 203-317-2226
Editor Name: Ralph Tomaselli
Editor Email: rtomaselli@record-journal.com
Editor Phone: 203-317-2220
Advertising Executive Name: Jim Mizener
Advertising Executive Email: jmizener@record-journal.com
Advertising Executive Phone: 203-317-2312

THE NORTH HAVEN CITIZEN

Corporate/Parent Company: The Record-Journal Publishing Co.
Street Address: 500 S Broad St
City: Meriden
State: CT
Postal Code: 06450-6643
Office phone: (203) 235-1661
Publication Website: www.myrecordjournal.com/news/north-haven-citizen/north-haven-citizen-epaper
General E-mail: newsroom@record-journal.com
Publisher Name: Liz White Notarangelo
Publisher Email: lwhite@record-journal.com
Publisher Phone: 203-317-2226
Editor Name: Ralph Tomaselli
Editor Email: rtomaselli@record-journal.com
Editor Phone: 203-317-2220
Advertising Executive Name: Jim Mizener
Advertising Executive Email: jmizener@record-journal.com
Advertising Executive Phone: 203-317-2312

THE PLAINVILLE CITIZEN

Corporate/Parent Company: The Record-Journal Publishing Co.
Street Address: 500 S Broad St
City: Meriden
State: CT
Postal Code: 06450-6643
Office phone: (203) 235-1661
Publication Website: www.myrecordjournal.com/news/plainville-citizen/plainville-citizen-epaper
General E-mail: newsroom@record-journal.com
Publisher Name: Liz White Notarangelo
Publisher Email: lwhite@record-journal.com
Publisher Phone: 203-317-2226
Editor Name: Ralph Tomaselli
Editor Email: rtomaselli@record-journal.com
Editor Phone: 203-317-2220
Advertising Executive Name: Jim Mizener
Advertising Executive Email: jmizener@record-journal.com
Advertising Executive Phone: 203-317-2312
Year Established: 2002
Own Printing Facility?: Y
Published Days: Thur
Avg Free Circ: 9200
Audit Company: Sworn/Estimate/Non-Audited
Audit Date: 6 10 2019

THE SOUTHINGTON CITIZEN

Corporate/Parent Company: The Record-Journal Publishing Co.
Street Address: 500 S Broad St
City: Meriden
State: CT
Postal Code: 06450-6643
Office phone: (203) 235-1661
Publication Website: www.myrecordjournal.com/news/southington/southington-citizen-epaper
General E-mail: newsroom@record-journal.com
Publisher Name: Liz White Notarangelo
Publisher Email: lwhite@record-journal.com
Publisher Phone: 203-317-2226
Editor Name: Ralph Tomaselli
Editor Email: rtomaselli@record-journal.com
Editor Phone: 203-317-2220
Advertising Executive Name: Jim Mizener
Advertising Executive Email: jmizener@record-journal.com
Advertising Executive Phone: 203-317-2312
Published Days: Fri
Avg Free Circ: 9800
Audit Company: Sworn/Estimate/Non-Audited
Audit Date: 6 10 2019

NEW CANAAN

NEW CANAAN ADVERTISER

Corporate/Parent Company: HAN Network
Street Address: 42 Vitti St
City: New Canaan
State: CT
Postal Code: 06840-4823
Office phone: (203) 966-9541
Publication Website: www.ncadvertiser.com
Editor Name: John Kovach
Editor Email: editor@ncadvertiser.com
Advertising Executive Name: Elizabeth Cote
Advertising Executive Email: ecote@hersamacorn.com
Advertising Executive Phone: 203-966-9541, ext. 106
Year Established: 1908
Delivery Methods: Mail`Newsstand`Racks
Own Printing Facility?: Y
Commercial printers?: Y
Mechanical specifications: Type page 10.75 x 21; E - 6 cols, 1 7/8, between; A - 6 cols, 1 7/8, between; C - 9 cols, 1 1/8, between.
Published Days: Thur
Avg Paid Circ: 4236
Audit Company: Sworn/Estimate/Non-Audited
Audit Date: 6 10 2019

NEW HAVEN

HAMDEN AND NORTH HAVEN POST-CHRONICLE

Corporate/Parent Company: Hearst Corp.
Street Address: 100 Gando Drive
City: New Haven
State: CT
Postal Code: 0 6513
Office phone: 203-789-5200
Publication Website: www.ctpostchronicle.com
General E-mail: letters@nhregister.com

SHORELINE TIMES

Corporate/Parent Company: Hearst Corp.
Street Address: 100 Gando Drive
City: New Haven
State: CT
Postal Code: 0 6513
Office phone: 1-203-789-5200
Publication Website: www.shorelinetimes.com

NORWALK

THE RIDGEFIELD PRESS

Corporate/Parent Company: Hearst Corp.
Street Address: 301 Merritt 7 – Suite 1
City: Norwalk
State: CT
Postal Code: 0 6851-1075

Non-Daily Newspapers in the U.S.

Office phone: 20 3 7313316
Publication Website: www.theridgefieldpress.com

RIDGEFIELD

RIDGEFIELD PRESS

Corporate/Parent Company: HAN Network
Street Address: 16 Bailey Ave
City: Ridgefield
State: CT
Postal Code: 06877-4512
Office phone: (203) 438-6544
Publication Website: www.theridgefieldpress.com
Editor Name: Steve Coulter
Editor Email: news@theridgefieldpress.com
Editor Phone: 203-731-3316
Advertising Executive Name: Laurie Campbell
Advertising Executive Email: lcampbell@hersamacorn.com
Advertising Executive Phone: 203-424-1302
Year Established: 1875
Delivery Methods: Mail`Newsstand
Own Printing Facility?: Y
Commercial printers?: Y
Mechanical specifications: Type page 10.75 x 21; E - 6 cols, 1 7/8, between; A - 6 cols, 1 7/8, between; C - 9 cols, 1 1/8, between.
Published Days: Thur
Avg Paid Circ: 5528
Audit Company: Sworn/Estimate/Non-Audited
Audit Date: 6 10 2019

SHELTON

MILFORD MIRROR

Corporate/Parent Company: HAN Network
Street Address: 1000 Bridgeport Ave
City: Shelton
State: CT
Postal Code: 06484-4660
Office phone: 203-402-2315
Publication Website: www.milfordmirror.com
Editor Name: Jill Dion
Editor Email: editor@milfordmirror.com
Editor Phone: 203-402-2315
Advertising Executive Name: Jim Chiappa
Advertising Executive Email: jchiappa@hersamacorn.com
Advertising Executive Phone: 203-402-2335
Year Established: 1985
Delivery Methods: Mail`Newsstand
Own Printing Facility?: Y
Commercial printers?: Y
Mechanical specifications: Type page 10.75 x 21; E - 6 cols, 1 7/8, between; A - 6 cols, 1 7/8, between; C - 9 cols, 1 1/8, between.
Published Days: Thur
Avg Paid Circ: 2932
Avg Free Circ: 591
Audit Company: Sworn/Estimate/Non-Audited
Audit Date: 6 10 2019

WATERTOWN

TOWN TIMES

Corporate/Parent Company: Prime Publisher's Inc.
Street Address: 449 Main Street
City: Watertown
State: CT
Postal Code: 6795
Office phone: (860) 274-6721
Publication Website: www.myrecordjournal.com/news/town-times
General E-mail: newsroom@record-journal.com
Publisher Name: Liz White Notarangelo
Publisher Email: lwhite@record-journal.com
Publisher Phone: 203-317-2226
Editor Name: Ralph Tomaselli
Editor Email: rtomaselli@record-journal.com
Editor Phone: 203-317-2220
Advertising Executive Name: Jim Mizener
Advertising Executive Email: jmizener@record-journal.com
Advertising Executive Phone: 203-317-2312

Year Established: 2002
Published Days: Thur
Avg Paid Circ: 96
Avg Free Circ: 12859
Audit Company: AAM
Audit Date: 24 01 2020

DISTRICT OF COLUMBIA

WASHINGTON

METRO WEEKLY

Corporate/Parent Company: Jansi LLC
Street Address: 1775 I Street NW, Suite 1150
City: Washington
State: DC
Postal Code: 20006
Office phone: (202) 638-6830
Publication Website: www.metroweekly.com
General E-mail: editor@metroweekly.com
Editor Name: Randy Shulman
Editor Email: rshulman@metroweekly.com

DELAWARE

DOVER

DELAWARE STATE NEWS

Corporate/Parent Company: Independent Newsmedia Inc USA
Street Address: 110 Galaxy Dr
City: Dover
State: DE
Postal Code: 19903
Office phone: (302) 674-3600
Publication Website: https://delawarestatenews.net/
General E-mail: newsroom@newszap.com
Publisher Name: Darel La Prade
Publisher Email: dlaprade@newszap.com
Editor Name: Ashley Dawson
Editor Email: adawson@newszap.com
Advertising Executive Name: Konrad La Prade
Advertising Executive Email: klaprade@newszap.com
Year Established: 1953
Delivery Methods: Newsstand`Carrier`Racks
Own Printing Facility?: Y
Commercial printers?: Y
Mechanical specifications: Printed page size 10.75 x 12. 4 columns. Width of 1 column = 2.343. Width of column rule: 0.125.
Published Days: Mon`Tues`Wed`Thur`Fri`Sat`Sun
Weekday Frequency: m
Saturday Frequency: m
Avg Paid Circ: 8588
Avg Free Circ: 491
Audit Company: AAM
Audit Date: 16 08 2019
Pressroom Equipment: Lines – Koenig & Bauer AG Colora Press;

DOVER POST

Corporate/Parent Company: Gannett
Street Address: 1196 South Little Creek Road
City: Dover
State: DE
Postal Code: 19901
Office phone: (302) 678-3616
Publication Website: https://www.doverpost.com/
General E-mail: ben.mace@doverpost.com
Publisher Name: Amy Dotson-Newton
Publisher Email: amy.dotsonnewton@doverpost.com
Publisher Phone: (302) 346-5449
Advertising Executive Name: Brigitte McKinney
Advertising Executive Email: brigitte.mckinney@doverpost.com
Advertising Executive Phone: (302) 346-5434
Year Established: 1975
Delivery Methods: Mail`Carrier`Racks
Own Printing Facility?: Y
Commercial printers?: Y
Mechanical specifications: Type page 10.33" x 11"; 6 cols
Published Days: Wed
Avg Paid Circ: 660
Avg Free Circ: 21088
Audit Company: CVC
Audit Date: 30 06 2016

SUSSEX COUNTIAN

Street Address: 1196 S. Little Creek Rd.
City: Dover
State: DE
Postal Code: 19901
Office phone: (302) 678-3616
Publication Website: https://www.sussexcountian.com/
General E-mail: ben.mace@doverpost.com
Publisher Name: Amy Dotson-Newton
Publisher Email: amy.dotsonnewton@doverpost.com
Publisher Phone: (302) 346-5449
Advertising Executive Name: Bettene Pereira
Advertising Executive Email: bettene.pereira@doverpost.com
Advertising Executive Phone: (302) 346-5442
Year Established: 1886
Delivery Methods: Mail`Carrier`Racks
Own Printing Facility?: Y
Mechanical specifications: Type page 10.32" x 11"; 6 cols
Published Days: Thur
Avg Paid Circ: 202
Avg Free Circ: 1637
Audit Company: CVC
Audit Date: 30 06 2016
Buisness Software: PBS
Note: Special Events - W3 What Women Want Fest (April); Best Friends Pet Expo (Oct) Maryland-Delaware-DC Press Association Editorial and Advertising Awards
Total Circulation: 14507

MIDDLETOWN

COMMUNITY NEWS

Corporate/Parent Company: Media News Group
Street Address: 24 W. Main St.
City: Middletown
State: DE
Postal Code: 19709
Office phone: 302-378-9531
Publication Website: www.hockessincommunitynews.com
General E-mail: editor@communitypub.com
Publisher Name: Amy Dotson-Newton
Publisher Email: amy.dotsonnewton@doverpost.com
Publisher Phone: 302-346-5449
Editor Name: Ben Mace
Editor Email: ben.mace@doverpost.com
Editor Phone: 302-346-5421
Advertising Executive Name: Lynn Kris
Advertising Executive Email: lynn.kris@doverpost.com
Advertising Executive Phone: 302-346-5428
Total Circulation: 21748

MIDDLETOWN TRANSCRIPT

Corporate/Parent Company: Gannett
Street Address: 24 W. Main St.
City: Middletown
State: DE
Postal Code: 19709

Office phone: (302) 378-9531
Publication Website: https://www.middletowntranscript.com/
General E-mail: ben.mace@doverpost.com
Publisher Name: Amy Dotson-Newton
Publisher Email: amy.dotsonnewton@doverpost.com
Publisher Phone: (302) 346-5449
Advertising Executive Name: Deb Kalinowski
Advertising Executive Email: debra.kalinowski@doverpost.com
Advertising Executive Phone: (302) 346-5435
Year Established: 1868
Delivery Methods: Mail`Carrier`Racks
Own Printing Facility?: Y
Mechanical specifications: Type page 10.33" x 11"; 6 cols
Published Days: Thur
Avg Paid Circ: 498
Avg Free Circ: 13200
Audit Company: CVC
Audit Date: 30 06 2016
Total Circulation: 13704

MILFORD

SUSSEX POST

Corporate/Parent Company: Independent Newsmedia Inc. Usa
Street Address: 37A N WALNUT ST
City: Milford
State: DE
Postal Code: 19964
Office phone: (302) 674-3600
Publication Website: https://sussexcountypost-de.newsmemory.com
General E-mail: adsonline@newszap.com
Publisher Name: Darel La Prade
Publisher Email: dlaprade@newszap.com
Editor Name: Andrew West
Editor Email: newsroom@newszap.com
Year Established: 1972
Delivery Methods: Carrier`Racks
Mechanical specifications: Type page 11 5/8 x 21 1/4; E - 6 cols, 1 3/4, 1/16 between; A - 6 cols, 1 3/4, 1/16 between; C - 9 cols, 1 1/3, 1/6 between.
Published Days: Wed
Avg Free Circ: 13000
Audit Company: Sworn/Estimate/Non-Audited
Audit Date: 6 10 2019
Total Circulation: 1839

THE CHRONICLE

Corporate/Parent Company: Gannett
Street Address: 37A N WALNUT ST
City: Milford
State: DE
Postal Code: 19963
Office phone: (302) 674-3600
Publication Website: https://milfordchronicle-de.newsmemory.com
General E-mail: adsonline@newszap.com
Publisher Name: Darel La Prade
Publisher Email: dlaprade@newszap.com
Editor Name: Andrew West
Editor Email: newsroom@newszap.com

FLORIDA

APALACHICOLA

APALACHICOLA TIMES (THE)

Street Address: 129 Commerce St.
City: Apalachicola
State: FL
Postal Code: 32320
Office phone: (850) 653-8868
Publication Website: www.apalachtimes.com
Publisher Name: Tim Thompson
Publisher Email: tthompson@pcnh.com

Editor Name: Tim Croft
Editor Email: tcroft@starfl.com
Editor Phone: 850-227-7827

BUNNELL
FLAGLER PENNYSAVER

Corporate/Parent Company: Florida Pennysavers
Street Address: 2729 E Moody Blvd
City: Bunnell
State: FL
Postal Code: 32110-5963
Office phone: (386) 437-5971
Publication Website: www.floridapennysavers.com/SiteDefault.aspx?edition=FL
General E-mail: Beatrix.deBoer@psavers.com
Publisher Name: Romaine Fine
Publisher Phone: (386) 615-2535
Advertising Executive Name: Beatrix deBoer
Advertising Executive Email: Beatrix.deBoer@psavers.com
Advertising Executive Phone: (386) 313-5378

CHIEFLAND
CEDAR KEY BEACON

Corporate/Parent Company: Landmark Community Newspapers
Street Address: 624 W. Park Ave
City: Chiefland
State: FL
Postal Code: 32626
Office phone: 352-493-4796
Publication Website: www.cedarkeybeacon.com
Publisher Name: Gerry Mulligan
Editor Name: Sean Arnold
Editor Email: editor@cedarkeybeacon.com
Total Circulation: 14334

CHIPLEY
HOLMES COUNTY TIMES-ADVERTISER

Street Address: 1364 N Railroad Ave
City: Chipley
State: FL
Postal Code: 32428-1456
Office phone: (850) 638-0212
Publication Website: www.chipleypaper.com
Publisher Name: Nicole Barefield
Editor Name: Jacqueline Bostick
Editor Email: jbostick@chipleypaper.com
Advertising Executive Name: Cathrine Lamb
Advertising Executive Email: clamb@chipleypaper.com
Advertising Executive Phone: (850) 638-0212
Own Printing Facility?: Y
Mechanical specifications: Type page 13 x 21 1/2; E - 6 cols, 2 1/6 between; A - 6 cols, 2, 1/6 between; C - 9 cols, 1 1/3, 1/6 between.
Published Days: Wed
Avg Paid Circ: 4200
Audit Company: Sworn/Estimate/Non-Audited
Audit Date: 6 10 2019
Total Circulation: 12100

WASHINGTON COUNTY NEWS

Corporate/Parent Company: Gannett
Street Address: 1364 N. Railroad Avenue
City: Chipley
State: FL
Postal Code: 32428
Office phone: (850) 638-0212
Publication Website: www.chipleypaper.com
Publisher Name: Nicole Barefield
Editor Name: Jacqueline Bostick
Editor Email: jbostick@chipleypaper.com
Advertising Executive Name: Famie Bush
Advertising Executive Email: fbush@chipleypaper.com
Advertising Executive Phone: (850) 703-3348

CLERMONT
CLERMONT NEWS LEADER

Corporate/Parent Company: DR Media and Investments
Street Address: 637 Eighth Street
City: Clermont
State: FL
Postal Code: 34711
Publication Website: www.midfloridanewspapers.com/clermont_news_leader
General E-mail: circulation@midfloridanewspapers.com
Publisher Name: Jay Kemp
Publisher Email: jkemp@clermontnewsleader.com
Editor Name: Andrew Fister
Editor Email: afister@d-r.media
Editor Phone: 352-242-9818
Advertising Executive Name: Ashley Abear
Advertising Executive Email: aabear@clermontnewsleader.com

SUMTER SHOPPER

Corporate/Parent Company: DR Media and Investments
Street Address: 637 8th St.
City: Clermont
State: FL
Postal Code: 34711-2159
Office phone: (352) 748-2424
Publication Website: www.midfloridanewspapers.com/sumter_county_shopper
General E-mail: circulation@midfloridanewspapers.com

DAYTONA
DAYTONA PENNYSAVER

Corporate/Parent Company: Florida Pennysavers
Street Address: 901 6th St.
City: Daytona
State: FL
Postal Code: 32117
Office phone: (386) 681-2200
Publication Website: www.floridapennysavers.com/SiteDefault.aspx?edition=DB
General E-mail: Romaine.Fine@PSavers.com
Publisher Name: Romaine Fine
Publisher Phone: (386) 615-2536

DEERFIELD BEACH
BOCA NEWSPAPER

Corporate/Parent Company: Four Story Media Group
Street Address: 1701 Green Rd
City: Deerfield Beach
State: FL
Postal Code: 33064
Office phone: (954) 356-4000
Publication Website: bocanewspaper.com
Editor Name: Marisa Herman
Editor Email: marisa@fourstorymg.com
Editor Phone: 954-695-9228
Advertising Executive Name: Kelly McCabe
Advertising Executive Email: Kelly@fourstorymg.com
Advertising Executive Phone: 828-260-1950
Buisness Equipment: PC
Buisness Software: Pre1
Classified Equipment: Mac
Classified Software: Pre1
Editorial Equipment: Mac
Editorial Software: InDesign
Production Equipment: Mac
Production Software: InDesign
Total Circulation: 25241

DELRAY TIMES

Corporate/Parent Company: Four Story Media Group
Street Address: 1702 Green Rd
City: Deerfield Beach
State: FL
Postal Code: 33065
Office phone: (954) 356-4000
Publication Website: delraynewspaper.com
Editor Name: Marisa Herman
Editor Email: marisa@fourstorymg.com
Editor Phone: 954-695-9229
Advertising Executive Name: Kylee Treyz
Advertising Executive Email: Kylee@fourstorymg.com
Advertising Executive Phone: 561-542-3838
Delivery Methods: Mail`Carrier`Racks
Mechanical specifications: Type page 10.5" x 10.5"; 6 cols
Published Days: Wed
Avg Free Circ: 27869
Audit Company: CVC
Audit Date: 6/31/2018

DELAND
WEST VOLUSIA PENNYSAVER

Corporate/Parent Company: Florida Pennysavers
Street Address: West Volusia
City: Deland
State: FL
Postal Code: 32720-2260
Office phone: (386) 736-2880
Publication Website: www.floridapennysavers.com/SiteDefault.aspx?edition=WV
General E-mail: mary.morrissey@psavers.com
Publisher Name: Romaine Fine
Publisher Phone: (386) 615-2535
Advertising Executive Name: Mary Morrissey
Advertising Executive Email: mary.morrissey@psavers.com

FORT MYERS
FLORIDA WEEKLY

Corporate/Parent Company: Florida Media Group LLC
Street Address: 2891 Center Pointe Drive, Suite 300
City: Fort Myers
State: FL
Postal Code: 33916
Office phone: 239.333.2135
Publication Website: www.floridaweekly.com
General E-mail: info@floridaweekly.com
Publisher Name: Angela Schivinski
Publisher Email: angela@floridaweekly.com
Editor Name: Betty Wells
Editor Email: bwells@floridaweekly.com
Total Circulation: 27869

FORT MYERS BEACH
FORT MYERS BEACH OBSERVER

Corporate/Parent Company: Ogden Newspapers Inc.
Street Address: 19260 San Carlos Blvd, Bldg. C
City: Fort Myers Beach
State: FL
Postal Code: 33931
Office phone: 239-463-4421
Publication Website: www.fortmyersbeachtalk.com
General E-mail: customerservice@breezenewspapers.com
Publisher Name: Scott Blonde
Publisher Email: sblonde@breezenewspapers.com
Publisher Phone: 574-1110 Ex 110
Editor Name: Valarie Harring
Editor Email: vharring@breezenewspapers.com
Editor Phone: 574-1110 Ex 119
Advertising Executive Name: Danielle Papoi
Advertising Executive Email: dpapoi@breezenewspapers.com

Total Circulation: 19421

ISLAND SAND PAPER

Street Address: 450 Old San Carlos Blvd., Unit G-108
City: Fort Myers Beach
State: FL
Postal Code: 33931
Office phone: (239) 463-4461
Publication Website: www.fortmyersbeach.news
General E-mail: Info@fortmyersbeach.news
Advertising Executive Name: Sandy Sandness
Advertising Executive Email: sandy2.sandpaper@gmail.com

FT. MYERS
LEHIGH ACRES CITIZEN

Corporate/Parent Company: Ogden Newspapers, Inc.
Street Address: 14051 Jetport Loop
City: Ft. Myers
State: FL
Postal Code: 33913
Office phone: 239-368-3944
Publication Website: www.lehighacrescitizen.com
Publisher Name: Scott Blonde
Publisher Email: sblonde@breezenewspapers.com
Publisher Phone: 574-1110 Ex 110
Editor Name: Valarie Harring
Editor Email: vharring@breezenewspapers.com
Editor Phone: 574-1110 Ex 119
Advertising Executive Name: Joe Trupo
Advertising Executive Email: jtrupo@breezenewspapers.com
Advertising Executive Phone: 574-1110 Ex 171

KEYSTONE HEIGHTS
LAKE REGION MONITOR

Street Address: 7382 State Rd 21
City: Keystone Heights
State: FL
Postal Code: 32656
Office phone: 904-964-6305
Publication Website: www.starkejournal.com
General E-mail: monitoreditor@bctelegraph.com
Editor Name: Mark Crawford
Editor Email: editor@BcTelegraph.com
Editor Phone: 904-964-6305

LABELLE
CALOOSA BELLE

Corporate/Parent Company: Independent NewsMedia
Street Address: PO Box 518
City: Labelle
State: FL
Postal Code: 33975-0518
Office phone: (863) 675-2541
Publication Website: caloosabelle-fl.newsmemory.com
General E-mail: cbnews@newszap.com
Publisher Name: Katrina Elsken
Publisher Email: kelsken@newszap.com
Advertising Executive Name: Barbara Calfee
Advertising Executive Email: bcalfee@newszap.com
Published Days: Thur
Audit Company: Sworn/Estimate/Non-Audited
Audit Date: 6 10 2019

LAND O' LAKES
LAKER / LUTZ NEWS (THE)

Corporate/Parent Company: Community Newspapers Inc.
Street Address: 3632 Land O' Lakes Blvd.,

Non-Daily Newspapers in the U.S.

Suite 102
City: Land O' Lakes
State: FL
Postal Code: 34639
Office phone: 813-909-2800
Publication Website: www.lakerlutznews.com
General E-mail: news@lakerlutznews.com
Publisher Name: Diane Kortus
Publisher Email: dkortus@lakerlutznews.com
Editor Name: B.C. Manion
Editor Email: bcmanion@lakerlutznews.com
Advertising Executive Name: Rachel Thompson
Advertising Executive Email: rthompson@lakerlutznews.com

MILTON

SANTA ROSA PRESS GAZETTE

Corporate/Parent Company: Gannett
Street Address: 6576 Caroline St
City: Milton
State: FL
Postal Code: 32570-4759
Office phone: (850) 623-2120
Publication Website: www.srpressgazette.com
Publisher Name: Jim Fletcher
Publisher Email: jfletcher@srpressgazette.com
Editor Name: Jason Blakeney
Editor Email: jblakeney@nwfdailynews.com
Advertising Executive Name: Tracie Smelstoys
Advertising Executive Email: tsmelstoys@srpressgazette.com
Year Established: 1908
Delivery Methods: Mail
Own Printing Facility?: Y
Commercial printers?: N
Mechanical specifications: Type page 9.90 x 20; E - 6 cols, 2, 1/6 between; A - 6 cols, 2, 1/6 between; C - 9 cols, 1 1/3, 1/12 between.
Published Days: Wed`Sat
Avg Paid Circ: 5000
Audit Company: Sworn/Estimate/Non-Audited
Audit Date: 6 10 2019
Total Circulation: 4200

MONTICELLO

JEFFERSON COUNTY JOURNAL

Corporate/Parent Company: ECB Publishing, Inc
Street Address: P.O. Box 428180 W. Washington St.
City: Monticello
State: FL
Postal Code: 32345
Office phone: 850-997-3568
Publication Website: www.ecbpublishing.com
Publisher Name: Emerald Greene Parsons
Publisher Email: emerald@greenepublishing.com
Publisher Phone: 850-997-3568

MT. DORA

THE TRIANGLE NEWS LEADER

Corporate/Parent Company: DR Media and Investments
Street Address: 4645 Hwy 19-A
City: Mt. Dora
State: FL
Postal Code: 32757
Office phone: 352-589-8211
Publication Website: www.midfloridanewspapers.com/triangle_news_leader
General E-mail: circulation@midfloridanewspapers.com
Advertising Executive Name: Ann Yager
Advertising Executive Email: ayager@trianglenewsleader.com

OKEECHOBEE

OKEECHOBEE NEWS

Corporate/Parent Company: Independent NewsMedia
Street Address: 107 SW 17th St
City: Okeechobee
State: FL
Postal Code: 34974-6110
Office phone: (863) 763-3134
Publication Website: okeechobeenews-fl.newsmemory.com
General E-mail: okeenews@newszap.com
Publisher Name: Katrina Elsken
Publisher Email: kelsken@newszap.com
Year Established: 1915
Delivery Methods: Mail`Newsstand`Carrier`Racks
Own Printing Facility?: N
Commercial printers?: Y
Mechanical specifications: Type page 11 5/8 x 21 1/2; E - 6 cols, 1 5/8, between; A - 6 cols, 1 5/8, between; C - 9 cols, 1 1/5, between.
Published Days: Wed`Fri`Sun
Weekday Frequency: m
Saturday Frequency: m
Avg Paid Circ: 2583
Avg Free Circ: 4000
Audit Company: Sworn/Estimate/Non-Audited
Audit Date: 6 10 2019

LAKE OKEECHOBEE NEWS

Corporate/Parent Company: Independent Newsmedia Inc.
Street Address: 107 S.W. 17th Street
City: Okeechobee
State: FL
Postal Code: 34974
Office phone: 863-763-3134
Publication Website: www.lakeokeechobeenews.com
General E-mail: okeenews@newszap.com
Publisher Name: Katrina Elsken
Publisher Email: kelsken@newszap.com

ORLANDO

EL SENTINEL

Street Address: 633 N. Orange Ave.
City: Orlando
State: FL
Postal Code: 32801
Office phone: (407) 420-5000
Publication Website: www.elsentinel.com
General E-mail: social@orlandosentinel.com
Publisher Name: Nancy A. Meyer
Publisher Email: nmeyer@tribpub.com
Editor Name: Roger Simmons
Editor Email: rsimmons@orlandosentinel.com
Advertising Executive Name: Erika Cooper
Advertising Executive Email: ecooper@orlandosentinel.com
Advertising Executive Phone: (407) 420-5101
Total Circulation: 10000

ORMOND BEACH

ORMOND BEACH OBSERVER

Corporate/Parent Company: Observer Media Group
Street Address: 175 W Granada Blvd
City: Ormond Beach
State: FL
Postal Code: 32174
Office phone: 386-492-2784
Publication Website: www.ormondbeachobserver.com
General E-mail: info@palmcoastobserver.com
Publisher Name: John Walsh
Publisher Email: jwalsh@palmcoastobserver.com
Editor Name: Brian McMillan
Editor Email: bmcmillan@palmcoastobserver.com
Advertising Executive Name: Jaclyn Centofanti
Advertising Executive Email: jaclyn@palmcoastobserver.com

PORT ORANGE OBSERVER

Corporate/Parent Company: Observer Media Group
Street Address: 175 W Granada Blvd
City: Ormond Beach
State: FL
Postal Code: 32174
Office phone: 386-492-2784
Publication Website: www.portorangeobserver.com
General E-mail: bonnie@palmcoastobserver.com
Publisher Name: John Walsh
Publisher Email: jwalsh@palmcoastobserver.com
Editor Name: Brian McMillan
Editor Email: bmcmillan@palmcoastobserver.com
Advertising Executive Name: Jaclyn Centofanti
Advertising Executive Email: jaclyn@palmcoastobserver.com

PERRY

PERRY NEWS-HERALD/TACO TIMES

Street Address: 123 S. Jefferson Street
City: Perry
State: FL
Postal Code: 32347
Office phone: (850) 584-5513
Publication Website: www.perrynewspapers.com
General E-mail: newsdesk@perrynewspapers.com
Publisher Name: Aaron Portwood

POMPANO BEACH

NEW PELICAN

Street Address: 1634 E. Atlantic Blvd.
City: Pompano Beach
State: FL
Postal Code: 33060
Office phone: (954) 783-8700
Publication Website: www.pelicannewspaper.com
Editor Name: John Geer
Editor Email: johngeer@newpelican.com
Editor Phone: (954) 783-8700 ext 101
Advertising Executive Name: Michael Sobel
Advertising Executive Email: michael@newpelican.com
Advertising Executive Phone: (954) 465-8006
Total Circulation: 24316

PORT RICHEY

SPRING HILL BEACON

Corporate/Parent Company: Tampa Bay Newspapers
Street Address: 11321 U.S. Hwy 19 North
City: Port Richey
State: FL
Postal Code: 34668
Office phone: 727-815-1023
Publication Website: www.suncoastnews.com
General E-mail: dpleus@SuncoastNews.com
Publisher Name: Dan Autrey
Publisher Email: dautrey@tbnweekly.com
Publisher Phone: 397-5563
Editor Name: Bob Hibbs
Editor Email: rhibbs@suncoastnews.com
Editor Phone: 815-1064
Advertising Executive Name: Doug Pleus
Advertising Executive Email: dpleus@suncoastnews.com
Advertising Executive Phone: 359-1803

SUN COAST NEWS CENTRAL

Corporate/Parent Company: Tampa Bay Newspapers
Street Address: 11321 U.S. Hwy 19 North
City: Port Richey
State: FL
Postal Code: 34668
Office phone: 727-815-1023
Publication Website: www.suncoastnews.com
General E-mail: dpleus@SuncoastNews.com
Publisher Name: Dan Autrey
Publisher Email: dautrey@tbnweekly.com
Publisher Phone: 397-5563
Editor Name: Bob Hibbs
Editor Email: rhibbs@suncoastnews.com
Editor Phone: 815-1064
Advertising Executive Name: Doug Pleus
Advertising Executive Email: dpleus@suncoastnews.com
Advertising Executive Phone: 359-1803

SUN COAST NEWS NORTH

Corporate/Parent Company: Tampa Bay Newspapers
Street Address: 11321 U.S. Hwy 19 North
City: Port Richey
State: FL
Postal Code: 34668
Office phone: 727-815-1023
Publication Website: www.suncoastnews.com
General E-mail: dpleus@SuncoastNews.com
Publisher Name: Dan Autrey
Publisher Email: dautrey@tbnweekly.com
Publisher Phone: 397-5563
Editor Name: Bob Hibbs
Editor Email: rhibbs@suncoastnews.com
Editor Phone: 815-1064
Advertising Executive Name: Doug Pleus
Advertising Executive Email: dpleus@suncoastnews.com
Advertising Executive Phone: 359-1803
Editorial Equipment: Hardware – APP/Mac
Editorial Software: Microsoft/Word, QPS/QuarkXPress.
Total Circulation: 6583

SUN COAST NEWS NORTH PINELLAS

Corporate/Parent Company: Tampa Bay Newspapers
Street Address: 11321 U.S. Hwy 19 North
City: Port Richey
State: FL
Postal Code: 34668
Office phone: 727-815-1023
Publication Website: www.suncoastnews.com
General E-mail: dpleus@SuncoastNews.com
Publisher Name: Dan Autrey
Publisher Email: dautrey@tbnweekly.com
Publisher Phone: 397-5563
Editor Name: Bob Hibbs
Editor Email: rhibbs@suncoastnews.com
Editor Phone: 815-1064
Advertising Executive Name: Doug Pleus
Advertising Executive Email: dpleus@suncoastnews.com
Advertising Executive Phone: 359-1803

SUN COAST NEWS SOUTH

Corporate/Parent Company: Tampa Bay Newspapers
Street Address: 11321 U.S. Hwy 19 North
City: Port Richey
State: FL
Postal Code: 34668
Office phone: 727-815-1023
Publication Website: www.suncoastnews.com
General E-mail: dpleus@SuncoastNews.com
Publisher Name: Dan Autrey
Publisher Email: dautrey@tbnweekly.com
Publisher Phone: 397-5563
Editor Name: Bob Hibbs
Editor Email: rhibbs@suncoastnews.com
Editor Phone: 815-1064

Advertising Executive Name: Doug Pleus
Advertising Executive Email: dpleus@suncoastnews.com
Advertising Executive Phone: 359-1803
Total Circulation: 24563

SUNCOAST NEWS - PASCO SOUTH

Corporate/Parent Company: Tampa Bay Newspapers
Street Address: 11321 U.S. Hwy 19 N.
City: Port Richey
State: FL
Postal Code: 34668
Office phone: 727-815-1023
Publication Website: www.suncoastnews.com/news/pasco
General E-mail: rhibbs@suncoastnews.com
Editor Name: Jeff Rosenfield
Editor Email: jrosenfield@suncoastnews.com
Total Circulation: 5000

PORT SAINT JOE

THE STAR

Corporate/Parent Company: Gannett
Street Address: 135 W Highway 98
City: Port Saint Joe
State: FL
Postal Code: 32456-1871
Office phone: (850) 227-1278
Publication Website: www.starfl.com
Editor Name: Tim Croft
Editor Email: tcroft@starfl.com
Published Days: Thur
Avg Free Circ: 2600
Audit Company: Sworn/Estimate/Non-Audited
Audit Date: 6 10 2019

SANIBEL

ISLAND SUN

Street Address: 1640 Periwinkle Way, Suite 2
City: Sanibel
State: FL
Postal Code: 33957
Office phone: 239-395-1213
Publication Website: www.islandsunnews.com
General E-mail: Press@IslandSunNews.com

SANTA ROSA BEACH

THE WALTON SUN

Corporate/Parent Company: Gannett
Street Address: 5597 US Highway 98 W
City: Santa Rosa Beach
State: FL
Postal Code: 32459-3283
Office phone: (850) 267-4555
Publication Website: waltonsun.com
General E-mail: news@waltonsunonline.com
Editor Name: Tina Harbuck
Mechanical specifications: Type page 9 2/3 x 16; E - 5 cols, 1 13/16, between; A - 5 cols, 1 13/16, between; C - 7 cols, 1 3/8, between.
Published Days: Sat
Avg Free Circ: 12000
Audit Company: Sworn/Estimate/Non-Audited
Audit Date: 6 10 2019

SEMINOLE

BELLEAIR BEE

Corporate/Parent Company: Times Publishing Company
Street Address: 9911 Seminole Blvd
City: Seminole
State: FL
Postal Code: 33772-2536
Office phone: (727) 397-5563
Publication Website: www.tbnweekly.com/belleair_bee
Publisher Name: Dan Autrey
Publisher Email: dautrey@tbnweekly.com
Publisher Phone: 397-55634
Editor Name: Tom Germond
Editor Email: tgermond@tbnweekly.com
Editor Phone: 397-5563, ext. 330
Advertising Executive Name: Karla Neuhaus
Advertising Executive Email: sales@tbnweekly.com
Advertising Executive Phone: 397-5563, ext. 312
Year Established: 1975
Delivery Methods: Newsstand`Carrier`Racks
Own Printing Facility?: Y
Mechanical specifications: 6 col. (11.5") x 21"
Published Days: Fri
Avg Free Circ: 12100
Audit Company: Sworn/Estimate/Non-Audited
Audit Date: 6 10 2019

CLEARWATER BEACON

Corporate/Parent Company: Times Publishing Company
Street Address: 9911 Seminole Blvd
City: Seminole
State: FL
Postal Code: 33772-2536
Office phone: (727) 397-5563
Publication Website: www.tbnweekly.com/clearwater_beacon
Publisher Name: Dan Autrey
Publisher Email: dautrey@tbnweekly.com
Publisher Phone: 397-5563
Editor Name: Logan Mosby
Editor Email: lmosby@tbnweekly.com
Editor Phone: 397-5563, ext. 304
Advertising Executive Name: Karla Neuhaus
Advertising Executive Email: sales@tbnweekly.com
Advertising Executive Phone: 397-5563, ext. 312
Year Established: 1950
Delivery Methods: Newsstand`Carrier`Racks
Own Printing Facility?: Y
Mechanical specifications: 6 col. (11.5") x 21"
Published Days: Fri
Avg Free Circ: 25241
Audit Company: CVC
Audit Date: 30 09 2017
Total Circulation: 5000

DUNEDIN BEACON

Corporate/Parent Company: Times Publishing Company
Street Address: 9911 Seminole Blvd
City: Seminole
State: FL
Postal Code: 33772-2536
Office phone: (727) 397-5563
Publication Website: www.tbnweekly.com/north_county/dunedin_beacon
Publisher Name: Dan Autrey
Publisher Email: dautrey@tbnweekly.com
Publisher Phone: 397-5566
Editor Name: Tom Germond
Editor Email: tgermond@tbnweekly.com
Editor Phone: 397-5563, ext. 330
Advertising Executive Name: Karla Neuhaus
Advertising Executive Email: sales@tbnweekly.com
Advertising Executive Phone: 397-5563, ext. 312
Year Established: 2009
Delivery Methods: Newsstand`Carrier`Racks
Own Printing Facility?: Y
Mechanical specifications: 10.5" x 11" (6 col.)
Published Days: Mthly
Avg Free Circ: 19421
Audit Company: CVC
Audit Date: 30 09 2017
Total Circulation: 27708

LARGO LEADER

Corporate/Parent Company: Times Publishing Company
Street Address: 9911 Seminole Blvd
City: Seminole
State: FL
Postal Code: 33772-2536
Office phone: (727) 397-5563
Publication Website: www.tbnweekly.com/largo_leader
Publisher Name: Dan Autrey
Publisher Email: dautrey@tbnweekly.com
Publisher Phone: 397-5564
Editor Name: Christopher George
Editor Email: cgeorge@TBNweekly.com
Editor Phone: 397-5563, ext. 316
Advertising Executive Name: Karla Neuhaus
Advertising Executive Email: sales@tbnweekly.com
Advertising Executive Phone: 397-5563, ext. 312
Year Established: 1977
Delivery Methods: Newsstand`Carrier`Racks
Own Printing Facility?: Y
Mechanical specifications: 6 col. (11.5") x 21"
Published Days: Thur
Avg Free Circ: 24316
Audit Company: CVC
Audit Date: 30 09 2017
Total Circulation: 18000

PALM HARBOR BEACON

Corporate/Parent Company: Tampa Bay Newspapers
Street Address: 9911 Seminole Blvd.
City: Seminole
State: FL
Postal Code: 33772
Office phone: (727) 397-5563
Publication Website: www.tbnweekly.com
Publisher Name: Dan Autrey
Publisher Email: dautrey@tbnweekly.com
Publisher Phone: 397-5563
Advertising Executive Name: Jay Rey
Advertising Executive Email: jrey@tbnweekly.com
Advertising Executive Phone: 397-5563, ext. 313
Year Established: 2011
Delivery Methods: Newsstand`Carrier`Racks
Own Printing Facility?: Y
Mechanical specifications: 10.5" x 11" (6 column)
Published Days: Mthly
Avg Free Circ: 24563
Audit Company: CVC
Audit Date: 17 12 2017

PINELLAS PARK BEACON

Corporate/Parent Company: Tampa Bay Newspapers
Street Address: 9911 Seminole Blvd
City: Seminole
State: FL
Postal Code: 33772-2536
Office phone: (727) 397-5563
Publication Website: www.tbnweekly.com/north_county/pinellas_park_beacon
Publisher Name: Dan Autrey
Publisher Email: dautrey@tbnweekly.com
Publisher Phone: 397-5566
Editor Name: Suzette Porter
Editor Email: sporter@tbnweekly.com

SEMINOLE BEACON

Corporate/Parent Company: Times Publishing Company
Street Address: 9911 Seminole Blvd
City: Seminole
State: FL
Postal Code: 33772-2536
Office phone: (727) 397-5563
Publication Website: www.tbnweekly.com/seminole_beacon
Publisher Name: Dan Autrey
Publisher Email: dautrey@tbnweekly.com
Publisher Phone: 397-5565
Editor Name: Tiffany Razzano
Editor Email: trazzano@tbnweekly.com
Editor Phone: 397-5563, ext. 306
Advertising Executive Name: Karla Neuhaus
Advertising Executive Email: sales@tbnweekly.com
Advertising Executive Phone: 397-5563, ext. 312
Year Established: 1977
Delivery Methods: Newsstand`Carrier`Racks
Own Printing Facility?: Y
Mechanical specifications: 6 col. (11.5") x 21"
Published Days: Thur
Avg Free Circ: 27708
Audit Company: CVC
Audit Date: 30 09 2017

SOUTH MIAMI

KENDALL GAZETTE

Corporate/Parent Company: Community Newspapers, Inc.
Street Address: 6796 SW 62nd Ave
City: South Miami
State: FL
Postal Code: 33143-3306
Office phone: (305) 669-7355
Publication Website: https://communitynewspapers.com/kendallgazette/
General E-mail: michael@communitynewspapers.com
Own Printing Facility?: Y
Published Days: Tues
Avg Free Circ: 10000
Audit Company: Sworn/Estimate/Non-Audited
Audit Date: 6 10 2019

PALMETTO BAY NEWS

Corporate/Parent Company: Community Newspapers, Inc.
Street Address: 6796 SW 62nd Ave
City: South Miami
State: FL
Postal Code: 33143-3306
Office phone: (305) 669-7355
Publication Website: communitynewspapers.com/palmetto-bay
General E-mail: michael@communitynewspapers.com
Year Established: 1958
Own Printing Facility?: Y
Published Days: Tues
Avg Free Circ: 5000
Audit Company: Sworn/Estimate/Non-Audited
Audit Date: 6 10 2019

SOUTH MIAMI NEWS

Corporate/Parent Company: Community Newspapers, Inc.
Street Address: 6796 SW 62nd Ave
City: South Miami
State: FL
Postal Code: 33143-3306
Office phone: (305) 667-7481
Publication Website: communitynewspapers.com/south-miami
General E-mail: michael@communitynewspapers.com
Own Printing Facility?: Y
Published Days: Tues
Avg Free Circ: 18000
Audit Company: Sworn/Estimate/Non-Audited
Audit Date: 6 10 2019

STUART

JUPITER COURIER

Street Address: 1939 SE Federal Hwy
City: Stuart
State: FL
Postal Code: 34994-3915
Office phone: (772) 287-1550

Non-Daily Newspapers in the U.S.

Publication Website: https://www.tcpalm.com/
Editor Name: Brightman Brock
Editor Email: brightman.brock@tcpalm.com

TAMPA

CENTRO TAMPA

Corporate/Parent Company: Poynter Institute
Street Address: 1000 N Ashley Drive, 7th floor
City: Tampa
State: FL
Postal Code: 33602
Office phone: (813) 226-3300
Publication Website: www.centrotampa.com
General E-mail: custserv@tampabay.com
Publisher Name: Joe DeLuca
Publisher Phone: 727-397-5563
Editor Name: Myriam Silva-Warren

WINTER GARDEN

WINDERMERE OBSERVER

Corporate/Parent Company: Observer Media Group
Street Address: "661 Garden Commerce Parkway Suite 180"
City: Winter Garden
State: FL
Postal Code: 34787
Office phone: 407-656-2121
Publication Website: www.orangeobserver.com
General E-mail: contact@orangeobserver.com
Publisher Name: Michael Eng
Publisher Email: meng@OrangeObserver.com
Editor Name: Tim Freed
Editor Email: tfreed@OrangeObserver.com
Advertising Executive Name: Ann Carpenter
Advertising Executive Email: acarpenter@OrangeObserver.com

WINTER HAVEN

FOUR CORNERS NEWS SUN

Corporate/Parent Company: DR Media and Investments
Street Address: 99 Third St. NW
City: Winter Haven
State: FL
Postal Code: 34285
Office phone: 863-533-4183
Publication Website: www.midfloridanewspapers.com/four_corners_news_sun
Publisher Name: Vinnie Grassia
Publisher Email: vgrassia@d-r.media
Editor Name: Steven Ryzewski
Editor Phone: sryzewski@d-r.media
Advertising Executive Name: Barbara Rakoczy
Advertising Executive Email: brakoczy@d-r.media

POLK NEWS SUN

Corporate/Parent Company: DR Media and Investments
Street Address: 99 Third St. NW
City: Winter Haven
State: FL
Postal Code: 34285
Office phone: 863-533-4183
Publication Website: www.midfloridanewspapers.com/polk_news_sun
General E-mail: news@scmginc.com
Editor Name: Steven Ryzewski
Editor Email: sryzewski@scmginc.com
Advertising Executive Name: Barbara Rakoczy
Advertising Executive Email: brakoczy@scmginc.com

WINTER HAVEN SUN (THE)

Corporate/Parent Company: DR Media and Investments
Street Address: 99 Third St. NW
City: Winter Haven
State: FL
Postal Code: 33881
Office phone: 863-533-4183
Publication Website: www.winterhavensun.com
Editor Name: Steven Ryzewski
Editor Email: sryzewski@d-r.media

BEACH BEACON

Corporate/Parent Company: Times Publishing Company
State: FL
Publication Website: www.tbnweekly.com/beach_beacon
Publisher Name: Dan Autrey
Publisher Email: dautrey@tbnweekly.com
Publisher Phone: 397-5563
Editor Name: Tom Germond
Editor Email: tgermond@tbnweekly.com
Editor Phone: 397-5563, ext. 330
Advertising Executive Name: Karla Neuhaus
Advertising Executive Email: sales@tbnweekly.com
Advertising Executive Phone: 397-5563, ext. 312
Year Established: 1980
Delivery Methods: Newsstand`Carrier`Racks
Own Printing Facility?: Y
Commercial printers?: Y
Mechanical specifications: 6 col. (11.5") x 21"
Published Days: Thur
Avg Free Circ: 14334
Audit Company: Sworn/Estimate/Non-Audited
Audit Date: 6 10 2019

SUNCOAST NEWS - PINELLAS NORTH

Corporate/Parent Company: Tampa Bay Newspapers
State: FL
Publication Website: www.suncoastnews.com/news/pinellas
General E-mail: dpleus@SuncoastNews.com
Editor Name: Robert Hibbs
Editor Email: rhibbs@suncoastnews.com
Editor Phone: 727-815-1023

FERNANDINA BEACH

FERNANDINA BEACH NEWS LEADER

Corporate/Parent Company: Community Newspapers, Incorporated
Street Address: 511 Ash Street?
City: Fernandina Beach
State: FL
Postal Code: 32034
Office phone: (904) 261-3696
Publication Website: www.fbNewsLeader.com
Publisher Name: Foy R. Maloy
Publisher Email: fmaloy@fbnewsleader.com
Editor Name: Peg Davis
Editor Email: pegdavis@fbnewsleader.com
Advertising Executive Name: Candy Hammer
Advertising Executive Email: chammer@fbnewsleader.com

GEORGIA

ADEL

ADEL NEWS-TRIBUNE

Street Address: 131 S. Hutchinson Ave. P.O. Box 1500
City: Adel
State: GA
Postal Code: 31620
Office phone: 229-896-2233
Publication Website: adelnewstribune.com
Editor Name: Charles Shiver
Editor Email: charles_cpc@runbox.com
Advertising Executive Name: Deborah Farmer
Advertising Executive Email: charles_cpc@runbox.com

ALBANY

THE ALBANY HERALD

Corporate/Parent Company: Southern Community Newspapers, Inc.
Street Address: 126 N Washington St
City: Albany
State: GA
Postal Code: 31701
Office phone: (229) 888-9300
Publication Website: https://www.albanyherald.com/
General E-mail: scot.morrissey@albanyherald.com
Publisher Name: Scot Morrissey
Publisher Email: scot.morrissey@albanyherald.com
Publisher Phone: (229) 438-3219
Editor Name: Carlton Fletcher
Editor Email: carlton.fletcher@albanyherald.com
Editor Phone: (229) 888-9360
Advertising Executive Name: Amber Jeffcoat
Advertising Executive Email: amber.jeffcoat@albanyherald.com
Advertising Executive Phone: (229) 888-9343

ALMA

THE ALMA TIMES

Street Address: 227 W. 12th Street
City: Alma
State: GA
Postal Code: 31510
Office phone: 912-632-7201
Publication Website: thealmatimes.com
General E-mail: mail@thealmatimes.com
Publisher Name: Robert M. Williams
Publisher Email: rwilliams@thealmatimes.com
Editor Name: Rick Head
Editor Email: editor@thealmatimes.com
Advertising Executive Name: Benny Boatright
Advertising Executive Email: advertising@thealmatimes.com
Total Circulation: 3490

BARNESVILLE

THE HERALD-GAZETTE

Corporate/Parent Company: Walter Geiger
Street Address: "509 Greenwood Street P.O. Box 220"
City: Barnesville
State: GA
Postal Code: 30204
Office phone: 770-358-NEWS (6397)
Publication Website: barnesville.com
Publisher Name: Walter Geiger
Publisher Email: news@barnesville.com
Total Circulation: 4000

BAXLEY

THE BAXLEY NEWS-BANNER

Street Address: 241 E Parker St
City: Baxley
State: GA
Postal Code: 31513
Office phone: 912-367-2468
Publication Website: baxleynewsbanner.com
General E-mail: mail@baxleynewsbanner.com
Publisher Name: Jamie Gardner
Mailroom Equipment: Counter Stackers – 1/BG; Tying Machines – 2-/Bu; Address Machine – 1-/Ch.;
Editorial Equipment: Hardware – COM/One Sys.
Production Equipment: Hardware – 11-COM/8400; Cameras – 1-C/17 x 24, 1-K/Vertical 16 x 22.
Total Circulation: 8273

BLAKELY

EARLY COUNTY NEWS

Street Address: 529 College St.
City: Blakely
State: GA
Postal Code: 39823
Office phone: 229-723-4376
Publication Website: earlycountynews.com
General E-mail: news@earlycountynews.com
Publisher Name: William W.Fleming
Publisher Email: publisher@earlycountynews.com
Editor Name: Brenda Wall
Editor Email: editor@earlycountynews.com
Advertising Executive Name: Judy Fleming

BUENA VISTA

THE JOURNAL

Street Address: 71 Webb Lane
City: Buena Vista
State: GA
Postal Code: 31803
Office phone: 229-649-6397
Publication Website: tjournal.com
General E-mail: tjournal@windstream.net
Advertising Executive Name: Richard Harris
Advertising Executive Email: tjournal@windstream.net

CLAYTON

THE CLAYTON TRIBUNE

Corporate/Parent Company: Community Newspapers, Inc.
Street Address: 120 N Main St
City: Clayton
State: GA
Postal Code: 30525
Office phone: (706) 782-3312
Publication Website: https://www.theclaytontribune.com/
General E-mail: thetribune@theclaytontribune.com
Publisher Name: Wayne Knuckles
Publisher Email: wknuckles@theclaytontribune.com
Year Established: 1897
Published Days: Thur
Avg Paid Circ: 8000
Audit Company: Sworn/Estimate/Non-Audited
Audit Date: 6 10 2019

COCHRAN

THE COCHRAN JOURNAL

Corporate/Parent Company: The Dublin Courier Herald Publishing Co
Street Address: 131 N Second St.
City: Cochran
State: GA
Postal Code: 31014
Office phone: (478) 934-6303
Publication Website: cochrannewstoday.com
General E-mail: advertisingtch@gmail.com
Publisher Name: Griffin Lovett
Editor Name: DuBose Porter
Total Circulation: 2195

CONYERS

THE ROCKDALE CITIZEN

Corporate/Parent Company: Southern Community Newspapers, Inc.
Street Address: 969 S Main St NE
City: Conyers
State: GA
Postal Code: 30012-4501
Office phone: (770) 483-7108

Publication Website: https://www.rockdalenewtoncitizen.com/
General E-mail: news@rockdalecitizen.com
Editor Name: Alice Queen
Editor Email: alice.queen@rockdalecitizen.com
Editor Phone: (770) 483-7108, ext : 226
Advertising Executive Name: Alicia Goss
Advertising Executive Email: alicia.goss@rockdalecitizen.com
Advertising Executive Phone: (706) 255-6745
Year Established: 1953
Mechanical specifications: Type page 12 x 21 1/2; E - 6 cols, 1 7/8, 1/8 between; A - 6 cols, 1 7/8, 1/8 between; C - 10 cols, 1/8 between.
Published Days: Wed`Fri`Sat
Weekday Frequency: m
Avg Paid Circ: 4267
Avg Free Circ: 452
Audit Company: CVC
Audit Date: 31 12 2016
Pressroom Equipment: Lines – 12-G/Urbanite 1997; Enkel/Splicers; 16-DEM/430; Press Drive – 2-A/B; Pasters –Enkel/G WebRegistration System – Stoesser/Pin System through Platebender.
Mailroom Equipment: Counter Stackers – KAN, SLS; Inserters & Stuffers – KAN, SLS;
Buisness Equipment: PC
Buisness Software: Baseview
Classified Equipment: Hardware – APP/iMacs; Printers – APP/Macs;
Classified Software: Baseview, QPS/QuarkXPress 4.0.
Editorial Equipment: Hardware – APP/Macs; Printers – APP/Mac
Editorial Software: Baseview.
Production Equipment: Hardware – ECR
Production Software: QPS/QuarkXPress 4.0.
Total Circulation: 384

DAHLONEGA

THE DAHLONEGA NUGGET

Corporate/Parent Company: Community Newspapers, Inc.
Street Address: P.O. Box 36,
City: Dahlonega
State: GA
Postal Code: 30533
Office phone: (706) 864-3613
Publication Website: https://www.thedahloneganugget.com/
General E-mail: cutterback@thedahloneganugget.com
Publisher Name: Matt Aiken
Publisher Email: maiken@thedahloneganugget.com
Advertising Executive Name: Keith Hart
Advertising Executive Email: ads@thedahloneganugget.com
Published Days: Wed
Avg Paid Circ: 5025
Avg Free Circ: 25
Audit Company: Sworn/Estimate/Non-Audited
Audit Date: 6 10 2019
Total Circulation: 2504

DARIEN

THE DARIEN NEWS

Street Address: P.O. Box 496
City: Darien
State: GA
Postal Code: 31305
Office phone: (912) 437-4251
Publication Website: thedariennews.net
General E-mail: news@thedariennews.net
Publisher Name: Kathleen Williamson Russell
Publisher Email: kathleen@thedariennews.net
Advertising Executive Name: Molly Duckworth
Advertising Executive Email: molly@thedariennews.net

DAWSONVILLE

DAWSON NEWS & ADVERTISER

(OOB)
Corporate/Parent Company: Community Newspapers, Inc.
Street Address: 40 Highway 9 N
City: Dawsonville
State: GA
Postal Code: 30534
Office phone: (706) 265-2345
Publication Website: https://www.dawsonnews.com/
General E-mail: jtaylor@dawsonnews.com
Publisher Name: Stephanie Woody
Publisher Email: swoody@dawsonnews.com
Publisher Phone: (770) 205-8945
Editor Name: Alex Popp
Editor Email: apopp@dawsonnews.com
Editor Phone: (706) 265-3384, ext : 1

EASTMAN

THE DODGE COUNTY NEWS

Street Address: 226 W Main St
City: Eastman
State: GA
Postal Code: 31023
Office phone: 478-374-NEWS (6397)
Publication Website: dodgecountynews.com
General E-mail: dcn@dodgecountynews.com
Publisher Name: Mr. Chuck Eckles
Publisher Email: publisher@dodgecountynews.com

EATONTON

THE EATONTON MESSENGER

Street Address: "100 N. Jefferson Ave. P.O. Box 4027"
City: Eatonton
State: GA
Postal Code: 31024
Office phone: (706) 485-3501
Publication Website: msgr.com
Publisher Name: A. Mark Smith
Editor Name: Josh Lurie
Editor Email: editor@msgr.com
Advertising Executive Name: Amy Hood

FORSYTH

MONROE COUNTY REPORTER

Street Address: P.O. Box 795 50 N. Jackson St
City: Forsyth
State: GA
Postal Code: 31029
Office phone: (478) 994-2358
Publication Website: mymcr.net
Publisher Name: Will Davis
Publisher Email: publisher@mymcr.net
Editor Name: Richard Dumas
Editor Email: forsyth@mymcr.net
Advertising Executive Name: Carolyn Martel
Advertising Executive Email: ads@mymcr.net

FORT VALLEY

THE LEADER TRIBUNE

Corporate/Parent Company: Peach Publishing, Inc
Street Address: 109 Anderson Avenue
City: Fort Valley
State: GA
Postal Code: 31030
Office phone: (478) 825-2432
Publication Website: theleadertribune.net
General E-mail: news@theleadertribune.net
Publisher Name: Judy Robinson
Editor Name: Victor Kulkosky
Advertising Executive Name: Emily Griffin

GREENSBORO

LAKE OCONEE NEWS

Street Address: 1106 Market St.
City: Greensboro
State: GA
Postal Code: 30642
Office phone: (706) 454-1290
Publication Website: www.lakeoconeenews.us
General E-mail: news@lakeoconeenews.us
Editor Name: Justin Hubbard
Editor Email: justin@lakeoconeenews.us
Total Circulation: 65391

HOMER

BANKS COUNTY NEWS

Corporate/Parent Company: MainStreet Newspapers, Inc
Street Address: 935 Historic Homer Hwy.
City: Homer
State: GA
Postal Code: 30547
Office phone: 706-612-5327
Publication Website: www.mainstreetnews.com/banks
General E-mail: news@mainstreetnews.com
Editor Name: Angela Gary
Year Established: 1968
Own Printing Facility?: Y
Commercial printers?: Y
Mechanical specifications: Type page 13 x 21 1/2; E - 6 cols, 2, 1/6 between; A - 6 cols, 2, 1/6 between; C - 6 cols, 2, 1/6 between.
Published Days: Wed
Avg Paid Circ: 3400
Avg Free Circ: 90
Audit Company: Sworn/Estimate/Non-Audited
Audit Date: 6 10 2019

IRWINTON

THE WILKINSON COUNTY POST

Corporate/Parent Company: The Dublin Courier Herald Publishing Co
Street Address: 103 Bacon St
City: Irwinton
State: GA
Postal Code: 31042
Office phone: (478) 946-7272
Publication Website: wilkinsonnewstoday.com
General E-mail: advertisingtch@gmail.com
Publisher Name: Griffin Lovett
Editor Name: DuBose Porter

JASPER

PICKENS COUNTY PROGRESS

Street Address: 94 N. Main Street
City: Jasper
State: GA
Postal Code: 30143
Office phone: 706-253-2457
Publication Website: pickensprogress.com
General E-mail: news@pickensprogress.com
Editor Name: Dan Pool
Editor Email: dpool@pickensprogress.com

JEFFERSONVILLE

THE TWIGGS TIMES NEW ERA

Corporate/Parent Company: The Dublin Courier Herald Publishing Co
Street Address: 505 Railroad St N
City: Jeffersonville
State: GA
Postal Code: 31044
Office phone: 478-945-6037
Publication Website: twiggsnewstoday.com
General E-mail: advertisingtch@gmail.com
Publisher Name: Griffin Lovett
Editor Name: DuBose Porter

JONESBORO

CLAYTON NEWS DAILY

Corporate/Parent Company: Southern Community Newspapers, Inc.
Street Address: 148 Courthouse Street
City: Jonesboro
State: GA
Postal Code: 30236
Office phone: (770) 478-5753
Publication Website: news-daily.com
General E-mail: dgoodson@news-daily.com
Editor Name: Alice Queen
Editor Email: alice.queen@rockdalecitizen.com
Advertising Executive Email: legals@news-daily.com
Year Established: 1970
Mechanical specifications: Type page 13 x 21 1/2; E - 6 cols, 2 1/16, 1/8 between; A - 6 cols, 2 1/16, 1/8 between; C - 6 cols, 2 1/16, 1/8 between.
Published Days: Wed`Thur`Fri`Sat
Weekday Frequency: m
Saturday Frequency: m
Avg Paid Circ: 1600
Avg Free Circ: 6673
Audit Company: CAC
Audit Date: 30 09 2012
Pressroom Equipment: Lines – 6-KP/News King; 8-KP/News King; Reels & Stands – 6;

LAGRANGE

TROUP COUNTY NEWS

Street Address: P.O. Box 1365 500 New Franklin Road
City: LaGrange
State: GA
Postal Code: 30240
Office phone: (706) 884-1151
Publication Website: troupcountynews.net
General E-mail: info@troupcountynews.net
Advertising Executive Name: John West
Total Circulation: 8000

LAKELAND

THE LANIER COUNTY ADVOCATE

Street Address: P.O.Box 476 5 South Center Str
City: Lakeland
State: GA
Postal Code: 31635
Office phone: 229-482-1045
Publication Website: laniercountyadvocate.com
Publisher Name: Len Robbins, III
Publisher Email: publisher@laniercountyadvocate.com
Advertising Executive Name: Lorene Warren
Advertising Executive Email: advertising@laniercountyadvocate.com

LAVONIA

THE FRANKLIN COUNTY CITIZEN

Corporate/Parent Company: Community Newspapers, Inc.
Street Address: P.O. Box 580, 12150 Augusta Road
City: Lavonia
State: GA
Postal Code: 30553
Office phone: 706-356-8557
Publication Website: franklincountycitizen.com
General E-mail: fcc@franklincountycitizen.com
Publisher Name: Shane Scoggins
Publisher Email: sscoggins@franklincountycitizen.com
Publisher Phone: 706-356-8557
Advertising Executive Name: Diane Rice
Advertising Executive Email: sales@franklincountycitizen.com
Total Circulation: 5050

LAWRENCEVILLE

GWINNETT DAILY POST

Corporate/Parent Company: Southern Community Newspapers, Inc.
Street Address: 725 Old Norcross Rd
City: Lawrenceville
State: GA

Non-Daily Newspapers in the U.S.

Postal Code: 30046-4317
Office phone: (770) 963-9205
Publication Website: http://www.gwinnettdailypost.com/
General E-mail: circulation@gwinnettdailypost.com
Editor Name: Todd Cline
Editor Phone: (770) 963-9205, ext : 1300
Advertising Executive Name: Janet McCray
Advertising Executive Phone: (770) 963-9205, ext : 1214
Year Established: 1970
Delivery Methods: Mail`Carrier`Racks
Own Printing Facility?: N
Commercial printers?: Y
Mechanical specifications: Type page 11.83 x 21.5 - 6 cols
Published Days: Wed`Fri`Sun
Weekday Frequency: m
Saturday Frequency: m
Avg Paid Circ: 335
Avg Free Circ: 49
Audit Company: CVC
Audit Date: 30 09 2016
Pressroom Equipment: Lines – 10-G/Urbanite 1997 DGM 2003; Folders – G/Urbanite.;

LEESBURG

THE LEE COUNTY LEDGER

Street Address: 126 Fourth Street
City: Leesburg
State: GA
Postal Code: 31763
Office phone: 229-759-2413
Publication Website: leecountyledger.com
Publisher Name: Jim Quinn
Publisher Email: jim@leecountyledger.com

LOUISVILLE

JEFFERSON REPORTER/NEWS & FARMER

Corporate/Parent Company: Gannett
Street Address: 615 Mulberry Street
City: Louisville
State: GA
Postal Code: 30434
Office phone: (478) 625-7722
Publication Website: thenewsandfarmer.com
General E-mail: news@thenewsandfarmer.com
Editor Name: Parish Howard
Editor Email: phoward@chroniclemedia.com
Editor Phone: (478) 625-7722

MANCHESTER

MANCHESTER STAR-MERCURY

Corporate/Parent Company: SmallTownPapers, Inc.
Street Address: PO Box 426
City: Manchester
State: GA
Postal Code: 31816
Office phone: (706) 846-3188
Publication Website: http://www.smalltownpapers.com/newspapers/newspaper.php?id=272
General E-mail: news@star-mercury.com
Editor Name: John Kuykendall

MC RAE

THE TELFAIR ENTERPRISE

Corporate/Parent Company: Community Newspapers, Inc.
Street Address: 31 W Oak St
City: Mc Rae
State: GA
Postal Code: 31055
Office phone: (229) 868-6015
Publication Website: http://www.thetelfairenterprise.com/
General E-mail: telfairenterprise@windstream.net

Publisher Name: Eric Denty
Publisher Email: edenty@thetelfairenterprise.com
Editor Name: Jamie Hussey
Editor Email: telfaireditor@windstream.net
Advertising Executive Name: Daisy McCauley
Advertising Executive Email: telfairads@windstream.net
Mechanical specifications: Type page 13 x 21; E - 6 cols, 2, 1/6 between; A - 6 cols, 2, 1/6 between; C - 6 cols, 2, 1/6 between.
Published Days: Wed
Avg Paid Circ: 3200
Avg Free Circ: 55
Audit Company: Sworn/Estimate/Non-Audited
Audit Date: 6 10 2019

MCDONOUGH

HENRY DAILY HERALD

Corporate/Parent Company: Southern Community Newspapers, Inc.
Street Address: 38 Sloan St
City: McDonough
State: GA
Postal Code: 30253-3102
Office phone: (770) 957-9161
Publication Website: https://www.henryherald.com
Published Days: Wed`Fri`Sat
Avg Paid Circ: 2493
Avg Free Circ: 11
Audit Company: Sworn/Estimate/Non-Audited
Audit Date: 6 10 2019

HENRY HERALD

Corporate/Parent Company: Southern Community Newspapers, Inc
Street Address: 38 Sloan Street
City: McDonough
State: GA
Postal Code: 30253
Office phone: 770-957-9161
Publication Website: henryherald.com
Editor Name: Alice Queen
Editor Email: Alice.queen@rockdalecitizen.com
Advertising Executive Name: Mary Ann Holland
Advertising Executive Email: maryann.holland@henryherald.com

MILLEDGEVILLE

THE BALDWIN BULLETIN

Street Address: 136 S Wayne St
City: Milledgeville
State: GA
Postal Code: 31061
Office phone: (478) 452-1777
Publication Website: www.bbnews.today
Publisher Name: A. Mark Smith Sr.
Publisher Email: amsmith@bbnews.today
Publisher Phone: 706-485-3501 x9
Editor Name: Wil Petty
Editor Email: wil@bbnews.today
Editor Phone: 478-452-1777
Advertising Executive Name: Brandi Harrison
Advertising Executive Email: brandi@bbnews.today

PEARSON

THE ATKINSON COUNTY CITIZEN

Corporate/Parent Company: Blalock, Lovett, & Associates, Inc
Street Address: 302 Austin Avenue E.
City: Pearson
State: GA
Postal Code: 31642
Office phone: 912-422-3824
Publication Website: atkinsoncountycitizennewspaper.com
Publisher Name: Len Robbins
Publisher Email: lrobbins@theclinchcountynews.com

Publisher Phone: 912-218-2255
Editor Name: Blake Pittman
Editor Email: atcocitizen@mchsi.com
Editor Phone: 912-520-8831

RICHMOND HILL

BRYAN COUNTY NEWS

Corporate/Parent Company: Morris Multimedia, Inc.
Street Address: 9998 Ford Ave
City: Richmond Hill
State: GA
Postal Code: 31324
Office phone: (912) 756-2668
Publication Website: http://www.bryancountynews.com/
General E-mail: m.swendra@bryancountynews.com
Publisher Name: Patty Leon
Publisher Email: pleon@coastalcourier.com
Publisher Phone: (912) 756-2668
Editor Name: Jeff Whitten
Editor Email: jwhitten@bryancountynews.com
Editor Phone: (912) 644-9263
Advertising Executive Name: Hollie Lewis
Advertising Executive Email: hlewis@bryancountynews.com
Advertising Executive Phone: (912) 756-2668, ext : 1102
Delivery Methods: Mail`Racks
Published Days: Wed`Thur`Sat
Avg Paid Circ: 3000
Avg Free Circ: 1000
Audit Company: Sworn/Estimate/Non-Audited
Audit Date: 6 10 2019

RINCON

EFFINGHAM HERALD

Corporate/Parent Company: Morris Multimedia, Inc.
Street Address: 1204 N. Columbia Ave
City: Rincon
State: GA
Postal Code: 31326
Office phone: "(912) 826-5012
"
Publication Website: https://www.effinghamherald.net/
General E-mail: kdennis@effinghamherald.net
Publisher Name: Kim Dennis
Publisher Email: kdennis@effinghamherald.net
Publisher Phone: (912) 826-5012
Editor Name: Mark Lastinger
Editor Email: mlastinger@effinghamherald.net
Editor Phone: (912) 826-5012
Advertising Executive Name: Jacquelyn Williams
Advertising Executive Email: jwilliams@effinghamherald.net
Advertising Executive Phone: (912) 826-5012
Year Established: 1908
Delivery Methods: Mail`Racks
Mechanical specifications: Type page 10.5 x 21; E - 6 cols, 1 13/16, 1/6 between; A & C- 6 cols, 1 13/16, 1/6 between.
Published Days: Wed
Avg Paid Circ: 2129
Avg Free Circ: 76
Audit Company: AAM
Audit Date: 7 05 2019
Mailroom Equipment: Counter Stackers – 2/KAN, 1-/Gammler; Inserters & Stuffers – 2-KAN/480; Tying Machines – 3-/StraPak.;
Buisness Equipment: APP/Mac Power Mac
Buisness Software: Baseview
Classified Equipment: Hardware – APP/Power Mac; Printers – APP/Mac, HP;
Classified Software: Baseview/ClassFlow 1.1.2.
Editorial Equipment: Hardware – APP/Power Mac; Printers – APP/Mac
Editorial Software: Baseview/NewsEdit Pro.
Production Equipment: Hardware – 2-ECR/VRL-80, SCREEN/220; Cameras – SCREEN/C-670-D; Scanners – 1-Nu/2024V-C, 4-Microtek/II HR
Production Software: QPS/QuarkXPress 4.0.
Total Circulation: 4719

SAVANNAH

CONNECT SAVANNAH

Corporate/Parent Company: Morris Multimedia, Inc.
Street Address: "611 East Bay Street
"
City: Savannah
State: GA
Postal Code: 31401
Office phone: (912) 238-2040
Publication Website: https://www.connectsavannah.com
General E-mail: sales@connectsavannah.com
Publisher Name: Chris Griffin
Publisher Phone: (912) 721-4378
Editor Name: Jim Morekis
Editor Phone: (912) 721-4360

SAVANNAH PENNYSAVER

Corporate/Parent Company: Morris Multimedia, Inc.
Street Address: 1464 E Victory Dr
City: Savannah
State: GA
Postal Code: 31404-4108
Office phone: (912) 238-2040
Publication Website: http://www.savpennysaver.com
Audit Company: AAM
Audit Date: 5 02 2020
Total Circulation: 3255

SYLVANIA

THE SYLVANIA TELEPHONE

Corporate/Parent Company: Gannett
Street Address: 208 N. Main St.
City: Sylvania
State: GA
Postal Code: 30467
Office phone: (912) 564-2045
Publication Website: sylvaniatelephone.com
Editor Name: Enoch Autry
Editor Email: enoch.autry@sylvaniatelephone.com
Editor Phone: (912) 564-2045
Total Circulation: 7200

THOMASTON

UPSON BEACON

Street Address: 108 East Gordon Street
City: Thomaston
State: GA
Postal Code: 30286
Office phone: 706-646-2382
Publication Website: www.upsonbeacon.com
Publisher Name: Debbie Lord
Publisher Email: dlord@upsonbeacon.com
Editor Name: Josh Gish
Editor Email: jmgish94@uga.edu
Advertising Executive Name: Bridge Turner
Advertising Executive Email: bturner@upsonbeacon.com

TOCCOA

THE TOCCOA RECORD

Corporate/Parent Company: Community Newspapers, Inc.
Street Address: 151 W Doyle St
City: Toccoa
State: GA
Postal Code: 30577
Office phone: (706) 886-9476
Publication Website: https://www.thetoccoarecord.com
Own Printing Facility?: Y
Published Days: Thur
Avg Paid Circ: 7200
Audit Company: Sworn/Estimate/Non-Audited
Audit Date: 6 10 2019

WRIGHTSVILLE

THE JOHNSON JOURNAL

Corporate/Parent Company: The Dublin Courier Herald Publishing Co
Street Address: 8664 S Marcus St
City: Wrightsville
State: GA
Postal Code: 31096-2000
Office phone: (478) 864-0007
Publication Website: johnsonnewstoday.com
General E-mail: advertisingtch@gmail.com
Publisher Name: Griffin Lovett
Editor Name: DuBose Porter

HAWAII

HILO

HAWAII TRIBUNE-HERALD

Corporate/Parent Company: Black Press Media Ltd.
Street Address: 355 Kinoole St
City: Hilo
State: HI
Postal Code: 96720
Office phone: (808) 935-6621
Publication Website: https://www.hawaiitribune-herald.com
General E-mail: dbock@hawaiitribune-herald.com
Publisher Name: David Bock
Publisher Email: dbock@hawaiitribune-herald.com
Publisher Phone: (808) 930-7323
Editor Name: David Bock
Editor Email: dbock@hawaiitribune-herald.com
Editor Phone: (808) 930-7323
Advertising Executive Name: Linda Woo
Advertising Executive Email: lwoo@staradvertiser.co
Advertising Executive Phone: (808) 529-4355
Delivery Methods: Newsstand`Carrier`Racks
Mechanical specifications: Type page 12 x 21 1/2; E - 6 cols, 1 7/8, 1/6 between; A - 6 cols, 1 7/8, 1/6 between; C - 9 cols, 1 1/4, 2/15 between.
Published Days: Mon`Tues`Wed`Thur`Fri`Sat`Sun
Weekday Frequency: m
Saturday Frequency: m
Avg Paid Circ: 11910
Avg Free Circ: 1475
Audit Company: AAM
Audit Date: 31 03 2018

HONOLULU

KAUAI MIDWEEK

Corporate/Parent Company: Black Press Media Ltd.
Street Address: 500 Ala Moana Blvd
City: Honolulu
State: HI
Postal Code: 96813
Office phone: (808) 529-4700
Publication Website: http://www.midweekkauai.com/
General E-mail: bmossman@midweek.com
Publisher Name: Dennis Francis
Editor Name: Bill Mossman
Editor Email: bmossman@midweek.com
Advertising Executive Phone: (808) 529-4700
Year Established: 2010
Delivery Methods: Carrier
Own Printing Facility?: Y
Commercial printers?: N
Mechanical specifications: Type page 11 x 21; E - 6 cols, 1 - 1/2", 1/8 between; A - 6 cols, 1 - 1/2, 1/8 between; C - 10 cols, 7/8", 3/32"between; tab page size 9.7"w x 10" depth, DT is 20"w x 10"depth.
Published Days: Wed

Avg Free Circ: 23294
Audit Company: AAM
Audit Date: 31 12 2017

MIDWEEK OAHU

Corporate/Parent Company: Black Press Media Ltd.
Street Address: 500 Ala Moana Blvd
City: Honolulu
State: HI
Postal Code: 96813
Office phone: (808) 529-4700
Publication Website: http://www.midweek.com/
General E-mail: dkennedy@staradvertiser.com
Publisher Name: Dennis Francis
Editor Name: Bill Mossman
Editor Email: bmossman@midweek.com
Editor Phone: (808) 529-4863
Advertising Executive Name: Darin Nakakura
Advertising Executive Email: dnakakura@staradvertiser.com
Advertising Executive Phone: (808) 529-4726
Year Established: 1984
Delivery Methods: Mail
Own Printing Facility?: Y
Commercial printers?: N
Mechanical specifications: Type page 11 x 21; 1/8 pg 4.787" x 2.5" 1/4 pg 4.787 x 5" 1/2 pg horizontal 9.7" x 5" 1/2 pg vertical 4.787" x 10" full pg 9.7" x 10" front pg banner 9.7" x 2" double truck 20" x 10"
Published Days: Wed
Avg Free Circ: 269041
Audit Company: AAM
Audit Date: 31 12 2017
Mailroom Equipment: Inserters & Stuffers – MM/227; Tying Machines – Sig LB2330; Address Machine – Videojet 7300;
Buisness Software: MPA
Classified Equipment: APP/Mac; Printers – NewGen, HP/1300 CP, Epson/1520, ;
Classified Software: Baseview/Ad Manager Pro. Adicio
Editorial Equipment: APP/Mac, QPS/QuarkXPress 4.11, Baseview/News Edit Pro 3.2.3/Nikon/LS 1000, Epson/1200 Scanners; Printers – LaserMaster/, APP/Mac, Epson/3000
Editorial Software: NewsEngin Adobe/InDesign.

STREET PULSE

Corporate/Parent Company: Black Press Media Ltd.
Street Address: 500 Ala Moana Blvd
City: Honolulu
State: HI
Postal Code: 96813-4930
Office phone: (808) 529-4700
Publication Website: http://www.honolulustreetpulse.com/
Year Established: 2012
Delivery Methods: Racks
Own Printing Facility?: Y
Published Days: Fri
Avg Free Circ: 44843
Audit Company: AAM
Audit Date: 31 12 2017

USA TODAY HAWAII EDITION

Corporate/Parent Company: Gannett
Street Address: 500 Ala Moana Blvd
City: Honolulu
State: HI
Postal Code: 96813-4930
Office phone: (808) 529-4700
Publication Website: https://mauinow.com/tag/usa-today-hawaii-edition/
Year Established: 2012
Delivery Methods: Newsstand`Carrier`Racks
Own Printing Facility?: Y

Mechanical specifications: Type Page 11 x 21; 6 cols 1-1/2", 1/8 between; 5 cols 1-7/8", 1/8 between
Published Days: Mon`Tues`Wed`Thur`Fri
Weekday Frequency: m
Avg Paid Circ: 5531
Audit Company: AAM
Audit Date: 24 10 2018

KAILUA KONA

WEST HAWAII TODAY

Corporate/Parent Company: Black Press Media Ltd.
Street Address: 75-5580 Kuakini Hwy
City: Kailua Kona
State: HI
Postal Code: 96740
Office phone: (808) 329-9311
Publication Website: https://www.westhawaiitoday.com/
General E-mail: cjensen@westhawaiitoday.com
Editor Name: Chelsea Jensen
Editor Email: cjensen@westhawaiitoday.com
Editor Phone: (808) 930-8618
Advertising Executive Name: Linda Woo
Advertising Executive Email: lwoo@staradvertiser.co
Advertising Executive Phone: (808) 529-4355
Year Established: 1968
Delivery Methods: Newsstand`Carrier`Racks
Own Printing Facility?: Y
Mechanical specifications: Type page 11 5/8 x 21 1/2; E - 6 cols, 1 3/4, 3/16 between; A - 6 cols, 1 3/4, 3/16 between; C - 9 cols, 1 3/16, 1/8 between.
Published Days: Mon`Tues`Wed`Thur`Fri`Sat`Sun
Weekday Frequency: m
Saturday Frequency: m
Avg Paid Circ: 6663
Avg Free Circ: 699
Audit Company: AAM
Audit Date: 31 03 2018
Pressroom Equipment: Lines – 8-G/Community; Press Drive – 2-Fin/60 h.p.; Folders – 1-G/SC.;

KAMUELA

NORTH HAWAII NEWS

Corporate/Parent Company: Black Press Media Ltd.
Street Address: 65-1279 Kawaihae Rd
City: Kamuela
State: HI
Postal Code: 96743
Office phone: (808) 930-8675
Publication Website: http://northhawaiinews.com/
Editor Name: Landry Fuller
Year Established: 2000
Delivery Methods: Mail
Own Printing Facility?: Y
Published Days: Wed
Avg Paid Circ: 1798
Audit Company: Sworn/Estimate/Non-Audited
Audit Date: 6 10 2019

KAUNAKAKAI

MOLOKAI ADVERTISER-NEWS

Street Address: 10254 Kamehameha V Hwy
City: Kaunakakai
State: HI
Postal Code: 96748-7000
Office phone: 808-558-8253
Publication Website: www.molokaiadvertisernews.com
Editor Name: George Peabody

LIHUE

THE GARDEN ISLAND, KAUAI

Corporate/Parent Company: Black Press Media Ltd.
Street Address: 3-3137 Kuhio Hwy
City: Lihue
State: HI
Postal Code: 96766
Office phone: (808) 245-3681
Publication Website: https://www.thegardenisland.com/
General E-mail: jelse@thegardenisland.com
Editor Name: Jessica Else
Editor Email: jelse@thegardenisland.com
Editor Phone: (808) 245-0452
Advertising Executive Name: Linda Woo
Advertising Executive Email: nationals@thegardenisland.com
Advertising Executive Phone: (808) 529-4355
Year Established: 1902
Delivery Methods: Mail`Newsstand`Carrier`Racks
Own Printing Facility?: Y
Commercial printers?: Y
Mechanical specifications: Type page 11 x 21; E - 6 cols, 1 - 1/2", 1/8 between; A - 6 cols, 1 - 1/2, 1/8 between; C - 10 cols, 7/8", 3/32"between.
Published Days: Mon`Tues`Wed`Thur`Fri`Sun
Weekday Frequency: m
Avg Paid Circ: 6493
Avg Free Circ: 2631
Audit Company: AAM
Audit Date: 31 03 2016
Pressroom Equipment: Lines – 6 Towers Man Roland Regioman 2004; 6 Towers Man Roland Regioman 2004; Press Drive – VFD - Shaftless; Folders – KFZ 80 (2-3-3) Jaw Folder System; Pasters –CD-13Reels & Stands – CD-13; Control System – PECOM; Registration System – PECOM
Mailroom Equipment: Counter Stackers – 4 - Quipp 501 1 - Quipp 401 4 - Muller Martini Combi Stacks; Inserters & Stuffers – 2 - GMA/SLS 2000; Tying Machines - 4-Dynaric NP 3000 4-Dynaric NP 1500; Control System – SAM; News Grip Links; Address Machine – Videojet BX 6500 ink jet printer.

THE GARDEN ISLAND, LIHUE

Corporate/Parent Company: Black Press Media Ltd.
Street Address: 3-3137 Kuhio Highway
City: Lihue
State: HI
Postal Code: 96766
Office phone: (808) 245-3681
Publication Website: https://www.thegardenisland.com/
General E-mail: jelse@thegardenisland.com
Editor Name: Jessica Else
Editor Email: jelse@thegardenisland.com
Editor Phone: (808) 245-0452
Advertising Executive Name: Linda Woo
Advertising Executive Email: nationals@thegardenisland.com
Advertising Executive Phone: (808) 529-4355

SCHOFIELD BARRACKS

HAWAII ARMY WEEKLY-OOB

Corporate/Parent Company: Black Press Media Ltd.
Street Address: 745 Wright Ave., Waaf
City: Schofield Barracks
State: HI
Postal Code: 96857
Office phone: (808) 656-3155
Publication Website: http://www.hawaiiarmyweekly.com/
Editor Name: JR Reese
Editor Email: news@hawaiiarmyweekly.com
Editor Phone: (808) 656-3488
Advertising Executive Email: onlineads@staradvertiser.com
Advertising Executive Phone: (808) 525-7439

Non-Daily Newspapers in the U.S.

IOWA

ADEL

NORTHEAST DALLAS COUNTY RECORD (OOB)

Street Address: 1316 2nd Street Suite B
City: Adel
State: IA
Postal Code: 50220
Office phone: (515) 465-4666
Publication Website: https://www.adelnews.com/
General E-mail: news@adelnews.com
Publisher Name: kim fowler
Publisher Email: kfowler@amestrib.com
Publisher Phone: (515) 663-6943
Editor Name: Allison Ullmann
Editor Email: news@adelnews.com
Editor Phone: (515) 465-4666
Advertising Executive Email: ads@adelnews.com
Advertising Executive Phone: (515) 465-4666
Mailroom Equipment: Counter Stackers – MM/310; Inserters & Stuffers – MM/227; Tying Machines – 2-MLN/Strapper; Address Machine – 3/Wm.;
Classified Equipment: Hardware – APP/Mac; Printers – HP;
Classified Software: Baseview/AdManager Pro, QPS/QuarkXPress.
Editorial Equipment: Hardware – APP/Mac; Printers – 1-Xante/Accel-a-Writer 3N
Editorial Software: Adobe/Illustrator CS2, Adobe/InDesign CS2, Adobe/Photoshop CS2, Baseview.
Production Equipment: Hardware – 1-Pre Press/Panther Pro 36-HS, 1-Mon/Ultra 36; Cameras – 1-LE/490 vertical
Production Software: Adobe/CS2.

AFTON

STAR ENTERPRISE

Street Address: 274 N Douglas St
City: Afton
State: IA
Postal Code: 50830
Office phone: 641-347-8721
Publication Website: www.aftoniowa.com
Publisher Name: Wayne Hill

ALGONA

KOSSUTH COUNTY ADVANCE

Street Address: 14 E. Nebraska Street
City: Algona
State: IA
Postal Code: 50511
Office phone: (515) 295-3535
Publication Website: www.algona.com
General E-mail: news@algona.com
Publisher Name: Brad Hicks
Publisher Email: publisher@algona.com
Publisher Phone: 515-295-3535 x 223
Editor Name: Alan Van Ormer
Editor Email: avanormer@algona.com
Editor Phone: 515-295-3535 x 230
Advertising Executive Name: Nancy Steburg
Advertising Executive Email: nsteburg@algona.com
Advertising Executive Phone: 515-295-3535 x 226

AMES

STORY COUNTY ADVERTISER

Street Address: 317 5th St, P.O. Box 380
City: Ames
State: IA
Postal Code: 50010-6101
Office phone: (515) 232-2160
Publication Website: https://www.amestrib.com/storycountysun
General E-mail: kfowler@amestrib.com
Publisher Name: Becky Bjork
Publisher Email: rbjork@amestrib.com
Publisher Phone: (515) 663-6947
Editor Name: Michael Crumb
Editor Email: mcrumb@amestrib.com
Editor Phone: (515) 663-6961
Advertising Executive Name: Kim Fowler
Advertising Executive Email: kfowler@amestrib.com
Advertising Executive Phone: (515) 663-6943

THE TRI-COUNTY TIMES

Corporate/Parent Company: Gannett
Street Address: 317 6th St., Suite B
City: Ames
State: IA
Postal Code: 50010-6101
Office phone: (515) 232-2160
Publication Website: https://www.tricountytimes.com/
General E-mail: ldodd@nevadaiowajournal.com
Publisher Name: Kim Fowler
Publisher Email: kfowler@amestrib.com
Advertising Executive Name: Lauri Dodd
Advertising Executive Email: ldodd@nevadaiowajournal.com
Advertising Executive Phone: (515) 663-6902
Published Days: Thur
Avg Paid Circ: 2500
Audit Company: Sworn/Estimate/Non-Audited
Audit Date: 6 10 2019
Total Circulation: 1875

ANAMOSA

THE JOURNAL-EUREKA

Street Address: P.O. Box 108
City: Anamosa
State: IA
Postal Code: 52205
Office phone: (319) 462-3511
Publication Website: www.journal-eureka.com
General E-mail: publisher@journal-eureka.com
Publisher Name: Mary Ungs-Sogaard
Publisher Email: mungs-sogaard@wcinet.com
Editor Name: Beth Lutgen
Editor Email: blutgen@wcinet.com
Advertising Executive Name: Wendy Geerts
Advertising Executive Email: wendy.geerts@wcinet.com

ARKON

THE AKRON HOMETOWNER

Street Address: PO Box 797
City: Arkon
State: IA
Postal Code: 51001
Office phone: 712-568-2208
Publication Website: www.akronhometowner.com
General E-mail: akronht@arkonhometowner.com
Publisher Name: Dodie Hook

BAYARD

THE NEWS GAZETTE

Street Address: 409 Main Street P. O. Box 130
City: Bayard
State: IA
Postal Code: 50029-0130
Office phone: 712-651-2321
Publication Website: www.BayardNewsGazette.com
Editor Name: Luann Waldo
Total Circulation: 3950

BELMOND

BELMOND INDEPENDENT

Street Address: 215 E. Main Street
City: Belmond
State: IA
Postal Code: 50421
Office phone: 641-444-3333
Publication Website: www.belmondnews.com
General E-mail: belmondnews@frontiernet.net
Year Established: 1885
Delivery Methods: Mail`Newsstand
Commercial printers?: Y
Mechanical specifications: Type page 13 wide x 21 tall; 6 columns, 12 picas per col. with one pica gutter.
Published Days: Thur
Avg Paid Circ: 1400
Avg Free Circ: 5
Audit Company: Sworn/Estimate/Non-Audited
Audit Date: 6 10 2019

CASCADE

CASCADE PIONEER

Corporate/Parent Company: Woodward Communications, Inc.
Street Address: 716 1st Ave. E, PO Box 9
City: Cascade
State: IA
Postal Code: 52033-0009
Office phone: (563) 852-3217
Publication Website: https://www.cpioneer.com/
General E-mail: pioneer@wcinet.com
Publisher Name: Mary Ungs-Sogaard
Publisher Email: mungs-sogaard@wcinet.com
Editor Name: Beth Lutgen
Editor Email: blutgen@wcinet.com
Advertising Executive Name: Linda Vorwald
Advertising Executive Email: pioneer@wcinet.com
Year Established: 1876
Delivery Methods: Mail`Newsstand
Own Printing Facility?: Y
Commercial printers?: N
Published Days: Wed
Avg Paid Circ: 1875
Audit Company: Sworn/Estimate/Non-Audited
Audit Date: 6 10 2019

CLARINDA

THE HERALD-JOURNAL

Street Address: 114 W Main St
City: Clarinda
State: IA
Postal Code: 51632
Office phone: 712-542-2181
Publication Website: www.clarindaherald.com
Publisher Name: John VanNostrand
Editor Name: Kent Dinnebier
Editor Email: news@clarindaherald.com
Advertising Executive Name: Jennifer Johnson
Advertising Executive Email: ads@clarindaherald.com

CLARION

THE WRIGHT COUNTY MONITOR

Corporate/Parent Company: Mid-America Publishing
Street Address: P.O. Box 153 107 2nd Avenue N.E.
City: Clarion
State: IA
Postal Code: 50525
Office phone: 515-532-2871
Publication Website: www.clarionnewsonline.com
General E-mail: cmonitor@mchsi.com
Editor Name: Bridget Shileny
Editor Email: wrightcomonitor@gmail.com
Advertising Executive Name: Shelbie Fisher
Advertising Executive Email: wrightcosales@midamericapub.com

CRESCO

TIMES PLAIN DEALER

Street Address: 214 N. Elm Street
City: Cresco
State: IA
Postal Code: 52136
Office phone: 563-547-3601
Publication Website: www.crescotimes.com
Publisher Name: Daniel Evans
Publisher Email: devansppc@mediacombb.net
Editor Name: Marcie Klomp
Editor Email: tpdeditor@crescotimes.com
Advertising Executive Name: Betty Schmitt
Advertising Executive Email: ads1@crescotimes.com
Total Circulation: 2600

DANBURY

THE DANBURY REVIEW

Street Address: Box 207
City: Danbury
State: IA
Postal Code: 51019
Office phone: 712-893-2001
Publication Website: www.danbury-ia.com
Editor Name: Michael Buth
Total Circulation: 1100

DAVENPORT

AD EXTRA

Street Address: 500 E. 3rd St.
City: Davenport
State: IA
Postal Code: 52801
Office phone: (309) 764-4344
Publication Website: https://qconline.com/
General E-mail: crockwell@qctimes.com
Publisher Name: Deb Anselm
Publisher Phone: (563) 383-2224
Editor Name: Matt Christensen
Editor Email: mchristensen@qctimes.com
Editor Phone: (563) 383-2264
Advertising Executive Name: Cathy Rockwell
Advertising Executive Email: crockwell@qctimes.com
Advertising Executive Phone: (563) 383-2306

MOLINE DISPATCH PUBLISHING COMPANY, L.L.C

Street Address: 500 E. 3rd St.
City: Davenport
State: IA
Postal Code: 52801
Office phone: (309) 764-4344
Publication Website: https://qconline.com/
General E-mail: crockwell@qctimes.com
Publisher Name: Deb Anselm
Publisher Email: danselm@qctimes.com
Publisher Phone: (563) 383-2224
Editor Name: Matt Christensen
Editor Email: mchristensen@qctimes.com
Editor Phone: (563) 383-2264
Advertising Executive Name: Cathy Rockwell
Advertising Executive Email: crockwell@qctimes.com
Advertising Executive Phone: (563) 383-2306

DAYTON

DAYTON LEADER

Street Address: 37 S MAIN ST
City: Dayton
State: IA
Postal Code: 50530
Office phone: 515 571 1666
Publication Website: www.daytonleader.wix.com/daytonleader
General E-mail: daytonleader@gmail.com
Editor Name: Kendra Breitsprecher

DENVER

THE FORUM

Corporate/Parent Company: Horizon Publishing Company
Street Address: PO Box 509
City: Denver
State: IA
Postal Code: 50622-0509
Office phone: 319-984-6179
Publication Website: www.denveriaforum.com
General E-mail: news@denveriaforum.com
Publisher Name: Kim Edward Adams
Total Circulation: 2219

DES MOINES

BUSINESS RECORD

Corporate/Parent Company: Business Publication Corp.
Street Address: The Depot at Fourth, 100 4th Street
City: Des Moines
State: IA
Postal Code: 50309
Office phone: (515) 288-3336
Publication Website: www.businessrecord.com
General E-mail: newsroom@bpcdm.com
Publisher Name: Chris Conetzkey
Publisher Email: chrisconetzkey@bpcdm.com
Publisher Phone: (515) 661-6081
Editor Name: Emily Barske
Editor Email: emilybarske@bpcdm.com
Editor Phone: (515) 661-6085

HERALD-INDEX

Street Address: 715 Locust Street
City: Des Moines
State: IA
Postal Code: 50309
Office phone: 515-699-7000
Publication Website: www.altoonaherald.com
General E-mail: newsubs@dmreg.com
Editor Name: Carol Hunter
Editor Email: chunter@registermedia.com

THE RECORD-HERALD & INDIANOLA TRIBUNE

Street Address: 400 Locust Street Suite 500
City: Des Moines
State: IA
Postal Code: 50309
Office phone: (515) 961-2511
Publication Website: www.indianolarecordherald.com
Editor Name: Carol Hunter
Editor Email: chunter@registermedia.com

DUBUQUE

MOUNT VERNON-LISBON SUN

Corporate/Parent Company: Woodward Communications, Inc.
Street Address: 801 Bluff Street
City: Dubuque
State: IA
Postal Code: 52001-4661
Office phone: (319) 895-6216
Publication Website: https://www.mvlsun.com/
General E-mail: advertising@mtvernonlisbonsun.com
Publisher Email: publisher@mtvernonlisbonsun.com
Publisher Phone: (800) 562-1825
Editor Name: Margaret Stevens
Editor Email: news@mtvernonlisbonsun.com
Advertising Executive Name: Rich Eskelsen
Advertising Executive Email: advertising@mtvernonlisbonsun.com
Year Established: 1869

Delivery Methods: Mail`Newsstand
Mechanical specifications: Type page 11 x 21 1/2; E - 6 cols, 1.5, 1/6 between; A - 6 cols, 1.5, 1/6 between; C - 6 cols, 1 1/2, 1/6 between.
Published Days: Thur
Avg Paid Circ: 2500
Avg Free Circ: 3000
Audit Company: Sworn/Estimate/Non-Audited
Audit Date: 6 10 2019

DYERSVILLE

DYERSVILLE COMMERCIAL

Corporate/Parent Company: Woodward Communications, Inc.
Street Address: 223 1st Ave E, P.O. Box 350
City: Dyersville
State: IA
Postal Code: 52040-1202
Office phone: (563) 875-7131
Publication Website: https://www.dyersvillecommercial.com/
General E-mail: lvorwald@wcinet.com
Publisher Name: Mary Ungs-Sogaard
Publisher Email: mungs-sogaard@wcinet.com
Editor Name: Beth Lutgen
Editor Email: blutgen@wcinet.com
Advertising Executive Name: Linda Vorwald
Advertising Executive Email: lvorwald@wcinet.com
Year Established: 1873
Delivery Methods: Mail`Carrier
Mechanical specifications: Type page 13 x 21 1/2; E - 6 cols, 2 1/32, 1/8 between; A - 6 cols, 2 1/32, 1/8 between; C - 6 cols, 2 1/32, 1/8 between.
Published Days: Wed
Avg Paid Circ: 3950
Audit Company: Sworn/Estimate/Non-Audited
Audit Date: 6 10 2019
Total Circulation: 1200

EASTERN IOWA SHOPPING NEWS

Corporate/Parent Company: Woodward Communications, Inc.
Street Address: 223 1st Ave E
City: Dyersville
State: IA
Postal Code: 52040-1202
Office phone: (563) 875-7131
Publication Website: http://www.easterniowashoppingnews.com/
General E-mail: lvorwald@wcinet.com
Publisher Name: Mary Ungs-Sogaard
Publisher Email: mungs-sogaard@wcinet.com
Editor Name: Beth Lutgen
Editor Email: blutgen@wcinet.com
Advertising Executive Name: Linda Vorwald
Advertising Executive Email: lvorwald@wcinet.com

ELDORA

ELDORA HERALD-LEDGER

Corporate/Parent Company: Mid-America Publishing
Street Address: 1254 Edgington Ave.
City: Eldora
State: IA
Postal Code: 50627
Office phone: 641-939-5051
Publication Website: www.eldoranewspapers.com
General E-mail: ads@eldoranewspaper.com
Publisher Name: Betty Gotto
Editor Name: Rick Patrie
Advertising Executive Name: Pam Warren
Total Circulation: 4800

ELKADER

THE CLAYTON COUNTY REGISTER

Corporate/Parent Company: Courier Press

Street Address: P.O. Box 130
City: Elkader
State: IA
Postal Code: 52043-9078
Office phone: (563) 245-1311
Publication Website: http://www.claytoncountyregister.com/articles/clayton-county-register
General E-mail: ccrfront@alpinecom.net
Year Established: 1878
Delivery Methods: Mail`Newsstand`Racks
Mechanical specifications: Type page 12 1/2 x 21 1/2; E - 7 cols, 1 1/2, 1/6 between; A - 7 cols, 1 1/2, 1/6 between; C - 7 cols, 1 1/2, 1/6 between.
Published Days: Wed
Avg Paid Circ: 1200
Avg Free Circ: 21000
Audit Company: Sworn/Estimate/Non-Audited
Audit Date: 6 10 2019

GOWRIE

THE GOWRIE NEWS

Street Address: 1107 Market St
City: Gowrie
State: IA
Postal Code: 50543
Office phone: (515) 352-3325
Publication Website: gowrienews.com
General E-mail: gnews@wccta.net
Editor Name: Glenn Schreiber

GRUNDY CENTER

THE GRUNDY REGISTER

Corporate/Parent Company: Mid-America Publishing
Street Address: 601 G. Avenue - P.O. Box 245
City: Grundy Center
State: IA
Postal Code: 50638
Office phone: 1-319-824-6958
Publication Website: www.thegrundyregister.com
Publisher Name: Robert Maharry
Publisher Email: grundypublisher@midamericapub.com
Editor Name: Michaela Kendall
Editor Email: grundyeditor@midamericapub.com

GUTTENBERG

GUTTENBERG PRESS

Corporate/Parent Company: Courier Press
Street Address: 10 Schiller St
City: Guttenberg
State: IA
Postal Code: 52052-9057
Office phone: (563) 252-2421
Publication Website: http://www.claytoncountyregister.com/articles/guttenberg-press
General E-mail: ads@guttenbergpress.com
Advertising Executive Email: ads@guttenbergpress.com
Year Established: 1896
Delivery Methods: Mail`Newsstand`Racks
Own Printing Facility?: Y
Commercial printers?: Y
Mechanical specifications: Type page 10 1/2 x 16; E - 4 cols, 2 1/2, 1/6 between; A - 4 cols, 2 1/2, 1/6 between; C - 5 cols, 1 11/12, 1/6 between.
Published Days: Wed
Avg Paid Circ: 2600
Audit Company: Sworn/Estimate/Non-Audited
Audit Date: 6 10 2019

HAMBURG

HAMBURG REPORTER

Corporate/Parent Company: Gannett
Street Address: 1009 Main St., P.O. Box 99
City: Hamburg

State: IA
Postal Code: 51640
Office phone: (712)382-1234
Publication Website: www.hamburgreporter.com
Editor Name: Kirt Manion
Editor Email: kmanion@ncnewspress.com
Editor Phone: 402-873-3334
Advertising Executive Name: Theresa Kaven
Advertising Executive Email: tkaven@ncnewspress.com
Advertising Executive Phone: 402-269-2135
Delivery Methods: Mail`Racks
Commercial printers?: Y
Published Days: Thur
Avg Paid Circ: 1100
Audit Company: Sworn/Estimate/Non-Audited
Audit Date: 6 10 2019

HARLAN

HARLAN - THE HARLAN TRIBUNE

Corporate/Parent Company: Harlan Newspapers
Street Address: 1114 7th St., PO Box 721
City: Harlan
State: IA
Postal Code: 51537
Office phone: 712-755-3111
Publication Website: www.harlanonline.com
Editor Name: Bob Bjoin
Editor Email: news2@harlanonline.com
Advertising Executive Name: Al Hazelton
Advertising Executive Email: adsales@harlanonline.com
Advertising Executive Phone: 712-755-3111

HARLAN

THE HARLAN NEWS-ADVERTISER

Corporate/Parent Company: Harlan Newspapers
Street Address: 1114 7th St., PO Box 721
City: Harlan
State: IA
Postal Code: 51537
Office phone: 712-755-3111
Publication Website: www.harlanonline.com
Editor Name: Bob Bjoin
Editor Email: news2@harlanonline.com
Advertising Executive Name: Al Hazelton
Advertising Executive Email: adsales@harlanonline.com
Advertising Executive Phone: 712-755-3111
Total Circulation: 5500

HOLSTEIN

THE ADVANCE

Corporate/Parent Company: Mid-America Publishing
Street Address: 523 S. Main Street
City: Holstein
State: IA
Postal Code: 51025
Office phone: 712-364-3131
Publication Website: www.holsteinadvance.com
General E-mail: holsteinadvance@gmail.com
Advertising Executive Name: Karla Meier
Advertising Executive Email: nwiasales@midamericapub.com

HULL

SIOUX COUNTY (HULL) INDEX

Corporate/Parent Company: New Century Press
Street Address: Box 420, 1013 First Street
City: Hull
State: IA
Postal Code: 51239
Office phone: (712) 439-1075
Publication Website: http://siouxcountyindex.com/
General E-mail: kjurrens@ncppub.com
Publisher Name: Lisa Miller
Publisher Email: lmiller@ncppub.com
Editor Name: Jessica Jensen
Editor Email: jjensen@ncppub.com
Advertising Executive Name: Kari Jurrens

Non-Daily Newspapers in the U.S.   III-37

Advertising Executive Email: kjurrens@ncppub.com
Total Circulation: 925

IDA GROVE
IDA COUNTY COURIER
Corporate/Parent Company: Mid-America Publishing
Street Address: 214 Main Street PO Box 249
City: Ida Grove
State: IA
Postal Code: 51445
Office phone: 712-364-3131
Publication Website: www.idacountycourier.com
General E-mail: idacourier@frontiernet.net
Publisher Name: Ryan Harvey
Advertising Executive Name: Karla Meier
Advertising Executive Email: nwiasales@midamericapub.com
Year Established: 1975
Delivery Methods: Mail
Mechanical specifications: Type page 11 1/2 x 21; E - 6 cols, 1 13/16, 1/8 between; A - 6 cols, 1 13/16, 1/8 between; C - 6 cols, 1 13/16, 1/8 between.
Published Days: Wed
Avg Paid Circ: 2099
Avg Free Circ: 120
Audit Company: Sworn/Estimate/Non-Audited
Audit Date: 6 10 2019

INWOOD
WEST LYON HERALD
Corporate/Parent Company: New Century Press
Street Address: Box 340, 211 South Main
City: Inwood
State: IA
Postal Code: 51240-7807
Office phone: (712) 753-2258
Publication Website: http://www.ncppub.com/pages/?cat=23
General E-mail: kjurrens@ncppub.com
Publisher Name: Lisa Miller
Publisher Email: lmiller@ncppub.com
Editor Name: Jessica Jensen
Editor Email: jjensen@ncppub.com
Advertising Executive Name: Kari Jurrens
Advertising Executive Email: kjurrens@ncppub.com
Year Established: 1890
Delivery Methods: Mail`Newsstand`Racks
Mechanical specifications: Type page 10 5/8 x 15; E - 5 cols, 2, 1/6 between; A - 5 cols, 2, 1/6 between; C - 5 cols, 2, 1/6 between.
Published Days: Wed
Avg Paid Circ: 1400
Audit Company: Sworn/Estimate/Non-Audited
Audit Date: 6 10 2019

KALONA
JOURNAL-EUREKA
Corporate/Parent Company: Anamosa Publications
Street Address: 405 E. Main Street, P.O. Box 108
City: Kalona
State: IA
Postal Code: 52205
Office phone: (319) 462-3511
Publication Website: https://www.journal-eureka.com/
General E-mail: wendy.geerts@wcinet.com
Publisher Name: Mary Ungs-Sogaard
Publisher Email: mungs-sogaard@wcinet.com
Editor Name: Beth Lutgen
Editor Email: blutgen@wcinet.com
Advertising Executive Name: Wendy Geerts
Advertising Executive Email: wendy.geerts@wcinet.com
Total Circulation: 1270

THE KALONA NEWS
Corporate/Parent Company: Johnson Iowa Media Inc
Street Address: 419 B Ave.
City: Kalona
State: IA
Postal Code: 52247
Office phone: 319-656-227
Publication Website: http://thenews-ia.com/kalona/
General E-mail: adsales@thenews-ia.com
Publisher Name: Jim Johnson
Publisher Email: publisher@kalonanews.com
Editor Name: James Jennings
Editor Email: news@thenews-ia.com
Advertising Executive Name: Bridget Johnson
Advertising Executive Email: adsales@thenews-ia.com
Year Established: 1891
Delivery Methods: Mail`Newsstand
Published Days: Thur
Avg Paid Circ: 2360
Audit Company: Sworn/Estimate/Non-Audited
Audit Date: 6 10 2019

KNOXVILLE
JOURNAL-EXPRESS
Street Address: 122 E. Robinson
City: Knoxville
State: IA
Postal Code: 50138
Office phone: 641-842-2155
Publication Website: www.journalexpress.net
General E-mail: editor@journalexpress.net
Publisher Name: Becky Maxwell
Publisher Email: publisher@journalexpress.net
Publisher Phone: 641-842-2155, ext. 14
Editor Name: Regional Editor
Editor Email: kocker@dailyiowegian.com
Editor Phone: 641-856-6336, ext. 35

MANCHESTER
MANCHESTER PRESS
Corporate/Parent Company: Woodward Communications, Inc.
Street Address: 109 East Delaware St.
City: Manchester
State: IA
Postal Code: 52057
Office phone: (563) 927-2020
Publication Website: http://www.manchesterpress.com/
General E-mail: blutgen@wcinet.com
Publisher Name: Mary Ungs-Sogaard
Publisher Email: mungs-sogaard@wcinet.com
Editor Name: Beth Lutgen
Editor Email: blutgen@wcinet.com
Advertising Executive Name: Kim Ronnebaum
Advertising Executive Email: kim.ronnebaum@wcinet.com
Delivery Methods: Mail`Newsstand`Racks
Published Days: Tues
Avg Paid Circ: 4800
Audit Company: Sworn/Estimate/Non-Audited
Audit Date: 6 10 2019

MANSON
THE CALHOUN COUNTY JOURNAL-HERALD
Street Address: 931 MAIN - P.O. BOX 40
City: MANSON
State: IA
Postal Code: 50563
Office phone: 712-469-3581
Publication Website: www.journalherald.com
General E-mail: journal@journalherald.com
Publisher Name: Jason Major
Editor Name: Ron Sturgis
Advertising Executive Name: Adeline Gutz
Advertising Executive Phone: 712-469-3581

MARENGO
THE PIONEER-REPUBLICAN
Street Address: 1152 Marengo Ave
City: Marengo
State: IA
Postal Code: 52301
Office phone: 319-642-5506
Publication Website: www.yourweeklypaper.com
General E-mail: customerservice@press-citizen.com
Editor Name: Tory Brecht
Editor Email: tbrecht@press-citizen.com

MARION
MARION TIMES
Corporate/Parent Company: Woodward Communications, Inc.
Street Address: 808 6th St. Suite 1
City: Marion
State: IA
Postal Code: 52302
Office phone: (319) 377-7037
Publication Website: https://www.mariontoday.org/times/
General E-mail: advertising@mariontimesonline.com

MCGREGOR
MCGREGOR - NORTH IOWA TIMES
Corporate/Parent Company: Courier Press
Street Address: P.O. Box M
City: McGregor
State: IA
Postal Code: 52157
Office phone: 563-873-2210
Publication Website: www.northiowatimes.com
General E-mail: niteditor@mhtc.net
Editor Name: Audrey Posten
Total Circulation: 22200

MONONA
MONONA - THE OUTLOOK
Corporate/Parent Company: Mid-America Publishing
Street Address: 116 West Center Street
City: Monona
State: IA
Postal Code: 52159
Office phone: 563-539-4554
Publication Website: http://www.outlooknewspaper.com/
General E-mail: mononaoutlook.map@gmail.com
Editor Name: John Jensen
Advertising Executive Name: Nicole Vega
Advertising Executive Email: outlook@neitel.net

MORAVIA
MORAVIA UNION
Street Address: 108 E King St
City: Moravia
State: IA
Postal Code: 52571
Office phone: 641-724-3224
Publication Website: moraviaiowa.com/community/newspaper
General E-mail: moravianews@gmail.com
Editor Name: Vicki Baty

MOVILLE
MOVILLE - THE RECORD
Corporate/Parent Company: Baker Newspapers, Inc.
Street Address: 238 Main Street
City: Moville
State: IA
Postal Code: 51039
Office phone: 712-873-3141
Publication Website: www.movillerecord.com
General E-mail: record@wiatel.net
Editor Name: Blake Stubbs

OSKALOOSA
THE OSKALOOSA HERALD
Corporate/Parent Company: CNHI, LLC
Street Address: 1901 A Avenue West
City: Oskaloosa
State: IA
Postal Code: 52577
Office phone: 641-672-2581
Publication Website: www.oskaloosa.com
General E-mail: oskynews@oskyherald.com
Publisher Name: Deb Van Engelenhoven
Publisher Email: debve@oskyherald.com
Publisher Phone: Ext. 413
Editor Name: Angie Holland
Editor Email: aholland@oskyherald.com
Editor Phone: Ext. 425
Advertising Executive Name: Barb Knox
Advertising Executive Email: adstwo@oskyherald.com
Advertising Executive Phone: Ext. 414

PARKERSBURG
ECLIPSE-NEWS-REVIEW
Corporate/Parent Company: Mid-America Publishing
Street Address: 503 Coates St.
City: Parkersburg
State: IA
Postal Code: 50665
Office phone: 319-346-1461
Publication Website: www.parkersburgeclipse.com
General E-mail: eclipse@midamericapub.com
Publisher Name: Jake Ryder
Editor Name: Bethany Carson
Advertising Executive Name: Clint Poock

PERRY
THE DALLAS COUNTY NEWS
Corporate/Parent Company: Gannett
Street Address: 1316 2nd Street Suite B
City: Perry
State: IA
Postal Code: 50220
Office phone: 515-465-4666
Publication Website: www.adelnews.com
General E-mail: ads@adelnews.com
Editor Name: Allison Ullmann
Editor Email: news@adelnews.com
Editor Phone: 515-465-4666

ROCK RAPIDS
LYON COUNTY REPORTER
Corporate/Parent Company: New Century Press
Street Address: Box 28, 310 First Avenue
City: Rock Rapids
State: IA
Postal Code: 51246-1595
Office phone: (712) 472-2525
Publication Website: http://www.lyoncountyreporter.com/pages/
General E-mail: kjurrens@ncppub.com
Publisher Name: Lisa Miller
Publisher Email: lmiller@ncppub.com
Editor Name: Jessica Jensen
Editor Email: jjensen@ncppub.com
Advertising Executive Name: Kari Jurrens
Advertising Executive Email: kjurrens@ncppub.com
Delivery Methods: Mail`Newsstand
Commercial printers?: Y
Mechanical specifications: Type page 11 5/8 x 21 1/2; E - 6 cols, 1 13/16, 1/6 between; A - 6 cols, 1 13/16, 1/6 between; C - 6 cols, 1 13/16, 1/6 between.
Published Days: Wed
Avg Paid Circ: 1200

Audit Company: Sworn/Estimate/Non-Audited
Audit Date: 6 10 2019

THE NORTHWEST IOWA EXTRA

Corporate/Parent Company: New Century Press
Street Address: Box 28, 310 First Avenue
City: Rock Rapids
State: IA
Postal Code: 51246-1595
Office phone: (712) 472-2525
Publication Website: http://www.ncppub.com/pages/?cat=102
General E-mail: kjurrens@ncppub.com
Publisher Name: Lisa Miller
Publisher Email: lmiller@ncppub.com
Editor Name: Jessica Jensen
Editor Email: jjensen@ncppub.com
Advertising Executive Name: Kari Jurrens
Advertising Executive Email: kjurrens@ncppub.com

SAINT ANSGAR

ENTERPRISE JOURNAL

Corporate/Parent Company: Enterprise Media Group, LLC
Street Address: 204 East 4th Street PO Box 310
City: Saint Ansgar
State: IA
Postal Code: 50472
Office phone: (641) 713-4541
Publication Website: www.staej.com
General E-mail: editor@staej.com
Total Circulation: 2360

SIOUX CENTER

THE SIOUX CENTER NEWS

Corporate/Parent Company: Iowa Information, Inc.
Street Address: 67 Third Street NE
City: Sioux Center
State: IA
Postal Code: 51250
Office phone: 712-722-0741
Publication Website: www.nwestiowa.com/scnews
General E-mail: editor@siouxcenternews.com
Publisher Name: Peter W. Wagner
Publisher Email: pwagner@iowainformation.com
Publisher Phone: 712-631-4830
Editor Name: Renee Wielenga
Editor Email: rwielenga@nwestiowa.com
Editor Phone: 712-722-5059
Advertising Executive Name: Amber Everson
Advertising Executive Email: aeverson@iowainformation.com
Advertising Executive Phone: 712-722-5054

SOLON

NORTH LIBERTY LEADER

Corporate/Parent Company: Woodward Communications, Inc.
Street Address: 206 E Main St
City: Solon
State: IA
Postal Code: 52333
Office phone: (319) 624-2233
Publication Website: http://www.northlibertyleader.com/
General E-mail: advertising@economistleader.com
Publisher Name: Doug Lindner
Publisher Email: doug.lindner@economistleader.com
Publisher Phone: (319) 624-2233
Advertising Executive Name: Jennifer Maresh
Advertising Executive Email: advertising@economistleader.com
Advertising Executive Phone: (319) 624-2233
Delivery Methods: Mail`Newsstand`Racks
Published Days: Thur

Avg Paid Circ: 925
Audit Company: Sworn/Estimate/Non-Audited
Audit Date: 6 10 2019

SOLON ECONOMIST

Corporate/Parent Company: Woodward Communications, Inc.
Street Address: 206 E. Main St.
City: Solon
State: IA
Postal Code: 52333
Office phone: (319) 624-2233
Publication Website: http://www.soloneconomist.com/
General E-mail: advertising@economistleader.com
Publisher Name: Doug Lindner
Publisher Email: doug.lindner@economistleader.com
Publisher Phone: (319) 624-2233
Advertising Executive Name: Jennifer Maresh
Advertising Executive Email: advertising@economistleader.com
Advertising Executive Phone: (319) 624-2233
Year Established: 1896
Delivery Methods: Mail`Newsstand`Racks
Published Days: Thur
Avg Paid Circ: 1270
Audit Company: Sworn/Estimate/Non-Audited
Audit Date: 6 10 2019

STATE CENTER

MID IOWA ENTERPRISE

Corporate/Parent Company: Chris Davis
Street Address: 201 West Main Street
City: State Center
State: IA
Postal Code: 50247
Office phone: 641-483-2120
Publication Website: www.midiaenterprise.com
Editor Name: Jamie Burdorf

SULLY

HOMETOWN PRESS

Street Address: 301 7th Ave., Suite 101
City: Sully
State: IA
Postal Code: 50251
Office phone: 641-594-3200
Publication Website: https://www.hometownpressia.com
General E-mail: press@netins.net
Publisher Name: Faye Brand
Publisher Email: fbrand@colinemfg.com
Editor Name: Margaret Vander Weerdt
Editor Email: press@netins.net
Advertising Executive Email: adshometownpress@netins.net

SUMNER

SUMNER GAZETTE

Street Address: 106 E 1st St
City: Sumner
State: IA
Postal Code: 50674
Office phone: 563-578-3351
Publication Website: www.sumnergazette.com
General E-mail: sumnergazette@gmail
Publisher Name: Doug Daniels

SWEA CITY

THE SWEA CITY HERALD-PRESS

Street Address: P.O. Box 428
City: Swea City
State: IA
Postal Code: 50590
Office phone: 515-272-4660
Publication Website: www.statelinepubs.com

Publisher Name: Kristin Grabinoski
Publisher Email: krisg@armstrongjournal.com
Editor Name: Kim Meyer
Editor Email: bancroftregister@yahoo.com

VINTON

CEDAR VALLEY TIMES

Street Address: PO Box 468 108 E 5th
City: Vinton
State: IA
Postal Code: 52349
Office phone: (319) 472-2311
Publication Website: www.vintonnewspapers.com
General E-mail: news@vintonnewspapers.com
Publisher Name: Deb Weigel
Editor Name: Anelia K. Dimitrova

THE VINTON EAGLE

Street Address: PO Box 468 108 E 5th
City: Vinton
State: IA
Postal Code: 52349
Office phone: (319) 472-2311
Publication Website: www.vintonnewspapers.com
General E-mail: news@vintonnewspapers.com
Publisher Name: Deb Weigel
Editor Name: Anelia K. Dimitrova
Total Circulation: 2500

WAVERLY

WAVERLY - BREMER COUNTY INDEPENDENT

Street Address: 311 West Bremer Avenue
City: Waverly
State: IA
Postal Code: 50677
Office phone: (319) 352-3334
Publication Website: www.waverlynewspapers.com
General E-mail: news@waverlynewspapers.com
Publisher Name: Deb Weigel
Publisher Email: debweigel@oelweindailyregister.com
Editor Name: Anelia K. Dimitrova
Editor Email: editorcft@gmail.com
Advertising Executive Name: Karen Wedeking
Advertising Executive Email: ads.waverlypaper@gmail.com

WAVERLY - WAVERLY DEMOCRAT

Street Address: 311 West Bremer Avenue
City: Waverly
State: IA
Postal Code: 50677
Office phone: (319) 352-3334
Publication Website: www.waverlynewspapers.com
General E-mail: news@waverlynewspapers.com
Publisher Name: Deb Weigel
Publisher Email: debweigel@oelweindailyregister.com
Editor Name: Anelia K. Dimitrova
Editor Email: editorcft@gmail.com
Advertising Executive Name: Karen Wedeking
Advertising Executive Email: ads.waverlypaper@gmail.com

WEST BRANCH

WEST BRANCH TIMES

Corporate/Parent Company: Woodward Communications, Inc.
Street Address: P.O. Box 368, 124 W. Main Street
City: West Branch

State: IA
Postal Code: 52358
Office phone: (319) 643-2131
Publication Website: https://www.westbranchtimes.com/
General E-mail: wbtimes@lcom.net
Publisher Name: Stu Clark
Editor Name: Gregory Norfleet
Editor Email: rob@westbranchtimes.com
Advertising Executive Name: Annie Schroder
Advertising Executive Email: aschroder79@gmail.com
Advertising Executive Phone: (319) 643-2131
Year Established: 1875
Delivery Methods: Mail`Newsstand`Racks
Published Days: Thur
Avg Paid Circ: 1153
Audit Company: Sworn/Estimate/Non-Audited
Audit Date: 6 10 2019

WEST LIBERTY

WEST LIBERTY INDEX

Corporate/Parent Company: Woodward Communications, Inc.
Street Address: 219 N. Calhoun St.
City: West Liberty
State: IA
Postal Code: 52776
Office phone: (319) 627-2814
Publication Website: https://www.westlibertyindex.com/
General E-mail: indexnews@lcom.net
Publisher Name: Derek Sawvell
Editor Name: Jacob Lane
Advertising Executive Name: Carissa Hoekstra
Published Days: Thur
Audit Company: Sworn/Estimate/Non-Audited
Audit Date: 6 10 2019

WEST UNION

THE OSSIAN BEE

Corporate/Parent Company: Fayette County Union
Street Address: Box 153
City: West Union
State: IA
Postal Code: 52175
Office phone: 563.422.3888
Publication Website: www.fayettecountynewspapers.com
General E-mail: lanews@thefayettecountyunion.com
Publisher Name: LeAnn Larson
Publisher Email: lanews@thefayettecountyunion.com
Advertising Executive Name: Jennifer Olsen
Advertising Executive Email: jolsen@fayettepublishing.com

WINTERSET

MADISONIAN

Street Address: 215 N. 1st Ave. PO Box 350
City: Winterset
State: IA
Postal Code: 50273
Office phone: 515-462-2101
Publication Website: www.wintersetmadisonian.com
General E-mail: life.madisonian@gmail.com
Editor Name: Charlotte Underwood
Total Circulation: 1153

WINTHROP

INDEPENDENCE - THE NEWS/BUCHANAN COUNTY REVIEW

Street Address: PO Box 9
City: Winthrop
State: IA
Postal Code: 50682
Office phone: 319-935-3027
Publication Website: www.thenews-guide.com

Non-Daily Newspapers in the U.S.

General E-mail: contactus@thenews-guide.com

IDAHO

ABERDEEN

THE ABERDEEN TIMES

Corporate/Parent Company: Crompton Publishing Inc.
Street Address: PO Box 856 31 S. Main
City: Aberdeen
State: ID
Postal Code: 83210
Office phone: (208) 397-4440
Publication Website: www.press-times.com
General E-mail: press1@press-times.com
Publisher Name: Brett Crompton
Publisher Email: press1@press-times.com
Editor Name: Vicki Gamble
Editor Email: times1@dcdi.net
Advertising Executive Name: Debbie Crompton
Advertising Executive Email: press3@press-times.com
Year Established: 1912
Delivery Methods: Mail`Newsstand
Mechanical specifications: Seven columns: 11 picas wide (approximately 1 3/4 ") Classidied: eight columns, 9 picas wide (1 1/2") Page height: 21.5 inches
Published Days: Wed
Avg Paid Circ: 900
Avg Free Circ: 30
Audit Company: Sworn/Estimate/Non-Audited
Audit Date: 6 10 2019
Total Circulation: 1400

BONNERS FERRY

BONNERS FERRY HERALD

Corporate/Parent Company: Hagadone Corp.
Street Address: 7183 Main St
City: Bonners Ferry
State: ID
Postal Code: 83805
Office phone: (208) 267-5521
Publication Website: https://www.bonnersferryherald.com/
General E-mail: bdavis@bonnercountydailybee.com
Year Established: 1891
Delivery Methods: Mail`Newsstand`Racks
Published Days: Thur
Avg Paid Circ: 3200
Avg Free Circ: 200
Audit Company: Sworn/Estimate/Non-Audited
Audit Date: 6 10 2019

ISLAND PARK

ISLAND PARK NEWS

Street Address: 4261 Stevenson
City: Island Park
State: ID
Postal Code: 83429
Office phone: 208-558-5250
Publication Website: www.islandparknews.com
General E-mail: ipnews@mac.com
Editor Name: Ann Marie Anthony

MONTPELIER

MONTPELIER NEWS-EXAMINER

Street Address: 847 Washington Street
City: Montpelier
State: ID
Postal Code: 83254
Office phone: (208) 847-0552
Publication Website: www.news-examiner.net
General E-mail: newseditor@news-examiner.net
Editor Name: Michelle Highley
Editor Email: mhigley@news-examiner.net

RIGBY

JEFFERSON STAR

Corporate/Parent Company: Adams Publishing Group
Street Address: 134 W. Main • P.O. Box 37
City: Rigby
State: ID
Postal Code: 83442
Office phone: 208.745.8701
Publication Website: www.jeffersonstarnews.com
General E-mail: info@jeffersonstarnews.com
Advertising Executive Name: Earlene Poole
Advertising Executive Email: epoole@jeffersonstarnews.com
Advertising Executive Phone: 208-970-9838

SANDPOINT

PRIEST RIVER TIMES

Corporate/Parent Company: Hagadone Corp.
Street Address: Po Box 159
City: Sandpoint
State: ID
Postal Code: 83864
Office phone: (208) 263-9534
Publication Website: http://www.priestrivertimes.com
General E-mail: bdavis@bonnercountydailybee.com
Publisher Name: Bill Davis
Publisher Email: bdavis@bonnercountydailybee.com
Editor Name: Caroline Lobsinger
Editor Email: clobsinger@bonnercountydailybee.com
Advertising Executive Name: Bill Davis
Advertising Executive Email: bdavis@bonnercountydailybee.com
Year Established: 1914
Delivery Methods: Mail`Newsstand`Racks
Mechanical specifications: Type page 12 1/2 x 21 1/2; E - 6 cols, 1 7/8, between; A - 6 cols, 1 7/8, between; C - 9 cols, between.
Published Days: Wed
Avg Paid Circ: 1427
Avg Free Circ: 9000
Audit Company: Sworn/Estimate/Non-Audited
Audit Date: 6 10 2019
Total Circulation: 10427

ST. MARIES

ST. MARIE'S GAZETTE RECORD

Street Address: 610 Main Avenue
City: St. Maries
State: ID
Postal Code: 83861
Office phone: 208-245-4538
Publication Website: www.gazetterecord.com
General E-mail: devon@smgazette.com
Publisher Name: Dan Hammes

ILLINOIS

PITTSFIELD

PIKE PRESS

Corporate/Parent Company: Campbell Publishing Co., Inc.
Street Address: 115 W. Jefferson Street
City: Pittsfield
State: IL
Postal Code: 62363
Office phone: 217-285-2345
Publication Website: www.pikepress.com
General E-mail: ppnews@campbellpublications.net
Publisher Name: Nichole Liehr
Publisher Email: nliehr@campbellpublications.net
Advertising Executive Name: Nichole Liehr
Advertising Executive Email: nliehr@campbellpublications.net

WINCHESTER

SCOTT COUNTY TIMES

Corporate/Parent Company: Campbell Publishing Co., Inc.
Street Address: P.O. Box 64
City: Winchester
State: IL
Postal Code: 62694
Office phone: 217-742-3313
Publication Website: www.scottcountytimes.com
General E-mail: sctnews@campbellpublications.net
Publisher Name: Nichole Liehr
Publisher Email: nliehr@campbellpublications.net
Advertising Executive Name: Nichole Liehr
Advertising Executive Email: nliehr@campbellpublications.net

ALEDO

ALEDO TIMES RECORD

Street Address: 219 S. College Ave.
City: Aledo
State: IL
Postal Code: 61231
Office phone: 309-582-5112
Publication Website: www.aledotimesrecord.com
General E-mail: editor@aledotimesrecord.com
Publisher Name: Shawn Fox
Publisher Email: sfox@pjstar.com
Editor Name: John Pulliam
Editor Email: jpulliam@aledotimesrecord.com
Advertising Executive Name: Teresa Welch
Advertising Executive Email: twelch@aledotimesrecord.com
Advertising Executive Phone: 309-582-5112

AMBOY

THE AMBOY NEWS

Corporate/Parent Company: News Media Grouip
Street Address: PO Box 162
City: Amboy
State: IL
Postal Code: 61310
Office phone: (815) 857-2311
Publication Website: https://www.amboynews.com/
General E-mail: tgreenfield@amboynews.com
Publisher Name: Kip Cheek
Publisher Email: kcheek@mendotareporter.com
Publisher Phone: (815) 539-9396
Editor Name: Bonnie Morris
Editor Email: bmorris@mendotareporter.com
Editor Phone: (815) 539-9396
Advertising Executive Name: Tonja Greenfield
Advertising Executive Email: tgreenfield@amboynews.com
Advertising Executive Phone: (815) 857-2311

ASHTON

ASHTON GAZETTE

Corporate/Parent Company: News Media Grouip
Street Address: 813 Main St
City: Ashton
State: IL
Postal Code: 61006
Office phone: (815) 453-2551
Publication Website: http://www.ashtongazette.com/
General E-mail: tgreenfield@amboynews.com
Publisher Name: Mike Felts
Publisher Email: mike@oglecountylife.com
Editor Name: Monetta Young
Editor Email: myoung@ashtongazette.com
Editor Phone: (815) 453-2551

THE ASHTON GAZETTE

Corporate/Parent Company: News Media Grouip
Street Address: 813 Main Street
City: Ashton
State: IL
Postal Code: 61006
Office phone: 815-453-2551
Publication Website: www.ashtongazette.com
General E-mail: myoung@ashtongazette.com
Editor Name: Monetta Young
Editor Email: myoung@ashtongazette.com
Editor Phone: 815-453-2551

AUBURN

NEW BERLIN BEE

Corporate/Parent Company: South County Publications
Street Address: 110 N 5th St
City: Auburn
State: IL
Postal Code: 62615
Office phone: (217) 438-6155
Publication Website: https://www.southcountypublications.net/site/about.html
General E-mail: southco@royell.org
Publisher Name: Joe Michelich, Jr.
Publisher Email: southco@royell.org

PAWNEE POST

Corporate/Parent Company: South County Publications
Street Address: 110 N 5th St
City: Auburn
State: IL
Postal Code: 62615
Office phone: (217) 438-6155
Publication Website: https://www.southcountypublications.net/site/about.html
General E-mail: southco@royell.org
Publisher Name: Joe Michelich Jr.
Publisher Email: southco@royell.org

PLEASANT PLAINS PRESS

Corporate/Parent Company: South County Publications
Street Address: 110 N 5th St
City: Auburn
State: IL
Postal Code: 62615
Office phone: (217) 438-6155
Publication Website: https://www.southcountypublications.net/site/about.html
General E-mail: southco@royell.org
Publisher Name: Joe Michelich Jr.
Publisher Email: southco@royell.org

ROCHESTER TIMES

Corporate/Parent Company: South County Publications
Street Address: 110 N 5th St
City: Auburn
State: IL
Postal Code: 62615
Office phone: (217) 438-6155
Publication Website: https://www.southcountypublications.net/rochester_times/news/
General E-mail: southco@royell.org
Publisher Name: Joe Michelich Jr.
Publisher Email: southco@royell.org

AURORA

THE VOICE

Corporate/Parent Company: The Voice Publications, Inc
Street Address: P.O. Box 123
City: Aurora
State: IL
Postal Code: 60507
Office phone: 630-966-Voice (8642)
Publication Website: www.thevoice.us
General E-mail: news@thevoice.us
Publisher Name: Carter Crane
Publisher Email: cartercrane@thevoice.us
Editor Name: Donna Crane
Editor Email: news@thevoice.us

BARTLETT

EXAMINER PUBLICATIONS, INC.

Corporate/Parent Company: Examiner Publications, Inc.
Street Address: 4N781 Gerber Rd
City: Bartlett
State: IL
Postal Code: 60103
Office phone: (630) 830-4145
Publication Website: http://www.examinerpublications.com/
General E-mail: ads@examinerpublications.com
Publisher Name: Randy Petrik
Publisher Email: randy@examinerpublications.com
Publisher Phone: randy@examinerpublications.com
Editor Name: Randy Petrik
Editor Email: randy@examinerpublications.com
Advertising Executive Email: ads@examinerpublications.com

THE EXAMINER OF BARTLETT

Corporate/Parent Company: Examiner Publications, Inc.
Street Address: 4N781 Gerber Rd
City: Bartlett
State: IL
Postal Code: 60103
Office phone: (630) 830-4145
Publication Website: http://www.examinerpublications.com/
General E-mail: ads@examinerpublications.com
Publisher Name: Randy Petrik
Publisher Email: randy@examinerpublications.com
Advertising Executive Email: ads@examinerpublications.com

THE EXAMINER OF CAROL STREAM

Corporate/Parent Company: Examiner Publications, Inc.
Street Address: 4N781 Gerber Rd
City: Bartlett
State: IL
Postal Code: 60103
Office phone: (630) 830-4145
Publication Website: http://www.examinerpublications.com/
General E-mail: ads@examinerpublications.com
Publisher Name: Randy Petrik
Publisher Email: randy@examinerpublications.com
Advertising Executive Email: ads@examinerpublications.com

THE EXAMINER OF HANOVER PARK

Corporate/Parent Company: Examiner Publications, Inc.
Street Address: 4N781 Gerber Rd
City: Bartlett
State: IL
Postal Code: 60103
Office phone: (630) 830-4145
Publication Website: http://www.examinerpublications.com/
General E-mail: ads@examinerpublications.com
Publisher Name: Randy Petrik
Publisher Email: randy@examinerpublications.com
Advertising Executive Email: ads@examinerpublications.com

THE EXAMINER OF SOUTH ELGIN

Corporate/Parent Company: Examiner Publications, Inc.
Street Address: 4N781 Gerber Rd
City: Bartlett
State: IL
Postal Code: 60103
Office phone: (630) 830-4145
Publication Website: http://www.examinerpublications.com/
General E-mail: ads@examinerpublications.com
Publisher Name: Randy Petrik
Publisher Email: randy@examinerpublications.com
Advertising Executive Email: ads@examinerpublications.com

THE EXAMINER OF STREAMWOOD

Corporate/Parent Company: Examiner Publications, Inc.
Street Address: 4N781 Gerber Rd
City: Bartlett
State: IL
Postal Code: 60103
Office phone: (630) 830-4145
Publication Website: http://www.examinerpublications.com/
General E-mail: ads@examinerpublications.com
Publisher Name: Randy Petrik
Publisher Email: randy@examinerpublications.com
Advertising Executive Email: ads@examinerpublications.com

THE EXAMINER OF WAYNE

Corporate/Parent Company: Examiner Publications, Inc.
Street Address: 4N781 Gerber Rd
City: Bartlett
State: IL
Postal Code: 60103
Office phone: (630) 830-4145
Publication Website: http://www.examinerpublications.com/
General E-mail: ads@examinerpublications.com
Publisher Name: Randy Petrik
Publisher Email: randy@examinerpublications.com
Advertising Executive Email: ads@examinerpublications.com

BEARDSTOWN

STAR-GAZETTE EXTRA

Corporate/Parent Company: DHI Media, Inc.
Street Address: 1210 Wall St, PO Box 79
City: Beardstown
State: IL
Postal Code: 62618-2327
Office phone: (217) 323-1010
Publication Website: https://www.beardstownnewspapers.com/contact
General E-mail: sgclassifieds@casscomm.com
Publisher Name: Pat Wellenkamp
Publisher Email: pwell@casscomm.com
Editor Name: Janet Martin
Editor Email: editor@casscomm.com

BELLEVILLE

THE LEGAL REPORTER

Street Address: 120 South Illinois PO Box 427
City: Belleville
State: IL
Postal Code: 62222
Office phone: 618-234-1000
Publication Website: www.bnd.com/ofallon-progress/
General E-mail: newsroom@bnd.com
Editor Name: Jeffry Couch
Editor Email: jcouch@bnd.com
Editor Phone: (618) 239-2551
Advertising Executive Name: Liz Rowland
Advertising Executive Email: lrowland@bnd.com
Advertising Executive Phone: (618) 239-2602

THE NEWS LEADER

Corporate/Parent Company: Gannett
Street Address: 120 South Illinois PO Box 427
City: Belleville
State: IL
Postal Code: 62222
Office phone: 618-234-1000
Publication Website: www.highlandnl.com
General E-mail: newsroom@bnd.com
Editor Name: Jeffry Couch
Editor Email: jcouch@bnd.com
Editor Phone: (618) 239-2551
Advertising Executive Name: Liz Rowland
Advertising Executive Email: lrowland@bnd.com
Advertising Executive Phone: (618) 239-2602

BELVIDERE

MCHENRY COUNTY NEWS

Corporate/Parent Company: Rock Valley Publishing LLC
Street Address: 130 S. State St., Suite 101
City: Belvidere
State: IL
Postal Code: 61008
Office phone: 815-547-0084
Publication Website: www.rvpublishing.com
General E-mail: info@rvpublishing.com
Publisher Name: Pete Cruger
Publisher Email: pete@rvpublishing.com
Editor Name: Anne Eickstadt
Editor Email: bdrnews@rvpublishing.com
Advertising Executive Name: Maxine Bayer
Advertising Executive Email: mbayer@rvpublishing.com

THE BELVIDERE DAILY REPUBLICAN

Corporate/Parent Company: Rock Valley Publishing LLC
Street Address: 130 S. State St., Suite 101
City: Belvidere
State: IL
Postal Code: 61008-3772
Office phone: (815) 547-0084
Publication Website: http://rvpnews.com/?cat=7
General E-mail: mbayer@rvpublishing.com
Publisher Name: Pete Cruger
Publisher Email: pete@rvpublishing.com
Editor Name: Anne Eickstadt
Editor Email: bdrnews@rvpublishing.com
Advertising Executive Name: Maxine Bayer
Advertising Executive Email: mbayer@rvpublishing.com

CAMP POINT

CAMP POINT JOURNAL

Corporate/Parent Company: Elliott Publishing, Inc.
Street Address: 202 E State St
City: Camp Point
State: IL
Postal Code: 62320-1114
Office phone: (217) 593-6515
Publication Website: http://www.elliott-publishing.com/
General E-mail: cpjournal@adams.net
Publisher Name: James Elliott
Publisher Email: cpjournal@adams.net
Editor Name: Marcia Elliott
Editor Email: cpjournal@adams.net
Advertising Executive Email: lisa@elliott-publishing.com

GOLDEN-CLAYTON NEW ERA

Corporate/Parent Company: Elliott Publishing, Inc.
Street Address: 202 E State St
City: Camp Point
State: IL
Postal Code: 62320-1114
Office phone: (217) 593-6515
Publication Website: http://www.elliott-publishing.com/
General E-mail: jim@elliott-publishing.com
Publisher Name: James Elliott
Publisher Email: cpjournal@adams.net
Editor Name: Marcia Elliott
Editor Email: cpjournal@adams.net
Advertising Executive Email: lisa@elliott-publishing.com

MENDON DISPATCH-TIMES

Corporate/Parent Company: Elliott Publishing, Inc.
Street Address: 202 E State St
City: Camp Point
State: IL
Postal Code: 62320-1114
Office phone: (217) 593-6515
Publication Website: http://www.elliott-publishing.com/
General E-mail: cpjournal@adams.net
Publisher Name: James Elliott
Publisher Email: cpjournal@adams.net
Editor Name: Marcia Elliott
Editor Email: cpjournal@adams.net
Advertising Executive Email: lisa@elliott-publishing.com

CARLOCK

THE QUILL, CARLOCK

Corporate/Parent Company: The Normalite Newspaper Group
Street Address: P.O. Box 217
City: Carlock
State: IL
Postal Code: 61725
Office phone: 309-365-8668
Publication Website: www.normalite.com
General E-mail: thenormalite@gmail.com
Publisher Name: Ed Pyne
Publisher Email: thenormalite@gmail.com

CARMI

CARMI CHRONICLE

Corporate/Parent Company: S&R Media, LLC
Street Address: 105A East Main Street
City: Carmi
State: IL
Postal Code: 62821
Office phone: 618-382-7155
Publication Website: www.carmichronicle.com
General E-mail: chronicleeditor2016@gmail.com
Publisher Name: Jerry Reppert
Publisher Email: jlreppert@annanews.com
Editor Name: Brandon Siegert
Editor Email: carmichronicle@yahoo.com

Non-Daily Newspapers in the U.S.

III-41

CARROLLTON

GREENE PRAIRIE PRESS

Corporate/Parent Company: Campbell Publishing Co., Inc.
Street Address: 516 N Main St
City: Carrollton
State: IL
Postal Code: 62016-1027
Office phone: (217) 942-9100
Publication Website: https://greeneprairiepress.com/
General E-mail: ppnews@campbellpublications.net
Publisher Name: Nichole Liehr
Publisher Email: nliehr@campbellpublications.net
Publisher Phone: (217) 285-2345
Editor Name: Jarad Jarmon
Editor Email: jcjnews@campbellpublications.net
Advertising Executive Name: Nichole Liehr
Advertising Executive Email: nliehr@campbellpublications.net
Advertising Executive Phone: (217) 285-2345

CARTHAGE

HANCOCK COUNTY JOURNAL-PILOT

Street Address: 31 N Washington St
City: Carthage
State: IL
Postal Code: 62321
Office phone: (217) 357-2149
Publication Website: http://www.mississippivalleypublishing.com/journalpilot/
General E-mail: editor@journalpilot.com
Publisher Name: Steve Helenthal
Publisher Email: steveh@dailygate.com
Editor Name: David M. Cox
Editor Email: editor@journalpilot.com
Advertising Executive Name: Bobbi Cleesen
Advertising Executive Email: classified@journalpilot.com

CHAMPAIGN

MAHOMET CITIZEN

Street Address: 15 Main St.
City: Champaign
State: IL
Postal Code: 61853
Office phone: (217) 351-5252
Publication Website: https://www.mcitizen.com/
General E-mail: ssmith@news-gazette.media
Publisher Name: Greg Perotto
Publisher Email: gperrotto@rensselaerrepublican.com
Editor Name: Penny Weaver
Editor Email: pweaver@news-gazette.media
Editor Phone: (217) 586-2512
Advertising Executive Name: Sue Smith
Advertising Executive Email: ssmith@news-gazette.media

CHATHAM

CHATHAM CLARION

Corporate/Parent Company: South County Publications
Street Address: Main Plaza
City: Chatham
State: IL
Postal Code: 62629
Office phone: (217) 483-2614
Publication Website: https://www.southcountypublications.net/chatham_clarion/
General E-mail: chatmclarion@royell.org
Publisher Name: Joe Michelich, Jr.
Publisher Email: southco@royell.org
Editor Name: Joe Pritchett
Editor Email: chathamclarion@royell.org
Advertising Executive Name: Connie Michelich
Advertising Executive Email: southco@royell.org

CHENOA

CHENOA TOWN CRIER

Corporate/Parent Company: The Normalite Newspaper Group
Street Address: P.O. Box 206
City: Chenoa
State: IL
Postal Code: 61726
Office phone: 815-945-7388
Publication Website: www.normalite.com
General E-mail: thenormalite@gmail.com
Publisher Name: Ed Pyne
Publisher Email: thenormalite@gmail.com
Editor Name: Laurie Sleetr
Editor Email: lexingtonian@frontier.com

CHICAGO

ARLINGTON HEIGHTS POST

Street Address: 160 N. Stetson Ave.
City: Chicago
State: IL
Postal Code: 60601
Office phone: (847) 599-6900
Publication Website: https://www.chicagotribune.com/suburbs/arlington-heights/
General E-mail: rhgillespie@chicagotribune.com
Publisher Name: Par Ridder (GM)
Publisher Email: pridder@tribpub.com
Editor Name: Rhonda Gillespie
Editor Email: rhgillespie@chicagotribune.com
Advertising Executive Email: ecom@tribpub.com
Advertising Executive Phone: (800) 974-7520

BARRINGTON COURIER-REVIEW

Street Address: 160 N. Stetson Ave.
City: Chicago
State: IL
Postal Code: 60601
Office phone: (847) 599-6900
Publication Website: https://www.chicagotribune.com/suburbs/barrington/
General E-mail: rhgillespie@chicagotribune.com
Publisher Name: Par Ridder (GM)
Publisher Email: pridder@tribpub.com
Editor Name: Rhonda Gillespie
Editor Email: rhgillespie@chicagotribune.com
Advertising Executive Email: ecom@tribpub.com
Advertising Executive Phone: (800) 974-7520

BUFFALO GROVE COUNTRYSIDE

Street Address: 160 N. Stetson Ave.
City: Chicago
State: IL
Postal Code: 60601
Office phone: (847) 599-6900
Publication Website: https://www.chicagotribune.com/suburbs/buffalo-grove/
General E-mail: rhgillespie@chicagotribune.com
Publisher Name: Par Ridder (GM)
Publisher Email: pridder@tribpub.com
Editor Name: Rhonda Gillespie
Editor Email: rhgillespie@chicagotribune.com
Advertising Executive Email: ecom@tribpub.com
Advertising Executive Phone: (800) 974-7520

CITIZEN SUBURBAN TIMES WEEKLY

Street Address: 8741 So. Greenwood
City: Chicago
State: IL
Postal Code: 60619
Office phone: 773.783.1251
Publication Website: www.cstweekly.com
General E-mail: editorial@cstweekly.com
Publisher Name: Darrell Garth
Publisher Email: dgarth@citizennewspapergroup.com

CROWN POINT STAR

Street Address: 160 N. Stetson Ave.
City: Chicago
State: IL
Postal Code: 60601
Office phone: (847) 599-6900
Publication Website: https://www.chicagotribune.com/suburbs/franklin-park/
General E-mail: cnance@post-trib.com
Publisher Name: Par Ridder (GM)
Publisher Email: pridder@tribpub.com
Editor Name: Christin Nance Lazerus
Editor Email: cnance@post-trib.com
Advertising Executive Email: ecom@tribpub.com
Advertising Executive Phone: (800) 974-7520

DEERFIELD REVIEW

Street Address: 160 N. Stetson Ave.
City: Chicago
State: IL
Postal Code: 60601
Office phone: (847) 599-6900
Publication Website: https://www.chicagotribune.com/suburbs/deerfield/
General E-mail: sdibenedetto@tribpub.com
Publisher Name: Par Ridder (GM)
Publisher Email: pridder@tribpub.com
Editor Name: Stephen Di Benedetto
Editor Email: sdibenedetto@tribpub.com
Advertising Executive Email: ecom@tribpub.com
Advertising Executive Phone: (800) 974-7520

ELMWOOD PARK LEAVES

Street Address: 160 N. Stetson Ave.
City: Chicago
State: IL
Postal Code: 60601
Office phone: (847) 599-6900
Publication Website: https://www.chicagotribune.com/suburbs/elmwood-park/
General E-mail: pdefiglio@chicagotribune.com
Publisher Name: Par Ridder (GM)
Publisher Email: pridder@tribpub.com
Editor Name: Pam DeFiglio
Editor Email: pdefiglio@chicagotribune.com
Advertising Executive Email: ecom@tribpub.com
Advertising Executive Phone: (800) 974-7520

EVANSTON REVIEW

Street Address: 160 N. Stetson Ave
City: Chicago
State: IL
Postal Code: 60601
Office phone: 847-486-9200
Publication Website: www.evanstonreview.com
General E-mail: evanston@aggrego.com
Publisher Name: Par Ridder (GM)
Publisher Email: pridder@tribpub.com
Editor Name: Dan Lambert
Editor Email: dalambert@chicagotribune.com

FRANKLIN PARK HERALD-JOURNAL

Street Address: 160 N. Stetson Ave.
City: Chicago
State: IL
Postal Code: 60601
Office phone: (847) 599-6900
Publication Website: https://www.chicagotribune.com/suburbs/franklin-park/
General E-mail: pdefiglio@chicagotribune.com
Publisher Name: Par Ridder (GM)
Publisher Email: pridder@tribpub.com
Editor Name: Pam DeFiglio
Editor Email: pdefiglio@chicagotribune.com
Advertising Executive Email: ecom@tribpub.com
Advertising Executive Phone: (800) 974-7520

NAPERVILLE SUN

Street Address: 160 N. Stetson Ave
City: Chicago
State: IL
Postal Code: 60601
Office phone: 630-230-8959
Publication Website: www.napersun.com
General E-mail: napervillesunservice@tribpub.com
Publisher Name: Par Ridder (GM)
Editor Name: Karen Sorensen
Editor Email: ksorensen@tribpub.com
Editor Phone: 630-978-8147

THE BEVERLY REVIEW

Corporate/Parent Company: The Beverly Review
Street Address: 10546 S. Western Ave.
City: Chicago
State: IL
Postal Code: 60643
Office phone: 773-238-3366
Publication Website: www.beverlyreview.net
General E-mail: kgarmes@beverlyreview.net
Publisher Name: Robert Olszewski, Jr.
Publisher Email: bobo@beverlyreview.net
Editor Name: Kyle Garmes
Editor Email: kgarmes@beverlyreview.net
Advertising Executive Name: Ericka Swanson
Advertising Executive Email: eswanson@beverlyreview.net

THE DOINGS - CLARENDON HILLS

Corporate/Parent Company: Tribune Publishing
Street Address: 160 N. Stetson Ave
City: Chicago
State: IL
Postal Code: 60601
Office phone: 630-230-8959
Publication Website: www.thedoings-clarendonhills.com
General E-mail: letters@chicagotribune.com
Publisher Name: Par Ridder (GM)
Publisher Email: pridder@chicagotribune.com
Editor Name: Larry Smith
Editor Email: lasmith@chicagotribune.com

THE DOINGS - HINSDALE

Corporate/Parent Company: Tribune Publishing
Street Address: 160 N. Stetson Ave
City: Chicago
State: IL
Postal Code: 60601
Office phone: 630-230-8959
Publication Website: www.thedoings-hinsdale.com
General E-mail: letters@chicagotribune.com
Publisher Name: Par Ridder (GM)
Publisher Email: pridder@chicagotribune.com
Editor Name: Larry Smith
Editor Email: lasmith@chicagotribune.com

THE DOINGS - LA GRANGE

Corporate/Parent Company: Tribune Publishing
Street Address: 160 N. Stetson Ave
City: Chicago

State: IL
Postal Code: 60601
Office phone: 630-230-8959
Publication Website: www.thedoings-lagrange.com
General E-mail: letters@chicagotribune.com
Publisher Name: Par Ridder (GM)
Publisher Email: pridder@chicagotribune.com
Editor Name: Larry Smith
Editor Email: lasmith@chicagotribune.com

THE DOINGS - OAK BROOK

Corporate/Parent Company: Tribune Publishing
Street Address: 160 N. Stetson Ave
City: Chicago
State: IL
Postal Code: 60601
Office phone: 630-230-8959
Publication Website: www.thedoings-oakbrook.com
General E-mail: letters@chicagotribune.com
Publisher Name: Par Ridder (GM)
Publisher Email: pridder@chicagotribune.com
Editor Name: Larry Smith
Editor Email: lasmith@chicagotribune.com

THE DOINGS - WEEKLY

Corporate/Parent Company: Tribune Publishing
Street Address: 160 N. Stetson Ave
City: Chicago
State: IL
Postal Code: 60601
Office phone: 630-230-8959
Publication Website: www.thedoings-weekly.com
General E-mail: letters@chicagotribune.com
Publisher Name: Par Ridder (GM)
Publisher Email: pridder@chicagotribune.com
Editor Name: Larry Smith
Editor Email: lasmith@chicagotribune.com

THE DOINGS - WESTERN SPRINGS

Corporate/Parent Company: Tribune Publishing
Street Address: 160 N. Stetson Ave
City: Chicago
State: IL
Postal Code: 60601
Office phone: 630-230-8959
Publication Website: www.thedoings-westernsprings.com
General E-mail: letters@chicagotribune.com
Publisher Name: Par Ridder (GM)
Publisher Email: pridder@chicagotribune.com
Editor Name: Larry Smith
Editor Email: lasmith@chicagotribune.com

CLINTON

CLINTON JOURNAL

Corporate/Parent Company: News Media Grouip
Street Address: 111 S Monroe St
City: Clinton
State: IL
Postal Code: 61727
Office phone: (217) 935-3171
Publication Website: https://theclintonjournal.com/
General E-mail: kpyne@theclintonjournal.com
Publisher Name: Katy O'Grady-Pyne
Publisher Email: kpyne@theclintonjournal.com
Editor Name: Gordon Woods
Editor Email: gwoods@theclintonjournal.com
Editor Phone: (217) 935-3171
Advertising Executive Name: Tom Zalabak
Advertising Executive Email: tzalabak@theclintonjournal.com
Advertising Executive Phone: (217) 935-3171

COLFAX

THE RIDGEVIEW REVIEW

Corporate/Parent Company: The Normalite Newspaper Group
Street Address: P.O. Box 402
City: Colfax
State: IL
Postal Code: 61728
Office phone: 309-723-2052
Publication Website: www.normalite.com
General E-mail: thenormalite@gmail.com
Publisher Name: Ed Pyne
Publisher Email: thenormalite@gmail.com

COLLINSVILLE

ILLINOIS SUBURBAN JOURNALS

Street Address: 2 Eastport Executive Dr
City: Collinsville
State: IL
Postal Code: 62234
Office phone: (618) 344-0264
Publication Website: https://www.stltoday.com/suburban-journals/illinois/
General E-mail: metroeastnews@yourjournal.com
Editor Name: Greg Uptain
Editor Email: guptain@yourjournal.com
Advertising Executive Email: advertising@post-dispatch.com

CRYSTAL LAKE

MCHENRY COUNTY MAGAZINE

Street Address: 7717 S IL Route 31
City: Crystal Lake
State: IL
Postal Code: 60014
Office phone: (815) 459-4040
Publication Website: https://www.nwherald.com/e-edition/mcm/
General E-mail: classified@shawsuburban.com
Publisher Name: Jim Ringness
Publisher Email: jringness@shawmedia.com
Editor Name: Scott Helmchen
Editor Email: shelmchen@shawmedia.com
Editor Phone: (815) 459-4122
Advertising Executive Name: Norm Fossmeyer
Advertising Executive Email: nfossmeyer@shawmedia.com
Advertising Executive Phone: (815) 459-4040

DANVILLE

INDEPENDENT NEWS

Corporate/Parent Company: Community Media Group
Street Address: 839 E. Vorhees St.
City: Danville
State: IL
Postal Code: 61832
Office phone: (217) 443-8484
Publication Website: https://www.the-independent-news.com/
General E-mail: news@the-independent-news.com
Publisher Name: Greg Perrotto
Publisher Email: gperrotto@rensselaerrepublican.com
Editor Name: Katie Morrow
Editor Email: kmarrow@news-gazette.com
Advertising Executive Name: Breanna Zimmerman
Advertising Executive Email: bzimmerman@news-gazette.media
Advertising Executive Phone: (217) 351-5650

THE INDEPENDENT NEWS

Corporate/Parent Company: Community Media Group
Street Address: 839 E. Vorhees St.
City: Danville
State: IL
Postal Code: 61832
Office phone: 217-443-8484
Publication Website: www.the-independent-news.com
General E-mail: news@the-independent-news.com
Publisher Name: Greg Perrotto
Publisher Email: gperrotto@rensselaerrepublican.com
Editor Name: Katie Morrow
Editor Email: kmarrow@news-gazette.com
Advertising Executive Name: Breanna Zimmerman
Advertising Executive Email: bzimmerman@news-gazette.media
Advertising Executive Phone: 217-351-5650

DEKALB

THE MIDWEEK

Corporate/Parent Company: Shaw Media
Street Address: 1586 Barber Greene Rd
City: Dekalb
State: IL
Postal Code: 60115
Office phone: (815) 756-4841
Publication Website: https://www.midweeknews.com/
General E-mail: readit@midweeknews.com
Editor Name: Inger Koch
Editor Email: ikoch@shawmedia.com
Editor Phone: (815) 756-4841, ext : 2220
Advertising Executive Phone: (815) 756-4841, ext : 2217

DEKALB

VALLEY LIFE

Street Address: 1586 Barber Greene Rd
City: Dekalb
State: IL
Postal Code: 60115
Office phone: (815) 756-4841
Publication Website: https://www.valleylifepress.com/
General E-mail: news@valleylifepress.com
Editor Name: Inger Koch
Editor Email: ikoch@shawmedia.com
Editor Phone: (815) 756-4841, ext : 2220
Advertising Executive Name: Rob Dancey
Advertising Executive Email: rdancey@shawsuburban.com
Advertising Executive Phone: (815) 756-4841, ext : 2251

DES PLAINES

ARLINGTON HEIGHTS JOURNAL

Corporate/Parent Company: Journal & Topics Online Media Group
Street Address: 622 Graceland Ave
City: Des Plaines
State: IL
Postal Code: 60016
Office phone: 847-299-5511
Publication Website: www.Journal-topics.com
General E-mail: journalnews@journal-topics.info
Publisher Name: Todd Wessell
Publisher Email: toddwessell@journal-topics.info
Editor Name: Todd Wessell
Editor Email: tomwessell@journal-topics.info

BUFFALO GROVE JOURNAL & TOPICS

Corporate/Parent Company: Journal & Topics Online Media Group
Street Address: 622 Graceland Ave
City: Des Plaines
State: IL
Postal Code: 60016
Office phone: 847-299-5511
Publication Website: www.Journal-topics.com
General E-mail: journalnews@journal-topics.info
Publisher Name: Todd Wessell
Publisher Email: toddwessell@journal-topics.info
Editor Name: Todd Wessell
Editor Email: tomwessell@journal-topics.info
Advertising Executive Name: Rick Wessell
Advertising Executive Email: rwessell@journal-topics.info

DES PLAINES JOURNAL

Corporate/Parent Company: Journal & Topics Online Media Group
Street Address: 622 Graceland Ave
City: Des Plaines
State: IL
Postal Code: 60016
Office phone: 847-299-5511
Publication Website: www.Journal-topics.com
General E-mail: journalnews@journal-topics.info
Publisher Name: Todd Wessell
Publisher Email: toddwessell@journal-topics.info
Editor Name: Todd Wessell
Editor Email: tomwessell@journal-topics.info
Advertising Executive Name: Rick Wessell
Advertising Executive Email: rwessell@journal-topics.info

ELK GROVE JOURNAL

Corporate/Parent Company: Journal & Topics Online Media Group
Street Address: 622 Graceland Ave
City: Des Plaines
State: IL
Postal Code: 60016
Office phone: 847-299-5511
Publication Website: www.Journal-topics.com
General E-mail: journalnews@journal-topics.info
Publisher Name: Todd Wessell
Publisher Email: toddwessell@journal-topics.info
Editor Name: Todd Wessell
Editor Email: tomwessell@journal-topics.info

GOLF MILL JOURNAL

Corporate/Parent Company: Journal & Topics Online Media Group
Street Address: 622 Graceland Ave
City: Des Plaines
State: IL
Postal Code: 60016
Office phone: 847-299-5511
Publication Website: www.Journal-topics.com
General E-mail: journalnews@journal-topics.info
Publisher Name: Todd Wessell
Publisher Email: tomwessell@journal-topics.info
Editor Name: Todd Wessell
Editor Email: tomwessell@journal-topics.info

NILES JOURNAL

Corporate/Parent Company: Journal & Topics Online Media Group
Street Address: 622 Graceland Ave
City: Des Plaines
State: IL
Postal Code: 60016
Office phone: 847-299-5511
Publication Website: www.Journal-topics.com
General E-mail: journalnews@journal-topics.info

Non-Daily Newspapers in the U.S.

III-43

Publisher Name: Todd Wessell
Publisher Email: toddwessell@journal-topics.info
Editor Name: Tom Wessell
Editor Email: tomwessell@journal-topics.info

NORTHWEST JOURNAL

Corporate/Parent Company: Journal & Topics Online Media Group
Street Address: 622 Graceland Ave
City: Des Plaines
State: IL
Postal Code: 60016
Office phone: 847-299-5511
Publication Website: www.Journal-topics.com
General E-mail: journalnews@journal-topics.info
Publisher Name: Todd Wessell
Publisher Email: toddwessell@journal-topics.info
Editor Name: Tom Wessell
Editor Email: tomwessell@journal-topics.info

PALATINE JOURNAL

Corporate/Parent Company: Journal & Topics Online Media Group
Street Address: 622 Graceland Ave
City: Des Plaines
State: IL
Postal Code: 60016
Office phone: 847-299-5511
Publication Website: www.Journal-topics.com
General E-mail: journalnews@journal-topics.info
Publisher Name: Todd Wessell
Publisher Email: toddwessell@journal-topics.info
Editor Name: Tom Wessell
Editor Email: tomwessell@journal-topics.info

PARK RIDGE JOURNAL & TOPICS

Corporate/Parent Company: Journal & Topics Online Media Group
Street Address: 622 Graceland Ave
City: Des Plaines
State: IL
Postal Code: 60016
Office phone: 847-299-5511
Publication Website: www.Journal-topics.com
General E-mail: journalnews@journal-topics.info
Publisher Name: Todd Wessell
Publisher Email: toddwessell@journal-topics.info
Publisher Phone: toddwessell@journal-topics.info
Editor Name: Tom Wessell
Editor Email: tomwessell@journal-topics.info

DIXON

FORRESTON JOURNAL

Corporate/Parent Company: Shaw Media
Street Address: 113 S Peoria Ave
City: Dixon
State: IL
Postal Code: 61021
Office phone: (815) 732-6166
Publication Website: https://www.oglecountynews.com/
General E-mail: news@oglecountynews.com
Publisher Name: Earleen Hinton
Publisher Email: ehinton@oglecountynews.com
Publisher Phone: (815) 632-2591
Editor Name: Earleen Hinton
Editor Email: ehinton@oglecountynews.com
Editor Phone: (815) 632-2591
Advertising Executive Name: Lori Walker
Advertising Executive Email: lwalker@oglecountynews.com
Advertising Executive Phone: (815) 632-2555

MT. MORRIS TIMES

Corporate/Parent Company: Shaw Media
Street Address: 113 S Peoria Ave
City: Dixon
State: IL
Postal Code: 61021
Office phone: (815) 732-6166
Publication Website: https://www.oglecountynews.com/
General E-mail: news@oglecountynews.com
Publisher Name: Earleen Hinton
Publisher Email: ehinton@oglecountynews.com
Publisher Phone: (815) 632-2591
Advertising Executive Name: Lori Walker
Advertising Executive Email: lwalker@oglecountynews.com
Advertising Executive Phone: (815) 632-2555

OREGON REPUBLICAN REPORTER

Corporate/Parent Company: Shaw Media
Street Address: 113 S Peoria Ave
City: Dixon
State: IL
Postal Code: 61021
Office phone: (815) 732-6166
Publication Website: https://www.oglecountynews.com/
General E-mail: news@oglecountynews.com
Publisher Name: Earleen Hinton
Publisher Email: ehinton@oglecountynews.com
Publisher Phone: (815) 632-2591
Advertising Executive Name: Lori Walker
Advertising Executive Email: lwalker@oglecountynews.com
Advertising Executive Phone: (815) 632-2555

THE PRAIRIE ADVOCATE NEWS

Street Address: 113 S. Peoria Ave.
City: Dixon
State: IL
Postal Code: 61021
Office phone: (815) 284-2224
Publication Website: https://www.prairieadvocate.com/
General E-mail: news@prairieadvocate.com
Publisher Name: Earleen Hinton
Publisher Email: ehinton@oglecountynews.com
Publisher Phone: (815) 632-2591
Editor Name: Kathleen Schultz
Editor Email: kschultz@saukvalley.com
Advertising Executive Name: Angelica Martinez
Advertising Executive Email: jheintzelman@saukvalley.com
Advertising Executive Phone: (815) 632-2560

TRI-COUNTY PRESS

Corporate/Parent Company: Shaw Media
Street Address: 113 S Peoria Ave
City: Dixon
State: IL
Postal Code: 61021
Office phone: (815) 732-6166
Publication Website: https://www.oglecountynews.com/
General E-mail: news@oglecountynews.com
Publisher Name: Earleen Hinton
Publisher Email: ehinton@oglecountynews.com
Publisher Phone: (815) 632-2591
Advertising Executive Name: Lori Walker
Advertising Executive Email: lwalker@oglecountynews.com
Advertising Executive Phone: (815) 632-2555

DOWNERS GROVE

ADDISON SUBURBAN LIFE

Street Address: 1101 31st St
City: Downers Grove
State: IL
Postal Code: 60515
Office phone: (630) 368-1100
Publication Website: https://www.mysuburbanlife.com/
General E-mail: circulation@mysuburbanlife.com
Publisher Name: Ryan Wells
Publisher Email: rwells@shawmedia.com
Editor Name: Bob Rakow
Editor Email: brakow@shawmedia.com
Editor Phone: (630) 427-6259
Advertising Executive Name: Norm Fossmeyer
Advertising Executive Email: nfossmeyer@shawmedia.com
Advertising Executive Phone: (815) 526-4645

BERWYN SUBURBAN LIFE

Street Address: 2001 Butterfield Road
City: Downers Grove
State: IL
Postal Code: 60515
Office phone: (844) 368-1100
Publication Website: https://www.mysuburbanlife.com/
General E-mail: circulation@mysuburbanlife.com
Publisher Name: Ryan Wells
Publisher Email: rwells@shawmedia.com
Editor Name: Bob Rakow
Editor Email: brakow@shawmedia.com
Editor Phone: (630) 427-6259
Advertising Executive Name: Norm Fossmeyer
Advertising Executive Email: nfossmeyer@shawmedia.com
Advertising Executive Phone: (815) 526-4645

CAROL STREAM SUBURBAN LIFE

Street Address: 1101 31st St
City: Downers Grove
State: IL
Postal Code: 60515
Office phone: (630) 368-1100
Publication Website: https://www.mysuburbanlife.com/
General E-mail: circulation@mysuburbanlife.com
Publisher Name: Ryan Wells
Publisher Email: rwells@shawmedia.com
Editor Name: Bob Rakow
Editor Email: brakow@shawmedia.com
Editor Phone: (630) 427-6259
Advertising Executive Name: Norm Fossmeyer
Advertising Executive Email: nfossmeyer@shawmedia.com
Advertising Executive Phone: (815) 526-4645

DOWNERS GROVE SUBURBAN LIFE

Street Address: 1101 31st St
City: Downers Grove
State: IL
Postal Code: 60515
Office phone: (630) 368-1100
Publication Website: https://www.mysuburbanlife.com/
General E-mail: circulation@mysuburbanlife.com
Publisher Name: Ryan Wells
Publisher Email: rwells@shawmedia.com
Editor Name: Bob Rakow
Editor Email: brakow@shawmedia.com
Editor Phone: (630) 427-6259
Advertising Executive Name: Norm Fossmeyer
Advertising Executive Email: nfossmeyer@shawmedia.com
Advertising Executive Phone: (815) 526-4645

ELMHURST SUBURBAN LIFE

Street Address: 2001 Butterfield Rd
City: Downers Grove
State: IL
Postal Code: 60515
Office phone: (630) 368-1100
Publication Website: https://www.mysuburbanlife.com/
General E-mail: circulation@mysuburbanlife.com
Publisher Name: Ryan Wells
Publisher Email: rwells@shawmedia.com
Editor Name: Bob Rakow
Editor Email: brakow@shawmedia.com
Editor Phone: (630) 427-6259
Advertising Executive Name: Norm Fossmeyer
Advertising Executive Email: nfossmeyer@shawmedia.com
Advertising Executive Phone: (815) 526-4645

GLEN ELLYN SUBURBAN LIFE

Street Address: 1101 31st St
City: Downers Grove
State: IL
Postal Code: 60515
Office phone: (630) 368-1100
Publication Website: https://www.mysuburbanlife.com/
General E-mail: circulation@mysuburbanlife.com
Publisher Name: Ryan Wells
Publisher Email: rwells@shawmedia.com
Editor Name: Bob Rakow
Editor Email: brakow@shawmedia.com
Editor Phone: (630) 427-6259
Advertising Executive Name: Norm Fossmeyer
Advertising Executive Email: nfossmeyer@shawmedia.com
Advertising Executive Phone: (815) 526-4645

HINSDALE SUBURBAN LIFE

Street Address: 1101 31st St
City: Downers Grove
State: IL
Postal Code: 60515
Office phone: (630) 368-1100
Publication Website: https://www.mysuburbanlife.com/
General E-mail: circulation@mysuburbanlife.com
Publisher Name: Ryan Wells
Publisher Email: rwells@shawmedia.com
Editor Name: Bob Rakow
Editor Email: brakow@shawmedia.com
Editor Phone: (630) 427-6259
Advertising Executive Name: Norm Fossmeyer
Advertising Executive Email: nfossmeyer@shawmedia.com
Advertising Executive Phone: (815) 526-4645

LAGRANGE SUBURBAN LIFE

Street Address: 2001 Butterfield Rd
City: Downers Grove
State: IL
Postal Code: 60515
Office phone: (630) 368-1100
Publication Website: https://www.mysuburbanlife.com/
General E-mail: circulation@mysuburbanlife.com
Publisher Name: Ryan Wells
Publisher Email: rwells@shawmedia.com
Editor Name: Bob Rakow
Editor Email: brakow@shawmedia.com
Editor Phone: (630) 427-6259
Advertising Executive Name: Norm Fossmeyer
Advertising Executive Email: nfossmeyer@shawmedia.com
Advertising Executive Phone: (815) 526-4645

LEMONT SUBURBAN LIFE

Street Address: 2001 Butterfield Road, Suite 105
City: Downers Grove
State: IL
Postal Code: 60515
Office phone: (630) 368-1100
Publication Website: https://www.mysuburbanlife.com/lemont/
General E-mail: circulation@mysuburbanlife.com
Publisher Name: Ryan Wells
Publisher Email: rwells@shawmedia.com
Editor Name: Sherri Dauskurdas
Editor Email: sdauskurdas@shawmedia.com
Editor Phone: (630) 427-6263
Advertising Executive Name: Norm Fossmeyer
Advertising Executive Email: nfossmeyer@shawmedia.com
Advertising Executive Phone: (815) 526-4645

LOMBARD SUBURBAN LIFE

Street Address: 2001 Butterfield Road, Suite 105
City: Downers Grove
State: IL
Postal Code: 60515
Office phone: (630) 368-1100
Publication Website: https://www.mysuburbanlife.com/lombard/
General E-mail: circulation@mysuburbanlife.com
Publisher Name: Ryan Wells
Publisher Email: rwells@shawmedia.com
Editor Name: Sherri Dauskurdas
Editor Email: sdauskurdas@shawmedia.com
Editor Phone: (630) 427-6263
Advertising Executive Name: Norm Fossmeyer
Advertising Executive Email: nfossmeyer@shawmedia.com
Advertising Executive Phone: (815) 526-4645

RIVERSIDE & BROOKFIELD SUBURBAN LIFE

Street Address: 2001 Butterfield Rd
City: Downers Grove
State: IL
Postal Code: 60515
Office phone: (630) 368-1100
Publication Website: https://www.mysuburbanlife.com/
General E-mail: circulation@mysuburbanlife.com
Publisher Name: Ryan Wells
Publisher Email: rwells@shawmedia.com
Editor Name: Bob Rakow
Editor Email: brakow@shawmedia.com
Editor Phone: (630) 427-6259
Advertising Executive Name: Norm Fossmeyer
Advertising Executive Email: nfossmeyer@shawmedia.com
Advertising Executive Phone: (815) 526-4645

VILLA PARK SUBURBAN LIFE

Street Address: 1101 31st St
City: Downers Grove
State: IL
Postal Code: 60515
Office phone: (630) 368-1100
Publication Website: https://www.mysuburbanlife.com/
General E-mail: circulation@mysuburbanlife.com
Publisher Name: Ryan Wells
Publisher Email: rwells@shawmedia.com
Editor Name: Bob Rakow
Editor Email: brakow@shawmedia.com
Editor Phone: (630) 427-6259
Advertising Executive Name: Norm Fossmeyer
Advertising Executive Email: nfossmeyer@shawmedia.com
Advertising Executive Phone: (815) 526-4645

WEST CHICAGO SUBURBAN LIFE

Street Address: 2001 Butterfield Road
City: Downers Grove
State: IL
Postal Code: 60515
Office phone: (844) 368-1100
Publication Website: https://www.mysuburbanlife.com/
General E-mail: circulation@mysuburbanlife.com
Publisher Name: Ryan Wells
Publisher Email: rwells@shawmedia.com
Editor Name: Bob Rakow
Editor Email: brakow@shawmedia.com
Editor Phone: (630) 427-6259
Advertising Executive Name: Norm Fossmeyer
Advertising Executive Email: nfossmeyer@shawmedia.com
Advertising Executive Phone: (815) 526-4645

WESTMONT SUBURBAN LIFE

Street Address: 1101 31st St
City: Downers Grove
State: IL
Postal Code: 60515
Office phone: (630) 368-1100
Publication Website: https://www.mysuburbanlife.com/
General E-mail: circulation@mysuburbanlife.com
Publisher Name: Ryan Wells
Publisher Email: rwells@shawmedia.com
Editor Name: Bob Rakow
Editor Email: brakow@shawmedia.com
Editor Phone: (630) 427-6259
Advertising Executive Name: Norm Fossmeyer
Advertising Executive Email: nfossmeyer@shawmedia.com
Advertising Executive Phone: (815) 526-4645

WHEATON SUBURBAN LIFE

Street Address: 2001 Butterfield Road, Suite 105
City: Downers Grove
State: IL
Postal Code: 60515
Office phone: (630) 368-1100
Publication Website: https://www.mysuburbanlife.com/wheaton/
General E-mail: circulation@mysuburbanlife.com
Publisher Name: Ryan Wells
Publisher Email: rwells@shawmedia.com
Editor Name: Sherri Dauskurdas
Editor Email: sdauskurdas@shawmedia.com
Editor Phone: (630) 427-6259
Advertising Executive Name: Norm Fossmeyer
Advertising Executive Email: nfossmeyer@shawmedia.com
Advertising Executive Phone: (815) 526-4645

WOODRIDGE SUBURBAN LIFE

Street Address: 2001 Butterfield Road, Suite 105
City: Downers Grove
State: IL
Postal Code: 60515
Office phone: (630) 368-1100
Publication Website: https://www.mysuburbanlife.com/woodridge/
General E-mail: circulation@mysuburbanlife.com
Publisher Name: Ryan Wells
Publisher Email: rwells@shawmedia.com
Editor Name: Sherri Dauskurdas
Editor Email: sdauskurdas@shawmedia.com
Editor Phone: (630) 427-6263
Advertising Executive Name: Norm Fossmeyer
Advertising Executive Email: nfossmeyer@shawmedia.com
Advertising Executive Phone: (815) 526-4645

DWIGHT

THE PAPER

Street Address: 204 E Chippewa St
City: Dwight
State: IL
Postal Code: 60420
Office phone: 815-584-1901
Publication Website: www.thepaper1901.com
General E-mail: thepaper1901@sbcglobal.net
Publisher Name: Mary Boma
Publisher Email: thepaper1901@sbcglobal.net
Editor Name: Rachel Reynolds-Soucie
Editor Email: rachaelreynoldssoucie@gmail.com

EARLVILLE

THE EARLVILLE POST

Street Address: P. O. Box 487
City: Earlville
State: IL
Postal Code: 60518
Office phone: (815) 246-4600
Publication Website: www.earlvillepost.com
General E-mail: publisher@earlvillepost.com
Publisher Name: Stu Bloom
Publisher Email: editor@earlvillepost.com
Editor Name: Andrea Bloom
Editor Email: abloom@earlvillepost.com

EDWARDSVILLE

ON THE EDGE OF THE WEEKEND

Corporate/Parent Company: Hearst Corp.
Street Address: 116 N. Main St.
City: Edwardsville
State: IL
Postal Code: 62025
Office phone: (618) 656-4700
Publication Website: www.theintelligencer.com/specialsections/article/090116-Edge-of-the-Weekend10647990.php
General E-mail: lbarnett@edwpub.net
Publisher Name: Denise VonderHaar
Publisher Email: dvonderhaar@hearstnp.com
Publisher Phone: 618-659-5731
Editor Name: Brittany Johnson
Editor Email: bjohnson@edwpub.com
Editor Phone: 618-659-5734

EFFINGHAM

EFFINGHAM & TEUTOPOLIS NEWS REPORT

Street Address: 1901 South Fourth St.; Suite 223
City: Effingham
State: IL
Postal Code: 62401
Office phone: (217) 342-5583
Publication Website: www.etnewsreport.com
General E-mail: news@etnewsreport.com
Publisher Name: Steve Raymond
Publisher Email: stever@etnewsreport.com
Publisher Phone: Ex 21
Editor Name: Herb Meeker
Editor Email: herbm@etnewsreport.com
Editor Phone: Ex 24
Advertising Executive Name: Denny Ricketts
Advertising Executive Email: dennyr@etnewsreport.com
Advertising Executive Phone: Ex 28

ELIZABETHTOWN

HARDIN COUNTY INDEPENDENT

Street Address: PO Box 328 196 W 1st Street
City: Elizabethtown
State: IL
Postal Code: 61540-0328
Office phone: (618) 287-2361
Publication Website: www.hardincountyindependentillinois.com
General E-mail: etownnews@yahoo.com
Publisher Name: Jennifer Lane
Publisher Email: etownnews@yahoo.com
Editor Name: Julie Hurford Farley
Editor Email: etownnews@yahoo.com

ELMHURST

BENSENVILLE INDEPENDENT

Corporate/Parent Company: The Independent Newspapers
Street Address: 240 N. West Avenue
City: Elmhurst
State: IL
Postal Code: 60126
Office phone: (630) 834-8244
Publication Website: www.theindependentnewspapers.com
General E-mail: Independent@rvpublishing.com
Publisher Name: Pete Cruger
Publisher Email: pete@rvpublishing.com

THE ADDISON INDEPENDENT

Corporate/Parent Company: The Independent Newspapers
Street Address: 240 N. West Avenue
City: Elmhurst
State: IL
Postal Code: 60126
Office phone: (630) 834-8244
Publication Website: www.theindependentnewspapers.com
General E-mail: Independent@rvpublishing.com
Publisher Name: Pete Cruger
Publisher Email: pete@rvpublishing.com

VILLA PARK INDEPENDENT

Corporate/Parent Company: The Independent Newspapers
Street Address: 240 N. West Avenue
City: Elmhurst
State: IL
Postal Code: 60126
Office phone: (630) 834-8244
Publication Website: www.theindependentnewspapers.com
General E-mail: Independent@rvpublishing.com

ELMWOOD

THE WEEKLY POST

Corporate/Parent Company: LAMPLE Publications LLC
Street Address: PO Box 745
City: Elmwood
State: IL
Postal Code: 61529
Office phone: (309) 741-9790
Publication Website: www.wklypost.com
General E-mail: news@wklypost.com
Publisher Name: Jeff Lampe
Publisher Email: jeff@wklypost.com
Advertising Executive Name: Monica Lampe
Advertising Executive Email: monica@wklypost.com

Non-Daily Newspapers in the U.S.

FLORA

CLAY COUNTY ADVOCATE-PRESS
Street Address: 105 West North Avenue
City: Flora
State: IL
Postal Code: 62839
Office phone: 833-948-1200
Publication Website: www.advocatepress.com
General E-mail: editor@advocatepress.com
Publisher Name: Chip Barche
Publisher Email: cbarche@olneydailymail.com
Editor Name: Chip Barche
Editor Email: cbarche@olneydailymail.com
Editor Phone: 618-393-2931
Advertising Executive Name: Cathy Slunaker
Advertising Executive Email: advertising1@olneydailymail.com
Advertising Executive Phone: 618-393-2931

GALENA

THE GALENA GAZETTE
Street Address: 716 S. Bench St.
City: Galena
State: IL
Postal Code: 61036
Office phone: 815-777-0019
Publication Website: www.galenagazette.com
Publisher Name: Carter Newton
Publisher Email: cnewton@galgazette.com
Editor Name: Hillary Dickerson
Editor Email: hdickerson@galgazette.com
Advertising Executive Name: Jay Dickerson
Advertising Executive Email: jdickerson@galgazette.com

GALESBURG

KNOX COUNTY NEIGHBORS
Corporate/Parent Company: Gannett
Street Address: 140 S. Prairie St
City: Galesburg
State: IL
Postal Code: 61401
Office phone: 309-343-7181 Dial 0 for Operator
Publication Website: www.galesburg.com
General E-mail: tmartin@register-mail.com
Publisher Name: Shawn Fox
Publisher Email: sfox@pjstar.com
Publisher Phone: 309-343-7181 ext. 6063
Editor Name: Tom Martin
Editor Email: sfox@pjstar.com
Advertising Executive Name: Shelly Trueblood
Advertising Executive Email: strueblood@register-mail.com
Advertising Executive Phone: 309-315-6062

GENESEO

HENRY COUNTY REPUBLIC
Corporate/Parent Company: Gannett
Street Address: 108 W. First St.
City: Geneseo
State: IL
Postal Code: 61254
Office phone: (309) 944-2119
Publication Website: www.geneseorepublic.com
General E-mail: editor@geneseorepublic.com
Publisher Name: Jim Holm
Publisher Email: jholm@gatehousemedia.com
Editor Name: Lisa Depies
Editor Email: ldepies@geneseorepublic.com
Advertising Executive Name: Karol Clementz
Advertising Executive Email: kclementz@geneseorepublic.com

GLASFORD

GLASFORD GAZETTE
Street Address: 508 W. Main St.
City: Glasford
State: IL
Postal Code: 61533
Office phone: (309) 389-2811
Publication Website: www.glasfordgazette.net
General E-mail: jessica@glasfordgazette.net
Publisher Name: Jessica Westerman
Publisher Email: jessica@glasfordgazette.net
Editor Name: Jessica Westerman
Editor Email: jessica@glasfordgazette.net

GRAYSLAKE

LAKE COUNTY JOURNAL
Corporate/Parent Company: Shaw Media
Street Address: PO Box 343
City: Grayslake
State: IL
Postal Code: 60030
Office phone: (847) 223-8161
Publication Website: http://www.lakecountyjournal.com/
General E-mail: classified@shawsuburban.com
Editor Email: editorial@lakecountyjournal.com
Advertising Executive Phone: (847) 828-1878

GREENVILLE

THE GREENVILLE ADVOCATE
Corporate/Parent Company: Boone Newspapers, Inc.
Street Address: P.O. Box 9
City: Greenville
State: IL
Postal Code: 62246
Office phone: (618) 664-3144
Publication Website: www.thegreenvilleadvocate.com
General E-mail: advocateil@sbcglobal.net
Publisher Name: Adam Jeffers
Publisher Email: greenvilleadvocate@gmail.com
Editor Name: David Bell
Editor Email: greenvilleadvocate@gmail.com

GRIDLEY

GRIDLEY VILLAGE TIMES
Corporate/Parent Company: The Normalite Newspaper Group
Street Address: 204 E 4th St
City: Gridley
State: IL
Postal Code: 61744
Office phone: 309-747-3070
Publication Website: www.normalite.com
General E-mail: thenormalite@gmail.com
Publisher Name: Ed Pyne
Publisher Email: thenormalite@gmail.com
Editor Name: Ed Pyne
Editor Email: thenormalite@gmail.com

HARDIN

CALHOUN NEWS-HERALD
Corporate/Parent Company: Campbell Publishing Co., Inc.
Street Address: 310 S County Rd
City: Hardin
State: IL
Postal Code: 62047-4414
Office phone: (618) 576-2345
Publication Website: https://calhounnewsherald.com/
General E-mail: cnhnews@campbellpublications.net
Publisher Name: Nichole Liehr
Publisher Email: nliehr@campbellpublications.net
Publisher Phone: (217) 285-2345
Editor Name: Jarad Jarmon
Editor Email: jcjnews@campbellpublications.net
Advertising Executive Name: Nichole Liehr
Advertising Executive Email: nliehr@campbellpublications.net
Advertising Executive Phone: (217) 285-2345

HEYWORTH

THE HEYWORTH BUZZ
Corporate/Parent Company: The Normalite Newspaper Group
Street Address: P.O. Box 66
City: Heyworth
State: IL
Postal Code: 61745
Office phone: 309-242-9325
Publication Website: www.normalite.com
General E-mail: thenormalite@gmail.com
Publisher Name: Ed Pyne
Publisher Email: thenormalite@gmail.com

HINSDALE

THE HINSDALEAN
Corporate/Parent Company: Hinsdale Publishing Company, Inc.
Street Address: 7 W. First St.
City: Hinsdale
State: IL
Postal Code: 60521
Office phone: (630) 323-4422
Publication Website: www.thehinsdalean.com
General E-mail: info@thehinsdalean.com
Publisher Name: Jim Slonoff
Publisher Email: jslonoff@thehinsdalean.com
Publisher Phone: Ext. 105
Editor Name: Pamela Lannom
Editor Email: plannom@thehinsdalean.com
Editor Phone: Ext. 104
Advertising Executive Name: Lisa Skrapka
Advertising Executive Email: lskrapka@thehinsdalean.com
Advertising Executive Phone: Ext. 101

HOOPESTON

THE CHRONICLE
Corporate/Parent Company: Gannett
Street Address: 308 E Main St
City: Hoopeston
State: IL
Postal Code: 60942-1505
Office phone: (217) 283-5111
Publication Website: http://www.newsbug.info/hoopeston_chronicle/
General E-mail: chronoffice@frontier.com
Publisher Name: Greg Perrotto
Publisher Email: gperrotto@rensselaerrepublican.com
Advertising Executive Name: Misty Courtney
Advertising Executive Email: chronads@frontier.com

THE HOOPESTON CHRONICLE
Corporate/Parent Company: Community Media Group
Street Address: 308 E Main St
City: Hoopeston
State: IL
Postal Code: 60942
Office phone: (217) 283-5111
Publication Website: http://www.newsbug.info/hoopeston_chronicle/
General E-mail: chronoffice@frontier.com
Publisher Name: Greg Perrotto
Publisher Email: gperrotto@rensselaerrepublican.com
Editor Name: Jordan Crook
Editor Email: chronreporter@frontier.com
Advertising Executive Name: Misty Courtney
Advertising Executive Email: chronads@frontier.com

JACKSONVILLE

THE SOURCE
Corporate/Parent Company: Media News Group
Street Address: P. O. Box 730
City: Jacksonville
State: IL
Postal Code: 62650
Office phone: 217-243-3857
Publication Website: www.the-source.net
General E-mail: info@the-source.net
Publisher Name: Marcy Patterson
Publisher Email: marcy@the-source.net
Editor Name: Paige Lambie
Editor Email: paige@the-source.net

JERSEYVILLE

JERSEY COUNTY JOURNAL
Corporate/Parent Company: Campbell Publishing Co., Inc.
Street Address: 832 S. State St
City: Jerseyville
State: IL
Postal Code: 62052
Office phone: 618-498-1234
Publication Website: www.jerseycountyjournal.com
General E-mail: jcjnews@campbellpublications.net
Publisher Name: Nichole Liehr
Publisher Email: nliehr@campbellpublications.net
Editor Name: Jarad Jarmon
Editor Email: jcjnews@campbellpublications.net

THE JERSEY COUNTY STAR (OOB)
Corporate/Parent Company: South County Publications
Street Address: 722 W County Rd Ste B
City: Jerseyville
State: IL
Postal Code: 62052
Office phone: (618) 498-3377
Publication Website: http://www.thejcstar.com/

KANKAKEE

THE SOUTH SUBURBAN NEWS
Street Address: 200 East Court St. Ste 606
City: Kankakee
State: IL
Postal Code: 6090
Office phone: 815-370-7388
Publication Website: mytaylormedia.com
General E-mail: p.taylormedia@yahoo.com
Publisher Name: Michael Taylor
Publisher Email: m.upclose@yahoo.com

LEBANON

LEBANON ADVERTISER
Street Address: P.O. Box 126
City: Lebanon
State: IL
Postal Code: 62254
Office phone: 618-713-4230
Publication Website: www.facebook.com/lebanonadvertiser
General E-mail: publisher@lebanonadvertiser.com
Publisher Name: David Porter
Publisher Email: publisher@lebanonadvertiser.com

LENA

SHOPPER'S GUIDE
Corporate/Parent Company: Rock Valley Publishing LLC
Street Address: Mark Gregory
City: Lena
State: IL
Postal Code: 61048
Office phone: 815-369-4112
Publication Website: www.rvpublishing.com
General E-mail: scoopshopper@rvpublishing.

com
Editor Name: Tony Carton
Editor Email: scoopshopper@rvpublishing.com
Advertising Executive Name: Cyndee Stiefel
Advertising Executive Email: lenaads@rvpublishing.com

THE SCOOP TODAY

Corporate/Parent Company: Rock Valley Publishing LLC
Street Address: 213 S. Center
City: Lena
State: IL
Postal Code: 61048
Office phone: 815-369-4112
Publication Website: www.rvpublishing.com
General E-mail: info@rvpublishing.com
Publisher Name: Pete Cruger
Publisher Email: pete@rvpublishing.com
Editor Name: Tony Carton
Editor Email: scoopshopper@rvpublishing.com
Advertising Executive Name: Cyndee Stiefel
Advertising Executive Email: lenaads@rvpublishing.com

LEROY

THE LE ROY LEADER

Corporate/Parent Company: The Normalite Newspaper Group
Street Address: P.O. Box 92
City: LeRoy
State: IL
Postal Code: 61752
Office phone: 309-310-6832
Publication Website: www.normalite.com
General E-mail: thenormalite@gmail.com
Publisher Name: Ed Pyne
Publisher Email: thenormalite@gmail.com

LEXINGTON

THE LEXINGTONIAN

Corporate/Parent Company: The Normalite Newspaper Group
Street Address: P.O. Box 136
City: Lexington
State: IL
Postal Code: 61753
Office phone: 309-365-8668
Publication Website: www.normalite.com
General E-mail: thenormalite@gmail.com
Publisher Name: Ed Pyne
Publisher Email: thenormalite@gmail.com
Editor Name: Laurie Sleeter
Editor Email: lexingtonian@frontier.com

LIBERTY

THE LIBERTY BEE-TIMES

Corporate/Parent Company: Elliott Publishing, Inc.
Street Address: 103 E Hannibal St
City: Liberty
State: IL
Postal Code: 62347-1055
Office phone: (217) 645 -3033
Publication Website: http://www.elliott-publishing.com/
General E-mail: libertyb@adams.net
Publisher Name: James Elliott
Publisher Email: cpjournal@adams.net
Editor Name: Marcia Elliott
Editor Email: cpjournal@adams.net
Advertising Executive Email: leeanne@elliott-publishing.com

LOMBARD

DUPAGE COUNTY CHRONICLE

Corporate/Parent Company: Chronicle Media, LLC.
Street Address: 1920 S. Highland Avenue, #333
City: Lombard
State: IL
Postal Code: 60148
Office phone: 866-672-1600
Publication Website: www.dupagechronicle.com
General E-mail: editor@chronicleillinois.com
Publisher Name: Rick Hibbert
Publisher Email: rhibbert@chronicleillinois.com
Publisher Phone: 312.690.5341
Editor Name: Judy Harvey
Editor Email: jharvey@chronicleillinois.com
Editor Phone: 866-672-1600
Advertising Executive Name: Mark Doherty
Advertising Executive Email: mdoherty@chronicleillinois.com
Advertising Executive Phone: 866.672.1600 Ext. 256

LAKE COUNTY CHRONICLE

Corporate/Parent Company: Chronicle Media, LLC.
Street Address: 1920 S. Highland Avenue, #333
City: Lombard
State: IL
Postal Code: 60148
Office phone: 866-672-1600
Publication Website: chronicleillinois.com/category/news/lake-county-news
General E-mail: editor@chronicleillinois.com
Publisher Name: Rick Hibbert
Publisher Email: rhibbert@chronicleillinois.com
Publisher Phone: 312.690.5341
Editor Name: Judy Harvey
Editor Email: jharvey@chronicleillinois.com
Editor Phone: 866-672-1600
Advertising Executive Name: Mark Doherty
Advertising Executive Email: mdoherty@chronicleillinois.com
Advertising Executive Phone: 866.672.1600 Ext. 256

MCLEAN CHRONICLE

Corporate/Parent Company: Chronicle Media, LLC.
Street Address: 1920 S. Highland Avenue, #333
City: Lombard
State: IL
Postal Code: 60148
Office phone: 866-672-1600
Publication Website: www.mcleanchronicle.com
General E-mail: editor@chronicleillinois.com
Publisher Name: Rick Hibbert
Publisher Email: rhibbert@chronicleillinois.com
Publisher Phone: 312.690.5341
Editor Name: Judy Harvey
Editor Email: jharvey@chronicleillinois.com
Editor Phone: 866-672-1600
Advertising Executive Name: Mark Doherty
Advertising Executive Email: mdoherty@chronicleillinois.com
Advertising Executive Phone: 866.672.1600 Ext. 256

METRO EAST CHRONICLE

Corporate/Parent Company: Chronicle Media, LLC.
Street Address: 1920 S. Highland Avenue, #333
City: Lombard
State: IL
Postal Code: 60148
Office phone: 866-672-1600
Publication Website: www.metroeastchronicle.com
General E-mail: editor@chronicleillinois.com
Publisher Name: Rick Hibbert
Publisher Email: rhibbert@chronicleillinois.com
Publisher Phone: 312.690.5341
Editor Name: Judy Harvey
Editor Email: jharvey@chronicleillinois.com
Editor Phone: 866-672-1600
Advertising Executive Name: Mark Doherty
Advertising Executive Email: mdoherty@chronicleillinois.com
Advertising Executive Phone: 866.672.1600 Ext. 256

SUBURBAN CHRONICLE

Corporate/Parent Company: Chronicle Media, LLC.
Street Address: 1920 S. Highland Avenue, #333
City: Lombard
State: IL
Postal Code: 60148
Office phone: 866-672-1600
Publication Website: www.chronicleillinois.com
General E-mail: editor@chronicleillinois.com
Publisher Name: Rick Hibbert
Publisher Email: rhibbert@chronicleillinois.com
Publisher Phone: 312.690.5341
Editor Name: Jack McCarthy
Editor Email: jmccarthy@chronicleillinois.com
Editor Phone: 866-672-1600
Advertising Executive Name: Mark Doherty
Advertising Executive Email: mdoherty@chronicleillinois.com
Advertising Executive Phone: 866.672.1600

TAZEWELL CHRONICLE

Corporate/Parent Company: Chronicle Media, LLC.
Street Address: 1920 S. Highland Avenue, #333
City: Lombard
State: IL
Postal Code: 60148
Office phone: 866-672-1600
Publication Website: www.tazewellchronicle.com
General E-mail: editor@chronicleillinois.com
Publisher Name: Rick Hibbert
Publisher Email: rhibbert@chronicleillinois.com
Publisher Phone: 312.690.5341
Editor Name: Jack McCarthy
Editor Email: jmccarthy@chronicleillinois.com
Editor Phone: 866-672-1600
Advertising Executive Name: Mark Doherty
Advertising Executive Email: mdoherty@chronicleillinois.com
Advertising Executive Phone: 866.672.1600

WINNEBAGO CHRONICLE

Corporate/Parent Company: Chronicle Media, LLC.
Street Address: 1920 S. Highland Avenue, #333
City: Lombard
State: IL
Postal Code: 60148
Office phone: 866-672-1600
Publication Website: www.winnebagochronicle.com
General E-mail: editor@chronicleillinois.com
Publisher Name: Rick Hibbert
Publisher Email: rhibbert@chronicleillinois.com
Publisher Phone: 312.690.5341
Editor Name: Jack McCarthy
Editor Email: jmccarthy@chronicleillinois.com
Editor Phone: 866-672-1600
Advertising Executive Name: Mark Doherty
Advertising Executive Email: mdoherty@chronicleillinois.com
Advertising Executive Phone: 866.672.1600

WOODFORD CHRONICLE

Corporate/Parent Company: Chronicle Media, LLC.
Street Address: 1920 S. Highland Avenue, #333
City: Lombard
State: IL
Postal Code: 60148
Office phone: 866-672-1600
Publication Website: www.woodfordchronicle.com
General E-mail: editor@chronicleillinois.com
Publisher Name: Rick Hibbert
Publisher Email: rhibbert@chronicleillinois.com
Publisher Phone: 312.690.5341
Editor Name: Jack McCarthy
Editor Email: jmccarthy@chronicleillinois.com
Editor Phone: 866-672-1600
Advertising Executive Name: Mark Doherty
Advertising Executive Email: mdoherty@chronicleillinois.com
Advertising Executive Phone: 866.672.1600

LOVES PARK

POST JOURNAL

Corporate/Parent Company: Rock Valley Publishing LLC
Street Address: 7124 Windsor Lake Parkway, Suite 4
City: Loves Park
State: IL
Postal Code: 61111
Office phone: (815) 654-4850
Publication Website: http://rvpnews.com/?cat=6
General E-mail: mbayer@rvpublishing.com
Publisher Name: Pete Cruger
Publisher Email: pete@rvpublishing.com
Editor Name: Anne Eickstadt
Editor Email: bdrnews@rvpublishing.com
Advertising Executive Name: Maxine Bayer
Advertising Executive Email: mbayer@rvpublishing.com

ROCKFORD JOURNAL

Corporate/Parent Company: Rock Valley Publishing
Street Address: 7124 Windsor Lake Parkway, Suite 4
City: Loves Park
State: IL
Postal Code: 61111
Office phone: 815-654-4850
Publication Website: www.rvpublishing.com
General E-mail: bdrnews@rvpublishing.com
Publisher Name: Pete Cruger
Publisher Email: pete@rvpublishing.com
Editor Name: Anne Eickstadt
Editor Email: bdrnews@rvpublishing.com
Advertising Executive Name: Maxine Bayer
Advertising Executive Email: mbayer@rvpublishing.com

THE HERALD

Corporate/Parent Company: Paxton Media Group
Street Address: 7124 Windsor Lake Parkway, Suite 4
City: Loves Park
State: IL
Postal Code: 61111
Office phone: (815) 654-4850
Publication Website: http://rvpnews.com/?cat=5
General E-mail: mbayer@rvpublishing.com
Publisher Name: Pete Cruger
Publisher Email: pete@rvpublishing.com
Editor Name: Melanie Bradley
Editor Email: mbradley@rvpublishing.com
Advertising Executive Name: Maxine Bayer
Advertising Executive Email: mbayer@rvpublishing.com

MACOMB

EAGLE - SCRIBE

Street Address: 26 W. Side Square
City: Macomb
State: IL
Postal Code: 61455
Office phone: (309) 833-2114

Non-Daily Newspapers in the U.S.

Publication Website: www.mcdonoughvoice.com
General E-mail: tmartin@register-mail.com
Editor Name: Michelle Langhout
Editor Email: editor@mcdonoughvoice.com
Editor Phone: (309) 833-2114 ext. 253
Advertising Executive Name: Michelle Ringenberger
Advertising Executive Email: mringenberger@mcdonoughvoice.com
Advertising Executive Phone: (309) 833-2114 ext. 258

MARION

THE INDEPENDENT

Corporate/Parent Company: Gannett
Street Address: 1205 Tower Square Plaza
City: Marion
State: IL
Postal Code: 62959
Office phone: 618-997-7827
Publication Website: swinfordpublications.com
General E-mail: editor.independent@frontier.com
Publisher Name: BILL SWINFORD
Publisher Email: bill.publisher@frontier.com
Editor Name: Riley Swinford
Editor Email: rileyswinford@gmail.com
Advertising Executive Name: Melanie Craig
Advertising Executive Email: mel.courier@frontier.com

THE MARION STAR

Corporate/Parent Company: Gannett
Street Address: 163 E. Center St., Suite 100
City: Marion
State: IL
Postal Code: 43302
Office phone: 740-387-0400
Publication Website: www.marionstar.com
Publisher Name: Bill Swinford
Publisher Email: bill.publisher@frontier.com
Editor Name: Benjamin Lanka
Editor Email: blanka@gannett.com

MASCOUTAH

SCOTT AIR FORCE BASE FLIER

Corporate/Parent Company: Herald Publications
Street Address: 410 East Main P. O. Drawer C
City: Mascoutah
State: IL
Postal Code: 62258
Office phone: 618-566-8282
Publication Website: https://www.heraldpubs.com/scott-air-force-base/
General E-mail: heraldpubs@heraldpubs.com
Publisher Name: Greg Hoskins
Publisher Email: ghoskins@heraldpubs.com
Editor Name: Pamela Rensing
Editor Email: heraldpubs@heraldpubs.com
Advertising Executive Name: Charlie Huelsmann
Advertising Executive Email: adv@heraldpubs.com

THE TRIBUNE

Corporate/Parent Company: AIM Media
Street Address: 410 East Main P. O. Drawer C
City: Mascoutah
State: IL
Postal Code: 62258
Office phone: 618-566-8282
Publication Website: www.heraldpubs.com
General E-mail: ccn@heraldpubs.com
Publisher Name: Greg Hoskins
Publisher Email: ghoskins@heraldpubs.com
Editor Name: Pamela Rensing
Editor Email: tribune@heraldpubs.com
Advertising Executive Name: Charlie Huelsmann
Advertising Executive Email: adv@heraldpubs.com

MATTOON

JOURNAL GAZETTE & TIMES-COURIER

Corporate/Parent Company: Lee Enterprises
Street Address: 700 Broadway Ave East, Ste 9A
City: Mattoon
State: IL
Postal Code: 61938
Office phone: (217) 235-5656
Publication Website: https://jg-tc.com/
General E-mail: jreynolds@pantagraph.com
Publisher Name: Barry Winterland
Publisher Email: bwinterland@pantagraph.com
Editor Name: Eric Skalac
Editor Email: eskalac@jg-tc.com
Editor Phone: (217) 238-6863
Advertising Executive Name: Jaime Reynolds
Advertising Executive Email: jreynolds@pantagraph.com
Advertising Executive Phone: (309) 820-3337

MENDOTA

MENDOTA REPORTER

Corporate/Parent Company: News Media Grouip
Street Address: 703 Illinois Ave
City: Mendota
State: IL
Postal Code: 61342
Office phone: (815) 539-9396
Publication Website: https://www.mendotareporter.com/
General E-mail: kcheek@mendotareporter.com
Publisher Name: Kip Cheek
Publisher Email: kcheek@mendotareporter.com
Publisher Phone: (815) 539-9396
Editor Name: Bonnie Morris
Editor Email: bmorris@mendotareporter.com
Editor Phone: (815) 539-9396
Advertising Executive Name: Tonja Greenfield
Advertising Executive Email: tgreenfield@amboynews.com
Advertising Executive Phone: (815) 857-2311

MIDLOTHIAN

ALSIP EXPRESS

Corporate/Parent Company: Southwest Messenger Press, Inc.
Street Address: 3840 W. 147th Street
City: Midlothian
State: IL
Postal Code: 60445
Office phone: (708) 388-2425
Publication Website: southwestmessengerpress.com/alsip-express
General E-mail: info@southwestmessengerpress.com
Publisher Name: Lucinda Lysen
Publisher Email: lucindalon@aol.com
Editor Name: (708) 388-2425 x__

BEVERLY NEWS

Corporate/Parent Company: Southwest Messenger Press, Inc.
Street Address: 3840 147th St
City: Midlothian
State: IL
Postal Code: 60445-3452
Office phone: (708) 388-2425
Publication Website: https://southwestmessengerpress.com/beverly-news
General E-mail: info@southwestmessengerpress.com
Publisher Name: Lucinda Lysen
Publisher Email: lucindalon@aol.com
Editor Name: Lucinda Lysen
Editor Email: lucindalon@aol.com

BRIDGEVIEW INDEPENDENT

Corporate/Parent Company: Southwest Messenger Press, Inc.
Street Address: 3840 147th St
City: Midlothian
State: IL
Postal Code: 60445-3452
Office phone: (708) 388-2425
Publication Website: https://southwestmessengerpress.com/bridgeview-independent
General E-mail: info@southwestmessengerpress.com
Publisher Name: Lucinda Lysen
Publisher Email: lucindalon@aol.com
Editor Name: Lucinda Lysen
Editor Email: lucindalon@aol.com

BURBANK-STICKNEY INDEPENDENT

Corporate/Parent Company: Southwest Messenger Press, Inc.
Street Address: 3840 147th St
City: Midlothian
State: IL
Postal Code: 60445-3452
Office phone: (708) 388-2425
Publication Website: https://southwestmessengerpress.com/burbank-independent
General E-mail: info@southwestmessengerpress.com
Publisher Name: Lucinda Lysen
Publisher Email: lucindalon@aol.com
Editor Name: Lucinda Lysen
Editor Email: lucindalon@aol.com

BURBANK-STICKNEY INDEPENDENT - SCOTTSDALE EDITION

Corporate/Parent Company: Southwest Messenger Press, Inc.
Street Address: 3840 147th St
City: Midlothian
State: IL
Postal Code: 60445-3452
Office phone: (708) 388-2425
Publication Website: https://southwestmessengerpress.com/scottsdale-independent
General E-mail: info@southwestmessengerpress.com
Publisher Name: Lucinda Lysen
Publisher Email: lucindalon@aol.com
Editor Name: Lucinda Lysen
Editor Email: lucindalon@aol.com

CHICAGO RIDGE CITIZEN

Corporate/Parent Company: Southwest Messenger Press, Inc.
Street Address: 3840 147th St
City: Midlothian
State: IL
Postal Code: 60445-3452
Office phone: (708) 388-2425
Publication Website: https://southwestmessengerpress.com/chicago-ridge-citizen
General E-mail: info@southwestmessengerpress.com
Publisher Name: Lucinda Lysen
Publisher Email: lucindalon@aol.com
Editor Name: Lucinda Lysen
Editor Email: lucindalon@aol.com

EVERGREEN PARK COURIER

Corporate/Parent Company: Southwest Messenger Press, Inc.
Street Address: 3840 147th St
City: Midlothian
State: IL
Postal Code: 60445-3452
Office phone: (708) 388-2425
Publication Website: https://southwestmessengerpress.com/evergreen-park-courier-1
General E-mail: info@southwestmessengerpress.com
Publisher Name: Lucinda Lysen
Publisher Email: lucindalon@aol.com
Editor Name: Lucinda Lysen
Editor Email: lucindalon@aol.com

HICKORY HILLS CITIZEN

Corporate/Parent Company: Southwest Messenger Press, Inc.
Street Address: 3840 147th St
City: Midlothian
State: IL
Postal Code: 60445-3452
Office phone: (708) 388-2425
Publication Website: https://southwestmessengerpress.com/hickory-hills-citizen
General E-mail: info@southwestmessengerpress.com
Publisher Name: Lucinda Lysen
Publisher Email: lucindalon@aol.com
Editor Name: Lucinda Lysen
Editor Email: lucindalon@aol.com

MIDLOTHIAN-BREMEN MESSENGER

Corporate/Parent Company: Southwest Messenger Press, Inc.
Street Address: 3840 147th St
City: Midlothian
State: IL
Postal Code: 60445-3452
Office phone: (708) 388-2425
Publication Website: https://southwestmessengerpress.com/midlo-bremen-messenger
General E-mail: info@southwestmessengerpress.com
Publisher Name: Lucinda Lysen
Publisher Email: lucindalon@aol.com
Editor Name: Lucinda Lyson
Editor Email: lucindalon@aol.com

MOUNT GREENWOOD EXPRESS

Corporate/Parent Company: Southwest Messenger Press, Inc.
Street Address: 3840 147th St
City: Midlothian
State: IL
Postal Code: 60445-3452
Office phone: (708) 388-2425
Publication Website: https://southwestmessengerpress.com/mount-greenwood-express
General E-mail: info@southwestmessengerpress.com
Publisher Name: Lucinda Lysen
Publisher Email: lucindalon@aol.com
Editor Name: Lucinda Lysen
Editor Email: lucindalon@aol.com

MOUNT GREENWOOD EXPRESS -

ALSIP EDITION

Corporate/Parent Company: Southwest Messenger Press, Inc.
Street Address: 3840 147th St
City: Midlothian
State: IL
Postal Code: 60445-3452
Office phone: (708) 388-2425
Publication Website: https://southwestmessengerpress.com/mount-greenwood-express
General E-mail: info@southwestmessengerpress.com
Publisher Name: Lucinda Lysen
Publisher Email: lucindalon@aol.com
Editor Name: Lucinda Lysen
Editor Email: lucindalon@aol.com

OAK LAWN INDEPENDENT

Corporate/Parent Company: Southwest Messenger Press, Inc.
Street Address: 3840 147th St
City: Midlothian
State: IL
Postal Code: 60445-3452
Office phone: (708) 388-2425
Publication Website: https://southwestmessengerpress.com/oak-lawn-independent-1
General E-mail: info@southwestmessengerpress.com
Publisher Name: Lucinda Lysen
Publisher Email: lucindalon@aol.com
Editor Name: Lucinda Lysen
Editor Email: lucindalon@aol.com

ORLAND TOWNSHIP MESSENGER

Corporate/Parent Company: Southwest Messenger Press, Inc.
Street Address: 3840 147th St
City: Midlothian
State: IL
Postal Code: 60445-3452
Office phone: (708) 388-2425
Publication Website: https://southwestmessengerpress.com/orland-township-msngr-1
General E-mail: info@southwestmessengerpress.com
Publisher Name: Lucinda Lysen
Publisher Email: lucindalon@aol.com

PALOS CITIZEN

Corporate/Parent Company: Southwest Messenger Press, Inc.
Street Address: 3840 147th St
City: Midlothian
State: IL
Postal Code: 60445-3452
Office phone: (708) 388-2425
Publication Website: https://southwestmessengerpress.com/palos-citizen
General E-mail: info@southwestmessengerpress.com
Publisher Name: Lucinda Lysen
Publisher Email: lucindalon@aol.com

SCOTTSDALE ASHBURN INDEPENDENT

Corporate/Parent Company: Arthur Publishing
Street Address: 3840 147th St
City: Midlothian
State: IL
Postal Code: 60445
Office phone: 708-388-2425
Publication Website: southwestmessengerpress.com/scottsdale-independent
General E-mail: info@southwestmessengerpress.com
Publisher Name: Lucinda Lysen
Publisher Email: lucindalon@aol.com
Editor Name: Dana Mayfield

WORTH CITIZEN

Corporate/Parent Company: Southwest Messenger Press, Inc.
Street Address: 3840 147th St
City: Midlothian
State: IL
Postal Code: 60445-3452
Office phone: (708) 388-2425
Publication Website: https://southwestmessengerpress.com/worth-citizen
General E-mail: info@southwestmessengerpress.com
Publisher Name: Lucinda Lysen
Publisher Email: lucindalon@aol.com

MONTICELLO

PIATT COUNTY JOURNAL-REPUBLICAN

Street Address: 118 E Washington St
City: Monticello
State: IL
Postal Code: 61856
Office phone: (217) 762-2511
Publication Website: https://www.journal-republican.com/
General E-mail: news@journal-republican.com
Publisher Name: Greg Perrotto
Publisher Email: gperrotto@rensselaerrepublican.com
Editor Name: Steve Hoffman
Editor Email: shoffman@news-gazette.media
Editor Phone: (217) 762-2511
Advertising Executive Name: Sue Smith
Advertising Executive Email: ssmith@news-gazette.media

MORRIS

HERALD LIFE

Corporate/Parent Company: Shaw Media
Street Address: 909 Liberty St.
City: Morris
State: IL
Postal Code: 60450
Office phone: (815) 280-4100
Publication Website: www.heraldlife.com
General E-mail: news@morrisdailyherald.com
Publisher Name: "Steve Vanisko
Publisher Email: svanisko@shawmedia.com
Publisher Phone: 815-280-4103
Editor Name: "Marney Simon
"
Editor Email: msimon@shawmedia.com

MORRIS

MORRIS HERALD-NEWS

Street Address: 909 Liberty St.
City: MORRIS
State: IL
Postal Code: 60450
Office phone: (815) 280-4100
Publication Website: https://www.morrisherald-news.com/
General E-mail: news@morrisherald-news.com
Publisher Name: Steve Vanisko
Publisher Email: bsvanisko@shawmedia.com
Publisher Phone: (815) 280-4103
Editor Name: Marney Simon
Editor Email: msimon@shawmedia.com
Advertising Executive Name: Steve Vanisko
Advertising Executive Email: svanisko@shawmedia.com
Advertising Executive Phone: (815) 280-4100

MOUNT PROSPECT

MT. PROSPECT JOURNAL

Corporate/Parent Company: Journal & Topics Online Media Group
Street Address: 622 Graceland Ave
City: Mount Prospect
State: IL
Postal Code: 60016-4519
Office phone: 847-299-5511
Publication Website: www.Journal-topics.com
General E-mail: newsjournal@journal-topics.com
Publisher Name: Todd Wessell
Publisher Email: toddwessell@journal-topics.info
Editor Name: Tom Wessell
Editor Email: tomwessell@journal-topics.info

ROLLING MEADOWS JOURNAL & TOPICS

Corporate/Parent Company: Journal & Topics Online Media Group
Street Address: IL
City: Mount Prospect
State: IL
Postal Code: 60016-4519
Office phone: 847-299-5511
Publication Website: www.Journal-topics.com
General E-mail: journalnews@journal-topics.info
Publisher Name: Todd Wessell
Publisher Email: toddwessell@journal-topics.info
Editor Name: Tom Wessell
Editor Email: tomwessell@journal-topics.info

SUBURBAN JOURNAL & TOPICS

Corporate/Parent Company: Journal & Topics Online Media Group
Street Address: 622 Graceland Ave
City: Mount Prospect
State: IL
Postal Code: 60016-4519
Office phone: 847-299-5511
Publication Website: www.journal-topics.com
General E-mail: journalnews@journal-topics.info
Publisher Name: Todd Wessell
Publisher Email: toddwessell@journal-topics.info
Editor Name: Tom Wessell
Editor Email: tomwessell@journal-topics.info

WHEELING JOURNAL & TOPICS

Corporate/Parent Company: Journal & Topics Online Media Group
Street Address: 622 Graceland Ave
City: Mount Prospect
State: IL
Postal Code: 60016-4519
Office phone: 847-299-5511
Publication Website: www.Journal-topics.com
General E-mail: journalnews@journal-topics.com
Publisher Name: Todd Wessell
Publisher Email: toddwessell@journal-topics.info
Editor Name: Tom Wessell
Editor Email: tomwessell@journal-topics.info

MT. CARMEL

MT. CARMEL REGISTER

Street Address: 217 E. 9th St.
City: Mt. Carmel
State: IL
Postal Code: 62863
Office phone: (618) 262-5144
Publication Website: www.mtcarmelregister.com
General E-mail: news@mtcarmelregister.com
Publisher Name: Mike Weafer
Publisher Email: mweafer@messenger-inquirer.com
Editor Name: Andrea Howe
Editor Email: news@mtcarmelregister.com
Advertising Executive Name: Courtney Shuttle
Advertising Executive Email: courtney@pdclarion.com

NEWTON

JASPER COUNTY NEWS EAGLE

Street Address: 700 W. Washington St
City: Newton
State: IL
Postal Code: 62448
Office phone: 833-948-1200
Publication Website: www.pressmentor.com
General E-mail: cbarche@olneydailymail.com
Editor Name: Chip Barche
Editor Email: cbarche@olneydailymail.com
Editor Phone: 618-393-2931
Advertising Executive Name: Cathy Slunaker
Advertising Executive Email: advertising1@olneydailymail.com
Advertising Executive Phone: 618-393-2931

NOKOMIS

NOKOMIS FREE PRESS-PROGRESS

Street Address: 112 W State St
City: Nokomis
State: IL
Postal Code: 62075
Office phone: (217) 563-2115
Publication Website: www.nokomisonline.com
General E-mail: freepress@consolidated.net
Publisher Name: Stefanie Anderson (GM)
Publisher Email: sanderson@localsouthernnews.com
Editor Name: John Broux
Editor Email: jbroux@pananewsgroup.com

NORMAL

THE NORMALITE

Corporate/Parent Company: The Normalite Newspaper Group
Street Address: 1702 W College Ave. Suite G
City: Normal
State: IL
Postal Code: 61761
Office phone: 309 454 5476
Publication Website: www.normalite.com
General E-mail: thenormalite@gmail.com
Publisher Name: Ed Pyne
Publisher Email: thenormalite@gmail.com

OAK PARK

ELM LEAVES

Street Address: 1140 Lake Street
City: Oak Park
State: IL
Postal Code: 60301
Office phone: 312-222-3232
Publication Website: www.elmwoodpark-leaves.com
General E-mail: pdefiglio@chicagotribune.com
Publisher Name: Par Ridder (GM)
Publisher Email: pridder@tribpub.com
Editor Name: Pam DeFiglio
Editor Email: pdefiglio@chicagotribune.com

Non-Daily Newspapers in the U.S.

RIVERSIDE-BROOKFIELD LANDMARK
Corporate/Parent Company: Wednesday Journal Publications
Street Address: 141 S. Oak Park Ave
City: Oak Park
State: IL
Postal Code: 60302
Office phone: 708-442-6739
Publication Website: www.rblandmark.com
General E-mail: buphues@rblandmark.com
Publisher Name: Dan Haley
Publisher Email: dhaley@wjinc.com
Editor Name: Bob Uphues
Editor Email: buphues@rblandmark.com
Editor Phone: 708-442-6739
Advertising Executive Name: Dawn Ferencak
Advertising Executive Email: dawn@oakpark.com

OAKLAND
OAKLAND INDEPENDENT
Street Address: P.O. Box 346, 26 E. Main St.,
City: Oakland
State: IL
Postal Code: 61943
Office phone: 217-346-2050
Publication Website: www.oaklandindependentnews.com
General E-mail: oaklandindependentnews@gmail.com
Publisher Name: Janice Hunt
Publisher Email: oaklandindependentnews@gmail.com

O'FALLON
O'FALLON WEEKLY
Street Address: P.O. Box 662
City: O'Fallon
State: IL
Postal Code: 62269
Office phone: 618-622-2525
Publication Website: www.OFallonWeekly.com
General E-mail: news@ofallonweekly.com
Editor Name: Nick Miller
Editor Email: nick@ofallonweekly.com

OLNEY
OLNEY GAZETTE
Street Address: 309 E Main St
City: Olney
State: IL
Postal Code: 62450
Office phone: 618-392-6397
Publication Website: www.olneygazette.com
General E-mail: olneygazettenews@gmail.com
Publisher Name: Mark Allen
Publisher Email: olneygazettenews@gmail.com
Editor Name: Mark Allen
Editor Email: olneygazettenews@gmail.com
Advertising Executive Name: Heather Shultz

OREGON
OGLE COUNTY LIFE
Corporate/Parent Company: News Media Grouip
Street Address: 311 E Washington St
City: Oregon
State: IL
Postal Code: 61061
Office phone: (815) 732-2156
Publication Website: http://www.oglecountylife.com
General E-mail: bjennings@oglecountylife.com
Publisher Name: John Shank
Publisher Email: jshank@rochellenews-leader.com
Editor Name: Brad Jennings
Editor Email: bjennings@oglecountylife.com

THE OGLE COUNTY LIFE
Corporate/Parent Company: News Media Grouip
Street Address: 311 W. Washington St
City: Oregon
State: IL
Postal Code: 61061
Office phone: 815-732-2156
Publication Website: www.oglecountylife.com
General E-mail: office@oglecountylife.com
Publisher Name: John Shank
Publisher Email: jshank@rochellenews-leader.com
Editor Name: Brad Jennings
Editor Email: bjennings@oglecountylife.com

ORLAND PARK
THE FRANKFORT STATION
Corporate/Parent Company: 22nd Century Media, LLC
Street Address: 11516 183rd Pl
City: Orland Park
State: IL
Postal Code: 60467
Office phone: (708) 326-9170
Publication Website: http://www.frankfortstation.com/
General E-mail: a.nicks@22ndcenturymedia.com
Publisher Name: Joe Coughlin
Publisher Email: j.coughlin@22ndcenturymedia.com
Editor Name: Nuria Mathog
Editor Email: nuria@frankfortstation.com

THE GLENCOE ANCHOR
Corporate/Parent Company: 22nd Century Media, LLC
Street Address: 11516 183rd Pl
City: Orland Park
State: IL
Postal Code: 60467
Office phone: (708) 326-9170
Publication Website: https://www.glencoeanchor.com
General E-mail: a.nicks@22ndcenturymedia.com
Publisher Name: Joe Coughlin
Publisher Email: j.coughlin@22ndcenturymedia.com
Editor Name: Aleksandra Ivanisevic
Editor Email: alex@glencoeanchor.com

THE GLENVIEW LANTERN
Corporate/Parent Company: 22nd Century Media, LLC
Street Address: 11516 183rd Pl
City: Orland Park
State: IL
Postal Code: 60467
Office phone: (708) 326-9170
Publication Website: https://www.glenviewlantern.com
General E-mail: a.nicks@22ndcenturymedia.com
Publisher Name: Joe Coughlin
Publisher Email: j.coughlin@22ndcenturymedia.com
Editor Name: Jason Addy
Editor Email: jason@glenviewlantern.com

ORLAND PARK
THE HIGHLAND PARK LANDMARK
Corporate/Parent Company: 22nd Century Media, LLC
Street Address: 11516 183rd Pl
City: Orland Park
State: IL
Postal Code: 60467
Office phone: (708) 326-9170
Publication Website: http://www.frankfortstation.com/
General E-mail: a.nicks@22ndcenturymedia.com
Publisher Name: Joe Coughlin
Publisher Email: j.coughlin@22ndcenturymedia.com
Editor Name: Erin Yarnall
Editor Email: erin@hplandmark.com

ORLAND PARK
THE LAKE FOREST LEADER
Corporate/Parent Company: 22nd Century Media, LLC
Street Address: 11516 183rd Pl
City: Orland Park
State: IL
Postal Code: 60467
Office phone: (708) 326-9170
Publication Website: http://www.frankfortstation.com/
General E-mail: a.nicks@22ndcenturymedia.com
Publisher Name: Joe Coughlin
Publisher Email: j.coughlin@22ndcenturymedia.com
Editor Name: Peter Kaspari
Editor Email: peter@lakeforestleader.com

PAXTON
FORD COUNTY RECORD
Corporate/Parent Company: Community Media Group
Street Address: 208 N Market St
City: Paxton
State: IL
Postal Code: 60957
Office phone: (217) 379-2356
Publication Website: https://www.fordcountyrecord.com/
General E-mail: news@fordcountyrecord.com
Publisher Name: Paul Barrett
Publisher Email: pmbpub@aol.com
Advertising Executive Name: Sheryl Schunke
Advertising Executive Email: sschunke@news-gazette.com

PINCKNEYVILLE
PINCKNEYVILLE PRESS
Street Address: 111 South Walnut Street
City: Pinckneyville
State: IL
Postal Code: 62274
Office phone: 618-357-6397
Publication Website: www.pinckneyvillepress.com
Publisher Name: Jeff Egbert
Editor Name: Eric Lambert
Editor Email: News@PinckneyvillePress.com

PITTSFIELD
THE WEEKLY MESSENGER
Corporate/Parent Company: Campbell Publishing Co., Inc
Street Address: 115 W Jefferson St
City: Pittsfield
State: IL
Postal Code: 62363-1424
Office phone: (217) 285-2345
Publication Website: https://pikepress.com/index107.htm
General E-mail: ppnews@campbellpublications.net
Publisher Name: Nichole Liehr
Publisher Email: nliehr@campbellpublications.net
Publisher Phone: (217) 285-2345
Advertising Executive Name: Nichole Liehr
Advertising Executive Email: nliehr@campbellpublications.net
Advertising Executive Phone: (217) 285-2345

PLAINFIELD
SHOREWOOD SENTINEL
Corporate/Parent Company: Enterprise Newspapers, Inc
Street Address: 23856 W. Andrew Rd., suite 104
City: Plainfield
State: IL
Postal Code: 60585
Office phone: (815) 436-2431
Publication Website: www.buglenewspapers.com
General E-mail: mark@buglenewspapers.com
Editor Name: Mark Gregory
Editor Email: mark@buglenewspapers.com
Editor Phone: 015-430-2431
Advertising Executive Name: Andrew Samaan
Advertising Executive Email: andrew@buglenewspapers.com
Advertising Executive Phone: 815-436-2431

THE BOLINGBROOK BUGLE
Corporate/Parent Company: Enterprise Newspapers, Inc
Street Address: 23856 W. Andrew Rd., suite 104
City: Plainfield
State: IL
Postal Code: 60585
Office phone: (815) 436-2431
Publication Website: www.buglenewspapers.com
General E-mail: mark@buglenewspapers.com
Editor Name: Mark Gregory
Editor Email: mark@buglenewspapers.com
Editor Phone: 815-436-2431
Advertising Executive Name: Andrew Samaan
Advertising Executive Email: andrew@buglenewspapers.com
Advertising Executive Phone: 815-436-2431

THE ENTERPRISE
Corporate/Parent Company: Gannett
Street Address: 23856 W. Andrew Rd., suite 104
City: Plainfield
State: IL
Postal Code: 60585
Office phone: (815) 436-2431
Publication Website: www.buglenewspapers.com
Publisher Name: Andrew Saman (GM)
Publisher Email: andrew@buglenewspapers.com
Editor Name: Mark Gregory
Editor Email: mark@buglenewspapers.com
Editor Phone: 815-436-2431 ext.102
Advertising Executive Name: Andrew Samaan
Advertising Executive Email: andrew@buglenewspapers.com
Advertising Executive Phone: 815-436-2431 ext. 104

THE JOLIET BUGLE
Corporate/Parent Company: Enterprise Newspapers, Inc
Street Address: 23856 W. Andrew Rd., suite 104
City: Plainfield
State: IL
Postal Code: 60585
Office phone: (815) 436-2431
Publication Website: www.buglenewspapers.com
General E-mail: news@enterprisepublications.com
Publisher Name: Michael James (GM)
Publisher Email: mjames@voyagermediaonline.com
Editor Name: Mark Gregory
Editor Email: mark@buglenewspapers.com

Editor Phone: 815-436-2431 ext.102
Advertising Executive Name: Andrew Samaan
Advertising Executive Email: andrew@buglenewspapers.com
Advertising Executive Phone: 815-436-2431 ext. 104

THE NILES BUGLE

Corporate/Parent Company: Enterprise Newspapers, Inc
Street Address: 23856 W. Andrew Rd., suite 104
City: Plainfield
State: IL
Postal Code: 60585
Office phone: (815) 436-2431
Publication Website: www.buglenewspapers.com
General E-mail: news@enterprisepublications.com
Publisher Name: Andrew Saman (GM)
Publisher Email: andrew@buglenewspapers.com
Editor Name: Mark Gregory
Editor Email: mark@buglenewspapers.com
Editor Phone: 815-436-2431 ext.102
Advertising Executive Name: Andrew Samaan
Advertising Executive Email: andrew@buglenewspapers.com
Advertising Executive Phone: 815-436-2431 ext. 104

THE ROMEOVILLE BUGLE

Corporate/Parent Company: Enterprise Newspapers, Inc
Street Address: 23856 W. Andrew Rd., suite 104
City: Plainfield
State: IL
Postal Code: 60585
Office phone: (815) 436-2431
Publication Website: www.buglenewspapers.com
General E-mail: webmaster@buglenewspapers.com
Publisher Name: Andrew Saman (GM)
Publisher Email: andrew@buglenewspapers.com
Editor Name: Mark Gregory
Editor Email: mark@buglenewspapers.com
Editor Phone: 815-436-2431 ext.102
Advertising Executive Name: Andrew Samaan
Advertising Executive Email: andrew@buglenewspapers.com
Advertising Executive Phone: 815-436-2431 ext. 104

PONTIAC

THE BLADE

Street Address: 318 N. Main Street
City: Pontiac
State: IL
Postal Code: 61764
Office phone: (815) 842-1153
Publication Website: www.pontiacdailyleader.com
General E-mail: emurphy@pontiacdailyleader.com
Editor Name: Erich Murphy
Editor Email: emurphy@pontiacdailyleader.com
Advertising Executive Name: Judy Sweitzer
Advertising Executive Email: jsweitzer@pontiacdailyleader.com

PRINCETON

BUREAU COUNTY REPUBLICAN

Corporate/Parent Company: Shaw Media
Street Address: 526 S. Bureau Valley Parkway, Suite F
City: Princeton
State: IL
Postal Code: 61356
Office phone: (815) 875-4461
Publication Website: https://www.bcrnews.com/
General E-mail: customerservice@bcrnews.com
Publisher Name: Jim Dunn
Publisher Email: jdunn@bcrnews.com
Editor Name: Jim Dunn
Editor Email: jdunn@bcrnews.com
Advertising Executive Name: Lou Romanelli
Advertising Executive Email: lromanelli@shawmedia.com

PUTNAM COUNTY RECORD

Corporate/Parent Company: Shaw Media
Street Address: 526 S. Bureau Valley Parkway, Suite F
City: Princeton
State: IL
Postal Code: 61356
Office phone: (815) 875-4461
Publication Website: https://www.putnamcountyrecord.com/
General E-mail: news@putnamcountyrecord.com
Publisher Name: Jim Dunn
Publisher Email: jdunn@bcrnews.com
Publisher Phone: (815) 875-4461, ext : 6330
Editor Name: Jim Dunn
Editor Email: jdunn@bcrnews.com
Editor Phone: (815) 875-4461, ext : 6330
Advertising Executive Name: Ashley Oliver
Advertising Executive Email: advertising@putnamcountyrecord.com
Advertising Executive Phone: (815) 875-4461, ext : 6345

THE PUTNAM COUNTY RECORD

Corporate/Parent Company: Shaw Media
Street Address: 526 S. Bureau Valley Parkway, Suite F
City: Princeton
State: IL
Postal Code: 61356
Office phone: (815) 875-4461
Publication Website: www.putnamcountyrecord.com
General E-mail: news@putnamcountyrecord.com
Editor Name: Jim Dunn
Editor Email: jdunn@bcrnews.com
Editor Phone: 815-875-4461, ext. 6330
Advertising Executive Name: Jennifer Heintzelman
Advertising Executive Email: jheintzelman@saukvalley.com

TONICA NEWS

Corporate/Parent Company: Shaw Media
Street Address: 800 Ace Rd
City: Princeton
State: IL
Postal Code: 61356
Office phone: (815) 875-4461
Publication Website: https://www.tonicanews.com/
General E-mail: news@tonicanews.com
Publisher Name: Jim Dunn
Publisher Email: jdunn@bcrnews.com
Publisher Phone: (815) 875-4461, ext : 6330
Editor Name: Jim Dunn
Editor Email: jdunn@bcrnews.com
Editor Phone: (815) 875-4461, ext : 6330
Advertising Executive Name: Ashley Oliver
Advertising Executive Email: advertising@tonicanews.com
Advertising Executive Phone: (815) 875-4461, ext : 6345

RANTOUL

RANTOUL PRESS

Corporate/Parent Company: Community Media Group
Street Address: 216 E Sangamon Ave
City: Rantoul
State: IL
Postal Code: 61866
Office phone: (217) 892-9613
Publication Website: https://www.rantoulpress.com/
General E-mail: news@rantoulpress.com
Publisher Name: Greg Perotto
Publisher Email: gperrotto@rensselaerrepublican.com
Editor Name: Dave Hinton
Editor Email: news@rantoulpress.com
Editor Phone: (217) 892-9613
Advertising Executive Name: Breanna Zimmerman
Advertising Executive Email: bzimmerman@news-gazette.media
Advertising Executive Phone: (217) 351-5650

RIVERTON

RIVERTON REGISTER

Corporate/Parent Company: South County Publications
Street Address: 715 N 7th St
City: Riverton
State: IL
Postal Code: 62561
Office phone: (217) 629-9221
Publication Website: https://www.southcountypublications.net/riverton_register/news/
General E-mail: southco@royell.org
Publisher Name: Joe Michelich Jr.
Publisher Email: southco@royell.org
Editor Name: Byron Painter
Editor Email: southcountypub@att.net
Editor Phone: (217) 629-9221

SUN-TIMES (SERVING WILLIAMSVILLE AND SHERMAN)

Corporate/Parent Company: South County Publications
Street Address: 715 N 7th St
City: Riverton
State: IL
Postal Code: 62561
Office phone: (217) 629-9221
Publication Website: https://www.southcountypublications.net/the_sun_times/news/
General E-mail: southco@royell.org
Publisher Name: Joe Michelich Jr.
Publisher Email: southco@royell.org
Editor Name: Byron Painter
Editor Email: southcountypub@att.net
Editor Phone: (217) 629-9221

TRI-CITY REGISTER

Corporate/Parent Company: South County Publications
Street Address: 715 N 7th St
City: Riverton
State: IL
Postal Code: 62561
Office phone: (217) 629-9221
Publication Website: https://www.southcountypublications.net/site/about.html
General E-mail: southco@royell.org
Publisher Name: Joe Michelich Jr.
Publisher Email: southco@royell.org
Editor Name: Byron Painter
Editor Email: southcountypub@att.net
Editor Phone: (217) 629-9221

ROCHELLE

THE ROCHELLE NEWS LEADER

Corporate/Parent Company: News Media Grouip
Street Address: 211 E Il Route 38
City: Rochelle
State: IL
Postal Code: 61068
Office phone: (815) 562-4171
Publication Website: https://rochellenews-leader.com/
General E-mail: jshank@rochellenews-leader.com
Publisher Name: John Shank
Publisher Email: jshank@rochellenews-leader.com
Publisher Phone: (815) 561-2111
Editor Name: Jennifer Simmons
Editor Email: jsimmons@rochellenews-leader.com
Editor Phone: (815) 561-2151
Advertising Executive Name: Mike Feltes
Advertising Executive Email: mfeltes@oglecountylife.com
Advertising Executive Phone: (815) 561-2124

SAINT CHARLES

KANE COUNTY CHRONICLE

Corporate/Parent Company: Shaw Media
Street Address: 333 N Randall Rd
City: Saint Charles
State: IL
Postal Code: 60174
Office phone: (630) 232-9222
Publication Website: https://www.kcchronicle.com/
General E-mail: editorial@kcchronicle.com
Publisher Name: Ryan Wells
Publisher Email: rwells@shawmedia.com
Editor Name: Aimee Barrows
Editor Email: abarrows@shawmedia.com
Editor Phone: (630) 845-5368
Advertising Executive Name: Brad Hanahan
Advertising Executive Email: bhanahan@shawmedia.com
Advertising Executive Phone: (630) 845-5284

KANE COUNTY MAGAZINE

Corporate/Parent Company: Shaw Media
Street Address: 333 N Randall Rd
City: Saint Charles
State: IL
Postal Code: 60174
Office phone: (630) 232-9222
Publication Website: https://www.kcchronicle.com/magazine/about/index.xml
General E-mail: editorial@kcchronicle.com
Publisher Name: Ryan Wells
Publisher Email: rwells@shawmedia.com
Editor Name: Aimee Barrows
Editor Email: abarrows@shawmedia.com
Editor Phone: (630) 845-5368
Advertising Executive Name: Brad Hanahan
Advertising Executive Email: bhanahan@shawmedia.com
Advertising Executive Phone: (630) 845-5284

SAINT JOSEPH

THE LEADER

Corporate/Parent Company: Adams Publishing Group
Street Address: 429 W WARREN ST
City: Saint Joseph
State: IL
Postal Code: 61873
Office phone: (217) 469-0045
Publication Website: http://www.leaderlandnews.com/

Non-Daily Newspapers in the U.S.

SIDELL

THE SIDELL REPORTER

Street Address: 116 E. Market, P.O. Box 475
City: Sidell
State: IL
Postal Code: 61876
Office phone: (217) 288-9365
Publication Website: www.thesidellreporter.com
General E-mail: editor@thesidellreporter.com
Publisher Name: Rinda Maddox
Publisher Email: editor@thesidellreporter.com
Editor Name: Rinda Maddox
Editor Email: editor@thesidellreporter.com

ST CHARLES

BATAVIA CHRONICLE

Street Address: 333 N Randall Rd
City: St Charles
State: IL
Postal Code: 60174
Office phone: (630) 232-9222
Publication Website: https://www.kcchronicle.com/batavia/
General E-mail: editorial@kcchronicle.com
Publisher Name: Ryan Wells
Publisher Email: rwells@shawmedia.com
Editor Name: Aimee Barrows
Editor Email: abarrows@shawmedia.com
Editor Phone: (630) 845-5368
Advertising Executive Name: Brad Hanahan
Advertising Executive Email: bhanahan@shawmedia.com
Advertising Executive Phone: (630) 845-5284

GENEVA CHRONICLE

Street Address: 333 N. Randall Road, Suite 1
City: St Charles
State: IL
Postal Code: 60174
Office phone: (630)232-9222
Publication Website: https://www.kcchronicle.com/
General E-mail: editorial@kcchronicle.com
Publisher Name: Ryan Wells
Publisher Email: rwells@shawmedia.com
Editor Name: Aimee Barrows
Editor Email: abarrows@shawmedia.com
Advertising Executive Name: Ryan Wells
Advertising Executive Email: rwells@shawmedia.com

ST. CHARLES CHRONICLE

Street Address: 333 N Randall Rd
City: St Charles
State: IL
Postal Code: 60174
Office phone: (630) 232-9222
Publication Website: https://www.kcchronicle.com
General E-mail: subscriptions@shawsuburban.com
Editor Name: Aimee Barrows
Editor Email: abarrows@shawmedia.com
Advertising Executive Name: Ryan Wells
Advertising Executive Email: rwells@shawmedia.com

THE ELBURN HERALD

Corporate/Parent Company: Shaw Media
Street Address: 333 N Randall Rd
City: St Charles
State: IL
Postal Code: 60174
Office phone: (630) 365-6446
Publication Website: https://www.kcchronicle.com/e-edition/elh/
General E-mail: subscriptions@shawsuburban.com
Publisher Name: Ryan Wells
Publisher Email: rwells@shawmedia.com
Editor Email: editorial@kcchronicle.com
Editor Phone: (630) 845-5355
Advertising Executive Name: Ryan Wells
Advertising Executive Email: rwells@shawmedia.com
Advertising Executive Phone: (630) 845-5284

STRONGHURST

THE HENDERSON COUNTY QUILL

Street Address: P.O. Box 149
City: Stronghurst
State: IL
Postal Code: 61480-0149
Office phone: 309-924-1871
Publication Website: www.quillnewspaper.com
General E-mail: quill@hcil.net
Publisher Name: Dessa Rodeffer
Publisher Email: dessa@hcil.net
Editor Name: Shirley Linder
Editor Email: quillnewspaper@frontier.com

SUMMIT

CLEAR-RIDGE REPORTER & NEWSHOUND

Corporate/Parent Company: Southwest Community News Group, LLC.
Street Address: 7674 West 63rd Street
City: Summit
State: IL
Postal Code: 60501
Office phone: (708) 496-0265
Publication Website: https://swnewsherald.com/clients/swnewsherald/Reporter.pdf
General E-mail: mhornung@cmgms.com
Publisher Name: Mark Hornung
Publisher Email: mhornung@cmgms.com
Editor Name: Tim Hadac
Editor Email: editor@archerjournalnews.com
Advertising Executive Name: Donna Brown
Advertising Executive Email: donna_brn@yahoo.com

DESPLAINES VALLEY NEWS

Street Address: 7676 W. 63rd St.
City: Summit
State: IL
Postal Code: 60501
Office phone: 708-594-9340
Publication Website: www.desplainesvalleynews.com
General E-mail: editor@desplainesvalleynews.com
Publisher Name: Mark Hornung
Publisher Email: mhornung@cmgms.com
Editor Name: Bob Bong
Editor Email: editor@desplainesvalleynews.com
Editor Phone: 708-496-0265

GREATER SOUTHWEST NEWS-HERALD

Corporate/Parent Company: Southwest Community News Group, LLC.
Street Address: 7676 W. 63rd St.
City: Summit
State: IL
Postal Code: 60501
Office phone: 708-496-0265
Publication Website: www.swnewsherald.com
Publisher Name: Mark Hornung
Publisher Email: mhornung@cmgms.com
Editor Name: Tim Hadac
Editor Email: editor@archerjournalnews.com

TROY

TIMES-TRIBUNE

Street Address: 201 E. Market Street
City: Troy
State: IL
Postal Code: 62294
Office phone: 618-667-3111
Publication Website: www.thetroytimestribune.com
General E-mail: news@timestribunenews.com
Publisher Name: Greg Hoskins
Publisher Email: ghoskins@heraldpubs.com
Editor Name: Steve Rensberry

TUSCOLA

THE TUSCOLA JOURNAL

Street Address: 115 W. Sale Street
City: Tuscola
State: IL
Postal Code: 61953
Office phone: 217-253-5086
Publication Website: www.thetuscolajournal.com
General E-mail: office@thetuscolajournal.com
Publisher Name: Greg Hoskins
Publisher Email: ghoskins@heraldpubs.com
Editor Name: Kendra Hennis
Editor Email: kendra@thetuscolajournal.com
Advertising Executive Name: Stephanie Wierman
Advertising Executive Email: stephanie@thetuscolajournal.com

TRI-COUNTY JOURNAL

Street Address: 115 W. Sale Street
City: Tuscola
State: IL
Postal Code: 61953
Office phone: 217-253-5086
Publication Website: www.thetuscolajournal.com
General E-mail: office@thetuscolajournal.com
Publisher Name: Greg Hoskins
Publisher Email: ghoskins@heraldpubs.com
Editor Name: Kendra Hennis
Editor Email: kendra@thetuscolajournal.com
Advertising Executive Name: Stephanie Wierman
Advertising Executive Email: stephanie@thetuscolajournal.com
Advertising Executive Phone: 217-620-7460

TUSCOLA REVIEW

Street Address: P.O. Box 11
City: Tuscola
State: IL
Postal Code: 61953
Office phone: 217-991-0935
Publication Website: www.tuscolareview.com
General E-mail: jennie@tuscolareview.com
Publisher Name: David Porter
Publisher Email: publisher@tuscolareview.com

VIRDEN

THE PANHANDLE PRESS

Corporate/Parent Company: Gold Nugget Publications Inc
Street Address: 169 W. Jackson St
City: Virden
State: IL
Postal Code: 62690
Office phone: (217) 965-3355
Publication Website: https://gnnews.net/
General E-mail: editor@gnnews.net
Publisher Name: Dorothy A. Jones
Editor Name: Sandy Webb
Editor Email: editor@gnnews.net
Editor Phone: (217) 227-4425
Advertising Executive Email: ads@gnnews.net
Advertising Executive Phone: (217) 965-4512

WARREN

THE FLASH

Street Address: 157 E. Main Street
City: Warren
State: IL
Postal Code: 61037
Office phone: (815) 745-3819
Publication Website: www.theflashonline.com
General E-mail: FlashMail@mchsi.com
Publisher Name: Mark Mahoney
Publisher Email: flashpub1@mchsi.com
Editor Name: Mark E Mahoney
Editor Email: FlashPub1@mchsi.com

WASHINGTON

MORTON COURIER

Corporate/Parent Company: Courier Newspapers
Street Address: 100 Ford Lane
City: Washington
State: IL
Postal Code: 61571
Office phone: 309-444-3139
Publication Website: www.courierpapers.com
General E-mail: joi67@mtco.com
Publisher Name: Joi Hagel-DeArmond
Publisher Email: joi67@courierpapers.com
Publisher Phone: 309-444-3139, x12
Editor Name: James Strauss
Editor Email: haglnews@mtco.com

WASHINGTON COURIER

Corporate/Parent Company: Courier Newspapers
Street Address: 100 Ford Lane
City: Washington
State: IL
Postal Code: 61571
Office phone: 309-444-3139
Publication Website: www.courierpapers.com
Publisher Name: Joi Hagel-DeArmond
Publisher Email: joi67@courierpapers.com
Publisher Phone: 309-444-3139, x12
Editor Name: James Strauss
Editor Email: haglnews@mtco.com

THE BRAIDWOOD JOURNAL

Corporate/Parent Company: Free Press Newspapers
Street Address: 111 S. Water Street
City: Wilmington
State: IL
Postal Code: 60481
Office phone: 815 476-7966
Publication Website: www.braidwoodjournal.com
General E-mail: fpnads@cbcast.com
Publisher Name: Eric Fisher
Publisher Email: efisher@fpnusa.com
Editor Name: Ann Gill
Editor Email: agill@fpnusa.com

THE FREE PRESS ADVOCATE

Corporate/Parent Company: Free Press Newspapers
Street Address: 111 S. Water Street
City: Wilmington
State: IL
Postal Code: 60481
Office phone: 815 476-7966
Publication Website: www.freepressnewspapers.com
General E-mail: news@fpnusa.com
Publisher Name: Eric Fisher
Publisher Email: efisher@fpnusa.com

WOODSTOCK

THE WOODSTOCK INDEPENDENT

Street Address: 671 E. Calhoun St.
City: Woodstock
State: IL
Postal Code: 60098
Office phone: 815.338.8040
Publication Website: www.thewoodstockindependent.com
General E-mail: news@thewoodstockindependent.com
Publisher Name: Cheryl Wormley
Publisher Email: c.wormley@thewoodstockindependent.com
Editor Name: Larry Lough
Editor Email: larry@thewoodstockindependent.com
Advertising Executive Name: Jen Wilson
Advertising Executive Email: jen@thewoodstockindependent.com

YORKVILLE

OSWEGO LEDGER

Corporate/Parent Company: Shaw Media
Street Address: 109 W. Veterans Parkway.
City: Yorkville
State: IL
Postal Code: Yorkville
Office phone: (630) 553-7034
Publication Website: https://www.kendallcountynow.com/oswego/
General E-mail: news@kendallcountynow.com
Publisher Name: Ryan Wells
Publisher Email: rwells@shawmedia.com
Editor Name: John Etheredge
Editor Email: jetheredge@shawmedia.com
Editor Phone: (630) 553-7034

ADVERTISING EXECUTIVE EMAIL: ADSALES@KENDALLCOUNTYNOW.COM%C2%A0

PLANO RECORD

Corporate/Parent Company: Shaw Media
Street Address: 109 W. Veterans Parkway.
City: Yorkville
State: IL
Postal Code: Yorkville
Office phone: (630) 553-7034
Publication Website: https://www.kendallcountynow.com/plano/
General E-mail: news@kendallcountynow.com
Publisher Name: Ryan Wells
Publisher Email: rwells@shawmedia.com
Editor Name: John Etheredge
Editor Email: jetheredge@shawmedia.com
Editor Phone: (630) 553-7034

ADVERTISING EXECUTIVE EMAIL: ADSALES@KENDALLCOUNTYNOW.COM%C2%A0

SANDWICH RECORD

Corporate/Parent Company: Shaw Media
Street Address: 109 W. Veterans Parkway.
City: Yorkville
State: IL
Postal Code: Yorkville
Office phone: (630) 553-7034
Publication Website: https://www.kendallcountynow.com/sandwich/
General E-mail: news@kendallcountynow.com
Publisher Name: Ryan Wells
Publisher Email: rwells@shawmedia.com
Editor Name: John Etheredge
Editor Email: jetheredge@shawmedia.com
Editor Phone: (630) 553-7034

ADVERTISING EXECUTIVE EMAIL: ADSALES@KENDALLCOUNTYNOW.COM%C2%A0

INDIANA

ALBION

ALBION NEW ERA

Corporate/Parent Company: KPC Media Group, Inc.
Street Address: 407 S Orange St
City: Albion
State: IN
Postal Code: 46701-1132
Office phone: (260) 636-2727
Publication Website: https://www.kpcnews.com/albionnewera/
General E-mail: drigas@kpcmedia.com
Publisher Name: Bob Allman
Publisher Email: rallman@kpcmedia.com
Publisher Phone: (260) 636-2727, ext : 2603
Editor Name: Matt Getts
Editor Email: mgetts@kpcmedia.com
Editor Phone: (260) 636-2727, ext : 2602
Advertising Executive Name: David Rigas
Advertising Executive Email: drigas@kpcmedia.com
Advertising Executive Phone: (260) 347-0400, ext : 1002
Year Established: 1876
Delivery Methods: Mail`Newsstand`Racks
Own Printing Facility?: Y
Commercial printers?: Y
Mechanical specifications: Type page 10 1/2 x 15 1/2; E - 6 cols, 1 1/2, 3/16 between; A - 6 cols, 1 1/2, 3/16 between; C - 6 cols, 1 1/2, 3/16 between.
Published Days: Wed
Avg Paid Circ: 6004
Audit Company: Sworn/Estimate/Non-Audited
Audit Date: 6 10 2019

ANGOLA

THE HERALD REPUBLICAN

Corporate/Parent Company: KPC Media Group, Inc.
Street Address: 107 N. Martha Street
City: Angola
State: IN
Postal Code: 46703-1926
Office phone: (260) 665-3117
Publication Website: https://www.kpcnews.com/heraldrepublican/
General E-mail: drigas@kpcmedia.com
Publisher Name: Terry Housholder
Publisher Email: thousholder@kpcmedia.com
Publisher Phone: (260) 347-0400 Ext. 1176
Editor Name: Mike Marturello
Editor Email: mmarturello@kpcmedia.com
Editor Phone: (260) 665-3117, ext : 2140
Advertising Executive Name: David Rigas
Advertising Executive Email: drigas@kpcmedia.com
Advertising Executive Phone: (260) 347-0400, ext : 1002
Year Established: 1857
Delivery Methods: Mail`Newsstand`Carrier`Racks
Own Printing Facility?: Y
Commercial printers?: Y
Mechanical specifications: Type page 13 x 21 1/2; E - 6 cols, 2, 1/6 between; A - 6 cols, 2 1/16, 1/6 between; C - 9 cols, 1 3/8, 1/6 between.
Published Days: Mon`Tues`Wed`Thur`Fri`Sat`Sun
Weekday Frequency: m
Saturday Frequency: m
Avg Paid Circ: 4070
Audit Company: AAM
Audit Date: 31 12 2014
Pressroom Equipment: Lines – 6-G/Community.;
Total Circulation: 6004

AUBURN

THE BUTLER BULLETIN

Corporate/Parent Company: KPC Media Group, Inc.
Street Address: 118 W 9th St
City: Auburn
State: IN
Postal Code: 46706-2225
Office phone: (260) 925-2611, ext : 2547
Publication Website: https://www.kpcnews.com/butlerbulletin/
General E-mail: jjones@kpcmedia.com
Publisher Name: Terry Housholder
Publisher Email: thousholder@kpcmedia.com
Publisher Phone: (260) 347-0400 Ext. 1176
Advertising Executive Name: Jeff Jones
Advertising Executive Email: jjones@kpcmedia.com
Advertising Executive Phone: (260) 925-2611, ext : 2547
Year Established: 1976
Delivery Methods: Mail`Newsstand`Racks
Published Days: Tues
Avg Paid Circ: 52
Audit Company: AAM
Audit Date: 31 12 2018
Total Circulation: 2000

AUBURN

THE GARRETT CLIPPER

Corporate/Parent Company: KPC Media Group, Inc.
Street Address: 118 W 9th St
City: Auburn
State: IN
Postal Code: 46706-2225
Office phone: (260) 925-2611, ext : 2547
Publication Website: https://www.kpcnews.com/garrettclipper/
General E-mail: drigas@kpcmedia.com
Publisher Name: Terry Housholder
Publisher Email: thousholder@kpcmedia.com
Publisher Phone: (260) 347-0400, ext : 1176
Editor Name: Sue Carpenter
Editor Email: scarpenter@kpcmedia.com
Editor Phone: (260) 925-2611, ext : 2545
Advertising Executive Name: David Rigas
Advertising Executive Email: drigas@kpcmedia.com
Advertising Executive Phone: (260) 347-0400, ext : 1002
Year Established: 1885
Delivery Methods: Mail`Newsstand`Carrier`Racks
Own Printing Facility?: Y
Commercial printers?: Y
Mechanical specifications: Type page 13 x 21 1/2; E - 6 cols, 2 1/16, 1/12 between; A - 6 cols, 4 3/16, 1/12 between; C - 6 cols, 6 1/16, 1/12 between.
Published Days: Mon`Thur
Avg Paid Circ: 141
Audit Company: AAM
Audit Date: 31 12 2018
Mailroom Equipment: Counter Stackers – BG/105, Rima/RS 2517; Inserters & Stuffers – 2-KAN/420; Tying Machines – 3/Bu, 1-/MLN; Wrapping Singles – Power Strap/Bottom Wrap.;
Classified Equipment: Hardware – 4-PC, 1-MS 2000 Server; Printers – Lexmark T520;
Classified Software: QPS/QuarkXPress 4.11, ACT.
Editorial Equipment: Hardware – 10-PC, 2-APT/PC fileservers, 12-PC, MS 2000 Server/Umax/Power Look IV, AP/Mac G4; Printers – ECR/VR 36, ECR/4550
Editorial Software: QPS/QuarkXPress 4.11, Microsoft/Word 2.0.
Production Equipment: Hardware – APP/Mac LaserWriter II NT, ECR/VR 36, Unity/1200 XLO, APP/Mac LaserWriter IIg, ECR/4550;
Scanners – Umax/Power Look III
Production Software: APT, QPS/QuarkXPress 4.11.
Total Circulation: 11240

BEDFORD

THE TIMES-MAIL

Corporate/Parent Company: Gannett
Street Address: 813 16th St
City: Bedford
State: IN
Postal Code: 47421-3822
Office phone: (812) 275-3355
Publication Website: https://www.hoosiertimes.com/tmnews/
General E-mail: cgiddens@heraldt.com
Publisher Name: Larry D. Hensley
Publisher Email: lhensley@heraldt.com
Publisher Phone: (812) 331-4259
Editor Name: Brian Kaufman
Editor Phone: (812) 277-7258
Advertising Executive Name: Chad Giddens
Advertising Executive Email: cgiddens@heraldt.com
Advertising Executive Phone: (812) 331-4292
Year Established: 1884
Delivery Methods: Mail`Newsstand`Carrier`Racks
Mechanical specifications: Type page 13 x 21; E - 6 cols, 2 1/16, 1/8 between; A - 6 cols, 2 1/16, 1/8 between; C - 9 cols, 1 3/8, 1/16 between.
Published Days: Mon`Tues`Wed`Thur`Fri`Sat`Sun
Weekday Frequency: m
Audit Company: Sworn/Estimate/Non-Audited
Audit Date: 7 12 2019
Pressroom Equipment: Lines – 15-G/Community single width (Color); Folders – 1-G/SC1045 Balloon Double Former, 1-G/SC1045.;

BLOOMINGTON

THE HERALD TIMES

Street Address: 1900 S Walnut St
City: Bloomington
State: IN
Postal Code: 47401-7720
Office phone: (812) 332-4401
Publication Website: https://www.hoosiertimes.com/herald_times_online/
General E-mail: cgiddens@heraldt.com
Publisher Name: Larry Hensley
Publisher Email: lhensley@heraldt.com
Publisher Phone: (812) 331-4259
Editor Name: Rich Jackson
Editor Email: rjackson@heraldt.com
Editor Phone: (812) 331-4364
Advertising Executive Name: Chad Giddens
Advertising Executive Email: cgiddens@heraldt.com
Advertising Executive Phone: (812) 331-4292
Year Established: 1877
Delivery Methods: Mail`Newsstand`Carrier`Racks
Mechanical specifications: Type page 11 5/8 x 21; E - 6 cols, 1 5/6, 1/6 between; A - 6 cols, 1 5/6, 1/6 between; C - 9 cols, 1 1/4, 1/10 between.
Published Days: Mon`Tues`Wed`Thur`Fri`Sat`Sun
Weekday Frequency: m
Saturday Frequency: m
Avg Paid Circ: 25732
Audit Company: Sworn/Estimate/Non-Audited
Audit Date: 7 12 2019
Pressroom Equipment: Lines – 5-KB/(3 color humps) double width 1985; Folders – 2-KB/3:2 KF 80 Jaw; Pasters –MEG; Reels & Stands – 5-MEG.;

BROWNSTOWN

THE JACKSON COUNTY BANNER

Corporate/Parent Company: AIM Media Indiana
Street Address: 1200 W. Spring St.
City: Brownstown
State: IN
Postal Code: 47220-2011

Non-Daily Newspapers in the U.S.

Office phone: (812) 358-2111
Publication Website: http://www.thebanner.com/
General E-mail: slawson@thebanner.com
Editor Name: Aubrey Woods
Editor Email: awoods@thebanner.com
Editor Phone: (812) 523-7051
Advertising Executive Name: Sally Lawson
Advertising Executive Email: slawson@thebanner.com
Advertising Executive Phone: (812) 358-2111
Year Established: 1869
Delivery Methods: Mail`Newsstand`Racks
Mechanical specifications: Type page 11 x 21; E - 6 cols, 2, 1/6 between; C - 6 cols, between.
Published Days: Tues`Thur
Avg Paid Circ: 1730
Avg Free Circ: 4140
Audit Company: Sworn/Estimate/Non-Audited
Audit Date: 6 10 2019

CHURUBUSCO

CHURUBUSCO NEWS

Corporate/Parent Company: KPC Media Group, Inc.
Street Address: 123 N Main St
City: Churubusco
State: IN
Postal Code: 46723-1708
Office phone: (260) 693-3949
Publication Website: https://www.kpcnews.com/churubusconews/
General E-mail: news@kpcmedia.com
Publisher Name: Terry Housholder
Publisher Email: thousholder@kpcmedia.com
Publisher Phone: (260) 347-0400 Ext. 1176
Editor Name: Nicole Minier
Editor Email: nminier@kpcmedia.com
Editor Phone: (260) 693-3949, ext : 2702
Advertising Executive Email: classifieds@kpcmedia.com
Advertising Executive Phone: (260) 347-0400, ext : 1115
Year Established: 1872
Delivery Methods: Mail`Newsstand`Racks
Published Days: Wed
Avg Paid Circ: 2000
Audit Company: Sworn/Estimate/Non-Audited
Audit Date: 6 10 2019

COLUMBIA CITY

IN|WHITLEY COUNTY

Corporate/Parent Company: KPC Media Group, Inc.
Street Address: 128 W. Van Buren St.
City: Columbia City
State: IN
Postal Code: 46725
Office phone: (260) 693-3949
Publication Website: https://www.inwhitleycounty.com/
General E-mail: nminier@kpcnews.com
Publisher Name: Terry Housholder
Publisher Email: thousholder@kpcmedia.com
Publisher Phone: (260) 347-0400, ext : 1176
Editor Name: Nicole Minier
Editor Email: nminier@kpcmedia.com
Editor Phone: (260) 693-3949, ext : 2702
Advertising Executive Email: classifieds@kpcmedia.com
Advertising Executive Phone: (260) 347-0400, ext : 1115
Total Circulation: 1500

COLUMBUS

REPUBLIC EXTRA

Corporate/Parent Company: AIM Media Indiana
Street Address: 2980 N National Rd
City: Columbus
State: IN
Postal Code: 47201-3234
Office phone: (812) 372-7811
Publication Website: http://www.therepublic.com/
General E-mail: advertise@therepublic.com
Editor Name: Julie McClure
Editor Email: jmcclure@therepublic.com
Editor Phone: (812) 379-5631
Advertising Executive Email: advertise@therepublic.com
Advertising Executive Phone: (812) 379-5652
Total Circulation: 2400

COLUMBUS

THE (COLUMBUS) REPUBLIC

Corporate/Parent Company: AIM Media Indiana
Street Address: 2980 N National Rd
City: Columbus
State: IN
Postal Code: 47201-3234
Office phone: (812) 372-7811
Publication Website: http://www.therepublic.com/
General E-mail: advertise@therepublic.com
Editor Name: Julie McClure
Editor Email: jmcclure@therepublic.com
Editor Phone: (812) 379-5631
Advertising Executive Email: advertise@therepublic.com
Advertising Executive Phone: (812) 379-5652

FORT WAYNE

GREATER FORT WAYNE BUSINESS WEEKLY

Corporate/Parent Company: KPC Media Group, Inc.
Street Address: 3306 Independence Dr
City: Fort Wayne
State: IN
Postal Code: 46808-4510
Office phone: (260) 426-2640
Publication Website: https://www.fwbusiness.com/
General E-mail: drigas@kpcmedia.com
Publisher Name: Terry Housholder
Publisher Email: thousholder@kpcmedia.com
Publisher Phone: (260) 347-0400 Ext. 1176
Editor Name: Lisa Long
Editor Email: llong@kpcmedia.com
Editor Phone: (260) 426-2640, ext : 3311
Advertising Executive Name: David Rigas
Advertising Executive Email: drigas@kpcmedia.com
Advertising Executive Phone: (260) 426-2640, ext : 3324
Year Established: 2005
Delivery Methods: Mail
Own Printing Facility?: Y
Commercial printers?: Y
Published Days: Fri
Audit Company: Sworn/Estimate/Non-Audited
Audit Date: 6 10 2019

IN|FORT WAYNE PUBLICATIONS (5 ZONES)

Corporate/Parent Company: KPC Media Group, Inc.
Street Address: 3306 Independence Drive
City: Fort Wayne
State: IN
Postal Code: 46808
Office phone: (260) 426-2640, ext : 3321
Publication Website: https://www.infortwayne.com/
General E-mail: lwyatt@kpcmedia.com
Publisher Name: Terry Housholder
Publisher Email: thousholder@kpcmedia.com
Publisher Phone: (260) 347-0400, ext : 1176
Editor Name: Garth Snow
Editor Email: gsnow@kpcmedia.com
Editor Phone: (260) 426-2640, ext : 3321
Advertising Executive Email: classifieds@kpcmedia.com
Advertising Executive Phone: (260) 347-0400, ext : 1115

NORTHWEST NEWS

Corporate/Parent Company: KPC Media Group, Inc.
Street Address: 3306 Independence Drive
City: Fort Wayne
State: IN
Postal Code: 46808
Office phone: (260) 426-2640
Publication Website: https://www.kpcnews.com/northwestnews/
General E-mail: news@kpcmedia.com
Publisher Name: Terry Housholder
Publisher Email: thousholder@kpcmedia.com
Publisher Phone: (260) 347-0400, ext : 1176
Editor Name: Louis Wyatt
Editor Email: lwyatt@kpcmedia.com
Editor Phone: (260) 665-3117, ext : 2118
Advertising Executive Email: classifieds@kpcmedia.com
Advertising Executive Phone: (260) 347-0400, ext : 1115
Year Established: 1997
Delivery Methods: Mail
Published Days: Wed
Avg Paid Circ: 1500
Audit Company: Sworn/Estimate/Non-Audited
Audit Date: 6 10 2019

FRANKLIN

DAILY JOURNAL

Corporate/Parent Company: Gannett
Street Address: 30 S. Water St., Second floor, Suite A, P.O. Box 699
City: Franklin
State: IN
Postal Code: 46131-2316
Office phone: (317) 736-7101
Publication Website: http://www.dailyjournal.net/
General E-mail: newstips@dailyjournal.net
Editor Name: Michele Holtkamp
Editor Email: mholtkamp@dailyjournal.net
Editor Phone: (317) 736-2774
Advertising Executive Name: Christina Cosner
Advertising Executive Email: newstips@dailyjournal.net
Advertising Executive Phone: (317) 736-2750
Year Established: 1963
Delivery Methods: Mail`Newsstand`Carrier`Racks
Own Printing Facility?: Y
Commercial printers?: Y
Mechanical specifications: Type page 11 5/8 x 21;A 6 cols, 1.833"wide per column; Classifieds - 9 cols, 1.203" wide per
Published Days: Mon`Tues`Wed`Thur`Fri`Sat
Weekday Frequency: m
Saturday Frequency: m
Avg Paid Circ: 11240
Audit Company: CAC
Audit Date: 31 03 2014
Pressroom Equipment: Reels & Stands – 9-G/ Roll Stand.;
Total Circulation: 94

KENDALLVILLE

SMART SHOPPER

Corporate/Parent Company: KPC Media Group, Inc.
Street Address: 102 N Main St
City: Kendallville
State: IN
Postal Code: 46755-1714
Office phone: (260) 347-0400, ext : 1002
Publication Website: https://www.kpcnews.com/site/about.html
General E-mail: info@kpcmedia.com
Publisher Name: Terry Housholder
Publisher Email: thousholder@kpcmedia.com
Publisher Phone: (260) 347-0400, ext : 1176
Advertising Executive Name: David Rigas
Advertising Executive Email: drigas@kpcmedia.com
Advertising Executive Phone: (260) 347-0400, ext : 1002
Total Circulation: 52

THE ADVANCE LEADER

Corporate/Parent Company: KPC Media Group, Inc.
Street Address: 102 N Main St
City: Kendallville
State: IN
Postal Code: 46755-1714
Office phone: (260) 347-0400
Publication Website: https://www.kpcnews.com/advanceleader/
General E-mail: news@kpcmedia.com
Publisher Name: Terry Housholder
Publisher Email: thousholder@kpcmedia.com
Publisher Phone: (260) 347-0400 Ext. 1176
Editor Name: Steve Garbacz
Editor Email: sgarbacz@kpcmedia.com
Editor Phone: (260) 347-0400, ext : 1136
Advertising Executive Name: David Rigas
Advertising Executive Email: drigas@kpcmedia.com
Advertising Executive Phone: (260) 347-0400, ext : 1002
Year Established: 1880
Delivery Methods: Mail`Newsstand`Carrier`Racks
Published Days: Thur
Avg Paid Circ: 94
Audit Company: AAM
Audit Date: 31 12 2018

LACROSSE

WESTVILLE INDICATOR

Corporate/Parent Company: Kiel Media, LLC
Street Address: 16 E. Main Street
City: LaCrosse
State: IN
Postal Code: 46348
Office phone: 219-544-2060
Publication Website: kielmedia.com
General E-mail: wi@kielmedia.com
Publisher Name: Justin Kiel
Editor Name: Kelly Kiel
Total Circulation: 141

LAFAYETTE

THE LAFAYETTE LEADER

Corporate/Parent Company: Community Media Group
Street Address: 401 Main Street, Suite 2F
City: Lafayette
State: IN
Postal Code: 47901
Office phone: 574-583-5121
Publication Website: www.newsbug.info/lafayette_leader/site
Publisher Name: Greg Perrotto
Publisher Email: gperrotto@rensselaerrepublican.com
Editor Name: Gregory Myers
Editor Email: nceeditor@centurylink.net
Editor Phone: 219-474-5532
Advertising Executive Name: Michelle Knapp
Advertising Executive Email: ncesales@centurylink.net
Editorial Software: ACT.
Note: All production of the Herald-Republican is done at the central plant in Kendallville.
Total Circulation: 4070

LAWRENCEBURG

THE DEARBORN COUNTY REGISTER

Corporate/Parent Company: Register Publications group.
Street Address: 126 W High St
City: Lawrenceburg
State: IN
Postal Code: 47025-1908
Office phone: (812) 537-0063

Publication Website: https://www.thedcregister.com/
General E-mail: cmunich@registerpublications.com
Publisher Name: April Fritch
Publisher Email: afritch@registerpublications.com
Publisher Phone: (812) 537-0063
Editor Name: Joe Awad
Editor Email: jawad@registerpublications.com
Mailroom Equipment: Counter Stackers – 1-QWI/300, 1-Rima/RS30, 2-HL/Dual Carrier; Inserters & Stuffers – 1-KAN/480 6:1, 1/AM Graphics/NP 630 13:1; Tying Machines – 2-/Power Strap/PSN20; Address Machine – 1-/KR, 1-/Ch, 1-/Ink Jet.;
Buisness Equipment: 2-DEC/VAX 3900, Microsoft/Windows NT
Classified Equipment: Hardware – DEC/Alphasaver 2000;
Classified Software: APT.
Editorial Equipment: Hardware – 2-DEC/Micro VAX 3000/AU/OPI Server, 2-AU/3850; Printers – HP/4MV
Editorial Software: Dewar/View, Microsoft/Windows, Microsoft/Word 2.0, QPS/QuarkXPress 3.2.
Production Equipment: Hardware – 2-AU/3850, 1-Nu/Flip Top FT40V6UPNS; Cameras – Nu/Horizontal; Scanners – 2-Linotype-Hell/Saphire, 1-Linotype-Hell/S3300 Drum
Production Software: Dewar.
Note: This publication shares a joint Sunday edition with the Bedford (IN) Times-Mail (mS) and the Martinsville (IN) Reporter-Times (eS).
Total Circulation: 25732

THE RISING SUN RECORDER

Corporate/Parent Company: Register Publications Group
Street Address: 126 W. High St
City: Lawrenceburg
State: IN
Postal Code: 47025
Office phone: 812-537-0063
Publication Website: www.theohiocountynews.com
General E-mail: newsroom@registerpublications.com
Editor Name: Joe Awad
Editor Email: jawad@registerpublications.com
Editor Phone: 812-537-0063
Advertising Executive Name: Chip Munich
Advertising Executive Email: cmunich@registerpublications.com
Advertising Executive Phone: 812-537-0063
Total Circulation: 5870

MARTINSVILLE

THE MOORESVILLE-DECATUR TIMES

Street Address: 78 N. Main St.
City: Martinsville
State: IN
Postal Code: 46151-1968
Office phone: (317) 831-0280
Publication Website: https://www.hoosiertimes.com/reporter_times/
General E-mail: cgiddens@heraldt.com
Publisher Name: Larry Hensley
Publisher Email: lhensley@heraldt.com
Publisher Phone: (812) 331-4259
Editor Name: Stephen Crane
Editor Email: scrane@reporter-times.com
Editor Phone: (765) 342-3311, ext : 4409
Advertising Executive Name: Chad Giddens
Advertising Executive Email: cgiddens@heraldt.com
Advertising Executive Phone: (812) 331-4292
Year Established: 1879
Delivery Methods: Carrier
Own Printing Facility?: Y
Commercial printers?: Y
Mechanical specifications: Type page 14 1/4 x 21 1/2; E – 6 cols, 2 1/4, 3/16 between; A – 6 cols, 2 1/4, 3/16 between; C – 9 cols, 1 3/8, 1/8 between.
Published Days: Wed`Sat
Avg Paid Circ: 5700
Audit Company: Sworn/Estimate/Non-Audited
Audit Date: 6 10 2019

THE REPORTER TIMES

Street Address: 78 N. Main St.
City: Martinsville
State: IN
Postal Code: 46151-1968
Office phone: (765) 342-3311
Publication Website: https://www.hoosiertimes.com/reporter_times/
General E-mail: cgiddens@heraldt.com
Publisher Name: Larry Hensley
Publisher Email: lhensley@heraldt.com
Publisher Phone: (812) 331-4259
Editor Name: Stephen Crane
Editor Email: scrane@reporter-times.com
Editor Phone: (765) 342-3311, ext : 4409
Advertising Executive Name: Chad Giddens
Advertising Executive Email: cgiddens@heraldt.com
Advertising Executive Phone: (812) 331-4292
Year Established: 1889
Delivery Methods: Mail`Newsstand`Carrier`Racks
Mechanical specifications: Type page 13 x 21 1/2; E – 6 cols, 2, 1/8 between; A – 6 cols, 2, 1/8 between; C – 9 cols, 1 5/16, 1/16 between.
Published Days: Mon`Tues`Wed`Thur`Fri`Sat`Sun
Weekday Frequency: e
Saturday Frequency: m
Avg Paid Circ: 4714
Audit Company: Sworn/Estimate/Non-Audited
Audit Date: 7 12 2019
Pressroom Equipment: Lines – 7-G/Community (color unit); Folders – 1-G/2:1.;

MONROEVILLE

THE MONROEVILLE NEWS

Corporate/Parent Company: Decatur Publishing Co., Inc
Street Address: 115 E. South Street
City: Monroeville
State: IN
Postal Code: 46773-0429
Office phone: 260-623-3316
Publication Website: monroeville.com/community-services/newspaper
General E-mail: maintenance@monroevillein.com
Publisher Name: Rodd Hale
Editor Name: Lois A. Ternet
Total Circulation: 5700

MT. CARMEL

WEEKENDER

Corporate/Parent Company: Paxton Media Group, LLC
Street Address: 217 E. 9th St.
City: Mt. Carmel
State: IN
Postal Code: 62863
Office phone: (618) 262-5144
Publication Website: https://www.mtcarmelregister.com/
General E-mail: courtney@pdclarion.com
Publisher Name: Mike Weafer
Publisher Email: mweafer@messenger-inquirer.com
Editor Name: Andrea Howe
Editor Email: news@mtcarmelregister.com
Advertising Executive Name: Courtney Shuttle
Advertising Executive Email: courtney@pdclarion.com

NORTH VERNON

NORTH VERNON PLAIN DEALER

Street Address: PO Box 988, 528 East O&M Ave
City: North Vernon
State: IN
Postal Code: 47265
Office phone: 812.346.3973
Publication Website: plaindealer-sun.com
Publisher Name: Barbara King
Publisher Email: bking@northvernon.com
Editor Name: Bryce Mayer
Editor Email: bmayer@northvernon.com
Advertising Executive Name: Sue Ross
Advertising Executive Email: sross@northvernon.com
Mailroom Equipment: Tying Machines – 2/Bu.;
Buisness Software: Baseview
Editorial Equipment: Hardware – APP/Mac; Printers – APP/Mac LaserWriter.
Note: This publication shares a joint Sunday edition with the Bedford (IN) Times-Mail (mS) and the Bloomington (IN) Herald-Times (mS).
Total Circulation: 4714

PENDLETON

PENDLETON TIMES-POST

Corporate/Parent Company: AIM Media Indiana
Street Address: 104 W. High St.
City: Pendleton
State: IN
Postal Code: 46064-1034
Office phone: (765) 778-2324
Publication Website: http://www.pendletontimespost.com/
General E-mail: ptnews@pendletontimespost.com
Editor Name: Scott Slade
Editor Email: sslade@pendletontimespost.com
Editor Phone: (317) 640-2935
Advertising Executive Name: John Senger
Advertising Executive Email: jsenger@aimmediaindiana.com
Advertising Executive Phone: (317) 477-3208
Year Established: 1897
Delivery Methods: Mail`Newsstand`Racks
Published Days: Wed
Avg Paid Circ: 2400
Audit Company: Sworn/Estimate/Non-Audited
Audit Date: 6 10 2019

THE TIMES-POST

Corporate/Parent Company: AIM Media Indiana
Street Address: 104 West High Street
City: Pendleton
State: IN
Postal Code: 46064
Office phone: (765) 778-2324
Publication Website: www.pendletontimespost.com
General E-mail: ptnews@pendletontimespost.com
Editor Name: Scott Slade
Editor Email: sslade@pendletontimespost.com
Editor Phone: 317-477-3229
Advertising Executive Name: John Senger
Advertising Executive Email: jsenger@pendletontimespost.com
Advertising Executive Phone: 317-477-3208
Mailroom Equipment: Counter Stackers – 1-BG/Stabb Brick, Rima/RS25; Inserters & Stuffers – 2-KAN/480; Tying Machines – 1-FMC/APM2A, 1-Sa/SR2A, 2/Dynaric, 2-/Bu, 1-/Interlake, Sterling; Address Machine – Ch, KR;
Buisness Equipment: 1-DEC/VAX, 1-DEC/Rainbow, IBM
Classified Equipment: Hardware – Novell/Server; Printers – 1-Dataproducts/LZR 1580;
Classified Software: Baseview/Ad Manager Pro.
Editorial Equipment: Hardware – APP/Mac 9150-120 Workgroup Server; Printers – 2-Dataproducts/LZR 1580
Editorial Software: Baseview/IQUE Server.
Production Equipment: Hardware – 2-Hardot/15.75 Imagesetter, Pre Press/Panther Pro 46, Pre Press/Panther Pro 46 HS, Adobe/PageMaker, Macromedia/Freehand, Multi-Ad; Cameras – 1-Screen/C-260-D; Scanners – 1-Lf/Leafscan 45, 3-Kk/RFE 2035, APP/Mac
Production Software: QPS/QuarkXPress, Ba
Note: This publication shares a joint Sunday edition with the Bloomington (IN) Herald-Times (mS) and the Martinsville (IN) Reporter-Times (eS).

RISING SUN

THE OHIO COUNTY NEWS/RISING SUN RECORDER

Corporate/Parent Company: Register Publications group.
Street Address: 235 Main St
City: Rising Sun
State: IN
Postal Code: 47040-1224
Office phone: (812) 438-2011
Publication Website: https://www.theohiocountynews.com/
General E-mail: cmunich@registerpublications.com
Publisher Name: April Fritch
Publisher Email: afritch@registerpublications.com
Publisher Phone: (812) 537-0063
Editor Name: Joe Awad
Editor Email: jawad@registerpublications.com

SEYMOUR

THE (SEYMOUR) TRIBUNE

Corporate/Parent Company: AIM Media Indiana
Street Address: 100 St. Louis Ave
City: Seymour
State: IN
Postal Code: 47274
Office phone: (812) 522-4871
Publication Website: http://www.tribtown.com/
General E-mail: tribuneadvertising@tribtown.com
Advertising Executive Email: tribuneadvertising@tribtown.com
Advertising Executive Phone: (812) 523-7052

WARSAW

THE TRIBUNE-NEWS

Street Address: P.O. Box 1448
City: Warsaw
State: IN
Postal Code: 46581-1448
Office phone: (574) 267-3111
Publication Website: www.timesuniononline.com
General E-mail: news@timesuniononline.com

KANSAS

ATWOOD

RAWLINS COUNTY SQUARE DEAL

Street Address: 114 S. 4th Street
City: Atwood
State: KS
Postal Code: 67730
Office phone: 785-626-3600
Publication Website: www.squaredealnews.com
General E-mail: squaredeal114@sbcglobal.net

BALDWIN CITY

BALDWIN CITY COMMUNITY NEWS

Street Address: PO Box 426

Non-Daily Newspapers in the U.S.

City: Baldwin City
State: KS
Postal Code: 66006
Office phone: 785-433-9096
Publication Website: www.baldwincitycommunitynews.com
General E-mail: baldwincitycommunitynews@yahoo.com

BAXTER SPRINGS

CHEROKEE COUNTY NEWS-ADVOCATE

Corporate/Parent Company: Gannett
Street Address: 1242 Military Ave
City: Baxter Springs
State: KS
Postal Code: 66713
Office phone: (620) 429-2773
Publication Website: https://www.sekvoice.com/
General E-mail: jleong@gatehousemedia.com
Publisher Name: Joe Leong
Publisher Email: jleong@gatehousemedia.com
Publisher Phone: (620) 231-2600, ext : 140
Editor Name: Patrick Richardson
Editor Email: prichardson@morningsun.net
Editor Phone: (620) 231-2600, ext : 140
Advertising Executive Name: Michelle Bradley
Advertising Executive Email: mbradley@morningsun.net
Advertising Executive Phone: (913) 938-2991
Year Established: 1882
Delivery Methods: Racks
Own Printing Facility?: N
Commercial printers?: N
Published Days: Tues`Fri
Weekday Frequency: m
Avg Paid Circ: 3300
Audit Company: Sworn/Estimate/Non-Audited
Audit Date: 6 10 2019

CAWKER CITY

CAWKER CITY LEDGER

Street Address: 728 Wisconsin St
City: Cawker City
State: KS
Postal Code: 67430
Office phone: 785-781-4831
Publication Website: www.mainstreetmedia.us
Editor Name: LaRhea Cole

CHAPMAN

DICKINSON COUNTY NEWS-TIMES

Street Address: PO Box 469
City: Chapman
State: KS
Postal Code: 67431
Office phone: (785) 922-6450
Publication Website: www.dickinsonnewstimes.com
General E-mail: office@dickinsonnewstimes.com
Total Circulation: 568

CHENEY

CONWAY SPRINGS STAR AND ARGONIA ARGOSY

Corporate/Parent Company: Times-Sentinel Newspapers, LLC
Street Address: P.O. Box 544
City: Cheney
State: KS
Postal Code: 67025
Office phone: 316-540-0500
Publication Website: www.tsnews.com
Publisher Name: Paul Rhodes
Publisher Email: prhodes@tsnews.com
Editor Name: Travis Mounts
Editor Email: news@tsnews.com

Advertising Executive Name: Valorie Castor
Advertising Executive Email: vjcastor@yahoo.com

COLBY

COLBY FREE PRESS

Corporate/Parent Company: Haynes Publishing Co.
Street Address: 155 W 5th St
City: Colby
State: KS
Postal Code: 67701-2312
Office phone: (785) 462-3963
Publication Website: http://nwkansas.com/
Year Established: 1888
Delivery Methods: Mail`Newsstand`Carrier`Racks
Own Printing Facility?: Y
Commercial printers?: Y
Mechanical specifications: Type page 13 x 21 ; E - 6 cols, 1 column 1.892, 2 column 3.916, 3 column 5.9375, 4 column 7.958, 5 column 9.979, 6 column 12.0
Published Days: Mon`Wed`Thur`Fri
Weekday Frequency: e
Avg Paid Circ: 1954
Audit Company: Sworn/Estimate/Non-Audited
Audit Date: 7 12 2019
Pressroom Equipment: Lines – none;
Mailroom Equipment: Address Machine – Automecha/Accufast PUM.;
Buisness Equipment: Pentium/PC
Buisness Software: ListMaster, Interlink-Subscriptions
Classified Equipment: Hardware – Pentium/PC.;
Editorial Equipment: Hardware – 4-APP/Mac; Printers – HP/LaserJet II, HP/LaserJet III, HP/LaserJet 4MV
Editorial Software: QPS/QuarkXPress.
Production Equipment: Hardware – B; Cameras – Acti; Scanners – Microtek, Umax.
Total Circulation: 3300

COUNTRY ADVOCATE

Corporate/Parent Company: Haynes Publishing Co.
Street Address: 155 W 5th St
City: Colby
State: KS
Postal Code: 67701-2312
Office phone: (785) 462-3963
Publication Website: http://nwkansas.com/
Buisness Equipment: IBM/AT, IBM/PC-2
Classified Equipment: Hardware – 1-APP/Mac.;
Editorial Equipment: Hardware – Apple Mac
Editorial Software: inDesign, neoOffice, PhotoShop
Total Circulation: 1954

DOWNS

DOWNS NEWS AND TIMES

Corporate/Parent Company: Main Street Media, Inc.
Street Address: 717 Railroad St
City: Downs
State: KS
Postal Code: 67437
Office phone: (785) 454-3514
Publication Website: https://www.mainstreetnewsgroup.com/downnewstimes
General E-mail: downsnews@ruraltel.net
Publisher Name: Michael Crawford
Advertising Executive Name: Beth Williamson
Advertising Executive Email: ads@windsornews.net
Delivery Methods: Mail
Published Days: Thur
Avg Paid Circ: 1155
Audit Company: Sworn/Estimate/Non-Audited
Audit Date: 6 10 2019

EMPORIA

LA VOZ

Street Address: 517 Merchant St.
City: Emporia
State: KS
Postal Code: 66801
Office phone: 620-342-4800
Publication Website: www.emporiagazette.com
General E-mail: news@emporia.com
Publisher Name: Chris Walker
Editor Name: Regina Murphy

FORT LEAVENWORTH

FORT LEAVENWORTH LAMP

Corporate/Parent Company: Gannett
Street Address: 296 Grant Ave
City: Fort Leavenworth
State: KS
Postal Code: 66027
Office phone: (913) 682-0305
Publication Website: https://www.ftleavenworthlamp.com/
General E-mail: editor@ftleavenworthlamp.com
Editor Name: Bob Kerr
Editor Email: editor@ftleavenworthlamp.com
Editor Phone: (913) 684-5267
Advertising Executive Name: Lisa Sweet
Advertising Executive Email: ads@ftleavenworthlamp.com
Advertising Executive Phone: (913) 682-0305

GALENA

SENTINEL-TIMES (GALENA)

Street Address: 511 S. Main St
City: Galena
State: KS
Postal Code: 66739
Office phone: 620-783-5034
Publication Website: www.sentineltimes.com
General E-mail: news@sentineltimes.com
Editor Name: Machelle Smith
Total Circulation: 1155

GARDNER

GARDNER NEWS

Corporate/Parent Company: Gannett
Street Address: 936 E Santa Fe St
City: Gardner
State: KS
Postal Code: 66030
Office phone: 913 856 7615
Publication Website: www.gardnernews.com
General E-mail: submissions@gardnernews.com
Publisher Name: Rhonda Humble

GARNETT

ANDERSON COUNTY AREA COMMUNITY NEWS

Street Address: 117 E. 4th Avenue PO Box 403
City: Garnett
State: KS
Postal Code: 66032
Office phone: 785-448-7000
Publication Website: www.garnett-andersoncountykscommunitynews.com
General E-mail: garnettadvocate@yahoo.com
Advertising Executive Name: Barbara Thompson
Advertising Executive Phone: 785-448-7000

GIRARD

HOMETOWN GIRARD

Street Address: 112 W. St. John, Lower Level
City: Girard
State: KS

Postal Code: 66743
Office phone: 620-249-7462
Publication Website: www.hometowngirard.com
Publisher Name: Jerod Norris
Publisher Email: publisher@hometowngirard.com

GOODLAND

GOODLAND STAR-NEWS

Corporate/Parent Company: Haynes Publishing Co.
Street Address: 1205 Main Ave
City: Goodland
State: KS
Postal Code: 67735-2946
Office phone: (785) 899-2338
Publication Website: http://nwkansas.com/
Year Established: 1993
Delivery Methods: Mail`Newsstand`Carrier`Racks
Own Printing Facility?: Y
Commercial printers?: Y
Mechanical specifications: Type page 12 x 21 1/2; E - 6 cols, 2, 1/8 between; A - 6 cols, 2, 1/8 between; C - 6 cols, 2, 1/8 between.
Published Days: Tues`Fri
Weekday Frequency: e
Avg Paid Circ: 2004
Audit Company: Sworn/Estimate/Non-Audited
Audit Date: 6 10 2019
Total Circulation: 2004

GREENSBURG

KIOWA COUNTY SIGNAL

Corporate/Parent Company: Gannett
Street Address: 320 S Main St
City: Greensburg
State: KS
Postal Code: 67054
Office phone: (620) 723-2115
Publication Website: https://www.kiowacountysignal.com/
General E-mail: jguy@kiowacountysignal.com
Publisher Name: Dena Sattler
Publisher Email: dsattler@gctelegram.com
Publisher Phone: (620) 672-5511
Editor Name: Jeff Guy
Editor Email: jguy@kiowacountysignal.com
Editor Phone: (620) 672-5511
Advertising Executive Name: Christy Nemec
Advertising Executive Email: cnemec@pratttribune.com
Advertising Executive Phone: (620) 672-5511
Year Established: 1886
Delivery Methods: Mail
Published Days: Wed
Avg Free Circ: 900
Audit Company: Sworn/Estimate/Non-Audited
Audit Date: 6 10 2019
Total Circulation: 6900

HOLTON

HOLTON RECORDER

Street Address: 109 W. Fourth St
City: Holton
State: KS
Postal Code: 66436
Office phone: 785-364-3141
Publication Website: www.holtonrecorder.net
Editor Name: David Powls
Editor Email: holtonrecorder@giantcomm.net
Year Established: 1867
Delivery Methods: Mail`Newsstand`Racks
Own Printing Facility?: Y
Commercial printers?: Y
Mechanical specifications: call for details
Published Days: Mon`Wed
Published Other: Thursday - non-duplicating shopper
Avg Paid Circ: 4200
Avg Free Circ: 2700
Audit Company: Sworn/Estimate/Non-Audited
Audit Date: 6 10 2019

HOXIE

HOXIE TIMES

Street Address: PO Box 436
City: Hoxie
State: KS
Postal Code: 67740
Office phone: (970) 768-5964
Publication Website: hoxietimes.com
General E-mail: thehoxietimes@outlook.com
Editor Phone: (785) 762-5000 ext. 112
Advertising Executive Name: Robin Phelan

JUNCTION CITY

FORT RILEY -THE 1ST INFANTRY DIVISION

Corporate/Parent Company: The Junction City Union
Street Address: 222 W Sixth Street
City: Junction City
State: KS
Postal Code: 66441
Office phone: 785-762-5000
Publication Website: www.junctioncityunion.com/news/fort_riley_news
General E-mail: info@jcdailyunion.com
Publisher Name: Ned Seaton
Editor Name: Lydia Kautz
Editor Phone: (785) 762-5000 ext. 112
Advertising Executive Name: Sherry Keck
Advertising Executive Phone: (785)762-5000 Ext: 103
Total Circulation: 900

LARNED

LARNED TILLER & TOILER

Corporate/Parent Company: Main Street Media, Inc.
Street Address: 115 W 5th St,
City: Larned
State: KS
Postal Code: 67550
Office phone: 620-285-3111
Publication Website: www.mainstreetnewsgroup.com/larnedstillertoiler
General E-mail: tiller@mainstreetmedia.us
Editor Name: John Settle

MARYSVILLE

ADVOCATE

Street Address: 107 S. Ninth St.
City: Marysville
State: KS
Postal Code: 66508
Office phone: 785-562-2317
Publication Website: www.marysvilleonline.net
Editor Name: Sarah Kessinger
Editor Email: skessinger@marysvilleonline.net
Editor Phone: 785-562-2317
Advertising Executive Name: Wayne Kruse
Advertising Executive Email: wkruse@marysvilleonline.net

THE MARYSVILLE ADVOCATE

Street Address: 107 S. Ninth St.
City: Marysville
State: KS
Postal Code: 66508
Office phone: 785-562-2317
Publication Website: www.marysvilleonline.net
Editor Name: Sarah Kessinger
Editor Email: skessinger@marysvilleonline.net
Editor Phone: 785-562-2317
Advertising Executive Name: Wayne Kruse
Advertising Executive Email: wkruse@marysvilleonline.net

MCPHERSON

MCPHERSON NEWS-LEDGER

Corporate/Parent Company: Kansas Publishing Ventures
Street Address: PO Box 649
City: McPherson
State: KS
Postal Code: 67460
Office phone: (620) 241-4290
Publication Website: mcphersonweeklynews.com
Editor Name: Jessie Wagoner
Editor Email: editor@mcphersonweeklynews.com
Total Circulation: 5150

NEWTON

NEWTON NOW

Street Address: 706 N. MAIN
City: NEWTON
State: KS
Postal Code: 67114
Office phone: 316-281-7899
Publication Website: harveycountynow.com
Publisher Name: Lindsey Young
Publisher Email: lindsey@kspublishingventures.com
Editor Name: Adam Strunk
Editor Email: adam@harveycountynow.com

NORTON

THE NORTON TELEGRAM

Corporate/Parent Company: Haynes Publishing Co.
Street Address: 215 S Kansas Ave
City: Norton
State: KS
Postal Code: 67654-2131
Office phone: (785) 877-3361
Publication Website: https://www.facebook.com/nortontelegram/
Delivery Methods: Mail
Mechanical specifications: Type page 13 3/4 x 22 3/4; E - 6 cols, 2 1/16, 3/16 between; A - 6 cols, 2 1/16, 3/16 between; C - 6 cols, 2 1/16, 3/16 between.
Published Days: Tues`Fri
Avg Paid Circ: 2704
Audit Company: Sworn/Estimate/Non-Audited
Audit Date: 6 10 2019
Total Circulation: 1815

OBERLIN

OBERLIN HERALD, THE

Corporate/Parent Company: Haynes Publishing Co.
Street Address: 170 S Penn Ave
City: Oberlin
State: KS
Postal Code: 67749-2243
Office phone: (785) 475-2206
Publication Website: http://nwkansas.com/
Year Established: 1879
Delivery Methods: Mail`Newsstand`Carrier`Racks
Own Printing Facility?: Y
Commercial printers?: Y
Mechanical specifications: Type page 13 x 21 1/2; E - 6 cols, 2 1/16, 1/8 between; A - 6 cols, 2 1/16, 1/8 between; C - 6 cols, 2 1/16, 1/8 between.
Published Days: Wed
Avg Paid Circ: 1724
Avg Free Circ: 91
Audit Company: Sworn/Estimate/Non-Audited
Audit Date: 6 10 2019
Total Circulation: 2000

OTTAWA

THE OTTAWA HERALD

Corporate/Parent Company: Gannett
Street Address: 214 S Hickory St
City: Ottawa
State: KS
Postal Code: 66067
Office phone: (785) 242-4700
Publication Website: https://www.ottawaherald.com/
General E-mail: circulation@ottawaherald.com
Editor Name: Jennifer McDaniel
Editor Email: jmcdaniel@ottawaherald.com
Editor Phone: (785) 242-4700, ext : 105
Advertising Executive Name: Sheila Holle
Advertising Executive Email: jtaylor@ottawaherald.com
Advertising Executive Phone: (785) 242-4700, ext : 110
Year Established: 1869
Delivery Methods: Mail`Newsstand`Racks
Own Printing Facility?: N
Commercial printers?: Y
Mechanical specifications: Type page 12 13/16 x 21 1/2; E - 6 cols, 2, 3/16 between; A - 6 cols, 2, 3/16 between; C - 6 cols, 1 15/16, 3/16 between.
Published Days: Tues`Thur`Sat
Weekday Frequency: m
Saturday Frequency: m
Avg Paid Circ: 4100
Avg Free Circ: 700
Audit Company: Sworn/Estimate/Non-Audited
Audit Date: 6 10 2019
Total Circulation: 1240

PAOLA

MIAMI COUNTY REPUBLIC

Corporate/Parent Company: News-Press & Gazette Co.
Street Address: 121 S. Pearl St.
City: Paola
State: KS
Postal Code: 66071
Office phone: (913) 294-2311
Publication Website: www.republic-online.com
General E-mail: republic@miconews.com
Publisher Name: Sandy Nelson
Publisher Email: sandy.nelson@miconews.com
Editor Name: Brian McCauley
Editor Email: brian.mccauley@miconews.com
Year Established: 1866
Delivery Methods: Mail`Racks
Mechanical specifications: Type page 11 5/8 x 21; E - 6 cols, 1 5/6, 1/8 between; A - 6 cols, 1 5/6, 1/8 between; C - 6 cols, 1 5/6, 1/8 between.
Published Days: Wed
Avg Paid Circ: 5140
Avg Free Circ: 10
Audit Company: Sworn/Estimate/Non-Audited
Audit Date: 6 10 2019

PHILLIPSBURG

PHILLIPS COUNTY REVIEW

Corporate/Parent Company: Main Street Media, Inc.
Street Address: 683 3rd St
City: Phillipsburg
State: KS
Postal Code: 67661
Office phone: (785) 543-5242
Publication Website: http://www.phillipscountyreview.com/
General E-mail: news@phillipscountyreview.com
Editor Name: Kirby Ross
Editor Email: kross@phillipscountyreview.com
Editor Phone: (785) 543-5242
Advertising Executive Name: Ronda Hueneke
Advertising Executive Email: ronda@phillipscountyreview.com
Advertising Executive Phone: (785) 543-5242
Year Established: 1889
Delivery Methods: Mail
Own Printing Facility?: Y
Mechanical specifications: Type page 13 x 21; E - 6 cols, 1 13/16, 1/6 between; A - 6 cols, 1 13/16, 1/6 between; C - 6 cols, 1 13/16, 1/6 between.
Published Days: Wed
Avg Paid Circ: 2000
Audit Company: Sworn/Estimate/Non-Audited
Audit Date: 6 10 2019

PLAINVILLE

PLAINVILLE TIMES

Corporate/Parent Company: Main Street Media, Inc.
Street Address: PO Box 40
City: Plainville
State: KS
Postal Code: 67663
Office phone: (785) 434-4525
Publication Website: https://www.mainstreetnewsgroup.com/plainvilletimes
General E-mail: pvtimes@ruraltel.net
Publisher Name: Michael Crawford
Advertising Executive Name: Beth Williamson
Advertising Executive Email: ads@windsornews.net
Delivery Methods: Mail`Newsstand
Published Days: Thur
Avg Paid Circ: 1200
Avg Free Circ: 40
Audit Company: Sworn/Estimate/Non-Audited
Audit Date: 6 10 2019

SAINT FRANCIS

BIRD CITY TIMES

Corporate/Parent Company: Haynes Publishing Co.
Street Address: PO Box 1050
City: Saint Francis
State: KS
Postal Code: 67756-1050
Office phone: (785) 332-3162
Publication Website: http://nwkansas.com/
Delivery Methods: Mail
Own Printing Facility?: Y
Commercial printers?: Y
Mechanical specifications: Type page 13 x 21 1/2; E - 6 cols, 2 1/16, 1/8 between; A - 6 cols, 2 1/16, 1/8 between; C - 6 cols, 2 1/16, 1/8 between.
Published Days: Thur
Avg Paid Circ: 565
Avg Free Circ: 3
Audit Company: Sworn/Estimate/Non-Audited
Audit Date: 6 10 2019

ST. FRANCIS HERALD

Corporate/Parent Company: Haynes Publishing Co.
Street Address: 310 W Washington St
City: Saint Francis
State: KS
Postal Code: 67756-9606
Office phone: (785) 332-3162
Publication Website: http://nwkansas.com/
Year Established: 1912
Delivery Methods: Mail`Newsstand
Own Printing Facility?: Y
Commercial printers?: Y
Mechanical specifications: Type page 13 x 21 1/2; E - 6 cols, 2 1/16, 1/8 between; A - 6 cols, 2 1/16, 1/8 between; C - 6 cols, 2 1/16, 1/8 between.
Published Days: Thur
Avg Paid Circ: 1288
Avg Free Circ: 4
Audit Company: Sworn/Estimate/Non-Audited
Audit Date: 6 10 2019

Non-Daily Newspapers in the U.S.

SCOTT CITY
SCOTT COUNTY RECORD
Street Address: PO Box 377
City: Scott City
State: KS
Postal Code: 67871
Office phone: 620-872-2090
Publication Website: www.scottcountyrecord.com
Publisher Name: Rod Haxton
Editor Name: Kathy Haxton
Editor Email: editor@screcord.com

SENECA
SENECA COURIER-TRIBUNE
Street Address: 512 Main
City: Seneca
State: KS
Postal Code: 66538
Office phone: 785-336-2175
Publication Website: www.couriertribuneonline.com
General E-mail: ctseneca@nvcs.com
Editor Name: Matt Diehl
Total Circulation: 1292

SHARON SPRINGS
WESTERN TIMES
Street Address: 126 N Main St / PO Box 279
City: Sharon Springs
State: KS
Postal Code: 67758
Publication Website: www.thewesterntimes.com
Editor Name: Lace David
Editor Email: editor@TheWesternTimes.com

SMITH CENTER
SMITH COUNTY PIONEER
Corporate/Parent Company: Main Street Media Group
Street Address: 201 S Main St
City: Smith Center
State: KS
Postal Code: 66967
Office phone: 785-282-3371
Publication Website: www.mainstreetnewsgroup.com/smithcountypioneer
General E-mail: pioneer@ruraltel.net
Total Circulation: 2704

WELLINGTON
WELLINGTON DAILY NEWS
Corporate/Parent Company: Gannett
Street Address: 113 W Harvey Ave
City: Wellington
State: KS
Postal Code: 67152
Office phone: (620) 326-3326
Publication Website: https://www.wellingtondailynews.com/
General E-mail: jwilson@butlercountytimesgazette.com
Publisher Name: Jennifer Wilson
Publisher Email: jwilson@butlercountytimesgazette.com
Publisher Phone: (620) 326-3326
Editor Name: Adam Catlin
Editor Email: acatlin@wellingtondailynews.com
Editor Phone: (620) 326-3326
Year Established: 1901
Delivery Methods: Mail`Racks
Own Printing Facility?: N
Commercial printers?: N
Mechanical specifications: Type page 11 x 10.5, E - 6 cols, 2, 1/8 between; A - 6 cols, 2, 1/8 between; C - 6 cols, 2, 1/8 between.
Published Days: Wed
Weekday Frequency: e
Avg Paid Circ: 2000

Audit Company: Sworn/Estimate/Non-Audited
Audit Date: 6 10 2019
Buisness Equipment: 5-PC
Buisness Software: Microsoft/Office, Newzware
Classified Equipment: Hardware – APP/Mac ; Printers – APP/Mac LaserWriter II, Epson/740;
Editorial Equipment: Hardware – APP/Mac APP/Mac G4, APP/Mac 7200, APP/Mac 7100, APP/Mac 7500; Printers – APP/Mac LaserWriter NTX, Xante/Accel-a-writer, HP/LaserJet 4V
Editorial Software: InDesign, InCopy
Production Equipment: Hardware – Caere/OmniPage Direct, Xante/Accel-A-Writer, HP/LaserJet 4V; Scanners – Microtek/Scanner, Linotype-HEII, Poloroid/SprintScan 35
Production Software: QPS/QuarkXPress.
Note: STudio 104/in-house advertising agency; The Shopper – TMC (13,800 dist. Tuesdays)
Total Circulation: 4800

WICHITA
SEDGWICK COUNTY POST
Street Address: 400 N. Woodlawn Suite 10
City: Wichita
State: KS
Postal Code: 67208
Office phone: (316) 691-8553
Publication Website: www.thesedgwickcountypost.com
General E-mail: notices@thesedgwickcountypost.com
Mailroom Equipment: Tying Machines – Manual; Address Machine – Dispensa-matic.;
Classified Equipment: Hardware – APP/Mac G3; Printers – Xante/Accel-a-Writer 3G.;
Editorial Equipment: Hardware – 3-APP/Mac G4, APP/Mac IIci, 3-APP/Mac G3; Printers – Xante/Accel-a-Writer 3G
Editorial Software: Baseview/NewsEdit, QPS/QuarkXPress.
Production Equipment: Cameras – SCREEN.
Total Circulation: 2000

KENTUCKY

BARDSTOWN
KENTUCKY STANDARD
Corporate/Parent Company: Landmark Community Newspapers
Street Address: 110 W Stephen Foster Ave
City: Bardstown
State: KY
Postal Code: 40004-1416
Office phone: (502) 348-9003
Publication Website: https://www.kystandard.com/
General E-mail: news@kystandard.com
Publisher Name: Alfred S. Wathen
Year Established: 1900
Delivery Methods: Mail`Newsstand`Carrier`Racks
Own Printing Facility?: Y
Published Days: Wed`Fri`Sun
Avg Paid Circ: 7536
Audit Company: Sworn/Estimate/Non-Audited
Audit Date: 6 10 2019

BEDFORD
TRIMBLE BANNER
Corporate/Parent Company: Landmark Community Newspapers
Street Address: 68 Wentworth Drive
City: Bedford
State: KY
Postal Code: 40006-7621
Office phone: (502) 255-3205
Publication Website: https://www.mytrimblenews.com/
General E-mail: dgarrett@mytrimblenews.com
Publisher Name: Jeff Moore
Publisher Email: jmoore@mycarrollnews.com
Editor Name: Dave Taylor
Editor Email: editor@mytrimblenews.com
Advertising Executive Name: Deborah Garrett
Advertising Executive Email: dgarrett@mytrimblenews.com
Year Established: 1879
Delivery Methods: Mail
Mechanical specifications: Type page 10.38 x 21 1/2.
Published Days: Thur
Avg Paid Circ: 1325
Avg Free Circ: 5
Audit Company: Sworn/Estimate/Non-Audited
Audit Date: 6 10 2019

BOONEVILLE
BOONEVILLE SENTINEL
Street Address: P. O. Box 129
City: Booneville
State: KY
Postal Code: 41314
Office phone: (606) 593-6627
Publication Website: facebook.com/boonesentinel
General E-mail: boonevillesentinel@gmail.com
Publisher Name: Jessica Butler
Editor Name: Douglas Brandenbury

CADIZ
THE CADIZ RECORD
Corporate/Parent Company: Paxton Media Group, LLC
Street Address: 58 Nunn Blvd
City: Cadiz
State: KY
Postal Code: 42211
Office phone: (270) 522-6605
Publication Website: https://www.kentuckynewera.com/cadiz_record/
General E-mail: news@cadizrecord.com
Delivery Methods: Mail
Mechanical specifications: Type page 13 x 21 1/2; E - 6 cols, 1 5/6, between; A - 6 cols, 3, between; C - 9 cols, 1 1/6, between.
Published Days: Wed
Avg Paid Circ: 4800
Avg Free Circ: 97
Audit Company: Sworn/Estimate/Non-Audited
Audit Date: 6 10 2019

CAMPBELLSVILLE
CENTRAL KENTUCKY NEWS-JOURNAL
Corporate/Parent Company: Landmark Community Newspapers
Street Address: 200 Albion Way, P.O. Box 1138
City: Campbellsville
State: KY
Postal Code: 42718-1565
Office phone: (270) 465-8111
Publication Website: https://www.cknj.com/
General E-mail: publisher@cknj.com
Publisher Name: John Overby
Publisher Email: publisher@cknj.com
Editor Name: John Overby
Editor Email: publisher@cknj.com
Advertising Executive Name: Geoff Botkin
Advertising Executive Email: gbotkin@cknj.com
Year Established: 1910
Delivery Methods: Mail
Own Printing Facility?: Y
Commercial printers?: Y
Mechanical specifications: Type page 13 x 21 1/2; E - 6 cols, 2, 5/16 between; A - 6 cols, 2, 5/16 between; C - 8 cols, 1 1/2, 1/48 between.
Published Days: Mon`Thur
Avg Paid Circ: 7600
Avg Free Circ: 12000
Audit Company: Sworn/Estimate/Non-Audited
Audit Date: 6 10 2019

CARLISLE
ROBERTSON COUNTY NEWS
Street Address: 240 E. Main St.
City: Carlisle
State: KY
Postal Code: 40311
Office phone: 859-289-6425
Publication Website: https://www.robconews.com
Publisher Name: Melissa Mitchell
Advertising Executive Name: Jeremiah Brown

CARROLLTON
CARROLLTON NEWS-DEMOCRAT
Corporate/Parent Company: Landmark Community Newspapers
Street Address: 122 6th St, P.O. Box 60
City: Carrollton
State: KY
Postal Code: 41008-1009
Office phone: (502) 732-4261
Publication Website: https://www.mycarrollnews.com/
General E-mail: editor@mycarrollnews.com
Publisher Name: Jeff Moore
Publisher Email: jmoore@mycarrollnews.com
Editor Name: Jacob Blair
Editor Email: editor@mycarrollnews.com
Advertising Executive Name: Deborah Garrett
Year Established: 1868
Delivery Methods: Mail
Own Printing Facility?: Y
Mechanical specifications: Type page 10.38 x 21 1/2; E - 6 cols, 2, 1/8 between; A - 6 cols, 2, 1/8 between; C - 8 cols, 1 1/2, 1/8 between.
Published Days: Wed
Avg Paid Circ: 2841
Avg Free Circ: 17
Audit Company: Sworn/Estimate/Non-Audited
Audit Date: 6 10 2019

THE NEWS-DEMOCRAT
Street Address: P. O. Box 60
City: Carrollton
State: KY
Postal Code: 41008
Office phone: (502) 732-4261
Publication Website: www.mycarrollnews.com
General E-mail: ckidwell@mycarrollnews.com
Publisher Name: Jeff Moore
Publisher Email: jmoore@mycarrollnews.com
Editor Name: Jacob Blair
Editor Email: editor@mycarrollnews.com
Advertising Executive Name: Jeff Moore

COLUMBIA
THE FARMER'S PRIDE
Street Address: P. O. Box 159
City: Columbia
State: KY
Postal Code: 42728
Office phone: 270-384-9454
Publication Website: thefarmerspride.com
General E-mail: newsroom@thefarmerspride.com
Publisher Name: Sharon Burton
Advertising Executive Name: Diana Withers

CYNTHIANA
CYNTHIANA DEMOCRAT
Corporate/Parent Company: Landmark Community Newspapers
Street Address: 302 Webster Ave, P.O. Box 160
City: Cynthiana
State: KY
Postal Code: 41031-1647

Office phone: (859) 234-1035
Publication Website: https://www.cynthianademocrat.com/
General E-mail: pjenkins@cynthianademocrat.com
Publisher Name: Patricia Jenkins
Publisher Email: pjenkins@cynthianademocrat.com
Editor Name: Becky Barnes
Editor Email: bbarnes@cynthianademocrat.com
Advertising Executive Name: Patricia Jenkins
Advertising Executive Email: pjenkins@cynthianademocrat.com
Delivery Methods: Mail`Newsstand`Racks
Own Printing Facility?: Y
Commercial printers?: Y
Mechanical specifications: Type page 11 5/8 x 21 1/2; E - 6 cols, 1 5/6, between; A - 6 cols, 1 5/6, between; C - 6 cols, 1 5/6, between.
Published Days: Thur
Avg Paid Circ: 5500
Audit Company: Sworn/Estimate/Non-Audited
Audit Date: 6 10 2019

EMINENCE

HENRY COUNTY LOCAL

Corporate/Parent Company: Landmark Community Newspapers
Street Address: 18 S Penn Ave
City: Eminence
State: KY
Postal Code: 40019-1036
Office phone: (502) 845-2858
Publication Website: https://www.hclocal.com/
General E-mail: kelli@sentinelnews.com
Publisher Name: Anna St. Charles
Publisher Email: publisher@hclocal.com
Editor Name: Aaron K. Nelson
Editor Email: editor@hclocal.com
Advertising Executive Name: Kelli Borders
Advertising Executive Email: kelli@sentinelnews.com
Delivery Methods: Mail
Published Days: Wed
Avg Paid Circ: 4500
Audit Company: Sworn/Estimate/Non-Audited
Audit Date: 6 10 2019

FALMOUTH

FALMOUTH OUTLOOK

Corporate/Parent Company: DHI Media, Inc.
Street Address: 210 Main St
City: Falmouth
State: KY
Postal Code: 41040-1265
Office phone: (859) 654-3332
Publication Website: https://www.falmouthoutlook.com/
General E-mail: news@falmouthoutlook.com
Publisher Name: Neil Belcher
Editor Name: Keith Smith

FLEMINGSBURG

FLEMINGSBURG GAZETTE

Street Address: P. O. Box 32
City: Flemingsburg
State: KY
Postal Code: 41041
Office phone: (606) 845-9211
Publication Website: www.fleminggazette.com
General E-mail: monica@kynewsgroup.com
Publisher Name: Melissa Mitchell

FRANKLIN

FRANKLIN FAVORITE

Corporate/Parent Company: Paxton Media Group, LLC
Street Address: 103 North High Street
City: Franklin
State: KY
Postal Code: 42134

Office phone: (270) 586-4481
Publication Website: https://www.franklinfavorite.com
General E-mail: editor@franklinfavorite.com
Publisher Name: Brandon Cox
Publisher Email: generalmanager@franklinfavorite.com
Editor Name: Megan Purazrang
Editor Email: editor@franklinfavorite.com
Advertising Executive Name: Brian Talley
Advertising Executive Email: btalley@franklinfavorite.com
Year Established: 1859
Delivery Methods: Mail`Newsstand`Racks
Own Printing Facility?: Y
Commercial printers?: Y
Mechanical specifications: Type page 13 1/2 x 21 1/2; E - 6 cols, 1 5/8, 1/6 between; A - 6 cols, 1 5/8, 1/6 between; C - 8 cols, 1 1/4, 1/8 between.
Published Days: Thur
Avg Paid Circ: 4000
Audit Company: Sworn/Estimate/Non-Audited
Audit Date: 6 10 2019

FULTON

THE CURRENT

Street Address: PO Box 1200
City: Fulton
State: KY
Postal Code: 42041
Office phone: (270) 472-1121
Publication Website: www.fultonleader.com
General E-mail: news@thecurrent.press
Publisher Name: Benita Fuzzell
Publisher Email: benita@thecurrent.press
Advertising Executive Name: Clay McWherther
Advertising Executive Email: clay@thecurrent.press

GLASGOW

BARREN COUNTY PROGRESS

Corporate/Parent Company: Jobe Publishing, Inc.
Street Address: 101 N Public Square
City: Glasgow
State: KY
Postal Code: 42141
Office phone: 270-659-2146
Publication Website: www.jpinews.com
General E-mail: progress@jpinews.com
Publisher Name: Jeffrey S. Jobe
Publisher Email: jobe@jobeinc.com
Publisher Phone: 270.590.6625
Advertising Executive Name: Jessica O'Banion

HARDINSBURG

BRECKINRIDGE HERALD-NEWS

Street Address: P.O. Box 31
City: Hardinsburg
State: KY
Postal Code: 40143
Office phone: 270-756-2109
Publication Website: breckheraldnews.com
General E-mail: bcheraldthn@bbtel.com
Editor Name: Austin Weedman
Editor Email: editorialthn@bbtel.com
Advertising Executive Name: Leslie Gedling

HARTFORD

THE OHIO COUNTY TIMES

Corporate/Parent Company: DHI Media, Inc.
Street Address: 314 S Main St
City: Hartford
State: KY
Postal Code: 42347-1129
Office phone: (270) 298-7100
Publication Website: https://www.octimesnews.com/
General E-mail: ads@octimesnews.com
Editor Name: Dana Brantley
Editor Email: editor@octimesnews.com

HODGENVILLE

LARUE COUNTY HERALD NEWS

Street Address: 40 Shawnee Dr
City: Hodgenville
State: KY
Postal Code: 42748-1639
Office phone: (270) 358-3118
Publication Website: https://www.laruecountyherald.com
General E-mail: publisher@laruecountyherald.com
Publisher Name: Allison Shepherd
Publisher Email: ashepherd@laruecountyherald.com
Editor Name: Zackerie Fairfax
Editor Email: editor@laruecountyherald.com
Year Established: 1885
Delivery Methods: Mail`Newsstand`Carrier`Racks
Own Printing Facility?: N
Commercial printers?: N
Mechanical specifications: Type page 13 x 21 1/2; E - 6 cols, 2, 1/6 between; A - 6 cols, 2, 1/6 between; C - 8 cols, 1 1/2, 1/6 between.
Published Days: Wed
Avg Paid Circ: 2842
Avg Free Circ: 3900
Audit Company: Sworn/Estimate/Non-Audited
Audit Date: 6 10 2019

IRVINE

ESTILL COUNTY TRIBUNE

Street Address: 6135 Winchester Road
City: Irvine
State: KY
Postal Code: 40336
Office phone: (606) 723-5012
Publication Website: www.estilltribune.com
General E-mail: news@estilltribune.com
Publisher Name: Tracy Patrick
Editor Name: Delores Rowland

JACKSON

BREATHITT ADVOCATE

Street Address: 1118 Main Street / PO Box 1015
City: Jackson
State: KY
Postal Code: 41339
Office phone: 606-693-0170
Publication Website: breathitt.news
General E-mail: news@breathittadvocate.com
Editor Name: Bobby Thorpe
Advertising Executive Name: Kimberly Thorpe

THE JACKSON-BREATHITT COUNTY TIMES-VOICE

Corporate/Parent Company: Nolan Group Media
Street Address: 22 Howell Lane
City: Jackson
State: KY
Postal Code: 41339
Office phone: 606-666-2451
Publication Website: jacksontimesvoice.com
General E-mail: advertising@jacksontimesky.com
Publisher Name: Glenn Gray
Editor Name: Jeff Noble
Advertising Executive Name: Cheryl Campbell

LA CENTER

ADVANCE YEOMAN

Corporate/Parent Company: Kentucky Publishing Inc.
Street Address: 114 W. Kentucky Dr.
City: La Center
State: KY
Postal Code: 42056

Office phone: (270) 908-2001
Publication Website: ky-news.com
Publisher Name: Greg LeNeave
Publisher Email: greg007@ky-news.com
Publisher Phone: 270-442-7389
Editor Name: Kelly Paul
Advertising Executive Name: Larrah Workman
Advertising Executive Email: larrah@ky-news.com
Advertising Executive Phone: 270-442-7389
Year Established: 1889
Delivery Methods: Mail
Published Days: Wed
Avg Paid Circ: 4300
Avg Free Circ: 45
Audit Company: Sworn/Estimate/Non-Audited
Audit Date: 6 10 2019

LA GRANGE

OLDHAM ERA

Corporate/Parent Company: Landmark Community Newspapers
Street Address: 202 S 1st Ave
City: La Grange
State: KY
Postal Code: 40031-2208
Office phone: (502) 222-7183
Publication Website: https://www.oldhamera.com/
General E-mail: barbara@oldhamera.com
Publisher Name: Jane Ashley Pace
Publisher Email: publisher@oldhamera.com
Editor Name: Chris Brooke
Editor Email: editor@oldhamera.com
Advertising Executive Name: Barbara Duncan
Advertising Executive Email: barbara@oldhamera.com
Year Established: 1876
Delivery Methods: Mail`Newsstand
Mechanical specifications: Type page 12 15/16 x 29 1/2; E - 6 cols, 2, 1/6 between; A - 6 cols, 2, 1/6 between; C - 6 cols, 2, 1/6 between.
Published Days: Thur
Avg Paid Circ: 3134
Audit Company: Sworn/Estimate/Non-Audited
Audit Date: 6 10 2019

LAWRENCEBURG

THE ANDERSON NEWS

Corporate/Parent Company: Landmark Community Newspapers
Street Address: PO Box 410, 504 W. Broadway, Suite D
City: Lawrenceburg
State: KY
Postal Code: 40342-0410
Office phone: (502) 839-6906
Publication Website: https://www.theandersonnews.com/
General E-mail: advertising@theandersonnews.com
Publisher Name: Ben Carlson
Editor Name: Ben Carlson
Editor Phone: (502) 839-6906
Advertising Executive Email: advertising@theandersonnews.com
Year Established: 1877
Delivery Methods: Mail`Racks
Mechanical specifications: Call for details
Published Days: Wed
Avg Paid Circ: 5200
Audit Company: Sworn/Estimate/Non-Audited
Audit Date: 6 10 2019

LEBANON

LEBANON ENTERPRISE

Corporate/Parent Company: Landmark Community Newspapers
Street Address: 119 S Proctor Knott Ave
City: Lebanon
State: KY
Postal Code: 40033-1259
Office phone: (270) 692-6026
Publication Website: https://www.

Non-Daily Newspapers in the U.S.

lebanonenterprise.com/
General E-mail: editor@lebanonenterprise.com
Publisher Name: Stevie Lowery
Editor Name: Stevie Lowery
Editor Email: editor@lebanonenterprise.com
Published Days: Wed
Avg Paid Circ: 5806
Audit Company: Sworn/Estimate/Non-Audited
Audit Date: 6 10 2019

LEITCHFIELD

GRAYSON COUNTY NEWS-GAZETTE

Corporate/Parent Company: Paxton Media Group, LLC
Street Address: 52 Public Square
City: Leitchfield
State: KY
Postal Code: 42754
Office phone: (270) 259-9622
Publication Website: https://www.gcnewsgazette.com/
General E-mail: editor@gcnewsgazette.com
Editor Name: Matt Lasley
Editor Email: mlasley@gcnewsgazette.com
Editor Phone: (270) 971-4295
Advertising Executive Name: Tracey Collins
Advertising Executive Email: tcollins@gcnewsgazette.com
Advertising Executive Phone: (270) 971-4290
Year Established: 1890
Delivery Methods: Mail
Published Days: Wed`Sat
Avg Paid Circ: 3000
Audit Company: Sworn/Estimate/Non-Audited
Audit Date: 6 10 2019

LEXINGTON

BUSINESS LEXINGTON

Corporate/Parent Company: Smiley Pete Publishing
Street Address: 434 Old Vine Street
City: Lexington
State: KY
Postal Code: 40507
Office phone: 859-266-6537
Publication Website: www.bizlex.com
Publisher Name: Chris Eddie
Publisher Email: chris@smileypete.com
Publisher Phone: (859) 266-6537 ext. 23
Editor Name: Saraya Brewer
Editor Email: saraya@smileypete.com

CHEVY CHASER MAGAZINE

Corporate/Parent Company: Smiley Pete Publishing
Street Address: 434 Old Vine Street
City: Lexington
State: KY
Postal Code: 40507
Office phone: 859-266-6537
Publication Website: www.chevychaser.com
Publisher Name: Chris Eddie
Publisher Email: chris@smileypete.com
Publisher Phone: (859) 266-6537 ext. 23
Editor Name: Saraya Brewer
Editor Email: saraya@smileypete.com

LIBERTY

CASEY COUNTY NEWS

Corporate/Parent Company: Landmark Community Newspapers
Street Address: 720 Campbellsville St
City: Liberty
State: KY
Postal Code: 42539-3106
Office phone: (606) 787-7171
Publication Website: https://www.caseynews.net/
General E-mail: cvanleuven@caseynews.net
Publisher Name: Charlie VanLeuven

Publisher Email: cvanleuven@caseynews.net
Editor Name: Charlie VanLeuven
Editor Email: cvanleuven@caseynews.net
Delivery Methods: Mail`Racks
Published Days: Wed
Avg Paid Circ: 6000
Avg Free Circ: 14
Audit Company: Sworn/Estimate/Non-Audited
Audit Date: 6 10 2019

MAYFIELD

THE MAYFIELD MESSENGER

Corporate/Parent Company: Paxton Media Group, LLC
Street Address: 111 S 7th St
City: Mayfield
State: KY
Postal Code: 42066-2341
Office phone: (270) 247-5223
Publication Website: https://www.mayfield-messenger.com
General E-mail: mellen@mayfield-messenger.com
Publisher Name: Areia Hathcock
Publisher Email: ahathcock@mayfield-messenger.com
Publisher Phone: (270) 247-5229
Editor Name: Eric Walker
Editor Email: ewalker@mayfield-messenger.com
Editor Phone: (270) 247-4607
Advertising Executive Name: Mary Ellen Matthews
Advertising Executive Email: mellen@mayfield-messenger.com
Advertising Executive Phone: (270) 804-4585
Year Established: 1900
Delivery Methods: Mail`Carrier`Racks
Own Printing Facility?: N
Commercial printers?: N
Published Days: Wed`Fri`Sun
Weekday Frequency: e
Avg Paid Circ: 2000
Audit Company: Sworn/Estimate/Non-Audited
Audit Date: 6 10 2019

MORGANTOWN

BUTLER COUNTY BANNER

Corporate/Parent Company: Jobe Publishing, Inc.
Street Address: P. O. Box 219
City: Morgantown
State: KY
Postal Code: 42261
Office phone: (270) 526-4151
Publication Website: jpinews.com
Publisher Name: Jeffrey S. Jobe
Publisher Email: jobe@jobeinc.com
Publisher Phone: 270.590.6625
Advertising Executive Name: Perlina Anderkin

MT. VERNON

MOUNT VERNON SIGNAL

Street Address: P.O. Box 185
City: Mt. Vernon
State: KY
Postal Code: 40456
Office phone: (606) 256-2244

OWENSBORO

MCLEAN COUNTY NEWS

Corporate/Parent Company: Paxton Media Group, LLC
Street Address: 1401 Frederica St.
City: Owensboro
State: KY
Postal Code: 42301
Office phone: (270) 926-0123
Publication Website: https://www.messenger-inquirer.com/mclean_county/
General E-mail: csr@messenger-inquirer.com
Publisher Name: Mike Weafer

Publisher Email: mweafer@messenger-inquirer.com
Publisher Phone: (270) 691-7285
Editor Name: Matt Francis
Editor Email: mfrancis@messenger-inquirer.com
Editor Phone: (270) 691-7292
Advertising Executive Name: Angela Mayes
Advertising Executive Email: amayes@messenger-inquirer
Advertising Executive Phone: (270) 691-7239
Year Established: 1884
Delivery Methods: Mail`Racks
Own Printing Facility?: Y
Commercial printers?: Y
Published Days: Thur
Avg Paid Circ: 3000
Avg Free Circ: 350
Audit Company: Sworn/Estimate/Non-Audited
Audit Date: 6 10 2019

OWENTON

OWENTON NEWS-HERALD

Corporate/Parent Company: Landmark Community Newspapers
Street Address: 154 W. Bryan St., P.O. Box 219
City: Owenton
State: KY
Postal Code: 40359-1440
Office phone: (502) 484-3431
Publication Website: https://www.owentonnewsherald.com/
General E-mail: mhaines@owentonnewsherald.com
Editor Name: Molly Haines
Editor Email: mhaines@owentonnewsherald.com
Year Established: 1868
Delivery Methods: Mail
Mechanical specifications: Type page 13 x 21 1/2; E - 6 cols, 2, 1/6 between; A - 6 cols, 2, 1/6 between; C - 8 cols, 1 1/2, 1/12 between.
Published Days: Wed
Avg Paid Circ: 4129
Audit Company: Sworn/Estimate/Non-Audited
Audit Date: 6 10 2019

THE NEWS HERALD

Corporate/Parent Company: Gannett
Street Address: 154 W. Bryan St., Suite 1 / P.O. Box 219
City: Owenton
State: KY
Postal Code: 40359
Office phone: (502) 484-3431
Publication Website: owentonnewsherald.com
General E-mail: SLYONS@OWENTONNEWSHERALD.COM
Editor Name: Molly Haines
Editor Email: mhaines@owentonnewsherald.com

PADUCAH

WEST KY NEWS

Corporate/Parent Company: Kentucky Publishing Inc
Street Address: 1540 McCracken Blvd.
City: Paducah
State: KY
Postal Code: 42001
Office phone: 270-442-7389
Publication Website: ky-news.com
General E-mail: kpilayout@gmail.com
Publisher Name: Greg LeNeave
Publisher Email: greg007@ky-news.com
Publisher Phone: 270-442-7389
Advertising Executive Name: Larrah Workman
Advertising Executive Email: larrah@ky-news.com
Advertising Executive Phone: 270-442-7389

PRESTONSBURG

FLOYD COUNTY TIMES

Corporate/Parent Company: Lancaster Management, Inc.
Street Address: 197 South Lake Drive
City: Prestonsburg
State: KY
Postal Code: 41653-1958
Office phone: (606) 886-8506
Publication Website: http://www.floydct.com/
General E-mail: news@floydchronicle.com
Publisher Name: Jeff Vanderbeck
Editor Name: Russ Cassidy
Year Established: 1927
Own Printing Facility?: Y
Mechanical specifications: Type page 11 3/4 x 21 1/4; E - 6 cols, 1 5/6, 1/6 between; A - 6 cols, 1 5/6, 1/6 between; C - 8 cols, 1 1/3, 1/6 between.
Published Days: Wed`Fri
Avg Paid Circ: 8200
Avg Free Circ: 110
Audit Company: Sworn/Estimate/Non-Audited
Audit Date: 6 10 2019

RADCLIFF

SENTINEL

Corporate/Parent Company: Lee Enterprises
Street Address: 1558 Hill Street
City: Radcliff
State: KY
Postal Code: 40160
Office phone: (270) 351-4407
Editor Name: O.J. Royalty

RUSSELL

GREENUP BEACON

Street Address: 1407 Beth Ann Drive
City: Russell
State: KY
Postal Code: 41169
Office phone: (606) 356-7509
Publication Website: greenupbeacon.com
Editor Name: Hank Bond
Editor Email: hank@greenupbeacon.com
Advertising Executive Name: Marilyn Bond

SEBREE

SEBREE BANNER

Corporate/Parent Company: CPC Newspaper Group
Street Address: P.O. Box 36
City: Sebree
State: KY
Postal Code: 42455
Office phone: (270) 318-5038
Publication Website: cpcnewspapers.com
General E-mail: sebreebanner@bellsouth.net
Editor Name: Anthony L. Catlett
Editor Email: tcatlett101@bellsouth.net
Advertising Executive Name: Regina A. Catlett
Advertising Executive Email: rcatlett222@bellsouth.net

SHELBYVILLE

SENTINEL NEWS PLUS

Street Address: 703 Taylorsville Rd
City: Shelbyville
State: KY
Postal Code: 40065-9125
Office phone: (502) 633-2526
Publication Website: https://www.sentinelnews.com/
General E-mail: tmartin@sentinelnews.com
Editor Name: Todd Martin
Editor Email: tmartin@sentinelnews.com
Editor Phone: (502) 633-2526

THE SENTINEL-NEWS

Corporate/Parent Company: Landmark Community Newspapers
Street Address: 703 Taylorsville Rd
City: Shelbyville
State: KY
Postal Code: 40065-9125
Office phone: (502) 633-2526
Publication Website: https://www.sentinelnews.com/
General E-mail: tmartin@sentinelnews.com
Editor Name: Todd Martin
Editor Email: tmartin@sentinelnews.com
Editor Phone: (502) 633-2526
Year Established: 1866
Delivery Methods: Mail
Own Printing Facility?: Y
Commercial printers?: Y
Mechanical specifications: Type page 11 5/8 x 21 1/2; E - 6 cols, 1 7/8, 1/8 between; A - 6 cols, 1 7/8, 1/8 between; C - 8 cols, 1 1/3, between.
Published Days: Wed`Fri
Avg Paid Circ: 7500
Avg Free Circ: 18000
Audit Company: Sworn/Estimate/Non-Audited
Audit Date: 6 10 2019

SHEPHERDSVILLE

PIONEER NEWS

Corporate/Parent Company: Landmark Community Newspapers
Street Address: 455 N Buckman St
City: Shepherdsville
State: KY
Postal Code: 40165-5902
Office phone: (502) 543-2288
Publication Website: https://www.pioneernews.net/
General E-mail: editor@pioneernews.net
Year Established: 1882
Delivery Methods: Mail`Newsstand`Racks
Own Printing Facility?: Y
Commercial printers?: Y
Mechanical specifications: Type page 13 x 21 1/2; E - 6 cols, 2 1/16, between; A - 6 cols, 2 1/16, between; C - 8 cols, 1 1/2, between.
Published Days: Mon`Wed
Avg Paid Circ: 5300
Audit Company: Sworn/Estimate/Non-Audited
Audit Date: 6 10 2019

SPRINGFIELD

SPRINGFIELD SUN

Corporate/Parent Company: Landmark Community Newspapers
Street Address: 108 Progress Ave
City: Springfield
State: KY
Postal Code: 40069-1400
Office phone: (859) 336-3716
Publication Website: https://www.thespringfieldsun.com/
General E-mail: editor@thespringfieldsun.com
Publisher Name: Alice Walker
Publisher Email: awalker@thespringfieldsun.com
Editor Name: Kelly McKinney
Editor Email: editor@thespringfieldsun.com
Delivery Methods: Mail`Newsstand`Racks
Mechanical specifications: Type page 9.89 x 21 1/2;
Published Days: Wed
Avg Paid Circ: 3500
Audit Company: Sworn/Estimate/Non-Audited
Audit Date: 6 10 2019

STURGIS

STURGIS NEWS

Corporate/Parent Company: CPC Newspaper Group
Street Address: P.O. Box 218
City: Sturgis
State: KY
Postal Code: 42459
Office phone: (270) 318-5038
Publication Website: cpcnewspapers.com
General E-mail: sebreebanner@bellsouth.net
Editor Name: Anthony L. Catlett
Editor Email: tcatlett101@bellsouth.net
Advertising Executive Name: Regina A. Catlett
Advertising Executive Email: rcatlett222@bellsouth.net

TAYLORSVILLE

SPENCER MAGNET

Corporate/Parent Company: Landmark Community Newspapers
Street Address: 100 W Main St
City: Taylorsville
State: KY
Postal Code: 40071-8624
Office phone: (502) 477-2239
Publication Website: https://www.spencermagnet.com/
General E-mail: anna.stcharles.sentinelnews.com
Publisher Name: Anna St.Charles
Publisher Email: anna.stcharles.sentinelnews.com
Editor Name: John Shindlebower
Editor Email: editor@spencermagnet.com
Year Established: 1867
Delivery Methods: Mail`Newsstand`Racks
Published Days: Wed
Avg Paid Circ: 3600
Audit Company: Sworn/Estimate/Non-Audited
Audit Date: 6 10 2019

WEST LIBERTY

LICKING VALLEY COURIER

Street Address: P.O. Box 187
City: West Liberty
State: KY
Postal Code: 41472
Office phone: 606.743.3551
Publication Website: www.thelickingvalleycourier.com
General E-mail: courier@mrtc.com
Publisher Name: Earl Kinner
Editor Name: Miranda Cantrell
Advertising Executive Name: Rick Adkins

WILLIAMSTOWN

GRANT COUNTY NEWS AND EXPRESS

Corporate/Parent Company: Landmark Community Newspapers
Street Address: 1406 N Main St
City: Williamstown
State: KY
Postal Code: 41097-8500
Office phone: (859) 824-3343
Publication Website: https://www.grantky.com
General E-mail: amappler@grantky.com
Publisher Name: Bryan Marshall
Publisher Email: bmarshall@grantky.com
Editor Name: Bryan Marshall
Editor Email: bmarshall@grantky.com
Advertising Executive Name: Anita Appler
Advertising Executive Email: amappler@grantky.com
Year Established: 1906
Delivery Methods: Mail
Own Printing Facility?: N
Commercial printers?: N
Mechanical specifications: Full Page = 9.89" x 21.5" (6 col.) Classified Full page = 8 col. 1 col. ROP = 1.56" 1 col. Class. = 1.14"
Published Days: Mon
Avg Paid Circ: 5000
Avg Free Circ: 12900
Audit Company: Sworn/Estimate/Non-Audited
Audit Date: 6 10 2019

LOUISIANA

ABBEVILLE

ABBEVILLE MERIDIONAL

Corporate/Parent Company: LSN Publishing Company LLC
Street Address: 318 N Main St
City: Abbeville
State: LA
Postal Code: 70510-4608
Office phone: (337) 893-4223
Publication Website: https://www.vermiliontoday.com/
General E-mail: kathy.cormier@vermiliontoday.com
Publisher Name: Katherine E. Cormier
Publisher Email: kathy.cormier@vermiliontoday.com
Editor Name: Christopher P. Rosa
Editor Email: chris.rosa@vermiliontoday.com
Advertising Executive Name: Katherine E. Cormier
Advertising Executive Email: kathy.cormier@vermiliontoday.com
Year Established: 1856
Delivery Methods: Mail`Newsstand`Carrier`Racks
Mechanical specifications: Type page 11 11/16 x 21 1/2; E - 6 cols, 1 4/5, 1/8 between; A - 6 cols, 1 4/5, 1/16 between; C - 9 cols, 1 3/20, 1/8 between.
Published Days: Tues`Wed`Thur`Fri
Weekday Frequency: m
Avg Paid Circ: 5379
Audit Company: Sworn/Estimate/Non-Audited
Audit Date: 7 12 2019

ALEXANDRIA

THE TOWN TALK

Corporate/Parent Company: Gannett
Street Address: 1201 3rd St
City: Alexandria
State: LA
Postal Code: 71301-8246
Office phone: (318) 487-6397
Publication Website: thetowntalk.com
General E-mail: yourmail@thetowntalk.com
Editor Name: Jim Smilie
Editor Email: jsmilie@thetowntalk.com
Editor Phone: 318-487-6348
Advertising Executive Name: Patrick Denofrio
Advertising Executive Email: pdenofrio@localiq.com
Advertising Executive Phone: 337-289-6388
Year Established: 1883
Delivery Methods: Mail`Newsstand`Carrier`Racks
Own Printing Facility?: Y
Commercial printers?: N
Mechanical specifications: Type page 11 5/8 x 21; E - 6 cols, 1 13/16, 1/8 between; A - 6 cols, 1 13/16, 1/8 between; C - 9 cols, 1 13/16, 1/16 between.
Published Days: Mon`Tues`Wed`Thur`Fri`Sat`Sun
Weekday Frequency: m
Saturday Frequency: m
Avg Paid Circ: 10888
Avg Free Circ: 22
Audit Company: AAM
Audit Date: 10 06 2019

ARABI

ST. BERNARD VOICE

Corporate/Parent Company: Georges Media
Street Address: 234 Mehle Street
City: Arabi
State: LA
Postal Code: 70032
Office phone: 504-279-7488
Publication Website: www.thestbernardvoice.com
Publisher Name: Norris Babin
Publisher Email: norris@thestbernardvoice.com
Publisher Phone: 504-279-7488
Editor Name: Edwin Roy
Editor Email: edroy@thestbernardvoice.com
Editor Phone: 504-279-7488
Year Established: 1890
Delivery Methods: Mail`Newsstand`Racks
Mechanical specifications: 11.25 inches wide x 21.5 inches deep six columns 1 column = 1.7361 inches 1 gutter= 0.1667 inches
Published Days: Fri
Avg Paid Circ: 3150
Audit Company: Sworn/Estimate/Non-Audited
Audit Date: 6 10 2019

ARCADIA

BIENVILLE DEMOCRAT

Corporate/Parent Company: Natchitoches Times Newspapers
Street Address: 1952 N Railroad Ave
City: Arcadia
State: LA
Postal Code: 71001-3422
Office phone: (318) 263-2922
Publication Website: https://www.facebook.com/The-Bienville-Democrat-147645275970554/?__tn__=%2Cd%2CP-R&eid=ARBqCLCPvae1fjrFQBcnHw6vdHA6Id2IAbeH_JyvanegGM0BMhJ0_FWtlj64GjllUku4DeV9c7KEPtuN
Mechanical specifications: Type page 13 x 21; E - 6 cols, between.
Published Days: Thur
Avg Paid Circ: 1903
Audit Company: Sworn/Estimate/Non-Audited
Audit Date: 6 10 2019

BASILE

THE BASILE WEEKLY

Corporate/Parent Company: LSN Publishing Company LLC
Street Address: P.O. Box 145
City: Basile
State: LA
Postal Code: 70515
Office phone: (337) 432-6807
Publication Website: https://www.evangelinetoday.com
General E-mail: kathy.gazette@yahoo.com
Publisher Name: Garland Forman
Publisher Email: garland.forman@evangelinetoday.com
Editor Name: Tony Marks
Editor Email: editor@evangelinetoday.com
Advertising Executive Name: Kathy Longino
Advertising Executive Email: kathy.gazette@yahoo.com
Year Established: 1964
Delivery Methods: Mail
Mechanical specifications: Type page 12 1/4 x 21 1/2; E - 6 cols, 2, 1/2 between; A - 6 cols, 2, 1/2 between; C - 6 cols, 2, 1/2 between.
Published Days: Thur
Avg Paid Circ: 800
Audit Company: Sworn/Estimate/Non-Audited
Audit Date: 6 10 2019

BERNICE

THE BANNER

Corporate/Parent Company: Georges Media
Street Address: 227 Boyette RD
City: Bernice
State: LA
Postal Code: 712222
Office phone: 318-285-7424
Publication Website: bernicebanner.weebly.com
General E-mail: bannerlady@oeccwildblue.com
Advertising Executive Name: Danielle Harkins
Advertising Executive Email: danihark@oeccwildblue.com

Non-Daily Newspapers in the U.S.

BUNKIE

BUNKIE RECORD
Corporate/Parent Company: Avoyelles Publishing Company
Street Address: 803 Evergreen Hwy
City: Bunkie
State: LA
Postal Code: 71322
Office phone: (318) 346-7251
Publication Website: https://www.avoyellestoday.com/
General E-mail: newsonline@avoyelles.com
Publisher Name: Randy DeCuir
Advertising Executive Name: Kathie Lipe
Advertising Executive Email: ads@avoyelles.com
Year Established: 1888
Delivery Methods: Mail`Newsstand`Racks
Own Printing Facility?: Y
Published Days: Thur
Avg Paid Circ: 1500
Avg Free Circ: 18000
Audit Company: Sworn/Estimate/Non-Audited
Audit Date: 6 10 2019

CHURCH POINT

CHURCH POINT NEWS
Corporate/Parent Company: LSN Publishing Company LLC
Street Address: 315 North Main Street
City: Church Point
State: LA
Postal Code: 70525
Office phone: (337) 684-5711
Publication Website: https://www.acadiaparishtoday.com/
General E-mail: liz.horecky@churchpointtoday.com
Editor Name: Claudette Olivier
Editor Email: news@churchpointtoday.com
Advertising Executive Name: Liz Horecky
Advertising Executive Email: liz.horecky@churchpointtoday.com

COLFAX

COLFAX CHRONICLE
Street Address: 305 Main Street
City: Colfax
State: LA
Postal Code: 71417
Office phone: (318) 627-3737
Publication Website: www.colfaxchronicle.com

COLUMBIA

CALDWELL WATCHMAN
Street Address: 241 Martin Luther St.
City: Columbia
State: LA
Postal Code: 71418
Office phone: (318) 649-7136
Publication Website: www.caldwellwatchman.com
General E-mail: caldwellwatchman@bellsouth.net
Editor Name: Terri Crockett
Editor Email: caldwelleditor@bellsouth.net
Editor Phone: (318) 649-7136

COVINGTON

ST. TAMMANY FARMER
Corporate/Parent Company: Georges Media
Street Address: 321 North New Hampshire Street
City: Covington
State: LA
Postal Code: 70434
Office phone: 985-892-2323
Publication Website: www.nola.com/news/communities/st_tammany
Editor Name: Peter Kovacs
Editor Email: pkovacs@theadvocate.com
Editor Phone: 225.388.0277
Advertising Executive Name: Connie Settle
Advertising Executive Email: csettle@theadvocate.com
Advertising Executive Phone: 225.388.0250

CROWLEY

THE CROWLEY POST-SIGNAL
Corporate/Parent Company: LSN Publishing Company LLC
Street Address: 602 N Parkerson Ave
City: Crowley
State: LA
Postal Code: 70526-4354
Office phone: (337) 783-3450
Publication Website: https://www.acadiaparishtoday.com/
General E-mail: advertising@crowleytoday.com
Publisher Name: Harold Gonzales
Publisher Email: haroldgonzalesjr@yahoo.com
Editor Name: Steve Bandy
Editor Email: steve.bandy@crowleytoday.com
Advertising Executive Name: Janet Doucet
Advertising Executive Email: advertising@crowleytoday.com
Year Established: 1885
Delivery Methods: Mail`Newsstand`Carrier`Racks
Mechanical specifications: Type page 13 x 21 1/2; E - 6 cols, 1 3/4, 1/8 between; A - 6 cols, 1 3/4, 1/8 between; C - 6 cols, 1 3/4, 1/8 between.
Published Days: Tues`Wed`Thur`Fri`Sun
Weekday Frequency: m
Avg Paid Circ: 4476
Audit Company: Sworn/Estimate/Non-Audited
Audit Date: 7 12 2019

DEQUINCY

CAMERON PARISH PILOT
Corporate/Parent Company: Wise Newspapers, Inc.
Street Address: ??203 Harrison St., P. O. Box 995
City: DeQuincy
State: LA
Postal Code: 70633
Office phone: 800-256-7323
Publication Website: www.cameronpilot.com/whoswho/pilot.htm
General E-mail: dequincynews@centurytel.net
Publisher Name: Jeffra Wise DeViney
Publisher Email: jdeviney@centurytel.net
Editor Name: Dustin Royer
Editor Email: webmaster@cameronpilot.com

EUNICE

THE EUNICE NEWS
Corporate/Parent Company: LSN Publishing Company LLC
Street Address: 465 Aymond St
City: Eunice
State: LA
Postal Code: 70535
Office phone: (337) 457-3061
Publication Website: https://www.eunicetoday.com/
General E-mail: misty.deaville@eunicetoday.com
Publisher Name: Darrell J. Guillory
Publisher Email: darrell.guillory@eunicetoday.com
Editor Name: Harlan Kirgan
Editor Email: harlan.kirgan@eunicetoday.com
Advertising Executive Name: Misty D. Gilley
Advertising Executive Email: misty.deaville@eunicetoday.com
Year Established: 1903
Delivery Methods: Mail`Newsstand`Carrier`Racks
Published Days: Thur`Sun
Avg Paid Circ: 3000
Audit Company: Sworn/Estimate/Non-Audited
Audit Date: 6 10 2019

FRANKLIN

FRANKLIN BANNER-TRIBUNE
Corporate/Parent Company: LSN Publishing Company LLC
Street Address: P.O. Box 566
City: Franklin
State: LA
Postal Code: 70538
Office phone: (337) 828-3706
Publication Website: https://www.daily-review.com/
General E-mail: classifieds@banner-tribune.com
Publisher Name: Allan R. Von Werder
Publisher Email: pub@banner-tribune.com
Editor Name: Roger Emile Stouff
Editor Email: editor@banner-tribune.com
Advertising Executive Name: Tanya Sonnier
Advertising Executive Email: classifieds@banner-tribune.com
Year Established: 1885
Delivery Methods: Mail`Newsstand`Carrier
Mechanical specifications: 11.75 w x 21 h
Published Days: Mon`Tues`Wed`Thur`Fri
Weekday Frequency: e
Avg Paid Circ: 3500
Avg Free Circ: 1500
Audit Company: USPS
Audit Date: 28 09 2012

FRANKLIN

ST. MARY AND FRANKLIN BANNER-TRIBUNE
Corporate/Parent Company: Georges Media
Street Address: P.O. Box 566
City: Franklin
State: LA
Postal Code: 70538
Office phone: 337-828-3706
Publication Website: www.stmarynow.com
Publisher Name: Allan Von Werder
Publisher Email: pub@daily-review.com
Editor Name: Bill Decker
Editor Email: bdecker@daily-review.com

GUEYDAN

GUEYDAN JOURNAL
Corporate/Parent Company: LSN Publishing Company LLC
Street Address: 311 Main St
City: Gueydan
State: LA
Postal Code: 70542-3631
Office phone: (337) 536-6016
Publication Website: https://www.vermiliontoday.com/
General E-mail: judy.leblanc@vermiliontoday.com
Delivery Methods: Mail
Own Printing Facility?: Y
Commercial printers?: Y
Mechanical specifications: Type page 13 x 21 1/2.
Published Days: Thur
Avg Paid Circ: 1200
Avg Free Circ: 15
Audit Company: Sworn/Estimate/Non-Audited
Audit Date: 6 10 2019

KAPLAN

THE KAPLAN HERALD
Corporate/Parent Company: LSN Publishing Company LLC
Street Address: 219 N Cushing Ave
City: Kaplan
State: LA
Postal Code: 70548-4119
Office phone: (337) 643-8002
Publication Website: https://www.vermiliontoday.com/
General E-mail: ejbheart@hotmail.com
Publisher Name: Katherine E. Cormier
Publisher Email: kathy.cormier@vermiliontoday.com
Advertising Executive Name: Elizabeth Breaux
Advertising Executive Email: ejbheart@hotmail.com
Delivery Methods: Mail
Published Days: Wed
Avg Paid Circ: 2000
Audit Company: Sworn/Estimate/Non-Audited
Audit Date: 6 10 2019

KINDER

KINDER COURIER NEWS
Corporate/Parent Company: LSN Publishing Company LLC
Street Address: 1024 3rd Ave
City: Kinder
State: LA
Postal Code: 70648-3413
Office phone: (337) 738-5642
Publication Website: https://www.kindernow.com/
Year Established: 1979
Delivery Methods: Mail`Newsstand
Mechanical specifications: Type page 11 3/5 x 21 1/2; E - 6 cols, 1 4/5, 1/8 between; A - 6 cols, 1 4/5, 1/8 between; C - 9 cols, 1 1/5, 1/8 between.
Published Days: Thur
Avg Paid Circ: 880
Audit Company: Sworn/Estimate/Non-Audited
Audit Date: 6 10 2019

LOUISIANA

BAYOU PIONEER
Corporate/Parent Company: LSN Publishing Company LLC
Street Address: 3409 Highway 70 S Pierre Part
City: Louisiana
State: LA
Postal Code: 70339
Office phone: (985) 252-0501
Publication Website: www.bayoujournal.com
General E-mail: bayoujournal@teche.net
Editor Name: Michelle Baker
Editor Email: bayoujournalmichelle@teche.net
Editor Phone: (985) 252-0501

BAYOU PIONEER
Street Address: 3409 Highway 70 S Pierre Part
City: Louisiana
State: LA
Postal Code: 70339
Office phone: (985) 252-0501
Publication Website: www.bayoujournal.com
General E-mail: bayoujournal@teche.net
Editor Name: Michelle Baker
Editor Email: bayoujournalmichelle@teche.net
Editor Phone: (985) 252-0501

CALDWELL WATCHMAN-OOB
Corporate/Parent Company: LSN Publishing Company LLC
Street Address: 241 Martin Luther St.
City: Columbia
State: LA
Postal Code: 71418
Office phone: (318) 649-7136
Publication Website: https://www.caldwellwatchman.com/
Editor Name: Terri Crockett
Editor Email: caldwelleditor@bellsouth.net

LUTCHER

NEWS EXAMINER-ENTERPRISE

Corporate/Parent Company: Georges Media
Street Address: 2290 Texas St.
City: Lutcher
State: LA
Postal Code: 70071
Office phone: (225) 869-5784
Publication Website: www.stjamesparishtoday.com
Editor Name: David Reynaud
Editor Email: ruhrvalley@earthlink.net
Editor Phone: 225-869-5784
Advertising Executive Name: Jennifer Glidden
Advertising Executive Email: jennglidden985@gmail.com
Advertising Executive Phone: 985-224-9718

MANSFIELD

THE ENTERPRISE & INTERSTATE PROGRESS

Corporate/Parent Company: Natchitoches Times Newspapers
Street Address: 202 Adams St
City: Mansfield
State: LA
Postal Code: 71052-2430
Office phone: (318) 872-4120
Publication Website: https://www.mansfieldenterprise.com/contact
General E-mail: advertising@mansfieldenterprise.com
Editor Name: Raley Pellittieri
Editor Email: news@mansfieldenterprise.com
Advertising Executive Name: Martha Rivers
Advertising Executive Email: advertising@mansfieldenterprise.com
Year Established: 1889
Delivery Methods: Mail`Newsstand
Own Printing Facility?: Y
Mechanical specifications: Type page 13 x 21; E - 6 cols, 2 1/16, 1/8 between; A - 6 cols, 2 1/16, 1/8 between; C - 8 cols, 1 8/2, 1/8 between.
Published Days: Thur
Avg Paid Circ: 4000
Audit Company: Sworn/Estimate/Non-Audited
Audit Date: 6 10 2019

MARKSVILLE

AVOYELLES JOURNAL

Corporate/Parent Company: Avoyelles Publishing Company
Street Address: PO Box 36
City: Marksville
State: LA
Postal Code: 71351
Office phone: (318) 253-5413
Publication Website: https://www.avoyellestoday.com/
General E-mail: newsonline@avoyelles.com
Publisher Name: Randy DeCuir
Advertising Executive Name: Kathie Lipe
Advertising Executive Email: ads@avoyelles.com
Advertising Executive Phone: (318) 253-5413
Year Established: 1978
Delivery Methods: Mail
Own Printing Facility?: Y
Published Days: Wed`Sun
Avg Free Circ: 16000
Audit Company: Sworn/Estimate/Non-Audited
Audit Date: 6 10 2019

THE MARKSVILLE WEEKLY NEWS

Corporate/Parent Company: Avoyelles Publishing Company
Street Address: PO Box 36
City: Marksville
State: LA
Postal Code: 71351-0036
Office phone: (318) 253-5413
Publication Website: https://www.avoyellestoday.com/
General E-mail: newsonline@avoyelles.com
Publisher Name: Randy DeCuir
Advertising Executive Name: Kathie Lipe
Advertising Executive Email: ads@avoyelles.com
Delivery Methods: Mail
Own Printing Facility?: Y
Published Days: Thur
Avg Paid Circ: 3500
Audit Company: Sworn/Estimate/Non-Audited
Audit Date: 6 10 2019

WEEKLY NEWS

Street Address: 105 N Main St
City: Marksville
State: LA
Postal Code: 71351
Office phone: (318) 253-9247
Publication Website: www.avoyellestoday.com
Editor Name: Randy DeCuir
Editor Email: newsonline@avoyelles.com
Advertising Executive Name: Marissa DeCuir
Advertising Executive Email: marissa@avoyelles.com

MORGAN CITY

THE DAILY REVIEW

Corporate/Parent Company: LSN Publishing Company LLC
Street Address: 1014 Front St
City: Morgan City
State: LA
Postal Code: 70380-3226
Office phone: (985) 384-8370
Publication Website: https://www.daily-review.com/
General E-mail: advertising@daily-review.com
Publisher Name: Allan Von Werder
Publisher Email: pub@daily-review.com
Editor Name: Bill Decker
Editor Email: bdecker@daily-review.com
Advertising Executive Email: advertising@daily-review.com
Year Established: 1872
Mechanical specifications: Type page 13 x 21 1/2; E - 6 cols, 2 1/16, 1/8 between; A - 6 cols, 2 1/16, 1/8 between; C - 8 cols, 1 1/2, 1/8 between.
Published Days: Mon`Tues`Wed`Thur`Fri
Weekday Frequency: e
Avg Paid Circ: 5946
Audit Company: Sworn/Estimate/Non-Audited
Audit Date: 7 12 2019

OAK GROVE

THE WEST CARROLL GAZETTE

Corporate/Parent Company: LSN Publishing Company LLC
Street Address: 512 S Constitution Ave
City: Oak Grove
State: LA
Postal Code: 71263-2514
Office phone: (318) 428-3207
Publication Website: https://www.westcarrollgazette.com/
Year Established: 1910
Delivery Methods: Mail
Mechanical specifications: Type page 13 x 21; E - 4 cols, 3 1/8, between; A - 6 cols, 2, between; C - 9 cols, 1 5/16, between.
Published Days: Wed
Avg Paid Circ: 2000
Avg Free Circ: 100
Audit Company: Sworn/Estimate/Non-Audited
Audit Date: 6 10 2019

OAKDALE

THE OAKDALE JOURNAL

Corporate/Parent Company: LSN Publishing Company LLC
Street Address: 231 E 6th Ave
City: Oakdale
State: LA
Postal Code: 71463-2617
Office phone: (318) 335-0635
Publication Website: https://www.oakdaletoday.com/
Year Established: 1913
Delivery Methods: Mail
Own Printing Facility?: Y
Published Days: Thur
Avg Paid Circ: 1700
Avg Free Circ: 12939
Audit Company: Sworn/Estimate/Non-Audited
Audit Date: 6 10 2019

PIERRE PART

THE BAYOU JOURNAL

Corporate/Parent Company: LSN Publishing Company LLC
Street Address: 3409 Highway 70 S
City: Pierre Part
State: LA
Postal Code: 70339
Office phone: (985) 252-0501
Publication Website: https://www.bayoujournal.com/
General E-mail: tracy@bayoujournal.com
Publisher Name: Tracy Hebert
Publisher Email: tracy@bayoujournal.com

PLAQUEMINE

PLAQUEMINE POST SOUTH

Street Address: 23520 Eden St. Suite E
City: Plaquemine
State: LA
Postal Code: 70764
Office phone: (225) 687-3288
Publication Website: www.postsouth.com
Editor Name: Greg Fischer
Editor Email: gfischer@weeklycitizen.com
Editor Phone: 225.687.3288
Advertising Executive Name: Crystal Barrett
Advertising Executive Email: cbarrett@gatehousemedia.com
Advertising Executive Phone: 225.644.6397

RAYNE

THE RAYNE-ACADIAN TRIBUNE

Corporate/Parent Company: LSN Publishing Company LLC
Street Address: 108 N Adams Ave
City: Rayne
State: LA
Postal Code: 70578-5918
Office phone: (337) 334-3186
Publication Website: https://www.acadiaparishtoday.com/
General E-mail: jah1126@yahoo.com
Editor Name: Lisa Soileaux
Editor Email: raynenewslife@cox-internet.com
Advertising Executive Name: Josie Henry
Advertising Executive Email: jah1126@yahoo.com
Year Established: 1904
Delivery Methods: Mail`Newsstand`Carrier
Own Printing Facility?: Y
Mechanical specifications: Type page 11 3/5 x 21 1/2; E - 6 cols, 1 4/5, between; A - 6 cols, 2 1/16, between; C - 9 cols, 2 1/16, between.
Published Days: Thur
Published Other: First Sunday of each month
Avg Paid Circ: 4105
Avg Free Circ: 8400
Audit Company: Sworn/Estimate/Non-Audited
Audit Date: 6 10 2019

RAYVILLE

RICHLAND BEACON-NEWS

Corporate/Parent Company: LSN Publishing Company LLC
Street Address: P.O. BOX 209
City: Rayville
State: LA
Postal Code: 71269
Office phone: (318) 728-6467
Publication Website: https://www.richlandtoday.com/
Year Established: 1868
Mechanical specifications: Type page 13 x 21; E - 6 cols, 2 1/16, 1/6 between; A - 6 cols, 2 1/16, 1/6 between; C - 9 cols, 1 1/4, 1/6 between.
Published Days: Thur
Avg Paid Circ: 3000
Avg Free Circ: 10000
Audit Company: Sworn/Estimate/Non-Audited
Audit Date: 6 10 2019

SAINT MARTINVILLE

TECHE NEWS

Corporate/Parent Company: LSN Publishing Company LLC
Street Address: 214 N Main St, P.O. Box 69
City: Saint Martinville
State: LA
Postal Code: 70582-4028
Office phone: (337) 394-6232
Publication Website: https://www.techetoday.com/
General E-mail: advertise@techetoday.com
Publisher Name: Mary Terry
Publisher Email: mary.terry@techetoday.com
Advertising Executive Name: Kristy Bourque
Advertising Executive Email: advertise@techetoday.com
Year Established: 1886
Delivery Methods: Mail
Published Days: Wed
Audit Company: Sworn/Estimate/Non-Audited
Audit Date: 6 10 2019

VILLE PLATTE

THE MAMOU ACADIAN PRESS

Corporate/Parent Company: LSN Publishing Company LLC
Street Address: 145 Court Street
City: Ville Platte
State: LA
Postal Code: 70586
Office phone: (337) 363-3939
Publication Website: https://www.evangelinetoday.com/
General E-mail: kathy.gazette@yahoo.com
Publisher Name: Garland Forman
Publisher Email: garland.forman@evangelinetoday.com
Advertising Executive Name: Kathy Longino
Advertising Executive Email: kathy.gazette@yahoo.com
Delivery Methods: Mail
Mechanical specifications: Type page 13 x 21 1/2; E - 6 cols, between; A - 6 cols, between; C - 9 cols, between.
Published Days: Tues
Avg Free Circ: 3000
Audit Company: Sworn/Estimate/Non-Audited
Audit Date: 6 10 2019

VILLE PLATTE GAZETTE

Corporate/Parent Company: LSN Publishing Company LLC
Street Address: 145 Court St
City: Ville Platte
State: LA
Postal Code: 70586-4409
Office phone: (337) 363-3939
Publication Website: https://www.villeplattetoday.com/
General E-mail: kathy.gazette@yahoo.com
Publisher Name: Garland Forman
Publisher Email: garland.forman@evangelinetoday.com
Advertising Executive Name: Kathy Longino
Advertising Executive Email: kathy.gazette@yahoo.com

Non-Daily Newspapers in the U.S.

Year Established: 1913
Delivery Methods: Mail`Carrier`Racks
Mechanical specifications: Type page 12 1/2 x 22; E - 6 cols, 1 4/5, 1/6 between; A - 6 cols, 1 4/5, 1/6 between; C - 9 cols, 1 3/16, between.
Published Days: Thur`Sun
Avg Paid Circ: 3000
Audit Company: Sworn/Estimate/Non-Audited
Audit Date: 6 10 2019

WINNFIELD

WINN PARISH ENTERPRISE-NEWS AMERICAN

Corporate/Parent Company: Natchitoches Times Newspapers
Street Address: P.O. Box 750
City: Winnfield
State: LA
Postal Code: 71483
Office phone: (318) 628-2712
Publication Website: https://www.winnparishenterprise.com/
General E-mail: advertising@winnparishenterprise.com
Advertising Executive Name: Shana Chandler
Advertising Executive Email: adsales@winnparishenterprise.com
Year Established: 1924
Delivery Methods: Mail
Own Printing Facility?: Y
Mechanical specifications: Type page 13 x 21; E - 6 cols, 2, 1/4 between; A - 6 cols, 2, between; C - 8 cols, 1 1/2, between.
Published Days: Wed
Avg Paid Circ: 3995
Avg Free Circ: 75
Audit Company: Sworn/Estimate/Non-Audited
Audit Date: 6 10 2019

MASSACHUSETTS

BARRE

BARRE GAZETTE

Corporate/Parent Company: Turley Publications, Inc.
Street Address: 5 Exchange St
City: Barre
State: MA
Postal Code: 01005-8702
Office phone: (978) 355-6274
Publication Website: http://barregazette.turley.com/
General E-mail: edowner@turley.com
Editor Name: Ellenor Downer
Editor Email: edowner@turley.com
Advertising Executive Name: Tim Mara
Advertising Executive Email: tmara@turley.com
Year Established: 1834
Delivery Methods: Mail
Own Printing Facility?: Y
Commercial printers?: Y
Published Days: Thur
Avg Paid Circ: 2666
Audit Company: Sworn/Estimate/Non-Audited
Audit Date: 6 10 2019

BELCHERTOWN

THE SENTINEL

Corporate/Parent Company: Lee Enterprises
Street Address: 1 Main St #100
City: Belchertown
State: MA
Postal Code: 01007-8829
Office phone: (413) 323-5999
Publication Website: http://sentinel.turley.com/
General E-mail: cgriswold@turley.com
Editor Name: Wyatt Aloisio
Editor Email: waloisio@turley.com

Editor Phone: (413) 283-8393
Advertising Executive Name: Maureen McGarrett Hall
Advertising Executive Email: mmcgarrett@turley.com
Advertising Executive Phone: (413) 323-5999
Year Established: 1915
Delivery Methods: Mail`Racks
Own Printing Facility?: Y
Commercial printers?: Y
Mechanical specifications: Type page 10 x 16; E - 6 cols, 1 1/2, between.
Published Days: Thur
Avg Free Circ: 10054
Audit Company: Sworn/Estimate/Non-Audited
Audit Date: 6 10 2019
Total Circulation: 6500

BOSTON

THE BEACON HILL TIMES

Street Address: 385 Broadway, Suite 105
City: Boston
State: MA
Postal Code: 02114-4509
Office phone: (781) 485-0588
Publication Website: https://beaconhilltimes.com/
General E-mail: webmaster@beaconhillonline.com
Editor Name: Stephen Quigley
Editor Email: stephen.quigley@reverejournal.com
Year Established: 1995
Mechanical specifications: Type page 10 x 15 3/8; E - 5 cols, 1 7/8, between.
Published Days: Tues
Avg Free Circ: 10500
Audit Company: Sworn/Estimate/Non-Audited
Audit Date: 6 10 2019
Total Circulation: 146

BROCKTON

EAST BRIDGEWATER STAR

Street Address: 1324 Belmont St., Unit 102
City: Brockton
State: MA
Postal Code: 2301
Office phone: (508) 427-4000
Publication Website: https://bridgewatereast.wickedlocal.com/
General E-mail: features@enterprisenews.com
Editor Name: Steve Damish
Editor Email: sdamish@enterprisenews.com
Editor Phone: (617) 786-4022
Advertising Executive Email: salesteam@wickedlocal.com
Total Circulation: 2666

HANSON TOWN CRIER

Street Address: 1324 Belmont St., Unit 102
City: Brockton
State: MA
Postal Code: 2301
Office phone: (508) 427-4000
Publication Website: https://hanson.wickedlocal.com/
General E-mail: features@enterprisenews.com
Editor Name: Steve Damish
Editor Email: sdamish@enterprisenews.com
Editor Phone: (617) 786-4022
Advertising Executive Email: salesteam@wickedlocal.com

THE LAKEVILLE CALL

Street Address: 1324 Belmont St., Unit 102
City: Brockton
State: MA
Postal Code: 2301
Office phone: (508) 427-4000
Publication Website: https://lakeville.

wickedlocal.com/
General E-mail: features@enterprisenews.com
Editor Name: Steve Damish
Editor Email: sdamish@enterprisenews.com
Editor Phone: (617) 786-4022
Advertising Executive Email: salesteam@wickedlocal.com
Delivery Methods: Mail`Racks
Published Days: Wed
Audit Company: Sworn/Estimate/Non-Audited
Audit Date: 6 10 2019

WEST BRIDGEWATER TIMES

Street Address: 1324 Belmont St., Unit 102
City: Brockton
State: MA
Postal Code: 2301
Office phone: (508) 427-4000
Publication Website: https://bridgewaterwest.wickedlocal.com/
General E-mail: features@enterprisenews.com
Editor Name: Steve Damish
Editor Email: sdamish@enterprisenews.com
Editor Phone: (617) 786-4022
Advertising Executive Email: salesteam@wickedlocal.com
Total Circulation: 4500

WHITMAN TIMES

Street Address: 1324 Belmont St., Unit 102
City: Brockton
State: MA
Postal Code: 2301
Office phone: (508) 427-4000
Publication Website: https://whitman.wickedlocal.com/
Advertising Executive Email: classifieds@wickedlocal.com
Total Circulation: 3317

CHICOPEE

THE HOLYOKE SUN

Corporate/Parent Company: Turley Publications, Inc.
Street Address: 333 Front St
City: Chicopee
State: MA
Postal Code: 01013-3194
Office phone: (413) 536-5333
Publication Website: https://sun.turley.com/
General E-mail: sun@turley.com
Editor Name: Lisa Redmond
Editor Email: thesun@turley.com
Editor Phone: (413) 536-5333
Advertising Executive Name: Maureen McGarrett
Advertising Executive Email: mmcgarrett@turley.com
Advertising Executive Phone: (413) 323-5999
Year Established: 1995
Delivery Methods: Racks
Own Printing Facility?: Y
Published Days: Fri
Avg Free Circ: 10000
Audit Company: Sworn/Estimate/Non-Audited
Audit Date: 6 10 2019
Total Circulation: 2725

FALMOUTH

THE BOURNE ENTERPRISE

Corporate/Parent Company: Enterprise Newspapers
Street Address: 50 Depot Ave
City: Falmouth
State: MA
Postal Code: 02540-2302
Office phone: (508) 548-4700
Publication Website: https://www.capenews.net/bourne/
General E-mail: newsroom@capenews.net

Editor Name: James Kinsella
Editor Email: kinsella@capenews.net
Editor Phone: (508) 548-4700, ext. 243
Advertising Executive Email: ads@capenews.net
Year Established: 1895
Published Days: Thur
Audit Company: Sworn/Estimate/Non-Audited
Audit Date: 6 10 2019
Total Circulation: 8000

THE FALMOUTH ENTERPRISE

Corporate/Parent Company: Enterprise Newspapers
Street Address: 50 Depot Ave
City: Falmouth
State: MA
Postal Code: 02540-2302
Office phone: (508) 548-4700
Publication Website: https://www.capenews.net/falmouth/
General E-mail: newsroom@capenews.net
Publisher Name: Bill Hough
Publisher Email: bhough@capenews.net
Publisher Phone: (508) 548-4700, ext. 214
Editor Name: Bill Hough
Editor Email: bhough@capenews.net
Editor Phone: (508) 548-4700, ext. 214
Year Established: 1895
Delivery Methods: Mail`Newsstand`Carrier`Racks
Published Days: Fri
Avg Paid Circ: 7759
Avg Free Circ: 66
Audit Company: AAM
Audit Date: 30 09 2016

THE MASHPEE ENTERPRISE

Corporate/Parent Company: Enterprise Newspapers
Street Address: 50 Depot Ave
City: Falmouth
State: MA
Postal Code: 02540-2302
Office phone: (508) 548-4700
Publication Website: https://www.capenews.net/mashpee/
General E-mail: entertainment@capenews.net
Editor Name: Jim Kinsella
Editor Email: kinsella@capenews.net
Editor Phone: (508) 548-4700, ext. 243
Year Established: 1895
Published Days: Fri
Audit Company: Sworn/Estimate/Non-Audited
Audit Date: 6 10 2019
Total Circulation: 12500

THE SANDWICH ENTERPRISE

Corporate/Parent Company: Enterprise Newspapers
Street Address: 50 Depot Ave
City: Falmouth
State: MA
Postal Code: 02540-2302
Office phone: (508) 548-4700
Publication Website: https://www.capenews.net/sandwich/
General E-mail: newsroom@capenews.net
Editor Name: John Paradise
Editor Email: paradise@capenews.net
Editor Phone: (508) 548-4700, ext. 228
Year Established: 1895
Published Days: Fri
Audit Company: Sworn/Estimate/Non-Audited
Audit Date: 6 10 2019

FEEDING HILLS

AGAWAM ADVERTISER NEWS

Corporate/Parent Company: Turley Publications, Inc.

Street Address: 23 Southwick St
City: Feeding Hills
State: MA
Postal Code: 1030
Office phone: (413) 786-7747
Publication Website: https://agawamadvertisernews.turley.com/
General E-mail: cgriswold@turley.com
Editor Name: Michael J. Ballway
Editor Email: mballway@turley.com
Advertising Executive Name: John Baskin
Advertising Executive Email: jbaskin@turley.com
Advertising Executive Phone: (413) 786-7747
Year Established: 1965
Delivery Methods: Mail`Newsstand
Own Printing Facility?: Y
Published Days: Thur
Avg Paid Circ: 6500
Audit Company: Sworn/Estimate/Non-Audited
Audit Date: 6 10 2019
Total Circulation: 751

SOUTHWICK SUFFIELD NEWS

Corporate/Parent Company: Turley Publications, Inc.
Street Address: 23 Southwick St
City: Feeding Hills
State: MA
Postal Code: 01030-2023
Office phone: (413) 786-7747
Year Established: 1967
Delivery Methods: Racks
Own Printing Facility?: Y
Published Days: Fri
Avg Free Circ: 9000
Audit Company: Sworn/Estimate/Non-Audited
Audit Date: 6 10 2019

FRAMINGHAM

ALLSTON-BRIGHTON TAB

Street Address: 1 Speen St
City: Framingham
State: MA
Postal Code: 1701
Office phone: (781) 433-6700
Publication Website: https://allston.wickedlocal.com/
General E-mail: allston-brighton@wickedlocal.com
Editor Name: Anne Brennan
Editor Email: abrennan@wickedlocal.com
Editor Phone: (508) 626-3871
Advertising Executive Email: classified@wickedlocal.com
Year Established: 1996
Published Days: Fri
Avg Paid Circ: 146
Audit Company: Sworn/Estimate/Non-Audited
Audit Date: 6 10 2019
Total Circulation: 1304

NORWOOD BULLETIN

Corporate/Parent Company: Gannett Company, Inc.
Street Address: 1 Speen St., Suite 200
City: Framingham
State: MA
Postal Code: 0 1701
Office phone: 781-433-6700
Publication Website: norwood.wickedlocal.com
General E-mail: norwood@wickedlocal.com

WALPOLE TIMES

Corporate/Parent Company: Gannett Company, Inc.
Street Address: 1 Speen St., Suite 200
City: Framingham
State: MA
Postal Code: 0 1701

Office phone: 781-433-6700
Publication Website: walpole.wickedlocal.com
General E-mail: walpole@wickedlocal.com
Editor Name: Alison Bosma
Delivery Methods: Mail`Newsstand`Racks
Mechanical specifications: Type page 12 7/8 x 21; E - 6 cols, between; A - 6 cols, between; C - 10 cols, between.
Published Days: Thur
Avg Paid Circ: 460
Audit Company: AAM
Audit Date: 31 12 2017

HUNTINGTON

COUNTRY JOURNAL

Corporate/Parent Company: Turley Publications, Inc.
Street Address: 5 Main St
City: Huntington
State: MA
Postal Code: 01050-9678
Office phone: (413) 667-3211
Publication Website: http://countryjournal.turley.com/
General E-mail: countryjournal@turley.com
Editor Name: Mike Ballway
Editor Email: countryjournal@turley.com
Editor Phone: (413) 667-3211
Advertising Executive Name: John Baskin
Advertising Executive Email: jbaskin@turley.com
Year Established: 1979
Delivery Methods: Mail`Newsstand
Mechanical specifications: Type page 10 1/4 x 16; E - 5 cols, 1 11/12, 1/6 between; A - 5 cols, 1 11/12, 1/6 between; C - 6 cols, 1 7/12, 5/36 between.
Published Days: Thur
Avg Free Circ: 3317
Audit Company: Sworn/Estimate/Non-Audited
Audit Date: 6 10 2019

HYANNIS

BOURNE COURIER

Corporate/Parent Company: Gannett
Street Address: 319 Main Street
City: Hyannis
State: MA
Postal Code: 0 2601
Office phone: 508-375-4925
Publication Website: bourne.wickedlocal.com
General E-mail: classifieds@wickedlocal.com
Publisher Name: Peter Meyer
Publisher Email: pmeyer@capecodonline.com
Publisher Phone: 508-862-1111
Editor Name: Paul Pronovost
Editor Email: ppronovost@capecodonline.com
Editor Phone: 508-862-1166
Advertising Executive Name: Molly Evans
Delivery Methods: Mail`Newsstand`Racks
Published Days: Wed
Audit Company: Sworn/Estimate/Non-Audited
Audit Date: 6 10 2019
Total Circulation: 1275

SANDWICH BROADSIDER

Corporate/Parent Company: Gannett
Street Address: 319 Main St
City: Hyannis
State: MA
Postal Code: 2601
Office phone: (508) 375-4925
Publication Website: https://sandwich.wickedlocal.com/
General E-mail: mevans@capecodonline.com
Publisher Name: Peter Meyer
Publisher Email: pmeyer@capecodonline.com
Publisher Phone: (508) 862-1111
Editor Name: Paul Pronovost
Editor Email: ppronovost@capecodonline.com
Editor Phone: (508) 862-1166
Advertising Executive Name: Molly Evans
Advertising Executive Email: mevans@capecodonline.com
Advertising Executive Phone: (508) 862-1377
Year Established: 2007
Published Days: Wed
Avg Paid Circ: 2332
Audit Company: Sworn/Estimate/Non-Audited
Audit Date: 6 10 2019

THE SANDWICH BROADSIDER

Corporate/Parent Company: Gannett
Street Address: 319 Main Street
City: Hyannis
State: MA
Postal Code: 0 2601
Office phone: 508-375-4925
Publication Website: sandwich.wickedlocal.com
General E-mail: classifieds@wickedlocal.com
Publisher Name: Peter Meyer
Publisher Email: pmeyer@capecodonline.com
Publisher Phone: 508-862-1111
Editor Name: Paul Pronovost
Editor Email: ppronovost@capecodonline.com
Editor Phone: 508-862-1166
Advertising Executive Name: Molly Evans

JAMAICA PLAIN

JAMAICA PLAIN CITIZEN

Street Address: 7 Harris Avenue
City: Jamaica Plain
State: MA
Postal Code: 2130
Office phone: (617) 524-2626
Publication Website: http://jamaicaplaingazette.com/
General E-mail: classifieds@jamaicaplaingazette.com
Editor Name: Stephen Quigley
Editor Email: stephen.quigley@reverejournal.com
Advertising Executive Name: Patricia DeOliveira
Advertising Executive Email: localads@jamaicaplaingazette.com

LEXINGTON

CAMBRIDGE CHRONICLE

Corporate/Parent Company: Gannett Company, Inc.
Street Address: 9 Meriam Street
City: Lexington
State: MA
Postal Code: 0 2420
Office phone: 781-433-6700
Publication Website: cambridge.wickedlocal.com
General E-mail: cambridge@wickedlocal.com
Editor Name: Amy Saltzman
Editor Email: asaltzman@wickedlocal.com
Editor Phone: 781-674-7733
Advertising Executive Name: John Lamp
Total Circulation: 1064

WATERTOWN TAB & PRESS

Corporate/Parent Company: Gannett
Street Address: 9 Meriam Street
City: Lexington
State: MA
Postal Code: 0 2420
Office phone: 781-433-6700
Publication Website: watertown.wickedlocal.com
General E-mail: watertown@wickedlocal.com
Editor Name: Kathleen Cordeiro
Editor Email: kcordeiro@wickedlocal.com
Editor Phone: 978-371-5736
Advertising Executive Name: Jenn Mann
Total Circulation: 2332

NEW BEDFORD

FALL RIVER SPIRIT

Corporate/Parent Company: Gannett Company, Inc.
Street Address: 25 Elm St.
City: New Bedford
State: MA
Postal Code: 0 2740
Office phone: (508) 979-4378
Publication Website: www.southcoasttoday.com/spirit
Editor Name: Mick Colageo
Editor Email: editor@fallriverspirit.com

NORWELL

PEMBROKE MARINER & EXPRESS

Street Address: 600 Cordwainer Drive
City: Norwell
State: MA
Postal Code: 2061
Office phone: (781) 837-4500
Publication Website: https://pembroke.wickedlocal.com/
General E-mail: pembroke@wickedlocal.com
Publisher Name: Mark Olivieri
Publisher Email: molivieri@wickedlocal.com
Publisher Phone: (781) 837-4504
Advertising Executive Name: Chris Avis
Advertising Executive Email: cavis@wickedlocal.com
Advertising Executive Phone: (781) 837-4503
Year Established: 1983
Own Printing Facility?: Y
Commercial printers?: Y
Published Days: Fri
Avg Paid Circ: 1275
Audit Company: Sworn/Estimate/Non-Audited
Audit Date: 6 10 2019
Total Circulation: 9000

PEMBROKE MARINER-REPORTER

Corporate/Parent Company: Gannett Company, Inc.
Street Address: 600 Cordwainer Drive
City: Norwell
State: MA
Postal Code: 0 2061
Office phone: 781-837-4500
Publication Website: pembroke.wickedlocal.com
General E-mail: pembroke@wickedlocal.com
Publisher Name: Mark Olivieri
Publisher Email: molivieri@wickedlocal.com
Publisher Phone: 781-837-4504
Editor Name: Gregory Mathis
Editor Email: gmathis@wickedlocal.com
Editor Phone: 508-591-6618
Advertising Executive Name: Chris Avis

ROCKLAND STANDARD

Street Address: 600 Cordwainer Drive
City: Norwell
State: MA
Postal Code: 2061
Office phone: (781) 837-4500
Publication Website: https://rockland.wickedlocal.com/
General E-mail: rockland@wickedlocal.com
Publisher Name: Mark Olivieri
Publisher Email: molivieri@wickedlocal.com
Publisher Phone: (781) 837-4504
Advertising Executive Name: Rafal Lipowicz
Advertising Executive Email: classifieds@wickedlocal.com
Own Printing Facility?: Y
Commercial printers?: Y
Mechanical specifications: Type page 10 9/16 x 16; E - 6 cols, between; A - 6 cols, between; C - 7 cols, between.
Published Days: Thur

Non-Daily Newspapers in the U.S.

Avg Free Circ: 1064
Audit Company: Sworn/Estimate/Non-Audited
Audit Date: 6 10 2019
Total Circulation: 10500

ORLEANS

HARWICH ORACLE

Street Address: 5 Namskaket Rd
City: Orleans
State: MA
Postal Code: 02653-02645
Office phone: (508) 247-3266
Publication Website: https://harwich.wickedlocal.com/
General E-mail: salesteam@wickedlocal.com
Publisher Name: Mark Olivieri
Publisher Email: molivieri@wickedlocal.com
Publisher Phone: (508) 247-3260
Editor Name: Carol Dumas
Editor Email: cdumas@wickedlocal.com
Editor Phone: (508) 247-3255
Advertising Executive Name: Louise Porter
Advertising Executive Email: lporter@wickedlocal.com
Advertising Executive Phone: (508) 247-3225
Year Established: 1986
Own Printing Facility?: Y
Commercial printers?: Y
Published Days: Wed
Avg Paid Circ: 1304
Audit Company: Sworn/Estimate/Non-Audited
Audit Date: 6 10 2019

UPPER CAPE CODDER

Street Address: 5 Namskaket Rd
City: Orleans
State: MA
Postal Code: 02653-02645
Office phone: (508) 247-3266
Publication Website: https://capecod.wickedlocal.com/
General E-mail: mevans@capecodonline.com
Publisher Name: Peter Meyer
Publisher Email: pmeyer@capecodonline.com
Publisher Phone: (508) 862-1111
Editor Name: Paul Pronovost
Editor Email: ppronovost@capecodonline.com
Editor Phone: (508) 862-1166
Advertising Executive Name: Molly Evans
Advertising Executive Email: mevans@capecodonline.com
Advertising Executive Phone: (508) 862-1377
Total Circulation: 4500

PALMER

NEW ENGLAND ANTIQUES JOURNAL

Corporate/Parent Company: Turley Publications, Inc.
Street Address: 24 Water St
City: Palmer
State: MA
Postal Code: 1069
Office phone: (800) 432-3505
Publication Website: https://antiquesjournal.com/
General E-mail: antiquesjournal@gmail.com
Editor Name: John Fiske
Editor Email: jfiske39@gmail.com
Advertising Executive Name: Mark Ehrlich
Advertising Executive Email: markantiques@cox.net
Total Circulation: 17000

SHOPPING GUIDE

Corporate/Parent Company: Turley Publications, Inc.
Street Address: 24 Water St
City: Palmer
State: MA

Postal Code: 01069-1885
Office phone: (413) 283-8393
Publication Website: http://newspapers.turley.com/shoppingguide/
General E-mail: lmarulli@turley.com
Total Circulation: 7825

THE CHICOPEE REGISTER

Corporate/Parent Company: Turley Publications, Inc.
Street Address: 24 Water Street
City: Palmer
State: MA
Postal Code: 1069
Office phone: (413) 592-3599
Publication Website: http://chicopeeregister.turley.com/
General E-mail: chicopeeregister@turley.com
Editor Name: Tyler Witkop
Editor Email: twitkop@turley.com
Editor Phone: (413) 283-8393
Advertising Executive Name: Wendy Delcamp
Advertising Executive Email: wdelcamp@turley.com
Advertising Executive Phone: (413) 237-4245
Year Established: 1970
Delivery Methods: Racks
Own Printing Facility?: Y
Published Days: Thur
Avg Free Circ: 17000
Audit Company: Sworn/Estimate/Non-Audited
Audit Date: 6 10 2019
Total Circulation: 10000

THE JOURNAL REGISTER

Corporate/Parent Company: Turley Publications, Inc.
Street Address: 24 Water St
City: Palmer
State: MA
Postal Code: 01069-1885
Office phone: (413) 283-8393
Publication Website: https://journalregister.turley.com/
Year Established: 1850
Delivery Methods: Mail
Own Printing Facility?: Y
Commercial printers?: Y
Published Days: Thur
Avg Paid Circ: 5200
Audit Company: Sworn/Estimate/Non-Audited
Audit Date: 6 10 2019
Total Circulation: 5200

PLYMOUTH

DUXBURY REPORTER

Street Address: 182 Standish Avenue
City: Plymouth
State: MA
Postal Code: 2360
Office phone: (508) 591-6623
Publication Website: https://duxbury.wickedlocal.com/
General E-mail: duxbury@wickedlocal.com
Publisher Name: Mark Olivieri
Publisher Email: molivieri@wickedlocal.com
Publisher Phone: (781) 837-4504
Advertising Executive Name: Chris Avis
Advertising Executive Email: cavis@wickedlocal.com
Advertising Executive Phone: (781) 837-4503
Year Established: 1987
Own Printing Facility?: Y
Commercial printers?: Y
Published Days: Fri
Avg Free Circ: 2725
Audit Company: Sworn/Estimate/Non-Audited
Audit Date: 6 10 2019

HALIFAX-PLYMPTON REPORTER

Street Address: 182 Standish Avenue
City: Plymouth
State: MA
Postal Code: 2360
Office phone: (508) 591-6623
Publication Website: https://halifax.wickedlocal.com/
General E-mail: molivieri@wickedlocal.com
Publisher Name: Mark Olivieri
Publisher Email: molivieri@wickedlocal.com
Publisher Phone: (781) 837-4504
Advertising Executive Name: Chris Avis
Advertising Executive Email: cavis@wickedlocal.com
Advertising Executive Phone: (781) 837-4503
Year Established: 1983
Own Printing Facility?: Y
Commercial printers?: Y
Published Days: Fri
Avg Paid Circ: 750
Avg Free Circ: 1
Audit Company: Sworn/Estimate/Non-Audited
Audit Date: 6 10 2019
Total Circulation: 10000

WAREHAM COURIER

Corporate/Parent Company: Gannett Company, Inc.
Street Address: 182 Standish Avenue
City: Plymouth
State: MA
Postal Code: 0 2360
Office phone: 508-591-6628
Publication Website: wareham.wickedlocal.com
General E-mail: wareham@wickedlocal.com
Editor Name: Gregory Mathis
Editor Email: gmathis@wickedlocal.com
Editor Phone: 508-591-6618
Advertising Executive Name: Chris Avis
Year Established: 1964
Published Days: Thur
Avg Paid Circ: 925
Audit Company: AAM
Audit Date: 31 03 2018

REVERE

CHELSEA RECORD

Street Address: 385 Broadway, Suite 105
City: Revere
State: MA
Postal Code: 02151-3049
Office phone: (781) 485-0588
Publication Website: http://chelsearecord.com/
Editor Name: Stephen Quigley
Editor Email: stephen.quigley@reverejournal.com
Year Established: 1890
Delivery Methods: Mail`Newsstand
Own Printing Facility?: N
Commercial printers?: Y
Mechanical specifications: Type page 13 x 21; E - 6 cols, 2 1/16, 1/8 between; A - 6 cols, 2 1/16, 1/8 between; C - 6 cols, 1 5/16, 1/8 between.
Published Days: Thur
Avg Paid Circ: 4500
Audit Company: Sworn/Estimate/Non-Audited
Audit Date: 6 10 2019
Total Circulation: 12500

EAST BOSTON TIMES

Street Address: 385 Broadway, Suite 105
City: Revere
State: MA
Postal Code: 02151-3049
Office phone: (781) 485-0588
Publication Website: http://eastietimes.com/
General E-mail: editor@eastietimes.com

Editor Email: editor@eastietimes.com
Own Printing Facility?: N
Commercial printers?: Y
Mechanical specifications: Type page 13 x 21 1/2; E - 6 cols, 2 1/16, 1/8 between; A - 6 cols, 2 1/16, 1/8 between; C - 6 cols, 1 5/16, 1/8 between.
Published Days: Wed`Thur
Avg Free Circ: 8000
Audit Company: Sworn/Estimate/Non-Audited
Audit Date: 6 10 2019
Total Circulation: 7500

EVERETT INDEPENDENT

Street Address: 385 Broadway, Suite 105
City: Revere
State: MA
Postal Code: 02151-3049
Office phone: (781) 485-0588
Publication Website: http://everettindependent.com/
General E-mail: editor@everettindependent.com
Editor Name: Stephen Quigley
Editor Email: stephen.quigley@reverejournal.com
Published Days: Wed
Avg Free Circ: 12500
Audit Company: Sworn/Estimate/Non-Audited
Audit Date: 6 10 2019

THE BACK BAY SUN

Street Address: 385 Broadway, Suite 105
City: Revere
State: MA
Postal Code: 02151-3049
Office phone: (781) 485-0588
Publication Website: https://thebostonsun.com/
General E-mail: deb@thebostonsun.com
Publisher Name: Debra DiGregorio
Publisher Email: deb@thebostonsun.com
Editor Name: Phil Orlandella
Published Days: Fri
Audit Company: Sworn/Estimate/Non-Audited
Audit Date: 6 10 2019

THE CHARLESTOWN PATRIOT-BRIDGE

Street Address: 385 Broadway, Suite 105
City: Revere
State: MA
Postal Code: 2151
Office phone: (781) 485-0588
Publication Website: https://charlestownbridge.com/
General E-mail: charlestownads@hotmail.com
Editor Email: editor@charlestownbridge.com
Mechanical specifications: Type page 10 1/4 x 16; E - 6 cols, 1 1/2, 1/4 between; A - 6 cols, 1 1/2, 1/4 between; C - 6 cols, 1 1/2, 1/4 between.
Published Days: Thur
Avg Paid Circ: 4500
Audit Company: Sworn/Estimate/Non-Audited
Audit Date: 6 10 2019

THE LYNN JOURNAL

Street Address: 385 Broadway, Suite 105
City: Revere
State: MA
Postal Code: 02151-3049
Office phone: (781) 485-0588
Publication Website: http://lynnjournal.com/
General E-mail: editor@lynnjournal.com
Editor Name: Cary Shuman
Editor Email: editor@lynnjournal.com
Editor Phone: (781) 485-0588

Year Established: 1998
Delivery Methods: Mail Racks
Published Days: Tues
Avg Free Circ: 10000
Audit Company: Sworn/Estimate/Non-Audited
Audit Date: 6 10 2019

THE REVERE JOURNAL

Street Address: 385 Broadway, Suite 105
City: Revere
State: MA
Postal Code: 02151-3049
Office phone: (781) 485-0588
Publication Website: http://reverejournal.com/
General E-mail: promo@reverejournal.com
Own Printing Facility?: Y
Commercial printers?: Y
Mechanical specifications: Type page 13 x 21 1/2; E - 6 cols, 2 1/16, 1/8 between; A - 6 cols, 2 1/16, 1/8 between; C - 6 cols, 1 5/16, 1/8 between.
Published Days: Wed
Avg Paid Circ: 7500
Audit Company: Sworn/Estimate/Non-Audited
Audit Date: 6 10 2019

WINTHROP SUN-TRANSCRIPT

Street Address: 385 Broadway, Suite 105
City: Revere
State: MA
Postal Code: 02151-3049
Office phone: (781) 485-0588
Publication Website: http://winthroptranscript.com/
General E-mail: editor@winthroptranscript.com
Editor Name: Cary Shuman
Editor Email: editor@winthroptranscript.com
Own Printing Facility?: Y
Commercial printers?: Y
Published Days: Thur
Avg Paid Circ: 4300
Audit Company: Sworn/Estimate/Non-Audited
Audit Date: 6 10 2019

ROWLEY

TOWN COMMON

Street Address: 77 Wethersfield St
City: Rowley
State: MA
Postal Code: 01969-1713
Office phone: (978) 948-8696
Publication Website: http://www.thetowncommon.com
General E-mail: advertise@thetowncommon.com
Editor Name: Marc Maravalli
Editor Email: editor@thetowncommon.com
Advertising Executive Email: advertise@thetowncommon.com
Year Established: 2004
Delivery Methods: Newsstand Racks
Published Days: Wed
Audit Company: Sworn/Estimate/Non-Audited
Audit Date: 6 10 2019

SOUTH HADLEY

TOWN REMINDER

Corporate/Parent Company: Turley Publications, Inc.
Street Address: 138 College St Ste 2
City: South Hadley
State: MA
Postal Code: 01075-1402
Office phone: (413) 536-5333
Publication Website: https://townreminder.turley.com/
General E-mail: townreminder@turley.com
Editor Name: Wyatt Aloisio
Editor Email: waloisio@turley.com
Editor Phone: (800) 824-6548

Advertising Executive Name: Maureen McGarrett Hall
Advertising Executive Email: mmcgarrett@turley.com
Year Established: 1968
Delivery Methods: Racks
Own Printing Facility?: Y
Published Days: Fri
Avg Free Circ: 12000
Audit Company: Sworn/Estimate/Non-Audited
Audit Date: 6 10 2019

WARE

QUABOAG CURRENT

Corporate/Parent Company: Turley Publications, Inc.
Street Address: 80 Main St
City: Ware
State: MA
Postal Code: 1082
Office phone: (413) 967-3505
Publication Website: https://quaboagcurrent.turley.com/
General E-mail: ekennedy@turley.com
Editor Name: Eileen Kennedy
Editor Email: ekennedy@turley.com
Editor Phone: (413) 967-3505
Advertising Executive Name: Dan Flynn
Advertising Executive Email: dflynn@turley.com
Advertising Executive Phone: (413) 967-3505
Delivery Methods: Mail Racks
Published Days: Thur
Audit Company: Sworn/Estimate/Non-Audited
Audit Date: 6 10 2019

WARE RIVER NEWS

Corporate/Parent Company: Turley Publications, Inc.
Street Address: 80 Main St
City: Ware
State: MA
Postal Code: 01082-1318
Office phone: (413) 967-3505
Publication Website: https://warerivernews.turley.com/
General E-mail: warerivernews@turley.com
Advertising Executive Name: Dan Flynn
Advertising Executive Email: dflynn@turley.com
Advertising Executive Phone: (413) 967-3505
Year Established: 1887
Delivery Methods: Mail
Own Printing Facility?: Y
Published Days: Thur
Avg Paid Circ: 4429
Audit Company: Sworn/Estimate/Non-Audited
Audit Date: 6 10 2019

WESTFIELD

PENNYSAVER

Corporate/Parent Company: The Westfield News Group LLC
Street Address: 62 School St
City: Westfield
State: MA
Postal Code: 01085-2835
Office phone: (413) 562-4181

WILBRAHAM

THE REGISTER

Corporate/Parent Company: Gannett
Street Address: 2341 Boston Rd
City: Wilbraham
State: MA
Postal Code: 01095-1244
Office phone: (413) 682-0007
Publication Website: http://register.turley.com/
General E-mail: ludlowregister@turley.com
Editor Name: Rich J. Wirth
Editor Email: rwirth@turley.com
Advertising Executive Name: Lisa Marulli

Advertising Executive Email: lmarulli@turley.com
Advertising Executive Phone: (413) 283-8393
Year Established: 1946
Delivery Methods: Racks
Published Days: Wed
Avg Free Circ: 12500
Audit Company: Sworn/Estimate/Non-Audited
Audit Date: 6 10 2019

WILBRAHAM-HAMPDEN TIMES

Corporate/Parent Company: Turley Publications, Inc.
Street Address: 2341 Boston Rd
City: Wilbraham
State: MA
Postal Code: 1095
Office phone: (413) 682-0007
Publication Website: http://wilbrahamhampdentimes.turley.com/
General E-mail: twitkop@turley.com
Editor Name: Tyler Witkop
Editor Email: twitkop@turley.com
Editor Phone: (413) 682-0007
Advertising Executive Name: Jocelyn Walker
Advertising Executive Email: jwalker@turley.com
Advertising Executive Phone: (800) 824-6548
Year Established: 2002
Delivery Methods: Mail
Own Printing Facility?: Y
Published Days: Thur
Avg Free Circ: 9300
Audit Company: Sworn/Estimate/Non-Audited
Audit Date: 6 10 2019

MARYLAND

ANNAPOLIS

BOWIE NEWS

Street Address: 888 Bestgate Rd
City: Annapolis
State: MD
Postal Code: 21401
Office phone: 410-280-5955
Publication Website: www.capitalgazette.com/maryland/bowie
General E-mail: bowiephoto@capgaznews.com
Editor Name: Rick Hutzell
Editor Email: rhutzell@bladenews.com
Advertising Executive Name: Lois Windsor
Advertising Executive Phone: 443-482-3145

BALTIMORE

HAVRE DE GRACE NEWS

Street Address: 300 E. Cromwell Street
City: Baltimore
State: MD
Postal Code: 21230
Office phone: (443) 692-9011
Publication Website: www.baltimoresun.com/news/maryland/harford/aberdeen-havre-de-grace
General E-mail: customersatisfaction@baltsun.com
Editor Name: Trif Alatzas
Editor Email: trif.alatzas@baltsun.com
Editor Phone: 410-332-6154

OWINGS MILLS NEWS

Street Address: 300 E. Cromwell Street
City: Baltimore
State: MD
Postal Code: 21230
Office phone: (443) 692-9011

Publication Website: www.baltimoresun.com/news/maryland/baltimore-county/owings-mills
General E-mail: newstips@baltimoresun.com
Editor Name: Trif Alatzas
Editor Email: trif.alatzas@baltsun.com
Editor Phone: 410-332-6154

CALIFORNIA

CHARLES NEWS

Street Address: P.O. Box 257
City: California
State: MD
Postal Code: 20619
Office phone: 301-200-1812
Publication Website: https://smnewsnet.com
General E-mail: news@smnewsnet.com

CENTREVILLE

RECORD OBSERVER

Corporate/Parent Company: Adams Publishing Group
Street Address: 114 Broadway
City: Centreville
State: MD
Postal Code: 21617
Office phone: 410-758-1400
Publication Website: www.myeasternshoremd.com/qa/record_observer
General E-mail: subscribe@chespub.com
Publisher Name: Jim Normandin
Publisher Email: jim.normandin@adamspg.com
Editor Name: Angela Price
Editor Email: aprice@chespub.com
Advertising Executive Name: Brandon Silverstein
Advertising Executive Email: bsilverstein@chespub.com
Advertising Executive Phone: 410-200-6469

CHESTER

QUEEN ANNES COUNTY NEWS

Street Address: 700-C Abruzzi Drive
City: Chester
State: MD
Postal Code: 21619
Office phone: 410-643-7770
Publication Website: www.myeasternshoremd.com/qa
General E-mail: baytimes@kibaytimes.com
Publisher Name: Jim Normandin
Publisher Email: jim.normandin@adamspg.com
Editor Name: Angela Price
Editor Email: aprice@chespub.com
Editor Phone: 443-239-0218
Advertising Executive Name: Brandon Silverstein
Advertising Executive Email: bsilverstein@chespub.com
Advertising Executive Phone: 410-200-6469

THE KENT ISLAND BAY TIMES

Street Address: 700-C Abruzzi Drive
City: Chester
State: MD
Postal Code: 21619
Office phone: 410-643-7770
Publication Website: www.myeasternshoremd.com/qa/bay_times
General E-mail: baytimes@kibaytimes.com
Publisher Name: Jim Normandin
Publisher Email: jim.normandin@adamspg.com
Editor Name: Angela Price
Editor Email: aprice@chespub.com
Editor Phone: 443-239-0218
Advertising Executive Name: Brandon Silverstein
Advertising Executive Email: bsilverstein@chespub.com
Advertising Executive Phone: 410-200-6469

Non-Daily Newspapers in the U.S.

EMMITSBURG

EMMITSBURG NEWS-JOURNAL
Street Address: 1 East Main Street
City: Emmitsburg
State: MD
Postal Code: 21727
Office phone: 301.471.3306
Publication Website: www.emmitsburg.com
General E-mail: advertising@emmitsburg.com
Editor Name: Michael Hillman
Editor Email: editor@emmitsburg.com

THE CATOCTIN BANNER
Street Address: 515B East Main Street
City: Emmitsburg
State: MD
Postal Code: 21727
Office phone: 240-288-0108
Publication Website: www.thecatoctinbanner.com
Editor Name: Deb Spalding
Editor Email: news@thecatoctinbanner.com

LA PLATA

URBAN SENTINEL
Street Address: 102 Discovery Ct.
City: La Plata
State: MD
Postal Code: 20646
Office phone: 301-661-3989
Publication Website: www.urbansentinel.com
Publisher Name: Reginald Kearney
Publisher Email: reginald.kearney@marylanddailyexaminer.com

OWINGS MILLS

BALTIMORE JEWISH TIMES
Street Address: 11459 Cronhill Drive Suite A
City: Owings Mills
State: MD
Postal Code: 21117
Office phone: 410-902-2300
Publication Website: www.jewishtimes.com
Publisher Name: Craig Burke
Publisher Email: cburke@midatlanticmedia.com
Publisher Phone: 410-902-2310
Editor Name: Selah Maya Zighelboim
Editor Email: Szighelboim@midatlanticmedia.com
Editor Phone: 410-902-2305
Advertising Executive Name: Michelle Weinstein

ROCKVILLE

THE SENTINEL (MONTGOMERY COUNTY)
Corporate/Parent Company: Berlyn, Inc.
Street Address: 22 W. Jefferson Street, Suite 309
City: Rockville
State: MD
Postal Code: 20850
Office phone: 301-838-0788
Publication Website: mont.thesentinel.com
Publisher Name: Lynn G. Kapiloff
Publisher Email: lynn@thesentinel.com
Editor Name: Daniel J. Kucin, Jr.
Editor Email: editor-mc@thesentinel.com

SALISBURY

WORCHESTER COUNTY TIMES
Street Address: 115 S. Division St.
City: Salisbury
State: MD
Postal Code: 21801
Office phone: 410-749-7171
Publication Website: www.delmarvanow.com/news/maryland
Editor Name: Laura Benedict Sileo
Editor Email: lbenedic@dmg.gannett.com
Editor Phone: 410-845-4632
Advertising Executive Name: Ron Pousson
Advertising Executive Email: rpousson@localiq.com
Advertising Executive Phone: 410-845-4609

SEABROOK

THE SENTINEL (PRINCE GEORGE)
Corporate/Parent Company: Berlyn, Inc.
Street Address: 9458 Lanham-Severn Road
City: Seabrook
State: MD
Postal Code: 20706
Office phone: 301-306-9500
Publication Website: pgs.thesentinel.com
General E-mail: editor-pg@thesentinel.com
Publisher Name: Lynn G. Kapiloff
Publisher Email: lynn@thesentinel.com

SILVER SPRING

WASHINGTON HISPANIC
Street Address: 8701 Georgia Ave. Suite 700
City: Silver Spring
State: MD
Postal Code: 20910
Office phone: 240-450-1779
Publication Website: washingtonhispanic.com/portal
Editor Name: Johnny A Yataco
Editor Email: jy@washingtonhispanic.com

WOODSBORO

WOODSBORO-WALKERSVILLE TIMES
Street Address: PO Box 502
City: Woodsboro
State: MD
Postal Code: 21798
Office phone: (240) 446-9797
Publication Website: www.woodsborotimes.com
Editor Name: Ken Kellar
Editor Email: WoodsboroEditor@gmail.com

EL IMPARCIAL NEWS
State: MD
Office phone: 571-332-8404
Publication Website: elimparcialnews.com
General E-mail: info@elimparcialnews.com
Editor Name: Antonio Ayuso Valdivieso
Editor Email: elimparcialusa@yahoo.com

MAINE

BELFAST

THE REPUBLICAN JOURNAL
Corporate/Parent Company: Courier Publications, LLC
Street Address: 156 High St
City: Belfast
State: ME
Postal Code: 04915-6548
Office phone: (207) 338-3333
Publication Website: https://knox.villagesoup.com/p/the-republican-journal/374732
General E-mail: insidesaleswaldo@villagesoup.com
Editor Name: Sarah Reynolds
Advertising Executive Name: Tim Hurlburt

THE WALDO INDEPENDENT
Corporate/Parent Company: Courier Publications, LLC
Street Address: 71 High St.
City: Belfast
State: ME
Postal Code: 4915
Office phone: (207) 338-5100
Publication Website: https://waldo.villagesoup.com/

BETHEL

THE BETHEL CITIZEN
Corporate/Parent Company: Masthead Maine
Street Address: 19 Main St
City: Bethel
State: ME
Postal Code: 04217-4014
Office phone: (207) 824-2444
Publication Website: https://www.sunjournal.com/the-bethel-citizen/
General E-mail: news@bethelcitizen.com
Publisher Name: Lisa DeSisto
Publisher Email: lisa@mainetoday.com
Publisher Phone: (207) 791-6630
Editor Name: Alison Aloisio
Editor Email: news@bethelcitizen.com
Editor Phone: (207) 824-2444

CAMDEN

THE CAMDEN HERALD
Corporate/Parent Company: Courier Publications, LLC
Street Address: 6 Virginia Ave, 2nd floor
City: Camden
State: ME
Postal Code: 04843-1076
Office phone: (207) 236-8511
Publication Website: https://waldo.villagesoup.com/p/the-camden-herald/801499
General E-mail: insidesalesknox@villagesoup.com
Editor Name: Susan Mustapich
Editor Email: smustapich@villagesoup.com
Editor Phone: (207) 236-8511
Advertising Executive Name: Jody McKee
Advertising Executive Email: jmckee@villagesoup.com
Advertising Executive Phone: (207) 236-8511

THE COURIER-GAZETTE
Corporate/Parent Company: Courier Publications, LLC
Street Address: PO Box 1076
City: Camden
State: ME
Postal Code: 04843-1076
Office phone: 207-594-4401
Publication Website: knox.villagesoup.com
General E-mail: news@villagesoup.com
Editor Name: Emma Testerman
Advertising Executive Name: Dave Libby

FARMINGTON

FRANKLIN JOURNAL
Corporate/Parent Company: MaineToday Media
Street Address: 187 Wilton Rd
City: Farmington
State: ME
Postal Code: 04938-6120
Office phone: (207) 778-2075
Publication Website: https://www.sunjournal.com/weeklies/the-franklin-journal/
General E-mail: info@thefranklinjournal.com
Publisher Name: Lisa DeSisto
Publisher Email: lisa@mainetoday.com
Publisher Phone: (207) 791-6630

LIVERMORE FALLS ADVERTISER
Corporate/Parent Company: MaineToday Media
Street Address: 187 Wilton Road
City: Farmington
State: ME
Postal Code: 4938
Office phone: (207) 780-2075
Publication Website: https://www.sunjournal.com/weeklies/livermore-falls-advertiser/
General E-mail: editor@thefranklinjournal.com
Publisher Name: Lisa DeSisto
Publisher Email: lisa@mainetoday.com
Publisher Phone: (207) 791-6630
Editor Name: Barry Matulaitis
Editor Email: editor@thefranklinjournal.com

LEWISTON

SUN JOURNAL
Corporate/Parent Company: Gannett
Street Address: 104 Park St
City: Lewiston
State: ME
Postal Code: 04240-7202
Office phone: (207) 784-5411
Publication Website: https://www.sunjournal.com/
General E-mail: tips@sunjournal.com
Publisher Name: Lisa DeSisto
Publisher Email: lisa@mainetoday.com
Publisher Phone: (207) 791-6630
Editor Name: Mark Mogensen
Editor Email: mmogensen@sunjournal.com
Editor Phone: (207) 689-2805
Advertising Executive Name: Mike Blanchet
Advertising Executive Email: mblanchet@sunjournal.com
Advertising Executive Phone: (800) 482-0759, ext : 4102

MACHIAS

COUNTY WIDE NEWSPAPER
Street Address: 26 Main St
City: Machias
State: ME
Postal Code: 0 4654
Office phone: 207-255-6397
Publication Website: https://www.facebook.com/County-Wide-Newspaper-183223331840680
General E-mail: countywidenews@hotmail.com

MADAWASKA

FIDDLEHEAD FOCUS
Corporate/Parent Company: Bangor Publishing Company
Street Address: 328 Main Street., Suite 102
City: Madawaska
State: ME
Postal Code: 4756
Office phone: 207-728-3336
Publication Website: fiddleheadfocus.com
General E-mail: story@fiddleheadfocus.com
Editor Name: Julie Harris
Editor Email: nepeditors@nepublish.com
Advertising Executive Name: Jessica Blalock
Advertising Executive Email: jblalock@bangordailynews.com

OLD TOWN

PENOBSCOT TIMES
Corporate/Parent Company: MaineToday Media
Street Address: 282 Main St
City: Old Town
State: ME
Postal Code: 04468-1529
Office phone: (207) 827-4451
Publication Website: https://thepenobscottimes.com/
General E-mail: news@thepenobscottimes.com

Publisher Name: Lynn Higgins
Publisher Email: lhiggins@thepenobscottimes.com
Publisher Phone: (207) 827-4451
Editor Name: Greg Fish
Editor Email: gfish@thepenobscottimes.com
Editor Phone: (207) 827-4451

OLD TOWN MAINE

THE PENOBSCOT TIMES

Street Address: 282 Main Street
City: Old Town Maine
State: ME
Postal Code: 4468
Office phone: 207-827-4451
Publication Website: thepenobscottimes.com
General E-mail: news@thepenobscottimes.com
Editor Name: Greg Fish

PORTLAND

THE FORECASTER

Corporate/Parent Company: Masthead Maine
Street Address: One City Center, 4th floor
City: Portland
State: ME
Postal Code: 4101
Office phone: (207) 781-3661
Publication Website: https://www.pressherald.com/forecaster/
General E-mail: support@pressherald.com
Publisher Name: Lisa DeSisto
Publisher Email: lisa@mainetoday.com
Publisher Phone: (207) 791-6630
Editor Name: John Swinconeck
Editor Email: jswinconeck@timesrecord.com
Editor Phone: (207) 504-8209
Advertising Executive Name: Courtney Spencer
Advertising Executive Email: cspencer@masthead.me
Advertising Executive Phone: (207) 791-6203

PRESQUE ISLE

THE STAR-HERALD

Corporate/Parent Company: Bangor Publishing Company
Street Address: 260 Missile St
City: Presque Isle
State: ME
Postal Code: 4769
Office phone: 207-764-4471
Publication Website: thecounty.me
General E-mail: story@thecounty.me
Editor Name: Julie Harris
Editor Email: nepeditors@nepublish.com

RANGELEY

THE RANGELEY HIGHLANDER

Corporate/Parent Company: MaineToday Media
Street Address: 2579 Main St
City: Rangeley
State: ME
Postal Code: 4970
Office phone: 207-864-3756
Publication Website: therangeleyhighlander.com
General E-mail: info@therangeleyhighlander.com
Publisher Name: Lisa DeSisto
Publisher Email: lisa@mainetoday.com
Publisher Phone: (207) 791-6630
Editor Name: Cliff Schechtman
Editor Email: cschechtman@mainetoday.com
Editor Phone: (207) 791-6693
Advertising Executive Name: Rick DeBruin
Advertising Executive Email: rdebruin@pressherald.com
Advertising Executive Phone: (207) 791-6091

MICHIGAN

ADRIAN

SIENA HEIGHTS UNIVERSITY/ SPECTRA

Street Address: 1247 E. Siena Heights Dr.
City: Adrian
State: MI
Postal Code: 49221
Office phone: (517) 264-7141
Publication Website: www.shuspectra.com
General E-mail: shuspectra@gmail.com
Editor Name: Jordyn Scholz

ALLEGAN

THE ALLEGAN COUNTY NEWS

Street Address: 241 Hubbard St. P.O. Box 189
City: Allegan
State: MI
Postal Code: 49010
Office phone: (269) 673-5534
Publication Website: www.allegannews.com
General E-mail: editor@allegannews.com
Editor Name: Ryan Lewis
Editor Email: rmlewis@allegannews.com
Advertising Executive Name: Robin Clark
Advertising Executive Email: robinclark@allegannews.com
Total Circulation: 24288

ALLEN PARK

CHELSEA GUARDIAN

Corporate/Parent Company: Hamilton Publishing Guardian Newspapers
Street Address: 15239 Horger
City: Allen Park
State: MI
Postal Code: 48101
Office phone: (734) 636-6577
Publication Website: www.guardiannewspapersmi.com/chelsea
Editor Name: Charla Hamilton
Editor Email: charlachelseaguardian@gmail.com
Total Circulation: 18391

ALMA

GRAND TRAVERSE INSIDER

Corporate/Parent Company: MediaNews Group, Inc.
Street Address: 311 E. Superior St.
City: Alma
State: MI
Postal Code: 48801
Office phone: (989) 779-6000
Publication Website: http://www.grandtraverseinsider.com/?fbclid=IwAR3755ocJvC6d1CHOBEFXcYQROkimNM02jPrwipTaVX_8etIYHhsDaEfbtA
General E-mail: customerservice@oakpress.com
Publisher Name: Greg Mazanec
Publisher Email: mipublisher@digitalfirstmedia.com
Editor Name: Jeff Hoard
Editor Email: jeff.hoard@oakpress.com
Advertising Executive Name: Tammy Fisher
Advertising Executive Email: tfisher@michigannewspapers.com
Advertising Executive Phone: (989) 779-6110

ANN ARBOR

THE CENTER FOR MICHIGAN

Street Address: 4100 N. Dixboro Road
City: Ann Arbor
State: MI
Postal Code: 48105
Office phone: 734 769 4625
Publication Website: thecenterformichigan.net
General E-mail: info@thecenterformichigan.net
Editor Name: John Bebow
Editor Email: jbebow@thecenterformichigan.net

WASHTENAW COUNTY LEGAL NEWS

Corporate/Parent Company: Detroit Legal News Publishing LLC
Street Address: PO Box 1367
City: Ann Arbor
State: MI
Postal Code: 48106
Office phone: (734) 477-0201
Publication Website: www.legalnews.com/washtenaw
Publisher Name: Ban Ibrahim
Publisher Email: ban@legalnews.com
Publisher Phone: (248) 577-6110
Editor Name: Tom Kirvan
Editor Email: tkirvan@legalnews.com
Editor Phone: (248) 556-7703
Advertising Executive Name: Suzanne Ketner
Advertising Executive Email: advertising@legalnews.com
Advertising Executive Phone: (734) 477-0247
Total Circulation: 33334

BALDWIN

LAKE COUNTY STAR

Corporate/Parent Company: Pioneer Group
Street Address: 851 Michigan Ave
City: Baldwin
State: MI
Postal Code: 49304-8140
Office phone: (231) 745-4635
Publication Website: https://www.lakecountystar.com
General E-mail: lcstar@pioneergroup.com
Year Established: 1873
Delivery Methods: Mail
Own Printing Facility?: Y
Commercial printers?: Y
Mechanical specifications: Type page 10 x 16; E - 5 cols, 2, between; A - 5 cols, 2, between; C - 5 cols, 2, between.
Published Days: Thur
Avg Paid Circ: 2976
Audit Company: Sworn/Estimate/Non-Audited
Audit Date: 6 10 2019

BATTLE CREEK

BATTLE CREEK SHOPPER NEWS

Corporate/Parent Company: J-Ad Graphics
Street Address: 1001 Columbia Ave E
City: Battle Creek
State: MI
Postal Code: 49014-4401
Office phone: (269) 965-3955
Publication Website: http://thebattlecreekshopper.com/index1.htm
General E-mail: shopperads@j-adgraphics.com
Editor Name: Shelly Sulser
Advertising Executive Name: Sue Camburn
Advertising Executive Email: scamburn@j-adgraphics.com
Advertising Executive Phone: (269) 965-3955, ext. 235
Total Circulation: 15000

BELLAIRE

THE ANTRIM REVIEW

Street Address: 4470 S. M-88 Hwy.
City: Bellaire
State: MI
Postal Code: 49615
Office phone: 231-533-5651
Publication Website: www.antrimreview.net
General E-mail: manager@antrimreview.net
Publisher Name: John Tarrant
Publisher Email: publisher@antrimreview.net
Publisher Phone: 231-533-5651 ext. 202
Editor Name: Chris Dorbrowlski
Editor Email: editor@antrimreview.net
Editor Phone: 231-533-5651 ext. 209
Advertising Executive Name: Jackie White
Advertising Executive Email: advertising@antrimreview.net
Advertising Executive Phone: 231-533-5651 ext. 204

BELLEVILLE

THE BELLEVILLE ENTERPRISE

Corporate/Parent Company: Associated Newspapers of Michigan
Street Address: 152 Main St., Suite 9
City: Belleville
State: MI
Postal Code: 48111-3911
Office phone: (734) 699-9020
Publication Website: http://bellevilleareaindependent.com/
General E-mail: mail@bellevilleareaindependent.com
Editor Name: Rosemary K. Otzman
Editor Email: rotzman@ameritech.net
Advertising Executive Name: Bob Mytych
Own Printing Facility?: Y
Commercial printers?: Y
Published Days: Thur
Avg Paid Circ: 1900
Audit Company: Sworn/Estimate/Non-Audited
Audit Date: 6 10 2019

BIG RAPIDS

HERALD REVIEW

Corporate/Parent Company: Pioneer Group
Street Address: 115 N Michigan Ave
City: Big Rapids
State: MI
Postal Code: 49307
Office phone: (231) 796-4831
Publication Website: https://www.theheraldreview.com
General E-mail: hrnews@herald-review.com
Year Established: 1862
Delivery Methods: Mail
Own Printing Facility?: Y
Commercial printers?: Y
Mechanical specifications: Type page 12 x 21 1/2; E - 6 cols, 1 7/8, between; A - 6 cols, 1 7/8, between; C - 6 cols, 1 7/8, between.
Published Days: Wed
Avg Paid Circ: 3500
Avg Free Circ: 15
Audit Company: Sworn/Estimate/Non-Audited
Audit Date: 6 10 2019

TRI-COUNTY SHOPPERS GUIDE

Street Address: 115 N Michigan Ave
City: Big Rapids
State: MI
Postal Code: 49307-1401
Office phone: (231) 796-4831
Total Circulation: 11800

BOYNE CITY

THE BOYNE CITY GAZETTE

Street Address: 5 W Main St., Ste. 7
City: Boyne City
State: MI
Postal Code: 49712
Office phone: (231) 582-2799
Publication Website: www.boynegazette.com
General E-mail: editor@boynegazette.com
Publisher Name: Christopher Faulknor
Publisher Phone: (231) 582-2799 EXT 1
Editor Name: Benjamin J. Gohs

Non-Daily Newspapers in the U.S.

Editor Phone: (231) 582-2799 EXT 2

CENTRAL LAKE
CENTRAL LAKE NEWS
Street Address: P.O. Box 201 / 1966 S. Main St.
City: Central Lake
State: MI
Postal Code: 49622
Office phone: (231) 350-1778
Publication Website: centrallakenews.com
Total Circulation: 2419

CHATHAM
UP MAGAZINE/ PORCUPINE PRESS
Street Address: P.O. Box 200 E3724 Autrain St.
City: Chatham
State: MI
Postal Code: 49816
Office phone: (906) 439-5111
Publication Website: www.upmag.net
Editor Name: CAPTAIN MIKE VAN DEN BRANDEN
Editor Email: mike@upmag.net

CHESANING
THE TOWNSHIP VIEW
Corporate/Parent Company: View Newspaper Group
Street Address: 110 S. Chapman St.
City: Chesaning
State: MI
Postal Code: 48616
Office phone: (989) 341-4806
Publication Website: townshipview.mihomepaper.com
General E-mail: twpviewnews@mihomepaper.com
Editor Name: KEITH SALISBURY
Editor Email: ksalisbury@mihomepaper.com

CLARKSTON
CLARKSTON NEWS
Corporate/Parent Company: Sherman Publications, Inc.
Street Address: 5 S Main St
City: Clarkston
State: MI
Postal Code: 48346-1597
Office phone: (248) 625-3370
Publication Website: https://clarkstonnews.com/
General E-mail: clarkstonnews@gmail.com
Publisher Name: Don Rush
Publisher Email: dontrushdon@gmail.com
Editor Name: Phil Custodio
Year Established: 1929
Delivery Methods: Mail
Own Printing Facility?: Y
Commercial printers?: Y
Mechanical specifications: Type page 10 x 11; E - 8 cols, 3 1/5, 1/5 between; A - 6 cols, 1 8/15, 1/5 between; C - 6 cols, 1 8/15, 1/5 between.
Published Days: Wed
Avg Paid Circ: 2419
Audit Company: CVC
Audit Date: 30 06 2018

CLINTON TOWNSHIP
MACOMB NOW MAGAZINE
Street Address: 18901 15 Mile Rd.
City: Clinton Township
State: MI
Postal Code: 48035
Office phone: 855.622.6621
Publication Website: macombnowmagazine.com
Editor Name: Tracey Moro
Editor Email: Editor@macombnowmagazine.com

CLIO
BIRCH RUN/BRIDGEPORT HERALD
Street Address: 10098 N. Dort Hwy.
City: Clio
State: MI
Postal Code: 48420
Office phone: (810) 686-3840
Publication Website: www.MyHerald.net
Publisher Name: Michael J. Harrington
Publisher Email: publisher@myherald.net
Editor Name: Megan Decker
Editor Email: editor@myherald.net

GENESEE COUNTY LEGAL NEWS
Corporate/Parent Company: Detroit Legal News Publishing LLC
Street Address: 111 W. Young St.
City: Clio
State: MI
Postal Code: 48420
Office phone: (810) 686-2080
Publication Website: www.legalnews.com/flintgenesee
Publisher Name: Ban Ibrahim
Publisher Email: ban@legalnews.com
Publisher Phone: (248) 577-6110
Editor Name: Tom Kirvan
Editor Email: tkirvan@legalnews.com
Editor Phone: (248) 556-7703
Advertising Executive Name: Suzanne Ketner
Advertising Executive Email: advertising@legalnews.com
Advertising Executive Phone: (734) 477-0247

DAVISON
BURTON VIEW
Corporate/Parent Company: View Newspaper Group
Street Address: 217 Shopper's Alley
City: Davison
State: MI
Postal Code: 48423
Office phone: 810-653-3511
Publication Website: burtonview.mihomepaper.com
General E-mail: lettersbuv@mihomepaper.com
Editor Name: Gary Gould
Editor Email: buveditor@mihomepaper.com
Total Circulation: 37805

DETROIT
DETROIT NATIVE SUN
Street Address: 17800 E. Warren Ave
City: Detroit
State: MI
Postal Code: 48224
Office phone: (313)457-5944
Publication Website: www.detroitnativesunonline.com
General E-mail: DETROITNATIVESUNNEWS@GMAIL.COM
Publisher Name: Valerie Lockhart
Publisher Email: publisher@detroitnativesun.com

ISSUE MEDIA GROUP
Street Address: 4470 2nd Ave
City: Detroit
State: MI
Postal Code: 48201
Office phone: 313-832-4621
Publication Website: www.issuemediagroup.com
Editor Name: Dorothy Hernandez

METROMODE
Corporate/Parent Company: Issue Media Group
Street Address: Model D 4470 2nd Ave
City: Detroit
State: MI
Postal Code: 48201
Publication Website: www.secondwavemedia.com/metromode
General E-mail: feedback@metromodemedia.com
Editor Name: Nina Ignaczak
Editor Email: nina@metromodemedia.com

MODEL D
Corporate/Parent Company: Issue Media Group
Street Address: 4470 2nd Ave
City: Detroit
State: MI
Postal Code: 48201
Office phone: 313-288-6681
Publication Website: www.modelmedia.com
General E-mail: tips@modelmedia.com
Editor Name: Dorothy Hernandez
Total Circulation: 32409

RAPID GROWTH
Corporate/Parent Company: Issue Media Group
Street Address: 4470 2nd Ave
City: Detroit
State: MI
Postal Code: 48201
Publication Website: www.rapidgrowthmedia.com
General E-mail: info@rapidgrowthmedia.com
Publisher Name: Tommy Allen
Publisher Email: RapidGSync@gmail.com
Editor Name: Lauren Fay Carlson
Editor Email: LaurenRapidGrowth@gmail.com

SANDRA SVOBODA
Street Address: 5401 Woodward Ave
City: Detroit
State: MI
Postal Code: 48202
Office phone: (248) 305-3788
Publication Website: www.greatlakesnow.org
General E-mail: ssvoboda@dptv.org

THE PULSE INSTITUTE (INSTITUTE FOR PUBLIC LEADERSHIP AND SOCIAL EQUITY)
Street Address: 615 Griswold St. Suite 700
City: Detroit
State: MI
Postal Code: 48226
Office phone: (313) 800-0142
Publication Website: thepulseinstitute.org
General E-mail: info@thepulseinstitute.org
Editor Name: Bankole Thompson

DRUMMOND ISLAND
DRUMMOND ISLAND DIGEST
Street Address: PO Box 469
City: Drummond Island
State: MI
Postal Code: 49726
Office phone: 906-493-5353
Publication Website: drummondislanddigest.com
Editor Name: Julie Covert
Editor Email: editor@drummondislanddigest.com

DUNDEE
THE INDEPENDENT
Corporate/Parent Company: Gannett
Street Address: 112 Park
City: Dundee
State: MI
Postal Code: 48131
Office phone: 734-529-2688
Publication Website: dundeeonline.com
General E-mail: sean@dundee.net
Editor Name: Tanya Whitaker

FOWLERVILLE
FOWLERVILLE NEWS AND VIEWS
Street Address: 206 E. Grand River : P.O. Box 937
City: Fowlerville
State: MI
Postal Code: 48836-0937
Office phone: 517-223-8760
Publication Website: www.fowlervillenewsandviews.com
Publisher Name: Steve Horton
Total Circulation: 18810

FRANKFORT
THE BENZIE COUNTY RECORD-PATRIOT
Corporate/Parent Company: Pioneer Group
Street Address: 417 Main St
City: Frankfort
State: MI
Postal Code: 49635
Office phone: (231) 352-9659
Publication Website: https://www.recordpatriot.com/
General E-mail: recpat@pioneergroup.com
Editor Name: Michelle Graves
Editor Email: mgraves@pioneergroup.com
Advertising Executive Name: Sandy Card
Advertising Executive Email: scard@pioneergroup.com
Year Established: 1888
Delivery Methods: Mail
Own Printing Facility?: Y
Mechanical specifications: Type page 10 3/16 x 16; E - 5 cols, 1 7/8, between; A - 5 cols, 1 7/8, between; C - 5 cols, 1 7/8, between.
Published Days: Wed
Avg Paid Circ: 4500
Audit Company: Sworn/Estimate/Non-Audited
Audit Date: 6 10 2019

FREMONT
TIMES INDICATOR
Street Address: 44 West Main Street - P.O. Box 7
City: Fremont
State: MI
Postal Code: 49412
Office phone: (231) 924-4400
Publication Website: www.timesindicator.com
General E-mail: tinews@comcast.net
Editor Name: Richard C. Wheater, Sr.
Advertising Executive Name: Debby Reinhold
Total Circulation: 3515

GLEN ARBOR
GLEN ARBOR SUN NEWSPAPER
Street Address: P.O. Box 615
City: Glen Arbor
State: MI
Postal Code: 49636
Office phone: (612) 804-5975
Publication Website: glenarborsun.com

GRAND RAPIDS

GRAND RAPIDS LEGAL NEWS

Corporate/Parent Company: Detroit Legal News Publishing LLC
Street Address: 1430 Monroe Ave N.W. Suite 140
City: Grand Rapids
State: MI
Postal Code: 49505
Office phone: (616) 454-9293
Publication Website: www.LegalNews.com/grandrapids
Publisher Name: Ban Ibrahim
Publisher Email: ban@legalnews.com
Publisher Phone: (248) 577-6110
Editor Name: Tom Kirvan
Editor Email: tkirvan@legalnews.com
Editor Phone: (248) 556-7703
Advertising Executive Name: Suzanne Ketner
Advertising Executive Email: advertising@legalnews.com
Advertising Executive Phone: (734) 477-0247

GRASS LAKE

THE GRASS LAKE TIMES

Street Address: PO Box 189
City: Grass Lake
State: MI
Postal Code: 49240
Office phone: 844-458-4637
Publication Website: www.thegrasslaketimes.com
General E-mail: news@thegrasslaketimes.com
Publisher Name: Raymond Tucker Cordani
Publisher Email: rtc@thegrasslaketimes.com

HAMTRAMCK

HAMTRAMCK REVIEW

Street Address: 3020 Caniff
City: Hamtramck
State: MI
Postal Code: 48212
Office phone: 313-874-2100
Publication Website: www.thehamtramckreview.com
General E-mail: news@thehamtramckreview.com
Publisher Name: John Ulaj
Editor Name: Charles Sercombe

HARRISON

CLARE COUNTY CLEAVER

Street Address: 183 West Main Street
City: Harrison
State: MI
Postal Code: 48625
Office phone: 989-539-7496
Publication Website: www.ClareCountyCleaver.net
Editor Name: Angela Kellogg
Editor Email: editor@clarecountycleaver.net

HASTINGS

LAKEWOOD NEWS

Street Address: 1351 N M 43 Hwy
City: Hastings
State: MI
Postal Code: 49058
Office phone: 269-945-9554
Publication Website: hastingsreminder.com
General E-mail: bonnie@j-adgraphics.com
Editor Name: Doug VanderLaan

Editor Name: Jacob Wheeler and Norm Wheeler
Editor Email: editorial@glenarborsun.com

MAPLE VALLEY NEWS

Corporate/Parent Company: J-Ad Graphics
Street Address: 1351 N M 43 Hwy
City: Hastings
State: MI
Postal Code: 49058-8499
Office phone: (269) 945-9554 ext.229
Publication Website: https://www.facebook.com/maplevalleynews/
General E-mail: maplevalleynews@j-adgraphics.com
Year Established: 1873
Delivery Methods: Newsstand`Carrier
Own Printing Facility?: Y
Commercial printers?: Y
Mechanical specifications: Type page 10 1/2 x 16; E - 6 cols, 1 2/3, 1/36 between.
Published Days: Sat
Avg Paid Circ: 160
Avg Free Circ: 4226
Audit Company: Sworn/Estimate/Non-Audited
Audit Date: 6 10 2019

THE HASTINGS BANNER

Corporate/Parent Company: J-Ad Graphics
Street Address: 1351 N M-43 Hwy
City: Hastings
State: MI
Postal Code: 49058
Office phone: (269) 945-9554
Publication Website: https://hastingsbanner.com/
Year Established: 1856
Delivery Methods: Mail`Newsstand
Own Printing Facility?: Y
Commercial printers?: Y
Mechanical specifications: Type page 14 3/4 x 22 3/4; E - 5 cols, 2 1/2, 1/2 between.
Published Days: Thur
Avg Paid Circ: 4998
Avg Free Circ: 30000
Audit Company: Sworn/Estimate/Non-Audited
Audit Date: 6 10 2019

HIGHLAND

OAKLAND LAKEFRONT LIFESTYLE MAGAZINE

Street Address: 1103 S. Milford Road
City: Highland
State: MI
Postal Code: 48357
Office phone: (248) 360-7355
Publication Website: www.oaklandlakefront.com
Publisher Name: Jim Stevenson
Publisher Email: jimstevenson@scnmail.com
Publisher Phone: 248-360-7355 ext. 21
Editor Name: Ali Armstrong
Editor Email: editor@scnmail.com
Editor Phone: 248-360-7355 ext. 12
Advertising Executive Name: Pat Collins
Advertising Executive Email: patcollins@scnmail.com
Advertising Executive Phone: 586-215-1400

HOWARD CITY

RIVER VALLEY NEWS SHOPPER

Corporate/Parent Company: Pioneer Group
Street Address: 491 W Shaw St
City: Howard City
State: MI
Postal Code: 49329-9401
Office phone: (231) 937-4740
Publication Website: http://www.rivervalleyshopper.com/
Editor Name: Tim Rath
Editor Phone: (231) 937-4740
Total Circulation: 32888

HUDSON

HUDSON POST-GAZETTE

Street Address: PO Box 70
City: Hudson
State: MI
Postal Code: 49247
Office phone: (517) 448-2611
Publication Website: www.HudsonPG.net
General E-mail: hudsonpost@gmail.com
Publication Name: Barbara Ireland
Editor Name: Rachel Stiverson
Total Circulation: 2976

IRON RIVER

IRON COUNTY REPORTER

Street Address: P.O. Box 311
City: Iron River
State: MI
Postal Code: 49935
Office phone: (906) 265-9927
Publication Website: www.ironcountyreporter.com
Editor Name: Jerry DeRoche
Editor Email: news@ironcountyreporter.com
Advertising Executive Name: Sari Jacobson
Advertising Executive Email: adsales@ironcountyreporter.com

JACKSON

JACKSON COUNTY LEGAL NEWS

Corporate/Parent Company: Detroit Legal News Publishing LLC
Street Address: 404 S Jackson Street
City: Jackson
State: MI
Postal Code: 49201
Office phone: (517) 782-0825
Publication Website: www.legalnews.com/jackson
Publisher Name: Ban Ibrahim
Publisher Email: ban@legalnews.com
Publisher Phone: (248) 577-6110
Editor Name: Tom Kirvan
Editor Email: tkirvan@legalnews.com
Editor Phone: (248) 556-7703
Advertising Executive Name: Suzanne Ketner
Advertising Executive Email: advertising@legalnews.com
Advertising Executive Phone: (734) 477-0247

LAKE CITY

THE MISSAUKEE SENTINEL

Street Address: 130 N. Main Street
City: Lake City
State: MI
Postal Code: 49651
Office phone: 231-839-5400
Publication Website: www.MissaukeeSentinel.com
General E-mail: sales@missaukeesentinel.com

LAKE ORION

THE LAKE ORION REVIEW

Corporate/Parent Company: Sherman Publications, Inc.
Street Address: 30 N Broadway St
City: Lake Orion
State: MI
Postal Code: 48362
Office phone: (248) 693-8331
Publication Website: http://www.lakeorionreview.com/
General E-mail: lakeorionreview@gmail.com
Publisher Name: Jim Sherman
Editor Name: Jim Newell
Advertising Executive Name: Eric Lewis
Year Established: 1881
Delivery Methods: Mail`Newsstand

Own Printing Facility?: Y
Commercial printers?: Y
Mechanical specifications: Type page 10 x11; 8, 1/5 between; between.
Published Days: Wed
Weekday Frequency: m
Avg Paid Circ: 2500
Avg Free Circ: 66
Audit Company: Sworn/Estimate/Non-Audited
Audit Date: 6 10 2019

LAKEVIEW

LAKEVIEW AREA NEWS

Street Address: 960 S. Lincoln Ave. Suite B / PO Box 439
City: Lakeview
State: MI
Postal Code: 48850
Office phone: (989) 352-5111
Publication Website: www.lakeviewareanewspaper.com
General E-mail: lannewsroom@gmail.com
Editor Name: Linda Huckins

LANSING

COMMUNITY VOICES MAGAZINE

Corporate/Parent Company: Season Press LLC
Street Address: 827 N. Washington Ave.
City: Lansing
State: MI
Postal Code: 48906
Office phone: 517.372.2424
Publication Website: www.comvoicesonline.com
General E-mail: ads@comvoicesonline.com
Editor Name: Sonya Bernard-Hollins
Editor Email: editor@comvoicesonline.com

GREAT LAKES BEACON

Street Address: 215 S Washington Square #150
City: Lansing
State: MI
Postal Code: 48933
Publication Website: www.greatlakesbeacon.org
General E-mail: contact@greatlakesbeacon.org

INSIDE MICHIGAN POLITICS

Street Address: 601 W. SHIAWASSEE ST
City: LANSING
State: MI
Postal Code: 48933
Office phone: 517.285.9659
Publication Website: www.insidemichiganpolitics.com
Publisher Name: Jake Davison
Publisher Email: insidemipolitics@gmail.com
Publisher Phone: 517-285-9659
Total Circulation: 29747

LANSING CITY PULSE

Street Address: 1905 E. Michigan Ave.
City: Lansing
State: MI
Postal Code: 48912
Office phone: (517) 371-5600
Publication Website: www.LansingCityPulse.com
Publisher Name: Berl Schwartz
Publisher Email: publisher@lansingcitypulse.com
Publisher Phone: (517) 999-5061
Advertising Executive Name: Lee Purdy
Advertising Executive Email: lee@lansingcitypulse.com
Advertising Executive Phone: (517) 999-5064

Non-Daily Newspapers in the U.S.

LAPEER

FLUSHING VIEW
Corporate/Parent Company: View Newspaper Group
Street Address: 1521 Imlay City Rd.
City: Lapeer
State: MI
Postal Code: 48446
Office phone: 810-664-0811
Publication Website: flushingview.mihomepaper.com
General E-mail: lettersbcb@mihomepaper.com
Editor Name: Jeff Hogan
Editor Email: bcbeditor@mihomepaper.com

LAPEER AREA VIEW
Corporate/Parent Company: View Newspaper Group
Street Address: 1521 Imlay City Rd.
City: Lapeer
State: MI
Postal Code: 48446
Office phone: 810-245-9343
Publication Website: LapeerAreaView.mihomepaper.com
General E-mail: letterslav@mihomepaper.com
Editor Name: Jeff Hogan
Editor Email: jhogan@mihomepaper.com
Total Circulation: 19202

VIEW NEWSPAPER GROUP
Corporate/Parent Company: View Newspaper Group
Street Address: P.O. Box 220 1521 Imlay City Road
City: Lapeer
State: MI
Postal Code: 48446
Office phone: 810-664-0811
Publication Website: www.viewnewspapers.net
General E-mail: info@mihomepaper.com
Publisher Name: Wes Smith
Publisher Email: wsmith@mihomepaper.com
Editor Name: Gary Gould
Editor Email: ggould@mihomepaper.com
Total Circulation: 4386

LOWELL

LOWELL BUYERS GUIDE
Corporate/Parent Company: J-Ad Graphics
Street Address: 105 N Broadway, PO Box 128
City: Lowell
State: MI
Postal Code: 49331
Office phone: (616) 897-9261
Publication Website: https://lowellbuyersguide.com/
General E-mail: ledger@lowellbuyersguide.com

MANCHESTER

THE MANCHESTER MIRROR
Street Address: PO Box 696
City: Manchester
State: MI
Postal Code: 48158
Office phone: (734) 328-1386
Publication Website: themanchestermirror.com
General E-mail: themanchestermirror@gmail.com
Editor Name: Marsha Chartrand
Editor Email: marshajc@gmail.com.

MANISTEE

WEST SHORE SHOPPER'S GUIDE
Street Address: 75 Maple St
City: Manistee
State: MI
Postal Code: 49660-1554
Office phone: (231) 723-3592

MARSHALL

AD-VISOR AND CHRONICLE
Corporate/Parent Company: J-Ad Graphics
Street Address: 514 S Kalamazoo Ave
City: Marshall
State: MI
Postal Code: 49068-1719
Office phone: (269) 781-5444
Publication Website: https://advisor-chronicle.com/index1.htm
General E-mail: alison@j-adgraphics.com
Editor Name: John Hendler
Editor Email: jhendler@j-adgraphics.com
Editor Phone: (269) 781-5444
Advertising Executive Name: Deb Miller
Advertising Executive Email: advisor@j-adgraphics.com
Year Established: 1985
Delivery Methods: Carrier`Racks
Mechanical specifications: Type page 10.5" x 16"; 6 cols
Published Days: Sat
Avg Paid Circ: 191
Avg Free Circ: 18200
Audit Company: Sworn/Estimate/Non-Audited
Audit Date: 6 10 2019

MASON

INGHAM COUNTY LEGAL NEWS
Corporate/Parent Company: Detroit Legal News Publishing LLC
Street Address: 157 West Maple Street
City: Mason
State: MI
Postal Code: 48854
Office phone: (517) 676-3395
Publication Website: www.LegalNews.com/Ingham
Publisher Name: Ban Ibrahim
Publisher Email: ban@legalnews.com
Publisher Phone: (248) 577-6110
Editor Name: Tom Kirvan
Editor Email: tkirvan@legalnews.com
Editor Phone: (248) 556-7703
Advertising Executive Name: Suzanne Ketner
Advertising Executive Email: advertising@legalnews.com
Advertising Executive Phone: (734) 477-0247

MIDLAND

MACKINAC CENTER FOR PUBLIC POLICY
Street Address: 140 W. Main Street
City: Midland
State: MI
Postal Code: 48640
Office phone: (989) 631-0900
Publication Website: www.mackinac.org
General E-mail: mcpp@mackinac.org
Editor Name: John LaPlante
Editor Email: author@mackinac.org
Total Circulation: 4662

MILAN

THE MILAN EAGLE
Street Address: 903 Dexter St.
City: Milan
State: MI
Postal Code: 48160
Office phone: (734) 649-6799
Publication Website: themilaneagle.com
General E-mail: editor@themilaneagle.com

MONROE

MONROE COUNTY COMMUNITY COLLEGE/ THE AGORA
Street Address: 1555 S. Raisinville Rd.
City: Monroe
State: MI
Postal Code: 48144
Office phone: (734) 384-4186
Publication Website: www.mcccagora.com
General E-mail: agora@monroeccc.edu
Editor Name: Todd Salisbury

MT. CLEMENS

MACOMB COUNTY LEGAL NEWS
Corporate/Parent Company: Detroit Legal News Publishing LLC
Street Address: 148 South Main Street, Suite 100
City: Mt. Clemens
State: MI
Postal Code: 48043
Office phone: (586) 463-4300
Publication Website: www.LegalNews.com
Publisher Name: Ban Ibrahim
Publisher Email: ban@legalnews.com
Publisher Phone: (248) 577-6110
Editor Name: Tom Kirvan
Editor Email: tkirvan@legalnews.com
Editor Phone: (248) 556-7703
Advertising Executive Name: Suzanne Ketner
Advertising Executive Email: advertising@legalnews.com
Advertising Executive Phone: (734) 477-0247

MUSKEGON

MUSKEGON COUNTY LEGAL NEWS
Corporate/Parent Company: Detroit Legal News Publishing LLC
Street Address: 950 W. Norton Ave. Suite 200
City: Muskegon
State: MI
Postal Code: 49441
Office phone: (231) 739-6397
Publication Website: www.legalnews.com/Muskegon
Publisher Name: Ban Ibrahim
Publisher Email: ban@legalnews.com
Publisher Phone: (248) 577-6110
Editor Name: Tom Kirvan
Editor Email: tkirvan@legalnews.com
Editor Phone: (248) 556-7703
Advertising Executive Name: Suzanne Ketner
Advertising Executive Email: advertising@legalnews.com
Advertising Executive Phone: (734) 477-0247
Total Circulation: 2397

MUSKEGON HEIGHTS

THE MUSKEGON TRIBUNE
Street Address: 260 E Broadway Ave
City: Muskegon Heights
State: MI
Postal Code: 49444
Office phone: 231-739-7253
Publication Website: muskegontribune.com
General E-mail: muskegontribune@gmail.com

NILES

LEADER PUBLICATIONS
Street Address: 217 N. 4th St.
City: Niles
State: MI
Postal Code: 49120
Office phone: 269-683-2100
Publication Website: www.leaderpub.com
General E-mail: classifieds@leaderpub.com
Editor Name: Sarah Culton
Editor Email: sarah.culton@leaderpub.com
Editor Phone: (269) 687-7712
Advertising Executive Name: Phil Langer
Advertising Executive Email: phil.langer@leaderpub.com
Advertising Executive Phone: (269) 687-7725
Total Circulation: 6000

NOVI

ITC HOLDINGS CORP
Street Address: 27175 Energy Way
City: Novi
State: MI
Postal Code: 48377
Office phone: 248-946-3000
Publication Website: www.itc-holdings.com
General E-mail: general@itctransco.com

WAYNE-WESTLAND OBSERVER
Street Address: 29725 Hudson Dr.
City: Novi
State: MI
Postal Code: 48377
Office phone: (866) 887-2737
Publication Website: www.hometownlife.com
General E-mail: livoenewstip@hometownlife.com

ORTONVILLE

CITIZEN
Corporate/Parent Company: Lee Enterprises
Street Address: 12 South St
City: Ortonville
State: MI
Postal Code: 48462-7717
Office phone: (248) 627-4332
Publication Website: http://www.thecitizenonline.com
General E-mail: citads@citnewspaper.com
Editor Name: David Fleet
Advertising Executive Name: Jackie Nowicki
Year Established: 1995
Delivery Methods: Mail
Commercial printers?: Y
Mechanical specifications: Type page 10 x 11; E - 6 cols, between.
Published Days: Sat
Avg Free Circ: 11800
Audit Company: Sworn/Estimate/Non-Audited
Audit Date: 6 10 2019
Total Circulation: 39362

OWOSSO

INDEPENDENT NEWSPAPERS
Street Address: 1907 W. M-21
City: Owosso
State: MI
Postal Code: 48867
Office phone: (989) 723-1118
Publication Website: www.owossoindependent.com
Editor Name: Graham Sturgeon
Editor Email: news@owossoindependent.com

THE NORTH INDEPENDENT
Street Address: 1907 W. M-21
City: Owosso
State: MI
Postal Code: 48867
Office phone: (989) 723-1118
Publication Website: owossoindependent.com
Editor Name: Graham Sturgeon
Editor Email: news@owossoindependent.com

THE SOUTH INDEPENDENT
Street Address: 1907 W. M-21
City: Owosso
State: MI
Postal Code: 48867
Office phone: (989) 723-1118
Publication Website: www.owossoindependent.com
Editor Name: Graham Sturgeon
Editor Email: news@owossoindependent.com

OXFORD

OXFORD LEADER
Corporate/Parent Company: Sherman Publications, Inc.
Street Address: 666 S Lapeer Rd
City: Oxford
State: MI
Postal Code: 48371-5034
Office phone: (248) 628-4801
Publication Website: http://www.oxfordleader.com/
General E-mail: eric@shermanpublications.org
Publisher Name: Jim Sherman
Editor Name: C.J.Carnacchio
Advertising Executive Name: Eric Lewis
Advertising Executive Email: eric@shermanpublications.org
Year Established: 1889
Delivery Methods: Mail
Own Printing Facility?: N
Commercial printers?: N
Mechanical specifications: Type page 10 x 11 A -8 cols, 1 1/8 between.1/8
Published Days: Wed
Weekday Frequency: m
Avg Paid Circ: 2300
Avg Free Circ: 97
Audit Company: Sworn/Estimate/Non-Audited
Audit Date: 6 10 2019

P.O. BOX 28

TINA NORRIS FIELDS
Corporate/Parent Company: Fields Media LLC
Street Address: P.O. Box 28
City: P.O. Box 28
State: MI
Postal Code: 49676
Office phone: (231) 322-2787
Publication Website: www.northwestmivoice.com
General E-mail: debbieomi@hotmail.com
Editor Name: Tina Norris
Editor Email: tina.fieldsmedia@gmail.com

PINCONNING

PINCONNING JOURNAL
Corporate/Parent Company: Issue Media Group
Street Address: 110 E. Third St. / P.O. Box 626
City: Pinconning
State: MI
Postal Code: 48650
Office phone: (989) 879-3811
Publication Website: www.pinconningjournal.com
General E-mail: editor@pinconningjournal.com

PLYMOUTH

CANTON EAGLE
Corporate/Parent Company: Associated Newspapers of Michigan
Street Address: P.O. Box 6320
City: Plymouth
State: MI
Postal Code: 48170-1752
Office phone: (734) 467-1900
Publication Website: http://associatednewspapers.net/
General E-mail: ads@journalgroup.com
Publisher Name: Susan Willett
Publisher Email: swillett@journalgroup.com
Publisher Phone: (734) 729-4000
Editor Name: Scott Spielman
Editor Phone: (734) 729-4000
Advertising Executive Email: ads@journalgroup.com
Year Established: 2002
Delivery Methods: Mail`Newsstand`Carrier`Racks
Own Printing Facility?: Y
Commercial printers?: Y
Mechanical specifications: 11.125" x 20.5 "
Published Days: Thur
Avg Paid Circ: 15000
Audit Company: Sworn/Estimate/Non-Audited
Audit Date: 6 10 2019

NEWS HUB MEDIA
Street Address: 14492 N. Sheldon Rd., Ste. 310
City: Plymouth
State: MI
Postal Code: 48170
Office phone: (248) 412-8810
Publication Website: www.pfmediatech.com
General E-mail: contact@newshubmedia.com

NORTHVILLE EAGLE
Corporate/Parent Company: Associated Newspapers of Michigan
Street Address: P.O. Box 6320
City: Plymouth
State: MI
Postal Code: 48170-1752
Office phone: (734) 467-1900
Publication Website: http://associatednewspapers.net/
General E-mail: ads@journalgroup.com
Publisher Name: Susan Willett
Publisher Email: swillett@journalgroup.com
Publisher Phone: (734) 729-4000
Editor Name: Scott Spielman
Editor Phone: (734) 729-4000
Advertising Executive Email: ads@journalgroup.com
Year Established: 2002
Delivery Methods: Mail`Carrier`Racks
Commercial printers?: Y
Published Days: Thur
Avg Paid Circ: 4662
Audit Company: Sworn/Estimate/Non-Audited
Audit Date: 6 10 2019

PLYMOUTH EAGLE
Corporate/Parent Company: Associated Newspapers of Michigan
Street Address: P.O. Box 6320
City: Plymouth
State: MI
Postal Code: 48170-1752
Office phone: (734) 467-1900
Publication Website: http://associatednewspapers.net/
General E-mail: ads@journalgroup.com
Publisher Name: Susan Willett
Publisher Email: swillett@journalgroup.com
Publisher Phone: (734) 729-4000
Editor Name: Scott Spielman
Editor Phone: (734) 729-4000
Advertising Executive Email: ads@journalgroup.com
Year Established: 2000
Delivery Methods: Mail`Newsstand`Carrier`Racks
Mechanical specifications: 11.125" x 20.5 "
Published Days: Thur
Avg Paid Circ: 6000
Audit Company: Sworn/Estimate/Non-Audited
Audit Date: 6 10 2019

THE EAGLE
Corporate/Parent Company: Lee Enterprises
Street Address: P.O. Box 6320
City: Plymouth
State: MI
Postal Code: 48170
Publication Website: www.associatednewspapers.net
General E-mail: swillett@journalgroup.com

THE ROMULUS ROMAN
Corporate/Parent Company: Associated Newspapers of Michigan
Street Address: P.O. Box 6320
City: Plymouth
State: MI
Postal Code: 48170-1752
Office phone: (734) 467-1900
Publication Website: http://associatednewspapers.net/
General E-mail: ads@journalgroup.com
Publisher Name: Susan Willett
Publisher Email: swillett@journalgroup.com
Publisher Phone: (734) 729-4000
Editor Name: Scott Spielman
Editor Phone: (734) 729-4000
Advertising Executive Email: ads@journalgroup.com
Year Established: 1885
Delivery Methods: Mail`Newsstand`Carrier`Racks
Own Printing Facility?: Y
Commercial printers?: Y
Mechanical specifications: 11.125" x 20.5"
Published Days: Thur
Avg Paid Circ: 1163
Avg Free Circ: 307
Audit Company: Sworn/Estimate/Non-Audited
Audit Date: 6 10 2019

THE WAYNE EAGLE
Corporate/Parent Company: Associated Newspapers of Michigan
Street Address: 502 Forest Ave
City: Plymouth
State: MI
Postal Code: 48170-1752
Office phone: (734) 467-1900
Publication Website: http://associatednewspapers.net/
General E-mail: ads@journalgroup.com
Publisher Name: Susan Willett
Publisher Email: swillett@journalgroup.com
Publisher Phone: (734) 729-4000
Editor Name: Scott Spielman
Editor Phone: (734) 729-4000
Advertising Executive Email: ads@journalgroup.com
Delivery Methods: Mail`Newsstand`Carrier`Racks
Mechanical specifications: 11/125" x 20.5 "
Published Days: Thur
Avg Paid Circ: 1253
Avg Free Circ: 998
Audit Company: Sworn/Estimate/Non-Audited
Audit Date: 6 10 2019

THE WESTLAND EAGLE
Corporate/Parent Company: Associated Newspapers of Michigan
Street Address: P.O. Box 6320
City: Plymouth
State: MI
Postal Code: 48170-1752
Office phone: (734) 467-1900
Publication Website: http://associatednewspapers.net/
General E-mail: ads@journalgroup.com
Publisher Name: Susan Willett
Publisher Email: swillett@journalgroup.com
Publisher Phone: (734) 729-4000
Editor Name: Scott Spielman
Editor Phone: (734) 729-4000
Advertising Executive Email: ads@journalgroup.com
Year Established: 1885
Delivery Methods: Mail`Newsstand`Carrier`Racks
Mechanical specifications: 11,125" x 20.5 "
Published Days: Thur
Avg Paid Circ: 100
Avg Free Circ: 1300
Audit Company: Sworn/Estimate/Non-Audited
Audit Date: 6 10 2019

PORTAGE

THE JOYFUL NOISELETTER
Street Address: P.O. Box 895
City: Portage
State: MI
Postal Code: 49081-0895
Office phone: 800-877-2757
Publication Website: www.joyfulnoiseletter.com/index.asp
General E-mail: JoyfulNZ@aol.com
Editor Name: Cal Samra

ROCHESTER

OAKLAND UNIVERSITY/ THE OAKLAND POST
Street Address: Room 63 312 Meadow Brook Road
City: Rochester
State: MI
Postal Code: 48309-4454
Office phone: (248) 370-2537
Publication Website: OaklandPostOnline.com
Editor Name: Trevor Tyle
Editor Email: editor@oaklandpostonline.com

ROSCOMMON

UP NORTH VOICE
Corporate/Parent Company: AuSable Media Group
Street Address: 709 Lake Street
City: Roscommon
State: MI
Postal Code: 48653
Office phone: (989) 275-1170
Publication Website: www.upnorthvoice.com
General E-mail: info@upnorthvoice.com
Editor Name: Theresa Ekdom
Editor Email: theresa@ausablemedia.com
Advertising Executive Name: Tracy Constance
Advertising Executive Email: tracy@ausablemedia.com
Advertising Executive Phone: 419-236-0359

SAGINAW

CATALYST MIDLAND
Corporate/Parent Company: Issue Media Group
Street Address: 5090 State St., Ste. D104
City: Saginaw
State: MI
Postal Code: 48603
Publication Website: www.secondwavemedia.com/midland
General E-mail: catalyst@catalystmidland.com
Editor Name: Courtney Soule

ROUTE BAY CITY
Corporate/Parent Company: Issue Media Group
Street Address: 5090 State St., Ste. D104
City: Saginaw
State: MI

Non-Daily Newspapers in the U.S.

Postal Code: 48603
Publication Website: www.secondwavemedia.com/Baycity
General E-mail: contact@routebaycity.com
Editor Email: editor@routebaycity.com

SECOND WAVE MICHIGAN
Corporate/Parent Company: Issue Media Group
Street Address: 5090 State St., Ste. D104
City: Saginaw
State: MI
Postal Code: 48603
Publication Website: www.secondwavemedia.com
General E-mail: feedback@secondwavemedia.com
Editor Name: Kathy Jennings

SOUTHWEST MICHIGAN SECOND WAVE
Corporate/Parent Company: Issue Media Group
Street Address: 5090 State St., Ste. D-104
City: Saginaw
State: MI
Postal Code: 48603
Publication Website: www.secondwavemedia.com/southwest-michigan
General E-mail: feedback@secondwavemedia.com
Editor Name: Kathy Jennings
Editor Email: kathy@secondwavemedia.com

THE KEEL
Corporate/Parent Company: Issue Media Group
Street Address: 5090 State St., Ste. D104
City: Saginaw
State: MI
Postal Code: 48603
Publication Website: www.secondwavemedia.com/the-keel
General E-mail: feedback@thekeelph.com
Editor Name: Jodi Rempala

SANDUSKY

SANDUSKY TRIBUNE & DECKERVILLE RECORDER & MARLETTE LEADER
Street Address: 43 S. Elk St.
City: Sandusky
State: MI
Postal Code: 48471
Office phone: (810) 648-5282
Publication Website: www.tribunerecorderleader.com
General E-mail: sandusky.tribune@gmail.com
Editor Name: William Dixon

SCHOOLCRAFT

SOUTH COUNTY NEWS
Street Address: P.O. Box 723
City: Schoolcraft
State: MI
Postal Code: 49087
Office phone: (269) 649-2453
Publication Website: southcountynews.org
General E-mail: sue@suemoore.com
Editor Name: Sue Moore
Advertising Executive Name: Sheri Freeland

TROY

OAKLAND COUNTY LEGAL NEWS
Corporate/Parent Company: Detroit Legal News Publishing LLC
Street Address: 1409 Allen Rd, Suite B
City: Troy
State: MI
Postal Code: 48083
Office phone: (248) 577-6100
Publication Website: www.legalnews.com/oakland
Publisher Name: Ban Ibrahim
Publisher Email: ban@legalnews.com
Publisher Phone: (248) 577-6110
Editor Name: Tom Kirvan
Editor Email: tkirvan@legalnews.com
Editor Phone: (248) 556-7703
Advertising Executive Name: Suzanne Ketner
Advertising Executive Email: advertising@legalnews.com
Advertising Executive Phone: (734) 477-0247

UNION CITY

HOMETOWN GAZETTE
Street Address: 220 N Broadway St.
City: Union City
State: MI
Postal Code: 49094
Office phone: (517) 741-7646
Publication Website: www.thehometowngazette.com

WARREN

ADVERTISER TIMES
Corporate/Parent Company: C & G Newspapers
Street Address: 13650 E 11 Mile Rd
City: Warren
State: MI
Postal Code: 48089-1422
Office phone: (586) 498-8000
Publication Website: https://www.candgnews.com/newspaper/advertisertimes
General E-mail: mail@candgnews.com
Editor Name: David Wallace
Editor Email: dwallace@candgnews.com
Editor Phone: (586) 498-1053
Advertising Executive Phone: (586) 924-9193
Year Established: 1981
Delivery Methods: Mail
Mechanical specifications: Type page 10 4/5 x 13 1/2; E - 5 cols, 2, 1/6 between; A - 5 cols, 2, 1/6 between; C - 6 cols, 1 1/2, 1/6 between.
Published Days: Wed
Avg Free Circ: 24588
Audit Company: Sworn/Estimate/Non-Audited
Audit Date: 6 10 2019

BIRMINGHAM-BLOOMFIELD EAGLE
Corporate/Parent Company: C & G Newspapers
Street Address: 13650 E 11 Mile Rd
City: Warren
State: MI
Postal Code: 48089-1422
Office phone: (586) 498-8000
Publication Website: https://www.candgnews.com/newspaper/birminghambloomfieldeagle
General E-mail: mail@candgnews.com
Editor Name: Annie Bates
Editor Email: abates@candgnews.com
Editor Phone: (586) 498-1071
Advertising Executive Phone: (586) 924-9193
Year Established: 2003
Delivery Methods: Mail Racks
Published Days: Wed
Avg Free Circ: 33334
Audit Company: AAM
Audit Date: 31 03 2018

FARMINGTON PRESS
Corporate/Parent Company: C & G Newspapers
Street Address: 13650 E 11 Mile Rd
City: Warren
State: MI
Postal Code: 48089-1422
Office phone: (586) 498-8000
Publication Website: https://www.candgnews.com/newspaper/farmingtonpress
General E-mail: mail@candgnews.com
Editor Name: Annie Bates
Editor Email: abates@candgnews.com
Editor Phone: (586) 498-1071
Advertising Executive Phone: (586) 924-9193
Year Established: 2008
Delivery Methods: Mail
Published Days: Wed
Avg Free Circ: 37805
Audit Company: AAM
Audit Date: 31 03 2018

FRASER-CLINTON CHRONICLE
Corporate/Parent Company: C & G Newspapers
Street Address: 13650 E 11 Mile Rd
City: Warren
State: MI
Postal Code: 48089-1422
Office phone: (586) 498-8000
Publication Website: https://www.candgnews.com/newspaper/fraserclintonchronicle
General E-mail: mail@candgnews.com
Editor Name: Jon Malavolti
Editor Email: jmalavolti@candgnews.com
Editor Phone: (586) 498-1059
Advertising Executive Phone: (586) 924-9193
Year Established: 1989
Delivery Methods: Mail
Own Printing Facility?: Y
Commercial printers?: N
Mechanical specifications: Type page 9.5 x 11; E - 5 cols, 5/16, 3/16 between; A - 5 cols, 5/16, 3/16 between; C - 5 cols, 1/4, 3/16 between.
Published Days: Wed
Avg Free Circ: 32409
Audit Company: CVC
Audit Date: 30 03 2018

GROSSE POINTE TIMES
Corporate/Parent Company: C & G Newspapers
Street Address: 13650 E 11 Mile Rd
City: Warren
State: MI
Postal Code: 48089-1422
Office phone: (586) 498-8000
Publication Website: https://www.candgnews.com/newspaper/grossepointetimes
General E-mail: mail@candgnews.com
Editor Name: David Wallace
Editor Email: dwallace@candgnews.com
Editor Phone: (586) 498-1053
Advertising Executive Phone: (586) 924-9193
Year Established: 1982
Delivery Methods: Mail Racks
Mechanical specifications: Type page 10 5/16 x 12 5/8; E - 5 cols, 2, 1/6 between; A - 5 cols, 2, 1/6 between; C - 6 cols, 1 1/2, 1/6 between.
Published Days: Wed
Avg Free Circ: 18810
Audit Company: AAM
Audit Date: 30 09 2018

JOURNAL
Corporate/Parent Company: C & G Newspapers
Street Address: 13650 E 11 Mile Rd
City: Warren
State: MI
Postal Code: 48089-1422
Office phone: (586) 498-8000
Publication Website: https://www.candgnews.com/newspaper/cgjournal
General E-mail: mail@candgnews.com
Editor Name: Jon Malavolti
Editor Email: jmalavolti@candgnews.com
Editor Phone: (586) 498-1059
Advertising Executive Phone: (586) 924-9193
Year Established: 1988
Delivery Methods: Mail
Mechanical specifications: Type page 10 4/5 x 13 1/6; E - 5 cols, 2, 1/6 between; A - 5 cols, 2, 1/6 between; C - 6 cols, 1 1/2, 1/6 between.
Published Days: Wed
Avg Free Circ: 32888
Audit Company: AAM
Audit Date: 31 03 2018

MACOMB CHRONICLE
Corporate/Parent Company: C & G Newspapers
Street Address: 13650 E 11 Mile Rd
City: Warren
State: MI
Postal Code: 48089-1422
Office phone: (586) 498-8000
Publication Website: https://www.candgnews.com/newspaper/macombchronicle
General E-mail: mail@candgnews.com
Editor Name: Jon Malavolti
Editor Email: jmalavolti@candgnews.com
Editor Phone: (586) 498-1059
Advertising Executive Phone: (586) 924-9193
Year Established: 1989
Delivery Methods: Mail Racks
Commercial printers?: Y
Published Days: Thur
Avg Free Circ: 29747
Audit Company: AAM
Audit Date: 31 03 2018

MADISON-PARK NEWS
Corporate/Parent Company: C & G Newspapers
Street Address: 13650 E 11 Mile Rd
City: Warren
State: MI
Postal Code: 48089-1422
Office phone: (586) 498-8000
Publication Website: https://www.candgnews.com/newspaper/madisonparknews
General E-mail: mail@candgnews.com
Editor Name: Jon Malavolti
Editor Email: jmalavolti@candgnews.com
Editor Phone: (586) 498-1059
Advertising Executive Phone: (586) 924-9193
Year Established: 1982
Delivery Methods: Mail Racks
Mechanical specifications: Type page 10 5/16 x 12 5/8; E - 5 cols, 2, 1/6 between; A - 5 cols, 2, 1/6 between; C - 6 cols, 1 1/2, 1/6 between.
Published Days: Wed
Avg Free Circ: 19292
Audit Company: AAM
Audit Date: 30 09 2018

ROCHESTER POST
Corporate/Parent Company: C & G Newspapers
Street Address: 13650 E 11 Mile Rd
City: Warren
State: MI
Postal Code: 48089-1422
Office phone: (586) 498-8000
Publication Website: https://www.candgnews.com/newspaper/rochester-post
General E-mail: mail@candgnews.com
Editor Name: Annie Bates
Editor Email: abates@candgnews.com
Editor Phone: (586) 498-1071
Advertising Executive Phone: (586) 924-9193
Year Established: 2005
Delivery Methods: Mail
Mechanical specifications: Type page 9.5" x

11"; 5 cols
Published Days: Thur
Avg Free Circ: 39362
Audit Company: AAM
Audit Date: 30 09 2018

ROSEVILLE-EASTPOINTE EASTSIDER

Corporate/Parent Company: C & G Publishing
Street Address: 13650 E. Eleven Mile Rd.
City: Warren
State: MI
Postal Code: 48089
Office phone: (586) 498-8000
Publication Website: www.candgnews.com
Editor Name: David Wallace
Editor Email: dwallace@candgnews.com
Editor Phone: (586) 498-1053

ROYAL OAK REVIEW

Corporate/Parent Company: C & G Newspapers
Street Address: 13650 E 11 Mile Rd
City: Warren
State: MI
Postal Code: 48089-1422
Office phone: (586) 498-8000
Publication Website: https://www.candgnews.com/newspaper/royaloak-review
General E-mail: mail@candgnews.com
Editor Name: David Wallace
Editor Email: dwallace@candgnews.com
Editor Phone: (586) 498-1053
Advertising Executive Phone: (586) 924-9193
Year Established: 2003
Delivery Methods: Mail
Published Days: Wed
Avg Free Circ: 32006
Audit Company: AAM
Audit Date: 31 03 2018

SHELBY-UTICA NEWS

Corporate/Parent Company: C & G Newspapers
Street Address: 13650 E 11 Mile Rd
City: Warren
State: MI
Postal Code: 48089-1422
Office phone: (586) 498-8000
Publication Website: https://www.candgnews.com/newspaper/shelbyuticanews
General E-mail: mail@candgnews.com
Editor Name: David Wallace
Editor Email: dwallace@candgnews.com
Editor Phone: (586) 498-1053
Advertising Executive Phone: (586) 924-9193
Year Established: 1992
Delivery Methods: Mail
Mechanical specifications: Type page 10 5/16 x 12 5/8; E - 4 cols, 2 7/16, 3/16 between; A - 4 cols, 2 7/16, 3/16 between; C - 6 cols, 1 9/16, 3/16 between.
Published Days: Wed
Avg Free Circ: 31103
Audit Company: AAM
Audit Date: 31 03 2018

SOUTHFIELD SUN

Corporate/Parent Company: C & G Newspapers
Street Address: 13650 E 11 Mile Rd
City: Warren
State: MI
Postal Code: 48089-1422
Office phone: (586) 498-8000
Publication Website: https://www.candgnews.com/newspaper/southfieldsun
General E-mail: mail@candgnews.com
Editor Name: Annie Bates
Editor Email: abates@candgnews.com

Editor Phone: (586) 498-1071
Advertising Executive Phone: (586) 924-9193
Year Established: 2004
Delivery Methods: Mail
Published Days: Thur
Avg Free Circ: 32135
Audit Company: AAM
Audit Date: 31 03 2018

ST. CLAIR SHORES SENTINEL

Corporate/Parent Company: C & G Newspapers
Street Address: 13650 E 11 Mile Rd
City: Warren
State: MI
Postal Code: 48089-1422
Office phone: (586) 498-8000
Publication Website: https://www.candgnews.com/newspaper/stclairshoressentinel
General E-mail: mail@candgnews.com
Editor Name: Jon Malavolti
Editor Email: jmalavolti@candgnews.com
Editor Phone: (586) 498-1059
Advertising Executive Phone: (586) 924-9193
Year Established: 1981
Delivery Methods: Mail`Racks
Mechanical specifications: Type page 10 5/16 x 12 5/8; E - 5 cols, 2, 1/6 between; A - 5 cols, 2, 1/6 between; C - 6 cols, 1 1/2, 1/6 between.
Published Days: Wed
Avg Free Circ: 27151
Audit Company: AAM
Audit Date: 31 03 2018

STERLING HEIGHTS SENTRY

Corporate/Parent Company: C & G Newspapers
Street Address: 13650 E 11 Mile Rd
City: Warren
State: MI
Postal Code: 48089-1422
Office phone: (586) 498-8000
Publication Website: https://www.candgnews.com/newspaper/sterlingheightssentry
General E-mail: mail@candgnews.com
Editor Name: Annie Bates
Editor Email: abates@candgnews.com
Editor Phone: (586) 498-1071
Advertising Executive Phone: (586) 924-9193
Year Established: 1990
Delivery Methods: Mail
Own Printing Facility?: Y
Commercial printers?: N
Mechanical specifications: Type page 9.5 x 11; E - 5 cols, 2, 1/6 between; A - 5 cols, 2, 1/6 between; C - 6 cols, 1 1/2, 1/6 between.
Published Days: Wed
Avg Free Circ: 48431
Audit Company: AAM
Audit Date: 31 03 2018

THE EASTSIDER

Corporate/Parent Company: C & G Newspapers
Street Address: 13650 E 11 Mile Rd
City: Warren
State: MI
Postal Code: 48089-1422
Office phone: (586) 498-8000
Publication Website: https://www.candgnews.com/newspaper/eastsider
General E-mail: mail@candgnews.com
Editor Name: David Wallace
Editor Email: dwallace@candgnews.com
Editor Phone: (586) 498-1053
Advertising Executive Phone: (586) 924-9193
Year Established: 1982
Delivery Methods: Mail`Racks
Mechanical specifications: Type page 10 4/5 x 13 1/6; E - 5 cols, 2, 1/6 between; A - 5 cols, 2, 1/6 between; C - 6 cols, 1 1/2, 1/6 between.
Published Days: Wed
Avg Free Circ: 31035
Audit Company: AAM

Audit Date: 30 09 2018

TROY TIMES

Corporate/Parent Company: C & G Newspapers
Street Address: 13650 E 11 Mile Rd
City: Warren
State: MI
Postal Code: 48089-1422
Office phone: (586) 498-8000
Publication Website: https://www.candgnews.com/newspaper/troytimes
General E-mail: mail@candgnews.com
Editor Name: Annie Bates
Editor Email: abates@candgnews.com
Editor Phone: (586) 498-1071
Advertising Executive Phone: (586) 924-9193
Year Established: 1985
Delivery Methods: Mail`Carrier`Racks
Mechanical specifications: Type page 10 5/16 x 12 5/8; E - 4 cols, 2 7/16, 3/16 between; A - 4 cols, 2 7/16, 3/16 between; C - 6 cols, 1 9/16, 3/16 between.
Published Days: Thur
Avg Free Circ: 31455
Audit Company: CVC
Audit Date: 31 03 2018

WARREN WEEKLY

Corporate/Parent Company: C & G Newspapers
Street Address: 13650 E 11 Mile Rd
City: Warren
State: MI
Postal Code: 48089-1422
Office phone: (586) 498-8000
Publication Website: https://www.candgnews.com/newspaper/warrenweekly
General E-mail: mail@candgnews.com
Editor Name: Jon Malavolti
Editor Email: jmalavolti@candgnews.com
Editor Phone: (586) 498-1059
Advertising Executive Phone: (586) 924-9193
Year Established: 1981
Delivery Methods: Mail`Racks
Mechanical specifications: Type page 10 5/16 x 12 5/8; E - 5 cols, 2, 1/6 between; A - 5 cols, 2, 1/6 between; C - 6 cols, 1 1/2, 1/6 between.
Published Days: Wed
Avg Free Circ: 55976
Audit Company: AAM
Audit Date: 31 03 2018

WEST BLOOMFIELD BEACON

Corporate/Parent Company: C & G Publishing
Street Address: 13650 E. Eleven Mile Rd.
City: Warren
State: MI
Postal Code: 48089
Office phone: (586) 498-8000
Publication Website: www.candgnews.com
General E-mail: skolade@candgnews.com
Editor Name: Annie Bates
Editor Email: mail@candgnews.com
Year Established: 2004
Delivery Methods: Mail
Published Days: Wed
Avg Free Circ: 27536
Audit Company: AAM
Audit Date: 30 09 2018

WOODWARD TALK

Corporate/Parent Company: C & G Newspapers
Street Address: 13650 E 11 Mile Rd
City: Warren
State: MI
Postal Code: 48089-1422
Office phone: (586) 498-8000
Publication Website: https://www.candgnews.

com/newspaper/woodwardtalk
General E-mail: mail@candgnews.com
Editor Name: David Wallace
Editor Email: dwallace@candgnews.com
Editor Phone: (586) 498-1053
Advertising Executive Phone: (586) 924-9193
Year Established: 2004
Delivery Methods: Mail
Published Days: Wed
Avg Free Circ: 20028
Audit Company: CVC
Audit Date: 31 03 2018

WASHINGTON

THE RECORD NEWSPAPER

Street Address: PO Box 708
City: Washington
State: MI
Postal Code: 48094
Office phone: 586-752-3524
Publication Website: www.myrecordnewspaper.com
General E-mail: publisher@myrecordnewspaper.com
Editor Name: LARRY SOBCZAK

CONCENTRATE

Corporate/Parent Company: Issue Media Group
State: MI
Publication Website: www.secondwavemedia.com/concentrate
General E-mail: feedback@concentratemedia.com
Editor Name: Patrick Dunn
Editor Email: patrickpdunn@gmail.com

EPICENTER MT. PLEASANT

Corporate/Parent Company: Issue Media Group
State: MI
Publication Website: www.secondwavemedia.com/epicenter
General E-mail: contact@epicentermtpleasant.com
Editor Name: GABRIELLE HAIDERER
Editor Email: editor@epicentermtpleasant.com

ERIC YOUNG

State: MI
Office phone: 989-513-2740
Publication Website: www.dreambiggermedia.com
Publisher Name: Eric Young
Publisher Email: Eric@dreambiggermedia.com

FLINTSIDE

Corporate/Parent Company: Issue Media Group
State: MI
Publication Website: www.flintside.com
General E-mail: contact@flintside.com
Editor Name: Alexandria Brown
Editor Email: abrown@flintside.com

MINNESOTA

ADRIAN

ADRIAN - NOBLES COUNTY REVIEW

Street Address: P.O. Box 160; 108 Maine

Non-Daily Newspapers in the U.S.

Avenue
City: Adrian
State: MN
Postal Code: 56110-0160
Office phone: (507) 483-2213
Publication Website: www.noblescountyreview.net
Publisher Name: Gerald D. Johnson
Editor Name: Kathy Burzlaf
Editor Email: ncreview@frontier.com

AITKIN

AITKIN INDEPENDENT AGE

Corporate/Parent Company: Adams Publishing Group
Street Address: 213 Minnesota Ave N
City: Aitkin
State: MN
Postal Code: 56431
Office phone: (218) 927-3761
Publication Website: https://www.messagemedia.co/aitkin/
General E-mail: news@aitkinage.com
Year Established: 1883
Delivery Methods: Mail`Newsstand
Commercial printers?: Y
Published Days: Wed
Avg Paid Circ: 3800
Audit Company: Sworn/Estimate/Non-Audited
Audit Date: 6 10 2019

ALBANY

ALBANY ENTERPRISE

Corporate/Parent Company: Star Publications
Street Address: 561 Railroad Ave.
City: Albany
State: MN
Postal Code: 56307
Office phone: (320) 845-2700
Publication Website: star-pub.com
General E-mail: logan@saukherald.com
Editor Name: Liz Vos
Editor Email: liz@albanyenterprise.com
Total Circulation: 3800

ALDEN

ALDEN ADVANCE

Street Address: P.O. Box 485; 150 East Main
City: Alden
State: MN
Postal Code: 56009-0485
Office phone: (507) 383-9001
Publication Website: www.aldenadvance.com
Editor Name: Shelly Zeller
Editor Email: editor@aldenadvance.com

ALEXANDRIA

ALEXANDRA ECHO PRESS

Corporate/Parent Company: Echo Press and Forum Communications Company
Street Address: P.O. Box 549; 225 Seventh Avenue East
City: Alexandria
State: MN
Postal Code: 56308-0549
Office phone: (320) 763-3133
Publication Website: www.echopress.com
General E-mail: echo@echopress.com
Publisher Name: Jody Hanson
Publisher Email: jhanson@echopress.com
Publisher Phone: (320) 763-1222
Editor Name: Ross Evavold
Editor Email: revavold@echopress.com
Editor Phone: (320) 763-1211
Advertising Executive Name: Karen Jennissen
Advertising Executive Email: kjennissen@echopress.com
Advertising Executive Phone: (320) 763-1215

APPLE VALLEY

APPLE VALLEY/FARMIGHTON/ROESEMOUNT-DAKOTA COUNTY TRIBUNE

Street Address: 15322 Galaxie Avenue, Suite 219
City: Apple Valley
State: MN
Postal Code: 55124
Office phone: (952) 894-1111
Publication Website: www.sunthisweek.com
Editor Name: Tad Johnson
Editor Email: tad.johnson@ecm-inc.com
Editor Phone: 952-846-2033
Advertising Executive Name: Steve Gall
Advertising Executive Email: ads.thisweek@ecm-inc.com

DAKOTA COUNTY TRIBUNE

Corporate/Parent Company: Adams Publishing Group
Street Address: 15322 Galaxie Ave
City: Apple Valley
State: MN
Postal Code: 55124
Office phone: (952) 894-1111
Publication Website: https://www.hometownsource.com/sun_thisweek/
General E-mail: servicecenter@ecm-inc.com
Editor Name: Tad Johnson
Editor Email: tad.johnson@ecm-inc.com
Editor Phone: (952) 846-2033
Advertising Executive Name: Steve Gall
Advertising Executive Email: steve.gall@ecm-inc.com
Advertising Executive Phone: (952) 392-6844
Year Established: 1887
Own Printing Facility?: Y
Commercial printers?: Y
Published Days: Thur
Avg Paid Circ: 19
Avg Free Circ: 12687
Audit Company: Sworn/Estimate/Non-Audited
Audit Date: 6 10 2019

EAGAPPLE VALLEY/ROSEMOUNT SUN THISWEEK

Street Address: 15322 Galaxie Ave., Suite 219
City: Apple Valley
State: MN
Postal Code: 55124
Office phone: (952) 894-1111
Publication Website: https://www.hometownsource.com/sun_thisweek/
General E-mail: servicecenter@ecm-inc.com
Editor Name: Andy Rogers
Editor Email: andy.rogers@ecm-inc.com
Editor Phone: (952) 846-2027
Advertising Executive Name: Steve Gall
Advertising Executive Email: steve.gall@ecm-inc.com
Advertising Executive Phone: (952) 392-6844

LAKEVILLE- SUN THISWEEK

Street Address: 15322 Galaxie Ave., Suite 219
City: Apple Valley
State: MN
Postal Code: 55124
Office phone: 952-894-1111
Publication Website: www.hometownsource.com/sun_thisweek
General E-mail: servicecenter@ecm-inc.com
Editor Name: Tad Johnson
Editor Email: tad.johnson@ecm-inc.com
Editor Phone: 952-846-2033
Advertising Executive Name: Steve Gall
Advertising Executive Email: steve.gall@ecm-inc.com
Advertising Executive Phone: 952-392-6844
Total Circulation: 3736

SUN THISWEEK APPLE VALLEY

Street Address: 15322 Galaxie Ave
City: Apple Valley
State: MN
Postal Code: 55124
Office phone: (952) 894-1111
Publication Website: https://www.hometownsource.com/sun_thisweek/
General E-mail: servicecenter@ecm-inc.com
Advertising Executive Name: Steve Gall
Advertising Executive Email: steve.gall@ecm-inc.com
Advertising Executive Phone: (952) 392-6844
Year Established: 1979
Delivery Methods: Carrier
Own Printing Facility?: Y
Commercial printers?: Y
Mechanical specifications: Type page 6 x 21; E - 5 cols, 2, 3/16 between; A - 5 cols, 2, 3/16 between; C - 8 cols, 1 1/8, 1/8 between.
Published Days: Thur
Avg Paid Circ: 25
Avg Free Circ: 11248
Audit Company: Sworn/Estimate/Non-Audited
Audit Date: 6 10 2019

SUN THISWEEK LAKEVILLE

Street Address: 15322 Galaxie Ave
City: Apple Valley
State: MN
Postal Code: 55124
Office phone: (952) 894-1111
Publication Website: https://www.hometownsource.com/sun_thisweek/
General E-mail: servicecenter@ecm-inc.com
Editor Name: Tad Johnson
Editor Email: tad.johnson@ecm-inc.com
Editor Phone: (952) 846-2033
Advertising Executive Name: Steve Gall
Advertising Executive Email: steve.gall@ecm-inc.com
Advertising Executive Phone: (952) 392-6844
Year Established: 1979
Delivery Methods: Carrier
Own Printing Facility?: N
Commercial printers?: N
Published Days: Thur
Avg Paid Circ: 22
Avg Free Circ: 16807
Audit Company: Sworn/Estimate/Non-Audited
Audit Date: 6 10 2019

THISWEEK BURNSVILLE-EAGAN SUN

Street Address: 15322 Galaxie Ave
City: Apple Valley
State: MN
Postal Code: 55124
Office phone: (952) 894-1111
Publication Website: https://www.hometownsource.com/sun_thisweek/
General E-mail: servicecenter@ecm-inc.com
Editor Name: John Gessner
Editor Email: john.gessner@ecm-inc.com
Editor Phone: (952) 846-2031
Advertising Executive Name: Steve Gall
Advertising Executive Email: steve.gall@ecm-inc.com
Advertising Executive Phone: (952) 392-6844
Year Established: 1979
Delivery Methods: Carrier
Own Printing Facility?: Y
Commercial printers?: Y
Mechanical specifications: Type page 10 x 15; E - 5 cols, 2, 3/16 between; A - 5 cols, 2, 1/8 between; C - 8 cols, 1 1/8, 1/8 between.
Published Days: Thur
Avg Paid Circ: 77
Avg Free Circ: 25733
Audit Company: Sworn/Estimate/Non-Audited
Audit Date: 6 10 2019

BAGLEY

BAGLEY-FARMERS INDEPENDENT

Street Address: P.O. Box 130; 102 North Main
City: Bagley
State: MN
Postal Code: 56621-0130
Office phone: (218) 694-6265
Publication Website: www.bagleymnnews.com
General E-mail: farmpub@gvtel.com
Editor Name: Tom Burford

BECKER

BECKER/CLEARWATER-CITIZEN-TRIBUNE

Corporate/Parent Company: Meyer Group
Street Address: 14054 Bank Street/P.O. Box 217
City: Becker
State: MN
Postal Code: 55308
Office phone: 763-261-5880
Publication Website: www.citizennewspaper.com
Publisher Name: Gary W. Meyer
Publisher Email: citizennewspaper@midconetwork.com
Advertising Executive Name: Mary Nehring
Advertising Executive Email: citizenads@midconetwork.com
Total Circulation: 15901

BLOOMING PRAIRIE

BLOOMING PRAIRIE- STEELE COUNTY TIMER

Corporate/Parent Company: Bussler Publishing, Inc.
Street Address: P.O. Box 247; 411 East Main Street
City: Blooming Prairie
State: MN
Postal Code: 55917-0247
Office phone: (507) 583-4431
Publication Website: www.steeledodgenews.com
General E-mail: bptimes@frontiernet.net
Publisher Name: Rick Bussler
Advertising Executive Name: Annie Anderson
Advertising Executive Phone: 507-319-1549

BOVEY

BOVEY- SCENIC RANGE NEWS FORUM

Street Address: PO Box 70
City: Bovey
State: MN
Postal Code: 55709
Office phone: (218) 245-1422
Publication Website: www.scenicrangenews.com
General E-mail: copy@scenicrangenewsforum.com
Editor Name: Mary Beth Bily
Advertising Executive Name: Ronald Brochu
Total Circulation: 24882

CALEDONIA

THE CALEDONIA ARGUS

Corporate/Parent Company: Adams Publishing Group

Non-Daily Newspapers in the U.S.

Street Address: 225 S. Kingston
City: Caledonia
State: MN
Postal Code: 55921
Office phone: (507) 724-3475
Publication Website: https://www.hometownsource.com/caledonia/
General E-mail: greg.petersen@ecm-inc.com
Editor Name: Jordan Gerard
Editor Email: jordan.gerard@ecm-inc.com
Editor Phone: (507) 556-1701
Year Established: 1875
Delivery Methods: Mail`Newsstand
Mechanical specifications: Type page 12 3/4 x 21 1/2; E - 6 cols, 2, 1/4 between; A - 6 cols, 2, between; C - 6 cols, 2, between.
Published Days: Wed
Avg Paid Circ: 2094
Avg Free Circ: 3748
Audit Company: Sworn/Estimate/Non-Audited
Audit Date: 6 10 2019

CAMBRIDGE

CAMBRIDGE/ NORTH BRANCH- COUNTY NEWS REVIEW

Street Address: 234 South Main Street
City: Cambridge
State: MN
Postal Code: 55008
Office phone: (763) 691-6000
Publication Website: www.hometownsource.com/county_news_review
Editor Name: Rachel Kytonen
Advertising Executive Name: Jerry Gloe
Advertising Executive Email: jerry.gloe@ecm-inc.com

ISANTI COUNTY NEWS

Street Address: 234 Main St S
City: Cambridge
State: MN
Postal Code: 55008
Office phone: (763) 691-6000
Publication Website: https://www.hometownsource.com/county_news_review/
General E-mail: servicecenter@ecm-inc.com
Editor Name: Rachel Kytonen
Editor Email: editor.countynews@ecm-inc.com
Editor Phone: (763) 691-6012
Advertising Executive Name: Jerry Gloe
Advertising Executive Email: jerry.gloe@ecm-inc.com
Advertising Executive Phone: (763) 712-3553
Year Established: 1900
Mechanical specifications: Type page: 10.4 x 21; 6 col
Published Days: Wed
Avg Paid Circ: 125
Avg Free Circ: 12948
Audit Company: Sworn/Estimate/Non-Audited
Audit Date: 6 10 2019

THE POST REVIEW

Corporate/Parent Company: Adams Publishing Group
Street Address: 234 Main St S
City: Cambridge
State: MN
Postal Code: 55008
Office phone: (763) 691-6000
Publication Website: https://www.hometownsource.com/county_news_review/
General E-mail: servicecenter@ecm-inc.com
Editor Name: Rachel Kytonen
Editor Email: editor.countynews@ecm-inc.com
Editor Phone: (763) 691-6012
Advertising Executive Name: Jerry Gloe
Advertising Executive Email: jerry.gloe@ecm-inc.com
Advertising Executive Phone: (763) 712-3553

Year Established: 1875
Delivery Methods: Mail
Mechanical specifications: Type page: 10.4 x 21; 6 col
Published Days: Wed
Avg Paid Circ: 1259
Audit Company: Sworn/Estimate/Non-Audited
Audit Date: 6 10 2019

CHASKA

CHANHASSEN VILLAGER

Street Address: 123 W 2nd St
City: Chaska
State: MN
Postal Code: 55318-1907
Office phone: (952) 934-5045
Publication Website: https://www.swnewsmedia.com/chanhassen_villager/
General E-mail: schacherer@hutchinsonleader.com
Publisher Name: Laurie Hartmann
Publisher Email: lhartmann@swnewsmedia.com
Publisher Phone: (952) 345-6878
Editor Name: Mark Olson
Editor Email: editor@chanvillager.com
Editor Phone: (952) 345-6574
Delivery Methods: Mail
Published Days: Thur
Avg Free Circ: 4532
Audit Company: Sworn/Estimate/Non-Audited
Audit Date: 6 10 2019
Total Circulation: 7031

CHASKA

CHASKA HERALD

Street Address: 123 W 2nd St
City: Chaska
State: MN
Postal Code: 55318-1907
Office phone: (952) 448-2650
Publication Website: https://www.swnewsmedia.com/chaska_herald/
General E-mail: schacherer@hutchinsonleader.com
Publisher Name: Laurie Hartmann
Publisher Email: lhartmann@swnewsmedia.com
Publisher Phone: (952) 345-6878
Editor Name: Mark Olson
Editor Email: editor@chanvillager.com
Editor Phone: (952) 345-6574
Year Established: 1862
Delivery Methods: Mail
Mechanical specifications: Type page 6 x 21 1/2; E - 6 cols, 2, 1/60 between; A - 6 cols, 2, 1/60 between; C - 8 cols, 1 1/2, 1/8 between.
Published Days: Thur
Avg Paid Circ: 4532
Avg Free Circ: 290
Audit Company: Sworn/Estimate/Non-Audited
Audit Date: 6 10 2019

CLOQUET

CLOQUET - PINE KNOT NEWS

Street Address: 122 Avenue C
City: Cloquet
State: MN
Postal Code: 55720
Office phone: (218) 213-1231
Publication Website: www.pineknotnews.com
Publisher Name: Pete Radosevich
Editor Name: Jana Peterson
Editor Email: news@pineknotnews.com
Advertising Executive Name: Ivan Hohnstadt
Advertising Executive Email: ads@pineknotnews.com
Advertising Executive Phone: (218) 391-3696

COKATO

COKATO- DASSEL-COKATO

ENTERPRISE DISPATCH

Corporate/Parent Company: Herald Journal Publishing
Street Address: 185 3rd St SW, PO Box 969
City: Cokato
State: MN
Postal Code: 55321
Office phone: 320-286-2118
Publication Website: www.dasselcokato.com
General E-mail: news@dasselcokato.com
Publisher Name: Chris Schultz
Publisher Email: cschultz@heraldjournal.com
Publisher Phone: 320-485-2535
Editor Name: Gabe Licht
Editor Email: glicht@heraldjournal.com
Editor Phone: 763-972-1028
Total Circulation: 44

COON RAPIDS

ANOKA COUNTY SHOPPER

Street Address: 4095 Coon Rapids Blvd.
City: Coon Rapids
State: MN
Postal Code: 55433
Office phone: (763) 421-4444
Publication Website: https://www.hometownsource.com/abc_newspapers/
General E-mail: servicecenter@ecm-inc.com
Editor Name: Jonathan Young
Editor Email: jonathan.young@ecm-inc.com
Editor Phone: (763) 712-3514
Advertising Executive Name: Jeremy Bradfield
Advertising Executive Email: jeremy.bradfield@ecm-inc.com
Advertising Executive Phone: (952) 392-6841
Total Circulation: 6261

ANOKA COUNTY UNION HERALD

Street Address: 4095 Coon Rapids Blvd.
City: Coon Rapids
State: MN
Postal Code: 55433
Office phone: (763) 421-4444
Publication Website: https://www.hometownsource.com/abc_newspapers/
General E-mail: servicecenter@ecm-inc.com
Editor Name: Jonathan Young
Editor Email: jonathan.young@ecm-inc.com
Editor Phone: (763) 712-3514
Advertising Executive Name: Jeremy Bradfield
Advertising Executive Email: jeremy.bradfield@ecm-inc.com
Advertising Executive Phone: (952) 392-6841
Year Established: 1865
Delivery Methods: Mail`Newsstand`Racks
Own Printing Facility?: Y
Commercial printers?: Y
Mechanical specifications: Type page 10 x 21; E - 6 cols, 1 3/4, 1/8 between; A - 6 cols, 1 3/4, 1/8 between; C - 8 cols, 1 1/2, 1/8 between.
Published Days: Fri
Avg Paid Circ: 3563
Avg Free Circ: 173
Audit Company: Sworn/Estimate/Non-Audited
Audit Date: 6 10 2019
Total Circulation: 4532

BLAINE-SPRING LAKE PARK LIFE

Street Address: 4095 Coon Rapids Blvd.
City: Coon Rapids
State: MN
Postal Code: 55433
Office phone: (763) 421-4444
Publication Website: https://www.hometownsource.com/abc_newspapers/
General E-mail: servicecenter@ecm-inc.com
Editor Name: Jonathan Young
Editor Email: jonathan.young@ecm-inc.com
Editor Phone: (763) 712-3514
Advertising Executive Name: Jeremy Bradfield

Advertising Executive Email: jeremy.bradfield@ecm-inc.com
Advertising Executive Phone: (952) 392-6841
Year Established: 1969
Delivery Methods: Carrier
Own Printing Facility?: Y
Commercial printers?: Y
Mechanical specifications: Type page 10 x 21; E - 6 cols, 1 3/4, 1/8 between; A - 6 cols, 1 3/4, 1/8 between; C - 8 cols, 1 1/2, 1/8 between.
Published Days: Fri
Avg Paid Circ: 145
Avg Free Circ: 15756
Audit Company: Sworn/Estimate/Non-Audited
Audit Date: 6 10 2019
Total Circulation: 4822

COLUMBIA HEIGHTS/FRIDLEY SUN FOCUS

Street Address: 4095 Coon Rapids Blvd.
City: Coon Rapids
State: MN
Postal Code: 55433
Office phone: (763) 421-4444
Publication Website: https://www.hometownsource.com/abc_newspapers/
General E-mail: servicecenter@ecm-inc.com
Editor Name: Jonathan Young
Editor Email: jonathan.young@ecm-inc.com
Editor Phone: (763) 712-3514
Advertising Executive Name: Jeremy Bradfield
Advertising Executive Email: jeremy.bradfield@ecm-inc.com
Advertising Executive Phone: (952) 392-6841
Year Established: 1968
Delivery Methods: Carrier
Own Printing Facility?: Y
Mechanical specifications: Type page 4 x 10; E - 5 cols, between; A - 5 cols, 1 5/8, between; C - 8 cols, between.
Published Days: Thur
Avg Paid Circ: 36
Avg Free Circ: 14254
Audit Company: Sworn/Estimate/Non-Audited
Audit Date: 6 10 2019

MOUNT/LONG LAKE- THE LAKER PIONEER

Street Address: 4095 Coon Rapids Blvd.
City: Coon Rapids
State: MN
Postal Code: 55421
Office phone: (952) 442-4414
Publication Website: www.hometownsource.com/laker_pioneer
Editor Name: Jason Schmucker
Editor Email: jason.schmucker@ecm-inc.com
Editor Phone: (952) 442-6810
Advertising Executive Name: Norma Carstensen
Advertising Executive Email: norma.carstensen@ecm-inc.com
Advertising Executive Phone: (952) 442-6820

EAST GRAND FORKS

EAST GRAND FORKS- THE EXPONENT

Corporate/Parent Company: Page 1 Publications
Street Address: P.O. Box 285; 207 Second Avenue NE
City: East Grand Forks
State: MN
Postal Code: 56721-0285
Office phone: (218) 773-2808
Publication Website: www.page1publications.com
Editor Name: Bruce Brierley
Editor Email: Bruce@page1publications.com
Editor Phone: 218.773.2808
Advertising Executive Name: Oliver Francies

Non-Daily Newspapers in the U.S.   III-77

Advertising Executive Email: oliver@page1publications.com
Advertising Executive Phone: 218.773.2808

EDEN PRAIRIE

BLOOMINGTON SUN-CURRENT
Street Address: 10917 Valley View Rd
City: Eden Prairie
State: MN
Postal Code: 55344
Office phone: (952) 392-6800
Publication Website: https://www.hometownsource.com/sun_current/
General E-mail: servicecenter@ecm-inc.com
Editor Name: Mike Hanks
Editor Email: mike.hanks@ecm-inc.com
Editor Phone: (952) 392-6852
Advertising Executive Name: Sharon Brauer
Advertising Executive Email: sharon.brauer@ecm-inc.com
Advertising Executive Phone: (952) 392-6855
Year Established: 1954
Delivery Methods: Carrier
Mechanical specifications: Type page 4 x 10; E - 4 cols, 2 1/2, 1/4 between; A - 5 cols, 1 5/8, between; C - 8 cols, 1 1/6, 5/24 between.
Published Days: Thur
Avg Paid Circ: 391
Avg Free Circ: 24491
Audit Company: Sworn/Estimate/Non-Audited
Audit Date: 6 10 2019
Total Circulation: 14290

BLOOMINGTON SUN-CURRENT
Street Address: 10917 Valley View Rd
City: Eden Prairie
State: MN
Postal Code: 55344-3730
Office phone: (952) 392-6800
Publication Website: https://www.hometownsource.com/sun_current/
General E-mail: advertise@ecm-inc.com
Editor Name: Matthew Hankey
Editor Email: matthew.hankey@ecm-inc.com

CRYSTAL/ROBBINSDALE/NEW HOPE/GOLDEN VALLEY SUN POST
Street Address: 10917 Valley View Road
City: Eden Prairie
State: MN
Postal Code: 55344
Office phone: (952) 829-0797
Publication Website: www.mnsun.com
Editor Name: Gretchen Schlosser
Editor Email: gretchen.schlosser@ecm-inc.com
Editor Phone: 763-424-7375
Advertising Executive Name: Steve Gall
Advertising Executive Email: steve.gall@ecm-inc.com
Advertising Executive Phone: 952-392-6844

EDEN PRAIRIE NEWS
Street Address: 250 Prairie Center Dr Ste 211
City: Eden Prairie
State: MN
Postal Code: 55344-7911
Office phone: (952) 942-7885
Publication Website: https://www.swnewsmedia.com/eden_prairie_news/
General E-mail: schacherer@hutchinsonleader.com
Publisher Name: Laurie Hartmann
Publisher Email: lhartmann@swnewsmedia.com
Publisher Phone: (952) 345-6378
Editor Name: Melissa Turtinen
Editor Email: mturtinen@swpub.com
Year Established: 1976

EDEN PRAIRIE SUN-CURRENT
Street Address: 10917 Valley View Rd
City: Eden Prairie
State: MN
Postal Code: 55344
Office phone: (952) 392-6800
Publication Website: https://www.hometownsource.com/sun_current/
General E-mail: advertise@ecm-inc.com
Editor Name: Matthew Hankey
Editor Email: matthew.hankey@ecm-inc.com
Editor Phone: (952) 392-6848
Advertising Executive Name: Sharon Brauer
Advertising Executive Email: sharon.brauer@ecm-inc.com
Advertising Executive Phone: (952) 392-6855
Year Established: 1954
Delivery Methods: Carrier
Published Days: Thur
Avg Paid Circ: 86
Avg Free Circ: 14760
Audit Company: Sworn/Estimate/Non-Audited
Audit Date: 6 10 2019
Total Circulation: 12706

EDINA SUN-CURRENT
Street Address: 10917 Valley View Rd
City: Eden Prairie
State: MN
Postal Code: 55369
Office phone: (952) 392-6800
Publication Website: https://www.hometownsource.com/sun_current/
General E-mail: advertise@ecm-inc.com
Editor Name: Matthew Hankey
Editor Email: matthew.hankey@ecm-inc.com
Editor Phone: (952) 392-6848
Advertising Executive Name: Sharon Brauer
Advertising Executive Email: sharon.brauer@ecm-inc.com
Advertising Executive Phone: (952) 392-6855
Year Established: 1954
Delivery Methods: Carrier
Mechanical specifications: Type page 4 x 10; E - 4 cols, 2 1/2, 1/4 between; A - 5 cols, 2, 1/8 between; C - 8 cols, 1 1/6, 5/24 between.
Published Days: Thur
Avg Paid Circ: 219
Avg Free Circ: 15755
Audit Company: Sworn/Estimate/Non-Audited
Audit Date: 6 10 2019

HOPKINS/ MINNENTOKA/ EXCELSIOR SUN SAILOR
Street Address: 10917 Valley View Road;
City: Eden Prairie
State: MN
Postal Code: 55344
Office phone: (952) 829-0797
Publication Website: www.mnsun.com
Editor Name: Gretchen Schlosser
Editor Email: gretchen.schlosser@ecm-inc.com
Advertising Executive Name: Steve Gall
Advertising Executive Email: advertise@ecm-inc.com

LAKEVILLE SUN-CURRENT
Street Address: 10917 Valley View Rd
City: Eden Prairie
State: MN
Postal Code: 55344
Office phone: (952) 392-6800
Publication Website: https://www.hometownsource.com/sun_current/
General E-mail: advertise@ecm-inc.com
Editor Name: Matthew Hankey
Editor Email: matthew.hankey@ecm-inc.com
Editor Phone: (952) 392-6848
Advertising Executive Name: Sharon Brauer
Advertising Executive Email: sharon.brauer@ecm-inc.com
Advertising Executive Phone: (952) 392-6855
Total Circulation: 9297

MOUNDS VIEW/NEW BRIGHTON SUN FOCUS
Street Address: 10917 Valley View Rd
City: Eden Prairie
State: MN
Postal Code: 55344
Office phone: (952) 392-6800
Publication Website: https://www.hometownsource.com/sun_focus/community/newbrighton/
General E-mail: advertise@ecm-inc.com
Advertising Executive Name: Steve Gall
Advertising Executive Email: steve.gall@ecm-inc.com
Advertising Executive Phone: (952) 392-6844
Year Established: 1968
Delivery Methods: Carrier
Own Printing Facility?: Y
Mechanical specifications: Type page 4 x 10; E - 4 cols, 2 1/2, 1/4 between; A - 5 cols, 1 5/8, between; C - 8 cols, 1 1/6, 5/24 between.
Published Days: Thur
Avg Paid Circ: 12
Avg Free Circ: 9309
Audit Company: Sworn/Estimate/Non-Audited
Audit Date: 6 10 2019
Total Circulation: 11632

PLYMOUTH/ WAYZATA SUN SAILOR
Street Address: 10917 Valley View Road
City: Eden Prairie
State: MN
Postal Code: 55344
Office phone: (952) 829-0797
Publication Website: www.mnsun.com
Editor Name: Gretchen Schlosser
Editor Email: gretchen.schlosser@ecm-inc.com
Editor Phone: 763-424-7375
Advertising Executive Name: Steve Gall
Advertising Executive Email: advertise@ecm-inc.com
Total Circulation: 14846

RICHFIELD SUN-CURRENT
Street Address: 10917 Valley View Rd
City: Eden Prairie
State: MN
Postal Code: 55344
Office phone: (952) 392-6800
Publication Website: https://www.hometownsource.com/sun_current/
General E-mail: servicecenter@ecm-inc.com
Editor Name: Ray Rivard
Editor Email: cam.bonelli@ecm-inc.com
Editor Phone: (763) 424-7381
Advertising Executive Name: Nicole Jorgenson
Advertising Executive Email: jorgensonnicole@hotmail.com
Advertising Executive Phone: (612) 961-2705
Year Established: 1954
Delivery Methods: Carrier
Mechanical specifications: Type page 4 x 10; E - 4 cols, 2 1/2, 1/4 between; A - 5 cols, 1 5/8, between; C - 8 cols, 1 1/6, 5/24 between.
Published Days: Thur
Avg Paid Circ: 163

Avg Free Circ: 9831
Audit Company: Sworn/Estimate/Non-Audited
Audit Date: 6 10 2019

SUN CURRENT- BLOOMINGTON
Street Address: 10917 Valley View Rd
City: Eden Prairie
State: MN
Postal Code: 55344
Office phone: (952) 392-6800
Publication Website: https://www.hometownsource.com/sun_current/
General E-mail: advertise@ecm-inc.com
Editor Name: Matthew Hankey
Editor Email: matthew.hankey@ecm-inc.com
Editor Phone: (952) 392-6848
Advertising Executive Name: Sharon Brauer
Advertising Executive Email: sharon.brauer@ecm-inc.com
Advertising Executive Phone: (952) 392-6855
Year Established: 1938
Delivery Methods: Carrier
Mechanical specifications: Type page 10 3/8 x 15; E - 4 cols, 2 1/2, 1/4 between; A - 5 cols, 1 5/8, between; C - 8 cols, 1 1/6, 5/24 between.
Published Days: Thur
Avg Paid Circ: 19
Avg Free Circ: 12099
Audit Company: CVC
Audit Date: 31 03 2018
Total Circulation: 15974

EDEN VALLEY

EDEN VALLEY WATKINS VOICE
Street Address: P.O. Box 7; 103 Stearns Avenue
City: Eden Valley
State: MN
Postal Code: 55329
Office phone: (320) 453-8642
Publication Website: www.evvvoice.com
General E-mail: news@evvvoice.com
Editor Name: Michael Jacobson
Editor Email: editor@evvvoice.com
Total Circulation: 6023

ELK RIVER

STAR NEWS
Corporate/Parent Company: Gannett
Street Address: 506 Freeport Ave NW
City: Elk River
State: MN
Postal Code: 55330
Office phone: (763) 441-3500
Publication Website: https://www.hometownsource.com/elk_river_star_news/
General E-mail: class@ecm-inc.com
Editor Name: Jim Boyle
Editor Email: editor.erstarnews@ecm-inc.com
Editor Phone: (763) 241-3670
Advertising Executive Name: Jerry Gloe
Advertising Executive Email: jerry.gloe@ecm-inc.com
Advertising Executive Phone: (763)-712-3533

FARIBAULT

FARIBAULT AREA SHOPPER
Street Address: 514 Central Ave N
City: Faribault
State: MN
Postal Code: 55021
Office phone: (507) 333-3100
Publication Website: https://www.southernminn.com/eedition/faribaultshopper/
General E-mail: chjellming@northfieldnews.com
Total Circulation: 1412

MINNESOTA RIVER VALLEY

SHOPPER
Street Address: 514 Central Ave.
City: Faribault
State: MN
Postal Code: 55021
Office phone: (507) 333-3111
Publication Website: https://www.southernminn.com/eedition/valleyshopper/
General E-mail: chjellming@northfieldnews.com
Total Circulation: 11642

NORTHFIELD WEEKENDER
Street Address: 514 Central Ave.
City: Faribault
State: MN
Postal Code: 55021
Office phone: (507) 333-3111
Publication Website: https://www.southernminn.com/eedition/northfield_weekender/
General E-mail: chjellming@northfieldnews.com
Total Circulation: 13076

FOREST LAKE

FOREST LAKE TIMES
Corporate/Parent Company: Adams Publishing Group
Street Address: 20 N. Lake Street, Suite 312
City: Forest Lake
State: MN
Postal Code: 55025
Office phone: (651) 464-4601
Publication Website: https://www.hometownsource.com/forest_lake_times/
General E-mail: servicecenter@ecm-inc.com
Editor Name: Ryan Howard
Editor Email: ryan.howard@ecm-inc.com
Editor Phone: (763) 233-0714
Advertising Executive Name: Jerry Gloe
Advertising Executive Email: jerry.gloe@ecm-inc.com
Advertising Executive Phone: (763)-712-3533
Year Established: 1903
Own Printing Facility?: Y
Commercial printers?: Y
Mechanical specifications: Type page 10 2/5 x 21; E - 6 cols, 1 3/4, 1/8 between; A - 6 cols, 1 3/4, 1/8 between; C - 8 cols, 1 3/4, 1/12 between.
Published Days: Thur
Avg Paid Circ: 175
Avg Free Circ: 12901
Audit Company: Sworn/Estimate/Non-Audited
Audit Date: 6 10 2019
Total Circulation: 700

ST. CROIX VALLEY PEACH
Street Address: 20 N. Lake Street, Suite 312
City: Forest Lake
State: MN
Postal Code: 55025
Office phone: (651) 464-4601
Publication Website: https://www.hometownsource.com/forest_lake_times/st-croix-valley-peach/
General E-mail: servicecenter@ecm-inc.com
Editor Name: Ryan Howard
Editor Email: ryan.howard@ecm-inc.com
Editor Phone: (763) 233-0714
Advertising Executive Name: Jerry Gloe
Advertising Executive Email: jerry.gloe@ecm-inc.com
Advertising Executive Phone: (763)-712-3533

GLENWOOD

ALEXANDRIA / ST. CLOUD / WILLMAR / MANKATO / MOORHEAD

- SENIOR
Street Address: PO Box 1
City: Glenwood
State: MN
Postal Code: 56334
Office phone: (320) 334-3344
Publication Website: www.srperspective.com
General E-mail: info@srperspective.com
Publisher Name: Jim Palmer
Advertising Executive Name: Jen Bergerson

GRYGLA

GRYGLA EAGLE
Corporate/Parent Company: Richards Publishing
Street Address: PO Box 17; 127 N Main Ave.
City: Grygla
State: MN
Postal Code: 56727
Office phone: 218-294-6220
Publication Website: www.tricocanary.com
General E-mail: grygla.eagle@gmail.com
Publisher Name: Richard D. Richards
Publisher Email: richards@gvtel.com
Editor Name: Kari Sundberg
Own Printing Facility?: Y
Commercial printers?: Y
Published Days: Wed
Avg Paid Circ: 700
Audit Company: Sworn/Estimate/Non-Audited
Audit Date: 6 10 2019
Total Circulation: 4365

HIBBING

THE CHISHOLM TRIBUNE PRESS
Street Address: 2142 1st Ave
City: Hibbing
State: MN
Postal Code: 55746
Office phone: (218) 262-1011
Publication Website: https://www.hibbingmn.com/
General E-mail: news@hibbingdailytribune.net
Publisher Name: Chris Knight
Publisher Email: cknight@mesabidailynews.net
Editor Name: Eric Killelea
Editor Email: cmanner@hibbingdailytribune.net
Advertising Executive Name: Tom Aune
Advertising Executive Email: taune@hibbingdailytribune.net
Delivery Methods: Mail
Own Printing Facility?: Y
Commercial printers?: Y
Published Days: Wed
Avg Paid Circ: 900
Avg Free Circ: 143
Audit Company: Sworn/Estimate/Non-Audited
Audit Date: 6 10 2019

HUTCHINSON

HUTCHINSON LEADER
Street Address: 170 Shady Ridge Rd NW
City: Hutchinson
State: MN
Postal Code: 55350-2440
Office phone: (320) 753-3635
Publication Website: https://www.crowrivermedia.com/hutchinsonleader/
General E-mail: news@hutchinsonleader.com
Publisher Name: Brent Schacherer
Publisher Email: schacherer@hutchinsonleader.com
Publisher Phone: (320) 753-3637
Editor Name: Stephen Wiblemo
Editor Email: wiblemo@hutchinsonleader.com
Editor Phone: (320) 753-3638
Advertising Executive Name: Kevin True
Advertising Executive Email: true@hutchinsonleader.com
Advertising Executive Phone: (320) 753-3649
Year Established: 1880
Delivery Methods: Mail`Carrier
Own Printing Facility?: Y
Commercial printers?: Y
Mechanical specifications: Type page 6 x 21 1/2; E - 6 cols, 2, between; A - 6 cols, 2, between; C - 6 cols, 2, between.
Published Days: Tues`Thur
Avg Paid Circ: 3986
Avg Free Circ: 379
Audit Company: Sworn/Estimate/Non-Audited
Audit Date: 6 10 2019

HUTCHINSON

HUTCHINSON LEADER AND LEADER SHOPPER
Street Address: 170 Shady Ridge Rd NW Ste 100
City: Hutchinson
State: MN
Postal Code: 55350-2440
Office phone: (320) 753-3635
Publication Website: https://www.crowrivermedia.com/hutchinsonleader/
General E-mail: news@hutchinsonleader.com
Publisher Name: Brent Schacherer
Publisher Email: schacherer@hutchinsonleader.com
Publisher Phone: (320) 753-3637
Editor Name: Stephen Wiblemo
Editor Email: wiblemo@hutchinsonleader.com
Editor Phone: (320) 753-3638
Advertising Executive Name: Kevin True
Advertising Executive Email: true@hutchinsonleader.com
Advertising Executive Phone: (320) 753-3649
Total Circulation: 13073

INTERNATIONAL FALLS

INTERNATIONAL FALLS JOURNAL
Street Address: 1602 Highway 71
City: International Falls
State: MN
Postal Code: 56649
Office phone: (218) 285-7411
Publication Website: https://www.ifallsjournal.com/
General E-mail: nikki@ifallsjournal.com
Publisher Name: Rob Davenport
Publisher Email: rob@ifallsjournal.com
Publisher Phone: (218) 285-7411 extension 2250
Editor Name: Laurel Beager
Editor Email: laurel@ifallsjournal.com
Editor Phone: (218) 285-7411 extension 2230
Advertising Executive Name: Karley Mastin
Advertising Executive Email: karley@ifallsjournal.com
Advertising Executive Phone: (218) 285-7411 extension 2225

THE INTERNATIONAL FALLS JOURNAL
Corporate/Parent Company: Media News Group
Street Address: 1602 Highway 71
City: International Falls
State: MN
Postal Code: 56649
Office phone: (218) 285-7411
Publication Website: https://www.ifallsjournal.com/
General E-mail: nikki@ifallsjournal.com
Publisher Name: Rob Davenport
Publisher Email: rob@ifallsjournal.com
Publisher Phone: (218) 285-7411, ext : 2250
Editor Name: Laurel Beager
Editor Email: laurel@ifallsjournal.com
Editor Phone: (218) 285-7411, ext : 2230
Advertising Executive Name: Karley Mastin
Advertising Executive Email: karley@ifallsjournal.com
Advertising Executive Phone: (218) 285-7411, ext : 2225
Year Established: 1911
Delivery Methods: Mail`Carrier`Racks
Own Printing Facility?: Y
Commercial printers?: Y
Mechanical specifications: Type page 6x 21 1/2; E - 6 cols, 2 1/16, 1/8 between; A - 6 cols, 2 1/16, 1/8 between; C - 8 cols, 1 1/2, 1/8 between.
Published Days: Wed`Sat
Weekday Frequency: m
Saturday Frequency: m
Avg Paid Circ: 3109
Audit Company: AAM
Audit Date: 2 07 2018
Pressroom Equipment: Lines – 6-G/Community.;
Total Circulation: 1709

IRONTON

BRAINERD-NEWSHOOPER
Street Address: P.O. Box 562
City: Ironton
State: MN
Postal Code: 56455
Office phone: (218) 772-0300
Publication Website: www.newshopper.net
Editor Name: Eric Heglund
Editor Email: hopper@crosbyironton.net
Total Circulation: 2970

ISLE

BARGAIN HUNTER
Street Address: PO Box 26
City: Isle
State: MN
Postal Code: 56342
Office phone: (320) 676-3123
Publication Website: https://www.messagemedia.co/
General E-mail: age@aitkinage.com

ISLE

MILLE LACS MESSENGER
Corporate/Parent Company: Adams Publishing Group
Street Address: PO Box 26
City: Isle
State: MN
Postal Code: 56342
Office phone: (320) 676-3123
Publication Website: https://www.messagemedia.co/millelacs/
General E-mail: mlm@millelacsmessenger.com
Year Established: 1913
Delivery Methods: Mail`Newsstand
Own Printing Facility?: N
Commercial printers?: N
Mechanical specifications: Type page 6 x 14.75; E - 6 cols, 1 5/8, 1/6 between; A - 6 cols, 1 5/8, 1/6 between; C - 7 cols, 1 3/8, 1/6 between.
Published Days: Wed
Avg Paid Circ: 3800
Audit Company: Sworn/Estimate/Non-Audited
Audit Date: 6 10 2019

JORDAN

JORDAN INDEPENDENT
Street Address: 109 Rice St S
City: Jordan
State: MN
Postal Code: 55352-1513
Office phone: (952) 492-2224
Publication Website: https://www.swnewsmedia.com/jordan_independent/
General E-mail: schacherer@hutchinsonleader.com
Publisher Name: Laurie Hartmann
Publisher Email: lhartmann@swnewsmedia.com
Publisher Phone: (952) 345-6878
Editor Name: Rachel Minske
Editor Email: rminske@swpub.com
Editor Phone: (952) 345-6679
Delivery Methods: Mail
Published Days: Thur
Avg Paid Circ: 1709
Audit Company: Sworn/Estimate/Non-Audited
Audit Date: 6 10 2019

Non-Daily Newspapers in the U.S.

KENYON

KENYON LEADER
Corporate/Parent Company: Adams Publishing Group
Street Address: 638 2nd St
City: Kenyon
State: MN
Postal Code: 55946-1334
Office phone: (507) 789-6161
Publication Website: https://www.southernminn.com/the_kenyon_leader/
General E-mail: editor@thekenyonleader.com
Publisher Name: Chad Hjellming
Publisher Email: chjellming@faribault.com
Publisher Phone: (507) 333-3105
Editor Name: Suzanne Rook
Editor Email: srook@faribault.com
Editor Phone: (507) 333-3134
Advertising Executive Name: Mark Nelson
Advertising Executive Email: mnelson@faribault.com
Advertising Executive Phone: (507) 333-3109
Year Established: 1885
Delivery Methods:
  Mail Newsstand Carrier Racks
Own Printing Facility?: Y
Commercial printers?: Y
Mechanical specifications: Type page 6 x 21 1/2; E - 6 cols, 1 5/16, between; A - 6 cols, 1 5/16, between; C - 6 cols, 1 5/16, between.
Published Days: Wed
Avg Paid Circ: 636
Avg Free Circ: 2334
Audit Company: Sworn/Estimate/Non-Audited
Audit Date: 6 10 2019

LAKE BENTON

LAKE BENTON VALLEY JOURNAL
Street Address: P.O. Box 328; 120 North Center Street
City: Lake Benton
State: MN
Postal Code: 56149
Office phone: 507-368-4604
Publication Website: http://lbvalleyjournal.com
General E-mail: valleyjournaloffice@gmail.com
Publisher Name: Chuck Hunt
Editor Name: Shelly Finzen
Editor Email: lbnews@itctel.com
Advertising Executive Name: Amber Casperson
Total Circulation: 909

LE CENTER

LE SUEUR NEWS-HERALD
Corporate/Parent Company: Adams Publishing Group
Street Address: P.O. Box 142
City: Le Center
State: MN
Postal Code: 56058
Office phone: (507) 665-3332
Publication Website: https://www.southernminn.com/le_sueur_county_news/
General E-mail: editor@lesueurcountynews.com
Publisher Name: Chad Hjellming
Publisher Email: chjellming@northfieldnews.com
Publisher Phone: (507) 645-1110
Editor Name: Philip Weyhe
Editor Email: editor@lesueurcountynews.com
Editor Phone: (507) 931-8567
Advertising Executive Name: Tom Kelling
Advertising Executive Email: tkelling@owatonna.com
Advertising Executive Phone: (507) 444-2390
Delivery Methods: Mail
Own Printing Facility?: Y
Mechanical specifications: Type page 6 x 21 1/2; E - 6 cols, 1 5/6, between; A - 6 cols, 1 5/6, between; C - 6 cols, 1 5/6, between.
Published Days: Wed
Avg Paid Circ: 864
Avg Free Circ: 45

THE LE CENTER LEADER-OOB
Street Address: P.O. Box 142
City: Le Center
State: MN
Postal Code: 56058
Office phone: (507) 665-3332
Publication Website: https://www.southernminn.com/le_sueur_county_news/
General E-mail: editor@lesueurcountynews.com
Publisher Name: Chad Hjellming
Publisher Email: chjellming@northfieldnews.com
Publisher Phone: (507) 645-1110
Editor Name: Philip Weyhe
Editor Email: editor@lesueurcountynews.com
Editor Phone: (507) 931-8567
Advertising Executive Name: Tom Kelling
Advertising Executive Email: tkelling@owatonna.com
Advertising Executive Phone: (507) 444-2390
Total Circulation: 2462

LE SUEUR

LE SUEUR COUNTY NEWS
Corporate/Parent Company: Adams Publishing Group
Street Address: P.O. Box 142
City: Le Sueur
State: MN
Postal Code: 56058
Office phone: 507-665-3332
Publication Website: www.southernminn.com/le_sueur_county_news
Publisher Name: Chad Hjellming
Publisher Email: chjellming@northfieldnews.com
Publisher Phone: 507-645-1110
Editor Name: Philip Weyhe
Editor Email: editor@lesueurcountynews.com
Editor Phone: 507-931-8567
Advertising Executive Name: Tom Kelling
Advertising Executive Email: tkelling@owatonna.com
Advertising Executive Phone: 507-444-2390
Total Circulation: 2555

LITTLE FALLS

MORRISON COUNTY RECORD
Corporate/Parent Company: Adams Publishing Group
Street Address: 216 1st St SE
City: Little Falls
State: MN
Postal Code: 56345
Office phone: (320) 632-2345
Publication Website: https://www.hometownsource.com/morrison_county_record/
General E-mail: mcr@mcrecord.com
Publisher Name: Carmen Meyer
Publisher Email: carmen.meyer@mcrecord.com
Publisher Phone: (320) 616-1913
Editor Name: Terry Lehrke
Editor Email: terry.lehrke@mcrecord.com
Editor Phone: (320) 616-1917
Advertising Executive Name: Tena Wensman
Advertising Executive Email: tena.wensman@ecm-inc.com
Advertising Executive Phone: (320) 616-1932
Year Established: 1969
Delivery Methods: Carrier
Mechanical specifications: ROP Type page 6 col x 21; Col width 9p4 (1.55"); 0p8 gutter between cols. Classified page 7 col x 21; Col width 7p10 (1.30") 0p8 gutter.
Published Days: Sun
Avg Paid Circ: 350
Avg Free Circ: 18114
Audit Company: CAC
Audit Date: 6/31/2017
Total Circulation: 4590

MINNEAPOLIS

MINNEAPOLIS - MINNESOTA WOMEN'S PRESS
Street Address: 800 West Broadway #3A
City: Minneapolis
State: MN
Postal Code: 55411
Office phone: 651-646-3968
Publication Website: www.womenspress.com
General E-mail: ads@womenspress.com
Editor Name: Mikki Morrissette
Editor Email: editor@womenspress.com
Advertising Executive Name: Shelle Eddy
Advertising Executive Email: ashlee@womenspress.com
Total Circulation: 1559

MINNEAPOLIS / ST PAUL BUSINESS JOURNAL
Corporate/Parent Company: American City Business Journals
Street Address: 100 South 5th Street Suite 1800
City: Minneapolis
State: MN
Postal Code: 55402
Office phone: 612-288-2100
Publication Website: www.bizjournals.com/twincities
General E-mail: twincities@bizjournals.com
Publisher Name: Kathy Robideau
Publisher Email: krobideau@bizjournals.com
Publisher Phone: 612-288-2135
Editor Name: Dirk DeYoung
Editor Email: ddeyoung@bizjournals.com
Editor Phone: 612-288-2111
Advertising Executive Name: Gina Sundeen
Advertising Executive Email: gsundeen@bizjournals.com
Advertising Executive Phone: 612-288-2131
Total Circulation: 3800

ST. PAUL LEGAL LEDGER- MINNESOTA LAWYER
Corporate/Parent Company: BridgeTower Media
Street Address: 222 South Ninth Street, Suite 900, Campbell Mithun Tower
City: Minneapolis
State: MN
Postal Code: 55402
Office phone: (612) 333-4244
Publication Website: www.minnlawyer.com
Publisher Name: Bill Gaier
Publisher Email: bgaier@finance-commerce.com
Publisher Phone: 612-584-1537
Editor Name: Barbara Jones
Editor Email: bjones@minnlawyer.com
Editor Phone: 612-584-1543
Advertising Executive Name: Alex Yermishkin
Advertising Executive Email: ayermishkin@finance-commerce.com
Advertising Executive Phone: 612-584-1545

MONTICELLO

MONTICELLO TIMES
Corporate/Parent Company: Adams Publishing Group
Street Address: 540 Walnut St
City: Monticello
State: MN
Postal Code: 55362
Office phone: (763) 295-3131
Publication Website: https://www.hometownsource.com/monticello_times/
General E-mail: norma.carstensen@ecm-inc.com
Editor Name: Jeff Hage
Editor Email: jeff.hage@ecm-inc.com
Editor Phone: (763) 271-6469
Advertising Executive Name: Jeremy Bradfield
Advertising Executive Email: jeremy.bradfield@ecm-inc.com
Advertising Executive Phone: (763) 295-3131
Mechanical specifications: Type page 6 x 21 1/2; E - 6 cols, 2, 1/4 between; A - 6 cols, 2, 1/4 between.
Published Days: Thur
Avg Paid Circ: 1312
Avg Free Circ: 18
Audit Company: Sworn/Estimate/Non-Audited
Audit Date: 6 10 2019

MOORHEAD

MOORHEAD - THE EXTRA NEWSPAPER
Street Address: P.O. Box 1026
City: Moorhead
State: MN
Postal Code: 56561
Office phone: (218) 284-1288
Publication Website: www.thefmextra.com
Editor Name: Tammy Finney
Editor Email: tfinney@ncppub.com
Advertising Executive Name: DIANE STROM
Advertising Executive Email: DIANERRVADSALES@GMAIL.COM

NEVIS

NEVIS- NORTHWOODS PRESS
Corporate/Parent Company: Bloomquist Group
Street Address: P.O. Box 28; 108 Main Street
City: Nevis
State: MN
Postal Code: 56467-0028
Office phone: (218) 652-3475
Publication Website: www.northwoodspress.com
General E-mail: info@northwoodspress.com
Editor Name: Tim Bloomquist
Advertising Executive Name: David Hanson
Advertising Executive Email: shooterreviewmessenger@gmail.com
Advertising Executive Phone: 218-252-3356

NEW LONDON

NEW LONDON/SPICER - LAKES AREA REVIEW
Street Address: 106 Norwood Street Southwest
City: New London
State: MN
Postal Code: 56273
Office phone: (320) 354-2945
Publication Website: lakes-area-review.business.site
Publisher Name: Kari Jo & T.J. Almen
Editor Name: Brett Blocker
Editor Email: lakesareareview@tds.net
Advertising Executive Name: Ashley Baker
Total Circulation: 18164

NEW RICHLAND

NEW RICHLAND- NRHEG STAR EAGLE
Street Address: PO Box 248
City: New Richland
State: MN
Postal Code: 56072
Office phone: 507-463-8112
Publication Website: www.newrichlandstar.com/jnews
General E-mail: steagle@hickorytech.net
Publisher Name: Jim Lutgens

NEW YORK MILLS

NEW YORK MILLS DISPATCH
Corporate/Parent Company: Henning Publications
Street Address: 17 E Centennial 84 Dr. Suite B; PO Box 297
City: New York Mills
State: MN
Postal Code: 56567
Office phone: (218) 385-7720
Publication Website: www.nymdispatch.com
General E-mail: nymdispatch@arvig.net
Publisher Name: Chad Koenen
Publisher Email: chad@henningadvocate.com
Editor Name: Connie Vandermay
Editor Email: news@nymdispatch.com
Total Circulation: 1330

NORTH SAINT PAUL

MAPLEWOOD REVIEW
Corporate/Parent Company: Lillie Suburban Newspapers, Inc.
Street Address: 2515 7th Ave E
City: North Saint Paul
State: MN
Postal Code: 55109
Office phone: (651) 777-8800
Publication Website: https://www.lillienews.com/articles/ramsey-county-maplewood-review?page=998
General E-mail: review@lillienews.com
Editor Name: Mike Munzenrider
Editor Email: mmunzenrider@lillienews.com
Editor Phone: (651) 748-7813
Advertising Executive Name: Tony Fragnito
Advertising Executive Email: tfragnito@lillienews.com
Advertising Executive Phone: (651) 777-8800
Own Printing Facility?: Y
Commercial printers?: Y
Mechanical specifications: Type page 12 7/8 x 21; E - 6 cols, 1 13/16, between; A - 6 cols, 1 13/16, between; C - 10 cols, 1 13/16, between.
Published Days: Wed
Avg Paid Circ: 36
Avg Free Circ: 4554
Audit Company: VAC
Audit Date: 30 09 2017

NEW BRIGHTON-MOUNDS VIEW BULLETIN
Corporate/Parent Company: Lillie Suburban Newspapers, Inc.
Street Address: 2515 7th Ave E
City: North Saint Paul
State: MN
Postal Code: 55109
Office phone: (651) 777-8800
Publication Website: https://lillienews.com/articles/new-brighton-mounds-view-bulletin-news
General E-mail: bulletin@lillienews.com
Editor Name: Mike Munzenrider
Editor Email: mmunzenrider@lillienews.com
Editor Phone: (651) 748-7813
Advertising Executive Name: Tony Fragnito
Advertising Executive Email: tfragnito@lillienews.com
Advertising Executive Phone: (651) 777-8800
Delivery Methods: Mail
Own Printing Facility?: Y
Commercial printers?: Y
Mechanical specifications: Type page 12 7/8 x 21; E - 6 cols, 1 13/16, between; A - 6 cols, 1 13/16, between; C - 10 cols, 1 13/16, between.
Published Days: Wed
Avg Paid Circ: 230
Avg Free Circ: 26000
Audit Company: Sworn/Estimate/Non-Audited
Audit Date: 6 10 2019
Note: Additional Free Circulation of Classified and Farm Sections total 3,729

Total Circulation: 18464

OAKDALE LAKE ELMO REVIEW
Corporate/Parent Company: Lillie Suburban Newspapers, Inc.
Street Address: 2515 7th Ave E
City: North Saint Paul
State: MN
Postal Code: 55109
Office phone: (651) 777-8800
Publication Website: https://www.lillienews.com/articles/oakdale-lake-elmo-review-0
General E-mail: oakdale-lakeelmo@lillienews.com
Editor Name: Mike Munzenrider
Editor Email: mmunzenrider@lillienews.com
Editor Phone: (651) 748-7813
Advertising Executive Name: Tony Fragnito
Advertising Executive Email: tfragnito@lillienews.com
Advertising Executive Phone: (651) 777-8800
Year Established: 1986
Delivery Methods: Carrier
Own Printing Facility?: Y
Commercial printers?: Y
Mechanical specifications: Type page 10" x 21; Display - 6 cols,, between; Classified - 10 cols, .
Published Days: Wed
Avg Paid Circ: 37
Avg Free Circ: 6710
Audit Company: VAC
Audit Date: 30 09 2017
Total Circulation: 9321

RAMSEY COUNTY REVIEW
Corporate/Parent Company: Lillie Suburban Newspapers, Inc.
Street Address: 2515 7th Ave E
City: North Saint Paul
State: MN
Postal Code: 55109
Office phone: (651) 777-8800
Publication Website: https://www.lillienews.com/articles/ramsey-county-maplewood-review?page=998
General E-mail: review@lillienews.com
Editor Name: Mike Munzenrider
Editor Email: mmunzenrider@lillienews.com
Editor Phone: (651) 748-7813
Advertising Executive Name: Tony Fragnito
Advertising Executive Email: tfragnito@lillienews.com
Advertising Executive Phone: (651) 777-8800
Year Established: 1938
Delivery Methods: Carrier
Own Printing Facility?: Y
Commercial printers?: Y
Mechanical specifications: Type page 6 x 21; Display - 6 cols, Classified - 10 cols.
Published Days: Wed
Avg Paid Circ: 39
Avg Free Circ: 2503
Audit Company: VAC
Audit Date: 30 09 2017

REVIEW PERSPECTIVES
Corporate/Parent Company: Lillie Suburban Newspapers, Inc.
Street Address: 2515 7th Ave E
City: North Saint Paul
State: MN
Postal Code: 55109
Office phone: (651) 777-8800
Publication Website: https://lillienews.com/perspectives
General E-mail: lillieontheweb@lillienews.com
Delivery Methods: Mail
Own Printing Facility?: Y
Commercial printers?: Y
Mechanical specifications: Type page 11 1/2 x 20 3/4; E - 6 cols, 1 13/16, 3/16 between; A - 6 cols, 1 13/16, 13/16 between; C - 10 cols, between.
Published Days: Mon
Avg Free Circ: 6613
Audit Company: Sworn/Estimate/Non-Audited
Audit Date: 6 10 2019

ROSEVILLE REVIEW
Corporate/Parent Company: Lillie Suburban Newspapers, Inc.
Street Address: 2515 7th Ave E
City: North Saint Paul
State: MN
Postal Code: 55109
Office phone: (651) 777-8800
Publication Website: https://lillienews.com/roseville-little-canada-review
General E-mail: roseville@lillienews.com
Editor Name: Mike Munzenrider
Editor Email: mmunzenrider@lillienews.com
Editor Phone: (651) 748-7813
Advertising Executive Name: Tony Fragnito
Advertising Executive Email: tfragnito@lillienews.com
Advertising Executive Phone: (651) 777-8800
Year Established: 1938
Delivery Methods: Carrier
Own Printing Facility?: Y
Commercial printers?: Y
Mechanical specifications: Type page 6 x 21; Display - 6 cols, Classified - 10 cols.
Published Days: Tues
Avg Paid Circ: 18
Avg Free Circ: 12276
Audit Company: VAC
Audit Date: 30 09 2017
Total Circulation: 5257

SHOREVIEW ARDEN HILLS BULLETIN
Corporate/Parent Company: Lillie Suburban Newspapers, Inc.
Street Address: 2515 7th Ave E
City: North Saint Paul
State: MN
Postal Code: 55109
Office phone: (651) 777-8800
Publication Website: https://lillienews.com/articles/shoreview-arden-hills-bulletin-news
General E-mail: bulletin@lillienews.com
Editor Name: Mike Munzenrider
Editor Email: mmunzenrider@lillienews.com
Editor Phone: (651) 748-7813
Advertising Executive Name: Tony Fragnito
Advertising Executive Email: tfragnito@lillienews.com
Advertising Executive Phone: (651) 777-8800
Delivery Methods: Carrier
Own Printing Facility?: Y
Commercial printers?: Y
Mechanical specifications: 10" x 21" display spread over 6 columns and classified spread over 10 columns
Published Days: Wed
Avg Paid Circ: 38
Avg Free Circ: 19683
Audit Company: Sworn/Estimate/Non-Audited
Audit Date: 6 10 2019
Total Circulation: 26230

SOUTH-WEST REVIEW
Corporate/Parent Company: Lillie Suburban Newspapers, Inc.
Street Address: 2515 7th Ave E
City: North Saint Paul
State: MN
Postal Code: 55109
Office phone: (651) 777-8800
Publication Website: https://lillienews.com/south-west-review
General E-mail: southwest@lillienews.com
Editor Name: Mike Munzenrider
Editor Email: mmunzenrider@lillienews.com
Editor Phone: (651) 748-7813
Advertising Executive Name: Tony Fragnito
Advertising Executive Email: tfragnito@lillienews.com
Advertising Executive Phone: (651) 777-8800
Year Established: 1938
Delivery Methods: Carrier
Own Printing Facility?: Y
Commercial printers?: Y
Mechanical specifications: Type page 10 x 21; E - 6 cols, between; A - 6 cols, between; C - 10 cols, between.
Published Days: Mon
Avg Paid Circ: 46
Avg Free Circ: 10975
Audit Company: Sworn/Estimate/Non-Audited
Audit Date: 6 10 2019

ST. ANTHONY BULLETIN
Corporate/Parent Company: Lillie Suburban Newspapers, Inc.
Street Address: 2515 7th Ave E
City: North Saint Paul
State: MN
Postal Code: 55109
Office phone: (651) 777-8800
Publication Website: http://www.lillienews.com/articles/st-anthony-bulletin-news?page=68
General E-mail: bulletin@lillienews.com
Editor Name: Mike Munzenrider
Editor Email: mmunzenrider@lillienews.com
Editor Phone: (651) 748-7813
Advertising Executive Name: Tony Fragnito
Advertising Executive Email: tfragnito@lillienews.com
Advertising Executive Phone: (651) 777-8800
Own Printing Facility?: Y
Commercial printers?: Y
Mechanical specifications: Type page 13 1/2 x 21; E - 6 cols, 1 13/16, 1/4 between; A - 6 cols, 1 13/16, 1/4 between; C - 10 cols, 1 13/16, 1/8 between.
Published Days: Wed
Avg Paid Circ: 1
Avg Free Circ: 2046
Audit Company: VAC
Audit Date: 30 09 2017

WOODBURY-SOUTH MAPLEWOOD REVIEW
Corporate/Parent Company: Lillie Suburban Newspapers, Inc.
Street Address: 2515 7th Ave. E.
City: North Saint Paul
State: MN
Postal Code: 55109
Office phone: (651) 777-8800
Publication Website: https://lillienews.com/perspectives
General E-mail: lillieontheweb@lillienews.com

NORTH ST PAUL

EAST SIDE REVIEW
Corporate/Parent Company: Lillie Suburban Newspapers
Street Address: 2515 7th Ave E
City: North St Paul
State: MN
Postal Code: 55109
Office phone: (651) 777-8800
Publication Website: https://lillienews.com/east-side-review
General E-mail: eastside@lillienews.com
Editor Name: Mike Munzenrider
Editor Email: mmunzenrider@lillienews.com
Editor Phone: (651) 748-7813
Advertising Executive Name: Tony Fragnito

Non-Daily Newspapers in the U.S.   III-81

Advertising Executive Email: tfragnito@lillienews.com
Advertising Executive Phone: (651) 777-8800
Year Established: 1938
Delivery Methods: Carrier
Own Printing Facility?: Y
Commercial printers?: Y
Mechanical specifications: Type page 6 x 21; Display - 6 cols, Classified - 10 cols.
Published Days: Mon
Avg Paid Circ: 20
Avg Free Circ: 9277
Audit Company: VAC
Audit Date: 31 05 2017
Total Circulation: 9194

NEW BRIGHTON BULLETIN

Corporate/Parent Company: Lillie Suburban Newspapers, Inc.
Street Address: 2515 7th Ave E
City: North St Paul
State: MN
Postal Code: 55109
Office phone: (651) 777-8800
Publication Website: https://lillienews.com/articles/new-brighton-mounds-view-bulletin-news
General E-mail: bulletin@lillienews.com
Editor Name: Mike Munzenrider
Editor Email: mmunzenrider@lillienews.com
Editor Phone: (651) 748-7813
Advertising Executive Name: Tony Fragnito
Advertising Executive Email: tfragnito@lillienews.com
Advertising Executive Phone: (651) 777-8800
Delivery Methods: Mail
Published Days: Wed
Avg Paid Circ: 12
Avg Free Circ: 5245
Audit Company: VAC
Audit Date: 30 09 2016
Total Circulation: 2850

SOUTH ST. PAUL - SOUTH WEST REVIEW

Corporate/Parent Company: Lillie Suburban Newspapers, Inc.
Street Address: 2515 7th Ave E
City: North St Paul
State: MN
Postal Code: 55109
Office phone: (651) 777-8800
Publication Website: https://lillienews.com/south-west-review
General E-mail: southwest@lillienews.com
Editor Name: Mike Munzenrider
Editor Email: mmunzenrider@lillienews.com
Editor Phone: (651) 748-7813
Advertising Executive Name: Tony Fragnito
Advertising Executive Email: tfragnito@lillienews.com
Advertising Executive Phone: (651) 777-8800
Year Established: 1938
Delivery Methods: Carrier
Mechanical specifications: 10"x21 spread over 6 column for display and 10 column for classified
Published Days: Mon
Avg Paid Circ: 21
Avg Free Circ: 4696
Audit Company: VAC
Audit Date: 30 09 2017

ST. PAUL - EAST SIDE REVIEW

Corporate/Parent Company: Lillie Suburban Newspapers, Inc.
Street Address: 2515 E. Seventh Ave
City: North St. Paul
State: MN
Postal Code: 55109
Office phone: (651) 748-7800

Publication Website: www.lillienews.com
Editor Name: Mike Munzenrider
Editor Email: mmunzenrider@lillienews.com
Editor Phone: (651) 748-7813
Advertising Executive Name: Tony Fragnito
Advertising Executive Email: tfragnito@lillienews.com
Advertising Executive Phone: 651-748-7860
Total Circulation: 2591

NORTHFIELD
LONSDALE AREA NEWS-REVIEW

Corporate/Parent Company: Adams Publishing Group
Street Address: 115 Fifth St. W
City: Northfield
State: MN
Postal Code: 55057
Office phone: (507) 744-2551
Publication Website: https://www.southernminn.com/lonsdale_area_news_review/
General E-mail: mschwab@lonsdalenewsreview.com
Publisher Name: Chad Hjellming
Publisher Email: chjellming@northfieldnews.com
Publisher Phone: (507) 645-1110
Editor Name: Suzanne Rook
Editor Email: srook@faribault.com
Editor Phone: (507) 333-3134
Advertising Executive Name: Jay Petsche
Advertising Executive Email: jpetsche@northfieldnews.com
Advertising Executive Phone: (507) 645-1120
Published Days: Tues
Avg Paid Circ: 17
Avg Free Circ: 2445
Audit Company: Sworn/Estimate/Non-Audited
Audit Date: 6 10 2019
Total Circulation: 6747

LONSDALE NEWS - REVIEW

Street Address: 115 Fifth St. W
City: Northfield
State: MN
Postal Code: 55057
Office phone: (507) 744-2551
Publication Website: https://www.southernminn.com/lonsdale_area_news_review/
General E-mail: mschwab@lonsdalenewsreview.com
Publisher Name: Chad Hjellming
Publisher Email: chjellming@northfieldnews.com
Publisher Phone: (507) 645-1110
Editor Name: Suzanne Rook
Editor Email: srook@faribault.com
Editor Phone: (507) 333-3134
Advertising Executive Name: Mark Nelson
Advertising Executive Email: mnelson@faribault.com
Advertising Executive Phone: (507) 333-3109
Year Established: 2006
Delivery Methods: Carrier
Mechanical specifications: Type page: 10.25 x 21; 6 col
Published Days: Tues
Avg Free Circ: 2555
Audit Company: Sworn/Estimate/Non-Audited
Audit Date: 6 10 2019

NORTHFIELD NEWS

Corporate/Parent Company: Adams Publishing Group
Street Address: 115 5th St W
City: Northfield
State: MN
Postal Code: 55057
Office phone: (507) 645-5615
Publication Website: https://www.southernminn.com/northfield_news/
General E-mail: advertising@northfieldnews.com

Publisher Name: Chad Hjellming
Publisher Email: chjellming@northfieldnews.com
Publisher Phone: (507) 645-1110
Editor Name: Suzanne Rook
Editor Email: srook@faribault.com
Editor Phone: (507) 333-3134
Advertising Executive Name: Jay Petsche
Advertising Executive Email: jpetsche@northfieldnews.com
Advertising Executive Phone: (507) 645-1120
Year Established: 1876
Delivery Methods: Mail
Own Printing Facility?: Y
Mechanical specifications: Type page 6 x 21 1/2; E - 6 cols, 1 5/6, between; A - 6 cols, 1 5/6, between; C - 6 cols, 1 5/6, between.
Published Days: Wed`Sat
Avg Paid Circ: 2850
Audit Company: Sworn/Estimate/Non-Audited
Audit Date: 6 10 2019
Total Circulation: 9494

ORTONVILLE
ORTHOVILLE INDEPENDENT

Street Address: 789 U.S. Hwy. 75
City: Ortonville
State: MN
Postal Code: 56278
Office phone: (320) 839-6163
Publication Website: www.ortonvilleindependent.com/Ortonville_Independent.html
General E-mail: mail@ortonvilleindependent.com
Publisher Name: Philip Blake

OSSEO
BROOKLYN CENTER/BROOKLYN PARK SUN-POST

Street Address: 33 2nd St NE
City: Osseo
State: MN
Postal Code: 55369
Office phone: (763) 425-3323
Publication Website: https://www.hometownsource.com/sun_post/
General E-mail: servicecenter@ecm-inc.com
Editor Name: Matt Hankey
Editor Email: matthew.hankey@ecm-inc.com
Editor Phone: (952) 392-6848
Advertising Executive Name: Lisa Nollen
Advertising Executive Email: dennis.thomsen@ecm-inc.com
Advertising Executive Phone: (952) 392-6886
Year Established: 1938
Delivery Methods: Carrier
Mechanical specifications: Type page 4 x 10; E - 4 cols, 2 1/2, 1/4 between; A - 5 cols, 1 5/8, 1/4 between; C - 8 cols, 1 1/6, 5/24 between.
Published Days: Thur
Avg Paid Circ: 62
Avg Free Circ: 6969
Audit Company: Sworn/Estimate/Non-Audited
Audit Date: 6 10 2019

BROOKLYN CENTER/BROOKLYN PARK SUN-POST

Street Address: 33 2nd St NE
City: Osseo
State: MN
Postal Code: 55369-1252
Office phone: (763) 425-3323
Publication Website: https://www.hometownsource.com/sun_post/
General E-mail: advertise@ecm-inc.com
Editor Name: Matt Hankey
Editor Email: matthew.hankey@ecm-inc.com

Publisher Name: Chad Hjellming
Publisher Email: chjellming@northfieldnews.com

CHAMPLIN-DAYTON PRESS

Corporate/Parent Company: Adams Publishing Group
Street Address: 33 2nd St NE
City: Osseo
State: MN
Postal Code: 55369
Office phone: (763) 425-3323
Publication Website: https://www.hometownsource.com/press_and_news/
General E-mail: jeremy.bradfield@ecm-inc.com
Advertising Executive Name: Jeremy Bradfield
Advertising Executive Email: jeremy.bradfield@ecm-inc.com
Advertising Executive Phone: (952) 392-6841
Own Printing Facility?: Y
Commercial printers?: Y
Mechanical specifications: Type page 6 x 21; E - 7 cols, 2 5/8, 1/8 between; A - 7 cols, 2 5/8, 1/8 between; C - 7 cols, 2 5/8, 1/8 between.
Published Days: Thur
Avg Paid Circ: 47
Avg Free Circ: 6214
Audit Company: Sworn/Estimate/Non-Audited
Audit Date: 6 10 2019

EXCELSIOR/SHOREWOOD/ CHANHASSEN SUN SAILOR

Street Address: 33 Second St. N.E
City: Osseo
State: MN
Postal Code: 55369
Office phone: (763) 425-3323
Publication Website: https://www.hometownsource.com/sun_sailor/
General E-mail: servicecenter@ecm-inc.com
Editor Name: Gretchen Schlosser
Editor Email: gretchen.schlosser@ecm-inc.com
Editor Phone: (763) 424-7375
Advertising Executive Name: Steve Gall
Advertising Executive Email: steve.gall@ecm-inc.com
Advertising Executive Phone: (952) 392-6844
Year Established: 1970
Delivery Methods: Carrier
Mechanical specifications: Type page 4 x 10; E - 4 cols, 2 1/2, 1/4 between; A - 5 cols, 1 5/8, 1/4 between; C - 8 cols, 1 1/6, 5/24 between.
Published Days: Thur
Avg Paid Circ: 60
Avg Free Circ: 5963
Audit Company: Sworn/Estimate/Non-Audited
Audit Date: 6 10 2019
Total Circulation: 1806

MINNETONKA/DEEPHAVEN/ HOPKINS SUN SAILOR

Street Address: 33 Second St. N.E
City: Osseo
State: MN
Postal Code: 55369
Office phone: (763) 425-3323
Publication Website: https://www.hometownsource.com/sun_sailor/
General E-mail: servicecenter@ecm-inc.com
Editor Name: Gretchen Schlosser
Editor Email: gretchen.schlosser@ecm-inc.com
Editor Phone: (763) 424-7375
Advertising Executive Name: Steve Gall
Advertising Executive Email: steve.gall@ecm-inc.com
Advertising Executive Phone: (952) 392-6844
Year Established: 1970
Delivery Methods: Carrier
Mechanical specifications: Type page 4 x 10; E - 4 cols, 2 1/2, 1/4 between; A - 5 cols, 1 5/8, 1/4 between; C - 8 cols, 1 1/6, 5/24 between.
Published Days: Thur
Avg Paid Circ: 88

MINNETONKA/DEEPHAVEN/ HOPKINS SUN SAILOR

Avg Free Circ: 18076
Audit Company: Sworn/Estimate/Non-Audited
Audit Date: 6 10 2019

Street Address: 33 Second St. N.E.
City: Osseo
State: MN
Postal Code: 55369
Office phone: (763) 425-3323
Publication Website: https://www.hometownsource.com/sun_sailor/
General E-mail: advertise@ecm-inc.com
Editor Name: Gretchen Schlosser
Editor Email: gretchen.schlosser@ecm-inc.com
Total Circulation: 9080

NORTH CROW RIVER NEWS

Street Address: 33 2nd St NE
City: Osseo
State: MN
Postal Code: 55369
Office phone: (763) 425-3323
Publication Website: https://www.hometownsource.com/press_and_news/
General E-mail: jeremy.bradfield@ecm-inc.com
Advertising Executive Name: Jeremy Bradfield
Advertising Executive Email: jeremy.bradfield@ecm-inc.com
Advertising Executive Phone: (952) 392-6841
Year Established: 1963
Own Printing Facility?: Y
Commercial printers?: Y
Mechanical specifications: Type page 6 x 21; E - 6 cols, 1 5/6, 1/8 between; A - 6 cols, 1 5/6, 1/8 between; C - 9 cols, 1 3/16, 1/8 between.
Published Days: Thur
Avg Paid Circ: 3280
Avg Free Circ: 6214
Audit Company: Sworn/Estimate/Non-Audited
Audit Date: 6 10 2019
Total Circulation: 6695

OSSEO-MAPLE GROVE PRESS

Corporate/Parent Company: Adams Publishing Group
Street Address: 33 2nd St NE
City: Osseo
State: MN
Postal Code: 55369
Office phone: (763) 425-3323
Publication Website: https://www.hometownsource.com/press_and_news/
General E-mail: jeremy.bradfield@ecm-inc.com
Advertising Executive Name: Jeremy Bradfield
Advertising Executive Email: jeremy.bradfield@ecm-inc.com
Advertising Executive Phone: (952) 392-6841
Year Established: 1924
Delivery Methods: Mail
Own Printing Facility?: Y
Commercial printers?: Y
Mechanical specifications: Type page 6 x 21; E - 6 cols, 1 5/6, 1/8 between; A - 6 cols, 1 5/6, 1/8 between; C - 9 cols, 1 3/16, 1/8 between.
Published Days: Thur
Avg Paid Circ: 3280
Avg Free Circ: 6214
Audit Company: Sworn/Estimate/Non-Audited
Audit Date: 6 10 2019
Total Circulation: 2542

ROCKFORD AREA NEWS LEADER

Street Address: 33 2nd St NE
City: Osseo
State: MN
Postal Code: 55369
Office phone: (763) 425-3323
Publication Website: https://www.hometownsource.com/press_and_news/
General E-mail: sunpressnews@ecm-inc.com
Advertising Executive Name: Jeremy Bradfield
Advertising Executive Email: jeremy.bradfield@ecm-inc.com
Advertising Executive Phone: (952) 392-6841
Year Established: 1963
Own Printing Facility?: Y
Commercial printers?: Y
Mechanical specifications: Type page 6 x 21; E - 6 cols, 1 5/6, 1/8 between; A - 6 cols, 1 5/6, 1/8 between; C - 9 cols, 1 3/16, 1/8 between.
Published Days: Mon
Avg Paid Circ: 780
Avg Free Circ: 3149
Audit Company: Sworn/Estimate/Non-Audited
Audit Date: 6 10 2019

SOUTH CROW RIVER NEWS

Street Address: 33 2nd St NE
City: Osseo
State: MN
Postal Code: 55369
Office phone: (763) 425-3323
Publication Website: https://www.hometownsource.com/press_and_news/
General E-mail: sunpressnews@ecm-inc.com
Editor Name: Aaron Brom
Editor Email: aaron.brom@ecm-inc.com
Editor Phone: (763) 424-7359
Advertising Executive Name: Jeremy Bradfield
Advertising Executive Email: jeremy.bradfield@ecm-inc.com
Advertising Executive Phone: (952) 392-6841
Year Established: 1963
Own Printing Facility?: Y
Commercial printers?: Y
Mechanical specifications: Type page 11 5/8 x 21; E - 6 cols, 1 5/6, 1/8 between; A - 6 cols, 1 5/6, 1/8 between; C - 9 cols, 1 3/16, 1/8 between.
Published Days: Thur
Avg Paid Circ: 715
Avg Free Circ: 420
Audit Company: Sworn/Estimate/Non-Audited
Audit Date: 6 10 2019
Total Circulation: 6613

ST. LOUIS PARK SUN SAILOR

Corporate/Parent Company: Adams Publishing Group
Street Address: 33 2nd St NE
City: Osseo
State: MN
Postal Code: 55369
Office phone: (763) 425-3323
Publication Website: https://www.hometownsource.com/sun_sailor/community/stlouispark/
General E-mail: servicecenter@ecm-inc.com
Editor Name: Gretchen Schlosser
Editor Email: gretchen.schlosser@ecm-inc.com
Editor Phone: (763) 424-7375
Advertising Executive Name: Steve Gall
Advertising Executive Email: steve.gall@ecm-inc.com
Advertising Executive Phone: (952) 392-6844
Year Established: 1970
Delivery Methods: Carrier
Published Days: Thur
Avg Paid Circ: 148
Avg Free Circ: 10821
Audit Company: Sworn/Estimate/Non-Audited
Audit Date: 6 10 2019
Total Circulation: 9994

ST. MICHAEL/ ROCKFORD CROW RIVER NEWS

Street Address: 33 Second St. N.E.
City: Osseo
State: MN
Postal Code: 55369
Office phone: (763) 425-3323
Publication Website: https://www.hometownsource.com/press_and_news
General E-mail: sunpressnews@ecm-inc.com
Editor Name: Aaron Brom
Editor Email: aaron.brom@ecm-inc.com
Editor Phone: 763-424-7359
Advertising Executive Name: Jeremy Bradfield
Advertising Executive Email: jeremy.bradfield@ecm-inc.com
Advertising Executive Phone: 952-392-6841
Total Circulation: 3929

WAYZATA/ORONO/PLYMOUTH/LONG LAKE SUN SAILOR

Street Address: 33 Second St. N.E
City: Osseo
State: MN
Postal Code: 55369
Office phone: (763) 425-3323
Publication Website: https://www.hometownsource.com/sun_sailor/
General E-mail: servicecenter@ecm-inc.com
Editor Name: Gretchen Schlosser
Editor Email: gretchen.schlosser@ecm-inc.com
Editor Phone: (763) 424-7375
Advertising Executive Name: Steve Gall
Advertising Executive Email: steve.gall@ecm-inc.com
Advertising Executive Phone: (952) 392-6844
Year Established: 1970
Delivery Methods: Carrier
Mechanical specifications: Type page 4 x 10; E - 4 cols, 2 1/2, 1/4 between; A - 5 cols, 1 5/8, 1/4 between; C - 8 cols, 1 1/6, 5/24 between.
Published Days: Thur
Avg Paid Circ: 146
Avg Free Circ: 18039
Audit Company: Sworn/Estimate/Non-Audited
Audit Date: 6 10 2019
Total Circulation: 12294

OWATONNA

OWATONNA AREA SHOPPER

Street Address: 135 W Pearl St
City: Owatonna
State: MN
Postal Code: 55060
Office phone: (507) 451-2840
Publication Website: https://www.southernminn.com/eedition/owatonnashopper/
General E-mail: advertising@owatonna.com
Publisher Name: Steve Fisher
Publisher Email: sfisher@owatonna.com
Publisher Phone: (507) 444-2367
Editor Name: Jeffrey Jackson
Editor Email: jjackson@owatonna.com
Editor Phone: (507) 444-2371
Advertising Executive Name: Tom Kelling
Advertising Executive Email: tkelling@owatonna.com
Advertising Executive Phone: (507) 444-2390

PIPESTONE

JASPER JOURNAL

Street Address: P.O. Box 277; 115 Second Street NE
City: Pipestone
State: MN
Postal Code: 56164-0277
Office phone: (507) 825-3333
Publication Website: www.pipestonestar.com/category/news/jasper-news
General E-mail: journal@pipestonestar.com
Publisher Name: John Draper
Advertising Executive Name: Paul Lorang
Total Circulation: 5614

PLAINVIEW

PLAINVIEW NEWS

Corporate/Parent Company: GMD Media Inc.
Street Address: 409 West Broadway
City: Plainview
State: MN
Postal Code: 55964
Office phone: (507) 534-3121
Publication Website: www.gmdmedia.net
Publisher Name: Daniel Stumpf
Editor Name: Cheryl Nymann
Editor Email: news@stumpfpublishing.net
Advertising Executive Name: Lynn Abbot

PRINCETON

MILLE LACS COUNTY TIMES

Street Address: 208 N Rum River Dr
City: Princeton
State: MN
Postal Code: 55371
Office phone: (763) 389-1222
Publication Website: https://www.hometownsource.com/union_times/
General E-mail: class@ecm-inc.com
Editor Name: Tim Hennagir
Editor Email: tim.hennagir@ecm-inc.com
Editor Phone: (763) 231-3249
Advertising Executive Name: Brigitte Alday
Advertising Executive Email: brigitte.alday@ecm-inc.com
Advertising Executive Phone: (763) 231-3247
Delivery Methods: Mail`Newsstand
Own Printing Facility?: Y
Published Days: Thur
Avg Paid Circ: 1559
Audit Company: Sworn/Estimate/Non-Audited
Audit Date: 6 10 2019
Total Circulation: 4602

PRINCETON UNION-EAGLE

Street Address: 208 N Rum River Dr
City: Princeton
State: MN
Postal Code: 55371
Office phone: (763) 389-1222
Publication Website: https://www.hometownsource.com/union_times/news/welcome-to-the-new-princeton-union-eagle/article_232652a8-b405-544e-9156-539350e40c89.html
General E-mail: servicecenter@ecm-inc.com
Editor Name: Tim Hennagir
Editor Email: tim.hennagir@ecm-inc.com
Editor Phone: (763) 231-3249
Advertising Executive Name: Cindy Collins
Advertising Executive Email: cindy.collins@ecm-inc.com
Advertising Executive Phone: (763) 231-3248
Year Established: 1876
Own Printing Facility?: Y
Commercial printers?: Y
Mechanical specifications: Type page 10.3339 x 21; E - 6 cols, 1 11/12, 1/6 between; A - 6 cols, 1 11/12, 1/6 between; C - 8 cols, 1 1/2, 1/12 between.
Published Days: Thur
Avg Paid Circ: 1806
Audit Company: Sworn/Estimate/Non-Audited
Audit Date: 6 10 2019
Total Circulation: 19721

PRINCETON/ MILACA- UNION TIMES

Street Address: 208 North Rum River Drive
City: Princeton
State: MN
Postal Code: 55371-0278
Office phone: (763) 389-1222
Publication Website: www.hometownsource.

Non-Daily Newspapers in the U.S.

com/union_times
Editor Name: Tim Hennagir
Editor Email: tim.hennagir@ecm-inc.com
Editor Phone: (763) 231-3249
Advertising Executive Name: Jerry Gloe
Advertising Executive Email: jerry.gloe@ecm-inc.com

RED WING

PIERCE COUNTY HERALD

Corporate/Parent Company: Forum Communications
Street Address: 2760 N Service Drive
City: Red Wing
State: MN
Postal Code: 55066
Office phone: 800) 535-1660
Publication Website: www.piercecountyherald.com
General E-mail: news@rivertowns.net
Publisher Name: Neal Ronquist
Publisher Email: nronquist@rivertowns.net
Publisher Phone: (651) 301-7855
Editor Name: Michael Brun
Editor Email: mbrun@rivertowns.net
Editor Phone: (651) 301-7875
Advertising Executive Name: Megan Keller
Advertising Executive Email: mkeller@rivertowns.net
Advertising Executive Phone: (651) 301-7801

RED WING REPUBLICAN EAGLE

Corporate/Parent Company: Forum Communications
Street Address: P.O. Box 15; 2760 North Service Drive
City: Red Wing
State: MN
Postal Code: 55066-0015
Office phone: (651) 388-8235
Publication Website: www.rivertowns.net
Publisher Name: Neal Ronquist
Publisher Email: nronquist@rivertowns.net
Publisher Phone: (218) 723-5235
Editor Name: Anne Jacobson
Editor Email: ajacobson@rivertowns.net
Editor Phone: (651) 301-7870
Advertising Executive Name: Megan Wedel
Advertising Executive Email: mkeller@rivertowns.net
Advertising Executive Phone: (651) 301-7801
Total Circulation: 1135

SAINT CHARLES

LEWISTON JOURNAL

Corporate/Parent Company: GMD Media Inc.
Street Address: 924 Whitewater Ave
City: Saint Charles
State: MN
Postal Code: 55972
Office phone: (507) 523-2119
Publication Website: https://www.sunjournal.com/
General E-mail: scpress@stumpfpublishing.net
Own Printing Facility?: Y
Published Days: Thur
Avg Paid Circ: 974
Audit Company: Sworn/Estimate/Non-Audited
Audit Date: 6 10 2019

ST. CHARLES PRESS

Corporate/Parent Company: GMD Media Inc.
Street Address: 924 Whitewater Ave
City: Saint Charles
State: MN
Postal Code: 55972
Office phone: (507) 932-3663
Publication Website: http://www.gmdmedia.net/st-charles-press
General E-mail: scpress@stumpfpublishing.net

Own Printing Facility?: Y
Commercial printers?: Y
Published Days: Thur
Avg Paid Circ: 1475
Audit Company: Sworn/Estimate/Non-Audited
Audit Date: 6 10 2019
Total Circulation: 11021

SAINT PETER

ST. PETER HERALD

Corporate/Parent Company: Adams Publishing Group
Street Address: 311 S Minnesota Ave
City: Saint Peter
State: MN
Postal Code: 56082
Office phone: (507) 931-4520
Publication Website: https://www.southernminn.com/st_peter_herald/
General E-mail: news@stpeterherald.com
Publisher Name: Chad Hjellming
Publisher Email: chjellming@northfieldnews.com
Publisher Phone: (507) 645-1110
Editor Name: Philip Weyhe
Editor Email: editor@stpeterherald.com
Editor Phone: (507) 931-8567
Advertising Executive Name: Kathleen Davies
Advertising Executive Email: kdavies@stpeterherald.com
Advertising Executive Phone: (507) 931-8564
Delivery Methods: Mail
Own Printing Facility?: Y
Mechanical specifications: Type page 6 x 21 1/2; E - 6 cols, 1 5/6, between; A - 6 cols, 1 5/6, between; C - 6 cols, 1 5/6, between.
Published Days: Thur
Avg Paid Circ: 1191
Avg Free Circ: 200
Audit Company: Sworn/Estimate/Non-Audited
Audit Date: 6 10 2019
Total Circulation: 1114

SAUK CENTRE

DAIRYLAND PEACH

Street Address: 601 Sinclair Lewis Ave
City: Sauk Centre
State: MN
Postal Code: 56378
Office phone: (320) 352-6569
Publication Website: https://www.hometownsource.com/dairyland_peach/
General E-mail: print.saukcentre@ecm-inc.com
Publisher Name: Carmen Meyer
Publisher Email: carmen.meyer@ecm-inc.com
Publisher Phone: (320) 616-1913
Advertising Executive Name: Tena Wensman
Advertising Executive Email: tena.wensman@ecm-inc.com
Advertising Executive Phone: (320) 611-1932
Total Circulation: 1219

SAUK RAPIDS

SAUK RAPIDS HERALD

Corporate/Parent Company: Star Publications
Street Address: 11 2nd Avenue North, Suite 103
City: Sauk Rapids
State: MN
Postal Code: 56379
Office phone: (320) 251-1971
Publication Website: www.saukrapidsherald.com
Editor Name: Natasha Barber
Editor Email: natasha@saukherald.com
Advertising Executive Name: Tim Vos
Advertising Executive Email: tim@saukherald.com
Advertising Executive Phone: (320) 492-6987
Total Circulation: 2047

SAVAGE

PRIOR LAKE AMERICAN

Street Address: 12925 Eagle Creek Pkwy
City: Savage
State: MN
Postal Code: 55378
Office phone: (952) 447-6669
Publication Website: https://www.swnewsmedia.com/prior_lake_american/
General E-mail: schacherer@hutchinsonleader.com
Publisher Name: Laurie Hartmann
Publisher Email: lhartmann@swnewsmedia.com
Publisher Phone: (952) 345-6878
Editor Name: Dan Holtmeyer
Editor Email: editor@plamerican.com
Editor Phone: (952) 345-6376
Year Established: 1960
Delivery Methods: Mail
Published Days: Sat
Avg Paid Circ: 740
Avg Free Circ: 8340
Audit Company: Sworn/Estimate/Non-Audited
Audit Date: 6 10 2019
Total Circulation: 1475

SAVAGE PACER

Street Address: 12925 Eagle Creek Pkwy
City: Savage
State: MN
Postal Code: 55378-1271
Office phone: (952) 440-1234
Publication Website: https://www.swnewsmedia.com/savage_pacer/
General E-mail: schacherer@hutchinsonleader.com
Publisher Name: Laurie Hartmann
Publisher Email: lhartmann@swnewsmedia.com
Publisher Phone: (952) 345-6878
Editor Name: Dan Holtmeyer
Editor Email: editor@plamerican.com
Editor Phone: (952) 345-6376
Delivery Methods: Mail`Newsstand
Published Days: Sat
Avg Free Circ: 5614
Audit Company: Sworn/Estimate/Non-Audited
Audit Date: 6 10 2019

SHAKOPEE VALLEY NEWS

Street Address: 12925 Eagle Creek Pkwy
City: Savage
State: MN
Postal Code: 55378
Office phone: (952) 445-3333
Publication Website: https://www.swnewsmedia.com/shakopee_valley_news/
General E-mail: schacherer@hutchinsonleader.com
Publisher Name: Laurie Hartmann
Publisher Email: lhartmann@swnewsmedia.com
Publisher Phone: (952) 345-6878
Editor Name: Rachel Minske
Editor Email: rminske@swpub.com
Editor Phone: (952) 345-6679
Delivery Methods: Mail`Newsstand
Published Days: Thur
Avg Paid Circ: 4602
Audit Company: Sworn/Estimate/Non-Audited
Audit Date: 6 10 2019

SCANDIA

SCANDIA - COUNTRY MESSENGER

Corporate/Parent Company: Sentinel Publications
Street Address: PO Box 96
City: Scandia
State: MN
Postal Code: 55073
Office phone: (651) 433-3845
Publication Website: www.countrymessenger.com

General E-mail: office@osceolasun.com
Publisher Name: Tom Stangl
Publisher Email: tstangl@theameryfreepress.com
Editor Name: Phillip Bock
Editor Email: editor@countrymessenger.com
Editor Phone: 651-433-3845
Advertising Executive Name: Elise Bourne
Advertising Executive Email: ads@osceolasun.com
Total Circulation: 10969

SLEEPY EYE

SLEEPY EYE HERALD - DISPATCH

Street Address: 119 Main Street East, (PO box 499)
City: Sleepy Eye
State: MN
Postal Code: 56085
Office phone: (507) 794-3511
Publication Website: www.sleepyeyenews.com
Publisher Name: Lisa Drafall
Publisher Email: ldrafall@sleepyeyenews.com
Publisher Phone: 507-794-3511 ext. 18
Editor Name: Deb Moldaschel
Editor Email: dmoldaschel@sleepyeyenews.com
Editor Phone: 507-794-3511 ext. 20
Advertising Executive Name: Cassie Walker
Advertising Executive Email: cwalker1@gatehousemedia.com

SPRING VALLEY

BLUFF COUNTRY READER

Corporate/Parent Company: Bluff Country Newspaper Group
Street Address: 101 South Broadway Ave
City: Spring Valley
State: MN
Postal Code: 55975
Office phone: (507) 346-7365
Publication Website: https://www.bluffcountrynews.com/category/bluff-country-reader
General E-mail: info@bluffcountrynews.com

FILLMORE COUNTY NEWS LEADER

Corporate/Parent Company: Bluff Country Newspaper Group
Street Address: 101 South Broadway Ave
City: Spring Valley
State: MN
Postal Code: 55975
Office phone: (507) 346-7365
Publication Website: https://www.bluffcountrynews.com/category/news-leader
General E-mail: info@bluffcountrynews.com
Delivery Methods: Mail
Published Days: Thur
Avg Paid Circ: 1412
Audit Company: Sworn/Estimate/Non-Audited
Audit Date: 6 10 2019

SPRING GROVE HERALD

Corporate/Parent Company: Bluff Country Newspaper Group
Street Address: 101 South Broadway Ave
City: Spring Valley
State: MN
Postal Code: 55975
Office phone: (507) 346-7365
Publication Website: https://www.bluffcountrynews.com/category/spring-grove-herald
General E-mail: info@bluffcountrynews.com
Year Established: 1892
Delivery Methods: Mail
Own Printing Facility?: N
Commercial printers?: Y

Mechanical specifications: Type page 6 x 21; E - 6 cols, 1.95", 1/8 between; A - 6 cols, 1 5/6, .16" between; C - 6 cols
Published Days: Wed
Avg Paid Circ: 1099
Avg Free Circ: 15
Audit Company: Sworn/Estimate/Non-Audited
Audit Date: 6 10 2019

SPRING VALLEY TRIBUNE
Corporate/Parent Company: Bluff Country Newspaper Group
Street Address: 101 South Broadway Ave
City: Spring Valley
State: MN
Postal Code: 55975
Office phone: (507) 346-7265
Publication Website: https://www.bluffcountrynews.com/category/spring-valley-tribune
General E-mail: info@bluffcountrynews.com
Year Established: 1880
Delivery Methods: Mail`Racks
Mechanical specifications: Type page 6 x 21 1/2; E - 6 cols, between; A - 6 cols, between; C - 6 cols, between.
Published Days: Wed
Avg Paid Circ: 1219
Audit Company: Sworn/Estimate/Non-Audited
Audit Date: 6 10 2019

THE CHATFIELD NEWS
Corporate/Parent Company: Bluff Country Newspaper Group
Street Address: 101 South Broadway Ave
City: Spring Valley
State: MN
Postal Code: 55975
Office phone: (507) 346-7265
Publication Website: https://www.bluffcountrynews.com/category/chatfield-news
General E-mail: chatfieldnews@bluffcountrynews.com
Delivery Methods: Mail
Published Days: Tues
Avg Paid Circ: 1413
Audit Company: Sworn/Estimate/Non-Audited
Audit Date: 6 10 2019

TRI-COUNTY RECORD
Corporate/Parent Company: Bluff Country Newspaper Group
Street Address: 101 South Broadway Ave
City: Spring Valley
State: MN
Postal Code: 55975
Office phone: (507) 346-7265
Publication Website: https://www.bluffcountrynews.com/category/tri-county-record
General E-mail: info@bluffcountrynews.com
Year Established: 1915
Delivery Methods: Mail`Newsstand
Mechanical specifications: Type page 6 x 21 1/2; E - 6 cols, 1/32, 1/6 between; A - 6 cols, 2 3/16, 1/6 between; C - 6 cols, 2 3/16, 1/6 between.
Published Days: Thur
Avg Paid Circ: 1063
Avg Free Circ: 53
Audit Company: Sworn/Estimate/Non-Audited
Audit Date: 6 10 2019
Total Circulation: 1391

ST. PAUL
MINNESOTA LEGIONNAIRE
Corporate/Parent Company: The American Legion Department of Minnesota
Street Address: 20 West 12th Street, Room 300A
City: St. Paul
State: MN
Postal Code: 55155-2069
Office phone: (651) 291-1800
Publication Website: mnlegion.org
Editor Name: Al Zdon
Editor Email: azdon@mnlegion.org

ST. PAUL- ACCESS PRESS
Street Address: 161 St. Anthony Avenue, Ste 910
City: St. Paul
State: MN
Postal Code: 55103
Office phone: (651) 644-2133
Publication Website: www.accesspress.org
Editor Name: Tim Benjamin
Editor Email: tim@accesspress.org
Advertising Executive Name: Michelle Hegarty
Advertising Executive Email: michelle@accesspress.org
Mailroom Equipment: Tying Machines – 1/Bu; Address Machine – 1-/Am.;
Classified Equipment: Hardware – Baseview.;
Editorial Equipment: Hardware – CText.
Production Equipment: Hardware – 1-Nu/FT40L; Cameras – 1-B/1822.
Total Circulation: 1615

ST. PAUL- THE PARK BUGLE
Street Address: P.O. Box 8126
City: St. Paul
State: MN
Postal Code: 55108
Office phone: 651-646-5369
Publication Website: www.parkbugle.org
Editor Name: Scott Carlson
Editor Email: editor@parkbugle.org
Editor Phone: 651-646-5369
Advertising Executive Name: Bradley Max Wolfe
Advertising Executive Email: bradley.wolfe@parkbugle.org
Advertising Executive Phone: 952-393-6814
Total Circulation: 12118

STILLWATER
STILLWATER GAZETTE
Street Address: 225 North Second St. Suite 100
City: Stillwater
State: MN
Postal Code: 55082
Office phone: (651) 439-3130
Publication Website: https://www.hometownsource.com/stillwater_gazette/
General E-mail: servicecenter@ecm-inc.com
Editor Name: Alicia Lebens
Editor Email: alicia.lebens@ecm-inc.com
Editor Phone: (651) 796-1118
Advertising Executive Name: Steve Gall
Advertising Executive Email: steve.gall@ecm-inc.com
Advertising Executive Phone: (952) 392-6844
Year Established: 1870
Delivery Methods: Mail`Carrier
Mechanical specifications: Type page 6 x 21; E - 6 cols, 2 1/16, 1/8 between; A - 6 cols, 2 1/16, 1/8 between; C - 9 cols, 1 3/8, 1/16 between.
Published Days: Wed`Fri
Weekday Frequency: e
Avg Paid Circ: 1591
Avg Free Circ: 24
Audit Company: Sworn/Estimate/Non-Audited
Audit Date: 6 10 2019
Pressroom Equipment: Lines – 4-HI/V-15A;
Total Circulation: 11273

WABASHA
WABASHA COUNTY HERALD
Corporate/Parent Company: GMD Media Inc.
Street Address: 200 Industrial Ct.
City: Wabasha
State: MN
Postal Code: 55981
Office phone: (651) 565-3368
Publication Website: http://www.gmdmedia.net/wabasha-county-herald
General E-mail: gmdmedia@gmdmedia.net
Total Circulation: 16829

WACONIA
CARVER COUNTY NEWS
Corporate/Parent Company: Adams Publishing Group
Street Address: 8 S Elm St
City: Waconia
State: MN
Postal Code: 55387
Office phone: (952) 442-4414
Publication Website: https://www.hometownsource.com/sun_patriot/
General E-mail: servicecenter@ecm-inc.com
Editor Name: Megan Glenn
Editor Email: megan.glenn@ecm-inc.com
Editor Phone: (952) 442-2521
Year Established: 1976
Published Days: Thur
Avg Free Circ: 44
Audit Company: Sworn/Estimate/Non-Audited
Audit Date: 6 10 2019
Total Circulation: 5842

NORWOOD YOUNG AMERICA TIMES
Corporate/Parent Company: Adams Publishing Group
Street Address: PO Box 5
City: Waconia
State: MN
Postal Code: 55387
Office phone: (952) 442-4414
Publication Website: https://www.hometownsource.com/sun_patriot/community/nya/
General E-mail: servicecenter@ecm-inc.com
Editor Name: Jason Schmucker
Editor Email: jason.schmucker@ecm-inc.com
Editor Phone: (952) 442-4186
Delivery Methods: Mail
Published Days: Thur
Avg Paid Circ: 2550
Avg Free Circ: 41
Audit Company: Sworn/Estimate/Non-Audited
Audit Date: 6 10 2019
Total Circulation: 1413

THE LAKER
Street Address: 8 S Elm St
City: Waconia
State: MN
Postal Code: 55387
Office phone: (952) 442-4414
Publication Website: https://www.hometownsource.com/laker_pioneer/
General E-mail: servicecenter@ecm-inc.com
Editor Name: Elizabeth Hustad
Editor Email: laker.reporter@ecm-inc.com
Editor Phone: (952) 442-6800
Delivery Methods: Mail
Published Days: Sat
Avg Paid Circ: 10
Avg Free Circ: 6499
Audit Company: Sworn/Estimate/Non-Audited
Audit Date: 6 10 2019
Total Circulation: 1043

THE PIONEER
Street Address: 8 S Elm St
City: Waconia
State: MN
Postal Code: 55387
Office phone: (952) 442-4414
Publication Website: https://www.hometownsource.com/laker_pioneer/
General E-mail: servicecenter@ecm-inc.com
Editor Name: Elizabeth Hustad
Editor Email: laker.reporter@ecm-inc.com
Editor Phone: (952) 442-6800
Delivery Methods: Mail
Published Days: Sat
Avg Paid Circ: 15
Avg Free Circ: 11459
Audit Company: Sworn/Estimate/Non-Audited
Audit Date: 6 10 2019
Note: The Citizen serves the cities of Hugo, Centerville and the eastern third of Lino Lakes, Minnesota
Total Circulation: 8262

THE WACONIA PATRIOT
Corporate/Parent Company: Adams Publishing Group
Street Address: 8 S Elm St
City: Waconia
State: MN
Postal Code: 55387
Office phone: (952) 442-4414
Publication Website: https://www.hometownsource.com/sun_patriot/
General E-mail: servicecenter@ecm-inc.com
Editor Name: Jason Schmucker
Editor Email: jason.schmucker@ecm-inc.com
Editor Phone: (952) 442-4186
Year Established: 1976
Delivery Methods: Mail
Published Days: Thur
Avg Paid Circ: 4640
Avg Free Circ: 6528
Audit Company: Sworn/Estimate/Non-Audited
Audit Date: 6 10 2019
Mailroom Equipment: Tying Machines – Bu; Address Machine – KR.;
Buisness Equipment: IBM/PS-2 Model 50
Buisness Software: MSSI, Quattro/Pro
Classified Equipment: Hardware – APP/Mac;
Classified Software: Baseview.
Editorial Equipment: Hardware – APP/Mac; Printers – APP/Mac
Editorial Software: NewsEdit/Pro.
Production Equipment: Hardware – APP/Mac; Cameras – SCREEN/Companica 690E; Scanners – APP/Mac, HP.
Total Circulation: 16244

WALKER
CO-PILOT
Street Address: 408 Minnesota Ave
City: Walker
State: MN
Postal Code: 56484
Office phone: (218) 547-1000
Publication Website: https://www.walkermn.com/co_pilot_shopper/
General E-mail: pilotnews@pilotindependent.com
Publisher Name: Terri Fierstine
Publisher Email: tfierstine@pilotindependent.com
Editor Name: Dean Morrill
Editor Email: dmorrill@pilotindependent.com
Advertising Executive Name: Michelle Bruns
Advertising Executive Email: pilotads@pilotindependent.com
Total Circulation: 6509

WALKER PILOT - INDEPENDENT

Street Address: P.O. Box 190; 408 Minnesota Avenue West
City: Walker
State: MN
Postal Code: 56484-0190
Office phone: (218) 547-1000
Publication Website: www.walkermn.com
Publisher Name: Terri Fierstine
Publisher Email: tfierstine@pilotindependent.com
Editor Name: Dean Morrill
Editor Email: dmorrill@pilotindependent.com
Advertising Executive Name: Michelle Bruns
Advertising Executive Email: pilotads@pilotindependent.com

WASECA

WASECA AREA SHOPPER

Street Address: 213 2nd St NW
City: Waseca
State: MN
Postal Code: 56093
Office phone: (507) 835-3380
Publication Website: https://www.southernminn.com/waseca_county_news/
General E-mail: news@wasecacountynews.com
Editor Name: Jeffrey Jackson
Editor Email: editor@wasecacountynews.com
Editor Phone: (507) 837-5402
Advertising Executive Name: Tom Kelling
Advertising Executive Email: tkelling@owatonna.com
Advertising Executive Phone: (507) 444-2390
Total Circulation: 2985

WASECA COUNTY NEWS

Corporate/Parent Company: Adams Publishing Group
Street Address: 213 2nd St NW
City: Waseca
State: MN
Postal Code: 56093
Office phone: (507) 835-3380
Publication Website: https://www.southernminn.com/waseca_county_news/
General E-mail: news@wasecacountynews.com
Editor Name: Jeffrey Jackson
Editor Email: editor@wasecacountynews.com
Editor Phone: (507) 837-5402
Advertising Executive Name: Tom Kelling
Advertising Executive Email: tkelling@owatonna.com
Advertising Executive Phone: (507) 444-2390
Year Established: srook@wasecacountynews.com
Mechanical specifications: Type page 6 x 21 1/2; E - 6 cols, 1 5/6, between; A - 6 cols, 1 5/6, between; C - 6 cols, 1 5/6, between.
Published Days: Fri
Avg Paid Circ: 1907
Avg Free Circ: 100
Audit Company: Sworn/Estimate/Non-Audited
Audit Date: 6 10 2019
Total Circulation: 2975

WATERVILLE

WATERVILLE - LAKE REGION LIFE

Corporate/Parent Company: Suel Printing Co.
Street Address: 115 South Third Street
City: Waterville
State: MN
Postal Code: 56096
Office phone: 507-362-4495
Publication Website: www.watervillemnnews.com
Publisher Name: Chuck Wann
Editor Name: Jay Schneider
Editor Email: lrlife@frontiernet.net
Advertising Executive Name: Mark Slavik
Total Circulation: 11474

WEST ST. PAUL

ST. PAUL VOICE

Corporate/Parent Company: St. Paul Publishing Co
Street Address: 1643 South Robert Street Suite 60B
City: West St. Paul
State: MN
Postal Code: 55118
Office phone: 651-457-1177
Publication Website: www.stpaulpublishing.com
General E-mail: info@stpaulpublishing.com
Editor Name: Tim Spitzack
Editor Email: tim@stpaulpublishing.com
Total Circulation: 1259

WHITE BEAR LAKE

CIRCLE PINES- QUAD COMMUNITY PRESS

Corporate/Parent Company: Press Publications
Street Address: 4779 Bloom Avenue
City: White Bear Lake
State: MN
Postal Code: 55110
Office phone: 651-407-1200
Publication Website: www.quadcommunitypress.com
General E-mail: news@presspubs.com
Publisher Name: Carter Johnson
Editor Name: Shannon Granholm
Editor Email: quadnews@presspubs.com
Editor Phone: 651-407-1227
Advertising Executive Name: Patty Steele
Advertising Executive Email: wbpressad2@presspubs.com
Advertising Executive Phone: 651-407-1213
Total Circulation: 11168

FOREST LAKE LOWDOWN

Corporate/Parent Company: Press Publications
Street Address: 4779 Bloom Ave
City: White Bear Lake
State: MN
Postal Code: 55110
Office phone: (651) 407-1200
Publication Website: https://www.presspubs.com/forest_lake/
General E-mail: news@presspubs.com
Publisher Name: Carter C. Johnson
Publisher Email: ppinfo@presspubs.com
Publisher Phone: (651) 407-1200
Editor Name: Debra Neutkens
Editor Email: news@presspubs.com
Editor Phone: (651) 407-1226
Advertising Executive Name: Patty Steele
Advertising Executive Email: marketing@presspubs.com
Advertising Executive Phone: (651) 407-1208
Year Established: 1903
Delivery Methods: Mail`Newsstand`Carrier`Racks
Own Printing Facility?: Y
Commercial printers?: Y
Mechanical specifications: Type page 6 x 21; E - 6 cols, 1.57", 1/6 between; A - 6 cols, 1.57", 1/6 between; C - 9 cols, 1.037, 1/12 between.
Published Days: Fri`Bi-Mthly
Avg Paid Circ: 58
Avg Free Circ: 11584
Audit Company: VAC
Audit Date: 28 09 2017
Total Circulation: 25810

HUGO- THE CITIZEN

Corporate/Parent Company: Press Publications
Street Address: 4779 Bloom Avenue
City: White Bear Lake
State: MN
Postal Code: 55110
Office phone: (651) 407-1200
Publication Website: www.readthecitizen.com
General E-mail: ppinfo@presspubs.com
Publisher Name: Carter Johnson
Editor Name: Shannon Granholm
Editor Email: citizen@presspubs.com
Editor Phone: 651-407-1227
Advertising Executive Name: Jeanne Kuenzli
Advertising Executive Email: citizenrep@presspubs.com
Advertising Executive Phone: 651-407-1224
Total Circulation: 1116

QUAD COMMUNITY PRESS

Corporate/Parent Company: Press Publications
Street Address: 4779 Bloom Ave
City: White Bear Lake
State: MN
Postal Code: 55110
Office phone: (365) 407-1200
Publication Website: https://www.presspubs.com/quad/
General E-mail: news@presspubs.com
Editor Name: Shannon Granholm
Editor Email: quadnews@presspubs.com
Editor Phone: (651) 407-1227
Advertising Executive Name: Patty Steele
Advertising Executive Email: wbpressad2@presspubs.com
Advertising Executive Phone: (651) 407-1213
Year Established: 1981
Delivery Methods: Mail`Carrier
Own Printing Facility?: Y
Commercial printers?: Y
Mechanical specifications: Type page 11 1/2 x 21; E - 6 cols, 1 13/16, between; A - 6 cols, 1 13/16, between; C - 10 cols, 1 1/4, 1/2 between.
Published Days: Tues
Avg Paid Circ: 708
Avg Free Circ: 5987
Audit Company: VAC
Audit Date: 30 09 2017
Total Circulation: 3538

SHOREVIEW PRESS

Corporate/Parent Company: Press Publications
Street Address: 4779 Bloom Avenue
City: White Bear Lake
State: MN
Postal Code: 55110
Office phone: (651) 407-1200
Publication Website: www.shoreviewpress.com
Publisher Name: Carter C. Johnson
Publisher Email: ppinfo@presspubs.com
Publisher Phone: 651-407-1200
Editor Name: Debra Neutkens
Editor Email: news@presspubs.com
Editor Phone: 651-407-1226
Advertising Executive Name: Patty Steele
Advertising Executive Email: marketing@presspubs.com
Advertising Executive Phone: (651) 407-1208

ST. CROIX VALLEY LOWDOWN

Corporate/Parent Company: Press Publications
Street Address: 4779 Bloom Avenue
City: White Bear Lake
State: MN
Postal Code: 55110
Office phone: (651) 407-1200
Publication Website: www.presspubs.com/st_croix
Publisher Name: Carter C. Johnson
Publisher Email: ppinfo@presspubs.com
Publisher Phone: 651-407-1200
Editor Name: Debra Neutkens
Editor Email: news@presspubs.com
Editor Phone: 651-407-1226
Advertising Executive Name: Patty Steele
Advertising Executive Email: marketing@presspubs.com
Advertising Executive Phone: 651-407-1208

THE HUGO CITIZEN

Corporate/Parent Company: Press Publications
Street Address: 4779 Bloom Ave
City: White Bear Lake
State: MN
Postal Code: 55110
Office phone: (651) 407-1200
Publication Website: https://www.presspubs.com/citizen/
General E-mail: news@presspubs.com
Editor Name: Shannon Granholm
Editor Email: citizen@presspubs.com
Editor Phone: (651) 407-1227
Advertising Executive Name: Jeanne Kuenzli
Advertising Executive Email: wbpressad3@presspubs.com
Advertising Executive Phone: (651) 407-1224
Year Established: 1998
Delivery Methods: Mail
Published Days: Thur
Published Other: Thursdays, bi-weekly
Avg Free Circ: 8262
Audit Company: Sworn/Estimate/Non-Audited
Audit Date: 6 10 2019

THE LOWDOWN - FOREST LAKE AREA

Corporate/Parent Company: Press Publications
Street Address: 4779 Bloom Ave
City: White Bear Lake
State: MN
Postal Code: 55110
Office phone: (651) 407-1200
Publication Website: https://www.presspubs.com/forest_lake/
General E-mail: news@presspubs.com
Editor Name: Elizabeth Callen
Editor Email: lowdownnews@presspubs.com
Editor Phone: (651) 407-1229
Advertising Executive Email: lowdown3@presspubs.com
Advertising Executive Phone: (651) 407-1210
Year Established: 1996
Delivery Methods: Mail`Racks
Own Printing Facility?: Y
Commercial printers?: Y
Mechanical specifications: Type page 11 1/2 x 21 1/2; E - 6 cols, 1 13/16, 1/6 between; A - 6 cols, 1 13/16, 1/6 between; C - 10 cols, 1 1/4, 1/12 between.
Published Days: Fri
Avg Paid Circ: 62
Avg Free Circ: 2923
Audit Company: Sworn/Estimate/Non-Audited
Audit Date: 6 10 2019

THE LOWDOWN - ST. CROIX VALLEY AREA

Corporate/Parent Company: Press Publications
Street Address: 4779 Bloom Ave
City: White Bear Lake
State: MN
Postal Code: 55110
Office phone: (365) 407-1200
Publication Website: https://www.presspubs.com/st_croix/
General E-mail: news@presspubs.com
Editor Name: Debra Neutkens
Editor Email: reporter@presspubs.com
Editor Phone: (651) 407-1230
Advertising Executive Name: Sharon Schuler
Advertising Executive Email: lowdown2@presspubs.com
Advertising Executive Phone: (651) 407-1219
Year Established: 1903

Non-Daily Newspapers in the U.S.

Delivery Methods:
  Mail`Newsstand`Carrier`Racks
Own Printing Facility?: Y
Commercial printers?: Y
Mechanical specifications: Type page 6 x 21; E - 6 cols, 1.57", 1/6 between; A - 6 cols, 1.57", 1/6 between; C - 9 cols, 1.037, 1/12 between.
Published Days: Fri
Avg Paid Circ: 125
Avg Free Circ: 2850
Audit Company: VAC
Audit Date: 30 09 2017

VADNAIS HEIGHTS PRESS
Corporate/Parent Company: Press Publications
Street Address: 4779 Bloom Ave
City: White Bear Lake
State: MN
Postal Code: 55110
Office phone: (365) 407-1200
Publication Website: https://www.presspubs.com/vadnais/
General E-mail: news@presspubs.com
Editor Name: Sara Marie Moore
Editor Email: vadnaisheightsnews@presspubs.com
Editor Phone: (651) 407-1235
Advertising Executive Name: Vicki Dobson
Advertising Executive Email: svpressad1@presspubs.com
Advertising Executive Phone: (651) 407-1211
Year Established: 1975
Delivery Methods: Mail`Newsstand`Carrier
Own Printing Facility?: Y
Commercial printers?: Y
Mechanical specifications: Type page 10 x 21 1/2; E - 6 cols, 1.57", between; A - 6 cols, 1,57", between; C - 10 cols, 1 1/4, 3/4 between.
Published Days: Wed
Avg Paid Circ: 226
Avg Free Circ: 3312
Audit Company: VAC
Audit Date: 30 09 2017

WHITE BEAR LAKE - WHITE BEAR PRESS
Corporate/Parent Company: Press Publications
Street Address: 4779 Bloom Avenue
City: White Bear Lake
State: MN
Postal Code: 55110
Office phone: (651) 407-1200
Publication Website: www.presspubs.com
General E-mail: ppinfo@presspubs.com
Editor Name: Debra Neutkens
Editor Email: whitebearnews@presspubs.com
Editor Phone: 651-407-1233
Advertising Executive Name: Patty Steele
Advertising Executive Email: wbpressad2@presspubs.com
Advertising Executive Phone: 651-407-1213

WHITE BEAR PRESS
Corporate/Parent Company: Press Publications
Street Address: 4779 Bloom Ave
City: White Bear Lake
State: MN
Postal Code: 55110
Office phone: (365) 407-1200
Publication Website: https://www.presspubs.com/white_bear/
General E-mail: news@presspubs.com
Editor Name: Debra Neutkens
Editor Email: news@presspubs.com
Editor Phone: (651) 407-1230
Advertising Executive Name: Patty Steele
Advertising Executive Email: wbpressad2@presspubs.com
Advertising Executive Phone: (651) 407-1213

Year Established: 1903
Delivery Methods:
  Mail`Newsstand`Carrier`Racks
Own Printing Facility?: Y
Commercial printers?: Y
Mechanical specifications: Type page 6 x 21; E - 6 cols, 1.57", 1/6 between; A - 6 cols, 1.57", 1/6 between; C - 9 cols, 1.037, 1/12 between.
Published Days: Wed
Avg Paid Circ: 2477
Avg Free Circ: 11370
Audit Company: VAC
Audit Date: 30 09 2017

MISSOURI

BELLE
MARIES COUNTY ADVOCATE
Street Address: 1110 Hwy. 28 Unit B
City: Belle
State: MO
Postal Code: 65013
Office phone: (573) 859-3323
Publication Website: mariescountyadvocate.com
Publisher Name: Dennis Warden
Editor Name: Dave Marner
Editor Email: news@wardpub.com

BELTON
NORTH CASS HERALD
Street Address: 120 Main Street
City: Belton
State: MO
Postal Code: 64012
Office phone: 816-322-2375
Publication Website: www.northcassherald.com
Publisher Name: Laurie Bassett Edmonds
Publisher Email: laurie@northcassherald.com
Editor Name: Allen Edmonds
Editor Email: allen@northcassherald.com
Advertising Executive Name: Angela Kraft
Advertising Executive Email: angela@northcassherald.com

BOONVILLE
BOONSLICK WEEKLY
Street Address: 412 High St
City: Boonville
State: MO
Postal Code: 65233
Office phone: (660) 882-5335
Publication Website: www.BoonvilleDailyNews.com
General E-mail: afennewald@gatehousemedia.com
Publisher Name: Terri Leifeste
Editor Name: Allen Fennewald
Editor Email: afennewald@gatehousemedia.com
Editor Phone: 573-815-1788

BRANSON
TANEY COUNTY TIMES
Street Address: 704 Veterans Boulevard
City: Branson
State: MO
Postal Code: 65615
Office phone: 417-334-2285
Publication Website: www.taneycounty.org
Publisher Name: Kurt J. Lewis
Editor Name: Craig Donze
Editor Email: omneditor@yahoo.com

CAPE GIRARDEAU
SOUTHEAST MISSOURIAN PLUS
Corporate/Parent Company: Rust Communications
Street Address: 301 Broadway St
City: Cape Girardeau
State: MO
Postal Code: 63701-7330
Office phone: (573) 388-3680
Publication Website: https://www.semissourian.com/
General E-mail: ddenson@semissourian.com
Publisher Name: Jon K. Rust
Publisher Email: jrust@semissourian.com
Editor Name: Rick Fahr
Editor Email: rfahr@semissourian.com
Editor Phone: (573) 388-3656
Advertising Executive Name: Donna Denson
Advertising Executive Email: ddenson@semissourian.com
Advertising Executive Phone: (573) 388-2751
Total Circulation: 3000

CARROLLTON
CARROLLTON DEMOCRAT
Street Address: 102 East Benton Street
City: Carrollton
State: MO
Postal Code: 64633
Office phone: 660-542-0881
Publication Website: carolnet.com/cdn
Publisher Name: Frank Mercer
Editor Name: Janet Zullig
Editor Email: democrat@carolnet.com

CARUTHERSVILLE
THE DEMOCRAT ARGUS
Corporate/Parent Company: Rust Communications
Street Address: 1011C Truman Blvd.
City: Caruthersville
State: MO
Postal Code: 63830
Office phone: (573) 333-4336
Publication Website: https://www.pemiscotpress.com
General E-mail: news@democratargus.com
Publisher Name: Sheila Rouse
Publisher Email: srouse@stategazette.com
Editor Name: Christina Williams
Editor Email: cwilliams@pemiscotpress.com
Advertising Executive Name: Terri Coleman
Advertising Executive Email: tcoleman@blythevillecourier.com
Year Established: 1868
Commercial printers?: Y
Mechanical specifications: Type page 13 x 21 1/2; E - 6 cols, between; A - 6 cols, between; C - 9 cols, between.
Published Days: Thur
Avg Paid Circ: 2417
Avg Free Circ: 30
Audit Company: Sworn/Estimate/Non-Audited
Audit Date: 6 10 2019

THE STEELE ENTERPRISE
Corporate/Parent Company: Rust Communications
Street Address: 1011C Truman Blvd.
City: Caruthersville
State: MO
Postal Code: 63830
Office phone: (573) 333-4336
Publication Website: https://www.pemiscotpress.com
General E-mail: news@democratargus.com
Publisher Name: Sheila Rouse
Publisher Email: srouse@stategazette.com
Editor Name: Christina Williams
Editor Email: cwilliams@pemiscotpress.com
Advertising Executive Name: Terri Coleman
Advertising Executive Email: tcoleman@blythevillecourier.com
Year Established: 1922
Delivery Methods: Mail`Newsstand`Racks
Commercial printers?: Y
Mechanical specifications: Type page 11 5/8 x 21; E - 6 cols, 1 4/5, between; A - 6 cols, 1 4/5, between; C - 6 cols, 1 4/5, between.
Published Days: Thur
Avg Paid Circ: 2250
Audit Company: Sworn/Estimate/Non-Audited
Audit Date: 6 10 2019
Total Circulation: 4000

CASSVILLE
CASSVILLE DEMOCRAT
Corporate/Parent Company: Rust Communications
Street Address: P.O. Box 486
City: Cassville
State: MO
Postal Code: 65625
Office phone: (417) 847-2610
Publication Website: https://www.cassville-democrat.com/
General E-mail: editor@cassville-democrat.com
Publisher Name: Lisa Craft
Publisher Email: community@monett-times.com
Editor Name: Kyle Troutman
Editor Email: editor@cassville-democrat.com
Year Established: 1871
Delivery Methods: Mail`Newsstand`Racks
Published Days: Wed
Avg Paid Circ: 3000
Audit Company: Sworn/Estimate/Non-Audited
Audit Date: 6 10 2019

CHESTERFIELD
WEST NEWSMAGAZINE
Street Address: 754 Spirit 40 Park Dr.
City: Chesterfield
State: MO
Postal Code: 63005
Office phone: 636-591-0010
Publication Website: www.westnewsmagazine.com
Editor Name: Kate Uptergrove
Editor Email: editor@westnewsmagazine.com
Total Circulation: 2500

CONCORDIA
THE CONCORDIAN
Corporate/Parent Company: Rust Communications
Street Address: 714 S Main St
City: Concordia
State: MO
Postal Code: 64020
Office phone: (660) 463-7522
Publication Website: http://www.theconcordianonline.com/
General E-mail: amilligan@marshallnews.com
Year Established: 1893
Mechanical specifications: Type page 13 x 21; E - 6 cols, 2, 1/6 between; A - 6 cols, 2, 1/6 between; C - 6 cols, 2, 1/6 between.
Published Days: Wed
Avg Paid Circ: 2635
Audit Company: Sworn/Estimate/Non-Audited
Audit Date: 6 10 2019

EAST PRAIRIE
CHARLESTON ENTERPRISE-COURIER
Street Address: 101 East Main Street
City: East Prairie
State: MO
Postal Code: 63845
Office phone: 573-649-9500
Publication Website: www.EnterpriseCourier.com
Publisher Name: Carlin Bennett

Non-Daily Newspapers in the U.S.

Editor Name: Adam Rhodes
Editor Email: news@enterprisecourier.com

ELLINGTON

REYNOLDS COUNTY COURIER

Street Address: 370 Main Street
City: Ellington
State: MO
Postal Code: 63638
Office phone: 573-663-2243
Publication Website: www.ReynoldsCountyCourier.com
Publisher Name: Greg Hoskins
Editor Name: Kim Combs
Editor Email: rccreporter@mac.com
Advertising Executive Name: Addison Gipson
Advertising Executive Email: Addison.gipson@waynecojournalbanner.com

EMINENCE

SHANNON COUNTY CURRENT WAVE

Street Address: 102 N Plum St
City: Eminence
State: MO
Postal Code: 65466
Office phone: (573)226-5229
Publication Website: www.ShannonCountyCurrentWave.com
Editor Name: Roger Dillon
Editor Email: cwave1282@gmail.com

FESTUS

WEST SIDE LEADER

Corporate/Parent Company: Leader Publications
Street Address: 503 N. Second St.
City: Festus
State: MO
Postal Code: 63028
Office phone: 6369377501
Publication Website: www.myleaderpaper.com
General E-mail: peggyscott@leaderpublications.biz
Publisher Name: Pam LaPlant
Publisher Email: pamlaplant@leaderpublications.biz
Editor Name: Peggy Bess
Editor Email: peggybess@leaderpublications.biz
Advertising Executive Name: Glenda O'Tool Potts
Advertising Executive Email: composing@leaderpublications.biz

GREENFIELD

GREENFIELD VEDETTE

Street Address: 7 N Main St
City: Greenfield
State: MO
Postal Code: 65661
Office phone: (417) 637-2712
Publication Website: www.GreenfieldVedette.com
Editor Name: Gina Langston
Editor Email: editor@greenfieldvedette.com

HERMITAGE

HERMITAGE INDEX

Corporate/Parent Company: Vernon Publishing Inc.
Street Address: 109 Polk St
City: Hermitage
State: MO
Postal Code: 65668
Office phone: 417-745-6404
Publication Website: www.VernonPublishing.com/Index
General E-mail: theindex@vernonpublishing.com
Publisher Name: Trevor Vernon
Publisher Email: tvernon@vernonpublishing.com
Publisher Phone: 573-392-5658
Editor Name: Jeremy Hulshof
Editor Email: jhulshof@vernonpublishing.com
Editor Phone: 417-745-6404

HOLDEN

HOLDEN IMAGE

Street Address: 117 East Second Street
City: Holden
State: MO
Postal Code: 64040
Office phone: 816-732-5552
Publication Website: www.HoldenImage.com
Editor Name: Dana Raker
Editor Email: holdenimage@embarqmail.com

IRONTON

IRONTON MOUNTAIN ECHO

Street Address: 110 N Main St
City: Ironton
State: MO
Postal Code: 63650
Office phone: 573-546-3917
Publication Website: www.myironcountynews.com
Editor Name: Amy Patterson
Editor Email: news@myironcountynews.com
Advertising Executive Name: Addison Gipson
Advertising Executive Email: advertising@myironcountynews.com

JACKSON

JACKSON CASH-BOOK JOURNAL

Street Address: 210 W. Main
City: Jackson
State: MO
Postal Code: 63755
Office phone: 573-243-3515
Publication Website: www.TheCash-Book.com
Publisher Name: Gina Raffety
Publisher Email: gina.raffety@thecash-book.com
Editor Name: Gregory Dullum
Editor Email: greg.dullum@thecash-book.com
Advertising Executive Name: Stephanie Watkins
Advertising Executive Email: cashbookjournal@gmail.com

KAHOKA

HOMETOWN JOURNAL

Street Address: 258 West Main Streeet
City: Kahoka
State: MO
Postal Code: 63445
Office phone: 660-727-3583
Publication Website: www.htjournal.net
Editor Name: Joe Roberts
Editor Email: Htjournal91@gmail.com

KANSAS CITY

CASS-CO MISSOURIAN

Street Address: 1601 McGee Street
City: Kansas City
State: MO
Postal Code: 64108
Office phone: 877-962-7827
Publication Website: www.Demo-MO.com
Editor Name: Mike Fannin
Editor Email: mfannin@kcstar.com
Editor Phone: 816-234-4545

KENNETT

DAILY DUNKLIN DEMOCRAT EXTRA

Corporate/Parent Company: Rust Communications
Street Address: 203 1st St
City: Kennett
State: MO
Postal Code: 63857
Office phone: (573) 888-4505
Publication Website: https://www.dddnews.com/
General E-mail: jdorris@dddnews.com
Publisher Name: Shelia Rouse
Publisher Email: srouse@stategazette.com
Publisher Phone: (731) 285-4091
Editor Name: Jeffrey Dorris
Editor Email: jdorris@dddnews.com
Advertising Executive Name: Terri Coleman
Advertising Executive Email: tcoleman@dddnews.com
Total Circulation: 1700

DELTA NEWS CITIZEN

Corporate/Parent Company: Rust Communications
Street Address: PO Box 669
City: Kennett
State: MO
Postal Code: 63857
Office phone: (573) 888-4505
Publication Website: https://www.dddnews.com/
General E-mail: jdorris@dddnews.com
Publisher Name: Shelia Rouse
Publisher Email: srouse@stategazette.com
Publisher Phone: (731) 285-4091
Editor Name: Jeffrey Dorris
Editor Email: jdorris@dddnews.com
Advertising Executive Name: Terri Coleman
Advertising Executive Email: tcoleman@dddnews.com
Year Established: 1997
Own Printing Facility?: Y
Published Days: Wed
Avg Paid Circ: 2500
Audit Company: Sworn/Estimate/Non-Audited
Audit Date: 6 10 2019
Total Circulation: 13050

KING CITY

TRI-COUNTY NEWS

Street Address: 110 East Vermont Street
City: King City
State: MO
Postal Code: 64463
Office phone: 320-398-5000
Publication Website: tricountynews.mn
General E-mail: news@tricountynews.mn
Editor Name: Matthew Pearl
Editor Email: editor@tricountynews.mn

LIBERTY

COURIER TRIBUNE

Street Address: 104 N. Main St.
City: Liberty
State: MO
Postal Code: 64068
Office phone: (816) 781-4941
Publication Website: https://www.mycouriertribune.com
General E-mail: news@mycouriertribune.com
Advertising Executive Email: advertise@mycouriertribune.com
Advertising Executive Phone: (816) 454-9660
Published Days: Thur
Avg Paid Circ: 4000
Audit Company: Sworn/Estimate/Non-Audited
Audit Date: 6 10 2019

MACON

MACON COUNTY HOME PRESS

Street Address: 115 N. Rubey
City: Macon
State: MO
Postal Code: 63552
Office phone: 660) 395-4663
Publication Website: www.MaconHomePress.com
Editor Name: Sharon Coram
Editor Email: shon@maconhomepress.com

MANILA

THE TOWN CRIER

Street Address: 100 West Lake Street
City: Manila
State: MO
Postal Code: 72442
Office phone: 870-561-4634
Publication Website: www.TheTown-Crier.com
Editor Name: Nancy Kemp
Editor Email: towncrier@centurytel.net
Total Circulation: 4306

MARBLE HILL

MARBLE HILL BANNER PRESS

Street Address: 103 Walnut St
City: Marble Hill
State: MO
Postal Code: 63764
Office phone: (573) 238-2821
Publication Website: www.thebannerpress.com
Editor Name: Linda Redeffer
Editor Email: news@thebannerpress.com

THE BANNER-PRESS

Corporate/Parent Company: Rust Communications
Street Address: 103 WALNUT ST
City: Marble Hill
State: MO
Postal Code: 63764
Office phone: (573) 238-2821
Publication Website: https://www.thebannerpress.com/
General E-mail: news@thebannerpress.com
Year Established: 1881
Delivery Methods: Mail`Newsstand`Racks
Own Printing Facility?: Y
Commercial printers?: Y
Published Days: Wed
Avg Paid Circ: 4200
Audit Company: Sworn/Estimate/Non-Audited
Audit Date: 6 10 2019

MONROE CITY

LAKE GAZETTE

Street Address: 304 S. Main St.
City: Monroe City
State: MO
Postal Code: 63456
Office phone: 573-735-3300
Publication Website: www.LakeGazette.com
Editor Name: Consetta Gottman
Editor Email: lgbkkpr@lakegazette.net

MOUNTAIN GROVE

MOUNTAIN GROVE NEWS-JOURNAL

Corporate/Parent Company: Lebanon Publishing Co.
Street Address: 150 E 1st St
City: Mountain Grove
State: MO
Postal Code: 65711
Office phone: (417) 926-5148
Publication Website: http://www.news-journal.net/
General E-mail: fsmfarms@hughes.net
Year Established: 1882
Delivery Methods: Mail
Own Printing Facility?: Y
Mechanical specifications: Type page 13 x 21; E - 6 cols, 2 1/16, between; A - 6 cols, 2 1/16,

between; C - 6 cols, 2 1/16, between.
Published Days: Wed
Avg Paid Circ: 3200
Avg Free Circ: 9850
Audit Company: Sworn/Estimate/Non-Audited
Audit Date: 6 10 2019

O'FALLON

ST. LOUIS COUNTY /ST. CHARLES COUNTY COMMUNITY NEWS

Street Address: 2139 Bryan Valley Commercial Drive
City: O'Fallon
State: MO
Postal Code: 63366
Office phone: (636) 379-1775
Publication Website: www.mycnews.com
General E-mail: info@mycnews.com
Publisher Name: Bob Huneke
Editor Name: Matthew DeKinder
Editor Email: editor@mycnews.com
Advertising Executive Name: Brooke Tolle

PLATTE CITY

PLATTE COUNTY LANDMARK

Street Address: 252 Main Street
City: Platte City
State: MO
Postal Code: 64079
Office phone: 816-858-0363
Publication Website: www.PlatteCountyLandmark.com
Editor Name: Ivan Foley
Editor Email: news@plattecountylandmark.com

POPLAR BLUFF

PUXICO PRESS

Corporate/Parent Company: Rust Communications
Street Address: 208 Poplar St.
City: Poplar Bluff
State: MO
Postal Code: 63901
Office phone: (573) 785-1414
Publication Website: https://www.darnews.com/
General E-mail: ads@darnews.com
Publisher Name: Chris Pruett
Publisher Email: cpruett@darnews.com
Publisher Phone: (573) 772-7275
Editor Name: Donna Farley
Editor Email: dfarley@darnews.com
Editor Phone: (573) 772-7392
Advertising Executive Name: Christy Pierce
Advertising Executive Email: ads@darnews.com
Advertising Executive Phone: (573) 772-7386
Year Established: 1884
Mechanical specifications: Type page 13 x 21; E - 6 cols, 2, between; A - 6 cols, 2, between; C - 6 cols, 2, between.
Published Days: Wed
Avg Paid Circ: 1285
Avg Free Circ: 3021
Audit Company: Sworn/Estimate/Non-Audited
Audit Date: 6 10 2019

PORTAGEVILLE

MISSOURIAN-NEWS

Corporate/Parent Company: Rust Communications
Street Address: 413 E Main St
City: Portageville
State: MO
Postal Code: 63873
Office phone: (573) 471-1137
Publication Website: https://standard-democrat.com/
General E-mail: news@standard-democrat.com
Publisher Name: DeAnna Nelson
Publisher Email: dnelson@standard-democrat.com
Editor Name: David Jenkins
Editor Email: news@standard-democrat.com
Advertising Executive Name: DeAnna Nelson
Advertising Executive Email: dnelson@standard-democrat.com
Mechanical specifications: Type page 11 3/5 x 21 1/2; E - 6 cols, 1 4/5, 1/5 between; A - 6 cols, 1 4/5, 1/5 between; C - 6 cols, 1 4/5, 1/5 between.
Published Days: Thur
Avg Paid Circ: 1700
Audit Company: Sworn/Estimate/Non-Audited
Audit Date: 6 10 2019

POTOSI

INDEPENDENT JOURNAL

Street Address: 119 E. High Street
City: Potosi
State: MO
Postal Code: 63664
Office phone: 573-438-5141
Publication Website: www.TheIJNews.com
Editor Name: Neil Richards
Editor Email: ijnews@centurytel.net

QUEEN CITY

SCHUYLER COUNTY TIMES

Street Address: 20447 New Hope Rd
City: Queen City
State: MO
Postal Code: 63561
Office phone: 660-457-8555
Publication Website: www.SchuylerCountyTimes.com
Editor Name: Lorraine Austin
Editor Email: news@schuylercountytimes.com

RAYMORE

RAYMORE JOURNAL

Street Address: 108 N. Madison St
City: Raymore
State: MO
Postal Code: 64083
Office phone: (785) 989-4415
Publication Website: www.TheRaymoreJournal.com
Editor Name: Christian D. Orr
Editor Email: theraymorejournal@gmail.com

SALISBURY

CHARITON COUNTY JOURNAL

Street Address: 317 S. Broadway
City: Salisbury
State: MO
Postal Code: 65281
Office phone: 660-388-6131
Publication Website: charitoncountyjournal.com
Editor Name: Glenda Weiseman
Editor Email: ps@cvalley.net

SHELBINA

SHELBINA WEEKLY

Street Address: 217 East Maple St
City: Shelbina
State: MO
Postal Code: 63468
Office phone: 573-588-0051
Publication Website: www.ShelbinaWeekly.com
Editor Name: Mark & Thad Requet
Editor Email: shelbinaweekly@gmail.com

SIKESTON

PORTAGEVILLE MISSOURIAN NEWS

Corporate/Parent Company: Standard Democrat
Street Address: 205 S New Madrid St
City: Sikeston
State: MO
Postal Code: 63801
Office phone: (573) 471-1137
Publication Website: www.PVMoNews.com
Editor Name: David Jenkins
Editor Email: news@standard-democrat.com
Advertising Executive Name: DeAnna Nelson
Advertising Executive Email: dnelson@standard-democrat.com

ST. JAMES

SAINT JAMES PRESS

Street Address: 120 S. Jefferson
City: St. James
State: MO
Postal Code: 65559
Office phone: 573-899-2345
Publication Website: www.ThreeRiversPublishing.com
General E-mail: advertising@threeriverspublishing.com
Publisher Name: Rob Viehman
Publisher Email: rviehman@cubafreepress.com
Publisher Phone: 573-885-7460
Editor Name: Chris Daniels
Editor Email: cdaniels@saintjamespress.com
Editor Phone: 573-899-2345
Advertising Executive Name: Kelli Rapp
Advertising Executive Email: kelli@threeriverspublishing.com
Advertising Executive Phone: 573-885-7460

ST. LOUIS

ST. LOUIS CALL NEWSPAPERS

Corporate/Parent Company: Call Newspapers
Street Address: 9977 Lin Ferry Dr.
City: St. Louis
State: MO
Postal Code: 63123
Office phone: 314-843-0102
Publication Website: www.CallNewspapers.com
Publisher Name: Deborah Baker
Publisher Email: dbaker@callnewspapers.com
Editor Name: Gloria Lloyd
Editor Email: glorialloyd@callnewspapers.com
Advertising Executive Name: Colleen Drewes
Advertising Executive Email: sales1@callnewspapers.com

ST. LOUIS LABOR TRIBUNE

Street Address: 505 South Ewing Avenue
City: St. Louis
State: MO
Postal Code: 63103
Office phone: 314-256-4136
Publication Website: www.LaborTribune.com
Publisher Name: Edward M. Finkelstein
Publisher Email: publisher@labortribune.com
Editor Name: Tim Rowden
Editor Email: news@labortribune.com
Advertising Executive Name: Dan Braun
Advertising Executive Email: advertising@labortribune.com

ST. LOUIS MISSOURI LAWYERS WEEKLY

Corporate/Parent Company: Missouri Lawyers Media
Street Address: 319 N Fourth St.
City: St. Louis
State: MO
Postal Code: 63102
Office phone: (314) 421-1880
Publication Website: www.MoLawyersMedia.com
Publisher Name: Liz Irwin
Publisher Email: lirwin@molawyersmedia.com
Editor Name: Cindi Lash
Editor Email: clash@molawyersmedia.com
Advertising Executive Name: Johnny Aguirre
Advertising Executive Email: jaguirre@molawyersmedia.com

ST. LOUIS RIVERFRONT TIMES

Street Address: 308 N. 21st Street, Ste. 300
City: St. Louis
State: MO
Postal Code: 63103
Office phone: 314-754-5966
Publication Website: www.RiverfrontTimes.com
Editor Name: Doyle Murphy
Editor Email: doyle.murphy@riverfronttimes.com
Advertising Executive Name: Colin Bell
Advertising Executive Email: Colin.Bell@riverfronttimes.com
Total Circulation: 4200

ST. LOUIS WEBSTER – KIRKWOOD TIMES / S CO. TIMES

Corporate/Parent Company: Webster-Kirkwood Times, Inc.
Street Address: 122 W. Lockwood Ave
City: St. Louis
State: MO
Postal Code: 63119
Office phone: 314-968-2699
Publication Website: www.timesnewspapers.com
General E-mail: delivery@timesnewspapers.com
Publisher Name: Dwight Bitikofer
Publisher Email: bitikofer@timesnewspapers.com
Editor Name: Don Corrigan
Editor Email: corrigan@timesnewspapers.com
Advertising Executive Name: Terry Cassidy
Advertising Executive Email: terry@timesnewspapers.com
Total Circulation: 2635

THE COUNTIAN (LEGAL PUBLICATION)

Corporate/Parent Company: Missouri Lawyers Media
Street Address: 319 N Fourth St.
City: St. Louis
State: MO
Postal Code: 63102
Office phone: (314) 421-1880
Publication Website: www.MoLawyersMedia.com
Publisher Name: Liz Irwin
Publisher Email: lirwin@molawyersmedia.com
Editor Name: Cindi Lash
Editor Email: clash@molawyersmedia.com
Advertising Executive Name: Johnny Aguirre
Advertising Executive Email: jaguirre@molawyersmedia.com

SUMMERSVILLE

SUMMERSVILLE BEACON

Street Address: 205 Richards St.
City: Summersville
State: MO
Postal Code: 65571
Office phone: 417-932-4700
Publication Website: www.SummersvilleBeacon.com
Editor Name: Sharon Vaughn
Editor Email: sbeaconeditor@centurytel.net
Total Circulation: 2447

Non-Daily Newspapers in the U.S.

SWEET SPRINGS

SWEET SPRINGS HERALD

Street Address: 238 W Main St
City: Sweet Springs
State: MO
Postal Code: 65351
Office phone: 660-335-6366
Publication Website: www.ssherald.com
Editor Name: Kathy Dohrman
Editor Email: ssherald@embarqmail.com
Total Circulation: 2250

THAYER

THAYER SOUTH MISSOURIAN NEWS

Street Address: 109 Chestnut Street
City: Thayer
State: MO
Postal Code: 65791
Office phone: (417) 264-3814
Publication Website: www.AreaWideNews.com
Editor Name: Kim Break
Editor Email: news@areawidenews.com

WASHINGTON

ST. CLAIR MISSOURIAN

Corporate/Parent Company: The Missourian Publishing Company
Street Address: 14 W. Main Street
City: Washington
State: MO
Postal Code: 63090
Office phone: 888-239-7701
Publication Website: www.Emissourian.com
Editor Name: Bill Miller
Editor Email: billmiller@emissourian.com
Advertising Executive Name: Jeanine York
Advertising Executive Email: yorkj@emissourian.com
Advertising Executive Phone: 636-390-3013

WASHINGTON

UNION MISSOURIAN

Corporate/Parent Company: The Missourian Publishing Company
Street Address: 14 W. Main Street
City: Washington
State: MO
Postal Code: 63090
Office phone: 888-239-7701
Publication Website: www.Emissourian.com
General E-mail: circulation@emissourian.com
Editor Name: Bill Miller
Editor Email: billmiller@emissourian.com
Advertising Executive Name: Jeanine York
Advertising Executive Email: yorkj@emissourian.com
Advertising Executive Phone: 636-390-3013

WILLOW SPRINGS

HOWELL COUNTY NEWS

Corporate/Parent Company: KDR Publishing / Howell County News
Street Address: 125 E. Main St.
City: Willow Springs
State: MO
Postal Code: 65793
Office phone: 417-469-1167
Publication Website: www.HowellCountyNews.com
Editor Name: Kim Rich
Editor Email: editor@howellcountynews.com
Editor Phone: 417-469-1167

MISSISSIPPI

ACKERMAN

THE CHOCTAW PLAINDEALER

Corporate/Parent Company: Emmerich Newspapers
Street Address: 48 N LOUISVILLE ST
City: Ackerman
State: MS
Postal Code: 39735
Office phone: (662) 285-6248
Publication Website: https://www.redhillsmsnews.com/
General E-mail: sales@winstoncountyjournal.com
Publisher Name: Joseph Mccain
Publisher Email: newsroom@winstoncountyjournal.com
Publisher Phone: (662) 773-6241, ext : 105
Editor Name: Russell Hood
Editor Email: rhood@websterprogresstimes.com
Editor Phone: (662) 258-7532
Advertising Executive Name: Kathy Johnson
Advertising Executive Email: sales@winstoncountyjournal.com
Advertising Executive Phone: (662) 773-6241, ext : 104
Own Printing Facility?: Y
Commercial printers?: Y
Mechanical specifications: Type page 13 x 21 1/2.
Published Days: Wed
Avg Paid Circ: 1200
Avg Free Circ: 100
Audit Company: Sworn/Estimate/Non-Audited
Audit Date: 6 10 2019

AMORY

MONROE COUNTY JOURNAL

Corporate/Parent Company: Journal Inc
Street Address: 115 Main St S, PO Box 519
City: Amory
State: MS
Postal Code: 38821-3407
Office phone: (662) 256-5647
Publication Website: https://www.djournal.com/monroe/
General E-mail: advertising@monroecountyjournal.com
Publisher Name: Emily Tubb
Publisher Email: emily.tubb@journalinc.com
Publisher Phone: (662) 256-5647
Editor Name: Ray Van Dusen
Editor Email: ray.vandusen@journalinc.com
Editor Phone: (662) 256-5647
Advertising Executive Email: advertising@monroecountyjournal.com
Mechanical specifications: Type page 13 1/2 x 21 1/2; E - 6 cols, 2 1/4, 1/8 between; A - 6 cols, 2 1/4, 1/8 between; C - 8 cols, 1 7/8, 1/8 between.
Published Days: Wed
Avg Paid Circ: 7300
Avg Free Circ: 132
Audit Company: Sworn/Estimate/Non-Audited
Audit Date: 6 10 2019

MONROE JOURNAL

Corporate/Parent Company: Journal Inc
Street Address: 115 S. Main Street
City: Amory
State: MS
Postal Code: 38821
Office phone: 662-256-5647
Publication Website: monroecountyjournal.com
General E-mail: webmonroe@journalinc.com
Editor Name: Ray Van Dusen
Editor Email: ray.vandusen@journalinc.com
Advertising Executive Name: Paul Fullerton
Advertising Executive Email: paul.fullerton@journalinc.com

MONROE JOURNAL

Corporate/Parent Company: Journal, Inc.
Street Address: 115 S. Main Street
City: Amory
State: MS
Postal Code: 38821
Office phone: 662-256-5647
Publication Website: monroecountyjournal.com
General E-mail: webmonroe@journalinc.com
Editor Name: Ray Van Dusen
Editor Email: ray.vandusen@journalinc.com
Advertising Executive Name: Paul Fullerton
Advertising Executive Email: paul.fullerton@journalinc.com
Total Circulation: 12500

BAY ST. LOUIS

"THE SEA COAST ECHO

Corporate/Parent Company: "
"
Street Address: 124 Court Street
City: Bay St. Louis
State: MS
Postal Code: 39520
Office phone: 228-467-5473
Publication Website: seacoastecho.com
General E-mail: gbelcher@seacoastecho.com
Editor Name: Cassandra Favre
Editor Email: cassandra@seacoastecho.com
Advertising Executive Name: Nathan Schuver
Advertising Executive Email: classifieds@seacoastecho.com
Total Circulation: 3785

"THE SEA COAST ECHO
"
Street Address: 124 Court Street
City: Bay St. Louis
State: MS
Postal Code: 39520
Office phone: 228-467-5473
Publication Website: seacoastecho.com
General E-mail: gbelcher@seacoastecho.com
Editor Name: Cassandra Favre
Editor Email: cassandra@seacoastecho.com
Advertising Executive Name: Nathan Schuver
Advertising Executive Email: classifieds@seacoastecho.com

BILOXI

"COASTAL BREEZE
"
Corporate/Parent Company: Coastal Breeze, LLC
Street Address: 996 Howard Ave
City: Biloxi
State: MS
Postal Code: 39530
Office phone: 228-435-0720
Publication Website: https://www.coastalbreezenews.com
Editor Name: Gaylon Parker
Total Circulation: 5234

OCEAN SPRINGS GAZETTE & RECORD

Corporate/Parent Company: Campbell Newspapers
Street Address: 819 Jackson Street
City: Biloxi
State: MS
Postal Code: 39531
Office phone: 228-435-0720
Publication Website: www.coastalbreezems.com
Publisher Name: Vickie Townsend
Editor Name: Gaylon Parker
Editor Email: business.thecoastalbreeze@gmail.com
Total Circulation: 7250

CHARLESTON

CHARLESTON SUN SENTINEL

Corporate/Parent Company: Emmerich Newspapers
Street Address: 149 Court Square, P.O. BOX 250
City: Charleston
State: MS
Postal Code: 38921
Office phone: (662) 647-8462
Publication Website: https://www.tallahatchienews.ms/
General E-mail: rista@charlestonsun.net
Publisher Name: Clay Mcferrin
Publisher Email: lay@charlestonsun.net
Editor Name: Clay Mcferrin
Editor Email: lay@charlestonsun.net
Advertising Executive Name: Krista Mcferrin
Advertising Executive Email: rista@charlestonsun.net

THE CHARLESTON SUN-SENTINEL

Corporate/Parent Company: Emmerich Newspapers
Street Address: 149 Court Square, P.O. BOX 250
City: Charleston
State: MS
Postal Code: 38921
Office phone: (662) 647-8462
Publication Website: https://www.tallahatchienews.ms/
General E-mail: rista@charlestonsun.net
Publisher Name: Clay Mcferrin
Publisher Email: lay@charlestonsun.net
Editor Name: Clay Mcferrin
Editor Email: lay@charlestonsun.net
Advertising Executive Name: Krista Mcferrin
Advertising Executive Email: rista@charlestonsun.net
Year Established: 1856
Delivery Methods: Mail`Newsstand`Racks
Own Printing Facility?: Y
Commercial printers?: N
Mechanical specifications: Berliner format
Published Days: Thur
Avg Paid Circ: 1526
Avg Free Circ: 123
Audit Company: Sworn/Estimate/Non-Audited
Audit Date: 6 10 2019
Total Circulation: 7432

THE SUN-SENTINEL

Corporate/Parent Company: Emmerich Newspapers
Street Address: 149 S. Court Square
City: Charleston
State: MS
Postal Code: 38921
Office phone: 662-647-8462
Publication Website: tallahatchienews.ms
Editor Name: CLAY McFERRIN
Editor Email: clay@charlestonsun.net

CLARKSDALE

THE CLARKSDALE PRESS REGISTER

Corporate/Parent Company: Emmerich Newspapers
Street Address: 128 E 2nd St
City: Clarksdale
State: MS

Postal Code: 38614-4206
Office phone: (662) 627-2201
Publication Website: https://www.pressregister.com/
General E-mail: bkeller@pressregister.com
Publisher Name: Floyd Ingram
Publisher Email: floyd@pressregister.com
Editor Name: Josh Troy
Editor Email: jtroy@pressregister.com
Advertising Executive Name: Brenda Keller
Advertising Executive Email: bkeller@pressregister.com
Year Established: 1826
Delivery Methods: Mail`Newsstand`Racks
Mechanical specifications: Type page 13 x 21 1/2; E - 6 cols, 2 1/16, 1/8 between; A - 6 cols, 2 1/16, 1/8 between; C - 8 cols, 1 1/2, 1/8 between.
Published Days: Wed
Weekday Frequency: e
Avg Paid Circ: 3175
Audit Company: Sworn/Estimate/Non-Audited
Audit Date: 6 10 2019
Pressroom Equipment: Lines – 6-KP/Daily King; Reels & Stands – 6;

COLUMBIA
THE COLUMBIAN-PROGRESS

Corporate/Parent Company: Emmerich Newspapers
Street Address: 318 Second St
City: Columbia
State: MS
Postal Code: 39429-2954
Office phone: (601) 736-2611
Publication Website: https://www.columbianprogress.com/
General E-mail: aclark@columbianprogress.com
Publisher Name: Charlie Smith
Publisher Email: csmith@columbianprogress.com
Editor Name: Charlie Smith
Editor Email: csmith@columbianprogress.com
Advertising Executive Name: Ashley Clark
Advertising Executive Email: aclark@columbianprogress.com
Year Established: 1882
Delivery Methods: Mail`Newsstand`Racks
Own Printing Facility?: N
Commercial printers?: N
Mechanical specifications: Type page 13 x 21 1/2; E - 6 cols, 2, between; A - 6 cols, 2, between; C - 8 cols, 1 1/2, between.
Published Days: Thur`Sat
Avg Paid Circ: 5700
Audit Company: Sworn/Estimate/Non-Audited
Audit Date: 6 10 2019

COLUMBUS
THE PACKET

Street Address: 425 COLLEGE ST
City: COLUMBUS
State: MS
Postal Code: 39701
Office phone: (662) 329-1741
Publication Website: packet-media.com
Editor Name: Brian Jones
Editor Email: columbuspacket@cableone.net
Total Circulation: 11692

FOREST
SCOTT COUNTY TIMES

Corporate/Parent Company: Emmerich Newspapers
Street Address: 311 Smith Ave
City: Forest
State: MS
Postal Code: 39074-4159
Office phone: (601) 469-2561
Publication Website: https://www.sctonline.net/
General E-mail: ckelly@sctonline.net
Publisher Name: Tim Beeland
Publisher Email: tbeeland@sctonline.net
Editor Name: James Phillips
Editor Email: jphillips@sctonline.net
Advertising Executive Name: Christian Kelly
Advertising Executive Email: ckelly@sctonline.net
Own Printing Facility?: Y
Mechanical specifications: Type page 13 1/4 x 21 1/2; E - 6 cols, 2, between; A - 6 cols, 2, between; C - 8 cols, 1 1/2, between.
Published Days: Wed
Avg Paid Circ: 5500
Avg Free Circ: 4000
Audit Company: Sworn/Estimate/Non-Audited
Audit Date: 6 10 2019

FULTON
THE ITAWAMBA COUNTY TIMES

Corporate/Parent Company: Journal Inc
Street Address: 106 W Main St
City: Fulton
State: MS
Postal Code: 38843-1146
Office phone: (662) 862-3141
Publication Website: https://www.djournal.com/itawamba/
General E-mail: itawamba.times@journalinc.com
Advertising Executive Email: itawamba.advertising@journalinc.com
Year Established: 1945
Mechanical specifications: Type page 11 5/8 x 21 1/2; E - 6 cols, 1 2/3, 1/6 between; A - 6 cols, 1 2/3, 1/6 between; C - 9 cols, 1 1/6, 1/6 between.
Published Days: Wed
Avg Paid Circ: 4850
Avg Free Circ: 45
Audit Company: Sworn/Estimate/Non-Audited
Audit Date: 6 10 2019
Total Circulation: 8021

GREENVILLE
DELTA DEMOCRAT TIMES

Corporate/Parent Company: Emmerich Newspapers
Street Address: 988 N Broadway St
City: Greenville
State: MS
Postal Code: 38701-2349
Office phone: (662) 335-1155
Publication Website: https://www.ddtonline.com/
General E-mail: keithwilliams@ddtonline.com
Publisher Name: Jon Alverson
Publisher Email: jalverson@ddtonline.com
Publisher Phone: (662) 378-0761
Editor Name: Catherine Kirk
Editor Email: ckirk@ddtonline.com
Editor Phone: (662) 378-0716
Advertising Executive Name: Keith Williams
Advertising Executive Email: keithwilliams@ddtonline.com
Advertising Executive Phone: (662) 378-0748
Year Established: 1938
Delivery Methods: Mail`Carrier`Racks
Mechanical specifications: Type page 13 x 21 1/2; E - 6 cols, 2 1/16, 1/8 between; A - 6 cols, 2 1/16, 1/8 between; C - 8 cols, 1 1/2, 1/16 between.
Published Days: Mon`Tues`Wed`Thur`Fri`Sun
Weekday Frequency: e
Saturday Frequency: m
Avg Paid Circ: 4864
Avg Free Circ: 370
Audit Company: AAM
Audit Date: 30 09 2016
Total Circulation: 9500

HATTIESBURG
THE HATTIESBURG POST

Corporate/Parent Company: Emmerich Newspapers
Street Address: 525 N. Main St., Suite C
City: Hattiesburg
State: MS
Postal Code: 39401-6606
Office phone: (601) 268-2331
Publication Website: http://hubcityspokes.com/
General E-mail: rick@hubcityspokes.com
Publisher Name: David Gustafson
Publisher Email: david@hubcityspokes.com
Editor Name: Joshua Wilson
Editor Email: joshua@hubcityspokes.com
Advertising Executive Name: Rick Jarman
Advertising Executive Email: rick@hubcityspokes.com
Year Established: 2013
Published Days: Thur
Avg Paid Circ: 9000
Audit Company: Sworn/Estimate/Non-Audited
Audit Date: 6 10 2019
Total Circulation: 3790

THE PETAL NEWS

Corporate/Parent Company: Emmerich Newspapers
Street Address: 525 N. Main St., Suite C
City: Hattiesburg
State: MS
Postal Code: 39401-6606
Office phone: (601) 268-2331
Publication Website: https://www.hubcityspokes.com/petal
General E-mail: rick@hubcityspokes.com
Publisher Name: David Gustafson
Publisher Email: david@hubcityspokes.com
Editor Name: Joshua Wilson
Editor Email: joshua@hubcityspokes.com
Advertising Executive Name: Rick Jarman
Advertising Executive Email: rick@hubcityspokes.com
Delivery Methods: Mail`Newsstand`Racks
Published Days: Thur
Avg Paid Circ: 3000
Audit Company: Sworn/Estimate/Non-Audited
Audit Date: 6 10 2019
Total Circulation: 1600

THE PINE BELT NEWS

Corporate/Parent Company: Emmerich Newspapers
Street Address: 103 N. 40th Avenue
City: Hattiesburg
State: MS
Postal Code: 39401
Office phone: 601-268-2331
Publication Website: hubcityspokes.com
Publisher Name: David Gustafson
Publisher Email: david@hubcityspokes.com
Editor Name: Joshua Wilson
Editor Email: joshua@HubCitySPOKES.com
Advertising Executive Name: Rick Jarman
Advertising Executive Email: rick@HubCitySPOKES.com
Total Circulation: 6800

HOUSTON
CHICKASAW JOURNAL

Corporate/Parent Company: Journal Inc
Street Address: 225 E Madison St, PO Box 629
City: Houston
State: MS
Postal Code: 38851-2320
Office phone: (662) 456-3771
Publication Website: https://www.djournal.com/chickasaw/
General E-mail: charlotte.wolfe@journalinc.com
Advertising Executive Email: charlotte.wolfe@journalinc.com
Published Days: Wed
Avg Paid Circ: 2000
Avg Free Circ: 10500
Audit Company: Sworn/Estimate/Non-Audited
Audit Date: 6 10 2019

INDIANOLA
THE ENTERPRISE-TOCSIN

Corporate/Parent Company: Emmerich Newspapers
Street Address: 114 Main St
City: Indianola
State: MS
Postal Code: 38751-2844
Office phone: (662) 887-2222
Publication Website: https://www.enterprise-tocsin.com/
General E-mail: advertising@enterprise-tocsin.com
Publisher Name: Bryan Davis
Publisher Email: bdavis@enterprise-tocsin.com
Advertising Executive Name: Mary Howard Gary
Advertising Executive Email: advertising@enterprise-tocsin.com
Year Established: 1888
Delivery Methods: Mail`Newsstand`Racks
Mechanical specifications: Type page 10 x 16 1/2; E - 6 cols, between; C - 6 cols, between.
Published Days: Thur
Avg Paid Circ: 4000
Avg Free Circ: 50
Audit Company: Sworn/Estimate/Non-Audited
Audit Date: 6 10 2019
Total Circulation: 8500

JACKSON
NORTHSIDE SUN

Corporate/Parent Company: Emmerich Newspapers
Street Address: 246 Briarwood Dr
City: Jackson
State: MS
Postal Code: 39206-3027
Office phone: (601) 957-1122
Publication Website: https://www.northsidesun.com/
General E-mail: jennifer@northsidesun.com
Publisher Name: Wyatt Emmerich
Publisher Email: wyatt@northsidesun.com
Editor Name: Jimmye Sweat
Editor Email: jimmye@northsidesun.com
Advertising Executive Name: Jennifer Stribling
Advertising Executive Email: jennifer@northsidesun.com
Published Days: Thur
Avg Paid Circ: 11144
Avg Free Circ: 548
Audit Company: Sworn/Estimate/Non-Audited
Audit Date: 6 10 2019

THE MADISON COUNTY HERALD

Street Address: PO Box 40
City: Jackson
State: MS
Postal Code: 39205-0040
Office phone: 601-853-2899
Publication Website: mcherald.com
Editor Name: Mary Irby-Jones
Editor Email: mirbyjones@jackson.gannett.com
Editor Phone: (601) 961-7064
Advertising Executive Name: Adrianne Dunn
Advertising Executive Email: adunn@localiq.com
Advertising Executive Phone: (601) 961-7169
Total Circulation: 1649

KOSCIUSKO
KOSCIUSKO STAR-HERALD

Corporate/Parent Company: Emmerich Newspapers
Street Address: 207 N Madison St
City: Kosciusko
State: MS
Postal Code: 39090-3626
Office phone: (662) 289-2251
Publication Website: https://www.starherald.net/
General E-mail: kwhite@starherald.net
Publisher Name: Karen Fioretti

Non-Daily Newspapers in the U.S.

Publisher Email: kfioretti@starherald.net
Publisher Phone: (662) 289-2251, ext : 15
Editor Name: Karen Fioretti
Editor Email: kfioretti@starherald.net
Editor Phone: (662) 289-2251, ext : 15
Advertising Executive Name: Laurie White
Advertising Executive Email: kwhite@starherald.net
Advertising Executive Phone: (662) 289-2251, ext : 14
Total Circulation: 1300

THE STAR-HERALD

Corporate/Parent Company: Emmerich Newspapers
Street Address: 207 N Madison St
City: Kosciusko
State: MS
Postal Code: 39090-3626
Office phone: (662) 289-2251
Publication Website: https://www.starherald.net/
General E-mail: kwhite@starherald.net
Publisher Name: Karen Fioretti
Publisher Email: kfioretti@starherald.net
Publisher Phone: (662) 289-2251, ext : 15
Editor Name: Karen Fioretti
Editor Email: kfioretti@starherald.net
Editor Phone: (662) 289-2251, ext : 15
Advertising Executive Name: Laurie White
Advertising Executive Email: kwhite@starherald.net
Advertising Executive Phone: (662) 289-2251, ext : 14
Year Established: 1866
Delivery Methods: Mail`Carrier`Racks
Own Printing Facility?: N
Mechanical specifications: 6 Columns; 11" x 21 1/2"
Published Days: Thur
Avg Paid Circ: 4800
Avg Free Circ: 100
Audit Company: Sworn/Estimate/Non-Audited
Audit Date: 6 10 2019
Mailroom Equipment: Tying Machines – 3-/Bu; Address Machine – 1-/PB.;
Buisness Equipment: 1-ATT/Unix
Classified Equipment: Hardware – 2-IBM; Printers – Xante/3G;
Classified Software: Synaptic.
Editorial Equipment: Hardware – 7-IBM/Lf/AP Leaf Picture Desk; Printers – Xante/3G
Editorial Software: QPS/QuarkXPress.
Production Equipment: Hardware – 1-B, 1-Kodamatic/425 Processor; Cameras – 1-B
Total Circulation: 3175

LAUREL

THE LAUREL CHRONICLE

Corporate/Parent Company: Emmerich Newspapers
Street Address: 130 Leontyne Price Blvd
City: Laurel
State: MS
Postal Code: 39440-4428
Office phone: (601) 651-2000
Publication Website: http://thechronicle.ms/
Year Established: 2012
Published Days: Tues
Audit Company: Sworn/Estimate/Non-Audited
Audit Date: 6 10 2019
Total Circulation: 5700

LOUISVILLE

WINSTON COUNTY JOURNAL

Corporate/Parent Company: Emmerich Newspapers
Street Address: 233 N Court Ave
City: Louisville
State: MS
Postal Code: 39339-2648
Office phone: (662) 773-6241
Publication Website: https://www.redhillsmsnews.com/
General E-mail: sales@winstoncountyjournal.com
Publisher Name: Joseph Mccain
Publisher Email: newsroom@winstoncountyjournal.com
Publisher Phone: (662) 773-6241, ext : 105
Editor Name: Russell Hood
Editor Email: rhood@websterprogresstimes.com
Editor Phone: (662) 258-7532
Advertising Executive Name: Kathy Johnson
Advertising Executive Email: sales@winstoncountyjournal.com
Advertising Executive Phone: (662) 773-6241, ext : 104
Published Days: Wed
Avg Paid Circ: 2703
Avg Free Circ: 20
Audit Company: Sworn/Estimate/Non-Audited
Audit Date: 6 10 2019
Total Circulation: 1364

MAGEE

SIMPSON COUNTY NEWS

Corporate/Parent Company: Emmerich Newspapers
Street Address: 206 Main Ave N
City: Magee
State: MS
Postal Code: 39111-3536
Office phone: (601) 849-3434
Publication Website: https://www.simpsoncounty.ms/
General E-mail: nbrown@mageecourier.ms
Publisher Name: Pat Brown
Publisher Email: pbrown@mageecourier.ms
Editor Name: Marlan Jones
Editor Email: mjones@mageecourier.ms
Advertising Executive Name: Nancy Brown
Advertising Executive Email: nbrown@mageecourier.ms
Own Printing Facility?: Y
Commercial printers?: Y
Mechanical specifications: Type page 13 x 21 1/2; E - 6 cols, between; A - 6 cols, between; C - 8 cols, between.
Published Days: Thur
Avg Paid Circ: 3750
Avg Free Circ: 40
Audit Company: Sworn/Estimate/Non-Audited
Audit Date: 6 10 2019
Total Circulation: 4050

THE MAGEE COURIER

Corporate/Parent Company: Emmerich Newspapers
Street Address: PO Box 338
City: Magee
State: MS
Postal Code: 39111-0338
Office phone: (601) 849-3434
Publication Website: https://www.simpsoncounty.ms/
General E-mail: nbrown@mageecourier.ms
Publisher Name: Pat Brown
Publisher Email: pbrown@mageecourier.ms
Editor Name: Marlan Jones
Editor Email: mjones@mageecourier.ms
Advertising Executive Name: Nancy Brown
Advertising Executive Email: nbrown@mageecourier.ms
Year Established: 1899
Delivery Methods: Mail`Racks
Own Printing Facility?: Y
Commercial printers?: Y
Mechanical specifications: Type page 10.246x15.5 ; E - 6 cols, 2 1/16, 1/8 between; A - 6 cols, 2 1/16, 1/8 between; C - 7 cols, 2 1/6, 1/8 between.
Published Days: Thur
Avg Paid Circ: 3750
Avg Free Circ: 125
Audit Company: Sworn/Estimate/Non-Audited
Audit Date: 6 10 2019

MCCOMB

ENTERPRISE-JOURNAL

Corporate/Parent Company: Emmerich Newspapers
Street Address: 112 Oliver Emmerich Dr, P.O. Box 2009
City: McComb
State: MS
Postal Code: 39648-6330
Office phone: (601) 684-2421
Publication Website: http://www.enterprise-journal.com
General E-mail: advertising@enterprise-journal.com
Publisher Name: Jack Ryan
Publisher Email: publisher@enterprise-journal.com
Publisher Phone: (601) 684-2421, ext : 232
Editor Name: Jack Ryan
Editor Phone: (601) 684-2421, ext : 232
Advertising Executive Email: advertising@enterprise-journal.com
Advertising Executive Phone: (601) 684-2421
Year Established: 1889
Delivery Methods: Mail`Carrier`Racks
Own Printing Facility?: Y
Commercial printers?: Y
Mechanical specifications: Type page 13 x 21 1/2; E - 6 cols, 2, 1/8 between; A - 6 cols, 2, 1/8 between; C - 8 cols, 1 1/2, 1/8 between.
Published Days: Mon`Tues`Wed`Thur`Fri`Sun
Weekday Frequency: e
Avg Paid Circ: 7128
Avg Free Circ: 122
Audit Company: AAM
Audit Date: 30 06 2017
Pressroom Equipment: Folders – 1, 1-KP/JK8.
Total Circulation: 9000

SOUTHWEST SUN

Corporate/Parent Company: Emmerich Newspapers
Street Address: 112 Oliver Emmerich Dr.
City: McComb
State: MS
Postal Code: 39648
Office phone: (601) 684-2421
Publication Website: http://www.enterprise-journal.com/?
General E-mail: advertising@enterprise-journal.com
Publisher Name: Jack Ryan
Publisher Email: publisher@enterprise-journal.com
Publisher Phone: (601) 684-2421, ext : 232
Editor Name: Jack Ryan
Editor Phone: (601) 684-2421, ext : 232
Advertising Executive Email: advertising@enterprise-journal.com
Advertising Executive Phone: (601) 684-2421
Own Printing Facility?: Y
Commercial printers?: Y
Mechanical specifications: Type page 13 x 21 1/2; E - 6 cols, 2 1/16, 1/6 between; A - 6 cols, 2 1/16, 1/6 between; C - 8 cols, 2 1/16, 1/6 between.
Published Days: Wed
Avg Free Circ: 8500
Audit Company: Sworn/Estimate/Non-Audited
Audit Date: 6 10 2019
Total Circulation: 4895

NEWTON

NEWTO COUNTY APPEAL

Corporate/Parent Company: Emmerich Newspapers
Street Address: 124 North Main Street • P.O. Box 37
City: Newton
State: MS
Postal Code: 39345
Office phone: (601) 683-7810
Publication Website: https://www.newtoncountyappeal.com/
General E-mail: hcollins@newtoncountyappeal.com
Publisher Name: Brent Maze
Publisher Email: bmaze@newtoncountyappeal.com
Editor Name: Thomas Howard
Editor Email: thoward@newtoncountyappeal.com
Advertising Executive Name: Heather Collins
Advertising Executive Email: hcollins@newtoncountyappeal.com

PASS CHRISTIAN

"THE GAZEBO GAZETTE

Street Address: 300 Davis Ave., Suite G
City: Pass Christian
State: MS
Postal Code: 39571
Office phone: 228-224-6781
Publication Website: thegazebogazette.com
General E-mail: editor@thegazebogazette.com
Publisher Name: Hunter Dawkins

PONTOTOC

PONTOTOC PROGRESS

Corporate/Parent Company: Journal Inc
Street Address: 13 E Jefferson St, PO Box 210
City: Pontotoc
State: MS
Postal Code: 38863-2807
Office phone: (662) 489-3511
Publication Website: https://www.djournal.com/pontotoc/
General E-mail: pontotoc.news@journalinc.com
Advertising Executive Email: pontotoc.advertising@journalinc.com
Year Established: 1929
Published Days: Wed
Avg Paid Circ: 7800
Avg Free Circ: 221
Audit Company: Sworn/Estimate/Non-Audited
Audit Date: 6 10 2019

QUITMAN

CLARKE COUNTY TRIBUNE

Corporate/Parent Company: Emmerich Newspapers
Street Address: 101 Main St, P.O. Box 900
City: Quitman
State: MS
Postal Code: 39355-2119
Office phone: (601) 776-3726
Publication Website: https://www.clarkecountytrib.com/
General E-mail: jbozeman@clarkecountytrib.com
Publisher Name: Jennifer Bozeman
Publisher Email: jbozeman@clarkecountytrib.com
Publisher Phone: (601) 776-3726
Mechanical specifications: Type page 10.25 x 16; E - 6 cols, 2, between; A - 6 cols, 2, between.
Published Days: Thur
Avg Paid Circ: 3735
Avg Free Circ: 50
Audit Company: Sworn/Estimate/Non-Audited
Audit Date: 6 10 2019
Total Circulation: 3875

RIPLEY

SOUTHERN ADVOCATE

Corporate/Parent Company: Journal Inc
Street Address: 1701 City Ave N, PO Box 558
City: Ripley
State: MS
Postal Code: 38663-1124
Office phone: (662) 837-8111
Publication Website: https://www.djournal.com/benton/
General E-mail: advertising@tippah360.com

Advertising Executive Email: advertising@tippah360.com
Mechanical specifications: Type page 13 x 21; E - 6 cols, 2, 1/6 between; A - 6 cols, 2, 1/6 between; C - 8 cols, 1 7/16, 1/6 between.
Published Days: Thur
Avg Paid Circ: 1600
Audit Company: Sworn/Estimate/Non-Audited
Audit Date: 6 10 2019
Total Circulation: 3200

SOUTHERN SENTINEL

Corporate/Parent Company: Journal Inc
Street Address: 1701 City Ave N, PO Box 558
City: Ripley
State: MS
Postal Code: 38663-1124
Office phone: (662) 837-8111
Publication Website: https://www.djournal.com/tippah/
General E-mail: advertising@tippah360.com
Advertising Executive Email: advertising@tippah360.com
Year Established: 1879
Mechanical specifications: Type page 11 1/2 x 21 1/2; E - 6 cols, 1 13/16, 2/3 between; A - 6 cols, 1 13/16, 2/3 between; C - 9 cols, 1 1/6, 2/3 between.
Published Days: Wed`Sat
Avg Paid Circ: 6800
Audit Company: Sworn/Estimate/Non-Audited
Audit Date: 6 10 2019

SOUTHERN SENTINES

Corporate/Parent Company: Journal Inc
Street Address: 1701 City Avenue
City: Ripley
State: MS
Postal Code: 38663
Office phone: 662-837-8111
Publication Website: southern-sentinel.com
General E-mail: web@tippah360.com
Editor Name: Elizabeth Walters
Editor Email: elizabeth.walters@journalinc.com
Editor Phone: 662-678-1586
Total Circulation: 3000

SENATOBIA

TATE RECORD

Street Address: 219 E. Main Street
City: Senatobia
State: MS
Postal Code: 38668
Office phone: 662-562-4414
Publication Website: taterecord.com
Publisher Name: Joe Lee

TUPELO

THE LEE COUNTY COURIER

Street Address: 303 W. Main Street
City: Tupelo
State: MS
Postal Code: 38804
Office phone: 662-840-8819
Publication Website: leecountycourier.net
Publisher Name: Jim Clark
Editor Name: Linda Clark
Editor Email: courierl@bellsouth.net

UNION

THE NEWTON COUNTY APPEAL

Corporate/Parent Company: Emmerich Newspapers
Street Address: 105 Main St. • P.O. Box 287
City: Union
State: MS
Postal Code: 39365-2519

Office phone: (601) 774-9433
Publication Website: https://www.newtoncountyappeal.com/
General E-mail: hcollins@newtoncountyappeal.com
Publisher Name: Brent Maze
Publisher Email: bmaze@newtoncountyappeal.com
Editor Name: Thomas Howard
Editor Email: thoward@newtoncountyappeal.com
Advertising Executive Name: Heather Collins
Advertising Executive Email: hcollins@newtoncountyappeal.com
Year Established: 1910
Own Printing Facility?: Y
Published Days: Wed
Avg Paid Circ: 3200
Audit Company: Sworn/Estimate/Non-Audited
Audit Date: 6 10 2019

WINONA

CARROLLTON CONSERVATIVE

Corporate/Parent Company: Emmerich Newspapers
Street Address: 401 Summit St
City: Winona
State: MS
Postal Code: 38967-2240
Office phone: (662) 283-1131
Publication Website: https://www.winonatimes.com/conservative
General E-mail: lodom@winonatimes.com
Publisher Name: Amanda Sexton Ferguson
Publisher Email: publisher@winonatimes.com
Editor Name: Amanda Sexton Ferguson
Editor Email: publisher@winonatimes.com
Advertising Executive Name: Lacey Odom
Advertising Executive Email: lodom@winonatimes.com
Total Circulation: 4900

THE CONSERVATIVE

Corporate/Parent Company: Emmerich Newspapers
Street Address: 401 Summit St
City: Winona
State: MS
Postal Code: 38967-2240
Office phone: (662) 283-1131
Publication Website: https://www.winonatimes.com/
General E-mail: lodom@winonatimes.com
Publisher Name: Amanda Sexton Ferguson
Publisher Email: publisher@winonatimes.com
Editor Name: Amanda Sexton Ferguson
Editor Email: publisher@winonatimes.com
Advertising Executive Name: Lacey Odom
Advertising Executive Email: lodom@winonatimes.com
Year Established: 1865
Published Days: Thur
Avg Paid Circ: 1350
Avg Free Circ: 14
Audit Company: Sworn/Estimate/Non-Audited
Audit Date: 6 10 2019

THE WINONA TIMES

Corporate/Parent Company: Emmerich Newspapers
Street Address: 401 Summit St
City: Winona
State: MS
Postal Code: 38967-2240
Office phone: (662) 283-1131
Publication Website: https://www.winonatimes.com/
General E-mail: lodom@winonatimes.com
Publisher Name: Amanda Sexton Ferguson
Publisher Email: publisher@winonatimes.com
Editor Name: Amanda Sexton Ferguson
Editor Email: publisher@winonatimes.com
Advertising Executive Name: Lacey Odom

Advertising Executive Email: lodom@winonatimes.com
Year Established: 1881
Published Days: Thur
Avg Paid Circ: 3650
Avg Free Circ: 61
Audit Company: Sworn/Estimate/Non-Audited
Audit Date: 6 10 2019
Total Circulation: 3711

YAZOO CITY

THE YAZOO HERALD

Corporate/Parent Company: Emmerich Newspapers
Street Address: 1025 GRAND AVE
City: Yazoo City
State: MS
Postal Code: 39194-2946
Office phone: (662) 746-4911
Publication Website: https://www.yazooherald.net/
General E-mail: sheila@yazooherald.net
Publisher Name: Jason Patterson
Publisher Email: jason@yazooherald.net
Editor Name: Jamie Patterson
Editor Email: jamie@yazooherald.net
Advertising Executive Name: Sheila Trimm Young
Advertising Executive Email: sheila@yazooherald.net
Year Established: 1871
Delivery Methods: Mail`Newsstand`Racks
Own Printing Facility?: N
Mechanical specifications: Type page 10.25x16; E - 6 cols, 2, 1/6 between; A - 6 cols, 2, 1/6 between; C - 9 cols, 1 1/4, 1/6 between.
Published Days: Wed`Sat
Avg Paid Circ: 3200
Avg Free Circ: 25
Audit Company: Sworn/Estimate/Non-Audited
Audit Date: 6 10 2019
Total Circulation: 3225

MONTANA

BIG SKY

LONE PEAK LOOKOUT

Street Address: 235 Snowy Mtn Circle
City: Big Sky
State: MT
Postal Code: 59716
Office phone: 406-465-2937
Publication Website: www.lonepeaklookout.com
Publisher Name: SUSANNE HILL
Publisher Email: shill@lonepeaklookout.com
Editor Name: JOLENE PALMER
Editor Email: editor@lonepeaklookout.com
Advertising Executive Name: Cori Koenig
Advertising Executive Email: sales@lonepeaklookout.com
Advertising Executive Phone: 406.579.6877
Total Circulation: 2723

BIG TIMBER

THE BIG TIMBER PIONEER

Corporate/Parent Company: Yellowstone Newspapers
Street Address: 105 E 2nd Ave, PO Box 830
City: Big Timber
State: MT
Postal Code: 59011-8800
Office phone: (406) 932-5298
Publication Website: https://www.bigtimberpioneer.net/
General E-mail: editor@bigtimberpioneer.net
Editor Name: Jeffrey Durham
Editor Email: editor@bigtimberpioneer.net
Year Established: 1890
Delivery Methods: Mail`Newsstand`Racks
Own Printing Facility?: Y

Commercial printers?: Y
Published Days: Thur
Avg Paid Circ: 1768
Audit Company: Sworn/Estimate/Non-Audited
Audit Date: 6 10 2019
Total Circulation: 2250

BROADUS

POWDER RIVER EXAMINER

Street Address: P.O. Box 328
City: Broadus
State: MT
Postal Code: 59317
Office phone: (406) 436-2244
Publication Website: www.powderriverexaminer.com
Editor Name: Billy Stuver
Editor Email: prexaminer@rangeweb.net

CHINOOK

BLAINE COUNTY JOURNAL NEWS-OPINION

Street Address: P.O. Box 279
City: Chinook
State: MT
Postal Code: 59523
Office phone: (406) 357-3573
Publication Website: www.blainecountyjournal.com
General E-mail: bcjnews@itstriangle.com
Publisher Name: Keith & Keri Hanson
Publisher Email: bcjnews@mtintouch.net
Editor Name: "
Keith Hanson"
Editor Email: bcjreporter@mtintouch.net
Advertising Executive Name: Paula Reynolds
Advertising Executive Email: bcjads@mtintouch.net

COLUMBUS

THE STILLWATER COUNTY NEWS

Corporate/Parent Company: Yellowstone Newspapers
Street Address: 38 N 4th St
City: Columbus
State: MT
Postal Code: 59019-7364
Office phone: (406) 322-5212
Publication Website: https://www.stillwatercountynews.com/
General E-mail: ads@stillwatercountynews.com
Editor Name: Marlo Pronovost
Editor Email: editor@stillwatercountynews.com
Advertising Executive Email: ads@stillwatercountynews.com
Delivery Methods: Mail`Newsstand`Racks
Mechanical specifications: Type page 13 x 21; E - 6 cols, 2, 1/6 between; A - 6 cols, 2, 1/6 between; C - 6 cols, 2, 1/6 between.
Published Days: Thur
Avg Paid Circ: 2100
Avg Free Circ: 5
Audit Company: Sworn/Estimate/Non-Audited
Audit Date: 6 10 2019

DILLON

DILLON TRIBUNE

Corporate/Parent Company: Yellowstone Newspapers
Street Address: 31 S Idaho St, P.O. Box 911
City: Dillon
State: MT
Postal Code: 59725-2509
Office phone: (406) 683-2331
Publication Website: https://www.dillontribune.com/
General E-mail: publisher@dillontribune.com
Publisher Name: J.P. Plutt
Publisher Email: publisher@dillontribune.com
Editor Name: J.P. Plutt
Advertising Executive Name: Paul Tatarka

Non-Daily Newspapers in the U.S.

III-93

Year Established: 1881
Delivery Methods: Mail`Newsstand`Carrier`Racks
Mechanical specifications: Column Widths: DisplayÃ‚Â– 1.81 inches with 1-pica (1/6 inch) gutter (6 columns per page) Classified DisplayÃ‚Â– 1.35 inches with 9-point gutter (8 columns per page) Page Size: 11.7 inches wide by 21 inches deep Unit of Measure: Column inch (1 column wide by one inch deep)
Published Days: Wed
Avg Paid Circ: 2700
Audit Company: Sworn/Estimate/Non-Audited
Audit Date: 6 10 2019
Total Circulation: 3600

GLENDIVE

GLENDIVE RANGER-REVIEW

Corporate/Parent Company: Yellowstone Newspapers
Street Address: PO Box 61 | 118 W. Benham St
City: Glendive
State: MT
Postal Code: 59330-1614
Office phone: (406) 377-3303
Publication Website: https://www.rangerreview.com/
General E-mail: rrads@rangerreview.com
Advertising Executive Email: rrads@rangerreview.com
Year Established: 1881
Delivery Methods: Mail`Newsstand`Carrier
Commercial printers?: Y
Mechanical specifications: Type page 13 x 21 1/2; E - 6 cols, 2 1/15, 1/6 between; A - 6 cols, 2 1/15, 1/6 between; C - 8 cols, 1/6 between.
Published Days: Thur`Sun
Avg Paid Circ: 3200
Avg Free Circ: 20
Audit Company: Sworn/Estimate/Non-Audited
Audit Date: 6 10 2019
Total Circulation: 2700

HARDIN

BIG HORN COUNTY NEWS

Corporate/Parent Company: Yellowstone Newspapers
Street Address: 204 N Center Ave, P.O. Box 926
City: Hardin
State: MT
Postal Code: 59034-1908
Office phone: (406) 665-1008
Publication Website: https://www.bighorncountynews.com/
General E-mail: news@bighorncountynews.com
Publisher Name: Luella N. Brien
Publisher Email: publisher@bighorncountynews.com
Editor Name: Luella N. Brien
Advertising Executive Name: Luella N. Brien
Year Established: 1908
Delivery Methods: Mail`Carrier`Racks
Own Printing Facility?: Y
Mechanical specifications: Type page 11 5/8 x 21; E - 6 cols, 1 5/6, 1/6 between; A - 6 cols, 1 5/6, 1/6 between; C - 6 cols, 1 5/6, 1/6 between.
Published Days: Thur
Avg Paid Circ: 2200
Avg Free Circ: 50
Audit Company: Sworn/Estimate/Non-Audited
Audit Date: 6 10 2019
Total Circulation: 3220

LAUREL

LAUREL OUTLOOK

Corporate/Parent Company: Yellowstone Newspapers
Street Address: 415 E Main St
City: Laurel
State: MT
Postal Code: 59044-3120
Office phone: (406) 628-4412
Publication Website: https://www.laureloutlook.com/
General E-mail: classifieds@laureloutlook.com
Editor Name: Kathleen Gilluly
Editor Email: news@laureloutlook.com
Editor Phone: (406) 628-4412, ext : 7113
Advertising Executive Name: Tonya Morgan
Advertising Executive Email: classifieds@laureloutlook.com
Advertising Executive Phone: (406) 628-4412, ext : 7111
Year Established: 1906
Delivery Methods: Mail`Newsstand`Carrier`Racks
Own Printing Facility?: Y
Commercial printers?: Y
Mechanical specifications: Type page 13 x 21; E - 6 cols, 2, 1/6 between; A - 6 cols, 2, 1/6 between; C - 6 cols, 2, 1/6 between.
Published Days: Thur
Avg Paid Circ: 2500
Avg Free Circ: 100
Audit Company: Sworn/Estimate/Non-Audited
Audit Date: 6 10 2019
Total Circulation: 500

LEWISTOWN

JUDITH BASIN PRESS

Corporate/Parent Company: Yellowstone Newspapers
Street Address: P.O. Box 524
City: Lewistown
State: MT
Postal Code: 59457-0900
Office phone: (406) 566-2471
Publication Website: https://www.judithbasinpress.net/
General E-mail: pressoffice@itstriangle.com
Advertising Executive Email: pressoffice@itstriangle.com
Year Established: 1909
Delivery Methods: Mail`Newsstand
Commercial printers?: Y
Published Days: Thur
Avg Paid Circ: 500
Audit Company: Sworn/Estimate/Non-Audited
Audit Date: 6 10 2019
Total Circulation: 2600

LEWISTOWN NEWS-ARGUS

Corporate/Parent Company: Yellowstone Newspapers
Street Address: 521 W Main St, P.O. Box 900
City: Lewistown
State: MT
Postal Code: 59457-2603
Office phone: (406) 535-3401
Publication Website: https://www.lewistownnews.com/
General E-mail: advertising1@lewistownnews.com
Publisher Name: Jacques Rutten
Publisher Email: publisher@lewistownnews.com
Editor Name: Jacques Rutten
Editor Email: editor@lewistownnews.com
Advertising Executive Email: advertising1@lewistownnews.com
Year Established: 1883
Delivery Methods: Mail`Newsstand`Racks
Own Printing Facility?: Y
Commercial printers?: Y
Mechanical specifications: Type page 11 11/16 x 21 1/2; E - 6 cols, 1 13/16, 3/16 between; A - 6 cols, 1 13/16, 3/16 between; C - 6 cols, 1 13/16, 3/16 between.
Published Days: Wed`Sat
Avg Paid Circ: 4551
Avg Free Circ: 108
Audit Company: Sworn/Estimate/Non-Audited
Audit Date: 6 10 2019
Total Circulation: 4659

LINCOLN

BLACKFOOT VALLEY DISPATCH

Street Address: 506 Main St.
City: Lincoln
State: MT
Postal Code: 59639
Office phone: (406) 362-4131
Publication Website: www.blackfootvalleydispatch.com
General E-mail: info@blackfootvalleydispatch.com
Editor Name: Roger Dey
Advertising Executive Name: Erin Dey

LIVINGSTON

MONTANA PIONEER

Street Address: PO Box 411
City: Livingston
State: MT
Postal Code: 59047
Office phone: (406) 222-1355
Publication Website: www.montanapioneer.com
General E-mail: montanapioneer@gmail.com
Mailroom Equipment: Tying Machines – 1/Bu String tie 2 Signod strappers; Address Machine – 1-/Am.;
Buisness Equipment: BFM
Classified Equipment: Hardware – APP/Mac; Printers – LaserMaster/XLO, Okidata;
Classified Software: Baseview/Class Manager Plus.
Editorial Equipment: Hardware – APP/Mac; Printers – APP/Mac LaserPrinter, LaserMaster/XLO, PrePress/Panther Pro Imagesetter
Editorial Software: QPS, Baseview/NewsEdit.
Production Equipment: Hardware – APP/Mac, LaserMaster, Adobe/Photosho Indesign; Cameras – 1-K
Production Software: Baseview/NewsEdit.
Total Circulation: 4029

PARK COUNTY SUPER SHOPPER

Corporate/Parent Company: Yellowstone Newspapers
Street Address: 401 S Main St, P.O. Box 2000
City: Livingston
State: MT
Postal Code: 59047-3418
Office phone: (406) 222-2000
Publication Website: https://www.livingstonenterprise.com/
General E-mail: ejones@livent.net
Publisher Name: John Sullivan
Publisher Email: execoffice@livent.net
Editor Name: Justin Post
Editor Email: jpost@livent.net
Advertising Executive Name: Emily Jones
Advertising Executive Email: ejones@livent.net

MILES CITY

MILES CITY STAR

Corporate/Parent Company: Yellowstone Communications
Street Address: 818 Main St, P.O. Box 1216
City: Miles City
State: MT
Postal Code: 59301-3221
Office phone: (406) 234-0450
Publication Website: https://www.milescitystar.com/
General E-mail: advsales@midrivers.com
Publisher Name: Andy Prutsok
Editor Name: Ashley Wise
Editor Email: starnews@midrivers.com
Advertising Executive Name: Kara Stewart
Advertising Executive Email: advsales@midrivers.com
Year Established: 1911

Delivery Methods: Mail`Newsstand`Carrier
Commercial printers?: Y
Mechanical specifications: Type page 12 x 21 1/2; E - 6 cols, 2 1/16, 1/8 between; A - 6 cols, 2 1/16, 1/8 between; C - 8 cols, 1 1/2, 1/8 between.
Published Days: Mon`Tues`Wed`Thur`Fri
Weekday Frequency: e
Avg Paid Circ: 4000
Avg Free Circ: 29
Audit Company: Sworn/Estimate/Non-Audited
Audit Date: 7 12 2019
Pressroom Equipment: Lines – 6-G/Community.;

RED LODGE

CARBON COUNTY NEWS

Corporate/Parent Company: Yellowstone Newspapers
Street Address: 202 S Hauser Ave, P.O. Box 970
City: Red Lodge
State: MT
Postal Code: 59068-9128
Office phone: (406) 446-2222
Publication Website: https://www.carboncountynews.com/
General E-mail: ads@carboncountynews.com
Publisher Name: Alastair Baker
Publisher Email: news@carboncountynews.com
Publisher Phone: (406) 446-2222
Editor Name: Alastair Baker
Editor Email: news@carboncountynews.com
Editor Phone: (406) 446-2222
Advertising Executive Name: Tina Williamson
Advertising Executive Email: classifieds@carboncountynews.com
Advertising Executive Phone: (406) 446-2222
Year Established: 1909
Delivery Methods: Mail`Carrier
Mechanical specifications: Type page 13 x 21; E - 6 cols, 2, 1/6 between; A - 6 cols, 2, 1/6 between; C - 6 cols, 2, 1/6 between.
Published Days: Thur
Avg Paid Circ: 3100
Avg Free Circ: 500
Audit Company: Sworn/Estimate/Non-Audited
Audit Date: 6 10 2019

TERRY

THE TERRY TRIBUNE

Corporate/Parent Company: Yellowstone Newspapers
Street Address: 204 S Logan Ave
City: Terry
State: MT
Postal Code: 59349
Office phone: (406) 635-5513
Publication Website: https://www.terrytribune.com/
Year Established: 1907
Mechanical specifications: Type page 10 1/4 x 13; A - 5 cols, 2, 1/4 between; C - 6 cols, 3/16 between.
Published Days: Wed
Avg Paid Circ: 856
Avg Free Circ: 17
Audit Company: Sworn/Estimate/Non-Audited
Audit Date: 6 10 2019
Total Circulation: 1768

TOWNSEND

BROADWATER REPORTER

Street Address: 303 Broadway
City: Townsend
State: MT
Postal Code: 59644
Office phone: 406-266-4455
Publication Website: www.broadwaterreporter.com
General E-mail: broadwaterrptr@mt.net
Editor Name: Bobbi Cross
Total Circulation: 2105

NORTH CAROLINA

AYDEN

THE TIMES-LEADER

Corporate/Parent Company: Cox
Street Address: 574 E. Third Street
City: Ayden
State: NC
Postal Code: 28513
Office phone: (252) 746-6261
Year Established: 1912
Delivery Methods: Mail`Newsstand`Racks
Commercial printers?: Y
Mechanical specifications: Type page 11 5/8 x 21 1/2; E - 6 cols, 1 7/8, 1/8 between; A - 6 cols, 1 7/8, 1/8 between; C - 6 cols, 1 7/8, 1/8 between.
Published Days: Wed
Avg Paid Circ: 2200
Audit Company: Sworn/Estimate/Non-Audited
Audit Date: 6 10 2019
Total Circulation: 873

CHAPEL HILL

PENNSYLVANIA CAPITAL-STAR

Corporate/Parent Company: States Newsroom
Street Address: 1450 Raleigh Rd, St. 200
City: Chapel Hill
State: NC
Postal Code: 27517
Publication Website: www.penncapital-star.com
General E-mail: info@penncapital-star.com
Editor Name: JOHN L. MICEK
Editor Email: jmicek@penncapital-star.com
Total Circulation: 4200

CLEMMONS

THE CLEMMONS COURIER

Corporate/Parent Company: Boone Newspapers, Inc.
Street Address: 3600 Clemmons Rd
City: Clemmons
State: NC
Postal Code: 27012-9104
Office phone: (336) 766-4126
Publication Website: www.clemmonscourier.net
Note: County seat newspaper serving Duplin County, North Carolina, southern Lenoir County and wesern Onslow County, ... and incorporating the former Wallace Enterprise, Warsaw-Faison News, and Richlands-Beulaville Advertiser News
Total Circulation: 17225

EDENTON

THE CHOWAN HERALD

Corporate/Parent Company: Cox
Street Address: 423 S Broad St
City: Edenton
State: NC
Postal Code: 27932-1935
Office phone: (252) 332-2123
Publication Website: http://www.dailyadvance.com
Publisher Name: Mike Goodman
Publisher Email: mgoodman@dailyadvance.com
Editor Name: Mike Goodman
Editor Email: mgoodman@dailyadvance.com
Editor Phone: (252) 329-9680
Advertising Executive Name: Sean O'Brien
Advertising Executive Email: Sean O'Brien
Advertising Executive Phone: sobrien@dailyadvance.com
Own Printing Facility?: Y
Commercial printers?: Y
Mechanical specifications: Type page 13 x 21 1/2; E - 6 cols, 2 1/4, between; A - 6 cols, 2 1/4, between; C - 8 cols, 1 1/2, between.
Published Days: Tues`Thur`Sat
Avg Paid Circ: 5000
Audit Company: Sworn/Estimate/Non-Audited
Audit Date: 6 10 2019
Total Circulation: 5121

FARMVILLE

THE FARMVILLE ENTERPRISE

Corporate/Parent Company: Cox
Street Address: 3754 S Main St
City: Farmville
State: NC
Postal Code: 27828-8546
Office phone: (252) 753-4126
Year Established: 1910
Delivery Methods: Mail
Mechanical specifications: Type page 13 x 21 1/2.
Published Days: Wed
Avg Paid Circ: 2500
Audit Company: Sworn/Estimate/Non-Audited
Audit Date: 6 10 2019

HAVELOCK

THE HAVELOCK NEWS

Corporate/Parent Company: Gannett
Street Address: 230 Stonebridge Sq
City: Havelock
State: NC
Postal Code: 28532-9505
Office phone: (252) 444-1999
Publication Website: www.havenews.com
Editor Name: Chris Segal
Editor Email: Chris.Segal@newbernsj.com
Editor Phone: 252-635-5663
Advertising Executive Name: Taylor Shannon
Advertising Executive Email: taylor.shannon@havenews.com
Advertising Executive Phone: 252-444-1999 x105
Total Circulation: 1733

HERTFORD

PERQUIMANS WEEKLY

Corporate/Parent Company: Cox
Street Address: 111 W Market St
City: Hertford
State: NC
Postal Code: 27944-1150
Office phone: (252) 426-5728
Publisher Name: Mike Goodman
Publisher Email: mgoodman@dailyadvance.com
Editor Name: Julian Eure
Editor Email: jeure@dailyadvance.com
Editor Phone: (252) 329-9680
Advertising Executive Name: Sean O'Brien
Advertising Executive Email: sobrien@dailyadvance.com
Year Established: 1932
Delivery Methods: Mail`Carrier`Racks
Own Printing Facility?: Y
Commercial printers?: Y
Mechanical specifications: Type page 11 5/8 x 21; E - 6 cols, 1 5/6, 1/8 between; C - 9 cols, 1 3/16, 1/8 between.
Published Days: Wed
Avg Paid Circ: 1733
Audit Company: Sworn/Estimate/Non-Audited
Audit Date: 6 10 2019
Total Circulation: 5000

KENANSVILLE

DUPLIN TIMES

Corporate/Parent Company: Cox
Street Address: 102 Front St
City: Kenansville
State: NC
Postal Code: 28349
Office phone: (910) 296-0239
Publication Website: theduplintimes.com
Publisher Name: Jim Sills
Publisher Email: jsills@ncweeklies.com
Editor Name: Trevor Normile
Editor Email: tnormile@ncweeklies.com
Advertising Executive Name: Alan Wells
Advertising Executive Email: awells@ncweeklies.com
Year Established: 1935
Delivery Methods: Mail`Newsstand`Racks
Mechanical specifications: 6 column format, 10.125" x 21" Classified is 8 col format, 10.125" x 21"
Published Days: Thur
Avg Paid Circ: 6100
Avg Free Circ: 11125
Audit Company: Sworn/Estimate/Non-Audited
Audit Date: 6 10 2019

ROCKY MOUNT

THE TARBORO WEEKLY

Corporate/Parent Company: Adams Publishing Group
Street Address: 1151 FALLS ROAD SUITE 2008
City: Rocky Mount
State: NC
Postal Code: 27804
Publication Website: www.rmtelegram.com/tarboro
General E-mail: website@tarboroweekly.com
Publisher Name: Kyle Stephens
Publisher Email: kstephens@rmtelegram.com
Publisher Phone: 252-366-8146
Editor Name: Gene Metrick
Editor Email: gmetrick@rmtelegram.com
Editor Phone: 252-366-8141
Advertising Executive Name: Chris Taylor
Advertising Executive Email: ctaylor@rmtelegram.com
Advertising Executive Phone: 252-366-8134
Total Circulation: 2500

SNOW HILL

THE STANDARD LACONIC

Corporate/Parent Company: Cox
Street Address: PO BOX 128
City: Snow Hill
State: NC
Postal Code: 28580-1643
Office phone: (252) 747-3882
Editor Email: aharne@ncweeklies.com
Advertising Executive Name: Angela Harne
Advertising Executive Email: dwilliams@ncweeklies.com

SPRUCE PINE

THE MITCHELL NEWS-JOURNAL

Corporate/Parent Company: Community Newspapers, Inc.
Street Address: P.O. Box 339
City: Spruce Pine
State: NC
Postal Code: 28777
Office phone: 828-765-7169
Publication Website: www.mitchellnews.com
Publisher Name: Brandon Roberts
Publisher Email: editor@mitchellnews.com

WILLIAMSTON

ENTERPRISE & WEEKLY HERALD

Street Address: 106 W Main St
City: Williamston
State: NC
Postal Code: 27892-2471
Office phone: (252) 792-1181
General E-mail: mleicester@ncweeklies.com
Publisher Name: Kyle Stephens
Publisher Email: kstephens@ncweeklies.com
Editor Name: Nita Smith
Advertising Executive Name: Lou Ann VanLandingham
Advertising Executive Email: lavan@ncweeklies.com
Year Established: 1899
Delivery Methods: Mail`Newsstand`Carrier`Racks
Own Printing Facility?: Y
Commercial printers?: Y
Mechanical specifications: Type page 11 5/8 x 21; E - 6 cols, 1 5/6, 1/6 between; A - 6 cols, 1 5/6, 1/6 between; C - 9 cols, 1 18/100, 1/6 between.
Published Days: Tues`Fri
Avg Paid Circ: 5100
Avg Free Circ: 21
Audit Company: Sworn/Estimate/Non-Audited
Audit Date: 6 10 2019

WINDSOR

BERTIE LEDGER-ADVANCE

Corporate/Parent Company: Cox
Street Address: 109 S. KING STREET
City: Windsor
State: NC
Postal Code: 27983-6753
Office phone: 252-794-3185
Publication Website: http://www.dailyadvance.com
General E-mail: mleicester@ncweeklies.com
Publisher Name: Kyle Stephens
Publisher Email: kstephens@ncweeklies.com
Editor Name: Thadd White
Editor Email: twhite@ncweeklies.com
Advertising Executive Name: Jessica Mobley
Advertising Executive Email: jmobley@ncweeklies.com
Year Established: 1930
Delivery Methods: Mail`Newsstand`Carrier`Racks
Mechanical specifications: Type page 12 3/4 x 21; E - 6 cols, 2 1/16, 1/8 between; A - 6 cols, 2 1/16, 1/8 between; C - 9 cols, 1 3/8, 1/8 between.
Published Days: Wed
Avg Paid Circ: 4200
Audit Company: Sworn/Estimate/Non-Audited
Audit Date: 6 10 2019

NORTH DAKOTA

BEULAH

BEULAH BEACON

Corporate/Parent Company: BHG, Inc.
Street Address: 324 2nd Ave. NE
City: Beulah
State: ND
Postal Code: 58523
Office phone: (701) 873-4381
Publication Website: https://www.bhgnews.com/newspapers/beulahbeacon/
General E-mail: beacon@bhgnews.com
Publisher Name: BHG, Inc
Editor Name: Michael W. Sasser
Total Circulation: 2200

CENTER REPUBLICAN

Corporate/Parent Company: BHG, Inc.
Street Address: 324 2nd Ave. NE
City: Beulah
State: ND
Postal Code: 58523
Office phone: (701) 873-4381
Publication Website: https://www.bhgnews.com/newspapers/centerrepublican/
General E-mail: coalnews@westriv.com
Publisher Name: BHG, Inc
Editor Name: Jarann Johnson
Editor Email: coalsports@bhgnews.com

Non-Daily Newspapers in the U.S.

DICKINSON

ADVERTIZER
Corporate/Parent Company: Forum Communications
Street Address: 1815 1st St W
City: Dickinson
State: ND
Postal Code: 58601-2463
Office phone: (701) 225-8111

FARGO

INFORUM
Corporate/Parent Company: Forum Communications
Street Address: 101 5th St N
City: Fargo
State: ND
Postal Code: 58102
Office phone: (701) 235-7311
Publication Website: http://www.inforum.com/
General E-mail: news@forumcomm.com
Editor Name: Matthew Von Pinnon
Editor Email: mvonpinnon@forumcomm.com
Editor Phone: (701) 241-5579
Advertising Executive Name: Mark Von Bank
Advertising Executive Email: mvonbank@forumcomm.com
Advertising Executive Phone: (701) 241-5561

THE METRO WEEKLY-OOB
Corporate/Parent Company: Forum Communications
Street Address: 101 5th St N
City: Fargo
State: ND
Postal Code: 58102-4826
Office phone: (701) 451-5774

GARRISON

MCLEAN COUNTY INDEPENDENT
Corporate/Parent Company: BHG, Inc.
Street Address: P.O. Box 309
City: Garrison
State: ND
Postal Code: 58540
Office phone: (701) 463-2201
Publication Website: https://www.bhgnews.com/newspapers/mcleancountyindependent/
General E-mail: independ@restel.net
Publisher Name: BHG, Inc
Editor Name: Diane Newberry
Editor Email: editors@bhgnews.com

GRAFTON

WALSH COUNTY RECORD
Street Address: 402 Hill Avenue
City: Grafton
State: ND
Postal Code: 58237
Office phone: 701-352-0641
Publication Website: www.wcrecord.com
Publisher Name: Jackie L. Thompson
Publisher Email: jackie@wcrecord.com
Editor Name: Todd Morgan
Editor Email: todd@wcrecord.com
Advertising Executive Name: Tim S. Martin
Advertising Executive Email: advertising@wcrecord.com

GRAND FORKS

AGWEEK
Corporate/Parent Company: Forum Communications
Street Address: 375 2nd Ave N
City: Grand Forks
State: ND
Postal Code: 58206
Office phone: (701) 780-1245
Publication Website: http://www.agweek.com/
General E-mail: subscriptions@agweek.com
Publisher Name: Kathryn Pinke
Publisher Phone: (701) 241-5571
Editor Name: Kathryn Pinke
Editor Phone: (701) 241-5571
Advertising Executive Email: customercare@agweek.com
Advertising Executive Phone: (888) 239-4089

HAZEN

THE HAZEN STAR
Corporate/Parent Company: BHG, Inc.
Street Address: PO Box 508
City: Hazen
State: ND
Postal Code: 58545
Office phone: (701) 748-2255
Publication Website: https://www.bhgnews.com/newspapers/hazenstar/
General E-mail: star@westriv.com
Publisher Name: BHG, Inc
Editor Name: Daniel Arens

JAMESTOWN

THE JAMESTOWN SUN
Corporate/Parent Company: Forum Communications
Street Address: 121 3rd St NW
City: Jamestown
State: ND
Postal Code: 58401-3127
Office phone: (701) 252-3120
Publication Website: www.jamestownsun.com
General E-mail: rkeller@jamestownsun.com
Publisher Name: Rob Keller
Publisher Email: rkeller@jamestownsun.com
Publisher Phone: (701) 952-8431
Editor Name: Kathy Steiner
Editor Email: ksteiner@jamestownsun.comq
Editor Phone: (701) 952-8449
Advertising Executive Name: Rob Keller
Advertising Executive Email: rkeller@jamestownsun.com
Advertising Executive Phone: (701) 952-8430

MCCLUSKY

MCCLUSKY GAZETTE
Corporate/Parent Company: BHG, Inc.
Street Address: PO Box 619
City: McClusky
State: ND
Postal Code: 58463
Office phone: (701) 363-2492
Publication Website: https://www.bhgnews.com/newspapers/mccluskygazette/
General E-mail: gazette@westriv.com
Publisher Name: BHG, Inc
Editor Name: Allan Tinker

NEW TOWN

MOUNTRAIL COUNTY RECORD
Corporate/Parent Company: BHG, Inc.
Street Address: PO Box 730
City: New Town
State: ND
Postal Code: 58763
Office phone: (701) 627-4829
Publication Website: https://www.bhgnews.com/newspapers/mountrailcountyrecord/
General E-mail: ntnews@restel.net
Publisher Name: BHG, Inc
Editor Name: Jerry Kram

NEW TOWN NEWS
Corporate/Parent Company: BHG, Inc.
Street Address: PO Box 730
City: New Town
State: ND
Postal Code: 58763
Office phone: (701) 627-4829
Publication Website: https://www.bhgnews.com/newspapers/newtownnews/
General E-mail: ntnews@restel.net
Publisher Name: BHG, Inc
Editor Name: Jerry Kram

ROLLA

TURTLE MOUNTAIN STAR
Corporate/Parent Company: Nordmark Publishing
Street Address: 11 1st Ave NE
City: Rolla
State: ND
Postal Code: 58367
Office phone: (701) 477-6495
Publication Website: https://www.tmstarnews.com/
General E-mail: tmstar@utma.com
Publisher Name: Jason Nordmark
Editor Name: Jason Nordmark

TOWNER

THE MOUSE RIVER JOURNAL
Corporate/Parent Company: Nordmark Publishing
Street Address: PO Box 268
City: Towner
State: ND
Postal Code: 58788
Office phone: (701) 537-5610
Publication Website: https://mouseriverjournal.weebly.com/
General E-mail: mrjads@srt.com
Publisher Name: Jason Nordmark
Editor Name: Billi Jo Eriksmoen

VELVA

VELVA AREA VOICE
Corporate/Parent Company: Ted Bolton
Street Address: PO Box 630
City: Velva
State: ND
Postal Code: 58790
Office phone: (701) 338-2599
Publication Website: https://www.bhgnews.com/newspapers/
General E-mail: vavads@srt.com
Publisher Name: Ted Bolton

WAHPETON

NEWS-MONITOR
Street Address: 601 Dakota Avenue
City: Wahpeton
State: ND
Postal Code: 58074
Office phone: (701) 642-8585
Publication Website: wahpetondailynews.com/news_monitor
General E-mail: newsmonitor@wahpetondailynews.com
Publisher Name: Tara Klostreich
Publisher Email: tarak@wahpetondailynews.com
Publisher Phone: (701) 642-8585
Editor Name: Carrie McDermott
Editor Email: editor@wahpetondailynews.com
Editor Phone: (701) 642-8585
Advertising Executive Name: Diana Hermes
Advertising Executive Email: dianah@wahpetondailynews.com
Advertising Executive Phone: (701) 642-8585

WASHBURN

WASHBURN LEADER-NEWS
Corporate/Parent Company: BHG, Inc.
Street Address: PO Box 340
City: Washburn
State: ND
Postal Code: 58577
Office phone: (701) 462-8126
Publication Website: https://www.bhgnews.com/newspapers/leader-news
Publisher Name: BHG, Inc
Editor Name: Alyssa Meier
Editor Email: washburned@bhgnews.com
Advertising Executive Name: Don Winter

CENTRAL MCLEAN NEWS-JOURNAL
Corporate/Parent Company: BHG, Inc.
Street Address: PO Box 340
City: Washburn
State: ND
Postal Code: 58577
Office phone: (701) 442-5535
Publication Website: www.bhgnews.com/newspapers/central-mclean-news-journal
General E-mail: centralmclean@westriv.com
Publisher Name: BHG, Inc
Editor Name: Suzanne Were

WEST FARGO

WEST FARGO PIONEER
Corporate/Parent Company: Forum Communications
Street Address: 101 5th Street North
City: West Fargo
State: ND
Postal Code: 58102
Office phone: (701) 451-5718
Publication Website: https://www.westfargopioneer.com/
Editor Name: Matthew Von Pinnon
Editor Phone: (701) 241-5579

NEBRASKA

AINSWORTH

STAR-JOURNAL
Street Address: 921 E. 4th St.
City: Ainsworth
State: NE
Postal Code: 69210
Office phone: (402) 387-2844
Publication Website: www.ainsworthnews.com
Editor Name: Kathy Worrell
Editor Email: ainsworthnews@ainsworthnews.com

ARNOLD

SENTINEL
Corporate/Parent Company: Lee Enterprises
Street Address: 113 S Walnut St
City: Arnold
State: NE
Postal Code: 69120
Office phone: 308-848-2511
Publication Website: arnoldsentinel.com
Editor Name: Janet Larreau
Editor Email: arnoldsentinel@gpcom.net

ATKINSON

GRAPHIC
Corporate/Parent Company: Gannett

Street Address: 207 E. State St.
City: Atkinson
State: NE
Postal Code: 68713
Office phone: 402-925-5411
Publication Website: www.atkinsongraphic.com
Editor Name: Brook D. Curtiss
Editor Email: editor@atkinsongraphic.com

BELLEVUE

BELLEVUE LEADER

Street Address: 604 Fort Crook Rd N
City: Bellevue
State: NE
Postal Code: 68005-4500
Office phone: (402) 733-7300
Publication Website: https://www.omaha.com/sarpy/bellevue/
General E-mail: classifieds@bellevueleader.com
Publisher Name: Paul Swanson
Publisher Email: paul.swanson@owh.com
Publisher Phone: (402) 444-1248
Editor Name: Ron Petak
Editor Email: ron.petak@bellevueleader.com
Editor Phone: (402) 505-3620
Advertising Executive Name: Eric Mayberry
Advertising Executive Email: eric.mayberry@owh.com
Advertising Executive Phone: (402) 444-1110
Year Established: 1971
Delivery Methods: Mail`Newsstand`Carrier`Racks
Own Printing Facility?: Y
Commercial printers?: Y
Published Days: Wed
Avg Paid Circ: 3100
Audit Company: Sworn/Estimate/Non-Audited
Audit Date: 6 10 2019

GRETNA BREEZE

Street Address: 604 Fort Crook Rd N
City: Bellevue
State: NE
Postal Code: 68005-4557
Office phone: (402) 733-7300
Publication Website: https://www.omaha.com/sarpy/gretna/
General E-mail: rachel.george@gretnabreeze.com
Publisher Name: Todd Sears
Publisher Email: todd.sears@owh.com
Publisher Phone: (402) 444-1179
Editor Name: Paul Goodsell
Editor Email: goodsell@owh.com
Editor Phone: (402) 444-1114
Advertising Executive Name: Eric Mayberry
Advertising Executive Email: eric.mayberry@owh.com
Advertising Executive Phone: (402) 444-1110
Year Established: 1971
Delivery Methods: Mail`Newsstand`Carrier`Racks
Own Printing Facility?: Y
Commercial printers?: Y
Published Days: Wed
Avg Paid Circ: 1241
Audit Company: Sworn/Estimate/Non-Audited
Audit Date: 6 10 2019

PAPILLION TIMES

Street Address: 604 Fort Crook Rd N
City: Bellevue
State: NE
Postal Code: 68005-4557
Office phone: (402) 733-7300
Publication Website: https://www.omaha.com/sarpy/papillion/
General E-Mail: eric.taylor@papilliontimes.com
Publisher Name: Shon Barenklau
Publisher Email: shon.barenklau@papilliontimes.com

Publisher Phone: (402) 537-4840
Editor Name: Paul Goodsell
Editor Email: goodsell@owh.com
Editor Phone: (402) 444-1114
Advertising Executive Name: Eric Mayberry
Advertising Executive Email: eric.mayberry@owh.com
Advertising Executive Phone: (402) 444-1110
Year Established: 1874
Delivery Methods: Mail`Newsstand`Carrier`Racks
Own Printing Facility?: Y
Commercial printers?: Y
Mechanical specifications: Full Size Broadsheet 11.5x20.75; full page width 6 columns 11 1/2; full page depth 20 3/4; agate line per column inch 14;
Published Days: Wed
Avg Paid Circ: 2298
Audit Company: Sworn/Estimate/Non-Audited
Audit Date: 6 10 2019
Classified Software: Mactive

RALSTON RECORDER

Street Address: 604 Fort Crook Rd N
City: Bellevue
State: NE
Postal Code: 68005-4557
Office phone: (402) 733-7300
Publication Website: https://www.omaha.com/sarpy/ralston/
General E-mail: eric.taylor@papilliontimes.com
Publisher Name: Todd Sears
Publisher Email: todd.sears@owh.com
Publisher Phone: (402) 444-1179
Editor Name: Paul Goodsell
Editor Email: goodsell@owh.com
Editor Phone: (402) 444-1114
Advertising Executive Name: Eric Mayberry
Advertising Executive Email: eric.mayberry@owh.com
Advertising Executive Phone: (402) 444-1110
Year Established: 1963
Delivery Methods: Mail`Newsstand`Carrier`Racks
Own Printing Facility?: Y
Commercial printers?: Y
Published Days: Wed
Avg Paid Circ: 778
Audit Company: Sworn/Estimate/Non-Audited
Audit Date: 6 10 2019

RECORDER

Street Address: 604 Fort Crook Rd N
City: Bellevue
State: NE
Postal Code: 68005
Office phone: 402-444-1000
Publication Website: www.omaha.com/sarpy/ralston
Publisher Name: Todd Sears
Publisher Email: todd.sears@owh.com
Publisher Phone: 402-444-1179
Editor Name: Paul Goodsell
Editor Email: goodsell@owh.com
Editor Phone: 402-444-1114
Advertising Executive Name: Eric Mayberry
Advertising Executive Email: eric.mayberry@owh.comA
Advertising Executive Phone: 402-444-1110

TIMES/SUN

Street Address: 604 Fort Crook Rd N
City: Bellevue
State: NE
Postal Code: 68005
Office phone: 402-444-1000
Publication Website: www.omaha.com/sarpy/papillion
Publisher Name: Todd Sears
Publisher Email: todd.sears@owh.com

Publisher Phone: 402-444-1179
Editor Name: Paul Goodsell
Editor Email: goodsell@owh.com
Editor Phone: 402-444-1114
Advertising Executive Name: Eric Mayberry
Advertising Executive Email: eric.mayberry@owh.comA
Advertising Executive Phone: 402-444-1110

BLAIR

ARLINGTON CITIZEN

Corporate/Parent Company: Enterprise Publishing Co.
Street Address: 138 N 16th St
City: Blair
State: NE
Postal Code: 68008
Office phone: (402) 426-2121
Publication Website: http://www.enterprisepub.com/news/arlington/
General E-mail: editor@enterprisepub.com
Publisher Name: Mark Rhoades
Publisher Email: mrhoades@enterprisepub.com
Editor Name: Katie Rohman
Editor Email: editor@enterprisepub.com
Advertising Executive Name: Lynette Hansen
Advertising Executive Email: lhansen@enterprisepub.com
Year Established: 1954
Delivery Methods: Mail
Published Days: Thur
Avg Paid Circ: 575
Audit Company: Sworn/Estimate/Non-Audited
Audit Date: 6 10 2019

CITIZEN

Corporate/Parent Company: Lee Enterprises
Street Address: 138 N. 16th St
City: Blair
State: NE
Postal Code: 68008
Office phone: 402-426-2121
Publication Website: www.enterprisepub.com
General E-mail: editor@enterprisepub.com
Publisher Name: Mark Rhoades
Publisher Email: mrhoades@enterprisepub.com
Editor Name: Leeanna Ellis
Editor Email: editor@enterprisepub.com
Advertising Executive Name: Lynette Hansen
Advertising Executive Email: lhansen@enterprisepub.com

THE PILOT TRIBUNE / ENTERPRISE

Corporate/Parent Company: Enterprise Publishing Co.
Street Address: 138 N 16th St
City: Blair
State: NE
Postal Code: 68008
Office phone: (402) 426-2121
Publication Website: http://www.enterprisepub.com/site/contact.html
General E-mail: editor@enterprisepub.com
Publisher Name: Mark Rhoades
Publisher Email: mrhoades@enterprisepub.com
Editor Name: Katie Rohman
Editor Email: editor@enterprisepub.com
Advertising Executive Name: Lynette Hansen
Advertising Executive Email: lhansen@enterprisepub.com
Year Established: 1869
Delivery Methods: Mail`Newsstand
Own Printing Facility?: Y
Commercial printers?: Y
Mechanical specifications: Type page 11.62 x 21 1/2; E - 6 cols, 2 1/16, 1/6 between; A - 6 cols, 2 1/16, 1/6 between; C - 6 cols, 2 1/16, 1/6 between.
Published Days: Tues`Fri
Published Other: (Tues - Pilot Tribune / Fri - Enterprise)
Avg Paid Circ: 14900

Avg Free Circ: 11700
Audit Company: Sworn/Estimate/Non-Audited
Audit Date: 6 10 2019

WASHINGTON CO. PILOT-TRIBUNE

Corporate/Parent Company: Enterprise Publishing Co.
Street Address: 138 N. 16th St.
City: Blair
State: NE
Postal Code: 68008
Office phone: 402-426-2121
Publication Website: www.enterprisepub.com
Publisher Name: Mark Rhoades
Publisher Email: mrhoades@enterprisepub.com
Editor Name: Leeanna Ellis
Editor Email: editor@enterprisepub.com
Advertising Executive Name: Lynette Hansen
Advertising Executive Email: lhansen@enterprisepub.com

WASHINGTON COUNTY ENTERPRISE

Corporate/Parent Company: Enterprise Publishing Co.
Street Address: 138 N 16th St
City: Blair
State: NE
Postal Code: 68008
Office phone: (402) 426-2121
Publication Website: http://www.enterprisepub.com/site/contact.html
General E-mail: editor@enterprisepub.com
Publisher Name: Mark Rhoades
Publisher Email: mrhoades@enterprisepub.com
Editor Name: Katie Rohman
Editor Email: editor@enterprisepub.com
Advertising Executive Name: Lynette Hansen
Advertising Executive Email: lhansen@enterprisepub.com
Year Established: 1892
Delivery Methods: Mail`Newsstand
Own Printing Facility?: Y
Commercial printers?: Y
Mechanical specifications: Type page 13 x 21 1/2; E - 6 cols, 2 1/16, 1/6 between; A - 6 cols, 2 1/16, 1/6 between; C - 6 cols, 2 1/16, 1/6 between.
Published Days: Fri
Avg Paid Circ: 3300
Avg Free Circ: 8400
Audit Company: Sworn/Estimate/Non-Audited
Audit Date: 6 10 2019

BLOOMFIELD

KNOX COUNTY NEWS

Corporate/Parent Company: Pitzer Digital LLC
Street Address: 110 N Broadway St
City: Bloomfield
State: NE
Postal Code: 68718
Office phone: 402-373-2332
Publication Website: www.myknoxcountynews.com
General E-mail: news@myknoxconews.com
Publisher Name: Carrie Pitzer
Publisher Email: carrie@pitzerdigital.com
Editor Name: Trisha Zach
Editor Email: trisha@mylocalcountynews.com
Advertising Executive Name: Judy Forbes
Advertising Executive Email: jforbes@creightonnews.com
Own Printing Facility?: Y
Commercial printers?: Y
Mechanical specifications: Type page 13 3/4 x 22 3/4; E - 6 cols, 2 1/12, 1/8 between; A - 6 cols, 2 1/12, 1/8 between; C - 6 cols, 2 1/12, 1/8 between.
Published Days: Thur
Avg Paid Circ: 1810
Avg Free Circ: 73
Audit Company: Sworn/Estimate/Non-Audited
Audit Date: 6 10 2019

Non-Daily Newspapers in the U.S.

MONITOR
Corporate/Parent Company: AIM Media
Street Address: 110 N. Broadway
City: Bloomfield
State: NE
Postal Code: 68718
Office phone: 402-373-2332
Publication Website: www.myknoxconews.com
General E-mail: news@myknoxconews.com
Publisher Name: Carrie Pitzer
Publisher Email: carrie@pitzerdigital.com
Advertising Executive Name: Wade Pitzer

BROKEN BOW

CHIEF
Street Address: 305 South 10th Avenue
City: Broken Bow
State: NE
Postal Code: 68822
Office phone: 308-872-2471
Publication Website: www.custercountychief.com
Publisher Name: Donnis Hueftle-Bullock
Publisher Email: publisher@custercountychief.com
Editor Name: Mona Weatherly
Editor Email: chiefnews@custercountychief.com
Advertising Executive Name: Renee Payne
Advertising Executive Email: chiefcomp@custercountychief.com

COLERIDGE

COLERIDGE BLADE
Corporate/Parent Company: Northeast Nebraska News Co.
Street Address: 107 W Broadway St
City: Coleridge
State: NE
Postal Code: 68727
Office phone: (402) 283-4267
Publication Website: https://www.northeastnebraskanews.us/coleridge-blade
Delivery Methods: Mail`Newsstand`Racks
Mechanical specifications: Type page 10 1/4 x 15; E - 5 cols, between; A - 5 cols, 2, 1/8 between.
Published Days: Wed
Avg Paid Circ: 445
Avg Free Circ: 35
Audit Company: Sworn/Estimate/Non-Audited
Audit Date: 6 10 2019

COLUMBUS

BANNER-PRESS
Street Address: 1254 27th Ave
City: Columbus
State: NE
Postal Code: 68601
Office phone: 402-564-2741
Publication Website: columbustelegram.com/community/banner-press
Publisher Name: Vincent Laboy
Publisher Email: vincent.laboy@lee.net
Publisher Phone: 402-563-7501
Editor Name: Matt Lindberg
Editor Email: mlindberg@columbustelegram.com
Editor Phone: 402-563-7502
Advertising Executive Name: Kelly Muchmore
Advertising Executive Email: kmuchmore@columbustelegram.com
Advertising Executive Phone: 402-563-7554
Classified Software: Mactive

DONIPHAN

HERALD
Corporate/Parent Company: Paxton Media Group
Street Address: PO BOX 211
City: Doniphan
State: NE
Postal Code: 68832
Office phone: (402) 845-2937
Publication Website: www.doniphanherald.com
General E-mail: info@doniphanherald.com
Publisher Name: Randy Sadd
Publisher Email: randy.sadd@doniphanherald.com
Editor Name: Christine Hollister
Editor Email: christine.hollister@doniphanherald.com

ELGIN

REVIEW
Corporate/Parent Company: Shaw Media
Street Address: PO Box 359
City: Elgin
State: NE
Postal Code: 68636
Office phone: 402-843-5500
Publication Website: www.elginreview.com
Editor Name: Dennis and Lynell Morgan
Editor Email: elginreview@yahoo.com

FAIRBURY

JOURNAL-NEWS
Street Address: 510 C Street
City: Fairbury
State: NE
Postal Code: 68352
Office phone: (402) 729-6141
Publication Website: www.fairburyjournalnews.com
General E-mail: info@fairburyjournalnews.com
Publisher Name: Timothy Linscott
Publisher Email: Timothylinscott1@gmail.com

FREMONT

JOURNAL
Street Address: 135 N. Main St
City: Fremont
State: NE
Postal Code: 68025
Office phone: 402-721-5000
Publication Website: www.cass-news.com
General E-mail: newsroom@fremonttribune.com
Publisher Name: Vincent Laboy
Publisher Email: vlaboy@fremonttribune.com
Publisher Phone: 402.941.1422
Editor Name: Tony Gray
Editor Email: tgray@fremonttribune.com
Editor Phone: 402.941.1436
Advertising Executive Name: Andrew Zeplin
Advertising Executive Email: azeplin@fremonttribune.com
Advertising Executive Phone: 402-941-1403

GORDON

SHERIDAN CO. JOURNAL-STAR
Street Address: 400 N Main St
City: Gordon
State: NE
Postal Code: 69343
Office phone: 308-282-0118
Publication Website: www.sheridancountyjournalstar.net
General E-mail: scjsnews@gmail.com
Editor Name: Jordan Huether
Editor Email: jordan.scjs@gmail.com
Advertising Executive Name: Rachael Huether
Advertising Executive Email: scjsads@gmail.com

GRAND ISLAND

THE GRAND ISLAND INDEPENDENT
Corporate/Parent Company: Lee Enterprises
Street Address: 422 W 1st St
City: Grand Island
State: NE
Postal Code: 68801-5802
Office phone: (308) 382-1000
Publication Website: https://www.theindependent.com/
General E-mail: circulation@theindependent.com
Delivery Methods: Mail`Newsstand`Carrier`Racks
Own Printing Facility?: Y
Commercial printers?: Y
Mechanical specifications: Type page 10 1/2 x 21 1/2; E - 6 cols, 1 5/8, 1/8 between; A - 6 cols, 1 5/8, 1/8 between; C - 8 cols, 1 3/16, 1/8 between.
Published Days: Mon`Tues`Wed`Thur`Fri`Sat`Sun
Weekday Frequency: m
Saturday Frequency: m
Avg Paid Circ: 13254
Avg Free Circ: 693
Audit Company: CAC
Audit Date: 30 06 2018
Pressroom Equipment: Lines – 10-G/Urbanite double width; Press Drive – 2-Fin/100 h.p.; Folders – 1-G/2:1.;

GRANT

TRIBUNE-SENTINEL
Street Address: 327 Central Ave
City: Grant
State: NE
Postal Code: 69140
Office phone: 308-352-4311
Publication Website: www.granttribune.com
General E-mail: tribads@gpcom.net
Editor Name: Brooke Robertson
Editor Email: granttribune@gpcom.net

GRETNA

GUIDE & NEWS
Street Address: 620 N. Hwy 6
City: Gretna
State: NE
Postal Code: 68028
Office phone: 402-332-3232
Publication Website: www.gretnaguide.com
General E-mail: frontdesk@gretnaguide.com
Publisher Name: Darren Ivy
Publisher Email: darren@gretnaguide.com
Advertising Executive Name: Wendy Doyle
Advertising Executive Email: gretnaguide@gretnaguide.com

HARTINGTON

CEDAR COUNTY NEWS
Corporate/Parent Company: Northeast Nebraska News Co.
Street Address: 102 W Main St, PO Box 977
City: Hartington
State: NE
Postal Code: 68739-3005
Office phone: (402) 254-3997
Publication Website: https://www.hartington.net/
Year Established: 1898
Delivery Methods: Mail`Newsstand`Racks
Own Printing Facility?: Y
Commercial printers?: Y
Published Days: Wed
Avg Paid Circ: 1640
Audit Company: Sworn/Estimate/Non-Audited
Audit Date: 6 10 2019

HEBRON

JOURNAL-REGISTER
Street Address: 318 Lincoln Ave.
City: Hebron
State: NE
Postal Code: 68370
Office phone: 402-768-6602
Publication Website: www.hebronjournalregister.com
General E-mail: hebronjr@windstream.net
Publisher Name: Nancy McGill

HEMINGFORD

LEDGER
Corporate/Parent Company: Gannett
Street Address: 714 Box Butte Avenue
City: Hemingford
State: NE
Postal Code: 69348
Office phone: (308) 487-3334
Publication Website: www.starherald.com/hemingford
General E-mail: news@starherald.com
Publisher Name: Rich Macke
Publisher Email: rich.macke@starherald.com
Editor Name: Kay Bakkehaug
Editor Email: kay.bakkehaug@hemingfordledger.com
Advertising Executive Name: Holly Wade
Advertising Executive Email: holly.wade@hemingfordledger.com

LAUREL

LAUREL ADVOCATE
Corporate/Parent Company: Northeast Nebraska News Co.
Street Address: 106 E 2nd St, PO Box 688
City: Laurel
State: NE
Postal Code: 68745-1990
Office phone: (402) 256-3200
Publication Website: https://www.northeastnebraskanews.us/laurel-advocate
Advertising Executive Name: JoAnn Wiebelhaus
Advertising Executive Phone: (402) 254-3997
Delivery Methods: Mail`Newsstand`Racks
Published Days: Wed
Avg Paid Circ: 950
Audit Company: Sworn/Estimate/Non-Audited
Audit Date: 6 10 2019

LEXINGTON

CLIPPER-HERALD
Street Address: 114 W 5th St
City: Lexington
State: NE
Postal Code: 68850
Office phone: 308-324-5511
Publication Website: lexch.com
General E-mail: news@lexch.com
Editor Name: Benjamin Arrowood
Editor Email: benjamin.arrowood@lexch.com
Editor Phone: 308-217-7036
Advertising Executive Name: Pat Hart Tysdal
Advertising Executive Email: pat.tysdal@lexch.com
Advertising Executive Phone: 308-217-7035

LEXINGTON CLIPPER-HERALD
Corporate/Parent Company: Lee Enterprises
Street Address: P.O. Box 599
City: Lexington
State: NE
Postal Code: 68850-1903
Office phone: (308) 324-5511
Publication Website: https://lexch.com/
General E-mail: news@lexch.com
Publisher Name: Heather Heinemann
Publisher Email: heather.heinemann@lexch.com
Publisher Phone: (308) 217-7040
Advertising Executive Name: Carol Meyer
Advertising Executive Email: carol.meyer@lexch.com
Advertising Executive Phone: (308) 217-7032
Delivery Methods: Mail`Carrier`Racks
Mechanical specifications: Type page 11 1/2 x 21; E - 6 cols, 1 3/16, 1/8 between; A - 6 cols, 1 1/8, 1/8 between; C - 9 cols, 1 3/16, 1/8 between.
Published Days: Wed`Sat

Avg Paid Circ: 3000
Avg Free Circ: 5200
Audit Company: Sworn/Estimate/Non-Audited
Audit Date: 6 10 2019

LINCOLN

REGISTER

Corporate/Parent Company: Gannett
Street Address: 3700 Sheridan Blvd
City: Lincoln
State: NE
Postal Code: 68506
Office phone: 402-488-0090
Publication Website: www.lincolndiocese.org/snr
Editor Name: Mrs. Cathy Blankenau Bender

LIVINGSTON

LIVINGSTON ENTERPRISE

Street Address: 203 S. Church Street
City: Livingston
State: NE
Postal Code: 38570
Office phone: 931-823-1274
Publication Website: www.livingstonenterprise.net

NELIGH

ANTELOPE COUNTY NEWS

Corporate/Parent Company: Pitzer Digital LLC
Street Address: 314 M Street
City: Neligh
State: NE
Postal Code: 68756
Office phone: 402-887-4000
Publication Website: www.antelopecountynews.com
General E-mail: news@myantelopecountynews.com
Publisher Name: Carrie Pitzer
Publisher Email: news@myantelopecountynews.com
Editor Name: Jenny Higgins
Editor Email: news@myantelopecountynews.com
Classified Software: Mactive

RECORD-NEWS

Corporate/Parent Company: Pitzer Digital LLC
Street Address: 419 Main Street
City: Neligh
State: NE
Postal Code: 68756
Office phone: 402-887-4000
Publication Website: www.nelighnews.com/clearwater_ewing
General E-mail: news@myantelopecountynews.com
Editor Name: Carrie Pitzer
Editor Email: news@myantelopecountynews.com

NORTH BEND

EAGLE

Corporate/Parent Company: Lee Enterprises
Street Address: 730 Main Street
City: North Bend
State: NE
Postal Code: 68649
Office phone: 402-652-8312
Publication Website: www.northbendeagle.com
Editor Name: Nathan Arneal
Editor Email: eagleads@gmail.com
Classified Software: Mactive

NORTH PLATTE

BULLETIN

Corporate/Parent Company: Gannett
Street Address: 1300 E 4th St F
City: North Platte
State: NE
Postal Code: 69101
Office phone: 308-696-0052
Publication Website: www.northplattebulletin.com
General E-mail: adcopy@northplattebulletin.com
Editor Name: George Lauby
Editor Email: george@northplattebulletin.com

THE NORTH PLATTE TELEGRAPH

Corporate/Parent Company: Lee Enterprises
Street Address: 621 N Chestnut St, P.O. Box 370
City: North Platte
State: NE
Postal Code: 69103-4131
Office phone: (308) 532-6000
Publication Website: https://www.nptelegraph.com/
General E-mail: dee.klein@nptelegraph.com
Publisher Name: Dee Klein
Publisher Email: dee.klein@nptelegraph.com
Publisher Phone: (308) 535-4708
Editor Name: Joan von Kampen
Editor Email: joan.vonkampen@nptelegraph.com
Editor Phone: (308) 535-4707
Year Established: 1881
Mechanical specifications: Type page 11 63/100 x 21 3/4; E - 6 cols, 1 5/6, 1/8 between; A - 6 cols, 1 5/6, 1/8 between; C - 9 cols, 1 5/6, 1/16 between.
Published Days: Tues`Wed`Thur`Fri`Sat`Sun
Weekday Frequency: m
Saturday Frequency: m
Avg Paid Circ: 6655
Avg Free Circ: 442
Audit Company: CAC
Audit Date: 30 06 2018
Pressroom Equipment: Lines – 9-HI/V-22 1965.;

OAKLAND

LYONS MIRROR-SUN

Corporate/Parent Company: Enterprise Publishing Co.
Street Address: 217 N Oakland Ave
City: Oakland
State: NE
Postal Code: 68045
Office phone: (402) 685-5624
Publication Website: http://enterprisepub.biz/publications/lyons-mirror-sun/
General E-mail: editorcurt@gmail.com
Publisher Name: Mark Rhoades
Publisher Email: mrhoades@enterprisepub.com
Editor Email: editorcurt@gmail.com
Advertising Executive Name: Paige Anderson
Advertising Executive Email: paige@enterprisepub.com
Advertising Executive Phone: (402) 870-2230
Delivery Methods: Mail`Newsstand`Racks
Mechanical specifications: Type page 13 x 21; E - 3 cols, 4 1/3, 1/6 between; A - 6 cols, 2 1/12, 1/6 between; C - 6 cols, 2 1/12, 1/6 between.
Published Days: Thur
Avg Paid Circ: 900
Avg Free Circ: 30
Audit Company: Sworn/Estimate/Non-Audited
Audit Date: 6 10 2019

OAKLAND INDEPENDENT

Corporate/Parent Company: Enterprise Publishing Co.
Street Address: 217 N Oakland Ave
City: Oakland
State: NE
Postal Code: 68045
Office phone: (402) 685-5624
Publication Website: http://enterprisepub.biz/publications/oakland-independent/
General E-mail: editorcurt@gmail.com
Publisher Name: Mark Rhoades
Publisher Email: mrhoades@enterprisepub.com
Editor Email: editorcurt@gmail.com
Advertising Executive Name: Paige Anderson
Advertising Executive Email: paige@enterprisepub.com
Advertising Executive Phone: (402) 870-2230
Delivery Methods: Mail`Newsstand`Racks
Published Days: Thur
Audit Company: Sworn/Estimate/Non-Audited
Audit Date: 6 10 2019

OMAHA

MIDLANDS NEWSPAPERS, INC.

Corporate/Parent Company: Lee Enterprises
Street Address: 1314 Douglas St.
City: Omaha
State: NE
Postal Code: 68102
Office phone: (402) 444-1233
Publication Website: https://www.omaha.com/contact-us/

ORD

QUIZ

Street Address: 305 South 16 St.
City: Ord
State: NE
Postal Code: 68862
Office phone: 308-728-3261
Publication Website: www.theordquiz.com/about
General E-mail: quizmain@frontier.com
Publisher Phone: Lacy Griffith
Editor Name: quizeditor@frontier.com

OSMOND

THE OSMOND REPUBLICAN

Corporate/Parent Company: Northeast Nebraska News Co.
Street Address: 340 N State St, PO Box 428
City: Osmond
State: NE
Postal Code: 68765-5723
Office phone: (402) 748-3666
Publication Website: https://www.northeastnebraskanews.us/osmond-republican
General E-mail: osmondnews@abbnebraska.com
Advertising Executive Name: JoAnn Wiebelhaus
Advertising Executive Phone: (402) 254-3997
Year Established: 1890
Delivery Methods: Mail`Newsstand`Racks
Own Printing Facility?: Y
Commercial printers?: Y
Published Days: Wed
Avg Paid Circ: 510
Audit Company: Sworn/Estimate/Non-Audited
Audit Date: 6 10 2019

PONCA

NEBRRASKA JOURNAL-LEADER

Street Address: 110 N East St
City: Ponca
State: NE
Postal Code: 68770
Office phone: 402-755-2203
Publication Website: www.nebnjl.com
General E-mail: deditor@gpcom.net

RANDOLPH

THE RANDOLPH TIMES

Corporate/Parent Company: Northeast Nebraska News Co.
Street Address: 121 W Broadway St, PO Box 97
City: Randolph
State: NE
Postal Code: 68771-2516
Office phone: (402) 337-0488
Publication Website: https://www.northeastnebraskanews.us/randolph-times
Advertising Executive Name: JoAnn Wiebelhaus
Advertising Executive Phone: (402) 254-3997
Delivery Methods: Mail`Newsstand`Racks
Published Days: Wed
Audit Company: Sworn/Estimate/Non-Audited
Audit Date: 6 10 2019

SCOTTSBLUFF

COURIER

Corporate/Parent Company: Lee Enterprises
Street Address: 1405 Broadway
City: Scottsbluff
State: NE
Postal Code: 69361
Office phone: (308) 436-2222
Publication Website: www.geringcourier.com
General E-mail: class@starherald.com
Editor Name: Lauren Brant
Editor Email: lauren.brant@starherald.com

GERING COURIER

Street Address: 1405 Broadway
City: Scottsbluff
State: NE
Postal Code: 69361-3151
Office phone: (308) 436-2222
Publication Website: https://www.starherald.com/gering/
General E-mail: circ@starherald.com
Publisher Name: Rich Macke
Publisher Email: rich.macke@starherald.com
Editor Name: Brad Staman
Editor Email: brad.staman@starherald.com
Advertising Executive Name: Russ Todd
Advertising Executive Email: russ.todd@starherald.com
Year Established: 1887
Delivery Methods: Mail`Newsstand`Racks
Own Printing Facility?: Y
Commercial printers?: Y
Published Days: Thur
Avg Paid Circ: 2118
Audit Company: Sworn/Estimate/Non-Audited
Audit Date: 6 10 2019

SEWARD

SEWARD COUNTY CONNECTION

Corporate/Parent Company: Enterprise Publishing Co.
Street Address: 129 S 6th St
City: Seward
State: NE
Postal Code: 68434-2003
Office phone: (402) 643-3676
Publication Website: http://sewardindependent.com/
General E-mail: scinews@sewardindependent.com
Publisher Name: Kevin L. Zadina
Publisher Email: kevinzadina@sewardindependent.com
Editor Name: Emily Hemphill
Editor Email: emily@sewardindependent.com
Advertising Executive Name: Nichole Javorsky
Advertising Executive Email: nichole@sewardindependent.com
Mailroom Equipment: Counter Stackers – 1-ld/440, 1-ld/Marathoner; Inserters & Stuffers – KM Rotary 14/Pocket; Tying Machines – 2-MLN/2A; Address Machine –

1-KAN/550.;
Buisness Equipment: HP
Buisness Software: APT
Classified Equipment: Hardware – APP/Power HP; Printers – APP/Mac LaserWriter;
Classified Software: APT

SHELTON

THE SHELTON CLIPPER

Corporate/Parent Company: Clipper Publishing, Inc.
Street Address: 113 C St
City: Shelton
State: NE
Postal Code: 68876
Office phone: 308-647-5158
Publication Website: www.clipperpubco.com
General E-mail: info@clipperpubco.com
Publisher Name: Steve Glenn
Publisher Email: sglenn@clipperpubco.com
Editor Name: Barb Berglund
Editor Email: bberglund@clipperpubco.com
Mailroom Equipment: Counter Stackers – TMSI; Inserters & Stuffers – 24-HI/6; Tying Machines – MLN/MLEE; Address Machine – Miller/Bevco/1 up Labeler.;
Buisness Equipment: Gateway, 8-Gateway/PS-100, 6-E/3200
Classified Equipment: Hardware – 2-Gateway/GP6-350, 1-Gateway/GP6-333, 1-Epson/Perfection 1200u Flatbed Scanner; Printers – 6-HP;
Classified Software: ACT.

SUPERIOR

SUPERIOR EXPRESS

Corporate/Parent Company: Superior Publishing Company, Inc.
Street Address: P.O. Box 408
City: Superior
State: NE
Postal Code: 68978
Office phone: (402) 879-3291
Publication Website: www.superiorne.com
Editor Name: Bill Blauvelt
Editor Email: tse@superiorne.com
Year Established: 1900
Delivery Methods: Mail`Newsstand`Racks
Own Printing Facility?: Y
Commercial printers?: Y
Mechanical specifications: Type page 15 x 21; E - 7 cols, 2, 1/6 between; A - 7 cols, 2, 1/6 between; C - 7 cols, 2, 1/6 between.
Published Days: Thur
Avg Paid Circ: 2900
Avg Free Circ: 116
Audit Company: Sworn/Estimate/Non-Audited
Audit Date: 6 10 2019

THE SUPERIOR EXPRESS

Corporate/Parent Company: Superior Publishing Co; Superior Publishing Company
Street Address: 148 E 3rd St
City: Superior
State: NE
Postal Code: 68978-1705
Office phone: (402) 879-3291
Publication Website: https://www.superiorne.com/
General E-mail: tse@superiorne.com
Year Established: 1900
Delivery Methods: Mail`Newsstand`Racks
Own Printing Facility?: Y
Commercial printers?: Y
Mechanical specifications: Type page 15 x 21; E - 7 cols, 2, 1/6 between; A - 7 cols, 2, 1/6 between; C - 7 cols, 2, 1/6 between.
Published Days: Thur
Avg Paid Circ: 2900
Avg Free Circ: 116
Audit Company: Sworn/Estimate/Non-Audited
Audit Date: 6 10 2019

SYRACUSE

JOURNAL-DEMOCRAT

Street Address: 123 W. 17th St.
City: Syracuse
State: NE
Postal Code: 68446
Office phone: 402-269-2135
Publication Website: www.ncnewspress.com
Editor Name: Kirt Manion
Editor Email: kmanion@ncnewspress.com
Editor Phone: 402-873-3334
Advertising Executive Name: Karisa Bryan
Advertising Executive Email: kbryan@ncnewspress.com
Advertising Executive Phone: 402-209-8020

TECUMSEH

CHIEFTAIN

Street Address: 241 Clay St.
City: Tecumseh
State: NE
Postal Code: 68450
Office phone: 402-335-3394
Publication Website: www.tecumsehchieftain.com
General E-mail: locals@tecumsehchieftain.com
Advertising Executive Name: Elaine Karel
Advertising Executive Email: ads@tecumsehchieftain.com
Advertising Executive Phone: 402-335-3394

WAHOO

GAZETTE

Corporate/Parent Company: Adams Publishing Group
Street Address: 564 N. Broadway St.
City: Wahoo
State: NE
Postal Code: 68066
Office phone: 402-944-3397
Publication Website: www.wahoo-ashland-waverly.com/ashland
General E-mail: news@ashland-gazette.com
Editor Name: Suzi Nelson
Editor Email: suzi.nelson@ashland-gazette.com
Editor Phone: 402-277-5512
Advertising Executive Name: Dawn Roth
Advertising Executive Email: dawn.roth@wahoonewspaper.com
Advertising Executive Phone: 402-277-5500

THE ASHLAND GAZETTE

Street Address: 564 N. Broadway St.
City: Wahoo
State: NE
Postal Code: 68066
Office phone: (402) 944-3397
Publication Website: https://www.wahoo-ashland-waverly.com/ashland/site/contact.html
General E-mail: amy.prohaska@wahoonewspaper.com
Publisher Name: Paul Swanson
Publisher Email: paul.swanson@owh.com
Publisher Phone: (402) 444-1248
Editor Name: Suzi Nelson
Editor Email: lisa.brichacek@wahoonewspaper.com
Editor Phone: (402) 443-4162
Advertising Executive Name: Amy Prohaska
Advertising Executive Email: amy.prohaska@wahoonewspaper.com
Advertising Executive Phone: (402) 277-5503
Year Established: 1879
Delivery Methods: Mail`Newsstand`Racks
Published Days: Thur
Avg Paid Circ: 1800
Audit Company: Sworn/Estimate/Non-Audited
Audit Date: 6 10 2019

WAHOO NEWSPAPER

Corporate/Parent Company: Lee Enterprises
Street Address: 564 N Broadway St
City: Wahoo
State: NE
Postal Code: 68066-1653
Office phone: (402) 443-4162
Publication Website: https://www.wahoo-ashland-waverly.com/
General E-mail: advertising@wahoonewspaper.com
Publisher Name: Paul Swanson
Publisher Email: paul.swanson@owh.com
Publisher Phone: (402) 444-1248
Editor Name: Suzi Nelson
Editor Email: lisa.brichacek@wahoonewspaper.com
Editor Phone: (402) 443-4162
Advertising Executive Email: advertising@wahoonewspaper.com
Year Established: 1886
Delivery Methods: Mail`Newsstand`Carrier`Racks
Own Printing Facility?: N
Commercial printers?: Y
Mechanical specifications: Type page 11 5/8 x 21 1/4; E - 6 cols, between; A - 8 cols, 1 1/3, between; C - 8 cols, 1 1/3, between.
Published Days: Thur
Avg Paid Circ: 2850
Audit Company: Sworn/Estimate/Non-Audited
Audit Date: 6 10 2019

WAUSA

THE WAUSA GAZETTE

Corporate/Parent Company: Northeast Nebraska News Co.
Street Address: 603 E Broadway, PO Box G,
City: Wausa
State: NE
Postal Code: 68586-1558
Office phone: (402) 586-2661
Publication Website: https://www.northeastnebraskanews.us/wausa-gazette
Advertising Executive Name: JoAnn Wiebelhaus
Advertising Executive Phone: (402) 254-3997
Delivery Methods: Mail`Newsstand`Racks
Own Printing Facility?: Y
Commercial printers?: Y
Mechanical specifications: Type page 13 1/4 x 21 1/2; E - 6 cols, 2, 1/6 between; A - 6 cols, 2, 1/6 between; C - 6 cols, 2, 1/6 between.
Published Days: Thur
Avg Paid Circ: 963
Avg Free Circ: 2
Audit Company: Sworn/Estimate/Non-Audited
Audit Date: 6 10 2019

WAVERLY

THE WAVERLY NEWS

Corporate/Parent Company: Lee Enterprises
Street Address: 14541 Castlewood St, Suite 300 P.O. Box 100
City: Waverly
State: NE
Postal Code: 68462-1526
Office phone: (402) 786-2344
Publication Website: https://www.wahoo-ashland-waverly.com/waverly/
General E-mail: advertising@newswaverly.com
Publisher Name: Paul Swanson
Publisher Email: paul.swanson@owh.com
Publisher Phone: (402) 444-1248
Editor Name: Suzi Nelson
Editor Email: lisa.brichacek@wahoonewspaper.com
Editor Phone: (402) 443-4162
Advertising Executive Email: advertising@newswaverly.com
Delivery Methods: Mail
Published Days: Thur
Avg Paid Circ: 925
Audit Company: Sworn/Estimate/Non-Audited
Audit Date: 6 10 2019

WOOD RIVER

SUNBEAM

Corporate/Parent Company: Clipper Publishing, Inc
Street Address: 113 C St., Shelton
City: Wood River
State: NE
Postal Code: 68876
Office phone: 308-647-5158
Publication Website: www.clipperpubco.com
Publisher Name: Steve Glenn
Publisher Email: sglenn@clipperpubco.com
Editor Name: Barb Berglund
Editor Email: bberglund@clipperpubco.com

WYMORE

ARBOR STATE

Street Address: PO Box 327
City: Wymore
State: NE
Postal Code: 68466
Office phone: 402-645-3344
Publication Website: www.wymorearborstate.com
General E-mail: wymorearborstate@gmail.com

YORK

YORK NEWS-TIMES

Corporate/Parent Company: Lee Enterprises
Street Address: 327 N Platte Ave
City: York
State: NE
Postal Code: 68467-3547
Office phone: (402) 362-4478
Publication Website: https://www.yorknewstimes.com/
General E-mail: carrie.colburn@yorknewstimes.com
Publisher Name: Carrie Colburn
Publisher Email: carrie.colburn@yorknewstimes.com
Publisher Phone: (402) 204-7001
Editor Name: Melanie Wilkinson
Editor Email: melanie.wilkinson@yorknewstimes.com
Editor Phone: (402) 204-7018
Advertising Executive Name: Maddie Elder
Advertising Executive Email: maddie.elder@yorknewstimes.com
Advertising Executive Phone: (402) 204-7010
Year Established: 1867
Delivery Methods: Mail`Newsstand`Carrier`Racks
Own Printing Facility?: Y
Commercial printers?: N
Mechanical specifications: Type page 13 x 21; E - 6 cols, 2 1/12, 1/8 between; A - 6 cols, 2 1/12, 1/8 between; C - 6 cols, 2 1/12, 1/8 between.
Published Days: Tues`Wed`Thur`Fri`Sat
Weekday Frequency: m
Saturday Frequency: m
Avg Paid Circ: 3589
Audit Company: Sworn/Estimate/Non-Audited
Audit Date: 7 12 2019

NEW HAMPSHIRE

BERLIN

THE BERLIN SUN

Corporate/Parent Company: Country News Club
Street Address: 164 Main Street
City: Berlin
State: NH
Postal Code: 0 3570
Office phone: (603) 752-5858
Publication Website: www.conwaydailysun.com/berlin_sun

BOW

BOW TIMES
Street Address: 40 Stone Sled Lane
City: Bow
State: NH
Postal Code: 0 3304
Publication Website: thebowtimes.com/news

CLAREMONT

E-TICKER NEWS OF CLAREMONT
Street Address: 6 Osgood Ave.
City: Claremont
State: NH
Postal Code: 0 3743
Office phone: 603-542-7319
Publication Website: www.etickernewsofclaremont.com
General E-mail: etickernews@gmail.com

COLEBROOK

COLEBROOK NEWS AND SENTINEL
Street Address: 6 Bridge Street, PO Box 39
City: Colebrook
State: NH
Postal Code: 0 3576
Office phone: 603-237-5501
Publication Website: www.colbsent.com

LANCASTER

CARROLL COUNTY INDEPENDENT
Corporate/Parent Company: Salmon Press
Street Address: 79 Main Street
City: Lancaster
State: NH
Postal Code: 3584
Office phone: (603) 788-4939
Publication Website: http://www.newhampshirelakesandmountains.com/
General E-mail: cathy@salmonpress.news

THE BERLIN REPORTER
Corporate/Parent Company: Salmon Press
Street Address: 79 Main St
City: Lancaster
State: NH
Postal Code: 03584-3027
Office phone: (603) 788-4939
Publication Website: http://www.newhampshirelakesandmountains.com/
General E-mail: cathy@salmonpress.news

THE COOS COUNTY DEMOCRAT
Corporate/Parent Company: Salmon Press
Street Address: 79 Main St
City: Lancaster
State: NH
Postal Code: 03584-3027
Office phone: (603) 788-4939
Publication Website: http://www.newhampshirelakesandmountains.com/
General E-mail: cathy@salmonpress.news

MEREDITH

GRANITE STATE NEWS
Corporate/Parent Company: Salmon Press
Street Address: 5 Water Street
City: Meredith

State: NH
Postal Code: 3253
Office phone: (603) 279-4516
Publication Website: http://www.newhampshirelakesandmountains.com/
General E-mail: cathy@salmonpress.news

LITTLETON COURIER
Corporate/Parent Company: Salmon Press
Street Address: 5 Water St.
City: Meredith
State: NH
Postal Code: 3253
Office phone: (603) 279-4516
Publication Website: http://www.newhampshirelakesandmountains.com/
General E-mail: tracy@salmonpress.news

MEREDITH NEWS
Corporate/Parent Company: Salmon Press
Street Address: 5 Water St
City: Meredith
State: NH
Postal Code: 03253-6233
Office phone: (603) 279-4516
Publication Website: http://www.newhampshirelakesandmountains.com/
General E-mail: lori@salmonpress.news

THE BAYSIDER
Corporate/Parent Company: Salmon Press
Street Address: 5 Water Street
City: Meredith
State: NH
Postal Code: 3253
Office phone: (603) 279-4516
Publication Website: http://www.newhampshirelakesandmountains.com/
General E-mail: cathy@salmonpress.news

THE GILFORD STEAMER
Corporate/Parent Company: Salmon Press
Street Address: 5 Water St
City: Meredith
State: NH
Postal Code: 03253-6233
Office phone: (603) 279-4516
Publication Website: http://www.newhampshirelakesandmountains.com/
General E-mail: lori@salmonpress.news

THE RECORD-ENTERPRISE (OOB)
Corporate/Parent Company: Salmon Press
Street Address: 5 Water St.
City: Meredith
State: NH
Postal Code: 03253-6233
Office phone: (603) 279-4516
Publication Website: http://www.newhampshirelakesandmountains.com/
General E-mail: tracy@salmonpress.news

WINNISQUAM ECHO
Corporate/Parent Company: Salmon Press
Street Address: 5 Water St.
City: Meredith
State: NH
Postal Code: 03253-6233
Office phone: (603) 279-4516

Publication Website: http://www.newhampshirelakesandmountains.com/
General E-mail: tracy@salmonpress.news

NEW JERSEY

BAYONNE

BAYONNE COMMUNITY NEWS
Corporate/Parent Company: Newspaper Media Group
Street Address: 447 Broadway
City: Bayonne
State: NJ
Postal Code: 07002-3623
Office phone: (201) 798-7800
Publication Website: https://hudsonreporter.com/
General E-mail: info@hudsonreporter.com
Editor Name: Gene Ritchings
Editor Email: gener@hudsonreporter.com
Editor Phone: (201) 798-7800, ext : 610
Advertising Executive Name: Tish Kraszyk
Advertising Executive Email: tishk@hudsonreporter.com
Advertising Executive Phone: (201) 798-7800, ext : 601

THE HOBOKEN REPORTER
Corporate/Parent Company: Newspaper Media Group
Street Address: 447 Broadway
City: Bayonne
State: NJ
Postal Code: 07002-3623
Office phone: (201) 798-7800
Publication Website: https://hudsonreporter.com/
General E-mail: info@hudsonreporter.com
Editor Name: Gene Ritchings
Editor Email: gener@hudsonreporter.com
Editor Phone: (201) 798-7800, ext : 610
Advertising Executive Name: Tish Kraszyk
Advertising Executive Email: tishk@hudsonreporter.com
Advertising Executive Phone: (201) 798-7800, ext : 601

THE NORTH BERGEN REPORTER
Corporate/Parent Company: Newspaper Media Group
Street Address: 447 Broadway
City: Bayonne
State: NJ
Postal Code: 07002-3623
Office phone: (201) 798-7800
Publication Website: https://hudsonreporter.com/
General E-mail: info@hudsonreporter.com
Editor Name: Gene Ritchings
Editor Email: gener@hudsonreporter.com
Editor Phone: (201) 798-7800, ext : 610
Advertising Executive Name: Tish Kraszyk
Advertising Executive Email: tishk@hudsonreporter.com
Advertising Executive Phone: (201) 798-7800, ext : 601

THE WEEHAWKEN REPORTER
Corporate/Parent Company: Newspaper Media Group
Street Address: 447 Broadway
City: Bayonne
State: NJ

Postal Code: 07002-3623
Office phone: (201) 798-7800
Publication Website: https://hudsonreporter.com/
General E-mail: info@hudsonreporter.com
Editor Name: Gene Ritchings
Editor Email: gener@hudsonreporter.com
Editor Phone: (201) 798-7800, ext : 610
Advertising Executive Name: Tish Kraszyk
Advertising Executive Email: tishk@hudsonreporter.com
Advertising Executive Phone: (201) 798-7800, ext : 601

CHERRY HILL

LOWER BUCKS TIMES
Corporate/Parent Company: Newspaper Media Group
Street Address: Two Executive Campus, Suite 135
City: Cherry Hill
State: NJ
Postal Code: 0 8002
Office phone: 856-779-3800
Publication Website: lowerbuckstimes.com
General E-mail: info@lowerbuckstimes.com
Editor Name: Tom Waring
Editor Email: TWaring@bsmphilly.com
Advertising Executive Name: Kevin Stuski
Advertising Executive Email: kstuski@bsmphilly.com

EGG HARBOR TWP.

THE CURRENT OF HAMILTON TOWNSHIP & EGG HARBOR CITY
Street Address: 3129 Fire Road, Suite 2
City: Egg Harbor Twp.
State: NJ
Postal Code: 0 8234
Office phone: 609-383-8994
Publication Website: www.shorenewstoday.com/hamilton township/
Publisher Name: Mark L. Blum
Publisher Email: MBlum@pressofac.com
Publisher Phone: 609-272-7110
Editor Name: Buzz Keough
Editor Email: WKeough@pressofac.com
Editor Phone: 609-272-7238
Advertising Executive Name: Michelle Rice
Advertising Executive Email: MRice@pressofac.com
Advertising Executive Phone: 609-272-7100

FAIR LAWN

THE RIDGEWOOD NEWS
Corporate/Parent Company: Gannett Company Inc.
Street Address: " 12-38 River Road"
City: Fair Lawn
State: NJ
Postal Code: 0 7410
Office phone: 201-791-8994
Publication Website: www.northjersey.com
Editor Name: Daniel Sforza
Editor Email: sforza@northjersey.com

FLANDERS

BLACK RIVER NEWS
Corporate/Parent Company: New View Media Group LLC
Street Address: 5 Vista Dr
City: Flanders
State: NJ
Postal Code: 7836
Office phone: (973) 252-9889
Publication Website: https://www.mypaperonline.com/
General E-mail: joe@mylifepublications.com

FLEMINGTON

THE CITIZEN OF MORRIS COUNTY

Corporate/Parent Company: Recorder Publishing Company
Street Address: 200 Route 31, 2nd Fl.
City: Flemington
State: NJ
Postal Code: 0 8822
Office phone: 908-782-4747
Publication Website: www.denvillecitizen.com
General E-mail: ourtown@lehighvalleylive.com
Editor Name: Kevin Shea
Editor Email: kshea@njadvancemedia.com
Editor Phone: 609-819-2390
Advertising Executive Name: Michael Mancuso
Advertising Executive Email: mmancuso@njadvancemedia.com
Advertising Executive Phone: 609-989-5710

THE WARREN REPORTER

Corporate/Parent Company: Advance Newspapers
Street Address: 200 Route 31, 2nd Fl.
City: Flemington
State: NJ
Postal Code: 0 8822
Office phone: 908-782-4747
Publication Website: www.nj.com
Editor Name: Kevin Shea
Editor Email: kshea@njadvancemedia.com
Editor Phone: 609-819-2390
Advertising Executive Name: Michael Mancuso
Advertising Executive Email: mmancuso@njadvancemedia.com
Advertising Executive Phone: 609-989-5710

HASBROUCK HEIGHTS

THE GAZETTE NEWSPAPER

Street Address: 345 Boulevard
City: Hasbrouck Heights
State: NJ
Postal Code: 7604
Office phone: 201-288-8656
Publication Website: www.the-gazette-newspaper.com
General E-mail: fritz@hasbrouck-heights.com

HOBOKEN

WEST NEW YORK/UNION CITY REPORTER

Corporate/Parent Company: Newspaper Media Group
Street Address: 1400 Washington St
City: Hoboken
State: NJ
Postal Code: 07030-9402
Office phone: (201) 798-7800
Publication Website: https://hudsonreporter.com/
General E-mail: info@hudsonreporter.com
Editor Name: Gene Ritchings
Editor Email: gener@hudsonreporter.com
Editor Phone: (201) 798-7800, ext : 610
Advertising Executive Name: Tish Kraszyk
Advertising Executive Email: tishk@hudsonreporter.com
Advertising Executive Phone: (201) 798-7800, ext : 601

MARMORA

THE CAPE MAY GAZETTE

Street Address: 507 S. Shore Road
City: Marmora
State: NJ
Postal Code: 0 8223
Office phone: 609-624-8900
Publication Website: www.shorenewstoday.com/cape may
Publisher Name: Mark L. Blum
Publisher Email: MBlum@pressofac.com
Publisher Phone: 609-272-7110
Editor Name: Buzz Keough
Editor Email: WKeough@pressofac.com
Editor Phone: 609-272-7238
Advertising Executive Name: Michelle Rice
Advertising Executive Email: MRice@pressofac.com
Advertising Executive Phone: 609-272-7100

THE OCEAN CITY GAZETTE

Street Address: 507 S. Shore Road
City: Marmora
State: NJ
Postal Code: 0 8223
Office phone: 609-624-8900
Publication Website: www.shorenewstoday.com/ocean city
Publisher Name: Mark L. Blum
Publisher Email: MBlum@pressofac.com
Publisher Phone: 609-272-7110
Editor Name: Buzz Keough
Editor Email: WKeough@pressofac.com
Editor Phone: 609-272-7238
Advertising Executive Name: Michelle Rice
Advertising Executive Email: MRice@pressofac.com
Advertising Executive Phone: 609-272-7100

MONTCLAIR

MONTCLAIR DISPATCH

Street Address: 423 Bloomfield Ave
City: Montclair
State: NJ
Postal Code: 7042
Office phone: 973-509-8861
Publication Website: Montclair Dispatch
General E-mail: Newsdesk@MontclairDispatch.com
Publisher Name: Scott F. Kennedy
Editor Name: Catherine Baxter

OCEAN CITY

THE OCEAN STAR

Corporate/Parent Company: Coast Star, Inc
Street Address: 801 Asbury Ave., Suite 310, P.O. Box 238
City: Ocean City
State: NJ
Postal Code: 0 8226
Office phone: 609-399-5411
Publication Website: www.starnewsgroup.com
General E-mail: ocsentinelfb@gmail.com
Editor Name: David Nahan

PLEASANTVILLE

THE CURRENT DOWNBEACH-VENTNOR, MARGATE AND LONGPORT

City: Pleasantville
State: NJ
Office phone: 877-773-7730
Publication Website: www.shorenewstoday.com/downbeach
General E-mail: SubscriberServices@pressofac.com
Publisher Name: Mark L. Blum
Publisher Email: MBlum@pressofac.com
Publisher Phone: 609-272-7116
Editor Name: Buzz Keough
Editor Email: bkeough@pressofac.com
Editor Phone: 609-272-7244
Advertising Executive Name: Kevin Post
Advertising Executive Email: kpost@pressofac.com
Advertising Executive Phone: 609-272-7256

THE CURRENT OF ABSECON AND PLEASANTVILLE

City: Pleasantville
State: NJ
Office phone: 877-773-7725
Publication Website: www.shorenewstoday.com/pleasantville absecon
General E-mail: SubscriberServices@pressofac.com
Publisher Name: Mark L. Blum
Publisher Email: MBlum@pressofac.com
Publisher Phone: 609-272-7111
Editor Name: Buzz Keough
Editor Email: bkeough@pressofac.com
Editor Phone: 609-272-7239
Advertising Executive Name: Kevin Post
Advertising Executive Email: kpost@pressofac.com
Advertising Executive Phone: 609-272-7251

THE CURRENT OF EGG HARBOR TOWNSHIP

City: Pleasantville
State: NJ
Office phone: 877-773-7726
Publication Website: www.shorenewstoday.com/egg harbor township
General E-mail: SubscriberServices@pressofac.com
Publisher Name: Mark L. Blum
Publisher Email: MBlum@pressofac.com
Publisher Phone: 609-272-7112
Editor Name: Buzz Keough
Editor Email: bkeough@pressofac.com
Editor Phone: 609-272-7240
Advertising Executive Name: Kevin Post
Advertising Executive Email: kpost@pressofac.com
Advertising Executive Phone: 609-272-7252

THE CURRENT OF GALLOWAY, EGG HARBOR CITY AND PORT REPUBLIC

City: Pleasantville
State: NJ
Office phone: 877-773-7727
Publication Website: www.shorenewstoday.com/galloway township/
General E-mail: SubscriberServices@pressofac.com
Publisher Name: Mark L. Blum
Publisher Email: MBlum@pressofac.com
Publisher Phone: 609-272-7113
Editor Name: Buzz Keough
Editor Email: bkeough@pressofac.com
Editor Phone: 609-272-7241
Advertising Executive Name: Kevin Post
Advertising Executive Email: kpost@pressofac.com
Advertising Executive Phone: 609-272-7253

THE CURRENT OF LINWOOD, NORTHFIELD AND SOMERS POINT

City: Pleasantville
State: NJ
Office phone: 877-773-7729
Publication Website: www.shorenewstoday.com/mainland
General E-mail: SubscriberServices@pressofac.com
Publisher Name: Mark L. Blum
Publisher Email: MBlum@pressofac.com
Publisher Phone: 609-272-7115
Editor Name: Buzz Keough
Editor Email: bkeough@pressofac.com
Editor Phone: 609-272-7243
Advertising Executive Name: Kevin Post
Advertising Executive Email: kpost@pressofac.com
Advertising Executive Phone: 609-272-7255

THE MIDDLE TOWNSHIP GAZETTE

City: Pleasantville
State: NJ
Office phone: 877-773-7731
Publication Website: www.shorenewstoday.com/middle township/
General E-mail: SubscriberServices@pressofac.com
Publisher Name: Mark L. Blum
Publisher Email: MBlum@pressofac.com
Publisher Phone: 609-272-7117
Editor Name: Buzz Keough
Editor Email: bkeough@pressofac.com
Editor Phone: 609-272-7245
Advertising Executive Name: Kevin Post
Advertising Executive Email: kpost@pressofac.com
Advertising Executive Phone: 609-272-7257
Total Circulation: 20619

THE UPPER TOWNSHIP GAZETTE

City: Pleasantville
State: NJ
Office phone: 877-773-7733
Publication Website: www.shorenewstoday.com/upper township
General E-mail: SubscriberServices@pressofac.com
Publisher Name: Mark L. Blum
Publisher Email: MBlum@pressofac.com
Publisher Phone: 609-272-7119
Editor Name: Buzz Keough
Editor Email: bkeough@pressofac.com
Editor Phone: 609-272-7247
Advertising Executive Name: Kevin Post
Advertising Executive Email: kpost@pressofac.com
Advertising Executive Phone: 609-272-7259

POINT PLEASANT BEACH

THE SANDPAPER

Corporate/Parent Company: The SandPaper, Inc.
Street Address: 421 River Ave.
City: Point Pleasant Beach
State: NJ
Postal Code: 0 8742
Office phone: 732-899-7606
Publication Website: www.thesandpaper.net
General E-mail: info@theoceanstar.com
Publisher Name: Alison Manser Ertl
Publisher Email: gm@starnewsgroup.com
Publisher Phone: (732) 223-0076, ext. 38
Editor Name: Gloria Stravelli
Editor Email: gstravelli@theoceanstar.com
Editor Phone: (732) 899-7606, ext. 112
Advertising Executive Name: Margaret Scheiderman
Advertising Executive Email: sales@theoceanstar.com
Advertising Executive Phone: (732) 223-0076, ext. 35

RED BANK

THE TWO RIVER TIMES

Corporate/Parent Company: The SandPaper, Inc.
Street Address: 75 West Front Street
City: Red Bank
State: NJ
Postal Code: 7701
Office phone: 732-219-5788
Publication Website: www.thesandpaper.net
General E-mail: Editor@TwoRiverTimes.com
Publisher Name: Lynette Wojcik
Editor Name: Judy O'Gorman Alvarez
Advertising Executive Name: Renée Mitchell

RIDGEWOOD

THE SUNDAY DEMOCRAT

Corporate/Parent Company: Advance Publications, Inc.
Street Address: 41 Oak Street
City: Ridgewood
State: NJ
Postal Code: 0 7450
Office phone: 201-612-5400
Publication Website: www.nj.com
Editor Name: Daniel Sforza
Editor Email: sforza@northjersey.com

RIO GRANDE

CAPE MAY COUNTY HERALD TIMES

Corporate/Parent Company: Seawave Corporation
Street Address: 1508 Route 47
City: Rio Grande
State: NJ
Postal Code: 8242
Office phone: 609-886-8600
Publication Website: www.capemaycountyherald.com
General E-mail: admin@cmcherald.com

SOUTHAMPTON

PINE BARRENS TRIBUNE

Corporate/Parent Company: Pine Barrens Media LLC
Street Address: 219 Burrs Mill Rd
City: Southampton
State: NJ
Postal Code: 8088
Office phone: (609) 801-2392
Publication Website: https://pinebarrenstribune.com

SPARTA

SPARTA INDEPENDENT

Corporate/Parent Company: Straus News
Street Address: 1A Main St
City: Sparta
State: NJ
Postal Code: 7871
Office phone: (973) 300-0890
Publication Website: http://www.spartaindependent.com/
General E-mail: editor.si@strausnews.com
Editor Name: Chris Sagona
Editor Email: editor.si@strausnews.com

THE ADVERTISER-NEWS (NORTH)

Corporate/Parent Company: Straus News
Street Address: 1A Main St
City: Sparta
State: NJ
Postal Code: 7871
Office phone: (973) 300-0890
Publication Website: http://www.advertisernewsnorth.com/
General E-mail: editor.ann@strausnews.com
Editor Name: Mike Zummo
Editor Email: editor.ann@strausnews.com
Commercial printers?: Y
Mechanical specifications: Type page 10 1/4 x 14; E - 6 cols, 1 1/2, between; A - 6 cols, between; C - 6 cols, between.
Published Days: Thur
Avg Free Circ: 20619
Audit Company: Sworn/Estimate/Non-Audited
Audit Date: 6 10 2019

TOWNSHIP JOURNAL

Corporate/Parent Company: Straus News
Street Address: 1A Main St
City: Sparta
State: NJ
Postal Code: 7871
Office phone: (973) 300-0890
Publication Website: www.townshipjournal.com
General E-mail: editor.tj@strausnews.com
Editor Name: Chris Sagona
Editor Email: editor.tj@strausnews.com

UNION

BELLEVILLE POST

Corporate/Parent Company: Worrall Community Newspapers, Inc.
Street Address: "1291 Stuyvesant Avenue P.O. Box 3639"
City: Union
State: NJ
Postal Code: 7083
Office phone: (908) 686-7700
Publication Website: https://essexnewsdaily.com/
General E-mail: webmaster@thelocalsource.com

IRVINGTON HERALD

Corporate/Parent Company: Worrall Community Newspapers, Inc.
Street Address: "1291 Stuyvesant Avenue P.O. Box 3639"
City: Union
State: NJ
Postal Code: 7083
Office phone: (908) 686-7700
Publication Website: https://essexnewsdaily.com/
General E-mail: webmaster@thelocalsource.com

NEWS-RECORD OF MAPLEWOOD & SOUTH ORANGE

Corporate/Parent Company: Worrall Community Newspapers, Inc.
Street Address: "1291 Stuyvesant Avenue P.O. Box 3639"
City: Union
State: NJ
Postal Code: 7083
Office phone: (908) 686-7700
Publication Website: https://essexnewsdaily.com/
General E-mail: webmaster@thelocalsource.com

NUTLEY JOURNAL

Corporate/Parent Company: Worrall Community Newspapers, Inc.
Street Address: "1291 Stuyvesant Avenue P.O. Box 3639"
City: Union
State: NJ
Postal Code: 7083
Office phone: (908) 686-7700
Publication Website: https://essexnewsdaily.com/
General E-mail: webmaster@thelocalsource.com

RECORD-TRANSCRIPT OF EAST ORANGE AND ORANGE

Corporate/Parent Company: Worrall Community Newspapers, Inc.
Street Address: "1291 Stuyvesant Avenue P.O. Box 3639"
City: Union
State: NJ
Postal Code: 7083
Office phone: (908) 686-7700
Publication Website: https://essexnewsdaily.com/
General E-mail: webmaster@thelocalsource.com

THE INDEPENDENT PRESS OF BLOOMFIELD

Corporate/Parent Company: Worrall Community Newspapers, Inc.
Street Address: "1291 Stuyvesant Avenue P.O. Box 3639"
City: Union
State: NJ
Postal Code: 7083
Office phone: (908) 686-7700
Publication Website: https://essexnewsdaily.com/
General E-mail: webmaster@thelocalsource.com

UNION COUNTY LOCAL SOURCE

Corporate/Parent Company: Worrall Community Newspapers, Inc.
Street Address: "1291 Stuyvesant Avenue P.O. Box 3639"
City: Union
State: NJ
Postal Code: 7083
Office phone: (908) 686-7700
Publication Website: https://essexnewsdaily.com/
General E-mail: webmaster@thelocalsource.com

VAILSBURG LEADER

Corporate/Parent Company: Worrall Community Newspapers, Inc.
Street Address: "1291 Stuyvesant Avenue P.O. Box 3639"
City: Union
State: NJ
Postal Code: 7083
Office phone: (908) 686-7700
Publication Website: https://essexnewsdaily.com/
General E-mail: webmaster@thelocalsource.com

WEST ORANGE CHRONICLE

Corporate/Parent Company: Worrall Community Newspapers, Inc.
Street Address: "1291 Stuyvesant Avenue P.O. Box 3639"
City: Union
State: NJ
Postal Code: 7083
Office phone: (908) 686-7700
Publication Website: https://essexnewsdaily.com/
General E-mail: webmaster@thelocalsource.com

WEST CAPE MAY

CAPE MAY STAR & WAVE

Corporate/Parent Company: Sample Media, Inc.
Street Address: 600 Park Blvd # 28
City: West Cape May
State: NJ
Postal Code: 8204
Office phone: 609-884-3466
Publication Website: www.starandwave.com
General E-mail: cmstarwave@comcast.net
Advertising Executive Name: Alaine
Advertising Executive Email: capemayalaine@gmail.com
Advertising Executive Phone: 609-289-2619

WHIPPANY

ECHOES-SENTINEL

Corporate/Parent Company: New Jersey Hills Media Group
Street Address: "Suite 104 100 South Jefferson Road"
City: Whippany
State: NJ
Postal Code: 7981
Office phone: (908) 766-3900
Publication Website: https://www.newjerseyhills.com/echoes-sentinel/
General E-mail: bjohnson@newjerseyhills.com
Editor Name: Alex Parker-Magyar
Editor Email: aparkermagyar@newjerseyhills.com
Editor Phone: (908) 766-3900, ext : 226
Advertising Executive Name: Jerry O'Donnell
Advertising Executive Email: jodonnell@newjerseyhills.com
Advertising Executive Phone: (908) 766-3900, ext : 230

FLORHAM PARK EAGLE

Corporate/Parent Company: New Jersey Hills Media Group
Street Address: "Suite 104 100 South Jefferson Road"
City: Whippany
State: NJ
Postal Code: 7981
Office phone: (908) 766-3900
Publication Website: https://www.newjerseyhills.com/florham_park_eagle/
General E-mail: jwinter@newjerseyhills.com
Editor Name: Jesse Winter
Editor Email: jwinter@newjerseyhills.com
Editor Phone: (908) 766-3900, ext : 246
Advertising Executive Name: Jerry O'Donnell
Advertising Executive Email: jodonnell@newjerseyhills.com
Advertising Executive Phone: (908) 766-3900, ext : 230

HANOVER EAGLE

Corporate/Parent Company: New Jersey Hills Media Group
Street Address: "Suite 104 100 South Jefferson Road"
City: Whippany
State: NJ
Postal Code: 7981
Office phone: (908) 766-3900
Publication Website: https://www.newjerseyhills.com/hanover_eagle/
General E-mail: jlent@newjerseyhills.com
Editor Name: Jim Lent
Editor Email: jlent@newjerseyhills.com
Editor Phone: (908) 766-3900, ext : 245
Advertising Executive Name: Jerry O'Donnell
Advertising Executive Email: jodonnell@newjerseyhills.com
Advertising Executive Phone: (908) 766-3900, ext : 230

HUNTERDON REVIEW

Corporate/Parent Company: New Jersey Hills Media Group
Street Address: "Suite 104 100 South Jefferson Road"
City: Whippany

State: NJ
Postal Code: 7981
Office phone: (908) 766-3900
Publication Website: https://www.newjerseyhills.com/hunterdon_review/
General E-mail: wobrien@newjerseyhills.com
Editor Name: Walter O'Brien
Editor Email: wobrien@newjerseyhills.com
Editor Phone: (908) 766-3900, ext : 255
Advertising Executive Name: Jerry O'Donnell
Advertising Executive Email: jodonnell@newjerseyhills.com
Advertising Executive Phone: (908) 766-3900, ext : 230

MADISON EAGLE

Corporate/Parent Company: New Jersey Hills Media Group
Street Address: "Suite 104 100 South Jefferson Road"
City: Whippany
State: NJ
Postal Code: 7981
Office phone: (908) 766-3900
Publication Website: https://www.newjerseyhills.com/madison_eagle/
General E-mail: melissad@newjerseyhills.com
Editor Name: Garry Herzog
Editor Email: gherzog@newjerseyhills.com
Editor Phone: (908) 766-3900, ext : 240
Advertising Executive Name: Jerry O'Donnell
Advertising Executive Email: jodonnell@newjerseyhills.com
Advertising Executive Phone: (908) 766-3900, ext : 230

OBSERVER TRIBUNE

Corporate/Parent Company: New Jersey Hills Media Group
Street Address: "Suite 104 100 South Jefferson Road"
City: Whippany
State: NJ
Postal Code: 7981
Office phone: (908) 766-3900
Publication Website: https://www.newjerseyhills.com/observer-tribune/
General E-mail: pgfarrell@newjerseyhills.com
Editor Name: Phil Garber
Editor Email: pgarber@newjerseyhills.com
Editor Phone: (908) 766-3900, ext : 251
Advertising Executive Name: Jerry O'Donnell
Advertising Executive Email: jodonnell@newjerseyhills.com
Advertising Executive Phone: (908) 766-3900, ext : 230

ROXBURY REGISTER

Corporate/Parent Company: New Jersey Hills Media Group
Street Address: "Suite 104 100 South Jefferson Road"
City: Whippany
State: NJ
Postal Code: 7981
Office phone: (908) 766-3900
Publication Website: https://www.newjerseyhills.com/roxbury_register/
General E-mail: mcondon@newjerseyhills.com
Editor Name: Mike Condon
Editor Email: mcondon@newjerseyhills.com
Editor Phone: (908) 766-3900, ext : 223
Advertising Executive Name: Jerry O'Donnell
Advertising Executive Email: jodonnell@newjerseyhills.com
Advertising Executive Phone: (908) 766-3900, ext : 230

THE CITIZEN

Corporate/Parent Company: Lee Enterprises
Street Address: "Suite 104 100 South Jefferson Road"
City: Whippany
State: NJ
Postal Code: 7981
Office phone: (908) 766-3900
Publication Website: https://www.newjerseyhills.com/the_citizen/
General E-mail: mcondon@newjerseyhills.com
Editor Name: Mike Condon
Editor Email: mcondon@newjerseyhills.com
Editor Phone: (908) 766-3900, ext : 223
Advertising Executive Name: Jerry O'Donnell
Advertising Executive Email: jodonnell@newjerseyhills.com
Advertising Executive Phone: (908) 766-3900, ext : 230

THE RANDOLPH REPORTER

Corporate/Parent Company: New Jersey Hills Media Group
Street Address: "Suite 104 100 South Jefferson Road"
City: Whippany
State: NJ
Postal Code: 7981
Office phone: (908) 766-3900
Publication Website: https://www.newjerseyhills.com/randolph_reporter/
General E-mail: lkieffer@newjerseyhills.com
Editor Name: Pat Robinson
Editor Email: probinson@newjerseyhills.com
Editor Phone: (908) 766-3900, ext : 219
Advertising Executive Name: Jerry O'Donnell
Advertising Executive Email: jodonnell@newjerseyhills.com
Advertising Executive Phone: (908) 766-3900, ext : 230

THE SENTINEL OF SOMERS POINT, LINWOOD AND NORTHFIELD

Corporate/Parent Company: Sample Media, Inc.
Street Address: Suite 104 100 South Jefferson Road
City: Whippany
State: NJ
Postal Code: 0 7981
Office phone: 908-766-3900
Publication Website: www.oceancitysentinel.com
Editor Name: Mike Condon
Editor Email: mcondon@Newjerseyhills.com
Editor Phone: 908-766-3900, ext. 223
Advertising Executive Name: Loretta Kieffer
Advertising Executive Email: lkieffer@newjerseyhills.com
Advertising Executive Phone: 908 766 3900 ext. 217

TODAY IN HUNTERDON (OOB)

Corporate/Parent Company: New Jersey Hills Media Group
Street Address: "Suite 104 100 South Jefferson Road"
City: Whippany
State: NJ
Postal Code: 7981
Office phone: (908) 766-3900
Publication Website: https://www.newjerseyhills.com/the_citizen/
General E-mail: heatherh@newjerseyhills.com
Editor Name: Walter O'Brien
Editor Email: wobrien@newjerseyhills.com
Editor Phone: (908) 766-3900, ext : 255
Advertising Executive Name: Jerry O'Donnell
Advertising Executive Email: jodonnell@newjerseyhills.com
Advertising Executive Phone: (908) 766-3900, ext : 230

NEW MEXICO

CARLSBAD

CARLSBAD CURRENT -ARGUS

Street Address: 620 South Main Street
City: Carlsbad
State: NM
Postal Code: 88220
Office phone: (575) 628-5501
Publication Website: www.currentargus.com
General E-mail: jonsurez@currentargus.com
Editor Name: Jessica Onsurez
Editor Email: jonsurez@currentargus.com
Editor Phone: (575) 628-5531

GALLUP

GALLUP SUN

Street Address: PO Box 1212
City: Gallup
State: NM
Postal Code: 87305
Office phone: (505) 722-8994
Publication Website: www.gallupsun.com
General E-mail: gallupsunreporters@gmail.com

GRANTS

CIBOLA CITIZEN

Street Address: 200 W Santa Fe Ave.
City: Grants
State: NM
Postal Code: 87020
Office phone: (505) 287-3840
Publication Website: www.cibolacitizen.com
General E-mail: ads@cibolacitizen.com
Editor Name: Scott Ford
Editor Email: editor@cibolacitizen.com

LAS CRUCES

LAS CRUCES BULLETIN

Corporate/Parent Company: Osteen Publishing
Street Address: 1740-A Calle de Mercado
City: Las Cruces
State: NM
Postal Code: 88005
Office phone: 575-524-8061
Publication Website: lascrucesbulletin.com
Publisher Name: Richard Coltharp
Publisher Email: richard@lascrucesbulletin.com
Publisher Phone: 575-526-4712
Editor Name: Jess Williams
Editor Email: jess@lascrucesbulletin.com
Editor Phone: 575-680-1977
Advertising Executive Name: Angel McKellar
Advertising Executive Email: angel@lascrucesbulletin.com
Advertising Executive Phone: 575-680-1982
Year Established: 1969
Delivery Methods:
    Mail`Newsstand`Carrier`Racks
Mechanical specifications: Type page 10 5/16 x 12 7/8; E - 6 cols, 1 9/16, 3/16 between; A - 6 cols, 1 9/16, 3/16 between; C - 8 cols, 1 1/8, 3/16 between.
Published Days: Fri
Avg Paid Circ: 1000
Avg Free Circ: 20000
Audit Company: Sworn/Estimate/Non-Audited
Audit Date: 6 10 2019

RATON

THE WORLD JOURNAL

Street Address: 113 N. 2nd St
City: Raton
State: NM
Postal Code: 87740
Office phone: 575-707-3928
Publication Website: huerfanoworldjournal.com/category/raton/
General E-mail: editor.worldjournal@gmail.com
Total Circulation: 21 000

NEVADA

CARSON CITY

NEVADA APPEAL

Street Address: 580 Mallory Way
City: Carson City
State: NV
Postal Code: 89701
Office phone: (775) 882-2111
Publication Website: https://www.nevadaappeal.com/
General E-mail: classifieds@nevadanewsgroup.com
Publisher Name: Peter Bernhard
Editor Name: Adam Trumble
Editor Email: atrumble@nevadaappeal.com
Editor Phone: (775) 881-1221
Advertising Executive Name: Robert Glenn
Advertising Executive Email: rglenn@nevadaappeal.com

ELKO

WELLS PROGRESS

Street Address: 1053 Idaho Street
City: Elko
State: NV
Postal Code: 89801
Office phone: 775-738-2334
Publication Website: wellsprogress.com
Editor Name: Michael A. Bail
Editor Email: editor@wellsprogress.com
Advertising Executive Name: Beth Woodbury
Advertising Executive Email: advertising@wellsprogress.com

ELY

ELY TIMES

Corporate/Parent Company: Battle Born Media LLC
Street Address: 515 Murry St
City: Ely
State: NV
Postal Code: 89315
Office phone: (775) 289-4491
Publication Website: https://elynews.com/
General E-mail: shermfrederick@gmail.com
Publisher Name: Sherman Frederick
Publisher Email: shermfrederick@gmail.com
Advertising Executive Name: Sherman Frederick
Advertising Executive Email: shermfrederick@gmail.com

THE EUREKA SENTINEL

Corporate/Parent Company: Battle Born Media LLC
Street Address: PO Box 150820
City: Ely
State: NV
Postal Code: 89315
Office phone: (775) 289-4491
Publication Website: https://eurekasentinel.com/

General E-mail: shermfrederick@gmail.com
Publisher Name: Sherman Frederick
Publisher Email: shermfrederick@gmail.com
Advertising Executive Name: Sherman Frederick
Advertising Executive Email: shermfrederick@gmail.com

FALLON

LAHONTAN VALLEY NEWS & FALLON EAGLE STANDARD

Corporate/Parent Company: Nevada News Group
Street Address: 37 S Maine St
City: Fallon
State: NV
Postal Code: 89406-3301
Office phone: (775) 423-6041
Publication Website: https://www.nevadaappeal.com/news/lahontan-valley/
General E-mail: classifieds@nevadanewsgroup.com
Publisher Name: Peter Bernhard
Advertising Executive Email: classifieds@nevadanewsgroup.com

GARDNERVILLE

THE RECORD-COURIER

Corporate/Parent Company: Gannett
Street Address: 1503 US Highway 395 N
City: Gardnerville
State: NV
Postal Code: 89410
Office phone: (775) 881-1201
Publication Website: https://www.recordcourier.com/
General E-mail: taddeo@recordcourier.com
Publisher Name: Peter Bernhard
Editor Name: Kurt Hildebrand
Editor Email: khildebrand@recordcourier.com
Editor Phone: 775-782-5121, ext : 21
Advertising Executive Name: Tara Addeo
Advertising Executive Email: taddeo@recordcourier.com

HAWTHORNE

MINERAL COUNTY INDEPENDENT NEWS

Corporate/Parent Company: Battle Born Media LLC
Street Address: 420 3rd St
City: Hawthorne
State: NV
Postal Code: 89415
Office phone: (775) 945-2414
Publication Website: https://mcindependentnews.com/
General E-mail: ben@nvcmedia.com

HENDERSON

VEGAS INC.

Corporate/Parent Company: Greenspun Media Group
Street Address: 2275 Corporate Circle, Ste. 300Ie, Third Floor
City: Henderson
State: NV
Postal Code: 89074
Office phone: 702-990-2550
Publication Website: vegasinc.com
Publisher Name: Gordon Prouty

MESQUITE

MESQUITE LOCAL NEWS

Corporate/Parent Company: Battle Born Media LLC
Street Address: 550 W. Pioneer Blvd. Suite 140-208
City: Mesquite

State: NV
Postal Code: 89024
Office phone: (702) 346-6397
Publication Website: https://mesquitelocalnews.com/
General E-mail: advertising.mln@gmail.com
Advertising Executive Name: Pam Mulligan
Advertising Executive Email: advertising.mln@gmail.com

PIOCHE

LINCOLN COUNTY RECORD

Corporate/Parent Company: Ben Rowley
Street Address: PO Box 485
City: Pioche
State: NV
Postal Code: 89043
Office phone: (775) 725-3232
Publication Website: https://lccentral.com/
General E-mail: contact.lcrecord@gmail.com
Editor Name: Ben Rowley
Editor Email: ben@NVCmedia.com
Editor Phone: (775) 327-6761

RENO

MASON VALLEY NEWS

Street Address: 955 Kuenzli St.
City: Reno
State: NV
Postal Code: 89502
Office phone: (775) 441-8588
Publication Website: masonvalleynews.com
Editor Name: Brian Duggan
Editor Email: bduggan@rgj.com

NORTHERN NEVADA BUSINESS VIEW

Corporate/Parent Company: Nevada News Group
Street Address: NV
City: Reno
State: NV
Postal Code: 89501
Office phone: 775-770-1173
Publication Website: nnbusinessview.com
General E-mail: circulation@nevadanewsgroup.com
Publisher Name: Peter Bernhard
Publisher Email: pbernhard@nevadanewsgroup.com
Editor Name: Kevin MacMillan
Editor Email: kmacmillan@nevadanewsgroup.com
Advertising Executive Name: Susan Anderson
Advertising Executive Email: sanderson@nevadanewsgroup.com

THE LEADER-COURIER

Street Address: 955 Kuenzli Street
City: Reno
State: NV
Postal Code: 89502
Office phone: (775) 441-8588
Publication Website: masonvalleynews.com
Editor Name: Brian Duggan
Editor Email: bduggan@rgj.com

TRUCKEE

NORTH LAKE TAHOE BONANZA

Street Address: NV
City: Truckee
State: NV
Postal Code: 96160
Office phone: 530-587-6061
Publication Website: tahoebonanza.com
General E-mail: classifieds@sierrasun.com
Publisher Name: Don Rogers

Publisher Email: drogers@theunion.com
Publisher Phone: 530-550-2641
Editor Name: Brian Hamilton
Editor Email: bhamilton@sierrasun.com
Editor Phone: 530-477-4249
Advertising Executive Name: Stephanie Azevedo
Advertising Executive Email: sazevedo@theunion.com

WENDOVER

THE WENDOVER TIMES

Street Address: P.O. Box 2716
City: Wendover
State: NV
Postal Code: 89883
Office phone: 775-664-2101
Publication Website: wendovertimes.com
General E-mail: news@wendovertimes.com
Publisher Name: Randy Croasmun
Publisher Phone: 775-408-0011

WINNEMUCCA

THE HUMBOLDT SUN

Corporate/Parent Company: Nevada News Group
Street Address: 1022 Grass Valley Rd.
City: Winnemucca
State: NV
Postal Code: 89445
Office phone: (866) 644-5011
Publication Website: insidenorthernnevada.com
Publisher Name: Peter Bernhard
Publisher Email: peterbernhard@yahoo.com
Publisher Phone: (925) 683-0439
Editor Name: Jen Anderson
Editor Email: jen.anderson@winnemuccapublishing.net
Editor Phone: 775) 623-5011
Advertising Executive Name: Rhonda Coleman
Advertising Executive Email: r.coleman@winnemuccapublishing.net

THE NEVADA RANCHER

Corporate/Parent Company: Nevada News Group
Street Address: 1022 Grass Valley Rd.
City: Winnemucca
State: NV
Postal Code: 89445
Office phone: (866) 644-5011
Publication Website: insidenorthernnevada.com
Publisher Name: Peter Bernhard
Publisher Email: peterbernhard@yahoo.com
Publisher Phone: (925) 683-0439
Editor Name: Jen Anderson
Editor Email: jen.anderson@winnemuccapublishing.net
Editor Phone: 775) 623-5011
Advertising Executive Name: Rhonda Coleman
Advertising Executive Email: r.coleman@winnemuccapublishing.net

NEW YORK

BATAVIA

THE DRUMMER PENNYSAVER

Corporate/Parent Company: Johnson Newspaper Corp.
Street Address: 2 Apollo Dr
City: Batavia
State: NY
Postal Code: 14020-3002
Office phone: (585) 343-2055
Year Established: 1979
Delivery Methods: Carrier Racks
Mechanical specifications: Type page 9.3 x 10.7; 5 cols, 1.625
Published Days: Sun

Avg Free Circ: 15200
Audit Company: Sworn/Estimate/Non-Audited
Audit Date: 6 10 2019

BRONX

THE RIVERDALE PRESS

Corporate/Parent Company: Richner Communications, Inc.
Street Address: 5676 Riverdale Avenue, Suite 311
City: Bronx
State: NY
Postal Code: 10471
Office phone: (718) 543-6065
Publication Website: https://riverdalepress.com/
General E-mail: cortiz@riverdalepress.com
Publisher Name: Stuart Richner
Publisher Phone: (516) 569-4000, ext. 230
Editor Name: Michael Hinman
Editor Email: mhinman@riverdalepress.com
Advertising Executive Name: Cheryl Ortiz
Advertising Executive Email: cortiz@riverdalepress.com
Year Established: 1950
Delivery Methods: Mail Newsstand Racks
Mechanical specifications: Type page 13 x 21; E - 6 cols, 1 7/8, 1/6 between; A - 6 cols, 1 7/8, 1/6 between; C - 8 cols, 1 3/8, between.
Published Days: Thur
Avg Paid Circ: 8140
Avg Free Circ: 2500
Audit Company: Sworn/Estimate/Non-Audited
Audit Date: 6 10 2019

BROOKLYN

BAY NEWS

Corporate/Parent Company: Schneps Media
Street Address: One Metrotech Center, Third Floor
City: Brooklyn
State: NY
Postal Code: 11235-3606
Office phone: (718) 660-2500
Publication Website: https://www.brooklynpaper.com/
General E-mail: ads@schnepsmedia.com
Editor Name: Colin Mixson
Editor Email: CMixson@SchnepsMedia.com
Editor Phone: (718) 260-4505
Advertising Executive Name: Ralph D'Onofrio
Advertising Executive Email: ads@schnepsmedia.com
Advertising Executive Phone: (718) 260-2510
Delivery Methods: Carrier Racks
Mechanical specifications: Type page 9.75 x 11; 6 cols, 1.5, 0.125 between
Published Days: Fri
Avg Free Circ: 32000
Audit Company: Sworn/Estimate/Non-Audited
Audit Date: 7 12 2019
Total Circulation: 30000

BAY RIDGE COURIER-OOB

Corporate/Parent Company: Schneps Media
Street Address: One Metrotech Center, Third Floor
City: Brooklyn
State: NY
Postal Code: 11235-3606
Office phone: (718) 660-2500
Publication Website: https://www.brooklynpaper.com/
General E-mail: ads@schnepsmedia.com
Editor Name: Colin Mixson
Editor Email: CMixson@SchnepsMedia.com
Editor Phone: (718) 260-4505
Advertising Executive Name: Ralph D'Onofrio
Advertising Executive Email: ads@schnepsmedia.com
Advertising Executive Phone: (718) 260-2510
Total Circulation: 5291

Non-Daily Newspapers in the U.S.

BROOKLYN COURIER
Corporate/Parent Company: Schneps Media
Street Address: One Metrotech Center, Third Floor
City: Brooklyn
State: NY
Postal Code: 11235-3606
Office phone: (718) 660-2500
Publication Website: https://www.brooklynpaper.com/
General E-mail: ads@schnepsmedia.com
Editor Name: Colin Mixson
Editor Email: CMixson@SchnepsMedia.com
Editor Phone: (718) 260-4505
Advertising Executive Name: Ralph D'Onofrio
Advertising Executive Email: ads@schnepsmedia.com
Advertising Executive Phone: (718) 260-2510
Delivery Methods: Carrier`Racks
Published Days: Thur
Audit Company: Sworn/Estimate/Non-Audited
Audit Date: 6 10 2019
Total Circulation: 32000

BROOKLYN GRAPHIC
Corporate/Parent Company: Schneps Media
Street Address: One Metrotech Center, Third Floor
City: Brooklyn
State: NY
Postal Code: 11235-3606
Office phone: (718) 660-2500
Publication Website: https://www.brooklynpaper.com/
General E-mail: ads@schnepsmedia.com
Editor Name: Colin Mixson
Editor Email: CMixson@SchnepsMedia.com
Editor Phone: (718) 260-4505
Advertising Executive Name: Ralph D'Onofrio
Advertising Executive Email: ads@schnepsmedia.com
Advertising Executive Phone: (718) 260-2510

CHELSEA NOW-OOB
Corporate/Parent Company: Schneps Media
Street Address: One Metrotech Center North
City: Brooklyn
State: NY
Postal Code: 11201
Office phone: (212) 229-1890
Publication Website: https://www.thevillager.com/
General E-mail: news@thevillager.com
Publisher Name: Victoria Schneps-Yunis
Editor Name: Robert Pozarycki
Editor Email: rpozarycki@qns.com
Editor Phone: (718) 260-4549
Advertising Executive Name: Ralph D'Onofrio
Advertising Executive Email: rdonofrio@schnepsmedia.com
Advertising Executive Phone: (718) 260-2510
Total Circulation: 5251

GAY CITY NEWS
Corporate/Parent Company: Schneps Media
Street Address: One Metrotech Center North, Suite 1001
City: Brooklyn
State: NY
Postal Code: 11201
Office phone: (212) 229-1890
Publication Website: https://www.gaycitynews.com/
General E-mail: editor@gaycitynews.com
Publisher Name: Victoria Schneps-Yunis
Editor Name: Paul Schindler
Editor Email: editor@gaycitynews.com
Editor Phone: (646) 452-2503
Advertising Executive Name: Ralph D'Onofrio
Advertising Executive Email: rdonofrio@schnepsmedia.com
Advertising Executive Phone: (718) 260-2510

MILL-MARINE COURIER & CANARSIE DIGEST
Corporate/Parent Company: Schneps Media
Street Address: One Metrotech Center, Third Floor
City: Brooklyn
State: NY
Postal Code: 11235-3606
Office phone: (718) 660-2500
Publication Website: https://www.brooklynpaper.com/
General E-mail: ads@schnepsmedia.com
Year Established: 1959
Delivery Methods: Carrier`Racks
Mechanical specifications: Type page 11 1/4 x 15; E - 6 cols, 1 1/2, 1/4 between; A - 6 cols, 1 1/2, 1/4 between; C - 7 cols, 1, between.
Published Days: Thur
Avg Paid Circ: 8645
Avg Free Circ: 1490
Audit Company: Sworn/Estimate/Non-Audited
Audit Date: 6 10 2019

THE DOWNTOWN EXPRESS
Corporate/Parent Company: Schneps Media
Street Address: One Metrotech Center North
City: Brooklyn
State: NY
Postal Code: 11201
Office phone: (212) 229-1890
Publication Website: https://www.thevillager.com/
General E-mail: news@thevillager.com
Publisher Name: Victoria Schneps-Yunis
Editor Name: Robert Pozarycki
Editor Email: rpozarycki@qns.com
Editor Phone: (718) 260-4549
Advertising Executive Name: Ralph D'Onofrio
Advertising Executive Email: rdonofrio@schnepsmedia.com
Advertising Executive Phone: (718) 260-2510
Mechanical specifications: Type page 10 x 14; E - 4 cols, 2 1/4, between; A - 6 cols, 2 1/2, between; C - 6 cols, 1 1/2, between.
Published Days: Fri
Avg Free Circ: 40000
Audit Company: Sworn/Estimate/Non-Audited
Audit Date: 6 10 2019
Total Circulation: 15000

THE VILLAGER
Corporate/Parent Company: Schneps Media
Street Address: One Metrotech Center North
City: Brooklyn
State: NY
Postal Code: 11201
Office phone: (212) 229-1890
Publication Website: https://www.thevillager.com/
General E-mail: news@thevillager.com
Publisher Name: Victoria Schneps-Yunis
Editor Name: Robert Pozarycki
Editor Email: rpozarycki@qns.com
Editor Phone: (718) 260-4549
Advertising Executive Name: Ralph D'Onofrio
Advertising Executive Email: rdonofrio@schnepsmedia.com
Advertising Executive Phone: (718) 260-2510
Year Established: 1933
Mechanical specifications: Type page 10 x 14; E - 4 cols, 2 1/4, between; A - 6 cols, 1 1/2, between; C - 6 cols, 1 1/2, between.
Published Days: Thur
Avg Paid Circ: 20000
Audit Company: Sworn/Estimate/Non-Audited
Audit Date: 6 10 2019

CHESTER

DIRT MAGAZINE
Corporate/Parent Company: Straus News
Street Address: 20 West Ave
City: Chester
State: NY
Postal Code: 10918-1032
Office phone: (845) 469-9000
Publication Website: http://www.dirt-mag.com/
General E-mail: nyoffice@strausnews.com
Editor Name: Becca Tucker
Editor Email: editor.dirt@strausnews.com
Year Established: 2011
Delivery Methods: Mail
Published Days: Bi-Mthly
Avg Free Circ: 20233
Audit Company: Sworn/Estimate/Non-Audited
Audit Date: 6 10 2019
Total Circulation: 104

PHOTO NEWS
Corporate/Parent Company: Straus News
Street Address: 20 West Ave
City: Chester
State: NY
Postal Code: 10918-1053
Office phone: (845) 469-9000
Publication Website: www.thephoto-news.com
General E-mail: nyoffice@strausnews.com
Editor Name: Bob Quinn
Editor Email: nyoffice@strausnews.com
Year Established: 1986
Mechanical specifications: Type page 10 1/4 x 14; E - 6 cols, 1 1/2, between; A - 6 cols, 1 1/2, between; C - 6 cols, 1 1/2, between.
Published Days: Fri
Avg Free Circ: 6701
Audit Company: Sworn/Estimate/Non-Audited
Audit Date: 6 10 2019
Total Circulation: 1200

WARWICK ADVERTISER
Corporate/Parent Company: Straus News
Street Address: 20 West Ave
City: Chester
State: NY
Postal Code: 10918-1053
Office phone: (845) 469-9000
Publication Website: www.warwickadvertiser.com
General E-mail: nyoffice@strausnews.com
Editor Name: Bob Quinn
Editor Email: nyoffice@strausnews.com
Year Established: 1866
Mechanical specifications: Type page 10 1/4 x 14; E - 6 cols, 1 1/2, between; A - 6 cols, 1 1/2, between; C - 6 cols, 1 1/2, between.
Published Days: Fri
Avg Free Circ: 6617
Audit Company: Sworn/Estimate/Non-Audited
Audit Date: 6 10 2019
Total Circulation: 1800

COBLESKILL

MY SHOPPER
Corporate/Parent Company: Snyder Communications
Street Address: 2403 State Route 7 Ste 4
City: Cobleskill
State: NY
Postal Code: 12043
Office phone: (518) 234-8215
Publication Website: https://pennysaveronline.com/
General E-mail: info@myshopperonline.com

ELIZABETHTOWN

THE ADIRONDACK JOURNAL SUN
Corporate/Parent Company: Sun Community News
Street Address: 14 Hand Ave
City: Elizabethtown
State: NY
Postal Code: 12932
Office phone: (518) 873-6368
Publication Website: suncommunitynews.com
General E-mail: dan@suncommunitynews.com
Publisher Name: Daniel E. Alexander
Year Established: 1948
Delivery Methods: Mail`Racks
Mechanical specifications: Type page: 10 x 16; 6 col
Published Days: Sat
Avg Paid Circ: 94
Avg Free Circ: 8087
Audit Company: CVC
Audit Date: 30 09 2017

THE BURGH SUN
Corporate/Parent Company: Sun Community News
Street Address: 14 Hand Ave
City: Elizabethtown
State: NY
Postal Code: 12932
Office phone: (518) 873-6368
Publication Website: suncommunitynews.com
General E-mail: dan@suncommunitynews.com
Publisher Name: Daniel E. Alexander
Total Circulation: 3716

THE EAGLE
Corporate/Parent Company: Lee Enterprises
Street Address: 14 Hand Ave
City: Elizabethtown
State: NY
Postal Code: 12932
Office phone: (518) 873-6368
Publication Website: suncommunitynews.com
General E-mail: dan@suncommunitynews.com
Publisher Name: Daniel E. Alexander
Delivery Methods: Mail`Newsstand`Carrier
Mechanical specifications: Type page 10 x 16; 6 cols, 1.5, 0.25 between
Published Days: Wed`Thur
Avg Paid Circ: 1
Avg Free Circ: 4850
Audit Company: Sworn/Estimate/Non-Audited
Audit Date: 6 10 2019

THE NEWS ENTERPRISE SUN
Corporate/Parent Company: Sun Community News
Street Address: 14 Hand Ave
City: Elizabethtown
State: NY
Postal Code: 12932
Office phone: (518) 873-6368
Publication Website: suncommunitynews.com
General E-mail: dan@suncommunitynews.com
Publisher Name: Daniel E. Alexander
Editor Name: Andy Flynn
Editor Email: andy@denpubs.com
Editor Phone: (518) 873-6368, ext. 213
Year Established: 1948
Delivery Methods: Mail`Racks
Mechanical specifications: Type page 10 x 16; E - 6 cols, 1 1/2, between; A - 6 cols, 1 1/2, between.
Published Days: Sat
Avg Paid Circ: 39
Avg Free Circ: 3414
Audit Company: VAC
Audit Date: 30 09 2016
Total Circulation: 3700

THE NORTH COUNTRYMAN SUN

Corporate/Parent Company: Sun Community News
Street Address: 14 Hand Ave
City: Elizabethtown
State: NY
Postal Code: 12932
Office phone: (518) 873-6368
Publication Website: suncommunitynews.com
General E-mail: dan@suncommunitynews.com
Publisher Name: Daniel E. Alexander
Year Established: 1927
Delivery Methods: Mail`Racks
Own Printing Facility?: Y
Commercial printers?: Y
Mechanical specifications: Type page 10 x 10; E - 4 cols, 1 1/2, 1/3 between.
Published Days: Sat
Weekday Frequency: All day
Saturday Frequency: All day
Avg Paid Circ: 37
Avg Free Circ: 8281
Audit Company: VAC
Audit Date: 30 09 2016
Pressroom Equipment: Goss Community 17 Units
Total Circulation: 20233

THE TIMES OF TI SUN

Corporate/Parent Company: Sun Community News
Street Address: 14 Hand Ave
City: Elizabethtown
State: NY
Postal Code: 12932
Office phone: (518) 873-6368
Publication Website: suncommunitynews.com
General E-mail: dan@suncommunitynews.com
Publisher Name: Daniel E. Alexander
Year Established: 1948
Delivery Methods: Mail`Racks
Own Printing Facility?: Y
Commercial printers?: Y
Mechanical specifications: Type page 10 x 16; E - 6 cols, 1 1/2, between; A - 6 cols, 1 1/2, between.
Published Days: Sat
Avg Paid Circ: 77
Avg Free Circ: 7214
Audit Company: CVC
Audit Date: 30 09 2017
Total Circulation: 2100

THE VALLEY NEWS SUN

Corporate/Parent Company: Sun Community News
Street Address: 14 Hand Ave
City: Elizabethtown
State: NY
Postal Code: 12932
Office phone: (518) 873-6368
Publication Website: suncommunitynews.com
General E-mail: dan@suncommunitynews.com
Publisher Name: Daniel E. Alexander
Year Established: 1948
Delivery Methods: Mail`Racks
Own Printing Facility?: Y
Commercial printers?: Y
Mechanical specifications: Type page 10 x 10; E - 4 cols, 1 1/2, 1/3 between.
Published Days: Sat
Avg Paid Circ: 67
Avg Free Circ: 15249
Audit Company: CVC
Audit Date: 30 09 2017
Total Circulation: 5600

GARDEN CITY

BALDWIN HERALD

Corporate/Parent Company: Richner Communications
Street Address: 2 Endo Blvd
City: Garden City
State: NY
Postal Code: 11530-6707
Office phone: (516) 569-4000
Publication Website: https://www.liherald.com/baldwin/
General E-mail: baldwineditor@liherald.com
Publisher Name: Stuart Richner
Publisher Phone: (516) 569-4000, ext. 230
Editor Name: Bridget Downes
Editor Email: baldwineditor@liherald.com
Editor Phone: (516) 569-4000, ext. 269
Advertising Executive Name: Ellen Reynolds
Advertising Executive Phone: (516) 569-4000, ext. 286
Delivery Methods: Mail`Newsstand`Racks
Own Printing Facility?: Y
Commercial printers?: Y
Mechanical specifications: Type page 9 3/4 x 13 3/4; E - 4 cols, 2 1/3, 1/6 between; A - 6 cols, 1 1/2, 1/6 between; C - 6 cols, 1 1/2, 1/6 between.
Published Days: Thur
Avg Paid Circ: 5291
Audit Company: Sworn/Estimate/Non-Audited
Audit Date: 6 10 2019
Total Circulation: 4293

BELLMORE HERALD

Corporate/Parent Company: Richner Communications
Street Address: 2 Endo Blvd
City: Garden City
State: NY
Postal Code: 11530-6707
Office phone: (516) 569-4000
Publication Website: https://www.liherald.com/bellmore/
General E-mail: belleditor@liherald.com
Publisher Name: Stuart Richner
Publisher Phone: (516) 569-4000, ext. 230
Editor Name: Alyssa Seidman
Editor Email: belleditor@liherald.com
Editor Phone: (516) 569-4000, ext. 207
Advertising Executive Name: Ellen Reynolds
Advertising Executive Phone: (516) 569-4000, ext. 286
Delivery Methods: Mail`Newsstand`Racks
Own Printing Facility?: Y
Commercial printers?: Y
Mechanical specifications: Type page 9 3/4 x 13 3/4; E - 4 cols, 2 1/3, 1/6 between; A - 6 cols, 1 1/2, 1/6 between; C - 6 cols, 1 1/2, 1/6 between.
Published Days: Thur
Avg Paid Circ: 5251
Audit Company: Sworn/Estimate/Non-Audited
Audit Date: 6 10 2019
Total Circulation: 5130

BETHPAGE NEWSGRAM

Street Address: 821 Franklin Ave, Suite 208
City: Garden City
State: NY
Postal Code: 11530
Office phone: (516) 294-8900
Publication Website: https://www.bethpagenewsgram.com/
General E-mail: production@gcnews.com
Publisher Name: Meg Morgan Norris
Editor Name: Meg Morgan Norris
Editor Email: editor@gcnews.com
Advertising Executive Name: Matt Merlis
Advertising Executive Email: mmerlis@gcnews.com

EAST MEADOW BEACON

Corporate/Parent Company: Richner Communications, Inc.
Street Address: 2 Endo Blvd
City: Garden City
State: NY
Postal Code: 11530-6707
Office phone: (516) 569-4000
Publication Website: https://www.liherald.com/eastmeadow/
General E-mail: marketing@liherald.com
Publisher Name: Stuart Richner
Publisher Phone: (516) 569-4000, ext. 230
Editor Name: Brian Stieglitz
Editor Phone: (516) 569-4000, ext. 246
Advertising Executive Name: Ellen Reynolds
Advertising Executive Phone: (516) 569-4000, ext. 286
Mechanical specifications: Type page 10 x 14.
Published Days: Fri
Avg Paid Circ: 5600
Audit Company: Sworn/Estimate/Non-Audited
Audit Date: 6 10 2019
Total Circulation: 18165

EAST MEADOW HERALD

Corporate/Parent Company: Richner Communications
Street Address: 2 Endo Blvd
City: Garden City
State: NY
Postal Code: 11530-6707
Office phone: (516) 569-4000
Publication Website: http://www.liherald.com/eastmeadow/
General E-mail: emeadoweditor@liherald.com
Publisher Name: Stuart Richner
Publisher Phone: (516) 569-4000, ext. 230
Editor Name: Brian Stieglitz
Editor Email: emeadoweditor@liherald.com
Editor Phone: (516) 569-4000, ext. 246
Advertising Executive Name: Ellen Reynolds
Advertising Executive Phone: (516) 569-4000, ext. 286
Delivery Methods: Mail`Newsstand`Racks
Own Printing Facility?: Y
Commercial printers?: Y
Mechanical specifications: Type page 9 3/4 x 13 3/4; E - 4 cols, 2 1/3, 1/6 between; A - 6 cols, 1 1/2, 1/6 between; C - 6 cols, 1 1/2, 1/6 between.
Published Days: Thur
Avg Paid Circ: 4068
Avg Free Circ: 225
Audit Company: Sworn/Estimate/Non-Audited
Audit Date: 6 10 2019
Total Circulation: 6096

FRANKLIN SQUARE/ELMONT HERALD

Corporate/Parent Company: Richner Communications, Inc.
Street Address: 2 Endo Blvd
City: Garden City
State: NY
Postal Code: 11530-6707
Office phone: (516) 569-4000
Publication Website: https://www.liherald.com/franklinsquare/
General E-mail: fseditor@liherald.com
Publisher Name: Stuart Richner
Publisher Phone: (516) 569-4000, ext. 230
Editor Name: Peter Belfiore
Editor Email: fseditor@liherald.com
Editor Phone: (516) 569-4000, ext. 282
Advertising Executive Name: Ellen Reynolds
Advertising Executive Phone: (516) 569-4000, ext. 286
Delivery Methods: Mail`Newsstand`Carrier`Racks
Mechanical specifications: Type page 9 3/4 x 13 3/4; E - 4 cols, 2 1/3, 1/6 between; A - 6 cols, 1 1/2, 1/6 between; C - 6 cols, 1 1/2, 1/6 between.
Published Days: Thur
Avg Paid Circ: 6096
Audit Company: Sworn/Estimate/Non-Audited
Audit Date: 6 10 2019
Total Circulation: 6010

GARDEN CITY NEWS

Corporate/Parent Company: Litmor Publishing
Street Address: 821 Franklin Ave, Suite 208
City: Garden City
State: NY
Postal Code: 11530
Office phone: (516) 294-8900
Publication Website: https://www.gcnews.com/
General E-mail: production@gcnews.com
Publisher Name: Meg Morgan Norris
Editor Name: Meg Morgan Norris
Editor Email: editor@gcnews.com
Advertising Executive Name: Matt Merlis
Advertising Executive Email: mmerlis@gcnews.com
Delivery Methods: Mail`Racks
Own Printing Facility?: Y
Mechanical specifications: Type page 8.75 x 11.5; 6 cols, 1.325, 0.183 between
Published Days: Fri
Avg Paid Circ: 8481
Audit Company: Sworn/Estimate/Non-Audited
Audit Date: 6 10 2019
Total Circulation: 8481

GOLD COAST GAZETTE

Corporate/Parent Company: Richner Communications, Inc.
Street Address: 2 Endo Blvd
City: Garden City
State: NY
Postal Code: 11530-6707
Office phone: (516) 671-2360
Publication Website: http://www.goldcoastgazette.net/
General E-mail: circ@liherald.com
Publisher Name: Stuart Richner
Publisher Phone: (516) 569-4000, ext. 230
Editor Name: Laura Lane
Editor Phone: (516) 569-4000, ext. 327
Advertising Executive Name: Ellen Reynolds
Advertising Executive Phone: (516) 569-4000, ext. 286
Published Days: Thur
Audit Company: Sworn/Estimate/Non-Audited
Audit Date: 6 10 2019

HERALD COMMUNITY NEWSPAPERS (OOB)

Corporate/Parent Company: Richner Communications, Inc.
Street Address: 2 Endo Blvd
City: Garden City
State: NY
Postal Code: 11530-6707
Office phone: (516) 569-4000
Publication Website: http://www.liherald.com/
General E-mail: circ@liherald.com
Publisher Name: Stuart Richner
Publisher Phone: (516) 569-4000, ext. 230
Advertising Executive Name: Ellen Reynolds
Advertising Executive Phone: (516) 569-4000, ext. 286
Total Circulation: 6472

HICKSVILLE MID-ISLAND TIMES

Corporate/Parent Company: Litmor Publishing
Street Address: 821 Franklin Ave, Suite 208

Non-Daily Newspapers in the U.S.

City: Garden City
State: NY
Postal Code: 11530
Office phone: (516) 294-8900
Publication Website: https://www.midislandtimes.com/
General E-mail: production@gcnews.com
Publisher Name: Meg Morgan Norris
Editor Name: Meg Morgan Norris
Editor Email: editor@gcnews.com
Advertising Executive Name: Matt Merlis
Advertising Executive Email: mmerlis@gcnews.com
Delivery Methods: Mail`Racks
Own Printing Facility?: Y
Commercial printers?: Y
Mechanical specifications: Type page 8.75 x 11.5; 6 cols, 1.325, 0.183 between
Published Days: Fri
Avg Paid Circ: 2765
Audit Company: Sworn/Estimate/Non-Audited
Audit Date: 6 10 2019
Total Circulation: 1485

JERICHO NEWS JOURNAL

Corporate/Parent Company: Litmor Publishing
Street Address: 821 Franklin Ave, Suite 208
City: Garden City
State: NY
Postal Code: 11530
Office phone: (516) 294-8900
Publication Website: https://www.jericho-news-journal.com/
General E-mail: production@gcnews.com
Publisher Name: Meg Morgan Norris
Editor Name: Meg Morgan Norris
Editor Email: editor@gcnews.com
Advertising Executive Name: Matt Merlis
Advertising Executive Email: mmerlis@gcnews.com
Delivery Methods: Mail`Racks
Own Printing Facility?: Y
Mechanical specifications: Type page 8.75 x 11.5; 6 cols, 1.325, 0.183 between
Published Days: Fri
Avg Paid Circ: 2727
Audit Company: Sworn/Estimate/Non-Audited
Audit Date: 6 10 2019

LONG BEACH HERALD

Corporate/Parent Company: Richner Communications
Street Address: 2 Endo Blvd
City: Garden City
State: NY
Postal Code: 11530-6707
Office phone: (516) 569-4000
Publication Website: http://www.liherald.com/longbeach/
General E-mail: lbeditor@liherald.com
Publisher Name: Stuart Richner
Publisher Phone: (516) 569-4000, ext. 230
Editor Name: Anthony Rifilato
Editor Email: lbeditor@liherald.com
Editor Phone: (516) 569-4000, ext. 213
Advertising Executive Name: Ellen Reynolds
Advertising Executive Phone: (516) 569-4000, ext. 286
Delivery Methods: Mail`Newsstand`Racks
Own Printing Facility?: Y
Commercial printers?: Y
Mechanical specifications: Type page 9 3/4 x 13 3/4; E - 4 cols, 2 1/3, 1/6 between; A - 6 cols, 1 1/2, 1/6 between; C - 6 cols, 1 1/2, 1/6 between.
Published Days: Thur
Avg Paid Circ: 6544
Avg Free Circ: 1356
Audit Company: Sworn/Estimate/Non-Audited
Audit Date: 6 10 2019
Total Circulation: 7986

LYNBROOK/EAST ROCKAWAY

HERALD

Corporate/Parent Company: Richner Communications, Inc.
Street Address: 2 Endo Blvd
City: Garden City
State: NY
Postal Code: 11530-6707
Office phone: (516) 569-4000
Publication Website: https://www.liherald.com/lynbrook/
General E-mail: lyn-ereditor@liherald.com
Publisher Name: Stuart Richner
Publisher Phone: (516) 569-4000, ext. 230
Editor Name: Michael Smollins
Editor Email: lyn-ereditor@liherald.com
Editor Phone: (516) 569-4000, ext. 265
Advertising Executive Name: Ellen Reynolds
Advertising Executive Phone: (516) 569-4000, ext. 286
Delivery Methods: Mail`Newsstand`Racks
Own Printing Facility?: Y
Commercial printers?: Y
Mechanical specifications: Type page 9 3/4 x 13 3/4; E - 4 cols, 2 1/3, 1/6 between; A - 6 cols, 1 1/2, 1/6 between; C - 6 cols, 1 1/2, 1/6 between.
Published Days: Thur
Avg Paid Circ: 5272
Avg Free Circ: 1293
Audit Company: Sworn/Estimate/Non-Audited
Audit Date: 6 10 2019
Total Circulation: 15000

MALVERNE/WEST HEMPSTEAD

HERALD

Corporate/Parent Company: Richner Communications, Inc.
Street Address: 2 Endo Blvd
City: Garden City
State: NY
Postal Code: 11530-6707
Office phone: (516) 569-4000
Publication Website: https://www.liherald.com/malverne/
General E-mail: mal-wheditor@liherald.com
Publisher Name: Stuart Richner
Publisher Phone: (516) 569-4000, ext. 230
Editor Name: Nakeem Grant
Editor Email: mal-wheditor@liherald.com
Editor Phone: (516) 569-4000, ext. 298
Advertising Executive Name: Ellen Reynolds
Advertising Executive Phone: (516) 569-4000, ext. 286
Delivery Methods: Mail`Newsstand`Racks
Own Printing Facility?: Y
Commercial printers?: Y
Mechanical specifications: Type page 9 3/4 x 13 3/4; E - 4 cols, 2 1/3, 1/6 between; A - 6 cols, 1 1/2, 1/6 between; C - 6 cols, 1 1/2, 1/6 between.
Published Days: Thur
Avg Paid Circ: 3286
Audit Company: Sworn/Estimate/Non-Audited
Audit Date: 6 10 2019

MERRICK HERALD

Corporate/Parent Company: Richner Communications
Street Address: 2 Endo Blvd
City: Garden City
State: NY
Postal Code: 11530-6707
Office phone: (516) 569-4000
Publication Website: https://www.liherald.com/merrick/
General E-mail: merrickeditor@liherald.com
Publisher Name: Stuart Richner
Publisher Phone: (516) 569-4000, ext. 230
Editor Name: Alyssa Seidman
Editor Email: merrickeditor@liherald.com
Editor Phone: (516) 569-4000, ext. 207
Advertising Executive Name: Ellen Reynolds
Advertising Executive Phone: (516) 569-4000, ext. 286
Delivery Methods: Mail`Newsstand`Racks
Own Printing Facility?: Y
Commercial printers?: Y
Mechanical specifications: Type page 9 1/2 x 13 3/4; E - 4 cols, 2 1/3, 1/6 between; A - 6 cols, 1 1/2, 1/6 between; C - 6 cols, 1 1/2, 1/6 between.
Published Days: Thur
Avg Paid Circ: 3846
Audit Company: Sworn/Estimate/Non-Audited
Audit Date: 6 10 2019

NASSAU HERALD

Corporate/Parent Company: Richner Communications, Inc.
Street Address: 2 Endo Blvd
City: Garden City
State: NY
Postal Code: 11530-6707
Office phone: (516) 569-4000
Publication Website: https://www.liherald.com/nassau.html
General E-mail: nassaueditor@liherald.com
Publisher Name: Stuart Richner
Publisher Phone: (516) 569-4000, ext. 230
Editor Name: Jeff Bessen
Editor Email: nassaueditor@liherald.com
Editor Phone: (516) 569-4000, ext. 201
Advertising Executive Name: Ellen Reynolds
Advertising Executive Phone: (516) 569-4000, ext. 286
Delivery Methods: Mail`Newsstand`Racks
Mechanical specifications: Type page 9 3/4 x 13 3/4; E - 4 cols, 2 1/3, 1/6 between; A - 6 cols, 1 1/2, 1/6 between; C - 6 cols, 1 1/2, 1/6 between.
Published Days: Thur
Avg Paid Circ: 8771
Audit Company: Sworn/Estimate/Non-Audited
Audit Date: 6 10 2019

OCEANSIDE-ISLAND PARK HERALD

Corporate/Parent Company: Richner Communications, Inc.
Street Address: 2 Endo Blvd
City: Garden City
State: NY
Postal Code: 11530-6707
Office phone: (516) 569-4000
Publication Website: http://www.liherald.com/oceanside/
General E-mail: oceaneditor@liherald.com
Publisher Name: Stuart Richner
Publisher Phone: (516) 569-4000, ext. 230
Editor Name: Michael Smollins
Editor Email: oceaneditor@liherald.com
Editor Phone: (516) 569-4000, ext. 265
Advertising Executive Name: Ellen Reynolds
Advertising Executive Phone: (516) 569-4000, ext. 286
Delivery Methods: Mail`Newsstand`Racks
Own Printing Facility?: Y
Commercial printers?: Y
Mechanical specifications: Type page 9 3/4 x 13 3/4; E - 4 cols, 2 1/3, 1/6 between; A - 6 cols, 1 1/2, 1/6 between; C - 6 cols, 1 1/2, 1/6 between.
Published Days: Thur
Avg Paid Circ: 5015
Avg Free Circ: 1281
Audit Company: Sworn/Estimate/Non-Audited
Audit Date: 6 10 2019
Total Circulation: 5000

OYSTER BAY GUARDIAN

Corporate/Parent Company: Richner Communications, Inc.
Street Address: 2 Endo Blvd
City: Garden City
State: NY
Postal Code: 11530-6707
Office phone: (516) 922-4215 X327
Publication Website: http://www.liherald.com/oysterbay
General E-mail: circ@liherald.com
Publisher Name: Stuart Richner
Publisher Phone: (516) 569-4000, ext. 230
Editor Name: Laura Lane
Editor Phone: (516) 569-4000, ext. 327
Advertising Executive Name: Ellen Reynolds
Advertising Executive Phone: (516) 569-4000, ext. 286
Year Established: 1899
Delivery Methods: Mail`Newsstand
Published Days: Fri
Avg Paid Circ: 3500
Avg Free Circ: 50
Audit Company: Sworn/Estimate/Non-Audited
Audit Date: 6 10 2019
Total Circulation: 2765

PRIMETIME

Corporate/Parent Company: Richner Communications, Inc.
Street Address: 2 Endo Blvd
City: Garden City
State: NY
Postal Code: 11530
Office phone: 516-569-4444
Publication Website: http://www.liprimetime.com/
General E-mail: marketing@liherald.com
Publisher Name: Stuart Richner
Publisher Phone: (516) 569-4000, ext. 230
Advertising Executive Name: Lori Berger
Advertising Executive Email: lberger@liprimetime.com
Advertising Executive Phone: (516) 569-4444, ext. 228

ROCKVILLE CENTRE HERALD

Corporate/Parent Company: Richner Communications
Street Address: 2 Endo Blvd
City: Garden City
State: NY
Postal Code: 11530-6707
Office phone: (516) 569-4000
Publication Website: http://www.liherald.com/rockvillecentre/
General E-mail: rvceditor@liherald.com
Publisher Name: Stuart Richner
Publisher Phone: (516) 569-4000, ext. 230
Editor Name: Jill Nossa
Editor Email: rvceditor@liherald.com
Editor Phone: (516) 569-4000, ext. 205
Advertising Executive Name: Ellen Reynolds
Advertising Executive Phone: (516) 569-4000, ext. 286
Delivery Methods: Mail`Newsstand`Racks
Own Printing Facility?: Y
Commercial printers?: Y
Mechanical specifications: Type page 9 3/4 x 13 3/4; E - 4 cols, 2 1/3, 1/6 between; A - 6 cols, 1 1/2, 1/6 between; C - 6 cols, 1 1/2, 1/6 between.
Published Days: Thur
Avg Paid Circ: 6367
Avg Free Circ: 1646
Audit Company: Sworn/Estimate/Non-Audited
Audit Date: 6 10 2019
Total Circulation: 2727

SOUTH SHORE RECORD (OOB)

Corporate/Parent Company: Richner Communications, Inc.
Street Address: 2 Endo Blvd
City: Garden City
State: NY
Postal Code: 11530-6707
Office phone: (516) 569-4000
Publication Website: https://www.liherald.com/nassau.html
General E-mail: circ@liherald.com

Publisher Name: Stuart Richner
Publisher Phone: (516) 569-4000, ext. 230
Advertising Executive Name: Ellen Reynolds
Advertising Executive Phone: (516) 569-4000, ext. 286
Total Circulation: 4128

SYOSSET ADVANCE

Street Address: 821 Franklin Ave, Suite 208
City: Garden City
State: NY
Postal Code: 11530
Office phone: (516) 294-8900
Publication Website: https://www.syossetadvance.com/
General E-mail: production@gcnews.com
Publisher Name: Meg Morgan Norris
Editor Name: Meg Morgan Norris
Editor Email: editor@gcnews.com
Advertising Executive Name: Matt Merlis
Advertising Executive Email: mmerlis@gcnews.com
Total Circulation: 1810

WEST HEMPSTEAD BEACON

Corporate/Parent Company: Richner Communications, Inc.
Street Address: 2 Endo Blvd
City: Garden City
State: NY
Postal Code: 11530-6707
Office phone: (516) 569-4000
Publication Website: https://www.liherald.com/westhempstead/
Publisher Name: Stuart Richner
Publisher Phone: (516) 569-4000, ext. 230
Editor Name: Nakeem Grant
Editor Phone: (516) 569-4000, ext. 298
Advertising Executive Name: Ellen Reynolds
Advertising Executive Phone: (516) 569-4000, ext. 286
Published Days: Fri
Avg Paid Circ: 5200
Audit Company: Sworn/Estimate/Non-Audited
Audit Date: 6 10 2019
Total Circulation: 1550

GRANVILLE

LAKES REGION FREE PRESS – POULTNEY

Corporate/Parent Company: Manchester Newspapers Inc.
Street Address: P.O. Box 330
City: Granville
State: NY
Postal Code: 12832
Office phone: 518-642-1234
Publication Website: manchesternewspapers.com/category/lakes-region-freepress/lakes-region-freepress-e-edition
General E-mail: news@manchesternewspapers.com
Publisher Name: Mark Vinciguerra
Advertising Executive Name: Jane Cosey

NORTH COUNTRY FREE PRESS

Corporate/Parent Company: Manchester Newspapers, Inc.
Street Address: 14 E Main St
City: Granville
State: NY
Postal Code: 12832-1334
Office phone: (518) 642-1234
Publication Website: https://manchesternewspapers.com/category/lakes-region-freepress/
General E-mail: advertising@manchesternewspapers.com

Publisher Name: Mark Vinciguerra
Advertising Executive Name: Jane E. Cosey
Advertising Executive Email: advertising@manchesternewspapers.com
Year Established: 1995
Delivery Methods: Mail`Racks
Mechanical specifications: Type page 10.5 x 16; 5 cols, 2, 0.125 between
Published Days: Fri
Avg Free Circ: 17172
Audit Company: CVC
Audit Date: 30 09 2017

NORTHSHIRE FREE PRESS – MANCHESTER

Corporate/Parent Company: Manchester Newspapers
Street Address: 14 East Main Street
City: Granville
State: NY
Postal Code: 12832
Office phone: 518-642-1234
Publication Website: manchesternewspapers.com/category/northshire-freepress
General E-mail: news@manchesternewspapers.com
Publisher Name: Mark Vinciguerra
Advertising Executive Name: Jane E. Cosey
Total Circulation: 4054

THE GRANVILLE SENTINEL

Corporate/Parent Company: Manchester Newspapers, Inc.
Street Address: 14 E Main St
City: Granville
State: NY
Postal Code: 12832-1334
Office phone: (518) 642-1234
Publication Website: https://manchesternewspapers.com/category/lakes-region-freepress/
General E-mail: advertising@manchesternewspapers.com
Publisher Name: Mark Vinciguerra
Editor Name: Matt Saari
Advertising Executive Name: Jane E. Cosey
Advertising Executive Email: advertising@manchesternewspapers.com
Year Established: 1875
Delivery Methods: Mail`Newsstand
Mechanical specifications: Type page 10.5 x 16; 5 cols, 2, 0.125 between
Published Days: Wed`Thur
Avg Paid Circ: 2800
Audit Company: Sworn/Estimate/Non-Audited
Audit Date: 6 10 2019
Total Circulation: 7900

THE LAKES REGION FREE PRESS

Corporate/Parent Company: Manchester Newspapers, Inc.
Street Address: 14 E Main St
City: Granville
State: NY
Postal Code: 12832-1334
Office phone: (518) 642-1234
Publication Website: https://manchesternewspapers.com/category/lakes-region-freepress/
General E-mail: advertising@manchesternewspapers.com
Publisher Name: Mark Vinciguerra
Advertising Executive Name: Jane E. Cosey
Advertising Executive Email: advertising@manchesternewspapers.com
Year Established: 1995
Delivery Methods: Mail
Mechanical specifications: Type page 10.5 x 16; 5 cols, 2, 0.125 between
Published Days: Fri

Avg Free Circ: 8039
Audit Company: CVC
Audit Date: 30 09 2017
Total Circulation: 18100

THE NORTH COUNTRY FREE PRESS

Corporate/Parent Company: Manchester Newspapers, Inc.
Street Address: 14 E Main St
City: Granville
State: NY
Postal Code: 12832-1334
Office phone: (518) 642-1234
Publication Website: https://manchesternewspapers.com/category/lakes-region-freepress/
General E-mail: advertising@manchesternewspapers.com
Publisher Name: Mark Vinciguerra
Advertising Executive Name: Jane E. Cosey
Advertising Executive Email: advertising@manchesternewspapers.com
Year Established: 1995
Delivery Methods: Mail`Racks
Mechanical specifications: Type page 10.5 x 16; 5 cols, 2, 0.125 between
Published Days: Fri
Avg Free Circ: 17172
Audit Company: VAC
Audit Date: 30 09 2017
Total Circulation: 6565

THE WEEKENDER

Corporate/Parent Company: Manchester Newspapers, Inc.
Street Address: 14 E Main St
City: Granville
State: NY
Postal Code: 12832-1334
Office phone: (518) 642-1234
Publication Website: https://manchesternewspapers.com/category/lakes-region-freepress/
General E-mail: advertising@manchesternewspapers.com
Publisher Name: Mark Vinciguerra
Editor Name: PJ Ferguson
Advertising Executive Name: Jane E. Cosey
Advertising Executive Email: advertising@manchesternewspapers.com
Year Established: 1995
Delivery Methods: Mail`Racks
Mechanical specifications: Type page 10.5 x 16; 5 cols, 2, 0.125 between
Published Days: Fri
Avg Free Circ: 5517
Audit Company: CVC
Audit Date: 30 09 2017
Total Circulation: 3286

THE WHITEHALL TIMES

Corporate/Parent Company: Manchester Newspapers, Inc.
Street Address: 14 E Main St
City: Granville
State: NY
Postal Code: 12832-1334
Office phone: (518) 642-1234
Publication Website: https://manchesternewspapers.com/category/lakes-region-freepress/
General E-mail: advertising@manchesternewspapers.com
Publisher Name: Mark Vinciguerra
Advertising Executive Name: Jane E. Cosey
Advertising Executive Email: advertising@manchesternewspapers.com
Year Established: 1815
Delivery Methods: Mail`Newsstand
Mechanical specifications: Type page 10.5 x 16; 5 cols, 2, 0.125 between
Published Days: Thur

Avg Paid Circ: 1400
Audit Company: Sworn/Estimate/Non-Audited
Audit Date: 6 10 2019
Total Circulation: 4105

HEMPSTEAD

THE HEMPSTEAD BEACON

Corporate/Parent Company: Nassau County Publications
Street Address: 5 Centre St
City: Hempstead
State: NY
Postal Code: 11550-2422
Office phone: (516) 481-5400
Published Days: Fri
Avg Paid Circ: 4800
Audit Company: Sworn/Estimate/Non-Audited
Audit Date: 6 10 2019
Total Circulation: 5551

THE MERRICK BEACON

Corporate/Parent Company: Nassau County Publications
Street Address: 5 Centre St
City: Hempstead
State: NY
Postal Code: 11550-2422
Office phone: (516) 481-5400
Editor Name: Barbara Yohe
Year Established: 1950
Published Days: Fri
Avg Paid Circ: 3700
Audit Company: Sworn/Estimate/Non-Audited
Audit Date: 6 10 2019
Total Circulation: 3846

THE UNIONDALE BEACON

Corporate/Parent Company: Nassau County Publications
Street Address: 5 Centre St
City: Hempstead
State: NY
Postal Code: 11550-2422
Office phone: (516) 481-5400
Published Days: Fri
Avg Paid Circ: 5000
Audit Company: Sworn/Estimate/Non-Audited
Audit Date: 6 10 2019
Total Circulation: 10135

HUDSON

CHATHAM COURIER

Corporate/Parent Company: Johnson Newspaper Corp.
Street Address: 1 Hudson City Ctr
City: Hudson
State: NY
Postal Code: 12534-2355
Office phone: (518) 828-1616
Publication Website: https://www.hudsonvalley360.com/site/contact.html
General E-mail: editorial@registerstar.com
Editor Name: Ray Pignone
Editor Email: rpignone@registerstar.com
Editor Phone: (518) 828-1616, ext : 2469
Advertising Executive Name: Patricia McKenna
Advertising Executive Email: pmckenna@registerstar.com
Advertising Executive Phone: (518) 828-1616, ext : 2413
Year Established: 1862
Delivery Methods: Mail`Newsstand`Carrier`Racks
Published Days: Thur
Avg Paid Circ: 1200
Audit Company: Sworn/Estimate/Non-Audited
Audit Date: 6 10 2019
Total Circulation: 4873

Non-Daily Newspapers in the U.S.

ITHACA

GROTON INDEPENDENT
Corporate/Parent Company: Finger Lakes Community Newspapers
Street Address: 109 N Cayuga St
City: Ithaca
State: NY
Postal Code: 14850
Office phone: (607) 277-7000
Publication Website: http://www.ithaca.com/news/groton/
General E-mail: production@ithacatimes.com
Publisher Name: Jim Bilinski
Publisher Email: jbilinski@ithacatimes.com
Publisher Phone: (607) 277-7000, ext. 212
Editor Name: Jaime Cone
Editor Email: southreporter@flcn.org
Editor Phone: (607) 277-7000
Advertising Executive Name: Jim Bilinski
Advertising Executive Email: jbilinski@ithacatimes.com
Advertising Executive Phone: (607) 277-7000, ext. 212

NEWFIELD NEWS
Corporate/Parent Company: Finger Lakes Community Newspapers
Street Address: 109 N Cayuga St
City: Ithaca
State: NY
Postal Code: 14850
Office phone: (607) 277-7000
Publication Website: http://www.ithaca.com/news/newfield/
General E-mail: southreporter@flcn.org
Publisher Name: Jim Bilinski
Publisher Email: jbilinski@ithacatimes.com
Publisher Phone: (607) 277-7000, ext. 212
Editor Name: Jaime Cone
Editor Email: southreporter@flcn.org
Editor Phone: (607) 277-7000
Advertising Executive Name: Jim Bilinski
Advertising Executive Email: jbilinski@ithacatimes.com
Advertising Executive Phone: (607) 277-7000, ext. 212
Delivery Methods: Mail
Published Days: Wed
Avg Paid Circ: 475
Avg Free Circ: 30
Audit Company: Sworn/Estimate/Non-Audited
Audit Date: 6 10 2019
Total Circulation: 8771

OVID GAZETTE
Corporate/Parent Company: Finger Lakes Community Newspapers
Street Address: 109 N Cayuga St
City: Ithaca
State: NY
Postal Code: 14850-4341
Office phone: (607) 277-7000
Publication Website: http://www.ithaca.com/news/south_seneca/
General E-mail: production@ithacatimes.com
Publisher Name: Jim Bilinski
Publisher Email: jbilinski@ithacatimes.com
Publisher Phone: (607) 277-7000, ext. 212
Editor Name: Jaime Cone
Editor Email: editor@flcn.org
Editor Phone: (607) 277-7000
Advertising Executive Name: Jim Bilinski
Advertising Executive Email: jbilinski@ithacatimes.com
Advertising Executive Phone: (607) 277-7000, ext. 212
Year Established: 1801
Delivery Methods: Mail
Published Days: Wed
Avg Paid Circ: 575
Avg Free Circ: 63
Audit Company: Sworn/Estimate/Non-Audited
Audit Date: 6 10 2019
Total Circulation: 5047

SPENCER RANDOM HARVEST WEEKLY
Corporate/Parent Company: Finger Lakes Community Newspapers
Street Address: 109 N Cayuga St
City: Ithaca
State: NY
Postal Code: 14850
Office phone: (607) 277-7000
Publication Website: http://www.ithaca.com/news/spencer_van_etten/
General E-mail: production@ithacatimes.com
Publisher Name: Jim Bilinski
Publisher Email: jbilinski@ithacatimes.com
Publisher Phone: (607) 277-7000, ext. 212
Editor Name: Matt Butler
Editor Email: editor@ithacatimes.com
Editor Phone: (607) 277-7000, ext. 224
Advertising Executive Name: Jim Bilinski
Advertising Executive Email: jbilinski@ithacatimes.com
Advertising Executive Phone: (607) 277-7000, ext. 212
Year Established: 1980
Delivery Methods: Mail
Published Days: Wed
Avg Paid Circ: 826
Audit Company: Sworn/Estimate/Non-Audited
Audit Date: 6 10 2019
Total Circulation: 4850

THE CANDOR CHRONICLE
Corporate/Parent Company: Finger Lakes Community Newspapers
Street Address: 109 N Cayuga St
City: Ithaca
State: NY
Postal Code: 14850
Office phone: (607) 277-7700
Publication Website: http://www.ithaca.com/news/candor/
General E-mail: production@ithacatimes.com
Publisher Name: Jim Bilinski
Publisher Email: jbilinski@ithacatimes.com
Publisher Phone: (607) 277-7000, ext. 212
Editor Name: Jaime Cone
Editor Email: southreporter@flcn.org
Editor Phone: (607) 277-7000
Advertising Executive Name: Jim Bilinski
Advertising Executive Email: jbilinski@ithacatimes.com
Advertising Executive Phone: (607) 277-7000, ext. 212
Published Days: Wed
Audit Company: Sworn/Estimate/Non-Audited
Audit Date: 6 10 2019
Total Circulation: 505

THE DRYDEN COURIER
Corporate/Parent Company: Finger Lakes Community Newspapers
Street Address: 109 N Cayuga St
City: Ithaca
State: NY
Postal Code: 14850
Office phone: (607) 277-7700
Publication Website: http://www.ithaca.com/news/dryden/
General E-mail: production@ithacatimes.com
Publisher Name: Jim Bilinski
Publisher Email: jbilinski@ithacatimes.com
Publisher Phone: (607) 277-7000, ext. 212
Editor Name: Jaime Cone
Editor Email: southreporter@flcn.org
Editor Phone: (607) 277-7000

Advertising Executive Name: Jim Bilinski
Advertising Executive Email: jbilinski@ithacatimes.com
Advertising Executive Phone: (607) 277-7000, ext. 212
Published Days: Wed
Audit Company: Sworn/Estimate/Non-Audited
Audit Date: 6 10 2019
Total Circulation: 17172

THE INTERLAKEN REVIEW
Corporate/Parent Company: Finger Lakes Community Newspapers
Street Address: 109 N Cayuga St
City: Ithaca
State: NY
Postal Code: 14850
Office phone: (607) 277-7000
Publication Website: http://www.ithaca.com/news/south_seneca/
General E-mail: production@ithacatimes.com
Publisher Name: Jim Bilinski
Publisher Email: jbilinski@ithacatimes.com
Publisher Phone: (607) 277-7000, ext. 212
Editor Name: Jaime Cone
Editor Email: southreporter@flcn.org
Editor Phone: (607) 277-7000
Advertising Executive Name: Jim Bilinski
Advertising Executive Email: jbilinski@ithacatimes.com
Advertising Executive Phone: (607) 277-7000, ext. 212
Delivery Methods: Mail
Published Days: Wed
Avg Paid Circ: 351
Avg Free Circ: 42
Audit Company: Sworn/Estimate/Non-Audited
Audit Date: 6 10 2019

THE LANSING LEDGER
Corporate/Parent Company: Finger Lakes Community Newspapers
Street Address: 109 N Cayuga St
City: Ithaca
State: NY
Postal Code: 14850
Office phone: (607) 277-7700
Publication Website: http://www.ithaca.com/news/lansing/
General E-mail: production@ithacatimes.com
Publisher Name: Jim Bilinski
Publisher Email: jbilinski@ithacatimes.com
Publisher Phone: (607) 277-7000, ext. 212
Editor Name: Jaime Cone
Editor Email: southreporter@flcn.org
Editor Phone: (607) 277-7000
Advertising Executive Name: Jim Bilinski
Advertising Executive Email: jbilinski@ithacatimes.com
Advertising Executive Phone: (607) 277-7000, ext. 212
Published Days: Wed
Audit Company: Sworn/Estimate/Non-Audited
Audit Date: 6 10 2019
Total Circulation: 6296

THE TRUMANSBURG FREE PRESS
Corporate/Parent Company: Finger Lakes Community Newspapers
Street Address: 109 N Cayuga St
City: Ithaca
State: NY
Postal Code: 14850-4341
Office phone: (607) 277-7000
Publication Website: http://www.ithaca.com/news/trumansburg/
General E-mail: production@ithacatimes.com
Publisher Name: Jim Bilinski
Publisher Email: jbilinski@ithacatimes.com
Publisher Phone: (607) 277-7000, ext. 212

Editor Name: Jaime Cone
Editor Email: southreporter@flcn.org
Editor Phone: (607) 277-7000
Advertising Executive Name: Jim Bilinski
Advertising Executive Email: jbilinski@ithacatimes.com
Advertising Executive Phone: (607) 277-7000, ext. 212
Year Established: 1865
Delivery Methods: Mail
Published Days: Wed
Avg Paid Circ: 1100
Avg Free Circ: 85
Audit Company: Sworn/Estimate/Non-Audited
Audit Date: 6 10 2019

KINGSTON

ALMANAC WEEKLY
Corporate/Parent Company: Ulster Publishing
Street Address: PO Box 3329
City: Kingston
State: NY
Postal Code: 12402
Office phone: (845) 334-8200
Publication Website: https://hudsonvalleyone.com/paper/almanac-weekly/
General E-mail: almanacweekly@gmail.com
Publisher Name: Geddy Sveikauskas
Publisher Email: gsveikauskas@ulsterpublishing.com
Publisher Phone: (845) 334-8201
Editor Name: Julie O'Connor
Advertising Executive Name: Genia Wickwire
Total Circulation: 2140

KINGSTON TIMES
Corporate/Parent Company: Ulster Publishing
Street Address: 322 Wall St
City: Kingston
State: NY
Postal Code: 12402
Office phone: (845) 334-8200
Publication Website: https://hudsonvalleyone.com/paper/kingston-times/
General E-mail: kingstontimes@gmail.com
Publisher Name: Geddy Sveikauskas
Publisher Email: gsveikauskas@ulsterpublishing.com
Publisher Phone: (845) 334-8201
Editor Name: Dan Barton
Advertising Executive Name: Genia Wickwire
Mechanical specifications: Type page 10 x 15.5; 3 cols, 3, 0.5 between
Published Days: Thur
Avg Paid Circ: 1550
Audit Company: Sworn/Estimate/Non-Audited
Audit Date: 6 10 2019

NEW PALTZ TIMES
Corporate/Parent Company: Ulster Publishing
Street Address: 322 Wall St
City: Kingston
State: NY
Postal Code: 12402
Office phone: (845) 334-8200
Publication Website: https://hudsonvalleyone.com/paper/new-paltz-times/
General E-mail: newpaltztimes@ulsterpublishing.com
Publisher Name: Geddy Sveikauskas
Publisher Email: gsveikauskas@ulsterpublishing.com
Publisher Phone: (845) 334-8201
Editor Name: Debbie Alexsa
Advertising Executive Name: Genia Wickwire
Mechanical specifications: Type page 10 x 15.5; 3 cols, 3, 0.5 between
Published Days: Thur
Avg Paid Circ: 4850
Audit Company: Sworn/Estimate/Non-Audited
Audit Date: 6 10 2019
Total Circulation: 19999

SAUGERTIES TIMES

Corporate/Parent Company: Ulster Publishing
Street Address: 322 Wall St
City: Kingston
State: NY
Postal Code: 12402
Office phone: (845) 334-8200
Publication Website: https://hudsonvalleyone.com/paper/saugerties-times/
General E-mail: saugertiestimes@gmail.com
Publisher Name: Geddy Sveikauskas
Publisher Email: gsveikauskas@ulsterpublishing.com
Publisher Phone: (845) 334-8201
Editor Name: Dan Barton
Advertising Executive Name: Genia Wickwire
Mechanical specifications: Type page 10 x 15.5; 3 cols, 3, 0.5 between
Published Days: Thur
Avg Paid Circ: 1700
Audit Company: Sworn/Estimate/Non-Audited
Audit Date: 6 10 2019
Total Circulation: 638

WOODSTOCK TIMES

Corporate/Parent Company: Ulster Publishing
Street Address: 322 Wall St
City: Kingston
State: NY
Postal Code: 12402
Office phone: (845) 334-8200
Publication Website: https://hudsonvalleyone.com/paper/woodstock-times/
General E-mail: wtedit@gmail.com
Publisher Name: Geddy Sveikauskas
Publisher Email: gsveikauskas@ulsterpublishing.com
Publisher Phone: (845) 334-8201
Editor Name: Brian Hollander
Advertising Executive Name: Genia Wickwire
Mechanical specifications: Type page 10 x 15.5; 3 cols, 3, 0.5 between
Published Days: Thur
Avg Paid Circ: 4400
Audit Company: Sworn/Estimate/Non-Audited
Audit Date: 6 10 2019
Total Circulation: 2384

LOWVILLE

CARTHAGE REPUBLICAN TRIBUNE

Corporate/Parent Company: Johnson Newspaper Corp.
Street Address: 7567 S STATE ST
City: LOWVILLE
State: NY
Postal Code: 13367-1512
Office phone: (315) 493-1270
Year Established: 1860
Delivery Methods: Mail`Newsstand`Carrier
Mechanical specifications: Type page 13 1/8 x 20 1/4; E - 6 cols, 2, 1/6 between; A - 6 cols, 2, 1/6 between; C - 6 cols, 2, 1/6 between.
Published Days: Thur
Avg Paid Circ: 104
Audit Company: AAM
Audit Date: 31 12 2017
Total Circulation: 3550

JOURNAL AND REPUBLICAN

Corporate/Parent Company: Johnson Newspaper Corp.
Street Address: 7840 NY-26
City: Lowville
State: NY
Postal Code: 13367
Office phone: (315) 755-1540
Publication Website: https://www.nny360.com/site/about.html
General E-mail: generalnews@lowville.com
Publisher Name: Alec Johnson
Publisher Email: aej@wdt.net
Publisher Phone: (315) 661-2351
Editor Name: Alec Johnson
Editor Email: aej@wdt.net
Editor Phone: (315) 661-2351
Advertising Executive Name: Michelle Bowers
Advertising Executive Email: mbowers@wdt.net
Advertising Executive Phone: (315) 661-2456
Year Established: 1830
Delivery Methods: Mail`Newsstand`Carrier
Mechanical specifications: Type page 13 x 21; E - 6 cols, 2, 3/8 between; A - 6 cols, 2, 3/8 between; C - 9 cols, 1 5/8, 1/8 between.
Published Days: Wed
Avg Paid Circ: 4106
Avg Free Circ: 22
Audit Company: Sworn/Estimate/Non-Audited
Audit Date: 6 10 2019
Total Circulation: 6701

MASSENA

DAILY COURIER-OBSERVER

Corporate/Parent Company: Johnson Newspaper Corp.
Street Address: 1 Harrowgate Commons
City: Massena
State: NY
Postal Code: 13662
Office phone: (315) 769-2451
Publication Website: https://www.nny360.com/site/about.html
General E-mail: courier@ogd.com
Publisher Name: Alec Johnson
Publisher Email: aej@wdt.net
Publisher Phone: (315) 661-2351
Editor Name: Alec Johnson
Editor Email: aej@wdt.net
Editor Phone: (315) 661-2351
Advertising Executive Name: Michelle Bowers
Advertising Executive Email: mbowers@wdt.net
Advertising Executive Phone: (315) 661-2456
Total Circulation: 3672

MINEOLA

FARMINGDALE OBSERVER

Corporate/Parent Company: Anton Media Group
Street Address: 132 E 2nd St
City: Mineola
State: NY
Postal Code: 11501-3522
Office phone: (516) 747-8282
Publication Website: https://farmingdale-observer.com/
General E-mail: farmingdale@antonmediagroup.com
Publisher Name: Angela Susan Anton
Publisher Email: aanton@antonmediagroup.com
Editor Name: CHRIS BIRSNER
Editor Email: cbirsner@antonmediagroup.com
Editor Phone: (516) 403-5167
Year Established: 1960
Delivery Methods: Mail`Newsstand
Own Printing Facility?: Y
Commercial printers?: Y
Published Days: Thur
Avg Paid Circ: 5130
Audit Company: Sworn/Estimate/Non-Audited
Audit Date: 6 10 2019
Total Circulation: 6830

FLORAL PARK DISPATCH

Corporate/Parent Company: Anton Media Group
Street Address: 132 E 2nd St
City: Mineola
State: NY
Postal Code: 11501-3522
Office phone: (516) 747-8282
Publication Website: https://floralparkdispatch.com/
General E-mail: floralpark@antonmediagroup.com
Publisher Name: Angela Susan Anton
Publisher Email: aanton@antonmediagroup.com
Editor Name: Anthony Murray
Editor Email: amurray@antonmediagroup.com
Editor Phone: (516) 403-5190

GARDEN CITY LIFE

Corporate/Parent Company: Anton Media Group
Street Address: 132 E 2nd St
City: Mineola
State: NY
Postal Code: 11501-3522
Office phone: (516) 747-8282
Publication Website: https://gardencity-life.com/
General E-mail: gardencity@antonmediagroup.com
Publisher Name: Angela Susan Anton
Publisher Email: aanton@antonmediagroup.com
Editor Name: William E. Lucano
Editor Email: wlucano@antonmediagroup.com
Editor Phone: (516) 403-5156
Year Established: 1985
Delivery Methods: Mail`Newsstand
Own Printing Facility?: Y
Commercial printers?: Y
Published Days: Thur
Avg Paid Circ: 6010
Audit Company: Sworn/Estimate/Non-Audited
Audit Date: 6 10 2019
Total Circulation: 10890

GLEN COVE RECORD-PILOT

Corporate/Parent Company: Anton Media Group
Street Address: 132 E 2nd St
City: Mineola
State: NY
Postal Code: 11501-3522
Office phone: (516) 747-8282
Publication Website: https://glencoverecordpilot.com/
General E-mail: glencove@antonmediagroup.com
Publisher Name: Angela Susan Anton
Publisher Email: aanton@antonmediagroup.com
Editor Name: Christy Hinko
Editor Email: chinko@antonmediagroup.com
Editor Phone: (516) 747-8282
Year Established: 1953
Delivery Methods: Mail`Newsstand
Own Printing Facility?: Y
Commercial printers?: Y
Published Days: Thur
Avg Paid Circ: 5344
Avg Free Circ: 1128
Audit Company: Sworn/Estimate/Non-Audited
Audit Date: 6 10 2019
Total Circulation: 8013

GREAT NECK RECORD

Corporate/Parent Company: Anton Media Group
Street Address: 132 E 2nd St
City: Mineola
State: NY
Postal Code: 11501-3522
Office phone: (516) 747-8282
Publication Website: https://greatneckrecord.com/
General E-mail: greatneck@antonmediagroup.com
Publisher Name: Angela Susan Anton
Publisher Email: aanton@antonmediagroup.com
Editor Name: MIKE ADAMS
Editor Email: madams@antonmediagroup.com
Editor Phone: (516) 403-5153
Year Established: 1933
Delivery Methods: Mail`Newsstand
Own Printing Facility?: Y
Commercial printers?: Y
Mechanical specifications: Type page 10 1/4 x 14; E - 4 cols, 2 3/8, 3/8 between; A - 4 cols, 2 3/8, 3/8 between; C - 6 cols, 1 9/16, 3/16 between.
Published Days: Thur
Avg Paid Circ: 6998
Avg Free Circ: 988
Audit Company: Sworn/Estimate/Non-Audited
Audit Date: 6 10 2019
Total Circulation: 5621

HICKSVILLE ILLUSTRATED NEWS

Corporate/Parent Company: Anton Media Group
Street Address: 132 E 2nd St
City: Mineola
State: NY
Postal Code: 11501-3522
Office phone: (516) 747-8282
Publication Website: https://www.hicksvillenews.com/
General E-mail: hicksville@antonmediagroup.com
Publisher Name: Angela Susan Anton
Publisher Email: aanton@antonmediagroup.com
Editor Name: Dave Gil de Rubio
Editor Email: dgilderubio@antonmediagroup.com
Editor Phone: (516) 403-5164
Year Established: 1986
Delivery Methods: Mail`Newsstand
Own Printing Facility?: Y
Commercial printers?: Y
Published Days: Thur
Avg Paid Circ: 5000
Audit Company: Sworn/Estimate/Non-Audited
Audit Date: 6 10 2019
Total Circulation: 1700

LEVITTOWN TRIBUNE

Corporate/Parent Company: Anton Media Group
Street Address: 132 E 2nd St
City: Mineola
State: NY
Postal Code: 11501-3522
Office phone: (516) 747-8282
Publication Website: https://levittown-tribune.com/
General E-mail: levittown@antonmediagroup.com
Publisher Name: Angela Susan Anton
Publisher Email: aanton@antonmediagroup.com
Editor Name: Joe Wolkin
Editor Email: jwolkin@antonmediagroup.com
Editor Phone: (516) 403-5104
Year Established: 1948
Delivery Methods: Mail`Newsstand
Own Printing Facility?: Y
Commercial printers?: Y
Published Days: Thur
Avg Paid Circ: 3290
Avg Free Circ: 764
Audit Company: Sworn/Estimate/Non-Audited
Audit Date: 6 10 2019

MANHASSET PRESS

Corporate/Parent Company: Anton Media Group
Street Address: 132 E 2nd St
City: Mineola
State: NY
Postal Code: 11501-3522
Office phone: (516) 747-8282
Publication Website: https://manhassetpress.com/
General E-mail: manhasset@antonmediagroup.com
Publisher Name: Angela Susan Anton
Publisher Email: aanton@antonmediagroup.com

Non-Daily Newspapers in the U.S.

Editor Name: MARCO SCHADEN
Editor Email: mschaden@antonmediagroup.com
Editor Phone: (516) 403-5152
Year Established: 1934
Delivery Methods: Mail`Newsstand
Own Printing Facility?: Y
Commercial printers?: Y
Published Days: Thur
Avg Paid Circ: 3801
Avg Free Circ: 304
Audit Company: Sworn/Estimate/Non-Audited
Audit Date: 6 10 2019

MASSAPEQUAN OBSERVER

Corporate/Parent Company: Anton Media Group
Street Address: 132 E 2nd St
City: Mineola
State: NY
Postal Code: 11501-3522
Office phone: (516) 747-8282
Publication Website: https://www.massapequaobserver.com
General E-mail: massapequa@antonmediagroup.com
Publisher Name: Angela Susan Anton
Publisher Email: aanton@antonmediagroup.com
Editor Name: Dave Gil de Rubio
Editor Email: dgilderubio@antonmediagroup.com
Editor Phone: (516) 403-5164
Year Established: 1959
Delivery Methods: Mail`Newsstand
Own Printing Facility?: Y
Commercial printers?: Y
Published Days: Thur
Avg Paid Circ: 4920
Avg Free Circ: 631
Audit Company: Sworn/Estimate/Non-Audited
Audit Date: 6 10 2019
Total Circulation: 826

MINEOLA AMERICAN

Corporate/Parent Company: Anton Media Group
Street Address: 132 E 2nd St
City: Mineola
State: NY
Postal Code: 11501-3522
Office phone: (516) 747-8282
Publication Website: https://mineolaamerican.com
General E-mail: mineolaamerican@antonmediagroup.com
Publisher Name: Angela Susan Anton
Publisher Email: aanton@antonmediagroup.com
Editor Name: ANTHONY MURRAY
Editor Email: amurray@antonmediagroup.com
Editor Phone: (516) 403-5190
Year Established: 1952
Delivery Methods: Mail`Newsstand
Published Days: Wed
Avg Paid Circ: 4873
Audit Company: Sworn/Estimate/Non-Audited
Audit Date: 6 10 2019

NEW HYDE PARK ILLUSTRATED

Corporate/Parent Company: Anton Media Group
Street Address: 132 E 2nd St
City: Mineola
State: NY
Postal Code: 11501-3522
Office phone: (516) 747-8282
Publication Website: https://newhydeparkillustrated.com/
General E-mail: newhydepark@antonmediagroup.com
Publisher Name: Angela Susan Anton
Publisher Email: aanton@antonmediagroup.com

Editor Name: ANTHONY MURRAY
Editor Email: amurray@antonmediagroup.com
Editor Phone: (516) 403-5190
Year Established: 1930
Delivery Methods: Mail`Newsstand
Own Printing Facility?: Y
Commercial printers?: Y
Published Days: Thur
Avg Paid Circ: 4200
Avg Free Circ: 847
Audit Company: Sworn/Estimate/Non-Audited
Audit Date: 6 10 2019
Total Circulation: 4973

OYSTER BAY ENTERPRISE PILOT

Corporate/Parent Company: Anton Media Group
Street Address: 132 E 2nd St
City: Mineola
State: NY
Postal Code: 11501-3522
Office phone: (516) 747-8282
Publication Website: https://oysterbayenterprisepilot.com/
General E-mail: oysterbay@antonmediagroup.com
Publisher Name: Angela Susan Anton
Publisher Email: aanton@antonmediagroup.com
Editor Name: Christy Hinko
Editor Email: chinko@antonmediagroup.com
Year Established: 1882
Delivery Methods: Mail`Newsstand
Own Printing Facility?: Y
Commercial printers?: Y
Published Days: Thur
Avg Paid Circ: 1892
Avg Free Circ: 492
Audit Company: Sworn/Estimate/Non-Audited
Audit Date: 6 10 2019
Total Circulation: 8181

PLAINVIEW/OLD BETHPAGE HERALD

Corporate/Parent Company: Anton Media Group
Street Address: 132 E 2nd St
City: Mineola
State: NY
Postal Code: 11501-3522
Office phone: (516) 747-8282
Publication Website: https://plainviewoldbethpageherald.com/
General E-mail: plainview@antonmediagroup.com
Publisher Name: Angela Susan Anton
Publisher Email: aanton@antonmediagroup.com
Editor Name: CHRIS BIRSNER
Editor Email: cbirsner@antonmediagroup.com
Editor Phone: (516) 403-5167
Year Established: 1956
Delivery Methods: Mail`Newsstand
Own Printing Facility?: Y
Commercial printers?: Y
Published Days: Thur
Avg Paid Circ: 3225
Avg Free Circ: 447
Audit Company: Sworn/Estimate/Non-Audited
Audit Date: 6 10 2019

ROSLYN NEWS

Corporate/Parent Company: Anton Media Group
Street Address: 132 E 2nd St
City: Mineola
State: NY
Postal Code: 11501-3522
Office phone: (516) 747-8282
Publication Website: https://roslyn-news.com/
General E-mail: roslyn@antonmediagroup.com
Publisher Name: Angela Susan Anton

Publisher Email: aanton@antonmediagroup.com
Editor Name: MICHAEL ADAMS
Editor Email: madams@antonmediagroup.com
Editor Phone: (516) 403-5153
Year Established: 1877
Delivery Methods: Mail`Newsstand
Own Printing Facility?: Y
Commercial printers?: Y
Published Days: Thur
Avg Paid Circ: 4800
Avg Free Circ: 821
Audit Company: Sworn/Estimate/Non-Audited
Audit Date: 6 10 2019

SYOSSET/JERICHO TRIBUNE

Corporate/Parent Company: Anton Media Group
Street Address: 132 E 2nd St
City: Mineola
State: NY
Postal Code: 11501-3522
Office phone: (516) 747-8282
Publication Website: https://syossetjerichotribune.com/
General E-mail: syossetjericho@antonmediagroup.com
Publisher Name: Angela Susan Anton
Publisher Email: aanton@antonmediagroup.com
Editor Name: Joe Wolkin
Editor Email: jwolkin@antonmediagroup.com
Editor Phone: (516) 403-5164
Year Established: 1958
Delivery Methods: Mail`Newsstand
Own Printing Facility?: Y
Commercial printers?: Y
Published Days: Thur
Avg Paid Circ: 4220
Avg Free Circ: 753
Audit Company: Sworn/Estimate/Non-Audited
Audit Date: 6 10 2019
Total Circulation: 40000

WESTBURY TIMES

Corporate/Parent Company: Anton Media Group
Street Address: 132 E 2nd St
City: Mineola
State: NY
Postal Code: 11501-3522
Office phone: (516) 747-8282
Publication Website: https://thewestburytimes.com/
General E-mail: westbury@antonmediagroup.com
Publisher Name: Angela Susan Anton
Publisher Email: aanton@antonmediagroup.com
Editor Name: FRANK RIZZO
Editor Email: frizzo@antonmediagroup.com
Editor Phone: (516) 403-5154
Year Established: 1933
Delivery Methods: Mail`Newsstand
Own Printing Facility?: Y
Commercial printers?: Y
Published Days: Thur
Avg Paid Circ: 3445
Audit Company: Sworn/Estimate/Non-Audited
Audit Date: 6 10 2019
Total Circulation: 15200

NEW BERLIN

THE NEW BERLIN GAZETTE-OOB

Corporate/Parent Company: Snyder Communications
Street Address: PO Box A
City: New Berlin
State: NY
Postal Code: 13411
Office phone: (607) 847-6131
Publication Website: https://pennysaveronline.com/about/us

NEW YORK

CHELSEA NEWS/CHELSEA CLINTON NEWS

Corporate/Parent Company: Straus News
Street Address: 505 8th Ave. Ste. 804
City: New York
State: NY
Postal Code: 10018
Office phone: (212) 868-0190
Publication Website: http://www.chelseanewsny.com/
General E-mail: nyoffice@strausnews.com
Editor Name: Alexis Gelber
Editor Email: nyoffice@strausnews.com
Advertising Executive Name: Fred Almonte
Total Circulation: 4851

OUR TOWN DOWNTOWN

Corporate/Parent Company: Straus News
Street Address: 505 8th Ave. Ste. 804
City: New York
State: NY
Postal Code: 10018
Office phone: (212) 868-0190
Publication Website: http://www.otdowntown.com/
General E-mail: nyoffice@strausnews.com
Editor Name: Alexis Gelber
Editor Email: nyoffice@strausnews.com
Advertising Executive Name: Fred Almonte
Total Circulation: 2800

OUR TOWN EASTSIDE

Corporate/Parent Company: Straus News
Street Address: 505 8th Ave. Ste. 804
City: New York
State: NY
Postal Code: 10018
Office phone: (212) 868-0190
Publication Website: http://www.ourtownny.com/
General E-mail: nyoffice@strausnews.com
Editor Name: Alexis Gelber
Editor Email: nyoffice@strausnews.com
Advertising Executive Name: Fred Almonte
Year Established: 1970
Own Printing Facility?: Y
Commercial printers?: Y
Mechanical specifications: Type page 10.333 x 11
Published Days: Thur
Avg Free Circ: 19999
Audit Company: Sworn/Estimate/Non-Audited
Audit Date: 6 10 2019
Total Circulation: 4800

WEST SIDE SPIRIT

Corporate/Parent Company: Straus News
Street Address: 505 8th Ave. Ste. 804
City: New York
State: NY
Postal Code: 10018
Office phone: (212) 868-0190
Publication Website: http://www.westsidespirit.com/
General E-mail: nyoffice@strausnews.com
Editor Name: Alexis Gelber
Editor Email: nyoffice@strausnews.com
Advertising Executive Name: Fred Almonte
Year Established: 1985
Mechanical specifications: Type page 10.333 x 11
Published Days: Thur
Audit Company: Sworn/Estimate/Non-Audited
Audit Date: 6 10 2019
Total Circulation: 393

NORWICH

WHARTON VALLEY PENNYSAVER

Corporate/Parent Company: Snyder Communications
Street Address: PO Box 111
City: Norwich
State: NY
Postal Code: 13815-0111
Office phone: (607) 965-8179
Publication Website: https://pennysaveronline.com/about/contact/
General E-mail: info@pennysaveronline.com
Total Circulation: 8039

PORT WASHINGTON

PORT WASHINGTON NEWS

Corporate/Parent Company: Anton Media Group
Street Address: 270 Main St
City: Port Washington
State: NY
Postal Code: 11050-2753
Office phone: (516) 747-8282
Publication Website: https://portwashington-news.com/
General E-mail: portwashington@antonmediagroup.com
Publisher Name: Angela Susan Anton
Publisher Email: aanton@antonmediagroup.com
Editor Name: CAROLINE RYAN
Editor Email: cryan@antonmediagroup.com
Editor Phone: (516) 403-5128
Year Established: 1903
Delivery Methods: Mail`Newsstand
Own Printing Facility?: Y
Published Days: Thur
Avg Paid Circ: 6501
Avg Free Circ: 329
Audit Company: Sworn/Estimate/Non-Audited
Audit Date: 30 09 2017

RAVENA

THE RAVENA NEWS-HERALD

Corporate/Parent Company: Johnson Newspaper Corp.
Street Address: 164 Main St.
City: Ravena
State: NY
Postal Code: 12143
Office phone: (518) 756-2030
Publication Website: https://ravenanews.com/
General E-mail: ravenanewsroom@gmail.com
Year Established: 2010
Delivery Methods: Mail`Racks
Own Printing Facility?: N
Commercial printers?: N
Published Days: Thur
Avg Paid Circ: 514
Audit Company: Sworn/Estimate/Non-Audited
Audit Date: 6 10 2019
Total Circulation: 25000

RICHFIELD SPRINGS

HALL OF FAME PENNYSAVER

Corporate/Parent Company: Snyder Communications
Street Address: 3178 US Highway 20
City: Richfield Springs
State: NY
Postal Code: 13439-2808
Office phone: (315) 858-1730
Publication Website: https://pennysaveronline.com/about/contact/
General E-mail: info@pennysaveronline.com
Total Circulation: 3700

SIDNEY

SIDNEY PENNYSAVER

Corporate/Parent Company: Snyder Communications
Street Address: 36 Main Street
City: Sidney
State: NY
Postal Code: 13838
Office phone: (607) 563-3761
Publication Website: https://pennysaveronline.com/about/contact/
General E-mail: info@pennysaveronline.com

WATERTOWN

JEFFERSON COUNTY PENNYSAVER

Corporate/Parent Company: Johnson Newspaper Corp.
Street Address: 260 Washington St
City: Watertown
State: NY
Postal Code: 13601-4669
Office phone: (315) 782-1000
Total Circulation: 3453

WILLIAMSVILLE

AMHERST BEE

Corporate/Parent Company: Bee Group Newspapers
Street Address: 5564 Main St
City: Williamsville
State: NY
Postal Code: 14221-5473
Office phone: (716) 632-4700
Publication Website: https://www.amherstbee.com/
Publisher Name: Trey Measer
Publisher Email: tmeaser@BeeNews.com
Publisher Phone: (716) 204-4900
Editor Name: Anna Derosa
Editor Email: aderosa@beenews.com
Editor Phone: (716) 204-4920
Advertising Executive Name: Brenda Denk
Advertising Executive Email: brendad@beenews.com
Advertising Executive Phone: (716) 204-4933
Year Established: 1879
Delivery Methods: Mail`Newsstand`Racks
Mechanical specifications: Type page 10 1/2 x 14; E - 5 cols, 2, 1/8 between; A - 5 cols, 2, 1/8 between; C - 6 cols, between.
Published Days: Wed
Avg Paid Circ: 5000
Avg Free Circ: 25000
Audit Company: Sworn/Estimate/Non-Audited
Audit Date: 6 10 2019
Total Circulation: 17172

CHEEKTOWAGA BEE

Corporate/Parent Company: Bee Group Newspapers
Street Address: 5564 Main St
City: Williamsville
State: NY
Postal Code: 14221-5410
Office phone: (716) 632-4700
Publication Website: https://www.cheektowagabee.com/
Publisher Name: Trey Measer
Publisher Email: tmeaser@BeeNews.com
Publisher Phone: (716) 204-4900
Editor Name: Bryan Jackson
Editor Email: bjackson@beenews.com
Editor Phone: (716) 204-4915
Advertising Executive Name: Brenda Denk
Advertising Executive Email: brendad@beenews.com
Advertising Executive Phone: (716) 204-4933
Year Established: 1977
Delivery Methods: Mail`Newsstand`Racks
Mechanical specifications: Type page 10 1/2 x 14; E - 5 cols, 2, 1/8 between; A - 5 cols, 2, 1/8 between; C - 6 cols, between.
Published Days: Thur
Avg Paid Circ: 1800
Audit Company: Sworn/Estimate/Non-Audited

Audit Date: 6 10 2019
Mailroom Equipment: Kirk Rudy 12 into 1 P-Note Labels
Buisness Equipment: Total Ad Vision Data
Buisness Software: Vision Data
Classified Equipment: Vision Data Total Ad
Classified Software: Vision Data
Editorial Software: InDsign InCopy
Total Circulation: 8318

CLARENCE BEE

Corporate/Parent Company: Bee Group Newspapers
Street Address: 5564 Main St
City: Williamsville
State: NY
Postal Code: 14221-5410
Office phone: (716) 632-4700
Publication Website: https://www.clarencebee.com/
Publisher Name: Trey Measer
Publisher Email: tmeaser@BeeNews.com
Publisher Phone: (716) 204-4900
Editor Name: Ethan Powers
Editor Email: epowers@beenews.com
Editor Phone: (716) 204-4921
Advertising Executive Name: Brenda Denk
Advertising Executive Email: brendad@beenews.com
Advertising Executive Phone: (716) 204-4933
Year Established: 1937
Delivery Methods: Mail`Newsstand`Racks
Mechanical specifications: Type page 10 1/2 x 14; E - 5 cols, 2, 1/8 between; A - 5 cols, 2, 1/8 between; C - 6 cols, between.
Published Days: Wed
Avg Paid Circ: 3700
Avg Free Circ: 16
Audit Company: Sworn/Estimate/Non-Audited
Audit Date: 6 10 2019
Total Circulation: 17000

DEPEW BEE

Corporate/Parent Company: Bee Group Newspapers
Street Address: 5564 Main St
City: Williamsville
State: NY
Postal Code: 14221-5410
Office phone: (716) 632-4700
Publication Website: https://www.lancasterbee.com/
Publisher Name: Trey Measer
Publisher Email: tmeaser@BeeNews.com
Publisher Phone: (716) 204-4900
Editor Name: Holly Lipka
Editor Email: hlipka@beenews.com
Editor Phone: (716) 204-4924
Advertising Executive Name: Brenda Denk
Advertising Executive Email: brendad@beenews.com
Advertising Executive Phone: (716) 204-4933
Year Established: 1893
Delivery Methods: Mail`Newsstand`Racks
Mechanical specifications: Type page 10 1/2 x 14; E - 5 cols, 2, 1/8 between; A - 5 cols, 2, 1/8 between; C - 6 cols, between.
Published Days: Thur
Avg Paid Circ: 3700
Audit Company: Sworn/Estimate/Non-Audited
Audit Date: 6 10 2019
Total Circulation: 514

EAST AURORA BEE

Corporate/Parent Company: Bee Group Newspapers
Street Address: 5564 Main St
City: Williamsville
State: NY
Postal Code: 14221-5410
Office phone: (716) 632-4700
Publication Website: https://www.eastaurorabee.com/
Publisher Name: Trey Measer
Publisher Email: tmeaser@BeeNews.com
Publisher Phone: (716) 204-4900
Editor Name: Kate Pelczynski
Editor Email: katep@beenews.com
Editor Phone: (716) 204-4918
Advertising Executive Name: Brenda Denk
Advertising Executive Email: brendad@beenews.com
Advertising Executive Phone: (716) 204-4933
Year Established: 1987
Delivery Methods: Mail`Newsstand`Racks
Mechanical specifications: Type page 10 1/2 x 14; E - 5 cols, 2, 1/8 between; A - 5 cols, 2, 1/8 between; C - 6 cols, between.
Published Days: Thur
Avg Paid Circ: 2100
Audit Company: Sworn/Estimate/Non-Audited
Audit Date: 6 10 2019
Total Circulation: 10640

KEN-TON BEE

Corporate/Parent Company: Bee Group Newspapers
Street Address: 5564 Main St
City: Williamsville
State: NY
Postal Code: 14221-5410
Office phone: (716) 632-4700
Publication Website: https://www.kentonbee.com/
Publisher Name: Trey Measer
Publisher Email: tmeaser@BeeNews.com
Publisher Phone: (716) 204-4900
Editor Name: Alan Rizzo
Editor Email: arizzo@beenews.com
Editor Phone: (716) 204-4920
Advertising Executive Name: Brenda Denk
Advertising Executive Email: brendad@beenews.com
Advertising Executive Phone: (716) 204-4933
Year Established: 1982
Delivery Methods: Mail`Newsstand`Racks
Mechanical specifications: Type page 10 1/2 x 14; E - 5 cols, 2, 1/8 between; A - 5 cols, 2, 1/8 between; C - 6 cols, between.
Published Days: Wed
Avg Paid Circ: 1800
Avg Free Circ: 10
Audit Company: Sworn/Estimate/Non-Audited
Audit Date: 6 10 2019
Total Circulation: 7291

LANCASTER BEE

Corporate/Parent Company: Bee Group Newspapers
Street Address: 5564 Main St
City: Williamsville
State: NY
Postal Code: 14221-5410
Office phone: (716) 632-4700
Publication Website: https://www.lancasterbee.com/
Publisher Name: Trey Measer
Publisher Email: tmeaser@BeeNews.com
Publisher Phone: (716) 204-4900
Editor Name: Holly Lipka
Editor Email: hlipka@beenews.com
Editor Phone: (716) 204-4924
Advertising Executive Name: Brenda Denk
Advertising Executive Email: brendad@beenews.com
Advertising Executive Phone: (716) 204-4933
Year Established: 1877
Delivery Methods: Mail`Newsstand`Racks
Published Days: Thur
Audit Company: Sworn/Estimate/Non-Audited
Audit Date: 6 10 2019
Total Circulation: 1185

Non-Daily Newspapers in the U.S.

ORCHARD PARK BEE

Corporate/Parent Company: Bee Group Newspapers
Street Address: 5564 Main St
City: Williamsville
State: NY
Postal Code: 14221-5410
Office phone: (716) 632-4700
Publication Website: https://www.orchardparkbee.com/
Publisher Name: Trey Measer
Publisher Email: tmeaser@BeeNews.com
Publisher Phone: (716) 204-4900
Editor Name: Chris Graham
Editor Email: cgraham@beenews.com
Editor Phone: (716) 204-4902
Advertising Executive Name: Dave Tiebor
Advertising Executive Email: dtiebor@beenews.com
Advertising Executive Phone: (716) 204-4932
Year Established: 1986
Delivery Methods: Mail`Newsstand`Racks
Mechanical specifications: Type page 10 1/2 x 14; E - 5 cols, 2, 1/8 between; A - 5 cols, 2, 1/8 between; C - 6 cols, between.
Published Days: Thur
Avg Paid Circ: 2140
Audit Company: Sworn/Estimate/Non-Audited
Audit Date: 6 10 2019
Total Circulation: 5000

WEST SENECA BEE

Corporate/Parent Company: Bee Group Newspapers
Street Address: 5564 Main St
City: Williamsville
State: NY
Postal Code: 14221-5410
Office phone: (716) 632-4700
Publication Website: https://www.westsenecabee.com/
Publisher Name: Trey Measer
Publisher Email: tmeaser@BeeNews.com
Publisher Phone: (716) 204-4900
Editor Name: Taylor Nigrelli
Editor Email: tnigrelli@beenews.com
Editor Phone: (716) 204-4922
Advertising Executive Name: Brenda Denk
Advertising Executive Email: brendad@beenews.com
Advertising Executive Phone: (716) 204-4933
Year Established: 1980
Delivery Methods: Mail`Newsstand`Racks
Own Printing Facility?: Y
Mechanical specifications: Type page 10 1/2 x 14; E - 5 cols, 2, 1/8 between; A - 5 cols, 2, 1/8 between; C - 6 cols, between.
Published Days: Thur
Avg Paid Circ: 5200
Avg Free Circ: 14
Audit Company: Sworn/Estimate/Non-Audited
Audit Date: 6 10 2019
Note: Same As North Countryman Equipment
Total Circulation: 15316

WOODSIDE

BROOKLYN DOWNTOWN STAR

Corporate/Parent Company: BQE Publishing Inc.
Street Address: 4523 47th St
City: Woodside
State: NY
Postal Code: 11377
Office phone: (718) 639-7000
Publication Website: http://www.brooklyndowntownstar.com/
General E-mail: ads@queensledger.com
Publisher Name: Walter H. Sanchez
Publisher Email: wsanchez@queensledger.com
Editor Name: Shane Miller
Editor Email: smiller@queensledger.com
Year Established: 2004
Delivery Methods: Mail`Newsstand`Racks
Commercial printers?: Y
Mechanical specifications: 13"high by 10"wide
Published Days: Thur
Avg Paid Circ: 500
Avg Free Circ: 14500
Audit Company: Sworn/Estimate/Non-Audited
Audit Date: 6 10 2019
Total Circulation: 20000

FOREST HILLS/REGO PARK TIMES

Corporate/Parent Company: BQE Publishing Inc.
Street Address: 45-23 47 St
City: Woodside
State: NY
Postal Code: 11377
Office phone: (718) 039-7000
Publication Website: http://www.foresthillstimes.com/
General E-mail: ads@queensledger.com
Publisher Name: Walter H. Sanchez
Publisher Email: wsanchez@queensledger.com
Editor Name: Shane Miller
Editor Email: smiller@queensledger.com
Year Established: 1995
Delivery Methods: Mail`Newsstand`Racks
Published Days: Thur
Avg Paid Circ: 18000
Avg Free Circ: 165
Audit Company: Sworn/Estimate/Non-Audited
Audit Date: 6 10 2019
Total Circulation: 5517

GLENDALE REGISTER

Corporate/Parent Company: BQE Publishing Inc.
Street Address: 45-23 47 St
City: Woodside
State: NY
Postal Code: 11377
Office phone: (718) 639-7000
Publication Website: http://www.glendaleregister.com/
General E-mail: ads@queensledger.com
Publisher Name: Walter H. Sanchez
Publisher Email: wsanchez@queensledger.com
Editor Name: Shane Miller
Editor Email: smiller@queensledger.com
Year Established: 1935
Delivery Methods: Mail`Newsstand`Racks
Mechanical specifications: Type page 10 x 14; E - 4 cols, 2 3/8, 1/4 between; A - 4 cols, 2 3/8, 1/4 between; C - 5 cols, 1 15/16, 1/4 between.
Published Days: Thur
Avg Paid Circ: 1320
Avg Free Circ: 165
Audit Company: Sworn/Estimate/Non-Audited
Audit Date: 6 10 2019
Total Circulation: 1400

GREENPOINT STAR & NORTHSIDE WEEKLY NEWS

Corporate/Parent Company: BQE Publishing Inc.
Street Address: 4523 47th St
City: Woodside
State: NY
Postal Code: 11377
Office phone: (718) 639-7000
Publication Website: http://www.greenpointstar.com/
General E-mail: ads@queensledger.com
Publisher Name: Walter H. Sanchez
Publisher Email: wsanchez@queensledger.com
Editor Name: Shane Miller
Editor Email: smiller@queensledger.com
Year Established: 1898
Delivery Methods: Mail`Newsstand`Racks
Mechanical specifications: 13" high by 10" high
Published Days: Thur
Avg Paid Circ: 2000
Avg Free Circ: 13000
Audit Company: Sworn/Estimate/Non-Audited
Audit Date: 6 10 2019
Total Circulation: 6617

LONG ISLAND CITY/ASTORIA/JACKSON HEIGHTS JOURNAL

Corporate/Parent Company: BQE Publishing Inc.
Street Address: 4523 47th St
City: Woodside
State: NY
Postal Code: 11377
Office phone: (718) 639-7000
Publication Website: http://www.licjournal.com/
General E-mail: ads@queensledger.com
Publisher Name: Walter H. Sanchez
Publisher Email: wsanchez@queensledger.com
Editor Name: Shane Miller
Editor Email: smiller@queensledger.com
Year Established: 1986
Delivery Methods: Mail`Newsstand`Racks
Mechanical specifications: 13" high by 10" wide
Published Days: Thur
Avg Paid Circ: 1100
Avg Free Circ: 17000
Audit Company: Sworn/Estimate/Non-Audited
Audit Date: 6 10 2019
Total Circulation: 5200

QUEENS LEDGER

Corporate/Parent Company: BQE Publishing Inc.
Street Address: 45-23 47 St
City: Woodside
State: NY
Postal Code: 11377
Office phone: (718) 639-7000
Publication Website: http://queensledger.com/
General E-mail: ads@queensledger.com
Publisher Name: Walter H. Sanchez
Publisher Email: wsanchez@queensledger.com
Editor Name: Shane Miller
Editor Email: smiller@queensledger.com
Year Established: 1873
Delivery Methods: Mail`Newsstand`Racks
Commercial printers?: Y
Published Days: Thur
Avg Paid Circ: 10890
Audit Company: Sworn/Estimate/Non-Audited
Audit Date: 6 10 2019
Total Circulation: 5214

THE LEADER-OBSERVER OF WOODHAVEN

Corporate/Parent Company: BQE Publishing Inc.
Street Address: 45-23 47 St
City: Woodside
State: NY
Postal Code: 11377
Office phone: (718) 639-7000
Publication Website: http://www.leaderobserver.com/
General E-mail: ads@queensledger.com
Publisher Name: Walter H. Sanchez
Publisher Email: wsanchez@queensledger.com
Editor Name: Shane Miller
Editor Email: smiller@queensledger.com
Year Established: 1909
Delivery Methods: Mail`Newsstand`Racks
Published Days: Thur
Avg Paid Circ: 25000
Audit Company: Sworn/Estimate/Non-Audited
Audit Date: 6 10 2019

THE QUEENS EXAMINER

Corporate/Parent Company: BQE Publishing Inc.
Street Address: 454-23 47 Street
City: Woodside
State: NY
Postal Code: 11377
Office phone: (718) 639-7000
Publication Website: http://www.queensexaminer.com/
General E-mail: ads@queensledger.com
Publisher Name: Walter H. Sanchez
Publisher Email: wsanchez@queensledger.com
Editor Name: Shane Miller
Editor Email: smiller@queensledger.com
Year Established: 1999
Delivery Methods: Mail`Newsstand`Racks
Mechanical specifications: 13" high by 10" high
Published Days: Thur
Avg Paid Circ: 5000
Avg Free Circ: 12000
Audit Company: Sworn/Estimate/Non-Audited
Audit Date: 6 10 2019
Total Circulation: 3445

OGDENSBURG JOURNAL

Corporate/Parent Company: Johnson Newspaper Corp.
State: NY

OHIO

ALLIANCE

THE NEWS LEADER

Corporate/Parent Company: Gannett
Street Address: 40 South Linden Ave.
City: Alliance
State: OH
Postal Code: 44601
Office phone: 330-821-1200
Publication Website: www.the-review.com/news/minerva
Editor Name: Laura Kessel
Editor Email: lkessel@the-review.com
Total Circulation: 4400

ADA

THE ADA HERALD

Corporate/Parent Company: Delphos Herald, Inc.
Street Address: 229 N Main St
City: Ada
State: OH
Postal Code: 45810-1109
Office phone: (419) 634-6055
Publication Website: https://adaherald.com/
General E-mail: candres@putnamsentinel.com
Editor Name: Steven Coburn-Griffis
Editor Email: news@putnamsentinel.com

ANTWERP

WEST BEND NEWS

Street Address: 101 N Main St
City: Antwerp
State: OH
Postal Code: 45813
Office phone: 419-258-2000
Publication Website: www.westbendnews.net/autonews
General E-mail: info@westbendnews.net
Publisher Name: Bryce Steiner

CHAGRIN FALLS

CHAGRIN VALLEY TIMES

Corporate/Parent Company: Chagrin Valley Publishing Co
Street Address: 525 Washington St

City: Chagrin Falls
State: OH
Postal Code: 44022-4455
Office phone: (440) 247-5335
Publication Website: http://www.chagrinvalleytoday.com/
General E-mail: news@chagrinvalleytimes.com
Publisher Name: H. Kenneth Douthit
Editor Name: Ellen Kleinerman
Editor Email: editor@chagrinvalleytimes.com

GEAUGA COURIER

Corporate/Parent Company: Chagrin Valley Publishing Co
Street Address: 525 Washington St
City: Chagrin Falls
State: OH
Postal Code: 44022-4455
Office phone: (440) 247-5335
Publication Website: http://www.chagrinvalleytoday.com/site/contact.html
General E-mail: news@chagrinvalleytimes.com
Publisher Name: H. Kenneth Douthit
Editor Name: Ellen Kleinerman
Editor Email: editor@chagrinvalleytimes.com

SOLON TIMES

Corporate/Parent Company: Chagrin Valley Publishing Co
Street Address: 525 Washington St
City: Chagrin Falls
State: OH
Postal Code: 44022-4455
Office phone: (440) 247-5335
Publication Website: http://www.chagrinvalleytoday.com/site/contact.html
General E-mail: news@chagrinvalleytimes.com
Publisher Name: H. Kenneth Douthit
Editor Name: Ellen Kleinerman
Editor Email: editor@chagrinvalleytimes.com

THE PRESS

Corporate/Parent Company: Gannett
Street Address: 525 Washington St
City: Chagrin Falls
State: OH
Postal Code: 44022-4455
Office phone: (440) 247-5335
Publication Website: http://www.chagrinvalleytoday.com/site/contact.html
General E-mail: news@chagrinvalleytimes.com
Publisher Name: H. Kenneth Douthit
Editor Name: Ellen Kleinerman
Editor Email: editor@chagrinvalleytimes.com

COLUMBUS

THISWEEK BEXLEY NEWS

Street Address: 5300 Crosswind Drive
City: Columbus
State: OH
Postal Code: 43228
Office phone: (740) 888-6000
Publication Website: https://www.thisweeknews.com/bexley
General E-mail: vbarnette@dispatch.com
Editor Name: Lisa Proctor
Editor Email: lproctor@thisweeknews.com

THISWEEK CLINTONVILLE BOOSTER

Street Address: 5300 Crosswind Drive
City: Columbus
State: OH
Postal Code: 43228
Office phone: (740) 888-6000
Publication Website: https://www.thisweeknews.com/clintonville
General E-mail: sleitch@dispatch.com

THISWEEK DELAWARE NEWS

Street Address: 5300 Crosswind Drive
City: Columbus
State: OH
Postal Code: 43228
Office phone: (740) 888-6000
Publication Website: https://www.thisweeknews.com/delaware
General E-mail: aabrams@dispatch.com
Editor Name: Dennis Laycock
Editor Email: dlaycock@thisweeknews.com

THISWEEK DUBLIN VILLAGER

Street Address: 5300 Crosswind Drive
City: Columbus
State: OH
Postal Code: 43228
Office phone: (740) 888-6000
Publication Website: https://www.thisweeknews.com/dublin
General E-mail: khinch@dispatch.com
Editor Name: Tim Krumlauf
Editor Email: tkrumlauf@thisweeknews.com

THISWEEK GERMAN VILLAGE GAZETTE

Street Address: 5300 Crosswind Drive
City: Columbus
State: OH
Postal Code: 43228
Office phone: (740) 888-6000
Publication Website: https://www.thisweeknews.com/germanvillage
General E-mail: cjoseph@dispatch.com
Editor Name: Tim Krumlauf
Editor Email: tkrumlauf@thisweeknews.com

THISWEEK GROVE CITY RECORD

Street Address: 5300 Crosswind Drive
City: Columbus
State: OH
Postal Code: 43228
Office phone: (740) 888-6000
Publication Website: https://www.thisweeknews.com/grovecity
General E-mail: kshockey@dispatch.com
Editor Name: Lisa Proctor
Editor Email: lproctor@thisweeknews.com

THISWEEK HILLIARD NORTHWEST NEWS

Street Address: 5300 Crosswind Drive
City: Columbus
State: OH
Postal Code: 43228
Office phone: (740) 888-6000
Publication Website: https://www.thisweeknews.com/hilliard
General E-mail: mvpardi@dispatch.com
Editor Name: Neil Thompson
Editor Email: nthompson@thisweeknews.com

THISWEEK JOHNSTOWN

INDEPENDENT

Street Address: 5300 Crosswind Drive
City: Columbus
State: OH
Postal Code: 43228
Office phone: (740) 888-6000
Publication Website: https://www.thisweeknews.com/johnstown
General E-mail: blanier@dispatch.com

THISWEEK LICKING COUNTY NEWS

Street Address: 5300 Crosswind Drive
City: Columbus
State: OH
Postal Code: 43228
Office phone: (740) 888-6000
Publication Website: http://www.thisweeknews.com/lickingcounty
General E-mail: blanier@dispatch.com

THISWEEK MARYSVILLE NEWS

Street Address: 5300 Crosswind Drive
City: Columbus
State: OH
Postal Code: 43228
Office phone: (740) 888-6000
Publication Website: http://www.thisweeknews.com/marysville
General E-mail: aabrams@dispatch.com

THISWEEK NEW ALBANY NEWS

Street Address: 5300 Crosswind Drive
City: Columbus
State: OH
Postal Code: 43228
Office phone: (740) 888-6000
Publication Website: https://www.thisweeknews.com/newalbany
General E-mail: blanier@dispatch.com
Editor Name: Neil Thompson
Editor Email: nthompson@thisweeknews.com

THISWEEK NORTHLAND NEWS

Street Address: 5300 Crosswind Drive
City: Columbus
State: OH
Postal Code: 43228
Office phone: (740) 888-6000
Publication Website: https://www.thisweeknews.com/northland
General E-mail: rroork@dispatch.com

THISWEEK NORTHWEST NEWS

Street Address: 5300 Crosswind Drive
City: Columbus
State: OH
Postal Code: 43228
Office phone: (740) 888-6000
Publication Website: https://www.thisweeknews.com/northwest
General E-mail: tkrumlauf@thisweeknews.com
Editor Name: Tim Krumlauf
Editor Email: tkrumlauf@thisweeknews.com

THISWEEK OLENTANGY VALLEY NEWS

Street Address: 5300 Crosswind Drive
City: Columbus
State: OH
Postal Code: 43228
Office phone: (740) 888-6000
Publication Website: https://www.thisweeknews.com/olentangy
General E-mail: dlaycock@thisweeknews.com
Editor Name: Dennis Laycock
Editor Email: dlaycock@thisweeknews.com

THISWEEK PICKERINGTON TIMES-SUN

Street Address: 5300 Crosswind Drive
City: Columbus
State: OH
Postal Code: 43228
Office phone: (740) 888-6000
Publication Website: https://www.thisweeknews.com/pickerington
General E-mail: vbarnette@dispatch.com
Editor Name: Tim Krumlauf
Editor Email: tkrumlauf@thisweeknews.com

THISWEEK REYNOLDSBURG NEWS

Street Address: 5300 Crosswind Drive
City: Columbus
State: OH
Postal Code: 43228
Office phone: (740) 888-6000
Publication Website: https://www.thisweeknews.com/reynoldsburg
General E-mail: vbarnette@dispatch.com

THISWEEK ROCKY FORK ENTERPRISE

Street Address: 5300 Crosswind Drive
City: Columbus
State: OH
Postal Code: 43228
Office phone: (740) 888-6000
Publication Website: https://www.thisweeknews.com/gahanna
General E-mail: blanier@dispatch.com
Editor Name: Lisa Proctor
Editor Email: lproctor@thisweeknews.com

THISWEEK THE CANAL WINCHESTER TIMES

Street Address: 5300 Crosswind Drive
City: Columbus
State: OH
Postal Code: 43228
Office phone: (740) 888-6000
Publication Website: https://www.thisweeknews.com/canalwinchester
General E-mail: bjameson@dispatch.com

THISWEEK TRI-VILLAGE NEWS

Street Address: 5300 Crosswind Drive
City: Columbus
State: OH
Postal Code: 43228
Office phone: (740) 888-6000
Publication Website: https://www.thisweeknews.com/news/grandview
General E-mail: ewilson@dispatch.com
Editor Name: Dennis Laycock
Editor Email: dlaycock@thisweeknews.com

Non-Daily Newspapers in the U.S.

THISWEEK UPPER ARLINGTON NEWS
Street Address: 5300 Crosswind Drive
City: Columbus
State: OH
Postal Code: 43228
Office phone: (740) 888-6000
Publication Website: https://www.thisweeknews.com/upperarlington
General E-mail: ewilson@dispatch.com

THISWEEK WEST SIDE NEWS
Street Address: 5300 Crosswind Drive
City: Columbus
State: OH
Postal Code: 43228
Office phone: (740) 888-6000
Publication Website: https://www.thisweeknews.com/westside
General E-mail: kshockey@dispatch.com

THISWEEK WESTERVILLE NEWS & PUBLIC OPINION
Street Address: 5300 Crosswind Drive
City: Columbus
State: OH
Postal Code: 43228
Office phone: (740) 888-6000
Publication Website: https://www.thisweeknews.com/westerville
General E-mail: kbrown@dispatch.com

THISWEEK WHITEHALL NEWS
Street Address: 5300 Crosswind Drive
City: Columbus
State: OH
Postal Code: 43228
Office phone: (740) 888-6000
Publication Website: https://www.thisweeknews.com/whitehall
General E-mail: vbarnette@dispatch.com

THISWEEK WORTHINGTON NEWS
Street Address: 5300 Crosswind Drive
City: Columbus
State: OH
Postal Code: 43228
Office phone: (740) 888-6000
Publication Website: https://www.thisweeknews.com/worthington
General E-mail: sleitch@dispatch.com

DAYTON

TODAY'S PULSE OF BUTLER COUNTY
Corporate/Parent Company: Cox Media Group
Street Address: 1611 S Main Street
City: Dayton
State: OH
Postal Code: 45409
Office phone: 513-420-0097
Publication Website: www.journal-news.com
General E-mail: newsdesk@cmgohio.com
Editor Name: Jim Bebbington
Editor Email: jim.bebbington@coxinc.com

TODAY'S PULSE OF WARREN COUNTY
Corporate/Parent Company: Cox Media Group
Street Address: 1611 S Main Street
City: Dayton
State: OH
Postal Code: 45409
Office phone: 513-420-0097
Publication Website: www.journal-news.com
General E-mail: newsdesk@cmgohio.com
Editor Name: Jim Bebbington
Editor Email: jim.bebbington@coxinc.com

DELPHOS

DELPHOS DAILY HERALD
Corporate/Parent Company: DHI Media, Inc.
Street Address: 405 N Main St
City: Delphos
State: OH
Postal Code: 45833-1577
Office phone: (419) 695-0015
Publication Website: https://www.delphosherald.com/
General E-mail: classifieds@delphosherald.com
Editor Name: Nancy Spencer
Editor Email: nspencer@delphosherald.com

HARRISON

THE HARRISON PRESS
Street Address: 112 Harrison Ave.
City: Harrison
State: OH
Postal Code: 45030
Office phone: 1-513-367-4582
Publication Website: www.theharrison-press.com
General E-mail: frontoffice@registerpublications.com
Editor Name: Joe Awad
Editor Email: jawad@registerpublications.com

KENT

NORDONIA NEWS LEADER
Corporate/Parent Company: Gannett
Street Address: 1050 W. Main St.
City: Kent
State: OH
Postal Code: 44240
Office phone: 330-541-9400
Publication Website: www.mytownneo.com/the-news-leader
Editor Name: Michael Shearer
Editor Email: mshearer@recordpub.com

LOUDONVILLE

LOUDONVILLE MOHICAN AREA TIMES-SHOPPER
Street Address: 263 West Main Street
City: Loudonville
State: OH
Postal Code: 44842
Office phone: (419) 994-5600
Publication Website: www.times-gazette.com/news/loudonville
Publisher Name: Bill Albrecht
Publisher Email: balbrecht@gatehousemedia.com
Publisher Phone: 330-996-3782
Editor Name: Rick Armon
Editor Email: rarmon@times-gazette.com

MCARTHUR

VINTON JACKSON COURIER
Street Address: 103 S. Market St.
City: McArthur
State: OH
Postal Code: 45651
Office phone: 740-596-5393
Publication Website: www.vintonjacksoncourier.com
General E-mail: info@vintonjacksoncourier.com
Editor Name: Sydney Dawes
Editor Email: sdawes@vintoncourier.com;

MT. GILEAD

MT. GILEAD
Corporate/Parent Company: AIM Media Midwest
Street Address: 46 S. Main Street
City: Mt. Gilead
State: OH
Postal Code: 43338
Office phone: 419-946-3010
Publication Website: www.morrowcountysentinel.com
Editor Name: Kristine Collier
Editor Email: aconchel@aimmediamidwest.com

OTTAWA

PUTNAM COUNTY SENTINEL
Corporate/Parent Company: DHI Media, Inc.
Street Address: 224 E Main St
City: Ottawa
State: OH
Postal Code: 45875-1944
Office phone: (419) 523-5709
Publication Website: https://putnamsentinel.com/
General E-mail: advertising@putnamsentinel.com
Editor Name: Martin Verni
Editor Email: martin@putnamsentinel.com

OTTAWA

PUTNAM COUNTY VIDETTE
Corporate/Parent Company: DHI Media, Inc.
Street Address: 1502 N. Perry St., P.O. Box 149
City: Ottawa
State: OH
Postal Code: 45875
Office phone: (419) 523-5709
Publication Website: https://putnamsentinel.com/
General E-mail: advertising@putnamsentinel.com
Editor Name: Martin Verni
Editor Email: martin@putnamsentinel.com

PAULDING

THE PAULDING PROGRESS
Corporate/Parent Company: DHI Media, Inc.
Street Address: 113 S Williams St
City: Paulding
State: OH
Postal Code: 45879-1429
Office phone: (419) 399-4015
Publication Website: https://progressnewspaper.org/
General E-mail: sbohner@progressnewspaper.org
Editor Name: Jennifer Dempsey
Editor Email: progress@progressnewspaper.org

ROCKY RIVER

WEST LIFE
Corporate/Parent Company: Chagrin Valley Publishing Co
Street Address: 19071 Old Detroit Rd
City: Rocky River
State: OH
Postal Code: 44116-1767
Office phone: (440) 871-5797
Publication Website: https://www.westlifenews.com/
General E-mail: editor@westlifenews.com
Publisher Name: H. Kenneth Douthit
Editor Name: Susan Condon Love
Editor Email: editor@westlfenews.com

SWANTON

SWANTON ENTERPRISE
Corporate/Parent Company: AIM Media Midwest
Street Address: PO Box 180
City: Swanton
State: OH
Postal Code: 43558
Office phone: 419-335-2010
Publication Website: www.swantonenterprise.com
General E-mail: tsenews@aimmediamidwest.com
Editor Name: Drew Stambaugh

URBANA

LOGAN COUNTY INDIAN LAKE CURRENT
Corporate/Parent Company: AIM Media Midwest
Street Address: 1637 E US Hwy 36
City: Urbana
State: OH
Postal Code: 43078
Office phone: 937-652-1331
Publication Website: www.weeklycurrents.com
Publisher Name: Lane Moon
Publisher Email: lmoon@aimmediamidwest.com
Editor Name: Kathleen Fox
Editor Email: kfox@aimmediamidwest.com

VAN WERT

THE TIMES BULLETIN
Corporate/Parent Company: DHI Media, Inc.
Street Address: 1167 Westwood Drive
City: Van Wert
State: OH
Postal Code: 45891
Office phone: (419) 238-2285
Publication Website: https://timesbulletin.com/
General E-mail: nswaney@timesbulletin.com
Editor Name: Kirsten Barnhart
Editor Email: kbarnhart@timesbulletin.com

WILLARD

THE TIMES JUNCTION
Corporate/Parent Company: SDGNewsgroup
Street Address: 211 S Myrtle Ave
City: Willard
State: OH
Postal Code: 44890
Office phone: 419-935-0184
Publication Website: www.sdgnewsgroup.com
General E-mail: globe@sdgnewsgroup.com
Editor Name: Jane Ernsberger

WOODSFIELD

MONROE COUNTY BEACON
Corporate/Parent Company: DHI Media, Inc.
Street Address: 103 E Court St
City: Woodsfield
State: OH
Postal Code: 43793-1110
Office phone: (740) 472-0734
Publication Website: https://www.mcbeacon.com/
General E-mail: monroecountybeacon@sbcglobal.net
Publisher Name: Kreg Robinson
Editor Name: Martha Ackerman

MONROE COUNTY SENTINEL

Corporate/Parent Company: DHI Media, Inc.
Street Address: 103 E Court St
City: Woodsfield
State: OH
Postal Code: 43793-1110
Office phone: (740) 472-0734
Publication Website: https://www.mcbeacon.com/
General E-mail: monroecountybeacon@sbcglobal.net
Publisher Name: Kreg Robinson
Editor Name: Martha Ackerman

OKLAHOMA

ADA

CHICKASAW NATION MEDIA RELATIONS

Street Address: 520 E. Arlington
City: Ada
State: OK
Postal Code: 74820
Office phone: (580) 559-0921
Publication Website: www.chickasaw.net
Editor Name: Tony Choate
Editor Email: Tony.Choate@chickasaw.net

ALVA

ALVA REVIEW-COURIER

Street Address: 620 Choctaw Street
City: Alva
State: OK
Postal Code: 73717
Office phone: (580) 327-2200
Publication Website: www.alvareviewcourier.com
General E-mail: manager@alvareviewcourier.net
Publisher Name: Lynn Martin
Publisher Email: lynn@lynnmartin.net
Editor Name: Marione Martin
Editor Email: marione@alvareviewcourier.net

BUFFALO

BUFFALO WEEKLY NEWS

Street Address: 201 North Hoy
City: Buffalo
State: OK
Postal Code: 73834
Office phone: 580-727-1094
Publication Website: www.buffaloweeklynews.com/index.html
Publisher Name: Kayla Williams
Publisher Email: kayla@buffaloweeklynews.com

BUFFALO

BUFFALO WEEKLY NEWS

Street Address: 201 North Hoy
City: Buffalo
State: OK
Postal Code: 73834
Office phone: 580-727-1094
Publication Website: www.buffaloweeklynews.com/index.html
Publisher Name: Kayla Williams
Publisher Email: kayla@buffaloweeklynews.com

CHECOTAH

MCINTOSH COUNTY DEMOCRAT

Street Address: 300-A S. Broadway
City: Checotah
State: OK
Postal Code: 74426
Office phone: (918) 473-2313
Publication Website: www.mcintoshdemocrat.com
General E-mail: demonews@bigbasinllc.com

CHECOTAH

MCINTOSH COUNTY DEMOCRAT

Street Address: 300-A S. Broadway
City: Checotah
State: OK
Postal Code: 74426
Office phone: (918) 473-2313
Publication Website: www.mcintoshdemocrat.com
General E-mail: demonews@bigbasinllc.com

CHEYENNE

THE CHEYENNE STAR

Street Address: 417 E Broadway
City: Cheyenne
State: OK
Postal Code: 73628
Office phone: 580-497-3324
Publication Website: cheyennestar.online
Editor Name: Melanie Anspaugh
Editor Email: cheystar@mydobson.net

THE CHEYENNE STAR

Street Address: 417 E Broadway
City: Cheyenne
State: OK
Postal Code: 73628
Office phone: 580-497-3324
Publication Website: cheyennestar.online
Editor Name: Melanie Anspaugh
Editor Email: cheystar@mydobson.net

CHOCTAW

CHOCTAW TIMES

Street Address: 2424 Main St
City: Choctaw
State: OK
Postal Code: 73020
Office phone: 405-390-0390
Publication Website: www.choctawtimes.com
Editor Name: Ryan Horton
Editor Email: choctawtimes@sbcglobal.net

DURANT

CHOCTAW NATION OF OKLAHOMA

Street Address: PO Box 1210
City: Durant
State: OK
Postal Code: 74702-1210
Office phone: (800) 522-6170
Publication Website: www.choctawnation.com
General E-mail: help@choctawnation.com
Editor Name: Ronni Pierce

EAKLY

THE COUNTRY CONNECTION NEWS

Street Address: 317 Main St.
City: Eakly
State: OK
Postal Code: 73033
Office phone: 405-797-3648
Publication Website: www.countryconnectionnews.com
General E-mail: countryconnectionnews@yahoo.com

THE COUNTRY CONNECTION NEWS

Street Address: 317 Main St.
City: Eakly
State: OK
Postal Code: 73033
Office phone: 405-797-3648
Publication Website: www.countryconnectionnews.com
General E-mail: countryconnectionnews@yahoo.com

EDMOND

EDMOND LIFE & LEISURE

Street Address: 107 S. Broadway
City: Edmond
State: OK
Postal Code: 73034
Office phone: 405-340-3311
Publication Website: www.edmondlifeandleisure.com
Publisher Name: Ray Hibbard Jr.
Publisher Email: ray@edmondpaper.com
Editor Name: Steve Gust
Editor Email: news@edmondpaper.com

EL RENO

CHEYENNE & ARAPAHO TRIBAL TRIBUNE

Street Address: 700 North Black Kettle Blvd
City: El Reno
State: OK
Postal Code: 73036
Office phone: (918) 453-5269
Publication Website: www.c-a-tribes.org
Editor Name: Rosemary Stephens
Editor Email: rmstephens@c-a-tribes.org

ELGIN

THE CHRONICLE

Corporate/Parent Company: Gannett
Street Address: 7602 US Highway 277, Suite A
City: Elgin
State: OK
Postal Code: 73538
Office phone: 580-529-6397
Publication Website: www.thechronicle.news
General E-mail: thechronicle@hillcom.net

THE CHRONICLE

Corporate/Parent Company: Gannett
Street Address: 7602 US Highway 277, Suite A
City: Elgin
State: OK
Postal Code: 73538
Office phone: 580-529-6397
Publication Website: www.thechronicle.news
General E-mail: thechronicle@hillcom.net

EUFAULA

THE EUFAULA INDIAN JOURNAL

Street Address: 109 S. Main
City: Eufaula
State: OK
Postal Code: 74432
Office phone: 918) 689-2191
Publication Website: www.eufaulaindianjournal.com
General E-mail: ijdemolegals@bigbasinllc.com

THE EUFAULA INDIAN JOURNAL

Street Address: 109 S. Main
City: Eufaula
State: OK
Postal Code: 74432
Office phone: 918) 689-2191
Publication Website: www.eufaulaindianjournal.com
General E-mail: ijdemolegals@bigbasinllc.com

HASKELL

THE HASKELL NEWS

Street Address: 108 East Main Street
City: Haskell
State: OK
Postal Code: 74436
Office phone: 918) 482-5619
Publication Website: haskellweekly.news
General E-mail: info@haskellweekly.news.

THE HASKELL NEWS

Street Address: 108 East Main Street
City: Haskell
State: OK
Postal Code: 74436
Office phone: 918) 482-5619
Publication Website: haskellweekly.news
General E-mail: info@haskellweekly.news.

HISTORIC HUGO

THE EXAMINER

Corporate/Parent Company: Gannett
Street Address: 104 North Broadway
City: Historic Hugo
State: OK
Postal Code: 73160
Office phone: (580) 326-3926
Publication Website: examinernewspaper.net
Publisher Name: John M. Brewer
Editor Name: Jim L. Smith
Editor Email: redriverpublishing@att.net

THE EXAMINER

Corporate/Parent Company: Gannett
Street Address: 104 North Broadway
City: Historic Hugo
State: OK
Postal Code: 73160
Office phone: (580) 326-3926
Publication Website: examinernewspaper.net
Publisher Name: John M. Brewer
Editor Name: Jim L. Smith
Editor Email: redriverpublishing@att.net

HOBART

THE HOBART DEMOCRAT-CHIEF

Street Address: 407 S Main St
City: Hobart
State: OK
Postal Code: 73651
Office phone: (580) 726-3333
Publication Website: www.hobartdemocratchief.com

THE HOBART DEMOCRAT-CHIEF

Street Address: 407 S Main St
City: Hobart
State: OK
Postal Code: 73651
Office phone: (580) 726-3333

Non-Daily Newspapers in the U.S.

III-117

Publication Website: www.hobartdemocratchief.com

INOLA

INOLA INDEPENDENT

Street Address: 113 W Commercial
City: Inola
State: OK
Postal Code: 74036
Office phone: 918 543-3134
Publication Website: www.theindependentnewspapers.net
Publisher Name: John and Martha Brock
Editor Name: Marci Shanks
Editor Email: Inolanewspaper@tds.net

MORRIS

THE MORRIS NEWS

Street Address: 421 E Ozark St
City: Morris
State: OK
Postal Code: 74445
Office phone: (918) 733-4898
Publication Website: themorrisnews.wordpress.com
Editor Name: Barry Thompson

THE MORRIS NEWS

Street Address: 421 E Ozark St
City: Morris
State: OK
Postal Code: 74445
Office phone: (918) 733-4898
Publication Website: themorrisnews.wordpress.com
Editor Name: Barry Thompson

MUSTANG

MINCO-UNION CITY TIMES

Street Address: 553 North Mustang Rd.
City: Mustang
State: OK
Postal Code: 73064
Office phone: (405) 376-6688
Publication Website: www.mincounioncitytimes.com
Editor Name: Jon Watje
Editor Email: us81@sbcglobal.net

MUSTANG TIMES

Street Address: 553 North Mustang Rd.
City: Mustang
State: OK
Postal Code: 73064
Office phone: (405) 376-6688
Publication Website: www.mustangpaper.com
Editor Name: Jess Kelsey
Editor Email: mustangtimesnews@sbcglobal.net

OKEENE

THE CANTON TIMES

Street Address: 114 W Main St
City: Okeene
State: OK
Postal Code: 73763
Office phone: (580) 822-4101
Publication Website: www.canton-times.com
General E-mail: cantonnews@trailmiller.com

OKLAHOMA CITY

GRIFFIN, ANDREW

Street Address: 717 NW 17th St
City: Oklahoma City
State: OK
Postal Code: 73103
Office phone: (405) 702-7667
Publication Website: www.reddirtreport.com/users/andrew-w-griffin
Editor Name: Andrew West Griffin
Editor Email: reddirtreport@gmail.com

ONE GAS

Street Address: P.O. Box 401
City: Oklahoma City
State: OK
Postal Code: 73101
Office phone: (800) 664-5463
Publication Website: www.oneok.com

SALLISAW

SEQUOYAH COUNTY TIMES

Street Address: 111 N Oak St
City: Sallisaw
State: OK
Postal Code: 74955
Office phone: (918) 775-4433
Publication Website: https://www.sequoyahcountytimes.com/
General E-mail: webeditor@seqcotimes.com
Editor Email: webeditor@seqcotimes.com

SHATTUCK

NORTHWEST OKLAHOMAN & ELLIS COUNTY NEWS

Street Address: 329 Main St
City: Shattuck
State: OK
Postal Code: 73858
Office phone: 580-938-2533
Publication Website: www.northwestoklahoman.com
General E-mail: nwopaper@pldi.net

TAHLEQUAH

CHEROKEE PHOENIX

Street Address: PO Box 948
City: Tahlequah
State: OK
Postal Code: 74465
Office phone: 918-207-3825
Publication Website: www.cherokeephoenix.org
Editor Name: TYLER THOMAS
Editor Email: tyler-thomas@cherokee.org

TISHOMINGO

JOHNSTON COUNTY SENTINEL

Street Address: 706 W Main Street
City: Tishomingo
State: OK
Postal Code: 73460
Office phone: 580-371-0275
Publication Website: johnstoncosentinel.com
Publisher Name: Tom and Mary Lokey
Editor Name: John Small
Editor Email: jcsentinel@yahoo.com

TULSA

TULSA PEOPLE

Street Address: 1603 S. Boulder
City: Tulsa
State: OK
Postal Code: 74119
Office phone: 918-585-9924
Publication Website: www.tulsapeople.com
General E-mail: contactus@langdonpublishing.com
Publisher Name: Jim Langdon
Publisher Email: jim@langdonpublishing.com
Editor Name: Anne Brockman
Editor Email: anne@langdonpublishing.com

VIAN

EASTERN TIMES-REGISTER

Street Address: 603 W. Schley
City: Vian
State: OK
Postal Code: 74962
Office phone: (918) 427-3636
Publication Website: www.easterntimesregister.com
General E-mail: news@bigbasinllc.com
Publisher Name: Jeff Mayo and Jack Mayo

VIAN TENKILLER NEWS

Street Address: 603 W. Schley
City: Vian
State: OK
Postal Code: 74962
Office phone: 918-773-8000
Publication Website: www.viannews.com
Editor Name: Amie Remer
Editor Email: news@bigbasinllc.com

VINITA

GRAND RIVER DAM AUTHORITY

Street Address: 226 W. Dwain Willis
City: Vinita
State: OK
Postal Code: 74301
Office phone: 918-256-5545
Publication Website: www.grda.com
General E-mail: questions@grda.com

WASHINGTON

LOGICO IMAGES

Street Address: PO Box 238
City: Washington
State: OK
Postal Code: 73093
Office phone: (405) 206-7412
Publication Website: dorman.photo

WAURIKA

WAURIKA NEWS JOURNAL & THE RYAN LEADER

Street Address: 114 S Main St
City: Waurika
State: OK
Postal Code: 73573
Office phone: 580-228-2545
Publication Website: waurikanewsjournal.com
Editor Name: Curtis Plant
Editor Email: waurikanewsjournal@gmail.com

WAYNOKA

WOODS COUNTY ENTERPRISE

Street Address: 1543 Main St
City: Waynoka
State: OK
Postal Code: 73860
Office phone: 580-824-2171
Publication Website: www.woodscountyenterprise.com
Editor Name: Mark Carson

Editor Email: wcepaper@pldi.net

WETUMKA

HUGHES COUNTY TRIBUNE

Street Address: 114 N. Broadway
City: WETUMKA
State: OK
Postal Code: 74883
Office phone: 405-379-5184
Publication Website: www.hughescountytribune.com
Publisher Name: Dayna Robinson
Publisher Email: robpublishing@sbcglobal.net
Editor Name: Jade Robinson

YALE

YALE NEWS

Street Address: 108 N. Main St
City: Yale
State: OK
Postal Code: 74085
Office phone: 918-232-8709
Publication Website: www.facebook.com/YaleNews
General E-mail: yalenews@drumrightgusher.com

YUKON

YUKON PROGRESS

Street Address: 508 W. Vandament
City: Yukon
State: OK
Postal Code: 73099
Office phone: (405) 577-6208
Publication Website: yukonprogressnews.com
Publisher Name: Randy K. Anderson
Publisher Email: randyk.anderson@sbcglobal.net
Editor Name: Conrad Dudderar
Editor Email: editor@yukonprogress.com

OREGON

BAKER CITY

BAKER CITY HERALD

Corporate/Parent Company: EO Media Group
Street Address: 1668 Resort St.
City: Baker City
State: OR
Postal Code: 97814
Office phone: (541) 523-3673
Publication Website: https://www.bakercityherald.com/
General E-mail: news@bakercityherald.com
Publisher Name: Karrine Brogoitti
Publisher Email: kbrogoitti@lagrandeobserver.com
Editor Name: Jayson Jacoby
Editor Email: jferdig@bakercityherald.com
Year Established: 1870
Delivery Methods:
 Mail`Newsstand`Carrier`Racks
Own Printing Facility?: Y
Commercial printers?: Y
Mechanical specifications: Type page 11.75 x 21 1/2; E – 6 cols, 2 1/16, 1/8 between; A – 6 cols, 2 1/16, 1/8 between; C – 6 cols, 1 9/16, 1/16 between.
Published Days: Mon`Wed`Fri
Weekday Frequency: e
Avg Paid Circ: 1858
Avg Free Circ: 73
Audit Company: Sworn/Estimate/Non-Audited
Audit Date: 6 10 2019
Pressroom Equipment: Lines – 6-G/Community; Folders – 1-G/SSC.;

BEND

THE BULLETIN
Corporate/Parent Company: Gannett
Street Address: 1777 SW Chandler Ave
City: Bend
State: OR
Postal Code: 97702-3200
Office phone: (541) 382-1811
Publication Website: https://www.bendbulletin.com/
General E-mail: bjackson@bendbulletin.com
Publisher Name: Heidi Wright
Publisher Phone: (541) 383-0388
Editor Name: Smith, Camile
Editor Email: csmith@bendbulletin.com
Editor Phone: (541) 383-0379
Advertising Executive Name: Jackson, Bret
Advertising Executive Email: bjackson@bendbulletin.com
Advertising Executive Phone: (541) 617-7824
Year Established: 1903
Delivery Methods: Mail`Newsstand`Carrier`Racks
Own Printing Facility?: Y
Commercial printers?: Y
Mechanical specifications: Type page: Broadsheet 10.71"w x 20.25"h; Editorial and Advertising: 6 columns are 1.65"w (with .17" gutter); Classified 9 columns are 1.12"w (with .08" gutter).
Published Days: Mon`Tues`Wed`Thur`Fri`Sat`Sun
Weekday Frequency: m
Saturday Frequency: m
Avg Paid Circ: 18424
Avg Free Circ: 3075
Audit Company: AAM
Audit Date: 6 08 2020
Pressroom Equipment: Lines – 1-KBA Comet 3 1/2 Tower (14 printing couples); Press Drive – 2-KBA/Shaftless; Folders – KBA/64; Reels & Stands – 5-AMAL/AR60; Control System – KBA/Ergotronic; Registration System – KBA/Ergotronic.
Mailroom Equipment: Tying Machines – MLN/Single strap; Address Machine – Wm.;
Buisness Software: Newscycle
Classified Equipment: Hardware – APP/Mac; Printers – Okidata/591;
Classified Software: MediaSpan Ad Manager Pro 4, version 1.9
Editorial Equipment: Hardware – APP/Mac
Editorial Software: InDesign
Production Equipment: Cameras – Canon
Note: Published cooperatively with The Observer. Unique local A sections, shared B sections and some special sections.
Total Circulation: 1931

CANBY

MOLALLA PIONEER-OOB
Corporate/Parent Company: Pamplin Media Group
Street Address: 911 SW 4th Ave
City: Canby
State: OR
Postal Code: 97013
Office phone: (503) 266-6831
Publication Website: https://pamplinmedia.com/molalla-pioneer-home/
General E-mail: circulation@commnewspapers.com
Publisher Name: Sandy Storey
Publisher Email: sstorey@pamplinmedia.com
Publisher Phone: (503) 266-6831
Editor Name: John Baker
Editor Email: jbaker@canbyherald.com
Editor Phone: (503) 829-2301
Advertising Executive Name: Sandy Storey
Advertising Executive Email: sstorey@pamplinmedia.com
Advertising Executive Phone: (503) 266-6831
Total Circulation: 3575

THE CANBY HERALD
Corporate/Parent Company: Pamplin Media Group
Street Address: 911 SW 4th Ave
City: Canby
State: OR
Postal Code: 97013
Office phone: (503) 266-6831
Publication Website: https://pamplinmedia.com/canby-herald-home/
General E-mail: dguinther@pamplinmedia.com
Publisher Name: Sandy Storey
Publisher Email: sstorey@pamplinmedia.com
Publisher Phone: (503) 266-6831
Editor Name: John Baker
Editor Email: jbaker@canbyherald.com
Editor Phone: (503) 266-6831
Advertising Executive Name: Sandy Storey
Advertising Executive Email: sstorey@pamplinmedia.com
Advertising Executive Phone: (503) 266-6831
Year Established: 1906
Delivery Methods: Mail`Newsstand
Own Printing Facility?: Y
Mechanical specifications: Type page 13 x 21 1/2; E - 6 cols, 2 1/12, 1/3 between; A - 6 cols, 2 1/12, 1/3 between; C - 9 cols, 1 1/3, 1/6 between.
Published Days: Wed
Avg Paid Circ: 5100
Audit Company: Sworn/Estimate/Non-Audited
Audit Date: 6 10 2019

CLATSKANIE

THE CHIEF
Corporate/Parent Company: Country Media Inc.
Street Address: 148 N Nehalem St
City: Clatskanie
State: OR
Postal Code: 97016
Office phone: (503) 728-3350
Publication Website: https://www.thechiefnews.com/
General E-mail: circulation@countrymedia.net
Publisher Name: Frank Perea
Publisher Email: frankperea@countrymedia.net
Editor Name: Jeremy Ruark
Editor Email: jruark@countrymedia.net
Advertising Executive Name: Amy Trull
Advertising Executive Email: atrull@countrymedia.net
Year Established: 1891
Delivery Methods: Mail`Newsstand
Mechanical specifications: Type page 12 3/4 x 21; E - 6 cols, 2, 1/6 between; A - 6 cols, 2, 1/6 between; C - 8 cols, 1 1/2, 1/6 between.
Published Days: Fri
Avg Paid Circ: 2750
Audit Company: Sworn/Estimate/Non-Audited
Audit Date: 6 10 2019
Total Circulation: 51693

DALLAS

THE POLK COUNTY ITEMIZER-OBSERVER
Corporate/Parent Company: Eagle Newspapers (OR)
Street Address: 147 SE Court St
City: Dallas
State: OR
Postal Code: 97338-3158
Office phone: (503) 623-2373
Publication Website: https://www.polkio.com/
General E-mail: ionews@polkio.com
Year Established: 1875
Delivery Methods: Mail
Own Printing Facility?: Y
Commercial printers?: N
Published Days: Wed
Avg Paid Circ: 4800
Avg Free Circ: 8500
Audit Company: Sworn/Estimate/Non-Audited
Audit Date: 6 10 2019
Total Circulation: 3753

ENTERPRISE

WALLOWA COUNTY CHIEFTAIN
Corporate/Parent Company: EO Media Group
Street Address: 209 NW First St
City: Enterprise
State: OR
Postal Code: 97828
Office phone: (541) 426-4567
Publication Website: https://www.wallowa.com/
General E-mail: editor@wallowa.com
Publisher Name: Chris Rush
Publisher Email: crush@eomediagroup.com
Publisher Phone: (541) 575-0710
Editor Name: Ellen Morris Bishop
Editor Email: editor@wallowa.com
Editor Phone: (541) 426-4567
Year Established: 1884
Mechanical specifications: Type page 12 3/4 x 21; E - 6 cols, 2 1/12, 1/6 between; A - 6 cols, 2 1/12, 1/6 between; C - 9 cols, 1 1/2, 1/6 between.
Published Days: Wed
Avg Paid Circ: 4000
Audit Company: Sworn/Estimate/Non-Audited
Audit Date: 6 10 2019

ESTACADA

ESTACADA NEWS
Corporate/Parent Company: Pamplin Media Group
Street Address: 307 SW Highway 224
City: Estacada
State: OR
Postal Code: 97023
Office phone: (503) 630-3241
Publication Website: https://pamplinmedia.com/estacada-news-home/
General E-mail: swells@theoutlookonline.com
Publisher Name: Steve Brown
Publisher Email: sbrown@theoutlookonline.com
Publisher Phone: (503) 492-5119
Editor Name: Anne Endicott
Editor Email: aendicott@theoutlookonline.com
Editor Phone: (503) 492-5118
Advertising Executive Name: Alisa Applegate
Advertising Executive Email: aapplegate@theoutlookonline.com
Advertising Executive Phone: (503) 492-5111
Year Established: 1904
Commercial printers?: Y
Published Days: Thur
Avg Paid Circ: 2000
Avg Free Circ: 35
Audit Company: Sworn/Estimate/Non-Audited
Audit Date: 6 10 2019
Mailroom Equipment: 1 STI stacker 1 12:2 SLS 1000 inserter with inline ink jet print labeler 1 10:1 Mueller -Martini 227 E Inserter 2 Quipp 400 Stackers 1 Goval Strapmaster strapper 1 Dynaric ST1strapper 1 Cowart-Gagnon offline inkjet print labeler 1 Rosback Stitcher Trimmer
Buisness Equipment: Macs
Buisness Software: Brainworks
Classified Equipment: Macs
Classified Software: Brainworks
Editorial Equipment: Macs
Editorial Software: Town News
Production Equipment: 2 Kodak Trendsetter 800 platesetters CtP units
Production Software: InDesign
Note: First Place Winner of the Oregon Newspaper Publishers Association General Excellence award, 2011-13 and 2015-18
Total Circulation: 4377

FOREST GROVE

FOREST GROVE NEWS-TIMES
Corporate/Parent Company: Pamplin Media Group
Street Address: 2004 Main St, Suite 309
City: Forest Grove
State: OR
Postal Code: 97116
Office phone: (503) 357-3181
Publication Website: https://pamplinmedia.com/forest-grove-news-times-home/
General E-mail: circulation@commnewspapers.com
Publisher Name: Nikki DeBuse
Publisher Email: ndebuse@fgnewstimes.com
Publisher Phone: (503) 357-3181
Editor Name: Mark Miller
Editor Email: mmiller@pamplinmedia.com
Editor Phone: (971) 762-1170
Advertising Executive Name: Toni Ashby
Advertising Executive Email: tashby@pamplinmedia.com
Advertising Executive Phone: (971) 762-1167
Year Established: 1886
Delivery Methods: Mail`Newsstand`Racks
Own Printing Facility?: Y
Commercial printers?: Y
Published Days: Wed
Avg Paid Circ: 3800
Avg Free Circ: 600
Audit Company: Sworn/Estimate/Non-Audited
Audit Date: 6 10 2019
Total Circulation: 2035

THE HILLSBORO TRIBUNE
Corporate/Parent Company: Pamplin Media Group
Street Address: 2004 Main St, Suite 309
City: Forest Grove
State: OR
Postal Code: 97116
Office phone: (503) 357-3181
Publication Website: https://pamplinmedia.com/hillsboro-tribune-home/
General E-mail: circulation@commnewspapers.com
Publisher Name: Nikki DeBuse
Publisher Email: ndebuse@fgnewstimes.com
Publisher Phone: (503) 357-3181
Editor Name: Mark Miller
Editor Email: mmiller@pamplinmedia.com
Editor Phone: (971) 762-1170
Advertising Executive Name: Toni Ashby
Advertising Executive Email: tashby@pamplinmedia.com
Advertising Executive Phone: (971) 762-1167
Year Established: 2012
Delivery Methods: Mail`Racks
Published Days: Fri
Avg Paid Circ: 3500
Avg Free Circ: 2500
Audit Company: Sworn/Estimate/Non-Audited
Audit Date: 6 10 2019
Total Circulation: 4400

GRESHAM

SANDY POST
Corporate/Parent Company: Pamplin Media Group
Street Address: 1584 NE Eighth St
City: Gresham
State: OR
Postal Code: 97030
Office phone: (503) 665-2181
Publication Website: https://pamplinmedia.com/sandy-post-home/
General E-mail: circulation@commnewspapers.com
Publisher Name: Steve Brown
Publisher Email: sbrown@theoutlookonline.com
Publisher Phone: (503) 492-5119
Editor Name: Anne Endicott
Editor Email: aendicott@theoutlookonline.com
Editor Phone: (503) 492-5118
Advertising Executive Name: Alisa Applegate
Advertising Executive Email: aapplegate@theoutlookonline.com
Advertising Executive Phone: (503) 492-5111
Year Established: 1937
Commercial printers?: Y
Mechanical specifications: Type page 13 x 21 1/2; E - 6 cols, 2 1/16, 1/6 between; A - 6 cols, 2 1/16, 1/6 between.
Published Days: Wed
Avg Paid Circ: 3500

Non-Daily Newspapers in the U.S.

Avg Free Circ: 28
Audit Company: Sworn/Estimate/Non-Audited
Audit Date: 6 10 2019

HERMISTON

HERMISTON HERALD-OOB

Corporate/Parent Company: EO Media Group
Street Address: 333 E Main St
City: Hermiston
State: OR
Postal Code: 97838-1869
Office phone: (541) 567-6457
Publication Website: https://www.hermistonherald.com/
General E-mail: jjewett@hermistonherald.com
Publisher Name: Christopher Rush
Publisher Email: crush@eomediagroup.com
Publisher Phone: (541) 278-2669
Editor Name: Jade McDowell
Editor Email: jmcdowell@eastoregonian.com
Editor Phone: (541) 564-4536
Advertising Executive Name: Jeanne Jewett
Advertising Executive Email: jjewett@hermistonherald.com
Advertising Executive Phone: (541) 564-4531
Total Circulation: 5398

HOOD RIVER

HOOD RIVER NEWS

Corporate/Parent Company: Eagle Newspapers (OR)
Street Address: 419 State St
City: Hood River
State: OR
Postal Code: 97031-2075
Office phone: (541) 386-1234
Publication Website: https://www.hoodrivernews.com/
General E-mail: hrnews@hoodrivernews.com
Year Established: 1905
Delivery Methods: Mail`Newsstand`Carrier`Racks
Own Printing Facility?: Y
Mechanical specifications: 6 columns - Each column 1.583 inches wide with 0.125 inch gutters. Depth: 21 inches.
Published Days: Wed`Sat
Avg Paid Circ: 5300
Avg Free Circ: 98
Audit Company: Sworn/Estimate/Non-Audited
Audit Date: 6 10 2019

JOHN DAY

BLUE MOUNTAIN EAGLE

Corporate/Parent Company: EO Media Group
Street Address: 195 N. Canyon Blvd.
City: John Day
State: OR
Postal Code: 97845
Office phone: (541) 575-0710
Publication Website: https://www.bluemountaineagle.com/
General E-mail: kim@bmeagle.com
Publisher Name: Chris Rush
Publisher Email: crush@eomediagroup.com
Publisher Phone: (541) 575-0710
Editor Name: Sean Hart
Editor Email: editor@bmeagle.com
Editor Phone: (541) 575-0710
Advertising Executive Name: Kim Kell
Advertising Executive Email: kim@bmeagle.com
Advertising Executive Phone: (541) 575-0710
Year Established: 1868
Own Printing Facility?: Y
Mechanical specifications: Type page 12 x 21 1/2; E - 6 cols, 1 3/4, 1/6 between; A - 6 cols, 1 3/4, 1/6 between; C - 6 cols, 1 3/4, 1/6 between.
Published Days: Wed
Avg Paid Circ: 3500
Avg Free Circ: 75
Audit Company: Sworn/Estimate/Non-Audited
Audit Date: 6 10 2019
Total Circulation: 1250

LA GRANDE

THE LAGRANE OBSERVER

Corporate/Parent Company: EO Media Group
Street Address: 1406 5th St
City: La Grande
State: OR
Postal Code: 97850-2402
Office phone: (541) 963-3161
Publication Website: https://www.lagrandeobserver.com/
General E-mail: dmathson@lagrandeobserver.com
Publisher Name: Karrine Brogoitti
Publisher Email: kbrogoitti@lagrandeobserver.com
Editor Name: Phil Wright
Editor Email: pwright@lagrandeobserver.com
Advertising Executive Name: Devi Mathson
Advertising Executive Email: dmathson@lagrandeobserver.com
Year Established: 1896
Delivery Methods: Mail`Newsstand`Carrier`Racks
Own Printing Facility?: Y
Commercial printers?: Y
Mechanical specifications: Type page 11.75 x 21 1/2; E - 6 cols, 2 1/16, 1/8 between; A - 6 cols, 2 1/16, 1/8 between; C - 6 cols, 1 9/16, 1/16 between.
Published Days: Mon`Wed`Fri
Weekday Frequency: e
Avg Paid Circ: 3371
Avg Free Circ: 166
Audit Company: CVC
Audit Date: 31 12 2018
Pressroom Equipment: Lines – 6-G/Community; Folders – 1-G/SSC.;
Total Circulation: 3500

LAKE OSWEGO

SOUTHWEST COMMUNITY CONNECTION

Corporate/Parent Company: Pamplin Media Group
Street Address: 400 2nd St
City: Lake Oswego
State: OR
Postal Code: 97034
Office phone: (503) 636-1281
Publication Website: https://pamplinmedia.com/southwest-community-connection-home/
General E-mail: circulation@commnewspapers.com
Publisher Name: Brian Monihan
Publisher Email: bmonihan@pamplinmedia.com
Publisher Phone: (971) 204-7784
Editor Name: Bill Gallagher
Editor Email: bgallagher@pamplinmedia.com
Advertising Executive Name: Christine Moore
Advertising Executive Email: cmoore@commnewspapers.com
Advertising Executive Phone: (971) 204-7771
Year Established: 1994
Delivery Methods: Mail`Newsstand`Racks
Published Days: Thur`Mthly
Audit Company: Sworn/Estimate/Non-Audited
Audit Date: 6 10 2019
Total Circulation: 17000

THE LAKE OSWEGO REVIEW

Corporate/Parent Company: Pamplin Media Group
Street Address: 400 2nd St
City: Lake Oswego
State: OR
Postal Code: 97034
Office phone: (503) 635-8811
Publication Website: https://pamplinmedia.com/lake-oswego-review-home/
General E-mail: circulation@commnewspapers.com
Publisher Name: Brian Monihan
Publisher Email: bmonihan@pamplinmedia.com
Publisher Phone: (971) 204-7784

Editor Name: Patrick Malee
Editor Email: pmalee@pamplinmedia.com
Editor Phone: (503) 635-8811
Advertising Executive Name: Christine Moore
Advertising Executive Email: cmoore@commnewspapers.com
Advertising Executive Phone: (971) 204-7771
Year Established: 1920
Delivery Methods: Mail`Newsstand
Commercial printers?: Y
Published Days: Thur
Avg Paid Circ: 7600
Audit Company: Sworn/Estimate/Non-Audited
Audit Date: 6 10 2019
Total Circulation: 3528

WEST LINN TIDINGS

Corporate/Parent Company: Pamplin Media Group
Street Address: 400 2nd St
City: Lake Oswego
State: OR
Postal Code: 97034
Office phone: (503) 635-8811
Publication Website: https://pamplinmedia.com/west-linn-tidings-home/
General E-mail: circulation@commnewspapers.com
Publisher Name: Brian Monihan
Publisher Email: bmonihan@pamplinmedia.com
Publisher Phone: (971) 204-7784
Editor Name: Leslie Pugmire Hole
Editor Email: lhole@pamplinmedia.com
Editor Phone: (503) 635-8811
Advertising Executive Name: Jesse Marichalar
Advertising Executive Email: jessem@pamplinmedia.com
Advertising Executive Phone: (971) 204-7774
Year Established: 1981
Delivery Methods: Mail`Newsstand
Published Days: Thur
Avg Paid Circ: 3750
Audit Company: Sworn/Estimate/Non-Audited
Audit Date: 6 10 2019
Total Circulation: 3500

WILSONVILLE SPOKESMAN

Corporate/Parent Company: Pamplin Media Group
Street Address: 400 2nd St
City: Lake Oswego
State: OR
Postal Code: 97034
Office phone: (503) 635-8811
Publication Website: https://pamplinmedia.com/wilsonville-spokesman-home/
General E-mail: circulation@commnewspapers.com
Publisher Name: Brian Monihan
Publisher Email: bmonihan@pamplinmedia.com
Publisher Phone: (971) 204-7784
Editor Name: Leslie Pugmire Hole
Editor Email: lhole@pamplinmedia.com
Editor Phone: (503) 635-8811
Advertising Executive Name: Jesse Marichalar
Advertising Executive Email: jessem@pamplinmedia.com
Advertising Executive Phone: (971) 204-7774
Year Established: 1985
Mechanical specifications: Type page 11 7/8 x 21 1/2; E - 6 cols, 1 7/8, 1/8 between; A - 6 cols, 1 7/8, 1/8 between; C - 9 cols, 1 1/4, 1/8 between.
Published Days: Wed
Avg Paid Circ: 3350
Avg Free Circ: 2500
Audit Company: Sworn/Estimate/Non-Audited
Audit Date: 6 10 2019

LINCOLN CITY

OREGON COAST TODAY

Corporate/Parent Company: EO Media Group
Street Address: 4741 SW Highway 101
City: Lincoln City
State: OR
Postal Code: 97367-2755
Office phone: (541) 921-0413
Publication Website: http://oregoncoasttoday.com/
General E-mail: lyaeger@oregoncoasttoday.com
Publisher Name: Patrick Alexander
Publisher Email: patrick alexander
Publisher Phone: (541) 921-0413
Editor Name: Patrick Alexander
Editor Email: Patrick Alexander
Editor Phone: (541) 921-0413
Advertising Executive Name: Larayne Yaeger
Advertising Executive Email: lyaeger@oregoncoasttoday.com
Advertising Executive Phone: (541) 992-1920
Published Days: Fri
Avg Free Circ: 17000
Audit Company: Sworn/Estimate/Non-Audited
Audit Date: 6 10 2019
Total Circulation: 7000

THE NEWS GUARD

Corporate/Parent Company: Country Media Inc.
Street Address: 1818 N E. 21st St.
City: Lincoln City
State: OR
Postal Code: 97367
Office phone: (541) 994-2178
Publication Website: https://www.thenewsguard.com/
General E-mail: circulation@countrymedia.net
Publisher Name: Frank Perea
Publisher Email: frankperea@countrymedia.net
Editor Name: Max Kirkendall
Editor Email: newsguardeditor@countrymedia.net
Advertising Executive Name: Nicole Clarke
Advertising Executive Email: newsguardads@countrymedia.net
Year Established: 1927
Delivery Methods: Mail`Newsstand`Racks
Mechanical specifications: Type page 11 1/8 x 21 1/2; E - 6 cols, 1 5/6, 1/8 between; A - 6 cols, 1 5/6, 1/8 between; C - 9 cols, 1 5/6, 1/8 between.
Published Days: Wed
Avg Paid Circ: 6000
Audit Company: Sworn/Estimate/Non-Audited
Audit Date: 6 10 2019

LONG BEACH

COAST RIVER BUSINESS JOURNAL

Corporate/Parent Company: EO Media Group
Street Address: 205 Bolstad S. Suite 2, P.O. Box 427
City: Long Beach
State: OR
Postal Code: 98631
Office phone: (360) 642-8181
Publication Website: https://www.coastriverbusinessjournal.com/
General E-mail: editor@crbizjournal.com
Publisher Name: Matt Winters
Editor Name: Matt Winters
Editor Email: editor@crbizjournal.com
Mailroom Equipment: Counter Stackers – 1-MM/388, 1-BG/105, 1/MM, 2-QWI/400, 1-Gammerler/KL 50 7/1; Inserters & Stuffers – 16-MM/375, 12-MM/375, 4-MM/227; Tying Machines – 1-/MLN, 1-Dynaric/NPI, 1-Dynaric/NPI;
Buisness Equipment: PCs
Buisness Software: DTI 5.5
Classified Equipment: Hardware – PCs; Printers – HP, Canon;
Classified Software: DTI 5.5
Editorial Equipment: Hardware – PCs; Printers – Canon, HP
Editorial Software: DTI 6.5
Production Equipment: Hardware – Kodak EVO
Production Software: Adobe/InDesign.
Total Circulation: 26934

MADRAS

THE MADRAS PIONEER

Corporate/Parent Company: Pamplin Media Group
Street Address: 345 SE 5th St
City: Madras
State: OR
Postal Code: 97741
Office phone: (541) 475-2275
Publication Website: https://pamplinmedia.com/madras-pioneer-home/
General E-mail: jgrant@madraspioneer.com
Publisher Name: Tony Ahern
Publisher Email: tahern@madraspioneer.com
Publisher Phone: (541) 475-2275
Editor Name: Teresa Jackson
Editor Email: tjackson@madraspioneer.com
Editor Phone: (541) 475-2275
Advertising Executive Name: Joy DeHaan
Advertising Executive Email: jdehaan@madraspioneer.com
Advertising Executive Phone: (541) 475-2275
Year Established: 1904
Own Printing Facility?: Y
Published Days: Wed
Avg Paid Circ: 3300
Avg Free Circ: 125
Audit Company: Sworn/Estimate/Non-Audited
Audit Date: 6 10 2019
Total Circulation: 5100

NEWBERG

THE NEWBERG GRAPHIC

Corporate/Parent Company: Pamplin Media Group
Street Address: 1505 Portland Rd.
City: Newberg
State: OR
Postal Code: 97132
Office phone: (503) 538-2181
Publication Website: https://pamplinmedia.com/newberg-graphic-home/
General E-mail: circulation@commnewspapers.com
Publisher Name: Allen Herriges
Publisher Email: aherriges@newberggraphic.com
Publisher Phone: (503) 538-2181
Editor Name: Gary Allen
Editor Email: gallen@newberggraphic.com
Editor Phone: (503) 538-2181
Advertising Executive Name: Paula Becker
Advertising Executive Email: pbecker@newberggraphic.com
Advertising Executive Phone: (503) 538-2181
Year Established: 1888
Mechanical specifications: Type page 11 7/8 x 21 1/2; E - 6 cols, 1 7/8, 1/6 between; A - 6 cols, 1 7/8, 1/6 between; C - 9 cols, 1 3/16, 1/6 between.
Published Days: Wed`Sat
Avg Paid Circ: 5500
Audit Company: Sworn/Estimate/Non-Audited
Audit Date: 6 10 2019
Total Circulation: 2750

PENDLETON

EAST OREGONIAN

Corporate/Parent Company: EO Media Group
Street Address: 211 SE Byers Ave
City: Pendleton
State: OR
Postal Code: 97801-2346
Office phone: (541) 276-2211
Publication Website: https://www.eastoregonian.com
General E-mail: atreadwell@eastoregonian.com
Publisher Name: Christopher Rush
Publisher Email: crush@eomediagroup.com
Publisher Phone: (541) 278-2669
Editor Name: Andrew Cutler
Editor Email: acutler@eastoregonian.com
Editor Phone: (541) 278-2673
Advertising Executive Name: Angela Treadwell
Advertising Executive Email: atreadwell@eastoregonian.com
Advertising Executive Phone: (541) 966-0827
Year Established: 1875
Delivery Methods: Mail`Newsstand`Racks
Own Printing Facility?: Y
Commercial printers?: Y
Published Days: Tues`Wed`Thur`Fri`Sat
Weekday Frequency: m
Saturday Frequency: m
Avg Paid Circ: 4155
Avg Free Circ: 222
Audit Company: AAM
Audit Date: 31 03 2019
Pressroom Equipment: 2 Tensor T-1400 color towers 1 Goss Community color tower 1 Re-aliner to add page count. A combination ribbon deck for all three towers in one assembly. 1 Goss Community half folder 1 DGM quarter folder 3 Jardis splicers
Total Circulation: 34300

PORTLAND

OREGON CITY NEWS

Corporate/Parent Company: Pamplin Media Group
Street Address: 6605 SE Lake Rd
City: Portland
State: OR
Postal Code: 97222
Office phone: (503) 684-0360
Publication Website: https://pamplinmedia.com/oregon-city-news-home/
General E-mail: rmansfield@pamplinmedia.com
Publisher Name: Angela Fox
Publisher Email: afox@clackamasreview.com
Publisher Phone: (971) 204-7717
Editor Name: Raymond Rendleman
Editor Email: rrendleman@clackamasreview.com
Editor Phone: (971) 204-7742
Advertising Executive Name: Rebecca Mansfield
Advertising Executive Email: rmansfield@pamplinmedia.com
Advertising Executive Phone: (971) 204-7757
Commercial printers?: Y
Published Days: Wed
Avg Paid Circ: 3500
Audit Company: Sworn/Estimate/Non-Audited
Audit Date: 6 10 2019
Buisness Equipment: 19-Magitonic
Buisness Software: QuarkXPress, Synaptic, Microsoft/Office, Adobe/Photoshop, Adobe/Illustratoe, Archetype/Corel Draw (PC Software/Bus. Applications)
Classified Equipment: Hardware – 2-ScrippSat; Printers – QMS/810 Turbo, Okidata/Microline 393 P14S;
Classified Software: Synaptic.
Editorial Equipment: Hardware – Sun; Printers – QMS/810 T, 2-PS, Elite, IBM
Editorial Software: Sun.
Production Equipment: Hardware – 2-QMS/810 Turbo, PostScript/Printer; Cameras – Nikon, Kk/Digital.
Total Circulation: 5067

THE BEAVERTON VALLEY TIMES

Corporate/Parent Company: Pamplin Media Group
Street Address: 6605 SE Lake Rd
City: Portland
State: OR
Postal Code: 97222
Office phone: (503) 684-0360
Publication Website: https://pamplinmedia.com/beaverton-valley-times-home/
General E-mail: cmoore@commnewspapers.com
Publisher Name: Christine Moore
Publisher Email: cmoore@commnewspapers.com
Publisher Phone: (971) 204-7771
Editor Name: Mark Miller
Editor Email: mmiller@pamplinmedia.com
Editor Phone: (503) 913-0450
Advertising Executive Name: Christine Moore
Advertising Executive Email: cmoore@commnewspapers.com
Advertising Executive Phone: (971) 204-7771
Year Established: 1921
Delivery Methods: Mail`Newsstand`Racks
Own Printing Facility?: Y
Commercial printers?: Y
Published Days: Thur
Avg Paid Circ: 7000
Audit Company: Sworn/Estimate/Non-Audited
Audit Date: 6 10 2019
Total Circulation: 6000

THE BEE

Corporate/Parent Company: Pamplin Media Group
Street Address: 1837 SE Harold St
City: Portland
State: OR
Postal Code: 97202
Office phone: (503) 232-2326
Publication Website: https://pamplinmedia.com/the-sellwood-bee-home/
General E-mail: readthebee@myexcel.com
Publisher Name: Brian Monihan
Publisher Email: bmonihan@pamplinmedia.com
Publisher Phone: (503) 546-0784
Editor Name: Eric Norberg
Editor Email: readthebee@myexcel.com
Editor Phone: (503) 232-2326
Advertising Executive Name: Rebecca Mansfield
Advertising Executive Email: rmansfield@pamplinmedia.com
Advertising Executive Phone: (971) 204-7757
Year Established: ReadTheBee@myexcel.com
Published Days: Wed`Mthly
Audit Company: Sworn/Estimate/Non-Audited
Audit Date: 6 10 2019
Mailroom Equipment: Tying Machines – MLN; MS-B; Address Machine – 4/Wm, 1-/Dispensa-Matic/16 label picker.;
Buisness Equipment: 2-Packard Bell/Microsphere
Buisness Software: Newscycle
Classified Equipment: Hardware – IMAC; 1-IBM/Selectric; Printers – B/W LASER PRINTER;
Classified Software: Media Span Ad Mgr Pro
Editorial Equipment: Hardware – G4 1.25 MAC/1-IBM/Selectric
Editorial Software: InDesign APP/Mac Sys 7.1.
Production Equipment: Hardware – 1-KYOCERA B/W LASER PRINT AND 1 TRENDSETTER; Cameras – SCREEN/670 D Auto.
Note: Published cooperatively with Baker City Herald. Unique local A section, shared B section and some special sections.
Total Circulation: 3537

THE CLACKAMAS REVIEW

Corporate/Parent Company: Pamplin Media Group
Street Address: 6605 SE Lake Rd
City: Portland
State: OR
Postal Code: 97222
Office phone: (503) 684-0360
Publication Website: https://pamplinmedia.com/clackamas-review-home/
General E-mail: circulation@commnewspapers.com
Publisher Name: Angela Fox
Publisher Email: afox@clackamasreview.com
Publisher Phone: (971) 204-7717
Editor Name: Raymond Rendleman
Editor Email: rrendleman@clackamasreview.com
Editor Phone: (971) 204-7742
Advertising Executive Name: Kathy Schaub
Advertising Executive Email: kschaub@clackamasreview.com
Advertising Executive Phone: (971) 204-7779
Mechanical specifications: Type page 9 3/4 x 15; E - 5 cols, 1 13/16, 1/4 between; A - 5 cols, 1 13/16, 1/4 between; C - 7 cols, 1 1/4, between.
Published Days: Wed
Avg Paid Circ: 1000
Avg Free Circ: 33300
Audit Company: Sworn/Estimate/Non-Audited
Audit Date: 6 10 2019
Total Circulation: 7600

THE PORTLAND TRIBUNE

Corporate/Parent Company: Pamplin Media Group
Street Address: 6605 SE Lake Rd
City: Portland
State: OR
Postal Code: 97222
Office phone: (503) 684-0360
Publication Website: https://pamplinmedia.com/
General E-mail: circulation@commnewspapers.com
Publisher Name: Mark Garber
Publisher Email: mgarber@commnewspapers.com
Publisher Phone: (971) 204-7714
Editor Name: Dana Haynes
Editor Email: dhaynes@pamplinmedia.com
Editor Phone: (971) 204-7735
Advertising Executive Name: Christine Moore
Advertising Executive Email: cmoore@commnewspapers.com
Advertising Executive Phone: (971) 204-7771
Year Established: 2001
Delivery Methods: Mail`Newsstand`Racks
Published Days: Thur
Audit Company: Sworn/Estimate/Non-Audited
Audit Date: 6 10 2019
Total Circulation: 3425

THE TIMES (TIGARD/TUALATIN TIMES)

Corporate/Parent Company: Pamplin Media Group
Street Address: 6605 SE Lake Rd
City: Portland
State: OR
Postal Code: 97222
Office phone: (503) 684-0360
Publication Website: https://pamplinmedia.com/the-times-home/
General E-mail: circulation@commnewspapers.com
Publisher Name: Christine Moore
Publisher Email: cmoore@commnewspapers.com
Publisher Phone: (503) 546-0771
Editor Name: Mark Miller
Editor Email: mmiller@pamplinmedia.com
Editor Phone: (503) 913-0450
Advertising Executive Name: Christine Moore
Advertising Executive Email: cmoore@commnewspapers.com
Advertising Executive Phone: (503) 546-0771
Year Established: 1956
Delivery Methods: Mail`Newsstand`Racks
Own Printing Facility?: Y
Published Days: Thur
Avg Paid Circ: 7000
Audit Company: Sworn/Estimate/Non-Audited
Audit Date: 6 10 2019
Total Circulation: 5500

PRINEVILLE

CENTRAL OREGONIAN

Corporate/Parent Company: Pamplin Media Group
Street Address: 558 N Main St
City: Prineville
State: OR
Postal Code: 97754
Office phone: (541) 447-6205
Publication Website: https://pamplinmedia.com/central-oregonian-home/
General E-mail: advertising@centraloregonian.com

Non-Daily Newspapers in the U.S.

Publisher Name: Tony Ahern
Publisher Email: tahern@centraloregonian.com
Publisher Phone: (541) 447-6205
Editor Name: Jason Chaney
Editor Email: jchaney@centraloregonian.com
Editor Phone: (541) 447-6205
Advertising Executive Name: Heidi Howard
Advertising Executive Email: advertising@centraloregonian.com
Advertising Executive Phone: (541) 447-6205
Year Established: 1881
Delivery Methods: Mail
Own Printing Facility?: Y
Mechanical specifications: Type page 11 5/8 x 21; E - 6 cols, 1 5/6, 1/10 between; A - 6 cols, 1 5/6, 1/10 between; C - 8 cols, 1 1/5, 1/10 between.
Published Days: Tues`Fri
Avg Paid Circ: 3753
Audit Company: Sworn/Estimate/Non-Audited
Audit Date: 6 10 2019
Total Circulation: 6000

REDMOND

THE REDMOND SPOKESMAN

Corporate/Parent Company: EO Media Group
Street Address: 226 NW 6th St
City: Redmond
State: OR
Postal Code: 97756-1718
Office phone: (541) 548-2184
Publication Website: https://www.redmondspokesman.com/
General E-mail: jdeboard@redmondspokesman.com
Advertising Executive Name: Jeremy DeBoard
Advertising Executive Email: jdeboard@redmondspokesman.com
Advertising Executive Phone: (541) 385-5809
Year Established: 1911
Delivery Methods: Mail`Carrier`Racks
Mechanical specifications: Type page 11 5/6 x 20 1/2; E - 6 cols, 1 4/5, 3/16 between; A - 6 cols, 1 4/5, 3/16 between; C - 9 cols, 1 2/9, 1/8 between.
Published Days: Wed
Avg Paid Circ: 1962
Avg Free Circ: 725
Audit Company: CVC
Audit Date: 31 12 2018
Total Circulation: 13300

SALEM

CAPITAL PRESS

Corporate/Parent Company: EO Media Group
Street Address: 2870 Broadway St. NE
City: Salem
State: OR
Postal Code: 97301
Office phone: (800) 882-6789
Publication Website: https://www.capitalpress.com/
General E-mail: kblodgett@capitalpress.com
Publisher Name: Joe Beach
Publisher Email: jbeach@capitalpress.com
Editor Name: Carl Sampson
Editor Email: csampson@capitalpress.com
Editor Phone: (800) 882-6789
Advertising Executive Name: Kevin Blodgett
Advertising Executive Email: kblodgett@capitalpress.com
Year Established: 1924
Delivery Methods: Mail`Newsstand`Racks
Mechanical specifications: Type page 10 1/2 x 21 1/4; E - 6 cols, 3/16; A - 6 cols, C - 8 cols
Published Days: Fri
Avg Paid Circ: 24332
Avg Free Circ: 27361
Audit Company: AAM
Audit Date: 31 12 2018

SCAPPOOSE

THE SOUTH COUNTY SPOTLIGHT

Corporate/Parent Company: Pamplin Media Group
Street Address: 52490 SE Second St., Suite 140
City: Scappoose
State: OR
Postal Code: 97056
Office phone: (503) 543-6387
Publication Website: https://pamplinmedia.com/south-county-spotlight-home/
General E-mail: circulation@commnewspapers.com
Publisher Name: Darryl Swan
Publisher Email: dswan@spotlightnews.net
Publisher Phone: (503) 543-6387
Advertising Executive Name: Dawn Britton
Advertising Executive Email: dbritton@spotlightnews.net
Advertising Executive Phone: (503) 543-6387
Year Established: 1961
Delivery Methods: Mail`Newsstand`Racks
Commercial printers?: Y
Mechanical specifications: Type page 11 3/4 x 17 1/2; E - 5 cols, 1/6, between; C - 6 cols, 1/12 between.
Published Days: Fri
Avg Paid Circ: 4500
Audit Company: Sworn/Estimate/Non-Audited
Audit Date: 6 10 2019
Total Circulation: 2687

SEASIDE

SEASIDE SIGNAL

Corporate/Parent Company: EO Media Group
Street Address: 1555 N. Roosevelt Drive
City: Seaside
State: OR
Postal Code: 97138-7143
Office phone: (503) 738-5561
Publication Website: https://www.seasidesignal.com/
General E-mail: ssilver@dailyastorian.com
Publisher Name: Kari Borgen
Publisher Email: kborgen@dailyastorian.com
Publisher Phone: (503) 523-4955
Editor Name: R.J. Marx
Editor Email: rmarx@seasidesignal.com
Editor Phone: (971) 320-4557
Advertising Executive Name: Sarah Silver
Advertising Executive Email: ssilver@dailyastorian.com
Advertising Executive Phone: (971) 704-1712
Year Established: 1905
Commercial printers?: Y
Mechanical specifications: Type page 10 1/4 x 16 1/2; E - 5 cols, 2, 1/6 between; A - 5 cols, 2, 1/6 between; C - 7 cols, 1 1/2, 1/6 between.
Published Days: Thur
Avg Paid Circ: 3500
Audit Company: Sworn/Estimate/Non-Audited
Audit Date: 6 10 2019
Total Circulation: 4500

THE DALLES

THE DALLES DAILY CHRONICLE

Corporate/Parent Company: Eagle Newspapers, Inc.
Street Address: 315 Federal St
City: The Dalles
State: OR
Postal Code: 97058-2115
Office phone: (541) 296-2141
Publication Website: https://www.thedalleschronicle.com/
General E-mail: tdchron@thedalleschronicle.com
Year Established: 1890
Mechanical specifications: Type page 13 x 21; E - 6 cols, 2, 1/8 between; A - 6 cols, 2, 1/8 between; C - 6 cols, 2, 1/8 between.
Published Days: Tues`Wed`Thur`Fri`Sun
Weekday Frequency: e
Avg Paid Circ: 5067
Audit Company: Sworn/Estimate/Non-Audited
Audit Date: 7 12 2019
Total Circulation: 7000

TILLAMOOK

CANNON BEACH GAZETTE

Corporate/Parent Company: Country Media Inc.
Street Address: 1906 Second Street
City: Tillamook
State: OR
Postal Code: 97141
Office phone: (503) 842-7535
Publication Website: https://www.cannonbeachgazette.com/
General E-mail: jwarren@countrymedia.net
Advertising Executive Name: Katherine Mace
Advertising Executive Email: headlightads@countrymedia.net
Advertising Executive Phone: (503) 842-7535
Total Circulation: 4000

TILLAMOOK

NORTH COAST CITIZEN

Corporate/Parent Company: Country Media Inc.
Street Address: 1906 2nd St.
City: Tillamook
State: OR
Postal Code: 97141
Office phone: (503) 842-7535
Publication Website: https://www.northcoastcitizen.com/
General E-mail: admin@countrymedia.net
Publisher Name: Joe Warren
Publisher Email: jwarren@countrymedia.net
Publisher Phone: (503) 842-7535
Editor Email: editor@northcoastcitizen.com
Advertising Executive Name: Katherine Mace
Advertising Executive Email: headlightads@countrymedia.net
Advertising Executive Phone: (503) 842-7535
Year Established: 1996
Delivery Methods: Mail`Newsstand`Racks
Published Days: Thur`Bi-Mthly
Avg Paid Circ: 1200
Avg Free Circ: 50
Audit Company: Sworn/Estimate/Non-Audited
Audit Date: 6 10 2019
Total Circulation: 3750

WOODBURN

WOODBURN INDEPENDENT

Corporate/Parent Company: Pamplin Media Group
Street Address: 1585H N. Pacific Hwy
City: Woodburn
State: OR
Postal Code: 97071
Office phone: (503) 981-3441
Publication Website: https://pamplinmedia.com/woodburn-independent-home/
General E-mail: circulation@commnewspapers.com
Publisher Name: Al Herriges
Publisher Email: aherriges@pamplinmedia.com
Publisher Phone: (503) 981-3441
Editor Name: Phil Hawkins
Editor Email: Phawkins@woodburnindependent.com
Editor Phone: (503) 981-3441
Advertising Executive Name: Susan Vetter
Advertising Executive Email: svetter@woodburnindependent.com
Advertising Executive Phone: (503) 981-3441
Year Established: 1888
Own Printing Facility?: Y
Published Days: Wed
Avg Paid Circ: 4692
Avg Free Circ: 163
Audit Company: Sworn/Estimate/Non-Audited
Audit Date: 6 10 2019
Total Circulation: 5850

PENNSYLVANIA

ALLENTOWN

LEHIGH VALLEY PRESS

Corporate/Parent Company: Levigh Valley Press
Street Address: 1633 N 26th St
City: Allentown
State: PA
Postal Code: 18104
Office phone: 610-740-0944 Ext 3711
Publication Website: www.thelehighvalleypress.com
General E-mail: lvpfsocialmedia@tnonline.com
Editor Name: George Taylor
Total Circulation: 4855

CORRY

THE CORRY JOURNAL

Corporate/Parent Company: Sample News Group
Street Address: 28 W South St
City: Corry
State: PA
Postal Code: 16407-1810
Office phone: (814) 665-8291
Publication Website: www.thecorryjournal.com
General E-mail: tim@thecorryjournal.com
Publisher Name: Bob Williams
Publisher Email: bwilliams@thecorryjournal.com
Publisher Phone: (814) 665-8291, Ext : 35
Editor Name: Kathleen Spinazzola
Editor Email: kathleen@thecorryjournal.com
Editor Phone: (814) 665-8291, Ext : 35
Advertising Executive Name: Tim Joncas
Advertising Executive Email: tim@thecorryjournal.com
Advertising Executive Phone: (814) 665-8291, Ext : 22

EPHRATA

HOCKING PRINTING CO., INC.

Street Address: 615 EAST MAIN STREET, P.O. BOX 456
City: EPHRATA
State: PA
Postal Code: 17522
Office phone: 717-738-1151
Publication Website: www.snews.com
General E-mail: SNEWS@PTD.NET
Publisher Name: Julie A. Hocking

EXTON

MAIN LINE MEDIA NEWS

Corporate/Parent Company: Media News Group
Street Address: 390 Eagleview Blvd.
City: Exton
State: PA
Postal Code: 19341
Office phone: (610) 642-4300
Publication Website: http://www.mainlinemedianews.com/
General E-mail: bdouglas@21st-centurymedia.com
Publisher Name: Edward S. Condra
Publisher Email: econdra@21st-centurymedia.com
Editor Name: Cheryl Rodgers
Editor Email: crodgers@timesherald.com
Advertising Executive Name: Beth Douglas
Advertising Executive Email: bdouglas@21st-centurymedia.com

SOUTHERN BERKS NEWS

Street Address: 390 Eagleview Blvd.
City: Exton

State: PA
Postal Code: 19341
Office phone: 610-970-3218
Publication Website: www.berksmontnews.com/news/southern_berks_news
Publisher Name: Edward S. Condra
Publisher Email: econdra@21st-centurymedia.com
Editor Name: Lisa Mitchell
Editor Email: lmitchell@21st-centurymedia.com
Advertising Executive Name: Toni Morressey
Advertising Executive Email: tonim@berksmontnews.com

SOUTHERN CHESTER COUNTY WEEKLIES

Corporate/Parent Company: Media News Group
Street Address: 390 Eagleview Blvd.
City: Exton
State: PA
Postal Code: 19341
Office phone: 610-696-1775
Publication Website: www.southernchestercountyweeklies.com
Publisher Name: Edward S. Condra
Publisher Email: econdra@21st-centurymedia.com
Editor Name: Fran Maye
Editor Email: fmaye@21st-centurymedia.com
Advertising Executive Name: Beth Douglas
Advertising Executive Email: bdouglas@21st-centurymedia.com

THE PHOENIX REPORTER & ITEM

Corporate/Parent Company: Media News Group
Street Address: 390 Eagleview Blvd.
City: Exton
State: PA
Postal Code: 19341
Office phone: (610) 850-0269
Publication Website: https://www.phoenixvillenews.com/
General E-mail: classified@pottsmerc.com
Editor Name: Tony Phyrillas
Editor Email: tphyrillas@pottsmerc.com
Editor Phone: (610) 850-0270
Year Established: 2013
Delivery Methods: Mail`Newsstand`Racks
Own Printing Facility?: Y
Mechanical specifications: Type page 12 3/4 x 21 1/2; E - 6 cols, 2, 1/6 between; A - 6 cols, 2, 1/6 between; C - 10 cols, 1 1/3, 1/6 between.
Published Days: Sun
Weekday Frequency: m
Saturday Frequency: m
Avg Paid Circ: 2566
Audit Company: Sworn/Estimate/Non-Audited
Audit Date: 6 10 2019

GLENOLDEN

DELAWARE COUNTY SPIRIT

Corporate/Parent Company: Sample News Group LLC
Street Address: P.O 464
City: Glenolden
State: PA
Postal Code: 19036
Office phone: 610-447-8484
Publication Website: www.chesterspirit.com
Editor Name: PAUL A. BENNETT
Editor Email: pbennett@myspiritnews.com
Total Circulation: 2735

SPIRIT MEDIA GROUP, INC.

Corporate/Parent Company: Sample News Group LLC
Street Address: P.O 464
City: Glenolden
State: PA
Postal Code: 19036
Office phone: 610-447-8484
Publication Website: www.myspiritnews.com
Editor Name: PAUL A. BENNETT
Editor Email: pbennett@myspiritnews.com

HARRISBURG

CAUCUS

Corporate/Parent Company: LNP Media Group
Street Address: 211 State Street, Suite #100
City: Harrisburg
State: PA
Postal Code: 17101
Office phone: 717-291-8811
Publication Website: caucuspa.com
General E-mail: info@caucuspa.com
Editor Name: TOM MURSE
Editor Email: tmurse@caucuspa.com

THEBURG

Street Address: 920 N. Third Street Suite 101
City: Harrisburg
State: PA
Postal Code: 17102
Publication Website: www.theburgnews.com
Editor Name: Lawrance Binda
Editor Email: lbinda@theburgnews.com
Editor Phone: 717-695-2576
Advertising Executive Name: Lauren Maurer
Advertising Executive Email: lmills@theburgnews.com
Advertising Executive Phone: 717-695-2621

HUMMELSTOWN

SUN

Corporate/Parent Company: Paxton Media Group
Street Address: 18 E. Main St.
City: Hummelstown
State: PA
Postal Code: 17036
Office phone: 717-566-3251
Publication Website: www.thesunontheweb.com
General E-mail: ads@thesunontheweb.com
Editor Name: David Buffington
Editor Email: news@thesunontheweb.com
Year Established: 1871
Delivery Methods: Mail`Newsstand`Racks
Mechanical specifications: Type page 13 3/4 x 21 1/2; E - 8 cols, 1 7/12, 1/6 between; A - 8 cols, 1 7/12, 1/6 between; C - 8 cols, 1 7/12, 1/6 between.
Published Days: Thur
Avg Paid Circ: 8000
Audit Company: Sworn/Estimate/Non-Audited
Audit Date: 6 10 2019

LANCASTER

STEINMAN COMMUNICATIONS

Corporate/Parent Company: LNP Media Group
Street Address: 8 W King St
City: Lancaster
State: PA
Postal Code: 17603
Office phone: (717) 291-8811
Publication Website: steinmancommunications.com

LANSDALE

MONTGOMERY MEDIA NETWORK

Street Address: 307 Derstine Ave.
City: Lansdale
State: PA
Postal Code: 19446
Office phone: 215-542-0200
Publication Website: www.montgomerynews.com
General E-mail: editorial@montgomerynews.com
Publisher Name: Edward S. Condra
Publisher Email: econdra@21st-centurymedia.com
Editor Name: Nancy March
Editor Email: nmarch@thereporteronline.com
Advertising Executive Name: Beth Douglas
Advertising Executive Email: bdouglas@21st-centurymedia.com
Total Circulation: 4945

ROXBOROUGH REVIEW

Street Address: 307 Derstine Ave.
City: Lansdale
State: PA
Postal Code: 19446
Office phone: 215-542-0200
Publication Website: www.roxreview.com
General E-mail: editorial@montgomerynews.com
Publisher Name: Edward S. Condra
Publisher Email: econdra@21st-centurymedia.com
Editor Name: Phil Heron
Editor Email: pheron@delcotimes.com
Advertising Executive Name: Beth Douglas
Advertising Executive Email: bdouglas@21st-centurymedia.com

LATROBE

LATROBE PRINTING & PUBLISHING, INC.

Street Address: 1211 Ligonier Street
City: Latrobe
State: PA
Postal Code: 15650
Office phone: (724) 537-3351
Publication Website: latrobebulletinnews.com
Publisher Name: Gary Siegel
Publisher Email: garysiegel1@verizon.net
Publisher Phone: 724-537-3351 Ext. 19
Editor Name: Steve Kittey
Editor Email: lb.editor@verizon.net
Editor Phone: 724-537-3351 Ext. 27
Advertising Executive Name: Joyce Lynn Helmetzi
Advertising Executive Email: latbull@gmail.com
Advertising Executive Phone: 724-537-3351 Ext. 24

MIDDLETOWN

PRESS AND JOURNAL PUBLICATIONS

Street Address: 20 S. Union Street
City: Middletown
State: PA
Postal Code: 17057-1445
Office phone: 717-944-4628
Publication Website: www.pressandjournal.com
General E-mail: info@pressandjournal.com
Publisher Name: Louise Sukle
Publisher Email: louisesukle@pressandjournal.com
Editor Name: Jason Maddux
Editor Email: jasonmaddux@pressandjournal.com
Advertising Executive Name: Dave Brown
Advertising Executive Email: davebrown@pressandjournal.com

MONROEVILLE

NORTH JOURNAL

Corporate/Parent Company: Trib Total Media, Inc.
Street Address: 610 Beatty Rd
City: Monroeville
State: PA
Postal Code: 15146-1558
Office phone: (412) 856-7400
Publication Website: https://northjournal.triblive.com/
General E-mail: dmcelhinny@tribweb.com
Editor Name: Dave Mcelhinny
Editor Email: dmcelhinny@tribweb.com
Editor Phone: (724) 772-6362
Delivery Methods: Mail`Newsstand
Own Printing Facility?: Y
Mechanical specifications: Type page 10 13/16 x 16; A - 5 cols, 2 1/16, between; C - 7 cols, 1 5/16, between.
Published Days: Sun
Avg Paid Circ: 59
Avg Free Circ: 18759
Audit Company: Sworn/Estimate/Non-Audited
Audit Date: 6 10 2019

PENN-TRAFFORD STAR

Corporate/Parent Company: Trib Total Media, LLC
Street Address: 610 Beatty Road
City: Monroeville
State: PA
Postal Code: 15146
Office phone: (412) 856-7400
Publication Website: https://triblive.com/local/penn-trafford/
General E-mail: bpoole@tribweb.com
Editor Name: Rebecca Poole
Editor Email: bpoole@tribweb.com
Editor Phone: (724) 838-5146
Delivery Methods: Mail`Newsstand
Published Days: Thur
Avg Paid Circ: 170
Avg Free Circ: 8138
Audit Company: Sworn/Estimate/Non-Audited
Audit Date: 6 10 2019
Total Circulation: 11367

MONTROSE

SUSQUEHANNA COUNTY INDEPENDENT

Street Address: 231 Church Street
City: Montrose
State: PA
Postal Code: 18801
Office phone: (570) 278-6397
Publication Website: www.independentweekender.com
Editor Name: Staci Wilson
Editor Email: indynews@independentweekender.com
Advertising Executive Name: Dan Tompkins
Advertising Executive Email: dtompkins@independentweekender.com
Year Established: 1816
Delivery Methods: Mail`Newsstand
Mechanical specifications: Type page 10 3/8 x 15 1/2.
Published Days: Wed
Avg Paid Circ: 3700
Avg Free Circ: 173
Audit Company: Sworn/Estimate/Non-Audited
Audit Date: 6 10 2019

MORGANTOWN

TRI-COUNTY RECORD

Corporate/Parent Company: MediaNews Group, Inc.
Street Address: 150 Morview Blvd.
City: Morgantown
State: PA
Postal Code: 19543
Office phone: (610) 286-0162
Publication Website: https://www.berksmontnews.com/
General E-mail: tonim@berksmontnews.com
Publisher Name: Edward S. Condra
Publisher Email: econdra@21st-centurymedia.com
Editor Name: Justin Finneran
Editor Phone: (610) 286-0162, ext : 25
Advertising Executive Name: Toni Morressey
Advertising Executive Email: tonim@

Non-Daily Newspapers in the U.S.

berksmontnews.com
Delivery Methods:
    Mail`Newsstand`Carrier`Racks
Mechanical specifications: Type page 10 3/8 x 13; E - 6 cols, 1 2/3, between; A - 6 cols, 1 2/3, between.
Published Days: Tues
Avg Free Circ: 20100
Audit Company: Sworn/Estimate/Non-Audited
Audit Date: 6 10 2019

NEW BETHLEHEM

LEADER-VINDICATOR

Street Address: 435 Broad St
City: New Bethlehem
State: PA
Postal Code: 16242
Office phone: 814-275-3131
Publication Website: www.thecourierexpress.com/the_leader_vindicator
Publisher Name: Pat Patterson
Publisher Email: dhamilton@thecourierexpress.com
Publisher Phone: 814-503-8860
Editor Name: Josh Walzak
Editor Email: jwalzak@thecourierexpress.com
Editor Phone: 814-275-3131 ext 225
Advertising Executive Name: Deb Huffman
Advertising Executive Email: dhuffman@thecourierexpress.com
Advertising Executive Phone: 814-275-3131 ext 224
Year Established: 1873
Delivery Methods:
    Mail`Newsstand`Carrier`Racks
Own Printing Facility?: Y
Commercial printers?: Y
Mechanical specifications: Type page 12 x 21; E - 6 cols, 1 13/16, 1/7 between; A - 6 cols, 1 13/16, 1/7 between; C - 6 cols, 1 13/16, 1/7 between.
Published Days: Wed
Avg Paid Circ: 4899
Avg Free Circ: 46
Audit Company: Sworn/Estimate/Non-Audited
Audit Date: 6 10 2019
Total Circulation: 18818

OIL CITY

DERRICK

Street Address: 1510 West First Street
City: Oil City
State: PA
Postal Code: 16301
Office phone: 814-676-7444
Publication Website: www.thederrick.com
General E-mail: newsroom.thederrick@gmail.com
Editor Name: Luka Krneta
Editor Email: lukakrneta.thederrick@gmail.com
Editor Phone: 814-677-8367
Advertising Executive Name: Paul Hess
Advertising Executive Email: ad_man_no1958@yahoo.com
Advertising Executive Phone: 814-677-8313
Total Circulation: 16304

PITTSBURGH

BRIDGEVILLE AREA NEWS

Corporate/Parent Company: Trib Total Media, Inc.
Street Address: 1964 Greentree Rd
City: Pittsburgh
State: PA
Postal Code: 15220-1813
Office phone: (412) 388-5800
Publication Website: https://triblive.com/local/carlynton/
General E-mail: nmiller@tribweb.com
Editor Name: Natalie Miller
Editor Email: nmiller@tribweb.com
Editor Phone: (412) 324-1408

NEW PITTSBURGH COURIER

Street Address: 315 East Carson Street
City: Pittsburgh
State: PA
Postal Code: 15219
Office phone: 412-481-8302
Publication Website: www.newpittsburghcourier.com
General E-mail: ads@newpittsburghcourier.com
Editor Name: Rob Taylor Jr.
Editor Email: rtaylor@newpittsburghcourier.com
Editor Phone: 412-481-8302, ext. 135
Total Circulation: 8308

SCOTTDALE

THE INDEPENDENT-OBSERVER

Street Address: 228 Pittsburgh Street
City: Scottdale
State: PA
Postal Code: 15683
Publication Website: http://www.theindependentobserver.com/
General E-mail: ioreporter@theindependentobserver.com
Total Circulation: 9928

SCRANTON

TIMES-SHAMROCK COMMUNITY NEWSPAPER GROUP

Corporate/Parent Company: Times-Shamrock Communications
Street Address: 149 Penn Ave.
City: Scranton
State: PA
Postal Code: 18503
Office phone: 855-614-5440
Publication Website: timesshamrock.com
General E-mail: customer_relations@tscsdirect.com
Publisher Name: Donald Farley

TIMES-SHAMROCK CREATIVE SERVICES

Corporate/Parent Company: Times-Shamrock Communications
Street Address: 149 Penn Ave.
City: Scranton
State: PA
Postal Code: 18503
Office phone: 855-614-5440
Publication Website: www.TSCSdirect.com
General E-mail: customer_relations@tscsdirect.com
Publisher Name: Donald Farley
Total Circulation: 10752

TIMES-SHAMROCK WEEKLY GROUP

Corporate/Parent Company: Times-Shamrock Communications
Street Address: 149 Penn Ave.
City: Scranton
State: PA
Postal Code: 18503
Office phone: 855-614-5440
Publication Website: timesshamrock.com
General E-mail: customer_relations@tscsdirect.com
Publisher Name: Donald Farley

SEWICKLEY

SEWICKLEY HERALD

Corporate/Parent Company: Trib Total Media, LLC
Street Address: 504 Beaver St
City: Sewickley
State: PA
Postal Code: 15143-1753
Office phone: (412) 324-1400
Publication Website: https://sewickley.triblive.com/
General E-mail: nmiller@tribweb.com
Editor Name: Natalie Miller
Editor Email: nmiller@tribweb.com
Editor Phone: (412) 324-1408
Year Established: 1903
Delivery Methods: Mail`Newsstand
Own Printing Facility?: Y
Commercial printers?: Y
Mechanical specifications: Type page 10 13/16 x 16; A - 5 cols, 2 1/16, between; C - 7 cols, 1 5/16, between.
Published Days: Thur
Avg Paid Circ: 431
Avg Free Circ: 7981
Audit Company: Sworn/Estimate/Non-Audited
Audit Date: 6 10 2019

SHIPPENSBURG

NEWVILLE VALLEY TIMES-STAR

Corporate/Parent Company: Sample News Group LLC
Street Address: 825 W. King St., Front
City: Shippensburg
State: PA
Postal Code: 17257
Office phone: 717-532-4101
Publication Website: www.shipnc.com/valley_times_star
Editor Name: Denise Bonura
Editor Email: editor@shipnc.com
Editor Phone: 717-532-4101 ext. 222
Advertising Executive Name: John Zimmerman
Advertising Executive Email: sales@shipnc.com
Advertising Executive Phone: 717-532-4101 ext. 225
Total Circulation: 8412

STATE COLLEGE

CENTRE COUNTY GAZETTE

Street Address: 403 S. Allen Street
City: State College
State: PA
Postal Code: 16801
Office phone: (814) 238-3500
Publication Website: www.centrecountygazette.com
General E-mail: info@statecollege.com
Editor Name: Kerry Webster
Editor Email: editor@centrecountygazette.com
Advertising Executive Name: Laurie Linton
Advertising Executive Email: llinton@centrecountygazette.com

SWARTHMORE

DELAWARE COUNTY NEWS NETWORK

Street Address: 639 S. Chester Road
City: Swarthmore
State: PA
Postal Code: 19081
Office phone: 610-915-2248
Publication Website: www.delconewsnetwork.com
Publisher Name: Edward S. Condra
Publisher Email: econdra@21st-centurymedia.com
Editor Name: Peg DeGrassa
Editor Email: pdegrassa@delconewsnetwork.com
Advertising Executive Name: Richard Crowe
Advertising Executive Email: rcrowe@21st-centurymedia.com

Total Circulation: 3114

GARNET VALLEY PRESS

Street Address: 639 South Chester Road
City: Swarthmore
State: PA
Postal Code: 19081
Office phone: 610-915-2248
Publication Website: www.delconewsnetwork.com/garnetvalleypress
Publisher Name: Edward S. Condra
Publisher Email: econdra@21st-centurymedia.com
Editor Name: Peg DeGrassa
Editor Email: pdegrassa@delconewsnetwork.com
Advertising Executive Name: Richard Crowe
Advertising Executive Email: rcrowe@21st-centurymedia.com

TARENTUM

HAMPTON JOURNAL

Corporate/Parent Company: Trib Total Media, Inc.
Street Address: 210 Wood Street
City: Tarentum
State: PA
Postal Code: 15084
Office phone: (800) 909-8742
Publication Website: https://hampton.triblive.com/
Editor Name: Dave Mcelhinny
Editor Email: dmcelhinny@tribweb.com
Editor Phone: (724) 772-6362

MURRYSVILLE STAR

Corporate/Parent Company: Trib Total Media, Inc.
Street Address: 210 Wood Street
City: Tarentum
State: PA
Postal Code: 15084
Office phone: (800) 909-8742
Publication Website: https://triblive.com/local/murrysville/
General E-mail: bpoole@tribweb.com
Editor Name: Rebecca Poole
Editor Email: bpoole@tribweb.com
Editor Phone: (724) 838-5146
Delivery Methods: Mail`Newsstand
Own Printing Facility?: Y
Commercial printers?: Y
Mechanical specifications: Type page 13 x 21 1/2; A - 6 cols, 2 1/16, between; C - 9 cols, 1 5/16, between.
Published Days: Thur
Avg Paid Circ: 68
Avg Free Circ: 11299
Audit Company: Sworn/Estimate/Non-Audited
Audit Date: 6 10 2019

NORWIN STAR

Corporate/Parent Company: Trib Total Media, Inc.
Street Address: 210 Wood Street
City: Tarentum
State: PA
Postal Code: 15084
Office phone: (800) 909-8742
Publication Website: https://triblive.com/local/norwin/
General E-mail: bpoole@tribweb.com
Editor Name: Rebecca Poole
Editor Email: bpoole@tribweb.com
Editor Phone: (724) 838-5146
Delivery Methods: Mail`Newsstand
Own Printing Facility?: Y
Commercial printers?: Y
Mechanical specifications: Type page 13 x 21 1/2; A - 6 cols, 2 1/16, between; C - 9 cols, 1 5/16, between.
Published Days: Thur

Avg Paid Circ: 134
Avg Free Circ: 16170
Audit Company: Sworn/Estimate/Non-Audited
Audit Date: 6 10 2019

PENN HILLS PROGRESS
Corporate/Parent Company: Trib Total Media, Inc.
Street Address: 210 Wood Street
City: Tarentum
State: PA
Postal Code: 15084
Office phone: (724) 226-4666
Publication Website: https://pennhills.triblive.com/
General E-mail: kgreen@tribweb.com
Editor Name: Katie Green
Editor Email: kgreen@tribweb.com
Total Circulation: 8000

PINE CREEK JOURNAL
Corporate/Parent Company: Trib Total Media, LLC
Street Address: 210 Wood Street
City: Tarentum
State: PA
Postal Code: 15084
Office phone: (800) 909-8742
Publication Website: https://pinecreek.triblive.com/
General E-mail: dmcelhinny@tribweb.com
Editor Name: Dave Mcelhinny
Editor Email: dmcelhinny@tribweb.com
Editor Phone: (724) 772-6362
Delivery Methods: Mail`Newsstand
Published Days: Sun
Avg Paid Circ: 309
Avg Free Circ: 9619
Audit Company: Sworn/Estimate/Non-Audited
Audit Date: 6 10 2019
Total Circulation: 3873

PLUM ADVANCE LEADER
Corporate/Parent Company: Trib Total Media, LLC
Street Address: 210 Wood Street
City: Tarentum
State: PA
Postal Code: 15084
Office phone: (724) 226-4666
Publication Website: https://plum.triblive.com/
General E-mail: nmiller@tribweb.com
Editor Name: Natalie Miller
Editor Email: nmiller@tribweb.com
Editor Phone: (412) 324-1408
Delivery Methods: Mail`Newsstand
Published Days: Thur
Avg Paid Circ: 95
Avg Free Circ: 10657
Audit Company: Sworn/Estimate/Non-Audited
Audit Date: 6 10 2019

SHALER JOURNAL
Corporate/Parent Company: Trib Total Media, Inc.
Street Address: 210 Wood Street
City: Tarentum
State: PA
Postal Code: 15084
Office phone: (800) 909-8742
Publication Website: https://shaler.triblive.com/
Editor Name: Dave Mcelhinny
Editor Email: dmcelhinny@tribweb.com
Editor Phone: (724) 772-6362

SOUTH HILLS RECORD
Corporate/Parent Company: Trib Total Media, LLC
Street Address: 210 Wood Street
City: Tarentum
State: PA
Postal Code: 15084
Office phone: (800) 909-8742
Publication Website: https://triblive.com/local/south-hills/
General E-mail: kgreen@tribweb.com
Editor Name: Katie Green
Editor Email: kgreen@tribweb.com
Delivery Methods: Mail`Newsstand
Own Printing Facility?: Y
Commercial printers?: Y
Mechanical specifications: Type page 10 13/16 x 16; A - 5 cols, 2 1/16, between; C - 7 cols, 1 5/16, between.
Published Days: Thur
Avg Paid Circ: 3114
Audit Company: Sworn/Estimate/Non-Audited
Audit Date: 6 10 2019

THE TIMES EXPRESS
Corporate/Parent Company: Trib Total Media, Inc.
Street Address: 210 Wood Street
City: Tarentum
State: PA
Postal Code: 15084
Office phone: (800) 909-8742
Publication Website: https://triblive.com/
General E-mail: nmiller@tribweb.com
Editor Name: Natalie Miller
Editor Email: nmiller@tribweb.com
Editor Phone: (412) 324-1408
Delivery Methods: Mail`Newsstand
Own Printing Facility?: Y
Commercial printers?: Y
Mechanical specifications: Type page 13 x 21 1/2; A - 6 cols, 2 1/16, between; C - 9 cols, 1 5/16, between.
Published Days: Thur
Avg Paid Circ: 137
Avg Free Circ: 15766
Audit Company: Sworn/Estimate/Non-Audited
Audit Date: 6 10 2019
Buisness Equipment: PC Network
Buisness Software: MSSI, ADP
Classified Equipment: Hardware – 1-Fax Telecopier.;
Editorial Equipment: Hardware – Baseview, APP/iMacs
Editorial Software: Baseview.
Production Equipment: Hardware – Intertext, V/600, Linotron/202; Cameras – 1-LE/5000H, 1-Spartan/III, C/1270, Autokon; Scanners – Nikon/Coolscan
Production Software: QPS/QuarkXPress 4.0.
Note: The Phoenix is printed by Journal Register Offset in Exton, PA.
Total Circulation: 2566

TRIBLIVE
Corporate/Parent Company: Trib Total Media, LLC
Street Address: 210 Wood Street
City: Tarentum
State: PA
Postal Code: 15084
Office phone: 800-909-8742
Publication Website: triblive.com
General E-mail: gateeds@tribweb.com
Editor Name: Susan K. McFarland
Editor Email: smcfarland@tribweb.com
Total Circulation: 15903

VALLEY NEWS DISPATCH
Corporate/Parent Company: Trib Total Media, Inc.
Street Address: 210 E 4th Ave
City: Tarentum
State: PA
Postal Code: 15084-1766
Office phone: (724) 224-4321
Publication Website: https://triblive.com/local/valley-news-dispatch/
General E-mail: tribliving@tribweb.com
Editor Name: LUIS FÁBREGA
Editor Email: lfabregas@tribweb.com
Editor Phone: (724) 226-4687
Total Circulation: 5500

TOWANDA

TOWANDA PRINTING COMPANY
Street Address: " 116 Main St Ste 5"
City: Towanda
State: PA
Postal Code: 18848
Office phone: 570-265-2151
Publication Website: www.thedailyreview.com
Editor Name: Matt Hicks
Editor Email: mhicks@thedailyreview.com
Editor Phone: Ext 1628

WELLSBORO

FREE PRESS-COURIER
Corporate/Parent Company: Tioga Publishing Company
Street Address: 25 East Ave
City: Wellsboro
State: PA
Postal Code: 16901-1618
Office phone: (814) 367-2230
Publication Website: http://www.tiogapublishing.com/free_press_courier/
General E-mail: gazette@tiogapublishing.com
Delivery Methods: Mail`Newsstand`Racks
Own Printing Facility?: Y
Commercial printers?: Y
Published Days: Wed
Avg Paid Circ: 2735
Audit Company: Sworn/Estimate/Non-Audited
Audit Date: 6 10 2019

MOUNTAIN HOME
Street Address: 39 Water St
City: Wellsboro
State: PA
Postal Code: 16901
Office phone: (570) 724-3838
Publication Website: www.mountainhomemag.com
Publisher Name: Teresa Banik Capuzzo
Publisher Email: teresac@mountainhomemag.com
Editor Name: Mike Capuzzo
Editor Email: mikec@mountainhomemag.com
Advertising Executive Name: Amy Packard
Advertising Executive Email: amyp@mountainhomemag.com

THE WELLSBORO GAZETTE
Corporate/Parent Company: Community Media Group
Street Address: 25 East Ave
City: Wellsboro
State: PA
Postal Code: 16901-1618
Office phone: (570) 724-2287
Publication Website: http://www.tiogapublishing.com/the_wellsboro_mansfield_gazette/
General E-mail: gazette@tiogapublishing.com
Publisher Name: David Sullens
Editor Name: David Sullens
Advertising Executive Name: Larry McCullen
Advertising Executive Phone: (585) 313-0938
Year Established: 1874
Delivery Methods: Mail`Newsstand`Racks
Own Printing Facility?: Y
Commercial printers?: Y
Mechanical specifications: Type page 13 x 21 1/2; E - 6 cols, 2 1/16, 1/6 between; A - 6 cols, 2, 1/6 between; C - 8 cols, 1 3/8, 1/6 between.

Published Days: Thur
Avg Paid Circ: 5500
Audit Company: Sworn/Estimate/Non-Audited
Audit Date: 6 10 2019

WHITE HAVEN

JOURNAL OF PENN-KIDDER
Corporate/Parent Company: Journal-Herald
Street Address: 211 Main Street
City: White Haven
State: PA
Postal Code: 18661
Office phone: 570-215-0204
Publication Website: pocononewspapers.com
Editor Name: Ruth Isenberg
Editor Email: journalruth@gmail.com

WILKES-BARRE

PITTSDON DISPATCH
Corporate/Parent Company: Avant Publications
Street Address: 90 E. Market St.
City: Wilkes-Barre
State: PA
Postal Code: 18640
Office phone: (570) 829-5000
Publication Website: https://www.psdispatch.com/
General E-mail: mmurray@timesleader.com
Publisher Name: Mike Murray
Publisher Email: mmurray@timesleader.com
Publisher Phone: (570) 704-3986
Editor Name: Dotty Martin
Editor Email: dmartin@timesleader.com
Editor Phone: (570) 704-3982
Advertising Executive Name: Kerry Miscavage
Advertising Executive Email: kmiscavage@timesleader.com
Advertising Executive Phone: (570) 704-3953

THE ABINGTON JOURNAL
Corporate/Parent Company: Avant Publications
Street Address: 90 E. Market St
City: Wilkes-Barre
State: PA
Postal Code: 18701
Office phone: (570) 991-6405
Publication Website: https://www.theabingtonjournal.com
General E-mail: bjackson@timesleader.com
Total Circulation: 20100

RHODE ISLAND

BRISTOL

BARRINGTON TIMES
Corporate/Parent Company: East Bay Newspapers
Street Address: 1 Bradford St
City: Bristol
State: RI
Postal Code: 02809-1906
Office phone: (401) 253-6000
Publication Website: https://www.eastbayri.com/barrington/
General E-mail: info@eastbaynewspapers.com
Editor Name: Josh Bickford
Editor Email: jbickford@eastbaymediagroup.com
Advertising Executive Name: Scott Pickering
Advertising Executive Email: spickering@eastbaymediagroup.com
Advertising Executive Phone: (401) 424-9144
Year Established: 1958
Delivery Methods: Mail`Newsstand
Own Printing Facility?: Y
Mechanical specifications: Type page 10 3/4 x

Non-Daily Newspapers in the U.S.

16 3/4.
Published Days: Wed
Avg Paid Circ: 2497
Audit Company: Sworn/Estimate/Non-Audited
Audit Date: 6 10 2019

BRISTOL PHOENIX

Corporate/Parent Company: East Bay Newspapers
Street Address: 1 Bradford St
City: Bristol
State: RI
Postal Code: 02809-1906
Office phone: (401) 253-6000
Publication Website: https://www.eastbayri.com/bristol/
General E-mail: info@eastbaynewspapers.com
Editor Name: Scott Pickering
Editor Email: spickering@eastbaymediagroup.com
Advertising Executive Name: Scott Pickering
Advertising Executive Email: spickering@eastbaymediagroup.com
Advertising Executive Phone: (401) 424-9144
Year Established: 1837
Delivery Methods: Mail`Newsstand
Own Printing Facility?: Y
Mechanical specifications: Type page 10 3/4 x 16 3/4; E - 5 cols, 2 1/16, between; A - 5 cols, 2 1/16, between; C - 6 cols, 1 5/8, between.
Published Days: Thur
Avg Paid Circ: 3284
Avg Free Circ: 15
Audit Company: CVC
Audit Date: 30 06 2018

PORTSMOUTH TIMES

Corporate/Parent Company: East Bay Newspapers
Street Address: 1 Bradford St
City: Bristol
State: RI
Postal Code: 02809-1906
Office phone: (401) 253-6000
Publication Website: https://www.eastbayri.com/portsmouth/
General E-mail: info@eastbaynewspapers.com
Editor Name: Jim McGaw
Editor Email: jmcgaw@eastbaymediagroup.com
Advertising Executive Name: Scott Pickering
Advertising Executive Email: spickering@eastbaymediagroup.com
Advertising Executive Phone: (401) 424-9144
Year Established: 1837
Delivery Methods: Newsstand
Published Days: Thur
Avg Free Circ: 3814
Audit Company: CVC
Audit Date: 30 06 2018

SAKONNET TIMES

Corporate/Parent Company: East Bay Newspapers
Street Address: 1 Bradford St
City: Bristol
State: RI
Postal Code: 02809-1906
Office phone: (401) 253-6000
Publication Website: eastbayri.com
General E-mail: info@eastbaynewspapers.com
Editor Name: Bruce Burdett
Editor Email: bburdett@eastbaymediagroup.com
Advertising Executive Name: Scott Pickering
Advertising Executive Email: spickering@eastbaymediagroup.com
Advertising Executive Phone: (401) 424-9144
Year Established: 1967
Delivery Methods: Mail`Newsstand`Racks
Own Printing Facility?: Y
Mechanical specifications: Type page 10 3/4 x 16 3/4; E - 5 cols, 2 1/16, between; A - 5 cols, 2 1/16, between; C - 6 cols, 1 5/8, between.
Published Days: Thur
Avg Paid Circ: 2842
Audit Company: CVC
Audit Date: 30 06 2016

THE POST

Street Address: 1 Bradford St
City: Bristol
State: RI
Postal Code: 02809-1906
Office phone: (401) 253-6000
Publication Website: eastbayri.com
General E-mail: info@eastbaynewspapers.com
Delivery Methods: Newsstand
Mechanical specifications: Type page 10 3/4 x 16 3/4.
Published Days: Thur
Avg Free Circ: 8324
Audit Company: VAC
Audit Date: 30 06 2016

TIMES-GAZETTE OF WARREN

Street Address: 1 Ford St
City: Bristol
State: RI
Postal Code: 0 2809
Office phone: 401-253-6000
Publication Website: eastbayri.com/warren
Editor Name: Ted Hayes
Editor Email: thayes@eastbaynewspapers.com
Advertising Executive Name: Matt Hayes
Advertising Executive Email: mhayes@eastbaymediagroup.com
Advertising Executive Phone: (401) 424-9140

WARREN TIMES-GAZETTE

Corporate/Parent Company: East Bay Newspapers
Street Address: 1 Bradford St
City: Bristol
State: RI
Postal Code: 02809-1906
Office phone: (401) 253-6000
Publication Website: https://www.eastbayri.com/warren/
General E-mail: info@eastbaynewspapers.com
Editor Name: Ted Hayes
Editor Email: jmcgaw@eastbaymediagroup.com
Advertising Executive Name: Scott Pickering
Advertising Executive Email: spickering@eastbaymediagroup.com
Advertising Executive Phone: (401) 424-9144
Year Established: 1837
Delivery Methods: Mail`Newsstand
Own Printing Facility?: Y
Commercial printers?: Y
Mechanical specifications: Type page 10 3/4 x 16 3/4; E - 5 cols, 2 1/16, between; A - 5 cols, 2 1/16, between; C - 6 cols, 1 5/8, between.
Published Days: Wed
Avg Paid Circ: 1426
Audit Company: CVC
Audit Date: 30 06 2018

WESTPORT SHORELINES

Corporate/Parent Company: East Bay Newspapers
Street Address: 1 Bradford St
City: Bristol
State: RI
Postal Code: 02809-1906
Office phone: (401) 253-6000
Publication Website: https://www.eastbayri.com/westport/
General E-mail: info@eastbaynewspapers.com
Editor Name: Bruce Burdett
Editor Email: bburdett@eastbaymediagroup.com
Advertising Executive Name: Scott Pickering
Advertising Executive Email: spickering@eastbaymediagroup.com
Advertising Executive Phone: (401) 424-9144
Year Established: 1837
Delivery Methods: Mail`Newsstand
Mechanical specifications: Type page 10 3/4 x 16 3/4.
Published Days: Thur
Avg Paid Circ: 1103
Audit Company: CVC
Audit Date: 30 06 2018

LINCOLN

THE VALLEY BREEZE OF NORTH SMITHFIELD AND WOONSOCKET, PROVIDENCE COUNTY; BLACKSTONE, MASSACHUSETTS

Corporate/Parent Company: Breeze Publications, Inc
Street Address: 6 Blackstone Valley Place, Suite 204
City: Lincoln
State: RI
Postal Code: 0 2865
Office phone: (401) 334-9555
Publication Website: valleybreeze.com
General E-mail: news@valleybreeze.com
Publisher Name: Tom Ward
Publisher Email: tward@valleybreeze.com
Publisher Phone: Extension 123
Editor Name: Ethan Shorey
Editor Email: ethan@valleybreeze.com
Editor Phone: Extension 130
Advertising Executive Name: Tammy Austin
Advertising Executive Email: tammy@valleybreeze.com
Advertising Executive Phone: Extension 121

WAKEFIELD

CHARIHO TIMES

Corporate/Parent Company: Southern Rhode Island Newspapers
Street Address: 187 Main St
City: Wakefield
State: RI
Postal Code: 02879-3504
Office phone: (401) 789-9744
Publication Website: https://www.ricentral.com/chariho_times/
General E-mail: info@ricentral.com
Publisher Name: Jody A. Boucher
Publisher Email: jboucher@ricentral.com
Publisher Phone: (401) 789-9744, ext : 105
Editor Name: Gabrielle Falletta
Editor Email: gfalletta@ricentral.com
Editor Phone: (401) 789-9744, ext : 139
Advertising Executive Name: Esther Diggins
Advertising Executive Email: ediggins@ricentral.com
Advertising Executive Phone: (401) 789-9744, ext : 117
Year Established: 1992
Delivery Methods: Mail`Newsstand`Racks
Published Days: Thur
Avg Paid Circ: 426
Avg Free Circ: 117
Audit Company: AAM
Audit Date: 24 10 2019

COVENTRY COURIER

Corporate/Parent Company: Southern Rhode Island Newspapers
Street Address: 187 Main St
City: Wakefield
State: RI
Postal Code: 02879-3504
Office phone: (401) 789-9744
Publication Website: https://www.ricentral.com/coventry_courier/
General E-mail: info@ricentral.com
Publisher Name: Jody A. Boucher
Publisher Email: jboucher@ricentral.com
Publisher Phone: (401) 789-9744, ext : 105
Editor Name: Gabrielle Falletta
Editor Email: gfalletta@ricentral.com
Editor Phone: (401) 789-9744, ext : 139
Advertising Executive Name: Esther Diggins
Advertising Executive Email: ediggins@ricentral.com
Advertising Executive Phone: (401) 789-9744, ext : 117
Year Established: 1996
Delivery Methods: Mail`Newsstand`Racks
Published Days: Fri
Avg Paid Circ: 282
Avg Free Circ: 58
Audit Company: AAM
Audit Date: 24 10 2019

EAST GREENWICH PENDULUM

Corporate/Parent Company: Southern Rhode Island Newspapers
Street Address: 187 Main St
City: Wakefield
State: RI
Postal Code: 02879-3504
Office phone: (401) 789-9744
Publication Website: https://www.ricentral.com/east_greenwich_pendulum/
General E-mail: info@ricentral.com
Publisher Name: Jody A. Boucher
Publisher Email: jboucher@ricentral.com
Publisher Phone: (401) 789-9744, ext : 105
Editor Name: Gabrielle Falletta
Editor Email: gfalletta@ricentral.com
Editor Phone: (401) 789-9744, ext : 139
Advertising Executive Name: Esther Diggins
Advertising Executive Email: ediggins@ricentral.com
Advertising Executive Phone: (401) 789-9744, ext : 117
Year Established: 1854
Delivery Methods: Newsstand`Carrier`Racks
Own Printing Facility?: N
Commercial printers?: N
Published Days: Thur
Avg Paid Circ: 741
Avg Free Circ: 61
Audit Company: AAM
Audit Date: 24 10 2019

NARRAGANSETT TIMES

Corporate/Parent Company: Southern Rhode Island Newspapers
Street Address: 187 Main St
City: Wakefield
State: RI
Postal Code: 02879-3504
Office phone: (401) 789-9744
Publication Website: https://www.ricentral.com/narragansett_times/
General E-mail: info@ricentral.com
Publisher Name: Jody A. Boucher
Publisher Email: jboucher@ricentral.com
Publisher Phone: (401) 789-9744, ext : 105
Editor Name: Gabrielle Falletta
Editor Email: gfalletta@ricentral.com
Editor Phone: (401) 789-9744, ext : 139
Advertising Executive Name: Esther Diggins
Advertising Executive Email: ediggins@ricentral.com
Advertising Executive Phone: (401) 789-9744, ext : 117
Year Established: 1855
Delivery Methods: Mail`Newsstand`Racks
Own Printing Facility?: N
Commercial printers?: N
Published Days: Wed`Fri
Avg Paid Circ: 1613
Avg Free Circ: 110
Audit Company: AAM

Audit Date: 24 10 2019

STANDARD-TIMES
Corporate/Parent Company: Gannett
Street Address: 187 Main St
City: Wakefield
State: RI
Postal Code: 02879-3504
Office phone: (401) 789-9744
Publication Website: https://www.ricentral.com/nk_standard_times/
General E-mail: info@ricentral.com
Publisher Name: Jody A. Boucher
Publisher Email: jboucher@ricentral.com
Publisher Phone: (401) 789-9744, ext : 105
Editor Name: Gabrielle Falletta
Editor Email: gfalletta@ricentral.com
Editor Phone: (401) 789-9744, ext : 139
Advertising Executive Name: Esther Diggins
Advertising Executive Email: ediggins@ricentral.com
Advertising Executive Phone: (401) 789-9744, ext : 117
Year Established: 1888
Delivery Methods: Newsstand`Carrier`Racks
Own Printing Facility?: N
Commercial printers?: N
Mechanical specifications: Type page 12 x 21; E - 6 cols, 1 15/16, 1/8 between; A - 6 cols, 1 15/16, 1/8 between; C - 8 cols, 1 5/8, 1/8 between.
Published Days: Thur
Avg Paid Circ: 1197
Avg Free Circ: 1205
Audit Company: AAM
Audit Date: 31 03 2019

WARWICK

CRANSTON HERALD
Corporate/Parent Company: Beacon Communications
Street Address: 1944 Warwick Ave
City: Warwick
State: RI
Postal Code: 02889-2448
Office phone: (401) 732-3100
Publication Website: http://cranstononline.com/
General E-mail: timf@rhodybeat.com
Publisher Name: John Howell
Publisher Email: johnh@rhodybeat.com
Advertising Executive Name: Lisa Bourque Yuettner
Year Established: 1928
Delivery Methods: Mail`Newsstand`Carrier
Mechanical specifications: 6 cols. x 21" (10.5" x 21") each column 1.65"
Published Days: Thur
Avg Paid Circ: 1901
Avg Free Circ: 94
Audit Company: CVC
Audit Date: 30 06 2018

JOHNSTON SUN RISE
Corporate/Parent Company: Beacon Communications
Street Address: 1944 Warwick Ave
City: Warwick
State: RI
Postal Code: 02889-2448
Office phone: (401) 732-3100
Publication Website: http://johnstonsunrise.net/
General E-mail: timf@rhodybeat.com
Publisher Name: John Howell
Publisher Email: johnh@rhodybeat.com
Advertising Executive Name: Lisa Bourque Yuettner
Year Established: 1998
Delivery Methods: Mail`Newsstand`Carrier
Published Days: Thur
Avg Free Circ: 8175
Audit Company: CVC

Audit Date: 30 06 2018

RHODY BEAT
Corporate/Parent Company: Beacon Communications
Street Address: 1944 Warwick Avenue
City: Warwick
State: RI
Postal Code: 02889-2448
Office phone: (401) 732-3100
Publication Website: http://rhodybeat.com/
General E-mail: timf@rhodybeat.com
Publisher Name: John Howell
Publisher Email: johnh@rhodybeat.com
Advertising Executive Name: Lisa Bourque Yuettner

WARWICK BEACON
Corporate/Parent Company: Beacon Communications
Street Address: 1944 Warwick Ave
City: Warwick
State: RI
Postal Code: 02889-2400
Office phone: (401) 732-3100
Publication Website: http://warwickonline.com/
General E-mail: timf@rhodybeat.com
Publisher Name: John Howell
Publisher Email: johnh@rhodybeat.com
Editor Name: Ethan Hartley
Advertising Executive Name: Lisa Bourque Yuettner
Year Established: 1954
Delivery Methods: Mail`Newsstand`Carrier
Own Printing Facility?: N
Commercial printers?: N
Mechanical specifications: 6 cols. x 21" (10.5" wide) Each column measures 1.65"
Published Days: Tues`Thur
Weekday Frequency: m
Avg Paid Circ: 5275
Avg Free Circ: 423
Audit Company: CVC
Audit Date: 30 06 2018

SOUTH CAROLINA

AIKEN

AIKEN STANDARD
Corporate/Parent Company: Evening Post Industries
Street Address: 326 Rutland Dr NW
City: Aiken
State: SC
Postal Code: 29801-4010
Office phone: 803648-2311
Publication Website: www.aikenstandard.com
General E-mail: support@aikenstandard.com
Publisher Name: Rhonda Overbey
Publisher Email: roverbey@aikenstandard.com
Publisher Phone: (803) 644-2345
Editor Name: John Boyette
Editor Email: jboyette@aikenstandard.com
Editor Phone: (803) 644-2364
Advertising Executive Name: Lisa Glass
Advertising Executive Email: lglass@aikenstandard.com
Advertising Executive Phone: (803) 644-2358

CHARLESTON

MOULTRIE NEWS
Corporate/Parent Company: Evening Post Industries
Street Address: 134 Columbus St

City: Charleston
State: SC
Postal Code: 29403-4809
Office phone: (843) 958-7480
Publication Website: www.moultrienews.com
General E-mail: editor@moultrienews.com
Publisher Name: Vickey Boyd
Publisher Email: vboyd@moultrienews.com
Publisher Phone: (843) 958-7480
Editor Name: Cecilia Brown
Editor Email: editor@moultrienews.com
Editor Phone: (843) 958-7482
Year Established: 1964
Delivery Methods: Mail`Carrier`Racks

GEORGETOWN

SOUTH STRAND NEWS
Corporate/Parent Company: Evening Post Industries
Street Address: 615 Front St
City: Georgetown
State: SC
Postal Code: 29440-3623
Office phone: (843) 546-4148
Publication Website: www.southstrandnews.com
General E-mail: digital@southstrandnews.com
Publisher Name: Susan Kelly-Gilbert
Publisher Email: skelly-gilbert@journalscene.com
Publisher Phone: 843.873.9424 (Ext 211)
Editor Name: Peter Banko
Editor Email: pbanko@southstrandnews.com
Editor Phone: 843.546.4148 (Ext. 243)
Advertising Executive Name: Kevin Hardy
Advertising Executive Email: khardy@southstrandnews.com
Advertising Executive Phone: 843.546.4148 (Ext 237)
Year Established: 1798
Delivery Methods: Mail`Racks

THE GEORGETOWN TIMES
Corporate/Parent Company: Evening Post Industries
Street Address: 615 Front St
City: Georgetown
State: SC
Postal Code: 29440-3623
Office phone: (843) 546-4148
Publication Website: www.southstrandnews.com
General E-mail: digital@southstrandnews.com
Publisher Name: Susan Kelly-Gilbert
Publisher Email: skelly-gilbert@journalscene.com
Publisher Phone: 843.873.9424 (Ext 211)
Editor Name: Peter Banko
Editor Email: pbanko@southstrandnews.com
Editor Phone: 843.546.4148 (Ext. 243)
Advertising Executive Name: Kevin Hardy
Advertising Executive Email: khardy@southstrandnews.com
Advertising Executive Phone: 843.546.4148 (Ext 237)
Year Established: 1798
Delivery Methods: Mail`Racks
Own Printing Facility?: Y
Commercial printers?: Y

KINGSTREE

THE NEWS
Corporate/Parent Company: Paxton Media Group
Street Address: 511 N Longstreet St
City: Kingstree
State: SC
Postal Code: 29556-3301
Office phone: (843) 355-6397
Publication Website: www.kingstreenews.com
General E-mail: news@kingstreenews.com
Publisher Name: Tami Rodgers
Publisher Email: trodgers@kingstreenews.com
Editor Name: Michaele Duke

Editor Email: news@kingstreenews.com
Advertising Executive Name: Casey McElveen
Advertising Executive Email: advertising@kingstreenews.com
Delivery Methods: Mail`Newsstand
Own Printing Facility?: Y

NORTH AUGUSTA

THE STAR
Corporate/Parent Company: Gannett
Street Address: 406 West Avenue
City: North Augusta
State: SC
Postal Code: 29841
Office phone: (803) 279-2793
Publication Website: www.northaugustastar.com
General E-mail: support@aikenstandard.com
Editor Name: Holly Kemp
Editor Email: editor@northaugustastar.com
Advertising Executive Name: Lindsey McCullough
Advertising Executive Email: lmccullough@aikenstandard.com
Advertising Executive Phone: (803) 644-2373
Year Established: 1954
Delivery Methods: Mail`Newsstand
Commercial printers?: Y

SUMMERVILLE

BERKELEY INDEPENDENT
Corporate/Parent Company: Evening Post Industries
Street Address: 104 E Doty Ave
City: Summerville
State: SC
Postal Code: 29483-6300
Office phone: (843) 761-6397
Publication Website: www.berkeleyind.com
General E-mail: online@berkeleyind.com
Editor Name: David Kennard
Editor Email: dkennard@journalscene.com
Advertising Executive Name: Ann Mack
Advertising Executive Email: amack@berkeleyind.com
Year Established: 1987
Delivery Methods: Mail`Racks
Commercial printers?: Y

THE GAZETTE
Corporate/Parent Company: Adams Publishing Group
Street Address: 104 E Doty Ave
City: Summerville
State: SC
Postal Code: 29483-6300
Office phone: (843) 873-9424
Publication Website: www.ourgazette.com
General E-mail: online@ourgazette.com
Editor Name: David Kennard
Editor Email: dkennard@journalscene.com
Advertising Executive Name: Ann Mack
Advertising Executive Email: amack@berkeleyind.com
Delivery Methods: Mail`Racks
Own Printing Facility?: Y

SOUTH DAKOTA

ALCESTER

ALCESTER UNION
Street Address: PO Box 227, Alcester, SD 57001-0227
City: Alcester
State: SD
Office phone: 605-934-2640
General E-mail: parapub@alliancecom.net
Publisher Name: Shane & Allyson Hill

Non-Daily Newspapers in the U.S.

III-127

ALEXANDRIA
ALEXANDRIA HERALD
Corporate/Parent Company: Anderson Publications
Street Address: PO Box 456, Alexandria, SD 57311-456
City: Alexandria
State: SD
Office phone: 605-239-4521
Publication Website: http://andersonpublications.com/
General E-mail: ementerprise@triotel.net
Publisher Name: Matt Anderson
Delivery Methods: Mail`Newsstand
Own Printing Facility?: Y
Commercial printers?: Y
Mechanical specifications: Type page 9 3/4 x 16; E - 5 cols, 1 13/16, 3/16 between.
Published Days: Thur
Avg Paid Circ: 430
Avg Free Circ: 15
Audit Company: Sworn/Estimate/Non-Audited
Audit Date: 6 10 2019

ARLINGTON
ARLINGTON SUN
Corporate/Parent Company: RFD News Group
Street Address: PO Box 370, Arlington, SD 57212-0370
City: Arlington
State: SD
Office phone: 605-983-5491
Publication Website: www.rfdnewsgroup.com
General E-mail: thearlingtonsun@gmail.com
Publisher Name: Ken Reiste
Editor Name: Frank Crisler
Year Established: 1885
Delivery Methods: Mail`Newsstand`Racks
Own Printing Facility?: Y
Commercial printers?: Y
Published Days: Thur
Avg Paid Circ: 900
Audit Company: Sworn/Estimate/Non-Audited
Audit Date: 6 10 2019

ARMOUR
ARMOUR CHRONICLE
Corporate/Parent Company: Douglas County Publishing
Street Address: PO Box 129, Armour, SD 57313-0129
City: Armour
State: SD
Office phone: 605-724-2747
General E-mail: chronicle@unitelsd.com
Publisher Name: Gerri Olson
Delivery Methods: Mail`Racks
Published Days: Tues
Avg Paid Circ: 913
Avg Free Circ: 10
Audit Company: Sworn/Estimate/Non-Audited
Audit Date: 6 10 2019

AVON
AVON CLARION
Street Address: PO Box 345, Avon, SD 57315-0345
City: Avon
State: SD
Office phone: 605-286-3919
General E-mail: theavonclarion@yahoo.com
Publisher Name: Slater Brodeen
Delivery Methods: Mail`Racks
Own Printing Facility?: Y
Commercial printers?: Y
Published Days: Wed
Avg Paid Circ: 800
Audit Company: Sworn/Estimate/Non-Audited
Audit Date: 6 10 2019

BERESFORD
BERESFORD REPUBLIC
Corporate/Parent Company: Star Publishing Co.
Street Address: 103 Main Street, Beresford, SD 57004
City: Beresford
State: SD
Office phone: 605-763-2006
General E-mail: republic@bmtc.net
Publisher Name: Shane & Allyson Hill
Year Established: 1894
Delivery Methods: Mail`Newsstand`Racks
Published Days: Thur
Avg Paid Circ: 1200
Audit Company: Sworn/Estimate/Non-Audited
Audit Date: 6 10 2019

BISON
BISON COURIER
Corporate/Parent Company: Ravellette Publications
Street Address: PO Box 429, Bison, SD 57620-0429
City: Bison
State: SD
Office phone: 605-244-7199
Publication Website: www.ravellettepublications.com
General E-mail: courier@sdplains.com
Publisher Name: Beau Ravellette
Editor Name: Arlis Seim
Delivery Methods: Mail`Racks
Mechanical specifications: Type page 12 x 16; A - 2 cols, between.
Published Days: Thur
Avg Paid Circ: 750
Avg Free Circ: 25
Audit Company: Sworn/Estimate/Non-Audited
Audit Date: 6 10 2019

BONESTEEL
BONESTEEL ENTERPRISE
Street Address: PO Box 200, Bonesteel, SD 57317
City: Bonesteel
State: SD
Office phone: 605-654-2678
Publication Website: www.thebonesteelenterprise.com
General E-mail: info@bonesteelenterprise.com
Publisher Name: Kelly Wollman

BOWDLE
PRIDE OF THE PRAIRIE
Corporate/Parent Company: Pride Publications
Street Address: PO Box 514, Bowdle, SD 57428
City: Bowdle
State: SD
Office phone: 605-285-6161
General E-mail: prideoffice@gmail.com
Publisher Name: Tara Beitelspacher

BRANDON
BRANDON VALLEY CHALLENGER
Street Address: PO Box 257, Brandon, SD 57005
City: Brandon
State: SD
Office phone: 605-582-6025
Publication Website: www.argusleader.com/news/brandon.com
General E-mail: editor@brandoninfo.com
Delivery Methods: Mail`Racks
Published Days: Wed
Avg Paid Circ: 1200
Avg Free Circ: 5700
Audit Company: Sworn/Estimate/Non-Audited
Audit Date: 6 10 2019

BRANDON VALLEY JOURNAL
Street Address: PO Box 842, Brandon, SD 57005
City: Brandon
State: SD
Office phone: 605-582-9999
Publication Website: http://brandonvalleyjournal.com
General E-mail: bvjournal@bvjournal.com
Publisher Name: Jill Meier
Publisher Email: editor@brandoninfo.com

BRIDGEWATER
BRIDGEWATER TRIBUNE
Street Address: PO Box 220, Salem, SD 57058
City: Bridgewater
State: SD
Office phone: 605-425-2361
Publication Website: www.salemspecial.com
General E-mail: tschwans@triotel.net
Publisher Name: Troy Schwans
Delivery Methods: Mail
Published Days: Thur
Avg Paid Circ: 350
Avg Free Circ: 50
Audit Company: Sworn/Estimate/Non-Audited
Audit Date: 6 10 2019

BRITTON
BRITTON JOURNAL
Street Address: PO Box 69, Britton, SD 57430-0069
City: Britton
State: SD
Office phone: 605-448-2281
Publication Website: www.marshallcountyjournal.com
General E-mail: journal@brittonsd.com
Publisher Name: Douglas Card
Advertising Executive Name: Ann Stiegelmeier
Delivery Methods: Mail`Racks
Published Days: Wed
Avg Paid Circ: 1779
Avg Free Circ: 50
Audit Company: Sworn/Estimate/Non-Audited
Audit Date: 6 10 2019

BRYANT
BRYANT DAKOTAN
Street Address: PO Box 127, Bryant, SD 57221
City: Bryant
State: SD
Office phone: 605-628-6397
General E-mail: BryantDakotan@itctel.com
Publisher Name: Stephanie Sauder
Year Established: 1979
Delivery Methods: Mail
Mechanical specifications: Type page 9 3/4 x 13 3/4.
Published Days: Wed
Avg Paid Circ: 504
Avg Free Circ: 30
Audit Company: Sworn/Estimate/Non-Audited
Audit Date: 6 10 2019

BUFFALO
NATION'S CENTER NEWS
Corporate/Parent Company: Seaton Publishing
Street Address: PO Box 107, Buffalo, SD 57720-0107
City: Buffalo
State: SD
Office phone: 605-375-3228
General E-mail: ncn@sdplains.com
Publisher Name: Letitia Lister
Publisher Email: letti@bhpioneer.com
Editor Name: Mark Watson
Editor Email: mark@bhpioneer.com
Advertising Executive Name: Sona O'Connell
Advertising Executive Email: sona@bhpioneer.com
Year Established: 1978
Delivery Methods: Mail`Racks
Published Days: Wed
Avg Paid Circ: 1200
Audit Company: Sworn/Estimate/Non-Audited
Audit Date: 6 10 2019

BURKE
BURKE GAZETTE
Street Address: PO Box 359, Burke, SD 57523-0359
City: Burke
State: SD
Office phone: 605-775-2612
General E-mail: burkegaz@gwtc.net
Publisher Name: C.J. Fahrenbacher
Year Established: 1904
Delivery Methods: Mail`Newsstand
Mechanical specifications: Type page 10 1/2 x 13; E - 5 cols, 2 , 1/8 between; A - 5 cols, 2 , 1/8 between; C - 5 cols, 2 , 1/8 between.
Published Days: Wed
Avg Paid Circ: 1250
Audit Company: Sworn/Estimate/Non-Audited
Audit Date: 6 10 2019

CANISTOTA
CANISTOTA CLIPPER
Corporate/Parent Company: Anderson Publications
Street Address: PO Box 128, Canistota, SD 57012-0128
City: Canistota
State: SD
Office phone: 605-296-3181
Publication Website: http://andersonpublications.com/
General E-mail: news@andersonpublications.com
Publisher Name: Matt Anderson
Delivery Methods: Mail`Racks
Published Days: Thur
Avg Paid Circ: 625
Audit Company: Sworn/Estimate/Non-Audited
Audit Date: 6 10 2019

CANTON
SIOUX VALLEY NEWS
Street Address: PO Box 255, Canton SD 57013-0255
City: Canton
State: SD
Office phone: 605-764-2000
Publication Website: www.siouxvalleynewsonline.com
General E-mail: svn@siouxvalleynewsonline.com
Publisher Name: Teresa Wilox
Year Established: 1872
Delivery Methods: Mail`Newsstand`Racks
Own Printing Facility?: Y
Commercial printers?: Y
Published Days: Thur
Avg Paid Circ: 1680
Audit Company: Sworn/Estimate/Non-Audited
Audit Date: 6 10 2019

CASTLEWOOD
HAMLIN COUNTY REPUBLICAN
Corporate/Parent Company: Hamlin County Publishing
Street Address: PO Box 50, Castlewood, SD 57223-0050
City: Castlewood
State: SD
Office phone: 605-793-2293
Publication Website: www.hamlincountypublishing.com
General E-mail: hcp@itctel.com
Publisher Name: LeeAnne Dufek

Delivery Methods: Mail
Commercial printers?: Y
Published Days: Wed
Avg Paid Circ: 800
Audit Company: Sworn/Estimate/Non-Audited
Audit Date: 6 10 2019

CENTERVILLE

CENTERVILLE JOURNAL

Corporate/Parent Company: Star Publishing Co.
Street Address: PO Box H, Centerville, SD 57014
City: Centerville
State: SD
Office phone: 605-563-2351
General E-mail: journal@iw.net
Publisher Name: Shane & Allyson Hill
Delivery Methods: Mail
Mechanical specifications: Type page 10 x 15; E - 5 cols, 1 5/6, 1/6 between; A - 5 cols, 1 5/6, 1/6 between; C - 5 cols, 1 5/6, 1/6 between.
Published Days: Thur
Avg Paid Circ: 810
Audit Company: Sworn/Estimate/Non-Audited
Audit Date: 6 10 2019

CHAMBERLAIN

CENTRAL DAKOTA TIMES

Street Address: PO Box 125, Chamberlain, SD 57325-0125
City: Chamberlain
State: SD
Office phone: 605-234-0266
Publication Website: www.centraldakotatimes.org
General E-mail: cdt@midstatesd.net
Publisher Name: Debi Ruiz

CHAMBERLAIN/OACOMA SUN

Street Address: 116 S. Main Street, Chamberlain, SD 57325
City: Chamberlain
State: SD
Office phone: 605-234-1444
Publication Website: www.chamberlainsun.com
General E-mail: news@chamberlainsun.com
Publisher Name: Lucy & Kim Halverson
Editor Name: Lucy Halverson

CLARK

CLARK COUNTY COURIER

Street Address: 119 1st Avenue East, Clark, SD 57225
City: Clark
State: SD
Office phone: 605-532-3654
Publication Website: www.clarkcountypublishing.com
General E-mail: courier@itctel.com
Publisher Name: William Krikac
Year Established: 1885
Delivery Methods: Mail`Newsstand`Racks
Commercial printers?: Y
Published Days: Wed
Avg Paid Circ: 2400
Avg Free Circ: 33
Audit Company: Sworn/Estimate/Non-Audited
Audit Date: 6 10 2019

CLEAR LAKE

CLEAR LAKE COURIER

Street Address: PO Box 830, Clear Lake, SD 57226-0830
City: Clear Lake
State: SD

Office phone: 605-874-2499
General E-mail: clprint@itctel.com
Publisher Name: Ken Reiste
Delivery Methods: Mail`Newsstand
Mechanical specifications: Type page 13 x 21 1/2; E - 6 cols, 2 1/16, 1/6 between; A - 6 cols, 2 1/16, 1/6 between; C - 6 cols, 2 1/16, 1/6 between.
Published Days: Wed
Avg Paid Circ: 1500
Avg Free Circ: 25
Audit Company: Sworn/Estimate/Non-Audited
Audit Date: 6 10 2019

CONDE

CONDE NEWS

Street Address: 165 2nd St., Conde, SD 57434
City: Conde
State: SD
Office phone: 605-382-5627
General E-mail: eastarea@nvc.net
Publisher Name: Tina Sanderson

CORSICA

CORSICA GLOBE

Corporate/Parent Company: Douglas County Publishing
Street Address: PO Box 45, Corsica, SD 57328-0045
City: Corsica
State: SD
Office phone: 605-946-5489
General E-mail: globe@siouxvalley.net
Publisher Name: Gerri Olson
Delivery Methods: Mail`Racks
Published Days: Tues
Avg Paid Circ: 1093
Avg Free Circ: 51
Audit Company: Sworn/Estimate/Non-Audited
Audit Date: 6 10 2019

CUSTER

CUSTER COUNTY CHRONICLE

Corporate/Parent Company: Southern Hills Publishing
Street Address: PO Box 551, Custer, SD 57730-0551
City: Custer
State: SD
Office phone: 605-673-2217
Publication Website: www.custercountychronicle.com
General E-mail: custerchronicle@gwtc.net
Publisher Name: Charley Najacht
Year Established: 1880
Delivery Methods: Mail`Newsstand
Mechanical specifications: Type page 10 x 21; E - 6 cols, 1.5, 1/6 between; A - 6 cols, 1.5, 1/6 between; C - 6 cols, 1.5, 1/6 between.
Published Days: Wed
Avg Paid Circ: 1800
Audit Company: Sworn/Estimate/Non-Audited
Audit Date: 6 10 2019

DE SMET

KINGSBURY JOURNAL

Street Address: 220 Calumet Ave, De Smet, SD 57231
City: De Smet
State: SD
Office phone: 605-854-3331
Publication Website: www.kingsburyjournal.com
General E-mail: tim@kingsburynews.com
Publisher Name: Tim Aughenbaugh
Publisher Email: tim@kingsburynews.com
Advertising Executive Name: Snookie Stoddard
Advertising Executive Email: snookie@kingsburynews.com

DELL RAPIDS

DELL RAPIDS TRIBUNE

Street Address: PO Box 99, Dell Rapids, SD 57022-0099
City: Dell Rapids
State: SD
Office phone: 605-428-5992
Publication Website: www.argusleader.com/news/dellrapids.com
General E-mail: editor@dellrapidsinfo.com
Delivery Methods: Mail`Newsstand`Racks
Published Days: Wed
Avg Paid Circ: 1300
Avg Free Circ: 34
Audit Company: Sworn/Estimate/Non-Audited
Audit Date: 6 10 2019

DELLS CITY JOURNAL

Corporate/Parent Company: New Century Press
Street Address: 501 1/2 E. 4th St., Suite 1, Dell Rapids, SD 57022
City: Dell Rapids
State: SD
Office phone: 605-428-5600
Publication Website: www.ncppub.com
General E-mail: news@dellscityjournal.com
Publisher Name: Lisa Miller

DELMONT

DELMONT RECORD

Corporate/Parent Company: Douglas County Publishing
Street Address: PO Box 129, Armour, SD 57313-0129
City: Delmont
State: SD
Office phone: 605-724-2747
General E-mail: chronicle@unitelsd.com
Publisher Name: Gerri Olson
Delivery Methods: Mail`Racks
Published Days: Tues
Avg Paid Circ: 220
Avg Free Circ: 10
Audit Company: Sworn/Estimate/Non-Audited
Audit Date: 6 10 2019

DOLAND

DOLAND TIMES-RECORD

Street Address: PO Box 102, Conde, SD 57434
City: Doland
State: SD
Office phone: 605-382-5627
General E-mail: eastarea@nvc.net
Publisher Name: Tina Sanderson

EAGLE BUTTE

WEST RIVER EAGLE

Corporate/Parent Company: Bridge City Publishing, Inc.
Street Address: PO Box 210, Eagle Butte, SD 57625-0210
City: Eagle Butte
State: SD
Office phone: 605-964-2100
Publication Website: www.westrivereagle.com
General E-mail: wreagle@westrivereagle.com
Publisher Name: Kelsey Majeske
Publisher Email: kelsey@mobridgetribune.com
Editor Name: Alaina Beautiful Bald Eagle
Editor Email: alaina@westrivereagle.com
Year Established: 1910
Delivery Methods: Mail`Newsstand`Racks
Mechanical specifications: Type page 11 x 16; E - 5 cols, 2 1/12, 5/36 between; A - 5 cols, 2 1/12, 5/36 between; C - 5 cols, 2 1/12, 5/36 between.
Published Days: Thur

Avg Paid Circ: 2100
Audit Company: Sworn/Estimate/Non-Audited
Audit Date: 6 10 2019

ELK POINT

SOUTHERN UNION COUNTY LEADER-COURIER

Street Address: PO Box 310, Elk Point, SD 57025-0310
City: Elk Point
State: SD
Office phone: 605-356-2632
Publication Website: www.leadercourier-times.com
General E-mail: leader1@iw.net
Publisher Name: Bruce Odson
Editor Name: Susan Odson
Delivery Methods: Mail
Published Days: Thur
Avg Paid Circ: 1150
Avg Free Circ: 19
Audit Company: Sworn/Estimate/Non-Audited
Audit Date: 6 10 2019

ELKTON

ELKTON RECORD

Corporate/Parent Company: RFD News Group
Street Address: PO Box K, Elkton, SD 57026
City: Elkton
State: SD
Office phone: 605-542-4831
Publication Website: www.rfdnewsgroup.com
General E-mail: ern@itctel.com
Publisher Name: Ken Reiste
Editor Name: Jessica J. Jensen
Year Established: 1884
Delivery Methods: Mail`Newsstand`Racks
Mechanical specifications: Type page 9 3/4 x 15; E - 5 cols, 1/6 between; A - 5 cols, 1/6 between; C - 5 cols, 1/6 between.
Published Days: Thur
Avg Paid Circ: 600
Avg Free Circ: 57
Audit Company: Sworn/Estimate/Non-Audited
Audit Date: 6 10 2019

EMERY

EMERY ENTERPRISE

Corporate/Parent Company: Anderson Publications
Street Address: PO Box 244, Emery, SD 57332-0244
City: Emery
State: SD
Office phone: 605-449-4420
Publication Website: http://andersonpublications.com/
General E-mail: ementerprise@triotel.net
Publisher Name: Matt Anderson

ESTELLINE

ESTELLINE JOURNAL

Corporate/Parent Company: Hamlin County Publishing
Street Address: PO Box 159, Estelline, SD 57234-0159
City: Estelline
State: SD
Office phone: 605-873-2475
Publication Website: www.hamlincountypublishing.com
General E-mail: hcp@itctel.com
Publisher Name: LeeAnne Dufek
Delivery Methods: Mail`Racks
Commercial printers?: Y
Published Days: Wed
Avg Paid Circ: 650
Audit Company: Sworn/Estimate/Non-Audited
Audit Date: 6 10 2019

Non-Daily Newspapers in the U.S.

EUREKA

NORTHWEST BLADE
Corporate/Parent Company: Pride Publications
Street Address: PO Box 797, Eureka, SD 57437-0797
City: Eureka
State: SD
Office phone: 605-284-2631
General E-mail: nwblade@valleytel.net
Publisher Name: Tara Beitelspacher
Delivery Methods: Mail`Newsstand
Own Printing Facility?: Y
Commercial printers?: Y
Mechanical specifications: Type page 13 1/2 x 21 1/2.
Published Days: Thur
Avg Paid Circ: 1125
Avg Free Circ: 25
Audit Company: Sworn/Estimate/Non-Audited
Audit Date: 6 10 2019

FAITH

FAITH INDEPENDENT
Corporate/Parent Company: Ravellette Publications
Street Address: PO Box 38, Faith, SD 57626-0038
City: Faith
State: SD
Office phone: 605-967-2161
Publication Website: www.ravellettepublications.com
General E-mail: faithind@faithsd.com
Publisher Name: Beau Ravellette
Editor Name: Krissy Johnson
Delivery Methods: Mail`Racks
Commercial printers?: Y
Published Days: Wed
Avg Paid Circ: 1000
Audit Company: Sworn/Estimate/Non-Audited
Audit Date: 6 10 2019

FAULKTON

FAULK COUNTY RECORD
Street Address: PO Box 68, Faulkton, SD 57438-0068
City: Faulkton
State: SD
Office phone: 605-598-6525
Publication Website: www.faulkcountyrecord.com
General E-mail: info@faulkcountyrecord.com
Publisher Name: Val & Dan Ramsdell
Editor Name: Val Ramsdell
Year Established: 1882
Delivery Methods: Mail`Newsstand
Mechanical specifications: 5 columns, tab, page size 10.5" x 13.75"
Published Days: Wed
Avg Paid Circ: 1420
Avg Free Circ: 8
Audit Company: Sworn/Estimate/Non-Audited
Audit Date: 6 10 2019

FLANDREAU

MOODY COUNTY ENTERPRISE
Corporate/Parent Company: News Media Grouip
Street Address: PO Box 71, Flandreau, SD 57028-0071
City: Flandreau
State: SD
Office phone: 605-997-3725
Publication Website: www.moodycountyenterprise.com
General E-mail: mce6@mcisweb.com
Publisher Name: William McMacken
Publisher Email: bmcmacken@brookingsregister.com
Editor Name: M.L. Headrick
Year Established: 1878
Delivery Methods: Mail`Newsstand`Racks
Commercial printers?: Y
Mechanical specifications: Type page 13 x 21; E - 6 cols, between.
Published Days: Wed
Avg Paid Circ: 3300
Avg Free Circ: 1200
Audit Company: Sworn/Estimate/Non-Audited
Audit Date: 6 10 2019

FREEMAN

FREEMAN COURIER
Corporate/Parent Company: Second Century Publishing Inc.
Street Address: PO Box 950, Freeman, SD 57029-0950
City: Freeman
State: SD
Office phone: 605-925-7033
Publication Website: www.freemansd.com
General E-mail: courier@gwtc.net
Publisher Name: Jeremy Waltner
Advertising Executive Name: Jason Scharberg
Year Established: 1901
Delivery Methods: Mail`Newsstand
Own Printing Facility?: Y
Commercial printers?: N
Published Days: Thur
Avg Paid Circ: 1500
Audit Company: Sworn/Estimate/Non-Audited
Audit Date: 6 10 2019

GARRETSON

GARRETSON GAZETTE
Street Address: PO Box 327, Garretson, SD 57030
City: Garretson
State: SD
Office phone: 605-594-2006
Publication Website: https://www.garretsongazette.com/
General E-mail: info@garretsongazette.com
Publisher Name: Garrick & Carrie Moritz
Editor Name: Garrick Moritz

GEDDES

CHARLES MIX COUNTY NEWS
Street Address: PO Box 257, Geddes, SD 57342-0257
City: Geddes
State: SD
Office phone: 605-337-2571
General E-mail: cmcountynews@midstatesd.net
Publisher Name: Rhonda & Wayne Blair
Delivery Methods: Mail`Racks
Published Days: Thur
Avg Paid Circ: 685
Avg Free Circ: 1
Audit Company: Sworn/Estimate/Non-Audited
Audit Date: 6 10 2019

GETTYSBURG

POTTER COUNTRY NEWS
Street Address: 110 S Exene St., Gettysburg, SD 57442
City: Gettysburg
State: SD
Office phone: 605-765-2464
Publication Website: www.pottercountynews.com
General E-mail: pcnews@pottercountynews.com
Publisher Name: Kelsey Majeske
Publisher Email: kelsey@mobridgetribune.com
Editor Name: Molly McRoberts
Editor Email: molly@pottercountynews.com

GREGORY

GREGORY TIMES-ADVOCATE
Street Address: PO Box 378, Gregory, SD 57533-0378
City: Gregory
State: SD
Office phone: 605-835-8089
Publication Website: www.gregorynews.com
General E-mail: gregorynews@gregorynews.com
Publisher Name: Cheryl Sperl
Year Established: 1904
Delivery Methods: Mail`Newsstand`Racks
Commercial printers?: Y
Published Days: Wed
Avg Paid Circ: 2000
Audit Company: Sworn/Estimate/Non-Audited
Audit Date: 6 10 2019

GROTON

GROTON INDEPENDENT
Corporate/Parent Company: Next Generation Publications, Inc.; Finger Lakes Community Newspapers
Street Address: PO Box 34, Groton, SD 57445
City: Groton
State: SD
Office phone: 605-397-6397
Publication Website: www.397news.com
General E-mail: paperpaul@grotonsd.net
Publisher Name: Paul Kosel
Publisher Email: paperpaul@grotonsd.net
Year Established: 1883
Delivery Methods: Mail`Newsstand
Mechanical specifications: Type page 13 1/4 x 21 1/2; E - 6 cols, 2 1/16, 1/8 between; A - 6 cols, 2 1/16, 1/8 between; C - 6 cols, 2 1/16, 1/8 between.
Published Days: Wed
Avg Paid Circ: 400
Audit Company: Sworn/Estimate/Non-Audited
Audit Date: 6 10 2019

HARTFORD

MINNEHAHA MESSENGER
Corporate/Parent Company: New Century Press
Street Address: PO Box 474, Hartford, SD 57033
City: Hartford
State: SD
Office phone: 605-296-3181
Publication Website: www.ncppub.com
General E-mail: news@andersonpublications.com
Publisher Name: Lisa Miller
Editor Name: Melissa Voss
Editor Email: mvoss@ncppub.com

HAYTI

HAMLIN COUNTY HERALD ENTERPRISE
Corporate/Parent Company: Hamlin County Publishing
Street Address: PO Box 207, Hayti, SD 57241-0207
City: Hayti
State: SD
Office phone: 605-783-3636
Publication Website: www.hamlincountypublishing.com
General E-mail: hcp@itctel.com
Publisher Name: LeeAnne Dufek

HIGHMORE

HIGHMORE HERALD
Street Address: PO Box 435, Highmore, SD 57345-0435
City: Highmore
State: SD
Office phone: 605-852-2927
General E-mail: hiherald@venturecomm.net
Publisher Name: Mary Ann Morford
Year Established: 1882
Delivery Methods: Mail`Racks
Published Days: Thur
Avg Paid Circ: 1450
Audit Company: Sworn/Estimate/Non-Audited
Audit Date: 6 10 2019

HILL CITY

HILL CITY PREVAILER NEWS
Corporate/Parent Company: Southern Hills Publishing
Street Address: PO Box 266, Hill City, SD 57745-0266
City: Hill City
State: SD
Office phone: 605-574-2538
Publication Website: www.hillcityprevailernews.com
General E-mail: prevailer@hillcityprevailernews.com
Publisher Name: Charley Najacht
Editor Name: Gray Hughes

HOT SPRINGS

FALL RIVER COUNTY HERALD-STAR
Corporate/Parent Company: Scherer Publishing, LLC
Street Address: 334 South Chicago, Hot Springs, SD 57747
City: Hot Springs
State: SD
Office phone: 605-745-3930
Publication Website: www.fallrivercountyherald.com
General E-mail: ads.frcherald@gmail.com
Publisher Name: Mandy Scherer
Editor Name: Brett Nachtigall
Editor Email: brett.nachtigall@gmail.com

HOVEN

HOVEN REVIEW
Street Address: PO Box 37, Hoven, SD 57450
City: Hoven
State: SD
Office phone: 605-948-2110
General E-mail: hoven@venturecomm.net
Publisher Name: Sara Johnson
Delivery Methods: Mail
Published Days: Thur
Avg Paid Circ: 650
Avg Free Circ: 9
Audit Company: Sworn/Estimate/Non-Audited
Audit Date: 6 10 2019

HOWARD

MINER COUNTY PIONEER
Street Address: PO Box 220, Howard, SD 57349-0220
City: Howard
State: SD
Office phone: 605-772-5644
General E-mail: news@minercountypioneer.com
Publisher Name: Carla Poulson
Advertising Executive Name: Heather Poulson
Delivery Methods: Mail`Racks
Published Days: Thur
Avg Paid Circ: 1902
Avg Free Circ: 65
Audit Company: Sworn/Estimate/Non-Audited
Audit Date: 6 10 2019

IPSWICH

IPSWICH TRIBUNE
Street Address: PO Box 7, Ipswich, SD 57451-0007
City: Ipswich
State: SD
Office phone: 605-426-6471
General E-mail: iptribune@valleytel.net
Publisher Name: Tena Gibson
Delivery Methods: Mail`Racks
Own Printing Facility?: Y

Commercial printers?: Y
Mechanical specifications: Type page 9 3/4 x 13; E - 5 cols, 1 3/4, 1 pica between; A - 5 cols, 1 3/4, 1 pica between; C - 5 cols, 1 3/4, 1 pica between.
Published Days: Wed
Avg Paid Circ: 941
Avg Free Circ: 3
Audit Company: Sworn/Estimate/Non-Audited
Audit Date: 6 10 2019

IRENE

IRENE TRI-COUNTY NEWS

Street Address: PO Box 6, Irene, SD 57037
City: Irene
State: SD
Office phone: 605-263-3339
General E-mail: thenews@iw.net
Publisher Name: Shane & Allyson Hill

KADOKA

KADOKA PRESS

Corporate/Parent Company: Ravellette Publications
Street Address: PO Box 309, Kadoka, SD 57543-0309
City: Kadoka
State: SD
Office phone: 605-837-2259
Publication Website: www.ravellettepublications.com
General E-mail: press@kadokatelco.com
Publisher Name: Beau Ravellette
Editor Name: Robyn Jones
Delivery Methods: Mail`Racks
Published Days: Thur
Avg Paid Circ: 1100
Audit Company: Sworn/Estimate/Non-Audited
Audit Date: 6 10 2019

LAKE ANDES

LAKE ANDES WAVE

Corporate/Parent Company: Star Publishing Co.
Street Address: 209 S. Main, Wagner, SD 57380
City: Lake Andes
State: SD
Office phone: 605-384-5616
Publication Website: www.postandwave.com
General E-mail: announcer@hcinet.net
Publisher Name: Barbra Pechous
Delivery Methods: Mail
Published Days: Wed
Avg Paid Circ: 440
Audit Company: Sworn/Estimate/Non-Audited
Audit Date: 6 10 2019

LANGFORD

LANGFORD BUGLE

Street Address: PO Box 69, Britton, SD 57430-0069
City: Langford
State: SD
Office phone: 605-448-2281
Publication Website: www.marshallcountyjournal.com
General E-mail: journal@brittonsd.com
Publisher Name: Douglas Card
Advertising Executive Name: Ann Stiegelmeier
Delivery Methods: Mail`Racks
Published Days: Wed
Avg Paid Circ: 485
Audit Company: Sworn/Estimate/Non-Audited
Audit Date: 6 10 2019

LEMMON

DAKOTA HERALD

Street Address: PO Box 207, Lemmon, SD 57638
City: Lemmon
State: SD
Office phone: 605-374-9628
Publication Website: www.dakotaherald.net
General E-mail: dakotaherald@sdplains.com
Publisher Name: LaQuita Shockley

LENNOX

LENNOX INDEPENDENT

Corporate/Parent Company: Independent Publishing Co.
Street Address: PO Box 76, Lennox, SD 57039-0076
City: Lennox
State: SD
Office phone: 605-647-2284
Publication Website: www.lennoxnews.com
General E-mail: editor@lennoxnews.com
Publisher Name: Debbie Schmidt & Kelli Bultena
Editor Name: Kelli Bultena
Advertising Executive Name: Kelli Bultena
Year Established: 1885
Delivery Methods: Mail`Newsstand
Own Printing Facility?: Y
Commercial printers?: N
Mechanical specifications: Type page 12 1/2 x 22 1/2; E - 6 cols, 1, between.
Published Days: Thur
Avg Paid Circ: 1500
Avg Free Circ: 35
Audit Company: Sworn/Estimate/Non-Audited
Audit Date: 6 10 2019

LEOLA

MCPHERSON COUNTY HERALD

Street Address: PO Box 170, Leola, SD 57456
City: Leola
State: SD
Office phone: 605-439-3131
General E-mail: herald@valleytel.net
Publisher Name: Jeremy Cox
Year Established: 1890
Delivery Methods: Mail
Published Days: Wed
Avg Paid Circ: 375
Audit Company: Sworn/Estimate/Non-Audited
Audit Date: 6 10 2019

MARION

MARION RECORD

Corporate/Parent Company: New Century Press
Street Address: PO Box 298, Marion, SD 57043-0298
City: Marion
State: SD
Office phone: 605-648-3821
Publication Website: www.ncppub.com
General E-mail: mrecord@gwtc.net
Publisher Name: Lisa Miller
Delivery Methods: Mail
Mechanical specifications: Type page 13 1/8 x 21; E - 6 cols, 2 1/16, 1/8 between; A - 6 cols, 2 1/16, 1/8 between; C - 6 cols, 2 1/16, 1/8 between.
Published Days: Thur
Avg Paid Circ: 500
Audit Company: Sworn/Estimate/Non-Audited
Audit Date: 6 10 2019

MARTIN

BENNETT COUNTY BOOSTER II

Corporate/Parent Company: Scherer Publishing, LLC
Street Address: PO Box 610, Martin, SD 57551-0610
City: Martin
State: SD
Office phone: 605-685-6866
Publication Website: www.bennettcountyboostersd.com
General E-mail: booster@gwtc.net
Publisher Name: Mandy Scherer
Editor Name: Mandy Scherer
Delivery Methods: Mail`Newsstand`Racks
Own Printing Facility?: Y
Commercial printers?: Y
Published Days: Wed
Avg Paid Circ: 2250
Audit Company: Sworn/Estimate/Non-Audited
Audit Date: 6 10 2019

LAKOTA TIMES

Street Address: PO Box 386, Martin SD 57551
City: Martin
State: SD
Office phone: 605-685-1868
Publication Website: www.lakotacountrytimes.com
General E-mail: connie@lakotacountrytimes.com
Publisher Name: Connie Smith
Editor Name: Vi Waln
Advertising Executive Name: Jenni Giovannetti

MCLAUGHLIN

CORSON/SIOUX COUNTY NEWS-MESSENGER

Street Address: PO Box 788, McLaughlin, SD 57642-0788
City: McLaughlin
State: SD
Office phone: 605-823-4490
General E-mail: macnews@westriv.com
Publisher Name: Zach Buechler

MILBANK

GRANT COUNTY REVIEW

Street Address: PO Box 390, Milbank, SD 57252-0390
City: Milbank
State: SD
Office phone: 605-432-4516
Publication Website: www.grantcountyreview.com
General E-mail: gcreview@itcmilbank.com
Publisher Name: Debbie Hemmer & Holli Seehafer
Editor Name: Debbie Hemmer
Advertising Executive Name: Holli Seehafer
Year Established: 1880
Delivery Methods: Mail
Mechanical specifications: Type page 13 5/6 x 21 1/2; E - 6 cols, 2 1/6, 1/6 between; A - 6 cols, 1/6 between; C - 6 cols, 1/6 between.
Published Days: Wed
Avg Paid Circ: 3600
Avg Free Circ: 68
Audit Company: Sworn/Estimate/Non-Audited
Audit Date: 6 10 2019

MILLER

MILLER PRESS

Street Address: 114 E. 3rd St., Miller, SD 57263
City: Miller
State: SD
Office phone: 605-853-3575
Publication Website: www.themillerpress.com
General E-mail: advertising@themillerpress.com
Publisher Name: Mike Caviness
Publisher Email: publisher@themillerpress.com
Editor Name: Janet Kittelson
Editor Email: jank@midconetwork.com
Advertising Executive Name: Kim Sporrer
Advertising Executive Email: advertising@themillerpress.com
Year Established: 1882
Delivery Methods: Mail`Newsstand
Mechanical specifications: Type page 13 x 21 1/2; E - 6 cols, 2 1/16, 1/6 between; A - 6 cols, 2 1/16, 1/6 between; C - 8 cols, 1 1/2, 1/8 between.
Published Days: Wed
Avg Paid Circ: 2050
Audit Company: Sworn/Estimate/Non-Audited
Audit Date: 6 10 2019

MISSION

TODD COUNTY TRIBUNE

Corporate/Parent Company: Scherer Publishing, LLC
Street Address: PO Box 229, Mission, SD 57555-0229
City: Mission
State: SD
Office phone: 605-856-4469
Publication Website: www.trib-news.com
General E-mail: tribnews@gwtc.net
Publisher Name: Mandy Scherer
Editor Name: Kevin Throw
Delivery Methods: Mail`Newsstand`Racks
Mechanical specifications: Type page 13 x 21 1/2; E - 6 cols, 2 1/16, 1/8 between; A - 6 cols, 2 1/16, 1/8 between.
Published Days: Wed
Avg Paid Circ: 2200
Audit Company: Sworn/Estimate/Non-Audited
Audit Date: 6 10 2019

MITCHELL

MITCHELL DAILY REPUBLIC

Corporate/Parent Company: Forum Communications
Street Address: PO Box 1288, Mitchell, SD 570301-1288
City: Mitchell
State: SD
Office phone: 605-996-5514
Publication Website: www.mitchellrepublic.com
General E-mail: jharms@mitchellrepublic.com
Publisher Name: Joni Harms
Publisher Email: jharms@mitchellrepublic.com
Editor Name: Luke Hagen
Editor Email: lhagen@mitchellrepublic.com
Advertising Executive Name: Lorie Hansen
Advertising Executive Email: lhansen@mitchellrepublic.com

MOBRIDGE

MOBRIDGE TRIBUNE

Corporate/Parent Company: Bridge City Publishing, Inc.
Street Address: PO Box 250, Mobridge, SD 57601-0250
City: Mobridge
State: SD
Office phone: 605-845-3646
Publication Website: www.mobridgetribune.com
General E-mail: news@mobridgetribune.com
Publisher Name: Kelsey Majeske
Publisher Email: kelsey@mobridgetribune.com
Editor Name: Katie Zerr
Editor Email: katie@mobridgetribune.com
Advertising Executive Name: Linda Meyer
Advertising Executive Email: linda@mobridgetribune.com
Year Established: 1909
Delivery Methods: Mail`Newsstand`Carrier`Racks
Own Printing Facility?: Y
Commercial printers?: Y
Mechanical specifications: Type page 10 3/4 x 16; E - 5 cols, 2 1/6, 1/8 between; A - 5 cols, 2 1/6, 1/8 between; C - 5 cols, 2 1/6, 1/8 between.
Published Days: Wed
Avg Paid Circ: 2012
Avg Free Circ: 46
Audit Company: Sworn/Estimate/Non-Audited
Audit Date: 6 10 2019

Non-Daily Newspapers in the U.S.

MONTROSE

MONTROSE HERALD
Corporate/Parent Company: Anderson Publications
Street Address: PO Box 128, Canistota, SD 57012-0128
City: Montrose
State: SD
Office phone: 605-296-3181
Publication Website: http://andersonpublications.com/
General E-mail: news@andersonpublications.com
Publisher Name: Matt Anderson
Delivery Methods: Mail`Racks
Published Days: Thur
Avg Paid Circ: 518
Audit Company: Sworn/Estimate/Non-Audited
Audit Date: 6 10 2019

MURDO

MURDO COYOTE
Corporate/Parent Company: Ravellette Publications
Street Address: PO Box 465, Murdo, SD 57559-0465
City: Murdo
State: SD
Office phone: 605-669-2271
Publication Website: www.ravellettepublications.com
General E-mail: mcoyote@gwtc.net
Publisher Name: Beau Ravellette
Editor Name: Rylee Metzger
Year Established: 1906
Delivery Methods: Mail`Racks
Own Printing Facility?: Y
Commercial printers?: Y
Mechanical specifications: Type page 13 x 21 1/2.
Published Days: Thur
Avg Paid Circ: 550
Avg Free Circ: 10
Audit Company: Sworn/Estimate/Non-Audited
Audit Date: 6 10 2019

NORTH SIOUX CITY/DAKOTA DUNES

DAKOTA DUNES NORTH SIOUX CITY TIMES
Street Address: PO Box 1340, North Sioux City, SD 57049-1340
City: North Sioux City/Dakota Dunes
State: SD
Office phone: 605-232-3539
Publication Website: www.leadercourier-times.com
General E-mail: leader2@iw.net
Publisher Name: Bruce Odson

ONIDA

ONIDA WATCHMAN
Street Address: PO Box 245, Onida, SD 57564-0245
City: Onida
State: SD
Office phone: 605-258-2604
Publication Website: www.onidawatchman.com
General E-mail: watchman@venturecomm.net
Publisher Name: Curt Olson
Editor Name: Sheila Ring
Year Established: 1883
Delivery Methods: Mail
Mechanical specifications: Type page 13 x 21 1/2.
Published Days: Thur
Avg Paid Circ: 1037
Avg Free Circ: 30
Audit Company: Sworn/Estimate/Non-Audited
Audit Date: 6 10 2019

PARKER

NEW ERA
Corporate/Parent Company: New Century Press
Street Address: PO Box 579, Parker, SD 57053-0579
City: Parker
State: SD
Office phone: 605-297-4419
Publication Website: www.ncppub.com
General E-mail: sebeling@ncppub.com
Publisher Name: Lisa Miller
Editor Name: Sarah Ebeling

PARKSTON

PARKSTON ADVANCE
Street Address: PO Box J, Parkston, SD 57366
City: Parkston
State: SD
Office phone: 605-928-3111
Publication Website: www.parkstonadvance.com
General E-mail: advance@santel.net
Publisher Name: Scott Ehler
Delivery Methods: Mail`Racks
Published Days: Wed
Avg Paid Circ: 1100
Audit Company: Sworn/Estimate/Non-Audited
Audit Date: 6 10 2019

PHILIP

PIONEER REVIEW
Corporate/Parent Company: Ravellette Publications
Street Address: PO Box 788, Philip, SD 57567-0788
City: Philip
State: SD
Office phone: 605-859-2516
Publication Website: www.pioneer-review.com
General E-mail: newsdesk@pioneer-review.com
Publisher Name: Beau Ravellette
Editor Name: Beau Ravellette

PIERRE

CAPITAL JOURNAL
Corporate/Parent Company: Wick Communications
Street Address: PO Box 878, Pierre, SD 57501-0878
City: Pierre
State: SD
Office phone: 605-224-7301
Publication Website: www.capjournal.com
General E-mail: jeffrey.hartley@capjournal.com
Publisher Name: Jeffrey Hartley
Publisher Email: jeffrey.hartley@capjournal.com
Editor Name: Casey Junkins
Editor Email: casey.junkins@capjournal.com
Advertising Executive Name: Julie Furchner
Advertising Executive Email: julie.furchner@capjournal.com
Year Established: 1889
Mechanical specifications: Type page 13 x 21 1/2; E - 6 cols, 2 1/16, 1/8 between; A - 6 cols, 2 1/16, 1/8 between; C - 8 cols, 1 9/16, 1/8 between.
Published Days: Mon`Tues`Wed`Thur`Fri
Weekday Frequency: e
Avg Paid Circ: 4100
Avg Free Circ: 21000
Audit Company: Sworn/Estimate/Non-Audited
Audit Date: 7 12 2019

PLANKINTON

SOUTH DAKOTA MAIL
Street Address: PO Box 367, Plankinton, SD 57368-0367
City: Plankinton
State: SD
Office phone: 605-942-7770

General E-mail: sdmail@siouxvalley.net
Publisher Name: Gayle Van Genderen & J.P. Studeny Jr
Editor Name: Gayle Van Genderen
Delivery Methods: Mail`Racks
Published Days: Thur
Avg Paid Circ: 950
Audit Company: Sworn/Estimate/Non-Audited
Audit Date: 6 10 2019

PLATTE

PLATTE ENTERPRISE
Street Address: PO Box 546, Platte, SD 57369-0546
City: Platte
State: SD
Office phone: 605-337-3101
General E-mail: eprise@midstatesd.net
Publisher Name: Sharon Huizenga
Year Established: 1900
Delivery Methods: Mail`Racks
Commercial printers?: Y
Published Days: Thur
Avg Paid Circ: 1890
Audit Company: Sworn/Estimate/Non-Audited
Audit Date: 6 10 2019

POLLOCK

POLLOCK PRAIRIE PIONEER
Street Address: PO Box 218, Pollock, SD 57648-0218
City: Pollock
State: SD
Office phone: 605-889-2320
Publication Website: www.ppioneer.com
General E-mail: pioneer@valleytel.net
Publisher Name: Leah Burke

PRESHO

LYMAN COUNTY HERALD
Street Address: PO Box 518, Presho, SD 57568
City: Presho
State: SD
Office phone: 605-895-6397
Publication Website: www.lcherald.com
General E-mail: news@lcherald.com
Publisher Name: Lucy & Kim Halverson
Editor Name: Lucy Halverson
Delivery Methods: Mail
Published Days: Wed
Avg Paid Circ: 962
Audit Company: Sworn/Estimate/Non-Audited
Audit Date: 6 10 2019

RAPID CITY

NATIVE SUN NEWS
Street Address: PO Box 1716, Rapid City, SD 57709
City: Rapid City
State: SD
Office phone: 605-721-1266
Publication Website: www.nativesunnews.today
General E-mail: editor@nativesunnews.today
Publisher Name: Christy Tibbitts
Editor Name: Tim Giago

RECORD
Corporate/Parent Company: Media News Group
Street Address: 507 Main Street
City: Rapid City
State: SD
Postal Code: 57701
Office phone: 605-394-8300
Publication Website: www.thechadronnews.com
Publisher Name: Matthew Tranquill
Publisher Email: matthew.tranquill@rapidcityjournal.com
Publisher Phone: 605-394-8301

Editor Name: Kent Bush
Editor Email: kbush@rapidcityjournal.com
Editor Phone: 605-394-8428
Advertising Executive Name: Brad Casto
Advertising Executive Email: brad.casto@rapidcityjournal.com
Advertising Executive Phone: 605-394-8356

REDFIELD

REDFIELD PRESS
Corporate/Parent Company: News Media Grouip
Street Address: PO Box 440, Redfield, SD 57469-0440
City: Redfield
State: SD
Office phone: 605-472-0822
Publication Website: www.redfieldpress.com
General E-mail: kunderstock@redfieldpress.com
Publisher Name: Mark Davis
Publisher Email: mdavis@plainsman.com
Editor Name: Shiloh Appel
Advertising Executive Name: Kayla Understock
Advertising Executive Email: kunderstock@redfieldpress.com
Delivery Methods: Mail`Newsstand`Racks
Mechanical specifications: Type page 11 1/4 x 13 3/4; E - 5 cols, 1 7/8, between.
Published Days: Wed
Avg Paid Circ: 1950
Audit Company: Sworn/Estimate/Non-Audited
Audit Date: 6 10 2019

ROSCOE

ROSCOE-HOSMER INDEPENDENT
Street Address: PO Box 7, Ipswich, SD 57451-0007
City: Roscoe
State: SD
Office phone: 605-426-6471
General E-mail: iptribune@valleytel.net
Publisher Name: Tena Gibson
Delivery Methods: Mail`Racks
Mechanical specifications: Type page 9 3/4 x 13; E - 5 cols, 1 3/4, 1 pica between; A - 5 cols, 1 3/4, 1 pica between; C - 5 cols, 1 3/4, 1 pica between.
Published Days: Wed
Avg Paid Circ: 605
Audit Company: Sworn/Estimate/Non-Audited
Audit Date: 6 10 2019

ROSHOLT

ROSHOLT REVIEW
Street Address: PO Box 136, Rosholt, SD 57260-0136
City: Rosholt
State: SD
Office phone: 605-537-4276
General E-mail: review@tnics.com
Publisher Name: Calvin F. Ceroll
Delivery Methods: Mail`Racks
Published Days: Wed
Avg Paid Circ: 1280
Avg Free Circ: 25
Audit Company: Sworn/Estimate/Non-Audited
Audit Date: 6 10 2019

SALEM

SALEM SPECIAL
Street Address: PO Box 220, Salem, SD 57058-0220
City: Salem
State: SD
Office phone: 605-425-2361
Publication Website: www.salemspecial.com
General E-mail: tschwans@triotel.net
Publisher Name: Troy Schwans
Year Established: 1890
Delivery Methods: Mail`Newsstand`Racks
Published Days: Thur
Avg Paid Circ: 1200

SCOTLAND

SCOTLAND JOURNAL
Corporate/Parent Company: B&H Publishing, Inc.
Street Address: PO Box 388, Scotland, SD 57059-0388
City: Scotland
State: SD
Office phone: 605-583-4419
General E-mail: scotnews@gwtc.net
Publisher Name: Becky Tycz
Year Established: 1894
Delivery Methods: Mail
Mechanical specifications: Type page 13 x 21 1/2.
Published Days: Wed
Avg Paid Circ: 900
Avg Free Circ: 60
Audit Company: Sworn/Estimate/Non-Audited
Audit Date: 6 10 2019

SELBY

SELBY RECORD
Street Address: PO Box 421, Selby, SD 57472-0421
City: Selby
State: SD
Office phone: 605-649-7866
General E-mail: selbyrec@venturecomm.net
Publisher Name: Sharon Wolff
Delivery Methods: Mail`Newsstand`Racks
Published Days: Thur
Avg Paid Circ: 1000
Avg Free Circ: 10
Audit Company: Sworn/Estimate/Non-Audited
Audit Date: 6 10 2019

SISSETON

SISSETON COURIER
Street Address: PO Box 169, Sisseton, SD 57262-0169
City: Sisseton
State: SD
Office phone: 605-698-7642
Publication Website: www.sissetoncourier.com
General E-mail: news@sissetoncourier.com
Publisher Name: Sylvia Deutsch
Delivery Methods: Mail`Newsstand`Racks
Own Printing Facility?: Y
Commercial printers?: Y
Published Days: Tues
Avg Paid Circ: 3201
Avg Free Circ: 90
Audit Company: Sworn/Estimate/Non-Audited
Audit Date: 6 10 2019

SOUTH SHORE

SOUTH SHORE GAZETTE
Street Address: PO Box 96, South Shore, SD 57263-0096
City: South Shore
State: SD
Office phone: 605-756-4247
General E-mail: elmo@sstel.net
Publisher Name: Glenn & Corrine Elmore

SPRINGFIELD

SPRINGFIELD TIMES
Street Address: PO Box 465, Springfield, SD 57062-0465
City: Springfield
State: SD
Office phone: 605-369-2441
General E-mail: times@gwtc.net
Publisher Name: Becky Tycz
Year Established: 1871
Delivery Methods: Mail`Racks
Published Days: Wed
Avg Paid Circ: 850
Audit Company: Sworn/Estimate/Non-Audited
Audit Date: 6 10 2019

STICKNEY

STICKNEY ARGUS
Corporate/Parent Company: Standard Publishing Inc.
Street Address: PO Box 98, Stickney, SD 57383
City: Stickney
State: SD
Office phone: 605-249-2166
General E-mail: info@auroracountynews.net
Publisher Name: Barb Becker
Year Established: 1906
Delivery Methods: Mail`Racks
Own Printing Facility?: Y
Commercial printers?: Y
Published Days: Wed
Avg Paid Circ: 400
Avg Free Circ: 31
Audit Company: Sworn/Estimate/Non-Audited
Audit Date: 6 10 2019

TEA

TEA WEEKLY
Street Address: PO Box 98, Tea, SD 57064
City: Tea
State: SD
Office phone: 605-213-0049
Publication Website: www.teaweekly.com
General E-mail: news@teaweekly.com
Publisher Name: Debbie Schmidt & Kelli Bultena
Editor Name: Kelli Bultena
Advertising Executive Name: Kelli Bultena

TIMBER LAKE

TIMBER LAKE TOPIC
Street Address: PO Box 10, Timber Lake, SD 57656-0010
City: Timber Lake
State: SD
Office phone: 605-865-3546
Publication Website: www.timberlakesouthdakota.com
General E-mail: timtopic@lakotanetwork.com
Publisher Name: Kathy Nelson & Robert Slocum
Editor Name: Kathy Nelson & Robert Slocum
Advertising Executive Name: Robert Slocum
Year Established: 1910
Delivery Methods: Mail`Newsstand`Racks
Published Days: Thur
Avg Paid Circ: 1450
Avg Free Circ: 31
Audit Company: Sworn/Estimate/Non-Audited
Audit Date: 6 10 2019

TRIPP

TRIPP STAR-LEDGER
Street Address: PO Box J, Parkston, SD 57366
City: Tripp
State: SD
Office phone: 605-928-3111
Publication Website: www.parkstonadvance.com
General E-mail: advance@santel.net
Publisher Name: Scott Ehler
Delivery Methods: Mail`Racks
Own Printing Facility?: Y
Commercial printers?: Y
Published Days: Wed
Avg Paid Circ: 606
Audit Company: Sworn/Estimate/Non-Audited
Audit Date: 6 10 2019

TYNDALL

TYNDALL TRIBUNE & REGISTER
Street Address: PO Box 520, Tyndall, SD 57066-0520
City: Tyndall
State: SD
Office phone: 605-589-3242
General E-mail: tyndalltribune@gmail.com
Publisher Name: Becky Tycz

VERMILLION

PLAIN TALK
Street Address: 201 West Cherry Street, Vermillion, SD 57069
City: Vermillion
State: SD
Office phone: 605-624-2695
Publication Website: www.plaintalk.net
General E-mail: penny.ascheman@plaintalk.net
Publisher Name: Gary Wood
Publisher Email: gary.wood@yankton.net
Editor Name: David Lias
Editor Email: david.lias@plaintalk.net
Advertising Executive Name: Penny Ascheman
Advertising Executive Email: penny.ascheman@plaintalk.net

VIBORG

VIBORG ENTERPRISE
Street Address: 100 N Main Street, Viborg, SD 57070
City: Viborg
State: SD
Office phone: 605-766-7827
General E-mail: enterprise@iw.net
Publisher Name: Shane & Allyson Hill

VOLGA

VOLGA TRIBUNE
Corporate/Parent Company: RFD News Group
Street Address: PO Box 18, Volga, SD 57071-0018
City: Volga
State: SD
Office phone: 605-627-9471
Publication Website: www.rfdnewsgroup.com
General E-mail: rfd@rfdnewsgroup.com
Publisher Name: Ken Reiste
Editor Name: Mary Ford
Year Established: 1882
Delivery Methods: Mail`Racks
Published Days: Thur
Avg Paid Circ: 1800
Audit Company: Sworn/Estimate/Non-Audited
Audit Date: 6 10 2019

WAGNER

WAGNER POST
Street Address: 209 South Main, Wagner, SD 57380
City: Wagner
State: SD
Office phone: 605-384-5616
Publication Website: www.postandwave.com
General E-mail: announcer@hcinet.net
Publisher Name: Barbra Pechous
Delivery Methods: Mail`Racks
Published Days: Wed
Avg Paid Circ: 1800
Avg Free Circ: 6500
Audit Company: Sworn/Estimate/Non-Audited
Audit Date: 6 10 2019

WALL

PENNINGTON COUNTY COURANT
Corporate/Parent Company: Ravellette Publications
Street Address: PO Box 435, Wall, SD 57790-0435
City: Wall
State: SD
Office phone: 605-279-2565
Publication Website: www.ravellettepublications.com
General E-mail: courant@gwtc.net
Publisher Name: Beau Ravellette
Editor Name: Tracie Crawford

WAUBAY

WAUBAY CLIPPER
Street Address: PO Box 47, Waubay, SD 57273-0047
City: Waubay
State: SD
Office phone: 605-947-4501
General E-mail: linda@waubayclipper.com
Publisher Name: Linda Walters
Delivery Methods: Mail`Newsstand
Published Days: Sat
Avg Paid Circ: 875
Avg Free Circ: 26
Audit Company: Sworn/Estimate/Non-Audited
Audit Date: 6 10 2019

WEBSTER

REPORTER & FARMER
Street Address: PO Box 30, Webster, SD 57274
City: Webster
State: SD
Office phone: 605-345-3356
Publication Website: www.reporterandfarmer.com
General E-mail: news@reporterandfarmer.com
Publisher Name: John & LeAnn Suhr
Publisher Email: suhrs@reporterandfarmer.com
Editor Name: John Suhr
Editor Email: suhrs@reporterandfarmer.com
Advertising Executive Name: John Suhr
Advertising Executive Email: suhrs@reporterandfarmer.com
Year Established: 1881
Delivery Methods: Mail`Newsstand`Racks
Own Printing Facility?: Y
Commercial printers?: Y
Published Days: Mon
Avg Paid Circ: 3200
Audit Company: Sworn/Estimate/Non-Audited
Audit Date: 6 10 2019

WESSINGTON SPRINGS

TRUE DAKOTAN
Corporate/Parent Company: Kristi Publishing, Inc.
Street Address: PO Box 358, Wessington Springs, SD 57382
City: Wessington Springs
State: SD
Office phone: 605-539-1281
Publication Website: www.truedakotan.com
General E-mail: kristi@truedakotan.com
Publisher Name: Kristi Kine
Year Established: 1975
Delivery Methods: Mail`Newsstand`Racks
Published Days: Tues
Avg Paid Circ: 1400
Audit Company: Sworn/Estimate/Non-Audited
Audit Date: 6 10 2019

WHITE

TRI-CITY STAR
Corporate/Parent Company: RFD News Group
Street Address: PO Box 341, White, SD 57276
City: White
State: SD
Office phone: 605-629-2052
Publication Website: www.rfdnewsgroup.com
General E-mail: T.C.S@mchsi.com
Publisher Name: Ken Reiste
Editor Name: Paul Ekern
Year Established: 1884

Non-Daily Newspapers in the U.S.

Delivery Methods: Mail`Racks
Published Days: Thur
Avg Paid Circ: 1800
Audit Company: Sworn/Estimate/Non-Audited
Audit Date: 6 10 2019

WHITE LAKE

AURORA COUNTY STANDARD

Street Address: PO Box 215, White Lake, SD 57383
City: White Lake
State: SD
Office phone: 605-249-2166
General E-mail: info@auroracountynews.net
Publisher Name: Barb Becker

WHITE RIVER

MELLETTE COUNTY NEWS

Street Address: PO Box F, White River, SD 57579
City: White River
State: SD
Office phone: 605-259-3642
Publication Website: www.mellettecountynews.com
General E-mail: mcnews@gwtc.net
Publisher Name: Mandy Scherer
Editor Name: Gina Adrian
Year Established: 1912
Delivery Methods: Mail
Mechanical specifications: Type page 11.75 x 21; 1 pica gutter; 1 col - 1.82"
Published Days: Wed
Avg Paid Circ: 500
Audit Company: Sworn/Estimate/Non-Audited
Audit Date: 6 10 2019

WILMOT

WILMOT ENTERPRISE

Street Address: PO Box 6, Wilmot, SD 57279-0037
City: Wilmot
State: SD
Office phone: 605-938-4651
General E-mail: wilnews@tnics.com
Publisher Name: Terry O'Keefe
Year Established: 1884
Delivery Methods: Mail
Published Days: Thur
Avg Paid Circ: 850
Audit Company: Sworn/Estimate/Non-Audited
Audit Date: 6 10 2019

WINNER

WINNER ADVOCATE

Street Address: 125 West Third Street, Winner, SD 57580-1707
City: Winner
State: SD
Office phone: 605-842-1481
Publication Website: www.thewinneradvocate.com
General E-mail: winneradvocate@hotmail.com
Publisher Name: Charley Najacht
Editor Name: Dan Bechtold
Advertising Executive Name: Laura Brown
Year Established: 1910
Delivery Methods: Mail`Newsstand`Racks
Published Days: Wed
Avg Paid Circ: 2600
Audit Company: Sworn/Estimate/Non-Audited
Audit Date: 6 10 2019

WOONSOCKET

SANBORN WEEKLY JOURNAL

Street Address: PO Box 218, Woonsocket, SD 57385-0218
City: Woonsocket
State: SD

Office phone: 605-796-4221
Publication Website: www.sanbornjournal.com
General E-mail: swj4221@icloud.com
Publisher Name: Tara Weber
Editor Name: Carrie Howard
Year Established: 1883
Delivery Methods: Mail`Racks
Mechanical specifications: Type page 13 x 21; E - 6 cols, 2, 1/6 between; A - 6 cols, 2, 1/6 between; C - 6 cols, 2, 1/6 between.
Published Days: Thur
Avg Paid Circ: 1201
Avg Free Circ: 38
Audit Company: Sworn/Estimate/Non-Audited
Audit Date: 6 10 2019

YANKTON

YANKTON COUNTY OBSERVER

Street Address: 308 Douglas, Yankton, SD 57077
City: Yankton
State: SD
Office phone: 605-665-0484
Publication Website: www.ycobserver.com
General E-mail: kathy@ycobserver.net
Publisher Name: Kathy Church
Publisher Email: kathy@ycobserver.net
Editor Name: Kathy Church
Editor Email: kathy@ycobserver.net
Advertising Executive Name: Jim Anderson
Advertising Executive Email: ads@ycobserver.net
Year Established: 1978
Delivery Methods: Mail`Newsstand`Racks
Commercial printers?: Y
Mechanical specifications: Type page 10.3 x 15.875; All pages - 5 cols, 1.926, 1/6 between.
Published Days: Fri
Avg Paid Circ: 2700
Avg Free Circ: 60
Audit Company: Sworn/Estimate/Non-Audited
Audit Date: 6 10 2019

TENNESSEE

ARDMORE

YOUR COMMUNITY SHOPPER

Street Address: 26297 Savings Center Dr
City: Ardmore
State: TN
Postal Code: 38449
Office phone: 931-427-2198
Publication Website: www.yourcommunityshopper.com

BARTLETT

THE COLLIERVILLE HERALD

Corporate/Parent Company: Magic Valley Publishing Co. Inc.
Street Address: 2850 Stage Village Cove, No. 5
City: Bartlett
State: TN
Postal Code: 38017
Office phone: (901) 433-9138
Publication Website: http://www.colliervilleherald.net/

BROWNSVILLE

BROWNSVILLE PRESS

Corporate/Parent Company: Wireless Group Inc.
Street Address: 42 S Washington Ave, Second Floor
City: Brownsville
State: TN
Postal Code: 38012
Office phone: (731) 772-9962
Publication Website: www.brownsvillepress.com

CELINA

CITIZEN-STATESMAN

Street Address: 801 East Lake Avenue
City: Celina
State: TN
Postal Code: 38551
Office phone: (931) 243-2235
Publication Website: www.citizen-statesman.com

DALE HOLLOW HORIZON

Corporate/Parent Company: Upper Cumberland Media Group
Street Address: 121 Donaldson Avenue, P O Box 69
City: Celina
State: TN
Postal Code: 38551
Office phone: 931-243-4710
Publication Website: www.dalehollowhorizon.com

CENTERVILLE

HICKMAN COUNTY TIMES

Street Address: 104 N Central Ave
City: Centerville
State: TN
Postal Code: 37033
Office phone: 931-729-4282
Publication Website: www.hickmancountytimes.net

CLARKSVILLE

STEWART-HOUSTON TIMES

Street Address: 200 Commerce St
City: Clarksville
State: TN
Postal Code: 37040
Office phone: (931) 552-1808
Publication Website: https://www.theleafchronicle.com/news/stewart-houston-times/

COVINGTON

THE LEADER

Corporate/Parent Company: Adams Publishing Group
Street Address: 111 S. Munford Street
City: Covington
State: TN
Postal Code: 37204
Office phone: 615-966-5180
Publication Website: www.covingtonleader.com

DAYTON

THE HERALD-NEWS (DAYTON)

Street Address: 916 Market St
City: Dayton
State: TN
Postal Code: 37321
Office phone: (423) 775-6111
Publication Website: http://www.rheaheraldnews.com/

DOVER

STEWART COUNTY STANDARD

Street Address: PO Box 543
City: Dover
State: TN
Postal Code: 37058
Office phone: (931) 232-3801
Publication Website: stewartcountystandard.com

DRESDEN

DRESDEN ENTERPRISE

Corporate/Parent Company: Tri-County Publishing, Inc
Street Address: 113 S Wilson St
City: Dresden
State: TN
Postal Code: 38225
Office phone: 731-364-2234
Publication Website: www.dresdenenterprise.com

FAYETTEVILLE

THE ELK VALLEY TIMES

Corporate/Parent Company: Lakeway Publishers, Inc.
Street Address: 418 Elk Ave N
City: Fayetteville
State: TN
Postal Code: 37334
Office phone: (931) 433-6151
Publication Website: https://www.elkvalleytimes.com/

GAINESBORO

JACKSON COUNTY SENTINEL

Street Address: South Main Street
City: Gainesboro
State: TN
Postal Code: 38562
Office phone: (931) 268-9725
Publication Website: www.jacksoncountysentinel.net

GALLATIN

GALLATIN NEWS EXAMINER

Street Address: 333 W Main St Suite E
City: Gallatin
State: TN
Postal Code: 37066
Office phone: (615) 452-4940
Publication Website: https://www.gallatinnews.com/

PORTLAND SUN

Corporate/Parent Company: Main Street Media of Tennessee
Street Address: 333 W Main St. Suite E
City: Gallatin
State: TN
Postal Code: 37066
Office phone: 615-452-4940
Publication Website: www.theportlandsun.com

THE GALLATIN NEWS

Corporate/Parent Company: Main Street Media of Tennessee
Street Address: 333 W Main St. Suite E
City: Gallatin
State: TN
Postal Code: 37066
Office phone: (615) 452-4940
Publication Website: www.gallatinnews.com

THE HENDERSONVILLE STAR NEWS

Street Address: 1 Examiner Ct
City: Gallatin
State: TN
Postal Code: 37066
Office phone: (615) 313-2726
Publication Website: https://www.tennessean.

HENDERSON

CHESTER COUNTY INDEPENDENT

Corporate/Parent Company: Magic Valley Publishing Co. Inc.
Street Address: 218 S Church Ave
City: Henderson
State: TN
Postal Code: 38340-2638
Office phone: (731) 989-4624
Publication Website: https://chestercountyindependent.com/

LAFAYETTE

MACON COUNTY CHRONICLE

Street Address: 109 Public Square
City: Lafayette
State: TN
Postal Code: 37083
Office phone: 615 688-6397
Publication Website: www.maconcountychronicle.com

LYNCHBURG

MOORE COUNTY NEWS

Corporate/Parent Company: Lakeway Publishers, Inc.
Street Address: P.O. Box 500
City: Lynchburg
State: TN
Postal Code: 37352
Office phone: (931) 759-7302
Publication Website: https://www.themoorecountynews.com/

MANCHESTER

MANCHESTER TIMES

Corporate/Parent Company: Lakeway Publishers, Inc.
Street Address: 300 N Spring St
City: Manchester
State: TN
Postal Code: 37355
Office phone: (931) 728-7577
Publication Website: https://www.manchestertimes.com/

MARYVILLE

THE DAILY TIMES (MARYVILLE)

Corporate/Parent Company: The Daily News Publishing Co.
Street Address: 307 E. Harper Ave
City: Maryville
State: TN
Postal Code: 37804
Office phone: (865) 981-1100
Publication Website: https://www.thedailytimes.com/

MEMPHIS

NEW TRI STATE DEFENDER

Street Address: 203 Beale Street, Suite 200
City: Memphis
State: TN
Postal Code: 38103
Office phone: 901-523-1818
Publication Website: tri-statedefender.com

MORISTOWN

THE CIVIL WAR COURIER

Corporate/Parent Company: Lakeway Publishers, Inc.
Street Address: 1609 W. 1st N. Street
City: Moristown
State: TN
Postal Code: 37815
Office phone: (423) 581-5630
Publication Website: https://www.timelinesmagazine.com/publication/civil_war_courier/

NASHVILLE

ASHLAND CITY TIMES

Street Address: 1801 West End, 17th Floor
City: Nashville
State: TN
Postal Code: 37203
Office phone: (615) 259-8300
Publication Website: http://www.ashlandcitytimes.com

DICKSON SHOPPER

Street Address: 1801 West End, 17th Floor
City: Nashville
State: TN
Postal Code: 37203
Office phone: (615) 259-8300
Publication Website: http://www.dicksonshopper.com/

FAIRVIEW OBSERVER

Street Address: 1801 West End, 17th Floor
City: Nashville
State: TN
Postal Code: 37203
Office phone: (615) 259-8300
Publication Website: https://www.tennessean.com/counties/williamson/

ROBERTSON COUNTY TIMES

Street Address: 1801 West End, 17th Floor
City: Nashville
State: TN
Postal Code: 37203
Office phone: (615) 259-8300
Publication Website: https://www.tennessean.com/counties/robertson/

THE DICKSON HERALD

Street Address: 1801 West End, 17th Floor
City: Nashville
State: TN
Postal Code: 37203
Office phone: (615) 259-8300
Publication Website: https://www.tennessean.com/counties/dickson/

THE KNOXVILLE LEDGER

Corporate/Parent Company: The Daily News Publishing Co
Street Address: 222 2nd Ave N., Suite 101
City: Nashville
State: TN
Postal Code: 37201
Office phone: 615.254.5522
Publication Website: www.tnledger.com/knoxville

NEWPORT

THE NEWPORT PLAIN TALK

Corporate/Parent Company: Adams Publishing Group
Street Address: 145 East Broadway
City: Newport
State: TN
Postal Code: 37821
Office phone: (423) 623-6171
Publication Website: http://www.newportplaintalk.com/

ONEIDA

INDEPENDENT HERALD

Corporate/Parent Company: Liberty Press Inc
Street Address: 19391 ALBERTA ST
City: ONEIDA
State: TN
Postal Code: 37841
Office phone: (423) 569-6343
Publication Website: www.ihoneida.com

ROGERSVILLE

THE ROGERSVILLE REVIEW

Corporate/Parent Company: Adams Publishing Group
Street Address: P.O. Box 100 316 East Main Street
City: Rogersville
State: TN
Postal Code: 37857
Office phone: (423) 272-7422
Publication Website: http://www.therogersvillereview.com/

SELMER

INDEPENDENT APPEAL

Corporate/Parent Company: McNairy County Publishing Co. LLC.
Street Address: 111 North 2nd Street Selmer
City: Selmer
State: TN
Postal Code: 38375
Office phone: (731)645-5346
Publication Website: www.independentappeal.com

SPARTA

THE SPARTA EXPOSITOR

Street Address: 34 West Bockman Way
City: Sparta
State: TN
Postal Code: 38583
Office phone: (931) 836-3284
Publication Website: www.spartalive.com

SPRINGFIELD

CHEATHAM COUNTY EXCHANGE

Corporate/Parent Company: Main Street Media of Tennessee
Street Address: 803 Memorial Blvd
City: Springfield
State: TN
Postal Code: 37172
Office phone: 615-384-6212
Publication Website: www.cheathamcountyexchange.com

ROBERTSON COUNTY CONNECTION

Corporate/Parent Company: Main Street Media of Tennessee
Street Address: 803 Memorial Dr.
City: Springfield
State: TN
Postal Code: 37172
Office phone: 615-384-6212
Publication Website: www.robertsoncountyconnection.com

SWEETWATER

THE ADVOCATE & DEMOCRAT (SWEETWATER)

Corporate/Parent Company: Jones Media Inc.
Street Address: PO Box 389
City: Sweetwater
State: TN
Postal Code: 37874
Office phone: (423) 337-7101
Publication Website: http://www.advocateanddemocrat.com/

TRACY CITY

GRUNDY COUNTY HERALD

Corporate/Parent Company: Lakeway Publishers, Inc.
Street Address: 65 Oak St
City: Tracy City
State: TN
Postal Code: 37387
Office phone: (931) 592-2781
Publication Website: https://www.grundycountyherald.com/

TRENTON

THE GAZETTE

Corporate/Parent Company: Adams Publishing Group
Street Address: PO Box 7
City: Trenton
State: TN
Postal Code: 38382
Office phone: 731-855-1711
Publication Website: www.trentongazette.com

TULLAHOMA

THE TULLAHOMA NEWS

Corporate/Parent Company: Lakeway Publishers, Inc.
Street Address: 505 Lake Way Pl
City: Tullahoma
State: TN
Postal Code: 37388
Office phone: (931) 455-4545
Publication Website: https://www.tullahomanews.com/

WINCHESTER

THE HERALD-CHRONICLE

Corporate/Parent Company: Lakeway Publishers, Inc.
Street Address: 906 Dinah Shore Blvd
City: Winchester
State: TN
Postal Code: 37398
Office phone: 931-967-2272
Publication Website: www.heraldchronicle.com

WOODBURY

CANNON COURIER

Street Address: 113 Main Street
City: Woodbury
State: TN
Postal Code: 37190
Office phone: 615-563-2512
Publication Website: www.cannoncourier.com

TEXAS

ABERNATHY

ABERNATHY ADVOCATE
Street Address: 420 9th St
City: Abernathy
State: TX
Postal Code: 79311
Office phone: 806.632.3822
Publication Website: www.abernathyadvocate.com
General E-mail: abernathyadvocate@windstream.net
Publisher Name: Kristina Janet

ALVIN

ALVIN ADVERTISER
Corporate/Parent Company: Hartman Newspapers, L.P.
Street Address: 570 DULA STREET
City: Alvin
State: TX
Postal Code: 77511
Office phone: (281) 331-4421
Publication Website: http://www.alvinsun.net/
General E-mail: publisher@alvinsun.net
Publisher Name: David Rupkalvis
Publisher Email: publisher@alvinsun.net
Editor Name: DAVID RUPKALVIS
Editor Email: publisher@alvinsun.net
Advertising Executive Name: Brenda Groves
Advertising Executive Email: ads@alvinsun.net

ALVIN SUN
Corporate/Parent Company: Hartman Newspapers, L.P.
Street Address: 570 Dula St.
City: Alvin
State: TX
Postal Code: 77511
Office phone: 281-331-4421
Publication Website: alvinsun.net
Publisher Name: DAVID RUPKALVIS
Publisher Email: publisher@alvinsun.net
Editor Name: DAVID RUPKALVIS
Editor Email: editor@alvinsun.net
Advertising Executive Name: KOBIE LEE
Advertising Executive Email: advertising@alvinsun.net
Total Circulation: 28987

BALLINGER

RUNNELS COUNTY REGISTER
Corporate/Parent Company: Gannett
Street Address: 709 Hutchins Ave.
City: Ballinger
State: TX
Postal Code: 76821
Office phone: (325) 365-3501
Publication Website: runnelscountyregister.com
Editor Name: Derrick Stuckly
Editor Email: dstuckly@brownwoodbulletin.com
Editor Phone: 325-641-3112
Advertising Executive Name: Kendra Chism
Advertising Executive Email: kchism@brownwoodbulletin.com
Advertising Executive Phone: 325-641-3119

BANDERA

BANDERA BULLETIN
Corporate/Parent Company: Fenice Community Media
Street Address: 606 Hwy 16 South
City: Bandera
State: TX
Postal Code: 78003
Office phone: (830) 796-3718
Publication Website: https://www.banderabulletin.com/
General E-mail: publisher@banderabulletin.com
Publisher Name: Jonathan Deeley
Publisher Email: publisher@banderabulletin.com
Editor Name: Bill Pack
Editor Email: bill@banderabulletin.com
Year Established: 1945
Delivery Methods: Mail`Newsstand
Own Printing Facility?: Y
Published Days: Wed
Avg Paid Circ: 2193
Audit Company: Sworn/Estimate/Non-Audited
Audit Date: 6 10 2019

BAY CITY

THE BAY CITY TRIBUNE
Corporate/Parent Company: Southern Newspapers Inc.
Street Address: 2901 Carey Smith Blvd
City: Bay City
State: TX
Postal Code: 77414
Office phone: (979) 245-5555
Publication Website: http://baycitytribune.com/
General E-mail: support@baycitytribune.com
Publisher Name: Brenda Burr
Publisher Email: brenda.burr@baycitytribune.com
Editor Name: Brenda Burr
Editor Email: brenda.burr@baycitytribune.com
Advertising Executive Name: Dena Matthews
Advertising Executive Email: classified@baycitytribune.com
Year Established: 1845
Delivery Methods: Newsstand`Carrier`Racks
Mechanical specifications: Type page 13 x 21 1/2; E - 6 cols, 2 1/16, 1/8 between; A - 6 cols, 2 1/16, 1/8 between; C - 9 cols, 1 7/16, 1/16 between.
Published Days: Wed`Sun
Avg Paid Circ: 2385
Avg Free Circ: 708
Audit Company: AAM
Audit Date: 15 08 2019
Total Circulation: 2193

BEEVILLE

THE NEWS OF SAN PATRICIO
Corporate/Parent Company: MYSoutx.com
Street Address: 111 N. Washington St.
City: Beeville
State: TX
Postal Code: 78387
Office phone: (361) 358-2550
Publication Website: https://www.mysoutex.com/san_patricio_county/
General E-mail: media@mysoutex.com
Editor Name: media@mysoutex.com
Advertising Executive Email: ads@mysoutex.com
Year Established: 1924
Delivery Methods: Mail`Newsstand`Carrier`Racks
Own Printing Facility?: Y
Commercial printers?: Y
Published Days: Thur
Avg Paid Circ: 2000
Avg Free Circ: 35
Audit Company: Sworn/Estimate/Non-Audited
Audit Date: 6 10 2019

BOERNE

BOERNE STAR
Corporate/Parent Company: Fenice Community Media
Street Address: 941 N School St
City: Boerne
State: TX
Postal Code: 78006
Office phone: (830) 249-2441
Publication Website: https://www.boernestar.com/
General E-mail: news@boernestar.com
Publisher Name: Jeffrey Parra
Publisher Email: publisher@boernestar.com
Editor Name: Keith E. Domke
Editor Email: keith@boernestar.com
Advertising Executive Name: Kolleen Roe
Advertising Executive Email: accounting@boernestar.com
Year Established: 1906
Delivery Methods: Mail`Newsstand`Racks
Mechanical specifications: Type page 13 x 21; E - 6 cols, 1 5/6, 1/8 between
Published Days: Tues`Fri
Avg Paid Circ: 4179
Avg Free Circ: 1401
Audit Company: Sworn/Estimate/Non-Audited
Audit Date: 6 10 2019
Total Circulation: 5580

BRENHAM

BRENHAM BANNER-PRESS
Corporate/Parent Company: Hartman Newspapers, L.P.
Street Address: P.O. Box 585
City: Brenham
State: TX
Postal Code: 77834
Office phone: (979) 836-7956
Publication Website: http://www.brenhambanner.com/
General E-mail: circ@brenhambanner.com
Publisher Name: Derek Hall
Publisher Email: derek@brenhambanner.com
Editor Name: Derek Hall
Editor Email: derek@brenhambanner.com
Advertising Executive Name: Helen Nowicki
Advertising Executive Email: helen@brenhambanner.com
Year Established: 1866
Delivery Methods: Mail`Newsstand`Carrier`Racks
Own Printing Facility?: Y
Commercial printers?: Y
Mechanical specifications: Type page 11.625 x 21, 6 cols.
Published Days: Tues`Wed`Thur`Fri`Sun
Weekday Frequency: e
Avg Paid Circ: 5730
Avg Free Circ: 295
Audit Company: CVC
Audit Date: 30 06 2015
Pressroom Equipment: Lines – 5-WPC/Leader.;
Mailroom Equipment: Counter Stackers – BG; Inserters & Stuffers – 3/KAN; Tying Machines – 2-/MLN.;
Buisness Equipment: APP/Mac
Buisness Software: Baseview
Classified Equipment: Hardware – APP/Mac; Imagesetter; Printers – APP/Mac LaserWriter II NTX, Okidata/Microline 320;
Classified Software: Baseview, QPS.
Editorial Equipment: Hardware – APP/Mac/Imagesetter; Printers – APP/Mac LaserWriter II NTX
Editorial Software: Baseview, QPS.
Production Equipment: Hardware – B; Cameras – C/Spartan II
Production Software: QPS/QuarkXPress.
Total Circulation: 6025

CANTON

CANTON HERALD
Corporate/Parent Company: Van Zandt Newspapers LLC
Street Address: 103 E. Tyler
City: Canton
State: TX
Postal Code: 75103
Office phone: (903) 567-4000
Publication Website: https://www.thecantonherald.com/
General E-mail: editor@vanzandtnews.com
Publisher Name: Brad Blakemore
Publisher Email: brad@vanzandtnews.com
Publisher Phone: (903) 567-4000
Editor Name: Britne Hammons
Editor Email: editor@vanzandtnews.com
Editor Phone: (903) 567-4000
Advertising Executive Name: David Barber
Advertising Executive Email: sales@vanzandtnews.com
Advertising Executive Phone: (903) 567-4000
Year Established: 1882
Delivery Methods: Mail`Newsstand
Published Days: Thur
Avg Paid Circ: 5000
Audit Company: Sworn/Estimate/Non-Audited
Audit Date: 6 10 2019
Total Circulation: 5000

VAN BANNER
Corporate/Parent Company: Van Zandt Newspapers LLC
Street Address: 103 E. Tyler
City: Canton
State: TX
Postal Code: 75103
Office phone: (903) 567-4000
Publication Website: https://www.vanzandtnews.com/
General E-mail: editor@vanzandtnews.com
Publisher Name: Brad Blakemore
Publisher Email: brad@vanzandtnews.com
Publisher Phone: (903) 567-4000
Editor Name: Britne Hammons
Editor Email: editor@vanzandtnews.com
Editor Phone: (903) 567-4000
Advertising Executive Name: David Barber
Advertising Executive Email: sales@vanzandtnews.com
Advertising Executive Phone: (903) 567-4000
Year Established: 1998
Delivery Methods: Mail
Published Days: Thur
Avg Paid Circ: 694
Audit Company: Sworn/Estimate/Non-Audited
Audit Date: 6 10 2019

VAN ZANDT NEWS
Corporate/Parent Company: Van Zandt Newspapers LLC
Street Address: 103 E. Tyler
City: Canton
State: TX
Postal Code: 75103
Office phone: (903) 567-4000
Publication Website: https://www.vanzandtnews.com/
General E-mail: editor@vanzandtnews.com
Publisher Name: Brad Blakemore
Publisher Email: brad@vanzandtnews.com
Publisher Phone: (903) 567-4000
Editor Name: Britne Hammons
Editor Email: editor@vanzandtnews.com
Editor Phone: (903) 567-4000
Advertising Executive Name: David Barber
Advertising Executive Email: sales@vanzandtnews.com
Advertising Executive Phone: (903) 567-4000
Year Established: 1982
Delivery Methods: Mail`Newsstand
Mechanical specifications: Type page 11 1/2 x 21 1/2; E - 6 cols, 1 13/16, between; A - 6 cols, 1 13/16, between; C - 8 cols, 1 5/16, between.
Published Days: Sun
Avg Paid Circ: 5500
Avg Free Circ: 100
Audit Company: Sworn/Estimate/Non-Audited
Audit Date: 6 10 2019
Total Circulation: 2022

CEDAR PARK

HILL COUNTRY NEWS
Corporate/Parent Company: Fenice Community Media
Street Address: 715 Discovery Blvd

City: Cedar Park
State: TX
Postal Code: 78613
Office phone: (512) 259-4449
Publication Website: http://hillcountrynews.com/
General E-mail: editor@hillcountrynews.com
Publisher Name: Scott W. Coleman
Editor Name: Scott W. Coleman
Editor Email: editor@hillcountrynews.com
Advertising Executive Name: Roger Munford
Year Established: 1968
Delivery Methods: Mail`Newsstand`Carrier`Racks
Mechanical specifications: Type page 10 x 21 1/2; E - 6 cols, 2 1/16, between; A - 6 cols, 2 1/16, between; C - 9 cols, 1 3/8, between.
Published Days: Thur
Avg Paid Circ: 988
Avg Free Circ: 15910
Audit Company: Sworn/Estimate/Non-Audited
Audit Date: 6 10 2019
Total Circulation: 371

CENTER

THE LIGHT & CHAMPION

Corporate/Parent Company: Fenice Community Media
Street Address: 137 San Augustine St
City: Center
State: TX
Postal Code: 75935
Office phone: (936) 598-3377
Publication Website: https://www.lightandchampion.com/
General E-mail: news@lightandchampion.com
Publisher Name: Mike Elswick
Publisher Email: publisher@lightandchampion.com
Editor Name: Mike Elswick
Advertising Executive Name: Stephanie Elswick
Advertising Executive Email: advertising@lightandchampion.com
Year Established: 1877
Delivery Methods: Mail`Newsstand`Racks
Published Days: Tues`Fri
Avg Paid Circ: 2496
Avg Free Circ: 29
Audit Company: Sworn/Estimate/Non-Audited
Audit Date: 6 10 2019

CHILDRESS

THE RED RIVER SUN

Street Address: PO Box 1260
City: Childress
State: TX
Postal Code: 79201
Office phone: 888-400-1083
Publication Website: redriversun.com
Publisher Name: Bruce W. Green
Editor Name: Kalin Bentley
Editor Email: news@redriversun.com
Advertising Executive Name: Stormi Clifton
Total Circulation: 965

COLUMBUS

THE COLORADO COUNTY CITIZEN

Corporate/Parent Company: Granite Publications
Street Address: 2024 Highway 71 S
City: Columbus
State: TX
Postal Code: 78934
Office phone: (979) 732-2304
Publication Website: https://www.coloradocountycitizen.com/
General E-mail: publisher@coloradocountycitizen.com
Publisher Email: publisher@coloradocountycitizen.com
Editor Email: editor@coloradocountycitizen.com
Year Established: 1857
Delivery Methods: Mail`Newsstand
Published Days: Wed
Avg Paid Circ: 2868

Avg Free Circ: 50
Audit Company: Sworn/Estimate/Non-Audited
Audit Date: 6 10 2019
Total Circulation: 9490

CROCKETT

HOUSTON COUNTY COURIER

Corporate/Parent Company: Polk County Publishing Co.
Street Address: 102 S 7th St
City: Crockett
State: TX
Postal Code: 75835
Office phone: (936) 544-2238
Publication Website: https://hccourier.com/
General E-mail: manager@hccourier.com
Publisher Email: manager@hccourier.com
Year Established: 1890
Delivery Methods: Mail`Newsstand`Racks
Own Printing Facility?: Y
Commercial printers?: Y
Published Days: Thur`Sun
Avg Paid Circ: 5763
Audit Company: Sworn/Estimate/Non-Audited
Audit Date: 6 10 2019

DRIPPING SPRINGS

DRIPPING SPRINGS CENTURY NEWS

Street Address: P.O. Box 732
City: Dripping Springs
State: TX
Postal Code: 78620
Office phone: (512) 858-4163
Publication Website: drippingspringsnews.com
Editor Name: John Pacheco
Editor Email: jpacheco@drippingspringsnews.com
Advertising Executive Name: Suzanne Warmack
Advertising Executive Email: swarmack@drippingspringsnews.com
Total Circulation: 1000

EASTLAND

CISCO PRESS

Corporate/Parent Company: Eastland County Newspapers
Street Address: 215 S Seaman St
City: Eastland
State: TX
Postal Code: 76448
Office phone: (254) 629-1707
Publication Website: https://www.eastlandcountytoday.com/cisco-press
General E-mail: ecn@att.net
Publisher Name: H.V. O'Brien
Publisher Email: ecn@att.net
Advertising Executive Email: ecnads@yahoo.com
Year Established: 1919
Delivery Methods: Mail`Newsstand
Published Days: Thur
Avg Paid Circ: 965
Audit Company: Sworn/Estimate/Non-Audited
Audit Date: 6 10 2019

EASTLAND COUNTY TODAY

Street Address: 215 S. Seaman St.
City: Eastland
State: TX
Postal Code: 76448
Office phone: (254) 629-1707
Publication Website: eastlandcountytoday.com
Publisher Name: H.V. O'Brien
Publisher Email: ecn@att.net
Advertising Executive Name: Sheila Hickox
Advertising Executive Email: ecnads@yahoo.com
Total Circulation: 1825

EASTLAND TELEGRAM

Corporate/Parent Company: Eastland County Newspapers
Street Address: 215 S Seaman St
City: Eastland
State: TX
Postal Code: 76448
Office phone: (254) 629-1707
Publication Website: https://www.eastlandcountytoday.com/eastland-telegram
General E-mail: ecn@att.net
Publisher Name: H.V. O'Brien
Publisher Email: ecn@att.net
Advertising Executive Email: ecnads@yahoo.com
Year Established: 1925
Delivery Methods: Mail`Racks
Own Printing Facility?: Y
Commercial printers?: Y
Mechanical specifications: Type page 14 x 21; E - 8 cols, 1 7/12, 1 between; A - 8 cols, 1 7/12, 1 between.
Published Days: Thur
Avg Paid Circ: 1825
Audit Company: Sworn/Estimate/Non-Audited
Audit Date: 6 10 2019
Total Circulation: 4698

GORMAN PROGRESS

Corporate/Parent Company: Eastland County Newspapers
Street Address: 215 S Seaman St
City: Eastland
State: TX
Postal Code: 76448
Office phone: (254) 629-1707
Publication Website: https://www.eastlandcountytoday.com/gorman-progress
General E-mail: ecn@att.net
Publisher Name: H.V. O'Brien
Publisher Email: ecn@att.net
Advertising Executive Email: ecnads@yahoo.com
Total Circulation: 2227

RANGER TIMES

Corporate/Parent Company: Eastland County Newspapers
Street Address: 215 S Seaman St
City: Eastland
State: TX
Postal Code: 76448
Office phone: (254) 629-1707
Publication Website: https://www.eastlandcountytoday.com/ranger-times
General E-mail: ecn@att.net
Publisher Name: H.V. O'Brien
Publisher Email: ecn@att.net
Advertising Executive Email: ecnads@yahoo.com
Year Established: 1919
Delivery Methods: Mail`Newsstand
Published Days: Thur
Avg Paid Circ: 538
Audit Company: Sworn/Estimate/Non-Audited
Audit Date: 6 10 2019
Total Circulation: 25043

RISING STAR

Corporate/Parent Company: Eastland County Newspapers
Street Address: 215 S Seaman St
City: Eastland
State: TX
Postal Code: 76448
Office phone: (254) 629-1707
Publication Website: https://www.eastlandcountytoday.com/rising-star
General E-mail: ecn@att.net
Publisher Name: H.V. O'Brien

Publisher Email: ecn@att.net
Advertising Executive Email: ecnads@yahoo.com
Delivery Methods: Mail`Racks
Mechanical specifications: Type page 14 x 23; E - 8 cols, 1 1/2, 1/4 between; A - 8 cols, 1 1/2, 1/4 between; C - 8 cols, 1 1/2, 1/4 between.
Published Days: Thur
Avg Paid Circ: 550
Avg Free Circ: 41
Audit Company: Sworn/Estimate/Non-Audited
Audit Date: 6 10 2019

EL CAMPO

EL CAMPO LEADER-NEWS

Corporate/Parent Company: Hartman Newspapers, L.P.
Street Address: 203 E Jackson St
City: El Campo
State: TX
Postal Code: 77437
Office phone: (979) 543-3363
Publication Website: http://www.leader-news.com/
General E-mail: publisher@leader-news.com
Publisher Name: Shannon Crabtree
Publisher Email: publisher@leader-news.com
Editor Email: scrabtree@leader-news.com
Advertising Executive Name: Haley Orsak
Advertising Executive Email: advertise@leader-news.com
Year Established: 1885
Delivery Methods: Mail`Newsstand`Racks
Mechanical specifications: Type page 13 x 21; E - 6 cols, 2 1/20, 1/6 between; A - 6 cols, 2 1/20, 1/6 between; C - 6 cols, 2 1/20, 1/6 between.
Published Days: Wed`Sat
Avg Paid Circ: 4583
Avg Free Circ: 115
Audit Company: Sworn/Estimate/Non-Audited
Audit Date: 6 10 2019
Total Circulation: 26744

ELGIN

ELGIN COURIER

Corporate/Parent Company: Granite Publications
Street Address: 105 N Main St
City: Elgin
State: TX
Postal Code: 78621
Office phone: (512) 285-3333
Publication Website: https://www.elgincourier.com/
General E-mail: ads@elgincourier.com
Publisher Name: Jim Beaver
Publisher Email: publisher@elgincourier.com
Advertising Executive Name: Heather Ott
Advertising Executive Email: ads@elgincourier.com
Year Established: 1890
Delivery Methods: Mail`Newsstand`Racks
Published Days: Wed
Avg Paid Circ: 2007
Avg Free Circ: 220
Audit Company: Sworn/Estimate/Non-Audited
Audit Date: 6 10 2019

FORT STOCKTON

THE FORT STOCKTON PIONEER

Corporate/Parent Company: Fenice Community Media
Street Address: 6210 N. Nelson
City: Fort Stockton
State: TX
Postal Code: 79735
Office phone: (432) 336-2281
Publication Website: http://fortstocktonpioneer.com/
General E-mail: publisher@fspioneer.com
Publisher Name: Steve Fountain
Publisher Email: steve.fountain@fortstocktonpioneer.com
Editor Name: Steve Fountain
Editor Email: steve.fountain@

fortstocktonpioneer.com
Advertising Executive Name: Laci Belovsky
Advertising Executive Email: laci.belovsky@fortstocktonpioneer.com
Year Established: 1908
Delivery Methods: Mail`Newsstand`Racks
Mechanical specifications: Type page 11 1/2 x 21 1/2; E - 6 cols, 1 5/6, 1/10 between; A - 6 cols, 1 5/6, 1/10 between; C - 9 cols, 1 1/6, 1/10 between.
Published Days: Thur
Avg Paid Circ: 3365
Audit Company: Sworn/Estimate/Non-Audited
Audit Date: 6 10 2019
Total Circulation: 16898

FORT WORTH
TARRANT COUNTY COMMERCIAL RECORD

Street Address: 201 Main Street, Suite 600
City: Fort Worth
State: TX
Postal Code: 76102
Office phone: 817.549-4846
Publication Website: tarrantcountycommercialrecord.com
General E-mail: notices@tarrantcountycommercialrecord.com
Publisher Name: E. Nuel Cates Jr.
Editor Name: Emily Cates
Advertising Executive Name: Chasity Johnson
Advertising Executive Email: chasity@tarrantcountycommercialrecord.com
Total Circulation: 5763

GONZALES
THE GONZALES INQUIRER

Corporate/Parent Company: Fenice Community Media
Street Address: 622 Saint Paul St
City: Gonzales
State: TX
Postal Code: 78629
Office phone: (830) 672-2861
Publication Website: http://gonzalesinquirer.com/
General E-mail: publisher@gonzalesinquirer.com
Publisher Email: publisher@gonzalesinquirer.com
Year Established: 1853
Delivery Methods: Mail`Newsstand`Racks
Own Printing Facility?: Y
Published Days: Tues`Fri
Published Other: semi-weekly
Avg Paid Circ: 1189
Avg Free Circ: 1088
Audit Company: Sworn/Estimate/Non-Audited
Audit Date: 6 10 2019

HEBBRONVILLE
THE ENTERPRISE

Corporate/Parent Company: Gannett
Street Address: 304 E. Galbraith
City: Hebbronville
State: TX
Postal Code: 78361-3406
Office phone: 361-460-9493
Publication Website: enterrprisenews.info
Editor Name: Poncho Hernandez
Editor Email: enterprise78361@aol.com
Editorial Equipment: Windows10
Editorial Software: InDesign PhotoShop
Production Equipment: Windows10
Production Software: InDesign PhotoShop
Total Circulation: 983

HENDERSON
THE HENDERSON NEWS

Corporate/Parent Company: Hartman Newspapers, L.P.
Street Address: 1711 US Highway 79 S
City: Henderson
State: TX
Postal Code: 75653
Office phone: (903) 657-2501
Publication Website: http://www.thehendersonnews.com/
General E-mail: publisher@thehendersonnews.com
Publisher Name: Dan Moore
Publisher Email: publisher@thehendersonnews.com
Editor Name: Kent Mahoney
Editor Email: agriffin@hendersondailynews.com
Advertising Executive Name: Valerie Reese
Advertising Executive Email: marketing@thehendersonnews.com
Year Established: 1930
Delivery Methods: Mail`Newsstand`Carrier`Racks
Own Printing Facility?: Y
Commercial printers?: Y
Mechanical specifications: Type page 13 x 21 1/2; E - 6 cols, 2 1/16, 1/8 between; A - 6 cols, 2 1/16, 1/8 between; C - 8 cols, 1 3/8, 1/16 between.
Published Days: Wed`Sun
Weekday Frequency: e
Avg Paid Circ: 4500
Audit Company: Sworn/Estimate/Non-Audited
Audit Date: 6 10 2019
Pressroom Equipment: Lines – 6-HI/V-15A (upper former).;
Total Circulation: 26000

HUMBLE
NEWS ADVOCATE

Corporate/Parent Company: Hartman Newspapers, L.P.
Street Address: 19245 Kenswick Dr #200
City: Humble
State: TX
Postal Code: 77338
Office phone: 713.362.1581
Publication Website: chron.com/cleveland
Publisher Name: Howard Decker
Editor Name: Chris Shelton
Editor Email: newstips@chron.com
Advertising Executive Name: Diane Heinricks
Advertising Executive Email: dheinricks@hcnonline.com
Total Circulation: 5371

JACKSONVILLE
JACKSONVILLE PROGRESS

Corporate/Parent Company: CNHI, LLC
Street Address: 525 E. Commerce St
City: Jacksonville
State: TX
Postal Code: 75766
Office phone: (903) 586-2236
Publication Website: jacksonvilleprogress.com
Publisher Name: Lange Svehlak
Publisher Email: publisher@jacksonvilleprogress.com
Editor Name: April Barbe
Editor Email: editor@jacksonvilleprogress.com
Editor Phone: 903-586-2236
Advertising Executive Name: Sharon Claxton
Advertising Executive Email: sclaxton@jacksonvilleprogress.com
Advertising Executive Phone: 903-586-2236
Total Circulation: 11552

KATY
THE KATY TIMES

Corporate/Parent Company: Hartman Newspapers, L.P.
Street Address: 5507 Morton Road, Ste. 103
City: Katy
State: TX
Postal Code: 77493
Office phone: (281) 391-3141
Publication Website: http://katytimes.com/
General E-mail: publisher@katytimes.com
Publisher Email: publisher@katytimes.com
Advertising Executive Name: Terri Richard
Advertising Executive Email: terri.richard@katytimes.com
Year Established: 1912
Delivery Methods: Mail`Newsstand`Carrier`Racks
Own Printing Facility?: Y
Commercial printers?: N
Published Days: Thur
Avg Paid Circ: 4300
Audit Company: Sworn/Estimate/Non-Audited
Audit Date: 6 10 2019
Total Circulation: 6031

KAUFMAN
THE KAUFMAN HERALD

Corporate/Parent Company: Hartman Newspapers, L.P.
Street Address: 300 N Washington St
City: Kaufman
State: TX
Postal Code: 75142
Office phone: (972) 932-2171
Publication Website: http://www.kaufmanherald.com/
General E-mail: mmazur@kaufmanherald.com
Publisher Name: Melanie Mazur
Publisher Email: mlewis@kaufmanherald.com
Editor Name: Andrew Burnes
Editor Email: news@kaufmanherald.com
Advertising Executive Name: Amy Fowler
Advertising Executive Email: ads@kaufmanherald.com
Year Established: 1885
Delivery Methods: Mail`Racks
Mechanical specifications: Full page 21.50 inches by 11.25
Published Days: Thur
Avg Paid Circ: 2972
Avg Free Circ: 277
Audit Company: Sworn/Estimate/Non-Audited
Audit Date: 6 10 2019

KYLE
NEWS-DISPATCH

Street Address: 113 W. Center St
City: Kyle
State: TX
Postal Code: 78640
Office phone: 512-268-7862
Publication Website: haysnewsdispatch.com
Publisher Name: Cyndy Slovak-Barton
Publisher Email: csb@haysfreepress.com
Editor Name: Anita Miller
Editor Email: anita@bartonpublicationsinc.com
Advertising Executive Name: Tracy Mack
Advertising Executive Email: tracy@haysfreepress.com
Total Circulation: 1234

LA PORTE
BAY AREA OBSERVER

Street Address: PO Box 82
City: La Porte
State: TX
Postal Code: 77572
Office phone: 281-907-3140
Publication Website: bayareaobserver.com
Editor Name: Rebecca Collins
Editor Email: editor@bayareaobserver.com
Mailroom Equipment: Counter Stackers – 1/BG; Tying Machines – 1-/Bu.;
Buisness Equipment: IBM
Classified Equipment: Hardware – 5-APP/Mac; Printers – APP/Mac;
Classified Software: Baseview/Class Manager.
Editorial Equipment: Hardware – 5-APP/Mac; Printers – APP/Mac
Editorial Software: Baseview/NewsEdit Pro, QPS/QuarkXPress 4.0.
Production Equipment: Hardware – 1-LE/24 Q; Cameras – 1-Acti; Scanners – B
Production Software: QPS/QuarkXPress 4.0.
Total Circulation: 30135

LIBERTY
THE VINDICATOR

Corporate/Parent Company: Granite Publications
Street Address: 1939 Trinity St
City: Liberty
State: TX
Postal Code: 77575
Office phone: (936) 336-3611
Publication Website: https://www.thevindicator.com/
General E-mail: publisher@thevindicator.com
Publisher Name: Jennifer Richardson
Publisher Email: publisher@thevindicator.com
Editor Name: Casey Stinnett
Editor Email: editor@thevindicator.com
Advertising Executive Name: Kim Marlow
Advertising Executive Email: ads@thevindicator.com
Year Established: 1887
Delivery Methods: Mail`Racks
Mechanical specifications: Type page 10.25 x 21; E - 6 cols, 1.625", 1.250" between; A - 6 cols, 1.625", 1.25" between; C - 9 cols, 9.000", 1.250" between.
Published Days: Thur
Avg Paid Circ: 1019
Avg Free Circ: 732
Audit Company: Sworn/Estimate/Non-Audited
Audit Date: 6 10 2019
Total Circulation: 23637

LIVINGSTON
POLK COUNTY ENTERPRISE

Corporate/Parent Company: Polk County Publishing Co.
Street Address: 100 S Calhoun
City: Livingston
State: TX
Postal Code: 77351
Office phone: (936) 327-4357
Publication Website: https://polkenterprise.com/
General E-mail: manager@polkcountypublishing.com
Publisher Email: manager@polkcountypublishing.com
Year Established: 1904
Delivery Methods: Mail`Newsstand`Carrier`Racks
Own Printing Facility?: Y
Commercial printers?: Y
Published Days: Thur`Sun
Avg Paid Circ: 7673
Avg Free Circ: 83
Audit Company: Sworn/Estimate/Non-Audited
Audit Date: 6 10 2019
Mailroom Equipment: Tying Machines – 2/Bu; Address Machine – 1-/KAN.;
Buisness Equipment: PC
Buisness Software: BMF
Classified Equipment: Hardware – PC; Printers – APP/Mac LaserWriter
Classified Software: BMF.
Editorial Equipment: Hardware – PC; Printers – APP/Mac LaserWriter
Editorial Software: WordPerfect.
Production Equipment: Hardware – APP/Mac LaserWriter.
Total Circulation: 2500

SAN JACINTO NEWS-TIMES

Corporate/Parent Company: Polk County Publishing Co.
Street Address: 11010 TX-150 Shepherd
City: Livingston
State: TX
Postal Code: 77371
Office phone: (936) 628-6851
Publication Website: https://sanjacnews.com/
General E-mail: editor@sanjacnews.com
Editor Email: editor@sanjacnews.com
Year Established: 1904
Delivery Methods: Mail`Racks

Published Days: Thur
Avg Paid Circ: 2450
Avg Free Circ: 17
Audit Company: Sworn/Estimate/Non-Audited
Audit Date: 6 10 2019

MABANK

KERENS TRIBUNE

Corporate/Parent Company: Media-One, L.L.C
Street Address: 1316 S. Third Street, Suite 108
City: Mabank
State: TX
Postal Code: 75147
Office phone: (903) 887-4511
Publication Website: https://www.themonitor.net/article/news-monitor-and-kerens-tribune-launches-new-website
General E-mail: publisher@themonitor.net
Publisher Email: publisher@themonitor.net
Advertising Executive Name: Janice Grubbs-Vincik
Advertising Executive Email: janice@themonitor.net
Advertising Executive Phone: (903) 887-4511
Year Established: 1892
Delivery Methods: Mail`Newsstand
Own Printing Facility?: N
Commercial printers?: Y
Published Days: Fri
Avg Paid Circ: 905
Avg Free Circ: 78
Audit Company: Sworn/Estimate/Non-Audited
Audit Date: 6 10 2019

LAKE AREA LEADER

Corporate/Parent Company: Media-One, L.L.C
Street Address: 1316 S. Third Street, Suite 108
City: Mabank
State: TX
Postal Code: 75147
Office phone: (903) 887-4511
Publication Website: https://www.themonitor.net/
General E-mail: publisher@themonitor.net
Publisher Email: publisher@themonitor.net
Advertising Executive Name: Janice Grubbs-Vincik
Advertising Executive Email: janice@themonitor.net
Advertising Executive Phone: (903) 887-4511
Year Established: 1974
Delivery Methods: Mail
Published Days: Wed
Avg Free Circ: 26000
Audit Company: Sworn/Estimate/Non-Audited
Audit Date: 6 10 2019

MABANK MONITOR

Corporate/Parent Company: Media-One, L.L.C
Street Address: 1316 S. Third Street, Suite 108
City: Mabank
State: TX
Postal Code: 75147
Office phone: (903) 887-4511
Publication Website: https://www.themonitor.net/
General E-mail: publisher@themonitor.net
Publisher Email: publisher@themonitor.net
Advertising Executive Name: Janice Grubbs-Vincik
Advertising Executive Email: janice@themonitor.net
Advertising Executive Phone: (903) 887-4511

THE NEWS (ATHENS / MALAKOFF)

Corporate/Parent Company: Media-One, L.L.C
Street Address: 1316 S. Third Street, Suite 108
City: Mabank
State: TX
Postal Code: 75147
Office phone: (903) 887-4511
Publication Website: https://www.themonitor.net/article/news-monitor-and-kerens-tribune-launches-new-website
General E-mail: publisher@themonitor.net
Publisher Email: publisher@themonitor.net
Advertising Executive Name: Janice Grubbs-Vincik
Advertising Executive Email: janice@themonitor.net
Advertising Executive Phone: (903) 887-4511
Total Circulation: 45039

MADISONVILLE

MADISONVILLE METEOR

Corporate/Parent Company: Fenice Community Media
Street Address: 205 N Madison St
City: Madisonville
State: TX
Postal Code: 77864
Office phone: (936) 348-3505
Publication Website: http://madisonvillemeteor.com/
General E-mail: publisher@madisonvillemeteor.com
Publisher Name: Roy Reynolds
Publisher Email: publisher@madisonvillemeteor.com
Editor Name: Roy Reynolds
Editor Email: editor@madisonvillemeteor.com
Advertising Executive Email: classifieds@madisonvillemeteor.com
Advertising Executive Phone: (936) 348-3505
Year Established: 1894
Delivery Methods: Mail
Mechanical specifications: 10" x 21"
Published Days: Wed
Avg Paid Circ: 1197
Avg Free Circ: 37
Audit Company: CVC
Audit Date: 12 12 2017
Total Circulation: 7756

MOUNT PLEASANT

MOUNT PLEASANT DAILY TRIBUNE

Corporate/Parent Company: Moser Media
Street Address: 202 S. Van Buren
City: Mount Pleasant
State: TX
Postal Code: 75455
Office phone: (903) 572-1705
Publication Website: https://www.tribnow.com/
General E-mail: accounting@tribnow.com
Publisher Name: Toni Rowan
Publisher Email: trowan@tribnow.com
Editor Name: Miranda Oglesby
Editor Email: miranda@tribnow.com
Advertising Executive Name: Leslie Brosnan
Advertising Executive Email: leslie@tribnow.com
Year Established: 1941
Own Printing Facility?: N
Commercial printers?: N
Mechanical specifications: Type page 13 x 21; E - 6 cols, 2 1/16, 1/8 between; A - 6 cols, 2 1/16, 1/8 between; C - 8 cols, 1 9/16, 1/16 between.
Published Days: Tues`Wed`Thur`Fri`Sun
Weekday Frequency: e
Avg Paid Circ: 2500
Audit Company: Sworn/Estimate/Non-Audited
Audit Date: 7 12 2019
Pressroom Equipment: Lines – 5-HI/V-15A 1984; 2-HI/V-15A 1993.;
Total Circulation: 6500

NAVASOTA

THE NAVASOTA EXAMINER

Corporate/Parent Company: Fenice Community Media
Street Address: 115 Railroad Street
City: Navasota
State: TX
Postal Code: 77868
Office phone: (936) 825-6484
Publication Website: https://www.navasotaexaminer.com/
General E-mail: editor@navasotaexaminer.com
Publisher Name: Ana Cosino
Publisher Email: publisher@navasotaexaminer.com
Advertising Executive Name: Angela Scurlock
Advertising Executive Email: sales@navasotaexaminer.com
Year Established: 1894
Delivery Methods: Mail`Newsstand`Carrier`Racks
Own Printing Facility?: Y
Commercial printers?: Y
Mechanical specifications: Type page 11 5/8 x 21; E - 6 cols, 1 5/6, between; A - 6 cols, 1 5/6, between; C - 9 cols, 1 1/4, between.
Published Days: Wed
Avg Paid Circ: 3616
Avg Free Circ: 370
Audit Company: Sworn/Estimate/Non-Audited
Audit Date: 6 10 2019
Total Circulation: 3000

PARIS

THE PARIS NEWS

Corporate/Parent Company: Southern Newspapers Inc.
Street Address: 5050 SE Loop 286
City: Paris
State: TX
Postal Code: 75460
Office phone: (903) 785-8744
Publication Website: http://theparisnews.com/
General E-mail: support@theparisnews.com
Publisher Name: Relan Walker
Publisher Email: relan.walker@theparisnews.com
Publisher Phone: (903) 785-6970
Editor Name: Klark Byrd
Editor Email: klark.byrd@theparisnews.com
Editor Phone: (903) 785-6960, ext : 243
Advertising Executive Name: Clay Carsner
Advertising Executive Email: clay.carsner@theparisnews.com
Advertising Executive Phone: (903) 785-6924, ext : 233
Year Established: 1869
Delivery Methods: Mail`Newsstand`Carrier`Racks
Own Printing Facility?: Y
Commercial printers?: Y
Mechanical specifications: Type page 11 5/8 x 21 1/2; E - 6 cols, 2 5/8, 1/8 between; A - 6 cols, 2 5/8, 1/8 between; C - 9 cols, 1 3/8, 1/8 between.
Published Days: Mon`Tues`Wed`Thur`Fri`Sun
Weekday Frequency: e
Avg Paid Circ: 4335
Avg Free Circ: 134
Audit Company: AAM
Audit Date: 30 04 2019
Pressroom Equipment: Lines – 8-G/Community 1974.;
Total Circulation: 538

PASADENA

THE PASADENA CITIZEN

Corporate/Parent Company: Hearst Corp.
Street Address: 102 S. Shaver
City: Pasadena
State: TX
Postal Code: 77506
Office phone: 713.477.0221
Publication Website: chron.com/pasadena
Editor Name: Roy Kent
Editor Email: tcurtis@HCNonline.com
Advertising Executive Name: Tom Curtis
Advertising Executive Email: tcurtis@HCNonline.com
Total Circulation: 591

PEARLAND

FRIENDSWOOD REPORTER NEWS

Corporate/Parent Company: My Reporter News
Street Address: 2407 S. Park
City: Pearland
State: TX
Postal Code: 77581
Office phone: 281-485-7501
Publication Website: myreporternews.com
Publisher Name: Laura Emmons
Publisher Email: laurae3009@yahoo.com
Editor Name: Kelly Yung

PITTSBURG

THE STEEL COUNTRY BEE

Street Address: 112 Quitman
City: Pittsburg
State: TX
Postal Code: 75686
Office phone: 903-645-3948
Publication Website: steelcountrybee.com
Publisher Name: Toni Rowan
Publisher Email: trowan@tribnow.com
Editor Name: Toni Walker
Editor Email: news@steelcountrybee.com
Advertising Executive Name: Trisha Carey
Advertising Executive Email: advertising@campcountynow.com
Total Circulation: 6426

PLANO

ALLEN AMERICAN

Corporate/Parent Company: Star Local Media
Street Address: 3501 E Plano Parkway #200
City: Plano
State: TX
Postal Code: 75074
Office phone: (972) 398-4200
Publication Website: https://starlocalmedia.com/allenamerican/
General E-mail: jdittrich@starlocalmedia.com
Publisher Name: Joani Dittrich
Publisher Email: jdittrich@starlocalmedia.com
Publisher Phone: (972) 398-4472
Editor Name: Liz McGathey
Editor Email: lmcgathey@starlocalmedia.com
Editor Phone: (972) 398-4206
Advertising Executive Name: Joani Dittrich
Advertising Executive Email: jdittrich@starlocalmedia.com
Advertising Executive Phone: (972) 398-4472
Year Established: 1969
Delivery Methods: Mail`Newsstand
Mechanical specifications: Type page 13 x 21 1/2; E - 6 cols, 2 1/16, 1/8 between; A - 6 cols, 2 1/16, 1/8 between; C - 8 cols, 1 1/2, 1/8 between.
Published Days: Thur
Avg Paid Circ: 753
Avg Free Circ: 28234
Audit Company: Sworn/Estimate/Non-Audited
Audit Date: 6 10 2019

CARROLLTON LEADER

Corporate/Parent Company: Star Local Media
Street Address: 3501 E Plano Parkway #200
City: Plano
State: TX
Postal Code: 75074
Office phone: (972) 398-4200
Publication Website: https://starlocalmedia.com/carrolltonleader/
General E-mail: jdittrich@starlocalmedia.com
Publisher Name: Joani Dittrich
Publisher Email: jdittrich@starlocalmedia.com
Publisher Phone: (972) 398-4472
Editor Name: Chris Roark
Editor Email: croark@starlocalmedia.com
Editor Phone: (972) 398-4462
Advertising Executive Name: Joani Dittrich
Advertising Executive Email: jdittrich@

Non-Daily Newspapers in the U.S.

starlocalmedia.com
Advertising Executive Phone: (972) 398-4472
Year Established: 2001
Delivery Methods: Mail`Newsstand
Mechanical specifications: Type page 13 x 21 1/2; E - 6 cols, 2 1/16, 1/8 between; A - 6 cols, 2 1/16, 1/8 between; C - 8 cols, 1 1/2, 1/8 between.
Published Days: Sun
Avg Paid Circ: 209
Avg Free Circ: 1813
Audit Company: CVC
Audit Date: 31 12 2018

CELINA RECORD

Corporate/Parent Company: Star Local Media
Street Address: 3501 E Plano Parkway #200
City: Plano
State: TX
Postal Code: 75074
Office phone: (972) 398-4200
Publication Website: https://starlocalmedia.com/celinarecord/
General E-mail: jdittrich@starlocalmedia.com
Publisher Name: Joani Dittrich
Publisher Email: jdittrich@starlocalmedia.com
Publisher Phone: (972) 398-4472
Editor Name: Liz McGathey
Editor Email: lmcgathey@starlocalmedia.com
Editor Phone: (972) 398-4206
Advertising Executive Name: Joani Dittrich
Advertising Executive Email: jdittrich@starlocalmedia.com
Advertising Executive Phone: (972) 398-4472
Year Established: 1901
Delivery Methods: Mail`Newsstand
Mechanical specifications: Type page 13 x 21 1/2; E - 6 cols, 2 1/16, 1/8 between; A - 6 cols, 2 1/16, 1/8 between; C - 8 cols, 1 1/2, 1/8 between.
Published Days: Fri
Avg Paid Circ: 284
Avg Free Circ: 87
Audit Company: CVC
Audit Date: 31 12 2018
Total Circulation: 2467

COPPELL GAZETTE

Corporate/Parent Company: Star Local Media
Street Address: 3501 E Plano Parkway #200
City: Plano
State: TX
Postal Code: 75074
Office phone: (972) 398-4200
Publication Website: https://starlocalmedia.com/coppellgazette/
General E-mail: jdittrich@starlocalmedia.com
Publisher Name: Joani Dittrich
Publisher Email: jdittrich@starlocalmedia.com
Publisher Phone: (972) 398-4472
Editor Name: Chris Roark
Editor Email: croark@starlocalmedia.com
Editor Phone: (972) 398-4462
Advertising Executive Name: Joani Dittrich
Advertising Executive Email: jdittrich@starlocalmedia.com
Advertising Executive Phone: (972) 398-4472
Year Established: 1981
Delivery Methods: Mail`Newsstand
Mechanical specifications: Type page 13 x 21 1/2; E - 6 cols, 2 1/16, 1/8 between; A - 6 cols, 2 1/16, 1/8 between; C - 8 cols, 1 1/2, 1/8 between.
Published Days: Sun
Avg Paid Circ: 185
Avg Free Circ: 9305
Audit Company: CVC
Audit Date: 31 12 2018
Mailroom Equipment: Wrapping Singles – BY HAND;
Production Equipment: Cameras – canon
Total Circulation: 2500

FLOWER MOUND LEADER

Corporate/Parent Company: Star Local Media
Street Address: 3501 E Plano Parkway #200
City: Plano
State: TX
Postal Code: 75074
Office phone: (972) 398-4200
Publication Website: https://starlocalmedia.com/theleader/
General E-mail: jdittrich@starlocalmedia.com
Publisher Name: Joani Dittrich
Publisher Email: jdittrich@starlocalmedia.com
Publisher Phone: (972) 398-4472
Editor Name: Chris Roark
Editor Email: croark@starlocalmedia.com
Editor Phone: (972) 398-4462
Advertising Executive Name: Joani Dittrich
Advertising Executive Email: jdittrich@starlocalmedia.com
Advertising Executive Phone: (972) 398-4472
Delivery Methods: Mail`Newsstand
Mechanical specifications: Type page 13 x 21 1/2; E - 6 cols, 2 1/16, 1/8 between; A - 6 cols, 2 1/16, 1/8 between; C - 8 cols, 1 1/2, 1/8 between.
Published Days: Sun
Avg Paid Circ: 176
Avg Free Circ: 24867
Audit Company: CVC
Audit Date: 31 12 2018
Total Circulation: 2857

FRISCO ENTERPRISE

Corporate/Parent Company: Star Local Media
Street Address: 3501 E Plano Parkway #200
City: Plano
State: TX
Postal Code: 75074
Office phone: (972) 398-4200
Publication Website: https://starlocalmedia.com/friscoenterprise/
General E-mail: jdittrich@starlocalmedia.com
Publisher Name: Joani Dittrich
Publisher Email: jdittrich@starlocalmedia.com
Publisher Phone: (972) 398-4472
Editor Name: Chris Roark
Editor Email: croark@starlocalmedia.com
Editor Phone: (972) 398-4462
Advertising Executive Name: Joani Dittrich
Advertising Executive Email: jdittrich@starlocalmedia.com
Advertising Executive Phone: (972) 398-4472
Year Established: 1957
Delivery Methods: Mail`Newsstand
Mechanical specifications: Type page 13 x 21 1/2; E - 6 cols, 2 1/16, 1/8 between; A - 6 cols, 2 1/16, 1/8 between; C - 8 cols, 1 1/2, 1/8 between.
Published Days: Fri
Avg Paid Circ: 534
Avg Free Circ: 26210
Audit Company: CVC
Audit Date: 31 12 2018

LAKE CITIES SUN

Corporate/Parent Company: Star Local Media
Street Address: 3501 E Plano Parkway #200
City: Plano
State: TX
Postal Code: 75074
Office phone: (972) 398-4200
Publication Website: https://starlocalmedia.com/lakecitiessun/
General E-mail: jdittrich@starlocalmedia.com
Publisher Name: Joani Dittrich
Publisher Email: jdittrich@starlocalmedia.com
Publisher Phone: (972) 398-4472
Editor Name: Chris Roark
Editor Email: croark@starlocalmedia.com
Editor Phone: (972) 398-4462
Advertising Executive Name: Joani Dittrich

Advertising Executive Email: jdittrich@starlocalmedia.com
Advertising Executive Phone: (972) 398-4472
Year Established: 1974
Delivery Methods: Mail`Newsstand
Published Days: Sun
Avg Paid Circ: 163
Avg Free Circ: 5208
Audit Company: CVC
Audit Date: 31 12 2018

LEWISVILLE LEADER

Corporate/Parent Company: Star Local Media
Street Address: 3501 E Plano Parkway #200
City: Plano
State: TX
Postal Code: 75074
Office phone: (972) 398-4200
Publication Website: https://starlocalmedia.com/lewisvilleleader/
General E-mail: jdittrich@starlocalmedia.com
Publisher Name: Joani Dittrich
Publisher Email: jdittrich@starlocalmedia.com
Publisher Phone: (972) 398-4472
Editor Name: Chris Roark
Editor Email: croark@starlocalmedia.com
Editor Phone: (972) 398-4462
Advertising Executive Name: Joani Dittrich
Advertising Executive Email: jdittrich@starlocalmedia.com
Advertising Executive Phone: (972) 398-4472
Delivery Methods: Mail`Newsstand
Mechanical specifications: Type page 13 x 21 1/2; E - 6 cols, 2 1/16, 1/8 between; A - 6 cols, 2 1/16, 1/8 between; C - 8 cols, 1 1/2, 1/8 between.
Published Days: Sun
Avg Paid Circ: 207
Avg Free Circ: 11345
Audit Company: CVC
Audit Date: 31 12 2018
Mailroom Equipment: Counter Stackers – 1-BG/Count-O-Veyor; Inserters & Stuffers – 1-KAN/320 with quarterfold; Tying Machines – 1/Malow; Address Machine – 1-/KR.;
Buisness Equipment: 1-IBM/System 34
Classified Equipment: Hardware – 2-APP/Mac, 1-IBM;
Classified Software: Baseview,
Editorial Equipment: Hardware – 5-APP/Mac; Printers – Konica/Imagesetter, ECR/Imagesetter
Editorial Software: QPS/Indesign CS Cloud
Production Equipment: Hardware – 1-Nu/Flip Top, Konica/Imagesetter, ECR/Imagesetter; Cameras - 1-C/Spartan III; Scanners - 1-GAM
Production Software: QPS/Indesign CS Cloud
Total Circulation: 2405

LITTLE ELM JOURNAL

Corporate/Parent Company: Star Local Media
Street Address: 3501 E Plano Parkway #200
City: Plano
State: TX
Postal Code: 75074
Office phone: (972) 398-4200
Publication Website: https://starlocalmedia.com/littleelmjournal/
General E-mail: jdittrich@starlocalmedia.com
Publisher Name: Joani Dittrich
Publisher Email: jdittrich@starlocalmedia.com
Publisher Phone: (972) 398-4472
Editor Name: Chris Roark
Editor Email: croark@starlocalmedia.com
Editor Phone: (972) 398-4462
Advertising Executive Name: Joani Dittrich
Advertising Executive Email: jdittrich@starlocalmedia.com
Advertising Executive Phone: (972) 398-4472
Year Established: 1993
Delivery Methods: Mail`Newsstand
Mechanical specifications: Type page 13 x 21 1/2; E - 6 cols, 2 1/16, 1/8 between; A - 6 cols, 2 1/16, 1/8 between; C - 8 cols, 1 1/2,

1/8 between.
Published Days: Fri
Avg Paid Circ: 110
Avg Free Circ: 5921
Audit Company: CVC
Audit Date: 31 12 2018
Total Circulation: 3859

MCKINNEY COURIER GAZETTE

Corporate/Parent Company: Star Local Media
Street Address: 3501 E Plano Parkway #200
City: Plano
State: TX
Postal Code: 75074
Office phone: (972) 398-4200
Publication Website: https://starlocalmedia.com/mckinneycouriergazette/
General E-mail: jdittrich@starlocalmedia.com
Publisher Name: Joani Dittrich
Publisher Email: jdittrich@starlocalmedia.com
Publisher Phone: (972) 398-4472
Editor Name: Liz McGathey
Editor Email: lmcgathey@starlocalmedia.com
Editor Phone: (972) 398-4206
Advertising Executive Name: Joani Dittrich
Advertising Executive Email: jdittrich@starlocalmedia.com
Advertising Executive Phone: (972) 398-4472
Year Established: 1991
Delivery Methods: Mail`Newsstand
Mechanical specifications: Type page 13 x 21 1/2; E - 6 cols, 2 1/16, 1/8 between; A - 6 cols, 2 1/16, 1/8 between; C - 8 cols, 1 1/2, 1/8 between.
Published Days: Sun
Weekday Frequency: e
Avg Paid Circ: 684
Avg Free Circ: 29451
Audit Company: CVC
Audit Date: 14 12 2018
Pressroom Equipment: Lines – 6-HI/V-15A; Folders – 1-HI.;
Total Circulation: 7024

MESQUITE NEWS

Corporate/Parent Company: Star Local Media
Street Address: 3501 E Plano Parkway #200
City: Plano
State: TX
Postal Code: 75074
Office phone: (972) 398-4200
Publication Website: https://starlocalmedia.com/mesquitenews/
General E-mail: jdittrich@starlocalmedia.com
Publisher Name: Joani Dittrich
Publisher Email: jdittrich@starlocalmedia.com
Publisher Phone: (972) 398-4472
Advertising Executive Name: Joani Dittrich
Advertising Executive Email: jdittrich@starlocalmedia.com
Advertising Executive Phone: (972) 398-4472
Year Established: 1882
Delivery Methods: Mail`Newsstand
Mechanical specifications: Type page 13 x 21 1/2; E - 6 cols, 2 1/16, 1/8 between; A - 6 cols, 2 1/16, 1/8 between; C - 8 cols, 1 1/2, 1/8 between.
Published Days: Thur
Avg Paid Circ: 284
Avg Free Circ: 23353
Audit Company: CVC
Audit Date: 31 12 2018
Total Circulation: 2918

PLANO STAR COURIER

Corporate/Parent Company: Star Local Media
Street Address: 3501 E Plano Parkway #200
City: Plano
State: TX
Postal Code: 75074
Office phone: (972) 398-4200

Publication Website: https://starlocalmedia.com/planocourier/
General E-mail: jdittrich@starlocalmedia.com
Publisher Name: Joani Dittrich
Publisher Email: jdittrich@starlocalmedia.com
Publisher Phone: (972) 398-4472
Editor Name: Matt Welch
Editor Email: mwelch@starlocalmedia.com
Editor Phone: (972) 398-4268
Advertising Executive Name: Joani Dittrich
Advertising Executive Email: jdittrich@starlocalmedia.com
Advertising Executive Phone: (972) 398-4472
Year Established: 1889
Delivery Methods: Mail`Newsstand
Mechanical specifications: Type page 13 x 21 1/2; E - 6 cols, 2 1/16, 1/8 between; A - 6 cols, 2 1/16, 1/8 between; C - 8 cols, 1 1/2, 1/8 between.
Published Days: Thur`Sun
Avg Paid Circ: 993
Avg Free Circ: 44046
Audit Company: CVC
Audit Date: 31 12 2018

ROWLETT LAKESHORE TIMES

Corporate/Parent Company: Star Local Media
Street Address: 3501 E Plano Parkway #200
City: Plano
State: TX
Postal Code: 75074
Office phone: (972) 398-4200
Publication Website: https://starlocalmedia.com/rowlettlakeshoretimes/
General E-mail: jdittrich@starlocalmedia.com
Publisher Name: Joani Dittrich
Publisher Email: jdittrich@starlocalmedia.com
Publisher Phone: (972) 398-4472
Advertising Executive Name: Joani Dittrich
Advertising Executive Email: jdittrich@starlocalmedia.com
Advertising Executive Phone: (972) 398-4472
Year Established: 1982
Delivery Methods: Mail`Newsstand
Mechanical specifications: Type page 13 x 21 1/2; E - 6 cols, 2 1/16, 1/8 between; A - 6 cols, 2 1/16, 1/8 between; C - 8 cols, 1 1/2, 1/8 between.
Published Days: Thur
Avg Paid Circ: 174
Avg Free Circ: 6252
Audit Company: CVC
Audit Date: 31 12 2018
Total Circulation: 3365

THE COLONY COURIER LEADER

Corporate/Parent Company: Star Local Media
Street Address: 3501 E Plano Parkway #200
City: Plano
State: TX
Postal Code: 75074
Office phone: (972) 398-4200
Publication Website: https://starlocalmedia.com/thecolonycourierleader/
General E-mail: jdittrich@starlocalmedia.com
Publisher Name: Joani Dittrich
Publisher Email: jdittrich@starlocalmedia.com
Publisher Phone: (972) 398-4472
Editor Name: Chris Roark
Editor Email: croark@starlocalmedia.com
Editor Phone: (972) 398-4462
Advertising Executive Name: Joani Dittrich
Advertising Executive Email: jdittrich@starlocalmedia.com
Advertising Executive Phone: (972) 398-4472
Year Established: 1981
Delivery Methods: Mail`Newsstand
Mechanical specifications: Type page 13 x 21 1/2; E - 6 cols, 2 1/16, 1/8 between; A - 6 cols, 2 1/16, 1/8 between; C - 8 cols, 1 1/2, 1/8 between.
Published Days: Sun
Avg Paid Circ: 223
Avg Free Circ: 6801
Audit Company: CVC

Audit Date: 31 12 2018
Total Circulation: 2277

PORT LAVACA

PORT LAVACA WAVE

Corporate/Parent Company: Hartman Newspapers, L.P.
Street Address: 107 E Austin St
City: Port Lavaca
State: TX
Postal Code: 77979
Office phone: (361) 552-9788
Publication Website: http://www.portlavacawave.com/
General E-mail: publisher@plwave.com
Publisher Name: Tania French
Publisher Email: tmartinez@plwave.com
Advertising Executive Email: classads@plwave.com
Year Established: 1890
Delivery Methods: Mail`Newsstand`Racks
Own Printing Facility?: Y
Commercial printers?: Y
Published Days: Wed`Sat
Avg Paid Circ: 4200
Avg Free Circ: 2300
Audit Company: Sworn/Estimate/Non-Audited
Audit Date: 6 10 2019
Mailroom Equipment: Tying Machines – 1-Bu/64808.;
Classified Software: Baseview/Class Manager.
Editorial Equipment: Hardware – APP/Mac/4-APP/Mac.
Production Equipment: Hardware – 3-APP/Mac LaserWriter Plus; Cameras – R/500; Scanners – 2-COM/MDR.
Total Circulation: 4500

RAYMONDVILLE

CHRONICLE/WILLACY COUNTY NEWS

Street Address: 192 N. 4th Street
City: Raymondville
State: TX
Postal Code: 78580
Office phone: 956-689-6575
Publication Website: raymondville-chronicle.com
Publisher Name: Diana Whitworth Nelson
Publisher Email: diana@raymondville-chronicle.com
Total Circulation: 6600

ROCKPORT

THE ROCKPORT PILOT

Corporate/Parent Company: Hartman Newspapers, L.P.
Street Address: 1002 E Wharf St
City: Rockport
State: TX
Postal Code: 78382
Office phone: (361) 729-9900
Publication Website: http://www.rockportpilot.com/
General E-mail: displayadvertising@rockportpilot.com
Publisher Name: Mike Probst
Publisher Email: publisher@rockportpilot.com
Editor Name: Mike Probst
Editor Email: publisher@rockportpilot.com
Year Established: 1869
Delivery Methods: Mail`Newsstand`Racks
Published Days: Wed`Sat
Audit Company: Sworn/Estimate/Non-Audited
Audit Date: 6 10 2019
Total Circulation: 4300

ROUND ROCK

ROUND ROCK LEADER

Corporate/Parent Company: Gannett
Street Address: 1111 N. Interstate Ste 230

City: Round Rock
State: TX
Postal Code: 78664-5807
Office phone: 512-255-5827
Publication Website: rrleader.com
Publisher Name: Patrick Dorsey
Publisher Email: publisher@statesman.com
Publisher Phone: 512-445-3555
Editor Name: John Bridges
Editor Email: jbridges@statesman.com
Editor Phone: 512-912-2952
Advertising Executive Name: Scott Pompe
Advertising Executive Email: spompe@statesman.com
Advertising Executive Phone: 512-445-3715
Total Circulation: 3249

ROXTON

ROXTON PROGRESS

Street Address: PO Box 343
City: Roxton
State: TX
Postal Code: 75477
Office phone: 903-502-0795
Publication Website: theroxtonprogress.com
Publisher Name: Kristopher & Karen Rutherford
Publisher Email: publisher@theroxtonprogress.com
Total Circulation: 2525

SCHULENBURG

SCHULENBURG STICKER

Street Address: P. O. Box 160
City: Schulenburg
State: TX
Postal Code: 78956
Office phone: 979-743-3450
Publication Website: schulenburgsticker.com
Publisher Name: Maxine Vyvjala
Editor Name: Diane Prause/Darrell Vyvjala
Editor Email: news@schulenburgsticker.com
Advertising Executive Name: Carla Ricicar
Advertising Executive Email: ads@schulenburgsticker.com
Year Established: 1894
Delivery Methods: Mail`Newsstand
Mechanical specifications: Type page 13 x 21; E - 6 cols, 2 1/16, 1/8 between; A - 6 cols, 2 1/16, 1/8 between; C - 6 cols, 2 1/16, 1/8 between.
Published Days: Thur
Avg Paid Circ: 2823
Avg Free Circ: 34
Audit Company: Sworn/Estimate/Non-Audited
Audit Date: 6 10 2019
Total Circulation: 3986

SEALY

THE SEALY NEWS

Corporate/Parent Company: Fenice Community Media
Street Address: 193 Schmidt Rd
City: Sealy
State: TX
Postal Code: 77474
Office phone: (979) 885-3562
Publication Website: http://sealynews.com/
General E-mail: publisher@sealynews.com
Publisher Name: Amy Lieb
Publisher Email: publisher@sealynews.com
Editor Name: Joe Southern
Editor Email: editor@sealynews.com
Advertising Executive Email: sales@sealynews.com
Year Established: 1887
Delivery Methods: Mail`Newsstand
Mechanical specifications: Type page 13 x 21 1/2; E - 6 cols, 2 1/16, 1/8 between; A - 6 cols, 2 1/16, 1/8 between; C - 9 cols, 1 3/8, 1/16 between.
Published Days: Thur
Avg Paid Circ: 3972
Avg Free Circ: 94
Audit Company: Sworn/Estimate/Non-Audited
Audit Date: 6 10 2019

SEGUIN

THE SEGUIN GAZETTE

Corporate/Parent Company: Southern Newspapers Inc.
Street Address: 1012 Schriewer
City: Seguin
State: TX
Postal Code: 78155
Office phone: (830) 379-5404
Publication Website: http://seguingazette.com/
General E-mail: support@seguingazette.com
Publisher Name: Elizabeth Engelhardt
Publisher Email: elizabeth.engelhardt@seguingazette.com
Publisher Phone: (830) 379-5441, ext : 206
Editor Name: Felicia Frazar
Editor Email: felicia.frazar@seguingazette.com
Editor Phone: (830) 379-5441, ext : 218
Year Established: 1888
Delivery Methods: Mail`Newsstand`Carrier`Racks
Own Printing Facility?: N
Commercial printers?: N
Published Days: Tues`Wed`Thur`Fri`Sun
Weekday Frequency: m
Avg Paid Circ: 2591
Avg Free Circ: 1025
Audit Company: CAC
Audit Date: 31 03 2017
Total Circulation: 2035

SHERMAN

VAN ALSTYNE LEADER

Corporate/Parent Company: Gannett
Street Address: 603 S Sam Rayburn Fwy
City: Sherman
State: TX
Postal Code: 75090
Office phone: 903-893-8181
Publication Website: vanalstyneleader.com
Publisher Name: Nate Rodriguez
Publisher Email: nrodriguez@heralddemocrat.com
Publisher Phone: 903-893-8181 ext. 1100
Editor Name: William C. Wadsack
Editor Email: wwadsack@heralddemocrat.com
Editor Phone: 903-893-8181 ext. 1138
Advertising Executive Name: Teresa Young
Advertising Executive Email: tyoung@heralddemocrat.com
Advertising Executive Phone: 903-893-8181 ext. 1120
Mailroom Equipment: Tying Machines – MLN/ML2 Et; Address Machine – Uarco/4930.;
Buisness Equipment: 1-Compaq/Proliant 1600, 5-HP/Vectra VL2
Buisness Software: Netware, Circ
Classified Equipment: Hardware – APP/Mac; Printers – APP/Mac LaserWriter II NTX;
Classified Software: Baseview.
Editorial Equipment: Hardware – APP/Mac/AG/Accuset 1000, Microtek/ScanMaker III, Polaroid/SprintScan; Printers – APP/Mac LaserWriter
Editorial Software: QPS/QuarkXPress, Baseview/NewsEdit.
Production Equipment: Hardware – Caere/OmniPage Pro, AG/Accuset 1000, APP/Mac LaserWriter 1600-600; Cameras – LE, R/500; Scanners – Microtek/ScanMaker III, Microtek/ScanMaker II, Polaroid/SprintScan
Production Software: QPS/QuarkXPress 3.32.
Total Circulation: 4927

SINTON

SAN PATRICIO COUNTY NEWS

Corporate/Parent Company: MYSoutx.com
Street Address: 104 N Sehorn St
City: Sinton
State: TX
Postal Code: 78387
Office phone: (361) 364-1270
Publication Website: https://www.mysoutex.com/san_patricio_county/

Non-Daily Newspapers in the U.S.

General E-mail: sintonoffice@mysoutex.com
Editor Email: media@mysoutex.com
Advertising Executive Email: ads@mysoutex.com
Year Established: 1901
Delivery Methods: Mail`Newsstand`Racks
Own Printing Facility?: Y
Commercial printers?: Y
Mechanical specifications: Type page 10 7/8 x 21 1/2
Published Days: Thur
Weekday Frequency: All day
Saturday Frequency: All day
Avg Paid Circ: 2500
Audit Company: Sworn/Estimate/Non-Audited
Audit Date: 6 10 2019

SULPHUR SPRINGS

NEWS TELEGRAM

Street Address: 401 Church St., Suite B
City: Sulphur Springs
State: TX
Postal Code: 75482
Office phone: (903) 885-8663
Publication Website: https://www.ssnewstelegram.com/
General E-mail: publisher@ssnewstelegram.com
Publisher Name: Clark Smith
Publisher Email: publisher@ssnewstelegram.com
Editor Name: Jillian Smith
Editor Email: jillian.smith@ssnewstelegram.com
Advertising Executive Name: Dave Shabaz
Advertising Executive Email: dshabaz@ssnewstelegram.com

NEWS-TELEGRAM

Street Address: 401 Church St., Suite B
City: Sulphur Springs
State: TX
Postal Code: 75482
Office phone: 903-885-8663
Publication Website: ssnewstelegram.com
Publisher Name: Clark Smith
Publisher Email: publisher@ssnewstelegram.com
Editor Name: Jillian Smith
Editor Email: jillian.smith@ssnewstelegram.com
Advertising Executive Name: Dave Shabaz
Advertising Executive Email: dshabaz@ssnewstelegram.com

TAYLOR

TAYLOR PRESS

Corporate/Parent Company: Granite Publications
Street Address: 211 W 3rd St
City: Taylor
State: TX
Postal Code: 76574
Office phone: (512) 3528535
Publication Website: https://taylorpress.net/
General E-mail: news@taylorpress.net
Publisher Name: Jason Hennington
Publisher Email: news@taylorpress.net
Editor Name: Jason Hennington
Advertising Executive Name: Regina Taylor
Advertising Executive Email: regina.taylor@taylorpress.net
Year Established: 1911
Delivery Methods: Mail`Newsstand`Racks
Own Printing Facility?: Y
Commercial printers?: Y
Mechanical specifications: Type page 10 x 21; E - 6 cols, 2 1/16, 1/8 between; A - 6 cols, 2 1/16, 1/8 between; C - 9 cols, 1 3/8, 1/16 between.
Published Days: Wed`Sun
Weekday Frequency: m
Saturday Frequency: m
Avg Paid Circ: 2233
Avg Free Circ: 172
Audit Company: CVC

Audit Date: 30 09 2016
Pressroom Equipment: Lines – 7-G/Community;

THE HUTTO NEWS

Corporate/Parent Company: Granite Publications
Street Address: 211 W 3rd St
City: Taylor
State: TX
Postal Code: 76574
Office phone: (512) 352-8535
Publication Website: https://taylorpress.net/thehuttonews/
General E-mail: news@taylorpress.net
Publisher Name: Jason Hennington
Publisher Email: news@taylorpress.net
Editor Name: Jason Hennington
Advertising Executive Name: Regina Taylor
Advertising Executive Email: regina.taylor@taylorpress.net
Delivery Methods: Carrier`Racks
Mechanical specifications: Type page 11 5/8 x 21 1/2; E - 6 cols, between; A - 6 cols, between; C - 6 cols, between.
Published Days: Wed
Avg Paid Circ: 100
Avg Free Circ: 6500
Audit Company: Sworn/Estimate/Non-Audited
Audit Date: 6 10 2019
Total Circulation: 4066

TEXAS CITY

THE POST NEWSPAPER

Street Address: 501-6th Street
City: Texas City
State: TX
Postal Code: 77591
Office phone: 409-943-4265
Publication Website: thepostnewspaper.net
General E-mail: info@thepostnewspaper.net
Publisher Name: David Day
Publisher Email: publisher@thepostnewspaper.net
Editor Name: Brandon Williams
Advertising Executive Name: Ulanda Bounds
Total Circulation: 3616

TRINITY

THE TRINITY STANDARD

Corporate/Parent Company: Polk County Publishing Co.
Street Address: 112 E Main Trinity
City: Trinity
State: TX
Postal Code: 75862
Office phone: (936) 594-2126
Publication Website: https://trinityconews.com/
General E-mail: editor@trinityconews.com
Editor Email: editor@trinityconews.com
Year Established: 1928
Delivery Methods: Mail`Newsstand`Racks
Mechanical specifications: Type page 13 x 21; E - 6 cols, between; A - 6 cols, between; C - 6 cols, between.
Published Days: Thur
Avg Paid Circ: 2800
Audit Company: Sworn/Estimate/Non-Audited
Audit Date: 6 10 2019

TRINITY COUNTY NEWS-STANDARD

Street Address: 112 E Main
City: Trinity
State: TX
Postal Code: 75862
Office phone: (936) 594-2126
Publication Website: trinityconews.com
General E-mail: trinity.standard@gmail.com
Publisher Name: Alvin Holley
Editor Name: Jason Chlapek
Editor Email: editor@trinityconews.com
Advertising Executive Name: Eddie Wilson

Total Circulation: 2800

TURKEY

CAPROCK COURIER

Street Address: 904 Childress Ave
City: Turkey
State: TX
Postal Code: 79261
Office phone: 806-620-5244
Publication Website: caprockcourier.com
Publisher Name: Tori Leigh Minick
Publisher Email: caprockcourier@gmail.com
Total Circulation: 1751

WHARTON

EAST BERNARD EXPRESS

Corporate/Parent Company: Hartman Newspapers, L.P.
Street Address: 115 W Burleson St
City: Wharton
State: TX
Postal Code: 77488
Office phone: (979) 532-8840
Publication Website: http://www.journal-spectator.com/east_bernard_express/
General E-mail: news@journal-spectator.com
Publisher Name: Bill Wallace
Publisher Email: bwallace@journal-spectator.com
Editor Name: Bill Wallace
Editor Email: bwallace@journal-spectator.com
Advertising Executive Name: Helen Halvorson
Advertising Executive Email: classified@journal-spectator.com
Year Established: 1949
Delivery Methods: Mail`Racks
Published Days: Thur
Avg Paid Circ: 1000
Audit Company: Sworn/Estimate/Non-Audited
Audit Date: 6 10 2019

WHARTON JOURNAL-SPECTATOR

Corporate/Parent Company: Hartman Newspapers, L.P.
Street Address: 115 W Burleson St
City: Wharton
State: TX
Postal Code: 77488
Office phone: (979) 532-8840
Publication Website: http://www.journal-spectator.com/
General E-mail: news@journal-spectator.com
Publisher Name: Bill Wallace
Publisher Email: bwallace@journal-spectator.com
Editor Name: Bill Wallace
Editor Email: bwallace@journal-spectator.com
Advertising Executive Name: Helen Halvorson
Advertising Executive Email: classified@journal-spectator.com
Year Established: 1889
Delivery Methods: Mail`Newsstand`Carrier`Racks
Mechanical specifications: 1 - column = 1.833 inches 2 - column = 3.792 inches 3 - column = 5.750 inches 4 - column = 7.708 inches 5 - column = 9.667 inches 6 - column = 11.625 inches
Published Days: Wed`Sat
Avg Paid Circ: 4500
Audit Company: Sworn/Estimate/Non-Audited
Audit Date: 6 10 2019
Total Circulation: 4750

WILLS POINT

QUINLAN-TAWAKONI NEWS

Corporate/Parent Company: Van Zandt Newspapers LLC
Street Address: 109 N. 5th Street
City: Wills Point
State: TX

Postal Code: 75169
Office phone: (903) 567-4000
Publication Website: https://www.quinlan-tawakoninews.com
General E-mail: editor@vanzandtnews.com
Publisher Name: Brad Blakemore
Publisher Email: brad@vanzandtnews.com
Publisher Phone: (903) 567-4000
Editor Name: Britne Hammons
Editor Email: editor@vanzandtnews.com
Editor Phone: (903) 567-4000
Advertising Executive Name: David Barber
Advertising Executive Email: sales@vanzandtnews.com
Advertising Executive Phone: (903) 567-4000
Year Established: 1963
Delivery Methods: Mail`Newsstand
Published Days: Fri
Avg Paid Circ: 3000
Audit Company: Sworn/Estimate/Non-Audited
Audit Date: 6 10 2019

WILLS POINT CHRONICLE

Corporate/Parent Company: Van Zandt Newspapers LLC
Street Address: 109 N. 5th Street
City: Wills Point
State: TX
Postal Code: 75169
Office phone: (903) 567-4000
Publication Website: https://www.willspointchronicle.com/
General E-mail: editor@vanzandtnews.com
Publisher Name: Brad Blakemore
Publisher Email: brad@vanzandtnews.com
Publisher Phone: (903) 567-4000
Editor Name: Britne Hammons
Editor Email: editor@vanzandtnews.com
Editor Phone: (903) 567-4000
Advertising Executive Name: David Barber
Advertising Executive Email: sales@vanzandtnews.com
Advertising Executive Phone: (903) 567-4000
Year Established: 1879
Delivery Methods: Mail`Newsstand`Racks
Published Days: Fri
Avg Paid Circ: 3051
Avg Free Circ: 500
Audit Company: Sworn/Estimate/Non-Audited
Audit Date: 6 10 2019
Total Circulation: 694

WINNIE

SEABREEZE BEACON

Street Address: 1354 SH 124
City: Winnie
State: TX
Postal Code: 77665
Office phone: (409) 296-2102
Publication Website: theseabreezebeacon.com
Editor Name: Gloria Roemer
Editor Email: seabreezebeacon@gmail.com
Total Circulation: 5600

WOODVILLE

TYLER COUNTY BOOSTER

Corporate/Parent Company: Polk County Publishing Co.
Street Address: 205 W Bluff St
City: Woodville
State: TX
Postal Code: 75979
Office phone: (409) 283-2516
Publication Website: https://tylercountybooster.com/
General E-mail: manager@tylercountybooster.com
Publisher Name: manager@tylercountybooster.com
Year Established: 1930
Delivery Methods: Mail`Newsstand`Racks
Published Days: Thur
Avg Paid Circ: 3750

Avg Free Circ: 1000
Audit Company: Sworn/Estimate/Non-Audited
Audit Date: 6 10 2019
Total Circulation: 4500

UTAH

BEAVER

BEAVER COUNTY JOURNAL

Street Address: 55 S Main St
City: Beaver
State: UT
Postal Code: 84713
Office phone: 435-438-5950
Publication Website: www.beavercountyjournal.com
General E-mail: bcjnews@infowest.com
Total Circulation: 3551

CEDAR CITY

IRON COUNTY TODAY

Corporate/Parent Company: R. Gail Stahle
Street Address: 389 North 100 West, Suite 12
City: Cedar City
State: UT
Postal Code: 84721
Office phone: 435-867-1865
Publication Website: ironcountytoday.com
Publisher Name: R. Gail Stahle
Publisher Email: gail@ironcountytoday.com
Publisher Phone: 801-295-2251 Ext. 114

ESCALANTE

THE INSIDER

Corporate/Parent Company: Snapshot Multimedia, LLC
Street Address: P.O. Box 105
City: Escalante
State: UT
Postal Code: 84726
Office phone: 435-826-4400
Publication Website: www.insiderutah.com
General E-mail: snapshot@live.com
Publisher Name: Erica Walz

HEBER CITY

SUMMIT COUNTY NEWS

Street Address: 165 S. 100 West
City: Heber City
State: UT
Postal Code: 84032
Office phone: 435-654-1471
Publication Website: www.wasatchwave.com

KANAB

SOUTHERN UTAH NEWS

Street Address: 245 S. 200 E.
City: Kanab
State: UT
Postal Code: 84741
Office phone: 435-644-2900
Publication Website: www.sunews.net

MOAB

TIMES-INDEPENDENT

Street Address: 35 East Center Street
City: Moab
State: UT
Postal Code: 84532
Office phone: 435-259-7525
Publication Website: www.moabtimes.com
General E-mail: advertising@moabtimes.com

MONTICELLO

SAN JUAN RECORD

Street Address: PO Box 879 49 S. Main St
City: Monticello
State: UT
Postal Code: 84535
Office phone: 435-587-2277
Publication Website: www.sjrnews.com
General E-mail: sjrnews@frontiernet.net

MORGAN

MORGAN COUNTY NEWS

Corporate/Parent Company: Landmark Community Newspapers
Street Address: PO Box 190
City: Morgan
State: UT
Postal Code: 84050
Office phone: 801-829-3451
Publication Website: morgannews.com
General E-mail: gstahle@davisclipper.com
Publisher Name: Gail Stahle

MURRAY

INTERMOUNTAIN COMMERCIAL RECORD/ SALT LAKE TIMES

Corporate/Parent Company: Utah Legal Publishing LLC
Street Address: 111 E 5600 S #202
City: Murray
State: UT
Postal Code: 84107
Office phone: 801.972.5642
Publication Website: slcrecord.com
General E-mail: icr@slcrecord.com

PROVO

PYRAMID

Corporate/Parent Company: Herald Communications
Street Address: 86 N. University Ave. #300
City: Provo
State: UT
Postal Code: 84604
Office phone: 801-375-5103
Publication Website: www.heraldextra.com/sanpete-county
General E-mail: pyramid@heraldextra.com
Publisher Name: SCOTT BLONDE
Publisher Email: sblonde@standard.net
Publisher Phone: 801-344-2935

ROOSEVELT

UINTAH BASIN STANDARD

Corporate/Parent Company: Brehm Communications Inc.
Street Address: 268 Main St
City: Roosevelt
State: UT
Postal Code: 84066
Office phone: 435-722-5131
Publication Website: ubmedia.biz/live-content/uintah-basin-standard
General E-mail: editor@ubmedia.biz

TOOELE

TOOELE TRANSCRIPT-BULLETIN

Corporate/Parent Company: Transcript Bulletin Publishing
Street Address: 58 N Main St
City: Tooele
State: UT
Postal Code: 84074
Office phone: 435-882-0050
Publication Website: tooeleonline.com
Publisher Name: Scott Dunn
Publisher Email: tbp@tooeletranscript.com

VERNAL

VERNAL EXPRESS

Corporate/Parent Company: Brehm Communications Inc.
Street Address: 60 East 100 North
City: Vernal
State: UT
Postal Code: 84078
Office phone: (435)938-7112
Publication Website: ubmedia.biz/live-content/vernal-express

WENDOVER

WENDOVER TIMES

Street Address: P.O. Box 805
City: Wendover
State: UT
Postal Code: 84083
Office phone: 775-664-2101
Publication Website: www.wendovertimes.com
General E-mail: news@wendovertimes.com
Publisher Name: Randy Croasmun
Publisher Phone: 775-408-0011

THE CROSSROADS JOURNAL

State: UT
Publication Website: www.thecrossroadsjournal.com
Publisher Name: Wendy Visser Lojik

VIRGINIA

VIRGINIA BEACH

PRINCESS ANNE INDEPENDENT NEWS, THE

Street Address: P.O. Box 7064
City: Virginia Beach
State: VA
Postal Code: 23457
Office phone: 757-502-5393
Publication Website: princessanneindy.com
Editor Name: John Doucette
Editor Email: jhd@princessanneindy.com

ACCOMAC

CHINCOTEAGUE BEACON-OOB

Street Address: 23079 Courthouse Ave
City: Accomac
State: VA
Postal Code: 23301
Office phone: (757) 787-1200
Publication Website: https://www.delmarvanow.com/
General E-mail: sbyclass@gannett.com
Advertising Executive Name: Ron Pousson
Advertising Executive Email: rpousson@localiq.com
Advertising Executive Phone: (410) 845-4609

ALEXANDRIA

ALEXANDRIA GAZETTE PACKET

Corporate/Parent Company: Ogden Newspapers Inc.
Street Address: 1606 King St
City: Alexandria
State: VA
Postal Code: 22314
Office phone: (703) 778-9431
Publication Website: http://www.alexandriagazette.com/
General E-mail: gazette@connectionnewspapers.com
Publisher Name: Mary Kimm
Publisher Email: mkimm@connectionnewspapers.com
Editor Name: Mary Kimm
Editor Email: mkimm@connectionnewspapers.com
Year Established: 1784
Delivery Methods: Mail Newsstand
Published Days: Thur
Avg Paid Circ: 105
Avg Free Circ: 10114
Audit Company: Sworn/Estimate/Non-Audited
Audit Date: 6 10 2019
Total Circulation: 10219

ARLINGTON CONNECTION

Corporate/Parent Company: Connection Newspapers
Street Address: 1606 King St
City: Alexandria
State: VA
Postal Code: 22314
Office phone: (703) 778-9431
Publication Website: http://www.arlingtonconnection.com/
General E-mail: gazette@connectionnewspapers.com
Publisher Name: Mary Kimm
Publisher Email: mkimm@connectionnewspapers.com
Editor Name: Mary Kimm
Editor Email: mkimm@connectionnewspapers.com
Year Established: 1988
Delivery Methods: Mail Newsstand
Published Days: Thur
Avg Free Circ: 5556
Audit Company: Sworn/Estimate/Non-Audited
Audit Date: 6 10 2019
Total Circulation: 16320

BURKE CONNECTION

Corporate/Parent Company: Connection Newspapers
Street Address: 1606 King St
City: Alexandria
State: VA
Postal Code: 22314
Office phone: (703) 778-9431
Publication Website: http://burkeconnection.com/
General E-mail: gazette@connectionnewspapers.com
Publisher Name: Mary Kimm
Publisher Email: mkimm@connectionnewspapers.com
Editor Name: Mary Kimm
Editor Email: mkimm@connectionnewspapers.com
Year Established: 1988
Delivery Methods: Mail Newsstand
Published Days: Thur
Avg Free Circ: 5963
Audit Company: Sworn/Estimate/Non-Audited
Audit Date: 6 10 2019
Total Circulation: 5556

CENTRE VIEW

Corporate/Parent Company: Connection Newspapers
Street Address: 1606 King St
City: Alexandria
State: VA
Postal Code: 22314

Non-Daily Newspapers in the U.S.

Office phone: (703) 778-9431
Publication Website: http://centre-view.com/
General E-mail: gazette@connectionnewspapers.com
Publisher Name: Mary Kimm
Publisher Email: mkimm@connectionnewspapers.com
Editor Name: Mary Kimm
Editor Email: mkimm@connectionnewspapers.com
Year Established: 1988
Delivery Methods: Mail`Newsstand
Published Days: Thur
Avg Paid Circ: 2
Avg Free Circ: 4745
Audit Company: Sworn/Estimate/Non-Audited
Audit Date: 6 10 2019

FAIRFAX CONNECTION

Corporate/Parent Company: Connection Newspapers
Street Address: 1606 King St
City: Alexandria
State: VA
Postal Code: 22314
Office phone: (703) 778-9431
Publication Website: http://fairfaxconnection.com/
General E-mail: gazette@connectionnewspapers.com
Publisher Name: Mary Kimm
Publisher Email: mkimm@connectionnewspapers.com
Editor Name: Mary Kimm
Editor Email: mkimm@connectionnewspapers.com
Year Established: 1986
Delivery Methods: Mail`Newsstand
Published Days: Thur
Avg Free Circ: 4952
Audit Company: Sworn/Estimate/Non-Audited
Audit Date: 6 10 2019

FAIRFAX STATION/CLIFTON/LORTON CONNECTION

Corporate/Parent Company: Connection Newspapers
Street Address: 1606 King St
City: Alexandria
State: VA
Postal Code: 22314
Office phone: (703) 778-9431
Publication Website: http://fairfaxstationconnection.com/
General E-mail: gazette@connectionnewspapers.com
Publisher Name: Mary Kimm
Publisher Email: mkimm@connectionnewspapers.com
Editor Name: Mary Kimm
Editor Email: mkimm@connectionnewspapers.com
Year Established: 1988
Delivery Methods: Mail`Newsstand
Published Days: Thur
Avg Free Circ: 6594
Audit Company: Sworn/Estimate/Non-Audited
Audit Date: 6 10 2019

GREAT FALLS CONNECTION

Corporate/Parent Company: Connection Newspapers
Street Address: 1606 King St
City: Alexandria
State: VA
Postal Code: 22314
Office phone: (703) 778-9410
Publication Website: http://greatfallsconnection.com/
General E-mail: gazette@connectionnewspapers.com
Publisher Name: Mary Kimm
Publisher Email: mkimm@connectionnewspapers.com
Editor Name: Mary Kimm
Editor Email: mkimm@connectionnewspapers.com
Year Established: 1988
Delivery Methods: Mail`Newsstand
Published Days: Thur
Avg Paid Circ: 1
Avg Free Circ: 6088
Audit Company: Sworn/Estimate/Non-Audited
Audit Date: 6 10 2019

MCLEAN CONNECTION

Corporate/Parent Company: Connection Newspapers
Street Address: 1606 King St
City: Alexandria
State: VA
Postal Code: 22314
Office phone: (703) 778-9431
Publication Website: http://www.mcleanconnection.com/
General E-mail: gazette@connectionnewspapers.com
Publisher Name: Mary Kimm
Publisher Email: mkimm@connectionnewspapers.com
Editor Name: Mary Kimm
Editor Email: mkimm@connectionnewspapers.com
Year Established: 1988
Delivery Methods: Mail`Newsstand
Published Days: Thur
Avg Free Circ: 6987
Audit Company: Sworn/Estimate/Non-Audited
Audit Date: 6 10 2019
Total Circulation: 5963

MOUNT VERNON GAZETTE

Corporate/Parent Company: Connection Newspapers
Street Address: 1606 King St
City: Alexandria
State: VA
Postal Code: 22314
Office phone: (703) 778-9431
Publication Website: http://www.mountvernongazette.com/
General E-mail: gazette@connectionnewspapers.com
Publisher Name: Mary Kimm
Publisher Email: mkimm@connectionnewspapers.com
Editor Name: Mary Kimm
Editor Email: mkimm@connectionnewspapers.com
Year Established: 1989
Delivery Methods: Mail`Newsstand
Published Days: Thur
Avg Paid Circ: 27
Avg Free Circ: 8724
Audit Company: Sworn/Estimate/Non-Audited
Audit Date: 6 10 2019
Total Circulation: 4747

OAK HILL/HERNDON CONNECTION

Corporate/Parent Company: Connection Newspapers
Street Address: 1606 King St
City: Alexandria
State: VA
Postal Code: 22314
Office phone: (703) 778-9431
Publication Website: http://herndonconnection.com/
General E-mail: gazette@connectionnewspapers.com
Publisher Name: Mary Kimm
Publisher Email: mkimm@connectionnewspapers.com
Editor Name: Mary Kimm
Editor Email: mkimm@connectionnewspapers.com
Year Established: 1988
Delivery Methods: Mail`Newsstand
Published Days: Thur
Avg Free Circ: 3450
Audit Company: Sworn/Estimate/Non-Audited
Audit Date: 6 10 2019

POTOMAC ALMANAC

Corporate/Parent Company: Connection Newspapers
Street Address: 1606 King St
City: Alexandria
State: VA
Postal Code: 22314
Office phone: (703) 778-9431
Publication Website: http://www.potomacalmanac.com/
General E-mail: gazette@connectionnewspapers.com
Publisher Name: Mary Kimm
Publisher Email: mkimm@connectionnewspapers.com
Editor Name: Mary Kimm
Editor Email: mkimm@connectionnewspapers.com
Year Established: 1957
Delivery Methods: Mail`Newsstand
Published Days: Thur
Avg Free Circ: 6528
Audit Company: Sworn/Estimate/Non-Audited
Audit Date: 6 10 2019

RESTON CONNECTION

Corporate/Parent Company: Connection Newspapers
Street Address: 1606 King St
City: Alexandria
State: VA
Postal Code: 22314
Office phone: (703) 778-9431
Publication Website: http://www.reston-connection.com/
General E-mail: gazette@connectionnewspapers.com
Publisher Name: Mary Kimm
Publisher Email: mkimm@connectionnewspapers.com
Editor Name: Mary Kimm
Editor Email: mkimm@connectionnewspapers.com
Year Established: 1988
Delivery Methods: Mail`Newsstand
Published Days: Thur
Avg Free Circ: 6650
Audit Company: Sworn/Estimate/Non-Audited
Audit Date: 6 10 2019
Total Circulation: 8755

SPRINGFIELD CONNECTION

Corporate/Parent Company: Connection Newspapers
Street Address: 1606 King St
City: Alexandria
State: VA
Postal Code: 22314
Office phone: (703) 778-9431
Publication Website: http://springfieldconnection.com/
General E-mail: gazette@connectionnewspapers.com
Publisher Name: Mary Kimm
Publisher Email: mkimm@connectionnewspapers.com
Editor Name: Mary Kimm
Editor Email: mkimm@connectionnewspapers.com
Year Established: 1995
Delivery Methods: Mail`Newsstand
Published Days: Thur
Avg Paid Circ: 3
Avg Free Circ: 4610
Audit Company: Sworn/Estimate/Non-Audited
Audit Date: 6 10 2019

VIENNA/OAKTON CONNECTION

Corporate/Parent Company: Connection Newspapers
Street Address: 1606 King St
City: Alexandria
State: VA
Postal Code: 22314
Office phone: (703) 778-9431
Publication Website: http://viennaconnection.com/
General E-mail: gazette@connectionnewspapers.com
Publisher Name: Mary Kimm
Publisher Email: mkimm@connectionnewspapers.com
Editor Name: Mary Kimm
Editor Email: mkimm@connectionnewspapers.com
Year Established: 1988
Delivery Methods: Mail`Newsstand
Published Days: Thur
Avg Paid Circ: 1
Avg Free Circ: 6180
Audit Company: Sworn/Estimate/Non-Audited
Audit Date: 6 10 2019
Total Circulation: 4952

ALTAVISTA

ALTAVISTA JOURNAL

Corporate/Parent Company: Womack Publishing Co.
Street Address: 1007 Main St
City: Altavista
State: VA
Postal Code: 24517
Office phone: (434) 369-6688
Publication Website: http://www.altavistajournal.com/
General E-mail: editor@altavistajournal.com
Editor Name: Don Richeson
Year Established: 1909
Delivery Methods: Mail`Newsstand`Racks
Mechanical specifications: Type page 6 x 21 1/2.
Published Days: Wed
Avg Paid Circ: 16200
Avg Free Circ: 120
Audit Company: Sworn/Estimate/Non-Audited
Audit Date: 6 10 2019
Total Circulation: 6594

APPOMATTOX

TIMES-VIRGINIAN

Corporate/Parent Company: Womack Publishing Co.
Street Address: 589 COURT ST
City: Appomattox
State: VA
Postal Code: 24522
Office phone: (434) 352-8215
Publication Website: http://www.timesvirginian.com/
General E-mail: editor@timesvirginian.com
Editor Name: C.E. Adams
Editor Email: editor@timesvirginian.com
Year Established: 1892
Delivery Methods: Mail`Racks
Own Printing Facility?: Y
Published Days: Wed
Avg Paid Circ: 4000
Avg Free Circ: 4800
Audit Company: Sworn/Estimate/Non-Audited
Audit Date: 6 10 2019

BEDFORD

BEDFORD BULLET

Corporate/Parent Company: Landmark

Communications, Inc.
Street Address: 233 W Depot St
City: Bedford
State: VA
Postal Code: 24523
Office phone: (540) 586-8612
Publication Website: https://www.bedfordbulletin.com/
General E-mail: news@bedfordbulletin.com
Publisher Name: Jay Bondurant
Publisher Email: jaybondurant@bedfordbulletin.com
Editor Name: Tom Wilmoth
Editor Email: news@bedfordbulletin.com
Advertising Executive Name: Jay Bondurant
Advertising Executive Email: jaybondurant@bedfordbulletin.com

BROOKNEAL

THE UNION STAR

Corporate/Parent Company: Womack Publishing Co.
Street Address: 241 MAIN ST
City: Brookneal
State: VA
Postal Code: 24528
Office phone: (434) 376-2795
Publication Website: http://www.theunionstar.com/
General E-mail: news@theunionstar.com
Editor Name: Don Richeson
Editor Email: aletterman@theunionstar.com
Year Established: 1906
Delivery Methods: Mail`Racks
Mechanical specifications: Type page 11 11/16 x 21; E - 6 cols, 1 5/6, 1/8 between; A - 6 cols, 1 5/6, 1/8 between; C - 6 cols, 1 5/6, 1/8 between.
Published Days: Wed
Avg Paid Circ: 2850
Avg Free Circ: 50
Audit Company: Sworn/Estimate/Non-Audited
Audit Date: 6 10 2019

CHASE CITY

THE NEWS PROGRESS

Corporate/Parent Company: Womack Publishing Co.
Street Address: 850 E. Second Street
City: Chase City
State: VA
Postal Code: 23924
Office phone: 434-372-5156
Publication Website: http://www.thenewsprogress.com
Total Circulation: 6089

CHATHAM

STAR-TRIBUNE

Corporate/Parent Company: Womack Publishing Co.
Street Address: 30 S Main St
City: Chatham
State: VA
Postal Code: 24531
Office phone: (434) 432-2791
Publication Website: http://www.chathamstartribune.com
General E-mail: office@chathamstartribune.com
Publisher Name: Leigh Ann Shields
Publisher Phone: news@chathamstartribune.com
Advertising Executive Name: Rachel Nanney
Advertising Executive Email: advertising@chathamstartribune.com
Year Established: 1869
Delivery Methods: Mail`Racks
Mechanical specifications: Type page 13 x 21 1/2; E - 6 cols, 2 1/16, between; A - 6 cols, 2 1/16, between; C - 6 cols, 2 1/16, between.
Published Days: Wed
Avg Paid Circ: 8217
Avg Free Circ: 275
Audit Company: Sworn/Estimate/Non-Audited

Audit Date: 6 10 2019

CHRISTIANSBURG

THE NEWS-MESSENGER

Corporate/Parent Company: Gannett
Street Address: 302 W. Main Street
City: Christiansburg
State: VA
Postal Code: 24073
Office phone: (540) 382-6171
Publication Website: montcova.com
Editor Name: Liz Kirchner
Editor Email: editor@ourvalley.org
Editor Phone: 540-382-6171

CHURCH

LAS AMERICAS NEWSPAPER

Street Address: 3809 Bell Manor Court Falls
City: Church
State: VA
Postal Code: 22041
Office phone: 703-256-4200
Publication Website: www.lasamericasnews.com
General E-mail: contacto@lasamericasnews.com

CLARKSVILLE

THE MECKLENBURG SUN

Corporate/Parent Company: The News & Record
Street Address: PO BOX 997/602 Virginia Avenue
City: Clarksville
State: VA
Postal Code: 23927
Office phone: 434-447-4823
Publication Website: www.sovanow.com/index.php?/mecklenburg
Editor Name: Eva Cassada
Editor Email: news@themecklenburgsun.com

DANVILLE

EVINCE MAGAZINE

Street Address: 753 Main Street #3
City: Danville
State: VA
Postal Code: 24541
Office phone: 877.638.8685
Publication Website: evincemagazine.com
General E-mail: info@evincemagazine.com
Publisher Name: Andrew Scott Brooks
Editor Name: Joyce Wilburn
Editor Phone: 434.799.3160

SHOWCASE MAGAZINE

Corporate/Parent Company: Andrew Brooks Media Group
Street Address: 753 Main Street, Ste 3
City: Danville
State: VA
Postal Code: 24541
Office phone: 434-709-7349
Publication Website: showcasemagazine.com
General E-mail: info@showcasemagazine.com
Editor Name: Paul Seiple
Editor Email: Paul@showcaseMagazine.com
Advertising Executive Name: Lee Vogler
Advertising Executive Email: lee@ShowcaseMagazine.com

ELKTON

THE VALLEY BANNER

Corporate/Parent Company: Daily News Record
Street Address: 157 W Spotswood Ave
City: Elkton

State: VA
Postal Code: 22827-1118
Office phone: (540) 298-9444
Publication Website: https://www.dnronline.com/the_valley_banner/
General E-mail: vbnews@comcast.net
Year Established: 1966
Delivery Methods: Mail`Racks
Own Printing Facility?: Y
Commercial printers?: Y
Mechanical specifications: Type page 11 5/8 x 21 1/4; E - 6 cols, 1 5/6, 1/8 between; A - 6 cols, 1 5/6, 1/8 between; C - 9 cols, 1 1/4, 1/10 between.
Published Days: Thur
Avg Paid Circ: 29896
Audit Company: Sworn/Estimate/Non-Audited
Audit Date: 6 10 2019

EMPORIA

INDEPENDENT MESSENGER

Corporate/Parent Company: Womack Publishing Co.
Street Address: 111 Baker St.
City: Emporia
State: VA
Postal Code: 23847
Office phone: (434) 634-4153
Publication Website: http://www.emporiaindependentmessenger.com/
General E-mail: news@imnewspaper.com
Publisher Name: Mark Mathews
Publisher Email: editor@imnewspaper.com
Advertising Executive Name: Darian Liles
Advertising Executive Email: becky@imnewspaper.com

INDEPENDENT-MESSENGER

Corporate/Parent Company: Womack Publishing Co.
Street Address: 111 Baker St.
City: Emporia
State: VA
Postal Code: 23847
Office phone: 434-634-4153
Publication Website: www.emporiaindependentmessenger.com
General E-mail: news@imnewspaper.com
Editor Name: Mark Mathews
Editor Email: editor@imnewspaper.com
Advertising Executive Name: Darian Liles
Advertising Executive Email: advertising@imnewspaper.com
Total Circulation: 6987

FARMVILLE

THE ROTUNDA

Street Address: Box 2901, 201 High Street
City: Farmville
State: VA
Postal Code: 23909
Publication Website: www.therotundaonline.com
General E-mail: therotundaonline@gmail.com
Editor Name: Rachael Poole
Editor Email: rotundaeditor@gmail.com
Total Circulation: 8751

FORT BELVOIR

BELVOIR EAGLE-OOB

Corporate/Parent Company: Northern Virginia Media Services
Street Address: 9820 Flagler Rd
City: Fort Belvoir
State: VA
Postal Code: 22060
Office phone: (703) 805-2382
Publication Website: http://www.belvoireagleonline.com
General E-mail: editor@belvoireagleonline.com
Editor Email: editor@belvoireagleonline.com
Editor Phone: 703-805-2019

Advertising Executive Name: Connie Fields
Advertising Executive Email: cfields@princewilliamtoday.com
Advertising Executive Phone: (703) 303-8713

FRONT ROYAL

THE WARREN COUNTY REPORT

Street Address: 213 E Main St
City: Front Royal
State: VA
Postal Code: 22630
Office phone: 540-636-1014
Publication Website: wcrnews.wordpress.com
Editor Name: Dan McDermott
Editor Email: editor@warrencountyreport.com
Editor Phone: (540) 305-3000

GALAX

THE GAZETTE

Corporate/Parent Company: Adams Publishing Group
Street Address: 108 W. Stuart Drive
City: Galax
State: VA
Postal Code: 24333
Office phone: 276-236-5178
Publication Website: www.galaxgazette.com
General E-mail: news@galaxgazette.com
Editor Name: Brian Funk
Editor Email: editor@galaxgazette.com

GLOUCESTE

GLOUCESTER-MATHEWS GAZETTE-JOURNAL

Street Address: 6625 Main Street, P.O. Box 2060
City: Glouceste
State: VA
Postal Code: 23061
Office phone: (804) 693-3101
Publication Website: www.gazettejournal.net
General E-mail: info@gazettejournal.net
Publisher Name: Elsa Verbyla
Publisher Email: everbyla@gazettejournal.net
Editor Name: Charlie Koenig
Editor Email: ckoenig@gazettejournal.net
Advertising Executive Name: Kim Andrews
Advertising Executive Email: kandrews@gazettejournal.net
Total Circulation: 3450

HARRISONBURG

NUEVAS RAICES

Street Address: PO Box 1281
City: Harrisonburg
State: VA
Postal Code: 22803
Office phone: 877-683-8277
Publication Website: www.nuevasraices.com
General E-mail: info@nuevasraices.com

HENRICO

HENRICO CITIZEN

Corporate/Parent Company: T3 Media, LLC
Street Address: 6924 Lakeside Avenue Suite 307
City: Henrico
State: VA
Postal Code: 23228
Office phone: (804) 262-1700
Publication Website: www.henricocitizen.com
General E-mail: citizen@henricocitizen.com
Publisher Name: Tom Lappas
Publisher Email: tlappas@henricocitizen.com
Editor Name: Patty Kruszewski
Editor Email: patty@henricocitizen.com
Total Circulation: 6528

Non-Daily Newspapers in the U.S.

KEYSVILLE

THE SOUTHSIDE MESSENGER

Street Address: PO Box 849
City: Keysville
State: VA
Postal Code: 23947
Office phone: 434-736-0152
Publication Website: southsidemessenger.com
General E-mail: ads@southsidemessenger.com
Editor Name: Averett Jones
Editor Email: editor@southsidemessenger.com

KILMARNOCK

RAPPAHANNOCK RECORD

Street Address: P.O. Box 400, 27 N Main St.
City: Kilmarnock
State: VA
Postal Code: 22482
Office phone: (804) 435-1701
Publication Website: rrecord.com
General E-mail: mail@rapprecord.com
Editor Name: Robert D. Mason Jr
Editor Email: editor@rapprecord.com
Editor Phone: ext. 25
Advertising Executive Name: Jessica Bell
Advertising Executive Email: JessicaBell@RappRecord.com
Advertising Executive Phone: ext. 13

LAWRENCEVILLE

BRUNSWICK TIMES-GAZETTE

Corporate/Parent Company: Womack Publishing Co.
Street Address: 213 N Main St
City: Lawrenceville
State: VA
Postal Code: 23868
Office phone: (434) 848-2114
Publication Website: http://www.brunswicktimes-gazette.com/
General E-mail: news@brunswicktimes-gazette.com
Editor Name: Sylvia Allen
Editor Email: news@brunswicktimes-gazette.com
Year Established: 1894
Delivery Methods: Mail`Newsstand`Racks
Published Days: Wed
Audit Company: Sworn/Estimate/Non-Audited
Audit Date: 6 10 2019

LEBANON

THE LEBANON NEWS

Street Address: 20 Clinch Mountain Ave
City: Lebanon
State: VA
Postal Code: 24266
Office phone: 276-889-2112
Publication Website: www.thelebanonnews.com
Editor Name: Jerry E. Lark
Editor Email: lebnews@verizon.net
Editor Phone: 276-889-2112

LEESBURG

LOUDOUN NOW

Street Address: 15 N. King St., Suite 101
City: Leesburg
State: VA
Postal Code: 20176
Office phone: (703) 770-9723
Publication Website: loudounnow.com
Editor Name: Norman K. Styer
Editor Email: nstyer@loudounnow.com
Advertising Executive Name: Susan Styer
Advertising Executive Email: sstyer@loudounnow.com
Total Circulation: 6650

LOUDOUN TIMES-MIRROR

Corporate/Parent Company: Times Community Media
Street Address: 108 Church Street, SE 2nd Floor
City: Leesburg
State: VA
Postal Code: 20175
Office phone: 703-777-1111
Publication Website: www.loudountimes.com
General E-mail: LTMEditor@loudountimes.com
Editor Name: Trevor Baratko
Editor Email: tbaratko@loudountimes.com
Editor Phone: 937-286-5154
Advertising Executive Name: Bruce Donaldson
Advertising Executive Email: bdonaldson@loudountimes.com
Advertising Executive Phone: 703-669-3020

LEXINGTON

THE ROCKBRIDGE ADVOCATE

Street Address: 7 E Washington St
City: Lexington
State: VA
Postal Code: 24450
Office phone: 540-463-2062
Publication Website: rockbridgeadvocate.com
Editor Name: Douglas J. Harwood
Editor Email: rbadvocate@embarqmail.com

MANASSAS

THE OLD BRIDGE OBSERVER

Corporate/Parent Company: Randall Publishing Corporation
Street Address: 8803 Sudley Road, Ste. 201
City: Manassas
State: VA
Postal Code: 20110
Office phone: 703.369.5253
Publication Website: www.theoldbridgeobserver.info
General E-mail: advertising@observernow.com
Editor Name: Randi Reid
Editor Email: editor@observernow.com
Editor Phone: 703-369-5253

MC LEAN

SUN GAZETTE

Corporate/Parent Company: Northern Virginia Media Services
Street Address: 6704 Old McLean Village Dr
City: Mc Lean
State: VA
Postal Code: 22101-3906
Office phone: (703) 738-2520
Publication Website: http://sungazette.net/
Year Established: 1935
Delivery Methods: Mail`Newsstand`Racks
Own Printing Facility?: Y
Commercial printers?: Y
Mechanical specifications: Type page 10 x 13; E - 5 cols, 1 7/8, 1/6 between; A - 5 cols, 1 7/8, 1/6 between; C - 6 cols, 1 5/12, 1/6 between.
Published Days: Thur
Avg Paid Circ: 37
Avg Free Circ: 34420
Audit Company: Sworn/Estimate/Non-Audited
Audit Date: 6 10 2019
Total Circulation: 4613

COMMUNITY NEWS

Corporate/Parent Company: Media News Group
Street Address: 7950 Jones Branch Drive
City: McLean
State: VA
Postal Code: 22107-0150
Office phone: 703-854-6000
Publication Website: www.hockessincommunitynews.com
General E-mail: 24 W. Main St.
Publisher Name: Middletown
Publisher Email: DE
Publisher Phone: 19709
Editor Name: 302-378-9531
Editor Email: editor@communitypub.com
Editor Phone: Amy Dotson-Newton
Advertising Executive Name: amy.dotsonnewton@doverpost.com
Advertising Executive Email: 302-346-5449
Advertising Executive Phone: Ben Mace
Total Circulation: 8492

YORK WEEKLY

Corporate/Parent Company: Gannett
Street Address: 7950 Jones Branch Drive
City: McLean
State: VA
Postal Code: 22107-0150
Office phone: 703-854-6000
Publication Website: www.seacoastonline.com/YorkWeekly
General E-mail: P.O. Box 7
Publisher Name: York
Publisher Email: ME
Publisher Phone: 3909
Editor Name: 207-985-2961
Advertising Executive Phone: Altschiller, Howard
Total Circulation: 34457

MONTEREY

THE RECORDER

Street Address: P.O. Box 10
City: Monterey
State: VA
Postal Code: 24465
Office phone: 540-468-2147
Publication Website: www.therecorderonline.com
Editor Name: Anne Witschey Adams
Editor Email: RecorderAnne@gmail.com
Editor Phone: 540-468-2147
Advertising Executive Name: Jessica Rogers
Advertising Executive Email: RecorderJessie@gmail.com
Advertising Executive Phone: 540-499-2239

NEWPORT NEWS

OYSTER POINTER

Street Address: 733 Thimble Shoals Blvd Suite 170
City: Newport News
State: VA
Postal Code: 23606
Office phone: 757-873-4523
Publication Website: oysterpointer.net
Editor Name: Sylvia Weinstein
Editor Email: editor@oysterpointer.net
Editor Phone: 757.873.4523

PEARISBURG

VIRGINIAN LEADER

Street Address: 511 Mountain Lake Ave.
City: Pearisburg
State: VA
Postal Code: 24134
Office phone: 540-921-3434
Publication Website: www.virginianleader.com
Publisher Name: Kenneth L. Rakes
Editor Name: Amy R. Burdette
Editor Email: aburdette@virginianleader.com
Advertising Executive Name: Kirsten O'Neill
Advertising Executive Email: ads@virginianleader.com

PULASKI

THE PATRIOT

Street Address: P.O. Box 2416
City: Pulaski
State: VA
Postal Code: 24301
Office phone: (540) 808-3949
Publication Website: pcpatriot.com
General E-mail: news@pcpatriot.com

RICHMOND

NORTH OF THE JAMES MAGAZINE

Street Address: 3122 West Clay St Ste 6
City: Richmond
State: VA
Postal Code: 23230
Office phone: (804) 908-4742
Publication Website: northofthejames.com

RICHMOND MAGAZINE

Corporate/Parent Company: Target Communications Inc.
Street Address: 2201 W. Broad St., Suite 105
City: Richmond
State: VA
Postal Code: 23220
Office phone: 804-355-0111
Publication Website: richmondmagazine.com
Publisher Name: Susan Winiecki
Publisher Email: susanw@richmag.com
Editor Name: Tina Eshleman
Editor Email: tinae@richmag.com

THE LEGACY

Street Address: 105 1/2 E Clay St
City: Richmond
State: VA
Postal Code: 23219
Office phone: (804) 644-1550
Publication Website: issuu.com/jackgreensvoice

VIRGINIA BUSINESS

Street Address: 1207 E. Main St.
City: Richmond
State: VA
Postal Code: 23219
Publication Website: www.virginiabusiness.com
Publisher Name: Bernie Niemeier
Publisher Email: bniemeier@va-business.com
Publisher Phone: (804) 225-1366
Editor Name: Richard Foster
Editor Email: rfoster@va-business.com
Editor Phone: 804-225-8859
Advertising Executive Name: Lori Collier Waran
Advertising Executive Email: lwaran@va-business.com
Advertising Executive Phone: (804) 225-0078

VIRGINIA LAWYERS WEEKLY

Corporate/Parent Company: Gannett
Street Address: 801 E. Main St. Suite 302
City: Richmond
State: VA
Postal Code: 23219
Office phone: (800) 456-5297
Publication Website: valawyersweekly.com
Publisher Name: Paul Fletcher
Publisher Email: editor@valawyersmedia.com
Editor Name: Peter Vieth
Editor Email: pvieth@valawyersmedia.com
Advertising Executive Name: Renée Baldwin
Advertising Executive Email: rbaldwin@valawyersmedia.com

Advertising Executive Phone: 800-456-5297, ext. 7412

SALEM

THE NEW CASTLE RECORD

Street Address: 1633 W. Main St.
City: Salem
State: VA
Postal Code: 24153
Office phone: (540) 389-9355
Publication Website: www.newcastlerecord.com
Editor Name: Shawn Nowlin
Editor Email: shawn.nowlin@ourvalley.org

THE VINTON MESSENGER

Street Address: P.O. Box 1125
City: Salem
State: VA
Postal Code: 24153
Publication Website: www.vintonmessenger.com
Editor Name: Ed McCoy
Editor Email: edmccoy@ourvalley.org
Editor Phone: 540-473-2741
Advertising Executive Name: James "Tucker" Frye
Advertising Executive Email: tfrye@ourvalley.org
Advertising Executive Phone: 540-473-2741

SMITHFIELD

THE SMITHFIELD TIMES

Street Address: 228 Main Street; P.O. Box 366
City: Smithfield
State: VA
Postal Code: 23431
Office phone: 757-357-3288
Publication Website: www.smithfieldtimes.com
Publisher Name: Steve Stewart
Publisher Email: steve.stewart@smithfieldtimes.com
Editor Name: Diana McFarland
Editor Email: news@smithfieldtimes.com
Advertising Executive Name: Amanda Gwaltney
Advertising Executive Email: agwaltney@smithfieldtimes.com

SOUTH BOSTON

THE NEWS & RECORD

Corporate/Parent Company: Lee Enterprises
Street Address: P.O. Drawer 100; 511 Broad Street
City: South Boston
State: VA
Postal Code: 24592
Office phone: (434) 572-2928
Publication Website: www.thenewsrecord.com
Editor Name: Sylvia O. McLaughlin
Editor Email: mail@thenewsrecord.com

SOUTH HILL

SOUTH HILL ENTERPRISE

Corporate/Parent Company: Womack Publishing Co.
Street Address: 914 W Danville St
City: South Hill
State: VA
Postal Code: 23970
Office phone: (434) 447-3178
Publication Website: http://www.southhillenterprise.com
General E-mail: editor@southhillenterprise.com
Publisher Name: Randy Velvin
Publisher Email: r.velvin@womackpublishing.com
Editor Email: editor@southhillenterprise.com
Published Days: Wed
Audit Company: Sworn/Estimate/Non-Audited
Audit Date: 6 10 2019

THE NEWS-PROGRESS

Street Address: 914 W. Danville St
City: South Hill
State: VA
Postal Code: 23970
Office phone: 434-447-3178
Publication Website: www.thenewsprogress.com
General E-mail: news@thenewsprogress.com
Editor Name: Dallas Weston
Editor Email: dallas@thenewsprogress.com
Advertising Executive Name: Mary Lou Cheek
Advertising Executive Email: advertising@thenewsprogress.com

SPRINGFIELD

FEDERAL TIMES

Street Address: 6883 Commercial Dr
City: Springfield
State: VA
Postal Code: 22159
Office phone: (703) 642-7330
Publication Website: www.federaltimes.com
General E-mail: advertisingsales@sightlinemg.com
Publisher Name: David Steinhafel
Editor Name: Andrew Tilghman
Editor Email: atilghman@militarytimes.com
Year Established: 1965
Delivery Methods: Mail`Newsstand`Racks
Published Days: Mon
Audit Company: Sworn/Estimate/Non-Audited
Audit Date: 6 10 2019

TASLEY

EASTERN SHORE NEWS

Street Address: PO Box 288
City: Tasley
State: VA
Postal Code: 23441
Office phone: (757) 787-1200
Publication Website: https://www.delmarvanow.com/
General E-mail: newshub@delmarvanow.com
Advertising Executive Name: Ron Pousson
Advertising Executive Email: rpousson@localiq.com
Advertising Executive Phone: (410) 845-4609
Year Established: 1897
Delivery Methods: Mail`Newsstand`Racks
Mechanical specifications: Type page 13 x 20 1/2; E - 6 cols, 2, 1/6 between; A - 6 cols, 2, 1/6 between; C - 9 cols, 1 1/3, 1/6 between.
Published Days: Wed`Sat
Avg Paid Circ: 8700
Avg Free Circ: 55
Audit Company: Sworn/Estimate/Non-Audited
Audit Date: 6 10 2019

VIENNA

AIR FORCE TIMES

Street Address: 1919 Gallows Rd
City: Vienna
State: VA
Postal Code: 22182
Office phone: (703) 750-7400
Publication Website: https://www.airforcetimes.com/
General E-mail: advertisingsales@sightlinemg.com
Publisher Name: David Steinhafel
Editor Name: Andrew Tilghman
Editor Email: atilghman@militarytimes.com

ARMY TIMES

Street Address: 1919 Gallows Rd
City: Vienna
State: VA
Postal Code: 22182
Office phone: (703) 750-7400
Publication Website: https://www.armytimes.com/
General E-mail: advertisingsales@sightlinemg.com
Publisher Name: David Steinhafel
Editor Name: Andrew Tilghman
Editor Email: atilghman@militarytimes.com
Year Established: 1940
Delivery Methods: Mail`Newsstand`Racks
Published Days: Mon

MARINE CORPS TIMES

Street Address: 1919 Gallows Rd
City: Vienna
State: VA
Postal Code: 22182-4038
Office phone: (703) 750-7400
Publication Website: https://www.marinecorpstimes.com/
General E-mail: advertisingsales@sightlinemg.com
Publisher Name: David Steinhafel
Editor Name: Andrew Tilghman
Editor Email: atilghman@militarytimes.com
Year Established: 1999
Delivery Methods: Mail`Newsstand`Racks
Published Days: Mon
Audit Company: Sworn/Estimate/Non-Audited
Audit Date: 6 10 2019
Total Circulation: 14000

WARRENTON

IN AND AROUND HORSE COUNTRY

Street Address: 60 Alexandria Pike
City: Warrenton
State: VA
Postal Code: 20186-2808
Office phone: 540-347-3141
Publication Website: www.horsecountrylife.com/aboutpaper.html
General E-mail: IAHC@horsecountrylife.com
Publisher Name: Marion Maggiolo
Editor Name: J. Harris Anderson
Advertising Executive Name: Kim Gray

PRINCE WILLIAM/GAINESVILLE TIMES

Corporate/Parent Company: Piedmont Media LLC
Street Address: 41 Culpeper St.
City: Warrenton
State: VA
Postal Code: 20186
Office phone: 540-347-4222
Publication Website: www.princewilliamtimes.com
General E-mail: news@fauquier.com
Publisher Name: Catherine M. Nelson
Publisher Email: cnelson@fauquier.com
Editor Name: Jill Palermo
Editor Email: jpalermo@fauquier.com

WASHINGTON

FAIRFAX SUN GAZETTE

Corporate/Parent Company: Rappahannock Media LLC
Street Address: PO Box 59 / 309 Jett Street
City: Washington
State: VA
Postal Code: 22747
Office phone: 703-738-2520
Publication Website: www.insidenova.com/news/fairfax
Editor Name: Scott McCaffrey
Editor Email: smccaffrey@sungazette.net
Advertising Executive Name: Vicky Mashaw
Advertising Executive Email: vmashaw@sungazette.net

Advertising Executive Phone: 571-333-6272

RAPPAHANNOCK NEWS

Corporate/Parent Company: Rappahannock Media LLC
Street Address: PO Box 59
City: Washington
State: VA
Postal Code: 22747
Office phone: 540-675-3338
Publication Website: rappnews.com
General E-mail: info@rappnews.com
Publisher Name: DENNIS BRACK
Publisher Email: publisher@rappnews.com
Editor Name: JOHN McCASLIN
Editor Email: editor@rappnews.com

WILLIAMSBURG

THE VIRGINIA GAZETTE

Street Address: 1430 High St., Unit 504
City: Williamsburg
State: VA
Postal Code: 23188
Office phone: 757-220-1736
Publication Website: www.dailypress.com/virginiagazette
Editor Name: Kris Worrell
Editor Email: kworrell@dailypress.com
Editor Phone: 757-446-2321
Year Established: 1930
Delivery Methods: Mail`Newsstand`Carrier`Racks
Published Days: Wed`Sat
Avg Paid Circ: 14000
Audit Company: Sworn/Estimate/Non-Audited
Audit Date: 6 10 2019

WOODSTOCK

MOUNTAIN COURIER

Street Address: PO Box 542
City: Woodstock
State: VA
Postal Code: 22664
Office phone: 540-335-9793
Publication Website: www.facebook.com/mountaincourier
Publisher Name: Jeff DeVito
Publisher Email: mtncourier@gmail.com
Publisher Phone: 540-335-9793
Editor Name: Joan Anderson
Editor Email: joanstar@shentel.net

VERMONT

BRANDON

BRANDON REPORTER

Street Address: Second Floor, 4 Union St
City: Brandon
State: VT
Postal Code: 0 5733
Office phone: 802-388-4944
Publication Website: thereportervt.wordpress.com/
Publisher Name: Angelo Lynn
Editor Name: Lee Kahrs
Editor Email: news@brandonreporter.com
Advertising Executive Name: Mike French
Advertising Executive Email: ads@brandonreporter.com

BURLINGTON

NORTH AVENUE NEWS INC.

Corporate/Parent Company: North Avenue News

Non-Daily Newspapers in the U.S.

Inc.
Street Address: P.O. Box 3178
City: Burlington
State: VT
Postal Code: 0 5408-0031
Office phone: 802 864 7530
Publication Website: www.northavenuenews.com
General E-mail: noavenews@aol.com

CASTLETON

LAKESIDE NEWS & THE RUTLAND SUN

Corporate/Parent Company: Lakeside News & The Rutland Sun
Street Address: PO Box 71
City: Castleton
State: VT
Postal Code: 0 5735
Office phone: 802-353-0573
Publication Website: www.lakesidenews.org
Publisher Name: Roy Newton
Publisher Email: roy@lakesidenews.org

CHARLOTTE

CHARLOTTE NEWS

Corporate/Parent Company: The Charlotte News, Inc
Street Address: P.O. Box 251 2848 Greenbush Road
City: Charlotte
State: VT
Postal Code: 0 5445
Office phone: (802) 425-4949
Publication Website: www.charlottenewsvt.org
General E-mail: news@thecharlottenews.org
Editor Name: CHEA WATERS EVANS
Editor Email: chea@thecharlottenews.org
Advertising Executive Name: ELIZABETH LANGFELDT
Advertising Executive Email: ads@thecharlottenews.org

CHESTER

MESSAGE FOR THE WEEK

Street Address: 287 Main Street Suite 1C
City: Chester
State: VT
Postal Code: 0 5143
Office phone: (802) 875-1350

DANVILLE

NORTH STAR MONTHLY

Corporate/Parent Company: Northstar Publishing LLC
Street Address: 29 Hill St - PO Box 319
City: Danville
State: VT
Postal Code: 0 5828
Office phone: 802-684-1056
Publication Website: www.northstarmonthly.com
General E-mail: info@northstarmonthly.com
Publisher Name: Justin & Ginni Lavely
Editor Name: Justin Lavely
Editor Email: justin@northstarmonthly.com
Advertising Executive Name: Vicki Moore
Advertising Executive Email: vicki@northstarmonthly.com

FAIRFAX

FAIRFAX NEWS

Street Address: P.O. Box 86
City: Fairfax
State: VT
Postal Code: 0 5454
Office phone: (802) 782-0406
General E-mail: thefairfaxnews@gmail.com

HINESBURG

HINESBURG RECORD

Street Address: P.O.Box 304
City: Hinesburg
State: VT
Postal Code: 0 5461
Office phone: 802-482-2350
Publication Website: hinesburgrecord.org
General E-mail: news@hinesburgrecord.org
Editor Name: June Giroux
Editor Email: junegiroux2@aol.com
Editor Phone: 802-482-2350
Advertising Executive Name: Kristin Wahner
Advertising Executive Email: ads@hinesburgrecord.org
Advertising Executive Phone: (802) 482-7227

LUDLOW

THE SHOPPER

Corporate/Parent Company: Eagle Newspapers Inc.
Street Address: 8 High St
City: Ludlow
State: VT
Postal Code: 0 5149
Office phone: 802-228-3600
Publication Website: www.vermontjournal.com
General E-mail: editor@vermontjournal.com
Publisher Name: Robert Miller
Publisher Email: publisher@vermontjournal.com
Editor Name: Amanda Wedegis
Editor Email: editor@vermontjournal.com

VERMONT JOURNAL

Corporate/Parent Company: Journal LLC/Bob Miller
Street Address: 8 High St
City: Ludlow
State: VT
Postal Code: 0 5149
Office phone: 802-228-3600
Publication Website: www.vermontjournal.com
General E-mail: editor@vermontjournal.com
Publisher Name: Robert Miller
Publisher Email: publisher@vermontjournal.com
Editor Name: Amanda Wedegis
Editor Email: editor@vermontjournal.com

MIDDLEBURY

ADDISON EAGLE

Corporate/Parent Company: Denton Publications Inc
Street Address: 16 Creek Road Suite 5A
City: Middlebury
State: VT
Postal Code: 0 5753
Office phone: (802) 388-6397
Publication Website: www.addison-eagle.com
General E-mail: info@suncommunitynews.com
Editor Name: Mr. Ed Coats

VALLEY VOICE

Street Address: 656 Exchange Street, Suite 2
City: Middlebury
State: VT
Postal Code: 0 5753
Office phone: 802-388-6366
Publication Website: www.vvoice.org
General E-mail: info@vvoice.org

MONTPELIER

THE BRIDGE

Street Address: PO Box 1143
City: Montpelier
State: VT
Postal Code: 0 5601
Office phone: 802-223-5112
Publication Website: montpelierbridge.org
Editor Name: Mara Brooks
Editor Email: mara@montpelierbridge.com
Advertising Executive Name: Rick McMahan
Advertising Executive Email: rick@vtbridge.com

MORRISVILLE

NEWS AND CITIZEN

Corporate/Parent Company: Vermont Community Newspaper Group LLC
Street Address: 92 Lower Main St.
City: Morrisville
State: VT
Postal Code: 0 5661
Office phone: 802-888-2212
Publication Website: www.newsandcitizen.com
Publisher Name: Greg Popa
Publisher Phone: Ext. 29
Editor Name: Tom Kearney
Editor Email: news@newsandcitizen.com
Editor Phone: Ext. 22
Advertising Executive Name: Judy Kearns
Advertising Executive Email: judy@otherpapersbvt.com
Advertising Executive Phone: 802-864-6670, Ext. 21

NORTH HERO

THE ISLANDER

Street Address: 2355 U.S. Route 2
City: North Hero
State: VT
Postal Code: 0 5474
Office phone: (802) 372-5600
Publication Website: www.theislandernewspaper.com
Editor Name: Tonya L. Poutry
Editor Email: islander@vermontislander.com

RICHMOND

THE TIMES INK

Street Address: P.O. Box 532
City: Richmond
State: VT
Postal Code: 0 5407
Office phone: (802) 434-2690
Publication Website: timesinkvt.org
General E-mail: news@timesinkvt.org
Editor Name: Heidi Racht
Editor Email: news@timesinkvt.org
Editor Phone: 434-2690
Advertising Executive Name: Meg Howard
Advertising Executive Email: advertising@timesinkvt.org

SOUTH BURLINGTON

CHARLOTTE CITIZEN

Corporate/Parent Company: Vermont Community Newspaper Group LLC
Street Address: 1340 Williston Road
City: South Burlington
State: VT
Postal Code: 0 5403
Office phone: 802-985-3091
Publication Website: www.vtcng.com/thecitizenvt
General E-mail: news@thecitizenvt.com
Publisher Name: Greg Popa
Publisher Phone: 802-253-2101, Ext. 29
Editor Name: Tom Kearney
Editor Phone: 802-253-2101, Ext. 18
Advertising Executive Name: Judy Kearns
Advertising Executive Email: judy@otherpapersbvt.com
Advertising Executive Phone: 802-864-6670, Ext. 21

SOUTH HERO

VERMONT WOMAN

Street Address: P.O. Box 490 | 307 Route 2
City: South Hero
State: VT
Postal Code: 0 5486
Office phone: 802-372-3201
Publication Website: www.vermontwoman.com
Publisher Name: Sue Gillis
Publisher Email: suegillis2@vermontwoman.com
Editor Name: Rickey Gard Diamond

SPRINGFIELD

SPRINGFIELD REPORTER

Street Address: 151 Summer St
City: Springfield
State: VT
Postal Code: 0 5156
Office phone: (802) 885-2246
Editor Name: Rodney W. Arnold
Editor Email: reporter@vermontel.net

STARKSBORO

MOUNTAIN GAZETTE

Street Address: 6558 VT Rt. 116,
City: Starksboro
State: VT
Postal Code: 0 5487
Office phone: 802-453-6354
Publication Website: www.mtngazettevt.com
General E-mail: mtngazette@gmavt.net
Publisher Name: Brenda Boutin

WILMINGTON

DEERFIELD VALLEY NEWS

Corporate/Parent Company: Vermont Media Publishing Co
Street Address: 797 VT Route 100 North
City: Wilmington
State: VT
Postal Code: 0 5363
Office phone: 802-464-3388
Publication Website: www.dvalnews.com
Publisher Name: Randy Capitani
Publisher Email: RandyC@vermontmedia.com
Editor Name: Mike Eldred
Editor Email: MikeE@vermontmedia.com

WASHINGTON

BELLEVUE

BELLEVUE REPORTER

Corporate/Parent Company: Sound Publishing, Inc.
Street Address: 2700 Richards Rd
City: Bellevue
State: WA
Postal Code: 98005
Office phone: (425) 453-4270
Publication Website: https://www.bellevuereporter.com/
General E-mail: ralcott@soundpublishing.com
Editor Name: Corey Morris
Editor Email: cmorris@soundpublishing.com
Advertising Executive Name: Pili Linares
Advertising Executive Email: plinares@soundpublishing.com
Year Established: 1930
Delivery Methods: Mail Newsstand Racks
Published Days: Fri
Avg Paid Circ: 42
Avg Free Circ: 34892
Audit Company: Sworn/Estimate/Non-Audited
Audit Date: 6 10 2019

ISSAQUAH/SAMMAMISH REPORTER

Corporate/Parent Company: Sound Publishing, Inc.
Street Address: 2700 Richards Rd
City: Bellevue
State: WA
Postal Code: 98005
Office phone: (425) 391-0363
Publication Website: https://www.issaquahreporter.com/
General E-mail: ralcott@soundpublishing.com
Editor Name: Corey Morris
Editor Email: cmorris@soundpublishing.com
Advertising Executive Name: Pili Linares
Advertising Executive Email: plinares@soundpublishing.com
Delivery Methods: Mail`Newsstand`Racks
Published Days: Fri
Avg Paid Circ: 50
Avg Free Circ: 24020
Audit Company: AAM
Audit Date: 31 03 2018

BELLINGHAM

BELLINGHAM BUSINESS JOURNAL

Corporate/Parent Company: Sound Publishing, Inc.
Street Address: 1909 Cornwall Ave
City: Bellingham
State: WA
Postal Code: 98225
Office phone: (360) 647-8805
Publication Website: http://bbjtoday.com/
General E-mail: editor@bbjtoday.com
Editor Name: Mathew Roland
Editor Email: editor@bbjtoday.com
Advertising Executive Email: sales@bbjtoday.com
Advertising Executive Phone: (360) 312-4380
Year Established: 1994
Delivery Methods: Mail`Newsstand`Racks
Published Days: Thur`Mthly
Audit Company: Sworn/Estimate/Non-Audited
Audit Date: 6 10 2019

CHEHALIS

DEVAUL PUBLISHING, INC

Corporate/Parent Company: DeVaul Publishing, Inc
Street Address: 429 N Market Blvd
City: Chehalis
State: WA
Postal Code: 98532
Office phone: 360-748-6848
Publication Website: www.devaulpublishing.com

CHENEY

FREE PRESS PUBLISHING

Corporate/Parent Company: Free Press Publishing Inc.
Street Address: 1616 W. First St.
City: Cheney
State: WA
Postal Code: 99004
Office phone: (509) 235-6184
Publication Website: www.cheneyfreepress.com
General E-mail: info@cheneyfreepress.com
Publisher Name: Roger Harnack
Advertising Executive Name: DeeAnn Gibb
Advertising Executive Email: dgibb@cheneyfreepress.com
Advertising Executive Phone: (509) 235-6184

CHEWELAH

CHEWELAH INDEPENDENT

Street Address: 401 South Park Street, Ste A PO Box 5
City: Chewelah
State: WA
Postal Code: 99109
Office phone: 509-935-8422
Publication Website: www.chewelahindependent.com
Publisher Name: Jared Arnold
Publisher Email: publisher@chewelahindependent.com
Publisher Phone: 509-935-8422
Editor Name: Brandon Hansen
Editor Email: brandon@chewelahindependent.com
Editor Phone: 509-935-8422
Advertising Executive Name: Andrea Arnold
Advertising Executive Email: theindependent@centurytel.net
Advertising Executive Phone: 509-935-8422

CONCRETE

CONCRETE HERALD

Street Address: P.O. Box 682
City: Concrete
State: WA
Postal Code: 98237
Office phone: 360.853.8213
Publication Website: www.concrete-herald.com
Editor Name: Jason Miller
Editor Email: editor@concrete-herald.com

COUPEVILLE

SOUTH WHIDBEY RECORD

Corporate/Parent Company: Sound Publishing, Inc.
Street Address: PO Box 1200
City: Coupeville
State: WA
Postal Code: 98239
Office phone: (360) 675-6611
Publication Website: https://www.southwhidbeyrecord.com/
General E-mail: editor@whidbeynewsgroup.com
Editor Email: editor@whidbeynewsgroup.com
Year Established: 1921
Delivery Methods: Mail`Newsstand`Racks
Published Days: Wed`Sat
Avg Paid Circ: 2623
Avg Free Circ: 3
Audit Company: AAM
Audit Date: 31 03 2018

THE WHIDBEY EXAMINER

Corporate/Parent Company: Sound Publishing, Inc.
Street Address: P.O. Box 1200
City: Coupeville
State: WA
Postal Code: 98239
Office phone: (360) 675-6611
Publication Website: https://www.whidbeynewstimes.com/
General E-mail: editor@whidbeynewsgroup.com
Editor Email: editor@whidbeynewsgroup.com
Editor Phone: (360) 675-6611, ext : 5056
Year Established: 1994
Delivery Methods: Mail`Newsstand`Racks
Commercial printers?: N
Published Days: Wed
Avg Paid Circ: 983
Avg Free Circ: 40
Audit Company: Sworn/Estimate/Non-Audited
Audit Date: 6 10 2019

WHIDBEY CROSSWIND

Corporate/Parent Company: Sound Publishing, Inc.
Street Address: P.O. Box 1200
City: Coupeville
State: WA
Postal Code: 98239-1200
Office phone: (360) 675-6611
Publication Website: https://www.whidbeynewstimes.com/crosswind/
General E-mail: editor@whidbeynewsgroup.com
Delivery Methods: Mail`Racks
Published Days: Mthly
Avg Paid Circ: 5
Avg Free Circ: 5650
Audit Company: AAM
Audit Date: 31 03 2018

WHIDBEY NEWS TIMES

Corporate/Parent Company: Sound Publishing, Inc.
Street Address: PO Box 1200
City: Coupeville
State: WA
Postal Code: 98239
Office phone: (360) 675-6611
Publication Website: https://www.whidbeynewstimes.com/
General E-mail: editor@whidbeynewsgroup.com
Editor Email: editor@whidbeynewsgroup.com
Editor Phone: (360) 675-6611, ext : 5056
Year Established: 1908
Delivery Methods: Mail`Newsstand`Racks
Published Days: Wed`Sat
Weekday Frequency: m
Saturday Frequency: m
Avg Paid Circ: 3576
Avg Free Circ: 309
Audit Company: AAM
Audit Date: 31 03 2018

EASTSOUND

THE ISLANDS' SOUNDER

Corporate/Parent Company: Sound Publishing, Inc.
Street Address: 217 Main St
City: Eastsound
State: WA
Postal Code: 98245
Office phone: (360) 376-4500
Publication Website: https://www.islandssounder.com/
Year Established: 1964
Delivery Methods: Mail
Published Days: Wed
Avg Paid Circ: 1269
Avg Free Circ: 8
Audit Company: AAM
Audit Date: 31 03 2018

THE ISLANDS' WEEKLY

Corporate/Parent Company: Sound Publishing, Inc.
Street Address: Box 758
City: Eastsound
State: WA
Postal Code: 98245
Office phone: (360) 376-4500
Publication Website: https://www.islandsweekly.com/
Year Established: 1982
Delivery Methods: Mail
Commercial printers?: Y
Published Days: Tues
Avg Paid Circ: 44
Avg Free Circ: 1863
Audit Company: AAM
Audit Date: 31 03 2018

ENUMCLAW

THE COURIER-HERALD

Corporate/Parent Company: Sound Publishing, Inc.
Street Address: 1186 Myrtle Ave.
City: Enumclaw
State: WA
Postal Code: 98022
Office phone: (360) 825-2555
Publication Website: https://www.courierherald.com/
General E-mail: khanson@soundpublishing.com
Editor Name: Ray Miller-Still
Editor Email: rstill@soundpublishing.com
Advertising Executive Name: Rudi Alcott
Advertising Executive Email: ralcott@soundpublishing.com
Year Established: 2003
Delivery Methods: Mail`Newsstand`Racks
Published Days: Wed
Avg Paid Circ: 924
Avg Free Circ: 24468
Audit Company: Sworn/Estimate/Non-Audited
Audit Date: 6 10 2019

THE ENUMCLAW COURIER-HERALD

Corporate/Parent Company: Sound Publishing, Inc.
Street Address: 1186 Myrtle Ave.
City: Enumclaw
State: WA
Postal Code: 98022
Office phone: (360) 825-2555
Publication Website: https://www.courierherald.com/
General E-mail: ahobbs@soundpublishing.com
Editor Name: Ray Miller-Still
Editor Email: rstill@soundpublishing.com
Advertising Executive Name: Rudi Alcott
Advertising Executive Email: ralcott@soundpublishing.com
Delivery Methods: Mail`Newsstand`Racks
Published Days: Wed
Avg Paid Circ: 967
Avg Free Circ: 23854
Audit Company: AAM
Audit Date: 31 03 2018

EPHRATA

GRANT COUNTY JOURNAL

Street Address: 29 Alder St SW
City: Ephrata
State: WA
Postal Code: 98823
Office phone: 509-754-4636
Publication Website: www.facebook.com/kerrycmo
Publisher Name: Jeff Fletcher
Publisher Email: moser@gcjournal.net
Editor Name: Randy Bracht
Editor Email: news@gcjournal.net
Advertising Executive Name: Jennifer DeChenne
Advertising Executive Email: advertising@gcjournal.net

EVERETT

THE DAILY HERALD

Corporate/Parent Company: Sound Publishing, Inc.
Street Address: 1800 41st St., S-300
City: Everett
State: WA
Postal Code: 98201-3445
Office phone: (425) 339-3000
Publication Website: https://www.heraldnet.com/
General E-mail: cradcliff@soundpublishing.com
Publisher Name: Josh O'Connor
Publisher Email: publisher@heraldnet.com
Publisher Phone: (425) 339-3007
Editor Name: Eric Stevickq
Editor Email: stevick@heraldnet.com
Editor Phone: (425) 339-3446
Advertising Executive Name: Carrie Radcliff
Advertising Executive Email: cradcliff@soundpublishing.com
Advertising Executive Phone: (425) 339-3052
Year Established: 1901
Delivery Methods: Newsstand`Carrier`Racks
Own Printing Facility?: Y

Non-Daily Newspapers in the U.S.

Commercial printers?: Y
Mechanical specifications: Type page 13 x 21; E - 6 cols, 2 1/16, 1/8 between; A - 6 cols, 2 1/16, 1/8 between; C - 10 cols, 1 3/16, 1/8 between.
Published Days: Mon`Tues`Wed`Thur`Fri`Sat`Sun
Weekday Frequency: m
Saturday Frequency: m
Avg Paid Circ: 27824
Audit Company: AAM
Audit Date: 31 03 2018

FEDERAL WAY

AUBURN REPORTER

Corporate/Parent Company: Auburn Reporter and Sound Publishing, Inc.
Street Address: 1010 S 336th St, Suite 330
City: Federal Way
State: WA
Postal Code: 98003
Office phone: 253.833.0218
Publication Website: www.auburn-reporter.com
General E-mail: editor@federalwaymirror.com
Editor Name: Mark Klaas
Editor Email: mklaas@soundpublishing.com
Editor Phone: 253.833.0218
Advertising Executive Name: Rudi Alcott
Advertising Executive Email: ralcott@soundpublishing.com
Advertising Executive Phone: 253.833.0218

COVINGTON-MAPLE VALLEY-BLACK DIAMOND REPORTER

Corporate/Parent Company: Sound Publishing, Inc.
Street Address: 1010 S 336th St, Suite 330
City: Federal Way
State: WA
Postal Code: 98003
Office phone: (425) 432-1209
Publication Website: https://www.covingtonreporter.com/
General E-mail: ahobbs@soundpublishing.com
Editor Name: Danielle Chastaine
Editor Email: dchastaine@soundpublishing.com
Advertising Executive Name: Rudi Alcott
Advertising Executive Email: ralcott@soundpublishing.com
Year Established: 2005
Delivery Methods: Mail`Newsstand`Racks
Published Days: Fri
Avg Paid Circ: 11
Avg Free Circ: 24024
Audit Company: AAM
Audit Date: 31 03 2018

FEDERAL WAY MIRROR

Corporate/Parent Company: Sound Publishing, Inc.
Street Address: 1010 S 336th St, Suite 330
City: Federal Way
State: WA
Postal Code: 98003
Office phone: (253) 925-5565
Publication Website: https://www.federalwaymirror.com
General E-mail: ahobbs@soundpublishing.com
Editor Name: Carrie Rodriguez
Editor Email: crodriguez@soundpublishing.com
Advertising Executive Name: Rudi Alcott
Advertising Executive Email: ralcott@soundpublishing.com
Year Established: 1998
Delivery Methods: Mail`Newsstand`Racks
Own Printing Facility?: Y
Mechanical specifications: Type page 13 x 21 1/2; E - 5 cols, 2 1/8, 1/8 between; A - 6 cols, 1 3/4, 1/8 between; C - 10 cols, 1 1/16, 1/16 between.
Published Days: Fri
Avg Paid Circ: 918
Avg Free Circ: 27964
Audit Company: AAM
Audit Date: 31 03 2018

TUKWILA REPORTER

Corporate/Parent Company: Sound Publishing, Inc.
Street Address: 1010 S 336th St, Suite 330
City: Federal Way
State: WA
Postal Code: 98003
Office phone: (253) 872-6600
Publication Website: https://www.tukwilareporter.com
General E-mail: kangel@soundpublishing.com
Editor Name: Sarah Brenden
Editor Email: sbrenden@soundpublishing.com
Published Days: Mthly
Avg Paid Circ: 9383
Avg Free Circ: 385
Audit Company: AAM
Audit Date: 31 03 2018

FORKS

FORKS FORUM

Corporate/Parent Company: Sound Publishing, Inc.
Street Address: 490 S Forks Ave
City: Forks
State: WA
Postal Code: 98331
Office phone: (360) 374-3311
Publication Website: https://www.forksforum.com/
General E-mail: tward@soundpublishing.com
Publisher Name: Terry Ward
Publisher Email: tward@soundpublishing.com
Editor Name: Christi Baron
Editor Email: cbaron@soundpublishing.com
Year Established: 1930
Delivery Methods: Mail`Racks
Mechanical specifications: 5X12.5 1/col. = 11p0 (1.83")
Published Days: Thur
Avg Paid Circ: 157
Avg Free Circ: 4287
Audit Company: AAM
Audit Date: 31 03 2018

FRIDAY HARBOR

THE JOURNAL OF THE SAN JUAN ISLANDS

Corporate/Parent Company: Sound Publishing, Inc.
Street Address: 640 Mullis St
City: Friday Harbor
State: WA
Postal Code: 98250
Office phone: (360) 378-5696
Publication Website: https://www.sanjuanjournal.com/
Year Established: 1906
Delivery Methods: Mail`Racks
Own Printing Facility?: Y
Mechanical specifications: Type page 10 3/4 x 16; E - 5 cols, 1 11/12, 1/6 between; A - 5 cols, 1 11/12, 1/6 between; C - 5 cols, 1 11/12, 1/6 between.
Published Days: Wed
Avg Paid Circ: 1264
Avg Free Circ: 35
Audit Company: AAM
Audit Date: 31 03 2018

GRANDVIEW

GRANDVIEW HERALD

Street Address: 308 Division St.
City: Grandview
State: WA
Postal Code: 98930
Office phone: (509) 882-3712
Publication Website: thenewsatvalleypublishing.com
General E-mail: legals@recordbulletin.com

KENT

KENT REPORTER

Corporate/Parent Company: Sound Publishing, Inc.
Street Address: 19426 68th Ave S
City: Kent
State: WA
Postal Code: 98032
Office phone: (253) 872-6600
Publication Website: https://www.kentreporter.com/
General E-mail: ralcott@soundpublishing.com
Editor Name: Mark Klaas
Editor Email: mklaas@soundpublishing.com
Advertising Executive Name: Rudi Alcott
Advertising Executive Email: ralcott@soundpublishing.com
Year Established: 1998
Delivery Methods: Mail`Newsstand`Racks
Published Days: Fri
Avg Paid Circ: 168
Avg Free Circ: 24660
Audit Company: AAM
Audit Date: 31 03 2018

RENTON REPORTER

Corporate/Parent Company: Sound Publishing, Inc.
Street Address: 19426 68th Ave S
City: Kent
State: WA
Postal Code: 98032
Office phone: (253) 255-3484
Publication Website: https://www.rentonreporter.com/
General E-mail: ahobbs@soundpublishing.com
Editor Name: Danielle Chastaine
Editor Email: dchastaine@soundpublishing.com
Advertising Executive Name: Rudi Alcott
Advertising Executive Email: ralcott@soundpublishing.com
Delivery Methods: Mail`Carrier`Racks
Published Days: Fri
Avg Paid Circ: 31
Avg Free Circ: 24257
Audit Company: AAM
Audit Date: 31 03 2018

KIRKLAND

BOTHELL/KENMORE REPORTER

Corporate/Parent Company: Sound Publishing, Inc.
Street Address: 11630 Slater Ave NE
City: Kirkland
State: WA
Postal Code: 98034
Office phone: (425) 483-3732
Publication Website: https://www.bothell-reporter.com/
General E-mail: ralcott@soundpublishing.com
Editor Name: Corey Morris
Editor Email: cmorris@soundpublishing.com
Advertising Executive Name: Pili Linares
Advertising Executive Email: plinares@soundpublishing.com
Delivery Methods: Mail`Newsstand`Racks
Published Days: Bi-Mthly
Avg Paid Circ: 38
Avg Free Circ: 19547
Audit Company: AAM
Audit Date: 31 03 2018

KIRKLAND REPORTER

Corporate/Parent Company: Sound Publishing, Inc.
Street Address: 11630 Slater Ave NE
City: Kirkland
State: WA
Postal Code: 98034
Office phone: (425) 822-9166
Publication Website: https://www.kirklandreporter.com/
General E-mail: ralcott@soundpublishing.com
Editor Name: Corey Morris
Editor Email: cmorris@soundpublishing.com
Advertising Executive Name: Pili Linares
Advertising Executive Email: plinares@soundpublishing.com
Year Established: 1978
Delivery Methods: Mail`Newsstand`Racks
Published Days: Fri
Avg Paid Circ: 24
Avg Free Circ: 24676
Audit Company: AAM
Audit Date: 31 03 2018

MERCER ISLAND REPORTER

Corporate/Parent Company: Sound Publishing, Inc.
Street Address: 11630 Slater Ave. N.E.
City: Kirkland
State: WA
Postal Code: 98034
Office phone: (206) 232-1215
Publication Website: https://www.mi-reporter.com/
General E-mail: ralcott@soundpublishing.com
Editor Name: Corey Morris
Editor Email: cmorris@soundpublishing.com
Advertising Executive Name: Pili Linares
Advertising Executive Email: plinares@soundpublishing.com
Year Established: 1947
Delivery Methods: Mail
Mechanical specifications: Type page 13 1/2 x 23; E - 6 cols, 2 1/5, between; A - 6 cols, 2 1/5, between.
Published Days: Wed
Avg Paid Circ: 2613
Audit Company: AAM
Audit Date: 31 03 2018

REDMOND REPORTER

Corporate/Parent Company: Sound Publishing, Inc.
Street Address: 11630 Slater Ave NE
City: Kirkland
State: WA
Postal Code: 98034
Office phone: (425) 867-0353
Publication Website: https://www.redmond-reporter.com/
General E-mail: ralcott@soundpublishing.com
Editor Name: Corey Morris
Editor Email: cmorris@soundpublishing.com
Advertising Executive Name: Pili Linares
Advertising Executive Email: plinares@soundpublishing.com

LYNNWOOD

LYNNWOOD TIMES
Street Address: 19200 44th Ave W
City: Lynnwood
State: WA
Postal Code: 98087
Office phone: 425-308-8371
Publication Website: www.lynnwoodtimes.com
General E-mail: tips@lynnwoodtimes.com
Publisher Name: Mario Lotmore
Editor Name: Teresa Wippel
Editor Email: editorial@lynnwoodtimes.com
Year Established: 2001
Delivery Methods: Mail`Newsstand`Racks
Published Days: Fri
Avg Paid Circ: 9
Avg Free Circ: 22224
Audit Company: AAM
Audit Date: 31 03 2018

MARYSVILLE

THE ARLINGTON TIMES
Corporate/Parent Company: Sound Publishing, Inc.
Street Address: 1085 Cedar Ave
City: Marysville
State: WA
Postal Code: 98270
Office phone: (360) 659-1300
Publication Website: https://www.arlingtontimes.com/
Year Established: 1887
Delivery Methods: Mail`Newsstand`Racks
Own Printing Facility?: Y
Commercial printers?: Y
Mechanical specifications: Type page 12 7/8 x 21 1/2; E - 6 cols, 2, 1/8 between; A - 6 cols, 2, 1/8 between; C - 9 cols, 1 3/8, 1/8 between.
Published Days: Wed`Sun
Avg Paid Circ: 137
Avg Free Circ: 4949
Audit Company: AAM
Audit Date: 17 03 2016

THE MARYSVILLE GLOBE
Corporate/Parent Company: Sound Publishing, Inc.
Street Address: PO Box 145
City: Marysville
State: WA
Postal Code: 98270
Office phone: (360) 659-1300
Publication Website: https://www.marysvilleglobe.com/
Year Established: 1892
Delivery Methods: Mail`Newsstand`Carrier`Racks
Published Days: Sun
Avg Paid Circ: 74
Avg Free Circ: 15000
Audit Company: AAM
Audit Date: 16 03 2016

MONTESANO

THE VIDETTE
Corporate/Parent Company: Sound Publishing, Inc.
Street Address: 109 W Marcy Ave
City: Montesano
State: WA
Postal Code: 98563-3615
Office phone: (360) 249-3311
Publication Website: https://www.thevidette.com/
General E-mail: editor@thevidette.com
Publisher Name: Michael Hrycko
Publisher Email: publisher@thedailyworld.com
Editor Name: Michael Lang
Editor Email: mlang@thevidette.com
Editor Phone: (360) 537-3936
Advertising Executive Name: Brent Hunter
Advertising Executive Email: bhunter@thedailyworld.com
Year Established: 1883
Delivery Methods: Mail`Newsstand`Racks
Published Days: Thur
Avg Paid Circ: 5583
Avg Free Circ: 749
Audit Company: AAM
Audit Date: 31 03 2016

MOUNT VERNON

THE ARGUS
Corporate/Parent Company: Adams Publishing Group
Street Address: 1215 Anderson Rd
City: Mount Vernon
State: WA
Postal Code: 98274
Office phone: (360) 424-3251
Publication Website: https://www.goskagit.com/
General E-mail: news@skagitpublishing.com
Advertising Executive Name: Duby Petit
Advertising Executive Email: dpetit@skagitpublishing.com
Advertising Executive Phone: (360) 416-2128
Delivery Methods: Mail
Mechanical specifications: Type page 10 1/4 x 16 1/2; E - 5 cols, 2 1/12, between; A - 5 cols, 2 1/12, between; C - 5 cols, 2 1/12, between.
Published Days: Wed
Avg Paid Circ: 3200
Avg Free Circ: 6300
Audit Company: Sworn/Estimate/Non-Audited
Audit Date: 6 10 2019

OLYMPIA

OLYMPIA NEWS BUREAU
Street Address: 522 Franklin Street SE
City: Olympia
State: WA
Postal Code: 98501
Office phone: 360-754-5400
Publication Website: www.theolympian.com
Editor Name: Dusti Demarest
Editor Email: ddemarest@theolympian.com
Editor Phone: (360) 357-0206
Advertising Executive Name: Kim Fuller
Advertising Executive Email: kim.fuller@thenewstribune.com
Advertising Executive Phone: (253) 597-8417

OROVILLE

OKANOGAN VALLEY GAZETTE-TRIBUNE
Corporate/Parent Company: Sound Publishing, Inc.
Street Address: 1422 Main St
City: Oroville
State: WA
Postal Code: 98844
Office phone: (509) 476-3602
Publication Website: http://www.gazette-tribune.com/
Year Established: 1905
Delivery Methods: Mail`Newsstand
Published Days: Thur
Avg Paid Circ: 1309
Audit Company: AAM
Audit Date: 31 03 2018

POULSBO

BAINBRIDGE ISLAND REVIEW
Corporate/Parent Company: Sound Publishing, Inc.
Street Address: PO Box 278
City: Poulsbo
State: WA
Postal Code: 98370
Office phone: (206) 842-6613
Publication Website: https://www.bainbridgereview.com/
Publisher Name: Terry Ward
Publisher Email: tward@soundpublishing.com
Editor Name: Brian Kelly
Editor Email: bkelly@soundpublishing.com
Year Established: 1923
Delivery Methods: Mail`Newsstand`Racks
Published Days: Fri
Avg Paid Circ: 1925
Avg Free Circ: 55
Audit Company: Sworn/Estimate/Non-Audited
Audit Date: 6 10 2019

BREMERTON PATRIOT-OOB
Corporate/Parent Company: Sound Publishing, Inc.
Street Address: 19351 8th Ave. NE, Suite #S-135
City: Poulsbo
State: WA
Postal Code: 98370
Office phone: (360) 779-4464
Publication Website: https://www.kitsapdailynews.com/print-editions-bremerton/
General E-mail: tward@soundpublishing.com
Publisher Name: Terry R. Ward
Publisher Email: tward@soundpublishing.com
Editor Name: Robert Monteith
Advertising Executive Name: Eran Kennedy
Advertising Executive Phone: (360) 779-4464, ext : 15049

CENTRAL KITSAP REPORTER
Corporate/Parent Company: Sound Publishing, Inc.
Street Address: 19351 8th Ave NE
City: Poulsbo
State: WA
Postal Code: 98370
Office phone: (360) 779-4464
Publication Website: https://www.kitsapdailynews.com/print-editions-central-kitsap/
General E-mail: tward@soundpublishing.com
Publisher Name: Terry R. Ward
Publisher Email: tward@soundpublishing.com
Publisher Phone: (360) 779-4464
Editor Name: Robert Monteith
Editor Phone: (360) 779-4464
Advertising Executive Name: Eran Kennedy
Advertising Executive Phone: (360) 779-4464, ext : 15049
Delivery Methods: Newsstand`Carrier
Own Printing Facility?: Y
Commercial printers?: Y
Mechanical specifications: Type page 10 1/4 x 15; E - 6 cols, 1 9/16, 1/6 between; A - 6 cols, 1 9/16, 1/6 between; C - 7 cols, 1 3/8, 1/12 between.
Published Days: Fri
Avg Paid Circ: 271
Avg Free Circ: 14487
Audit Company: AAM
Audit Date: 31 03 2018

KINGSTON COMMUNITY NEWS
Corporate/Parent Company: Sound Publishing, Inc.
Street Address: Box 278, 19351 8th Ave. NE, Suite #S-135
City: Poulsbo
State: WA
Postal Code: 98370
Office phone: (360) 779-4464
Publication Website: https://www.kitsapdailynews.com/print-editions-kingston/
General E-mail: tward@soundpublishing.com
Publisher Name: Terry R. Ward
Publisher Email: tward@soundpublishing.com
Publisher Phone: (360) 779-4464
Editor Name: Robert Monteith
Editor Phone: (360) 779-4464
Advertising Executive Name: Eran Kennedy
Advertising Executive Phone: (360) 779-4464, ext : 15049
Delivery Methods: Mail
Published Days: Mthly
Avg Free Circ: 8988
Audit Company: AAM
Audit Date: 31 03 2018

NORTH KITSAP HERALD
Corporate/Parent Company: Sound Publishing, Inc.
Street Address: 19351 8th Ave. NE, S-135
City: Poulsbo
State: WA
Postal Code: 98370
Office phone: (360) 779-4464
Publication Website: https://www.kitsapdailynews.com/print-editions-north-kitsap/
General E-mail: tward@soundpublishing.com
Publisher Name: Terry R. Ward
Publisher Email: tward@soundpublishing.com
Editor Name: Robert Monteith
Advertising Executive Name: Eran Kennedy
Advertising Executive Phone: (360) 779-4464, ext : 15049
Year Established: 1901
Delivery Methods: Mail`Newsstand`Carrier`Racks
Own Printing Facility?: Y
Commercial printers?: Y
Mechanical specifications: Type page 10 3/8 x 15; E - 6 cols, 1 3/5, 1/6 between; A - 6 cols, 1 3/5, 1/6 between; C - 7 cols, 1 2/5, 1/12 between.
Published Days: Fri
Avg Paid Circ: 509
Avg Free Circ: 10565
Audit Company: AAM
Audit Date: 31 03 2018

PORT ORCHARD INDEPENDENT
Corporate/Parent Company: Sound Publishing, Inc.
Street Address: Box 278, 19351 8th Ave. NE, Suite #S-135
City: Poulsbo
State: WA
Postal Code: 98370
Office phone: (360) 876-4414
Publication Website: https://www.kitsapdailynews.com/print-editions-port-orchard/
General E-mail: tward@soundpublishing.com
Publisher Name: Terry R. Ward
Publisher Email: tward@soundpublishing.com
Publisher Phone: (360) 779-4464
Editor Name: Robert Monteith
Editor Phone: (360) 779-4464
Advertising Executive Name: Eran Kennedy
Advertising Executive Phone: (360) 779-4464, ext : 15049
Year Established: 1890
Delivery Methods: Newsstand`Carrier
Own Printing Facility?: Y
Published Days: Fri
Avg Paid Circ: 837
Avg Free Circ: 16382
Audit Company: AAM
Audit Date: 31 03 2018

REPUBLIC

FERRY COUNTY VIEW
Street Address: 771 S Keller St
City: Republic
State: WA
Postal Code: 99166
Office phone: 509-775-2425
Publication Website: www.ferrycountyview.com

Non-Daily Newspapers in the U.S.

Editor Name: Mr. Greg Sheffield
Editor Email: editor@ferrycountyview.com

SEQUIM

THE SEQUIM GAZETTE

Corporate/Parent Company: Sound Publishing, Inc.
Street Address: 147 W Washington St
City: Sequim
State: WA
Postal Code: 98382
Office phone: (360) 683-3311
Publication Website: https://www.sequimgazette.com
General E-mail: tward@soundpublishing.com
Publisher Name: Terry Ward
Publisher Email: tward@soundpublishing.com
Editor Name: Michael Dashiell
Editor Email: mdashiell@soundpublishing.com
Year Established: 1988
Delivery Methods:
    Mail`Newsstand`Carrier`Racks
Commercial printers?: Y
Mechanical specifications: Type page 10 1/2 x 21 1/col. = 9p8 (1.61")
Published Days: Wed
Avg Paid Circ: 3547
Audit Company: AAM
Audit Date: 31 03 2018

SNOQUALMIE

SNOQUALMIE VALLEY RECORD

Corporate/Parent Company: Sound Publishing, Inc.
Street Address: 8124 Falls Ave SE
City: Snoqualmie
State: WA
Postal Code: 98065
Office phone: (425) 888-2311
Publication Website: https://www.valleyrecord.com/
General E-mail: plinares@soundpublishing.com
Publisher Name: William Shaw
Editor Name: Samantha Pak
Editor Email: spak@soundpublishing.com
Advertising Executive Name: Pili Linares
Advertising Executive Email: plinares@soundpublishing.com
Year Established: 1913
Delivery Methods: Mail`Newsstand`Racks
Mechanical specifications: Type page 11 3/5 x 21; E - 6 cols, 2, 1/6 between; A - 6 cols, 2, 1/6 between; C - 7 cols, 1 7/12, 1/6 between.
Published Days: Wed
Avg Paid Circ: 351
Avg Free Circ: 10810
Audit Company: AAM
Audit Date: 31 03 2018

SPOKANE

GONZAGA BULLETIN

Street Address: 502 East Boone MSC 2476
City: Spokane
State: WA
Postal Code: 99258
Office phone: (509) 313-6606
Publication Website: www.gonzagabulletin.com
General E-mail: adoffice@gonzaga.edu
Editor Name: Arcelia Martin
Editor Email: bulletin@zagmail.gonzaga.edu

STANWOOD

STANWOOD CAMANO ADVERTISER

Corporate/Parent Company: Skagit Publishing Co.
Street Address: 9005 271st St NW
City: Stanwood
State: WA
Postal Code: 98292
Office phone: (360) 629-2155
Publication Website: https://www.goskagit.com/scnews/
General E-mail: newsroom@scnews.com
Publisher Name: Kathy Boyd
Publisher Email: kboyd@scnews.com
Publisher Phone: (360) 629-2155, ext : 2217
Editor Name: Kathy Boyd
Editor Email: kboyd@scnews.com
Editor Phone: (360) 629-2155, ext : 2217
Advertising Executive Name: Jenny Baehm
Advertising Executive Email: jbaehm@scnews.com
Advertising Executive Phone: (360) 629-2155, ext : 2134

SUNNYSIDE

SUNNYSIDE SUN

Corporate/Parent Company: Sunnyside Sun Media, LLC
Street Address: 600 S. Sixth Street
City: Sunnyside
State: WA
Postal Code: 98944
Office phone: 509-837-4500
Publication Website: www.sunnysidesun.com
General E-mail: news@sunnysidesun.com
Editor Name: Patrick Shelby
Editor Email: pshelby@sunnysidesun.com
Editor Phone: 509-837-4500 Ext. 110
Advertising Executive Name: Matt Sagen
Advertising Executive Email: msagen@sunnysidesun.com
Advertising Executive Phone: 509-837-4500 Ext. 101

TACOMA

THE HERALD (PUYALLUP)

Street Address: 1950 South State Street
City: Tacoma
State: WA
Postal Code: 98405
Office phone: 253-597-8742
Publication Website: www.thenewstribune.com/news/local/community/puyallup-herald
Publisher Name: Rebecca Poynter
Publisher Email: rebecca.poynter@thenewstribune.com
Publisher Phone: (253) 597-8554
Editor Name: Dale Phelps
Editor Email: dale.phelps@thenewstribune.com
Editor Phone: (253) 597-8681
Advertising Executive Name: Rebecca Poynter
Advertising Executive Email: rpoynter@mcclatchy.com
Advertising Executive Phone: (253) 597-8554

VASHON

VASHON-MAURY ISLAND BEACHCOMBER

Corporate/Parent Company: Sound Publishing, Inc.
Street Address: 17141 Vashon Hwy SW
City: Vashon
State: WA
Postal Code: 98070
Office phone: (206) 463-9195
Publication Website: https://www.vashonbeachcomber.com/
General E-mail: ahobbs@soundpublishing.com
Editor Name: Kevin Opsahl
Editor Email: kopsahl@soundpublishing.com
Advertising Executive Name: Rudi Alcott
Advertising Executive Email: ralcott@soundpublishing.com
Year Established: 1957
Delivery Methods:
    Mail`Newsstand`Carrier`Racks
Own Printing Facility?: Y
Mechanical specifications: Type page 10 1/4 x 21; E - 6 cols, 1 7/12, between; A - 6 cols, 1 7/12, between; C - 10 cols, 1 1/3, between.
Published Days: Wed
Avg Paid Circ: 2606
Avg Free Circ: 30

VAUGHN

KEY PENINSULA NEWS

Street Address: Key Peninsula News P.O. Box 3
City: Vaughn
State: WA
Postal Code: 98394
Office phone: 253-884-4699
Publication Website: keypennews.com
Editor Name: Scott Turner
Editor Email: editor@keypennews.org

YAKIMA

YAKIMA HERALD-REPUBLIC

Corporate/Parent Company: Yakima Herald-Republic
Street Address: 114 N 4th St
City: Yakima
State: WA
Postal Code: 98901
Office phone: (509) 248-1251
Publication Website: https://www.yakimaherald.com/
General E-mail: advertising@yakimaherald.com
Publisher Name: Bob Crider
Publisher Email: bcrider@yakimaherald.com
Publisher Phone: (509) 577-7701
Editor Name: Greg Halling
Editor Email: ghalling@yakimaherald.com
Editor Phone: (509) 577-7703
Advertising Executive Name: Carmela Solorzano
Advertising Executive Email: csolorzano@yakimaherald.com
Advertising Executive Phone: (509) 577-7676
Year Established: 1889
Delivery Methods:
    Mail`Newsstand`Carrier`Racks
Own Printing Facility?: Y
Commercial printers?: Y
Mechanical specifications: Tyoe Page Thru Feb 2018 - 12.5 x 20.5 March 2018 - 10.125 x 20.5 6 Columns, 1/8" gutter
Published Days: Mon`Tues`Wed`Thur`Fri`Sat`Sun
Weekday Frequency: m
Saturday Frequency: m
Avg Paid Circ: 21661
Audit Company: AAM
Audit Date: 31 12 2016

WISCONSIN

ABBOTSFORD

THE RECORD-REVIEW

Street Address: 103 W. Spruce Street Abbotsford
City: Abbotsford
State: WI
Postal Code: 54405
Office phone: 715-223-2342
Publication Website: www.centralwinews.com/record-review
General E-mail: rr@tpprinting.com

THE STAR NEWS

Corporate/Parent Company: Gannett
Street Address: 103 W Spruce St
City: Abbotsford
State: WI
Postal Code: 54405
Office phone: 715-748-2626
Publication Website: centralwinews.com/star-news
General E-mail: starnews@centralwinews.com

ADAMS

ADAMS-FRIENDSHIP TIMES REPORTER

Corporate/Parent Company: Adams Friendship Newspapers
Street Address: 116 S. Main/P.O. Box 99
City: Adams
State: WI
Postal Code: 53910
Office phone: 608-339-7844
Publication Website: afnewspapers.com
General E-mail: media@afnewspapers.com
Advertising Executive Name: Jody McManus
Advertising Executive Email: rrsales@afnewspapers.com
Advertising Executive Phone: 608-339-7844

ARCADIA

THE BLAIR PRESS

Street Address: 109 Gilbert St
City: Arcadia
State: WI
Postal Code: 54616
Office phone: 608-989-2531
Publication Website: www.blairpress.com
Editor Name: Alex Reitz
Editor Email: blairprs@triwest.net

ARGYLE

PECATONICA VALLEY LEADER

Corporate/Parent Company: Reilly & Reilly, Inc
Street Address: 101 N. State St.
City: Argyle
State: WI
Postal Code: 53504
Office phone: 608-543-9500
Publication Website: www.thedodgevillechronicle.com
Publisher Name: Mike Reilly
Publisher Email: mreilly@thedodgevillechronicle.com
Publisher Phone: 608-935-2331
Editor Name: Gary McKenzie
Editor Email: blade@tds.net
Advertising Executive Name: Shelly Roh
Advertising Executive Email: ad@thedodgevillechronicle.com
Advertising Executive Phone: 608-935-2331

ASHLAND

THE COUNTY JOURNAL

Street Address: 122 West 3rd Street
City: Ashland
State: WI
Postal Code: 54806
Office phone: 715-682-2313
Publication Website: www.bayfieldtoday.com
General E-mail: pressclass@ashlanddailypress.net
Advertising Executive Name: Steve Furuta
Advertising Executive Email: (steve.furuta@ecpc.com
Advertising Executive Phone: 715-830-5823
Total Circulation: 8701

BALSAM LAKE

COUNTY LEDGER PRESS

Corporate/Parent Company: Ledger Publications, Inc
Street Address: 105 Main Street, P.O. Box 129
City: Balsam Lake
State: WI
Postal Code: 54810
Office phone: 715-485-3121
Publication Website: www.pc-ledger.com
General E-mail: pcledger@lakeland.ws

BEAVER DAM

COLUMBUS JOURNAL
Street Address: 805 Park Ave
City: Beaver Dam
State: WI
Postal Code: 53916-2205
Office phone: (920) 623-3160
Publication Website: http://www.wiscnews.com/columbusjournal/
General E-mail: kpremo-rake@wiscnews.com
Editor Name: Kevin Damask
Editor Email: kdamask@wiscnews.com
Editor Phone: (608) 963-7323
Advertising Executive Name: Kara Premo Rake
Advertising Executive Email: kpremo-rake@wiscnews.com
Advertising Executive Phone: (920) 356-6772
Year Established: 1855
Delivery Methods: Mail`Racks
Own Printing Facility?: Y
Commercial printers?: Y
Published Days: Sat
Avg Paid Circ: 1736
Audit Company: Sworn/Estimate/Non-Audited
Audit Date: 6 10 2019

BLACK EARTH

MIDDLETON TIMES-TRIBUNE
Corporate/Parent Company: News Publishing Company, Inc
Street Address: 1126 Mills St, PO BOX 286
City: Black Earth
State: WI
Postal Code: 53515-9419
Office phone: (608) 767-3655
Publication Website: http://www.middletontimes.com/
General E-mail: classifieds@newspubinc.com
Editor Name: Matt Geiger
Editor Email: mgeiger@newspubinc.com
Editor Phone: (608) 437-5553
Delivery Methods: Mail`Newsstand
Published Days: Thur
Avg Paid Circ: 1694
Audit Company: Sworn/Estimate/Non-Audited
Audit Date: 6 10 2019

NEWS-SICKLE-ARROW
Corporate/Parent Company: News Publishing, Co., Inc.
Street Address: 1126 Mills St
City: Black Earth
State: WI
Postal Code: 53515-9419
Office phone: (608) 767-3655
Publication Website: https://www.nsarrow.com/
General E-mail: spseditor@newspubinc.com
Editor Name: Joe Block
Editor Email: spseditor@newspubinc.com
Advertising Executive Name: Amanda Henning
Advertising Executive Email: starnewssales@newspubinc.com
Advertising Executive Phone: (608) 509-4548
Delivery Methods: Mail`Newsstand
Own Printing Facility?: Y
Commercial printers?: Y
Mechanical specifications: Type page 10 1/4 x 16; E - 5 cols, 2, 1/3 between; A - 5 cols, 2, 1/3 between; C - 5 cols, 2, 1/3 between.
Published Days: Thur
Avg Paid Circ: 2012
Audit Company: Sworn/Estimate/Non-Audited
Audit Date: 6 10 2019
Total Circulation: 1736

BLACK RIVER FALLS

BANNER JOURNAL
Street Address: 409 East Main Street
City: Black River Falls
State: WI
Postal Code: 54615
Office phone: 715-284-4304
Publication Website: bannerjournal.com

BURLINGTON

BURLINGTON STANDARD PRESS
Corporate/Parent Company: Southern Lakes Newspapers LLC
Street Address: 209 N. Dodge St.
City: Burlington
State: WI
Postal Code: 53105-1472
Office phone: (262) 763-3330
Publication Website: http://southernlakesnewspapers.com/
General E-mail: dbrooks@southernlakesnewspapers.com
Publisher Name: Sue Z. Lange
Publisher Email: suez@standardpress.com
Publisher Phone: (262) 728-3411, ext : 114
Editor Name: Jason Arndt
Editor Email: jarndt@southernlakesnewspapers.com
Editor Phone: (262) 763-3330, ext : 148
Advertising Executive Name: Donna Sylvester Brooks
Advertising Executive Email: dbrooks@southernlakesnewspapers.com
Advertising Executive Phone: (262) 763-2575, ext : 138
Delivery Methods: Mail
Own Printing Facility?: Y
Commercial printers?: Y
Mechanical specifications: Type page 13 x 21.
Published Days: Thur
Avg Paid Circ: 3900
Avg Free Circ: 4801
Audit Company: Sworn/Estimate/Non-Audited
Audit Date: 6 10 2019

STANDARD-PRESS
Street Address: 209 N Dodge St
City: Burlington
State: WI
Postal Code: 53105
Office phone: (262) 763-3330
Publication Website: myracinecounty.com
Editor Name: Jason Arndt
Editor Email: jarndt@southernlakesnewspapers.com
Editor Phone: (262) 763-3330, ext. 148
Advertising Executive Name: Donna Sylvester Brooks
Advertising Executive Email: dbrooks@southernlakesnewspapers.com
Advertising Executive Phone: (262) 763-2575, ext. 138

CEDARBURG

NEWS GRAPHIC
Corporate/Parent Company: Conley Media LLC
Street Address: W61 N306 Washington Ave. Suite L1
City: Cedarburg
State: WI
Postal Code: 53012-2451
Office phone: (262) 306-5000
Publication Website: http://www.gmtoday.com/promotions/cust_service/mkelifestyle.htm
General E-mail: webmaster@conleynet.com
Editor Name: Ashley Haynes
Editor Email: ahaynes@conleynet.com
Advertising Executive Name: Jim Baumgart
Advertising Executive Email: jbaumgart@conleynet.com
Year Established: 1883
Delivery Methods: Mail`Newsstand`Racks
Published Days: Tues`Thur
Avg Paid Circ: 7218
Avg Free Circ: 232
Audit Company: Sworn/Estimate/Non-Audited
Audit Date: 6 10 2019

OZAUKEE COUNTY NEWS GRAPHIC
Corporate/Parent Company: Conley Media LLC
Street Address: W61 N306 Washington Ave. Suite L1
City: Cedarburg
State: WI
Postal Code: 53012-2451
Office phone: (262) 306-5000
Publication Website: http://www.gmtoday.com/promotions/cust_service/newsgraphic.asp
General E-mail: webmaster@conleynet.com

CLINTONVILLE

CLINTONVILLE CHRONICLE
Street Address: 10 N. Main Street
City: Clintonville
State: WI
Postal Code: 54929
Office phone: 715-823-7323
Publication Website: www.clintonvillechronicle.com
General E-mail: clintonville@clintonvillewi.org
Editor Name: Tricia Rose
Editor Email: trose@clintonvillechronicle.com

CLINTONVILLE TRIBUNE GAZETTE
Corporate/Parent Company: Multi Media Channels, LLC
Street Address: 17 9th St
City: Clintonville
State: WI
Postal Code: 54929
Office phone: 715-823-3151
Publication Website: www.clintonvilletribunegazette.com
General E-mail: clintonville.news@mmclocal.com
Advertising Executive Name: Bernice Fuhrmann
Advertising Executive Email: bfuhrmann@mmclocal.com
Advertising Executive Phone: 715-377-3641

COCHRANE

BUFFALO COUNTY JOURNAL
Corporate/Parent Company: Conley Media LLC
Street Address: P.O. Box 40
City: Cochrane
State: WI
Postal Code: 54622
Office phone: 608-248-2451
Publication Website: www.gmdmedia.net/buffalo-county-journal
General E-mail: Recorder@mwt.net
Total Circulation: 2771

COCHRANE-FOUNTAIN CITY RECORDER
Corporate/Parent Company: Conley Media LLC
Street Address: P.O. Box 40
City: Cochrane
State: WI
Postal Code: 54622
Office phone: 608-248-2451
Publication Website: www.gmdmedia.net/cochrane-fountain-city-record
General E-mail: Recorder@mwt.net
Total Circulation: 653

DELAVAN

LAKE GENEVA TIMES
Corporate/Parent Company: Southern Lakes Newspapers LLC
Street Address: 1102 Ann St
City: Delavan
State: WI
Postal Code: 53115-1938
Office phone: (262) 728-3411
Publication Website: http://southernlakesnewspapers.com/
General E-mail: tamera@southernlakesnewspapers.com
Publisher Name: Heather Ruenz
Publisher Email: delavaneditor@southernlakesnewspapers.com
Publisher Phone: (262) 725-3411, ext : 125
Editor Name: Heather Perkins
Editor Email: delavanassistant@southernlakesnewspapers.com
Editor Phone: (262) 728-3411
Advertising Executive Name: Tamera Hamilton
Advertising Executive Email: tamera@southernlakesnewspapers.com
Advertising Executive Phone: (262) 725-7701, ext : 132
Delivery Methods: Mail
Published Days: Thur
Avg Free Circ: 1206
Audit Company: Sworn/Estimate/Non-Audited
Audit Date: 6 10 2019

PADDOCK LAKE REPORT
Corporate/Parent Company: Southern Lakes Newspapers LLC
Street Address: 1102 Ann St
City: Delavan
State: WI
Postal Code: 53115-1938
Office phone: (262) 728-3411
Publication Website: http://southernlakesnewspapers.com/
General E-mail: lucia@southernlakesnewspapers.com
Publisher Name: Sue Z. Lange
Publisher Email: suez@standardpress.com
Publisher Phone: (262) 728-3411, ext : 114
Editor Name: Jason Arndt
Editor Email: jarndt@southernlakesnewspapers.com
Editor Phone: (262) 763-3330, ext : 148
Advertising Executive Name: Lucia Crivello
Advertising Executive Email: lucia@southernlakesnewspapers.com
Advertising Executive Phone: (262) 728-3411, ext : 145
Delivery Methods: Mail
Published Days: Sat
Avg Free Circ: 1496
Audit Company: Sworn/Estimate/Non-Audited
Audit Date: 6 10 2019
Total Circulation: 5050

PALMYRA ENTERPRISE
Corporate/Parent Company: Southern Lakes Newspapers LLC
Street Address: 1102 Ann St
City: Delavan
State: WI
Postal Code: 53115-1938
Office phone: (262) 728-3411
Publication Website: http://southernlakesnewspapers.com/
General E-mail: phansen@standardpress.com
Publisher Name: Sue Z. Lange
Publisher Email: suez@standardpress.com
Publisher Phone: (262) 728-3411, ext : 114
Editor Name: Todd Mishler
Editor Email: todd.mishler@southernlakesnewspapers.com
Editor Phone: (262) 725-7701, ext : 140
Advertising Executive Name: Pete Hansen
Advertising Executive Email: phansen@standardpress.com
Advertising Executive Phone: (414) 801-2360
Delivery Methods: Mail`Newsstand
Own Printing Facility?: Y
Commercial printers?: Y
Published Days: Fri
Avg Paid Circ: 1400
Avg Free Circ: 700

Non-Daily Newspapers in the U.S.

Audit Company: Sworn/Estimate/Non-Audited
Audit Date: 6 10 2019
Total Circulation: 1206

THE DELAVAN ENTERPRISE

Corporate/Parent Company: Southern Lakes Newspapers LLC
Street Address: 1102 Ann St
City: Delavan
State: WI
Postal Code: 53115-1938
Office phone: (262) 728-3411
Publication Website: http://southernlakesnewspapers.com/
General E-mail: tamera@southernlakesnewspapers.com
Publisher Name: Heather Ruenz
Publisher Email: delavaneditor@southernlakesnewspapers.com
Publisher Phone: (262) 725-3411, ext : 125
Editor Name: Heather Perkins
Editor Email: delavanassistant@southernlakesnewspapers.com
Editor Phone: (262) 728-3411
Advertising Executive Name: Tamera Hamilton
Advertising Executive Email: tamera@southernlakesnewspapers.com
Advertising Executive Phone: (262) 725-7701, ext : 132
Year Established: 1878
Delivery Methods: Mail`Newsstand
Own Printing Facility?: Y
Mechanical specifications: Type page 13 x 21 1/2.
Published Days: Thur
Avg Paid Circ: 4500
Audit Company: Sworn/Estimate/Non-Audited
Audit Date: 6 10 2019

WATERFORD POST

Corporate/Parent Company: Southern Lakes Newspapers LLC
Street Address: 1102 Ann St.
City: Delavan
State: WI
Postal Code: 53115
Office phone: (262) 728-3411
Publication Website: http://southernlakesnewspapers.com/
General E-mail: vicki@southernlakesnewspapers.com
Publisher Name: Sue Z. Lange
Publisher Email: suez@standardpress.com
Publisher Phone: (262) 728-3411, ext : 114
Editor Name: Edward Nadolski
Editor Email: enadolski@standardpress.com
Editor Phone: (262) 728-3411, ext : 126
Advertising Executive Name: Vicki Vanderwerff
Advertising Executive Email: vicki@southernlakesnewspapers.com
Advertising Executive Phone: (262) 728-3411, ext : 134
Delivery Methods: Mail
Own Printing Facility?: Y
Mechanical specifications: Type page 13 x 21.
Published Days: Fri
Avg Paid Circ: 1900
Avg Free Circ: 527
Audit Company: Sworn/Estimate/Non-Audited
Audit Date: 6 10 2019

EAGLE RIVER

NORTH WOODS TRADER

Corporate/Parent Company: DHI Media, Inc.
Street Address: 425 W Mill St
City: Eagle River
State: WI
Postal Code: 54521-8002
Office phone: (715) 479-4421
Publication Website: https://vcnewsreview.com/
General E-mail: jod@vcnewsreview.com
Publisher Name: Kurt Krueger
Publisher Email: kurtk@vcnewsreview.com
Editor Name: Gary Ridderbusch
Editor Email: garyr@vcnewsreview.com
Total Circulation: 1694

THREE LAKES NEWS

Corporate/Parent Company: Register Publications group.
Street Address: 425 W Mill St
City: Eagle River
State: WI
Postal Code: 54521-8002
Office phone: (715) 479-4421
Publication Website: https://vcnewsreview.com/
General E-mail: jod@vcnewsreview.com
Publisher Name: Kurt Krueger
Publisher Email: kurtk@vcnewsreview.com
Editor Name: Gary Ridderbusch
Editor Email: garyr@vcnewsreview.com

ELKHORN

THE ELKHORN INDEPENDENT

Corporate/Parent Company: Southern Lakes Newspapers LLC
Street Address: 812 N Wisconsin St
City: Elkhorn
State: WI
Postal Code: 53121-1137
Office phone: (262) 723-2250
Publication Website: http://southernlakesnewspapers.com/
General E-mail: phansen@standardpress.com
Publisher Name: Sue Z. Lange
Publisher Email: suez@standardpress.com
Publisher Phone: (262) 728-3411, ext : 114
Editor Name: Heather Ruenz
Editor Email: elkinde@elkhornindependent.com
Editor Phone: (262) 728-3411, ext. 125
Advertising Executive Name: Pete Hansen
Advertising Executive Email: phansen@standardpress.com
Advertising Executive Phone: (262) 723-2250
Year Established: 1853
Delivery Methods: Mail`Racks
Own Printing Facility?: Y
Commercial printers?: Y
Mechanical specifications: Type page 13 x 21.
Published Days: Thur
Avg Paid Circ: 2911
Avg Free Circ: 18
Audit Company: Sworn/Estimate/Non-Audited
Audit Date: 6 10 2019

GREEN BAY

THE PRESS TIMES

Corporate/Parent Company: Multi Media Channels, LLC
Street Address: 400 Security Blvd
City: Green Bay
State: WI
Postal Code: 54313
Office phone: 715-258-4360
Publication Website: gopresstimes.com
Editor Name: Ben Rodgers
Editor Email: brodgers@mmclocal.com
Advertising Executive Name: Mick Gotta
Advertising Executive Email: mgotta@mmlocal.com

HARTLAND

KETTLE MORAINE INDEX

Street Address: 1010 Richards Rd
City: Hartland
State: WI
Postal Code: 53029-8301
Office phone: (262) 367-3272
Publication Website: https://www.jsonline.com/communities/lakecountry/
General E-mail: class@journalsentinel.com
Editor Name: George Stanley
Editor Email: george.stanley@jrn.com
Editor Phone: (414) 224-2248
Advertising Executive Email: class@journalsentinel.com
Advertising Executive Phone: (414) 224-2121
Delivery Methods: Mail`Newsstand
Published Days: Thur
Avg Paid Circ: 653
Audit Company: AAM
Audit Date: 31 03 2016

LAKE COUNTRY REPORTER

Street Address: 1010 Richards Rd
City: Hartland
State: WI
Postal Code: 53029-8301
Office phone: (262) 367-3272
Publication Website: https://www.jsonline.com/communities/lakecountry/
General E-mail: class@journalsentinel.com
Editor Name: George Stanley
Editor Email: george.stanley@jrn.com
Editor Phone: (414) 224-2248
Advertising Executive Email: class@journalsentinel.com
Advertising Executive Phone: (414) 224-2121
Delivery Methods: Mail`Newsstand
Own Printing Facility?: Y
Commercial printers?: Y
Mechanical specifications: Type page 9 3/4 x 13 3/4; E - 4 cols, 2 1/4, 1/6 between; A - 4 cols, 2 1/4, 1/6 between.
Published Days: Tues`Wed`Thur
Avg Paid Circ: 5050
Audit Company: AAM
Audit Date: 31 03 2016

OCONOMOWOC FOCUS

Street Address: 1010 Richards Rd
City: Hartland
State: WI
Postal Code: 53029-8301
Office phone: (262) 367-3272
Publication Website: https://www.jsonline.com/communities/lakecountry/
General E-mail: class@journalsentinel.com
Editor Name: George Stanley
Editor Email: george.stanley@jrn.com
Editor Phone: (414) 224-2248
Advertising Executive Email: class@journalsentinel.com
Advertising Executive Phone: (414) 224-2121
Delivery Methods: Mail`Newsstand
Published Days: Tues`Thur
Avg Paid Circ: 1303
Audit Company: AAM
Audit Date: 31 03 2016
Total Circulation: 7450

LA CROSSE

COURIER-LIFE

Street Address: 401 N. Third Street
City: La Crosse
State: WI
Postal Code: 54601
Office phone: 608-782-9710
Publication Website: www.courierlifenews.com
General E-mail: wsm.news@lee.net
Publisher Name: Sean Burke
Publisher Email: sean.burke@lee.net
Publisher Phone: 608-791-8237
Advertising Executive Name: Paul Pehler
Advertising Executive Email: paul.pehler@lee.net
Advertising Executive Phone: 608-791-8300
Total Circulation: 2012

LA CRESCENT- HOUSTON COUNTY NEWSPAPERS

Street Address: 401 3rd St N
City: La Crosse
State: WI
Postal Code: 54601
Office phone: 608-782-9710
Publication Website: lacrossetribune.com
Publisher Name: Sean Burke
Publisher Email: sean.burke@lee.net
Publisher Phone: 608-791-8237
Editor Name: Avery Wehrs
Editor Email: avery.wehrs@lee.net
Editor Phone: 608-791-8413
Advertising Executive Name: Paul Pehler
Advertising Executive Email: paul.pehler@lee.net
Advertising Executive Phone: 608-791-8300

LAKE MILLS

THE COURIER

Corporate/Parent Company: Gannett
Street Address: 320 N. Main St.
City: Lake Mills
State: WI
Postal Code: 53551
Office phone: 920-478-2188
Publication Website: www.courierenews.com
General E-mail: wmcourier@hngnews.com
Editor Name: Amber Gerber
Editor Email: agerber@hngnews.com
Editor Phone: 920-478-2188
Advertising Executive Name: Mary Jo Currie
Advertising Executive Email: classifieds@hngnews.com
Advertising Executive Phone: 608-478-2509
Total Circulation: 3844

MADISON

THE PROGRESSIVE

Street Address: 30 West Mifflin Street, Suite 703
City: Madison
State: WI
Postal Code: 53703
Office phone: (608)257-4626
Publication Website: progressive.org
General E-mail: info@progressive.org
Publisher Name: Norman Stockwell
Editor Name: Bill Lueders
Editor Email: editorial@progressive.org
Total Circulation: 1303

MAUSTON

JUNEAU COUNTY STAR-TIMES

Street Address: 201 E State St
City: Mauston
State: WI
Postal Code: 53948-1390
Office phone: (608)847-7341
Publication Website: https://www.wiscnews.com/juneaucountystartimes/
Year Established: 1857
Delivery Methods: Mail`Racks
Own Printing Facility?: Y
Published Days: Wed`Sat
Avg Paid Circ: 2771
Audit Company: Sworn/Estimate/Non-Audited
Audit Date: 6 10 2019

REEDSBURG TIMES-PRESS

Street Address: 201 E. State St.
City: Mauston
State: WI
Postal Code: 53948
Office phone: (608) 847-7341
Publication Website: https://www.wiscnews.com/reedsburgtimespress/
General E-mail: szeinemann@madison.com
Editor Name: Aaron Holbrook
Editor Email: aholbrook@wiscnews.com
Editor Phone: (920) 356-6752

Advertising Executive Name: Scott Zeinemann
Advertising Executive Email: szeinemann@madison.com
Advertising Executive Phone: (608) 745-3571
Delivery Methods: Mail`Newsstand`Carrier`Racks
Published Days: Wed`Sat
Avg Paid Circ: 966
Audit Company: Sworn/Estimate/Non-Audited
Audit Date: 6 10 2019

SAUK PRAIRIE EAGLE

Street Address: 201 E. State St.
City: Mauston
State: WI
Postal Code: 53948
Office phone: (608) 847-7341
Publication Website: https://www.wiscnews.com/saukprairieeagle/
General E-mail: szeinemann@madison.com
Editor Name: Aaron Holbrook
Editor Email: aholbrook@wiscnews.com
Editor Phone: (920) 356-6752
Advertising Executive Name: Scott Zeinemann
Advertising Executive Email: szeinemann@madison.com
Advertising Executive Phone: (608) 252-6092
Delivery Methods: Mail`Newsstand`Carrier`Racks
Own Printing Facility?: Y
Published Days: Wed
Avg Paid Circ: 2000
Audit Company: Sworn/Estimate/Non-Audited
Audit Date: 6 10 2019
Total Circulation: 1496

WISCONSIN DELLS EVENTS

Street Address: 201 E. State St.
City: Mauston
State: WI
Postal Code: 53948
Office phone: (608) 847-7341
Publication Website: https://www.wiscnews.com/wisconsindellsevents/
General E-mail: szeinemann@madison.com
Editor Name: Aaron Holbrook
Editor Email: aholbrook@wiscnews.com
Editor Phone: (920) 356-6752
Advertising Executive Name: Scott Zeinemann
Advertising Executive Email: szeinemann@madison.com
Advertising Executive Phone: (608) 745-3571
Year Established: 1903
Delivery Methods: Mail`Newsstand`Carrier`Racks
Commercial printers?: N
Mechanical specifications: Type page 11 x 22 1/2; E - 6 cols, 2 1/4, 2/9 between; A - 6 cols, 2 1/4, 2/9 between; C - 8 cols, between.
Published Days: Wed`Sat
Avg Paid Circ: 2305
Avg Free Circ: 100
Audit Company: Sworn/Estimate/Non-Audited
Audit Date: 6 10 2019
Total Circulation: 2100

MILWAUKEE

CONQUISTADOR

Street Address: 4531 West Forest Home Avenue
City: Milwaukee
State: WI
Postal Code: 53219
Office phone: 4143831000
Publication Website: conquistadornews.com
General E-mail: conquistador@bizwi.rr.com
Publisher Name: Victor Huyke
Editor Name: Yadira Sanchez Olson

FRANKLIN-GREENDALE-HALES CORNERS-OAK CREEK NOW

Street Address: 333 W State St
City: Milwaukee
State: WI
Postal Code: 53203
Office phone: 414-224-2000
Publication Website: www.mycommunitynow.com
General E-mail: jsmetro@journalsentinel.com
Editor Name: George Stanley
Editor Email: george.stanley@jrn.com

GERMANTOWN-MENOMONEE FALLS NOW

Street Address: 333 W. State St.
City: Milwaukee
State: WI
Postal Code: 53022
Office phone: 414-224-2100
Publication Website: www.MyNorthwestNow.com
General E-mail: milwaukeejournalsentinel@gannett.com
Editor Name: George Stanley
Editor Email: george.stanley@jrn.com
Editor Phone: 414-224-2248
Total Circulation: 1217

MILWAUKEE POST

Corporate/Parent Company: Conley Media LLC
Street Address: 3397 S Howell Ave
City: Milwaukee
State: WI
Postal Code: 53207-2743
Office phone: (414)744-6370
Publication Website: http://www.gmtoday.com/
General E-mail: webmaster@conleynet.com
Published Days: Fri
Audit Company: Sworn/Estimate/Non-Audited
Audit Date: 6 10 2019

SOUTH SHORE NOW

Street Address: 333 W State St
City: Milwaukee
State: WI
Postal Code: 53203
Office phone: 414-224-2000
Publication Website: www.mycommunitynow.com
General E-mail: jsmetro@journalsentinel.com
Editor Name: George Stanley
Editor Email: george.stanley@jrn.com

WAUKESHA NOW

Street Address: 333 W State St
City: Milwaukee
State: WI
Postal Code: 53203
Office phone: 414-224-2000
Publication Website: www.mycommunitynow.com
General E-mail: jsmetro@journalsentinel.com
Editor Name: George Stanley
Editor Email: george.stanley@jrn.com

MONDOVI

MONDOVI HERALD NEWS

Corporate/Parent Company: Conley Media LLC
Street Address: 123 W. Main St.
City: Mondovi
State: WI
Postal Code: 54755
Office phone: 715-926-4970
Publication Website: www.gmdmedia.net/mondovi-herald-news
General E-mail: mhnewscopy@media-md.net
Editor Name: Beth Kraft
Editor Email: mheditor@media-md.net

MOUNT HOREB

MOUNT HOREB MAIL

Corporate/Parent Company: News Publishing, Co., Inc.
Street Address: 114 East Main Street PO Box 88
City: Mount Horeb
State: WI
Postal Code: 53572
Office phone: 608-437-5553
Publication Website: www.newspubinc.com
General E-mail: mhclassies@newspubinc.com
Editor Name: Matt Geiger
Editor Email: mgeiger@newspubinc.com
Advertising Executive Name: Marc Mickelson
Advertising Executive Email: marc@newspubinc.com
Advertising Executive Phone: 608-225-9515

MUKWONAGO

LIVING - KETTLE MORAINE SUNDAY-OOB

Street Address: 111 N Rochester St
City: Mukwonago
State: WI
Postal Code: 53149-1309
Office phone: (262) 368-2966
Publication Website: https://www.jsonline.com/communities/lakecountry/
General E-mail: class@journalsentinel.com
Editor Name: George Stanley
Editor Email: george.stanley@jrn.com
Editor Phone: (414) 224-2248
Advertising Executive Email: class@journalsentinel.com
Advertising Executive Phone: (414) 224-2121

MUKWONAGO CHIEF

Street Address: 555 Bayview Rd #1
City: Mukwonago
State: WI
Postal Code: 53149
Office phone: 262-363-4045
Publication Website: www.lakecountrynow.com
Editor Name: George Stanley
Editor Email: george.stanley@jrn.com
Editor Phone: 414-224-2248

NEW GLARUS

POST MESSENGER RECORDER

Corporate/Parent Company: News Publishing, Co., Inc.
Street Address: 109 5th Ave., Suite A
City: New Glarus
State: WI
Postal Code: 53574
Office phone: (608) 527-5252
Publication Website: https://www.postmessengerrecorder.com/
General E-mail: khenning@newspubinc.com
Editor Name: Sue Moen
Editor Email: pmreditor@newspubinc.com
Editor Phone: (608) 527-5252
Advertising Executive Name: Karin Henning
Advertising Executive Email: khenning@newspubinc.com
Advertising Executive Phone: (608) 358-7958
Delivery Methods: Mail`Newsstand
Own Printing Facility?: Y
Published Days: Thur
Avg Paid Circ: 1217
Audit Company: Sworn/Estimate/Non-Audited
Audit Date: 6 10 2019

NEW LONDON

NEW LONDON PRESS STAR

Corporate/Parent Company: Multi Media Channels, LLC
Street Address: 301 S Pearl St
City: New London
State: WI
Postal Code: 54961
Office phone: 920-982-2511
Publication Website: https://waupacanow.com
General E-mail: ebuchinger@mmclocal.com
Advertising Executive Name: Bernice Fuhrmann
Advertising Executive Email: bfuhrmann@mmclocal.com
Advertising Executive Phone: 715-377-3641

OSSEO

AUGUSTA AREA TIMES

Corporate/Parent Company: Conley Media LLC
Street Address: P.O. Box 460
City: Osseo
State: WI
Postal Code: 54758
Office phone: 715-597-3313
Publication Website: www.gmdmedia.net/augusta-area-times
General E-mail: erika@media-md.net

PESHTIGO

PESHTIGO TIMES

Corporate/Parent Company: Peshtigo Times Printers & Publishers
Street Address: 841 Maple St PO Box 187
City: Peshtigo
State: WI
Postal Code: 54157
Office phone: 715-582-4541
Publication Website: www.peshtigotimes.com
General E-mail: News@PeshtigoTimes.com

RACINE

THE TIMES

Corporate/Parent Company: Gannett
Street Address: 212 Fourth St
City: Racine
State: WI
Postal Code: 53401
Office phone: 262-634-3322
Publication Website: www.journaltimes.com
Editor Name: Tom Farley
Editor Email: tom.farley@journaltimes.com
Editor Phone: 262-631-1723
Advertising Executive Name: David Habrat
Advertising Executive Email: david.habrat@journaltimes.com
Advertising Executive Phone: 262-631-1709

REEDSBURG

REEDSBURG INDEPENDENT

Corporate/Parent Company: News Publishing Company, Inc
Street Address: 222 N Walnut St
City: Reedsburg
State: WI
Postal Code: 53959
Office phone: 608-524-0387
Publication Website: www.facebook.com/reedsburgindy
General E-mail: classifieds@newspubinc.com
Editor Name: Heather Stanek
Editor Email: reedindy@newspubinc.com
Editor Phone: (608) 495-9301
Advertising Executive Name: Karen Schrank
Advertising Executive Email: reedsales@newspubinc.com

Non-Daily Newspapers in the U.S.

Advertising Executive Phone: 608-393-3913

RICE LAKE

THE CHRONOTYPE

Corporate/Parent Company: Adams Publishing Group
Street Address: 28 S. Main Street
City: Rice Lake
State: WI
Postal Code: 54868
Office phone: 715-234-2121
Publication Website: www.chronotype.com
General E-mail: citynews@chronotype.com
Editor Name: Urban Ryan
Editor Email: citynews@chronotype.com
Editor Phone: 715-790-1331
Advertising Executive Name: Page Pam
Advertising Executive Email: ppage@chronotype.com
Advertising Executive Phone: 715-790-1555

SAUK CITY

SAUK PRAIRIE STAR

Corporate/Parent Company: News Publishing, Co., Inc.
Street Address: 801 Water St
City: Sauk City
State: WI
Postal Code: 53583-1502
Office phone: (608) 643-3444
Publication Website: http://www.newspubinc.com/
General E-mail: classifieds@newspubinc.com
Editor Name: Joe Block
Editor Email: spseditor@newspubinc.com
Advertising Executive Email: classifieds@newspubinc.com
Delivery Methods: Mail
Own Printing Facility?: Y
Commercial printers?: Y
Published Days: Thur
Avg Paid Circ: 2800
Avg Free Circ: 40
Audit Company: Sworn/Estimate/Non-Audited
Audit Date: 6 10 2019

SHAWANO

OCONTO COUNTY TIMES-HERALD

Corporate/Parent Company: New Media Inc.
Street Address: 1464 E. Green Bay St
City: Shawano
State: WI
Postal Code: 54166
Office phone: 715-526-2121
Publication Website: www.newmedia-wi.com
General E-mail: editorial@newmedia-wi.com
Publisher Name: Greg Mellis
Publisher Email: gmellis@newmedia-wi.com
Editor Name: Carol Ryczek
Editor Email: cryczek@newmedia-wi.com
Advertising Executive Name: Chris Kennedy
Advertising Executive Email: ckennedy@newmedia-wi.com

SPRING GREEN

HOME NEWS

Corporate/Parent Company: News Publishing Company, Inc
City: Spring Green
State: WI
Postal Code: 53588
Office phone: 608-767-3655
Publication Website: newspubinc.com
Editor Name: Linda Schwanke
Editor Email: homenewseditor@newspubinc.com
Advertising Executive Name: Dave Pronold
Advertising Executive Email: homenewssales@newspubinc.com
Advertising Executive Phone: 608-588-4777

SPRING GREEN HOME NEWS

Corporate/Parent Company: News Publishing, Co., Inc.
Street Address: 120 N Worcester St
City: Spring Green
State: WI
Postal Code: 53588-8015
Office phone: (608) 588-4777
Publication Website: http://www.newspubinc.com/
General E-mail: homenewssales@newspubinc.com
Editor Name: Linda Schwanke
Editor Email: homenewseditor@newspubinc.com
Advertising Executive Name: Dave Pronold
Advertising Executive Email: homenewssales@newspubinc.com
Advertising Executive Phone: (608) 588-4777
Delivery Methods: Mail`Racks
Published Days: Wed
Avg Paid Circ: 2700
Audit Company: Sworn/Estimate/Non-Audited
Audit Date: 6 10 2019

TWIN LAKES

WESTOSHA REPORT

Corporate/Parent Company: Southern Lakes Newspapers LLC
Street Address: 147 E Main St
City: Twin Lakes
State: WI
Postal Code: 53181-9679
Office phone: (262) 877-2813
Publication Website: http://southernlakesnewspapers.com/
General E-mail: lucia@southernlakesnewspapers.com
Publisher Name: Sue Z. Lange
Publisher Email: suez@standardpress.com
Publisher Phone: (262) 728-3411, ext : 114
Editor Name: Jason Arndt
Editor Email: jarndt@southernlakesnewspapers.com
Editor Phone: (262) 763-3330, ext : 148
Advertising Executive Name: Lucia Crivello
Advertising Executive Email: lucia@southernlakesnewspapers.com
Advertising Executive Phone: (262) 728-3411, ext : 145
Delivery Methods: Mail`Newsstand
Own Printing Facility?: Y
Commercial printers?: Y
Published Days: Sat
Avg Free Circ: 1208
Audit Company: Sworn/Estimate/Non-Audited
Audit Date: 6 10 2019

WAUKESHA

GREATER MILWAUKEE JOBS-OOB

Corporate/Parent Company: Conley Media LLC
Street Address: 801 N Barstow St
City: Waukesha
State: WI
Postal Code: 53186-4801
Office phone: (262) 542-2500
Publication Website: http://www.gmtoday.com/
General E-mail: webmaster@conleynet.com
Publisher Name: Bill Yorth
Publisher Email: byorth@conleynet.com
Publisher Phone: (262) 513-2671
Editor Name: Katherine Beck
Editor Email: kbeck@conleynet.com
Editor Phone: (262) 513-2644
Advertising Executive Name: Jim Baumgart
Advertising Executive Email: jbaumgart@conleynet.com
Advertising Executive Phone: (262) 513-2621

OCONOMOWOC ENTERPRISE

Corporate/Parent Company: Conley Media LLC
Street Address: 801 N Barstow St, P.O. Box 7
City: Waukesha
State: WI
Postal Code: 53186-4801
Office phone: (262) 542-2500
Publication Website: http://www.gmtoday.com/promotions/cust_service/enterprise.asp
General E-mail: webmaster@conleynet.com
Year Established: 1888
Mechanical specifications: Type page: 10.6 x 21; 6 col
Published Days: Thur
Avg Paid Circ: 3804
Avg Free Circ: 40
Audit Company: CVC
Audit Date: 31 12 2018

WAUNAKEE

LODI ENTERPRISE AND POYNETTE PRESS

Street Address: 204 Moravian Valley Rd., Suite F
City: Waunakee
State: WI
Postal Code: 53597
Office phone: 608-592-3261
Publication Website: www.lodinews.com
General E-mail: lodi@hngnews.com
Editor Name: Brian Sheridan
Editor Email: LPedit@hngnews.com
Editor Phone: 608-729-3366
Advertising Executive Name: Mary Jo Currie
Advertising Executive Email: classifieds@hngnews.com
Advertising Executive Phone: 608-478-2509

WAUTOMA

WAUSHARA ARGUS

Corporate/Parent Company: DHI Media, Inc.
Street Address: W7781 Hwy 21 & 73 E
City: Wautoma
State: WI
Postal Code: 54982
Office phone: (920) 787-3334
Publication Website: https://www.wausharaargus.com/
General E-mail: argus@wausharaargus.com
Publisher Name: Mary Kunasch
Publisher Email: argusmary@wausharaargus.com
Publisher Phone: (920) 787-3334
Editor Name: Sara Ann Mihor
Editor Email: argus@wausharaargus.com

WEST BEND

THE HARTFORD TIMES PRESS

Corporate/Parent Company: Conley Media LLC
Street Address: 100 S 6th Ave
City: West Bend
State: WI
Postal Code: 53095-3309
Office phone: (262) 375-5100
Publication Website: http://www.gmtoday.com/
General E-mail: webmaster@conleynet.com
Editor Name: Ashley Haynes
Editor Email: ahaynes@conleynet.com
Editor Phone: (262) 513-2681
Advertising Executive Name: Jim Baumgart
Advertising Executive Email: jbaumgart@conleynet.com
Advertising Executive Phone: (262) 513-2621
Year Established: 1867
Delivery Methods: Mail
Mechanical specifications: Type page: 10.6 x 10.5; 6 col
Published Days: Sun
Avg Free Circ: 13779
Audit Company: Sworn/Estimate/Non-Audited
Audit Date: 6 10 2019

WASHINGTON COUNTY POST

Corporate/Parent Company: Conley Media LLC
Street Address: 100 S 6th Ave, P.O. Box 478
City: West Bend
State: WI
Postal Code: 53095-3309
Office phone: (262) 306-5000
Publication Website: http://www.gmtoday.com/promotions/cust_service/sunday_post.asp
General E-mail: customerservice_ls@conleynet.com
Advertising Executive Name: Jim Baumgart
Advertising Executive Email: jbaumgart@conleynet.com
Year Established: 1950
Delivery Methods: Carrier
Published Days: Sun
Avg Free Circ: 44279
Audit Company: Sworn/Estimate/Non-Audited
Audit Date: 6 10 2019

WHITEHALL

TREMPEALEAU COUNTY TIMES

Street Address: 36435 Main St. P.O. Box 95
City: Whitehall
State: WI
Postal Code: 54773
Office phone: 715-538-4765
Publication Website: www.arrow-times.com
Editor Name: Andrew Danneh
Editor Email: andrew@trempcotimes.com
Advertising Executive Name: Karla Demaske
Advertising Executive Email: karla@arrowshopper.com

WINTER

SAWYER COUNTY GAZETTE

Street Address: P.O. Box 245
City: Winter
State: WI
Postal Code: 54896
Office phone: 715.266.2204
Publication Website: www.winterwi.com
General E-mail: gazette@centurytel.net
Publisher Name: Sue Johnston

WITTENBERG

THE WITTENBERG ENTERPRISE AND BIRNAMWOOD NEWS

Corporate/Parent Company: New Media Inc.
Street Address: 511 S Webb St
City: Wittenberg
State: WI
Postal Code: 54499
Office phone: (715) 253-2737
Publication Website: www.wittenbergenterprise.com
Editor Name: Miriam Nelson
Editor Email: mnelson@newmedia-wi

WEST VIRGINIA

HUNTINGTON

PUTNAM HERALD

Corporate/Parent Company: HD Media Company LLC
Street Address: 946 5th Ave
City: Huntington
State: WV
Postal Code: 25701-2004
Office phone: (304) 526-4000
Publication Website: https://www.herald-dispatch.com/news/putnam_news/

General E-mail: hdnews@hdmediallc.com
Editor Name: Les Smith
Editor Email: lessmith@hdmediallc.com
Editor Phone: (304) 526-2779
Advertising Executive Name: Jerry Briggs
Advertising Executive Email: jwbriggs@hdmediallc.com
Advertising Executive Phone: (304) 526-2820
Delivery Methods: Mail Racks
Published Days: Sat
Avg Free Circ: 3203
Audit Company: AAM
Audit Date: 31 12 2018

MADISON

COAL VALLEY NEWS

Corporate/Parent Company: HD Media
Street Address: 350 Main St
City: Madison
State: WV
Postal Code: 25130-1293
Office phone: (304) 369-1165
Publication Website: https://www.coalvalleynews.com/
General E-mail: pperry@hdmediallc.com
Advertising Executive Name: Melissa Blair
Advertising Executive Email: mblair@hdmediallc.com
Advertising Executive Phone: (304) 236-3543
Year Established: 1925
Delivery Methods: Mail Racks
Published Days: Wed
Avg Paid Circ: 5000
Audit Company: Sworn/Estimate/Non-Audited
Audit Date: 6 10 2019
Total Circulation: 5000

MOUNDSVILLE

GREEN TAB

Corporate/Parent Company: Ogden Newspapers Inc.
Street Address: 605 Court Ave
City: Moundsville
State: WV
Postal Code: 26041-2139
Office phone: (304) 845-4050
Publication Website: http://www.greentab.com/

NEW MARTINSVILLE

WETZEL CHRONICLE

Corporate/Parent Company: Ogden Newspapers Inc.
Street Address: 1100 3rd St
City: New Martinsville
State: WV
Postal Code: 26155-1500
Office phone: (304) 455-3300
Publication Website: http://www.wetzelchronicle.com/
Delivery Methods: Mail Newsstand
Mechanical specifications: Type page 13 x 22; E - 6 cols, 2 1/8, 1/8 between; A - 6 cols, 2 1/8, 1/8 between; C - 6 cols, 2 1/8, 1/8 between.
Published Days: Wed
Avg Paid Circ: 6000
Avg Free Circ: 106
Audit Company: Sworn/Estimate/Non-Audited
Audit Date: 6 10 2019
Total Circulation: 3203

PINEVILLE

THE INDEPENDENT HERALD

Corporate/Parent Company: HD Media Company LLC
Street Address: 127 Main Ave.
City: Pineville
State: WV
Postal Code: 24874
Office phone: (304) 732-6060
Publication Website: https://www.williamsondailynews.com/
General E-mail: mblair@hdmediallc.com
Publisher Name: NA
Editor Name: NA
Advertising Executive Name: Melissa Blair
Advertising Executive Email: mblair@hdmediallc.com
Advertising Executive Phone: (304) 236-3543
Year Established: 1968
Delivery Methods: Mail Racks
Published Days: Wed
Avg Paid Circ: 2500
Audit Company: Sworn/Estimate/Non-Audited
Audit Date: 6 10 2019
Total Circulation: 2500

SHEPHERDSTOWN

THE SHEPHERDSTOWN CHRONICLE

Corporate/Parent Company: Ogden Newspapers Inc.
Street Address: P.O. Box 2088
City: Shepherdstown
State: WV
Postal Code: 25443-2088
Office phone: (304) 876-3380
Publication Website: http://www.shepherdstownchronicle.com/
General E-mail: edit@shepherdstownchronicle.com
Editor Name: Tabitha Johnston
Editor Email: tjohnston@shepherdstownchronicle.com
Advertising Executive Name: Judy Gelestor
Advertising Executive Email: jgelestor@journal-news.net
Advertising Executive Phone: (304) 263-8931, ext : 110
Delivery Methods: Mail Newsstand Racks
Published Days: Fri
Audit Company: Sworn/Estimate/Non-Audited
Audit Date: 6 10 2019

SISTERSVILLE

TYLER STAR NEWS

Corporate/Parent Company: Ogden Newspapers Inc.
Street Address: 720 Wells St
City: Sistersville
State: WV
Postal Code: 26175-1326
Office phone: (304) 652-4141
Publication Website: http://www.tylerstarnews.com/
Delivery Methods: Mail Newsstand
Mechanical specifications: Type page 13 x 22; E - 6 cols, 2 1/8, 1/8 between; A - 6 cols, 2 1/8, 1/8 between; C - 6 cols, 2 1/8, 1/8 between.
Published Days: Wed
Avg Paid Circ: 4000
Audit Company: Sworn/Estimate/Non-Audited
Audit Date: 6 10 2019
Total Circulation: 4000

ONLINE ONLY

AMANDLA NEWS

Publication Website: http://amandlanews.com

AUBURN CITIZEN

Corporate/Parent Company: South County Publications
Publication Website: https://www.southcountypublications.net/auburn_citizen/news/
General E-mail: southco@royell.org
Publisher Name: Joe Michelich, Jr.
Publisher Email: southco@royell.org
Editor Name: Joseph M. Michelich
Advertising Executive Name: Connie Michelich
Advertising Executive Email: southco@royell.org

DISCOVERING BULLOCH

Corporate/Parent Company: Morris Multimedia, Inc.
Publication Website: https://www.discoveringbulloch.com/news/

HIGHLANDS CURRENT

Publication Website: highlandscurrent.org

LEDGER LOCAL

Corporate/Parent Company: Advance Publications, Inc.
Office phone: 800-300-9321
Publication Website: https://www.nj.com/independentpress/
General E-mail: ledgerlocal@njadvancemedia.com

MONTCLAIR LOCAL

Publication Website: https://www.montclairlocal.news
Editor Name: Kevin Meacham
Editor Email: meacham@montclairlocal.news
Editor Phone: 862-277-5202
Advertising Executive Name: Scott Drukker
Advertising Executive Email: drukker@montclairlocal.news
Advertising Executive Phone: 862-277-5022

SOMERSET OBSERVER

Corporate/Parent Company: Advance Publications, Inc.
Office phone: 800-300-9321
Publication Website: www.nj.com
General E-mail: somerset@njnpublishing.com

STATESBORO PENNYSAVER

Corporate/Parent Company: Morris Multimedia, Inc.
Publication Website: https://www.statesboroherald.com/pennysaver/

THE ADVERTISER-NEWS (SOUTH)

Corporate/Parent Company: Straus News
Publication Website: https://www.advertisernewssouth.com/
General E-mail: editor.ans@strausnews.com
Editor Name: Mike Zummo
Editor Email: editor.ans@strausnews.com

THE QUODDY TIDES

Publication Website: www.quoddytides.com
General E-mail: P.O. Box 213
Publisher Name: Eastport
Publisher Email: ME
Publisher Phone: 4631
Editor Name: 207-853-4806
Editor Email: qtides@midmaine.com
Advertising Executive Phone: Edward French

UNION SUN & JOURNAL

Corporate/Parent Company: CNHI, LLC
Publication Website: www.lockportjournal.com

UPPER TOWNSHIP SENTINEL

Corporate/Parent Company: Press of Atlantic City
Office phone: 877-773-7724
Publication Website: https://www.pressofatlanticcity.com/currents_gazettes/upper_township/
General E-mail: SubscriberServices@pressofac.com
Publisher Name: Mark L. Blum
Publisher Email: MBlum@pressofac.com
Publisher Phone: 609-272-7119
Editor Name: Buzz Keough
Editor Email: bkeough@pressofac.com
Editor Phone: 609-272-7247
Advertising Executive Name: Kevin Post
Advertising Executive Email: kpost@pressofac.com
Advertising Executive Phone: 609-272-7259

COMMUNITY NEWSPAPERS IN THE U.S.

ALASKA

ANCHORAGE

THE ARCTIC SOUNDER

Street Address: 500 W Intl Airport Rd
City: Anchorage
State: AK
ZIP Code: 99518-1175
General Phone: (907) 770-0820
General Email: ads@reportalaska.com
Publication Website: https://reportalaska.com/
Parent Company: Alaska Media LLC
Editor Name: Carey Restino
Mechanical specifications: Type page 10 3/16 x 15 1/2; E - 5 cols, 1 15/16, between; A - 5 cols, 1 15/16, between; C - 5 cols, 1 15/16, between.
Published Days: Thur
Avg. Paid Circ.: 2000
Audit Company: Sworn/Estimate/Non-Audited
Audit Date: 43626

ANCHORAGE

THE BRISTOL BAY TIMES

Street Address: 500 W Intl Airport Rd
City: Anchorage
State: AK
ZIP Code: 99518-1175
General Phone: (907) 770-0820
General Email: ads@reportalaska.com
Publication Website: https://reportalaska.com/
Parent Company: Alaska Media LLC
Editor Name: Carey Restino
Published Days: Thur
Avg. Paid Circ.: 2000
Avg. Free Circ.: 552
Audit Company: Sworn/Estimate/Non-Audited
Audit Date: 43626

ANCHORAGE

THE DUTCH HARBOR FISHERMAN

Street Address: 500 W Intl Airport Rd
City: Anchorage
State: AK
ZIP Code: 99518-1175
General Phone: (907) 770-0820
General Email: ads@reportalaska.com
Publication Website: https://reportalaska.com/
Parent Company: Alaska Media LLC
Editor Name: Carey Restino
Published Days: Thur
Avg. Paid Circ.: 2000
Avg. Free Circ.: 74
Audit Company: Sworn/Estimate/Non-Audited
Audit Date: 43626

CORDOVA

THE CORDOVA TIMES

Street Address: 110 Nicholoff Way
City: Cordova
State: AK
ZIP Code: 99574
General Phone: (907) 424-7181
General Email: apotter@thecordovatimes.com
Publication Website: https://www.thecordovatimes.com/
Parent Company: Alaska Newspapers, Inc. (OOB)
Editor Name: Annette Potter
Editor Email: apotter@thecordovatimes.com
Advertising Executive Name: Vivian Kennedy
Advertising Executive Email: advertising@thecordovatimes.com
Advertising Executive Phone: (907) 424-2236
Delivery Methods: Mail`Racks
Year Established: 1906
Published Days: Thur
Avg. Paid Circ.: 919
Avg. Free Circ.: 50
Audit Company: Sworn/Estimate/Non-Audited
Audit Date: 43626

EAGLE RIVER

ALASKA STAR

Street Address: 11401 Old Glenn Hwy
City: Eagle River
State: AK
ZIP Code: 99577
General Phone: (907) 694-2727
General Email: editor@alaskastar.com
Publication Website: https://www.alaskastar.com/
Parent Company: Binkley Co.
Editor Name: Matt Tunseth
Editor Email: editor@alaskastar.com
Editor Phone: (907) 257-4274
Advertising Executive Name: Jada Nowling
Advertising Executive Email: jada.nowling@alaskajournal.com
Advertising Executive Phone: (907) 257-4268
Mechanical specifications: Type page 11 1/4 x 17 1/2; E - 5 cols, 1 11/12, 1/6 between; A - 6 cols, 1 7/12, 1/6 between; C - 6 cols, 1 7/12, 1/6 between.
Published Days: Thur
Avg. Paid Circ.: 4800
Audit Company: Sworn/Estimate/Non-Audited
Audit Date: 43626

HAINES

CHILKAT VALLEY NEWS

Street Address: PO Box 630
City: Haines
State: AK
ZIP Code: 99827
General Phone: (907) 766-2688
General Email: cvn@chilkatvalleynews.com
Publication Website: https://www.chilkatvalleynews.com/
Publisher Name: Kyle Clayton
Advertising Executive Name: Jasmine Taylor
Delivery Methods: Mail`Carrier`Racks
Year Established: 1966
Mechanical specifications: Type page 10 x 15; E - 5 cols, 1 5/6, 3/16 between; A - 5 cols, 1 5/6, 3/16 between; C - 5 cols, 1 5/6, 3/16 between.
Published Days: Thur
Avg. Paid Circ.: 1200
Avg. Free Circ.: 11
Audit Company: Sworn/Estimate/Non-Audited
Audit Date: 43626

JUNEAU

JUNEAU EMPIRE

Street Address: 3100 Channel Drive
City: Juneau
State: AK
ZIP Code: 99801
General Phone: (907) 586-3740
General Email: editor@juneauempire.com
Publication Website: https://www.juneauempire.com/
Parent Company: Black Press Media Ltd.
Publisher Name: Terry Ward
Publisher Email: tward@soundpublishing.com
Publisher Phone: (360) 417-3500
Editor Email: editor@juneauempire.com
Delivery Methods: Mail`Racks
Year Established: 1980
Mechanical specifications: Tabloid size.
Published Days: Wed
Avg. Free Circ.: 30000
Audit Company: Sworn/Estimate/Non-Audited
Audit Date: 43626

NOME

THE NOME NUGGET

City: Nome
State: AK
ZIP Code: 99672-0610
General Phone: (907) 443-5235
General Email: ads@nomenugget.com
Publication Website: http://www.nomenugget.com/
Editor Name: Diana Haecker
Editor Email: diana@nomenugget.com
Advertising Executive Name: Nils Hahn
Advertising Executive Email: ads@nomenugget.com
Delivery Methods: Mail`Carrier
Year Established: 1897
Own Printing Facility?: Y
Commercial printers?: N
Mechanical specifications: Type page 9 3/4 x 15 1/2; E - 5 cols, 1 3/4, 1/25 between; A - 5 cols, 1 3/4, 1/25 between; C - 5 cols, 1 3/4, between.
Published Days: Thur
Avg. Paid Circ.: 6000
Audit Company: Sworn/Estimate/Non-Audited
Audit Date: 43626

PETERSBURG

PETERSBURG PILOT

Street Address: 207 N Nordic Dr
City: Petersburg
State: AK
ZIP Code: 99833
General Phone: (907) 772-9393
General Email: pilotpub@gmail.com
Publication Website: http://www.petersburgpilot.com/
Parent Company: Pilot Publishing, Inc.
Publisher Name: Anne M. Ioesch
Delivery Methods: Mail`Newsstand`Racks
Year Established: 1974
Own Printing Facility?: Y
Commercial printers?: Y
Mechanical specifications: Type page 9 7/8 x 16 1/2.
Published Days: Thur
Avg. Paid Circ.: 1800
Avg. Free Circ.: 34
Audit Company: Sworn/Estimate/Non-Audited
Audit Date: 43626

SEWARD

THE SEWARD PHOENIX LOG

Street Address: 301 Calista Court
City: Seward
State: AK
ZIP Code: 99518
General Phone: (907) 272-9830
General Email: banderson@alaskanewspapers.com
Publication Website: http://www.thesewardphoenixlog.com/
Parent Company: Alaska Newspapers Inc.
Publisher Name: Margaret Nelson
Publisher Email: mnelson@alaskanewspapers.com
Editor Name: Tony Hall
Editor Email: ahall@alaskanewspapers.com
Advertising Executive Name: Barry Anderson
Advertising Executive Email: banderson@alaskanewspapers.com
Advertising Executive Phone: (907) 348-2423
Delivery Methods: Mail`Newsstand
Year Established: 1966
Own Printing Facility?: Y
Commercial printers?: Y
Mechanical specifications: Type page 10 1/4 x 15 1/2; E - 5 cols, 1 14/15, 1/6 between; A - 5 cols, 1 14/15, 1/6 between; C - 5 cols, 1 14/15, 1/6 between.
Published Days: Thur
Avg. Paid Circ.: 700
Avg. Free Circ.: 50
Audit Company: Sworn/Estimate/Non-Audited
Audit Date: 43626

SEWARD

THE TUNDRA DRUMS

Street Address: 232 4th Ave
City: Seward
State: AK
ZIP Code: 99664
General Phone: (907) 224-4888
Publication Website: http://www.thetundradrums.com/
Parent Company: Alaska Newspapers Inc.
Editor Name: Annette Shacklett
Delivery Methods: Mail`Racks
Year Established: 1974
Mechanical specifications: Type page 10 1/4 x 15; E - 5 cols, 1 11/12, 1/6 between; A - 5 cols, 1 11/12, 1/6 between; C - 5 cols, 1 11/12, 1/6 between.
Published Days: Thur
Avg. Paid Circ.: 700
Avg. Free Circ.: 1000
Audit Company: Sworn/Estimate/Non-Audited
Audit Date: 43626

VALDEZ

VALDEZ STAR

Street Address: 310 Pioneer St
City: Valdez
State: AK
ZIP Code: 99686
General Phone: (907) 835-2405
General Email: editor@valdezstar.net
Publication Website: https://www.valdezstar.net/
Published Days: Wed
Avg. Paid Circ.: 2020
Audit Company: Sworn/Estimate/Non-Audited

Audit Date: 43626

WASILLA

FRONTIERSMAN

Street Address: 5751 E Mayflower Ct
City: Wasilla
State: AK
ZIP Code: 99654
General Phone: (907) 352-2250
General Email: dennis.anderson@frontiersman.com
Publication Website: http://www.frontiersman.com/
Publisher Name: Dennis Anderson
Publisher Email: dennis.anderson@frontiersman.com
Publisher Phone: (970) 252-7099
Editor Name: Jeremiah Bartz
Editor Email: editor@frontiersman.com
Editor Phone: (907) 352-2273
Advertising Executive Name: Petra Albecker
Advertising Executive Email: petra.albecker@frontiersman.com
Advertising Executive Phone: (907) 352-2262
Delivery Methods: Mail`Racks
Year Established: 1947
Published Days: Wed`Fri`Sun
Avg. Paid Circ.: 1925
Avg. Free Circ.: 2352
Audit Company: AAM
Audit Date: 43622

WRANGELL

WRANGELL SENTINEL

Street Address: 205 Front St
City: Wrangell
State: AK
ZIP Code: 99929
General Phone: (907) 874-2301
General Email: wrgsent@gmail.com
Publication Website: http://www.wrangellsentinel.com/
Parent Company: Pilot Publishing, Inc.
Publisher Name: Anne M. Ioesch
Year Established: 1902
Mechanical specifications: Type page 9 4/5 x 14 1/4; E - 5 cols, 1 5/6, 1/6 between; A - 5 cols, 1 5/6, 1/6 between.
Published Days: Thur
Avg. Paid Circ.: 1500
Avg. Free Circ.: 20
Audit Company: Sworn/Estimate/Non-Audited
Audit Date: 43626

ALABAMA

ABBEVILLE

ABBEVILLE HERALD

Street Address: 135 Kirkland St
City: Abbeville
State: AL
ZIP Code: 63610
General Phone: (334) 585-2331
General Email: heraldnews@centurytel.net
Publication Website: https://theabbevilleherald.com/
Delivery Methods: Mail`Racks
Year Established: 1912
Published Days: Thur
Avg. Paid Circ.: 2350
Audit Company: Sworn/Estimate/Non-Audited
Audit Date: 43626

ALBERTVILLE

SAND MOUNTAIN REPORTER

Street Address: 1603 Progress Dr
City: Albertville
State: AL
ZIP Code: 35950
General Phone: (256) 840-3000
General Email: support@sandmountainreporter.com
Publication Website: http://www.sandmountainreporter.com/
Parent Company: Southern Newspapers, Inc.
Publisher Name: Kimberly Patterson
Publisher Email: kim.patterson@sandmountainreporter.com
Publisher Phone: (256) 840-3000, ext : 111
Editor Name: Taylor Beck
Editor Email: taylor.beck@sandmountainreporter.com
Editor Phone: (256) 840-3000, ext : 113
Advertising Executive Name: Sherrie Hall
Advertising Executive Email: sherrie.hall@sandmountainreporter.com
Advertising Executive Phone: (256) 840-3000, ext : 122
Delivery Methods: Mail`Carrier`Racks
Year Established: 1955
Own Printing Facility?: Y
Commercial printers?: Y
Mechanical specifications: Type page 11 9/16 x 21 1/2; E - 6 cols, 1/8 between; A - 6 cols, 1/8 between; C - 9 cols, 1/16 between.
Published Days: Tues`Thur`Sat
Avg. Paid Circ.: 4280
Avg. Free Circ.: 261
Audit Company: AAM
Audit Date: 43806

ARAB

THE ARAB TRIBUNE

Street Address: 619 S Brindlee Mountain Pkwy
City: Arab
State: AL
ZIP Code: 35016
General Phone: (256) 586-3188
General Email: tribadss@otelco.net
Publication Website: http://www.thearbtribune.com/
Editor Name: Charles Whisenant
Editor Email: tribnews@otelco.net
Advertising Executive Email: tribadss@otelco.net
Delivery Methods: Mail`Carrier`Racks
Year Established: 1958
Own Printing Facility?: Y
Commercial printers?: Y
Mechanical specifications: 21.29 x 10.96 inches; 6 columns; column = 1.69 inches x 1 inch deep
Published Days: Wed`Sat
Avg. Paid Circ.: 6500
Audit Company: Sworn/Estimate/Non-Audited
Audit Date: 43626

ATMORE

ATMORE NEWS

Street Address: 128 S Main St
City: Atmore
State: AL
ZIP Code: 36502-2446
General Phone: (251) 368-6397
General Email: sherry@atmorenews.com
Publication Website: http://atmorenews.com/
Delivery Methods: Mail`Carrier`Racks
Year Established: 2005
Own Printing Facility?: N
Commercial printers?: Y
Published Days: Wed
Avg. Paid Circ.: 1500
Avg. Free Circ.: 50
Audit Company: Sworn/Estimate/Non-Audited

Audit Date: 43626

AUBURN

AUBURN VILLAGER

Street Address: 687 N Dean Rd
City: Auburn
State: AL
ZIP Code: 36831
General Phone: (334) 501-0600
General Email: editorial@auburnvillager.com
Publication Website: https://www.auburnvillager.com/
Editor Name: Allison Blankenship
Editor Email: allison@auburnvillager.com
Advertising Executive Email: advertising@auburnvillager.com
Delivery Methods: Mail`Racks
Year Established: 2006
Mechanical specifications: 21" x 11.625" -- 6 cols (1 1/2" x 1 1/2" each)
Published Days: Thur
Avg. Paid Circ.: 3000
Avg. Free Circ.: 1000
Audit Company: Sworn/Estimate/Non-Audited
Audit Date: 43626

BIRMINGHAM

THE BIRMINGHAM NEWS

Street Address: 1731 1st Ave N
City: Birmingham
State: AL
ZIP Code: 35203
General Phone: (205) 325.4444
General Email: advertise@al.com
Publication Website: https://www.alabamamediagroup.com/
Parent Company: Advance Newspapers
Advertising Executive Email: advertise@al.com
Delivery Methods: Carrier`Racks
Own Printing Facility?: Y
Commercial printers?: Y
Mechanical specifications: Type page 12 1/2 x 21 3/4; E - 6 cols, 2 1/16, 1/8 between; A - 6 cols, 2 1/16, 1/8 between; C - 10 cols, 1 3/8, 1/16 between.
Published Days: Wed`Fri`Sun
Weekday Frequency: m
Saturday Frequency: m
Avg. Paid Circ.: 30136
Audit Company: AAM
Audit Date: 44077
Pressroom Equipment: Lines -- 21-G/Metroliner w/12 half decks; Folders -- 4-G/3:2; Control System -- EAE/Print 4 System.;
Mailroom Equipment: Counter Stackers -- 3-HL/DUK-Carriers, 4-HL/Monitor, 6-QWI/401; Inserters & Stuffers -- 3-S/72P; Tying Machines -- 14-Dynaric/1500, 4/Power Strap.;
Business Equipment: 1-V/8545-II, Dec/Alpha, Compaq/2100
Business Software: CJAIMS
Classified Equipment: Hardware -- CSI/Sys 2400, 2-Compaq/4100; 54-CSI/112 B, 75-MS/NT workstations; Printers -- HP/4100;
Classified Software: PPI/Classified 3.0.
Editorial Equipment: Hardware -- 2-CSI/1170, 2-APP/Mac Plus, 30-HI/Newsmaker, 4-HI/Sun Sparc 20/7-HI/Page Layout Sys, 62-CSI/EDIT 112, 41-CSI/EDIT 90, 110-PC; Printers -- HP/2100 PLC
Editorial Software: HI/Informix Database.
Production Equipment: Hardware -- 2-WL/III, 1-AU/APS 6, 1-LE/LD24AC, 2-LE/24L, Micro/3; Scanners -- 2-ECR/Autokon 1000, 1-LE/480, Kk/RSF 2035+
Production Software: HI.

CAMDEN

WILCOX PROGRESSIVE ERA

Street Address: 16 Water St
City: Camden
State: AL
ZIP Code: 36726
General Phone: (334) 682-4422
General Email: ethanvansice@gmail.com
Publication Website: https://www.thewilcoxprogressiveera.com/
Delivery Methods: Mail`Newsstand`Racks
Mechanical specifications: 1 col wide = 1.833" 2 col wide = 3.792" 3 col wide = 5.75" 4 col wide = 7.708" 5 col wide = 9.667" 6 col wide = 11.625"
Published Days: Wed
Avg. Paid Circ.: 2000
Audit Company: Sworn/Estimate/Non-Audited
Audit Date: 43626

CARROLLTON

PICKENS COUNTY HERALD

Street Address: 215 REFORM ST
City: Carrollton
State: AL
ZIP Code: 35447
General Phone: (205) 367-2217
General Email: pickenscnty@centurytel.net
Publication Website: https://www.pcherald.com/
Parent Company: Mid-South Newspapers Inc
Editor Name: Brian Hamilton
Delivery Methods: Mail`Racks
Year Established: 1848
Mechanical specifications: Type page 11 5/8 x 21 1/2; E - 6 cols, 2 1/16, between; A - 6 cols, 2 1/16, between; C - 9 cols, 2 1/16, between.
Published Days: Wed
Avg. Paid Circ.: 4000
Avg. Free Circ.: 27
Audit Company: Sworn/Estimate/Non-Audited
Audit Date: 43626

CHATOM

WASHINGTON COUNTY NEWS

Street Address: PO Box 510
City: Chatom
State: AL
ZIP Code: 36518
General Phone: (251) 847-2599
General Email: news@washcountynews.com
Publication Website: https://www.washcountynews.com
Parent Company: Gannett
Publisher Name: Jason Boothe
Publisher Email: Jason@washcountynews.com
Mechanical specifications: Type page 13 x 21 1/2; E - 6 cols, 2, 1/6 between; A - 6 cols, 2, 1/6 between; C - 8 cols, 3/20 between.
Published Days: Fri
Avg. Paid Circ.: 4000
Avg. Free Circ.: 75
Audit Company: Sworn/Estimate/Non-Audited
Audit Date: 43626

CITRONELLE

CALL NEWS

Street Address: 7870 State St
City: Citronelle
State: AL
ZIP Code: 36522
General Phone: (251) 866-5998
General Email: rhondagray@thecallnews.com
Publication Website: https://www.thecallnews.com/
Parent Company: Willie T. Gray / Gray & Gray Inc.

Community Newspapers in the U.S.

Publisher Name: Willie Gray
Publisher Email: williegray@thecallnews.com
Editor Name: Tommy Hicks
Editor Email: tommyhicks@thecallnews.com
Advertising Executive Name: William Gray
Advertising Executive Email: williamgray@thecallnews.com
Published Days: Wed
Avg. Paid Circ.: 4550
Audit Company: Sworn/Estimate/Non-Audited
Audit Date: 43626

CLANTON

CHILTON COUNTY NEWS

Street Address: 1203 7th St S
City: Clanton
State: AL
ZIP Code: 35045-3723
General Phone: (205) 755-0110
General Email: news@chiltoncountynews.com
Publication Website: http://www.chiltoncountynews.com/
Editor Email: editor@chiltoncountynews.com
Published Days: Thur
Avg. Paid Circ.: 3000
Audit Company: Sworn/Estimate/Non-Audited
Audit Date: 43626

DECATUR

REDSTON ROCKET

Street Address: 201 1st Ave SE
City: Decatur
State: AL
ZIP Code: 35808
General Phone: (256) 340-2463
General Email: online@theredstonerocket.com
Publication Website: https://www.theredstonerocket.com/
Parent Company: Tennessee Valley Media Co., Inc.
Publisher Name: French Salter
Publisher Email: french.salter@theredstonerocket.com
Publisher Phone: (256) 340-2463
Editor Name: Kelsey Smith
Advertising Executive Name: Donna Counts
Advertising Executive Email: donna.counts@theredstonerocket.com
Advertising Executive Phone: (256) 714-7152
Published Days: Wed
Audit Company: Sworn/Estimate/Non-Audited
Audit Date: 43626

DOTHAN

DOTHAN PROGRESS

Street Address: 227 N Oates St
City: Dothan
State: AL
ZIP Code: 36303
General Phone: (334) 792-3141
General Email: advertising@dothaneagle.com
Publication Website: https://www.dothaneagle.com/news/dothan_progress/
Advertising Executive Email: advertising@dothaneagle.com
Own Printing Facility?: Y
Commercial printers?: Y
Mechanical specifications: Type page 13 1/2 x 21 1/2; E - 6 cols, 2 1/16, between; A - 6 cols, 2 1/16, between; C - 6 cols, 2 1/6, between.
Published Days: Thur
Avg. Paid Circ.: 25000
Audit Company: Sworn/Estimate/Non-Audited
Audit Date: 43626

ELBA

THE ELBA CLIPPER

Street Address: 417 Buford St
City: Elba
State: AL
ZIP Code: 36323
General Phone: (334) 897-2823
General Email: clipper@troycable.net
Publication Website: https://www.elba-clipper.com/
Parent Company: HF Enterprises, Inc.
Publisher Name: Ferrin Cox
Publisher Email: clipper@troycable.net
Editor Name: Linda Hodge
Editor Email: clipperace@troycable.net
Delivery Methods: Mail Racks
Year Established: 1897
Own Printing Facility?: Y
Commercial printers?: N
Mechanical specifications: 21.5 X 10 wide - 6 column format
Published Days: Thur
Avg. Paid Circ.: 2650
Audit Company: Sworn/Estimate/Non-Audited
Audit Date: 43626

EUFAULA

EUFAULA TRIBUNE

Street Address: 514 E Barbour St
City: Eufaula
State: AL
ZIP Code: 36027
General Phone: (334) 687-3506
General Email: webmaster@eufaulatribune.com
Publication Website: https://www.dothaneagle.com/eufaula_tribune/
Editor Email: editorial@eufaulatribune.com
Editor Phone: (334) 687-3229
Advertising Executive Name: Dennis Shelley
Advertising Executive Phone: (334) 687-3506, ext : 105
Delivery Methods: Mail Racks
Year Established: 1929
Commercial printers?: N
Mechanical specifications: Full Page 9.88 x 19.75
Published Days: Wed Sun
Avg. Paid Circ.: 3500
Audit Company: Sworn/Estimate/Non-Audited
Audit Date: 43626

FAYETTE

THE TIMES-RECORD

Street Address: 106 1st St SE
City: Fayette
State: AL
ZIP Code: 35555
General Phone: (205) 932-6271
Publication Website: https://www.pressherald.com/times-record/
Parent Company: Adams Publishing Group
Publisher Name: Jesse Ayres
Editor Name: Dean Maddox
Advertising Executive Name: Gina Lynn
Delivery Methods: Mail Carrier Racks
Year Established: 1977
Published Days: Wed
Avg. Paid Circ.: 5000
Audit Company: Sworn/Estimate/Non-Audited
Audit Date: 43626

FLOMATON

THE TRI-CITY LEDGER

Street Address: 20766 Hwy 31
City: Flomaton
State: AL
ZIP Code: 36441
General Phone: (251) 296-3491
General Email: newsroom@tricityledger.com
Publication Website: https://www.tricityledger.com/
Publisher Name: Joe Thomas
Editor Name: Joe Thomas
Advertising Executive Name: Tommy Standefer
Published Days: Thur
Avg. Paid Circ.: 5300
Audit Company: Sworn/Estimate/Non-Audited
Audit Date: 43626

FLORENCE

COURIER JOURNAL

Street Address: 219 W Tennessee St
City: Florence
State: AL
ZIP Code: 35630
General Phone: (256) 764-4268
General Email: sadonna@courierjournal.net
Publication Website: https://www.courierjournal.net/
Parent Company: Gannett
Publisher Name: Thomas V. Magazzu
Editor Name: Thomas V. Magazzu
Editor Email: editor@courierjournal.net
Advertising Executive Name: Sadonna B. Magazzu
Advertising Executive Email: sadonna@courierjournal.net
Delivery Methods: Mail
Year Established: 1884
Mechanical specifications: Type page 13 x 21 1/2; E - 6 cols, 1 7/8, 1/8 between; A - 6 cols, 1 7/8, 1/6 between; C - 9 cols, 1 1/4, between.
Published Days: Wed
Avg. Paid Circ.: 19
Avg. Free Circ.: 73211
Audit Company: CVC
Audit Date: 44024

GADSDEN

GADSDEN MESSENGER

Street Address: 408 Broad St
City: Gadsden
State: AL
ZIP Code: 35901
General Phone: (256) 547-1049
General Email: info@gadsdenmessenger.com
Publication Website: https://gadsdenmessenger.com/
Advertising Executive Name: Teri Chupp
Advertising Executive Email: tchupp@gadsdenmessenger.com
Published Days: Fri
Avg. Paid Circ.: 8000
Audit Company: Sworn/Estimate/Non-Audited
Audit Date: 43626

GENEVA

GENEVA COUNTY REAPER

Street Address: 506 S Commerce St
City: Geneva
State: AL
ZIP Code: 36340
General Phone: (334) 684-2280
General Email: moe@pujolprint.com
Publication Website: https://www.oppnewsonline.com/
Parent Company: Pujol Printing and Publishing LLC
Publisher Name: Moe Pujol
Publisher Email: moe@pujolprint.com

Editor Name: Katherine Hepperle
Editor Email: genevaeditor@gmail.com
Delivery Methods: Racks
Year Established: 1899
Mechanical specifications: Type page 13 x 21 1/2; E - 6 cols, 2, 1/8 between; A - 6 cols, 2, 1/8 between; C - 6 cols, 2, 1/8 between.
Published Days: Wed
Avg. Paid Circ.: 2500
Audit Company: Sworn/Estimate/Non-Audited
Audit Date: 43626

GILBERTOWN

CHOCTAW SUN-ADVOCATE

Street Address: PO Box 269
City: Gilbertown
State: AL
ZIP Code: 36908
General Phone: (251) 843-6397
General Email: choctawsun@millry.net
Publication Website: https://www.choctawsun.org/
Publisher Name: Dee Ann Campbell
Publisher Email: choctawsun@millry.net
Publisher Phone: (205) 604-9849
Editor Name: Dee Ann Campbell
Editor Email: choctawsun@millry.net
Editor Phone: (205) 604-9849
Advertising Executive Name: Dan Melvin
Advertising Executive Phone: (251) 843-6397
Delivery Methods: Mail Newsstand Racks
Year Established: 1890
Published Days: Wed
Published Other: Paper is available online through e-Paper Plus subscriptions
Avg. Paid Circ.: 4800
Audit Company: Sworn/Estimate/Non-Audited
Audit Date: 43626
Note: We also operate SunLite Online Radio, a fully licensed commercial internet radio. Log on at www.live365.com/stations/sunliteonline

GROVE HILL

CLARKE COUNTY DEMOCRAT

Street Address: P.O. Box 39
City: Grove Hill
State: AL
ZIP Code: 36451
General Phone: (251) 275-3375
General Email: clarkecountydem@tds.net
Publication Website: https://www.clarkecountydemocrat.com/
Parent Company: Jim Cox
Publisher Name: Jim Cox
Editor Name: Jim Cox
Delivery Methods: Mail Racks
Year Established: 1856
Own Printing Facility?: Y
Commercial printers?: Y
Mechanical specifications: Type page 10 inches x 21 6 cols. per page
Published Days: Thur
Avg. Paid Circ.: 3700
Audit Company: Sworn/Estimate/Non-Audited
Audit Date: 43626

GUNTERSVILLE

THE ADVERTISER-GLEAM

Street Address: 2218 Taylor St
City: Guntersville
State: AL
ZIP Code: 35976
General Phone: (256) 582-3232
General Email: ads@advertisergleam.com
Publication Website: https://www.advertisergleam.com/
Parent Company: Tennessee Valley Media

Co., Inc.
Publisher Name: Christine Hammers
Publisher Email: christine.hammers@advertisergleam.com
Editor Name: Anthony Campbell
Editor Email: news@advertisergleam.com
Advertising Executive Name: John Cagle
Advertising Executive Email: john.cagle@advertisergleam.com
Delivery Methods: Mail`Newsstand`Racks
Mechanical specifications: Type page 13 x 21 1/2; E - 6 cols, 2 1/16, 1/8 between; A - 6 cols, 2 1/16, 1/8 between; C - 6 cols, 2 1/16, 1/8 between.
Published Days: Wed`Sat
Avg. Paid Circ.: 8140
Audit Company: Sworn/Estimate/Non-Audited
Audit Date: 43626

HALEYVILLE

NORTHWEST ALABAMIAN

Street Address: 1530 21st St
City: Haleyville
State: AL
ZIP Code: 35565
General Phone: (205) 486-9461
General Email: nwaads@centurytel.net
Publication Website: https://www.mynwapaper.com/
Parent Company: Mid-South Newspapers Inc
Publisher Name: Horace Moore
Editor Name: Shelly Hess
Advertising Executive Name: Roger Carden
Delivery Methods: Mail`Racks
Year Established: 1915
Own Printing Facility?: Y
Commercial printers?: Y
Mechanical specifications: Type page 13 1/4 x 21 1/4; E - 6 cols, 2 1/16, 1/8 between; A - 6 cols, 2 1/16, 1/8 between; C - 6 cols, 2 1/16, 1/8 between.
Published Days: Wed`Sat
Avg. Paid Circ.: 7500
Avg. Free Circ.: 78
Audit Company: Sworn/Estimate/Non-Audited
Audit Date: 43626

HAMILTON

JOURNAL RECORD

Street Address: 401 State Highway 17
City: Hamilton
State: AL
ZIP Code: 35570-1477
General Phone: (205) 921-3104
General Email: jrads@centurytel.net
Publication Website: https://www.mynwapaper.com/
Parent Company: Gannett
Publisher Name: Les Walters
Editor Name: Scott Johnson
Advertising Executive Name: Kristi White
Delivery Methods: Mail`Newsstand
Year Established: 1970
Own Printing Facility?: Y
Commercial printers?: Y
Mechanical specifications: Type page 13 1/8 x 21 1/2; E - 6 cols, 1 1/16, 1/8 between; A - 6 cols, 2 1/16, 1/8 between; C - 6 cols, 2 1/16, 1/8 between.
Published Days: Wed
Avg. Paid Circ.: 5841
Avg. Free Circ.: 126
Audit Company: Sworn/Estimate/Non-Audited
Audit Date: 43626

HUNTSVILLE

THE HUNTSVILLE TIMES

Street Address: 200 Westside Sq
City: Huntsville
State: AL
ZIP Code: 35801
General Phone: (256) 532-4000
General Email: circulation@htimes.com
Publication Website: https://www.al.com/huntsville/
Parent Company: Advance Newspapers
Advertising Executive Email: advertise@al.com
Mechanical specifications: Type page 12 x 21; E - 6 cols, 2, 3/16 between; A - 6 cols, 2, 3/16 between; C - 10 cols, 1 1/4, 1/6 between.
Published Days: Wed`Fri`Sun
Weekday Frequency: m
Saturday Frequency: m
Avg. Paid Circ.: 34196
Audit Company: AAM
Audit Date: 44077
Pressroom Equipment: Lines -- 8-TKS/M-72 black units; 4-TKS/M-72 Half Decks Spot Color Unit; 1-TKS/M-72 4 Color Satellite Unit; 1-TKS/M-72 Standalone Black Unit; Reels & Stands -- 9-TKS/M-72 Reels & Stands & Stands; Control System -- TKS/Press Control;
Mailroom Equipment: Counter Stackers -- 4-QWI/200, 1-Id/440; Inserters & Stuffers -- 2-HI/1372 Inserters; Tying Machines -- 4-Dynaric/Strapper NP-1; Wrapping Singles -- 4-QWI/Bottom Wrap; Address Machine -- 2/KR.;
Business Equipment: 1-IBM/400-RISC 500
Business Software: INSI/OS400 2.1.0
Classified Equipment: Hardware -- Tandem/CLX, 12-IBM/286-30; PC; Printers -- Genicom/LW455 Linewriter, HP/4;
Classified Software: SII/ICP Sys, Northwood/Class Page.
Editorial Equipment: Hardware -- Tandem/CLX, 54-IBM/286-30, 6-Compaq/386-25/APP/Mac Graphics System, Merlin/T1; Printers -- HP/III, HP/IV, Compaq/PageMarq 15
Editorial Software: SII/INL Sys, Decade, Coyote III.
Production Equipment: Hardware -- WL/Litho Plater, AP Server, 2-AII/APS 3850; Scanners -- 1-ECR/Autokon 1030, ECR/Autokon 1000, CD/6306 Scanner, 4-AG/Argus II, 4-Polaroid/SprintScan
Production Software: QPS/QuarkXPress.

JACKSON

THE SOUTH ALABAMIAN

Street Address: 1525 College Ave
City: Jackson
State: AL
ZIP Code: 36545
General Phone: (251) 246-4494
General Email: ads@thesouthalabamian.com
Publication Website: https://www.southalabamian.com/
Parent Company: Jim Cox
Advertising Executive Email: ads@thesouthalabamian.com
Mechanical specifications: Type page 13 x 21; E - 6 cols, 2, 3/8 between; A - 6 cols, 2, 3/8 between; C - 6 cols, 2, 3/8 between.
Published Days: Thur
Avg. Paid Circ.: 4200
Avg. Free Circ.: 58
Audit Company: Sworn/Estimate/Non-Audited
Audit Date: 43626

LAFAYETTE

LAFAYETTE SUN

Street Address: 116 S Lafayette St
City: Lafayette
State: AL
ZIP Code: 36862
General Phone: (334) 864-8885
Publication Website: http://thelafayettesun.com/

Year Established: 1880
Mechanical specifications: Type page 13 x 21 1/2; E - 6 cols, 2, between; A - 6 cols, 2, between.
Published Days: Wed
Avg. Paid Circ.: 2605
Avg. Free Circ.: 33
Audit Company: Sworn/Estimate/Non-Audited
Audit Date: 43626

LINEVILLE

CLAY TIMES-JOURNAL

Street Address: 60132 Hwy 49
City: Lineville
State: AL
ZIP Code: 36266
General Phone: (256) 396-5760
General Email: claytimes97@gmail.com
Publication Website: https://www.claytimesjournal.com/
Publisher Name: David Proctor
Editor Name: David Proctor
Mechanical specifications: Type page 13 x 21 1/2; E - 6 cols, 2 1/16, 1/8 between; A - 6 cols, 2 1/16, 1/8 between; C - 6 cols, 2 1/16, 1/8 between.
Published Days: Thur
Avg. Paid Circ.: 3800
Avg. Free Circ.: 99
Audit Company: Sworn/Estimate/Non-Audited
Audit Date: 43626

LIVINGSTON

SUMTER COUNTY RECORD-JOURNAL

Street Address: 210 S Washington St
City: Livingston
State: AL
ZIP Code: 35470
General Phone: (205) 652-6100
General Email: scrjmedia@yahoo.com
Publication Website: http://www.recordjournal.net/
Publisher Name: Tommy McGraw
Editor Name: Kasey DeCastra
Advertising Executive Name: Herman B. Ward
Mechanical specifications: Type page 13 x 21 1/2; E - 6 cols, 2, 1/6 between; A - 6 cols, 2, 1/6 between; C - 6 cols, 2, 1/6 between.
Published Days: Thur
Avg. Paid Circ.: 5200
Avg. Free Circ.: 200
Audit Company: Sworn/Estimate/Non-Audited
Audit Date: 43626

MONROEVILLE

THE MONROE JOURNAL

Street Address: P.O. Box 826
City: Monroeville
State: AL
ZIP Code: 36461
General Phone: (251) 575-3282
General Email: news@monroejournal.com
Publication Website: https://www.monroejournal.com/
Publisher Name: Bo Bolton
Publisher Email: publisher@monroejournal.com
Editor Name: Mike Qualls
Editor Email: monjoured@yahoo.com
Advertising Executive Name: Michael Lambeth
Advertising Executive Email: advertising@monroejournal.com
Own Printing Facility?: Y
Commercial printers?: Y
Published Days: Thur

Avg. Paid Circ.: 7800
Avg. Free Circ.: 11900
Audit Company: Sworn/Estimate/Non-Audited
Audit Date: 43626

MONTGOMERY

PRATTVILLE PROGRESS

Street Address: 425 Molton St.
City: Montgomery
State: AL
ZIP Code: 36104
General Phone: (334) 262-1611
General Email: info@prattvilleprogress.com
Publication Website: https://www.montgomeryadvertiser.com/news/prattville/
Published Days: Sat
Avg. Paid Circ.: 8500
Avg. Free Circ.: 88
Audit Company: Sworn/Estimate/Non-Audited
Audit Date: 43626

MOULTON

THE MOULTON ADVERTISER

Street Address: 659 Main St
City: Moulton
State: AL
ZIP Code: 35650
General Phone: (256) 974-1114
General Email: teresa@moultonadvertiser.com
Publication Website: https://www.moultonadvertiser.com/
Parent Company: Tennessee Valley Media Co., Inc.
Publisher Name: Teresa Woodruff
Publisher Email: teresa@moultonadvertiser.com
Advertising Executive Email: classified@moultonadvertiser.com
Delivery Methods: Mail`Newsstand`Carrier`Racks
Year Established: 1828
Mechanical specifications: Type page 10.25 x 21; E - 6 cols, between; A - 6 cols, between; C - 6 cols, between.
Published Days: Thur
Avg. Paid Circ.: 4123
Avg. Free Circ.: 9550
Audit Company: Sworn/Estimate/Non-Audited
Audit Date: 43626

MOUNDVILLE

MOUNDVILLE TIMES

Street Address: 46 2ND AVE
City: Moundville
State: AL
ZIP Code: 35474
General Phone: (205) 371-2488
General Email: times@mound.net
Publication Website: http://moundvilletimes.net/
Published Days: Wed
Avg. Paid Circ.: 1300
Audit Company: Sworn/Estimate/Non-Audited
Audit Date: 43626

NORTHPORT

THE NORTHPORT GAZETTE

Street Address: 401 20th Ave
City: Northport
State: AL
ZIP Code: 35476
General Phone: (205) 759-3091
General Email: northportgazette@

Community Newspapers in the U.S.

northportgazette.com
Publication Website: http://www.northportgazette.com/
Delivery Methods: Mail`Newsstand`Racks
Year Established: 1998
Published Days: Wed
Avg. Paid Circ.: 4500
Audit Company: Sworn/Estimate/Non-Audited
Audit Date: 43626

ONEONTA

THE BLOUNT COUNTIAN

Street Address: 217 3rd St S
City: Oneonta
State: AL
ZIP Code: 35121
General Phone: (205) 625-3231
General Email: news@blountcountian.com
Publication Website: https://www.blountcountian.com/
Publisher Name: Aimee Wilson
Editor Name: Aimee Wilson
Editor Email: editor@blountcountian.com
Advertising Executive Name: Melanie Skillman
Mechanical specifications: Type page 13 x 21 1/2; E - 4 cols, 3 1/8, 1/8 between; A - 6 cols, 2 1/16, 1/8 between; C - 6 cols, 2 1/16, 1/8 between.
Published Days: Wed
Avg. Paid Circ.: 6900
Avg. Free Circ.: 13000
Audit Company: Sworn/Estimate/Non-Audited
Audit Date: 43626

OPP

THE OPP NEWS

Street Address: 200 W Covington Ave
City: Opp
State: AL
ZIP Code: 36467
General Phone: (334) 493-3595
General Email: opppublisher@centurytel.net
Publication Website: https://www.oppnewsonline.com/
Parent Company: Pujol Printing and Publishing LLC
Publisher Name: Moe Pujol
Publisher Email: moe@pujolprint.com
Editor Name: Katherine Hepperle
Editor Email: editor@pujolprint.com
Own Printing Facility?: Y
Commercial printers?: Y
Published Days: Thur
Avg. Paid Circ.: 5200
Audit Company: Sworn/Estimate/Non-Audited
Audit Date: 43626

PHENIX CITY

THE CITIZEN OF EAST ALABAMA

Street Address: 2401 Sportsman Dr
City: Phenix City
State: AL
ZIP Code: 36867-5402
General Phone: (334) 664-0145
Publication Website: https://citizenofeastalabama.com/
Publisher Name: Denise DuBois
Editor Name: Denise DuBois
Advertising Executive Name: Darlene Spears
Delivery Methods: Mail`Racks
Year Established: 1954
Mechanical specifications: Type page 11 5/8 x 21; E - 6 cols, 1 2/3, between; A - 6 cols, 1 2/3, between; C - 6 cols, 1 2/3, between.
Published Days: Thur
Avg. Paid Circ.: 13500
Audit Company: Sworn/Estimate/Non-Audited

Audit Date: 43626

RED BAY

THE RED BAY NEWS

Street Address: 120 4th Ave SE
City: Red Bay
State: AL
ZIP Code: 35582-4191
General Phone: (256) 356-2148
General Email: rbaynews@gmail.com
Publication Website: http://trbnews.net/main/
Delivery Methods: Mail`Newsstand`Racks
Year Established: 1963
Published Days: Wed
Avg. Paid Circ.: 2600
Audit Company: Sworn/Estimate/Non-Audited
Audit Date: 43626

ROANOKE

THE RANDOLPH LEADER

Street Address: 524 Main St
City: Roanoke
State: AL
ZIP Code: 36274
General Phone: (334) 863-2819
General Email: vanessa@therandolphleader.com
Publication Website: https://www.therandolphleader.com/
Parent Company: Randolph Publishers, Inc
Publisher Name: Tim Altork
Publisher Email: tim@therandolphleader.com
Editor Name: Tim Altork
Editor Email: tim@therandolphleader.com
Advertising Executive Name: Danielle Tooker
Advertising Executive Email: danielle@therandolphleader.com
Delivery Methods: Mail`Racks
Year Established: 1892
Mechanical specifications: Type page 13 x 21 1/4; E - 6 cols, 2 1/20, between; A - 6 cols, 2 1/20, between; C - 6 cols, 2 1/20, between.
Published Days: Wed
Avg. Paid Circ.: 7000
Audit Company: Sworn/Estimate/Non-Audited
Audit Date: 43626

ROCKFORD

COOSA COUNTY NEWS

Street Address: 296 School Street
City: Rockford
State: AL
ZIP Code: 35136
General Phone: (256) 377-2211
General Email: office@coosaso.com
Publication Website: http://www.coosacountyso.org/
Published Days: Fri
Avg. Paid Circ.: 1400
Avg. Free Circ.: 300
Audit Company: Sworn/Estimate/Non-Audited
Audit Date: 43626

STEVENSON

NORTH JACKSON PROGRESS

Street Address: 128 Oak Hill Cir
City: Stevenson
State: AL
ZIP Code: 35772-5411
General Phone: (256) 437-2395
General Email: njprogresslog@aol.com
Publication Website: http://www.northjacksonprogress.com/

Published Days: Mon`Thur
Avg. Paid Circ.: 6000
Audit Company: Sworn/Estimate/Non-Audited
Audit Date: 43626

THOMASVILLE

THE THOMASVILLE TIMES

Street Address: 24 W. Front St S.
City: Thomasville
State: AL
ZIP Code: 36784
General Phone: (334) 636-2214
General Email: newsroom@thethomasvilletimes.net
Publication Website: https://www.thethomasvilletimes.com/
Advertising Executive Name: Renee Campbell
Advertising Executive Email: ads@thethomasvilletimes.net
Year Established: 1921
Mechanical specifications: Type page 13 x 21 1/2; E - 6 cols, 2, 1/6 between; A - 6 cols, 2, 1/6 between; C - 6 cols, 2, 1/6 between.
Published Days: Tues`Thur`Sat
Avg. Paid Circ.: 3700
Audit Company: Sworn/Estimate/Non-Audited
Audit Date: 43626

TUSKEGEE

THE TUSKEGEE NEWS

Street Address: 103 S Main St
City: Tuskegee
State: AL
ZIP Code: 36083
General Phone: (334) 727-3020
General Email: tuskegeenews@bellsouth.net
Publication Website: http://www.thetuskegeenews.com/
Publisher Name: Guy Rhodes
Publisher Email: guynrhodes@bellsouth.net
Editor Name: Guy Rhodes
Editor Email: guynrhodes@bellsouth.net
Advertising Executive Name: Scott Richardson
Advertising Executive Email: tuskegeenews@bellsouth.net
Delivery Methods: Mail`Newsstand`Carrier`Racks
Year Established: 1865
Own Printing Facility?: N
Commercial printers?: N
Mechanical specifications: 1 Column 1.555" 2 Columns 3.222" 3 Columns 4.888" 4 Columns 6.555" 5 Columns 8.222" 6 Columns 9.888" Depth 20"
Published Days: Thur
Avg. Paid Circ.: 2500
Audit Company: Sworn/Estimate/Non-Audited
Audit Date: 43626

ARKANSAS

AMITY

THE STANDARD

Street Address: P.O. Box 171
City: Amity
State: AR
ZIP Code: 71921
General Phone: (870) 342-5007
General Email: southernstandard@yahoo.com
Publication Website: http://

thesouthernstandard.com/
Editor Name: Joe May

ARKADELPHIA

THE GURDON TIMES

Street Address: 205 S 26th St
City: Arkadelphia
State: AR
ZIP Code: 71923
General Phone: (870) 353-4482
General Email: lmartin@picayune-times.com
Publication Website: http://thegurdontimes.gatehousecontests.com/Ultimate-Summer-Vacation-Giveaway/

ASHDOWN

LITTLE RIVER NEWS

Street Address: P.O. Box 608
City: Ashdown
State: AR
ZIP Code: 71822
General Phone: (870) 667 – 0108
General Email: editor@lrnews1898.com
Publication Website: https://lrnews1898.com/
Parent Company: Red River Media

BEEBE

THE BEEBE NEWS

Street Address: 107 E Center St
City: Beebe
State: AR
ZIP Code: 72012
General Phone: (501) 882-5414
General Email: tbn@beebenews.com
Publication Website: https://beebenews.com/
Publisher Name: Lee McLane
Publisher Email: tbn@beebenews.com
Editor Name: Lee McLane

BENTONVILLE

THE WEEKLY VISTA

Street Address: 13026 Frontage Road
City: Bentonville
State: AR
ZIP Code: 72712
General Phone: (479) 855-3724
General Email: weeklyvista@nwadg.com
Publication Website: https://bvwv.nwaonline.com/
Parent Company: WEHCO Media, Inc.
Editor Name: Rusty Turner

BERRYVILLE

CARROLL COUNTY NEWS

Street Address: 1105 S Main St
City: Berryville
State: AR
ZIP Code: 72616-4332
General Phone: (870) 423-6636
General Email: rhonda.w@cox-internet.com
Publication Website: https://www.carrollconews.com/
Parent Company: Rust Communications
Publisher Name: Bob Moore
Publisher Email: b.moore@cox-internet.com
Publisher Phone: (870) 423-6636
Editor Name: Scott Loftis

BLYTHEVILLE

III-161

NEA TOWN CRIER

Street Address: PO Box 1108
City: Blytheville
State: AR
ZIP Code: 72316
General Phone: (870) 763-4461
General Email: srouse@stategazette.com
Publication Website: http://www.thetown-crier.com/
Parent Company: Rust Communications
Publisher Name: Shelia Rouse
Publisher Email: srouse@stategazette.com
Publisher Phone: (731) 285-4091
Editor Name: Mark Brasfield

BOONEVILLE

BOONEVILLE DEMOCRAT

Street Address: P.O. Box 208
City: Booneville
State: AR
ZIP Code: 72927-4043
General Phone: (479) 675-4455
General Email: ccoffee@boonevilledemocrat.com
Publication Website: https://www.boonevilledemocrat.com/
Parent Company: Gannett
Publisher Name: Kristyn Sims
Publisher Email: ksims@boonevilledemocrat.com
Publisher Phone: (833) 675-4455, ext : 1372
Editor Name: Glenn Parrish

BRINKLEY

MONROE COUNTY HERALD

Street Address: 322 W Cypress St
City: Brinkley
State: AR
ZIP Code: 72021
General Phone: (870) 589-5055
General Email: monroecountyherald@gmail.com
Publication Website: https://www.monroecountyherald.news/

CALICO ROCK

WHITE RIVER CURRENT

Street Address: 15 W 1st St
City: Calico Rock
State: AR
ZIP Code: 72519
General Phone: (870) 297-3010
General Email: news@whiterivercurrent.com
Publication Website: https://www.whiterivercurrent.com/
Publisher Name: Charles Francis
Publisher Phone: (870) 373-2693
Editor Name: Tabitha West

CLARKSVILLE

JOHNSON COUNTY GRAPHIC

Street Address: 203 E Cherry St
City: Clarksville
State: AR
ZIP Code: 72830
General Phone: (479) 754-2005
General Email: ron@thegraphic.org
Publication Website: http://www.thegraphic.org/
Publisher Name: Ron Wylie
Publisher Email: ron@thegraphic.org
Editor Name: Margaret Wylie

CLINTON

VAN BUREN COUNTY DEMOCRAT

Street Address: 197 COURT ST
City: Clinton
State: AR
ZIP Code: 72031
General Phone: (501) 745-5175
General Email: ads@vanburencountydem.com
Publication Website: http://www.vanburencountydem.com/
Publisher Name: Frank Leto
Publisher Email: fleto@thecabin.net
Publisher Phone: (501) 505-1213
Editor Name: Nick Stahl

CORNING

CLAY COUNTY COURIER

Street Address: 810 N Missouri Ave
City: Corning
State: AR
ZIP Code: 72422-0085
General Phone: (870) 857-3531
Publication Website: https://www.claycountyliving.com/

CROSSETT

ASHLEY NEWS OBSERVER

Street Address: 106 E Second St
City: Crossett
State: AR
ZIP Code: 71635
General Phone: (870) 364-5186
General Email: kcaldwell@ashleynewsobserver.com
Publication Website: https://www.ashleynewsobserver.com
Parent Company: Lancaster Management Inc.
Publisher Name: Barney White
Publisher Email: bwhite@ashleynewsobserver.com
Publisher Phone: (870) 364-5186

DE QUEEN

DEQUEEN BEE

Street Address: 404 W Dequeen Ave
City: De Queen
State: AR
ZIP Code: 71832
General Phone: (870) 642-2111
General Email: editor@dequeenbee.com
Publication Website: http://www.dequeenbee.com/
Parent Company: Lancaster Management Inc.
Publisher Name: Tom Byrd
Publisher Phone: (479) 394-1900
Editor Name: Marty Bachman

DE WITT

DE WITT ERA-ENTERPRISE

Street Address: 140 Court Sq
City: De Witt
State: AR
ZIP Code: 72042-2049
General Phone: (870) 946-3933
General Email: manager@dewitt-ee.com
Publication Website: https://www.dewitt-ee.com/
Parent Company: Kingsett, LLC
Publisher Email: everyone@dewitt-ee.com

EUREKA SPRINGS

LOVELY COUNTY CITIZEN

Street Address: 3022 E Van Buren
City: Eureka Springs
State: AR
ZIP Code: 72632-9800
General Phone: (479) 253-0070
General Email: b.moore@cox-internet.com
Publication Website: https://www.lovelycitizen.com
Parent Company: Rust Communications
Publisher Name: Bob Moore
Publisher Email: b.moore@cox-internet.com
Publisher Phone: (870) 423-6636
Editor Name: Scott Loftis

FAIRFIELD BAY

LAKE AREA WEEKLY

Street Address: PO Box 1370
City: Fairfield Bay
State: AR
ZIP Code: 72088
General Phone: (501) 884-6010
General Email: editor@lakeareaweekly.com
Publication Website: https://fairfieldbaynews.com/
Parent Company: Fairfield Bay Community Club

FARMINGTON

WASHINGTON COUNTY ENTERPRISE-LEADER

Street Address: 128 Southwinds Rd
City: Farmington
State: AR
ZIP Code: 72730
General Phone: (479) 571-6418
General Email: rturner@nwaonline.net
Publication Website: https://wcel.nwaonline.com/
Parent Company: NWA Media
Editor Name: Lynn Kutter

FLIPPIN

THE MOUNTAINEER ECHO

Street Address: 1277 Highway 178 N
City: Flippin
State: AR
ZIP Code: 72634
General Phone: (870) 453-3731
General Email: mtnecho@gmail.com
Publication Website: https://www.flippinonline.com/
Parent Company: Jade Media, Inc.

GRAVETTE

WESTSIDE EAGLE OBSERVER

Street Address: PO Box 640
City: Gravette
State: AR
ZIP Code: 72736
General Phone: (800) 641-6882
General Email: rturner@nwaonline.com
Publication Website: https://www.eagleobserver.com/
Parent Company: WEHCO Media, Inc.
Editor Name: Rusty Turner

GREENWOOD

CHARLESTON EXPRESS

Street Address: 38 TOWN SQ
City: Greenwood
State: AR
ZIP Code: 72936
General Phone: (479) 965-7368
General Email: ksims@charlestonexpress.com
Publication Website: https://www.charlestonexpress.com/
Parent Company: Gannett
Publisher Name: Kristyn Sims
Publisher Email: ksims@charlestonexpress.com
Publisher Phone: (479) 965-7368
Editor Name: Paul Gramlich

GREENWOOD

GREENWOOD DEMOCRAT

Street Address: 38 TOWN SQ
City: Greenwood
State: AR
ZIP Code: 72936
General Phone: (479) 996-4494
General Email: rbenner@swtimes.com
Publication Website: http://www.greenwooddemocrat.com/
Publisher Name: Ronald Benner
Publisher Email: rbenner@swtimes.com
Publisher Phone: (479) 785-7700, ext : 1300

HAMBURG

ASHLEY COUNTY LEDGER

Street Address: PO Box 471
City: Hamburg
State: AR
ZIP Code: 71646
General Phone: (870) 853-2424
General Email: the_ledger@att.net
Publication Website: http://www.ashleycountyledger.com
Parent Company: Ashley Publishing Inc.
Publisher Email: the_ledger@att.net
Publisher Phone: (870) 853-2424

HAZEN

HERALD PUBLISHING CO.

Street Address: PO Box 370
City: Hazen
State: AR
ZIP Code: 72064
General Phone: (870) 255-4538
General Email: heraldpublishing@gmail.com
Publication Website: http://herald-publishing.com/
Parent Company: Herald Publishing Co.
Editor Name: Roxanne Bradow

HEBER SPRINGS

THE SUN-TIMES

Street Address: 107 N 4th St
City: Heber Springs
State: AR
ZIP Code: 72543
General Phone: (501) 362-2425
General Email: advertising@thesuntimes.com
Publication Website: https://www.thesuntimes.com
Parent Company: Paxton Media Group, LLC
Publisher Name: Shane Allen

HELENA

THE HELENA ARKANSAS DAILY WORLD

Street Address: 417 YORK ST
City: HELENA
State: AR
ZIP Code: 72342
General Phone: (870) 338-9181
General Email: thicks@gatehousemedia.com
Publication Website: https://www.helena-arkansas.com/

Community Newspapers in the U.S.

Publisher Name: Teresa Hicks
Publisher Email: thicks@gatehousemedia.com
Editor Name: Rick Wright

HOT SPRINGS VILLAGE

HOT SPRINGS VILLAGE VOICE

Street Address: 3576 N Highway 7
City: Hot Springs Village
State: AR
ZIP Code: 71909
General Phone: (501) 623-6397
General Email: jallen@hsvvoice.com
Publication Website: https://www.hsvvoice.com/
Publisher Name: Jennifer Allen
Publisher Email: jallen@gatehousemedia.com
Publisher Phone: (501) 623-6397
Editor Name: Misty Castile

HUNTSVILLE

THE MADISON COUNTY RECORD

Street Address: 201 Church St
City: Huntsville
State: AR
ZIP Code: 72740
General Phone: (479) 738-2141
General Email: loripollock@mcrecordonline.com
Publication Website: http://www.mcrecordonline.com/
Parent Company: Boone Newspapers
Publisher Name: Ellen Kreth
Editor Name: Rod Harrington

JACKSONVILLE

THE LEADER

Street Address: 404 Graham Rd
City: Jacksonville
State: AR
ZIP Code: 72076
General Phone: (501) 982-9421
General Email: johnhenderson@leaderpublishing.com
Publication Website: https://www.arkansasleader.com/
Parent Company: Adams Publishing Group
Publisher Name: Garrick Feldman
Publisher Email: gfeldman@arkansasleader.com
Editor Name: Jonathan Feldman

LAKE VILLAGE

CHICOT SPECTATOR

Street Address: 105 N Court St
City: Lake Village
State: AR
ZIP Code: 71653
General Phone: (870) 265-2071
General Email: news@chicotnewspapers.com
Publication Website: https://www.chicotnewspapers.com/
Parent Company: Lancaster Management, Inc.
Publisher Name: Barney White
Publisher Phone: (870) 265-2071

LAKE VILLAGE

EUDORA ENTERPRISE

Street Address: 105 N Court St
City: Lake Village
State: AR
ZIP Code: 71653
General Phone: (870) 265-2071
General Email: news@chicotnewspapers.com
Publication Website: https://www.chicotnewspapers.com/
Parent Company: Chicot County Newspapers LLC
Publisher Name: Barney White
Publisher Phone: (870) 265-2071

LITTLE ROCK

ARKANSAS TIMES

Street Address: 201 E Markham St
City: Little Rock
State: AR
ZIP Code: 72201
General Phone: (501) 375-2985
General Email: arktimes@arktimes.com
Publication Website: https://arktimes.com/
Parent Company: Arkansas Times Limited Partnership
Publisher Name: Alan Leveritt
Publisher Email: alanleveritt@arktimes.com
Editor Name: Lindsey Millar

MC CRORY

WOODRUFF COUNTY MONITOR-LEADER-ADVOCATE

Street Address: 112 W 2nd St
City: Mc Crory
State: AR
ZIP Code: 72101-8062
General Phone: (870) 731-2263
General Email: wcm@centurytel.net
Publication Website: http://www.wcmla.net/

MENA

THE MENA STAR

Street Address: 501 Mena St
City: Mena
State: AR
ZIP Code: 71953
General Phone: (479) 394-1900
General Email: editor@menastar.com
Publication Website: http://www.menastar.com/
Parent Company: Lancaster Management Inc.
Publisher Name: Clark Smith
Publisher Email: clark@menastar.com
Editor Name: Sarah Wilson

MONTICELLO

ADVANCE-MONTICELLONIAN

Street Address: 314 N Main St
City: Monticello
State: AR
ZIP Code: 7165
General Phone: (870) 367-5325
General Email: publisher@monticellonews.net
Publication Website: https://www.mymonticellonews.net/
Parent Company: Smith Newspapers
Publisher Name: Tom White
Publisher Email: publisher@monticellonews.net
Publisher Phone: (870) 367-5325
Editor Name: Harold Coggins

MORRILTON

CONWAY COUNTY PETIT JEAN COUNTRY HEADLIGHT

Street Address: 908 W Broadway St
City: Morrilton
State: AR
ZIP Code: 72110
General Phone: (501) 354-2451
General Email: pjch@suddenlinkmail.com
Publication Website: https://www.headlightnews.com/
Parent Company: Yell County Publishing, Inc.

MORRILTON

PERRY COUNTY PETIT JEAN COUNTRY HEADLIGHT

Street Address: 908 W Broadway St
City: Morrilton
State: AR
ZIP Code: 72110
General Phone: (501) 354-2451
General Email: pjch@suddenlinkmail.com
Publication Website: https://www.headlightnews.com/
Parent Company: Yell County Publishing, Inc.

MOUNTAIN VIEW

STONE COUNTY LEADER

Street Address: 104 W Main St
City: Mountain View
State: AR
ZIP Code: 72560
General Phone: (870) 269-3841
General Email: leader@mvtel.net
Publication Website: http://stonecountyleader.com/
Publisher Name: James R. Fraser
Publisher Email: rusty@stonecountyleader.com
Editor Name: Lori Freeze

NASHVILLE

GLENWOOD HERALD

Street Address: 119 N Main St
City: Nashville
State: AR
ZIP Code: 71852
General Phone: (870) 356-2111
General Email: contact@swarkansasnews.com
Publication Website: https://www.swarkansasnews.com/digital-newspapers/glenwood-herald-news/
Parent Company: Nashville News Leader
Publisher Name: Louie Graves
Publisher Email: louie@nashvilleleader.com
Editor Name: John Robert Schirmer

NASHVILLE

MONTGOMERY COUNTY NEWS

Street Address: 119 N Main St.
City: Nashville
State: AR
ZIP Code: 71852
General Phone: (870) 867-2821
General Email: contact@swarkansasnews.com
Publication Website: https://www.swarkansasnews.com/digital-newspapers/montgomery-county-news/
Parent Company: Nashville News Leader
Publisher Name: Louie Graves
Publisher Email: louie@nashvilleleader.com
Editor Name: John Robert Schirmer

NASHVILLE

MURFREESBORO DIAMOND

Street Address: 119 N Main St.
City: Nashville
State: AR
ZIP Code: 71852
General Phone: (870) 285-2723
General Email: contact@swarkansasnews.com
Publication Website: https://www.swarkansasnews.com/digital-newspapers/murfreesboro-diamond-news/
Publisher Name: Louie Graves
Publisher Email: louie@nashvilleleader.com
Editor Name: John Robert Schirmer

NASHVILLE

THE NASHVILLE NEWS-LEADER

Street Address: 119 N Main St
City: Nashville
State: AR
ZIP Code: 71852
General Phone: (870) 845-0600
General Email: contact@swarkansasnews.com
Publication Website: https://www.swarkansasnews.com/digital-newspapers/nashville-news-leader/
Parent Company: Nashville News Leader
Publisher Name: Louie Graves
Publisher Email: louie@nashvilleleader.com
Editor Name: John Robert Schirmer

NEWPORT

NEWPORT INDEPENDENT

Street Address: 2408 Highway 367 N
City: Newport
State: AR
ZIP Code: 72112
General Phone: (870) 523-5855
General Email: ads@newportindependent.com
Publication Website: https://newportarcity.org/
Parent Company: Gatehouse Media, LLC

OSCEOLA

THE OSCEOLA TIMES

Street Address: 105 North Walnut
City: Osceola
State: AR
ZIP Code: 72370
General Phone: (870) 563-2615
General Email: timesnews@osceolatimes.com
Publication Website: https://www.osceolatimes.com/
Parent Company: Rust Communications
Publisher Name: Mike Smith
Editor Name: Sandra Brand

OZARK

THE SPECTATOR

Street Address: 207 W Main St
City: Ozark
State: AR
ZIP Code: 72949
General Phone: (479) 667-2136
General Email: spectator@centurytel.net
Publication Website: https://www.ozarkspectator.net/
Parent Company: Gannett
Publisher Name: Bob Bevil
Editor Name: Joselyn Eveld

PEA RIDGE

THE TIMES OF NORTHEAST BENTON COUNTY

Street Address: 981 N Curtis Ave
City: Pea Ridge
State: AR
ZIP Code: 72751
General Phone: (479) 451-1196
General Email: prtnews@nwaonline.com
Publication Website: https://tnebc.nwaonline.com/
Parent Company: NWA Media
Editor Name: Annette Beard

PIGGOTT

CLAY COUNTY TIMES-DEMOCRAT

Street Address: 270 W Court St
City: Piggott
State: AR
ZIP Code: 72454
General Phone: (870) 598-2201
General Email: piggotttimes@centurytel.net
Publication Website: https://www.cctimesdemocrat.com/
Parent Company: Rust Communications
Publisher Name: Sheila Rouse
Publisher Email: srouse@stategazette.com
Publisher Phone: (731) 285-4091

POCAHONTAS

POCAHONTAS STAR HERALD

Street Address: 109 N Van Bibber St
City: Pocahontas
State: AR
ZIP Code: 72455
General Phone: (870) 892-4451
General Email: anita@starheraldnews.com
Publication Website: https://www.starheraldnews.com/

RISON

CLEVELAND COUNTY HERALD

Street Address: 215 N MAIN ST
City: Rison
State: AR
ZIP Code: 71665
General Phone: (870) 325-6412
General Email: contact@clevelandcountyherald.com
Publication Website: http://www.clevelandcountyherald.com/
Parent Company: Talent Publishing LLC
Publisher Name: Britt Talent
Editor Name: Britt Talent

SALEM

THE NEWS

Street Address: 388 Highway 62 E
City: Salem
State: AR
ZIP Code: 72576
General Phone: (800) 995-3209
General Email: news@areawidenews.com
Publication Website: https://www.areawidenews.com/
Parent Company: Paxton Media Group
Publisher Name: Patti Sanders
Editor Name: Kim Break

SHERIDAN

SHERIDAN HEADLIGHT

Street Address: 101 N Rose St
City: Sheridan
State: AR
ZIP Code: 72150
General Phone: (870) 942-2142
General Email: info@thesheridanheadlight.com
Publication Website: http://thesheridanheadlight.com/
Publisher Name: Byron Tate
Publisher Email: byron@thesheridanheadlight.com
Editor Name: Millie McClain

STAMPS

LAFAYETTE COUNTY PRESS

Street Address: 221 Main St
City: Stamps
State: AR
ZIP Code: 71860
General Phone: (870) 533-4708
General Email: lcpress@sbcglobal.net
Publication Website: https://www.lafayettecountypress.com/
Publisher Name: Lucy Goodwin
Editor Name: Tommy Goodwin

TRUMANN

POINSETT COUNTY DEMOCRAT TRIBUNE

Street Address: 201 Highway 463 N
City: Trumann
State: AR
ZIP Code: 72472-3503
General Phone: (870) 483-6317
General Email: ronkemp@centurytel.net
Publication Website: https://www.democrattribune.com
Publisher Name: Sheila Rouse
Publisher Email: ronkemp@centurytel.net
Editor Name: Phillip Patterson

WALDRON

THE CITIZEN

Street Address: 200 S MAIN ST
City: Waldron
State: AR
ZIP Code: 72958
General Phone: (479) 637-4161
General Email: publisher@menastar.com
Publication Website: https://www.waldronnews.com/eedition/the_citizen/
Parent Company: Lee Enterprises

WALDRON

THE WALDRON NEWS

Street Address: 200 S MAIN ST
City: Waldron
State: AR
ZIP Code: 72958
General Phone: (479) 637-4161
General Email: ads@waldronnews.com
Publication Website: https://www.waldronnews.com/eedition/waldron_news/
Parent Company: The Waldron News

WALNUT RIDGE

THE TIMES DISPATCH

Street Address: 225 W Main St
City: Walnut Ridge
State: AR
ZIP Code: 72476
General Phone: (870) 886-2464
General Email: editor@thetd.com
Publication Website: http://www.thetd.com/

ARIZONA

AJO

AJO COPPER NEWS

Street Address: P.O. Box 39
City: Ajo
State: AZ
ZIP Code: 85321-2435
General Phone: (520) 387-7688
General Email: cunews@cunews.info
Publication Website: http://www.cunews.info/
Parent Company: ANA Advertising Services, Inc. (Arizona Newspaper Association)
Publisher Name: H.J. David
Publisher Email: hopd@cunews.info
Editor Name: Gabrielle David
Editor Email: editor@cunews.info
Advertising Executive Email: advertising@cunews.info
Delivery Methods: Mail/Newsstand
Year Established: 1916
Commercial printers?: Y
Mechanical specifications: Type page 9 5/6 x 16; E - 5 cols, 1 4/5, 1/6 between; A - 5 cols, 1 4/5, 1/6 between; C - 5 cols, 1 4/5, 1/6 between.
Published Days: Tues
Avg. Paid Circ.: 1000
Avg. Free Circ.: 45
Audit Company: Sworn/Estimate/Non-Audited
Audit Date: 43626

APACHE JUNCTION

QUEEN CREEK INDEPENDENT

Street Address: 2066 W Apache Trl
City: Apache Junction
State: AZ
ZIP Code: 85120-3733
General Phone: (480) 982-7799
General Email: qcnews@newszap.com
Publication Website: https://www.yourvalley.net/queen-creek-independent/
Parent Company: Independent NewsMedia
Delivery Methods: Carrier
Year Established: 2004
Published Days: Wed
Avg. Free Circ.: 10000
Audit Company: Sworn/Estimate/Non-Audited
Audit Date: 43626

APACHE JUNCTION

THE APACHE JUNCTION/GOLD CANYON NEWS

Street Address: 879 N. Plaza Dr. Building C, Suite 101
City: Apache Junction
State: AZ
ZIP Code: 85120
General Phone: (480) 982-6397
General Email: ajnews@ajnews.com
Publication Website: https://www.ajnews.com/eedition
Parent Company: Foothills Publishing, Inc.
Publisher Name: Robin Barker
Publisher Email: robin@ajnews.com
Advertising Executive Name: Trish Beltran
Advertising Executive Email: tbeltran@ajnews.com
Year Established: 1997
Published Days: Mon
Audit Company: Sworn/Estimate/Non-Audited
Audit Date: 43626

BISBEE

THE BISBEE OBSERVER

Street Address: 7 Bisbee Rd Ste L
City: Bisbee
State: AZ
ZIP Code: 85603-1140
General Phone: (520) 432-7254
General Email: bisbeeobserver@cableone.net
Publication Website: https://thebisbeeobserver.com/default.aspx
Parent Company: ANA Advertising Services, Inc. (Arizona Newspaper Association)
Delivery Methods: Mail/Newsstand
Year Established: 1985
Mechanical specifications: Type page 10 1/4 x 15 1/2; E - 5 cols, 1 19/20, 1/8 between; A - 5 cols, 1 19/20, 1/8 between; C - 5 cols, 1 19/20, 1/8 between.
Published Days: Thur
Avg. Paid Circ.: 2100
Avg. Free Circ.: 45
Audit Company: Sworn/Estimate/Non-Audited
Audit Date: 43626

BUCKEYE

THE BUCKEYE STAR

Street Address: 108 N 4th St
City: Buckeye
State: AZ
ZIP Code: 85326-2402
General Phone: (623) 374-4303
General Email: info@thebuckeyestar.com
Publication Website: https://www.thebuckeyestar.net/
Editor Name: Nathan Stein
Editor Email: nstein@thebuckeyestar.com
Year Established: 2010
Published Days: Wed/Bi-Mthly
Audit Company: Sworn/Estimate/Non-Audited
Audit Date: 43626

BULLHEAD CITY

LAUGHLIN ENTERTAINER

Street Address: 2435 Miracle Mile
City: Bullhead City
State: AZ
ZIP Code: 86442-7311
General Phone: (928) 763-2505
General Email: entertainerstaff@gmail.com
Publication Website: http://laughlinentertainer.com/
Parent Company: Brehm Communications, Inc.
Year Established: 1985
Published Days: Wed
Avg. Free Circ.: 55000
Audit Company: Sworn/Estimate/Non-Audited
Audit Date: 43626

BULLHEAD CITY

LAUGHLIN NEVADA TIMES

Street Address: 2435 Miracle Mile
City: Bullhead City
State: AZ
ZIP Code: 86442-7311
General Phone: (928) 296-8455
General Email: wells@nwppub.com
Publication Website: http://www.mohavedailynews.com/laughlin_times/
Parent Company: Brehm Communications, Inc.; News West Publishing Company Inc. (OOB)
Publisher Name: Larry Kendrick
Publisher Email: larry@nwppub.com
Publisher Phone: (928) 296-8455, ext : 7122
Editor Name: Bill McMillen
Editor Email: bmcmillen@mohavedailynews.com

Community Newspapers in the U.S.

Editor Phone: (928) 296-8455, ext : 5144
Delivery Methods: Newsstand`Carrier`Racks
Year Established: 1990
Own Printing Facility?: Y
Published Days: Wed
Avg. Paid Circ.: 4300
Audit Company: Sworn/Estimate/Non-Audited
Audit Date: 43626

CAMP VERDE

THE CAMP VERDE JOURNAL

Street Address: 406 S. First St.
City: Camp Verde
State: AZ
ZIP Code: 86322
General Phone: (928) 567-3341
General Email: editor@larsonnewspapers.com
Publication Website: https://www.journalaz.com/news/camp-verde.html
Parent Company: Larson Newspapers
Publisher Name: Kyle Larson
Publisher Email: klarson@larsonnewspapers.com
Publisher Phone: (928) 282-7795, ext : 114
Editor Name: Christopher Fox Graham
Editor Email: editor@larsonnewspapers.com
Editor Phone: (928) 282-7795, ext : 129
Advertising Executive Phone: (928) 282-7795, ext : 114
Year Established: 1980
Own Printing Facility?: Y
Commercial printers?: Y
Mechanical specifications: Type page 13 x 21; E - 6 cols, 2, 1/6 between; A - 6 cols, 2, 1/6 between; C - 6 cols, 2, 1/6 between.
Published Days: Wed
Avg. Paid Circ.: 2000
Avg. Free Circ.: 125
Audit Company: Sworn/Estimate/Non-Audited
Audit Date: 43626

CAVE CREEK

SONORAN NEWS

Street Address: 6702 E Cave Creek Rd
City: Cave Creek
State: AZ
ZIP Code: 85331-8659
General Phone: (480) 488-2021
General Email: sonnews@aol.com
Publication Website: http://sonorannews.com/
Publisher Name: Don Sorchych
Publisher Email: sonnews@aol.com
Publisher Phone: (480) 488-2021, ext : 25
Editor Name: Don Sorchych
Editor Email: sonnews@aol.com
Editor Phone: (480) 488-2021, ext : 25
Advertising Executive Name: Charlie Blankenship
Advertising Executive Email: advertising@sonorannews.com
Advertising Executive Phone: (480) 488-2021, ext : 23
Delivery Methods: Mail
Mechanical specifications: Type page 11 5/8 x 21; E - 6 cols, 1 4/5, between; A - 6 cols, 1 4/5, between; C - 6 cols, 1 4/5, between.
Published Days: Wed
Avg. Paid Circ.: 62
Avg. Free Circ.: 43000
Audit Company: Sworn/Estimate/Non-Audited
Audit Date: 43626

COTTONWOOD

COTTONWOOD JOURNAL EXTRA

Street Address: 830 S Main St
City: Cottonwood
State: AZ
ZIP Code: 86326-4621
General Phone: (928) 634-8551
General Email: jhechta@larsonnewspapers.com
Publication Website: https://www.journalaz.com/news/cottonwood.html
Parent Company: Larson Newspapers
Editor Name: Jon Hecht
Editor Email: jhechta@larsonnewspapers.com
Editor Phone: (928) 634-8551
Own Printing Facility?: Y
Commercial printers?: Y
Mechanical specifications: Type page 13 x 21; E - 6 cols, 2, 1/6 between; A - 6 cols, 2, 1/6 between; C - 6 cols, 2, 1/6 between.
Published Days: Wed
Avg. Paid Circ.: 548
Avg. Free Circ.: 8500
Audit Company: Sworn/Estimate/Non-Audited
Audit Date: 43626

FLAGSTAFF

FLAGSTAFF LIVE!

Street Address: 1751 S Thompson St
City: Flagstaff
State: AZ
ZIP Code: 86001-8716
General Phone: (928) 774-4545
General Email: cbrady@azdailysun.com
Publication Website: https://azdailysun.com/
Publisher Name: Colleen Brady
Publisher Email: cbrady@azdailysun.com
Publisher Phone: (928) 556-2279
Editor Name: MacKenzie Chase
Editor Email: mchase@azdailysun.com
Editor Phone: (928) 556-2262
Advertising Executive Name: Ian Logan
Advertising Executive Email: ilogan@azdailysun.com
Advertising Executive Phone: (928) 913-8023
Delivery Methods: Racks
Year Established: 1995
Own Printing Facility?: Y
Published Days: Thur
Avg. Free Circ.: 8300
Audit Company: Sworn/Estimate/Non-Audited
Audit Date: 43626

FOUNTAIN HILLS

LET'S GO

Street Address: 16508 E Laser Dr., Suite 101
City: Fountain Hills
State: AZ
ZIP Code: 85268-6512
General Phone: (480) 837-1925
General Email: duke@fhtimes.com
Publication Website: https://www.fhtimes.com/lets_go/
Parent Company: Western States Publishers, Inc.
Publisher Name: Brent Cruikshank
Publisher Email: brent@fhtimes.com
Editor Name: Ryan Winslett
Editor Email: ryan@fhtimes.com
Advertising Executive Name: Duke Kirkendoll
Advertising Executive Email: duke@fhtimes.com
Delivery Methods: Mail`Newsstand
Year Established: 1999
Published Days: Thur`Mthly
Avg. Free Circ.: 17000
Audit Company: Sworn/Estimate/Non-Audited
Audit Date: 43626

FOUNTAIN HILLS

THE FOUNTAIN HILL TIMES

Street Address: 16508 E Laser Dr., Suite 101
City: Fountain Hills
State: AZ
ZIP Code: 85268-6512
General Phone: (480) 837-1925
General Email: duke@fhtimes.com
Publication Website: https://www.fhtimes.com/
Parent Company: Western States Publishers, Inc.
Publisher Name: Brent Cruikshank
Publisher Email: brent@fhtimes.com
Editor Name: Ryan Winslett
Editor Email: ryan@fhtimes.com
Advertising Executive Name: Duke Kirkendoll
Advertising Executive Email: duke@fhtimes.com
Delivery Methods: Mail`Newsstand`Carrier
Year Established: 1974
Published Days: Wed
Avg. Paid Circ.: 5300
Audit Company: Sworn/Estimate/Non-Audited
Audit Date: 43626

GLENDALE

THE GLENDALE STAR

Street Address: 7122 N 59th Ave
City: Glendale
State: AZ
ZIP Code: 85301-2436
General Phone: (623) 842-6000
General Email: lmeehan@star-times.com
Publication Website: https://www.glendalestar.com/
Parent Company: Times Media Group
Publisher Name: Steve Strickbine
Editor Name: Christina Fuoco-Karasinski
Editor Email: christina@star-times.com
Editor Phone: (623) 777-1492
Advertising Executive Name: Laura Meehan
Advertising Executive Email: lmeehan@star-times.com
Advertising Executive Phone: (623) 777-1042
Delivery Methods: Mail`Newsstand
Year Established: 1978
Own Printing Facility?: Y
Mechanical specifications: Type page 10 5/16 x 16; E - 6 cols, 1 9/16, 1/6 between; A - 6 cols, 1 9/16, 1/6 between; C - 6 cols, 1 9/16, 1/6 between.
Published Days: Thur
Avg. Paid Circ.: 6000
Avg. Free Circ.: 1000
Audit Company: Sworn/Estimate/Non-Audited
Audit Date: 43626

HOLBROOK

SILVER CREEK HERALD

Street Address: 200 E Hopi Dr
City: Holbrook
State: AZ
ZIP Code: 86025-2628
General Phone: (928) 524-6203
General Email: mbarger@cableone.net
Publication Website: http://www.tribunenewsnow.com/
Parent Company: Navajo County Publishers, Inc.
Publisher Name: Linda Kor
Editor Name: Linda Kor
Advertising Executive Name: Matthew Barger
Delivery Methods: Mail`Racks
Year Established: 1909
Published Days: Wed`Fri
Avg. Free Circ.: 3200
Audit Company: Sworn/Estimate/Non-Audited
Audit Date: 43626

HOLBROOK

THE TRIBUNE-NEWS

Street Address: 200 E Hopi Dr
City: Holbrook
State: AZ
ZIP Code: 86025-2628
General Phone: (928) 524-6203
General Email: mikenilsson.adv@gmail.com
Publication Website: http://www.tribunenewsnow.com/
Parent Company: Navajo County Publishers, Inc.
Publisher Name: Linda Kor
Editor Name: Linda Kor
Advertising Executive Name: Matthew Barger
Delivery Methods: Mail`Newsstand
Mechanical specifications: Type page 9.8889 x 21; E - 6 cols, .1111 between; A - 6 cols, .1111 between; C - 6 cols, .1111 between.
Published Days: Wed`Fri
Avg. Paid Circ.: 2490
Avg. Free Circ.: 1538
Audit Company: Sworn/Estimate/Non-Audited
Audit Date: 43626

KEARNY

COPPER BASIN NEWS

Street Address: 366 W Alden Rd
City: Kearny
State: AZ
ZIP Code: 85137-1208
General Phone: (520) 363-5554
General Email: copperbasinnews@gmail.com
Publication Website: http://www.copperarea.com/pages/category/publications/copper-basin-news/
Parent Company: Copper Area News Publishers
Year Established: 1958
Mechanical specifications: Type page 13 x 20 3/4.
Published Days: Wed
Avg. Paid Circ.: 2403
Avg. Free Circ.: 23
Audit Company: Sworn/Estimate/Non-Audited
Audit Date: 43626

KEARNY

SAN MANUEL MINER

Street Address: 366 W Alden Rd
City: Kearny
State: AZ
ZIP Code: 85137-1208
General Phone: (520) 385-2266
General Email: copperbasinnews@gmail.com
Publication Website: http://www.copperarea.com/pages/category/publications/san-manuel-miner/
Parent Company: Copper Area News Publishers
Published Days: Wed
Avg. Paid Circ.: 3310
Avg. Free Circ.: 36
Audit Company: Sworn/Estimate/Non-Audited
Audit Date: 43626

KEARNY

THE PINAL NUGGET

Street Address: 366 W Alden Rd
City: Kearny
State: AZ
ZIP Code: 85137-1208
General Phone: (520) 385-2266
General Email: copperbasinnews@gmail.com
Publication Website: http://www.copperarea.com/pages/category/publications/nugget/
Parent Company: Copper Area News

Publishers
Year Established: 2007
Published Days: Wed
Audit Company: Sworn/Estimate/Non-Audited
Audit Date: 43626

KINGMAN

THE STANDARD

Street Address: 221 E Beale St
City: Kingman
State: AZ
ZIP Code: 86401-5829
General Phone: (928) 753-1143
General Email: editor@thestandardnewspaper.net
Publication Website: https://www.thestandardnewspaper.net/
Editor Email: editor@thestandardnewspaper.net
Year Established: 1990
Published Days: Wed
Audit Company: Sworn/Estimate/Non-Audited
Audit Date: 43626

NEW RIVER

FOOTHILLS FOCUS

Street Address: 46641 N Black Canyon Hwy
City: New River
State: AZ
ZIP Code: 85087-6941
General Phone: (623) 465-5808
General Email: foothillsfocus@qwestoffice.net
Publication Website: https://thefoothillsfocus.com/
Publisher Name: John Alexander
Publisher Email: foothillsfocus@qwestoffice.net
Editor Name: Tracy Demetropolis
Editor Email: editor@thefoothillsfocus.com
Advertising Executive Email: foothillsfocus@qwestoffice.net
Year Established: 2002
Published Days: Wed
Audit Company: Sworn/Estimate/Non-Audited
Audit Date: 43626

NOGALES

SANTA CRUZ VALLEY SUN

Street Address: 268 W View Point Dr
City: Nogales
State: AZ
ZIP Code: 85621-4114
General Phone: (520) 375-5760
General Email: publisher@nogalesinternational.com
Publication Website: https://www.nogalesinternational.com/santa_cruz_valley_sun/
Publisher Name: Manuel Coppola
Publisher Email: publisher@nogalesinternational.com
Publisher Phone: (520) 415-1836
Editor Name: Jonathan Clark
Editor Email: editorial@nogalesinternational.com
Editor Phone: (520) 415-1837
Published Days: Wed
Avg. Free Circ.: 18079
Audit Company: Sworn/Estimate/Non-Audited
Audit Date: 43626

NOGALES

THE WEEKLY BULLETIN

Street Address: 268 W View Point Dr
City: Nogales
State: AZ
ZIP Code: 85621-4114
General Phone: (520) 375-5760
General Email: publisher@nogalesinternational.com
Publication Website: https://www.nogalesinternational.com/the_bulletin/
Parent Company: Wick Communications
Publisher Name: Manuel Coppola
Publisher Email: publisher@nogalesinternational.com
Publisher Phone: (520) 415-1836
Editor Name: Jonathan Clark
Editor Email: editorial@nogalesinternational.com
Editor Phone: (520) 415-1837
Year Established: 1991
Published Days: Wed
Avg. Paid Circ.: 515
Audit Company: Sworn/Estimate/Non-Audited
Audit Date: 43626

PAYSON

THE PAYSON ROUNDUP

Street Address: 708 N Beeline Hwy
City: Payson
State: AZ
ZIP Code: 85541-3770
General Phone: (928) 474-5251
General Email: abechman@payson.com
Publication Website: https://www.paysonroundup.com/
Parent Company: Kramer Media
Publisher Name: Brian Kramer
Publisher Email: bkramer@wmicentral.com
Advertising Executive Name: Alexis Bechman
Advertising Executive Email: abechman@payson.com
Advertising Executive Phone: (928) 474-5251, ext : 112
Delivery Methods: Mail`Newsstand`Carrier`Racks
Year Established: 1937
Own Printing Facility?: Y
Commercial printers?: Y
Mechanical specifications: Type page 12 19/20 x 21 1/2; A - 6 cols, between; C - 8 cols, between.
Published Days: Tues`Wed`Fri
Avg. Paid Circ.: 5166
Avg. Free Circ.: 169
Audit Company: Sworn/Estimate/Non-Audited
Audit Date: 43626

PHOENIX

APACHE JUNCTION/GOLD CANYON INDEPENDENT

Street Address: 23043 N 16th Ln
City: Phoenix
State: AZ
ZIP Code: 85027-1331
General Phone: (480) 982-7799
General Email: azads@newszap.com
Publication Website: https://www.yourvalley.net/apache-junction-independent/
Parent Company: Independent NewsMedia
Advertising Executive Email: iniclassads@newszap.com
Advertising Executive Phone: (623) 972-6101
Delivery Methods: Carrier`Racks
Year Established: 1959
Published Days: Wed
Avg. Free Circ.: 20000
Audit Company: Sworn/Estimate/Non-Audited
Audit Date: 43626

PHOENIX

ARIZONA BUSINESS GAZETTE

Street Address: 200 E Van Buren St
City: Phoenix
State: AZ
ZIP Code: 85004-2238
General Phone: (602) 444-8838
General Email: javier.arce@lavozarizona.com
Publication Website: https://www.azcentral.com/
Editor Name: Javier Arce
Editor Email: javier.arce@lavozarizona.com
Advertising Executive Phone: (602) 444-4444
Published Days: Thur
Audit Company: Sworn/Estimate/Non-Audited
Audit Date: 43626

PHOENIX

ARIZONA CAPITOL TIMES

Street Address: MN
City: Phoenix
State: AZ
ZIP Code: 85007-2603
General Phone: (602) 258-7026
General Email: lsimpson@azcapitoltimes.com
Publication Website: https://azcapitoltimes.com/
Parent Company: Bridgetower Media
Publisher Name: Luige del Puert
Publisher Email: ldelpuerto@azcapitoltimes.com
Publisher Phone: (602) 889-7131
Editor Name: Gary Grado
Editor Email: ggrado@azcapitoltimes.com
Editor Phone: (602) 889-7111
Advertising Executive Name: Lisa Simpson
Advertising Executive Email: lsimpson@azcapitoltimes.com
Advertising Executive Phone: (602) 889-7125
Delivery Methods: Mail`Newsstand`Racks
Year Established: 1906
Mechanical specifications: Type page 10 1/4 x 12 1/4; E - 4 cols, 2 3/8, 1/4 between; A - 4 cols, 2 3/8, 1/4 between; C - 4 cols, 2 3/8, 1/4 between.
Published Days: Fri
Avg. Paid Circ.: 1675
Avg. Free Circ.: 26
Audit Company: Sworn/Estimate/Non-Audited
Audit Date: 43626

PHOENIX

SCOTTSDALE INDEPENDENT

Street Address: 23043 N 16th Ln
City: Phoenix
State: AZ
ZIP Code: 85027-1331
General Phone: (623) 445-2777
General Email: azads@newszap.com
Publication Website: https://www.yourvalley.net/scottsdale-independent/
Parent Company: Independent NewsMedia
Delivery Methods: Carrier`Racks
Year Established: 1984
Own Printing Facility?: Y
Mechanical specifications: Full page: 10" wide by 10.625" high
Published Days: Wed
Avg. Free Circ.: 10000
Audit Company: Sworn/Estimate/Non-Audited
Audit Date: 43626

PHOENIX

THE BUSINESS JOURNAL

Street Address: 101 N 1st Ave Ste 2300
City: Phoenix
State: AZ
ZIP Code: 85003-1903
General Phone: (602) 230-8400
General Email: phoenix@bizjournals.com
Publication Website: https://www.bizjournals.com/
Parent Company: American City Business Journals
Publisher Name: Ray Schey
Publisher Email: rschey@bizjournals.com
Editor Name: Patrick O'Grady
Editor Email: pogrady@bizjournals.com
Advertising Executive Name: Amy Lindsey
Advertising Executive Email: alindsey@bizjournals.com
Published Days: Fri
Audit Company: Sworn/Estimate/Non-Audited
Audit Date: 43626

SEDONA

SEDONA RED ROCK NEWS

Street Address: 298 Van Deren Rd
City: Sedona
State: AZ
ZIP Code: 86336-4826
General Phone: (928) 282-7795
General Email: klarson@larsonnewspapers.com
Publication Website: https://redrocknews.com/
Parent Company: Larson Newspapers
Publisher Name: Kyle Larson
Publisher Email: klarson@larsonnewspapers.com
Publisher Phone: (928) 282-7795, ext : 114
Editor Name: Christopher Fox Graham
Editor Email: editor@larsonnewspapers.com
Editor Phone: (928) 282-7795, ext : 129
Year Established: 1963
Published Days: Wed`Fri
Audit Company: Sworn/Estimate/Non-Audited
Audit Date: 43626

SHOW LOW

WHITE MOUNTAIN INDEPENDENT

Street Address: 3191 S White Mountain Rd
City: Show Low
State: AZ
ZIP Code: 85901
General Phone: (928) 537-5721
General Email: postmaster@wmicentral.com
Publication Website: https://www.wmicentral.com/
Parent Company: Kramer Media
Publisher Name: Brian Kramer
Publisher Email: bkramer@wmicentral.com
Editor Name: Trudy Balcom
Editor Email: tbalcom@wmicentral.com
Editor Phone: (928) 537-5721, ext : 225
Advertising Executive Name: Mark Ruiz
Advertising Executive Email: mruiz@wmicentral.com
Advertising Executive Phone: (928) 537-5721, ext : 238
Delivery Methods: Mail`Newsstand`Racks
Year Established: 1888
Own Printing Facility?: N
Commercial printers?: N
Mechanical specifications: Type page 13 x 21 1/2; E - 6 cols, 2 1/16, 1/8 between; A - 6 cols, 2 1/16, 1/8 between; C - 6 cols, 2 1/16, 1/8 between.
Published Days: Tues`Fri
Avg. Paid Circ.: 11494
Avg. Free Circ.: 17
Audit Company: Sworn/Estimate/Non-Audited
Audit Date: 43626

SUN CITY

GLENDALE TODAY

Street Address: 17220 N Boswell Blvd

Community Newspapers in the U.S.

City: Sun City
State: AZ
ZIP Code: 85373-2065
General Phone: (623) 977-8351
General Email: azads@newszap.com
Publication Website: https://www.yourvalley.net/glendale-independent/
Parent Company: Independent NewsMedia
Delivery Methods: Mail`Newsstand`Carrier`Racks
Year Established: 1995
Own Printing Facility?: Y
Commercial printers?: Y
Mechanical specifications: Type page 10" x 12.75"; 6 cols
Published Days: Fri
Avg. Paid Circ.: 1
Avg. Free Circ.: 22384
Audit Company: Sworn/Estimate/Non-Audited
Audit Date: 43626

TEMPE

WRANGLER NEWS

Street Address: 2145 E Warner Rd
City: Tempe
State: AZ
ZIP Code: 85284-3497
General Phone: (480) 966-0837
General Email: tracy.doren@wranglernews.com
Publication Website: https://www.wranglernews.com/
Editor Email: editor@wranglernews.com
Advertising Executive Email: joyce.coronel@wranglernews.com
Delivery Methods: Carrier`Racks
Year Established: 1991
Published Days: Sat
Avg. Free Circ.: 20000
Audit Company: Sworn/Estimate/Non-Audited
Audit Date: 43626
Note: Bi-weekly, driveway delivered to 20,000 homes and racks in Tempe and west Chandler, Ariz. News and features focusing on people who live, work and do business in this high-demographic area of families and executives. Voted Best Community Newspaper by Phoenix magazine.

TOMBSTONE

THE TOMBSTONE NEWS

Street Address: 525 E Allen St.
City: Tombstone
State: AZ
ZIP Code: 85638
General Phone: (520) 457-3086
General Email: tombstonenews@hotmail.com
Publication Website: http://thetombstonenews.com/
Year Established: 2005
Published Days: Fri
Audit Company: Sworn/Estimate/Non-Audited
Audit Date: 43626

TUCSON

EXPLORER

Street Address: 7225 N Mona Lisa Rd
City: Tucson
State: AZ
ZIP Code: 85741-2581
General Phone: (520) 797-4384
General Email: tucsoneditor@tucsonlocalmedia.com
Publication Website: https://www.tucsonlocalmedia.com/explorernews/
Parent Company: Tucson Local Media
Publisher Name: Jason Joseph
Publisher Email: jjoseph@azlocalmedia.com

Editor Name: Logan Burtch-Buus
Editor Email: logan@tucsonlocalmedia.com
Editor Phone: (520) 797-4384, ext : 36
Advertising Executive Name: Casey Anderson
Advertising Executive Email: casey@tucsonlocalmedia.com
Advertising Executive Phone: (520) 797-4384, ext : 22
Delivery Methods: Newsstand`Racks
Year Established: 1993
Mechanical specifications: Type page 10" x 12.75"; 5 cols
Published Days: Wed
Avg. Paid Circ.: 14
Avg. Free Circ.: 43114
Audit Company: CVC
Audit Date: 43988

TUCSON

FOOTHILLS NEWS

Street Address: 7225 N Mona Lisa Rd
City: Tucson
State: AZ
ZIP Code: 85741-2581
General Phone: (520) 797-4384
General Email: tucsoneditor@tucsonlocalmedia.com
Publication Website: https://www.tucsonlocalmedia.com/foothillsnews/
Parent Company: Tucson Local Media
Publisher Name: Jason Joseph
Publisher Email: jjoseph@azlocalmedia.com
Editor Name: Logan Burtch-Buus
Editor Email: logan@tucsonlocalmedia.com
Editor Phone: (520) 797-4384, ext : 36
Advertising Executive Name: Casey Anderson
Advertising Executive Email: casey@tucsonlocalmedia.com
Advertising Executive Phone: (520) 797-4384, ext : 22
Published Days: Mthly
Audit Company: Sworn/Estimate/Non-Audited
Audit Date: 43626

WICKENBURG

WICKENBURG SUN

Street Address: 180 N Washington St
City: Wickenburg
State: AZ
ZIP Code: 85390-2263
General Phone: (928) 684-5454
General Email: publisher@wickenburgsun.com
Publication Website: http://www.wickenburgsun.com/
Parent Company: Brehm Communications Inc.
Delivery Methods: Mail`Newsstand`Racks
Year Established: 1934
Own Printing Facility?: Y
Commercial printers?: N
Published Days: Wed
Avg. Paid Circ.: 3000
Avg. Free Circ.: 3200
Audit Company: Sworn/Estimate/Non-Audited
Audit Date: 43626

CALIFORNIA

12ROSEVILLE

THE PRESS-TRIBUNE

Street Address: 901 Sunrise Ave. Suite A-12
City: 12Roseville

State: CA
ZIP Code: 95661
General Phone: (916) 624-9713
General Email: johnl@goldcountrymedia.com
Publication Website: https://goldcountrymedia.com/live-content/the-press-tribune/
Parent Company: Brehm Communications Inc.
Publisher Name: Bill Sullivan
Publisher Email: bills@goldcountrymedia.com
Publisher Phone: (916) 351-3750
Advertising Executive Name: John Love
Advertising Executive Email: johnl@goldcountrymedia.com

AGOURA HILLS

SIMI VALLEY ACORN

Street Address: 30423 Canwood St
City: Agoura Hills
State: CA
ZIP Code: 91301
General Phone: (805) 367-8232
General Email: adrep@theacorn.com
Publication Website: https://www.simivalleyacorn.com/
Parent Company: J. Bee NP Publishing, Ltd.
Editor Name: Sylvie Belmond
Editor Email: simi@theacorn.com
Advertising Executive Email: adrep@theacorn.com

AGOURA HILLS

THE ACORN

Street Address: 30423 Canwood St
City: Agoura Hills
State: CA
ZIP Code: 91301
General Phone: (818) 706-0266
General Email: adrep@theacorn.com
Publication Website: https://www.theacorn.com/
Parent Company: J. Bee NP Publishing, Ltd.
Editor Name: John Loesing
Editor Email: newstip@theacorn.com
Advertising Executive Email: adrep@theacorn.com

AGOURA HILLS

THOUSAND OAKS ACORN

Street Address: 30423 Canwood St
City: Agoura Hills
State: CA
ZIP Code: 91301
General Phone: (805) 367-8232
General Email: tonewstip@theacorn.com
Publication Website: https://www.toacorn.com/
Parent Company: J. Bee NP Publishing, Ltd.
Editor Name: Kyle Jorrey
Advertising Executive Email: adrep@theacorn.com

ALAMEDA

PIEDMONTER

Street Address: 1516 Oak St
City: Alameda
State: CA
ZIP Code: 94501-2907
General Phone: (510) 748-1666
General Email: editor@bayareanewsgroup.com
Publication Website: https://www.eastbaytimes.com/location/piedmont/
Publisher Name: Sharon Ryan
Publisher Email: publisher@bayareanewsgroup.com

Editor Name: Mario Dianda
Editor Email: mdianda@bayareanewsgroup.com
Editor Phone: (650) 391-1342
Advertising Executive Name: Michael Turpin
Advertising Executive Email: mturpin@bayareanewsgroup.com

ALAMEDA

THE MONTCLARION

Street Address: 1516 Oak St
City: Alameda
State: CA
ZIP Code: 94501
General Phone: (510) 748-1666
General Email: editor@bayareanewsgroup.com
Publication Website: https://www.eastbaytimes.com/location/montclair/
Publisher Name: Sharon Ryan
Publisher Email: publisher@bayareanewsgroup.com
Editor Name: Mario Dianda
Editor Email: mdianda@bayareanewsgroup.com
Editor Phone: (650) 391-1342
Advertising Executive Name: Michael Turpin
Advertising Executive Email: mturpin@bayareanewsgroup.com

ALPINE

ALPINE SUN

Street Address: 2144 Alpine Blvd
City: Alpine
State: CA
ZIP Code: 91901
General Phone: (619) 445-3288
General Email: info@thealpinesun.com
Publication Website: https://thealpinesun.com/
Publisher Name: Jennifer Tschida
Publisher Email: jennifer@thealpinesun.com
Editor Name: Carlos Davalos
Editor Email: carlos@thestarnews.com
Editor Phone: (619) 427-3000, ext : 807
Advertising Executive Email: legals@eccalifornian.com

ALTURAS

THE MODOC COUNTY RECORD

Street Address: 201 W Carlos St
City: Alturas
State: CA
ZIP Code: 96101
General Phone: (530) 233-2632
General Email: record1@modocrecord.com
Publication Website: https://www.modocrecord.com/

ANAHEIM

LAGUNA NIGUEL NEWS

Street Address: 2190 S. Towne Centre Place
City: Anaheim
State: CA
ZIP Code: 92806
General Phone: (714) 796-7000
General Email: service@scng.com
Publication Website: https://www.ocregister.com/location/california/orange-county/laguna-niguel/
Publisher Name: Ron Hasse
Publisher Email: publisher@scng.com
Publisher Phone: (818) 713-3883
Editor Name: Carlos Aviles
Editor Email: caviles@scng.com
Editor Phone: (951) 368-9330
Advertising Executive Name: Kyla Rodriguez
Advertising Executive Email: krodriguez@

ANAHEIM

LAGUNA WOODS GLOBE

Street Address: 2190 S. Towne Centre Place
City: Anaheim
State: CA
ZIP Code: 92806
General Phone: (714) 796-7000
General Email: service@scng.com
Publication Website: https://www.ocregister.com/location/california/orange-county/laguna-woods/
Publisher Name: Ron Hasse
Publisher Email: publisher@scng.com
Publisher Phone: (818) 713-3883
Editor Name: Carlos Aviles
Editor Email: caviles@scng.com
Editor Phone: (951) 368-9330
Advertising Executive Name: Kyla Rodriguez
Advertising Executive Email: krodriguez@scng.com

APPLE VALLEY

APPLE VALLEY NEWS

Street Address: 21940 HWY 18 unit B
City: Apple Valley
State: CA
ZIP Code: 92307
General Phone: (760) 242-1930
General Email: questions@valleywidenewspaper.com
Publication Website: http://www.valleywidenewspaper.com/
Parent Company: Valley Wide Newspapers
Advertising Executive Email: classified@valleywidenewspaper.com

ATASCADERO

ATASCADERO NEWS

Street Address: 5860 El Camino Real, Suite G
City: Atascadero
State: CA
ZIP Code: 93422
General Phone: (805) 466-2585
General Email: sales@atascaderonews.com
Publication Website: https://atascaderonews.com/
Parent Company: 13 Stars Media
Publisher Name: Nic Mattson
Publisher Email: nic@atascaderonews.com
Editor Name: Luke Phillips
Editor Email: luke@atascaderonews.com
Advertising Executive Name: Carmen Kessler
Advertising Executive Email: carmen@atascaderonews.com

AVALON

THE CATALINA ISLANDER

Street Address: 635 Crescent Ave
City: Avalon
State: CA
ZIP Code: 90704
General Phone: (310) 510-0500
General Email: info@thecatalinaislander.com
Publication Website: https://thecatalinaislander.com/
Parent Company: CommunityMedia Corp.
Publisher Name: Steven Remery
Publisher Phone: (310) 510-0550, ext : 510
Editor Name: Ted Apodaca
Editor Email: editor@thecatalinaislander.com
Editor Phone: (562) 317-1100
Advertising Executive Name: Jennifer Hartinger
Advertising Executive Email: jennifer@thecatalinaislander.com

BEVERLY HILLS

BEVERLY HILLS COURIER

Street Address: 499 Canon Drive
City: Beverly Hills
State: CA
ZIP Code: 90210
General Phone: (310) 278-1322
General Email: eportugal@bhcourier.com
Publication Website: http://www.bhcourier.com/
Publisher Name: John Bendheim
Editor Name: Carole Dixon
Editor Email: cdixon@bhcourier.com
Editor Phone: (310) 278-1322, ext : 112
Advertising Executive Name: Pat Wilkins
Advertising Executive Email: pwilkins@bhcourier.com

BEVERLY HILLS

BEVERLY HILLS WEEKLY

Street Address: 140 S Beverly Dr
City: Beverly Hills
State: CA
ZIP Code: 90212
General Phone: (310) 887-0788
General Email: josh@bhweekly.com
Publication Website: https://bhweekly.com/
Parent Company: Beverly Hills Weekly
Publisher Name: Josh Gross
Publisher Email: josh@bhweekly.com
Editor Email: editor@bhweekly.com
Editor Phone: (310) 887-0788

BISHOP

INYO REGISTER

Street Address: 407 W Line St
City: Bishop
State: CA
ZIP Code: 93514
General Phone: (760) 873-3535
General Email: advertising@inyoregister.com
Publication Website: https://inyoregister.com/
Parent Company: Horizon Publications Inc.
Editor Email: editor@inyoregister.com
Advertising Executive Email: advertising@inyoregister.com

BLYTHE

PALO VERDE VALLEY TIMES

Street Address: 400 W Hobsonway
City: Blythe
State: CA
ZIP Code: 92225
General Phone: (760) 922-3181
General Email: webmaster@pvvt.com
Publication Website: https://www.pvvt.com/
Parent Company: Western News&Info, Inc.
Advertising Executive Email: advertising@pvvt.com

BLYTHE

QUARTZSITE TIMES

Street Address: 400 W. Hobsonway
City: Blythe
State: CA
ZIP Code: 92225
General Phone: (760) 922-3181
General Email: webmaster@pvvt.com
Publication Website: https://www.pvvt.com/
Parent Company: Western News&Info, Inc.
Advertising Executive Email: advertising@pvvt.com

BOONVILLE

ANDERSON VALLEY ADVERTISER

Street Address: PO Box 459
City: Boonville
State: CA
ZIP Code: 95415
General Phone: (707) 895-3016
General Email: editor@theava.com
Publication Website: https://www.theava.com/
Publisher Name: Bruce Anderson
Publisher Email: editor@theava.com
Editor Name: Bruce Anderson
Editor Email: editor@theava.com

BRENTWOOD

THE PRESS

Street Address: 248 Oak St
City: Brentwood
State: CA
ZIP Code: 94513
General Phone: (925) 634-1441
General Email: grobinson@brentwoodpress.com
Publication Website: https://www.thepress.net/
Parent Company: Brentwood Press & Publishing Corporation
Publisher Name: Greg Robinson
Publisher Email: greg@brentwoodpress.com
Editor Name: Ruth Roberts
Editor Email: rroberts@brentwoodpress.com
Advertising Executive Name: Connie O'Neill
Advertising Executive Email: coneill@brentwoodpress.com

BURNEY

THE INTERMOUNTAIN NEWS

Street Address: PO Box 1030
City: Burney
State: CA
ZIP Code: 96013
General Phone: (530) 725-0925
General Email: news@northstate.news
Publication Website: http://northstate.news/
Parent Company: Cright, Inc.

CALIFORNIA CITY

MOJAVE DESERT NEWS

Street Address: 8016 California City Blvd St #7
City: California City
State: CA
ZIP Code: 93505
General Phone: (760) 373-4812
General Email: sales@desertnews.com
Publication Website: http://www.desertnews.com/
Parent Company: Times Media Group
Editor Email: editor@desertnews.com

CALISTOGA

THE WEEKLY CALISTOGAN

Street Address: PO Box 385
City: Calistoga
State: CA
ZIP Code: 94515
General Phone: (707) 942-4035
General Email: nkostecka@napanews.com
Publication Website: https://napavalleyregister.com/community/calistogan/
Publisher Name: Davis Taylor
Publisher Email: davis.taylor@lee.net
Publisher Phone: (707) 256-2234
Editor Name: Cynthia Sweeney
Editor Email: editor@weeklycalistogan.com
Editor Phone: (707) 942-4035
Advertising Executive Name: Norma Kostecka
Advertising Executive Email: nkostecka@napanews.com

CAMARILLO

CAMARILLO ACORN

Street Address: 1203 Flynn Rd
City: Camarillo
State: CA
ZIP Code: 93012
General Phone: (805) 484-1949
General Email: camarillo@theacorn.com
Publication Website: https://www.thecamarilloacorn.com/
Parent Company: J. Bee NP Publishing, Ltd.
Editor Name: Daniel Wolowicz
Editor Email: camarillo@theacorn.com
Editor Phone: (805) 484-1949

CAMARILLO

MOORPARK ACORN

Street Address: 1203 Flynn Rd
City: Camarillo
State: CA
ZIP Code: 93012
General Phone: (818) 706-0266
General Email: moorpark@theacorn.com
Publication Website: https://www.mpacorn.com/
Parent Company: J. Bee NP Publishing, Ltd.
Editor Name: Daniel Wolowicz
Editor Email: moorpark@theacorn.com
Advertising Executive Email: adrep@theacorn.com

CAMPBELL

CAMPBELL EXPRESS

Street Address: 334 E Campbell Ave
City: Campbell
State: CA
ZIP Code: 95008
General Phone: (408) 374-9700
General Email: info@campbellexpress.com
Publication Website: https://www.campbellexpress.com/

CANYON LAKE

THE FRIDAY FLYER

Street Address: 31558 Railroad Canyon Rd
City: Canyon Lake
State: CA
ZIP Code: 92587
General Phone: (951) 244-1966
General Email: news@goldingpublications.com
Publication Website: http://www.fridayflyer.com/
Parent Company: Golding Publications

CAPISTRANO BEACH

DANA POINT TIMES

Street Address: 34932 Calle Del Sol
City: Capistrano Beach
State: CA
ZIP Code: 92624
General Phone: (949) 388-7700
General Email: info@danapointtimes.com

Community Newspapers in the U.S.

Publication Website: https://www.danapointtimes.com/
Parent Company: Picket Fence Media
Publisher Name: Norb Garrett
Publisher Email: ngarrett@picketfencemedia.com
Editor Name: Lillian Boyd
Editor Email: lboyd@picketfencemedia.com
Editor Phone: (949) 388-7700, ext : 113
Advertising Executive Name: Lauralyn Loynes
Advertising Executive Email: lloynes@picketfencemedia.com

CAPISTRANO BEACH

SAN CLEMENTE TIMES

Street Address: 34932 Calle Del Sol
City: Capistrano Beach
State: CA
ZIP Code: 92624
General Phone: (949) 388-7700
General Email: info@picketfencemedia.com
Publication Website: https://www.sanclementetimes.com/
Parent Company: Picket Fence Media
Publisher Name: Norb Garrett
Publisher Email: ngarrett@picketfencemedia.com
Editor Name: Shawn Raymundo
Editor Email: sraymundo@picketfencemedia.com
Editor Phone: (949) 388-7700, ext : 108
Advertising Executive Name: Traci Kelly
Advertising Executive Email: tkelly@picketfencemedia.com

CAPISTRANO BEACH

THE CAPISTRANO DISPATCH

Street Address: 34932 Calle Del Sol
City: Capistrano Beach
State: CA
ZIP Code: 92624
General Phone: (949) 388-7700
General Email: info@picketfencemedia.com
Publication Website: http://www.thecapistranodispatch.com/
Parent Company: Picket Fence Media
Publisher Name: Norb Garrett
Publisher Email: ngarrett@picketfencemedia.com
Editor Name: Collin Breaux
Editor Email: cbreaux@picketfencemedia.com
Editor Phone: (949) 388-7700, ext : 109
Advertising Executive Name: Debra Wells
Advertising Executive Email: debra@wellsadsolutions.com

CARMICHAEL

CARMICHAEL TIMES

Street Address: 7144 Fair Oaks Blvd
City: Carmichael
State: CA
ZIP Code: 95608
General Phone: (916) 773-1111
General Email: publisher@mpg8.com
Publication Website: http://www.carmichaeltimes.com/
Parent Company: Messenger Publishing Group
Publisher Name: Paul V. Scholl
Publisher Email: publisher@mpg8.com

CARMICHAEL

THE GRIDLEY HERALD

Street Address: 7144 Fair Oaks Blvd Suite #5
City: Carmichael
State: CA
ZIP Code: 95608
General Phone: (916) 773-1111
General Email: publisher@mpg8.com
Publication Website: http://www.gridleyherald.com/
Parent Company: Messenger Publishing Group
Publisher Name: Paul V. Scholl
Publisher Email: publisher@mpg8.com

CARPINTERIA

COASTAL VIEW NEWS

Street Address: 4856 Carpinteria Ave
City: Carpinteria
State: CA
ZIP Code: 93013
General Phone: (805) 684-4428
General Email: news@coastalview.com
Publication Website: http://www.coastalview.com/
Parent Company: RMG VENTURES, LLC

CHINO

CHINO CHAMPION

Street Address: 13179 9th St
City: Chino
State: CA
ZIP Code: 91710
General Phone: (909) 628-5501
General Email: ads@championnewspapers.com
Publication Website: https://www.championnewspapers.com/
Parent Company: Champion Newspapers
Publisher Name: William H. Fleet
Editor Name: Brenda Dunkle
Advertising Executive Name: Will Fleet
Advertising Executive Email: ads@championnewspapers.com

CHULA VISTA

THE STAR-NEWS

Street Address: 296 3rd Ave
City: Chula Vista
State: CA
ZIP Code: 91910
General Phone: (619) 427-3000
General Email: info@thestarnews.com
Publication Website: https://www.thestarnews.com/
Parent Company: CommunityMedia Corp.
Publisher Name: Linda Rosas Townson
Publisher Phone: (619) 427-3000, ext : 806
Editor Name: Carlos R. Davalos
Editor Phone: (619) 427-3000, ext : 807

CLAREMONT

CLAREMONT COURIER

Street Address: 114 Olive St
City: Claremont
State: CA
ZIP Code: 91711
General Phone: (909) 621-4761
General Email: editor@claremont-courier.com
Publication Website: https://www.claremont-courier.com/
Publisher Name: Peter Weinberger
Publisher Email: pweinberger@claremont-courier.com
Editor Name: Kathryn Dunn
Editor Email: editor@claremont-courier.com
Advertising Executive Name: Mary Rose
Advertising Executive Email: maryrose@claremont-courier.com

CORCORAN

THE CORCORAN JOURNAL

Street Address: 1012 Hale Ave
City: Corcoran
State: CA
ZIP Code: 93212
General Phone: (559) 992-3115
General Email: tbotill@hotmail.com
Publication Website: https://thecorcoranjournal.net/
Publisher Name: Jeanette Todd
Editor Name: Jeanette Todd
Advertising Executive Email: tbotill@hotmail.com

CORONADO

CORONADO EAGLE & JOURNAL

Street Address: 1224 Tenth Street, Ste 103
City: Coronado
State: CA
ZIP Code: 92118
General Phone: (619) 437-8800
General Email: editor@eaglenewsca.com
Publication Website: http://www.coronadonewsca.com/
Parent Company: Eagle Newspapers
Publisher Name: Dean Eckenroth
Publisher Email: publisher@eaglenewsca.com
Publisher Phone: (619) 437-8800, ext : 208
Editor Name: Dean Eckenroth
Editor Email: editor@eaglenewsca.com
Editor Phone: (619) 437-8800, ext : 208
Advertising Executive Name: Patricia Ross
Advertising Executive Email: patricia@eaglenewsca.com

CORONADO

IMPERIAL BEACH EAGLE & TIMES

Street Address: 1116 Teneth Street
City: Coronado
State: CA
ZIP Code: 92118
General Phone: (619) 437-8800
General Email: editor@eaglenewsca.com
Publication Website: http://www.imperialbeachnewsca.com/
Editor Email: editor@eaglenewsca.com

CRESCENT CITY

THE DEL NORTE TRIPLICATE

Street Address: 501 H Street
City: Crescent City
State: CA
ZIP Code: 95531
General Phone: (707) 460-6727
General Email: triplicateofficemgr@countrymedia.net
Publication Website: https://www.triplicate.com/
Parent Company: Country Media, Inc.
Advertising Executive Email: triplicateads1@countrymedia.net

DIXON

DIXON'S INDEPENDENT VOICE

Street Address: PO Box 1106
City: Dixon
State: CA
ZIP Code: 95620
General Phone: (707) 678-8917
General Email: staff@independentvoice.com
Publication Website: https://independentvoice.com/

EL CAJON

THE EAST COUNTY CALIFORNIAN

Street Address: 119 N Magnolia Ave
City: El Cajon
State: CA
ZIP Code: 92020
General Phone: (619) 441-0400
General Email: info@eccalifornian.com
Publication Website: https://eccalifornian.com/
Publisher Name: Linda Rosas Townson
Publisher Phone: (619) 427-3000, ext : 806
Editor Name: Mary York
Editor Email: editor@eccalifornian.com
Editor Phone: (619) 441-0400, ext : 1203
Advertising Executive Name: Marcela Aguayo

EL CENTRO

ADELANTE VALLE

Street Address: 205 N 8th St
City: El Centro
State: CA
ZIP Code: 92243
General Phone: (760) 337-3418
General Email: webmaster@ivpressonline.com
Publication Website: https://www.ivpressonline.com/
Parent Company: Imperial Valley Press, Inc.
Editor Name: Arturo Bojorquez
Editor Email: abojorquez@ivpressonline.com
Editor Phone: (760) 335-4646
Advertising Executive Name: Alexis Singh
Advertising Executive Email: asingh@ivpressonline.com

EL CENTRO

HOLTVILLE TRIBUNE

Street Address: 1239 W Main St.
City: El Centro
State: CA
ZIP Code: 92243
General Phone: (760) 339-4899
General Email: holtvillenews@aol.com
Publication Website: https://holtvilletribune.com/
Parent Company: Calexico Chronicle

EL SEGUNDO

EL SEGUNDO HERALD

Street Address: 500 Center St
City: El Segundo
State: CA
ZIP Code: 90245
General Phone: (310) 322-1830
General Email: pr@heraldpublications.com
Publication Website: http://www.heraldpublications.com/herald/el-segundo-herald/
Parent Company: Herald Publications

ENCINITAS

RANCHO SANTA FE NEWS

Street Address: 315 S Coast Highway 101
City: Encinitas
State: CA
ZIP Code: 92024
General Phone: (760) 436-9737
General Email: advertising@coastnewsgroup.com
Publication Website: https://www.thecoastnews.com/#/
Parent Company: Coast News Group, Inc.
Publisher Name: Chris Kydd
Publisher Email: ckydd@coastnewsgroup.com
Editor Name: Abraham Jewett

ENCINITAS

THE COAST NEWS

Street Address: 315 S Coast Highway 101
City: Encinitas
State: CA
ZIP Code: 92024
General Phone: (760) 436-9737
General Email: advertising@coastnewsgroup.com
Publication Website: https://www.thecoastnews.com/
Parent Company: Coast News Group, Inc.
Publisher Name: Chris Kydd
Publisher Email: ckydd@coastnewsgroup.com
Editor Name: Abraham Jewett
Editor Email: abraham@coastnewsgroup.com
Advertising Executive Name: Sue Otto
Advertising Executive Email: sue@coastnewsgroup.com

ESCONDIDO

TIMES-ADVOCATE

Street Address: 720 N Broadway
City: Escondido
State: CA
ZIP Code: 92025
General Phone: (760) 546-4000
General Email: news@times-advocate.com
Publication Website: https://www.times-advocate.com/
Parent Company: Roadrunner Publications, Inc.
Publisher Name: Justin Salter
Editor Name: David Ross

EUREKA

NORTH COAST JOURNAL

Street Address: 310 F St
City: Eureka
State: CA
ZIP Code: 95501-1006
General Phone: (707) 442-1400
General Email: newsroom@northcoastjournal.com
Publication Website: https://www.northcoastjournal.com/
Parent Company: C-VILLE Holdings LLC
Editor Name: Thadeus Greenson
Editor Email: thad@northcoastjournal.com
Advertising Executive Name: Kyle Windham
Advertising Executive Email: kyle@northcoastjournal.com

EUREKA

THE HUMBOLDT BEACON

Street Address: 930 6th St
City: Eureka
State: CA
ZIP Code: 95501
General Phone: (707) 441-0500
General Email: jrichmond@times-standard.com
Publication Website: http://www.humboldtbeacon.com/
Publisher Name: John Richmond
Publisher Email: jrichmond@times-standard.com
Publisher Phone: (707) 441-0584
Editor Name: Marc Valles
Editor Email: mvalles@times-standard.com

Editor Email: abraham@coastnewsgroup.com
Advertising Executive Name: Sue Otto
Advertising Executive Email: sue@coastnewsgroup.com

EXETER

THE FOOTHILLS SUN-GAZETTE

Street Address: PO Box 7
City: Exeter
State: CA
ZIP Code: 93221-0007
General Phone: (559) 592-3171
General Email: publisher@thesungazette.com
Publication Website: https://thesungazette.com/
Parent Company: Mineral King Publishing, Inc.
Publisher Name: Reggie Ellis
Publisher Email: publisher@thesungazette.com
Publisher Phone: (559) 592-3171
Editor Name: Paul Myers
Editor Email: editor@thesungazette.com

FALL RIVER MILLS

THE MOUNTAIN ECHO

Street Address: P. O. Box 224
City: Fall River Mills
State: CA
ZIP Code: 96028
General Phone: (530) 336-6262
General Email: mtecho@frontiernet.net
Publication Website: http://www.mountainecho.com/

FERNDALE

THE FERNDALE ENTERPRISE

Street Address: 207 Francis St
City: Ferndale
State: CA
ZIP Code: 95536
General Phone: (707) 786-3068
General Email: editor@ferndaleenterprise.us
Publication Website: https://www.ferndaleenterprise.com/
Parent Company: Cages Publishing, Inc.
Publisher Name: Caroline Titus
Editor Name: Caroline Titus
Editor Email: editor@ferndaleenterprise.us

FORT BRAGG

FORT BRAGG ADVOCATE-NEWS

Street Address: 690 S Main St
City: Fort Bragg
State: CA
ZIP Code: 95437
General Phone: (707) 964-5642
General Email: mrahm@advocate-news.com
Publication Website: https://www.advocate-news.com/
Parent Company: Media News Group
Publisher Name: K.C. Meadows
Publisher Email: publisher@advocate-news.com
Editor Email: editor@advocate-news.com
Advertising Executive Email: mrahm@advocate-news.com

FORT BRAGG

THE MENDOCINO BEACON

Street Address: 690 S Main St
City: Fort Bragg
State: CA

ZIP Code: 95437
General Phone: (707) 964-5642
General Email: mrahm@advocate-news.com
Publication Website: https://www.mendocinobeacon.com/
Parent Company: Media News Group
Publisher Name: K.C. Meadows
Publisher Email: publisher@advocate-news.com
Editor Email: editor@advocate-news.com
Advertising Executive Email: mrahm@advocate-news.com

FOUNTAIN VALLEY

THE LOG NEWSPAPER

Street Address: 18475 Bandilier Cir
City: Fountain Valley
State: CA
ZIP Code: 92708-7000
General Phone: (949) 660-6150
General Email: susanne@thelog.com
Publication Website: https://www.thelog.com/
Parent Company: Duncan McIntosh Co., Inc.

FREMONT

TRI-CITY VOICE

Street Address: 39737 Paseo Padre Pkwy
City: Fremont
State: CA
ZIP Code: 94538
General Phone: (510) 494-1999
General Email: tricityvoice@aol.com
Publication Website: https://tricityvoice.com/
Advertising Executive Name: Sharon Marshak
Advertising Executive Email: tricityvoice@aol.com

FRESNO

THE BUSINESS JOURNAL

Street Address: 1315 Van Ness Ave
City: Fresno
State: CA
ZIP Code: 93721
General Phone: (559) 490-3400
General Email: kaysi@thebusinessjournal.com
Publication Website: https://thebusinessjournal.com/
Parent Company: Pacific Publishing Group, Inc.
Publisher Name: Gordon Webster
Advertising Executive Name: Abner Garcia

GARDEN GROVE

WESTMINSTER HERALD

Street Address: 7441 Garden Grove Blvd
City: Garden Grove
State: CA
ZIP Code: 92841
General Phone: (714) 895-3484
General Email: info@westminsterhj.com
Publication Website: https://westminsterhj.com/
Parent Company: CommunityMedia Corp.
Publisher Name: Steven Remery
Publisher Email: publisher@localnewspapers.org
Publisher Phone: (562) 799-0615, ext : 510
Editor Name: Brady Rhoades
Editor Email: brhoades@localnewspapers.org
Editor Phone: (657) 233-2550, ext : 105
Advertising Executive Name: Carlos Munoz
Advertising Executive Email: cmunoz@localnewspapers.org

GARDENA

GARDENA VALLEY NEWS

Street Address: 15005 S Vermont Ave
City: Gardena
State: CA
ZIP Code: 90247
General Phone: (310) 329-6351
General Email: info@gardenavalleynews.org
Publication Website: https://gardenavalleynews.org/
Parent Company: CommunityMedia Corp.
Publisher Name: Alan Moskal
Publisher Email: publisher@gardenavalleynews.org
Publisher Phone: (310) 437-4401
Editor Name: Gary Kohatsu
Editor Email: editor@gardenavalleynews.org
Editor Phone: (310) 329-6351, ext : 121

GEORGETOWN

GEORGETOWN GAZETTE

Street Address: 2775 Miners Flat Rd
City: Georgetown
State: CA
ZIP Code: 95634
General Phone: (530) 333-4481
General Email: editor@gtgazette.com
Publication Website: https://www.gtgazette.com/
Parent Company: McNaughton Newspapers, Inc.

GUALALA

INDEPENDENT COAST OBSERVER

Street Address: PO Box 1200
City: Gualala
State: CA
ZIP Code: 95445-1200
General Phone: (707) 884-3501
General Email: display@mendonoma.com
Publication Website: http://www.mendonoma.com/
Publisher Name: J. Stephen McLaughlin
Publisher Email: publisher@mendonoma.com
Publisher Phone: (707) 884-3501, ext : 13
Editor Name: Chris McManus
Editor Email: editor@mendonoma.com
Editor Phone: (707) 884-3501, ext : 16
Advertising Executive Name: Ayla Nicholas
Advertising Executive Email: display@mendonoma.com

HALF MOON BAY

HALF MOON BAY REVIEW

Street Address: 714 Kelly St
City: Half Moon Bay
State: CA
ZIP Code: 94019
General Phone: (650) 726-4424
General Email: karin@hmbreview.com
Publication Website: https://www.hmbreview.com/
Publisher Name: Barbara Anderson
Publisher Email: barbanderson@hmbreview.com
Publisher Phone: (650) 726-4424, ext : 303
Editor Name: Clay Lambert
Editor Email: clay@hmbreview.com
Editor Phone: (650) 726-4424, ext : 304
Advertising Executive Name: Karin Litcher
Advertising Executive Email: karin@hmbreview.com

HANFORD

Community Newspapers in the U.S.

THE KINGSBURG RECORDER

Street Address: 300 W 6th St
City: Hanford
State: CA
ZIP Code: 93230
General Phone: (559) 582-0471
General Email: publisher@hanfordsentinel.com
Publication Website: https://hanfordsentinel.com/community/kingsburg_recorder/
Publisher Name: Davis Taylor
Publisher Email: publisher@hanfordsentinel.com
Publisher Phone: (559) 583-2400
Editor Name: Chris Aguirre
Editor Email: caguirre@hanfordsentinel.com
Editor Phone: (559) 583-2405
Advertising Executive Name: Mark Daniel
Advertising Executive Email: mdaniel@hanfordsentinel.com

HANFORD

THE SELMA ENTERPRISE

Street Address: 300 W 6th St
City: Hanford
State: CA
ZIP Code: 93230
General Phone: (559) 582-0471
General Email: publisher@hanfordsentinel.com
Publication Website: https://hanfordsentinel.com/community/selma_enterprise/
Publisher Name: Davis Taylor
Publisher Email: publisher@hanfordsentinel.com
Publisher Phone: (559) 583-2400
Editor Name: Chris Aguirre
Editor Email: caguirre@hanfordsentinel.com
Editor Phone: (559) 583-2405
Advertising Executive Name: Mark Daniel
Advertising Executive Email: mdaniel@hanfordsentinel.com

HEALDSBURG

THE WINDSOR TIMES

Street Address: 230 Center St
City: Healdsburg
State: CA
ZIP Code: 95448
General Phone: (707) 838-9211
General Email: editor@wdsrtimes.com
Publication Website: http://www.sonomawest.com/the_windsor_times/
Parent Company: Sonoma West Publishers
Publisher Name: Rollie Atkinson
Publisher Email: rollie@sonomawest.com
Editor Name: Heather Bailey
Editor Email: heather@sonomawest.com

HESPERIA

HESPERIA RESORTER

Street Address: 16925 Main St
City: Hesperia
State: CA
ZIP Code: 92345
General Phone: (760) 244-0021
General Email: questions@valleywidenewspaper.com
Publication Website: http://www.valleywidenewspaper.com/
Parent Company: Valley Wide Newspapers
Advertising Executive Email: classified@valleywidenewspaper.com

HOLLISTER

HOLLISTER FREE LANCE

Street Address: 615 San Benito Street
City: Hollister
State: CA
ZIP Code: 95023
General Phone: (831) 637-5566
General Email: bholtzclaw@newsvmedia.com
Publication Website: https://sanbenito.com/
Parent Company: New SV Media, Inc.

IDYLLWILD

IDYLLWILD TOWN CRIER

Street Address: 54405 North Circle Dr
City: Idyllwild
State: CA
ZIP Code: 92549
General Phone: (951) 659-2145
General Email: lisa@towncrier.com
Publication Website: https://idyllwildtowncrier.com/
Parent Company: Idyllwild House Publishing Co., Ltd.
Publisher Name: Becky Clark
Publisher Email: becky@towncrier.com
Editor Name: Melissa Diaz Hernandez
Editor Email: melissa@towncrier.com
Advertising Executive Name: Lisa Streeter
Advertising Executive Email: lisa@towncrier.com

INVERNESS

POINT REYES LIGHT

Street Address: 12781 Sir Francis Drake Blvd
City: Inverness
State: CA
ZIP Code: 94937-9736
General Phone: (415) 669-1200
General Email: editor@ptreyeslight.com
Publication Website: https://www.ptreyeslight.com/
Publisher Name: Tess Elliott
Editor Name: Anna Guth
Editor Email: aftitzguth@gmail.com
Advertising Executive Name: David Briggs
Advertising Executive Email: davidcharlesbriggs@gmail.com

JULIAN

JULIAN NEWS

Street Address: PO Box 639
City: Julian
State: CA
ZIP Code: 92036
General Phone: (760) 765-2231
General Email: publisher@juliannews.com
Publication Website: http://www.juliannews.com/
Publisher Name: Michael Hart
Publisher Email: publisher@juliannews.com
Editor Email: editor@juliannews.com

KERMAN

THE KERMAN NEWS

Street Address: 652 S Madera Ave
City: Kerman
State: CA
ZIP Code: 93630
General Phone: (559) 846-6689
General Email: kerwest@msn.com
Publication Website: https://kerwestnewspapers.com/
Parent Company: Kerwest Newspapers
Editor Name: Mark O. Kilen
Advertising Executive Name: Merlyn Wilcox

KING CITY

GONZALES TRIBUNE

Street Address: 522-B Broadway
City: King City
State: CA
ZIP Code: 93930
General Phone: (831) 385-4880
General Email: jjohnson@southcountynewspapers.com
Publication Website: https://gonzalestribune.com/
Parent Company: New SV Media, Inc.
Publisher Name: Jeanie Johnson
Publisher Email: jjohnson@newsvmedia.com
Publisher Phone: (831) 385-4880
Editor Name: Ryan Cronk
Editor Email: rcronk@newsvmedia.com
Editor Phone: (831) 385-4880, ext : 15
Advertising Executive Name: Sheryl Bailey
Advertising Executive Email: sbailey@newsvmedia.com

KING CITY

GREENFIELD NEWS

Street Address: 522-B Broadway
City: King City
State: CA
ZIP Code: 93930
General Phone: (831) 385-4880
General Email: jjohnson@southcountynewspapers.com
Publication Website: https://greenfieldnews.com/
Parent Company: New SV Media, Inc.
Publisher Name: Jeanie Johnson
Publisher Email: jjohnson@newsvmedia.com
Publisher Phone: (831) 385-4880
Editor Name: Ryan Cronk
Editor Email: rcronk@newsvmedia.com
Editor Phone: (831) 385-4880, ext : 15
Advertising Executive Name: Sheryl Bailey
Advertising Executive Email: sbailey@newsvmedia.com

KING CITY

SOLEDAD BEE

Street Address: 522-B Broadway
City: King City
State: CA
ZIP Code: 93930
General Phone: (831) 385-4880
General Email: jjohnson@southcountynewspapers.com
Publication Website: https://soledadbee.com/
Parent Company: New SV Media, Inc.
Publisher Name: Jeanie Johnson
Publisher Email: jjohnson@newsvmedia.com
Publisher Phone: (831) 385-4880
Editor Name: Ryan Cronk
Editor Email: rcronk@newsvmedia.com
Editor Phone: (831) 385-4880, ext : 15
Advertising Executive Name: Sheryl Bailey
Advertising Executive Email: sbailey@newsvmedia.com

KING CITY

THE RUSTLER

Street Address: 522-B Broadway
City: King City
State: CA
ZIP Code: 93930
General Phone: (831) 385-4880
General Email: rcronk@newsvmedia.com
Publication Website: https://kingcityrustler.com/
Parent Company: New SV Media, Inc.
Publisher Name: Jeanie Johnson
Publisher Email: jjohnson@newsvmedia.com
Publisher Phone: (831) 385-4880
Editor Name: Ryan Cronk
Editor Email: rcronk@newsvmedia.com
Editor Phone: (831) 385-4880, ext : 15
Advertising Executive Name: Sheryl Bailey
Advertising Executive Email: sbailey@newsvmedia.com

LA JOLLA

LA JOLLA LIGHT

Street Address: 565 Pearl St
City: La Jolla
State: CA
ZIP Code: 92037
General Phone: (858) 459-4201
General Email: editor@lajollalight.com
Publication Website: https://www.lajollalight.com/
Parent Company: San Diego Union-Tribune, LLC
Publisher Name: Phyllis Pfeiffer
Publisher Email: ppfeiffer@lajollalight.com
Publisher Phone: (858) 875-5940
Editor Name: Susan DeMaggio
Editor Email: susandemaggio@lajollalight.com
Editor Phone: (858) 875-5950
Advertising Executive Name: Don Parks

LAKE ISABELLA

KERN VALLEY SUN

Street Address: 6416 LAKE ISABELLA BLVD
City: Lake Isabella
State: CA
ZIP Code: 93240
General Phone: (760) 379-3667
General Email: publisher@kvsun.com
Publication Website: https://kernvalleysun.com/
Publisher Email: publisher@kvsun.com
Publisher Phone: (760) 379-3667, ext : 1011
Editor Email: editor@kvsun.com
Editor Phone: (760) 379-3667, ext : 1004
Advertising Executive Name: Michele Lynn
Advertising Executive Email: michelel@kvsun.com

LAKEPORT

CLEAR LAKE OBSERVER-AMERICAN

Street Address: 2150 S Main St
City: Lakeport
State: CA
ZIP Code: 95453-5620
General Phone: (707) 263-5636
General Email: ahansmith@record-bee.com
Publication Website: https://www.record-bee.com/
Publisher Name: Kevin McConnell
Publisher Email: udjpublisher@ukiahdj.com
Publisher Phone: (707) 900-2012
Editor Name: Ariel Carmona
Editor Email: arielcarmona@record-bee.com
Editor Phone: (707) 900-2016
Advertising Executive Name: Amy Hansmith
Advertising Executive Email: ahansmith@record-bee.com

LAKEPORT

SOUTH COUNTY NEWS

Street Address: 2150 S Main St
City: Lakeport
State: CA
ZIP Code: 95453-5620
General Phone: (707) 263-5636
General Email: udjpublisher@ukiahdj.com
Publication Website: https://www.record-bee.com/
Publisher Name: Kevin McConnell
Publisher Email: udjpublisher@ukiahdj.com
Publisher Phone: (707) 900-2012
Editor Name: Ariel Carmona

Editor Email: arielcarmona@record-bee.com
Editor Phone: (707) 900-2016
Advertising Executive Name: Amy Hansmith
Advertising Executive Email: ahansmith@record-bee.com

LIVERMORE

THE INDEPENDENT

Street Address: 2250 1st St
City: Livermore
State: CA
ZIP Code: 94550
General Phone: (925) 447-8700
General Email: editmail@compuserve.com
Publication Website: https://www.independentnews.com/
Parent Company: Gannett
Publisher Name: Joan Seppala
Editor Email: editmail@compuserve.com
Advertising Executive Name: Kim Contente
Advertising Executive Email: kim@independentnews.com

LONG BEACH

DOWNTOWN GAZETTE

Street Address: 5225 E 2nd St
City: Long Beach
State: CA
ZIP Code: 90803
General Phone: (562) 433-2000
General Email: advertising@gazettes.com
Publication Website: https://www.gazettes.com/
Publisher Name: Simon Grieve
Publisher Email: sgrieve@gazettes.com
Editor Name: Harry Saltzgaver
Editor Email: hsalt@gazettes.com
Advertising Executive Name: Susan Stehno
Advertising Executive Email: spilgram@gazettes.com

LONG BEACH

GRUNION GAZETTE

Street Address: 5225 E 2nd St
City: Long Beach
State: CA
ZIP Code: 90803
General Phone: (562) 433-2000
General Email: advertising@gazettes.com
Publication Website: https://www.gazettes.com/
Publisher Name: Simon Grieve
Publisher Email: sgrieve@gazettes.com
Editor Name: Harry Saltzgaver
Editor Email: hsalt@gazettes.com
Advertising Executive Name: Susan Stehno
Advertising Executive Email: spilgram@gazettes.com

LONG BEACH

UPTOWN GAZETTE

Street Address: 5225 E 2nd St
City: Long Beach
State: CA
ZIP Code: 90803
General Phone: (562) 433-2000
General Email: advertising@gazettes.com
Publication Website: https://www.gazettes.com/e_edition/uptown/
Publisher Name: Simon Grieve
Publisher Email: sgrieve@gazettes.com
Editor Name: Harry Saltzgaver
Editor Email: hsalt@gazettes.com
Advertising Executive Name: Susan Stehno
Advertising Executive Email: spilgram@gazettes.com

LOS ALTOS

LOS ALTOS TOWN CRIER

Street Address: 138 Main St
City: Los Altos
State: CA
ZIP Code: 94022
General Phone: (650) 948-9000
General Email: info@latc.com
Publication Website: https://www.losaltosonline.com/
Parent Company: LATC Media Inc
Publisher Name: Dennis Young
Editor Name: Pete Borello
Advertising Executive Name: Kathy Lera

LOS ANGELES

LOS ANGELES WAVE

Street Address: 3731 Wilshire Blvd
City: Los Angeles
State: CA
ZIP Code: 90010
General Phone: (323) 556-5720
General Email: newsroom@wavepublication.com
Publication Website: http://wavenewspapers.com/
Advertising Executive Name: Linda Lodder
Advertising Executive Email: llodder@wavepublication.com

MADERA

THE MADERA TRIBUNE

Street Address: 2591 Mitchell Ct
City: Madera
State: CA
ZIP Code: 93637
General Phone: (559) 674-2424
Publication Website: http://www.maderatribune.com/
Publisher Phone: (559) 674-8134

MALIBU

THE MALIBU SURFSIDE NEWS

Street Address: PO Box 6854
City: Malibu
State: CA
ZIP Code: 90264
General Phone: (708) 326-9170
General Email: mary@malibusurfsidenews.com
Publication Website: https://www.malibusurfsidenews.com/
Parent Company: 22nd Century Media, LLC
Publisher Name: Joe Coughlin
Publisher Email: j.coughlin@22ndcenturymedia.com
Editor Name: Bill Jones
Editor Email: bill@opprairie.com

MALIBU

THE MALIBU TIMES

Street Address: 3864 Las Flores Canyon Rd
City: Malibu
State: CA
ZIP Code: 90265
General Phone: (310) 456-5507
General Email: webeditor@malibutimes.com
Publication Website: http://www.malibutimes.com
Publisher Name: Arnold Grant York
Publisher Email: agyork@malibutimes.com
Publisher Phone: (310) 456-5507, ext : 101
Editor Name: Emily Sawicki
Editor Email: emily@malibutimes.com
Editor Phone: (310) 456-5507, ext : 109
Advertising Executive Name: Teresa Gelbman
Advertising Executive Email: classads@malibutimes.com

MAMMOTH LAKES

MAMMOTH TIMES

Street Address: 645 Old Mammoth Road, Suite A
City: Mammoth Lakes
State: CA
ZIP Code: 93546
General Phone: (760) 934-3929
Publication Website: https://mammothtimes.com/
Parent Company: The Mammoth Times

MARIPOSA

MARIPOSA GAZETTE

Street Address: 5108 Highway 140, Suite B, P.O. Box 38
City: Mariposa
State: CA
ZIP Code: 95338
General Phone: (209) 966-2500
General Email: ads@mariposagazette.com
Publication Website: https://www.mariposagazette.com/
Parent Company: The Mariposa Gazette and Miner
Publisher Name: Nicole W. Little
Publisher Email: nicole@mariposagazette.com
Editor Name: Greg Little
Editor Email: greg@mariposagazette.com
Advertising Executive Name: Shantel Sojka
Advertising Executive Email: shantel@mariposagazette.com

MARTINEZ

MARTINEZ NEWS-GAZETTE

Street Address: 802 Alhambra Ave
City: Martinez
State: CA
ZIP Code: 94553-1604
General Phone: (925) 228-6400
General Email: editor@martinezgazette.com
Publication Website: https://martinezgazette.com/
Parent Company: Gibson Publishing
Editor Name: Rick Jones
Editor Email: editor@martinezgazette.com
Editor Phone: (925) 293-9471

MARYSVILLE

COLUSA COUNTY SUN-HERALD

Street Address: 1530 Ellis Lake Dr
City: Marysville
State: CA
ZIP Code: 95901
General Phone: (530) 749-4700
General Email: info@appealdemocrat.com
Publication Website: https://www.appeal-democrat.com/colusa_sun_herald/
Parent Company: Times Media Group
Publisher Name: Glenn Stifflemire
Publisher Email: gstifflemire@appealdemocrat.com
Publisher Phone: (530) 749-4705
Editor Name: Steve Miller
Editor Email: smiller@appealdemocrat.com
Editor Phone: (530) 749-4767
Advertising Executive Name: Jamie Keith
Advertising Executive Email: lnash@appealdemocrat.com

MARYSVILLE

CORNING OBSERVER

Street Address: 1530 Ellis Lake Dr
City: Marysville
State: CA
ZIP Code: 95901-4258
General Phone: (530) 824-5464
General Email: adnewsroom@appealdemocrat.com
Publication Website: https://www.appeal-democrat.com/corning_observer/
Parent Company: Times Media Group
Advertising Executive Email: adclass@appealdemocrat.com

MENLO PARK

PALO ALTO DAILY NEWS

Street Address: 255 Constitution Dr
City: Menlo Park
State: CA
ZIP Code: 94025-1108
General Phone: (650) 391-1000
General Email: letters@bayareanewsgroup.com
Publication Website: https://www.mercurynews.com/location/peninsula/
Publisher Name: Sharon Ryan
Publisher Email: publisher@bayareanewsgroup.com
Editor Name: Bert Robinson
Editor Email: jhrobinson@bayareanewsgroup.com
Editor Phone: (408) 920-5970
Advertising Executive Name: Michael Turpin
Advertising Executive Email: mturpin@bayareanewsgroup.com

MENLO PARK

THE ALMANAC

Street Address: 3525 Alameda De Las Pulgas
City: Menlo Park
State: CA
ZIP Code: 94025-6544
General Phone: (650) 854-2626
General Email: ads@almanacnews.com
Publication Website: https://www.almanacnews.com/
Parent Company: Embarcadero Media
Editor Name: Renee Batti
Editor Phone: (650) 223-6528
Advertising Executive Name: Tom Zahiralis

MONROVIA

AZUSA HERALD HIGHLANDER

Street Address: 605 E Huntington Dr
City: Monrovia
State: CA
ZIP Code: 91016-6353
General Phone: (626) 962-8811
General Email: mark.welches@sgvn.com
Publication Website: https://www.sgvtribune.com/location/california/los-angeles-county/san-gabriel-valley/azusa/
Publisher Name: Ron Hasse
Publisher Email: publisher@scng.com
Publisher Phone: (818) 713-3883
Editor Name: Penny Arevalo,
Editor Email: parevalo@scng.com
Editor Phone: (626) 544-0981
Advertising Executive Name: Melene Alfonso
Advertising Executive Email: malfonso@scng.com

MONROVIA

COVINA PRESS COURIER HIGHLANDER

Community Newspapers in the U.S.

III-173

Street Address: 605 E Huntington Dr
City: Monrovia
State: CA
ZIP Code: 91016-6353
General Phone: (626) 962-8811
General Email: jim.maurer@sgvn.com
Publication Website: https://www.sgvtribune.com/location/california/los-angeles-county/san-gabriel-valley/covina/
Publisher Name: Ron Hasse
Publisher Email: publisher@scng.com
Publisher Phone: (818) 713-3883
Editor Name: Penny Arevalo,
Editor Email: parevalo@scng.com
Editor Phone: (626) 544-0981
Advertising Executive Name: Melene Alfonso
Advertising Executive Email: malfonso@scng.com

MONROVIA

GAN GABRIEL VALLEY TRIBUNE

Street Address: 605 E Huntington Dr
City: Monrovia
State: CA
ZIP Code: 91016-6353
General Phone: (626) 962-8811
General Email: malfonso@scng.com
Publication Website: https://www.sgvtribune.com/
Publisher Name: Ron Hasse
Publisher Email: publisher@scng.com
Publisher Phone: (818) 713-3883
Editor Name: Frank Pine
Editor Email: editor@scng.com
Editor Phone: (909) 483-9360
Advertising Executive Name: Melene Alfonso
Advertising Executive Email: malfonso@scng.com

MONROVIA

LA PUENTE HIGHLANDER

Street Address: 605 E Huntington Dr
City: Monrovia
State: CA
ZIP Code: 91016-6353
General Phone: (626) 962-8811
General Email: malfonso@scng.com
Publication Website: https://www.sgvtribune.com/location/california/los-angeles-county/san-gabriel-valley/la-puente/
Publisher Name: Ron Hasse
Publisher Email: publisher@scng.com
Publisher Phone: (818) 713-3883
Editor Name: Penny Arevalo,
Editor Email: parevalo@scng.com
Editor Phone: (626) 544-0981
Advertising Executive Name: Melene Alfonso
Advertising Executive Email: malfonso@scng.com

MONROVIA

ROWLAND HEIGHTS HIGHLANDER

Street Address: 605 E Huntington Dr
City: Monrovia
State: CA
ZIP Code: 91016-6353
General Phone: (626) 962-8811
General Email: highlanders@sgvn.com
Publication Website: https://www.sgvtribune.com/location/california/los-angeles-county/san-gabriel-valley/rowland-heights/
Publisher Name: Ron Hasse
Publisher Email: publisher@scng.com
Publisher Phone: (818) 713-3883
Editor Name: Penny Arevalo,
Editor Email: parevalo@scng.com
Editor Phone: (626) 544-0981

Advertising Executive Name: Melene Alfonso
Advertising Executive Email: malfonso@scng.com

MONROVIA

THE HIGHLANDER - GLENDORA EDITION

Street Address: 605 E Huntington Dr
City: Monrovia
State: CA
ZIP Code: 91016-6353
General Phone: (626) 962-8811
General Email: malfonso@scng.com
Publication Website: https://www.sgvtribune.com/location/california/los-angeles-county/san-gabriel-valley/glendora/
Publisher Name: Ron Hasse
Publisher Email: publisher@scng.com
Publisher Phone: (818) 713-3883
Editor Name: Penny Arevalo,
Editor Email: parevalo@scng.com
Editor Phone: (626) 544-0981
Advertising Executive Name: Melene Alfonso
Advertising Executive Email: malfonso@scng.com

MONROVIA

THE HIGHLANDER - LA PUENTE EDITION

Street Address: 605 E Huntington Dr
City: Monrovia
State: CA
ZIP Code: 91016
General Phone: (626) 962-8811
General Email: malfonso@scng.com
Publication Website: https://www.sgvtribune.com/location/california/los-angeles-county/san-gabriel-valley/la-puente/
Publisher Name: Ron Hasse
Publisher Email: publisher@scng.com
Publisher Phone: (818) 713-3883
Editor Name: Penny Arevalo
Editor Email: parevalo@scng.com
Editor Phone: (626) 544-0981
Advertising Executive Name: Melene Alfonso
Advertising Executive Email: malfonso@scng.com

MONROVIA

THE HIGHLANDER - ROWLAND HEIGHTS EDITION

Street Address: 605 E Huntington Dr
City: Monrovia
State: CA
ZIP Code: 91016-6353
General Phone: (626) 962-8811
General Email: malfonso@scng.com
Publication Website: https://www.sgvtribune.com/location/california/los-angeles-county/san-gabriel-valley/rowland-heights/
Publisher Name: Ron Hasse
Publisher Email: publisher@scng.com
Publisher Phone: (818) 713-3883
Editor Name: Penny Arevalo,
Editor Email: parevalo@scng.com
Editor Phone: (626) 544-0981
Advertising Executive Name: Melene Alfonso
Advertising Executive Email: malfonso@scng.com

MORGAN HILL

MORGAN HILL TIMES

Street Address: 17500 Depot St
City: Morgan Hill
State: CA
ZIP Code: 95037-3886
General Phone: (408) 963-0120
General Email: editor@morganhilltimes.com
Publication Website: https://morganhilltimes.com/
Parent Company: New SV Media, Inc.
Publisher Name: Jeanette Close
Publisher Email: jclose@newsvmedia.com
Publisher Phone: (408) 842-8313
Editor Name: Michael Moore
Editor Email: mmoore@newsvmedia.com
Editor Phone: (408) 963-0121

MOUNT SHASTA

DUNSMUIR NEWS

Street Address: 924 N Mount Shasta Blvd
City: Mount Shasta
State: CA
ZIP Code: 96067-8700
General Phone: (530) 926-5214
General Email: news@mtshastanews.com
Publication Website: https://www.mtshastanews.com/
Parent Company: Gannett
Publisher Name: Amy Lanier
Publisher Email: alanier@mtshastanews.com
Editor Name: Skye Kinkade
Editor Email: news@mtshastanews.com
Advertising Executive Name: Cathy Athens
Advertising Executive Email: classifieds@mtshastanews.com

MOUNT SHASTA

MT. SHASTA HERALD

Street Address: 924 N Mount Shasta Blvd
City: Mount Shasta
State: CA
ZIP Code: 96067-8700
General Phone: (530) 926-5214
General Email: news@mtshastanews.com
Publication Website: https://www.mtshastanews.com/
Publisher Name: Amy Lanier
Publisher Email: alanier@mtshastanews.com
Editor Name: Skye Kinkade
Editor Email: news@mtshastanews.com
Advertising Executive Name: Cathy Athens
Advertising Executive Email: classifieds@mtshastanews.com

MOUNT SHASTA

MT. SHASTA NEWS

Street Address: 924 N Mount Shasta Blvd
City: Mount Shasta
State: CA
ZIP Code: 96067-8700
General Phone: (530) 926-5214
General Email: news@mtshastanews.com
Publication Website: https://www.mtshastanews.com/
Publisher Name: Amy Lanier
Publisher Email: alanier@mtshastanews.com
Editor Name: Skye Kinkade
Editor Email: news@mtshastanews.com
Advertising Executive Name: Cathy Athens
Advertising Executive Email: classifieds@mtshastanews.com

NAPA

AMERICAN CANYON EAGLE

Street Address: 1615 Soscol Ave
City: Napa
State: CA
ZIP Code: 94559-1901
General Phone: (707) 256-2269

Publication Website: https://napavalleyregister.com/community/eagle/
Publisher Name: Davis Taylor
Publisher Email: davis.taylor@lee.net
Publisher Phone: (707) 256-2234
Editor Name: Sean Scully
Editor Email: sscully@napanews.com
Editor Phone: (707) 256-2246
Advertising Executive Name: Norma Kostecka
Advertising Executive Email: nkostecka@napanews.com

NAPA

ST HELENA STAR

Street Address: 1615 Soscol Ave.
City: Napa
State: CA
ZIP Code: 94559
General Phone: (707) 226-3711
General Email: dstoneberg@sthelenastar.com
Publication Website: https://napavalleyregister.com/community/star/
Publisher Name: Davis Taylor
Publisher Email: davis.taylor@lee.net
Publisher Phone: (707) 256-2234
Editor Name: David Stoneberg
Editor Email: dstoneberg@sthelenastar.com
Editor Phone: (707) 967-6800

NEWMAN

TUESDAY REVIEW

Street Address: 1021 Fresno St
City: Newman
State: CA
ZIP Code: 95360-1303
General Phone: (209) 862-2222
General Email: advertising@mattosnews.com
Publication Website: http://mattosnews.com/
Parent Company: Mattos Newspapers

OAKDALE

ESCALON TIMES

Street Address: 122 S 3rd Ave
City: Oakdale
State: CA
ZIP Code: 95361-3935
General Phone: (209) 847-3021
General Email: ads@oakdaleleader.com
Publication Website: https://www.escalontimes.com/
Parent Company: Morris Multimedia, Inc.
Publisher Name: Hank Vander Veen
Publisher Email: hvanderveen@turlockjournal.com
Publisher Phone: (209) 249-3503
Editor Name: Marg Jackson
Editor Email: mjackson@oakdaleleader.com
Editor Phone: (209) 845-4080
Advertising Executive Name: Michelle Kendig
Advertising Executive Email: mkendig@oakdaleleader.com

OAKDALE

OAKDALE LEADER

Street Address: 122 S 3rd Ave
City: Oakdale
State: CA
ZIP Code: 95361-3993
General Phone: (209) 847-3021
General Email: mjackson@oakdaleleader.com
Publication Website: https://www.oakdaleleader.com/
Parent Company: Morris Multimedia, Inc.

Publisher Name: Hank Vander Veen
Publisher Email: hvanderveen@turlockjournal.com
Publisher Phone: (209) 249-3503
Editor Name: Marg Jackson
Editor Email: mjackson@oakdaleleader.com
Editor Phone: (209) 845-4080
Advertising Executive Name: Michelle Kendig
Advertising Executive Email: mkendig@oakdaleleader.com

OAKDALE

THE RIVERBANK NEWS

Street Address: 122 S 3rd Ave
City: Oakdale
State: CA
ZIP Code: 95361-3935
General Phone: (209) 847-3021
General Email: news@oakdaleleader.com
Publication Website: https://www.theriverbanknews.com/
Parent Company: Morris Multimedia, Inc.
Publisher Name: Hank Vander Veen
Publisher Email: hvanderveen@turlockjournal.com
Publisher Phone: (209) 249-3503
Editor Name: Marg Jackson
Editor Email: mjackson@oakdaleleader.com
Editor Phone: (209) 845-4080
Advertising Executive Name: Michelle Kendig
Advertising Executive Email: mkendig@oakdaleleader.com

OAKLAND

JOINT FORCES JOURNAL

Street Address: PO Box 13283
City: Oakland
State: CA
ZIP Code: 94661-0283
General Phone: (510) 428-2000
General Email: cardchron@aol.com
Publication Website: https://jointforcesjournal.com/

OAKLAND

MARIN COUNTY POST

Street Address: 405 14th St
City: Oakland
State: CA
ZIP Code: 94612-2707
General Phone: (510) 287-8200
General Email: contact@postnewsgroup.com
Publication Website: http://lajonesmedia.com/news/the-post-news-group/
Parent Company: Post News Group

OJAI

OJAI VALLEY NEWS

Street Address: 101 Vallerio Ave
City: Ojai
State: CA
ZIP Code: 93023-3631
General Phone: (805) 646-1476
General Email: team@ojaivalleynews.com
Publication Website: https://www.ojaivalleynews.com/
Parent Company: Downhome Publishing LLC
Publisher Name: Laura Rearwin Ward
Publisher Email: publisher@ojaivalleynews.com

PACIFIC PALISADES

PALISADIAN-POST

Street Address: 881 Alma Real Dr
City: Pacific Palisades
State: CA
ZIP Code: 90272-3737
General Phone: (310) 454-1321
General Email: classifieds@palipost.com
Publication Website: https://www.palipost.com/
Editor Name: Gina Kernan
Editor Email: gina@palipost.com
Advertising Executive Name: Lia Asher
Advertising Executive Email: lia@palipost.com

PALO ALTO

MOUNTAIN VIEW VOICE

Street Address: 450 Cambridge Ave
City: Palo Alto
State: CA
ZIP Code: 94306-1507
General Phone: (650) 964-6300
General Email: ads@mv-voice.com
Publication Website: https://www.mv-voice.com/
Parent Company: Embarcadero Media
Editor Name: Andrea Gemmet
Editor Phone: (650) 223-6537
Advertising Executive Name: Tom Zahiralis

PARADISE

PARADISE POST

Street Address: PO Box 70
City: Paradise
State: CA
ZIP Code: 95967-0070
General Phone: (530) 879-7888
General Email: rsilva@paradisepost.com
Publication Website: https://www.paradisepost.com/
Parent Company: Media News Group
Editor Name: Rick Silva
Editor Email: rsilva@paradisepost.com
Editor Phone: (530) 876-3014
Advertising Executive Name: Darren Holden
Advertising Executive Email: dholden@chicoer.com

PARAMOUNT

THE PARAMOUNT JOURNAL

Street Address: 8007 Somerset Blvd
City: Paramount
State: CA
ZIP Code: 90723-4334
General Phone: (800) 540-1870
General Email: info@paramountjournal.org
Publication Website: https://paramountjournal.org/
Publisher Name: Steven Remery
Publisher Email: publisher@localnewspapers.org
Publisher Phone: (562) 430-7555
Editor Name: Charles M. Kelly
Editor Email: ckelly@localnewspapers.org
Editor Phone: (562) 430-8895
Advertising Executive Name: Angelina Blackhawk
Advertising Executive Email: pjlegals@localnewspapers.org

PASADENA

PASADENA WEEKLY

Street Address: 161 South Pasadena Ave, Suite B
City: Pasadena
State: CA
ZIP Code: 91030
General Phone: (626) 584-1500
General Email: jon@pasadenaweekly.com
Publication Website: https://pasadenaweekly.com/
Parent Company: Times Media Group
Publisher Name: Kevin Uhrich
Publisher Email: kevinu@pasadenaweekly.com

PASO ROBLES

PASO ROBLES PRESS

Street Address: 935 Riverside Ave.
City: Paso Robles
State: CA
ZIP Code: 93446
General Phone: (805) 237-6060
General Email: spotruch@pasoroblespress.com
Publication Website: https://pasoroblespress.com/
Parent Company: 13 Stars Media
Publisher Name: Nic Mattson
Publisher Email: nic@pasoroblespress.com
Editor Name: Luke Phillips
Editor Email: luke@pasoroblespress.com
Advertising Executive Name: Carmen Kessler
Advertising Executive Email: armen@pasoroblespress.com

PATTERSON

PATTERSON IRRIGATOR

Street Address: 26 N 3rd St
City: Patterson
State: CA
ZIP Code: 95363-2507
General Phone: (209) 892-6187
General Email: news@pattersonirrigator.com
Publication Website: https://www.ttownmedia.com/patterson_irrigator/
Parent Company: TankTown Media
Editor Name: Jenifer West
Editor Email: jenifer@pattersonirrigator.com
Advertising Executive Name: Marybeth Bragdon
Advertising Executive Email: marybeth@pattersonirrigator.com

PERRIS

PERRIS PROGRESS

Street Address: 277 E 4th St
City: Perris
State: CA
ZIP Code: 92570-2256
General Phone: (951) 737-9784
General Email: sentinelweekly@aol.com
Publication Website: http://www.theperrisprogress.com/

PETALUMA

PETALUMA ARGUS-COURIER

Street Address: 1372 E North McDowell Blvd
City: Petaluma
State: CA
ZIP Code: 94954-8004
General Phone: (707) 762-4541
General Email: matt.brown@arguscourier.com
Publication Website: https://www.petaluma360.com/
Parent Company: Sonoma Media Investments
Publisher Name: Emily Charrier
Publisher Email: emily.charrier@arguscourier.com
Publisher Phone: (707) 776-8450
Editor Name: Matt Brown
Editor Email: matt.brown@arguscourier.com
Editor Phone: (707) 776-8458
Advertising Executive Name: Joanne Herrfeldt
Advertising Executive Email: joanne.herrfeldt@pressdemocrat.com

PLACERVILLE

MOUNTAIN DEMOCRAT

Street Address: 2889 Ray Lawyer Dr
City: Placerville
State: CA
ZIP Code: 95667-3914
General Phone: (530) 622-1255
General Email: mtdemo@mtdemocrat.net
Publication Website: https://www.mtdemocrat.com/
Parent Company: Mountain Democrat, Inc.
Publisher Name: Richard Esposito
Publisher Email: resposito@mtdemocrat.net
Publisher Phone: (530) 344-5055
Editor Name: Krysten Kellum
Editor Email: kkellum@mtdemocrat.net
Editor Phone: (530) 344-5072
Advertising Executive Name: Ian Balentine
Advertising Executive Email: ibalentine@mtdemocrat.net

PLEASANTON

PLEASANTON WEEKLY

Street Address: 5506 Sunol Blvd
City: Pleasanton
State: CA
ZIP Code: 94566
General Phone: (925) 600-0840
General Email: ads@pleasantonweekly.com
Publication Website: https://www.pleasantonweekly.com/
Parent Company: Embarcadero Media
Publisher Name: Gina Channell
Publisher Phone: (925) 600-0840, ext : 119
Editor Name: Jeremy Walsh
Editor Phone: (925) 600-0840, ext : 118
Advertising Executive Name: Carol Cano

POWAY

POWAY NEWS CHIEFTAIN

Street Address: 13426 Community Road, Suite C
City: Poway
State: CA
ZIP Code: 92064-3959
General Phone: (858) 221-9202
General Email: news@pomeradonews.com
Publication Website: https://www.sandiegouniontribune.com/pomerado-news/
Parent Company: San Diego Union-Tribune, LLC
Editor Name: Steve Dreyer
Editor Email: editor@pomeradonews.com
Editor Phone: (858) 218-7207

POWAY

RANCHO BERNARDO NEWS-JOURNAL

Street Address: 13426 Community Road, Suite C
City: Poway
State: CA
ZIP Code: 92064-3959
General Phone: (858) 221-9202
General Email: rbnews@pomeradonews.com
Publication Website: https://www.sandiegouniontribune.com/pomerado-news/
Parent Company: The San Diego Union-Tribune
Editor Name: Steve Dreyer
Editor Email: editor@pomeradonews.com
Editor Phone: (858) 218-7207

Community Newspapers in the U.S.

III-175

REEDLEY

THE REEDLEY EXPONENT

Street Address: 1130 G Street
City: Reedley
State: CA
ZIP Code: 93654-0432
General Phone: (559) 638-2244
General Email: janie@midvalleypublishing.com
Publication Website: http://www.reedleyexponent.com/
Parent Company: Mid-Valley Publications
Publisher Name: Fred Hall
Editor Name: Jon Earnest

RICHMOND

THE BERKELEY VOICE

Street Address: 1050 Marina Way S
City: Richmond
State: CA
ZIP Code: 94804-3741
General Phone: (510) 262-2784
General Email: editor@bayareanewsgroup.com
Publication Website: https://www.eastbaytimes.com/location/berkeley/
Publisher Name: Sharon Ryan
Publisher Email: publisher@bayareanewsgroup.com
Editor Name: Mario Dianda
Editor Email: mdianda@bayareanewsgroup.com
Editor Phone: (650) 391-1342
Advertising Executive Name: Michael Turpin
Advertising Executive Email: mturpin@bayareanewsgroup.com

RIDGECREST

THE NEWS REVIEW

Street Address: 109 N Sanders St
City: Ridgecrest
State: CA
ZIP Code: 93555-3848
General Phone: (760) 371-4301
General Email: rsvp.mccarthy@mail.house.gov
Publication Website: http://www.news-ridgecrest.com/news/category.pl

RIO VISTA

THE RIVER NEWS-HERALD & ISLETON JOURNAL

Street Address: 21 S Front St
City: Rio Vista
State: CA
ZIP Code: 94571-1822
General Phone: (707) 374-6431
General Email: rvads@citlink.net
Publication Website: https://rivernewsherald.com/

ROHNERT PARK

THE COMMUNITY VOICE

Street Address: 100 Professional Center Dr
City: Rohnert Park
State: CA
ZIP Code: 94928-2137
General Phone: (707) 584-2222
General Email: publisher@thecommunityvoice.com
Publication Website: http://www.thecommunityvoice.com/
Advertising Executive Name: Yatin Shah

ROLLING HILLS ESTATES

PALOS VERDES PENINSULA NEWS

Street Address: 609 Deep Valley Dr
City: Rolling Hills Estates
State: CA
ZIP Code: 90274
General Phone: (310) 377-6877
General Email: lisa.jacobs@tbrnews.com
Publication Website: http://pvnews.com/
Editor Name: Lisa Jacobs
Editor Email: lisa.jacobs@tbrnews.com

SACRAMENTO

INSIDE EAST SACRAMENTO

Street Address: 3104 O St
City: Sacramento
State: CA
ZIP Code: 95816
General Phone: (916) 443-5087
General Email: editor@insidepublications.com
Publication Website: https://insidesacramento.com/
Parent Company: Inside Publications
Publisher Name: Cecily Hastings
Publisher Email: cecily@insidepublications.com
Editor Name: Cathryn Rakich
Editor Email: editor@insidepublications.com
Advertising Executive Name: Michele Mazzera
Advertising Executive Email: ads@insidepublications.com

SACRAMENTO

SACRAMENTO BUSINESS JOURNAL

Street Address: 555 Capitol Mall, Suite 200
City: Sacramento
State: CA
ZIP Code: 95814-4557
General Phone: (916) 447-7661
General Email: sacramento@bizjournals.com
Publication Website: https://www.bizjournals.com/sacramento/
Parent Company: American City Business Journals
Publisher Name: David Lichtman
Publisher Email: dlichtman@bizjournals.com
Editor Name: Sam Boykin
Editor Email: sboykin@bizjournals.com
Editor Phone: (916) 558-7865
Advertising Executive Name: Joann Kurtyak
Advertising Executive Email: jkurtyak@bizjournals.com

SACRAMENTO

SACRAMENTO GAZETTE

Street Address: 770 L St
City: Sacramento
State: CA
ZIP Code: 95814-3361
General Phone: (916) 567-9654
General Email: sacgazette@aol.com
Publication Website: http://www.sacgazette.com/

SALINAS

THE SALINAS CALIFORNIAN

Street Address: 1093 S MAIN ST STE 101
City: Salinas
State: CA
ZIP Code: 93901
General Phone: (831) 424-2221
General Email: tdean@gannett.com
Publication Website: https://www.thecalifornian.com/
Parent Company: Gannett
Publisher Name: Paula Goudreau
Publisher Email: pgoudreau@thecalifornian.com
Publisher Phone: (831) 754-4100
Editor Name: Silas Lyons
Editor Email: sjlyons@gannett.com
Editor Phone: (530) 225-8210
Advertising Executive Name: Trey Dean
Advertising Executive Email: tdean@gannett.com

SAN ANDREAS

CALAVERAS ENTERPRISE

Street Address: 15 Main St
City: San Andreas
State: CA
ZIP Code: 95249-9548
General Phone: (209) 754-3861
General Email: news@calaverasenterprise.com
Publication Website: http://www.calaverasenterprise.com/
Parent Company: Calaveras First Co.
Publisher Name: Ralph Alldredge
Publisher Email: publisher@calaverasenterprise.com
Publisher Phone: (209) 754-3861
Editor Name: Marc Lutz
Editor Email: editor@calaverasenterprise.com
Editor Phone: (209) 500-6182
Advertising Executive Name: Jason Currier
Advertising Executive Email: jcurrier@calaverasenterprise.com

SAN DIEGO

BEACH & BAY PRESS

Street Address: 1621 Grand Ave
City: San Diego
State: CA
ZIP Code: 92109-4458
General Phone: (858) 270-3103
General Email: julie@sdnews.com
Publication Website: http://www.sdnews.com/pages/home?site=bbp
Parent Company: San Diego Community Newspaper Group
Publisher Name: Julie Main
Publisher Email: julie@sdnews.com
Publisher Phone: (858) 270-3103, ext : 106
Editor Name: Thomas Melville
Editor Email: tom@sdnews.com
Editor Phone: (858) 270-3103, ext : 131
Advertising Executive Name: Heather Long
Advertising Executive Email: heather@sdnews.com

SAN DIEGO

LA JOLLA VILLAGE NEWS

Street Address: 1621 Grand Ave
City: San Diego
State: CA
ZIP Code: 92109-4458
General Phone: (858) 270-3103
General Email: julie@sdnews.com
Publication Website: http://www.sdnews.com/pages/home?site=ljvn
Parent Company: San Diego Community Newspaper Group
Publisher Name: Julie Main
Publisher Email: julie@sdnews.com
Publisher Phone: (858) 270-3103, ext : 106
Editor Name: Thomas Melville
Editor Email: tom@sdnews.com
Editor Phone: (858) 270-3103, ext : 131
Advertising Executive Name: Heather Long
Advertising Executive Email: heather@sdnews.com

SAN DIEGO

PENINSULA BEACON

Street Address: 1621 Grand Ave
City: San Diego
State: CA
ZIP Code: 92109-4458
General Phone: (858) 270-3103
General Email: heather@sdnews.com
Publication Website: http://www.sdnews.com/pages/home?site=pb
Parent Company: San Diego Community Newspaper Group
Publisher Name: Julie Main
Publisher Email: julie@sdnews.com
Publisher Phone: (858) 270-3103, ext : 106
Editor Name: Thomas Melville
Editor Email: tom@sdnews.com
Editor Phone: (858) 270-3103, ext : 131
Advertising Executive Name: Heather Long
Advertising Executive Email: heather@sdnews.com

SAN DIEGO

UPTOWN SAN DIEGO EXAMINER

Street Address: 3601 30th St
City: San Diego
State: CA
ZIP Code: 92104-3508
General Phone: (619) 955-8960
General Email: kevin@uptownexaminer.com
Publication Website: https://uptownexaminer.com/

SAN FRANCISCO

EAST BAY BUSINESS TIMES

Street Address: 275 Battery St
City: San Francisco
State: CA
ZIP Code: 94111-3332
General Phone: (415) 989-2522
General Email: mfernald@bizjournals.com
Publication Website: https://www.bizjournals.com/sanfrancisco/
Parent Company: American City Business Journals
Publisher Name: Mary Huss
Publisher Email: mhuss@bizjournals.com
Publisher Phone: (415) 288-4934
Editor Name: Jim Gardner
Editor Email: jgardner@bizjournals.com
Editor Phone: (415) 288-4955
Advertising Executive Name: Michael S. Fernald
Advertising Executive Email: mfernald@bizjournals.com

SAN FRANCISCO

SAN FRANCISCO EXAMINER

Street Address: 835 Market St.
City: San Francisco
State: CA
ZIP Code: 94103
General Phone: (415) 359-2600
General Email: jcurran@sfmediaco.com
Publication Website: https://www.sfexaminer.com/
Parent Company: San Francisco Media Company
Publisher Name: Jay Curran
Publisher Email: jcurran@sfmediaco.com
Editor Name: Sara Gaiser
Editor Email: sgaiser@sfmediaco.com
Advertising Executive Name: Emma Mai
Advertising Executive Email: emai@sfmediaco.com

SAN JOSE

ALMADEN RESIDENT

Street Address: 1095 the Alameda
City: San Jose
State: CA
ZIP Code: 95126-3142
General Phone: (408) 200-1000
General Email: mturpin@bayareanewsgroup.com
Publication Website: https://www.mercurynews.com/location/california/bay-area/east-bay/alameda-county/
Publisher Name: Sharon Ryan
Publisher Email: publisher@bayareanewsgroup.com
Editor Name: Randall Keith
Editor Email: rkeith@bayareanewsgroup.com
Editor Phone: (408) 271-3747
Advertising Executive Name: Michael Turpin
Advertising Executive Email: mturpin@bayareanewsgroup.com

SAN JOSE

CAMPBELL REPORTER

Street Address: 1095 the Alameda
City: San Jose
State: CA
ZIP Code: 95126-3142
General Phone: (408) 200-1000
General Email: mturpin@bayareanewsgroup.com
Publication Website: https://www.mercurynews.com/location/campbell/
Publisher Name: Sharon Ryan
Publisher Email: publisher@bayareanewsgroup.com
Editor Name: Randall Keith
Editor Email: rkeith@bayareanewsgroup.com
Editor Phone: (408) 271-3747
Advertising Executive Name: Michael Turpin
Advertising Executive Email: mturpin@bayareanewsgroup.com

SAN JOSE

FREMONT BULLETIN

Street Address: 4 N. Second Street, Suite 800
City: San Jose
State: CA
ZIP Code: 95113
General Phone: (408) 920-5000
General Email: jgeha@bayareanewsgroup.com
Publication Website: https://www.mercurynews.com/location/fremont/
Publisher Name: Sharon Ryan
Publisher Email: publisher@bayareanewsgroup.com
Editor Name: Bert Robinson
Editor Email: jhrobinson@bayareanewsgroup.com
Editor Phone: (408) 920-5970
Advertising Executive Name: Michael Turpin
Advertising Executive Email: mturpin@bayareanewsgroup.com

SAN JOSE

ROSE GARDEN RESIDENT

Street Address: 1095 the Alameda
City: San Jose
State: CA
ZIP Code: 95126-3142
General Phone: (408) 200-1000
General Email: mturpin@bayareanewsgroup.com
Publication Website: https://www.mercurynews.com/location/rose-garden/
Publisher Name: Sharon Ryan
Publisher Email: publisher@bayareanewsgroup.com
Editor Name: Randall Keith
Editor Email: rkeith@bayareanewsgroup.com
Editor Phone: (408) 271-3747
Advertising Executive Name: Michael Turpin
Advertising Executive Email: mturpin@bayareanewsgroup.com

SAN JOSE

SAN JOSE BUSINESS JOURNAL

Street Address: 125 S Market St
City: San Jose
State: CA
ZIP Code: 95113-2292
General Phone: (408) 295-5028
General Email: wkupiec@bizjournals.com
Publication Website: https://www.bizjournals.com/sanjose/
Parent Company: American City Business Journals

SAN JOSE

SARATOGA NEWS

Street Address: 4 N. Second Street
City: San Jose
State: CA
ZIP Code: 95113
General Phone: (408) 920-5000
General Email: mturpin@bayareanewsgroup.com
Publication Website: http://www.mercurynews.com/saratoga
Publisher Name: Sharon Ryan
Publisher Email: publisher@bayareanewsgroup.com
Editor Name: Randall Keith
Editor Email: rkeith@bayareanewsgroup.com
Editor Phone: (408) 271-3747
Advertising Executive Name: Michael Turpin
Advertising Executive Email: mturpin@bayareanewsgroup.com

SAN JOSE

THE CUPERTINO COURIER

Street Address: 1095 the Alameda
City: San Jose
State: CA
ZIP Code: 95126-3142
General Phone: (408) 200-1000
General Email: jkohler@bayareanewsgroup.com
Publication Website: https://www.mercurynews.com/location/cupertino/
Publisher Name: Sharon Ryan
Publisher Email: publisher@bayareanewsgroup.com
Editor Name: Randall Keith
Editor Email: rkeith@bayareanewsgroup.com
Editor Phone: (408) 271-3747
Advertising Executive Name: Jenny Kohler
Advertising Executive Email: jkohler@bayareanewsgroup.com

SANTA ANA

ANAHEIM BULLETIN

Street Address: 625 N Grand Ave
City: Santa Ana
State: CA
ZIP Code: 92701-4347
General Phone: (714) 634-1567
General Email: anaheimhillsnews@ocregister.com
Publication Website: https://www.ocregister.com/location/california/orange-county/anaheim/
Publisher Name: Ron Hasse
Publisher Email: publisher@scng.com
Publisher Phone: (818) 713-3883
Editor Name: Leo Smith
Editor Email: leosmith@scng.com
Editor Phone: (714) 796-7835
Advertising Executive Name: Kyla Rodriguez
Advertising Executive Email: krodriguez@scng.com

SANTA ANA

FOUNTAIN VALLEY VIEW

Street Address: 625 N Grand Ave
City: Santa Ana
State: CA
ZIP Code: 92701-4347
General Phone: (877) 469-7344
General Email: advertising@scng.com
Publication Website: https://www.ocregister.com/2005/11/14/fountain-valley-view/
Publisher Name: Ron Hasse
Publisher Email: publisher@scng.com
Publisher Phone: (818) 713-3883
Editor Name: Carlos Aviles
Editor Email: caviles@scng.com
Editor Phone: (951) 368-9330
Advertising Executive Name: Kyla Rodriguez
Advertising Executive Email: krodriguez@scng.com

SANTA ANA

FULLERTON NEWS-TRIBUNE

Street Address: 625 N Grand Ave
City: Santa Ana
State: CA
ZIP Code: 92701
General Phone: (877) 469-7344
General Email: jeongpark@scng.com
Publication Website: https://www.ocregister.com/location/california/orange-county/fullerton/
Publisher Name: Ron Hasse
Publisher Email: publisher@scng.com
Publisher Phone: (818) 713-3883
Editor Name: Leo Smith
Editor Email: leosmith@scng.com
Editor Phone: (714) 796-7835
Advertising Executive Name: Kyla Rodriguez
Advertising Executive Email: krodriguez@scng.com

SANTA ANA

HUNTINGTON BEACH WAVE

Street Address: 625 N Grand Ave
City: Santa Ana
State: CA
ZIP Code: 92701-4347
General Phone: (877) 469-7344
General Email: advertising@scng.com
Publication Website: http://ocregister.com/huntington?fbclid=IwAR2THX7GPa56SNVlpc81MJjbvVR754cDQynCxd20JZv7weRhCwUaDc8kL5c
Publisher Name: Ron Hasse
Publisher Email: publisher@scng.com
Publisher Phone: (818) 713-3883
Editor Name: Carlos Aviles
Editor Email: caviles@scng.com
Editor Phone: (951) 368-9330
Advertising Executive Name: Kyla Rodriguez
Advertising Executive Email: krodriguez@scng.com

SANTA ANA

IRVINE WORLD NEWS

Street Address: 625 N Grand Ave
City: Santa Ana
State: CA
ZIP Code: 92701-4347
General Phone: (877) 469-7344
General Email: advertising@scng.com
Publication Website: https://www.ocregister.com/location/california/orange-county/irvine/
Publisher Name: Ron Hasse
Publisher Email: publisher@scng.com
Publisher Phone: (818) 713-3883
Editor Name: Carlos Aviles
Editor Email: caviles@scng.com
Editor Phone: (951) 368-9330
Advertising Executive Name: Kyla Rodriguez
Advertising Executive Email: krodriguez@scng.com

SANTA ANA

LAGUNA BEACH NEWS POST

Street Address: 625 N Grand Ave
City: Santa Ana
State: CA
ZIP Code: 92701-4347
General Phone: (877) 469-7344
General Email: advertising@scng.com
Publication Website: https://www.ocregister.com/location/california/orange-county/laguna-beach/
Publisher Name: Ron Hasse
Publisher Email: publisher@scng.com
Publisher Phone: (818) 713-3883
Editor Name: Carlos Aviles
Editor Email: caviles@scng.com
Editor Phone: (951) 368-9330
Advertising Executive Name: Kyla Rodriguez
Advertising Executive Email: krodriguez@scng.com

SANTA ANA

LAGUNA NEWS-POST

Street Address: 625 N Grand Ave
City: Santa Ana
State: CA
ZIP Code: 92701-4347
General Phone: (714) 796-7954
General Email: lagunanewspost@ocregister.com
Publication Website: https://www.ocregister.com/location/california/orange-county/laguna-beach/
Publisher Name: Ron Hasse
Publisher Email: publisher@scng.com
Publisher Phone: (818) 713-3883
Editor Name: Leo Smith
Editor Email: leosmith@scng.com
Editor Phone: (714) 796-7835
Advertising Executive Name: Kyla Rodriguez
Advertising Executive Email: krodriguez@scng.com

SANTA ANA

ORANGE CITY NEWS

Street Address: 625 N Grand Ave
City: Santa Ana
State: CA
ZIP Code: 92701-4347
General Phone: (714) 796-7954
General Email: jeongpark@scng.com
Publication Website: https://www.ocregister.com/location/california/orange-county/orange/
Publisher Name: Ron Hasse
Publisher Email: publisher@scng.com
Publisher Phone: (818) 713-3883
Editor Name: Leo Smith
Editor Email: leosmith@scng.com
Editor Phone: (714) 796-7835
Advertising Executive Name: Kyla Rodriguez
Advertising Executive Email: krodriguez@scng.com

SANTA ANA

PLACENTIA NEWS TIMES

Community Newsforms in the U.S.

SANTA ANA

Street Address: 625 N Grand Ave
City: Santa Ana
State: CA
ZIP Code: 92701-4347
General Phone: (877) 469-7344
General Email: advertising@scng.com
Publication Website: https://www.ocregister.com/location/california/orange-county/placentia/
Publisher Name: Ron Hasse
Publisher Email: publisher@scng.com
Publisher Phone: (818) 713-3883
Editor Name: Carlos Aviles
Editor Email: caviles@scng.com
Editor Phone: (951) 368-9330
Advertising Executive Name: Kyla Rodriguez
Advertising Executive Email: krodriguez@scng.com

SANTA ANA

SADDLEBACK VALLEY NEWS - MISSION VIEJO

Street Address: 625 N Grand Ave
City: Santa Ana
State: CA
ZIP Code: 92701-4347
General Phone: (877) 469-7344
General Email: advertising@scng.com
Publication Website: https://www.ocregister.com/2006/07/31/saddleback-valley-news/
Publisher Name: Ron Hasse
Publisher Email: publisher@scng.com
Publisher Phone: (818) 713-3883
Editor Name: Carlos Aviles
Editor Email: caviles@scng.com
Editor Phone: (951) 368-9330
Advertising Executive Name: Patty Roberts
Advertising Executive Email: proberts@scng.com

SANTA ANA

SAN CLEMENTE SUN POST

Street Address: 625 N Grand Ave
City: Santa Ana
State: CA
ZIP Code: 92701-4347
General Phone: (877) 469-7344
General Email: advertising@scng.com
Publication Website: https://www.ocregister.com/location/california/orange-county/san-clemente/
Publisher Name: Ron Hasse
Publisher Email: publisher@scng.com
Publisher Phone: (818) 713-3883
Editor Name: Carlos Aviles
Editor Email: caviles@scng.com
Editor Phone: (951) 368-9330
Advertising Executive Name: Patty Roberts
Advertising Executive Email: proberts@scng.com

SANTA ANA

SUN-POST NEWS

Street Address: 625 N Grand Ave
City: Santa Ana
State: CA
ZIP Code: 92701-4347
General Phone: (949) 492-4316
General Email: advertising@scng.com
Publication Website: https://www.ocregister.com/2008/04/09/where-to-pick-up-the-sun-post-news/
Publisher Name: Ron Hasse
Publisher Email: publisher@scng.com
Publisher Phone: (818) 713-3883
Editor Name: Carlos Aviles
Editor Email: caviles@scng.com
Editor Phone: (951) 368-9330
Advertising Executive Name: Patty Roberts
Advertising Executive Email: proberts@scng.com

SANTA ANA

YORBA LINDA STAR

Street Address: 625 N Grand Ave
City: Santa Ana
State: CA
ZIP Code: 92701
General Phone: (714) 634-1567
General Email: iwheeler@scng.com
Publication Website: https://www.ocregister.com/
Publisher Name: Ron Hasse
Publisher Email: publisher@scng.com
Publisher Phone: (818) 713-3883
Editor Name: Tom Bray
Editor Email: tbray@scng.com
Editor Phone: (310) 543-6601
Advertising Executive Name: Kyla Rodriguez
Advertising Executive Email: krodriguez@scng.com

SANTA CLARITA

SANTA CLARITA VALLEY SIGNAL

Street Address: 26330 Diamond Place
City: Santa Clarita
State: CA
ZIP Code: 91350
General Phone: (661) 259-1234
General Email: rbudman@signalscv.com
Publication Website: https://signalscv.com/
Parent Company: Paladin Multi-Media Group, Inc.
Publisher Name: Richard Budman
Publisher Email: rbudman@signalscv.com
Publisher Phone: (661) 287-5501
Editor Name: Tim Whyte
Editor Email: twhyte@signalscv.com
Editor Phone: (661) 287-5591
Advertising Executive Name: Maureen Daniels
Advertising Executive Email: mdaniels@signalscv.com

SANTA MARIA

ADOBE PRESS

Street Address: 3200 Skyway Dr
City: Santa Maria
State: CA
ZIP Code: 93455
General Phone: (888) 422-8822
General Email: gtamayo@leecentralcoastnews.com
Publication Website: http://theadobepress.com/
Publisher Name: Davis Taylor
Publisher Email: publisher@leecentralcoastnews.com
Publisher Phone: (805) 739-2154
Editor Name: Emily Slater
Editor Email: eslater@theadobepress.com
Editor Phone: (805) 739-2217
Advertising Executive Name: Marie Schaefer
Advertising Executive Email: mschaefer@leecentralcoastnews.com

SANTA MARIA

THE LOMPOC RECORD

Street Address: 3200 Skyway Dr
City: Santa Maria
State: CA
ZIP Code: 93455
General Phone: (888) 422-8822
General Email: gtamayo@leecentralcoastnews.com
Publication Website: https://lompocrecord.com/
Publisher Name: Davis Taylor
Publisher Email: publisher@leecentralcoastnews.com
Publisher Phone: (805) 739-2154
Editor Name: Emily Slater
Editor Email: eslater@theadobepress.com
Editor Phone: (805) 739-2217
Advertising Executive Name: Marie Schaefer
Advertising Executive Email: mschaefer@leecentralcoastnews.com

SANTA MONICA

BRENTWOOD NEWS

Street Address: 2116 Wilshire Blvd
City: Santa Monica
State: CA
ZIP Code: 90403
General Phone: (310) 310-2637
General Email: advertising@mirrormediagroupla.com
Publication Website: https://brentwoodnewsla.com/
Editor Name: Sam Cantanzaro
Editor Email: sam@mirrormediagroupla.com
Editor Phone: (310) 310-2637, ext : 103
Advertising Executive Email: advertising@mirrormediagroupla.com/

SANTA MONICA

CENTURY CITY NEWS

Street Address: 2116 Wilshire Blvd
City: Santa Monica
State: CA
ZIP Code: 90403
General Phone: (310) 310-2637
General Email: advertising@mirrormediagroupla.com/
Publication Website: https://centurycity-westwoodnews.com/
Parent Company: Mirror Media Group
Editor Name: Sam Cantanzaro
Editor Email: sam@mirrormediagroupla.com
Editor Phone: (310) 310-2637, ext : 103
Advertising Executive Email: advertising@mirrormediagroupla.com/

SANTA MONICA

LA PRIDE

Street Address: 2116 Wilshire Blvd
City: Santa Monica
State: CA
ZIP Code: 90403
General Phone: (310) 310-2637
General Email: advertising@mirrormediagroupla.com/
Publication Website: https://thepridela.com/masthead/
Parent Company: Mirror Media Group
Publisher Name: Tj Montemer
Editor Name: Henry Giardina
Editor Email: henry@smmirror.com
Editor Phone: (413) 320-7081
Advertising Executive Name: Judy Swarz
Advertising Executive Email: judy@smmirror.com

SANTA MONICA

SANTA MONICA MIRROR

Street Address: 2116 Wilshire Blvd
City: Santa Monica
State: CA
ZIP Code: 90403
General Phone: (310) 310-2637
General Email: advertising@mirrormediagroupla.com
Publication Website: https://smmirror.com/
Parent Company: Mirror Media Group
Editor Name: Sam Cantanzaro
Editor Email: sam@mirrormediagroupla.com
Editor Phone: (310) 310-2637x103
Advertising Executive Name: Max Montemer
Advertising Executive Email: max@mirrormediagroupla.com

SANTA MONICA

WESTSIDE TODAY

Street Address: 2116 Wilshire Blvd
City: Santa Monica
State: CA
ZIP Code: 90403
General Phone: (310) 310-2637
General Email: advertising@mirrormediagroupla.com
Publication Website: https://westsidetoday.com/
Parent Company: Mirror Media Group
Editor Name: Sam Cantanzaro
Editor Email: sam@mirrormediagroupla.com
Advertising Executive Name: Max Montemer
Advertising Executive Email: max@smmirror.com

SANTA MONICA

YO! VENICE

Street Address: 2116 Wilshire Blvd
City: Santa Monica
State: CA
ZIP Code: 90403
General Phone: (310) 310-2637
General Email: advertising@mirrormediagroupla.com
Publication Website: https://yovenice.com/
Parent Company: Mirror Media Group
Editor Name: Sam Cantanzaro
Editor Email: sam@mirrormediagroupla.com
Advertising Executive Name: Max Montemer
Advertising Executive Email: max@smmirror.com

SCOTTS VALLEY

PRESS BANNER

Street Address: 5215 Scotts Valley Dr
City: Scotts Valley
State: CA
ZIP Code: 95066
General Phone: (831) 438-2500
General Email: pbads@pressbanner.com
Publication Website: https://www.ttownmedia.com/press_banner/
Parent Company: TankTown Media
Editor Name: Cherie Anderson
Editor Email: pbeditor@pressbanner.com
Advertising Executive Name: Cherie Anderson
Advertising Executive Email: pbeditor@pressbanner.com

SEAL BEACH

LEISURE WORLD GOLDEN RAIN NEWS

Street Address: 13533 Seal Beach Blvd.
City: Seal Beach
State: CA
ZIP Code: 90740
General Phone: (562) 430-0534
General Email: davesaunders@lwsbnews.com
Publication Website: https://www.lwsb.com/
Parent Company: Golden Rain Foundations

SEAL BEACH

NEWS ENTERPRISE

Street Address: 216 Main St
City: Seal Beach
State: CA
ZIP Code: 90740

General Phone: (562) 431-1397
General Email: info@newsenterprise.net
Publication Website: https://event-newsenterprise.com/
Parent Company: CommunityMedia Corp.
Publisher Name: Steven Remery
Publisher Email: publisher@localnewspapers.org
Publisher Phone: (562) 431-1397
Editor Name: David Young
Editor Email: editor@event-newsenterprise.com
Editor Phone: (562) 251-6628
Advertising Executive Name: Carlos Munoz
Advertising Executive Email: carlos@sunnews.org

SEASIDE

MONTEREY COUNTY WEEKLY

Street Address: 668 Williams Ave
City: Seaside
State: CA
ZIP Code: 93955
General Phone: (831) 394-5656
General Email: erik@mcweekly.com
Publication Website: https://www.montereycountyweekly.com/
Parent Company: Milestones, Inc.
Publisher Name: Erik Cushman
Publisher Email: erik@mcweekly.com
Publisher Phone: (831) 394-5656, ext : 125
Editor Name: Sara Rubin
Editor Email: sara@mcweekly.com
Editor Phone: (831) 394-5656, ext : 120
Advertising Executive Name: George Kassal
Advertising Executive Email: george@mcweekly.com

SEBASTOPOL

SONOMA WEST TIMES AND NEWS

Street Address: 1070 Gravenstein Highway South Suite 220
City: Sebastopol
State: CA
ZIP Code: 95472
General Phone: (707) 823-7845
General Email: laura@sonomawest.com
Publication Website: http://www.sonomawest.com/
Parent Company: Sonoma West Publishers
Publisher Name: Rollie Atkinson
Publisher Email: rollie@sonomawest.com
Editor Name: Laura Hagar Rush
Editor Email: laura@sonomawest.com
Editor Phone: (707) 322-8696

SOLANA BEACH

CARMEL VALLEY NEWS

Street Address: 380 Stevens Ave
City: Solana Beach
State: CA
ZIP Code: 92075
General Phone: (858) 876-7997
General Email: editor@delmartimes.net
Publication Website: https://www.delmartimes.net/carmel-valley
Parent Company: NantMedia Holdings, LLC
Publisher Name: Phyllis Pfeiffer
Publisher Email: ppfeiffer@lajollalight.com
Publisher Phone: (858) 875-5940
Editor Name: Lorine Wright
Editor Email: editor@delmartimes.net
Editor Phone: (858) 876-8945

SOLANA BEACH

DEL MAR TIMES

Street Address: 380 Stevens Ave
City: Solana Beach
State: CA
ZIP Code: 92075
General Phone: (858) 876-7997
General Email: editor@delmartimes.net
Publication Website: https://www.delmartimes.net/
Parent Company: San Diego Union-Tribune, LLC
Publisher Name: Phyllis Pfeiffer
Publisher Email: ppfeiffer@lajollalight.com
Publisher Phone: (858) 875-5940
Editor Name: Lorine Wright
Editor Email: editor@delmartimes.net
Editor Phone: (858) 876-8945
Advertising Executive Name: Don Parks

SOLANA BEACH

ENCINITAS ADVOCATE

Street Address: 380 Stevens Ave
City: Solana Beach
State: CA
ZIP Code: 92075-2069
General Phone: (858) 876-7997
General Email: editor@delmartimes.net
Publication Website: https://www.encinitasadvocate.com/
Parent Company: San Diego Union-Tribune, LLC
Publisher Name: Phyllis Pfeiffer
Publisher Email: ppfeiffer@lajollalight.com
Publisher Phone: (858) 875-5940
Editor Name: Lorine Wright
Editor Email: editor@delmartimes.net
Editor Phone: (858) 876-8945

SOLANA BEACH

RANCHO SANTA FE REVIEW

Street Address: 380 Stevens Ave Ste 316
City: Solana Beach
State: CA
ZIP Code: 92075
General Phone: (858) 876-7997
General Email: editor@rsfreview.com
Publication Website: https://www.ranchosantafereview.com/
Parent Company: NantMedia Holdings, LLC
Publisher Name: Phyllis Pfeiffer
Publisher Email: ppfeiffer@lajollalight.com
Publisher Phone: (858) 875-5940
Editor Name: Lorine Wright
Editor Email: editor@delmartimes.net
Editor Phone: (858) 876-8945
Advertising Executive Name: Don Parks

SOLANA BEACH

SOLANA BEACH SUN

Street Address: 380 Stevens Ave
City: Solana Beach
State: CA
ZIP Code: 92075
General Phone: (858) 876-7997
General Email: editor@delmartimes.net
Publication Website: https://www.delmartimes.net/solana-beach-sun
Parent Company: NantMedia Holdings, LLC
Publisher Name: Phyllis Pfeiffer
Publisher Email: ppfeiffer@lajollalight.com
Publisher Phone: (858) 875-5940
Editor Name: Lorine Wright
Editor Email: editor@delmartimes.net
Editor Phone: (858) 876-8945
Advertising Executive Name: Don Parks

SOLVANG

SANTA YNEZ VALLEY NEWS/EXTRA

Street Address: 423 2nd St
City: Solvang
State: CA
ZIP Code: 93463
General Phone: (805) 688-5522
General Email: publisher@leecentralcoastnews.com
Publication Website: https://syvnews.com/
Publisher Name: Davis Taylor
Publisher Email: publisher@leecentralcoastnews.com
Publisher Phone: (805) 739-2154
Editor Name: Marga Cooley
Editor Email: mcooley@leecentralcoastnews.com
Editor Phone: (805) 739-2143
Advertising Executive Name: Claudia Delgado
Advertising Executive Email: cdelgado@leecentralcoastnews.com

SONOMA

THE SONOMA INDEX-TRIBUNE

Street Address: 117 W Napa St
City: Sonoma
State: CA
ZIP Code: 95476
General Phone: (707) 938-2111
General Email: robert.lee@sonomanews.com
Publication Website: https://www.sonomanews.com/
Parent Company: Sonoma Media Investments
Publisher Name: EMILY CHARRIER
Publisher Email: emily.charrier@sonomanews.com
Publisher Phone: (707) 933-2711
Editor Name: Jason Walsh
Editor Email: jason.walsh@sonomanews.com
Editor Phone: (707) 933-2734
Advertising Executive Name: ROBERT LEE
Advertising Executive Email: robert.lee@sonomanews.com

SOUTH LAKE TAHOE

TAHOE DAILY TRIBUNE

Street Address: 3079 Harrison Ave
City: South Lake Tahoe
State: CA
ZIP Code: 96150
General Phone: (530) 541-3880
General Email: legals@tahoedailytribune.com
Publication Website: https://www.tahoedailytribune.com/
Parent Company: Swift Communications
Publisher Name: Rob Galloway
Publisher Email: rgalloway@tahoedailytribune.com
Publisher Phone: (530) 542-8046
Editor Name: Bill Rozak
Editor Email: brozak@tahoedailytribune.com
Editor Phone: (530) 542-8010
Advertising Executive Name: Annemarie Prudente
Advertising Executive Email: aprudente@tahoedailytribune.com

SOUTH PASADENA

LOS ANGELES DOWNTOWN NEWS

Street Address: 161 S. Pasadena Ave., Suite B
City: South Pasadena
State: CA
ZIP Code: 91030
General Phone: (626) 584-1500
General Email: michael@downtownnews.com
Publication Website: http://www.ladowntownnews.com/
Parent Company: Southland Publishing
Advertising Executive Name: Michael Lamb
Advertising Executive Email: michael@downtownnews.com

SOUTH PASADENA

SOUTH PASADENA REVIEW

Street Address: 1020 Mission St
City: South Pasadena
State: CA
ZIP Code: 91030
General Phone: (626) 799-1161
General Email: mhong@gavilanmedia.com
Publication Website: http://southpasadenareview.com/
Publisher Name: Charles Champion
Editor Name: Kevin Kenney
Editor Email: kkenney@gavilanmedia.com
Editor Phone: (626) 792-4914
Advertising Executive Name: Joelle Grossi
Advertising Executive Email: jgrossi@sanmarinotribune.com

SOUTH PASADENA

THE ARGONAUT

Street Address: 161 S. Pasadena Ave., Suite B
City: South Pasadena
State: CA
ZIP Code: 91030
General Phone: (310) 822-1629
General Email: jpiasecki@timespublications.com
Publication Website: https://argonautnews.com/
Parent Company: Times Media Group
Publisher Name: Rebecca Bermudez
Publisher Phone: (310) 574-7655
Editor Name: Joe Piasecki
Editor Email: jpiasecki@timespublications.com
Editor Phone: (310) 574-7652
Advertising Executive Name: Kay Christy

TAFT

DAILY MIDWAY DRILLER

Street Address: 800 Center St
City: Taft
State: CA
ZIP Code: 93268
General Phone: (661) 763-3171
General Email: cthompson@taftmidwaydriller.com
Publication Website: https://www.taftmidwaydriller.com/
Publisher Name: John Watkins
Publisher Email: jwatkins@ridgecrestca.com
Publisher Phone: (760) 375-4481
Editor Name: Doug Keeler
Editor Email: dkeeler@taftmidwaydriller.com
Advertising Executive Name: Christine Thompson
Advertising Executive Email: cthompson@taftmidwaydriller.com

TIBURON

THE ARK

Street Address: 1550 Tiburon Blvd
City: Tiburon
State: CA
ZIP Code: 94920
General Phone: (415) 435-2652
General Email: ads@thearknewspaper.com
Publication Website: http://www.thearknewspaper.com/
Parent Company: AMMI Publishing Co Inc
Publisher Name: Alison T. Gray
Editor Name: Kevin Hessel
Editor Email: editor@thearknewspaper.com
Editor Phone: (415) 435-2652
Advertising Executive Name: Henriette Corn
Advertising Executive Email: hcorn@thearknewspaper.com

Community Newspapers in the U.S.

TRACY

TRACY PRESS

Street Address: 145 W 10th St
City: Tracy
State: CA
ZIP Code: 95376
General Phone: (209) 835-3030
General Email: tpads@tracypress.com
Publication Website: https://www.ttownmedia.com/
Parent Company: TankTown Media

TURLOCK

THE CERES COURIER

Street Address: 121 S. Center Street, Second Floor
City: Turlock
State: CA
ZIP Code: 95380
General Phone: (209) 537-5032
General Email: hvanderveen@morrismultimedia.com
Publication Website: https://www.cerescourier.com/
Parent Company: Morris Multimedia, Inc.
Publisher Name: Hank Vander Veen
Publisher Email: hvanderveen@morrismultimedia.com
Publisher Phone: (209) 249-3503
Editor Name: Jeff Benziger
Editor Email: jbenziger@cerescourier.com
Editor Phone: (209) 633-3583
Advertising Executive Name: Charles Webber
Advertising Executive Email: cwebber@cerescourier.com

TURLOCK

TURLOCK JOURNAL

Street Address: 121 S. Center Street, Second Floor
City: Turlock
State: CA
ZIP Code: 95380
General Phone: (209) 634-9141
General Email: circulation@turlockjournal.com
Publication Website: https://www.turlockjournal.com/
Parent Company: Morris Multimedia, Inc.
Publisher Name: Hank Vander Veen
Publisher Email: hvanderveen@turlockjournal.com
Publisher Phone: (209) 249-3503
Editor Name: Kristina Hacker
Editor Email: khacker@turlockjournal.com
Editor Phone: (209) 633-1421
Advertising Executive Name: Beth Flanagan
Advertising Executive Email: bflanagan@turlockjournal.com

UKIAH

THE WILLITS NEWS

Street Address: 617 S. State St.
City: Ukiah
State: CA
ZIP Code: 95482
General Phone: (707) 459-4643
General Email: advertising@willitsnews.com
Publication Website: https://www.willitsnews.com/
Parent Company: Media News Group
Editor Name: Aura Whittaker
Editor Email: awhittaker@willitsnews.com
Editor Phone: (707) 841-2123
Advertising Executive Name: Sarah Delk-Pritchard
Advertising Executive Email: sdelk@record-bee.com

VALLEY CENTER

VALLEY ROADRUNNER

Street Address: 29115 Valley Center Rd
City: Valley Center
State: CA
ZIP Code: 92082
General Phone: (760) 749-1112
General Email: advertising@valleycenter.com
Publication Website: http://www.valleycenter.com/
Parent Company: Roadrunner Publications, Inc.
Publisher Name: Justin Salter
Editor Name: David Ross

VENTURA

VENTURA COUNTY REPORTER

Street Address: 700 E Main St
City: Ventura
State: CA
ZIP Code: 93001
General Phone: (805) 648-2244
General Email: diane@vcreporter.com
Publication Website: http://vcreporter.com/
Parent Company: Times Media Group
Editor Name: Michael Sullivan
Editor Email: editor@vcreporter.com

VICTORVILLE

HESPERIA STAR

Street Address: 13891 Park Ave
City: Victorville
State: CA
ZIP Code: 92392
General Phone: (760) 241-7744
General Email: snakutin@vvdailypress.com
Publication Website: https://www.vvdailypress.com/hesperia-star
Parent Company: Gannett
Publisher Name: Steve Nakutin
Publisher Email: snakutin@vvdailypress.com
Publisher Phone: (760) 951-6288
Editor Name: Matthew Cabe
Editor Email: mcabe@vvdailypress.com
Editor Phone: (760) 490-0052
Advertising Executive Name: Steve Nakutin
Advertising Executive Email: snakutin@vvdailypress.com

VICTORVILLE

VICTORVILLE DAILY PRESS

Street Address: 13891 Park Ave
City: Victorville
State: CA
ZIP Code: 92392
General Phone: (760) 241-7744
General Email: snakutin@vvdailypress.com
Publication Website: https://www.vvdailypress.com/
Parent Company: Gannett
Publisher Name: Steve Nakutin
Publisher Email: snakutin@vvdailypress.com
Publisher Phone: (760) 951-6288
Editor Name: Matthew Cabe
Editor Email: mcabe@vvdailypress.com
Editor Phone: (760) 490-0052
Advertising Executive Name: Steve Nakutin
Advertising Executive Email: snakutin@vvdailypress.com

WALNUT

EASTVALE COMMUNITY NEWS

Street Address: 385 S. Lemon Ave., Suite H
City: Walnut
State: CA
ZIP Code: 91789
General Phone: (909) 464-1200
General Email: info@anapr.com
Publication Website: https://anapr.com/
Parent Company: ANAPR
Editor Email: editor@anapr.com
Advertising Executive Email: design@anapr.com

WALNUT CREEK

ALAMEDA JOURNAL

Street Address: 2850 Shadelands Dr
City: Walnut Creek
State: CA
ZIP Code: 94598
General Phone: (925) 935-2525
General Email: publisher@bayareanewsgroup.com
Publication Website: https://www.eastbaytimes.com/
Publisher Name: Sharon Ryan
Publisher Email: publisher@bayareanewsgroup.com
Editor Name: Frank Pine
Editor Email: editor@bayareanewsgroup.com
Editor Phone: (408) 920-5456
Advertising Executive Name: Michael Turpin
Advertising Executive Email: mturpin@bayareanewsgroup.com

WALNUT CREEK

EAST BAY TIMES

Street Address: 2850 Shadelands Dr
City: Walnut Creek
State: CA
ZIP Code: 94598
General Phone: (925) 935-2525
General Email: publisher@bayareanewsgroup.com
Publication Website: https://www.eastbaytimes.com/
Publisher Name: Sharon Ryan
Publisher Email: publisher@bayareanewsgroup.com
Editor Name: Frank Pine
Editor Email: editor@bayareanewsgroup.com
Editor Phone: (408) 920-5456
Advertising Executive Name: Michael Turpin
Advertising Executive Email: mturpin@bayareanewsgroup.com

WALNUT CREEK

LAMORINDA SUN

Street Address: 2850 Shadelands Dr
City: Walnut Creek
State: CA
ZIP Code: 94598
General Phone: (925) 935-2525
General Email: publisher@bayareanewsgroup.com
Publication Website: https://www.eastbaytimes.com/
Publisher Name: Sharon Ryan
Publisher Email: publisher@bayareanewsgroup.com
Editor Name: Frank Pine
Editor Email: editor@bayareanewsgroup.com
Editor Phone: (408) 920-5456
Advertising Executive Name: Michael Turpin
Advertising Executive Email: mturpin@bayareanewsgroup.com

WEAVERVILLE

TRINITY JOURNAL

Street Address: 500 Main St
City: Weaverville
State: CA
ZIP Code: 96093
General Phone: (530) 623-2055
General Email: editor@trinityjournal.com
Publication Website: http://www.trinityjournal.com/
Parent Company: WRA Enterprises, Inc.
Editor Name: Wayne R. Agner
Editor Email: editor@trinityjournal.com

WEST SACRAMENTO

THE NEWS-LEDGER

Street Address: 1040 W Capitol Ave
City: West Sacramento
State: CA
ZIP Code: 95691
General Phone: (916) 371-8030
General Email: editor@news-ledger.com
Publication Website: http://www.westsac.com/news-ledger/
Editor Name: Monica Stark
Editor Email: editor@news-ledger.com
Editor Phone: (916) 371-8030

WRIGHTWOOD

MOUNTAINEER PROGRESS

Street Address: 3407 State Highway 2
City: Wrightwood
State: CA
ZIP Code: 92397
General Phone: (760) 249-3245
General Email: newsroom@mtprogress.net
Publication Website: http://www.mtprogress.net/

COLORADO

AKRON

AKRON NEWS-REPORTER

Street Address: 69 Main Ave
City: Akron
State: CO
ZIP Code: 80720-1439
General Phone: (970) 345-2296
General Email: jbusing@akronnewsreporter.com
Publication Website: http://www.akronnewsreporter.com/

ASPEN

SNOWMASS SUN

Street Address: 314 E Hyman Ave
City: Aspen
State: CO
ZIP Code: 81611-1918
General Phone: (970) 925-3414
General Email: mail@aspentimes.com
Publication Website: https://www.aspentimes.com/
Parent Company: Swift Communications

AURORA

AURORA SENTINEL

Street Address: 12100 E Iliff Ave Ste 102
City: Aurora
State: CO
ZIP Code: 80014-1277
General Phone: (303) 750-7555
General Email: legals@sentinelcolorado.com

Publication Website: http://www.aurorasentinel.com/

BOULDER

BROOMFIELD ENTERPRISE

Street Address: 2500 55th St
City: Boulder
State: CO
ZIP Code: 80301-5740
General Phone: (970) 215-4943
General Email: clabozan@prairiemountainmedia.com
Publication Website: https://www.broomfieldenterprise.com/
Parent Company: Media News Group

BOULDER

COLORADO HOMETOWN WEEKLY

Street Address: 2500 55th St
City: Boulder
State: CO
ZIP Code: 80301
General Phone: (303) 684-5218
General Email: clabozan@prairiemountainmedia.com
Publication Website: https://www.coloradohometownweekly.com/
Parent Company: Media News Group

BRIGHTON

BRIGHTON STANDARD BLADE

Street Address: 143 S. 2nd Place
City: Brighton
State: CO
ZIP Code: 80601-1626
General Phone: (303) 659-2522
Publication Website: https://www.thebrightonblade.com/
Parent Company: Landmark Community Newspapers

BRIGHTON

COMMERCE CITY SENTINEL EXPRESS

Street Address: 143 S. 2nd Place
City: Brighton
State: CO
ZIP Code: 80601-1626
General Phone: (303) 659-2522
Publication Website: https://www.commercecitysentinel.com/
Parent Company: Landmark Community Newspapers

BRIGHTON

FORT LUPTON PRESS

Street Address: 143 S. 2nd Place
City: Brighton
State: CO
ZIP Code: 80601-1626
General Phone: (303) 659-2522
Publication Website: https://www.ftluptonpress.com
Parent Company: Landmark Community Newspapers

BRUSH

THE BRUSH NEWS-TRIBUNE

Street Address: 216 Clayton St
City: Brush
State: CO
ZIP Code: 80723
General Phone: (970) 842-5516
General Email: horner@brushnewstribune.com
Publication Website: https://www.brushnewstribune.com/
Parent Company: Digital First Media

BUENA VISTA

THE CHAFFEE COUNTY TIMES

Street Address: 209 W Main St
City: Buena Vista
State: CO
ZIP Code: 81211
General Phone: (719) 395-8621
General Email: ckennedy@chaffeecountytimes.com
Publication Website: http://www.chaffeecountytimes.com
Parent Company: Arkansas Valley Publishing

BURLINGTON

BURLINGTON RECORD

Street Address: 202 S 14th St
City: Burlington
State: CO
ZIP Code: 80807
General Phone: (719) 346-5381
General Email: brecordadvertising@plainstel.com
Publication Website: https://www.burlington-record.com/
Parent Company: Media News Group

CARBONDALE

THE SOPRIS SUN

Street Address: PO Box 399
City: Carbondale
State: CO
ZIP Code: 81623
General Phone: (970) 510-3003
General Email: news@soprissun.com
Publication Website: https://www.soprissun.com/

COLORADO SPRINGS

COLORADO SPRINGS BUSINESS JOURNAL

Street Address: 235 S. Nevada Ave.
City: Colorado Springs
State: CO
ZIP Code: 80903
General Phone: (719) 634-5905
General Email: amy.sweet@csbj.com
Publication Website: https://www.csbj.com/
Parent Company: Colorado Community Media

CORTEZ

CORTEZ JOURNAL

Street Address: 8 W Main St
City: Cortez
State: CO
ZIP Code: 81321
General Phone: (970) 565-8527
General Email: news@the-journal.com
Publication Website: https://the-journal.com/tags/cortez
Parent Company: Ballantine Communications, Inc.

CORTEZ

DOLORES STAR

Street Address: 8 W Main St
City: Cortez
State: CO
ZIP Code: 81321-3141
General Phone: (970) 565-8527
General Email: news@the-journal.com
Publication Website: https://the-journal.com/tags/dolores

CORTEZ

MANCOS TIMES

Street Address: 8 W Main St
City: Cortez
State: CO
ZIP Code: 81321-3141
General Phone: (970) 565-8527
General Email: news@the-journal.com
Publication Website: https://the-journal.com/tags/mancos

CRESTED BUTTE

CRESTED BUTTE NEWS

Street Address: 301 Belleview
City: Crested Butte
State: CO
ZIP Code: 81224
General Phone: (970) 349-0500
General Email: nolan@crestedbuttenews.com
Publication Website: http://crestedbuttenews.com/
Parent Company: John Leonardi

DENVER

COLORADO STATESMAN

Street Address: 30 E. Pikes Peak Avenue, Suite #100
City: Denver
State: CO
ZIP Code: 80903
General Phone: (303) 837-8600
General Email: info@coloradopolitics.com
Publication Website: https://www.coloradopolitics.com/
Parent Company: Colorado Politics LLC

DENVER

DENVER BUSINESS JOURNAL

Street Address: 1660 Lincoln Street, Suite 1700
City: Denver
State: CO
ZIP Code: 80290
General Phone: (303) 803-9200
General Email: denver@bizjournals.com
Publication Website: https://www.bizjournals.com/denver/
Parent Company: American City Business Journals

DURANGO

PINE RIVER TIMES

Street Address: 1275 Main Avenue
City: Durango
State: CO
ZIP Code: 81301
General Phone: (970) 274-3504
General Email: prt@pinerivertimes.com
Publication Website: https://pinerivertimes.com/
Parent Company: Ballantine Communications, Inc.

EADS

KIOWA COUNTY PRESS

Street Address: 1208 Maine St
City: Eads
State: CO
ZIP Code: 81036
General Phone: (719) 438-5800
General Email: kiowacountypress@gmail.com
Publication Website: http://kiowacountypress.net/
Parent Company: Chris Sorensen

EAGLE

THE EAGLE VALLEY ENTERPRISE

Street Address: Post Office Box 450
City: Eagle
State: CO
ZIP Code: 81631
General Phone: (970) 328-6656
General Email: cbukovich@vaildaily.com
Publication Website: https://www.swiftcom.com/brands/eagle-valley-enterprise
Parent Company: Swift Communications

EATON

NORTH WELD HERALD

Street Address: PO Box 775
City: Eaton
State: CO
ZIP Code: 80615-3598
General Phone: (970) 454-5551
General Email: nwherald@qwestoffice.net
Publication Website: http://www.smalltownpapers.com/newspapers/newspaper.php?id=295

ENGLEWOOD

THE LITTLETON INDEPENDENT

Street Address: 750 W. Hampden Ave., Suite 225
City: Englewood
State: CO
ZIP Code: 80110
General Phone: (303) 566-4100
General Email: circulation@coloradocommunitymedia.com
Publication Website: https://littletonindependent.net/
Parent Company: Colorado Community Media

ESTES PARK

ESTES PARK TRAIL-GAZETTE

Street Address: 351 Moraine Avenue
City: Estes Park
State: CO
ZIP Code: 80517
General Phone: (970) 586-3356
General Email: romerom@eptrail.com
Publication Website: https://www.eptrail.com/
Parent Company: Media News Group

EVERGREEN

COLUMBINE COURIER

Street Address: 27902 Meadow Dr
City: Evergreen
State: CO

Community Newspapers in the U.S.

ZIP Code: 80439
General Phone: (303) 674-5534
General Email: kristin@evergreenco.com
Publication Website: https://www.columbinecourier.com/

EVERGREEN

THE CANYON COURIER

Street Address: 27972 Meadow Dr
City: Evergreen
State: CO
ZIP Code: 80439
General Phone: (303) 350-1039
General Email: kristin@evergreenco.com
Publication Website: https://www.canyoncourier.com/
Parent Company: Landmark Community Newspapers

FORT COLLINS

WINDSOR BEACON

Street Address: 1300 Riverside Ave, Suite 200
City: Fort Collins
State: CO
ZIP Code: 80524-4353
General Phone: (970) 493-6397
General Email: jkurtyak@coloradoan.com
Publication Website: https://www.coloradoan.com/windsor-beacon/

FORT MORGAN

MORGAN TIMES REVIEW

Street Address: CO
City: Fort Morgan
State: CO
ZIP Code: 80701
General Phone: (970) 867-5651
General Email: porterb@brushnewstribune.com
Publication Website: https://www.fortmorgantimes.com/
Parent Company: Digital First Media

FOUNTAIN

EL PASO COUNTY ADVERTISER & NEWS

Street Address: 120 E Ohio Ave
City: Fountain
State: CO
ZIP Code: 80817
General Phone: (719) 382-5611
General Email: news@epcan.com
Publication Website: https://www.epcan.com/
Parent Company: Shopper Press, Inc.

GLENWOOD SPRINGS

POST INDEPENDENT

Street Address: 824 Grand Ave
City: Glenwood Springs
State: CO
ZIP Code: 81601-3557
General Phone: (970) 945-8515
General Email: jraehal@postindependent.com
Publication Website: https://www.postindependent.com/

GRANBY

SKY-HI NEWS

Street Address: 424 E Agate Ave
City: Granby
State: CO
ZIP Code: 80446
General Phone: (970) 887-3334
General Email: etrainor@skyhinews.com
Publication Website: https://www.skyhinews.com/
Parent Company: Swift Communications

GUNNISON

GUNNISON COUNTRY TIMES

Street Address: 218 N Wisconsin St
City: Gunnison
State: CO
ZIP Code: 81230
General Phone: (970) 641-1414
General Email: publisher@gunnisontimes.com
Publication Website: http://www.gunnisontimes.com/

HAXTUN

HAXTUN-FLEMING HERALD

Street Address: 217 S COLORADO AVE
City: Haxtun
State: CO
ZIP Code: 80731
General Phone: (970) 774-6118
General Email: news@hfherald.com
Publication Website: http://www.hfherald.com/

HOLYOKE

HOLYOKE ENTERPRISE

Street Address: 130 N Interocean Ave
City: Holyoke
State: CO
ZIP Code: 80734-1013
General Phone: (970) 854-2811
Publication Website: http://www.holyokeenterprise.com/
Parent Company: Johnson Publications

IDAHO SPRINGS

CLEAR CREEK COURANT

Street Address: 1639 Miner St.
City: Idaho Springs
State: CO
ZIP Code: 80452
General Phone: (303) 567-4491
Publication Website: https://www.clearcreekcourant.com/
Parent Company: Landmark Community Newspapers

JOHNSTOWN

THE JOHNSTOWN BREEZE

Street Address: 7 S Parish Ave
City: Johnstown
State: CO
ZIP Code: 80534
General Phone: (970) 587-4525
General Email: editor@johnstownbreeze.com
Publication Website: http://myjohnstownbreeze.com/
Parent Company: Paul and Joyce Williams

JULESBURG

JULESBURG ADVOCATE

Street Address: 114 W 1st St
City: Julesburg
State: CO
ZIP Code: 80737
General Phone: (970) 474-3388
General Email: advertising@julesburgadvocate.com
Publication Website: http://www.julesburgadvocate.com/
Parent Company: Digital First Media

LA JUNTA

AG JOURNAL

Street Address: 422 Colorado Ave
City: La Junta
State: CO
ZIP Code: 81050
General Phone: (719) 384-4475
General Email: jhamilton@ljtdmail.com
Publication Website: https://www.agjournalonline.com/
Parent Company: Gannett

LA JUNTA

THE FOWLER TRIBUNE

Street Address: 422 Colorado Avenue
City: La Junta
State: CO
ZIP Code: 81050
General Phone: (719) 384-4475
General Email: jzemba@ljtdmail.com
Publication Website: https://www.fowlertribune.com/
Parent Company: Gannett

LAMAR

THE LAMAR LEDGER

Street Address: 222 S Main St
City: Lamar
State: CO
ZIP Code: 81052
General Phone: (719) 336-2266
General Email: rstagner@lamarledger.com, blasley@lamarledger.com
Publication Website: https://www.lamarledger.com/
Parent Company: Media News Group

LAS ANIMAS

BENT COUNTY DEMOCRAT

Street Address: 510 Carson Ave
City: Las Animas
State: CO
ZIP Code: 81054
General Phone: (719) 456-1333
General Email: jzemba@ljtdmail.com
Publication Website: http://www.bcdemocratonline.com/
Parent Company: Gannett

LEADVILLE

HERALD DEMOCRAT

Street Address: 717 Harrison Ave
City: Leadville
State: CO
ZIP Code: 80461
General Phone: (719) 486-0641
General Email: heraldweb@leadvilleherald.com
Publication Website: http://www.leadvilleherald.com/
Parent Company: Arkansas Valley Publishing

LIMON

THE LIMON LEADER

Street Address: P.O. Box 1300
City: Limon
State: CO
ZIP Code: 80828
General Phone: (719) 775-2064
General Email: publisher@thelimonleader.com
Publication Website: https://thelimonleader.com/
Parent Company: SMH Publications LLC

LYONS

THE LYONS RECORDER

Street Address: 454 Main St
City: Lyons
State: CO
ZIP Code: 80540
General Phone: (303) 823-6625
General Email: lyonsrecorder.editor@gmail.com.
Publication Website: http://www.lyonsrecorder.com/

MEEKER

THE RIO BLANCO HERALD TIMES

Street Address: 592 Main St
City: Meeker
State: CO
ZIP Code: 81641
General Phone: (970) 878-4017
General Email: ads@theheraldtimes.com
Publication Website: https://www.theheraldtimes.com/
Parent Company: Solas Publications, Inc.

MONTE VISTA

CENTER POST-DISPATCH

Street Address: 835 1st Ave
City: Monte Vista
State: CO
ZIP Code: 81144-1474
General Phone: (719) 852-3531
General Email: tspaulding@valleypublishinginc.com
Publication Website: https://centerpostdispatch.com/
Parent Company: Valley Publishing, Inc.

MONTE VISTA

THE CONEJOS COUNTY CITIZEN

Street Address: 835 1st Ave
City: Monte Vista
State: CO
ZIP Code: 81144-1474
General Phone: (719) 852-3531
General Email: tspaulding@valleypublishinginc.com
Publication Website: https://www.conejoscountycitizen.com/
Parent Company: News Media Grouip

MONTE VISTA

THE DEL NORTE PROSPECTOR

Street Address: 835 1st Ave
City: Monte Vista
State: CO
ZIP Code: 81144-1474
General Phone: (719) 852-3531
General Email: tspaulding@

MONTE VISTA

THE MINERAL COUNTY MINER

Street Address: 835 1st Ave
City: Monte Vista
State: CO
ZIP Code: 81144-1474
General Phone: (719) 852-3531
General Email: tspaulding@valleypublishinginc.com
Publication Website: https://mineralcountyminer.com/
Parent Company: News Media Grouip

MONTE VISTA

THE MONTE VISTA JOURNAL

Street Address: 835 1st Ave
City: Monte Vista
State: CO
ZIP Code: 81144-1474
General Phone: (719) 852-3531
General Email: tspaulding@valleypublishinginc.com
Publication Website: https://montevistajournal.com/
Parent Company: News Media Grouip

MONTE VISTA

THE SOUTH FORK TINES

Street Address: 835 1st Ave
City: Monte Vista
State: CO
ZIP Code: 81144-1474
General Phone: (719) 852-3531
General Email: tspaulding@valleypublishinginc.com
Publication Website: https://www.southforktines.com/
Parent Company: News Media Grouip

NUCLA

SAN MIGUEL BASIN FORUM

Street Address: PO Box 9
City: Nucla
State: CO
ZIP Code: 81424-0009
General Phone: (970) 864-7425
General Email: ads@nntcwireless.com
Publication Website: http://www.smalltownpapers.com/newspapers/newspaper.php?id=357

PAGOSA SPRINGS

THE PAGOSA SPRINGS SUN

Street Address: 466 Pagosa St
City: Pagosa Springs
State: CO
ZIP Code: 81147-9955
General Phone: (970) 264-2100
General Email: tjay@pagosasun.com
Publication Website: http://www.pagosasun.com/pagosa-springs-sun-staff-contact

SALIDA

MOUNTAIN GUIDE

Street Address: 125 E 2nd St
City: Salida
State: CO
ZIP Code: 81201
General Phone: (719) 539-6691
General Email: mmweb@themountainmail.com
Publication Website: http://www.themountainmail.com/
Parent Company: Arkansas Valley Publishing

SILVERTON

SILVERTON STANDARD AND THE MINER

Street Address: 1316 Snowden St.
City: Silverton
State: CO
ZIP Code: 81433
General Phone: (970) 387-5477
General Email: silvertonads@gmail.com
Publication Website: http://www.silvertonstandard.com/

SIMLA

RANCHLAND NEWS

Street Address: 115 Sioux Ave
City: Simla
State: CO
ZIP Code: 80835
General Phone: (719) 541-2288
General Email: ranchland@bigsandytelco.com
Publication Website: http://www.ranchland-news.com/

STEAMBOAT SPRINGS

STEAMBOAT PILOT

Street Address: 32 10th St.
City: Steamboat Springs
State: CO
ZIP Code: 80487
General Phone: (970) 879-1502
General Email: lmolen@steamboatpilot.com
Publication Website: https://www.steamboatpilot.com/

STRASBURG

EASTERN COLORADO NEWS

Street Address: P.O. Box 829
City: Strasburg
State: CO
ZIP Code: 80136
General Phone: (303) 622-9796
General Email: dclaussen@i-70scout.com
Publication Website: http://i-70scout.com/

TELLURIDE

THE NORWOOD POST

Street Address: PO Box 2315
City: Telluride
State: CO
ZIP Code: 81435
General Phone: (970) 728-9788
General Email: dusty@telluridedailyplanet.com
Publication Website: https://www.telluridenews.com/

WALSENBURG

THE SIGNATURE

Street Address: 508 Main Street
City: Walsenburg
State: CO
ZIP Code: 81089
General Phone: (719) 738-1415
General Email: editor.worldjournal@gmail.com
Publication Website: https://huerfanoworldjournal.com/

WESTCLIFFE

WET MOUNTAIN TRIBUNE

Street Address: 404 E Main St
City: Westcliffe
State: CO
ZIP Code: 81252
General Phone: (719) 783-2361
General Email: ads@wetmountaintribune.com
Publication Website: https://wetmountaintribune.com/
Parent Company: Little Publishing Company, Inc.

WINDSOR

WINDSOR NOW

Street Address: 423 Main St
City: Windsor
State: CO
ZIP Code: 80550
General Phone: (970) 674-1431
General Email: information@windsorchamber.net
Publication Website: http://www.mywindsornow.com/

CONNECTICUT

BRIDGEPORT

DARIEN NEWS

Street Address: 410 State St
City: Bridgeport
State: CT
ZIP Code: 6604
General Phone: (203) 333-0161
General Email: dariennews@hearstmediact.com
Publication Website: https://www.darientimes.com
Parent Company: Hearst Corp.
Editor Name: Susan Shultz
Editor Phone: (203) 912-4564
Advertising Executive Name: Lauren Spicehandler
Advertising Executive Phone: (203) 842-2734
Mechanical specifications: Type page 10 x 16; E - 5 cols, between; A - 5 cols, between; C - 5 cols, between.
Published Days: Fri
Avg. Paid Circ.: 784
Avg. Free Circ.: 12
Audit Company: Sworn/Estimate/Non-Audited
Audit Date: 43626

BRIDGEPORT

NEW CANAAN NEWS

Street Address: 410 State St
City: Bridgeport
State: CT
ZIP Code: 6604
General Phone: (203) 330-6245
General Email: agonzalez@scni.com
Publication Website: http://www.newcanaannewsonline.com/
Parent Company: Hearst Corp.
Editor Name: John Kovach
Editor Phone: (203) 966-9541
Advertising Executive Phone: (203) 333-4151
Delivery Methods: Mail`Newsstand
Published Days: Thur
Avg. Paid Circ.: 2710
Audit Company: Sworn/Estimate/Non-Audited
Audit Date: 43626

BRIDGEPORT

WESTPORT NEWS

Street Address: 410 State St
City: Bridgeport
State: CT
ZIP Code: 6604
General Phone: (203) 337-4877
General Email: lteixeira@ctpost.com
Publication Website: https://www.westport-news.com/
Parent Company: Hearst Corp.
Editor Name: Liana Teixeira
Editor Email: lteixeira@ctpost.com
Editor Phone: (203) 842-2582
Advertising Executive Email: advertise@hearstmediact.com
Advertising Executive Phone: (203) 330-6245
Mechanical specifications: Type page 10 1/4 x 15 1/2; A - 5 cols, 1 7/8, between.
Published Days: Wed`Fri
Avg. Paid Circ.: 2505
Audit Company: Sworn/Estimate/Non-Audited
Audit Date: 43626

CHESHIRE

THE CHESHIRE HERALD

Street Address: 195 South Main Street
City: Cheshire
State: CT
ZIP Code: 6410
General Phone: (203) 272-5316
General Email: circulation@cheshireherald.com
Publication Website: https://www.cheshireherald.com/
Parent Company: The Cheshire Herald
Publisher Name: Elizabeth White
Publisher Email: lwhite@rjmediagroup.com
Publisher Phone: (203) 317-2226
Editor Name: John Rook
Editor Email: jrook@cheshireherald.com
Advertising Executive Name: Jim Mizener
Advertising Executive Email: jmizener@rjmediagroup.com
Year Established: 1953
Mechanical specifications: Type page 10 x 15.5; 5 cols, 1.875, 0.125 between
Published Days: Thur
Avg. Paid Circ.: 7200
Avg. Free Circ.: 197
Audit Company: Sworn/Estimate/Non-Audited
Audit Date: 43626

GLASTONBURY

GLASTONBURY CITIZEN

Street Address: 87 Nutmeg Ln
City: Glastonbury
State: CT
ZIP Code: 6033
General Phone: (860) 633-4691
General Email: rivereast@snet.com
Publication Website: http://www.glcitizen.com/
Parent Company: The Glastonbury Citizen, Inc.
Publisher Name: Jim Hallas
Publisher Email: jim@glcitizen.com
Publisher Phone: (860) 633-4691, ext : 226

Community Newspapers in the U.S.

Editor Name: Mike Thompson
Editor Email: bulletin@glcitizen.com
Editor Phone: (860) 633-4691, ext : 225
Advertising Executive Name: Carole Saucier
Advertising Executive Email: bulletin@glcitizen.com
Advertising Executive Phone: (860) 633-4691, ext : 237
Own Printing Facility?: Y
Mechanical specifications: Type page 10 1/2 x 15 1/2; E - 4 cols, 2 3/4, 1/6 between; A - 8 cols, 1 1/6, 1/6 between; C - 8 cols, 1 1/6, 1/6 between.
Published Days: Thur
Avg. Paid Circ.: 7792
Audit Company: Sworn/Estimate/Non-Audited
Audit Date: 43626

GLASTONBURY

RIVEREAST NEWS BULLETIN

Street Address: 87 Nutmeg Ln
City: Glastonbury
State: CT
ZIP Code: 6033
General Phone: (860) 633-4691
General Email: jim@glcitizen.com
Publication Website: http://glcitizen.com/
Parent Company: The Glastonbury Citizen, Inc.
Publisher Name: Jim Hallas
Publisher Email: jim@glcitizen.com
Publisher Phone: (860) 633-4691, ext : 226
Editor Name: Jim Hallas
Editor Email: jim@glcitizen.com
Editor Phone: (860) 633-4691, ext : 226
Advertising Executive Name: Carole Saucier
Advertising Executive Email: bulletin@glcitizen.com
Advertising Executive Phone: (860) 633-4691, ext : 237
Mechanical specifications: Type page 10 1/2 x 15 1/2; E - 8 cols, 1 3/16, between; A - 8 cols, 1 3/16, between; C - 8 cols, 1 3/16, between.
Published Days: Fri
Avg. Free Circ.: 27050
Audit Company: Sworn/Estimate/Non-Audited
Audit Date: 43626

HAMDEN

THE HAMDEN JOURNAL

Street Address: PO Box 187101
City: Hamden
State: CT
ZIP Code: 6518
General Phone: (203) 687-3075
General Email: office@goodnewspublishing.solutions
Publication Website: https://www.goodnewspublishing.solutions/?fbclid=IwAR1FVF59DISNP7fQ6W8Vaqf2hBm7QeTEvGGs1QwCdLzNiYfoS0RoCJMTOVo
Parent Company: Good News Publishing LLC
Publisher Name: Shala J. LaTorraca
Publisher Phone: (203) 687-3075
Advertising Executive Name: Chris LaTorraca
Advertising Executive Phone: (203) 687-3075
Delivery Methods: Carrier`Racks
Year Established: 2010
Own Printing Facility?: Y
Commercial printers?: Y
Mechanical specifications: Type page 12 x 21; E - 6 cols, 1 7/8, 1/8 between; A - 6 cols, 1 7/8, 1/8 between; C - 10 cols, 1 1/8, between.
Published Days: Mthly
Published Other: Semi-Monthly
Avg. Free Circ.: 7500
Audit Company: Sworn/Estimate/Non-Audited
Audit Date: 43626

HARTFORD

COURANT COMMUNITY - COLCHESTER

Street Address: 285 Broad St
City: Hartford
State: CT
ZIP Code: 6115
General Phone: (860) 241-6200
General Email: custserv@courant.com
Publication Website: https://www.courant.com/community/colchester/
Publisher Name: Andrew Julien
Publisher Email: ajulien@courant.com
Publisher Phone: (000) 241-0007
Editor Name: Andrew Julien
Editor Email: ajulien@courant.com
Editor Phone: (860) 241-3997
Advertising Executive Email: mtingley@courant.com
Advertising Executive Phone: (860) 647-5401
Delivery Methods:
  Mail`Newsstand`Carrier`Racks
Published Days: Thur
Avg. Free Circ.: 13620
Audit Company: Sworn/Estimate/Non-Audited
Audit Date: 43626

HARTFORD

COURANT COMMUNITY - EAST HARTFORD

Street Address: 285 Broad St
City: Hartford
State: CT
ZIP Code: 6115
General Phone: (860) 241-6200
General Email: custserv@courant.com
Publication Website: https://www.courant.com/community/east-hartford
Publisher Name: Andrew Julien
Publisher Email: ajulien@courant.com
Publisher Phone: (860) 241-3997
Editor Name: Andrew Julien
Editor Email: ajulien@courant.com
Editor Phone: (860) 241-3997
Advertising Executive Email: mtingley@courant.com
Advertising Executive Phone: (860) 647-5401
Delivery Methods:
  Mail`Newsstand`Carrier`Racks
Mechanical specifications: Type page 9.875" x 11.25"; 4 cols
Published Days: Thur
Avg. Free Circ.: 13289
Audit Company: Sworn/Estimate/Non-Audited
Audit Date: 43626

HARTFORD

COURANT COMMUNITY - ENFIELD

Street Address: 285 Broad St
City: Hartford
State: CT
ZIP Code: 6115
General Phone: (860) 241-6200
General Email: custserv@courant.com
Publication Website: https://www.courant.com/community/enfield/
Publisher Name: Andrew Julien
Publisher Email: ajulien@courant.com
Publisher Phone: (860) 241-3997
Editor Name: Andrew Julien
Editor Email: ajulien@courant.com
Editor Phone: (860) 241-3997
Advertising Executive Email: mtingley@courant.com
Advertising Executive Phone: (860) 647-5401
Delivery Methods:
  Mail`Newsstand`Carrier`Racks
Published Days: Thur
Avg. Free Circ.: 18829

HARTFORD

COURANT COMMUNITY - GLASTONBURY

Street Address: 285 Broad St
City: Hartford
State: CT
ZIP Code: 6115
General Phone: (860) 241-6200
General Email: custserv@courant.com
Publication Website: https://www.courant.com/community/glastonbury/
Publisher Name: Andrew Julien
Publisher Email: ajulien@courant.com
Publisher Phone: (860) 241-3997
Editor Name: Andrew Julien
Editor Email: ajulien@courant.com
Editor Phone: (860) 241-3997
Advertising Executive Email: mtingley@courant.com
Advertising Executive Phone: (860) 647-5401
Delivery Methods:
  Mail`Newsstand`Carrier`Racks
Published Days: Thur
Avg. Free Circ.: 9856
Audit Company: Sworn/Estimate/Non-Audited
Audit Date: 43626

HARTFORD

COURANT COMMUNITY - HEBRON

Street Address: 285 Broad St
City: Hartford
State: CT
ZIP Code: 6115
General Phone: (860) 241-6200
General Email: custserv@courant.com
Publication Website: https://www.courant.com/community/hebron
Publisher Name: Andrew Julien
Publisher Email: ajulien@courant.com
Publisher Phone: (860) 241-3997
Editor Name: Andrew Julien
Editor Email: ajulien@courant.com
Editor Phone: (860) 241-3997
Advertising Executive Email: mtingley@courant.com
Advertising Executive Phone: (860) 647-5401
Delivery Methods:
  Mail`Newsstand`Carrier`Racks
Published Days: Thur
Avg. Free Circ.: 7867
Audit Company: Sworn/Estimate/Non-Audited
Audit Date: 43626

HARTFORD

COURANT COMMUNITY - KILLINGLY

Street Address: 285 Broad St
City: Hartford
State: CT
ZIP Code: 6115
General Phone: (860) 241-6200
General Email: custserv@courant.com
Publication Website: https://www.courant.com/community/killingly
Publisher Name: Andrew Julien
Publisher Email: ajulien@courant.com
Publisher Phone: (860) 241-3997
Editor Name: Andrew Julien
Editor Email: ajulien@courant.com
Editor Phone: (860) 241-3997
Advertising Executive Email: mtingley@courant.com
Advertising Executive Phone: (860) 647-5401
Delivery Methods:
  Mail`Newsstand`Carrier`Racks
Published Days: Thur
Avg. Free Circ.: 16076
Audit Company: Sworn/Estimate/Non-Audited
Audit Date: 43626

HARTFORD

COURANT COMMUNITY - MANCHESTER

Street Address: 285 Broad St
City: Hartford
State: CT
ZIP Code: 6115
General Phone: (860) 241-6200
General Email: custserv@courant.com
Publication Website: https://www.courant.com/community/manchester
Publisher Name: Andrew Julien
Publisher Email: ajulien@courant.com
Publisher Phone: (860) 241-3997
Editor Name: Andrew Julien
Editor Email: ajulien@courant.com
Editor Phone: (860) 241-3997
Advertising Executive Email: mtingley@courant.com
Advertising Executive Phone: (860) 647-5401
Delivery Methods:
  Mail`Newsstand`Carrier`Racks
Published Days: Thur
Avg. Free Circ.: 15633
Audit Company: Sworn/Estimate/Non-Audited
Audit Date: 43626

HARTFORD

COURANT COMMUNITY - PUTNAM

Street Address: 285 Broad St
City: Hartford
State: CT
ZIP Code: 6115
General Phone: (860) 241-6200
General Email: custserv@courant.com
Publication Website: https://www.courant.com/community/putnam/
Publisher Name: Andrew Julien
Publisher Email: ajulien@courant.com
Publisher Phone: (860) 241-3997
Editor Name: Andrew Julien
Editor Email: ajulien@courant.com
Editor Phone: (860) 241-3997
Advertising Executive Email: mtingley@courant.com
Advertising Executive Phone: (860) 647-5401
Delivery Methods:
  Mail`Newsstand`Carrier`Racks
Published Days: Thur
Avg. Free Circ.: 9598
Audit Company: Sworn/Estimate/Non-Audited
Audit Date: 43626

HARTFORD

COURANT COMMUNITY - SOUTH WINDSOR

Street Address: 285 Broad St
City: Hartford
State: CT
ZIP Code: 6115
General Phone: (860) 241-6200
General Email: custserv@courant.com
Publication Website: https://www.courant.com/community/south-windsor/
Publisher Name: Andrew Julien
Publisher Email: ajulien@courant.com
Publisher Phone: (860) 241-3997
Editor Name: Andrew Julien
Editor Email: ajulien@courant.com
Editor Phone: (860) 241-3997
Advertising Executive Email: mtingley@courant.com
Advertising Executive Phone: (860) 647-5401
Delivery Methods:
  Mail`Newsstand`Carrier`Racks
Published Days: Thur

Avg. Free Circ.: 7604
Audit Company: Sworn/Estimate/Non-Audited
Audit Date: 43626

HARTFORD

COURANT COMMUNITY - STAFFORD

Street Address: 285 Broad St
City: Hartford
State: CT
ZIP Code: 6115
General Phone: (860) 241-6200
General Email: custserv@courant.com
Publication Website: https://www.courant.com/community/stafford/
Publisher Name: Andrew Julien
Publisher Email: ajulien@courant.com
Publisher Phone: (860) 241-3997
Editor Name: Andrew Julien
Editor Email: ajulien@courant.com
Editor Phone: (860) 241-3997
Advertising Executive Email: mtingley@courant.com
Advertising Executive Phone: (860) 647-5401
Delivery Methods:
    Mail`Newsstand`Carrier`Racks
Published Days: Thur
Avg. Free Circ.: 7607
Audit Company: Sworn/Estimate/Non-Audited
Audit Date: 43626

HARTFORD

COURANT COMMUNITY - VERNON

Street Address: 285 Broad St
City: Hartford
State: CT
ZIP Code: 6115
General Phone: (860) 241-6200
General Email: custserv@courant.com
Publication Website: https://www.courant.com/community/vernon/
Publisher Name: Andrew Julien
Publisher Email: ajulien@courant.com
Publisher Phone: (860) 241-3997
Editor Name: Andrew Julien
Editor Email: ajulien@courant.com
Editor Phone: (860) 241-3997
Advertising Executive Email: mtingley@courant.com
Advertising Executive Phone: (860) 647-5401
Delivery Methods:
    Mail`Newsstand`Carrier`Racks
Published Days: Thur
Avg. Free Circ.: 15816
Audit Company: Sworn/Estimate/Non-Audited
Audit Date: 43626

HARTFORD

COURANT COMMUNITY - WEST HARTFORD

Street Address: 285 Broad St
City: Hartford
State: CT
ZIP Code: 6115
General Phone: (860) 241-6200
General Email: custserv@courant.com
Publication Website: https://www.courant.com/community/west-hartford/
Publisher Name: Andrew Julien
Publisher Email: ajulien@courant.com
Publisher Phone: (860) 241-3997
Editor Name: Andrew Julien
Editor Email: ajulien@courant.com
Editor Phone: (860) 241-3997
Advertising Executive Email: mtingley@courant.com
Advertising Executive Phone: (860) 647-5401
Published Days: Thur
Audit Company: Sworn/Estimate/Non-Audited

Audit Date: 43626

HARTFORD

COURANT COMMUNITY - WETHERSFIELD

Street Address: 285 Broad St
City: Hartford
State: CT
ZIP Code: 6115
General Phone: (860) 241-6200
General Email: custserv@courant.com
Publication Website: https://www.courant.com//community/wethersfield
Publisher Name: Andrew Julien
Publisher Email: ajulien@courant.com
Publisher Phone: (860) 241-3997
Editor Name: Andrew Julien
Editor Email: ajulien@courant.com
Editor Phone: (860) 241-3997
Advertising Executive Email: mtingley@courant.com
Advertising Executive Phone: (860) 647-5401
Published Days: Thur
Audit Company: Sworn/Estimate/Non-Audited
Audit Date: 43626

HARTFORD

COURANT COMMUNITY - WINDHAM

Street Address: 285 Broad St
City: Hartford
State: CT
ZIP Code: 6115
General Phone: (860) 241-6200
General Email: custserv@courant.com
Publication Website: https://www.courant.com/community/windham/
Publisher Name: Andrew Julien
Publisher Email: ajulien@courant.com
Publisher Phone: (860) 241-3997
Editor Name: Andrew Julien
Editor Email: ajulien@courant.com
Editor Phone: (860) 241-3997
Advertising Executive Email: mtingley@courant.com
Advertising Executive Phone: (860) 647-5401
Delivery Methods:
    Mail`Newsstand`Carrier`Racks
Published Days: Thur
Avg. Free Circ.: 12734
Audit Company: Sworn/Estimate/Non-Audited
Audit Date: 43626

HARTFORD

COURANT COMMUNITY - WINDSOR

Street Address: 285 Broad St
City: Hartford
State: CT
ZIP Code: 6115
General Phone: (860) 241-6200
General Email: custserv@courant.com
Publication Website: https://www.courant.com/community/windsor/
Publisher Name: Andrew Julien
Publisher Email: ajulien@courant.com
Publisher Phone: (860) 241-3997
Editor Name: Andrew Julien
Editor Email: ajulien@courant.com
Editor Phone: (860) 241-3997
Advertising Executive Email: mtingley@courant.com
Advertising Executive Phone: (860) 647-5401
Delivery Methods:
    Mail`Newsstand`Carrier`Racks
Published Days: Thur
Avg. Free Circ.: 9689
Audit Company: Sworn/Estimate/Non-Audited
Audit Date: 43626

HARTFORD

COURANT COMMUNITY - WINDSOR LOCKS

Street Address: 285 Broad St
City: Hartford
State: CT
ZIP Code: 6115
General Phone: (860) 241-6200
General Email: custserv@courant.com
Publication Website: https://www.courant.com/community/windsor-locks/
Publisher Name: Andrew Julien
Publisher Email: ajulien@courant.com
Publisher Phone: (860) 241-3997
Editor Name: Andrew Julien
Editor Email: ajulien@courant.com
Editor Phone: (860) 241-3997
Advertising Executive Email: mtingley@courant.com
Advertising Executive Phone: (860) 647-5401
Delivery Methods:
    Mail`Newsstand`Carrier`Racks
Published Days: Thur
Avg. Free Circ.: 9887
Audit Company: Sworn/Estimate/Non-Audited
Audit Date: 43626

HARTFORD

HARTFORD BUSINESS JOURNAL

Street Address: 15 Lewis St
City: Hartford
State: CT
ZIP Code: 6103
General Phone: (860) 236-9998
General Email: hartfordbusiness.com@cambeywest.com
Publication Website: https://www.hartfordbusiness.com/
Parent Company: New England Business Media
Publisher Name: Donna Collins
Publisher Email: dcollins@hartfordbusiness.com
Publisher Phone: (860) 236-9998, ext : 121
Editor Name: Greg Bordonaro
Editor Email: gbordonaro@hartfordbusiness.com
Editor Phone: (860) 236-9998, ext : 139
Advertising Executive Email: advertising@hartfordbusiness.com
Delivery Methods: Mail`Newsstand
Year Established: 1992
Published Days: Mon
Avg. Paid Circ.: 608
Avg. Free Circ.: 8662
Audit Company: CVC
Audit Date: 43622

MADISON

EAST HAVEN COURIER

Street Address: 724 Boston Post Rd
City: Madison
State: CT
ZIP Code: 6443
General Phone: (203) 245-1877
General Email: r.collins@shorepublishing.com
Publication Website: https://www.zip06.com/Assets/iMag/EastHavenCourier-01302020/
Parent Company: Shore Publishing
Publisher Name: Robyn Wolcott
Publisher Email: collins@shorepublishing.com
Publisher Phone: (203) 245-1877, ext : 6142
Advertising Executive Name: Lee Poruban
Advertising Executive Email: l.poruban@shorepublishing.com
Advertising Executive Phone: (203) 245-1877, ext : 6158
Delivery Methods: Carrier`Racks
Year Established: 1996
Mechanical specifications: Type page 9.7 x 10.25; 5 cols, 1.80, 0.20 between
Published Days: Thur
Avg. Free Circ.: 9347
Audit Company: CVC
Audit Date: 43988

MADISON

GUILFORD COURIER

Street Address: 724 Boston Post Rd
City: Madison
State: CT
ZIP Code: 6443
General Phone: (203) 245-1877
General Email: r.collins@shorepublishing.com
Publication Website: https://www.zip06.com/Assets/iMag/GuilfordCourier-01302020/
Parent Company: Shore Publishing
Publisher Name: Robyn Wolcott
Publisher Email: collins@shorepublishing.com
Publisher Phone: (203) 245-1877, ext : 6142
Advertising Executive Name: Mary Lyons
Advertising Executive Email: m.lyons@shorepublishing.com
Advertising Executive Phone: (203) 245-1877, ext : 6168
Delivery Methods: Carrier`Racks
Mechanical specifications: Type page 9.7 x 10.25; 5 cols, 1.80, 0.20 between
Published Days: Thur
Avg. Free Circ.: 7777
Audit Company: CVC
Audit Date: 43988

MADISON

HARBOR NEWS

Street Address: 724 Boston Post Rd
City: Madison
State: CT
ZIP Code: 6443
General Phone: (203) 245-1877
General Email: r.collins@shorepublishing.com
Publication Website: https://www.zip06.com/Assets/iMag/HarborNews-01302020/
Parent Company: Shore Publishing
Publisher Name: Robyn Wolcott
Publisher Email: collins@shorepublishing.com
Publisher Phone: (203) 245-1877, ext : 6142
Advertising Executive Name: Stephanie Chang
Advertising Executive Email: s.chang@shorepublishing.com
Advertising Executive Phone: (203) 245-1877, ext : 6144
Delivery Methods: Mail`Carrier`Racks
Own Printing Facility?: Y
Mechanical specifications: Type page 9.7 x 10.25; 5 cols, 1.80, 0.20 between
Published Days: Thur
Avg. Free Circ.: 10467
Audit Company: CVC
Audit Date: 43988

MADISON

NORTH HAVEN COURIER

Street Address: 724 Boston Post Rd
City: Madison
State: CT
ZIP Code: 6443
General Phone: (203) 245-1877
General Email: r.collins@shorepublishing.com
Publication Website: https://www.zip06.com/Assets/iMag/NorthHavenCourier-01302020/
Parent Company: Shore Publishing
Publisher Name: Robyn Wolcott
Publisher Email: collins@shorepublishing.com
Publisher Phone: (203) 245-1877, ext : 6142

Community Newspapers in the U.S.

III-185

Advertising Executive Name: Lee Poruban
Advertising Executive Email: l.poruban@shorepublishing.com
Advertising Executive Phone: (203) 245-1877, ext : 6158
Delivery Methods: Carrier`Racks
Mechanical specifications: Type page 9.7 x 10.25; 5 cols, 1.80, 0.20 between
Published Days: Thur
Avg. Free Circ.: 8518
Audit Company: CVC
Audit Date: 43988

MADISON

SHORE PUBLISHING

Street Address: 724 Boston Post Rd
City: Madison
State: CT
ZIP Code: 6443
General Phone: (203) 245-1877
General Email: news@shorepublishing.com
Publication Website: https://www.zip06.com/
Parent Company: Shore Publishing
Publisher Name: Robyn Wolcott
Publisher Email: collins@shorepublishing.com
Publisher Phone: (203) 245-1877, ext : 6142
Editor Name: Brian Boyd
Editor Email: b.boyd@shorepublishing.com
Editor Phone: (203) 245-1877, ext : 6136
Advertising Executive Name: Stephanie Chang
Advertising Executive Email: s.chang@shorepublishing.com
Advertising Executive Phone: (203) 245-1877, ext : 6144
Own Printing Facility?: Y
Mechanical specifications: Type page 9.7 x 10.25; 5 cols, 1.80, 0.20 between
Published Days: Thur`Fri
Avg. Free Circ.: 8546
Audit Company: Sworn/Estimate/Non-Audited
Audit Date: 43626

MADISON

SOURCE

Street Address: 724 Boston Post Rd
City: Madison
State: CT
ZIP Code: 6443
General Phone: (203) 245-1877
General Email: r.collins@shorepublishing.com
Publication Website: https://www.zip06.com/Assets/iMag/TheSource-01302020/
Parent Company: Media News Group
Publisher Name: Robyn Wolcott
Publisher Email: collins@shorepublishing.com
Publisher Phone: (203) 245-1877, ext : 6142
Advertising Executive Name: Stephanie Chang
Advertising Executive Email: s.chang@shorepublishing.com
Advertising Executive Phone: (203) 245-1877, ext : 6144
Delivery Methods: Carrier`Racks
Year Established: 1996
Mechanical specifications: Type page 9.7 x 10.25; 5 cols, 1.80, 0.20 between
Published Days: Thur
Avg. Free Circ.: 8483
Audit Company: CVC
Audit Date: 43988

MADISON

THE SOUND

Street Address: 724 Boston Post Rd
City: Madison
State: CT
ZIP Code: 6443
General Phone: (203) 245-1877
General Email: r.collins@shorepublishing.com
Publication Website: https://www.zip06.com/Assets/iMag/TheSound-01302020/
Parent Company: Shore Publishing
Publisher Name: Robyn Wolcott
Publisher Email: collins@shorepublishing.com
Publisher Phone: (203) 245-1877, ext : 6142
Advertising Executive Name: Melissa Nicholson
Advertising Executive Email: m.nicholson@shorepublishing.com
Advertising Executive Phone: (203) 245-1877, ext : 6113
Year Established: 1994
Mechanical specifications: Type page 9.7 x 10.25; 5 cols, 1.80, 0.20 between
Published Days: Thur
Avg. Free Circ.: 12657
Audit Company: CVC
Audit Date: 43988

MADISON

VALLEY COURIER

Street Address: 724 Boston Post Rd
City: Madison
State: CT
ZIP Code: 6443
General Phone: (203) 245-1877
General Email: r.collins@shorepublishing.com
Publication Website: https://www.zip06.com/Assets/iMag/ValleyCourier-01302020/
Parent Company: News Media Grouip
Publisher Name: Robyn Wolcott
Publisher Email: collins@shorepublishing.com
Publisher Phone: (203) 245-1877, ext : 6142
Advertising Executive Name: Lori Gregan
Advertising Executive Email: l.gregan@shorepublishing.com
Advertising Executive Phone: (203) 245-1877, ext : 6167
Delivery Methods: Carrier`Racks
Mechanical specifications: Type page 9.7 x 10.25; 5 cols, 1.80, 0.20 between
Published Days: Thur
Avg. Free Circ.: 6043
Audit Company: CVC
Audit Date: 43988

NEW BRITAIN

NEWINGTON TOWN CRIER

Street Address: 1 Herald Sq
City: New Britain
State: CT
ZIP Code: 06051-5009
General Phone: (860) 225-4601
General Email: editor@centralctcommunications.com
Publication Website: http://www.newingtontowncrier.com/
Parent Company: Central Connecticut Communications LLC
Publisher Name: Michael E. Schroeder
Publisher Phone: (860) 801-5099
Editor Name: Michael E. Schroeder
Editor Phone: (860) 801-5099
Advertising Executive Name: Gary Curran
Advertising Executive Phone: (860) 801-5073
Delivery Methods: Mail
Published Days: Fri
Audit Company: Sworn/Estimate/Non-Audited
Audit Date: 43626

NEW HAVEN

SHORELINE TIMES

Street Address: 100 Gando Dr
City: New Haven
State: CT
ZIP Code: 6513
General Phone: (203) 789-5200
General Email: sbraden@ctcentral.com
Publication Website: http://www.shorelinetimes.com/
Parent Company: Hearst Corp.
Editor Name: Susan Braden
Editor Email: sbraden@ctcentral.com
Advertising Executive Name: Elliot Huron
Advertising Executive Email: ehuron@newhavenregister.com
Advertising Executive Phone: (203) 680-9924
Mechanical specifications: Type page 10 1/4 x 16; E - 4 cols, 2 3/8, 1/6 between; A - 6 cols, 1 5/8, 1/6 between; C - 6 cols, 1 5/8, 1/6 between.
Published Days: Fri
Avg. Paid Circ.: 42709
Audit Company: AAM
Audit Date: 43625

NEW HAVEN

THE LITCHFIELD COUNTY TIMES

Street Address: 100 Gando Drive
City: New Haven
State: CT
ZIP Code: 6513
General Phone: (860) 294-0157
General Email: news@countytimes.com
Publication Website: http://www.countytimes.com/
Parent Company: Hearst Corp.
Editor Name: Catherine Guarnieri
Editor Email: catherine.guarnieri@hearstmediact.com
Editor Phone: (860) 294-0157
Advertising Executive Phone: (800) 922-7066
Year Established: 1981
Mechanical specifications: Type page 11.63 x 21; 6 cols, 1.80, 0.20 between
Published Days: Fri
Avg. Paid Circ.: 3335
Avg. Free Circ.: 25
Audit Company: Sworn/Estimate/Non-Audited
Audit Date: 43626

NEW HAVEN

WEST HARTFORD NEWS

Street Address: 100 Gando Dr
City: New Haven
State: CT
ZIP Code: 6513
General Phone: (860) 294-0157
General Email: westhartfordnews@ctcentral.com
Publication Website: http://www.westhartfordnews.com/
Parent Company: Hearst Corp.
Editor Name: Catherine Guarnieri
Editor Email: catherine.guarnieri@hearstmediact.com
Editor Phone: (860) 294-0157
Advertising Executive Name: Lisa Basile
Advertising Executive Email: lbasile@ctcentral.com
Advertising Executive Phone: (860) 685-9121
Delivery Methods: Mail`Newsstand
Year Established: 1931
Mechanical specifications: Type page 11.63 x 21; 6 cols, 1.80, 0.20 between
Published Days: Fri
Avg. Free Circ.: 10000
Audit Company: Sworn/Estimate/Non-Audited
Audit Date: 43626

NEW LONDON

NEW LONDON TIMES

Street Address: 47 Eugene Oneill Dr
City: New London
State: CT
ZIP Code: 06320-1231
General Phone: (860) 442-2200
General Email: memberservices@theday.com
Publication Website: https://www.theday.com/article/99999999/STATIC01/140719869
Parent Company: The Day Publishing Co.
Publisher Name: Tim Dwyer
Publisher Email: t.dwyer@theday.com
Publisher Phone: (860) 701-4379
Editor Name: Greg Smith
Editor Email: g.smith@theday.com
Editor Phone: (860) 701-4326
Advertising Executive Name: Shawn Palmer
Advertising Executive Email: s.palmer@theday.com
Advertising Executive Phone: (860) 701-4264
Commercial printers?: Y
Mechanical specifications: Type page 9.7 x 10.25; 5 cols, 1.80, 0.20 between
Published Days: Thur`Fri
Avg. Free Circ.: 11261
Audit Company: Sworn/Estimate/Non-Audited
Audit Date: 43626

NEW LONDON

THE GROTON TIMES

Street Address: 47 Eugene Oneill Dr
City: New London
State: CT
ZIP Code: 06320-6306
General Phone: (860) 442-2200
General Email: memberservices@theday.com
Publication Website: https://www.theday.com/
Parent Company: The Day Publishing Co.
Publisher Name: Tim Dwyer
Publisher Email: t.dwyer@theday.com
Publisher Phone: (860) 701-4379
Advertising Executive Name: Shawn Palmer
Advertising Executive Email: s.palmer@theday.com
Advertising Executive Phone: (860) 701-4264
Year Established: 1995
Commercial printers?: Y
Mechanical specifications: Type page 9.7 x 10.25; 5 cols, 1.80, 0.20 between
Published Days: Thur`Fri
Avg. Free Circ.: 11687
Audit Company: Sworn/Estimate/Non-Audited
Audit Date: 43626

NEW LONDON

THE LYME TIMES

Street Address: 47 Eugene Oneill Dr
City: New London
State: CT
ZIP Code: 06320-6306
General Phone: (860) 701-4480
General Email: k.drelich@theday.com
Publication Website: https://www.theday.com/section/nwsbytown&profile=1001
Parent Company: The Day Publishing Co.
Publisher Name: Tim Dwyer
Publisher Email: t.dwyer@theday.com
Publisher Phone: (860) 701-4379
Editor Name: M. Dirk Langeveld
Editor Email: d.langeveld@theday.com
Editor Phone: (860) 701-4301
Advertising Executive Name: Rich Swanson
Advertising Executive Email: r.swanson@theday.com
Advertising Executive Phone: (860) 701-4263
Own Printing Facility?: Y
Mechanical specifications: Type page 9.7 x 10.25; 5 cols, 1.80, 0.20 between
Published Days: Thur
Avg. Free Circ.: 14591
Audit Company: Sworn/Estimate/Non-Audited
Audit Date: 43626

NEW LONDON

THE MONTVILLE TIMES

Street Address: 47 Eugene Oneill Dr
City: New London
State: CT
ZIP Code: 06320-6306
General Phone: (860) 701-4367
General Email: b.kail@theday.com
Publication Website: https://www.theday.com/section/nwsbytown&profile=1031
Parent Company: The Day Publishing Co.
Publisher Name: Tim Dwyer
Publisher Email: t.dwyer@theday.com
Publisher Phone: (860) 701-4379
Editor Name: M. Dirk Langeveld
Editor Email: d.langeveld@theday.com
Editor Phone: (860) 701-4301
Advertising Executive Name: Rich Swanson
Advertising Executive Email: r.swanson@theday.com
Advertising Executive Phone: (860) 701-4263
Mechanical specifications: Type page 9.7 x 10.25; 5 cols, 1.80, 0.20 between
Published Days: Thur`Fri
Avg. Free Circ.: 6980
Audit Company: Sworn/Estimate/Non-Audited
Audit Date: 43626

NEW LONDON

THE MYSTIC TIMES

Street Address: 47 Eugene Oneill Dr
City: New London
State: CT
ZIP Code: 06320-6306
General Phone: (860) 701-4494
General Email: j.wojtas@theday.com
Publication Website: https://www.theday.com/section/nwsbytown&profile=1084
Parent Company: The Day Publishing Co.
Publisher Name: Tim Dwyer
Publisher Email: t.dwyer@theday.com
Publisher Phone: (860) 701-4379
Editor Name: M. Dirk Langeveld
Editor Email: d.langeveld@theday.com
Editor Phone: (860) 701-4301
Advertising Executive Name: Rich Swanson
Advertising Executive Email: r.swanson@theday.com
Advertising Executive Phone: (860) 701-4263
Own Printing Facility?: Y
Mechanical specifications: Type page 9.7 x 10.25; 5 cols, 1.80, 0.20 between
Published Days: Thur
Avg. Free Circ.: 7465
Audit Company: Sworn/Estimate/Non-Audited
Audit Date: 43626

NEW LONDON

THE THAMES RIVER TIMES

Street Address: 47 Eugene Oneill Dr
City: New London
State: CT
ZIP Code: 06320-6306
General Phone: (860) 442-2200
General Email: memberservices@theday.com
Publication Website: https://www.theday.com/article/20130328/nws01/303289687
Parent Company: The Day Publishing Co.
Publisher Name: Tim Dwyer
Publisher Email: t.dwyer@theday.com
Publisher Phone: (860) 701-4379
Editor Name: M. Dirk Langeveld
Editor Email: d.langeveld@theday.com
Editor Phone: (860) 701-4301
Advertising Executive Name: Rich Swanson
Advertising Executive Email: r.swanson@theday.com
Advertising Executive Phone: (860) 701-4263
Year Established: 1986
Mechanical specifications: Type page 9.7 x 10.25; 5 cols, 1.80, 0.20 between
Published Days: Thur
Avg. Free Circ.: 7626
Audit Company: Sworn/Estimate/Non-Audited
Audit Date: 43626

NEW MILFORD

NEW MILFORD SPECTRUM

Street Address: 43E Main Street
City: New Milford
State: CT
ZIP Code: 6776
General Phone: (203) 731-3340
General Email: ktorres@ctpost.com
Publication Website: https://www.newmilfordspectrum.com/
Parent Company: Hearst Corp.
Editor Name: Deborah Rose
Editor Email: drose@newstimes.com
Editor Phone: (203) 355-7324
Advertising Executive Phone: (203) 333-4151
Published Days: Fri
Avg. Paid Circ.: 19771
Avg. Free Circ.: 20598
Audit Company: Sworn/Estimate/Non-Audited
Audit Date: 43626

NEWTOWN

THE NEWTOWN BEE

Street Address: 5 Church Hill Rd
City: Newtown
State: CT
ZIP Code: 6470
General Phone: (203) 426-3141
General Email: ellen@thebee.com
Publication Website: https://www.newtownbee.com/
Parent Company: Bee Publishing Co., Inc.
Publisher Name: R. Scudder Smith
Editor Name: Nancy K. Crevier
Editor Email: editor@thebee.com
Advertising Executive Name: Sherri Baggett
Advertising Executive Email: sherri@thebee.com
Delivery Methods: Mail`Newsstand
Year Established: 1877
Own Printing Facility?: Y
Published Days: Fri
Avg. Paid Circ.: 8000
Avg. Free Circ.: 6300
Audit Company: Sworn/Estimate/Non-Audited
Audit Date: 43626

NORWALK

FAIRFIELD CITIZEN

Street Address: 301 Merritt 7-Suite 1
City: Norwalk
State: CT
ZIP Code: 06851-1075
General Phone: (203) 842-2500
General Email: fairfieldnews@hearstmediact.com
Publication Website: https://www.fairfieldcitizenonline.com/
Parent Company: Hearst Corp.
Editor Name: Thomas Henry
Editor Email: thomas.henry@hearstmediact.com
Editor Phone: (203) 842-2509
Advertising Executive Email: advertise@hearstmediact.com
Advertising Executive Phone: (203) 330-6245
Published Days: Wed`Fri
Avg. Paid Circ.: 1823
Audit Company: Sworn/Estimate/Non-Audited
Audit Date: 43626

NORWALK

WESTPORT MINUTEMAN

Street Address: 301 Merritt 7 - Suite 1
City: Norwalk
State: CT
ZIP Code: 6851
General Phone: (203) 842-2500
General Email: advertise@hearstmediact.com
Publication Website: http://minutemannewscenter.com
Parent Company: Hearst Corp.
Editor Name: Thomas Henry
Editor Email: thomas.henry@hearstmediact.com
Editor Phone: (203) 842-2509
Advertising Executive Email: advertise@hearstmediact.com
Advertising Executive Phone: (203) 330-6245
Delivery Methods: Mail
Year Established: 1992
Mechanical specifications: Type page 10.25 x 15.25; 5 cols, 1.875, 0.25 between
Published Days: Thur
Avg. Free Circ.: 11215
Audit Company: Sworn/Estimate/Non-Audited
Audit Date: 43626

PAWCATUCK

CHARLESTOWN PRESS

Street Address: 99 Mechanic Street
City: Pawcatuck
State: CT
ZIP Code: 6379
General Phone: (401) 348-1000
General Email: circulation@ricentral.com
Publication Website: https://www.thewesterlysun.com/news/charlestown/
Parent Company: Sun Publishing Company
Publisher Name: Jody Boucher
Publisher Email: jboucher@ricentral.com
Publisher Phone: (860) 495-8277
Editor Name: Corey Fyke
Editor Email: cfyke@thewesterlysun.com
Editor Phone: (860) 495-8248
Advertising Executive Name: Kathy Enders
Advertising Executive Email: kenders@thewesterlysun.com
Advertising Executive Phone: (860) 495-8274
Delivery Methods: Mail`Racks
Published Days: Thur
Audit Company: Sworn/Estimate/Non-Audited
Audit Date: 43626

PAWCATUCK

THE RESIDENT

Street Address: 252 S Broad St
City: Pawcatuck
State: CT
ZIP Code: 6378
General Phone: (860) 599-1221
General Email: alexisinmystic@aol.com
Publication Website: http://www.theresident.com/
Editor Email: editor@theresident.com
Advertising Executive Email: alexisinmystic@aol.com
Delivery Methods: Racks
Year Established: 1990
Mechanical specifications: Type page 10 x 13; E - 5 cols, 1 7/8, 1/4 between.
Published Days: Wed
Avg. Free Circ.: 29251
Audit Company: CVC
Audit Date: 43136

SIMSBURY

THE VALLEY PRESS

Street Address: 540 Hopmeadow St
City: Simsbury
State: CT
ZIP Code: 6070
General Phone: (860) 651-4700
General Email: lisa@turleyct.com
Publication Website: https://www.valleypressextra.com/
Parent Company: TurleyCT Community Publications
Mechanical specifications: Type page 10 x 14; 5 cols, 1.875, 0.125 between
Published Days: Thur
Avg. Free Circ.: 39500
Audit Company: Sworn/Estimate/Non-Audited
Audit Date: 43626

SIMSBURY

THE WEST HARTFORD PRESS

Street Address: 540 Hopmeadow St
City: Simsbury
State: CT
ZIP Code: 6070
General Phone: (860) 651-4700
General Email: lisa@turleyct.com
Publication Website: https://www.valleypressextra.com/
Parent Company: TurleyCT Community Publications
Mechanical specifications: Type page 10 x 14; 5 cols, 1.875, 0.125 between
Published Days: Thur
Avg. Free Circ.: 12000
Audit Company: Sworn/Estimate/Non-Audited
Audit Date: 43626

SOUTHBURY

VOICES

Street Address: PO Box 383
City: Southbury
State: CT
ZIP Code: 6488
General Phone: (203) 262-6631
General Email: webmaster@ctvoices.com
Publication Website: https://www.primepublishers.com/voicesnews/site/contact.html
Parent Company: Prime Publisher's Inc.
Publisher Name: Rudy Mazurosky
Publisher Email: rmazurosky@ctvoices.com
Editor Name: Pattie Wesley
Editor Email: pwesley@ctvoices.com
Advertising Executive Name: Randa Dobos
Advertising Executive Email: rdobos@ctvoices.com
Published Days: Wed
Avg. Paid Circ.: 352
Avg. Free Circ.: 27650
Audit Company: AAM
Audit Date: 44531

SOUTHINGTON

THE OBSERVER

Street Address: 213 Spring St
City: Southington
State: CT
ZIP Code: 6489
General Phone: (860) 621-6751
General Email: info@stepsaver.com
Publication Website: https://southingtonobserver.com/
Parent Company: Republican American
Editor Name: John Goralski
Editor Email: jgoralski@southingtonobserver.com
Advertising Executive Email: sales@stepsaver.com
Advertising Executive Phone: (860) 628-9645
Own Printing Facility?: Y
Commercial printers?: Y
Mechanical specifications: Type page 13 x 22 1/2; E - 5 cols, 2 1/2, 1/6 between;

A - 6 cols, 2, 1/6 between; C - 6 cols, 2, 1/6 between.
Published Days: Fri
Avg. Paid Circ.: 5394
Avg. Free Circ.: 46
Audit Company: Sworn/Estimate/Non-Audited
Audit Date: 43626

TORRINGTON

THE FOOTHILLS TRADER

Street Address: 59 Field St
City: Torrington
State: CT
ZIP Code: 6790
General Phone: (860) 489-3121
General Email: dnaparstek@adtaxi.com
Publication Website: http://www.foothillstrader.com/
Parent Company: Hearst Corp.
Editor Name: Helen Bennett Harvey
Editor Email: helen.bennett@hearstmediact.com
Editor Phone: (203) 789-5730
Advertising Executive Email: advertise@hearstmediact.com
Published Days: Wed
Audit Company: Sworn/Estimate/Non-Audited
Audit Date: 43626

WINSTED

THE WINSTED JOURNAL

Street Address: 452 Main St
City: Winsted
State: CT
ZIP Code: 06098-1537
General Phone: (860) 738-4418
General Email: advertising@lakevillejournal.com
Publication Website: http://www.tricornernews.com/winstedjournal
Parent Company: The Lakeville Journal
Year Established: 1996
Own Printing Facility?: Y
Commercial printers?: Y
Mechanical specifications: Type page 15 7/16 x 21; E - 7 cols, 2 1/16, 1/8 between; A - 7 cols, 2 1/16, 1/8 between; C - 8 cols, 1 3/4, 1/8 between.
Published Days: Fri
Avg. Paid Circ.: 592
Audit Company: Sworn/Estimate/Non-Audited
Audit Date: 43626

DELAWARE

BETHANY BEACH

THE DELAWARE WAVE

Street Address: Route 1 Lem Hickman Plaza
City: Bethany Beach
State: DE
ZIP Code: 19930
General Phone: (302) 537-1881
General Email: rpousson@gannett.com
Publication Website: https://www.delmarvanow.com/
Parent Company: Gannett Company Inc.
Advertising Executive Name: Ron Pousson
Advertising Executive Email: rpousson@localiq.com
Advertising Executive Phone: (410) 845-4609
Own Printing Facility?: Y
Commercial printers?: Y
Published Days: Tues
Avg. Free Circ.: 20328
Audit Company: AAM
Audit Date: 43893

DOVER

MILFORD BEACON

Street Address: 1196 S Little Creek Rd
City: Dover
State: DE
ZIP Code: 19901
General Phone: (302) 678-3616
General Email: ben.mace@doverpost.com
Publication Website: https://www.milfordbeacon.com/
Parent Company: Gannett
Publisher Name: Amy Dotson-Newton
Publisher Email: amy.dotsonnewton@doverpost.com
Publisher Phone: (302) 346-5449
Advertising Executive Name: Traci McKnight
Advertising Executive Email: traci.mcknight@doverpost.com
Advertising Executive Phone: (302) 345-5456
Delivery Methods: Mail`Racks
Year Established: 2004
Mechanical specifications: Type page 10.3125" x 11"; 6 cols
Published Days: Wed
Avg. Paid Circ.: 235
Avg. Free Circ.: 6149
Audit Company: CVC
Audit Date: 43257

DOVER

THE SUSSEX COUNTIAN

Street Address: 1196 S Little Creek Rd
City: Dover
State: DE
ZIP Code: 19901-4727
General Phone: (302) 678-3616
General Email: ben.mace@doverpost.com
Publication Website: https://www.sussexcountian.com/
Publisher Name: Amy Dotson-Newton
Publisher Email: amy.dotsonnewton@doverpost.com
Publisher Phone: (302) 346-5449
Advertising Executive Name: Bettene Pereira
Advertising Executive Email: bettene.pereira@doverpost.com
Advertising Executive Phone: (302) 346-5442
Delivery Methods: Mail`Carrier`Racks
Year Established: 1886
Own Printing Facility?: Y
Mechanical specifications: Type page 10.32" x 11"; 6 cols
Published Days: Thur
Avg. Paid Circ.: 202
Avg. Free Circ.: 1637
Audit Company: CVC
Audit Date: 43257

LEWES

CAPE GAZETTE

Street Address: 17585 Nassau Commons Blvd
City: Lewes
State: DE
ZIP Code: 19958
General Phone: (302) 645-7700
General Email: adsales@capegazette.com
Publication Website: http://capegazette.com/
Publisher Name: Dennis Forney
Publisher Email: dennisforney@capegazette.com
Publisher Phone: (302) 645-7700, ext : 303
Editor Name: Trish Vernon
Editor Email: thv@capegazette.com
Editor Phone: (302) 645-7700 ext: 315
Advertising Executive Name: Amanda Neafie
Advertising Executive Email: aneafie@capegazette.com
Advertising Executive Phone: (302) 645-7700, ext : 306
Published Days: Tues`Fri
Avg. Paid Circ.: 12000
Audit Company: Sworn/Estimate/Non-Audited
Audit Date: 43626

MIDDLETOWN

HOCKESSIN COMMUNITY NEWS

Street Address: 24 W Main St
City: Middletown
State: DE
ZIP Code: 19709
General Phone: (302) 378-9531
General Email: ben.mace@doverpost.com
Publication Website: https://www.hockessincommunitynews.com/
Publisher Name: Amy Dotson-Newton
Publisher Email: amy.dotsonnewton@doverpost.com
Publisher Phone: (302) 346-5449
Advertising Executive Name: Amanda Neafie
Advertising Executive Email: aneafie@capegazette.com
Advertising Executive Phone: (302) 645-7700, ext : 306
Delivery Methods: Mail`Carrier`Racks
Year Established: 1983
Published Days: Fri
Avg. Paid Circ.: 6
Avg. Free Circ.: 13626
Audit Company: CVC
Audit Date: 43257

MIDDLETOWN

SMYRNA/CLAYTON SUN-TIMES

Street Address: 24 W Main St
City: Middletown
State: DE
ZIP Code: 19709
General Phone: (302) 378-9531
General Email: ben.mace@doverpost.com
Publication Website: https://www.scsuntimes.com/
Parent Company: The Hays Daily News
Publisher Name: Amy Dotson-Newton
Publisher Email: amy.dotsonnewton@doverpost.com
Publisher Phone: (302) 346-5449
Advertising Executive Name: Bettene Pereira
Advertising Executive Email: bettene.pereira@doverpost.com
Advertising Executive Phone: (302) 346-5442
Delivery Methods: Carrier`Racks
Year Established: 1854
Own Printing Facility?: Y
Mechanical specifications: Type page 10.33" x 11"; 6 cols
Published Days: Wed
Avg. Paid Circ.: 1768
Avg. Free Circ.: 955
Audit Company: CVC
Audit Date: 43257

MIDDLETOWN

THE MIDDLETOWN TRANSCRIPT

Street Address: 24 W Main St
City: Middletown
State: DE
ZIP Code: 19709
General Phone: (302) 378-9531
General Email: ben.mace@doverpost.com
Publication Website: https://www.middletowntranscript.com/
Parent Company: Gannett
Publisher Name: Amy Dotson-Newton
Publisher Email: amy.dotsonnewton@doverpost.com
Publisher Phone: (302) 346-5449
Advertising Executive Name: Deb Kalinowski
Advertising Executive Email: debra.kalinowski@doverpost.com
Advertising Executive Phone: (302) 346-5435
Delivery Methods: Mail`Carrier`Racks
Year Established: 1868
Own Printing Facility?: Y
Mechanical specifications: Type page 10.33" x 11"; 6 cols
Published Days: Thur
Avg. Paid Circ.: 498
Avg. Free Circ.: 13206
Audit Company: CVC
Audit Date: 43257

OCEAN VIEW

COASTAL POINT

Street Address: 111 Atlantic Ave
City: Ocean View
State: DE
ZIP Code: 19970
General Phone: (302) 539-1788
General Email: susan.lyons@coastalpoint.com
Publication Website: http://www.coastalpoint.com
Delivery Methods: Newsstand`Racks
Year Established: 2004
Mechanical specifications: column inch 2.312 x 1 inch 4 col x 13 for a full page
Published Days: Fri
Avg. Paid Circ.: 40
Avg. Free Circ.: 18000
Audit Company: Sworn/Estimate/Non-Audited
Audit Date: 43626

FLORIDA

ALACHUA

ALACHUA COUNTY TODAY

Street Address: 14804 Main St
City: Alachua
State: FL
ZIP Code: 32615-8590
General Phone: (386) 462-3355
General Email: ads@alachuatoday.com
Publication Website: alachuatoday.com
Publisher Name: Bryan Boukari
Publisher Email: editor@alachuatoday.com
Editor Name: Ellen Boukari
Editor Email: ellen@alachuatoday.com
Delivery Methods: Mail`Newsstand`Racks
Year Established: 2000
Mechanical specifications: Type page 10 x 20; A - 6 cols, 1.55
Published Days: Thur
Avg. Paid Circ.: 5000
Audit Company: Sworn/Estimate/Non-Audited
Audit Date: 43626

ANNA MARIA

ANNA MARIA ISLAND SUN

Street Address: 9801 Gulf Drive
City: Anna Maria
State: FL
ZIP Code: 34216
General Phone: (941) 778-3986
General Email: ads@amisun.com
Publication Website: amisun.com
Publisher Name: Mike Field
Publisher Email: mfield@amisun.com
Editor Name: Mike Field
Editor Email: mfield@amisun.com
Year Established: 2000

APALACHICOLA

THE APALACHICOLA CARRABELLE TIMES

Street Address: 129 Commerce St
City: Apalachicola
State: FL
ZIP Code: 32320-1717
General Phone: (850) 653-8868
General Email: rhoxie@starfl.com
Publication Website: apalachtimes.com
Editor Name: David Adlerstein
Editor Email: dadlerstein@starfl.com
Editor Phone: 850-653-8894
Published Days: Thur
Avg. Paid Circ.: 5100
Audit Company: Sworn/Estimate/Non-Audited
Audit Date: 43626

APOPKA

APOPKA CHIEF (THE)

Street Address: 400 N Park Ave
City: Apopka
State: FL
ZIP Code: 32712-4152
General Phone: (407) 886-2777
General Email: news@theapopkachief.com
Publication Website: theapopkachief.com
Publisher Name: John Ricketson
Publisher Email: jr@theapopkachief.com
Editor Name: John Peery
Editor Email: news@theapopkachief.com
Advertising Executive Name: Jackie Trefcer
Advertising Executive Email: jackie@theapopkachief.com
Delivery Methods: Mail`Newsstand`Racks
Year Established: 1923
Commercial printers?: N
Mechanical specifications: Type page 11 1/4 x 21 1/2; E - 6 cols, 1 13/16, 1/8 between; A - 6 cols, 1 13/16, 1/8 between; C - 9 cols, 1 3/16, 1/8 between.
Published Days: Fri
Avg. Paid Circ.: 5000
Avg. Free Circ.: 100
Audit Company: Sworn/Estimate/Non-Audited
Audit Date: 43626

APOPKA

THE PLANTER

Street Address: 400 N Park Ave
City: Apopka
State: FL
ZIP Code: 32712-4152
General Phone: (407) 886-2777
General Email: news@theapopkachief.com
Publication Website: theapopkachief.com
Publisher Name: John Ricketson
Publisher Email: jr@theapopkachief.com
Editor Name: John Peery
Editor Email: news@theapopkachief.com
Advertising Executive Name: Jackie Trefcer
Advertising Executive Email: jackie@theapopkachief.com
Delivery Methods: Newsstand`Carrier`Racks
Year Established: 1965
Own Printing Facility?: Y
Mechanical specifications: Type page 13 x 21 1/2; E - 6 cols, 2 1/16, 1/8 between; A - 6 cols, 2 1/16, 1/8 between; C - 9 cols, 1 5/16, 1/8 between.
Published Days: Thur
Avg. Free Circ.: 8500
Audit Company: Sworn/Estimate/Non-Audited

Published Days: Wed
Avg. Free Circ.: 16000
Audit Company: Sworn/Estimate/Non-Audited
Audit Date: 43626

Audit Date: 43626

ARCADIA

ARCADIAN

Street Address: 108 S Polk Ave
City: Arcadia
State: FL
ZIP Code: 34266-3952
General Phone: (863) 494-7600
General Email: majoraccts@sun-herald.com
Publication Website: yoursun.net
Parent Company: Adams Publishing Group
Publisher Name: Glen Nickerson
Publisher Email: gnickerson@sun-herald.com
Editor Name: Jim Gouvellis
Editor Email: jim.gorvellis@yoursun.com
Editor Phone: (941) 206-1134
Advertising Executive Name: Omar Zucco
Advertising Executive Email: omar.zucco@yoursun.com
Published Days: Thur
Audit Company: Sworn/Estimate/Non-Audited
Audit Date: 43626

BELLEVIEW

VOICE OF SOUTH MARION

Street Address: 5513 SE 113th St
City: Belleview
State: FL
ZIP Code: 34420-4039
General Phone: (352) 245-3161
General Email: vosm@aol.com
Publication Website: thevosm.net
Editor Name: Sandy Waldron
Delivery Methods: Mail`Newsstand`Racks
Year Established: 1969
Mechanical specifications: Type page 10 x 16.
Published Days: Thur
Avg. Paid Circ.: 2800
Audit Company: Sworn/Estimate/Non-Audited
Audit Date: 43626

BLOUNTSTOWN

THE COUNTY RECORD

Street Address: PO Box 366
City: Blountstown
State: FL
ZIP Code: 32424-0366
General Phone: (850) 674-5041
General Email: displayads@thecountyrecord.net
Publication Website: thecountyrecord.net
Editor Name: Ciara Davis
Editor Email: editor@thecountyrecord.net
Year Established: 1907
Published Days: Wed
Audit Company: Sworn/Estimate/Non-Audited
Audit Date: 43626

BOCA GRANDE

BOCA BEACON

Street Address: 431 Park Ave
City: Boca Grande
State: FL
ZIP Code: 33921
General Phone: (941) 964-2995
General Email: info@bocabeacon.com
Publication Website: bocabeacon.com
Parent Company: Hopkins & Daughter Publishing
Publisher Name: Dusty Hopkins
Publisher Phone: 800-749-2995
Editor Name: Marcy Shortuse

Editor Email: mshortuse@bocabeacon.com
Editor Phone: 800-749-2995
Advertising Executive Name: Julianne Greenberg
Year Established: 1980
Commercial printers?: Y
Published Days: Fri
Avg. Paid Circ.: 3000
Avg. Free Circ.: 4000
Audit Company: Sworn/Estimate/Non-Audited
Audit Date: 43626

BRISTOL

THE CALHOUN LIBERTY JOURNAL

Street Address: 11493 NW Summers Rd
City: Bristol
State: FL
ZIP Code: 32321-3364
General Phone: (850) 643-3333
General Email: thejournal@fairpoint.net
Publication Website: cljnews.com
Editor Name: Teresa Eubanks
Delivery Methods: Mail`Newsstand`Racks
Year Established: 1981
Commercial printers?: Y
Mechanical specifications: Type page 11 x 16; E - 5 cols, 2, 1/6 between; A - 5 cols, 2, 1/6 between; C - 5 cols, 2, 1/6 between.
Published Days: Wed
Avg. Paid Circ.: 5200
Avg. Free Circ.: 18
Audit Company: Sworn/Estimate/Non-Audited
Audit Date: 43626

BROOKSVILLE

HERNANDO SUN

Street Address: 13491 Simmons Lake Road
City: Brooksville
State: FL
ZIP Code: 34601
General Phone: (352) 238-5454
Publication Website: www.hernandosun.com
Parent Company: Hernando Sun
Editor Name: Julie Maglio
Editor Email: editor@hernandosun.com
Published Days: Fri
Avg. Paid Circ.: 1207
Avg. Free Circ.: 975
Audit Company: AAM
Audit Date: 44292

BUSHNELL

SUMTER COUNTY TIMES

Street Address: 204 E McCollum Ave
City: Bushnell
State: FL
ZIP Code: 33513-6145
General Phone: (352) 793-2161
General Email: mtaylor@sctnews.com
Publication Website: sumtercountytimes.com
Parent Company: Landmark Community Newspapers
Editor Name: Bob Reichman
Editor Phone: (352) 793-2161
Delivery Methods: Mail`Newsstand
Year Established: 1881
Own Printing Facility?: Y
Commercial printers?: Y
Mechanical specifications: Type page 11 x 21 1/2; E - 6 cols, 1.555, 1/8 between; A - 6 cols, 1.555, 1/8 between; C - 9 cols, 1, 1/8 between.
Published Days: Thur
Avg. Paid Circ.: 2600
Audit Company: Sworn/Estimate/Non-Audited
Audit Date: 43626

CALLAHAN

NASSAU COUNTY RECORD

Street Address: 617317 Brandies Ave
City: Callahan
State: FL
ZIP Code: 32011-3704
General Phone: (904) 879-2727
General Email: advertising@nassaucountyrecord.com
Publication Website: nassaucountyrecord.com
Parent Company: Community Newspapers, Incorporated
Editor Name: Amanda Ream
Editor Email: editor@nassaucountyrecord.com
Advertising Executive Name: Samantha Coxwell
Advertising Executive Email: advertising@nassaucountyrecord.com
Delivery Methods: Mail`Newsstand`Carrier`Racks
Year Established: 1930
Own Printing Facility?: Y
Commercial printers?: Y
Published Days: Thur
Avg. Paid Circ.: 3000
Audit Company: Sworn/Estimate/Non-Audited
Audit Date: 43626

CAPE CORAL

CAPE CORAL BREEZE

Street Address: 2510 Del Prado Blvd S
City: Cape Coral
State: FL
ZIP Code: 33904-5750
General Phone: (239) 574-1110
Publication Website: breezenewspapers.com
Parent Company: Ogden Newspapers Inc.
Publisher Name: Raymond. M. Eckenrode
Publisher Email: reckenrode@breezenewspapers.com
Publisher Phone: 239-574-1110 Ext 110
Editor Name: Valarie Harring
Editor Email: vharring@breezenewspapers.com
Editor Phone: 239-574-1110 Ext 119
Advertising Executive Name: Laurie Ragle
Advertising Executive Email: jkonig@breezenewspapers.com
Delivery Methods: Mail`Newsstand`Carrier`Racks
Year Established: 1951
Own Printing Facility?: N
Commercial printers?: Y
Mechanical specifications: Type page 11 3/4 x 21 1/2; E - 6 cols, 2 1/16, 1/4 between; A - 8 cols, 1 3/8, 3/16 between; C - 8 cols, 1 3/8, 3/16 between.
Published Days: Wed
Weekday Frequency: m
Saturday Frequency: m
Avg. Paid Circ.: 1742
Avg. Free Circ.: 71872
Audit Company: CVC
Audit Date: 43625
Pressroom Equipment: Lines -- 20 unit DGM 430 Single Wide. 4- 4 Color Towers Standard Ink and 1- 4 Color Tower UV ; Press Drive -- 4- Fincor 150 H.P. Drive Motors; Folders -- 2-DGM 1035; Reels & Stands -- 8-Jardis/Splicers. 5-jardis infeeds; Control System -- Microcolor 2 Automatic Remote Inking; Registration System -- Quad Tech Register Motorization System 2000
Mailroom Equipment: Counter Stackers -- 2-Rima/RS2510, ; Inserters & Stuffers -- K & M 1472 Rotary Inserter; Tying Machines -- Dynaric D2400, Samuel NT 440; Address Machine -- Kirf Rudy Ink Jet Labeler;
Business Equipment: NCR
Classified Equipment: Hardware -- Daktech/52X Max; Printers -- HP/LaserJet 2100TN;
Classified Software: ONI/Class 0.5.4.

Community Newspapers in the U.S.

Editorial Equipment: Hardware -- APP/Power Mac G3; Printers -- HP/LaserJet 4MV
Editorial Software: QPS/QuarkXPress 3.32.
Production Hardware -- Kodak Prinergy Evo and Kodak Trendsetter computer-to-plate
Production Software: QPS/QuarkXPress 3.32.

CAPE CORAL

NORTH FORT MYERS NEIGHBOR

Street Address: 2510 Del Prado Blvd S
City: Cape Coral
State: FL
ZIP Code: 33904-5750
General Phone: (239) 574-1110
General Email: mjohnson@breezenewspapers.com
Publication Website: northfortmyersneighbor.com
Parent Company: Ogden Newspapers Inc.
Publisher Name: Scott Blonde
Publisher Email: sblonde@breezenewspapers.com
Publisher Phone: 574-1110 Ext 110
Editor Name: Valarie Harring
Editor Email: vharring@breezenewspapers.com
Editor Phone: 574-1110 Ex 119
Advertising Executive Name: Beth Zedek
Advertising Executive Email: bzedek@breezenewspapers.com
Year Established: 1999
Published Days: Wed
Avg. Paid Circ.: 8
Avg. Free Circ.: 5626
Audit Company: CVC
Audit Date: 43658

CAPE CORAL

SANIBEL-CAPTIVA ISLANDER

Street Address: 2510 Del Prado Blvd S
City: Cape Coral
State: FL
ZIP Code: 33904-5750
General Phone: (239)-574-1110
General Email: dpapoi@breezenewspapers.com
Publication Website: captivasanibel.com
Parent Company: Ogden Newspapers Inc.
Publisher Name: Scott Blonde
Publisher Email: sblonde@breezenewspapers.com
Publisher Phone: 574-1110 Ext 110
Editor Name: Tiffany Repecki
Editor Email: trepecki@breezenewspapers.com
Editor Phone: 472-8398
Advertising Executive Name: Mark Martens
Advertising Executive Email: mmartens@breezenewspapers.com
Year Established: 1960
Mechanical specifications: Type page 9 3/4 x 12 5/8; E - 4 cols, between; A - 6 cols, between; C - 6 cols, between.
Published Days: Wed
Avg. Paid Circ.: 424
Avg. Free Circ.: 6606
Audit Company: CVC
Audit Date: 43658

CAPE CORAL

THE PINE ISLAND EAGLE

Street Address: 2510 Del Prado Blvd
City: Cape Coral
State: FL
ZIP Code: 33904
General Phone: (239) 283-2022
General Email: cgallagher@breezenewspapers.com
Publication Website: pineisland-eagle.com
Parent Company: Ogden Newspapers Inc.
Publisher Name: Ray Eckenrode
Publisher Email: reckenrode@breezenewspapers.com
Publisher Phone: 574-1110 Ex 110
Editor Name: Paulette LeBlanc
Editor Email: pleblanc@breezenewspapers.com
Editor Phone: 283-2022
Advertising Executive Name: Charlene Russ
Advertising Executive Email: cruss@breezenewspapers.com
Year Established: 1976
Published Days: Wed
Avg. Paid Circ.: 185
Avg. Free Circ.: 7967
Audit Company: CVC
Audit Date: 43628

CHIEFLAND

CHIEFLAND CITIZEN

Street Address: 624 W Park Ave
City: Chiefland
State: FL
ZIP Code: 32626-0430
General Phone: (352) 493-4796
General Email: circulation@chieflandcitizen.com
Publication Website: chieflandcitizen.com
Parent Company: Landmark Community Newspapers
Publisher Name: Gerry Mulligan
Editor Name: David Davis
Editor Email: editor@chieflandcitizen.com
Delivery Methods: Mail`Newsstand`Racks
Year Established: 1950
Published Days: Thur
Avg. Paid Circ.: 6000
Audit Company: Sworn/Estimate/Non-Audited
Audit Date: 43626

CLEARWATER

BUSINESS OBSERVER-PINELLAS

Street Address: 14004 Roosevelt Blvd
City: Clearwater
State: FL
ZIP Code: 33762-3850
General Phone: (727) 447-7784
General Email: dschaefer@BusinessObserverFL.com
Publication Website: businessobserverfl.com
Parent Company: Observer Media Group Inc.
Publisher Name: Matt Walsh
Publisher Email: mwalsh@BusinessObserverFL.com
Publisher Phone: 941-362-4848
Editor Name: Kat Hughes
Editor Email: khughes@BusinessObserverFL.com
Editor Phone: 941-362-4848
Advertising Executive Name: Kristen Boothroyd
Advertising Executive Email: kboothroyd@BusinessObserverFL.com
Delivery Methods: Mail`Newsstand`Racks
Year Established: 1997
Mechanical specifications: 10.375" x 16"
Published Days: Fri
Avg. Paid Circ.: 185
Avg. Free Circ.: 696
Audit Company: Sworn/Estimate/Non-Audited
Audit Date: 43626

CRAWFORDVILLE

THE WAKULLA NEWS

Street Address: 3119A Crawfordville Hwy
City: Crawfordville
State: FL
ZIP Code: 32327-3148
General Phone: (850) 926-7102
General Email: lkinsey@thewakullanews.net
Publication Website: thewakullanews.com
Parent Company: Landmark Community Newspapers
Editor Name: William Snowden
Editor Email: editor@thewakullanews.net
Advertising Executive Name: Lynda Kinsey
Delivery Methods: Mail`Newsstand`Racks
Year Established: 1897
Own Printing Facility?: N
Commercial printers?: Y
Mechanical specifications: Type Page 9.888 x 21.5; E - 6 cols, 1.555, .111 between; A - 6 cols, 1.555, .111 between; C - 9 cols, 1, .111 between.
Published Days: Thur
Avg. Paid Circ.: 4500
Audit Company: Sworn/Estimate/Non-Audited
Audit Date: 43626

CRESCENT CITY

PUTNAM COUNTY COURIER JOURNAL

Street Address: 320 N Summit St
City: Crescent City
State: FL
ZIP Code: 32112-2300
General Phone: (386) 698-1644
General Email: ads@cjnewsfl.com
Publication Website: cjnewsfl.com
Parent Company: Lakestreet Publishing Company
Publisher Name: Laura Turner
Editor Name: William "B.J." Laurie
Editor Email: news@cjnewsfl.com
Advertising Executive Name: Mike Jones
Delivery Methods: Mail`Newsstand`Racks
Year Established: 1898
Commercial printers?: Y
Published Days: Wed
Avg. Paid Circ.: 3000
Audit Company: Sworn/Estimate/Non-Audited
Audit Date: 43626

CRESTVIEW

CRESTVIEW NEWS BULLETIN

Street Address: 1911 N 13th St
City: Crestview
State: FL
ZIP Code: 32536-2170
General Phone: (850) 682-6524
Publication Website: crestviewbulletin.com
Parent Company: Gannett
Publisher Name: Jim Fletcher
Publisher Email: jfletcher@crestviewbulletin.com
Editor Name: Jason Blakeney
Editor Email: jblakeney@nwfdailynews.com
Advertising Executive Name: Diana Baker
Advertising Executive Email: dbaker@crestviewbulletin.comm
Delivery Methods: Mail`Carrier`Racks
Year Established: 1975
Own Printing Facility?: Y
Commercial printers?: Y
Mechanical specifications: Type page 11 9/16 x 21; E - 6 cols, 1 29/36, 1/6 between; A - 6 cols, 1 29/36, 1/6 between; C - 10 cols, 1 1/72, 1/6 between.
Published Days: Wed`Sat
Avg. Paid Circ.: 4000
Avg. Free Circ.: 13000
Audit Company: Sworn/Estimate/Non-Audited
Audit Date: 43626

DEERFIELD BEACH

OBSERVER NEWSPAPER

Street Address: 201 N Federal Hwy
City: Deerfield Beach
State: FL
ZIP Code: 33441-3621
General Phone: (954) 428-9045
General Email: observerart@comcast.net
Publication Website: observernewspaperonline.com
Publisher Name: Dana Eller
Editor Name: Rachel Galvin
Delivery Methods: Mail`Newsstand`Racks
Year Established: 1962
Commercial printers?: Y
Mechanical specifications: Type page 10 1/4 x 16; E - 6 cols, 1 1/2, 1/8 between; A - 6 cols, 1 1/2, 1/8 between; C - 5 cols, 1 3/4, 1/8 between.
Published Days: Thur
Avg. Free Circ.: 15000
Audit Company: Sworn/Estimate/Non-Audited
Audit Date: 43626

DELAND

THE WEST VOLUSIA BEACON

Street Address: 110 W New York Ave
City: Deland
State: FL
ZIP Code: 32720-5416
General Phone: (386) 734-4622
General Email: adsales@beacononlinenews.com
Publication Website: beacononlinenews.com
Editor Name: Anthony DeFeo
Delivery Methods: Mail`Newsstand
Year Established: 1992
Commercial printers?: Y
Mechanical specifications: Type page 13 x 21 1/2; E - 6 cols, 2 1/16, 1/8 between; A - 6 cols, 2 1/16, 1/8 between; C - 8 cols, 1 1/2, 1/8 between.
Published Days: Mon`Thur
Avg. Paid Circ.: 5000
Avg. Free Circ.: 9050
Audit Company: Sworn/Estimate/Non-Audited
Audit Date: 43626

DUNNELLON

RIVERLAND NEWS

Street Address: 20441 E Pennsylvania Ave
City: Dunnellon
State: FL
ZIP Code: 34432-6035
General Phone: (352) 489-2731
General Email: editor@riverlandnews.com
Publication Website: riverlandnews.com
Parent Company: Landmark Community Newspapers
Editor Name: Jeff Bryan
Editor Email: editor@riverlandnews.com
Year Established: 1982
Mechanical specifications: Type page 11 5/8 x 21 1/2; E - 6 cols, 1 5/6, 1/8 between; A - 6 cols, 1 5/6, 1/8 between; C - 10 cols, 1 1/16, 1/8 between.
Published Days: Thur
Avg. Paid Circ.: 3000
Audit Company: Sworn/Estimate/Non-Audited
Audit Date: 43626

FERNANDINA BEACH

NEWS-LEADER

Street Address: 511 Ash St
City: Fernandina Beach
State: FL
ZIP Code: 32034-3930
General Phone: (904) 261-3696
General Email: ads@fbnewsleader.com
Publication Website: fbnewsleader.com
Parent Company: CNHI, LLC
Publisher Name: Foy R. Maloy
Publisher Email: fmaloy@fbnewsleader.com
Editor Name: Peg Davis

Editor Email: pegdavis@fbnewsleader.com
Advertising Executive Name: April Butler
Advertising Executive Email: abutler@fbnewsleader.com
Delivery Methods: Mail
Year Established: 1854
Mechanical specifications: Type page 11 5/8 x 21 1/4; E - 6 cols, between; A - 6 cols, between; C - 6 cols, between.
Published Days: Wed`Fri
Avg. Paid Circ.: 10000
Audit Company: Sworn/Estimate/Non-Audited
Audit Date: 43626

FLEMING ISLAND

CLAY TODAY

Street Address: 3513 US Highway 17
City: Fleming Island
State: FL
ZIP Code: 32003-7122
General Phone: (904) 264-3200
General Email: jon@opcfla.com
Publication Website: claytodayonline.com
Parent Company: Osteen Publishing Company
Publisher Name: Jon Cantrell
Publisher Email: jon@opcfla.com
Editor Name: Don Coble
Editor Email: don@opcfla.com
Advertising Executive Name: Peggy Oddy
Advertising Executive Email: peg@opcfla.com
Delivery Methods: Mail`Newsstand`Carrier`Racks
Year Established: 1950
Own Printing Facility?: N
Commercial printers?: N
Mechanical specifications: Type page 10 x 12 3/4; E - 4 cols, 2 1/2, 1/16 between; A - 4 cols, 2 1/2, 1/16 between; C - 4 cols, 2 1/2, 1/16 between.
Published Days: Thur
Published Other: TMC - Weekly FREE 7,000
Avg. Paid Circ.: 3637
Avg. Free Circ.: 838
Audit Company: VAC
Audit Date: 42837
Note: (3) County Wide Newspapers - Clay Today, Clay County Leader (TMC) and the OAKLEAF Monthly

FORT LAUDERDALE

THE GAZETTE - PEMBROKE PINES & MIRAMAR

Street Address: 500 E Broward Blvd
City: Fort Lauderdale
State: FL
ZIP Code: 33394-3000
General Phone: (954) 698-6397
General Email: Kenwilliams@tribpub.com
Publication Website: forumpubs.com
Parent Company: Sun-Sentinal
Editor Name: Dana Banker
Editor Email: dbanker@sunsentinel.com
Editor Phone: 954-356-4681
Published Days: Mthly
Audit Company: Sworn/Estimate/Non-Audited
Audit Date: 43626

FORT MYERS

FORT MYERS FLORIDA WEEKLY

Street Address: 4300 Ford St
City: Fort Myers
State: FL
ZIP Code: 33916-9318
General Phone: (239) 333-2135
General Email: advertise@floridaweekly.com
Publication Website: floridaweekly.com
Parent Company: Florida Media Group LLC
Publisher Name: Angela Schivinski

Publisher Email: angela@floridaweekly.com
Editor Name: Betty Wells
Editor Email: bwells@floridaweekly.com
Delivery Methods: Mail`Newsstand
Year Established: 2007
Published Days: Wed
Avg. Paid Circ.: 35646
Audit Company: Sworn/Estimate/Non-Audited
Audit Date: 43626

FORT MYERS BEACH

FORT MYERS BEACH BULLETIN

Street Address: 19260 San Carlos Blvd
City: Fort Myers Beach
State: FL
ZIP Code: 33931-2266
General Phone: (239) 463-4421
General Email: beachbulletin@breezenewspapers.com
Publication Website: fortmyersbeachtalk.com
Parent Company: Ogden Newspapers Inc.
Publisher Name: Scott Blonde
Publisher Email: sblonde@breezenewspapers.com
Publisher Phone: 574-1110 Ext 110
Editor Name: Jessica Salmond
Editor Email: jsalmond@breezenewspapers.com
Editor Phone: 765-0400
Advertising Executive Name: Danielle Papoi
Advertising Executive Email: dpapoi@breezenewspapers.com
Year Established: 1951
Own Printing Facility?: Y
Commercial printers?: Y
Mechanical specifications: Type page 10 5/8 x 16; E - 6 cols, between; A - 6 cols, between; C - 6 cols, between.
Published Days: Wed
Avg. Paid Circ.: 35
Avg. Free Circ.: 6923
Audit Company: Sworn/Estimate/Non-Audited
Audit Date: 43626

FORT WALTON BEACH

THE DESTIN LOG

Street Address: 2 Eglin Parkway NE
City: Fort Walton Beach
State: FL
ZIP Code: 32548
General Phone: (850) 315-4306
General Email: jkirkland@pcnh.com
Publication Website: thedestinlog.com
Parent Company: Gannett
Editor Name: Dusty Ricketts
Editor Email: dricketts@nwfdailynews.com
Editor Phone: 850-315-4448
Advertising Executive Name: Jennifer Hoda
Advertising Executive Email: jhoda@nwfdailynews.com
Published Days: Wed`Sat
Audit Company: Sworn/Estimate/Non-Audited
Audit Date: 43626

GULF BREEZE

GULF BREEZE NEWS

Street Address: 913 Gulf Breeze Pkwy
City: Gulf Breeze
State: FL
ZIP Code: 32561-4754
General Phone: (850) 932-8986
General Email: bob@gulfbreezenews.com
Publication Website: gulfbreezenews.com
Parent Company: Gulf Breeze News, Inc.
Publisher Name: Lisa Newell
Publisher Email: lisa@gulfbreezenews.com
Publisher Phone: Ext. 101
Advertising Executive Name: Bob Newell

Advertising Executive Email: bob@gulfbreezenews.com
Delivery Methods: Mail`Newsstand
Year Established: 2001
Mechanical specifications: Display column inch: 1.799" Classified column inch: 1.02"
Published Days: Thur
Avg. Paid Circ.: 2000
Avg. Free Circ.: 1000
Audit Company: Sworn/Estimate/Non-Audited
Audit Date: 43626

HAVANA

THE HERALD

Street Address: 103 W 7th Ave
City: Havana
State: FL
ZIP Code: 32333-1660
General Phone: (850) 539-6586
General Email: colleen@prioritynews.net
Publication Website: theherald.online
Parent Company: Paxton Media Group
Editor Name: Brian Dekle
Delivery Methods: Mail`Newsstand`Racks
Year Established: 1947
Published Days: Thur
Avg. Paid Circ.: 3500
Audit Company: Sworn/Estimate/Non-Audited
Audit Date: 43626

HOLMES BEACH

THE ISLANDER

Street Address: 3218 E Bay Dr
City: Holmes Beach
State: FL
ZIP Code: 34217-2039
General Phone: (941) 778-7978
General Email: toni@islander.org
Publication Website: islander.org
Publisher Name: Bonner Joy
Publisher Email: news@islander.org
Editor Name: Lisa Neff
Editor Email: lisa@islander.org
Advertising Executive Name: Toni Lyon
Advertising Executive Email: toni@islander.org
Delivery Methods: Mail`Newsstand`Carrier`Racks
Year Established: 1992
Published Days: Wed
Avg. Paid Circ.: 2900
Avg. Free Circ.: 15000
Audit Company: Sworn/Estimate/Non-Audited
Audit Date: 43626
Note: News of record for cities of Anna Maria, Bradenton Beach and Holmes Beach, Fla., and communities adjacent to Anna Maria Island.

HOMESTEAD

SOUTH DADE NEWS LEADER

Street Address: 125 NE 8th St.
City: Homestead
State: FL
ZIP Code: 33030
General Phone: (305) 245-2311
General Email: mdill@calkins-media.com
Publication Website: southdadenewsleader.com
Parent Company: South Dade News Inc.
Publisher Name: Dale Machesic
Publisher Email: dale@newsleadermail.com
Editor Name: Ann Machesic
Editor Email: ann@newsleadermail.com
Year Established: 1912
Own Printing Facility?: Y
Mechanical specifications: Type page 12 1/2 x 21 1/2; E - 6 cols, 2, 3/16 between; A - 6 cols, 2, 3/16 between; C - 9 cols, 1 1/4, 1/8

between.
Published Days: Tues`Thur`Fri
Avg. Paid Circ.: 24000
Audit Company: Sworn/Estimate/Non-Audited
Audit Date: 43626

JACKSONVILLE

FOLIO WEEKLY

Street Address: 91731 Overseas Hwy
City: Jacksonville
State: FL
ZIP Code: 32202-3632
General Phone: (904) 860-2465
General Email: sam@folioweekly.com
Publication Website: folioweekly.com
Publisher Name: Sam Taylor
Publisher Email: sam@folioweekly.com
Publisher Phone: (904) 860-2465
Editor Name: Georgio Valentino
Editor Email: georgio@folioweekly.com
Editor Phone: Ext. #115
Delivery Methods: Racks
Year Established: 1987
Mechanical specifications: Type page 10 x 13; E - 4 cols, 2 3/8, between; A - 4 cols, 2 3/8, between; C - 4 cols, 2 3/8, between.
Published Days: Wed
Avg. Free Circ.: 25349
Audit Company: Sworn/Estimate/Non-Audited
Audit Date: 43626

JACKSONVILLE

JACKSONVILLE BUSINESS JOURNAL

Street Address: 200 W Forsyth St
City: Jacksonville
State: FL
ZIP Code: 32202-4349
General Phone: (904) 396-3502
Publication Website: bizjournals.com/jacksonville
Parent Company: American City Business Journals
Publisher Name: Sara Leutzinger
Publisher Email: sleutzinger@bizjournals.com
Publisher Phone: 904-265-2203
Editor Name: James Cannon
Editor Email: jcannon@bizjournals.com
Editor Phone: 904-521-9234
Advertising Executive Name: Traig Kaszyk
Advertising Executive Email: tkaszyk@bizjournals.com
Delivery Methods: Mail`Newsstand
Published Days: Fri
Audit Company: Sworn/Estimate/Non-Audited
Audit Date: 43626

JACKSONVILLE

MANDARIN NEWSLINE

Street Address: 12443 San Jose Blvd
City: Jacksonville
State: FL
ZIP Code: 32223-8650
General Phone: (904) 886-4919
General Email: Linda@floridanewsline.com
Publication Website: mandarinnewsline.com
Parent Company: Green Publishing Inc.
Editor Name: Martie Thompson
Editor Email: editor@floridanewsline.com
Advertising Executive Name: Linda Gay
Advertising Executive Email: Linda@floridanewsline.com
Delivery Methods: Mail
Year Established: 2007
Mechanical specifications: 11 x 17 tabloid. visit www.rtpublishinginc.com for rate card with ad specs.
Published Days: Mthly

Community Newspapers in the U.S.

III-191

Avg. Free Circ.: 27178
Audit Company: CVC
Audit Date: 43658

JACKSONVILLE

OCEAN BREEZE

Street Address: 12443 San Jose Blvd
City: Jacksonville
State: FL
ZIP Code: 32223-8650
General Phone: (904) 886-4919
General Email: publisher@rtpublishinginc.com
Publication Website: floridanewsline.com
Parent Company: Local Community News
Editor Name: Martie Thompson
Editor Email: editor@floridanewsline.com
Advertising Executive Name: Linda Gay
Advertising Executive Email: Linda@floridanewsline.com
Delivery Methods: Mail
Year Established: 2001
Mechanical specifications: 11' X 14" see media kit at www.rtpublishinginc.com for ad and color specifications
Published Days: Wed`Bi-Mthly
Published Other: Quaterly (Mar, Jun, Sept, Dec)
Avg. Free Circ.: 1800
Audit Company: Sworn/Estimate/Non-Audited
Audit Date: 43626

JACKSONVILLE

PLAYERS JOURNAL

Street Address: 12443 San Jose Blvd
City: Jacksonville
State: FL
ZIP Code: 32223-8650
General Phone: (904) 886-4919
General Email: publisher@rtpublishinginc.com
Publication Website: floridanewsline.com
Parent Company: Local Community News
Editor Name: Martie Thompson
Editor Email: editor@floridanewsline.com
Advertising Executive Name: Linda Gay
Advertising Executive Email: Linda@floridanewsline.com
Delivery Methods: Mail
Year Established: 2001
Mechanical specifications: 11" x 14". See www.rtpublishinginc.com media kit for specifications.
Published Days: Thur`Bi-Mthly
Published Other: Quarterly (Jan, Apr, Jul, Oct)
Avg. Free Circ.: 1850
Audit Company: Sworn/Estimate/Non-Audited
Audit Date: 43626

JACKSONVILLE

PONTE VEDRA NEWSLINE

Street Address: 12443 San Jose Blvd
City: Jacksonville
State: FL
ZIP Code: 32223-8650
General Phone: (904) 886-4919
General Email: Linda@floridanewsline.com
Publication Website: floridanewsline.com
Parent Company: Local Community News
Editor Name: Martie Thompson
Editor Email: editor@floridanewsline.com
Advertising Executive Name: Linda Gay
Advertising Executive Email: Linda@floridanewsline.com
Delivery Methods: Mail
Year Established: 2014
Mechanical specifications: 11" x 17" tabloid. VIsit www.rtpublishinginc.com for the full media kit with specifications.

Published Days: Mthly
Avg. Free Circ.: 22321
Audit Company: CVC
Audit Date: 43658

JACKSONVILLE

THE CREEKLINE

Street Address: 12443 San Jose Blvd
City: Jacksonville
State: FL
ZIP Code: 32223-8650
General Phone: (904) 886-4919
General Email: linda@floridanewsline.com
Publication Website: floridanewsline.com
Parent Company: Florida NewsLine
Editor Name: Martie Thompson
Editor Email: editor@floridanewsline.com
Advertising Executive Name: Linda Gay
Advertising Executive Email: Linda@floridanewsline.com
Delivery Methods: Mail
Year Established: 2000
Mechanical specifications: 11" x 17" tabloid. Visit www.rtpublishinginc.com for the media kit with specifications or call 904-886-4919.
Published Days: Mthly
Avg. Free Circ.: 27299
Audit Company: CVC
Audit Date: 43658

JACKSONVILLE BEACH

THE BEACHES LEADER

Street Address: 1372 Beach Blvd
City: Jacksonville Beach
State: FL
ZIP Code: 32250-3447
General Phone: (904) 249-9033
General Email: Sales@beachesleader.com
Publication Website: BeachesLeader.com
Editor Name: Kathleen Feindt Bailey
Editor Email: editor@beachesleader.com
Advertising Executive Name: Marie Adams
Advertising Executive Email: classified@beachesleader.com
Delivery Methods: Mail`Newsstand`Racks
Year Established: 1963
Published Days: Thur
Avg. Paid Circ.: 7500
Audit Company: Sworn/Estimate/Non-Audited
Audit Date: 43626

KEY BISCAYNE

ISLANDER NEWS

Street Address: 104 Crandon Blvd
City: Key Biscayne
State: FL
ZIP Code: 33149-1556
General Phone: (305) 361-3333
General Email: lia@islandernews.com
Publication Website: islandernews.com
Publisher Name: Justo Rey
Publisher Email: jrey@islandernews.com
Publisher Phone: Extension 13
Editor Name: Raquel Garcia
Editor Email: rqgarcia@islandernews.com
Editor Phone: Extension 12
Advertising Executive Name: Mariella Oliva
Advertising Executive Email: moliva@islandernews.com
Year Established: 1966
Published Days: Thur
Avg. Paid Circ.: 3900
Avg. Free Circ.: 690
Audit Company: Sworn/Estimate/Non-Audited
Audit Date: 43626

KEY WEST

KEY WEST WEEKLY

Street Address: 5450 Macdonald Ave
City: Key West
State: FL
ZIP Code: 33040
General Phone: (305) 453-6928
Publication Website: keysweekly.com
Parent Company: Keys Weekly Newspapers
Publisher Name: BRITT MYERS
Publisher Email: BRITT@KEYSWEEKLY.COM
Publisher Phone: 305.453.6928
Published Days: Thur
Avg. Free Circ.: 6977
Audit Company: AAM
Audit Date: 43991

KISSIMMEE

EL OSCEOLA STAR

Street Address: 1970 Main St
City: Kissimmee
State: FL
ZIP Code: 34741-5752
General Phone: (407) 933-0174
General Email: ad@elosceolastar.com
Publication Website: elosceolastar.com
Editor Name: Guillermo Hansen
Editor Email: artstarnews@aol.com
Delivery Methods: Racks
Mechanical specifications: Type page 9 3/4 x 16; E - 2 cols, 2 1/4, 1/4 between; A - 2 cols, 4 3/4, 1/4 between; C - 3 cols, 1 1/2, 3/25 between.
Published Days: Fri
Avg. Free Circ.: 15000
Audit Company: Sworn/Estimate/Non-Audited
Audit Date: 43626

KISSIMMEE

OSCEOLA NEWS-GAZETTE

Street Address: 108 Church St
City: Kissimmee
State: FL
ZIP Code: 34741-5055
General Phone: (407) 846-7600
General Email: bberry@osceolanewsgazette.com
Publication Website: aroundosceola.com
Parent Company: Lakeway Publishers, Inc.
Publisher Name: Rochelle Stidham
Publisher Email: toverton@osceolanewsgazette.com
Publisher Phone: 407-846-7600
Editor Name: Brian McBride
Editor Email: bmcbride@osceolanewsgazette.com
Editor Phone: 321-402-0436
Advertising Executive Name: Jaime Sousse
Advertising Executive Email: jsousse@osceolanewsgazette.com
Delivery Methods: Mail`Carrier`Racks
Year Established: 1897
Commercial printers?: Y
Mechanical specifications: Type page 11.75" x 21"; 6 cols
Published Days: Thur`Sat
Avg. Paid Circ.: 582
Avg. Free Circ.: 39371
Audit Company: CVC
Audit Date: 43628

LABELLE

IMMOKALEE BULLETIN

Street Address: 22 Fort Thompson Ave.
City: Labelle
State: FL
ZIP Code: 33975
General Phone: (863) 675-2541
Publication Website: immokaleebulletin.com
Parent Company: Independent NewsMedia
Publisher Name: Katrina Elsken

Publisher Email: kelsken@newszap.com
Advertising Executive Name: Barbara Calfee
Advertising Executive Email: bcalfee@newszap.com
Published Days: Thur
Audit Company: Sworn/Estimate/Non-Audited
Audit Date: 43626

LAKE WORTH

COASTAL/GREENACRES OBSERVER

Street Address: 1857 San Marco Rd
City: Lake Worth
State: FL
ZIP Code: 33460-1835
General Phone: (561) 585-9387
General Email: Adsales@lwherald.com
Publication Website: lwherald.com
Parent Company: Lake Worth Herald Press, Inc.
Editor Name: Mark Easton
Editor Email: Editor@lwherald.com
Delivery Methods: Mail`Newsstand`Carrier`Racks
Year Established: 1912
Published Days: Thur
Avg. Paid Circ.: 1200
Avg. Free Circ.: 28000
Audit Company: Sworn/Estimate/Non-Audited
Audit Date: 43626

LAKE WORTH

THE LAKE WORTH HERALD

Street Address: 1313 Central Ter
City: Lake Worth
State: FL
ZIP Code: 33460-1835
General Phone: (561) 585-9387
General Email: Adsales@lwherald.com
Publication Website: lwherald.com
Parent Company: Lake Worth Herald Press, Inc.
Editor Name: Mark Easton
Editor Email: Editor@lwherald.com
Delivery Methods: Mail`Newsstand`Carrier`Racks
Year Established: 1912
Own Printing Facility?: Y
Commercial printers?: Y
Published Days: Thur
Avg. Paid Circ.: 918
Avg. Free Circ.: 16000
Audit Company: Sworn/Estimate/Non-Audited
Audit Date: 43626

LAND O LAKES

LAND O LAKES LAKER

Street Address: 3632 Land O Lakes Blvd
City: Land O Lakes
State: FL
ZIP Code: 34639-4407
General Phone: (813) 909-2800
General Email: dkortus@lakerlutznews.com
Publication Website: lakerlutznews.com
Parent Company: Community News Publications
Publisher Name: Diane Kortus
Publisher Email: dkortus@lakerlutznews.com
Editor Name: B.C. Manion
Editor Email: bcmanion@lakerlutznews.com
Advertising Executive Name: Beth Ross
Advertising Executive Email: bross@lakerlutznews.com
Delivery Methods: Carrier`Racks
Year Established: 1981
Mechanical specifications: Full Page: 9.916 X 15.1 1/2 Page Vertical: 4.875 X 15.5 1/2 page Horizontal: 9.916 X 7.675 1/3 Page Vertical: 4.875 X 10 1/3 Page Horizontal: 15.5 X 5 1/4 Page Vertical: 4.875 X 7.675

1/4 Page Horizontal: 9.916 X 3.75 1/6 Page Vertical: 4.75 X 3.75 1/6 Page Horizontal: 9.916 X 2.5 1/8 Page: 4.875 X 3.75 1/12 Page Horizontal: 4.875 X 2.5 Font Page Panel: 2.354 X 4
Published Days: Wed
Avg. Free Circ.: 13795
Audit Company: CVC
Audit Date: 43628

LAND O LAKES

THE LUTZ NEWS

Street Address: 3632 Land O Lakes Blvd
City: Land O Lakes
State: FL
ZIP Code: 34639-4407
General Phone: (813) 909-2800
General Email: dkortus@lakerlutznews.com
Publication Website: lakerlutznews.com
Parent Company: Community News Publications
Publisher Name: Diane Kortus
Publisher Email: dkortus@lakerlutznews.com
Editor Name: B.C. Manion
Editor Email: bcmanion@lakerlutznews.com
Advertising Executive Name: Rachel Thompson
Advertising Executive Email: rthompson@lakerlutznews.com
Delivery Methods: Carrier`Racks
Year Established: 1965
Mechanical specifications: Full Page: 9.916 X 15.1 1/2 Page Vertical: 4.875 X 15.5 1/2 page Horizontal: 9.916 X 7.675 1/3 Page Vertical: 4.875 X 10 1/3 Page Horizontal: 15.5 X 5 1/4 Page Vertical: 4.875 X 7.675 1/4 Page Horizontal: 9.916 X 3.75 1/6 Page Vertical: 4.75 X 3.75 1/6 Page Horizontal: 9.916 X 2.5 1/8 Page: 4.875 X 3.75 1/12 Page Horizontal: 4.875 X 2.5 Font Page Panel: 2.354 X 4
Published Days: Wed
Avg. Free Circ.: 8510
Audit Company: CVC
Audit Date: 43628

LAND O LAKES

WESLEY CHAPEL LAKER

Street Address: 3632 Land O Lakes Blvd
City: Land O Lakes
State: FL
ZIP Code: 34639-4407
General Phone: (813) 909-2800
General Email: sales@lakerlutznews.com
Publication Website: lakerlutznews.com
Parent Company: Community News Publications
Publisher Name: Diane Kortus
Publisher Email: dkortus@lakerlutznews.com
Editor Name: B.C. Manion
Editor Email: bcmanion@lakerlutznews.com
Advertising Executive Name: Carolyn Bennett
Advertising Executive Email: cbennett@lakerlutznews.com
Delivery Methods: Carrier`Racks
Year Established: 1981
Mechanical specifications: Full Page: 9.916 X 15.1 1/2 Page Vertical: 4.875 X 15.5 1/2 page Horizontal: 9.916 X 7.675 1/3 Page Vertical: 4.875 X 10 1/3 Page Horizontal: 15.5 X 5 1/4 Page Vertical: 4.875 X 7.675 1/4 Page Horizontal: 9.916 X 3.75 1/6 Page Vertical: 4.75 X 3.75 1/6 Page Horizontal: 9.916 X 2.5 1/8 Page: 4.875 X 3.75 1/12 Page Horizontal: 4.875 X 2.5 Font Page Panel: 2.354 X 4
Published Days: Wed
Avg. Free Circ.: 13570
Audit Company: CVC
Audit Date: 43624

LIVE OAK

JASPER NEWS

Street Address: 521 Demorest St SE
City: Live Oak
State: FL
ZIP Code: 32064-3320
General Phone: (386) 792-2487
General Email: jaspernews1@windstream.net
Publication Website: nflaonline.com
Parent Company: CNHI, LLC
Publisher Name: Jeff Masters
Publisher Email: jmasters@cnhi.com
Editor Name: Jamie Wachter
Editor Email: jamie.wachter@gaflnews.com
Editor Phone: 386-362-1734 x131
Advertising Executive Name: Monja Slater
Advertising Executive Email: monja.slater@gaflnews.com
Year Established: 1870
Own Printing Facility?: Y
Mechanical specifications: Type page 11 x 21 1/2; E - 6 cols, between; A - 6 cols, between; C - 10 cols, between.
Published Days: Thur
Avg. Paid Circ.: 1450
Avg. Free Circ.: 30
Audit Company: Sworn/Estimate/Non-Audited
Audit Date: 43626

LIVE OAK

MAYO FREE PRESS

Street Address: PO Box 370
City: Live Oak
State: FL
ZIP Code: 32064-0370
General Phone: (386) 362-1734
General Email: mayofreepress@windstream.net
Publication Website: suwanneedemocrat.com/mayo
Parent Company: CNHI, LLC
Publisher Name: Jeff Masters
Publisher Email: jmasters@cnhi.com
Editor Name: Jamie Wachter
Editor Email: jamie.wachter@gaflnews.com
Editor Phone: 386-362-1734 x131
Advertising Executive Name: Monja Slater
Advertising Executive Email: monja.slater@gaflnews.com
Year Established: 1888
Published Days: Thur
Avg. Paid Circ.: 900
Avg. Free Circ.: 50
Audit Company: Sworn/Estimate/Non-Audited
Audit Date: 43626

LIVE OAK

SUWANNEE DEMOCRAT

Street Address: 521 Demorest St SE
City: Live Oak
State: FL
ZIP Code: 32064-3320
General Phone: (386) 362-1734
General Email: monja.slater@gaflnews.com
Publication Website: suwanneedemocrat.com
Parent Company: CNHI, LLC
Publisher Name: Jeff Masters
Publisher Email: jmasters@cnhi.com
Editor Name: Jamie Wachter
Editor Email: jamie.wachter@gaflnews.com
Editor Phone: 386-362-1734 x131
Advertising Executive Name: Monja Slater
Advertising Executive Email: monja.slater@gaflnews.com
Delivery Methods: Mail`Newsstand`Racks
Year Established: 1884
Own Printing Facility?: N
Commercial printers?: N
Published Days: Wed`Fri
Avg. Paid Circ.: 3215
Audit Company: Sworn/Estimate/Non-Audited
Audit Date: 43626

MACCLENNY

THE BAKER COUNTY PRESS

Street Address: 104 S 5th St
City: Macclenny
State: FL
ZIP Code: 32063-2304
General Phone: (904) 259-2400
General Email: advertising@bakercountypress.com
Publication Website: bakercountypress.com
Publisher Name: James McGauley
Publisher Email: editor@bakercountypress.com
Editor Name: Joel Addington
Editor Email: reporter@bakercountypress.com
Advertising Executive Name: Jessica Prevatt
Advertising Executive Email: advertising@bakercountypress.com
Delivery Methods: Mail`Racks
Year Established: 1929
Own Printing Facility?: Y
Mechanical specifications: Type page 13 x 21; E - 6 cols, 1.95, 0.267 between.
Published Days: Thur
Avg. Paid Circ.: 5400
Audit Company: Sworn/Estimate/Non-Audited
Audit Date: 43626

MADISON

MADISON COUNTY CARRIER

Street Address: 1695 S State Road 53
City: Madison
State: FL
ZIP Code: 32340-3331
General Phone: (850) 973-4141
General Email: greenepub@greenepublishing.com
Publication Website: greenepublishing.com
"Parent Company: Green Publishing Inc.
"
Publisher Name: Emerald Greene Parsons
Publisher Email: emerald@greenepublishing.com
Editor Name: Savannah Reams
Editor Email: editor@greenepublishing.com
Advertising Executive Name: Jeanette Dunn
Advertising Executive Email: jeanette@greenepublishing.com
Year Established: 1964
Own Printing Facility?: Y
Mechanical specifications: Type page 13 x 21 1/2; E - 6 cols, 2 1/16, between; A - 6 cols, 2 1/16, between; C - 6 cols, 2 1/16, between.
Published Days: Wed
Avg. Paid Circ.: 3700
Audit Company: Sworn/Estimate/Non-Audited
Audit Date: 43626

MADISON

MADISON ENTERPRISE-RECORDER

Street Address: 1695 S State Road 53
City: Madison
State: FL
ZIP Code: 32340-3331
General Phone: (850) 973-4141
General Email: greenepub@greenepublishing.com
Publication Website: greenepublishing.com
"Parent Company: Green Publishing Inc.
"
Publisher Name: Emerald Greene Parsons
Publisher Email: emerald@greenepublishing.com
Editor Name: Savannah Reams
Editor Email: editor@greenepublishing.com
Advertising Executive Name: Jeanette Dunn
Advertising Executive Email: jeanette@greenepublishing.com
Mechanical specifications: Type page 13 x 21 1/2; E - 6 cols, 2, between; A - 6 cols, 2, between; C - 6 cols, 2, between.
Published Days: Fri
Avg. Paid Circ.: 3700
Audit Company: Sworn/Estimate/Non-Audited
Audit Date: 43626

MARCO ISLAND

COASTAL BREEZE NEWS

Street Address: 3513 US Highway 17
City: Marco Island
State: FL
ZIP Code: 34145-6742
General Phone: (239) 393-4991
General Email: val@coastalbreezenews.com
Publication Website: coastalbreezenews.com
Publisher Name: Val Simon
Publisher Email: val@coastalbreezenews.com
Advertising Executive Name: Mary Quinton
Advertising Executive Email: mary@coastalbreezenews.com
Delivery Methods: Carrier`Racks
Year Established: 2010
Mechanical specifications: Page 11" X 17" Image area 10" X 15.5"
Published Days: Fri`Other
Avg. Free Circ.: 17500
Audit Company: CVC
Audit Date: 43009

MARIANNA

JACKSON COUNTY TIMES

Street Address: 2866 Madison St
City: Marianna
State: FL
ZIP Code: 32448-4610
General Phone: (850) 526-1501
General Email: bo.jctimes@gmail.com
Publication Website: jacksoncountytimes.net
Parent Company: Hatcher Publications
Publisher Name: Woodrow Hatcher
Editor Name: Shelia Mader
Editor Email: editor@jacksoncountytimes.net
Editor Phone: (850) 718-6674
Delivery Methods: Mail`Racks
Year Established: 2006
Mechanical specifications: Type page 10.25 x 21; E - 6 cols 1.596, 0.117 between
Published Days: Thur
Avg. Paid Circ.: 2500
Audit Company: Sworn/Estimate/Non-Audited
Audit Date: 43626
Note: Weekly Newspaper that publishes on Thursday

MELBOURNE

BEST - CENTRAL

Street Address: 1 Gannett Plaza
City: Melbourne
State: FL
ZIP Code: 32940
General Phone: (321) 242-3500
General Email: advertising@floridatoday.com
Publication Website: floridatoday.com
Editor Name: Mara Bellaby
Editor Email: mbellaby@floridatoday.com
Editor Phone: 321-242-3573
Advertising Executive Name: Brian Wallace
Advertising Executive Email: BWALLACE@floridatoday.com
Delivery Methods: Mail
Own Printing Facility?: Y
Commercial printers?: Y
Mechanical specifications: Type page 11 5/8 x 21; 6 cols, 1.75, 0.225 between
Published Days: Wed

Community Newspapers in the U.S.

Avg. Paid Circ.: 45000
Audit Company: Sworn/Estimate/Non-Audited
Audit Date: 43626

MELBOURNE

BEST - NORTH

Street Address: 1 Gannett Plaza
City: Melbourne
State: FL
ZIP Code: 32940
General Phone: (321) 242-3500
General Email: advertising@floridatoday.com
Publication Website: floridatoday.com
Editor Name: Mara Bellaby
Editor Email: mbellaby@floridatoday.com
Editor Phone: 321-242-3573
Advertising Executive Name: Brian Wallace
Advertising Executive Email: BWALLACE@floridatoday.com
Delivery Methods: Mail
Mechanical specifications: Type page 11 5/8 x 21; 6 cols, 1.75, 0.225 between
Published Days: Wed
Avg. Paid Circ.: 55000
Audit Company: Sworn/Estimate/Non-Audited
Audit Date: 43626

MELBOURNE

BEST - SOUTH

Street Address: 1 Gannett Plaza
City: Melbourne
State: FL
ZIP Code: 32940
General Phone: (321) 242-3500
General Email: advertising@floridatoday.com
Publication Website: floridatoday.com
Editor Name: Mara Bellaby
Editor Email: mbellaby@floridatoday.com
Editor Phone: 321-242-3573
Advertising Executive Name: Brian Wallace
Advertising Executive Email: BWALLACE@floridatoday.com
Delivery Methods: Mail
Own Printing Facility?: Y
Commercial printers?: Y
Mechanical specifications: Type page 11 5/8 x 21; 6 cols, 1.75, 0.225 between
Published Days: Wed
Avg. Paid Circ.: 55000
Audit Company: Sworn/Estimate/Non-Audited
Audit Date: 43626

MIAMI

MIAMI TODAY

Street Address: 2000 S Dixie Hwy
City: Miami
State: FL
ZIP Code: 33133-2451
General Phone: (305) 358-2663
General Email: cblewis@miamitodaynews.com
Publication Website: miamitodaynews.com
Parent Company: Today Enterprises Inc.
Editor Name: Michael Lewis
Editor Email: editor@miamitodaynews.com
Delivery Methods: Carrier
Year Established: 1983
Own Printing Facility?: N
Commercial printers?: N
Published Days: Thur
Avg. Paid Circ.: 172
Avg. Free Circ.: 27229
Audit Company: BPA
Audit Date: 43622

MIAMI

SOUTH FLORIDA BUSINESS JOURNAL

Street Address: 80 SW 8th St
City: Miami
State: FL
ZIP Code: 33130-3057
General Phone: (954) 949-7600
General Email: southflorida@bizjournals.com
Publication Website: bizjournals.com/southflorida
Parent Company: American City Business Journals
Publisher Name: Melanie Dickinson
Publisher Email: mdickinson@bizjournals.com
Publisher Phone: 786-533-8201
Editor Name: Michael Adams
Editor Email: madams@bizjournals.com
Editor Phone: 786-533-8216
Advertising Executive Name: Yasmine Gahed
Advertising Executive Email: ygahed@bizjournals.com
Published Days: Fri
Avg. Free Circ.: 9000
Audit Company: Sworn/Estimate/Non-Audited
Audit Date: 43626

MONTICELLO

MONTICELLO NEWS

Street Address: 180 W Washington St
City: Monticello
State: FL
ZIP Code: 32344-1954
General Phone: (850) 997-3568
General Email: glendaslater@embarqmail.com
Publication Website: ecbpublishing.com
Publisher Name: Emerald Parsons
Publisher Email: emerald@greenepublishing.com
Publisher Phone: (850)997-3568
Delivery Methods: Mail`Racks
Published Days: Wed`Sat
Avg. Paid Circ.: 3000
Avg. Free Circ.: 30
Audit Company: Sworn/Estimate/Non-Audited
Audit Date: 43626

NAPLES

BONITA SPRINGS FLORIDA WEEKLY

Street Address: 9051 Tamiami Trl N
City: Naples
State: FL
ZIP Code: 34108-2520
General Phone: (239) 325-1960
General Email: advertise@floridaweekly.com
Publication Website: floridaweekly.com
Parent Company: Florida Media Group LLC
Publisher Name: Shelley Hobbs
Publisher Email: shobbs@floridaweekly.com
Editor Name: Eric Strachan
Editor Email: eric.strachan@floridaweekly.com
Delivery Methods: Mail`Newsstand
Published Days: Thur
Avg. Paid Circ.: 35646
Audit Company: Sworn/Estimate/Non-Audited
Audit Date: 43626

NAPLES

BUSINESS OBSERVER-COLLIER

Street Address: 501 Goodlette Rd N
City: Naples
State: FL
ZIP Code: 34102-5666
General Phone: (239) 263-0122
General Email: dschaefer@BusinessObserverFL.com
Publication Website: businessobserverfl.com
Parent Company: Observer Media Group Inc.
Publisher Name: Matt Walsh
Publisher Email: mwalsh@BusinessObserverFL.com
Publisher Phone: 941-362-4848
Editor Name: Kat Hughes
Editor Email: khughes@BusinessObserverFL.com
Editor Phone: 941-362-4848
Advertising Executive Name: Kristen Boothroyd
Advertising Executive Email: kboothroyd@BusinessObserverFL.com
Delivery Methods: Mail`Newsstand`Carrier`Racks
Year Established: 1997
Mechanical specifications: 10.375" x 16"
Published Days: Fri
Avg. Paid Circ.: 145
Avg. Free Circ.: 446
Audit Company: Sworn/Estimate/Non-Audited
Audit Date: 43626

NAPLES

MARCO EAGLE

Street Address: 1100 Immokalee Rd
City: Naples
State: FL
ZIP Code: 34110-4810
General Phone: (239) 213-6000
General Email: JLFuenmayor@Naplesnews.com
Publication Website: naplesnews.com/community/marco-eagle
Parent Company: Local Community News
Editor Name: Bill Green
Editor Email: Bill.Green@naplesnews.com
Editor Phone: 239-213-5329
Delivery Methods: Mail`Racks
Published Days: Wed`Fri`Sat
Avg. Free Circ.: 15900
Audit Company: Sworn/Estimate/Non-Audited
Audit Date: 43626

NAPLES

NAPLES FLORIDA WEEKLY

Street Address: 9051 Tamiami Trl N
City: Naples
State: FL
ZIP Code: 34108-2520
General Phone: (239) 325-1960
General Email: advertise@floridaweekly.com
Publication Website: www.floridaweekly.com
Parent Company: Florida Media Group LLC
Publisher Name: Shelley Hobbs
Publisher Email: shobbs@floridaweekly.com
Editor Name: Eric Strachan
Editor Email: eric.strachan@floridaweekly.com
Delivery Methods: Mail`Newsstand
Published Days: Thur
Avg. Paid Circ.: 35646
Audit Company: Sworn/Estimate/Non-Audited
Audit Date: 43626

NAPLES

THE COLLIER CITIZEN

Street Address: 1100 Immokalee Rd
City: Naples
State: FL
ZIP Code: 34110-4810
General Phone: (239) 213-6000
Publication Website: colliercitizen.com
Editor Name: Vonna Keomanyvong
Editor Email: vonna.keomanyvong@naplesnews.com
Delivery Methods: Mail`Racks
Year Established: 2005
Own Printing Facility?: Y
Mechanical specifications: Type page 10 1/4 x 16; E - 5 cols, 2 1/4, between; A - 5 cols, 2 1/4, between; C - 8 cols, 2 1/4, between.
Published Days: Sat
Avg. Free Circ.: 52118
Audit Company: Sworn/Estimate/Non-Audited
Audit Date: 43626

NAVARRE

NAVARRE PRESS

Street Address: 7502 Harvest Village Ct
City: Navarre
State: FL
ZIP Code: 32566-7319
General Phone: (850) 939-8040
General Email: ads@navarrepress.com
Publication Website: navarrepress.com
Publisher Name: Sandi Kemp
Publisher Email: skemp@navarrepress.com
Publisher Phone: (850) 939-8040
Editor Name: Gail Acosta
Editor Email: ads@navarrepress.com
Editor Phone: (850) 939-8040 ext. 103
Mechanical specifications: Type page 11 x 21; E - 6 cols, 1.55
Published Days: Thur
Avg. Paid Circ.: 4000
Audit Company: Sworn/Estimate/Non-Audited
Audit Date: 43626

NEW PORT RICHEY

THE SUNCOAST NEWS

Street Address: 6214 US Highway 19
City: New Port Richey
State: FL
ZIP Code: 34652-2528
General Phone: (727) 815-1000
General Email: dpleus@suncoastnews.com
Publication Website: suncoastnews.com
Parent Company: Times Publishing Company
Editor Name: Robert Hibbs
Editor Email: rhibbs@suncoastnews.com
Own Printing Facility?: Y
Commercial printers?: Y
Mechanical specifications: Type page 10 3/4 x 15; E - 5 cols, 2 1/16, between; A - 5 cols, 2 1/16, between; C - 9 cols, 1 1/16, between.
Published Days: Wed`Sat
Avg. Free Circ.: 90433
Audit Company: Sworn/Estimate/Non-Audited
Audit Date: 43626

NICEVILLE

THE BAY BEACON

Street Address: 1181 John Sims Pkwy E
City: Niceville
State: FL
ZIP Code: 32578-2752
General Phone: (850) 678-1080
General Email: info@baybeacon.com
Publication Website: baybeacon.com
Editor Name: Stephen Kent
Delivery Methods: Carrier
Year Established: 1992
Own Printing Facility?: N
Commercial printers?: N
Mechanical specifications: Type page 11.6" x 20"; 6 cols, 1.83", 0.167" between; C - 6 cols, 1.167", 0.167" between.
Published Days: Wed
Avg. Free Circ.: 15000
Audit Company: Sworn/Estimate/Non-Audited
Audit Date: 43626

OCEAN RIDGE

THE COASTAL STAR

Street Address: 5114 N Ocean Blvd
City: Ocean Ridge
State: FL
ZIP Code: 33435-7031
General Phone: (561) 337-1553
General Email: sales@thecoastalstar.com
Publication Website: thecoastalstar.com
Publisher Name: Jerry Lower
Publisher Email: publisher@thecoastalstar.com
Editor Name: Mary Thurwachter
Editor Email: maryt@thecoastalstar.com
Advertising Executive Name: Chris Bellard
Advertising Executive Email: sales@thecoastalstar.com
Delivery Methods: Mail`Newsstand`Carrier`Racks
Year Established: 2008
Mechanical specifications: Full page 10" x 15.85"; 5 cols, 1.85", 0.18 between
Published Days: Mthly
Avg. Paid Circ.: 400
Avg. Free Circ.: 17000
Audit Company: Sworn/Estimate/Non-Audited
Audit Date: 43626
Note: Two editions, delivered free during the first weekend of the month to every occupied home and condo in: South Palm Beach, Hypoluxo Island, Manalapan, Ocean Ridge, Briny Breezes, Gulf Stream, Coastal Delray Beach / Highland Beach and Coastal Boca Raton This target market is one of the most affluent in America Special sections include: ArtsPaper section Oct., Nov., Dec., Jan., Feb., March, & April Holiday Gift Guide December Summer Camp Guide April All special sections are mini tabs full page size 7.5" X 10" tall

ORLANDO

ORLANDO BUSINESS JOURNAL

Street Address: 255 S Orange Ave
City: Orlando
State: FL
ZIP Code: 32801-5007
General Phone: (407) 649-8470
General Email: rbobroff@bizjournals.com
Publication Website: bizjournals.com/orlando
Parent Company: American City Business Journals
Publisher Name: Donna Dyson
Publisher Email: ddyson@bizjournals.com
Editor Name: Susan Lundine
Editor Email: slundine@bizjournals.com
Advertising Executive Name: Drew Schrimsher
Advertising Executive Email: dschrimsher@bizjournals.com
Delivery Methods: Mail`Newsstand`Racks
Year Established: 1984
Mechanical specifications: Type page 11 x 14; cols 2.375
Published Days: Wed
Avg. Paid Circ.: 9496
Audit Company: Sworn/Estimate/Non-Audited
Audit Date: 43626

ORLANDO

WINTER PARK-MAITLAND OBSERVER

Street Address: 1500 Park Center Dr
City: Orlando
State: FL
ZIP Code: 32835-5705
General Phone: (407) 563-7000
Publication Website: wpmobserver.com
Parent Company: Observer Media Group
Publisher Name: Michael Eng
Publisher Email: meng@OrangeObserver.com
Editor Name: Tim Freed
Editor Email: tfreed@OrangeObserver.com
Advertising Executive Name: Ann Carpenter
Advertising Executive Email: acarpenter@OrangeObserver.com
Delivery Methods: Mail`Newsstand`Racks
Year Established: 1989
Commercial printers?: Y
Mechanical specifications: Type page: 10.25x16, E - 5 cols , 1.91", 0.18 between
Published Days: Thur
Avg. Paid Circ.: 5300
Audit Company: Sworn/Estimate/Non-Audited
Audit Date: 43626

PALM BEACH GARDENS

PALM BEACH GARDENS FLORIDA WEEKLY

Street Address: 11380 Prosperity Farms Rd
City: Palm Beach Gardens
State: FL
ZIP Code: 33410-3450
General Phone: (561) 904-6470
General Email: advertise@floridaweekly.com
Publication Website: floridaweekly.com
Parent Company: Florida Media Group LLC
Publisher Name: Cindy Giles
Publisher Email: cindy.giles@floridaweekly.com
Editor Name: Scott Simmons
Editor Email: ssimmons@floridaweekly.com
Delivery Methods: Mail`Newsstand
Published Days: Thur
Avg. Paid Circ.: 35646
Audit Company: Sworn/Estimate/Non-Audited
Audit Date: 43626

PALM COAST

PALM COAST OBSERVER

Street Address: 1 Florida Park Dr N
City: Palm Coast
State: FL
ZIP Code: 32137-3843
General Phone: (386) 447-9723
General Email: jaclyn@palmcoastobserver.com
Publication Website: palmcoastobserver.com
Parent Company: Observer Media Group Inc.
Publisher Name: John Walsh
Publisher Email: jwalsh@palmcoastobserver.com
Editor Name: Brian McMillan
Editor Email: bmcmillan@palmcoastobserver.com
Advertising Executive Name: Jaclyn Centofanti
Advertising Executive Email: jaclyn@palmcoastobserver.com
Delivery Methods: Newsstand`Carrier`Racks
Year Established: 2010
Mechanical specifications: Type page 10.375 x 16; 4 cols, 2.45, 0.19 between
Published Days: Thur
Avg. Paid Circ.: 11
Avg. Free Circ.: 26787
Audit Company: VAC
Audit Date: 43284

PANAMA CITY

BAY COUNTY BULLET

Street Address: 1714 W 23rd St
City: Panama City
State: FL
ZIP Code: 32405-2924
General Phone: (850) 640-0855
General Email: ads@baybullet.com
Publication Website: baybullet.com
Editor Name: Linda O. Lucas
Editor Email: llucas@baybullet.com
Editor Phone: 850-640-0855
Delivery Methods: Mail`Newsstand`Carrier`Racks
Year Established: 2009
Mechanical specifications: Type page 9.54 x 12.147
Published Days: Fri
Avg. Paid Circ.: 3300
Avg. Free Circ.: 2700
Audit Company: Sworn/Estimate/Non-Audited
Audit Date: 43626

PENSACOLA

ESCAMBIA SUN PRESS

Street Address: 220 E Monument Ave
City: Pensacola
State: FL
ZIP Code: 32507-2129
General Phone: (850) 456-3121
General Email: stories@escambiasunpress.com
Publication Website: escambiasunpress.com
Publisher Name: Michael J. Driver
Editor Name: Michael P. Driver
Delivery Methods: Mail`Racks
Year Established: 1948
Own Printing Facility?: Y
Mechanical specifications: Type page 15.75 x 21; 9 cols, 1.75
Published Days: Thur
Avg. Paid Circ.: 1600
Audit Company: Sworn/Estimate/Non-Audited
Audit Date: 43626

PERRY

TACO TIMES

Street Address: 123 S Jefferson St
City: Perry
State: FL
ZIP Code: 32347-3232
General Phone: (850) 584-5513
General Email: ads@perrynewspapers.com
Publication Website: perrynewspapers.com
Editor Name: Angela M. Castelucci
Year Established: 1961
Own Printing Facility?: Y
Mechanical specifications: Type page 10.1.25 x 21.5; 6 cols, 1.56, 0.15 between
Published Days: Wed
Avg. Paid Circ.: 5346
Audit Company: Sworn/Estimate/Non-Audited
Audit Date: 43626

PLANT CITY

PLANT CITY OBSERVER

Street Address: 1507 S Alexander St
City: Plant City
State: FL
ZIP Code: 33563-8413
General Phone: (813) 704-6850
General Email: vprostko@PlantCityObserver.com
Publication Website: PlantCityObserver.com
Parent Company: Plant City Media LLC
Publisher Name: Karen Berry
Publisher Email: kberry@plantcityobserver.com
Editor Name: Sarah Holt
Editor Email: sholt@plantcityobserver.com
Delivery Methods: Mail`Newsstand`Racks
Mechanical specifications: Type page 10 13/16 x 15; E - 5 cols, 2, 1/6 between; A - 5 cols, 2, 1/6 between; C - 8 cols, 1 1/4, 1/6 between.
Published Days: Fri
Avg. Free Circ.: 13246
Audit Company: VAC
Audit Date: 43651

POMPANO BEACH

THE SENTRY

Street Address: 2500 SE 5th Ct
City: Pompano Beach
State: FL
ZIP Code: 33062-6108
General Phone: (954) 532-2000
General Email: advertise@flsentry.com
Publication Website: flsentry.com
Editor Name: Ross Schulmister
Editor Email: Editor@flsentry.com
Year Established: 1980
Commercial printers?: Y
Mechanical specifications: Type page 13 x 21 1/2; A - 6 cols, 2 7/50, 1/6 between; C - 10 cols, 1 3/10, between.
Published Days: Thur
Avg. Paid Circ.: 5000
Audit Company: Sworn/Estimate/Non-Audited
Audit Date: 43626

PONTE VEDRA BEACH

PONTE VEDRA RECORDER

Street Address: 1102 A1A N
City: Ponte Vedra Beach
State: FL
ZIP Code: 32082-4098
General Phone: (904) 285-8831
General Email: susan@opcfla.com
Publication Website: pontevedrarecorder.com
Parent Company: Osteen Publishing Company
Publisher Name: Susan Griffin
Publisher Email: susan@opcfla.com
Publisher Phone: (904) 686-3938
Editor Name: Maggie FitzRoy
Editor Email: maggie@opcfla.com
Editor Phone: (904) 686-3939
Delivery Methods: Mail`Newsstand`Racks
Year Established: 1969
Own Printing Facility?: Y
Mechanical specifications: Type page 9 3/4 x 16; E - 4 cols, 2 5/16, between; A - 4 cols, between; C - 6 cols, 1 1/2, between.
Published Days: Fri
Avg. Paid Circ.: 1814
Avg. Free Circ.: 8000
Audit Company: CVC
Audit Date: 43628

PUNTA GORDA

PUNTA GORDA/PORT CHARLOTTE FLORIDA WEEKLY

Street Address: 1205 Elizabeth St
City: Punta Gorda
State: FL
ZIP Code: 33950-6054
General Phone: (941) 621-3422
General Email: advertise@floridaweekly.com
Publication Website: floridaweekly.com
Parent Company: Florida Media Group LLC
Publisher Name: Brandi Riede
Publisher Email: brandi.riede@floridaweekly.com
Editor Name: Bob Massey
Editor Email: bmassey@floridaweekly.com
Delivery Methods: Mail`Newsstand
Published Days: Thur
Avg. Paid Circ.: 35646
Audit Company: Sworn/Estimate/Non-Audited
Audit Date: 43626

QUINCY

Community Newspapers in the U.S.

GADSDEN COUNTY TIMES

Street Address: 112 E Washington St
City: Quincy
State: FL
ZIP Code: 32351-2415
General Phone: (904) 627-7649
General Email: poconnell@gadcotimes.com
Publication Website: gadcotimes.com
Parent Company: Landmark Community Newspapers
Editor Name: Scott J. Bryan
Editor Email: editor@gadcotimes.com
Advertising Executive Name: Amy Rooks
Advertising Executive Email: arooks@gadcotimes.com
Delivery Methods: Mail`Racks
Year Established: 1901
Mechanical specifications: Type page 10.389 x 21; A - 6 cols, 1.627, .125 between; C - 8 cols, 1.152, 0.169 between
Published Days: Thur
Avg. Paid Circ.: 3500
Avg. Free Circ.: 50
Audit Company: Sworn/Estimate/Non-Audited
Audit Date: 43626

RUSKIN

OBSERVER NEWS

Street Address: 210 Woodland Estates Ave
City: Ruskin
State: FL
ZIP Code: 33570-4591
General Phone: (813) 645-3111
General Email: desi@observernews.net
Publication Website: observernews.net
Parent Company: M&M Printing Co. Inc.
Editor Name: Chere Simmons
Editor Email: chere@observernews.net
Advertising Executive Name: Desi Ferreira
Advertising Executive Email: desi@observernews.net
Delivery Methods: Carrier`Racks
Year Established: 1958
Mechanical specifications: Type page 10.25 x 15.8; 5 cols, 1.875, 0.25 between
Published Days: Thur
Avg. Free Circ.: 51260
Audit Company: CVC
Audit Date: 44015

SAINT PETERSBURG

SOUTH TAMPA NEWS & TRIBUNE

Street Address: 490 First Avenue South
City: Saint Petersburg
State: FL
ZIP Code: 33701
General Phone: (800) 888-7012
General Email: rmcghan@tampabay.com
Publication Website: tampabay.com
Parent Company: Poynter Institute
Publisher Name: Dan Autrey
Publisher Email: dautrey@tbnweekly.com
Publisher Phone: 727-397-5563
Delivery Methods: Mail
Own Printing Facility?: Y
Mechanical specifications: Type page 10 13/16 x 15; E - 5 cols, 2 1/16, between; A - 5 cols, 2 1/16, between; C - 8 cols, 1, between.
Published Days: Wed
Avg. Paid Circ.: 18680
Avg. Free Circ.: 26334
Audit Company: Sworn/Estimate/Non-Audited
Audit Date: 43626

SANFORD

SANFORD HERALD

Street Address: 217 E 1st St
City: Sanford
State: FL
ZIP Code: 32771-1376
General Phone: (407) 322-2611
General Email: rlavender@mysanfordherald.com
Publication Website: mysanfordherald.com
Parent Company: North Carolina Press Service, Inc.
Publisher Name: Susan Wenner
Publisher Email: swenner@mysanfordherald.com
Editor Name: Rachel Graeser
Editor Email: rgraeser@mysanfordherald.com
Advertising Executive Name: Roxzie Lavender
Advertising Executive Email: RLavender@MySanfordHerald.com
Delivery Methods: Mail
Year Established: 1908
Own Printing Facility?: N
Mechanical specifications: Type page 13 x 21 1/2; E - 6 cols, 2 1/16, 1/8 between; A - 6 cols, 2 1/16, 1/8 between; C - 8 cols, 1 1/2, 1/8 between.
Published Days: Wed`Sun
Avg. Paid Circ.: 6500
Audit Company: Sworn/Estimate/Non-Audited
Audit Date: 43626

SANIBEL

CAPTIVA CURRENT

Street Address: 695 Tarpon Bay Rd Unit 13
City: Sanibel
State: FL
ZIP Code: 33957-3135
General Phone: (239) 472-1587
General Email: dpapoi@breezenewspapers.com
Publication Website: captivasanibel.com
Parent Company: Ogden Newspapers Inc.
Publisher Name: Scott Blonde
Publisher Email: sblonde@breezenewspapers.com
Publisher Phone: 574-1110 Ext 110
Editor Name: Tiffany Repecki
Editor Email: trepecki@breezenewspapers.com
Editor Phone: 472-8398
Advertising Executive Name: Mark Martens
Advertising Executive Email: mmartens@breezenewspapers.com
Year Established: 1990
Own Printing Facility?: Y
Commercial printers?: Y
Mechanical specifications: Type page 10 5/16 x 16; E - 6 cols, 1 9/16, between; A - 6 cols, 1 9/16, between; C - 6 cols, 1 9/16, between.
Published Days: Fri
Avg. Paid Circ.: 142
Avg. Free Circ.: 466
Audit Company: Sworn/Estimate/Non-Audited
Audit Date: 43626

SANIBEL

ISLAND REPORTER

Street Address: 2340 Periwinkle Way
City: Sanibel
State: FL
ZIP Code: 33957-3220
General Phone: (239) 472-1587
General Email: dpapoi@breezenewspapers.com
Publication Website: captivasanibel.com
Parent Company: Ogden Newspapers Inc.
Publisher Name: Scott Blonde
Publisher Email: sblonde@breezenewspapers.com
Publisher Phone: 574-1110 Ext 110
Editor Name: Tiffany Repecki
Editor Email: trepecki@breezenewspapers.com
Editor Phone: 472-8398
Advertising Executive Name: Mark Martens
Advertising Executive Email: mmartens@breezenewspapers.com
Delivery Methods: Mail`Racks
Year Established: 1973
Own Printing Facility?: Y
Commercial printers?: Y
Mechanical specifications: Type page 9 3/4 x 12 5/8; E - 4 cols, between; A - 6 cols, between; C - 6 cols, between.
Published Days: Fri
Avg. Paid Circ.: 789
Avg. Free Circ.: 4752
Audit Company: Sworn/Estimate/Non-Audited
Audit Date: 43626

SARASOTA

BUSINESS OBSERVER

Street Address: 1970 Main St
City: Sarasota
State: FL
ZIP Code: 34236-5923
General Phone: (941) 362-4848
General Email: dschaefer@BusinessObserverFL.com
Publication Website: businessobserverfl.com
Parent Company: Observer Media Group
Publisher Name: Matt Walsh
Publisher Email: mwalsh@BusinessObserverFL.com
Publisher Phone: 941-362-4848
Editor Name: Kat Hughes
Editor Email: khughes@BusinessObserverFL.com
Editor Phone: 941-362-4848
Advertising Executive Name: Kristen Boothroyd
Advertising Executive Email: kboothroyd@BusinessObserverFL.com
Delivery Methods: Mail`Newsstand`Carrier
Year Established: 1997
Mechanical specifications: 10.375" x 16"
Published Days: Fri
Avg. Paid Circ.: 1515
Avg. Free Circ.: 5139
Audit Company: VAC
Audit Date: 43260

SARASOTA

BUSINESS OBSERVER-HILLSBOROUGH-PASCO

Street Address: 1970 Main St
City: Sarasota
State: FL
ZIP Code: 34236-5921
General Phone: (941) 362-4848
General Email: dschaefer@BusinessObserverFL.com
Publication Website: businessobserverfl.com
Parent Company: Observer Media Group Inc.
Publisher Name: Matt Walsh
Publisher Email: mwalsh@BusinessObserverFL.com
Publisher Phone: 941-362-4848
Editor Name: Kat Hughes
Editor Email: khughes@BusinessObserverFL.com
Editor Phone: 941-362-4848
Advertising Executive Name: Kristen Boothroyd
Advertising Executive Email: kboothroyd@BusinessObserverFL.com
Delivery Methods: Mail`Newsstand`Racks
Year Established: 1997
Mechanical specifications: 10.375" x 16"
Published Days: Fri
Avg. Paid Circ.: 403
Avg. Free Circ.: 1112
Audit Company: Sworn/Estimate/Non-Audited
Audit Date: 43626

SARASOTA

BUSINESS OBSERVER-LEE

Street Address: 1970 Main St
City: Sarasota
State: FL
ZIP Code: 34236-5923
General Phone: (941) 906-9386
General Email: dschaefer@BusinessObserverFL.com
Publication Website: businessobserverfl.com
Parent Company: Observer Media Group Inc.
Publisher Name: Matt Walsh
Publisher Email: mwalsh@BusinessObserverFL.com
Publisher Phone: 941-362-4848
Editor Name: Kat Hughes
Editor Email: khughes@BusinessObserverFL.com
Editor Phone: 941-362-4848
Advertising Executive Name: Kristen Boothroyd
Advertising Executive Email: kboothroyd@BusinessObserverFL.com
Delivery Methods: Mail`Newsstand`Racks
Year Established: 1997
Mechanical specifications: 10.375" x 16"
Published Days: Fri
Avg. Paid Circ.: 202
Avg. Free Circ.: 590
Audit Company: Sworn/Estimate/Non-Audited
Audit Date: 43626

SARASOTA

EAST COUNTY OBSERVER

Street Address: 174 NE Highway 351
City: Sarasota
State: FL
ZIP Code: 34236-5921
General Phone: (941) 366-3468
General Email: mwalsh@yourobserver.com
Publication Website: yourobserver.com
Parent Company: Observer Media Group
Publisher Name: Emily Walsh
Publisher Email: ewalsh@yourobserver.com
Editor Name: Jay Heater
Editor Email: jheater@yourobserver.com
Delivery Methods: Newsstand`Carrier`Racks
Year Established: 1998
Mechanical specifications: 6 col x 16"
Published Days: Thur
Avg. Paid Circ.: 3
Avg. Free Circ.: 22250
Audit Company: VAC
Audit Date: 43651

SARASOTA

LONGBOAT OBSERVER

Street Address: 1970 Main St
City: Sarasota
State: FL
ZIP Code: 34236-5921
General Phone: (941) 366-3468
General Email: jraleigh@yourobserver.com
Publication Website: yourobserver.com
Parent Company: Observer Media Group
Publisher Name: Emily Walsh
Publisher Email: ewalsh@yourobserver.com
Editor Name: Eric Garwood
Editor Email: egarwood@yourobserver.com
Delivery Methods: Mail`Newsstand`Carrier`Racks
Year Established: 1978
Mechanical specifications: 6 col x 16"
Published Days: Thur
Avg. Paid Circ.: 271
Avg. Free Circ.: 10409
Audit Company: VAC
Audit Date: 43651

SARASOTA

SARASOTA OBSERVER

Street Address: 1970 Main St
City: Sarasota
State: FL
ZIP Code: 34236-5921
General Phone: (941) 366-3468
General Email: mwalsh@yourobserver.com
Publication Website: yourobserver.com
Parent Company: Observer Media Group
Publisher Name: Emily Walsh
Publisher Email: ewalsh@yourobserver.com
Editor Name: Eric Garwood
Editor Email: egarwood@yourobserver.com
Delivery Methods: Newsstand`Carrier`Racks
Year Established: 2004
Mechanical specifications: 6 col x 16"
Published Days: Thur
Avg. Paid Circ.: 26
Avg. Free Circ.: 16743
Audit Company: VAC
Audit Date: 43651

SARASOTA

SIESTA KEY OBSERVER

Street Address: 1970 Main St
City: Sarasota
State: FL
ZIP Code: 34236-5921
General Phone: (941) 366-3468
General Email: advertise@yourobserver.com
Publication Website: yourobserver.com
Parent Company: Observer Media Group
Publisher Name: Emily Walsh
Publisher Email: ewalsh@yourobserver.com
Editor Name: Eric Garwood
Editor Email: egarwood@yourobserver.com
Delivery Methods: Newsstand`Carrier`Racks
Year Established: 1972
Mechanical specifications: 6 col x 16"
Published Days: Thur
Avg. Free Circ.: 5109
Audit Company: VAC
Audit Date: 43651

SEMINOLE

TARPON SPRINGS BEACON

Street Address: 9911 Seminole Blvd
City: Seminole
State: FL
ZIP Code: 33772-2536
General Phone: (727) 397-5563
General Email: dautrey@tbnweekly.com
Publication Website: tbnweekly.com
Parent Company: Tampa Bay Newspapers
Publisher Name: Dan Autrey
Publisher Email: dautrey@tbnweekly.com
Publisher Phone: 397-5563
Advertising Executive Name: Jay Rey
Advertising Executive Email: jrey@tbnweekly.com
Delivery Methods: Newsstand`Carrier`Racks
Own Printing Facility?: Y
Published Days: Wed
Avg. Free Circ.: 21,7
Audit Company: Sworn/Estimate/Non-Audited
Audit Date: 43626
Business Equipment: PC
Business Software: Pre1
Classified Equipment: Mac
Classified Software: Pre1
Editorial Equipment: Mac
Editorial Software: InDesign
Production Equipment: Mac
Production Software: InDesign

SOUTH PASADENA

THE ISLAND REPORTER

Street Address: 1331 Sea Gull Dr S
City: South Pasadena
State: FL
ZIP Code: 33707-3833
General Phone: (727) 631-4730

General Email: info@theislandreporter.com
Publication Website: theislandreporter.com
Delivery Methods: Mail`Racks
Year Established: 2003
Published Days: Wed`Mthly
Avg. Free Circ.: 30175
Audit Company: CVC
Audit Date: 43284

STARKE

BRADFORD COUNTY TELEGRAPH

Street Address: 135 W Call St
City: Starke
State: FL
ZIP Code: 32091-3210
General Phone: (904) 964-6305
General Email: darlene@bctelegraph.com
Publication Website: bctelegraph.com
Editor Name: Mark Crawford
Editor Email: editor@bctelegraph.com
Advertising Executive Name: John Ryan
Advertising Executive Email: johnryan@bctelegraph.com
Year Established: 1879
Own Printing Facility?: Y
Commercial printers?: Y
Mechanical specifications: Type Page 11 x 21; SAU - 6 cols, 1.83" C - 9 cols, 1.181"
Published Days: Thur
Avg. Paid Circ.: 5825
Avg. Free Circ.: 1000
Audit Company: Sworn/Estimate/Non-Audited
Audit Date: 43626

STARKE

UNION COUNTY TIMES

Street Address: 131 W Call St
City: Starke
State: FL
ZIP Code: 32091-3210
General Phone: (904) 964-6305
General Email: kmiller@bctelegraph.com
Publication Website: starkejournal.com
Editor Name: Mark Crawford
Editor Email: editor@BcTelegraph.com
Editor Phone: 904-964-6305
Year Established: 1912
Own Printing Facility?: Y
Mechanical specifications: Type Page 11 x 21; SAU - 6 cols, 1.83" C - 9 cols, 1.181"
Published Days: Thur
Avg. Paid Circ.: 1000
Avg. Free Circ.: 1750
Audit Company: Sworn/Estimate/Non-Audited
Audit Date: 43626

STUART

JUPITER COURIER

Street Address: 1939 SE Federal Hwy
City: Stuart
State: FL
ZIP Code: 34994-3915
General Phone: (772) 287-1550
General Email: jess.mcallister@scripps.com
Publication Website: tcpalm.com
Editor Name: Adam L. Neal
Editor Email: adam.neal@tcpalm.com
Year Established: 1957
Own Printing Facility?: Y
Published Days: Wed`Sun
Avg. Paid Circ.: 8500
Avg. Free Circ.: 8500
Audit Company: Sworn/Estimate/Non-Audited
Audit Date: 43284

TAMPA

BRANDON NEWS & TRIBUNE

Street Address: 202 S Parker St
City: Tampa
State: FL
ZIP Code: 33606-2379
General Phone: (813) 259-7711
General Email: adsolutions@tampatrib.com
Publication Website: tbo.com/brandon
Parent Company: Tampa Bay Newspapers
Publisher Name: Dan Autrey
Publisher Email: dautrey@tbnweekly.com
Publisher Phone: 727-397-5563
Delivery Methods: Mail
Year Established: 1956
Own Printing Facility?: Y
Mechanical specifications: Type page 10 1/4 x 15; E - 5 cols, 2 1/16, between; A - 5 cols, 2 1/16, between; C - 8 cols, 1 5/12, between.
Published Days: Wed
Avg. Paid Circ.: 16682
Avg. Free Circ.: 41318
Audit Company: Sworn/Estimate/Non-Audited
Audit Date: 43626

TAMPA

CARROLLWOOD NEWS & TRIBUNE

Street Address: 202 S Parker St
City: Tampa
State: FL
ZIP Code: 33606-2379
General Phone: (813) 259-7711
General Email: adsolutions@tampatrib.com
Publication Website: tbo.com/carrollwood
Parent Company: Tampa Bay Newspapers
Publisher Name: Dan Autrey
Publisher Email: dautrey@tbnweekly.com
Publisher Phone: 727-397-5563
Delivery Methods: Mail
Own Printing Facility?: Y
Mechanical specifications: Type page 10 1/4 x 15; E - 5 cols, 2 1/16, between; A - 5 cols, 2 1/16, between; C - 8 cols, 1 5/12, between.
Published Days: Wed
Avg. Paid Circ.: 12851
Avg. Free Circ.: 35800
Audit Company: Sworn/Estimate/Non-Audited
Audit Date: 43626

TAMPA

CREATIVE LOAFING TAMPA BAY

Street Address: 1313 Central Ter
City: Tampa
State: FL
ZIP Code: 33605-3652
General Phone: (813) 739-4800
General Email: kelly.moroni@creativeloafing.com
Publication Website: cltampa.com
Parent Company: Euclid Media Group LLC
Publisher Name: James Howard
Publisher Email: james.howard@cltampa.com
Publisher Phone: 813-739-4800
Editor Name: Ray Roa
Editor Email: rroa@cltampa.com
Editor Phone: 813-739-4800
Advertising Executive Name: Anthony Carbone
Advertising Executive Email: ANTHONY.CARBONE@CLTAMPA.COM
Year Established: 1988
Published Days: Thur
Avg. Free Circ.: 33976
Audit Company: VAC
Audit Date: 43284

TAMPA

PLANT CITY COURIER & TRIBUNE

Street Address: 202 S Parker St
City: Tampa
State: FL
ZIP Code: 33606-2379
General Phone: (813) 259-7711
General Email: adsolutions@tampatrib.com
Publication Website: tbo.com/plant-city
Parent Company: Poynter Institute
Publisher Name: Dan Autrey
Publisher Email: dautrey@tbnweekly.com
Publisher Phone: 727-397-5563
Delivery Methods: Mail
Own Printing Facility?: Y
Commercial printers?: Y
Mechanical specifications: Type page 10 13/16 x 15; E - 5 cols, 2, 1/6 between; A - 5 cols, 2, 1/6 between; C - 8 cols, 1 1/4, 1/6 between.
Published Days: Wed
Avg. Paid Circ.: 6621
Avg. Free Circ.: 2336
Audit Company: Sworn/Estimate/Non-Audited
Audit Date: 43626

TAVERNIER

FLORIDA KEYS FREE PRESS

Street Address: 605 S Old Corry Field Rd
City: Tavernier
State: FL
ZIP Code: 33070-2649
General Phone: (305) 853-7277
General Email: sales@keysnews.com
Publication Website: keysnews.com
Parent Company: Adams Publishing Group
Publisher Name: Richard Tamborrino
Publisher Email: rtamborrino@keysnews.com
Editor Name: Dan Campbell
Editor Email: dcampbell@keysnews.com
Advertising Executive Name: Jill Jones
Advertising Executive Email: jjones@keysnews.com
Own Printing Facility?: N
Published Days: Wed
Avg. Paid Circ.: 210
Avg. Free Circ.: 14000
Audit Company: Sworn/Estimate/Non-Audited
Audit Date: 43626

TAVERNIER

THE REPORTER

Street Address: 171 Hood Ave
City: Tavernier
State: FL
ZIP Code: 33070-2645
General Phone: (305) 852-3216
General Email: jdarden@keysreporter.com
Publication Website: flkeysnews.com
Parent Company: Media News Group
Editor Name: David Goodhue
Editor Email: dgoodhue@flkeysnews.com
Advertising Executive Name: Glenn Brandt
Advertising Executive Email: gbrandt@flkeysnews.com
Delivery Methods: Mail`Newsstand`Carrier`Racks
Year Established: 1973
Published Days: Fri
Avg. Paid Circ.: 7094
Avg. Free Circ.: 500
Audit Company: Sworn/Estimate/Non-Audited
Audit Date: 43626

TRENTON

GILCHRIST COUNTY JOURNAL

Street Address: 207 N Main St
City: Trenton
State: FL
ZIP Code: 32693-3439
General Phone: (352) 463-7135

Community Newspapers in the U.S.

III-197

General Email: gcjads@bellsouth.net
Publication Website: gilchristcountyjournal.net
Publisher Name: John M. Ayers II
Publisher Email: gilchristjournal@bellsouth.net
Editor Name: Carrie A. Mizell
Editor Email: gcjreport@bellsouth.net
Advertising Executive Name: Chris Rogers
Advertising Executive Email: gcjads@bellsouth.net
Mechanical specifications: Type page 13 x 21; 6 cols, 2", 0.25 between
Published Days: Thur
Avg. Paid Circ.: 4000
Audit Company: Sworn/Estimate/Non-Audited
Audit Date: 43626

UMATILLA

NORTH LAKE OUTPOST

Street Address: PO Box 1099
City: Umatilla
State: FL
ZIP Code: 32784-1099
General Phone: (352) 669-2430
General Email: northlakeoutpost@aol.com
Publication Website: thenorthlakeoutpost.com
Publisher Name: Holly Palmer-Newby
Delivery Methods: Mail`Racks
Year Established: 1979
Mechanical specifications: one column = 9.5 picas
Published Days: Thur
Avg. Paid Circ.: 3000
Audit Company: Sworn/Estimate/Non-Audited
Audit Date: 43626

VENICE

VENICE GONDOLIER SUN

Street Address: 200 E Venice Ave
City: Venice
State: FL
ZIP Code: 34285-1998
General Phone: (941) 207-1000
General Email: majoraccts@sun-herald.com
Publication Website: venicegondolier.com
Parent Company: Adams Publishing Group
Publisher Name: Glen Nickerson
Publisher Email: glen.nickerson@yoursun.com
Publisher Phone: (941) 207-1010
Editor Name: Scott Lawson
Editor Email: scott.lawson@yoursun.com
Editor Phone: (941) 429-3010
Delivery Methods: Mail`Newsstand`Carrier`Racks
Year Established: 1946
Own Printing Facility?: Y
Mechanical specifications: Type page 6 x 21; E - 6 cols, 2 1/16, between; A - 6 cols, 2 1/16, Classy-6Cols
Published Days: Wed`Sun
Avg. Paid Circ.: 14000
Avg. Free Circ.: 13000
Audit Company: Sworn/Estimate/Non-Audited
Audit Date: 43626

WAUCHULA

THE HERALD-ADVOCATE

Street Address: 115 S 7th Ave
City: Wauchula
State: FL
ZIP Code: 33873-2801
General Phone: (863) 773-3255
General Email: publisher@theheraldadvocate.com
Publication Website: theheraldadvocate.com
Editor Name: Cynthia Krahl

Year Established: 1955
Mechanical specifications: Type page 11 x 21.5; 6 cols, 1.75, 0.1 between
Published Days: Thur
Avg. Paid Circ.: 4750
Avg. Free Circ.: 50
Audit Company: Sworn/Estimate/Non-Audited
Audit Date: 43626

WELLINGTON

THE TOWN CRIER

Street Address: 12794 Forest Hill Blvd
City: Wellington
State: FL
ZIP Code: 33414-4758
General Phone: (561) 793-7606
General Email: news@gotowncrier.com
Publication Website: gotowncrier.com
Parent Company: Newspaper Publishers LLC
Publisher Name: Barry S. Manning
Editor Name: Joshua I. Manning
Advertising Executive Name: Betty Buglio
Delivery Methods: Mail`Newsstand`Racks
Year Established: 1980
Mechanical specifications: Type page 9 1/2 x 16; E - 5 cols, 1 3/4, 1/4 between; A - 5 cols, 1 3/4, 1/4 between; C - 5 cols, 1 3/4, 1/4 between.
Published Days: Thur
Avg. Free Circ.: 25000
Audit Company: Sworn/Estimate/Non-Audited
Audit Date: 43626

WILLISTON

WILLISTON PIONEER SUN NEWS

Street Address: 607 SW 1st Ave
City: Williston
State: FL
ZIP Code: 32696-2515
General Phone: (352) 528-3343
General Email: Chad.Thompson@chieflandcitizen.com
Publication Website: willistonpioneer.com
Parent Company: Landmark Community Newspapers
Editor Name: Carolyn Ten Broeck
Editor Email: editor@willistonpioneer.com
Advertising Executive Name: Nicole Walker
Advertising Executive Email: nwalker@willistonpioneer.com
Delivery Methods: Mail`Newsstand`Racks
Year Established: 1879
Own Printing Facility?: Y
Mechanical specifications: Type page 9.888 x 21.25; 6 cols, 1.639
Published Days: Thur
Avg. Paid Circ.: 1500
Audit Company: Sworn/Estimate/Non-Audited
Audit Date: 43626

WINTER GARDEN

THE WEST ORANGE TIMES & OBSERVER

Street Address: 720 S Dillard St
City: Winter Garden
State: FL
ZIP Code: 34787-3908
General Phone: (407) 656-2121
General Email: advertising@orangeobserver.com
Publication Website: orangeobserver.com
Parent Company: Observer Media Group
Publisher Name: Michael Eng
Publisher Email: meng@OrangeObserver.com
Editor Name: Tim Freed
Editor Email: tfreed@OrangeObserver.com
Advertising Executive Name: Ann Carpenter

Advertising Executive Email: acarpenter@OrangeObserver.com
Delivery Methods: Mail`Racks
Year Established: 1905
Published Days: Thur
Avg. Paid Circ.: 22000
Audit Company: Sworn/Estimate/Non-Audited
Audit Date: 43626

WINTER HAVEN

THE POLK COUNTY NEWS AND DEMOCRAT

Street Address: 99 3rd St NW
City: Winter Haven
State: FL
ZIP Code: 33881-4609
General Phone: (863) 533-4183
General Email: kedwards@scmginc.com
Publication Website: polkcountydemocrat.com
Parent Company: Sun Coast Media Group
Editor Name: Steven Ryzewski
Advertising Executive Name: Anita Swain
Advertising Executive Email: aswain@scmginc.com
Delivery Methods: Mail`Newsstand`Carrier`Racks
Year Established: 1931
Own Printing Facility?: Y
Commercial printers?: Y
Mechanical specifications: Type page 15 1/8 x 21; E - 7 cols, 2 1/16, 1/8 between; A - 7 cols, 2 1/16, 1/8 between; C - 9 cols, 1 1/2, 1/8 between.
Published Days: Wed`Mthly`Other
Weekday Frequency: All day
Avg. Paid Circ.: 2500
Avg. Free Circ.: 18000
Audit Company: Sworn/Estimate/Non-Audited
Audit Date: 43626

GEORGIA

ALPHARETTA

JOHN'S CREEK HERALD

Street Address: 319 N Main St
City: Alpharetta
State: GA
ZIP Code: 30009-2321
General Phone: (770)442-3278
General Email: carson@appenmediagroup.com
Publication Website: https://www.northfulton.com/johnscreek/
Parent Company: Appen Media Group
Publisher Name: Ray Appen
Publisher Email: ray@appenmediagroup.com
Publisher Phone: (770) 442-3278, ext : 101
Advertising Executive Name: Kimberly Tyson
Advertising Executive Email: kimberly@appenmediagroup.com
Advertising Executive Phone: (770) 442-3278
Published Days: Other
Avg. Free Circ.: 19975
Audit Company: Sworn/Estimate/Non-Audited
Audit Date: 43626

ALPHARETTA

MILTON HERALD

Street Address: 319 N Main St
City: Alpharetta
State: GA
ZIP Code: 30009-2321
General Phone: (770)442-3278

General Email: joe@appenmediagroup.com
Publication Website: https://www.northfulton.com/johnscreek/
Parent Company: Appen Media Group
Publisher Name: Ray Appen
Publisher Email: ray@appenmediagroup.com
Publisher Phone: (770) 442-3278, ext : 101
Editor Name: Joe Parker
Editor Email: joe@appenmediagroup.com
Editor Phone: (770) 442-3278, ext : 139
Advertising Executive Name: Kimberly Tyson
Advertising Executive Email: kimberly@appenmediagroup.com
Advertising Executive Phone: (770) 442-3278
Published Days: Other
Avg. Free Circ.: 9308
Audit Company: Sworn/Estimate/Non-Audited
Audit Date: 43626

ALPHARETTA

THE FORSYTH HERALD

Street Address: 319 N Main St
City: Alpharetta
State: GA
ZIP Code: 30009-2321
General Phone: (770) 442-3278
General Email: kathleen@appenmediagroup.com
Publication Website: https://www.northfulton.com/johnscreek/
Parent Company: Appen Media Group
Publisher Name: Ray Appen
Publisher Email: ray@appenmediagroup.com
Publisher Phone: (770) 442-3278, ext : 101
Editor Name: Kathleen Sturgeon
Editor Email: kathleen@appenmediagroup.com
Editor Phone: (770) 442-3278, ext : 143
Advertising Executive Name: Kimberly Tyson
Advertising Executive Email: kimberly@appenmediagroup.com
Advertising Executive Phone: (770) 442-3278
Year Established: 1998
Published Days: Other
Avg. Free Circ.: 16975
Audit Company: CVC
Audit Date: 43628

ALPHARETTA

THE REVUE & NEWS

Street Address: 319 N Main St
City: Alpharetta
State: GA
ZIP Code: 30009-2321
General Phone: (770) 442-3278
General Email: pat@appenmediagroup.com
Publication Website: https://www.northfulton.com/johnscreek/
Parent Company: Appen Media Group
Publisher Name: Ray Appen
Publisher Email: ray@appenmediagroup.com
Publisher Phone: (770) 442-3278, ext : 101
Editor Name: Patrick Fox
Editor Email: pat@appenmediagroup.com
Editor Phone: (770) 442-3278, ext : 118
Advertising Executive Name: Kimberly Tyson
Advertising Executive Email: kimberly@appenmediagroup.com
Advertising Executive Phone: (770) 442-3278
Mechanical specifications: Type page 10 x 12 3/8; E - 5 cols, 1 7/8, 9/16 between; A - 5 cols, 1 7/8, 9/16 between; C - 8 cols, 1 1/8, 1/8 between.
Published Days: Other
Avg. Paid Circ.: 350
Avg. Free Circ.: 27625
Audit Company: Sworn/Estimate/Non-Audited
Audit Date: 43626

ASHBURN

WIREGRASS FARMER

Street Address: 109 N Gordon St
City: Ashburn
State: GA
ZIP Code: 31714-5208
General Phone: (229) 567-3655
General Email: circulation_cpc@runbox.com
Publication Website: https://www.thewiregrassfarmer.com/
Publisher Name: Ben Baker
Publisher Email: wiregrassfarmer@yahoo.com
Delivery Methods: Mail`Newsstand`Racks
Year Established: 1902
Published Days: Wed
Avg. Paid Circ.: 2000
Avg. Free Circ.: 100
Audit Company: Sworn/Estimate/Non-Audited
Audit Date: 43626

ATLANTA

ATLANTA BUSINESS CHRONICLE

Street Address: 3384 Peachtree Road NE, Suite 900
City: Atlanta
State: GA
ZIP Code: 30326-2828
General Phone: (404) 249-1000
General Email: atlanta@bizjournals.com
Publication Website: https://www.bizjournals.com/atlanta
Parent Company: American City Business Journals
Publisher Name: David Rubinger
Publisher Email: drubinger@bizjournals.com
Publisher Phone: (404) 249-1009
Editor Name: Jessica Saunders
Editor Email: jessicasaunders@bizjournals.com
Advertising Executive Name: Joey Powell
Advertising Executive Email: jpowell@bizjournals.com
Advertising Executive Phone: (404) 249-1011
Delivery Methods: Mail`Newsstand`Racks
Year Established: 1978
Published Days: Fri
Audit Company: Sworn/Estimate/Non-Audited
Audit Date: 43626

ATLANTA

NORTHSIDE NEIGHBOR

Street Address: 5290 Roswell Rd., N.W., Suite M
City: Atlanta
State: GA
ZIP Code: 30342-1978
General Phone: (404) 256-3100
General Email: nside@neighbornewspapers.com
Publication Website: https://www.mdjonline.com/neighbor_newspapers/northside_sandy_springs/
Parent Company: MDJ
Editor Name: Everett Catts
Advertising Executive Name: Stephanie DeJarnette
Advertising Executive Email: sdejarnette@neighbornewspapers.com
Advertising Executive Phone: (404) 256-3100, ext : 725
Own Printing Facility?: Y
Commercial printers?: Y
Mechanical specifications: Type page 13 x 21; E - 6 cols, 2 1/16, between; A - 6 cols, 2 1/16, between; C - 10 cols, 1 3/16, between.
Published Days: Wed
Audit Company: Sworn/Estimate/Non-Audited
Audit Date: 43626

ATLANTA

REPORTER NEWSPAPERS

Street Address: 6065 Roswell Rd Ste 225
City: Atlanta
State: GA
ZIP Code: 30328-4012
General Phone: (404) 917-2200
General Email: amyarno@reporternewspapers.com
Publication Website: https://www.reporternewspapers.net/
Parent Company: Springs Publishing LLC
Publisher Name: Steve Levene
Publisher Email: stevelevene@reporternewspapers.net
Publisher Phone: (404) 917-2200, ext : 111
Editor Name: John Ruch
Editor Email: johnruch@reporternewspapers.net
Editor Phone: (404) 917-2200, ext : 113
Advertising Executive Name: Deborah Davis
Advertising Executive Email: deborahdavis@reporternewspapers.net
Advertising Executive Phone: (404) 917-2200, ext : 110
Delivery Methods: Carrier`Racks
Year Established: 2006
Own Printing Facility?: N
Commercial printers?: Y
Published Days: Fri
Published Other: Bi-weekly
Avg. Free Circ.: 100000
Audit Company: Sworn/Estimate/Non-Audited
Audit Date: 43626

BAINBRIDGE

THE POST-SEARCHLIGHT

Street Address: 301 N Crawford St
City: Bainbridge
State: GA
ZIP Code: 39817-3612
General Phone: (229) 246-2827
General Email: powell.cobb@thepostsearchlight.com
Publication Website: https://www.thepostsearchlight.com/
Parent Company: Boone Newspapers
Publisher Name: Mark Pope
Publisher Email: mark.pope@thepostsearchlight.com
Publisher Phone: (229) 246-2827, ext : 112
Editor Name: Powell Cobb
Editor Email: powell.cobb@thepostsearchlight.com
Editor Phone: (229) 246-2827, ext : 104
Advertising Executive Name: Jason Smith
Advertising Executive Email: jason.smith@thepostsearchlight.com
Advertising Executive Phone: (229) 246-2827, ext : 109
Own Printing Facility?: Y
Commercial printers?: Y
Published Days: Wed`Sat
Avg. Paid Circ.: 7167
Avg. Free Circ.: 242
Audit Company: Sworn/Estimate/Non-Audited
Audit Date: 43626

BLACKSHEAR

THE BLACKSHEAR TIMES

Street Address: 121 SW Central Ave
City: Blackshear
State: GA
ZIP Code: 31516-2259
General Phone: (912) 449-6693
General Email: mail@theblacksheartimes.com
Publication Website: http://www.theblacksheartimes.com/
Parent Company: SouthFire Newspapers
Publisher Name: Matt Gardner
Publisher Email: mgardner@theblacksheartimes.com
Editor Name: Sarah Tarr Gove
Editor Email: cwilliams@theblacksheartimes.com
Advertising Executive Name: Matt Gardner
Advertising Executive Email: mgardner@theblacksheartimes.com
Delivery Methods: Mail`Newsstand
Mechanical specifications: Type page 11 1/16 x 21 1/2; E - 6 cols, 1 5/6, between; A - 6 cols, 1 5/6, between; C - 6 cols, 1 5/6, between.
Published Days: Wed
Avg. Paid Circ.: 3650
Audit Company: Sworn/Estimate/Non-Audited
Audit Date: 43626

BLAIRSVILLE

NORTH GEORGIA NEWS

Street Address: 266 Cleveland St
City: Blairsville
State: GA
ZIP Code: 30512-8537
General Phone: (706) 745-6343
General Email: northgeorgianews@hotmail.com
Publication Website: https://www.nganews.com/
Publisher Name: Kenneth West
Editor Name: Shawn Jarrard
Mechanical specifications: Type page 13 x 21 1/2.
Published Days: Wed
Avg. Paid Circ.: 10400
Audit Company: Sworn/Estimate/Non-Audited
Audit Date: 43626

BLUE RIDGE

THE NEWS-OBSERVER

Street Address: 5748 Appalachian Hwy
City: Blue Ridge
State: GA
ZIP Code: 30513-4240
General Phone: (706) 632-2019
General Email: news@thenewsobserver.com
Publication Website: https://www.thenewsobserver.com/
Parent Company: Community Newspapers Inc.
Publisher Name: Glenn Harbison
Publisher Email: glenn@thenewsobserver.com
Editor Name: Lauren Bearden
Editor Email: lauren@thenewsobserver.com
Advertising Executive Email: ads@thenewsobserver.com
Mechanical specifications: Type page 13 x 21 1/2; E - 6 cols, 2 1/8, 1/6 between; A - 6 cols, 2 1/8, 1/6 between; C - 6 cols, 2 1/8, 1/6 between.
Published Days: Wed
Avg. Paid Circ.: 2372
Audit Company: Sworn/Estimate/Non-Audited
Audit Date: 43626

BRUNSWICK

THE ISLANDER

Street Address: 1604B Newcastle St
City: Brunswick
State: GA
ZIP Code: 31520-6729
General Phone: (912) 265-9654
General Email: ssislander@bellsouth.net
Publication Website: https://www.theislanderonline.com/
Delivery Methods: Mail
Year Established: 1972
Own Printing Facility?: N
Commercial printers?: N
Mechanical specifications: Type page 10 x 13; E - 4 cols, 2 1/3, between; A - 4 cols, 2 1/3, between; C - 5 cols, 1 2/3, between.
Published Days: Mon
Avg. Paid Circ.: 3500
Avg. Free Circ.: 500
Audit Company: Sworn/Estimate/Non-Audited
Audit Date: 43626

CAIRO

THE CAIRO MESSENGER

Street Address: P.O. Box 30
City: Cairo
State: GA
ZIP Code: 39828-2102
General Phone: (229) 377-2032
General Email: news@cairomessenger.com
Publication Website: https://www.cairomessenger.com/
Advertising Executive Email: advertising@cairomessenger.com
Year Established: 1904
Published Days: Wed
Avg. Paid Circ.: 500
Avg. Free Circ.: 2750
Audit Company: Sworn/Estimate/Non-Audited
Audit Date: 43626

CALHOUN

CALHOUN TIMES AND GORDON COUNTY NEWS

Street Address: 210 S. King St., Suite D
City: Calhoun
State: GA
ZIP Code: 30701-1815
General Phone: (706) 629-2231
General Email: calhountimes@calhountimes.com
Publication Website: http://www.northwestgeorgianews.com/calhoun_times
Parent Company: Times Journal Inc.
Editor Name: Daniel Bell
Editor Email: dbell@calhountimes.com
Advertising Executive Name: Billy Steele
Advertising Executive Email: bsteele@calhountimes.com
Delivery Methods: Mail`Newsstand`Carrier`Racks
Year Established: 1870
Own Printing Facility?: Y
Commercial printers?: Y
Mechanical specifications: Type page 13 x 21 1/4; E - 6 cols, 2, 1/6 between; A - 6 cols, 2, 1/6 between; C - 9 cols, 1 1/3, 1/10 between.
Published Days: Wed`Sat
Avg. Paid Circ.: 8500
Audit Company: Sworn/Estimate/Non-Audited
Audit Date: 43626

CARROLLTON

TALLAPOOSA JOURNAL

Street Address: 901 Hays Mill Rd
City: Carrollton
State: GA
ZIP Code: 30117-9576
General Phone: (770) 834-6631
General Email: melissa@times-georgian.com
Publication Website: https://times-georgian.com/news-category/tallapoosa-journal/25/
Parent Company: Times-Georgian
Publisher Name: Rachael Raney
Publisher Email: publisher@times-georgian.com
Publisher Phone: (470) 729-3234
Advertising Executive Name: Melissa Wilson
Advertising Executive Email: melissa@times-georgian.com
Advertising Executive Phone: (470) 729-3237
Delivery Methods: Mail`Newsstand`Racks
Published Days: Thur

CARROLLTON

THE VILLA RICAN

Street Address: 901 Hays Mill Rd
City: Carrollton
State: GA
ZIP Code: 30117-9576
General Phone: (770) 834-6631
General Email: ken@times-georgian.com
Publication Website: https://times-georgian.com/news-category/villa-rican/22/
Parent Company: Paxton Media Group, LLC
Publisher Name: Rachael Raney
Publisher Email: publisher@times-georgian.com
Publisher Phone: (470) 729-3234
Editor Name: Ken Denney
Editor Email: ken@times-georgian.com
Editor Phone: (470) 729-3254
Advertising Executive Name: Angie Glasscock
Advertising Executive Email: angie@times-georgian.com
Advertising Executive Phone: (470) 729-3238
Delivery Methods: Carrier`Racks
Own Printing Facility?: Y
Commercial printers?: Y
Published Days: Thur
Avg. Free Circ.: 8200
Audit Company: Sworn/Estimate/Non-Audited
Audit Date: 43626

CEDARTOWN

THE POLK COUNTY STANDARD JOURNAL

Street Address: 213 Main St
City: Cedartown
State: GA
ZIP Code: 30125-3048
General Phone: (770) 748-1520
General Email: kmyrick@npco.com
Publication Website: http://www.northwestgeorgianews.com/polk_standard_journal/
Parent Company: Times Journal Inc.
Delivery Methods: Mail`Carrier`Racks
Year Established: 1869
Own Printing Facility?: Y
Commercial printers?: Y
Published Days: Wed
Avg. Paid Circ.: 3679
Audit Company: Sworn/Estimate/Non-Audited
Audit Date: 43626

CHATSWORTH

CHATSWORTH TIMES

Street Address: 224 N 3rd Ave
City: Chatsworth
State: GA
ZIP Code: 30705-2536
General Phone: (706) 695-4646
General Email: sherri.jenkins@chatsworthtimes.com
Publication Website: http://www.chatsworthtimes.com/
Parent Company: Pittsburgh Post Gazette
Editor Name: Kyle Presley
Editor Email: kyle.presley@chatsworthtimes.com
Advertising Executive Name: Sherri Jenkins
Advertising Executive Email: sherri.jenkins@chatsworthtimes.com
Advertising Executive Phone: (706) 695-4646
Mechanical specifications: Type page 13 x 21 1/2; E - 6 cols, 2 1/16, 1/8 between; A - 6 cols, 2 1/16, 1/8 between; C - 6 cols, 2 1/16, 1/8 between.
Published Days: Wed
Avg. Paid Circ.: 6000
Audit Company: Sworn/Estimate/Non-Audited
Audit Date: 43626

CLAXTON

CLAXTON ENTERPRISE

Street Address: 24 S Newton St
City: Claxton
State: GA
ZIP Code: 30417-2044
General Phone: (912) 739-2132
General Email: editor@claxtonenterprise.com
Publication Website: https://www.claxtonenterprise.com/
Publisher Name: Pamela Peace
Publisher Email: papeace@claxtonenterprise.com
Editor Name: Julie Braly
Editor Email: editor@claxtonenterprise.com
Advertising Executive Name: Paula McNeely
Advertising Executive Email: paula@claxtonenterprise.com
Delivery Methods: Mail`Racks
Mechanical specifications: Type page 13 x 21; E - 6 cols, 2 1/6 between; A - 6 cols, 2, 1/6 between; C - 6 cols, 2, 1/6 between.
Published Days: Wed
Avg. Paid Circ.: 4200
Avg. Free Circ.: 50
Audit Company: Sworn/Estimate/Non-Audited
Audit Date: 43626

CLEVELAND

WHITE COUNTY NEWS

Street Address: 13 E Jarrard St
City: Cleveland
State: GA
ZIP Code: 30528-1228
General Phone: (706) 865-4718
General Email: subs@whitecountynews.net
Publication Website: https://www.whitecountynews.net/
Parent Company: Community Newspapers, Inc.
Publisher Name: Wayne Hardy
Publisher Email: publisher@whitecountynews.net
Publisher Phone: (706) 865-4718
Delivery Methods: Mail`Racks
Year Established: 1968
Own Printing Facility?: Y
Published Days: Thur
Avg. Paid Circ.: 5000
Audit Company: Sworn/Estimate/Non-Audited
Audit Date: 43626

COLQUITT

MILLER COUNTY LIBERAL

Street Address: 157 E. Main St.
City: Colquitt
State: GA
ZIP Code: 39837-0037
General Phone: (229) 758-5549
General Email: millercountyliberal@gmail.com
Publication Website: https://www.millercountyliberal.com/
Publisher Name: Betty Jo Toole
Editor Name: Terry Toole
Advertising Executive Name: Wanda Griffin
Delivery Methods: Mail`Newsstand`Carrier`Racks
Year Established: 1897
Own Printing Facility?: Y
Published Days: Wed
Avg. Paid Circ.: 3000
Audit Company: Sworn/Estimate/Non-Audited
Audit Date: 43626

CONYERS

THE NEWTON CITIZEN

Street Address: 969 S Main St NE
City: Conyers
State: GA
ZIP Code: 30012-4501
General Phone: (770) 483-7108
General Email: alicia.goss@rockdalecitizen.com
Publication Website: https://www.rockdalenewtoncitizen.com/
Parent Company: Southern Community Newspapers, Inc.
Editor Name: Alice Queen
Editor Email: alice.queen@rockdalecitizen.com
Editor Phone: (770) 483-7108, ext : 226
Advertising Executive Name: Alicia Goss
Advertising Executive Email: alicia.goss@rockdalecitizen.com
Advertising Executive Phone: (706) 255-6745
Published Days: Wed`Fri`Sat
Weekday Frequency: m
Avg. Paid Circ.: 1863
Avg. Free Circ.: 246
Audit Company: CVC
Audit Date: 43293

CORDELE

CORDELE DISPATCH

Street Address: 306 West 13th Avenue
City: Cordele
State: GA
ZIP Code: 31015-1669
General Phone: (229) 273-2277
General Email: gabe.jordan@cordeledispatch.com
Publication Website: https://www.cordeledispatch.com/
Parent Company: Boone Newspapers
Editor Name: Erica O'Neal
Advertising Executive Name: Chris Lewis
Advertising Executive Email: chris.lewis@cordeledispatch.com
Year Established: 1908
Mechanical specifications: Type page 13 x 21 1/2; E - 6 cols, 2 1/16, 1/8 between; A - 6 cols, 2 1/16, 1/8 between; C - 9 cols, 1 3/8, 1/16 between.
Published Days: Wed`Sat
Weekday Frequency: m
Avg. Paid Circ.: 4590
Audit Company: Sworn/Estimate/Non-Audited
Audit Date: 43626
Pressroom Equipment: Registration System -- Duarte/Pin Registration System.
Mailroom Equipment: Tying Machines -- 1/Midstates, 1-MLN/SP300; Address Machine -- 1-/El, 1-/Am.;
Business Equipment: ATT
Business Software: Lotus 1-2-3, WordPerfect
Classified Equipment: Hardware -- APP/Mac Centris 610;
Classified Software: FSI.
Editorial Equipment: Hardware -- 1-APP/Mac Quadra 950, 4-APP/Mac LC III, 2-APP/Mac Centris 610, 1-APP/Mac IIcx/TI/Omni 800
Editorial Software: FSI.
Production Equipment: Hardware -- Caere/OmniPage, V/5060, V/5300, DEC/VT-820; Cameras -- 1-R; Scanners -- Lf/Leafscan 35, AG/Arcus Plus
Production Software: QPS/QuarkXPress 3.3.

CORNELIA

THE NORTHEAST GEORGIAN

Street Address: 2440 Old Athens Hwy
City: Cornelia
State: GA
ZIP Code: 30531-5364
General Phone: (706) 778-4215
General Email: advertising@thenortheastgeorgian.com
Publication Website: https://www.thenortheastgeorgian.com/
Parent Company: Community Newspapers, Inc.
Publisher Name: Alan NeSmith
Publisher Email: anesmith@thenortheastgeorgian.com
Editor Name: Matthew Osborne
Editor Email: editor@thenortheastgeorgian.com
Advertising Executive Name: Tom Tucker
Advertising Executive Email: ttucker@cninewspapers.com
Year Established: 1892
Own Printing Facility?: Y
Commercial printers?: Y
Published Days: Wed`Fri
Avg. Paid Circ.: 9000
Avg. Free Circ.: 50
Audit Company: Sworn/Estimate/Non-Audited
Audit Date: 43626

COVINGTON

THE COVINGTON NEWS

Street Address: 1166 Usher St NW
City: Covington
State: GA
ZIP Code: 30014-2451
General Phone: (770) 787-6397
General Email: cbwarren@covnews.com
Publication Website: https://www.covnews.com/
Parent Company: Morris Multimedia, Inc.
Publisher Name: Madison Graham
Publisher Email: madison@covnews.com
Publisher Phone: (770) 728-1409
Editor Name: Darryl Welch
Editor Email: dwelch@covnews.com
Editor Phone: (770) 728-1401
Advertising Executive Name: Cynthia Blackshear Warren
Advertising Executive Email: cbwarren@covnews.com
Advertising Executive Phone: (770) 728-1407
Delivery Methods: Newsstand`Carrier`Racks
Year Established: 1865
Mechanical specifications: Type page 12 1/2 x 21 1/2; E - 6 cols, 2 1/24, 1/6 between; A - 6 cols, 2 1/4, 1/6 between; C - 9 cols, 1 7/24, 1/6 between.
Published Days: Sun
Avg. Paid Circ.: 5500
Avg. Free Circ.: 43500
Audit Company: Sworn/Estimate/Non-Audited
Audit Date: 43656

CUMMING

FORSYTH COUNTY NEWS

Street Address: 302 Veterans Memorial Blvd
City: Cumming
State: GA
ZIP Code: 30040-2644
General Phone: (770) 887-3126
General Email: marketing@forsythnews.com
Publication Website: https://www.forsythnews.com/
Parent Company: Metro Market Media
Publisher Name: Stephanie Woody
Publisher Email: swoody@forsythnews.com
Publisher Phone: (770) 205-8945
Editor Name: Brian Paglia
Editor Email: bpaglia@forsythnews.com
Editor Phone: (770) 205-8970
Advertising Executive Name: Nathan Schutter
Advertising Executive Email: nschutter@forsythnews.com
Advertising Executive Phone: (770) 205-8960
Delivery Methods: Carrier`Racks

Year Established: 1908
Own Printing Facility?: N
Commercial printers?: Y
Published Days: Wed`Fri`Sun
Weekday Frequency: m
Avg. Paid Circ.: 12500
Audit Company: Sworn/Estimate/Non-Audited
Audit Date: 43626

DALLAS

DALLAS NEW ERA

Street Address: 121 W Spring St
City: Dallas
State: GA
ZIP Code: 30132-4138
General Phone: (770) 445-3379
General Email: newerapr@bellsouth.net
Publication Website: https://www.thedallasnewera.com/
Own Printing Facility?: Y
Commercial printers?: Y
Published Days: Thur
Avg. Paid Circ.: 6500
Audit Company: Sworn/Estimate/Non-Audited
Audit Date: 43626

DANIELSVILLE

THE MADISON COUNTY JOURNAL

Street Address: PO Box 658, 438 Court House Square
City: Danielsville
State: GA
ZIP Code: 30633
General Phone: (800) 795-2581
General Email: news@mainstreetnews.com
Publication Website: https://www.mainstreetnews.com/
Year Established: 1997
Mechanical specifications: Type page 13 x 21 1/2; E - 6 cols, 2, 1/6 between; A - 6 cols, 2, 1/6 between; C - 6 cols, 2, 1/6 between.
Published Days: Wed
Avg. Paid Circ.: 3900
Avg. Free Circ.: 210
Audit Company: Sworn/Estimate/Non-Audited
Audit Date: 43626

DAWSON

THE DAWSON NEWS

Street Address: 139 W Lee St
City: Dawson
State: GA
ZIP Code: 39842-1624
General Phone: (229) 995-2175
Publication Website: http://www.thedawsonnews.com/
Delivery Methods: Mail
Year Established: 1866
Own Printing Facility?: Y
Mechanical specifications: Type page 11.625 x 21.5; E - 6 cols, 1 5/6, 1/8 between; A - 6 cols, 1 5/6, 1/8 between; C - 6 cols, 1 5/6, 1/8 between.
Published Days: Thur
Avg. Paid Circ.: 2800
Audit Company: Sworn/Estimate/Non-Audited
Audit Date: 43626

DAWSONVILLE

DAWSON COUNTY NEWS

Street Address: 30 SHOAL CREEK RD
City: Dawsonville
State: GA

ZIP Code: 30534
General Phone: (706) 265-3384
General Email: jtaylor@dawsonnews.com
Publication Website: https://www.dawsonnews.com
Parent Company: Swartz Media, LLC
Publisher Name: Stephanie Woody
Publisher Email: swoody@dawsonnews.com
Publisher Phone: (770) 205-8945
Editor Name: Alex Popp
Editor Email: apopp@dawsonnews.com
Editor Phone: (706) 265-3384, ext : 1
Published Days: Wed
Avg. Paid Circ.: 4024
Avg. Free Circ.: 8
Audit Company: Sworn/Estimate/Non-Audited
Audit Date: 43626

DECATUR

CROSSROADSNEWS

Street Address: 2346 Candler Rd
City: Decatur
State: GA
ZIP Code: 30032-6406
General Phone: (404) 284-1888
General Email: editor@crossroadsnews.com
Publication Website: http://crossroadsnews.com/
Publisher Name: Jennifer Parker
Publisher Email: editor@crossroadsnews.com
Editor Name: Jennifer Parker
Editor Email: editor@crossroadsnews.com
Delivery Methods: Carrier`Racks
Year Established: 1995
Mechanical specifications: 10.5 inches wide x 16 inches deep [4-column grid]
Published Days: Sat
Avg. Paid Circ.: 11
Avg. Free Circ.: 27908
Audit Company: VAC
Audit Date: 43293
Note:

DECATUR

THE CHAMPION

Street Address: 114 New St
City: Decatur
State: GA
ZIP Code: 30030-5356
General Phone: (404) 373-7779
General Email: johnh@dekalbchamp.com
Publication Website: http://thechampionnewspaper.com/
Publisher Name: Carolyn Glenn
Publisher Email: cfjglenn@dekalbchamp.com
Publisher Phone: (404) 373-7779
Editor Name: Asia Ashley
Editor Email: asia@dekalbchamp.com
Editor Phone: (404) 373-7779, ext : 110
Advertising Executive Name: John Hewitt
Advertising Executive Email: johnh@dekalbchamp.com%20
Advertising Executive Phone: (404) 373-7779, ext : 110
Delivery Methods: Mail`Newsstand`Racks
Mechanical specifications: Type page 10 1/4 x 14 1/4; E - 5 cols, 2, 3/16 between; A - 5 cols, 2, 3/16 between; C - 7 cols, 1 5/16, 3/16 between.
Published Days: Thur
Avg. Paid Circ.: 443
Avg. Free Circ.: 97
Audit Company: CVC
Audit Date: 43991

DONALSONVILLE

DONALSONVILLE NEWS

Street Address: 216 Cherry St
City: Donalsonville
State: GA

ZIP Code: 39845-1616
General Phone: (229) 524-2343
General Email: news@donalsonvillenews.com
Publication Website: https://www.donalsonvillenews.com/
Published Days: Thur
Avg. Paid Circ.: 3500
Audit Company: Sworn/Estimate/Non-Audited
Audit Date: 43626

DOUGLAS

THE DOUGLAS ENTERPRISE

Street Address: 1823 Peterson Ave S
City: Douglas
State: GA
ZIP Code: 31535-4013
General Phone: (912) 384-2323
Publication Website: https://www.douglasenterprise.net/
Year Established: 1888
Own Printing Facility?: Y
Commercial printers?: Y
Mechanical specifications: Type page 11.5 x 21; E - 6 cols, 2 1/16, 1/16 between; A - 6 cols, 2 1/16, 1/16 between; C - 8 cols, 1 7/12, 1/16 between.
Published Days: Wed`Sun
Avg. Paid Circ.: 8000
Avg. Free Circ.: 5
Audit Company: Sworn/Estimate/Non-Audited
Audit Date: 43626

DOUGLASVILLE

DOUGLAS COUNTY SENTINEL

Street Address: 8501 Bowden St
City: Douglasville
State: GA
ZIP Code: 30134-1705
General Phone: (770) 942-6571
General Email: publisher@douglascountysentinel.com
Publication Website: https://douglascountysentinel.com/
Parent Company: Paxton Media Group, LLC
Publisher Name: Rachael Raney
Publisher Email: publisher@douglascountysentinel.com
Publisher Phone: (470) 729-3234
Editor Name: Ron Daniel
Editor Email: ron@douglascountysentinel.com
Editor Phone: (470) 336-5224
Advertising Executive Name: Wende LaPierre
Advertising Executive Email: wlapierre@douglascountysentinel.com
Advertising Executive Phone: (470) 336-5594
Delivery Methods: Mail`Newsstand`Carrier`Racks
Year Established: 1902
Own Printing Facility?: Y
Commercial printers?: N
Mechanical specifications: Type page 10 x 21; E - 6 cols, 1 9/16, 1/8 between; A - 6 cols, 1 9/16, 1/8 between; C - 6 cols, 1 9/16, 1/8 between.
Published Days: Wed`Fri`Sun
Weekday Frequency: m
Avg. Paid Circ.: 1608
Avg. Free Circ.: 1013
Audit Company: Sworn/Estimate/Non-Audited
Audit Date: 43626
Classified Equipment: Hardware -- 3-PC.;
Editorial Equipment: Hardware -- 1-EKI, 7-EKI/Televideo.

DUNWOODY

DUNWOODY CRIER

Street Address: 5064 Nandina Ln
City: Dunwoody
State: GA
ZIP Code: 30338-4115
General Phone: (770) 451-4147
General Email: thecrier@mindspring.com
Publication Website: http://www.thecrier.net/
Parent Company: Crier Newspapers LLC
Publisher Name: Hans Appen
Publisher Email: hans@appenmediagroup.com
Editor Name: Patrick Fox
Editor Email: pat@appenmediagroup.com
Advertising Executive Name: Jim Hart
Advertising Executive Email: jim@appenmediagroup.com
Delivery Methods: Carrier`Racks
Year Established: 1976
Own Printing Facility?: N
Commercial printers?: Y
Mechanical specifications: Type page 10 1/4 x 14.
Published Days: Wed
Avg. Free Circ.: 15564
Audit Company: Sworn/Estimate/Non-Audited
Audit Date: 43626

ELBERTON

THE ELBERTON STAR

Street Address: 25 N Public Sq
City: Elberton
State: GA
ZIP Code: 30635-2416
General Phone: (706) 283-8500
General Email: bslay@elberton.com
Publication Website: https://www.elberton.com/
Parent Company: Community Newspapers, Inc.
Publisher Name: Gary Jones
Publisher Email: gjones@elberton.com
Advertising Executive Name: Valerie Evans
Advertising Executive Email: vevans@elberton.com
Delivery Methods: Mail`Newsstand`Racks
Mechanical specifications: Type page 13 x 21 1/4; E - 6 cols, 2, 1/6 between; A - 6 cols, 2, 1/6 between; C - 6 cols, 2, 1/6 between.
Published Days: Wed
Avg. Paid Circ.: 5650
Avg. Free Circ.: 159
Audit Company: Sworn/Estimate/Non-Audited
Audit Date: 43626

ELLIJAY

TIMES-COURIER

Street Address: 47 River St
City: Ellijay
State: GA
ZIP Code: 30540-3174
General Phone: (706) 635-4313
General Email: news@timescourier.com
Publication Website: https://www.timescourier.com/
Parent Company: Community Newspapers Inc.
Publisher Name: Andy Ashurst
Publisher Email: publisher@timescourier.com
Advertising Executive Name: Kathy Aker
Advertising Executive Email: kathyaker@timescourier.com%e2%80%8b
Delivery Methods: Mail`Newsstand`Racks
Year Established: 1875
Mechanical specifications: Type page 12 x 21; E - 6 cols, 2 1/8, 1/8 between; A - 6 cols, 2 1/8, 1/8 between; C - 6 cols, 2 1/8, 1/8 between.
Published Days: Wed
Avg. Paid Circ.: 6600
Avg. Free Circ.: 60
Audit Company: Sworn/Estimate/Non-Audited
Audit Date: 43626

Community Newspapers in the U.S.

FAYETTEVILLE

THE CITIZEN

Street Address: 310 B. North Glynn Street
City: Fayetteville
State: GA
ZIP Code: 30214-1105
General Phone: (770) 719-1880
General Email: editor@thecitizen.com
Publication Website: https://thecitizen.com/
Parent Company: Fayette Publishing
Delivery Methods: Newsstand`Carrier`Racks
Year Established: 1993
Published Days: Wed`Thur
Avg. Free Circ.: 32992
Audit Company: CAC
Audit Date: 44015

FITZGERALD

THE HERALD-LEADER

Street Address: 202 E Central Ave
City: Fitzgerald
State: GA
ZIP Code: 31750-2503
General Phone: (229) 423-9331
General Email: andersonherald@gmail.com
Publication Website: http://www.herald-leader.net/
Parent Company: Community Newspapers Inc.
Advertising Executive Name: Becky Anderson
Advertising Executive Email: andersonherald@gmail.com
Year Established: 1916
Own Printing Facility?: Y
Commercial printers?: Y
Published Days: Wed
Avg. Paid Circ.: 5300
Audit Company: Sworn/Estimate/Non-Audited
Audit Date: 43626

FOLKSTON

CHARLTON COUNTY HERALD

Street Address: 3781 Main St
City: Folkston
State: GA
ZIP Code: 31537-7572
General Phone: (912) 496-3585
General Email: editor@charltonherald.com
Publication Website: http://www.charltoncountyherald.com/
Parent Company: Gannett
Publisher Name: Marla Ogletree
Editor Name: Marla Ogletree
Editor Email: editor@charltonherald.com
Delivery Methods: Mail`Racks
Year Established: 1898
Mechanical specifications: Type page 13 x 21; E - 6 cols, 2, 1/8 between; A - 6 cols, 2, 1/8 between; C - 6 cols, 2, 1/8 between.
Published Days: Wed
Avg. Paid Circ.: 3000
Avg. Free Circ.: 100
Audit Company: Sworn/Estimate/Non-Audited
Audit Date: 43626

GRAY

THE JONES COUNTY NEWS

Street Address: 102 Stewart Ave
City: Gray
State: GA
ZIP Code: 31032-5219
General Phone: (478) 986-3929
Publication Website: http://www.jcnews.com/

Year Established: 1895
Mechanical specifications: Type page 13 x 21 1/2; E - 6 cols, 2, 1/6 between; A - 6 cols, 2, 1/6 between; C - 6 cols, 2, 1/6 between.
Published Days: Thur
Avg. Paid Circ.: 4300
Audit Company: Sworn/Estimate/Non-Audited
Audit Date: 43626

HARTWELL

THE HARTWELL SUN

Street Address: 8 Benson St
City: Hartwell
State: GA
ZIP Code: 30643-1990
General Phone: (706) 376-8025
General Email: mhall@thehartwellsun.com
Publication Website: https://www.thehartwellsun.com/
Parent Company: Community Newspapers, Inc.
Publisher Name: Michael Hall
Publisher Email: mhall@thehartwellsun.com
Editor Name: Michael Hall
Editor Email: mhall@thehartwellsun.com
Delivery Methods: Mail
Year Established: 1874
Own Printing Facility?: Y
Commercial printers?: Y
Mechanical specifications: Type page 11.625 x 21 1/2; 1 column 1.833, 2 column 3.79, 3 column 5.75, 4 column 7.708, 5 column 9.667.
Published Days: Thur
Avg. Paid Circ.: 6771
Audit Company: Sworn/Estimate/Non-Audited
Audit Date: 43626

HAZLEHURST

JEFF DAVIS LEDGER

Street Address: 12 Latimer St
City: Hazlehurst
State: GA
ZIP Code: 31539-6110
General Phone: (912) 375-4225
General Email: news@jdledger.com
Publication Website: https://www.jdledger.com/
Published Days: Wed
Avg. Paid Circ.: 3850
Audit Company: Sworn/Estimate/Non-Audited
Audit Date: 43626

HIAWASSEE

TOWNS COUNTY HERALD

Street Address: 446 N MAIN ST
City: Hiawassee
State: GA
ZIP Code: 30546
General Phone: (706) 896-4454
General Email: tcherald@windstream.net
Publication Website: http://www.townscountyherald.net/
Publisher Name: Kenneth West
Editor Name: Shawn Jarrard
Published Days: Wed
Avg. Paid Circ.: 4200
Audit Company: Sworn/Estimate/Non-Audited
Audit Date: 43626

HINESVILLE

THE COASTAL COURIER

Street Address: 125 S Main St

City: Hinesville
State: GA
ZIP Code: 31313-3217
General Phone: (912) 876-0156
General Email: pleon@coastalcourier.com
Publication Website: http://coastalcourier.com/
Parent Company: Morris Multimedia, Inc.
Publisher Name: Patty Leon
Publisher Email: pleon@coastalcourier.com
Publisher Phone: (912) 876-0156, ext : 1013
Editor Name: Jeff Whitten
Editor Email: jwhitten@morrismultimedia.com
Editor Phone: (912) 876-0156
Advertising Executive Name: Cindy White
Advertising Executive Email: cwhite@coastalcourier.com
Advertising Executive Phone: (912) 876-0156, ext : 1035
Delivery Methods: Mail`Newsstand`Carrier`Racks
Mechanical specifications: Type page 13 x 21 1/2; E - 6 cols, 2 1/16, 1/6 between; A - 6 cols, 2 1/16, 1/6 between; C - 9 cols, 1 5/16, 1/6 between.
Published Days: Wed`Sun
Avg. Paid Circ.: 5000
Avg. Free Circ.: 192
Audit Company: Sworn/Estimate/Non-Audited
Audit Date: 43626

HOMER

THE BANKS COUNTY NEWS

Street Address: 935 Historic Homer Hwy.
City: Homer
State: GA
ZIP Code: 30547
General Phone: (706) 612-5327
General Email: news@mainstreetnews.com
Publication Website: https://www.mainstreetnews.com/
Year Established: 1968
Own Printing Facility?: Y
Commercial printers?: Y
Mechanical specifications: Type page 13 x 21 1/2; E - 6 cols, 2, 1/6 between; A - 6 cols, 2, 1/6 between; C - 6 cols, 2, 1/6 between.
Published Days: Wed
Avg. Paid Circ.: 3400
Avg. Free Circ.: 90
Audit Company: Sworn/Estimate/Non-Audited
Audit Date: 43626

HOMERVILLE

CLINCH COUNTY NEWS

Street Address: 113 E Dame Ave
City: Homerville
State: GA
ZIP Code: 31634-2456
General Phone: (912) 487-5337
General Email: clinnews@windstream.net
Publication Website: https://www.theclinchcountynews.com/
Publisher Name: A.I. Robbins
Publisher Email: lrobbins@theclinchcountynews.com
Editor Name: A.I. Robbins
Editor Email: lrobbins@theclinchcountynews.com
Delivery Methods: Mail`Newsstand
Own Printing Facility?: Y
Commercial printers?: Y
Published Days: Wed
Avg. Paid Circ.: 1800
Avg. Free Circ.: 70
Audit Company: Sworn/Estimate/Non-Audited
Audit Date: 43626

JACKSON

JACKSON PROGRESS-ARGUS

Street Address: 129 S Mulberry St
City: Jackson
State: GA
ZIP Code: 30233-2056
General Phone: (770) 775-3107
General Email: legals@myjpa.com
Publication Website: https://www.jacksonprogress-argus.com/
Parent Company: Southern Community Newspapers, Inc.
Advertising Executive Name: Sandra Thomas
Advertising Executive Email: sthomas@myjpa.com
Advertising Executive Phone: (770) 775-3107, ext : 104
Year Established: 1873
Mechanical specifications: Type page 13 x 21 1/2; E - 6 cols, 2, between; A - 6 cols, 2, between; C - 6 cols, 2, between.
Published Days: Wed
Avg. Paid Circ.: 4600
Audit Company: Sworn/Estimate/Non-Audited
Audit Date: 43626

JEFFERSON

THE JACKSON HERALD

Street Address: 33 Lee St
City: Jefferson
State: GA
ZIP Code: 30549-1345
General Phone: (706) 367-5233
General Email: news@mainstreetnews.com
Publication Website: https://www.mainstreetnews.com/
Own Printing Facility?: Y
Commercial printers?: Y
Mechanical specifications: Type page 13 x 21 1/2; E - 6 cols, 2, 1/6 between; A - 6 cols, 2, 1/6 between; C - 6 cols, 2, 1/6 between.
Published Days: Wed
Avg. Paid Circ.: 9500
Avg. Free Circ.: 210
Audit Company: Sworn/Estimate/Non-Audited
Audit Date: 43626

JESUP

THE PRESS-SENTINEL

Street Address: 252 W Walnut St
City: Jesup
State: GA
ZIP Code: 31545-1331
General Phone: (912) 427-3757
General Email: edenty@bellsouth.net
Publication Website: https://www.thepress-sentinel.com/
Parent Company: Community Newspapers Inc.
Publisher Name: Eric Denty
Publisher Email: edenty@bellsouth.net
Editor Name: Drew Davis
Editor Email: legals@thepress-sentinel.com
Advertising Executive Name: Melisa Mallard
Advertising Executive Email: thepsadvertising@bellsouth.net
Delivery Methods: Mail`Racks
Year Established: 1865
Own Printing Facility?: Y
Published Days: Wed`Sat
Avg. Paid Circ.: 7000
Audit Company: Sworn/Estimate/Non-Audited
Audit Date: 43626

LA FAYETTE

WALKER COUNTY MESSENGER

Street Address: 102 N Main St

City: La Fayette
State: GA
ZIP Code: 30728-2418
General Phone: (706) 638-1859
General Email: walkercountymessenger@npco.com
Publication Website: http://www.northwestgeorgianews.com/catoosa_walker_news/site/about.html
Parent Company: Times Journal Inc.
Editor Name: Augustus McHan
Own Printing Facility?: Y
Commercial printers?: Y
Mechanical specifications: Type page 13 x 21 1/4; E - 6 cols, 2 1/16, 1/8 between; A - 6 cols, 2 1/16, 1/8 between; C - 9 cols, 1 3/8, 1/12 between.
Published Days: Wed`Fri
Avg. Paid Circ.: 4700
Avg. Free Circ.: 50
Audit Company: Sworn/Estimate/Non-Audited
Audit Date: 43626

LAVONIA

FRANKLIN COUNTY CITIZEN LEADER

Street Address: 12150 Augusta Rd
City: Lavonia
State: GA
ZIP Code: 30553-1208
General Phone: (706) 356-8557
General Email: fcc@franklincountycitizen.com
Publication Website: https://www.franklincountycitizen.com/
Parent Company: Community Newspapers Inc.
Publisher Name: Shane Scoggins
Publisher Email: sscoggins@franklincountycitizen.com
Publisher Phone: (706) 356-8557
Advertising Executive Name: Diane Rice
Advertising Executive Email: sales@franklincountycitizen.com
Advertising Executive Phone: (706) 356-8557
Delivery Methods: Mail`Racks
Year Established: 1955
Own Printing Facility?: Y
Published Days: Thur
Avg. Paid Circ.: 4000
Avg. Free Circ.: 150
Audit Company: Sworn/Estimate/Non-Audited
Audit Date: 43626

LAVONIA

THE NEWS LEADER

Street Address: 12150 Augusta Rd
City: Lavonia
State: GA
ZIP Code: 30553-1208
General Phone: (706) 356-8557
General Email: fcc@franklincountycitizen.com
Publication Website: https://www.franklincountycitizen.com/
Parent Company: Community Newspapers, Inc.
Publisher Name: Shane Scoggins
Publisher Email: sscoggins@franklincountycitizen.com
Publisher Phone: (706) 356-8557
Advertising Executive Name: Diane Rice
Advertising Executive Email: sales@franklincountycitizen.com
Advertising Executive Phone: (706) 356-8557
Published Days: Thur
Avg. Paid Circ.: 1950
Audit Company: Sworn/Estimate/Non-Audited
Audit Date: 43626

LINCOLNTON

THE LINCOLN JOURNAL

Street Address: P.O. Box 399
City: Lincolnton
State: GA
ZIP Code: 30817-5884
General Phone: (706) 359-3229
Publication Website: https://www.lincolnjournalonline.com/
Publisher Name: Sparky Newsome
Editor Name: Sparky Newsome
Published Days: Thur
Avg. Paid Circ.: 2850
Audit Company: Sworn/Estimate/Non-Audited
Audit Date: 43626

MADISON

MORGAN COUNTY CITIZEN

Street Address: 259 N Second St
City: Madison
State: GA
ZIP Code: 30650-1317
General Phone: (706) 342-7440
General Email: morgancountycitizen@gmail.com
Publication Website: http://www.morgancountycitizen.com/
Editor Name: Patrick Yost
Published Days: Thur
Avg. Paid Circ.: 5000
Audit Company: Sworn/Estimate/Non-Audited
Audit Date: 43626

MANCHESTER

HOGANSVILLE HOME NEWS

Street Address: PO Box 426
City: Manchester
State: GA
ZIP Code: 31816-0426
General Phone: (706) 846-3188
Publication Website: http://www.smalltownpapers.com/newspapers/newspaper.php?id=175
Parent Company: SmallTownPapers, Inc.
Own Printing Facility?: Y
Commercial printers?: Y
Published Days: Fri
Avg. Paid Circ.: 4300
Audit Company: Sworn/Estimate/Non-Audited
Audit Date: 43626

MARIETTA

HENRY NEIGHBOR

Street Address: 47 Waddell Street
City: Marietta
State: GA
ZIP Code: 30060
General Phone: (678) 938-2387
Publication Website: https://www.mdjonline.com/neighbor_newspapers/south_metro/
Parent Company: Neighbor Newspapers
Editor Name: Christine Fonville
Editor Email: smetro@neighbornewspapers.com
Delivery Methods: Carrier
Own Printing Facility?: Y
Commercial printers?: Y
Mechanical specifications: Type page 13 x 21; E - 6 cols, 2 1/16, between; A - 6 cols, 2 1/16, between; C - 10 cols, 1 3/16, between.
Published Days: Wed`Thur
Avg. Paid Circ.: 2
Avg. Free Circ.: 40000
Audit Company: Sworn/Estimate/Non-Audited
Audit Date: 43626

METTER

THE METTER ADVERTISER

Street Address: 15 S Rountree St
City: Metter
State: GA
ZIP Code: 30439-4416
General Phone: (912) 685-6566
General Email: news@metteradvertiser.com
Publication Website: http://www.metteradvertiser.com/
Editor Name: Jerri Goodman
Advertising Executive Name: Mandi Carter
Year Established: 1912
Mechanical specifications: Type page 13 x 21 1/2; E - 6 cols, 2, 1/8 between; A - 6 cols, 2, 1/8 between; C - 6 cols, 2, 1/8 between.
Published Days: Wed
Avg. Paid Circ.: 3200
Audit Company: Sworn/Estimate/Non-Audited
Audit Date: 43626

MILLEDGEVILLE

LAKE OCONEE BREEZE

Street Address: 165 Garrett Way NW
City: Milledgeville
State: GA
ZIP Code: 31061-2318
General Phone: (478) 453-1432
General Email: breeze@unionrecorder.com
Publication Website: https://www.lakeoconeebreeze.net/
Parent Company: Community Newspaper Holdings, Inc.
Publisher Name: Keith Barlow
Publisher Email: kbarlow@unionrecorder.com
Publisher Phone: (478) 453-1441
Editor Name: Natalie Davis Linder
Editor Email: breeze@unionrecorder.com
Editor Phone: (478) 453-1462
Advertising Executive Name: Jennifer Garrett
Advertising Executive Email: jgresham@unionrecorder.com
Advertising Executive Phone: (478) 453-1431
Published Days: Thur
Avg. Paid Circ.: 6200
Audit Company: Sworn/Estimate/Non-Audited
Audit Date: 43626

MONROE

THE WALTON TRIBUNE

Street Address: 121 S Broad St
City: Monroe
State: GA
ZIP Code: 30655-2153
General Phone: (770) 267-8371
General Email: support@waltontribune.com
Publication Website: http://www.waltontribune.com/
Parent Company: Monroe Media Inc.
Publisher Name: David Clemons
Publisher Email: david.clemons@waltontribune.com
Publisher Phone: (770) 267-2492
Editor Name: David Clemons
Editor Email: david.clemons@waltontribune.com
Editor Phone: (770) 267-2492
Advertising Executive Name: Rose Thomas
Advertising Executive Email: rose.thomas@waltontribune.com
Advertising Executive Phone: (770) 267-2929
Delivery Methods: Mail`Newsstand`Carrier`Racks
Year Established: 1900
Mechanical specifications: Type page 11 5/8 x 21; E - 6 cols, 1 13/16, between; A - 6 cols, 1 13/16, between; C - 8 cols, 1 5/16, between.
Published Days: Wed`Sun
Avg. Paid Circ.: 4415
Avg. Free Circ.: 1013
Audit Company: AAM
Audit Date: 44143

MONTICELLO

THE MONTICELLO NEWS

Street Address: 247 W Washington St
City: Monticello
State: GA
ZIP Code: 31064-1241
General Phone: (706) 468-6511
General Email: news@themonticellonews.com
Publication Website: http://themonticellonews.com/
Editor Name: Kathy Mudd
Editor Email: editor@themonticellonews.com
Advertising Executive Name: Jenny Murphy
Advertising Executive Email: advertising@themonticellonews.com
Delivery Methods: Mail`Newsstand`Racks
Year Established: 1881
Mechanical specifications: Type page 13 x 21; E - 6 cols, 2 1/16, 1/8 between; A - 6 cols, 2 1/16, 1/8 between; C - 6 cols, 2 1/16, 1/8 between.
Published Days: Thur
Avg. Paid Circ.: 2600
Audit Company: Sworn/Estimate/Non-Audited
Audit Date: 43626

NASHVILLE

THE BERRIEN PRESS

Street Address: 200 E McPherson Ave
City: Nashville
State: GA
ZIP Code: 31639-2250
General Phone: (229) 686-3523
General Email: localnews@windstream.net
Publication Website: https://www.theberrienpress.com/
Publisher Name: Maria Hardman
Publisher Email: maria_hardman@yahoo.com
Editor Name: Janet Studstill
Editor Email: localnews@windstream.net
Advertising Executive Name: Christina Milton
Advertising Executive Email: localnews@windstream.net
Own Printing Facility?: Y
Commercial printers?: Y
Mechanical specifications: Type page 13 x 21; E - 6 cols, 2 1/8, between; A - 6 cols, 2 1/8, between; C - 6 cols, 2 1/8, between.
Published Days: Wed
Avg. Paid Circ.: 4200
Avg. Free Circ.: 50
Audit Company: Sworn/Estimate/Non-Audited
Audit Date: 43626

OCILLA

THE OCILLA STAR

Street Address: 102 E 4th St
City: Ocilla
State: GA
ZIP Code: 31774-1541
General Phone: (229) 468-5433
General Email: ocillastar@windstream.net
Publication Website: https://www.theocillastar.com/
Published Days: Wed
Avg. Paid Circ.: 2000
Audit Company: Sworn/Estimate/Non-Audited
Audit Date: 43626

PERRY

Community Newspapers in the U.S.

THE HOUSTON HOME JOURNAL

Street Address: 1210 Washington St
City: Perry
State: GA
ZIP Code: 31069-2556
General Phone: (478) 987-1823
General Email: kerriw@hhjnews.com
Publication Website: http://hhjonline.com/
Parent Company: Sun Multimedia Inc.
Publisher Name: Cheri Adams
Publisher Email: cadams@hhjnews.com
Publisher Phone: (478) 987-1823, ext : 227
Advertising Executive Name: Kerri Wright
Advertising Executive Email: kerriw@hhjnews.com
Advertising Executive Phone: (478) 987-1823, ext : 243
Delivery Methods: Mail
Year Established: 1870
Own Printing Facility?: Y
Commercial printers?: Y
Mechanical specifications: Type page 11 5/8 x 21; E - 6 cols, 5/6, between; A - 6 cols, 1 5/6, between; C - 8 cols, 1 5/16, between.
Published Days: Wed`Sat
Weekday Frequency: m
Saturday Frequency: m
Avg. Paid Circ.: 13000
Audit Company: Sworn/Estimate/Non-Audited
Audit Date: 43626

QUITMAN

QUITMAN FREE PRESS

Street Address: 112 N Lee St
City: Quitman
State: GA
ZIP Code: 31643-2124
General Phone: (229) 263-4615
General Email: maria_hardman@yahoo.com
Publication Website: https://www.thequitmanfreepress.com/
Parent Company: Cook Publishing Co.
Publisher Name: Maria Hardman
Publisher Email: maria_hardman@yahoo.com
Editor Name: Bonnell Holmes
Editor Email: quitmanpress@windstream.net
Advertising Executive Name: Jennifer Edwards
Advertising Executive Email: quitmanadvertising@gmail.com
Delivery Methods: Mail
Year Established: 1876
Commercial printers?: Y
Published Days: Wed
Avg. Paid Circ.: 3400
Avg. Free Circ.: 60
Audit Company: Sworn/Estimate/Non-Audited
Audit Date: 43626

RICHLAND

STEWART-WEBSTER JOURNAL

Street Address: 106 Broad St
City: Richland
State: GA
ZIP Code: 31825-6106
General Phone: (229) 887-3674
General Email: swjpc@bellsouth.net
Publication Website: http://swjpc.com/
Delivery Methods: Mail`Newsstand`Carrier`Racks
Mechanical specifications: Type page 13 x 21 1/2; E - 6 cols, 2 1/16, 1/6 between; A - 6 cols, 2 1/16, 1/6 between; C - 6 cols, 2 1/16, 1/6 between.
Published Days: Thur
Avg. Paid Circ.: 4654
Avg. Free Circ.: 20
Audit Company: Sworn/Estimate/Non-Audited
Audit Date: 43626

RICHMOND HILL

BRYAN COUNTY NEWS

Street Address: 9998 Ford Ave
City: Richmond Hill
State: GA
ZIP Code: 31324
General Phone: (912) 756-2668
General Email: m.swendra@bryancountynews.com
Publication Website: https://www.bryancountynews.com/
Parent Company: Morris Multimedia, Inc.
Publisher Name: Patty Leon
Publisher Email: pleon@coastalcourier.com
Publisher Phone: (912) 756-2668
Editor Name: Jeff Whitten
Editor Email: jwhitten@bryancountynews.com
Editor Phone: (912) 644-9263
Advertising Executive Name: Cindy White
Advertising Executive Email: cwhite@coastalcourier.com
Advertising Executive Phone: (912) 876-0156, ext : 1035
Delivery Methods: Mail`Racks
Published Days: Wed`Thur`Sat
Avg. Paid Circ.: 3000
Avg. Free Circ.: 1000
Audit Company: Sworn/Estimate/Non-Audited
Audit Date: 43626

RINGGOLD

CATOOSA COUNTY NEWS

Street Address: 7513 Nashville St
City: Ringgold
State: GA
ZIP Code: 30736-2357
General Phone: (706) 935-2621
General Email: catoosacountynews@npco.com
Publication Website: http://www.catoosanews.com/
Parent Company: Times Journal Inc.
Mechanical specifications: Type page 13 x 21 1/4; E - 6 cols, 2, 1/4 between; A - 6 cols, 2, 1/4 between; C - 9 cols, 1 3/8, 1/8 between.
Published Days: Wed
Avg. Paid Circ.: 4261
Audit Company: Sworn/Estimate/Non-Audited
Audit Date: 43626

ROSWELL

DEKALB NEIGHBOR

Street Address: 10930 Crabapple Rd
City: Roswell
State: GA
ZIP Code: 30075-5812
General Phone: (770) 454-9388
General Email: dekalb@neighbornewspapers.com
Publication Website: https://www.mdjonline.com/neighbor_newspapers/dekalb/
Parent Company: Neighbor Newspapers
Own Printing Facility?: Y
Published Days: Wed
Avg. Paid Circ.: 7
Avg. Free Circ.: 15552
Audit Company: Sworn/Estimate/Non-Audited
Audit Date: 43626

SAINT MARYS

TRIBUNE & GEORGIAN

Street Address: 206 Osborne St
City: Saint Marys
State: GA
ZIP Code: 31558-8400
General Phone: (912) 882-4927
General Email: classifieds@tribune-georgian.com
Publication Website: http://www.tribune-georgian.com/
Parent Company: Community Newspapers, Inc.
Publisher Name: Jill Helton
Editor Name: Jill Helton
Advertising Executive Name: Denise Carver
Year Established: 1894
Published Days: Thur
Avg. Paid Circ.: 6437
Avg. Free Circ.: 228
Audit Company: Sworn/Estimate/Non-Audited
Audit Date: 43626

SUMMERVILLE

THE SUMMERVILLE NEWS

Street Address: 20 Wildlife Lake Rd
City: Summerville
State: GA
ZIP Code: 30747-5300
General Phone: (706) 857-2494
General Email: news@thesummervillenews.com
Publication Website: https://www.thesummervillenews.com/
Delivery Methods: Mail`Newsstand`Racks
Year Established: 1886
Own Printing Facility?: Y
Commercial printers?: Y
Published Days: Thur
Avg. Paid Circ.: 7000
Avg. Free Circ.: 75
Audit Company: Sworn/Estimate/Non-Audited
Audit Date: 43626

SWAINSBORO

THE FOREST-BLADE

Street Address: 416 W Moring St
City: Swainsboro
State: GA
ZIP Code: 30401-3177
General Phone: (478) 237-9971
General Email: emanuelcountylive@gmail.com
Publication Website: https://emanuelcountylive.com/
Parent Company: Smith Newspapers
Publisher Name: Gail Williamson
Publisher Email: gail@emanuelcountylive.com
Editor Name: Trudie Kasper
Editor Email: advertising@forest-blade.com
Advertising Executive Name: Pam Akridge
Advertising Executive Email: pam@forest-blade.com
Delivery Methods: Mail`Newsstand`Racks
Year Established: 1861
Own Printing Facility?: Y
Commercial printers?: Y
Mechanical specifications: Type page 13 x 21; E - 6 cols, 2, between; A - 6 cols, 2, between; C - 6 cols, 2, between.
Published Days: Wed
Avg. Paid Circ.: 4200
Audit Company: Sworn/Estimate/Non-Audited
Audit Date: 43626

SYLVESTER

THE SYLVESTER LOCAL NEWS

Street Address: 103 E Kelly St
City: Sylvester
State: GA
ZIP Code: 31791-2159
General Phone: (229) 776-3991
General Email: info@thesylvesterlocal.com
Publication Website: https://thesylvesterlocal.com/
Year Established: 1884

Own Printing Facility?: Y
Commercial printers?: Y
Published Days: Wed
Avg. Paid Circ.: 3800
Avg. Free Circ.: 20
Audit Company: Sworn/Estimate/Non-Audited
Audit Date: 43626

THOMSON

THE MCDUFFIE MIRROR

Street Address: 108 Railroad St
City: Thomson
State: GA
ZIP Code: 30824-2733
General Phone: (706) 597-0335
General Email: bookkeeping@mcduffieprogress.com
Publication Website: https://www.mcduffieprogress.com/
Publisher Name: Wayne Parham
Publisher Email: wparham@mcduffieprogress.com
Editor Name: Wayne Parham
Editor Email: wparham@mcduffieprogress.com
Advertising Executive Name: Sally Adams
Published Days: Thur
Avg. Paid Circ.: 3700
Audit Company: Sworn/Estimate/Non-Audited
Audit Date: 43626

THOMSON

THE MCDUFFIE PROGRESS

Street Address: 101 Church St
City: Thomson
State: GA
ZIP Code: 30824-2613
General Phone: (706) 595-1601
General Email: bookkeeping@mcduffieprogress.com
Publication Website: https://www.mcduffieprogress.com/
Parent Company: Lancaster Management Inc.
Publisher Name: Wayne Parham
Publisher Email: wparham@mcduffieprogress.com
Advertising Executive Name: Brian Hobbs
Advertising Executive Email: composing@mcduffieprogress.com
Own Printing Facility?: Y
Commercial printers?: Y
Mechanical specifications: Type page 13 x 21 1/2; E - 6 cols, 2 1/16, between; A - 6 cols, 2 1/16, between; C - 9 cols, between.
Published Days: Wed`Sun
Avg. Paid Circ.: 5600
Avg. Free Circ.: 128
Audit Company: Sworn/Estimate/Non-Audited
Audit Date: 43626

WATKINSVILLE

OCONEE ENTERPRISE

Street Address: 26 S Barnett Shoals Rd
City: Watkinsville
State: GA
ZIP Code: 30677-2500
General Phone: (706) 769-5175
General Email: businessnews@oconeeenterprise.com
Publication Website: http://www.oconeeenterprise.com/
Publisher Name: Vinnie Williams
Publisher Email: oconeeenterprise@mindspring.com
Publisher Phone: (706) 769-5175, ext : 110
Editor Name: Maridee Williams
Editor Email: oconeeenterprise@mindspring.com

Editor Phone: (706) 769-5175, ext : 102
Advertising Executive Name: Maridee Williams
Advertising Executive Email: oconeeenterprise@mindspring.com
Advertising Executive Phone: (706) 769-5175, ext : 102
Mechanical specifications: Type page 13 x 21; E - 6 cols, 2 1/16, 1/8 between; A - 6 cols, 2 1/16, 1/8 between; C - 6 cols, 2 1/16, 1/8 between.
Published Days: Thur
Avg. Paid Circ.: 4000
Audit Company: Sworn/Estimate/Non-Audited
Audit Date: 43626

WAYNESBORO

THE TRUE CITIZEN

Street Address: 629 Shadrack St
City: Waynesboro
State: GA
ZIP Code: 30830-1451
General Phone: (706) 554-2111
General Email: truecitizennews@live.com
Publication Website: https://www.thetruecitizen.com/
Publisher Name: Roy Chalker
Publisher Email: rchalker@bellsouth.net
Editor Name: Roy Chalker
Editor Email: rchalker@bellsouth.net
Delivery Methods: Mail`Racks
Year Established: 1882
Own Printing Facility?: Y
Commercial printers?: Y
Mechanical specifications: Type page 13 x 21 1/2; E - 6 cols, 2 1/12, 1/4 between; A - 6 cols, 2 1/12, 1/4 between; C - 7 cols, 1 1/12, 1/4 between.
Published Days: Wed
Avg. Paid Circ.: 4200
Audit Company: Sworn/Estimate/Non-Audited
Audit Date: 43626

ZEBULON

PIKE COUNTY JOURNAL AND REPORTER

Street Address: 1 Courthouse Square
City: Zebulon
State: GA
ZIP Code: 30295
General Phone: (770) 567-3446
General Email: news@pikecountygeorgia.com
Publication Website: http://www.pikecountygeorgia.com/
Publisher Name: Walter Geiger
Publisher Email: news@barnesville.com
Editor Name: Rachel McDaniel
Editor Email: news@pikecountygeorgia.com
Advertising Executive Name: Brenda Sanchez
Advertising Executive Email: brenda@pikecountygeorgia.com
Own Printing Facility?: Y
Published Days: Wed
Avg. Paid Circ.: 3000
Audit Company: Sworn/Estimate/Non-Audited
Audit Date: 43626

HAWAII

KAUNAKAKAI

THE MOLOKAI DISPATCH

Street Address: 2 Kamoi St.
City: Kaunakakai
State: HI
ZIP Code: 96748
General Phone: (808) 552-2781
General Email: sales@themolokaidispatch.com
Publication Website: http://www.themolokaidispatch.com/
Editor Name: Catherine Cluett Pactol
Editor Email: editor@themolokaidispatch.com
Editor Phone: (808) 552-2781
Advertising Executive Name: Tirzah Pactol
Advertising Executive Email: sales@themolokaidispatch.com
Advertising Executive Phone: (808) 552-2781
Delivery Methods: Mail`Newsstand`Racks
Year Established: 1985
Commercial printers?: Y
Mechanical specifications: Type page 10 1/4 x 14 3/4; E - 4 cols, 2 3/8, 1/4 between; A - 4 cols, 2 3/8, 1/4 between; C - 4 cols, 2 3/8, 1/4 between.
Published Days: Wed
Avg. Paid Circ.: 300
Avg. Free Circ.: 3500
Audit Company: Sworn/Estimate/Non-Audited
Audit Date: 43626

KAUNAKAKAI

THE MOLOKAI DISPATCH

Street Address: 2 Kamoi St. Ste 5
City: Kaunakakai
State: HI
ZIP Code: 96748
General Phone: 808-552-2781
Publication Website: https://themolokaidispatch.com/
Editor Name: Catherine Cluett Pactol
Editor Email: editor@themolokaidispatch.com
Advertising Executive Name: Tirzah Pactol
Advertising Executive Email: sales@themolokaidispatch.com

WAILUKU

MAUI TIME

Street Address: 16 S Market Street
City: Wailuku
State: HI
ZIP Code: 96793
General Phone: (808) 244-0777
Publication Website: https://mauitime.com/
Parent Company: Ogden Newspapers Inc.
Publisher Name: Tommy Russo
Publisher Email: tommy@mauitime.com
Publisher Phone: (808) 283-0512
Editor Name: Axel Beers
Editor Email: editor@mauitime.com
Editor Phone: (808) 283-1308
Year Established: 1997
Published Days: Thur
Audit Company: Sworn/Estimate/Non-Audited
Audit Date: 43626

IOWA

ACKLEY

ACKLEY WORLD JOURNAL

Street Address: 736 Main St
City: Ackley
State: IA
ZIP Code: 50601-1538
General Phone: (641) 847-2592
General Email: jlovelace@iafalls.com
Publication Website: http://www.timescitizen.com/ackley_world_journal/
Parent Company: Times Citizen Communications
Publisher Name: John Goossen
Publisher Email: jgoossen@iafalls.com
Publisher Phone: (800) 798-2691, ext : 345
Editor Name: Becky Schipper
Editor Email: news@iafalls.com
Editor Phone: (641) 847-2592
Advertising Executive Name: Josh Lovelace
Advertising Executive Email: jlovelace@iafalls.com
Advertising Executive Phone: (800) 798-2691, ext : 356
Delivery Methods: Mail`Newsstand`Carrier
Published Days: Wed
Audit Company: Sworn/Estimate/Non-Audited
Audit Date: 43626

AKRON

AKRON HOMETOWNER

Street Address: 110 Reed St, P.O. Box. 797
City: Akron
State: IA
ZIP Code: 51001-7739
General Phone: (712) 568-2208
General Email: akronht@hickorytech.net
Publication Website: http://akronhometowner.com/
Parent Company: Dodie Hook
Publisher Name: Dodie Hook
Editor Name: Dodie Hook
Delivery Methods: Mail`Racks
Year Established: 2001
Mechanical specifications: Tab size - 16" long by 10.25" wide
Published Days: Wed
Avg. Paid Circ.: 1400
Audit Company: Sworn/Estimate/Non-Audited
Audit Date: 43626

ALBIA

ALBIA UNION-REPUBLICAN

Street Address: 109-111 Benton Avenue
City: Albia
State: IA
ZIP Code: 52531-2034
General Phone: (641) 932-7121
General Email: marilyn@albianews.com
Publication Website: http://www.albianews.com/
Parent Company: Dave Paxton
Publisher Name: Dave Paxton
Publisher Email: dave@albianews.com
Editor Name: Dave Paxton
Editor Email: dave@albianews.com
Advertising Executive Name: Marilyn Teno
Advertising Executive Email: marilyn@albianews.com
Year Established: 1862
Own Printing Facility?: Y
Commercial printers?: Y
Published Days: Thur
Avg. Paid Circ.: 3500
Avg. Free Circ.: 3000
Audit Company: Sworn/Estimate/Non-Audited
Audit Date: 43626

ALBIA

MONROE COUNTY NEWS

Street Address: 109-111 Benton Avenue
City: Albia
State: IA
ZIP Code: 52531-2034
General Phone: (641) 932-7121
General Email: marilyn@albianews.com
Publication Website: https://www.monroenews.com

Parent Company: Dave Paxton
Publisher Name: Dave Paxton
Publisher Email: dave@albianews.com
Editor Name: Dave Paxton
Editor Email: dave@albianews.com
Advertising Executive Name: Marilyn Teno
Advertising Executive Email: marilyn@albianews.com
Delivery Methods: Mail`Newsstand`Carrier`Racks
Published Days: Tues
Avg. Paid Circ.: 2850
Avg. Free Circ.: 900
Audit Company: Sworn/Estimate/Non-Audited
Audit Date: 43626

ALGONA

ALGONA UPPER DES MOINES

Street Address: 14 E Nebraska St
City: Algona
State: IA
ZIP Code: 50511-2630
General Phone: (515) 295-3535
General Email: ads@algona.com
Publication Website: http://www.algona.com/
Publisher Name: Brad Hicks
Publisher Email: publisher@algona.com
Publisher Phone: (515) 295-3535, ext : 223
Editor Name: Alan Van Ormer
Editor Email: avanormer@algona.com
Editor Phone: (515) 295-3535, ext : 230
Advertising Executive Name: Nancy Steburg
Advertising Executive Email: nsteburg@algona.com
Advertising Executive Phone: (515) 295-3535, ext : 226
Delivery Methods: Mail`Newsstand`Racks
Year Established: 1866
Own Printing Facility?: Y
Commercial printers?: Y
Mechanical specifications: Type page 11 1/2 x 21 1/2; E - 6 cols, 1.812 between; A - 6 cols, 1.812, between; C - 6 cols, 1.812, between.
Published Days: Thur
Avg. Paid Circ.: 3500
Audit Company: Sworn/Estimate/Non-Audited
Audit Date: 43626

ALLISON

BUTLER COUNTY TRIBUNE JOURNAL

Street Address: 422 N Main St
City: Allison
State: IA
ZIP Code: 50602-7710
General Phone: (319) 267-2731
General Email: tjstarnews@midamericapub.com
Publication Website: https://www.butlercountytribune.com/
"Parent Company: Mid-America Publishing http://mid-americapublishing.com IA"
Publisher Name: Bethany Carson
Publisher Email: tjstarnews@midamericapub.com
Publisher Phone: (319) 267-2731
Commercial printers?: Y
Published Days: Thur
Avg. Paid Circ.: 1600
Audit Company: Sworn/Estimate/Non-Audited
Audit Date: 43626

AMES

NEVADA JOURNAL

Street Address: 317 5th St
City: Ames

Community Newspapers in the U.S.

State: IA
ZIP Code: 50010-6101
General Phone: (515) 382-2160
General Email: ldodd@nevadaiowajournal.com
Publication Website: https://www.nevadaiowajournal.com/
Parent Company: Gannett
Publisher Name: Kim Fowler
Publisher Email: kfowler@amestrib.com
Advertising Executive Name: Lauri Dodd
Advertising Executive Email: ldodd@nevadaiowajournal.com
Advertising Executive Phone: (515) 663-6902
Published Days: Thur
Audit Company: Sworn/Estimate/Non-Audited
Audit Date: 43626

AMES

THE STORY CITY HERALD

Street Address: PO Box 380
City: Ames
State: IA
ZIP Code: 50010-0380
General Phone: (515)232-2160
General Email: rrong@amestrib.com
Publication Website: https://www.storycityherald.com/
Parent Company: Gannett
Publisher Name: Scott Anderson
Publisher Email: sanderson@amestrib.com
Publisher Phone: (515) 663-6943
Editor Name: Michael Crumb
Editor Email: mcrumb@amestrib.com
Editor Phone: (515) 663-6961
Advertising Executive Name: Rebecca Rong
Advertising Executive Email: rrong@amestrib.com
Advertising Executive Phone: (515) 663-6963
Delivery Methods: Mail
Year Established: 1881
Mechanical specifications: Type page 11 3/4 x 21 1/2; E - 6 cols, 1 7/8, 3/8 between; A - 6 cols, 1 7/8, 3/8 between; C - 6 cols, 1 7/8, 3/8 between.
Published Days: Wed
Avg. Paid Circ.: 1963
Audit Company: Sworn/Estimate/Non-Audited
Audit Date: 43626

ANITA

ANITA TRIBUNE

Street Address: 850 Main
City: Anita
State: IA
ZIP Code: 50020
General Phone: (712) 762-4188
General Email: gandrews@midlands.net
Publication Website: http://www.anitatribune.com/
Delivery Methods: Mail`Newsstand`Racks
Year Established: 1883
Mechanical specifications: 6 columns x 21 1/2 broadsheet
Published Days: Thur
Avg. Paid Circ.: 1100
Audit Company: Sworn/Estimate/Non-Audited
Audit Date: 43626

ARMSTRONG

ARMSTRONG JOURNAL

Street Address: 529 6th St, P.O. Box 289
City: Armstrong
State: IA
ZIP Code: 50514-7711
General Phone: (712) 868-3460
General Email: ads@armstrongjournal.com
Publication Website: http://statelinepubs.com/ringsted-dispatch

Parent Company: Stateline Publications
Publisher Name: Kristin Grabinoski
Publisher Email: krisg@armstrongjournal.com
Editor Name: Clinton Davis
Editor Email: clint@armstrongjournal.com
Delivery Methods: Mail`Racks
Own Printing Facility?: Y
Commercial printers?: Y
Published Days: Wed
Avg. Paid Circ.: 850
Audit Company: Sworn/Estimate/Non-Audited
Audit Date: 43626

ARMSTRONG

RINGSTED DISPATCH

Street Address: P.O. Box 188
City: Armstrong
State: IA
ZIP Code: 50514-7711
General Phone: (712) 868-3460
General Email: ads@armstrongjournal.com
Publication Website: http://statelinepubs.com/bancroft-register
Parent Company: Stateline Publications
Publisher Name: Kristin Grabinoski
Publisher Email: krisg@armstrongjournal.com
Editor Name: Clinton Davis
Editor Email: clint@armstrongjournal.com
Delivery Methods: Mail`Racks
Own Printing Facility?: Y
Commercial printers?: Y
Published Days: Wed
Avg. Paid Circ.: 400
Audit Company: Sworn/Estimate/Non-Audited
Audit Date: 43626

AUDUBON

AUDUBON COUNTY ADVOCATE JOURNAL

Street Address: 517 Leroy St, P.O. Box 268
City: Audubon
State: IA
ZIP Code: 50025-0268
General Phone: (712) 563-2741
General Email: jeannem@auduboncountynews.com
Publication Website: http://www.swiowanewssource.com/eeditioudubon_county_advocate_journal/
Publisher Name: Jeff Lundquist
Publisher Email: jrlund@ant-news.com
Publisher Phone: (712) 243-2624
Editor Name: Jeff Lundquist
Editor Email: jrlund@ant-news.com
Editor Phone: (712) 243-2624
Advertising Executive Name: Jeanne Meaike
Advertising Executive Email: jeannem@auduboncountynews.com
Advertising Executive Phone: (712) 563-2741
Delivery Methods: Mail`Newsstand`Racks
Year Established: 1879
Published Days: Tues`Fri
Avg. Paid Circ.: 2100
Avg. Free Circ.: 8022
Audit Company: Sworn/Estimate/Non-Audited
Audit Date: 43626

AURELIA

AURELIA STAR

Street Address: PO Box 248
City: Aurelia
State: IA
ZIP Code: 51005-0248
General Phone: (712) 229-5492
General Email: aurstar@gmail.com
Publication Website: http://www.aureliastar.com

"Parent Company: Mid-America Publishing
http://mid-americapublishing.com
IA"
Delivery Methods: Mail`Racks
Published Days: Wed
Avg. Paid Circ.: 380
Avg. Free Circ.: 20
Audit Company: Sworn/Estimate/Non-Audited
Audit Date: 43626

AVOCA

THE BEDFORD TIMES-PRESS

Street Address: 164 S Elm St
City: Avoca
State: IA
ZIP Code: 51521-4003
General Phone: (712) 343-2154
General Email: avocajh@iowatelecom.net
Publication Website: https://www.bedfordtimes-press.com/
Delivery Methods: Mail`Newsstand`Racks
Published Days: Wed
Avg. Paid Circ.: 1700
Audit Company: Sworn/Estimate/Non-Audited
Audit Date: 43626

BANCROFT

THE BANCROFT REGISTER

Street Address: P.O. Box 175, 103 Ramsey St. W
City: Bancroft
State: IA
ZIP Code: 50517-8012
General Phone: (515) 885-2531
General Email: ads@armstrongjournal.com
Publication Website: http://www.swiowanewssource.com/audubon/
Parent Company: Stateline Publications
Publisher Name: Kristin Grabinoski
Publisher Email: krisg@armstrongjournal.com
Editor Name: Kim Meyer
Editor Email: bancroftregister@yahoo.com
Delivery Methods: Mail`Racks
Own Printing Facility?: Y
Published Days: Wed
Avg. Paid Circ.: 800
Audit Company: Sworn/Estimate/Non-Audited
Audit Date: 43626

BEDFORD

STAR PRESS UNION

Street Address: 404 Main St, P.O. Box 108
City: Bedford
State: IA
ZIP Code: 50833-1357
General Phone: (712) 523-2525
General Email: btimespress@gmail.com
Publication Website: https://www.press-citizen.com/eastern-iowa/
Parent Company: Randy Larimer
Publisher Name: Randy Larimer
Delivery Methods: Mail`Newsstand`Racks
Own Printing Facility?: Y
Commercial printers?: Y
Mechanical specifications: Type page 10 1/4 x 14; E - 9 cols, 1 1/2, 1/6 between; A - 9 cols, 1 1/2, 1/6 between; C - 9 cols, 1 1/2, 1/6 between.
Published Days: Wed
Avg. Paid Circ.: 1348
Audit Company: Sworn/Estimate/Non-Audited
Audit Date: 43626

BELLEVUE

BELLEVUE HERALD-LEADER

Street Address: 118 S 2nd St
City: Bellevue
State: IA
ZIP Code: 52031-1318
General Phone: (563) 872-4159
General Email: bhleader@bellevueheraldleader.com
Publication Website: https://www.bellevueheraldleader.com
Parent Company: Sycamore Media
Editor Name: David Namanny
Editor Email: dnamanny@bellevueheraldleader.com
Advertising Executive Name: Dean Upmann
Advertising Executive Email: dupmann@bellevueheraldleader.com
Delivery Methods: Mail`Newsstand`Racks
Year Established: 1871
Mechanical specifications: Type page 10 1/2 x 16; E - 4 cols, between; A - 6 cols, 1 5/8, between; C - 6 cols, 1 5/8, between.
Published Days: Thur
Avg. Paid Circ.: 2770
Avg. Free Circ.: 12
Audit Company: Sworn/Estimate/Non-Audited
Audit Date: 43626

BELMOND

BELMOND NEWS

Street Address: 215 E Main St
City: Belmond
State: IA
ZIP Code: 50421-1122
General Phone: (641) 444-3333
General Email: belmondnews@frontiernet.net
Publication Website: http://www.belmondnews.com/

BLOOMFIELD

BLOOMFIELD DEMOCRAT

Street Address: 207 S Madison St
City: Bloomfield
State: IA
ZIP Code: 52537-1622
General Phone: (641) 664-2334
General Email: ads@bdemo.com
Publication Website: https://www.bdemo.com/
Parent Company: Sycamore Media
Publisher Name: Karen Spurgeon
Publisher Email: karen@bdemo.com
Editor Name: Scott Spurgeon
Editor Email: sspurg@netins.net
Advertising Executive Name: Laura Swarts
Advertising Executive Email: laura@bdemo.com
Delivery Methods: Mail
Year Established: 1869
Mechanical specifications: PDF or similar
Published Days: Wed
Avg. Paid Circ.: 1661
Audit Company: Sworn/Estimate/Non-Audited
Audit Date: 43626

BOONE

BOONE NEWS-REPUBLICAN

Street Address: 2136 Mamie Eisenhower Ave
City: Boone
State: IA
ZIP Code: 50036-4437
General Phone: (515) 432-6694
General Email: mscott@amestrib.com
Publication Website: https://www.newsrepublican.com/
Publisher Name: Kim Fowler
Publisher Email: kfowler@amestrib.com
Publisher Phone: (515) 663-6943
Editor Name: Logan Kahler

Editor Email: lkahler@newsrepublican.com
Editor Phone: (515) 432-6694
Advertising Executive Name: Mary Beth Scott
Advertising Executive Email: mscott@amestrib.com
Advertising Executive Phone: (515) 663-6951
Delivery Methods: Mail`Newsstand`Carrier`Racks
Year Established: 1888
Own Printing Facility?: N
Commercial printers?: N
Mechanical specifications: Type page 13 x 21 1/2; E - 6 cols, 2 1/16, 1/8 between; A - 6 cols, 2 1/16, 1/8 between; C - 9 cols, 1 1/3, 1/8 between.
Published Days: Tues`Thur`Sat
Weekday Frequency: m
Avg. Paid Circ.: 1399
Audit Company: Sworn/Estimate/Non-Audited
Audit Date: 43626
Editorial Software: .

BUFFALO CENTER

BUFFALO CENTER TRIBUNE

Street Address: 124 N Main St
City: Buffalo Center
State: IA
ZIP Code: 50424
General Phone: (641) 562-2606
General Email: bctrib@wctatel.net
Publication Website: https://thebuffalocentertribune.com/
Editor Name: Andrew Shaw
Delivery Methods: Mail`Newsstand`Racks
Own Printing Facility?: Y
Commercial printers?: Y
Published Days: Tues
Avg. Paid Circ.: 1595
Audit Company: Sworn/Estimate/Non-Audited
Audit Date: 43626

CALMAR

CALMAR COURIER

Street Address: PO Box 507
City: Calmar
State: IA
ZIP Code: 52132
General Phone: (563) 562-3488
General Email: calmarnews@midamericapub.com
Publication Website: https://calmarcourier.com/
Parent Company: Mid-America Publishing
Editor Name: Michael Hohenbrink
Delivery Methods: Mail
Year Established: 2005
Published Days: Tues
Avg. Paid Circ.: 1800
Audit Company: Sworn/Estimate/Non-Audited
Audit Date: 43626

CHARITON

THE CARLISLE CITIZEN

Street Address: P.O. Box 651, 908 Court Ave.
City: Chariton
State: IA
ZIP Code: 50049
General Phone: (641) 774-2137
General Email: charnews@charitonleader.com
Publication Website: http://crl.stparchive.com/
Parent Company: Mid-America Publishing
Delivery Methods: Mail`Racks
Year Established: 1926
Own Printing Facility?: Y
Commercial printers?: Y
Published Days: Thur

Avg. Paid Circ.: 1600
Audit Company: Sworn/Estimate/Non-Audited
Audit Date: 43626

CHEROKEE

THE CHARITON LEADER

Street Address: 111 S 2nd St
City: Cherokee
State: IA
ZIP Code: 51012
General Phone: (712) 225-5111
General Email: editor@ctimes.biz
Publication Website: http://www.charitonleader.com/
Parent Company: Chariton Newspapers
Editor Name: Paul Struck
Editor Email: pauls@ctimes.biz
Editor Phone: (712) 225-5111
Advertising Executive Name: Chris Reed
Advertising Executive Email: ads@ctimes.biz
Advertising Executive Phone: (712) 225-5111
Delivery Methods: Newsstand`Carrier`Racks
Published Days: Tues`Thur
Avg. Paid Circ.: 2500
Audit Company: Sworn/Estimate/Non-Audited
Audit Date: 43626

CLARION

CLARION WRIGHT COUNTY MONITOR

Street Address: 107 2nd Ave NE
City: Clarion
State: IA
ZIP Code: 50525
General Phone: (515) 532-2871
General Email: cmonitor@mchsi.com
Publication Website: https://clarionnewsonline.com/
Editor Email: wrightcomonitor@gmail.com
Published Days: Thur
Audit Company: Sworn/Estimate/Non-Audited
Audit Date: 43626

CLARKSVILLE

THE CLARKSVILLE STAR

Street Address: 101 N. Main St.
City: Clarksville
State: IA
ZIP Code: 50619
General Phone: (319) 278-4641
General Email: tjstarnews@midamericapub.com
Publication Website: https://www.butlercountytribune.com/
Parent Company: Mid-America Publishing
Publisher Name: Bethany Carson
Publisher Email: startjnews@midamericapub.com
Publisher Phone: (319) 278-4641
Delivery Methods: Mail`Newsstand`Racks
Year Established: 1865
Published Days: Thur
Avg. Paid Circ.: 1058
Avg. Free Circ.: 31
Audit Company: Sworn/Estimate/Non-Audited
Audit Date: 43626

CLEAR LAKE

CLEAR LAKE MIRROR REPORTER

Street Address: 12 N 4th St
City: Clear Lake
State: IA
ZIP Code: 50428
General Phone: (641) 357-2131

General Email: michelle@clreporter.com
Publication Website: http://clreporter.com/
Parent Company: Mid-America Publishing
Editor Name: Marianne Gasaway
Editor Email: marianne@clreporter.com
Delivery Methods: Mail
Year Established: 1869
Mechanical specifications: Type page 14 x 21; E - 6 cols, 2 1/4, 1/18 between; A - 6 cols, 2 1/4, 1/18 between; C - 6 cols, 2 1/4, 1/18 between.
Published Days: Wed
Avg. Paid Circ.: 2500
Avg. Free Circ.: 45
Audit Company: Sworn/Estimate/Non-Audited
Audit Date: 43626

COLFAX

JASPER COUNTY TRIBUNE

Street Address: 1 W Howard St
City: Colfax
State: IA
ZIP Code: 50054
General Phone: (515) 674-3591
General Email: news@jaspercountytribune.com
Publication Website: https://jaspercountytribune.shawcms.com/
Parent Company: Shaw Media
Publisher Name: Dan Goetz
Publisher Email: dgoetz@newtondailynews.com
Editor Name: Mike Mendenhall
Editor Email: mmendenhall@jaspercountytribune.com
Advertising Executive Email: ads@jaspercountytribune.com
Delivery Methods: Mail`Newsstand
Year Established: 1895
Published Days: Thur
Avg. Paid Circ.: 860
Audit Company: Sworn/Estimate/Non-Audited
Audit Date: 43626

COLUMBUS JUNCTION

COLUMBUS GAZETTE

Street Address: 209 Main St
City: Columbus Junction
State: IA
ZIP Code: 52738
General Phone: (319) 728-2413
General Email: cjgaz@windstream.net
Publication Website: http://www.thecolumbusgazette.com/
Publisher Name: Donna Carpenter
Editor Name: John Carpenter
Advertising Executive Name: Carmen Lawrence
Delivery Methods: Mail`Newsstand`Racks
Year Established: 1886
Own Printing Facility?: Y
Commercial printers?: Y
Mechanical specifications: Type page 13 x 21 1/2; E - 6 cols, 2, 1/3 between; A - 6 cols, 2, 1/3 between; C - 8 cols, 1 1/2, 1/3 between.
Published Days: Wed
Avg. Paid Circ.: 1370
Audit Company: Sworn/Estimate/Non-Audited
Audit Date: 43626

COON RAPIDS

COON RAPIDS ENTERPRISE

Street Address: 504 Main St
City: Coon Rapids
State: IA
ZIP Code: 50058
General Phone: (712) 999-6397
General Email: news@coonrapidsenterprise.com

Publication Website: https://www.coonrapidsenterprise.com/
Delivery Methods: Mail`Newsstand`Racks
Year Established: 1881
Published Days: Thur
Avg. Paid Circ.: 1700
Audit Company: Sworn/Estimate/Non-Audited
Audit Date: 43626

CORNING

ADAMS COUNTY FREE PRESS

Street Address: 618 Davis Ave
City: Corning
State: IA
ZIP Code: 50841
General Phone: (641)322-3161
General Email: editor@acfreepress.com
Publication Website: https://www.acfreepress.com
Publisher Name: Don Groves
Publisher Email: publisher@acfreepress.com
Publisher Phone: (641) 322-3161
Editor Name: Don Groves
Editor Email: editor@acfreepress.com
Editor Phone: (641) 322-3161
Advertising Executive Name: Christy Groves
Advertising Executive Email: advertising@acfreepress.com
Advertising Executive Phone: (641) 322-3161
Delivery Methods: Mail
Year Established: 1882
Mechanical specifications: Type page 13 x 21 1/2; E - 6 cols, 2 1/8, 1/6 between; A - 6 cols, 2 1/8, 1/6 between; C - 6 cols, 2 1/8, 1/6 between.
Published Days: Thur
Avg. Paid Circ.: 2000
Audit Company: Sworn/Estimate/Non-Audited
Audit Date: 43626

CORYDON

CORYDON TIMES REPUBLICAN

Street Address: 204 S Franklin St
City: Corydon
State: IA
ZIP Code: 50060
General Phone: (641) 872-1234
General Email: rbennett@corydontimes.com
Publication Website: https://www.corydontimes.com
Publisher Name: Rhonda Bennett
Publisher Email: rbennett@corydontimes.com
Delivery Methods: Mail`Newsstand
Year Established: 1865
Own Printing Facility?: Y
Published Days: Tues
Avg. Paid Circ.: 2000
Audit Company: Sworn/Estimate/Non-Audited
Audit Date: 43626

CRESCO

CRESCO TIMES-PLAIN DEALER

Street Address: 214 N Elm St
City: Cresco
State: IA
ZIP Code: 52136
General Phone: (563) 547-3601
General Email: ads1@crescotimes.com
Publication Website: http://crescotimes.com/
Parent Company: Evans Printing & Publishing, Inc.
Publisher Name: Daniel Evans
Publisher Email: devansppc@mediacombb.net
Editor Name: Marcie Klomp
Editor Email: tpdeditor@crescotimes.com

Community Newspapers in the U.S.

Advertising Executive Name: Betty Schmitt
Advertising Executive Email: ads1@crescotimes.com
Delivery Methods: Mail`Newsstand
Year Established: 1855
Own Printing Facility?: Y
Commercial printers?: Y
Published Days: Wed
Avg. Paid Circ.: 2500
Avg. Free Circ.: 6000
Audit Company: Sworn/Estimate/Non-Audited
Audit Date: 43626
Note: We are a weekly newspaper, but we're also affiliated with Evans Printing & Publishing, which owns the Riceville Recorder and Lime Springs Herald - two weeklies in Iowa, and the Meadow Area News (Grand Meadow) and LeRoy/Southland Independent in Minnesota. We basically cover all of Howard County and parts of Mitchell in Iowa and 2/3rds of Mower County and parts of Fillmore County in Minnesota.

DAVENPORT

BETTENDORF NEWS

Street Address: 500 E 3rd St
City: Davenport
State: IA
ZIP Code: 52801
General Phone: (563) 383-2200
General Email: bettnews@qctimes.com
Publication Website: https://qctimes.com/community/bettendorf/
Parent Company: Dispatch-Argus
Publisher Name: Deb Anselm
Publisher Email: danselm@qctimes.com
Publisher Phone: (563) 383-2224
Editor Name: Matt Christensen
Editor Email: mchristensen@qctimes.com
Editor Phone: (563) 383-2264
Advertising Executive Name: Cathy Rockwell
Advertising Executive Email: crockwell@qctimes.com
Advertising Executive Phone: (563) 383-2308
Delivery Methods: Mail`Newsstand`Carrier`Racks
Year Established: 1927
Own Printing Facility?: Y
Commercial printers?: Y
Published Days: Thur
Avg. Paid Circ.: 9700
Avg. Free Circ.: 2453
Audit Company: Sworn/Estimate/Non-Audited
Audit Date: 43626

DAYTON

DAYTON REVIEW

Street Address: PO Box 6
City: Dayton
State: IA
ZIP Code: 50530
General Phone: (515) 547-2811
General Email: daytonreview@lvcta.com
Publication Website: http://dyr.stparchive.com/
Delivery Methods: Mail`Newsstand`Racks
Year Established: 1877
Mechanical specifications: Type page 9 3/4 x 16; E - 3 cols, 3, 1/3 between; A - 6 cols, 1 7/12, 1/16 between; C - 6 cols, 1 7/12, 1/16 between.
Published Days: Wed
Avg. Paid Circ.: 1100
Avg. Free Circ.: 20
Audit Company: Sworn/Estimate/Non-Audited
Audit Date: 43626

DE WITT

THE OBSERVER

Street Address: 512 7th St
City: De Witt
State: IA
ZIP Code: 52742
General Phone: (563) 659-3121
General Email: news@dewittobserver.com
Publication Website: https://www.dewittobserver.com/
Parent Company: Sycamore Media
Advertising Executive Email: advertising@dewittobserver.com
Delivery Methods: Mail
Year Established: 1865
Own Printing Facility?: Y
Commercial printers?: N
Mechanical specifications: Type page 10 1/2 x 16; E - 4 cols, 2 1/2, 1/6 between; A - 4 cols, 2 1/2, 1/6 between; C - 6 cols, 1 5/8, 1/6 between.
Published Days: Wed`Sat
Avg. Paid Circ.: 4174
Audit Company: Sworn/Estimate/Non-Audited
Audit Date: 43626

DECORAH

DECORAH PUBLIC OPINION

Street Address: 107 E Water St
City: Decorah
State: IA
ZIP Code: 52101
General Phone: (563) 382-4221
General Email: fromm@decorahnewspapers.com
Publication Website: https://decorahnewspapers.com/
Parent Company: Sycamore Media
Editor Name: Rick Fromm
Editor Email: fromm@decorahnewspapers.com
Editor Phone: (563) 382-4221
Advertising Executive Name: Tanya O'Connor
Advertising Executive Email: oconnor@decorahnewspapers.com
Advertising Executive Phone: (563) 382-4221
Delivery Methods: Mail
Year Established: 1898
Mechanical specifications: Type page 13 1/2 x 23; E - 6 cols, 2, 1/6 between.
Published Days: Tues`Thur
Avg. Paid Circ.: 5200
Avg. Free Circ.: 80
Audit Company: Sworn/Estimate/Non-Audited
Audit Date: 43626

DECORAH

THE DECORAH JOURNAL

Street Address: 107 E Water St
City: Decorah
State: IA
ZIP Code: 52101
General Phone: (563) 382-4221
General Email: fromm@decorahnewspapers.com
Publication Website: https://decorahnewspapers.com/
Parent Company: Decorah Newspapers
Editor Name: Rick Fromm
Editor Email: fromm@decorahnewspapers.com
Editor Phone: (563) 382-4221
Advertising Executive Name: Tanya O'Connor
Advertising Executive Email: oconnor@decorahnewspapers.com
Advertising Executive Phone: (563) 382-4221
Delivery Methods: Mail`Newsstand`Racks
Year Established: 1895
Mechanical specifications: Type page 13 1/2 x 23; E - 6 cols, 2, 1/6 between; A - 6 cols, 2, between; C - 6 cols, 2, between.
Published Days: Thur

Avg. Paid Circ.: 5185
Avg. Free Circ.: 16000
Audit Company: Sworn/Estimate/Non-Audited
Audit Date: 43626

DENVER

ELDORA NEWSPAPERS

Street Address: PO Box 509
City: Denver
State: IA
ZIP Code: 50622-0509
General Phone: (319) 984-6179
General Email: ads@denveriaforum.com
Publication Website: http://www.denveriaforum.com/
Parent Company: Horizon Publishing Company
Delivery Methods: Mail`Newsstand`Racks
Year Established: 1860
Own Printing Facility?: N
Commercial printers?: N
Published Days: Tues`Fri
Avg. Paid Circ.: 1750
Audit Company: Sworn/Estimate/Non-Audited
Audit Date: 43626

DES MOINES

ALTOONA HERALD-INDEX

Street Address: 400 Locust St
City: Des Moines
State: IA
ZIP Code: 50309-2355
General Phone: (515) 699-7000
General Email: newsubs@dmreg.com
Publication Website: https://www.desmoinesregister.com/communities/altoona/
Parent Company: Decorah Newspapers
Editor Name: Carol Hunter
Editor Email: chunter@registermedia.com
Advertising Executive Phone: (515) 284-8141
Delivery Methods: Carrier
Published Days: Wed
Audit Company: Sworn/Estimate/Non-Audited
Audit Date: 43626

DES MOINES

ANKENY REGISTER & PRESS CITIZEN

Street Address: 400 Locust St
City: Des Moines
State: IA
ZIP Code: 50309-2355
General Phone: (515) 284-8000
General Email: newsubs@dmreg.com
Publication Website: https://www.desmoinesregister.com/communities/ankeny/
Editor Name: Carol Hunter
Editor Email: chunter@registermedia.com
Advertising Executive Phone: (515) 284-8141
Delivery Methods: Carrier
Year Established: 1953
Mechanical specifications: standard advertising units
Published Days: Tues`Fri
Avg. Free Circ.: 24000
Audit Company: Sworn/Estimate/Non-Audited
Audit Date: 43626

DOON

DOON PRESS

Street Address: 209 Hubbard Ave
City: Doon

State: IA
ZIP Code: 51235-7716
General Phone: (712) 726-3313
General Email: pressgal@premieronline.net
Publication Website: https://businessrecord.com/
Delivery Methods: Mail`Newsstand`Racks
Year Established: 1872
Published Days: Thur
Avg. Paid Circ.: 2600
Audit Company: Sworn/Estimate/Non-Audited
Audit Date: 43626

DYSART

THE DYSART REPORTER

Street Address: P.O. Box 70
City: Dysart
State: IA
ZIP Code: 52224
General Phone: (641) 484-2841
Publication Website: http://www.dysartreporter.com/
Parent Company: Ogden Newspapers Inc.
Mechanical specifications: Type page 13 1/2 x 21; E - 6 cols, 2, 1/4 between; A - 6 cols, 2, 1/4 between; C - 6 cols, 2, 1/4 between.
Published Days: Thur
Avg. Paid Circ.: 800
Avg. Free Circ.: 10
Audit Company: Sworn/Estimate/Non-Audited
Audit Date: 43626

EAGLE GROVE

EAGLE GROVE EAGLE

Street Address: 314 W Broadway St
City: Eagle Grove
State: IA
ZIP Code: 50533
General Phone: (515) 448-4745
General Email: egeagle@goldfieldaccess.net
Publication Website: https://theeaglegroveeagle.com/
Parent Company: Ogden Newspapers Inc.
Delivery Methods: Mail`Newsstand
Mechanical specifications: Type page 14 x 21; E - 6 cols, 2 1/8, 1/6 between; A - 6 cols, 2 1/8, 1/6 between; C - 6 cols, 2 1/8, 1/6 between.
Published Days: Thur
Avg. Paid Circ.: 2317
Audit Company: Sworn/Estimate/Non-Audited
Audit Date: 43626

EDGEWOOD

EDGEWOOD REMINDER

Street Address: 108 E Union
City: Edgewood
State: IA
ZIP Code: 52042
General Phone: (563) 928-6876
General Email: edgewood.reminder@yahoo.com
Publication Website: https://www.edgewoodreminder.net/
Parent Company: Mid-America Publishing
Delivery Methods: Mail`Newsstand
Published Days: Tues
Avg. Paid Circ.: 1100
Avg. Free Circ.: 17
Audit Company: Sworn/Estimate/Non-Audited
Audit Date: 43626

ELDORA

GOWRIE NEWS

Street Address: 1254 Edgington Ave.
City: Eldora
State: IA
ZIP Code: 50627-1623
General Phone: (641) 939-5051
General Email: news@eldoranewspaper.com
Publication Website: https://www.eldoranewspapers.com/
Parent Company: Mid-America Publishing
Publisher Name: Betty Gotto
Delivery Methods: Mail`Racks
Published Days: Wed
Audit Company: Sworn/Estimate/Non-Audited
Audit Date: 43626

ELDORA

OSCEOLA SENTINEL-TRIBUNE

Street Address: 1254 Edgington Ave.
City: Eldora
State: IA
ZIP Code: 50627-1623
General Phone: (641) 939-5051
General Email: news@eldoranewspaper.com
Publication Website: http://www.eldoranewspapers.com/
Parent Company: Shaw Media
Publisher Name: Betty Gotto
Delivery Methods: Mail`Newsstand
Own Printing Facility?: Y
Commercial printers?: Y
Mechanical specifications: Type page 11 x 21 1/2; E - 6 cols, 9 1/9, between; A - 7 cols, 9 1/9, between; C - 8 cols, 9 1/9, between.
Published Days: Thur
Avg. Paid Circ.: 3200
Avg. Free Circ.: 11000
Audit Company: CVC
Audit Date: 43226

ELDRIDGE

THE NORTH SCOTT PRESS

Street Address: 214 N 2nd St
City: Eldridge
State: IA
ZIP Code: 52748
General Phone: (563) 285-8111
General Email: adsales@northscottpress.com
Publication Website: http://www.northscottpress.com
Publisher Name: Linda Tubbs
Publisher Email: ltubbs@northscottpress.com
Editor Name: Scott Campbell
Editor Email: scampbell@northscottpress.com
Advertising Executive Name: Jeff Martens
Advertising Executive Email: advertising@northscottpress.com
Delivery Methods: Mail`Newsstand`Racks
Year Established: 1968
Own Printing Facility?: N
Commercial printers?: N
Mechanical specifications: Type page 10.2 x 16; E - 4 cols, 2.5, 1/6 between; A - 4 cols, 2.5, 1/6 between; C - 6 cols, 1.67, 1/6 between.
Published Days: Wed
Avg. Paid Circ.: 5000
Audit Company: Sworn/Estimate/Non-Audited
Audit Date: 43626

EMMETSBURG

REPORTER-DEMOCRAT

Street Address: PO Box 73
City: Emmetsburg
State: IA
ZIP Code: 50536
General Phone: (712) 852-2323
General Email: mduhn@emmetsburgnews.com
Publication Website: http://www.emmetsburgnews.com/
Parent Company: Ogden Newspapers Inc.
Publisher Name: Dan McCain
Publisher Email: dmccain@emmetsburgnews.com
Advertising Executive Name: Karmen Gappa
Advertising Executive Email: kgappa@emmetsburgnews.com
Delivery Methods: Mail`Newsstand`Racks
Own Printing Facility?: Y
Commercial printers?: Y
Mechanical specifications: Type page 11 1/2 x 21 1/2; E - 6 cols, 1 7/8, 1/12 between; A - 6 cols, 1 7/8, 1/12 between; C - 6 cols, 1 7/8, 1/12 between.
Published Days: Thur
Avg. Paid Circ.: 2700
Audit Company: Sworn/Estimate/Non-Audited
Audit Date: 43626

EMMETSBURG

THE DEMOCRAT

Street Address: PO Box 73
City: Emmetsburg
State: IA
ZIP Code: 50536
General Phone: (712) 852-2323
General Email: mduhn@emmetsburgnews.com
Publication Website: http://www.emmetsburgnews.com/
Parent Company: Ogden Newspapers Inc.
Publisher Name: Dan McCain
Publisher Email: dmccain@emmetsburgnews.com
Advertising Executive Name: Karmen Gappa
Advertising Executive Email: kgappa@emmetsburgnews.com
Delivery Methods: Mail`Newsstand`Racks
Year Established: 1882
Published Days: Thur
Audit Company: Sworn/Estimate/Non-Audited
Audit Date: 43626

EMMETSBURG

THE EMMETSBURG REPORTER

Street Address: PO Box 73
City: Emmetsburg
State: IA
ZIP Code: 50536
General Phone: (712) 852-2323
General Email: mduhn@emmetsburgnews.com
Publication Website: http://www.emmetsburgnews.com/
Parent Company: Ogden Newspapers Inc.
Publisher Name: Dan McCain
Publisher Email: dmccain@emmetsburgnews.com
Advertising Executive Name: Karmen Gappa
Advertising Executive Email: kgappa@emmetsburgnews.com
Delivery Methods: Mail`Newsstand`Racks
Year Established: 1876
Own Printing Facility?: Y
Commercial printers?: Y
Mechanical specifications: Type page 11 1/2 x 21 1/2; E - 6 cols, 1 7/8, 1/12 between; A - 6 cols, 1 7/8, 1/12 between; C - 6 cols, 1 7/8, 1/12 between.
Published Days: Tues
Avg. Paid Circ.: 2400
Audit Company: Sworn/Estimate/Non-Audited
Audit Date: 43626

FOREST CITY

BRITT NEWS-TRIBUNE

Street Address: 105 S Clark St
City: Forest City
State: IA
ZIP Code: 50436
General Phone: (641) 585-2112
General Email: news@brittnewstribune.com
Publication Website: https://globegazette.com/community/brittnewstribune/
Parent Company: Ogden Newspapers Inc.
Delivery Methods: Mail`Newsstand`Racks
Published Days: Wed
Audit Company: Sworn/Estimate/Non-Audited
Audit Date: 43626

FOREST CITY

FOREST CITY SUMMIT

Street Address: 105 S Clark St
City: Forest City
State: IA
ZIP Code: 50436
General Phone: (641) 585-2112
General Email: news@forestcitysummit.com
Publication Website: https://globegazette.com/community/forestcitysummit/#tracking-source=menu-nav
Delivery Methods: Mail`Newsstand`Racks
Published Days: Wed
Audit Company: Sworn/Estimate/Non-Audited
Audit Date: 43626

GARNER

THE LEADER

Street Address: 365 State St
City: Garner
State: IA
ZIP Code: 50438
General Phone: (641) 923-2684
General Email: glads@qwestoffice.net
Publication Website: http://theleaderonline.net/
Parent Company: Adams Publishing Group
Publisher Name: Ana Olsthoorn
Publisher Email: glads@qwestoffice.net
Publisher Phone: (641) 529-3088
Editor Name: Rebecca Peter
Editor Email: gleadernews@qwestoffice.net
Editor Phone: (641) 923-2684
Advertising Executive Email: winnehancocksales@midamericapub.com
Advertising Executive Phone: (712) 898-4834
Delivery Methods: Mail`Newsstand
Own Printing Facility?: Y
Commercial printers?: Y
Published Days: Wed
Avg. Paid Circ.: 2500
Avg. Free Circ.: 40
Audit Company: Sworn/Estimate/Non-Audited
Audit Date: 43626

GEORGE

LYON COUNTY NEWS

Street Address: 113 E Michigan Ave
City: George
State: IA
ZIP Code: 51237-7751
General Phone: (712) 475-3351
General Email: lyonconews@mtcnet.net
Publication Website: https://lyoncountynews.com/
Parent Company: Mid-America Publishing
Delivery Methods: Mail
Year Established: 1906
Mechanical specifications: Type page 15 x 21 1/2; E - 7 cols, 2, 1/6 between; A - 7 cols, 2, 1/6 between; C - 7 cols, 2, 1/6 between.
Published Days: Thur
Avg. Paid Circ.: 750

Avg. Free Circ.: 80
Audit Company: Sworn/Estimate/Non-Audited
Audit Date: 43626

GLADBROOK

NORTHERN-SUN PRINT

Street Address: P.O. Box 340
City: Gladbrook
State: IA
ZIP Code: 50635
General Phone: (641) 484-2841
General Email: editor@northernsunprint.com
Publication Website: http://www.northernsunprint.com/
Parent Company: Ogden Newspapers Inc.
Editor Name: Betty Dahms
Editor Email: editor@northernsunprint.com
Editor Phone: (641) 484-2841
Delivery Methods: Mail`Newsstand
Mechanical specifications: Type page 10 1/4 x 14 1/2; E - 5 cols, 1 11/12, 1/6 between; A - 5 cols, 1 11/12, 1/6 between; C - 5 cols, 1 11/12, 1/6 between.
Published Days: Fri
Avg. Paid Circ.: 1100
Audit Company: Sworn/Estimate/Non-Audited
Audit Date: 43626

GOWRIE

HARDIN COUNTY INDEX

Street Address: 1107 Market St
City: Gowrie
State: IA
ZIP Code: 50543
General Phone: (515) 352-3325
General Email: gnews@wccta.net
Publication Website: https://gowrienews.com/
Parent Company: Mid-America Publishing
Delivery Methods: Mail
Year Established: 1865
Published Days: Tues`Fri
Avg. Paid Circ.: 1500
Audit Company: Sworn/Estimate/Non-Audited
Audit Date: 43626

GREENE

GREENE RECORDER

Street Address: PO Box 370
City: Greene
State: IA
ZIP Code: 50636
General Phone: (641) 816-4525
General Email: news@greenerecorder.com
Publication Website: https://www.opinion-tribune.com/
Parent Company: Ogden Newspapers Inc.
Delivery Methods: Mail`Newsstand`Racks
Year Established: 1901
Published Days: Wed
Avg. Paid Circ.: 1250
Avg. Free Circ.: 20
Audit Company: Sworn/Estimate/Non-Audited
Audit Date: 43626

GRINNELL

POWESHIEK COUNTY CHRONICLE-REPUBLICAN

Street Address: 925 Broad St
City: Grinnell
State: IA
ZIP Code: 50112-2047
General Phone: (641) 522-7155
General Email: powcr@dmreg.com

Community Newspapers in the U.S.

Publication Website: https://www.greenerecorder.com/
Parent Company: SmugMug, Inc
Published Days: Wed
Audit Company: Sworn/Estimate/Non-Audited
Audit Date: 43626

GRISWOLD

GRISWOLD AMERICAN

Street Address: 519 MAIN ST
City: Griswold
State: IA
ZIP Code: 51535
General Phone: (712) 778-4337
General Email: grisamer@netins.net
Publication Website: http://www.griswoldamerican.com/
Delivery Methods: Mail`Racks
Year Established: 1880
Published Days: Wed
Published Other: Weekly
Avg. Paid Circ.: 900
Avg. Free Circ.: 30
Audit Company: Sworn/Estimate/Non-Audited
Audit Date: 43626

GRUNDY CENTER

GRUNDY CENTER REGISTER

Street Address: 601 G Ave
City: Grundy Center
State: IA
ZIP Code: 50638
General Phone: (319) 824-6958
General Email: grundypublisher@midamericapub.com
Publication Website: https://www.thegrundyregister.com/
Parent Company: Mid-America Publishing
Publisher Name: Robert Maharry
Publisher Email: grundypublisher@midamericapub.com
Editor Name: Michaela Kendall
Editor Email: grundyeditor@midamericapub.com
Delivery Methods: Mail`Newsstand`Racks
Published Days: Thur
Audit Company: Sworn/Estimate/Non-Audited
Audit Date: 43626

GUTHRIE CENTER

GUTHRIE CENTER TIMES

Street Address: 205 State St
City: Guthrie Center
State: IA
ZIP Code: 50115-1370
General Phone: (641) 332-2380
Publication Website: https://www.thegrundyregister.com/
Parent Company: Mid-America Publishing
Delivery Methods: Mail`Newsstand`Racks
Own Printing Facility?: Y
Commercial printers?: Y
Mechanical specifications: Type page 15 1/4 x 21 1/2; E - 8 cols, 1 3/4, 1/6 between; A - 8 cols, 1 3/4, 1/6 between; C - 8 cols, 1 3/4, 1/6 between.
Published Days: Wed
Avg. Paid Circ.: 1350
Avg. Free Circ.: 17
Audit Company: Sworn/Estimate/Non-Audited
Audit Date: 43626

HAMBURG

DENVER FORUM

Street Address: 1009 Main St
City: Hamburg
State: IA
ZIP Code: 51640-1231
General Phone: (712) 382-1234
General Email: hamburgreporter@qwestoffice.net
Publication Website: https://www.hamburgreporter.com/
Publisher Name: Tammy Schumacher
Publisher Email: tschumacher@ncnewspress.com
Publisher Phone: (402) 873-3334
Editor Name: Kirt Manion
Editor Email: kmanion@ncnewspress.com
Editor Phone: (402) 873-3334
Advertising Executive Name: Theresa Kaven
Advertising Executive Email: tkaven@ncnewsproc.com
Advertising Executive Phone: (402) 269-2135
Delivery Methods: Mail`Newsstand
Year Established: 1976
Mechanical specifications: Tabloid
Published Days: Wed
Avg. Paid Circ.: 600
Audit Company: Sworn/Estimate/Non-Audited
Audit Date: 43626

HARLAN

HAMPTON CHRONICLE

Street Address: 1114 7th St
City: Harlan
State: IA
ZIP Code: 51537-1338
General Phone: (712) 755-3111
General Email: news2@harlanonline.com
Publication Website: http://hamptonchronicle.com/
Published Days: Wed
Audit Company: Sworn/Estimate/Non-Audited
Audit Date: 43626

HAWARDEN

HAWARDEN INDEPENDENT/IRETON EXAMINER

Street Address: 700 7th Street
City: Hawarden
State: IA
ZIP Code: 51023
General Phone: (712) 551-1051
General Email: kanderson@nwestiowa.com
Publication Website: http://www.independentexaminer.net/
Parent Company: Iowa Information Publishers and Printers
Editor Name: Katie Anderson
Editor Email: kanderson@nwestiowa.com
Editor Phone: (712) 631-5727
Advertising Executive Email: ads@iowainformation.com
Delivery Methods: Mail`Newsstand
Year Established: 1878
Published Days: Thur
Avg. Paid Circ.: 1256
Avg. Free Circ.: 21
Audit Company: Sworn/Estimate/Non-Audited
Audit Date: 43626

HOPKINTON

DELAWARE COUNTY LEADER

Street Address: 101 1st St SE
City: Hopkinton
State: IA
ZIP Code: 52237
General Phone: (563) 926-2626
General Email: delcoleader@yahoo.com
Publication Website: https://delawarecountyleader.com/
Parent Company: Iowa Information Publishers and Printers
Published Days: Tues
Avg. Paid Circ.: 1420
Audit Company: Sworn/Estimate/Non-Audited
Audit Date: 43626

HOSPERS

HUMBOLDT INDEPENDENT

Street Address: 105 Ash St
City: Hospers
State: IA
ZIP Code: 51238
General Phone: (712) 752-8401
General Email: slpress@nethtc.net
Publication Website: http://humboldtnews.com/
Delivery Methods: Mail`Newsstand`Racks
Year Established: 1985
Mechanical specifications: Type page 11 3/4 x 21; E - 6 cols, 1 7/8, 1/8 between; A - 6 cols, 1 7/8, 1/8 between; C - 6 cols, 1 7/8, 1/8 between.
Published Days: Thur
Avg. Paid Circ.: 3623
Avg. Free Circ.: 197
Audit Company: Sworn/Estimate/Non-Audited
Audit Date: 43626

HULL

HUDSON HERALD

Street Address: PO Box 420
City: Hull
State: IA
ZIP Code: 51239
General Phone: (712) 439-1075
General Email: hulleditor@ncppub.com
Publication Website: http://www.hudherald.com/
Parent Company: Hudson Printing Company
Editor Email: hulleditor@ncppub.com
Delivery Methods: Mail`Newsstand
Year Established: 1911
Own Printing Facility?: Y
Commercial printers?: Y
Mechanical specifications: Type page 11x22; E - 5 cols, 1.89, 1/8 gutter; A - 5 cols, 1.89, 1/8 gutter; C - 5 cols, 1.89
Published Days: Thur
Avg. Paid Circ.: 900
Avg. Free Circ.: 25
Audit Company: Sworn/Estimate/Non-Audited
Audit Date: 43626

INDEPENDENCE

INDEPENDENCE BULLETIN JOURNAL

Street Address: 900 5th Ave NE
City: Independence
State: IA
ZIP Code: 50644-1464
General Phone: (319) 334-2557
General Email: debweigel@oelweindailyregister.com
Publication Website: http://www.communitynewspapergroup.com/independence_bulletin_journal/
Parent Company: Mid-America Publishing
Publisher Name: Deb Weigel
Publisher Email: debweigel@oelweindailyregister.com
Editor Name: John Klotzbach
Editor Email: editor@bulletinjournal.com
Advertising Executive Name: Tracy Cummings
Advertising Executive Email: tracy.cummings@oelweindailyregister.com
Delivery Methods: Mail
Published Days: Wed`Sat
Audit Company: Sworn/Estimate/Non-Audited
Audit Date: 43626

INDIANOLA

DM JUICE

Street Address: 112 N Howard St
City: Indianola
State: IA
ZIP Code: 50125-2510
General Phone: (515) 284-8000
Publication Website: https://www.dmjuice.com
Delivery Methods: Mail`Newsstand`Carrier`Racks
Year Established: 1856
Own Printing Facility?: Y
Commercial printers?: Y
Mechanical specifications: Type page 12 7/8 x 21; E - 6 cols, 2, 1/8 between; A - 6 cols, 2, 1/8 between; C - 10 cols, between.
Published Days: Wed
Avg. Paid Circ.: 7480
Audit Company: Sworn/Estimate/Non-Audited
Audit Date: 43626

JEFFERSON

IOWA FALLS IOWA FARM BUREAU SPOKESMAN

Street Address: 200 N Wilson Ave
City: Jefferson
State: IA
ZIP Code: 50129
General Phone: (515) 386-4161
General Email: news@beeherald.com
Publication Website: https://www.iowafarmbureau.com/News/Spokesman?listpage=5
Publisher Name: Ann Wilson
Publisher Email: management@carrollspaper.com
Editor Name: Andrew McGinn
Editor Email: news@beeherald.com
Advertising Executive Name: Deb Geisler
Advertising Executive Email: ads@beeherald.com
Delivery Methods: Mail
Published Days: Wed
Audit Company: Sworn/Estimate/Non-Audited
Audit Date: 43626

JEFFERSON

THE JEFFERSON HERALD

Street Address: 200 N Wilson Ave
City: Jefferson
State: IA
ZIP Code: 50129
General Phone: (515) 386-4161
General Email: news@beeherald.com
Publication Website: http://beeherald.com/
Publisher Name: Ann Wilson
Publisher Email: management@carrollspaper.com
Editor Name: Andrew McGinn
Editor Email: news@beeherald.com
Advertising Executive Name: Deb Geisler
Advertising Executive Email: ads@beeherald.com
Delivery Methods: Mail`Newsstand`Racks
Own Printing Facility?: Y
Commercial printers?: Y
Mechanical specifications: Type page 15 3/4 x 21; E - 7 cols, 2 1/12, 1 1/24 between; A - 7 cols, 2 1/12, 1 1/24 between; C - 7 cols, 2 1/12, between.
Published Days: Thur
Avg. Paid Circ.: 2294
Audit Company: Sworn/Estimate/Non-Audited
Audit Date: 43626

JEWELL

JESUP CITIZEN HERALD

Street Address: 602 Main St
City: Jewell
State: IA
ZIP Code: 50130-2012
General Phone: (515) 827-5931
General Email: shrecnew@netins.net
Publication Website: https://jesupcitizenherald.com/
Parent Company: Horizon Publishing Company
Delivery Methods: Mail`Newsstand
Year Established: 1899
Mechanical specifications: Type page 13 3/4 x 21 1/2; E - 6 cols, 2 1/10, 1/10 between; A - 6 cols, 2 1/10, 1/10 between; C - 6 cols, 2 1/10, 1/10 between.
Published Days: Wed
Avg. Paid Circ.: 1020
Audit Company: Sworn/Estimate/Non-Audited
Audit Date: 43626

KALONA

ANAMOSA PUBLICATIONS

Street Address: 405 E. Main Street, P.O. Box 108
City: Kalona
State: IA
ZIP Code: 52205
General Phone: (319) 462-3511
General Email: wendy.geerts@wcinet.com
Publication Website: https://www.journal-eureka.com/
Parent Company: Anamosa Publications
Publisher Name: Mary Ungs-Sogaard
Publisher Email: mungs-sogaard@wcinet.com
Editor Name: Beth Lutgen
Editor Email: blutgen@wcinet.com
Advertising Executive Name: Wendy Geerts
Advertising Executive Email: wendy.geerts@wcinet.com
Delivery Methods: Mail`Newsstand
Year Established: 1856
Mechanical specifications: Six-column tabloid 10 x 21 inches
Published Days: Thur
Published Other: Shopper on Tuesday
Avg. Paid Circ.: 2500
Avg. Free Circ.: 11223
Audit Company: Sworn/Estimate/Non-Audited
Audit Date: 43626

KALONA

THE BELMOND INDEPENDENT

Street Address: 419 B Ave
City: Kalona
State: IA
ZIP Code: 52247-7719
General Phone: (319) 656-2273
General Email: admin@thenews-ia.com
Publication Website: http://thenews-ia.com
Publisher Name: Jim Johnson
Publisher Email: publisher@kalonanews.com
Editor Name: James Jennings
Editor Email: news@thenews-ia.com
Advertising Executive Name: Bridget Johnson
Advertising Executive Email: adsales@thenews-ia.com
Delivery Methods: Mail`Newsstand
Year Established: 1885
Commercial printers?: Y
Mechanical specifications: Type page 13 wide x 21 tall; 6 columns, 12 picas per col. with one pica gutter.
Published Days: Thur
Avg. Paid Circ.: 1400
Avg. Free Circ.: 5
Audit Company: Sworn/Estimate/Non-Audited
Audit Date: 43626

KINGSLEY

KEOTA EAGLE

Street Address: 120 Main St
City: Kingsley
State: IA
ZIP Code: 51028-7725
General Phone: (712) 378-2770
General Email: knewest@evertek.net
Publication Website: http://www.keotaeagle.com/
Parent Company: Mid-America Publishing
Delivery Methods: Mail`Newsstand
Year Established: 1875
Published Days: Wed
Audit Company: Sworn/Estimate/Non-Audited
Audit Date: 43626

KNOXVILLE

THE KNOXVILLE JOURNAL-EXPRESS

Street Address: 122 E Robinson St
City: Knoxville
State: IA
ZIP Code: 50138
General Phone: (641) 842-2155
General Email: editor@journalexpress.net
Publication Website: http://www.journalexpress.net/
Parent Company: Raycom Media
Publisher Name: Becky Maxwell
Publisher Email: publisher@journalexpress.net
Publisher Phone: (641) 842-2155, ext : 14
Editor Name: Kyle Ocker
Editor Email: kocker@dailyiowegian.com
Editor Phone: (641) 856-6336, ext : 35
Advertising Executive Name: Gabrielle Rehard
Advertising Executive Email: grehard@journalexpress.net
Delivery Methods: Mail`Newsstand`Racks
Year Established: 1855
Mechanical specifications: Type page 13 x 21 1/2; E - 6 cols, 2 1/8, 1/8 between; A - 6 cols, 2 1/8, 1/8 between; C - 6 cols, 2 1/8, 1/8 between.
Published Days: Thur
Avg. Paid Circ.: 1800
Audit Company: Sworn/Estimate/Non-Audited
Audit Date: 43626

LA PORTE CITY

THE PROGRESS-REVIEW

Street Address: 213 Main St
City: La Porte City
State: IA
ZIP Code: 50651
General Phone: (319) 342-2429
General Email: news@theprogressreview.co
Publication Website: https://www.theprogressreview.co/
Delivery Methods: Mail`Newsstand`Racks
Year Established: 1865
Published Days: Wed
Avg. Paid Circ.: 1360
Audit Company: Sworn/Estimate/Non-Audited
Audit Date: 43626

LAKE CITY

THE GRAPHIC ADVOCATE

Street Address: 121 North Center St
City: Lake City
State: IA
ZIP Code: 51449
General Phone: (712) 464-3188
General Email: lcgraphic@iowatelecom.net
Publication Website: https://thegraphic-advocate.com/
Parent Company: Mid-America Publishing
Editor Name: Tyler Anderson
Advertising Executive Name: Toni Venteicher
Delivery Methods: Mail`Newsstand`Racks
Year Established: 1889
Published Days: Wed
Avg. Paid Circ.: 700
Audit Company: Sworn/Estimate/Non-Audited
Audit Date: 43626

LAKE CITY

THE LAKE CITY GRAPHIC-ADVOCATE

Street Address: 121 N Center St
City: Lake City
State: IA
ZIP Code: 51449
General Phone: (712) 464-3188
General Email: gaeditor@windstream.net
Publication Website: http://thegraphic-advocate.com/
Parent Company: Mid-America Publishing
Publisher Name: Jeri Wilson
Editor Name: Tyler Anderson
Editor Email: gaeditor@windstream.net
Advertising Executive Name: Toni Venteicher
Advertising Executive Email: toni.venteicher4@gmail.com
Delivery Methods: Mail`Newsstand`Racks
Published Days: Wed
Avg. Paid Circ.: 1150
Audit Company: Sworn/Estimate/Non-Audited
Audit Date: 43626

LONE TREE

REMSEN BELL-ENTERPRISE

Street Address: PO Box 13
City: Lone Tree
State: IA
ZIP Code: 52755-0013
General Phone: (319) 629-5207
General Email: ltnews@iowatelecom.net
Publication Website: https://www.lemarssentinel.com/remsen
Parent Company: Rust Communications
Delivery Methods: Mail`Newsstand
Year Established: 1887
Mechanical specifications: Type page 12 7/8 x 21; E - 6 cols, 2, 1/6 between; A - 6 cols, 2, 1/6 between; C - 6 cols, 2, 1/6 between.
Published Days: Thur
Avg. Paid Circ.: 1100
Avg. Free Circ.: 4
Audit Company: Sworn/Estimate/Non-Audited
Audit Date: 43626

MALVERN

THE LOGAN HERALD-OBSERVER

Street Address: PO Box 129
City: Malvern
State: IA
ZIP Code: 51551-0129
General Phone: (712) 624-8512
General Email: leaderbeacon@qwestoffice.net
Publication Website: https://www.loganwoodbine.com/
Mechanical specifications: Type page 15 x 21 1/2; E - 6 cols, 2 1/3, 1/6 between; A - 6 cols, 2 1/3, 1/6 between; C - 9 cols, 1 7/12, 1/6 between.
Published Days: Wed
Avg. Paid Circ.: 1400
Audited
Audit Date: 43626

MANCHESTER

THE MANCHESTER PRESS

Street Address: 109 E Delaware St
City: Manchester
State: IA
ZIP Code: 52057-2208
General Phone: (563) 927-2020
General Email: manpress@mchsi.com
Publication Website: https://www.manchesterpress.com/
Publisher Name: Mary Ungs-Sogaard
Publisher Email: mungs-sogaard@wcinet.com
Editor Name: Beth Lutgen
Editor Email: blutgen@wcinet.com
Advertising Executive Name: Kim Ronnebaum
Advertising Executive Email: lvorwald@wcinet.com
Delivery Methods: Mail`Newsstand`Racks
Published Days: Tues
Avg. Paid Circ.: 4800
Audit Company: Sworn/Estimate/Non-Audited
Audit Date: 43626

MANSON

MANILLA TIMES

Street Address: 931 Main St
City: Manson
State: IA
ZIP Code: 50563-5135
General Phone: (712) 469-3381
General Email: journal@journalherald.com
Parent Company: Kock Publishing
Delivery Methods: Mail`Newsstand
Year Established: 1899
Published Days: Thur
Avg. Paid Circ.: 782
Avg. Free Circ.: 18
Audit Company: Sworn/Estimate/Non-Audited
Audit Date: 43626

MAPLETON

MAPLETON PRESS

Street Address: 502 Main St
City: Mapleton
State: IA
ZIP Code: 51034-1215
General Phone: (712) 881-1101
General Email: news@mapletonpress.com
Publication Website: http://www.enterprisepub.com/mapleton/
Parent Company: Enterprise Publishing Co.
Publisher Name: Brad Swenson
Advertising Executive Name: Kathy Boehm
Delivery Methods: Mail`Newsstand
Year Established: 1874
Mechanical specifications: 1 column = 1.833" 2 columns = 3.792" 3 columns = 5.75" 4 columns = 7.708" 5 columns = 9.667" 6 columns = 11.625" Page height = 21.5"
Published Days: Thur
Avg. Paid Circ.: 1300
Audit Company: Sworn/Estimate/Non-Audited
Audit Date: 43626

MAQUOKETA

MAQUOKETA SENTINEL-PRESS

Street Address: 108 W Quarry St
City: Maquoketa

Community Newspapers in the U.S.

State: IA
ZIP Code: 52060-2244
General Phone: (563) 652-2441
General Email: mspress@mspress.net
Publication Website: https://www.maqnews.com
Parent Company: Sycamore Media
Delivery Methods: Mail`Newsstand
Own Printing Facility?: Y
Commercial printers?: Y
Published Days: Wed`Sat
Avg. Paid Circ.: 5050
Audit Company: Sworn/Estimate/Non-Audited
Audit Date: 43626

MARENGO

MARENGO PIONEER-REPUBLICAN

Street Address: 1152 Marengo Ave
City: Marengo
State: IA
ZIP Code: 52301-1523
General Phone: (319) 642-5506
General Email: publish@netins.net
Publication Website: https://www.press-citizen.com/eastern-iowa/
Delivery Methods: Mail`Newsstand`Racks
Own Printing Facility?: Y
Commercial printers?: Y
Mechanical specifications: Type page 14 1/4 x 21; E - 6 cols, 2 1/16, 1/8 between; A - 6 cols, 2 1/16, 1/8 between; C - 6 cols, 2 1/16, 1/8 between.
Published Days: Thur
Avg. Paid Circ.: 2542
Audit Company: Sworn/Estimate/Non-Audited
Audit Date: 43626

MC GREGOR

NORTH IOWA TIMES

Street Address: P.O. Box M
City: Mc Gregor
State: IA
ZIP Code: 52157-8718
General Phone: (563) 873-2210
General Email: niteditor@mhtc.net
Publication Website: http://www.claytoncountyregister.com/articles/north-iowa-times
Parent Company: Courier Press
Delivery Methods: Mail`Newsstand
Year Established: 1856
Own Printing Facility?: Y
Commercial printers?: Y
Mechanical specifications: Type page 10 x 15 1/2; E - 5 cols, 1 11/12, 1/6 between; A - 5 cols, 1 11/12, 1/6 between; C - 5 cols, 1 11/12, 1/6 between.
Published Days: Wed
Avg. Paid Circ.: 750
Avg. Free Circ.: 20000
Audit Company: Sworn/Estimate/Non-Audited
Audit Date: 43626

MEDIAPOLIS

MEDIAPOLIS NEWS

Street Address: 616 Main St
City: Mediapolis
State: IA
ZIP Code: 52637-7731
General Phone: (319) 394-3174
General Email: meponews@mepotelco.net
Publication Website: http://www.mediapolisnews.com/
Delivery Methods: Mail`Racks
Year Established: 1874
Published Days: Thur
Avg. Paid Circ.: 1000
Avg. Free Circ.: 600
Audit Company: Sworn/Estimate/Non-Audited
Audit Date: 43626

MISSOURI VALLEY

DUNLAP REPORTER

Street Address: 513 E. Erie St., P.O.Box 159
City: Missouri Valley
State: IA
ZIP Code: 51555
General Phone: (712) 642-2791
General Email: thedunlapreporter@gmail.com
Publication Website: https://www.dunlapiowa.com
Publisher Name: Brad Swenson
Delivery Methods: Mail`Newsstand`Racks
Year Established: 1870
Own Printing Facility?: Y
Commercial printers?: N
Mechanical specifications: Type page 15 x 21 1/2; E - 8 cols, 1 3/4, 1/6 between; A - 8 cols, 1 3/4, 1/6 between; C - 8 cols, 1 3/4, 1/6 between.
Published Days: Thur
Avg. Paid Circ.: 560
Avg. Free Circ.: 10
Audit Company: Sworn/Estimate/Non-Audited
Audit Date: 43626

MISSOURI VALLEY

MISSOURI VALLEY TIMES-NEWS

Street Address: 501 E Erie St
City: Missouri Valley
State: IA
ZIP Code: 51555-1646
General Phone: (712) 642-2791
General Email: news@missourivalleytimes.com
Publication Website: http://www.enterprisepub.com/movalley
Parent Company: Enterprise Publishing Co.
Publisher Name: Brad Swenson
Publisher Email: pub@missourivalleytimes.com
Advertising Executive Name: Lynette Hansen
Advertising Executive Email: lhansen@enterprisepub.com
Delivery Methods: Mail`Newsstand
Year Established: 1868
Mechanical specifications: Type page 11.625" x 21.5"; E - 6 cols, 2, 1/8 between; A - 6 cols, 2, 1/8 between; C - 6 cols, 2, 1/8 between.
Published Days: Wed`Fri
Avg. Paid Circ.: 1900
Audit Company: Sworn/Estimate/Non-Audited
Audit Date: 43626

MONROE

MONROE LEGACY

Street Address: 213 W Mills St
City: Monroe
State: IA
ZIP Code: 50170-7920
General Phone: (641) 259-2708
General Email: mmml@iowatelecom.net
Publication Website: http://www.monroelegacy.com/
Parent Company: Shaw Media
Delivery Methods: Mail`Newsstand`Racks
Year Established: 1873
Published Days: Thur
Audit Company: Sworn/Estimate/Non-Audited
Audit Date: 43626

MONTICELLO

THE MONTICELLO EXPRESS

Street Address: 111 E Grand St
City: Monticello
State: IA
ZIP Code: 52310-1688
General Phone: (319) 465-3555
General Email: advertising@monticelloexpress.com
Publication Website: http://monticelloexpress.com/
Publisher Name: Dan Goodyear
Publisher Email: dgoodyear@monticelloexpress.com
Editor Name: Kim Brooks
Editor Email: kbrooks@monticelloexpress.com
Advertising Executive Name: Mark Spensley
Advertising Executive Email: advertising@monticelloexpress.com
Delivery Methods: Mail`Newsstand`Racks
Year Established: 1865
Own Printing Facility?: Y
Commercial printers?: Y
Mechanical specifications: Type page 10 1/4 x 16; E - 6 cols, 1 7/12, 1/6 between; A - 6 cols, 1 7/12, 1/6 between; C - 6 cols, 1 7/12, 1/6 between.
Published Days: Wed
Avg. Paid Circ.: 3450
Audit Company: Sworn/Estimate/Non-Audited
Audit Date: 43626

MOUNT AYR

MOUNT AYR RECORD-NEWS

Street Address: 122 W Madison St
City: Mount Ayr
State: IA
ZIP Code: 50854-1630
General Phone: (641) 464-2440
General Email: staff@mtayrnews.com
Publication Website: https://www.mtayrnews.com/
Parent Company: Paragon Publications
Publisher Name: Tom Hawley
Editor Name: Tom Hawley
Advertising Executive Name: LuAnn Jackson
Delivery Methods: Mail`Racks
Year Established: 1864
Own Printing Facility?: N
Commercial printers?: Y
Mechanical specifications: Type page 11.5 x 21; E -6 cols, 1 5/8, 1/6 between; A - 6 cols, 1 5/8, 1/6 between; C - 6 cols, 1 5/8, 1/6 between.
Published Days: Thur
Avg. Paid Circ.: 2221
Avg. Free Circ.: 69
Audit Company: Sworn/Estimate/Non-Audited
Audit Date: 43626

MUSCATINE

THE MUSCATINE POST

Street Address: 301 E 3rd St
City: Muscatine
State: IA
ZIP Code: 52761-4116
General Phone: (563) 263-2331
General Email: david.hotle@muscatinejournal.com
Publication Website: https://muscatinejournal.com/
Parent Company: Baker Newspapers, Inc.
Publisher Name: Debbie Anselm
Publisher Email: deb.anselm@lee.net
Editor Name: David Hotle
Editor Email: david.hotle@muscatinejournal.com
Editor Phone: (563) 262-0545
Advertising Executive Name: Kayla Brix
Advertising Executive Email: kbrix@qctimes.com
Published Days: Tues
Avg. Paid Circ.: 1

Avg. Free Circ.: 14913
Audit Company: Sworn/Estimate/Non-Audited
Audit Date: 43626

NASHUA

NASHUA REPORTER

Street Address: PO Box 517
City: Nashua
State: IA
ZIP Code: 50658
General Phone: (641) 394-2111
General Email: nashuareporter@gmail.com
Publication Website: http://nhtrib.com/
Publisher Name: Kevin Brown
Publisher Email: publisher@nhtrib.com
Editor Name: Bob Fenske
Editor Email: editor@nhtrib.com
Advertising Executive Name: Tim Craig
Advertising Executive Email: ads@nhtrib.com
Delivery Methods: Mail`Newsstand`Racks
Published Days: Thur
Audit Company: Sworn/Estimate/Non-Audited
Audit Date: 43626

NEW HAMPTON

NEW HAMPTON TRIBUNE

Street Address: 10 N Chestnut Ave
City: New Hampton
State: IA
ZIP Code: 50659
General Phone: (641) 394-2111
General Email: tribune@nhtrib.com
Publication Website: http://www.nhtrib.com/
Publisher Name: Kevin Brown
Publisher Email: publisher@nhtrib.com
Editor Name: Bob Fenske
Editor Email: editor@nhtrib.com
Advertising Executive Name: Tim Craig
Advertising Executive Email: ads@nhtrib.com
Delivery Methods: Mail`Newsstand`Racks
Own Printing Facility?: Y
Commercial printers?: Y
Mechanical specifications: Type page 15 1/8 x 21 1/2; E - 6 cols, 2 5/16, between; A - 9 cols, 1 9/16, between; C - 9 cols, 1 9/16, between.
Published Days: Tues`Fri
Avg. Paid Circ.: 2600
Audit Company: Sworn/Estimate/Non-Audited
Audit Date: 43626

OGDEN

OGDEN REPORTER

Street Address: 222 W Walnut St
City: Ogden
State: IA
ZIP Code: 50212
General Phone: 515-275-2101
General Email: kspierce@netins.net
Publication Website: https://www.ogdenreporter.com
Delivery Methods: Mail`Newsstand`Racks
Year Established: 1884
Published Days: Tues`Wed
Avg. Paid Circ.: 1850
Audit Company: Sworn/Estimate/Non-Audited
Audit Date: 43626

ONAWA

ONAWA DEMOCRAT

Street Address: 720 Iowa Ave
City: Onawa

State: IA
ZIP Code: 51040-1628
General Phone: (712) 423-2411
General Email: democrat@longlines.com
Publication Website: https://www.facebook.com/TheOnawaDemocratNewspaper/
Delivery Methods: Mail Newsstand Racks
Published Days: Wed
Audit Company: Sworn/Estimate/Non-Audited
Audit Date: 43626

OSAGE

MITCHELL COUNTY PRESS-NEWS

Street Address: 112 N 6th St
City: Osage
State: IA
ZIP Code: 50461-1202
General Phone: (641) 732-3721
General Email: editor@mcpress.com
Publication Website: https://globegazette.com/community/mcpress/
Parent Company: Lee Enterprises
Editor Name: Jim Cross
Editor Email: jim.cross@globegazette.com
Advertising Executive Name: Jessica Hinman
Advertising Executive Email: jessica.hinman@globegazette.com
Delivery Methods: Mail Newsstand Racks
Own Printing Facility?: Y
Commercial printers?: Y
Mechanical specifications: Type page 13 x 21 1/2; E - 6 cols, 2, 1/6 between; A - 6 cols, 2, 1/6 between; C - 6 cols, 2, 1/6 between.
Published Days: Wed
Avg. Paid Circ.: 6900
Audit Company: Sworn/Estimate/Non-Audited
Audit Date: 43626

PANORA

GUTHRIE COUNTY VEDETTE

Street Address: 111 E Main St
City: Panora
State: IA
ZIP Code: 50216-1155
General Phone: (641) 755-2115
General Email: ads@gctimesnews.com
Publication Website: https://www.guthriecountynewspapers.com/
Editor Email: editor@gctimesnews.com
Delivery Methods: Mail Newsstand Racks
Published Days: Thur
Avg. Paid Circ.: 1200
Audit Company: Sworn/Estimate/Non-Audited
Audit Date: 43626

PARKERSBURG

PARKERSBURG ECLIPSE-NEWS-REVIEW

Street Address: 503 Coates St
City: Parkersburg
State: IA
ZIP Code: 50665-7733
General Phone: (319) 346-1461
General Email: butlersales.map@gmail.com
Publication Website: http://www.parkersburgeclipse.com/
Parent Company: Mid-America Publishing
Publisher Name: Jake Ryder
Editor Name: Bethany Carson
Advertising Executive Email: butlersales.map@gmail.com
Delivery Methods: Mail Newsstand Racks
Mechanical specifications: Type page 14 1/2 x 21 1/2; E - 8 cols, 1 3/4, 1/12 between; A - 8 cols, 1 3/4, 1/12 between; C - 8 cols, 1 3/4, 1/12 between.
Published Days: Wed

Avg. Paid Circ.: 1500
Avg. Free Circ.: 16
Audit Company: Sworn/Estimate/Non-Audited
Audit Date: 43626

PELLA

PELLA CHRONICLE

Street Address: 812 Main St
City: Pella
State: IA
ZIP Code: 50219-1522
General Phone: (641) 628-3882
General Email: editor@pellachronicle.com
Publication Website: https://www.pellachronicle.com/
Parent Company: CNHI, LLC
Publisher Name: Becky Maxwell
Publisher Email: publisher@pellachronicle.com
Publisher Phone: (641) 628-3882
Editor Name: Kyle Ocker
Editor Email: kocker@dailyiowegian.com
Delivery Methods: Mail Newsstand Racks
Year Established: 1866
Published Days: Thur
Avg. Paid Circ.: 2000
Audit Company: Sworn/Estimate/Non-Audited
Audit Date: 43626

PERRY

PERRY CHIEF

Street Address: 1316 2nd St
City: Perry
State: IA
ZIP Code: 50220-1549
General Phone: (515) 465-4666
General Email: publisher@theperrychief.com
Publication Website: https://www.theperrychief.com/
Parent Company: Gannett
Publisher Name: Kim Fowler
Publisher Email: kfowler@amestrib.com
Publisher Phone: (515) 663-6943
Editor Name: Allison Ullmann
Editor Email: aullmann@theperrychief.com
Editor Phone: (515) 465-4666
Advertising Executive Name: Linda Schumacher
Advertising Executive Email: ads@theperrychief.com
Advertising Executive Phone: (515) 465-4666
Delivery Methods: Mail Newsstand Racks
Year Established: 1874
Own Printing Facility?: Y
Commercial printers?: Y
Mechanical specifications: Type page 13 1/4 x 21; E - 6 cols, 2, 1/6 between; A - 6 cols, 2, 1/6 between; C - 6 cols, 2, 1/6 between.
Published Days: Fri
Avg. Paid Circ.: 1900
Avg. Free Circ.: 14500
Audit Company: Sworn/Estimate/Non-Audited
Audit Date: 43626

POCAHONTAS

LAKE MILLS GRAPHIC

Street Address: 218 N Main St
City: Pocahontas
State: IA
ZIP Code: 50574-1605
General Phone: (712) 335-3553
General Email: ads@laurenssun.com
Publication Website: http://www.lmgraphic.com/
Delivery Methods: Mail Newsstand Racks
Year Established: 1872
Published Days: Wed
Avg. Paid Circ.: 1650
Audit Company: Sworn/Estimate/Non-

Audited
Audit Date: 43626

POSTVILLE

POSTVILLE HERALD

Street Address: 101 N Lawler St
City: Postville
State: IA
ZIP Code: 52162-7799
General Phone: (563) 864-3333
General Email: ads@postvilleherald.com
Publication Website: http://postvilleherald.com/
Parent Company: Mid-America Publishing
Editor Name: Sharon Drahn
Editor Email: sharon@postvilleherald.com
Delivery Methods: Mail Newsstand
Year Established: 1892
Mechanical specifications: 27" Broadsheet, 23" Total Depth Each Page is 12.5" Wide, 21.5" Deep 7 Columns per Page Columns 1.625"; Gutter 0.1875"
Published Days: Wed
Avg. Paid Circ.: 1107
Audit Company: Sworn/Estimate/Non-Audited
Audit Date: 43626

PRAIRIE CITY

PRAIRIE CITY NEWS

Street Address: 200 1st Ave. E.
City: Prairie City
State: IA
ZIP Code: 50208
General Phone: (641) 792-3121
General Email: advertising@newtondailynews.com
Publication Website: http://www.newtondailynews.com/prairie-city-news/
"Parent Company: Shaw Media
"
Publisher Name: Kelly Vest
Publisher Email: kvest@newtondailynews.com
Editor Name: Pam Pratt
Editor Email: pampratt@newtondailynews.com
Delivery Methods: Mail Newsstand Racks
Year Established: 1874
Published Days: Thur
Audit Company: Sworn/Estimate/Non-Audited
Audit Date: 43626

PRESTON

PRESTON TIMES

Street Address: 4 N Stephens St
City: Preston
State: IA
ZIP Code: 52069-7742
General Phone: (563) 689-3841
General Email: prestontimes@netins.net
Publication Website: https://www.prestontimesonline.com
Editor Email: editor@prestontimesonline.com
Advertising Executive Email: sales@prestontimesonline.com
Delivery Methods: Mail Newsstand Racks
Year Established: 1847
Own Printing Facility?: Completed
Published Days: Wed
Avg. Paid Circ.: 1000
Avg. Free Circ.: 25
Audit Company: Sworn/Estimate/Non-Audited
Audit Date: 43626

REINBECK

REINBECK COURIER

Street Address: 107 Broad St
City: Reinbeck
State: IA
ZIP Code: 50669-1013
General Phone: (319) 345-2031
Publication Website: http://www.reinbeckcourier.com/
Parent Company: Ogden Newspapers Inc.
Editor Name: Betty Dahms
Editor Email: editor@reinbeckcourier.com
Editor Phone: (641) 484-2841
Delivery Methods: Mail Newsstand Racks
Own Printing Facility?: Y
Mechanical specifications: Type page 11 3/4 x 21 1/2; E - 6 cols, 1 7/8, 1/8 between; A - 6 cols, 1 7/8, 1/8 between; C - 6 cols, 1 7/8, 1/8 between.
Published Days: Thur
Avg. Paid Circ.: 1112
Audit Company: Sworn/Estimate/Non-Audited
Audit Date: 43626

RICHLAND

THE CLARION-PLAINSMAN

Street Address: 107 S Richland St
City: Richland
State: IA
ZIP Code: 52585-9226
General Phone: (319) 456-6641
General Email: lpc@louisacomm.net
Publication Website: https://www.facebook.com/ClarionPlainsman/
Delivery Methods: Mail Newsstand Racks
Year Established: 1881
Published Days: Thur
Audit Company: Sworn/Estimate/Non-Audited
Audit Date: 43626

ROCKWELL

ROCKWELL PIONEER ENTERPRISE

Street Address: PO Box 302
City: Rockwell
State: IA
ZIP Code: 50469-7755
General Phone: (641) 822-3193
General Email: regionalnews@midamericapub.com
Publication Website: https://www.thesheffieldpress.com/
Published Days: Thur
Audit Company: Sworn/Estimate/Non-Audited
Audit Date: 43626

SAC CITY

THE SAC SUN

Street Address: 406 Williams St
City: Sac City
State: IA
ZIP Code: 50583-1739
General Phone: (712) 662-7161
General Email: sacsuneditor@frontiernet.net
Publication Website: https://sacsun.smugmug.com/
Parent Company: Mid-America Publishing
Delivery Methods: Mail Newsstand
Year Established: 1871
Mechanical specifications: 15" x 21.5"
Published Days: Tues
Avg. Paid Circ.: 1400
Avg. Free Circ.: 85
Audit Company: Sworn/Estimate/Non-Audited
Audit Date: 43626

SAINT ANSGAR

ST. ANSGAR ENTERPRISE JOURNAL

Community Newspapers in the U.S.

Street Address: 204 E 4th St, PO Box 310
City: Saint Ansgar
State: IA
ZIP Code: 50472-9606
General Phone: (641) 713-4541
General Email: staej@iowatelecom.net
Publication Website: https://www.staej.com/
Parent Company: Enterprise Media Inc.
Editor Email: editor@staej.com
Mechanical specifications: Type page 15 x ; E - 6 cols, 2, 1/8 between; A - 6 cols, 2, 1/8 between.
Published Days: Sat
Avg. Paid Circ.: 1300
Audit Company: Sworn/Estimate/Non-Audited
Audit Date: 43626

SHEFFIELD

SHEFFIELD PRESS

Street Address: 305 Gilman St, PO Box 36
City: Sheffield
State: IA
ZIP Code: 50475-5007
General Phone: (641) 892-4636
General Email: regionalnews@midamericapub.com
Publication Website: https://www.thesheffieldpress.com/
Parent Company: Mid-America Publishing
Published Days: Thur
Audit Company: Sworn/Estimate/Non-Audited
Audit Date: 43626

SHELDON

N'WEST IOWA REVIEW

Street Address: 227 9th St
City: Sheldon
State: IA
ZIP Code: 51201-1419
General Phone: (712) 324-5347
General Email: ads@iowainformation.com
Publication Website: https://www.nwestiowa.com/
Parent Company: Mid-America Publishing
Publisher Name: Peter W. Wagner
Publisher Email: pwagner@iowainformation.com
Publisher Phone: (712) 631-4830
Editor Name: Ty Rushing
Editor Email: trushing@nwestiowa.com
Editor Phone: (712) 631-4842
Advertising Executive Name: Eli Anderson
Advertising Executive Email: eanderson@iowainformation.com
Advertising Executive Phone: (712) 631-4823
Delivery Methods: Mail`Newsstand`Carrier`Racks
Year Established: 1972
Own Printing Facility?: Y
Commercial printers?: Y
Mechanical specifications: Type page 13 x 21 1/2; E - 6 cols, 1 5/6, 1/6 between; A - 6 cols, 1 5/6, 1/6 between; C - 6 cols, 1 5/6, 1/6 between.
Published Days: Sat
Avg. Paid Circ.: 6647
Audit Company: Sworn/Estimate/Non-Audited
Audit Date: 43626

SHELDON

SHELDON MAIL-SUN

Street Address: 227 9th St
City: Sheldon
State: IA
ZIP Code: 51201-1419
General Phone: (712) 324-5347
General Email: ads@iowainformation.com
Publication Website: https://www.nwestiowa.com/

Parent Company: Iowa Information Publishers and Printers
Publisher Name: Peter W. Wagner
Publisher Email: pwagner@iowainformation.com
Publisher Phone: (712) 631-4830
Editor Name: Ty Rushing
Editor Email: trushing@nwestiowa.com
Editor Phone: (712) 631-4842
Advertising Executive Name: Eli Anderson
Advertising Executive Email: eanderson@iowainformation.com
Advertising Executive Phone: (712) 631-4823
Delivery Methods: Mail`Newsstand`Racks
Year Established: 1862
Own Printing Facility?: Y
Commercial printers?: Y
Mechanical specifications: Type page 13 x 21 1/2; E - 6 cols, 1 5/6, 1/6 between; A - 6 cols, 1 5/16, 1/6 between; C - 6 cols, 1 5/6, 1/6 between.
Published Days: Wed
Avg. Paid Circ.: 2220
Avg. Free Circ.: 13
Audit Company: Sworn/Estimate/Non-Audited
Audit Date: 43626

SHENANDOAH

THE CLARINDA HERALD-JOURNAL

Street Address: 617 W. Sheridan
City: Shenandoah
State: IA
ZIP Code: 51601
General Phone: (712) 542-2181
General Email: news@clarindaherald.com
Publication Website: https://www.clarindaherald.com/
Parent Company: Lee Enterprises
Publisher Name: John VanNostrand
Editor Name: Kent Dinnebier
Editor Email: news@clarindaherald.com
Advertising Executive Name: Jennifer Johnson
Advertising Executive Email: ads@clarindaherald.com
Delivery Methods: Mail`Newsstand`Racks
Year Established: 1859
Commercial printers?: Y
Published Days: Thur
Avg. Paid Circ.: 2250
Avg. Free Circ.: 75
Audit Company: Sworn/Estimate/Non-Audited
Audit Date: 43626

SHENANDOAH

THE ESSEX INDEPENDENT

Street Address: 617 W. Sheridan Ave.
City: Shenandoah
State: IA
ZIP Code: 51601
General Phone: (712) 246-3097
General Email: ads@valleynewstoday.com
Publication Website: https://www.valleynewstoday.com/essex_independent/
Publisher Name: John Van Nostrand
Publisher Email: john.vannostrand@clarindaherald.com
Publisher Phone: (712) 246-3097, ext : 2102
Editor Name: Heidi Hertensen
Editor Email: heidi.hertensen@valleynewstoday.com
Editor Phone: (712) 246-3097, ext : 2111
Advertising Executive Name: Beth Steeve
Advertising Executive Email: bethany.steeve@valleynewstoday.com
Advertising Executive Phone: (712) 246-3097, ext : 2115
Delivery Methods: Mail`Newsstand
Year Established: 1953
Mechanical specifications: Type page 13 x 21; E - 6 cols, 1 5/6, 1/6 between; A - 6 cols, 1 5/6, 1/6 between; C - 6 cols, 1 5/6, 1/6 between.
Published Days: Thur

Avg. Paid Circ.: 300
Avg. Free Circ.: 7
Audit Company: Sworn/Estimate/Non-Audited
Audit Date: 43626

SHENANDOAH

VALLEY NEWS TODAY

Street Address: 617 W Sheridan Ave
City: Shenandoah
State: IA
ZIP Code: 51601-1707
General Phone: (712) 246-3097
General Email: ads@valleynewstoday.com
Publication Website: https://www.valleynewstoday.com/
Publisher Name: John Van Nostrand
Publisher Email: john.vannostrand@clarindaherald.com
Publisher Phone: (712) 246-3097, ext : 2102
Editor Name: Heidi Hertensen
Editor Email: heidi.hertensen@valleynewstoday.com
Editor Phone: (712) 246-3097, ext : 2111
Advertising Executive Name: Beth Steeve
Advertising Executive Email: bethany.steeve@valleynewstoday.com
Advertising Executive Phone: (712) 246-3097, ext : 2115
Delivery Methods: Mail`Newsstand`Carrier`Racks
Year Established: 1882
Own Printing Facility?: N
Commercial printers?: N
Mechanical specifications: Type page 11 x 21 1/2; E - 6 cols, 2, 1/6 between; A - 6 cols, 2, 1/6 between; C - 6 cols, 2, 1/6 between.
Published Days: Mon`Wed`Sat
Weekday Frequency: e
Saturday Frequency: e
Avg. Paid Circ.: 2300
Avg. Free Circ.: 23000
Audit Company: Sworn/Estimate/Non-Audited
Audit Date: 43626
Business Equipment: Avis/500
Classified Equipment: Hardware -- APP/Mac;
Classified Software: Microsoft/Word.
Editorial Equipment: Hardware -- APP/Mac; Printers -- APP/Mac LaserWriter Pro 600, Lexmark/1200
Editorial Software: Microsoft/Word.
Production Equipment: Scanners -- HP.

SIDNEY

SIDNEY ARGUS-HERALD

Street Address: 614 Main St
City: Sidney
State: IA
ZIP Code: 51652
General Phone: 712-374-2251
General Email: news@argusherald.com
Publication Website: https://sidneyargusherald.wordpress.com/
Parent Company: Chris Godfredsen
Publisher Name: Ellen Longman
Editor Name: Tess Gruber Nelson
Delivery Methods: Mail`Racks
Year Established: 1927
Mechanical specifications: Type page Mechanicals, 9.75â (58 picas) x 21â (126.5 picas); E - 6 cols, 1 7/8, 1/8 between; A - 6 cols, 1 7/8, 1/8 between; C - 6 cols, 1 7/8, 1/8 between.
Published Days: Thur
Avg. Paid Circ.: 700
Audit Company: Sworn/Estimate/Non-Audited
Audit Date: 43626

SIGOURNEY

THE NEWS-REVIEW

Street Address: 120 East Washington
City: Sigourney
State: IA
ZIP Code: 52591
General Phone: (641) 622-3110
General Email: keokukconews@midamericapub.com
Publication Website: http://sigourneynewsreview.com/
Parent Company: Mid-America Publishing
Publisher Name: Charlie Comfort
Publisher Email: keokukconews@midamericapub.com
Publisher Phone: (641) 622-3110
Editor Name: Charlie Comfort
Editor Email: keokukconews@midamericapub.com
Editor Phone: (641) 622-3110
Delivery Methods: Mail`Newsstand`Racks
Year Established: 1860
Own Printing Facility?: Y
Mechanical specifications: Type page 13 1/4 x 21; E - 7 cols, 1 11/12, between; A - 7 cols, 1 11/12, between; C - 7 cols, 1 11/12, between.
Published Days: Wed
Avg. Paid Circ.: 2500
Audit Company: Sworn/Estimate/Non-Audited
Audit Date: 43626

STATE CENTER

STATE CENTER MID IOWA ENTERPRISE

Street Address: 201 West Main Street
City: State Center
State: IA
ZIP Code: 50247
General Phone: (641) 483-2120
General Email: midiaenterprise@partnercom.net
Publication Website: https://www.midiaenterprise.com/
Parent Company: Chris Davis
Editor Name: Jamie Burdorf
Delivery Methods: Mail`Newsstand
Published Days: Thur
Avg. Paid Circ.: 1000
Audit Company: Sworn/Estimate/Non-Audited
Audit Date: 43626

STORM LAKE

PILOT TRIBUNE

Street Address: 527 Cayuga St
City: Storm Lake
State: IA
ZIP Code: 50588
General Phone: (712) 732-3130
General Email: sledt@ncn.net
Publication Website: https://www.stormlakepilottribune.com/
Parent Company: Rust Communications
Publisher Name: Paula Buenger
Publisher Email: pbuenger@spencerdailyreporter.com
Publisher Phone: (800) 383-0964
Editor Name: Dana Larsen
Editor Email: dlarsen@stormlakepilottribune.com
Editor Phone: (712) 732-3130
Advertising Executive Name: Ely Gonzalez
Advertising Executive Email: egonzalez@stormlakepilottribune.com
Advertising Executive Phone: (712) 732-3130
Mechanical specifications: Type page 13 x 21 1/2; E - 6 cols, 2, 3/16 between; A - 8 cols, 1 1/2, 3/16 between; C - 8 cols, 1 1/2, 3/16 between.
Published Days: Tues`Thur`Sat
Avg. Paid Circ.: 3085
Audit Company: Sworn/Estimate/Non-Audited
Audit Date: 43626

STORM LAKE

THE STORM LAKE TIMES

Street Address: 220 W Railroad St
City: Storm Lake
State: IA
ZIP Code: 50588
General Phone: (712) 732-4991
General Email: times@stormlake.com
Publication Website: http://www.stormlake.com
Publisher Name: John Cullen
Editor Name: Art Cullen
Advertising Executive Name: Whitney Robinson
Delivery Methods: Mail`Newsstand`Racks
Year Established: 1990
Own Printing Facility?: Y
Commercial printers?: Y
Mechanical specifications: Type page 11 1/2 x 21; E - 6 cols, 1 5/6, 1/6 between; A - 6 cols, 1 5/6, 1/6 between; C - 6 cols, 1 5/6, 1/6 between.
Published Days: Wed`Fri
Avg. Paid Circ.: 2900
Audit Company: Sworn/Estimate/Non-Audited
Audit Date: 43626

STUART

STUART HERALD

Street Address: 119 NW 2nd St
City: Stuart
State: IA
ZIP Code: 50250
General Phone: (515) 523-1010
General Email: ads@thestuartherald.com
Publication Website: https://stuart-herald.business.site/
Delivery Methods: Mail`Newsstand`Racks
Year Established: 1871
Own Printing Facility?: N
Commercial printers?: N
Published Days: Thur
Weekday Frequency: e
Avg. Paid Circ.: 1100
Avg. Free Circ.: 200
Audit Company: Sworn/Estimate/Non-Audited
Audit Date: 43626

SULLY

SULLY HOMETOWN PRESS

Street Address: 301 7th Ave
City: Sully
State: IA
ZIP Code: 50251
General Phone: (641) 594-3200
General Email: press@netins.net
Publication Website: https://www.hometownpressia.com/
Parent Company: Co-Line
Publisher Name: Faye Brand
Publisher Email: fbrand@colinemfg.com
Editor Name: Margaret Vander Weerdt
Editor Email: press@netins.net
Advertising Executive Email: adshometownpress@netins.net
Delivery Methods: Mail`Newsstand`Racks
Year Established: 2009
Own Printing Facility?: N
Commercial printers?: Y
Mechanical specifications: 16" Tabloid, five 2" columns
Published Days: Thur
Avg. Paid Circ.: 1160
Audit Company: Sworn/Estimate/Non-Audited
Audit Date: 43626

TAMA

THE TAMA-TOLEDO NEWS CHRONICAL

Street Address: 220 W 3rd St
City: Tama
State: IA
ZIP Code: 52339
General Phone: (641) 484-2841
General Email: jspeer@tamatoledonews.com
Publication Website: http://www.tamatoledonews.com/
Parent Company: Ogden Newspapers Inc.
Editor Name: John Speer
Editor Email: jspeer@tamatoledonews.com
Advertising Executive Name: Darvin Graham
Advertising Executive Email: dgraham@tamatoledonews.com
Delivery Methods: Mail`Newsstand
Year Established: 1925
Mechanical specifications: Type page 9 13/16 x 12 1/2; E - 6 cols, 1 7/8, 1 1/2 between; A - 6 cols, 1 7/8, between; C - 6 cols, 1 7/8, between.
Published Days: Fri
Avg. Paid Circ.: 1951
Audit Company: Sworn/Estimate/Non-Audited
Audit Date: 43626

TAMA

TOLEDO CHRONICLE

Street Address: 220 W 3rd St
City: Tama
State: IA
ZIP Code: 52339
General Phone: (641) 484-2841
General Email: jspeer@tamatoledonews.com
Publication Website: http://www.tamatoledonews.com/
Parent Company: Ogden Newspapers Inc.
Editor Name: John Speer
Editor Email: jspeer@tamatoledonews.com
Advertising Executive Name: Darvin Graham
Advertising Executive Email: dgraham@tamatoledonews.com
Delivery Methods: Mail`Newsstand
Year Established: 1853
Mechanical specifications: Type page 9 13/16 x 12 1/2; E - 6 cols, 1 13/16, 1 1/2 between; A - 6 cols, 1 13/16, between; C - 6 cols, 1 13/16, between.
Published Days: Wed
Avg. Paid Circ.: 1950
Audit Company: Sworn/Estimate/Non-Audited
Audit Date: 43626

TIPTON

TIPTON CONSERVATIVE AND ADVERTISER

Street Address: 124 W 5th St
City: Tipton
State: IA
ZIP Code: 52772-0271
General Phone: (563) 886-2131
General Email: stuartc108@aol.com
Publication Website: https://www.tiptonconservative.com/
Publisher Name: Stuart Clark
Publisher Email: stuartc108@aol.com
Editor Name: Stuart Clark
Editor Email: stuartc108@aol.com
Advertising Executive Name: Annie Schroder
Advertising Executive Email: aschroder79@gmail.com
Year Established: 1853
Mechanical specifications: Type page 15 7/8 x 21; E - 9 cols, 1 2/3, 1/12 between; A - 9 cols, 1 2/3, 1/12 between; C - 9 cols, 1 2/3, 1/12 between.
Published Days: Wed
Avg. Paid Circ.: 4582
Avg. Free Circ.: 10
Audit Company: Sworn/Estimate/Non-Audited
Audit Date: 43626

TRAER

THE TRAER STAR-CLIPPER

Street Address: 625 2nd St
City: Traer
State: IA
ZIP Code: 50675
General Phone: (319) 478-2323
General Email: editor@traerstarclipper.com
Publication Website: http://www.traerstarclipper.com/
Parent Company: Ogden Newspapers Inc.
Editor Name: CJ Eilers
Editor Email: editor@traerstarclipper.com
Editor Phone: (641) 484-2841
Published Days: Thur
Avg. Paid Circ.: 2500
Audit Company: Sworn/Estimate/Non-Audited
Audit Date: 43626

VILLISCA

VILLISCA REVIEW

Street Address: 201 S 5th Ave
City: Villisca
State: IA
ZIP Code: 50864-1132
General Phone: (712) 826-2142
General Email: newspapr@netins.net; wordchick@villiscareview.com
Publication Website: https://www.facebook.com/Villisca-Review-Stanton-Viking-1703231826555199/
Year Established: 1871
Published Days: Thur
Avg. Paid Circ.: 1300
Audit Company: Sworn/Estimate/Non-Audited
Audit Date: 43626

WAUKON

THE STANDARD

Street Address: 15 1st St NW
City: Waukon
State: IA
ZIP Code: 52172
General Phone: (563) 568-3431
General Email: news@waukonstandard.com
Publication Website: https://waukonstandard.com/
Editor Name: Jeremy Troendle
Editor Email: news@waukonstandard.com
Editor Phone: (563) 568-3431
Advertising Executive Email: ads@waukonstandard.com
Advertising Executive Phone: (563) 568-3431
Delivery Methods: Mail`Racks
Year Established: 1858
Own Printing Facility?: Y
Commercial printers?: Y
Mechanical specifications: 12.5" x 21.5"
Published Days: Wed
Avg. Paid Circ.: 2850
Audit Company: Sworn/Estimate/Non-Audited
Audit Date: 43626

WAVERLY

BREMER COUNTY INDEPENDENT

Street Address: 311 W Bremer Ave
City: Waverly
State: IA
ZIP Code: 50677
General Phone: (319) 352-3334
General Email: debweigel@oelweindailyregister.com
Publication Website: http://www.communitynewspapergroup.com/waverly_newspapers/
Publisher Name: Deb Weigel
Publisher Email: debweigel@oelweindailyregister.com
Editor Name: Anelia K. Dimitrova
Editor Email: editorcft@gmail.com
Advertising Executive Name: Karen Wedeking
Advertising Executive Email: ads.waverlypaper@gmail.com
Delivery Methods: Mail`Newsstand`Carrier`Racks
Year Established: 1858
Published Days: Tues
Audit Company: Sworn/Estimate/Non-Audited
Audit Date: 43626

WEST UNION

FAYETTE COUNTY UNION

Street Address: 119 S Vine St
City: West Union
State: IA
ZIP Code: 52175-1354
General Phone: (563) 422-3888
General Email: jolsen@fayettepublishing.com
Publication Website: https://www.fayettecountynewspapers.com/
Parent Company: Community Media Group
Publisher Name: LeAnn Larson
Publisher Email: lanews@thefayettecountyunion.com
Advertising Executive Name: Jennifer Olsen
Advertising Executive Email: jolsen@fayettepublishing.com
Delivery Methods: Mail`Newsstand`Racks
Year Established: 1866
Published Days: Wed
Avg. Paid Circ.: 2600
Avg. Free Circ.: 4400
Audit Company: Sworn/Estimate/Non-Audited
Audit Date: 43626

WEST UNION

FAYETTE LEADER

Street Address: 119 S Vine St
City: West Union
State: IA
ZIP Code: 52175-1354
General Phone: (563) 422-5410
General Email: jolsen@fayettepublishing.com
Publication Website: https://www.fayettecountynewspapers.com/
Parent Company: Fayette County Newspapers
Publisher Name: LeAnn Larson
Publisher Email: lanews@thefayettecountyunion.com
Advertising Executive Name: Jennifer Olsen
Advertising Executive Email: jolsen@fayettepublishing.com
Delivery Methods: Mail`Racks
Published Days: Wed
Avg. Paid Circ.: 812
Audit Company: Sworn/Estimate/Non-Audited
Audit Date: 43626

WEST UNION

OSSIAN BEE

Street Address: 119 S Vine St
City: West Union
State: IA
ZIP Code: 52175-1354
General Phone: (563) 422-5410
General Email: jolsen@fayettepublishing.com
Publication Website: https://www.fayettecountynewspapers.com/
Parent Company: Fayette County Newspapers
Publisher Name: LeAnn Larson

Community Newspapers in the U.S.

III-215

Publisher Email: lanews@thefayettecountyunion.com
Advertising Executive Name: Jennifer Olsen
Advertising Executive Email: jolsen@fayettepublishing.com
Year Established: 1889
Mechanical specifications: Type page 15 x 21; E - 6 cols, 2 1/3, 1/4 between; A - 6 cols, 2 1/3, 1/4 between; C - 6 cols, 2 1/3, 1/4 between.
Published Days: Wed
Avg. Paid Circ.: 812
Audit Company: Sworn/Estimate/Non-Audited
Audit Date: 43626

WEST UNION

THE ELGIN ECHO

Street Address: 119 S Vine St
City: West Union
State: IA
ZIP Code: 52175-1354
General Phone: (563) 422-5410
General Email: jolsen@fayettepublishing.com
Publication Website: https://www.fayettecountynewspapers.com/
Parent Company: Fayette County Newspapers
Publisher Name: LeAnn Larson
Publisher Email: lanews@thefayettecountyunion.com
Advertising Executive Name: Jennifer Olsen
Advertising Executive Email: jolsen@fayettepublishing.com
Delivery Methods: Mail Newsstand
Year Established: 1886
Published Days: Wed
Avg. Paid Circ.: 875
Audit Company: Sworn/Estimate/Non-Audited
Audit Date: 43626

WESTSIDE

WESTSIDE OBSERVER

Street Address: 324 1st St
City: Westside
State: IA
ZIP Code: 51467
General Phone: (712) 663-4362
General Email: observer@win-4-u.net
Publication Website: https://www.westsideobserveronline.com/
Parent Company: Kock Publishing Inc.
Publisher Name: Janine L. Kock
Publisher Email: observer@win-4-u.net
Editor Name: Janine L. Kock
Editor Email: observer@win-4-u.net
Delivery Methods: Mail Newsstand
Published Days: Thur
Avg. Paid Circ.: 1140
Avg. Free Circ.: 35
Audit Company: Sworn/Estimate/Non-Audited
Audit Date: 43626

WHITTEMORE

WHITTEMORE INDEPENDENT

Street Address: 315 Fourth Street, P.O. Box 116
City: Whittemore
State: IA
ZIP Code: 50598-8512
General Phone: (515) 884-2265
General Email: whitcity@ncn.net
Publication Website: http://www.whittemoreiowa.com/
Delivery Methods: Mail Newsstand
Year Established: 1988
Published Days: Thur
Avg. Paid Circ.: 235
Audit Company: Sworn/Estimate/Non-Audited

Audit Date: 43626

WILLIAMSBURG

WILTON-DURANT ADVOCATE NEWS

Street Address: 208 W State St
City: Williamsburg
State: IA
ZIP Code: 52361-4708
General Phone: (319) 668-1240
General Email: adnews@netwtc.net
Publication Website: https://www.northscottpress.com/wdadvocatenews/
Delivery Methods: Mail Newsstand
Audit Company: Sworn/Estimate/Non-Audited
Audit Date: 43626

WILTON

WINFIELD BEACON / WAYLAND NEWS

Street Address: 410 Cedar St
City: Wilton
State: IA
ZIP Code: 52778-9495
General Phone: (563) 732-2029
General Email: anads@netwtc.net
Publication Website: https://www.northscottpress.com/wdadvocatenews/
Advertising Executive Name: Carissa Hoekstra
Advertising Executive Email: anads@netwtc.net
Advertising Executive Phone: (563) 732-2029
Published Days: Thur
Audit Company: Sworn/Estimate/Non-Audited
Audit Date: 43626

WINFIELD

WINTERSET MADISONIAN

Street Address: 107 E Elm St
City: Winfield
State: IA
ZIP Code: 52659-9780
General Phone: (319) 257-6813
General Email: life.madisonian@gmail.com
Publication Website: https://www.wintersetmadisonian.com/
Parent Company: North Scott Press
Year Established: 1856
Mechanical specifications: Type page 14 x 21 1/2; E - 6 cols, 2, 1/3 between; A - 6 cols, 2, 1/3 between; C - 6 cols, 2, 1/3 between.
Published Days: Wed
Avg. Paid Circ.: 3580
Audit Company: Sworn/Estimate/Non-Audited
Audit Date: 43626

WINTERSET

WINTHROP NEWS

Street Address: 215 N 1st Ave
City: Winterset
State: IA
ZIP Code: 50273-1506
General Phone: (515) 462-2101
General Email: life.madisonian@gmail.com
Publication Website: https://www.wintersetmadisonian.com/
Delivery Methods: Mail Newsstand Racks
Year Established: 1892
Mechanical specifications: Type page 10 1/4 x 14; E - 6 cols, 1 1/2, between.
Published Days: Thur
Avg. Paid Circ.: 3580
Audit Company: Sworn/Estimate/Non-

Audited
Audit Date: 43626

WINTHROP

THE WOODBINE TWINER

Street Address: 225 W Madison St
City: Winthrop
State: IA
ZIP Code: 50682-7705
General Phone: (319) 935-3027
General Email: news@thewinthropnews.com
Publication Website: https://www.thewinthropnews.com/
Delivery Methods: Mail Newsstand Racks
Year Established: 1878
Mechanical specifications: Type page 13 x 21 1/2; E - 6 cols, 1 3/4, 1/6 between; A - 6 cols, 1 3/4, between; C - 7 cols, 1 1/2, between.
Published Days: Wed
Avg. Paid Circ.: 1200
Audit Company: Sworn/Estimate/Non-Audited
Audit Date: 43626

WOODBINE

TWINER-HERALD

Street Address: 503 Walker St.
City: Woodbine
State: IA
ZIP Code: 51579-1267
General Phone: (712) 647-2821
General Email: ads@loganwoodbine.com
Publication Website: https://www.loganwoodbine.com/
Parent Company: Gannett
Editor Name: Jacob Snyder
Editor Email: jacob.snyder@loganwoodbine.com
Advertising Executive Email: ads@loganwoodbine.com
Delivery Methods: Mail Racks
Commercial printers?: Y
Published Days: Thur
Avg. Paid Circ.: 1100
Audit Company: Sworn/Estimate/Non-Audited
Audit Date: 43626

IDAHO

AMERICAN FALLS

THE POWER COUNTY PRESS

Street Address: 174 Idaho St
City: American Falls
State: ID
ZIP Code: 83211-1234
General Phone: (208) 226-5294
General Email: press5@press-times.com
Publication Website: https://www.press-times.com/
Parent Company: Crompton Publishing Inc.
Publisher Name: Brett Crompton
Publisher Email: press5@press-times.com
Advertising Executive Name: Debbie Crompton
Advertising Executive Email: press3@press-times.com
Delivery Methods: Mail Newsstand
Year Established: 1902
Own Printing Facility?: Y
Commercial printers?: Y
Mechanical specifications: Type page 13 1/2 x 21 1/2; E - 7 cols, 1 5/6, 1/6 between; A - 7 cols, 1 5/6, 1/6 between; C - 8 cols, 1 1/2, 1/6 between.
Published Days: Wed

Audited
Audit Date: 43626

Avg. Paid Circ.: 1600
Audit Company: Sworn/Estimate/Non-Audited
Audit Date: 43626

BOISE

IDAHO BUSINESS REVIEW

Street Address: 4696 W. Overland Road, Suite 180
City: Boise
State: ID
ZIP Code: 83705
General Phone: (208) 336-3768
General Email: advertising@idahobusinessreview.com
Publication Website: https://idahobusinessreview.com/
Parent Company: BridgeTower Media
Publisher Name: Cindy Suffa
Publisher Email: csuffa@idahobusinessreview.com
Publisher Phone: (208) 639-3517
Editor Name: Kim Burgess
Editor Email: kburgess@idahobusinessreview.com
Editor Phone: (208) 639-3518
Advertising Executive Email: advertising@idahobusinessreview.com
Advertising Executive Phone: (208) 639-3517
Delivery Methods: Mail
Published Days: Mon
Avg. Paid Circ.: 2600
Avg. Free Circ.: 75
Audit Company: Sworn/Estimate/Non-Audited
Audit Date: 43626

CHALLIS

THE CHALLIS MESSENGER

Street Address: 310 E Main Ave
City: Challis
State: ID
ZIP Code: 83226
General Phone: (208) 879-4445
General Email: tquast@apgwest.com
Publication Website: http://Challismessenger.com
Parent Company: Adams Publishing Group
Publisher Name: Travis Quast
Publisher Email: tquast@apgwest.com
Editor Name: Monte LaOrange
Editor Email: mlaorange@postregister.com
Editor Phone: (208) 542-6795
Advertising Executive Name: Donna Nims
Advertising Executive Email: dnims@postregister.com
Advertising Executive Phone: (208) 542-6701
Delivery Methods: Mail Newsstand Racks
Year Established: 1881
Published Days: Thur
Avg. Paid Circ.: 1600
Avg. Free Circ.: 200
Audit Company: Sworn/Estimate/Non-Audited
Audit Date: 43626

COTTONWOOD

COTTONWOOD CHRONICLE

Street Address: 503 King St
City: Cottonwood
State: ID
ZIP Code: 83522
General Phone: (208) 962-3851
General Email: editor@cottonwoodchronicle.com
Publication Website: http://www.cottonwoodchronicle.com/
Editor Email: editor@cottonwoodchronicle.com
Delivery Methods: Mail
Year Established: 1893
Mechanical specifications: 5 column page.

COUNCIL

THE ADAMS COUNTY RECORD

Street Address: 108 ILLINOIS AVE
City: Council
State: ID
ZIP Code: 83612
General Phone: (208) 253-6961
General Email: editor@theadamscountyrecord.com
Publication Website: https://www.theadamscountyrecord.com/
Publisher Name: Lyle Sall
Editor Name: Dale Fisk
Editor Email: editor@theadamscountyrecord.com
Advertising Executive Name: Kaitlynn Fallows
Advertising Executive Email: advertising@theadamscountyrecord.com
Advertising Executive Phone: (208) 253-6961
Delivery Methods: Mail`Newsstand
Year Established: 1908
Commercial printers?: Y
Mechanical specifications: Type page 13 x 21; E - 6 cols, 2 1/6, 1/6 between; A - 7 cols, 1 5/6, 1/6 between; C - 8 cols, 1 7/12, 1/6 between.
Published Days: Wed
Avg. Paid Circ.: 1200
Avg. Free Circ.: 75
Audit Company: Sworn/Estimate/Non-Audited
Audit Date: 43626

DRIGGS

TETON VALLEY NEWS

Street Address: 75 N Main St
City: Driggs
State: ID
ZIP Code: 83422
General Phone: (208) 231-8747
General Email: editor@tetonvalleynews.net
Publication Website: https://www.tetonvalleynews.net/
Parent Company: Adams Publishing Group
Publisher Name: Travis Quast
Publisher Email: tquast@apgwest.com
Editor Name: Jeannette Boner
Editor Email: editor@tetonvalleynews.net
Delivery Methods: Mail`Racks
Year Established: 1909
Own Printing Facility?: Y
Published Days: Thur
Avg. Paid Circ.: 2300
Avg. Free Circ.: 50
Audit Company: Sworn/Estimate/Non-Audited
Audit Date: 43626

EMMETT

MESSENGER-INDEX

Street Address: 120 N Washington Ave
City: Emmett
State: ID
ZIP Code: 83617
General Phone: (208) 365-6066
General Email: mdavison@idahopress.com
Publication Website: https://www.idahopress.com/emmett/
Publisher Name: Matt Davison
Publisher Email: mdavison@idahopress.com
Publisher Phone: (208) 465-8101
Editor Name: Holly Beech
Editor Email: hbeech@idahopress.com

Page size 10.25" wide by 13" tall.
Published Days: Thur
Avg. Paid Circ.: 577
Avg. Free Circ.: 10
Audit Company: Sworn/Estimate/Non-Audited
Audit Date: 43626

Advertising Executive Name: Michelle Robinson
Advertising Executive Email: mrobinson@idahopress.com
Advertising Executive Phone: (208) 465-8148
Delivery Methods: Mail`Newsstand`Carrier
Year Established: 1893
Own Printing Facility?: Y
Published Days: Wed`Sun
Avg. Paid Circ.: 1660
Avg. Free Circ.: 50
Audit Company: Sworn/Estimate/Non-Audited
Audit Date: 43626

GRANGEVILLE

IDAHO COUNTY FREE PRESS

Street Address: 900 W Main St
City: Grangeville
State: ID
ZIP Code: 83530
General Phone: (208) 983-1200
General Email: ifponline@idahocountyfreepress.com
Publication Website: https://www.idahocountyfreepress.com/
Parent Company: Eagle Newspapers (OR)
Publisher Name: Sarah Klement
Publisher Email: sklement@idahocountyfreepress.com
Publisher Phone: (208) 983-1200
Editor Name: David Rauzi
Editor Email: drauzi@idahocountyfreepress.com
Editor Phone: (208) 983-1200
Advertising Executive Name: Lisa Adkison
Advertising Executive Email: ladkison@idahocountyfreepress.com
Advertising Executive Phone: (208) 983-1200
Delivery Methods: Mail`Newsstand`Racks
Year Established: 1886
Own Printing Facility?: Y
Commercial printers?: N
Published Days: Wed
Avg. Paid Circ.: 3600
Avg. Free Circ.: 68
Audit Company: Sworn/Estimate/Non-Audited
Audit Date: 43626

HOMEDALE

THE OWYHEE AVALANCHE

Street Address: 20 E IDAHO AVE
City: Homedale
State: ID
ZIP Code: 83628
General Phone: (208) 337-4681
General Email: rob@owyhee.com
Publication Website: http://www.owyheepublishing.com/
Parent Company: Owyhee Publishing
Publisher Name: Joe Aman
Editor Name: Jon Brown
Delivery Methods: Mail
Year Established: 1865
Own Printing Facility?: Y
Published Days: Wed
Avg. Paid Circ.: 1800
Avg. Free Circ.: 34
Audit Company: Sworn/Estimate/Non-Audited
Audit Date: 43626

IDAHO CITY

IDAHO WORLD

Street Address: PO Box 220
City: Idaho City
State: ID
ZIP Code: 83631
General Phone: (208) 429-1606
General Email: editor@idahoworld.com
Publication Website: https://idahoworld.

com/
Editor Name: Eileen K. Capson
Editor Email: editor@idahoworld.com
Editor Phone: (208) 202-9288
Published Days: Wed
Avg. Paid Circ.: 1300
Audit Company: Sworn/Estimate/Non-Audited
Audit Date: 43626

KAMIAH

THE CLEARWATER PROGRESS

Street Address: 417 Main St
City: Kamiah
State: ID
ZIP Code: 83536
General Phone: (208) 935-0838
General Email: progress@clearwaterprogress.com
Publication Website: https://clearwaterprogress.com/
Publisher Name: Susan Bennett
Editor Name: Ben Jorgensen
Advertising Executive Name: Angela Berger
Delivery Methods: Mail`Newsstand
Year Established: 1905
Mechanical specifications: 9.5x17
Published Days: Thur
Avg. Paid Circ.: 400
Avg. Free Circ.: 3700
Audit Company: Sworn/Estimate/Non-Audited
Audit Date: 43626

KETCHUM

IDAHO MOUNTAIN EXPRESS

Street Address: 591 N 1st Ave
City: Ketchum
State: ID
ZIP Code: 83340
General Phone: (208) 726-8060
General Email: publisher@mtexpress.com
Publication Website: http://www.mtexpress.com/
Parent Company: Express Publishing, Inc.
Publisher Name: Pam Morris
Publisher Email: publisher@mtexpress.com
Publisher Phone: (208) 726-8060
Editor Name: Greg Foley
Editor Email: gfoley@mtexpress.com
Editor Phone: (208) 726-8060
Advertising Executive Name: Sara Adamiec
Advertising Executive Email: sadamiec@mtexpress.com
Advertising Executive Phone: (208) 726-8060
Delivery Methods: Mail`Newsstand`Racks
Published Days: Wed`Fri
Avg. Paid Circ.: 11
Avg. Free Circ.: 28394
Audit Company: Sworn/Estimate/Non-Audited
Audit Date: 43626

KUNA

KUNA MELBA NEWS

Street Address: 326 Avenue D
City: Kuna
State: ID
ZIP Code: 83634
General Phone: (208) 922-3008
General Email: editor@kunamelbanews.com
Publication Website: https://www.idahopress.com/kuna/
Parent Company: Adams Publishing Group
Publisher Name: Matt Davison
Publisher Email: mdavison@idahopress.com
Publisher Phone: (208) 465-8101
Editor Name: Scott McIntosh
Editor Email: smcintosh@idahopress.com
Editor Phone: (208) 465-8110
Advertising Executive Name: Michelle Robinson

Advertising Executive Email: mrobinson@idahopress.com
Advertising Executive Phone: (208) 465-8148
Delivery Methods: Mail`Newsstand`Racks
Year Established: 1983
Published Days: Wed
Avg. Paid Circ.: 408
Audit Company: CAC
Audit Date: 42800

MALAD CITY

IDAHO ENTERPRISE

Street Address: 100 E 90 S
City: Malad City
State: ID
ZIP Code: 83252
General Phone: (208) 766-4773
General Email: newsdesk1@atcnet.net
Publication Website: http://www.idahoenterprise.com/
Publisher Name: Kristine Smith
Publisher Email: idahoenterprise@atcnet.net
Publisher Phone: (208) 766-4773
Editor Name: Kristine Smith
Editor Email: idahoenterprise@atcnet.net
Editor Phone: (208) 766-4773
Advertising Executive Name: Sherrie Wise
Advertising Executive Email: enterpriseads@atcnet.net
Advertising Executive Phone: (208) 766-4773
Delivery Methods: Mail`Newsstand`Racks
Year Established: 1879
Commercial printers?: Y
Published Days: Thur
Avg. Paid Circ.: 1300
Audit Company: Sworn/Estimate/Non-Audited
Audit Date: 43626

MCCALL

THE STAR-NEWS

Street Address: 1000 N 1st St
City: McCall
State: ID
ZIP Code: 83638-3848
General Phone: (208) 634-2123
General Email: tomigrote@gmail.com
Publication Website: https://www.mccallstarnews.com/
Publisher Name: A.L. Alford
Delivery Methods: Mail`Newsstand`Racks
Year Established: 1915
Mechanical specifications: Image Area: 10.0 inches wide by 19.75 inches deep.
Published Days: Thur
Avg. Paid Circ.: 4000
Avg. Free Circ.: 20
Audit Company: Sworn/Estimate/Non-Audited
Audit Date: 43626

MONTPELIER

THE NEWS-EXAMINER

Street Address: 847 Washington St
City: Montpelier
State: ID
ZIP Code: 83254
General Phone: (208) 847-0552
General Email: newseditor@news-examiner.net
Publication Website: https://www.hjnews.com/montpelier/
Parent Company: Adams Publishing Group
Publisher Name: Ben Kenfield
Publisher Email: bkenfield@hjnews.com
Publisher Phone: (435) 752-2121, ext : 1000
Editor Name: Charles McCollum
Editor Email: cmccollum@hjnews.com
Editor Phone: (435) 752-2121, ext : 1004
Advertising Executive Name: Kaylee Butterfield
Advertising Executive Email: kbutterfield@

Community Newspapers in the U.S.

hjnews.com
Advertising Executive Phone: (435) 752-2121, ext : 1019
Delivery Methods: Mail`Racks
Year Established: 1895
Own Printing Facility?: Y
Mechanical specifications: Type page 9.88 x 20.5; 6 cols, 1.55, .111 gutter;
Published Days: Wed
Avg. Paid Circ.: 1400
Avg. Free Circ.: 30
Audit Company: Sworn/Estimate/Non-Audited
Audit Date: 43626

MOUNTAIN HOME

MOUNTAIN HOME NEWS

Street Address: 195 S 3rd E
City: Mountain Home
State: ID
ZIP Code: 83647
General Phone: (208) 587-3331
General Email: bfincher@mountainhomenews.com
Publication Website: http://www.mountainhomenews.com
Parent Company: Rust Communications
Publisher Name: Brenda M. Fincher
Publisher Email: bfincher@mountainhomenews.com
Publisher Phone: (208) 587-3331
Editor Name: Stephanie Root
Editor Email: editor@mountainhomenews.com
Editor Phone: (208) 587-3331
Advertising Executive Name: Peggy Engelhardt
Advertising Executive Email: advertising@mountainhomenews.com
Advertising Executive Phone: (208) 587-3331
Delivery Methods: Mail`Newsstand`Racks
Year Established: 1888
Own Printing Facility?: Y
Commercial printers?: Y
Mechanical specifications: Type page 13 1/4 x 21 1/2; E - 6 cols, 2 1/16, 1/6 between; A - 6 cols, 2 1/16, 1/6 between; C - 6 cols, 2 1/16, 1/6 between.
Published Days: Wed
Avg. Paid Circ.: 2800
Audit Company: Sworn/Estimate/Non-Audited
Audit Date: 43626

OROFINO

CLEARWATER TRIBUNE

Street Address: 161 Main St
City: Orofino
State: ID
ZIP Code: 83544
General Phone: (208) 476-4571
General Email: cleartrib@cbridge.net
Publication Website: https://www.clearwatertribune.com/
Publisher Name: Marcie Stanton
Advertising Executive Name: Anne Cermak
Delivery Methods: Mail`Newsstand`Racks
Year Established: 1912
Commercial printers?: Y
Published Days: Thur
Avg. Paid Circ.: 14
Avg. Free Circ.: 5061
Audit Company: Sworn/Estimate/Non-Audited
Audit Date: 43626

PAYETTE

INDEPENDENT-ENTERPRISE

Street Address: 124 S Main St
City: Payette
State: ID
ZIP Code: 83661-2851

General Phone: (208) 642-3357
General Email: andys@argusobserver.com
Publication Website: https://www.argusobserver.com/independent/
Parent Company: Wick Communications
Publisher Name: Stephanie Spiess
Publisher Email: stephanies@argusobserver.com
Publisher Phone: (541) 823-4830
Editor Name: Leslie Thompson
Editor Email: lesliet@argusobserver.com
Editor Phone: (541) 823-4818
Advertising Executive Name: Ali Thayer
Advertising Executive Email: alit@argusobserver.com
Advertising Executive Phone: (541) 823-4832
Delivery Methods: Mail`Newsstand`Carrier`Racks
Year Established: 1891
Own Printing Facility?: Y
Commercial printers?: Y
Mechanical specifications: Type page 13 x 21 1/2; E - 6 cols, 2 1/16, 1/8 between; A - 6 cols, 2 1/16, 1/8 between; C - 9 cols, 1 1/4, 1/8 between.
Published Days: Wed
Weekday Frequency: e
Avg. Paid Circ.: 1245
Avg. Free Circ.: 16
Audit Company: Sworn/Estimate/Non-Audited
Audit Date: 43626
Pressroom Equipment: Lines -- 6-G;
Business Equipment: DEC/Micro-VAX/3100
Business Software: Vision Data
Classified Equipment: Hardware -- APP/Mac; CtP; Printers -- 2-HP/LaserJet;
Classified Software: Baseview.
Editorial Equipment: Hardware -- APP/Mac/CtP; Printers -- HP/LaserJet
Production Equipment: Hardware -- Nu/Ultra Plus; Cameras -- SCREEN; Scanners -- Umax, Polaroid/SprintScan
Production Software: Baseview.

PRESTON

PRESTON CITIZEN

Street Address: 1250 Industrial Park Rd
City: Preston
State: ID
ZIP Code: 83263
General Phone: (208) 852-0155
General Email: editor@prestoncitizen.com
Publication Website: http://www.prestoncitizen.com/
Parent Company: Adams Publishing Group
Publisher Name: Ben Kenfield
Publisher Email: bkenfield@hjnews.com
Publisher Phone: (435) 752-2121, ext : 1000
Editor Name: Charles McCollum
Editor Email: cmccollum@hjnews.com
Editor Phone: (435) 752-2121, ext : 1004
Advertising Executive Name: Kaylee Butterfield
Advertising Executive Email: kbutterfield@hjnews.com
Advertising Executive Phone: (435) 752-2121, ext : 1019
Delivery Methods: Mail`Newsstand
Year Established: 1890
Own Printing Facility?: Y
Mechanical specifications: Type page 9.88 x 20 1/2; E - 6 cols.
Published Days: Wed
Avg. Paid Circ.: 3000
Avg. Free Circ.: 130
Audit Company: Sworn/Estimate/Non-Audited
Audit Date: 43626

SAINT MARIES

ST. MARIES GAZETTE-RECORD

Street Address: 610 Main Ave
City: Saint Maries
State: ID
ZIP Code: 83861-1838

General Phone: (208) 245-4538
General Email: dan@smgazette.com
Publication Website: http://www.gazetterecord.com/
Delivery Methods: Mail`Racks
Year Established: 1906
Published Days: Wed
Avg. Paid Circ.: 3500
Audit Company: Sworn/Estimate/Non-Audited
Audit Date: 43626

WEISER

WEISER SIGNAL AMERICAN

Street Address: 18 E Idaho St
City: Weiser
State: ID
ZIP Code: 83672-2530
General Phone: (208) 549-1717
General Email: ads@signalamerican.org
Publication Website: http://signalamerican.com/
Publisher Name: Sarah Imada
Editor Name: Steve Lyon
Advertising Executive Name: Tabitha Leija
Delivery Methods: Mail`Newsstand`Carrier`Racks
Year Established: 1882
Own Printing Facility?: Y
Mechanical specifications: Type page 10 x 21; E - 6 cols, 2 1/16, 1/3 between; A - 6 cols, 2 1/16, 1/3 between; C - 9 cols, 1 1/2, 1/6 between.
Published Days: Wed
Avg. Paid Circ.: 2200
Audit Company: Sworn/Estimate/Non-Audited
Audit Date: 43626

ILLINOIS

ALBION

THE NAVIGATOR

Street Address: 19 W Main St
City: Albion
State: IL
ZIP Code: 62806-1006
General Phone: (618) 445-2355
General Email: gatoreditor@nwcable.net
Publication Website: http://www.navigatorjournal.com/
Parent Company: S&R Media, LLC
Publisher Name: JoEllen Seil
Publisher Email: gatorbills1@yahoo.com
Publisher Phone: (618) 445-2355 x___
Editor Name: TJ Hug
Editor Email: gatoreditor1@gmail.com
Editor Phone: (618) 445-2355 x___
Advertising Executive Name: Steve Hartsock
Advertising Executive Email: gatoradvertising1@gmail.com
Advertising Executive Phone: (618) 445-2355 x___

ALBION

THE PRAIRIE POST

Street Address: 19 W Main St
City: Albion
State: IL
ZIP Code: 62806-1006
General Phone: (618) 445-2355
General Email: gatoreditor@nwcable.net
Publication Website: http://www.navigatorjournal.com/prairie_post/
Parent Company: S&R Media, LLC
Publisher Name: JoEllen Seil
Publisher Email: gatorbills1@yahoo.com

Publisher Phone: (618) 445-2355 x___
Editor Name: TJ Hug
Editor Email: gatoreditor1@gmail.com
Editor Phone: (618) 445-2355 x___
Advertising Executive Name: Steve Hartsock
Advertising Executive Email: gatoradvertising1@gmail.com
Advertising Executive Phone: (618) 445-2355 x___

ALEDO

THE TIMES RECORD

Street Address: 219 S College Ave
City: Aledo
State: IL
ZIP Code: 61231
General Phone: (309) 582-5112
General Email: twelch@aledotimesrecord.com
Publication Website: https://www.aledotimesrecord.com/
Parent Company: Gannett
Publisher Name: Shawn Fox
Publisher Email: sfox@pjstar.com
Publisher Phone: (309) 686-3000 x
Advertising Executive Name: Teresa Welch
Advertising Executive Email: twelch@aledotimesrecord.com
Advertising Executive Phone: (309) 582-5112

ALTAMONT

ST. ELMO BANNER

Street Address: 7 Do It Dr
City: Altamont
State: IL
ZIP Code: 62411
General Phone: (618) 483-6176
General Email: news@altnewsban.com
Publication Website: https://www.altnewsban.com/
Parent Company: Altamont News Banner
Publisher Name: Mark Hoskins
Publisher Email: news@altnewsban.com
Publisher Phone: (618) 483-6176 x___
Editor Name: Mark Hoskins
Editor Email: news@altnewsban.com
Editor Phone: (618) 483-6176 x___
Advertising Executive Name: Mark Hoskins
Advertising Executive Email: news@altnewsban.com
Advertising Executive Phone: (618) 483-6176 x___

ALTON

ADVANTAGE NEWS - EDWARDSVILLE

Street Address: 1000 W. Homer Adams Parkway, Godfrey
City: Alton
State: IL
ZIP Code: 62002
General Phone: (618) 463-0612
General Email: info@advantagenews.com
Publication Website: https://advantagenews.com/topics/edwardsville/
Parent Company: Advantage
Editor Name: Fred Pollard
Editor Email: fredpollard@advantagenews.com
Advertising Executive Email: advertising@advantagenews.com

ANNA

MONDAY'S PUB

Street Address: 112 Lafayette St
City: Anna
State: IL
ZIP Code: 62906

General Phone: (618) 833-2158
General Email: news@annanews.com
Publication Website: https://annanews.com/mondays-pub
Parent Company: North Scott Press
Publisher Name: Lonnie Hinton
Publisher Email: viennatimes@frontier.com
Publisher Phone: 618-658-4321
Editor Name: Bobby Mayberry
Editor Email: 618-658-4321
Advertising Executive Name: Lonnie Hinton
Advertising Executive Email: 618-658-4321
Advertising Executive Phone: 618-658-4321

ANNA

THE GAZETTE-DEMOCRAT

Street Address: 112 Lafayette St
City: Anna
State: IL
ZIP Code: 62906
General Phone: (618) 833-2158
General Email: news@annanews.com
Publication Website: https://annanews.com/
Publisher Name: Jerry L. Reppert
Publisher Email: jlreppert@annanews.com
Publisher Phone: (618) 833-2158 x__
Editor Name: Bobby Mayberry
Advertising Executive Name: Angel West
Advertising Executive Email: gazettegirl26@hotmail.com
Advertising Executive Phone: (618) 833-2158 x__

ARCOLA

ARCOLA RECORD-HERALD

Street Address: 118 E Main St
City: Arcola
State: IL
ZIP Code: 61910
General Phone: (217) 268-4950
General Email: slackpub@consolidated.net
Publication Website: http://www.arcolarecordherald.com/
Publisher Name: David Porter
Publisher Email: publisher@arcola.news
Editor Name: David Porter
Editor Email: publisher@arcola.news
Editor Phone: 217-268-4959
Advertising Executive Name: David Porter
Advertising Executive Email: publisher@arcola.news
Advertising Executive Phone: 217-268-4959

ARTHUR

ARTHUR GRAPHIC CLARION

Street Address: 113 E Illinois St
City: Arthur
State: IL
ZIP Code: 61911
General Phone: (217) 543-2151
General Email: arthurgraphic@consolidated.net
Publication Website: https://www.arthurgraphic.com/arthur-graphic-clarion-homepage/
Parent Company: The Miami Herald Publishing Co.
Publisher Name: Greg Hoskins
Publisher Email: ghoskins@heraldpubs.com
Publisher Phone: (618) 566-8282
Editor Name: Roger Bonham
Editor Email: arthurgraphic@consolidated.net
Editor Phone: (217) 543-2151
Advertising Executive Name: Stephanie Wierman
Advertising Executive Email: stephanie@thetuscolajournal.com

ASTORIA

THE ASTORIA SOUTH FULTON ARGUS

Street Address: 100 N Pearl St
City: Astoria
State: IL
ZIP Code: 61501
General Phone: (309) 329-2151
General Email: argus@kkspc.com
Publication Website: http://www.kkspc.com/argus/
Parent Company: K.K. Stevens Publishing Co.
Publisher Name: Thomas B. Stevens
Publisher Email: tomstevens@kkspc.com
Publisher Phone: (309) 329-2151 x__
Editor Name: Judy Beaird
Editor Email: argus@kkspc.com
Editor Phone: (309) 329-2151 x__
Advertising Executive Name: Ellen Stevens
Advertising Executive Email: argus@kkspc.com
Advertising Executive Phone: (309) 329-2151 x__

AVON

ARGUS-SENTINEL

Street Address: PO Box 143
City: Avon
State: IL
ZIP Code: 61415
General Phone: (309) 833-5534
General Email: argus@abingdon.net
Publication Website: https://www.eaglepublications.com/abingdon.html
Parent Company: Eagle Publications
Advertising Executive Phone: (309) 833-2114

BEARDSTOWN

CASS COUNTY STAR-GAZETTE

Street Address: 1210 Wall St
City: Beardstown
State: IL
ZIP Code: 62618
General Phone: (217) 323-1010
General Email: stargazette@casscomm.com
Publication Website: https://www.beardstownnewspapers.com/contact
Parent Company: Beardstown Newspapers, Inc
Publisher Name: Pat Wellenkamp
Publisher Email: pwell@casscomm.com
Publisher Phone: (217) 323-1010 x__
Editor Name: Sandy Haschemeyer
Editor Email: editor@casscomm.com
Editor Phone: (217) 323-1010 x__
Advertising Executive Name: Diane Kloker
Advertising Executive Email: sgbusiness@casscomm.com
Advertising Executive Phone: (217) 323-1010

BEECHER CITY

BEECHER CITY JOURNAL

Street Address: 104 S Charles St
City: Beecher City
State: IL
ZIP Code: 62414
General Phone: (618) 487-5634
General Email: bcj@frontiernet.net
Publication Website: https://herald-review.com
Publisher Name: P.J. Ryan
Publisher Email: news@beechercityjournal.com
Publisher Phone: (618) 487-5634
Editor Name: P.J. Ryan
Editor Email: news@beechercityjournal.com
Editor Phone: (618) 487-5634
Advertising Executive Name: Cherie Ryan
Advertising Executive Email: cherie@beechercityjournal.com
Advertising Executive Phone: (618) 487-5634

BELLEVILLE

O'FALLON PROGRESS

Street Address: 120 S Illinois St
City: Belleville
State: IL
ZIP Code: 62222
General Phone: (618) 234-1000
General Email: newsroom@bnd.com
Publication Website: https://www.bnd.com/news/local/community/ofallon-progress/
Publisher Name: Jeffry Couch
Publisher Email: jcouch@bnd.com
Publisher Phone: (618) 239-2551
Editor Name: Jeffry Couch
Editor Email: jcouch@bnd.com
Editor Phone: (618) 239-2551
Advertising Executive Name: Jeffry Couch
Advertising Executive Email: jcouch@bnd.com
Advertising Executive Phone: (618) 239-2550

BLUE MOUND

BLUE MOUND LEADER

Street Address: 205 W Niles St
City: Blue Mound
State: IL
ZIP Code: 62513
General Phone: (217) 692-2323
General Email: jreynolds@pantagraph.com
Publication Website: https://herald-review.com
Publisher Name: Stefanie Anderson (GM)
Publisher Email: sanderson@localsouthernnews.com
Publisher Phone: (618) 606-1208 x__
Editor Email: John Broux
Editor Phone: jbroux@pananewsgroup.com
Advertising Executive Name: Jaime Reynolds
Advertising Executive Email: jreynolds@pantagraph.com
Advertising Executive Phone: (309) 820-3337

BREESE

THE BREESE JOURNAL

Street Address: 8060 Old US Highway 50
City: Breese
State: IL
ZIP Code: 62230
General Phone: (618) 526-7211
General Email: info@thebreesejournal.com
Publication Website: https://www.thebreesejournal.com/
Parent Company: Breese Journal & Publishing Company
Publisher Name: Steve Mahlandt
Publisher Email: steve@breesepub.com
Publisher Phone: (618) 526-7211 x__
Editor Name: Bryan Hunt
Editor Email: editor@breesepub.com
Editor Phone: (618) 526-7211 x__
Advertising Executive Name: Mandy Ribbing
Advertising Executive Email: mandy@breesepub.com
Advertising Executive Phone: (618) 526-7211 x__

BUSHNELL

MCDONOUGH-DEMOCRAT

Street Address: 358 E Main St
City: Bushnell
State: IL
ZIP Code: 61422
General Phone: (309) 772-2129
General Email: info@themcdonoughdemocrat.com
Publication Website: http://www.themcdonoughdemocrat.com/
Publisher Name: David S. Norton
Publisher Email: davenorton@themcdonoughdemocrat.com
Publisher Phone: (309) 772-2129

BYRON

THE TEMPO

Street Address: 418 W Blackhawk Dr
City: Byron
State: IL
ZIP Code: 61010-8634
General Phone: (815) 234-4821
General Email: mbradley@rvpublishing.com
Publication Website: http://rvpnews.com/?cat=4
Parent Company: Rock Valley Publishing LLC
Publisher Name: Pete Cruger
Publisher Email: pete@rvpublishing.com
Publisher Phone: (815) 877-4044 x__
Editor Name: Melanie Bradley
Editor Email: mbradley@rvpublishing.com
Editor Phone: 815-877-4044
Advertising Executive Name: Rhonda Marshall
Advertising Executive Email: rmarshall@rvpublishing.com
Advertising Executive Phone: (815) 234-4821 x

CAIRO

THE CAIRO CITIZEN

Street Address: 231 16th St
City: Cairo
State: IL
ZIP Code: 62914
General Phone: (618) 734-4242
General Email: lvaughn@annanews.com
Publication Website: https://annanews.com/cairo-citizen
Parent Company: North Scott Press
Publisher Name: Jerry L. Reppert
Editor Name: Bobby Mayberry

CAMBRIDGE

CAMBRIDGE CHRONICLE IN ILLINOIS

Street Address: 119 W Exchange St
City: Cambridge
State: IL
ZIP Code: 61238
General Phone: (309) 944-2119
General Email: mcarls@cambridgechron.com
Publication Website: https://www.cambridgechron.com/
Editor Name: Mindy Carls
Editor Email: mcarls@cambridgechron.com
Editor Phone: (309) 944-2119

CANTON

FULTON DEMOCRAT

Street Address: 31 S Main St
City: Canton
State: IL
ZIP Code: 61520
General Phone: (309) 518-4444
General Email: fultondemocrat@gmail.com
Publication Website: https://www.democratnewspapers.com/rack-locations-fulton-democrat/
Parent Company: Martin Publishing Company
Publisher Name: Robert Martin
Publisher Email: bob@havanaprint.com
Publisher Phone: (309) 543-3311 x__
Editor Name: John Froehling
Editor Email: editor1855@gmail.com

Community Newspapers in the U.S.

III-219

Editor Phone: (309) 647-9501 x___
Advertising Executive Email: democratnewspaper@gmail.com

CARBONDALE

CARBONDALE TIMES

Street Address: 2015 W. Main St.
City: Carbondale
State: IL
ZIP Code: 62901
General Phone: (618) 549-2799
General Email: legals@localsouthernnews.com
Publication Website: http://www.carbondaletimes.com/
Parent Company: Paddock Publications, Inc.
Publisher Name: Stefanie Anderson (GM)
Publisher Email: sanderson@localsouthernnews.com
Publisher Phone: 618-438-5611
Editor Name: Geoffrey Ritter
Editor Email: gritter@localsouthernnews.com
Editor Phone: 618-438-5611
Advertising Executive Name: Devan Vaughn
Advertising Executive Email: dvaughn@localsouthernnews.com
Advertising Executive Phone: 618-542-2133

CARLINVILLE

COAL COUNTRY TIMES

Street Address: 125 E Main St
City: Carlinville
State: IL
ZIP Code: 62626
General Phone: (217) 854-2534
General Email: coalcountrytimes@gmail.com
Publication Website: http://enquirerdemocrat.com/coalcountytimes
Publisher Name: Paula Endress
Publisher Email: pjendress@gmail.com
Publisher Phone: (217) 854-2534 x___
Advertising Executive Name: Aimee Arseneaux-Payne
Advertising Executive Email: aapayne@enquirerdemocrat.com
Advertising Executive Phone: (217) 854-2534 x___

CARLINVILLE

MACOUPIN COUNTY ENQUIRER DEMOCRAT

Street Address: 125 E Main St
City: Carlinville
State: IL
ZIP Code: 62626
General Phone: (217) 854-2534
General Email: info@enquirerdemocrat.com
Publication Website: https://enquirerdemocrat.com/
Publisher Name: Paula Endress
Publisher Email: pjendress@gmail.com
Publisher Phone: (217) 854-2534 x___
Editor Name: Daniel Winningham
Editor Email: editorial@enquirerdemocrat.com
Editor Phone: (217) 839-2626 x
Advertising Executive Name: Aimee Arseneaux-Payne
Advertising Executive Email: mcednews@enquirerdemocrat.com
Advertising Executive Phone: (217) 854-2534, ext : 25

CHAMPAIGN

VILLA GROVE NEWS

Street Address: 15 Main St.
City: Champaign
State: IL

ZIP Code: 61956-1522
General Phone: (217) 351-5252
General Email: news@news-gazette.com
Publication Website: https://www.news-gazette.com/
Publisher Name: Paul Barrett
Publisher Phone: (217) 351-5252
Editor Name: Mike Goebel
Editor Email: mgoebel@news-gazette.media
Editor Phone: (217) 351-5258

CHICAGO

BRIDGEPORT NEWS

Street Address: 3506 S Halsted St
City: Chicago
State: IL
ZIP Code: 60609-1605
General Phone: (773) 927-0025
General Email: jrbridgeportnews@aol.com
Publication Website: https://www.bridgeportnews.com/
Publisher Name: Joseph Feldman
Editor Name: Jan Racinowski
Editor Email: jrbridgeportnews@aol.com
Editor Phone: (773) 927-0025 x___

CHICAGO

BRIGHTON PARK - MCKINLEY PARK LIFE

Street Address: 2949 W Pope John Paul II Dr
City: Chicago
State: IL
ZIP Code: 60632
General Phone: (773) 523-3663
General Email: brightonparklife@aol.com
Publication Website: http://brightonparklife.com/
Parent Company: Brighton Park - McKinley Park LIFE Newspaper
Publisher Name: Albert Slinski
Publisher Email: brightonparklife@aol.com
Publisher Phone: (773) 523-3663 x_
Advertising Executive Name: Donna Rooney
Advertising Executive Email: brightonparklife@aol.com
Advertising Executive Phone: 773-523-3663

CHICAGO

CHICAGO'S NORTHWEST SIDE PRESS

Street Address: 4937 N Milwaukee Ave
City: Chicago
State: IL
ZIP Code: 60630
General Phone: (773) 286-6100
General Email: nadignewspapers@aol.com
Publication Website: http://nadignewspapers.com/
Parent Company: Nadig Newspapers
Publisher Name: Glenn Nadig
Publisher Email: news@nadignewspapers.com
Publisher Phone: (773) 286-6100 x____
Editor Name: Brian Nadig
Editor Email: news@nadignewspapers.com
Editor Phone: 773-286-6100
Advertising Executive Name: Joe Czech
Advertising Executive Email: news@nadignewspapers.com
Advertising Executive Phone: 773-286-6100

CHICAGO

FOREST LEAVES

Street Address: 160 N. Stetson Ave.
City: Chicago
State: IL
ZIP Code: 60601
General Phone: (847) 599-6900

General Email: pdefiglio@chicagotribune.com
Publication Website: https://www.chicagotribune.com/suburbs/river-forest/
Publisher Name: Par Ridder (GM)
Publisher Email: pridder@tribpub.com
Editor Name: Pam DeFiglio
Editor Email: pdefiglio@chicagotribune.com
Advertising Executive Email: ecom@tribpub.com
Advertising Executive Phone: (800) 974-7520

CHICAGO

GLENCOE NEWS

Street Address: 160 N. Stetson Ave.
City: Chicago
State: IL
ZIP Code: 60601
General Phone: (847) 599-6900
General Email: dalambert@chicagotribune.com
Publication Website: https://www.chicagotribune.com/suburbs/glencoe/
Publisher Name: Par Ridder (GM)
Publisher Email: pridder@tribpub.com
Editor Name: Dan Lambert
Editor Email: dalambert@chicagotribune.com
Advertising Executive Email: ecom@tribpub.com
Advertising Executive Phone: (800) 974-7520

CHICAGO

GLENVIEW ANNOUNCEMENTS

Street Address: 160 N. Stetson Ave.
City: Chicago
State: IL
ZIP Code: 60601
General Phone: (847) 599-6900
General Email: rhgillespie@chicagotribune.com
Publication Website: https://www.chicagotribune.com/suburbs/glenview/
Publisher Name: Par Ridder (GM)
Publisher Email: pridder@tribpub.com
Editor Name: Rhonda Gillespie
Editor Email: rhgillespie@chicagotribune.com
Advertising Executive Email: ecom@tribpub.com
Advertising Executive Phone: (800) 974-7520

CHICAGO

HIGHLAND PARK NEWS

Street Address: 160 N. Stetson Ave.
City: Chicago
State: IL
ZIP Code: 60601
General Phone: (847) 599-6900
General Email: sdibenedetto@tribpub.com
Publication Website: https://www.chicagotribune.com/suburbs/highland-park/
Publisher Name: Par Ridder (GM)
Publisher Email: pridder@tribpub.com
Publisher Phone: (312) 222-3331 x____
Editor Name: Stephen Di Benedetto
Editor Email: sdibenedetto@tribpub.com
Advertising Executive Email: ecom@tribpub.com
Advertising Executive Phone: (800) 974-7520

CHICAGO

HYDE PARK HERALD

Street Address: 1525 E 53rd St
City: Chicago
State: IL
ZIP Code: 60615-4530
General Phone: (773) 643-8533

General Email: display@hpherald.com
Publication Website: https://hpherald.com/
Parent Company: Herald Newspapers, Inc.
Publisher Name: Randall F. Weissman
Publisher Email: r.weissman@hpherald.com
Publisher Phone: (773) 358-3132
Editor Name: Randall F. Weissman
Editor Email: r.weissman@hpherald.com
Editor Phone: (773) 358-3132
Advertising Executive Name: Susan Malone
Advertising Executive Email: malone@hpherald.com
Advertising Executive Phone: (773) 358-3124

CHICAGO

LAKE FORESTER

Street Address: 160 N. Stetson Ave.
City: Chicago
State: IL
ZIP Code: 60601
General Phone: (847) 599-6900
General Email: sdibenedetto@tribpub.com
Publication Website: https://www.chicagotribune.com/suburbs/lake-forest/
Publisher Name: Par Ridder (GM)
Publisher Email: pridder@tribpub.com
Publisher Phone: (312) 222-3331 x____
Editor Name: Stephen Di Benedetto
Editor Email: sdibenedetto@tribpub.com
Advertising Executive Email: ecom@tribpub.com
Advertising Executive Phone: (800) 974-7520

CHICAGO

LAKE ZURICH COURIER

Street Address: 160 N. Stetson Ave.
City: Chicago
State: IL
ZIP Code: 60601
General Phone: (847) 599-6900
General Email: sdibenedetto@tribpub.com
Publication Website: https://www.chicagotribune.com/suburbs/lake-zurich/
Publisher Name: Par Ridder (GM)
Publisher Email: pridder@tribpub.com
Publisher Phone: (312) 222-3331 x____
Editor Name: Stephen Di Benedetto
Editor Email: sdibenedetto@tribpub.com
Advertising Executive Email: ecom@tribpub.com
Advertising Executive Phone: (800) 974-7520

CHICAGO

LIBERTYVILLE REVIEW

Street Address: 160 N. Stetson Ave.
City: Chicago
State: IL
ZIP Code: 60601
General Phone: (847) 599-6900
General Email: sdibenedetto@tribpub.com
Publication Website: https://www.chicagotribune.com/suburbs/libertyville/
Publisher Name: Par Ridder (GM)
Publisher Email: pridder@tribpub.com
Editor Name: Stephen Di Benedetto
Editor Email: sdibenedetto@tribpub.com
Advertising Executive Email: ecom@tribpub.com
Advertising Executive Phone: (800) 974-7520

CHICAGO

LINCOLNSHIRE REVIEW

Street Address: 160 N. Stetson Ave.
City: Chicago
State: IL
ZIP Code: 60601
General Phone: (847) 599-6900
General Email: rhgillespie@chicagotribune.com

CHICAGO
MORTON GROVE CHAMPION

Street Address: 160 N. Stetson Ave.
City: Chicago
State: IL
ZIP Code: 60601
General Phone: (847) 599-6900
General Email: pdefiglio@chicagotribune.com
Publication Website: http://www.chicagotribune.com/suburbs/morton-grove/
Publisher Name: Par Ridder (GM)
Publisher Email: pridder@tribpub.com
Editor Name: Pam DeFiglio
Editor Email: pdefiglio@chicagotribune.com
Advertising Executive Email: ecom@tribpub.com
Advertising Executive Phone: (800) 974-7520

CHICAGO
MUNDELEIN REVIEW

Street Address: 160 N. Stetson Ave.
City: Chicago
State: IL
ZIP Code: 60601
General Phone: (847) 599-6900
General Email: sdibenedetto@tribpub.com
Publication Website: http://www.chicagotribune.com/suburbs/mundelein/
Publisher Name: Par Ridder (GM)
Publisher Email: pridder@tribpub.com
Editor Name: Stephen Di Benedetto
Editor Email: sdibenedetto@tribpub.com
Advertising Executive Email: ecom@tribpub.com
Advertising Executive Phone: (800) 974-7520

CHICAGO
NEWS-STAR

Street Address: 6221 N Clark St
City: Chicago
State: IL
ZIP Code: 60660
General Phone: (773) 465-9700
General Email: info@insideonline.com
Publication Website: https://www.insideonline.com/
Parent Company: Gannett
Publisher Name: Ronald Roenigk
Publisher Email: inside1958@gmail.com
Publisher Phone: (773) 465-9700 x_
Advertising Executive Name: Karen Sonnefeldt
Advertising Executive Email: inside1958@gmail.com

CHICAGO
NILES HERALD-SPECTATOR

Street Address: 160 N. Stetson Ave.
City: Chicago
State: IL
ZIP Code: 60601
General Phone: (847) 599-6900
General Email: pdefiglio@chicagotribune.com
Publication Website: http://www.chicagotribune.com/suburbs/niles/
Publisher Name: Par Ridder (GM)
Publisher Email: pridder@tribpub.com
Editor Name: Pam DeFiglio
Editor Email: pdefiglio@chicagotribune.com
Advertising Executive Email: ecom@tribpub.com
Advertising Executive Phone: (800) 974-7520

CHICAGO
NORRIDGE-HARWOOD HEIGHTS NEWS

Street Address: 160 N. Stetson Ave.
City: Chicago
State: IL
ZIP Code: 60601
General Phone: (847) 599-6900
General Email: chicagoland@chicagotribune.com
Publication Website: http://www.chicagotribune.com/suburbs/norridge/
Publisher Name: Par Ridder (GM)
Publisher Email: pridder@tribpub.com
Editor Name: Larry Smith
Editor Email: lasmith@chicagotribune.com
Advertising Executive Email: ecom@tribpub.com
Advertising Executive Phone: (800) 974-7520

CHICAGO
NORTHBROOK STAR

Street Address: 160 N. Stetson Ave.
City: Chicago
State: IL
ZIP Code: 60601
General Phone: (847) 599-6900
General Email: rhgillespie@chicagotribune.com
Publication Website: http://www.chicagotribune.com/suburbs/northbrook/
Publisher Name: Par Ridder (GM)
Publisher Email: pridder@tribpub.com
Editor Name: Rhonda Gillespie
Editor Email: rhgillespie@chicagotribune.com
Advertising Executive Email: ecom@tribpub.com
Advertising Executive Phone: (800) 974-7520

CHICAGO
OAK LEAVES

Street Address: 160 N. Stetson Ave.
City: Chicago
State: IL
ZIP Code: 60601
General Phone: (847) 599-6900
General Email: pdefiglio@chicagotribune.com
Publication Website: http://www.chicagotribune.com/suburbs/oak-park/
Publisher Name: Par Ridder (GM)
Publisher Email: pridder@tribpub.com
Editor Name: Pam DeFiglio
Editor Email: pdefiglio@chicagotribune.com
Advertising Executive Email: ecom@tribpub.com
Advertising Executive Phone: (800) 974-7520

CHICAGO
PARK RIDGE HERALD ADVOCATE

Street Address: 160 N. Stetson Ave.
City: Chicago
State: IL
ZIP Code: 60601
General Phone: (847) 599-6900
General Email: pdefiglio@chicagotribune.com
Publication Website: http://www.chicagotribune.com/suburbs/park-ridge/
Publisher Name: Par Ridder (GM)
Publisher Email: pridder@tribpub.com
Editor Name: Pam DeFiglio
Editor Email: pdefiglio@chicagotribune.com
Advertising Executive Email: ecom@tribpub.com
Advertising Executive Phone: (800) 974-7520

CHICAGO
REDEYE

Street Address: 435 N Michigan Ave
City: Chicago
State: IL
ZIP Code: 60611
General Phone: (312) 222-4970
General Email: redeye@tribune.com
Publication Website: https://www.chicagotribune.com/redeye/
Publisher Name: R. Bruce Dold
Publisher Email: editor@chicagotribune.com
Editor Name: Christine Taylor
Editor Email: cwolfram@chicagotribune.com

CHICAGO
REPORTER JOURNAL

Street Address: 4937 N Milwaukee Ave
City: Chicago
State: IL
ZIP Code: 60630
General Phone: (773) 286-6100
General Email: nadignewspapers@aol.com
Publication Website: http://nadignewspapers.com/
Parent Company: Nadig Newspapers
Publisher Name: Glenn Nadig
Publisher Email: news@nadignewspapers.com
Publisher Phone: (773) 286-6100 x_
Advertising Executive Name: Joe Czech
Advertising Executive Email: Joe@Nadignewspapers.com
Advertising Executive Phone: 773-286-6100

CHICAGO
SKOKIE REVIEW

Street Address: 160 N. Stetson Ave.
City: Chicago
State: IL
ZIP Code: 60601
General Phone: (847) 599-6900
General Email: dalambert@chicagotribune.com
Publication Website: http://www.chicagotribune.com/suburbs/skokie/
Publisher Name: Par Ridder (GM)
Publisher Email: pridder@tribpub.com
Editor Name: Dan Lambert
Editor Email: dalambert@chicagotribune.com
Advertising Executive Email: ecom@tribpub.com
Advertising Executive Phone: (800) 974-7520

CHICAGO
THE DOINGS - CLARENDON HILLS

Street Address: 435 N Michigan Ave
City: Chicago
State: IL
ZIP Code: 60611
General Phone: (866) 399-0537
General Email: jmcdermott@tribpub.com
Publication Website: https://www.chicagotribune.com/suburbs/clarendon-hills/
Parent Company: Tribune Publishing
Publisher Name: Par Ridder (GM)
Publisher Email: pridder@chicagotribune.com
Editor Name: Christine Taylor
Editor Email: cwolfram@chicagotribune.com

CHICAGO
THE DOINGS - HINSDALE

Street Address: 435 N Michigan Ave
City: Chicago
State: IL
ZIP Code: 60611
General Phone: (866) 399-0537
General Email: jmcdermott@tribpub.com
Publication Website: https://www.chicagotribune.com/suburbs/hinsdale/
Parent Company: Tribune Publishing
Publisher Name: Par Ridder (GM)
Publisher Email: pridder@chicagotribune.com
Editor Name: Christine Taylor
Editor Email: cwolfram@chicagotribune.com

CHICAGO
THE DOINGS - LA GRANGE

Street Address: 435 N Michigan Ave
City: Chicago
State: IL
ZIP Code: 60611
General Phone: (866) 399-0537
General Email: jmcdermott@tribpub.com
Publication Website: https://www.chicagotribune.com/suburbs/la-grange/
Parent Company: Tribune Publishing
Publisher Name: Par Ridder (GM)
Publisher Email: pridder@chicagotribune.com
Editor Name: Christine Taylor
Editor Email: cwolfram@chicagotribune.com

CHICAGO
THE DOINGS - OAK BROOK AND ELMHURST

Street Address: 435 N Michigan Ave
City: Chicago
State: IL
ZIP Code: 60611
General Phone: (866) 399-0537
General Email: jmcdermott@tribpub.com
Publication Website: https://www.chicagotribune.com/suburbs/oak-brook/
Parent Company: Tribune Publishing
Publisher Name: Par Ridder (GM)
Publisher Email: pridder@chicagotribune.com
Editor Name: Christine Taylor
Editor Email: cwolfram@chicagotribune.com

CHICAGO
THE DOINGS WEEKLY - BURR RIDGE

Street Address: 435 N Michigan Ave
City: Chicago
State: IL
ZIP Code: 60611
General Phone: (866) 399-0537
General Email: jmcdermott@tribpub.com
Publication Website: https://www.chicagotribune.com/suburbs/burr-ridge/
Parent Company: Tribune Publishing
Publisher Name: Par Ridder (GM)
Publisher Email: pridder@chicagotribune.com
Editor Name: Christine Taylor
Editor Email: cwolfram@chicagotribune.com

CHICAGO
THE DOINGS -WESTERN SPRINGS

Community Newspapers in the U.S.

III-221

Street Address: 435 N Michigan Ave
City: Chicago
State: IL
ZIP Code: 60611
General Phone: (866) 399-0537
General Email: jmcdermott@tribpub.com
Publication Website: https://www.chicagotribune.com/suburbs/western-springs/
Parent Company: Tribune Publishing
Publisher Name: Par Ridder (GM)
Publisher Email: pridder@chicagotribune.com
Editor Name: Christine Taylor
Editor Email: cwolfram@chicagotribune.com

CHICAGO

THE NAPERVILLE SUN

Street Address: 435 N Michigan Ave
City: Chicago
State: IL
ZIP Code: 60611
General Phone: (866) 399-0537
General Email: jmcdermott@tribpub.com
Publication Website: https://www.chicagotribune.com/suburbs/naperville-sun/
Parent Company: Tribune Publishing
Publisher Name: Par Ridder (GM)
Publisher Email: pridder@chicagotribune.com
Editor Name: Christine Taylor
Editor Email: cwolfram@chicagotribune.com

CHICAGO

VERNON HILLS REVIEW

Street Address: 160 N. Stetson Ave.
City: Chicago
State: IL
ZIP Code: 60601
General Phone: (847) 599-6900
General Email: sdibenedetto@tribpub.com
Publication Website: http://www.chicagotribune.com/suburbs/vernon-hills/
Publisher Name: Par Ridder (GM)
Publisher Email: pridder@tribpub.com
Editor Name: Stephen Di Benedetto
Editor Email: sdibenedetto@tribpub.com
Advertising Executive Email: ecom@tribpub.com
Advertising Executive Phone: (800) 974-7520

CHICAGO

WILMETTE LIFE

Street Address: 160 N. Stetson Ave.
City: Chicago
State: IL
ZIP Code: 60601
General Phone: (847) 599-6900
General Email: dalambert@chicagotribune.com
Publication Website: http://www.chicagotribune.com/suburbs/wilmette/
Publisher Name: Par Ridder (GM)
Publisher Email: pridder@tribpub.com
Editor Name: Dan Lambert
Editor Email: dalambert@chicagotribune.com
Advertising Executive Email: ecom@tribpub.com
Advertising Executive Phone: (800) 974-7520

CHICAGO

WINNETKA TALK

Street Address: 160 N. Stetson Ave.
City: Chicago
State: IL
ZIP Code: 60601
General Phone: (847) 599-6900
General Email: dalambert@chicagotribune.com
Publication Website: http://www.chicagotribune.com/suburbs/winnetka/
Publisher Name: Par Ridder (GM)
Publisher Email: pridder@tribpub.com
Editor Name: Dan Lambert
Editor Email: dalambert@chicagotribune.com
Advertising Executive Email: ecom@tribpub.com
Advertising Executive Phone: (800) 974-7520

COAL CITY

THE COAL CITY COURANT

Street Address: 271 S Broadway St
City: Coal City
State: IL
ZIP Code: 60416-1534
General Phone: (815) 634-0315
General Email: fpnads@cbcast.com
Publication Website: https://freepressnewspapers.com/category/coal-city-courant
Parent Company: Free Press Newspapers
Publisher Name: Eric Fisher
Publisher Email: efisher@fpnusa.com
Publisher Phone: (815) 476-7966 x209_
Editor Name: Ann Gill
Editor Email: agill@fpnusa.com
Editor Phone: (815) 634-0315 x_

COLLINSVILLE

ST. CHARLES COUNTY SUBURBAN JOURNALS

Street Address: 2 Eastport Executive Dr
City: Collinsville
State: IL
ZIP Code: 62234
General Phone: (618) 344-0264
General Email: goodnews@yourjournal.com
Publication Website: https://www.stltoday.com/
Editor Name: Greg Uptain
Editor Email: guptain@yourjournal.com

DECATUR

DECATUR TRIBUNE

Street Address: 132 S Water St
City: Decatur
State: IL
ZIP Code: 62523-6043
General Phone: (217) 422-9702
General Email: decaturtribune@aol.com
Publication Website: https://www.decaturtribune.com/
Publisher Name: Paul Osborne
Publisher Email: decaturtribune@aol.com
Publisher Phone: (217) 422-9702 x____
Editor Name: Paul Osborne
Editor Email: decaturtribune@aol.com
Editor Phone: (217) 422-9702 x____
Advertising Executive Name: Kathryn Bottrell
Advertising Executive Email: decaturtribune@aol.com

DES PLAINES

ARLINGTON HEIGHTS/BUFFALO GROVE/ROLLING MEADOWS/ WHEELING JOURNAL

Street Address: 622 Graceland Ave
City: Des Plaines
State: IL
ZIP Code: 60016
General Phone: (847) 299-5511
General Email: journalnews@journal-topics.info
Publication Website: https://www.journal-topics.com/category/news/arlington-heights-news/
Parent Company: Journal & Topics Online Media Group
Publisher Name: Todd Wessell
Publisher Email: toddwessell@journal-topics.info
Publisher Phone: (847) 299-5511
Editor Name: Tom Wessell
Editor Email: tomwessell@journal-topics.info
"Editor Phone: 847-299-5511
"
Advertising Executive Phone: (847) 299-5511

DES PLAINES

DES PLAINES JOURNAL

Street Address: 622 Graceland Ave
City: Des Plaines
State: IL
ZIP Code: 60016
General Phone: (847) 299-5511
General Email: journalnews@journal-topics.info
Publication Website: https://www.journal-topics.com/category/news/des-plaines-news/
Parent Company: Journal & Topics Online Media Group
Publisher Name: Todd Wessell
Publisher Email: toddwessell@journal-topics.info
Publisher Phone: (847) 299-5511 x_____
Editor Name: Tom Wessell
Editor Email: tomwessell@journal-topics.info
Editor Phone: 847-299-5511
Advertising Executive Name: Rick Wessell
Advertising Executive Email: rwessell@journal-topics.info
Advertising Executive Phone: (847) 299-5511

DES PLAINES

GLENVIEW JOURNAL

Street Address: 622 Graceland Ave
City: Des Plaines
State: IL
ZIP Code: 60016
General Phone: (847) 299-5511
General Email: journalnews@journal-topics.info
Publication Website: https://www.journal-topics.com/category/news/glenview-news/
Publisher Name: Todd Wessell
Publisher Email: toddwessell@journal-topics.info
Editor Name: Tom Wessell
Editor Email: tomwessell@journal-topics.info
Editor Phone: tomwessell@journal-topics.info
Advertising Executive Name: 847-299-5511
Advertising Executive Email: Rick Wessell
Advertising Executive Phone: rwessell@journal-topics.info

DES PLAINES

MOUNT PROSPECT JOURNAL

Street Address: 622 Graceland Ave
City: Des Plaines
State: IL
ZIP Code: 60016
General Phone: (847) 299-5511
General Email: journalnews@journal-topics.info
Publication Website: https://www.journal-topics.com/category/news/mount-prospect-news/
Publisher Name: Todd Wessell
Publisher Email: toddwessell@journal-topics.info
Publisher Phone: (847) 299-5511 x_
Editor Name: Tom Wessell
Editor Email: tomwessell@journal-topics.info
Editor Phone: 847-299-5511

Advertising Executive Name: Rick Wessell
Advertising Executive Email: rwessell@journal-topics.info
Advertising Executive Phone: (847) 299-5511

DES PLAINES

NILES JOURNAL

Street Address: 622 Graceland Ave
City: Des Plaines
State: IL
ZIP Code: 60016
General Phone: (847) 299-5511
General Email: journalnews@journal-topics.info
Publication Website: https://www.journal-topics.com/category/news/niles-journal-news/
Publisher Name: Todd Wessell
Publisher Email: toddwessell@journal-topics.info
Publisher Phone: (847) 299-5511 x_
Editor Name: Tom Wessell
Editor Email: tomwessell@journal-topics.info
Editor Phone: 847-299-5511
Advertising Executive Name: Rick Wessell
Advertising Executive Email: rwessell@journal-topics.info
Advertising Executive Phone: (847) 299-5511

DES PLAINES

PROSPECT HEIGHTS JOURNAL

Street Address: 622 Graceland Ave
City: Des Plaines
State: IL
ZIP Code: 60016
General Phone: (847) 299-5511
General Email: journalnews@journal-topics.info
Publication Website: https://www.journal-topics.com/category/news/prospect-heights-news/
Publisher Name: Todd Wessell
Publisher Email: toddwessell@journal-topics.info
Publisher Phone: (847) 299-5511 x_
Editor Name: Tom Wessell
Editor Email: tomwessell@journal-topics.info
Editor Phone: 847-299-5511
Advertising Executive Name: Rick Wessell
Advertising Executive Email: rwessell@journal-topics.info
Advertising Executive Phone: (847) 299-5511

DES PLAINES

ROSEMONT JOURNAL

Street Address: IL
City: Des Plaines
State: IL
ZIP Code: 60016-4519
General Phone: (847) 299-5511
General Email: journalads@mail.com
Publication Website: https://www.journal-topics.com/register/rosemont/
Parent Company: Journal & Topics Online Media Group
Publisher Name: Todd Wessell
Publisher Email: toddwessell@journal-topics.info
Publisher Phone: (847) 299-5511 x_
Editor Name: Tom Wessell
Editor Email: tomwessell@journal-topics.info
Editor Phone: 847-299-5511
Advertising Executive Name: Rick Wessell
Advertising Executive Email: rwessell@journal-topics.info
Advertising Executive Phone: 847-299-5511

DOWNERS GROVE

BENSENVILLE PRESS

DOWNERS GROVE

BOLINGBROOK SUBURBAN LIFE

Street Address: 2001 Butterfield Road, Suite 105
City: Downers Grove
State: IL
ZIP Code: 60515
General Phone: (630) 368-1100
General Email: circulation@mysuburbanlife.com
Publication Website: https://www.mysuburbanlife.com/bensenville/
Publisher Name: Ryan Wells
Publisher Email: rwells@shawmedia.com
Editor Name: Bob Rakow
Editor Email: brakow@shawmedia.com
Editor Phone: (630) 427-6259
Advertising Executive Name: Norm Fossmeyer
Advertising Executive Email: nfossmeyer@shawmedia.com
Advertising Executive Phone: (815) 526-4645

DOWNERS GROVE

BOLINGBROOK SUBURBAN LIFE

Street Address: 2001 Butterfield Road, Suite 105
City: Downers Grove
State: IL
ZIP Code: 60515
General Phone: (630) 368-1100
General Email: circulation@mysuburbanlife.com
Publication Website: https://www.mysuburbanlife.com/bolingbrook/
Publisher Name: Ryan Wells
Publisher Email: rwells@shawmedia.com
Editor Name: Bob Rakow
Editor Email: brakow@shawmedia.com
Editor Phone: (630) 427-6259
Advertising Executive Name: Norm Fossmeyer
Advertising Executive Email: nfossmeyer@shawmedia.com
Advertising Executive Phone: (815) 526-4645

DOWNERS GROVE

LISLE SUBURBAN LIFE

Street Address: 1101 W. 31st St., Suite 260
City: Downers Grove
State: IL
ZIP Code: 60515-5585
General Phone: (630) 368-1100
General Email: nfossmeyer@shawmedia.com
Publication Website: https://www.mysuburbanlife.com/lisle/
Publisher Name: Ryan Wells
Publisher Email: rwells@shawmedia.com
Editor Name: Sherri Dauskurdas
Editor Email: sdauskurdas@shawmedia.com
Editor Phone: (630) 427-6263
Advertising Executive Name: Norm Fossmeyer
Advertising Executive Email: nfossmeyer@shawmedia.com
Advertising Executive Phone: (815) 526-4645

DOWNERS GROVE

ROSELLE ITASCA PRESS

Street Address: 2001 Butterfield Road, Suite 105
City: Downers Grove
State: IL
ZIP Code: 60515
General Phone: (630) 368-1100
General Email: circulation@mysuburbanlife.com
Publication Website: https://www.mysuburbanlife.com/roselle/
Publisher Name: Ryan Wells
Publisher Email: rwells@shawmedia.com
Editor Name: Bob Rakow
Editor Email: brakow@shawmedia.com
Editor Phone: (630) 427-6259

Advertising Executive Name: Norm Fossmeyer
Advertising Executive Email: nfossmeyer@shawmedia.com
Advertising Executive Phone: (815) 526-4645

DU QUOIN

RANDOLPH COUNTY HERALD TRIBUNE

Street Address: 18 E. Main St
City: Du Quoin
State: IL
ZIP Code: 62832
General Phone: (616) 826-2385
General Email: editor@heraldtrib.com
Publication Website: http://www.randolphcountyheraldtribune.com/
Parent Company: Paddock Publications, Inc.
Publisher Name: Stefanie Anderson (GM)
Publisher Email: sanderson@localsouthernnews.com
Publisher Phone: (618) 606-1208 x_
Editor Name: Renee Trappe
Editor Email: editor@heraldtrib.com
Editor Phone: (847) 427-4630 x___
Advertising Executive Name: Devan Vaughn
Advertising Executive Email: dvaughn@localsouthernnews.com
Advertising Executive Phone: 618-542-2133

DU QUOIN

STEELEVILLE LEDGER

Street Address: 18 E. Main St
City: Du Quoin
State: IL
ZIP Code: 62832
General Phone: (616) 826-2385
General Email: editor@heraldtrib.com
Publication Website: http://www.randolphcountyheraldtribune.com/
Parent Company: Paddock Publications, Inc.
Editor Name: Renee Trappe
Editor Email: editor@heraldtrib.com
Advertising Executive Name: Norma Tackett
Advertising Executive Email: ntackett@duquoin.com

EFFINGHAM

REGISTER-NEWS

Street Address: PO Box 370
City: Effingham
State: IL
ZIP Code: 62401-0370
General Phone: (618) 242-0113
General Email: sheonna.hill@register-news.com
Publication Website: http://www.register-news.com/
Parent Company: CNHI, LLC

ELMHURST

THE ELMHURST INDEPENDENT

Street Address: 240 N. West Avenue
City: Elmhurst
State: IL
ZIP Code: 60126
General Phone: (630) 834-8244
General Email: independent@rvpublishing.com
Publication Website: http://theindependentnewspapers.com/
Parent Company: Rock Valley Publishing LLC
Publisher Name: Pete Cruger
Publisher Email: pete@rvpublishing.com
Publisher Phone: (815) 877-4044 x_
Advertising Executive Name: Debbie Hamilton

Advertising Executive Email: questpublishing@sbcglobal.net
Advertising Executive Phone: (630) 834-8355 x___

EUREKA

THE WOODFORD COUNTY JOURNAL

Street Address: 1926 S Main St
City: Eureka
State: IL
ZIP Code: 61530-1666
General Phone: (309) 467-3314
General Email: hbowman@pantagraph.com
Publication Website: https://www.pantagraph.com/community/wcj/
Publisher Name: Barry Winterland
Publisher Email: bwinterland@pantagraph.com
Publisher Phone: (309) 820-3205
Editor Name: Chris Coates
Editor Email: ccoates@herald-review.com
Editor Phone: (217) 421-8905
Advertising Executive Name: Jaime Reynolds
Advertising Executive Email: jreynolds@pantagraph.com
Advertising Executive Phone: (309) 820-3337

EUREKA

WOODFORD COUNTY JOURNAL ROANOKE-MINONK EDITION

Street Address: 1926 S Main St
City: Eureka
State: IL
ZIP Code: 61530-1666
General Phone: (309) 467-3314
General Email: hbowman@pantagraph.com
Publication Website: https://www.pantagraph.com/community/wcj/
Publisher Name: Barry Winterland
Publisher Email: bwinterland@pantagraph.com
Publisher Phone: (309) 820-3205
Editor Name: Chris Coates
Editor Email: ccoates@herald-review.com
Editor Phone: (217) 421-8905
Advertising Executive Name: Jaime Reynolds
Advertising Executive Email: jreynolds@pantagraph.com
Advertising Executive Phone: (309) 820-3337

FAIRFIELD

WAYNE COUNTY PRESS

Street Address: 213 E Main St
City: Fairfield
State: IL
ZIP Code: 62837-2028
General Phone: (618) 842-2662
General Email: news@waycopress.com
Publication Website: http://www.waycopress.com/
Publisher Name: Tom Matthews Jr.
Publisher Email: news@waycopress.com
Publisher Phone: (618) 842-2662 x__
Editor Name: N?A
Advertising Executive Name: Carol Tannahill
Advertising Executive Email: addesign@waycopress.com

FLORA

THE CLAY COUNTY ADVOCATE-PRESS

Street Address: 105 W North Ave
City: Flora
State: IL
ZIP Code: 62839-1613
General Phone: (833) 948-1200

General Email: advertising1@olneydailymail.com
Publication Website: https://www.advocatepress.com/
Publisher Name: Chip Barche
Publisher Email: cbarche@olneydailymail.com
Publisher Phone: (618) 393-2931
Editor Name: Chip Barche
Editor Email: cbarche@olneydailymail.com
Editor Phone: (618) 393-2931
Advertising Executive Name: Cathy Slunaker
Advertising Executive Email: advertising1@olneydailymail.com
Advertising Executive Phone: (618) 393-2931

GALVA

GALVA NEWS

Street Address: 348 Front St
City: Galva
State: IL
ZIP Code: 61434
General Phone: (309) 932-2103
General Email: dboock@galvanews.com
Publication Website: https://www.galvanews.com/
Publisher Name: Jim Holm
Publisher Email: jholm@gatehousemedia.com
Publisher Phone: (309) 944-2119
Editor Name: Doug Boock
Editor Email: dboock@galvanews.com
Editor Phone: (309) 932-2103

GENESEO

GENESEO REPUBLIC

Street Address: 108 W 1st St
City: Geneseo
State: IL
ZIP Code: 61254
General Phone: (309) 944-2119
General Email: ldepies@geneseorepublic.com
Publication Website: https://www.geneseorepublic.com/
Publisher Name: Jim Holm
Publisher Email: jholm@gatehousemedia.com
Publisher Phone: (309) 944-2119
Editor Name: Lisa Depies
Editor Email: ldepies@geneseorepublic.com
Editor Phone: (309) 944-2119
Advertising Executive Name: Karol Clementz
Advertising Executive Email: kclementz@geneseorepublic.com
Advertising Executive Phone: (309) 944-2119

GILMAN

THE GILMAN STAR

Street Address: 203 N Central St
City: Gilman
State: IL
ZIP Code: 60938
General Phone: (815) 265-7332
General Email: gstar7332@yahoo.com
Publication Website: http://www.thegilmanstar.com/
Publisher Name: John Elliott
Publisher Email: gstar7332@yahoo.com
Publisher Phone: (815) 265-7332 x_
Editor Name: John Elliott
Editor Email: gstar7332@yahoo.com
Editor Phone: (815) 265-7332 x_
Advertising Executive Name: Lisa Clark
Advertising Executive Email: gstar7332@yahoo.com
Advertising Executive Phone: 815-265-7332

GODFREY

Community Newspapers in the U.S.

ADVANTAGE NEWS - GRANITE CITY

Street Address: 1000 W. Homer M. Adams Pkwy
City: Godfrey
State: IL
ZIP Code: 62035
General Phone: (618) 462-0612
General Email: ericmcroy@advantagenews.com
Publication Website: https://advantagenews.com/topics/granite-city/
Parent Company: Advantage
Editor Name: Fred Pollard
Editor Email: fredpollard@advantagenews.com

GODFREY

ADVANTAGE NEWS-RIVERBEND

Street Address: 1000 W Homer Adams Pkwy
City: Godfrey
State: IL
ZIP Code: 62035
General Phone: (618) 463-0612
General Email: info@advantagenews.com
Publication Website: https://advantagenews.com/topics/river-bend/
Parent Company: Advantage
Publisher Name: Erin McRoy
Publisher Email: ericmcroy@advantagenews.com
Editor Name: Fred Pollard
Editor Email: fredpollard@advantagenews.com
Editor Phone: (618) 463-0612
Advertising Executive Name: Sharon Mcroy
Advertising Executive Email: advertising@advantagenews.com
Advertising Executive Phone: (618) 463-0612

HAVANA

MASON COUNTY DEMOCRAT

Street Address: 219 W Market St
City: Havana
State: IL
ZIP Code: 62644
General Phone: (309) 518-4445
General Email: democratnewspaper@gmail.com
Publication Website: https://www.democratnewspapers.com/
Publisher Name: Robert Martin
Publisher Email: bob@havanaprint.com
Publisher Phone: (309) 543-3311 x
Editor Name: Wendy Martin
Editor Email: democratnewspaper@gmail.com
Editor Phone: (309) 543-3311 x____

HERSCHER

HERSCHER PILOT

Street Address: 100 S Main St
City: Herscher
State: IL
ZIP Code: 60941
General Phone: (815) 426-2132
General Email: editor@herscherpilot.com
Publication Website: http://www.herscherpilot.com/
Publisher Name: Janet Mau
Publisher Email: editor@herscherpilot.com
Publisher Phone: (815) 426-2132 x____
Editor Name: Janet Mau
Editor Email: editor@herscherpilot.com
Editor Phone: (815) 426-2132 x____
Advertising Executive Name: Janet Mau
Advertising Executive Email: editor@herscherpilot.com
Advertising Executive Phone: (815) 426-2132 x____

HIGHLAND

HIGHLAND NEWS LEADER

Street Address: 1 Woodcrest Professional Park
City: Highland
State: IL
ZIP Code: 62249-1254
General Phone: (618) 654-2366
General Email: jcouch@bnd.com
Publication Website: https://www.bnd.com/news/local/community/highland-news-leader/
Parent Company: Belleville News-Democrat
Publisher Name: Jeff Couch
Publisher Email: jcouch@bnd.com
Publisher Phone: (618) 239-2550
Editor Name: Garen Vartanian
Editor Email: gvartanian@bnd.com
Editor Phone: (618) 239-2511
Advertising Executive Name: Jeffry Couch
Advertising Executive Email: jcouch@bnd.com
Advertising Executive Phone: (618) 239-2550

HILLSBORO

THE JOURNAL-NEWS

Street Address: 431 S Main St
City: Hillsboro
State: IL
ZIP Code: 62049
General Phone: (217) 532-3933
General Email: thejournal-news@consolidated.net
Publication Website: https://www.thejournal-news.net/
Parent Company: Hillsboro Journal, Inc.
Publisher Name: Michael Plunkett
Publisher Email: jnmike@consolidated.net
Publisher Phone: (217) 532-3933 x_
Editor Name: Mary Herschelman
Editor Email: jnmary@consolidated.net
Editor Phone: (217) 532-3933 x
Advertising Executive Name: Cheri Ozee
Advertising Executive Email: jnclassifieds@gmail.com
Advertising Executive Phone: (217) 532-3933 x___

ILLIOPOLIS

THE SENTINEL

Street Address: 311 W Matilda St
City: Illiopolis
State: IL
ZIP Code: 62539
General Phone: (217) 486-6496
General Email: thesentinel@comcast.net
Publication Website: http://www.illiopolis.com/pages/members/illiopolis_sentinel.htm
Parent Company: Lee Enterprises
Publisher Name: Cindy Wilson
Publisher Email: thesentinel@comcast.net
Publisher Phone: 217-486-6496
Editor Name: Cindy Wilson
Editor Email: thesentinel@comcast.net
Editor Phone: 217-486-6496
Advertising Executive Name: Maurice Wilson
Advertising Executive Email: thesentinel@comcast.net
Advertising Executive Phone: 217-486-6496

JOLIET

FARMERS WEEKLY REVIEW

Street Address: 100 Manhattan Rd
City: Joliet
State: IL
ZIP Code: 60433
General Phone: (815) 727-4811
General Email: debbie@willcfb.com
Publication Website: https://www.willcfb.com/home/weekly-review.html
Publisher Name: Michael J. Cleary
Publisher Email: farmersweekly@sbcglobal.net
Publisher Phone: (815) 727-4811 x___
Editor Name: Nick Reiher
Editor Email: nick.reiher@gmail.com
Editor Phone: (815) 727-4811 x___
Advertising Executive Name: Debbie Werner
Advertising Executive Email: debbie@willcfb.com
Advertising Executive Phone: (815) 727-4811 x___

JOLIET

THE TIMES WEEKLY

Street Address: 254 E Cass St
City: Joliet
State: IL
ZIP Code: 60432-2813
General Phone: (815) 723-0325
General Email: ads@thetimesweekly.com
Publication Website: http://thetimesweekly.com/
Parent Company: M.I.A. Media Group
Publisher Name: Jayme Cain
Publisher Email: jcain@thetimesweekly.com
Publisher Phone: (815) 723-0325
Editor Email: editor@thetimesweekly.com
Advertising Executive Name: Tamika Archibald
Advertising Executive Email: tarchibald@thetimesweekly.com

LACON

LACON HOME JOURNAL

Street Address: 204 S Washington St
City: Lacon
State: IL
ZIP Code: 61540
General Phone: (309) 246-2865
General Email: sonbtp@aol.com
Publication Website: https://www.laconhomejournal.com/
Publisher Name: William Sondag
Publisher Email: sonbtp@aol.com
Publisher Phone: (309) 246-2865 x___
Editor Name: William Sondag
Editor Email: sonbtp@aol.com
Editor Phone: (309) 246-2865 x___
Advertising Executive Name: Sally Lazam
Advertising Executive Email: sonbtp@aol.com
Advertising Executive Phone: (309) 246-2865 x____

LAWRENCEVILLE

LAWRENCE COUNTY NEWS

Street Address: 1209 State St
City: Lawrenceville
State: IL
ZIP Code: 62439-2332
General Phone: (618) 943-2331
General Email: syoung@lawdailyrecord.com
Publication Website: http://lawdailyrecord.com/
Parent Company: Lewis Newspapers
Publisher Name: Kathleen Lewis
Editor Name: Bill Richardson
Editor Phone: (618) 943-2331, ext : 103
Advertising Executive Name: Sandie Young
Advertising Executive Phone: (618) 943-2331, ext. 114

LOMBARD

LOMBARDIAN

Street Address: 929 S Main St
City: Lombard
State: IL
ZIP Code: 60148
General Phone: (630) 627-7010
General Email: lombardian@rvpublishing.com
Publication Website: http://theindependentnewspapers.com/
Parent Company: Rock Valley Publishing LLC
Publisher Name: Pete Cruger
Publisher Email: pete@rvpublishing.com
Publisher Phone: (815) 877-4044 x____
Editor Name: Jane Charmelo
Editor Email: lombardian@rvpublishing.com
Editor Phone: 630-627-7010
Advertising Executive Name: Betty Jesensky
Advertising Executive Email: lombardian@rvpublishing.com
Advertising Executive Phone: 630-627-7010

LOMBARD

VILLA PARK REVIEW

Street Address: 929 S Main St
City: Lombard
State: IL
ZIP Code: 60148
General Phone: (630) 627-7010
General Email: lombardian@rvpublishing.com
Publication Website: http://theindependentnewspapers.com/
Parent Company: Rock Valley Publishing LLC
Publisher Name: Pete Cruger
Publisher Email: pete@rvpublishing.com
Publisher Phone: pete@rvpublishing.com
Editor Name: Jane Charmelo
Editor Email: lombardian@rvpublishing.com
Editor Phone: 630-627-7010

MACOMB

MCDONOUGH COUNTY VOICE

Street Address: 26 W Side Sq
City: Macomb
State: IL
ZIP Code: 61455
General Phone: (309) 833-2114
General Email: editor@mcdonoughvoice.com
Publication Website: https://www.mcdonoughvoice.com/
Parent Company: Gannett
Publisher Name: Shawn Fox
Publisher Email: sfox@pjstar.com
Publisher Phone: (309) 686-3000 x_
Editor Name: Michelle Langhout
Editor Email: editor@mcdonoughvoice.com
Editor Phone: (309) 833-2114, ext : 253
Advertising Executive Name: Michelle Ringenberger
Advertising Executive Email: mringenberger@mcdonoughvoice.com
Advertising Executive Phone: (309) 833-2114, ext : 258

MARSHALL

CASEY WESTFIELD REPORTER

Street Address: 510 N. Michigan Avenue - P.O. Box 433
City: Marshall
State: IL
ZIP Code: 62441
General Phone: (217) 826-3600
General Email: strohmnewspapers@gmail.com
Publication Website: http://www.strohmnews.com/
Parent Company: Strohm Newspapers
Publisher Name: Melody Strohm
Publisher Email: strohmnews@joink.com
Publisher Phone: 217-826-3600
Advertising Executive Name: Debbie Pleij

MARSHALL

MARSHALL ADVOCATE

Street Address: 510 N. Michigan Avenue - P.O. Box 433
City: Marshall
State: IL
ZIP Code: 62441
General Phone: (217) 826-3600
General Email: strohmnewspapers@gmail.com
Publication Website: http://www.strohmnews.com/
Parent Company: Strohm Newspapers
Publisher Name: Melody Strohm
Publisher Email: strohmnews@joink.com
Publisher Phone: 217-826-3600
Advertising Executive Name: Debbie Pleij
Advertising Executive Email: strohmnews@joink.com
Advertising Executive Phone: 217-826-3600

MARSHALL

WEST VIGO TIMES

Street Address: 510 N. Michigan Avenue - P.O. Box 433
City: Marshall
State: IL
ZIP Code: 62441
General Phone: (217) 826-3600
General Email: strohmnewspapers@gmail.com
Publication Website: http://www.strohmnews.com/
Parent Company: Strohm Newspapers
Publisher Name: Melody Strohm
Advertising Executive Name: Debbie Pleij

MASCOUTAH

CLINTON COUNTY NEWS

Street Address: 410 East Main
City: Mascoutah
State: IL
ZIP Code: 62258
General Phone: (618) 566-8282
General Email: ccn@heraldpubs.com
Publication Website: https://www.heraldpubs.com/
Parent Company: Herald Publications
Publisher Name: Greg Hoskins
Publisher Email: ghoskins@heraldpubs.com
Publisher Phone: (618) 566-8282 x__
Editor Name: Pamela Rensing
Editor Email: mascherald@heraldpubs.com
Editor Phone: (618) 566-8282 x__
Advertising Executive Name: Charlie Huelsmann
Advertising Executive Email: adv@heraldpubs.com

MASCOUTAH

FAIRVIEW HEIGHTS TRIBUNE

Street Address: 410 East Main
City: Mascoutah
State: IL
ZIP Code: 62258
General Phone: (618) 566-8282
General Email: tribune@heraldpubs.com
Publication Website: https://www.heraldpubs.com/
Parent Company: Herald Publications
Publisher Name: Greg Hoskins
Publisher Email: ghoskins@heraldpubs.com
Publisher Phone: (618) 566-8282 x__
Editor Name: Pamela Rensing
Editor Email: mascherald@heraldpubs.com
Editor Phone: (618) 566-8282 x__
Advertising Executive Name: Charlie Huelsmann
Advertising Executive Email: adv@heraldpubs.com

MASCOUTAH

THE MASCOUTAH HERALD

Street Address: 410 East Main
City: Mascoutah
State: IL
ZIP Code: 62258
General Phone: (618) 566-8282
General Email: mascherald@heraldpubs.com
Publication Website: https://www.heraldpubs.com/
Parent Company: Herald Publications
Publisher Name: Greg Hoskins
Publisher Email: ghoskins@heraldpubs.com
Publisher Phone: (618) 566-8282 x__
Editor Name: Pamela Rensing
Editor Email: mascherald@heraldpubs.com
Editor Phone: (618) 566-8282 x__
Advertising Executive Name: Charlie Huelsmann
Advertising Executive Email: adv@heraldpubs.com
Advertising Executive Phone: 618-566-8282

METROPOLIS

METROPOLIS PLANET

Street Address: 111 E 5th St
City: Metropolis
State: IL
ZIP Code: 62960
General Phone: (618) 524-2141
General Email: ahathcock@metropolisplanet.com
Publication Website: https://www.metropolisplanet.com/
Parent Company: Paxton Media Group, LLC
Publisher Name: Areia Hathcock
Publisher Email: ahathcock@metropolisplanet.com
Publisher Phone: (618) 524-2141
Editor Name: Linda Kennedy
Editor Email: news@metropolisplanet.com
Editor Phone: (618) 524-2141

MIDLOTHIAN

SOUTHWEST MESSENGER PRESS, INC.

Street Address: 3840 147th St
City: Midlothian
State: IL
ZIP Code: 60445
General Phone: (708) 388-2425
General Email: info@southwestmessengerpress.com
Publication Website: http://www.southwestmessengerpress.com/
Parent Company: Southwest Messenger Press, Inc.

MOMENCE

THE MOMENCE PROGRESS REPORTER

Street Address: 110 W River St
City: Momence
State: IL
ZIP Code: 60954
General Phone: (815) 472-2000
General Email: m.reporter@mchsi.com
Publication Website: https://www.momenceprogressreporter.com/
Publisher Name: Gene Lincoln
Publisher Email: m.reporter@mchsi.com
Publisher Phone: (815) 472-2000 x__
Editor Name: Sue Lincoln
Editor Email: m.reporter@mchsi.com
Editor Phone: (815) 472-2000 x__
Advertising Executive Name: Anita Allison
Advertising Executive Email: m.reporter@mchsi.com
Advertising Executive Phone: (815) 472-2000 x__

MORRISON

WHITESIDE NEWS SENTINEL

Street Address: 100 E Main St
City: Morrison
State: IL
ZIP Code: 61270-2694
General Phone: (815) 772-7244
General Email: jlindsey@shawmedia.com
Publication Website: http://whitesidesentinel.com/
Parent Company: Shaw Media
Publisher Name: Jerry Lindsey
Publisher Email: jlindsey@shawmedia.com
Publisher Phone: 815-772-7244
Editor Name: Jerry Lindsey
Editor Email: jlindsey@shawmedia.com
Editor Phone: 815-772-7244

MOUNT CARROLL

CARROLL COUNTY MIRROR-DEMOCRAT

Street Address: 308 N Main St
City: Mount Carroll
State: IL
ZIP Code: 61053-1024
General Phone: (815) 244-2411
General Email: mirrordem@grics.net
Publication Website: http://www.mycarrollcountynews.com/
Parent Company: Mirror-Democrat Co
Publisher Name: Robert Watson
Publisher Email: mirrordem@grics.net
Publisher Phone: (815) 244-2411 x__

MOUNT ZION

THE MT. ZION REGION NEWS

Street Address: 433 N State Route 121, PO Box 79
City: Mount Zion
State: IL
ZIP Code: 62549-1514
General Phone: (217) 864-4212
General Email: mtzionregionnews@comcast.net
Publication Website: https://www.arthurgraphic.com/contact-us-mt-zion-region-news/
Parent Company: Arthur Publishing
Publisher Name: Greg Hoskins
Publisher Email: ghoskins@heraldpubs.com
Publisher Phone: (618) 566-8282 x__
Editor Name: Crystal Reed
Editor Email: mtzionregionnews@comcast.net
Editor Phone: 217-864-4212

MT STERLING

BROWN COUNTY DEMOCRAT MESSAGE

Street Address: 123 W MAIN ST
City: Mt Sterling
State: IL
ZIP Code: 62353-1223
General Phone: (217) 773-3371
General Email: thedmads@yahoo.com
Publication Website: http://browncountydm.com/index1.htm
Parent Company: Coulson Publications
Publisher Name: Dan Long
Publisher Email: thedmnews@yahoo.com
Publisher Phone: (217) 773-3371 x__

NASHVILLE

THE NASHVILLE NEWS

Street Address: 211 W Saint Louis St
City: Nashville
State: IL
ZIP Code: 62263
General Phone: (618) 327-3411
General Email: news@nashnews.net
Publication Website: https://www.nash-news.com/
Parent Company: The Nashville News
Publisher Name: Greg Hoskins
Publisher Email: ghoskins@heraldpubs.com
Publisher Phone: (618) 566-8282 x__
Editor Name: Leah Williams
Editor Email: news@nashnews.net
Advertising Executive Email: ads@nashnews.net

NEWMAN

THE NEWMAN INDEPENDENT

Street Address: 207 W Yates St
City: Newman
State: IL
ZIP Code: 61942
General Phone: (217) 837-2414
General Email: news1@tni-news.com
Publication Website: https://tni-news.com/
Parent Company: The Newman Independent
Publisher Name: Cathy Hales
Publisher Email: news1@tni-news.com
Publisher Phone: 217-837-2414
Editor Name: Cathy Hales
Editor Email: news1@tni-news.com
Editor Phone: 217-837-2414

NEWTON

NEWTON PRESS-MENTOR

Street Address: 700 W Washington St
City: Newton
State: IL
ZIP Code: 62448-1129
General Phone: (833) 948-1200
General Email: advertising1@olneydailymail.com
Publication Website: https://www.pressmentor.com/
Publisher Name: Chip Barche
Publisher Email: cbarche@olneydailymail.com
Publisher Phone: (618) 393-2931 x__
Editor Name: Chip Barche
Editor Email: cbarche@olneydailymail.com
Editor Phone: (618) 393-2931
Advertising Executive Name: Cathy Slunaker
Advertising Executive Email: advertising1@olneydailymail.com
Advertising Executive Phone: (618) 393-2931

NOKOMIS

FREE PRESS-PROGRESS

Street Address: 112 W State St
City: Nokomis
State: IL
ZIP Code: 62075-1657
General Phone: (217) 563-2115
General Email: freepress@consolidated.net
Publication Website: http://pananewsonline.com/
Publisher Name: Stefanie Anderson (GM)
Publisher Email: sanderson@localsouthernnews.com
Publisher Phone: (618) 606-1208 x__
Editor Name: John Broux

Community Newspapers in the U.S.

III-225

Editor Email: jbroux@pananewsgroup.com
Editor Phone: (217) 562-2111 x__

OAK PARK

AUSTIN WEEKLY NEWS

Street Address: 141 S Oak Park Ave
City: Oak Park
State: IL
ZIP Code: 60302
General Phone: (773) 626-6332
General Email: dawn@austinweeklynews.com
Publication Website: http://www.austinweeklynews.com/
Parent Company: Wednesday Journal Publications
Publisher Name: Dan Haley
Publisher Email: dhaley@wjinc.com
Publisher Phone: (708) 524-8300
Editor Name: Michael Romain
Editor Email: michael@austinweeklynews.com
Advertising Executive Name: Mary Ellen Nelligan
Advertising Executive Email: classifieds@austinweeklynews.com

OAK PARK

FOREST PARK REVIEW

Street Address: 141 S Oak Park Ave
City: Oak Park
State: IL
ZIP Code: 60302
General Phone: (708) 366-0600
General Email: maria@forestparkreview.com
Publication Website: https://www.forestparkreview.com/
Parent Company: Wednesday Journal Publications
Publisher Name: Dan Haley
Publisher Email: dhaley@wjinc.com
Publisher Phone: (708) 524-8300 x___
Editor Name: Maria Maxham
Editor Email: maria@forestparkreview.com
Advertising Executive Name: Mary Ellen Nelligan
Advertising Executive Email: classifieds@forestparkreview.com

OAK PARK

LANDMARK

Street Address: 141 S Oak Park Ave # 1
City: Oak Park
State: IL
ZIP Code: 60302-2972
General Phone: (708) 442-6739
General Email: dawn@oakpark.com
Publication Website: https://www.rblandmark.com/
Parent Company: Gannett
Publisher Name: Dan Haley
Publisher Email: dhaley@wjinc.com
Publisher Phone: (708) 524-8300 x___
Editor Name: Bob Uphues
Editor Email: buphues@rblandmark.com
Editor Phone: (708) 524-8300 x___
Advertising Executive Name: Dawn Ferencak
Advertising Executive Email: dawn@oakpark.com
Advertising Executive Phone: (708) 524-8300 x___

OAK PARK

WEDNESDAY JOURNAL OF OAK PARK & RIVER FOREST

Street Address: 141 S Oak Park Ave
City: Oak Park
State: IL
ZIP Code: 60302
General Phone: (708) 524-8300
General Email: dhaley@wjinc.com
Publication Website: https://www.oakpark.com/
Parent Company: Wednesday Journal Publications
Publisher Name: Dan Haley
Publisher Email: dhaley@wjinc.com
Publisher Phone: (708) 524-8300 x_
Editor Name: Michael Romain
Editor Email: michael@austinweeklynews.com
Advertising Executive Name: Mary Ellen Nelligan
Advertising Executive Email: classifieds@austinweeklynews.com

OKAWVILLE

THE OKAWVILLE TIMES

Street Address: 109 E Walnut St
City: Okawville
State: IL
ZIP Code: 62271-1883
General Phone: (618) 243-5563
General Email: press1@okawvilletimes.com
Publication Website: https://www.okawvilletimes.com/
Publisher Name: Debby Stricker
Publisher Email: press1@okawvilletimes.com
Publisher Phone: (618) 243-5563 x_
Editor Name: Debby Stricker
Editor Email: press1@okawvilletimes.com
Editor Phone: (618) 243-5563 x_

ORION

ORION GAZETTE

Street Address: P.O. Box 400
City: Orion
State: IL
ZIP Code: 61273-7731
General Phone: (309) 944-2119
General Email: mcarls@oriongazette.com
Publication Website: https://www.oriongazette.com/
Editor Name: Mindy Carls
Editor Email: mcarls@oriongazette.com
Editor Phone: (309) 944-2119

PALOS HEIGHTS

THE REGIONAL NEWS

Street Address: 12243 S Harlem Ave
City: Palos Heights
State: IL
ZIP Code: 60463-1431
General Phone: (708) 448-4000
General Email: theregional@comcast.net
Publication Website: https://theregionalnews.com/
Parent Company: Southwest Regional Publishing Co
Publisher Name: Mark Hornung
Publisher Email: mhornung@cmgms.com
Publisher Phone: 815-432-5227
Editor Name: Bob Bong

PALOS HEIGHTS

THE REPORTER

Street Address: 12243 S Harlem Ave
City: Palos Heights
State: IL
ZIP Code: 60463-1431
General Phone: (708) 448-6161
General Email: thereporter@comcast.net
Publication Website: http://www.thereporteronline.net/
Parent Company: Media News Group
Publisher Name: Mark Hornung
Publisher Email: mhornung@cmgms.com
Publisher Phone: 815-432-5227
Editor Name: Joe Boyle
Editor Email: thereporter@comcast.net
Editor Phone: (708) 448-6161 x__

PARIS

THE PRAIRIE PRESS

Street Address: 101 N Central Ave
City: Paris
State: IL
ZIP Code: 61944-1704
General Phone: (217) 921-3216
General Email: nzeman@prairiepress.net
Publication Website: http://prairiepress.net/
Publisher Name: Nancy Roberts Zeman
Publisher Email: nzeman@prairiepress.net
Publisher Phone: (217) 921-3216 x___
Editor Name: Gary Henry
Editor Email: ghenry@prairiepress.net
Editor Phone: 217-921-3216

PECATONICA

THE GAZETTE

Street Address: 217 Main Street
City: Pecatonica
State: IL
ZIP Code: 61063-7712
General Phone: (815) 239-1028
General Email: rmarshall@rvpublishing.com
Publication Website: http://rvpnews.com/?cat=3
Parent Company: Adams Publishing Group
Publisher Name: Pete Cruger
Publisher Email: pete@rvpublishing.com
Publisher Phone: (815) 877-4044 x_
Editor Name: Melanie Bradley
Editor Email: mbradley@rvpublishing.com
Editor Phone: 815-877-4044
Advertising Executive Name: Rhonda Marshall
Advertising Executive Email: rmarshall@rvpublishing.com
Advertising Executive Phone: (815) 234-4821 x_

PEKIN

EAST PEORIA TIMES-COURIER

Street Address: PO Box 430
City: Pekin
State: IL
ZIP Code: 61555-0430
General Phone: (309) 346-1111
General Email: snorbits@timestoday.com
Publication Website: https://www.eastpeoriatimescourier.com/
Parent Company: Gannett
Publisher Name: Shaw Fox
Publisher Email: sfox@pjstar.com
Publisher Phone: (309) 686-3000 x_
Editor Name: Chris Kaergard
Editor Email: ckaergard@pjstar.com
Editor Phone: (309) 686-3255 x_
Advertising Executive Name: Sandy Norbits
Advertising Executive Email: snorbits@timestoday.com
Advertising Executive Phone: (309) 686-3116

PEKIN

MORTON TIMES-NEWS

Street Address: 306 Court St
City: Pekin
State: IL
ZIP Code: 61554-3104
General Phone: (309) 346-1111
General Email: snorbits@timestoday.com
Publication Website: https://www.mortontimesnews.com/
Advertising Executive Name: Sandy Norbits
Advertising Executive Email: snorbits@timestoday.com
Advertising Executive Phone: (309) 686-3116

PEKIN

WASHINGTON TIMES REPORTER

Street Address: 306 Court St
City: Pekin
State: IL
ZIP Code: 61554-3104
General Phone: (833) 948-1200
General Email: snorbits@timestoday.com
Publication Website: https://www.washingtontimesreporter.com/
Parent Company: Gannett
Publisher Name: David Adams
Advertising Executive Name: Sandy Norbits
Advertising Executive Email: snorbits@timestoday.com
Advertising Executive Phone: (309) 686-3116

PEKIN

WOODFORD TIMES

Street Address: PO Box 430
City: Pekin
State: IL
ZIP Code: 61555-0430
General Phone: (309) 346-1111
General Email: snorbits@timestoday.com
Publication Website: https://www.woodfordtimes.com/
Parent Company: Gannett
Publisher Name: David Adams
Advertising Executive Name: Sandy Norbits
Advertising Executive Email: snorbits@timestoday.com
Advertising Executive Phone: (309) 686-3116

PEORIA

CHILLICOTHE TIMES-BULLETIN

Street Address: PO Box 9426
City: Peoria
State: IL
ZIP Code: 61612-9426
General Phone: (309) 274-2185
General Email: snorbits@timestoday.com
Publication Website: https://www.chillicothetimesbulletin.com/
Publisher Name: Shawn Fox
Publisher Email: sfox@pjstar.com
Publisher Phone: sfox@pjstar.com
Editor Name: Chris Kaergard
Editor Email: ckaergard@pjstar.com
Editor Phone: (309) 686-3255 x__
Advertising Executive Name: Sandy Norbits
Advertising Executive Email: snorbits@timestoday.com
Advertising Executive Phone: (309) 686-3116

PERCY

COUNTY JOURNAL

Street Address: 1101 E Pine St
City: Percy
State: IL
ZIP Code: 62272-1333
General Phone: (618) 497-8272
General Email: cjournal@egyptian.net
Publication Website: https://countyjournal.org/
Parent Company: Willis Publishing
Publisher Name: Larry Willis
Publisher Email: cjournal@egyptian.net
Publisher Phone: (618) 497-8272 x_
Editor Name: Jerry Willis
Editor Email: cjournal@egyptian.net
Editor Phone: (618) 497-8272 x_

Advertising Executive Name: John Falkenhein
Advertising Executive Email: cjournal@egyptian.net
Advertising Executive Phone: (618) 497-8272 x___

PETERSBURG

MENARD COUNTY REVIEW

Street Address: 235 E Sangamon Ave
City: Petersburg
State: IL
ZIP Code: 62675-1245
General Phone: (217) 632-2236
General Email: info@petersburgil.com
Publication Website: http://www.petersburgil.com/
Publisher Name: Jane Shaw Cutright
Publisher Email: observer@casscomm.com
Publisher Phone: (217) 632-2236
Editor Name: David Crosnoe

PETERSBURG

THE PETERSBURG OBSERVER

Street Address: 235 E Sangamon Ave
City: Petersburg
State: IL
ZIP Code: 62675-1245
General Phone: (217) 632-2236
General Email: info@petersburgil.com
Publication Website: http://www.petersburgil.com/
Parent Company: Petersburg Observer Corporation
Publisher Name: Jane Shaw Cutright
Publisher Email: observer@casscomm.com
Publisher Phone: (217) 632-2236 x_
Editor Name: David Crosnoe
Advertising Executive Name: Denise Boeker
Advertising Executive Email: observer@casscomm.com
Advertising Executive Phone: (217) 632-2236 x___

PITTSFIELD

PIKE COUNTY EXPRESS

Street Address: 129 N Madison St
City: Pittsfield
State: IL
ZIP Code: 62363-1405
General Phone: (217) 285-5415
General Email: pikecountyexpressnews@yahoo.com
Publication Website: http://pikecountyexpress.com/
Parent Company: Coulson Publications
Publisher Name: Dan Logn
Publisher Email: thedmnews@yahoo.com
Publisher Phone: (217) 773-3371 x___

PLAINFIELD

BUGLE NEWSPAPERS

Street Address: 23856 W Andrew Rd
City: Plainfield
State: IL
ZIP Code: 60585-8770
General Phone: (815) 436-2431
General Email: webmaster@buglenewspapers.com
Publication Website: https://www.buglenewspapers.com/
Parent Company: Enterprise Newspapers, Inc
Publisher Name: Andrew Samaan (GM)
Publisher Email: andrew@buglenewspapers.com
Publisher Phone: (815) 436-2431, ext : 104
Editor Name: Mark Gregory

Editor Email: mark@buglenewspapers.com
Editor Phone: (815) 955-7803 x___
Advertising Executive Name: Shelley Holmgren
Advertising Executive Email: sholmgren@buglenewspapers.com
Advertising Executive Phone: (815) 436-2431, ext : 107

PLAINFIELD

THE BUGLE

Street Address: 23856 W Andrew Rd
City: Plainfield
State: IL
ZIP Code: 60585-8771
General Phone: (815) 436-2431
General Email: webmaster@buglenewspapers.com
Publication Website: https://www.buglenewspapers.com/
Parent Company: Enterprise Newspapers, Inc
Publisher Name: Andrew Samaan
Publisher Email: andrew@buglenewspapers.com
Publisher Phone: (815) 436-2431, ext : 104
Editor Name: Mark Gregory
Editor Email: mark@buglenewspapers.com
Editor Phone: (815) 955-7803 x_
Advertising Executive Name: Shelley Holmgren
Advertising Executive Email: sholmgren@buglenewspapers.com
Advertising Executive Phone: (815) 436-2431, ext : 107

PROPHETSTOWN

PROPHETSTOWN ECHO

Street Address: 342 Washington St
City: Prophetstown
State: IL
ZIP Code: 61277-1115
General Phone: (815) 772-7244
General Email: echo@whitesidesentinel.com
Publication Website: http://whitesidesentinel.com/
Parent Company: Shaw Media
Publisher Name: Jerry Lindsey
Publisher Email: jlindsey@shawmedia.com
Publisher Phone: 815-772-7244

RAMSEY

RAMSEY NEWS-JOURNAL

Street Address: 223 S. Superior St
City: Ramsey
State: IL
ZIP Code: 62080
General Phone: (618) 423-4142
General Email: ramseynewsjournal@gmail.com
Publication Website: http://ramseynewsjournal.net/
Publisher Name: Stefanie Anderson (GM)
Publisher Email: sanderson@localsouthernnews.com
Publisher Phone: (618) 606-1208 x_
Editor Name: Tracy Strawn-Kunkel
Editor Email: ramseynewsjournal@gmail.com
Editor Phone: (618) 423-4142 x_

RED BUD

NORTH COUNTY NEWS

Street Address: 124 S Main St
City: Red Bud
State: IL
ZIP Code: 62278-1103
General Phone: (618) 282-3803
General Email: incnews@htc.net

Publication Website: http://www.northcountynews.org/
Publisher Name: Vic Mohr
Publisher Email: ncnews@htc.net
Publisher Phone: (618) 282-3803 x___
Editor Name: Mary Koester
Editor Email: ncnews@htc.net
Editor Phone: (618) 282-3803
Advertising Executive Name: Jesse Heidel
Advertising Executive Email: incnews@htc.net
Advertising Executive Phone: (618) 282-3803

RIVERTON

WILLIAMSVILLE-SHERMAN SUN TIMES

Street Address: 715 N 7th St
City: Riverton
State: IL
ZIP Code: 62561-1019
General Phone: (217) 629-9221
General Email: southcountypub@att.net
Publication Website: https://www.southcountypublications.net/the_sun_times/news/
Parent Company: South County Publications
Publisher Name: Joseph M. Michelich
Publisher Email: southco@royell.org
Publisher Phone: (217) 483-2614 x___
Editor Name: Byron Painter
Editor Email: southcountypub@att.net
Editor Phone: (217) 629-9221
Advertising Executive Name: Connie Michelich
Advertising Executive Email: southco@royell.org
Advertising Executive Phone: (217) 438-6155 x_

ROBINSON

THE ROBINSON CONSTITUTION

Street Address: P.O. Box 639
City: Robinson
State: IL
ZIP Code: 62454-2137
General Phone: (618) 544-2101
General Email: wpiper@robdailynews.com
Publication Website: http://robdailynews.com/
Parent Company: Lewis Newspapers
Editor Name: Greg Bilbrey
Editor Email: gbilbrey@robdailynews.com
Editor Phone: (618) 544-2101, ext : 111
Advertising Executive Name: Winnie Piper
Advertising Executive Email: wpiper@robdailynews.com
Advertising Executive Phone: (618) 544-2101, ext. 103

ROCKFORD

THE ROCK RIVER TIMES

Street Address: 128 N Church St
City: Rockford
State: IL
ZIP Code: 61101
General Phone: (815) 964-9767
General Email: contact@rockrivertimes.com
Publication Website: http://rockrivertimes.com/
Parent Company: The Rock River Times
Publisher Name: Josh Johnson
Publisher Email: josh.johnson@rockrivertimes.com
Publisher Phone: 815-964-9767
Editor Name: Shane Nicholson
Editor Email: shane.nicholson@rockrivertimes.com
Editor Phone: 815-964-9767
Advertising Executive Name: Donna George
Advertising Executive Email: donna.george@rockrivertimes.com
Advertising Executive Phone: 815-964-9767

ROSEVILLE

ROSEVILLE INDEPENDENT

Street Address: 145 South Chamberlain Street
City: Roseville
State: IL
ZIP Code: 61473
General Phone: (309) 255-7581
General Email: abingdonargus@gmail.com
Publication Website: https://www.eaglepublications.com/roseville.html
Parent Company: Eagle Publications
Advertising Executive Phone: (309) 833-2114

RUSHVILLE

THE RUSHVILLE TIMES

Street Address: 110 E Lafayette St
City: Rushville
State: IL
ZIP Code: 62681-1412
General Phone: (217) 322-3321
General Email: ads@rushvilletimes.com
Publication Website: http://www.rushvilletimes.com/
Publisher Name: Alan Icenogle
Publisher Email: editor@rushvilletimes.com
Publisher Phone: (217) 322-3321 x_
Editor Name: Alan Icenogle
Editor Email: editor@rushvilletimes.com
Editor Phone: (217) 322-3321 x_
Advertising Executive Name: Teresa Haines
Advertising Executive Email: ads@rushvilletimes.com
Advertising Executive Phone: (217) 322-3321 x

SAVANNA

SAVANNA TIMES-JOURNAL

Street Address: 315 Main St
City: Savanna
State: IL
ZIP Code: 61074-1629
General Phone: (815) 273-2277
General Email: savtj@grics.net
Publication Website: http://www.mycarrollcountynews.com/
Publisher Name: Robert Watson
Publisher Email: mirrordem@grics.net
Publisher Phone: (815) 244-2411 x_
Editor Name: Robert Watson
Editor Email: mirrordem@grics.net
Editor Phone: (815) 244-2411 x_
Advertising Executive Name: Pam Villalobos
Advertising Executive Email: savtj@grics.net
Advertising Executive Phone: 815-273-2277

SHELBYVILLE

DAILY UNION

Street Address: 201 N Banker St
City: Shelbyville
State: IL
ZIP Code: 62565-1652
General Phone: (217) 774-2161
General Email: deanna.sickles@shelbyvilledailyunion.com
Publication Website: https://www.shelbyvilledailyunion.com/
Parent Company: CNHI, LLC
Publisher Name: Amy Winter
Publisher Email: amy.winter@shelbyvilledailyunion.com
Publisher Phone: (217) 347-7151, ext : 112
Editor Name: Jeff Long
Editor Email: jeff.long@shelbyvilledailyunion.com
Editor Phone: (217) 347-7151, ext : 129
Advertising Executive Name: Deanna Sickles

Community Newspapers in the U.S.

III-227

Advertising Executive Email: deanna.
sickles@shelbyvilledailyunion.com
Advertising Executive Phone: (217) 519-2913

STAUNTON

STAUNTON STAR-TIMES

Street Address: 108 W Main St
City: Staunton
State: IL
ZIP Code: 62088-1453
General Phone: (618) 635-2000
General Email: startime@madisontelco.com
Publication Website: https://www.
stauntonstartimes.com/
Publisher Name: John Galer
Publisher Email: thejournal-news@
consolidated.net
Publisher Phone: (217) 532-3933 x_

STRONGHURST

THE HANCOCK-HENDERSON QUILL

Street Address: 102 N Broadway St
City: Stronghurst
State: IL
ZIP Code: 61480-5023
General Phone: (309) 924-1871
General Email: quill@hcil.net
Publication Website: http://quillnewspaper.
com/
Publisher Name: Dessa Bell Rodeffer
Publisher Email: dessa@hcil.net
Publisher Phone: (309) 924-1871 x_
Editor Name: Shirley Linder
Editor Email: quillnewspaper@frontier.com
Editor Phone: (309) 924-1871 x____

SULLIVAN

NEWS-PROGRESS

Street Address: 100 W Monroe St
City: Sullivan
State: IL
ZIP Code: 61951-1400
General Phone: (217) 728-7381
General Email: ads@newsprogress.com
Publication Website: http://newsprogress.
com/
Publisher Name: Stefanie Anderson (GM)
Publisher Email: sanderson@
localsouthernnews.com
Publisher Phone: (618) 606-1208 x_
Advertising Executive Name: Barry Morgan
Advertising Executive Email: ads@
newsprogress.com
Advertising Executive Phone: (217) 728-7381 x__

SUMMIT

SOUTHWEST NEWS-HERALD

Street Address: 7676 W 63rd St
City: Summit
State: IL
ZIP Code: 60501-1812
General Phone: (708) 496-0265
General Email: vonpub@aol.com
Publication Website: https://swnewsherald.
com/home-1.htm
Parent Company: Southwest Community
News Group, LLC.
Publisher Name: Mark Hornung
Publisher Email: mhornung@cmgms.com
Publisher Phone: 815-432-5277
Editor Name: Tim Hadac
Editor Email: editor@archerjournalnews.com
Editor Phone: (708) 496-0265 x
Advertising Executive Name: Donna Brown
Advertising Executive Email: donna_brn@
yahoo.com
Advertising Executive Phone: (708) 496-0265 x__

SUMMIT

SOUTHWEST SUBURBAN NEWS-HERALD

Street Address: 7676 W 63rd St
City: Summit
State: IL
ZIP Code: 60501
General Phone: (708) 496-0265
General Email: vonpub@aol.com
Publication Website: https://swnewsherald.
com/
Parent Company: Southwest Community
News Group, LLC.

TEUTOPOLIS

TEUTOPOLIS PRESS-DIETERICH SPECIAL GAZETTE

Street Address: 107 E Main St
City: Teutopolis
State: IL
ZIP Code: 62467
General Phone: (833) 948-1200
General Email: cbarche@olneydailymail.com
Publication Website: https://www.
teutopolispress.com/
Publisher Name: Chip Barche
Publisher Email: cbarche@olneydailymail.
com
Publisher Phone: (618) 393-2931 x__
Editor Name: Chip Barche
Editor Email: cbarche@olneydailymail.com
Editor Phone: (618) 393-2931
Advertising Executive Name: Cathy Slunaker
Advertising Executive Email: advertising1@
olneydailymail.com
Advertising Executive Phone: (618) 393-2931

TRENTON

THE TRENTON SUN

Street Address: 19 W. Broadway P.O. Box 118
City: Trenton
State: IL
ZIP Code: 62293
General Phone: (618) 224-9422
General Email: mike@trentonsun.net
Publication Website: https://trentonsun.net/
Parent Company: The Sun
Publisher Name: Sybil Conley
Publisher Email: sybil@trentonsun.net
Publisher Phone: (618) 224-9422 x
Editor Name: Michael L. Conley
Editor Email: mike@trentonsun.net
Editor Phone: (618) 224-9422 x_
Advertising Executive Name: Sybil Conley
Advertising Executive Email: sybil@
trentonsun.net
Advertising Executive Phone: (618) 224-9422 x_

VANDALIA

THE LEADER-UNION

Street Address: 229 S 5th St, P.O. Box 315
City: Vandalia
State: IL
ZIP Code: 62471-2703
General Phone: (618) 283-3374
General Email: sales@leaderunion.com
Publication Website: https://www.
leaderunion.com/
Publisher Name: Rich Bauer
Publisher Email: rbauer@leaderunion.com
Publisher Phone: (618) 283-3374 x_
Editor Name: Rich Bauer

VIENNA

GOREVILLE GAZETTE

Street Address: PO Box 457, 305 E. Main Street
City: Vienna
State: IL
ZIP Code: 62995-0457
General Phone: (618) 658-4321
General Email: viennatimes@frontier.com
Publication Website: https://theviennatimes.
com/
Parent Company: H&R Media, LLC
Publisher Name: Lonnie J. Hinton
Publisher Email: viennatimes@frontier.com
Publisher Phone: (618) 658-4321
Editor Name: Joseph Rehana
Editor Email: gorevillegazette@frontier.com
Editor Phone: 618-658-4321
Advertising Executive Name: Hillary Wright
Advertising Executive Email:
gorevillegazette@frontier.com
Advertising Executive Phone: (618) 995-9445 x__

VIENNA

THE VIENNA TIMES

Street Address: 305 E Main St
City: Vienna
State: IL
ZIP Code: 62995
General Phone: (618) 658-4321
General Email: viennatimes@frontier.com
Publication Website: https://theviennatimes.
com/
Publisher Name: Lonnie J. Hinton
Publisher Email: viennatimes@frontier.com
Publisher Phone: (618) 658-4321
Editor Name: Lonnie Hinton
Editor Email: viennatimes@frontier.com
Editor Phone: (618) 658-4321
Advertising Executive Name: Hilary Wright
Advertising Executive Email:
gorevillegazette@frontier.com
Advertising Executive Phone: (618) 995-9445 x

VILLA GROVE

SOUTHERN CHAMPAIGN CO. TODAY

Street Address: 5-7 S. Main Street
City: Villa Grove
State: IL
ZIP Code: 61956-1522
General Phone: (217) 832-4201
General Email: vgnews@mchsi.com
Publication Website: https://www.
arthurgraphic.com/home-southern-champaign-county-today/
Parent Company: Arthur Publishing
Publisher Name: Greg Hoskins
Publisher Email: ghoskins@heraldpubs.com
Publisher Phone: (618) 566-8282 x_

VIRDEN

NORTHWESTERN NEWS

Street Address: 169 E. Dean St., P.O. Box 440
City: Virden
State: IL
ZIP Code: 62690
General Phone: (217) 965-3355
General Email: ads@gnnews.net
Publication Website: https://gnnews.net/
Parent Company: Gold Nugget Publications Inc
Publisher Name: Stefanie Anderson (GM)
Publisher Email: sanderson@
localsouthernnews.com
Publisher Phone: (618) 606-1208 x_
Editor Name: Lisa Rascher

Editor Email: editor@gnnews.net
Editor Phone: (217) 436-2424
Advertising Executive Email: ads@gnnews.
net
Advertising Executive Phone: (217) 965-4512

VIRDEN

THE GIRARD GAZETTE

Street Address: 169 E. Dean St., P.O. Box 440
City: Virden
State: IL
ZIP Code: 62690
General Phone: (217) 965-3355
General Email: ads@gnnews.net
Publication Website: https://gnnews.net/
Parent Company: Gold Nugget Publications Inc
Publisher Name: Stefanie Anderson (GM)
Publisher Email: sanderson@
localsouthernnews.com
Publisher Phone: (618) 606-1208 x_
Editor Name: Janice Smith
Editor Email: mirrordem@grics.net
Editor Phone: (217) 627-2115
Advertising Executive Email: ads@gnnews.
net
Advertising Executive Phone: (217) 965-4512

VIRDEN

VIRDEN RECORDER

Street Address: 169 E. Dean St., P.O. Box 440
City: Virden
State: IL
ZIP Code: 62690
General Phone: (217) 965-3355
General Email: ads@gnnews.net
Publication Website: https://gnnews.net/
Parent Company: Paddock Publications
Publisher Name: Stefanie Anderson (GM)
Publisher Email: sanderson@
localsouthernnews.com
Publisher Phone: (618) 606-1208 x__
Editor Name: Judy Hendricks
Editor Phone: (217) 965-3355
Advertising Executive Name: Julie Westerhausen
Advertising Executive Email: ads@gnnews.
net
Advertising Executive Phone: (217) 965-4512

WASHINGTON

COURIER

Street Address: 100 Ford Ln
City: Washington
State: IL
ZIP Code: 61571-2668
General Phone: (309) 444-3139
General Email: joi67@courierpapers.com
Publication Website: https://www.
courierpapers.com/washington_courier/
Parent Company: Gannett
Publisher Name: Joi Hagel-DeArmond
Publisher Email: joi67@courierpapers.com
Publisher Phone: (309) 444-3139, ext : 12
Editor Name: James Strauss
Editor Email: haglnews@mtco.com
Editor Phone: (309) 444-3139 x____

WASHINGTON

WOODFORD COURIER

Street Address: 100 Ford Ln
City: Washington
State: IL
ZIP Code: 61571-2668
General Phone: (309) 444-3139
General Email: bookkper@courierpapers.

com
Publication Website: https://www.courierpapers.com/woodford_courier/
Parent Company: Courier Newspapers
Publisher Name: Joi Hagel-DeArmond
Publisher Email: joi67@courierpapers.com
Publisher Phone: (309) 444-3139, ext : 12
Editor Name: James Strauss
Editor Email: haglnews@mtco.com

YORKVILLE

KENDALL COUNTY RECORD, OSWEGO LEDGER, SANDWICH RECORD, PLANO RECORD

Street Address: 109 W Veterans Pkwy
City: Yorkville
State: IL
ZIP Code: 60560-1905
General Phone: (630) 553-7034
General Email: adsales@kendallcountynow.com
Publication Website: https://www.kendallcountynow.com/online-newspaper/
Publisher Name: Ryan Wells
Publisher Email: rwells@shawmedia.com
Publisher Phone: (630) 365-6446 x___
Editor Name: John Etheredge
Editor Email: jetheredge@shawmedia.com
Editor Phone: (630) 553-7034
Advertising Executive Email: classified@shawsuburban.com

YORKVILLE

LEDGER-SENTINEL

Street Address: 109 W Veterans Pkwy
City: Yorkville
State: IL
ZIP Code: 60560-1905
General Phone: (630) 553-7034
General Email: adsales@kendallcountynow.com
Publication Website: https://www.kendallcountynow.com/yorkville/
Publisher Name: Ryan Wells
Publisher Email: rwells@shawmedia.com
Publisher Phone: (630) 365-6446 x___
Editor Name: John Etheredge
Editor Email: jetheredge@shawmedia.com
Editor Phone: (630) 553-7034
Advertising Executive Name: Steve Vanisco
Advertising Executive Email: classified@shawsuburban.com

INDIANA

ATTICA

FOUNTAIN COUNTY NEIGHBOR

Street Address: 113 S Perry St
City: Attica
State: IN
ZIP Code: 47918
General Phone: (765) 762-2411
General Email: atticaeditor@gmail.com
Publication Website: http://www.newsbug.info/eedition/fountain_county_neighbor/
Editor Name: Wendy Davis
Editor Email: atticaeditor@gmail.com
Advertising Executive Name: Greg Willhite
Advertising Executive Email: generalmanageradman@gmail.com
Delivery Methods: Mail`Newsstand`Racks
Own Printing Facility?: Y
Commercial printers?: Y
Mechanical specifications: Type page 11 1/2 x 21; E - 6 cols, 1 9/16, between; A - 6 cols, 1 9/16, between; C - 6 cols, 1 9/16, between.
Published Days: Tues
Avg. Paid Circ.: 1803
Audit Company: Sworn/Estimate/Non-Audited
Audit Date: 43626

AVON

HENDRICKS COUNTY FLYER

Street Address: 8109 Kingston St
City: Avon
State: IN
ZIP Code: 46123-8211
General Phone: (317) 272-5800
General Email: david.johnson@flyergroup.com
Parent Company: CNHI, LLC
Delivery Methods: Mail`Newsstand`Carrier`Racks
Year Established: 1994
Own Printing Facility?: N
Commercial printers?: Y
Mechanical specifications: Type page 11 x 21 1/2; E - 6 cols, 1 5/6, 3/8 between; A - 6 cols, 1 5/6, 3/8 between; C - 6 cols, 1 5/6, 3/8 between.
Published Days: Wed`Sat
Avg. Paid Circ.: 2750
Avg. Free Circ.: 28800
Audit Company: Sworn/Estimate/Non-Audited
Audit Date: 43626

AVON

THE WEEKEND FLYER

Street Address: 8109 Kingston St
City: Avon
State: IN
ZIP Code: 46123-8211
General Phone: (317) 272-5800
General Email: flyer@flyergroup.com
Parent Company: Community Newspaper Holdings, Inc.
Mechanical specifications: Type page 13 x 21 1/2; E - 6 cols, 2 1/16, between; A - 6 cols, 2 1/16, between; C - 10 cols, 1 3/16, between.
Published Days: Wed`Sat
Avg. Free Circ.: 16000
Audit Company: Sworn/Estimate/Non-Audited
Audit Date: 43626

BATESVILLE

THE HERALD-TRIBUNE

Street Address: 475 N Huntersville Rd
City: Batesville
State: IN
ZIP Code: 47006
General Phone: (812) 934-4343
General Email: theheraldtribune@batesvilleheraldtribune.com
Publication Website: https://www.batesvilleheraldtribune.com/
Parent Company: Gannett
Publisher Name: Laura Welborn
Publisher Email: laura.welborn@indianamediagroup.com
Publisher Phone: (812) 663-3111, ext : 217001
Editor Name: Debbie Blank
Editor Email: theheraldtribune@batesvilleheraldtribune.com
Editor Phone: (812) 934-4343, ext : 220113
Advertising Executive Name: Marilyn Schwegman
Advertising Executive Email: marilyn.schwegman@batesvilleheraldtribune.com
Advertising Executive Phone: (812) 934-4343, ext : 220116
Delivery Methods: Mail`Newsstand`Racks
Year Established: 1891
Mechanical specifications: 6 column format - 1 col 1.6"; 2 col 3.31"; 3 col 5.0"; 4 col 6.71"; 5 col 8.43"; 6 col 10.15" - 21.25" tall
Published Days: Tues`Fri
Avg. Paid Circ.: 2000
Audit Company: Sworn/Estimate/Non-Audited
Audit Date: 43626

BERNE

BERNE TRI WEEKLY NEWS

Street Address: 153 S Jefferson St
City: Berne
State: IN
ZIP Code: 46711-2157
General Phone: (260) 589-2101
General Email: advertising@bernewitness.com
Publication Website: https://bernewitness.com/
Parent Company: Dynamic Resource Group
Publisher Name: Clint Anderson
Editor Name: Manda Arnold
Advertising Executive Name: Jessica Elzey
Advertising Executive Email: advertising@bernewitness.com
Delivery Methods: Mail`Newsstand`Carrier`Racks
Year Established: 1896
Mechanical specifications: Type page 12 3/4 x 20 1/2; E - 6 cols, 2, 1/6 between; A - 6 cols, 2, 1/6 between.
Published Days: Mon`Wed`Fri
Avg. Paid Circ.: 2000
Audit Company: Sworn/Estimate/Non-Audited
Audit Date: 43626

BOONVILLE

THE WARWICK COUNTY STANDARD

Street Address: 131 S. Warwick St.
City: Boonville
State: IN
ZIP Code: 47601
General Phone: (812) 897-2330
General Email: advertising@warricknews.com
Publication Website: https://www.warricknews.com/
Parent Company: Paxton Media Group, LLC
Editor Name: Megan Purazrang
Editor Email: editor@warricknews.com
Advertising Executive Name: Bob Rigg
Advertising Executive Email: brigg@warricknews.com
Delivery Methods: Mail`Racks
Year Established: 1874
Mechanical specifications: Type page 10.875 x 21 1/2; E - 6 cols, 1.712, between - .12; A - 6 cols, 1.712, between -0.12; C - 8 cols,1.25, between - .12.
Published Days: Thur
Avg. Paid Circ.: 4000
Avg. Free Circ.: 2000
Audit Company: Sworn/Estimate/Non-Audited
Audit Date: 43626

BOONVILLE

WARRICK COUNTY TODAY

Street Address: 204 W Locust St
City: Boonville
State: IN
ZIP Code: 47601
General Phone: (812) 897-2330
General Email: advertising@warricknews.com
Publication Website: https://www.warricknews.com/
Parent Company: Paxton Media Group, LLC
Editor Name: Megan Purazrang
Editor Email: editor@warricknews.com
Advertising Executive Name: Bob Rigg
Advertising Executive Email: brigg@warricknews.com
Delivery Methods: Mail`Newsstand`Carrier`Racks
Year Established: 1875
Own Printing Facility?: Y
Commercial printers?: Y
Mechanical specifications: Type page 10 x 21 1/2; E - 6 cols, 1.56, between, .111; A - 6 cols, 1.56, between, .111; C - 6 cols, 1.56, between, .111.
Published Days: Thur
Avg. Paid Circ.: 4000
Avg. Free Circ.: 12000
Audit Company: Sworn/Estimate/Non-Audited
Audit Date: 43626

BROOKVILLE

THE BROOKVILLE AMERICAN

Street Address: 531 Main St
City: Brookville
State: IN
ZIP Code: 47012
General Phone: (765) 647-4221
General Email: info@whitewaterpub.com
Publication Website: https://whitewaterpub.com/
Parent Company: Whitewater Publications
Delivery Methods: Mail`Newsstand`Racks
Year Established: 1838
Mechanical specifications: Type page 13 x 21; E - 6 cols, 2, 1/4 between; A - 6 cols, 2, 1/4 between; C - 8 cols, 1 1/2, 1/8 between.
Published Days: Wed
Avg. Paid Circ.: 5000
Avg. Free Circ.: 62
Audit Company: Sworn/Estimate/Non-Audited
Audit Date: 43626

CLAY CITY

THE CLAY CITY NEWS

Street Address: 717 Main St
City: Clay City
State: IN
ZIP Code: 47841
General Phone: (812) 829-2255
General Email: ccnews@claycitynews.com
Publication Website: http://digital.olivesoftware.com/Olive/ODN/ClayCityNews/
Parent Company: Gannett
Publisher Name: Larry Hensley
Delivery Methods: Mail
Year Established: 1912
Mechanical specifications: Type page 15 5/6 x 21; E - 7 cols, 2, 1/8 between; A - 7 cols, 2, 1/8 between; C - 7 cols, 2, 1/8 between.
Published Days: Wed
Avg. Paid Circ.: 1800
Audit Company: Sworn/Estimate/Non-Audited
Audit Date: 43626

CORYDON

CLARION NEWS

Street Address: 301 N Capitol Ave
City: Corydon
State: IN
ZIP Code: 47112
General Phone: (812) 738-2211
General Email: cadams@clarionnews.net
Publication Website: http://www.clarionnews.net/
Parent Company: O'Bannon Publishing Co., Inc.
Delivery Methods: Mail
Own Printing Facility?: Y
Commercial printers?: Y
Published Days: Wed
Avg. Free Circ.: 16600

Community Newspapers in the U.S.

Audit Company: Sworn/Estimate/Non-Audited
Audit Date: 43626

CORYDON

THE CORYDON DEMOCRAT

Street Address: 301 N Capitol Ave
City: Corydon
State: IN
ZIP Code: 47112
General Phone: (812) 738-2211
General Email: ctimberlake@corydondemocrat.com
Publication Website: http://www.corydondemocrat.com/
Parent Company: O'Bannon Publishing Co., Inc.
Delivery Methods: Mail`Newsstand`Carrier`Racks
Year Established: 1856
Own Printing Facility?: Y
Commercial printers?: Y
Mechanical specifications: Type page 13 x 21 1/4; E - 6 cols, between; A - 6 cols, between; C - 8 cols, between.
Published Days: Wed
Avg. Paid Circ.: 6800
Avg. Free Circ.: 17600
Audit Company: Sworn/Estimate/Non-Audited
Audit Date: 43626
Note: none

CROTHERSVILLE

CROTHERSVILLE TIMES

Street Address: 510 Moore St
City: Crothersville
State: IN
ZIP Code: 47229
General Phone: (812) 793-2188
General Email: ctimes@frontier.com
Publication Website: http://crothersvilletimes.com/
Editor Name: Curt Kovener
Delivery Methods: Mail`Racks
Year Established: 1980
Mechanical specifications: Type page 10 1/4 x 12.5; E - 6 cols, 1 5/8, 1/6 between; A - 6 cols, 1 5/8, 1/6 between; C - 6 cols, 1 5/8, 1/6 between.
Published Days: Wed
Avg. Paid Circ.: 1300
Avg. Free Circ.: 28
Audit Company: Sworn/Estimate/Non-Audited
Audit Date: 43626

DANVILLE

THE REPUBLICAN

Street Address: 6 E Main St
City: Danville
State: IN
ZIP Code: 46122
General Phone: (317) 745-2777
General Email: betty@therepublicannewspaper.com
Publication Website: https://www.therepublicannewspaper.com/
Parent Company: Advance Newspapers
Editor Name: Betty Bartley
Editor Email: betty@therepublicannewspaper.com
Advertising Executive Name: Beth
Advertising Executive Email: beth@therepublicannewspaper.com
Advertising Executive Phone: (317) 745-2777
Delivery Methods: Mail
Year Established: 1847
Own Printing Facility?: Y
Commercial printers?: Y
Mechanical specifications: Type page 11 1/4 x 21; E - 6 cols, 1 3/4, 1/8 between.

Published Days: Thur
Avg. Paid Circ.: 1600
Audit Company: Sworn/Estimate/Non-Audited
Audit Date: 43626

DEMOTTE

KANKAKEE VALLEY POST-NEWS

Street Address: 827 S Halleck St
City: Demotte
State: IN
ZIP Code: 46310
General Phone: (219) 987-5111
General Email: ggperrotto@rensselaerrepublican.com
Publication Website: http://www.newsbug.info/kankakee_valley_post_news/
Publisher Name: Greg Perrotto
Publisher Email: ggperrotto@rensselaerrepublican.com
Editor Name: Michael S. Johnson
Editor Email: editor@thehj.com
Advertising Executive Name: Cindy Teeter
Advertising Executive Email: kvpadvertisingworks@gmail.com
Advertising Executive Phone: (219) 474-5532
Delivery Methods: Mail`Newsstand`Racks
Year Established: 1932
Published Days: Thur
Avg. Paid Circ.: 2800
Avg. Free Circ.: 19000
Audit Company: Sworn/Estimate/Non-Audited
Audit Date: 43626

ELWOOD

ALEXANDRIA TIMES-TRIBUNE

Street Address: 317 S Anderson St
City: Elwood
State: IN
ZIP Code: 46036-2018
General Phone: (765) 724-4469
General Email: alextribune@elwoodpublishing.com
Publication Website: https://www.elwoodpublishing.com/alexandria-times-tribune-contact-us/
Parent Company: Elwood Publishing Co., Inc.
Publisher Name: Robert Nash
Editor Name: Jenny Renbarger
Advertising Executive Name: Cindy Tyner
Delivery Methods: Mail
Year Established: 1885
Own Printing Facility?: Y
Commercial printers?: Y
Mechanical specifications: Type page 10 x 21 1/2; E - 6 cols, 1 5/6, between; A - 6 cols, 1 5/6, between; C - 6 cols, 1 5/6, between.
Published Days: Wed
Avg. Paid Circ.: 1200
Audit Company: Sworn/Estimate/Non-Audited
Audit Date: 43626

FERDINAND

FERDINAND NEWS

Street Address: PO Box 38
City: Ferdinand
State: IN
ZIP Code: 47532
General Phone: (812) 367-2041
General Email: ferdnews@psci.net
Publication Website: https://www.ferdinandnews.com/
Parent Company: Dubois Spencer Counties Pubishing Co., Inc.
Advertising Executive Email: ads@psci.net
Delivery Methods: Mail`Newsstand`Racks
Year Established: 1906
Own Printing Facility?: Y

Commercial printers?: Y
Mechanical specifications: Type page 13 x 21 1/2; E - 3 cols, 4 1/4, 1/4 between; A - 6 cols, 2, 1/4 between; C - 6 cols, 2, 1/4 between.
Published Days: Wed
Avg. Paid Circ.: 2500
Audit Company: Sworn/Estimate/Non-Audited
Audit Date: 43626

FLORA

CARROLL COUNTY COMET

Street Address: 14 E Main St
City: Flora
State: IN
ZIP Code: 46929
General Phone: (574) 967-4135
General Email: comet@carrollcountycomet.com
Publication Website: https://www.carrollcountycomet.com/
Parent Company: Carroll Papers, Inc.
Publisher Name: Susan Scholl
Editor Name: Susan Scholl
Editor Email: editor@carrollcountycomet.com
Advertising Executive Name: Joe Moss
Advertising Executive Email: comet@carrollcountycomet.com
Delivery Methods: Mail`Newsstand`Racks
Year Established: 1974
Own Printing Facility?: Y
Commercial printers?: N
Mechanical specifications: 10.389 wide by 21.5 deep
Published Days: Wed
Avg. Paid Circ.: 3200
Avg. Free Circ.: 34
Audit Company: Sworn/Estimate/Non-Audited
Audit Date: 43626

FORT BRANCH

SOUTH GIBSON STAR TIMES

Street Address: 203 S McCreary St
City: Fort Branch
State: IN
ZIP Code: 47648
General Phone: (812) 753-3553
General Email: ads@sgstartimes.com
Publication Website: http://sgstartimes.com/
Parent Company: Pike Publishing
Editor Email: editor@sgstartimes.com
Advertising Executive Email: ads@sgstartimes.com
Delivery Methods: Mail
Year Established: 1955
Mechanical specifications: Type page 9 3/4 x 16; E - 6 cols, 1 1/2, 1/8 between; A - 6 cols, 1 1/2, 1/8 between; C - 6 cols, 1 1/2, 1/8 between.
Published Days: Tues
Avg. Paid Circ.: 4952
Avg. Free Circ.: 21
Audit Company: Sworn/Estimate/Non-Audited
Audit Date: 43626

FOWLER

THE BENTON REVIEW

Street Address: 205 E 5th St
City: Fowler
State: IN
ZIP Code: 47944
General Phone: (765) 884-1902
General Email: bentonreview@sbcglobal.net
Publication Website: http://bentonreview.com/
Parent Company: Hoosier Media Group, LLC
Advertising Executive Email: bentonreviewads@gmail.com

Delivery Methods: Mail`Newsstand`Racks
Year Established: 1875
Mechanical specifications: Type page 13 x 21; E - 6 cols, 2 1/12, 1/6 between; A - 6 cols, 2 1/12, 1/6 between; C - 6 cols, 2 1/12, 1/6 between.
Published Days: Wed
Avg. Paid Circ.: 3000
Avg. Free Circ.: 76
Audit Company: Sworn/Estimate/Non-Audited
Audit Date: 43626

FRENCH LICK

SPRINGS VALLEY HERALD

Street Address: 8481 W College St
City: French Lick
State: IN
ZIP Code: 47432
General Phone: (812) 936-9630
General Email: mflynn@ocpnews.com
Publication Website: https://www.hoosiertimes.com/springs_valley_herald/
Parent Company: Gannett
Delivery Methods: Mail`Newsstand
Year Established: 1903
Mechanical specifications: Type page 10 x 21; E - 6 cols, 2, between; A - 6 cols, 2, between; C - 6 cols, 2, between.
Published Days: Tues
Avg. Paid Circ.: 2200
Audit Company: Sworn/Estimate/Non-Audited
Audit Date: 43626

GREENFIELD

NEW PALESTINE PRESS

Street Address: 22 W New Rd
City: Greenfield
State: IN
ZIP Code: 46140
General Phone: (317) 467-6000
General Email: advert@newpalestinepress.com
Publication Website: http://www.greenfieldreporter.com
Parent Company: AIM Media Indiana
Advertising Executive Name: John Senger
Advertising Executive Email: jsenger@greenfieldreporter.com
Advertising Executive Phone: (317) 477-3208
Delivery Methods: Mail`Carrier
Own Printing Facility?: Y
Commercial printers?: Y
Published Days: Thur
Avg. Paid Circ.: 2500
Audit Company: Sworn/Estimate/Non-Audited
Audit Date: 43626

GREENSBURG

THE GREENSBURG TIMES

Street Address: 135 S Franklin St
City: Greensburg
State: IN
ZIP Code: 47240
General Phone: (812) 663-3111
General Email: news@greensburgdailynews.com
Publication Website: https://www.greensburgdailynews.com/
Parent Company: CNHI, LLC
Publisher Name: Laura Welborn
Publisher Email: laura.welborn@indianamediagroup.com
Publisher Phone: (812) 663-3111, ext : 217001
Editor Name: Kevin Green
Editor Email: melissa.conrad@greensburgdailynews.com
Editor Phone: (812) 663-3111, ext : 217056
Advertising Executive Name: Natalie Acra

Advertising Executive Email: natalie.acra@greensburgdailynews.com
Advertising Executive Phone: (812) 663-3111, ext : 217034
Delivery Methods: Mail`Racks
Year Established: 1894
Own Printing Facility?: Y
Commercial printers?: Y
Mechanical specifications: Type page 13 x 21 1/2; E - 6 cols, 2 1/4, between; A - 6 cols, 2 1/4, between; C - 8 cols, 1 1/2, between.
Published Days: Fri
Avg. Paid Circ.: 692
Avg. Free Circ.: 3
Audit Company: Sworn/Estimate/Non-Audited
Audit Date: 43626

HUNTINGBURG

THE HUNTINGBURG PRESS

Street Address: KY
City: Huntingburg
State: IN
ZIP Code: 47542-1337
General Phone: (812) 683-5899
General Email: huntingburgpress@frontier.com
Publication Website: http://www.ky-news.com/
Parent Company: Kentucky Publishing, Inc.
Delivery Methods: Mail`Newsstand`Carrier`Racks
Year Established: 1905
Mechanical specifications: 1 COLUMN IS 1.625" WIDE FULL PAGE IS 10.625" WIDE X 19.75" TALL
Published Days: Wed
Avg. Paid Circ.: 1100
Avg. Free Circ.: 8900
Audit Company: Sworn/Estimate/Non-Audited
Audit Date: 43626

INDIANAPOLIS

FRANKLIN TOWNSHIP INFORMER

Street Address: 8822 Southeastern Ave
City: Indianapolis
State: IN
ZIP Code: 46239
General Phone: (317) 862-1774
General Email: ftinformer@sbcglobal.net
Publication Website: http://www.ftcivicleague.org/informer
Parent Company: Franklin Township Civic League, Inc.
Delivery Methods: Mail
Year Established: 1971
Published Days: Wed
Avg. Paid Circ.: 1500
Audit Company: Sworn/Estimate/Non-Audited
Audit Date: 43626

INDIANAPOLIS

INDIANAPOLIS BUSINESS JOURNAL

Street Address: One Monument Circle, Suite 300
City: Indianapolis
State: IN
ZIP Code: 46204
General Phone: (317) 634-6200
General Email: gmorris@ibj.com
Publication Website: https://www.ibj.com/
Parent Company: IBJ Media Corporation
Publisher Name: Greg Morris
Publisher Email: gmorris@ibj.com
Publisher Phone: (317) 472-5320
Editor Name: Greg Andrews
Editor Email: gandrews@ibj.com
Editor Phone: (317) 472-5378
Advertising Executive Name: Lisa Bradley
Advertising Executive Email: lbradley@ibj.com
Advertising Executive Phone: (317) 472-5321
Delivery Methods: Mail
Year Established: 1980
Published Days: Mon
Avg. Paid Circ.: 10637
Avg. Free Circ.: 494
Audit Company: AAM
Audit Date: 42864

INDIANAPOLIS

SOUTHSIDE TIMES

Street Address: 7670 US 31 S
City: Indianapolis
State: IN
ZIP Code: 46227
General Phone: (317) 300-8782
General Email: rickm@ss-times.com
Publication Website: https://ss-times.com/
Parent Company: Times-Leader Publications
Delivery Methods: Mail`Newsstand`Carrier`Racks
Year Established: 1928
Own Printing Facility?: Y
Commercial printers?: N
Mechanical specifications: Type page 10.75 x 21; E - 6 cols, 1 13/16, 1/2 between; A - 6 cols, 1 13/16, 1/2 between; C - 9 cols, 1 13/16, 1/2 between.
Published Days: Thur
Avg. Free Circ.: 17500
Audit Company: Sworn/Estimate/Non-Audited
Audit Date: 43626

INDIANAPOLIS

THE INDIANAPOLIS RECORDER

Street Address: 2901 N Tacoma Ave
City: Indianapolis
State: IN
ZIP Code: 46218
General Phone: (317) 924-5143
General Email: newsroom@indyrecorder.com
Publication Website: http://www.indianapolisrecorder.com/
Parent Company: Recorder Media Group
Publisher Name: William G. Mays
Editor Name: Oseye Boyd
Editor Email: oseyeb@indyrecorder.com
Advertising Executive Name: Temica Key
Advertising Executive Email: temicak@indyrecorder.com
Delivery Methods: Mail
Year Established: 1895
Published Days: Fri
Avg. Paid Circ.: 4729
Avg. Free Circ.: 395
Audit Company: CVC
Audit Date: 43254

KENTLAND

MOROCCO COURIER

Street Address: 305 E Graham St
City: Kentland
State: IN
ZIP Code: 47951
General Phone: (219) 474-5532
General Email: daily@rensselaerrepublican.com
Publication Website: http://www.newsbug.info/newton_county_enterprise/
Publisher Name: Greg Perrotto
Publisher Email: gperrotto@rensselaerrepublican.com
Advertising Executive Name: Cindy Teeter
Advertising Executive Email: kvpadvertisingworks@gmail.com
Delivery Methods: Mail
Year Established: 1877
Published Days: Wed
Avg. Paid Circ.: 450
Avg. Free Circ.: 10
Audit Company: Sworn/Estimate/Non-Audited
Audit Date: 43626

KENTLAND

THE NEWTON COUNTY ENTERPRISE

Street Address: 305 E Graham St
City: Kentland
State: IN
ZIP Code: 47951-1235
General Phone: (219) 474-5532
General Email: nceditor@centurylink.net
Publication Website: http://www.newsbug.info/newton_county_enterprise/
Publisher Name: Greg Perrotto
Publisher Email: gperrotto@rensselaerrepublican.com
Editor Name: Gregory Myers
Editor Email: nceditor@centurylink.net
Advertising Executive Name: Cindy Teeter
Advertising Executive Email: kvpadvertisingworks@gmail.com
Delivery Methods: Mail`Newsstand`Carrier`Racks
Mechanical specifications: Type page 10 1/2 x 14; E - 6 cols, 1 9/16, between; A - 6 cols, 1 9/16, between; C - 6 cols, 1 9/16, between.
Published Days: Wed
Avg. Paid Circ.: 1600
Audit Company: Sworn/Estimate/Non-Audited
Audit Date: 43626

KNIGHTSTOWN

KNIGHTSTOWN BANNER

Street Address: 24 N Washington St
City: Knightstown
State: IN
ZIP Code: 46148
General Phone: (765) 345-2292
General Email: thebanner@embarqmail.com
Publication Website: http://thebanneronline.com/
Parent Company: Paxton Media Group, LLC
Publisher Name: Eric Cox
Publisher Email: thebanner@embarqmail.com
Editor Name: Eric Cox
Editor Email: thebanner@embarqmail.com
Delivery Methods: Mail`Newsstand
Year Established: 1867
Mechanical specifications: Type page 10 1/4 x 16; E - 5 cols, 1 11/12, 1/6 between; A - 5 cols, 1 11/12, 1/6 between; C - 5 cols, 1 11/12, 1/6 between.
Published Days: Wed
Avg. Paid Circ.: 1400
Avg. Free Circ.: 15
Audit Company: Sworn/Estimate/Non-Audited
Audit Date: 43626

KOKOMO

KOKOMO HERALD

Street Address: 300 N. Union St
City: Kokomo
State: IN
ZIP Code: 46901
General Phone: (765) 459-3121
General Email: webmaster@kokomotribune.com
Publication Website: https://www.kokomotribune.com/
Parent Company: CNHI, LLC
Publisher Name: Robyn McCloskey
Publisher Email: robyn.mccloskey@indianamediagroup.com
Publisher Phone: (765) 459-3121, ext : 288563
Editor Name: Sally Mahan
Editor Email: sally.mahan@kokomotribune.com
Editor Phone: (765) 454-8578
Advertising Executive Name: Joe Blaylock
Advertising Executive Email: joe.blaylock@kokomotribune.com
Advertising Executive Phone: (765) 454-8578, ext : 286716
Delivery Methods: Mail`Newsstand
Year Established: 1971
Published Days: Thur
Audit Company: Sworn/Estimate/Non-Audited
Audit Date: 43626

LAGRANGE

LAGRANGE NEWS

Street Address: PO Box 148
City: Lagrange
State: IN
ZIP Code: 46761
General Phone: (260) 463-2166
General Email: advertising@lagrangepublishing.com
Publication Website: http://lagrangepublishing.hosting-bnin.net/openpublish/
Parent Company: LaGrange Publishing, Co.
Publisher Email: publisher@lagrangepublishing.com
Editor Email: editor@lagrangepublishing.com
Advertising Executive Email: advertising@lagrangepublishing.com
Delivery Methods: Mail`Newsstand`Racks
Year Established: 1861
Own Printing Facility?: Y
Commercial printers?: Y
Mechanical specifications: Type page 7 x 21 1/2; E - 7 cols, 2 1/12, 6/7 between; A - 7 cols, 2 1/12, 6/7 between; C - 9 cols, 1 7/12, 1/6 between.
Published Days: Fri
Avg. Paid Circ.: 5000
Audit Company: Sworn/Estimate/Non-Audited
Audit Date: 43626

LAGRANGE

LAGRANGE STANDARD

Street Address: PO Box 148
City: Lagrange
State: IN
ZIP Code: 46761
General Phone: (260) 463-2166
General Email: advertising@lagrangepublishing.com
Publication Website: http://lagrangepublishing.hosting-bnin.net/openpublish/
Parent Company: LaGrange Publishing, Co.
Publisher Email: publisher@lagrangepublishing.com
Editor Email: editor@lagrangepublishing.com
Advertising Executive Email: advertising@lagrangepublishing.com
Delivery Methods: Mail`Newsstand`Racks
Year Established: 1856
Own Printing Facility?: Y
Commercial printers?: Y
Mechanical specifications: Type page 7 x 21 1/2; E - 7 cols, 2 1/12, 6/7 between; A - 7 cols, 2 1/12, 6/7 between; C - 9 cols, 1 7/12, 1/6 between.
Published Days: Mon
Avg. Paid Circ.: 5200
Audit Company: Sworn/Estimate/Non-Audited
Audit Date: 43626

LAGRANGE

THE MIDDLEBURY INDEPENDENT

Street Address: PO Box 148

Community Newspapers in the U.S.

City: Lagrange
State: IN
ZIP Code: 46761
General Phone: (260) 463-2166
General Email: advertising@lagrangepublishing.com
Publication Website: http://lagrangepublishing.hosting-bnin.net/openpublish/
Parent Company: LaGrange Publishing, Co.
Publisher Email: publisher@lagrangepublishing.com
Editor Email: editor@lagrangepublishing.com
Advertising Executive Email: advertising@lagrangepublishing.com
Delivery Methods: Mail˙Newsstand˙Racks
Year Established: 1946
Own Printing Facility?: Y
Commercial printers?: Y
Published Days: Wed
Avg. Paid Circ.: 890
Avg. Free Circ.: 44
Audit Company: Sworn/Estimate/Non-Audited
Audit Date: 43626

LAWRENCEBURG

HARRISON PRESS

Street Address: 126 W High St
City: Lawrenceburg
State: IN
ZIP Code: 47025
General Phone: (812) 537-0063
General Email: frontoffice@registerpublications.com
Publication Website: https://www.theharrison-press.com/
Parent Company: Register Publications Group
Publisher Name: April Fritch
Publisher Email: afritch@registerpublications.com
Publisher Phone: (812) 537-0063
Editor Name: Joe Awad
Editor Email: jawad@registerpublications.com
Editor Phone: (812) 537-0063
Advertising Executive Name: Chip Munich
Advertising Executive Email: cmunich@registerpublications.com
Advertising Executive Phone: (812) 537-0063
Delivery Methods: Mail˙Newsstand˙Racks
Year Established: 1928
Own Printing Facility?: Y
Commercial printers?: N
Mechanical specifications: 10.582"x21.0"
Published Days: Wed
Avg. Paid Circ.: 4000
Avg. Free Circ.: 110
Audit Company: Sworn/Estimate/Non-Audited
Audit Date: 43626

LAWRENCEBURG

THE DEARBORN COUNTY REGISTER

Street Address: 126 W High St
City: Lawrenceburg
State: IN
ZIP Code: 47025
General Phone: (812) 537-0063
General Email: frontoffice@registerpublications.com
Publication Website: https://www.thedcregister.com/
Parent Company: Register Publications Group
Publisher Name: April Fritch
Publisher Email: afritch@registerpublications.com
Publisher Phone: (812) 537-0063
Editor Name: Joe Awad
Editor Email: jawad@registerpublications.com
Editor Phone: (812) 537-0063
Advertising Executive Name: Chip Munich
Advertising Executive Email: cmunich@registerpublications.com
Advertising Executive Phone: (812) 537-0063
Year Established: 1841
Mechanical specifications: Type page 14 1/2 x 21; E - 6 cols, 2 3/16, between; A - 6 cols, 2 3/16, between; C - 8 cols, 1 9/16, between.
Published Days: Thur
Avg. Paid Circ.: 6000
Audit Company: Sworn/Estimate/Non-Audited
Audit Date: 43626

LAWRENCEBURG

THE JOURNAL-PRESS

Street Address: 126 W High St
City: Lawrenceburg
State: IN
ZIP Code: 47025
General Phone: (812) 537-0063
General Email: frontoffice@registerpublications.com
Publication Website: https://www.thedcregister.com/
Parent Company: Register Publications Group
Publisher Name: April Fritch
Publisher Email: afritch@registerpublications.com
Publisher Phone: (812) 537-0063
Editor Name: Joe Awad
Editor Email: jawad@registerpublications.com
Editor Phone: (812) 537-0063
Advertising Executive Name: Chip Munich
Advertising Executive Email: cmunich@registerpublications.com
Advertising Executive Phone: (812) 537-0063
Delivery Methods: Mail
Year Established: 1975
Own Printing Facility?: Y
Mechanical specifications: Type page 11 1/2 x 21; E - 6 cols, 2 3/16, between; A - 6 cols, 2 3/16, between; C - 8 cols, 1 9/16, between.
Published Days: Tues
Avg. Paid Circ.: 6300
Audit Company: Sworn/Estimate/Non-Audited
Audit Date: 43626

LOWELL

CEDAR LAKE JOURNAL

Street Address: 116 Clark St
City: Lowell
State: IN
ZIP Code: 46356-1702
General Phone: (219) 696-7711
General Email: pilcherpubco@comcast.net
Own Printing Facility?: Y
Commercial printers?: Y
Mechanical specifications: Type page 15 1/8 x 21; E - 8 cols, 1 3/4, 1/4 between; A - 8 cols, 1 3/4, 1/4 between; C - 8 cols, 1 3/4, 1/4 between.
Published Days: Tues
Avg. Paid Circ.: 1500
Audit Company: Sworn/Estimate/Non-Audited
Audit Date: 43626

LOWELL

LOWELL TRIBUNE

Street Address: PO Box 191
City: Lowell
State: IN
ZIP Code: 46356-0191
General Phone: (219) 696-7711
General Email: pilcherpubco@comcast.net
Delivery Methods: Mail
Own Printing Facility?: Y
Commercial printers?: Y
Mechanical specifications: Type page 15 1/8 x 21; E - 8 cols, 1 3/4, 1/4 between; A - 8 cols, 1 3/4, 1/4 between; C - 8 cols, 1 3/4, 1/4 between.
Published Days: Tues
Avg. Paid Circ.: 4650
Audit Company: Sworn/Estimate/Non-Audited
Audit Date: 43626

MICHIGAN CITY

HARBOR COUNTRY NEWS

Street Address: 422 Franklin St, Suite B
City: Michigan City
State: IN
ZIP Code: 46360
General Phone: (800) 726-5735
General Email: news@harborcountry-news.com
Publication Website: https://www.harborcountry-news.com/
Parent Company: Paxton Media Group, LLC
Publisher Name: Bill Hackney
Publisher Email: bhackney@thenewsdispatch.com
Publisher Phone: (800) 489-9292
Editor Name: David Johnson
Editor Email: djohnson@harborcountry-news.com
Editor Phone: (269) 469-1410
Advertising Executive Name: Isis Cains
Advertising Executive Email: icains@thenewsdispatch.com
Advertising Executive Phone: (800) 489-9292
Delivery Methods: Mail˙Newsstand˙Carrier˙Racks
Year Established: 1984
Own Printing Facility?: Y
Commercial printers?: Y
Mechanical specifications: Type page 10 1/4 x 13; E - 5 cols, between; A - 5 cols, between; C - 7 cols, between.
Published Days: Thur
Avg. Free Circ.: 9200
Audit Company: Sworn/Estimate/Non-Audited
Audit Date: 43626

MIDDLETOWN

THE MIDDLETOWN NEWS

Street Address: 106 N 5th St
City: Middletown
State: IN
ZIP Code: 47356
General Phone: (765) 354-2221
General Email: news@themiddletownnews.com
Publication Website: http://www.themiddletownnews.com/
Publisher Name: Sue Cooper
Publisher Email: sue@themiddletownnews.com
Editor Name: Sue Cooper
Editor Email: sue@themiddletownnews.com
Advertising Executive Email: michael@themiddletownnews.com
Delivery Methods: Mail
Year Established: 1885
Mechanical specifications: Type page 10 x 14; E - 5 cols, 2, between.
Published Days: Thur
Avg. Paid Circ.: 2000
Audit Company: Sworn/Estimate/Non-Audited
Audit Date: 43626

MILFORD

THE MAIL-JOURNAL

Street Address: 206 S Main St
City: Milford
State: IN
ZIP Code: 46542
General Phone: (574) 658-4111
General Email: kschumm@the-papers.com
Publication Website: http://www.the-papers.com/publication.aspx?pub=mailjournal
Parent Company: The Papers Incorporated
Publisher Name: Kip Schumm
Publisher Email: kschumm@the-papers.com
Publisher Phone: (800) 733-4111 ext. 2328
Editor Name: Deb Patterson
Editor Email: dpatterson@the-papers.com
Delivery Methods: Mail˙Newsstand
Year Established: 1888
Own Printing Facility?: Y
Commercial printers?: Y
Mechanical specifications: Type page 13 13/16 x 21 1/2; E - 7 cols, 1 13/16, between; A - 7 cols, 1 13/16, between.
Published Days: Wed
Avg. Paid Circ.: 3000
Audit Company: Sworn/Estimate/Non-Audited
Audit Date: 43626

MILFORD

THE PAPER - KOSCIUSKO EDITION

Street Address: 206 S Main St
City: Milford
State: IN
ZIP Code: 46542
General Phone: (574) 658-4111
General Email: kschumm@the-papers.com
Publication Website: http://www.the-papers.com/publication.aspx?pub=thepaper
Parent Company: The Papers Incorporated
Publisher Name: Kip Schumm
Publisher Email: kschumm@the-papers.com
Publisher Phone: (800) 733-4111 ext. 2328
Editor Name: Deb Patterson
Editor Email: dpatterson@the-papers.com
Delivery Methods: Newsstand˙Carrier
Year Established: 1971
Own Printing Facility?: Y
Commercial printers?: Y
Mechanical specifications: Type page 9 3/4 x 15 3/4.
Published Days: Tues
Avg. Free Circ.: 52641
Audit Company: CVC
Audit Date: 43896

MOUNT VERNON

MOUNT VERNON DEMOCRAT

Street Address: 132 E 2nd St
City: Mount Vernon
State: IN
ZIP Code: 47620
General Phone: (812) 838-4811
General Email: editor@mvdemocrat.com
Publication Website: https://www.mvdemocrat.com/
Editor Email: editor@mvdemocrat.com
Delivery Methods: Mail˙Newsstand˙Racks
Year Established: 1867
Own Printing Facility?: N
Commercial printers?: N
Mechanical specifications: Type page 13 x 21 1/2.
Published Days: Wed
Avg. Paid Circ.: 1500
Avg. Free Circ.: 6100
Audit Company: Sworn/Estimate/Non-Audited
Audit Date: 43626

NEW HARMONY

THE POSEY COUNTY NEWS

Street Address: 641 3rd St
City: New Harmony
State: IN
ZIP Code: 47631
General Phone: (812) 682-3950
General Email: news@poseycountynews.

com
Publication Website: https://poseycountynews.com/
Publisher Name: Dave Pearce
Publisher Email: dpearce263@poseycountynews.com
Editor Name: Theresa Bratcher
Editor Email: news@poseycountynews.com
Advertising Executive Email: office@poseycountynews.com
Advertising Executive Phone: (812) 682-3950
Delivery Methods: Mail
Year Established: 1955
Published Days: Tues
Avg. Paid Circ.: 4500
Audit Company: Sworn/Estimate/Non-Audited
Audit Date: 43626

NORTH VERNON

THE NORTH VERNON SUN

Street Address: 528 E O and M Ave
City: North Vernon
State: IN
ZIP Code: 47265
General Phone: (812) 346-3973
General Email: advertisingpds@northvernon.com
Publication Website: http://plaindealer-sun.com/
Parent Company: North Vernon Plain Dealer & Sun, Inc.
Publisher Name: Barbara King
Publisher Email: bking@northvernon.com
Editor Name: Bryce Mayer
Editor Email: bmayer@northvernon.com
Advertising Executive Name: Sue Ross
Advertising Executive Email: sross@northvernon.com
Delivery Methods: Mail`Newsstand
Year Established: 1872
Own Printing Facility?: Y
Commercial printers?: Y
Mechanical specifications: Type page 13 x 21 1/2; A - 6 cols, 2 1/16, 1/8 between; C - 7 cols, 1 3/4, 1/8 between.
Published Days: Tues
Avg. Paid Circ.: 5000
Avg. Free Circ.: 52
Audit Company: Sworn/Estimate/Non-Audited
Audit Date: 43626

ORLEANS

THE PROGRESS EXAMINER

Street Address: 233 S 2nd St
City: Orleans
State: IN
ZIP Code: 47452-1601
General Phone: (812) 865-3242
General Email: penews@blueriver.net
Delivery Methods: Mail`Newsstand
Year Established: 1879
Mechanical specifications: Type page 13 x 21; E - 6 cols, 2, 1/6 between; A - 6 cols, 2, 1/6 between; C - 6 cols, 2, 1/6 between.
Published Days: Wed
Avg. Paid Circ.: 1684
Avg. Free Circ.: 44
Audit Company: Sworn/Estimate/Non-Audited
Audit Date: 43626

PETERSBURG

THE PRESS-DISPATCH

Street Address: 820 E Poplar St
City: Petersburg
State: IN
ZIP Code: 47567
General Phone: (812) 354-8500
General Email: editor@pressdispatch.net
Publication Website: https://www.pressdispatch.net/#!/
Parent Company: Pike Publishing
Editor Email: editor@pressdispatch.net
Delivery Methods: Mail`Newsstand`Racks
Year Established: 1898
Own Printing Facility?: Y
Commercial printers?: N
Mechanical specifications: Page - 9.75" x 21"
Published Days: Wed
Avg. Paid Circ.: 5000
Audit Company: Sworn/Estimate/Non-Audited
Audit Date: 43626

PLYMOUTH

THE CULVER CITIZEN

Street Address: 214 N Michigan St
City: Plymouth
State: IN
ZIP Code: 46563
General Phone: (574) 936-3101
General Email: webmaster@thepilotnews.com
Publication Website: https://www.thepilotnews.com/
Parent Company: Horizon Publications
Publisher Name: Cindy Stockton
Publisher Email: cstockton@thepilotnews.com
Editor Name: James Master
Editor Email: news@starkecountyleader.com
Editor Phone: (574) 772-2101
Advertising Executive Name: Cindy Stockton
Advertising Executive Email: cstockton@thepilotnews.com
Delivery Methods: Mail`Newsstand`Carrier`Racks
Year Established: 1894
Own Printing Facility?: Y
Commercial printers?: Y
Mechanical specifications: Type page 13 x 21 1/2; E - 6 cols, 2 1/16, 1/8 between; A - 6 cols, 2 1/16, 1/8 between; C - 7 cols, 1 5/8, 1/8 between.
Published Days: Fri
Avg. Paid Circ.: 900
Audit Company: Sworn/Estimate/Non-Audited
Audit Date: 43626

RISING SUN

THE OHIO COUNTY NEWS/RISING SUN RECORDER

Street Address: 235 Main St
City: Rising Sun
State: IN
ZIP Code: 47040
General Phone: (812) 438-2011
General Email: afritch@registerpublications.com
Publication Website: https://www.theohiocountynews.com/
Parent Company: Register Publications Group
Publisher Name: April Fritch
Publisher Email: afritch@registerpublications.com
Publisher Phone: (812) 537-0063
Editor Name: Joe Awad
Editor Email: jawad@registerpublications.com
Editor Phone: (812) 537-0063
Advertising Executive Name: Chip Munich
Advertising Executive Email: cmunich@registerpublications.com
Advertising Executive Phone: (812) 537-0063
Delivery Methods: Mail`Newsstand
Year Established: 1833
Own Printing Facility?: Y
Published Days: Fri
Avg. Paid Circ.: 1700
Audit Company: Sworn/Estimate/Non-Audited
Audit Date: 43626

ROCKPORT

SPENCER COUNTY JOURNAL-DEMOCRAT

Street Address: 541 Main St
City: Rockport
State: IN
ZIP Code: 47635
General Phone: (812) 649-9197
General Email: editor@spencercountyjournal.com
Publication Website: https://www.spencercountyjournal.com/
Parent Company: Landmark Community Newspapers
Delivery Methods: Mail`Newsstand
Year Established: 1855
Published Days: Thur
Avg. Paid Circ.: 5700
Audit Company: Sworn/Estimate/Non-Audited
Audit Date: 43626

ROCKPORT

SPENCER COUNTY LEADER

Street Address: 314 Main Street
City: Rockport
State: IN
ZIP Code: 47635
General Phone: (812) 649-2800
General Email: sclreporter@psci.net
Publication Website: https://www.ferdinandnews.com/
Parent Company: Dubois Spencer Counties Pubishing Co., Inc.
Advertising Executive Email: ads@psci.net
Delivery Methods: Mail`Newsstand`Racks
Year Established: 1960
Own Printing Facility?: Y
Commercial printers?: Y
Mechanical specifications: Type page 13 x 21 1/2; E - 6 cols, 2, 1/4 between.
Published Days: Thur
Avg. Paid Circ.: 2100
Audit Company: Sworn/Estimate/Non-Audited
Audit Date: 43626

ROCKVILLE

PARKE COUNTY SENTINEL

Street Address: 125 W High St
City: Rockville
State: IN
ZIP Code: 47872
General Phone: (765) 569-2033
General Email: knelson@parkecountysentinel.com
Publication Website: https://www.parkecountysentinel.com/
Parent Company: Torch Newspapers, Inc.
Publisher Name: Mary Jo Harney
Editor Name: Larry Bemis
Editor Email: lbemis@parkecountysentinel.com
Advertising Executive Name: Kelly Nelson
Advertising Executive Email: knelson@parkecountysentinel.com
Delivery Methods: Mail
Year Established: 1977
Published Days: Wed
Avg. Paid Circ.: 3500
Avg. Free Circ.: 49
Audit Company: Sworn/Estimate/Non-Audited
Audit Date: 43626

RUSHVILLE

RUSHVILLE REPUBLICAN

Street Address: 315 N Main St
City: Rushville
State: IN
ZIP Code: 46173
General Phone: (765) 932-2222
General Email: aaron.kirchoff@rushvillerepublican.com
Publication Website: https://www.rushvillerepublican.com/
Parent Company: CNHI, LLC
Publisher Name: Laura Welborn
Publisher Email: laura.welborn@indianamediagroup.com
Publisher Phone: (812) 663-3111, ext : 7001
Editor Name: Aaron Kirchoff
Editor Email: aaron.kirchoff@rushvillerepublican.com
Editor Phone: (765) 932-2222, ext : 114
Advertising Executive Name: Marilyn Land
Advertising Executive Email: marilyn.land@rushvillerepublican.com
Advertising Executive Phone: (765) 932-2222, ext : 103
Delivery Methods: Mail`Newsstand`Carrier`Racks
Year Established: 1840
Mechanical specifications: Type page 13 x 21 1/2; E - 6 cols, 2 1/16, 1/8 between; A - 6 cols, 2 1/16, 1/8 between; C - 8 cols, 1 17/32, 1/8 between.
Published Days: Tues`Fri
Weekday Frequency: e
Saturday Frequency: m
Avg. Paid Circ.: 3682
Audit Company: Sworn/Estimate/Non-Audited
Audit Date: 43626
Pressroom Equipment: Lines -- G.;
Mailroom Equipment: Tying Machines -- 2/Bu; Address Machine -- ATT.;
Classified Equipment: Hardware -- APP/Mac SE30, APP/Mac IIsi, APP/Mac ImageWriter; Printers -- APP/Mac LaserWriter;
Classified Software: Baseview/Class Manager, QPS/QuarkXPress 3.0.
Editorial Equipment: Hardware -- 4-APP/Mac; Printers -- APP/Mac LaserPro 630, APP/Mac LaserWriter, APP/Mac LaserWriter Plus
Editorial Software: QPS/QuarkXPress 2.12, Baseview/NewsEdit.
Production Equipment: Hardware -- Caere/OmniPage, Microtek/ScanMaker II Flatbed; Cameras -- 1-Nu
Production Software: QPS/QuarkXPress, Adobe/Photoshop.

SALEM

THE SALEM DEMOCRAT

Street Address: 117-119 East Walnut Street, P.O. Box 506
City: Salem
State: IN
ZIP Code: 47167
General Phone: (812) 883-3281
General Email: rhonda@salemleader.com
Publication Website: http://salemleader.com/
Parent Company: Leader Publishing Company Of Salem, Inc.
Publisher Name: Nancy Grossman
Editor Name: Lana Hamilton
Editor Email: lana@salemleader.com
Delivery Methods: Mail`Newsstand
Year Established: 1827
Published Days: Thur
Avg. Paid Circ.: 6000
Audit Company: Sworn/Estimate/Non-Audited
Audit Date: 43626

SALEM

THE SALEM LEADER

Street Address: 117-119 East Walnut Street, P.O. Box 506
City: Salem
State: IN
ZIP Code: 47167

Community Newspapers in the U.S. — III-233

General Phone: (812) 883-3281
General Email: rhonda@salemleader.com
Publication Website: http://salemleader.com/
Parent Company: Leader Publishing Company Of Salem, Inc.
Publisher Name: Nancy Grossman
Editor Name: Lana Hamilton
Editor Email: lana@salemleader.com
Delivery Methods: Mail`Newsstand
Year Established: 1878
Own Printing Facility?: Y
Commercial printers?: Y
Published Days: Tues
Avg. Paid Circ.: 5800
Avg. Free Circ.: 324
Audit Company: Sworn/Estimate/Non-Audited
Audit Date: 43626

SALEM

YOUR ADVANTAGE

Street Address: 117 E Walnut St
City: Salem
State: IN
ZIP Code: 47167
General Phone: (812) 883-3281
General Email: rhonda@salemleader.com
Publication Website: http://salemleader.com/
Parent Company: Leader Publishing Company Of Salem, Inc.
Publisher Name: Nancy Grossman
Editor Name: Lana Hamilton
Editor Email: lana@salemleader.com
Own Printing Facility?: Y
Commercial printers?: Y
Mechanical specifications: Type page 13 3/4 x 22 3/4; E - 6 cols, 2 1/32, between; A - 6 cols, 2 1/32, between; C - 7 cols, 1 3/4, between.
Published Days: Thur
Avg. Free Circ.: 12400
Audit Company: Sworn/Estimate/Non-Audited
Audit Date: 43626

SCOTTSBURG

THE SCOTT CO. JOURNAL & CHRONICLE

Street Address: 183 E McClain Ave
City: Scottsburg
State: IN
ZIP Code: 47170-1845
General Phone: (812) 752-3171
General Email: sales@gbpnews.com
Delivery Methods: Mail`Racks
Year Established: 1899
Published Days: Sat
Avg. Paid Circ.: 4794
Audit Company: Sworn/Estimate/Non-Audited
Audit Date: 43626

SHOALS

THE SHOALS NEWS

Street Address: 311 High St
City: Shoals
State: IN
ZIP Code: 47581
General Phone: (812) 247-2828
General Email: steve@theshoalsnews.com
Publication Website: http://www.theshoalsnews.com
Publisher Name: Stephen A. Deckard
Publisher Email: steve@theshoalsnews.com
Editor Name: Stephen A. Deckard
Editor Email: steve@theshoalsnews.com
Delivery Methods: Mail`Newsstand
Year Established: 1888
Own Printing Facility?: Y
Mechanical specifications: 6 col. 11p3

Published Days: Wed
Avg. Paid Circ.: 2750
Avg. Free Circ.: 39
Audit Company: Sworn/Estimate/Non-Audited
Audit Date: 43626

SOUTH BEND

TRI-COUNTY NEWS

Street Address: 748 S 28th St
City: South Bend
State: IN
ZIP Code: 46615-2222
General Phone: (574) 232-8590
General Email: admin@tricountynewsinc.com
Delivery Methods: Mail
Mechanical specifications: Type page 10 1/4 x 16.
Published Days: Fri
Avg. Paid Circ.: 1000
Audit Company: Sworn/Estimate/Non-Audited
Audit Date: 43626

SPENCER

THE ELLETTSVILLE JOURNAL

Street Address: 114 E. Franklin St
City: Spencer
State: IN
ZIP Code: 47460
General Phone: (812) 829-2255
General Email: editor@spencereveningworld.com
Publication Website: http://digital.olivesoftware.com/Olive/ODN/EllettsvilleJournal/Default.aspx
Parent Company: Gannett
Publisher Name: Larry Hensley
Editor Email: editor@spencereveningworld.com
Advertising Executive Name: Casey Shively
Advertising Executive Email: cshively@spencereveningworld.com
Advertising Executive Phone: (812) 652-6103
Delivery Methods: Mail`Newsstand`Racks
Year Established: 1939
Published Days: Wed
Avg. Paid Circ.: 1500
Audit Company: Sworn/Estimate/Non-Audited
Audit Date: 43626

TELL CITY

PERRY COUNTY NEWS

Street Address: 537 Main Street
City: Tell City
State: IN
ZIP Code: 47586
General Phone: (812) 547-3424
General Email: publisher@perrycountynews.com
Publication Website: https://www.perrycountynews.com/
Parent Company: Landmark Community Newspapers
Delivery Methods: Mail`Newsstand`Racks
Year Established: 1891
Own Printing Facility?: Y
Commercial printers?: Y
Mechanical specifications: Type page 10.38 x 21
Published Days: Mon`Thur
Avg. Paid Circ.: 6792
Audit Company: Sworn/Estimate/Non-Audited
Audit Date: 43626

TIPTON

LEADER-TRIBUNE REVIEW EAST

City: Tipton
State: IN
ZIP Code: 46072-1864
General Phone: (765) 675-2115
General Email: tiptoneditor@elwoodpublishing.com
Publication Website: https://www.elwoodpublishing.com/
Parent Company: Elwood Publishing Co., Inc.
Publisher Name: Robert Nash
Editor Name: Jackie Henry
Editor Email: tiptoneditor@elwoodpublishing.com
Editor Phone: (765) 675-2115
Advertising Executive Name: Lori Nash
Delivery Methods: Mail`Newsstand`Carrier`Racks
Own Printing Facility?: Y
Commercial printers?: Y
Mechanical specifications: Type page 13 x 21 1/2; E - 6 cols, 2 1/16, 1/8 between; A - 6 cols, 2 1/16, 1/8 between; C - 8 cols, 1 1/2, 1/8 between.
Published Days: Wed
Weekday Frequency: m
Saturday Frequency: m
Avg. Paid Circ.: 5400
Avg. Free Circ.: 5298
Audit Company: Sworn/Estimate/Non-Audited
Audit Date: 43626

TIPTON

LEADER-TRIBUNE REVIEW WEST

City: Tipton
State: IN
ZIP Code: 46072-1864
General Phone: (765) 675-2115
General Email: tiptoneditor@elwoodpublishing.com
Publication Website: https://www.elwoodpublishing.com/
Parent Company: Elwood Publishing Co., Inc.
Publisher Name: Robert Nash
Editor Name: Jackie Henry
Editor Email: tiptoneditor@elwoodpublishing.com
Editor Phone: (765) 675-2115
Advertising Executive Name: Lori Nash
Delivery Methods: Mail`Newsstand`Carrier`Racks
Own Printing Facility?: Y
Commercial printers?: Y
Mechanical specifications: Type page 13 x 21 1/2; E - 6 cols, 2 1/16, 1/8 between; A - 6 cols, 2 1/16, 1/8 between; C - 8 cols, 1 1/2, 1/8 between.
Published Days: Wed
Weekday Frequency: m
Saturday Frequency: m
Avg. Paid Circ.: 5400
Avg. Free Circ.: 5298
Audit Company: Sworn/Estimate/Non-Audited
Audit Date: 43626

VERSAILLES

OSGOOD JOURNAL

Street Address: 115 S. Washington Street, P.O. Box 158
City: Versailles
State: IN
ZIP Code: 47042
General Phone: (812) 689-6364
General Email: publication@ripleynews.com
Publication Website: https://ripleynews.com/
Parent Company: Ripley Publishing
Publisher Name: Linda Chandler
Publisher Email: lchandler@ripleynews.com
Editor Name: Wanda Burnett
Editor Email: wburnett@ripleynews.com
Delivery Methods: Mail
Year Established: 1865
Own Printing Facility?: Y
Mechanical specifications: Type page 14 x 21; E - 6 cols, 2, 1/3 between; A - 6 cols, 2, 1/3 between; C - 8 cols, 1 1/2, 1/3 between.
Published Days: Tues
Avg. Paid Circ.: 5200
Avg. Free Circ.: 48
Audit Company: Sworn/Estimate/Non-Audited
Audit Date: 43626

VERSAILLES

VERSAILLES REPUBLICAN

Street Address: 115 S. Washington Street, P.O. Box 158
City: Versailles
State: IN
ZIP Code: 47042
General Phone: (812) 689-6364
General Email: publication@ripleynews.com
Publication Website: https://ripleynews.com/
Parent Company: Ripley Publishing
Publisher Name: Linda Chandler
Publisher Email: lchandler@ripleynews.com
Editor Name: Wanda Burnett
Editor Email: wburnett@ripleynews.com
Delivery Methods: Mail
Year Established: 1865
Own Printing Facility?: Y
Mechanical specifications: Type page 14 x 21; E - 6 cols, 2, 1/3 between; A - 6 cols, 2, 1/3 between; C - 8 cols, 1 1/2, 1/3 between.
Published Days: Thur
Avg. Paid Circ.: 5200
Avg. Free Circ.: 48
Audit Company: Sworn/Estimate/Non-Audited
Audit Date: 43626

VEVAY

THE SWITZERLAND DEMOCRAT

Street Address: 111 W Market St
City: Vevay
State: IN
ZIP Code: 47043
General Phone: (812) 427-2311
General Email: vevaynews@gmail.com
Publication Website: http://www.vevaynewspapers.com/
Parent Company: Vevay Newspapers, Inc.
Delivery Methods: Mail`Newsstand`Racks
Year Established: 1839
Mechanical specifications: Type page 13 x 21 1/2; E - 6 cols, 2 1/16, 1/8 between; A - 6 cols, 2 1/16, 1/8 between; C - 8 cols, 1 1/2, 1/8 between.
Published Days: Thur
Avg. Paid Circ.: 600
Audit Company: Sworn/Estimate/Non-Audited
Audit Date: 43626

VEVAY

VEVAY REVEILLE-ENTERPRISE

Street Address: 111 W Market St
City: Vevay
State: IN
ZIP Code: 47043
General Phone: (812) 427-2311
General Email: vevaynews@gmail.com
Publication Website: http://www.vevaynewspapers.com/
Parent Company: Vevay Newspapers, Inc.
Delivery Methods: Mail`Newsstand`Racks
Year Established: 1816
Mechanical specifications: Type page 13 x 21 1/2; E - 6 cols, 2 1/16, 1/8 between; A - 6 cols, 2 1/16, 1/8 between; C - 8 cols, 1 1/2, 1/8 between.
Published Days: Thur
Avg. Paid Circ.: 3000
Audit Company: Sworn/Estimate/Non-Audited

WABASH

THE NEWS-JOURNAL

Street Address: 606 N State Road 13
City: Wabash
State: IN
ZIP Code: 46992-7735
General Phone: (260) 982-6383
General Email: mreese@thepaperofwabash.com
Publication Website: https://www.thepaperofwabash.com/
Parent Company: The Paper of Wabash Co. Inc.
Publisher Name: Don L. Hurd
Editor Name: Joseph Slacian
Delivery Methods: Mail
Year Established: 1865
Mechanical specifications: Type page 10 3/8 x 15 1/2; E - 5 cols, 1 15/16, 1/8 between; A - 5 cols, 1 15/16, 1/8 between; C - 5 cols, 1 15/16, 1/8 between.
Published Days: Wed
Avg. Paid Circ.: 2000
Audit Company: Sworn/Estimate/Non-Audited
Audit Date: 43626

WINAMAC

THE PULASKI COUNTY JOURNAL

Street Address: 114 W Main St
City: Winamac
State: IN
ZIP Code: 46996
General Phone: (574) 946-6628
General Email: sales@pulaskijournal.com
Publication Website: http://www.pulaskijournal.com
Parent Company: Winamac Publishers, LLC
Advertising Executive Email: sales@pulaskijournal.com
Delivery Methods: Mail`Newsstand
Year Established: 1859
Mechanical specifications: Type page 10 1/4 x 15 3/4; E - 6 cols, 1 9/16, 1/8 between; A - 6 cols, 1 9/16, 1/8 between; C - 6 cols, 1/8 between.
Published Days: Wed
Avg. Paid Circ.: 3000
Audit Company: Sworn/Estimate/Non-Audited
Audit Date: 43626

ZIONSVILLE

ZIONSVILLE TIMES SENTINEL

Street Address: 250 S Elm St
City: Zionsville
State: IN
ZIP Code: 46077
General Phone: (317) 873-6397
General Email: rick.whiteman@timessentinel.com
Publication Website: https://www.timessentinel.com/
Parent Company: CNHI, LLC
Publisher Name: Beverly Joyce
Publisher Email: beverly.joyce@indianamediagroup.com
Publisher Phone: (765) 482-4650, ext : 121
Advertising Executive Name: Beverly Joyce
Advertising Executive Email: beverly.joyce@indianamediagroup.com
Advertising Executive Phone: (765) 482-4650, ext : 121
Delivery Methods: Mail`Newsstand`Racks
Year Established: 1860
Mechanical specifications: Type page 12 1/2 x 21; E - 6 cols, 1 4/5, 1/8 between; A - 6 cols, 1 4/5, 1/8 between; C - 6 cols, 1 4/5, 1/8 between.
Published Days: Wed

Avg. Paid Circ.: 4300
Audit Company: Sworn/Estimate/Non-Audited
Audit Date: 43626

KANSAS

ALMA

THE WABAUNSEE COUNTY SIGNAL-ENTERPRISE

Street Address: 323 Missouri Ave
City: Alma
State: KS
ZIP Code: 66401-9810
General Phone: (785) 765-3327
General Email: signal@embarqmail.com
Publication Website: http://signal-enterprise.com/
Delivery Methods: Mail`Racks
Year Established: 1884
Mechanical specifications: Type page 10 x 16; E - 5 cols, 2, between; A - 5 cols, 2, between; C - 5 cols, 2, between.
Published Days: Thur
Avg. Paid Circ.: 1300
Avg. Free Circ.: 12
Audit Company: Sworn/Estimate/Non-Audited
Audit Date: 43626

ANDALE

THE CLARION

Street Address: 314 N Main St
City: Andale
State: KS
ZIP Code: 67001-9700
General Phone: (316) 445-2444
General Email: marketingdesk@clarionpaper.com
Publication Website: https://clarionpaper.com/
Parent Company: JOEY YOUNG
Publisher Name: JOEY YOUNG
Editor Name: Lindsey Young
Editor Email: editor@clarionpaper.com
Delivery Methods: Mail`Newsstand`Racks
Own Printing Facility?: N
Commercial printers?: N
Mechanical specifications: Type page 10 1/4 x 16; E - 4 cols, 2 3/8, 1/6 between; A - 4 cols, 2 3/8, 1/6 between; C - 4 cols, 2 3/8, 1/6 between.
Published Days: Thur
Avg. Paid Circ.: 1500
Audit Company: Sworn/Estimate/Non-Audited
Audit Date: 43626
Note: Paper was recently sold to local ownership - Joey and Lindsey Young in June of 2012.

ANTHONY

ANTHONY REPUBLICAN

Street Address: 121 E. Main, P O Box 31
City: Anthony
State: KS
ZIP Code: 67003-2720
General Phone: (620) 842-5129
General Email: anthonyrepublican@att.net
Publication Website: http://www.anthonyrepublicannews.com/
Parent Company: LD Enterprises, Inc
Editor Name: Ross Downing
Delivery Methods: Mail`Racks
Year Established: 1878
Own Printing Facility?: Y
Commercial printers?: Y

Mechanical specifications: Type page 15 x 21 1/2; E - 7 cols, 2, between; A - 7 cols, 2, between; C - 7 cols, 1 2/3, between.
Published Days: Wed
Avg. Paid Circ.: 1900
Audit Company: Sworn/Estimate/Non-Audited
Audit Date: 43626

AUGUSTA

THE BUTLER COUNTY TIMES-GAZETTE

Street Address: 204 E 5th Ave
City: Augusta
State: KS
ZIP Code: 67010-1012
General Phone: (316) 321-1120
General Email: bpeters@butlercountytimesgazette.com
Publication Website: https://www.butlercountytimesgazette.com/
Parent Company: Gannett
Editor Name: Chad Frey
Editor Email: news@butlercountytimesgazette.com
Editor Phone: (316) 804-7728
Advertising Executive Name: Brittani Peters
Advertising Executive Email: bpeters@butlercountytimesgazette.com
Advertising Executive Phone: (316) 321-1120
Delivery Methods: Mail`Newsstand`Carrier
Year Established: 1902
Mechanical specifications: Type page 13 x 21; E - 6 cols, 2 3/4, 1/8 between; A - 6 cols, 2 3/4, 1/8 between; C - 6 cols, 2 3/4, 1/8 between.
Published Days: Tues`Thur`Sat
Weekday Frequency: e
Avg. Paid Circ.: 2247
Audit Company: Sworn/Estimate/Non-Audited
Audit Date: 43626
Pressroom Equipment: Lines -- 1-ATF/Chief 17, 1-ATF/Chief 117; SLN/17x22.;
Mailroom Equipment: Tying Machines -- Bu.;
Business Equipment: IBM, Quickbook
Business Software: NoMads 7.55
Classified Equipment: Hardware -- APP/Mac; Printers -- APP/Mac LaserPrinter;
Classified Software: QPS 3.2.
Editorial Equipment: Hardware -- Mk; Printers -- APP/Mac LaserPrinter.
Editorial Software: QPS 3.2.
Production Equipment: Hardware -- 1-B/MP2; Cameras -- 1-Acti/225.
Note: For printing and production information see the El Dorado Times listing.

BELLE PLAINE

THE BELLE PLAINE NEWS

Street Address: 402 N. Merchant
City: Belle Plaine
State: KS
ZIP Code: 67013-9117
General Phone: (620) 488-2234
General Email: newsbelleplaine@gmail.com
Publication Website: https://www.belleplainenews.com/
Parent Company: Main Street Publishing LLC
Delivery Methods: Mail`Newsstand
Own Printing Facility?: N
Commercial printers?: N
Mechanical specifications: Type page 11.5 x 21.5; E - 6 cols, 2, between; A - 5 cols, 2, between; C - 6 cols, 2, between.
Published Days: Thur
Avg. Paid Circ.: 500
Avg. Free Circ.: 48
Audit Company: Sworn/Estimate/Non-Audited
Audit Date: 43626

BELLE PLAINE

THE BELLE PLAINE NEWS & THE OXFORD REGISTER

Street Address: 217 W 5th Ave
City: Belle Plaine
State: KS
ZIP Code: 67013-9117
General Phone: (620) 488-2234
General Email: newsbelleplaine@gmail.com
Publication Website: https://www.belleplainenews.com/oxford-register
Parent Company: Main Street Publishing LLC
Delivery Methods: Mail`Newsstand
Year Established: 1879
Own Printing Facility?: Y
Commercial printers?: Y
Mechanical specifications: Type page 11.5 x 21.5; E - 6 cols, 1 7/8, 1/6 between; A - 5 cols, 1 7/8, 1/6 between; C - 6 cols, 1 7/8, 1/6 between.
Published Days: Thur
Avg. Paid Circ.: 500
Avg. Free Circ.: 24
Audit Company: Sworn/Estimate/Non-Audited
Audit Date: 43626

BELLEVILLE

THE BELLEVILLE TELESCOPE

Street Address: 1805 N St
City: Belleville
State: KS
ZIP Code: 66935
General Phone: (785) 527-2244
General Email: bellevilletelescope@gmail.com
Publication Website: https://www.thebellevilletelescope.com/
Publisher Name: Fred Arnold
Publisher Email: fred@mcbattascompanies.com
Editor Name: Tiffany Hansen
Editor Email: telescope_editor@hotmail.com
Advertising Executive Email: bellevilletelescope@gmail.com
Delivery Methods: Mail
Own Printing Facility?: Y
Commercial printers?: Y
Mechanical specifications: Type page 16 x 23; E - 6 cols, between.
Published Days: Wed
Avg. Paid Circ.: 3500
Audit Company: Sworn/Estimate/Non-Audited
Audit Date: 43626

BELOIT

BELOIT CALL

Street Address: 119 E Main St
City: Beloit
State: KS
ZIP Code: 67420-3234
General Phone: (785) 738-3537
General Email: beloitcall@nckcn.com
Publication Website: https://www.beloitcall.com/
Delivery Methods: Mail`Carrier`Racks
Published Days: Mon`Wed`Fri
Audit Company: Sworn/Estimate/Non-Audited
Audit Date: 43626

BURLINGTON

COFFEY COUNTY REPUBLICAN

Street Address: 324 Hudson, P.O. Box A
City: Burlington
State: KS
ZIP Code: 66839-1327
General Phone: (620) 364-5325
General Email: repubads1@gmail.com
Publication Website: https://www.

Community Newspapers in the U.S.

coffeycountyonline.com/
Parent Company: Faimon Publications, LLC
Publisher Name: Chris Faimon
Publisher Email: ccrepub@gmail.com
Editor Name: Mark Petterson
Editor Email: ccrepub@gmail.com
Advertising Executive Name: Bradley Rice
Advertising Executive Email: repubads1@gmail.com
Delivery Methods: Mail
Year Established: 1856
Own Printing Facility?: Y
Commercial printers?: Y
Mechanical specifications: Type page 13 x 21; E - 6 cols, 2 1/12, 1/8 between; A - 6 cols, 2 1/12, 1/8 between; C - 6 cols, 2 1/12, 1/8 between.
Published Days: Tues`Fri
Avg. Paid Circ.: 3000
Audit Company: Sworn/Estimate/Non-Audited
Audit Date: 43626

CANEY

MONTGOMERY COUNTY CHRONICLE

Street Address: 202 W. 4th, P.O. Box 186
City: Caney
State: KS
ZIP Code: 67333-1462
General Phone: (620) 879-2156
General Email: chronicle@taylornews.org
Publication Website: https://taylornews.org/newsm
Parent Company: Taylor Newspapers
Publisher Name: Rudy Taylor
Editor Name: Andy Taylor
Advertising Executive Name: Emalee Mikel
Delivery Methods: Mail`Newsstand`Racks
Published Days: Thur
Audit Company: Sworn/Estimate/Non-Audited
Audit Date: 43626

CHAPMAN

CHAPMAN & ENTERPRISE NEWS-TIMES

Street Address: PO Box 469
City: Chapman
State: KS
ZIP Code: 67431
General Phone: (785) 922-6450
General Email: chapmannewstimes@gmail.com
Publication Website: http://www.dickinsonnewstimes.com/
Parent Company: David Parker
Published Days: Thur
Audit Company: Sworn/Estimate/Non-Audited
Audit Date: 43626

CHENEY

TIMES SENTINEL

Street Address: 125 N Main St, P.O. Box 544
City: Cheney
State: KS
ZIP Code: 67025-8844
General Phone: (316) 540-0500
General Email: prhodes@tsnews.com
Publication Website: http://tsnews.com/tsnewswordpress/
Parent Company: Times-Sentinel Newspapers, LLC
Publisher Name: Paul Rhodes
Publisher Email: prhodes@tsnews.com
Editor Name: Travis Mounts
Editor Email: news@tsnews.com
Advertising Executive Name: Paul Rhodes
Advertising Executive Email: prhodes@tsnews.com
Delivery Methods: Mail
Year Established: 1894

Own Printing Facility?: Y
Commercial printers?: Y
Mechanical specifications: Type page 10 1/4 x 16; E - 5 cols, 10 1/4, 1/6 between; A - 5 cols, 10 1/4, 1/6 between; C - 5 cols, 10 1/4, 1/6 between.
Published Days: Thur
Avg. Paid Circ.: 3000
Audit Company: Sworn/Estimate/Non-Audited
Audit Date: 43626

COFFEYVILLE

COFFEYVILLE JOURNAL

Street Address: 716 Maple St
City: Coffeyville
State: KS
ZIP Code: 67337-5829
General Phone: (620) 251-3300
General Email: advertising@cj.kscoxmail.com
Delivery Methods: Mail
Year Established: 1875
Own Printing Facility?: Y
Mechanical specifications: Type page 13 x 21 1/2; E - 6 cols, 2 1/16, 1/8 between; A - 6 cols, 2 1/16, 1/8 between; C - 9 cols, 1 3/8, 1/8 between.
Published Days: Mon`Wed`Fri
Weekday Frequency: m
Avg. Paid Circ.: 4103
Avg. Free Circ.: 10000
Audit Company: Sworn/Estimate/Non-Audited
Audit Date: 43626
Pressroom Equipment: Lines -- 6-HI/Cotrell V-22; Folders -- 1-HI/2:1.;
Mailroom Equipment: Counter Stackers -- HI/RS 25; Tying Machines -- 2/Bu.;
Business Equipment: DPT
Classified Equipment: Hardware -- 1-Hx.;
Editorial Equipment: Hardware -- 2-DEC/PDP 11-34, Hx/Hs 46.
Production Equipment: Hardware -- 2-COM/Universal Videosetter; Cameras -- 1-R/480.

COLUMBUS

COLUMBUS NEWS REPORT

Street Address: 105 S Pennsylvania Ave
City: Columbus
State: KS
ZIP Code: 66725
General Phone: (620) 429-4684
Publication Website: https://www.columbusnews-report.com/
Delivery Methods: Mail
Year Established: 2010
Published Days: Mon`Wed`Fri
Avg. Paid Circ.: 1191
Audit Company: Sworn/Estimate/Non-Audited
Audit Date: 43626
Note: We livestream all city council, county commissioner, school board and sporting events over citylinktv.com-Columbus News Report KS. Channel.

DERBY

DERBY INFORMER

Street Address: 219 E Madison Ave
City: Derby
State: KS
ZIP Code: 67037-1711
General Phone: (316) 788-4006
General Email: mail@derbyinformer.com
Publication Website: http://www.derbyinformer.com/
Parent Company: Jeff Cott
Publisher Name: Jeff Cott
Publisher Email: jeff@derbyinformer.com
Editor Name: Adam Suderman
Editor Email: sports@derbyinformer.com

Advertising Executive Name: Jeff Cott
Advertising Executive Email: jeff@derbyinformer.com
Delivery Methods: Mail`Newsstand`Racks
Year Established: 1998
Mechanical specifications: Call
Published Days: Wed
Avg. Paid Circ.: 2789
Audit Company: Sworn/Estimate/Non-Audited
Audit Date: 43626

DODGE CITY

HIGH PLAINS JOURNAL

Street Address: 1500 E Wyatt Earp Blvd
City: Dodge City
State: KS
ZIP Code: 67801-7001
General Phone: (620) 227-7171
General Email: ads@hpj.com
Publication Website: https://www.hpj.com/
Parent Company: High Plains Pub., Inc.
Publisher Name: Nelson Spencer
Publisher Email: nspencer@hpj.com
Editor Name: Dave Bergmeier
Editor Email: dbergmeier@hpj.com
Editor Phone: (800) 452-7171
Advertising Executive Email: ads@hpj.com
Advertising Executive Phone: (800) 452-7171
Delivery Methods: Mail
Year Established: 1949
Published Days: Mon
Avg. Paid Circ.: 44232
Audit Company: Sworn/Estimate/Non-Audited
Audit Date: 43626

EFFINGHAM

NEWSLEAF

Street Address: 417 MAIN ST
City: Effingham
State: KS
ZIP Code: 66023
General Phone: (913) 833-4180
General Email: cap@thenewsleaf.com
Publication Website: http://www.thenewsleaf.com/
Parent Company: Caplingers, LLC
Editor Name: Steve Caplinger
Delivery Methods: Mail
Published Days: Tues
Audit Company: Sworn/Estimate/Non-Audited
Audit Date: 43626

ELLINWOOD

ELLINWOOD LEADER

Street Address: 105 N Main St
City: Ellinwood
State: KS
ZIP Code: 67526-1639
General Phone: (620) 564-3116
General Email: ellinwoodleader@gmail.com
Publication Website: https://www.mainstreetnewsgroup.com/ellinwoodleader/
Parent Company: Main Street Media, Inc.
Delivery Methods: Mail
Year Established: 1894
Own Printing Facility?: Y
Commercial printers?: Y
Mechanical specifications: Type page 13 x 21; E - 4 cols, 1/2 between; C - 6 cols, 2, 1/8 between.
Published Days: Fri
Avg. Paid Circ.: 1053
Avg. Free Circ.: 613
Audit Company: Sworn/Estimate/Non-Audited
Audit Date: 43626

ELLSWORTH

THE ELLSWORTH COUNTY INDEPENDENT-REPORTER

Street Address: 304 N Douglas Ave
City: Ellsworth
State: KS
ZIP Code: 67439-3218
General Phone: (785) 472-5085
General Email: eciads@yahoo.com
Publication Website: https://www.indyrepnews.com/
"Parent Company: Morris Multimedia, Inc.
"
Publisher Name: Linda Mowery-Denning
Publisher Email: indy@eaglecom.net
Publisher Phone: (785) 472-5085
Editor Name: Linda Mowery-Denning
Editor Email: indy@eaglecom.net
Editor Phone: (785) 472-5085
Advertising Executive Name: Alan Rusch
Advertising Executive Email: eciads@yahoo.com
Advertising Executive Phone: (785) 472-5085
Delivery Methods: Mail`Newsstand`Racks
Year Established: 1999
Published Days: Thur
Avg. Paid Circ.: 2700
Avg. Free Circ.: 45
Audit Company: Sworn/Estimate/Non-Audited
Audit Date: 43626

EUREKA

THE EUREKA HERALD

Street Address: 822 E River St
City: Eureka
State: KS
ZIP Code: 67045-2132
General Phone: (620) 583-5721
General Email: ads@eurekaherald.com
Publication Website: https://www.eurekaherald.com/
Parent Company: Robin Wunderlich
Editor Name: Robin Wunderlich
Editor Email: news@eurekaherald.com
Advertising Executive Name: Jen Thomsen
Advertising Executive Email: ads@eurekaherald.com
Advertising Executive Phone: (620) 583-5721
Delivery Methods: Mail
Year Established: 1868
Published Days: Wed
Avg. Paid Circ.: 2300
Avg. Free Circ.: 40
Audit Company: Sworn/Estimate/Non-Audited
Audit Date: 43626

FRANKFORT

FRANKFORT AREA NEWS

Street Address: 116 E 2nd St
City: Frankfort
State: KS
ZIP Code: 66427-1403
General Phone: (785) 292-4726
General Email: fan@bluevalley.net
Publication Website: https://frankfortareanews.com/
Delivery Methods: Mail`Racks
Year Established: 1991
Published Days: Thur
Avg. Paid Circ.: 700
Audit Company: Sworn/Estimate/Non-Audited
Audit Date: 43626

FREDONIA

WILSON COUNTY CITIZEN

Street Address: 406 N 7th St

City: Fredonia
State: KS
ZIP Code: 66736-1315
General Phone: (620) 378-4415
General Email: news@wilsoncountycitizen.com
Publication Website: http://www.wilsoncountycitizen.com/9634/1705/1/fpvonline-edition
Publisher Name: Joe Relph
Editor Name: Mina DeBerry
Delivery Methods: Mail
Year Established: 1870
Own Printing Facility?: Y
Commercial printers?: Y
Published Days: Mon`Thur
Avg. Paid Circ.: 3000
Avg. Free Circ.: 69
Audit Company: Sworn/Estimate/Non-Audited
Audit Date: 43626

GARDNER

SPRING HILL NEW ERA

Street Address: 936 E Santa Fe St
City: Gardner
State: KS
ZIP Code: 66030-1549
General Phone: (913) 856-7615
General Email: submissions@gardnernews.com
Publication Website: https://gardnernews.com/spring-hill-new-era-ceases-publication/
Published Days: Wed
Avg. Paid Circ.: 2000
Avg. Free Circ.: 10
Audit Company: Sworn/Estimate/Non-Audited
Audit Date: 43626

GARNETT

ANDERSON COUNTY ADVOCATE

Street Address: 117 E 4th Ave
City: Garnett
State: KS
ZIP Code: 66032-1502
General Phone: (785) 448-7000
General Email: garnettadvocate@yahoo.com
Publication Website: https://www.garnett-andersoncountykscommunitynews.com/
Advertising Executive Name: Barbara Thompson
Advertising Executive Phone: (785) 448-7000
Delivery Methods: Newsstand`Racks
Published Days: Fri
Audit Company: Sworn/Estimate/Non-Audited
Audit Date: 43626

HALSTEAD

HARVEY COUNTY INDEPENDENT

Street Address: 220 Main St
City: Halstead
State: KS
ZIP Code: 67056-1913
General Phone: (316) 835-2235
General Email: bruce@harveycountynow.com
Publication Website: https://harveycountynow.com/
Publisher Name: Joey Young
Publisher Email: joey@kspublishingventures.com
Editor Name: Jared Janzen
Editor Email: jared@hcindependent.com
Advertising Executive Name: Bruce Behymer
Advertising Executive Email: bruce@harveycountynow.com
Delivery Methods: Mail
Year Established: 1881

Published Days: Thur
Audit Company: Sworn/Estimate/Non-Audited
Audit Date: 43626

HARPER

HARPER ADVOCATE

Street Address: 907 Central St
City: Harper
State: KS
ZIP Code: 67058-1112
General Phone: (620) 896-7311
General Email: harperadvocate@sbcglobal.net
Delivery Methods: Mail`Newsstand
Year Established: 1882
Own Printing Facility?: N
Commercial printers?: N
Mechanical specifications: 8 col (1.75") x 21"
Published Days: Wed
Avg. Paid Circ.: 1200
Audit Company: Sworn/Estimate/Non-Audited
Audit Date: 43626

HAVEN

RURAL MESSENGER

Street Address: 115 S Kansas St
City: Haven
State: KS
ZIP Code: 67543-9261
General Phone: (620) 465-4636
General Email: malfers@ruralmessenger.com
Publication Website: https://www.ruralmessenger.com/
Publisher Name: Mike Alfers
Publisher Phone: (620) 801-3128
Year Established: 2004
Published Days: Tues
Avg. Free Circ.: 18000
Audit Company: Sworn/Estimate/Non-Audited
Audit Date: 43626

HAYSVILLE

HAYSVILLE SUN-TIMES

Street Address: 325 N Main St
City: Haysville
State: KS
ZIP Code: 67060-1159
General Phone: (316) 524-6868
General Email: graphicsdept@tsnews.com
Publication Website: http://www.tsnews.com/haysvillesuntimes.html
Parent Company: Times-Sentinel Newspapers LLC
Publisher Name: Paul Rhodes
Publisher Email: prhodes@tsnews.com
Editor Name: Travis Mounts
Editor Email: news@tsnews.com
Advertising Executive Name: Paul Rhodes
Advertising Executive Email: prhodes@tsnews.com
Delivery Methods: Mail`Newsstand`Racks
Published Days: Thur
Avg. Paid Circ.: 1100
Audit Company: Sworn/Estimate/Non-Audited
Audit Date: 43626

HERINGTON

THE HERINGTON TIMES

Street Address: 106 N Broadway
City: Herington
State: KS
ZIP Code: 67449-2225
General Phone: (785) 366-6186

General Email: editor@heringtontimes.com
Publication Website: https://www.heringtontimes.com/
Parent Company: Kansas Publishing Ventures
Publisher Name: Kristi Lovett
Publisher Email: editor@heringtontimes.com
Publisher Phone: (785) 366-6186
Delivery Methods: Mail`Racks
Year Established: 1889
Published Days: Thur
Avg. Paid Circ.: 800
Avg. Free Circ.: 50
Audit Company: Sworn/Estimate/Non-Audited
Audit Date: 43626

HESSTON

THE LEDGER

Street Address: 105 N Main St
City: Hesston
State: KS
ZIP Code: 67062-9143
General Phone: (620) 327-4831
General Email: ledg@mtelco.net
Publication Website: https://harveycountynow.com/public/kpv-to-acquire-the-harvey-county-independent-hesston-record
Parent Company: Gannett
Mechanical specifications: Type page 10 1/2 x 16; E - 5 cols, 2, 1/4 between; A - 5 cols, 2, 1/4 between; C - 5 cols, 2, 1/4 between.
Published Days: Thur
Avg. Paid Circ.: 1300
Audit Company: Sworn/Estimate/Non-Audited
Audit Date: 43626

HIAWATHA

HIAWATHA WORLD

Street Address: 607 Utah St
City: Hiawatha
State: KS
ZIP Code: 66434
General Phone: (785) 742-2111
General Email: tony.luke@newspressnow.com
Publication Website: https://www.hiawathaworldonline.com/
Parent Company: News-Press & Gazette Co.
Editor Name: Steve Booher
Editor Email: steve.booher@newspressnow.com
Editor Phone: (816) 271-8583
Delivery Methods: Mail
Year Established: 1908
Own Printing Facility?: Y
Mechanical specifications: Type page 13 x 21; E - 6 cols, 2 1/16, 1/8 between; A - 6 cols, 2 1/16, 1/8 between; C - 6 cols, 2 1/16, 1/8 between.
Published Days: Tues`Fri
Avg. Paid Circ.: 2300
Audit Company: Sworn/Estimate/Non-Audited
Audit Date: 43626

HILLSBORO

HILLSBORO FREE PRESS

Street Address: 116 S Main St
City: Hillsboro
State: KS
ZIP Code: 67063-1526
General Phone: (620) 947-5702
General Email: joey@hillsborofreepress.com
Publication Website: https://www.hillsborofreepress.com/
Parent Company: Kansas Publishing Ventures
Publisher Name: Joey Young
Advertising Executive Name: Natalie

Hoffman
Delivery Methods: Mail`Carrier`Racks
Year Established: 1998
Mechanical specifications: 6 col x 21
Published Days: Wed
Avg. Paid Circ.: 120
Avg. Free Circ.: 7140
Audit Company: Sworn/Estimate/Non-Audited
Audit Date: 43626

HOLTON

THE HOLTON RECORDER

Street Address: 109 W 4th St
City: Holton
State: KS
ZIP Code: 66436-1701
General Phone: (785) 364-3141
General Email: holtonrecorder@giantcomm.net
Publication Website: http://www.holtonrecorder.net/
Publisher Name: David Powls
Publisher Email: holtonrecorder@giantcomm.net
Publisher Phone: (785) 364 3141
Editor Name: David Powls
Editor Email: holtonrecorder@giantcomm.net
Editor Phone: (785) 364 3141
Delivery Methods: Mail`Newsstand`Racks
Year Established: 1867
Own Printing Facility?: Y
Commercial printers?: Y
Mechanical specifications: call for details
Published Days: Mon`Wed
Published Other: Thursday - non-duplicating shopper
Avg. Paid Circ.: 4200
Avg. Free Circ.: 2700
Audit Company: Sworn/Estimate/Non-Audited
Audit Date: 43626

HORTON

HORTON HEADLIGHT

Street Address: 133 W 8th St
City: Horton
State: KS
ZIP Code: 66439-1601
General Phone: (785) 486-2512
General Email: headlight@carsoncomm.com
Publication Website: https://www.cityofhorton.com/businesses.html
Delivery Methods: Mail`Racks
Own Printing Facility?: Y
Commercial printers?: Y
Mechanical specifications: Type page 14 x 21.
Published Days: Thur
Avg. Paid Circ.: 1300
Audit Company: Sworn/Estimate/Non-Audited
Audit Date: 43626

HOXIE

THE SHERIDAN SENTINEL

Street Address: 716 Main St
City: Hoxie
State: KS
ZIP Code: 67740-8800
General Phone: (785) 675-3321
General Email: advertising@sheridansentinel.com
Publication Website: https://www.sheridansentinel.com/
Parent Company: Sheridan Sentinel, LLC
Editor Email: editor@sheridansentinel.com
Advertising Executive Email: advertising@sheridansentinel.com
Delivery Methods: Mail`Newsstand`Racks
Year Established: 42550
Published Days: Thur

Community Newspapers in the U.S.

Avg. Paid Circ.: 800
Avg. Free Circ.: 50
Audit Company: Sworn/Estimate/Non-Audited
Audit Date: 43626
Editorial Equipment: PC
Editorial Software: InDesign & Photoshop

HUGOTON

THE HUGOTON HERMES

Street Address: 522 S Main St
City: Hugoton
State: KS
ZIP Code: 67951-2428
General Phone: (620) 544-4321
General Email: hermes10@pld.com
Publication Website: http://hugotonhermes.com/
Editor Name: RoGlenda Coulter
Editor Email: hermesro@pld.com
Advertising Executive Name: Kay McDaniels
Advertising Executive Email: hermes10@pld.com
Delivery Methods: Mail
Year Established: 1887
Mechanical specifications: Type page 12 3/4 x 20; E - 6 cols, 2, 1/6 between; A - 6 cols, 2, 1/6 between; C - 6 cols, 2, 1/6 between.
Published Days: Thur
Avg. Paid Circ.: 2300
Audit Company: Sworn/Estimate/Non-Audited
Audit Date: 43626

KANSAS CITY

WYANDOTTE COUNTY BUSINESS NEWS

Street Address: PO Box 13235
City: Kansas City
State: KS
ZIP Code: 66113-0235
General Phone: (913) 422-8232
General Email: notices@wyandottecountylegalnews.com
Publication Website: http://www.wybiznews.com/
Parent Company: Lewis Legal News, Inc.
Delivery Methods: Mail`Racks
Published Days: Mon
Audit Company: Sworn/Estimate/Non-Audited
Audit Date: 43626

KANSAS CITY

WYANDOTTE DAILY NEWS WEEKLY PRINT EDITION

Street Address: 2 S 14th St
City: Kansas City
State: KS
ZIP Code: 66102-5041
General Phone: (913) 788-5565
General Email: news@wyandottedaily.com
Publication Website: http://wyandottedaily.com/
Parent Company: TrulyLocal Media
Editor Name: Mary Rupert
Editor Email: maryr@wyandottedaily.com
Delivery Methods: Mail`Newsstand`Carrier`Racks
Year Established: 1968
Published Days: Thur
Avg. Paid Circ.: 1500
Avg. Free Circ.: 10000
Audit Company: Sworn/Estimate/Non-Audited
Audit Date: 43626
Note: Wyandotte Publishing operates TrulyLocal NewzMedia by converging online, print, mobile, email and broadcast channels into an integrated distribution system for news, information and commerce. The CentraMart Network provides local and regional eCommerce capability using a new business strategy for community media.

KINGMAN

KINGMAN LEADER-COURIER

Street Address: 140 N Main St
City: Kingman
State: KS
ZIP Code: 67068
General Phone: (620) 532-3151
General Email: advertise@kcnonline.com
Publication Website: https://www.kcnonline.com/
Publisher Name: Jason Jump
Editor Name: Jason Jump
Advertising Executive Name: Jason Jump
Delivery Methods: Mail`Newsstand
Year Established: 1878
Published Days: Thur
Avg. Paid Circ.: 2400
Avg. Free Circ.: 50
Audit Company: Sworn/Estimate/Non-Audited
Audit Date: 43626

KIOWA

THE KIOWA NEWS

Street Address: 614 Main St
City: Kiowa
State: KS
ZIP Code: 67070-1414
General Phone: (620) 825-4229
General Email: kionews@sctelcom.net
Publication Website: http://kiowanews.com/
Delivery Methods: Mail
Year Established: 1893
Published Days: Wed
Avg. Paid Circ.: 1250
Avg. Free Circ.: 34
Audit Company: Sworn/Estimate/Non-Audited
Audit Date: 43626

LAKIN

THE LAKIN INDEPENDENT

Street Address: 118 N Main St
City: Lakin
State: KS
ZIP Code: 67860-9474
General Phone: (620) 355-6162
General Email: indpndt@pld.com
Publication Website: http://www.lakinindependent.com/
Delivery Methods: Mail`Racks
Year Established: 1885
Published Days: Thur
Avg. Paid Circ.: 1450
Audit Company: Sworn/Estimate/Non-Audited
Audit Date: 43626

LINCOLN

LINCOLN SENTINEL-REPUBLICAN

Street Address: P.O. Box 67
City: Lincoln
State: KS
ZIP Code: 67455
General Phone: (785) 524-4200
General Email: lincolnksads@gmail.com
Publication Website: https://www.lincolnsentinel.com/
Delivery Methods: Mail`Racks
Published Days: Thur
Avg. Paid Circ.: 1750
Avg. Free Circ.: 1750
Audit Company: Sworn/Estimate/Non-Audited

Audit Date: 43626

MANHATTAN

GRASS & GRAIN

Street Address: 1531 Yuma St
City: Manhattan
State: KS
ZIP Code: 66502-4228
General Phone: (785) 539-7558
General Email: agpress2@agpress.com
Publication Website: https://www.grassandgrain.com/
Parent Company: AG Press
Editor Name: Donna Sullivan
Editor Email: gandgeditor@agpress.com
Editor Phone: (785) 539-7558
Advertising Executive Name: Kurtis Geisler
Advertising Executive Email: kurtis@agpress.com
Delivery Methods: Mail
Year Established: 1953
Own Printing Facility?: Y
Commercial printers?: Y
Published Days: Tues
Avg. Paid Circ.: 14000
Audit Company: Sworn/Estimate/Non-Audited
Audit Date: 43626

MARION

MARION COUNTY RECORD

Street Address: 117 S 3rd St
City: Marion
State: KS
ZIP Code: 66861
General Phone: (620) 382-2165
General Email: advertising@marionrecord.com
Publication Website: http://marionrecord.com/
Parent Company: Hoch Publishing Co. Inc.
Publisher Name: Eric Meyer
Publisher Email: eric@marioncountyrecord.com
Editor Name: Mindy Kepfield
Editor Email: mindy@marioncountyrecord.com
Advertising Executive Email: advertising@marioncountyrecord.com
Delivery Methods: Mail`Newsstand`Racks
Year Established: 1869
Own Printing Facility?: N
Commercial printers?: Y
Mechanical specifications: Page size 10.125 x 21 inches
Published Days: Wed
Avg. Paid Circ.: 2700
Avg. Free Circ.: 100
Audit Company: Sworn/Estimate/Non-Audited
Audit Date: 43626
Note: Special combo rates with Hillsboro Star-Journal and Peabody Gazette-Bulletin.

MARYSVILLE

MARYSVILLE ADVOCATE

Street Address: 107 S 9th St
City: Marysville
State: KS
ZIP Code: 66508
General Phone: (785) 562-2317
General Email: skessinger@marysvilleonline.net
Publication Website: http://www.marysvilleonline.net/
Parent Company: Advocate Publishing Co.
Publisher Name: Sarah Kessinger
Publisher Email: skessinger@marysvilleonline.net
Publisher Phone: (785) 562-2317
Editor Name: Sarah Kessinger
Editor Email: skessinger@marysvilleonline.net
Editor Phone: (785) 562-2317
Advertising Executive Name: Wayne Kruse
Advertising Executive Email: akracht@marysvilleonline.net
Advertising Executive Phone: (785) 562-2317
Delivery Methods: Mail`Newsstand`Racks
Year Established: 1885
Own Printing Facility?: N
Commercial printers?: N
Mechanical specifications: Type page 6 x 21.
Published Days: Thur
Weekday Frequency: All day
Avg. Paid Circ.: 3600
Avg. Free Circ.: 100
Audit Company: Sworn/Estimate/Non-Audited
Audit Date: 43626

MEADE

MEADE COUNTY NEWS

Street Address: 105 S Fowler St
City: Meade
State: KS
ZIP Code: 67864
General Phone: (620) 873-2118
General Email: mcnews@mcnewsonline.com
Publication Website: https://mcnewsonline.com/
Delivery Methods: Mail
Year Established: 1885
Own Printing Facility?: Y
Commercial printers?: Y
Published Days: Wed
Avg. Paid Circ.: 1300
Audit Company: Sworn/Estimate/Non-Audited
Audit Date: 43626

MEDICINE LODGE

THE GYP HILL PREMIERE

Street Address: 108 N Main St
City: Medicine Lodge
State: KS
ZIP Code: 67104-1317
General Phone: (620) 886-5654
General Email: rnoland@cyberlodg.com
Publication Website: http://www.gyphillpremiere.com/
Parent Company: Kevin Noland
Publisher Name: Kevin J. Noland
Publisher Email: knoland@cyberlodg.com
Editor Name: Joyce Noland
Editor Email: jnoland@cyberlodg.com
Advertising Executive Name: Ronda Noland
Advertising Executive Email: rnoland@cyberlodg.com
Delivery Methods: Mail
Own Printing Facility?: Y
Commercial printers?: Y
Published Days: Mon
Avg. Paid Circ.: 1200
Audit Company: Sworn/Estimate/Non-Audited
Audit Date: 43626

MINNEAPOLIS

MINNEAPOLIS MESSENGER

Street Address: 108 N Concord St
City: Minneapolis
State: KS
ZIP Code: 67467-2320
General Phone: (785) 392-2129
General Email: submit@mymessengerks.com
Publication Website: http://www.mymessengerks.com/
Delivery Methods: Mail
Mechanical specifications: Type page 13 x 21; E - 6 cols, 2 1/16, 1/6 between; A - 6 cols, 2 1/16, 1/6 between; C - 6 cols, 2 1/16, 1/6 between.

MINNEOLA

CLARK COUNTY GAZETTE

Street Address: PO Box 463
City: Minneola
State: KS
ZIP Code: 67865-0463
General Phone: (620) 339-9217
General Email: gazette@clarkcountygazette.com
Publication Website: https://clarkcountygazette.com/
Parent Company: Meade County News
Delivery Methods: Mail
Published Days: Wed
Audit Company: Sworn/Estimate/Non-Audited
Audit Date: 43626

NESS CITY

NESS COUNTY NEWS

Street Address: 110 S Kansas Ave
City: Ness City
State: KS
ZIP Code: 67560
General Phone: (785) 798-2213
General Email: nessnews@gbta.net
Publication Website: http://nesscountyks.com/
Delivery Methods: Mail
Published Days: Thur
Avg. Paid Circ.: 2200
Avg. Free Circ.: 48
Audit Company: Sworn/Estimate/Non-Audited
Audit Date: 43626

NEWTON

HESSTON RECORD

Street Address: 706 N. Main
City: Newton
State: KS
ZIP Code: 67062-0340
General Phone: 316-281-7899
General Email: ads@hesstonrecord.com
Publication Website: https://harveycountynow.com/public/kpv-to-acquire-the-harvey-county-independent-hesston-record
Parent Company: Kansas Publishing Ventures
Delivery Methods: Mail
Published Days: Thur
Avg. Paid Circ.: 1074
Avg. Free Circ.: 130
Audit Company: Sworn/Estimate/Non-Audited
Audit Date: 43626

OAKLEY

THE OAKLEY GRAPHIC

Street Address: 404 Front Street
City: Oakley
State: KS
ZIP Code: 67748
General Phone: (785) 672-3228
General Email: graphic@st-tel.net
Publication Website: http://kspress.com/viewRecord.php?recid=347
Parent Company: Kansas Press Association
Publisher Name: Anita Gabel
Editor Name: Anita Gabel

Published Days: Thur
Avg. Paid Circ.: 2300
Avg. Free Circ.: 33
Audit Company: Sworn/Estimate/Non-Audited
Audit Date: 43626

OLATHE

LEGAL RECORD

Street Address: 1701 E Cedar St
City: Olathe
State: KS
ZIP Code: 66062
General Phone: (913) 780-5790
General Email: notices@thelegalrecord.net
Publication Website: http://www.thelegalrecord.net/
Parent Company: Lewis Legal News Inc.
Delivery Methods: Mail
Published Days: Tues
Audit Company: Sworn/Estimate/Non-Audited
Audit Date: 43626

OSAGE CITY

THE OSAGE COUNTY HERALD-CHRONICLE

Street Address: 527 Market St
City: Osage City
State: KS
ZIP Code: 66523
General Phone: (785) 528-3511
General Email: ochnews@gmail.com
Publication Website: https://och-c.com/
Advertising Executive Email: ochcads@gmail.com
Delivery Methods: Mail Newsstand Racks
Year Established: 1869
Mechanical specifications: Type page 13 3/4 x 21 1/2; E - 6 cols, 2 1/12, between; A - 6 cols, 2 1/12, between.
Published Days: Thur
Avg. Paid Circ.: 4000
Audit Company: Sworn/Estimate/Non-Audited
Audit Date: 43626

OSKALOOSA

OSKALOOSA INDEPENDENT

Street Address: 607 Delaware St
City: Oskaloosa
State: KS
ZIP Code: 66066
General Phone: (785) 863-2520
General Email: independent@centurylink.net
Publication Website: https://www.jeffcountynews.com/
Parent Company: Davis Publications Inc.
Editor Name: Clarke Davis
Editor Email: independent@centurylink.net
Delivery Methods: Mail Newsstand
Year Established: 1860
Own Printing Facility?: N
Commercial printers?: Y
Published Days: Thur
Avg. Paid Circ.: 1530
Avg. Free Circ.: 29
Audit Company: Sworn/Estimate/Non-Audited
Audit Date: 43626

OSWEGO

LABETTE AVENUE

Street Address: 711 Fourth, P.O Box 269
City: Oswego
State: KS

Advertising Executive Name: Kerri Traynor
Delivery Methods: Mail
Own Printing Facility?: Y
Published Days: Wed
Avg. Paid Circ.: 1200
Audit Company: Sworn/Estimate/Non-Audited
Audit Date: 43626

ZIP Code: 67356-1601
General Phone: (620) 795-2550
General Email: labetteavenue@taylornews.org
Publication Website: https://taylornews.org/newsm
Parent Company: Taylor Newspapers
Publisher Name: Rudy Taylor
Editor Name: Rena Russell
Advertising Executive Name: Emalee Mikel
Delivery Methods: Mail Newsstand Racks
Year Established: 1879
Mechanical specifications: 10.5 x 21
Published Days: Wed
Avg. Paid Circ.: 1865
Avg. Free Circ.: 24
Audit Company: Sworn/Estimate/Non-Audited
Audit Date: 43626

PAOLA

THE MIAMI COUNTY REPUBLIC

Street Address: 121 S Pearl St
City: Paola
State: KS
ZIP Code: 66071
General Phone: (913) 294-2311
General Email: republic@miconew.com
Publication Website: https://www.republic-online.com/
Parent Company: News-Press & Gazette Co.
Publisher Name: Sandy Nelson
Publisher Email: sandy.nelson@miconews.com
Editor Name: Brian McCauley
Editor Email: brian.mccauley@miconews.com
Advertising Executive Name: Teresa Morrow
Advertising Executive Email: teresa.morrow@miconews.com
Delivery Methods: Mail Racks
Year Established: 1866
Mechanical specifications: Type page 11 5/8 x 21; E - 6 cols, 1 5/6, 1/8 between; A - 6 cols, 1 5/6, 1/8 between; C - 6 cols, 1 5/6, 1/8 between.
Published Days: Wed
Avg. Paid Circ.: 5140
Avg. Free Circ.: 10
Audit Company: Sworn/Estimate/Non-Audited
Audit Date: 43626

PARSONS

FARM TALK

Street Address: 1801 S US Highway 59
City: Parsons
State: KS
ZIP Code: 67357
General Phone: (800) 356-8255
General Email: info@farmtalknewspaper.com
Publication Website: https://www.farmtalknewspaper.com/
Parent Company: Farm Talk
Publisher Name: Lance Markley
Publisher Email: lance@farmtalknewspaper.com
Advertising Executive Name: Lance Markley
Advertising Executive Email: lance@farmtalknewspaper.com
Delivery Methods: Mail
Year Established: 1974
Published Days: Wed
Audit Company: Sworn/Estimate/Non-Audited
Audit Date: 43626

PEABODY

PEABODY GAZETTE-BULLETIN

Street Address: 113 N Walnut St
City: Peabody
State: KS

ZIP Code: 66866-1059
General Phone: (620) 382-2165
General Email: social@peabodykansas.com
Publication Website: http://www.peabodykansas.com
Parent Company: Hoch Publishing Co. Inc.
Publisher Name: Eric Meyer
Publisher Email: eric@peabodykansas.com
Editor Name: Mindy Kepfield
Editor Email: mindy@peabodykansas.com
Advertising Executive Email: advertising@peabodykansas.com
Delivery Methods: Mail Newsstand Racks
Published Days: Wed
Avg. Paid Circ.: 1400
Avg. Free Circ.: 9
Audit Company: Sworn/Estimate/Non-Audited
Audit Date: 43626

PLEASANTON

THE LINN COUNTY NEWS

Street Address: 808 Main St
City: Pleasanton
State: KS
ZIP Code: 66075-4077
General Phone: (913) 352-6235
General Email: raquel@linncountynews.net
Publication Website: https://linncountynews.net/
Parent Company: Linn County
Publisher Name: Jackie Taylor
Publisher Email: jackielcn@ckt.net
Publisher Phone: (913) 352-6235
Editor Name: Jackie Taylor
Editor Email: jackielcn@ckt.net
Editor Phone: (913) 352-6235
Delivery Methods: Mail
Published Days: Wed
Avg. Paid Circ.: 2600
Audit Company: Sworn/Estimate/Non-Audited
Audit Date: 43626

PRATT

ST. JOHN NEWS

Street Address: 320 S. Main St.
City: Pratt
State: KS
ZIP Code: 67124
General Phone: (620) 672-5511
General Email: dsattler@gctelegram.com
Publication Website: https://www.sjnewsonline.com/
Publisher Name: Dena Sattler
Publisher Email: dsattler@gctelegram.com
Publisher Phone: (620) 672-5511
Delivery Methods: Mail Newsstand Racks
Year Established: 1878
Mechanical specifications: Type page 13 x 21 1/2; E - 6 cols, 2 1/16, 1/8 between; A - 6 cols, 2 1/16, 1/8 between; C - 6 cols, 2 1/16, 1/8 between.
Published Days: Wed
Avg. Paid Circ.: 700
Avg. Free Circ.: 14
Audit Company: Sworn/Estimate/Non-Audited
Audit Date: 43626

PRATT

THE PRATT TRIBUNE

Street Address: 320 S Main St
City: Pratt
State: KS
ZIP Code: 67124
General Phone: (620) 672-5511
General Email: jstultz@pratttribune.com
Publication Website: https://www.pratttribune.com/
Parent Company: Gannett
Publisher Name: Stephen Wade

Community Newspapers in the U.S.

Publisher Email: stephen.wade@cjonline.com
Publisher Phone: (785) 295-1115
Editor Name: Jennifer Stultz
Editor Email: jstultz@pratttribune.com
Editor Phone: (620) 672-5511
Advertising Executive Name: Kim Smith
Advertising Executive Email: ksmith@pratttribune.com
Advertising Executive Phone: (620) 672-5511
Delivery Methods: Mail`Newsstand`Carrier
Year Established: 1917
Mechanical specifications: Type page 13 3/4 x 21 1/2; E - 6 cols, 2 1/16, 1/8 between; A - 6 cols, 2 1/16, 1/8 between; C - 8 cols, 2 1/16, 1/8 between.
Published Days: Tues`Thur`Sat
Weekday Frequency: e
Avg. Paid Circ.: 2000
Audit Company: Sworn/Estimate/Non-Audited
Audit Date: 43626
Pressroom Equipment: Lines -- 4-G/Community.;
Mailroom Equipment: Tying Machines -- 1/Bu; Address Machine -- 1-/Am.;
Business Equipment: 1-Bs
Classified Equipment: Hardware -- 1-Mk.;
Editorial Equipment: Hardware -- 6-Mk.
Production Equipment: Hardware -- 3-COM; Cameras -- 1-R.

QUINTER

GOVE COUNTY ADVOCATE

Street Address: 304 Main St
City: Quinter
State: KS
ZIP Code: 67752-9526
General Phone: (785) 754-3651
General Email: advocate@ruraltel.net
Publication Website: https://www.mainstreetnewsgroup.com/govecountyadvocate/
Parent Company: Main Street Media, Inc.
Delivery Methods: Mail
Own Printing Facility?: Y
Commercial printers?: Y
Published Days: Wed
Avg. Paid Circ.: 1800
Avg. Free Circ.: 100
Audit Company: Sworn/Estimate/Non-Audited
Audit Date: 43626

RILEY

RILEY COUNTIAN

Street Address: 207 S Broadway St
City: Riley
State: KS
ZIP Code: 66531-9559
General Phone: (785) 485-2290
General Email: countian@twinvalley.net
Publication Website: https://www.rileycountian.com/
Delivery Methods: Mail`Racks
Published Days: Wed
Avg. Paid Circ.: 1200
Audit Company: Sworn/Estimate/Non-Audited
Audit Date: 43626

SABETHA

THE SABETHA HERALD

Street Address: 1024 Main St
City: Sabetha
State: KS
ZIP Code: 66534-1831
General Phone: (785) 284-3300
General Email: advertising@sabethaherald.com
Publication Website: http://www.sabethaherald.com/home/about-us/

Editor Name: Tim Kellenberger
Editor Email: timmy@sabethaherald.com
Advertising Executive Name: Amber Deters
Advertising Executive Email: amber@sabethaherald.com
Delivery Methods: Mail
Year Established: 1884
Mechanical specifications: Type page 13 x 21; E - 6 cols, 2, 1/6 between; A - 6 cols, 2, 1/6 between; C - 6 cols, 2, 1/6 between.
Published Days: Wed
Avg. Paid Circ.: 2542
Avg. Free Circ.: 50
Audit Company: Sworn/Estimate/Non-Audited
Audit Date: 43626

SAINT MARYS

ST. MARYS STAR

Street Address: P.O. Box 190
City: Saint Marys
State: KS
ZIP Code: 66536
General Phone: (785) 430-6323
General Email: thesmstar@gmail.com
Publication Website: https://www.thesmstar.com/
Parent Company: The White Corporation
Editor Email: thesmstar@gmail.com
Delivery Methods: Mail`Racks
Year Established: 1884
Mechanical specifications: 6 column; 21 Inches Long
Published Days: Tues
Avg. Paid Circ.: 1850
Audit Company: Sworn/Estimate/Non-Audited
Audit Date: 43626

SEDAN

PRAIRIE STAR

Street Address: 226 E Main St
City: Sedan
State: KS
ZIP Code: 67361-1629
General Phone: (620) 725-3176
General Email: taylornews@taylornews.org
Publication Website: https://taylornews.org/newsm
Parent Company: Taylor Newspapers
Publisher Name: Rudy Taylor
Editor Name: Jenny Diveley
Advertising Executive Name: Emalee Mikel
Delivery Methods: Mail`Newsstand`Racks
Year Established: 1870
Mechanical specifications: Type page 13 x 21; E - 6 cols, 2, between; A - 6 cols, 2, between; C - 6 cols, 2, between.
Published Days: Wed
Avg. Paid Circ.: 1325
Avg. Free Circ.: 25
Audit Company: Sworn/Estimate/Non-Audited
Audit Date: 43626

SENECA

THE COURIER-TRIBUNE

Street Address: 512 Main St
City: Seneca
State: KS
ZIP Code: 66538
General Phone: (785) 336-2175
General Email: ctseneca@nvcs.com
Publication Website: https://www.couriertribuneonline.com/
Parent Company: Gannett
Delivery Methods: Mail`Carrier`Racks
Year Established: 1863
Mechanical specifications: 6 column 25" broadsheet
Published Days: Wed
Avg. Paid Circ.: 3100

Avg. Free Circ.: 1800
Audit Company: Sworn/Estimate/Non-Audited
Audit Date: 43626

SHAWNEE

SHAWNEE DISPATCH

Street Address: 6301 Pflumm Rd
City: Shawnee
State: KS
ZIP Code: 66216
General Phone: (913) 962-3001
General Email: bwoods@shawneedispatch.com
Publication Website: http://www.shawneedispatch.com/
Parent Company: Ogden Newspapers Inc.
Editor Name: Jennifer Bhargava
Editor Email: jbhargava@shawneedispatch.com
Editor Phone: (913) 962-3001
Advertising Executive Name: Kathleen Johnson
Advertising Executive Email: kjohnson@shawneedispatch.com
Advertising Executive Phone: (785) 832-7223
Delivery Methods: Mail`Carrier`Racks
Year Established: 2003
Published Days: Wed
Avg. Free Circ.: 20108
Audit Company: VAC
Audit Date: 43293

SPEARVILLE

SPEARVILLE NEWS

Street Address: 400 N Main St
City: Spearville
State: KS
ZIP Code: 67876-9501
General Phone: (620) 385-2200
General Email: spnews@ucom.net
Publication Website: http://spearville.fn.net/
Delivery Methods: Mail`Newsstand
Year Established: 1899
Own Printing Facility?: Y
Commercial printers?: Y
Mechanical specifications: Type page 11 1/2 x 17 1/2; E - 5 cols, 2, 1/6 between; A - 5 cols, 2, 1/6 between; C - 5 cols, 2, 1/6 between.
Published Days: Thur
Avg. Paid Circ.: 575
Avg. Free Circ.: 20
Audit Company: Sworn/Estimate/Non-Audited
Audit Date: 43626

STERLING

STERLING BULLETIN

Street Address: 107 N Broadway Ave
City: Sterling
State: KS
ZIP Code: 67579
General Phone: (620) 278-2114
General Email: ads@sterlingbulletin.com
Publication Website: http://sterlingbulletin.net/
Publisher Name: FRANK MERCER
Publisher Email: news@sterlingbulletin.com
Editor Name: Rene Wilson
Editor Email: news@sterlingbulletin.com
Advertising Executive Name: KONI HENDRICKS
Advertising Executive Email: ads@sterlingbulletin.com
Delivery Methods: Mail
Year Established: 1876
Own Printing Facility?: Y
Commercial printers?: N
Mechanical specifications: Type page 13 x 21; E - 6 cols, 2, 1/8 between; A - 6 cols, 2, 1/8 between; C - 6 cols, 2, 1/8 between.

Published Days: Thur
Avg. Paid Circ.: 1000
Avg. Free Circ.: 47
Audit Company: Sworn/Estimate/Non-Audited
Audit Date: 43626

STOCKTON

STOCKTON SENTINEL

Street Address: 414 Main St
City: Stockton
State: KS
ZIP Code: 67669-1930
General Phone: (785) 425-6354
General Email: stkpaper@ruraltel.net
Publication Website: http://www.stocktonsentinel.com/
Publisher Name: Bob Hamilton
Editor Name: Deb Dix
Advertising Executive Name: Bob Hamilton
Delivery Methods: Mail
Year Established: 1989
Published Days: Thur
Avg. Paid Circ.: 1851
Audit Company: Sworn/Estimate/Non-Audited
Audit Date: 43626

SUBLETTE

THE HASKELL COUNTY MONITOR-CHIEF

Street Address: 114 S. Inman St.
City: Sublette
State: KS
ZIP Code: 67877-0700
General Phone: (620) 675-2204
General Email: monitorchief27@gmail.com
Publication Website: http://kspress.com/viewRecord.php?recid=271
Parent Company: Golden Plains Publishing
Publisher Name: Mark Anderson
Editor Name: Kenneth Bell
Advertising Executive Name: Mikayla Blankenship
Delivery Methods: Mail
Year Established: 1891
Own Printing Facility?: Y
Commercial printers?: Y
Mechanical specifications: Type page 14 x 21; E - 6 cols, 2, 1/8 between; A - 6 cols, 2, 1/8 between.
Published Days: Wed
Avg. Paid Circ.: 800
Audit Company: Sworn/Estimate/Non-Audited
Audit Date: 43626

SYRACUSE

THE SYRACUSE JOURNAL

Street Address: 123 N. Main St
City: Syracuse
State: KS
ZIP Code: 67878
General Phone: (620) 384-5640
General Email: sjournal@pld.com
Publication Website: https://thesyracusejournal.com/
Parent Company: Michele Boy
Editor Name: Michele Boy
Delivery Methods: Mail`Racks
Year Established: 1885
Published Days: Wed
Avg. Paid Circ.: 650
Avg. Free Circ.: 17
Audit Company: Sworn/Estimate/Non-Audited
Audit Date: 43626

TONGANOXIE

THE MIRROR

Street Address: P.O. Box 71
City: Tonganoxie
State: KS
ZIP Code: 66086
General Phone: (913) 845-2222
General Email: classifieds@tongnoxiemirror.com
Publication Website: http://www.tonganoxiemirror.com
Parent Company: Ogden Newspapers Inc.
Editor Name: Shawn Linenberger
Editor Email: slinenberger@tonganoxiemirror.com
Advertising Executive Name: Kathleen Johnson
Advertising Executive Email: kjohnson@ljworld.com
Advertising Executive Phone: (785) 832-7223
Delivery Methods: Mail
Year Established: 1882
Mechanical specifications: Type page 11 3/4 x 20 7/8; E - 6 cols, 1 1/6, 1/5 between; A - 6 cols, 1 1/6, 1/5 between; C - 9 cols, 1 1/4, 1/5 between.
Published Days: Wed
Avg. Paid Circ.: 2256
Avg. Free Circ.: 299
Audit Company: Sworn/Estimate/Non-Audited
Audit Date: 43626

TOPEKA

TOPEKA METRO NEWS

Street Address: P.O. Box 1794
City: Topeka
State: KS
ZIP Code: 66612
General Phone: (785) 232-8600
General Email: legal@topekametronews.com
Publication Website: http://www.topekametronews.com
Parent Company: Lewis Legal News, Inc.
Delivery Methods: Mail`Racks
Published Days: Mon
Audit Company: Sworn/Estimate/Non-Audited
Audit Date: 43626

TRIBUNE

GREELEY COUNTY REPUBLICAN

Street Address: 507 Broadway Ave
City: Tribune
State: KS
ZIP Code: 67879
General Phone: (620) 376-4264
General Email: newspaper@sunflowertelco.com
Publication Website: http://gcrnews.com/
Advertising Executive Email: gcrnews@gcrnews.com
Delivery Methods: Mail
Published Days: Wed
Avg. Paid Circ.: 900
Avg. Free Circ.: 14
Audit Company: Sworn/Estimate/Non-Audited
Audit Date: 43626

TURON

THE RECORD

Street Address: 107 S Burns St
City: Turon
State: KS
ZIP Code: 67583-0038
General Phone: (620) 497-6448
General Email: record@sctelcom.net
Parent Company: Media News Group
Publisher Name: Stephen Green
Editor Name: Erin Green
Advertising Executive Name: Erin Green

Delivery Methods: Mail
Own Printing Facility?: Y
Commercial printers?: Y
Published Days: Thur
Avg. Paid Circ.: 550
Avg. Free Circ.: 26
Audit Company: Sworn/Estimate/Non-Audited
Audit Date: 43626

ULYSSES

THE ULYSSES NEWS

Street Address: 218 N Main St
City: Ulysses
State: KS
ZIP Code: 67880
General Phone: (620) 356-1201
General Email: ulynews3@pld.com
Publication Website: https://ulyssesnews.com/
Parent Company: Southwest Kansas Publications Inc.
Publisher Name: Shayla Jaquez
Publisher Email: ulynews2@pld.com
Editor Name: Shayla Jaquez
Editor Email: ulynews2@pld.com
Advertising Executive Name: Alyssa Hammond
Advertising Executive Email: ulynews3@pld.com
Delivery Methods: Mail`Newsstand
Own Printing Facility?: Y
Commercial printers?: Y
Published Days: Thur
Avg. Paid Circ.: 2200
Avg. Free Circ.: 16
Audit Company: Sworn/Estimate/Non-Audited
Audit Date: 43626

VALLEY CENTER

ARK VALLEY NEWS

Street Address: PO Box 120
City: Valley Center
State: KS
ZIP Code: 67147
General Phone: (316) 755-0821
General Email: ads@arkvalleynews.com
Publication Website: http://www.arkvalleynews.com/
Advertising Executive Name: Christie Newman
Advertising Executive Email: ads@arkvalleynews.com
Advertising Executive Phone: (316) 755-0821
Delivery Methods: Mail
Mechanical specifications: Type page 10 1/2 x 16; E - 4 cols, 2 5/12, 1/6 between; A - 4 cols, 2 5/12, 1/6 between; C - 4 cols, 2 5/12, 1/6 between.
Published Days: Thur
Avg. Paid Circ.: 3000
Avg. Free Circ.: 93
Audit Company: Sworn/Estimate/Non-Audited
Audit Date: 43625

VALLEY FALLS

VALLEY FALLS VINDICATOR

Street Address: 416 Broadway St
City: Valley Falls
State: KS
ZIP Code: 66088
General Phone: (785) 945-3257
General Email: vindicator@embarqmail.com
Publication Website: https://www.jeffcountynews.com/category/valley-falls-vindicator/
Parent Company: Davis Publications Inc.
Editor Name: Clarke Davis
Delivery Methods: Mail`Newsstand
Year Established: 1890

Own Printing Facility?: Y
Commercial printers?: Y
Mechanical specifications: Type page 15 1/2 x 21; E - 7 cols, 2 1/12, 1/6 between; A - 7 cols, 2 1/12, 1/6 between.
Published Days: Thur
Avg. Paid Circ.: 1865
Avg. Free Circ.: 35
Audit Company: Sworn/Estimate/Non-Audited
Audit Date: 43626

WAKEENEY

WESTERN KANSAS WORLD

Street Address: 205 N Main St
City: Wakeeney
State: KS
ZIP Code: 67661
General Phone: (785) 743-2155
General Email: westernkansasworld@yahoo.com
Publication Website: https://www.mainstreetnewsgroup.com/westernkansasworld/
Parent Company: Main Street Media, Inc.
Delivery Methods: Mail
Mechanical specifications: Type page 13 1/8 x 21; E - 6 cols, 1 3/4, between; A - 6 cols, 1 3/4, between; C - 8 cols, 1 3/8, between.
Published Days: Thur
Avg. Paid Circ.: 1700
Avg. Free Circ.: 400
Audit Company: Sworn/Estimate/Non-Audited
Audit Date: 43626

WAMEGO

THE WAMEGO TIMES

Street Address: 407 Lincoln Ave
City: Wamego
State: KS
ZIP Code: 66547
General Phone: (785) 456-2602
General Email: office@wamegonews.com
Publication Website: http://www.wamegotimes.com/
Parent Company: Wamego Times
Publisher Name: Ned Seaton
Editor Name: Beth Day
Advertising Executive Name: Shannon Fritz
Advertising Executive Email: advertising@wamegonews.com
Delivery Methods: Mail
Year Established: 1889
Own Printing Facility?: N
Commercial printers?: N
Published Days: Thur
Avg. Paid Circ.: 950
Audit Company: Sworn/Estimate/Non-Audited
Audit Date: 43626

WAMEGO

WAMEGO SMOKE SIGNAL

Street Address: 407 Lincoln Ave
City: Wamego
State: KS
ZIP Code: 66547
General Phone: (785) 456-2602
General Email: office@wamegonews.com
Publication Website: http://www.wamegotimes.com/eedition_smoke_signal/
Parent Company: Wamego Times
Publisher Name: Ned Seaton
Editor Name: Beth Day
Advertising Executive Name: Shannon Fritz
Advertising Executive Email: advertising@wamegonews.com
Delivery Methods: Mail
Published Days: Wed
Avg. Free Circ.: 9823
Audit Company: Sworn/Estimate/Non-

Audited
Audit Date: 43626

WASHINGTON

WASHINGTON COUNTY NEWS

Street Address: P.O. Box 316
City: Washington
State: KS
ZIP Code: 66968-1908
General Phone: (785) 325-2219
General Email: editor@bluevalley.net
Publication Website: https://www.backroadsnews.com
Parent Company: Gannett
Publisher Name: Dan Thalmann
Editor Email: editor@bluevalley.net
Advertising Executive Email: sales@bluevalley.net
Delivery Methods: Mail`Racks
Year Established: 1869
Own Printing Facility?: Y
Commercial printers?: Y
Published Days: Thur
Avg. Paid Circ.: 2300
Avg. Free Circ.: 10
Audit Company: Sworn/Estimate/Non-Audited
Audit Date: 43626

WHITE CITY

THE PRAIRIE POST

Street Address: PO Box 326
City: White City
State: KS
ZIP Code: 66872
General Phone: (785) 349-5516
General Email: ppost@tctelco.net
Publication Website: http://tpp.stparchive.com/
Parent Company: SmallTownPapers, Inc
Delivery Methods: Mail`Newsstand
Year Established: 1993
Own Printing Facility?: N
Commercial printers?: N
Mechanical specifications: Type page 10.5 x 21; E - 5 cols, 2, 1/6 between; A - 5 cols, 2, 1/6 between; C - 5 cols, 2, 1/6 between.
Published Days: Thur
Avg. Paid Circ.: 750
Avg. Free Circ.: 15
Audit Company: Sworn/Estimate/Non-Audited
Audit Date: 43626

WICHITA

WICHITA BUSINESS JOURNAL

Street Address: 121 N Mead St
City: Wichita
State: KS
ZIP Code: 67202
General Phone: (316) 267-6406
General Email: wichita@bizjournals.com
Publication Website: https://www.bizjournals.com/wichita/
Parent Company: American City Business Journals
Publisher Name: John Ek
Publisher Email: jek@bizjournals.com
Editor Name: Bill Roy
Editor Email: broy@bizjournals.com
Editor Phone: (316) 266-6184
Advertising Executive Name: Stacie Myers
Advertising Executive Email: smyers@bizjournals.com
Advertising Executive Phone: (316) 266-6174
Delivery Methods: Mail
Year Established: 1986
Published Days: Fri
Audit Company: Sworn/Estimate/Non-Audited
Audit Date: 43626

Community Newspapers in the U.S.

WINFIELD

COWLEY COURIER TRAVELER

Street Address: PO Box 543
City: Winfield
State: KS
ZIP Code: 67156-0543
General Phone: (620) 221-1050
General Email: daseaton@ctnewsonline.com
Publication Website: ctnewsonline.com
Parent Company: Winfield Publishing Co., Inc.
Publisher Name: David Allen Seaton
Publisher Email: daseaton@ctnewsonline.com
Publisher Phone: 620-442-4200 ext. 122
Advertising Executive Name: Arty Hicks
Advertising Executive Email: advertising1@ctnewsonline.com
Advertising Executive Phone: 620-442-4200 ext. 103
Delivery Methods: Mail
Published Days: Tues`Wed`Thur`Fri`Sat
Weekday Frequency: m
Saturday Frequency: m
Audit Company: Sworn/Estimate/Non-Audited
Audit Date: 43626

O

ATCHISON GLOBE

State: KS
Publication Website: https://www.atchisonglobenow.com
Delivery Methods: Mail`Newsstand`Carrier
Year Established: 1877
Own Printing Facility?: Y
Commercial printers?: Y
Mechanical specifications: Type page 13 x 21 1/2; E - 6 cols, 2 1/16, 1/8 between; A - 6 cols, 2 1/16, 1/8 between; C - 8 cols, 1 1/2, 1/8 between.
Published Days: Wed`Sat
Weekday Frequency: e
Saturday Frequency: m
Avg. Paid Circ.: 3293
Audit Company: Sworn/Estimate/Non-Audited
Audit Date: 43626
Pressroom Equipment: Lines -- 5-HI/V-15A 1977.;
Mailroom Equipment: Tying Machines -- OVL.;
Business Equipment: MIS 486
Business Software: Lotus 1-2-3
Classified Equipment: Hardware -- APP/Mac; Printers -- APP/Mac LaserWriter Plus;
Classified Software: CAMS.
Editorial Equipment: Hardware -- APP/Mac; Printers -- 2-APP/Mac LaserWriter Plus
Editorial Software: Microsoft/Word.
Production Equipment: Hardware -- Nu/UP; Cameras -- SCREEN/Companica 680 C.

KENTUCKY

ALBANY

CLINTON COUNTY NEWS

Street Address: 116 N Washington St, P.O. Box 360
City: Albany
State: KY
ZIP Code: 42602-1302
General Phone: (606) 387-5144
General Email: gpcompany@kih.net
Publication Website: http://clintonnews.net/
Publisher Name: Al Gibson
Editor Name: Al Gibson
Advertising Executive Name: Erika Roe
Delivery Methods: Mail`Newsstand
Year Established: 1949
Published Days: Thur
Avg. Paid Circ.: 3100
Audit Company: Sworn/Estimate/Non-Audited
Audit Date: 43626

ASHLAND

GRAYSON JOURNAL-ENQUIRER

Street Address: 224 17th Street
City: Ashland
State: KY
ZIP Code: 41101-1355
General Phone: (606) 474-5101
General Email: newsroom@journal-times.com
Publication Website: https://www.journal-times.com/
Parent Company: CNHI, LLC
Publisher Email: publisher@journal-times.com
Advertising Executive Name: Sharon Fitzpatrick
Advertising Executive Email: sfitzpatrick@journal-times.com
Delivery Methods: Mail`Newsstand`Racks
Year Established: 1916
Commercial printers?: Y
Mechanical specifications: Type page 9.889 x 21; 6 cols, .111 between
Published Days: Wed
Avg. Paid Circ.: 2700
Avg. Free Circ.: 100
Audit Company: Sworn/Estimate/Non-Audited
Audit Date: 43626

BARBOURVILLE

THE MOUNTAIN ADVOCATE

Street Address: 214 Knox St
City: Barbourville
State: KY
ZIP Code: 40906-1428
General Phone: (606) 546-9225
General Email: advertising@mountainadvocate.com
Publication Website: https://www.nolangroupmedia.com/mountain_advocate/
Parent Company: Nolan Group Media
Publisher Name: Charles Myrick
Editor Name: Charles Myrick
Advertising Executive Name: Tim Terrell
Delivery Methods: Mail
Published Days: Thur
Avg. Paid Circ.: 4200
Avg. Free Circ.: 25
Audit Company: Sworn/Estimate/Non-Audited
Audit Date: 43626

BEATTYVILLE

BEATTYVILLE ENTERPRISE

Street Address: 149 Main Street
City: Beattyville
State: KY
ZIP Code: 41311-7491
General Phone: (606) 464-2444
General Email: thebeattyvilleenterprise@gmail.com
Publication Website: https://www.nolangroupmedia.com/beattyville_enterprise/
Parent Company: Nolan Group Media
Publisher Name: Jessica Butler
Editor Name: Doug Brandenburg
Year Established: 1883
Own Printing Facility?: Y
Published Days: Thur
Avg. Paid Circ.: 4000
Audit Company: Sworn/Estimate/Non-Audited
Audit Date: 43626

BENTON

MARSHALL COUNTY TRIBUNE-COURIER

Street Address: 86A Commerce Blvd
City: Benton
State: KY
ZIP Code: 42025
General Phone: (270) 527-3162
General Email: editor@tribunecourier.com
Publication Website: https://www.tribunecourier.com/
Parent Company: Paxton Media Group, LLC
Publisher Name: Venita Fritz
Publisher Email: vfritz@tribunecourier.com
Editor Name: Rachel Keller Collins
Editor Email: editor@tribunecourier.com

BEREA

THE BEREA CITIZEN

Street Address: 711 Chestnut St
City: Berea
State: KY
ZIP Code: 40403-1916
General Phone: (859) 986-0959
General Email: bereacitizen@windstream.net
Publication Website: https://www.nolangroupmedia.com/berea_citizen/
Parent Company: Nolan Group Media
Publisher Name: Teresa Scenters
Advertising Executive Name: Sheila Johnson
Delivery Methods: Mail`Racks
Mechanical specifications: Type page 13 x 21 1/2; E - 6 cols, 2 1/8, 3/20 between; A - 6 cols, 2 1/8, 3/20 between; C - 6 cols, 2 1/8, 3/20 between.
Published Days: Thur
Avg. Paid Circ.: 4000
Audit Company: Sworn/Estimate/Non-Audited
Audit Date: 43626

BRANDENBURG

THE MEADE COUNTY MESSENGER

Street Address: 138 Broadway St
City: Brandenburg
State: KY
ZIP Code: 40108-1272
General Phone: (270) 422-2155
General Email: mcmeditor@bbtel.com
Publication Website: https://www.meadecountymessenger.com/
Editor Email: mcmeditor@bbtel.com
Advertising Executive Email: mcmads@bbtel.com
Delivery Methods: Mail`Newsstand`Racks
Year Established: 1882
Own Printing Facility?: Y
Commercial printers?: Y
Mechanical specifications: Type page 13 x 25; E - 6 cols, 2, between; A - 6 cols, 2, between; C - 8 cols, 1 1/2, between.
Published Days: Thur
Avg. Paid Circ.: 5460
Avg. Free Circ.: 142
Audit Company: Sworn/Estimate/Non-Audited
Audit Date: 43626

BROOKSVILLE

THE BRACKEN COUNTY NEWS

Street Address: P.O. Box 68 | 216 Frankfort Street
City: Brooksville
State: KY
ZIP Code: 41004-8306
Audited
Audit Date: 43626
General Phone: (606) 735-2198
General Email: brackencountynews@gmail.com
Publication Website: http://thebrackencountynews.com/index.html
Publisher Name: Kathy Bay
Editor Name: Vanessa Ferrell
Advertising Executive Name: Shelly Hargett
Delivery Methods: Mail`Newsstand
Year Established: 1927
Mechanical specifications: Type page 11 5/8 x 21; E - 6 cols, 1/4 between; A - 6 cols, 5/6, 1/4 between; C - 6 cols, 1/4 between.
Published Days: Thur
Avg. Paid Circ.: 3000
Avg. Free Circ.: 114
Audit Company: Sworn/Estimate/Non-Audited
Audit Date: 43626

BROWNSVILLE

EDMONSON NEWS

Street Address: 101 S Main St, PO BOX 94
City: Brownsville
State: KY
ZIP Code: 42210-7233
General Phone: (270) 597-3115
General Email: ednews@windstream.net
Publication Website: https://www.jpinews.com/the-edmonson-news-home/
Parent Company: Jobe Publishing, Inc.
Publisher Name: Jeffrey S. Jobe
Publisher Email: jobe@jobeinc.com
Publisher Phone: (270) 590-6625
Advertising Executive Name: Anissa Meredith
Advertising Executive Email: anissameredith@jpinews.com
Advertising Executive Phone: (270) 786-2676
Delivery Methods: Mail
Own Printing Facility?: Y
Commercial printers?: Y
Published Days: Tues
Avg. Paid Circ.: 4200
Audit Company: Sworn/Estimate/Non-Audited
Audit Date: 43626

BURKESVILLE

CUMBERLAND COUNTY NEWS

Street Address: 412 Courthouse Sq., PO Box 307
City: Burkesville
State: KY
ZIP Code: 42717
General Phone: (270) 864-3891
General Email: ads@burkesville.com
Publication Website: https://www.cumberlandcountynewspaper.com/
Publisher Name: Patsy Judd
Editor Name: Cyndi Pritchett
Editor Email: ccn@burkesville.com
Advertising Executive Name: Kimberly Johnson
Advertising Executive Email: ads@burkesville.com
Delivery Methods: Mail
Mechanical specifications: Type page 13 x 21; E - 6 cols, 2 1/25, 1/6 between; A - 6 cols, 2 1/25, 1/6 between; C - 6 cols, 2 1/25, 1/6 between.
Published Days: Wed
Avg. Paid Circ.: 2900
Audit Company: Sworn/Estimate/Non-Audited
Audit Date: 43626

CALVERT CITY

THE LAKE NEWS

Street Address: 153 E 5th Ave
City: Calvert City
State: KY

ZIP Code: 42029-9998
General Phone: (270) 395-5858
General Email: news@thelakenews.com
Publication Website: https://www.thelakenews.com/
Publisher Name: Loyd W. Ford
Editor Name: Loyd W. Ford
Delivery Methods: Mail`Newsstand`Racks
Year Established: 1984
Published Days: Thur
Audit Company: Sworn/Estimate/Non-Audited
Audit Date: 43626

CENTRAL CITY

CENTRAL CITY LEADER NEWS

Street Address: 1730 W EVERLY BROTHERS BLVD
City: Central City
State: KY
ZIP Code: 42330
General Phone: (270) 754-3000
General Email: advp@ky-leadernews.com
Publication Website: https://ky-leadernews.com/
Parent Company: Andy Anderson Corporation
Publisher Name: Jowanna Band
Publisher Phone: (270) 754-3000
Editor Name: C. Josh Givens
Editor Phone: (270) 754-3000
Advertising Executive Name: Luba Baxter
Advertising Executive Phone: (270) 754-3000
Delivery Methods: Mail`Newsstand`Racks
Published Days: Tues
Audit Company: Sworn/Estimate/Non-Audited
Audit Date: 43626

CENTRAL CITY

THE TIMES-ARGUS

Street Address: 202 W Broad St, P.O. Box 31
City: Central City
State: KY
ZIP Code: 42330-1540
General Phone: (270) 754-2331
General Email: timesargus@bellsouth.net
Publication Website: https://www.timesargus.com/
Parent Company: Brunswick Publishing, LLC
Publisher Name: Mark Stephen Stone
Editor Name: Charlotte Ball
Delivery Methods: Mail
Year Established: 1906
Mechanical specifications: Type page 13 x 21; E - 6 cols, 2, 1/6 between; A - 6 cols, 2, 1/6 between; C - 6 cols, 2, 1/6 between.
Published Days: Wed
Avg. Paid Circ.: 2600
Audit Company: Sworn/Estimate/Non-Audited
Audit Date: 43626

CLAY CITY

THE CLAY CITY TIMES

Street Address: 4477 Main St
City: Clay City
State: KY
ZIP Code: 40380
General Phone: (606) 663-5540
General Email: cctads@hatfieldnewspapers.com
Publication Website: http://www.claycity-times.com/
Parent Company: Hatfield Newspapers Inc.
Publisher Name: Teresa Hatfield-Barger
Publisher Email: teresa@hatfieldnewspapers.com
Editor Name: Cecil Pergram
Advertising Executive Name: Cheyenne Young
Advertising Executive Email: cctads@hatfieldnewspapers.com
Advertising Executive Phone: (606) 723-5161
Delivery Methods: Mail`Newsstand
Year Established: 1899
Published Days: Thur
Avg. Paid Circ.: 3200
Audit Company: Sworn/Estimate/Non-Audited
Audit Date: 43626

CLINTON

THE HICKMAN COUNTY GAZETTE

Street Address: 308 S Washington St
City: Clinton
State: KY
ZIP Code: 42031-1340
General Phone: (270) 653-3381
General Email: gazette3322@bellsouth.net
Publication Website: http://www.hickmancountygazette.com/
Parent Company: Magic Valley Publishing Co., Inc
Publisher Name: Benita Fuzzell
Publisher Email: benita@thecurrent.press
Year Established: 1843
Mechanical specifications: Type page 11 5/8 x 21; E - 6 cols, 1 5/6, 1/8 between; A - 6 cols, 1 5/6, 1/8 between; C - 6 cols, 1 5/6, 1/8 between.
Published Days: Wed
Avg. Paid Circ.: 2000
Avg. Free Circ.: 25
Audit Company: Sworn/Estimate/Non-Audited
Audit Date: 43626

CLINTON

THE HICKMAN COUNTY TIMES

Street Address: 104 S Jefferson St
City: Clinton
State: KY
ZIP Code: 42031-1318
General Phone: (270) 653-4040
General Email: gaye@thehctimes.com
Publication Website: http://thehctimes.com/
Publisher Name: Gaye Bencini
Publisher Email: gaye@thehctimes.com
Delivery Methods: Mail`Racks
Year Established: 2011
Published Days: Tues
Audit Company: Sworn/Estimate/Non-Audited
Audit Date: 43626

COLUMBIA

ADAIR COUNTY COMMUNITY VOICE

Street Address: 316 Public Sq
City: Columbia
State: KY
ZIP Code: 42728-1456
General Phone: (270) 384-9454
General Email: snburton@duo-county.com
Publication Website: https://adairvoice.com/
Publisher Name: Sharon Burton
Publisher Email: snburton@adairvoice.com
Editor Name: Sharon Burton
Editor Email: snburton@adairvoice.com
Delivery Methods: Mail`Newsstand`Racks
Year Established: 1989
Published Days: Thur
Avg. Paid Circ.: 3200
Audit Company: Sworn/Estimate/Non-Audited
Audit Date: 43626

COLUMBIA

ADAIR PROGRESS

Street Address: 98 Grant Ln
City: Columbia
State: KY
ZIP Code: 42728-2233
General Phone: (270) 384-6471
General Email: advertising@adairprogress.com
Publication Website: https://www.adairprogress.com/
Publisher Name: Donna Hancock
Publisher Email: donna@adairprogress.com
Editor Name: Jeff Neagle
Editor Email: jeff@adairprogress.com
Advertising Executive Name: Ann Melton
Advertising Executive Email: advertising@adairprogress.com
Delivery Methods: Mail
Year Established: 1987
Own Printing Facility?: Y
Commercial printers?: Y
Mechanical specifications: Type page 13 x 21; E - 6 cols, 1/4 between; A - 6 cols, 1/4 between; C - 6 cols, 1/4 between.
Published Days: Thur
Avg. Paid Circ.: 4900
Audit Company: Sworn/Estimate/Non-Audited
Audit Date: 43626

CORBIN

NEWS JOURNAL

Street Address: 215 N Main St
City: Corbin
State: KY
ZIP Code: 40701-1451
General Phone: (606) 528-9767
General Email: advertising@corbinnewsjournal.com
Publication Website: https://www.thenewsjournal.net/
Parent Company: AIM Media
Publisher Name: Trent Knuckles
Publisher Email: tknuckles@corbinnewsjournal.com
Editor Name: Mark White
Editor Email: mwhite@corbinnewsjournal.com
Advertising Executive Name: Melissa Hudson
Advertising Executive Email: mhudson@corbinnewsjournal.com
Delivery Methods: Mail`Racks
Year Established: 1908
Own Printing Facility?: Y
Commercial printers?: Y
Mechanical specifications: Type page 11.25 x 21 1/2; 1 col-1.75, 2 col.- 3.56, 3 col. 5.5- 4 col. 7.45, 5 col.- 9.35, 6 col.- 11.25
Published Days: Mon`Thur
Avg. Paid Circ.: 7774
Audit Company: Sworn/Estimate/Non-Audited
Audit Date: 43626

CROMONA

THE LETCHER COUNTY COMMUNITY PRESS

Street Address: P. O. Box 217
City: Cromona
State: KY
ZIP Code: 41810-9000
General Phone: (606) 855-4541
General Email: paul@superiorprinting.org
Publication Website: http://lch.stparchive.com/
Delivery Methods: Mail
Year Established: 1959
Own Printing Facility?: Y
Commercial printers?: Y
Published Days: Wed
Avg. Paid Circ.: 2000
Avg. Free Circ.: 20
Audit Company: Sworn/Estimate/Non-Audited
Audit Date: 43626

DAWSON SPRINGS

THE DAWSON SPRINGS PROGRESS

Street Address: 131 S Main St, P.O. Box 460
City: Dawson Springs
State: KY
ZIP Code: 42408-1745
General Phone: (270) 797-3271
General Email: progress@vci.net
Publication Website: https://www.dawsonspringsprogress.com/
Parent Company: Paxton Media Group, LLC
Editor Name: Melissa Larimore
Editor Email: melissa@dawsonspringsprogress.com
Editor Phone: (270) 797-3271
Advertising Executive Name: Erik Waywood
Advertising Executive Email: ewaywood@dawsonspringsprogress.com
Advertising Executive Phone: (270) 797-3271
Delivery Methods: Mail
Year Established: 1919
Mechanical specifications: Type page 13 x 21; E - 6 cols, 2, 1/6 between; A - 6 cols, 2, 1/6 between; C - 8 cols, 1 5/12, 1/6 between.
Published Days: Wed
Avg. Paid Circ.: 1800
Avg. Free Circ.: 35
Audit Company: Sworn/Estimate/Non-Audited
Audit Date: 43626

EDDYVILLE

THE HERALD-LEDGER

Street Address: 143 W Main St
City: Eddyville
State: KY
ZIP Code: 42038-7762
General Phone: (270) 388-2269
General Email: sales@heraldledger.com
Publication Website: https://www.heraldledger.com/
Parent Company: Paxton Media Group, LLC
Advertising Executive Name: Becky Murphy
Advertising Executive Email: sales@heraldledger.com
Delivery Methods: Mail`Newsstand`Racks
Year Established: 1901
Published Days: Wed
Avg. Paid Circ.: 2000
Audit Company: Sworn/Estimate/Non-Audited
Audit Date: 43626

EDMONTON

THE EDMONTON HERALD-NEWS

Street Address: 116 S MAIN ST
City: Edmonton
State: KY
ZIP Code: 42129
General Phone: (270) 432-3291
General Email: heraldnews@jpinews.com
Publication Website: https://www.jpinews.com/
Parent Company: Jobe Publishing, Inc.
Publisher Name: Jennifer Moonsong
Publisher Email: jupitermoonsong@yahoo.com
Publisher Phone: (270) 670-9233
Advertising Executive Email: print@jpinews.com
Advertising Executive Phone: (270) 786-2676
Delivery Methods: Mail`Newsstand`Racks
Year Established: 1894
Mechanical specifications: Type page 13 x 21; E - 6 cols, 2 1/8, 1/8 between; A - 6 cols, 2 1/8, 1/8 between; C - 6 cols, 2 1/8, 1/8 between.
Published Days: Wed
Avg. Paid Circ.: 2500
Audit Company: Sworn/Estimate/Non-Audited
Audit Date: 43626

Community Newspapers in the U.S.

FALMOUTH

FALMOUTH OUTLOOK

Street Address: 210 Main St, P.O. Box 111
City: Falmouth
State: KY
ZIP Code: 41040-1265
General Phone: (859) 654-3332
General Email: ads@falmouthoutlook.com
Publication Website: https://www.falmouthoutlook.com/
Parent Company: Delphos Herald, Inc.
Publisher Name: Neil Belcher
Editor Name: Keith Smith
Advertising Executive Name: Sarah Tackett
Delivery Methods: Mail`Newsstand`Racks
Year Established: 1907
Own Printing Facility?: N
Commercial printers?: N
Mechanical specifications: 1 col. 1.56 2 col. 3.22 3 col. 4.89 4 col. 6.56 5 col. 8.22 6 col. 9.89
Published Days: Tues
Avg. Paid Circ.: 2244
Avg. Free Circ.: 5200
Audit Company: Sworn/Estimate/Non-Audited
Audit Date: 43626

FLATWOODS

GREENUP COUNTY NEWS-TIMES

Street Address: 1407 Beth Ann Dr
City: Flatwoods
State: KY
ZIP Code: 41139
General Phone: (606) 356-7509
General Email: hank@greenupbeacon.com
Publication Website: http://greenupbeacon.com/
Parent Company: CNHI, LLC
Publisher Name: Hank Bond
Publisher Email: hank@greenupbeacon.com
Editor Name: Hank Bond
Editor Email: hank@greenupbeacon.com
Delivery Methods: Mail`Newsstand
Own Printing Facility?: Y
Commercial printers?: Y
Published Days: Thur
Avg. Paid Circ.: 3600
Audit Company: Sworn/Estimate/Non-Audited
Audit Date: 43626

FORT KNOX

THE GOLD STANDARD

Street Address: 125 Sixth Avenue, Bldg. 1110, 2nd Floor, Wing B, PO Box 1000
City: Fort Knox
State: KY
ZIP Code: 40121-5199
General Phone: (502) 624-1095
General Email: eric.b.pilgrim.civ@mail.mil
Publication Website: https://www.fkgoldstandard.com/
Editor Name: Eric Pilgrim
Editor Email: eric.b.pilgrim.civ@mail.mil
Editor Phone: (502) 624-1095
Delivery Methods: Mail
Published Days: Thur
Audit Company: Sworn/Estimate/Non-Audited
Audit Date: 43626

FORT MITCHELL

BOONE COMMUNITY RECORDER

Street Address: 226 Grandview Dr
City: Fort Mitchell
State: KY
ZIP Code: 41017-2702
General Phone: (859) 578-5501
General Email: jkey@enquirer.com
Publication Website: https://www.cincinnati.com/communities/boone-county/
Editor Name: Jennie Key
Editor Email: jkey@enquirer.com
Delivery Methods: Mail
Year Established: 2001
Published Days: Thur
Avg. Paid Circ.: 15
Avg. Free Circ.: 5907
Audit Company: Sworn/Estimate/Non-Audited
Audit Date: 43626

FORT MITCHELL

CAMPBELL COUNTY RECORDER

Street Address: 654 Highland Ave., Suite 27
City: Fort Mitchell
State: KY
ZIP Code: 41075
General Phone: (859) 283-0404
General Email: kynews@communitypress.com
Publication Website: http://www.communitypress.com/
Delivery Methods: Mail
Year Established: 2001
Published Days: Thur
Avg. Paid Circ.: 1747
Avg. Free Circ.: 7898
Audit Company: Sworn/Estimate/Non-Audited
Audit Date: 43626

FORT MITCHELL

FLORENCE RECORDER

Street Address: 226 Grandview Dr
City: Fort Mitchell
State: KY
ZIP Code: 41017-2702
General Phone: (859) 578-5501
General Email: jkey@enquirer.com
Publication Website: https://www.cincinnati.com/communities/florence/
Editor Name: Jennie Key
Editor Email: jkey@enquirer.com
Delivery Methods: Mail
Year Established: 2001
Published Days: Thur
Avg. Paid Circ.: 1398
Avg. Free Circ.: 13304
Audit Company: Sworn/Estimate/Non-Audited
Audit Date: 43626

FORT MITCHELL

FORT THOMAS RECORDER

Street Address: 226 Grandview Dr
City: Fort Mitchell
State: KY
ZIP Code: 41017-2702
General Phone: (859) 283-0404
General Email: jkey@enquirer.com
Publication Website: https://www.cincinnati.com/communities/ft-thomas/
Editor Name: Jennie Key
Editor Email: jkey@enquirer.com
Delivery Methods: Mail
Year Established: 2001
Published Days: Thur
Avg. Paid Circ.: 1024
Avg. Free Circ.: 4294
Audit Company: Sworn/Estimate/Non-Audited
Audit Date: 43626

FORT MITCHELL

SOUTH KENTON RECORDER

Street Address: 226 Grandview Dr
City: Fort Mitchell
State: KY
ZIP Code: 41017-2702
General Phone: (859) 283-0404
General Email: jkey@enquirer.com
Publication Website: https://www.cincinnati.com/communities/kentoncounty/
Editor Name: Jennie Key
Editor Email: jkey@enquirer.com
Delivery Methods: Mail
Year Established: 2011
Mechanical specifications: Type page 13 x 21 1/2; E - 6 cols, 2, 1/8 between; A - 6 cols, 2, 1/8 between; C - 10 cols, 1 1/4, 1/8 between.
Published Days: Thur
Avg. Paid Circ.: 911
Avg. Free Circ.: 13423
Audit Company: Sworn/Estimate/Non-Audited
Audit Date: 43626

FORT MITCHELL

THE ERLANGER RECORDER

Street Address: 226 Grandview Dr
City: Fort Mitchell
State: KY
ZIP Code: 41017-2702
General Phone: (859) 283-0404
General Email: jkey@enquirer.com
Publication Website: https://www.cincinnati.com/communities/ft-thomas/
Editor Name: Jennie Key
Editor Email: jkey@enquirer.com
Delivery Methods: Mail
Year Established: 2001
Published Days: Thur
Avg. Paid Circ.: 130
Avg. Free Circ.: 7201
Audit Company: Sworn/Estimate/Non-Audited
Audit Date: 43626

FORT MITCHELL

UNION RECORDER

Street Address: 226 Grandview Dr
City: Fort Mitchell
State: KY
ZIP Code: 41017-2702
General Phone: (859) 578-5501
General Email: kynews@communitypress.com
Publication Website: http://www.communitypress.com/
Delivery Methods: Mail
Year Established: 2001
Published Days: Thur
Audit Company: Sworn/Estimate/Non-Audited
Audit Date: 43626

FRANKFORT

KENTUCKY MONTHLY

Street Address: 100 Consumer Ln, PO Box 559
City: Frankfort
State: KY
ZIP Code: 40601-8489
General Phone: (502) 227-0053
General Email: ads@kentuckymonthly.com
Publication Website: http://www.kentuckymonthly.com
Parent Company: Vested Interest Publications, Inc.
Publisher Name: Stephen M. Vest
Publisher Email: steve@kentuckymonthly.com
Editor Name: Stephen M. Vest
Editor Email: steve@kentuckymonthly.com
Delivery Methods: Mail`Newsstand
Year Established: 1998
Published Days: Mthly
Avg. Paid Circ.: 35000
Avg. Free Circ.: 5000
Audit Company: Sworn/Estimate/Non-Audited
Audit Date: 43626

FULTON

THE FULTON LEADER

Street Address: 214 Main St
City: Fulton
State: KY
ZIP Code: 42041
General Phone: (270) 472-1121
General Email: fultonleader@bellsouth.net
Publication Website: https://www.thecurrent.press/about
Parent Company: Magic Valley Publishing Co., Inc
Publisher Name: Benita Fuzzell
Publisher Email: benita@thecurrent.press
Delivery Methods: Mail`Newsstand
Year Established: 1898
Mechanical specifications: Type page 11 5/8 x 21; E - 6 cols, 1 5/6, 1/8 between; A - 6 cols, 1 5/6, 1/8 between; C - 8 cols, 1 1/3, 1/6 between.
Published Days: Wed
Avg. Paid Circ.: 2261
Avg. Free Circ.: 31
Audit Company: Sworn/Estimate/Non-Audited
Audit Date: 43626

GEORGETOWN

GEORGETOWN NEWS-GRAPHIC

Street Address: 1481 Cherry Blossom Way
City: Georgetown
State: KY
ZIP Code: 40324-8953
General Phone: (502) 863-1111
General Email: mscogin@news-graphic.com
Publication Website: http://www.news-graphic.com/
Parent Company: Lancaster Management, Inc.
Publisher Name: Mike Scogin
Publisher Email: mscogin@news-graphic.com
Advertising Executive Name: Sean McDonald
Advertising Executive Email: smcdonald@news-graphic.com
Delivery Methods: Mail`Newsstand`Racks
Year Established: 1867
Own Printing Facility?: Y
Commercial printers?: Y
Published Days: Tues`Thur`Sat
Avg. Paid Circ.: 5780
Avg. Free Circ.: 622
Audit Company: Sworn/Estimate/Non-Audited
Audit Date: 43626

GREENSBURG

GREENSBURG RECORD-HERALD

Street Address: 102 W Court St
City: Greensburg
State: KY
ZIP Code: 42743-1564
General Phone: (270) 932-4381
General Email: advertising@record-herald.com
Publication Website: https://www.record-herald.com/
Publisher Name: Walt Gorin
Publisher Email: waltgorin@aol.com
Editor Name: Tom Mills
Editor Email: news@record-herald.com
Advertising Executive Name: Walt Gorin

Advertising Executive Email: advertising@record-herald.com
Delivery Methods: Mail`Newsstand
Year Established: 1895
Own Printing Facility?: N
Commercial printers?: N
Published Days: Wed
Avg. Paid Circ.: 3500
Avg. Free Circ.: 3300
Audit Company: Sworn/Estimate/Non-Audited
Audit Date: 43626

HARRODSBURG

THE HARRODSBURG HERALD

Street Address: 101 W Broadway St
City: Harrodsburg
State: KY
ZIP Code: 40330-1527
General Phone: (859) 734-2726
General Email: advertising@harrodsburgherald.com
Publication Website: https://www.harrodsburgherald.com/
Publisher Name: April Ellis
Publisher Email: april@harrodsburgherald.com
Publisher Phone: (859) 734-2726, ext : 102
Editor Name: Robert Moore
Editor Email: rmoore@harrodsburgherald.com
Editor Phone: (859) 734-2726, ext : 111
Advertising Executive Name: Stacy Baker
Advertising Executive Email: sbaker@harrodsburgherald.com
Advertising Executive Phone: (859) 734-2726, ext : 109
Delivery Methods: Mail
Year Established: 1884
Own Printing Facility?: Y
Commercial printers?: Y
Mechanical specifications: Type page 11 1/2 x 21 1/2; E - 6 cols, 1 3/4, 1/4 between; A - 6 cols, 1 3/4, 1/4 between; C - 8 cols, 1 1/4, 1/4 between.
Published Days: Thur
Avg. Paid Circ.: 3326
Audit Company: Sworn/Estimate/Non-Audited
Audit Date: 43626

HARTFORD

THE OHIO COUNTY TIMES

Street Address: 314 S Main St
City: Hartford
State: KY
ZIP Code: 42347-1129
General Phone: (270) 298-7100
General Email: ads@octimesnews.com
Publication Website: https://www.octimesnews.com/
Parent Company: Andy Anderson Corporation
Editor Name: Dana Brantley
Editor Email: editor@octimesnews.com
Advertising Executive Name: Sarah Carroll
Advertising Executive Email: ads@octimesnews.com
Delivery Methods: Mail`Newsstand`Racks
Own Printing Facility?: Y
Commercial printers?: Y
Published Days: Thur
Avg. Paid Circ.: 6700
Avg. Free Circ.: 75
Audit Company: Sworn/Estimate/Non-Audited
Audit Date: 43626

HAWESVILLE

THE HANCOCK CLARION

Street Address: 230 Main St
City: Hawesville
State: KY
ZIP Code: 42348-2626
General Phone: (270) 927-6945
General Email: hancockclarion@bellsouth.net
Publication Website: https://www.hancockclarion.com/
Publisher Name: Donn K. Wimmer
Publisher Email: hancockclarion@gmail.com
Publisher Phone: (270) 927-6945
Editor Name: Dave Taylor
Editor Email: dave.hancockclarion@gmail.com
Editor Phone: (270) 927-6945
Advertising Executive Name: Ralph Dickerson
Advertising Executive Email: ralph.hancockclarion@gmail.com
Advertising Executive Phone: (270) 927-6945
Delivery Methods: Mail
Year Established: 1893
Mechanical specifications: Type page 11 5/8 x 21; E - 6 cols, 1 7/8, 1/6 between; A - 6 cols, 1 7/8, 1/6 between; C - 6 cols, 1 7/8, 1/6 between.
Published Days: Thur
Avg. Paid Circ.: 3683
Audit Company: Sworn/Estimate/Non-Audited
Audit Date: 43626

HAZARD

THE HAZARD HERALD

Street Address: 439 High St
City: Hazard
State: KY
ZIP Code: 41701-1701
General Phone: (606) 436-5771
General Email: bskeens@hazard-herald.com
Publication Website: https://www.hazard-herald.com/
Parent Company: Lancaster Management, Inc.
Publisher Name: Joshua Byers
Editor Name: Cris Ritchie
Delivery Methods: Mail`Newsstand`Racks
Year Established: 1911
Mechanical specifications: Type page 13 x 21 1/2; E - 6 cols, 2 1/12, 5/8 between; A - 6 cols, 2 1/12, between; C - 6 cols, 2 1/12, between.
Published Days: Thur
Avg. Paid Circ.: 4000
Audit Company: Sworn/Estimate/Non-Audited
Audit Date: 43626

HINDMAN

TROUBLESOME CREEK TIMES

Street Address: 27 Main St E
City: Hindman
State: KY
ZIP Code: 41822-9998
General Phone: (606) 785-5134
General Email: shall@troublesomecreektimes.com
Publication Website: http://troublesomecreektimes.com/
Parent Company: Knott County Publishing Co., Inc.
Delivery Methods: Mail`Newsstand`Carrier`Racks
Year Established: 1980
Mechanical specifications: Type page 10 x 21 1/2; E - 6 cols, 1.53, 1/6 between; A - 6 cols, 1.53, 1/6 between; C - 6 cols, 1.53, 1/6 between.
Published Days: Thur
Avg. Paid Circ.: 4000
Avg. Free Circ.: 250
Audit Company: Sworn/Estimate/Non-Audited
Audit Date: 43626

HOPKINSVILLE

EAGLE POST

Street Address: 1618 E 9th St
City: Hopkinsville
State: KY
ZIP Code: 42240-4430
General Phone: (270) 887-3241
General Email: ads@kentuckynewera.com
Publication Website: https://www.kentuckynewera.com/ep/
Parent Company: Paxton Media Group, LLC
Publisher Name: Taylor W. Hayes
Editor Name: Jon Russelburg
Editor Email: jrusselburg@kentuckynewera.com
Editor Phone: (270) 887-3241
Advertising Executive Name: Richard Wimsatt
Advertising Executive Email: ads@kentuckynewera.com
Advertising Executive Phone: (270) 887-3275
Delivery Methods: Mail`Carrier`Racks
Year Established: 2008
Published Days: Wed
Avg. Paid Circ.: 5490
Avg. Free Circ.: 12000
Audit Company: Sworn/Estimate/Non-Audited
Audit Date: 43626

HORSE CAVE

HART COUNTY NEWS HERALD

Street Address: 570 S Dixie St
City: Horse Cave
State: KY
ZIP Code: 42749-1253
General Phone: (270) 786-2676
General Email: print@jpinews.com
Publication Website: https://www.jpinews.com/
Parent Company: Jobe Publishing, Inc.
Publisher Name: Jeffrey S. Jobe
Publisher Email: jobe@jobeinc.com
Publisher Phone: (270) 590-6625
Advertising Executive Email: print@jpinews.com
Advertising Executive Phone: (270) 786-2676
Delivery Methods: Mail`Newsstand`Racks
Own Printing Facility?: Y
Commercial printers?: Y
Mechanical specifications: Type page 12 7/8 x 21 1/2; E - 8 cols, 1 1/2, 1/6 between; A - 8 cols, 1 1/2, 1/6 between; C - 8 cols, 1 1/2, 1/6 between.
Published Days: Thur
Avg. Paid Circ.: 8000
Avg. Free Circ.: 4000
Audit Company: Sworn/Estimate/Non-Audited
Audit Date: 43626

IRVINE

CITIZEN VOICE & TIMES

Street Address: 108 S Court St, P.O. Box 660
City: Irvine
State: KY
ZIP Code: 40336-1079
General Phone: (606) 723-5161
General Email: cvtads@windstream.net
Publication Website: http://www.cvt-news.com/
Parent Company: Hatfield Newspapers Inc.
Publisher Name: Teresa Hatfield-Barger
Publisher Email: teresa@hatfieldnewspapers.com
Editor Name: Lisa Bicknell
Editor Email: lisa@hatfieldnewspapers.com
Advertising Executive Name: Cheyenne Young
Advertising Executive Email: cvtads@windstream.net
Advertising Executive Phone: (606) 723-5161
Delivery Methods: Mail`Newsstand
Year Established: 1973
Published Days: Thur
Avg. Paid Circ.: 3600

Audit Company: Sworn/Estimate/Non-Audited
Audit Date: 43626

JACKSON

JACKSON TIMES-VOICE

Street Address: 22 Howell Lane
City: Jackson
State: KY
ZIP Code: 41339-1036
General Phone: (606) 666-2451
General Email: advertising@jacksontimesky.com
Publication Website: https://www.nolangroupmedia.com/jackson_times_voice/
Parent Company: Nolan Group Media
Editor Name: Fletcher Long
Advertising Executive Name: Cheryl Campbell
Delivery Methods: Mail`Newsstand
Year Established: 1893
Mechanical specifications: Type page 6 x 21; E - 6 cols, between; A - 6 cols, between.
Published Days: Wed
Avg. Paid Circ.: 4000
Audit Company: Sworn/Estimate/Non-Audited
Audit Date: 43626

LANCASTER

GARRARD CENTRAL RECORD

Street Address: 106 Richmond St, P.O. Box 800
City: Lancaster
State: KY
ZIP Code: 40444-1158
General Phone: (859) 792-2831
General Email: ads@garrardcentralrecord.com
Publication Website: http://garrardcentralrecord.com/
Publisher Name: Ted Cox
Editor Name: Ted Cox
Delivery Methods: Mail`Newsstand`Racks
Year Established: 1889
Mechanical specifications: Type page 13 x 21; E - 6 cols, 2 1/12, 1/8 between; A - 6 cols, 2 1/12, 1/8 between; C - 8 cols, 1 3/8, 1/8 between.
Published Days: Thur
Avg. Paid Circ.: 3993
Avg. Free Circ.: 95
Audit Company: Sworn/Estimate/Non-Audited
Audit Date: 43626

LEITCHFIELD

THE RECORD

Street Address: 20 Public Square
City: Leitchfield
State: KY
ZIP Code: 42754-5816
General Phone: (270) 259-6061
General Email: circulation@graysonrecord.com
Publication Website: https://www.graysonrecord.com/
Parent Company: Media News Group
Publisher Name: Rebecca Morris
Publisher Email: rmorris@graysonrecord.com
Editor Name: Rebecca Morris
Editor Email: rmorris@graysonrecord.com
Advertising Executive Name: Michaela Priddy
Advertising Executive Email: mpriddy@graysonrecord.com
Delivery Methods: Mail`Racks
Year Established: 1980
Published Days: Thur
Avg. Paid Circ.: 3167

Community Newspapers in the U.S.

III-245

Avg. Free Circ.: 6
Audit Company: Sworn/Estimate/Non-Audited
Audit Date: 43626

LONDON

THE SENTINEL-ECHO

Street Address: 123 W 5th St
City: London
State: KY
ZIP Code: 40741-1837
General Phone: (606) 878-7400
General Email: advertising@sentinel-echo.com
Publication Website: https://www.sentinel-echo.com/
Parent Company: CNHI, LLC
Publisher Name: Mark Walker
Publisher Email: mwalker@sentinel-echo.com
Editor Name: Erin Cox
Editor Email: editor@sentinel-echo.com
Advertising Executive Email: advertising@sentinel-echo.com
Delivery Methods: Mail
Year Established: 1873
Mechanical specifications: Type page 11 5/8 x 21 1/2; E - 6 cols, 1 13/16, 1/8 between; A - 6 cols, 1 13/16, 1/8 between; C - 9 cols, 1 1/8, 1/16 between.
Published Days: Mon`Wed`Fri
Avg. Paid Circ.: 9800
Avg. Free Circ.: 10000
Audit Company: Sworn/Estimate/Non-Audited
Audit Date: 43626

LOUISA

THE BIG SANDY NEWS

Street Address: PO Box 766
City: Louisa
State: KY
ZIP Code: 41230-0766
General Phone: (606) 638-4581
General Email: bcrum@bigsandynews.com
Publication Website: http://www.bigsandynews.com/
Publisher Name: Melissa Mitchell
Delivery Methods: Mail
Year Established: 1885
Mechanical specifications: Type page 11 1/2 x 21 1/4; E - 6 cols, 1 13/16, between; A - 6 cols, 1 13/16, between; C - 10 cols, 1 1/16, between.
Published Days: Wed
Avg. Paid Circ.: 12000
Audit Company: Sworn/Estimate/Non-Audited
Audit Date: 43626

LOUISVILLE

LOUISVILLE BUSINESS FIRST

Street Address: 462 S 4th St
City: Louisville
State: KY
ZIP Code: 40202-4403
General Phone: (502) 583-1731
General Email: louisville@bizjournals.com
Publication Website: https://www.bizjournals.com/louisville/
Parent Company: American City Business Journals
Publisher Name: Lisa Benson
Publisher Email: lisabenson@bizjournals.com
Publisher Phone: (502) 498-1958
Editor Name: Jason Thomas
Editor Email: jthomas@bizjournals.com
Editor Phone: (502) 498-1968
Advertising Executive Name: Doug James
Advertising Executive Email: djames@bizjournals.com

Advertising Executive Phone: (502) 498-1970
Delivery Methods: Mail
Year Established: 1984
Published Days: Fri
Avg. Paid Circ.: 9749
Audit Company: AAM
Audit Date: 43983

LOUISVILLE

THE VOICE-TRIBUNE

Street Address: 735 E. Main St.
City: Louisville
State: KY
ZIP Code: 40202
General Phone: (502) 897-8900
General Email: smitchell@voice-tribune.com
Publication Website: https://voice-tribune.com/
Parent Company: Red Pin Media Co
Publisher Name: Janice Carter Levitch
Publisher Email: janice@redpinmedia.com
Editor Name: Mariah Kline
Editor Email: mkline@redpinmedia.com
Advertising Executive Name: Eric Clark
Advertising Executive Email: eclark@redpinmedia.com
Delivery Methods: Mail`Racks
Year Established: 1987
Published Days: Thur
Avg. Paid Circ.: 11587
Avg. Free Circ.: 1850
Audit Company: Sworn/Estimate/Non-Audited
Audit Date: 43626

MANCHESTER

THE MANCHESTER ENTERPRISE

Street Address: 103 3rd St
City: Manchester
State: KY
ZIP Code: 40962-1119
General Phone: (606) 598-2319
General Email: mhoskins@themanchesterenterprise.com
Publication Website: https://www.nolangroupmedia.com/manchester_enterprise/
Parent Company: Nolan Group Media
Editor Name: Mark Hoskins
Editor Email: mhoskins@themanchesterenterprise.com
Advertising Executive Name: Jessica Bowling
Advertising Executive Email: jbowling@themanchesterenterprise.com
Own Printing Facility?: Y
Commercial printers?: Y
Published Days: Thur
Avg. Paid Circ.: 6500
Audit Company: Sworn/Estimate/Non-Audited
Audit Date: 43626

MARION

THE CRITTENDEN PRESS

Street Address: 125 E Bellville St
City: Marion
State: KY
ZIP Code: 42064-1409
General Phone: (270) 965-3191
General Email: advertising@the-press.com
Publication Website: http://crittendenpress.blogspot.com/
Publisher Name: Chris Evans
Publisher Email: evans@the-press.com
Editor Name: Chris Evans
Editor Email: evans@the-press.com
Advertising Executive Name: Allison Mick-Evans
Advertising Executive Email: advertising@the-press.com
Delivery Methods: Mail

Own Printing Facility?: Y
Commercial printers?: Y
Mechanical specifications: Type page 13 1/4 x 21 1/2; E - 6 cols, 2, 1/6 between; A - 6 cols, 2, 1/6 between; C - 8 cols, 1 1/2, 1/6 between.
Published Days: Thur
Avg. Paid Circ.: 3800
Avg. Free Circ.: 64
Audit Company: Sworn/Estimate/Non-Audited
Audit Date: 43626

MC KEE

JACKSON COUNTY SUN

Street Address: 101 Main St, PO Box 130
City: Mc Kee
State: KY
ZIP Code: 40447
General Phone: (606) 287-7197
General Email: jcsunad@prtcnet.org
Publication Website: https://www.nolangroupmedia.com/jackson_county_sun/
Parent Company: Nolan Group Media
Publisher Name: Carmen Abner
Delivery Methods: Mail
Year Established: 1926
Mechanical specifications: Type page 13 x 21 1/2; E - 6 cols, between; A - 6 cols, between; C - 6 cols, between.
Published Days: Thur
Avg. Paid Circ.: 4050
Audit Company: Sworn/Estimate/Non-Audited
Audit Date: 43626

MONTICELLO

THE WAYNE COUNTY OUTLOOK

Street Address: 45 E Columbia Ave
City: Monticello
State: KY
ZIP Code: 42633-1293
General Phone: (606) 348-3338
General Email: advertising@wcoutlook.com
Publication Website: https://www.wcoutlook.com/
Parent Company: CNHI, LLC
Publisher Name: Melinda Jones
Editor Name: Melodie Phelps
Advertising Executive Name: Melinda Jones
Delivery Methods: Mail
Published Days: Wed
Avg. Paid Circ.: 5800
Audit Company: Sworn/Estimate/Non-Audited
Audit Date: 43626

MOREHEAD

THE MOREHEAD NEWS

Street Address: 710 W 1st St
City: Morehead
State: KY
ZIP Code: 40351-1436
General Phone: (606) 784-4116
General Email: dduncan@themoreheadnews.com
Publication Website: https://www.themoreheadnews.com/
Parent Company: CNHI, LLC
Publisher Name: Patricia Bennett
Publisher Email: publisher@themoreheadnews.com
Editor Name: Stephanie Ockerman
Editor Email: sockerman@themoreheadnews.com
Advertising Executive Name: Kim Harper
Advertising Executive Email: kharper@dailyindependent.com
Delivery Methods: Mail`Newsstand`Racks
Year Established: 1883
Own Printing Facility?: Y

Commercial printers?: Y
Published Days: Tues`Fri
Avg. Paid Circ.: 4200
Avg. Free Circ.: 100
Audit Company: Sworn/Estimate/Non-Audited
Audit Date: 43626

MORGANFIELD

UNION COUNTY ADVOCATE

Street Address: 214 W Main St, 270-827-2000
City: Morganfield
State: KY
ZIP Code: 42437-1479
General Phone: (270) 389-1833
General Email: uca@ucadvocate.com
Publication Website: https://hendersongleanernews-ky.newsmemory.com/
Delivery Methods: Mail
Year Established: 1885
Mechanical specifications: Type page 13 x 21 1/2; E - 6 cols, between; A - 6 cols, between; C - 8 cols, between.
Published Days: Wed
Avg. Paid Circ.: 5000
Avg. Free Circ.: 11
Audit Company: Sworn/Estimate/Non-Audited
Audit Date: 43626

MORGANTOWN

THE BUTLER COUNTY BANNER-REPUBLICAN

Street Address: PO Box 219, 120 E. Ohio Street
City: Morgantown
State: KY
ZIP Code: 42261-0219
General Phone: (270) 526-4151
General Email: banner@jpinews.com
Publication Website: https://www.jpinews.com/
Parent Company: Jobe Publishing, Inc.
Publisher Name: Jeffrey S. Jobe
Publisher Email: jobe@jobeinc.com
Publisher Phone: (270) 590-6625
Advertising Executive Email: print@jpinews.com
Advertising Executive Phone: (270) 786-2676
Delivery Methods: Mail`Newsstand`Racks
Year Established: 1864
Mechanical specifications: Type page 13 x 21; E - 6 cols, 2, 1/4 between; C - 6 cols, 2, 1/4 between.
Published Days: Wed
Avg. Paid Circ.: 5900
Avg. Free Circ.: 6100
Audit Company: Sworn/Estimate/Non-Audited
Audit Date: 43626

MOUNT STERLING

MT. STERLING ADVOCATE

Street Address: 219 Midland Trl, P.O. Box 406
City: Mount Sterling
State: KY
ZIP Code: 40353-9070
General Phone: (859) 498-2222
General Email: advertising@msadvocate.com
Publication Website: http://msadvocate.com/
Parent Company: Hasco Inc
Editor Name: Jamie Vinson
Editor Email: news@msadvocate.com
Editor Phone: (859) 498-2222
Advertising Executive Name: Sharon Manning
Advertising Executive Email: advertising@

msadvocate.com
Advertising Executive Phone: (859) 498-2222
Delivery Methods: Mail
Year Established: 1890
Own Printing Facility?: Y
Commercial printers?: Y
Published Days: Thur
Avg. Paid Circ.: 7500
Avg. Free Circ.: 38
Audit Company: Sworn/Estimate/Non-Audited
Audit Date: 43626

NICHOLASVILLE

THE JESSAMINE JOURNAL

Street Address: 507 N Main St
City: Nicholasville
State: KY
ZIP Code: 40356-1156
General Phone: (859) 885-5381
General Email: lana.johnson@jessaminejournal.com
Publication Website: https://www.jessaminejournal.com/
Parent Company: Boone Newspapers, Inc.
Publisher Name: Mike Caldwell
Publisher Email: mike.caldwell@jessaminejournal.com
Publisher Phone: (859) 759-0095
Editor Name: Whitney Leggett
Editor Email: whitney.leggett@jessaminejournal.com
Editor Phone: (859) 759-0049
Advertising Executive Name: Lana Johnson
Advertising Executive Email: lana.johnson@jessaminejournal.com
Advertising Executive Phone: (859) 595-4779
Delivery Methods: Mail
Year Established: 1873
Mechanical specifications: Type page 11 5/8 x 21; E - 6 cols, 1 5/6, 3/16 between; A - 6 cols, 1 5/6, 3/16 between; C - 6 cols, 1 5/6, 3/16 between.
Published Days: Thur
Avg. Paid Circ.: 3500
Audit Company: Sworn/Estimate/Non-Audited
Audit Date: 43626

OLIVE HILL

OLIVE HILL TIMES

Street Address: 187 RAILROAD ST
City: Olive Hill
State: KY
ZIP Code: 41164
General Phone: (606) 286-4201
General Email: dduncan@journal-times.com
Publication Website: https://www.journal-times.com/
Parent Company: CNHI, LLC
Publisher Name: Eddie Blakeley
Publisher Email: publisher@journal-times.com
Editor Name: Tim Preston
Editor Email: tpreston@journal-times.com
Advertising Executive Name: Dan Duncan
Advertising Executive Email: dduncan@journal-times.com
Delivery Methods: Mail`Newsstand`Racks
Year Established: 1935
Own Printing Facility?: N
Commercial printers?: Y
Published Days: Wed
Avg. Paid Circ.: 1800
Avg. Free Circ.: 100
Audit Company: Sworn/Estimate/Non-Audited
Audit Date: 43626

PADUCAH

THE ADVANCE YEOMAN

Street Address: 1540 McCracken Blvd
City: Paducah
State: KY
ZIP Code: 42001-9192
General Phone: (270) 519-3395
General Email: larrah@ky-news.com
Publication Website: http://www.ky-news.com/section/the-advance-yeoman
Parent Company: Kentucky Publishing, Inc.
Publisher Name: Greg LeNeave
Publisher Email: greg007@ky-news.com
Editor Name: Teresa Ann Pearson
Editor Email: advanceyeoman@gmail.com
Delivery Methods: Mail
Year Established: 1889
Published Days: Wed
Avg. Paid Circ.: 4300
Avg. Free Circ.: 45
Audit Company: Sworn/Estimate/Non-Audited
Audit Date: 43626

PADUCAH

THE CARLISLE COUNTY NEWS

Street Address: 1540 McCracken Blvd
City: Paducah
State: KY
ZIP Code: 42001-9192
General Phone: (270) 628-5490
General Email: ccn1@galaxycable.net
Publication Website: http://www.ky-news.com/section/the-carlisle-county-news
Parent Company: Kentucky Publishing, Inc.
Publisher Name: Greg LeNeave
Publisher Email: greg007@ky-news.com
Delivery Methods: Mail`Newsstand`Carrier`Racks
Year Established: 1894
Published Days: Thur
Avg. Paid Circ.: 1625
Avg. Free Circ.: 77
Audit Company: Sworn/Estimate/Non-Audited
Audit Date: 43626

PAINTSVILLE

THE PAINTSVILLE HERALD

Street Address: 978 Broadway St
City: Paintsville
State: KY
ZIP Code: 41240-1346
General Phone: (606) 789-5315
General Email: ads@paintsvilleherald.com
Publication Website: https://www.paintsvilleherald.com/
Parent Company: Lancaster Management, Inc.
Publisher Name: Jeff Vanderbeck
Publisher Email: jvanderbeck@news-expressky.com
Publisher Phone: (606) 437-4054
Editor Name: Aaron K. Nelson
Editor Email: anelson@paintsvilleherald.com
Editor Phone: (606) 789-5315
Advertising Executive Name: Danny Coleman
Advertising Executive Email: dcoleman@news-expressky.com
Advertising Executive Phone: (606) 437-4054
Delivery Methods: Mail`Newsstand`Carrier`Racks
Year Established: 1901
Mechanical specifications: Type page 12 1/2 x 21 1/2; E - 6 cols, 2, 1/2 between; A - 6 cols, 2, 1/2 between; C - 8 cols, 1 1/2, 1/3 between.
Published Days: Wed`Fri
Avg. Paid Circ.: 5200
Audit Company: Sworn/Estimate/Non-Audited
Audit Date: 43626

PARIS

BOURBON COUNTY CITIZEN

Street Address: 123 West Eighth Street - P.O. Box 158
City: Paris
State: KY
ZIP Code: 40361-1343
General Phone: (859) 987-1870
General Email: ads@citizenadvertiser.com
Publication Website: https://www.bourboncountycitizen.com/
Editor Name: James Brannon
Delivery Methods: Mail
Year Established: 1984
Mechanical specifications: Type page 13 x 21.
Published Days: Wed
Avg. Paid Circ.: 3000
Audit Company: Sworn/Estimate/Non-Audited
Audit Date: 43626

PIKEVILLE

THE APPALACHIAN NEWS-EXPRESS

Street Address: 129 Caroline Ave
City: Pikeville
State: KY
ZIP Code: 41501-1101
General Phone: (606) 437-4054
General Email: mkeller@news-expressky.com
Publication Website: http://www.news-expressky.com/
Parent Company: Lancaster Management, Inc.
Publisher Name: Jeff Vanderbeck
Publisher Email: jvanderbeck@news-expressky.com
Editor Name: Russ Cassady
Editor Email: editor@news-expressky.com
Advertising Executive Name: Danny Coleman
Advertising Executive Email: dcoleman@news-expressky.com
Delivery Methods: Mail
Mechanical specifications: Type page 12 x 21 1/2; E - 6 cols, 1 5/6, 1/4 between; A - 6 cols, 1 5/6, 1/4 between; C - 9 cols, 1 1/6, 1/4 between.
Published Days: Wed`Fri`Sat
Avg. Paid Circ.: 11000
Audit Company: Sworn/Estimate/Non-Audited
Audit Date: 43626

PINEVILLE

PINEVILLE SUN

Street Address: 210 Virginia Avenue, PO Box 250
City: Pineville
State: KY
ZIP Code: 40977-0250
General Phone: (606) 337-2333
General Email: news@thepinevillesun.com
Publication Website: https://www.nolangroupmedia.com/pineville_suncourier/
Parent Company: Nolan Group Media
Editor Name: Jay Compton
Editor Email: jay@thepinevillesun.com
Published Days: Thur
Avg. Paid Circ.: 3500
Avg. Free Circ.: 41
Audit Company: Sworn/Estimate/Non-Audited
Audit Date: 43626

PRINCETON

TIMES LEADER

Street Address: 607 W Washington St
City: Princeton
State: KY
ZIP Code: 42445-1941
General Phone: (270) 365-5588
General Email: advertising@timesleader.net
Publication Website: https://www.timesleader.net/
Parent Company: Paxton Media Group, LLC
Publisher Name: Venita Fritz
Advertising Executive Name: Kayla Stevenson
Advertising Executive Email: kayla@timesleader.net
Advertising Executive Phone: (270) 365-5588
Delivery Methods: Mail`Newsstand`Racks
Year Established: 1871
Own Printing Facility?: Y
Commercial printers?: Y
Mechanical specifications: Type page 13 x 21 1/2; E - 6 cols, 2, 1/6 between; A - 6 cols, 2, 1/6 between; C - 9 cols, 1 3/10, 1/6 between.
Published Days: Wed`Sat
Avg. Paid Circ.: 5490
Avg. Free Circ.: 45
Audit Company: Sworn/Estimate/Non-Audited
Audit Date: 43626

PROVIDENCE

THE JOURNAL ENTERPRISE

Street Address: 114 N. Broadway
City: Providence
State: KY
ZIP Code: 42450-1220
General Phone: (270) 667-2068
General Email: tpruitt@journalenterprise.com
Publication Website: https://www.journalenterprise.com/
Parent Company: Paxton Media Group, LLC
Publisher Name: Matt Hughes
Publisher Email: matt@journalenterprise.com
Publisher Phone: (270) 667-2068
Editor Name: Matt Hughes
Editor Email: matt@journalenterprise.com
Editor Phone: (270) 667-2068
Advertising Executive Name: Tina Pruitt
Advertising Executive Email: tpruitt@journalenterprise.com
Advertising Executive Phone: (270) 667-2068
Delivery Methods: Mail
Year Established: 1905
Mechanical specifications: Type page 13 x 21 1/2; E - 6 cols, 2, between; A - 6 cols, 2, between; C - 6 cols, 2, between.
Published Days: Thur
Avg. Paid Circ.: 4500
Audit Company: Sworn/Estimate/Non-Audited
Audit Date: 43626

RICHMOND

THE MADISON COUNTY ADVERTISER

Street Address: 380 Big Hill Ave
City: Richmond
State: KY
ZIP Code: 40475-2012
General Phone: (859) 623-1669
General Email: gtyler@richmondregister.com
Publication Website: https://www.richmondregister.com/?fbclid=IwAR3-rtyoYe02mniSJbSUri4PwLvJMFRi3AeuLWbzO9PEy78R4nI3XB2qUVQ
Parent Company: CNHI, LLC
Publisher Name: Bill Hanson
Editor Name: Jonathan Greene
Editor Email: editor@richmondregister.com
Editor Phone: (859) 624-6690
Advertising Executive Name: Gary Tyler
Advertising Executive Email: gtyler@richmondregister.com
Advertising Executive Phone: (859) 624-6682
Delivery Methods: Mail`Racks
Own Printing Facility?: Y
Commercial printers?: Y
Mechanical specifications: Type page 13 x 21; E - 6 cols, between; A - 6 cols, between; C - 9 cols, between.
Published Days: Wed

Community Newspapers in the U.S.

III-247

Avg. Free Circ.: 28000
Audit Company: Sworn/Estimate/Non-Audited
Audit Date: 43626

RUSSELL SPRINGS

THE RUSSELL COUNTY NEWS-REGISTER

Street Address: 120 Wilson St
City: Russell Springs
State: KY
ZIP Code: 42642-4315
General Phone: (270) 866-3191
General Email: advertising@russellcountynewspapers.com
Publication Website: http://russellcountynewspapers.com/
Parent Company: Russell County Newspaper, LLC
Publisher Name: Stephanie Smith
Publisher Email: stephanie@russellcountynewspapers.com
Advertising Executive Email: advertising@russellcountynewspapers.com
Own Printing Facility?: Y
Commercial printers?: Y
Mechanical specifications: Type page 13 x 21; E - 6 cols, 2 1/16, 1/8 between; A - 6 cols, 2 1/16, 1/8 between; C - 6 cols, 2 1/16, 1/8 between.
Published Days: Sat
Avg. Free Circ.: 10000
Audit Company: Sworn/Estimate/Non-Audited
Audit Date: 43626

RUSSELL SPRINGS

THE TIMES JOURNAL

Street Address: 120 Wilson St
City: Russell Springs
State: KY
ZIP Code: 42642-4315
General Phone: (270) 866-3191
General Email: advertising@russellcountynewspapers.com
Publication Website: http://russellcountynewspapers.com/
Parent Company: Russell County Newspaper, LLC
Publisher Name: Stephanie Smith
Publisher Email: stephanie@russellcountynewspapers.com
Advertising Executive Email: advertising@russellcountynewspapers.com
Delivery Methods: Mail
Year Established: 1949
Own Printing Facility?: Y
Commercial printers?: Y
Mechanical specifications: Type page 13 x 21; E - 6 cols, 2 1/16, 1/8 between; A - 6 cols, 2 1/16, 1/8 between; C - 6 cols, 2 1/16, 1/8 between.
Published Days: Thur`Sat
Avg. Paid Circ.: 5000
Avg. Free Circ.: 235
Audit Company: Sworn/Estimate/Non-Audited
Audit Date: 43626

RUSSELLVILLE

THE NEWS DEMOCRAT & LEADER

Street Address: 250 N Main St
City: Russellville
State: KY
ZIP Code: 42276-1841
General Phone: (270) 726-8394
General Email: ostapleton@newsdemocratleader.com
Publication Website: http://www.newsdemocratleader.com/
Parent Company: Paxton Media Group, LLC
Publisher Name: Lola Nash

Editor Name: OJ Stapleton
Editor Email: ostapleton@newsdemocratleader.com
Delivery Methods: Mail
Own Printing Facility?: Y
Commercial printers?: Y
Mechanical specifications: Type page 13 x 21 1/2; E - 6 cols, 2, 1/4 between; A - 6 cols, 2, 1/4 between; C - 8 cols, between.
Published Days: Tues`Fri
Avg. Paid Circ.: 6000
Audit Company: Sworn/Estimate/Non-Audited
Audit Date: 43626

SALYERSVILLE

SALYERSVILLE INDEPENDENT

Street Address: P.O. Box 29
City: Salyersville
State: KY
ZIP Code: 41465-9251
General Phone: (606) 349-2915
General Email: vanessa@salyersvilleindependent.com
Publication Website: https://www.salyersvilleindependent.com/
Parent Company: Mortimer Media Group
Editor Name: Heather Oney
Editor Email: heather@salyersvilleindependent.com
Advertising Executive Name: Vanessa Castle
Advertising Executive Email: vanessa@salyersvilleindependent.com
Delivery Methods: Mail
Year Established: 1821
Published Days: Thur
Audit Company: Sworn/Estimate/Non-Audited
Audit Date: 43626

SCOTTSVILLE

THE CITIZEN-TIMES

Street Address: 611 E Main St, P.O. Box 310
City: Scottsville
State: KY
ZIP Code: 42164-1628
General Phone: (270) 237-3441
General Email: ctines@nctc.com
Publication Website: http://thecitizen-times.com/
Delivery Methods: Mail
Year Established: 1918
Mechanical specifications: Type page 11.5 x 21; E - 6 cols, 1/8 between;
Published Days: Thur
Avg. Paid Circ.: 6000
Avg. Free Circ.: 212
Audit Company: Sworn/Estimate/Non-Audited
Audit Date: 43626

SMITHLAND

LIVINGSTON LEDGER

Street Address: 130 E Adair St
City: Smithland
State: KY
ZIP Code: 42081-9998
General Phone: (270) 442-7389
General Email: kpiads@ky-news.com
Publication Website: http://www.ky-news.com/section/livingston-ledger
Parent Company: Kentucky Publishing, Inc.
Publisher Name: Greg LeNeave
Publisher Email: greg007@ky-news.com
Delivery Methods: Mail`Racks
Own Printing Facility?: Y
Commercial printers?: Y
Published Days: Thur
Avg. Paid Circ.: 3400
Avg. Free Circ.: 30
Audit Company: Sworn/Estimate/Non-Audited

Audit Date: 43626

STANFORD

THE INTERIOR JOURNAL

Street Address: 301 W Main St
City: Stanford
State: KY
ZIP Code: 40484-1215
General Phone: (606) 365-2104
General Email: lee.smith@theinteriorjournal.com
Publication Website: https://www.theinteriorjournal.com/
Parent Company: Boone Newspapers, Inc.
Publisher Name: Mike Caldwell
Publisher Email: mike.caldwell@winchestersun.com
Publisher Phone: (859) 759-0095
Editor Name: Nancy Leedy
Editor Email: nancy.leedy@theinteriorjournal.com
Editor Phone: (859) 469-6416
Advertising Executive Name: Lee Smith
Advertising Executive Email: lee.smith@theinteriorjournal.com
Advertising Executive Phone: (859) 469-6429
Delivery Methods: Mail`Newsstand`Racks
Year Established: 1860
Own Printing Facility?: N
Commercial printers?: N
Mechanical specifications: Type page 13 x 21 1/2; E - 6 cols, 2 1/16, 1/6 between; A - 6 cols, 2, 1/6 between; C - 8 cols, 1 1/2, 1/6 between.
Published Days: Thur
Weekday Frequency: m
Avg. Paid Circ.: 2400
Audit Company: Sworn/Estimate/Non-Audited
Audit Date: 43626

TOMPKINSVILLE

THE MONROE COUNTY CITIZEN

Street Address: 201 N Main St
City: Tompkinsville
State: KY
ZIP Code: 42167-1685
General Phone: (270) 487-8666
General Email: citizen@jpinews.com
Publication Website: https://www.jpinews.com/the-monroe-county-citizen/
Parent Company: Jobe Publishing, Inc.
Publisher Name: Jennifer Moonsong
Publisher Email: jupitermoonsong@yahoo.com
Publisher Phone: (270) 670-9233
Advertising Executive Email: print@jpinews.com
Advertising Executive Phone: (270) 786-2676
Delivery Methods: Mail`Newsstand`Racks
Own Printing Facility?: Y
Commercial printers?: Y
Mechanical specifications: Type page 14 x 22 3/8; E - 8 cols, 1 1/2, 1/8 between; A - 8 cols, 1 1/2, 1/8 between; C - 8 cols, 1 1/2, 1/8 between.
Published Days: Thur
Avg. Paid Circ.: 1026
Avg. Free Circ.: 4874
Audit Company: Sworn/Estimate/Non-Audited
Audit Date: 43626

TOMPKINSVILLE

TOMPKINSVILLE NEWS

Street Address: 105 N Main St
City: Tompkinsville
State: KY
ZIP Code: 42167-1507
General Phone: (270) 487-5576
General Email: admanager@tompkinsvillenews.com

Publication Website: https://www.tompkinsvillenews.com
Parent Company: Monroe County Press, Inc.
Publisher Name: Blanche Trimble
Publisher Email: btrimble@tompkinsvillenews.com
Editor Name: Ronda Jordan-Elam
Editor Email: relam@tompkinsvillenews.com
Advertising Executive Name: Ronda Chandler
Advertising Executive Email: admanager@tompkinsvillenews.com
Delivery Methods: Mail`Newsstand`Racks
Year Established: 1903
Own Printing Facility?: Y
Commercial printers?: Y
Mechanical specifications: Type page 12 3/4 x 21; E - 6 cols, 2 1/16, 1/6 between; A - 6 cols, 2 1/16, 1/6 between; C - 6 cols, 2 1/16, 1/6 between.
Published Days: Thur
Avg. Paid Circ.: 3594
Avg. Free Circ.: 488
Audit Company: Sworn/Estimate/Non-Audited
Audit Date: 43626

VANCEBURG

LEWIS COUNTY HERALD

Street Address: 187 Main St
City: Vanceburg
State: KY
ZIP Code: 41179-1031
General Phone: (606) 796-2331
General Email: heraldadvertising@yahoo.com
Publication Website: http://www.lewiscountyherald.com/
Parent Company: The Lewis County Herald Publishing Company, Inc.
Publisher Name: Dennis K. Brown
Delivery Methods: Mail
Published Days: Tues
Avg. Paid Circ.: 4400
Audit Company: Sworn/Estimate/Non-Audited
Audit Date: 43626

VERSAILLES

WOODFORD SUN

Street Address: 184 South Main Street
City: Versailles
State: KY
ZIP Code: 40383-0029
General Phone: (859) 873-4131
General Email: ads@woodfordsun.com
Publication Website: https://www.woodfordsun.com/
Publisher Name: Whitney Chandler
Editor Name: John McGary
Editor Email: john@woodfordsun.com
Editor Phone: (859) 873-4131, ext : 13
Advertising Executive Name: Jennifer Cardwell
Advertising Executive Email: jennifer@woodfordsun.com
Advertising Executive Phone: (859) 873-4131, ext : 15
Delivery Methods: Mail`Racks
Year Established: 1869
Published Days: Thur
Audit Company: Sworn/Estimate/Non-Audited
Audit Date: 43626

WARSAW

THE GALLATIN COUNTY NEWS

Street Address: 211 Third Street, P.O. Box 435
City: Warsaw
State: KY
ZIP Code: 41095-2002

General Phone: (859) 567-5051
General Email: galnews@zoomtown.com
Publication Website: https://www.thegallatincountynews.com/pages/index.php
Publisher Name: Denny Kelley-Warnick
Editor Name: Kelley Warnick
Advertising Executive Name: Clay Warnick
Delivery Methods: Mail`Newsstand
Year Established: 1880
Published Days: Wed
Avg. Paid Circ.: 2400
Avg. Free Circ.: 37
Audit Company: Sworn/Estimate/Non-Audited
Audit Date: 43626

WHITESBURG

THE MOUNTAIN EAGLE

Street Address: 41 N Webb St
City: Whitesburg
State: KY
ZIP Code: 41858-7324
General Phone: (606) 633-2252
General Email: mtneagle@bellsouth.net
Publication Website: https://www.themountaineagle.com/
Parent Company: The Mountain Eagle LP
Publisher Name: Thomas E. Gish
Editor Name: Benjamin T. Gish
Editor Email: bengish@mac.com
Advertising Executive Name: Freddy D. Oakes
Advertising Executive Email: foakes@bellsouth.net
Advertising Executive Phone: (859) 294-6063
Delivery Methods: Mail
Year Established: 1907
Mechanical specifications: Type page 13 x 21; E - 6 cols, 2 1/16, 1/8 between.
Published Days: Wed
Avg. Paid Circ.: 4748
Avg. Free Circ.: 92
Audit Company: AAM
Audit Date: 43506

WHITLEY CITY

THE MCCREARY COUNTY VOICE

Street Address: 57 Oaks Ln
City: Whitley City
State: KY
ZIP Code: 42653-6173
General Phone: (606) 376-5500
General Email: susie@tmcvoice.com
Publication Website: https://www.themccrearyvoice.com/
Editor Email: editor@tmcvoice.com
Delivery Methods: Mail`Newsstand`Racks
Year Established: 2000
Published Days: Thur
Audit Company: Sworn/Estimate/Non-Audited
Audit Date: 43626

LOUISIANA

ALEXANDRIA

CENLA FOCUS MAGAZINE

Street Address: 3911 Parliament Dr
City: Alexandria
State: LA
ZIP Code: 71303-3016
General Phone: (318) 442-8277
General Email: contact@cenlafocus.com
Publication Website: https://www.cenlafocus.com/
Delivery Methods: Newsstand`Racks

Year Established: 1997
Published Days: Wed`Mthly
Audit Company: Sworn/Estimate/Non-Audited
Audit Date: 43626

ARABI

THE ST. BERNARD VOICE

Street Address: 234 Mehle St
City: Arabi
State: LA
ZIP Code: 70032-1054
General Phone: (504) 279-7488
General Email: ads@thestbernardvoice.com
Publication Website: https://www.thestbernardvoice.com/
Publisher Name: Norris Babin
Publisher Email: norris@thestbernardvoice.com
Publisher Phone: (504) 279-7488
Editor Name: Edwin Roy
Editor Email: edroy@thestbernardvoice.com
Editor Phone: (504) 279-7488
Advertising Executive Email: ads@thestbernardvoice.com
Delivery Methods: Mail`Newsstand`Racks
Year Established: 1890
Mechanical specifications: 11.25 inches wide x 21.5 inches deep six columns 1 column = 1.7361 inches 1 gutter= 0.1667 inches
Published Days: Fri
Avg. Paid Circ.: 3150
Audit Company: Sworn/Estimate/Non-Audited
Audit Date: 43626

BATON ROUGE

COUNTRY ROADS MAGAZINE

Street Address: 758 Saint Charles St
City: Baton Rouge
State: LA
ZIP Code: 70802-6446
General Phone: (225) 343-3714
General Email: sales@countryroadsmag.com
Publication Website: https://countryroadsmagazine.com/
Publisher Name: James Fox-Smith
Publisher Phone: (225) 343-3714, ext. 107
Editor Name: Jordan LaHaye
Editor Phone: (225) 343-3714, ext : 110
Delivery Methods: Mail`Racks
Year Established: 1983
Published Days: Wed`Mthly
Avg. Free Circ.: 27000
Audit Company: Sworn/Estimate/Non-Audited
Audit Date: 43626

BATON ROUGE

LOUISIANA FOOTBALL MAGAZINE

Street Address: PO Box 86638
City: Baton Rouge
State: LA
ZIP Code: 70879-6638
General Phone: (225) 262-7667
General Email: info@lafootballmagazine.com
Publication Website: https://www.lafootballmagazine.com/
Year Established: 1996
Published Days: Mon
Audit Company: Sworn/Estimate/Non-Audited
Audit Date: 43626

BATON ROUGE

THE ZACHARY PLAINSMAN-NEWS

Street Address: PO Box 588

City: Baton Rouge
State: LA
ZIP Code: 70821-0588
General Phone: (225) 654-6841
General Email: newstips@theadvocate.com
Publication Website: https://www.theadvocate.com/baton_rouge/news/communities/zachary/
Parent Company: Capital City Press, LLC
Delivery Methods: Mail`Racks
Year Established: 1953
Published Days: Wed
Avg. Paid Circ.: 2000
Audit Company: Sworn/Estimate/Non-Audited
Audit Date: 43626

BELLE CHASSE

PLAQUEMINES GAZETTE

Street Address: 7962 Highway 23
City: Belle Chasse
State: LA
ZIP Code: 70037-2432
General Phone: (504) 392-1619
General Email: ads@plaqueminesgazette.com
Publication Website: https://www.plaqueminesgazette.com/
Publisher Name: Norris Babin
Publisher Email: norris@plaqueminesgazette.com
Publisher Phone: (504) 392-1619
Editor Name: Norris Babin
Editor Email: norris@plaqueminesgazette.com
Editor Phone: (504) 392-1619
Delivery Methods: Mail`Newsstand`Racks
Year Established: 1928
Own Printing Facility?: Y
Commercial printers?: Y
Mechanical specifications: Type page 11.25 x 21.5 6 columns Column = 1.7361 in Gutter = 0.1667 in
Published Days: Tues
Avg. Paid Circ.: 2846
Avg. Free Circ.: 26
Audit Company: Sworn/Estimate/Non-Audited
Audit Date: 43626

BERNICE

THE BERNICE BANNER

Street Address: 227 Boyette Rd
City: Bernice
State: LA
ZIP Code: 71222-5327
General Phone: (318) 285-7420
General Email: bernicebanner@oeccwildblue.com
Publication Website: https://bernicebanner.weebly.com/
Advertising Executive Email: bannerlady@oeccwildblue.com
Delivery Methods: Mail`Newsstand
Year Established: 1995
Published Days: Thur
Audit Company: Sworn/Estimate/Non-Audited
Audit Date: 43626

BOGALUSA

BOGALUSA DAILY NEWS

Street Address: 525 Avenue V
City: Bogalusa
State: LA
ZIP Code: 70427-4493
General Phone: (985) 732-2565
General Email: justin.schuver@bogalusadailynews.com
Publication Website: https://www.bogalusadailynews.com/
Parent Company: Boone Newspapers, Inc.

Publisher Name: Justin Schuver
Publisher Email: justin.schuver@bogalusadailynews.com
Editor Name: Justin Schuver
Editor Email: justin.schuver@bogalusadailynews.com
Advertising Executive Name: Carol Case
Advertising Executive Email: carol.case@bogalusadailynews.com
Delivery Methods: Mail
Year Established: 1927
Mechanical specifications: Type page 13 x 21 1/2; E - 6 cols, 2, 1/6 between; A - 6 cols, 2, 1/6 between; C - 9 cols, between.
Published Days: Wed`Sat
Weekday Frequency: m
Avg. Paid Circ.: 5195
Audit Company: Sworn/Estimate/Non-Audited
Audit Date: 43626

BOSSIER CITY

BOSSIER PRESS-TRIBUNE

Street Address: 6346 Venecia Dr
City: Bossier City
State: LA
ZIP Code: 71111-7454
General Phone: (318) 747-7900
General Email: rbrown@bossierpress.com
Publication Website: https://bossierpress.com/
Parent Company: Bossier Newspaper Publishing Company, Inc.
Publisher Name: Randy Brown
Publisher Email: rbrown@bossierpress.com
Publisher Phone: (318) 747-7900, ext. 111
Editor Name: Sean Green
Editor Email: sean@bossierpress.com
Editor Phone: (318) 747-7900, ext : 113
Delivery Methods: Mail`Newsstand`Racks
Year Established: 1927
Mechanical specifications: Type page 10.5 x 21; E - 6 cols, 2, 1/6 between; A - 6 cols, 1.6, 1/6 between; C - 9 cols, 1, 1/6 between.
Published Days: Wed
Avg. Paid Circ.: 5000
Audit Company: Sworn/Estimate/Non-Audited
Audit Date: 43626

BOUTTE

ST. CHARLES HERALD-GUIDE

Street Address: 14236 Highway 90
City: Boutte
State: LA
ZIP Code: 70039-3516
General Phone: (985) 758-2795
General Email: jonathanm@heraldguide.com
Publication Website: https://www.heraldguide.com/
Parent Company: LSN Publishing Company LLC
Publisher Name: Jonathan Menard
Publisher Email: ydunn@lasmag.com
Editor Name: Anna Thibodeaux
Editor Email: annat@heraldguide.com
Advertising Executive Name: Yvette Dunn
Delivery Methods: Mail`Newsstand
Year Established: 1993
Mechanical specifications: Type page 13 x 21; E - 6 cols, 2 1/16, 1/8 between.
Published Days: Thur
Avg. Paid Circ.: 4600
Audit Company: Sworn/Estimate/Non-Audited
Audit Date: 43626

DENHAM SPRINGS

THE LIVINGSTON PARISH NEWS

Street Address: 688 Hatchell Ln
City: Denham Springs

Community Newspapers in the U.S.

State: LA
ZIP Code: 70726-3015
General Phone: (225) 665-5176
General Email: subscriptions@lpn1898.com
Publication Website: https://www.livingstonparishnews.com
Publisher Name: McHugh David
Publisher Email: mchugh@lpn1898.com
Editor Name: McHugh David
Editor Email: mchugh@lpn1898.com
Advertising Executive Name: Karen Brooks
Advertising Executive Email: karen@lpn1898.com
Delivery Methods: Mail`Newsstand
Year Established: 1898
Own Printing Facility?: N
Commercial printers?: N
Mechanical specifications: Type page 13 3/4 x 21; E - 6 cols, 2 1/30, 5/6 between; A - 6 cols, 2 1/30, 5/6 between; C - 6 cols, 2 1/30, 5/6 between.
Published Days: Thur`Sun
Avg. Paid Circ.: 30000
Audit Company: Sworn/Estimate/Non-Audited
Audit Date: 43626

DEQUINCY

THE DEQUINCY NEWS

Street Address: 203 E Harrison St
City: Dequincy
State: LA
ZIP Code: 70633-3545
General Phone: (337) 786-8004
General Email: jdeviney@centurytel.net
Publication Website: https://dequincynews.com/
Parent Company: Wise Newspapers, Inc.
Publisher Name: Jeffra Wise DeViney
Publisher Email: jdeviney@centurytel.net
Advertising Executive Name: Jeffra Wise DeViney
Advertising Executive Email: jdeviney@centurytel.net
Delivery Methods: Mail`Racks
Year Established: 1923
Mechanical specifications: Type page 11 1/2 x 21; E - 6 cols, 1 3/4, 1/8 between; A - 6 cols, 1 3/4, 1/8 between; C - 6 cols, 1 3/4, 1/8 between.
Published Days: Wed
Avg. Paid Circ.: 3600
Audit Company: Sworn/Estimate/Non-Audited
Audit Date: 43626

DERIDDER

BEAUREGARD DAILY NEWS

Street Address: 903 W 1st St (P.O. Box 698)
City: Deridder
State: LA
ZIP Code: 70634-3701
General Phone: (337) 462-0616
General Email: csherman@beauregarddailynews.net
Publication Website: https://www.beauregarddailynews.net/
Parent Company: Gannett
Publisher Name: Joann Zollo
Publisher Email: jzollo@gatehousemedia.com
Editor Name: Lauren Blankenship
Editor Email: lblankenship@beauregarddailynews.net
Advertising Executive Name: Cindy Sherman
Advertising Executive Email: csherman@beauregarddailynews.net
Delivery Methods: Mail`Newsstand`Carrier`Racks
Year Established: 1945
Mechanical specifications: Type page 13 x 21; E - 6 cols, 2 1/16, 1/8 between; C - 8 cols, 1 7/16, 1/8 between.
Published Days: Wed`Fri`Sun
Weekday Frequency: m
Avg. Paid Circ.: 2800
Avg. Free Circ.: 5500
Audit Company: Sworn/Estimate/Non-Audited
Audit Date: 43626

DONALDSONVILLE

THE DONALDSONVILLE CHIEF

Street Address: 120 420 Mississippi St. Ste. B
City: Donaldsonville
State: LA
ZIP Code: 70346-2520
General Phone: (225) 473-3101
General Email: cbarrett@gatehousemedia.com
Publication Website: https://www.donaldsonvillechief.com/
Parent Company: Gannett
Editor Name: Greg Fischer
Editor Email: news@donaldsonvillechief.com
Editor Phone: (225) 473-3102
Advertising Executive Name: Crystal Barrett
Advertising Executive Email: cbarrett@gatehousemedia.com
Advertising Executive Phone: (225) 473-3102
Delivery Methods: Mail`Newsstand`Carrier`Racks
Year Established: 1871
Own Printing Facility?: N
Commercial printers?: Y
Published Days: Thur
Avg. Paid Circ.: 1000
Avg. Free Circ.: 50
Audit Company: Sworn/Estimate/Non-Audited
Audit Date: 43626

FERRIDAY

CONCORDIA SENTINEL

Street Address: 421 North 1st Street
City: Ferriday
State: LA
ZIP Code: 71334-2847
General Phone: (318) 757-3646
General Email: gerry@concordiasentinel.com
Publication Website: https://www.hannapub.com/concordiasentinel/
Parent Company: Hanna Newspapers
Publisher Name: Lesley Capdepon
Publisher Email: lesley@concordiasentinel.com
Editor Name: Stanley Nelson
Editor Email: stanley@concordiasentinel.com
Advertising Executive Name: Gerry Meraz
Advertising Executive Email: barbara@concordiasentinel.com
Delivery Methods: Mail`Racks
Year Established: 1876
Own Printing Facility?: Y
Commercial printers?: Y
Mechanical specifications: Type page 13 3/8 x 21; E - 6 cols, 2, 1/6 between; A - 6 cols, 2, 1/6 between; C - 6 cols, 2, 1/6 between.
Published Days: Wed
Avg. Paid Circ.: 4700
Audit Company: Sworn/Estimate/Non-Audited
Audit Date: 43626

FRANKLINTON

THE ERA-LEADER

Street Address: 1137 Main St
City: Franklinton
State: LA
ZIP Code: 70438-2083
General Phone: (985) 839-9077
General Email: info@era-leader.com
Publication Website: https://www.era-leader.com/
Parent Company: Emmerich Newspapers
Publisher Name: Steve Kuperstock
Publisher Email: steve@era-leader.com
Editor Name: Steve Kuperstock
Editor Email: steve@era-leader.com
Advertising Executive Name: Casey Gulsby
Advertising Executive Email: casey@era-leader.com
Delivery Methods: Mail`Newsstand`Racks
Year Established: 1910
Own Printing Facility?: Y
Commercial printers?: Y
Mechanical specifications: Type page 13 x 21; E - 6 cols, 2 1/16, 1/8 between; A - 6 cols, 2 1/16, 1/8 between.
Published Days: Wed
Avg. Paid Circ.: 4088
Audit Company: Sworn/Estimate/Non-Audited
Audit Date: 43626

GONZALES

GONZALES WEEKLY CITIZEN

Street Address: 231 W Cornerview St
City: Gonzales
State: LA
ZIP Code: 70737-2841
General Phone: (225) 644-6397
General Email: cbarrett@gatehousemedia.com
Publication Website: https://www.weeklycitizen.com/
Parent Company: Gannett
Publisher Name: Stephanie Schexnaydre
Publisher Email: sschexnaydre@gatehousemedia.com
Editor Name: Greg Fischer
Editor Email: editor@weeklycitizen.com
Advertising Executive Name: Crystal Barrett
Advertising Executive Email: cbarrett@gatehousemedia.com
Delivery Methods: Mail`Newsstand`Carrier`Racks
Year Established: 1998
Own Printing Facility?: Y
Commercial printers?: Y
Mechanical specifications: Type page 11 5/8 x 21; E - 6 cols, 2 1/16, between; A - 6 cols, 2 1/16, between; C - 6 cols, 2 1/16, between.
Published Days: Thur
Avg. Paid Circ.: 2500
Avg. Free Circ.: 250
Audit Company: Sworn/Estimate/Non-Audited
Audit Date: 43626

GREENSBURG

ST. HELENA ECHO

Street Address: Corner of Main and Lafette
City: Greensburg
State: LA
ZIP Code: 70441
General Phone: (225) 222-4541
General Email: echo@tangilena.com
Delivery Methods: Mail
Year Established: 1857
Mechanical specifications: Type page 13 x 21; E - 6 cols, between; A - 6 cols, between; C - 9 cols, between.
Published Days: Wed
Avg. Paid Circ.: 1150
Avg. Free Circ.: 4438
Audit Company: Sworn/Estimate/Non-Audited
Audit Date: 43626

GREENWELL SPRINGS

CENTRAL CITY NEWS

Street Address: PO Box 1
City: Greenwell Springs
State: LA
ZIP Code: 70739
General Phone: (225) 261-5055
General Email: centralcitynews@hotmail.com
Publication Website: http://www.centralcitynews.net/
Parent Company: Boone Newspapers
Published Days: Thur
Audit Company: Sworn/Estimate/Non-Audited
Audit Date: 43626

HOMER

HOMER GUARDIAN-JOURNAL

Street Address: 620 N Main St
City: Homer
State: LA
ZIP Code: 71040-3847
General Phone: (318) 927-3541
General Email: guardian-journal@claiborneone.com
Delivery Methods: Mail
Mechanical specifications: Type page 13 x 21; E - 6 cols, 2 1/16, between; A - 6 cols, 2 1/16, between; C - 8 cols, 1 1/2, between.
Published Days: Thur
Avg. Paid Circ.: 3200
Audit Company: Sworn/Estimate/Non-Audited
Audit Date: 43626

HOMER

THE HAYNESVILLE NEWS

Street Address: 604 N Main St
City: Homer
State: LA
ZIP Code: 71040-3806
General Phone: (318) 927-3721
General Email: webmaster@claiborneone.org
Publication Website: http://www.claiborneone.org/haynesville/
Delivery Methods: Mail
Year Established: 1924
Published Days: Tues`Thur
Avg. Paid Circ.: 1200
Avg. Free Circ.: 8233
Audit Company: Sworn/Estimate/Non-Audited
Audit Date: 43626

HOUMA

POINT OF VUE

Street Address: 6160 W Park Ave
City: Houma
State: LA
ZIP Code: 70364-1700
General Phone: (985) 868-7515
General Email: sales@rushing-media.com
Publication Website: https://www.houmatimes.com/lifestyles/point-of-vue/
Publisher Name: Brian Rushing
Publisher Email: brian@rushing-media.com
Publisher Phone: (985) 868-7515
Editor Name: Mary Ditch
Editor Email: mary@rushing-media.com
Editor Phone: (985) 868-7515
Advertising Executive Name: Deanne Ratliff
Advertising Executive Email: deanne@rushing-media.com
Advertising Executive Phone: (985) 868-7515
Delivery Methods: Mail`Newsstand
Year Established: 2007
Published Days: Thur`Mthly
Audit Company: Sworn/Estimate/Non-Audited
Audit Date: 43626

HOUMA

TRI-PARISH TIMES & BUSINESS NEWS

Street Address: 6160 West Park Avenue

City: Houma
State: LA
ZIP Code: 70364
General Phone: (985) 868-7515
General Email: mail@rushing-media.com
Publication Website: http://www.houmatimes.com/
Parent Company: Rushing Media
Publisher Name: Brian Rushing
Publisher Email: brian@rushing-media.com
Publisher Phone: (985) 868-7515
Editor Name: Mary Ditch
Editor Email: mary@rushing-media.com
Editor Phone: (985) 868-7515
Advertising Executive Name: Deanne Ratliff
Advertising Executive Email: deanne@rushing-media.com
Advertising Executive Phone: (985) 868-7515
Delivery Methods: Mail`Racks
Year Established: 1997
Published Days: Wed
Avg. Paid Circ.: 5076
Avg. Free Circ.: 943
Audit Company: Sworn/Estimate/Non-Audited
Audit Date: 43626

JENA

THE JENA-TIMES/OLLA-TULLOS-URANIA SIGNAL

Street Address: 1509 N 3RD ST
City: Jena
State: LA
ZIP Code: 71342
General Phone: (318) 992-4121
General Email: sales@thejenatimes.com
Publication Website: https://www.thejenatimes.net/
Publisher Name: Sammy J. Franklin
Publisher Email: editor@thejenatimes.net
Editor Name: Sammy J. Franklin
Editor Email: editor@thejenatimes.net
Advertising Executive Name: Libby Warwick
Advertising Executive Email: sales@thejenatimes.net
Delivery Methods: Mail`Newsstand
Year Established: 1905
Mechanical specifications: Type page 13 x 21; E - 6 cols, 2, 1/6 between; A - 6 cols, 2, 1/6 between; C - 8 cols, 1 1/2, 1/6 between.
Published Days: Wed
Avg. Paid Circ.: 4000
Audit Company: Sworn/Estimate/Non-Audited
Audit Date: 43626

JONESVILLE

CATAHOULA NEWS BOOSTER

Street Address: 103 Third St
City: Jonesville
State: LA
ZIP Code: 71343-2339
General Phone: (318) 339-7242
General Email: catahoulanewsmedia@gmail.com
Publication Website: https://www.catahoulanewsbooster.com/
Delivery Methods: Mail
Year Established: 1853
Mechanical specifications: Type page 13 1/4 x 21; E - 6 cols, 2, between; A - 6 cols, 2, between; C - 6 cols, 2, between.
Published Days: Wed
Avg. Paid Circ.: 3200
Avg. Free Circ.: 10
Audit Company: Sworn/Estimate/Non-Audited
Audit Date: 43626

KENTWOOD

THE KENTWOOD NEWS-LEDGER

Street Address: 234 Avenue F
City: Kentwood
State: LA
ZIP Code: 70444-2522
General Phone: (985) 229-8607
General Email: editor.newsledger@tangilena.com
Delivery Methods: Mail
Year Established: 1934
Own Printing Facility?: Y
Mechanical specifications: Type page 13 x 21 1/2; E - 6 cols, 2, between; A - 6 cols, 2, between.
Published Days: Wed
Avg. Paid Circ.: 1525
Audit Company: Sworn/Estimate/Non-Audited
Audit Date: 43626

LA PLACE

L'OBSERVATEUR

Street Address: 116 Newspaper Dr
City: La Place
State: LA
ZIP Code: 70068-4509
General Phone: (985) 652-9545
General Email: lobads@lobservateur.com
Publication Website: https://www.lobservateur.com/
Parent Company: Boone Newspapers
Advertising Executive Email: lobads@lobservateur.com
Delivery Methods: Mail`Carrier
Own Printing Facility?: Y
Commercial printers?: Y
Published Days: Wed`Thur`Sat
Avg. Paid Circ.: 5000
Audit Company: Sworn/Estimate/Non-Audited
Audit Date: 43626

LAROSE

LAFOURCHE GAZETTE

Street Address: 12958 E MAIN ST
City: Larose
State: LA
ZIP Code: 70373
General Phone: (985) 693-7229
General Email: ads@tlgnewspaper.com
Publication Website: http://www.tlgnewspaper.com/
Delivery Methods: Carrier
Year Established: 1965
Own Printing Facility?: Y
Commercial printers?: N
Mechanical specifications: Type page 11 x 22; E - 6 cols, 1.73, between; A - 6 cols, 1.73, between; C - 9 cols, 1.11, between.
Published Days: Wed`Sun
Avg. Free Circ.: 15675
Audit Company: CVC
Audit Date: 43344

LEESVILLE

THE LEESVILLE DAILY LEADER

Street Address: 206 E Texas St
City: Leesville
State: LA
ZIP Code: 71446-4056
General Phone: (337) 239-3444
General Email: egreen@leesvilledailyleader.com
Publication Website: https://www.leesvilledailyleader.com/
Parent Company: Gannett
Publisher Name: Joann Zollo
Publisher Email: jzollo@gatehousemedia.com
Editor Name: Lauren Blankenship
Editor Email: lblankenship@beauregarddailynews.net
Advertising Executive Name: Erik Green
Advertising Executive Email: egreen@leesvilledailyleader.com
Delivery Methods: Mail`Newsstand`Carrier`Racks
Year Established: 1898
Mechanical specifications: Type page 12 1/2 x 21; E - 6 cols, 2 1/16, 1/8 between; A - 6 cols, 2 1/16, 1/8 between; C - 8 cols, 1 1/2, 1/8 between.
Published Days: Wed`Fri`Sun
Weekday Frequency: m
Avg. Paid Circ.: 2800
Avg. Free Circ.: 5000
Audit Company: Sworn/Estimate/Non-Audited
Audit Date: 43626

MANY

THE SABINE INDEX

Street Address: 875 San Antonio Ave
City: Many
State: LA
ZIP Code: 71449-3140
General Phone: (318) 256-3495
General Email: sales@sabineindex.net
Publication Website: https://www.sabinetoday.com/
Editor Name: Daniel Jones
Editor Email: news@sabineindex.net
Advertising Executive Name: Debbie Rose
Advertising Executive Email: sales@sabineindex.net
Delivery Methods: Mail
Year Established: 1879
Mechanical specifications: Type page 13 x ; E - 6 cols, 2, between; A - 6 cols, 2, between; C - 6 cols, 2, between.
Published Days: Wed
Avg. Paid Circ.: 6130
Avg. Free Circ.: 25
Audit Company: Sworn/Estimate/Non-Audited
Audit Date: 43626

METAIRIE

NEW ORLEANS CITY BUSINESS

Street Address: 3350 Ridgelake Drive
City: Metairie
State: LA
ZIP Code: 70002-3768
General Phone: (504) 834-9292
General Email: lbaldini@nopg.com
Publication Website: https://neworleanscitybusiness.com/
Publisher Name: Lisa Blossman
Publisher Email: lblossman@nopg.com
Editor Name: Lance Traweek
Editor Email: ltraweek@nopg.com
Advertising Executive Name: Liz Baldini
Advertising Executive Email: lbaldini@nopg.com
Published Days: Mon
Avg. Paid Circ.: 3311
Avg. Free Circ.: 2380
Audit Company: Sworn/Estimate/Non-Audited
Audit Date: 43626

NATCHITOCHES

NATCHITOCHES TIMES

Street Address: 904 South Dr
City: Natchitoches
State: LA
ZIP Code: 71457-3053
General Phone: (318) 352-3618
General Email: news@natchitochestimes.com
Publication Website: https://www.natchitochestimes.com/
Advertising Executive Email: advertising@natchitochestimes.com
Delivery Methods: Mail`Racks
Year Established: 1903
Own Printing Facility?: Y
Commercial printers?: Y
Mechanical specifications: Type page 13 x 21; A - 6 cols, 2, between.
Published Days: Thur`Sat
Weekday Frequency: All day
Saturday Frequency: All day
Avg. Paid Circ.: 4805
Audit Company: Sworn/Estimate/Non-Audited
Audit Date: 43626

NEW ROADS

THE POINTE COUPEE BANNER

Street Address: 123 Saint Mary St
City: New Roads
State: LA
ZIP Code: 70760-3529
General Phone: (225) 638-7155
General Email: gail.pcbanner@gmail.com
Publication Website: https://www.thepointecoupeebanner.com/
Publisher Name: Ashleigh David Vasquez
Publisher Email: ash.pcbanner@gmail.com
Editor Name: John Dupont
Editor Email: john.pcbanner@gmail.com
Advertising Executive Name: Gail Hurst
Advertising Executive Email: gail.pcbanner@gmail.com
Delivery Methods: Mail
Year Established: 1880
Own Printing Facility?: Y
Commercial printers?: Y
Published Days: Thur
Avg. Paid Circ.: 5000
Audit Company: Sworn/Estimate/Non-Audited
Audit Date: 43626

OPELOUSAS

DAILY WORLD

Street Address: 5367 I 49 S Service Rd
City: Opelousas
State: LA
ZIP Code: 70570-0743
General Phone: (337) 942-4971
General Email: cmcross@gannett.com
Publication Website: https://www.dailyworld.com/
Parent Company: Gannett
Delivery Methods: Mail`Newsstand`Carrier`Racks
Year Established: 1939
Own Printing Facility?: Y
Commercial printers?: Y
Mechanical specifications: Type page 13 x 21 1/2; E - 6 cols, 2 1/16, 3/16 between; A - 6 cols, 2 1/16, 3/16 between; C - 9 cols, 1 3/8, 1/8 between.
Published Days: Mon`Tues`Wed`Thur`Fri`Sat`Sun
Weekday Frequency: m
Saturday Frequency: m
Avg. Paid Circ.: 2329
Audit Company: AAM
Audit Date: 44380

PLAQUEMINE

POST SOUTH

Street Address: 23520 Eden St.
City: Plaquemine
State: LA
ZIP Code: 70764
General Phone: (225) 687-3288
General Email: cbarrett@gatehousemedia.com
Publication Website: https://www.postsouth.com/
Parent Company: Gannett
Editor Name: Greg Fischer
Editor Email: gfischer@weeklycitizen.com
Editor Phone: (225) 687-3288

Community Newspapers in the U.S.

III-251

Advertising Executive Name: Crystal Barrett
Advertising Executive Email: cbarrett@gatehousemedia.com
Advertising Executive Phone: (225) 644-6397
Delivery Methods: Mail
Year Established: 1957
Own Printing Facility?: Y
Commercial printers?: Y
Mechanical specifications: Type page 11 5/8 x 21; E - 6 cols, 1 5/8, 3/16 between; A - 6 cols, 1 5/6, 3/16 between; C - 6 cols, 1 5/6, 3/16 between.
Published Days: Thur
Avg. Paid Circ.: 5500
Avg. Free Circ.: 12
Audit Company: Sworn/Estimate/Non-Audited
Audit Date: 43626

PORT ALLEN

RIVERSIDE READER

Street Address: 570 N Jefferson Ave
City: Port Allen
State: LA
ZIP Code: 70767-2412
General Phone: (225) 336-0749
General Email: advertising@riversidereader.com
Publication Website: https://riversidereader.com/
Published Days: Wed
Audit Company: Sworn/Estimate/Non-Audited
Audit Date: 43626

PORT ALLEN

WEST SIDE JOURNAL

Street Address: 668 N Jefferson Ave
City: Port Allen
State: LA
ZIP Code: 70767-2414
General Phone: (225) 343-2540
General Email: advertising@thewestsidejournal.com
Publication Website: https://www.thewestsidejournal.com/
Parent Company: Venture Capital Publishing
Publisher Email: publisher@thewestsidejournal.com
Editor Email: editor@thewestsidejournal.com
Advertising Executive Email: shelli@thewestsidejournal.com
Delivery Methods: Mail
Year Established: 1937
Published Days: Thur
Avg. Paid Circ.: 2473
Audit Company: Sworn/Estimate/Non-Audited
Audit Date: 43626

SAINT FRANCISVILLE

ST. FRANCISVILLE DEMOCRAT

Street Address: 4749 Johnson St
City: Saint Francisville
State: LA
ZIP Code: 70775-4330
General Phone: (225) 635-3366
General Email: sfdemocrat@bellsouth.net
Publication Website: https://www.theadvocate.com/baton_rouge/news/communities/west_feliciana/
Parent Company: Georges Media
Own Printing Facility?: Y
Commercial printers?: Y
Published Days: Thur
Avg. Paid Circ.: 2000
Audit Company: Sworn/Estimate/Non-Audited
Audit Date: 43626

SHREVEPORT

THE FORUM

Street Address: 1158 Texas Ave
City: Shreveport
State: LA
ZIP Code: 71101-3343
General Phone: (318) 222-0409
General Email: virginia@theforumnews.com
Publication Website: https://theforumnews.com
Parent Company: Venture Publishing Inc.
Publisher Name: Jay Covington
Publisher Email: editor@theforumnews.com
Publisher Phone: (318) 222-0409, ext : 101
Editor Name: Jay Covington
Editor Email: editor@theforumnews.com
Editor Phone: (318) 222-0409, ext : 101
Advertising Executive Name: Virginia St. John
Advertising Executive Email: virginia@theforumnews.com
Advertising Executive Phone: (318) 222-0409, ext : 112
Year Established: 1988
Published Days: Wed
Avg. Paid Circ.: 43
Avg. Free Circ.: 22755
Audit Company: Sworn/Estimate/Non-Audited
Audit Date: 43626

SULPHUR

SOUTHWEST DAILY NEWS

Street Address: 120 S Huntington St
City: Sulphur
State: LA
ZIP Code: 70663-3332
General Phone: (337) 527-7075
General Email: sdneditorial@yahoo.com
Publication Website: http://www.sulphurdailynews.com/
Parent Company: Lake Charles American Press
Editor Name: Brian Trahan
Editor Email: btrahan@sulphurdailynews.com
Advertising Executive Name: Traci Bumgardner
Advertising Executive Email: tbumgardner@sulphurdailynews.com
Delivery Methods: Mail`Newsstand`Carrier`Racks
Year Established: 1930
Own Printing Facility?: Y
Commercial printers?: Y
Mechanical specifications: Type page 13 x 21; E - 6 cols, 2 1/16, 1/8 between; A - 6 cols, 2 1/16, 1/8 between; C - 8 cols, 1 1/2, 1/8 between.
Published Days: Wed`Fri`Sun
Weekday Frequency: m
Avg. Paid Circ.: 4631
Audit Company: Sworn/Estimate/Non-Audited
Audit Date: 43626

TALLULAH

MADISON JOURNAL

Street Address: 300 S Chestnut St
City: Tallulah
State: LA
ZIP Code: 71282-4206
General Phone: (318) 574-1404
General Email: publisher@madisonjournal.com
Publication Website: under maintenance
Parent Company: 1976
Published Days: Thur
Avg. Paid Circ.: 2000
Audit Company: Sworn/Estimate/Non-Audited
Audit Date: 43626

VACHERIE

THE ENTERPRISE

Street Address: 2677 HIGHWAY 20
City: Vacherie
State: LA
ZIP Code: 70090
General Phone: (225) 265-2120
General Email: karenenterprise@bellsouth.net
Parent Company: Gannett
Published Days: Wed
Avg. Paid Circ.: 1800
Audit Company: Sworn/Estimate/Non-Audited
Audit Date: 43626

VIVIAN

CADDO CITIZEN

Street Address: 203 S Spruce St
City: Vivian
State: LA
ZIP Code: 71082-2841
General Phone: (318) 375-3294
General Email: caddocitizen@centurytel.net
Parent Company: Natchitoches Times newspaper
Published Days: Thur
Avg. Paid Circ.: 1350
Audit Company: Sworn/Estimate/Non-Audited
Audit Date: 43626

WELSH

THE WELSH CITIZEN

Street Address: 119 S Elms St
City: Welsh
State: LA
ZIP Code: 70591-4211
General Phone: (337) 734-2891
General Email: welshcitizen@centurytel.net
Year Established: 1958
Published Days: Tues
Avg. Paid Circ.: 1000
Audit Company: Sworn/Estimate/Non-Audited
Audit Date: 43626

WEST MONROE

THE OUACHITA CITIZEN

Street Address: 4423 Cypress St
City: West Monroe
State: LA
ZIP Code: 71291-7405
General Phone: (318) 396-0602
General Email: news@ouachitacitizen.com
Publication Website: https://www.hannapub.com/ouachitacitizen/
Parent Company: Hanna Newspapers
Publisher Name: Sam Hanna
Publisher Email: rick@ouachitacitizen.com
Publisher Phone: (318) 396-0602, ext : 202
Editor Name: Zachary Parker
Editor Email: zach@ouachitacitizen.com
Editor Phone: (318) 396-0602, ext : 205
Advertising Executive Name: Rick Day
Advertising Executive Email: rick@ouachitacitizen.com
Advertising Executive Phone: (318) 396-0602, ext : 203
Delivery Methods: Mail
Year Established: 1924
Own Printing Facility?: Y
Commercial printers?: Y
Mechanical specifications: 10x21.5 image size on 6 columns with standard gutter.
Published Days: Thur
Avg. Paid Circ.: 5200
Audit Company: Sworn/Estimate/Non-Audited
Audit Date: 43626

WINNSBORO

THE FRANKLIN SUN

Street Address: 514 Prairie St
City: Winnsboro
State: LA
ZIP Code: 71295-2737
General Phone: (318) 435-4521
General Email: monica@franklinsun.com
Publication Website: https://www.hannapub.com/franklinsun/
Parent Company: Hanna Newspapers
Editor Name: Joe Curtis
Advertising Executive Name: Monica Huff
Advertising Executive Email: monica@franklinsun.com
Delivery Methods: Mail`Racks
Year Established: 1856
Own Printing Facility?: Y
Mechanical specifications: Type page 13 x 21; E - 2 cols, 4 1/4, 1/8 between; A - 6 cols, 1/8 between; C - 6 cols, 1/8 between.
Published Days: Wed
Avg. Paid Circ.: 6200
Audit Company: Sworn/Estimate/Non-Audited
Audit Date: 43626

MASSACHUSETTS

ANDOVER

ANDOVER TOWNSMAN

Street Address: 33 Chestnut St
City: Andover
State: MA
ZIP Code: 1810
General Phone: (978) 475-7000
General Email: townsman@andovertownsman.com
Publication Website: https://www.andovertownsman.com/
Parent Company: CNHI, LLC
Delivery Methods: Mail`Newsstand
Year Established: 1887
Mechanical specifications: Type page 11 5/8 x 21 1/2; E - 6 cols, 1 5/6, 1/8 between; A - 6 cols, 1 5/6, 1/8 between; C - 10 cols, 1 1/16, 1/16 between.
Published Days: Thur
Avg. Paid Circ.: 5000
Avg. Free Circ.: 500
Audit Company: Sworn/Estimate/Non-Audited
Audit Date: 43626

BELLINGHAM

BELLINGHAM BULLETIN

Street Address: 36 Rakeville Cir
City: Bellingham
State: MA
ZIP Code: 2019
General Phone: (508) 883-3252
General Email: email@bellinghambulletin.com
Publication Website: http://www.bellinghambulletin.com/
Advertising Executive Name: Cyndy Rogers
Advertising Executive Email: cyndyrogers@charter.net
Advertising Executive Phone: (508) 529-4437
Year Established: 1994
Published Days: Thur`Mthly
Audit Company: Sworn/Estimate/Non-Audited
Audit Date: 43626

BEVERLY

AMESBURY NEWS

Street Address: 48 Dunham Road, Suite 3100
City: Beverly
State: MA
ZIP Code: 1915
General Phone: (978) 388-2406
General Email: amesbury@wickedlocal.com
Publication Website: https://amesbury.wickedlocal.com/
Advertising Executive Name: Linc Murphy
Advertising Executive Email: rmurphy@wickedlocal.com
Advertising Executive Phone: (978) 739-1371
Own Printing Facility?: Y
Commercial printers?: Y
Published Days: Fri
Avg. Paid Circ.: 7767
Avg. Free Circ.: 295
Audit Company: Sworn/Estimate/Non-Audited
Audit Date: 43626

BEVERLY

BEVERLY CITIZEN

Street Address: 48 Dunham Road, Suite 3100
City: Beverly
State: MA
ZIP Code: 1915
General Phone: (978) 927-2777
General Email: beverly@wickedlocal.com
Publication Website: https://beverly.wickedlocal.com/
Advertising Executive Name: Nancy Prag
Advertising Executive Email: nprag@wickedlocal.com
Advertising Executive Phone: (978) 739-1310
Year Established: 1851
Own Printing Facility?: Y
Commercial printers?: Y
Mechanical specifications: Type page 10 13/16 x 16; E - 5 cols, 2 1/16, between; A - 5 cols, 2 1/16, between; C - 8 cols, 1 7/32, between.
Published Days: Thur
Avg. Paid Circ.: 6284
Avg. Free Circ.: 470
Audit Company: AAM
Audit Date: 44015

BEVERLY

CAPE ANN BEACON

Street Address: 48 Dunham Road, Suite 3100
City: Beverly
State: MA
ZIP Code: 0 1915
General Phone: 978-739-1300
General Email: capeann@wickedlocal.com
Publication Website: gloucester.wickedlocal.com
Parent Company: Gannett
Editor Name: Kathleen Cordeiro
Editor Email: kcordeiro@wickedlocal.com
Editor Phone: 978-371-5736
Advertising Executive Name: Nancy Prag
Published Days: Fri
Avg. Free Circ.: 5500
Audit Company: AAM
Audit Date: 43284

BEVERLY

GEORGETOWN RECORD

Street Address: 48 Dunham Road, Suite 3100
City: Beverly
State: MA
ZIP Code: 1915
General Phone: (978) 739-8506
General Email: georgetown@wickedlocal.com
Publication Website: https://georgetown.wickedlocal.com/
Editor Name: Bryan McGonigle
Editor Email: bmcgonigle@wickedlocal.com
Editor Phone: (978) 739-1331
Advertising Executive Name: Nancy Prag
Advertising Executive Email: nprag@wickedlocal.com
Advertising Executive Phone: (978) 739-1310
Commercial printers?: Y
Mechanical specifications: Type page 10 13/16 x 16; E - 5 cols, 2 1/16, between; A - 5 cols, 2 1/16, between; C - 8 cols, 1 7/32, between.
Published Days: Thur
Avg. Paid Circ.: 592
Audit Company: AAM
Audit Date: 44015

BEVERLY

HAMILTON-WENHAM CHRONICLE

Street Address: 48 Dunham Road, Suite 3100
City: Beverly
State: MA
ZIP Code: 1915
General Phone: (978) 739-8542
General Email: hamilton-wenham@wickedlocal.com
Publication Website: https://hamilton.wickedlocal.com/
Advertising Executive Name: Nancy Prag
Advertising Executive Email: nprag@wickedlocal.com
Advertising Executive Phone: (978) 739-1310
Own Printing Facility?: Y
Commercial printers?: Y
Mechanical specifications: Type page 10 13/16 x 16; E - 5 cols, 2 1/16, between; A - 5 cols, 2 1/16, between; C - 8 cols, 1 7/32, between.
Published Days: Thur
Avg. Paid Circ.: 942
Audit Company: AAM
Audit Date: 44015

BEVERLY

IPSWICH CHRONICLE

Street Address: 48 Dunham Road, Suite 3100
City: Beverly
State: MA
ZIP Code: 1915
General Phone: (978) 739-1303
General Email: ipswich@wickedlocal.com
Publication Website: https://ipswich.wickedlocal.com/
Advertising Executive Name: Nancy Prag
Advertising Executive Email: nprag@wickedlocal.com
Advertising Executive Phone: (978) 739-1310
Own Printing Facility?: Y
Commercial printers?: Y
Mechanical specifications: Type page 10 13/16 x 16; E - 5 cols, 2 1/16, between; A - 5 cols, 2 1/16, between; C - 8 cols, 1 7/32, between.
Published Days: Thur
Avg. Paid Circ.: 2233
Avg. Free Circ.: 2
Audit Company: Sworn/Estimate/Non-Audited
Audit Date: 43626

BEVERLY

MALDEN OBSERVER

Street Address: 48 Dunham Road, Suite 3100
City: Beverly
State: MA
ZIP Code: 1915
General Phone: (781) 393-1827
General Email: malden@wickedlocal.com
Publication Website: https://malden.wickedlocal.com/
Advertising Executive Name: Nancy Prag
Advertising Executive Email: nprag@wickedlocal.com
Advertising Executive Phone: (978) 739-1310
Own Printing Facility?: Y
Commercial printers?: Y
Mechanical specifications: Type page 10 13/16 x 16; E - 5 cols, 2 1/16, between; A - 5 cols, 2 1/16, between; C - 8 cols, 1 7/32, between.
Published Days: Fri
Avg. Paid Circ.: 809
Audit Company: AAM
Audit Date: 44015

BEVERLY

MARBLEHEAD REPORTER

Street Address: 48 Dunham Road, Suite 3100
City: Beverly
State: MA
ZIP Code: 1915
General Phone: (781) 639-4800
General Email: marblehead@wickedlocal.com
Publication Website: https://marblehead.wickedlocal.com/
Parent Company: Gannett
Advertising Executive Name: Nancy Prag
Advertising Executive Email: nprag@wickedlocal.com
Advertising Executive Phone: (978) 739-1310
Own Printing Facility?: Y
Commercial printers?: Y
Mechanical specifications: Type page 10 13/16 x 16; E - 5 cols, 2 1/16, between; A - 5 cols, 2 1/16, between; C - 8 cols, 1 7/32, between.
Published Days: Thur
Avg. Paid Circ.: 3239
Avg. Free Circ.: 68
Audit Company: AAM
Audit Date: 44015

BEVERLY

MEDFORD TRANSCRIPT

Street Address: 48 Dunham Road, Suite 3100
City: Beverly
State: MA
ZIP Code: 1915
General Phone: (781) 396-1982
General Email: medford@wickedlocal.com
Publication Website: https://medford.wickedlocal.com/
Parent Company: Gannett
Advertising Executive Name: Nancy Prag
Advertising Executive Email: nprag@wickedlocal.com
Advertising Executive Phone: (978) 739-1310
Own Printing Facility?: Y
Commercial printers?: Y
Mechanical specifications: Type page 13 x 21; E - 6 cols, 2 1/16, between; A - 6 cols, 2 1/16, between; C - 10 cols, 1 7/32, between.
Published Days: Thur
Avg. Paid Circ.: 2036
Audit Company: AAM
Audit Date: 44015

BEVERLY

NEWBURYPORT CURRENT

Street Address: 48 Dunham Road, Suite 3100
City: Beverly
State: MA
ZIP Code: 1915
General Phone: (978) 739-1347
General Email: newburyport@wickedlocal.com
Publication Website: https://newburyport.wickedlocal.com/
Parent Company: Gannett
Advertising Executive Name: Nancy Prag
Advertising Executive Email: nprag@wickedlocal.com
Advertising Executive Phone: (978) 739-1310
Own Printing Facility?: Y
Commercial printers?: Y
Mechanical specifications: Type page 10 13/16 x 16; E - 5 cols, 2 1/16, between; A - 5 cols, 2 1/16, between; C - 8 cols, 1 7/32, between.
Published Days: Fri
Avg. Paid Circ.: 7428
Audit Company: Sworn/Estimate/Non-Audited
Audit Date: 43626

BEVERLY

NORTH ANDOVER CITIZEN

Street Address: 48 Dunham Road, Suite 3100
City: Beverly
State: MA
ZIP Code: 1915
General Phone: (978) 685-5128
General Email: northandover@wickedlocal.com
Publication Website: https://northandover.wickedlocal.com/
Advertising Executive Name: Nancy Prag
Advertising Executive Email: nprag@wickedlocal.com
Advertising Executive Phone: (978) 739-1310
Own Printing Facility?: Y
Commercial printers?: Y
Mechanical specifications: Type page 10 13/16 x 16; E - 5 cols, 2 1/16, between; A - 5 cols, 2 1/16, between; C - 8 cols, 1 7/32, between.
Published Days: Fri
Avg. Paid Circ.: 513
Audit Company: AAM
Audit Date: 44015

BEVERLY

SALEM GAZETTE

Street Address: 48 Dunham Road, Suite 3100
City: Beverly
State: MA
ZIP Code: 0 1915
General Phone: 978-739-1300
General Email: salem@wickedlocal.com
Publication Website: salem.wickedlocal.com
Parent Company: Gannett
Editor Name: Kathleen Cordeiro
Editor Email: kcordeiro@wickedlocal.com
Editor Phone: 978-371-5736
Advertising Executive Name: Jenn Mann
Published Days: Fri
Audit Company: Sworn/Estimate/Non-Audited
Audit Date: 43626

BEVERLY

SOMERVILLE JOURNAL

Street Address: 48 Dunham Road
City: Beverly
State: MA
ZIP Code: 1915
General Phone: (617) 433-6700
General Email: somerville@wickedlocal.com
Publication Website: https://somerville.wickedlocal.com/
Parent Company: Gannett
Advertising Executive Name: Linc Murphy
Advertising Executive Email: rmurphy@

Community Newspapers in the U.S.

III-253

wickedlocal.com
Advertising Executive Phone: (978) 739-1371
Year Established: 1870
Published Days: Wed
Avg. Paid Circ.: 1085
Audit Company: AAM
Audit Date: 44015

BEVERLY

SWAMPSCOTT REPORTER

Street Address: 48 Dunham Road, Suite 3100
City: Beverly
State: MA
ZIP Code: 1915
General Phone: (781) 639-4800
General Email: swampscott@wickedlocal.com
Publication Website: https://swampscott.wickedlocal.com/
Parent Company: Gannett
Advertising Executive Name: Linc Murphy
Advertising Executive Email: rmurphy@wickedlocal.com
Advertising Executive Phone: (978) 739-1371
Delivery Methods: Mail`Carrier
Year Established: 1850
Own Printing Facility?: Y
Commercial printers?: Y
Mechanical specifications: Type page 10 13/16 x 16; E - 5 cols, 2 1/16, between; A - 5 cols, 2 1/16, between; C - 8 cols, 1 7/32, between.
Published Days: Thur
Avg. Paid Circ.: 94
Avg. Free Circ.: 1228
Audit Company: AAM
Audit Date: 44015

BEVERLY

TRI-TOWN TRANSCRIPT

Street Address: 48 Dunham Road, Suite 3100
City: Beverly
State: MA
ZIP Code: 1915
General Phone: (978) 739-1393
General Email: tritown@wickedlocal.com
Publication Website: https://boxford.wickedlocal.com/
Advertising Executive Name: Nancy Prag
Advertising Executive Email: nprag@wickedlocal.com
Advertising Executive Phone: (978) 739-1310
Own Printing Facility?: Y
Commercial printers?: Y
Mechanical specifications: Type page 10 13/16 x 16; E - 5 cols, 2 1/16, between; A - 5 cols, 2 1/16, between; C - 8 cols, 1 7/32, between.
Published Days: Fri
Avg. Paid Circ.: 2604
Audit Company: Sworn/Estimate/Non-Audited
Audit Date: 43626

BEVERLY

WAKEFIELD OBSERVER

Street Address: 48 Dunham Road, Suite 3100
City: Beverly
State: MA
ZIP Code: 1915
General Phone: (978) 739-8504
General Email: wakefield@wickedlocal.com
Publication Website: https://wakefield.wickedlocal.com/
Advertising Executive Name: Nancy Prag
Advertising Executive Email: nprag@wickedlocal.com
Advertising Executive Phone: (978) 739-1310
Own Printing Facility?: Y
Commercial printers?: Y
Mechanical specifications: Type page 10 13/16 x 16; E - 5 cols, 2 1/16, between; A - 5 cols, 2 1/16, between; C - 8 cols, 1 7/32, between.
Published Days: Thur
Avg. Paid Circ.: 200
Audit Company: AAM
Audit Date: 44015

BOSTON

BOSTON BUSINESS JOURNAL

Street Address: 70 Franklin St., 8th Floor
City: Boston
State: MA
ZIP Code: 2110
General Phone: (617) 330-1000
General Email: boston@bizjournals.com
Publication Website: https://www.bizjournals.com/boston/
Parent Company: American City Business Journals
Publisher Name: Carolyn M. Jones
Publisher Email: cmjones@bizjournals.com
Publisher Phone: (617) 316-3220
Editor Name: Don Seiffert
Editor Email: dseiffert@bizjournals.com
Editor Phone: (617) 316-3271
Advertising Executive Name: Cheryl Maier
Advertising Executive Email: cmaier@bizjournals.com
Advertising Executive Phone: (617) 316-3217
Year Established: 1981
Published Days: Thur
Audit Company: Sworn/Estimate/Non-Audited
Audit Date: 43626

BOSTON

MASSACHUSETTS LAWYERS WEEKLY

Street Address: 40 Court Street
City: Boston
State: MA
ZIP Code: 02108-4620
General Phone: (617) 451-7300
General Email: sziegler@lawyersweekly.com
Publication Website: https://masslawyersweekly.com/
Parent Company: Gannett
Publisher Name: Susan Bocamazo
Publisher Email: sbocamazo@lawyersweekly.com
Publisher Phone: (617) 218-8191
Editor Name: Henriette Campagne
Editor Email: hcampagne@lawyersweekly.com
Editor Phone: (617) 218-8192
Advertising Executive Name: Scott Ziegler
Advertising Executive Email: sziegler@lawyersweekly.com
Advertising Executive Phone: (617) 218-8211
Delivery Methods: Mail`Carrier
Year Established: 1972
Published Days: Mon
Audit Company: Sworn/Estimate/Non-Audited
Audit Date: 43626

BOSTON

RHODE ISLAND LAWYERS WEEKLY

Street Address: 40 Court St., 5th Floor
City: Boston
State: MA
ZIP Code: 2108
General Phone: (617) 451-7300
General Email: sziegler@lawyersweekly.com
Publication Website: https://rilawyersweekly.com/
Parent Company: Gannett
Publisher Name: Susan A. Bocamazo
Publisher Email: sbocamazo@lawyersweekly.com
Publisher Phone: (617) 218-8191
Editor Name: Susan A. Bocamazo
Editor Email: sbocamazo@lawyersweekly.com
Editor Phone: (617) 218-8191
Advertising Executive Name: Scott Ziegler
Advertising Executive Email: sziegler@lawyersweekly.com
Advertising Executive Phone: (617) 218-8211
Delivery Methods: Mail`Carrier
Published Days: Mon
Audit Company: Sworn/Estimate/Non-Audited
Audit Date: 43626

BROCKTON

AVON MESSENGER

Street Address: 1324 Belmont St
City: Brockton
State: MA
ZIP Code: 02301-4435
General Phone: (508) 427-4000
General Email: newsroom@enterprisenews.com
Publication Website: https://avon.wickedlocal.com/
Editor Name: Steve Damish
Editor Email: sdamish@enterprisenews.com
Editor Phone: (617) 786-4022
Own Printing Facility?: Y
Commercial printers?: Y
Mechanical specifications: Type page 10 9/16 x 16; E - 6 cols, between; A - 6 cols, between; C - 7 cols, between.
Published Days: Thur
Avg. Paid Circ.: 1022
Audit Company: Sworn/Estimate/Non-Audited
Audit Date: 43626

CANTON

CANTON CITIZEN

Street Address: 866 Washington St
City: Canton
State: MA
ZIP Code: 2021
General Phone: (781) 821-4418
General Email: submissions@thecantoncitizen.com
Publication Website: https://www.thecantoncitizen.com/
Publisher Name: Connor Erickson
Editor Name: Jay Turner
Editor Phone: (617) 827-4987
Advertising Executive Name: Connor Erickson
Delivery Methods: Mail`Newsstand
Year Established: 1987
Own Printing Facility?: Y
Published Days: Thur
Avg. Paid Circ.: 3600
Avg. Free Circ.: 20
Audit Company: Sworn/Estimate/Non-Audited
Audit Date: 43626

CARLISLE

CARLISLE MOSQUITO

Street Address: 662A Bedford Rd
City: Carlisle
State: MA
ZIP Code: 1741
General Phone: (978) 369-8313
General Email: ads@carlislemosquito.org
Publication Website: http://www.carlislemosquito.org/
Publisher Name: Susan Emmons
Publisher Phone: (978) 369-8313
Editor Name: Penny Zezima
Editor Phone: (978) 369-8313
Advertising Executive Name: Susan Mills
Advertising Executive Email: ads@carlislemosquito.org
Advertising Executive Phone: (978) 369-8313
Delivery Methods: Mail
Year Established: 1972
Published Days: Fri
Avg. Free Circ.: 2100
Audit Company: Sworn/Estimate/Non-Audited
Audit Date: 43626

CHATHAM

THE CAPE COD CHRONICLE

Street Address: 60 Munson Meeting Way
City: Chatham
State: MA
ZIP Code: 02633-1992
General Phone: (508) 945-2220
General Email: info@capecodchronicle.com
Publication Website: https://capecodchronicle.com/
Publisher Name: Henry C. Hyora
Publisher Email: hank@capecodchronicle.com
Publisher Phone: (508) 348-5112
Editor Name: Bill Galvin
Editor Email: billy@capecodchronicle.com
Editor Phone: (508) 348-5102
Advertising Executive Name: Debra DeCosta
Advertising Executive Email: debbie@capecodchronicle.com
Advertising Executive Phone: (508) 348-5106
Delivery Methods: Mail`Newsstand
Mechanical specifications: Type page 10 1/4 x 16.
Published Days: Thur
Avg. Paid Circ.: 27404
Avg. Free Circ.: 721
Audit Company: Sworn/Estimate/Non-Audited
Audit Date: 43626

CLINTON

THE BANNER

Street Address: 156 Church St
City: Clinton
State: MA
ZIP Code: 01510-2563
General Phone: (508) 835-4865
General Email: mfroimson@telegram.com
Publication Website: https://www.telegram.com/
Publisher Name: Gary Hutner
Publisher Email: gary.hutner@telegram.com
Publisher Phone: (508) 793-9329
Editor Name: Jan Gottesman
Editor Email: jan.gottesman@telegram.com
Editor Phone: (508) 793-9345
Advertising Executive Name: Marita Froimson
Advertising Executive Email: mfroimson@telegram.com
Advertising Executive Phone: (508) 793-9314
Delivery Methods: Mail`Newsstand
Year Established: 1978
Mechanical specifications: Type page 9 2/3 x 12; E - 5 cols, 2 1/16, between; A - 5 cols, 2 1/16, between; C - 5 cols, 2 1/16, between.
Published Days: Fri
Avg. Paid Circ.: 1800
Audit Company: Sworn/Estimate/Non-Audited
Audit Date: 43626

CLINTON

THE ITEM

Street Address: 156 Church St
City: Clinton
State: MA
ZIP Code: 01510-2563
General Phone: (978) 368-0176

General Email: itemads@telegram.com
Publication Website: https://www.telegram.com/theitem
Publisher Name: Gary Hutner
Publisher Email: gary.hutner@telegram.com
Publisher Phone: (508) 793-9329
Editor Name: Jan Gottesman
Editor Email: jan.gottesman@telegram.com
Editor Phone: (508) 793-9345
Advertising Executive Name: Marita Froimson
Advertising Executive Email: mfroimson@telegram.com
Advertising Executive Phone: (508) 793-9314
Delivery Methods: Mail Carrier
Year Established: 1893
Mechanical specifications: Type page 9.667X12.75 E - 5 cols
Published Days: Fri
Avg. Paid Circ.: 5100
Avg. Free Circ.: 100
Audit Company: Sworn/Estimate/Non-Audited
Audit Date: 43626

CONCORD

BEDFORD MINUTEMAN

Street Address: 150 Baker Avenue Ext
City: Concord
State: MA
ZIP Code: 1742
General Phone: (978) 371-5796
General Email: bedford@wickedlocal.com
Publication Website: https://bedford.wickedlocal.com/
Parent Company: Gannett
Advertising Executive Name: Pam Calder
Advertising Executive Email: pcalder@wickedlocal.com
Advertising Executive Phone: (978) 371-5723
Delivery Methods: Mail
Year Established: 1956
Own Printing Facility?: Y
Commercial printers?: Y
Published Days: Thur
Avg. Paid Circ.: 7996
Avg. Free Circ.: 5815
Audit Company: Sworn/Estimate/Non-Audited
Audit Date: 43626

CONCORD

BILLERICA MINUTEMAN

Street Address: 150 Baker Avenue Ext
City: Concord
State: MA
ZIP Code: 1742
General Phone: (781) 674-7729
General Email: billerica@wickedlocal.com
Publication Website: https://billerica.wickedlocal.com/
Parent Company: Gannett
Advertising Executive Email: classifieds@wickedlocal.com
Own Printing Facility?: Y
Commercial printers?: Y
Published Days: Thur
Avg. Paid Circ.: 7996
Avg. Free Circ.: 3360
Audit Company: AAM
Audit Date: 44015

CONCORD

BURLINGTON UNION

Street Address: 150 Baker Avenue Ext
City: Concord
State: MA
ZIP Code: 1742
General Phone: (617) 629-3390
General Email: burlington@wickedlocal.com
Publication Website: https://burlington.wickedlocal.com/
Parent Company: Gannett
Advertising Executive Email: classifieds@wickedlocal.com
Delivery Methods: Mail Newsstand
Year Established: 1963
Own Printing Facility?: Y
Commercial printers?: Y
Published Days: Thur
Avg. Paid Circ.: 1319
Audit Company: AAM
Audit Date: 44015

CONCORD

CHELMSFORD INDEPENDENT

Street Address: 150 Baker Avenue Ext., Suite 101
City: Concord
State: MA
ZIP Code: 01742-2126
General Phone: (978) 371-5751
General Email: chelmsford@wickedlocal.com
Publication Website: https://chelmsford.wickedlocal.com/
Advertising Executive Email: classifieds@wickedlocal.com
Advertising Executive Phone: (781) 433-6925
Own Printing Facility?: Y
Commercial printers?: Y
Published Days: Thur
Avg. Paid Circ.: 1336
Audit Company: AAM
Audit Date: 44015

CONCORD

LINCOLN JOURNAL

Street Address: 150 Baker Avenue Ext., Suite 101
City: Concord
State: MA
ZIP Code: 01742-2199
General Phone: (978) 371-5759
General Email: lincoln@wickedlocal.com
Publication Website: https://lincoln.wickedlocal.com/
Advertising Executive Name: Linc Murphy
Advertising Executive Email: rmurphy@wickedlocal.com
Advertising Executive Phone: (978) 739-1371
Published Days: Thur
Avg. Paid Circ.: 439
Avg. Free Circ.: 37
Audit Company: AAM
Audit Date: 44015

CONCORD

LITTLETON INDEPENDENT

Street Address: 150 Baker Avenue Ext., Suite 101
City: Concord
State: MA
ZIP Code: 01742-2199
General Phone: (978) 371-5713
General Email: littleton@wickedlocal.com
Publication Website: https://littleton.wickedlocal.com/
Advertising Executive Name: Pam Calder
Advertising Executive Email: pcalder@wickedlocal.com
Advertising Executive Phone: (978) 371-5723
Commercial printers?: Y
Published Days: Thur
Avg. Paid Circ.: 779
Avg. Free Circ.: 225
Audit Company: AAM
Audit Date: 44015

CONCORD

TEWKSBURY ADVOCATE

Street Address: 150 Baker Ave. Ext., Suite 101
City: Concord
State: MA
ZIP Code: 1742
General Phone: (978) 371-5744
General Email: tewksbury@wickedlocal.com
Publication Website: https://tewksbury.wickedlocal.com/
Advertising Executive Email: classifieds@wickedlocal.com
Advertising Executive Phone: (781) 433-6925
Published Days: Thur
Avg. Paid Circ.: 247
Audit Company: AAM
Audit Date: 44015

CONCORD

THE BEACON-VILLAGER

Street Address: 150 Baker Avenue Ext, Suite 101
City: Concord
State: MA
ZIP Code: 1742
General Phone: (978) 371-5759
General Email: beacon-villager@wickedlocal.com
Publication Website: https://maynard.wickedlocal.com/
Parent Company: Gannett
Advertising Executive Name: Pam Calder
Advertising Executive Email: pcalder@wickedlocal.com
Advertising Executive Phone: (978) 371-5723
Published Days: Thur
Avg. Paid Circ.: 1939
Avg. Free Circ.: 971
Audit Company: AAM
Audit Date: 44015

CONCORD

THE BOLTON COMMON

Street Address: 150 Baker Avenue Ext
City: Concord
State: MA
ZIP Code: 1742
General Phone: (978) 371-5759
General Email: delivery@mypapertoday.com
Publication Website: https://bolton.wickedlocal.com/
Advertising Executive Email: classifieds@wickedlocal.com
Year Established: 1988
Published Days: Fri
Avg. Paid Circ.: 1141
Audit Company: Sworn/Estimate/Non-Audited
Audit Date: 43626

CONCORD

THE CONCORD JOURNAL

Street Address: 150 Baker Avenue Ext
City: Concord
State: MA
ZIP Code: 1742
General Phone: (978) 371-5742
General Email: pcalder@wickedlocal.com
Publication Website: https://concord.wickedlocal.com/
Parent Company: Gannett
Advertising Executive Name: Pam Calder
Advertising Executive Email: pcalder@wickedlocal.com
Advertising Executive Phone: (978) 371-5723
Published Days: Thur
Avg. Paid Circ.: 3002
Avg. Free Circ.: 714
Audit Company: AAM
Audit Date: 44015

CONCORD

THE HARVARD POST

Street Address: 150 Baker Avenue Ext
City: Concord
State: MA
ZIP Code: 1742
General Phone: (978) 371-5759
General Email: classifieds@wickedlocal.com
Publication Website: https://harvard.wickedlocal.com/
Parent Company: Gannett Co., Inc
Advertising Executive Email: classifieds@wickedlocal.com
Advertising Executive Phone: (781) 433-6925
Year Established: 1973
Published Days: Fri
Avg. Free Circ.: 83
Audit Company: Sworn/Estimate/Non-Audited
Audit Date: 43626

CONCORD

TIMES & COURIER

Street Address: 150 Baker Avenue Ext, Suite 101
City: Concord
State: MA
ZIP Code: 01742-2199
General Phone: (978) 371-5759
General Email: classifieds@wickedlocal.com
Publication Website: https://clinton.wickedlocal.com/contact
Advertising Executive Email: classifieds@wickedlocal.com
Advertising Executive Phone: (781) 433-6925
Delivery Methods: Mail Newsstand Racks
Mechanical specifications: Type page 12 x 12; E - 5 cols
Published Days: Thur
Avg. Paid Circ.: 2809
Audit Company: Sworn/Estimate/Non-Audited
Audit Date: 43626

CONCORD

WESTFORD EAGLE

Street Address: 150 Baker Avenue Ext
City: Concord
State: MA
ZIP Code: 01742-2199
General Phone: (978) 371-5729
General Email: westford@wickedlocal.com
Publication Website: https://westford.wickedlocal.com/
Advertising Executive Name: Pam Calder
Advertising Executive Email: pcalder@wickedlocal.com
Advertising Executive Phone: (978) 371-5723
Own Printing Facility?: Y
Commercial printers?: Y
Published Days: Fri
Avg. Paid Circ.: 1477
Avg. Free Circ.: 536
Audit Company: AAM
Audit Date: 44015

CONCORD

WILMINGTON ADVOCATE

Street Address: 150 Baker Avenue Ext
City: Concord
State: MA
ZIP Code: 01742-2199
General Phone: (978) 371-5744
General Email: wilmington@wickedlocal.com
Publication Website: https://wilmington.wickedlocal.com/
Advertising Executive Email: classifieds@wickedlocal.com
Advertising Executive Phone: (781) 433-6925
Own Printing Facility?: Y
Commercial printers?: Y
Published Days: Fri

Community Newspapers in the U.S.

III-255

Avg. Free Circ.: 685
Audit Company: AAM
Audit Date: 44015

CONCORD

WOBURN ADVOCATE

Street Address: 150 Baker Ave. Ext., Suite 101,
City: Concord
State: MA
ZIP Code: 01742-2117
General Phone: (978) 371-5744
General Email: woburn@wickedlocal.com
Publication Website: https://woburn.wickedlocal.com/
Advertising Executive Email: classifieds@wickedlocal.com
Advertising Executive Phone: (781) 433-6925
Published Days: Thur
Avg. Free Circ.: 3627
Audit Company: AAM
Audit Date: 44015

DANVERS

DANVERS HERALD

Street Address: 75 Sylvan St
City: Danvers
State: MA
ZIP Code: 01923-2765
General Phone: (978) 774-0505
General Email: danvers@wickedlocal.com
Publication Website: http://danvers.wickedlocal.com/
Editor Name: Jeff Pope
Advertising Executive Name: Linc Murphy
Advertising Executive Email: rmurphy@wickedlocal.com
Advertising Executive Phone: (978) 739-1371
Own Printing Facility?: Y
Commercial printers?: Y
Mechanical specifications: Type page 10 13/16 x 16; E - 5 cols, 2 1/16, between; A - 5 cols, 2 1/16, between; C - 8 cols, 1 7/32, between.
Published Days: Thur
Avg. Paid Circ.: 1465
Avg. Free Circ.: 192
Audit Company: AAM
Audit Date: 44015

DANVERS

MELROSE FREE PRESS

Street Address: 75 Sylvan St, C 105
City: Danvers
State: MA
ZIP Code: 01923-2765
General Phone: (978) 739-1314
General Email: melrose@wickedlocal.com
Publication Website: https://melrose.wickedlocal.com/
Parent Company: Gannett
Advertising Executive Name: Nancy Prag
Advertising Executive Email: nprag@wickedlocal.com
Advertising Executive Phone: (978) 739-1310
Year Established: 1901
Own Printing Facility?: Y
Commercial printers?: Y
Mechanical specifications: Type page 13 x 21; E - 6 cols, 2 1/16, between; A - 6 cols, 2 1/16, between; C - 10 cols, 1 7/32, between.
Published Days: Thur
Avg. Paid Circ.: 1372
Audit Company: AAM
Audit Date: 44015

DANVERS

READING ADVOCATE

Street Address: 48 Dunham Road
City: Danvers
State: MA
ZIP Code: 1915
General Phone: (781) 942-2252
General Email: reading@wickedlocal.com
Publication Website: https://reading.wickedlocal.com/
Advertising Executive Name: Nancy Prag
Advertising Executive Email: nprag@wickedlocal.com
Advertising Executive Phone: (978) 739-1310
Published Days: Wed
Avg. Paid Circ.: 520
Audit Company: AAM
Audit Date: 44015

DANVERS

SAUGUS ADVERTISER

Street Address: 48 Dunham Road
City: Danvers
State: MA
ZIP Code: 1915
General Phone: (978) 739-1395
General Email: saugus@wickedlocal.com
Publication Website: https://saugus.wickedlocal.com/
Parent Company: Gannett
Advertising Executive Name: Nancy Prag
Advertising Executive Email: nprag@wickedlocal.com
Advertising Executive Phone: (978) 739-1310
Own Printing Facility?: Y
Commercial printers?: Y
Mechanical specifications: Type page 13 x 21; E - 6 cols, 2 1/16, between; A - 6 cols, 2 1/16, between; C - 10 cols, 1 7/32, between.
Published Days: Thur
Avg. Paid Circ.: 1362
Audit Company: AAM
Audit Date: 44015

DEVENS

PEPPERELL FREE PRESS

Street Address: 78 Barnum Rd
City: Devens
State: MA
ZIP Code: 01434-3508
General Phone: (978) 772-0777
General Email: news@nashobavalleyvoice.com
Publication Website: https://www.nashobavalleyvoice.com/location/connecticut/middlesex-county/pepperell/
Publisher Name: Kevin Corrado
Publisher Email: kcorrado@medianewsgroup.com
Publisher Phone: (978) 970-4807
Advertising Executive Name: Eddie R. Najeeullah
Advertising Executive Email: enajeeullah@mediaonene.com
Advertising Executive Phone: (978) 970-4715
Year Established: 1869
Mechanical specifications: Type page 12 x 21; E - 6 cols, between; A - 6 cols, between; C - 9 cols, between.
Published Days: Fri
Avg. Paid Circ.: 1023
Audit Company: Sworn/Estimate/Non-Audited
Audit Date: 43626

DEVENS

TOWNSEND TIMES

Street Address: 78 Barnum Rd
City: Devens
State: MA
ZIP Code: 01434-3508
General Phone: (978) 772-0777
General Email: news@nashobavalleyvoice.com
Publication Website: https://www.nashobavalleyvoice.com/location/connecticut/middlesex-county/townsend/
Publisher Name: Kevin Corrado
Publisher Email: kcorrado@medianewsgroup.com
Publisher Phone: (978) 970-4807
Advertising Executive Name: Eddie R. Najeeullah
Advertising Executive Email: enajeeullah@mediaonene.com
Advertising Executive Phone: (978) 970-4715
Delivery Methods: Mail`Newsstand`Racks
Mechanical specifications: Type page 12 x 21; E - 6 cols, between; A - 6 cols, between; C - 9 cols, between.
Published Days: Fri
Avg. Paid Circ.: 643
Audit Company: Sworn/Estimate/Non-Audited
Audit Date: 43626

DORCHESTER

BOSTON HAITIAN REPORTER

Street Address: 150 Mount Vernon St
City: Dorchester
State: MA
ZIP Code: 02125-3135
General Phone: (617) 436-1222
General Email: addesk@dotnews.com
Publication Website: https://www.bostonhaitian.com/
Parent Company: Boston Neighborhood News, Inc.
Publisher Name: William P. Forry
Publisher Email: bforry@dotnews.com
Editor Name: William P. Forry
Editor Email: bforry@dotnews.com
Advertising Executive Name: Jack Conboy
Advertising Executive Email: addesk@dotnews.com
Advertising Executive Phone: (617) 436-1222, ext : 14
Delivery Methods: Mail
Year Established: 1983
Published Days: Mthly
Audit Company: Sworn/Estimate/Non-Audited
Audit Date: 43626

DORCHESTER

BOSTON IRISH REPORTER

Street Address: 150 Mount Vernon St
City: Dorchester
State: MA
ZIP Code: 2125
General Phone: (617) 436-1222
General Email: news@dotnews.com
Publication Website: https://www.bostonirish.com/
Parent Company: Boston Neighborhood News, Inc.
Publisher Name: William P. Forry
Publisher Email: bforry@dotnews.com
Editor Name: William P. Forry
Editor Email: bforry@dotnews.com
Advertising Executive Name: Jack Conboy
Advertising Executive Email: addesk@dotnews.com
Advertising Executive Phone: (617) 436-1222, ext : 14
Delivery Methods: Mail
Year Established: 1983
Published Days: Mthly
Audit Company: Sworn/Estimate/Non-Audited
Audit Date: 43626

DORCHESTER

MATTAPAN REPORTER

Street Address: 150 Mount Vernon St
City: Dorchester
State: MA
ZIP Code: 02125-3135
General Phone: (617) 436-1222
General Email: addesk@dotnews.com
Publication Website: https://www.dotnews.com/mattapan
Parent Company: Boston Neighborhood News, Inc.
Publisher Name: Edward W. Forry
Publisher Email: eforry@dotnews.com
Editor Name: William P. Forry
Editor Email: bforry@dotnews.com
Advertising Executive Name: Jack Conboy
Advertising Executive Email: addesk@dotnews.com
Delivery Methods: Mail
Year Established: 1983
Published Days: Thur
Audit Company: Sworn/Estimate/Non-Audited
Audit Date: 43626

DORCHESTER

THE DORCHESTER REPORTER

Street Address: 150 Mount Vernon St
City: Dorchester
State: MA
ZIP Code: 2125
General Phone: (617) 436-1222
General Email: addesk@dotnews.com
Publication Website: https://www.dotnews.com/
Publisher Name: William P. Forry
Publisher Email: bforry@dotnews.com
Editor Name: William P. Forry
Editor Email: bforry@dotnews.com
Advertising Executive Name: Jack Conboy
Advertising Executive Email: addesk@dotnews.com
Advertising Executive Phone: (617) 436-1222, ext : 14
Delivery Methods: Mail`Newsstand
Year Established: 1983
Published Days: Thur
Avg. Paid Circ.: 22000
Audit Company: Sworn/Estimate/Non-Audited
Audit Date: 43626

DUXBURY

DUXBURY CLIPPER

Street Address: 11 S Station St
City: Duxbury
State: MA
ZIP Code: 02332-4534
General Phone: (781) 934-2811
General Email: ads@duxburyclipper.com
Publication Website: http://www.duxburyclipper.com/
Parent Company: Duxbury Clipper
Editor Name: Matthew Nadler
Editor Email: editor@duxburyclipper.com
Editor Phone: (781) 934-2811, ext : 31
Advertising Executive Name: Robin Nudd
Advertising Executive Email: robin@duxburyclipper.com
Advertising Executive Phone: (781) 934-2811, ext : 21
Year Established: 1950
Published Days: Wed
Avg. Paid Circ.: 4500
Audit Company: Sworn/Estimate/Non-Audited
Audit Date: 43626

EAST LONGMEADOW

REMINDER METROWEST / CHICOPEE HERALD

Street Address: 280 N Main St
City: East Longmeadow
State: MA

ZIP Code: 1085
General Phone: (413) 525-6661
General Email: pressreleases@thelongmeadownews.com
Publication Website: http://www.thelongmeadownews.com/
Parent Company: Reminder Publications
Publisher Name: Fran Smith
Publisher Email: fran@thereminder.com
Editor Name: G. Michael Dobbs
Editor Email: news@thereminder.com
Editor Phone: (413) 525-6661, ext : 103
Delivery Methods: Mail`Carrier
Year Established: 1962
Mechanical specifications: Type page 10 x 13; E - 5 cols, 2, 1/8 between; A - 5 cols, 2, 1/8 between; C - 5 cols, 2, 1/8 between.
Published Days: Fri
Avg. Paid Circ.: 2
Avg. Free Circ.: 8926
Audit Company: Sworn/Estimate/Non-Audited
Audit Date: 43626

EAST LONGMEADOW

SPRINGFIELD REMINDER

Street Address: 280 N Main St
City: East Longmeadow
State: MA
ZIP Code: 01028-1868
General Phone: (413) 525-3247
General Email: marketing@reminderpublications.com
Publication Website: https://www.thereminder.com/Localnews/springfield/
Parent Company: Reminder Publications
Editor Name: G. Michael Dobbs
Editor Email: news@thereminder.com
Editor Phone: (413) 525-3247, ext : 103
Advertising Executive Name: Barb Perry
Advertising Executive Phone: (413) 525-6661x135
Delivery Methods: Mail`Carrier
Year Established: 1962
Mechanical specifications: Type page 10 x 13; E - 5 cols, 2, 1/8 between; A - 5 cols, 2, 1/8 between; C - 5 cols, 2, 1/8 between.
Published Days: Fri
Avg. Paid Circ.: 8
Avg. Free Circ.: 5931
Audit Company: Sworn/Estimate/Non-Audited
Audit Date: 43626

EAST LONGMEADOW

THE REMINDER

Street Address: 280 N Main St
City: East Longmeadow
State: MA
ZIP Code: 1028
General Phone: (413) 525-3247
General Email: marketing@reminderpublications.com
Publication Website: https://www.thereminder.com/
Parent Company: Reminder Publications
Editor Name: G. Michael Dobbs
Editor Email: news@thereminder.com
Editor Phone: (413) 525-3247, ext : 103
Advertising Executive Name: Paula Dimauro
Advertising Executive Email: pdimauro@thereminder.com
Advertising Executive Phone: (413) 525-6661, ext : 111
Delivery Methods: Mail`Carrier
Year Established: 1962
Mechanical specifications: Type page 10 x 13; E - 5 cols, 2, 1/8 between; A - 5 cols, 2, 1/8 between; C - 5 cols, 2, 1/8 between.
Published Days: Thur`Fri
Avg. Paid Circ.: 8
Avg. Free Circ.: 94904
Audit Company: CVC
Audit Date: 43081

EDGARTOWN

VINEYARD GAZETTE

Street Address: 34 S Summer St
City: Edgartown
State: MA
ZIP Code: 02539-8104
General Phone: (508) 627-4311
General Email: news@mvgazette.com
Publication Website: https://vineyardgazette.com/
Parent Company: Martha's Vineyard Online
Publisher Name: Jane Seagrave
Publisher Email: jseagrave@mvgazette.com
Editor Name: Julia Wells
Editor Email: jwells@mvgazette.com
Advertising Executive Name: Jane McTeigue
Advertising Executive Email: jmcteigue@mvgazette.com
Delivery Methods: Mail`Newsstand`Racks
Year Established: 1846
Own Printing Facility?: Y
Commercial printers?: N
Mechanical specifications: Type page 16 1/4 x 20 3/4; E - 7 cols, 2 1/8, 1/4 between; A - 7 cols, 2 1/8, 1/4 between; C - 7 cols, 2 1/8, 1/4 between.
Published Days: Fri
Avg. Paid Circ.: 9000
Avg. Free Circ.: 150
Audit Company: Sworn/Estimate/Non-Audited
Audit Date: 43626

EVERETT

EVERETT LEADER HERALD NEWS GAZETTE

Street Address: 28 Church St
City: Everett
State: MA
ZIP Code: 02149-2719
General Phone: (617) 387-4570
General Email: everettleader@comcast.net
Publication Website: https://everettleader.com/
Parent Company: Dorchester Publishing Company
Publisher Name: Joshua Resnek
Editor Name: Joshua Resnek
Delivery Methods: Carrier
Year Established: 1885
Mechanical specifications: Type page 13 5/8 x 21; E - 6 cols, 2, between; A - 6 cols, 2, between; C - 9 cols, 1 5/16, between.
Published Days: Thur
Avg. Free Circ.: 15000
Audit Company: Sworn/Estimate/Non-Audited
Audit Date: 43626

FOXBORO

THE FOXBORO REPORTER

Street Address: 36 Mechanic St
City: Foxboro
State: MA
ZIP Code: 02035-2073
General Phone: (508) 543-4851
General Email: mfulcher@thesunchronicle.com
Publication Website: https://www.thesunchronicle.com/foxboro_reporter/
Parent Company: Triboro Massachusetts News Media Inc.
Advertising Executive Name: Michelle Fulcher
Advertising Executive Email: mfulcher@thesunchronicle.com
Advertising Executive Phone: (508) 236-0328
Delivery Methods: Mail`Newsstand
Mechanical specifications: Type page 11 5/8 x 21 1/4; E - 6 cols, 1 7/8, between.
Published Days: Thur
Avg. Paid Circ.: 2500
Audit Company: Sworn/Estimate/Non-Audited
Audit Date: 43626

FRAMINGHAM

ASHLAND TAB

Street Address: 33 New York Ave
City: Framingham
State: MA
ZIP Code: 1701
General Phone: (508) 626-3800
General Email: obits@wickedlocal.com
Publication Website: https://ashland.wickedlocal.com/
Editor Name: Anne Brennan
Editor Email: abrennan@wickedlocal.com
Editor Phone: (508) 626-3871
Advertising Executive Email: classifieds@wickedlocal.com
Published Days: Fri
Avg. Paid Circ.: 987
Audit Company: Sworn/Estimate/Non-Audited
Audit Date: 43626

FRAMINGHAM

BROOKLINE TAB

Street Address: 1 Speen St
City: Framingham
State: MA
ZIP Code: 1701
General Phone: (781) 433-6700
General Email: brookline@wickedlocal.com
Publication Website: https://brookline.wickedlocal.com/
Parent Company: Gannett
Editor Name: Anne Brennan
Editor Email: abrennan@wickedlocal.com
Editor Phone: (508) 626-3871
Advertising Executive Email: classifieds@wickedlocal.com
Published Days: Thur
Avg. Free Circ.: 14302
Audit Company: AAM
Audit Date: 44015

FRAMINGHAM

FRAMINGHAM TAB

Street Address: 1 Speen St.
City: Framingham
State: MA
ZIP Code: 01701-8857
General Phone: (508) 626-3800
General Email: framingham@wickedlocal.com
Publication Website: https://framingham.wickedlocal.com/
Editor Name: Anne Brennan
Editor Email: abrennan@wickedlocal.com
Editor Phone: (508) 626-3871
Advertising Executive Email: classifieds@wickedlocal.com
Advertising Executive Phone: (781) 433-6925
Published Days: Fri
Avg. Free Circ.: 4536
Audit Company: AAM
Audit Date: 44015

FRAMINGHAM

HOLLISTON TAB

Street Address: 33 New York Ave
City: Framingham
State: MA
ZIP Code: 01701-8857
General Phone: (508) 626-3800
General Email: classifieds@wickedlocal.com
Publication Website: https://holliston.wickedlocal.com/
Editor Name: Anne Brennan
Editor Email: abrennan@wickedlocal.com
Editor Phone: (508) 626-3871
Advertising Executive Email: classifieds@wickedlocal.com
Advertising Executive Phone: (781) 433-6925
Published Days: Thur
Avg. Paid Circ.: 1343
Audit Company: Sworn/Estimate/Non-Audited
Audit Date: 43626

FRAMINGHAM

HOPKINTON CRIER

Street Address: 1 Speen St
City: Framingham
State: MA
ZIP Code: 1701
General Phone: (508) 626-3800
General Email: classifieds@wickedlocal.com
Publication Website: https://hopkinton.wickedlocal.com/
Editor Name: Anne Brennan
Editor Email: abrennan@wickedlocal.com
Editor Phone: (508) 626-3871
Advertising Executive Email: classifieds@wickedlocal.com
Advertising Executive Phone: (781) 433-6925
Delivery Methods: Mail`Newsstand`Racks
Year Established: 1987
Own Printing Facility?: Y
Published Days: Fri
Avg. Paid Circ.: 195
Audit Company: AAM
Audit Date: 44015

FRAMINGHAM

HUDSON SUN

Street Address: 1 Speen St
City: Framingham
State: MA
ZIP Code: 1701
General Phone: (508) 626-3800
General Email: hudson@wickedlocal.com
Publication Website: https://hudson.wickedlocal.com/
Parent Company: Gannett
Editor Name: Anne Brennan
Editor Email: abrennan@wickedlocal.com
Editor Phone: (508) 626-3871
Advertising Executive Email: classifieds@wickedlocal.com
Advertising Executive Phone: (781) 433-6925
Delivery Methods: Mail
Published Days: Thur
Avg. Paid Circ.: 726
Audit Company: AAM
Audit Date: 44015

FRAMINGHAM

MARLBOROUGH ENTERPRISE

Street Address: 1 Speen St
City: Framingham
State: MA
ZIP Code: 1701
General Phone: (508) 626-3800
General Email: classifieds@wickedlocal.com
Publication Website: https://marlborough.wickedlocal.com/
Parent Company: Gannett
Editor Name: Anne Brennan
Editor Email: abrennan@wickedlocal.com
Editor Phone: (508) 626-3871
Advertising Executive Email: classifieds@wickedlocal.com
Advertising Executive Phone: (781) 433-6925
Own Printing Facility?: Y
Commercial printers?: Y
Published Days: Thur
Avg. Paid Circ.: 1746
Audit Company: Sworn/Estimate/Non-Audited
Audit Date: 43626

Community Newspapers in the U.S.

FRAMINGHAM
MEDFIELD PRESS
Street Address: 1 Speen St., Suite 200
City: Framingham
State: MA
ZIP Code: 1701
General Phone: (781) 433-6700
General Email: medfield@wickedlocal.com
Publication Website: https://medfield.wickedlocal.com/
Advertising Executive Email: classifieds@wickedlocal.com
Advertising Executive Phone: (781) 433-6925
Published Days: Fri
Avg. Paid Circ.: 491
Audit Company: AAM
Audit Date: 44015

FRAMINGHAM
NATICK BULLETIN & TAB
Street Address: 1 Speen St
City: Framingham
State: MA
ZIP Code: 1701
General Phone: (508) 626-3800
General Email: natick@wickedlocal.com
Publication Website: https://natick.wickedlocal.com/
Editor Name: Anne Brennan
Editor Email: abrennan@wickedlocal.com
Editor Phone: (508) 626-3871
Advertising Executive Email: classifieds@wickedlocal.com
Advertising Executive Phone: (781) 433-6925
Year Established: 1986
Published Days: Fri
Avg. Paid Circ.: 4696
Audit Company: Sworn/Estimate/Non-Audited
Audit Date: 43626

FRAMINGHAM
NEEDHAM TIMES
Street Address: 1 Speen St
City: Framingham
State: MA
ZIP Code: 1701
General Phone: (781) 433-6700
General Email: needham@wickedlocal.com
Publication Website: https://needham.wickedlocal.com/
Parent Company: Gannett
Editor Name: Anne Brennan
Editor Email: abrennan@wickedlocal.com
Editor Phone: (508) 626-3871
Advertising Executive Email: classifieds@wickedlocal.com
Advertising Executive Phone: (781) 433-6925
Year Established: 1874
Published Days: Wed`Thur`Fri
Avg. Free Circ.: 9687
Audit Company: AAM
Audit Date: 44015

FRAMINGHAM
NEWTON TAB
Street Address: 1 Speen St.
City: Framingham
State: MA
ZIP Code: 1701
General Phone: (781) 433-6700
General Email: newton@wickedlocal.com
Publication Website: https://newton.wickedlocal.com/
Parent Company: Gannett
Editor Name: Anne Brennan
Editor Email: abrennan@wickedlocal.com
Editor Phone: (508) 626-3871
Advertising Executive Email: classifieds@wickedlocal.com
Advertising Executive Phone: (781) 433-6925
Published Days: Wed
Avg. Free Circ.: 27884
Audit Company: AAM
Audit Date: 44015

FRAMINGHAM
NORWOOD TRANSCRIPT & BULLETIN
Street Address: 1 Speen St.
City: Framingham
State: MA
ZIP Code: 1701
General Phone: (781) 433-6700
General Email: norwood@wickedlocal.com
Publication Website: https://norwood.wickedlocal.com/
Advertising Executive Email: classifieds@wickedlocal.com
Published Days: Fri
Avg. Paid Circ.: 628
Audit Company: AAM
Audit Date: 44015

FRAMINGHAM
ROSLINDALE TRANSCRIPT
Street Address: 1 Speen St.
City: Framingham
State: MA
ZIP Code: 1701
General Phone: (781) 433-6700
General Email: jmann@wickedlocal.com
Publication Website: https://roslindale.wickedlocal.com/
Editor Name: Anne Brennan
Editor Email: abrennan@wickedlocal.com
Editor Phone: (508) 626-3871
Advertising Executive Email: classifieds@wickedlocal.com
Own Printing Facility?: Y
Commercial printers?: Y
Mechanical specifications: Type page 10 1/4 x 13 5/8; E - 5 cols, 1 11/12, 1/6 between; A - 5 cols, 1 11/12, between; C - 8 cols, 1 1/8, between.
Published Days: Thur
Avg. Paid Circ.: 191
Audit Company: AAM
Audit Date: 44015

FRAMINGHAM
SHARON ADVOCATE
Street Address: 1 Speen St.
City: Framingham
State: MA
ZIP Code: 1701
General Phone: (617) 433-6700
General Email: sharon@wickedlocal.com
Publication Website: https://sharon.wickedlocal.com/
Advertising Executive Email: classifieds@wickedlocal.com
Published Days: Fri
Avg. Paid Circ.: 215
Audit Company: AAM
Audit Date: 43658

FRAMINGHAM
SHREWSBURY CHRONICLE
Street Address: 1 Speen St.
City: Framingham
State: MA
ZIP Code: 1701
General Phone: (508) 626-3800
General Email: shrewsbury@wickedlocal.com
Publication Website: https://shrewsbury.wickedlocal.com/
Editor Name: Anne Brennan
Editor Email: abrennan@wickedlocal.com
Editor Phone: (508) 626-3871
Advertising Executive Email: classifieds@wickedlocal.com
Delivery Methods: Mail`Newsstand
Published Days: Fri
Avg. Paid Circ.: 1904
Avg. Free Circ.: 2146
Audit Company: AAM
Audit Date: 44015

FRAMINGHAM
SUDBURY TOWN CRIER
Street Address: 1 Speen St.
City: Framingham
State: MA
ZIP Code: 1701
General Phone: (508) 626-3800
General Email: subury@wickedlocal.com
Publication Website: https://sudbury.wickedlocal.com/
Parent Company: Gannett
Editor Name: Anne Brennan
Editor Email: abrennan@wickedlocal.com
Editor Phone: (508) 626-3871
Advertising Executive Email: classifieds@wickedlocal.com
Advertising Executive Phone: (781) 433-6925
Delivery Methods: Mail`Newsstand
Published Days: Thur
Avg. Paid Circ.: 3969
Audit Company: Sworn/Estimate/Non-Audited
Audit Date: 43626

FRAMINGHAM
THE DEDHAM TRANSCRIPT
Street Address: 1 Speen St.
City: Framingham
State: MA
ZIP Code: 1701
General Phone: (781) 433-6700
General Email: dedham@wickedlocal.com
Publication Website: https://dedham.wickedlocal.com/
Advertising Executive Email: classifieds@wickedlocal.com
Advertising Executive Phone: (781) 433-6925
Delivery Methods: Mail`Newsstand`Racks
Year Established: 1873
Published Days: Wed
Avg. Paid Circ.: 453
Audit Company: AAM
Audit Date: 44015

FRAMINGHAM
THE VILLAGER
Street Address: 33 New York Ave
City: Framingham
State: MA
ZIP Code: 01701-8857
General Phone: (508) 490-7454
General Email: crobinso@wickedlocal.com
Publication Website: wickedlocal.com/northborough
Parent Company: Schneps Media
Publisher Name: Chuck Goodrich
Editor Name: Glenda Hazard
Editor Email: ghazard@wickedlocal.com
Own Printing Facility?: Y
Commercial printers?: Y
Published Days: Fri
Avg. Paid Circ.: 429
Avg. Free Circ.: 4
Audit Company: Sworn/Estimate/Non-Audited
Audit Date: 43626

FRAMINGHAM
THE WALPOLE TIMES
Street Address: 1 Speen St.
City: Framingham
State: MA
ZIP Code: 1701
General Phone: (781) 433-6700
General Email: walpole@wickedlocal.com
Publication Website: https://walpole.wickedlocal.com/
Advertising Executive Email: classifieds@wickedlocal.com
Advertising Executive Phone: (781) 433-6925
Delivery Methods: Mail`Newsstand`Racks
Mechanical specifications: Type page 12 7/8 x 21; E - 6 cols, between; A - 6 cols, between; C - 10 cols, between.
Published Days: Thur
Avg. Paid Circ.: 460
Audit Company: AAM
Audit Date: 43658

FRAMINGHAM
THE WESTBOROUGH NEWS
Street Address: 1 Speen St
City: Framingham
State: MA
ZIP Code: 0 1701
General Phone: 508-490-7459
General Email: westboroevents@wickedlocal.com
Publication Website: www.wickedlocal.com/westborough
Parent Company: Gannett Company, Inc.
Editor Name: Sandy Meindersma
Editor Email: smeindersma@wickedlocal.com
Editor Phone: 508-490-7459
Published Days: Fri
Avg. Paid Circ.: 986
Audit Company: AAM
Audit Date: 44015

FRAMINGHAM
WAYLAND TOWN CRIER
Street Address: 1 Speen St.
City: Framingham
State: MA
ZIP Code: 1701
General Phone: (508) 626-3800
General Email: wayland@wickedlocal.com
Publication Website: https://wayland.wickedlocal.com/
Parent Company: Gannett
Editor Name: Anne Brennan
Editor Email: abrennan@wickedlocal.com
Editor Phone: (508) 626-3871
Advertising Executive Email: classifieds@wickedlocal.com
Advertising Executive Phone: (781) 433-6925
Published Days: Thur
Avg. Paid Circ.: 2362
Audit Company: Sworn/Estimate/Non-Audited
Audit Date: 43626

FRAMINGHAM
WELLESLEY TOWNSMAN
Street Address: 1 Spleen St.
City: Framingham
State: MA
ZIP Code: 1701
General Phone: (781) 433-6700
General Email: wellesley@wickedlocal.com
Publication Website: https://wellesley.wickedlocal.com/
Editor Name: Anne Brennan
Editor Email: abrennan@wickedlocal.com
Editor Phone: (508) 626-3871

FRAMINGHAM

WEST ROXBURY TRANSCRIPT

Advertising Executive Email: classifieds@wickedlocal.com
Advertising Executive Phone: (781) 433-6925
Own Printing Facility?: Y
Mechanical specifications: Type page 13 x 21 1/2; E - 6 cols, 2, 1/6 between; A - 6 cols, 2, 1/6 between; C - 10 cols, 1 1/8, between.
Published Days: Thur
Avg. Paid Circ.: 2948
Avg. Free Circ.: 129
Audit Company: AAM
Audit Date: 44015

FRAMINGHAM

WEST ROXBURY TRANSCRIPT

Street Address: 1 Spleen St.
City: Framingham
State: MA
ZIP Code: 1701
General Phone: (781) 433-6700
General Email: west-roxbury@wickedlocal.com
Publication Website: https://west-roxbury.wickedlocal.com/
Editor Name: Anne Brennan
Editor Email: abrennan@wickedlocal.com
Editor Phone: (508) 626-3871
Advertising Executive Email: classifieds@wickedlocal.com
Advertising Executive Phone: (781) 433-6925
Own Printing Facility?: Y
Commercial printers?: Y
Mechanical specifications: Type page 10 1/4 x 13 5/8; E - 5 cols, 1 11/12, 1/6 between; A - 5 cols, 1 11/12, 1/6 between; C - 8 cols, 1 1/8, between.
Published Days: Thur
Avg. Paid Circ.: 508
Audit Company: AAM
Audit Date: 44015

FRAMINGHAM

WESTON TOWN CRIER

Street Address: 1 Speen St.
City: Framingham
State: MA
ZIP Code: 1701
General Phone: (508) 626-3800
General Email: weston@wickedlocal.com
Publication Website: https://weston.wickedlocal.com/
Parent Company: Gannett
Editor Name: Anne Brennan
Editor Email: abrennan@wickedlocal.com
Editor Phone: (508) 626-3871
Advertising Executive Email: classifieds@wickedlocal.com
Advertising Executive Phone: (781) 433-6925
Own Printing Facility?: Y
Commercial printers?: Y
Published Days: Thur
Avg. Free Circ.: 1131
Audit Company: AAM
Audit Date: 44015

FRAMINGHAM

WESTWOOD PRESS

Street Address: 1 Speen St.
City: Framingham
State: MA
ZIP Code: 1701
General Phone: (781) 433-6700
General Email: westwood@wickedlocal.com
Publication Website: https://westwood.wickedlocal.com/
Advertising Executive Email: classifieds@wickedlocal.com
Advertising Executive Phone: (781) 433-6925
Published Days: Fri
Avg. Paid Circ.: 440
Audit Company: AAM

Audit Date: 44015

GREAT BARRINGTON

THE BERKSHIRE RECORD

Street Address: 21 Elm St
City: Great Barrington
State: MA
ZIP Code: 01230-1516
General Phone: (413) 528-5380
General Email: news@berkshirerecord.net
Publication Website: http://berkshirerecord.net/
Parent Company: Limestone Communications Inc
Advertising Executive Email: production@berkshirerecord.net
Advertising Executive Phone: (413) 528-5380, ext : 31
Delivery Methods: Mail`Newsstand`Racks
Published Days: Thur
Avg. Paid Circ.: 14000
Audit Company: Sworn/Estimate/Non-Audited
Audit Date: 43626

HANSON

PLYMPTON-HALIFAX EXPRESS

Street Address: PO Box 60
City: Hanson
State: MA
ZIP Code: 2341
General Phone: (781) 293-0420
General Email: ads@whphexpress.com
Publication Website: http://www.plymptonhalifaxexpress.com/
Parent Company: Anderson Newspapers, Inc., d/b/a Express Newspapers
Editor Name: Deborah Anderson
Editor Email: deb@whphexpress.com
Advertising Executive Email: ads@whphexpress.com
Delivery Methods: Mail
Year Established: 2014
Published Days: Fri
Avg. Paid Circ.: 528
Avg. Free Circ.: 23
Audit Company: Sworn/Estimate/Non-Audited
Audit Date: 43626

HANSON

WHITMAN-HANSON EXPRESS

Street Address: 1000 Main St
City: Hanson
State: MA
ZIP Code: 02341-1560
General Phone: (781) 293-0420
General Email: ads@whitmanhansonexpress.com
Publication Website: http://whitmanhansonexpress.com/
Parent Company: Anderson Newspapers, Inc., d/b/a Express Newspapers
Editor Name: Tracy Seelye
Editor Email: editor@whitmanhansonexpress.com
Advertising Executive Email: ads@whitmanhansonexpress.com
Delivery Methods: Mail`Newsstand
Year Established: 2002
Own Printing Facility?: N
Published Days: Thur
Avg. Paid Circ.: 2022
Avg. Free Circ.: 58
Audit Company: Sworn/Estimate/Non-Audited
Audit Date: 43626

HARVARD

THE HARVARD PRESS

Street Address: 1 Still River Rd
City: Harvard
State: MA
ZIP Code: 1451
General Phone: (978) 456-3700
General Email: ben.myers43@gmail.com
Publication Website: https://www.harvardpress.com/
Advertising Executive Name: Ben Myers
Advertising Executive Email: ben.myers43@gmail.com
Advertising Executive Phone: (978) 844-8312
Delivery Methods: Mail`Racks
Published Days: Fri
Audit Company: Sworn/Estimate/Non-Audited
Audit Date: 43626

HULL

THE HULL TIMES

Street Address: 412 Nantasket Ave
City: Hull
State: MA
ZIP Code: 2045
General Phone: (781) 925-9266
General Email: office@hulltimes.com
Publication Website: http://www.hulltimes.com/
Publisher Name: Patricia Abbate
Editor Name: Patricia Abbate
Advertising Executive Email: office@hulltimes.com
Delivery Methods: Mail`Newsstand
Year Established: 1930
Mechanical specifications: Type page 10 x 15 3/4.
Published Days: Thur
Avg. Paid Circ.: 3000
Audit Company: Sworn/Estimate/Non-Audited
Audit Date: 43626

HYANNIS

BARNSTABLE PATRIOT

Street Address: 4 Ocean Ave
City: Hyannis
State: MA
ZIP Code: 2601
General Phone: (508) 771-1427
General Email: editor@barnstablepatriot.com
Publication Website: https://www.barnstablepatriot.com/
Parent Company: Gannett
Editor Name: Bronwen Howells Walsh
Editor Email: bwalsh@barnstablepatriot.com
Editor Phone: (508) 862-1137
Advertising Executive Name: April Miller
Advertising Executive Email: aprilm@capecodonline.com
Advertising Executive Phone: (508) 862-1128
Delivery Methods: Mail`Newsstand
Year Established: 1830
Mechanical specifications: Type page 11.625 x 21.25; E - 6 cols, 1.83, between.
Published Days: Fri
Avg. Paid Circ.: 4905
Avg. Free Circ.: 350
Audit Company: Sworn/Estimate/Non-Audited
Audit Date: 43626

HYANNIS

THE BULLETIN

Street Address: 319 Main Street
City: Hyannis
State: MA
ZIP Code: 2601
General Phone: (508) 375-4925
General Email: mevans@capecodonline.com
Publication Website: https://falmouth.wickedlocal.com/
Parent Company: Gannett
Publisher Name: Peter Meyer
Publisher Email: pmeyer@capecodonline.com
Publisher Phone: (508) 862-1111
Editor Name: Paul Pronovost
Editor Email: ppronovost@capecodonline.com
Editor Phone: (508) 862-1166
Advertising Executive Name: Molly Evans
Advertising Executive Email: mevans@capecodonline.com
Advertising Executive Phone: (508) 862-1377
Year Established: 2007
Published Days: Thur
Avg. Paid Circ.: 6525
Audit Company: Sworn/Estimate/Non-Audited
Audit Date: 43626

HYDE PARK

WEST ROXBURY/ROSINDALE BULLETIN

Street Address: 1 Westinghouse Plz
City: Hyde Park
State: MA
ZIP Code: 02136-2075
General Phone: (617) 361-8400
General Email: news@westroxburybulletin.com; news@bulletinnewspapers.com
Publication Website: https://bulletinnewspapers.weebly.com/
Parent Company: Bulletin Newspapers, Inc
Publisher Name: Paul DiModica
Publisher Email: pdimodica@bulletinnewspapers.com
Editor Name: Dennis Cawley
Editor Email: dcawley@bulletinnewspapers.com
Advertising Executive Name: Jennifer Ferri
Advertising Executive Email: bulletingraphics@aol.com
Delivery Methods: Mail`Newsstand`Racks
Year Established: 1992
Published Days: Thur
Avg. Free Circ.: 11500
Audit Company: Sworn/Estimate/Non-Audited
Audit Date: 43626

LENOX DALE

BERKSHIRE BEACON

Street Address: PO Box 312
City: Lenox Dale
State: MA
ZIP Code: 01242-0312
General Phone: (413) 637-2250
General Email: ads@berkshirebeacon.com?Ç¬†
Publication Website: http://berkshirebeacon.com/
Publisher Name: George C. Jordan
Publisher Email: george@berkshirebeacon.com
Editor Name: George C. Jordan
Editor Email: george@berkshirebeacon.com
Advertising Executive Name: Tim Davis
Advertising Executive Email: tdavis@berkshirebeacon.com
Delivery Methods: Newsstand`Racks
Year Established: 2011
Mechanical specifications: tab 10.5 by 12.5
Published Days: Thur
Published Other: weekly
Audit Company: Sworn/Estimate/Non-Audited
Audit Date: 43626
Note: Tourist publication: Berkshire Sonata

LEOMINSTER

LEOMINSTER CHAMPION

Community Newspapers in the U.S.

Street Address: 100 Front St., 5th Floor
City: Leominster
State: MA
ZIP Code: 1608
General Phone: (978) 534-6006
General Email: lceditor@gatehousemedia.com
Publication Website: https://www.leominsterchamp.com/
Parent Company: Gannett
Editor Name: David Dore
Editor Email: ddore@gatehousemedia.com
Editor Phone: (508) 767-6006
Advertising Executive Name: Jeremy Wardwell
Advertising Executive Email: cngsales@gatehousemedia.com
Advertising Executive Phone: (508) 767-9574
Delivery Methods: Racks
Year Established: 2006
Mechanical specifications: Type page 9.5" x 10.75"; 6 cols
Published Days: Fri
Avg. Free Circ.: 5984
Audit Company: Sworn/Estimate/Non-Audited
Audit Date: 43626

LEOMINSTER

MILLBURY-SUTTON CHRONICLE

Street Address: 100 Front St., 5th Floor
City: Leominster
State: MA
ZIP Code: 1608
General Phone: (508) 865-1645
General Email: editor@millburysutton.com
Publication Website: https://www.millburysutton.com/
Editor Name: Paula Owen
Editor Email: powen@gatehousemedia.com
Editor Phone: (508) 865-1645
Advertising Executive Name: Henry Rosenthal
Advertising Executive Email: hrosenthal@gatehousemedia.com
Advertising Executive Phone: (508) 767-9578
Delivery Methods: Mail`Newsstand
Published Days: Thur
Audit Company: Sworn/Estimate/Non-Audited
Audit Date: 43626

LEXINGTON

ARLINGTON ADVOCATE

Street Address: 9 Meriam St
City: Lexington
State: MA
ZIP Code: 2420
General Phone: (781) 674-7734
General Email: arlington@wickedlocal.com
Publication Website: https://arlington.wickedlocal.com/
Parent Company: Gannett
Advertising Executive Name: Philip Gaudette
Advertising Executive Email: pgaudette@wickedlocal.com
Advertising Executive Phone: (978) 371-5717
Own Printing Facility?: Y
Commercial printers?: Y
Mechanical specifications: Type page 13 x 21 1/2; E - 6 cols, 2, 1/6 between; A - 6 cols, 2, 1/6 between.
Published Days: Wed`Thur`Fri
Avg. Paid Circ.: 6624
Avg. Free Circ.: 2830
Audit Company: Sworn/Estimate/Non-Audited
Audit Date: 43626

LEXINGTON

BELMONT CITIZEN HERALD

Street Address: 9 Meriam St.
City: Lexington
State: MA
ZIP Code: 2420
General Phone: (781) 674-7723
General Email: belmont@wickedlocal.com
Publication Website: https://belmont.wickedlocal.com/
Advertising Executive Email: classifieds@wickedlocal.com
Published Days: Thur
Avg. Free Circ.: 2305
Audit Company: Sworn/Estimate/Non-Audited
Audit Date: 43626

LEXINGTON

CAMBRIDGE CHRONICLE & TAB

Street Address: 9 Meriam St.
City: Lexington
State: MA
ZIP Code: 2420
General Phone: (781) 433-6700
General Email: cambridge@wickedlocal.com
Publication Website: https://cambridge.wickedlocal.com/
Advertising Executive Email: classifieds@wickedlocal.com
Year Established: 1846
Published Days: Thur
Avg. Paid Circ.: 659
Avg. Free Circ.: 4500
Audit Company: AAM
Audit Date: 44015

LEXINGTON

LEXINGTON MINUTEMAN

Street Address: 9 Meriam St
City: Lexington
State: MA
ZIP Code: 02420-5300
General Phone: (781) 674-7722
General Email: lexington@wickedlocal.com
Publication Website: https://lexington.wickedlocal.com/
Parent Company: Gannett
Advertising Executive Name: Philip Gaudette
Advertising Executive Phone: (978) 731-5717
Delivery Methods: Mail`Newsstand
Year Established: 1870
Own Printing Facility?: Y
Commercial printers?: Y
Published Days: Thur
Avg. Paid Circ.: 2840
Avg. Free Circ.: 1454
Audit Company: AAM
Audit Date: 44015

LEXINGTON

WALTHAM NEWS TRIBUNE

Street Address: 9 Meriam St.
City: Lexington
State: MA
ZIP Code: 2420
General Phone: (781) 433-6700
General Email: waltham@wickedlocal.com
Publication Website: https://waltham.wickedlocal.com/
Parent Company: Gannett
Advertising Executive Email: classifieds@wickedlocal.com
Advertising Executive Phone: (781) 433-6925
Published Days: Fri
Weekday Frequency: m
Avg. Paid Circ.: 2005
Audit Company: AAM
Audit Date: 44015

LEXINGTON

WATERTOWN TAB

Street Address: 9 Meriam Street
City: Lexington
State: MA
ZIP Code: 2420
General Phone: (781) 433-6700
General Email: watertown@wickedlocal.com
Publication Website: https://watertown.wickedlocal.com/
Advertising Executive Email: classifieds@wickedlocal.com
Advertising Executive Phone: (781) 433-6925
Own Printing Facility?: Y
Published Days: Fri
Avg. Paid Circ.: 1386
Audit Company: AAM
Audit Date: 44015

LEXINGTON

WINCHESTER STAR

Street Address: 9 Meriam St
City: Lexington
State: MA
ZIP Code: 02420-5300
General Phone: (781) 674-7740
General Email: winchester@wickedlocal.com
Publication Website: https://winchester.wickedlocal.com/
Parent Company: Gannett
Advertising Executive Name: Philip Gaudette
Advertising Executive Phone: (978) 371-5717
Own Printing Facility?: Y
Commercial printers?: Y
Published Days: Thur
Avg. Paid Circ.: 2032
Avg. Free Circ.: 489
Audit Company: AAM
Audit Date: 44015

LOWELL

NASHOBA VALLEY VOICE

Street Address: 491 Dutton St
City: Lowell
State: MA
ZIP Code: 01854-4290
General Phone: (978) 459-1300
General Email: news@nashobavalleyvoice.com
Publication Website: https://www.nashobavalleyvoice.com/
Parent Company: Media News Group
Publisher Name: Kevin Corrado
Publisher Email: kcorrado@medianewsgroup.com
Publisher Phone: (978) 970-4807
Advertising Executive Name: Eddie R. Najeeullah
Advertising Executive Email: enajeeullah@mediaonene.com
Advertising Executive Phone: (508) 366-5500, ext : 12
Delivery Methods: Mail`Newsstand
Year Established: 2015
Own Printing Facility?: N
Commercial printers?: Y
Published Days: Fri
Avg. Paid Circ.: 3500
Avg. Free Circ.: 15000
Audit Company: Sworn/Estimate/Non-Audited
Audit Date: 43626
Note: Nashoba Publishing became the Nashoba Valley Voice on Sept. 25, 2015

LOWELL

THE DISPATCH NEWS

Street Address: 491 Dutton St
City: Lowell
State: MA
ZIP Code: 1854

General Phone: (978) 458-7100
General Email: fsplaine@mediaone.com
Publication Website: https://www.thevalleydispatch.com/
Publisher Name: Kevin Corrado
Publisher Email: kcorrado@digitalfirstmedia.com
Publisher Phone: (978) 970-4807
Editor Name: Kris Pisarik
Editor Email: kpisarik@lowellsun.com
Editor Phone: (978) 970-4637
Advertising Executive Name: Eddie R. Najeeullah
Advertising Executive Email: enajeeullah@mediaonene.com
Advertising Executive Phone: (978) 970-4715
Mechanical specifications: Type page 10 x 16; E - 6 cols, 1 1/4, 1/4 between; A - 6 cols, 1 1/4, 1/4 between; C - 6 cols, 1 1/4, 1/4 between.
Published Days: Fri
Avg. Free Circ.: 18000
Audit Company: Sworn/Estimate/Non-Audited
Audit Date: 43626

LYNN

ITEM LIVE

Street Address: 110 Munroe St.
City: Lynn
State: MA
ZIP Code: 1901
General Phone: (781) 593-7700
General Email: advertising@itemlive.com
Publication Website: https://www.itemlive.com/location/lynn/
Parent Company: Essex Media Group
Delivery Methods: Mail`Newsstand`Racks
Mechanical specifications: Type page 10 x 15 3/4; E - 5 cols, 2 1/16, 1/8 between; A - 5 cols, 2 1/16, 1/8 between; C - 6 cols, 1 11/16, 5/16 between.
Published Days: Thur
Avg. Free Circ.: 19263
Audit Company: Sworn/Estimate/Non-Audited
Audit Date: 43626

MANCHESTER

THE MANCHESTER CRICKET

Street Address: 50 Summer St, PO Box 379
City: Manchester
State: MA
ZIP Code: 01944-1518
General Phone: (978) 526-7171
General Email: ads@cricketpress.com
Publication Website: http://cricketpress.com/
Parent Company: The Cricket Press, Inc.
Advertising Executive Email: classifieds@cricketpress.com
Delivery Methods: Mail`Newsstand
Year Established: 1888
Mechanical specifications: Type page 11 x 23; E - 6 cols, 1.625, .082 between; A - 6 cols, 1.625, .083 between; C - 6 cols, 1.65, .083 between.
Published Days: Fri
Avg. Paid Circ.: 2500
Audit Company: Sworn/Estimate/Non-Audited
Audit Date: 43626

MATTAPOISETT

THE WANDERER

Street Address: 55 County Rd
City: Mattapoisett
State: MA
ZIP Code: 2739
General Phone: (508) 758-9055
General Email: office@wanderer.com
Publication Website: https://www.wanderer.

com/
Editor Email: news@wanderer.com
Advertising Executive Email: office@wanderer.com
Delivery Methods: Racks
Year Established: 1992
Mechanical specifications: Type page 8 1/2 x 11; E - 2 cols, 4, 1/2 between; A - 2 cols, 4, 1/2 between; C - 3 cols, 2 1/2, 1/2 between.
Published Days: Thur
Avg. Free Circ.: 4700
Audit Company: Sworn/Estimate/Non-Audited
Audit Date: 43626

MIDDLEBORO

MIDDLEBORO GAZETTE

Street Address: 148 W Grove St
City: Middleboro
State: MA
ZIP Code: 02346-1457
General Phone: (508) 947-1760
General Email: news@gazettenewsonline.com
Publication Website: https://www.southcoasttoday.com/Gazette
Parent Company: Gannett
Editor Name: Jon Haglof
Advertising Executive Name: Chris Rohland
Advertising Executive Email: crohland@s-t.com
Advertising Executive Phone: (508) 979-4360
Delivery Methods: Mail`Newsstand
Year Established: 1852
Own Printing Facility?: Y
Commercial printers?: Y
Published Days: Thur
Avg. Paid Circ.: 4802
Avg. Free Circ.: 184
Audit Company: Sworn/Estimate/Non-Audited
Audit Date: 43626

MILFORD

THE COUNTRY GAZETTE

Street Address: 197 Main St
City: Milford
State: MA
ZIP Code: 1757
General Phone: (508) 634-7522
General Email: gazette@wickedlocal.com
Publication Website: https://bellingham.wickedlocal.com/
Parent Company: Gannett
Editor Name: Anne Brennan
Editor Email: abrennan@wickedlocal.com
Editor Phone: (508) 626-3871
Advertising Executive Email: classifieds@wickedlocal.com
Year Established: 1985
Published Days: Fri
Avg. Free Circ.: 20114
Audit Company: AAM
Audit Date: 44015

MILTON

MILTON TIMES

Street Address: 3 Boulevard St
City: Milton
State: MA
ZIP Code: 02186-5400
General Phone: (617) 696-7758
General Email: webeditor@miltontimes.com
Publication Website: https://www.miltontimes.com/
Publisher Name: Pat Desmond
Publisher Email: pat@miltontimes.com
Editor Name: Lisa Connell
Editor Email: editor@miltontimes.com
Advertising Executive Name: Nadine Leary
Advertising Executive Email: ads@miltontimes.com
Delivery Methods: Mail`Newsstand
Year Established: 1995
Mechanical specifications: Tabloid, 6 col. 1 and 5/8" per column, 16" depth available.
Published Days: Thur
Published Other: online - special issues when appropriate
Avg. Paid Circ.: 4600
Audit Company: Sworn/Estimate/Non-Audited
Audit Date: 43626

NANTUCKET

NANTUCKET TODAY

Street Address: The Inquirer and Mirror, 1 Old South Rd
City: Nantucket
State: MA
ZIP Code: 02554-2836
General Phone: (508) 228-0001
General Email: mstanton@inkym.com
Publication Website: https://nantuckettodayonline.com/
Parent Company: Dow Jones Local Media Group-OOB
Publisher Name: Marianne R. Stanton
Publisher Email: mstanton@inkym.com
Publisher Phone: (508) 228-0001, ext : 11
Published Days: Mthly`Other
Audit Company: Sworn/Estimate/Non-Audited
Audit Date: 43626

NANTUCKET

THE INQUIRER AND MIRROR

Street Address: 1 Old South Rd
City: Nantucket
State: MA
ZIP Code: 2554
General Phone: (508) 228-0001
General Email: advertising@inkym.com
Publication Website: https://www.ack.net/
Publisher Name: Marianne R. Stanton
Publisher Email: mstanton@inkym.com
Publisher Phone: (508) 228-0001, ext : 11
Editor Name: Joshua H. Balling
Editor Email: jballing@inkym.com
Editor Phone: (508) 228-0001, ext : 14
Advertising Executive Name: Mary Sharpe
Advertising Executive Email: advertising@inkym.com
Advertising Executive Phone: (508) 228-0001x27
Delivery Methods: Mail`Newsstand
Year Established: 1865
Own Printing Facility?: Y
Commercial printers?: Y
Published Days: Thur
Avg. Paid Circ.: 8903
Avg. Free Circ.: 162
Audit Company: Sworn/Estimate/Non-Audited
Audit Date: 43626

NEEDHAM

DOVER-SHERBORN PRESS

Street Address: 254 2nd Ave
City: Needham
State: MA
ZIP Code: 02494-2829
General Phone: (781) 433-6700
General Email: sherborn@wickedlocal.com
Publication Website: https://sherborn.wickedlocal.com/
Advertising Executive Email: classifieds@wickedlocal.com
Advertising Executive Phone: (781) 433-6925
Published Days: Thur
Avg. Paid Circ.: 400
Audit Company: AAM
Audit Date: 44015

NEW BEDFORD

THE ADVOCATE

Street Address: 25 Elm Street
City: New Bedford
State: MA
ZIP Code: 2740
General Phone: (508) 997-7411
General Email: theadvocatenewspaper@yahoo.com; editor@advocatenewsonline.com
Publication Website: http://advocate.southcoasttoday.com/
Editor Name: Jennifer Driscoll
Editor Email: jdriscoll@s-t.com
Editor Phone: (508) 979-4466
Advertising Executive Name: Chris Rohland
Advertising Executive Email: crohland@s-t.com
Advertising Executive Phone: (508) 979-4360
Published Days: Thur
Avg. Paid Circ.: 1518
Avg. Free Circ.: 141
Audit Company: Sworn/Estimate/Non-Audited
Audit Date: 43626

NEW BEDFORD

THE CHRONICLE

Street Address: 25 Elm St
City: New Bedford
State: MA
ZIP Code: 2740
General Phone: (508) 997-7411
General Email: chronnews@aol.com
Publication Website: https://www.southcoasttoday.com/Chronicle
Parent Company: Gannett
Editor Name: Phil Devitt
Editor Email: pdevitt@hathawaypublishing.com
Editor Phone: (508) 979-4492
Advertising Executive Name: Chris Rohland
Advertising Executive Email: crohland@s-t.com
Advertising Executive Phone: (508) 979-4360
Published Days: Wed
Avg. Paid Circ.: 3995
Avg. Free Circ.: 196
Audit Company: Sworn/Estimate/Non-Audited
Audit Date: 43626

NEW BEDFORD

THE SPECTATOR

Street Address: 25 Elm St
City: New Bedford
State: MA
ZIP Code: 2740
General Phone: (508) 674-7411
General Email: crohland@s-t.com
Publication Website: https://www.southcoasttoday.com/spectator
Parent Company: Gannett
Editor Name: George Austin
Editor Email: gaustin@hathawaypublishing.com
Editor Phone: (508) 979-4338
Advertising Executive Name: Chris Rohland
Advertising Executive Email: crohland@s-t.com
Advertising Executive Phone: (508) 979-4360
Year Established: 1932
Published Days: Wed
Avg. Paid Circ.: 4338
Avg. Free Circ.: 105
Audit Company: Sworn/Estimate/Non-Audited
Audit Date: 43626

NORTH ANDOVER

THE HAVERHILL GAZETTE

Street Address: 100 Turnpike St
City: North Andover
State: MA
ZIP Code: 1845
General Phone: (978) 946-2000
General Email: ewholley@eagletribune.com
Publication Website: https://www.hgazette.com/
Parent Company: CNHI, LLC
Publisher Name: Karen Andreas
Publisher Email: kandreas@hgazette.com
Publisher Phone: (978) 946-2241
Editor Name: Bill Cantwell
Editor Email: bcantwell@hgazette.com
Editor Phone: (978) 946-2215
Advertising Executive Name: Mark Zappala
Advertising Executive Email: mzappala@hgazette.com
Advertising Executive Phone: (978) 946-2154
Delivery Methods: Newsstand`Carrier`Racks
Year Established: 1821
Mechanical specifications: Type page 11 5/8 x 21 1/2; E - 6 cols, 1 5/6, 1/8 between; A - 6 cols, 1 5/6, 1/8 between; C - 10 cols, 1 1/16, 1/16 between.
Published Days: Thur
Avg. Paid Circ.: 3590
Avg. Free Circ.: 292
Audit Company: Sworn/Estimate/Non-Audited
Audit Date: 43626

NORTH ATTLEBORO

NORTH ATTLEBORO FREE PRESS

Street Address: 31 N Washington St
City: North Attleboro
State: MA
ZIP Code: 02760-1650
General Phone: (508) 634-7584
General Email: ads@nafreepress.com
Publication Website: https://northattleborough.wickedlocal.com/
Editor Name: Anne Brennan
Editor Email: abrennan@wickedlocal.com
Editor Phone: (508) 626-3871
Advertising Executive Email: classifieds@wickedlocal.com
Advertising Executive Phone: (781) 433-6925
Year Established: 1987
Mechanical specifications: Type page 10 1/2 x 15 3/4; E - 4 cols, 2 3/8, 1/6 between; A - 4 cols, 2 3/8, 1/6 between; C - 6 cols, 1 5/8, 1/6 between.
Published Days: Wed
Avg. Free Circ.: 16993
Audit Company: Sworn/Estimate/Non-Audited
Audit Date: 43626

NORTHAMPTON

AMHERST BULLETIN

Street Address: 115 Conz St
City: Northampton
State: MA
ZIP Code: 1060
General Phone: (413) 584-5000
General Email: classifieds@gazettenet.com
Publication Website: https://www.amherstbulletin.com/
Parent Company: Newspapers of New England
Publisher Email: publisher@gazettenet.com
Editor Email: webeditor@gazettenet.com
Advertising Executive Email: sales@gazettenet.com
Delivery Methods: Mail`Carrier`Racks
Year Established: 1786
Own Printing Facility?: Y
Commercial printers?: Y
Published Days: Fri
Avg. Paid Circ.: 108
Avg. Free Circ.: 12750
Audit Company: Sworn/Estimate/Non-Audited

Community Newspapers in the U.S.

Audit Date: 43626

NORWELL

ABINGTON MARINER

Street Address: 600 Cordwainer Drive
City: Norwell
State: MA
ZIP Code: 2061
General Phone: (781) 837-4500
General Email: classifieds@wickedlocal.com
Publication Website: https://abington.wickedlocal.com/
Publisher Name: Mark Olivieri
Publisher Email: molivieri@wickedlocal.com
Publisher Phone: (781) 837-4504
Advertising Executive Name: Karen Willette
Advertising Executive Email: kwillette@wickedlocal.com
Advertising Executive Phone: (508) 638-5578
Own Printing Facility?: Y
Commercial printers?: Y
Published Days: Fri
Avg. Paid Circ.: 609
Audit Company: Sworn/Estimate/Non-Audited
Audit Date: 43626

NORWELL

BRAINTREE FORUM

Street Address: 600 Cordwainer Drive
City: Norwell
State: MA
ZIP Code: 2061
General Phone: (781) 837-4500
General Email: braintree@wickedlocal.com
Publication Website: https://braintree.wickedlocal.com/
Parent Company: Gannett
Publisher Name: Mark Olivieri
Publisher Email: molivieri@wickedlocal.com
Publisher Phone: (781) 837-4504
Advertising Executive Name: Donna Warren
Advertising Executive Email: dwarren@wickedlocal.com
Advertising Executive Phone: (617) 786-7188
Commercial printers?: Y
Published Days: Thur
Avg. Paid Circ.: 1471
Audit Company: AAM
Audit Date: 44015

NORWELL

COHASSET MARINER

Street Address: 600 Cordwainer Drive
City: Norwell
State: MA
ZIP Code: 2061
General Phone: (781) 837-4500
General Email: coliver@wickedlocal.com
Publication Website: https://cohasset.wickedlocal.com/
Parent Company: Gannett
Publisher Name: Mark Olivieri
Publisher Email: molivieri@wickedlocal.com
Publisher Phone: (781) 837-4504
Editor Name: Mark Burridge
Editor Email: mburridge@wickedlocal.com
Editor Phone: (781) 837-4559
Advertising Executive Name: Chris Avis
Advertising Executive Email: cavis@wickedlocal.com
Advertising Executive Phone: (781) 837-4503
Own Printing Facility?: Y
Commercial printers?: Y
Published Days: Fri
Avg. Paid Circ.: 1449
Avg. Free Circ.: 36
Audit Company: AAM
Audit Date: 44015

NORWELL

HANOVER MARINER

Street Address: 600 Cordwainer Drive
City: Norwell
State: MA
ZIP Code: 2061
General Phone: (781) 837-4560
General Email: molivieri@wickedlocal.com
Publication Website: https://hanover.wickedlocal.com/
Publisher Name: Mark Olivieri
Publisher Email: molivieri@wickedlocal.com
Publisher Phone: (781) 837-4504
Editor Name: Mark Burridge
Editor Email: mburridge@wickedlocal.com
Editor Phone: (781) 837-4559
Advertising Executive Name: Chris Avis
Advertising Executive Email: cavis@wickedlocal.com
Advertising Executive Phone: (781) 837-4503
Year Established: 1980
Commercial printers?: Y
Published Days: Wed
Avg. Paid Circ.: 939
Audit Company: AAM
Audit Date: 44015

NORWELL

HINGHAM JOURNAL

Street Address: 600 Cordwainer Drive
City: Norwell
State: MA
ZIP Code: 2061
General Phone: (781) 837-4500
General Email: classifieds@wickedlocal.com
Publication Website: https://hingham.wickedlocal.com/
Parent Company: Gannett
Publisher Name: Mark Olivieri
Publisher Email: molivieri@wickedlocal.com
Publisher Phone: (781) 837-4504
Advertising Executive Name: Chris Avis
Advertising Executive Email: cavis@wickedlocal.com
Advertising Executive Phone: (781) 837-4503
Published Days: Thur
Avg. Paid Circ.: 3414
Avg. Free Circ.: 235
Audit Company: AAM
Audit Date: 44015

NORWELL

MARSHFIELD MARINER

Street Address: 600 Cordwainer Drive
City: Norwell
State: MA
ZIP Code: 2061
General Phone: (781) 837-4500
General Email: classifieds@wickedlocal.com
Publication Website: https://marshfield.wickedlocal.com/
Parent Company: Gannett
Publisher Name: Mark Olivieri
Publisher Email: molivieri@wickedlocal.com
Publisher Phone: (781) 837-4504
Editor Name: Mark Burridge
Editor Email: mburridge@wickedlocal.com
Editor Phone: (781) 837-4559
Advertising Executive Name: Chris Avis
Advertising Executive Email: cavis@wickedlocal.com
Advertising Executive Phone: (781) 837-4503
Own Printing Facility?: Y
Commercial printers?: Y
Mechanical specifications: Type page 10 3/4 x 16; E - 5 cols, 2, between; A - 5 cols, 2, between.
Published Days: Wed
Avg. Paid Circ.: 2409
Avg. Free Circ.: 142
Audit Company: AAM
Audit Date: 44015

NORWELL

NORWELL MARINER

Street Address: 600 Cordwainer Drive
City: Norwell
State: MA
ZIP Code: 2061
General Phone: (781) 837-4500
General Email: sjacobson@wickedlocal.com
Publication Website: https://norwell.wickedlocal.com/
Publisher Name: Mark Olivieri
Publisher Email: molivieri@wickedlocal.com
Publisher Phone: (781) 837-4504
Editor Name: Mark Burridge
Editor Email: mburridge@wickedlocal.com
Editor Phone: (781) 837-4559
Advertising Executive Name: Chris Avis
Advertising Executive Email: cavis@wickedlocal.com
Advertising Executive Phone: (781) 837-4503
Year Established: 1974
Own Printing Facility?: Y
Commercial printers?: Y
Published Days: Thur
Avg. Paid Circ.: 962
Audit Company: AAM
Audit Date: 44015

NORWELL

SCITUATE MARINER

Street Address: 600 Cordwainer Drive
City: Norwell
State: MA
ZIP Code: 2061
General Phone: (781) 837-4500
General Email: scituate@wickedlocal.com
Publication Website: https://scituate.wickedlocal.com/
Parent Company: Gannett
Publisher Name: Mark Olivieri
Publisher Email: molivieri@wickedlocal.com
Publisher Phone: (781) 837-4504
Advertising Executive Name: Chris Avis
Advertising Executive Email: cavis@wickedlocal.com
Advertising Executive Phone: (781) 837-4503
Own Printing Facility?: Y
Commercial printers?: Y
Published Days: Thur
Avg. Paid Circ.: 2088
Avg. Free Circ.: 211
Audit Company: AAM
Audit Date: 44015

NORWOOD

HYDE PARK BULLETIN

Street Address: 661 Washington St, Ste 202
City: Norwood
State: MA
ZIP Code: 02062-3529
General Phone: (617) 361-8400
General Email: news@bulletinnewspapers.com
Publication Website: https://bulletinnewspapers.weebly.com/
Parent Company: Bulletin Newspapers, Inc
Publisher Name: Paul DiModica
Publisher Email: pdimodica@bulletinnewspapers.com
Editor Name: Dennis Cawley
Editor Email: dcawley@bulletinnewspapers.com
Advertising Executive Name: Jennifer Ferri
Advertising Executive Email: bulletingraphics@aol.com
Delivery Methods: Mail`Newsstand`Racks
Year Established: 1992
Own Printing Facility?: Y
Published Days: Thur
Avg. Free Circ.: 5500
Audit Company: Sworn/Estimate/Non-Audited
Audit Date: 43626

NORWOOD

THE BOSTON BULLETIN

Street Address: 661 Washington Street
City: Norwood
State: MA
ZIP Code: 2062
General Phone: (617) 361-8400
General Email: info@bulletinnewspapers.com
Publication Website: https://bulletinnewspapers.weebly.com/
Publisher Name: Paul DiModica
Publisher Email: pdimodica@bulletinnewspapers.com
Editor Name: Dennis Cawley
Editor Email: dcawley@bulletinnewspapers.com
Advertising Executive Name: Jennifer Ferri
Advertising Executive Email: bulletingraphics@aol.com
Delivery Methods: Mail`Newsstand
Commercial printers?: Y
Published Days: Thur
Avg. Free Circ.: 3000
Audit Company: Sworn/Estimate/Non-Audited
Audit Date: 43626

ORLEANS

THE CAPE CODDER

Street Address: 5 Namskaket Rd
City: Orleans
State: MA
ZIP Code: 02653-3202
General Phone: (508) 247-3255
General Email: codder@cnc.com
Publication Website: https://orleans.wickedlocal.com/
Parent Company: Gannett
Publisher Name: Peter Meyer
Publisher Email: pmeyer@capecodonline.com
Publisher Phone: (508) 862-1111
Editor Name: Donna Tunney
Editor Email: dtunney@wickedlocal.com
Advertising Executive Name: Molly Evans
Advertising Executive Email: mevans@capecodonline.com
Advertising Executive Phone: (508) 862-1377
Year Established: 1946
Own Printing Facility?: Y
Commercial printers?: Y
Published Days: Wed`Thur`Fri`Sat
Avg. Paid Circ.: 10653
Avg. Free Circ.: 10587
Audit Company: AAM
Audit Date: 44015

PALMER

THE TANTASQUA TOWN COMMON

Street Address: 24 Water St
City: Palmer
State: MA
ZIP Code: 1069
General Phone: (413) 283-8393
General Email: jbonsall@turley.com
Publication Website: thetantasquatowncommon.com
Delivery Methods: Racks
Published Days: Thur
Audit Company: Sworn/Estimate/Non-Audited
Audit Date: 43626

PITTSFIELD

THE PITTSFIELD GAZETTE

Street Address: 10 Wendell Avenue Extension
City: Pittsfield
State: MA
ZIP Code: 01201-6284
General Phone: (413) 443-2010
General Email: info@pittsfieldgazette.com

Publication Website: http://pittsfieldgazette.com/
Editor Name: Jonathan Levine
Editor Email: gazette@berkshire.net
Delivery Methods: Mail`Newsstand`Racks
Year Established: 1991
Mechanical specifications: Type page 10 1/4 x 16; E - 5 cols, 1 11/12, between; A - 5 cols, 1 11/12, between.
Published Days: Thur
Avg. Paid Circ.: 1500
Audit Company: Sworn/Estimate/Non-Audited
Audit Date: 43626

PLYMOUTH

CARVER REPORTER

Street Address: 182 Standish Ave
City: Plymouth
State: MA
ZIP Code: 2360
General Phone: (508) 591-6623
General Email: salesteam@wickedlocal.com
Publication Website: https://carver.wickedlocal.com/
Parent Company: Gannett
Publisher Name: Mark Olivieri
Publisher Email: molivieri@wickedlocal.com
Publisher Phone: (781) 837-4504
Advertising Executive Name: Chris Avis
Advertising Executive Email: cavis@wickedlocal.com
Advertising Executive Phone: (781) 837-4503
Year Established: 1980
Commercial printers?: Y
Mechanical specifications: Type page 10 3/4 x 16; E - 5 cols, 2, between; A - 5 cols, 2, between.
Published Days: Fri
Avg. Paid Circ.: 651
Audit Company: AAM
Audit Date: 43101

PLYMOUTH

KINGSTON REPORTER

Street Address: 182 Standish Ave
City: Plymouth
State: MA
ZIP Code: 02360-4162
General Phone: (508) 591-6623
General Email: kingston@wickedlocal.com
Publication Website: https://kingston.wickedlocal.com/
Parent Company: Gannett
Publisher Name: Mark Olivieri
Publisher Email: molivieri@wickedlocal.com
Publisher Phone: (781) 837-4504
Advertising Executive Name: Chris Avis
Advertising Executive Email: cavis@wickedlocal.com
Advertising Executive Phone: (781) 837-4503
Own Printing Facility?: Y
Commercial printers?: Y
Mechanical specifications: Type page 10 3/4 x 16; E - 5 cols, 2, between; A - 5 cols, 2, between.
Published Days: Fri
Avg. Paid Circ.: 195
Audit Company: AAM
Audit Date: 43649

PLYMOUTH

OLD COLONY MEMORIAL

Street Address: 182 Standish Ave
City: Plymouth
State: MA
ZIP Code: 2360
General Phone: (508) 591-6623
General Email: ocm@wickedlocal.com
Publication Website: https://plymouth.wickedlocal.com/
Parent Company: Gannett
Publisher Name: Mark Olivieri
Publisher Email: molivieri@wickedlocal.com
Publisher Phone: (781) 837-4504
Advertising Executive Name: Chris Avis
Advertising Executive Email: cavis@wickedlocal.com
Advertising Executive Phone: (781) 837-4503
Own Printing Facility?: Y
Commercial printers?: Y
Mechanical specifications: Type page 13 x 21 1/2; E - 6 cols, 2, between; A - 6 cols, 2, between.
Published Days: Wed`Sat
Avg. Paid Circ.: 4572
Avg. Free Circ.: 22
Audit Company: Sworn/Estimate/Non-Audited
Audit Date: 43626

PROVINCETOWN

PROVINCETOWN BANNER

Street Address: P.O. Box 977
City: Provincetown
State: MA
ZIP Code: 2657
General Phone: (508) 487-7400
General Email: sales@provincetownbanner.com
Publication Website: https://provincetown.wickedlocal.com/
Parent Company: Gannett
Publisher Name: Peter Meyer
Publisher Email: pmeyer@capecodonline.com
Publisher Phone: (508) 862-1111
Editor Name: Paul Pronovost
Editor Email: ppronovost@capecodonline.com
Editor Phone: (508) 862-1166
Advertising Executive Name: Molly Evans
Advertising Executive Email: mevans@capecodonline.com
Year Established: 1995
Published Days: Thur
Avg. Paid Circ.: 3199
Avg. Free Circ.: 316
Audit Company: AAM
Audit Date: 44015

QUINCY

THE QUINCY SUN

Street Address: 1372 Hancock St
City: Quincy
State: MA
ZIP Code: 02169-5107
General Phone: (617) 471-3100
General Email: quincysunads@verizon.net
Publication Website: https://thequincysun.com/
Publisher Name: Robert H. Bosworth
Publisher Email: thequincysun@verizon.net
Editor Name: Robert H. Bosworth
Editor Email: thequincysun@verizon.net
Advertising Executive Name: Robert Bosworth
Advertising Executive Email: quincysunads@verizon.net
Delivery Methods: Mail`Newsstand`Carrier`Racks
Year Established: 1968
Published Days: Thur
Avg. Paid Circ.: 7000
Audit Company: Sworn/Estimate/Non-Audited
Audit Date: 43626

RANDOLPH

HOLBROOK SUN

Street Address: 15 Pacella Park Dr
City: Randolph
State: MA
ZIP Code: 02368-1700
General Phone: (508) 967-3535
General Email: molivieri@wickedlocal.com
Publication Website: https://holbrook.wickedlocal.com/
Publisher Name: Mark Olivieri
Publisher Email: molivieri@wickedlocal.com
Publisher Phone: (781) 837-4504
Advertising Executive Name: Rafal Lipowicz
Delivery Methods: Mail`Carrier
Year Established: 1958
Own Printing Facility?: Y
Commercial printers?: Y
Published Days: Fri
Weekday Frequency: m
Saturday Frequency: m
Avg. Paid Circ.: 330
Audit Company: AAM
Audit Date: 44015

RANDOLPH

RANDOLPH HERALD

Street Address: 15 Pacella Park Dr
City: Randolph
State: MA
ZIP Code: 2368
General Phone: (508) 967-3515
General Email: ccrimmins@wickedlocal.com
Publication Website: https://randolph.wickedlocal.com/
Publisher Name: Mark Olivieri
Publisher Email: molivieri@wickedlocal.com
Publisher Phone: (781) 837-4504
Advertising Executive Name: Karen Willette
Advertising Executive Email: kwillette@wickedlocal.com
Advertising Executive Phone: (508) 638-5578
Year Established: 1924
Commercial printers?: Y
Mechanical specifications: Type page 10 9/16 x 16; E - 6 cols, 1 9/16, 1/6 between; A - 6 cols, between; C - 7 cols, between.
Published Days: Wed
Avg. Paid Circ.: 107
Avg. Free Circ.: 2513
Audit Company: AAM
Audit Date: 44015

RANDOLPH

WEYMOUTH NEWS

Street Address: 15 Pacella Park Dr
City: Randolph
State: MA
ZIP Code: 02368-1700
General Phone: (781) 682-4850
General Email: weymouth@wickedlocal.com
Publication Website: https://weymouth.wickedlocal.com/
Parent Company: Gannett
Publisher Name: Mark Olivieri
Publisher Email: molivieri@wickedlocal.com
Publisher Phone: (781) 837-4504
Advertising Executive Name: Dona Bula-Bula
Advertising Executive Email: dbula@wickedlocal.com
Advertising Executive Phone: (508) 638-5573
Commercial printers?: Y
Published Days: Wed
Avg. Paid Circ.: 1740
Audit Company: AAM
Audit Date: 44015

RAYNHAM

BRIDGEWATER INDEPENDENT

Street Address: 370 Paramount Dr
City: Raynham
State: MA
ZIP Code: 2767
General Phone: (508) 967-3518
General Email: dteehan@wickedlocal.com
Publication Website: https://bridgewater.wickedlocal.com/
Publisher Name: Mark Olivieri
Publisher Email: molivieri@wickedlocal.com
Publisher Phone: (781) 837-4504
Editor Name: Rebecca Hyman
Editor Email: rhyman@gatehousemedia.com
Editor Phone: (508) 967-3150
Advertising Executive Name: Rafal Lipowicz
Advertising Executive Email: classifieds@wickedlocal.com
Year Established: 1875
Own Printing Facility?: Y
Commercial printers?: Y
Published Days: Wed
Avg. Paid Circ.: 310
Avg. Free Circ.: 1530
Audit Company: AAM
Audit Date: 44015

RAYNHAM

CANTON JOURNAL

Street Address: 15 Pacella Park Drive
City: Raynham
State: MA
ZIP Code: 2368
General Phone: (508) 967-3515
General Email: sgreen@wickedlocal.com
Publication Website: https://canton.wickedlocal.com/
Publisher Name: Mark Olivieri
Publisher Email: molivieri@wickedlocal.com
Publisher Phone: (781) 837-4504
Advertising Executive Name: Rafal Lipowicz
Advertising Executive Email: classifieds@wickedlocal.com
Year Established: 1876
Own Printing Facility?: Y
Commercial printers?: Y
Published Days: Fri
Avg. Free Circ.: 169
Audit Company: AAM
Audit Date: 43658

RAYNHAM

EASTON JOURNAL

Street Address: 370 Paramount Dr
City: Raynham
State: MA
ZIP Code: 02767-5419
General Phone: (508) 967-3510
General Email: molivieri@wickedlocal.com
Publication Website: https://easton.wickedlocal.com/
Publisher Name: Mark Olivieri
Publisher Email: molivieri@wickedlocal.com
Publisher Phone: (781) 837-4504
Advertising Executive Name: Rafal Lipowicz
Published Days: Fri
Avg. Paid Circ.: 301
Audit Company: AAM
Audit Date: 44024

RAYNHAM

NORTON MIRROR

Street Address: 370 Paramount Dr, Suite 3
City: Raynham
State: MA
ZIP Code: 02767-5419
General Phone: (508) 967-3510
General Email: classifieds@wickedlocal.com
Publication Website: https://norton.wickedlocal.com/
Publisher Name: Mark Olivieri
Publisher Email: molivieri@wickedlocal.com
Publisher Phone: (781) 837-4504
Advertising Executive Email: classifieds@wickedlocal.com
Advertising Executive Phone: (781) 433-6925
Year Established: 1987
Own Printing Facility?: Y
Commercial printers?: Y
Published Days: Fri
Avg. Paid Circ.: 721

Community Newspapers in the U.S.

Audit Company: Sworn/Estimate/Non-Audited
Audit Date: 43626

RAYNHAM

STOUGHTON JOURNAL

Street Address: 370 Paramount Dr
City: Raynham
State: MA
ZIP Code: 02767-5419
General Phone: (508) 967-3515
General Email: classifieds@wickedlocal.com
Publication Website: https://stoughton.wickedlocal.com/
Publisher Name: Mark Olivieri
Publisher Email: molivieri@wickedlocal.com
Publisher Phone: (781) 837-4504
Advertising Executive Name: Mike Coyne
Advertising Executive Email: mcoyne@wickedlocal.com
Advertising Executive Phone: (508) 638-5572
Year Established: 1989
Own Printing Facility?: Y
Commercial printers?: Y
Published Days: Fri
Avg. Paid Circ.: 156
Audit Company: AAM
Audit Date: 44024

ROWLEY

THE TOWN COMMON

Street Address: 77 Wethersfield St
City: Rowley
State: MA
ZIP Code: 01969-1713
General Phone: (978) 948-8696
General Email: advertise@thetowncommon.com
Publication Website: http://www.thetowncommon.com/
Publisher Name: Marc Maravalli
Editor Name: Marc Maravalli
Editor Email: editor@thetowncommon.com
Advertising Executive Email: advertise@thetowncommon.com
Delivery Methods: Newsstand Racks
Year Established: 2004
Published Days: Wed
Audit Company: Sworn/Estimate/Non-Audited
Audit Date: 43626

SHELBURNE FALLS

WEST COUNTY NEWS

Street Address: 87 Bridge St
City: Shelburne Falls
State: MA
ZIP Code: 01370-1102
General Phone: (413) 625-4660
General Email: wcnews@turley.com
Year Established: 1979
Mechanical specifications: Type page 10 1/4 x 16; E - 5 cols, 1 7/8, 1/8 between.
Published Days: Thur
Avg. Free Circ.: 21629
Audit Company: Sworn/Estimate/Non-Audited
Audit Date: 43626

SOMERVILLE

STONEHAM SUN

Street Address: 20 Holland St
City: Somerville
State: MA
ZIP Code: 02144-2749
General Phone: (781) 279-1051
General Email: stoneham@wickedlocal.com
Publication Website: https://stoneham.wickedlocal.com/
Advertising Executive Name: Linc Murphy
Advertising Executive Email: rmurphy@wickedlocal.com
Advertising Executive Phone: (978) 739-1371
Own Printing Facility?: Y
Commercial printers?: Y
Mechanical specifications: Type page 10 13/16 x 16; E - 5 cols, 2 1/16, between; A - 5 cols, 2 1/16, between; C - 8 cols, 1 7/32, between.
Published Days: Wed
Avg. Free Circ.: 3821
Audit Company: Sworn/Estimate/Non-Audited
Audit Date: 43626

SOMERVILLE

THE SOMERVILLE TIMES

Street Address: 699 Broadway
City: Somerville
State: MA
ZIP Code: 2144
General Phone: (617) 666-4010
General Email: ads@thesomervilletimes.com
Publication Website: https://www.thesomervilletimes.com/
Editor Name: Jim Clark
Editor Email: jclark@thesomervilletimes.com
Editor Phone: (617) 666-4010
Advertising Executive Name: Bobbie Toner
Advertising Executive Email: bobbie@thesomervilletimes.com
Advertising Executive Phone: (617) 666-4010
Delivery Methods: Mail Racks
Year Established: 1969
Published Days: Wed
Audit Company: Sworn/Estimate/Non-Audited
Audit Date: 43626

SOUTHBRIDGE

AUBURN NEWS

Street Address: 25 Elm St
City: Southbridge
State: MA
ZIP Code: 01550-2605
General Phone: (508) 764-4325
General Email: jsima@stonebridgepress.news
Publication Website: http://www.southbridgeeveningnews.com/
Parent Company: Stonebridge Press, Inc.
Advertising Executive Name: June Simakauskas
Advertising Executive Email: jsima@stonebridgepress.news
Advertising Executive Phone: (508) 909-4062
Delivery Methods: Mail
Own Printing Facility?: Y
Mechanical specifications: Type page 11 1/2 x 21; E - 6 cols, 1 1/2, 1/4 between; A - 8 cols, 1 5/4, 1/4 between.
Published Days: Wed
Avg. Paid Circ.: 1600
Avg. Free Circ.: 8
Audit Company: Sworn/Estimate/Non-Audited
Audit Date: 43626

SOUTHBRIDGE

BLACKSTONE VALLEY TRIBUNE

Street Address: 25 Elm St
City: Southbridge
State: MA
ZIP Code: 01550-2605
General Phone: (508) 764-4325
General Email: patricia@stonebridgepress.news
Publication Website: http://www.southbridgeeveningnews.com/
Parent Company: Stonebridge Press, Inc.

SOUTHBRIDGE

CHARLTON VILLAGER

Street Address: 25 Elm St
City: Southbridge
State: MA
ZIP Code: 01550-2605
General Phone: (508) 764-4325
General Email: jsima@stonebridgepress.news
Publication Website: http://www.southbridgeeveningnews.com/
Parent Company: Stonebridge Press, Inc.
Advertising Executive Name: June Simakauskas
Advertising Executive Email: jsima@stonebridgepress.news
Advertising Executive Phone: (508) 909-4062
Delivery Methods: Mail
Published Days: Fri
Audit Company: Sworn/Estimate/Non-Audited
Audit Date: 43626

SOUTHBRIDGE

KILLINGLY VILLAGER

Street Address: 25 Elm Street, PO Box 90
City: Southbridge
State: MA
ZIP Code: 1550
General Phone: (508) 764-4325
General Email: kerri@stonebridgepress.news
Publication Website: http://www.southbridgeeveningnews.com/
Publisher Name: Brendan Berube
Publisher Email: news@stonebridgepress.news
Publisher Phone: (508) 909-4106
Advertising Executive Name: June Simakauskas
Advertising Executive Email: jsima@stonebridgepress.news
Advertising Executive Phone: (508) 909-4062
Mechanical specifications: Type page 11 x 20.7; 8 cols, 1.25, 0.14 between
Published Days: Fri
Avg. Free Circ.: 9418
Audit Company: Sworn/Estimate/Non-Audited
Audit Date: 43626

SOUTHBRIDGE

SPENCER NEW LEADER

Street Address: 25 Elm St
City: Southbridge
State: MA
ZIP Code: 01550-2605
General Phone: (508) 764-4325
General Email: jsima@stonebridgepress.news
Publication Website: http://www.southbridgeeveningnews.com/
Parent Company: Stonebridge Press, Inc.
Advertising Executive Name: June Simakauskas
Advertising Executive Email: jsima@stonebridgepress.news
Delivery Methods: Mail
Own Printing Facility?: Y
Commercial printers?: Y
Published Days: Thur
Avg. Free Circ.: 17200
Audit Company: Sworn/Estimate/Non-Audited
Audit Date: 43626
Year Established: 1949
Own Printing Facility?: Y
Commercial printers?: Y
Published Days: Fri
Avg. Paid Circ.: 15000
Audit Company: Sworn/Estimate/Non-Audited
Audit Date: 43626

SOUTHBRIDGE

STURBRIDGE VILLAGER

Street Address: 25 Elm St
City: Southbridge
State: MA
ZIP Code: 01550-2605
General Phone: (508) 764-4325
General Email: news@stonbridgepress.news
Publication Website: http://www.southbridgeeveningnews.com/
Parent Company: Stonebridge Press, Inc.
Publisher Name: Frank G. Chilinski
Editor Name: Brendan Berube
Editor Phone: (508) 909-4106
Advertising Executive Name: Kerri Peterson
Advertising Executive Email: kerri@stonebridgepress.news
Advertising Executive Phone: (508) 909-4103
Delivery Methods: Mail
Published Days: Fri
Audit Company: Sworn/Estimate/Non-Audited
Audit Date: 43626

SOUTHBRIDGE

THE WEBSTER TIMES

Street Address: 25 Elm St
City: Southbridge
State: MA
ZIP Code: 1550
General Phone: (508) 764-4325
General Email: patricia@stonebridgepress.news
Publication Website: http://www.southbridgeeveningnews.com/
Parent Company: Stonebridge Press, Inc.
Advertising Executive Name: Patricia Owens
Advertising Executive Email: patricia@stonebridgepress.news
Advertising Executive Phone: (508) 909-4135
Delivery Methods: Mail
Own Printing Facility?: Y
Published Days: Fri
Avg. Paid Circ.: 15200
Avg. Free Circ.: 17000
Audit Company: Sworn/Estimate/Non-Audited
Audit Date: 43626

STONEHAM

THE STONEHAM INDEPENDENT

Street Address: 200F Main St
City: Stoneham
State: MA
ZIP Code: 02180-1619
General Phone: (781) 438-1660
General Email: news@stonehamindependent.com
Publication Website: http://homenewshere.com/stoneham_independent/
Parent Company: Woburn Daily Times, Inc.
Advertising Executive Email: advertising@dailytimesinc.com
Delivery Methods: Mail Newsstand Racks
Year Established: 1870
Own Printing Facility?: Y
Mechanical specifications: Type page 11 5/8 x 21; E - 6 cols, 1 13/16, between; A - 6 cols, 1 13/16, between; C - 9 cols, 1 1/6, between.
Published Days: Wed
Avg. Paid Circ.: 3000
Audit Company: Sworn/Estimate/Non-Audited
Audit Date: 43626

TAUNTON

MANSFIELD NEWS

Street Address: 5 Cohannet St.
City: Taunton
State: MA
ZIP Code: 2780
General Phone: (508) 967-3510
General Email: cavis@wickedlocal.com
Publication Website: https://mansfield.wickedlocal.com/
Publisher Name: Mark Olivieri
Publisher Email: molivieri@wickedlocal.com
Publisher Phone: (781) 837-4504
Advertising Executive Name: Chris Avis
Advertising Executive Email: cavis@wickedlocal.com
Advertising Executive Phone: (781) 837-4503
Year Established: 1872
Own Printing Facility?: Y
Published Days: Fri
Avg. Paid Circ.: 236
Audit Company: AAM
Audit Date: 44024

TAUNTON

THE RAYNHAM CALL

Street Address: 5 Cohannet St
City: Taunton
State: MA
ZIP Code: 2780
General Phone: (508) 967-3518
General Email: ccrimmins@wickedlocal.com
Publication Website: https://raynham.wickedlocal.com/
Publisher Name: Mark Olivieri
Publisher Email: molivieri@wickedlocal.com
Publisher Phone: (781) 837-4504
Advertising Executive Name: Cyndy Taylor
Advertising Executive Email: ctaylor@wickedlocal.com
Advertising Executive Phone: (508) 638-5585
Published Days: Wed
Avg. Paid Circ.: 136
Avg. Free Circ.: 1700
Audit Company: AAM
Audit Date: 44015

VINEYARD HAVEN

THE MARTHA'S VINEYARD TIMES

Street Address: 30 Beach Rd
City: Vineyard Haven
State: MA
ZIP Code: 02568-5582
General Phone: (508) 693-6100
General Email: carrie@mvtimes.com
Publication Website: https://www.mvtimes.com/
Publisher Name: Peter Oberfest
Publisher Phone: (508) 693-6100, ext : 17
Editor Name: George Brennan
Editor Phone: (508) 693-6100, ext : 11
Advertising Executive Name: Jenna Lambert
Advertising Executive Phone: (508) 693-6100, ext : 35
Year Established: 1984
Published Days: Thur
Avg. Paid Circ.: 250
Avg. Free Circ.: 16000
Audit Company: Sworn/Estimate/Non-Audited
Audit Date: 43626

WAKEFIELD

NORTH READING TRANSCRIPT

Street Address: 26 Albion St
City: Wakefield
State: MA
ZIP Code: 01880-2803
General Phone: (781) 245-0080
General Email: ads@wakefielditem.com
Publication Website: https://www.localheadlinenews.com/
Editor Name: Robert Burgess
Advertising Executive Email: ads@wakefielditem.com
Delivery Methods: Mail`Newsstand`Carrier
Year Established: 1956
Mechanical specifications: Type page 10 13/16 x 16; E - 5 cols, 2 1/16, 1/8 between; A - 5 cols, 2 1/16, 1/8 between; C - 5 cols, 2 1/16, 1/8 between.
Published Days: Thur
Avg. Paid Circ.: 4000
Avg. Free Circ.: 290
Audit Company: Sworn/Estimate/Non-Audited
Audit Date: 43626

WAKEFIELD

THE LYNNFIELD VILLAGER

Street Address: 26 Albion St
City: Wakefield
State: MA
ZIP Code: 01880-2803
General Phone: (781) 245-0080
General Email: ads@wakefielditem.com
Publication Website: https://www.localheadlinenews.com/
Editor Name: Robert Burgess
Advertising Executive Email: ads@wakefielditem.com
Delivery Methods: Mail`Newsstand`Carrier
Year Established: 1973
Own Printing Facility?: Y
Commercial printers?: N
Mechanical specifications: Type page 10 13/16 x 16; E - 5 cols, 2 1/16, 1/8 between; A - 5 cols, 2 1/16, 1/8 between; C - 5 cols, 2 1/16, 1/8 between.
Published Days: Wed
Avg. Paid Circ.: 1615
Avg. Free Circ.: 207
Audit Company: Sworn/Estimate/Non-Audited
Audit Date: 43626

WEST SPRINGFIELD

WEST SPRINGFIELD RECORD

Street Address: 516 Main St
City: West Springfield
State: MA
ZIP Code: 01089-3973
General Phone: (413) 736-1587
General Email: wsrecord@comcast.net
Delivery Methods: Mail`Newsstand`Racks
Year Established: 1953
Commercial printers?: Y
Published Days: Thur
Avg. Paid Circ.: 5600
Audit Company: Sworn/Estimate/Non-Audited
Audit Date: 43626

WESTBOROUGH

COMMUNITY ADVOCATE

Street Address: 32 South St
City: Westborough
State: MA
ZIP Code: 01581-1619
General Phone: (508) 366-5500
General Email: news@communityadvocate.com
Publication Website: https://www.communityadvocate.com/
Publisher Name: David Bagdon
Editor Name: Bonnie Adams
Editor Email: news@communityadvocate.com
Editor Phone: (508) 366-5500, ext : 14
Advertising Executive Name: Diane Sabatini
Advertising Executive Email: diane@communityadvocate.com
Year Established: 1974
Mechanical specifications: Type page 10 x 13; E - 5 cols, 1 5/8, between; A - 5 cols, 1 5/8, between; C - 7 cols, 1 3/16, between.
Published Days: Fri
Avg. Paid Circ.: 16000
Avg. Free Circ.: 5194
Audit Company: Sworn/Estimate/Non-Audited
Audit Date: 43626

WOBURN

TOWN CRIER

Street Address: 1 Arrow Dr
City: Woburn
State: MA
ZIP Code: 01801-2039
General Phone: (978) 658-2346 ext 100
General Email: office@yourtowncrier.com
Publication Website: http://homenewshere.com/wilmington_town_crier/
Parent Company: Woburn Daily Times, Inc.
Advertising Executive Name: Bruce Hilliard
Advertising Executive Email: bruce.hilliard@verizon.net
Delivery Methods: Mail`Newsstand`Carrier`Racks
Year Established: 1955
Own Printing Facility?: Y
Mechanical specifications: Type page 11 x 21; E - 6 cols, 2 1/16, between; A - 6 cols, 2 1/16, between; C - 6 cols, 2 1/16, between.
Published Days: Wed
Avg. Paid Circ.: 6000
Avg. Free Circ.: 500
Audit Company: Sworn/Estimate/Non-Audited
Audit Date: 43626

WORCESTER

THE LANDMARK

Street Address: 100 Front St., 5th Floor
City: Worcester
State: MA
ZIP Code: 01615-0012
General Phone: (508) 767-9555
General Email: sales@holdenlandmark.com
Publication Website: https://www.thelandmark.com/
Parent Company: Gannett
Editor Name: Kristen Payson
Editor Email: kpayson@gatehousemedia.com
Editor Phone: (508) 767-9555, ext : 4555
Advertising Executive Email: classifieds@gatehousemedia.com
Advertising Executive Phone: (888) 254-3466
Delivery Methods: Mail`Racks
Year Established: 1976
Commercial printers?: Y
Mechanical specifications: Type page 11 x 16; E - 4 cols, 2 3/8, 3/16 between; A - 6 cols, 1 9/16, 3/16 between; C - 6 cols, 1 9/16, 3/16 between.
Published Days: Thur
Avg. Paid Circ.: 8909
Avg. Free Circ.: 350
Audit Company: Sworn/Estimate/Non-Audited
Audit Date: 43626

WORCESTER

WORCESTER BUSINESS JOURNAL

Street Address: 172 Shrewsbury St
City: Worcester
State: MA
ZIP Code: 01604-4636
General Phone: (508) 755-8004
General Email: wbjournal@cambeywest.com
Publication Website: https://www.wbjournal.com/
Parent Company: New England Business Media
Publisher Name: Peter Stanton
Publisher Email: pstanton@wbjournal.com
Publisher Phone: (508) 755-8004, ext : 223
Editor Name: Brad Kane
Editor Email: bkane@wbjournal.com
Editor Phone: (508) 755-8004, ext : 256
Advertising Executive Name: Mark Murray
Advertising Executive Email: mmurray@wbjournal.com
Advertising Executive Phone: (508) 755-8004, ext : 227
Delivery Methods: Mail`Newsstand
Year Established: 1990
Published Days: Mon
Published Other: every other week
Avg. Paid Circ.: 453
Avg. Free Circ.: 8465
Audit Company: CVC
Audit Date: 43081

MARYLAND

ANNAPOLIS

BAY WEEKLY

Street Address: 1160 Spa Rd
City: Annapolis
State: MD
ZIP Code: 21403-1097
General Phone: (410) 626-9888
General Email: ads@bayweekly.com
Publication Website: https://www.bayweekly.com/
Parent Company: New Bay Enterprises
Publisher Name: J. Alex Knoll
Publisher Email: jak@bayweekly.com
Editor Name: Sandra Olivetti Martin
Editor Email: editor@bayweekly.com
Advertising Executive Name: Audrey Broomfield
Advertising Executive Email: audrey@bayweekly.com

ANNAPOLIS

BOWIE BLADE-NEWS

Street Address: 2000 Capital Dr
City: Annapolis
State: MD
ZIP Code: 21401-3155
General Phone: (410) 268-5000
General Email: classifieds@capgaznews.com
Publication Website: https://www.capitalgazette.com/

ANNAPOLIS

CROFTON-WEST COUNTY GAZETTE

Street Address: 2000 Capital Dr
City: Annapolis
State: MD
ZIP Code: 21401-3155
General Phone: (410) 268-5000
General Email: classifieds@capgaznews.com
Publication Website: https://www.capitalgazette.com/

BALTIMORE

ARBUTUS TIMES

Street Address: 501 N Calvert St
City: Baltimore
State: MD
ZIP Code: 21278-1000
General Phone: (410) 332-6000
General Email: advertise@baltsun.com

BALTIMORE

Community Newspapers in the U.S.

BALTIMORE BUSINESS JOURNAL

Street Address: 36 S Charles St
City: Baltimore
State: MD
ZIP Code: 21201-3107
General Phone: (410) 576-1161
General Email: baltimore@bizjournals.com
Publication Website: https://www.bizjournals.com/baltimore/
Parent Company: American City Business Journals
Publisher Name: Rhonda Pringle
Publisher Email: rpringle@bizjournals.com
Editor Name: Jessica Iannetta
Editor Email: jiannetta@bizjournals.com
Editor Phone: 410-454-0511
Advertising Executive Name: Annie Payne
Advertising Executive Email: apayne@bizjournals.com
Advertising Executive Phone: (410) 454-0521

BALTIMORE

BALTIMORE GUIDE SOUTH

Street Address: 2935 Odonnell St
City: Baltimore
State: MD
ZIP Code: 21224-4823
General Phone: (410) 732-6600
General Email: lnemec@baltimoreguide.com

BALTIMORE

CATONSVILLE TIMES

Street Address: 501 N Calvert St
City: Baltimore
State: MD
ZIP Code: 21278-1000
General Phone: (410) 788-4500
General Email: catonsvilletimes@patuxent.com
Publication Website: https://www.baltimoresun.com/maryland/baltimore-county/catonsville/
Publisher Name: Triffon G. Alatzas
Publisher Email: trif.alatzas@baltsun.com
Editor Name: Ron Fritz
Editor Email: rtfritz@baltsun.com
Editor Phone: 410-468-2622

BALTIMORE

LAUREL LEADER

Street Address: 501 N Calvert St
City: Baltimore
State: MD
ZIP Code: 21278-1000
General Phone: (410) 332-6594
General Email: jduchman@baltsun.com
Publication Website: https://www.baltimoresun.com/maryland/laurel/
Publisher Name: Triffon G. Alatzas
Publisher Email: trif.alatzas@baltsun.com
Editor Name: Ron Fritz
Editor Email: rtfritz@baltsun.com
Editor Phone: 410-468-2622

BALTIMORE

THE AEGIS

Street Address: 501 North Calvert Street
City: Baltimore
State: MD
ZIP Code: 21278
General Phone: (410) 838-4400
General Email: news@theaegis.com
Publication Website: https://www.baltimoresun.com/maryland/harford/aegis/
Parent Company: tronc, Inc.
Publisher Name: Triffon G. Alatzas
Publisher Email: trif.alatzas@baltsun.com

Editor Name: Ron Fritz
Editor Email: rtfritz@baltsun.com
Editor Phone: 410-468-2622

BERLIN

MARYLAND COAST DISPATCH

Street Address: 10012 Old Ocean City Blvd
City: Berlin
State: MD
ZIP Code: 21811-1145
General Phone: (410) 641-4561
General Email: editor@mdcoastdispatch.com
Publication Website: http://www.mdcoastdispatch.com/
Publisher Name: J. Steven Green
Publisher Email: editor@mdcoastdispatch.com
Editor Name: Shawn J. Soper

BERLIN

OCEAN PINES INDEPENDENT

Street Address: 11021 Nicholas Ln
City: Berlin
State: MD
ZIP Code: 21811-3244
General Phone: (401) 600-0434
General Email: info@oceanpines.org
Publication Website: https://www.oceanpines.org/
Publisher Name: John Viola
Publisher Email: gm@oceanpines.org
Publisher Phone: (410) 641-7717, ext : 3001

BRUNSWICK

THE VALLEY CITIZEN

Street Address: 101 W Potomac St
City: Brunswick
State: MD
ZIP Code: 21716-1114
General Phone: (301) 834-7722
General Email: citizen@mip.net
Publication Website: http://www.citizennewspapers.com/
Parent Company: Citizen Newspapers

CALIFORNIA

THE ENTERPRISE

Street Address: 22685 Three Notch Road, Suite D
City: California
State: MD
ZIP Code: 20619
General Phone: (301) 862-2111
General Email: chesads@chespub.com
Publication Website: https://www.somdnews.com/enterprise/
Parent Company: Gannett
Editor Name: Donnie Morgan
Editor Email: dmorgan@somdnews.com
Editor Phone: 301-866-6446
Advertising Executive Name: Brook Ash
Advertising Executive Email: bash@somdnews.com
Advertising Executive Phone: (240) 561-1390

CAMBRIDGE

DORCHESTER BANNER

Street Address: 103 Cedar St
City: Cambridge
State: MD
ZIP Code: 21613-2361
General Phone: (410) 228-3131
General Email: bannernews@newszap.com
Publication Website: https://www.dorchesterbanner.com/
Parent Company: Independent NewsMedia
Publisher Name: Darel LaPrade
Publisher Email: dlaprade@newszap.com
Editor Name: Dave Ryan
Editor Email: dryan@newszap.com

CAMBRIDGE

THE DORCHESTER STAR

Street Address: 511 Poplar St
City: Cambridge
State: MD
ZIP Code: 21613
General Phone: (410) 228-0222
General Email: news@dorchesterstar.com
Publication Website: https://www.myeasternshoremd.com/dorchester_star
Parent Company: Adams Publishing Group
Publisher Name: Jim Normandin
Publisher Email: jim.normandin@adamspg.com
Editor Name: Hannah Combs
Editor Email: hcombs@chespub.com
Editor Phone: 443-239-9169
Advertising Executive Name: Brandon Silverstein
Advertising Executive Email: bsilverstein@chespub.com
Advertising Executive Phone: (410) 200-6469

CENTREVILLE

QUEEN ANNE'S RECORD OBSERVER

Street Address: 114 Broadway
City: Centreville
State: MD
ZIP Code: 21617-1006
General Phone: (410) 758-1400
General Email: recordobserver@chespub.com
Publication Website: https://www.myeasternshoremd.com/qa/record_observer/
Publisher Name: Jim Normandin
Publisher Email: jim.normandin@adamspg.com
Editor Name: Angela Price
Editor Email: aprice@chespub.com
Editor Phone: 443-239-0218
Advertising Executive Name: Brandon Silverstein
Advertising Executive Email: bsilverstein@chespub.com
Advertising Executive Phone: (410) 200-6469

CHESTER

THE BAY TIMES

Street Address: 700-C Abruzzi Drive
City: Chester
State: MD
ZIP Code: 21619
General Phone: (410) 643-7770
General Email: baytimes@kibaytimes.com
Publication Website: https://www.myeasternshoremd.com/qa/bay_times/
Parent Company: Adams Publishing Group
Publisher Name: James F. Normandin
Editor Name: Angela Price
Editor Email: aprice@chespub.com
Editor Phone: 443-239-0218
Advertising Executive Name: Brandon Silverstein
Advertising Executive Email: bsilverstein@chespub.com
Advertising Executive Phone: (410) 200-6469

CHESTERTOWN

KENT COUNTY NEWS

Street Address: 223 High Street
City: Chestertown
State: MD
ZIP Code: 21620
General Phone: (410) 778-2011
General Email: bsilverstein@chespub.com
Publication Website: https://www.myeasternshoremd.com/kent_county_news
Parent Company: Adams Publishing Group
Editor Name: Dan Divilio
Editor Email: ddivilio@thekentcountynews.com
Editor Phone: 443-239-1456
Advertising Executive Name: Brandon Silverstein
Advertising Executive Email: bsilverstein@chespub.com
Advertising Executive Phone: (410) 200-6469

COLUMBIA

COLUMBIA FLIER

Street Address: 10750 Little Patuxent Pkwy
City: Columbia
State: MD
ZIP Code: 21044-3106
General Phone: (443) 692-9011
General Email: wartuscooper@baltsun.com
Publication Website: https://www.baltimoresun.com/maryland/howard/columbia/
Publisher Name: Triffon G. Alatzas
Publisher Email: trif.alatzas@baltsun.com
Editor Name: Ron Fritz
Editor Email: rtfritz@baltsun.com
Editor Phone: 410-468-2622

COLUMBIA

HOWARD COUNTY TIMES

Street Address: 10750 Little Patuxent Pkwy
City: Columbia
State: MD
ZIP Code: 21044-3106
General Phone: (410) 730-3620
General Email: mcimino@baltsun.com
Publication Website: https://www.baltimoresun.com/maryland/howard/
Publisher Name: Triffon G. Alatzas
Publisher Email: trif.alatzas@baltsun.com
Editor Name: Ron Fritz
Editor Email: rtfritz@baltsun.com
Editor Phone: 410-468-2622

CRISFIELD

CRISFIELD-SOMERSET COUNTY TIMES

Street Address: 914 W Main St
City: Crisfield
State: MD
ZIP Code: 21817-1016
General Phone: (410) 968-1188
General Email: adsales@newszap.com
Publication Website: https://www.csctimes.com/
Parent Company: Independent NewsMedia
Publisher Name: Darel LaPrade
Publisher Email: dlaprade@newszap.com
Editor Name: Richard Crumbacker,
Editor Email: crisfieldnews@newszap.com
Advertising Executive Name: Karen Riggin
Advertising Executive Email: kriggin@newszap.com

CUMBERLAND

THE GARRETT COUNTY WEEKENDER

Street Address: 19 Baltimore St
City: Cumberland
State: MD
ZIP Code: 21502-3023
General Phone: (301) 722-4600

General Email: advertising@times-news.com
Publication Website: https://www.times-news.com/
Parent Company: CNHI, LLC
Publisher Name: Robert Forcey
Publisher Phone: (301) 784-2514
Advertising Executive Name: Meaghan Beem
Advertising Executive Email: mbeem@times-news.com
Advertising Executive Phone: (301) 784-2505

DUNDALK

THE AVENUE NEWS

Street Address: 4 N Center Pl
City: Dundalk
State: MD
ZIP Code: 21222-4300
General Phone: (410) 687-7775
General Email: jneill@chespub.com
Publication Website: https://www.avenuenews.com/
Parent Company: Adams Publishing Group
Publisher Name: Jim Normandin
Publisher Email: jim.normandin@adamspg.com
Editor Name: Kaitlin Kulich
Editor Email: kkulich@chespub.com
Editor Phone: 443-963-6004
Advertising Executive Name: Jason O'Neill
Advertising Executive Email: jneill@chespub.com
Advertising Executive Phone: (443) 963-6006

DUNDALK

THE DUNDALK EAGLE

Street Address: 4 N Center Pl
City: Dundalk
State: MD
ZIP Code: 21222-4300
General Phone: (410) 288-6060
General Email: joneill@chespub.com
Publication Website: https://www.dundalkeagle.com/
Parent Company: Adams Publishing Group
Editor Name: Mike Ursery
Editor Email: mursery@chespub.com
Editor Phone: 443-786-2809
Advertising Executive Name: Jason O'Neill
Advertising Executive Email: joneill@chespub.com
Advertising Executive Phone: (443) 963-6006

EASTON

EASTERN SHORE BARGAINEER

Street Address: 29088 Airpark Dr
City: Easton
State: MD
ZIP Code: 21601-7000
General Phone: (410) 822-1500
General Email: bsilverstein@chespub.com
Publication Website: https://www.stardem.com/
Publisher Name: Jim Normandin
Publisher Email: jim.normandin@adamspg.com
Editor Name: Connie Connolly
Editor Email: cconnolly@chespub.com
Editor Phone: 443-786-1060
Advertising Executive Name: Brandon Silverstein
Advertising Executive Email: bsilverstein@chespub.com
Advertising Executive Phone: (410) 200-6469

ELKTON

CECIL WHIG

Street Address: 601 N Bridge St
City: Elkton
State: MD
ZIP Code: 21921-5307
General Phone: (410) 398-3311
General Email: mfoglio@chespub.com
Publication Website: https://www.cecildaily.com/
Parent Company: Adams Publishing Group
Publisher Name: Jim Normandin
Publisher Email: jim.normandin@adamspg.com
Editor Name: B. Rae Perryman
Editor Email: bperryman@chespub.com
Editor Phone: 443-963-6007
Advertising Executive Name: Lisa Minto
Advertising Executive Email: lminto@chespub.com
Advertising Executive Phone: (443) 239-1598

ELKTON

NEWARK POST

Street Address: 601 N Bridge St
City: Elkton
State: MD
ZIP Code: 21921-5307
General Phone: (302) 737-0724
General Email: news@newarkpostonline.com
Publication Website: https://www.newarkpostonline.com/
Parent Company: Adams Publishing Group
Publisher Name: Jim Normandin
Publisher Email: jim.normandin@adamspg.com
Editor Name: Josh Shannon
Editor Email: jshannon@chespub.com
Editor Phone: 443-907-8437
Advertising Executive Name: Lisa Minto
Advertising Executive Email: lminto@chespub.com
Advertising Executive Phone: (443) 239-1598

GREENBELT

GREENBELT NEWS REVIEW

Street Address: 15 Crescent Road, Suite 100
City: Greenbelt
State: MD
ZIP Code: 20770-0807
General Phone: (301) 474-4131
General Email: newsreview@verizon.net
Publication Website: https://www.greenbeltnewsreview.com/
Editor Name: Gary Childs
Editor Email: editor@greenbeltnewsreview.com
Advertising Executive Email: ads@greenbeltnewsreview.com

HANCOCK

THE HANCOCK NEWS

Street Address: 263 N Pennsylvania Ave
City: Hancock
State: MD
ZIP Code: 21750
General Phone: (301) 678-6255
General Email: ads@morganmessenger.com
Publication Website: https://www.hancocknews.us/
Parent Company: The Morgan Messenger
Editor Name: Kate Shunney
Editor Email: editor@morganmessenger.com
Advertising Executive Name: Jody Crouse
Advertising Executive Email: ads@morganmessenger.com

LA PLATA

THE ENQUIRER-GAZETTE

Street Address: 204 Washington Ave
City: La Plata
State: MD
ZIP Code: 20645
General Phone: (443) 231-3387
General Email: princegeorges@gazette.net
Publication Website: https://www.somdnews.com/enquirer_gazette/
Parent Company: Southern Maryland Newspapers
Editor Name: Darwin Weigel
Editor Email: dweigel@somdnews.com
Editor Phone: 240-561-0327
Advertising Executive Name: John Rives
Advertising Executive Email: jrives@chespub.com
Advertising Executive Phone: (301) 848-0175

OCEAN CITY

BAYSIDE GAZETTE

Street Address: 8200 Coastal Hwy
City: Ocean City
State: MD
ZIP Code: 21842
General Phone: (410) 723-6397
General Email: ebrady@baysidegazette.com
Publication Website: https://baysideoc.com/
Publisher Name: Elaine Brady
Publisher Email: ebrady@baysidegazette.com
Editor Name: Lisa Capitelli
Editor Email: editor@baysidegazette.com

OCEAN CITY

OCEAN CITY TODAY

Street Address: 8200 Coastal Hwy
City: Ocean City
State: MD
ZIP Code: 21842-2834
General Phone: (410) 723-6397
General Email: webeditor@oceancitytoday.net
Publication Website: https://www.oceancitytoday.com/
Publisher Name: Christine Brown
Publisher Email: cbrown@oceancitytoday.net
Editor Name: Lisa Capitelli
Editor Email: editor@oceancitytoday.net

PRINCE FREDERICK

THE CALVERT RECORDER

Street Address: 134 Main St
City: Prince Frederick
State: MD
ZIP Code: 20678-6150
General Phone: (410) 535-1234
General Email: bash@chespub.com
Publication Website: https://www.somdnews.com/recorder/
Parent Company: Adams Publishing Group
Publisher Name: James F. Normandin
Editor Name: Michael Reid
Editor Email: mreid@somdnews.com
Editor Phone: 240-561-0427
Advertising Executive Name: Brook Ash
Advertising Executive Email: bash@somdnews.com
Advertising Executive Phone: (240) 561-1390

ROCKVILLE

MONTGOMERY COUNTY SENTINEL

Street Address: 22 W. Jefferson Street, Suite 309
City: Rockville
State: MD
ZIP Code: 20850-4259
General Phone: (301) 838-0788
General Email: editor-mc@thesentinel.com
Publication Website: https://mont.thesentinel.com/
Parent Company: Berlyn, Inc.
Advertising Executive Name: Lonnie Johnson
Advertising Executive Email: lonnie@thesentinel.com
Advertising Executive Phone: (301) 306-9500

SALISBURY

DELAWARE COAST PRESS

Street Address: 115 S. Division St.
City: Salisbury
State: MD
ZIP Code: 21801
General Phone: (410) 749-7171
General Email: rpousson@localiq.com
Publication Website: https://www.delmarvanow.com/
Advertising Executive Name: Ron Pousson
Advertising Executive Email: rpousson@localiq.com
Advertising Executive Phone: (410) 845-4609

SALISBURY

SALISBURY INDEPENDENT

Street Address: PO Box 1385
City: Salisbury
State: MD
ZIP Code: 21802-1385
General Phone: (410) 543-4500
General Email: salisburysales@newszap.com
Publication Website: https://salisburyindependent.net/
Parent Company: Independent NewsMedia
Publisher Name: Darel La Prade
Publisher Email: dlaprade@newszap.com
Editor Name: Greg Bassett
Editor Email: gbassett@newszap.com
Advertising Executive Email: adsonline@newszap.com

SEABROOK

THE PRINCE GEORGE'S SENTINEL

Street Address: 9458 Lanham Severn Rd
City: Seabrook
State: MD
ZIP Code: 20706-2661
General Phone: (301) 306-9500
General Email: lonnie@thesentinel.com
Publication Website: http://www.thesentinel.com/
Editor Email: editor-pg@thesentinel.com
Advertising Executive Name: Sherry Sanderson
Advertising Executive Email: sherry@thesentinel.com
Advertising Executive Phone: (301) 838-0788

UPPER MARLBORO

PRINCE GEORGE'S POST

Street Address: 15207 Marlboro Pike
City: Upper Marlboro
State: MD
ZIP Code: 20772-3112
General Phone: (301) 627-0900
General Email: pgpost@gmail.com
Publication Website: http://www.pgpost.com/
Publisher Name: Legusta Floyd
Editor Name: Lisa Duan
Advertising Executive Name: Brenda Boice

WHITE PLAINS

THE MARYLAND INDEPENDENT

Street Address: 4475 Regency Pl

City: White Plains
State: MD
ZIP Code: 20695-3077
General Phone: (301) 645-9480
General Email: kminopoli@somdnews.com
Publication Website: https://www.somdnews.com/independent/
Parent Company: Adams Publishing Group
Editor Name: Darwin Weigel
Editor Email: dweigel@somdnews.com
Editor Phone: 240-561-0327

MAINE

BAR HARBOR

MOUNT DESERT ISLANDER

Street Address: 310 Main St
City: Bar Harbor
State: ME
ZIP Code: 04609-1638
General Phone: (207) 288-0556
General Email: news@mdislander.com
Publication Website: https://www.mdislander.com/
Parent Company: Mount Desert Islander
Editor Name: Faith DeAmbrose
Advertising Executive Name: Kelley Wescott
Advertising Executive Email: kwescott@ellsworthamerican.com
Advertising Executive Phone: (207) 667-2576

BIDDEFORD

KENNEBUNK POST

Street Address: 180 Main St
City: Biddeford
State: ME
ZIP Code: 04005-2410
General Phone: (207) 282-4337
Publication Website: https://www.pressherald.com/kennebunk-post/
Parent Company: MaineToday Media, Inc.

BIDDEFORD

SOUTH PORTLAND-CAPE/ELIZABETH SENTRY

Street Address: 180 Main St
City: Biddeford
State: ME
ZIP Code: 04005-2410
General Phone: (207) 282-4337
Publication Website: https://www.pressherald.com/mainely-media/south-portland-sentry/
Parent Company: Masthead Maine

BLUE HILL

CASTINE PATRIOT

Street Address: 13 Main St
City: Blue Hill
State: ME
ZIP Code: 04614-5985
General Phone: (207) 326-9300
General Email: news@pbp.me
Publication Website: http://castinepatriot.com/
Parent Company: Penobscot Bay Press, Inc.
Publisher Name: Nat Barrows
Editor Name: Nat Barrows

BLUE HILL

THE WEEKLY PACKET

Street Address: 13 Main St
City: Blue Hill
State: ME
ZIP Code: 04614-5985
General Phone: (207) 374-2341
General Email: news@pbp.me
Publication Website: http://weeklypacket.com/
Parent Company: Penobscot Bay Press, Inc.
Publisher Name: Nat Barrows
Editor Name: Nat Barrows

BOOTHBAY HARBOR

BOOTHBAY REGISTER

Street Address: 97 Townsend Ave
City: Boothbay Harbor
State: ME
ZIP Code: 04538-1843
General Phone: (207) 633-4620
General Email: subscriptions@boothbayregister.com
Publication Website: https://www.boothbayregister.com/
Parent Company: Maine-OK Enterprises
Editor Name: Kevin Burnham
Editor Email: kevinburnham@boothbayregister.com
Editor Phone: (207) 633-4620, ext : 112

BOOTHBAY HARBOR

WISCASSET NEWSPAPER

Street Address: 97 Townsend Ave
City: Boothbay Harbor
State: ME
ZIP Code: 04538-1843
General Phone: (207) 633-4620
General Email: editorkburnham@boothbayregister.com
Publication Website: https://www.wiscassetnewspaper.com/
Parent Company: Maine-OK Enterprises, Inc.
Editor Name: Kevin Burnham
Editor Email: kevinburnham@boothbayregister.com
Editor Phone: (207) 633-4620, ext : 112
Advertising Executive Name: Kathy Frizzell
Advertising Executive Email: kathyfrizzell@boothbayregister.com
Advertising Executive Phone: (207) 633-4620, ext : 107

BRIDGTON

THE BRIDGTON NEWS

Street Address: 118 Main St
City: Bridgton
State: ME
ZIP Code: 04009-1127
General Phone: (207) 647-2851
General Email: bnews@roadrunner.com
Publication Website: http://www.bridgton.com/
Publisher Name: Wayne E. Rivet
Editor Name: Wayne E. Rivet
Editor Email: bnewseditor@roadrunner.com
Advertising Executive Name: Eric C. Gulbrandsen
Advertising Executive Email: bnewsads@roadrunner.com

BRUNSWICK

COASTAL JOURNAL

Street Address: 3 Business Parkway
City: Brunswick
State: ME
ZIP Code: 4011
General Phone: (207) 386-5230
General Email: circulation@pressherald.com
Publication Website: https://www.pressherald.com/coastal-journal/
Parent Company: MaineToday Media
Editor Name: John Swinconeck
Editor Email: jswinconeck@timesrecord.com
Editor Phone: (207) 504-8209
Advertising Executive Name: Dennis Gears
Advertising Executive Email: dgears@timesrecord.com
Advertising Executive Phone: (207) 807-3408

BUCKSPORT

THE BUCKSPORT ENTERPRISE

Street Address: 105 Main St
City: Bucksport
State: ME
ZIP Code: 04416-4028
General Phone: (207) 469-6722
General Email: theenterpr@aol.com
Publication Website: https://www.bucksportenterprise.com/
Publisher Name: Don Houghton
Publisher Email: theenterpr@aol.com
Editor Name: Don Houghton
Editor Email: theenterpr@aol.com

CALAIS

THE CALAIS ADVERTISER

Street Address: 23 Church St
City: Calais
State: ME
ZIP Code: 04619-1639
General Phone: (207) 454-3561
General Email: info@calais.news
Publication Website: http://www.calais.news/

DEXTER

EASTERN GAZETTE

Street Address: 97 Church St
City: Dexter
State: ME
ZIP Code: 04930-1332
General Phone: (207) 924-7402
General Email: info@easterngazette.com
Publication Website: http://www.easterngazette.com/
Parent Company: The Gazette Inc.
Publisher Name: Robert Shank
Editor Name: India Shank Quiambao

DOVER FOXCROFT

THE PISCATAQUIS OBSERVER

Street Address: 12 E Main St
City: Dover Foxcroft
State: ME
ZIP Code: 04426-1414
General Phone: (207) 564-8355
General Email: observer@nepublish.com
Publication Website: https://observer-me.com/
Parent Company: Bangor Publishing Company
Editor Name: Mike Dowd
Editor Email: contact@observer-me.com

ELLSWORTH

THE ELLSWORTH AMERICAN

Street Address: 30 Water St
City: Ellsworth
State: ME
ZIP Code: 04605-2033
General Phone: (207) 667-2576
General Email: news@ellsworthamerican.com
Publication Website: https://www.ellsworthamerican.com/
Parent Company: Ellsworth American, Inc.
Publisher Name: Kathy Cook
Editor Name: Cyndi Wood
Advertising Executive Name: Julie Clark
Advertising Executive Email: jclark@mdislander.com
Advertising Executive Phone: (207) 288-0556

KENNEBUNK

YORK COUNTY COAST STAR

Street Address: 85 Main Street
City: Kennebunk
State: ME
ZIP Code: 4043
General Phone: (207) 985-5901
Publication Website: https://www.seacoastonline.com/YorkStar
Parent Company: Gannett

LINCOLN

LINCOLN NEWS

Street Address: PO Box 35
City: Lincoln
State: ME
ZIP Code: 04457-0035
General Phone: (207) 794-6532
General Email: katsports@lincnews.com
Publication Website: http://www.lincnews.com/
Publisher Name: David R. Whalen
Editor Name: David R. Whalen
Advertising Executive Name: Avern Danforth
Advertising Executive Email: danforthab@myfairpoint.net

MACHIAS

MACHIAS VALLEY NEWS OBSERVER

Street Address: 41 Broadway
City: Machias
State: ME
ZIP Code: 04654-1105
General Phone: (207) 255-6561
Publication Website: https://www.machiasnews.com/

MADAWASKA

ST. JOHN VALLEY TIMES

Street Address: 328 Main St
City: Madawaska
State: ME
ZIP Code: 04756-1166
General Phone: (207) 728-3336
General Email: nepeditors@nepublish.com
Publication Website: https://fiddleheadfocus.com/
Parent Company: Bangor Publishing Company
Editor Name: Julie Harris
Editor Email: nepeditors@nepublish.com
Advertising Executive Name: Jessica Blalock
Advertising Executive Email: jblalock@bangordailynews.com

NEWCASTLE

THE LINCOLN COUNTY NEWS

Street Address: 116 Mills Rd
City: Newcastle
State: ME
ZIP Code: 04553-3408

General Phone: (207) 563-3171
General Email: info@lcnme.com
Publication Website: http://lcnme.com/
Editor Name: J.W. Oliver
Editor Email: joliver@lcnme.com
Advertising Executive Name: Sarah Caton
Advertising Executive Email: ads@lcnme.com

NEWPORT

ROLLING THUNDER EXPRESS

Street Address: 134A Main St
City: Newport
State: ME
ZIP Code: 04953-3105
General Phone: (207) 368-2028
General Email: info@rollingthunderexpress.com
Publication Website: https://www.rollingthunderexpress.com/
Parent Company: The Rolling Thunder Express

NORWAY

ADVERTISER DEMOCRAT

Street Address: 220 Main Street
City: Norway
State: ME
ZIP Code: 04268-4350
General Phone: (207) 743-7011
General Email: newsteam@advertiserdemocrat.com
Publication Website: https://advertiserdemocrat.com/
Parent Company: MaineToday Media
Publisher Name: Lisa DeSisto
Publisher Email: lisa@mainetoday.com
Publisher Phone: (207) 791-6630
Editor Name: Judith Meyer
Editor Email: jmeyer@sunjournal.com
Editor Phone: (207) 689-2902
Advertising Executive Name: Robert Pond
Advertising Executive Email: bpond@sunjournal.com
Advertising Executive Phone: (207) 491-7800

PORTLAND

MAINEBIZ

Street Address: 48 Free St
City: Portland
State: ME
ZIP Code: 04101-3874
General Phone: (207) 761-8379
General Email: mainebiz@cambeywest.com
Publication Website: https://www.mainebiz.biz/
Parent Company: New England Business Media
Publisher Name: Donna Brassard
Publisher Email: dbrassard@mainebiz.biz
Publisher Phone: (207) 761-8379
Editor Name: Peter Van Allen
Editor Email: pvanallen@mainebiz.biz
Editor Phone: (207) 761-8379, ext : 325

PRESQUE ISLE

AROOSTOOK REPUBLICAN AND NEWS

Street Address: 260 Missile Street • Box 510
City: Presque Isle
State: ME
ZIP Code: 04769-0510
General Phone: (207) 496-3251
General Email: cbouchard@bangordailynews.com
Publication Website: https://thecounty.me/category/aroostook-republican/
Parent Company: Bangor Publishing Company
Editor Name: Julie Harris
Editor Email: nepeditors@nepublish.com
Advertising Executive Name: Anita Adams
Advertising Executive Email: aadams@bangordailynews.com

ROCKLAND

FREE PRESS

Street Address: 8 N Main St
City: Rockland
State: ME
ZIP Code: 04841-3154
General Phone: (207) 596-0055
General Email: ethan@freepressonline.com
Publication Website: https://freepressonline.com/
Parent Company: Gannett
Publisher Name: Steve Davis
Publisher Email: admanager@freepressonline.com
Editor Name: Wendell Greer
Editor Email: freepress@freepressonline.com
Advertising Executive Name: Glenn Billington
Advertising Executive Email: glenn@freepressonline.com

RUMFORD

RUMFORD FALLS TIMES

Street Address: 69 Congress St
City: Rumford
State: ME
ZIP Code: 04276-2015
General Phone: (207) 364-7893
General Email: bfarrin@sunmediagroup.net
Publication Website: http://rumfordfallstimes.com/
Parent Company: MaineToday Media, Inc.
Editor Name: Bruce Farrin
Editor Email: bfarrin@sunmediagroup.net
Editor Phone: (207) 364-7893, ext : 5208

SOUTH PORTLAND

CENTRAL MAINE SUNDAY

Street Address: 295 Gannett Drive
City: South Portland
State: ME
ZIP Code: 4106
General Phone: (207) 791-6204
General Email: support@centralmaine.com
Publication Website: https://www.centralmaine.com/
Parent Company: MaineToday Media
Publisher Name: Lisa DeSisto
Publisher Email: lisa@mainetoday.com
Publisher Phone: (207) 791-6630
Editor Name: Judith Meyer
Editor Email: jmeyer@sunjournal.com
Editor Phone: (207) 689-2902
Advertising Executive Name: Robert Pond
Advertising Executive Email: bpond@sunjournal.com
Advertising Executive Phone: (207) 491-7800

STONINGTON

ISLAND AD-VANTAGES

Street Address: 69 Main St
City: Stonington
State: ME
ZIP Code: 4681
General Phone: (207) 367-2200
General Email: news@pbp.me
Publication Website: http://islandadvantages.com/
Parent Company: Penobscot Bay Press, Inc.
Publisher Name: Nat Barrows
Editor Name: Nat Barrows

WELLS

WEEKLY SENTINEL

Street Address: 952 Post Rd
City: Wells
State: ME
ZIP Code: 04090-4142
General Phone: (207) 646-8448
General Email: ads@theweeklysentinel.com
Publication Website: http://www.theweeklysentinel.com/
Publisher Name: Carol Brennan
Publisher Email: publisher@theweeklysentinel.com
Editor Email: editor@theweeklysentinel.com

WESTBROOK

THE LAKES REGION WEEKLY

Street Address: 840 Main St
City: Westbrook
State: ME
ZIP Code: 04092-2847
General Phone: (207) 854-2577
Publication Website: https://www.pressherald.com/lakes-region-weekly/
Parent Company: Masthead Maine

MICHIGAN

ALLEGAN

ALLEGAN COUNTY NEWS

Street Address: 241 Hubbard St, P.O. Box 189
City: Allegan
State: MI
ZIP Code: 49010-1320
General Phone: (269) 673-5534
General Email: robinclark@allegannews.com
Publication Website: https://www.allegannews.com/
Parent Company: Kaechele Publications, Inc.
Publisher Name: R. Michael Wilcox
Publisher Email: publisher@allegannews.com
Editor Name: Ryan Lewis
Editor Email: rmlewis@allegannews.com
Advertising Executive Name: Robin Clark
Advertising Executive Email: robinclark@allegannews.com
Delivery Methods: Mail`Newsstand
Year Established: 1858
Own Printing Facility?: N
Commercial printers?: N
Mechanical specifications: Full page image size 10.5" x 21 1/2"; 6 cols, 1.646", 1/8 between.
Published Days: Thur
Avg. Paid Circ.: 3361
Avg. Free Circ.: 83
Audit Company: Sworn/Estimate/Non-Audited
Audit Date: 43626

ANN ARBOR

ANN ARBOR OBSERVER

Street Address: 2390 Winewood Ave
City: Ann Arbor
State: MI
ZIP Code: 48103-3841
General Phone: (734) 769-3175
General Email: pg@aaobserver.com
Publication Website: https://annarborobserver.com/
Publisher Name: Patricia M. Garcia
Publisher Email: pg@aaobserver.com
Editor Name: John Hilton
Editor Email: pg@aaobserver.com
Delivery Methods: Mail
Year Established: 1976
Published Days: Mthly
Avg. Paid Circ.: 2125
Avg. Free Circ.: 28534
Audit Company: Sworn/Estimate/Non-Audited
Audit Date: 43626

ANN ARBOR

THE ANN ARBOR NEWS

Street Address: 111 N Ashley St
City: Ann Arbor
State: MI
ZIP Code: 48104-1307
General Phone: (734) 623-2500
General Email: advertise@mlive.com
Publication Website: https://www.mlive.com/ann-arbor/
Parent Company: Advance Newspapers
Publisher Name: Dan Gaydou
Advertising Executive Name: Anne Drummond
Advertising Executive Email: advertise@mlive.com
Delivery Methods: Mail`Newsstand`Carrier`Racks
Year Established: 2009
Mechanical specifications: Type page 11 5/8 x 22; E - 6 cols, 2 1/16, 1/8 between; A - 6 cols, 2 1/16, 1/8 between; C - 10 cols, 1 1/4, 1/16 between.
Published Days: Thur`Sun
Weekday Frequency: e
Avg. Paid Circ.: 12950
Avg. Free Circ.: 2481
Audit Company: AAM
Audit Date: 44049

ANN ARBOR

THE CURRENT

Street Address: 3003 Washtenaw Ave
City: Ann Arbor
State: MI
ZIP Code: 48104
General Phone: (734) 668-4044
General Email: cjacobs@toledocitypaper.com
Publication Website: https://www.ecurrent.com/
Parent Company: Adams Street Publishing Co
Publisher Name: Collette Jacobs
Publisher Email: cjacobs@toledocitypaper.com
Publisher Phone: (419) 244-9859, ext : 301
Editor Name: Collette Jacobs
Editor Email: cjacobs@toledocitypaper.com
Editor Phone: (419) 244-9859, ext : 301
Advertising Executive Name: Jack Tackett
Advertising Executive Email: jtackett@adamsstreetpublishing.com
Advertising Executive Phone: (734) 668-4044
Published Days: Wed
Avg. Paid Circ.: 1500
Avg. Free Circ.: 150
Audit Company: Sworn/Estimate/Non-Audited
Audit Date: 43626

ATLANTA

THE MONTMORENCY COUNTY TRIBUNE

Street Address: 12625 State St.
City: Atlanta
State: MI
ZIP Code: 49709
General Phone: (989) 785-4214

General Email: office@montmorencytribune.com
Publication Website: https://www.montmorencytribune.com/
Publisher Email: press@montmorencytribune.com
Editor Name: Michelle Pinson
Editor Email: editor@montmorencytribune.com
Advertising Executive Email: sales@montmorencytribune.com
Delivery Methods: Mail`Newsstand
Year Established: 1886
Own Printing Facility?: Y
Commercial printers?: Y
Mechanical specifications: Type page 10 1/4 x 16; E - 6 cols, 1 1/2, 1/6 between; A - 6 cols, 1 1/2, 1/6 between; C - 6 cols, 1 1/2, 1/6 between.
Published Days: Wed
Avg. Paid Circ.: 5200
Audit Company: Sworn/Estimate/Non-Audited
Audit Date: 43626

BAD AXE

HURON COUNTY VIEW

Street Address: 592 N. Port Crescent St.
City: Bad Axe
State: MI
ZIP Code: 48413
General Phone: 989-269-9918
General Email: lettershcp@mihomepaper.com
Publication Website: huroncountyview.mihomepaper.com
Parent Company: View Newspaper Group
Editor Name: Eric Levine
Editor Email: elevine@mihomepaper.com
Delivery Methods: Mail
Year Established: 1980
Own Printing Facility?: Y
Mechanical specifications: Tabloid Size: 9.5"X10" in four column format
Published Days: Thur
Avg. Free Circ.: 18457
Audit Company: CVC
Audit Date: 43993
Note: Thumb Blanket changed name to Huron County View March 2012, free TMC editorial newspaper

BELLEVILLE

BELLEVILLE-AREA INDEPENDENT

Street Address: 152 Main St
City: Belleville
State: MI
ZIP Code: 48111-3911
General Phone: (734) 699-9020
General Email: mail@bellevilleareaindependent.com
Publication Website: http://bellevilleareaindependent.com/
Editor Name: Rosemary K. Otzman
Editor Email: rotzman@ameritech.net
Advertising Executive Name: Bob Mytych
Delivery Methods: Mail`Racks
Year Established: 1995
Own Printing Facility?: N
Commercial printers?: N
Mechanical specifications: Type page 10 x 12 3/4; E - 4 cols, 2 3/8, 3/8 between; A - 4 cols, 2 3/8, 3/8 between; C - 4 cols, 2 3/8, 3/8 between.
Published Days: Thur
Avg. Paid Circ.: 342
Avg. Free Circ.: 6600
Audit Company: Sworn/Estimate/Non-Audited
Audit Date: 43626

BERRIEN SPRINGS

THE JOURNAL ERA

Street Address: 101 W Ferry St
City: Berrien Springs
State: MI
ZIP Code: 49103
General Phone: (269) 473-5421
General Email: thejournalera@yahoo.com
Publication Website: https://www.thejournalera.com/
Publisher Name: Tim Pullano
Editor Name: Kathy Pullano
Advertising Executive Name: Francie VanderMolen
Delivery Methods: Mail`Newsstand
Year Established: 1874
Own Printing Facility?: Y
Commercial printers?: N
Published Days: Wed
Avg. Paid Circ.: 2000
Audit Company: Sworn/Estimate/Non-Audited
Audit Date: 43626

BIG RAPIDS

PIONEER EAST

Street Address: 115 N Michigan Ave
City: Big Rapids
State: MI
ZIP Code: 49307-1401
General Phone: (231) 796-4831
General Email: advertising@pioneergroup.com
Publication Website: http://pioneergroup.com/
Parent Company: Hearst Corp.
Editor Name: Tim Rath
Editor Email: trath@pioneergroup.com
Editor Phone: (231) 592-8386
Advertising Executive Name: Danette Doyle
Advertising Executive Email: advertising@pioneergroup.com
Delivery Methods: Mail
Commercial printers?: Y
Mechanical specifications: Type page 10 1/16 x 16; A - 7 cols, 1 3/8, 1/2 between.
Published Days: Mon
Avg. Free Circ.: 8000
Audit Company: Sworn/Estimate/Non-Audited
Audit Date: 43626

BROOKLYN

THE EXPONENT

Street Address: 160 S Main St
City: Brooklyn
State: MI
ZIP Code: 49230
General Phone: (517) 592-2122
General Email: news@theexponent.com
Publication Website: http://theexponent.com/
Publisher Name: Matt Schepeler
Publisher Email: news@theexponent.com
Advertising Executive Email: dorothy@theexponent.com
Delivery Methods: Mail
Year Established: 1881
Own Printing Facility?: Y
Commercial printers?: Y
Published Days: Tues
Avg. Paid Circ.: 5000
Audit Company: Sworn/Estimate/Non-Audited
Audit Date: 43626

BUCHANAN

BERRIEN COUNTY RECORD

Street Address: PO BOX 191
City: Buchanan
State: MI
ZIP Code: 49107-1376
General Phone: (269) 695-3878
Publication Website: https://bcrnews.net/
Parent Company: Randy Hendrixson
Publisher Name: Randy Hendrixson
Editor Name: Jessica Hendrixson
Delivery Methods: Mail
Year Established: 1865
Mechanical specifications: Type page 13 x 21 1/2; E - 6 cols, 2 1/16, 1/4 between; A - 6 cols, 2 1/16, 1/4 between; C - 6 cols, 2 1/16, 1/4 between.
Published Days: Mon`Thur
Avg. Paid Circ.: 2600
Avg. Free Circ.: 176
Audit Company: Sworn/Estimate/Non-Audited
Audit Date: 43626

CADILLAC

NORTHERN MICHIGAN NEWS

Street Address: 130 N Mitchell St
City: Cadillac
State: MI
ZIP Code: 49601-1856
General Phone: (231) 775-6565
General Email: customerservice@cadillacnews.com
Publication Website: https://www.cadillacnews.com/
Publisher Name: Christopher Huckle
Publisher Phone: (231) 779-5200
Editor Name: Matthew Seward
Editor Phone: (231) 779-4126
Advertising Executive Phone: (231) 775-6565
Delivery Methods: Mail
Year Established: 1872
Own Printing Facility?: Y
Commercial printers?: Y
Mechanical specifications: Type page 11 5/8 x 22; E - 6 cols, 1 5/6, 1/8 between; A - 6 cols, 1 5/6, 1/8 between; C - 6 cols, 1 5/6, 1/8 between.
Published Days: Mon
Avg. Free Circ.: 28500
Audit Company: Sworn/Estimate/Non-Audited
Audit Date: 43626

CARO

TUSCOLA COUNTY ADVERTISER

Street Address: 344 N State St
City: Caro
State: MI
ZIP Code: 48723
General Phone: (989) 673-3181
General Email: ads@tcadvertiser.com
Publication Website: https://www.tuscolatoday.com/
Parent Company: Edwards Group
Publisher Name: Tim Murphy
Editor Name: John Schneider
Editor Email: john@tcadvertiser.com
Editor Phone: (989) 673-3181
Advertising Executive Name: Jean Norton
Advertising Executive Email: jnorton@tcadvertiser.com
Delivery Methods: Mail
Year Established: 1868
Own Printing Facility?: Y
Commercial printers?: Y
Mechanical specifications: Type page 11 1/2 x 20 1/2; E - 6 cols, 2, 1/3 between; A - 8 cols, 1 1/2, 1/3 between; C - 8 cols, 1 1/2, 1/3 between.
Published Days: Wed`Sat
Avg. Paid Circ.: 8220
Audit Company: Sworn/Estimate/Non-Audited
Audit Date: 43626

CASS CITY

CASS CITY CHRONICLE

Street Address: 6550 Main St, PO BOX 115
City: Cass City
State: MI
ZIP Code: 48726-1561
General Phone: (989) 872-2010
General Email: sales@ccchronicle.net
Publication Website: http://ccchronicle.net/
Publisher Name: Clarke Haire
Publisher Email: clarke@ccchronicle.net
Publisher Phone: (989) 872-2010
Editor Name: Tom Montgomery
Editor Email: tom@ccchronicle.net
Editor Phone: (989) 872-2010
Advertising Executive Name: Krysta Boyce
Advertising Executive Email: sales@ccchronicle.net
Advertising Executive Phone: (989) 872-2010
Delivery Methods: Mail`Newsstand
Year Established: 1899
Mechanical specifications: Type page 13 3/4 x 21 1/4; E - 8 cols, 1 1/2, 1/4 between; C - 8 cols, 1 1/2, 1/4 between.
Published Days: Wed
Avg. Paid Circ.: 2400
Audit Company: Sworn/Estimate/Non-Audited
Audit Date: 43626

CEDAR SPRINGS

CEDAR SPRINGS POST

Street Address: 36 E Maple
City: Cedar Springs
State: MI
ZIP Code: 49319-5143
General Phone: (616) 696-3655
General Email: news@cedarspringspost.com
Publication Website: https://cedarspringspost.com/
Delivery Methods: Mail`Newsstand
Year Established: 1988
Published Days: Thur
Avg. Free Circ.: 5000
Audit Company: Sworn/Estimate/Non-Audited
Audit Date: 43626

CHARLEVOIX

CHARLEVOIX COURIER

Street Address: 411 Bridge St
City: Charlevoix
State: MI
ZIP Code: 49720
General Phone: (231) 547-6558
General Email: adoyle@charlevoixcourier.com
Publication Website: https://www.petoskeynews.com/charlevoix/
Parent Company: Gannett
Editor Name: Jeremy McBain
Editor Phone: (231) 439-9316
Advertising Executive Name: Christy Lyons
Advertising Executive Phone: (231) 838-9949
Delivery Methods: Mail
Year Established: 1883
Mechanical specifications: Type page 10 13/16 x 13 5/8; E - 5 cols, 2 1/16, 1/8 between; A - 5 cols, 2 1/16, 1/8 between; C - 5 cols, 2 1/16, 1/8 between.
Published Days: Fri
Avg. Paid Circ.: 3500
Audit Company: Sworn/Estimate/Non-Audited
Audit Date: 43626

CHARLOTTE

THE COUNTY JOURNAL

Street Address: 241 S Cochran Ave
City: Charlotte
State: MI
ZIP Code: 48813-1584
General Phone: (517) 543-1099
General Email: advertising@county-journal.com
Publication Website: https://county-journal.

com/
Parent Company: Flashes Advertising & News
Publisher Name: Cindy Gaedert-Gearhart
Publisher Phone: (517) 543-1099
Editor Name: Carla Bumstead
Editor Phone: (517) 543-1099, ext : 227
Advertising Executive Email: advertising@county-journal.com
Delivery Methods: Carrier
Year Established: 2006
Mechanical specifications: Type page: 10.25 x 16; 6 col
Published Days: Sat
Avg. Paid Circ.: 15
Avg. Free Circ.: 18901
Audit Company: CVC
Audit Date: 43988

CHEBOYGAN

MACKINAW JOURNAL

Street Address: 308 N Main St
City: Cheboygan
State: MI
ZIP Code: 49721-1545
General Phone: (231) 627-7144
General Email: nkidder@mackinacjournal.com
Publication Website: https://www.mackinacjournal.com/
Publisher Name: Gary Lamberg
Publisher Email: gary@mackinacjournal.com
Advertising Executive Name: Nancy Kidder
Advertising Executive Email: nkidder@mackinacjournal.com
Published Days: Thur`Mthly
Audit Company: Sworn/Estimate/Non-Audited
Audit Date: 43626

CHELSEA

THE SUN TIMES NEWS

Street Address: 118 S Main St
City: Chelsea
State: MI
ZIP Code: 48118
General Phone: (734) 648-0837
General Email: info@thesuntimesnews.com
Publication Website: https://thesuntimesnews.com
Publisher Name: Robert Nester
Publisher Email: rnester@thesuntimesnews.com
Editor Name: Wendy Wood
Editor Email: wendy@thesuntimesnews.com
Advertising Executive Name: Tom Drinkwater
Advertising Executive Email: tomdrinkwater@thesuntimesnews.com
Delivery Methods: Mail`Newsstand`Racks
Year Established: 1878
Own Printing Facility?: Y
Commercial printers?: Y
Mechanical specifications: Type page 10.75 x 20.5; E - 2 cols, 1 5/8, 1/8 between; A - 6 cols, 1 5/8, 1/8 between; C - 1 cols, 1 5/8, 1/8 between.
Published Days: Tues
Avg. Paid Circ.: 358
Avg. Free Circ.: 16561
Audit Company: Sworn/Estimate/Non-Audited
Audit Date: 43626

CHESANING

TOWNSHIP VIEW

Street Address: 110 S Chapman St
City: Chesaning
State: MI
ZIP Code: 48616-1221
General Phone: (989) 393-4100
General Email: pclinton@mihomepaper.com
Publication Website: https://townshipview.mihomepaper.com/
Parent Company: View Newspaper Group
Editor Name: Keith Salisbury
Editor Email: ksalisbury@mihomepaper.com
Advertising Executive Email: ads@mihomepaper.com
Delivery Methods: Mail`Racks
Year Established: 2010
Mechanical specifications: Type page 9.75" x 10"; 4 cols
Published Days: Thur
Avg. Free Circ.: 20268
Audit Company: CVC
Audit Date: 43622

CHESANING

TRI-COUNTY CITIZEN

Street Address: 110 S. Chapman St.
City: Chesaning
State: MI
ZIP Code: 48616
General Phone: (989) 341-4806
General Email: tccsales@mihomepaper.com
Publication Website: https://tricountycitizen.mihomepaper.com/
Parent Company: View Newspaper Group
Editor Email: tccnews@mihomepaper.com
Advertising Executive Email: tccsales@mihomepaper.com
Advertising Executive Phone: (989) 341-4806
Delivery Methods: Carrier
Year Established: 1983
Mechanical specifications: Type page: 9.75 x 15.875; 6 col
Published Days: Sun
Avg. Free Circ.: 17844
Audit Company: Sworn/Estimate/Non-Audited
Audit Date: 43626

CLARE

THE CLARE COUNTY REVIEW

Street Address: 135 N McEwan St.
City: Clare
State: MI
ZIP Code: 48617
General Phone: (989) 386-4414
General Email: info@clarecountyreview.com
Publication Website: http://www.clarecountyreview.com/
Publisher Name: Michael Wilcox
Year Established: 1947
Mechanical specifications: Type page 11 1/2 x 21; E - 6 cols, 1 3/4, between; A - 6 cols, 1 3/4, between; C - 8 cols, 1 3/16, between.
Published Days: Fri
Avg. Paid Circ.: 473
Avg. Free Circ.: 9557
Audit Company: Sworn/Estimate/Non-Audited
Audit Date: 43626

CLIMAX

THE CLIMAX CRESCENT

Street Address: 150 N Main St
City: Climax
State: MI
ZIP Code: 49034
General Phone: (269) 746-4331
General Email: scribe@ctsmail.net
Publication Website: http://www.theclimaxcrescent.com/
Parent Company: The Rolfes
Delivery Methods: Mail`Newsstand
Year Established: 1912
Own Printing Facility?: Y
Commercial printers?: Y
Published Days: Fri
Avg. Paid Circ.: 1050
Audit Company: Sworn/Estimate/Non-Audited
Audit Date: 43626

CLINTON

THE CLINTON LOCAL

Street Address: Po Box B
City: Clinton
State: MI
ZIP Code: 49236-9507
General Phone: (517) 456-4100
General Email: editor@theclintonlocal.com
Publication Website: https://www.theclintonlocal.com/
Parent Company: The Clinton Local
Editor Email: editor@theclintonlocal.com
Delivery Methods: Mail`Newsstand`Racks
Year Established: 1884
Mechanical specifications: 10" wide x 16" deep
Published Days: Wed
Avg. Paid Circ.: 1500
Audit Company: Sworn/Estimate/Non-Audited
Audit Date: 43626
Note: Ginny Krauss, layout, news etc. Maryann Habrick continues as owner/editor. Also have Spencer Krauss as ad person, numerous other assignments.

CLINTON TOWNSHIP

BLUE WATER VOICE

Street Address: 19176 Hall Rd
City: Clinton Township
State: MI
ZIP Code: 48038-6914
General Phone: (586) 716-8100
General Email: classified.voice@voicenews.com
Publication Website: https://www.voicenews.com/
Publisher Name: Greg Mazanec
Publisher Email: mipublisher@digitalfirstmedia.com
Editor Name: Noelle Klomp
Editor Email: nklomp@21st-centurymedia.com
Editor Phone: (586) 783-0393
Advertising Executive Name: Noelle Klomp
Advertising Executive Email: nklomp@21st-centurymedia.com
Advertising Executive Phone: (586) 783-0393
Delivery Methods: Mail`Newsstand`Carrier`Racks
Year Established: 1983
Mechanical specifications: Type page 10 x 15; E - 5 cols, 1 15/16, 1/8 between; A - 5 cols, 1 15/16, 1/8 between; C - 6 cols, 1 7/10, 1/8 between.
Published Days: Wed
Avg. Paid Circ.: 40
Avg. Free Circ.: 9697
Audit Company: Sworn/Estimate/Non-Audited
Audit Date: 43626

CLINTON TOWNSHIP

DOWNRIVER VOICE

Street Address: 19176 Hall Rd
City: Clinton Township
State: MI
ZIP Code: 48038
General Phone: (586) 716-8100
General Email: classified.voice@voicenews.com
Publication Website: https://www.voicenews.com/
Publisher Name: Greg Mazanec
Publisher Email: mipublisher@digitalfirstmedia.com
Editor Name: Noelle Klomp
Editor Email: nklomp@21st-centurymedia.com
Editor Phone: (586) 783-0228
Advertising Executive Name: Noelle Klomp
Advertising Executive Email: nklomp@21st-centurymedia.com
Advertising Executive Phone: (586) 783-0393
Delivery Methods: Mail`Newsstand`Carrier`Racks
Year Established: 1983
Mechanical specifications: Type page 10 x 15; E - 5 cols, 1 15/16, 1/8 between; A - 5 cols, 1 15/16, 1/8 between; C - 6 cols, 1 7/10, 1/8 between.
Published Days: Wed
Avg. Free Circ.: 9234
Audit Company: Sworn/Estimate/Non-Audited
Audit Date: 43626

CLINTON TOWNSHIP

THE ADVISOR & SOURCE

Street Address: 19176 Hall Rd
City: Clinton Township
State: MI
ZIP Code: 48038-6914
General Phone: (586) 716-8100
General Email: noelle.klomp@oakpress.com
Publication Website: https://www.macombdaily.com/
Publisher Name: Greg Mazanec
Publisher Email: mipublisher@medianewsgroup.com
Editor Name: Jeff Payne
Editor Email: jpayne@medianewsgroup.com
Editor Phone: (586) 783-0228
Advertising Executive Name: Noelle Klomp
Advertising Executive Email: nklomp@medianewsgroup.com
Advertising Executive Phone: (586) 783-0393
Own Printing Facility?: Y
Commercial printers?: Y
Mechanical specifications: Type page 13 x 21 1/2; E - 6 cols, 2 1/16, 1/8 between; A - 6 cols, 2 1/16, 1/8 between; C - 10 cols, 1 7/32, 1/8 between.
Published Days: Sun
Avg. Free Circ.: 115389
Audit Company: Sworn/Estimate/Non-Audited
Audit Date: 43626

CLINTON TOWNSHIP

THE ARMADA TIMES

Street Address: 19176 Hall Rd
City: Clinton Township
State: MI
ZIP Code: 48038
General Phone: (586) 716-8100
General Email: jeff.payne@voicenews.com
Publication Website: https://www.voicenews.com/
Publisher Name: Greg Mazanec
Publisher Email: mipublisher@medianewsgroup.com
Editor Name: Jeff Payne
Editor Email: jpayne@medianewsgroup.com
Editor Phone: (586) 783-0228
Advertising Executive Name: Noelle Klomp
Advertising Executive Email: nklomp@medianewsgroup.com
Advertising Executive Phone: (586) 783-0393
Delivery Methods: Mail`Newsstand`Racks
Year Established: 1887
Mechanical specifications: Type page 10 x 15; E - 5 cols, 2, between; A - 5 cols, 2, between; C - 6 cols, 1 7/10, between.
Published Days: Wed
Avg. Free Circ.: 59500
Audit Company: Sworn/Estimate/Non-Audited
Audit Date: 43626

CLINTON TOWNSHIP

THE BAY VOICE

Community Newspapers in the U.S.

Street Address: 19176 Hall Rd
City: Clinton Township
State: MI
ZIP Code: 48038
General Phone: (586) 716-8100
General Email: jeff.payne@voicenews.com
Publication Website: https://www.voicenews.com/
Publisher Name: Greg Mazanec
Publisher Email: mipublisher@digitalfirstmedia.com
Editor Name: Noelle Klomp
Editor Email: nklomp@21st-centurymedia.com
Editor Phone: (586) 783-0228
Advertising Executive Name: Noelle Klomp
Advertising Executive Email: nklomp@21st-centurymedia.com
Advertising Executive Phone: (586) 783-0393
Delivery Methods: Mail`Newsstand`Carrier`Racks
Year Established: 1983
Mechanical specifications: Type page 10 x 15; E - 5 cols, 1 15/16, 1/8 between; A - 5 cols, 1 15/16, 1/8 between; C - 6 cols, 1 7/10, 1/8 between.
Published Days: Wed
Avg. Paid Circ.: 40
Avg. Free Circ.: 9697
Audit Company: Sworn/Estimate/Non-Audited
Audit Date: 43626

CLINTON TOWNSHIP

THE MACOMB VOICE

Street Address: 19176 Hall Rd
City: Clinton Township
State: MI
ZIP Code: 48038
General Phone: (586) 716-8100
General Email: jeff.payne@voicenews.com
Publication Website: https://www.voicenews.com/
Publisher Name: Greg Mazanec
Publisher Email: mipublisher@digitalfirstmedia.com
Editor Name: Noelle Klomp
Editor Email: nklomp@21st-centurymedia.com
Editor Phone: (586) 783-0228
Advertising Executive Name: Noelle Klomp
Advertising Executive Email: nklomp@21st-centurymedia.com
Advertising Executive Phone: (586) 783-0393
Delivery Methods: Mail`Newsstand`Carrier`Racks
Year Established: 1983
Mechanical specifications: Type page 10 x 15; E - 5 cols, 2, between; A - 5 cols, 2, between; C - 6 cols, 1 7/10, between.
Published Days: Wed
Avg. Paid Circ.: 4000
Audit Company: Sworn/Estimate/Non-Audited
Audit Date: 43626

CLINTON TOWNSHIP

THE NORTH MACOMB VOICE

Street Address: 19176 Hall Rd
City: Clinton Township
State: MI
ZIP Code: 48038
General Phone: (586) 716-8100
General Email: jeff.payne@voicenews.com
Publication Website: https://www.voicenews.com/
Publisher Name: Greg Mazanec
Publisher Email: mipublisher@digitalfirstmedia.com
Editor Name: Noelle Klomp
Editor Email: nklomp@21st-centurymedia.com
Editor Phone: (586) 783-0228
Advertising Executive Name: Noelle Klomp
Advertising Executive Email: nklomp@21st-centurymedia.com

Advertising Executive Phone: (586) 783-0393
Delivery Methods: Mail`Newsstand`Carrier`Racks
Year Established: 1983
Mechanical specifications: Type page 10 x 15; E - 5 cols, 2, between; A - 5 cols, 2, between; C - 6 cols, 1 7/10, between.
Published Days: Wed
Avg. Free Circ.: 9636
Audit Company: Sworn/Estimate/Non-Audited
Audit Date: 43626

CLINTON TOWNSHIP

THE VOICE

Street Address: 19176 Hall Rd
City: Clinton Township
State: MI
ZIP Code: 48038
General Phone: (586) 716-8100
General Email: editor@voicenews.com
Publication Website: https://www.voicenews.com/
Publisher Name: Greg Mazanec
Publisher Email: mipublisher@digitalfirstmedia.com
Editor Name: Noelle Klomp
Editor Email: nklomp@21st-centurymedia.com
Editor Phone: (586) 783-0228
Advertising Executive Name: Noelle Klomp
Advertising Executive Email: nklomp@21st-centurymedia.com
Advertising Executive Phone: (586) 783-0393
Published Days: Wed
Audit Company: Sworn/Estimate/Non-Audited
Audit Date: 43626

CLIO

GENESEE COUNTY HERALD, INC.

Street Address: G 10098 N Dort Hwy
City: Clio
State: MI
ZIP Code: 48420
General Phone: (810) 686-3840
General Email: publisher@myherald.net
Publication Website: https://myherald.net/
Publisher Name: Michael J. Harrington
Publisher Email: publisher@myherald.net
Editor Name: Megan Decker
Editor Email: editor@myherald.net
Advertising Executive Name: Jeff Harrington
Advertising Executive Email: advertising@myherald.net
Mechanical specifications: Type page 10 1/4 x 16; E - 6 cols, between.
Published Days: Mon
Avg. Free Circ.: 22153
Audit Company: Sworn/Estimate/Non-Audited
Audit Date: 43626

COLDWATER

REGISTER-TRIBUNE

Street Address: 15 W Pearl St
City: Coldwater
State: MI
ZIP Code: 49036
General Phone: (517) 278-2318
General Email: editor@thedailyreporter.com
Publication Website: https://www.thedailyreporter.com/
Publisher Name: Lisa Vickers
Publisher Email: lvickers@thedailyreporter.com
Publisher Phone: (517) 278-2318, ext : 19
Editor Name: Candice Phelps
Editor Email: cphelps@stugisjournal.com
Editor Phone: (517) 278-2318, ext : 23
Advertising Executive Name: Amy Crabtree
Advertising Executive Email: acrabtree@hillsdale.net

Advertising Executive Phone: (517) 278-2318
Mechanical specifications: Type page 13 x 21 1/2; E - 6 cols, 2 1/16, 1/6 between; A - 6 cols, 2 1/16, 1/6 between; C - 6 cols, 2 1/16, 1/6 between.
Published Days: Thur
Avg. Paid Circ.: 1150
Avg. Free Circ.: 125
Audit Company: Sworn/Estimate/Non-Audited
Audit Date: 43626

DAVISON

GRAND BLANC VIEW

Street Address: 217 Shopper's Alley
City: Davison
State: MI
ZIP Code: 48423
General Phone: (810) 653-3511
General Email: sales@mihomepaper.com
Publication Website: https://grandblancview.mihomepaper.com/
Parent Company: View Newspaper Group
Advertising Executive Email: sales@mihomepaper.com
Advertising Executive Phone: (810) 653-3511
Delivery Methods: Mail
Year Established: 2005
Mechanical specifications: Type page 9.75" x 10"; 4 cols
Published Days: Thur
Avg. Free Circ.: 27641
Audit Company: CVC
Audit Date: 43622

DAVISON

SWARTZ CREEK VIEW

Street Address: 220 N Main St
City: Davison
State: MI
ZIP Code: 48423-1432
General Phone: (810) 653-3511
General Email: ads@mihomepaper.com
Publication Website: https://swartzcreekview.mihomepaper.com/
Parent Company: View Newspaper Group
Advertising Executive Email: ads@mihomepaper.com
Delivery Methods: Mail
Year Established: 2010
Mechanical specifications: Type page 9.75" x 10"; 4 cols
Published Days: Thur
Avg. Free Circ.: 9418
Audit Company: CVC
Audit Date: 43257

DAVISON

THE DAVISON INDEX

Street Address: 217 Shopper's Alley
City: Davison
State: MI
ZIP Code: 48423-1432
General Phone: (810) 653-3511
General Email: ads@mihomepaper.com
Publication Website: https://davisonindex.mihomepaper.com/
Parent Company: View Newspaper Group
Editor Email: daveditor@mihomepaper.com
Advertising Executive Email: ads@mihomepaper.com
Delivery Methods: Mail
Year Established: 1889
Own Printing Facility?: Y
Commercial printers?: Y
Published Days: Thur
Avg. Free Circ.: 14593
Audit Company: VAC
Audit Date: 43622

DEARBORN

DEARBORN TIMES-HERALD

Street Address: 15630 Michigan Avenue
City: Dearborn
State: MI
ZIP Code: 48126
General Phone: (313) 584-4000
General Email: timesheraldads@yahoo.com
Publication Website: https://www.downriversundaytimes.com/
Delivery Methods: Mail`Newsstand`Carrier
Year Established: 1963
Mechanical specifications: Type page 13 x 21 1/2; E - 6 cols, 2 1/4, 1/6 between; A - 6 cols, 2 1/4, 1/6 between; C - 10 cols, 1 1/4, 1/6 between.
Published Days: Wed
Avg. Paid Circ.: 5639
Avg. Free Circ.: 847
Audit Company: Sworn/Estimate/Non-Audited
Audit Date: 43626

DETROIT

BIRMINGHAM ECCENTRIC

Street Address: 615 W Lafayette Blvd
City: Detroit
State: MI
ZIP Code: 48226-3124
General Phone: (866) 887-2737
General Email: livoenewstip@hometownlife.com
Publication Website: https://www.hometownlife.com/news/eccentric/
Delivery Methods: Newsstand`Carrier`Racks
Year Established: 1869
Mechanical specifications: Type page 11 5/8 x 21 1/4; E - 6 cols, 1 13/16, 1/8 between; A - 6 cols, 1 13/16, 1/16 between; C - 9 cols, 1 3/16, 1/16 between.
Published Days: Sun
Avg. Paid Circ.: 1748
Avg. Free Circ.: 4705
Audit Company: Sworn/Estimate/Non-Audited
Audit Date: 43626

DETROIT

CANTON OBSERVER

Street Address: 615 W Lafayette Blvd
City: Detroit
State: MI
ZIP Code: 48226-3124
General Phone: (866) 887-2737
General Email: livoenewstip@hometownlife.com
Publication Website: https://www.hometownlife.com/news/eccentric/
Delivery Methods: Newsstand`Carrier`Racks
Year Established: 1869
Mechanical specifications: Type page 11 5/8 x 21 1/4; E - 6 cols, 1 13/16, 1/8 between; A - 6 cols, 1 13/16, 1/16 between; C - 9 cols, 1 3/16, 1/16 between.
Published Days: Thur`Sun
Avg. Paid Circ.: 2232
Avg. Free Circ.: 4350
Audit Company: Sworn/Estimate/Non-Audited
Audit Date: 43626

EAST TAWAS

IOSCO COUNTY NEWS HERALD

Street Address: 110 W State St
City: East Tawas
State: MI
ZIP Code: 48730
General Phone: (989) 362-3456
General Email: advertising@iosconews.com

Publication Website: http://www.iosconews.com/
Publisher Name: Ray McGrew
Publisher Email: rmcgrew@cmgms.com
Editor Name: John Morris
Editor Email: editor@iosconews.com
Advertising Executive Name: Julie Carroll
Advertising Executive Email: advertising@iosconews.com
Delivery Methods: Mail`Racks
Own Printing Facility?: Y
Commercial printers?: Y
Mechanical specifications: Type page 10 x 16 1/2; E - 5 cols, 1 11/12, between; A - 5 cols, 1 11/12, between; C - 6 cols, between.
Published Days: Wed
Avg. Paid Circ.: 4800
Audit Company: Sworn/Estimate/Non-Audited
Audit Date: 43626

FENTON

TRI-COUNTY TIMES

Street Address: 256 N Fenway Dr
City: Fenton
State: MI
ZIP Code: 48430-2699
General Phone: (810) 629-8282
General Email: tallen@tctimes.com
Publication Website: https://www.tctimes.com/
Parent Company: Gannett
Publisher Name: Jennifer Ward
Publisher Email: jward@tctimes.com
Editor Name: Sharon Stone
Editor Email: sstone@tctimes.com
Advertising Executive Name: Vera Hogan
Advertising Executive Email: vhogan@tctimes.com
Delivery Methods: Mail`Newsstand`Carrier`Racks
Year Established: 1955
Own Printing Facility?: Y
Commercial printers?: Y
Mechanical specifications: Type page 10 x 14; A - 4 cols, 2 3/8, 1/4 between; C - 6 cols, 1 1/2, 3/16 between.
Published Days: Wed`Sun
Avg. Paid Circ.: 9881
Avg. Free Circ.: 19800
Audit Company: Sworn/Estimate/Non-Audited
Audit Date: 43626

FLINT

THE BURTON NEWS

Street Address: 200 E 1st St
City: Flint
State: MI
ZIP Code: 48502-1911
General Phone: (810) 766-6100
General Email: advertise@mlive.com
Publication Website: https://www.mlive.com/burton/
Parent Company: Advance Publications, Inc.
Advertising Executive Email: advertise@mlive.com
Delivery Methods: Mail
Year Established: 2002
Mechanical specifications: Type page 11 1/2 x 21; E - 6 cols, 1 3/16, between; A - 6 cols, 1 3/16, between; C - 10 cols, 1 3/16, between.
Published Days: Sun
Avg. Paid Circ.: 15000
Audit Company: Sworn/Estimate/Non-Audited
Audit Date: 43626

FRANKENMUTH

FRANKENMUTH NEWS

Street Address: 527 N Franklin St
City: Frankenmuth
State: MI
ZIP Code: 48734
General Phone: (989) 652-3246
General Email: frankenmuthnews@airadvantage.net
Publication Website: http://www.frankenmuthnews.com/
Publisher Name: Steve Grainger
Publisher Phone: (989) 652-3246
Editor Name: Vicky Hayden
Editor Email: vhayden@airadv.net
Advertising Executive Name: Vicky Hayden
Advertising Executive Email: vhayden@airadv.net
Delivery Methods: Mail`Newsstand
Year Established: 1906
Own Printing Facility?: Y
Commercial printers?: Y
Mechanical specifications: Type page 13 3/4 x 21 1/4; E - 6 cols, 2 1/8, between; A - 6 cols, 2 1/8, between; C - 8 cols, 1 5/8, between.
Published Days: Wed
Avg. Paid Circ.: 5000
Audit Company: Sworn/Estimate/Non-Audited
Audit Date: 43626

FREMONT

FREMONT TIMES-INDICATOR

Street Address: 44 W Main St
City: Fremont
State: MI
ZIP Code: 49412
General Phone: (231) 924-4400
General Email: tinews@comcast.net
Publication Website: http://www.timesindicator.com/
Publisher Name: Richard C. Wheater
Editor Name: Richard C. Wheater
Advertising Executive Name: Debby Reinhold
Delivery Methods: Mail
Year Established: 1878
Published Days: Tues`Fri
Avg. Paid Circ.: 7500
Audit Company: Sworn/Estimate/Non-Audited
Audit Date: 43626

GAYLORD

GAYLORD HERALD TIMES

Street Address: 2058 S Otsego Ave
City: Gaylord
State: MI
ZIP Code: 49735
General Phone: (989) 732-1111
General Email: editor@gaylordheraldtimes.com
Publication Website: http://www.gaylordheraldtimes.com
Parent Company: Gannett
Publisher Name: Christy Lyons
Publisher Phone: (231) 439-9329
Editor Name: Jeremy McBain
Editor Email: editor@gaylordheraldtimes.com
Editor Phone: (231) 439-9316
Advertising Executive Name: Louann Krone
Advertising Executive Phone: (989) 858-3411
Delivery Methods: Mail`Newsstand`Racks
Year Established: 1875
Mechanical specifications: Type page 10 5/8 x 21.
Published Days: Wed`Sat
Avg. Paid Circ.: 7000
Avg. Free Circ.: 13000
Audit Company: Sworn/Estimate/Non-Audited
Audit Date: 43626

GLADWIN

GLADWIN COUNTY RECORD

Street Address: 700 E Cedar Ave
City: Gladwin
State: MI
ZIP Code: 48624
General Phone: (989) 426-9411
General Email: info@thegladwincountyrecord.com
Publication Website: https://www.gladwinmi.com/
Publisher Name: Dawn Laidlaw
Publisher Email: dlaidlaw@thegladwincountyrecord.com
Editor Name: Max Milne
Editor Email: mmilne@thegladwincountyrecord.com
Delivery Methods: Mail`Newsstand
Year Established: 1877
Own Printing Facility?: Y
Mechanical specifications: Type page 11 1/4 x 20; E - 6 cols, 1/6 between; A - 6 cols, 1/6 between; C - 6 cols, 1/6 between.
Published Days: Wed
Avg. Paid Circ.: 4200
Avg. Free Circ.: 120
Audit Company: Sworn/Estimate/Non-Audited
Audit Date: 43626

GRAND RAPIDS

MIBIZ

Street Address: 1059 Wealthy St SE, Unit 202
City: Grand Rapids
State: MI
ZIP Code: 49506
General Phone: (616) 608-6170
General Email: sales@mibiz.com
Publication Website: https://mibiz.com/
Parent Company: Serenidipty Media LLC.
Publisher Name: Brian Edwards
Publisher Email: bedwards@mibiz.com
Editor Name: Joe Boomgaard
Editor Email: editor@mibiz.com
Advertising Executive Name: Shelly Keel
Advertising Executive Email: skeel@mibiz.com
Delivery Methods: Mail`Newsstand
Year Established: 1988
Own Printing Facility?: N
Commercial printers?: N
Published Days: Mon
Published Other: Every other week
Avg. Free Circ.: 11345
Audit Company: Sworn/Estimate/Non-Audited
Audit Date: 43626

GRAYLING

CRAWFORD COUNTY AVALANCHE

Street Address: Box 490
City: Grayling
State: MI
ZIP Code: 49738
General Phone: (989) 348-6811
General Email: information@crawfordcountyavalanche.com
Publication Website: http://www.crawfordcountyavalanche.com/
Publisher Name: Teresa Milliman Brandell
Publisher Email: caleb@crawfordcountyavalanche.com
Editor Name: Caleb Casey
Editor Email: caleb@crawfordcountyavalanche.com
Advertising Executive Name: Denis Mayowski
Advertising Executive Email: denis@crawfordcountyavalanche.com
Delivery Methods: Mail`Newsstand
Year Established: 1879
Published Days: Thur
Avg. Paid Circ.: 5000
Audit Company: Sworn/Estimate/Non-Audited
Audit Date: 43626

GROSSE POINTE

GROSSE POINTE NEWS

Street Address: 16980 Kercheval Ave
City: Grosse Pointe
State: MI
ZIP Code: 48230
General Phone: (313) 882-6900
General Email: schambers@grossepointenews.com
Publication Website: https://www.grossepointenews.com/
Publisher Name: John Minnis
Publisher Email: jminnis@grossepointenews.com
Publisher Phone: (313) 343-5596
Editor Name: Jody Mcveig
Editor Email: jmcveigh@grossepointenews.com
Editor Phone: (313) 343-5590
Advertising Executive Name: Shelley Owens
Advertising Executive Email: sowens@grossepointenews.com
Advertising Executive Phone: (313) 343-5584
Delivery Methods: Mail
Year Established: 1940
Mechanical specifications: Type page 11 5/8 x 21; E - 6 cols, 1 3/4, 3/20 between; A - 6 cols, 1 3/4, 3/20 between; C - 8 cols, 1 3/8, 1/10 between.
Published Days: Thur
Avg. Paid Circ.: 12014
Audit Company: Sworn/Estimate/Non-Audited
Audit Date: 43626

HARBOR SPRINGS

HARBOR LIGHT

Street Address: 293 W. Lake Street
City: Harbor Springs
State: MI
ZIP Code: 49740-1534
General Phone: (231) 526-2191
General Email: news@ncpublish.com
Publication Website: https://www.harborlightnews.com/
Editor Name: Kate Bassett
Advertising Executive Name: Michelle Ketterer
Delivery Methods: Mail`Newsstand`Racks
Year Established: 1970
Mechanical specifications: Type page 13 x 21; E - 6 cols, between.
Published Days: Wed
Avg. Paid Circ.: 2000
Avg. Free Circ.: 69
Audit Company: Sworn/Estimate/Non-Audited
Audit Date: 43626

HARRISVILLE

ALCONA COUNTY REVIEW

Street Address: P.O. Box 548
City: Harrisville
State: MI
ZIP Code: 48740-9696
General Phone: (989) 724-6384
General Email: editor@alconareview.com
Publication Website: https://www.alconareview.com/
Publisher Name: Cheryl Peterson
Editor Name: Cheryl Peterson
Editor Email: editor@alconareview.com
Delivery Methods: Mail`Newsstand
Year Established: 1877
Published Days: Wed
Avg. Paid Circ.: 3200
Audit Company: Sworn/Estimate/Non-Audited
Audit Date: 43626

Community Newspapers in the U.S.

III-273

HART

OCEANA'S HERALD-JOURNAL

Street Address: 123 South State St.
City: Hart
State: MI
ZIP Code: 49420
General Phone: (231) 873-5602
General Email: clerk@oceanaheraldjournal. com
Publication Website: www.shorelinemedia. net/oceanas_herald_journal
Parent Company: Community Media Group
Editor Name: Andrew Skinner
Editor Email: editor@oceanaheraldjournal. com
Delivery Methods: Mail`Newsstand`Racks
Mechanical specifications: Type page 14 1/4 x 21; E - 6 cols, 2 1/4, 3/16 between; A - 6 cols, 2 1/4, 3/16 between; C - 8 cols, 1 5/8, 1/8 between.
Published Days: Thur
Avg. Paid Circ.: 5525
Avg. Free Circ.: 15
Audit Company: Sworn/Estimate/Non-Audited
Audit Date: 43626

HOMER

THE HOMER INDEX

Street Address: 119 W Main St
City: Homer
State: MI
ZIP Code: 49245
General Phone: (517) 568-4646
General Email: ads@homerindex.com
Publication Website: http://www. homerindex.com/
Publisher Name: Mike Warner
Advertising Executive Name: Dan Mullaly
Delivery Methods: Mail`Newsstand
Year Established: 1872
Mechanical specifications: Type page 12 15/16 x 21; E - 6 cols, 2, 3/16 between; A - 6 cols, 2, 3/16 between; C - 6 cols, 2, 3/16 between.
Published Days: Wed
Avg. Paid Circ.: 1150
Avg. Free Circ.: 20
Audit Company: Sworn/Estimate/Non-Audited
Audit Date: 43626

HOUGHTON LAKE

THE HOUGHTON LAKE RESORTER

Street Address: 4049 W Houghton Lake Dr
City: Houghton Lake
State: MI
ZIP Code: 48629
General Phone: (989) 366-5341
General Email: news@houghtonlakeresorter. com
Publication Website: https://www. houghtonlakeresorter.com/
Publisher Name: Eric M. Hamp
Publisher Email: eric.hamp@ houghtonlakeresorter.com
Editor Name: Eric M. Hamp
Editor Email: eric.hamp@ houghtonlakeresorter.com
Advertising Executive Name: Patty Tribelhorn
Advertising Executive Email: ads@ houghtonlakeresorter.com
Delivery Methods: Mail`Newsstand`Racks
Year Established: 1939
Own Printing Facility?: Y
Commercial printers?: N
Mechanical specifications: Type page 13 1/2 x 21 3/8; E - 6 cols, 2, 1/6 between; A - 6 cols, 2, 1/6 between; C - 6 cols, 2, 1/6 between.
Published Days: Thur
Avg. Paid Circ.: 7800
Avg. Free Circ.: 58
Audit Company: Sworn/Estimate/Non-Audited
Audit Date: 43626

IMLAY CITY

TRI-CITY TIMES

Street Address: 594 N Almont Ave
City: Imlay City
State: MI
ZIP Code: 48444
General Phone: (810) 724-2615
General Email: rjorgensen@pageone-inc.com
Publication Website: https://tricitytimes-online.com/
Publisher Name: Delores Heim
Editor Name: Maria Brown
Advertising Executive Name: Randy Jorgensen
Delivery Methods: Mail`Newsstand
Published Days: Wed
Avg. Paid Circ.: 5771
Avg. Free Circ.: 1229
Audit Company: Sworn/Estimate/Non-Audited
Audit Date: 43626

IRON RIVER

REPORTER

Street Address: 801 W Adams St
City: Iron River
State: MI
ZIP Code: 49935
General Phone: (906) 265-9927
General Email: sales@ironcountyreporter. com
Publication Website: https://www. ironcountyreporter.com/
Parent Company: Media News Group
Publisher Name: Wendy Graham
Publisher Email: wendy@ironcountyreporter. com
Editor Name: Jerry DeRoche
Editor Email: news@ironcountyreporter.com
Delivery Methods: Mail
Year Established: 1885
Published Days: Wed
Avg. Paid Circ.: 5000
Audit Company: Sworn/Estimate/Non-Audited
Audit Date: 43626

ITHACA

GRATIOT COUNTY HERALD

Street Address: 123 N Main St
City: Ithaca
State: MI
ZIP Code: 48847-1131
General Phone: (989) 875-4151
General Email: gcherald@gcherald.com
Publication Website: https://gcherald.com/
Publisher Name: Tom MacDonald
Publisher Email: tom@gcherald.com
Editor Name: Michael MacDonald
Editor Email: editor@gcherald.com
Delivery Methods: Mail
Own Printing Facility?: Y
Commercial printers?: Y
Published Days: Thur
Avg. Paid Circ.: 6727
Audit Company: Sworn/Estimate/Non-Audited
Audit Date: 43626

LAKE LEELANAU

THE LEELANAU ENTERPRISE

Street Address: 7200 E Duck Lake Rd
City: Lake Leelanau
State: MI
ZIP Code: 49653
General Phone: (231) 256-9827
General Email: info@leelanaunews.com
Publication Website: https://www. leelanaunews.com/
Publisher Name: John Elchert
Publisher Email: john@leelanaunews.com
Advertising Executive Name: Kelli Ameling
Advertising Executive Email: kelli@ leelanaunews.com
Delivery Methods: Mail`Newsstand
Year Established: 1975
Own Printing Facility?: Y
Commercial printers?: Y
Mechanical specifications: Type page 10 x 16; E - 5 cols, 1 5/6, 1/6 between; A - 5 cols, 1 5/6, 1/6 between; C - 5 cols, 1 5/6, 1/6 between.
Published Days: Thur
Avg. Paid Circ.: 8100
Avg. Free Circ.: 24
Audit Company: Sworn/Estimate/Non-Audited
Audit Date: 43626

LANSE

L'ANSE SENTINEL

Street Address: 202 N Main St
City: Lanse
State: MI
ZIP Code: 49946-1118
General Phone: (906) 524-6194
General Email: sentinel1886@gmail.com
Publication Website: https://lansesentinel. net/
Delivery Methods: Mail`Newsstand
Year Established: 1880
Own Printing Facility?: Y
Commercial printers?: Y
Mechanical specifications: Type page 13 x 22; E - 6 cols, 2 1/4, 1/4 between.
Published Days: Wed
Avg. Paid Circ.: 2200
Audit Company: Sworn/Estimate/Non-Audited
Audit Date: 43626

LANSING

EATON RAPIDS COMMUNITY NEWS

Street Address: 300 S Washington Sq
City: Lansing
State: MI
ZIP Code: 48933-2102
General Phone: (517) 377-1000
General Email: lansingstatejournal@gannett. com
Publication Website: https://www. lansingstatejournal.com/news/communities-eaton-rapids/
Editor Name: Stephanie Angel
Editor Email: sangel@lsj.com
Advertising Executive Name: Staci Holmes
Advertising Executive Email: sholmes@ localiq.com
Delivery Methods: Mail
Year Established: 1856
Mechanical specifications: Type page: 10 x 10; 6 col
Published Days: Sun
Avg. Paid Circ.: 3
Avg. Free Circ.: 4321
Audit Company: Sworn/Estimate/Non-Audited
Audit Date: 43626

LANSING

INGHAM COUNTY COMMUNITY NEWS

Street Address: 300 S. Washington Square, Suite #300
City: Lansing
State: MI
ZIP Code: 48933
General Phone: (517) 377-1000
General Email: csmith@lsj.com
Publication Website: https://www. lansingstatejournal.com/
Publisher Name: Stephanie Angel
Publisher Email: sangel@lsj.com
Delivery Methods: Mail
Year Established: 1856
Mechanical specifications: Type page: 10 x 10; 6 col
Published Days: Sun
Avg. Free Circ.: 6993
Audit Company: Sworn/Estimate/Non-Audited
Audit Date: 43626

LANSING

LANSING CITY COMMUNITY NEWS

Street Address: 300 S Washington Sq
City: Lansing
State: MI
ZIP Code: 48933-2102
General Phone: (517) 377-1000
General Email: csmith@lsj.com
Publication Website: https://www. lansingstatejournal.com/
Editor Name: Stephanie Angel
Editor Email: sangel@lsj.com
Advertising Executive Name: Staci Holmes
Advertising Executive Email: sholmes@ localiq.com
Delivery Methods: Mail
Year Established: 1856
Mechanical specifications: Type page: 10 x 10; 6 col
Published Days: Sun
Avg. Paid Circ.: 3
Avg. Free Circ.: 27120
Audit Company: Sworn/Estimate/Non-Audited
Audit Date: 43626

LAPEER

BANNER

Street Address: 1521 Imlay City Rd
City: Lapeer
State: MI
ZIP Code: 48446
General Phone: (810) 664-0811
General Email: ads@mihomepaper.com
Publication Website: https:// browncitybanner.mihomepaper.com/
Parent Company: View Newspaper Group
Advertising Executive Email: sales@ mihomepaper.com
Delivery Methods: Mail
Published Days: Mon
Avg. Paid Circ.: 1814
Audit Company: Sworn/Estimate/Non-Audited
Audit Date: 43626

LAPEER

FLINT TOWNSHIP VIEW

Street Address: 1521 Imlay City Rd
City: Lapeer
State: MI
ZIP Code: 48446
General Phone: (810) 664-0811
General Email: wsmith@mihomepaper.com
Publication Website: https:// flinttownshipview.mihomepaper.com/
Parent Company: View Newspaper Group
Advertising Executive Email: sales@ mihomepaper.com
Delivery Methods: Mail
Year Established: 2010
Mechanical specifications: Type page 9.75" x 10"; 4 cols
Published Days: Thur

LAPEER

LA VIEW

Street Address: 1521 Imlay City Rd
City: Lapeer
State: MI
ZIP Code: 48446-3175
General Phone: (810) 664-0811
General Email: laveditor@mihomepaper.com
Publication Website: https://lapeerareaview.mihomepaper.com/
Parent Company: View Newspaper Group
Publisher Name: Wes Smith
Editor Name: Jeff Hogan
Editor Email: jhogan@mihomepaper.com
Advertising Executive Name: Pete Clinton
Advertising Executive Email: pclinton@mihomepaper.com
Delivery Methods: Mail
Year Established: 2003
Mechanical specifications: Type page 9.75" x 10"; 4 cols
Published Days: Thur
Avg. Free Circ.: 34904
Audit Company: CVC
Audit Date: 43257

LAPEER

THE COUNTY PRESS

Street Address: 1521 Imlay City Rd
City: Lapeer
State: MI
ZIP Code: 48446
General Phone: (810) 664-0811
General Email: thecountypress.mihomepaper.com
Publication Website: https://thecountypress.mihomepaper.com/
Parent Company: View Newspaper Group
Publisher Name: Wes Smith
Editor Name: Jeffrey Hogan
Editor Email: editor@mihomepaper.com
Advertising Executive Email: sales@mihomepaper.com
Advertising Executive Phone: (810) 664-0811, ext : 1100
Delivery Methods: Mail
Year Established: 1839
Own Printing Facility?: Y
Commercial printers?: Y
Mechanical specifications: Type page 10 5/8 x 21; A - 6 cols, 1 3/8, 1/6 between; C - 10 cols, 1 3/16, 1/6 between.
Published Days: Wed`Sun
Avg. Paid Circ.: 7941
Avg. Free Circ.: 233
Audit Company: AAM
Audit Date: 43658

MANISTIQUE

PIONEER TRIBUNE

Street Address: 212 Walnut St
City: Manistique
State: MI
ZIP Code: 49854-1445
General Phone: (906) 341-5200
General Email: ads@pioneertribune.com
Publication Website: https://www.pioneertribune.com/
Publisher Name: Lisa A. Demers
Publisher Email: ldemers@pioneertribune.com
Editor Name: Ashley Roberson-Smith
Editor Email: editor@pioneertribune.com
Advertising Executive Email: ads@pioneertribune.com
Delivery Methods: Mail`Newsstand`Carrier
Year Established: 1876
Own Printing Facility?: Y

Commercial printers?: Y
Mechanical specifications: Type page 15 x 21 1/2; A - 8 cols, 1 3/4, 1/6 between; C - 9 cols, 1 1/16, 1/6 between.
Published Days: Thur
Avg. Paid Circ.: 3500
Audit Company: Sworn/Estimate/Non-Audited
Audit Date: 43626

MARION

THE MARION PRESS

Street Address: 301 E. Mill St.
City: Marion
State: MI
ZIP Code: 49665
General Phone: (231) 743-2481
General Email: yourmarionpress@gmail.com
Publication Website: http://www.marion-press.com/
Published Days: Wed
Avg. Paid Circ.: 1941
Avg. Free Circ.: 10
Audit Company: Sworn/Estimate/Non-Audited
Audit Date: 43626

MONROE

BEDFORD NOW

Street Address: 20 W 1st St
City: Monroe
State: MI
ZIP Code: 48161-2333
General Phone: (734) 242-1100
General Email: trent@monroenews.com
Publication Website: https://www.bedfordnow.com/
Parent Company: Gannett
Publisher Name: Vince Bodiford
Publisher Email: vbodiford@monroenews.com
Publisher Phone: (734) 240-5795
Editor Name: Ray Kisonas
Editor Email: rkisonas@monroenews.com
Editor Phone: (734) 240-5778
Advertising Executive Name: Kristi Prater
Advertising Executive Email: kprater@monroenews.com
Advertising Executive Phone: (734) 240-5721
Own Printing Facility?: N
Commercial printers?: N
Published Days: Sat
Audit Company: Sworn/Estimate/Non-Audited
Audit Date: 43626

MORENCI

STATE LINE OBSERVER

Street Address: 120 North St
City: Morenci
State: MI
ZIP Code: 49256
General Phone: (517) 458-6811
General Email: editor@statelineobserver.com
Publication Website: https://statelineobserver.com/
Parent Company: The Green family
Editor Name: David Green
Editor Email: editor@statelineobserver.com
Editor Phone: (517) 458-6811
Delivery Methods: Mail`Newsstand
Year Established: 1872
Mechanical specifications: Type page 10 1/4 x 16; E - 4 cols, 2 1/2, 1/6 between; A - 6 cols, 1 1/2, 1/12 between; C - 6 cols, 1 1/2, 1/12 between.
Published Days: Wed
Avg. Paid Circ.: 2321
Audit Company: Sworn/Estimate/Non-Audited
Audit Date: 43626

MUNISING

THE MUNISING NEWS

Street Address: 132 E Superior St
City: Munising
State: MI
ZIP Code: 49862-1122
General Phone: (906) 387-3282
General Email: munisingnews@jamadots.com
Publication Website: https://www.themunisingnews.com/
Parent Company: Peterson Publishing, Inc
Delivery Methods: Mail`Newsstand
Year Established: 1896
Own Printing Facility?: N
Commercial printers?: Y
Mechanical specifications: Type page 15 x 21 1/2; E - 9 cols, 1 5/8, 1/6 between; A - 9 cols, 1 5/8, 1/6 between; C - 9 cols, 1 5/8, 1/6 between.
Published Days: Wed
Avg. Paid Circ.: 2250
Avg. Free Circ.: 5000
Audit Company: Sworn/Estimate/Non-Audited
Audit Date: 43626

NEW BUFFALO

NEW BUFFALO TIMES

Street Address: P.O. Box 369, 140 N. Whittaker St.
City: New Buffalo
State: MI
ZIP Code: 49117-1764
General Phone: (269) 469-1100
General Email: info@newbuffalotimes.com
Publication Website: http://www.newbuffalotimes.com/
Editor Name: Kristin E. Fatouros
Delivery Methods: Mail
Year Established: 1943
Published Days: Thur
Avg. Paid Circ.: 5000
Audit Company: Sworn/Estimate/Non-Audited
Audit Date: 43626

NEWBERRY

THE NEWBERRY NEWS

Street Address: P.O. Box 46
City: Newberry
State: MI
ZIP Code: 49868
General Phone: (906) 293-8401
General Email: nbynews@jamadots.com
Publication Website: https://newberry-news.com/
Delivery Methods: Mail`Newsstand
Year Established: 1886
Own Printing Facility?: Y
Commercial printers?: N
Mechanical specifications: Type page 11 5/8 x 21 1/2; E - 6 cols, 1 13/16, 1/8 between; A - 6 cols, 1 13/16, 1/8 between; C - 6 cols, 1 13/16, 1/8 between.
Published Days: Wed
Avg. Paid Circ.: 3600
Audit Company: Sworn/Estimate/Non-Audited
Audit Date: 43626

NILES

CASSOPOLIS VIGILANT

Street Address: 217 N 4th St
City: Niles
State: MI
ZIP Code: 49120-2301
General Phone: (269) 683-2101
General Email: classifieds@leaderpub.com

Publication Website: https://www.leaderpub.com/category/news/cassopolis-news/
Parent Company: Boone Newspapers, Inc.
Publisher Name: Ambrosia Neldon
Publisher Email: ambrosia.neldon@leaderpub.com
Publisher Phone: (269) 687-7700
Editor Name: Sarah Culton
Editor Email: sarah.culton@leaderpub.com
Editor Phone: (269) 687-7712
Advertising Executive Name: Phil Langer
Advertising Executive Email: phil.langer@leaderpub.com
Advertising Executive Phone: (269) 687-7725
Delivery Methods: Mail`Newsstand`Racks
Mechanical specifications: Type page 13 x 21 1/4; E - 8 cols, 1 1/2, between; A - 8 cols, 1 1/2, between; C - 8 cols, 1 1/2, between.
Published Days: Thur
Avg. Paid Circ.: 800
Audit Company: Sworn/Estimate/Non-Audited
Audit Date: 43626

NILES

EDWARDSBURG ARGUS

Street Address: 217 N 4th St
City: Niles
State: MI
ZIP Code: 49120
General Phone: (269) 683-2100
General Email: classifieds@leaderpub.com
Publication Website: https://www.leaderpub.com/
Parent Company: Boone Newspapers, Inc.
Publisher Name: Ambrosia Neldon
Publisher Email: ambrosia.neldon@leaderpub.com
Publisher Phone: (269) 687-7700
Editor Name: Sarah Culton
Editor Email: sarah.culton@leaderpub.com
Editor Phone: (269) 687-7712
Advertising Executive Name: Phil Langer
Advertising Executive Email: phil.langer@leaderpub.com
Advertising Executive Phone: (269) 687-7725
Delivery Methods: Mail`Newsstand`Racks
Own Printing Facility?: Y
Commercial printers?: Y
Mechanical specifications: Type page 13 x 21 1/4; E - 8 cols, 1 1/2, between; A - 8 cols, 1 1/2, between; C - 8 cols, 1 1/2, between.
Published Days: Thur
Avg. Paid Circ.: 800
Avg. Free Circ.: 21
Audit Company: Sworn/Estimate/Non-Audited
Audit Date: 43626

NOVI

FARMINGTON OBSERVER

Street Address: 29725 Hudson Drive
City: Novi
State: MI
ZIP Code: 48377
General Phone: (866) 887-2737
General Email: pallmen@hometownlife.com
Publication Website: https://www.hometownlife.com/news/observer-farmington/
Delivery Methods: Newsstand`Carrier`Racks
Mechanical specifications: Type page 11 5/8 x 21 1/4; E - 6 cols, 1 13/16, 1/8 between; A - 6 cols, 1 13/16, 1/16 between; C - 9 cols, 1 3/16, 1/16 between.
Published Days: Thur`Sun
Avg. Paid Circ.: 895
Avg. Free Circ.: 7190
Audit Company: AAM
Audit Date: 44024

NOVI

Community Newspapers in the U.S.

GRAND LEDGE INDEPENDENT

Street Address: 29725 Hudson Drive
City: Novi
State: MI
ZIP Code: 48377
General Phone: (866) 887-2737
General Email: lansingstatejournal@gannett.com
Publication Website: https://www.lansingstatejournal.com/news/communities-grand-ledge/
Editor Name: Stephanie Angel
Editor Email: sangel@lsj.com
Advertising Executive Name: Staci Holmes
Advertising Executive Email: sholmes@localiq.com
Delivery Methods: Mail
Year Established: 1856
Mechanical specifications: Type page 10 x 10; E - 6 cols, 1 9/16, 1/6 between; A - 6 cols, 1 9/16, 1/6 between; C - 6 cols, 1 9/16, 1/6 between.
Published Days: Sun
Avg. Paid Circ.: 6
Avg. Free Circ.: 7643
Audit Company: Sworn/Estimate/Non-Audited
Audit Date: 43626

NOVI

LIVONIA OBSERVER

Street Address: 29725 Hudson Drive
City: Novi
State: MI
ZIP Code: 48377
General Phone: (866) 887-2737
General Email: stankersle@hometownlife.com
Publication Website: https://www.hometownlife.com/
Delivery Methods: Mail`Newsstand`Carrier
Year Established: 1869
Mechanical specifications: Type page 11 5/8 x 21 1/4; E - 6 cols, 1 13/16, 1/8 between; A - 6 cols, 1 13/16, 1/16 between; C - 9 cols, 1 3/16, 1/16 between.
Published Days: Thur`Sun
Avg. Paid Circ.: 2892
Avg. Free Circ.: 6805
Audit Company: AAM
Audit Date: 43988

NOVI

MILFORD TIMES

Street Address: 29725 Hudson Drive
City: Novi
State: MI
ZIP Code: 48377
General Phone: (866) 887-2737
General Email: sbromley@hometownlife.com
Publication Website: https://www.hometownlife.com/
Delivery Methods: Mail
Published Days: Thur
Avg. Paid Circ.: 1720
Avg. Free Circ.: 210
Audit Company: AAM
Audit Date: 43988

NOVI

NORTHVILLE RECORD

Street Address: 29725 Hudson Drive
City: Novi
State: MI
ZIP Code: 48377
General Phone: (866) 887-2737
General Email: eawright@hometownlife.com
Publication Website: https://www.hometownlife.com/
Delivery Methods: Mail
Published Days: Thur
Avg. Paid Circ.: 1905
Avg. Free Circ.: 210
Audit Company: AAM
Audit Date: 43988

NOVI

NOVI NEWS

Street Address: 29725 Hudson Drive
City: Novi
State: MI
ZIP Code: 48377
General Phone: (866) 887-2737
General Email: sbromley@hometownlife.com
Publication Website: https://www.hometownlife.com/
Delivery Methods: Mail
Published Days: Thur
Avg. Paid Circ.: 1155
Avg. Free Circ.: 255
Audit Company: AAM
Audit Date: 43988

NOVI

OBSERVER & ECCENTRIC MEDIA

Street Address: 29725 Hudson Drive
City: Novi
State: MI
ZIP Code: 48377
General Phone: (866) 887-2737
General Email: pallmen@hometownlife.com
Publication Website: https://www.hometownlife.com/news/observer/
Published Days: Thur`Sun
Avg. Paid Circ.: 13871
Avg. Free Circ.: 39261
Audit Company: AAM
Audit Date: 43988

NOVI

PLYMOUTH OBSERVER

Street Address: 29725 Hudson Drive
City: Novi
State: MI
ZIP Code: 48377
General Phone: (866) 887-2737
General Email: eawright@hometownlife.com
Publication Website: https://www.hometownlife.com/news/observer/
Delivery Methods: Carrier
Year Established: 1869
Own Printing Facility?: Y
Commercial printers?: Y
Mechanical specifications: Type page 11 5/8 x 21 1/4; E - 6 cols, 1 13/16, 1/8 between; A - 6 cols, 1 13/16, 1/16 between; C - 9 cols, 1 3/16, 1/16 between.
Published Days: Thur`Sun
Avg. Paid Circ.: 1187
Avg. Free Circ.: 210
Audit Company: AAM
Audit Date: 43988

NOVI

SOUTH LYON HERALD

Street Address: 29725 Hudson Drive
City: Novi
State: MI
ZIP Code: 48377
General Phone: (866) 887-2737
General Email: sbromley@hometownlife.com
Publication Website: https://www.hometownlife.com/news/observer/
Delivery Methods: Mail
Published Days: Thur
Avg. Paid Circ.: 1790
Avg. Free Circ.: 210
Audit Company: AAM
Audit Date: 43988

NOVI

WESTLAND OBSERVER

Street Address: 29725 Hudson Drive
City: Novi
State: MI
ZIP Code: 48377
General Phone: (866) 887-2737
General Email: stankersle@hometownlife.com
Publication Website: https://www.hometownlife.com/news/observer/
Delivery Methods: Newsstand`Carrier`Racks
Own Printing Facility?: Y
Commercial printers?: Y
Mechanical specifications: Type page 11 5/8 x 21 1/4; E - 6 cols, 1 13/16, 1/8 between; A - 6 cols, 1 13/16, 1/16 between; C - 9 cols, 1 3/16, 1/16 between.
Published Days: Thur`Sun
Avg. Paid Circ.: 950
Avg. Free Circ.: 5400
Audit Company: AAM
Audit Date: 44024

ONTONAGON

THE ONTONAGON HERALD

Street Address: 326 River St
City: Ontonagon
State: MI
ZIP Code: 49953
General Phone: (906) 884-2826
General Email: maureen@ontonagonherald.com
Publication Website: https://ontonagonherald.com/
Delivery Methods: Mail
Year Established: 1881
Own Printing Facility?: Y
Commercial printers?: Y
Mechanical specifications: Type page 13 1/2 x 21; E - 6 cols, 2 1/16, 1/6 between; A - 6 cols, 2 1/16, 1/6 between; C - 9 cols, 1 1/3, 1/12 between.
Published Days: Wed
Avg. Paid Circ.: 3700
Avg. Free Circ.: 70
Audit Company: Sworn/Estimate/Non-Audited
Audit Date: 43626

OSCODA

OSCODA PRESS

Street Address: 311 S State St
City: Oscoda
State: MI
ZIP Code: 48750
General Phone: (989) 739-2054
General Email: comp@iosconews.com
Publication Website: http://www.iosconews.com/oscoda_press/
Parent Company: Community Media Group
Publisher Name: Ray McGrew
Publisher Email: rmcgrew@cmgms.com
Editor Name: Jason Ogden
Editor Email: editor1@oscodapress.com
Advertising Executive Name: Penny Essary
Advertising Executive Email: advertising@oscodapress.com
Delivery Methods: Mail`Newsstand`Racks
Year Established: 1879
Own Printing Facility?: Y
Commercial printers?: Y
Published Days: Wed
Avg. Paid Circ.: 3900
Audit Company: Sworn/Estimate/Non-Audited
Audit Date: 43626

OWOSSO

SUNDAY INDEPENDENT

Street Address: 1907 W. M-21
City: Owosso
State: MI
ZIP Code: 48867
General Phone: (989) 723-1118
General Email: news@owossoindependent.com
Publication Website: http://owossoindependent.com/
Delivery Methods: Mail`Carrier
Year Established: 1968
Mechanical specifications: Type page 10 x 15; E - 6 cols, 1 1/2, 1/8 between.
Published Days: Wed`Sun
Avg. Free Circ.: 32035
Audit Company: Sworn/Estimate/Non-Audited
Audit Date: 43626

PARMA

COUNTY PRESS

Street Address: PO Box 279
City: Parma
State: MI
ZIP Code: 49269-0279
General Phone: (517) 531-4542
General Email: advertising@jxncopress.com
Publication Website: http://www.jxncopress.com/
Editor Email: editor@jxncopress.com
Advertising Executive Email: advertising@jxncopress.com
Delivery Methods: Mail`Racks
Year Established: 1868
Mechanical specifications: Type page 10 x 15; E - 5 cols, 2, between; A - 5 cols, 2, between; C - 5 cols, 2, between.
Published Days: Wed
Avg. Paid Circ.: 1500
Audit Company: Sworn/Estimate/Non-Audited
Audit Date: 43626

PAW PAW

COURIER-LEADER

Street Address: 32280 E Red Arrow Hwy
City: Paw Paw
State: MI
ZIP Code: 49079
General Phone: (269) 657-3072
General Email: ads@vineyardpress.biz
Publication Website: http://www.pawpawcourierleader.com/
Editor Name: Robin Racette-Griffin
Editor Email: couriereditorial@vineyardpress.biz
Advertising Executive Email: ads@vineyardpress.biz
Delivery Methods: Mail`Newsstand`Carrier`Racks
Year Established: 1844
Own Printing Facility?: Y
Commercial printers?: Y
Mechanical specifications: Type page 13 x 21; E - 6 cols, 2 1/8, 1/8 between; A - 6 cols, 2 1/8, 1/8 between; C - 6 cols, 2 1/8, 1/8 between.
Published Days: Fri`Sun
Avg. Paid Circ.: 2987
Avg. Free Circ.: 16300
Audit Company: Sworn/Estimate/Non-Audited
Audit Date: 43626

PLAINWELL

UNION ENTERPRISE

Street Address: P.O. Box 483
City: Plainwell
State: MI
ZIP Code: 49080

General Phone: (269) 673-5534
General Email: publisher@allegannews.com
Publication Website: http://allegannews.com/union-enterprise
Parent Company: Kaechele Publications, Inc.
Publisher Name: R. Michael Wilcox
Publisher Email: publisher@allegannews.com
Editor Name: Ryan Lewis
Editor Email: rmlewis@allegannews.com
Advertising Executive Name: Robin Clark
Advertising Executive Email: robinclark@allegannews.com
Delivery Methods: Mail
Year Established: 1871
Own Printing Facility?: N
Commercial printers?: N
Mechanical specifications: Full page image size 10.5" X 16"; 6 cols, 1.646", 1/8 between columns
Published Days: Mon
Avg. Paid Circ.: 519
Avg. Free Circ.: 35
Audit Company: Sworn/Estimate/Non-Audited
Audit Date: 43626

ROCKFORD

ROCKFORD SQUIRE

Street Address: 331 Northland Dr NE
City: Rockford
State: MI
ZIP Code: 49341
General Phone: (616) 866-4465
General Email: squiremail@aol.com
Publication Website: http://rockfordsquire.com/
Editor Name: Beth Altena
Editor Email: squiremail@aol.com
Advertising Executive Email: squiresalesteam@gmail.com
Delivery Methods: Mail
Year Established: 1871
Published Days: Thur
Avg. Free Circ.: 11300
Audit Company: Sworn/Estimate/Non-Audited
Audit Date: 43626

ROGERS CITY

PRESQUE ISLE COUNTY ADVANCE

Street Address: P.O. Box 50
City: Rogers City
State: MI
ZIP Code: 49779-1710
General Phone: (989) 734-2105
General Email: editor@piadvance.com
Publication Website: https://piadvance.com/
Parent Company: Richard and Riconda Lamb
Delivery Methods: Mail`Newsstand
Year Established: 1878
Own Printing Facility?: N
Commercial printers?: N
Mechanical specifications: Type page 10.375 wide by 21 tall. 1.625 inch column, 6 column format
Published Days: Thur
Avg. Paid Circ.: 3800
Avg. Free Circ.: 50
Audit Company: Sworn/Estimate/Non-Audited
Audit Date: 43626

SAGINAW

SAGINAW PRESS

Street Address: 100 S Michigan Ave
City: Saginaw
State: MI
ZIP Code: 48602-2054
General Phone: (989) 793-8070
General Email: advertise@mlive.com
Publication Website: https://www.mlive.com/news/saginaw-bay-city/
Parent Company: Advance Publications, Inc.
Advertising Executive Name: Anne Drummond
Advertising Executive Email: advertise@mlive.com
Own Printing Facility?: Y
Commercial printers?: Y
Mechanical specifications: Type page 13 1/2 x 19 1/2; E - 6 cols, 2 2/3, 1/12 between; A - 6 cols, 2 2/3, 1/12 between; C - 6 cols, 2 2/3, 1/12 between.
Published Days: Fri
Avg. Paid Circ.: 448
Avg. Free Circ.: 6
Audit Company: Sworn/Estimate/Non-Audited
Audit Date: 43626

SAINT IGNACE

THE ST. IGNACE NEWS

Street Address: 359 Reagon St
City: Saint Ignace
State: MI
ZIP Code: 49781-1134
General Phone: (906) 643-9150
General Email: ads@saintignacenews.com
Publication Website: https://www.stignacenews.com
Publisher Name: Wesley H. Maurer
Publisher Email: wes@stignacenews.com
Editor Name: Ellen Paquin
Editor Email: news@stignacenews.com
Advertising Executive Name: Tammy Matson
Advertising Executive Email: ads@saintignacenews.com
Delivery Methods: Mail
Year Established: 1878
Own Printing Facility?: Y
Commercial printers?: Y
Mechanical specifications: Type page 12 1/2 x 20; E - 6 cols, 1 15/16, 1/8 between; A - 6 cols, 1 15/16, 1/8 between; C - 9 cols, 1 1/4, 1/8 between.
Published Days: Thur
Avg. Paid Circ.: 4985
Audit Company: Sworn/Estimate/Non-Audited
Audit Date: 43626

SANDUSKY

SANILAC COUNTY NEWS

Street Address: 65 S Elk St
City: Sandusky
State: MI
ZIP Code: 48471-1337
General Phone: (810) 648-4000
General Email: elevine@mihomepaper.com
Publication Website: https://sanilaccountynews.mihomepaper.com/
Parent Company: View Newspaper Group
Editor Email: scneditor@mihomepaper.com
Delivery Methods: Mail`Newsstand`Racks
Year Established: 1971
Own Printing Facility?: Y
Commercial printers?: Y
Mechanical specifications: Type page 11 67/500 x 20; E - 6 cols, 1 1/2, between; A - 6 cols, 1 1/2, between; C - 6 cols, 1 1/2, between.
Published Days: Wed
Avg. Paid Circ.: 4818
Avg. Free Circ.: 30
Audit Company: Sworn/Estimate/Non-Audited
Audit Date: 43626

SANDUSKY

THE JEFFERSONIAN

Street Address: 65 S Elk St
City: Sandusky
State: MI
ZIP Code: 48471-1337
General Phone: (810) 648-4000
General Email: jvanderpoel@mihomepaper.com
Publication Website: https://sanilaccountynews.mihomepaper.com/
Editor Name: Eric Levine
Editor Email: elevine@mihomepaper.com
Delivery Methods: Mail`Racks
Year Established: 1971
Mechanical specifications: Type page 11 67/500 x 20; E - 6 cols, 1 1/2, between; A - 6 cols, 1 1/2, between; C - 6 cols, 1 1/2, between.
Published Days: Fri
Avg. Paid Circ.: 262
Avg. Free Circ.: 151
Audit Company: AAM
Audit Date: 43991

SANDUSKY

TRIBUNE RECORDER LEADER

Street Address: 43 S Elk St
City: Sandusky
State: MI
ZIP Code: 48471-1353
General Phone: (810) 648-5282
Publication Website: http://www.tribunerecorderleader.com/about/
Publisher Name: William R. Dixon
Year Established: 1893
Commercial printers?: Y
Mechanical specifications: Type page 10 x 15; E - 6 cols, 1 1/2, 1/8 between; A - 6 cols, 1 1/2, 1/8 between; C - 6 cols, 1 1/2, 1/8 between.
Published Days: Tues
Avg. Paid Circ.: 1500
Avg. Free Circ.: 10
Audit Company: Sworn/Estimate/Non-Audited
Audit Date: 43626

SAUGATUCK

THE COMMERCIAL RECORD

Street Address: 3217 Blue Star Hwy
City: Saugatuck
State: MI
ZIP Code: 49453-9723
General Phone: (269) 857-2570
General Email: commrec@allegannews.com
Publication Website: http://allegannews.com/
Parent Company: Kaechele Publications, Inc.
Publisher Name: R. Michael Wilcox
Publisher Email: publisher@allegannews.com
Editor Name: Scott Sullivan
Editor Email: editor@allegannews.com
Advertising Executive Name: Robin Clark
Advertising Executive Email: robinclark@allegannews.com
Delivery Methods: Mail`Newsstand
Year Established: 1869
Own Printing Facility?: Y
Commercial printers?: N
Mechanical specifications: full page image size 10.5" x 21.5"; 6 cols, 1.646, 1/8 between
Published Days: Thur
Avg. Paid Circ.: 1020
Avg. Free Circ.: 21
Audit Company: Sworn/Estimate/Non-Audited
Audit Date: 43626

SOUTH HAVEN

SOUTH HAVEN TRIBUNE

Street Address: 308 Kalamazoo St
City: South Haven
State: MI
ZIP Code: 49090-1308
General Phone: (269) 637-1104
General Email: southhaventribune@yahoo.com
Publication Website: http://southhaventribune.net/
Parent Company: Paxton Media Group, LLC
Editor Name: Rebecca Burkert
Editor Email: news@southhaventribune.com
Editor Phone: (269) 637-1104, ext : 102
Advertising Executive Name: Jeanine Lesneski
Advertising Executive Email: jlesneski@thehp.com
Advertising Executive Phone: (269) 429-2400, ext : 405
Delivery Methods: Newsstand`Carrier`Racks
Year Established: 1899
Mechanical specifications: Type page 11 5/8 x 22; E - 6 cols, 1 5/6, 1/8 between; A - 6 cols, 1 5/6, 1/8 between; C - 9 cols, 1 13/16, 1/8 between.
Published Days: Sun
Avg. Free Circ.: 13665
Audit Company: Sworn/Estimate/Non-Audited
Audit Date: 43626

SOUTHGATE

NEWS-HERALD

Street Address: 1 Heritage Dr
City: Southgate
State: MI
ZIP Code: 48195
General Phone: (734) 246-0800
General Email: onlineads@21stcenturynewspapers.com
Publication Website: https://www.thenewsherald.com/
Parent Company: Media News Group
Publisher Name: Greg Mazanec
Publisher Email: mipublisher@digitalfirstmedia.com
Editor Name: Jason Alley
Editor Email: jalley@thenewsherald.com
Advertising Executive Email: onlineads@21stcenturynewspapers.com
Delivery Methods: Mail`Carrier
Year Established: 1986
Published Days: Wed`Fri`Sun
Avg. Paid Circ.: 17219
Avg. Free Circ.: 33120
Audit Company: AAM
Audit Date: 44413

SOUTHGATE

PRESS & GUIDE

Street Address: 1 Heritage Dr
City: Southgate
State: MI
ZIP Code: 48195-3047
General Phone: (734) 246-0800
General Email: editor@pressandguide.com
Publication Website: https://www.pressandguide.com/
Parent Company: Media News Group
Publisher Name: Greg Mazanec
Publisher Email: mipublisher@digitalfirstmedia.com
Editor Name: Jason Alley
Editor Email: jalley@thenewsherald.com
Advertising Executive Email: onlineads@21st-centurynewspapers.com
Delivery Methods: Mail`Carrier
Year Established: 1918
Published Days: Wed`Sun
Avg. Paid Circ.: 1256
Avg. Free Circ.: 7384
Audit Company: AAM
Audit Date: 44110

SPRINGPORT

Community Newspapers in the U.S.

SPRINGPORT

SPRINGPORT SIGNAL

Street Address: 123 W Main St
City: Springport
State: MI
ZIP Code: 49284
General Phone: (517) 857-2500
General Email: springportsignal@springcom.com
Publication Website: http://www.springportmi.com/
Publisher Name: Dawn Doner
Published Days: Thur
Avg. Paid Circ.: 1100
Avg. Free Circ.: 10
Audit Company: Sworn/Estimate/Non-Audited
Audit Date: 43626

STANDISH

ARENAC COUNTY INDEPENDENT

Street Address: 1010 W Cedar St
City: Standish
State: MI
ZIP Code: 48658-9421
General Phone: (989) 846-4531
General Email: sales@arenacindependent.com
Publication Website: https://www.arenacindependent.com/
Parent Company: Sunrise Printing & Publishing, Inc
Advertising Executive Name: Jenni Grezeszak
Advertising Executive Email: classifieds@ogemawherald.com
Delivery Methods: Mail
Year Established: 1883
Own Printing Facility?: Y
Commercial printers?: Y
Published Days: Wed
Avg. Paid Circ.: 6000
Audit Company: Sworn/Estimate/Non-Audited
Audit Date: 43625

TECUMSEH

THE TECUMSEH HERALD

Street Address: 110 E Logan St
City: Tecumseh
State: MI
ZIP Code: 49286
General Phone: (517) 423-2174
General Email: brian@tecumsehherald.com
Publication Website: https://tecumsehherald.com/
Publisher Name: James L. Lincoln
Publisher Email: jim@tecumsehherald.com
Editor Name: Suzanne Hayes
Editor Email: homefront@tecumsehherald.com
Advertising Executive Name: Sharon Maher
Advertising Executive Email: sharonm@tecumsehherald.com
Delivery Methods: Mail˙Newsstand
Year Established: 1850
Own Printing Facility?: Y
Commercial printers?: Y
Mechanical specifications: Type page 13 x 21; E - 6 cols, 2, 1/6 between; A - 6 cols, 2, 1/6 between; C - 6 cols, 2, 1/6 between.
Published Days: Mon˙Thur
Avg. Paid Circ.: 4000
Audit Company: Sworn/Estimate/Non-Audited
Audit Date: 43626

TRAVERSE CITY

NORTHERN EXPRESS

Street Address: 129 1/2 E Front St
City: Traverse City
State: MI
ZIP Code: 49684-2508
General Phone: (231) 947-8787
General Email: info@northernexpress.com
Publication Website: https://www.northernexpress.com/
Parent Company: Express Publications, Inc.
Advertising Executive Email: info@northernexpress.com
Delivery Methods: Mail˙Newsstand
Year Established: 1992
Published Days: Mon
Avg. Free Circ.: 34000
Audit Company: Sworn/Estimate/Non-Audited
Audit Date: 43626

WALKER

CADENCE

Street Address: 3102 Walker Ridge Dr NW
City: Walker
State: MI
ZIP Code: 49544-9125
General Phone: (616) 669-2700
General Email: advanceadvertising@mlive.com
Publication Website: https://www.mlive.com/community/
Parent Company: Advance Local Media LLC
Delivery Methods: Carrier
Year Established: 1965
Own Printing Facility?: Y
Commercial printers?: Y
Mechanical specifications: Type page 10 3/8 x 16; A - 6 cols, 1 5/8, 1/8 between.
Published Days: Sun
Avg. Free Circ.: 48302
Audit Company: Sworn/Estimate/Non-Audited
Audit Date: 43626

WALKER

GRAND VALLEY ADVANCE

Street Address: 3102 Walker Ridge Dr NW
City: Walker
State: MI
ZIP Code: 49544
General Phone: (616) 669-2700
General Email: advanceadvertising@mlive.com
Publication Website: https://www.mlivemediagroup.com/
Parent Company: Advance Publications, Inc.
Advertising Executive Email: advanceadvertising@mlive.com
Delivery Methods: Carrier
Own Printing Facility?: Y
Commercial printers?: Y
Published Days: Sun
Avg. Free Circ.: 37280
Audit Company: Sworn/Estimate/Non-Audited
Audit Date: 43626

WALKER

NORTHEAST ADVANCE

Street Address: 3102 Walker Ridge Dr NW
City: Walker
State: MI
ZIP Code: 49544
General Phone: (616) 669-2700
General Email: advanceadvertising@mlive.com
Publication Website: https://www.mlivemediagroup.com/
Parent Company: Advance Publications, Inc.
Advertising Executive Email: advanceadvertising@mlive.com
Delivery Methods: Carrier
Year Established: 1965
Own Printing Facility?: Y
Commercial printers?: Y
Mechanical specifications: Type page 10 3/8 x 16; A - 6 cols, 1 5/8, 1/8 between.
Published Days: Sun
Avg. Free Circ.: 22040
Audit Company: Sworn/Estimate/Non-Audited
Audit Date: 43626

WALKER

NORTHWEST ADVANCE

Street Address: 3102 Walker Ridge Dr NW
City: Walker
State: MI
ZIP Code: 49544
General Phone: (616) 669-2700
General Email: advanceadvertising@mlive.com
Publication Website: https://www.mlivemediagroup.com/
Parent Company: Advance Publications, Inc.
Advertising Executive Email: advanceadvertising@mlive.com
Delivery Methods: Carrier
Year Established: 1965
Own Printing Facility?: Y
Commercial printers?: Y
Mechanical specifications: Type page 10 3/8 x 16; A - 6 cols, 1 5/8, 1/8 between.
Published Days: Sun
Avg. Free Circ.: 44911
Audit Company: Sworn/Estimate/Non-Audited
Audit Date: 43626

WALKER

PENASEE GLOBE

Street Address: 3102 Walker Ridge Dr NW
City: Walker
State: MI
ZIP Code: 49544
General Phone: (616) 669-2700
General Email: advanceadvertising@mlive.com
Publication Website: https://www.mlivemediagroup.com/
Parent Company: Advance Publications, Inc.
Advertising Executive Email: advanceadvertising@mlive.com
Delivery Methods: Carrier
Year Established: 1884
Own Printing Facility?: Y
Commercial printers?: Y
Mechanical specifications: Type page 10 1/4 x 16; A - 6 cols, 1 1/2, 1/6 between; C - 6 cols, 1 1/2, 1/6 between.
Published Days: Sun
Avg. Free Circ.: 14000
Audit Company: Sworn/Estimate/Non-Audited
Audit Date: 43626

WALKER

SOUTHEAST ADVANCE

Street Address: 3102 Walker Ridge Dr NW
City: Walker
State: MI
ZIP Code: 49544
General Phone: (616) 669-2700
General Email: advanceadvertising@mlive.com
Publication Website: https://www.mlivemediagroup.com/
Parent Company: Advance Publications, Inc.
Advertising Executive Email: advanceadvertising@mlive.com
Delivery Methods: Carrier
Year Established: 1965
Own Printing Facility?: Y
Commercial printers?: Y
Mechanical specifications: Type page 10 3/8 x 16.
Published Days: Sun
Avg. Free Circ.: 29749
Audit Company: Sworn/Estimate/Non-Audited
Audit Date: 43626

WALKER

SOUTHWEST ADVANCE

Street Address: 3102 Walker Ridge Dr NW
City: Walker
State: MI
ZIP Code: 49544
General Phone: (616) 669-2700
General Email: advanceadvertising@mlive.com
Publication Website: https://www.mlivemediagroup.com/
Parent Company: Advance Publications, Inc.
Advertising Executive Email: advanceadvertising@mlive.com
Delivery Methods: Carrier
Year Established: 1965
Own Printing Facility?: Y
Commercial printers?: Y
Mechanical specifications: Type page 10 3/8 x 16; A - 6 cols, 1 5/8, 1/8 between.
Published Days: Sun
Avg. Free Circ.: 28705
Audit Company: Sworn/Estimate/Non-Audited
Audit Date: 43626

WEST BRANCH

OGEMAW COUNTY HERALD

Street Address: 215 W Houghton Ave
City: West Branch
State: MI
ZIP Code: 48661-1219
General Phone: (989) 345-0044
General Email: classifieds@ogemawherald.com
Publication Website: https://www.ogemawherald.com/
Parent Company: Sunrise Printing & Publishing, Inc
Publisher Name: Jenni Grezeszak
Advertising Executive Email: classifieds@ogemawherald.com
Delivery Methods: Mail˙Newsstand
Year Established: 1878
Own Printing Facility?: Y
Commercial printers?: Y
Published Days: Thur
Avg. Paid Circ.: 6700
Avg. Free Circ.: 76
Audit Company: Sworn/Estimate/Non-Audited
Audit Date: 43626

WHITEHALL

WHITE LAKE BEACON

Street Address: 432 E Spring St
City: Whitehall
State: MI
ZIP Code: 49461
General Phone: (231) 894-5356
General Email: editor@whitelakebeacon.com
Publication Website: https://www.shorelinemedia.net/white_lake_beacon/
Parent Company: Community Media Group
Editor Email: editor@whitelakebeacon.com
Advertising Executive Name: Mindy
Advertising Executive Email: mindy@whitelakebeacon.com
Delivery Methods: Mail˙Newsstand˙Carrier
Year Established: 1983
Own Printing Facility?: N
Commercial printers?: Y
Mechanical specifications: Type page 14 1/4 x 21; E - 6 cols, 2 1/4, 1/8 between; A - 6 cols, 2 1/4, 1/8 between; C - 8 cols, 1 5/8, 3/16 between.
Published Days: Sun
Avg. Paid Circ.: 4062

YALE

THE YALE EXPOSITOR

Street Address: 21 S Main St
City: Yale
State: MI
ZIP Code: 48097-3317
General Phone: (810) 387-2300
General Email: yaleexpositor@gmail.com
Publication Website: https://yaleexpositor.wixsite.com/
Publisher Name: James D. Brown
Editor Name: Barbara Brown Stasik
Advertising Executive Name: Melissa Hughes
Delivery Methods: Mail`Newsstand
Year Established: 1882
Own Printing Facility?: Y
Commercial printers?: Y
Published Days: Wed
Avg. Paid Circ.: 2500
Audit Company: Sworn/Estimate/Non-Audited
Audit Date: 43626

ZEELAND

ZEELAND RECORD

Street Address: 16 S Elm St
City: Zeeland
State: MI
ZIP Code: 49464-1751
General Phone: (616) 772-2131
General Email: kurt@zrgraphics.com
Publication Website: http://www.zrgraphics.com/
Editor Name: Kurt Van Koevering
Editor Email: kurt@zrgraphics.com
Delivery Methods: Mail
Year Established: 1893
Own Printing Facility?: Y
Commercial printers?: Y
Mechanical specifications: Type page 10 1/2 x 15; E - 5 cols, 2, 1/8 between; A - 5 cols, 2, 1/8 between; C - 5 cols, 2, 1/8 between.
Published Days: Thur
Avg. Paid Circ.: 1100
Audit Company: Sworn/Estimate/Non-Audited
Audit Date: 43626

MINNESOTA

ALEXANDRIA

ECHO-PRESS

Street Address: 225 7th Ave E
City: Alexandria
State: MN
ZIP Code: 56308
General Phone: (320) 763-3133
General Email: jhanson@echopress.com
Publication Website: https://www.echopress.com/
Parent Company: Forum Communications
Publisher Name: Jody Hanson
Publisher Email: jhanson@echopress.com
Publisher Phone: (320) 763-1222
Editor Name: Ross Evavold
Editor Email: revavold@echopress.com
Editor Phone: (320) 763-1211
Advertising Executive Name: Karen Jennissen
Advertising Executive Email: kjennissen@echopress.com

Advertising Executive Phone: (320) 763-1215
Delivery Methods: Mail`Newsstand`Carrier
Year Established: 1891
Own Printing Facility?: N
Commercial printers?: N
Published Days: Wed`Fri
Avg. Paid Circ.: 6920
Audit Company: Sworn/Estimate/Non-Audited
Audit Date: 43626

ALEXANDRIA

OSAKIS REVIEW

Street Address: PO Box 5
City: Alexandria
State: MN
ZIP Code: 56308
General Phone: (320) 859-2143
General Email: echo@echopress.com
Publication Website: https://www.theosakisreview.com/
Parent Company: Forum Communications
Publisher Name: Jody Hanson
Publisher Email: jhanson@echopress.com
Publisher Phone: (320) 763-1222
Editor Name: Al Edenloff
Editor Email: news@theosakisreview.com
Editor Phone: (320) 763-1236
Advertising Executive Name: Randy Jansen
Advertising Executive Email: rjansen@echopress.com
Advertising Executive Phone: (320) 763-1224
Delivery Methods: Mail`Carrier
Year Established: 1890
Mechanical specifications: Type page 5 x 16 1/2; E - 4 cols, 2 1/5, 1/60 between; A - 4 cols, 2 1/5, 1/60 between; C - 4 cols, 2 1/5, 1/60 between.
Published Days: Tues
Avg. Paid Circ.: 1147
Avg. Free Circ.: 28
Audit Company: Sworn/Estimate/Non-Audited
Audit Date: 43626

ANNANDALE

ANNANDALE ADVOCATE

Street Address: 73 Oak Ave S
City: Annandale
State: MN
ZIP Code: 55302-1205
General Phone: (320) 274-3052
General Email: ads@annandaleadvocate.com
Publication Website: http://annandaleadvocate.com/
Parent Company: Paw Publications LLC
Publisher Name: Michele Pawlenty
Editor Name: Tom Fenton
Advertising Executive Name: Allen Diel
Delivery Methods: Mail
Published Days: Wed
Avg. Paid Circ.: 2515
Audit Company: Sworn/Estimate/Non-Audited
Audit Date: 43626

APPLE VALLEY

THISWEEK NEWSPAPERS

Street Address: 15322 Galaxie Ave
City: Apple Valley
State: MN
ZIP Code: 55124
General Phone: (952) 894-1111
General Email: servicecenter@ecm-inc.com
Publication Website: https://www.hometownsource.com/sun_thisweek/
Editor Name: Tad Johnson
Editor Email: tad.johnson@ecm-inc.com
Editor Phone: (952) 846-2033
Advertising Executive Name: Steve Gall
Advertising Executive Email: steve.gall@ecm-inc.com
Advertising Executive Phone: (952) 392-6844
Year Established: 1884
Mechanical specifications: Type page 10 1/4 x 15; E - 4 cols, 1 5/12, 1/4 between; A - 4 cols, 1 5/12, 1/6 between; C - 6 cols, 1 7/12, 1/6 between.
Published Days: Sat
Avg. Free Circ.: 62000
Audit Company: Sworn/Estimate/Non-Audited
Audit Date: 43626

APPLETON

THE APPLETON PRESS

Street Address: 241 W Snelling Ave
City: Appleton
State: MN
ZIP Code: 56208
General Phone: (320) 289-1323
General Email: editor@appletonpress.com
Publication Website: http://www.appletonpress.com/
Parent Company: Ehrenberg Publishing, Inc.
Publisher Name: Leslie Ehrenberg
Publisher Email: editor@appletonpress.com
Editor Name: Leslie Ehrenberg
Editor Email: editor@appletonpress.com
Advertising Executive Name: April Ehrenberg
Advertising Executive Email: ads@appletonpress.com
Published Days: Wed
Avg. Paid Circ.: 2110
Audit Company: Sworn/Estimate/Non-Audited
Audit Date: 43626

ARLINGTON

ARLINGTON ENTERPRISE

Street Address: 402 W Alden St
City: Arlington
State: MN
ZIP Code: 55307
General Phone: (507) 964-5547
General Email: info@arlingtonmnnews.com
Publication Website: https://www.arlingtonmnnews.com/
Parent Company: McLeod Publishing, Inc.
Publisher Name: Karin Ramige
Editor Name: Kurt Menk
Editor Email: kurtm@arlingtonmnnews.com
Editor Phone: (507) 964-5547
Delivery Methods: Mail`Newsstand
Year Established: 1884
Published Days: Thur
Avg. Paid Circ.: 1040
Avg. Free Circ.: 400
Audit Company: Sworn/Estimate/Non-Audited
Audit Date: 43626

BAGLEY

FARMERS INDEPENDENT

Street Address: P.O. Box 130
City: Bagley
State: MN
ZIP Code: 56621
General Phone: (218) 694-6265
General Email: farmpubads@gvtel.com
Publication Website: https://www.bagleymnnews.com/
Advertising Executive Email: farmpubads@gvtel.com
Delivery Methods: Mail`Newsstand
Year Established: 1918
Own Printing Facility?: N
Commercial printers?: Y
Mechanical specifications: Type page 6 x 21 1/2; E - 6 cols, 1-5/8, 1/8 between; A - 6 cols, 1-5/8, 1/8 between; C - 6 cols, 1-5/8, 1/8 between.

Published Days: Wed
Avg. Paid Circ.: 2350
Audit Company: Sworn/Estimate/Non-Audited
Audit Date: 43626
Mailroom Equipment: label printer bundler
Mailroom Software: Satori
Business Equipment: laser and inkjet printers
Business Software: InDesign Micrsoft Word

BARNESVILLE

BARNESVILLE RECORD REVIEW

Street Address: 424 Front St S
City: Barnesville
State: MN
ZIP Code: 56514-3825
General Phone: (218) 354-2606
General Email: adsrecordreview@bvillemn.net
Publication Website: https://www.barnesvillerecordreview.net/
Parent Company: Prim Group
Editor Name: Gene Prim
Advertising Executive Email: adsrecordreview@bvillemn.net
Delivery Methods: Mail
Year Established: 1903
Published Days: Mon
Avg. Paid Circ.: 1725
Audit Company: Sworn/Estimate/Non-Audited
Audit Date: 43626

BATTLE LAKE

BATTLE LAKE REVIEW

Street Address: 114 N Lake Ave
City: Battle Lake
State: MN
ZIP Code: 56515
General Phone: (218) 864-5952
General Email: blreview@arvig.net
Publication Website: https://battlelakereview.com/
Parent Company: Ed Pawlenty
Publisher Name: Ed Pawlenty
Publisher Email: publisher@battlelakereview.com
Editor Name: Janet Widness
Editor Email: blreview@arvig.net
Year Established: 1884
Mechanical specifications: Type page 6 x 21; E - 7 cols, 2, between; A - 7 cols, 2, between; C - 7 cols, 2, between.
Published Days: Wed
Avg. Paid Circ.: 2026
Audit Company: Sworn/Estimate/Non-Audited
Audit Date: 43626

BAUDETTE

THE NORTHERN LIGHT REGION

Street Address: 420 North Main Avenue, PO Box 1132
City: Baudette
State: MN
ZIP Code: 56623
General Phone: (218) 634-2700
General Email: mikeh@wiktel.com
Publication Website: https://www.page1publications.com/
Parent Company: Page 1 Publications
Editor Name: Doris Knutson
Editor Email: norlight@wiktel.com
Editor Phone: (218) 634-2700
Advertising Executive Name: Mike Hovde
Advertising Executive Email: mikeh@wiktel.com
Advertising Executive Phone: (218) 634-2700
Delivery Methods: Mail
Mechanical specifications: Type page 6 x 20.75; E - 6 cols, 2, 1/6 between; A - 6 cols,

Community Newspapers in the U.S.

2, 1/6 between; C - 6 cols, 2, 1/6 between.
Published Days: Wed
Avg. Paid Circ.: 1415
Avg. Free Circ.: 38
Audit Company: Sworn/Estimate/Non-Audited
Audit Date: 43626

BELLE PLAINE

BELLE PLAINE HERALD

Street Address: 113 E Main St
City: Belle Plaine
State: MN
ZIP Code: 56011
General Phone: (952) 873-2261
General Email: belleplaineherald@icloud.com
Publication Website: http://www.belleplaineherald.com/
Parent Company: Belle Plaine Herald
Delivery Methods: Mail
Year Established: 1882
Published Days: Wed
Avg. Paid Circ.: 3834
Audit Company: Sworn/Estimate/Non-Audited
Audit Date: 43626

BENSON

SWIFT COUNTY MONITOR & NEWS

Street Address: 101 12th St S
City: Benson
State: MN
ZIP Code: 56215
General Phone: (320) 843-4111
General Email: ads@monitor-news.com
Publication Website: http://www.swiftcountymonitor.com/
Parent Company: Swift County Monitor-News
Delivery Methods: Mail`Carrier
Year Established: 1886
Commercial printers?: Y
Published Days: Wed
Avg. Paid Circ.: 2299
Audit Company: Sworn/Estimate/Non-Audited
Audit Date: 43626

BIG LAKE

WEST SHERBURNE TRIBUNE

Street Address: 29 Lake St S
City: Big Lake
State: MN
ZIP Code: 55309-4588
General Phone: (763) 263-3602
General Email: westrib@sherbtel.net
Publication Website: http://www.westsherburnetribune.com/
Year Established: Website can't open
Mechanical specifications: Type page: 12 x 21; 6 col
Published Days: Sat
Avg. Paid Circ.: 33
Avg. Free Circ.: 10920
Audit Company: CVC
Audit Date: 43260

BLOOMING PRAIRIE

PRAIRIE TIMES

Street Address: 411 E Main St
City: Blooming Prairie
State: MN
ZIP Code: 55917
General Phone: (507) 583-4431
General Email: bptimes@frontiernet.net
Publication Website: http://www.bloomingprairieonline.com/
Parent Company: Bussler Publishing, Inc

Delivery Methods: Mail
Published Days: Tues
Avg. Paid Circ.: 1073
Audit Company: Sworn/Estimate/Non-Audited
Audit Date: 43626

BLUE EARTH

FARIBAULT COUNTY REGISTER

Street Address: 125 N Main St
City: Blue Earth
State: MN
ZIP Code: 56013
General Phone: (507) 526-7324
General Email: lnauman@faribaultcountyregister.com
Publication Website: http://www.faribaultcountyregister.com
Parent Company: Ogden Newspapers Inc.
Publisher Name: Lori Nauman
Publisher Email: lnauman@faribaultcountyregister.com
Editor Name: Chuck Hunt
Editor Email: chunt@faribaultcountyregister.com
Advertising Executive Name: Lori Nauman
Advertising Executive Email: lnauman@faribaultcountyregister.com
Delivery Methods: Mail`Newsstand`Carrier`Racks
Year Established: 1868
Own Printing Facility?: Y
Commercial printers?: N
Published Days: Mon
Avg. Paid Circ.: 3000
Audit Company: Sworn/Estimate/Non-Audited
Audit Date: 43626

BRAINERD

ECHO JOURNAL

Street Address: 506 James St. / PO Box 974
City: Brainerd
State: MN
ZIP Code: 56401
General Phone: (218) 829-4705
Publication Website: https://www.pineandlakes.com/
Parent Company: Forum Communications
Publisher Name: Pete Mohs
Publisher Phone: (218) 855-5855
Editor Name: Nancy Vogt
Editor Phone: (218) 855-5877
Advertising Executive Name: Susie Alters
Advertising Executive Phone: (218) 855-5836
Published Days: Thur
Audit Company: Sworn/Estimate/Non-Audited
Audit Date: 43626

BRAINERD

NEWS HOPPER

Street Address: 21 Washington St
City: Brainerd
State: MN
ZIP Code: 56401
General Phone: (218) 454-4017
General Email: hopper@emily.net
Publication Website: http://www.newshopper.net/
Parent Company: NewsHopper Publications Inc.
Delivery Methods: Mail`Racks
Year Established: 2000
Mechanical specifications: Type page: 10.15 x 21.25; 6 col
Published Days: Sat
Avg. Free Circ.: 17141
Audit Company: CVC
Audit Date: 43991

BRAINERD

PINE AND LAKES ECHO JOURNAL

Street Address: 506 James St
City: Brainerd
State: MN
ZIP Code: 56401
General Phone: (218) 829-4705
Publication Website: https://www.pineandlakes.com/
Parent Company: Forum Communications
Publisher Name: Pete Mohs
Publisher Phone: (218) 855-5855
Editor Name: Nancy Vogt
Editor Phone: (218) 855-5877
Advertising Executive Name: Susie Alters
Advertising Executive Phone: (218) 855-5836
Delivery Methods: Mail`Racks
Year Established: 1935
Mechanical specifications: Type page: 10.25 x 14.75; 6 col
Published Days: Thur
Avg. Paid Circ.: 3400
Avg. Free Circ.: 52
Audit Company: Sworn/Estimate/Non-Audited
Audit Date: 43626

BROOTEN

BONANZA VALLEY VOICE

Street Address: 131 Central Ave N
City: Brooten
State: MN
ZIP Code: 56316
General Phone: (320) 346-2400
General Email: bonanzavalvoice@tds.net
Publication Website: https://www.bonanzavalleyvoice.com/
Delivery Methods: Mail`Racks
Year Established: 1969
Published Days: Thur
Avg. Paid Circ.: 1450
Audit Company: Sworn/Estimate/Non-Audited
Audit Date: 43626

BUFFALO

WRIGHT COUNTY JOURNAL-PRESS

Street Address: 108 Central Ave
City: Buffalo
State: MN
ZIP Code: 55313
General Phone: (763) 682-1221
General Email: business@thedrummer.com
Publication Website: http://www.thedrummer.com/
Editor Email: editor@thedrummer.com
Editor Phone: (763) 682-0660, ext : 22
Delivery Methods: Mail`Newsstand
Year Established: 1887
Own Printing Facility?: Y
Published Days: Thur
Avg. Paid Circ.: 5230
Audit Company: Sworn/Estimate/Non-Audited
Audit Date: 43626

CAMBRIDGE

ISANTI-CHISAGO COUNTY STAR

Street Address: 930 Cleveland St S
City: Cambridge
State: MN
ZIP Code: 55008
General Phone: (763) 698-1181
General Email: akrist@moraminn.com
Publication Website: http://www.isanti-chisagocountystar.com/
Parent Company: Northstar Media, Inc.
Publisher Name: Jeff Andres
Publisher Email: jeff@northstarmedia.net

Publisher Phone: (763) 689-1181
Editor Name: Bill Stickels
Editor Email: editor@countystar.com
Advertising Executive Name: Annette Krist
Advertising Executive Email: akrist@moraminn.com
Advertising Executive Phone: (320) 225-5124
Delivery Methods: Mail
Year Established: 1905
Own Printing Facility?: Y
Mechanical specifications: Type page 13 x 21.
Published Days: Thur
Avg. Free Circ.: 8263
Audit Company: VAC
Audit Date: 43622

CANNON FALLS

CANNON FALLS BEACON

Street Address: 120 South 4th Street, Box 366
City: Cannon Falls
State: MN
ZIP Code: 55009
General Phone: (507) 263-3991
General Email: beacon@cannonfalls.com
Publication Website: https://cannonfalls.com/
Editor Name: Dick Dalton
Editor Email: dick@cannonfalls.com
Advertising Executive Name: Dave Templin
Advertising Executive Email: dave@cannonfalls.com
Year Established: 1876
Own Printing Facility?: Y
Commercial printers?: Y
Mechanical specifications: Type page 6 x 21 1/2; E - 6 cols, 2, 1/36 between; A - 6 cols, 2, 1/36 between.
Published Days: Thur
Avg. Paid Circ.: 3900
Audit Company: Sworn/Estimate/Non-Audited
Audit Date: 43626

CASS LAKE

THE CASS LAKE TIMES

Street Address: PO Box 398
City: Cass Lake
State: MN
ZIP Code: 56633
General Phone: (218) 335-2290
General Email: cltimes1@arvig.net
Publication Website: https://www.lakeandpine.com/
Advertising Executive Name: Allan Olson
Advertising Executive Email: cltimes1@arvig.net
Advertising Executive Phone: (218) 689-7290
Delivery Methods: Mail`Newsstand
Own Printing Facility?: Y
Commercial printers?: N
Mechanical specifications: Type page 6 x 21 1/2; E - 6 cols, 1 5/8, 1/6 between; A - 6 cols, 1 5/8, 1/6 between; C - 6 cols, 1 5/8, 1/6 between.
Published Days: Thur
Avg. Paid Circ.: 1077
Avg. Free Circ.: 11
Audit Company: Sworn/Estimate/Non-Audited
Audit Date: 43626

CLARISSA

INDEPENDENT NEWS HERALD

Street Address: 310 Main St W
City: Clarissa
State: MN
ZIP Code: 56440
General Phone: (218) 756-2131
General Email: news@inhnews.com
Publication Website: https://www.inhnews.

com/
Parent Company: Benning Printing & Publishing
Publisher Name: Ray Benning
Publisher Email: ray@inhnews.com
Editor Name: Kathy Marquardt
Editor Email: kathy@inhnews.com
Advertising Executive Name: Jenny Krueger
Advertising Executive Email: ads@inhnews.com
Delivery Methods: Mail
Own Printing Facility?: Y
Commercial printers?: Y
Mechanical specifications: Type page 6x 21 1/2; E - 6 cols, 2, between; A - 6 cols, 2, between; C - 6 cols, 2, between.
Published Days: Tues
Avg. Paid Circ.: 2375
Avg. Free Circ.: 92
Audit Company: Sworn/Estimate/Non-Audited
Audit Date: 43626

COLD SPRING

COLD SPRING RECORD

Street Address: 403 Westwind Ct
City: Cold Spring
State: MN
ZIP Code: 56320
General Phone: (320) 685-8621
General Email: csrecord@midconetwork.com
Publication Website: http://csrecord.net/
Delivery Methods: Mail
Year Established: 1899
Own Printing Facility?: N
Commercial printers?: Y
Published Days: Tues
Avg. Paid Circ.: 3400
Avg. Free Circ.: 12
Audit Company: Sworn/Estimate/Non-Audited
Audit Date: 43626

COON RAPIDS

COON RAPIDS HERALD

Street Address: 4095 Coon Rapids Blvd.
City: Coon Rapids
State: MN
ZIP Code: 55433
General Phone: (763) 421-4444
General Email: servicecenter@ecm-inc.com
Publication Website: https://www.hometownsource.com/
Editor Name: Jonathan Young
Editor Email: jonathan.young@ecm-inc.com
Editor Phone: (763) 712-3514
Advertising Executive Name: Jeremy Bradfield
Advertising Executive Email: jeremy.bradfield@ecm-inc.com
Advertising Executive Phone: (952) 392-6841
Delivery Methods: Mail
Year Established: 1875
Own Printing Facility?: Y
Commercial printers?: Y
Mechanical specifications: Type page 10 x 21; E - 6 cols, 1 3/4, 1/8 between; A - 6 cols, 1 3/4, 1/8 between; C - 8 cols, 1 1/2, 1/8 between.
Published Days: Fri
Avg. Paid Circ.: 2650
Avg. Free Circ.: 76
Audit Company: Sworn/Estimate/Non-Audited
Audit Date: 43626

CROSSLAKE

NORTHLAND PRESS

Street Address: 13833 Riverwood Lane, Suite #2
City: Crosslake
State: MN
ZIP Code: 56442-2823
General Phone: (218) 692-5842
General Email: news@northlandpress.com
Publication Website: http://www.northlandpress.com/
Parent Company: Boblett Family
Publisher Name: Joanne Boblett
Editor Name: Paul Boblett
Delivery Methods: Mail
Year Established: 2005
Mechanical specifications: Type page 11.75 x 20.5; 6 col
Published Days: Tues
Avg. Free Circ.: 5331
Audit Company: CVC
Audit Date: 43991

DELANO

DELANO HERALD JOURNAL

Street Address: 127 Bridge Ave E
City: Delano
State: MN
ZIP Code: 55328
General Phone: (763) 972-1028
General Email: delano@heraldjournal.com
Publication Website: https://www.delanoheraldjournal.com/
Parent Company: Herald Journal Publishing
Publisher Name: Chris Schultz
Publisher Email: cschultz@heraldjournal.com
Publisher Phone: (320) 485-2535
Editor Name: Gabe Licht
Editor Email: glicht@heraldjournal.com
Editor Phone: (763) 972-1028
Delivery Methods: Mail`Newsstand
Year Established: 2006
Mechanical specifications: 6 col x 21.5"
Published Days: Fri
Avg. Paid Circ.: 1800
Audit Company: Sworn/Estimate/Non-Audited
Audit Date: 43626

DETROIT LAKES

DETROIT LAKES TRIBUNE

Street Address: 511 Washington Ave
City: Detroit Lakes
State: MN
ZIP Code: 56501
General Phone: (218) 847-3151
General Email: mswenson@dlnewspapers.com
Publication Website: https://www.dl-online.com/
Parent Company: Forum Communications
Publisher Name: Melissa Swenson
Publisher Email: mswenson@dlnewspapers.com
Publisher Phone: (218) 844-1451
Editor Name: J.J. Perry
Editor Email: jperry@dlnewspapers.com
Editor Phone: (218) 844-1466
Advertising Executive Name: Melissa Swenson
Advertising Executive Email: mswenson@dlnewspapers.com
Advertising Executive Phone: (218) 844-1451
Delivery Methods: Mail`Carrier
Published Days: Wed`Sun
Avg. Paid Circ.: 3400
Avg. Free Circ.: 59
Audit Company: VAC
Audit Date: 43619

DETROIT LAKES

LAKE AREA PRESS

Street Address: 511 Washington Ave
City: Detroit Lakes
State: MN
ZIP Code: 56501
General Phone: (218) 847-3151
General Email: mswenson@dlnewspapers.com
Publication Website: https://www.dl-online.com/
Parent Company: Forum Communications
Publisher Name: Melissa Swenson
Publisher Email: mswenson@dlnewspapers.com
Publisher Phone: (218) 844-1451
Editor Name: J.J. Perry
Editor Email: jperry@dlnewspapers.com
Editor Phone: (218) 844-1466
Advertising Executive Name: Melissa Swenson
Advertising Executive Email: mswenson@dlnewspapers.com
Advertising Executive Phone: (218) 844-1451
Delivery Methods: Mail`Carrier
Published Days: Sat
Avg. Free Circ.: 9958
Audit Company: VAC
Audit Date: 43619

DETROIT LAKES

THE DETROIT LAKES TRIBUNE

Street Address: 511 Washington Ave
City: Detroit Lakes
State: MN
ZIP Code: 56501
General Phone: (218) 847-3151
General Email: mswenson@dlnewspapers.com
Publication Website: https://www.dl-online.com/
Parent Company: Forum Communications
Publisher Name: Melissa Swenson
Publisher Email: mswenson@dlnewspapers.com
Publisher Phone: (218) 844-1451
Editor Name: J.J. Perry
Editor Email: jperry@dlnewspapers.com
Editor Phone: (218) 844-1466
Advertising Executive Name: Melissa Swenson
Advertising Executive Email: mswenson@dlnewspapers.com
Advertising Executive Phone: (218) 844-1451
Delivery Methods: Mail`Carrier
Own Printing Facility?: Y
Commercial printers?: Y
Published Days: Wed
Avg. Paid Circ.: 3584
Avg. Free Circ.: 94
Audit Company: Sworn/Estimate/Non-Audited
Audit Date: 43626

DULUTH

DULUTH BUDGETEER NEWS

Street Address: 424 W 1st St
City: Duluth
State: MN
ZIP Code: 55802
General Phone: (218) 723-5281
General Email: news@duluthnews.com
Publication Website: http://www.duluthnewstribune.com/
Parent Company: Forum Communications
Publisher Name: Neal Ronquist
Publisher Email: nronquist@duluthnews.com
Publisher Phone: (218) 723-5235
Editor Name: Katie Rohman
Editor Email: krohman@duluthnews.com
Editor Phone: (218) 723-5334
Advertising Executive Name: James Erickson
Advertising Executive Phone: (218) 720-4105
Delivery Methods: Carrier
Year Established: 1931
Published Days: Sun
Avg. Free Circ.: 21606
Audit Company: Sworn/Estimate/Non-Audited
Audit Date: 43626

DULUTH

DULUTH-ZENITH NEWS

Street Address: PO Box 3280
City: Duluth
State: MN
ZIP Code: 55803
General Phone: (218) 940-3132
General Email: zenithcityweekly@yahoo.com
Publication Website: https://www.zenithcitynews.com/
Publisher Name: Taylor Martin-Romme
Editor Name: Jennifer Martin-Romme
Year Established: 2007
Published Days: Tues
Published Other: Every three weeks
Avg. Free Circ.: 11000
Audit Company: Sworn/Estimate/Non-Audited
Audit Date: 43626

DULUTH

SUPERIOR TELEGRAM

Street Address: 424 W. First St.
City: Duluth
State: MN
ZIP Code: 55802
General Phone: (715) 395-5000
General Email: eolson@duluthnews.com
Publication Website: https://www.superiortelegram.com/
Parent Company: Forum Communications
Publisher Name: Neal Ronquist
Publisher Email: nronquist@duluthnews.com
Publisher Phone: (218) 723-5235
Editor Name: Jen Zettel-Vandenhouten
Editor Email: jzvandenhouten@duluthnews.com
Editor Phone: (218) 720-4102
Advertising Executive Name: Eric Olson
Advertising Executive Email: eolson@duluthnews.com
Advertising Executive Phone: (218) 720-4101
Delivery Methods: Mail`Newsstand`Carrier`Racks
Mechanical specifications: Type page 12 1/2 x 21 1/2; E - 6 cols, 2 1/16, 1/8 between; A - 6 cols, 2 1/16, 1/8 between; C - 9 cols, 1 3/8, 1/16 between.
Published Days: Tues`Fri
Weekday Frequency: e
Saturday Frequency: m
Avg. Paid Circ.: 4456
Audit Company: Sworn/Estimate/Non-Audited
Audit Date: 43626
Pressroom Equipment: Lines -- 5-G/Urbanite 1972.;
Mailroom Equipment: Counter Stackers -- Id; Inserters & Stuffers -- AM Graphics/848; Tying Machines -- EAM-Mosca, Dynaric; Control System -- HI/148NC; Address Machine -- Dispensa-Matic.;
Business Equipment: Vision Data, 10-PC
Business Software: Vision Data
Classified Equipment: Hardware -- DP, Cx, APP/Mac OS; Printers -- TI/820, QMS/LaserWriter;
Classified Software: DP, Cx, Baseview.
Editorial Equipment: Hardware -- DP, Cx, APP/Mac OS; Printers -- Okidata, QMS/8000S LaserJet
Editorial Software: DP, Cx, APP/Mac OS 5.0.
Production Equipment: Hardware -- 1-Nu, Nat/250-A, MON/ImageMaster 1000; Cameras -- R, R/with Carlson Exposure; Scanners -- ECR/Autokon, Umax/Astra 1200S, Umax/Vista 563, Autokon/1000 DE
Production Software: Baseview.

DULUTH

THE PINE JOURNAL

Street Address: 424 W 1st St
City: Duluth
State: MN
ZIP Code: 55802
General Phone: (218) 879-1950
General Email: news@pinejournal.com
Publication Website: http://www.pinejournal.com/
Parent Company: Forum Communications
Publisher Name: Neal Ronquist
Publisher Email: nronquist@duluthnews.com
Publisher Phone: (218) 723-5235
Editor Name: Rick Lubbers
Editor Email: rlubbers@duluthnews.com
Editor Phone: (218) 723-5301
Advertising Executive Name: Eric Olson
Advertising Executive Email: eolson@duluthnews.com
Advertising Executive Phone: (218) 720-4101
Year Established: 1884
Mechanical specifications: Type page 6x 21; E - 6 cols, 1 5/6, 1/6 between; A - 6 cols, 2, between; C - 6 cols, 1 5/6, 1/6 between.
Published Days: Wed
Avg. Paid Circ.: 4471
Audit Company: Sworn/Estimate/Non-Audited
Audit Date: 43626

EAST GRAND FORKS

THE EXPONENT

Street Address: 207 2nd Ave NE
City: East Grand Forks
State: MN
ZIP Code: 56721
General Phone: (218) 773-2808
General Email: exponent@page1publications.com
Publication Website: https://www.page1publications.com/
Parent Company: Page 1 Publications
Editor Name: Bruce Brierley
Editor Email: bruce@page1publications.com
Editor Phone: (218) 773-2808
Advertising Executive Name: Linda Forseide
Advertising Executive Email: designteam@page1publications.com
Advertising Executive Phone: (218) 773-2808
Published Days: Wed
Avg. Paid Circ.: 1343
Audit Company: Sworn/Estimate/Non-Audited
Audit Date: 43626

EDGERTON

EDGERTON ENTERPRISE

Street Address: 831 MAIN ST
City: Edgerton
State: MN
ZIP Code: 56128
General Phone: (507) 442-6161
General Email: edgent@iw.net
Publication Website: http://edgertonenterprise.com/
Publisher Name: Jill Fennema
Editor Name: Jill Fennema
Delivery Methods: Mail
Year Established: 1883
Mechanical specifications: Type page 6 x 21 1/2; E - 7 cols, 2 1/16, 3/16 between; A - 7 cols, 2 1/16, 3/16 between; C - 7 cols, 2 1/16, 3/16 between.
Published Days: Wed
Avg. Paid Circ.: 1679
Audit Company: Sworn/Estimate/Non-Audited
Audit Date: 43626

ELY

THE ELY ECHO

Street Address: 15 E Chapman St
City: Ely
State: MN
ZIP Code: 55731
General Phone: (218) 365-3141
General Email: thepub@elyecho.com
Publication Website: http://elyecho.com/
Parent Company: Nick Wognum
Publisher Name: Nick Wognum
Publisher Email: elyecho@aol.com
Editor Name: Tom Coombe
Editor Email: tcoombe@aol.com
Advertising Executive Name: Lisa Vidal
Advertising Executive Email: ads@elyecho.com
Delivery Methods: Mail Newsstand Racks
Year Established: 1972
Own Printing Facility?: Y
Commercial printers?: Y
Mechanical specifications: Type page 6 x 19; E - 6 cols, 1.59, 1/6 between
Published Days: Sat
Avg. Paid Circ.: 3329
Avg. Free Circ.: 32
Audit Company: Sworn/Estimate/Non-Audited
Audit Date: 43626

FAIRFAX

FAIRFAX STANDARD GAZETTE

Street Address: 102 SE First St.
City: Fairfax
State: MN
ZIP Code: 55332
General Phone: (507) 426-7235
General Email: fxstandardnews@gmail.com
Publication Website: http://standard-gazette.com/
Parent Company: D&D Publications LLC
Publisher Name: Dave Bonsack
Publisher Email: fxstandardnews@gmail.com
Editor Name: Dave Bonsack
Editor Email: fxstandardnews@gmail.com
Advertising Executive Name: Dave Bonsack
Advertising Executive Email: fxstandardnews@gmail.com
Year Established: 2000
Mechanical specifications: Type page 6 x 21 1/2; E - 7 cols, 2, 1/4 between; A - 7 cols, 2, 1/4 between; C - 7 cols, 2, 1/4 between.
Published Days: Wed
Avg. Paid Circ.: 1423
Audit Company: Sworn/Estimate/Non-Audited
Audit Date: 43626

FOLEY

BENTON COUNTY NEWS

Street Address: 1061 Hwy 23
City: Foley
State: MN
ZIP Code: 56329
General Phone: (320) 968-7220
General Email: natasha@saukherald.com
Publication Website: https://www.bentonconews.com/
Parent Company: Star Publications
Editor Name: Natasha Barber
Editor Email: natasha@saukherald.com
Advertising Executive Name: Daisy Perez
Advertising Executive Email: daisy.p@starpub.com
Delivery Methods: Mail Racks
Year Established: 1932
Published Days: Tues
Avg. Paid Circ.: 1300
Audit Company: Sworn/Estimate/Non-Audited
Audit Date: 43626

FOSSTON

THE THIRTEEN TOWNS

Street Address: 118 Johnson Ave N
City: Fosston
State: MN
ZIP Code: 56542
General Phone: (218) 435-1313
General Email: 13towns@gvtel.com
Publication Website: https://www.13towns.com/
Parent Company: Thirteen Towns of Fosston
Delivery Methods: Mail Newsstand Racks
Year Established: 1884
Commercial printers?: Y
Published Days: Tues
Avg. Paid Circ.: 1600
Audit Company: Sworn/Estimate/Non-Audited
Audit Date: 43626

FRAZEE

FRAZEE-VERGAS FORUM

Street Address: 112 W Main Ave
City: Frazee
State: MN
ZIP Code: 56544
General Phone: (218) 334-3566
General Email: fforum@loretel.net
Publication Website: http://www.frazeeforum.com/
Delivery Methods: Mail Newsstand
Year Established: 1960
Commercial printers?: Y
Mechanical specifications: Type page 6 x 21 1/2; E - 6 cols, 2, between; A - 6 cols, 2, between; C - 6 cols, 2, between.
Published Days: Thur
Published Other: Weekly
Avg. Paid Circ.: 1750
Avg. Free Circ.: 25
Audit Company: Sworn/Estimate/Non-Audited
Audit Date: 43626

FULDA

FULDA FREE PRESS

Street Address: 118 N St Paul Ave
City: Fulda
State: MN
ZIP Code: 56131
General Phone: (507) 425-2303
General Email: photo@fuldafreepress.net
Publication Website: http://www.fuldafreepress.net/
Delivery Methods: Mail
Year Established: 1879
Published Days: Wed
Avg. Paid Circ.: 1148
Audit Company: Sworn/Estimate/Non-Audited
Audit Date: 43626

GLENCOE

THE MCLEOD COUNTY CHRONICLE

Street Address: 716 E. 10th St.
City: Glencoe
State: MN
ZIP Code: 55336-2212
General Phone: (320) 864-5518
General Email: brendaf@glencoenews.com
Publication Website: http://www.glencoenews.com/
Parent Company: McLeod Publishing, Inc
Publisher Name: Karin Ramige
Publisher Email: karinr@glencoenews.com
Editor Name: John Mueller
Editor Email: johnm@glencoenews.com
Advertising Executive Name: Brenda Fogarty
Advertising Executive Email: brendaf@glencoenews.com
Delivery Methods: Mail
Mechanical specifications: Type page 13 x 21 1/2; E - 6 cols, 2, 1/4 between; A - 6 cols, 2, 1/4 between; C - 6 cols, 2, 1/4 between.
Published Days: Wed
Avg. Paid Circ.: 3367
Avg. Free Circ.: 50
Audit Company: Sworn/Estimate/Non-Audited
Audit Date: 43626

GLENWOOD

POPE COUNTY TRIBUNE

Street Address: 14 1st Ave SE
City: Glenwood
State: MN
ZIP Code: 56334
General Phone: (320) 634-4571
General Email: news@pctribune.com
Publication Website: https://pctribune.com/
Parent Company: Pope County Press, Inc.
Publisher Name: Tim Douglass
Publisher Email: tdouglass@pctribune.com
Publisher Phone: (320) 634-4571
Editor Name: Tim Douglass
Editor Email: tdouglass@pctribune.com
Editor Phone: (320) 634-4571
Advertising Executive Name: Erika Andreas
Advertising Executive Email: locals@pctribune.com
Advertising Executive Phone: (320) 634-4571
Delivery Methods: Mail Newsstand Racks
Year Established: 1920
Own Printing Facility?: Y
Commercial printers?: Y
Mechanical specifications: Type page 6 x 21 1/2; E - 6 cols, 2 1/4, 1/6 between; A - 6 cols, 2 1/4, 1/6 between; C - 6 cols, 2 1/4, 1/6 between.
Published Days: Mon
Avg. Paid Circ.: 3200
Audit Company: Sworn/Estimate/Non-Audited
Audit Date: 43626

GLENWOOD

THE STARBUCK TIMES

Street Address: 14 1st Ave SE
City: Glenwood
State: MN
ZIP Code: 56334-1621
General Phone: (320) 239-2244
General Email: ads@pctribune.com
Publication Website: http://pctribune.com/starbuck.php
Parent Company: Pope County Press, Inc
Publisher Name: Tim Douglass
Publisher Email: tdouglass@pctribune.com
Publisher Phone: (320) 634-4571
Editor Name: Zach Anderson
Editor Email: news.times@hcinet.net
Editor Phone: (320) 239-2244
Advertising Executive Name: Erika Andreas
Advertising Executive Email: locals@pctribune.com
Advertising Executive Phone: (320) 634-4571
Mechanical specifications: Type page 6 x 21 1/2; E - 6 cols, 2 1/4, 1/8 between; A - 6 cols, 2 1/4, 1/8 between; C - 6 cols, 2 1/4, 1/8 between.
Published Days: Tues
Avg. Paid Circ.: 1320
Audit Company: Sworn/Estimate/Non-Audited
Audit Date: 43626

GONVICK

LEADER RECORD

Street Address: 239 2ND AVE
City: Gonvick
State: MN
ZIP Code: 56644
General Phone: (218) 487-5225
General Email: richards@gvtel.com
Publication Website: http://www.tricocanary.com/leader-record

Parent Company: Richards Publishing
Publisher Name: Richard D. Richards
Publisher Email: richards@gvtel.com
Editor Name: Corrine Richards
Own Printing Facility?: Y
Commercial printers?: Y
Published Days: Wed
Avg. Paid Circ.: 1535
Audit Company: Sworn/Estimate/Non-Audited
Audit Date: 43626

GRAND MARAIS

COOK COUNTY NEWS-HERALD

Street Address: 15 1st Ave W
City: Grand Marais
State: MN
ZIP Code: 55604
General Phone: (218) 387-1025
General Email: star@boreal.org
Publication Website: https://www.cookcountynews-herald.com/
Parent Company: Hal & Deidre Kettunen
Publisher Name: Deidre Kettunen
Editor Name: Brian Larson
Advertising Executive Name: Laurie Johnson
Delivery Methods: Mail
Year Established: 1881
Published Days: Sat
Avg. Paid Circ.: 4010
Avg. Free Circ.: 66
Audit Company: Sworn/Estimate/Non-Audited
Audit Date: 43626

GRAND RAPIDS

GRAND RAPIDS HERALD-REVIEW

Street Address: 301 NW 1st Ave
City: Grand Rapids
State: MN
ZIP Code: 55744
General Phone: (218) 326-6623
General Email: webmaster@grandrapidsheraldreview.net
Publication Website: https://www.grandrapidsmn.com/
Parent Company: Adams Publishing Group
Publisher Name: Mark Roy
Publisher Email: mroy@grandrapidsheraldreview.net
Editor Name: Britta Arendt
Editor Email: barendt@grandrapidsheraldreview.net
Advertising Executive Name: Andrew Nintzel
Advertising Executive Email: anintzel@grandrapidsheraldreview.net
Delivery Methods: Mail Newsstand Carrier
Year Established: 1894
Own Printing Facility?: Y
Commercial printers?: Y
Published Days: Wed Sun
Avg. Paid Circ.: 7883
Audit Company: Sworn/Estimate/Non-Audited
Audit Date: 43626

GRANITE FALLS

GRANITE FALLS-CLARKFIELD ADVOCATE-TRIBUNE

Street Address: 713 Prentice St
City: Granite Falls
State: MN
ZIP Code: 56241
General Phone: (320) 564-2126
General Email: kklausing@granitefallsnews.com
Publication Website: https://www.granitefallsnews.com/
Editor Name: Kyle Klausing
Editor Email: kklausing@granitefallsnews.com
Advertising Executive Name: Bev Sommervold
Advertising Executive Email: bsommervold@granitefallsnews.com
Own Printing Facility?: Y
Published Days: Thur
Avg. Paid Circ.: 2108
Audit Company: Sworn/Estimate/Non-Audited
Audit Date: 43626

GREENBUSH

TRIBUNE

Street Address: 192 Hill St.
City: Greenbush
State: MN
ZIP Code: 56726
General Phone: (218) 782-2275
General Email: tribune@wiktel.com
Publication Website: https://www.page1publications.com/
Parent Company: AIM Media
Delivery Methods: Mail
Published Days: Wed
Avg. Paid Circ.: 986
Audit Company: Sworn/Estimate/Non-Audited
Audit Date: 43626

GRYGLA

THE GRYGLA EAGLE

Street Address: 127 N Main Ave.
City: Grygla
State: MN
ZIP Code: 56727
General Phone: (218) 294-6220
General Email: grygla.eagle@gmail.com
Publication Website: http://www.tricocanary.com/grygla-eagle
Parent Company: Richards Publishing
Publisher Name: Richard D. Richards
Editor Name: Kari Sundberg
Own Printing Facility?: Y
Commercial printers?: Y
Published Days: Wed
Avg. Paid Circ.: 700
Audit Company: Sworn/Estimate/Non-Audited
Audit Date: 43626

HALLOCK

KITTSON COUNTY ENTERPRISE

Street Address: 118 2nd St S
City: Hallock
State: MN
ZIP Code: 56728
General Phone: (218) 843-2868
General Email: kce@wiktel.com
Publication Website: https://www.kittsonarea.com/
Publisher Name: Myrna Moore
Editor Name: Margie Holmgren
Editor Email: kce@wiktel.com
Advertising Executive Name: Margie Holmgren
Advertising Executive Email: kce@wiktel.com
Delivery Methods: Mail Newsstand
Year Established: 1881
Own Printing Facility?: Y
Commercial printers?: Y
Mechanical specifications: Type page 13 x 21.
Published Days: Wed
Avg. Paid Circ.: 1000
Audit Company: Sworn/Estimate/Non-Audited
Audit Date: 43626

HASTINGS

WOODBURY BULLETIN

Street Address: PO Box 277
City: Hastings
State: MN
ZIP Code: 55033-0277
General Phone: (651) 319-4270
General Email: sengelhart@woodburybulletin.com
Publication Website: https://www.rivertowns.net/tags/THE_BULLETIN
Parent Company: Forum Communications
Publisher Name: Neal Ronquist
Publisher Email: nronquist@rivertowns.net
Publisher Phone: (651) 301-7855
Editor Name: Jake Pfeifer
Editor Email: jpfeifer@rivertowns.net
Editor Phone: (651) 301-7880
Advertising Executive Name: Megan Keller
Advertising Executive Email: mkeller@rivertowns.net
Advertising Executive Phone: (651) 301-7801
Delivery Methods: Mail Carrier
Own Printing Facility?: Y
Commercial printers?: Y
Mechanical specifications: Type page 6 x 21 1/2; E - 6 cols, 2 1/16, 1/16 between; A - 6 cols, 2 1/16, 1/16 between; C - 8 cols, 1 1/2, 1/16 between.
Published Days: Wed
Avg. Free Circ.: 4892
Audit Company: Sworn/Estimate/Non-Audited
Audit Date: 43626

HAWLEY

THE HAWLEY HERALD

Street Address: PO Box 709
City: Hawley
State: MN
ZIP Code: 56549
General Phone: (218) 483-3306
General Email: ads@hawleyherald.net
Publication Website: https://www.hawleyherald.net/
Editor Name: Marc Ness
Editor Email: marc@hawleyherald.net
Advertising Executive Name: Melissa Stock
Advertising Executive Email: ads@hawleyherald.net
Delivery Methods: Mail
Year Established: 1927
Published Days: Mon
Avg. Paid Circ.: 1712
Audit Company: Sworn/Estimate/Non-Audited
Audit Date: 43626

HENNING

CITIZEN'S ADVOCATE

Street Address: 412 Douglas Ave
City: Henning
State: MN
ZIP Code: 56551
General Phone: (218) 548-5585
General Email: news@henningadvocate.com
Publication Website: https://www.henningadvocate.com
Parent Company: Henning Publications, LLC
Publisher Name: Chad Koenen
Publisher Email: chad@henningadvocate.com
Delivery Methods: Mail Newsstand
Year Established: 1891
Published Days: Tues
Avg. Paid Circ.: 910
Avg. Free Circ.: 27
Audit Company: Sworn/Estimate/Non-Audited
Audit Date: 43626

HINCKLEY

HINCKLEY NEWS

Street Address: 115 Main St E
City: Hinckley
State: MN
ZIP Code: 55037-8763
General Phone: (320) 384-6188
General Email: hinckleynews@scicable.com
Publication Website: https://www.hinckleynews.com/
Parent Company: Franklin Newspapers Inc.
Delivery Methods: Mail Newsstand Racks
Year Established: 1891
Commercial printers?: Y
Mechanical specifications: Type page 6 x 21 1/2; E - 7 cols, 2, 1/4 between; A - 7 cols, 2, 1/4 between; C - 7 cols, 2, 1/4 between.
Published Days: Thur
Avg. Paid Circ.: 1600
Audit Company: Sworn/Estimate/Non-Audited
Audit Date: 43626

KARLSTAD

NORTH STAR NEWS

Street Address: 204 Main St S
City: Karlstad
State: MN
ZIP Code: 56732
General Phone: (218) 436-2157
General Email: nsads@wiktel.com
Publication Website: https://www.page1publications.com/
Parent Company: Page 1 Publications
Editor Name: Gretchen Baker
Editor Email: nsads@wiktel.com
Editor Phone: (218) 436-2157
Year Established: 1904
Commercial printers?: Y
Published Days: Thur
Avg. Paid Circ.: 1490
Audit Company: Sworn/Estimate/Non-Audited
Audit Date: 43626

LAFAYETTE

LAFAYETTE NICOLLET LEDGER

Street Address: 766 Main Avenue, PO Box 212
City: Lafayette
State: MN
ZIP Code: 56054
General Phone: (507) 228-8985
General Email: ledger@prairiepublishingmn.com
Publication Website: https://www.prairiepublishingmn.com/lafayette-nicollet-ledger-public-notices/
Parent Company: Prairie Publishing, Inc
Delivery Methods: Mail
Year Established: 1904
Published Days: Thur
Avg. Paid Circ.: 1263
Avg. Free Circ.: 11
Audit Company: Sworn/Estimate/Non-Audited
Audit Date: 43626

LAKEFIELD

LAKEFIELD STANDARD

Street Address: 403 Main St
City: Lakefield
State: MN
ZIP Code: 56150
General Phone: (507) 662-5555
General Email: standard@livewireprinting.com
Publication Website: https://www.lakefieldstandard.com/
Publisher Name: Justin R. Lessman
Publisher Email: justin@livewireprinting.com
Delivery Methods: Mail
Published Days: Thur
Avg. Paid Circ.: 1055

Community Newspapers in the U.S.

III-283

Avg. Free Circ.: 41
Audit Company: Sworn/Estimate/Non-Audited
Audit Date: 43626

LAMBERTON

LAMBERTON NEWS

Street Address: 218 S Main St
City: Lamberton
State: MN
ZIP Code: 56152-1389
General Phone: (507) 752-7181
Publication Website: https://lambertonmn.com/
Year Established: 1923
Mechanical specifications: Type page 6 x 21 1/4; E - 6 cols, 2, 1/6 between; A - 6 cols, 2, 1/6 between.
Published Days: Wed
Avg. Paid Circ.: 1700
Avg. Free Circ.: 4
Audit Company: Sworn/Estimate/Non-Audited
Audit Date: 43626

LINDSTROM

CHISAGO COUNTY PRESS

Street Address: 12631 Lake Blvd
City: Lindstrom
State: MN
ZIP Code: 55045-9344
General Phone: (651) 257-5115
General Email: chisago@citlink.net
Publication Website: https://chisagocountypress.com/
Publisher Name: Matt Silver
Editor Name: Denise Martin
Delivery Methods: Mail`Newsstand
Year Established: 1898
Own Printing Facility?: Y
Commercial printers?: N
Mechanical specifications: Type page 6 x 21 1/2; E - 6 cols, 2 1/16, 1/6 between; A - 6 cols, 2 1/16, 1/6 between; C - 6 cols, 2 1/16, 1/6 between.
Published Days: Thur
Avg. Paid Circ.: 3413
Avg. Free Circ.: 115
Audit Company: Sworn/Estimate/Non-Audited
Audit Date: 43626

LITCHFIELD

INDEPENDENT REVIEW

Street Address: 217 N Sibley Ave
City: Litchfield
State: MN
ZIP Code: 55355-2140
General Phone: (320) 693-3266
General Email: news@independentreview.net
Publication Website: https://crowrivermedia.com/independentreview/
Parent Company: Crow River Media
Publisher Name: Brent Schacherer
Publisher Email: schacherer@hutchinsonleader.com
Publisher Phone: (320) 693-3266
Advertising Executive Name: Kevin True
Advertising Executive Email: true@hutchinsonleader.com
Advertising Executive Phone: (320) 753-3649
Mechanical specifications: Type page 6 x 21 1/2; E - 8 cols, 1 3/4, between; A - 8 cols, 1 3/4, between; C - 8 cols, 1 3/4, between.
Published Days: Thur`Sun
Avg. Paid Circ.: 2659
Avg. Free Circ.: 11
Audit Company: Sworn/Estimate/Non-Audited
Audit Date: 43626

LONG PRAIRIE

THE LONG PRAIRIE LEADER

Street Address: 21 3rd St S
City: Long Prairie
State: MN
ZIP Code: 56347-1195
General Phone: (320) 732-2151
General Email: news@lpleader.com
Publication Website: http://www.lpleader.com/
Publisher Name: Jason C. Brown
Publisher Email: news@lpleader.com
Editor Name: Jason C. Brown
Editor Email: news@lpleader.com
Advertising Executive Name: Susan Lubbers
Advertising Executive Email: advertising@lpleader.com
Delivery Methods: Mail
Year Established: 1883
Published Days: Wed
Avg. Paid Circ.: 2392
Audit Company: Sworn/Estimate/Non-Audited
Audit Date: 43626

LONGVILLE

PINE CONE PRESS CITIZEN

Street Address: P.O Box 401
City: Longville
State: MN
ZIP Code: 56655
General Phone: (218) 363-2002
General Email: presscit@eot.com
Publication Website: https://pineconepresscitizen.com/main.asp?SectionID=11
Publisher Name: Dave Delost
Editor Name: Dave Delost
Delivery Methods: Mail`Newsstand
Year Established: 1984
Own Printing Facility?: Y
Commercial printers?: N
Published Days: Tues
Avg. Paid Circ.: 250
Avg. Free Circ.: 6986
Audit Company: Sworn/Estimate/Non-Audited
Audit Date: 43626

LUVERNE

HILLS CRESCENT

Street Address: 117 W Main St
City: Luverne
State: MN
ZIP Code: 56156-1843
General Phone: (507) 283-2333
General Email: editor@star-herald.com
Publication Website: http://www.star-herald.com/crescent
Publisher Name: Rick Peterson
Publisher Email: rick@star-herald.com
Editor Name: Glenda Mcgaffee
Editor Email: hceditor@star-herald.com
Advertising Executive Name: Chantel Connell
Delivery Methods: Mail
Own Printing Facility?: Y
Commercial printers?: Y
Published Days: Thur
Avg. Paid Circ.: 394
Audit Company: Sworn/Estimate/Non-Audited
Audit Date: 43626

LUVERNE

THE ROCK COUNTY STAR HERALD

Street Address: 117 W Main St
City: Luverne
State: MN
ZIP Code: 56156-1843
General Phone: (507) 283-2333
General Email: editor@star-herald.com
Publication Website: http://www.star-herald.com/
Parent Company: Tollefson Publishing
Publisher Name: Rick Peterson
Publisher Email: rick@star-herald.com
Editor Name: Lori Ehde
Editor Email: editor@star-herald.com
Advertising Executive Name: Chantel Connell
Advertising Executive Email: sales@star-herald.com
Delivery Methods: Mail
Year Established: 1940
Published Days: Thur
Avg. Paid Circ.: 2300
Audit Company: Sworn/Estimate/Non-Audited
Audit Date: 43626

MADELIA

MADELIA TIMES-MESSENGER

Street Address: 112 W Main St
City: Madelia
State: MN
ZIP Code: 56062-1440
General Phone: (507) 642-3636
General Email: michelle@tmpuregold.com
Publication Website: https://www.prairiepublishingmn.com/
Parent Company: Prairie Publishing, Inc
Delivery Methods: Mail
Year Established: 1871
Published Days: Thur
Avg. Paid Circ.: 875
Avg. Free Circ.: 16
Audit Company: Sworn/Estimate/Non-Audited
Audit Date: 43626

MADELIA

THE HANSKA HERALD

Street Address: 112 W Main St
City: Madelia
State: MN
ZIP Code: 56062-1440
General Phone: (507) 642-3636
General Email: michelle@tmpuregold.com
Publication Website: https://www.prairiepublishingmn.com/
Parent Company: Prairie Publishing, Inc
Delivery Methods: Mail
Mechanical specifications: Type page 6 x 21; E - 7 cols, 2 1/16, 1/6 between; A - 7 cols, 2 1/16, 1/6 between; C - 11 cols, 2 1/16, 1/6 between.
Published Days: Thur
Avg. Paid Circ.: 349
Audit Company: Sworn/Estimate/Non-Audited
Audit Date: 43626

MADISON

THE WESTERN GUARD

Street Address: 216 6th Ave
City: Madison
State: MN
ZIP Code: 56256-1309
General Phone: (320) 598-7521
General Email: news.thewesternguard@gmail.com
Publication Website: https://www.thewesternguardnews.com/
Parent Company: RBM News
Publisher Name: Adam Conroy
Editor Name: Tricia Groenhoff
Delivery Methods: Mail`Newsstand`Racks
Year Established: 1891
Commercial printers?: Y
Published Days: Tues

Avg. Paid Circ.: 1691
Avg. Free Circ.: 15
Audit Company: Sworn/Estimate/Non-Audited
Audit Date: 43626

MAHNOMEN

THE MAHNOMEN PIONEER

Street Address: 207 North Main Street
City: Mahnomen
State: MN
ZIP Code: 56557
General Phone: (218) 935-5296
General Email: mahpioneer@arvig.net
Publication Website: https://www.mahnomenpioneer.com/
Editor Name: Sue G Kraft
Editor Email: mahedit@arvig.net
Delivery Methods: Mail`Newsstand
Year Established: 1905
Own Printing Facility?: N
Mechanical specifications: Type page 10.5" x 21"
Published Days: Thur
Avg. Paid Circ.: 1600
Avg. Free Circ.: 100
Audit Company: Sworn/Estimate/Non-Audited
Audit Date: 43626

MAPLE LAKE

MAPLE LAKE MESSENGER

Street Address: 218 Division St W
City: Maple Lake
State: MN
ZIP Code: 55358-4576
General Phone: (320) 963-3813
General Email: ads@maplelakemessenger.com
Publication Website: https://maplelakemessenger.com/
Parent Company: Neal and Nikki Meyer
Publisher Name: Michele Pawlenty
Publisher Email: publisher@maplelakemessenger.com
Editor Name: Brenda Erdahl
Editor Email: news@maplelakemessenger.com
Advertising Executive Name: Bob Zimmerman
Advertising Executive Email: ads@maplelakemessenger.com
Delivery Methods: Mail
Mechanical specifications: Type page 6 x 21 1/2; E - 6 cols, 2, 1/12 between; A - 6 cols, 2, 1/12 between; C - 6 cols, 2, 1/12 between.
Published Days: Wed
Avg. Paid Circ.: 1113
Audit Company: Sworn/Estimate/Non-Audited
Audit Date: 43626

MAPLETON

MAPLE RIVER MESSENGER

Street Address: 309 Main St W
City: Mapleton
State: MN
ZIP Code: 56065-2062
General Phone: (507) 524-3212
General Email: editor@maplerivermessenger.com
Publication Website: https://www.maplerivermessenger.com/
Parent Company: Neal and Nikki Meyer
Publisher Name: Nikki Meyer
Publisher Email: publisher@maplerivermessenger.com
Editor Name: Koni Preston
Editor Email: editor@maplerivermessenger.com
Advertising Executive Name: Dennis Urban

MCINTOSH

MCINTOSH TIMES

Street Address: 115 Broadway NW
City: McIntosh
State: MN
ZIP Code: 56556-5777
General Phone: (218) 563-3585
General Email: mcintoshtimes@gmail.com
Publication Website: http://www.tricocanary.com/mcintosh-times
Parent Company: Richards Publishing
Publisher Name: Richard D. Richards
Editor Name: Kim Hedlund
Year Established: 1888
Published Days: Wed
Avg. Paid Circ.: 939
Audit Company: Sworn/Estimate/Non-Audited
Audit Date: 43626

MELROSE

MELROSE BEACON

Street Address: 408 E Main St
City: Melrose
State: MN
ZIP Code: 56352-1186
General Phone: (320) 351-6579
General Email: missy@saukherald.com
Publication Website: https://star-pub.com/
Parent Company: Star Publications
Advertising Executive Email: missy@saukherald.com
Advertising Executive Phone: (320) 352-6577
Delivery Methods: Mail
Mechanical specifications: Type page 6 x 21; E - 7 cols, 2, 1/8 between; A - 7 cols, 2, 1/8 between; C - 7 cols, 2, 1/8 between.
Published Days: Sat
Avg. Paid Circ.: 1900
Avg. Free Circ.: 2300
Audit Company: Sworn/Estimate/Non-Audited
Audit Date: 43626

MIDDLE RIVER

MIDDLE RIVER HONKER

Street Address: 655 2nd St N
City: Middle River
State: MN
ZIP Code: 56737-4136
General Phone: (218) 222-3501
General Email: honkernews@wiktel.com
Publication Website: https://www.thehonker.com/
Delivery Methods: Mail
Year Established: 2006
Published Days: Sat
Avg. Paid Circ.: 1100
Avg. Free Circ.: 15
Audit Company: Sworn/Estimate/Non-Audited
Audit Date: 43626

MINNEAPOLIS

NORTH NEWS

Street Address: 125 W Broadway Ave
City: Minneapolis
State: MN
ZIP Code: 55411-2245
General Phone: (651) 245-2647
General Email: kenzieo@pillsburyunited.org
Publication Website: https://mynorthnews.org/
Parent Company: Pillsbury United Communities
Editor Name: Kenzie O'Keefe
Editor Email: kenzieo@pillsburyunited.org
Delivery Methods: Racks
Year Established: 1991
Published Days: Thur`Mthly
Avg. Free Circ.: 10000
Audit Company: Sworn/Estimate/Non-Audited
Audit Date: 43626

MINNEAPOLIS

NORTHEASTER

Street Address: 2844 Johnson St NE
City: Minneapolis
State: MN
ZIP Code: 55418-3056
General Phone: (612) 788-9003
General Email: contact@mynortheaster.com
Publication Website: https://www.mynortheaster.com/
Parent Company: Pro Media, Inc
Publisher Name: Margo Ashmore
Editor Name: Cynthia Sowden
Advertising Executive Name: Vince Brown
Delivery Methods: Carrier
Year Established: 1978
Own Printing Facility?: N
Commercial printers?: N
Published Days: Wed
Published Other: Northeaster Bi-Weekly, NorthNews monthly
Avg. Paid Circ.: 31
Avg. Free Circ.: 32453
Audit Company: CVC
Audit Date: 44015

MINNEAPOLIS

SOUTHWEST JOURNAL

Street Address: 1115 Hennepin Ave
City: Minneapolis
State: MN
ZIP Code: 55403-1705
General Phone: (612) 825-9205
General Email: info@swjournal.com
Publication Website: https://www.southwestjournal.com/
Parent Company: Minnesota Premier Publications
Publisher Name: Janis Hall
Publisher Email: jhall@swjournal.com
Editor Name: Zac Farber
Editor Email: zfarber@mnpubs.com
Advertising Executive Name: Owen Davis
Advertising Executive Email: odavis@swjournal.com
Delivery Methods: Mail`Newsstand`Racks
Published Days: Mon`Mthly
Audit Company: Sworn/Estimate/Non-Audited
Audit Date: 43626

MINNEAPOLIS

THE BUSINESS JOURNAL

Street Address: 333 S 7th St
City: Minneapolis
State: MN
ZIP Code: 55402-2466
General Phone: (612) 288-2100
General Email: gsundeen@bizjournals.com
Publication Website: https://www.bizjournals.com/
Parent Company: American City Business Journals
Publisher Name: Kathy Robideau
Publisher Email: krobideau@bizjournals.com
Publisher Phone: (612) 288-2135
Editor Name: Mark Reilly
Editor Email: mreilly@bizjournals.com
Editor Phone: (612) 288-2110
Advertising Executive Name: Gina Sundeen
Advertising Executive Email: gsundeen@bizjournals.com
Advertising Executive Phone: (612) 288-2131
Delivery Methods: Mail
Year Established: 1983
Published Days: Fri
Audit Company: Sworn/Estimate/Non-Audited
Audit Date: 43626

MINNEAPOLIS

THE DOWNTOWN JOURNAL

Street Address: 1115 Hennepin Ave
City: Minneapolis
State: MN
ZIP Code: 55403-1705
General Phone: (612) 825-9205
General Email: sales@mnpubs.com
Publication Website: https://www.journalmpls.com/
Parent Company: Minnesota Premier Publications
Publisher Name: Janis Hall
Publisher Email: jhall@journalmpls.com
Editor Name: Dylan Thomas
Editor Email: dthomas@journalmpls.com
Advertising Executive Email: sales@mnpubs.com
Advertising Executive Phone: (612) 825-9205
Mechanical specifications: Type page 6 x 17; E - 4 cols, 2 3/8, between; A - 5 cols, 1 15/16, 3/16 between; C - 6 cols, 1 1/8, between.
Published Days: Mon`Bi-Mthly
Published Other: Every other mon
Avg. Paid Circ.: 220
Avg. Free Circ.: 30000
Audit Company: Sworn/Estimate/Non-Audited
Audit Date: 43626

MINNEOTA

MINNEOTA MASCOT

Street Address: 201 N. JEFFERSON ST
City: Minneota
State: MN
ZIP Code: 56264
General Phone: (507) 872-6492
General Email: office@minneotamascot.com
Publication Website: http://www.minneotamascot.com/
Parent Company: Byron Higgin
Editor Name: Brittany Moors
Editor Email: editor@minneotamascot.com
Delivery Methods: Mail`Newsstand
Year Established: 1891
Published Days: Wed
Avg. Paid Circ.: 1200
Audit Company: Sworn/Estimate/Non-Audited
Audit Date: 43626

MONTEVIDEO

MONTEVIDEO AMERICAN-NEWS

Street Address: P.O. Box 99
City: Montevideo
State: MN
ZIP Code: 56265
General Phone: (320) 269-2156
General Email: mbutzin@montenews.com
Publication Website: https://www.montenews.com/
Editor Name: Mike Milbrandt
Editor Email: mmilbrandt@montenews.com
Advertising Executive Name: Autumn Lee
Advertising Executive Email: alee@montenews.com

Own Printing Facility?: Y
Commercial printers?: Y
Mechanical specifications: Type page 6 x 21 1/2; E - 5 cols, 2 1/4, 1/8 between; A - 6 cols, 1 1/2, 1/8 between; C - 7 cols, 1 1/2, 1/8 between.
Published Days: Thur
Avg. Paid Circ.: 3257
Avg. Free Circ.: 41
Audit Company: Sworn/Estimate/Non-Audited
Audit Date: 43626

MONTGOMERY

MONTGOMERY MESSENGER

Street Address: 310 1st St S
City: Montgomery
State: MN
ZIP Code: 56069-1604
General Phone: (507) 364-8601
General Email: wade@montgomerymnnews.com
Publication Website: http://www.newpraguetimes.com/publication/montgomery-messenger
Parent Company: Suel Printing Co.
Publisher Name: E. Charles Wann
Editor Name: Wade Young
Advertising Executive Name: Mark Slavik
Delivery Methods: Mail`Newsstand
Published Days: Thur
Avg. Paid Circ.: 1777
Avg. Free Circ.: 15
Audit Company: Sworn/Estimate/Non-Audited
Audit Date: 43626

MOORHEAD

THE FM EXTRA

Street Address: 810 4th Ave S
City: Moorhead
State: MN
ZIP Code: 56560-2800
General Phone: (218) 284-1288
General Email: extra@ncppub.com
Publication Website: http://www.thefmextra.com/
Parent Company: New Century Press Inc.
Editor Name: Tammy Finney
Editor Email: extramediasales@aol.com
Advertising Executive Name: Diane Strom
Advertising Executive Email: dianerrvadsales@gmail.com
Year Established: 2001
Mechanical specifications: Type page: 10.02 x 10.5; 6 col
Published Days: Thur
Avg. Free Circ.: 5335
Audit Company: CVC
Audit Date: 43994

MOOSE LAKE

MOOSE LAKE STAR GAZETTE

Street Address: 321 Elm Ave.
City: Moose Lake
State: MN
ZIP Code: 55767-7706
General Phone: (218) 485-4406
General Email: evergreen@mlstargazette.com
Publication Website: https://www.mlstargazette.com/
Parent Company: Northstar Media LLC
Advertising Executive Phone: (218) 485-4406
Delivery Methods: Mail
Published Days: Thur
Avg. Paid Circ.: 3865
Audit Company: Sworn/Estimate/Non-Audited
Audit Date: 43626

Community Newspapers in the U.S.

MORA

KANABEC COUNTY TIMES

Street Address: 107 Park St S
City: Mora
State: MN
ZIP Code: 55051-1459
General Phone: (320) 679-2661
General Email: editor@moraminn.com
Publication Website: http://www.moraminn.com/
Parent Company: Kanabec Publications, Inc.
Publisher Name: Jeff Andres
Publisher Email: jeff@northstarmedia.net
Publisher Phone: (763) 689-1181, ext : 110
Editor Name: Kirsten Faurie
Editor Email: editor@moraminn.com
Editor Phone: (320) 225-5128
Advertising Executive Name: Annette Krist
Advertising Executive Email: akrist@moraminn.com
Advertising Executive Phone: (320) 225-5124
Delivery Methods: Mail
Commercial printers?: Y
Published Days: Thur
Avg. Paid Circ.: 3000
Audit Company: Sworn/Estimate/Non-Audited
Audit Date: 43626

MORRIS

STEVENS COUNTY TIMES

Street Address: 607 Pacific Avenue
City: Morris
State: MN
ZIP Code: 56267-1942
General Phone: (320) 589-2525
General Email: nancy@stevensctimes.com
Publication Website: https://www.stevenscountytimes.com/
Parent Company: Forum Communications
Publisher Name: Shelly Anfinson
Publisher Email: shelly@stevensctimes.com
Editor Name: Katie Erdman
Editor Email: katie@stevensctimes.com
Advertising Executive Name: Nancy Olson
Advertising Executive Email: nancy@stevensctimes.com
Delivery Methods: Mail`Newsstand`Racks
Year Established: 1899
Own Printing Facility?: Y
Commercial printers?: Y
Mechanical specifications: 6 column x 21"
1 column = 1.66 inches 2 columns = 3.451
3 columns = 5.243 4 columns = 7.035 5
columns = 8.826 6 columns = 10.625 inches
Published Days: Sat
Avg. Paid Circ.: 2400
Audit Company: Sworn/Estimate/Non-Audited
Audit Date: 43626

MOUNTAIN LAKE

MOUNTAIN LAKE/BUTTERFIELD OBSERVER-ADVOCATE

Street Address: P.O. Box 429 | 1025 2nd Avenue, Suite 2
City: Mountain Lake
State: MN
ZIP Code: 56159-1456
General Phone: (507) 427-2725
General Email: suef@mtlakenews.com
Publication Website: http://www.mtlakenews.com/
Publisher Name: Rahn Larson
Publisher Email: rahnl@windomnews.com
Delivery Methods: Mail`Carrier
Mechanical specifications: Type page 6 x 21 1/2; E - 6 cols, 2, 1/6 between; A - 6 cols, 2, 1/6 between; C - 6 cols, 2, 1/6 between.
Published Days: Wed
Avg. Paid Circ.: 1141
Audit Company: Sworn/Estimate/Non-Audited

Audit Date: 43626

NEW PRAGUE

THE NEW PRAGUE TIMES

Street Address: 200 Main St E
City: New Prague
State: MN
ZIP Code: 56071-2438
General Phone: (952) 758-4435
General Email: ads@newpraguetimes.com
Publication Website: http://www.newpraguetimes.com/
Parent Company: Suel Printing Co.
Publisher Name: E. Charles Wann
Editor Name: Jan Wann
Advertising Executive Name: Mark Slavik
Delivery Methods: Mail
Year Established: 1889
Published Days: Thur
Avg. Paid Circ.: 3700
Audit Company: Sworn/Estimate/Non-Audited
Audit Date: 43626

NEW RICHLAND

STAR EAGLE

Street Address: 128 Broadway Ave N, PO Box 248
City: New Richland
State: MN
ZIP Code: 56072-2020
General Phone: (507) 463-8112
General Email: steagle@hickorytech.net
Publication Website: http://www.newrichlandstar.com/
Parent Company: JDL Publications, Inc
Publisher Name: Jim Lutgens
Delivery Methods: Mail`Newsstand`Racks
Year Established: 1887
Published Days: Thur
Avg. Paid Circ.: 2000
Audit Company: Sworn/Estimate/Non-Audited
Audit Date: 43626

OKLEE

THE OKLEE HERALD

Street Address: 301 Main St, PO Box 9
City: Oklee
State: MN
ZIP Code: 56742
General Phone: (218) 796-5181
General Email: richards@gvtel.com
Publication Website: http://www.tricocanary.com/oklee-herald
Parent Company: Richards Publishing
Publisher Name: Richard D. Richards
Publisher Email: richards@gvtel.com
Editor Name: Bonny Cote
Own Printing Facility?: Y
Published Days: Wed
Avg. Paid Circ.: 895
Audit Company: Sworn/Estimate/Non-Audited
Audit Date: 43626

ORTONVILLE

THE ORTONVILLE INDEPENDENT

Street Address: 789 US Highway 75
City: Ortonville
State: MN
ZIP Code: 56278-4084
General Phone: (320) 839-6163
General Email: mail@ortonvilleindependent.com
Publication Website: https://www.ortonvilleindependent.com/
Parent Company: Kaercher Publications, Inc.

Delivery Methods: Mail`Newsstand
Year Established: 1920
Own Printing Facility?: Y
Commercial printers?: Y
Mechanical specifications: Type page 6 x 21 1/2; E - 6 cols, 2 1/8, 1/6 between; A - 6 cols, 2 1/8, 1/6 between; C - 6 cols, 2 1/8, 1/6 between.
Published Days: Tues
Avg. Paid Circ.: 2619
Avg. Free Circ.: 100
Audit Company: Sworn/Estimate/Non-Audited
Audit Date: 43626

PARK RAPIDS

PARK RAPIDS ENTERPRISE

Street Address: 203 Henrietta Ave N
City: Park Rapids
State: MN
ZIP Code: 56470-2617
General Phone: (218) 732-3364
General Email: cparks@parkrapidsenterprise.com
Publication Website: https://www.parkrapidsenterprise.com/
Publisher Name: Jody Hanson
Publisher Email: jhanson@echopress.com
Publisher Phone: (320) 763-3133
Editor Name: Shannon Geisen
Editor Email: sgeisen@parkrapidsenterprise.com
Editor Phone: (218) 237-1822
Advertising Executive Name: Candy Parks
Advertising Executive Email: cparks@parkrapidsenterprise.com
Advertising Executive Phone: (218) 237-1816
Delivery Methods: Mail`Newsstand
Published Days: Wed`Sat
Avg. Paid Circ.: 3341
Avg. Free Circ.: 73
Audit Company: VAC
Audit Date: 43625

PARKERS PRAIRIE

THE PARKERS PRAIRIE INDEPENDENT, LLC

Street Address: P.O. Box 42, 117 N Otter Ave
City: Parkers Prairie
State: MN
ZIP Code: 56361-4996
General Phone: (218) 338-2741
General Email: ppinews@me.com
Publication Website: https://www.ppindependent.net/
Publisher Name: Jennifer Marquardt
Editor Name: Jacquelyn Wehking
Delivery Methods: Mail`Newsstand
Year Established: 1902
Own Printing Facility?: Y
Commercial printers?: Y
Published Days: Thur
Avg. Paid Circ.: 950
Audit Company: Sworn/Estimate/Non-Audited
Audit Date: 43626

PAYNESVILLE

PAYNESVILLE PRESS

Street Address: 211 Washburne Ave, PO Box 54
City: Paynesville
State: MN
ZIP Code: 56362-1642
General Phone: (320) 243-3772
General Email: adsales@paynesvillepress.com
Publication Website: www.paynesvillearea.com
Editor Email: editor@paynesvillepress.com
Advertising Executive Email: adsales@paynesvillepress.com

Year Established: 1887
Own Printing Facility?: Y
Commercial printers?: Y
Mechanical specifications: Type page 6 x 20 3/4; E - 6 cols, 2, 1/8 between; A - 6 cols, 2, 1/8 between; C - 6 cols, 2, 1/8 between.
Published Days: Wed
Avg. Paid Circ.: 2142
Avg. Free Circ.: 177
Audit Company: Sworn/Estimate/Non-Audited
Audit Date: 43626

PELICAN RAPIDS

PELICAN RAPIDS PRESS

Street Address: 29 W Mill Ave
City: Pelican Rapids
State: MN
ZIP Code: 56572-4228
General Phone: (218) 863-1421
General Email: ads@pelicanrapidspress.com
Publication Website: https://pelicanrapidspress.com/
Parent Company: Jeff Meyer
Editor Name: Louis Hoglund
Advertising Executive Email: ads@pelicanrapidspress.com
Year Established: 1897
Mechanical specifications: Type page 6 x 11; E - 5 cols, 2 3/8, between; A - 6 cols, 2, between; C - 6 cols, 2, between.
Published Days: Wed
Avg. Paid Circ.: 2470
Audit Company: Sworn/Estimate/Non-Audited
Audit Date: 43626

PEQUOT LAKES

LAKE COUNTRY ECHO

Street Address: 4285 W Lake St
City: Pequot Lakes
State: MN
ZIP Code: 56472-3014
General Phone: (800) 432-3703
General Email: news@pequotlakesecho.com
Publication Website: https://www.pineandlakes.com/
Parent Company: Forum Communications
Publisher Name: Pete Mohs
Publisher Phone: (218) 855-5855
Editor Name: Nancy Vogt
Editor Phone: (218) 855-5877
Advertising Executive Name: Susie Alters
Advertising Executive Phone: (218) 855-5836
Delivery Methods: Mail`Racks
Year Established: 1972
Mechanical specifications: Type page: 10.25 x 14.75; 6 col
Published Days: Thur
Avg. Paid Circ.: 2820
Avg. Free Circ.: 59
Audit Company: CVC
Audit Date: 41275

PERHAM

ENTERPRISE BULLETIN

Street Address: 300 W. Main St. Suite C
City: Perham
State: MN
ZIP Code: 56573-1707
General Phone: (218) 346-5900
General Email: classifieds@perhamfocus.com
Publication Website: https://www.perhamfocus.com/
Parent Company: Forum Communications
Publisher Name: Melissa Swenson
Publisher Email: mswenson@dlnewspapers.com
Publisher Phone: (218) 844-1451
Editor Name: J.J. Perry
Editor Email: editor@perhamfocus.com

Editor Phone: (218) 844-1466
Advertising Executive Name: Melissa Swenson
Advertising Executive Email: mswenson@dlnewspapers.com
Advertising Executive Phone: (218) 844-1451
Delivery Methods: Mail`Carrier
Year Established: 1882
Own Printing Facility?: Y
Commercial printers?: Y
Mechanical specifications: Type page 13 x 21 1/2; E - 6 cols, 2 1/24, 1/6 between; A - 6 cols, 2 1/24, 1/6 between; C - 9 cols, between.
Published Days: Thur
Avg. Paid Circ.: 3200
Avg. Free Circ.: 50
Audit Company: Sworn/Estimate/Non-Audited
Audit Date: 43626

PERHAM

PERHAM FOCUS

Street Address: 300 W. Main St. Suite C
City: Perham
State: MN
ZIP Code: 56573-1707
General Phone: (218) 346-5900
General Email: classifieds@perhamfocus.com
Publication Website: https://www.perhamfocus.com/
Parent Company: Forum Communications
Publisher Name: Melissa Swenson
Publisher Email: mswenson@dlnewspapers.com
Publisher Phone: (218) 844-1451
Editor Name: J.J. Perry
Editor Email: editor@perhamfocus.com
Editor Phone: (218) 844-1466
Advertising Executive Name: Melissa Swenson
Advertising Executive Email: mswenson@dlnewspapers.com
Advertising Executive Phone: (218) 844-1451
Delivery Methods: Mail`Newsstand
Published Days: Thur
Avg. Paid Circ.: 2100
Audit Company: Sworn/Estimate/Non-Audited
Audit Date: 43626

PINE CITY

PINE CITY PIONEER

Street Address: 405 2nd Ave SE
City: Pine City
State: MN
ZIP Code: 55063-1504
General Phone: (320) 629-6771
General Email: ads@pinecitymn.com
Publication Website: http://www.pinecitymn.com/
Publisher Name: Jeff Andres
Publisher Email: jeff@northstarmedia.net
Publisher Phone: (763) 689-1181
Editor Name: Mike Gainor
Editor Email: editor@pinecitymn.com
Editor Phone: (320) 629-6771
Advertising Executive Email: ads@pinecitymn.com
Advertising Executive Phone: (320) 629-6771
Delivery Methods: Mail
Year Established: 1895
Own Printing Facility?: Y
Mechanical specifications: Type page 6 x 21 1/2; E - 6 cols, 2 1/8, 3/16 between; A - 6 cols, 2 1/8, 3/16 between; C - 9 cols, 1 3/8, 1/16 between.
Published Days: Thur
Avg. Paid Circ.: 2588
Avg. Free Circ.: 104
Audit Company: Sworn/Estimate/Non-Audited
Audit Date: 43626

PIPESTONE

PIPESTONE COUNTY STAR

Street Address: PO Box 277 | 115 2nd St. NE
City: Pipestone
State: MN
ZIP Code: 56164-1957
General Phone: (507) 825-3333
General Email: plorang@pipestonestar.com
Publication Website: https://www.pipestonestar.com/
Parent Company: Pipestone Publishing Co
Publisher Name: John Draper
Publisher Email: pipepub@pipestonestar.com
Editor Name: Debra Fitzgerald
Editor Email: editor@pipestonestar.com
Advertising Executive Name: Paul Lorang
Advertising Executive Email: plorang@pipestonestar.com
Delivery Methods: Mail`Newsstand`Carrier
Year Established: 1879
Mechanical specifications: Type page 6 x 21 1/2; E - 6 cols, 2 1/16, 1/8 between; A - 6 cols, 2 1/16, 1/8 between; C - 6 cols, 2 1/16, 1/8 between.
Published Days: Thur
Avg. Paid Circ.: 2445
Avg. Free Circ.: 15
Audit Company: Sworn/Estimate/Non-Audited
Audit Date: 43626

PRESTON

FILLMORE COUNTY JOURNAL

Street Address: 136 Saint Anthony St S
City: Preston
State: MN
ZIP Code: 55965-1151
General Phone: (507) 765-2151
General Email: jason@fillmorecountyjournal.com
Publication Website: http://fillmorecountyjournal.com/
Parent Company: Sethre Media Group, Inc.
Publisher Name: Jason Sethre
Publisher Email: jason@fillmorecountyjournal.com
Editor Name: Ellen Whalen
Editor Email: news@fillmorecountyjournal.com
Delivery Methods: Mail`Racks
Year Established: 1985
Own Printing Facility?: N
Commercial printers?: Y
Mechanical specifications: Type page 10 x 15; E - 5 cols, 2, between; A - 5 cols, 2, between; C - 5 cols, 2, between.
Published Days: Mon
Weekday Frequency: All day
Avg. Paid Circ.: 200
Avg. Free Circ.: 13026
Audit Company: CVC
Audit Date: 43991
Production Equipment: Mac computers
Production Software: Adobe Premium Creative Suite

PROCTOR

PROCTOR JOURNAL

Street Address: 215 5th St
City: Proctor
State: MN
ZIP Code: 55810-1628
General Phone: (218) 624-3344
General Email: journal@proctormn.com
Publication Website: http://www.proctorjournal.com/
Parent Company: Jake Benson
Publisher Name: Jake Benson
Delivery Methods: Mail`Newsstand
Year Established: 1906
Commercial printers?: Y
Mechanical specifications: 15 H x 9.75 w 5 column - 11 pica
Published Days: Thur
Avg. Paid Circ.: 1800
Audit Company: Sworn/Estimate/Non-Audited
Audit Date: 43626

RED WING

PIERCE COUNTY HERALD

Street Address: 2760 N Service Drive
City: Red Wing
State: MN
ZIP Code: 55066
General Phone: (800) 535-1660
General Email: mkeller@rivertowns.net
Publication Website: https://www.rivertowns.net/tags/FARMINGTON_INDEPENDENT
Parent Company: Forum Communications
Publisher Name: Neal Ronquist
Publisher Email: nronquist@rivertowns.net
Publisher Phone: (651) 301-7855
Editor Name: Jake Pfeifer
Editor Email: jpfeifer@rivertowns.net
Editor Phone: (651) 301-7880
Advertising Executive Name: Megan Keller
Advertising Executive Email: mkeller@rivertowns.net
Advertising Executive Phone: (651) 301-7801
Delivery Methods: Mail`Newsstand
Mechanical specifications: Type page 13 x 21 1/2; E - 6 cols, 2, 3/16 between; A - 6 cols, 2, 3/16 between; C - 6 cols, 2, 3/16 between.
Published Days: Wed
Avg. Paid Circ.: 3000
Avg. Free Circ.: 28
Audit Company: Sworn/Estimate/Non-Audited
Audit Date: 43626

RED WING

RIVER FALLS JOURNAL

Street Address: 2760 N. Service Drive
City: Red Wing
State: MN
ZIP Code: 55066
General Phone: (651) 388-8235
General Email: news@rivertowns.net
Publication Website: www.riverfallsjournal.com
Parent Company: Forum Communications
Publisher Name: Neal Ronquist
Publisher Email: nronquist@rivertowns.net
Publisher Phone: (651) 301-7855
Editor Email: news@rivertowns.net
Advertising Executive Name: Megan Keller
Advertising Executive Email: mkeller@rivertowns.net
Advertising Executive Phone: (651) 301-7801
Delivery Methods: Mail`Newsstand
Year Established: 1858
Published Days: Thur
Avg. Paid Circ.: 2839
Audit Company: Sworn/Estimate/Non-Audited
Audit Date: 43626

RED WING

THE FARMINGTON INDEPENDENT

Street Address: 2760 N Service Drive
City: Red Wing
State: MN
ZIP Code: 55066
General Phone: (800) 535-1660
General Email: mkeller@rivertowns.net
Publication Website: https://www.rivertowns.net/tags/FARMINGTON_INDEPENDENT
Parent Company: Forum Communications
Publisher Name: Neal Ronquist
Publisher Email: nronquist@rivertowns.net
Publisher Phone: (651) 301-7855
Editor Name: Jake Pfeifer
Editor Email: jpfeifer@rivertowns.net
Editor Phone: (651) 301-7880
Advertising Executive Name: Megan Keller
Advertising Executive Email: mkeller@rivertowns.net
Advertising Executive Phone: (651) 301-7801
Mechanical specifications: Type page 13 x 21; E - 6 cols, 2, 1/4 between; A - 6 cols, 2, 1/4 between; C - 8 cols, 2, 1/4 between.
Published Days: Thur
Avg. Paid Circ.: 2500
Audit Company: Sworn/Estimate/Non-Audited
Audit Date: 43626

RED WING

THE HUDSON STAR-OBSERVER

Street Address: 2760 N. Service Drive
City: Red Wing
State: MN
ZIP Code: 55066
General Phone: (651) 388-8235
General Email: news@rivertowns.net
Publication Website: www.riverfallsjournal.com
Parent Company: Forum Communications
Publisher Name: Neal Ronquist
Publisher Email: nronquist@rivertowns.net
Publisher Phone: (651) 301-7855
Editor Email: news@rivertowns.net
Advertising Executive Name: Megan Keller
Advertising Executive Email: mkeller@rivertowns.net
Advertising Executive Phone: (651) 301-7801
Delivery Methods: Mail`Newsstand
Year Established: 1854
Published Days: Thur
Avg. Paid Circ.: 7275
Avg. Free Circ.: 50
Audit Company: Sworn/Estimate/Non-Audited
Audit Date: 43626

REDWOOD FALLS

THE REDWOOD FALLS GAZETTE

Street Address: 219 South Washington Street, P.O. Box 299
City: Redwood Falls
State: MN
ZIP Code: 56283-1700
General Phone: (507) 637-2929
General Email: classified@redwoodfallsgazette.com
Publication Website: https://www.redwoodfallsgazette.com/
Publisher Name: Lisa Drafall
Publisher Email: ldrafall@redwoodfallsgazette.com
Editor Name: Troy Krause
Editor Email: tkrause@redwoodfallsgazette.com
Advertising Executive Email: classified@redwoodfallsgazette.com
Delivery Methods: Mail`Newsstand
Published Days: Mon`Thur
Avg. Paid Circ.: 1401
Audit Company: Sworn/Estimate/Non-Audited
Audit Date: 43626

ROSEAU

ROSEAU TIMES-REGION

Street Address: 1307 3rd St NE
City: Roseau
State: MN
ZIP Code: 56751-2105
General Phone: (218) 463-1521
General Email: rtr@mncable.net
Publication Website: https://www.roseautimes.com/

Community Newspapers in the U.S.

Parent Company: Jodi Wojciechowski
Publisher Name: Jodi Wojciechowski
Advertising Executive Name: Carrie Johnson
Year Established: 1892
Mechanical specifications: Type page 6 x 21 1/2; E - 6 cols, 2, between; A - 6 cols, 2, between; C - 6 cols, 2, between.
Published Days: Sat
Avg. Paid Circ.: 3191
Audit Company: Sworn/Estimate/Non-Audited
Audit Date: 43626

SAINT JAMES

ST JAMES PLAINDEALER

Street Address: 604 1st Ave S
City: Saint James
State: MN
ZIP Code: 56081-1729
General Phone: (507) 936-0186
General Email: knordhausen@stjamesnews.com
Publication Website: http://www.stjamesnews.com/
Parent Company: Gannett
Publisher Name: Lisa Drafall
Publisher Email: ldrafall@stjamesnews.com
Advertising Executive Name: Kyle Nordhausen
Advertising Executive Email: knordhausen@stjamesnews.com
Advertising Executive Phone: (507) 936-0315
Delivery Methods: Mail`Newsstand
Mechanical specifications: Type page 6 x 21 1/2.
Published Days: Thur
Avg. Paid Circ.: 1145
Avg. Free Circ.: 40
Audit Company: Sworn/Estimate/Non-Audited
Audit Date: 43626

SAINT JAMES

TOWN & COUNTRY SHOPPER

Street Address: 604 1st Ave S
City: Saint James
State: MN
ZIP Code: 56081-1729
General Phone: (507) 375-3161
General Email: knordhausen@stjamesnews.com
Publication Website: https://www.stjamesnews.com/
Publisher Name: Lisa Drafall
Publisher Email: ldrafall@stjamesnews.com
Advertising Executive Name: Kyle Nordhausen
Advertising Executive Email: knordhausen@stjamesnews.com
Advertising Executive Phone: (507) 936-0315
Delivery Methods: Mail`Carrier
Mechanical specifications: 10.375 X 15
Published Days: Mon
Avg. Free Circ.: 9648
Audit Company: CVC
Audit Date: 42981

SAINT PAUL

ACCESS PRESS

Street Address: 161 Saint Anthony Ave
City: Saint Paul
State: MN
ZIP Code: 55103-2454
General Phone: (651) 644-2133
General Email: access@accesspress.org
Publication Website: http://www.accesspress.org/
Editor Name: Tim Benjamin
Delivery Methods: Mail
Year Established: 1990
Published Days: Wed`Mthly
Published Other: 10th of every month

Avg. Paid Circ.: 550
Avg. Free Circ.: 12000
Audit Company: Sworn/Estimate/Non-Audited
Audit Date: 43626

SAINT PAUL

BIRD DOG & RETRIEVER NEWS

Street Address: 563 17th Ave NW, PO Box 120089
City: Saint Paul
State: MN
ZIP Code: 55112-6514
General Phone: (612) 868-9169
General Email: publisher@bird-dog-news.com
Publication Website: http://www.bird-dog-news.com/
Publisher Name: Dennis Guldan
Publisher Email: publisher@bird-dog-news.com
Delivery Methods: Mail
Year Established: 1992
Published Days: Bi-Mthly
Avg. Paid Circ.: 10000
Avg. Free Circ.: 17000
Audit Company: Sworn/Estimate/Non-Audited
Audit Date: 43626

SAINT PAUL

THE PARK BUGLE

Street Address: 2190 Como Ave
City: Saint Paul
State: MN
ZIP Code: 55108-1850
General Phone: (651) 646-5369
General Email: bradley.wolfe@parkbugle.org
Publication Website: https://www.parkbugle.org/
Parent Company: Park Press Inc.
Editor Email: editor@parkbugle.org
Advertising Executive Name: Fariba Sanikhatam
Advertising Executive Email: http://classifieds@parkbugle.org/
Advertising Executive Phone: (651) 440-8160
Delivery Methods: Carrier
Year Established: 1974
Published Days: Thur`Mthly
Audit Company: Sworn/Estimate/Non-Audited
Audit Date: 43626

SAINT PAUL

VILLAGER

Street Address: 757 Snelling Ave S
City: Saint Paul
State: MN
ZIP Code: 55116-2296
General Phone: (651) 699-1462
General Email: tcarroll@myvillager.com
Publication Website: http://www.myvillager.com/
Parent Company: Villager Communications, Inc
Publisher Name: Michael Mischke
Publisher Email: mmischke@myvillager.com
Advertising Executive Name: Tim Carroll
Advertising Executive Email: tcarroll@myvillager.com
Delivery Methods: Mail`Newsstand`Carrier
Year Established: 1953
Mechanical specifications: Type page: 10.3334 x 15; 6 col
Published Days: Wed
Published Other: every other week
Avg. Paid Circ.: 59
Avg. Free Circ.: 59830
Audit Company: CVC
Audit Date: 43619

SANDSTONE

PINE COUNTY COURIER

Street Address: 414 N. Main St.
City: Sandstone
State: MN
ZIP Code: 55072
General Phone: (320) 245-2368
General Email: courier@pinenet.com
Publication Website: https://www.pinecountycourier.com/
Publisher Name: Tim Franklin
Delivery Methods: Mail`Newsstand`Racks
Year Established: 1894
Mechanical specifications: 11.625 x 21
Published Days: Thur
Avg. Paid Circ.: 1744
Avg. Free Circ.: 90
Audit Company: Sworn/Estimate/Non-Audited
Audit Date: 43626

SAUK CENTRE

SAUK CENTRE HERALD

Street Address: 522 Sinclair Lewis Ave
City: Sauk Centre
State: MN
ZIP Code: 56378-1246
General Phone: (320) 352-6577
General Email: missy@saukherald.com
Publication Website: https://www.saukrapidsherald.com/
Parent Company: Star Publications
Editor Name: Natasha Barber
Editor Email: natasha@saukherald.com
Advertising Executive Name: Missy Traeger
Advertising Executive Email: missy@saukherald.com
Advertising Executive Phone: (320) 352-6577
Delivery Methods: Mail
Year Established: 1868
Published Days: Tues
Avg. Paid Circ.: 3276
Audit Company: Sworn/Estimate/Non-Audited
Audit Date: 43626

SAVAGE

LAKESHORE WEEKLY NEWS

Street Address: 12925 Eagle Creek Parkway
City: Savage
State: MN
ZIP Code: 55378
General Phone: (952) 445-3333
General Email: lhartmann@swnewsmedia.com
Publication Website: https://www.swnewsmedia.com/savage_pacer/
Publisher Name: Laurie Hartmann
Publisher Email: lhartmann@swnewsmedia.com
Publisher Phone: (952) 345-6878
Editor Name: Dan Holtmeyer
Editor Email: editor@plamerican.com
Editor Phone: (952) 345-6376
Published Days: Tues
Avg. Paid Circ.: 11
Avg. Free Circ.: 14280
Audit Company: CAC
Audit Date: 44351

SCANDIA

MESSENGER

Street Address: PO Box 96
City: Scandia
State: MN
ZIP Code: 55073
General Phone: (651) 433-3845
General Email: office@osceolasun.com
Publication Website: http://www.

countrymessenger.com/
Parent Company: Paxton Media Group
Editor Name: Matt Anderson
Editor Email: editor@countrymessenger.com
Advertising Executive Name: Elise Bourne
Advertising Executive Email: sales@osceolasun.com
Year Established: 1986
Mechanical specifications: Type page 6 x 14 1/2.
Published Days: Wed
Avg. Paid Circ.: 1600
Audit Company: Sworn/Estimate/Non-Audited
Audit Date: 43626

SEBEKA

THE REVIEW MESSENGER

Street Address: PO Box 309, 112 Minnesota Ave W
City: Sebeka
State: MN
ZIP Code: 56477-6004
General Phone: (218) 837-5558
General Email: remess@wcta.net
Publication Website: https://www.lakeandpine.com/
Parent Company: Lake and Pine Publications
Advertising Executive Name: Bernice Eckenrode
Advertising Executive Email: bernice@reviewmessenger.com
Advertising Executive Phone: (218) 837-5558
Delivery Methods: Mail`Newsstand
Year Established: 1898
Own Printing Facility?: N
Commercial printers?: N
Mechanical specifications: 6 col (10-5/8") x 21.5"
Published Days: Wed
Avg. Paid Circ.: 2958
Audit Company: Sworn/Estimate/Non-Audited
Audit Date: 43626

SLAYTON

MURRAY COUNTY NEWS

Street Address: 2627 Broadway Ave
City: Slayton
State: MN
ZIP Code: 56172-1311
General Phone: (507) 836-8929
General Email: mcn@murraycountynews.net
Publication Website: http://www.murraycountynews.net/
Delivery Methods: Mail`Racks
Published Days: Wed
Avg. Paid Circ.: 950
Audit Company: Sworn/Estimate/Non-Audited
Audit Date: 43626

SLEEPY EYE

SLEEPY EYE HERALD-DISPATCH

Street Address: 119 Main St E
City: Sleepy Eye
State: MN
ZIP Code: 56085-1352
General Phone: (507) 794-3511
General Email: ldrafall@sleepyeyenews.com
Publication Website: http://www.sleepyeyenews.com/
Publisher Name: Lisa Drafall
Publisher Email: ldrafall@sleepyeyenews.com
Publisher Phone: (507) 794-3511, ext : 18
Editor Name: Deb Moldaschel
Editor Email: dmoldaschel@sleepyeyenews.com
Editor Phone: (507) 794-3511, ext : 20
Delivery Methods: Mail`Newsstand

Year Established: 1880
Mechanical specifications: 6 col x 21.5"
Published Days: Thur
Avg. Paid Circ.: 1515
Audit Company: Sworn/Estimate/Non-Audited
Audit Date: 43626

SPRINGFIELD

SPRINGFIELD ADVANCE-PRESS

Street Address: 13 S Marshall Ave, PO Box 78
City: Springfield
State: MN
ZIP Code: 56087-1612
General Phone: (507) 723-4225
General Email: comp.aps@newulmtel.net
Publication Website: http://www.springfieldap.com/
Parent Company: Adam Conroy
Publisher Name: Adam Conroy
Advertising Executive Email: comp.aps@newulmtel.net
Year Established: 1888
Own Printing Facility?: Y
Mechanical specifications: Type page 6 x 21.
Published Days: Wed
Avg. Paid Circ.: 1813
Avg. Free Circ.: 39
Audit Company: Sworn/Estimate/Non-Audited
Audit Date: 43626

STAPLES

STAPLES WORLD

Street Address: 224 4th St NE, P.O. Box 100
City: Staples
State: MN
ZIP Code: 56479-2428
General Phone: (218) 894-1112
General Email: info@staplesworld.com
Publication Website: http://www.staplesworld.com/
Parent Company: RMM Publications LLC
Publisher Name: Rick Gail
Editor Name: Mark Anderson
Editor Email: editor@staplesworld.com
Delivery Methods: Mail`Newsstand
Year Established: 1890
Own Printing Facility?: Y
Commercial printers?: Y
Mechanical specifications: Type page 6 x 21 1/2; E - 6 cols, 1.6319, 1/6 between; A - 6 cols, 1.6319, 1/6 between; C - 6 cols, 1.6319, 1/6 between.
Published Days: Thur
Avg. Paid Circ.: 1800
Audit Company: Sworn/Estimate/Non-Audited
Audit Date: 43626

STEWARTVILLE

STEWARTVILLE STAR

Street Address: 101 4th Street NE #2, PO Box 35
City: Stewartville
State: MN
ZIP Code: 55976
General Phone: (507) 533-4271
General Email: starads@stewiestar.com
Publication Website: https://thinkstewartville.com/main.asp?SectionID=15
Parent Company: Galaxy Publications LLC
Delivery Methods: Mail`Newsstand
Year Established: 1891
Mechanical specifications: Type page 6 x 21; E - 6 cols, 2, 1/6 between; A - 6 cols, 2, 1/6 between; C - 6 cols, 2, 1/6 between.
Published Days: Tues
Avg. Paid Circ.: 1575

Avg. Free Circ.: 4800
Audit Company: Sworn/Estimate/Non-Audited
Audit Date: 43626

THIEF RIVER FALLS

NORTHERN WATCH

Street Address: 324 Main Ave N
City: Thief River Falls
State: MN
ZIP Code: 56701-1906
General Phone: (218) 681-4450
General Email: sales@trftimes.com
Publication Website: https://trftimes.com/
Parent Company: Page 1 Publications
Publisher Name: Kathy Svidal
Publisher Email: kathy@trftimes.com
Publisher Phone: (218) 681-4450
Editor Name: David Hill
Editor Email: dhill@trftimes.com
Editor Phone: (218) 681-4450
Advertising Executive Name: Dede Coltom
Advertising Executive Email: sales@trftimes.com
Advertising Executive Phone: (218) 681-4450
Year Established: 1910
Own Printing Facility?: Y
Commercial printers?: Y
Mechanical specifications: Type page 14 x 22 3/4; E - 6 cols, 2, 1/8 between; A - 6 cols, 2, 1/8 between; C - 6 cols, 2, 1/8 between.
Published Days: Sat
Avg. Free Circ.: 22000
Audit Company: Sworn/Estimate/Non-Audited
Audit Date: 43626

THIEF RIVER FALLS

THIEF RIVER FALLS TIMES

Street Address: 324 Main Ave N
City: Thief River Falls
State: MN
ZIP Code: 56701
General Phone: (218) 681-4450
General Email: sales@trftimes.com
Publication Website: https://trftimes.com/
Parent Company: Page 1 Publications
Publisher Name: Kathy Svidal
Publisher Email: kathy@trftimes.com
Publisher Phone: (218) 681-4450
Editor Name: David Hill
Editor Email: dhill@trftimes.com
Editor Phone: (218) 681-4450
Advertising Executive Name: Tom Williams
Advertising Executive Email: sales@trftimes.com
Advertising Executive Phone: (218) 681-4450
Delivery Methods: Mail`Newsstand
Year Established: 1910
Own Printing Facility?: Y
Commercial printers?: Y
Mechanical specifications: Type page 6 x 21 1/2; E - 6 cols, 2, 1/8 between; A - 6 cols, 2, 1/8 between; C - 6 cols, 2, 1/8 between.
Published Days: Wed
Avg. Paid Circ.: 4997
Avg. Free Circ.: 71
Audit Company: Sworn/Estimate/Non-Audited
Audit Date: 43626

TOWER

ELY TIMBERJAY

Street Address: PO Box 718
City: Tower
State: MN
ZIP Code: 55731
General Phone: (218) 365-3114
General Email: editor@timberjay.com
Publication Website: http://www.timberjay.com/

Editor Name: Keith Vandervort
Editor Email: ely@timberjay.com
Advertising Executive Email: editor@timberjay.com
Delivery Methods: Mail`Newsstand
Published Days: Fri
Avg. Paid Circ.: 1208
Audit Company: Sworn/Estimate/Non-Audited
Audit Date: 43626

TOWER

TIMBERJAY

Street Address: 414 Main St
City: Tower
State: MN
ZIP Code: 55790
General Phone: (218) 753-2950
General Email: editor@timberjay.com
Publication Website: http://www.timberjay.com/
Parent Company: Helmberger Group
Editor Email: editor@timberjay.com
Delivery Methods: Mail`Racks
Year Established: 1989
Published Days: Fri
Avg. Paid Circ.: 3430
Avg. Free Circ.: 80
Audit Company: Sworn/Estimate/Non-Audited
Audit Date: 43626

TRACY

TRACY HEADLIGHT-HERALD

Street Address: 207 4th St
City: Tracy
State: MN
ZIP Code: 56175
General Phone: (507) 629-4300
General Email: admanager@headlightherald.com
Publication Website: https://headlightherald.com/
Parent Company: Tracy Publishing Company, Inc
Publisher Name: Tara Brandl
Publisher Email: tara@headlightherald.com
Editor Name: Per Peterson
Editor Email: per@headlightherald.com
Advertising Executive Name: Lisa Sell
Advertising Executive Email: tara@headlightherald.com
Delivery Methods: Mail`Newsstand`Carrier`Racks
Year Established: 1879
Own Printing Facility?: Y
Commercial printers?: N
Published Days: Wed
Avg. Paid Circ.: 1685
Avg. Free Circ.: 4600
Audit Company: Sworn/Estimate/Non-Audited
Audit Date: 43626

TRUMAN

TRUMAN TRIBUNE

Street Address: 118 E Ciro St
City: Truman
State: MN
ZIP Code: 56088-2017
General Phone: (507) 776-2751
General Email: office@thetrumantribune.com
Publication Website: https://www.thetrumantribune.com/
Parent Company: Neal and Nikki Meyer
Publisher Name: Nikki Meyer
Publisher Email: nikki@thetrumantribune.com
Editor Name: Nikki Meyer
Editor Email: nikki@thetrumantribune.com
Advertising Executive Name: Neal Meyer
Advertising Executive Email: neal@

thetrumantribune.com
Delivery Methods: Mail`Racks
Year Established: 1899
Published Days: Wed
Avg. Paid Circ.: 821
Avg. Free Circ.: 250
Audit Company: Sworn/Estimate/Non-Audited
Audit Date: 43626

TWO HARBORS

LAKE COUNTY NEWS-CHRONICLE

Street Address: P.O. Box 158
City: Two Harbors
State: MN
ZIP Code: 55616
General Phone: (218) 834-2141
General Email: chronicle@lcnewschronicle.com
Publication Website: https://www.lcnewschronicle.com/
Parent Company: Forum Communications
Publisher Name: Neal Ronquist
Publisher Email: nronquist@duluthnews.com
Publisher Phone: (218) 723-5235
Editor Name: Rick Lubbers
Editor Email: rlubbers@duluthnews.com
Editor Phone: (218) 723-5301
Advertising Executive Name: Eric Olson
Advertising Executive Email: eolson@duluthnews.com
Advertising Executive Phone: (218) 720-4101
Delivery Methods: Mail`Newsstand`Carrier`Racks
Year Established: 1890
Published Days: Fri
Avg. Paid Circ.: 2031
Audit Company: Sworn/Estimate/Non-Audited
Audit Date: 43626

TYLER

TYLER TRIBUTE

Street Address: 124 N Tyler St
City: Tyler
State: MN
ZIP Code: 56178
General Phone: (507) 247-5502
General Email: tributeadvertising@gmail.com
Publication Website: http://www.tylertribute.com/
Parent Company: Buffalo Ridge Newspapers
Publisher Name: Mark Wilmes
Editor Name: Mark Wilmes
Editor Email: tributeeditor@gmail.com
Advertising Executive Email: tributeadvertising@gmail.com
Delivery Methods: Mail
Own Printing Facility?: Y
Commercial printers?: Y
Mechanical specifications: Type page 6 x 21 1/2; E - 6 cols, 2, 1/8 between; A - 6 cols, 2, 1/8 between; C - 6 cols, 2, 1/8 between.
Published Days: Wed
Avg. Paid Circ.: 1081
Avg. Free Circ.: 134
Audit Company: Sworn/Estimate/Non-Audited
Audit Date: 43626

ULEN

CLAY COUNTY UNION

Street Address: PO Box 248
City: Ulen
State: MN
ZIP Code: 56585
General Phone: (218) 596-8813
General Email: news@claycountyunion.net
Publication Website: https://www.hawleyherald.net/
Parent Company: Prim Group
Advertising Executive Name: Melissa Stock

Community Newspapers in the U.S.

III-289

Advertising Executive Email: news@claycountyunion.net
Delivery Methods: Mail
Published Days: Mon
Avg. Paid Circ.: 1226
Audit Company: Sworn/Estimate/Non-Audited
Audit Date: 43626

VERNDALE

THE VERNDALE SUN

Street Address: 121 W Farewell St
City: Verndale
State: MN
ZIP Code: 56481
General Phone: (218) 445-6397
General Email: verndalesun@inhnews.com
Publication Website: https://www.inhnews.com/verndalesun
Parent Company: Benning Printing & Publishing
Publisher Name: Ray Benning
Publisher Email: ray@inhnews.com
Editor Name: Kathy Marquardt
Editor Email: kathy@inhnews.com
Advertising Executive Name: Jenny Krueger
Advertising Executive Email: ads@inhnews.com
Delivery Methods: Mail
Published Days: Thur
Avg. Paid Circ.: 870
Audit Company: Sworn/Estimate/Non-Audited
Audit Date: 43626

WABASSO

WABASSO STANDARD

Street Address: 1034 Cedar St
City: Wabasso
State: MN
ZIP Code: 56293-1408
General Phone: (507) 342-5143
General Email: manderson@wabasso-standard.com
Publication Website: https://www.redwoodfallsgazette.com/news/20190716/wabasso-standard-is-not-closing
Publisher Name: Lisa Drafall
Publisher Email: ldrafall@gatehousemedia.com
Editor Name: Paul Zaid
Editor Email: phzaid@wabasso-standard.com
Published Days: Wed
Avg. Paid Circ.: 1200
Audit Company: Sworn/Estimate/Non-Audited
Audit Date: 43626

WADENA

WADENA PIONEER JOURNAL

Street Address: 314 Jefferson St S
City: Wadena
State: MN
ZIP Code: 56482
General Phone: (218) 631-2561
General Email: khelmbrecht@wadenapj.com
Publication Website: https://www.wadenapj.com/
Parent Company: Forum Communications
Publisher Name: Melissa Swenson
Publisher Email: mswenson@wadenapj.com
Publisher Phone: (218) 631-2561, ext : 1451
Editor Name: Michael Johnson
Editor Email: mjohnson@wadenapj.com
Editor Phone: (218) 631-2561, ext : 6111
Delivery Methods: Mail`Carrier`Racks
Own Printing Facility?: Y
Published Days: Thur
Avg. Paid Circ.: 1860
Avg. Free Circ.: 38
Audit Company: VAC

Audit Date: 43625

WALKER

THE PILOT-INDEPENDENT

Street Address: 408 MINNESOTA AVE
City: Walker
State: MN
ZIP Code: 56484
General Phone: (218) 547-1000
General Email: pilotads@pilotindependent.com
Publication Website: https://www.walkermn.com/
Parent Company: Adams Publishing Group
Publisher Name: Terri Fierstine
Publisher Email: tfierstine@pilotindependent.com
Editor Name: Dean Morrill
Editor Email: dmorrill@pilotindependent.com
Advertising Executive Name: Michelle Bruns
Advertising Executive Email: pilotads@pilotindependent.com
Delivery Methods: Mail`Racks
Year Established: 1900
Mechanical specifications: Type page 6 x 21; E - 6 cols, 1 4/5, 1/6 between; A - 6 cols, 1 4/5, 1/6 between; C - 6 cols, 1 4/5, 1/6 between.
Published Days: Wed
Avg. Paid Circ.: 2200
Audit Company: Sworn/Estimate/Non-Audited
Audit Date: 43626

WARREN

WARREN SHEAF

Street Address: 127 W Johnson Ave
City: Warren
State: MN
ZIP Code: 56762
General Phone: (218) 745-5174
General Email: news@warrensheaf.com
Publication Website: https://www.warrensheaf.com/
Parent Company: Warren Sheaf
Publisher Name: Eric Mattson
Delivery Methods: Mail
Year Established: 1880
Mechanical specifications: Type page 6 x 21; E - 6 cols, 2 1/8, 1/6 between; A - 6 cols, 2 1/8, 1/6 between.
Published Days: Wed
Avg. Paid Circ.: 1929
Audit Company: Sworn/Estimate/Non-Audited
Audit Date: 43626

WATERVILLE

LAKE REGION LIFE

Street Address: 115 South Third Street
City: Waterville
State: MN
ZIP Code: 56096
General Phone: (507) 362-4495
General Email: ads@newpraguetimes.com
Publication Website: https://www.newpraguetimes.com/
Parent Company: Suel Printing Co.
Publisher Name: E. Charles Wann
Editor Name: Jay Schneider
Advertising Executive Name: Mark Slavik
Year Established: 1970
Published Days: Thur
Avg. Paid Circ.: 1425
Avg. Free Circ.: 65
Audit Company: Sworn/Estimate/Non-Audited
Audit Date: 43626

WEST ST PAUL

THE ST. PAUL VOICE, DOWNTOWN ST. PAUL VOICE, SOUTH ST. PAUL VOICE AND LA VOZ LATINA

Street Address: 1643 Robert St S
City: West St Paul
State: MN
ZIP Code: 55118
General Phone: (651) 457-1177
General Email: info@stpaulpublishing.com
Publication Website: https://stpaulpublishing.com/
Parent Company: St. Paul Publishing Co.
Publisher Name: Tim Spitzack
Publisher Email: tim@stpaulpublishing.com
Editor Name: Tim Spitzack
Editor Email: tim@stpaulpublishing.com
Delivery Methods: Carrier`Racks
Year Established: 1966
Own Printing Facility?: N
Commercial printers?: N
Published Days: Mthly
Avg. Free Circ.: 37500
Audit Company: Sworn/Estimate/Non-Audited
Audit Date: 43626
Note: Publisher of the St. Paul Voice, Downtown St. Paul Voice, South St. Paul Voice and La Voz Latina

WESTBROOK

WESTBROOK SENTINEL TRIBUNE

Street Address: 611 1st Ave
City: Westbrook
State: MN
ZIP Code: 56183
General Phone: (507) 274-6136
General Email: jspielman@ncppub.com
Publication Website: http://www.ncppub.com/pages/?cat=60
Parent Company: New Century Press Inc.
Publisher Name: Carolyn Van Loh
Publisher Email: cvanloh@ncppub.com
Published Days: Wed
Avg. Paid Circ.: 997
Audit Company: Sworn/Estimate/Non-Audited
Audit Date: 43626

WINDOM

COTTONWOOD COUNTY CITIZEN

Street Address: 260 10th St
City: Windom
State: MN
ZIP Code: 56101-1411
General Phone: (507) 831-3455
General Email: citizen@windomnews.com
Publication Website: https://windomnews.com
Parent Company: Citizen Publishing Co.
Publisher Name: Trevor Slette
Publisher Email: trevors@windomnews.com
Editor Name: Rahn Larson
Editor Email: rahnl@windomnews.com
Advertising Executive Name: Trevor Slette
Advertising Executive Email: trevors@windomnews.com
Delivery Methods: Mail`Newsstand`Racks
Year Established: 1883
Published Days: Wed
Avg. Paid Circ.: 2579
Avg. Free Circ.: 188
Audit Company: Sworn/Estimate/Non-Audited
Audit Date: 43626

WINONA

WINONA POST

Street Address: 64 E 2nd St
City: Winona
State: MN
ZIP Code: 55987-3409

General Phone: (507) 452-1262
General Email: winpost@winonapost.com
Publication Website: https://www.winonapost.com/
Parent Company: Patrick Marek
Publisher Name: Patrick Marek
Publisher Email: pmarek@hbci.com
Publisher Phone: (507) 452-1262, ext : 110
Editor Name: Sarah Squires
Editor Email: winpost@winonapost.com
Editor Phone: (507) 452-1262, ext : 101
Advertising Executive Name: Kim Farkas
Advertising Executive Email: farkas@winonapost.com
Advertising Executive Phone: (507) 452-1262, ext : 111
Delivery Methods: Carrier
Year Established: 1971
Own Printing Facility?: Y
Commercial printers?: Y
Mechanical specifications: Type page 11.375 x 21 1/2; E - 6 cols, 2, 1/8 between; A - 6 cols, 2, 1/8 between; C - 8 cols, 1 1/2, 1/16 between.
Published Days: Wed`Sun
Avg. Paid Circ.: 75
Avg. Free Circ.: 21973
Audit Company: CVC
Audit Date: 43991

WINSTED

HERALD JOURNAL

Street Address: 120 6th St N
City: Winsted
State: MN
ZIP Code: 55395-1024
General Phone: (320) 485-2535
General Email: hj@heraldjournal.com
Publication Website: http://www.heraldjournal.com/c
Parent Company: Adams Publishing Group
Publisher Name: Chris Schultz
Publisher Email: cschultz@heraldjournal.com
Publisher Phone: (320) 485-2535
Editor Name: Ivan Raconteur
Editor Email: iraconteur@heraldjournal.com
Editor Phone: (320) 485-2535
Advertising Executive Email: ads@heraldjournal.com
Delivery Methods: Mail`Newsstand
Mechanical specifications: Type page 6 x 21 1/2; E - 7 cols, 2, 5/24 between; A - 7 cols, 2, 5/24 between; C - 7 cols, 2, 5/24 between.
Published Days: Fri
Avg. Paid Circ.: 2500
Audit Company: Sworn/Estimate/Non-Audited
Audit Date: 43626

WINTHROP

THE WINTHROP NEWS

Street Address: 110 N Carver St
City: Winthrop
State: MN
ZIP Code: 55396-2800
General Phone: (507) 647-5357
General Email: winthropnews@gmail.com
Publication Website: https://www.winthropnewsmn.com/
Publisher Name: Doug Hanson
Publisher Email: winthropnews@gmail.com
Editor Name: Michael Mattison
Editor Email: winthropnews@gmail.com
Advertising Executive Name: Dawn Fritz
Advertising Executive Email: winthropnewsdawn@gmail.com
Published Days: Wed
Avg. Paid Circ.: 1148
Audit Company: Sworn/Estimate/Non-Audited
Audit Date: 43626

ZUMBROTA

NEWS-RECORD

Street Address: 225 S Main St
City: Zumbrota
State: MN
ZIP Code: 55992-1698
General Phone: (507) 732-7617
General Email: news@zumbrota.com
Publication Website: https://www.zumbrota.com
Publisher Name: Peter Grimsrud
Editor Name: Matt Grimsrud
Delivery Methods: Mail
Published Days: Wed
Avg. Paid Circ.: 2733
Avg. Free Circ.: 10976
Audit Company: Sworn/Estimate/Non-Audited
Audit Date: 43626

MISSOURI

ALBANY

THE ALBANY LEDGER

Street Address: 213 W Clay St
City: Albany
State: MO
ZIP Code: 64402
General Phone: (660) 726-3998
General Email: taradodge@aledger.net
Publication Website: http://www.aledger.net/
Parent Company: Pearl Publishing
Delivery Methods: Mail`Racks
Year Established: 1868
Commercial printers?: N
Published Days: Wed
Avg. Paid Circ.: 1500
Avg. Free Circ.: 45
Audit Company: Sworn/Estimate/Non-Audited
Audit Date: 43626

ALMA

THE SANTA FE TIMES

Street Address: 106 3rd St.
City: Alma
State: MO
ZIP Code: 64001
General Phone: (660) 674-2250
General Email: safetnews@gmail.com
Publication Website: https://www.mainstreetnewsgroup.com/santafetimes/
Parent Company: Main Street Media of Tennessee
Publisher Name: Frank Mercer
Mechanical specifications: Type page 11 9/16 x 21; E - 6 cols, 1 13/16, 1/8 between; A - 6 cols, 1 13/16, 1/8 between; C - 6 cols, 2 13/16, 1/8 between.
Published Days: Thur
Avg. Paid Circ.: 800
Avg. Free Circ.: 20
Audit Company: Sworn/Estimate/Non-Audited
Audit Date: 43626

APPLETON CITY

APPLETON CITY JOURNAL

Street Address: 104 E 4th St
City: Appleton City
State: MO
ZIP Code: 64724
General Phone: (888) 646-2211
General Email: sacosagenews@centurytel.net
Publication Website: https://www.mainstreetnewsgroup.com/journal/
Parent Company: Main Street Media of Tennessee
Published Days: Fri
Avg. Paid Circ.: 1200
Avg. Free Circ.: 64
Audit Company: Sworn/Estimate/Non-Audited
Audit Date: 43626

ASH GROVE

ASH GROVE COMMONWEALTH

Street Address: 100 E Main St
City: Ash Grove
State: MO
ZIP Code: 65604-9096
General Phone: (417) 363-7025
General Email: recordadvertising@centurytel.net
Publication Website: http://greenecountycommonwealth.com/
Advertising Executive Email: recordadvertising@centurytel.net
Published Days: Wed
Avg. Paid Circ.: 2000
Avg. Free Circ.: 3725
Audit Company: Sworn/Estimate/Non-Audited
Audit Date: 43626

ASHLAND

BOONE COUNTY JOURNAL

Street Address: 201 S Henry Clay Blvd
City: Ashland
State: MO
ZIP Code: 65010
General Phone: (573) 657-2334
General Email: reporter@bocojo.com
Publication Website: http://bocojo.com/
Parent Company: Bruce and Sue Wallace
Year Established: 1969
Commercial printers?: Y
Mechanical specifications: Type page 13 x 21; E - 6 cols, 2 1/12, 1/8 between; A - 6 cols, 2 1/12, 1/8 between; C - 6 cols, 2 1/12, 1/8 between.
Published Days: Wed
Avg. Paid Circ.: 2000
Avg. Free Circ.: 150
Audit Company: Sworn/Estimate/Non-Audited
Audit Date: 43626

AURORA

AURORA ADVERTISER

Street Address: 33 W Olive St
City: Aurora
State: MO
ZIP Code: 65605
General Phone: (417) 451-1520
General Email: classifieds@auroraadvertiser.net
Publication Website: https://www.auroraadvertiser.net/
Parent Company: Gannett
Publisher Name: Joe Leong
Publisher Email: jleong@gatehousemedia.com
Editor Name: Patrick Richardson
Editor Email: prichardson@gatehousemedia.com
Advertising Executive Email: sbanta@bignickel.com
Delivery Methods: Mail`Racks
Year Established: 1886
Own Printing Facility?: Y
Commercial printers?: N
Mechanical specifications: Type page 13 x 21 1/2; E - 6 cols, 2 1/24, 1/6 between; A - 6 cols, 2 1/24, 1/6 between; C - 6 cols, 2 1/24, 1/6 between.
Published Days: Wed`Fri
Avg. Paid Circ.: 1100

Avg. Free Circ.: 7000
Audit Company: Sworn/Estimate/Non-Audited
Audit Date: 43626

AVA

DOUGLAS COUNTY HERALD

Street Address: 302 E Washington Ave
City: Ava
State: MO
ZIP Code: 65608
General Phone: (417) 683-4181
General Email: info@douglascountyherald.com
Publication Website: https://douglascountyherald.com/
Publisher Name: Sue Curry Jones
Publisher Email: scurry@douglascountyherald.com
Editor Name: Michael Boyink
Editor Email: michael@douglascountyherald.com
Advertising Executive Name: Mindy Johnson
Advertising Executive Email: admanager@douglascountyherald.com
Delivery Methods: Mail`Newsstand
Year Established: 1887
Own Printing Facility?: Y
Mechanical specifications: Type page 15 x 21; E - 7 cols, 2, 1/6 between; A - 7 cols, 2, 1/6 between; C - 7 cols, 2, 1/6 between.
Published Days: Thur
Avg. Paid Circ.: 3150
Avg. Free Circ.: 15
Audit Company: Sworn/Estimate/Non-Audited
Audit Date: 43626

BELLE

THE BELLE BANNER

Street Address: P.O. Box 711
City: Belle
State: MO
ZIP Code: 65013
General Phone: (573) 859-3328
General Email: tcnpub3@gmail.com
Publication Website: https://lifeinthearmy.com/the-belle-banner/
Year Established: 1906
Own Printing Facility?: Y
Commercial printers?: Y
Mechanical specifications: Type page 13 x 21; E - 6 cols, 2, 1/8 between; A - 6 cols, 2, 1/8 between; C - 6 cols, 2, 1/8 between.
Published Days: Wed
Avg. Paid Circ.: 2000
Avg. Free Circ.: 200
Audit Company: Sworn/Estimate/Non-Audited
Audit Date: 43626

BELLE

THE BLAND COURIER

Street Address: 217 S. Alvarado Ave.
City: Belle
State: MO
ZIP Code: 65013
General Phone: (573) 859-3328
General Email: kjl@sockets.net
Own Printing Facility?: Y
Commercial printers?: Y
Mechanical specifications: Type page 13 x 21 1/2; E - 6 cols, 2, 1/8 between; A - 6 cols, 2, 1/8 between; C - 6 cols, 2, 1/8 between.
Published Days: Wed
Avg. Paid Circ.: 728
Avg. Free Circ.: 30
Audit Company: Sworn/Estimate/Non-Audited
Audit Date: 43626

BETHANY

BETHANY REPUBLICAN-CLIPPER

Street Address: 202 N 16th St
City: Bethany
State: MO
ZIP Code: 64424
General Phone: (660) 425-6325
General Email: rclipper@grm.net
Publication Website: https://www.bethanyclipper.com/
Parent Company: Bethany Printing Company
Editor Name: Phil Conger
Editor Email: news1@grm.net
Advertising Executive Name: Kathy Conger
Advertising Executive Email: ad1@grm.net
Own Printing Facility?: Y
Commercial printers?: Y
Mechanical specifications: Type page 15 3/4 x 21; E - 7 cols, 2 1/4, 1/6 between; A - 7 cols, 2 1/4, 1/6 between.
Published Days: Wed
Avg. Paid Circ.: 3550
Avg. Free Circ.: 10000
Audit Company: Sworn/Estimate/Non-Audited
Audit Date: 43626

BOLIVAR

BOLIVAR HERALD-FREE PRESS

Street Address: 335 S Springfield Ave
City: Bolivar
State: MO
ZIP Code: 65613
General Phone: (417) 326-7636
General Email: news@bolivarmonews.com
Publication Website: https://bolivarmonews.com/
Parent Company: Phillips Media Group, LLC
Publisher Name: Jamey Honeycutt
Publisher Email: jameyh@phillipsmedia.com
Editor Name: Jessica Franklin Maull
Editor Email: jessicam@bolivarmonews.com
Advertising Executive Name: Deanna Moore
Advertising Executive Email: deannam@bolivarmonews.com
Year Established: 1868
Own Printing Facility?: Y
Commercial printers?: Y
Mechanical specifications: Type page 10.25 x 21; E - 6 cols, 1 4/5, 1/5 between; A - 6 cols, 1 4/5, 1/5 between; C - 7 cols, 1 1/2, 1/5 between.
Published Days: Wed`Fri
Avg. Paid Circ.: 5061
Avg. Free Circ.: 77
Audit Company: Sworn/Estimate/Non-Audited
Audit Date: 43626

BOONVILLE

BOONVILLE DAILY NEWS

Street Address: 412 High St
City: Boonville
State: MO
ZIP Code: 65233
General Phone: (660) 882-5335
General Email: bookkeeping@boonvilledailynews.com
Publication Website: https://www.boonvilledailynews.com/
Parent Company: Gannett
Publisher Name: Terri Leifeste
Editor Name: Allen Fennewald
Editor Email: afennewald@gatehousemedia.com
Editor Phone: (573) 815-1788
Advertising Executive Email: production@boonvilledailynews.com
Delivery Methods: Mail`Carrier`Racks
Year Established: 1919
Own Printing Facility?: Y
Mechanical specifications: Type page 13 x 21; E - 6 cols, 2 1/16, 1/8 between; A - 6

Community Newspapers in the U.S.

cols, 2 1/16, 1/8 between; C - 6 cols, 2 1/16, 1/8 between.
Published Days: Tues`Thur`Fri
Weekday Frequency: e
Avg. Paid Circ.: 2484
Audit Company: Sworn/Estimate/Non-Audited
Audit Date: 43626
Pressroom Equipment: Lines -- 4-G/Community;
Mailroom Equipment: Counter Stackers -- BG; Tying Machines -- 3/Bu; Address Machine -- 2-/Dispensa-Matic/16.;
Business Equipment: IBM, AT
Classified Equipment: Hardware -- APP/Mac SE, 1-APP/Power Mac; Printers -- APP/Mac LaserWriter 12-640;
Classified Software: QPS/QuarkXPress 3.32.
Editorial Equipment: Hardware -- APP/Mac Plus, APP/Mac Classic, APP/Power Mac; Printers -- 1-APP/Mac LaserPrinter, 1-APP/Mac LaserWriter 360, 1-HP/4MV
Editorial Software: QPS/QuarkXPress (3.32).
Production Equipment: Hardware -- Nu, 1-APP/Mac LaserPrinter; Cameras -- SCREEN
Production Software: QPS/QuarkXPress 3.32.

BOWLING GREEN

BOWLING GREEN TIMES

Street Address: 106 West Main Street
City: Bowling Green
State: MO
ZIP Code: 63334
General Phone: (573) 324-2222
General Email: slenk@pikecountynews.com
Publication Website: https://www.pikecountynews.com/
Parent Company: Lakeway Publishers, Inc.
Publisher Name: Tom Latos
Publisher Email: tlatos@pikecountynews.com
Editor Name: Stan Schwartz
Editor Email: sschwartz@pikecountynews.com
Advertising Executive Name: Julie House
Advertising Executive Email: jhouse@pikecountynews.com
Delivery Methods: Mail`Newsstand`Racks
Year Established: 1874
Own Printing Facility?: Y
Mechanical specifications: Type page 13 x 21; E - 6 cols, 2 1/16, between; A - 6 cols, 2 1/16, between; C - 6 cols, 2 1/16, between.
Published Days: Wed
Avg. Paid Circ.: 3125
Audit Company: Sworn/Estimate/Non-Audited
Audit Date: 43626

BOWLING GREEN

THE LOUISIANA PRESS-JOURNAL

Street Address: PO Box 110
City: Bowling Green
State: MO
ZIP Code: 63334-0110
General Phone: (573) 754-5566
General Email: lpjads@lcs.net
Publication Website: http://www.louisianapressjournal.com
Parent Company: Lakeway Publishers, Inc.
Year Established: 1855
Own Printing Facility?: Y
Commercial printers?: Y
Published Days: Wed
Avg. Paid Circ.: 3175
Avg. Free Circ.: 21
Audit Company: Sworn/Estimate/Non-Audited
Audit Date: 43626

BOWLING GREEN

THE PEOPLE'S TRIBUNE

Street Address: 17 N Main Cross St
City: Bowling Green
State: MO
ZIP Code: 63334
General Phone: (573) 324-6111
General Email: peoplestribune@sbcglobal.net
Publication Website: http://thepeoplestribune.com/
Year Established: 1996
Mechanical specifications: Type page 10 1/2 x 16; E - 5 cols, 1/8 between; A - 5 cols, 1/8 between; C - 5 cols, 1/8 between.
Published Days: Tues
Avg. Free Circ.: 8500
Audit Company: Sworn/Estimate/Non-Audited
Audit Date: 43626

BROOKFIELD

LINN COUNTY LEADER

Street Address: 314 N Main St
City: Brookfield
State: MO
ZIP Code: 64628
General Phone: (660) 258-7237
General Email: hjanssen@linncountyleader.com
Publication Website: https://www.linncountyleader.com/
Parent Company: Gannett
Editor Name: Matt Ragsdale
Editor Email: mragsdale@linncountyleader.com
Advertising Executive Name: Aaron Consalvi
Advertising Executive Email: aconsalvi@columbiatribune.com
Year Established: 2001
Published Days: Mon`Wed`Fri
Avg. Paid Circ.: 3300
Audit Company: Sworn/Estimate/Non-Audited
Audit Date: 43626

BUFFALO

BUFFALO REFLEX

Street Address: 114 E LINCOLN ST
City: Buffalo
State: MO
ZIP Code: 65622
General Phone: (417) 345-2224
General Email: news@buffaloreflex.com
Publication Website: https://buffaloreflex.com/
Parent Company: Phillips Media Group, LLC
Publisher Name: Jamey Honeycutt
Publisher Email: jameyh@phillipsmedia.com
Editor Name: Steve Johnson
Editor Email: stevej@buffaloreflex.com
Advertising Executive Name: Sherry Bennett
Advertising Executive Email: sherryb@buffaloreflex.com
Delivery Methods: Mail`Newsstand`Racks
Year Established: 1869
Mechanical specifications: Type page 10.25 x 21 1/2; E - 6 cols, 2, 1/6 between; A - 6 cols, 2, 1/6 between; C - 6 cols, 1 7/12, 1/6 between.
Published Days: Wed
Avg. Paid Circ.: 4000
Avg. Free Circ.: 380
Audit Company: Sworn/Estimate/Non-Audited
Audit Date: 43626

BUTLER

NEWS-XPRESS

Street Address: 5 N Main St
City: Butler
State: MO
ZIP Code: 64730
General Phone: (660) 679-6126
General Email: butlerxchanger@gmail.com
Publication Website: https://www.yourxgroup.com/
Parent Company: The X Group
Publisher Name: Jon Peters
Publisher Email: butlerxchanger@gmail.com
Editor Name: Abby Hamilton
Editor Email: butlerxchanger@gmail.com
Delivery Methods: Mail`Racks
Year Established: 1984
Own Printing Facility?: Y
Mechanical specifications: Type page 10.25 x 19.9; E - 1 col - 1.5672 6 col. 10.2567 x 19.905
Published Days: Fri
Avg. Paid Circ.: 2570
Avg. Free Circ.: 65
Audit Company: Sworn/Estimate/Non-Audited
Audit Date: 43626

CABOOL

CABOOL ENTERPRISE

Street Address: 525 Main St
City: Cabool
State: MO
ZIP Code: 65689
General Phone: (417) 962-4411
General Email: news@thecaboolenterprise.com
Publication Website: https://www.caboolenterprise.com/
Delivery Methods: Mail`Newsstand
Year Established: 1884
Mechanical specifications: Type page 13 x 21; E - 6 cols, 2 1/8, between; A - 6 cols, 2 1/8, between; C - 6 cols, 2 1/8, between.
Published Days: Thur
Avg. Paid Circ.: 1369
Avg. Free Circ.: 41
Audit Company: Sworn/Estimate/Non-Audited
Audit Date: 43626

CALIFORNIA

CALIFORNIA DEMOCRAT

Street Address: 319 S High St
City: California
State: MO
ZIP Code: 65018-1807
General Phone: (573) 796-2135
General Email: editor@californiademocrat.com
Publication Website: https://www.californiademocrat.com/
Parent Company: WEHCO Media, Inc.
Editor Name: Austin Hornbostel
Editor Email: editor@californiademocrat.com
Editor Phone: (573) 464-4170
Delivery Methods: Mail`Newsstand`Carrier`Racks
Year Established: 1858
Mechanical specifications: Type page 13 x 21 1/2; E - 6 cols, 2 1/30, 1/6 between; A - 6 cols, 2 1/30, 1/6 between; C - 6 cols, 2 1/30, 1/6 between.
Published Days: Wed
Avg. Paid Circ.: 2750
Audit Company: Sworn/Estimate/Non-Audited
Audit Date: 43626

CAMERON

THE CITIZEN OBSERVER

Street Address: P.O. Box 498
City: Cameron
State: MO
ZIP Code: 64429
General Phone: (816) 632-6543
General Email: advertising@mycameronnews.com
Publication Website: http://mycameronnews.com/
Parent Company: Smith Newspapers
Publisher Name: Tina Svoboda
Publisher Email: advertising@mycameronnews.com
Editor Name: Annette Bauer
Editor Email: editor@mycameronnews.com
Advertising Executive Name: Helen Guffey
Advertising Executive Email: composing@mycameronnews.com
Delivery Methods: Mail`Racks
Own Printing Facility?: Y
Commercial printers?: Y
Mechanical specifications: Type page 13 1/2 x 20 1/2; E - 6 cols, 2 1/6, 1/6 between; A - 8 cols, 1 7/12, 1/6 between; C - 8 cols, 1 7/12, 1/6 between.
Published Days: Thur
Avg. Paid Circ.: 2000
Avg. Free Circ.: 14000
Audit Company: Sworn/Estimate/Non-Audited
Audit Date: 43626

CASSVILLE

BARRY COUNTY ADVERTISER

Street Address: 904 West St
City: Cassville
State: MO
ZIP Code: 65625
General Phone: (417) 847-4475
General Email: ads@4bca.com
Publication Website: http://www.4bcaonline.com/
Parent Company: Melton Publications
Editor Name: Charlea Estes-Jones
Editor Email: editor@4bca.com
Advertising Executive Name: Adriana Keeton
Advertising Executive Email: sales@4bca.com
Delivery Methods: Mail
Year Established: 1966
Own Printing Facility?: Y
Commercial printers?: Y
Mechanical specifications: Type page 11 x 17; E - 6 cols, between; A - 6 cols, between; C - 6 cols, between.
Published Days: Wed
Avg. Paid Circ.: 200
Avg. Free Circ.: 13200
Audit Company: Sworn/Estimate/Non-Audited
Audit Date: 43626
Pressroom Equipment: Harris Color Web
Mailroom Equipment: USA Inserter
Business Equipment: Mac Computer
Business Software: Adobe Creative
Classified Equipment: Mac Computer
Classified Software: NewsCycle Media
Editorial Equipment: Mac Computer
Editorial Software: Adobe Creative
Production Equipment: Kodak CTP

CENTRALIA

THE CENTRALIA FIRESIDE GUARD

Street Address: 123 N Allen St
City: Centralia
State: MO
ZIP Code: 65240
General Phone: (573) 682-2133
General Email: cfgcomp@lcs.net
Publication Website: https://www.firesideguard.com/
Parent Company: Lakeway Publishers, Inc.
Advertising Executive Email: cfgads@lcs.net
Delivery Methods: Mail`Newsstand`Racks
Year Established: 1868
Published Days: Wed
Avg. Paid Circ.: 3700
Audit Company: Sworn/Estimate/Non-Audited
Audit Date: 43626

CHARLESTON

MISSISSIPPI COUNTY TIMES

Street Address: 207 S Main St
City: Charleston
State: MO
ZIP Code: 63834-1639
General Phone: (573) 683-6689
General Email: countytimes@sbcglobal.net
Publication Website: http://www.misscotimes.com/
Published Days: Tues
Avg. Free Circ.: 40000
Audit Company: Sworn/Estimate/Non-Audited
Audit Date: 43626

CLARENCE

CLARENCE COURIER

Street Address: 106 E Maple St
City: Clarence
State: MO
ZIP Code: 63437
General Phone: (660) 699-2344
General Email: advertising@shelbycountyherald.com
Publication Website: https://nemonews.net/shelby-county-news/
Publisher Name: Mike Scott
Publisher Email: themedia@centurytel.net
Advertising Executive Email: advertising@shelbycountyherald.com
Own Printing Facility?: Y
Commercial printers?: Y
Published Days: Wed
Avg. Paid Circ.: 1600
Avg. Free Circ.: 118
Audit Company: Sworn/Estimate/Non-Audited
Audit Date: 43626

CRANE

CRANE CHRONICLE/STONE COUNTY REPUBLICAN

Street Address: 114 Main St
City: Crane
State: MO
ZIP Code: 65633
General Phone: (417) 723-5248
General Email: screditor@centurylink.net
Publication Website: https://www.ccscrnews.com/
Parent Company: Stone County Publishing, Inc.
Editor Name: Isaac Estes-Jones
Editor Email: screditor@centurylink.net
Delivery Methods: Mail
Year Established: 1876
Commercial printers?: Y
Mechanical specifications: Type page 11 x 17; E - 5 cols, 2, between; A - 5 cols, 2, between; C - 5 cols, 2, between.
Published Days: Thur
Avg. Paid Circ.: 1104
Avg. Free Circ.: 45
Audit Company: Sworn/Estimate/Non-Audited
Audit Date: 43626
Editorial Software: InDesign

CUBA

THE CUBA FREE PRESS

Street Address: 501 E Washington St
City: Cuba
State: MO
ZIP Code: 65453
General Phone: (573) 885-7460
General Email: news@cubafreepress.com
Publication Website: https://www.threeriverspublishing.com/TRP3/
Parent Company: Three Rivers Publishing, Inc.
Publisher Name: Rob Viehman
Publisher Email: rviehman@cubafreepress.com
Publisher Phone: (573) 885-7460
Editor Name: Kelli Rapp
Editor Email: kelli@threeriverspublishing.com
Editor Phone: (573) 885-7460
Advertising Executive Email: advertising@threeriverspublishing.com
Delivery Methods: Mail Newsstand
Year Established: 1960
Own Printing Facility?: Y
Commercial printers?: Y
Mechanical specifications: 21.5 inches tall 1 col - 1.833 inches 2 col - 3.792 inches 3 col - 5.75 inches 4 col - 7.708 inches 5 col - 9.667 inches 6 col - 11.625 inches
Published Days: Thur
Avg. Paid Circ.: 3450
Audit Company: Sworn/Estimate/Non-Audited
Audit Date: 43626

DEXTER

THE NORTH-STODDARD COUNTIAN

Street Address: 909 Mallory St.
City: Dexter
State: MO
ZIP Code: 63841
General Phone: (573) 624-4545
General Email: news@dexterstatesman.com
Publication Website: https://www.dexterstatesman.com/
Parent Company: Rust Communications
Editor Name: Josh Ayers
Editor Email: jayers@dexterstatesman.com
Year Established: 1877
Published Days: Wed
Avg. Paid Circ.: 2000
Audit Company: Sworn/Estimate/Non-Audited
Audit Date: 43626

DIXON

DIXON PILOT NEWSPAPER AND PRINT SHOP

Street Address: 302 N Locust St
City: Dixon
State: MO
ZIP Code: 65459
General Phone: (573) 759-2127
General Email: dixonpilotnews@yahoo.com
Publication Website: https://www.dixonpilot.com/
Delivery Methods: Mail Racks
Year Established: 1915
Published Days: Wed
Avg. Paid Circ.: 2200
Audit Company: Sworn/Estimate/Non-Audited
Audit Date: 43626

DONIPHAN

THE PROSPECT-NEWS

Street Address: 110 Washington St
City: Doniphan
State: MO
ZIP Code: 63935
General Phone: (573) 996-2103
General Email: cpruett@darnews.com
Publication Website: https://www.theprospectnews.com/
Parent Company: Rust Communications
Publisher Name: Chris Pruett
Publisher Email: cpruett@darnews.com
Publisher Phone: (573) 772-7275
Editor Name: Barbie Rogers
Editor Email: brogers@theprospectnews.com
Delivery Methods: Mail Carrier Racks
Year Established: 1874

Own Printing Facility?: Y
Commercial printers?: Y
Mechanical specifications: 1.562 inches per column
Published Days: Wed
Avg. Paid Circ.: 3000
Audit Company: Sworn/Estimate/Non-Audited
Audit Date: 43626

EAST PRAIRIE

EAST PRAIRIE EAGLE & ENTERPRISE-COURIER

Street Address: 101 E Main St
City: East Prairie
State: MO
ZIP Code: 63845
General Phone: (573) 683-3351
General Email: news@enterprisecourier.com
Publication Website: https://www.enterprisecourier.com/
Advertising Executive Email: advertising@enterprisecourier.com
Published Days: Tues
Published Other: weekly
Avg. Paid Circ.: 2500
Audit Company: Sworn/Estimate/Non-Audited
Audit Date: 43626

EDINA

THE EDINA SENTINEL

Street Address: 207 N Main St
City: Edina
State: MO
ZIP Code: 63537
General Phone: (660) 397-2226
General Email: edinasentinel@att.net
Publication Website: https://nemonews.net/category/edina-sentinel/
Publisher Name: Mike Scott
Publisher Email: themedia@centurytel.net
Year Established: 1868
Own Printing Facility?: Y
Commercial printers?: Y
Published Days: Wed
Avg. Paid Circ.: 1600
Audit Company: Sworn/Estimate/Non-Audited
Audit Date: 43626

EL DORADO SPRINGS

EL DORADO SPRINGS SUN

Street Address: 125 N Main St
City: El Dorado Springs
State: MO
ZIP Code: 64744
General Phone: (417) 876-3841
General Email: sunnews@centurylink.net
Publication Website: https://eldoradospringsmo.com/
Parent Company: Kenny & Kimball Long
Delivery Methods: Mail Racks
Year Established: 1890
Mechanical specifications: Type page 11 2/3 x 21 1/2; E - 6 cols, 1 5/6, 1/8 between; A - 6 cols, 1 5/6, 1/8 between; C - 6 cols, 1 5/6, 1/8 between.
Published Days: Thur
Avg. Paid Circ.: 3800
Avg. Free Circ.: 3580
Audit Company: Sworn/Estimate/Non-Audited
Audit Date: 43626

ELDON

ELDON ADVERTISER

Street Address: 415 S Maple St, PO Box 315

City: Eldon
State: MO
ZIP Code: 65026-1856
General Phone: (573) 392-5658
General Email: advertisersales@vernonpublishing.com
Publication Website: https://www.vernonpublishing.com
Parent Company: Vernon Publishing
Publisher Name: Trevor Vernon
Publisher Email: tvernon@vernonpublishing.com
Publisher Phone: (573) 392-5658
Editor Name: Tim Flora
Editor Email: tflora@vernonpublishing.com
Editor Phone: (573) 392-5658
Advertising Executive Name: Benne Myers
Advertising Executive Email: advertisersales@vernonpublishing.com
Advertising Executive Phone: (573) 392-5658
Delivery Methods: Mail Newsstand Racks
Own Printing Facility?: Y
Commercial printers?: Y
Mechanical specifications: Type page 13 x 21; E - 6 cols, 2 1/16, 1/8 between; A - 6 cols, 2 1/16, 1/8 between; C - 7 cols, 1 23/32, 1/8 between.
Published Days: Thur
Avg. Paid Circ.: 4825
Avg. Free Circ.: 52
Audit Company: Sworn/Estimate/Non-Audited
Audit Date: 43626

ELDON

MILLER COUNTY AUTOGRAM SENTINEL

Street Address: 415 S Maple St
City: Eldon
State: MO
ZIP Code: 65026-1856
General Phone: (573) 392-5658
General Email: advertisersales@vernonpublishing.com
Publication Website: http://www.vernonpublishing.com/Autogram-Sentinel/Main/
Parent Company: Vernon Publishing
Publisher Name: Trevor Vernon
Publisher Email: tvernon@vernonpublishing.com
Publisher Phone: (573) 392-5658
Editor Name: Tim Flora
Editor Email: tflora@vernonpublishing.com
Editor Phone: (573) 392-5658
Advertising Executive Name: Benne Myers
Advertising Executive Email: advertisersales@vernonpublishing.com
Advertising Executive Phone: (573) 392-5658
Year Established: 1883
Own Printing Facility?: Y
Commercial printers?: Y
Mechanical specifications: Type page 13 x 21; E - 6 cols, 2 1/16, 1/8 between; A - 6 cols, 2 1/16, 1/8 between; C - 7 cols, 1 23/32, 1/8 between.
Published Days: Thur
Avg. Paid Circ.: 1875
Avg. Free Circ.: 20
Audit Company: Sworn/Estimate/Non-Audited
Audit Date: 43626

ELSBERRY

THE ELSBERRY DEMOCRAT

Street Address: 106 N 3rd St, PO Box 105
City: Elsberry
State: MO
ZIP Code: 63343-1344
General Phone: (573) 898-2318
General Email: sjenkinson@lincolncountyjournal.com
Publication Website: https://www.lincolnnewsnow.com
Parent Company: Lakeway Publishers, Inc.
Publisher Name: Michael Short

Community Newspapers in the U.S.

Publisher Email: mshort@elsberrydemocrat.com
Publisher Phone: (573) 898-2318
Year Established: 1901
Own Printing Facility?: Y
Published Days: Wed
Avg. Paid Circ.: 1350
Avg. Free Circ.: 5
Audit Company: Sworn/Estimate/Non-Audited
Audit Date: 43626

FAIRFAX

THE FAIRFAX FORUM

Street Address: 128 E. Main Street
City: Fairfax
State: MO
ZIP Code: 64446-9305
General Phone: (660) 686-2741
General Email: amail@rpt.coop
Publication Website: https://farmerpublishing.com/
Parent Company: W.C. & Shauna Farmer
Year Established: 1892
Mechanical specifications: Type page 12 1/2 x 20 1/2; E - 6 cols, 2 1/8, between; A - 6 cols, 2 1/8, between; C - 6 cols, 2 1/8, between.
Published Days: Thur
Avg. Paid Circ.: 800
Avg. Free Circ.: 14
Audit Company: Sworn/Estimate/Non-Audited
Audit Date: 43626

FARMINGTON

THE FARMINGTON PRESS

Street Address: 227 E Columbia St
City: Farmington
State: MO
ZIP Code: 63640-3106
General Phone: (573) 756-8927
General Email: mnicholson@farmingtonpressonline.com
Publication Website: http://www.farmingtonpress.com/
Editor Name: Shawnna Robinson
Editor Email: srobinson@farmingtonpressonline.com
Editor Phone: (573) 756-8927
Advertising Executive Name: Sarah Jones
Advertising Executive Email: sjones@dailyjournalonline.com
Year Established: 1928
Published Days: Wed
Audit Company: Sworn/Estimate/Non-Audited
Audit Date: 43626

FAYETTE

FAYETTE ADVERTISER

Street Address: 203 N Main St
City: Fayette
State: MO
ZIP Code: 65248-1421
General Phone: (660) 248-2235
General Email: advertising@fayettenews.com
Publication Website: https://www.fayettenewspapers.com/
Publisher Name: Justin Addison
Publisher Email: jaddison@fayettenews.com
Editor Name: Justin Addison
Editor Email: jaddison@fayettenews.com
Advertising Executive Email: advertising@fayettenews.com
Delivery Methods: Mail`Newsstand
Year Established: 1840
Commercial printers?: Y
Mechanical specifications: Type page 14 x 22; E - 6 cols, 2 1/16, between; A - 6 cols, 2 1/16, between; C - 6 cols, 2 1/16, between.
Published Days: Wed
Avg. Paid Circ.: 1800
Audit Company: Sworn/Estimate/Non-Audited
Audit Date: 43626

FAYETTE

THE FAYETTE ADVERTISER

Street Address: 203 N Main St
City: Fayette
State: MO
ZIP Code: 65248-1421
General Phone: (660) 248-2235
General Email: advertising@fayettenews.com
Publication Website: https://www.fayettenewspapers.com/
Publisher Name: Justin Addison
Publisher Email: jaddison@fayettenews.com
Editor Name: Justin Addison
Editor Email: jaddison@fayettenews.com
Advertising Executive Email: advertising@fayettenews.com
Year Established: 1840
Mechanical specifications: Type page 14 x 22; E - 6 cols, 2 1/16, 1/8 between; A - 6 cols, 2 1/16, 1/8 between; C - 6 cols, 2 1/16, 1/8 between.
Published Days: Wed`Sat
Avg. Paid Circ.: 2300
Audit Company: Sworn/Estimate/Non-Audited
Audit Date: 43626

FLORISSANT

INDEPENDENT NEWS

Street Address: 25 Saint Anthony Ln
City: Florissant
State: MO
ZIP Code: 63031-6720
General Phone: (314) 831-4645
General Email: independentnws@aol.com
Publication Website: http://www.flovalleynews.com/
Parent Company: Community Media Group
Delivery Methods: Carrier`Racks
Year Established: 1987
Mechanical specifications: Type page 10 x 16; E - 5 cols, 2, 3/8 between; A - 5 cols, 2, 3/8 between; C - 8 cols, 1 1/2, 1/8 between.
Published Days: Thur
Avg. Free Circ.: 25506
Audit Company: CVC
Audit Date: 43081

FORT LEONARD WOOD

FORT LEONARD WOOD GUIDON

Street Address: 4079 Illinois Ave
City: Fort Leonard Wood
State: MO
ZIP Code: 65473-9105
General Phone: (573) 563-5014
General Email: dgunter@gannett.com
Publication Website: https://www.myguidon.com/
Editor Name: Brian Hill
Editor Email: guidoneditor@myguidon.com
Editor Phone: (573) 563-5014
Advertising Executive Name: Joshwa McMullen
Advertising Executive Email: jmcmullen@gannett.com
Advertising Executive Phone: (417) 836-1168
Published Days: Thur
Audit Company: Sworn/Estimate/Non-Audited
Audit Date: 43626

FREDERICKTOWN

DEMOCRAT NEWS

Street Address: 131 S Main St
City: Fredericktown
State: MO
ZIP Code: 63645-1451
General Phone: (573) 783-3366
General Email: mmenley@dailyjournalonline.com
Publication Website: https://dailyjournalonline.com/democrat-news/
Publisher Name: Melissa Bellew
Publisher Email: mbellew@dailyjournalonline.com
Publisher Phone: (573) 518-3635
Editor Name: Teresa Ressel
Editor Email: tressel@dailyjournalonline.com
Editor Phone: (573) 518-3613
Advertising Executive Name: Michelle Menley
Advertising Executive Email: mmenley@dailyjournalonline.com
Advertising Executive Phone: (573) 518-3603
Delivery Methods: Mail`Newsstand`Carrier`Racks
Year Established: 1870
Own Printing Facility?: Y
Commercial printers?: Y
Published Days: Wed
Avg. Paid Circ.: 2300
Avg. Free Circ.: 300
Audit Company: Sworn/Estimate/Non-Audited
Audit Date: 43626

GAINESVILLE

OZARK COUNTY TIMES

Street Address: 504 Third Street
City: Gainesville
State: MO
ZIP Code: 65655
General Phone: (417) 679-4641
General Email: jenny@ozarkcountytimes.com
Publication Website: http://www.ozarkcountytimes.com/
Parent Company: Ozark County Media LLC
Publisher Name: Norene Prososki
Publisher Email: norene@ozarkcountytimes.com
Editor Name: Sue Ann Jones
Editor Email: sueann@ozarkcountytimes.com
Advertising Executive Name: Jenny Yarger
Advertising Executive Email: jenny@ozarkcountytimes.com
Delivery Methods: Mail`Racks
Year Established: 1876
Mechanical specifications: Type page 13 x 21 1/2; E - 6 cols, 2 1/12, 1/6 between; A - 6 cols, 2 1/12, 1/6 between; C - 6 cols, 2 1/12, 1/6 between.
Published Days: Wed
Avg. Paid Circ.: 3050
Audit Company: Sworn/Estimate/Non-Audited
Audit Date: 43626

GALLATIN

GALLATIN NORTH MISSOURIAN

Street Address: 609B S Main St
City: Gallatin
State: MO
ZIP Code: 64640-1447
General Phone: (660) 663-2154
General Email: gpc@gpcink.com
Publication Website: https://gallatinnorthmissourian.com/
Publisher Name: Darryl Wilkinson
Publisher Email: darryl@gpcink.com
Advertising Executive Name: Brooke Trussell
Advertising Executive Email: advertising@gpcink.com
Delivery Methods: Mail`Newsstand`Racks
Year Established: 1864
Own Printing Facility?: Y
Commercial printers?: Y
Mechanical specifications: Type page 10" x 16"; E - 5 cols, 1 5/6, 1/6 between; A - 5 cols, 1 5/6, 1/6 between; C - 5 cols, 1 5/6, 1/6 between.
Published Days: Wed
Avg. Paid Circ.: 1700
Audit Company: Sworn/Estimate/Non-Audited
Audit Date: 43626
Pressroom Equipment: 6-unit News King Web Press
Pressroom Software: RTI
Business Equipment: IBM compatibles
Business Software: Adobe InDesign CS5 Suite CorelDraw

GRANDVIEW

JACKSON COUNTY ADVOCATE

Street Address: 1102 Main St
City: Grandview
State: MO
ZIP Code: 64030-2480
General Phone: (816) 761-6200
General Email: mwilson@jcadvocate.com
Publication Website: http://www.jcadvocate.com/
Publisher Name: Mike Davis
Editor Name: Mary K. Wilson
Editor Email: mwilson@jcadvocate.com
Editor Phone: (816) 761-6200
Delivery Methods: Mail`Newsstand`Racks
Year Established: 1953
Own Printing Facility?: Y
Published Days: Thur
Avg. Paid Circ.: 6000
Avg. Free Circ.: 175
Audit Company: Sworn/Estimate/Non-Audited
Audit Date: 43626

GREENFIELD

THE VEDETTE

Street Address: 7 N Main St#2
City: Greenfield
State: MO
ZIP Code: 65661-1128
General Phone: (417) 637-2712
General Email: editor@greenfieldvedette.com
Publication Website: https://www.greenfieldvedette.com/
Parent Company: Phil Calian
Publisher Name: Gina Langston
Editor Name: Gina Langston
Editor Email: editor@greenfieldvedette.com
Delivery Methods: Mail`Racks
Year Established: 1866
Own Printing Facility?: N
Commercial printers?: N
Published Days: Thur
Avg. Paid Circ.: 1500
Audit Company: Sworn/Estimate/Non-Audited
Audit Date: 43626

HAMILTON

THE CALDWELL COUNTY NEWS

Street Address: 101 S Davis St
City: Hamilton
State: MO
ZIP Code: 64644-1405
General Phone: (816) 583-2116
General Email: ads@mycaldwellcounty.com
Publication Website: http://www.mycaldwellcounty.com/
Parent Company: L & L Publications, Inc
Delivery Methods: Mail`Newsstand`Racks
Year Established: 1869
Own Printing Facility?: N
Commercial printers?: N
Published Days: Wed
Avg. Paid Circ.: 1140
Avg. Free Circ.: 72
Audit Company: Sworn/Estimate/Non-Audited
Audit Date: 43626

HANNIBAL

SALT RIVER JOURNAL

Street Address: 200 N 3rd St
City: Hannibal
State: MO
ZIP Code: 63401-3504
General Phone: (573) 221-2800
General Email: saltriverjournal@quincymedia.com
Publication Website: http://www.hannibal.net/
Parent Company: Quincy Media Inc
Publisher Name: Ron Wallace
Publisher Email: rwallace@courierpost.com
Publisher Phone: (217) 221-3381
Editor Name: Doug Wilson
Editor Email: dwilson@courierpost.com
Editor Phone: (573) 248-2750
Advertising Executive Name: Shelly Bissell
Advertising Executive Email: sbissell@courierpost.com
Advertising Executive Phone: (217) 221-3337
Year Established: 1838
Own Printing Facility?: Y
Commercial printers?: Y
Mechanical specifications: Type page 11 3/4 x 21 1/2; E - 6 cols, 1 5/6, 1/8 between; A - 6 cols, 1 1/4, 1/8 between; C - 9 cols, 1 5/6, 1/12 between.
Published Days: Wed
Avg. Paid Circ.: 5383
Avg. Free Circ.: 9230
Audit Company: Sworn/Estimate/Non-Audited
Audit Date: 43626

HERMANN

THE HERMANN ADVERTISER-COURIER

Street Address: 136 E 4th St
City: Hermann
State: MO
ZIP Code: 65041-1177
General Phone: (573) 486-5418
General Email: info@hermannadvertisercourier.com
Publication Website: https://www.hermannadvertisercourier.com/
Parent Company: Lakeway Publishers, Inc.
Year Established: 1837
Mechanical specifications: Type page 13 x 21 1/2; E - 6 cols, 2 1/8, between; A - 6 cols, 2 1/8, between.
Published Days: Wed
Avg. Paid Circ.: 3900
Audit Company: Sworn/Estimate/Non-Audited
Audit Date: 43626

HERMITAGE

THE INDEX

Street Address: PO Box 127
City: Hermitage
State: MO
ZIP Code: 65668
General Phone: (417) 745-6404
General Email: jfoltz@vernonpublishing.com
Publication Website: https://www.vernonpublishing.com/Index/ContactUs
Parent Company: Vernon Publishing
Publisher Name: Trevor Vernon
Publisher Email: tvernon@vernonpublishing.com
Publisher Phone: (573) 392-5658
Editor Name: Jeremy Hulshof
Editor Email: jhulshof@vernonpublishing.com
Editor Phone: (417) 745-6404
Advertising Executive Email: theindex@vernonpublishing.com
Advertising Executive Phone: (417) 745-6404
Delivery Methods: Mail`Newsstand
Year Established: 1903
Own Printing Facility?: Y
Commercial printers?: Y
Mechanical specifications: 6 col x 21.5" 2" columns
Published Days: Wed
Avg. Paid Circ.: 4300
Audit Company: Sworn/Estimate/Non-Audited
Audit Date: 43626

HIGGINSVILLE

HIGGINSVILLE ADVANCE

Street Address: 3002 Highway 13 Blvd
City: Higginsville
State: MO
ZIP Code: 64037-1870
General Phone: (660) 584-3611
General Email: higvladv@ctcis.net
Publication Website: https://www.mainstreetnewsgroup.com/higginsvilleadvance/
Parent Company: Beverly Mackie
Publisher Name: Beverly Mackie
Publisher Email: bmackie@ctcis.net
Delivery Methods: Mail`Racks
Year Established: 1876
Own Printing Facility?: Y
Commercial printers?: Y
Published Days: Wed
Avg. Paid Circ.: 1700
Avg. Free Circ.: 15
Audit Company: Sworn/Estimate/Non-Audited
Audit Date: 43626

HOLLISTER

BRANSON TRI-LAKES NEWS

Street Address: 200 Industrial Park Dr
City: Hollister
State: MO
ZIP Code: 65672
General Phone: (417) 334-3161
General Email: internet@bransontrilakesnews.com
Publication Website: http://bransontrilakesnews.com
Parent Company: Branson Tri-Lakes News
Publisher Name: Robert Erickson
Publisher Email: rerickson@bransontrilakesnews.com
Editor Name: Cliff Sain
Editor Email: csain@bransontrilakesnews.com
Delivery Methods: Mail`Newsstand`Racks
Year Established: 1895
Own Printing Facility?: Y
Commercial printers?: Y
Mechanical specifications: Type page 11 1/2 x 21; E - 6 cols, 1 13/16, 1/8 between; A - 6 cols, 1 13/16, 1/8 between; C - 6 cols, 1 13/16, 1/8 between.
Published Days: Wed`Sat
Weekday Frequency: m
Avg. Paid Circ.: 9300
Avg. Free Circ.: 19000
Audit Company: Sworn/Estimate/Non-Audited
Audit Date: 43626
Pressroom Equipment: Lines -- 12-G/Community 1996.;
Mailroom Equipment: Counter Stackers -- KAN; Inserters & Stuffers -- KAN/480 5:1; Tying Machines -- Bu; Address Machine -- KAN;
Business Equipment: 5-PC, MSSI
Classified Equipment: Hardware -- APP/iMac, 2-APP/Mac Classic II; Printers -- APP/Mac LaserPrinter;
Classified Software: Baseview/Class Manager.
Editorial Equipment: Hardware -- APP/Mac G3; Printers -- APP/Mac LaserPrinter
Editorial Software: Baseview/NewsEdit, Baseview/Wire Manager.
Production Equipment: Hardware -- Caere/OmniPage; Cameras -- LE; Scanners -- Ofoto, APP/Mac One Scanner.

HOUSTON

HOUSTON HERALD

Street Address: 113 N Grand Ave
City: Houston
State: MO
ZIP Code: 65483-1223
General Phone: (417) 967-2000
General Email: news@houstonherald.com
Publication Website: https://www.houstonherald.com/
Publisher Name: Bradley G. Gentry
Publisher Email: bgentry@houstonherald.com
Advertising Executive Name: Doug Davison
Advertising Executive Email: ddavison@houstonherald.com
Delivery Methods: Mail`Newsstand`Carrier`Racks
Year Established: 1878
Own Printing Facility?: Y
Commercial printers?: Y
Mechanical specifications: Type page 11.625 x 21; E - 6 cols, 1.83, 1/6 between; A - 6 cols, 1.83, 1/6 between; C - 6 cols, 1.83, 1/6 between.
Published Days: Thur
Weekday Frequency: m
Avg. Paid Circ.: 4075
Avg. Free Circ.: 6100
Audit Company: Sworn/Estimate/Non-Audited
Audit Date: 43626

HUMANSVILLE

HUMANSVILLE STAR-LEADER

Street Address: 117 N Ohio St
City: Humansville
State: MO
ZIP Code: 65674-8734
General Phone: (417) 754-2228
General Email: humansvillestarleader@gmail.com
Parent Company: Main Street Media of Tennessee
Delivery Methods: Mail
Year Established: 1887
Commercial printers?: Y
Published Days: Fri
Avg. Paid Circ.: 1715
Avg. Free Circ.: 10
Audit Company: Sworn/Estimate/Non-Audited
Audit Date: 43626

IRONTON

THE MOUNTAIN ECHO

Street Address: P.O. Box 25
City: Ironton
State: MO
ZIP Code: 63650
General Phone: (573) 546-3917
General Email: kimg@waynecojournalbanner.com
Publication Website: http://www.mountainecho.com/
Publisher Name: Kimberly Combs
Editor Name: Amy Patterson
Editor Email: news@myironcountynews.com
Advertising Executive Name: Addison Gipson
Advertising Executive Email: addison.gipson@wayneco journalbanner.com
Delivery Methods: Mail`Newsstand`Racks
Year Established: 1937
Own Printing Facility?: N
Commercial printers?: N
Mechanical specifications: Type page 11 5/8 x 21 1/2; E - 6 cols, 1 1/8, 1/6 between; A - 6 cols, 1 1/8, 1/6 between; C - 6 cols, 1 1/8, 1/6 between.
Published Days: Wed
Avg. Paid Circ.: 1407
Avg. Free Circ.: 4976
Audit Company: Sworn/Estimate/Non-Audited
Audit Date: 43626

JACKSON

CASH-BOOK JOURNAL/THE WEEKENDER

Street Address: 210 W Main St
City: Jackson
State: MO
ZIP Code: 63755-1822
General Phone: (573) 243-3515
General Email: stephanie.watkins@thecash-book.com
Publication Website: https://www.thecash-book.com/
Publisher Name: Gina Raffety
Publisher Email: gina.raffety@thecash-book.com
Editor Name: Gregory Dullum
Editor Email: greg.dullum@thecash-book.com
Advertising Executive Name: Stephanie Watkins
Advertising Executive Email: cashbookjournal@gmail.com
Year Established: 1870
Own Printing Facility?: Y
Commercial printers?: Y
Published Days: Wed`Fri
Avg. Paid Circ.: 6000
Avg. Free Circ.: 4000
Audit Company: Sworn/Estimate/Non-Audited
Audit Date: 43626

KAHOKA

THE MEDIA

Street Address: 178 W Main St
City: Kahoka
State: MO
ZIP Code: 63445-1637
General Phone: (660) 727-3395
General Email: news@kahokamedia.com
Publication Website: https://www.kahokamedia.com/
Publisher Name: Sue Scott
Delivery Methods: Mail`Newsstand
Year Established: 1977
Mechanical specifications: Type page 13 x 21; E - 6 cols, 2, 1/6 between; A - 6 cols, 1/6 between; C - 8 cols, 1 1/2, 1/6 between.
Published Days: Wed
Avg. Paid Circ.: 2650
Audit Company: Sworn/Estimate/Non-Audited
Audit Date: 43626

KANSAS CITY

KANSAS CITY BUSINESS JOURNAL

Street Address: 1100 Main St, Suite 2450
City: Kansas City
State: MO
ZIP Code: 64105-5123
General Phone: (816) 421-5900
General Email: kansascity@bizjournals.com
Publication Website: https://www.bizjournals.com/kansascity/
Parent Company: American City Business Journals
Publisher Name: Stacie Prosser
Publisher Email: sprosser@bizjournals.com
Publisher Phone: (816) 777-2225
Editor Name: Russell Gray
Editor Email: rgray@bizjournals.com
Editor Phone: (816) 777-2246
Advertising Executive Name: Beth Collins
Advertising Executive Email: bcollins@

Community Newspapers in the U.S.

bizjournals.com
Delivery Methods: Mail˜Newsstand˜Racks
Year Established: 1982
Published Days: Fri
Published Other: Morning Briefing and Daily Updates available Monday thru Friday
Avg. Paid Circ.: 10500
Audit Company: Sworn/Estimate/Non-Audited
Audit Date: 43626

KANSAS CITY

LEE'S SUMMIT JOURNAL

Street Address: 1601 McGee St.
City: Kansas City
State: MO
ZIP Code: 64108
General Phone: (816) 234-4345
Publication Website: https://www.kansascity.com/news/local/community/lsjournal/
Editor Name: Greg Farmer
Editor Email: gfarmer@kcstar.com
Editor Phone: (816) 234-4321
Year Established: 1881
Mechanical specifications: Type page 13 x 21; E - 6 cols, 2 1/16, 1/8 between; A - 6 cols, 2 1/16, 1/8 between; C - 9 cols, 1 3/4, 1/8 between.
Published Days: Wed˜Fri
Avg. Paid Circ.: 3369
Avg. Free Circ.: 2521
Audit Company: Sworn/Estimate/Non-Audited
Audit Date: 43626

KANSAS CITY

THE NORTHEAST NEWS

Street Address: 5715 Saint John Ave
City: Kansas City
State: MO
ZIP Code: 64123-1819
General Phone: (816) 241-0765
General Email: northeastnews@socket.net
Publication Website: http://www.northeastnews.net/
Parent Company: Chris Adams
Publisher Name: Michael Bushnell
Publisher Email: mbushnell@northeastnews.net
Editor Name: Paul Thompson
Advertising Executive Name: Dorri Partain
Advertising Executive Email: advertising@northeastnews.net
Delivery Methods: Carrier
Year Established: 1932
Published Days: Wed
Avg. Paid Circ.: 28
Avg. Free Circ.: 10000
Audit Company: CVC
Audit Date: 43081

LA GRANGE

THE CANTON PRESS-NEWS JOURNAL

Street Address: 109 N 4th St
City: La Grange
State: MO
ZIP Code: 63448
General Phone: (573) 288-5668
General Email: ads@lewispnj.com
Publication Website: https://www.lewispnj.com/
Editor Email: rita@lewispnj.com
Advertising Executive Email: ads@lewispnj.com
Own Printing Facility?: Y
Commercial printers?: Y
Mechanical specifications: Type page 11 3/4 x 21; E - 6 cols, 1 3/4, 1/4 between; A - 6 cols, 1 3/4, 1/4 between; C - 6 cols, 1 3/4, 1/4 between.

Published Days: Thur
Avg. Paid Circ.: 3000
Audit Company: Sworn/Estimate/Non-Audited
Audit Date: 43626

LAMAR

LAMAR DEMOCRAT

Street Address: 100 E 11th St
City: Lamar
State: MO
ZIP Code: 64759
General Phone: (417) 682-5529
General Email: melissa@lamardemocrat.com
Publication Website: https://www.lamardemocrat.com/
Publisher Email: melodymetzger@lamardemocrat.com
Advertising Executive Email: melissa@lamardemocrat.com
Delivery Methods: Mail˜Racks
Year Established: 1920
Published Days: Wed˜Sat
Published Other: daily on the web
Avg. Paid Circ.: 3335
Audit Company: Sworn/Estimate/Non-Audited
Audit Date: 43626

LEES SUMMIT

LEE'S SUMMIT TRIBUNE

Street Address: 219 SE Douglas St
City: Lees Summit
State: MO
ZIP Code: 64063-2328
General Phone: (816) 524-0061
General Email: editor@lstribune.net
Publication Website: http://lstribune.net/
Parent Company: Linda Ahern
Publisher Name: Linda Ahern
Publisher Email: editor@lstribune.net
Editor Name: Linda Ahern
Editor Email: editor@lstribune.net
Delivery Methods: Mail˜Newsstand˜Racks
Year Established: 2002
Mechanical specifications: 10.5" wide by 21.5" tall
Published Days: Sat
Avg. Paid Circ.: 3500
Audit Company: Sworn/Estimate/Non-Audited
Audit Date: 43626

LIBERTY

GLADSTONE DISPATCH

Street Address: 104 N Main St
City: Liberty
State: MO
ZIP Code: 64068
General Phone: (816) 454-9660
General Email: sandy.nelson@npgco.com
Publication Website: http://www.gladstonedispatch.com/
Parent Company: News-Press & Gazette Co.
Publisher Name: Sandy Nelson
Publisher Email: sandy.nelson@npgco.com
Publisher Phone: (816) 389-6608
Editor Name: Kellie Houx
Editor Email: kellie.houx@npgco.com
Editor Phone: (816) 389-6630
Advertising Executive Name: Quinn Gregg
Advertising Executive Email: quinn.gregg@npgco.com
Advertising Executive Phone: (816) 389-6619
Published Days: Thur
Audit Company: Sworn/Estimate/Non-Audited
Audit Date: 43626

LIBERTY

THE COURIER TRIBUNE

Street Address: 104 N. Main St.
City: Liberty
State: MO
ZIP Code: 64068
General Phone: (816) 781-4941
General Email: advertise@mycouriertribune.com
Publication Website: https://www.mycouriertribune.com/
Delivery Methods: Mail˜Newsstand˜Racks
Year Established: 1888
Mechanical specifications: Type page 10 1/4 x 20; E - 6 cols, 2, 1/6 between; A - 6 cols, 2, 1/6 between; C - 6 cols, 2, 1/6 between.
Published Days: Wed
Avg. Paid Circ.: 2000
Audit Company: Sworn/Estimate/Non-Audited
Audit Date: 43626

LICKING

THE LICKING NEWS

Street Address: 115 S Main St
City: Licking
State: MO
ZIP Code: 65542
General Phone: (573) 674-2412
General Email: news_ads@thelickingnews.com
Publication Website: https://www.thelickingnews.com/
Parent Company: Shari Harris and Scott Hamilton
Publisher Name: Scott Hamilton
Publisher Email: publisher@thelickingnews.com
Editor Name: Katie Anderson
Editor Email: news_ads@thelickingnews.com
Year Established: 1893
Own Printing Facility?: Y
Commercial printers?: Y
Published Days: Thur
Avg. Paid Circ.: 2421
Audit Company: Sworn/Estimate/Non-Audited
Audit Date: 43626

LINN

UNTERRIFIED DEMOCRAT

Street Address: 300 E Main St
City: Linn
State: MO
ZIP Code: 65051
General Phone: (573) 897-3150
General Email: udnewslinn@gmail.com
Publication Website: https://www.unterrifieddemocrat.com/
Delivery Methods: Mail
Year Established: 1866
Mechanical specifications: Type page 15 3/4 x 21; E - 6 cols, 2 1/3, between; A - 8 cols, 1 5/6, between; C - 8 cols, 2, 1/6 between.
Published Days: Wed
Avg. Paid Circ.: 7100
Audit Company: Sworn/Estimate/Non-Audited
Audit Date: 43626

MACON

THE HOME PRESS

Street Address: 115 N. Rubey
City: Macon
State: MO
ZIP Code: 63552
General Phone: (660) 395-4663
General Email: shon@maconhomepress.com
Publication Website: https://www.maconhomepress.com/
Parent Company: Macon County Home Press

Publisher Email: shon@maconhomepress.com
Delivery Methods: Mail
Year Established: 1876
Commercial printers?: Y
Published Days: Wed
Audit Company: Sworn/Estimate/Non-Audited
Audit Date: 43626

MARSHFIELD

THE MARSHFIELD MAIL

Street Address: 225 N Clay St
City: Marshfield
State: MO
ZIP Code: 65706
General Phone: (417) 468-2013
General Email: news@marshfieldmail.com
Publication Website: http://marshfieldmail.com/
Parent Company: Phillips Media Group, LLC
Delivery Methods: Mail˜Newsstand
Year Established: 1891
Own Printing Facility?: Y
Commercial printers?: Y
Mechanical specifications: Type page 10.25 x 21; E - 6 cols, 2 1/6, 1/6 between; A - 6 cols, 2 1/6, 1/6 between; C - 8 cols, 1 1/2, 1/6 between.
Published Days: Wed
Avg. Paid Circ.: 4814
Avg. Free Circ.: 99
Audit Company: Sworn/Estimate/Non-Audited
Audit Date: 43626

MARYVILLE

NODAWAY NEWS LEADER

Street Address: 116 E 3rd St
City: Maryville
State: MO
ZIP Code: 64468
General Phone: (660) 562-4747
General Email: ldalton@nodawaynews.com
Publication Website: https://nodawaynews.com/
Parent Company: Kay Wilson
Publisher Name: Kay Wilson
Publisher Email: kwilson@nodawaynews.com
Editor Name: Kay Wilson
Editor Email: kwilson@nodawaynews.com
Editor Phone: (660) 562-8635
Advertising Executive Name: Lisa Dalton
Advertising Executive Email: ldalton@nodawaynews.com
Advertising Executive Phone: (660) 562-4421
Delivery Methods: Mail˜Newsstand
Year Established: 1996
Published Days: Thur
Avg. Paid Circ.: 2649
Audit Company: Sworn/Estimate/Non-Audited
Audit Date: 43626

MEMPHIS

MEMPHIS DEMOCRAT

Street Address: 121 S Main St
City: Memphis
State: MO
ZIP Code: 63555
General Phone: (660) 465-7016
General Email: news@memphisdemocrat.com
Publication Website: http://www.memphisdemocrat.com/
Publisher Name: Sue Scott
Publisher Email: news@memphisdemocrat.com
Publisher Phone: (660) 465-7016
Year Established: 1872
Published Days: Wed

III-295

Avg. Paid Circ.: 2780
Audit Company: Sworn/Estimate/Non-Audited
Audit Date: 43626

MOUND CITY

MOUND CITY NEWS

Street Address: 18121 Hwy. 59
City: Mound City
State: MO
ZIP Code: 64470
General Phone: (660) 442-5423
General Email: moundcitynews@socket.net
Publication Website: http://www.moundcitynews.com/
Parent Company: Adam Johnson
Publisher Name: Adam Johnson
Editor Name: Adam Johnson
Advertising Executive Name: Pam Kent
Year Established: 1879
Mechanical specifications: Type page 13 x 21 1/2; E - 6 cols, 2 1/16, 1/6 between; A - 6 cols, 2 1/16, 1/6 between; C - 7 cols, 1 4/5, 1/6 between.
Published Days: Thur
Avg. Paid Circ.: 2600
Audit Company: Sworn/Estimate/Non-Audited
Audit Date: 43626

MOUNT VERNON

LAWRENCE COUNTY RECORD

Street Address: 312 S Hickory St
City: Mount Vernon
State: MO
ZIP Code: 65712
General Phone: (417) 466-2185
General Email: recordadvertising@centurytel.net
Publication Website: http://www.lawrencecountyrecord.com/
Editor Email: thepaper@lawrencecountyrecord.com
Advertising Executive Email: recordadvertising@centurytel.net
Delivery Methods: Mail`Newsstand`Carrier`Racks
Year Established: 1876
Own Printing Facility?: Y
Mechanical specifications: Type page 11 5/8 x 21 1/2; E - 6 cols, 1 3/4, 1/6 between; A - 6 cols, 2 1/16, 1/6 between; C - 6 cols, 2 1/16, 1/6 between.
Published Days: Wed
Avg. Paid Circ.: 4000
Avg. Free Circ.: 7600
Audit Company: Sworn/Estimate/Non-Audited
Audit Date: 43626

NEOSHO

NEWTON COUNTY NEWS

Street Address: 200 S Jefferson St
City: Neosho
State: MO
ZIP Code: 64850
General Phone: (417) 455-6901
Publication Website: https://photos.newconews.com/
Published Days: Wed
Avg. Paid Circ.: 2500
Avg. Free Circ.: 10
Audit Company: Sworn/Estimate/Non-Audited
Audit Date: 43626

NEOSHO

SENECA NEWS-DISPATCH

Street Address: 212 E Main St.
City: Neosho
State: MO
ZIP Code: 64850
General Phone: (417) 451-3798
General Email: jimmy@thenewsdispatch.net
Publication Website: https://www.thenewsdispatch.net/
Parent Company: Sexton Media Group, Inc.
Publisher Name: Jimmy Sexton
Publisher Email: jimmy@thenewsdispatch.net
Editor Name: Madeleine Sexton
Year Established: 1882
Commercial printers?: Y
Mechanical specifications: Type page 11 2/3 x 21 1/2; E - 6 cols, 1 5/6, 1/8 between; A - 6 cols, 1 5/6, 1/8 between; C - 6 cols, 1 5/6, 1/8 between.
Published Days: Thur
Avg. Paid Circ.: 1800
Audit Company: Sworn/Estimate/Non-Audited
Audit Date: 43626

NEW MADRID

THE WEEKLY RECORD

Street Address: 218 Main St
City: New Madrid
State: MO
ZIP Code: 63869-1911
General Phone: (573) 748-2120
General Email: ed@weeklyrecord.net
Publication Website: http://www.weeklyrecord.net/
Delivery Methods: Mail`Newsstand`Racks
Year Established: 1866
Mechanical specifications: Type page 10 x 21 1/4; E - 6 cols, 3/16 between; A - 6 cols, .125 between; C - 6 cols, .125 between.
Published Days: Fri
Avg. Paid Circ.: 1000
Avg. Free Circ.: 60
Audit Company: Sworn/Estimate/Non-Audited
Audit Date: 43626

ODESSA

THE ODESSAN

Street Address: 212 W Mason St
City: Odessa
State: MO
ZIP Code: 64076
General Phone: (816) 230-5311
General Email: spaar@iland.net
Publication Website: http://www.theodessan.net/
Publisher Name: John Spaar
Publisher Email: spaar@iland.net
Editor Name: Hannah Spaar
Advertising Executive Name: John Spaar
Advertising Executive Email: spaar@iland.net
Delivery Methods: Mail`Racks
Year Established: 1880
Own Printing Facility?: Y
Commercial printers?: Y
Mechanical specifications: 22 inch web
Published Days: Thur
Avg. Paid Circ.: 4200
Audit Company: Sworn/Estimate/Non-Audited
Audit Date: 43626

OWENSVILLE

GASCONADE COUNTY REPUBLICAN

Street Address: 106 E Washington Ave
City: Owensville
State: MO
ZIP Code: 65066
General Phone: (573) 437-2323
General Email: news@wardpub.com
Publication Website: https://www.gasconadecountyrepublican.com/
Parent Company: Gasconade County Republican
Delivery Methods: Mail`Newsstand`Carrier`Racks
Year Established: 1905
Own Printing Facility?: Y
Mechanical specifications: Type page 13 x 21 1/2; E - 6 cols, 2 1/30, 1/6 between; A - 6 cols, 2 1/30, 1/6 between; C - 6 cols, 2 1/30, 1/6 between.
Published Days: Wed
Avg. Paid Circ.: 2800
Audit Company: Sworn/Estimate/Non-Audited
Audit Date: 43626

OZARK

CHRISTIAN COUNTY HEADLINER NEWS

Street Address: 114 N 2nd Ave
City: Ozark
State: MO
ZIP Code: 65721
General Phone: (417) 581-3541
General Email: news@ccheadliner.com
Publication Website: http://ccheadliner.com/
Delivery Methods: Mail`Newsstand`Racks
Year Established: 1961
Own Printing Facility?: Y
Mechanical specifications: Type page 10 1/2 x 21; E - 6 cols, 1 4/5, between; A - 6 cols, 1 4/5, between; C - 6 cols, 1 4/5, between.
Published Days: Wed
Avg. Paid Circ.: 3412
Avg. Free Circ.: 377
Audit Company: Sworn/Estimate/Non-Audited
Audit Date: 43626

PALMYRA

PALMYRA SPECTATOR

Street Address: 304 S Main St
City: Palmyra
State: MO
ZIP Code: 63461
General Phone: (573) 769-3111
General Email: editorial@palmyra-spectator.com
Publication Website: http://www.palmyra-spectator.com/
Publisher Name: Mark Cheffey
Publisher Email: editorial@palmyra-spectator.com
Editor Name: Mark Cheffey
Editor Email: editorial@palmyra-spectator.com
Advertising Executive Name: Chase Johnston
Advertising Executive Email: advertising@palmyra-spectator.com
Year Established: 1839
Own Printing Facility?: Y
Commercial printers?: Y
Published Days: Wed
Avg. Paid Circ.: 2628
Avg. Free Circ.: 75
Audit Company: Sworn/Estimate/Non-Audited
Audit Date: 43626

PARIS

MONROE COUNTY APPEAL

Street Address: 230 N Main St
City: Paris
State: MO
ZIP Code: 65275
General Phone: (660) 327-4192
General Email: editor@monroecountyappeal.com
Publication Website: https://www.monroecountyappeal.com/
Parent Company: Lewis County Press
Editor Email: editor@monroecountyappeal.com
Delivery Methods: Mail`Newsstand
Year Established: 1868
Commercial printers?: Y
Published Days: Thur
Avg. Paid Circ.: 1000
Audit Company: Sworn/Estimate/Non-Audited
Audit Date: 43626

PARK HILLS

FARMINGTON PRESS

Street Address: 1513 S Saint Joe Dr
City: Park Hills
State: MO
ZIP Code: 63601-2402
General Phone: (573) 431-2010
General Email: mmenley@dailyjournalonline.com
Publication Website: https://dailyjournalonline.com/democrat-news/
Publisher Name: Melissa Bellew
Publisher Email: mbellew@dailyjournalonline.com
Publisher Phone: (573) 518-3635
Editor Name: Teresa Ressel
Editor Email: tressel@dailyjournalonline.com
Editor Phone: (573) 518-3613
Advertising Executive Name: Michelle Menley
Advertising Executive Email: mmenley@dailyjournalonline.com
Advertising Executive Phone: (573) 518-3603
Published Days: Wed
Audit Company: Sworn/Estimate/Non-Audited
Audit Date: 43626

PIEDMONT

WAYNE COUNTY JOURNAL-BANNER

Street Address: 101 West Elm
City: Piedmont
State: MO
ZIP Code: 63957
General Phone: (573) 223-7122
General Email: kimg@waynecojournalbanner.com
Publication Website: http://www.waynecojournalbanner.com/
Parent Company: Better Newspapers
Publisher Name: Kimberly Combs
Publisher Email: kimg@waynecojournalbanner.com
Advertising Executive Name: Addison Gipson
Advertising Executive Email: addison.gipson@waynecojournalbanner.com
Delivery Methods: Mail`Newsstand
Year Established: 1876
Own Printing Facility?: Y
Commercial printers?: Y
Mechanical specifications: Type page 11.125 x 21.5; E - 6 cols, 1 5/6, 1/8 between; A - 6 cols, 1 5/6, 1/8 between; C - 6 cols, 1 5/6, 1/8 between.
Published Days: Thur
Avg. Paid Circ.: 3200
Avg. Free Circ.: 70
Audit Company: Sworn/Estimate/Non-Audited
Audit Date: 43626

PINEVILLE

MCDONALD COUNTY NEWS-GAZETTE

Street Address: 11248 US-71
City: Pineville
State: MO
ZIP Code: 64856

Community Newspapers in the U.S.

General Phone: (479) 855-3724
General Email: mcpress@nwadg.com
Publication Website: https://mdcp.nwaonline.com/
Parent Company: NWA Media
Editor Name: Rusty Turner
Editor Email: rturner@nwadg.com
Advertising Executive Name: Don Jones
Advertising Executive Email: djones@nwadg.com
Delivery Methods: Mail`Newsstand`Racks
Own Printing Facility?: Y
Published Days: Thur
Avg. Paid Circ.: 1431
Audit Company: Sworn/Estimate/Non-Audited
Audit Date: 43626

PINEVILLE

MCDONALD COUNTY PRESS

Street Address: 11248 US-71
City: Pineville
State: MO
ZIP Code: 64856
General Phone: (479) 855-3724
General Email: mcpress@nwadg.com
Publication Website: https://mdcp.nwaonline.com/
Parent Company: WEHCO Media, Inc.
Editor Name: Rusty Turner
Editor Email: rturner@nwadg.com
Advertising Executive Name: Don Jones
Advertising Executive Email: djones@nwadg.com
Delivery Methods: Mail
Own Printing Facility?: Y
Commercial printers?: Y
Published Days: Wed
Avg. Paid Circ.: 6127
Audit Company: Sworn/Estimate/Non-Audited
Audit Date: 43626

PLATTE CITY

THE PLATTE COUNTY CITIZEN

Street Address: PO Box 888
City: Platte City
State: MO
ZIP Code: 64079
General Phone: (816) 858-5154
General Email: advertising@plattecountycitizen.com
Publication Website: http://www.plattecountycitizen.com/
Editor Name: Cody Thorn
Editor Email: editor@plattecountycitizen.com
Advertising Executive Name: Bob Chizek
Advertising Executive Email: graphicdesign@plattecountycitizen.com
Delivery Methods: Mail`Newsstand`Racks
Year Established: 1962
Own Printing Facility?: Y
Commercial printers?: Y
Published Days: Wed
Avg. Paid Circ.: 3560
Avg. Free Circ.: 7300
Audit Company: Sworn/Estimate/Non-Audited
Audit Date: 43626

PLATTSBURG

THE CLINTON COUNTY LEADER

Street Address: 102 E Maple St
City: Plattsburg
State: MO
ZIP Code: 64477
General Phone: (816) 539-2111
General Email: leader@clintoncountyleader.com
Publication Website: http://www.clintoncountyleader.com/
Publisher Name: Steve Tinnen
Publisher Email: publisher@clintoncountyleader.com
Editor Name: Brett Adkison
Editor Email: leader@clintoncountyleader.com
Advertising Executive Name: Nikki Keling
Advertising Executive Email: nikki@clintoncountyleader.com
Delivery Methods: Mail
Year Established: 1895
Own Printing Facility?: Y
Commercial printers?: Y
Published Days: Thur
Avg. Paid Circ.: 2400
Audit Company: Sworn/Estimate/Non-Audited
Audit Date: 43626

PLEASANT HILL

PLEASANT HILL TIMES

Street Address: 126 S 1st St
City: Pleasant Hill
State: MO
ZIP Code: 64080-1604
General Phone: (816) 540-3500
General Email: advertising.phtimes@comcast.net
Publication Website: https://www.phtimes.net/
Publisher Name: Pat Roll
Publisher Email: plroll@hotmail.com
Editor Email: editor.phtimes@comcast.net
Advertising Executive Email: advertising.phtimes@comcast.net
Delivery Methods: Mail`Racks
Year Established: 1901
Mechanical specifications: The Times: 6 columns by 20.5 inches. Column widths are: 1 column, 1.611 inches
Published Days: Wed
Audit Company: Sworn/Estimate/Non-Audited
Audit Date: 43626

POTOSI

THE INDEPENDENT-JOURNAL

Street Address: 119 E High St
City: Potosi
State: MO
ZIP Code: 63664-1906
General Phone: (573) 438-5141
General Email: ijnews@centurytel.net
Publication Website: http://www.theijnews.com/news/
Parent Company: Kristopher Hugh Richards
Delivery Methods: Mail`Racks
Year Established: 1872
Own Printing Facility?: Y
Commercial printers?: Y
Mechanical specifications: Type page 13 x 21; E - 6 cols, 2 1/8, 1/16 between; A - 6 cols, 2 1/16, 1/16 between; C - 6 cols, 2 1/16, 1/8 between.
Published Days: Thur
Avg. Paid Circ.: 4485
Avg. Free Circ.: 425
Audit Company: Sworn/Estimate/Non-Audited
Audit Date: 43626

RICH HILL

RICH HILL MINING REVIEW

Street Address: P.O. Box 49
City: Rich Hill
State: MO
ZIP Code: 64776
General Phone: (417) 395-4131
General Email: sacosagenews@centurytel.net
Publication Website: https://www.mainstreetnewsgroup.com/richhillminingreview/contact-us/
Parent Company: Main Street Media of Tennessee
Commercial printers?: Y
Published Days: Fri
Avg. Paid Circ.: 1000
Audit Company: Sworn/Estimate/Non-Audited
Audit Date: 43626

RICHMOND

RICHMOND NEWS

Street Address: 204 W North Main St
City: Richmond
State: MO
ZIP Code: 64085-1610
General Phone: (816) 776-5454
General Email: marie@richmond-dailynews.com
Publication Website: https://www.richmond-dailynews.com/
Parent Company: Richmond News Inc.
Publisher Name: Brian K. Rice
Editor Name: Jack Ventimiglia
Advertising Executive Name: Wanda Rowe
Delivery Methods: Mail`Newsstand`Carrier
Year Established: 1914
Mechanical specifications: Type page 12 1/4 x 21 1/2; E - 4 cols, 2 31/32, 1/8 between; A - 7 cols, 1 5/8, 1/8 between; C - 7 cols, 1 5/8, 1/8 between.
Published Days: Tues`Wed`Fri
Weekday Frequency: e
Avg. Paid Circ.: 2050
Avg. Free Circ.: 8940
Audit Company: Sworn/Estimate/Non-Audited
Audit Date: 43626
Pressroom Equipment: Lines -- 5-G/Community; Pasters -- 1-HP/30Reels & Stands -- 5;
Mailroom Equipment: Counter Stackers -- 1-BG/Count-O-Veyor; Tying Machines -- 2/Bu.;
Business Equipment: IBM/5120
Classified Equipment: Hardware -- 1-Macintosh/iMac; Printers -- APP/Mac LaserWriter IIF.;
Editorial Equipment: Hardware -- 5-Macintosh/iMac; Printers -- APP/Mac LaserWriter IIF, APP/Mac Laserwriter Select, GCC/Elite XL 20/600
Editorial Software: QPS/QuarkXPress 4.0.
Production Equipment: Hardware -- 1-Nu; Cameras -- 1-R/400; Scanners -- Umax/2400, Nikon/CoolScan III.

ROCK PORT

ATCHISON COUNTY MAIL

Street Address: 300 S Main St
City: Rock Port
State: MO
ZIP Code: 64482-1534
General Phone: (660) 744-6245
General Email: amail@rpt.coop
Publication Website: https://farmerpublishing.com/
Parent Company: Farmer Publishing
Published Days: Thur
Avg. Paid Circ.: 2200
Avg. Free Circ.: 30
Audit Company: Sworn/Estimate/Non-Audited
Audit Date: 43626

SAINT LOUIS

SOUTH COUNTY TIMES

Street Address: 122 W Lockwood Ave
City: Saint Louis
State: MO
ZIP Code: 63119
General Phone: (314) 968-2699
General Email: advertising@timesnewspapers.com
Publication Website: https://www.timesnewspapers.com/southcountytimes/
Parent Company: Webster-Kirkwood Times, Inc.
Editor Email: editor@westendword.com
Advertising Executive Email: advertising@timesnewspapers.com
Advertising Executive Phone: (314) 968-2699
Delivery Methods: Carrier`Racks
Year Established: 1947
Mechanical specifications: see online rate card and media kit
Published Days: Fri
Avg. Free Circ.: 37489
Audit Company: CVC
Audit Date: 43658
Note: South County Times is owned by the independent, local company, Webster-Kirkwood Times, Inc. The company also publishes Webster-Kirkwood Times and West End Word

SAINT LOUIS

ST. LOUIS BUSINESS JOURNAL

Street Address: 815 Olive St
City: Saint Louis
State: MO
ZIP Code: 63101
General Phone: (314) 421-6200
General Email: stlouis@bizjournals.com
Publication Website: https://www.bizjournals.com/stlouis/
Parent Company: American City Business Journals
Publisher Name: Robert Bobroff
Publisher Email: rbobroff@bizjournals.com
Publisher Phone: (314) 421-8326
Editor Name: Erik Siemers
Editor Email: esiemers@bizjournals.com
Editor Phone: (314) 421-8324
Advertising Executive Name: Melissa Thomson
Advertising Executive Email: mtwall@bizjournals.com
Advertising Executive Phone: (314) 421-8340
Delivery Methods: Mail`Newsstand`Racks
Year Established: 1980
Published Days: Fri
Audit Company: Sworn/Estimate/Non-Audited
Audit Date: 43626

SAINT LOUIS

ST. LOUIS/SOUTHERN ILLINOIS LABOR TRIBUNE

Street Address: 505 S Ewing Ave
City: Saint Louis
State: MO
ZIP Code: 63103
General Phone: (314) 535-9660
General Email: info@labortribune.com
Publication Website: https://labortribune.com/
Parent Company: Labor Tribune
Publisher Email: publisher@labortribune.com
Advertising Executive Email: advertising@labortribune.com
Delivery Methods: Mail
Year Established: 1937
Mechanical specifications: Full page: 10 5/16" x 13" Half page: 5 1/16" 13" Quarter page: 5 1/16" x 6 1/2" Eighth page: 3 5/16" x 5"
Published Days: Thur
Published Other: Weekly
Avg. Paid Circ.: 31219
Avg. Free Circ.: 610
Audit Company: Sworn/Estimate/Non-Audited
Audit Date: 43626

SAINT LOUIS

WEBSTER-KIRKWOOD TIMES, INC.

Street Address: 122 W Lockwood Ave
City: Saint Louis
State: MO
ZIP Code: 63119
General Phone: (314) 968-2699
General Email: advertising@timesnewspapers.com
Publication Website: https://www.timesnewspapers.com/
Parent Company: Webster-Kirkwood Times, Inc.
Editor Email: editor@westendword.com
Advertising Executive Email: advertising@timesnewspapers.com
Advertising Executive Phone: (314) 968-2699
Delivery Methods: Carrier Racks
Year Established: 1978
Own Printing Facility?: Y
Mechanical specifications: Type page 10 x 15 3/4; E - 4 cols, 2 3/8, 1/4 between; A - 4 cols, 2 3/8, 1/4 between; C - 4 cols, 2 3/8, 1/4 between.
Published Days: Fri
Avg. Free Circ.: 40277
Audit Company: CVC
Audit Date: 43658
Note: Webster-Kirkwood Times, Inc. is independently owned. The company publishes Webster-Kirkwood Times, South County Times and West End Word

SAINT LOUIS

WEST END WORD

Street Address: 122 W Lockwood Ave
City: Saint Louis
State: MO
ZIP Code: 63119
General Phone: (314) 968-2699
General Email: advertising@timesnewspapers.com
Publication Website: https://www.timesnewspapers.com/
Parent Company: Webster-Kirkwood Times, Inc.
Editor Email: editor@westendword.com
Advertising Executive Email: advertising@timesnewspapers.com
Advertising Executive Phone: (314) 968-2699
Delivery Methods: Carrier Racks
Year Established: 1972
Own Printing Facility?: Y
Mechanical specifications: Type page 10 x 15 3/4; E - 4 cols, 2 3/8, 1/4 between; A - 4 cols, 2 3/8, 1/4 between; C - 4 cols, 2 3/8, 1/4 between.
Published Days: Fri
Published Other: Every two weeks on Friday
Avg. Free Circ.: 17211
Audit Company: CVC
Audit Date: 43988
Note: The West End Word is a publication of Webster-Kirkwood Times, Inc. The company also publishes Webster-Kirkwood Times and South County Times.

SAINTE GENEVIEVE

STE. GENEVIEVE HERALD

Street Address: 330 Market St
City: Sainte Genevieve
State: MO
ZIP Code: 63670-1638
General Phone: (573) 883-2222
General Email: jgettinger@stegenherald.com
Publication Website: http://www.stegenherald.com/
Parent Company: Ste. Genevieve Media, LLC
Publisher Name: Toby Carrig
Publisher Email: tcarrig@stegenherald.com
Editor Name: Toby Carrig
Editor Email: tcarrig@stegenherald.com
Advertising Executive Name: Jill Gettinger
Advertising Executive Email: jgettinger@stegenherald.com
Delivery Methods: Mail Newsstand
Year Established: 1882
Own Printing Facility?: Y
Mechanical specifications: Type page 11 x 20.5; E - 6 cols, 1 3/4, 1/8 between; A - 6 cols, 1 3/4, 1/8 between; C - 6 cols, 1 3/4, 1/8 between.
Published Days: Wed
Avg. Paid Circ.: 3665
Avg. Free Circ.: 76
Audit Company: Sworn/Estimate/Non-Audited
Audit Date: 43626

SALEM

THE SALEM NEWS

Street Address: PO Box 798
City: Salem
State: MO
ZIP Code: 65560
General Phone: (573) 729-4126
General Email: salemnews@thesalemnewsonline.com
Publication Website: https://www.thesalemnewsonline.com/
Parent Company: Ogden
Publisher Name: Donald Dodd
Publisher Email: donald@thesalemnewsonline.com
Publisher Phone: (573) 729-4126
Advertising Executive Name: Donna Purcell
Advertising Executive Email: donna@thesalemnewsonline.com
Delivery Methods: Mail Newsstand
Year Established: 1918
Own Printing Facility?: Y
Commercial printers?: Y
Mechanical specifications: Type page 13 x 21 1/2; E - 6 cols, 2 1/8, between; A - 6 cols, 2 1/8, between; C - 6 cols, 2 1/8, between.
Published Days: Tues
Avg. Paid Circ.: 3100
Avg. Free Circ.: 4400
Audit Company: Sworn/Estimate/Non-Audited
Audit Date: 43626

SHELBYVILLE

SHELBY COUNTY HERALD

Street Address: 109 E Main St
City: Shelbyville
State: MO
ZIP Code: 63469-1433
General Phone: (573) 633-2261
General Email: news@shelbycountyherald.com
Publication Website: https://www.shelbycountyherald.com/contact-us/
Parent Company: NEMOnews Media Group, LLC
Publisher Name: Sue Scott
Editor Name: Martha Jane East
Delivery Methods: Mail Newsstand
Mechanical specifications: Type page 13 x 21 1/2; A - 6 cols, between; C - 6 cols, between.
Published Days: Wed
Avg. Paid Circ.: 1500
Avg. Free Circ.: 40
Audit Company: Sworn/Estimate/Non-Audited
Audit Date: 43626

ST. LOUIS

NORTH SIDE JOURNAL

Street Address: 901 N. 10th St.
City: St. Louis
State: MO
ZIP Code: 63101
General Phone: (314) 340-8000
General Email: advertising@post-dispatch.com
Publication Website: https://www.stltoday.com/
Editor Name: Gilbert Bailon
Editor Email: gbailon@post-dispatch.com
Editor Phone: (314) 340-8387
Advertising Executive Email: advertising@post-dispatch.com
Own Printing Facility?: Y
Mechanical specifications: Type page 12 x 21 1/2; E - 6 cols, 1 7/8, 1/8 between; A - 6 cols, 1 7/8, 1/8 between; C - 10 cols, 1 1/4, 1/3 between.
Published Days: Wed
Avg. Free Circ.: 31000
Audit Company: Sworn/Estimate/Non-Audited
Audit Date: 43626

STEELVILLE

STEELVILLE STAR-CRAWFORD MIRROR

Street Address: 103 W MAIN ST
City: Steelville
State: MO
ZIP Code: 65565
General Phone: (573) 775-5454
General Email: advertising@threeriverspublishing.com
Publication Website: https://www.threeriverspublishing.com/TRP3/
Parent Company: Three Rivers Publishing, Inc.
Publisher Name: Rob Viehman
Publisher Email: rviehman@cubafreepress.com
Publisher Phone: (573) 885-7460
Editor Name: Kelli Rapp
Editor Email: kelli@threeriverspublishing.com
Editor Phone: (573) 885-7460
Advertising Executive Email: advertising@threeriverspublishing.com
Delivery Methods: Mail Newsstand
Year Established: 1872
Mechanical specifications: 1 col - 1.833 inches 2 col - 3.792 inches 3 col - 5.75 inches 4 col - 7.708 inches 5 col - 9.667 inches 6 col - 11.625 inches Page height - 21.5 inches
Published Days: Wed
Avg. Paid Circ.: 3500
Avg. Free Circ.: 2250
Audit Company: Sworn/Estimate/Non-Audited
Audit Date: 43626

STOCKTON

CEDAR COUNTY REPUBLICAN/ STOCKTON JOURNAL

Street Address: 26 Public Sq
City: Stockton
State: MO
ZIP Code: 65785
General Phone: (417) 276-4211
General Email: news@cedarrepublican.com
Publication Website: https://cedarrepublican.com/
Parent Company: Phillips Media Group, LLC
Publisher Name: Becky Jones
Publisher Email: marilyne@cedarrepublican.com
Editor Name: Miles Brite
Editor Email: milesb@cedarrepublican.com
Advertising Executive Name: Melanie Chance
Advertising Executive Email: melaniec@phillipsmedia.com
Year Established: 1885
Mechanical specifications: Type page: 10.25 x 21; 6 col
Published Days: Wed
Avg. Paid Circ.: 2714
Avg. Free Circ.: 267
Audit Company: Sworn/Estimate/Non-Audited
Audit Date: 43626

SULLIVAN

SULLIVAN INDEPENDENT NEWS

Street Address: 411 Scottsdale Dr
City: Sullivan
State: MO
ZIP Code: 63080
General Phone: (573) 468-6511
General Email: nuz4u@fidnet.com
Publication Website: https://www.mysullivannews.com/
Parent Company: Sullivan Independent Newspaper
Publisher Name: James Bartle
Editor Name: James Bartle
Delivery Methods: Mail Newsstand Racks
Year Established: 1964
Own Printing Facility?: Y
Published Days: Wed
Avg. Paid Circ.: 5960
Avg. Free Circ.: 240
Audit Company: Sworn/Estimate/Non-Audited
Audit Date: 43626
Note: Began a new publication in April 2017. The New Haven Independent News. Circulation 1,000. Covers Franklin and Gasconade Counties in Missouri. website: mynewhavennews.net

TIPTON

THE TIPTON TIMES

Street Address: 113 E Morgan St
City: Tipton
State: MO
ZIP Code: 65081-8322
General Phone: (660) 433-5721
General Email: times@vernonpublishing.com
Publication Website: https://www.vernonpublishing.com/Times/ContactUs
Parent Company: Vernon Publishing
Editor Name: Becky Holloway
Editor Email: bholloway@vernonpublishing.com
Editor Phone: (660) 433-5721
Delivery Methods: Mail Newsstand Racks
Year Established: 1875
Mechanical specifications: Type page 13 x 21; E - 6 cols, 2 1/16, 1/8 between; A - 6 cols, 2 1/16, 1/8 between; C - 7 cols, 1 23/32, 1/8 between.
Published Days: Thur
Avg. Paid Circ.: 1900
Audit Company: Sworn/Estimate/Non-Audited
Audit Date: 43626

TROY

THE LINCOLN COUNTY JOURNAL

Street Address: 20 Business Park Dr
City: Troy
State: MO
ZIP Code: 63379-2819
General Phone: (636) 528-9550
General Email: sjenkinson@lincolncountyjournal.com
Publication Website: https://www.lincolnnewsnow.com/
Parent Company: Lakeway Publishers, Inc.
Editor Name: Dan Fox
Editor Email: dfox@lincolncountyjournal.com
Editor Phone: (636) 528-9550
Delivery Methods: Mail Carrier Racks
Year Established: 1986
Published Days: Tues
Avg. Paid Circ.: 18900
Avg. Free Circ.: 18800
Audit Company: Sworn/Estimate/Non-Audited
Audit Date: 43626

TROY

Community Newspapers in the U.S.

TROY

TROY FREE PRESS

Street Address: 20 Business Park Dr
City: Troy
State: MO
ZIP Code: 63379-2819
General Phone: (636) 528-9550
General Email: sjenkinson@lincolncountyjournal.com
Publication Website: https://www.lincolnnewsnow.com/
Parent Company: Lakeway Publishers, Inc.
Editor Name: Dan Fox
Editor Email: dfox@lincolncountyjournal.com
Editor Phone: (636) 528-9550
Delivery Methods: Mail`Newsstand`Racks
Own Printing Facility?: Y
Commercial printers?: Y
Published Days: Wed
Avg. Paid Circ.: 1000
Audit Company: Sworn/Estimate/Non-Audited
Audit Date: 43626

UNIONVILLE

UNIONVILLE REPUBLICAN

Street Address: 111 S 16th St
City: Unionville
State: MO
ZIP Code: 63565
General Phone: (660) 947-2222
General Email: urep@nemr.net
Publication Website: http://www.unionvillerepublicanonline.com/
Advertising Executive Email: unionvillerepublican@mac.com
Delivery Methods: Mail`Newsstand
Year Established: 1865
Mechanical specifications: 6 col. SAU
Published Days: Wed
Avg. Paid Circ.: 1700
Avg. Free Circ.: 5000
Audit Company: Sworn/Estimate/Non-Audited
Audit Date: 43626

VAN BUREN

THE CURRENT LOCAL

Street Address: 504 Ash St
City: Van Buren
State: MO
ZIP Code: 63965
General Phone: (573) 323-4515
General Email: currentlocal@centurytel.net
Publication Website: https://www.currentlocal.com/
Parent Company: The Current Local
Delivery Methods: Mail`Newsstand`Racks
Year Established: 1884
Published Days: Thur
Avg. Paid Circ.: 1700
Audit Company: Sworn/Estimate/Non-Audited
Audit Date: 43626

VANDALIA

THE VANDALIA LEADER

Street Address: 108 W State St
City: Vandalia
State: MO
ZIP Code: 63382
General Phone: (573) 594-2222
General Email: tvlads@lcs.net
Publication Website: https://www.vandalialeader.com/
Parent Company: Lakeway Publishers, Inc.
Publisher Name: Ron Schott
Publisher Email: tvlgenmgr@lcs.net
Editor Name: Ron Schott
Editor Email: tvlgenmgr@lcs.net
Advertising Executive Email: tvlads@lcs.net
Year Established: 1874

Own Printing Facility?: Y
Commercial printers?: Y
Mechanical specifications: Type page 12 x 21 1/2; A - 6 cols, 2, 1/8 between; C - 8 cols, 1 7/16, 1/8 between.
Published Days: Wed
Avg. Paid Circ.: 2217
Avg. Free Circ.: 9
Audit Company: Sworn/Estimate/Non-Audited
Audit Date: 43626

VERSAILLES

MORGAN COUNTY PRESS

Street Address: 104 W Jasper Street
City: Versailles
State: MO
ZIP Code: 65084
General Phone: (573) 378-5441
General Email: news@morgancountypress.com
Publication Website: https://morgancountypress.com/
Delivery Methods: Mail`Newsstand`Racks
Year Established: 1911
Own Printing Facility?: Y
Mechanical specifications: Type page 10.875 x 21; E - 6 cols, 1.729 in., .1 in. between
Published Days: Wed
Avg. Paid Circ.: 1300
Avg. Free Circ.: 279
Audit Company: Sworn/Estimate/Non-Audited
Audit Date: 43626

VERSAILLES

THE VERSAILLES LEADER-STATESMAN

Street Address: 104 W Jasper St
City: Versailles
State: MO
ZIP Code: 65084
General Phone: (573) 378-5441
Publication Website: https://leader-statesman.com/
Parent Company: Leader Statesman
Delivery Methods: Mail`Newsstand`Racks
Year Established: 1878
Own Printing Facility?: Y
Mechanical specifications: Type page 10 1/4 x 21; E - 6 cols, 2 1/8, 1/8 between; A - 6 cols, 2 1/8, 1/8 between; C - 7 cols, 1 3/4, 1/8 between.
Published Days: Thur
Avg. Paid Circ.: 4100
Avg. Free Circ.: 100
Audit Company: Sworn/Estimate/Non-Audited
Audit Date: 43626

WARRENTON

WARREN COUNTY RECORD

Street Address: 103 E Booneslick Rd
City: Warrenton
State: MO
ZIP Code: 63383
General Phone: (636) 456-6397
General Email: jtodd@warrencountyrecord.com
Publication Website: https://www.warrencountyrecord.com/
Parent Company: Missourian Publishing Co.
Publisher Name: Tim Schmidt
Publisher Email: tim@mystandardnews.com
Delivery Methods: Mail`Newsstand`Racks
Year Established: 1896
Own Printing Facility?: Y
Mechanical specifications: Type page 12 1/2 x 21 1/2; E - 6 cols, 1 15/16, between; A - 6 cols, 1 15/16, between; C - 6 cols, 1 15/16, between.

Published Days: Thur
Avg. Paid Circ.: 3555
Audit Company: Sworn/Estimate/Non-Audited
Audit Date: 43626

WARSAW

BENTON COUNTY ENTERPRISE

Street Address: 107 Main St
City: Warsaw
State: MO
ZIP Code: 65355
General Phone: (660) 438-6312
General Email: janesalley@bentoncountyenterprise.com
Publication Website: http://www.bentoncountyenterprise.com
Publisher Name: James Mahlon White
Publisher Email: jameswhite@bentoncountyenterprise.com
Advertising Executive Name: Carrie Rieman
Advertising Executive Email: carrierieman@bentoncountyenterprise.com
Advertising Executive Phone: (660) 438-6312
Own Printing Facility?: Y
Commercial printers?: Y
Published Days: Thur
Avg. Paid Circ.: 5700
Avg. Free Circ.: 30
Audit Company: Sworn/Estimate/Non-Audited
Audit Date: 43626

WASHINGTON

WASHINGTON MISSOURIAN

Street Address: 14 W Main St
City: Washington
State: MO
ZIP Code: 63090
General Phone: (636) 239-7701
General Email: yorkj@emissourian.com
Publication Website: https://www.emissourian.com/
Parent Company: The Missourian Publishing Company
Editor Name: Bill Miller
Editor Email: billmiller@emissourian.com
Advertising Executive Name: Jeanine York
Advertising Executive Email: yorkj@emissourian.com
Advertising Executive Phone: (636) 390-3013
Delivery Methods: Mail`Carrier`Racks
Year Established: 1937
Own Printing Facility?: Y
Commercial printers?: Y
Mechanical specifications: Full Page 11.50 x 21.37", 1 col. - 1.812, 2 col. - 3.75", 3 col. - 5.687", 4 col. - 7.625", 5 col. - 9.562" 6 col. - 11.50"
Published Days: Wed`Sat
Avg. Paid Circ.: 11648
Avg. Free Circ.: 1849
Audit Company: AAM
Audit Date: 43962

WEBB CITY

WEBB CITY SENTINEL

Street Address: 8 S Main St
City: Webb City
State: MO
ZIP Code: 64870
General Phone: (417) 673-2421
General Email: sales@webbcity.net
Publication Website: https://www.webbcity.net/
Editor Name: Bob Foos
Advertising Executive Name: Betty Whipple
Delivery Methods: Mail`Carrier`Racks
Year Established: 1879
Own Printing Facility?: N
Mechanical specifications: Type page 11 5/8 x 21 1/2; E - 6 cols, 1 5/6, 1/8 between;

A - 6 cols, 1 5/6, 1/8 between; C - 6 cols, 1 5/6, 1/8 between.
Published Days: Wed
Avg. Paid Circ.: 2000
Avg. Free Circ.: 50
Audit Company: Sworn/Estimate/Non-Audited
Audit Date: 43626

WESTON

WESTON CHRONICLE

Street Address: 18275 Hwy. 45 N.
City: Weston
State: MO
ZIP Code: 64098
General Phone: (816) 640-2251
General Email: wcnews@embarqmail.com
Publication Website: http://www.plattechronicle.com/
Publisher Name: Jim McPherson
Publisher Email: wcads@embarqmail.com
Editor Name: Beth McPherson
Editor Email: wcnews@embarqmail.com
Advertising Executive Name: Jim McPherson
Advertising Executive Email: wcads@embarqmail.com
Year Established: 1872
Commercial printers?: Y
Mechanical specifications: Type page 12 3/4 x 21; E - 6 cols, 2, 1/8 between; A - 6 cols, 2, 1/8 between; C - 6 cols, 2, 1/8 between.
Published Days: Wed
Avg. Paid Circ.: 1600
Audit Company: Sworn/Estimate/Non-Audited
Audit Date: 43626

MISSISSIPPI

BALDWYN

BALDWYN NEWS

Street Address: 102 W Main St
City: Baldwyn
State: MS
ZIP Code: 38824-1814
General Phone: (662) 365-3232
General Email: thebaldwynnews@dixie-net.com
Publication Website: http://www.baldwynnews.com/main/
Mechanical specifications: Type page 13 x 21 1/2; E - 6 cols, 2 1/16, 1/6 between; A - 6 cols, 2 1/16, 1/6 between; C - 8 cols, 1 1/2, 1/6 between.
Published Days: Thur
Avg. Paid Circ.: 2500
Avg. Free Circ.: 20
Audit Company: Sworn/Estimate/Non-Audited
Audit Date: 43626

BATESVILLE

THE PANOLIAN

Street Address: 363 Highway 51 N
City: Batesville
State: MS
ZIP Code: 38606-2311
General Phone: (662) 563-4591
General Email: advertising@panolian.com
Publication Website: https://www.panolian.com/
Publisher Name: Delia Childers
Publisher Email: delia.childers@panolian.com
Editor Name: Jeremy Weldon
Editor Email: jeremy.weldon@panolian.com

Delivery Methods: Mail`Newsstand`Racks
Year Established: 1882
Own Printing Facility?: Y
Commercial printers?: Y
Mechanical specifications: Type page 11 1/2 x 21 1/4; E - 6 cols, 1 3/4, 1/6 between; A - 6 cols, 1 3/4, 1/6 between; C - 9 cols, 1 3/16, 1/6 between.
Published Days: Tues`Wed`Fri
Avg. Paid Circ.: 5650
Avg. Free Circ.: 5500
Audit Company: Sworn/Estimate/Non-Audited
Audit Date: 43626

BAY SAINT LOUIS

SEA COAST ECHO

Street Address: 124 Court St
City: Bay Saint Louis
State: MS
ZIP Code: 39520-4516
General Phone: (228) 467-5473
General Email: gbelcher@seacoastecho.com
Publication Website: https://www.seacoastecho.com/
Parent Company: Lancaster Management Inc.
Publisher Name: Geoff Belcher
Publisher Email: gbelcher@seacoastecho.com
Editor Name: Cassandra Favre
Editor Email: cassandra@seacoastecho.com
Delivery Methods: Mail`Newsstand`Carrier`Racks
Year Established: 1892
Own Printing Facility?: Y
Commercial printers?: Y
Mechanical specifications: Type page 10 x 21 1/2; E - 6 cols, 1.7between; A - 6 cols, 2 1/16, between; C - 6 cols, 2 1/16, between.
Published Days: Wed`Sat
Avg. Paid Circ.: 6100
Audit Company: Sworn/Estimate/Non-Audited
Audit Date: 43626

BAY SPRINGS

THE JASPER COUNTY NEWS

Street Address: 3362 HIGHWAY 15
City: Bay Springs
State: MS
ZIP Code: 39422-5181
General Phone: (601) 764-3104
General Email: news@jaspercountynews.net
Publication Website: https://impact601.com/
Parent Company: Buckley Newspapers Inc
Own Printing Facility?: Y
Commercial printers?: Y
Mechanical specifications: Type page 12 1/2 x 21 1/2.
Published Days: Wed
Avg. Paid Circ.: 2772
Avg. Free Circ.: 110
Audit Company: Sworn/Estimate/Non-Audited
Audit Date: 43626

BELZONI

THE BELZONI BANNER

Street Address: 115 E Jackson St, P.O. Box 610
City: Belzoni
State: MS
ZIP Code: 39038-3641
General Phone: (662) 247-3373
General Email: editor@thebelzonibanner.com
Publication Website: http://www.thebelzonibanner.com/
Editor Email: editor@thebelzonibanner.com
Delivery Methods: Mail`Newsstand`Carrier
Year Established: 1914
Own Printing Facility?: Y

Commercial printers?: Y
Mechanical specifications: Broadsheet-11" x 21.5"
Published Days: Wed
Avg. Paid Circ.: 950
Avg. Free Circ.: 25
Audit Company: Sworn/Estimate/Non-Audited
Audit Date: 43626

BOONEVILLE

BANNER INDEPENDENT

Street Address: 208 N Main St
City: Booneville
State: MS
ZIP Code: 38829-3317
General Phone: (662) 728-6214
General Email: admanager@dailycorinthian.com
Publication Website: https://www.dailycorinthian.com/booneville/
Parent Company: Paxton Media Group, LLC
Publisher Name: Reece Terry
Publisher Email: rterry@dailycorinthian.com
Publisher Phone: (662) 287-6111, ext : 337
Editor Name: Mark Boehler
Editor Email: editor@dailycorinthian.com
Editor Phone: (662) 287-6111, ext : 340
Advertising Executive Name: Derinda Nunley
Advertising Executive Email: admanager@dailycorinthian.com
Advertising Executive Phone: (662) 287-6111, ext : 339
Delivery Methods: Mail`Racks
Year Established: 1898
Commercial printers?: Y
Published Days: Thur
Avg. Paid Circ.: 4400
Avg. Free Circ.: 35
Audit Company: Sworn/Estimate/Non-Audited
Audit Date: 43626

BRANDON

RANKIN COUNTY NEWS

Street Address: 207 E Government St, P.O. Box 107
City: Brandon
State: MS
ZIP Code: 39042-3151
General Phone: (601) 825-8333
General Email: rankincn@bellsouth.net
Publication Website: https://www.rankincn.com/
Publisher Name: Marcus Bowers
Publisher Phone: (601) 825-8333
Year Established: 1852
Mechanical specifications: Type page 14 3/16 x 21 1/2; E - 6 cols, 2 1/6, between; A - 6 cols, 2 1/6, between; C - 6 cols, 2 1/6, between.
Published Days: Wed
Avg. Paid Circ.: 8000
Audit Company: Sworn/Estimate/Non-Audited
Audit Date: 43626

BRUCE

THE CALHOUN COUNTY JOURNAL

Street Address: PO Box 278
City: Bruce
State: MS
ZIP Code: 38915-0278
General Phone: (662) 983-2570
General Email: lisamcneece@gmail.com
Publication Website: https://calhouncountyjournal.com/
Publisher Name: Joel Mcneece
Publisher Email: joelmcneece@gmail.com
Editor Name: Celia Hillhouse
Editor Email: celiahillhouse@gmail.com
Advertising Executive Name: Lisa Mcneece

Advertising Executive Email: lisamcneece@gmail.com
Delivery Methods: Mail`Racks
Year Established: 1 08 1953
Published Days: Wed
Avg. Paid Circ.: 4700
Audit Company: Sworn/Estimate/Non-Audited
Audit Date: 43626

CARTHAGE

THE CARTHAGINIAN

Street Address: 123 E Main St
City: Carthage
State: MS
ZIP Code: 39051-4102
General Phone: (601) 267-4501
General Email: bobby@thecarthaginian.com
Publication Website: https://www.thecarthaginian.com/
Parent Company: The 'Ginian, LLC
Publisher Name: Waid Prather
Publisher Email: waid@thecarthaginian.com
Editor Name: Waid Prather
Editor Email: waid@thecarthaginian.com
Advertising Executive Name: Bobby Latham
Advertising Executive Email: bobby@thecarthaginian.com
Delivery Methods: Mail`Racks
Year Established: 1872
Published Days: Thur
Avg. Paid Circ.: 5700
Avg. Free Circ.: 59
Audit Company: Sworn/Estimate/Non-Audited
Audit Date: 43626

CRYSTAL SPRINGS

THE METEOR INC.

Street Address: 201 E Georgetown St, P.O. Box 353
City: Crystal Springs
State: MS
ZIP Code: 39059-2516
General Phone: (601) 892-2581
General Email: advertising@themeteor.com
Publication Website: https://www.themeteor.com/
Advertising Executive Email: advertising@themeteor.com
Year Established: 1881
Own Printing Facility?: Y
Commercial printers?: Y
Mechanical specifications: Type page 15 x 22 3/4; E - 6 cols, 2 1/6, 1/6 between; A - 6 cols, 2 1/6, between; C - 6 cols, 2 1/6, 1/6 between.
Published Days: Wed
Avg. Paid Circ.: 3615
Avg. Free Circ.: 1385
Audit Company: Sworn/Estimate/Non-Audited
Audit Date: 43626

DE KALB

KEMPER COUNTY MESSENGER

Street Address: 102 Main Ave, PO Box 546
City: De Kalb
State: MS
ZIP Code: 39328-6381
General Phone: (601) 743-5760
Publication Website: http://kempercountymessenger.com/
Editor Name: Steve Swogentinsky
Editor Phone: (601) 676-0993
Mechanical specifications: Type page 11 5/8 x 21 1/2; E - 6 cols, 1 1/8, 1/8 between.
Published Days: Thur
Avg. Paid Circ.: 2100
Avg. Free Circ.: 85
Audit Company: Sworn/Estimate/Non-Audited

Audit Date: 43626

EUPORA

WEBSTER PROGRESS-TIMES

Street Address: 58 N Dunn St
City: Eupora
State: MS
ZIP Code: 39744-2631
General Phone: (662) 773-6241
General Email: ads@websterprogresstimes.com
Publication Website: https://www.redhillsmsnews.com/
Parent Company: Emmerich Newspapers
Publisher Name: Joseph Mccain
Publisher Email: newsroom@winstoncountyjournal.com
Publisher Phone: (662) 773-6241, ext : 105
Editor Name: Russell Hood
Editor Email: rhood@websterprogresstimes.com
Editor Phone: (662) 258-7532
Advertising Executive Name: Kathy Johnson
Advertising Executive Email: sales@winstoncountyjournal.com
Advertising Executive Phone: (662) 773-6241, ext : 104
Year Established: 1968
Published Days: Thur
Avg. Paid Circ.: 2500
Avg. Free Circ.: 6500
Audit Company: Sworn/Estimate/Non-Audited
Audit Date: 43626

GLOSTER

WILK-AMITE RECORD

Street Address: PO Box 130, 243 E. Main Street
City: Gloster
State: MS
ZIP Code: 39638-9009
General Phone: (601) 841-5100
General Email: info@wilkamiterecord.com
Publication Website: http://www.wilkamiterecord.com/
Publisher Name: Greg Adams
Editor Name: Greg Adams
Year Established: 1892
Mechanical specifications: Type page 15 x 21; E - 7 cols, 1 3/4, 1/6 between; A - 7 cols, 1 3/4, 1/6 between; C - 7 cols, 1 3/4, 1/6 between.
Published Days: Fri
Avg. Paid Circ.: 2400
Avg. Free Circ.: 10
Audit Company: Sworn/Estimate/Non-Audited
Audit Date: 43626

GRENADA

GRENADA STAR

Street Address: 50 Corporate Row
City: Grenada
State: MS
ZIP Code: 38901-2823
General Phone: (662) 226-4321
General Email: sales1@grenadastar.com
Publication Website: https://www.grenadastar.com/
Publisher Name: Joe Lee
Publisher Email: publisher@grenadastar.com
Editor Name: Nanette Laster
Editor Email: editor@grenadastar.com
Advertising Executive Name: Lyne Shack
Advertising Executive Email: sales1@grenadastar.com
Delivery Methods: Mail`Carrier
Year Established: 1854
Mechanical specifications: Type page 13 x 21 1/2; E - 6 cols, 2 1/16, 1/8 between; A - 6 cols, 2 1/16, 1/8 between; C - 6 cols, 2

Community Newspapers in the U.S.

1/16, 1/8 between.
Published Days: Tues`Fri
Weekday Frequency: e
Avg. Paid Circ.: 5776
Audit Company: Sworn/Estimate/Non-Audited
Audit Date: 43626
Pressroom Equipment: Lines -- 6-KP/News King 1968.;
Business Software: Synaptic
Classified Equipment: Hardware -- PC;
Classified Software: Synaptic.
Editorial Equipment: Hardware -- ACT, APP/Mac, Gateway/2000; Printers -- Xante
Editorial Software: QPS, Microsoft/Word.
Production Equipment: Hardware -- Caere/OmniPage Pro 6.0; Cameras -- C/Spartan III; Scanners -- Umax
Production Software: QPS/QuarkXPress 3.31.

HATTIESBURG

HATTIESBURG AMERICAN

Street Address: 4200 Mamie St
City: Hattiesburg
State: MS
ZIP Code: 39402-1729
General Phone: (601) 582-4321
General Email: mmcleod@gannett.com
Publication Website: https://www.hattiesburgamerican.com/
Parent Company: Gannett
Editor Name: Sam R. Hall
Editor Email: srhall@gannett.com
Editor Phone: (601) 961-7163
Advertising Executive Name: Natasha Mcleod
Advertising Executive Email: mmcleod@gannett.com
Advertising Executive Phone: (601) 584-3032
Delivery Methods: Mail`Newsstand`Carrier`Racks
Year Established: 1897
Own Printing Facility?: Y
Commercial printers?: N
Mechanical specifications: Type page 13 x 21 1/2; E - 6 cols, 2 1/16, 1/8 between; A - 6 cols, 2 1/16, 1/8 between; C - 9 cols, 1 5/16, 1/8 between.
Published Days: Wed`Fri`Sun
Weekday Frequency: e
Saturday Frequency: m
Avg. Paid Circ.: 6722
Avg. Free Circ.: 61
Audit Company: AAM
Audit Date: 44200
Business Equipment: IBM/AS-400
Classified Equipment: Hardware -- Mactive;
Note: The Hattiesburg American is printed at the Clarion Ledger located at 201 S. Congress Street, Jackson, MS.

HATTIESBURG

THE LAMAR TIMES

Street Address: 103 N 40th Ave
City: Hattiesburg
State: MS
ZIP Code: 39401-6606
General Phone: (601) 268-2331
General Email: rick@hubcityspokes.com
Publication Website: https://www.hubcityspokes.com
Parent Company: Emmerich Newspapers
Publisher Name: David Gustafson
Publisher Email: david@hubcityspokes.com
Editor Name: Joshua Wilson
Editor Email: joshua@hubcityspokes.com
Advertising Executive Name: Rick Jarman
Advertising Executive Email: rick@hubcityspokes.com
Delivery Methods: Mail`Newsstand`Racks
Own Printing Facility?: Y
Published Days: Thur
Avg. Paid Circ.: 5000
Audit Company: Sworn/Estimate/Non-Audited
Audit Date: 43626

HAZLEHURST

COPIAH COUNTY COURIER

Street Address: 103 S Ragsdale Ave, P.O. Box 351
City: Hazlehurst
State: MS
ZIP Code: 39083-3037
General Phone: (601) 894-3141
General Email: publisher@copiahcountycourier.com
Publication Website: https://www.copiahcountycourier.com/
Publisher Name: John Carney
Publisher Email: publisher@copiahcountycourier.com
Advertising Executive Email: printing@copiahcountycourier.com
Delivery Methods: Mail`Newsstand`Racks
Year Established: 1874
Mechanical specifications: 6 columns, 10.8333 x 21
Published Days: Wed
Avg. Paid Circ.: 4400
Avg. Free Circ.: 1600
Audit Company: Sworn/Estimate/Non-Audited
Audit Date: 43626

HOLLY SPRINGS

SOUTH REPORTER

Street Address: 157 S Center St, P.O. Box 278
City: Holly Springs
State: MS
ZIP Code: 38635-3040
General Phone: (662) 252-4261
General Email: southreporter@dixie-net.com
Publication Website: https://www.southreporter.com/
Publisher Name: Barry Burleson
Editor Name: Barry Burleson
Year Established: 1865
Mechanical specifications: Type page 13 x 21; E - 6 cols, 2, 1/8 between; A - 6 cols, 2, 1/8 between; C - 8 cols, 1 1/2, 1/8 between.
Published Days: Thur
Avg. Paid Circ.: 5200
Avg. Free Circ.: 52
Audit Company: Sworn/Estimate/Non-Audited
Audit Date: 43626

JACKSON

MISSISSIPPI BUSINESS JOURNAL

Street Address: 200 N Congress St
City: Jackson
State: MS
ZIP Code: 39201-1902
General Phone: (601) 364-1011
General Email: tami.jones@msbusiness.com
Publication Website: https://msbusiness.com/
Parent Company: Journal Inc
Publisher Name: Tami Jones
Publisher Email: tami.jones@msbusiness.com
Publisher Phone: (601) 364-1011
Editor Name: Ross Reily
Editor Email: ross.reily@msbusiness.com
Editor Phone: (601) 364-1018
Delivery Methods: Mail`Newsstand
Year Established: 1978
Published Days: Fri
Avg. Paid Circ.: 3941
Avg. Free Circ.: 174
Audit Company: Sworn/Estimate/Non-Audited
Audit Date: 43626

LAUREL

LAUREL LEADER-CALL

Street Address: 318 N Magnolia St
City: Laurel
State: MS
ZIP Code: 39440-3932
General Phone: (601) 649-9388
General Email: ad2@leader-call.com
Publication Website: https://www.leader-call.com/
Parent Company: Gin Creek Publishing
Publisher Name: Jim Cegielski
Publisher Email: cigcar@comcast.net
Editor Name: Sean Murphy
Editor Email: murph@leader-call.com
Advertising Executive Name: Courtney Creel
Advertising Executive Email: ad2@leader-call.com
Delivery Methods: Mail`Newsstand`Racks
Year Established: 1911
Own Printing Facility?: Y
Commercial printers?: N
Mechanical specifications: Type page 13 x 21 1/2; E - 6 cols, 2 1/16, 1/8 between; A - 6 cols, 2 1/16, 1/8 between; C - 9 cols, 1 3/8, 1/16 between.
Published Days: Tues`Thur`Sat
Weekday Frequency: All day
Saturday Frequency: All day
Avg. Paid Circ.: 7500
Audit Company: Sworn/Estimate/Non-Audited
Audit Date: 43626
Mailroom Equipment: Tying Machines -- 1/Ms; Address Machine -- 1-Am/4000EP.;
Classified Equipment: Hardware -- APP/Mac.;
Editorial Equipment: Hardware -- APP/Mac.
Production Equipment: Hardware -- 2-APP/Mac LaserPrinter; Cameras -- 1-R/500.

LEAKESVILLE

GREENE COUNTY HERALD

Street Address: 431 Maine Street, P.O. BOX 220
City: Leakesville
State: MS
ZIP Code: 39451-6502
General Phone: (601) 394-5070
General Email: advertising_gcherald@tds.net
Publication Website: https://www.greenecountyheraldonline.org/
Parent Company: The Turner Group LLC
Publisher Name: Leola Turner
Editor Name: George R. Turner
Editor Email: herald@tds.net
Advertising Executive Name: Joni Cooley Mcmillon
Advertising Executive Email: advertising_gcherald@tds.net
Delivery Methods: Mail`Newsstand`Racks
Year Established: 1898
Mechanical specifications: 11.625 x 21
Published Days: Thur
Avg. Paid Circ.: 3100
Avg. Free Circ.: 52
Audit Company: Sworn/Estimate/Non-Audited
Audit Date: 43626

LELAND

LELAND PROGRESS

Street Address: 119 E 3rd St
City: Leland
State: MS
ZIP Code: 38756-2705
General Phone: (662) 771-4012
General Email: editor@thelelandprogress.com
Publication Website: https://thelelandprogress.com/
Publisher Name: Stephanie Patton
Editor Name: Stephanie Patton
Editor Email: editor@thelelandprogress.com
Delivery Methods: Mail`Newsstand
Year Established: 1897
Published Days: Thur
Avg. Paid Circ.: 1000
Avg. Free Circ.: 50
Audit Company: Sworn/Estimate/Non-Audited
Audit Date: 43626

LEXINGTON

HOLMES COUNTY HERALD

Street Address: 308 Court Square, P.O. Box 60
City: Lexington
State: MS
ZIP Code: 39095-3636
General Phone: (662) 834-1151
General Email: hcherald@gmail.com
Publication Website: https://www.holmescountyherald.com/
Publisher Name: Maria Edwards
Publisher Email: hcherald@gmail.com
Editor Name: Matthew Breazeale
Editor Email: hcherald@gmail.com
Delivery Methods: Mail`Racks
Year Established: 1959
Mechanical specifications: 10.25 x 16 full page
Published Days: Thur
Avg. Paid Circ.: 2000
Audit Company: Sworn/Estimate/Non-Audited
Audit Date: 43626

LUCEDALE

GEORGE COUNTY TIMES

Street Address: 5133 Main St, PO Box 238
City: Lucedale
State: MS
ZIP Code: 39452-6523
General Phone: (601) 947-2967
General Email: gctimes@bellsouth.net
Publication Website: https://www.gctimesonline.com/
Published Days: Thur
Avg. Paid Circ.: 6300
Audit Company: Sworn/Estimate/Non-Audited
Audit Date: 43626

MAGNOLIA

THE MAGNOLIA GAZETTE

Street Address: 280 Magnolia St
City: Magnolia
State: MS
ZIP Code: 39652-2828
General Phone: (601) 783-2441
General Email: magnoliagazette@bellsouth.net
Publication Website: http://www.magnoliagazette.com/
Publisher Name: Lucius M. Lampton
Editor Name: Donna Delee
Advertising Executive Name: Joy Gardner Reeves
Mechanical specifications: Type page 13 x 21 1/2; E - 6 cols, 2 1/16, 1/8 between; A - 6 cols, 2 1/16, 1/8 between; C - 6 cols, 2 1/16, 1/6 between.
Published Days: Thur
Avg. Paid Circ.: 1400
Audit Company: Sworn/Estimate/Non-Audited
Audit Date: 43626

MEADVILLE

FRANKLIN ADVOCATE

Street Address: 111 MAIN ST E
City: Meadville
State: MS
ZIP Code: 39653
General Phone: (601) 384-2484
General Email: publisher@franklinadvocate.com
Publication Website: https://www.franklinadvocate.com/
Publisher Email: publisher@franklinadvocate.com
Delivery Methods: Mail`Newsstand
Year Established: 1890
Mechanical specifications: Type page 15 x 21; E - 7 cols, 1 3/4, 1/6 between; A - 7 cols, 1 3/4, 1/6 between; C - 7 cols, 1 3/4, 1/6 between.
Published Days: Wed`Thur
Avg. Paid Circ.: 3200
Avg. Free Circ.: 12
Audit Company: Sworn/Estimate/Non-Audited
Audit Date: 43626

MONTICELLO

LAWRENCE COUNTY PRESS

Street Address: 296 F E Sellers Hwy, P.O. Box 549
City: Monticello
State: MS
ZIP Code: 39654-9555
General Phone: (601) 587-2781
General Email: ads@lawrencecountypress.com
Publication Website: https://www.lawrencecountypress.com/
Publisher Name: John Carney
Editor Name: Kelsey Wells Lambert
Delivery Methods: Mail`Racks
Year Established: 1888
Mechanical specifications: Type page 10.833 x 21; 6 cols, 1.6667 between
Published Days: Wed
Avg. Paid Circ.: 2814
Avg. Free Circ.: 34
Audit Company: Sworn/Estimate/Non-Audited
Audit Date: 43626

NESBIT

DESOTO TIMES-TRIBUNE

Street Address: 2342 Highway 51 North
City: Nesbit
State: MS
ZIP Code: 38651
General Phone: (662) 403-9380
General Email: legals@dttclick.com
Publication Website: http://www.desototimes.com/
Publisher Name: Dick Mathauer
Delivery Methods: Mail`Carrier`Racks
Year Established: 1839
Mechanical specifications: Type page 13 x 21; E - 6 cols, 2 3/100, 1/6 between; A - 6 cols, 2 3/100, 1/6 between; C - 8 cols, 1 1/2, 1/6 between.
Published Days: Tues`Thur`Sat
Weekday Frequency: m
Saturday Frequency: m
Avg. Paid Circ.: 7810
Audit Company: Sworn/Estimate/Non-Audited
Audit Date: 43626
Classified Equipment: Hardware -- APP/Mac;
Classified Software: Baseview/Ad Manager Pro.
Editorial Equipment: Hardware -- APP/Mac
Editorial Software: Baseview/News Edit.
Production Equipment: Hardware -- Pre Press/Panther Plus
Production Software: QPS/QuarkXPress.

NEW ALBANY

NEW ALBANY GAZETTE

Street Address: 713 Carter Avenue, PO Box 300
City: New Albany
State: MS
ZIP Code: 38652-0300
General Phone: (662) 534-6321
General Email: advertising@newalbanygazette.com
Publication Website: https://www.djournal.com/new-albany/
Parent Company: Journal Inc
Publisher Name: Lisa Bryant
Editor Name: David Johnson
Advertising Executive Name: Kim Surber
Delivery Methods: Mail`Newsstand`Racks
Year Established: 1889
Own Printing Facility?: Y
Commercial printers?: Y
Mechanical specifications: Type page 11 x 20.5; E - 6 cols, 2, 1/6 between; A - 6 cols, 2, 1/6 between; C - 6 cols, 2, 1/6 between.
Published Days: Wed`Fri
Avg. Paid Circ.: 4200
Avg. Free Circ.: 12000
Audit Company: Sworn/Estimate/Non-Audited
Audit Date: 43626

PASCAGOULA

THE MISSISSIPPI PRESS

Street Address: 909 CONVENT AVE
City: Pascagoula
State: MS
ZIP Code: 39567
General Phone: (228) 762-1111
General Email: msnews@themississippipress.com
Publication Website: https://www.gulflive.com/
Parent Company: Advance Publications, Inc.
Delivery Methods: Mail`Carrier
Year Established: 1964
Mechanical specifications: Type page 11 5/8 x 21 1/2; E - 6 cols, 1 13/16, 1/8 between; A - 6 cols, 1 13/16, 1/8 between; C - 10 cols, 1 1/16, 1/8 between.
Published Days: Wed`Fri`Sun
Weekday Frequency: m
Avg. Paid Circ.: 5749
Audit Company: Sworn/Estimate/Non-Audited
Audit Date: 43626
Pressroom Equipment: Lines -- 1-G/Urbanite 1013 single width (8 stacked units, 1 full color); Registration System -- KFM/Pin Registration System.
Mailroom Equipment: Counter Stackers -- 5-HL; Inserters & Stuffers -- 1-MM/227, 1-HI/1872; Tying Machines -- 1-Bu/68950, 2-Si/MLN2A.;
Business Equipment: 6-Compaq/Proline 450, 2-Compaq/Desk Pro
Classified Equipment: Hardware -- 6-APP/Super Mac C-500, 2-APP/iMac; Printers -- QMS/Laserwriter, APP/Mac LaserWriter Pro;
Classified Software: Baseview, QPS.
Editorial Equipment: Hardware -- 5-APP/Mac (with file server)/ScenicSoft/OPI Color Central 2,2; Printers -- AU/3850, AU/108C
Editorial Software: Baseview.
Production Equipment: Hardware -- Nu Plate Burner, AU/3850, Lf/AP Leaf Picture Desk; Cameras -- SCREEN/270-D; Scanners -- Lf/Leafscan, Microtek, Nikon/LS 2000
Production Software: QPS 4.0, Mk/Managing Editor.

PHILADELPHIA

THE NESHOBA DEMOCRAT

Street Address: 439 E Beacon St
City: Philadelphia
State: MS
ZIP Code: 39350-2950
General Phone: (601) 656-4000
General Email: joy@neshobademocrat.com
Publication Website: http://neshobademocrat.com/
Publisher Name: James E. Prince
Publisher Email: jprince@neshobademocrat.com
Publisher Phone: (601) 656-4000
Editor Name: Steve Swogetinsky
Editor Email: steve@neshobademocrat.com
Editor Phone: (601) 656-0993
Advertising Executive Name: Joy Stewart
Advertising Executive Email: joy@neshobademocrat.com
Advertising Executive Phone: (601) 676-0999
Mechanical specifications: Type page 14 x 21 1/2.
Published Days: Wed
Avg. Paid Circ.: 8000
Avg. Free Circ.: 70
Audit Company: Sworn/Estimate/Non-Audited
Audit Date: 43626

PRENTISS

PRENTISS HEADLIGHT

Street Address: 1020 Third St
City: Prentiss
State: MS
ZIP Code: 39474-6002
General Phone: (601) 792-4221
General Email: editor@prentissheadlight.com
Publication Website: https://www.prentissheadlight.com/
Parent Company: Boone Newspapers
Editor Name: Holley Cochran
Editor Email: holley.cochran@prentissheadlight.com
Delivery Methods: Mail`Newsstand`Carrier`Racks
Year Established: 1906
Own Printing Facility?: Y
Commercial printers?: N
Mechanical specifications: Type page 10.125 x 21 1/2; E - 6 cols, 2 1/16, 1/3 between; A - 6 cols, 2 1/16, 1/3 between.
Published Days: Wed
Avg. Paid Circ.: 1568
Avg. Free Circ.: 25
Audit Company: Sworn/Estimate/Non-Audited
Audit Date: 43626

RALEIGH

SMITH COUNTY REFORMER

Street Address: 153 MAIN ST
City: Raleigh
State: MS
ZIP Code: 39153
General Phone: (601) 782-4358
General Email: ads@smithcountyreformer.net
Publication Website: https://impact601.com/
Parent Company: Buckley Newspapers
Delivery Methods: Mail`Racks
Year Established: 1889
Own Printing Facility?: Y
Commercial printers?: Y
Published Days: Wed
Avg. Paid Circ.: 2965
Avg. Free Circ.: 720
Audit Company: Sworn/Estimate/Non-Audited
Audit Date: 43626

RICHTON

THE RICHTON DISPATCH

Street Address: 110 Walnut St, P. O. Box 429
City: Richton
State: MS
ZIP Code: 39476
General Phone: (601) 788-6031
General Email: news@therichtondispatch.com
Publication Website: https://www.therichtondispatch.com/
Delivery Methods: Mail`Racks
Year Established: 1905
Mechanical specifications: Type page 13 x 21; E - 6 cols, 2, 1/6 between; A - 6 cols, 2, 1/6 between; C - 6 cols, 2, 1/6 between.
Published Days: Thur
Avg. Paid Circ.: 1825
Avg. Free Circ.: 8
Audit Company: Sworn/Estimate/Non-Audited
Audit Date: 43626

RIDGELAND

MADISON COUNTY JOURNAL

Street Address: 293 Commerce Park Dr, P.O. Box 219
City: Ridgeland
State: MS
ZIP Code: 39157-2233
General Phone: (601) 853-4222
General Email: msimmons@onlinemadison.com
Publication Website: http://www.onlinemadison.com/
Parent Company: Prince Media Group
Publisher Name: James E. Prince
Publisher Email: jprince@onlinemadison.com
Publisher Phone: (601) 853-4222, ext : 31
Editor Name: James E. Prince
Editor Email: jprince@onlinemadison.com
Editor Phone: (601) 853-4222, ext : 31
Advertising Executive Name: Michael Simmons
Advertising Executive Email: msimmons@onlinemadison.com
Advertising Executive Phone: (601) 853-4222, ext : 32
Delivery Methods: Mail`Newsstand`Racks
Year Established: 1982
Mechanical specifications: Type page 11 x 21 1/2; E - 6 cols, 2 1/16, between; A - 6 cols, 2 1/16, between; C - 8 cols, 2 1/6, between.
Published Days: Thur
Avg. Paid Circ.: 3600
Audit Company: Sworn/Estimate/Non-Audited
Audit Date: 43626

ROLLING FORK

DEER CREEK PILOT

Street Address: 145 N First St
City: Rolling Fork
State: MS
ZIP Code: 39159-2749
General Phone: (662) 873-4354
General Email: deercreekpilot@bellsouth.net
Publication Website: http://deercreekpilot.com/
Published Days: Thur
Avg. Paid Circ.: 1500
Avg. Free Circ.: 50
Audit Company: Sworn/Estimate/Non-Audited
Audit Date: 43626

SENATOBIA

THE DEMOCRAT

Street Address: 219 E Main St
City: Senatobia
State: MS
ZIP Code: 38668-2123
General Phone: (662) 562-4414
General Email: strimm@taterecord.com
Publication Website: http://www.taterecord.com/
Mechanical specifications: Type page 13 x 21 1/2; E - 6 cols, 1 5/6, 1/6 between; A - 6 cols, 1 5/6, 1/6 between; C - 6 cols, 1 5/6,

Community Newspapers in the U.S.

1/8 between.
Published Days: Tues
Avg. Paid Circ.: 5200
Audit Company: Sworn/Estimate/Non-Audited
Audit Date: 43626

TUNICA

THE TUNICA TIMES

Street Address: P.O. Box 308/986 Magnolia Street
City: Tunica
State: MS
ZIP Code: 38676-9742
General Phone: (662) 363-1511
General Email: ads@tunicatimes.com
Publication Website: http://tunicatimes.com/
Delivery Methods: Mail`Racks
Year Established: 1904
Mechanical specifications: Type page 11 1/2 x 20 3/4; E - 6 cols, 1 7/10, 1/8 between; A - 6 cols, 1 7/10, 1/8 between; C - 8 cols, 1 1/3, 1/8 between.
Published Days: Fri
Avg. Paid Circ.: 2400
Audit Company: Sworn/Estimate/Non-Audited
Audit Date: 43626

TYLERTOWN

THE TYLERTOWN TIMES

Street Address: 727 Beulah Ave
City: Tylertown
State: MS
ZIP Code: 39667-2709
General Phone: (601) 876-5111
General Email: tylertowntimes@bellsouth.net
Publication Website: https://www.thetylertowntimes.org/
Delivery Methods: Mail
Year Established: 1907
Published Days: Thur
Avg. Paid Circ.: 3248
Avg. Free Circ.: 6729
Audit Company: Sworn/Estimate/Non-Audited
Audit Date: 43626

WATER VALLEY

NORTH MISSISSIPPI HERALD

Street Address: 416 N Main St, P.O. Box 648
City: Water Valley
State: MS
ZIP Code: 38965-2506
General Phone: (662) 473-1473
General Email: heralddads@bellsouth.net
Publication Website: http://yalnews.com/
Publisher Name: David Howell
Publisher Email: dhowl@bellsouth.net
Publisher Phone: (662) 473-8444
Editor Name: David Howell
Editor Email: dhowl@bellsouth.net
Editor Phone: (662) 473-8444
Delivery Methods: Mail`Racks
Mechanical specifications: Type page 12 3/4 x 21; E - 6 cols, 2, 1/6 between; A - 6 cols, 2, 1/6 between; C - 8 cols, 1 1/2, 1/6 between.
Published Days: Thur
Avg. Paid Circ.: 2900
Avg. Free Circ.: 102
Audit Company: Sworn/Estimate/Non-Audited
Audit Date: 43626

WAYNESBORO

THE WAYNE COUNTY NEWS

Street Address: 716 South St
City: Waynesboro
State: MS
ZIP Code: 39367-2727
General Phone: (601) 735-4341
General Email: advertising@thewaynecountynews.com
Publication Website: https://www.thewaynecountynews.com/
Parent Company: HD Media
Publisher Name: Paul Keane
Publisher Email: publisher@thewaynecountynews.com
Editor Name: Paul Keane
Editor Email: publisher@thewaynecountynews.com
Advertising Executive Name: Doris Keane
Advertising Executive Email: advertising@thewaynecountynews.com
Delivery Methods: Mail
Year Established: 1890
Own Printing Facility?: Y
Commercial printers?: Y
Published Days: Thur
Avg. Paid Circ.: 4000
Avg. Free Circ.: 79
Audit Company: Sworn/Estimate/Non-Audited
Audit Date: 43626

WIGGINS

STONE COUNTY ENTERPRISE

Street Address: 143 First St S
City: Wiggins
State: MS
ZIP Code: 39577-2733
General Phone: (601) 928-4802
General Email: publisher@stonecountyenterprise.com
Publication Website: https://www.stonecountyenterprise.com/
Parent Company: Lancaster Management Inc.
Publisher Email: publisher@stonecountyenterprise.com
Editor Email: editor@stonecountyenterprise.com
Delivery Methods: Mail`Newsstand`Racks
Year Established: 1916
Mechanical specifications: Type page 13 x 21 1/2.
Published Days: Wed
Avg. Paid Circ.: 3000
Avg. Free Circ.: 25
Audit Company: Sworn/Estimate/Non-Audited
Audit Date: 43626

MONTANA

BAKER

FALLON COUNTY TIMES

Street Address: 115 S Main St, PO Box 679
City: Baker
State: MT
ZIP Code: 59313-9013
General Phone: (406) 778-3344
General Email: fctimes@midrivers.com
Publication Website: https://www.falloncountyextra.com/
Parent Company: Country Media Inc.; Country Media, Inc
Delivery Methods: Mail`Newsstand
Year Established: 1916
Published Days: Fri
Avg. Paid Circ.: 1200
Avg. Free Circ.: 49
Audit Company: Sworn/Estimate/Non-Audited
Audit Date: 43626

BELGRADE

BELGRADE NEWS

Street Address: 29 W Main St
City: Belgrade
State: MT
ZIP Code: 59714-3716
General Phone: (406) 388-5101
General Email: ghoffman@belgrade-news.com
Publication Website: http://www.belgrade-news.com/
Parent Company: Adams Publishing Group
Editor Name: Michael Tucker
Editor Email: mtucker@belgrade-news.com
Editor Phone: (406) 388-5101, ext : 3
Advertising Executive Name: George Hoffman
Advertising Executive Email: ghoffman@belgrade-news.com
Advertising Executive Phone: (406) 388-5101, ext : 1
Delivery Methods: Mail`Newsstand`Racks
Year Established: 2004
Mechanical specifications: 1/8 4.75 x 3.9, 1/4 4.75 x 7.9, 1/2 9.667 x 7.9, full 9.667 x 15.75
Published Days: Tues`Fri
Avg. Paid Circ.: 300
Avg. Free Circ.: 4500
Audit Company: Sworn/Estimate/Non-Audited
Audit Date: 43626

BIG SANDY

THE MOUNTAINEER

Street Address: 122 Johannas Ave, P.O. Box 529
City: Big Sandy
State: MT
ZIP Code: 59520
General Phone: (406) 378-2176
General Email: bsmnews@mtintouch.net
Publication Website: https://www.bigsandymountaineer.com/
Publisher Name: Lorrie Merrill
Publisher Phone: (406) 378-2176
Delivery Methods: Mail`Newsstand
Year Established: 1911
Own Printing Facility?: Y
Commercial printers?: Y
Published Days: Wed
Avg. Paid Circ.: 926
Avg. Free Circ.: 99
Audit Company: Sworn/Estimate/Non-Audited
Audit Date: 43626

BIGFORK

THE BIGFORK EAGLE

Street Address: 8299 Mt Highway 35
City: Bigfork
State: MT
ZIP Code: 59911-3574
General Phone: (406) 758-4433
General Email: editor@bigforkeagle.com
Publication Website: https://www.bigforkeagle.com/
Editor Email: editor@bigforkeagle.com
Delivery Methods: Mail`Newsstand`Racks
Own Printing Facility?: Y
Commercial printers?: Y
Mechanical specifications: Type page 11 7/10 x 20 3/4; E - 6 cols, 1 4/5, 7/100 between; A - 6 cols, 1 4/5, 7/100 between; C - 6 cols, 1 4/5, 7/100 between.
Published Days: Wed
Avg. Paid Circ.: 14954
Avg. Free Circ.: 403
Audit Company: Sworn/Estimate/Non-Audited
Audit Date: 43626

BILLINGS

BILLINGS TIMES

Street Address: 2919 Montana Ave
City: Billings
State: MT
ZIP Code: 59101-2143
General Phone: (406) 245-4994
General Email: mail@billingstimes.net
Publication Website: https://billingstimes.net/
Delivery Methods: Mail
Year Established: 1891
Published Days: Thur
Audit Company: Sworn/Estimate/Non-Audited
Audit Date: 43626

BOULDER

THE BOULDER MONITOR

Street Address: 104 W Centennial Ave, PO Box 66
City: Boulder
State: MT
ZIP Code: 59632
General Phone: (406) 225-3822
General Email: info@boulder-monitor.com
Publication Website: https://www.boulder-monitor.com/
Parent Company: Response Media LLC
Publisher Name: Keith Hammonds
Publisher Email: keith@boulder-monitor.com
Editor Name: John Blodgett
Editor Email: john@boulder-monitor.com
Advertising Executive Email: ads@boulder-monitor.com
Delivery Methods: Mail`Newsstand`Racks
Own Printing Facility?: N
Commercial printers?: Y
Published Days: Wed
Audit Company: Sworn/Estimate/Non-Audited
Audit Date: 43626
Note: THIS IS NOT A DAILY OR FOUR DAYS OR MORE PER WEEK NEWSPAPER. WE PUBLISH ONCE PER WEEK AND ALREADY UPDATED THAT ENTRY.

BROWNING

GLACIER REPORTER

Street Address: 208 N PIEGAN ST, PO Box 349
City: Browning
State: MT
ZIP Code: 59417
General Phone: (406) 338-2090
General Email: glacrptr@3rivers.net
Publication Website: http://www.cutbankpioneerpress.com/glacier_reporter/
Publisher Name: Brian Kavanagh
Publisher Email: photos@cutbankpioneerpress.com
Editor Name: John McGill
Advertising Executive Name: Marlene Augare
Published Days: Wed
Avg. Paid Circ.: 2362
Audit Company: Sworn/Estimate/Non-Audited
Audit Date: 43626

BUTTE

THE BUTTE WEEKLY

Street Address: PO Box 4898
City: Butte
State: MT
ZIP Code: 59702-4898
General Phone: (406) 782-3820
General Email: butte.news@butteweekly.com
Publication Website: https://www.

butteweekly.com/
Parent Company: Butte Weekly
Publisher Name: Linda Anderson
Publisher Email: butte.news@butteweekly.com
Editor Name: Robin Jordan
Editor Email: editor@butteweekly.com
Advertising Executive Name: Linda Anderson
Advertising Executive Email: butte.news@butteweekly.com
Delivery Methods: Racks
Year Established: 1992
Commercial printers?: Y
Mechanical specifications: Type page 10 x 15 3/4; E - 4 cols, 2 5/12, 1/6 between; A - 4 cols, 2 5/12, 1/6 between; C - 4 cols, 2 5/12, 1/6 between.
Published Days: Wed
Avg. Free Circ.: 5500
Audit Company: Sworn/Estimate/Non-Audited
Audit Date: 43626

CASCADE

CASCADE COURIER

Street Address: P. O. Box 309
City: Cascade
State: MT
ZIP Code: 59421-4801
General Phone: (406) 468-9231
General Email: cascadecourier@mcn.net
Publication Website: https://www.cascadenewspaper.com/
Parent Company: Montana Newspaper Advertising Service, Inc.
Publisher Name: Toni M. Castellanos
Editor Name: Toni M. Castellanos
Year Established: 1910
Mechanical specifications: Type page 10 1/4 x 12 1/2.
Published Days: Thur
Avg. Paid Circ.: 560
Avg. Free Circ.: 13
Audit Company: Sworn/Estimate/Non-Audited
Audit Date: 43626

CHESTER

LIBERTY COUNTY TIMES

Street Address: 46 1st St E
City: Chester
State: MT
ZIP Code: 59522
General Phone: (406) 759-5355
General Email: lctimes@itstriangle.com
Publication Website: http://libertycountytimes.net/
Delivery Methods: Mail
Year Established: 1905
Published Days: Wed
Avg. Paid Circ.: 1202
Avg. Free Circ.: 17
Audit Company: Sworn/Estimate/Non-Audited
Audit Date: 43626

CHINOOK

JOURNAL NEWS OPINION

Street Address: 217 Indiana St
City: Chinook
State: MT
ZIP Code: 59523-9716
General Phone: (406) 357-3573
General Email: bcjnews@itstriangle.com
Publication Website: https://www.blainecountyjournal.com/
Delivery Methods: Mail Racks
Year Established: 1890
Own Printing Facility?: Y
Commercial printers?: Y
Published Days: Wed

Avg. Paid Circ.: 2150
Avg. Free Circ.: 48
Audit Company: Sworn/Estimate/Non-Audited
Audit Date: 43626

CHOTEAU

CHOTEAU ACANTHA

Street Address: 216 1st Ave NW, P.O. Box 320
City: Choteau
State: MT
ZIP Code: 59422-9269
General Phone: (406) 466-2403
General Email: tetonads@3rivers.net
Publication Website: http://www.choteauacantha.com/
Publisher Name: Jeff Martinsen
Editor Name: Melody Martinsen
Advertising Executive Name: Jeff Martinsen
Advertising Executive Email: tetonads@3rivers.net
Delivery Methods: Mail Newsstand
Year Established: 1893
Own Printing Facility?: N
Commercial printers?: Y
Mechanical specifications: type page is 6 col. wide by 21.75 inches deep. ROP col. width is 11.125". Classified page is 7 col. wide. 0p9 picas between each column
Published Days: Wed
Avg. Paid Circ.: 1600
Avg. Free Circ.: 20
Audit Company: Sworn/Estimate/Non-Audited
Audit Date: 43626

COLUMBIA FALLS

HUNGRY HORSE NEWS

Street Address: PO BOX 189, 926 Nucleus Avenue
City: Columbia Falls
State: MT
ZIP Code: 59912-0189
General Phone: (406) 892-2151
General Email: abrowning@hungryhorsenews.com
Publication Website: https://www.hungryhorsenews.com/
Parent Company: Flathead Publishing Group
Publisher Name: Rick Weaver
Publisher Email: publisher@dailyinterlake.com
Publisher Phone: (406) 755-7000
Editor Name: Chris Peterson
Editor Email: editor@hungryhorsenews.com
Editor Phone: (406) 892-2151
Advertising Executive Name: Andrea Browning
Advertising Executive Email: abrowning@hungryhorsenews.com
Advertising Executive Phone: (406) 892-2151
Delivery Methods: Mail Newsstand Racks
Year Established: 1947
Own Printing Facility?: Y
Commercial printers?: Y
Mechanical specifications: Type page 11 7/10 x 20 3/4; E - 6 cols, 1 4/5, 7/50 between; A - 6 cols, 1 4/5, 7/50 between; C - 6 cols, 2, 1/4 between.
Published Days: Wed
Avg. Paid Circ.: 1880
Audit Company: CAC
Audit Date: 44015

CONRAD

INDEPENDENT OBSERVER

Street Address: 7 3rd Ave SE
City: Conrad
State: MT
ZIP Code: 59425-2039
General Phone: (406) 271-5561

General Email: indobserv@3rivers.net
Publication Website: https://www.theindependentobserver.com/
Parent Company: The Independent-Observer
Delivery Methods: Mail Newsstand Carrier
Year Established: 1906
Own Printing Facility?: Y
Commercial printers?: Y
Mechanical specifications: 1 column - 1.83" 2 column - 3.79" 3 column - 5.75" 4 column - 7.708" 5 column - 9.66" 6 column - 11.625"
Published Days: Thur
Avg. Paid Circ.: 1900
Avg. Free Circ.: 60
Audit Company: Sworn/Estimate/Non-Audited
Audit Date: 43626

CUT BANK

CUT BANK PIONEER PRESS

Street Address: 19 S Central Ave, PO Box 847
City: Cut Bank
State: MT
ZIP Code: 59427-2914
General Phone: (406) 873-2201
General Email: news@cutbankpioneerpress.com
Publication Website: http://www.cutbankpioneerpress.com/cut_bank_pioneer_press/
Publisher Name: Brian Kavanagh
Publisher Email: photos@cutbankpioneerpress.com
Editor Name: LeAnne Kavanagh
Editor Email: editor@cutbankpioneerpress.com
Delivery Methods: Mail Newsstand Carrier Racks
Published Days: Wed
Avg. Paid Circ.: 1600
Audit Company: Sworn/Estimate/Non-Audited
Audit Date: 43626

CUT BANK

THE VALIERIAN

Street Address: 19 S Central Ave, PO Box 847
City: Cut Bank
State: MT
ZIP Code: 59427-2914
General Phone: (406) 279-3440
General Email: staff@thevalierian.com
Publication Website: http://www.cutbankpioneerpress.com/cut_bank_pioneer_press/
Publisher Name: Brian Kavanagh
Publisher Email: photos@cutbankpioneerpress.com
Delivery Methods: Mail Newsstand
Published Days: Wed
Audit Company: Sworn/Estimate/Non-Audited
Audit Date: 43626

DEER LODGE

SILVER STATE POST

Street Address: 312 Missouri Ave, P.O. Box 111
City: Deer Lodge
State: MT
ZIP Code: 59722-1077
General Phone: (406) 846-2424
General Email: ads@pburgmail.com
Publication Website: http://www.sspmt.com/
Editor Name: Michael Stafford
Editor Email: news@sspmt.com
Advertising Executive Name: Jesse Mullen
Advertising Executive Email: info@adedpro.com

Delivery Methods: Mail Newsstand Racks
Year Established: 1887
Commercial printers?: Y
Published Days: Wed
Avg. Paid Circ.: 1900
Avg. Free Circ.: 2200
Audit Company: Sworn/Estimate/Non-Audited
Audit Date: 43626

EKALAKA

THE EKALAKA EAGLE

Street Address: 307 N Main St, P.O. Box 66
City: Ekalaka
State: MT
ZIP Code: 59324
General Phone: (406) 775-6245
General Email: ekeagle@midrivers.com
Publication Website: https://www.ekalakaeagle.com/
Parent Company: Montana Newspaper Advertising Service, Inc.
Delivery Methods: Mail
Year Established: 1909
Commercial printers?: Y
Published Days: Fri
Avg. Paid Circ.: 1100
Audit Company: Sworn/Estimate/Non-Audited
Audit Date: 43626

ENNIS

THE MADISONIAN

Street Address: 65 Mt Highway 287
City: Ennis
State: MT
ZIP Code: 59729-9117
General Phone: (406) 682-7755
General Email: ads@madisoniannews.com
Publication Website: http://madisoniannews.com/
Editor Email: editor@madisoniannews.com
Advertising Executive Name: Erin Leonard
Advertising Executive Email: eleonard@madisoniannews.com
Delivery Methods: Mail Newsstand Carrier Racks
Year Established: 1873
Published Days: Thur
Avg. Paid Circ.: 2300
Audit Company: Sworn/Estimate/Non-Audited
Audit Date: 43626

EUREKA

TOBACCO VALLEY NEWS

Street Address: PO Box 307
City: Eureka
State: MT
ZIP Code: 59917
General Phone: (406) 297-2514
General Email: robnewman22@gmail.com
Publication Website: https://tobaccovalleynews.com/
Publisher Name: Steve Newman
Editor Name: Steve Newman
Editor Email: eurekaeditor@gmail.com
Advertising Executive Name: Robin Newman
Advertising Executive Email: robin.newman22@icloud.com
Delivery Methods: Mail Newsstand Carrier
Year Established: 1960
Published Days: Wed
Avg. Paid Circ.: 2101
Avg. Free Circ.: 13
Audit Company: Sworn/Estimate/Non-Audited
Audit Date: 43626

FAIRFIELD

Community Newspapers in the U.S.

FAIRFIELD

FAIRFIELD SUN TIMES

Street Address: PO Box 578
City: Fairfield
State: MT
ZIP Code: 59436-0578
General Phone: (406) 467-2334
General Email: suntimes@3rivers.net
Publication Website: https://www.fairfieldsuntimes.com/
Parent Company: Sun Times Printing & Publishing, LLC
Publisher Name: Darryl L. Flowers
Publisher Email: suntimes@3rivers.net
Editor Name: Darryl L. Flowers
Editor Email: suntimes@3rivers.net
Delivery Methods: Mail`Newsstand
Year Established: 1912
Own Printing Facility?: N
Commercial printers?: Y
Published Days: Thur
Avg. Paid Circ.: 760
Avg. Free Circ.: 10
Audit Company: Sworn/Estimate/Non-Audited
Audit Date: 43626

FORT BENTON

THE RIVER PRESS

Street Address: 1408 Front St.
City: Fort Benton
State: MT
ZIP Code: 59442
General Phone: (406) 622-3311
General Email: riverpressnews@gmail.com
Publication Website: http://www.riverpressnews.com/
Editor Name: Bethany Monroe DeBorde
Editor Email: riverpressbethany@gmail.com
Advertising Executive Email: riverpressads@gmail.com
Delivery Methods: Mail`Newsstand`Carrier
Year Established: 1880
Commercial printers?: Y
Mechanical specifications: Type page 13 x 21 1/2; E - 6 cols, 2, 1/6 between; A - 6 cols, 2, 1/6 between; C - 6 cols, 2, 1/6 between.
Published Days: Wed
Avg. Paid Circ.: 2000
Avg. Free Circ.: 50
Audit Company: Sworn/Estimate/Non-Audited
Audit Date: 43626

GLASGOW

THE GLASGOW COURIER

Street Address: 54226 US Highway 2
City: Glasgow
State: MT
ZIP Code: 59230-2401
General Phone: (406) 228-9301
General Email: courier@nemont.net
Publication Website: https://www.glasgowcourier.com/
Parent Company: Stevenson/Hicks Newspapers
Delivery Methods: Mail`Newsstand`Carrier
Year Established: 1913
Own Printing Facility?: Y
Published Days: Wed
Avg. Paid Circ.: 2707
Avg. Free Circ.: 95
Audit Company: Sworn/Estimate/Non-Audited
Audit Date: 43626

HUNTLEY

THE YELLOWSTONE COUNTY NEWS

Street Address: 113 Northern Ave
City: Huntley
State: MT
ZIP Code: 59037-9101
General Phone: (406) 348-2649
General Email: ads@yellowstonecountynews.com
Publication Website: https://www.yellowstonecountynews.com/
Editor Name: Jonathan McNiven
Delivery Methods: Mail`Newsstand`Racks
Year Established: 1976
Own Printing Facility?: Y
Commercial printers?: N
Mechanical specifications: Type page 10 x 16; E - 5 cols, 1 5/6, 5/24 between; C - 6 cols, between.
Published Days: Fri
Avg. Paid Circ.: 1900
Audit Company: Sworn/Estimate/Non-Audited
Audit Date: 43626

KALISPELL

FLATHEAD BEACON

Street Address: 17 Main St
City: Kalispell
State: MT
ZIP Code: 59901-4449
General Phone: (406) 257-9220
General Email: hunt@flatheadbeacon.com
Publication Website: https://flatheadbeacon.com/
Editor Name: Myers Reece
Editor Email: mreece@flatheadbeacon.com
Advertising Executive Name: Bob Hunt
Advertising Executive Email: hunt@flatheadbeacon.com
Delivery Methods: Newsstand`Carrier`Racks
Year Established: 2007
Own Printing Facility?: N
Commercial printers?: N
Published Days: Wed
Avg. Free Circ.: 25000
Audit Company: Sworn/Estimate/Non-Audited
Audit Date: 43626

LIBBY

THE MONTANIAN

Street Address: 317 California Ave
City: Libby
State: MT
ZIP Code: 59923-1937
General Phone: (406) 293-8202
General Email: news@montanian.com
Publication Website: http://montanian.com/
Delivery Methods: Newsstand
Year Established: 1989
Own Printing Facility?: Y
Commercial printers?: N
Mechanical specifications: on request
Published Days: Wed
Avg. Free Circ.: 3400
Audit Company: Sworn/Estimate/Non-Audited
Audit Date: 43626

LIBBY

THE WESTERN NEWS

Street Address: 311 California Ave
City: Libby
State: MT
ZIP Code: 59923-1937
General Phone: (406) 293-4124
General Email: sresch@thewesternnews.com
Publication Website: https://www.thewesternnews.com/
Parent Company: Hagadone Corporation
Publisher Name: Suzanne Resch
Publisher Email: sresch@thewesternnews.com
Publisher Phone: (406) 293-4124
Advertising Executive Email: classads@thewesternnews.com
Advertising Executive Phone: (406) 293-4124
Delivery Methods: Mail`Newsstand`Racks
Year Established: 1902
Commercial printers?: Y
Mechanical specifications: Type page 13 x 21; E - 6 cols, 2 1/18, 1/6 between; A - 6 cols, 2 1/18, 1/6 between; C - 6 cols, 2 1/18, 1/6 between.
Published Days: Tues`Fri
Avg. Paid Circ.: 1804
Audit Company: CAC
Audit Date: 44015

MALTA

THE PHILLIPS COUNTY NEWS

Street Address: 220 N CENTRAL AVE
City: Malta
State: MT
ZIP Code: 59538
General Phone: (406) 654-2020
General Email: adspcnews@gmail.com
Publication Website: https://www.phillipscountynews.com/
Parent Company: Glasgow Courier, Inc.
Publisher Name: Mark, Hebert
Publisher Email: markpcnews@gmail.com
Editor Name: Pierre Bibbs
Advertising Executive Name: Deb Solberg
Advertising Executive Email: adspcnews@gmail.com
Delivery Methods: Mail`Racks
Year Established: 1896
Own Printing Facility?: N
Commercial printers?: N
Published Days: Wed
Avg. Paid Circ.: 2324
Avg. Free Circ.: 52
Audit Company: Sworn/Estimate/Non-Audited
Audit Date: 43626

PHILIPSBURG

THE PHILIPSBURG MAIL

Street Address: 206 East Broadway
City: Philipsburg
State: MT
ZIP Code: 59858
General Phone: (406) 859-3223
General Email: ads@pburgmail.com
Publication Website: http://www.pburgmail.com/
Parent Company: Montana Newspaper Advertising Service, Inc.
Publisher Name: Jesse Mullen
Editor Name: Emily Petrovski
Delivery Methods: Mail`Newsstand`Racks
Year Established: 1887
Own Printing Facility?: N
Commercial printers?: Y
Mechanical specifications: Type page 10 1/2 x 16; E - 5 cols, 1 9/10, 1/6 between; A - 5 cols, 1 9/10, 1/6 between; C - 5 cols, 1 9/10, 1/6 between.
Published Days: Thur
Avg. Paid Circ.: 1400
Avg. Free Circ.: 13
Audit Company: Sworn/Estimate/Non-Audited
Audit Date: 43626

PLAINS

CLARK FORK VALLEY PRESS

Street Address: 105 Lynch St
City: Plains
State: MT
ZIP Code: 59859
General Phone: (406) 826-3402
General Email: llarson@vp-mi.com
Publication Website: https://vp-mi.com/contact-us
Parent Company: Hagadone Corp.
Publisher Name: Laurie Ramos
Publisher Email: lramos@leaderadvertiser.com
Advertising Executive Name: Lisa Larson
Advertising Executive Email: llarson@vp-mi.com
Advertising Executive Phone: (406) 826-3403
Delivery Methods: Mail`Racks
Published Days: Wed
Avg. Paid Circ.: 586
Audit Company: CAC
Audit Date: 44015

PLAINS

MINERAL INDEPENDENT

Street Address: 105 Lynch St
City: Plains
State: MT
ZIP Code: 59859
General Phone: (406) 826-3402
General Email: llarson@vp-mi.com
Publication Website: https://vp-mi.com/contact-us
Parent Company: Hagadone Corp.
Publisher Name: Laurie Ramos
Publisher Email: lramos@leaderadvertiser.com
Advertising Executive Name: Lisa Larson
Advertising Executive Email: llarson@vp-mi.com
Advertising Executive Phone: (406) 826-3403
Delivery Methods: Mail`Racks
Year Established: 1910
Published Days: Wed
Avg. Paid Circ.: 483
Audit Company: CAC
Audit Date: 44015

POLSON

LAKE COUNTY LEADER

Street Address: 108 1st St E
City: Polson
State: MT
ZIP Code: 59860
General Phone: (406) 883-4343
General Email: lramos@leaderadvertiser.com
Publication Website: https://www.leaderadvertiser.com/
Parent Company: Hagadone Corp.
Publisher Name: Laurie Ramos
Publisher Email: lramos@leaderadvertiser.com
Publisher Phone: (406) 883-4343
Editor Name: Matt Baldwin
Editor Email: editor@leaderadvertiser.com
Editor Phone: (406) 883-4343
Advertising Executive Name: Laurie Ramos
Advertising Executive Email: lramos@leaderadvertiser.com
Advertising Executive Phone: (406) 883-4343
Delivery Methods: Mail`Newsstand`Racks
Year Established: 1910
Own Printing Facility?: Y
Commercial printers?: Y
Mechanical specifications: Type page 12 1/2 x 21.
Published Days: Thur
Avg. Paid Circ.: 1486
Audit Company: CAC
Audit Date: 44015

RONAN

VALLEY JOURNAL

Street Address: 331 Main St SW
City: Ronan
State: MT
ZIP Code: 59864
General Phone: (406) 676-8989
General Email: boone@valleyjournal.net
Publication Website: http://www.valleyjournal.net/
Parent Company: The Valley Journal
Publisher Name: Summer Goddard

Publisher Email: summer@valleyjournal.net
Editor Name: Summer Goddard
Editor Email: summer@valleyjournal.net
Advertising Executive Name: Boone Goddard
Advertising Executive Email: boone@valleyjournal.net
Delivery Methods: Mail`Newsstand`Racks
Year Established: 2004
Mechanical specifications: Mission, Jocko and lower Flathead Valley
Published Days: Wed
Avg. Free Circ.: 8400
Audit Company: Sworn/Estimate/Non-Audited
Audit Date: 43626

ROUNDUP

THE ROUNDUP RECORD-TRIBUNE/ WINNETT TIMES

Street Address: 343 Main Street
City: Roundup
State: MT
ZIP Code: 59072
General Phone: (406) 320-0322
General Email: rrtnews@midrivers.com
Publication Website: https://www.rounduprecord.com/
Parent Company: Proclaim Good News, LLC
Publisher Name: David Ponte
Editor Name: Lura Moore
Advertising Executive Email: rrtnews@midrivers.com
Advertising Executive Phone: (406) 320-0322
Delivery Methods: Mail
Year Established: 1908
Own Printing Facility?: N
Commercial printers?: Y
Mechanical specifications: Type page 15 1/2 x 21.
Published Days: Wed
Avg. Paid Circ.: 2600
Avg. Free Circ.: 88
Audit Company: Sworn/Estimate/Non-Audited
Audit Date: 43626

SCOBEY

DANIELS COUNTY LEADER

Street Address: 214 Main St
City: Scobey
State: MT
ZIP Code: 59263
General Phone: (406) 487-5303
General Email: 2leader@nemont.net
Publication Website: http://danielscountyleader.com/
Publisher Name: Burley R. Bowler
Publisher Phone: (406) 487-5303
Editor Name: Milton Gunderson
Editor Phone: (406) 487-5303
Own Printing Facility?: Y
Commercial printers?: Y
Published Days: Thur
Avg. Paid Circ.: 1540
Audit Company: Sworn/Estimate/Non-Audited
Audit Date: 43626

SEELEY LAKE

SEELEY SWAN PATHFINDER

Street Address: 3166 Highway 83 N
City: Seeley Lake
State: MT
ZIP Code: 59868
General Phone: (406) 677-2022
General Email: pathfinder@seeleylake.com
Publication Website: https://www.seeleylake.com/
Parent Company: Pathfinder LLC
Advertising Executive Email: pathfinder@seeleylake.com

Advertising Executive Phone: (406) 677-2022
Delivery Methods: Mail`Newsstand
Year Established: 1984
Mechanical specifications: Type page 10 x 11 1/2; E - 5 cols, 1 3/4, 1/4 between; A - 5 cols, 1 3/4, 1/4 between; C - 5 cols, 1 3/4, 1/4 between.
Published Days: Thur
Avg. Paid Circ.: 1250
Avg. Free Circ.: 50
Audit Company: Sworn/Estimate/Non-Audited
Audit Date: 43626

SHELBY

THE SHELBY PROMOTER

Street Address: 119 2nd Ave S, PO Box 610
City: Shelby
State: MT
ZIP Code: 59474-1962
General Phone: (406) 434-5171
General Email: promoadmgr@3rivers.net
Publication Website: http://www.cutbankpioneerpress.com/shelby_promoter/
Parent Company: Montana Newspaper Advertising Service, Inc.
Publisher Name: Brian Kavanagh
Publisher Email: photos@cutbankpioneerpress.com
Delivery Methods: Mail`Newsstand`Carrier`Racks
Own Printing Facility?: Y
Published Days: Wed
Avg. Paid Circ.: 2125
Audit Company: Sworn/Estimate/Non-Audited
Audit Date: 43626

SIDNEY

SIDNEY HERALD

Street Address: 310 2nd Ave NE
City: Sidney
State: MT
ZIP Code: 59270
General Phone: (406) 433-2403
General Email: editor@sidneyherald.com
Publication Website: https://www.sidneyherald.com/
Parent Company: Wick Communications
Publisher Name: Kelly Miller
Publisher Email: publisher@sidneyherald.com
Editor Name: Eric Gill
Editor Email: editor@sidneyherald.com
Advertising Executive Name: Emily Wion
Advertising Executive Email: ewion@willistonherald.com
Delivery Methods: Mail`Newsstand`Carrier`Racks
Year Established: 1907
Commercial printers?: Y
Mechanical specifications: Type page 11 1/4 x 21; E - 6 cols, 1 5/8, between; A - 6 cols, 1 5/8, between; C - 9 cols, 1 3/16, between.
Published Days: Wed`Sun
Avg. Paid Circ.: 2192
Audit Company: VAC
Audit Date: 43260

SIDNEY

THE ROUNDUP

Street Address: P.O. Box 1207
City: Sidney
State: MT
ZIP Code: 59270
General Phone: (406) 433-3306
General Email: info@roundupweb.com
Publication Website: https://www.roundupweb.com/
Editor Name: Lois Kerr
Advertising Executive Name: Dianne

Swanson
Advertising Executive Phone: (406) 433-3306
Delivery Methods: Newsstand`Carrier
Year Established: 1994
Published Days: Wed
Avg. Free Circ.: 9500
Audit Company: Sworn/Estimate/Non-Audited
Audit Date: 43626

STEVENSVILLE

BITTERROOT STAR

Street Address: 215 Main St
City: Stevensville
State: MT
ZIP Code: 59870
General Phone: (406) 777-3928
General Email: editor@bitterrootstar.com
Publication Website: https://bitterrootstar.com/
Parent Company: Bitterroot Star
Publisher Name: Victoria Howell
Publisher Phone: (406) 777-3928
Editor Name: Victoria Howell
Editor Email: editor@bitterrootstar.com
Editor Phone: (406) 777-3928
Delivery Methods: Mail`Newsstand`Carrier`Racks
Year Established: 1985
Own Printing Facility?: Y
Commercial printers?: N
Mechanical specifications: Type page 12 7/8 x 21; E - 6 cols, 2, 1/6 between; A - 6 cols, 2, 1/6 between; C - 6 cols, 2, 1/6 between.
Published Days: Wed
Avg. Paid Circ.: 400
Avg. Free Circ.: 6800
Audit Company: Sworn/Estimate/Non-Audited
Audit Date: 43626

THOMPSON FALLS

SANDERS COUNTY LEDGER

Street Address: 603 W Main St
City: Thompson Falls
State: MT
ZIP Code: 59873
General Phone: (406) 827-3421
General Email: news@scledger.net
Publication Website: https://www.scledger.net/
Publisher Name: Annie Wooden
Editor Name: Annie Wooden
Editor Email: editor@scledger.net.
Advertising Executive Name: Sherry Hagerman-Benton
Advertising Executive Email: ledgerads@blackfoot.net
Delivery Methods: Mail`Newsstand`Racks
Year Established: 1983
Published Days: Thur
Avg. Paid Circ.: 28700
Audit Company: Sworn/Estimate/Non-Audited
Audit Date: 43626

WHITE SULPHUR SPRINGS

THE MEAGHER COUNTY NEWS

Street Address: P.O. Box 349
City: White Sulphur Springs
State: MT
ZIP Code: 59645-0349
General Phone: (406) 547-3831
General Email: mcnews@mtintouch.net
Publication Website: http://www.meagher-county-news.com/
Delivery Methods: Mail`Newsstand
Year Established: 1889
Mechanical specifications: Type page 10 3/4 x 13 1/2; E - 5 cols, 2 1/16, 1/8 between; A - 5 cols, 2 1/16, 1/8 between; C - 5 cols, 2 1/16, 1/8 between.

Published Days: Thur
Avg. Paid Circ.: 1200
Audit Company: Sworn/Estimate/Non-Audited
Audit Date: 43626

WHITEFISH

THE WHITEFISH PILOT

Street Address: 312 2nd St E
City: Whitefish
State: MT
ZIP Code: 59937
General Phone: (406) 862-3505
General Email: editor@whitefishpilot.com
Publication Website: https://www.whitefishpilot.com/
Parent Company: Hagadone Corp.
Publisher Name: Rick Weaver
Publisher Email: publisher@dailyinterlake.com
Publisher Phone: (406) 755-7000
Editor Name: Heidi Desch
Editor Email: editor@whitefishpilot.com
Advertising Executive Name: Anton Kaufer
Advertising Executive Email: dmactaggart@whitefishpilot.com
Delivery Methods: Mail`Newsstand`Racks
Year Established: 1904
Mechanical specifications: Type page 13 x 21; E - 6 cols, 2, 1/4 between; A - 6 cols, 2, 1/4 between; C - 6 cols, 2, 1/4 between.
Published Days: Wed
Avg. Paid Circ.: 1930
Audit Company: CAC
Audit Date: 44015

WHITEHALL

WHITEHALL LEDGER

Street Address: 15 W Legion St
City: Whitehall
State: MT
ZIP Code: 59759
General Phone: (406) 287-5301
General Email: info@whitehallledger.com
Publication Website: https://www.whitehallledger.com/
Parent Company: Montana Newspaper Advertising Service, Inc.
Advertising Executive Email: advertising@whitehallledger.com
Delivery Methods: Mail`Newsstand`Racks
Year Established: 1984
Mechanical specifications: Type page 9 7/8 x 15; E - 5 cols, 1 5/6, 1/8 between; A - 5 cols, 1 5/6, 1/8 between; C - 5 cols, 1 5/6, 1/8 between.
Published Days: Wed
Avg. Paid Circ.: 1400
Avg. Free Circ.: 16
Audit Company: Sworn/Estimate/Non-Audited
Audit Date: 43626

WOLF POINT

THE HERALD-NEWS

Street Address: 408 Main St
City: Wolf Point
State: MT
ZIP Code: 59201-1534
General Phone: (406) 653-2222
General Email: herald@nemontel.net
Publication Website: http://www.wolfpoint.com/herald.htm
Parent Company: Adams Publishing Group
Delivery Methods: Mail`Newsstand
Commercial printers?: Y
Mechanical specifications: Type page 11.125 x 21.5; 6 cols, .14" between
Published Days: Thur
Avg. Paid Circ.: 2000
Avg. Free Circ.: 30
Audit Company: Sworn/Estimate/Non-

Audited
Audit Date: 43626

NORTH CAROLINA

AHOSKIE

ROANOKE-CHOWAN NEWS-HERALD

Street Address: 801 Parker Ave E
City: Ahoskie
State: NC
ZIP Code: 27910-3641
General Phone: (252) 332-2123
General Email: judy.farmer@r-cnews.com
Publication Website: r-cnews.com
Parent Company: Boone Newspapers, Inc.
Publisher Name: Anthony Clark
Publisher Phone: (252) 332-2123
Editor Name: Cal Bryant
Editor Email: cal.bryant@r-cnews.com
Advertising Executive Name: Judy Farmer
Advertising Executive Email: judy.farmer@r-cnews.com
Delivery Methods: Mail`Carrier`Racks
Year Established: 1914
Own Printing Facility?: Y
Commercial printers?: Y
Published Days: Tues`Thur`Sat
Avg. Paid Circ.: 6800
Avg. Free Circ.: 5000
Audit Company: Sworn/Estimate/Non-Audited

ALBEMARLE

THE STANLY NEWS & PRESS

Street Address: 237 W North St
City: Albemarle
State: NC
ZIP Code: 28001-3923
General Phone: (704) 982-2121
General Email: talmond@stanlynewspress.com
Publication Website: thesnaponline.com
Parent Company: Boone Newspapers
Publisher Name: Roger Watson
Publisher Email: roger.watson@stanlynewspress.com
Publisher Phone: (704) 982-2121
Editor Name: B.J. Drye
Editor Email: bj.drye@stanlynewspress.com
Editor Phone: roger.watson@stanlynewspress.com
Advertising Executive Name: Debbie Holt
Advertising Executive Email: debbie.holt@stanlynewspress.com
Advertising Executive Phone: bj.drye@stanlynewspress.com
Delivery Methods: Mail`Newsstand`Carrier`Racks
Year Established: 1880
Own Printing Facility?: Y
Commercial printers?: N
Mechanical specifications: Type page 11 10/16 x 21 1/2; E - 6 cols, 1 13/16, between; A - 6 cols, 1 13/16, between; C - 6 cols, 1 13/16, between.
Published Days: Tues`Thur`Sun
Avg. Paid Circ.: 7000
Avg. Free Circ.: 13000
Audit Company: Sworn/Estimate/Non-Audited

BAYBORO

THE COUNTY COMPASS

Street Address: PO Box 460
City: Bayboro
State: NC
ZIP Code: 28515-0460
General Phone: (252) 745-3155
General Email: flora@compassnews360.com
Publication Website: compassnews360.com
Publisher Name: Jeff Aydelette
Publisher Email: 28515-0460
Publisher Phone: (252) 745-3155
Editor Name: flora@compassnews360.com
Editor Email: Jeff Aydelette
Editor Phone: Jeff@compassnews360.com
Advertising Executive Name: (252) 670-0447
Delivery Methods: Mail`Newsstand`Carrier`Racks
Year Established: 2009
Published Days: Thur
Published Other: Weekly
Avg. Paid Circ.: 500
Avg. Free Circ.: 19500
Audit Company: Sworn/Estimate/Non-Audited
Note: Our business model -- free to the reader -- with hard, local news is allowing us to grow while other publications are shrinking.

BENSON

FOUR OAKS-BENSON NEWS IN REVIEW

Street Address: 113 S Market St
City: Benson
State: NC
ZIP Code: 27504-1520
General Phone: (919) 894-3331
General Email: fobnews@aol.com
Publication Website: www.bensonfouroaksnews.com
Publisher Phone: (919) 894-3331
Editor Name: fobnews@aol.com
Advertising Executive Email: Mike Dart
Advertising Executive Phone: fobnews@bensonfouroaksnews.com
Delivery Methods: Mail`Newsstand
Published Days: Wed
Avg. Paid Circ.: 4500
Audit Company: Sworn/Estimate/Non-Audited

BLACK MOUNTAIN

BLACK MOUNTAIN NEWS

Street Address: 111 Richardson Blvd
City: Black Mountain
State: NC
ZIP Code: 28711-3526
General Phone: (828) 669-8727
General Email: lfprince@gannett.com
Publication Website: blackmountainnews.com
Publisher Name: Thomas Claybaugh
Publisher Phone: (828) 669-8727
Editor Name: Paul Clark
Advertising Executive Name: Lyn Price
Advertising Executive Email: Lyn@blackmountainnews.com
Delivery Methods: Mail`Newsstand`Carrier`Racks
Year Established: 1945
Commercial printers?: Y
Mechanical specifications: Type page 11 1/16 x 21; E - 6 cols, 1 13/16, 1/8 between; A - 6 cols, 1 13/16, 1/8 between; C - 8 cols, 1 5/16, 1/8 between.
Published Days: Thur
Avg. Paid Circ.: 3000
Avg. Free Circ.: 135
Audit Company: Sworn/Estimate/Non-Audited

BLOWING ROCK

THE BLOWING ROCKET

Street Address: 474 Industrial Park Drive
City: Blowing Rock
State: NC
ZIP Code: 28607

General Phone: (828) 264-6397
Publication Website: blowingrocket.com
Parent Company: Adams Publishing Group
Publisher Name: Gene Fowler
Publisher Email: gene.fowler@mountaintimes.com
Publisher Phone: (828) 264-6397
Editor Name: Tom Mayer
Editor Email: tom.mayer@mountaintimes.com
Advertising Executive Name: Charlie Price
Advertising Executive Email: charlie.price@mountaintimes.com
Advertising Executive Phone: charlie.price@mountaintimes.com
Delivery Methods: Mail`Newsstand`Carrier`Racks
Year Established: 1932
Own Printing Facility?: Y
Commercial printers?: Y
Mechanical specifications: Type page 13 1/2 x 21; E - 6 cols, 2, 3/16 between; A - 6 cols, 2, 3/16 between; C - 9 cols, 1 5/16, 1/8 between.
Published Days: Thur
Avg. Paid Circ.: 2700
Avg. Free Circ.: 36
Audit Company: Sworn/Estimate/Non-Audited

BOONE

WATAUGA DEMOCRAT

Street Address: 474 Industrial Park Dr
City: Boone
State: NC
ZIP Code: 28607-3937
General Phone: (828) 264-3612
General Email: charlie.price@mountaintimes.com
Publication Website: wataugademocrat.com
Parent Company: Adams Publishing Group
Publisher Name: Gene Fowler
Publisher Email: gene.fowler@mountaintimes.com
Publisher Phone: (828) 264-3612
Editor Name: Anna Oakes
Editor Email: anna.oakes@wataugademocrat.com
Advertising Executive Name: Charlie Price
Advertising Executive Email: charlie.price@mountaintimes.com
Delivery Methods: Mail`Newsstand`Carrier`Racks
Year Established: 1888
Own Printing Facility?: Y
Commercial printers?: Y
Mechanical specifications: Type page 13 x 21; E - 6 cols, 2 1/6, 1/8 between; A - 6 cols, 2 1/6, 1/8 between; C - 9 cols, 1 3/8, 1/8 between.
Published Days: Wed`Sun
Avg. Paid Circ.: 3800
Avg. Free Circ.: 296
Audit Company: Sworn/Estimate/Non-Audited

BREVARD

THE TRANSYLVANIA TIMES

Street Address: 37 N Broad St
City: Brevard
State: NC
ZIP Code: 28712-3725
General Phone: (828) 883-8156
General Email: shirsh@transylvaniatimes.com
Publication Website: transylvaniatimes.com
Publisher Name: Sean Trapp
Publisher Email: seantrapp@transylvaniatimes.com
Publisher Phone: (828) 883-8156
Editor Name: John Lanier
Editor Email: jlanier@transylvaniatimes.com
Advertising Executive Name: Leigh Trapp
Advertising Executive Email: leightrapp@transylvaniatimes.com
Advertising Executive Phone: leightrapp@transylvaniatimes.com
Delivery Methods: Mail`Newsstand`Racks
Year Established: 1887
Mechanical specifications: Type page 11 5/8 x 21; E - 6 cols, 1 13/16, 1/16 between; A - 6 cols, 1 13/16, 1/16 between; C - 6 cols, 1 13/16, 1/16 between.
Published Days: Mon`Thur
Avg. Paid Circ.: 8200
Avg. Free Circ.: 80
Audit Company: Sworn/Estimate/Non-Audited

BRYSON CITY

THE SMOKY MOUNTAIN TIMES

Street Address: 1 River St
City: Bryson City
State: NC
ZIP Code: 28713-6982
General Phone: (828) 488-2189
General Email: adrep@thesmokymountaintimes.com
Publication Website: thesmokymountaintimes.com
Parent Company: Community Newspapers Inc.
Publisher Name: Rachel Hoskins
Publisher Email: rhoskins@thefranklinpress.com
Publisher Phone: (828) 488-2189
Editor Name: Jessica Webb
Editor Email: editor@thesmokymountaintimes.com
Advertising Executive Name: Kristi Suess
Advertising Executive Email: classifieds@thesmokymountaintimes.com
Delivery Methods: Mail`Racks
Year Established: 1883
Commercial printers?: Y
Published Days: Thur
Avg. Paid Circ.: 3900
Audit Company: Sworn/Estimate/Non-Audited

BURGAW

PENDER-TOPSAIL POST & VOICE

Street Address: P.O. Box 955
City: Burgaw
State: NC
ZIP Code: 28425
General Phone: (910) 259-9111
General Email: advertising@post-voice.com
Publication Website: post-voice.com
Parent Company: Carteret Publishing Co.
Publisher Name: Andy Pettigrew
Publisher Email: posteditor@post-voice.com
Publisher Phone: (910) 259-9111
Editor Name: Andy Pettigrew
Editor Email: posteditor@post-voice.com
Advertising Executive Email: Katie Pettigrew
Advertising Executive Phone: advertising@post-voice.com
Mechanical specifications: Type page 13 x 21 1/2; E - 6 cols, 2, 1/6 between; A - 6 cols, 2, 1/6 between; C - 6 cols, 2, 1/6 between.
Published Days: Wed
Avg. Paid Circ.: 5000
Avg. Free Circ.: 400
Audit Company: Sworn/Estimate/Non-Audited

BURNSVILLE

YANCEY COMMON TIMES JOURNAL

Street Address: 22 N Main St
City: Burnsville
State: NC
ZIP Code: 28714-2925
General Phone: (828) 682-2120
General Email: pat@yanceypaper.com
Publication Website: yanceytimesjournal.com

Parent Company: Trib Publications
Publisher Name: Pat Randolph
Publisher Email: pat@yanceypaper.com
Publisher Phone: (828) 682-2120
Editor Name: Jody Higgins
Editor Email: editor@yanceypaper.com
Advertising Executive Name: Pat Randolph
Advertising Executive Email: pat@yanceypaper.com
Delivery Methods: Mail`Newsstand`Racks
Published Days: Wed
Audit Company: Sworn/Estimate/Non-Audited

CAROLINA BEACH

THE ISLAND GAZETTE

Street Address: 1003 Bennet Ln
City: Carolina Beach
State: NC
ZIP Code: 28428-5770
General Phone: (910) 458-8156
General Email: islandgazette@aol.com
Publication Website: islandgazette.net
Publisher Email: 28428-5770
Publisher Phone: (910) 458-8156
Editor Name: islandgazette@aol.com
Advertising Executive Email: Willard H. Killough III
Advertising Executive Phone: editor@islandgazette.net
Year Established: 1978
Mechanical specifications: Type page 13 x 21.
Published Days: Wed
Avg. Paid Circ.: 7000
Avg. Free Circ.: 325
Audit Company: Sworn/Estimate/Non-Audited

CASHIERS

CROSSROADS CHRONICLE

Street Address: 196 Burns St.
City: Cashiers
State: NC
ZIP Code: 28717
General Phone: (828) 743-5101
General Email: mhenry@CrossroadsChronicle.com
Publication Website: crossroadschronicle.com
Parent Company: Community Newspapers Inc.
Publisher Name: Brad Spaulding
Publisher Email: publisher@CrossroadsChronicle.com
Publisher Phone: (828) 743-5101
Editor Email: editor@CrossroadsChronicle.com
Editor Phone: publisher@CrossroadsChronicle.com
Advertising Executive Name: 828-743-5101, ext: 205
Advertising Executive Email: Randi VanGilder
Advertising Executive Phone: advertising@CrossroadsChronicle.com
Delivery Methods: Mail`Newsstand`Racks
Year Established: 1983
Own Printing Facility?: Y
Commercial printers?: N
Mechanical specifications: Ã¢€Â¢ CamEra rEady adsmust be a PDF, JPG or TIF file with all images, fonts, etc. embedded and RGB/PMS spot colors converted to either Grayscale or CMYK. InDesign files that are packaged with fonts and links may be submitted. Publisher and Word files will NOT be accepted. Ã¢€Â¢ Resolution for both submitted ads and photos should be a minimum of 300 dpi. The Chronicle will not be held responsible for ads and/or photos that do not print clearly as a result of low resolution. Width Picas Inches 1 Column 10p 1.667Ã¢€Â 2 Columns 20p9 3.458Ã¢€Â 3 Columns 31p6 5.25Ã¢€Â 4 Columns 42p3 7.042Ã¢€Â 5 Columns 52p12 8.833Ã¢€Â 6 Columns 63p9 10.625Ã¢€Â
Published Days: Wed
Avg. Paid Circ.: 2200
Audit Company: Sworn/Estimate/Non-Audited

CHAPEL HILL

THE DURHAM NEWS

Street Address: 505 W Franklin St
City: Chapel Hill
State: NC
ZIP Code: 27516-2315
General Phone: (919) 932-2003
General Email: kberkeley@newsobserver.com
Publication Website: thedurhamnews.com
Parent Company: The News & Observer Publishing Co.
Publisher Phone: (919) 932-2003
Editor Name: kberkeley@newsobserver.com
Editor Email: Sara Glines
Editor Phone: sglines@newsobserver.com (919) 829-4659"
Advertising Executive Email: Jane Elizabeth
Advertising Executive Phone: jelizabeth@newsobserver.com
Delivery Methods: Carrier
Published Days: Wed`Sun
Avg. Free Circ.: 75594
Audit Company: Sworn/Estimate/Non-Audited

CHARLOTTE

CHARLOTTE BUSINESS JOURNAL

Street Address: 550 S Caldwell St
City: Charlotte
State: NC
ZIP Code: 28202-2881
General Phone: (704) 973-1100
Publication Website: charlottebusinessjournal.com
Parent Company: American City Business Journals
Publisher Name: T.J. McCullough
Publisher Phone: (704) 973-1100
Editor Email: T.J. McCullough
Editor Phone: tmccullough@bizjournals.com
Advertising Executive Name: 704-973-1135
Advertising Executive Email: Robert Morris
Advertising Executive Phone: rmorris@bizjournals.com
Delivery Methods: Mail
Published Days: Fri
Audit Company: Sworn/Estimate/Non-Audited

CHARLOTTE

NORTH CAROLINA LAWYERS WEEKLY

Street Address: 130 N. McDowell St.
City: Charlotte
State: NC
ZIP Code: 28204
General Phone: (800) 876-5297
General Email: andrea.mounts@nclawyersweekly.com
Publication Website: nclawyersweekly.com
Parent Company: Gannett
Publisher Name: Grady Johnson
Publisher Email: gjohnson@scbiznews.com
Publisher Phone: (800) 876-5297
Editor Name: David Donovan
Editor Email: david.donovan@nclawyersweekly.com
Editor Phone: gjohnson@scbiznews.com
Advertising Executive Email: Andrea Mounts
Advertising Executive Phone: andrea.mounts@nclawyersweekly.com
Delivery Methods: Mail
Year Established: 1987
Published Days: Mon

Audit Company: Sworn/Estimate/Non-Audited

CHARLOTTE

THE CHARLOTTE POST

Street Address: 1531 Camden Rd
City: Charlotte
State: NC
ZIP Code: 28203-4753
General Phone: (704) 376-0496
General Email: advertising@thecharlottepost.com
Publication Website: thecharlottepost.com
Publisher Name: Gerald Johnson
Publisher Email: publisher@thecharlottepost.com
Publisher Phone: (704) 376-0496
Editor Name: Herbert White
Editor Email: Herb.White@thecharlottepost.com
Advertising Executive Name: Linda Johnson
Advertising Executive Email: linda.lanel@thecharlottepost.com
Advertising Executive Phone: herb.white@thecharlottepost.com
Delivery Methods: Mail`Newsstand`Racks
Year Established: 1974
Published Days: Thur
Avg. Paid Circ.: 10695
Avg. Free Circ.: 6083
Audit Company: Sworn/Estimate/Non-Audited

CHARLOTTE

THE MATTHEWS-MINT HILL

Street Address: 9506 Monroe Rd
City: Charlotte
State: NC
ZIP Code: 28270-1527
General Phone: (704) 849-2261
General Email: adsales@carolinaweeklynewspapers.com
Publication Website: matthewsminthillweekly.com
Parent Company: McElvy Media Group LLC
Publisher Name: Adrian Garson
Publisher Email: 28270-1527
Publisher Phone: (704) 849-2261
Editor Name: adsales@carolinaweeklynewspapers.com
Editor Email: Adrian Garson
Editor Phone: adrian@cmgweekly.com
Advertising Executive Email: Justin Vick
Advertising Executive Phone: justin@cmgweekly.com
Delivery Methods: Mail`Newsstand`Carrier`Racks
Year Established: 2007
Mechanical specifications: Type page: 9.875 x 12.5; 4 col
Published Days: Fri
Avg. Paid Circ.: 1
Avg. Free Circ.: 12976
Audit Company: VAC

CHARLOTTE

THE MECKLENBURG TIMES

Street Address: 130 N McDowell St
City: Charlotte
State: NC
ZIP Code: 28204-2268
General Phone: (704) 247-2900
General Email: andrea.mounts@nclawyersweekly.com
Publication Website: mecktimes.com
Parent Company: BridgeTower Media
Publisher Name: Grady Johnson
Publisher Email: 28204-2268
Publisher Phone: (704) 247-2900
Editor Name: andrea.mounts@nclawyersweekly.com
Editor Email: Grady Johnson

Editor Phone: gjohnson@scbiznews.com
Advertising Executive Email: Scott Baughman
Advertising Executive Phone: scott.baughman@mecktimes.com
Delivery Methods: Mail`Racks
Year Established: 1923
Own Printing Facility?: Y
Published Days: Tues`Fri
Avg. Paid Circ.: 965
Avg. Free Circ.: 45
Audit Company: Sworn/Estimate/Non-Audited

CHARLOTTE

THE UNION COUNTY WEEKLY

Street Address: 9506 Monroe Rd
City: Charlotte
State: NC
ZIP Code: 28270-1527
General Phone: (704) 849-2261
General Email: adrian@cmgweekly.com
Publication Website: unioncountyweekly.com
Parent Company: McElvy Media Group LLC
Publisher Name: Adrian Garson
Publisher Email: 28270-1527
Publisher Phone: (704) 849-2261
Editor Name: adrian@cmgweekly.com
Editor Email: Adrian Garson
Editor Phone: adrian@cmgweekly.com
Advertising Executive Name: Justin Vick
Advertising Executive Email: justin@cmgweekly.com
Advertising Executive Phone: justin@cmgweekly.com
Delivery Methods: Mail`Newsstand`Carrier`Racks
Year Established: 2005
Mechanical specifications: Type page: 9.875 x 12.5; 4 col
Published Days: Fri
Avg. Free Circ.: 18417
Audit Company: CVC

CHERRYVILLE

THE CHERRYVILLE EAGLE

Street Address: 107 E Main St
City: Cherryville
State: NC
ZIP Code: 28021-3406
General Phone: (704) 435-6752
General Email: michael.cherryvilleeagle@gmail.com
Publication Website: cherryvilleeagle.com
Parent Company: Community First Media
Publisher Name: Greg Ledford
Publisher Email: 28021-3406
Publisher Phone: (704) 435-6752
Editor Name: Michael Powell
Editor Email: michael.cherryvilleeagle@gmail.com
Advertising Executive Email: Mark Blanton
Advertising Executive Phone: mark@cfmedia.info
Delivery Methods: Mail`Carrier`Racks
Year Established: 1906
Own Printing Facility?: N
Commercial printers?: N
Mechanical specifications: Type page 13 x 21 1/2; E - 6 cols, 2, 3/16 between; A - 6 cols, 2, 3/16 between; C - 6 cols, 2, 3/16 between.
Published Days: Wed
Avg. Paid Circ.: 2750
Audit Company: Sworn/Estimate/Non-Audited

CLEMMONS

THE CLEMMONS COURIER

Street Address: 3600 Clemmons Rd
City: Clemmons

State: NC
ZIP Code: 27012-9104
General Phone: (336) 766-4126
General Email: courier9@bellsouth.net
Publication Website: clemmonscourier.com
Parent Company: Boone Newspapers, Inc.
Publisher Email: 27012-9104
Publisher Phone: (336) 766-4126
Editor Name: courier9@bellsouth.net
Own Printing Facility?: Y
Mechanical specifications: Type page 13 x 21; A - 6 cols, between; C - 6 cols, between.
Published Days: Thur
Avg. Paid Circ.: 2700
Avg. Free Circ.: 50
Audit Company: Sworn/Estimate/Non-Audited

CONCORD

INDEPENDENT TRIBUNE

Street Address: 363 Church St N STE 140
City: Concord
State: NC
ZIP Code: 28025-4589
General Phone: (704) 782-3155
General Email: bbarker@independenttribune.com
Publication Website: independenttribune.com
Parent Company: Lee Enterprises
Publisher Name: Eric Millsaps
Publisher Email: emillsaps@statesville.com
Publisher Phone: (704) 782-3155
Editor Name: Mark Plemmons
Editor Email: mplemmons@independenttribune.com
Advertising Executive Name: Bruce Barker
Advertising Executive Email: bbarker@independenttribune.com
Advertising Executive Phone: bbarker@independenttribune.com
Delivery Methods: Mail`Newsstand`Carrier`Racks
Year Established: 1996
Mechanical specifications: Type page 13 x 21 1/2; E - 6 cols, 2 1/16, 1/8 between; A - 6 cols, 2 1/16, 1/8 between; C - 9 cols, 1 3/8, 1/16 between.
Published Days: Wed`Fri`Sun
Avg. Paid Circ.: 6208
Avg. Free Circ.: 99
Audit Company: AAM
Pressroom Equipment: Lines -- 4-G/Urbanite.;
Mailroom Equipment: Counter Stackers -- 1/BG; Inserters & Stuffers -- MM; Tying Machines -- 1-/Bu; Address Machine -- Vista Data.;
Business Equipment: Convergent
Business Software: Vision Data
Classified Equipment: Hardware -- APP/Mac; Printers -- APP/Mac LaserPrinter;
Classified Software: Fox.
Editorial Equipment: Hardware -- APP/Mac, Ethernet; Printers -- APP/Mac LaserPrinter
Editorial Software: QPS/QuarkXPress, Baseview.
Production Equipment: Hardware -- 2-COM/8400S; Cameras -- C/Spartan III, AG/Repromaster 2100.

CREEDMOOR

THE BUTNER-CREEDMOOR NEWS

Street Address: 418 N Main St
City: Creedmoor
State: NC
ZIP Code: 27522-8809
General Phone: (919) 528-2393
General Email: advertising@buttercreedmoornews.com
Publication Website: butnercreedmoornews.com
Publisher Name: Keven Zepezauer
Publisher Email: 27522-8809
Publisher Phone: (919) 528-2393

Editor Name: advertising@buttercreedmoornews.com
Editor Email: Keven Zepezauer
Editor Phone: kzepezauer@wilsontimes.com
Advertising Executive Name: Logan Martinez
Advertising Executive Email: lmartinez@wakeweekly.com
Advertising Executive Phone: lmartinez@wakeweekly.com
Mechanical specifications: Type page 11 1/2 x 21 1/2; E - 6 cols, 1 3/4, 1/6 between; A - 6 cols, 1 3/4, 1/6 between; C - 6 cols, 1 3/4, 1/6 between.
Published Days: Thur
Avg. Paid Circ.: 5400
Audit Company: Sworn/Estimate/Non-Audited

DURHAM

INDY WEEK

Street Address: 201 W Main St
City: Durham
State: NC
ZIP Code: 27701-3228
General Phone: (919) 286-1972
General Email: eroberts@indyweek.com
Publication Website: indyweek.com
Publisher Name: Susan Harper
Publisher Email: sharper@indyweek.com
Publisher Phone: (919) 286-1972
Editor Name: Jeffrey Billman
Editor Email: jbillman@indyweek.com
Editor Phone: sharper@indyweek.com
Advertising Executive Name: John Hurld
Advertising Executive Email: jhurld@indyweek.com
Advertising Executive Phone: jhurld@indyweek.com
Published Days: Wed
Avg. Free Circ.: 45000
Audit Company: Sworn/Estimate/Non-Audited

ELIZABETHTOWN

BLADEN JOURNAL

Street Address: 138 W BROAD ST
City: Elizabethtown
State: NC
ZIP Code: 28337
General Phone: (910) 862-4163
General Email: ads@bladenjournal.com
Publication Website: bladenjournal.com
Parent Company: Champion Media
Publisher Name: Denise Ward
Publisher Email: dward@robesonian.com
Publisher Phone: (910) 862-4163
Editor Name: Alan Wooten
Editor Email: awooten@bladenjournal.com
Advertising Executive Name: Alan Wooten
Advertising Executive Email: awooten@bladenjournal.com
Delivery Methods: Mail`Carrier
Year Established: 1978
Commercial printers?: Y
Mechanical specifications: Type page 11 5/8 x 21 1/2; E - 6 cols, 1 4/5, 1/8 between; A - 6 cols, 1 4/5, 1/8 between; C - 9 cols, 1 5/16, 1/11 between.
Published Days: Tues`Fri
Avg. Paid Circ.: 4400
Avg. Free Circ.: 3800
Audit Company: Sworn/Estimate/Non-Audited

ELKIN

THE TRIBUNE

Street Address: 214 E Main St
City: Elkin
State: NC
ZIP Code: 28621-3431
General Phone: (336) 835-1513

General Email: hlamm@elkintribune.com
Publication Website: elkintribune.com
Parent Company: AIM Media
Publisher Name: Holly Lamm
Publisher Email: hlamm@elkintribune.com
Publisher Phone: (336) 835-1513
Editor Name: Wendy Byerly Wood
Editor Email: wbyerly-wood@elkintribune.com
Advertising Executive Name: Scott Belcher
Advertising Executive Email: sbelcher@elkintribune.com
Advertising Executive Phone: sbelcher@elkintribune.com
Delivery Methods: Carrier`Racks
Year Established: 1911
Own Printing Facility?: Y
Commercial printers?: Y
Published Days: Mon`Wed`Fri
Avg. Paid Circ.: 6000
Audit Company: Sworn/Estimate/Non-Audited

FAYETTEVILLE

UP & COMING WEEKLY

Street Address: 208 Rowan St
City: Fayetteville
State: NC
ZIP Code: 28301-4922
General Phone: (910) 484-6200
General Email: bbowman@upandcomingweekly.com
Publication Website: upandcomingweekly.com
Publisher Name: Bill Bowman
Publisher Email: bbowman@upandcomingweekly.com
Publisher Phone: (910) 484-6200
Editor Name: Stephanie Crider
Editor Email: editor@upandcomingweekly.com
Advertising Executive Name: Bill Bowman
Advertising Executive Email: bbowman@upandcomingweekly.com
Advertising Executive Phone: bbowman@upandcomingweekly.com
Year Established: 1996
Mechanical specifications: Type page 9 3/4 x 12; E - 6 cols, 2 1/4, 2/3 between; A - 4 cols, 2 1/4, 2/3 between; C - 6 cols, 1 1/2, 2/3 between.
Published Days: Wed
Avg. Free Circ.: 8648
Audit Company: CVC

FOREST CITY

RUTHERFORD WEEKLY

Street Address: 369 Butler Rd
City: Forest City
State: NC
ZIP Code: 28043-6106
General Phone: (828) 248-1408
General Email: mike@rutherfordweekly.com
Publication Website: rutherfordweekly.com
Parent Company: CNHI, LLC
Publisher Phone: (828) 248-1408
Editor Name: mike@rutherfordweekly.com
Delivery Methods: Racks
Year Established: 1991
Mechanical specifications: 6 columns 10.333 wide by 15 inches tall
Published Days: Thur
Published Other: online edition
Avg. Free Circ.: 15807
Audit Company: Sworn/Estimate/Non-Audited
Note: Buy our print added online no extra cost.

FRANKLIN

THE FRANKLIN PRESS

Street Address: 40 Depot St

City: Franklin
State: NC
ZIP Code: 28734-2704
General Phone: (828) 524-2010
General Email: addirector@thefranklinpress.com
Publication Website: thefranklinpress.com
Parent Company: Community Newspapers Inc.
Publisher Name: Rachel Hoskins
Publisher Email: rhoskins@thefranklinpress.com
Publisher Phone: (828) 524-2010
Editor Name: Lee Buchanen
Editor Email: editor@thefranklinpress.com
Advertising Executive Email: Rachel Hoskins
Advertising Executive Phone: rhoskins@thefranklinpress.com
Delivery Methods: Mail
Year Established: 1886
Own Printing Facility?: Y
Commercial printers?: Y
Mechanical specifications: Type page 13 1/2 x 21 1/2; E - 6 cols, 2, 1/6 between; A - 6 cols, 2, 1/6 between; C - 9 cols, 1 1/3, 1/8 between.
Published Days: Wed`Fri
Avg. Paid Circ.: 8524
Avg. Free Circ.: 21
Audit Company: Sworn/Estimate/Non-Audited

GRAHAM

THE ALAMANCE NEWS

Street Address: 114 W Elm St
City: Graham
State: NC
ZIP Code: 27253-2802
General Phone: (336) 228-7851
General Email: alamanacenews@mail.com
Publication Website: alamancenews.us
Publisher Name: Thomas Boney Jr.
Publisher Email: alamancenews@mail.com
Publisher Phone: (336) 228-7851
Editor Name: Thomas Boney Jr
Editor Email: alamancenews@mail.com
Advertising Executive Name: Joann Boone
Delivery Methods: Mail`Newsstand`Racks
Own Printing Facility?: Y
Mechanical specifications: Type page 11.6 x 21; E - 6 cols, 1.8;
Published Days: Thur
Avg. Paid Circ.: 4000
Audit Company: Sworn/Estimate/Non-Audited

GREENSBORO

THE BUSINESS JOURNAL

Street Address: 101 South Elm Street
City: Greensboro
State: NC
ZIP Code: 27401
General Phone: (336) 271-6539
General Email: amellott@bizjournals.com
Publication Website: bizjournals.com/triad
Parent Company: American City Business Journals
Publisher Name: Jason Christie
Publisher Email: jchristie@bizjournals.com
Publisher Phone: (336) 271-6539
Editor Name: Sougata Mukherjee
Editor Email: smukherjee@bizjournals.com
Advertising Executive Name: Courtney Bode
Delivery Methods: Mail`Newsstand`Racks
Year Established: 1998
Published Days: Fri
Audit Company: Sworn/Estimate/Non-Audited

GREENSBORO

YES! WEEKLY

Street Address: 5500 Adams Farm Ln

City: Greensboro
State: NC
ZIP Code: 27407-7059
General Phone: (336) 316-1231
General Email: publisher@yesweekly.com
Publication Website: yesweekly.com
Parent Company: Womack Publishing Co.
Publisher Name: CHARLES WOMACK
Publisher Email: Publisher@yesweekly.com
Publisher Phone: (336) 316-1231
Editor Name: Katie Murawski
Editor Email: katie@yesweekly.com
Advertising Executive Name: Charles Womack
Advertising Executive Email: publisher@yesweekly.com
Delivery Methods: Charles Womack
Year Established: 2005
Own Printing Facility?: Publisher@yesweekly.com
Commercial printers?: 336-316-1231
Mechanical specifications: 9.9 x 10.2
Published Days: Wed
Avg. Free Circ.: 20000
Audit Company: Sworn/Estimate/Non-Audited

HAVELOCK

THE HAVELOCK NEWS

Street Address: 230 Stonebridge Sq
City: Havelock
State: NC
ZIP Code: 28532-9505
General Phone: (252) 444-1999
General Email: taylor.shannon@havenews.com
Publication Website: havenews.com
Parent Company: Gannett
Publisher Email: 28532-9505
Publisher Phone: (252) 444-1999
Editor Name: Chris Segal
Editor Email: Chris.Segal@newbernsj.com
Advertising Executive Name: Taylor Shannon
Advertising Executive Email: taylor.shannon@havenews.com
Delivery Methods: Mail`Newsstand
Year Established: 1986
Own Printing Facility?: Y
Mechanical specifications: Type page 13 x 21 1/2.
Published Days: Thur
Avg. Paid Circ.: 1200
Avg. Free Circ.: 21
Audit Company: Sworn/Estimate/Non-Audited

HAYESVILLE

CLAY COUNTY PROGRESS

Street Address: 43 Main St
City: Hayesville
State: NC
ZIP Code: 28904-5808
General Phone: (828) 389-8431
General Email: ads@claycountyprogress.com
Publication Website: claycountyprogress.com
Parent Company: Community Newspapers Inc.
Publisher Name: Becky Long
Publisher Email: publisher@claycountyprogress.com
Publisher Phone: (828) 389-8431
Editor Name: Becky Long
Editor Email: publisher@claycountyprogress.com
Advertising Executive Name: 828-389-8431
Advertising Executive Email: Gary Corsair
Advertising Executive Phone: ads@claycountyprogress.com
Delivery Methods: Mail`Newsstand`Carrier
Year Established: 1980
Mechanical specifications: Type page 13 x 21; E - 6 cols, 2, between; A - 6 cols, 2, between; C - 6 cols, 2, between.

Published Days: Thur
Avg. Paid Circ.: 4400
Audit Company: Sworn/Estimate/Non-Audited

HIGH POINT

THOMASVILLE TIMES

Street Address: 213 Woodbine St
City: High Point
State: NC
ZIP Code: 27260-8339
General Phone: (336) 888-3590
General Email: aduncan@hpenews.com
Publication Website: tvilletimes.com
Parent Company: Paxton Media Group, LLC
Publisher Name: Nancy Baker
Publisher Email: 27260-8339
Publisher Phone: (336) 888-3590
Editor Name: aduncan@hpenews.com
Editor Email: Nancy Baker
Editor Phone: nbaker@hpenews.com
Advertising Executive Name: 336-888-3655
Advertising Executive Email: Megan Ward
Advertising Executive Phone: mward@hpenews.com
Delivery Methods: Mail`Newsstand`Racks
Year Established: 1890
Own Printing Facility?: Y
Commercial printers?: Y
Mechanical specifications: Type page 13 x 21; E - 6 cols, 2, 1/6 between; A - 6 cols, 2, 1/6 between; C - 9 cols, 1 1/3, 1/6 between.
Published Days: Wed`Sat
Avg. Paid Circ.: 5500
Avg. Free Circ.: 334
Audit Company: Sworn/Estimate/Non-Audited

HIGHLANDS

THE HIGHLANDER

Street Address: 34 N Fifth St
City: Highlands
State: NC
ZIP Code: 28741
General Phone: (828) 526-4114
General Email: ads@highlandsnews.com
Publication Website: highlandsnews.com
Parent Company: Community Newspapers Inc.
Publisher Name: Brad Spaulding
Publisher Email: publisher@highlandnews.com
Publisher Phone: (828) 526-4114
Editor Name: Brad Spaulding
Editor Email: editor@highlandnews.com
Advertising Executive Name: Josh Smith
Advertising Executive Email: ads@highlandnews.com
Delivery Methods: Mail
Year Established: 1958
Published Days: Thur
Avg. Paid Circ.: 3500
Avg. Free Circ.: 60
Audit Company: Sworn/Estimate/Non-Audited

HILLSBOROUGH

THE NEWS OF ORANGE COUNTY

Street Address: 109 E King St
City: Hillsborough
State: NC
ZIP Code: 27278-2570
General Phone: (919) 732-2171
General Email: k.coleman@newsoforange.com
Publication Website: newsoforange.com
Parent Company: Womack Publishing Co.
Publisher Email: 27278-2570
Publisher Phone: (919) 732-2171
Editor Name: Adam Powell
Editor Email: mebaneenterpriseeditor@yahoo.com

Advertising Executive Email: Dale Edwards
Advertising Executive Phone: newsofrangeeditor@yahoo.com
Year Established: 1893
Own Printing Facility?: Y
Commercial printers?: Y
Mechanical specifications: Type page 13 x 21 1/2; E - 6 cols, 1 5/6, 1/8 between; A - 6 cols, 1 5/6, 1/8 between; C - 6 cols, 1 5/6, 1/8 between.
Published Days: Wed
Avg. Paid Circ.: 4200
Audit Company: Sworn/Estimate/Non-Audited

JAMESTOWN

JAMESTOWN NEWS

Street Address: 206 E Main St
City: Jamestown
State: NC
ZIP Code: 27282-8005
General Phone: (336) 841-4933
General Email: publisher@yesweeekly.com
Publication Website: jamestownnews.com
Parent Company: Womack Publishing Co.
Publisher Name: Charles Womack
Publisher Phone: (336) 841-4933
Editor Name: publisher@yesweeekly.com
Editor Email: Charles Womack
Editor Phone: publisher@yesweekly.com
Delivery Methods: Norma B. Dennis
Year Established: 1978
Commercial printers?: Y
Published Days: Wed
Avg. Paid Circ.: 4000
Avg. Free Circ.: 10
Audit Company: Sworn/Estimate/Non-Audited

KENLY

JOHNSTONIAN NEWS

Street Address: 201 W 2ND ST
City: Kenly
State: NC
ZIP Code: 27542
General Phone: (919) 284-2295
General Email: debra@kenlynews.com
Publication Website: http://johnstoniannews.com
Parent Company: Restoration News Media
Publisher Name: Keven Zepezauer
Publisher Email: kzepezauer@restorationnewsmedia.com
Publisher Phone: (919) 284-2295
Editor Name: Scott Boljack
Editor Email: sbolejack@johnstoniannews.com
Advertising Executive Name: Shana Hoover
Advertising Executive Email: shana@wilsontimes.com
Advertising Executive Phone: shana@wilsontimes.com

KERNERSVILLE

KERNERSVILLE NEWS

Street Address: 300 E Mountain St
City: Kernersville
State: NC
ZIP Code: 27284-2943
General Phone: (336) 993-2161
General Email: ad_director@kernersvillenews.com
Publication Website: kernersvillenews.com
Publisher Name: John Owensby
Publisher Email: publisher@kernersvillenews.com
Publisher Phone: (336) 993-2161
Editor Name: John Owensby
Editor Email: editor@kernersvillenews.com
Editor Phone: publisher@kernersvillenews.com
Advertising Executive Name: Wendy Davis

Advertising Executive Email: wendy@kernersvillenews.com
Delivery Methods: Mail`Newsstand`Carrier`Racks
Year Established: 1938
Own Printing Facility?: Y
Commercial printers?: Y
Published Days: Tues`Thur`Sat
Avg. Paid Circ.: 6000
Avg. Free Circ.: 17850
Audit Company: Sworn/Estimate/Non-Audited

KING

THE STOKES NEWS

Street Address: 122 S Main St
City: King
State: NC
ZIP Code: 27021-9011
General Phone: (336) 591-8191
General Email: sstanley@civitasmedia.com
Publication Website: thestokesnews.com
Parent Company: Adams Publishing Group
Publisher Name: Sandra Hurley
Publisher Email: shurley@mtairynews.com
Publisher Phone: (336) 591-8191
Editor Name: Neill Caldwell
Editor Email: neill.caldwell@thestokesnews.com
Advertising Executive Name: Bob Ward
Advertising Executive Email: bward@mtairynews.com
Delivery Methods: Mail`Racks
Year Established: 1872
Own Printing Facility?: Y
Commercial printers?: Y
Mechanical specifications: Type page 11 9/16 x 21 1/2; E - 6 cols, 1 3/4, between; A - 6 cols, 1 3/4, between; C - 9 cols, 1 3/4, between.
Published Days: Thur
Avg. Paid Circ.: 8400
Avg. Free Circ.: 21
Audit Company: Sworn/Estimate/Non-Audited

LINCOLNTON

LINCOLN TIMES-NEWS

Street Address: 119 W Water St
City: Lincolnton
State: NC
ZIP Code: 28092-2623
General Phone: (704) 735-3031
General Email: advertising@lincolntimesnews.com
Publication Website: lincolntimesnews.com
Parent Company: Western Publishing Co
Publisher Name: Jerry Leedy
Publisher Email: jerryleedy@lincolntimesnews.com
Publisher Phone: (704) 735-3031
Editor Name: Michael Gebelein
Editor Email: editor@lincolntimesnews.com
Advertising Executive Email: advertising@lincolntimesnews.com
Advertising Executive Phone: advertising@lincolntimesnews.com
Delivery Methods: Mail`Newsstand`Carrier`Racks
Year Established: 1873
Own Printing Facility?: Y
Mechanical specifications: Type page 13 x 21 1/2; E - 6 cols, 2 1/16, 1/8 between; A - 6 cols, 2 1/16, 1/8 between; C - 9 cols, 1 5/12, 1/8 between.
Published Days: Mon`Wed`Fri
Avg. Paid Circ.: 10500
Audit Company: Sworn/Estimate/Non-Audited

LITTLETON

LAKE GASTON GAZETTE-OBSERVER

Community Newspapers in the U.S.

Street Address: 378 Lizard Creek Rd
City: Littleton
State: NC
ZIP Code: 27850-8390
General Phone: (252) 586-2700
General Email: ads@lakegastongazette-observer.com
Publication Website: lakegastongazette-observer.com
Parent Company: Womack Publishing Co.
Publisher Phone: (252) 586-2700
Editor Name: Della Rose
Editor Email: news@lakegastongazette-observer.com
Advertising Executive Name: Heather Abbott
Advertising Executive Email: ads@lakegastongazette-observer.com
Advertising Executive Phone: ads@lakegastongazette-observer.com
Delivery Methods: Heather Abbott
Year Established: 1955
Own Printing Facility?: ads@lakegastongazette-observer.com
Published Days: Wed
Audit Company: Sworn/Estimate/Non-Audited

MARSHALL

NEWS-RECORD AND SENTINEL

Street Address: 58 Back St.
City: Marshall
State: NC
ZIP Code: 28753
General Phone: (828) 649-1075
General Email: karen@newsrecordandsentinel.com
Publication Website: www.citizen-times.com/local/news-record-and-sentinel
Publisher Phone: (828) 649-1075
Editor Name: karen@newsrecordandsentinel.com
Advertising Executive Name: Lucas Calloway
Advertising Executive Email: tcalloway1@gannett.com
Delivery Methods: Mail`Racks
Year Established: 1901
Own Printing Facility?: Y
Published Days: Wed
Avg. Paid Circ.: 6500
Avg. Free Circ.: 50
Audit Company: Sworn/Estimate/Non-Audited

MEBANE

THE MEBANE ENTERPRISE

Street Address: 106 N Fourth St
City: Mebane
State: NC
ZIP Code: 27302-2428
General Phone: (919) 563-3555
General Email: j.brown@mebaneenterprise.com
Publication Website: mebaneenterprise.com
Parent Company: Womack Publishing Co.
Publisher Name: Chad Harrisom
Publisher Email: chadjourn@gmail.com
Publisher Phone: (919) 563-3555
Editor Name: Adam Powell
Editor Email: mebaneenterpriseeditor@yahoo.com
Advertising Executive Name: Charlie Pogacar
Advertising Executive Email: charliepogacar@gmail.com
Advertising Executive Phone: mebaneenterpriseeditor@yahoo.com
Delivery Methods: Connie Manion
Year Established: 1908
Own Printing Facility?: c.manion@mebaneenterprise.com
Mechanical specifications: 6 col x 21.5 " 1 col - 1.56 2 col - 3.25" 3 col - 4.93" 4 col - 6.63" 5 col - 8.31" 6 col - 10"
Published Days: Wed
Avg. Paid Circ.: 3100

Avg. Free Circ.: 81
Audit Company: Sworn/Estimate/Non-Audited

MOCKSVILLE

DAVIE COUNTY ENTERPRISE-RECORD

Street Address: 171 S Main St
City: Mocksville
State: NC
ZIP Code: 27028-2424
General Phone: (336) 751-2120
General Email: erads2@davie-enterprise.com
Publication Website: ourdavie.com
Parent Company: Boone Newspapers, Inc.
Publisher Name: Greg Anderson
Publisher Email: greg.anderson@salisburypost.com
Publisher Phone: (336) 751-2120
Editor Name: Mike Barnhardt
Editor Email: mike.barnhardt@davie-enterprise.com
Advertising Executive Name: Ray Tutterow
Advertising Executive Email: ray.tutterow@davie-enterprise.com
Delivery Methods: Mail`Racks
Year Established: 1899
Published Days: Thur
Avg. Paid Circ.: 8500
Avg. Free Circ.: 32
Audit Company: Sworn/Estimate/Non-Audited

MONROE

THE ENQUIRER-JOURNAL

Street Address: 1508 Skyway Dr
City: Monroe
State: NC
ZIP Code: 28110-3008
General Phone: (704) 289-1541
General Email: apurser@theej.com
Publication Website: enquirerjournal.com
Parent Company: Paxton Media Group, LLC
Publisher Name: Dale Morefield
Publisher Email: dmorefield@theej.com
Publisher Phone: (704) 289-1541
Editor Name: Jerry Snow
Editor Email: jerrysnow@theej.com
Advertising Executive Name: 704-261-2200
Advertising Executive Email: Dale Morefield
Advertising Executive Phone: dmorefield@theej.com
Delivery Methods: Mail`Newsstand`Carrier`Racks
Year Established: 1873
Own Printing Facility?: Y
Commercial printers?: N
Published Days: Wed`Fri`Sun
Weekday Frequency: m
Saturday Frequency: m
Avg. Paid Circ.: 5392
Avg. Free Circ.: 4000
Audit Company: Sworn/Estimate/Non-Audited
Classified Equipment: Printers -- ECR;
Editorial Equipment: Printers -- ECR

MOORESVILLE

MOORESVILLE TRIBUNE

Street Address: 147 E Center Ave
City: Mooresville
State: NC
ZIP Code: 28115-2513
General Phone: (704) 696-2950
General Email: advertising@mooresvilletribune.com
Publication Website: mooresvilletribune.com
Parent Company: Lee Enterprises
Publisher Phone: (704) 696-2950
Editor Name: Rea White
Editor Email: RWhite1@statesville.com
Advertising Executive Name: LeAnna Dunlap

Advertising Executive Email: ldunlap@mooresvilletribune.com
Delivery Methods: Mail`Newsstand`Carrier`Racks
Year Established: 1937
Published Days: Wed`Sun
Avg. Paid Circ.: 925
Avg. Free Circ.: 9500
Audit Company: AAM

MOREHEAD CITY

CARTERET COUNTY NEWS-TIMES

Street Address: 4206 Bridges St
City: Morehead City
State: NC
ZIP Code: 28557-2942
General Phone: (252) 726-7081
General Email: kim@thenewstimes.com
Publication Website: carolinacoastonline.com
Parent Company: Carteret Publishing Co.
Publisher Name: Lockwood Phillips
Publisher Email: lockwood@thenewstimes.com
Publisher Phone: (252) 726-7081
Editor Name: Richard Clark
Editor Email: richard@thenewstimes.com
Advertising Executive Name: Kim Moseley
Advertising Executive Email: kim@thenewstimes.com
Advertising Executive Phone: richard@thenewstimes.com
Delivery Methods: Mail`Newsstand`Carrier`Racks
Year Established: 1942
Own Printing Facility?: Y
Commercial printers?: N
Mechanical specifications: Type page 13 1/8 x 21 1/2; E - 6 cols, 2 1/16, 1/4 between; A - 6 cols, 2 1/16, 1/4 between; C - 8 cols, 1 1/2, 3/16 between.
Published Days: Wed`Fri`Sun
Avg. Paid Circ.: 10230
Audit Company: Sworn/Estimate/Non-Audited

MOUNT OLIVE

MOUNT OLIVE TRIBUNE

Street Address: 214 N Center St
City: Mount Olive
State: NC
ZIP Code: 28365-1702
General Phone: (919) 658-9456
General Email: ads@mountolivetribune.com
Publication Website: mountolivetribune.com
Publisher Name: Keven Zepezauer
Publisher Email: kzepezauer@restorationnewsmedia.com
Publisher Phone: (919) 658-9456
Editor Name: Emily Weaver
Editor Email: eweaver@mydailyrecord.com
Advertising Executive Name: Maria House
Advertising Executive Email: addirector@mydailyrecord.com
Delivery Methods: Mail`Newsstand`Carrier`Racks
Year Established: 1904
Own Printing Facility?: Y
Mechanical specifications: Type page 13 x 21 1/2; E - 6 cols, 2 1/16, between; A - 6 cols, 2 1/16, between; C - 6 cols, 2 1/16, between.
Published Days: Mon
Avg. Paid Circ.: 2000
Avg. Free Circ.: 49
Audit Company: Sworn/Estimate/Non-Audited

MURPHY

CHEROKEE SCOUT

Street Address: 89 Sycamore St
City: Murphy

State: NC
ZIP Code: 28906-2954
General Phone: (828) 837-5122
General Email: advertising@cherokeescout.com
Publication Website: cherokeescout.com
Parent Company: Community Newspapers Inc.
Publisher Name: David Brown
Publisher Email: dbrown@cherokeescout.com
Publisher Phone: (828) 837-5122
Editor Name: Charlene Kephart
Editor Email: news@cherokeescout.com
Advertising Executive Name: Debbie Dills
Advertising Executive Phone: ddills@cherokeescout.com
Delivery Methods: Mail`Newsstand`Racks
Year Established: 1889
Own Printing Facility?: Y
Commercial printers?: Y
Mechanical specifications: Type page 13 x 21 1/2; E - 6 cols, 2, 1/6 between; A - 6 cols, 2, 1/6 between; C - 6 cols, 2, 1/6 between.
Published Days: Wed
Avg. Paid Circ.: 8000
Avg. Free Circ.: 100
Audit Company: Sworn/Estimate/Non-Audited

NASHVILLE

THE NASHVILLE GRAPHIC

Street Address: 203 W Washington St
City: Nashville
State: NC
ZIP Code: 27856-1263
General Phone: (252) 459-7101
General Email: ads@nashvillegraphic.com
Publication Website: nashvillegraphic.com
Publisher Name: Jo Anne Cooper
Publisher Email: 27856-1263
Publisher Phone: (252) 459-7101
Editor Name: ads@nashvillegraphic.com
Editor Email: Jo Anne Cooper
Editor Phone: jcooper@nashvillegraphic.com
Advertising Executive Email: Amanda Clark
Advertising Executive Phone: news@nashvillegraphic.com
Delivery Methods: Mail`Newsstand`Racks
Year Established: 1895
Mechanical specifications: Type page 11 5/8 x 21 1/2; E - 6 cols, 2 1/16, 1/6 between; A - 6 cols, 2 1/16, 1/6 between.
Published Days: Thur
Avg. Paid Circ.: 3328
Avg. Free Circ.: 3800
Audit Company: Sworn/Estimate/Non-Audited

NEWLAND

THE AVERY JOURNAL-TIMES

Street Address: 335 Linville St
City: Newland
State: NC
ZIP Code: 28657-8037
General Phone: (828) 733-2448
General Email: cindy.zuerchertlaws@civitasmedia.com
Publication Website: averyjournal.com
Publisher Email: 28657-8037
Publisher Phone: (828) 733-2448
Editor Name: Jamie Shell
Editor Email: editor@averyjournal.com
Advertising Executive Name: Andy Gainey
Advertising Executive Email: andy.gainey@mountaintimes.com
Advertising Executive Phone: andy.gainey@mountaintimes.com
Delivery Methods: Mail`Newsstand`Racks
Year Established: 1959
Own Printing Facility?: Y
Mechanical specifications: Type page 13 x 21; E - 6 cols, 2, 1/6 between; A - 6 cols, 2, 1/6 between; C - 9 cols, 1 1/2, 1/12 between.

NORTH WILKESBORO

THE WILKES JOURNAL-PATRIOT

Street Address: 711 Main St
City: North Wilkesboro
State: NC
ZIP Code: 28659-4211
General Phone: (336) 838-4117
General Email: narchibald@journalpatriot.com
Publication Website: journalpatriot.com
Publisher Email: 28659-4211
Publisher Phone: (336) 838-4117
Editor Name: narchibald@journalpatriot.com
Advertising Executive Name: Jule Hubbard
Advertising Executive Email: wjpjule@wilkes.net
Advertising Executive Phone: wjpjule@wilkes.net
Delivery Methods: Mail`Newsstand`Carrier`Racks
Year Established: 1906
Own Printing Facility?: Y
Commercial printers?: Y
Mechanical specifications: Type page 13 x 21 1/2; A - 6 cols, 2 1/16, 1/8 between.
Published Days: Tues`Fri
Avg. Paid Circ.: 11000
Audit Company: Sworn/Estimate/Non-Audited

OXFORD

OXFORD PUBLIC LEDGER

Street Address: 200 W Spring St
City: Oxford
State: NC
ZIP Code: 27565-3247
General Phone: (919) 693-2646
General Email: oplronnieadvertising@earthlink.net
Publication Website: www.oxfordledger.com
Publisher Phone: (919) 693-2646
Editor Name: oplronnieadvertising@earthlink.net
Editor Email: Ronnie Critcher
Editor Phone: oplronnieadvertising@earthlink.net
Advertising Executive Email: Ronnie Critcher
Advertising Executive Phone: oplronnieadvertising@earthlink.net
Year Established: 1881
Own Printing Facility?: Y
Commercial printers?: Y
Published Days: Mon`Thur
Avg. Paid Circ.: 6500
Avg. Free Circ.: 60
Audit Company: Sworn/Estimate/Non-Audited

PILOT MOUNTAIN

THE PILOT

Street Address: 11 W. Main St.
City: Pilot Mountain
State: NC
ZIP Code: 27041
General Phone: (336) 415-4739
General Email: pilnews@civitasmedia.com
Publication Website: pilotmountainnews.com
Parent Company: Adams Publishing Group
Publisher Name: David Woronoff
Publisher Email: david@thepilot.com
Publisher Phone: (336) 415-4739
Editor Name: John Nagy
Editor Email: john@thepilot.com
Advertising Executive Name: Darlene Stark
Advertising Executive Email: darlene@thepilot.com
Published Days: Wed
Audit Company: Sworn/Estimate/Non-Audited

PLYMOUTH

THE ROANOKE BEACON

Street Address: 212 W Water St
City: Plymouth
State: NC
ZIP Code: 27962-1212
General Phone: (252) 793-2123
General Email: sales@roanokebeacon.com
Publication Website: roanokebeacon.com
Parent Company: Maypo Media, LLC
Publisher Name: Mary Wayt
Publisher Email: editor@roanokebeacon.com
Publisher Phone: (252) 793-2123
Editor Name: Mary Wyatt
Editor Email: editor@roanokebeacon.com
Advertising Executive Name: Mary Wyatt
Advertising Executive Email: sales@roanokebeacon.com
Delivery Methods: Mail`Newsstand`Racks
Year Established: 1889
Own Printing Facility?: N
Commercial printers?: N
Mechanical specifications: Type page 10.04 x 20 1/2; E - 6 cols, 1 4/5, 1/8 between; A - 6 cols, 1 4/5, 1/8 between; C - 6 cols, 1 4/5, 1/8 between.
Published Days: Wed
Avg. Paid Circ.: 2226
Avg. Free Circ.: 334
Audit Company: Sworn/Estimate/Non-Audited

RAEFORD

THE NEWS-JOURNAL

Street Address: 119 W Elwood Ave
City: Raeford
State: NC
ZIP Code: 28376-2801
General Phone: (910) 875-2121
General Email: ads@thenews-journal.com
Publication Website: thenews-journal.com
Parent Company: Dickson Press, Inc
Publisher Name: Ken MacDonald
Publisher Email: ken@thenews-journal.com
Publisher Phone: (910) 875-2121
Editor Phone: ken@thenews-journal.com
Delivery Methods: Mail`Newsstand`Racks
Year Established: 1905
Own Printing Facility?: Y
Commercial printers?: N
Mechanical specifications: Type page 13 x 21; E - 6 cols, 2 1/16, 1/6 between; A - 6 cols, 2 1/16, 1/6 between; C - 8 cols, 1 1/2, 1/6 between.
Published Days: Wed
Avg. Paid Circ.: 3100
Avg. Free Circ.: 10000
Audit Company: Sworn/Estimate/Non-Audited

RALEIGH

THE NEWS & OBSERVER

Street Address: 421 Fayetteville Street
City: Raleigh
State: NC
ZIP Code: 27601-1331
General Phone: (919) 829-4500
General Email: metroeds@newsobserver.com
Publication Website: newsobserver.com
Parent Company: McClatchy Company
Publisher Name: Jill Christensen
Publisher Email: jchristensen@mcclatchy.com
Publisher Phone: (919) 829-4500
Editor Name: Robyn Tomlin
Editor Email: rtomlin@newsobserver.com
Delivery Methods: Carrier
Year Established: 1925
Mechanical specifications: Type page 13 x 21 1/4; E - 6 cols, between; A - 6 cols, between; C - 10 cols, between.
Published Days: Wed`Sun
Avg. Paid Circ.: 7
Avg. Free Circ.: 24416
Audit Company: AAM

RALEIGH

TRIANGLE BUSINESS JOURNAL

Street Address: 3515 Glenwood Avenue
City: Raleigh
State: NC
ZIP Code: 27612
General Phone: (919) 878-0010
General Email: hrodgers@bizjournals.com
Publication Website: bizjournals.com/triangle
Parent Company: American City Business Journals Inc
Publisher Name: Jason Christie
Publisher Email: jchristie@bizjournals.com
Publisher Phone: (919) 878-0010
Editor Name: Sougata Mukherjee
Editor Email: smukherjee@bizjournals.com
Advertising Executive Name: Courtney Bode
Advertising Executive Email: cbode@bizjournals.com
Delivery Methods: Mail
Year Established: 1985
Published Days: Fri
Audit Company: Sworn/Estimate/Non-Audited

REIDSVILLE

ROCKINGHAM NOW

Street Address: 1921 Vance St
City: Reidsville
State: NC
ZIP Code: 27320-3254
General Phone: (800) 323-2951
Publication Website: rockinghamnow.com
Publisher Name: Alton Brown
Publisher Email: abrown@wsjournal.com
Publisher Phone: (800) 323-2951
Editor Name: Joe Dexter & Susan Spear
Editor Email: joe.dexter@RockinghamNow.com, sspear@RockinghamNow.com
Advertising Executive Name: Karl Miller
Advertising Executive Email: karl.miller@greensboro.com
Advertising Executive Phone: joe.dexter@RockinghamNow.com
Published Days: Wed`Sun
Audit Company: Sworn/Estimate/Non-Audited

REIDSVILLE

THE EDEN NEWS

Street Address: 1921 Vance St
City: Reidsville
State: NC
ZIP Code: 27320-3254
General Phone: (336) 349-4331
General Email: pdurham@reidsvillereview.com
Publication Website: rockinghamnow.com
Publisher Email: 27320-3254
Publisher Phone: (336) 349-4331
Editor Name: pdurham@reidsvillereview.com
Advertising Executive Email: Joe Dexter
Advertising Executive Phone: joe.dexter@RockinghamNow.com
Delivery Methods: Mail`Newsstand`Carrier`Racks
Published Days: Wed`Sun
Audit Company: Sworn/Estimate/Non-Audited

REIDSVILLE

THE MESSENGER

Street Address: 1921 Vance St
City: Reidsville
State: NC
ZIP Code: 27320-3254
General Phone: (336) 349-4331
General Email: karl.miller@greensboro.com
Publication Website: rockinghamnow.com
Parent Company: Paxton Media Group
Publisher Email: 27320-3254
Publisher Phone: (336) 349-4331
Editor Name: karl.miller@greensboro.com
Delivery Methods: Mail`Newsstand`Carrier`Racks
Year Established: 1915
Mechanical specifications: Type page 11 1/2 x 21 1/2; E - 6 cols, 1/8 between; A - 6 cols, 1/8 between; C - 9 cols, 1/8 between.
Published Days: Wed
Avg. Paid Circ.: 4475
Avg. Free Circ.: 75
Audit Company: Sworn/Estimate/Non-Audited

REIDSVILLE

THE REIDSVILLE REVIEW

Street Address: 1921 Vance St
City: Reidsville
State: NC
ZIP Code: 27320-3254
General Phone: (336) 349-4331
General Email: pdurham@reidsvillereview.com
Publication Website: news-record.com/rockingham_now
Publisher Email: 27320-3254
Publisher Phone: (336) 349-4331
Editor Name: pdurham@reidsvillereview.com
Delivery Methods: Mail`Newsstand`Carrier`Racks
Year Established: 1928
Mechanical specifications: Type page 13 x 21 1/2; E - 6 cols, 2 1/16, 1/8 between; A - 6 cols, 2 1/16, 1/8 between; C - 9 cols, 1 5/16, 1/8 between.
Published Days: Wed`Sun
Weekday Frequency: m
Avg. Paid Circ.: 5195
Audit Company: Sworn/Estimate/Non-Audited
Pressroom Equipment: Lines -- G/Community 1971; G/Community 1971; G/Community 1971; G/Community 1986; G/Community 1986.;
Business Equipment: IBM/Newzware, Smith Corona/PC 386SX HD
Business Software: IBM/Newzware
Classified Equipment: Hardware -- APP/Mac SE; Printers -- APP/Mac LaserWriter II;
Classified Software: Baseview/Class Manager.
Editorial Equipment: Hardware -- APP/Mac SE, APP/Mac IIcx/APP/Mac Scanner; Printers -- APP/Mac LaserWriter II
Editorial Software: QPS/QuarkXPress, Baseview/NewsEdit.
Production Equipment: Hardware -- APP/Mac IIcx; Cameras -- C/Marathon; Scanners -- APP/Mac.

ROBBINSVILLE

THE GRAHAM STAR

Street Address: 720 Tallulah Rd
City: Robbinsville
State: NC
ZIP Code: 28771-9461
General Phone: (828) 479-3383
General Email: ads@grahamstar.com
Publication Website: grahamstar.com
Parent Company: Community Newspapers Inc.
Publisher Name: Kevin Hensley

Community Newspapers in the U.S.

Publisher Email: editor@grahamstar.com
Publisher Phone: (828) 479-3383
Editor Name: Kevin Hensley
Editor Email: editor@grahamstar.com
Advertising Executive Name: Debbie Dills
Advertising Executive Email: ads@grahamstar.com
Year Established: 1955
Own Printing Facility?: Y
Published Days: Thur
Avg. Paid Circ.: 3500
Avg. Free Circ.: 24
Audit Company: Sworn/Estimate/Non-Audited

ROXBORO

THE COURIER-TIMES

Street Address: 109 Clayton Ave
City: Roxboro
State: NC
ZIP Code: 27573-4611
General Phone: (336) 599-0162
General Email: learussell@roxboro-courier.com
Publication Website: personcountylife.com
Publisher Name: Johnny Whitfield
Publisher Phone: (336) 599-0162
Editor Name: Johnny Whitfield
Advertising Executive Email: Lea Russell
Advertising Executive Phone: learussell@roxboro-courier.com
Year Established: 1881
Mechanical specifications: Type page 13 x 21 1/2; E - 6 cols, 2 1/16, 1/6 between; A - 6 cols, 2 1/16, 1/6 between; C - 8 cols, 1 1/2, 1/8 between.
Published Days: Wed`Sat
Avg. Paid Circ.: 8509
Avg. Free Circ.: 95
Audit Company: Sworn/Estimate/Non-Audited

SHALLOTTE

THE BRUNSWICK BEACON

Street Address: 208 Smith Ave
City: Shallotte
State: NC
ZIP Code: addirector@brunswickbeacon.com
General Phone: (910) 754-6890
Publication Website: brunswickbeacon.com
Parent Company: Landmark Community Newspapers
Publisher Name: Angie Sutton
Publisher Email: asutton@brunswickbeacon.com
Publisher Phone: (910) 754-6890
Editor Name: Angie Sutton
Editor Email: asutton@brunswickbeacon.com
Year Established: 1962
Own Printing Facility?: Y
Mechanical specifications: Type page 13 x 21; E - 6 cols, 2, 1/6 between; A - 6 cols, 2, 1/6 between; C - 6 cols, 2, 1/6 between.
Published Days: Thur
Avg. Paid Circ.: 17700
Avg. Free Circ.: 2
Audit Company: Sworn/Estimate/Non-Audited

SILER CITY

THE CHATHAM NEWS + RECORD

Street Address: 303 W Raleigh St
City: Siler City
State: NC
ZIP Code: 27344-3725
General Phone: (919) 663-3232
General Email: advertising@thechathamnews.com
Publication Website: thechathamnews.com
Parent Company: The Chatham News Publishing Co, Inc.
Publisher Name: Bill Horner III
Publisher Email: bhorner3@chathamnr.com
Publisher Phone: (919) 663-3232
Editor Name: Randall Rigsbee
Editor Email: rigsbee@chathamnr.com
Advertising Executive Email: Jason Justice
Advertising Executive Phone: jjustice@chathamnr.com

SOUTHPORT

THE STATE PORT PILOT

Street Address: 114 E Moore St
City: Southport
State: NC
ZIP Code: 28461-3926
General Phone: (910) 457-4568
General Email: carol@stateportpilot.com
Publication Website: stateportpilot.com
Parent Company: The State Port Pilot
Publisher Name: Morgan Harper
Publisher Email: mharper@stateportpilot.com
Publisher Phone: (910) 457-4568
Editor Name: Morgan Harper
Editor Email: pilot@stateportpilot.com
Advertising Executive Name: Carol Magnaniv
Advertising Executive Email: carol@stateportpilot.com
Delivery Methods: Mail`Newsstand`Racks
Year Established: 1928
Commercial printers?: Y
Mechanical specifications: Type page 11 1/2 x 21; E - 6 cols, 1 3/4, between; A - 6 cols, 1 3/4, between; C - 6 cols, 1 3/4, between.
Published Days: Wed
Avg. Paid Circ.: 7400
Audit Company: Sworn/Estimate/Non-Audited

SPARTA

THE ALLEGHANY NEWS

Street Address: 20 S Main St
City: Sparta
State: NC
ZIP Code: 28675-9643
General Phone: (336) 372-8999
General Email: ads@alleghanynews.com
Publication Website: alleghanynews.com
Publisher Name: Coby LaRue
Publisher Email: publisher@alleghanynews.com
Publisher Phone: (336) 372-8999
Editor Name: Bob Bamberg
Editor Email: news@alleghanynews.com
Editor Phone: publisher@alleghanynews.com
Advertising Executive Name: Coby LaRue
Advertising Executive Email: ads@alleghanynews.com
Advertising Executive Phone: ads@alleghanynews.com
Delivery Methods: Mail`Newsstand`Racks
Year Established: 1889
Own Printing Facility?: Y
Commercial printers?: N
Mechanical specifications: Type page 10.125"x 21.5"; E - 6 cols, A - 6 cols, 0.125 inches gutter
Published Days: Wed
Avg. Paid Circ.: 3800
Avg. Free Circ.: 50
Audit Company: Sworn/Estimate/Non-Audited

SPRING HOPE

THE ENTERPRISE

Street Address: 113 N Ash St
City: Spring Hope
State: NC
ZIP Code: 27882-7711
General Phone: (252) 478-3651
General Email: Springhopeads@embarqmail.com
Publication Website: springhopeenterprise.com
Parent Company: Gannett
Publisher Name: Keven Zepezauer
Publisher Email: kzepezauer@restorationnewsmedia.com
Publisher Phone: (252) 478-3651
Editor Name: Corey Friedman
Editor Email: cfriedman@restorationnewsmedia.com
Advertising Executive Name: 252-265-7812
Advertising Executive Email: Shana Hoover
Advertising Executive Phone: shana@wilsontimes.com
Delivery Methods: Mail`Racks
Year Established: 1947
Mechanical specifications: Type page 11 x 21 1/2; E - 6 cols, 2, 1/6 between; A - 6 cols, 2, 1/6 between.
Published Days: Thur
Avg. Paid Circ.: 2400
Avg. Free Circ.: 600
Audit Company: Sworn/Estimate/Non-Audited

SPRUCE PINE

MITCHELL NEWS-JOURNAL

Street Address: 261 Locust St
City: Spruce Pine
State: NC
ZIP Code: 28777-2713
General Phone: (828) 765-2071
General Email: adrep@mitchellnews.com
Publication Website: mitchellnews.com
Parent Company: Community Newspapers Inc.
Publisher Name: Brandon Roberts
Publisher Email: editor@mitchellnews.com
Publisher Phone: (828) 765-2071
Editor Name: adrep@mitchellnews.com
Editor Email: Brandon Roberts
Editor Phone: editor@mitchellnews.com
Advertising Executive Name: Kelli Beam
Advertising Executive Email: adrep@mitchellnews.com
Advertising Executive Phone: adrep@mitchellnews.com
Delivery Methods: Mail`Carrier
Year Established: 1927
Mechanical specifications: Type page 13 x 21 1/2; E - 6 cols, 2, 1/6 between; A - 6 cols, 2, 1/6 between; C - 6 cols, 2, 1/6 between.
Published Days: Wed
Avg. Paid Circ.: 4922
Avg. Free Circ.: 135
Audit Company: Sworn/Estimate/Non-Audited

SWANSBORO

TIDELAND NEWS

Street Address: 774 W Corbett Ave
City: Swansboro
State: NC
ZIP Code: 28584-8452
General Phone: (910) 326-5066
General Email: jennifer@tidelandnews.com
Publication Website: tidelandnews.com
Parent Company: Carteret Publishing Co.
Publisher Name: Lockwood Phillips
Publisher Email: lockwood@thenewstimes.com
Publisher Phone: (910) 326-5066
Editor Name: Richard Clark
Editor Email: richard@thenewstimes.com
Advertising Executive Name: Kim Moseley
Advertising Executive Email: kim@thenewstimes.com
Delivery Methods: Mail`Newsstand`Carrier`Racks
Year Established: 1979
Mechanical specifications: Type page 11 1/2 x 21 1/2; E - 6 cols, 1 3/4, 1/6 between; A - 6 cols, 1 3/4, 1/6 between; C - 8 cols, 1 1/2, 1/6 between.
Published Days: Wed
Avg. Paid Circ.: 3000
Avg. Free Circ.: 500
Audit Company: Sworn/Estimate/Non-Audited

SYLVA

THE SYLVA HERALD & RURALITE

Street Address: 539 W Main St
City: Sylva
State: NC
ZIP Code: 28779-5551
General Phone: (828) 586-2611
General Email: margo@thesylvaherald.com
Publication Website: thesylvaherald.com
Publisher Name: Steven B Gray
Publisher Email: sbg@thesylvaherald.com
Publisher Phone: (828) 586-2611
Editor Name: Jim Buchanan & Dave Russell
Editor Email: jim@thesylvaherald.com , dave@thesylvaherald.com
Advertising Executive Name: Margo Gray
Advertising Executive Email: margo@thesylvaherald.com
Delivery Methods: Mail`Newsstand
Year Established: 1926
Own Printing Facility?: Y
Commercial printers?: Y
Mechanical specifications: Type page 13 1/16 x 21 1/2; E - 6 cols, 2 1/16, 1/8 between; A - 6 cols, 2 1/16, 1/8 between; C - 6 cols, 2 1/16, 1/8 between.
Published Days: Thur
Avg. Paid Circ.: 7300
Avg. Free Circ.: 42
Audit Company: Sworn/Estimate/Non-Audited

TABOR CITY

TABOR-LORIS TRIBUNE

Street Address: PO Box 67
City: Tabor City
State: NC
ZIP Code: 28463-0067
General Phone: (910) 653-3153
General Email: tribpenny@tabor-loris.com
Publication Website: tabor-loris.com
Parent Company: Atlantic Corp.
Publisher Email: 28463-0067
Publisher Phone: (910) 653-3153
Editor Name: Duece Niven
Editor Email: tribdeuce@tabor-loris.com
Advertising Executive Email: Penny Holmes
Advertising Executive Phone: tribpenny@tabor-loris.com
Delivery Methods: Mail`Newsstand`Racks
Year Established: 1946
Own Printing Facility?: Y
Commercial printers?: Y
Mechanical specifications: Type page 13 x 21; E - 6 cols, 2, 1/6 between; A - 6 cols, 2, 1/6 between; C - 6 cols, 2, 1/6 between.
Published Days: Wed
Avg. Paid Circ.: 3000
Avg. Free Circ.: 200
Audit Company: Sworn/Estimate/Non-Audited
Note: First Pulitzer Prize winning weekly newspaper in the United States. Under founder W. Horace Carter, The Tabor City Tribune was awarded the Pulitzer Prize for Meritorious Public Service in 1953, with The News Reporter in neighboring Whiteville, for the crusade Carter waged to rein in the Ku Klux Klan.

TAYLORSVILLE

THE TAYLORSVILLE TIMES

Street Address: 24 E Main Ave
City: Taylorsville
State: NC
ZIP Code: 28681-2541

General Phone: (828) 632-2532
General Email: ads@taylorsvilletimes.com
Publication Website: taylorsvilletimes.com
Publisher Email: 28681-2541
Publisher Phone: (828) 632-2532
Editor Email: taylorsvilletimes@taylorsvilletimes.com
Advertising Executive Email: ads@taylorsvilletimes.com
Advertising Executive Phone: taylorsvilletimes@taylorsvilletimes.com
Delivery Methods: Mail`Newsstand`Racks
Year Established: 1886
Own Printing Facility?: Y
Mechanical specifications: Type page 10 x 21 1/2; E - 6 cols, 1/6 between; A - 6 cols, 1/6 between; C - 6 cols, 1/6 between.
Published Days: Wed
Avg. Paid Circ.: 5002
Avg. Free Circ.: 49
Audit Company: Sworn/Estimate/Non-Audited

TROY

MONTGOMERY HERALD

Street Address: 139 Bruton St
City: Troy
State: NC
ZIP Code: 27371-2815
General Phone: (910) 576-6051
General Email: advertise@montgomeryhrald.com
Publication Website: montgomeryherald.com
Parent Company: Womack Publishing Co.
Publisher Name: Tammy Dunn
Publisher Email: tdunn@montgomeryherald.com
Publisher Phone: (910) 576-6051
Editor Name: advertise@montgomeryhrald.com
Editor Email: Tammy Dunn
Editor Phone: tdunn@montgomeryherald.com
Advertising Executive Name: Tammy O'Brien
Advertising Executive Email: ads@montgomeryherald.com
Advertising Executive Phone: ads@montgomeryherald.com
Delivery Methods: Bailey Haywood
Year Established: 1880s
Own Printing Facility?: ads@montgomeryherald.com
Commercial printers?: N
Published Days: Wed
Avg. Paid Circ.: 4700
Avg. Free Circ.: 556
Audit Company: Sworn/Estimate/Non-Audited

WADESBORO

THE ANSON RECORD

Street Address: 123 E Martin St
City: Wadesboro
State: NC
ZIP Code: 28170-2276
General Phone: (704) 694-2161
General Email: dspencer@yourdailyjournal.com
Publication Website: ansonrecord.com
Parent Company: Champion Media
Publisher Name: Brian Bloom
Publisher Email: bbloom@yourdailyjournal.com
Publisher Phone: (704) 694-2161
Editor Name: Bob Leininger
Editor Email: rleininger@yourdailyjournal.com
Delivery Methods: Mail`Racks
Year Established: 1881
Commercial printers?: Y
Mechanical specifications: Type page 13 x 21 1/2; E - 6 cols, between; A - 6 cols, between; C - 6 cols, between.
Published Days: Wed
Avg. Paid Circ.: 5000
Avg. Free Circ.: 1000

Audit Company: Sworn/Estimate/Non-Audited

WAKE FOREST

THE WAKE WEEKLY

Street Address: 229 E Owen Ave
City: Wake Forest
State: NC
ZIP Code: 27587-2717
General Phone: (919) 556-3182
General Email: advertising@wakeweekly.com
Publication Website: wakeweekly.com
Publisher Name: Keven Zepezauer
Publisher Email: kzepezauer@wilsontimes.com
Publisher Phone: (919) 556-3182
Editor Name: Shawn Taylor
Editor Email: shawn@wakeweekly.com
Advertising Executive Name: April Phipps
Advertising Executive Email: april@wakeweekly.com
Advertising Executive Phone: april@wakeweekly.com
Delivery Methods: Mail`Newsstand`Racks
Year Established: 1947
Commercial printers?: Y
Published Days: Thur
Avg. Paid Circ.: 8900
Audit Company: Sworn/Estimate/Non-Audited
Note: Since 1947

WARRENTON

WARREN RECORD

Street Address: 112 N Main St
City: Warrenton
State: NC
ZIP Code: 27589-1922
General Phone: (252) 257-3341
General Email: ads@warrenrecord.com
Publication Website: warrenrecord.com
Parent Company: Womack Publishing Co.
Publisher Email: 27589-1922
Publisher Phone: (252) 257-3341
Editor Name: Jennifer Harris
Editor Email: editor@warrenrecord.com
Advertising Executive Name: Janie Miller
Advertising Executive Email: ads@warrenrecord.com
Advertising Executive Phone: ads@warrenrecord.com
Delivery Methods: Janie Miller
Year Established: 1896
Own Printing Facility?: ads@warrenrecord.com
Commercial printers?: Y
Mechanical specifications: Type page 13 x 21 1/2; E - 6 cols, 2, 1/6 between; A - 6 cols, 2, 1/6 between; C - 6 cols, 2, 1/6 between.
Published Days: Wed
Avg. Paid Circ.: 5600
Avg. Free Circ.: 113
Audit Company: Sworn/Estimate/Non-Audited

WAYNESVILLE

SMOKY MOUNTAIN NEWS

Street Address: PO BOX 629
City: Waynesville
State: NC
ZIP Code: 28786-0629
General Phone: (828) 452-4251
General Email: ads@smokymountainnews.com
Publication Website: smokymountainnews.com
Publisher Name: Scott McLeod
"Publisher Email: info@smokymountainnews.com
"
Publisher Phone: (828) 452-4251

Editor Name: Jessi Stone
Editor Email: jessi@smokymountainnews.com
Advertising Executive Name: 828.507.882
Advertising Executive Email: Greg Boothroyd
Advertising Executive Phone: greg@smokymountainnews.com
Delivery Methods: Racks
Published Days: Wed
Avg. Free Circ.: 16260
Audit Company: CVC

WAYNESVILLE

THE MOUNTAINEER

Street Address: 220 N Main St
City: Waynesville
State: NC
ZIP Code: 28786-3812
General Phone: (828) 452-0661
General Email: info@themountaineer.com
Publication Website: http://themountaineer.com
Publisher Name: Jonathan Key
Publisher Email: jkey@themountaineer.com
Publisher Phone: (828) 452-0661
Editor Name: Vicki Hyatt
Editor Email: news@themountaineer.com
Advertising Executive Name: 828.452.0661 ext. 110
Advertising Executive Email: Paula Lily
Advertising Executive Phone: plilly@themountaineer.com
Delivery Methods: Mail`Newsstand`Carrier`Racks
Published Days: Mon`Wed`Fri
Audit Company: Sworn/Estimate/Non-Audited

WEAVERVILLE

THE WEAVERVILLE TRIBUNE

Street Address: 113 N Main St
City: Weaverville
State: NC
ZIP Code: 28787-8444
General Phone: (828) 252-5804
General Email: starnesp@att.net
Publication Website: weavervilletribune.com
Publisher Name: Clint Parker
Publisher Email: editor@weavervilletribune.com
Publisher Phone: (828) 252-5804
Editor Name: Clint Parker
Editor Email: editor@weavervilletribune.com
Advertising Executive Name: Clint Parker
Advertising Executive Email: editor@weavervilletribune.com
Advertising Executive Phone: editor@weavervilletribune.com
Delivery Methods: Mail`Newsstand`Racks
Year Established: 2003
Published Days: Thur
Audit Company: Sworn/Estimate/Non-Audited

WEST JEFFERSON

ASHE POST & TIMES

Street Address: 203 S. 2nd Ave.
City: West Jefferson
State: NC
ZIP Code: 28694
General Phone: (336) 846-7164
General Email: tlaws@civitasmedia.com
Publication Website: https://www.ashepostandtimes.com
Parent Company: Adams Publishing Group
Publisher Phone: (336) 846-7164
Editor Name: Tom Mayer
Editor Email: tom.mayer@ashepostandtimes.com
Advertising Executive Name: Teresa Laws
Advertising Executive Email: teresa.laws@

ashepostandtimes.com

WEST JEFFERSON

THE ASHE MOUNTAIN TIMES

Street Address: 7 E Main St
City: West Jefferson
State: NC
ZIP Code: 28694
General Phone: (336) 246-6397
General Email: ron.brown@mountaintimes.com
Publication Website: ashepostandtimes.com
Publisher Email: 28694
Publisher Phone: (336) 246-6397
Editor Name: ron.brown@mountaintimes.com
Advertising Executive Name: Tom Mayer
Advertising Executive Email: tom.mayer@ashepostandtimes.com
Advertising Executive Phone: tom.mayer@ashepostandtimes.com
Published Days: Thur
Avg. Free Circ.: 9553
Audit Company: Sworn/Estimate/Non-Audited

WHITEVILLE

THE NEWS REPORTER

Street Address: 127 W Columbus St
City: Whiteville
State: NC
ZIP Code: 28472-4023
General Phone: (910) 642-4104
General Email: deanlewis@nrcolumbus.com
Publication Website: nrcolumbus.com
Publisher Email: 28472-4023
Publisher Phone: (910) 642-4104
Editor Name: deanlewis@nrcolumbus.com
Advertising Executive Email: Justin Smith
Delivery Methods: Mail`Newsstand`Carrier`Racks
Year Established: 1890
Own Printing Facility?: Y
Mechanical specifications: Type page 11 1/2 x 21; E - 6 cols, 1 13/16, 1/6 between; A - 6 cols, 1 13/16, 1/6 between; C - 6 cols, 1 13/16, 1/6 between.
Published Days: Mon`Thur
Avg. Paid Circ.: 10100
Avg. Free Circ.: 235
Audit Company: Sworn/Estimate/Non-Audited

WINSTON SALEM

THE CHRONICLE

Street Address: 1300 E. 5th St.
City: Winston Salem
State: NC
ZIP Code: 27101-2912
General Phone: (336) 722-8624
Publication Website: wschronicle.com
Parent Company: Gannett
Publisher Name: James Taylor, Jr.
Publisher Email: jtaylorjr@wschronicle.com
Publisher Phone: (336) 722-8624
Editor Name: Bridget Elam
Editor Email: news@wschronicle.com
Advertising Executive Name: 336-722-8624
Advertising Executive Email: Shayna Smith
Advertising Executive Phone: ssmith@wschronicle.com
Delivery Methods: Mail`Newsstand`Carrier`Racks
Year Established: 1974
Mechanical specifications: 9.889" X 21"
Published Days: Thur
Avg. Paid Circ.: 5000
Avg. Free Circ.: 2000
Audit Company: CVC

YADKINVILLE

Community Newspapers in the U.S.

THE YADKIN RIPPLE

Street Address: 115 S Jackson St
City: Yadkinville
State: NC
ZIP Code: 27055-7714
General Phone: (336) 679-2341
General Email: hlamm@civitasmedia.com
Publication Website: yadkinripple.com
Parent Company: Adams Publishing Group
Publisher Name: Sandra Hurley
Publisher Email: shurley@mtairynews.com
Publisher Phone: (336) 679-2341
Editor Name: Wendy Byerly Wood
Editor Email: wbyerly-wood@yadkinripple.com
Advertising Executive Name: Holly Lamm
Advertising Executive Email: hlamm@yadkinripple.com
Year Established: 1892
Commercial printers?: Y
Mechanical specifications: Type page 13 x 21 1/2; E - 6 cols, 2 1/20, between; A - 6 cols, 2 1/20, between; C - 6 cols, 2 1/20, between.
Published Days: Thur
Avg. Paid Circ.: 6000
Avg. Free Circ.: 40
Audit Company: Sworn/Estimate/Non-Audited

YANCEYVILLE

CASWELL MESSENGER

Street Address: 137 MAIN ST
City: Yanceyville
State: NC
ZIP Code: 27379
General Phone: (336) 694-4145
General Email: ads@caswellmessenger.com
Publication Website: caswellmessenger.com
Parent Company: Womack Publishing Co.
Publisher Phone: (336) 694-4145
Editor Name: Debra Ferrell
Editor Email: editor@caswellmessenger.com
Advertising Executive Email: advertising@caswellmessenger.com
Delivery Methods: Mail Newsstand Racks
Year Established: 1926
Own Printing Facility?: Y
Published Days: Wed
Avg. Paid Circ.: 4000
Avg. Free Circ.: 142
Audit Company: Sworn/Estimate/Non-Audited

NORTH DAKOTA

BOTTINEAU

BOTTINEAU COURANT

Street Address: 419 Main St
City: Bottineau
State: ND
ZIP Code: 58318-1229
General Phone: (701) 228-2605
General Email: courant@utma.com
Publication Website: https://www.bottineaunewspaper.com/
Advertising Executive Name: Lynn Evenson

BOWBELLS

BURKE COUNTY TRIBUNE

Street Address: 104 Railway St. SE
City: Bowbells
State: ND
ZIP Code: 58721
General Phone: (701) 377-2626
General Email: tribune@nccray.net
Publication Website: https://burkecountynd.com/
Parent Company: Kristi Bohl
Publisher Name: Kristi Bohl

BOWMAN

BOWMAN COUNTY PIONEER

Street Address: 18 S Main St.
City: Bowman
State: ND
ZIP Code: 58623
General Phone: (701) 523-5623
General Email: pioneerinfo@countrymedia.net
Publication Website: https://www.bowmanextra.com/
Parent Company: Country Media Inc.
Publisher Name: Joe Warren
Publisher Email: jwarren@countrymedia.net
Editor Name: Joe Warren
Editor Email: jwarren@countrymedia.net

CASSELTON

CASS COUNTY REPORTER

Street Address: 122 6th Ave N
City: Casselton
State: ND
ZIP Code: 58012-3232
General Phone: (701) 347-4493
General Email: ads@ccreporter.com
Publication Website: http://www.ccreporter.com/
Publisher Name: Kelsey Majeske
Advertising Executive Name: Retta Roach
Advertising Executive Email: retta@ccreporter.com

CAVALIER

THE CAVALIER CHRONICLE

Street Address: 207 Main St W
City: Cavalier
State: ND
ZIP Code: 58220-4503
General Phone: (701) 265-8844
General Email: lynn@cavchronicle.com
Publication Website: http://www.cavalierchronicle.com/
Publisher Name: Lynn Schroeder
Publisher Email: lynn@cavchronicle.com
Editor Name: Lynn Schroeder
Editor Email: lynn@cavchronicle.com
Advertising Executive Name: Delores Kemp

COOPERSTOWN

GRIGGS COUNTY COURIER

Street Address: 809 Burrel Ave NW
City: Cooperstown
State: ND
ZIP Code: 58425-7106
General Phone: (701) 797-3331
General Email: mcampbell@ncppub.com
Publication Website: http://www.ncppub.com/
Parent Company: New Century Press
Editor Name: Mara Campbell
Editor Email: mcampbell@ncppub.com
Advertising Executive Name: Catherine Albert

CROSBY

THE JOURNAL

Street Address: 117 North Main
City: Crosby
State: ND
ZIP Code: 58730
General Phone: (701) 965-6088
General Email: journal@crosbynd.com
Publication Website: https://www.journaltrib.com/
Parent Company: Journal Publishing
Publisher Name: Cecile Wehrman
Publisher Email: cecilew@crosbynd.com
Editor Name: Cecile Wehrman
Editor Email: cecilew@crosbynd.com
Advertising Executive Name: Cecile Wehrman

DRAYTON

VALLEY NEWS & VIEWS

Street Address: 206 Almeron Ave
City: Drayton
State: ND
ZIP Code: 58225
General Phone: (701) 454-6333
General Email: valleynv@polarcomm.com
Publication Website: https://www.valleynewsandviews.com/
Parent Company: Lesa Van Camp
Publisher Name: Lesa Van Camp
Editor Name: Lesa Van Camp

EDGELEY

EDGELEY MAIL

Street Address: 516 MAIN ST
City: Edgeley
State: ND
ZIP Code: 58433
General Phone: (701) 493-2261
General Email: edgeleymail@drtel.net
Publication Website: http://www.edgeleynd.com/
Publisher Name: Patty Wood Bartle
Publisher Email: edgeleymail@drtel.net
Editor Name: Patty Wood Bartle
Editor Email: edgeleymail@drtel.net

ELGIN

CARSON PRESS

Street Address: P.O. Box 100
City: Elgin
State: ND
ZIP Code: 58533
General Phone: (701) 584-2900
General Email: gcn@westriv.com
Publication Website: https://www.gspublishing.net/
Parent Company: GS Publishing
Publisher Name: Jill Friesz
Publisher Email: gcn@westriv.com
Editor Name: Jill Friesz

ELGIN

THE GRANT COUNTY NEWS

Street Address: P.O. Box 100
City: Elgin
State: ND
ZIP Code: 58533
General Phone: (701) 584-2900
General Email: gcn@westriv.com
Publication Website: https://www.gspublishing.net/
Parent Company: GS Publishing
Publisher Name: Jill Friesz
Publisher Email: gcn@westriv.com
Editor Name: Jill Friesz

FINLEY

STEELE COUNTY PRESS

Street Address: 215 4th St W
City: Finley
State: ND
ZIP Code: 58230-3000
General Phone: (701) 524-1640
General Email: calbert@ncppub.com
Publication Website: http://www.ncppub.com/
Parent Company: New Century Press
Editor Name: Mara Campbell
Editor Email: mcampbell@ncppub.com
Advertising Executive Name: Lisa Midstokke

FORDVILLE

ANETA STAR

Street Address: PO Box 157
City: Fordville
State: ND
ZIP Code: 58231-3134
General Phone: (701) 229-3641
General Email: nesspres@polarcomm.com
Parent Company: Ness Press, Inc.
Publisher Name: Ness Press
Publisher Email: nesspres@polarcomm.com
Editor Name: Ness Press
Editor Email: nesspres@polarcomm.com
Advertising Executive Name: Truman Ness

FORDVILLE

EDMORE HERALD

Street Address: PO Box 157
City: Fordville
State: ND
ZIP Code: 58231-3134
General Phone: (701) 229-3641
General Email: nesspres@polarcomm.com
Parent Company: Ness Press, Inc.
Publisher Name: Ness Press
Publisher Email: nesspres@polarcomm.com
Editor Name: Ness Press
Editor Email: nesspres@polarcomm.com
Advertising Executive Name: Truman Ness

FORDVILLE

FORDVILLE TRI-COUNTY SUN

Street Address: PO Box 157
City: Fordville
State: ND
ZIP Code: 58231-3134
General Phone: (701) 229-3641
General Email: nesspres@polarcomm.com
Parent Company: Ness Press, Inc.
Publisher Name: Ness Press
Publisher Email: nesspres@polarcomm.com
Editor Name: Ness Press
Editor Email: nesspres@polarcomm.com
Advertising Executive Name: Truman Ness

FORDVILLE

HATTON FREE PRESS

Street Address: PO Box 157
City: Fordville
State: ND
ZIP Code: 58231
General Phone: (701) 229-3641
General Email: nesspres@polarcomm.com
Parent Company: Ness Press, Inc.
Publisher Name: Ness Press
Publisher Email: nesspres@polarcomm.com
Editor Name: Ness Press
Editor Email: nesspres@polarcomm.com
Advertising Executive Name: Truman Ness

FORDVILLE

LARIMORE LEADER-TRIBUNE

Street Address: 122 Main St N
City: Fordville
State: ND
ZIP Code: 58231-3134
General Phone: (701) 229-3641
General Email: nesspres@polarcomm.com
Parent Company: Ness Press, Inc.
Publisher Name: Ness Press
Publisher Email: nesspres@polarcomm.com
Editor Name: Marvin Ness
Editor Email: nesspres@polarcomm.com
Advertising Executive Name: Truman Ness

FORDVILLE

MCVILLE MESSENGER

Street Address: PO Box 157
City: Fordville
State: ND
ZIP Code: 58231-3134
General Phone: (701) 229-3641
General Email: nesspres@polarcomm.com
Parent Company: Ness Press, Inc.
Publisher Name: Ness Press
Publisher Email: nesspres@polarcomm.com
Editor Name: Ness Press
Editor Email: nesspres@polarcomm.com
Advertising Executive Name: Truman Ness

FORDVILLE

NELSON COUNTY ARENA

Street Address: PO Box 157
City: Fordville
State: ND
ZIP Code: 58231-3134
General Phone: (701) 229-3641
General Email: nesspres@polarcomm.com
Parent Company: Ness Press, Inc.
Publisher Name: Ness Press
Publisher Email: nesspres@polarcomm.com
Editor Name: Ness Press
Editor Email: nesspres@polarcomm.com
Advertising Executive Name: Truman Ness

FORDVILLE

PEMBINA NEW ERA

Street Address: PO Box 157
City: Fordville
State: ND
ZIP Code: 58231-3134
General Phone: (701) 229-3641
General Email: nesspres@polarcomm.com
Parent Company: Ness Press, Inc.
Publisher Name: Ness Press
Publisher Email: nesspres@polarcomm.com
Editor Name: Ness Press
Editor Email: nesspres@polarcomm.com
Advertising Executive Name: Truman Ness

GACKLE

TRI COUNTY NEWS

Street Address: 321 Main St
City: Gackle
State: ND
ZIP Code: 58442-7109
General Phone: (701) 485-3550
General Email: tcnews@daktel.com
Parent Company: Art & Diane Hagebock
Publisher Name: Diane Hagebock
Publisher Email: tcnews@daktel.com
Editor Name: Tanya Metz

GLEN ULLIN

GLEN ULLIN TIMES

Street Address: PO Box 668
City: Glen Ullin
State: ND
ZIP Code: 58631-7110
General Phone: (701) 348-3325
General Email: gutimes@westriv.com
Publisher Name: Nancy Bittner
Publisher Email: gutimes@westriv.com
Editor Name: Nancy Bittner
Editor Email: gutimes@westriv.com

GRAFTON

THE WALSH COUNTY RECORD

Street Address: 402 Hill Ave
City: Grafton
State: ND
ZIP Code: 58237-1002
General Phone: (701) 352-0640
General Email: advertising@wcrecord.com
Publication Website: http://www.wcrecord.com
Publisher Name: Jackie L. Thompson
Publisher Email: jackie@wcrecord.com
Editor Name: Todd Morgan
Editor Email: todd@wcrecord.com
Advertising Executive Name: Tim S. Martin
Advertising Executive Email: advertising@wcrecord.com

HARVEY

THE HERALD-PRESS

Street Address: 913 Lincoln Ave
City: Harvey
State: ND
ZIP Code: 58341-1523
General Phone: (701) 324-4646
General Email: heraldpressonline@yahoo.com
Publication Website: https://www.heraldpressnd.com
Parent Company: Eldredge Publishing
Publisher Name: Anne Ehni
Publisher Email: heraldpress@midconetwork.com
Editor Name: Anne Ehni
Advertising Executive Name: Edie Schell

HEBRON

HEBRON HERALD

Street Address: PO Box 9
City: Hebron
State: ND
ZIP Code: 58638-0009
General Phone: (701) 878-4494
General Email: hherald@westriv.com
Publisher Name: Jane Brandt
Publisher Email: hherald@westriv.com
Editor Name: Jane Brandt
Editor Email: hherald@westriv.com

HETTINGER

ADAMS COUNTY RECORD

Street Address: 116 S Main St
City: Hettinger
State: ND
ZIP Code: 58639-7031
General Phone: (701) 567-2424
General Email: adamscountyrecord@countrymedia.net
Publication Website: https://www.gspublishing.net/
Parent Company: GS Publishing
Publisher Name: Jill Friesz
Publisher Email: adamscountyrecord@gspublishing.net
Editor Name: Jill Friesz
Advertising Executive Name: Cassidy Fosheim

HILLSBORO

HILLSBORO BANNER

Street Address: 502 West Caledonia Ave.
City: Hillsboro
State: ND
ZIP Code: 58045-4205
General Phone: (701) 636-4241
General Email: hbanner@rrv.net
Publication Website: http://www.hillsborobanner.com/
Parent Company: Sub-Zero Press, Inc.
Publisher Name: Sub-Zero Press, Inc.
Publisher Email: hbanner@rrv.net
Editor Name: Cole Short
Advertising Executive Name: Cory Erickson

KENMARE

THE KENMARE NEWS

Street Address: 20 2nd St NW
City: Kenmare
State: ND
ZIP Code: 58746-7114
General Phone: (701) 385-4275
General Email: news@kenmarend.com
Publication Website: http://www.kenmarend.com/
Publisher Name: Terry Froseth
Publisher Email: news@kenmarend.com
Editor Name: Terry Froseth

LANGDON

CAVALIER COUNTY REPUBLICAN

Street Address: 618 3rd St
City: Langdon
State: ND
ZIP Code: 58249
General Phone: (701) 256-5311
General Email: admin@countrymedia.net
Publication Website: https://www.cavaliercountyextra.com/
Parent Company: Country Media Inc.
Publisher Name: Lori Peterson
Publisher Email: ccr@utma.com
Editor Name: Melissa Anderson
Advertising Executive Name: Lori Peterson

LINTON

EMMONS COUNTY RECORD

Street Address: 201 N Broadway St
City: Linton
State: ND
ZIP Code: 58552
General Phone: (701) 254-4537
General Email: info@lintonnd.com
Publication Website: https://www.ecrecord.com/
Parent Company: Leah Burke
Publisher Name: Leah Burke
Publisher Email: leah@lintonnd.com
Editor Name: Leah Burke
Editor Email: leah@lintonnd.com
Advertising Executive Name: Julie Brandner
Advertising Executive Email: ads@valleytel.net

LISBON

THE RANSOM COUNTY GAZETTE

Street Address: 410 Main St
City: Lisbon
State: ND
ZIP Code: 58054
General Phone: (701) 683-4128
General Email: info@rcgazette.com
Publication Website: http://rcgazette.com/
Parent Company: NorDak Publishing LLC
Publisher Name: Kelsey Majeske
Publisher Email: info@rcgazette.com

LITCHVILLE

THE LITCHVILLE BULLETIN

Street Address: 505 3RD AVE
City: Litchville
State: ND
ZIP Code: 58461
General Phone: (701) 762-4267
General Email: bulletin@drtel.net
Parent Company: Art & Diane Hagebock
Publisher Name: Diane Hagebock
Publisher Email: bulletin@drtel.net

MAYVILLE

TRAILL COUNTY TRIBUNE

Street Address: 12 3rd St SE
City: Mayville
State: ND
ZIP Code: 58257
General Phone: (701) 788-3281
General Email: tom@tctribune.net
Publication Website: http://www.tctribune.net/
Parent Company: NorDak Publishing LLC
Publisher Name: Kelsey Majeske
Publisher Email: tribune@tctribune.net
Advertising Executive Name: Gail Mooney

MINNEWAUKAN

BENSON COUNTY FARMERS PRESS

Street Address: PO Box 98
City: Minnewaukan
State: ND
ZIP Code: 58351
General Phone: (701) 473-5436
General Email: farmerspress@gondtc.com
Publication Website: https://www.bensoncountynews.com/
Parent Company: Consolidated Newspapers Inc.
Publisher Name: Denise Westad
Publisher Email: farmerspress@gondtc.com
Editor Name: Kelly L. Glover
Advertising Executive Email: farmerspress@gondtc.com

NAPOLEON

NAPOLEON HOMESTEAD

Street Address: 323 Main Ave
City: Napoleon
State: ND
ZIP Code: 58561-7108
General Phone: (701) 754-2212
General Email: homestead@napoleonnd.com
Publication Website: https://www.centraldakotanews.com/newspapers/napoleon-homestead/
Parent Company: Central Dakota News
Publisher Name: Terry Schwartzenberger
Publisher Email: homestead@napoleonnd.com
Editor Name: Terry Scheartzenberger
Advertising Executive Name: Jessica Wald

NEW ROCKFORD

NEW ROCKFORD TRANSCRIPT

Street Address: 6 8th St N
City: New Rockford
State: ND
ZIP Code: 58356
General Phone: (701) 947-2417
General Email: nrtranscript@gmail.com

Community Newspapers in the U.S.

Publication Website: http://www.newrockfordtranscript.com/
Publisher Name: Amy Wobbema
Publisher Email: nrtranscript@gmail.com
Advertising Executive Name: Amy Wobbema

RUGBY

PIERCE COUNTY TRIBUNE

Street Address: 219 S Main Ave
City: Rugby
State: ND
ZIP Code: 58368
General Phone: (701) 776-5252
General Email: advertising@thepiercecountytribune.com
Publication Website: http://www.thepiercecountytribune.com/
Parent Company: Ogden Newspapers Inc.
Publisher Email: business@thepiercecountytribune.com
Advertising Executive Name: Megan Reichenberger
Advertising Executive Email: advertising@thepiercecountytribune.com

STANLEY

MOUNTRAIL COUNTY PROMOTER

Street Address: P.O. Box 99
City: Stanley
State: ND
ZIP Code: 58784
General Phone: (701) 628-2333
General Email: promoter@midstatetel.com
Publication Website: http://www.mountrailcountypromoter.com/
Parent Company: Stanley at the Mountrail County
Publisher Name: Mary Kilen
Publisher Email: promoter@midstatetel.com
Editor Name: Mary Kilen

STEELE

STEELE OZONE AND KIDDER COUNTY PRESS

Street Address: 115 1st Ave SE
City: Steele
State: ND
ZIP Code: 58482
General Phone: (701) 475-2513
General Email: sop@bektel.com
Publication Website: https://www.steeleozone.com/
Parent Company: Central Dakota News
Publisher Name: Paul Erdelt
Publisher Email: sop@bektel.com
Editor Name: Paul Erdelt
Advertising Executive Name: Shirley Morlock

TIOGA

TIOGA TRIBUNE

Street Address: 101 2nd Street
City: Tioga
State: ND
ZIP Code: 58852
General Phone: (701) 664-2222
General Email: advertising@tiogand.com
Publication Website: https://www.journaltrib.com
Parent Company: Journal Publishing
Publisher Name: Cecile Wehrman
Publisher Email: tribune@tiogand.com
Advertising Executive Name: Cecile Wehrman

WATFORD CITY

MCKENZIE COUNTY FARMER

Street Address: 109 N Main St
City: Watford City
State: ND
ZIP Code: 58854-7101
General Phone: (701) 842-2351
General Email: ads@watfordcitynd.com
Publication Website: http://www.watfordcitynd.com
Publisher Name: Neal A. Shipman
Publisher Email: mcf@watfordcitynd.com
Editor Name: Neal A. Shipman
Advertising Executive Name: Neal A. Shipman

WESTHOPE

WESTHOPE STANDARD

Street Address: 150 MAIN ST
City: Westhope
State: ND
ZIP Code: 58793
General Phone: (701) 245-6461
General Email: standard@srt.com
Publication Website: https://www.westhopestandard.com/
Parent Company: Steve & Ginny Heth
Publisher Name: Ginny Heth
Publisher Phone: (701) 263-7226
Editor Name: Ginny Heth
Editor Phone: (701) 263-7226

WISHEK

THE WISHEK STAR

Street Address: 24 N Centennial St
City: Wishek
State: ND
ZIP Code: 58495-0275
General Phone: (701) 452-2331
General Email: wishekstar@gmail.com
Parent Company: Central Dakota News
Publisher Name: Tony Bender
Editor Name: Tony Bender

NEBRASKA

AINSWORTH

AINSWORTH STAR-JOURNAL

Street Address: 921 E 4th St
City: Ainsworth
State: NE
ZIP Code: 69210
General Phone: (402) 387-2844
General Email: ainsworthnews@ainsworthnews.com
Publication Website: https://www.ainsworthnews.com/ainsworth-star-journal
Parent Company: Ainsworth News
Delivery Methods: Mail`Newsstand`Racks
Own Printing Facility?: Y
Commercial printers?: Y
Mechanical specifications: 6 column by 21.5" SAU
Published Days: Wed
Avg. Paid Circ.: 1375
Audit Company: Sworn/Estimate/Non-Audited
Audit Date: 43626
Pressroom Equipment: Newsking web press

ALBION

ALBION COUNTY NEWS

Street Address: 328 W Church St
City: Albion
State: NE
ZIP Code: 68620
General Phone: (402) 395-2115
General Email: ads@albionnewsonline.com
Publication Website: http://www.albionnewsonline.com/
Parent Company: Dickerson Newspapers, Inc.
Publisher Name: Jim Dickerson
Publisher Email: jim@albionnewsonline.com
Advertising Executive Email: ads@albionnewsonline.com
Delivery Methods: Mail`Newsstand`Racks
Year Established: 1879
Own Printing Facility?: N
Commercial printers?: Y
Mechanical specifications: Type page 15 1/2 x 21; E - 7 cols, 2 1/12, 1/6 between; A - 7 cols, 2 1/12, 1/6 between; C - 7 cols, 2 1/12, 1/6 between.
Published Days: Wed
Weekday Frequency: m
Avg. Paid Circ.: 1850
Audit Company: Sworn/Estimate/Non-Audited
Audit Date: 43626
Classified Software: Adobe Suite

ALBION

PETERSBURG PRESS

Street Address: 328 W Church St
City: Albion
State: NE
ZIP Code: 68620
General Phone: (402) 395-2115
General Email: ads@albionnewsonline.com
Publication Website: https://albionnewsonline.com/category/petersburg-press/
Parent Company: Dickerson Newspapers, Inc.
Advertising Executive Email: ads@albionnewsonline.com
Delivery Methods: Mail`Newsstand`Racks
Year Established: 1888
Published Days: Wed
Avg. Paid Circ.: 380
Audit Company: Sworn/Estimate/Non-Audited
Audit Date: 43626

ALMA

HARLAN COUNTY JOURNAL

Street Address: 711 Main St
City: Alma
State: NE
ZIP Code: 68620
General Phone: (308) 928-2143
General Email: journal@frontiernet.net
Publication Website: https://www.mainstreetnewsgroup.com/harlancountyjournal/
Parent Company: Main Street Media
Delivery Methods: Mail`Newsstand`Racks
Published Days: Thur
Avg. Paid Circ.: 1600
Avg. Free Circ.: 67
Audit Company: Sworn/Estimate/Non-Audited
Audit Date: 43626

ARAPAHOE

ARAPAHOE PUBLIC MIRROR

Street Address: 420 Nebraska Ave
City: Arapahoe
State: NE
ZIP Code: 68922
General Phone: (308) 962-7261
General Email: arapmir@atcjet.net
Publication Website: http://www.frappr.com/
Delivery Methods: Mail`Racks
Year Established: 18
Own Printing Facility?: Y
Commercial printers?: N
Mechanical specifications: Type page 13 x 21 1/2; E - 6 cols, 2, 1/3 between; A - 6 cols, 2, 1/3 between; C - 6 cols, 2, 1/3 between.
Published Days: Wed
Avg. Paid Circ.: 950
Audit Company: Sworn/Estimate/Non-Audited
Audit Date: 43626

ARNOLD

ARNOLD SENTINEL

Street Address: 113 S Walnut
City: Arnold
State: NE
ZIP Code: 69120
General Phone: (308) 848-2511
General Email: arnoldsentinel@gpcom.net
Publication Website: https://arnoldsentinel.com/
Parent Company: The Arnold Sentinel LLC
Delivery Methods: Mail`Newsstand`Racks
Mechanical specifications: Type page 11 x 23; E - 6 cols, between; A - 6 cols, between; C - 6 cols, between.
Published Days: Thur
Avg. Paid Circ.: 800
Audit Company: Sworn/Estimate/Non-Audited
Audit Date: 43626

ATKINSON

THE ATKINSON GRAPHIC

Street Address: 207 E Main St
City: Atkinson
State: NE
ZIP Code: 68713
General Phone: (402) 925-5411
General Email: news@atkinsongraphic.com
Publication Website: http://www.atkinsongraphic.com/
Publisher Name: Brook D. Curtiss
Editor Name: Brook D. Curtiss
Editor Email: editor@atkinsongraphic.com
Advertising Executive Name: Cindy Poessnecker
Advertising Executive Email: news@atkinsongraphic.com
Published Days: Thur
Avg. Paid Circ.: 2300
Audit Company: Sworn/Estimate/Non-Audited
Audit Date: 43626

AUBURN

NEMAHA COUNTY HERALD

Street Address: PO Box 250
City: Auburn
State: NE
ZIP Code: 6830
General Phone: (402) 274-3185
General Email: kendall@anewspaper.net
Publication Website: https://www.anewspaper.net/
Year Established: 1888
Own Printing Facility?: Y
Commercial printers?: Y
Published Days: Thur
Avg. Paid Circ.: 3245
Audit Company: Sworn/Estimate/Non-Audited
Audit Date: 43625

AURORA

AURORA NEWS-REGISTER

Street Address: 1320 K St
City: Aurora
State: NE
ZIP Code: 68818
General Phone: (402) 694-2131
General Email: advertising@hamilton.net
Publication Website: https://www.auroranewsregister.com/
Parent Company: Kurt and Paula Johnson
Advertising Executive Email: advertising@hamilton.net
Delivery Methods: Mail`Newsstand
Year Established: 1929
Own Printing Facility?: Y
Commercial printers?: Y
Mechanical specifications: Type page 14 1/4 x 21; E - 6 cols, 2 1/4, 1/6 between; A - 6 cols, 2 1/4, 1/6 between; C - 6 cols, 2 1/4, 1/6 between.
Published Days: Wed
Avg. Paid Circ.: 3000
Audit Company: Sworn/Estimate/Non-Audited
Audit Date: 43626

BENKELMAN

THE BENKELMAN POST AND NEWS-CHRONICLE

Street Address: 513 Chief St
City: Benkelman
State: NE
ZIP Code: 69021
General Phone: (308) 423-2337
General Email: cityben@bwtelcom.net
Publication Website: https://www.benkelmanusa.com/newresidents
Delivery Methods: Mail`Newsstand`Carrier`Racks
Year Established: 1993
Commercial printers?: Y
Published Days: Wed
Avg. Paid Circ.: 1245
Avg. Free Circ.: 35
Audit Company: Sworn/Estimate/Non-Audited
Audit Date: 43626

BLOOMFIELD

THE BLOOMFIELD MONITOR

Street Address: 110 N Broadway St
City: Bloomfield
State: NE
ZIP Code: 68718
General Phone: (402) 373-2332
General Email: news@bloomfieldmonitor.com
Publication Website: http://www.myknoxconews.com/
Parent Company: Pitzer Digital LLC
Publisher Name: Carrie Pitzer
Advertising Executive Name: Wade Pitzer
Delivery Methods: Mail`Newsstand
Year Established: 1890
Own Printing Facility?: Y
Commercial printers?: Y
Mechanical specifications: Type page 15 x 21; E - 7 cols, 2 1/12, 1/6 between; A - 7 cols, 2 1/12, 1/6 between; C - 7 cols, 2 1/12, 1/6 between.
Published Days: Thur
Avg. Paid Circ.: 1300
Audit Company: Sworn/Estimate/Non-Audited
Audit Date: 43626

BLUE HILL

BLUE HILL LEADER

Street Address: 565 W Gage St
City: Blue Hill
State: NE
ZIP Code: 68930
General Phone: (402) 756-2077

General Email: bluehillleader@gtmc.net
Publication Website: https://www.mainstreetnewsgroup.com/bluehillleader/
Parent Company: Main Street Media
Editor Name: Rick Houchin
Advertising Executive Name: Melissa Lounsbury
Delivery Methods: Mail`Newsstand`Racks
Year Established: 1887
Own Printing Facility?: Y
Commercial printers?: Y
Mechanical specifications: Type page 11 1/8 x 17; E - 5 cols, 1 15/16, 1/6 between; A - 5 cols, 1 15/16, 1/6 between; C - 5 cols, 1 15/16, 1/6 between.
Published Days: Thur
Avg. Paid Circ.: 950
Audit Company: Sworn/Estimate/Non-Audited
Audit Date: 43626

BRIDGEPORT

BRIDGEPORT NEWS-BLADE

Street Address: PO Box 400
City: Bridgeport
State: NE
ZIP Code: 69336
General Phone: (308) 262-0675
General Email: news@newsblade.net
Publication Website: https://www.newsblade.com/
Parent Company:
Editor Name: John Erickson
Editor Email: editor@newsblade.net
Advertising Executive Email: ads@newsblade.net
Delivery Methods: Mail`Newsstand
Year Established: 1900
Own Printing Facility?: Y
Commercial printers?: Y
Published Days: Wed
Avg. Paid Circ.: 1200
Avg. Free Circ.: 50
Audit Company: Sworn/Estimate/Non-Audited
Audit Date: 43626

BROKEN BOW

CUSTER COUNTY CHIEF

Street Address: 305 S 10th Ave
City: Broken Bow
State: NE
ZIP Code: 68822
General Phone: (308) 872-2471
General Email: chiefads@custercountychief.com
Publication Website: https://www.custercountychief.com/
Parent Company: Horizon Publications Inc.
Publisher Name: Donnis Hueftle-Bullock
Publisher Email: publisher@custercountychief.com
Editor Name: Mona Weatherly
Editor Email: chiefnews@custercountychief.com
Advertising Executive Name: Renee Payne
Advertising Executive Email: chiefads@custercountychief.com
Delivery Methods: Mail`Newsstand`Racks
Year Established: 1892
Own Printing Facility?: Y
Commercial printers?: Y
Mechanical specifications: Type page 13 x 21 1/2; E - 6 cols, 2 1/16, 1/72 between; A - 6 cols, 2 1/16, 1/72 between; C - 6 cols, 2 1/16, 1/72 between.
Published Days: Thur
Avg. Paid Circ.: 3900
Audit Company: Sworn/Estimate/Non-Audited
Audit Date: 43626

CAMBRIDGE

CAMBRIDGE CLARION

Street Address: 706 Patterson St
City: Cambridge
State: NE
ZIP Code: 69022
General Phone: (308) 697-3326
General Email: clarion@cambridgeclarion.com
Publication Website: http://www.cambridgeclarion.com/
Delivery Methods: Mail`Newsstand`Racks
Year Established: 1920
Commercial printers?: Y
Mechanical specifications: Type page 13 1/2 x 21; E - 6 cols, 2, 1/6 between; A - 6 cols, 2, 1/6 between; C - 6 cols, 2, 1/6 between.
Published Days: Thur
Avg. Paid Circ.: 1100
Avg. Free Circ.: 70
Audit Company: Sworn/Estimate/Non-Audited
Audit Date: 43626

CENTRAL CITY

REPUBLICAN-NONPAREIL

Street Address: 802 C Ave
City: Central City
State: NE
ZIP Code: 68826-1738
General Phone: (308) 946-3081
General Email: rnnews@hamilton.net
Publication Website: https://www.republicannonpareil.com/
Own Printing Facility?: Y
Commercial printers?: Y
Mechanical specifications: Type page 10 x 14; E - 4 cols, 2 1/4, 1/6 between; A - 4 cols, 2 1/4, 1/6 between; C - 4 cols, 2 1/4, 1/6 between.
Published Days: Thur
Avg. Paid Circ.: 1995
Audit Company: Sworn/Estimate/Non-Audited
Audit Date: 43626

CHADRON

THE CHADRON RECORD

Street Address: 248 W 2nd St
City: Chadron
State: NE
ZIP Code: 69337-2337
General Phone: (308) 432-5511
General Email: cdrrecord@bbc.net
Publication Website: https://rapidcityjournal.com/community/chadron/
Publisher Name: Matthew Tranquill
Publisher Email: matthew.tranquill@rapidcityjournal.com
Publisher Phone: (605) 394-8301
Editor Name: Pat Butler
Editor Email: patrick.butler@rapidcityjournal.com
Editor Phone: (605) 394-8434
Advertising Executive Name: Jesse Hendrickson
Advertising Executive Email: jhendrickson@rapidcityjournal.com
Advertising Executive Phone: (605) 394-8339
Delivery Methods: Mail`Newsstand`Carrier`Racks
Year Established: 1884
Own Printing Facility?: Y
Commercial printers?: N
Mechanical specifications: Type page 10x 20,5; E - 6 cols, 1 4/5, 1/8 between; A - 6 cols, 1 4/5, 1/8 between; C - 6 cols, 1 4/5, 1/8 between.
Published Days: Wed
Avg. Paid Circ.: 2100
Avg. Free Circ.: 4700
Audit Company: Sworn/Estimate/Non-Audited
Audit Date: 43626

CHAPPELL

CHAPPELL REGISTER

Street Address: 273 Vincent Ave
City: Chappell
State: NE
ZIP Code: 69129-9701
General Phone: (308) 874-2207
General Email: chapregister@embarqmail.com
Publication Website: https://www.starherald.com/marketplace/industry_manufacturing/paper_cardboard_boxes/chappell-register/business_b36f43aa-e415-5bf3-a049-d727143a1e55.html
Delivery Methods: Mail
Published Days: Thur
Avg. Paid Circ.: 1000
Audit Company: Sworn/Estimate/Non-Audited
Audit Date: 43626

COZAD

THE TRI-CITY TRIBUNE

Street Address: 320 W 8th St
City: Cozad
State: NE
ZIP Code: 69130
General Phone: (308) 784-3644
General Email: sports@tricitytrib.com
Publication Website: http://www.tricitytrib.com/
Delivery Methods: Mail`Newsstand`Racks
Year Established: 1965
Mechanical specifications: Type page 10 x 13; E - 6 cols, between.
Published Days: Wed`Thur
Avg. Paid Circ.: 3450
Audit Company: Sworn/Estimate/Non-Audited
Audit Date: 43626

CRAWFORD

CRAWFORD CLIPPER/HARRISON SUN LLC

Street Address: 427 2nd Street
City: Crawford
State: NE
ZIP Code: 69339-1099
General Phone: (308) 665-2310
General Email: crawfordclipper@gmail.com
Publication Website: https://crawfordclipper.com/
Delivery Methods: Mail`Newsstand`Racks
Year Established: 1979
Own Printing Facility?: N
Commercial printers?: N
Published Days: Wed
Avg. Paid Circ.: 1050
Avg. Free Circ.: 50
Audit Company: Sworn/Estimate/Non-Audited
Audit Date: 43626

CREIGHTON

CREIGHTON NEWS

Street Address: 816 Main St
City: Creighton
State: NE
ZIP Code: 68729
General Phone: (402) 358-5220
General Email: news@myknoxconews.com
Publication Website: http://www.myknoxcountynews.com/
Parent Company: Pitzer Digital LLC
Publisher Name: Carrie Pitzer
Publisher Email: carrie@pitzerdigital.com
Editor Name: Trisha Zach
Editor Email: trisha@mylocalcountynews.com

Community Newspapers in the U.S.

Advertising Executive Name: Judy Forbes
Advertising Executive Email: jforbes@creightonnews.com
Delivery Methods: Mail`Newsstand`Racks
Published Days: Wed
Avg. Paid Circ.: 1400
Audit Company: Sworn/Estimate/Non-Audited
Audit Date: 43626

CROFTON

THE CROFTON JOURNAL

Street Address: 108 W Main St
City: Crofton
State: NE
ZIP Code: 68730
General Phone: (402) 388-4255
General Email: journal@gpcom.net
Publication Website: http://www.croftonjournal.com/
Publisher Name: Brook D. Curtiss
Publisher Email: plainviewnews@nyecom.net
Editor Name: Brook D. Curtiss
Editor Email: plainviewnews@nyecom.net
Published Days: Tues
Avg. Paid Circ.: 1000
Audit Company: Sworn/Estimate/Non-Audited
Audit Date: 43626

DONIPHAN

THE DONIPHAN HERALD

Street Address: 206 W Walnut St
City: Doniphan
State: NE
ZIP Code: 68832-8903
General Phone: (402) 845-2937
General Email: info@doniphanherald.com
Publication Website: http://www.doniphanherald.com
Publisher Name: Randy Sadd
Publisher Email: randy.sadd@doniphanherald.com
Editor Name: Christine Hollister
Editor Email: christine.hollister@doniphanherald.com
Delivery Methods: Mail`Newsstand`Racks
Year Established: 1972
Published Days: Thur
Avg. Paid Circ.: 712
Avg. Free Circ.: 23
Audit Company: Sworn/Estimate/Non-Audited
Audit Date: 43626

ELGIN

THE ELGIN REVIEW

Street Address: PO Box 359
City: Elgin
State: NE
ZIP Code: 68636
General Phone: (402) 843-5500
General Email: elginreview@yahoo.com
Publication Website: http://www.elginreview.com/
Parent Company: Dennis and Lynell Morgan
Publisher Name: Dennis Morgan
Editor Name: Lynell Morgan
Delivery Methods: Mail
Year Established: 1897
Published Days: Wed
Avg. Paid Circ.: 1043
Audit Company: Sworn/Estimate/Non-Audited
Audit Date: 43626

FAIRBURY

FAIRBURY JOURNAL-NEWS

Street Address: 510 C St.
City: Fairbury
State: NE
ZIP Code: 68352
General Phone: (402) 729-6141
General Email: info@fairburyjournalnews.com
Publication Website: https://fairburyjournalnews.com/
Parent Company: Timothy Linscott
Publisher Name: Timothy Linscott
Publisher Email: timothylinscott1@gmail.com
Advertising Executive Name: Jennifer
Advertising Executive Email: info@fairburyjournalnews.com
Advertising Executive Phone: (402) 729-6141
Delivery Methods: Mail`Newsstand`Racks
Year Established: 1892
Own Printing Facility?: Y
Commercial printers?: Y
Published Days: Wed
Avg. Paid Circ.: 4500
Audit Company: Sworn/Estimate/Non-Audited
Audit Date: 43626

FALLS CITY

FALLS CITY JOURNAL

Street Address: 1709 Stone St
City: Falls City
State: NE
ZIP Code: 68355
General Phone: (402) 245-2431
General Email: fcjournalads@sentco.net
Publication Website: https://fcjournal.net/
Publisher Name: Richard Halbert
Advertising Executive Name: Nikki McKim
Delivery Methods: Mail`Newsstand`Carrier`Racks
Published Days: Tues
Avg. Paid Circ.: 4100
Audit Company: Sworn/Estimate/Non-Audited
Audit Date: 43626

FRIEND

FRIEND SENTINEL

Street Address: 108 S. Main St
City: Friend
State: NE
ZIP Code: 68359
General Phone: (402) 643-3676
General Email: nichole@sewardindependent.com
Publication Website: https://www.sewardindependent.com/friend/
Parent Company: Enterprise Publishing Co.
Publisher Name: Kevin L. Zadina
Publisher Email: kevinzadina@sewardindependent.com
Editor Name: Emily Hemphill
Editor Email: emily@sewardindependent.com
Advertising Executive Name: Nichole Javorsky
Advertising Executive Email: nichole@sewardindependent.com
Delivery Methods: Mail`Newsstand`Racks
Published Days: Wed
Audit Company: Sworn/Estimate/Non-Audited
Audit Date: 43626

GENEVA

NEBRASKA SIGNAL

Street Address: 131 N 9th St
City: Geneva
State: NE
ZIP Code: 68361
General Phone: (402) 759-3117
General Email: signal@thenebraskasignal.com
Publication Website: https://thenebraskasignal.com/
Parent Company: Tim Curran
Year Established: 1881
Mechanical specifications: Type page 13 x 21; E - 6 cols, 1, 1/6 between; A - 6 cols, 1, 1/6 between; C - 6 cols, 1, 1/6 between.
Published Days: Wed
Avg. Paid Circ.: 2500
Audit Company: Sworn/Estimate/Non-Audited
Audit Date: 43626

GORDON

SHERIDAN COUNTY JOURNAL STAR

Street Address: 400 N Main St
City: Gordon
State: NE
ZIP Code: 69343-1264
General Phone: (308) 282-0118
General Email: scjsads@gmail.com
Publication Website: https://sheridancountyjournalstar.net/
Parent Company: Jordan Huether
Editor Name: Jordan Huether
Editor Email: jordan.scjs@gmail.com
Advertising Executive Name: Rachael Huether
Advertising Executive Email: scjsads@gmail.com
Delivery Methods: Mail`Newsstand`Racks
Year Established: 1891
Published Days: Wed
Avg. Paid Circ.: 1700
Audit Company: Sworn/Estimate/Non-Audited
Audit Date: 43626

GOTHENBURG

GOTHENBURG TIMES

Street Address: P.O. Box 385
City: Gothenburg
State: NE
ZIP Code: 69138
General Phone: (308) 537-3636
General Email: ads@gothenburgtimes.com
Publication Website: https://www.gothenburgtimes.com/
Parent Company: Platte Valley Media LLC
Editor Name: John Verser
Editor Email: sports@gothenburgtimes.com
Advertising Executive Name: Amanda Long
Advertising Executive Email: ads@gothenburgtimes.com
Advertising Executive Phone: 308-537-3636
Delivery Methods: Mail`Newsstand`Racks
Year Established: 1908
Mechanical specifications: Type page 11 5/8 x 21; E - 6 cols, 1 5/6, 1/6 between; A - 6 cols, 1 5/6, 1/6 between; C - 8 cols, 1 1/3, 1/8 between.
Published Days: Wed
Avg. Paid Circ.: 1800
Audit Company: Sworn/Estimate/Non-Audited
Audit Date: 43626

GRANT

THE GRANT TRIBUNE SENTINEL

Street Address: PO Box 67
City: Grant
State: NE
ZIP Code: 69140
General Phone: (308) 352-4311
General Email: granttribune@gpcom.net
Publication Website: https://www.granttribune.com/
Parent Company: Johnson Publications
Advertising Executive Email: tribads@gpcom.net
Delivery Methods: Mail`Newsstand`Racks
Year Established: 1897
Published Days: Wed
Avg. Paid Circ.: 1200
Audit Company: Sworn/Estimate/Non-Audited
Audit Date: 43626

GRETNA

THE DOUGLAS COUNTY POST GAZETTE

Street Address: 620 No. Hwy. 6
City: Gretna
State: NE
ZIP Code: Gretna
General Phone: (402) 289-2329
General Email: info@dcpostgazette.com
Publication Website: https://dcpostgazette.com/
Publisher Name: Darren Ivy
Publisher Email: darren@dcpostgazette.com
Publisher Phone: (402) 289-2329
Advertising Executive Email: info@dcpostgazette.com
Delivery Methods: Mail`Newsstand
Year Established: 1984
Mechanical specifications: Type page 14 1/4 x 21 1/2; E - 6 cols, 2 1/6, between; A - 6 cols, 2 1/6, between; C - 6 cols, 2 1/6, between.
Published Days: Tues
Avg. Paid Circ.: 3400
Avg. Free Circ.: 12200
Audit Company: Sworn/Estimate/Non-Audited
Audit Date: 43626

GRETNA

THE GRETNA GUIDE & NEWS

Street Address: 620 N Highway 6
City: Gretna
State: NE
ZIP Code: 68028
General Phone: (402) 332-3232
General Email: frontdesk@gretnaguide.com
Publication Website: https://gretnaguide.com/
Publisher Name: Darren Ivy
Publisher Email: darren@gretnaguide.com
Advertising Executive Name: Wendy Doyle
Advertising Executive Email: gretnaguide@gretnaguide.com
Delivery Methods: Mail`Newsstand
Year Established: 1963
Mechanical specifications: Type page 11.5 x 21.5; E - 6 cols, 1 col: 1.778" 2 col: 3.722" 3 col: 5.667" 4 col: 7.611" 5 col: 9.556" 6 col: 11.5"
Published Days: Wed
Avg. Paid Circ.: 1170
Avg. Free Circ.: 3380
Audit Company: Sworn/Estimate/Non-Audited
Audit Date: 43626

HEBRON

HEBRON JOURNAL-REGISTER

Street Address: 318 Lincoln Ave
City: Hebron
State: NE
ZIP Code: 68370-0210
General Phone: (402) 768-6602
General Email: hebronjr@windstream.net
Publication Website: http://www.hebronjournalregister.com/
Delivery Methods: Mail`Newsstand`Racks
Published Days: Wed
Avg. Paid Circ.: 2500
Audit Company: Sworn/Estimate/Non-Audited
Audit Date: 43626

HEMINGFORD

THE HEMINGFORD LEDGER

Street Address: 714 Box Butte Ave
City: Hemingford
State: NE
ZIP Code: 69348
General Phone: (308) 487-3334
General Email: circ@starherald.com
Publication Website: https://www.starherald.com/hemingford/
Publisher Name: Rich Macke
Publisher Email: rich.macke@starherald.com
Editor Name: Kay Bakkehaug
Editor Email: kay.bakkehaug@hemingfordledger.com
Delivery Methods: Mail`Newsstand`Racks
Year Established: 1907
Published Days: Thur
Avg. Paid Circ.: 1400
Audit Company: Sworn/Estimate/Non-Audited
Audit Date: 43626

HICKMAN

VOICE NEWS

Street Address: 114 Locust St
City: Hickman
State: NE
ZIP Code: 68372
General Phone: (402) 792-2255
General Email: receptionist@voicenewsnebraska.com
Publication Website: https://voicenewsnebraska.com/
Parent Company: Media News Group
Publisher Name: Darren Ivy
Publisher Email: darren@voicenewsnebraska.com
Publisher Phone: (402) 792-2255, ext : 102
Advertising Executive Name: Wendy Doyle
Advertising Executive Email: marketing@voicenewsnebraska.com
Advertising Executive Phone: (402) 792-2255, ext : 111
Delivery Methods: Mail`Racks
Year Established: 1978
Published Days: Thur
Avg. Paid Circ.: 3304
Avg. Free Circ.: 260
Audit Company: Sworn/Estimate/Non-Audited
Audit Date: 43626

HOWELLS

HOWELLS JOURNAL

Street Address: 122 N 3rd St
City: Howells
State: NE
ZIP Code: 68641-3087
General Phone: (402) 986-1777
General Email: howellsjournal@msn.com
Publication Website: https://www.theindependent.com/marketplace/business_professional_services/advertising/newspaper/howells-journal-newspaper-office/business_1ad39ed9-1ebc-5ba8-ba45-8cc06de59e58.html
Publisher Name: Terrie Baker
Publisher Email: terrie.baker@theindependent.com
Publisher Phone: (308) 381-9410
Editor Name: Jim Faddis
Editor Email: jim.faddis@theindependent.com
Editor Phone: (308) 381-9413
Advertising Executive Name: Kim Sweetser
Advertising Executive Email: kimberly.sweester@theindependent.com
Advertising Executive Phone: (308) 381-9434
Published Days: Wed
Avg. Paid Circ.: 915
Audit Company: Sworn/Estimate/Non-Audited
Audit Date: 43626

HUMBOLDT

HUMBOLDT STANDARD

Street Address: 317 W Square St
City: Humboldt
State: NE
ZIP Code: 68376
General Phone: (402) 862-2200
General Email: hs40231@windstream.net
Publication Website: http://humboldtstandard.tripod.com/
Editor Name: Jack Cooper
Delivery Methods: Mail`Newsstand`Racks
Year Established: 1882
Mechanical specifications: Type page 13 x 21 1/2; E - 6 cols, 2 1/20, between; A - 6 cols, 2 1/20, between; C - 8 cols, 1 2/3, between.
Published Days: Thur
Avg. Paid Circ.: 750
Audit Company: Sworn/Estimate/Non-Audited
Audit Date: 43626

IMPERIAL

THE IMPERIAL REPUBLICAN

Street Address: 622 Broadway
City: Imperial
State: NE
ZIP Code: 69033-3136
General Phone: (308) 882-4453
General Email: imperialnews@jpipapers.com
Publication Website: https://www.imperialrepublican.com/
Editor Name: Russell Pankonin
Editor Email: imperialnews@jpipapers.com
Advertising Executive Email: adrep@jpipapers.com
Delivery Methods: Mail`Newsstand
Year Established: 1885
Own Printing Facility?: Y
Commercial printers?: Y
Published Days: Thur
Avg. Paid Circ.: 1614
Avg. Free Circ.: 36
Audit Company: Sworn/Estimate/Non-Audited
Audit Date: 43626

KIMBALL

WESTERN NEBRASKA OBSERVER

Street Address: 118 E 2nd St
City: Kimball
State: NE
ZIP Code: 69145-1209
General Phone: (308) 235-3631
General Email: editor@westernnebraskaobserver.net
Publication Website: https://www.westernnebraskaobserver.net/
Delivery Methods: Mail
Year Established: 1885
Mechanical specifications: Type page 11 5/8 x 21 1/2; E - 6 cols, 1 5/6, 1/8 between; A - 6 cols, 1 5/6, 1/8 between; C - 6 cols, 1 5/6, 1/8 between.
Published Days: Thur
Avg. Paid Circ.: 1910
Audit Company: Sworn/Estimate/Non-Audited
Audit Date: 43626

MADISON

THE MADISON STAR-MAIL

Street Address: 211 S Main St
City: Madison
State: NE
ZIP Code: 68748-6485
General Phone: (402) 454-3818
General Email: starmail@telebeep.com
Publication Website: https://www.madison-ne.com/business/madison-star-mail-/
Delivery Methods: Mail
Year Established: 1878
Mechanical specifications: Type page 13 1/4 x 21 1/2; E - 6 cols, 2 1/24, 1/6 between; A - 6 cols, 2 1/24, 1/6 between; C - 6 cols, 2 1/24, 1/6 between.
Published Days: Thur
Avg. Paid Circ.: 700
Avg. Free Circ.: 50
Audit Company: Sworn/Estimate/Non-Audited
Audit Date: 43626

MILFORD

MILFORD TIMES

Street Address: 607 1st Street
City: Milford
State: NE
ZIP Code: 68405
General Phone: (402) 761-2911
General Email: emily@sewardindependent.com
Publication Website: https://www.sewardindependent.com/milford/
Parent Company: Enterprise Publishing Co.
Publisher Name: Kevin L. Zadina
Publisher Email: kevinzadina@sewardindependent.com
Editor Name: Emily Hemphill
Editor Email: emily@sewardindependent.com
Advertising Executive Name: Nichole Javorsky
Advertising Executive Email: nichole@sewardindependent.com
Delivery Methods: Mail`Newsstand`Racks
Mechanical specifications: Type page 10 1/2 x 15; E - 5 cols, 2, 1/8 between; A - 5 cols, 2, 1/8 between; C - 5 cols, 2, 1/8 between.
Published Days: Wed
Avg. Paid Circ.: 1100
Avg. Free Circ.: 10
Audit Company: Sworn/Estimate/Non-Audited
Audit Date: 43626

MINDEN

THE MINDEN COURIER

Street Address: P.O. Box 379
City: Minden
State: NE
ZIP Code: 68959
General Phone: (308) 832-2220
General Email: mindencourier@gtmc.net
Publication Website: https://themindencourier.com/
Editor Name: Jim Edgecombe
Editor Email: mindencourier@gtmc.net
Delivery Methods: Mail`Newsstand`Racks
Year Established:
Mechanical specifications: Type page 13 x 21; E - 6 cols, 2, 1/6 between; A - 6 cols, 2, 1/6 between; C - 6 cols, 2, 1/6 between.
Published Days: Wed
Avg. Paid Circ.: 2300
Audit Company: Sworn/Estimate/Non-Audited
Audit Date: 43626

NEBRASKA CITY

NEBRASKA CITY NEWS-PRESS

Street Address: 823 Central Ave
City: Nebraska City
State: NE
ZIP Code: 68410-2408
General Phone: (402) 873-3334
General Email: tkaven@ncnewspress.com
Publication Website: https://www.ncnewspress.com/
Parent Company: Lee Enterprises
Publisher Name: Tammy Schumacher
Publisher Email: tschumacher@ncnewspress.com
Publisher Phone: (402) 873-3334
Editor Name: Kirt Manion
Editor Email: kmanion@ncnewspress.com
Editor Phone: (402) 873-3334
Advertising Executive Name: Theresa Kaven
Advertising Executive Email: tkaven@ncnewspress.com
Advertising Executive Phone: (402) 269-2135
Delivery Methods: Mail`Newsstand`Racks
Year Established: 1858
Mechanical specifications: Type page 12 1/4 x 21 1/2; E - 6 cols, 1 7/8, 3/16 between; A - 6 cols, 1 7/8, 3/16 between; C - 6 cols, 1 7/8, 3/16 between.
Published Days: Tues`Fri
Weekday Frequency: e
Avg. Paid Circ.: 2110
Audit Company: Sworn/Estimate/Non-Audited
Audit Date: 43626
Pressroom Equipment: 4-G; Control System -- 8-G.
Mailroom Equipment: Tying Machines -- 1/B; Address Machine -- Epson.;
Classified Equipment: Hardware -- APP/Mac G4; Printers -- APP/Mac LaserWriter Pro;
Classified Software: Baseview.

NELIGH

CLEARWATER RECORD-EWING NEWS

Street Address: PO Box 46, 419 Main Street Neligh
City: Neligh
State: NE
ZIP Code: 68756-1422
General Phone: (402) 887-4840
General Email: jwright@nelighnews.com
Publication Website: https://www.antelopecountynews.com/clearwater_ewing/
Parent Company: Pitzer Digital LLC
Publisher Name: Carrie Pitzer
Publisher Email: news@myantelopecountynews.com
Editor Name: Jenny Higgins
Editor Email: news@myantelopecountynews.com
Advertising Executive Email: news@myantelopecountynews.com
Delivery Methods: Mail`Newsstand`Racks
Published Days: Thur
Avg. Paid Circ.: 600
Audit Company: Sworn/Estimate/Non-Audited
Audit Date: 43626

NELIGH

THE NELIGH NEWS AND LEADER

Street Address: 314 M Street, Nelighq
City: Neligh
State: NE
ZIP Code: 68756
General Phone: (402) 887-4000
General Email: jpellatz@nelighnews.com
Publication Website: https://www.antelopecountynews.com/
Parent Company: Pitzer Digital LLC
Publisher Name: Carrie Pitzer
Publisher Email: news@myantelopecountynews.com
Editor Name: Jenny Higgins
Editor Email: news@myantelopecountynews.com
Advertising Executive Email: news@myantelopecountynews.com
Delivery Methods: Mail`Newsstand`Carrier`Racks
Own Printing Facility?: Y
Commercial printers?: Y
Published Days: Wed
Avg. Paid Circ.: 1500
Audit Company: Sworn/Estimate/Non-Audited

Audit Date: 43626

NIOBRARA

NIOBRARA TRIBUNE

Street Address: 254 Park Ave.
City: Niobrara
State: NE
ZIP Code: 68760-7073
General Phone: (402) 857-3737
General Email: niobraratribune@yahoo.com
Publication Website: http://www.niobraratribune.com/
Publisher Name: Brook D. Curtiss
Editor Name: Brook D. Curtiss
Editor Email: editor@atkinsongraphic.com
Advertising Executive Name: Valorie Zach
Published Days: Thur
Avg. Paid Circ.: 520
Audit Company: Sworn/Estimate/Non-Audited
Audit Date: 43626

NORTH BEND

NORTH BEND EAGLE

Street Address: 730 Main St, P.O. Box 100
City: North Bend
State: NE
ZIP Code: 68649-5003
General Phone: (402) 652-8312
General Email: nbeagle@gmail.com
Publication Website: http://www.northbendeagle.com/
Publisher Name: Nathan Arneal
Editor Name: Nathan Arneal
Advertising Executive Name: Mary Le Arneal
Delivery Methods: Mail`Newsstand
Year Established: 1897
Published Days: Wed
Avg. Paid Circ.: 1100
Avg. Free Circ.: 10
Audit Company: Sworn/Estimate/Non-Audited
Audit Date: 43626

O' NEILL

HOLT COUNTY INDEPENDENT

Street Address: 114 N 4th St
City: O' Neill
State: NE
ZIP Code: 68763-1503
General Phone: (402) 336-1220
General Email: ads@holtindependent.com
Publication Website: http://www.holtindependent.com/
Parent Company: Terry Miles
Publisher Name: Terry Miles
Publisher Email: news@holtindependent.com
Editor Name: Amanda Sindelar
Editor Email: editor@holtindependent.com
Advertising Executive Name: Crystal Matthews
Advertising Executive Email: ads@holtindependent.com
Delivery Methods: Mail`Racks
Year Established: 1880
Own Printing Facility?: Y
Commercial printers?: Y
Published Days: Thur
Avg. Paid Circ.: 2500
Avg. Free Circ.: 20
Audit Company: Sworn/Estimate/Non-Audited
Audit Date: 43626

OGALLALA

KEITH COUNTY NEWS

Street Address: 116 W A St, P.O. Box 359
City: Ogallala
State: NE
ZIP Code: 69153-2543
General Phone: (308) 284-4046
General Email: newsboy@ogallalakcnews.com
Publication Website: http://ogallalakcnews.com/Welcome.html
Publisher Name: Jeff Headley
Publisher Email: newsboy@ogallalakcnews.com
Advertising Executive Name: marilee perlinger
Delivery Methods: Mail`Newsstand`Carrier`Racks
Year Established: 1885
Mechanical specifications: Type page 11 5/8 x 21 1/2; E - 6 cols, 1 13/16, 1/8 between; A - 6 cols, 1 13/16, 1/8 between; C - 9 cols, 1 1/6, 1/8 between.
Published Days: Mon`Wed
Avg. Paid Circ.: 3900
Avg. Free Circ.: 200
Audit Company: Sworn/Estimate/Non-Audited
Audit Date: 43626

ORCHARD

THE ORCHARD NEWS

Street Address: 230 Windom St
City: Orchard
State: NE
ZIP Code: 68764-5077
General Phone: (402) 893-2535
General Email: orchardnews@juno.com
Publication Website: https://www.myantelopecountynews.com/orchard-news
Parent Company: Pitzer Digital LLC
Publisher Name: Carrie Pitzer
Publisher Email: carrie@pitzerdigital.com
Editor Name: Jenny Higgins
Editor Email: news@myantelopecountynews.com
Advertising Executive Name: Wade Pitzer
Advertising Executive Email: wade@pitzerdigital.com
Published Days: Thur
Avg. Paid Circ.: 600
Audit Company: Sworn/Estimate/Non-Audited
Audit Date: 43626

ORD

THE ORD QUIZ

Street Address: 237 South 15th Street
City: Ord
State: NE
ZIP Code: 68862-1752
General Phone: (308) 728-3261
General Email: quizadv@frontier.com
Publication Website: https://www.theordquiz.com/
Advertising Executive Email: quizadv@frontier.com
Delivery Methods: Mail`Racks
Year Established: 1882
Own Printing Facility?: Y
Commercial printers?: Y
Mechanical specifications: Type page 10 1/2 x 21; 6 cols
Published Days: Wed
Avg. Paid Circ.: 2050
Avg. Free Circ.: 40
Audit Company: Sworn/Estimate/Non-Audited
Audit Date: 43626

OSHKOSH

GARDEN COUNTY NEWS

Street Address: 204 Main St
City: Oshkosh
State: NE
ZIP Code: 69154-6130
General Phone: (308) 772-3555
General Email: gardencountynews@gmail.com
Publication Website: http://www.gardencountynews.com/
Parent Company: Kelly Reece
Editor Name: Kelly Reece
Editor Email: gcnews@embarqmail.com
Advertising Executive Name: Tessa Paulsen
Delivery Methods: Mail`Newsstand`Racks
Year Established: 1905
Published Days: Wed
Avg. Paid Circ.: 1300
Audit Company: Sworn/Estimate/Non-Audited
Audit Date: 43626

PAWNEE CITY

THE PAWNEE REPUBLICAN

Street Address: 600 G St
City: Pawnee City
State: NE
ZIP Code: 68420
General Phone: (402) 852-2575
General Email: ads@pawneenews.com
Publication Website: https://www.pawneenews.com/
Parent Company: Sunrise Publications, Inc
Publisher Name: Ronald Puhalla
Publisher Email: ronald@pawneenews.com
Publisher Phone: (402) 852-2575
Advertising Executive Name: Ronald Puhalla
Advertising Executive Email: ads@pawneenews.com
Advertising Executive Phone: (402) 852-2575
Delivery Methods: Mail`Newsstand`Racks
Year Established: 1867
Own Printing Facility?: Y
Commercial printers?: Y
Mechanical specifications: Type page 13 x 21; E - 6 cols, 2, 1/6 between; A - 6 cols, 2, 1/6 between; C - 6 cols, 2, 1/6 between.
Published Days: Thur
Avg. Paid Circ.: 1500
Avg. Free Circ.: 52
Audit Company: Sworn/Estimate/Non-Audited
Audit Date: 43626

PENDER

THE PENDER TIMES

Street Address: 313 Main St
City: Pender
State: NE
ZIP Code: 68047
General Phone: (402) 385-3013
General Email: ptimes@abbnebraska.com
Publication Website: http://www.penderthurston.com/
Parent Company: Sturek Media Inc.
Publisher Name: Jason Sturek
Mechanical specifications: Type page 10 1/2 x 21 1/2.
Published Days: Thur
Avg. Paid Circ.: 1450
Avg. Free Circ.: 75
Audit Company: Sworn/Estimate/Non-Audited
Audit Date: 43626

PLAINVIEW

THE PLAINVIEW NEWS

Street Address: 508 W Locust Ave, P.O. Box 9
City: Plainview
State: NE
ZIP Code: 68769-4119
General Phone: (402) 582-4921
General Email: plainviewnews@nyecom.net
Publication Website: http://www.theplainviewnews.com/
Publisher Name: Brook D. Curtiss
Publisher Email: plainviewnews@nyecom.net
Editor Name: Brook D. Curtiss
Editor Email: plainviewnews@nyecom.net
Advertising Executive Name: Brook D. Curtiss
Advertising Executive Email: plainviewnews@nyecom.net
Delivery Methods: Mail`Newsstand`Racks
Year Established: 1892
Mechanical specifications: Type page 15 1/2 x 21 1/4; E - 7 cols, 2 1/12, 1/6 between; A - 7 cols, 2 1/12, 1/6 between; C - 7 cols, 2 1/12, 1/6 between.
Published Days: Wed
Avg. Paid Circ.: 1900
Audit Company: Sworn/Estimate/Non-Audited
Audit Date: 43626

PLATTSMOUTH

THE PLATTSMOUTH JOURNAL

Street Address: 410 Main St
City: Plattsmouth
State: NE
ZIP Code: 68048-1960
General Phone: (402) 296-2141
General Email: placlassifieds@lee.net
Publication Website: https://fremonttribune.com/community/cass-news/#tracking-source=menu-nav
Publisher Name: Vincent Laboy
Publisher Email: vincent.laboy@lee.net
Publisher Phone: (402) 563-7501
Editor Name: Matt Lindberg
Editor Email: mlindberg@columbustelegram.com
Editor Phone: (402) 563-7502
Advertising Executive Name: Kelly Muchmore
Advertising Executive Email: kmuchmore@columbustelegram.com
Advertising Executive Phone: (402) 563-7554
Delivery Methods: Mail`Newsstand`Racks
Year Established: 1881
Mechanical specifications: Type page 14 x 21; E - 6 cols, 2 1/8, between; A - 6 cols, 2 1/8, between; C - 6 cols, 2 1/8, between.
Published Days: Thur
Avg. Paid Circ.: 5200
Avg. Free Circ.: 16250
Audit Company: Sworn/Estimate/Non-Audited
Audit Date: 43626

RAVENNA

THE RAVENNA NEWS

Street Address: 322 Grand Ave
City: Ravenna
State: NE
ZIP Code: 68869-1398
General Phone: (308) 452-3411
General Email: ranews@cornhusker.net
Publication Website: https://www.theravennanews.com/
Delivery Methods: Mail`Newsstand`Racks
Year Established: 1886
Mechanical specifications: Type page 11 1/2 x 21; E - 6 cols, 1 5/6, 1/8 between; A - 6 cols, 1 5/6, 1/8 between; C - 6 cols, 1 5/6, 1/8 between.
Published Days: Wed
Avg. Paid Circ.: 1152
Avg. Free Circ.: 3
Audit Company: Sworn/Estimate/Non-Audited
Audit Date: 43626

RED CLOUD

THE RED CLOUD CHIEF

Street Address: 413 N. Webster
City: Red Cloud
State: NE

ZIP Code: 68970
General Phone: (402) 746-3700
General Email: chief@gpcom.net
Publication Website: https://www.visitredcloud.com/business/red-cloud-chief
Parent Company: Main Street Media, Inc.
Delivery Methods: Mail`Newsstand`Racks
Published Days: Wed
Avg. Paid Circ.: 1682
Audit Company: Sworn/Estimate/Non-Audited
Audit Date: 43626

SAINT EDWARD

THE ST. EDWARD ADVANCE

Street Address: 105 N 3rd St
City: Saint Edward
State: NE
ZIP Code: 68660-4559
General Phone: (402) 395-2115
General Email: advance@gpcom.net
Publication Website: https://albionnewsonline.com/category/st-edward/
Advertising Executive Email: ads@albionnewsonline.com
Delivery Methods: Mail
Year Established: 1900
Own Printing Facility?: Y
Commercial printers?: Y
Mechanical specifications: Type page 13 x 21; E - 6 cols, 2 1/12, 1/6 between; A - 6 cols, 2 1/12, 1/6 between; C - 6 cols, 2 1/12, 1/6 between.
Published Days: Thur
Avg. Paid Circ.: 582
Avg. Free Circ.: 8
Audit Company: Sworn/Estimate/Non-Audited
Audit Date: 43626

SAINT PAUL

THE PHONOGRAPH-HERALD

Street Address: 408 Howard Ave
City: Saint Paul
State: NE
ZIP Code: 68873-2141
General Phone: (308) 754-4401
General Email: kimberly.sweester@theindependent.com
Publication Website: https://www.phonographherald.com/
Publisher Name: Terrie Baker
Publisher Email: terrie.baker@theindependent.com
Publisher Phone: (308) 381-9410
Editor Name: Jim Faddis
Editor Email: jim.faddis@theindependent.com
Editor Phone: (308) 381-9413
Advertising Executive Name: Kim Sweester
Advertising Executive Email: kimberly.sweester@theindependent.com
Advertising Executive Phone: (308) 381-9434
Delivery Methods: Mail`Newsstand`Racks
Year Established: 1873
Own Printing Facility?: Y
Commercial printers?: Y
Published Days: Wed
Avg. Paid Circ.: 2452
Audit Company: Sworn/Estimate/Non-Audited
Audit Date: 43626

SCOTTSBLUFF

THE BUSINESS FARMER

Street Address: 22 W 17th St
City: Scottsbluff
State: NE
ZIP Code: 69361-3156
General Phone: (308) 635-3110
General Email: farmads@thebusinessfarmer.com
Publication Website: https://www.thebusinessfarmer.com/
Parent Company: News Media Grouip
Publisher Name: Rob Mortimore
Publisher Email: rmort@thebusinessfarmer.com
Publisher Phone: (308) 635-3110
Editor Name: Andrew Brosig
Editor Email: abrosig@thebusinessfarmer.com
Editor Phone: (308) 635-3110
Delivery Methods: Mail`Newsstand`Racks
Mechanical specifications: Type page 10 x 13 1/2; E - 6 cols, 1 7/12, 1/6 between; A - 6 cols, 1 7/12, 1/6 between; C - 6 cols, 1 7/12, 1/6 between.
Published Days: Fri
Avg. Paid Circ.: 2300
Audit Company: Sworn/Estimate/Non-Audited
Audit Date: 43626

SEWARD

CRETE NEWS

Street Address: 129 S. 6th Street
City: Seward
State: NE
ZIP Code: 68434
General Phone: (402) 826-2147
General Email: scinews@sewardindependent.com
Publication Website: https://www.sewardindependent.com/crete/
Publisher Name: Kevin L. Zadina
Publisher Email: kevinzadina@sewardindependent.com
Editor Name: Emily Hemphill
Editor Email: emily@sewardindependent.com
Advertising Executive Name: Nichole Javorsky
Advertising Executive Email: nichole@sewardindependent.com
Delivery Methods: Mail`Newsstand`Racks
Year Established: 1871
Own Printing Facility?: Y
Commercial printers?: Y
Mechanical specifications: Type page 13 x 21 1/2; E - 6 cols, 1/6 between; A - 6 cols, 1/6 between; C - 6 cols, 3/8, 1/6 between.
Published Days: Wed
Avg. Paid Circ.: 3500
Audit Company: Sworn/Estimate/Non-Audited
Audit Date: 43626

SEWARD

SEWARD COUNTY INDEPENDENT

Street Address: 129 S 6th St
City: Seward
State: NE
ZIP Code: 68434-2078
General Phone: (402) 643-3676
General Email: scinews@sewardindependent.com
Publication Website: https://www.sewardindependent.com/
Parent Company: Enterprise Publishing Co.
Publisher Name: Kevin L. Zadina
Publisher Email: kevinzadina@sewardindependent.com
Editor Name: Emily Hemphill
Editor Email: emily@sewardindependent.com
Advertising Executive Name: Nichole Javorsky
Advertising Executive Email: nichole@sewardindependent.com
Delivery Methods: Mail`Newsstand`Racks
Year Established: 1893
Mechanical specifications: Type page 15 x 22; E - 6 cols, 2 1/30, 1/6 between; A - 6 cols, 2 1/30, 1/6 between; C - 6 cols, 2 1/30, 1/6 between.
Published Days: Wed
Avg. Paid Circ.: 3200
Avg. Free Circ.: 25
Audit Company: Sworn/Estimate/Non-Audited
Audit Date: 43626

SEWARD

WILBER REPUBLICAN

Street Address: 129 S. 6th Street
City: Seward
State: NE
ZIP Code: 68434
General Phone: (402) 821-2586
General Email: nichole@sewardindependent.com
Publication Website: https://www.sewardindependent.com/wilber/
Parent Company: Enterprise Publishing Co.
Publisher Name: Kevin L. Zadina
Publisher Email: kevinzadina@sewardindependent.com
Editor Name: Emily Hemphill
Editor Email: emily@sewardindependent.com
Advertising Executive Name: Nichole Javorsky
Advertising Executive Email: nichole@sewardindependent.com
Delivery Methods: Mail`Newsstand`Racks
Own Printing Facility?: Y
Commercial printers?: Y
Mechanical specifications: Type page 15 x 21; E - 6 cols, 2, 1/6 between; A - 6 cols, 2, 1/6 between; C - 6 cols, 2, 1/6 between.
Published Days: Wed
Avg. Paid Circ.: 2000
Avg. Free Circ.: 37
Audit Company: Sworn/Estimate/Non-Audited
Audit Date: 43626

SHELTON

SHELTON CLIPPER

Street Address: 113 C St, P.O. Box 620
City: Shelton
State: NE
ZIP Code: 68876-9688
General Phone: (308) 647-5158
General Email: info@clipperpubco.com
Publication Website: https://www.clipperpubco.com/
Parent Company: Clipper Publishing, Inc
Publisher Name: Steve Glenn
Publisher Email: sglenn@clipperpubco.com
Editor Name: Barb Berglund
Editor Email: bberglund@clipperpubco.com
Delivery Methods: Mail`Newsstand`Racks
Own Printing Facility?: Y
Commercial printers?: Y
Published Days: Thur
Avg. Paid Circ.: 1001
Audit Company: Sworn/Estimate/Non-Audited
Audit Date: 43626

SIDNEY

SIDNEY SUN-TELEGRAPH

Street Address: 817 12th Ave., P.O. Box 193
City: Sidney
State: NE
ZIP Code: 69162-1625
General Phone: (308) 254-2818
General Email: ads@suntelegraph.com
Publication Website: http://www.suntelegraph.com/
Parent Company: Stevenson Newspapers
Delivery Methods: Mail`Newsstand`Racks
Year Established: 1873
Own Printing Facility?: Y
Commercial printers?: Y
Mechanical specifications: Type page 12 x 21 1/2; E - 6 cols, 2, 1/3 between; A - 6 cols, 2, 1/3 between; C - 8 cols, 1/3 between.
Published Days: Wed`Fri
Weekday Frequency: m

Avg. Paid Circ.: 1476
Audit Company: Sworn/Estimate/Non-Audited
Audit Date: 43626
Pressroom Equipment: Lines -- 5-G/Community 1997; Press Drive -- RKW/25 h.p. electric 1997; Folders -- G/S 1997; Control System -- G/Community 1997; Registration System -- G/Dual-Pin.
Mailroom Equipment: Tying Machines -- Malow/Heavy Duty; Wrapping Singles -- St/String Tyer.;
Business Equipment: Dell, Pentium II
Business Software: Microsoft/Windows 98, QuickBooks Pro
Classified Equipment: Hardware -- APP/Power Mac 4400; Printers -- APP/Mac LaserWriter.;

SPENCER

THE SPENCER ADVOCATE

Street Address: 100 S Thayer St
City: Spencer
State: NE
ZIP Code: 68777-9784
General Phone: (402) 589-1010
General Email: advocate@nntc.net
Publication Website: http://www.spencerne.net/
Published Days: Thur
Avg. Paid Circ.: 1056
Avg. Free Circ.: 21
Audit Company: Sworn/Estimate/Non-Audited
Audit Date: 43626

SPRINGVIEW

SPRINGVIEW HERALD

Street Address: 102 S Main St
City: Springview
State: NE
ZIP Code: 68778-9603
General Phone: (402) 497-3651
General Email: editor@springviewherald.com
Publication Website: https://springviewherald.zenfolio.com/
Editor Email: editor@springviewherald.com
Delivery Methods: Mail`Newsstand`Racks
Year Established: 1886
Mechanical specifications: Type page 11 1/2 x 16; E - 5 cols, 2, 1/16 between; A - 5 cols, 2, 1/16 between; C - 5 cols, 2, 1/16 between.
Published Days: Wed
Avg. Paid Circ.: 750
Avg. Free Circ.: 25
Audit Company: Sworn/Estimate/Non-Audited
Audit Date: 43626

STAPLETON

STAPLETON ENTERPRISE

Street Address: 238 Main St, P.O. Box 98
City: Stapleton
State: NE
ZIP Code: 69163-9701
General Phone: (308) 636-2444
General Email: stapleton@bytz.net
Publication Website: https://creativeprintersonline.com/stapleton-enterprise
Parent Company: The Arnold Sentinel LLC
Delivery Methods: Mail`Newsstand`Racks
Year Established: 1912
Own Printing Facility?: Y
Commercial printers?: Y
Mechanical specifications: Type page 11 1/2 x 17; E - 6 cols, 2, 1/2 between; A - 6 cols, between; C - 6 cols, between.
Published Days: Thur
Avg. Paid Circ.: 650
Audit Company: Sworn/Estimate/Non-

Community Newspapers in the U.S.

III-323

Audited
Audit Date: 43626

STAPLETON

THOMAS COUNTY HERALD

Street Address: 238 Main St, P.O. Box 98
City: Stapleton
State: NE
ZIP Code: 69163-9701
General Phone: (308) 636-2444
General Email: creativeprinters@gpcom.net
Publication Website: https://creativeprintersonline.com/thomas-county-herald
Parent Company: The Arnold Sentinel LLC
Delivery Methods: Mail`Newsstand`Racks
Own Printing Facility?: Y
Commercial printers?: Y
Mechanical specifications: Type page 11 x 16; E - 5 cols, 2, between; A - 5 cols, 2, between; C - 5 cols, 2, between.
Published Days: Thur
Avg. Paid Circ.: 600
Audit Company: Sworn/Estimate/Non-Audited
Audit Date: 43626

STROMSBURG

POLK COUNTY NEWS

Street Address: PO Box 365
City: Stromsburg
State: NE
ZIP Code: 68666-0365
General Phone: (402) 764-5341
General Email: polkcountynews@yahoo.com
Publication Website: https://polkcountynewspaper.com/
Published Days: Thur
Avg. Paid Circ.: 1800
Avg. Free Circ.: 20
Audit Company: Sworn/Estimate/Non-Audited
Audit Date: 43626

SUTHERLAND

THE COURIER-TIMES

Street Address: 824 1st St
City: Sutherland
State: NE
ZIP Code: 69165-2155
General Phone: (308) 386-4617
General Email: suthcourier@gpcom.net
Publication Website: https://www.thecouriertimes.com/
Delivery Methods: Mail`Racks
Year Established: 1895
Mechanical specifications: Type page 10 x 20; E - 6 cols, 1.5, 1/6 between; A - 6 cols, 1.5, 1/6 between; C - 6 cols, 1.5, 1/6 between.
Published Days: Thur
Avg. Paid Circ.: 1200
Audit Company: Sworn/Estimate/Non-Audited
Audit Date: 43626

SUTTON

CLAY COUNTY NEWS

Street Address: 207 N Saunders Ave
City: Sutton
State: NE
ZIP Code: 68979-2511
General Phone: (402) 773-5576
General Email: ccntory@gmail.com
Publication Website: https://www.theclaycountynews.com/
Editor Name: Tory Duncan
Editor Email: ccntory@gmail.com
Editor Phone: (402) 773-5576
Advertising Executive Name: Ashley D. Swanson
Advertising Executive Email: ccnadvertising@gmail.com
Advertising Executive Phone: (402) 773-5576
Delivery Methods: Mail`Newsstand`Racks
Year Established: 1875
Mechanical specifications: Type page 12 7/8 x 21; E - 6 cols, 13, 1/6 between; A - 6 cols, 1/6 between; C - 6 cols, 1/6 between.
Published Days: Thur
Avg. Paid Circ.: 2805
Avg. Free Circ.: 50
Audit Company: Sworn/Estimate/Non-Audited
Audit Date: 43626

SYRACUSE

SYRACUSE JOURNAL-DEMOCRAT

Street Address: 123 W 17th St
City: Syracuse
State: NE
ZIP Code: 68446
General Phone: (402) 269-2135
General Email: tkaven@ncnewspress.com
Publication Website: https://www.journaldemocrat.com/
Publisher Name: Tammy Schumacher
Publisher Email: tschumacher@ncnewspress.com
Publisher Phone: (402) 873-3334
Editor Name: Kirt Manion
Editor Email: kmanion@ncnewspress.com
Editor Phone: (402) 873-3334
Advertising Executive Name: Theresa Kaven
Advertising Executive Email: tkaven@ncnewspress.com
Advertising Executive Phone: (402) 269-2135
Delivery Methods: Mail`Newsstand`Racks
Year Established: 1876
Own Printing Facility?: Y
Commercial printers?: Y
Published Days: Thur
Avg. Paid Circ.: 1550
Avg. Free Circ.: 74
Audit Company: Sworn/Estimate/Non-Audited
Audit Date: 43626

TECUMSEH

THE TECUMSEH CHIEFTAIN

Street Address: 241 Clay St
City: Tecumseh
State: NE
ZIP Code: 68450-2317
General Phone: (402) 335-3394
General Email: ads@tecumsehchieftain.com
Publication Website: https://www.tecumsehchieftain.com/
Parent Company: Sunrise Publications, Inc
Advertising Executive Name: Elaine Karel
Advertising Executive Email: ads@tecumsehchieftain.com
Advertising Executive Phone: (402) 335-3394
Delivery Methods: Mail`Newsstand`Racks
Own Printing Facility?: Y
Commercial printers?: Y
Mechanical specifications: Type page 13 x 21 1/2; E - 6 cols, 2 1/16, 1/8 between; A - 6 cols, 2 1/16, between; C - 6 cols, 2 1/16, between.
Published Days: Thur
Avg. Paid Circ.: 1630
Audit Company: Sworn/Estimate/Non-Audited
Audit Date: 43626

TEKAMAH

BURT COUNTY PLAINDEALER

Street Address: 707 S 13th St
City: Tekamah
State: NE
ZIP Code: 68061-1326
General Phone: (402) 374-2226
General Email: deanna.ray@lee.net
Publication Website: https://www.agupdate.com/community/burt_county/
Publisher Name: Mike Wood
Publisher Email: mike.wood@lee.net
Editor Name: Katy Moore
Editor Email: katy.moore@lee.net
Advertising Executive Name: Deanna Ray
Advertising Executive Email: deanna.ray@lee.net
Delivery Methods: Mail`Newsstand`Racks
Year Established: 1934
Own Printing Facility?: Y
Commercial printers?: Y
Mechanical specifications: Type page 9(13/16) x 21; 5-column.
Published Days: Wed
Avg. Paid Circ.: 1057
Avg. Free Circ.: 121
Audit Company: Sworn/Estimate/Non-Audited
Audit Date: 43626

TEKAMAH

MIDWEST MESSENGER

Street Address: 707 S 13th St
City: Tekamah
State: NE
ZIP Code: 68061-1326
General Phone: (402) 374-2226
General Email: deanna.ray@midwestmessenger.com
Publication Website: https://www.agupdate.com/midwestmessenger/
Publisher Name: Mike Wood
Publisher Email: mike.wood@lee.net
Editor Name: Katy Moore
Editor Email: katy.moore@lee.net
Advertising Executive Name: Deanna Ray
Advertising Executive Email: deanna.ray@lee.net
Delivery Methods: Mail`Racks
Year Established: 1968
Published Days: Bi-Mthly
Avg. Free Circ.: 100000
Audit Company: Sworn/Estimate/Non-Audited
Audit Date: 43626

TRENTON

HITCHOCK COUNTY NEWS

Street Address: 346 Main St
City: Trenton
State: NE
ZIP Code: 69044-1809
General Phone: (308) 334-5226
General Email: bpwebupdates@gmail.com
Publication Website: https://www.scoopmedianews.com/
Publisher Name: Amy Frederick
Publisher Phone: (308) 340-4648
Advertising Executive Name: Sally Hudson
Published Days: Wed
Avg. Paid Circ.: 1142
Avg. Free Circ.: 21
Audit Company: Sworn/Estimate/Non-Audited
Audit Date: 43626

VALENTINE

VALENTINE MIDLAND NEWS

Street Address: 146 W 2nd St, P.O. Box 448
City: Valentine
State: NE
ZIP Code: 69201-1822
General Phone: (402) 376-2833
General Email: valentinenews@valentinenews.com
Publication Website: https://www.ainsworthnews.com/valentine-midland-news
Parent Company: Ainsworth News
Publisher Name: Brook D. Curtiss
Editor Name: Laura Vroman
Editor Email: valentinenews@valentinenews.com
Advertising Executive Name: Cindy Poessnecker
Advertising Executive Email: news@atkinsongraphic.com
Year Established: 1989
Own Printing Facility?: Y
Commercial printers?: Y
Mechanical specifications: Type page 15 x 21 3/4; A - 7 cols, 2, 1/6 between; C - 7 cols, 2, 1/6 between.
Published Days: Wed
Avg. Paid Circ.: 2050
Audit Company: Sworn/Estimate/Non-Audited
Audit Date: 43626

WAKEFIELD

THE WAKEFIELD REPUBLICAN

Street Address: 201 Main St
City: Wakefield
State: NE
ZIP Code: 68784
General Phone: (402) 287-2323
General Email: wakenews@huntel.net
Publication Website: http://www.wakefieldrepublican.com/
Delivery Methods: Mail`Newsstand
Year Established: 1882
Mechanical specifications: Type page 10 x 15 1/2; E - 5 cols, 1 11/12, 1/8 between; A - 5 cols, 1 11/12, 1/8 between; C - 5 cols, 1 11/12, 1/8 between.
Published Days: Thur
Avg. Paid Circ.: 1050
Avg. Free Circ.: 50
Audit Company: Sworn/Estimate/Non-Audited
Audit Date: 43626

WAUNETA

THE WAUNETA BREEZE

Street Address: 324 N Tecumseh
City: Wauneta
State: NE
ZIP Code: 69045-9509
General Phone: (308) 394-5389
General Email: breeze.office@jpipapers.com
Publication Website: https://www.waunetanebraska.com/
Parent Company: Johnson Publications
Publisher Name: Lori Pankonin
Delivery Methods: Mail`Racks
Year Established: 1887
Own Printing Facility?: Y
Commercial printers?: Y
Published Days: Thur
Avg. Paid Circ.: 817
Audit Company: Sworn/Estimate/Non-Audited
Audit Date: 43626

WAYNE

THE WAYNE HERALD

Street Address: 114 Main St
City: Wayne
State: NE
ZIP Code: 68787-1940
General Phone: (402) 375-2600
General Email: melissa@wayneherald.com
Publication Website: http://mywaynenews.com/
Parent Company: Smith Newspapers
Publisher Name: Kevin Peterson
Publisher Email: kevin@wayneherald.com
Editor Name: Sarah Lentz

Community Newspapers in the U.S.

Editor Email: editor@wayneherald.com
Advertising Executive Name: Jan Stark
Advertising Executive Email: whclass@inebraska.com
Delivery Methods: Mail`Newsstand`Racks
Own Printing Facility?: Y
Mechanical specifications: Type page 13 x 21 1/2; E - 6 cols, 2, 1/16 between; A - 6 cols, 2, 1/16 between; C - 6 cols, 2, 1/16 between.
Published Days: Thur
Avg. Paid Circ.: 2100
Audit Company: Sworn/Estimate/Non-Audited
Audit Date: 43626

WEST POINT

WEST POINT NEWS

Street Address: 134 E Grove St
City: West Point
State: NE
ZIP Code: 68788-1823
General Phone: (402) 372-2461
General Email: admanager@wpnews.com
Publication Website: http://www.wpnews.com/
Parent Company: Tom Kelly
Publisher Name: Tom Kelly
Publisher Email: publisher@wpnews.com
Editor Name: Willis Mahannah
Editor Email: editor@wpnews.com
Advertising Executive Name: Karey Rahn
Advertising Executive Email: admanager@wpnews.com
Delivery Methods: Mail`Newsstand`Racks
Year Established: 1869
Own Printing Facility?: Y
Commercial printers?: Y
Published Days: Wed
Avg. Paid Circ.: 2500
Avg. Free Circ.: 165
Audit Company: Sworn/Estimate/Non-Audited
Audit Date: 43626

WISNER

WISNER NEWS-CHRONICLE

Street Address: 1014 Avenue E
City: Wisner
State: NE
ZIP Code: 68791-2248
General Phone: (402) 529-3228
General Email: admanager@wpnews.com
Publication Website: http://www.wpnews.com/
Parent Company: Tom Kelly
Publisher Name: Tom Kelly
Publisher Email: publisher@wpnews.com
Editor Name: Willis Mahannah
Editor Email: editor@wpnews.com
Advertising Executive Name: Karey Rahn
Advertising Executive Email: admanager@wpnews.com
Mechanical specifications: Type page 13 x 21 1/2; E - 6 cols, 2 1/12, 1/6 between; A - 6 cols, 2 1/12, 1/6 between; C - 6 cols, 2 1/12, 1/6 between.
Published Days: Thur
Avg. Paid Circ.: 1991
Avg. Free Circ.: 30
Audit Company: Sworn/Estimate/Non-Audited
Audit Date: 43626

NEW HAMPSHIRE

AMHERST

AMHERST CITIZEN

Street Address: 16 Pine Acres Rd
City: Amherst
State: NH
ZIP Code: 3031
General Phone: (603) 672-9444
General Email: ads@amherstcitizen.com
Publication Website: http://amherstcitizen.com/
Parent Company: None

BERLIN

THE BERLIN DAILY SUN

Street Address: 164 MAIN ST
City: BERLIN
State: NH
ZIP Code: 3570
General Phone: (603) 752-5858
General Email: bds@berlindailysun.com
Publication Website: https://www.conwaydailysun.com/berlin_sun/site/contact.html

COLEBROOK

THE NEWS AND SENTINEL

Street Address: 6 Bridge St
City: Colebrook
State: NH
ZIP Code: 3576
General Phone: (603) 237-5501
General Email: butchladd@colebrooknewsandsentinel.com
Publication Website: http://www.colbsent.com/
Parent Company: The Fort Wayne Daily News

DERRY

DERRY NEWS

Street Address: 46 W Broadway
City: Derry
State: NH
ZIP Code: 3038
General Phone: (603) 437-7000
General Email: advertising@derrynews.com
Publication Website: http://www.derrynews.com/
Parent Company: CNHI, LLC

HILLSBOROUGH

MESSENGER

Street Address: 246 W Main St
City: Hillsborough
State: NH
ZIP Code: 3244
General Phone: (603) 464-3388
General Email: granitequill@mcttelecom.com
Publication Website: http://granitequill.com/about/
Parent Company: Paxton Media Group

HUDSON

HUDSON-LITCHFIELD NEWS

Street Address: 17 Executive Drive, Suite One
City: Hudson
State: NH
ZIP Code: 3051
General Phone: (603) 880-1516
General Email: sales@areanewsgroup.com
Publication Website: http://www.areanewsgroup.com/
Parent Company: Area News Group

HUDSON

PELHAM/WINDHAM NEWS

Street Address: 17 Executive Drive, Suite One
City: Hudson
State: NH
ZIP Code: 3051
General Phone: (603) 880-1516
General Email: sales@areanewsgroup.com
Publication Website: http://www.areanewsgroup.com/
Parent Company: Area News Group

HUDSON

SALEM COMMUNITY PATRIOT

Street Address: 17 Executive Drive, Suite One
City: Hudson
State: NH
ZIP Code: 3051
General Phone: (603) 880-1516
General Email: news@areanewsgroup.com
Publication Website: http://www.areanewsgroup.com/
Parent Company: Area News Group

KEENE

MONADNOCK SHOPPER NEWS

Street Address: 445 West St
City: Keene
State: NH
ZIP Code: 3431
General Phone: (603) 352-5250
General Email: sales@shoppernews.com
Publication Website: http://www.shoppernews.com

KINGSTON

CARRIAGE TOWNE NEWS

Street Address: 14 Church St
City: Kingston
State: NH
ZIP Code: 3848
General Phone: (603) 642-4499
General Email: advertise@carriagetownenews.com
Publication Website: http://www.carriagetownenews.com/
Parent Company: North of Boston Media Group

LACONIA

THE WEIRS TIMES

Street Address: 515 Endicott St N
City: Laconia
State: NH
ZIP Code: 3246
General Phone: (603) 366-8463
General Email: advertise@weirs.com
Publication Website: https://weirs.com/
Parent Company: Weirs Publishing Company Inc

LONDONDERRY

LONDONDERRY TIMES

Street Address: 2 Litchfield Rd
City: Londonderry
State: NH
ZIP Code: 3053
General Phone: (603) 537-2760
General Email: dpaul@nutpub.com
Publication Website: http://londonderrytimes.net/
Parent Company: Nutfield Publishing, LLC

LONDONDERRY

NUTFIELD NEWS

Street Address: 2 Litchfield Rd
City: Londonderry
State: NH
ZIP Code: 3053
General Phone: (603) 537-2760
General Email: dpaul@nutpub.com
Publication Website: http://nutfieldnews.net/
Parent Company: Nutfield Publishing, LLC

LONDONDERRY

TRI-TOWN TIMES

Street Address: 2 Litchfield Rd
City: Londonderry
State: NH
ZIP Code: 3053
General Phone: (603) 537-2760
General Email: dpaul@nutpub.com
Publication Website: http://tritowntimes.net/
Parent Company: Nutfield Publishing, LLC

MANCHESTER

GOFFSTOWN NEWS

Street Address: 100 William Loeb Dr
City: Manchester
State: NH
ZIP Code: 3109
General Phone: (603) 206-7800
General Email: ul@unionleader.com
Publication Website: https://www.unionleader.com/nni/goffstown_news/
Parent Company: Union Leader Corp.

MEREDITH

PLYMOUTH RECORD ENTERPRISE

Street Address: 5 Water St
City: Meredith
State: NH
ZIP Code: 3253
General Phone: (603) 279-4516
General Email: courierstj@salmonpress.com
Publication Website: http://www.newhampshirelakesandmountains.com/Site.Home.html
Parent Company: Salmon Press LLC

NORTH SUTTON

INTERTOWN RECORD

Street Address: 1719 Route 114
City: North Sutton
State: NH
ZIP Code: 3260
General Phone: (603) 927-4028
General Email: info@intertownrecord.com
Publication Website: https://www.intertownrecord.com/

PETERBOROUGH

MONADNOCK LEDGER-TRANSCRIPT

Street Address: P.O. Box 36
City: Peterborough
State: NH
ZIP Code: 3458
General Phone: (603) 924-7172
General Email: ads@ledgertranscript.com

Community Newspapers in the U.S.

Publication Website: https://www.ledgertranscript.com/
Parent Company: Newspapers of New England

PORTSMOUTH

EXETER NEWS-LETTER

Street Address: 111 NH Ave
City: Portsmouth
State: NH
ZIP Code: 3801
General Phone: (800) 439-0303
General Email: sales@seacoastonline.com
Publication Website: https://www.seacoastonline.com/ExeterNewsLetter
Parent Company: Gannett

PORTSMOUTH

THE HAMPTON UNION

Street Address: 111 NH Ave
City: Portsmouth
State: NH
ZIP Code: 3801
General Phone: (800) 439-0303
General Email: hamptonunion@seacoastonline.com
Publication Website: https://www.seacoastonline.com/
Parent Company: Gannett

PORTSMOUTH

THE YORK WEEKLY

Street Address: 111 NH Ave
City: Portsmouth
State: NH
ZIP Code: 3801
General Phone: (800) 439-0303
General Email: adreps@seacoastonline.com
Publication Website: https://www.seacoastonline.com/yorkweekly
Parent Company: Gannett

NEW JERSEY

ASBURY PARK

COASTER

Street Address: 1011 Main St
City: Asbury Park
State: NJ
ZIP Code: 07712-5963
General Phone: (732) 775-3010
General Email: editor@thecoaster.net
Publication Website: http://thecoaster.net/wordpress/
Advertising Executive Name: Joe Garrett
Advertising Executive Email: joeg@thecoaster.net
Advertising Executive Phone: (973) 906-3488

BAYONNE

SECAUCUS REPORTER

Street Address: 447 Broadway
City: Bayonne
State: NJ
ZIP Code: 7002
General Phone: (201) 798-7800
General Email: info@hudsonreporter.com
Publication Website: https://hudsonreporter.com/category/news/secaucus-news/
Parent Company: Newspaper Media Group
Editor Name: Gene Ritchings
Editor Email: gener@hudsonreporter.com
Editor Phone: (201) 798-7800, ext : 610
Advertising Executive Name: Tish Kraszyk
Advertising Executive Email: tishk@hudsonreporter.com
Advertising Executive Phone: (201) 798-7800, ext : 601

CHERRY HILL

BURLINGTON TOWNSHIP SUN

Street Address: Two Executive Campus, Suite 400
City: Cherry Hill
State: NJ
ZIP Code: 8002
General Phone: (856) 779-3800
General Email: news@burlingtontownshipsun.com
Publication Website: https://thesunpapers.com/burlington-twp-sun/
Parent Company: Newspaper Media Group
Publisher Name: Arlene Reyes
Publisher Email: areyes@newspapermediagroup.com
Publisher Phone: (856) 282-1347
Editor Name: Arlene Reyes
Editor Email: areyes@newspapermediagroup.com
Editor Phone: (856) 282-1347
Advertising Executive Name: Kristen Dowd
Advertising Executive Email: kdowd@newspapermediagroup.com
Advertising Executive Phone: (856) 270-7037

CHERRY HILL

CHERRY HILL SUN

Street Address: Two Executive Campus, Suite 400
City: Cherry Hill
State: NJ
ZIP Code: 8002
General Phone: (856) 779-3800
General Email: news@cherryhillsun.com
Publication Website: https://thesunpapers.com/cherry-hill-sun/
Parent Company: Newspaper Media Group
Publisher Name: Arlene Reyes
Publisher Email: areyes@newspapermediagroup.com
Publisher Phone: (856) 282-1347
Editor Name: Arlene Reyes
Editor Email: areyes@newspapermediagroup.com
Editor Phone: (856) 282-1347
Advertising Executive Name: Kristen Dowd
Advertising Executive Email: kdowd@newspapermediagroup.com
Advertising Executive Phone: (856) 270-7037

CHERRY HILL

CINNAMINSON SUN

Street Address: Two Executive Campus, Suite 400
City: Cherry Hill
State: NJ
ZIP Code: 8002
General Phone: (856) 779-3800
General Email: news@cinnaminsonsun.com
Publication Website: https://thesunpapers.com/cinnaminson-sun/
Parent Company: Newspaper Media Group
Publisher Name: Arlene Reyes
Publisher Email: areyes@newspapermediagroup.com
Publisher Phone: (856) 282-1347
Editor Name: Arlene Reyes
Editor Email: areyes@newspapermediagroup.com
Editor Phone: (856) 282-1347
Advertising Executive Name: Kristen Dowd
Advertising Executive Email: kdowd@newspapermediagroup.com
Advertising Executive Phone: (856) 270-7037

CHERRY HILL

HADDONFIELD SUN

Street Address: Two Executive Campus, Suite 400
City: Cherry Hill
State: NJ
ZIP Code: 8002
General Phone: (856) 779-3800
General Email: news@haddonfieldsun.com
Publication Website: https://thesunpapers.com/haddonfield-sun/
Parent Company: Newspaper Media Group
Publisher Name: Arlene Reyes
Publisher Email: areyes@newspapermediagroup.com
Publisher Phone: (856) 282-1347
Editor Name: Arlene Reyes
Editor Email: areyes@newspapermediagroup.com
Editor Phone: (856) 282-1347
Advertising Executive Name: Kristen Dowd
Advertising Executive Email: kdowd@newspapermediagroup.com
Advertising Executive Phone: (856) 270-7037

CHERRY HILL

JEWISH VOICE

Street Address: 1301 Springdale Road, Suite 250
City: Cherry Hill
State: NJ
ZIP Code: 08003-2762
General Phone: (856) 751-9500, ext : 1217
General Email: jvoice@jfedsnj.org
Publication Website: http://www.jewishvoicesnj.org/
Parent Company: Jewish Federation of South New Jersey
Editor Name: David Portnoe
Editor Email: dportnoe@jfedsnj.org
Editor Phone: (856) 751-9500, ext : 1237
Advertising Executive Name: Sally Grossman
Advertising Executive Email: sgrossman@jfedsnj.org
Advertising Executive Phone: (856) 751-9500, ext : 1279

CHERRY HILL

MARLTON SUN

Street Address: Two Executive Campus, Suite 400
City: Cherry Hill
State: NJ
ZIP Code: 8002
General Phone: (856) 779-3800
General Email: news@marltonsun.com
Publication Website: https://thesunpapers.com/marlton-sun/
Parent Company: Newspaper Media Group
Publisher Name: Arlene Reyes
Publisher Email: areyes@newspapermediagroup.com
Publisher Phone: (856) 282-1347
Editor Name: Arlene Reyes
Editor Email: areyes@newspapermediagroup.com
Editor Phone: (856) 282-1347
Advertising Executive Name: Kristen Dowd
Advertising Executive Email: kdowd@newspapermediagroup.com
Advertising Executive Phone: (856) 270-7037

CHERRY HILL

MEDFORD SUN

Street Address: Two Executive Campus, Suite 400
City: Cherry Hill
State: NJ
ZIP Code: 8002
General Phone: (856) 779-3800
General Email: news@medfordsun.com
Publication Website: https://thesunpapers.com/medford-sun/
Parent Company: Newspaper Media Group
Publisher Name: Arlene Reyes
Publisher Email: areyes@newspapermediagroup.com
Publisher Phone: (856) 282-1347
Editor Name: Arlene Reyes
Editor Email: areyes@newspapermediagroup.com
Editor Phone: (856) 282-1347
Advertising Executive Name: Kristen Dowd
Advertising Executive Email: kdowd@newspapermediagroup.com
Advertising Executive Phone: (856) 270-7037

CHERRY HILL

MOORESTOWN SUN

Street Address: Two Executive Campus, Suite 400
City: Cherry Hill
State: NJ
ZIP Code: 8002
General Phone: (856) 779-3800
General Email: news@moorestownsun.com
Publication Website: https://thesunpapers.com/moorestown-sun/
Parent Company: Newspaper Media Group
Publisher Name: Arlene Reyes
Publisher Email: areyes@newspapermediagroup.com
Publisher Phone: (856) 282-1347
Editor Name: Arlene Reyes
Editor Email: areyes@newspapermediagroup.com
Editor Phone: (856) 282-1347
Advertising Executive Name: Kristen Dowd
Advertising Executive Email: kdowd@newspapermediagroup.com
Advertising Executive Phone: (856) 270-7037

CHERRY HILL

MT. LAUREL SUN

Street Address: Two Executive Campus, Suite 400
City: Cherry Hill
State: NJ
ZIP Code: 8002
General Phone: (856) 779-3800
General Email: news@mtlaurelsun.com
Publication Website: https://thesunpapers.com/mt-laurel-sun/
Parent Company: Newspaper Media Group
Publisher Name: Arlene Reyes
Publisher Email: areyes@newspapermediagroup.com
Publisher Phone: (856) 282-1347
Editor Name: Arlene Reyes
Editor Email: areyes@newspapermediagroup.com
Editor Phone: (856) 282-1347
Advertising Executive Name: Kristen Dowd
Advertising Executive Email: kdowd@newspapermediagroup.com
Advertising Executive Phone: (856) 270-7037

CHERRY HILL

NORTHEAST TIMES

Street Address: 2 Executive Campus, Suite 400
City: Cherry Hill
State: NJ
ZIP Code: 8002
General Phone: (215) 354-3000
General Email: kstuski@bsmphilly.com

CHERRY HILL

NORTHEAST TIMES

Street Address: 2 Executive Campus, Suite 400
City: Cherry Hill
State: NJ
ZIP Code: 8002
General Phone: (215) 355-9009
General Email: info@northeasttimes.com
Publication Website: https://northeasttimes.com/
Parent Company: Newspaper Media Group
Publisher Name: Brandon Chamberlain
Publisher Email: bchamberlain@bsmphilly.com
Editor Name: Melissa Mitman
Editor Email: mmitman@bsmphilly.com
Delivery Methods: Carrier
Year Established: 1937
Own Printing Facility?: Y
Commercial printers?: N
Mechanical specifications: 9.5"w x 10.66"h
Published Days: Wed
Avg. Paid Circ.: 1025
Avg. Free Circ.: 109074
Audit Company: Sworn/Estimate/Non-Audited
Audit Date: 43626

CHERRY HILL

PALMYRA SUN

Street Address: Two Executive Campus, Suite 400
City: Cherry Hill
State: NJ
ZIP Code: 8002
General Phone: (856) 779-3800
General Email: news@palmyrasun.com
Publication Website: https://thesunpapers.com/palmyra-sun/
Parent Company: Newspaper Media Group
Publisher Name: Arlene Reyes
Publisher Email: areyes@newspapermediagroup.com
Publisher Phone: (856) 282-1347
Editor Name: Arlene Reyes
Editor Email: areyes@newspapermediagroup.com
Editor Phone: (856) 282-1347
Advertising Executive Name: Kristen Dowd
Advertising Executive Email: kdowd@newspapermediagroup.com
Advertising Executive Phone: (856) 270-7037

CHERRY HILL

SHAMONG SUN

Street Address: Two Executive Campus, Suite 400
City: Cherry Hill
State: NJ
ZIP Code: 8002
General Phone: (856) 779-3800
General Email: news@shamongsun.com
Publication Website: https://thesunpapers.com/shamong-sun/
Parent Company: Newspaper Media Group
Publisher Name: Arlene Reyes
Publisher Email: areyes@newspapermediagroup.com
Publisher Phone: (856) 282-1347
Editor Name: Arlene Reyes
Editor Email: areyes@newspapermediagroup.com
Editor Phone: (856) 282-1347
Advertising Executive Name: Kristen Dowd
Advertising Executive Email: kdowd@newspapermediagroup.com
Advertising Executive Phone: (856) 270-7037

CHERRY HILL

SICKLERVILLE SUN

Street Address: Two Executive Campus, Suite 400
City: Cherry Hill
State: NJ
ZIP Code: 8002
General Phone: (856) 779-3800
General Email: news@sicklervillesun.com
Publication Website: https://thesunpapers.com/sicklerville-sun/
Parent Company: Newspaper Media Group
Publisher Name: Arlene Reyes
Publisher Email: areyes@newspapermediagroup.com
Publisher Phone: (856) 282-1347
Editor Name: Arlene Reyes
Editor Email: areyes@newspapermediagroup.com
Editor Phone: (856) 282-1347
Advertising Executive Name: Kristen Dowd
Advertising Executive Email: kdowd@newspapermediagroup.com
Advertising Executive Phone: (856) 270-7037

CHERRY HILL

SOUTH PHILLY REVIEW

Street Address: Two Executive Campus, Suite 135
City: Cherry Hill
State: NJ
ZIP Code: 8002
General Phone: (856) 779-3800
Publication Website: https://southphillyreview.com/
Parent Company: Newspaper Media Group
Advertising Executive Name: Deidre Simms
Advertising Executive Email: dsimms@newspapermediagroup.com
Advertising Executive Phone: (917) 692-3221

CHERRY HILL

STAR COMMUNITY NEWSWEEKLY

Street Address: 2 Executive Campus, Suite 135
City: Cherry Hill
State: NJ
ZIP Code: 8002
General Phone: (215) 354-3000
General Email: star@bsmphilly.com
Publication Website: https://starnewsphilly.com/
Parent Company: Newspaper Media Group
Publisher Name: Tom Waring
Publisher Email: twaring@bsmphilly.com
Editor Name: Melissa Mitman
Editor Email: mmitman@bsmphilly.com
Delivery Methods: Carrier
Year Established: 1982
Own Printing Facility?: N
Commercial printers?: N
Mechanical specifications: 10" x 10" full page
Published Days: Wed Thur
Avg. Free Circ.: 27275
Audit Company: Sworn/Estimate/Non-Audited
Audit Date: 43626

CHERRY HILL

TABERNACLE SUN

Street Address: Two Executive Campus, Suite 400
City: Cherry Hill
State: NJ
ZIP Code: 8002
General Phone: (856) 779-3800
General Email: news@tabernaclesun.com
Publication Website: https://thesunpapers.com/tabernacle-sun/
Parent Company: Newspaper Media Group
Publisher Name: Arlene Reyes
Publisher Email: areyes@newspapermediagroup.com
Publisher Phone: (856) 282-1347
Editor Name: Arlene Reyes
Editor Email: areyes@newspapermediagroup.com
Editor Phone: (856) 282-1347
Advertising Executive Name: Kristen Dowd
Advertising Executive Email: kdowd@newspapermediagroup.com
Advertising Executive Phone: (856) 270-7037

CHERRY HILL

THE BERLIN SUN

Street Address: Two Executive Campus, Suite 400
City: Cherry Hill
State: NJ
ZIP Code: 8002
General Phone: (856) 779-3800
General Email: news@theberlinsun.com
Publication Website: https://thesunpapers.com/berlin-sun/
Parent Company: Newspaper Media Group
Publisher Name: Arlene Reyes
Publisher Email: areyes@newspapermediagroup.com
Publisher Phone: (856) 282-1347
Editor Name: Arlene Reyes
Editor Email: areyes@newspapermediagroup.com
Editor Phone: (856) 282-1347
Advertising Executive Name: Kristen Dowd
Advertising Executive Email: kdowd@newspapermediagroup.com
Advertising Executive Phone: (856) 270-7037

CHERRY HILL

VOORHEES SUN

Street Address: Two Executive Campus, Suite 400
City: Cherry Hill
State: NJ
ZIP Code: 8002
General Phone: (856) 779-3800
General Email: news@voorheessun.com
Publication Website: https://thesunpapers.com/voorhees-sun/
Parent Company: Newspaper Media Group
Publisher Name: Arlene Reyes
Publisher Email: areyes@newspapermediagroup.com
Publisher Phone: (856) 282-1347
Editor Name: Arlene Reyes
Editor Email: areyes@newspapermediagroup.com
Editor Phone: (856) 282-1347
Advertising Executive Name: Kristen Dowd
Advertising Executive Email: kdowd@newspapermediagroup.com
Advertising Executive Phone: (856) 270-7037

COLLINGSWOOD

THE RETROSPECT

Street Address: 732 Haddon Ave
City: Collingswood
State: NJ
ZIP Code: 8108
General Phone: (856) 854-1400
General Email: publisher@theretrospect.com
Publication Website: http://theretrospect.com
Parent Company: Ainsworth Media, Inc
Publisher Name: Brett Ainsworth
Publisher Email: publisher@theretrospect.com
Publisher Phone: (856) 854-1400
Editor Name: Brett Ainsworth
Editor Email: publisher@theretrospect.com
Editor Phone: (856) 854-1400

ELMER

ELMER TIMES

Street Address: 21 State St
City: Elmer
State: NJ
ZIP Code: 8318
General Phone: (856) 358-6171
General Email: elmertimesco@aol.com
Publication Website: http://www.elmerboroughnj.com/ElmerTimes.html

FLEMINGTON

HUNTERDON OBSERVER

Street Address: 18 Minneakoning Rd
City: Flemington
State: NJ
ZIP Code: 08822-5725
General Phone: (800) 300-9321
General Email: news@hcdemocrat.com
Publication Website: https://www.nj.com/hunterdon-county-democrat/
Parent Company: Advance Local Media LLC

GLOUCESTER CITY

GLOUCESTER CITY NEWS

Street Address: 34 S Broadway, P.O. Box 151
City: Gloucester City
State: NJ
ZIP Code: 8030
General Phone: (856) 456-1199
General Email: gcneditor@verizon.net
Publication Website: https://gloucestercitynews.org/
Parent Company: Gloucester City News
Publisher Name: Albert Countryman
Editor Name: Albert Countryman
Editor Email: gcneditor@verizon.net

HAMMONTON

HAMMONTON NEWS

Street Address: 115 12th St.
City: Hammonton
State: NJ
ZIP Code: 8037
General Phone: (856) 563-5248
Publication Website: https://www.thehammontonnews.com/
Publisher Name: Joseph Calchi
Editor Name: John Garrahan
Advertising Executive Phone: (609) 561-2300

ISELIN

LEDGER SOMERSET OBSERVER

Street Address: 485 Route 1 S
City: Iselin
State: NJ
ZIP Code: 8830
General Phone: (732) 902-4372
General Email: northjerseymediagroup@gannett.com
Publication Website: nj.com
Advertising Executive Name: Jason Goldman
Advertising Executive Email: jgoldman@njadvancemedia.com

Community Newspapers in the U.S.

ISELIN

STAR-GAZETTE

Street Address: 485 Route 1 S
City: Iselin
State: NJ
ZIP Code: 8830
General Phone: (732) 902-4372
General Email: northjerseymediagroup@gannett.com
Publication Website: nj.com
Advertising Executive Name: Jason Goldman
Advertising Executive Email: jgoldman@njadvancemedia.com

KINGSTON

TOWN TOPICS

Street Address: 4438 Route 27
City: Kingston
State: NJ
ZIP Code: 08528-9613
General Phone: (609) 924-2200
General Email: editor@towntopics.com
Publication Website: http://www.towntopics.com/
Parent Company: Witherspoon Media Group
Publisher Name: Lynn Adams Smith
Editor Name: Laurie Pellichero
Editor Email: editor@towntopics.com
Editor Phone: (609) 924-2200, ext : 26
Advertising Executive Name: Monica Sankey
Advertising Executive Email: monica.sankey@witherspoonmediagroup.com
Advertising Executive Phone: (609) 924-5400, ext : 21

LAWRENCE

BORDENTOWN CURRENT

Street Address: 15 Princess Rd
City: Lawrence
State: NJ
ZIP Code: 08648-2301
General Phone: (609) 396-1511
General Email: advertise@communitynews.org
Publication Website: https://communitynews.org/bordentown-current/
Parent Company: Community News Service, LLC

LAWRENCE

COMMUNITY NEWS SERVICE - HAMILTON POST

Street Address: 15 Princess Rd
City: Lawrence
State: NJ
ZIP Code: 08648-2301
General Phone: (609) 396-1511
General Email: advertise@communitynews.org
Publication Website: https://communitynews.org/hamilton-post/
Parent Company: Community News Service, LLC

LAWRENCE

HAMILTON POST

Street Address: 15 Princess Road
City: Lawrence
State: NJ
ZIP Code: 8648
General Phone: (609) 396-1511
General Email: advertise@communitynews.org
Publication Website: https://communitynews.org/hamilton-post/
Parent Company: Community News Service, LLC
Advertising Executive Email: advertise@communitynews.org

LAWRENCE

LAWRENCE GAZETTE - COMMUNITY NEWS SERVICE

Street Address: 15 Princess Rd
City: Lawrence
State: NJ
ZIP Code: 08648-2301
General Phone: (609) 396-1511
General Email: advertise@communitynews.org
Publication Website: https://communitynews.org/lawrence-gazette/
Parent Company: Community News Service, LLC

LIVINGSTON

WEST ESSEX TRIBUNE

Street Address: 495 S Livingston Ave
City: Livingston
State: NJ
ZIP Code: 07039-0065
General Phone: (973) 992-1771
General Email: wetribune@gmail.com
Publication Website: https://www.westessextribune.net/
Parent Company: West Essex Tribune

MANALAPAN

ATLANTICVILLE

Street Address: 198 Route 9, Suite 100
City: Manalapan
State: NJ
ZIP Code: 7726
General Phone: (732) 358-5200
General Email: feedback@centraljersey.com
Publication Website: https://archive.centraljersey.com/category/atlanticville-news/
Parent Company: Newspaper Media Group
Publisher Name: Joe Eisele
Publisher Email: jeisele@newspapermediagroup.com
Publisher Phone: (732) 358-5200, ext : 8282
Editor Name: Jennifer Amato
Editor Email: jamato@newspapermediagroup.com
Editor Phone: (732) 358-5200, ext : 8223
Advertising Executive Name: Michelle Nesbihal
Advertising Executive Email: mnesbihal@centraljersey.com
Advertising Executive Phone: (856) 237-6025

MANALAPAN

CRANBURY PRESS

Street Address: 198 Route 9, Suite 100
City: Manalapan
State: NJ
ZIP Code: 7726
General Phone: (732) 358-5200
General Email: mnesbihal@centraljersey.com
Publication Website: https://centraljersey.com/cranbury-press/
Parent Company: Newspaper Media Group
Publisher Name: Joe Eisele
Publisher Email: jeisele@newspapermediagroup.com
Publisher Phone: (732) 358-5200, ext : 8282
Editor Name: Mark Rosman
Editor Email: mrosman@newspapermediagroup.com
Editor Phone: (732) 358-5200, ext : 8278
Advertising Executive Name: Michelle Nesbihal
Advertising Executive Email: mnesbihal@centraljersey.com
Advertising Executive Phone: (856) 237-6025

MANALAPAN

EAST BRUNSWICK SENTINEL

Street Address: 198 Route 9, Suite 100
City: Manalapan
State: NJ
ZIP Code: 7726
General Phone: (732) 358-5200
General Email: feedback@centraljersey.com
Publication Website: https://centraljersey.com/eb-sentinel/
Parent Company: Newspaper Media Group
Publisher Name: Joe Eisele
Publisher Email: jeisele@newspapermediagroup.com
Publisher Phone: (732) 358-5200, ext : 8282
Editor Name: Mark Rosman
Editor Email: mrosman@newspapermediagroup.com
Editor Phone: (732) 358-5200, ext : 8278
Advertising Executive Name: Michelle Nesbihal
Advertising Executive Email: mnesbihal@centraljersey.com
Advertising Executive Phone: (856) 237-6025

MANALAPAN

EDISON/NETUCHEN SENTINEL

Street Address: 198 Route 9, Suite 100
City: Manalapan
State: NJ
ZIP Code: 7726
General Phone: (732) 358-5200
General Email: feedback@centraljersey.com
Publication Website: https://centraljersey.com/em-sentinel/
Parent Company: Newspaper Media Group
Publisher Name: Joe Eisele
Publisher Email: jeisele@newspapermediagroup.com
Publisher Phone: (732) 358-5200, ext : 8282
Editor Name: Mark Rosman
Editor Email: mrosman@newspapermediagroup.com
Editor Phone: (732) 358-5200, ext : 8278
Advertising Executive Name: Michelle Nesbihal
Advertising Executive Email: mnesbihal@centraljersey.com
Advertising Executive Phone: (856) 237-6025

MANALAPAN

EXAMINER

Street Address: 198 Route 9, Suite 100
City: Manalapan
State: NJ
ZIP Code: 7726
General Phone: (732) 358-5200
General Email: feedback@centraljersey.com
Publication Website: https://centraljersey.com/examiner/
Parent Company: Gannett
Publisher Name: Joe Eisele
Publisher Email: jeisele@newspapermediagroup.com
Publisher Phone: (732) 358-5200, ext : 8282
Editor Name: Mark Rosman
Editor Email: mrosman@newspapermediagroup.com
Editor Phone: (732) 358-5200, ext : 8278
Advertising Executive Name: Michelle Nesbihal
Advertising Executive Email: mnesbihal@centraljersey.com
Advertising Executive Phone: (856) 237-6025

MANALAPAN

HILLSBOROUGH BEACON

Street Address: 198 Route 9, Suite 100
City: Manalapan
State: NJ
ZIP Code: 7726
General Phone: (732) 358-5200
General Email: feedback@centraljersey.com
Publication Website: https://centraljersey.com/hillsborough-beacon/
Parent Company: Newspaper Media Group
Publisher Name: Joe Eisele
Publisher Email: jeisele@newspapermediagroup.com
Publisher Phone: (732) 358-5200, ext : 8282
Editor Name: Mark Rosman
Editor Email: mrosman@newspapermediagroup.com
Editor Phone: (732) 358-5200, ext : 8278
Advertising Executive Name: Michelle Nesbihal
Advertising Executive Email: mnesbihal@centraljersey.com
Advertising Executive Phone: (856) 237-6025

MANALAPAN

HOPEWELL VALLEY NEWS

Street Address: 198 Route 9, Suite 100
City: Manalapan
State: NJ
ZIP Code: 7726
General Phone: (732) 358-5200
General Email: feedback@centraljersey.com
Publication Website: https://centraljersey.com/hopewell-valley-news/
Parent Company: Newspaper Media Group
Publisher Name: Joe Eisele
Publisher Email: jeisele@newspapermediagroup.com
Publisher Phone: (732) 358-5200, ext : 8282
Editor Name: Mark Rosman
Editor Email: mrosman@newspapermediagroup.com
Editor Phone: (732) 358-5200, ext : 8278
Advertising Executive Name: Michelle Nesbihal
Advertising Executive Email: mnesbihal@centraljersey.com
Advertising Executive Phone: (856) 237-6025

MANALAPAN

NEWS TRANSCRIPT

Street Address: 198 Route 9, Suite 100
City: Manalapan
State: NJ
ZIP Code: 7726
General Phone: (732) 358-5200
General Email: feedback@centraljersey.com
Publication Website: https://centraljersey.com/news-transcript/
"Parent Company: Newspaper Media Group
https://newspapermediagroup.com
NJ"
Publisher Name: Joe Eisele
Publisher Email: jeisele@newspapermediagroup.com
Publisher Phone: (732) 358-5200, ext : 8282
Editor Name: Mark Rosman
Editor Email: mrosman@newspapermediagroup.com
Editor Phone: (732) 358-5200, ext : 8278
Advertising Executive Name: Michelle Nesbihal
Advertising Executive Email: mnesbihal@centraljersey.com
Advertising Executive Phone: (856) 237-6025

MANALAPAN

NORTH/SOUTH BRUNSWICK SENTINEL

Street Address: 198 Route 9, Suite 100
City: Manalapan
State: NJ
ZIP Code: 7726
General Phone: (732) 358-5200
General Email: feedback@centraljersey.com
Publication Website: https://centraljersey.com/ns-sentinel/
Parent Company: Newspaper Media Group
Publisher Name: Joe Eisele
Publisher Email: jeisele@newspapermediagroup.com
Publisher Phone: (732) 358-5200, ext : 8282
Editor Name: Mark Rosman
Editor Email: mrosman@newspapermediagroup.com
Editor Phone: (732) 358-5200, ext : 8278
Advertising Executive Name: Michelle Nesbihal
Advertising Executive Email: mnesbihal@centraljersey.com
Advertising Executive Phone: (856) 237-6025

MANALAPAN

SUBURBAN

Street Address: 198 Route 9, Suite 100
City: Manalapan
State: NJ
ZIP Code: 7726
General Phone: (732) 358-5200
General Email: feedback@centraljersey.com
Publication Website: https://centraljersey.com/suburban/
Parent Company: Newspaper Media Group
Publisher Name: Joe Eisele
Publisher Email: jeisele@newspapermediagroup.com
Publisher Phone: (732) 358-5200, ext : 8282
Editor Name: Mark Rosman
Editor Email: mrosman@newspapermediagroup.com
Editor Phone: (732) 358-5200, ext : 8278
Advertising Executive Name: Michelle Nesbihal
Advertising Executive Email: mnesbihal@centraljersey.com
Advertising Executive Phone: (856) 237-6025

MANALAPAN

THE BEACON

Street Address: 198 Route 9, Suite 100
City: Manalapan
State: NJ
ZIP Code: 7726
General Phone: (732) 358-5200
General Email: feedback@centraljersey.com
Publication Website: https://centraljersey.com/hillsborough-beacon/
Parent Company: Gannett
Publisher Name: Joe Eisele
Publisher Email: jeisele@newspapermediagroup.com
Publisher Phone: (732) 358-5200, ext : 8282
Editor Name: Mark Rosman
Editor Email: mrosman@newspapermediagroup.com
Editor Phone: (732) 358-5200, ext : 8278
Advertising Executive Name: Michelle Nesbihal
Advertising Executive Email: mnesbihal@centraljersey.com
Advertising Executive Phone: (856) 237-6025

MANALAPAN

THE HUB

Street Address: 198 Route 9, Suite 100
City: Manalapan
State: NJ
ZIP Code: 7726
General Phone: (732) 358-5200
General Email: feedback@centraljersey.com
Publication Website: https://centraljersey.com/atlantic-hub/
Parent Company: Newspaper Media Group
Publisher Name: Joe Eisele
Publisher Email: jeisele@newspapermediagroup.com
Publisher Phone: (732) 358-5200, ext : 8282
Editor Name: Mark Rosman
Editor Email: mrosman@newspapermediagroup.com
Editor Phone: (732) 358-5200, ext : 8278
Advertising Executive Name: Michelle Nesbihal
Advertising Executive Email: mnesbihal@centraljersey.com
Advertising Executive Phone: (856) 237-6025

MANALAPAN

THE INDEPENDENT

Street Address: 198 Route 9, Suite 100
City: Manalapan
State: NJ
ZIP Code: 7726
General Phone: (732) 358-5200
General Email: feedback@centraljersey.com
Publication Website: https://centraljersey.com/independent/
Parent Company: Gannett
Publisher Name: Joe Eisele
Publisher Email: jeisele@newspapermediagroup.com
Publisher Phone: (732) 358-5200, ext : 8282
Editor Name: Mark Rosman
Editor Email: mrosman@newspapermediagroup.com
Editor Phone: (732) 358-5200, ext : 8278
Advertising Executive Name: Michelle Nesbihal
Advertising Executive Email: mnesbihal@centraljersey.com
Advertising Executive Phone: (856) 237-6025

MANALAPAN

THE LAWRENCE LEDGER

Street Address: 198 Route 9, Suite 100
City: Manalapan
State: NJ
ZIP Code: 7726
General Phone: (732) 358-5200
General Email: feedback@centraljersey.com
Publication Website: https://centraljersey.com/lawrence-ledger/
Parent Company: Newspaper Media Group
Publisher Name: Joe Eisele
Publisher Email: jeisele@newspapermediagroup.com
Publisher Phone: (732) 358-5200, ext : 8282
Editor Name: Mark Rosman
Editor Email: mrosman@newspapermediagroup.com
Editor Phone: (732) 358-5200, ext : 8278
Advertising Executive Name: Michelle Nesbihal
Advertising Executive Email: mnesbihal@centraljersey.com
Advertising Executive Phone: (856) 237-6025

MANALAPAN

TRI-TOWN NEWS

Street Address: 198 Route 9, Suite 100
City: Manalapan
State: NJ
ZIP Code: 7726
General Phone: (732) 358-5200
General Email: feedback@centraljersey.com
Publication Website: https://centraljersey.com/tri-town-news/
Parent Company: Newspaper Media Group
Publisher Name: Joe Eisele
Publisher Email: jeisele@newspapermediagroup.com
Publisher Phone: (732) 358-5200, ext : 8282
Editor Name: Mark Rosman
Editor Email: mrosman@newspapermediagroup.com
Editor Phone: (732) 358-5200, ext : 8278
Advertising Executive Name: Michelle Nesbihal
Advertising Executive Email: mnesbihal@centraljersey.com
Advertising Executive Phone: (856) 237-6025

MANALAPAN

WINDSOR-HIGHTS HERALD

Street Address: 198 Route 9, Suite 100
City: Manalapan
State: NJ
ZIP Code: 7726
General Phone: (732) 358-5200
General Email: feedback@centraljersey.com
Publication Website: https://centraljersey.com/windsor-hights-herald/
Parent Company: Newspaper Media Group
Publisher Name: Joe Eisele
Publisher Email: jeisele@newspapermediagroup.com
Publisher Phone: (732) 358-5200, ext : 8282
Editor Name: Mark Rosman
Editor Email: mrosman@newspapermediagroup.com
Editor Phone: (732) 358-5200, ext : 8278
Advertising Executive Name: Michelle Nesbihal
Advertising Executive Email: mnesbihal@centraljersey.com
Advertising Executive Phone: (856) 237-6025

MANASQUAN

THE COAST STAR

Street Address: 13 Broad St
City: Manasquan
State: NJ
ZIP Code: 8736
General Phone: (732) 223-0076
General Email: info@thecoaststar.com
Publication Website: http://www.starnewsgroup.com/
Parent Company: Star News Group
Publisher Name: Alison Manser Ertl
Publisher Email: gm@starnewsgroup.com
Publisher Phone: (732) 223-0076, ext : 38
Editor Name: Frederick J Tuccillo
Editor Email: ftuccillo@thecoaststar.com
Editor Phone: (732) 223-0076, ext : 27

MARMORA

BRIGANTINE BEACHCOMBER

Street Address: 507 S. Shore Road
City: Marmora
State: NJ
ZIP Code: 8223
General Phone: (609) 624-8900
General Email: adpro@thebeachcombernews.com
Publication Website: https://www.pressofatlanticcity.com/currents_gazettes/brigantine/
Parent Company: Lee Enterprises
Publisher Name: Mark L. Blum
Publisher Email: mblum@pressofac.com
Publisher Phone: (609) 272-7110
Editor Name: Kevin Post
Editor Email: letters@pressofac.com
Editor Phone: (609) 272-7267
Advertising Executive Name: Michelle Rice
Advertising Executive Email: mrice@pressofac.com
Advertising Executive Phone: (609) 272-7100

MAYWOOD

OUR TOWN

Street Address: 19 W Pleasant Ave
City: Maywood
State: NJ
ZIP Code: 07607-1320
General Phone: (201) 843-5700
General Email: rtownmaywoodrp@aol.com
Publication Website: http://www.ourtownnewsonline.com/
Parent Company: Jim Hornes
Editor Name: Camille Hornes

MEDFORD

THE CENTRAL RECORD

Street Address: P.O. Box 1027
City: Medford
State: NJ
ZIP Code: 8055
General Phone: (609) 654-5000
General Email: news@medfordcentralrecord.com
Publication Website: http://southjerseylocalnews.com/
Parent Company: Digital First Media
Publisher Name: Edward S. Condra
Publisher Email: econdra@21st-centurymedia.com
Advertising Executive Name: Beth Douglas
Advertising Executive Email: bdouglas@21st-centurymedia.com

MILLVILLE

CUMBERLAND REMINDER

Street Address: 2 West Vine St
City: Millville
State: NJ
ZIP Code: 8332
General Phone: (856) 825-8811
General Email: thereminderbeth@comcast.net
Publication Website: http://www.reminderusa.net/
Parent Company: Cohansey Cove Publishing Inc
Publisher Name: Darrell Kopp
Editor Name: Dan Podehl
Editor Email: editor@remindernewspaper.net
Advertising Executive Email: thereminderbeth@comcast.net

MILLVILLE

SNJ TODAY NEWSPAPER

Street Address: 600 G St
City: Millville
State: NJ
ZIP Code: 8332
General Phone: (856) 327-8800
General Email: news@snjtoday.com
Publication Website: http://snjtoday.com/?fbclid=IwAR0bDcA79vPt9tC17wm1GHxidMSTpwHEQ-vbJTahkhoG6F2XRR5abt4ODd8
Parent Company: SNJ Today

NEPTUNE

TOMS RIVER OBSERVER-REPORTER

Street Address: 3600 State Route 66
City: Neptune
State: NJ
ZIP Code: 07753-2605
General Phone: (800) 822-9770
General Email: htowns@gannettnj.com
Publication Website: http://www.ocobserver.com/
Publisher Name: Thomas M. Donovan
Publisher Phone: (800) 822-9770, ext : 4110
Editor Name: Paul D'ambrosio
Editor Email: pdambrosio@gannettnj.com

Editor Phone: (800) 822-9770, ext : 4261
Advertising Executive Name: Karen Guarasi
Advertising Executive Phone: (800) 822-9770, ext : 3644

OCEAN CITY

OCEAN CITY SENTINEL

Street Address: 112 E. 8th Street. Ocean City
City: Ocean City
State: NJ
ZIP Code: 08226-3641
General Phone: (609) 399-5411
General Email: oc-ads@comcast.net
Publication Website: http://www.ocsentinel.com/
Parent Company: Sample Media, Inc.

PLEASANTVILLE

WILDWOOD LEADER

Street Address: 1000 W. Washington Ave.
City: Pleasantville
State: NJ
ZIP Code: 08232-3806
General Phone: (609) 272-7231
General Email: subscriberservices@pressofac.com
Publication Website: https://www.pressofatlanticcity.com/currents_gazettes/wildwood/
Parent Company: Shore News Today
Publisher Name: Mark L. Blum
Publisher Email: mblum@pressofac.com
Publisher Phone: (609) 272-7110
Editor Name: Buzz Keough
Editor Email: wkeough@pressofac.com
Editor Phone: (609) 272-7238
Advertising Executive Name: Michelle Rice
Advertising Executive Email: mrice@pressofac.com
Advertising Executive Phone: (609) 272-7100

PRINCETON

THE PRINCETON PACKET

Street Address: PO Box 350
City: Princeton
State: NJ
ZIP Code: 08542-0350
General Phone: (609) 924-3244
General Email: dwillever@pacpub.com
Publication Website: https://centraljersey.com/princeton-packet/
Parent Company: Packet Media, LLC
Publisher Name: James B. Kilgore
Publisher Email: jkilgore@pacpub.com
Publisher Phone: (609) 924-3244, ext : 122
Editor Name: Aubrey Huston
Editor Email: ahuston@pacpub.com
Editor Phone: (609) 924-3244, ext : 336
Advertising Executive Name: Gerri Guld
Advertising Executive Email: advdir@pacpub.com
Advertising Executive Phone: (609) 924-3244, ext : 320

RAHWAY

NJTODAY.NET

Street Address: PO Box 1061
City: Rahway
State: NJ
ZIP Code: 07065-1061
General Phone: (908) 352-3100
General Email: ads@njtoday.net
Publication Website: http://njtoday.net/
Parent Company: CMD Media LLC
Publisher Name: Lisa McCormick
Editor Name: Paul W. Hadsall

RED BANK

THE MONMOUTH JOURNAL

Street Address: 212 Maple Ave
City: Red Bank
State: NJ
ZIP Code: 7701
General Phone: (732) 747-7007
General Email: ads@themonmouthjournal.com
Publication Website: https://themonmouthjournal.com/
Parent Company: The Monmouth Journal, LLC

RIDGEWOOD

MAHWAH SUBURBAN NEWS

Street Address: 41 Oak St
City: Ridgewood
State: NJ
ZIP Code: 7450
General Phone: (201) 612-5415
General Email: northjerseymediagroup@gannett.com
Publication Website: https://www.northjersey.com
Editor Name: Daniel Sforza
Editor Email: sforza@northjersey.com

RIDGEWOOD

RAMSEY SUBURBAN NEWS

Street Address: 41 Oak St
City: Ridgewood
State: NJ
ZIP Code: 07450-
General Phone: (800) 300-9321
General Email: union@njnpublishing.com
Publication Website: https://www.nj.com/suburbannews/
Editor Name: Daniel Sforza
Editor Email: sforza@northjersey.com
Advertising Executive Phone: (973) 569-7801

ROCKAWAY

AIM JEFFERSON

Street Address: 100 Commons Way
City: Rockaway
State: NJ
ZIP Code: 07866-2038
General Phone: (973) 586-8000
General Email: northjerseymediagroup@gannett.com
Publication Website: https://www.northjersey.com
Editor Name: Daniel Sforza
Editor Email: sforza@northjersey.com

ROCKAWAY

AIM VERNON

Street Address: 100 Commons Way
City: Rockaway
State: NJ
ZIP Code: 07866-2038
General Phone: (973) 586-8000
General Email: northjerseymediagroup@gannett.com
Publication Website: https://www.northjersey.com
Editor Name: Daniel Sforza
Editor Email: sforza@northjersey.com

ROCKAWAY

AIM WEST MILFORD

Street Address: 100 Commons Way
City: Rockaway
State: NJ
ZIP Code: 07866-2038
General Phone: (973) 586-8000
General Email: northjerseymediagroup@gannett.com
Publication Website: https://www.northjersey.com
Editor Name: Daniel Sforza
Editor Email: sforza@northjersey.com

ROCKAWAY

ARGUS

Street Address: 100 Commons Way
City: Rockaway
State: NJ
ZIP Code: 07866-2038
General Phone: (973) 586-8000
General Email: northjerseymediagroup@gannett.com
Publication Website: https://www.northjersey.com/
Parent Company: Gannett
Editor Name: Daniel Sforza
Editor Email: sforza@northjersey.com

ROCKAWAY

BELLEVILLE TIMES

Street Address: 100 Commons Way
City: Rockaway
State: NJ
ZIP Code: 07866-2038
General Phone: (973) 586-8000
General Email: northjerseymediagroup@gannett.com
Publication Website: https://www.northjersey.com
Editor Name: Daniel Sforza
Editor Email: sforza@northjersey.com

SOUTH PLAINFIELD

SOUTH PLAINFIELD OBSERVER

Street Address: 1110 Hamilton Blvd
City: South Plainfield
State: NJ
ZIP Code: 07080-2031
General Phone: (908) 668-0010
General Email: spobserver@comcast.net
Publication Website: https://www.spobserver.com/

SPARTA

SPARTA INDEPENDENT

Street Address: 1A Main St
City: Sparta
State: NJ
ZIP Code: 7871
General Phone: (845) 469-9000
General Email: njoffice@strausnews.com
Publication Website: http://spartaindependent.com/
Parent Company: Straus News
Editor Name: Chris Sagona
Editor Email: njoffice@strausnews.com

SPARTA

TOWNSHIP JOURNAL

Street Address: 1A Main St
City: Sparta
State: NJ
ZIP Code: 7871
General Phone: (845) 469-9000
General Email: sales@strausnews.com
Publication Website: http://www.townshipjournal.com/
Parent Company: Straus News
Editor Name: Chris Sagona
Editor Email: njoffice@strausnews.com

UNION

THE GLEN RIDGE PAPER

Street Address: 1291 Stuyvesant Ave
City: Union
State: NJ
ZIP Code: 7083
General Phone: (908) 686-7700
General Email: ads@thelocalsource.com
Publication Website: https://essexnewsdaily.com/category/news/glenridge
Parent Company: Worrall Community Newspapers, Inc.
Editor Email: essexcty@thelocalsource.com
Editor Phone: (908) 686-7700
Advertising Executive Email: ads@thelocalsource.com
Advertising Executive Phone: (908) 686-7700

UNION VALLEY RD.

THE WEST MILFORD MESSENGER

Street Address: 1499 Union Valley Rd
City: Union Valley Rd.
State: NJ
ZIP Code: 7480
General Phone: (973) 300-0890
General Email: njoffice@strausnews.com
Publication Website: http://www.westmilfordmessenger.com/
Parent Company: Straus News
Editor Name: Charlie Kim
Editor Email: njoffice@strausnews.com
Advertising Executive Name: Vincent A. Gardino
Advertising Executive Email: advertising@strausnews.com

VERNON

ADVERTISER NEWS (NORTH EDITION)

Street Address: 1A Main St Ste 9
City: Vernon
State: NJ
ZIP Code: 07871-1909
General Phone: (973) 300-0890
General Email: sales@strausnews.com
Publication Website: http://www.advertisernewsnorth.com/
Parent Company: Straus News
Editor Name: Mike Zummo
Editor Email: editor.ann@strausnews.com

VERNON

ADVERTISER NEWS (SOUTH EDITION)

Street Address: 1A Main St Ste 9
City: Vernon
State: NJ
ZIP Code: 07871-1909
General Phone: (973) 300-0890
General Email: sales@strausnews.com
Publication Website: http://www.advertisernewssouth.com/
Parent Company: Straus News
Editor Name: Mike Zummo
Editor Email: editor.ann@strausnews.com

WEST CAPE MAY

CAPE MAY STAR AND WAVE

Street Address: PO Box 2427
City: West Cape May
State: NJ
ZIP Code: 08204-7427
General Phone: (609) 884-3466
General Email: cmstarwave@comcast.net
Publication Website: https://www.starandwave.com/
Parent Company: Sample Media Inc
Advertising Executive Email: capemayalaine@gmail.com
Advertising Executive Phone: (609) 289-2619

WESTFIELD

THE TIMES OF SCOTCH PLAINS-FANWOOD

Street Address: 251 North Ave W
City: Westfield
State: NJ
ZIP Code: 7091
General Phone: (908) 232-4407
General Email: editor@goleader.com
Publication Website: http://www.goleader.com/
Parent Company: The Westfield Leader and The Scotch Plains-Fanwood Times
Publisher Name: Horace Corbin
Publisher Email: press@goleader.com

WESTFIELD

THE WESTFIELD LEADER

Street Address: 251 North Ave W
City: Westfield
State: NJ
ZIP Code: 7091
General Phone: (908) 232-4407
General Email: editor@goleader.com
Publication Website: https://www.goleader.com/20feb06/
Parent Company: The Westfield Leader and The Scotch Plains-Fanwood Times
Publisher Name: Horace Corbin
Publisher Email: press@goleader.com

WHIPPANY

BERNARDSVILLE NEWS

Street Address: 100 South Jefferson Road, Suite 104
City: Whippany
State: NJ
ZIP Code: 7981
General Phone: (908) 766-3900
General Email: jwinter@newjerseyhills.com
Publication Website: https://www.newjerseyhills.com/bernardsville_news/
Parent Company: New Jersey Hills Media Group
Publisher Name: Elizabeth K. Parker
Publisher Email: eparker@newjerseyhills.com
Publisher Phone: (908) 766-3900, ext : 241
Editor Name: Charlie Zavalick

WHIPPANY

CHATHAM COURIER

Street Address: 100 S. Jefferson Road
City: Whippany
State: NJ
ZIP Code: 7981
General Phone: (908) 766-3900
General Email: eparker@newjerseyhills.com
Publication Website: https://www.newjerseyhills.com/
Parent Company: New Jersey Hills Media Group
Publisher Name: Elizabeth K. Parker
Publisher Email: eparker@newjerseyhills.com

Publisher Phone: (908) 766-3900, ext : 241
Editor Name: Garry Herzog
Editor Email: gherzog@newjerseyhills.com
Editor Phone: (908) 766-3900, ext : 240
Advertising Executive Name: Jerry O'Donnell
Advertising Executive Email: jodonnell@newjerseyhills.com
Advertising Executive Phone: (908) 766-3900, ext : 230

WHIPPANY

MORRIS NEWS-BEE

Street Address: 100 S Jefferson Rd
City: Whippany
State: NJ
ZIP Code: 7981
General Phone: (908) 766-3900
General Email: eparker@newjerseyhills.com
Publication Website: https://www.newjerseyhills.com/
Parent Company: Newspaper Media Group
Publisher Name: Elizabeth K. Parker
Publisher Email: eparker@newjerseyhills.com
Publisher Phone: (908) 766-3900, ext : 241
Editor Name: Jim Lent
Editor Email: jlent@newjerseyhills.com
Editor Phone: (908) 766-3900, ext : 245
Advertising Executive Name: Jerry O'Donnell
Advertising Executive Email: jodonnell@newjerseyhills.com
Advertising Executive Phone: (908) 766-3900, ext : 230

WHIPPANY

MOUNT OLIVE CHRONICLE

Street Address: 100 S Jefferson Rd
City: Whippany
State: NJ
ZIP Code: 7981
General Phone: (908) 766-3900
General Email: eparker@newjerseyhills.com
Publication Website: https://www.newjerseyhills.com/
Parent Company: New Jersey Hills Media Group
Publisher Name: Elizabeth K. Parker
Publisher Email: eparker@newjerseyhills.com
Publisher Phone: (908) 766-3900, ext : 241
Editor Name: Phil Garber
Editor Email: pgarber@newjerseyhills.com
Editor Phone: (908) 766-3900, ext : 251
Advertising Executive Name: Jerry O'Donnell
Advertising Executive Email: jodonnell@newjerseyhills.com
Advertising Executive Phone: (908) 766-3900, ext : 230

WHIPPANY

THE PROGRESS

"Street Address: Suite 104 100 South Jefferson Road"
City: Whippany
State: NJ
ZIP Code: 7981
General Phone: (908) 766-3900
General Email: bmarmol@newjerseyhills.com
Publication Website: https://www.newjerseyhills.com/the_progress/
Parent Company: New Jersey Hills Media Group
Editor Name: Kathy Shwiff
Editor Email: kshwiff@newjerseyhills.com
Editor Phone: (908) 766-3900, ext : 247
Advertising Executive Name: Jerry O'Donnell
Advertising Executive Email: jodonnell@newjerseyhills.com

Advertising Executive Phone: (908) 766-3900, ext : 230

WOODLAND PARK

BLOOMFIELD LIFE

Street Address: 1 Garret Mountain Plz
City: Woodland Park
State: NJ
ZIP Code: 07424-3320
General Phone: (973) 569-7000
General Email: glenridgevoice@northjersey.com
Publication Website: https://www.northjersey.com/
Publisher Name: Daniel Sforza
Publisher Email: sforza@northjersey.com

WOODLAND PARK

BOGOTA BULLETIN

Street Address: 1 Garret Mountain Plz
City: Woodland Park
State: NJ
ZIP Code: 07424-3320
General Phone: (973) 569-7000
General Email: glenridgevoice@northjersey.com
Publication Website: http://www.northjersey.com/towns/Bogota.html
Publisher Name: Daniel Sforza
Publisher Email: sforza@northjersey.com

WOODLAND PARK

CLIFFSIDE PARK CITIZEN

Street Address: 1 Garret Mountain Plz
City: Woodland Park
State: NJ
ZIP Code: 07424-3320
General Phone: (973) 569-7000
General Email: glenridgevoice@northjersey.com
Publication Website: https://www.northjersey.com/
Publisher Name: Daniel Sforza
Publisher Email: sforza@northjersey.com

WOODLAND PARK

CLIFTON JOURNAL

Street Address: 1 Garret Mountain Plz
City: Woodland Park
State: NJ
ZIP Code: 07424-3320
General Phone: (973) 569-7000
General Email: glenridgevoice@northjersey.com
Publication Website: http://www.northjersey.com/
Publisher Name: Daniel Sforza
Publisher Email: sforza@northjersey.com

WOODLAND PARK

COMMUNITY NEWS

Street Address: 1 Garret Mountain Plz
City: Woodland Park
State: NJ
ZIP Code: 07424-3320
General Phone: (973) 569-7000
General Email: glenridgevoice@northjersey.com
Publication Website: https://www.northjersey.com/
Parent Company: Media News Group
Publisher Name: Daniel Sforza
Publisher Email: sforza@northjersey.com

WOODLAND PARK

EDGEWATER VIEW

Street Address: 1 Garret Mountain Plz
City: Woodland Park
State: NJ
ZIP Code: 07424-3320
General Phone: (973) 569-7000
General Email: glenridgevoice@northjersey.com
Publication Website: https://www.northjersey.com/
Publisher Name: Daniel Sforza
Publisher Email: sforza@northjersey.com

WOODLAND PARK

ENGLEWOOD SUBURBANITE

Street Address: 1 Garret Mountain Plz
City: Woodland Park
State: NJ
ZIP Code: 07424-3320
General Phone: (973) 569-7000
General Email: glenridgevoice@northjersey.com
Publication Website: https://www.northjersey.com/
Publisher Name: Daniel Sforza
Publisher Email: sforza@northjersey.com

WOODLAND PARK

FORT LEE SUBURBANITE

Street Address: 1 Garret Mountain Plz
City: Woodland Park
State: NJ
ZIP Code: 07424-3320
General Phone: (973) 569-7000
General Email: glenridgevoice@northjersey.com
Publication Website: https://www.northjersey.com/
Publisher Name: Daniel Sforza
Publisher Email: sforza@northjersey.com

WOODLAND PARK

FRANKLIN LAKES/OAKLAND SUBURBAN NEWS

Street Address: 1 Garret Mountain Plz
City: Woodland Park
State: NJ
ZIP Code: 07424-3320
General Phone: (973) 569-7000
General Email: glenridgevoice@northjersey.com
Publication Website: https://www.northjersey.com/
"Parent Company: Gannett
https://www.gannett.com
VA"
Publisher Name: Daniel Sforza
Publisher Email: sforza@northjersey.com

WOODLAND PARK

GLEN RIDGE VOICE

Street Address: 1 Garret Mountain Plz
City: Woodland Park
State: NJ
ZIP Code: 07424-3320
General Phone: (973) 569-7000
General Email: glenridgevoice@northjersey.com
Publication Website: http://northjersey.com/
Publisher Name: Daniel Sforza
Publisher Email: sforza@northjersey.com

WOODLAND PARK

Community Newspapers in the U.S.

GLEN ROCK GAZETTE

Street Address: 1 Garret Mountain Plz
City: Woodland Park
State: NJ
ZIP Code: 07424-3320
General Phone: (973) 569-7000
General Email: glenridgevoice@northjersey.com
Publication Website: http://www.northjersey.com/glenrock?fbclid=IwAR0Cy6aeW0fhv2TYafDKSIsZDVRlhuc8yXishKVCgL3zcxdcIWD620c6cY0
Publisher Name: Daniel Sforza
Publisher Email: sforza@northjersey.com

WOODLAND PARK

HACKENSACK CHRONICLE

Street Address: 1 Garret Mountain Plz
City: Woodland Park
State: NJ
ZIP Code: 07424-3320
General Phone: (973) 569-7000
General Email: glenridgevoice@northjersey.com
Publication Website: https://www.northjersey.com/local/hackensack
Publisher Name: Daniel Sforza
Publisher Email: sforza@northjersey.com

WOODLAND PARK

LEONIA LIFE

Street Address: 1 Garret Mountain Plz
City: Woodland Park
State: NJ
ZIP Code: 07424-3320
General Phone: (973) 569-7000
General Email: glenridgevoice@northjersey.com
Publication Website: http://northjersey.com/
Publisher Name: Daniel Sforza
Publisher Email: sforza@northjersey.com

WOODLAND PARK

MIDLAND PARK SUBURBAN NEWS

Street Address: 1 Garret Mountain Plz
City: Woodland Park
State: NJ
ZIP Code: 07424-3320
General Phone: (973) 569-7000
General Email: glenridgevoice@northjersey.com
Publication Website: https://www.northjersey.com/local/hackensack
Publisher Name: Daniel Sforza
Publisher Email: sforza@northjersey.com

WOODLAND PARK

NORTHERN VALLEY SUBURBANITE

Street Address: 1 Garret Mountain Plz
City: Woodland Park
State: NJ
ZIP Code: 07424-3320
General Phone: (973) 569-7000
General Email: glenridgevoice@northjersey.com
Publication Website: http://northjersey.com/
Publisher Name: Daniel Sforza
Publisher Email: sforza@northjersey.com

WOODLAND PARK

NUTLEY SUN

Street Address: 1 Garret Mountain Plz
City: Woodland Park
State: NJ
ZIP Code: 07424-3320
General Phone: (973) 569-7000
General Email: glenridgevoice@northjersey.com
Publication Website: https://www.northjersey.com/local/essex/
Publisher Name: Daniel Sforza
Publisher Email: sforza@northjersey.com

WOODLAND PARK

PARSIPPANY LIFE

Street Address: 1 Garret Mountain Plz
City: Woodland Park
State: NJ
ZIP Code: 07424-3320
General Phone: (973) 569-7000
General Email: glenridgevoice@northjersey.com
Publication Website: http://northjersey.com/
Publisher Name: Daniel Sforza
Publisher Email: sforza@northjersey.com

WOODLAND PARK

PASCACK VALLEY COMMUNITY LIFE

Street Address: 1 Garret Mountain Plz
City: Woodland Park
State: NJ
ZIP Code: 07424-3320
General Phone: (973) 569-7000
General Email: glenridgevoice@northjersey.com
Publication Website: http://northjersey.com/
Publisher Name: Daniel Sforza
Publisher Email: sforza@northjersey.com

WOODLAND PARK

PASSAIC VALLEY TODAY

Street Address: 1 Garret Mountain Plz
City: Woodland Park
State: NJ
ZIP Code: 07424-3320
General Phone: (973) 569-7000
General Email: glenridgevoice@northjersey.com
Publication Website: https://www.northjersey.com/local/passaic/
Publisher Name: Daniel Sforza
Publisher Email: sforza@northjersey.com

WOODLAND PARK

RIDGEFIELD PARK PATRIOT

Street Address: 1 Garret Mountain Plz
City: Woodland Park
State: NJ
ZIP Code: 07424-3320
General Phone: (973) 569-7000
General Email: glenridgevoice@northjersey.com
Publication Website: http://www.northjersey.com/towns/RidgefieldPark.html
Publisher Name: Daniel Sforza
Publisher Email: sforza@northjersey.com

WOODLAND PARK

SOUTH BERGENITE

Street Address: 1 Garret Mountain Plaza
City: Woodland Park
State: NJ
ZIP Code: 07424-0471
General Phone: (973) 569-7000
General Email: northjerseymediagroup@gannett.com
Publication Website: https://www.northjersey.com/
Editor Name: Daniel Sforza
Editor Email: sforza@northjersey.com
Advertising Executive Phone: (973) 569-7801

WOODLAND PARK

SUBURBAN TRENDS

Street Address: 1 Garret Mountain Plaza
City: Woodland Park
State: NJ
ZIP Code: 07424-0471
General Phone: (973) 569-7000
General Email: northjerseymediagroup@gannett.com
Publication Website: https://www.northjersey.com/
Editor Name: Daniel Sforza
Editor Email: sforza@northjersey.com
Advertising Executive Phone: (973) 569-7801

WOODLAND PARK

TEANECK SUBURBANITE

Street Address: 1 Garret Mountain Plaza
City: Woodland Park
State: NJ
ZIP Code: 07424-0471
General Phone: (973) 569-7000
General Email: northjerseymediagroup@gannett.com
Publication Website: https://www.northjersey.com/
Editor Name: Daniel Sforza
Editor Email: sforza@northjersey.com
Advertising Executive Phone: (973) 569-7801

WOODLAND PARK

TENAFLY SUBURBANITE

Street Address: 1 Garret Mountain Plaza
City: Woodland Park
State: NJ
ZIP Code: 07424-0471
General Phone: (973) 569-7000
General Email: northjerseymediagroup@gannett.com
Publication Website: https://www.northjersey.com/
Editor Name: Daniel Sforza
Editor Email: sforza@northjersey.com
Advertising Executive Phone: (973) 569-7801

WOODLAND PARK

THE GAZETTE

Street Address: 1 Garret Mountain Plaza
City: Woodland Park
State: NJ
ZIP Code: 07424-0471
General Phone: (973) 569-7000
General Email: northjerseymediagroup@gannett.com
Publication Website: https://www.northjersey.com/
Parent Company: Gannett
Editor Name: Daniel Sforza
Editor Email: sforza@northjersey.com
Advertising Executive Phone: (973) 569-7801

WOODLAND PARK

THE ITEM OF MILLBURN AND SHORT HILLS

Street Address: 1 Garret Mountain Plaza
City: Woodland Park
State: NJ
ZIP Code: 07424-0471
General Phone: (973) 569-7000
General Email: northjerseymediagroup@gannett.com
Publication Website: https://www.northjersey.com/
Editor Name: Daniel Sforza
Editor Email: sforza@northjersey.com
Advertising Executive Phone: (973) 569-7801

WOODLAND PARK

THE MONTCLAIR TIMES

Street Address: 1 Garret Mountain Plaza
City: Woodland Park
State: NJ
ZIP Code: 07424-0471
General Phone: (973) 569-7000
General Email: northjerseymediagroup@gannett.com
Publication Website: https://www.northjersey.com/local/montclair/
Editor Name: Daniel Sforza
Editor Email: sforza@northjersey.com
Advertising Executive Phone: (973) 569-7801

WOODLAND PARK

TOWN JOURNAL

Street Address: 1 Garret Mountain Plaza
City: Woodland Park
State: NJ
ZIP Code: 07424-0471
General Phone: (973) 569-7000
General Email: northjerseymediagroup@gannett.com
Publication Website: https://www.northjersey.com/
Editor Name: Daniel Sforza
Editor Email: sforza@northjersey.com
Advertising Executive Phone: (973) 569-7801

WOODLAND PARK

TOWN NEWS

Street Address: 1 Garret Mountain Plaza
City: Woodland Park
State: NJ
ZIP Code: 07424-0471
General Phone: (973) 569-7000
General Email: northjerseymediagroup@gannett.com
Publication Website: https://www.northjersey.com/
Editor Name: Daniel Sforza
Editor Email: sforza@northjersey.com
Advertising Executive Phone: (973) 569-7801

WOODLAND PARK

TWIN-BORO NEWS

Street Address: 1 Garret Mountain Plaza
City: Woodland Park
State: NJ
ZIP Code: 07424-0471
General Phone: (973) 569-7000
General Email: northjerseymediagroup@gannett.com
Publication Website: https://www.northjersey.com/
Editor Name: Daniel Sforza
Editor Email: sforza@northjersey.com
Advertising Executive Phone: (973) 569-7801

WOODLAND PARK

VERONA-CEDAR GROVE TIMES

Street Address: 1 Garret Mountain Plz
City: Woodland Park
State: NJ

ZIP Code: 07424-3320
General Phone: (973) 569-7000
General Email: glenridgevoice@northjersey.com
Publication Website: http://www.northjersey.com/
Publisher Name: Daniel Sforza
Publisher Email: sforza@northjersey.com

WOODLAND PARK

WALDWICK SUBURBAN NEWS

Street Address: 1 Garret Mountain Plaza
City: Woodland Park
State: NJ
ZIP Code: 07424-0471
General Phone: (973) 569-7000
General Email: northjerseymediagroup@gannett.com
Publication Website: https://www.northjersey.com/
Editor Name: Daniel Sforza
Editor Email: sforza@northjersey.com
Advertising Executive Phone: (973) 569-7801

WOODLAND PARK

WAYNE TODAY

Street Address: 1 Garret Mountain Plz
City: Woodland Park
State: NJ
ZIP Code: 07424-0471
General Phone: (973) 585-5633
General Email: northjerseymediagroup@gannett.com
Publication Website: http://www.northjersey.com/wayne?fbclid=IwAR3ilaet06mq4SRW-yqfu-SZ3_8FdcP4R4ojEJAQbr-X_p0e_T58UAqyZIs
Editor Name: Cindy Schweich Handler
Editor Email: handler@northjersey.com
Advertising Executive Phone: (973) 569-7801

NEW MEXICO

ALBUQUERQUE

ALBUQUERQUE BUSINESS FIRST

Street Address: 6565 Americas Pkwy NE, Suite 770
City: Albuquerque
State: NM
ZIP Code: 87110-8177
General Phone: (505) 768-7008
General Email: albuquerque@bizjournals.com
Publication Website: https://www.bizjournals.com/albuquerque/
Parent Company: American City Business Journals
Publisher Name: Candace Beeke
Publisher Email: cbeeke@bizjournals.com
Publisher Phone: (505) 348-8320
Editor Name: Will Martinez
Editor Email: wmartinez@bizjournals.com
Editor Phone: (505) 348-8312
Advertising Executive Name: Rachel Sams
Advertising Executive Email: rsams@bizjournals.com
Advertising Executive Phone: (505) 348-8322
Delivery Methods: Mail
Year Established: 1993
Published Days: Fri
Published Other: Digital Morning Edition - Monday thru Friday. Digital Afternoon Edition Monday thru Saturday
Avg. Paid Circ.: 5400
Audit Company: Sworn/Estimate/Non-Audited
Audit Date: 43626

ALBUQUERQUE

HEALTH CITY SUN

Street Address: 6300 Montano NW Ste.G3 Second Floor
City: Albuquerque
State: NM
ZIP Code: 87120
General Phone: (505) 242-3010
General Email: legal@healthcitysun.com
Publication Website: https://healthcitysun.com/
Delivery Methods: Mail
Year Established: 1929
Commercial printers?: Y
Published Days: Fri
Avg. Paid Circ.: 2000
Avg. Free Circ.: 250
Audit Company: Sworn/Estimate/Non-Audited
Audit Date: 43626

BELEN

VALENCIA COUNTY NEWS-BULLETIN

Street Address: 221 S. Main St., Suite B
City: Belen
State: NM
ZIP Code: 87002-2619
General Phone: (505) 864-4472
General Email: bchandler@news-bulletin.com
Publication Website: http://www.news-bulletin.com/
Parent Company: Albuquerque Publishing Co.
Publisher Name: Clara Garcia
Publisher Email: cgarcia@news-bulletin.com
Publisher Phone: (505) 966-8156
Editor Name: Clara Garcia
Editor Email: cgarcia@news-bulletin.com
Editor Phone: (505) 966-8156
Advertising Executive Name: Bobbi Chandler
Advertising Executive Email: bchandler@news-bulletin.com
Advertising Executive Phone: (505) 966-8154
Delivery Methods: Mail`Newsstand`Carrier`Racks
Year Established: 1910
Own Printing Facility?: N
Commercial printers?: Y
Mechanical specifications: Type page 13 x 21 1/2; E - 6 cols, 1 5/6, 1/6 between; A - 6 cols, 1 5/6, 1/6 between; C - 8 cols, 1 1/3, 1/6 between.
Published Days: Thur
Weekday Frequency: m
Avg. Paid Circ.: 2855
Avg. Free Circ.: 12174
Audit Company: Sworn/Estimate/Non-Audited
Audit Date: 43626

CLOVIS

EASTERN NEW MEXICO NEWS

Street Address: 521 Pile St
City: Clovis
State: NM
ZIP Code: 88101-6637
General Phone: (575) 763-3431
General Email: info@thenews.email
Publication Website: https://www.easternnewmexiconews.com
Parent Company: Clovis Media Inc
Delivery Methods: Mail`Newsstand`Carrier`Racks
Year Established: 1929
Own Printing Facility?: N
Commercial printers?: N
Mechanical specifications: Type page 11 x 21; E - 6 cols, 1 13/16, 1/8 between; A - 6 cols, 2 13/16, 1/8 between; C - 9 cols, 1 3/16, 1/8 between.
Published Days: Wed`Sun
Weekday Frequency: m
Avg. Paid Circ.: 5235
Audit Company: Sworn/Estimate/Non-Audited
Audit Date: 43626
Pressroom Equipment: Lines -- 8-HI/V-15A 1974. Quad Stack Color Press;
Mailroom Equipment: Tying Machines -- 2-/Bu.;
Business Equipment: Dell/HP
Business Software: Vision Data AR2000, Quickbooks Pro
Classified Equipment: Hardware -- APP/Mac;
Classified Software: Baseview.
Editorial Equipment: Hardware -- APP/Mac; Printers -- HP
Editorial Software: Baseview.
Production Equipment: Hardware -- App/MAC, Trendsetters; Cameras -- R/580; Scanners -- Umax Astra 1220U, Canon
Production Software: QPS/QuarkXPress 6.5

EDGEWOOD

THE INDEPENDENT

Street Address: 95 N.M. 344
City: Edgewood
State: NM
ZIP Code: 87015
General Phone: (505) 286-1212
General Email: news.ind.ads@gmail.com
Publication Website: https://edgewood.news/
Parent Company: Gannett
Publisher Name: Leota Harriman
Publisher Email: news.ind.editor@gmail.com
Editor Name: Leota Harriman
Editor Email: news.ind.editor@gmail.com
Advertising Executive Email: news.ind.ads@gmail.com
Delivery Methods: Mail`Newsstand`Racks
Year Established: 1999
Own Printing Facility?: N
Commercial printers?: N
Mechanical specifications: 10x13
Published Days: Fri
Avg. Paid Circ.: 3000
Avg. Free Circ.: 500
Audit Company: Sworn/Estimate/Non-Audited
Audit Date: 43626

ESPANOLA

RIO GRANDE SUN

Street Address: 123 N Railroad Ave
City: Espanola
State: NM
ZIP Code: 87532-2627
General Phone: (505) 753-2126
General Email: rgsun@cybermesa.com
Publication Website: http://www.riograndesun.com/
Publisher Name: Robert B. Trapp
Editor Name: Austin Fisher
Advertising Executive Name: Maria Lopez Garcia
Delivery Methods: Newsstand`Racks
Year Established: 1956
Published Days: Thur
Avg. Paid Circ.: 11500
Audit Company: Sworn/Estimate/Non-Audited
Audit Date: 43626

JAL

THE JAL RECORD

Street Address: PO box 548
City: Jal
State: NM
ZIP Code: 88252
General Phone: (575) 395-3530
General Email: adverising@jalrecord.net
Publication Website: https://jalrecord.net/
Editor Name: Kelly Dawson
Editor Email: adverising@jalrecord.net
Editor Phone: (575) 395-2516
Advertising Executive Email: adverising@jalrecord.net
Delivery Methods: Mail`Newsstand`Racks
Year Established: 1939
Own Printing Facility?: Y
Commercial printers?: Y
Mechanical specifications: page size 10 x 13
Published Days: Thur
Avg. Paid Circ.: 1475
Avg. Free Circ.: 26
Audit Company: Sworn/Estimate/Non-Audited
Audit Date: 43626

LAS CRUCES

THE LAS CRUCES BULLETIN

Street Address: 1740 Calle De Mercado
City: Las Cruces
State: NM
ZIP Code: 88005-8254
General Phone: (575) 524-8061
General Email: shellie@lascrucesbulletin.com
Publication Website: https://www.lascrucesbulletin.com
Parent Company: OPC News, LLC
Publisher Name: Richard Coltharp
Publisher Email: richard@lascrucesbulletin.com
Publisher Phone: (575) 526-4712
Editor Name: Jess Williams
Editor Email: jess@lascrucesbulletin.com
Editor Phone: (575) 680-1977
Advertising Executive Name: Angel McKellar
Advertising Executive Email: angel@lascrucesbulletin.com
Advertising Executive Phone: (575) 680-1982
Delivery Methods: Mail`Newsstand`Carrier`Racks
Year Established: 1969
Mechanical specifications: Type page 10 5/16 x 12 7/8; E - 6 cols, 1 9/16, 3/16 between; A - 6 cols, 1 9/16, 3/16 between; C - 8 cols, 1 1/8, 3/16 between.
Published Days: Fri
Avg. Paid Circ.: 1000
Avg. Free Circ.: 20000
Audit Company: Sworn/Estimate/Non-Audited
Audit Date: 43626

LAS VEGAS

LAS VEGAS OPTIC

Street Address: 720 University Ave
City: LAS VEGAS
State: NM
ZIP Code: 87701
General Phone: (505) 425-6796
General Email: optic@lasvegasoptic.com
Publication Website: https://www.lasvegasoptic.com/
Parent Company: Landmark Community Newspapers
Editor Name: Phil Scherer
Editor Email: pscherer@lasvegasoptic.com
Delivery Methods: Mail
Year Established: 1879
Own Printing Facility?: N
Commercial printers?: N
Mechanical specifications: Type page 10 1/2 x 22 1/2; E - 6 cols, 1 1/2, 1/8 between; A - 6 cols, 1 1/2, 1/8 between; C - 6 cols, 1 1/2, 1/8 between.
Published Days: Wed`Fri`Sun
Weekday Frequency: e
Avg. Paid Circ.: 3850
Audit Company: Sworn/Estimate/Non-Audited
Audit Date: 43626
Pressroom Equipment: Lines -- G/

Community 1975; G/Community 1975; G/Community 1975; G/Community 1975.;
Business Equipment: 2-PC
Business Software: AccPac, Interlink
Classified Equipment: Hardware -- Mk, APP/Mac; Printers -- APP/Mac LaserPrinter;
Classified Software: APT
Editorial Equipment: Hardware -- Mk, APP/Mac; Printers -- APP/Mac LaserPrinter
Editorial Software: PhotoShop 6 / InDesign 6
Production Equipment: Hardware -- 1-Nu, Vastec; Cameras -- AG.

LOVINGTON

LOVINGTON LEADER

Street Address: 14 W Avenue B
City: Lovington
State: NM
ZIP Code: 88260-4404
General Phone: (505) 396-2844
General Email: lovingtonleader@yahoo.com
Publication Website: http://www.lovingtonleaderonline.com
Editor Name: Phil Scherer
Editor Email: pscherer@lasvegasoptic.com
Mechanical specifications: Type page 13 x 21; E - 6 cols, 2 1/16, 1/8 between; A - 6 cols, 2 1/16, 1/8 between; C - 6 cols, 2 1/16, 1/8 between.
Published Days: Tues`Thur`Sat
Weekday Frequency: e
Avg. Paid Circ.: 1495
Audit Company: Sworn/Estimate/Non-Audited
Audit Date: 43626
Pressroom Equipment: Lines -- HI/Offset.;
Mailroom Equipment: Tying Machines -- 1/BU; Address Machine -- 1-/Am.;
Classified Equipment: Hardware -- Wyse.;
Editorial Equipment: Hardware -- APP/Mac; Printers -- APP/Mac LaserWriter Select 360, QMS/810 T
Editorial Software: Baseview/NewsEdit.
Production Equipment: Hardware -- Caere/OmniPage Pro; Cameras -- Nu; Scanners -- Umax
Production Software: QPS/QuarkXPress, Adobe/Photoshop.

RIO RANCHO

THE RIO RANCHO OBSERVER

Street Address: 409 NM 528 NE
City: Rio Rancho
State: NM
ZIP Code: 87124
General Phone: (505) 892-8080
General Email: mhartranft@rrobserver.com
Publication Website: https://www.abqjournal.com/rio-rancho-observer
Parent Company: Osteen Publishing
Publisher Name: Argen Marie Duncan
Publisher Phone: (505) 891-7172
Editor Name: Argen Marie Duncan
Editor Email: editor@rrobserver.com
Editor Phone: (505) 891-7172
Advertising Executive Name: Susan Saunier
Advertising Executive Email: ssaunier@abqjournal.com
Advertising Executive Phone: (505) 221-9881
Delivery Methods: Newsstand`Carrier`Racks
Year Established: 1973
Own Printing Facility?: Y
Mechanical specifications: Type page 11 5/8 x 21 1/2; E - 6 cols, 1 13/16, 1/8 between; A - 6 cols, 1 13/16, 1/8 between; C - 7 cols, 1 9/16, 13/100 between.
Published Days: Sun
Avg. Free Circ.: 23500
Audit Company: Sworn/Estimate/Non-Audited
Audit Date: 43626

RUIDOSO

THE RUIDOSO NEWS

Street Address: 104 Park Ave
City: Ruidoso
State: NM
ZIP Code: 88345-6154
General Phone: (575) 257-4001
General Email: jonsurez@gannett.com
Publication Website: https://www.ruidosonews.com/
Parent Company: Gannett
Advertising Executive Phone: (800) 764-5620
Delivery Methods: Mail`Newsstand`Racks
Year Established: 1946
Own Printing Facility?: Y
Mechanical specifications: Type page 12 1/2 x 21 1/4; E - 6 cols, 1 5/6, 1/6 between; A - 6 cols, 1 5/6, 1/6 between; C - 8 cols, 1 1/3, 1/6 between.
Published Days: Wed`Fri
Avg. Paid Circ.: 2214
Avg. Free Circ.: 45
Audit Company: AAM
Audit Date: 43354
Note: Vamono's is inserted into the Ruidoso News, Carlsbad Current Argus, and Alamogordo Daily News every Friday. Vamono's is an Arts and Entertainment tabloid that is inserted and racked for free at 60 locations throughout Lincoln, Otero, and Eddy Counties.

SANTA FE

SANTA FE REPORTER

Street Address: 132 E Marcy St
City: Santa Fe
State: NM
ZIP Code: 87501-2054
General Phone: (505) 988-5541
General Email: advertising@sfreporter.com
Publication Website: https://www.sfreporter.com/
Parent Company: City of Roses Newspaper Company
Publisher Name: Julie Ann Grimm
Publisher Phone: (505) 988-5541, ext : 1215
Editor Name: Julie Ann Grimm
Editor Email: editor@sfreporter.com
Editor Phone: (505) 988-5541, ext : 1215
Advertising Executive Name: Anna Maggiore
Advertising Executive Email: anna@sfreporter.com
Advertising Executive Phone: (505) 988-5541, ext : 1207
Delivery Methods: Racks
Year Established: 1974
Published Days: Wed
Avg. Free Circ.: 15000
Audit Company: Sworn/Estimate/Non-Audited
Audit Date: 43626

SOCORRO

EL DEFENSOR CHIEFTAIN

Street Address: 200 Winkler St
City: Socorro
State: NM
ZIP Code: 87801-4200
General Phone: (575) 835-0520
General Email: editorial@dchieftain.com
Publication Website: http://www.dchieftain.com/
Publisher Name: Wanda Moeller
Publisher Email: wmoeller@dchieftain.com
Publisher Phone: (575) 517-2701
Editor Name: Wanda Moeller
Editor Email: wmoeller@dchieftain.com
Editor Phone: (575) 517-2701
Advertising Executive Name: Stephanie McFadden
Advertising Executive Email: smcfadden@dchieftain.com
Advertising Executive Phone: (505) 517-2699
Year Established: 1860
Own Printing Facility?: Y
Mechanical specifications: Type page 11 5/6 x 21 1/2; E - 6 cols, 1 5/6, 1/6 between; A - 6 cols, 1 5/6, 1/6 between; C - 8 cols, 1, 1/6 between.
Published Days: Wed`Sat
Avg. Paid Circ.: 72020
Audit Company: Sworn/Estimate/Non-Audited
Audit Date: 43626

TAOS

THE TAOS NEWS

Street Address: 226 Albright St
City: Taos
State: NM
ZIP Code: 87571-6312
General Phone: (575) 758-2241
General Email: admanager@taosnews.com
Publication Website: https://www.taosnews.com
Publisher Name: Staci Matlock
Editor Name: Staci Matlock
Editor Email: editor@taosnews.com
Advertising Executive Name: Chris Wood
Advertising Executive Email: admanager@taosnews.com
Delivery Methods: Mail`Newsstand`Carrier`Racks
Year Established: 1959
Own Printing Facility?: Y
Commercial printers?: Y
Mechanical specifications: Type page 13 x 21 1/2; E - 6 cols, 2 1/16, between; A - 6 cols, 2 1/16, between; C - 9 cols, 1 1/4, between.
Published Days: Thur
Avg. Paid Circ.: 6871
Avg. Free Circ.: 14
Audit Company: VAC
Audit Date: 43625

TRUTH OR CONSEQUENCES

SIERRA COUNTY SENTINEL

Street Address: 1747 E 3rd Ave
City: Truth Or Consequences
State: NM
ZIP Code: 87901-2042
General Phone: (575) 894-3088
General Email: sentinel@gpkmedia.com
Publication Website: https://www.gpkmedia.com/
Parent Company: New Mexico Press Association
Publisher Name: Frances Luna
Publisher Email: francesfirecrackerluna@gmail.com
Editor Name: Chuck Wentworth
Editor Email: chuckw57@gmail.com
Delivery Methods: Mail`Newsstand`Carrier`Racks
Year Established: 1967
Own Printing Facility?: Y
Commercial printers?: N
Mechanical specifications: Type page 11 1/2 x 21; E - 8 cols, 1 5/8, 1/6 between; A - 8 cols, 1 5/8, 1/6 between; C - 8 cols, 1 5/8, 1/6 between.
Published Days: Fri
Avg. Paid Circ.: 4580
Avg. Free Circ.: 30
Audit Company: Sworn/Estimate/Non-Audited
Audit Date: 43626

TUCUMCARI

QUAY COUNTY SUN

Street Address: 902 S 1st St
City: Tucumcari
State: NM
ZIP Code: 88401-3217
General Phone: (575) 461-1952
General Email: info@qcsunonline.com
Publication Website: https://www.qcsunonline.com/
Parent Company: Clovis Media Inc.
Mechanical specifications: Type page 13 x 21 1/2; E - 6 cols, 2 1/16, 1/8 between; A - 6 cols, 2 1/16, 1/8 between; C - 9 cols, 1 3/8, 1/8 between.
Published Days: Wed`Sat
Avg. Paid Circ.: 4200
Avg. Free Circ.: 30
Audit Company: Sworn/Estimate/Non-Audited
Audit Date: 43626

NEVADA

BOULDER CITY

BOULDER CITY REVIEW

Street Address: 508 Nevada Way
City: Boulder City
State: NV
ZIP Code: 89005
General Phone: (702) 823-1457
General Email: volsen@bouldercityreview.com
Publication Website: https://bouldercityreview.com/
Parent Company: Las Vegas Review-Journal Inc.
Publisher Name: Noah Cusick
Publisher Email: ncusick@bouldercityreview.com
Editor Name: Hali Bernstein Saylor
Editor Email: hsaylor@bouldercityreview.com
Editor Phone: (702) 586-9523
Advertising Executive Name: Val Olsen
Advertising Executive Email: volsen@bouldercityreview.com

LAS VEGAS

LAS VEGAS BUSINESS PRESS

Street Address: 1111 W Bonanza Rd
City: Las Vegas
State: NV
ZIP Code: 89106-3545
General Phone: (702) 383-4617
General Email: adhelp@reviewjournal.com
Publication Website: https://businesspress.vegas/
Parent Company: Las Vegas Review-Journal, Inc.
Editor Name: Lyn Collier
Editor Email: lcollier@businesspress.vegas
Editor Phone: (702) 383-0299
Advertising Executive Email: adhelp@reviewjournal.com

LAS VEGAS

NIFTY NICKEL

Street Address: 1111 W Bonanza Rd
City: Las Vegas
State: NV
ZIP Code: 89106
General Phone: (702) 224-5500
Publication Website: http://thriftynickel.com/papers/las-vegas-las-vegas-nye-county-nifty-nickel-1489/about.html
Parent Company: Las Vegas Review-Journal, Inc.

LAS VEGAS

VIEW NEIGHBORHOOD NEWSPAPERS

Street Address: 1111 W Bonanza Rd

City: Las Vegas
State: NV
ZIP Code: 89106
General Phone: (702) 380-4589
General Email: kmoyer@reviewjournal.com
Publication Website: https://www.reviewjournal.com/local/local-las-vegas/downtown/view-neighborhood-newspapers-names-new-editor/
Parent Company: Las Vegas Review-Journal, Inc.
Publisher Name: J. Keith Moyer
Publisher Email: kmoyer@reviewjournal.com
Publisher Phone: (702) 477-3829
Editor Name: Anastasia Hendrix
Editor Email: ahendrix@reviewjournal.com
Editor Phone: (702) 383-0232

LOGANDALE

MOAPA VALLEY PROGRESS

Street Address: 2885 N Moapa Valley Blvd
City: Logandale
State: NV
ZIP Code: 89021
General Phone: (702) 397-6246
General Email: vrobison@mvprogress.com
Publication Website: https://mvprogress.com/
Publisher Name: Vernon Richardson
Publisher Email: vrobison@mvprogress.com
Editor Name: Vernon Robison
Editor Email: vrobison@mvprogress.com
Advertising Executive Name: Laura Robison
Advertising Executive Email: progress2@mvdsl.com

MESQUITE

DESERT VALLEY TIMES

Street Address: 355 W Mesquite Blvd
City: Mesquite
State: NV
ZIP Code: 89027-8128
General Phone: (702) 323-7922
General Email: ddemille@thespectrum.com
Publication Website: https://www.thespectrum.com/mesquite/
Publisher Name: David DeMille
Publisher Email: ddemille@thespectrum.com

PAHRUMP

PAHRUMP VALLEY TIMES

Street Address: 1570 E HIGHWAY 372
City: Pahrump
State: NV
ZIP Code: 89048
General Phone: (775) 727-5102
General Email: pvtads@pvtimes.com
Publication Website: https://pvtimes.com/
Parent Company: Las Vegas Review-Journal, Inc.
Publisher Name: Noah Cusick
Publisher Email: ncusick@pvtimes.com
Publisher Phone: (775) 727-5102, ext : 1015
Editor Name: Jeffrey Meehan
Editor Email: jmeehan@pvtimes.com
Editor Phone: (775) 727-5102, ext : 1011
Advertising Executive Email: pvtads@pvtimes.com

PAHRUMP

TONOPAH TIMES-BONANZA AND GOLDFIELD NEWS

Street Address: 1570 E HIGHWAY 372
City: Pahrump
State: NV
ZIP Code: 89048
General Phone: (775) 727-5102
General Email: pvtads@pvtimes.com
Publication Website: https://pvtimes.com/tonopah/
Parent Company: Las Vegas Review-Journal, Inc.
Publisher Name: Noah Cusick
Publisher Email: ncusick@pvtimes.com
Publisher Phone: (775) 727-5102, ext : 1015
Editor Name: Jeffrey Meehan
Editor Email: jmeehan@pvtimes.com
Editor Phone: (775) 727-5102, ext : 1011
Advertising Executive Email: pvtads@pvtimes.com

RENO

RENO NEWS & REVIEW

Street Address: 760 Margrave Drive
City: Reno
State: NV
ZIP Code: 89502
General Phone: (775) 324-4440
General Email: jobs@newsreview.com
Publication Website: https://www.newsreview.com/reno/home
Parent Company: Chico Community Publishing Inc.
Editor Name: Brad Bynum

SPARKS

SPARKS TRIBUNE

Street Address: 155 Glendale Ave
City: Sparks
State: NV
ZIP Code: 89431-5751
General Phone: (775) 358-8062
General Email: advertising@sparkstrib.com
Publication Website: https://sparkstrib.com/
Parent Company: Battle Born Media LLC
Publisher Name: Sherman Frederick
Publisher Email: shermfrederick@gmail.com
Publisher Phone: (702) 525-2440
Editor Name: Eric Dahlberg
Editor Email: sparkstribune.eric@gmail.com
Editor Phone: (775) 316-2265
Advertising Executive Email: advertising@sparkstrib.com

WENDOVER

HIGH DESERT ADVOCATE

Street Address: PO Box 2805
City: Wendover
State: NV
ZIP Code: 89883
General Phone: (775) 664-3415
General Email: advocate@wrecwireless.coop
Publication Website: https://www.coyote-tv.com/
Parent Company: Coyote TV

WINNEMUCCA

BATTLE MOUNTAIN BUGLE

Street Address: 1022 Grass Valley Rd
City: Winnemucca
State: NV
ZIP Code: 89445
General Phone: (775) 635-2230
General Email: k.koseck@winnemuccapublishing.net
Publication Website: https://nevadanewsgroup.com/
Parent Company: Winnemucca Publishing
Publisher Name: Peter Bernhard
Publisher Email: peterbernhard@yahoo.com
Publisher Phone: (925) 683-0439
Editor Name: Jen Anderson
Editor Email: jen.anderson@winnemuccapublishing.net
Editor Phone: (775) 623-5011, ext : 205
Advertising Executive Name: Rhonda Coleman
Advertising Executive Email: r.coleman@winnemuccapublishing.net

WINNEMUCCA

LOVELOCK REVIEW-MINER

Street Address: 1022 Grass Valley Rd
City: Winnemucca
State: NV
ZIP Code: 89445
General Phone: (775) 623-5011
General Email: l.enget@winnemuccapublishing.net
Publication Website: https://nevadanewsgroup.com/
Parent Company: Winnemucca Publishing
Publisher Name: Peter Bernhard
Publisher Email: peterbernhard@yahoo.com
Publisher Phone: (925) 683-0439
Editor Name: Jen Anderson
Editor Email: jen.anderson@winnemuccapublishing.net
Editor Phone: (775) 623-5011, ext : 205
Advertising Executive Name: Rhonda Coleman
Advertising Executive Email: r.coleman@winnemuccapublishing.net

WINNEMUCCA

THE HUMBOLDT SUN

Street Address: 1022 Grass Valley Rd
City: Winnemucca
State: NV
ZIP Code: 89445
General Phone: (775) 623-5011
General Email: r.coleman@winnemuccapublishing.net
Publication Website: https://nevadanewsgroup.com/
Parent Company: Winnemucca Publishing
Publisher Name: Peter Bernhard
Publisher Email: peterbernhard@yahoo.com
Publisher Phone: (925) 683-0439
Editor Name: Jen Anderson
Editor Email: jen.anderson@winnemuccapublishing.net
Editor Phone: (775) 623-5011, ext : 205
Advertising Executive Name: Rhonda Coleman
Advertising Executive Email: r.coleman@winnemuccapublishing.net

NEW YORK

AKRON

AKRON BUGLE

Street Address: 7263 Downey Rd
City: Akron
State: NY
ZIP Code: 14001-9714
General Phone: (716) 542-9615
General Email: akronbugleadvertising@gmail.com
Publication Website: http://www.akronbugle.com/
Advertising Executive Email: akronbugleadvertising@gmail.com
Delivery Methods: Mail Newsstand
Year Established: 1981
Own Printing Facility?: N
Mechanical specifications: Type page 10 x 15.85; 5 cols, 2
Published Days: Thur
Avg. Paid Circ.: 1895
Avg. Free Circ.: 15
Audit Company: Sworn/Estimate/Non-Audited
Audit Date: 43626

ALBANY

THE LEGISLATIVE GAZETTE

Street Address: PO Box 7329
City: Albany
State: NY
ZIP Code: 12224-0329
General Phone: (518) 486-6513
General Email: ads@legislativegazette.com
Publication Website: https://legislativegazette.com/
Parent Company: State University of New York at New Paltz
Publisher Name: Alan Chartock
Publisher Phone: (518) 465-5233, ext : 150
Editor Name: James Gormley
Editor Email: editor@legislativegazette.com
Editor Phone: (518) 257-2901
Year Established: 1978
Published Days: Tues
Audit Company: Sworn/Estimate/Non-Audited
Audit Date: 43626

ALDEN

ALDEN ADVERTISER

Street Address: 13200 Broadway St
City: Alden
State: NY
ZIP Code: 14004-1313
General Phone: (716) 937-9226
General Email: aldenadvertiser@rochester.rr.com
Publication Website: https://aldenadvertisernews.com/
Parent Company: Leonard A. Weisbeck Jr
Editor Name: Leonard A. Weisbeck
Advertising Executive Email: aldenadvertiser@rochester.rr.com
Advertising Executive Phone: (716) 937-9226
Year Established: 1914
Mechanical specifications: Type page 10 x 16; E - 5 cols, 1 11/12, 1/6 between; A - 5 cols, 1 11/12, 1/6 between.
Published Days: Thur
Avg. Paid Circ.: 3550
Avg. Free Circ.: 108
Audit Company: Sworn/Estimate/Non-Audited
Audit Date: 43626

ALEXANDRIA BAY

THOUSAND ISLAND SUN

Street Address: Route 12
City: Alexandria Bay
State: NY
ZIP Code: 13607
General Phone: (315) 482-2581
General Email: tisun@gisco.net
Publication Website: http://www.thousandislandssun.net/
Advertising Executive Email: tisun@gisco.net
Year Established: 1901
Mechanical specifications: Type page 16 x 21; E - 7 cols, 2, 1/6 between; A - 7 cols, 2, 1/6 between; C - 7 cols, 2, 1/6 between.
Published Days: Wed
Avg. Paid Circ.: 6397
Avg. Free Circ.: 25
Audit Company: Sworn/Estimate/Non-Audited
Audit Date: 43626

ALFRED

THE ALFRED SUN

Street Address: 764 State Rt 244

Community Newspapers in the U.S.

City: Alfred
State: NY
ZIP Code: 14802
General Phone: (607) 587-8110
General Email: alfredsun.news@gmail.com
Publication Website: https://aura.alfred.edu/
Parent Company: Alfred University
Publisher Name: Dave Snyder
Delivery Methods: Mail`Newsstand
Year Established: 1883
Mechanical specifications: Type page 11 x 14; E - 5 cols, 2, between; A - 5 cols, 2, between; C - 6 cols, 1 5/8, between.
Published Days: Thur
Avg. Paid Circ.: 959
Avg. Free Circ.: 50
Audit Company: Sworn/Estimate/Non-Audited
Audit Date: 43626

ALTAMONT

THE ALTAMONT ENTERPRISE & ALBANY COUNTY POST

Street Address: 120 Maple Ave
City: Altamont
State: NY
ZIP Code: 12009-7718
General Phone: (518) 861-4026
General Email: ads@altamontenterprise.com
Publication Website: https://altamontenterprise.com/
Parent Company: Melissa Hale-Spencer
Editor Name: Melissa Hale-Spencer
Editor Email: mhale-spencer@altamontenterprise.com
Editor Phone: (518)861-4026, ext : 102
Advertising Executive Email: ads@altamontenterprise.com
Delivery Methods: Mail`Newsstand
Year Established: 1884
Mechanical specifications: Type page 11 1/4 x 16; E - 5 cols, 1 7/8, 1/8 between; A - 5 cols, 1 7/8, 1/8 between; C - 5 cols, 1 7/8, 1/8 between.
Published Days: Thur
Avg. Paid Circ.: 4757
Avg. Free Circ.: 111
Audit Company: Sworn/Estimate/Non-Audited
Audit Date: 43626
Note: Award-winning coverage of local news

AMITYVILLE

MASSAPEQUA POST

Street Address: 85 Broadway
City: Amityville
State: NY
ZIP Code: 11701
General Phone: (516) 798-5100
General Email: acjads@optonline.net
Publication Website: https://www.massapequapost.com/
Parent Company: CJ Publishers Inc.
Publisher Name: Alfred James
Editor Name: Carolyn James
Advertising Executive Name: Maryann Heins
Advertising Executive Email: acjads@optonline.net
Delivery Methods: Mail`Newsstand
Year Established: 1954
Mechanical specifications: Type page 10 x 12; 6 cols, 1.5, 0.125 between
Published Days: Wed
Avg. Paid Circ.: 2800
Avg. Free Circ.: 400
Audit Company: Sworn/Estimate/Non-Audited
Audit Date: 43626

AMITYVILLE

THE AMITYVILLE RECORD

Street Address: 85 Broadway

City: Amityville
State: NY
ZIP Code: 11701
General Phone: (631) 264-0077
General Email: acjads@optonline.net
Publication Website: https://www.amityvillerecord.com/
Parent Company: CJ Publishers Inc.
Publisher Name: Alfred James
Editor Name: Carolyn James
Advertising Executive Name: Barbara Frisch
Delivery Methods: Mail`Newsstand
Year Established: 1904
Mechanical specifications: Type page 10 x 12; 6 cols, 1.5, 0.125 between
Published Days: Wed
Avg. Paid Circ.: 2800
Avg. Free Circ.: 300
Audit Company: Sworn/Estimate/Non-Audited
Audit Date: 43626

AMSTERDAM

COURIER STANDARD ENTERPRISE

Street Address: 1 Venner Rd
City: Amsterdam
State: NY
ZIP Code: 12010
General Phone: (518) 843-1100
General Email: support@mcclarymedia.com
Publication Website: https://www.courierstandardenterprise.com/
Parent Company: McClary Media, Inc.
Publisher Name: Kevin McClary
Publisher Email: kevin@mcclarymedia.com
Editor Name: Joshua Thomas
Editor Email: joshua.thomas@mcclarymedia.com
Advertising Executive Name: Elisha Gill
Advertising Executive Email: elisha.gill@mcclarymedia.com
Advertising Executive Phone: (518) 843-1100, ext : 123
Delivery Methods: Mail`Newsstand
Year Established: 1876
Own Printing Facility?: N
Commercial printers?: N
Published Days: Fri
Avg. Paid Circ.: 2000
Avg. Free Circ.: 100
Audit Company: Sworn/Estimate/Non-Audited
Audit Date: 43626

AMSTERDAM

SACANDAGA EXPRESS

Street Address: 1 Venner Rd
City: Amsterdam
State: NY
ZIP Code: 12010-5617
General Phone: (518) 843-1100
General Email: news@mcclarymedia.com
Publication Website: https://www.sacandagaexpress.com/
Parent Company: Port Jackson Media LLC
Publisher Name: Kevin McClary
Publisher Email: kevin@mcclarymedia.com
Advertising Executive Name: Elisha Gill
Advertising Executive Email: elisha.gill@mcclarymedia.com
Delivery Methods: Newsstand
Published Days: Wed`Fri
Avg. Free Circ.: 4500
Audit Company: Sworn/Estimate/Non-Audited
Audit Date: 43626

ARCADE

ARCADE HERALD

Street Address: 223 Main St
City: Arcade
State: NY

ZIP Code: 14009-1209
General Phone: (585) 492-2525
General Email: heraldads@roadrunner.com
Publication Website: https://www.arcadeherald.com/
Parent Company: Neighbor to Neighbor News, Inc.
Publisher Name: Grant Hamilton
Editor Name: Casey Dunlap
Advertising Executive Name: Tammy Hobson
Year Established: 1891
Mechanical specifications: Type page 10.5 x 19.5; 5 cols, 2, 0.125 between
Published Days: Thur
Avg. Paid Circ.: 5000
Audit Company: Sworn/Estimate/Non-Audited
Audit Date: 43626

ARKVILLE

CATSKILL MOUNTAIN NEWS

Street Address: 43414 State Hwy. 28, P. O. Box 515
City: Arkville
State: NY
ZIP Code: 12406
General Phone: (845) 586-2601
General Email: cnewsjlb@gmail.com
Publication Website: https://www.catskillmountainnews.com/
Publisher Name: Joan Lawrence-Bauer
Publisher Email: cnewsjlb@gmail.com
Editor Name: Joan Lawrence-Bauer
Editor Email: cnewsjlb@gmail.com
Advertising Executive Name: Dana Hensley
Advertising Executive Email: ads@catskillmountainnews.com
Year Established: 1863
Mechanical specifications: Type page 12 x 21; E - 6 cols, 1 7/8, 1/8 between; A - 6 cols, 1 7/8, 1/8 between; C - 9 cols, 1 1/4, 1/16 between.
Published Days: Wed
Avg. Paid Circ.: 4100
Avg. Free Circ.: 6
Audit Company: Sworn/Estimate/Non-Audited
Audit Date: 43626

BABYLON

THE BEACON

Street Address: 65 Deer Park Ave
City: Babylon
State: NY
ZIP Code: 11701
General Phone: (631) 587-5612
General Email: acjads@optonline.net
Publication Website: https://www.babylonbeacon.com/
Parent Company: Gannett
Publisher Name: Alfred James
Editor Name: Carolyn James
Advertising Executive Email: acjads@optonline.net
Delivery Methods: Mail`Newsstand`Racks
Year Established: 1966
Own Printing Facility?: N
Mechanical specifications: Type page 10 x 12; 6 cols, 1.5, 0.125 between
Published Days: Thur
Avg. Paid Circ.: 2800
Avg. Free Circ.: 400
Audit Company: Sworn/Estimate/Non-Audited
Audit Date: 43626

BALLSTON SPA

BALLSTON JOURNAL

Street Address: PO Box 319
City: Ballston Spa
State: NY

ZIP Code: 12020-0319
General Phone: (518) 885-5238
General Email: jpublisher@theballstonjournal.com
Publication Website: https://theballstonjournal.com/
Year Established: 1798
Mechanical specifications: Type page 9 3/4 x 14; E - 6 cols, 1 1/2, 1/3 between; A - 6 cols, between; C - 6 cols, between.
Published Days: Thur
Avg. Free Circ.: 151000
Audit Company: Sworn/Estimate/Non-Audited
Audit Date: 43626

BAYSIDE

ASTORIA TIMES

Street Address: 41-02 Bell Blvd
City: Bayside
State: NY
ZIP Code: 11361-2792
General Phone: (718) 229-0300
General Email: timesledgernews@cnglocal.com
Publication Website: https://qns.com/
Parent Company: Community News Group
Publisher Name: Steven Blank
Publisher Email: sblank@timesledger.com
Publisher Phone: (718) 229-0300, ext : 111
Editor Name: Roz Liston
Editor Email: liston@timesledger.com
Editor Phone: (718) 229-0300, Ext : 136
Delivery Methods: Mail`Racks
Mechanical specifications: Type page 10 1/3 x 14; E - 4 cols, 2 4/9, 1/6 between; A - 4 cols, 2 4/9, 1/6 between; C - 7 cols, 1 5/12, 1/8 between.
Published Days: Thur
Avg. Paid Circ.: 1983
Audit Company: Sworn/Estimate/Non-Audited
Audit Date: 43626

BAYSIDE

BAYSIDE TIMES

Street Address: 38-15 Bell Blvd.
City: Bayside
State: NY
ZIP Code: 11361-2794
General Phone: (718) 260-2500
General Email: bbrennan@queenscourier.com
Publication Website: https://qns.com/groups/bayside/
Parent Company: Les Goodstein, Jennifer Goodstein
Publisher Name: Victoria Schneps-Yunis
Publisher Email: vschneps@qns.com
Editor Name: Zach Gewelb
Editor Email: zgewelb@schnepsmedia.com
Editor Phone: (718) 260-8303
Advertising Executive Email: bbrennan@queenscourier.com
Advertising Executive Phone: (718) 260-2538
Delivery Methods: Mail`Racks
Year Established: 1935
Mechanical specifications: Type page 10 1/3 x 14; E - 4 cols, 2 4/9, 1/6 between; A - 4 cols, 2 4/9, 1/6 between; C - 8 cols, 1 1/8, 1/8 between.
Published Days: Fri
Avg. Paid Circ.: 11042
Audit Company: Sworn/Estimate/Non-Audited
Audit Date: 43626

BAYSIDE

FLUSHING TIMES

Street Address: 38-15 Bell Blvd.
City: Bayside
State: NY

ZIP Code: 11361
General Phone: (718) 260-2500
General Email: jschneps@qns.com
Publication Website: https://qns.com/groups/flushing/
Parent Company: Community News Group
Publisher Name: Victoria Schneps-Yunis
Publisher Email: vschneps@qns.com
Editor Name: Zach Gewelb
Editor Email: zgewelb@schnepsmedia.com
Editor Phone: (718) 260-8303
Advertising Executive Email: bbrennan@queenscourier.com
Advertising Executive Phone: (718) 260-2538
Delivery Methods: Mail`Newsstand`Racks
Year Established: 1992
Mechanical specifications: Type page 10 1/3 x 14; E - 4 cols, 2 4/9, 1/6 between; A - 4 cols, 2 4/9, 1/6 between; C - 8 cols, 1 1/8, 1/8 between.
Published Days: Thur
Avg. Paid Circ.: 5015
Audit Company: Sworn/Estimate/Non-Audited
Audit Date: 43626

BAYSIDE

FOREST HILLS LEDGER

Street Address: 38-15 Bell Blvd.
City: Bayside
State: NY
ZIP Code: 11361
General Phone: (718) 260-2500
General Email: jschneps@qns.com
Publication Website: https://qns.com/groups/forest-hills/
Parent Company: Community News Group
Publisher Name: Victoria Schneps-Yunis
Publisher Email: vschneps@qns.com
Editor Name: Zach Gewelb
Editor Email: zgewelb@schnepsmedia.com
Editor Phone: (718) 260-8303
Advertising Executive Email: bbrennan@queenscourier.com
Advertising Executive Phone: (718) 260-2538
Mechanical specifications: Type page 10 1/3 x 14; E - 4 cols, 2 4/9, 1/6 between; A - 4 cols, 2 4/9, 1/6 between; C - 7 cols, 1 5/12, 1/8 between.
Published Days: Thur
Avg. Paid Circ.: 2503
Audit Company: Sworn/Estimate/Non-Audited
Audit Date: 43626

BAYSIDE

FRESH MEADOWS TIMES

Street Address: 38-15 Bell Blvd.
City: Bayside
State: NY
ZIP Code: 11361
General Phone: (718) 260-2500
General Email: jschneps@qns.com
Publication Website: https://qns.com/groups/flushing/
Parent Company: Community News Group
Publisher Name: Victoria Schneps-Yunis
Publisher Email: vschneps@qns.com
Editor Name: Zach Gewelb
Editor Email: zgewelb@schnepsmedia.com
Editor Phone: (718) 260-8303
Advertising Executive Email: bbrennan@queenscourier.com
Advertising Executive Phone: (718) 260-2538
Delivery Methods: Newsstand`Racks
Mechanical specifications: Page- 9.75 x 11 (inches) E- 6 columns, 1.5 inches/column,1/4 inch between A-6 columns, 1.5 inches/ column,1/4 inch between C- 8 columns, 1.1367 inches/column
Published Days: Fri
Avg. Paid Circ.: 21000
Audit Company: Sworn/Estimate/Non-Audited
Audit Date: 43626

BAYSIDE

JACKSON HEIGHTS TIMES

Street Address: 38-15 Bell Blvd.
City: Bayside
State: NY
ZIP Code: 11361
General Phone: (718) 260-2500
General Email: jschneps@qns.com
Publication Website: https://qns.com/groups/jackson-heights/
Parent Company: Community News Group
Publisher Name: Victoria Schneps-Yunis
Publisher Email: vschneps@qns.com
Editor Name: Zach Gewelb
Editor Email: zgewelb@schnepsmedia.com
Editor Phone: (718) 260-8303
Advertising Executive Email: bbrennan@queenscourier.com
Advertising Executive Phone: (718) 260-2538
Delivery Methods: Newsstand`Racks
Mechanical specifications: Page- 9.75 x 11 (inches) E- 6 columns, 1.5 inches/column,1/4 inch between A-6 columns, 1.5 inches/ column,1/4 inch between C- 8 columns, 1.1367 inches/column
Published Days: Fri
Avg. Paid Circ.: 21000
Audit Company: Sworn/Estimate/Non-Audited
Audit Date: 43626

BAYSIDE

JAMAICA TIMES

Street Address: 38-15 Bell Blvd.
City: Bayside
State: NY
ZIP Code: 11361
General Phone: (718) 260-2500
General Email: jschneps@qns.com
Publication Website: https://qns.com/groups/jamaica/
Parent Company: Community News Group
Publisher Name: Victoria Schneps-Yunis
Publisher Email: vschneps@qns.com
Editor Name: Zach Gewelb
Editor Email: zgewelb@schnepsmedia.com
Editor Phone: (718) 260-8303
Advertising Executive Email: bbrennan@queenscourier.com
Advertising Executive Phone: (718) 260-2538
Delivery Methods: Newsstand`Racks
Mechanical specifications: Page- 9.75 x 11 (inches) E- 6 columns, 1.5 inches/column,1/4 inch between A-6 columns, 1.5 inches/ column,1/4 inch between C- 8 columns, 1.1367 inches/column
Published Days: Fri
Avg. Paid Circ.: 21000
Audit Company: Sworn/Estimate/Non-Audited
Audit Date: 43626

BAYSIDE

LAURELTON TIMES

Street Address: 38-15 Bell Blvd.
City: Bayside
State: NY
ZIP Code: 11361
General Phone: (718) 260-2500
General Email: jschneps@qns.com
Publication Website: https://qns.com/groups/laurelton/
Parent Company: Community News Group
Publisher Name: Victoria Schneps-Yunis
Publisher Email: vschneps@qns.com
Editor Name: Zach Gewelb
Editor Email: zgewelb@schnepsmedia.com
Editor Phone: (718) 260-8303
Advertising Executive Email: bbrennan@queenscourier.com
Advertising Executive Phone: (718) 260-2538
Delivery Methods: Newsstand`Racks
Mechanical specifications: Page- 9.75 x 11 (inches) E- 6 columns, 1.5 inches/column,1/4 inch between A-6 columns, 1.5 inches/ column,1/4 inch between C- 8 columns, 1.1367 inches/column
Published Days: Fri
Avg. Paid Circ.: 21000
Audit Company: Sworn/Estimate/Non-Audited
Audit Date: 43626

BAYSIDE

RIDGEWOOD LEDGER

Street Address: 38-15 Bell Blvd.
City: Bayside
State: NY
ZIP Code: 11361
General Phone: (718) 260-2500
General Email: jschneps@qns.com
Publication Website: https://qns.com/groups/ridgewood/
Parent Company: Les Goodstein, Jennifer Goodstein
Publisher Name: Victoria Schneps-Yunis
Publisher Email: vschneps@qns.com
Editor Name: Zach Gewelb
Editor Email: zgewelb@schnepsmedia.com
Editor Phone: (718) 260-8303
Advertising Executive Email: bbrennan@queenscourier.com
Advertising Executive Phone: (718) 260-2538
Delivery Methods: Newsstand`Racks
Mechanical specifications: Page- 9.75 x 11 (inches) E- 6 columns, 1.5 inches/column,1/4 inch between A-6 columns, 1.5 inches/ column,1/4 inch between C- 8 columns, 1.1367 inches/column
Published Days: Fri
Avg. Paid Circ.: 21000
Audit Company: Sworn/Estimate/Non-Audited
Audit Date: 43626

BAYSIDE

THE LITTLE NECK LEDGER

Street Address: 38-15 Bell Blvd.
City: Bayside
State: NY
ZIP Code: 11361-2794
General Phone: (718) 260-2500
General Email: bbrennan@queenscourier.com
Publication Website: https://qns.com/groups/little-neck/
Parent Company: Les Goodstein, Jennifer Goodstein
Publisher Name: Victoria Schneps-Yunis
Publisher Email: vschneps@qns.com
Editor Name: Zach Gewelb
Editor Email: zgewelb@schnepsmedia.com
Editor Phone: (718) 260-8303
Advertising Executive Email: bbrennan@queenscourier.com
Advertising Executive Phone: (718) 260-2538
Mechanical specifications: Type page 10 1/3 x 14; E - 4 cols, 2 4/9, 1/6 between; A - 4 cols, 2 4/9, 1/6 between; C - 7 cols, 1 5/12, 1/8 between.
Published Days: Thur
Avg. Paid Circ.: 1686
Audit Company: Sworn/Estimate/Non-Audited
Audit Date: 43626

BAYSIDE

THE QUEENS COURIER

Street Address: 38-15 Bell Blvd.
City: Bayside
State: NY
ZIP Code: 11361-2058
General Phone: (718) 224-5863
General Email: bbrennan@queenscourier.com
Publication Website: https://qns.com/
Parent Company: Les Goodstein, Jennifer Goodstein
Publisher Name: Victoria Schneps-Yunis
Publisher Email: vschneps@qns.com
Editor Name: Zach Gewelb
Editor Email: zgewelb@schnepsmedia.com
Editor Phone: (718) 260-8303
Advertising Executive Email: bbrennan@queenscourier.com
Advertising Executive Phone: (718) 260-2538
Delivery Methods: Mail`Newsstand`Racks
Year Established: 1985
Mechanical specifications: Full page 8.75 x 11.5 1/2 page Horizontal 8.75 x 5.6875 1/2 page Vertical 4.313 x 11.5 Strip 8.75 x 1.8125 Quarter page 4.313 x 5.6875 Eighth page 4.313 x 2.78125 Junior page 8.75 x 8.25
Published Days: Thur
Avg. Paid Circ.: 6000
Avg. Free Circ.: 70000
Audit Company: Sworn/Estimate/Non-Audited
Audit Date: 43626

BAYSIDE

THE WHITESTONE TIMES

Street Address: 38-15 Bell Blvd.
City: Bayside
State: NY
ZIP Code: 11361-2794
General Phone: (718) 260-2500
General Email: bbrennan@queenscourier.com
Publication Website: https://qns.com/groups/whitestone/
Parent Company: Les Goodstein, Jennifer Goodstein
Publisher Name: Victoria Schneps-Yunis
Publisher Email: vschneps@qns.com
Editor Name: Zach Gewelb
Editor Email: zgewelb@schnepsmedia.com
Editor Phone: (718) 260-8303
Advertising Executive Email: bbrennan@queenscourier.com
Advertising Executive Phone: (718) 260-2538
Delivery Methods: Mail`Newsstand`Racks
Mechanical specifications: Type page 10 1/3 x 14; E - 4 cols, 2 4/9, 1/6 between; A - 4 cols, 2 4/9, 1/6 between; C - 7 cols, 1 5/12, 1/8 between.
Published Days: Thur
Avg. Paid Circ.: 5015
Audit Company: Sworn/Estimate/Non-Audited
Audit Date: 43626

BAYSIDE

TIMES NEWSWEEKLY

Street Address: 3815 Bell Blvd
City: Bayside
State: NY
ZIP Code: 11361
General Phone: (718) 260-2500
General Email: bbrennan@queenscourier.com
Publication Website: https://qns.com/timesnewsweekly/
Parent Company: Les Goodstein
Publisher Name: Victoria Schneps-Yunis
Publisher Email: vschneps@qns.com
Editor Name: Zach Gewelb
Editor Email: zgewelb@schnepsmedia.com
Editor Phone: (718) 260-8303
Advertising Executive Email: bbrennan@queenscourier.com
Advertising Executive Phone: (718) 260-2538
Delivery Methods: Mail`Newsstand
Year Established: 1908
Own Printing Facility?: Y
Published Days: Thur
Avg. Paid Circ.: 20000
Audit Company: Sworn/Estimate/Non-Audited
Audit Date: 43626

Community Newspapers in the U.S.

BEDFORD HILLS

RECORD-REVIEW

Street Address: PO Box 455
City: Bedford Hills
State: NY
ZIP Code: 10507
General Phone: (914) 244-0533
General Email: flynch@scarsdalenews.com
Publication Website: http://www.record-review.com/record-review/Home.html
Publisher Name: Deborah G. White
Publisher Email: dwhite@scarsdalenews.com
Editor Name: Ed Baum
Editor Email: ebaum@record-review.com
Editor Phone: (914) 244-0533, ext : 15
Advertising Executive Name: Francesca Lynch
Advertising Executive Email: flynch@scarsdalenews.com
Delivery Methods: Mail
Year Established: 1995
Own Printing Facility?: N
Commercial printers?: N
Mechanical specifications: Type page 14 1/16 x 21; E - 6 cols, 2 1/6, 1/6 between; A - 9 cols, 1 5/12, 1/6 between; C - 9 cols, 1 5/12, 1/6 between.
Published Days: Fri
Avg. Paid Circ.: 3300
Avg. Free Circ.: 100
Audit Company: Sworn/Estimate/Non-Audited
Audit Date: 43626

BRONX

BRONX PRESS-REVIEW

Street Address: 5752 Fieldston Rd
City: Bronx
State: NY
ZIP Code: 10471-0620
General Phone: (718) 543-5200
General Email: bxny@aol.com
Publication Website: http://bronxpresspolitics.blogspot.com/p/
Parent Company: Metro North Media
Publisher Name: Andrew Wolf
Editor Name: Andrew Wolf
Year Established: 1942
Mechanical specifications: Type page 9 7/8 x 13; E - 5 cols, 5/6, 1/6 between; A - 5 cols, 1 5/6, 1/6 between; C - 5 cols, 1/6 between.
Published Days: Thur
Avg. Free Circ.: 20000
Audit Company: Sworn/Estimate/Non-Audited
Audit Date: 43626

BRONX

BRONX TIMES REPORTER

Street Address: 3602 East Tremont Avenue, Suite 205
City: Bronx
State: NY
ZIP Code: 10465-2050
General Phone: (718) 260-4593
General Email: bronxtimes@schnepsmedia.com
Publication Website: http://www.bxtimes.com/
Parent Company: Schneps Media
Publisher Name: Laura Guerriero
Publisher Email: lguerriero@schnepsmedia.com
Publisher Phone: (718) 260-4593
Editor Name: John Collazzi
Editor Email: jcollazzi@schnepsmedia.com
Editor Phone: (718) 260-4596
Advertising Executive Phone: (718) 260-2500
Mechanical specifications: Type page 9.75 x 11; 6 cols, 1.5, 0.125 between

Published Days: Fri
Avg. Free Circ.: 26000
Audit Company: Sworn/Estimate/Non-Audited
Audit Date: 43626

BRONX

CO-OP CITY TIMES

Street Address: 2049 Bartow Ave
City: Bronx
State: NY
ZIP Code: 10475
General Phone: (718) 320-3300
General Email: jflynn@riverbaycorp.com
Publication Website: http://www.riverbaycorp.com/
Parent Company: Riverbay Corporation
Delivery Methods: Carrier
Year Established: 1966
Published Days: Sat
Avg. Free Circ.: 18000
Audit Company: Sworn/Estimate/Non-Audited
Audit Date: 43626

BRONX

RIVERDALE REVIEW

Street Address: PO Box 1252
City: Bronx
State: NY
ZIP Code: 10471-0620
General Phone: (718) 543-5200
General Email: bxny@aol.com
Publication Website: http://riverdale.me/news/
Parent Company: Metro North Media
Publisher Name: Andrew Wolf
Editor Name: Andrew Wolf
Delivery Methods: Carrier`Racks
Year Established: 1993
Mechanical specifications: Type page 9 7/8 x 13; E - 5 cols, 1 5/6, 1/6 between; A - 5 cols, 1 5/6, 1/6 between; C - 5 cols, 1 5/6, 1/6 between.
Published Days: Thur
Avg. Free Circ.: 20000
Audit Company: Sworn/Estimate/Non-Audited
Audit Date: 43626

BROOKLYN

BROOKLYN HEIGHTS PRESS & COBBLE HILL NEWS

Street Address: 16 Court St
City: Brooklyn
State: NY
ZIP Code: 11241-1013
General Phone: (718) 422-7400
General Email: kat@brooklyneagle.com
Publication Website: https://brooklyneagle.com/
Parent Company: Everything Brooklyn Media Inc
Editor Name: Helen Klein
Editor Email: helen@brooklyneagle.com
Advertising Executive Name: Kat Ramus
Advertising Executive Email: kat@brooklyneagle.com
Year Established: 1937
Published Days: Thur
Avg. Paid Circ.: 12500
Audit Company: Sworn/Estimate/Non-Audited
Audit Date: 43626

BROOKLYN

CANARSIE COURIER

Street Address: 1142 E 92nd St
City: Brooklyn
State: NY
ZIP Code: 11236-3624
General Phone: (718) 257-0600
General Email: canarsiec@aol.com
Publication Website: https://canarsiecourier.com/
Publisher Name: Donna Marra
Delivery Methods: Mail`Newsstand
Year Established: 1921
Published Days: Thur
Avg. Paid Circ.: 10000
Audit Company: Sworn/Estimate/Non-Audited
Audit Date: 43626

BROOKLYN

SPRING CREEK SUN

Street Address: 1540 Van Siclen Ave
City: Brooklyn
State: NY
ZIP Code: 11239-2429
General Phone: (718) 642-2718
Publication Website: http://springcreeksunonline.com/
Parent Company: Starrett City Inc.
Publisher Name: Devorah L. Fong
Editor Name: Pamela Stern
Delivery Methods: Mail`Carrier`Racks
Year Established: 1974
Own Printing Facility?: N
Commercial printers?: Y
Mechanical specifications: Type page 10 x 14; E - 5 cols, 2, 1/8 between; A - 5 cols, 1/8 between; C - 5 cols, 2, 1/8 between.
Published Days: Fri`Bi-Mthly
Published Other: every other week
Avg. Free Circ.: 8500
Audit Company: Sworn/Estimate/Non-Audited
Audit Date: 43626

BROOKLYN

THE BROOKLYN PAPERS

Street Address: 1 Metrotech Ctr N
City: Brooklyn
State: NY
ZIP Code: 11201
General Phone: (718) 260-2500
General Email: ads@schnepsmedia.com
Publication Website: https://www.brooklynpaper.com/
Parent Company: Schneps Media
Editor Name: Colin Mixson
Editor Email: cmixson@schnepsmedia.com
Editor Phone: (718) 260-4505
Advertising Executive Name: Ralph D'Onofrio
Advertising Executive Email: ads@schnepsmedia.com
Advertising Executive Phone: (718) 260-2510
Mechanical specifications: Type page 11 x 20.125; 8 cols, 1.27, 0.12 between
Published Days: Fri
Avg. Free Circ.: 25600
Audit Company: Sworn/Estimate/Non-Audited
Audit Date: 43626

BROOKLYN

THE BROOKLYN SPECTATOR

Street Address: 7333 6th Avenue
City: Brooklyn
State: NY
ZIP Code: 11209-8104
General Phone: (718) 238-6600
General Email: clatorre@brooklynreporter.com
Publication Website: https://brooklynreporter.com/tag/brooklyn-spectator/
Parent Company: Schneps Communications

Publisher Name: Helen Klein
Publisher Email: hklein@brooklynreporter.com
Advertising Executive Email: kat@brooklyneagle.com
Advertising Executive Phone: (718) 643-9099, ext : 103
Delivery Methods: Mail`Newsstand`Racks
Published Days: Fri
Avg. Paid Circ.: 800
Avg. Free Circ.: 10000
Audit Company: Sworn/Estimate/Non-Audited
Audit Date: 43626

BROOKLYN

THE GREENPOINT GAZETTE

Street Address: 597 Manhattan Ave
City: Brooklyn
State: NY
ZIP Code: 11222-3924
General Phone: (718) 389-6067
General Email: jdh@brooklyneagle.com
Publication Website: http://greenpointnews.com/
Parent Company: Greenpoint Gazette
Publisher Name: JD Hasty
Publisher Email: jdh@brooklyneagle.com
Year Established: 1973
Mechanical specifications: Type page 10 x 14
Published Days: Wed
Avg. Paid Circ.: 9000
Audit Company: Sworn/Estimate/Non-Audited
Audit Date: 43626

BUFFALO

BUFFALO BUSINESS FIRST

Street Address: 465 Main St
City: Buffalo
State: NY
ZIP Code: 14203-1717
General Phone: (716) 854-5822
General Email: buffalo@bizjournals.com
Publication Website: https://www.bizjournals.com/buffalo/
Parent Company: American City Business Journals
Publisher Name: John Tebeau
Publisher Email: jtebeau@bizjournals.com
Publisher Phone: (716) 541-1601
Editor Name: Donna Collins
Editor Email: dcollins@bizjournals.com
Published Days: Fri
Audit Company: Sworn/Estimate/Non-Audited
Audit Date: 43626

BUFFALO

BUFFALO LAW JOURNAL

Street Address: 465 Main St
City: Buffalo
State: NY
ZIP Code: 14203-1717
General Phone: (716) 854-5822
General Email: buffalo@bizjournals.com
Publication Website: http://www.lawjournalbuffalo.com/?fbclid=IwAR031Oz6YXoV3x2WGOoEkW64yixwdPbm6bp3n3zVJKqIkiHuU9TcQqdgVuU
Parent Company: American City Business Journals
Publisher Name: John Tebeau
Publisher Email: jtebeau@bizjournals.com
Publisher Phone: (716) 541-1601
Editor Name: Donna Collins
Editor Email: dcollins@bizjournals.com
Published Days: Mon
Audit Company: Sworn/Estimate/Non-Audited

BUFFALO

BUFFALO ROCKET

Street Address: P.O. Box 271
City: Buffalo
State: NY
ZIP Code: 14031-1931
General Phone: (716) 873-2595
General Email: barbarag.gallagherprinting@gmail.com
Publication Website: http://www.buffalorocket.com/
Parent Company: Rocket Communications, Inc
Publisher Name: David H. Gallagher
Editor Name: Dennis Gallagher
Editor Email: editor.buffalorocket@gmail.com
Advertising Executive Name: Barbara Gilboy
Delivery Methods: Mail`Newsstand`Carrier
Year Established: 1969
Own Printing Facility?: Y
Commercial printers?: Y
Mechanical specifications: Type page 10 x 14; 5 cols, 2
Published Days: Thur
Avg. Free Circ.: 14100
Audit Company: Sworn/Estimate/Non-Audited
Audit Date: 43626

BUFFALO

BUSINESS FIRST OF BUFFALO

Street Address: 465 Main St
City: Buffalo
State: NY
ZIP Code: 14203-1717
General Phone: (716) 541-1600
General Email: buffalo@bizjournals.com
Publication Website: https://www.bizjournals.com/buffalo/about-us/
Parent Company: American City Business Journals
Publisher Name: John Tebeau
Publisher Email: jtebeau@bizjournals.com
Publisher Phone: (716) 541-1601
Editor Name: Donna Collins
Editor Email: dcollins@bizjournals.com
Delivery Methods: Mail`Newsstand
Year Established: 1984
Published Days: Fri
Audit Company: Sworn/Estimate/Non-Audited
Audit Date: 43626

CALLICOON

SULLIVAN COUNTY DEMOCRAT

Street Address: 5 Lower Main St
City: Callicoon
State: NY
ZIP Code: 12723
General Phone: (845) 887-5200
General Email: info@sc-democrat.com
Publication Website: http://www.scdemocratonline.com
Parent Company: Catskill-Delaware Publications
Publisher Email: publisher@sc-democrat.com
Editor Name: Matt Shortall
Editor Email: editor@sc-democrat.com
Advertising Executive Name: Liz Tucker
Advertising Executive Email: lizt@sc-democrat.com
Advertising Executive Phone: (845) 887-5200
Delivery Methods: Mail`Newsstand`Racks
Year Established: 1891
Mechanical specifications: Type page 11 1/4 x 21; E - 6 cols, 2, 1/6 between; A - 6 cols, 2, 1/6 between; C - 9 cols, 1 3/8, between.
Published Days: Tues`Fri
Avg. Paid Circ.: 9000

Audit Company: Sworn/Estimate/Non-Audited
Audit Date: 43626

CANANDAIGUA

BRIGHTON-PITTSFORD POST

Street Address: 73 Buffalo St
City: Canandaigua
State: NY
ZIP Code: 14424-1001
General Phone: (585) 394-0770
General Email: bkesel@messengerpostmedia.com
Publication Website: https://www.mpnnow.com/news/towns/canandaigua
Parent Company: Messenger Post Media
Editor Name: Jennifer Reed
Editor Email: jreed@messengerpostmedia.com
Editor Phone: (585) 337-4226
Advertising Executive Name: Beth Kesel
Advertising Executive Email: bkesel@messengerpostmedia.com
Advertising Executive Phone: (585) 337-4217
Own Printing Facility?: Y
Commercial printers?: Y
Mechanical specifications: Type page 13 x 20 1/2; E - 6 cols, 2 1/12, 1/6 between; A - 6 cols, 2 1/12, 1/6 between; C - 8 cols, 1 1/2, 1/6 between.
Published Days: Thur
Avg. Paid Circ.: 147
Avg. Free Circ.: 8305
Audit Company: Sworn/Estimate/Non-Audited
Audit Date: 43626

CANANDAIGUA

EAST ROCHESTER-FAIRPORT POST

Street Address: 73 Buffalo St
City: Canandaigua
State: NY
ZIP Code: 14424
General Phone: (585) 394-0770
General Email: bkesel@messengerpostmedia.com
Publication Website: https://www.monroecopost.com/fairport
Publisher Name: Beth Kesel
Publisher Email: bkesel@messengerpostmedia.com
Publisher Phone: (585) 337-4217
Editor Name: Jennifer Reed
Editor Email: jreed@messengerpostmedia.com
Editor Phone: (585) 337-4226
Advertising Executive Name: Beth Kesel
Advertising Executive Email: bkesel@messengerpostmedia.com
Advertising Executive Phone: (585) 337-4217
Delivery Methods: Mail
Published Days: Thur
Avg. Paid Circ.: 108
Avg. Free Circ.: 5179
Audit Company: Sworn/Estimate/Non-Audited
Audit Date: 43626

CANANDAIGUA

GATES-CHILI POST

Street Address: 73 Buffalo St
City: Canandaigua
State: NY
ZIP Code: 14424
General Phone: (585) 394-0770
General Email: bkesel@messengerpostmedia.com
Publication Website: https://www.monroecopost.com/gates-chili
Publisher Name: Beth Kesel
Publisher Email: bkesel@messengerpostmedia.com
Publisher Phone: (585) 337-4217
Editor Name: Jennifer Reed
Editor Email: jreed@messengerpostmedia.com
Editor Phone: (585) 337-4226
Advertising Executive Name: Beth Kesel
Advertising Executive Email: bkesel@messengerpostmedia.com
Advertising Executive Phone: (585) 337-4217
Delivery Methods: Mail
Own Printing Facility?: Y
Commercial printers?: Y
Mechanical specifications: Type page 11 7/8 x 20 1/2; E - 6 cols, 1 13/16, 1/8 between; A - 6 cols, 1 13/16, 1/8 between; C - 8 cols, 1 3/8, 1/8 between.
Published Days: Thur
Avg. Paid Circ.: 52
Avg. Free Circ.: 4973
Audit Company: Sworn/Estimate/Non-Audited
Audit Date: 43626

CANANDAIGUA

GREECE POST

Street Address: 73 Buffalo St
City: Canandaigua
State: NY
ZIP Code: 14424
General Phone: (585) 394-0770
General Email: bkesel@messengerpostmedia.com
Publication Website: https://www.monroecopost.com/greece
Publisher Name: Beth Kesel
Publisher Email: bkesel@messengerpostmedia.com
Publisher Phone: (585) 337-4217
Editor Name: Jennifer Reed
Editor Email: jreed@messengerpostmedia.com
Editor Phone: (585) 337-4226
Advertising Executive Name: Beth Kesel
Advertising Executive Email: bkesel@messengerpostmedia.com
Advertising Executive Phone: (585) 337-4217
Delivery Methods: Mail
Own Printing Facility?: Y
Commercial printers?: Y
Mechanical specifications: Type page 11 7/8 x 20 1/2; E - 6 cols, 1 13/16, 1/8 between; A - 6 cols, 1 13/16, 1/8 between; C - 8 cols, 1 3/8, 1/8 between.
Published Days: Thur
Avg. Paid Circ.: 88
Avg. Free Circ.: 14569
Audit Company: Sworn/Estimate/Non-Audited
Audit Date: 43626

CANANDAIGUA

IRONDEQUOIT POST

Street Address: 73 Buffalo St
City: Canandaigua
State: NY
ZIP Code: 14424
General Phone: (585) 394-0770
General Email: bkesel@messengerpostmedia.com
Publication Website: http://www.irondequoitpost.com/
Publisher Name: Beth Kesel
Publisher Email: bkesel@messengerpostmedia.com
Publisher Phone: (585) 337-4217
Editor Name: Jennifer Reed
Editor Email: jreed@messengerpostmedia.com
Editor Phone: (585) 337-4226
Advertising Executive Name: Beth Kesel
Advertising Executive Email: bkesel@messengerpostmedia.com
Advertising Executive Phone: (585) 337-4217
Delivery Methods: Mail
Own Printing Facility?: Y
Commercial printers?: Y

Published Days: Thur
Avg. Paid Circ.: 83
Avg. Free Circ.: 7104
Audit Company: Sworn/Estimate/Non-Audited
Audit Date: 43626

CANANDAIGUA

MESSENGER POST MEDIA

Street Address: 73 Buffalo St
City: Canandaigua
State: NY
ZIP Code: 14424-1001
General Phone: (585) 394-0770
General Email: messenger@messengerpostmedia.com
Publication Website: https://www.mpnnow.com/
Editor Name: Jennifer Reed
Editor Email: jreed@messengerpostmedia.com
Editor Phone: (585) 337-4226
Advertising Executive Name: Beth Kesel
Advertising Executive Email: bkesel@messengerpostmedia.com
Advertising Executive Phone: (585) 337-4217
Delivery Methods: Mail`Newsstand`Carrier`Racks
Year Established: 1970
Own Printing Facility?: Y
Mechanical specifications: Type page 10 1/4 x 12; E - 5 cols, 2 1/3, 1/6 between; A - 6 cols, 1 3/5, 1/6 between; C - 6 cols, 1 3/5, 1/6 between.
Published Days: Wed`Thur`Fri
Weekday Frequency: m
Avg. Free Circ.: 8975
Audit Company: Sworn/Estimate/Non-Audited
Audit Date: 43626

CANANDAIGUA

PENFIELD POST

Street Address: 73 Buffalo St
City: Canandaigua
State: NY
ZIP Code: 14424
General Phone: (585) 394-0770
General Email: bkesel@messengerpostmedia.com
Publication Website: https://www.monroecopost.com/penfield
Publisher Name: Beth Kesel
Publisher Email: bkesel@messengerpostmedia.com
Publisher Phone: (585) 337-4217
Editor Name: Jennifer Reed
Editor Email: jreed@messengerpostmedia.com
Editor Phone: (585) 337-4226
Advertising Executive Name: Beth Kesel
Advertising Executive Email: bkesel@messengerpostmedia.com
Advertising Executive Phone: (585) 337-4217
Delivery Methods: Mail
Year Established: 1971
Own Printing Facility?: Y
Commercial printers?: Y
Mechanical specifications: Type page 11 7/8 x 20 1/2; E - 6 cols, 1 13/16, 1/8 between; A - 6 cols, 1 13/16, 1/8 between; C - 8 cols, 1 3/8, 1/8 between.
Published Days: Thur
Avg. Paid Circ.: 94
Avg. Free Circ.: 3241
Audit Company: Sworn/Estimate/Non-Audited
Audit Date: 43626

CANANDAIGUA

RUSH-HENRIETTA POST

Street Address: 73 Buffalo St

Community Newspapers in the U.S.

City: Canandaigua
State: NY
ZIP Code: 14424
General Phone: (585) 394-0770
General Email: bkesel@messengerpostmedia.com
Publication Website: https://www.monroecopost.com/
Publisher Name: Beth Kesel
Publisher Email: bkesel@messengerpostmedia.com
Publisher Phone: (585) 337-4217
Editor Name: Jennifer Reed
Editor Email: jreed@messengerpostmedia.com
Editor Phone: (585) 337-4226
Advertising Executive Name: Beth Kesel
Advertising Executive Email: bkesel@messengerpostmedia.com
Advertising Executive Phone: (585) 337-4217
Delivery Methods: Mail
Own Printing Facility?: Y
Commercial printers?: Y
Mechanical specifications: Type page 11 7/8 x 20 1/2; E - 6 cols, 1 13/16, 1/8 between; A - 6 cols, 1 13/16, 1/8 between; C - 8 cols, 1 3/8, 1/8 between.
Published Days: Thur
Avg. Paid Circ.: 68
Avg. Free Circ.: 2924
Audit Company: Sworn/Estimate/Non-Audited
Audit Date: 43626

CANANDAIGUA

VICTOR POST

Street Address: 73 Buffalo St
City: Canandaigua
State: NY
ZIP Code: 14424-1001
General Phone: (585) 394-0770
General Email: messenger@messengerpostmedia.com
Publication Website: https://www.mpnnow.com/victor
Editor Name: Jennifer Reed
Editor Email: jreed@messengerpostmedia.com
Editor Phone: (585) 337-4226
Advertising Executive Name: Beth Kesel
Advertising Executive Email: bkesel@messengerpostmedia.com
Advertising Executive Phone: (585) 337-4217
Delivery Methods: Mail
Published Days: Fri
Avg. Paid Circ.: 16
Avg. Free Circ.: 3674
Audit Company: Sworn/Estimate/Non-Audited
Audit Date: 43626

CANANDAIGUA

WAYNE POST

Street Address: 73 Buffalo St
City: Canandaigua
State: NY
ZIP Code: 14424-1001
General Phone: (585) 394-0770
General Email: bkesel@messengerpostmedia.com
Publication Website: https://www.waynepost.com/
Editor Name: Jennifer Reed
Editor Email: jreed@messengerpostmedia.com
Editor Phone: (585) 337-4226
Advertising Executive Name: Beth Kesel
Advertising Executive Email: bkesel@messengerpostmedia.com
Advertising Executive Phone: (585) 337-4217
Delivery Methods: Mail
Year Established: 1876
Published Days: Wed
Avg. Paid Circ.: 1317
Avg. Free Circ.: 170
Audit Company: Sworn/Estimate/Non-Audited
Audit Date: 43626

CANANDAIGUA

WEBSTER POST

Street Address: 73 Buffalo St
City: Canandaigua
State: NY
ZIP Code: 14424
General Phone: (585) 394-0770
General Email: bkesel@messengerpostmedia.com
Publication Website: https://www.monroecopost.com/webster
Publisher Name: Beth Kesel
Publisher Email: bkesel@messengerpostmedia.com
Publisher Phone: (585) 337-4217
Editor Name: Jennifer Reed
Editor Email: jreed@messengerpostmedia.com
Editor Phone: (585) 337-4226
Advertising Executive Name: Beth Kesel
Advertising Executive Email: bkesel@messengerpostmedia.com
Advertising Executive Phone: (585) 337-4217
Delivery Methods: Mail
Own Printing Facility?: Y
Commercial printers?: Y
Mechanical specifications: Type page 13 x 20 1/2; E - 6 cols, 1 13/16, 1/8 between; A - 6 cols, 1 13/16, 1/8 between; C - 8 cols, 1 3/8, 1/8 between.
Published Days: Thur
Avg. Paid Circ.: 71
Avg. Free Circ.: 4750
Audit Company: Sworn/Estimate/Non-Audited
Audit Date: 43626

CANTON

ST. LAWRENCE PLAINDEALER

Street Address: 75 Main Street
City: Canton
State: NY
ZIP Code: 13617-1279
General Phone: (315) 386-8521
General Email: pdealer@ogd.com
Publication Website: http://www.stlawrencegop.com/
Parent Company: St. Lawrence County Republican Committee
Published Days: Tues
Avg. Paid Circ.: 156
Avg. Free Circ.: 1
Audit Company: Sworn/Estimate/Non-Audited
Audit Date: 43626

CATSKILL

WINDHAM JOURNAL

Street Address: 414 Main St
City: Catskill
State: NY
ZIP Code: 12414-1303
General Phone: (518) 943-2100
General Email: advertising@thedailymail.net
Publication Website: https://www.hudsonvalley360.com/windham_journal/
Parent Company: Johnson Newspaper Corp
Editor Name: Mary Dempsey
Editor Email: mdempsey@registerstar.com
Year Established: 1857
Published Days: Thur
Avg. Paid Circ.: 2400
Audit Company: Sworn/Estimate/Non-Audited
Audit Date: 43626

COBLESKILL

MY SHOPPER - MOHAWK VALLEY EDITION

Street Address: 2403 State Route 7
City: Cobleskill
State: NY
ZIP Code: 12043-5740
General Phone: (518) 234-8215
General Email: info@myshopperonline.com
Publication Website: http://pennysaveronline.com/
Parent Company: Snyder Communication Corp.
Advertising Executive Phone: (607) 334-4714
Delivery Methods: Carrier
Year Established: 1987
Mechanical specifications: 96 ad units per page 6 col. wide x 16" deep col. width 1 5/8" or 10 picas
Published Days: Sat`Sun
Avg. Free Circ.: 11499
Audit Company: CVC
Audit Date: 44086

COBLESKILL

TIMES-JOURNAL

Street Address: 108 Division St
City: Cobleskill
State: NY
ZIP Code: 12043
General Phone: (518) 234-2515
General Email: tjournalads@yahoo.com
Publication Website: https://www.timesjournalonline.com/
Publisher Name: Jim Poole
Editor Name: Patsy Nicosia
Advertising Executive Name: Bruce Tryon
Advertising Executive Email: tjournalads@yahoo.com
Delivery Methods: Mail`Newsstand
Year Established: 1877
Own Printing Facility?: Y
Mechanical specifications: Type page 10.5 x 21; A - 6 cols, 1.625, 0.0625 between; C - 8 cols, 1.25, 0.0625 between
Published Days: Wed
Avg. Paid Circ.: 6800
Avg. Free Circ.: 76
Audit Company: Sworn/Estimate/Non-Audited
Audit Date: 43626

COLD SPRING

PUTNAM COUNTY NEWS & RECORDER

Street Address: 3 Stone St
City: Cold Spring
State: NY
ZIP Code: 10516
General Phone: (845) 265-2468
General Email: editor@pcnr.com
Publication Website: https://www.pcnr.com/
Parent Company: Elizabeth Ailes of Garrison
Publisher Name: Douglas Cunningham
Publisher Email: doug@pcnr.com
Editor Name: Douglas Cunningham
Editor Email: doug@pcnr.com
Advertising Executive Email: ads@pcnr.com
Delivery Methods: Mail`Newsstand
Year Established: 1866
Published Days: Wed
Avg. Paid Circ.: 2100
Audit Company: Sworn/Estimate/Non-Audited
Audit Date: 43626

COLD SPRING

THE PUTNAM COUNTY COURIER

Street Address: 144 Main St
City: Cold Spring
State: NY
ZIP Code: 10516-2854
General Phone: (845) 265-2468
General Email: ads@pcnr.com
Publication Website: https://www.putnamcountycourier.com/
Parent Company: Douglas Cunningham
Publisher Name: Douglas Cunningham
Publisher Email: doug@pcnr.com
Editor Name: Douglas Cunningham
Editor Email: doug@pcnr.com
Advertising Executive Name: Joan Byrnes
Advertising Executive Email: ads@pcnr.com
Advertising Executive Phone: (845) 265-2468
Delivery Methods: Mail`Newsstand
Year Established: 1841
Own Printing Facility?: Y
Commercial printers?: Y
Mechanical specifications: Type page 1 1/4 x 21; E - 6 cols, 1 7/8, 1/8 between; A - 6 cols, 1 7/8, 1/8 between; C - 8 cols, 1 4/5, 1/8 between.
Published Days: Tues
Avg. Paid Circ.: 2100
Audit Company: Sworn/Estimate/Non-Audited
Audit Date: 43626

CONKLIN

VESTAL TOWN CRIER

Street Address: 1035 Conklin Rd
City: Conklin
State: NY
ZIP Code: 13748-1102
General Phone: (607) 775-0472
General Email: subscriptions@wecoverthetowns.com
Publication Website: https://wecoverthetowns.com/
Parent Company: Newspaper Publishers LLC
Advertising Executive Name: Elizabeth Einstein
Advertising Executive Email: subscriptions@wecoverthetowns.com
Advertising Executive Phone: (607) 775-0472
Delivery Methods: Mail
Year Established: 1979
Mechanical specifications: Type page 10 x 13.5; 6 cols, 1.5, 0.22 between
Published Days: Wed
Avg. Paid Circ.: 1200
Audit Company: Sworn/Estimate/Non-Audited
Audit Date: 43626

CORNING

STEUBEN COURIER-ADVOCATE

Street Address: 34 W. Pulteney St
City: Corning
State: NY
ZIP Code: 14830
General Phone: (607) 776-2121
General Email: jamiestopka@steubencourier.com
Publication Website: https://www.steubencourier.com/
Editor Name: Shawn Vargo
Editor Email: svargo@the-leader.com
Advertising Executive Name: Jennifer Gresham
Advertising Executive Email: jgresham@gatehousemedia.com
Delivery Methods: Mail`Carrier`Racks
Year Established: 1968
Own Printing Facility?: Y
Commercial printers?: N
Mechanical specifications: Type page 10 x 20.5; 6 cols
Published Days: Sun
Avg. Free Circ.: 11113
Audit Company: Sworn/Estimate/Non-Audited
Audit Date: 43626

CORNWALL

THE CORNWALL LOCAL

Street Address: P.O. Box 518
City: Cornwall
State: NY
ZIP Code: 12518
General Phone: (845) 534-7771
General Email: matthewlawney@thecornwalllocal.com
Publication Website: http://thecornwalllocal.com/
Parent Company: News of the Highlands Inc.
Editor Email: kencashman@thecornwalllocal.com
Advertising Executive Name: Laura McDermott
Advertising Executive Email: admin@thecornwalllocal.com
Delivery Methods: Mail`Newsstand
Year Established: 1888
Mechanical specifications: Type page 11 x 21; E & A - 6 cols, 1.625, 0.25 between; C - 7 cols, 1.4306, 0.1666 between
Published Days: Fri
Avg. Paid Circ.: 1676
Avg. Free Circ.: 67
Audit Company: Sworn/Estimate/Non-Audited
Audit Date: 43626

CORNWALL

THE NEWS OF THE HIGHLANDS

Street Address: P.O. Box 518
City: Cornwall
State: NY
ZIP Code: 12518
General Phone: (845) 534-7771
General Email: newsofthehighlands@gmail.com
Publication Website: http://wordpress.thenewsofthehighlands.com/
Parent Company: News of the Highlands Inc.
Advertising Executive Email: admin@thecornwalllocal.com
Delivery Methods: Mail`Newsstand
Year Established: 1891
Mechanical specifications: Type page 11 x 21; E & A - 6 cols, 1.625, 0.25 between; C - 7 cols, 1.4306, 0.1666 between
Published Days: Fri
Avg. Paid Circ.: 919
Avg. Free Circ.: 730
Audit Company: Sworn/Estimate/Non-Audited
Audit Date: 43626

CROPSEYVILLE

THE EASTWICK PRESS

Street Address: 34 Richmond Road
City: Cropseyville
State: NY
ZIP Code: 12052
General Phone: (518) 491-1613
General Email: ads@eastwickpress.com
Publication Website: https://eastwickpress.com/news/
Parent Company: Eastwick Press LLC
Publisher Name: Doug La Rocque
Editor Name: Doug La Rocque
Advertising Executive Email: ads@eastwickpress.com
Delivery Methods: Mail`Racks
Year Established: 2017
Published Days: Fri
Audit Company: Sworn/Estimate/Non-Audited
Audit Date: 43626

CUBA

CUBA PATRIOT & FREE PRESS

Street Address: 25 W Main St
City: Cuba
State: NY
ZIP Code: 14727-1403
General Phone: (585) 968-2580
General Email: mail@cubapatriot.com
Publication Website: https://cubapatriot.com/
Editor Name: Melodie Farwell
Editor Email: mail@cubapatriot.com
Advertising Executive Name: Donna Falandys
Advertising Executive Email: mail@cubapatriot.com
Year Established: 1862
Own Printing Facility?: Y
Commercial printers?: Y
Mechanical specifications: Type page 10 x 16; 5 cols, 1.891, 0.128 between
Published Days: Wed
Avg. Paid Circ.: 3870
Audit Company: Sworn/Estimate/Non-Audited
Audit Date: 43626

DELHI

THE REPORTER

Street Address: 97 Main St
City: Delhi
State: NY
ZIP Code: 13753-1231
General Phone: (607) 464-4009
General Email: editor@the-reporter.net
Publication Website: https://www.the-reporter.net/
Parent Company: Media News Group
Editor Email: editor@the-reporter.net
Advertising Executive Name: Bernice Bates
Advertising Executive Email: b.bates@waltonreporter.com
Year Established: 1881
Mechanical specifications: Type page 10 3/8 x 15 1/2; A - 5 cols, 1 7/8, 1/4 between; C - 6 cols, 1 1/2, 1/4 between.
Published Days: Wed
Avg. Paid Circ.: 6800
Avg. Free Circ.: 50
Audit Company: Sworn/Estimate/Non-Audited
Audit Date: 43626

DELMAR

COLONIE/LOUDONVILLE SPOTLIGHT

Street Address: 341 Delaware Ave
City: Delmar
State: NY
ZIP Code: 12054
General Phone: (518) 439-4949
General Email: advertise@spotlightnews.com
Publication Website: https://www.spotlightnews.com/
Parent Company: Community Media Group LLC.
Publisher Name: John McIntyre
Publisher Email: mcintyrej@spotlightnews.com
Publisher Phone: (518) 439-4949, ext : 420
Editor Name: Michael Hallisey
Editor Phone: (518) 439-4949 416
Advertising Executive Email: advertise@spotlightnews.com
Advertising Executive Phone: (518) 439-4949
Delivery Methods: Mail`Newsstand`Racks
Year Established: 1955
Mechanical specifications: Type page 10 x 15.5; 6 cols, 1.5625, 0.125 between
Published Days: Wed
Avg. Paid Circ.: 10000
Audit Company: Sworn/Estimate/Non-Audited
Audit Date: 43626

DELMAR

SPOTLIGHT NEWSPAPERS

Street Address: 341 Delaware Ave
City: Delmar
State: NY
ZIP Code: 12054-1920
General Phone: (518) 439-4949
General Email: news@spotlightnews.com
Publication Website: https://www.spotlightnews.com/
Parent Company: Community News Group
Publisher Name: John McIntyre
Publisher Email: mcintyrej@spotlightnews.com
Publisher Phone: (518) 439-4949, ext : 420
Editor Name: Michael Hallisey
Editor Phone: (518) 439-4949, ext : 420
Published Days: Wed
Avg. Paid Circ.: 5389
Avg. Free Circ.: 16371
Audit Company: CVC
Audit Date: 43628

DELMAR

THE SPOTLIGHT

Street Address: 341 Delaware Ave
City: Delmar
State: NY
ZIP Code: 12054
General Phone: (518) 439-4949
General Email: advertise@spotlightnews.com
Publication Website: https://www.spotlightnews.com/
Parent Company: Community Media Group LLC.
Publisher Name: John McIntyre
Publisher Email: mcintyrej@spotlightnews.com
Publisher Phone: (518) 439-4949, ext : 420
Editor Name: Michael Hallisey
Editor Phone: (518) 439-4949, ext : 416
Advertising Executive Email: advertise@spotlightnews.com
Advertising Executive Phone: (518) 439-4949
Delivery Methods: Mail`Newsstand`Racks
Year Established: 1955
Mechanical specifications: Type page 10 x 15.5; 6 cols, 1.5625, 0.125 between
Published Days: Wed
Avg. Paid Circ.: 7270
Avg. Free Circ.: 18983
Audit Company: Sworn/Estimate/Non-Audited
Audit Date: 43626

DEPOSIT

THE DEPOSIT COURIER

Street Address: 24 Laurel Bank Ave
City: Deposit
State: NY
ZIP Code: 13754-1251
General Phone: (607) 467-3600
General Email: couriernews@tds.net
Publication Website: http://www.4ever66.com/thedepositcourier/index.html
Parent Company: Evans Communications, Inc
Year Established: 1848
Own Printing Facility?: Y
Commercial printers?: Y
Published Days: Wed
Avg. Paid Circ.: 2050
Avg. Free Circ.: 32
Audit Company: Sworn/Estimate/Non-Audited
Audit Date: 43626

DOBBS FERRY

THE RIVERTOWNS ENTERPRISE

Street Address: 95 Main St
City: Dobbs Ferry
State: NY
ZIP Code: 10522-1673
General Phone: (914) 478-2787
General Email: displayads@rivertownsenterprise.net
Publication Website: http://www.rivertownsenterprise.net/Rivertowns_Enterprise/Home.html
Advertising Executive Name: Marilyn Petrosa
Advertising Executive Email: displayads@rivertownsenterprise.net
Year Established: 1975
Commercial printers?: Y
Mechanical specifications: Type page 9.3125 x 14; 4 cols, 2.1875, 0.25 between
Published Days: Fri
Avg. Paid Circ.: 6000
Avg. Free Circ.: 200
Audit Company: Sworn/Estimate/Non-Audited
Audit Date: 43626

DUNDEE

THE WATKINS REVIEW & EXPRESS

Street Address: P.O. Box 127
City: Dundee
State: NY
ZIP Code: 14537
General Phone: (607) 243-7600
General Email: obsrev@gmail.com
Publication Website: http://www.observer-review.com/
Parent Company: Finger Lakes Media. Inc.
Advertising Executive Email: theobserver@citlink.net
Delivery Methods: Mail`Newsstand
Year Established: 1854
Published Days: Wed
Avg. Paid Circ.: 1350
Avg. Free Circ.: 300
Audit Company: Sworn/Estimate/Non-Audited
Audit Date: 43626

EAST AURORA

EAST AURORA ADVERTISER

Street Address: 710 Main St
City: East Aurora
State: NY
ZIP Code: 14052
General Phone: (716) 652-0320
General Email: ads@eastaurorany.com
Publication Website: https://www.eastaurorany.com/
Parent Company: Neighbor to Neighbor News, Inc.
Publisher Name: Grant Hamilton
Advertising Executive Email: ads@eastaurorany.com
Year Established: 1872
Mechanical specifications: Type page 10.5 x 19.5; 5 cols, 2, 0.125 between
Published Days: Thur
Avg. Paid Circ.: 4440
Avg. Free Circ.: 340
Audit Company: Sworn/Estimate/Non-Audited
Audit Date: 43626

EAST AURORA

ELMA REVIEW

Street Address: 710 Main St
City: East Aurora
State: NY
ZIP Code: 14052
General Phone: (716) 652-0320
General Email: ads@eastaurorany.com
Publication Website: https://www.eastaurorany.com/
Parent Company: Neighbor to Neighbor News, Inc.
Publisher Name: Grant Hamilton
Advertising Executive Email: ads@eastaurorany.com

Community Newspapers in the U.S.

Year Established: 1979
Mechanical specifications: Type page 10.5 x 19.5; 5 cols, 2, 0.125 between
Published Days: Thur
Avg. Paid Circ.: 1030
Audit Company: Sworn/Estimate/Non-Audited
Audit Date: 43626

EAST HAMPTON

THE EAST HAMPTON STAR

Street Address: 153 Main Street - P.O. Box 5002
City: East Hampton
State: NY
ZIP Code: 11937-2716
General Phone: (631) 324-0002
General Email: ads@ehstar.com
Publication Website: https://www.easthamptonstar.com/
Parent Company: Rattray
Publisher Name: Helen S. Rattray
Editor Name: David E. Rattray
Editor Email: editor@easthamptonstar.com
Advertising Executive Email: ads@ehstar.com
Year Established: 1885
Mechanical specifications: Type page 13.667 x 20.917; 6 cols, 2.139, 0.166 between.
Published Days: Thur
Avg. Paid Circ.: 11000
Avg. Free Circ.: 612
Audit Company: Sworn/Estimate/Non-Audited
Audit Date: 43626

ELLENVILLE

SHAWANGUNK JOURNAL

Street Address: PO Box 669
City: Ellenville
State: NY
ZIP Code: 12428-0669
General Phone: (845) 647-9190
General Email: info@gunkjournal.com
Publication Website: https://www.shawangunkjournal.com/
Parent Company: Electric Valley Media LLC
Publisher Name: Amberly Jane Campbell
Publisher Email: amberly@gunkjournal.com
Editor Name: Lisa Reider
Editor Email: lisa@gunkjournal.com
Delivery Methods: Mail`Racks
Year Established: 1849
Mechanical specifications: Type page 10.25 x 15
Published Days: Thur
Audit Company: Sworn/Estimate/Non-Audited
Audit Date: 43626

FULTON

THE PALLADIUM-TIMES

Street Address: 67 S 2nd St
City: Fulton
State: NY
ZIP Code: 13069-1725
General Phone: (315) 592-2459
General Email: editor@palltimes.com
Publication Website: http://www.oswegocountynewsnow.com/
Parent Company: Sample News Group LLC
Publisher Name: Jon D. Spaulding
Publisher Email: jspaulding@palltimes.com
Publisher Phone: (315) 343-3800, ext : 2248
Editor Name: Seth Wallace
Editor Email: editor@palltimes.com
Editor Phone: (315) 343-3800, ext : 2245
Advertising Executive Name: Tiera Barnes
Advertising Executive Email: tbarnes@palltimes.com
Advertising Executive Phone: (315) 343-3800, ext : 2229
Delivery Methods: Mail
Mechanical specifications: Type page 10.3125 x 16; 6 cols
Published Days: Sat
Avg. Paid Circ.: 8230
Avg. Free Circ.: 5000
Audit Company: Sworn/Estimate/Non-Audited
Audit Date: 43626

FULTON

THE VALLEY NEWS

Street Address: 67 S 2nd St
City: Fulton
State: NY
ZIP Code: 13069-1259
General Phone: (315) 598-6397
General Email: editor@fultonvalleynews.com
Publication Website: http://www.oswegocountynewsnow.com/
Parent Company: Sample News Group LLC
Publisher Name: Jon D. Spaulding
Publisher Email: jspaulding@palltimes.com
Publisher Phone: (315) 343-3800, ext : 2248
Editor Name: Mike LeBoeuf
Editor Email: mike@fultonvalleynews.com
Editor Phone: (315) 343-3800, ext : 2256
Delivery Methods: Mail
Year Established: 1947
Own Printing Facility?: Y
Commercial printers?: Y
Mechanical specifications: Type page 10 1/4 x 15 3/4; E - 4 cols, 2 5/12, 1/3 between; A - 4 cols, 2 3/8, 1/3 between; C - 4 cols, 2 5/12, 1/3 between.
Published Days: Wed`Sat
Avg. Paid Circ.: 8105
Avg. Free Circ.: 5000
Audit Company: Sworn/Estimate/Non-Audited
Audit Date: 43626

GENESEO

THE LIVINGSTON COUNTY NEWS

Street Address: 122 Main St
City: Geneseo
State: NY
ZIP Code: 14454
General Phone: (585) 243-0296
General Email: news@livingstonnews.com
Publication Website: https://thelcn.com/
Parent Company: Johnson Newspaper Corporation
Publisher Name: Michael Messerly
Publisher Email: mmesserly@batavianews.com
Publisher Phone: (585) 343-8000
Editor Name: Ben Beagle
Editor Email: ben@livingstonnews.com
Editor Phone: (585) 243-0296
Advertising Executive Name: Jayme Qutermous
Advertising Executive Email: jqutermous@batavianews.com
Advertising Executive Phone: (585) 343-8000, ext : 2157
Delivery Methods: Mail`Newsstand`Racks
Published Days: Thur
Avg. Paid Circ.: 5789
Audit Company: Sworn/Estimate/Non-Audited
Audit Date: 43626

GHENT

THE COLUMBIA PAPER

Street Address: PO Box 482
City: Ghent
State: NY
ZIP Code: 12075-0482
General Phone: (518) 392-1122
General Email: ads@columbiapaper.com
Publication Website: https://www.columbiapaper.com/
Parent Company: The Columbia Paper
Publisher Name: Parry Teasdale
Publisher Email: pteasdale@columbiapaper.com
Editor Name: Parry Teasdale
Editor Email: pteasdale@columbiapaper.com
Advertising Executive Email: ads@columbiapaper.com
Delivery Methods: Mail`Newsstand
Year Established: 2009
Mechanical specifications: Type page 10 x 16; 5 cols, 1.83, 0.2 between
Published Days: Thur
Published Other: Regular web updates, Facebook, Twitter
Avg. Paid Circ.: 2200
Audit Company: Sworn/Estimate/Non-Audited
Audit Date: 43626

GLENS FALLS

THE CHRONICLE

Street Address: 15 Ridge St
City: Glens Falls
State: NY
ZIP Code: 12801-3608
General Phone: (518) 792-1126
General Email: chronicle@loneoak.com
Publication Website: https://www.glensfallschronicle.com/
Parent Company: Gannett
Publisher Name: Mark Frost
Editor Name: Cathy DeDe
Advertising Executive Name: Don Donofrio
Delivery Methods: Mail`Newsstand`Racks
Year Established: 1980
Own Printing Facility?: N
Mechanical specifications: Type page 10 x 16; E - 4 cols, 2 1/3, 1/4 between; A - 4 cols, 2 1/3, 1/4 between; C - 6 cols, 1 1/2, 1/4 between.
Published Days: Thur
Avg. Paid Circ.: 500
Avg. Free Circ.: 28000
Audit Company: Sworn/Estimate/Non-Audited
Audit Date: 43626

GOUVERNEUR

THE GOUVERNEUR TRIBUNE-PRESS

Street Address: 74 Trinity Ave
City: Gouverneur
State: NY
ZIP Code: 13642-1126
General Phone: (315) 287-2100
General Email: tribunepress@verizon.net
Publication Website: http://gouverneurtribunepress.com/
Editor Name: Rachel Riley
Advertising Executive Email: tribune@roadrunner.com
Published Days: Fri
Avg. Paid Circ.: 3724
Avg. Free Circ.: 301
Audit Company: Sworn/Estimate/Non-Audited
Audit Date: 43626

GRAND ISLAND

ISLAND DISPATCH

Street Address: 1859 Whitehaven Rd
City: Grand Island
State: NY
ZIP Code: 14072-1803
General Phone: (716) 773-7676
General Email: majoraccounts@wnypapers.com
Publication Website: https://www.wnypapers.com/content/pages/grand-island-dispatch
Parent Company: Niagara Frontier Publications
Publisher Name: Skip Mazenauer
Publisher Email: skip@wnypapers.com
Editor Name: Larry Austin
Editor Email: dispatch@wnypapers.com
Advertising Executive Name: Colleen Rebmann
Advertising Executive Email: grandislandsales@wnypapers.com
Delivery Methods: Mail`Newsstand
Year Established: 1944
Own Printing Facility?: N
Commercial printers?: N
Mechanical specifications: Type page 10 1/2 x 15.75; E - 5 cols, 2, 1/8 between; A - 5 cols, 2, 1/8 between; C - 5 cols, 2, 1/8 between.
Published Days: Fri
Avg. Paid Circ.: 1550
Audit Company: Sworn/Estimate/Non-Audited
Audit Date: 43626

GRAND ISLAND

LEWISTON-PORTER SENTINEL

Street Address: 1859 Whitehaven Rd
City: Grand Island
State: NY
ZIP Code: 14072-1803
General Phone: (716) 773-7676
General Email: majoraccounts@wnypapers.com
Publication Website: https://www.wnypapers.com/content/pages/lewiston-porter-sentinel
Parent Company: Niagara Frontier Publications
Publisher Name: Skip Mazenauer
Publisher Email: skip@wnypapers.com
Editor Name: Larry Austin
Advertising Executive Name: Marcy Lombardo
Advertising Executive Email: sentinelsales@wnypapers.com
Delivery Methods: Carrier`Racks
Year Established: 1987
Mechanical specifications: Type page 10 3/4 x 15.75; E - 5 cols, 2, 1/8 between; A - 5 cols, 2, 1/8 between; C - 5 cols, 2, 1/8 between.
Published Days: Sat
Avg. Free Circ.: 10800
Audit Company: Sworn/Estimate/Non-Audited
Audit Date: 43626

GRAND ISLAND

NIAGARA-WHEATFIELD TRIBUNE

Street Address: 1859 Whitehaven Rd
City: Grand Island
State: NY
ZIP Code: 14072-1803
General Phone: (716) 773-7676
General Email: majoraccounts@wnypapers.com
Publication Website: https://www.wnypapers.com/content/pages/niagara-wheatfield-tribune
Parent Company: Niagara Frontier Publications
Publisher Name: Skip Mazenauer
Publisher Email: skip@wnypapers.com
Editor Name: Larry Austin
Advertising Executive Name: Jeff Calarco
Advertising Executive Email: tribunesales@wnypapers.com
Delivery Methods: Carrier`Racks
Year Established: 1944
Mechanical specifications: Type page 10 .5 x 15.75; E - 5 cols, 2, 1/8 between; A - 5 cols, 2, 1/8 between; C - 5 cols, 2, 1/8 between.
Published Days: Thur
Avg. Free Circ.: 11500
Audit Company: Sworn/Estimate/Non-

GREENWICH

THE GREENWICH JOURNAL & SALEM PRESS

Street Address: PO Box 185, 171 Windy Hill Road
City: GREENWICH
State: NY
ZIP Code: 12834
General Phone: (518) 692-2266
General Email: gjpreporter@aol.com
Publication Website: http://www.greenwichjournalsalempress.com/
Parent Company: Greenwich Journal & Salem Press
Editor Email: editor@journalandpress.com
Delivery Methods: Mail`Newsstand`Carrier
Year Established: 1842
Published Days: Thur
Avg. Paid Circ.: 900
Audit Company: Sworn/Estimate/Non-Audited
Audit Date: 43626

HANCOCK

THE HANCOCK HERALD

Street Address: 102 E Front St
City: Hancock
State: NY
ZIP Code: 13783-1200
General Phone: (607) 637-3591
General Email: hancockherald@hancock.net
Publication Website: https://hancockherald.com/
Parent Company: Hancock Herald, LLC
Publisher Name: Sally Zegers
Editor Name: Sally Zegers
Advertising Executive Name: Louise Botsford
Delivery Methods: Mail`Newsstand
Year Established: 1873
Mechanical specifications: Type page 15 1/2 x 21 1/2; E - 8 cols, 1 5/6, 1/6 between; A - 8 cols, 1 5/6, 1/6 between; C - 8 cols, 1 5/6, 1/6 between.
Published Days: Wed
Avg. Paid Circ.: 2000
Audit Company: Sworn/Estimate/Non-Audited
Audit Date: 43626

HORNELL

GENESEE COUNTRY EXPRESS

Street Address: 32 Broadway Mall
City: Hornell
State: NY
ZIP Code: 14843
General Phone: (607) 324-1425
General Email: jcronk@gatehousemedia.com
Publication Website: https://local.dansvilleonline.com/dansville-ny/communication/newspapers-and-magazines/genesee-country-express-585-335-2271
Publisher Name: Rick Emanuel
Publisher Email: remanuel@the-leader.com
Publisher Phone: (607) 936-9231
Editor Name: Chris Potter
Editor Email: cpotter@gatehousemedia.com
Editor Phone: (607) 324-1425, ext : 205
Advertising Executive Name: Judy Smith-Cronk
Advertising Executive Email: jcronk@gatehousemedia.com
Advertising Executive Phone: (585) 447-0235
Delivery Methods: Mail`Newsstand
Year Established: 1851
Mechanical specifications: Type page 13 x 21; E - 6 cols, 1 7/8, 1/16 between; A - 6 cols, 1 7/8, 1/16 between; C - 6 cols, 1 7/8, 1/16 between.
Published Days: Thur
Avg. Paid Circ.: 2500
Avg. Free Circ.: 6
Audit Company: Sworn/Estimate/Non-Audited
Audit Date: 43626

HOWARD BEACH

THE FORUM

Street Address: 155-19 Lahn Street
City: Howard Beach
State: NY
ZIP Code: 11414-2858
General Phone: (718) 845-3221
General Email: forumsouth@gmail.com
Publication Website: http://theforumnewsgroup.com/
Parent Company: The Forum Newspaper, Inc.
Publisher Name: Patricia L. Adams
Editor Name: Michael V. Cusenza
Editor Email: michael@theforumnewsgroup.com
Mechanical specifications: Howard Beach, Ozone Park, Broad Channel, Richmond Hill, Woodhaven
Published Days: Thur
Avg. Free Circ.: 25000
Audit Company: Sworn/Estimate/Non-Audited
Audit Date: 43626

HUDSON

GREENE COUNTY NEWS

Street Address: 1 Hudson City Ctr
City: Hudson
State: NY
ZIP Code: 12534-2355
General Phone: (518) 828-1616
General Email: advertising@registerstar.com
Publication Website: https://www.hudsonvalley360.com/news/greenecounty/
Parent Company: Johnson Newspaper Corp.
Editor Name: Mary Dempsey
Editor Email: mdempsey@registerstar.com
Editor Phone: (518) 828-1616, ext : 2533
Delivery Methods: Mail`Newsstand`Carrier
Year Established: 1907
Own Printing Facility?: Y
Commercial printers?: Y
Published Days: Thur
Avg. Paid Circ.: 668
Audit Company: Sworn/Estimate/Non-Audited
Audit Date: 43626

HUNTINGTON

THE LONG-ISLANDER NEWS

Street Address: 14 Wall St
City: Huntington
State: NY
ZIP Code: 11743-7622
General Phone: (631) 427-7000
General Email: info@longislandernews.com
Publication Website: http://www.longislandernews.com/
Parent Company: Tribco LLC-OOB
Publisher Name: Pete Sloggatt
Publisher Email: psloggatt@longislandergroup.com
Publisher Phone: (631) 427-7000, ext : 11
Editor Name: Pete Sloggatt
Editor Email: psloggatt@longislandergroup.com
Editor Phone: (631) 427-7000, ext : 11
Delivery Methods: Mail`Newsstand
Year Established: 1838
Own Printing Facility?: N
Commercial printers?: Y
Mechanical specifications: Type page 10 1/4 x 13 7/8; E - 4 cols, 2 1/2, 1/4 between; A - 4 cols, 2 1/2, 1/4 between; C - 6 cols, 1 1/2, 1/6 between.
Published Days: Thur
Avg. Paid Circ.: 24000
Audit Company: Sworn/Estimate/Non-Audited
Audit Date: 43626

HYDE PARK

HUDSON VALLEY NEWS

Street Address: PO Box 268
City: Hyde Park
State: NY
ZIP Code: 12538
General Phone: (845) 233-4651
General Email: editorial@thehudsonvalleynews.com
Publication Website: https://thehudsonvalleynews.com
Publisher Name: Caroline M. Carey
Publisher Email: carolinemcarey@thehudsonvalleynews.com
Editor Name: Jim Langan
Editor Email: jimlangan@thehudsonvalleynews.com
Advertising Executive Email: advertising@thehudsonvalleynews.com
Mechanical specifications: Type page 11.375 x 12; 4 cols, 2.5
Published Days: Wed
Audit Company: Sworn/Estimate/Non-Audited
Audit Date: 43626

ITHACA

ITHACA TIMES

Street Address: 109 N Cayuga St
City: Ithaca
State: NY
ZIP Code: 14850
General Phone: (607) 277-7000
General Email: production@ithacatimes.com
Publication Website: https://www.ithaca.com/
Publisher Name: Jim Bilinski
Publisher Email: jbilinski@ithacatimes.com
Publisher Phone: (607) 277-7000, ext : 212
Editor Name: Matt Butler
Editor Email: editor@ithacatimes.com
Editor Phone: (607) 277-7000 ext. 224
Advertising Executive Name: Jim Bilinski
Advertising Executive Email: jbilinski@ithacatimes.com
Advertising Executive Phone: (607) 277-7000, ext : 212
Delivery Methods: Newsstand
Published Days: Wed
Avg. Free Circ.: 22936
Audit Company: Sworn/Estimate/Non-Audited
Audit Date: 43626

LAKE PLACID

THE LAKE PLACID NEWS

Street Address: 6179 Sentinel Rd
City: Lake Placid
State: NY
ZIP Code: 12946-3509
General Phone: (518) 523-4401
General Email: cswirsky@adirondackdailyenterprise.com
Publication Website: http://www.lakeplacidnews.com/
Parent Company: Ogden Newspapers Inc.
Publisher Name: Catherine Moore
Publisher Email: cmoore@adirondackdailyenterprise.com
Publisher Phone: (518) 891-2600
Editor Name: Andy Flynn
Editor Email: news@lakeplacidnews.com
Editor Phone: (518) 891-2600, ext : 34
Advertising Executive Name: Carol Swirsky
Advertising Executive Email: cswirsky@adirondackdailyenterprise.com
Advertising Executive Phone: (518) 891-2600
Delivery Methods: Mail`Newsstand`Racks
Year Established: 1905
Own Printing Facility?: N
Commercial printers?: Y
Mechanical specifications: Type page 11 4/5 x 21; E - 6 cols, 1 4/5, between; A - 6 cols, 3 4/5, between; C - 8 cols, 1 1/3, between.
Published Days: Fri
Avg. Paid Circ.: 2500
Audit Company: Sworn/Estimate/Non-Audited
Audit Date: 43626
Note: Advertising is done with in combination with the Adirondack Daily Enterprise for just $1.50 more per column inch.

LATHAM

ALBANY BUSINESS REVIEW

Street Address: 40 British American Blvd
City: Latham
State: NY
ZIP Code: 12110-1424
General Phone: (518) 640-6800
General Email: wthorne@bizjournals.com
Publication Website: https://www.bizjournals.com/albany/
Parent Company: American City Business Journals
Publisher Name: Cindy Applebaum
Publisher Email: capplebaum@bizjournals.com
Publisher Phone: (518) 640-6802
Editor Name: Melissa Mangini
Editor Email: mmangini@bizjournals.com
Editor Phone: (518) 640-6835
Advertising Executive Name: Walter Thorne
Advertising Executive Email: wthorne@bizjournals.com
Advertising Executive Phone: (518) 640-6833
Published Days: Fri
Audit Company: Sworn/Estimate/Non-Audited
Audit Date: 43626

LE ROY

LE ROY PENNYSAVER & NEWS

Street Address: 1 Church St
City: Le Roy
State: NY
ZIP Code: 14482
General Phone: (585) 768-2201
General Email: office@leroyny.com
Publication Website: http://www.leroyny.com/
Parent Company: Dray Enterprises Inc.
Editor Email: editor@leroyny.com
Advertising Executive Email: office@leroyny.com
Delivery Methods: Mail`Carrier
Year Established: 1935
Mechanical specifications: Type page 8.5 x 12, 4 cols, 1.75, 0.5 between
Published Days: Mon
Avg. Free Circ.: 6793
Audit Company: CVC
Audit Date: 43625

MAHOPAC

PUTNAM COUNTY PRESS

Street Address: PO Box 608
City: Mahopac
State: NY
ZIP Code: 10516
General Phone: (845) 628-8400
General Email: editor@pcnr.com
Publication Website: http://www.putnampresstimes.com/
Parent Company: Don Hall
Publisher Name: Douglas Cunningham

Community Newspapers in the U.S.

Publisher Email: doug@pcnr.com
Editor Name: Douglas Cunningham
Editor Email: doug@pcnr.com
Advertising Executive Email: ads@pcnr.com
Delivery Methods: Mail`Racks
Published Days: Wed
Avg. Paid Circ.: 3200
Audit Company: Sworn/Estimate/Non-Audited
Audit Date: 43626

MAHOPAC

PUTNAM COUNTY TIMES

Street Address: PO Box 608
City: Mahopac
State: NY
ZIP Code: 10516
General Phone: (845) 628-8400
General Email: editor@pcnr.com
Publication Website: http://www.putnampresstimes.com/
Parent Company: Don Hall
Publisher Name: Douglas Cunningham
Publisher Email: doug@pcnr.com
Editor Name: Douglas Cunningham
Editor Email: doug@pcnr.com
Advertising Executive Email: ads@pcnr.com
Delivery Methods: Mail`Racks
Published Days: Wed
Audit Company: Sworn/Estimate/Non-Audited
Audit Date: 43626

MATTITUCK

RIVERHEAD NEWS-REVIEW

Street Address: 7785 Main Rd
City: Mattituck
State: NY
ZIP Code: 11952-1518
General Phone: (631) 298-3200
General Email: jtumminello@timesreview.com
Publication Website: https://riverheadnewsreview.timesreview.com/
Parent Company: Times Review Media Group
Publisher Name: Andrew Olsen
Publisher Email: aolsen@timesreview.com
Publisher Phone: (631) 354-8031
Editor Name: Ambrose Clancy
Editor Email: a.clancy@timesreview
Editor Phone: (631) 749-1000
Delivery Methods: Mail`Racks
Year Established: 1868
Mechanical specifications: Type page 9.75 x 13.75; E&A - 4 cols, 2.25, 0.25 between; C - 5 cols, 1.875, 0.105 between.
Published Days: Thur
Avg. Paid Circ.: 5255
Avg. Free Circ.: 61
Audit Company: Sworn/Estimate/Non-Audited
Audit Date: 43626

MATTITUCK

SHELTER ISLAND REPORTER

Street Address: 7785 Main Rd
City: Mattituck
State: NY
ZIP Code: 11952
General Phone: (631) 298-3200
General Email: aolsen@timesreview.com
Publication Website: http://www.sireporter.com/
Parent Company: Times Review Media Group
Publisher Name: Andrew Olsen
Publisher Email: aolsen@timesreview.com
Publisher Phone: (631) 354-8031
Editor Name: Ambrose Clancy
Editor Email: a.clancy@timesreview
Editor Phone: (631) 749-1000

Delivery Methods: Mail`Newsstand
Mechanical specifications: Type page 9.75 x 13.75; E&A - 4 cols, 2.25, 0.25 between; C - 5 cols, 1.875, 0.105 between.
Published Days: Thur
Avg. Paid Circ.: 2191
Audit Company: Sworn/Estimate/Non-Audited
Audit Date: 43626

MATTITUCK

THE SUFFOLK TIMES

Street Address: 7785 Main Rd
City: Mattituck
State: NY
ZIP Code: 11952
General Phone: (631) 298-3200
General Email: aolsen@timesreview.com
Publication Website: https://suffolktimes.timesreview.com/
Parent Company: Times Review Newsgroup
Publisher Name: Andrew Olsen
Publisher Email: aolsen@timesreview.com
Publisher Phone: (631) 354-8031
Editor Name: Joe Werkmeister
Editor Email: joew@timesreview.com
Editor Phone: (631) 354-8049
Delivery Methods: Mail
Year Established: 1857
Mechanical specifications: Type page 9.75 x 13.75; E&A - 4 cols, 2.25, 0.25 between; C - 5 cols, 1.875, 0.105 between.
Published Days: Thur
Avg. Paid Circ.: 8723
Avg. Free Circ.: 200
Audit Company: Sworn/Estimate/Non-Audited
Audit Date: 43626

MECHANICVILLE

THE EXPRESS

Street Address: 30 Walnut St, P.O. Box 608
City: Mechanicville
State: NY
ZIP Code: 12118-1040
General Phone: (518) 664-3335
General Email: ads.expresspaper@gmail.com
Publication Website: http://www.theexpressweeklynews.com/
Parent Company: Gannett Company Inc.
Publisher Name: Tom Mahoney
Publisher Phone: (518) 664-3335
Editor Name: Cindy L. Mahoney
Editor Phone: (518) 664-3335
Delivery Methods: Mail`Newsstand
Year Established: 1981
Mechanical specifications: Type page 10.25 x 14; 6 cols, 1.5, 0.25 between
Published Days: Thur
Avg. Paid Circ.: 2700
Audit Company: AAM
Audit Date: 44356

MEXICO

THE CITIZEN OUTLET

Street Address: 80 N Jefferson St
City: Mexico
State: NY
ZIP Code: 13114-3001
General Phone: (315) 963-7813
General Email: ocwadvertising@cnymail.com
Publication Website: https://www.ocweekly.com/
Parent Company: OC Weekly News, Inc
Advertising Executive Name: Cynthia Rebolledo
Advertising Executive Phone: (714) 550-5900
Year Established: 1950
Own Printing Facility?: Y
Commercial printers?: Y
Published Days: Fri

Avg. Paid Circ.: 4889
Audit Company: Sworn/Estimate/Non-Audited
Audit Date: 43626

MILLERTON

THE LAKEVILLE JOURNAL

Street Address: 16 CENTURY BLVD
City: MILLERTON
State: NY
ZIP Code: 12541
General Phone: (860) 435-9873
General Email: jamesc@lakevillejournal.com
Publication Website: http://lakevillejournal.com/current/
Parent Company: The Lakeville Journal
Publisher Name: Janet Manko
Editor Name: Janet Manko
Editor Email: editor@millertonnews.com
Advertising Executive Name: Libby Hall-Abeel
Delivery Methods: Mail`Newsstand`Racks
Year Established: 1897
Own Printing Facility?: N
Commercial printers?: N
Mechanical specifications: Type page 11.5 x 21; 6 cols, 1.75"
Published Days: Thur
Avg. Paid Circ.: 2824
Avg. Free Circ.: 98
Audit Company: AAM
Audit Date: 44024

MILLERTON

THE MILLERTON NEWS

Street Address: 16 CENTURY BLVD
City: MILLERTON
State: NY
ZIP Code: 12541
General Phone: (860) 435-9873
General Email: jamesc@lakevillejournal.com
Publication Website: http://millertonnews.com/current/
Parent Company: The Lakeville Journal
Publisher Name: Janet Manko
Editor Name: Whitney Joseph
Editor Email: editor@millertonnews.com
Advertising Executive Name: Libby Hall-Abeel
Own Printing Facility?: Y
Commercial printers?: Y
Mechanical specifications: Type page 15 x 21; E - 7 cols, 2 1/16, between; A - 7 cols, 2 1/16, between; C - 8 cols, between.
Published Days: Thur
Avg. Paid Circ.: 1014
Avg. Free Circ.: 39
Audit Company: AAM
Audit Date: 44024

MOUNT KISCO

THE EXAMINER

Street Address: PO Box 611
City: Mount Kisco
State: NY
ZIP Code: 10549
General Phone: (914) 864-0878
General Email: advertising@theexaminernews.com
Publication Website: https://www.theexaminernews.com/
Parent Company: Gannett
Publisher Name: Adam Stone
Publisher Email: astone@theexaminernews.com
Editor Name: Martin Wilbur
Editor Email: mwilbur@theexaminernews.com
Editor Phone: (914) 419-0390
Advertising Executive Email: advertising@theexaminernews.com
Delivery Methods: Mail`Newsstand`Racks

Year Established: 2007
Published Days: Tues
Avg. Free Circ.: 6475
Audit Company: Sworn/Estimate/Non-Audited
Audit Date: 43626

MOUNT KISCO

THE NORTHERN WESTCHESTER EXAMINER

Street Address: PO Box 611
City: Mount Kisco
State: NY
ZIP Code: 10549
General Phone: (914) 864-0878
General Email: advertising@theexaminernews.com
Publication Website: https://www.theexaminernews.com/
Parent Company: Examiner Media
Publisher Name: Adam Stone
Publisher Email: astone@theexaminernews.com
Editor Name: Rick Pezzullo
Editor Email: rpezzullo@theexaminernews.com
Editor Phone: (914) 729-4242
Advertising Executive Email: advertising@theexaminernews.com
Delivery Methods: Mail`Newsstand`Racks
Year Established: 2007
Published Days: Tues
Avg. Free Circ.: 7360
Audit Company: Sworn/Estimate/Non-Audited
Audit Date: 43626

MOUNT KISCO

THE PUTNAM EXAMINER

Street Address: PO Box 611
City: Mount Kisco
State: NY
ZIP Code: 10549
General Phone: (914) 864-0878
General Email: advertising@theexaminernews.com
Publication Website: https://www.theexaminernews.com/
Parent Company: Examiner Media
Publisher Name: Adam Stone
Publisher Email: astone@theexaminernews.com
Editor Name: Holly Crocco
Editor Email: hcrocco@theexaminernews.com
Editor Phone: (607) 229-0599
Advertising Executive Email: advertising@theexaminernews.com
Delivery Methods: Mail`Newsstand`Racks
Year Established: 2007
Published Days: Tues
Avg. Free Circ.: 5841
Audit Company: Sworn/Estimate/Non-Audited
Audit Date: 43626

MOUNT KISCO

THE WHITE PLAINS EXAMINER

Street Address: PO Box 611
City: Mount Kisco
State: NY
ZIP Code: 10549
General Phone: (914) 864-0878
General Email: advertising@theexaminernews.com
Publication Website: https://www.theexaminernews.com/
Parent Company: Examiner Media
Publisher Name: Adam Stone
Publisher Email: astone@theexaminernews.com
Editor Name: Pat Casey

Editor Email: pcasey@theexaminernews.com
Editor Phone: (914) 588-5583
Advertising Executive Email: advertising@theexaminernews.com
Delivery Methods: Mail`Newsstand`Racks
Year Established: 2007
Published Days: Tues
Avg. Free Circ.: 5226
Audit Company: Sworn/Estimate/Non-Audited
Audit Date: 43626

NANUET

ROCKLAND COUNTY TIMES

Street Address: 119 Main St
City: Nanuet
State: NY
ZIP Code: 10954
General Phone: (845) 627-1414
General Email: editor@rocklandcountytimes.com
Publication Website: https://www.rocklandtimes.com/
Parent Company: Citizens Publishing Corporation of Rockland
Publisher Name: Dylan Skriloff
Editor Name: Dylan Skriloff
Editor Email: editor@rocklandcountytimes.com
Advertising Executive Name: Diane Kugel
Advertising Executive Email: diane@rocklandtimes.com
Advertising Executive Phone: (845) 627-1414
Delivery Methods: Mail`Newsstand`Carrier`Racks
Year Established: 1888
Mechanical specifications: Type page 13 x 20; E - 9 cols, 1 5/16, 1/6 between; A - 9 cols, 1 5/16, 1/6 between; C - 9 cols, 1 5/16, 1/6 between.
Published Days: Thur
Avg. Paid Circ.: 3100
Avg. Free Circ.: 4400
Audit Company: Sworn/Estimate/Non-Audited
Audit Date: 43626

NARROWSBURG

THE RIVER REPORTER

Street Address: PO Box 150, 93 Erie Ave
City: Narrowsburg
State: NY
ZIP Code: 12764-6423
General Phone: (845) 252-7414
General Email: sales@riverreporter.com
Publication Website: https://riverreporter.com/
Parent Company: Stuart Communications Inc.
Publisher Email: publisher@riverreporter.com
Editor Email: editor@riverreporter.com
Advertising Executive Email: sales@riverreporter.com
Delivery Methods: Mail
Year Established: 1975
Mechanical specifications: Type page 10 1/4 x 10 1/2; E - 6 cols, 1 1/2, between; A - 6 cols, 1 1/2, between; C - 6 cols, 1 1/2, between.
Published Days: Thur
Avg. Paid Circ.: 3000
Avg. Free Circ.: 265
Audit Company: Sworn/Estimate/Non-Audited
Audit Date: 43626

NEW PROVIDENCE

YORKTOWN NEWS, MAHOPAC NEWS, THE SOMERS RECORD, NORTH SALEM NEWS

Street Address: PO Box 794
City: New Providence
State: NY
ZIP Code: 7974
General Phone: (908) 279-0303
General Email: editor@tapinto.net
Publication Website: https://www.tapinto.net/towns/yorktown
Parent Company: Halston Media, LLC
Editor Name: Jodi Weinberger
Editor Email: somers@tapinto.net
Editor Phone: (914) 302-5830
Delivery Methods: Mail
Year Established: 2015
Own Printing Facility?: N
Commercial printers?: N
Published Days: Thur
Weekday Frequency: All day
Avg. Free Circ.: 25500
Audit Company: Sworn/Estimate/Non-Audited
Audit Date: 43626

NEW YORK

CHAIN DRUG REVIEW

Street Address: 126 Fifth Avenue
City: New York
State: NY
ZIP Code: 10011
General Phone: (212) 213-6000
General Email: pnavarre@racherpress.com
Publication Website: https://www.chaindrugreview.com/
Parent Company: Racher Press
Editor Name: David Pinto
Editor Email: dpinto@racherpress.com
Editor Phone: (212) 213-6000
Advertising Executive Name: Rick Kolinsky
Advertising Executive Email: rkolinsky@racherpress.com
Advertising Executive Phone: (908) 884-4592
Year Established: 1978
Published Days: Other
Avg. Paid Circ.: 87
Avg. Free Circ.: 42977
Audit Company: CVC
Audit Date: 43628

NEW YORK

CHELSEA CLINTON NEWS

Street Address: 505 8th Ave. Ste. 804
City: New York
State: NY
ZIP Code: 10018
General Phone: (212) 868-0190
General Email: advertising@strausnews.com
Publication Website: http://www.chelseanewsny.com/
Parent Company: Straus News
Editor Name: Alexis Gelber
Editor Email: nyoffice@strausnews.com
Advertising Executive Name: Vincent A. Gardino
Advertising Executive Email: advertising@strausnews.com
Year Established: 1939
Own Printing Facility?: Y
Mechanical specifications: Type page 10.333 x 11
Published Days: Thur
Avg. Paid Circ.: 138
Audit Company: Sworn/Estimate/Non-Audited
Audit Date: 43626

NEW YORK

FORWARD NEWSPAPER

Street Address: 125 Maiden Ln
City: New York
State: NY
ZIP Code: 10038
General Phone: (212) 889-8200
General Email: info@forward.com
Publication Website: https://forward.com/
Publisher Name: Rachel Fishman Feddersen
Publisher Email: rachel@forward.com
Publisher Phone: (212) 453-9401
Editor Name: Jodi Rudoren
Editor Email: rudoren@forward.com
Advertising Executive Email: info@forward.com
Year Established: 1897
Mechanical specifications: Type page 11.5 x 18.3; 6 cols, 1.78, 0.16 between
Published Days: Fri
Avg. Paid Circ.: 29479
Audit Company: Sworn/Estimate/Non-Audited
Audit Date: 43626

NEW YORK

MASS MARKET RETAILERS

Street Address: 126 Fifth Avenue, 12th Floor
City: New York
State: NY
ZIP Code: 10011
General Phone: (212) 213-6000
General Email: pnavarre@racherpress.com
Publication Website: https://www.massmarketretailers.com/
Parent Company: Racher Press, Inc
Publisher Name: Susan Schinitsky
Publisher Phone: (212) 213-6000
Editor Name: David Pinto
Editor Email: dpinto@racherpress.com
Editor Phone: (212) 213-6000
Advertising Executive Name: Peggy Navarre
Advertising Executive Email: pnavarre@racherpress.com
Advertising Executive Phone: (212) 699-2371
Year Established: 1983
Published Days: Mon`Other
Avg. Paid Circ.: 91
Avg. Free Circ.: 23276
Audit Company: CVC
Audit Date: 43658

NEW YORK

NEW JERSEY LAW JOURNAL

Street Address: 150 East 42nd Street, Mezzanine Level
City: New York
State: NY
ZIP Code: 07102-4005
General Phone: (720) 895-4985
General Email: njladvertising@alm.com
Publication Website: https://www.law.com/njlawjournal/?slreturn=20200106203328
Parent Company: ALM Media Properties, LLC
Editor Name: Lisa Helem

NEW YORK

THE BRONX FREE PRESS

Street Address: 5030 Broadway, Suite 801
City: New York
State: NY
ZIP Code: 10034-1666
General Phone: (212) 569-5800
General Email: editor@manhattantimesnews.com
Publication Website: https://thebronxfreepress.com/
Parent Company: Bronx Free Press
Publisher Name: Roberto Ramirez
Editor Name: Debralee Santos
Editor Email: editor@manhattantimesnews.com
Delivery Methods: Mail`Racks
Mechanical specifications: Type page 10 x 11.25; 4 cols
Published Days: Wed`Thur
Audit Company: Sworn/Estimate/Non-Audited
Audit Date: 43626

NEW YORK

THE NEW YORK OBSERVER

Street Address: 1 WHITEHALL STREET
City: New York
State: NY
ZIP Code: 10004
General Phone: (212) 755-2400
General Email: sales@observer.com
Publication Website: https://observer.com/
Parent Company: Observer Media
Publisher Name: Joseph Meyer
Editor Name: Max Gross
Editor Email: editorial@observer.com
Editor Phone: (212) 407-9302
Advertising Executive Email: sales@observer.com
Advertising Executive Phone: (212) 407-9389
Year Established: 1987
Published Days: Wed
Avg. Paid Circ.: 52000
Audit Company: Sworn/Estimate/Non-Audited
Audit Date: 43626

NEW YORK

THE WESTSIDER

Street Address: 505 8th Ave. Ste. 804
City: New York
State: NY
ZIP Code: 10018
General Phone: (212) 868-0190
General Email: sales@strausnews.com
Publication Website: http://www.westsidespirit.com/
Parent Company: Straus News
Publisher Name: Becca Tucker
Publisher Email: editor.dirt@strausnews.com
Editor Name: Alexis Gelber
Editor Email: nyoffice@strausnews.com
Advertising Executive Name: Mike Zummo
Advertising Executive Email: njoffice@strausnews.com
Year Established: 1972
Mechanical specifications: Type page 10.333 x 11
Published Days: Thur
Avg. Paid Circ.: 326
Audit Company: Sworn/Estimate/Non-Audited
Audit Date: 43626

NEWBURGH

HUDSON VALLEY PRESS

Street Address: PO Box 2160
City: Newburgh
State: NY
ZIP Code: 12550-0332
General Phone: (845) 562-1313
General Email: subscriptions@hvpress.net
Publication Website: https://hudsonvalleypress.com
Editor Email: editor@hvpress.net
Year Established: 1983
Mechanical specifications: Type page 11 x 12; 6 cols, 1.5, 0.2 between
Published Days: Wed
Audit Company: Sworn/Estimate/Non-Audited
Audit Date: 43626

NEWBURGH

MID-HUDSON TIMES

Street Address: 300 Stony Brook Ct
City: Newburgh
State: NY
ZIP Code: 12550
General Phone: (845) 561-0170
General Email: advertising@tcnewspapers.com

Publication Website: http://timeshudsonvalley.com/mid-hudson-times/index.html
Parent Company: Times Community Newspapers
Editor Email: editor@tcnewspapers.com
Advertising Executive Name: Carl Aiello
Advertising Executive Email: advertising@tcnewspapers.com
Delivery Methods: Mail`Newsstand`Racks
Year Established: 1989
Own Printing Facility?: Y
Commercial printers?: N
Mechanical specifications: Type page 10.25 x 11; 6 cols, 1.5, 0.25 between
Published Days: Wed
Avg. Paid Circ.: 2700
Avg. Free Circ.: 100
Audit Company: Sworn/Estimate/Non-Audited
Audit Date: 43626

NEWBURGH

WALLKILL VALLEY TIMES

Street Address: 300 Stony Brook Ct
City: Newburgh
State: NY
ZIP Code: 12550
General Phone: (845) 561-0170
General Email: advertising@tcnewspapers.com
Publication Website: http://timeshudsonvalley.com/wallkill-valley-times/index.html
Parent Company: Times Community Newspapers
Editor Email: editor@tcnewspapers.com
Advertising Executive Name: Diane Holbert
Advertising Executive Email: dholbert@tcnewspapers.com
Delivery Methods: Mail`Newsstand`Racks
Year Established: 1983
Own Printing Facility?: Y
Mechanical specifications: Type page 10.25 x 11; 6 cols, 1.5, 0.25 between
Published Days: Wed
Avg. Paid Circ.: 5000
Avg. Free Circ.: 53
Audit Company: Sworn/Estimate/Non-Audited
Audit Date: 43626

OGDENSBURG

NORTH COUNTRY CATHOLIC

Street Address: 622 Washington St
City: Ogdensburg
State: NY
ZIP Code: 13669
General Phone: (315) 608-7556
General Email: dfargo@rcdony.org
Publication Website: http://www.northcountrycatholic.org/
Parent Company: Roman Catholic Diocese of Ogdensburg
Publisher Name: Terry R. LaValley
Editor Name: Darcy Fargo
Editor Email: dfargo@rcdony.org
Editor Phone: (315) 393-2920, ext : 1370
Advertising Executive Name: Christine Ward
Advertising Executive Email: cward@rcdony.org
Year Established: 1946
Mechanical specifications: Type page 8.75 x 10.75; 5 cols, 1.75
Published Days: Wed
Audit Company: Sworn/Estimate/Non-Audited
Audit Date: 43626

OLD FORGE

THE WEEKLY ADIRONDACK

Street Address: P.O. Box 553
City: Old Forge
State: NY
ZIP Code: 13420
General Phone: (315) 369-9982
General Email: weeklyadk@yahoo.com
Publication Website: http://www.weeklyadk.com/
Delivery Methods: Mail`Racks
Published Days: Thur
Audit Company: Sworn/Estimate/Non-Audited
Audit Date: 43626

ONEIDA

THE ONEIDA DAILY DISPATCH

Street Address: 730 Lenox Avenue
City: Oneida
State: NY
ZIP Code: 13421
General Phone: (315) 363-5100
General Email: customerservice@oneidadispatch.com
Publication Website: https://www.oneidadispatch.com/
Parent Company: Media News Group
Publisher Name: Kevin Corrado
Publisher Email: kcorrado@medianewsgroup.com
Editor Name: Ron Rosner
Editor Email: rrosner@medianewsgroup.com
Editor Phone: (518) 290-3905
Advertising Executive Name: Karen Alvord
Advertising Executive Email: advertising@oneidadispatch.com
Advertising Executive Phone: (315) 231-5136
Delivery Methods: Mail`Newsstand`Carrier`Racks
Year Established: 1873
Own Printing Facility?: Y
Commercial printers?: N
Mechanical specifications: 1 col. 1.557", 2 col. 3.223", 3 col. 4.89", 4 col. 6.557", 5 col. 8.223", 6 col. 9.89"
Published Days: Tues`Thur`Sun
Weekday Frequency: m
Avg. Paid Circ.: 5396
Avg. Free Circ.: 1751
Audit Company: AAM
Audit Date: 44625
Business Equipment: IBM/60 fileserver, 1-IBM/30-286, 5-IBM/25
Business Software: Novell/MSSI
Classified Equipment: Hardware -- IBM/XT;
Classified Software: Cx.
Editorial Equipment: Hardware -- APP/Mac G3
Editorial Software: Cx, Baseview/News IQUE.
Production Equipment: Cameras -- B/Caravel, SCREEN/C-6500 D; Scanners -- HP/ScanJet 4C.

ONEONTA

COOPERSTOWN CRIER

Street Address: 102 Chestnut St
City: Oneonta
State: NY
ZIP Code: 13820
General Phone: (607) 432-1000
General Email: crier@coopercrier.com
Publication Website: https://www.coopercrier.com/
Parent Company: Community Media Group LLC.
Publisher Phone: (607) 432-1000, ext : 214
Advertising Executive Phone: (607) 432-1000, ext : 235
Published Days: Thur
Audit Company: Sworn/Estimate/Non-Audited
Audit Date: 43626

PALATINE BRIDGE

COUNTRY FOLKS - EAST ZONE

Street Address: 6113 State Highway 5
City: Palatine Bridge
State: NY
ZIP Code: 13428-2809
General Phone: (518) 673-3237
General Email: info@leepub.com
Publication Website: https://countryfolks.com/
Advertising Executive Name: Larry Price
Advertising Executive Email: lprice@leepub.com
Advertising Executive Phone: (518) 673-0106
Delivery Methods: Mail
Year Established: 1970
Mechanical specifications: Type page 10.25 x 13; 6 cols, 1.5625
Published Days: Mon
Avg. Paid Circ.: 8900
Avg. Free Circ.: 1100
Audit Company: Sworn/Estimate/Non-Audited
Audit Date: 43626

PATCHOGUE

ISLIP BULLETIN

Street Address: 20 Medford Ave
City: Patchogue
State: NY
ZIP Code: 11772
General Phone: (631) 475-1000
General Email: islipbulletineditorial@gmail.com
Publication Website: https://www.islipbulletin.net/
Publisher Name: Terry Tuthill
Publisher Phone: (631) 475-1000, ext : 25
Editor Name: Nicole Fuentes
Editor Phone: (631) 475-1000 ext. 21
Advertising Executive Name: Monica Musetti-Carlin
Advertising Executive Phone: (631) 475-1000, ext : 17
Delivery Methods: Mail`Newsstand`Racks
Year Established: 1948
Mechanical specifications: Type page 10 x 13.75; 4 cols, 2.25, 0.25 between
Published Days: Thur
Avg. Paid Circ.: 1500
Audit Company: Sworn/Estimate/Non-Audited
Audit Date: 43626

PATCHOGUE

LONG ISLAND ADVANCE

Street Address: 20 Medford Ave
City: Patchogue
State: NY
ZIP Code: 11772
General Phone: (631) 475-1000
General Email: liaeditorial@gmail.com
Publication Website: http://www.longislandadvance.net/
Parent Company: Terry Tuthill
Publisher Name: Terry Tuthill
Publisher Phone: (631) 475-1000, ext : 25
Editor Name: Nicole Fuentes
Editor Phone: (631) 475-1000 ext. 21
Advertising Executive Name: Vicki Ann Morales
Advertising Executive Phone: (631) 475-1000, ext : 23
Delivery Methods: Mail`Newsstand`Racks
Year Established: 1871
Own Printing Facility?: N
Commercial printers?: N
Mechanical specifications: Type page 10 x 13.75; 4 cols, 2.25, 0.25 between
Published Days: Thur
Avg. Paid Circ.: 5000
Audit Company: Sworn/Estimate/Non-Audited
Audit Date: 43626
Pressroom Equipment: Macs
Pressroom Software: Indesign

PATCHOGUE

SUFFOLK COUNTY NEWS

Street Address: 20 Medford Ave
City: Patchogue
State: NY
ZIP Code: 11772-1220
General Phone: (631) 475-1000
General Email: scnewseditorial@gmail.com
Publication Website: http://www.suffolkcountynews.net/
Parent Company: John T. Tuthill, III
Publisher Name: John T. Tuthill
Publisher Phone: (631) 475-1000, ext : 25
Editor Name: Nicole Fuentes
Editor Phone: (631) 475-1000, ext : 21
Advertising Executive Name: Lynn Halverson
Advertising Executive Phone: (631) 475-1000, ext : 10
Delivery Methods: Mail`Newsstand`Racks
Year Established: 1884
Own Printing Facility?: Y
Mechanical specifications: Type page 10 x 13.75; 4 cols, 2.25, 0.25 between
Published Days: Thur
Avg. Paid Circ.: 53000
Audit Company: Sworn/Estimate/Non-Audited
Audit Date: 43626

PENN YAN

THE CHRONICLE-EXPRESS

Street Address: 138 Main St
City: Penn Yan
State: NY
ZIP Code: 14527-1299
General Phone: (315) 536-4422
General Email: candyscutt@chronicle-express.com
Publication Website: https://www.chronicle-express.com/
Publisher Name: Karen Morris
Publisher Email: karenmorris@chronicle-express.com
Editor Name: Gwen Chamberlain
Editor Email: gwenchamberlain@chronicle-express.com
Advertising Executive Name: Candace Scutt
Advertising Executive Email: candyscutt@chronicle-express.com
Delivery Methods: Mail`Newsstand`Racks
Year Established: 1824
Own Printing Facility?: Y
Commercial printers?: Y
Mechanical specifications: Type page 10 x 16; 6 cols, 1.75
Published Days: Wed`Sun
Avg. Paid Circ.: 3200
Avg. Free Circ.: 11245
Audit Company: Sworn/Estimate/Non-Audited
Audit Date: 43626

PERRY

PERRY HERALD

Street Address: 75 South Main Street
City: Perry
State: NY
ZIP Code: 14530
General Phone: (585) 237-2212
General Email: ads@perryshopper.com
Publication Website: http://www.perryshopper.com/
Parent Company: Warsaw Pennysaver
Year Established: 1878
Own Printing Facility?: Y
Commercial printers?: Y
Published Days: Thur
Avg. Paid Circ.: 772
Avg. Free Circ.: 7
Audit Company: Sworn/Estimate/Non-Audited

Audit Date: 43626

PORT CHESTER

WESTMORE NEWS

Street Address: 38 Broad St
City: Port Chester
State: NY
ZIP Code: 10573
General Phone: (914) 939-6864
General Email: publisher@westmorenews.com
Publication Website: https://westmorenews.com/
Publisher Name: Richard Abel
Publisher Email: publisher@westmorenews.com
Editor Name: Jananne Abel
Editor Email: editor@westmorenews.com
Delivery Methods: Mail`Newsstand`Racks
Year Established: 1964
Mechanical specifications: Type page 10 x 16; E - 5 cols, 1 5/6, 1/6 between; A - 5 cols, 1 5/6, 1/6 between; C - 6 cols, 1 1/2, 1/6 between.
Published Days: Fri
Avg. Paid Circ.: 2433
Avg. Free Circ.: 983
Audit Company: Sworn/Estimate/Non-Audited
Audit Date: 43626

POTSDAM

NORTH COUNTRY THIS WEEK

Street Address: 4 Clarkson Ave.
City: Potsdam
State: NY
ZIP Code: 13676
General Phone: (315) 265-1000
General Email: thisweek@northcountrynow.com
Publication Website: https://northcountrynow.com/
Publisher Name: Bill Shumway
Publisher Email: bill@northcountrynow.com
Publisher Phone: (315) 265-1000, ext : 21
Editor Name: Jimmy Lawton
Editor Email: jimmy@northcountrynow.com
Editor Phone: (315) 265-1000, ext : 26
Advertising Executive Name: John Basham
Advertising Executive Email: john@northcountrynow.com
Advertising Executive Phone: (315) 265-1000, ext : 25
Delivery Methods: Mail`Carrier`Racks
Year Established: 1984
Own Printing Facility?: N
Commercial printers?: N
Mechanical specifications: Type page 10.8336 x 16; 5 cols, 2.014, 0.18 between
Published Days: Wed`Sat
Avg. Paid Circ.: 7
Avg. Free Circ.: 9745
Audit Company: CVC
Audit Date: 43070
Classified Equipment: Imac OSX 10.12.6
Classified Software: Pre-1
Editorial Equipment: Imac OSX 10.12.6
Editorial Software: InDesign Suite, Word
Production Equipment: Imac OSX 10.12.6
Production Software: InDesign Suite, Word
Note: We publish 2 editions: Potsdam-Canton Edition on Wednesday, 9,764circulation, and Massena-Ogdensburg Edition on Saturday, 7,740 circulation

ROCHESTER

ROCHESTER BUSINESS JOURNAL

Street Address: 16 W. Main St.
City: Rochester
State: NY
ZIP Code: 14614

General Phone: (866) 941-4130
General Email: service@bridgetowermedia.com
Publication Website: https://rbj.net/
Publisher Name: Kevin Momot
Publisher Email: kmomot@bridgetowermedia.com
Publisher Phone: (585) 363-7272
Editor Name: Ben Jacobs
Editor Email: bjacobs@bridgetowermedia.com
Editor Phone: (585) 232-6922
Advertising Executive Name: Jean Moorhouse
Advertising Executive Email: jmoorhouse@bridgetowermedia.com
Advertising Executive Phone: (585) 363-7273
Year Established: 1985
Mechanical specifications: Type page 10 x 14
Published Days: Fri
Avg. Paid Circ.: 4827
Avg. Free Circ.: 2526
Audit Company: CVC
Audit Date: 43658

ROCKAWAY BEACH

THE WAVE

Street Address: 8808 Rockaway Beach Blvd
City: Rockaway Beach
State: NY
ZIP Code: 11693-1608
General Phone: (718) 634-4000
General Email: editor@rockawave.com
Publication Website: https://www.rockawave.com/
Publisher Name: Walter H. Sanchez
Publisher Email: whs@rockawave.com
Editor Name: Mark C. Healey
Editor Email: editor@rockawave.com
Advertising Executive Name: Kenneth Good
Advertising Executive Email: kgood@rockawave.com
Delivery Methods: Mail`Newsstand
Year Established: 1893
Mechanical specifications: Type page 9 3/4 x 14; E - 4 cols, 2 1/3, 1/6 between; A - 4 cols, 2 1/3, 1/6 between; C - 5 cols, 1 5/6, 1/6 between.
Published Days: Fri
Avg. Paid Circ.: 9000
Avg. Free Circ.: 100
Audit Company: Sworn/Estimate/Non-Audited
Audit Date: 43626

RONKONKOMA

LONG ISLAND BUSINESS NEWS

Street Address: 2150 Smithtown Ave
City: Ronkonkoma
State: NY
ZIP Code: 11779
General Phone: (631) 737-1700
General Email: advertising@libn.com
Publication Website: https://libn.com/
Publisher Name: Joe Dowd
Publisher Email: jdowd@libn.com
Publisher Phone: (631) 913-4238
Editor Name: Joe Dowd
Editor Email: jdowd@libn.com
Editor Phone: (631) 913.4238
Advertising Executive Name: Barbara Pescuma
Advertising Executive Email: bpescuma@libn.com
Advertising Executive Phone: (631) 913-4249
Delivery Methods: Mail`Newsstand`Racks
Year Established: 1953
Published Days: Fri
Avg. Paid Circ.: 4000
Avg. Free Circ.: 1000
Audit Company: VAC
Audit Date: 43260

ROSLYN HEIGHTS

GREAT NECK NEWS

Street Address: 25 Red Ground Road
City: Roslyn Heights
State: NY
ZIP Code: 11577
General Phone: (516) 307-1045
General Email: hblank@theislandnow.com
Publication Website: https://theislandnow.com/category/community-news/great-neck-cn/
Parent Company: Blank Slate Media LLC
Advertising Executive Name: Wendy Kates
Advertising Executive Email: wkates@theislandnow.com
Advertising Executive Phone: (516) 307-1045, ext : 212
Delivery Methods: Mail`Newsstand`Racks
Year Established: 1926
Mechanical specifications: Type page 8.75 x 11.5; 6 cols, 1.325, 0.183 between
Published Days: Fri
Avg. Paid Circ.: 4033
Audit Company: Sworn/Estimate/Non-Audited
Audit Date: 43626

ROSLYN HEIGHTS

MANHASSET TIMES

Street Address: 25 Red Ground Road
City: Roslyn Heights
State: NY
ZIP Code: 11577
General Phone: (516) 307-1045
General Email: hblank@theislandnow.com
Publication Website: https://theislandnow.com/category/manhasset-107/
Parent Company: Blank Slate Media
Publisher Name: Steven Blank
Publisher Email: sblank@theislandnow.com
Publisher Phone: (516) 307-1045, ext : 201
Editor Name: STEVEN BLANK
Editor Email: sblank@theislandnow.com
Editor Phone: (516) 307-1045, ext : 201
Advertising Executive Email: proberts@theislandnow.com
Advertising Executive Phone: (516) 819-4097
Published Days: Mon`Tues`Fri
Audit Company: Sworn/Estimate/Non-Audited
Audit Date: 43626

ROSLYN HEIGHTS

NEW HYDE PARK HERALD COURIER

Street Address: 25 Red Ground Road
City: Roslyn Heights
State: NY
ZIP Code: 11577
General Phone: (516) 307-1045
General Email: sshaughnessy@theislandnow.com
Publication Website: https://theislandnow.com/category/new_hyde_park-108/
Parent Company: Blank Slate Media
Publisher Name: Steven Blank
Publisher Email: sblank@theislandnow.com
Publisher Phone: (516) 307-1045, ext : 201
Advertising Executive Name: Peter Roberts
Advertising Executive Email: proberts@theislandnow.com
Advertising Executive Phone: (516) 819-4097
Delivery Methods: Mail`Racks
Year Established: 1936
Commercial printers?: Y
Mechanical specifications: Type page 8.75 x 11.5; 6 cols, 1.325, 0.183 between
Published Days: Fri
Avg. Paid Circ.: 4381
Audit Company: Sworn/Estimate/Non-Audited
Audit Date: 43626

ROSLYN HEIGHTS

PORT WASHINGTON TIMES

Street Address: 25 Red Ground Road
City: Roslyn Heights
State: NY
ZIP Code: 11577
General Phone: (516) 307-1045
General Email: stabakin@theislandnow.com
Publication Website: https://theislandnow.com/category/port-washington/
Parent Company: Blank Slate Media
Publisher Name: Steven Blank
Publisher Email: sblank@theislandnow.com
Publisher Phone: (516) 307-1045, ext : 201
Editor Name: Steven Blank
Editor Email: sblank@theislandnow.com
Editor Phone: (516) 307-1045, ext : 201
Advertising Executive Email: proberts@theislandnow.com
Advertising Executive Phone: (516) 819-4097
Published Days: Mon`Wed`Fri
Audit Company: Sworn/Estimate/Non-Audited
Audit Date: 43626

ROSLYN HEIGHTS

ROSLYN TIMES

Street Address: 25 Red Ground Road
City: Roslyn Heights
State: NY
ZIP Code: 11577
General Phone: (516) 307-1045
General Email: hblank@theislandnow.com
Publication Website: https://theislandnow.com/category/roslyn-109/
Parent Company: Blank Slate Media
Publisher Name: Steven Blank
Publisher Email: sblank@theislandnow.com
Publisher Phone: (516) 307-1045, ext : 201
Editor Name: Steven Blank
Editor Email: sblank@theislandnow.com
Editor Phone: (516) 307-1045, ext : 201
Advertising Executive Email: proberts@theislandnow.com
Advertising Executive Phone: (516) 819-4097
Published Days: Wed
Audit Company: Sworn/Estimate/Non-Audited
Audit Date: 43626

ROSLYN HEIGHTS

WILLISTON TIMES

Street Address: 25 Red Ground Road
City: Roslyn Heights
State: NY
ZIP Code: 11577
General Phone: (516) 307-1045
General Email: pcamp@theislandnow.com
Publication Website: https://theislandnow.com/category/williston-110/
Parent Company: Blank Slate Media
Publisher Name: Steven Blank
Publisher Email: sblank@theislandnow.com
Publisher Phone: (516) 307-1045, ext : 201
Advertising Executive Name: Peter Roberts
Advertising Executive Email: proberts@theislandnow.com
Advertising Executive Phone: (516) 819-4097
Delivery Methods: Mail`Newsstand`Racks
Year Established: 1940
Own Printing Facility?: Y
Commercial printers?: Y
Mechanical specifications: Type page 8.75 x 11.5; 6 cols, 1.325, 0.183 between
Published Days: Fri
Avg. Paid Circ.: 4284
Audit Company: Sworn/Estimate/Non-Audited
Audit Date: 43626

RYE

WESTCHESTER MAGAZINE

Community Newspapers in the U.S.

Street Address: 2 Clinton Avenue
City: Rye
State: NY
ZIP Code: 10580
General Phone: (914) 345-0601
General Email: jdambrosio@westchestermagazine.com
Publication Website: https://westchestermagazine.com/
Parent Company: Today Media, LLC
Publisher Name: Samuel N. Wender
Publisher Email: swender@westchestermagazine.com
Editor Name: Amy R. Partridge
Editor Email: apartridge@westchestermagazine.com
Advertising Executive Email: sales@westchestermagazine.com
Advertising Executive Phone: (914) 345-0601, ext : 138
Published Days: Other
Avg. Paid Circ.: 698
Avg. Free Circ.: 17750
Audit Company: CVC
Audit Date: 43658

SALAMANCA

THE SALAMANCA PRESS

Street Address: 36 River St
City: Salamanca
State: NY
ZIP Code: 14779-1474
General Phone: (716) 945-1644
General Email: salpressads@gmail.com
Publication Website: http://www.salamancapress.com/
Parent Company: Community Media Group
Editor Name: Kellen M. Quigley
Editor Email: kquigleysp@gmail.com
Editor Phone: (716) 945-1644 x. 302
Delivery Methods: Mail Racks
Year Established: 1867
Published Days: Thur
Avg. Paid Circ.: 1200
Audit Company: Sworn/Estimate/Non-Audited
Audit Date: 43626

SARATOGA SPRINGS

COMMUNITY NEWS

Street Address: 20 Lake Ave
City: Saratoga Springs
State: NY
ZIP Code: 12866-2314
General Phone: (518) 290-3905
General Email: cnews@saratogian.com
Publication Website: http://www.cnweekly.com/
Parent Company: Media News Group
Publisher Name: Kevin Corrado
Publisher Email: kcorrado@digitalfirstmedia.com
Advertising Executive Name: Karen Alvord
Advertising Executive Email: kalvord@adtaxi.com
Advertising Executive Phone: (315) 231-5136
Mechanical specifications: Type page 12 x 21; E - 5 cols, 1/6 between; A - 6 cols, 1 7/8, 1/6 between; C - 9 cols, 1 1/5, 1/6 between.
Published Days: Fri
Avg. Free Circ.: 26000
Audit Company: Sworn/Estimate/Non-Audited
Audit Date: 43626

SARATOGA SPRINGS

SARATOGA TODAY

Street Address: 5 Case St
City: Saratoga Springs
State: NY
ZIP Code: 12866-3501
General Phone: (518) 581-2480
General Email: rmitchell@saratogapublishing.com
Publication Website: http://saratogatodaynewspaper.com/
Parent Company: Chad Beatty
Publisher Name: Chad Beatty
Publisher Email: cbeatty@saratogapublishing.com
Publisher Phone: (518) 581-2480, ext : 212
Editor Name: Chris Bushee
Editor Email: cbushee@saratogapublishing.com
Editor Phone: (518) 581-2480, ext : 201
Advertising Executive Name: JIM DALEY
Advertising Executive Email: jdaley@saratogapublishing.com
Advertising Executive Phone: (518) 581-2480, ext : 209
Delivery Methods: Mail Racks
Year Established: 2006
Mechanical specifications: Type page 10.5 x 13; 5 cols, 1.9, 0.3 between
Published Days: Fri
Avg. Free Circ.: 10000
Audit Company: Sworn/Estimate/Non-Audited
Audit Date: 43626

SETAUKET

THE PORT TIMES-RECORD

Street Address: 185 Main St
City: Setauket
State: NY
ZIP Code: 11733
General Phone: (631) 751-7744
General Email: kjm@tbrnewsmedia.com
Publication Website: http://tbrnewsmedia.com/port-times-record/
Parent Company: Times Beacon Record News Media
Publisher Name: Leah S. Dunaief
Publisher Email: pub@tbrnewsmedia.com
Publisher Phone: (631) 751-7744, ext : 116
Editor Name: Rita J. Egan
Editor Email: rita@tbrnewsmedia.com
Editor Phone: (631) 751-7744, ext. 130
Advertising Executive Name: Kathryn Mandracchia
Advertising Executive Email: kjm@tbrnewsmedia.com
Advertising Executive Phone: (631) 751-7744, ext : 118
Delivery Methods: Mail Newsstand
Year Established: 1989
Published Days: Thur
Avg. Paid Circ.: 8814
Audit Company: Sworn/Estimate/Non-Audited
Audit Date: 43626

SETAUKET

THE VILLAGE TIMES HERALD

Street Address: 185 Main St
City: Setauket
State: NY
ZIP Code: 11733
General Phone: (631) 751-7744
General Email: kjm@tbrnewsmedia.com
Publication Website: https://tbrnewsmedia.com/village-times-herald/
Parent Company: TBR NewsMedia
Publisher Name: Leah S. Dunaief
Publisher Email: pub@tbrnewsmedia.com
Publisher Phone: (631) 751-7744, ext : 116
Editor Name: Rita J. Egan
Editor Email: rita@tbrnewsmedia.com
Editor Phone: (631) 751-7744, ext. 130
Advertising Executive Name: Kathryn Mandracchia
Advertising Executive Email: kjm@tbrnewsmedia.com
Advertising Executive Phone: (631) 751-7744, ext : 118
Delivery Methods: Mail Newsstand
Year Established: 1976

Published Days: Thur
Avg. Paid Circ.: 10060
Audit Company: Sworn/Estimate/Non-Audited
Audit Date: 43626

SHERBURNE

SHERBURNE NEWS

Street Address: 17 E State St
City: Sherburne
State: NY
ZIP Code: 13460-9751
General Phone: (607) 674-6071
General Email: info@sherburnenews.net
Publication Website: http://www.sherburnenews.net/
Parent Company: Sherburne News
Advertising Executive Email: thesherburnenews@gmail.com
Advertising Executive Phone: (607) 674-6071
Delivery Methods: Mail Racks
Year Established: 1864
Mechanical specifications: Type page 12 x 20; E - 6 cols, 2, between; A - 6 cols, 2, between.
Published Days: Thur
Avg. Paid Circ.: 2000
Audit Company: Sworn/Estimate/Non-Audited
Audit Date: 43626

SIDNEY

TRI-TOWN NEWS

Street Address: 85 Main St., Ste. 1
City: Sidney
State: NY
ZIP Code: 13838
General Phone: (607) 561-3526
General Email: ttnews@tritownnews.com
Publication Website: https://tritownnewscom.wordpress.com/
Editor Name: Allison Collins
Editor Email: alliedcollins@frontier.com
Advertising Executive Name: Melissa Matthews
Advertising Executive Email: melissa@tritownnews.com
Advertising Executive Phone: (607) 208-4064
Delivery Methods: Mail Newsstand
Year Established: 1856
Own Printing Facility?: Y
Commercial printers?: Y
Published Days: Wed
Avg. Paid Circ.: 3400
Audit Company: Sworn/Estimate/Non-Audited
Audit Date: 43626

SMITHTOWN

SMITHTOWN MESSENGER

Street Address: 27 W Main St
City: Smithtown
State: NY
ZIP Code: 11787-2602
General Phone: (631) 265-3500
General Email: messenger127e@aol.com
Publication Website: http://www.smithtowninfo.com/
Parent Company: P & S News Group
Year Established: 1887
Own Printing Facility?: Y
Commercial printers?: Y
Published Days: Thur
Avg. Paid Circ.: 8500
Audit Company: Sworn/Estimate/Non-Audited
Audit Date: 43626

SOMERS

MAHOPAC NEWS

Street Address: 334 Route 202
City: Somers
State: NY
ZIP Code: 10589
General Phone: (845) 621-1115
General Email: freeman@halstonmedia.com
Publication Website: http://www.mahopacnews.com/
Parent Company: Halston Media, LLC
Publisher Name: Brett Freeman
Publisher Email: freeman@halstonmedia.com
Publisher Phone: (845) 208-8151
Editor Name: Brian Marschhauser
Editor Email: marschhauser@halstonmedia.com
Editor Phone: (914) 302-5628
Advertising Executive Name: Paul Forhan
Advertising Executive Email: forhan@halstonmedia.com
Advertising Executive Phone: (914) 202-2392
Delivery Methods: Mail Newsstand Racks
Published Days: Thur
Audit Company: Sworn/Estimate/Non-Audited
Audit Date: 43626

SOUTHAMPTON

DAN'S PAPERS LLC

Street Address: 158 County Road 39
City: Southampton
State: NY
ZIP Code: 11968
General Phone: (631) 537-0500
General Email: mcable@danshamptons.com
Publication Website: https://www.danspapers.com/
Parent Company: Manhattan Media LLC
Publisher Name: Maria Cable
Publisher Email: mcable@danshamptons.com
Editor Name: Eric Feil
Editor Email: editor@danspapers.com
Advertising Executive Email: mcable@danshamptons.com
Advertising Executive Phone: (631) 537-0500
Delivery Methods: Mail Racks
Year Established: 1960
Mechanical specifications: Type page 9.375 x 12.25
Published Days: Fri
Avg. Free Circ.: 32940
Audit Company: Sworn/Estimate/Non-Audited
Audit Date: 43626
Note: Dan's is now the largest luxury food & wine event company on Long Island's East End. Dan's also publishes a variety of niche print/online supplements annually.

SOUTHAMPTON

THE SOUTHAMPTON PRESS

Street Address: 135 Windmill Ln
City: Southampton
State: NY
ZIP Code: 11968
General Phone: (631) 283-4100
General Email: ads@pressnewsgroup.com
Publication Website: https://www.27east.com/southampton-press/
Parent Company: The Press News Group
Publisher Name: Gavin Menu
Publisher Email: gmenu@expressnewsgroup.com
Publisher Phone: (631) 283-4100, ext : 120
Editor Name: Bill Sutton
Editor Email: billsutton@expressnewsgroup.com
Editor Phone: (631) 283-4100. ext.111
Advertising Executive Name: Winifred Channing
Advertising Executive Email: wchanning@expressnewsgroup.com
Advertising Executive Phone: (631) 283-4100, ext : 147

Delivery Methods: Mail`Newsstand
Year Established: 1897
Mechanical specifications: Type page 11.125 x 20.5; 6 cols, 1.715, 0.167 between
Published Days: Thur
Avg. Paid Circ.: 8382
Avg. Free Circ.: 209
Audit Company: Sworn/Estimate/Non-Audited
Audit Date: 43626

SPECULATOR

HAMILTON COUNTY EXPRESS

Street Address: 2892 State Route 30
City: Speculator
State: NY
ZIP Code: 12164
General Phone: (518) 843-1100
General Email: briankrohn@recordernews.com
Publication Website: http://www.hamcoountyexpress.com/
Parent Company: Port Jackson Media LLC
Delivery Methods: Mail`Newsstand
Year Established: 1949
Own Printing Facility?: Y
Commercial printers?: Y
Mechanical specifications: Type page 11 x 17; E - 5 cols, 2, 3/5 between; A - 5 cols, 2, 3/5 between; C - 5 cols, 2, 3/5 between.
Published Days: Wed
Avg. Paid Circ.: 2681
Avg. Free Circ.: 81
Audit Company: Sworn/Estimate/Non-Audited
Audit Date: 43626

SPENCERPORT

HAMLIN CLARKSON HERALD

Street Address: 1776 Hilton Parma Corners Rd
City: Spencerport
State: NY
ZIP Code: 14559
General Phone: (585) 352-3411
General Email: info@westsidenewsny.com
Publication Website: https://www.westsidenewsny.com/
Parent Company: Westside News
Publisher Name: Keith Ryan
Publisher Phone: (585) 352-3411, ext : 125
Editor Name: Evelyn Dow
Advertising Executive Name: Karen Fien
Advertising Executive Email: production@westsidenewsny.com
Advertising Executive Phone: (585) 352-3411, ext : 128
Delivery Methods: Mail`Newsstand`Carrier`Racks
Year Established: 1988
Mechanical specifications: Type page 10.25 x 16; 6 cols, 1.5, 0.25 between
Published Days: Sun
Avg. Paid Circ.: 10
Avg. Free Circ.: 5915
Audit Company: CVC
Audit Date: 43625

SPENCERPORT

SUBURBAN NEWS NORTH

Street Address: 1776 Hilton Parma Corners Rd
City: Spencerport
State: NY
ZIP Code: 14559
General Phone: (585) 352-3411
General Email: info@westsidenewsny.com
Publication Website: https://www.westsidenewsny.com/
Parent Company: Westside News
Publisher Name: Keith Ryan
Publisher Phone: (585) 352-3411, ext : 125

Editor Name: Evelyn Dow
Advertising Executive Name: Karen Fien
Advertising Executive Email: production@westsidenewsny.com
Advertising Executive Phone: (585) 352-3411, ext : 128
Delivery Methods: Mail`Newsstand`Carrier`Racks
Year Established: 1953
Mechanical specifications: Type page 10.25 x 16; 6 cols, 1.5, 0.25 between
Published Days: Sun
Avg. Paid Circ.: 6
Avg. Free Circ.: 7094
Audit Company: CVC
Audit Date: 43625

SPENCERPORT

SUBURBAN NEWS SOUTH

Street Address: 1776 Hilton Parma Corners Rd
City: Spencerport
State: NY
ZIP Code: 14559
General Phone: (585) 352-3411
General Email: info@westsidenewsny.com
Publication Website: https://www.westsidenewsny.com/
Parent Company: Westside News
Publisher Name: Keith Ryan
Publisher Phone: (585) 352-3411, ext : 125
Editor Name: Evelyn Dow
Advertising Executive Name: Karen Fien
Advertising Executive Email: production@westsidenewsny.com
Advertising Executive Phone: (585) 352-3411, ext : 128
Delivery Methods: Mail`Newsstand`Carrier`Racks
Year Established: 1988
Mechanical specifications: Type page 10.25 x 16; 6 cols, 1.5, 0.25 between
Published Days: Sun
Avg. Paid Circ.: 38
Avg. Free Circ.: 11887
Audit Company: CVC
Audit Date: 43625

SPENCERPORT

SUBURBAN NEWS WEST

Street Address: 1776 Hilton Parma Corners Rd
City: Spencerport
State: NY
ZIP Code: 14559
General Phone: (585) 352-3411
General Email: production@westsidenewsny.com
Publication Website: https://www.westsidenewsny.com/
Parent Company: Westside News
Publisher Name: Keith Ryan
Publisher Phone: (585) 352-3411, ext : 125
Editor Name: Evelyn Dow
Advertising Executive Name: Karen Fien
Advertising Executive Email: production@westsidenewsny.com
Advertising Executive Phone: (585) 352-3411, ext : 128
Delivery Methods: Mail`Newsstand`Carrier`Racks
Year Established: 1989
Mechanical specifications: Type page 10.25 x 16; 6 cols, 1.5, 0.25 between
Published Days: Sun
Avg. Paid Circ.: 8
Avg. Free Circ.: 8817
Audit Company: CVC
Audit Date: 43625

SUNNYSIDE

WOODSIDE HERALD

Street Address: 4311 Greenpoint Ave
City: Sunnyside
State: NY
ZIP Code: 11104-2605
General Phone: (718) 729-3772
General Email: ssabba@woodsideherald.com
Publication Website: http://www.woodsideherald.com/
Editor Email: ssabba@woodsideherald.com
Advertising Executive Email: sherilynsabba@woodsideherald.com
Own Printing Facility?: Y
Commercial printers?: Y
Mechanical specifications: Type page 10 1/2 x 14; E - 2 cols, 4 1/4, 1/6 between.
Published Days: Fri
Avg. Paid Circ.: 14000
Avg. Free Circ.: 5000
Audit Company: Sworn/Estimate/Non-Audited
Audit Date: 43626

SYOSSET

LONG ISLAND PRESS

Street Address: 6901 Jericho Tpke, Suite 215
City: Syosset
State: NY
ZIP Code: 11791-4447
General Phone: (516) 284-3300
General Email: felice@longislandpress.com
Publication Website: https://www.longislandpress.com/
Parent Company: Schneps Media
Publisher Name: Joanna Austin
Editor Name: Timothy Bolger
Mechanical specifications: Type page 8.75 x 11.25
Published Days: Mthly
Avg. Free Circ.: 40000
Audit Company: Sworn/Estimate/Non-Audited
Audit Date: 43626

SYRACUSE

BALDWINSVILLE MESSENGER

Street Address: 2501 James St
City: Syracuse
State: NY
ZIP Code: 13206-2996
General Phone: (315) 434-8889
General Email: messenger@cnylink.com
Publication Website: https://www.eaglenewsonline.com
Parent Company: Eagle Newspapers (NY)
Publisher Name: Dave Tyler
Publisher Email: dtyler@eaglenewsonline.com
Publisher Phone: (315) 434-8889, ext : 302
Editor Name: Jennifer Wing
Editor Email: jwing@eaglenewsonline.com
Editor Phone: (315) 434-8889, ext : 340
Delivery Methods: Mail`Newsstand`Carrier
Own Printing Facility?: Y
Mechanical specifications: Type page 10 13/16 x 16; E - 5 cols, 2 1/16, 1/8 between; A - 5 cols, 2 1/16, 1/8 between; C - 7 cols, 1 1/2, between.
Published Days: Wed
Avg. Paid Circ.: 6100
Audit Company: Sworn/Estimate/Non-Audited
Audit Date: 43626

SYRACUSE

CAZENOVIA REPUBLICAN

Street Address: 2501 James St, Suite 100
City: Syracuse
State: NY
ZIP Code: 13206-2996
General Phone: (315) 434-8889
General Email: editor@cazenoviarepublican.com
Publication Website: https://www.eaglenewsonline.com
Parent Company: Eagle Newspapers (NY)
Publisher Name: Dave Tyler
Publisher Email: dtyler@eaglenewsonline.com
Publisher Phone: (315) 434-8889, ext : 302
Editor Name: Jennifer Wing
Editor Email: jwing@eaglenewsonline.com
Editor Phone: (315) 434-8889, ext : 340
Delivery Methods: Mail`Newsstand`Racks
Year Established: 1854
Own Printing Facility?: Y
Commercial printers?: Y
Mechanical specifications: Type page 10 13/16 x 16; E - 5 cols, 2 1/16, 1/8 between; A - 5 cols, 2 1/16, 1/8 between; C - 7 cols, 1 1/2, between.
Published Days: Wed
Avg. Paid Circ.: 103
Avg. Free Circ.: 3294
Audit Company: CVC
Audit Date: 43625

SYRACUSE

EAGLE BULLETIN

Street Address: 2501 James St
City: Syracuse
State: NY
ZIP Code: 13206
General Phone: (315) 434-8889
General Email: llewis@eaglenewsonline.com
Publication Website: https://www.eaglenewsonline.com
Parent Company: Eagle Newspapers (NY)
Publisher Name: Dave Tyler
Publisher Email: dtyler@eaglenewsonline.com
Publisher Phone: (315) 434-8889, ext : 302
Editor Name: Jennifer Wing
Editor Email: jwing@eaglenewsonline.com
Editor Phone: (315) 434-8889, ext 340
Advertising Executive Name: Luba Demkiv
Advertising Executive Email: ldemkiv@eaglenewsonline.com
Advertising Executive Phone: (315) 434-8889, ext : 330
Delivery Methods: Mail`Newsstand`Carrier
Own Printing Facility?: Y
Commercial printers?: Y
Mechanical specifications: Type page 10 13/16 x 16; E - 5 cols, 2 1/16, 1/8 between; A - 5 cols, 2 1/16, 1/8 between; C - 7 cols, 1 1/2, between.
Published Days: Wed
Avg. Paid Circ.: 56
Avg. Free Circ.: 5902
Audit Company: CVC
Audit Date: 43625

SYRACUSE

EAGLE OBSERVER

Street Address: 2501 James St
City: Syracuse
State: NY
ZIP Code: 13206
General Phone: (315) 434-8889
General Email: editor@eagle-observer.com
Publication Website: https://www.eaglenewsonline.com
Parent Company: Eagle Newspapers (NY)
Publisher Name: Dave Tyler
Publisher Email: dtyler@eaglenewsonline.com
Publisher Phone: (315) 434-8889, ext : 302
Editor Name: Jennifer Wing
Editor Email: jwing@eaglenewsonline.com
Editor Phone: (315) 434-8889 ext. 340
Advertising Executive Name: Luba Demkiv
Advertising Executive Email: ldemkiv@eaglenewsonline.com
Advertising Executive Phone: (315) 434-8889, ext : 330
Delivery Methods: Mail`Newsstand`Carrier
Published Days: Wed

Community Newspapers in the U.S.

Audit Company: Sworn/Estimate/Non-Audited
Audit Date: 43626

SYRACUSE

EAGLE STAR REVIEW

Street Address: 2501 James St
City: Syracuse
State: NY
ZIP Code: 13206
General Phone: (315) 434-8889
General Email: editor@eaglestarreview.com
Publication Website: https://www.eaglenewsonline.com
Parent Company: Eagle Newspapers (NY)
Publisher Name: Dave Tyler
Publisher Email: dtyler@eaglenewsonline.com
Publisher Phone: (315) 434-8889, ext : 302
Editor Name: Jennifer Wing
Editor Email: jwing@eaglenewsonline.com
Editor Phone: (315) 434-8889 ext. 340
Advertising Executive Name: Luba Demkiv
Advertising Executive Email: ldemkiv@eaglenewsonline.com
Advertising Executive Phone: (315) 434-8889, ext : 330
Delivery Methods: Mail
Own Printing Facility?: N
Commercial printers?: N
Mechanical specifications: Type page 10 13/16 x 16; E - 5 cols, 2 1/6, 1/8 between; A - 5 cols, 2 1/6, 1/8 between; C - 7 cols, 1 1/3, 1/8 between.
Published Days: Wed
Avg. Paid Circ.: 21
Avg. Free Circ.: 5542
Audit Company: CVC
Audit Date: 43625

SYRACUSE

SKANEATELES PRESS

Street Address: 2501 James St
City: Syracuse
State: NY
ZIP Code: 13206-2996
General Phone: (315) 685-8338
General Email: press_observer@cnylink.com
Publication Website: https://www.eaglenewsonline.com
Parent Company: Eagle Newspapers (NY)
Publisher Name: Dave Tyler
Publisher Email: dtyler@eaglenewsonline.com
Publisher Phone: (315) 434-8889, ext : 302
Editor Name: Jennifer Wing
Editor Email: jwing@eaglenewsonline.com
Editor Phone: (315) 434-8889, ext : 340
Advertising Executive Name: Luba Demkiv
Advertising Executive Email: ldemkiv@eaglenewsonline.com
Advertising Executive Phone: (315) 434-8889, ext : 303
Delivery Methods: Mail`Newsstand`Carrier
Year Established: 1808
Own Printing Facility?: Y
Commercial printers?: Y
Mechanical specifications: Type page 10 13/16 x 16; E - 5 cols, 2 1/6, 1/8 between; A - 5 cols, 2 1/16, 1/8 between; C - 7 cols, 1 1/3, 1/8 between.
Published Days: Wed
Avg. Paid Circ.: 146
Avg. Free Circ.: 2973
Audit Company: CVC
Audit Date: 43625

SYRACUSE

THE CENTRAL NEW YORK BUSINESS JOURNAL

Street Address: 211 W. Jefferson St
City: Syracuse
State: NY
ZIP Code: 13202-2334
General Phone: (315) 472-3104
General Email: news@cnybj.com
Publication Website: https://www.cnybj.com/
Parent Company: Central New York Business Journal
Publisher Name: Marny Nesher
Publisher Email: mnesher@cnybj.com
Publisher Phone: (315) 579-3925
Editor Name: Adam Rombel
Editor Email: arombel@cnybj.com
Editor Phone: (315) 579-3902
Advertising Executive Name: Dony K. Bardenett
Advertising Executive Email: dbardenett@cnybj.com
Advertising Executive Phone: (315) 579-3901
Mechanical specifications: Type page 10 x 12.75
Published Days: Fri
Audit Company: Sworn/Estimate/Non-Audited
Audit Date: 43626

TUPPER LAKE

TUPPER LAKE FREE PRESS

Street Address: 136 Park St
City: Tupper Lake
State: NY
ZIP Code: 12986
General Phone: (518) 359-2166
General Email: tlfreepress@roadrunner.com
Publication Website: https://tupperfreepress.com/
Year Established: 1931
Published Days: Wed
Avg. Paid Circ.: 3800
Avg. Free Circ.: 89
Audit Company: Sworn/Estimate/Non-Audited
Audit Date: 43626

UTICA

MID YORK WEEKLY

Street Address: 221 Oriskany St E
City: Utica
State: NY
ZIP Code: 13501
General Phone: (315) 792-5000
General Email: tcascioli@uticaod.com
Publication Website: https://www.uticaod.com/midyorkweekly
Publisher Name: Terry Cascioli
Publisher Email: tcascioli@uticaod.com
Publisher Phone: (315) 792-5002
Editor Name: Mike Jaquays
Editor Email: mjaquays@uticaod.com
Editor Phone: (315) 824-2150
Advertising Executive Name: Scott Rosenburgh
Advertising Executive Email: mjaquays@uticaod.com
Advertising Executive Phone: (315) 792-5082
Year Established: 2004
Published Days: Thur
Avg. Paid Circ.: 1984
Audit Company: CVC
Audit Date: 43625

UTICA

UTICA PHOENIX

Street Address: 1113 Linwood Pl
City: Utica
State: NY
ZIP Code: 13501
General Phone: (315) 797-2417
General Email: uticaphoenix@gmail.com
Publication Website: https://www.uticaphoenix.net/
Delivery Methods: Racks
Year Established: 2002
Mechanical specifications: Type page 9.75 x 15
Published Days: Mthly
Avg. Free Circ.: 365
Audit Company: Sworn/Estimate/Non-Audited
Audit Date: 43626

UTICA

YOUR VALLEY

Street Address: 221 Oriskany St E
City: Utica
State: NY
ZIP Code: 13501
General Phone: (315) 792-5000
General Email: tcascioli@uticaod.com
Publication Website: https://www.uticaod.com
Publisher Name: Terry Cascioli
Publisher Email: tcascioli@uticaod.com
Publisher Phone: (315) 792-5002
Editor Name: Ron Johns
Editor Email: rjohns1@uticaod.com
Editor Phone: (315) 792-5004
Advertising Executive Name: Scott Rosenburgh
Advertising Executive Email: srosenburgh@uticaod.com
Advertising Executive Phone: (315) 792-5082
Delivery Methods: Mail`Racks
Year Established: 2006
Mechanical specifications: Type page 10.12 x 21; 6 cols, 1.3125
Published Days: Thur
Avg. Free Circ.: 9895
Audit Company: CVC
Audit Date: 43625

VAILS GATE

ORANGE COUNTY POST

Street Address: PO Box 405
City: Vails Gate
State: NY
ZIP Code: 12584
General Phone: (845) 562-1218
General Email: ocpads@frontiernet.net
Publication Website: https://ocpostny.com/
Parent Company: EWSmith Publishing
Advertising Executive Email: ocpads@frontiernet.net
Delivery Methods: Mail`Newsstand`Carrier
Year Established: 1936
Own Printing Facility?: Y
Commercial printers?: Y
Published Days: Wed
Avg. Paid Circ.: 2400
Avg. Free Circ.: 150
Audit Company: Sworn/Estimate/Non-Audited
Audit Date: 43626

WAPPINGERS FALLS

BEACON FREE PRESS

Street Address: 84 E Main St
City: Wappingers Falls
State: NY
ZIP Code: 12590-2504
General Phone: (845) 297-3723
General Email: sdnadvertising@aol.com
Publication Website: http://www.sdutchessnews.com/about/about.htm#Beacon
Parent Company: Southern Dutchess News
Publisher Name: Ray Fashona
Publisher Email: newsplace@aol.com
Advertising Executive Name: Janet Way
Advertising Executive Email: sdnadvertising@aol.com
Delivery Methods: Mail
Own Printing Facility?: Y
Commercial printers?: Y
Mechanical specifications: Type page 9.875 x 16; E&A - 6 cols, 2.375, 0.125 between; C - 7 cols, 1.3125, 0.125 between
Published Days: Wed
Avg. Free Circ.: 8002
Audit Company: Sworn/Estimate/Non-Audited
Audit Date: 43626

WAPPINGERS FALLS

NORTHERN DUTCHESS NEWS

Street Address: 84 E Main St
City: Wappingers Falls
State: NY
ZIP Code: 12590-2599
General Phone: (845) 297-3723
General Email: northerndutchess@sdutchessnews.com
Publication Website: https://www.sdutchessnews.com/NDN/ndn.htm
Parent Company: Southern Dutchess News
Editor Name: Kate Goldsmith
Editor Email: northerndutchess@sdutchessnews.com
Advertising Executive Name: Richard Wambach
Advertising Executive Email: richard@wambachcommunications.com
Advertising Executive Phone: (845) 297-3723
Delivery Methods: Mail
Mechanical specifications: Type page 9.875 x 16; E&A - 6 cols, 2.375, 0.125 between; C - 7 cols, 1.3125, 0.125 between
Published Days: Wed
Audit Company: Sworn/Estimate/Non-Audited
Audit Date: 43626

WAPPINGERS FALLS

SOUTHERN DUTCHESS NEWS

Street Address: 84 E Main St
City: Wappingers Falls
State: NY
ZIP Code: 12590-2599
General Phone: (845) 297-3723
General Email: sdnadvertising@aol.com
Publication Website: http://www.sdutchessnews.com/
Parent Company: Southern Dutchess News
Editor Name: Ray Fashona
Editor Email: newsplace@aol.com
Advertising Executive Name: Janet Way
Advertising Executive Email: sdnadvertising@aol.com
Delivery Methods: Mail
Year Established: 1952
Own Printing Facility?: Y
Commercial printers?: Y
Mechanical specifications: Type page 9.875 x 16; E&A - 6 cols, 2.375, 0.125 between; C - 7 cols, 1.3125, 0.125 between
Published Days: Wed
Avg. Paid Circ.: 7947
Audit Company: Sworn/Estimate/Non-Audited
Audit Date: 43626

WARSAW

WARSAW PENNYSAVER

Street Address: 72 N Main St
City: Warsaw
State: NY
ZIP Code: 14569
General Phone: (585) 786-8161
General Email: ads@warsawpennysaver.com
Publication Website: http://www.warsawpennysaver.com/
Parent Company: Warsaw Pennysaver
Advertising Executive Email: ads@warsawpennysaver.com
Delivery Methods: Mail
Year Established: 1943

Mechanical specifications: Type page 7.5 x 11
Published Days: Sun
Avg. Paid Circ.: 9280
Audit Company: Sworn/Estimate/Non-Audited
Audit Date: 43626

WARSAW

WARSAW'S COUNTRY COURIER

Street Address: 11 S Main St
City: Warsaw
State: NY
ZIP Code: 14569
General Phone: (585) 786-3080
General Email: tammy-courierads@roadrunner.com
Publication Website: https://www.couriercountry.com/
Parent Company: Neighbor to Neighbor News, Inc.
Advertising Executive Email: tammy-courierads@roadrunner.com
Year Established: 1997
Mechanical specifications: Type page 10.5 x 19.5; 5 cols, 2, 0.125 between
Published Days: Thur
Audit Company: Sworn/Estimate/Non-Audited
Audit Date: 43626

WARWICK

WARWICK VALLEY DISPATCH

Street Address: 2 Oakland Ave
City: Warwick
State: NY
ZIP Code: 10990
General Phone: (845) 986-2216
General Email: ads@wvdispatch.com
Publication Website: https://www.wvdispatch.com/
Parent Company: F. Eugene Wright
Publisher Name: F. Eugene Wright
Editor Email: editor@wvdispatch.com
Advertising Executive Email: ads@wvdispatch.com
Year Established: 1885
Own Printing Facility?: Y
Commercial printers?: Y
Mechanical specifications: Type page 10 3/8 x 15; E - 6 cols, 1 5/8, 1/8 between; A - 6 cols, 1 5/8, 1/8 between; C - 6 cols, 1 5/8, 1/8 between.
Published Days: Wed
Avg. Paid Circ.: 2500
Avg. Free Circ.: 50
Audit Company: Sworn/Estimate/Non-Audited
Audit Date: 43626

WATERVILLE

THE WATERVILLE TIMES

Street Address: 129 W Main St
City: Waterville
State: NY
ZIP Code: 13480
General Phone: (315) 841-4105
General Email: advertising@cnymail.com
Publication Website: https://www.watervilletimes.com/
Parent Company: Patty Louise
Publisher Name: Patty Louise
Advertising Executive Email: advertising@cnymail.com
Delivery Methods: Mail
Year Established: 1856
Mechanical specifications: Type page 10 x 16; 5 cols, 1.8125, 0.1875 between
Published Days: Wed
Avg. Paid Circ.: 2516
Avg. Free Circ.: 73
Audit Company: Sworn/Estimate/Non-Audited
Audit Date: 43626

WEBSTER

WEBSTER HERALD

Street Address: 46 North Ave
City: Webster
State: NY
ZIP Code: 14580
General Phone: (585) 671-1533
General Email: websterherald@empirestateweeklies.com
Publication Website: http://empirestateweeklies.com/
Parent Company: Empire State Weeklies
Publisher Name: Lynn Tabak
Publisher Email: lynn@empirestateweeklies.com
Editor Name: Anna Hubbel
Editor Email: websterherald@empirestateweeklies.com
Advertising Executive Name: Laurie Zahn Herman
Advertising Executive Email: laurie@empirestateweeklies.com
Advertising Executive Phone: (585) 727-0269
Own Printing Facility?: Y
Commercial printers?: Y
Mechanical specifications: Type page 10 x 16; E - 4 cols, 2 2/5, between; C - 6 cols, between.
Published Days: Wed
Avg. Paid Circ.: 4000
Avg. Free Circ.: 800
Audit Company: Sworn/Estimate/Non-Audited
Audit Date: 43626

WESTFIELD

THE WESTFIELD REPUBLICAN

Street Address: 41 E Main St
City: Westfield
State: NY
ZIP Code: 14787-1303
General Phone: (716) 326-3163
General Email: jsaxton@westfieldrepublican.com
Publication Website: http://www.westfieldrepublican.com/
Parent Company: Ogden Newspapers Inc.
Editor Name: Jeff Keller
Published Days: Thur`Sat
Avg. Paid Circ.: 2100
Avg. Free Circ.: 5256
Audit Company: Sworn/Estimate/Non-Audited
Audit Date: 43626

WESTFIELD

WESTFIELD REPUBLICAN

Street Address: 41 E Main St
City: Westfield
State: NY
ZIP Code: 14787-1303
General Phone: (716) 326-3163
General Email: jsaxton@westfieldrepublican.com
Publication Website: http://www.westfieldrepublican.com/
Parent Company: Ogden Newspapers Inc.
Editor Name: Jeff Keller
Delivery Methods: Mail`Newsstand
Published Days: Thur
Avg. Paid Circ.: 900
Avg. Free Circ.: 25
Audit Company: Sworn/Estimate/Non-Audited
Audit Date: 43626

WHITE PLAINS

FAIRFIELD COUNTY BUSINESS JOURNAL

Street Address: 3 Gannett Dr
City: White Plains
State: NY
ZIP Code: 10604
General Phone: (914) 694-3600
General Email: dee@westfairinc.com
Publication Website: http://www.fairfieldcbj.com/
Parent Company: Westfair Communications Inc.
Delivery Methods: Mail`Newsstand`Racks
Published Days: Mon
Avg. Paid Circ.: 1453
Avg. Free Circ.: 3757
Audit Company: Sworn/Estimate/Non-Audited
Audit Date: 43626

WHITE PLAINS

WESTCHESTER COUNTY BUSINESS JOURNAL

Street Address: 701 Westchester Ave., Suite 100J
City: White Plains
State: NY
ZIP Code: 10604-3402
General Phone: (914) 694-3600
General Email: dee@westfairinc.com
Publication Website: https://westfaironline.com/
Parent Company: Westfair Communications Inc.
Publisher Name: Dee DelBello
Publisher Email: dee@westfairinc.com
Editor Name: Bob Rozycki
Editor Email: bobr@westfairinc.com
Advertising Executive Name: Anne Jordan
Advertising Executive Email: anne@westfairinc.com
Delivery Methods: Mail`Newsstand`Racks
Published Days: Mon
Avg. Paid Circ.: 1697
Avg. Free Circ.: 4496
Audit Company: Sworn/Estimate/Non-Audited
Audit Date: 43626

WHITESTONE

THE PRESS OF SOUTHEAST QUEENS

Street Address: 15050 14th Rd
City: Whitestone
State: NY
ZIP Code: 11357-2609
General Phone: (718) 357-7400
General Email: sales@queenstribune.com
Publication Website: http://www.queenstribune.com/
Parent Company: Tribco LLC-OOB
Published Days: Fri
Avg. Free Circ.: 25000
Audit Company: Sworn/Estimate/Non-Audited
Audit Date: 43626

WOODSIDE

ECUADOR NEWS

Street Address: 6403 Roosevelt Ave
City: Woodside
State: NY
ZIP Code: 11377
General Phone: (718) 205-7014
General Email: semanario@ecuadornews.us
Publication Website: http://ecuadornews.com.ec/
Year Established: 1996
Mechanical specifications: Type page 5 cols x 13.5
Published Days: Tues
Audit Company: Sworn/Estimate/Non-Audited
Audit Date: 43626

YONKERS

YONKERS RISING

Street Address: 25 Warburton Ave
City: Yonkers
State: NY
ZIP Code: 10701
General Phone: (914) 965-4000
General Email: pgerken@risingmediagroup.com
Publication Website: http://yonkersrising.com/
Parent Company: Rising Media Group
Publisher Name: Nick Sprayregen
Publisher Email: nsprayregen@risingmediagroup.com
Editor Name: Daniel J. Murphy
Editor Email: dmurphy@risingmediagroup.com
Advertising Executive Name: Paul Gerken
Advertising Executive Email: pgerken@risingmediagroup.com
Own Printing Facility?: Y
Mechanical specifications: Type page 13 x 21 1/2; E - 6 cols, 2 1/16, 1/8 between; A - 6 cols, 2 1/16, 1/8 between.
Published Days: Fri
Avg. Free Circ.: 16476
Audit Company: Sworn/Estimate/Non-Audited
Audit Date: 43626

OHIO

ALLIANCE

THE ALLIANCE REVIEW

Street Address: 40 South Linden Ave.
City: Alliance
State: OH
ZIP Code: 44601
General Phone: (330) 821-1200
General Email: pcochran@the-review.com
Publication Website: https://www.the-review.com/
Parent Company: Gannett
Editor Name: Laura Kessel
Editor Email: lkessel@the-review.com

AMHERST

AMHERST NEWS-TIMES

Street Address: P.O. Box 67
City: Amherst
State: OH
ZIP Code: 44001
General Phone: (440) 988-2801
General Email: news@lcnewspapers.com
Publication Website: https://www.lcnewspapers.com/
Parent Company: Lorain County Printing & Publishing Co.

ARCHBOLD

ARCHBOLD BUCKEYE

Street Address: 207 N Defiance St
City: Archbold
State: OH
ZIP Code: 43502
General Phone: (419) 445-4466
General Email: buckeye@archboldbuckeye.com
Publication Website: https://www.

Community Newspapers in the U.S.

archboldbuckeye.com/
Publisher Name: Mary Huber
Editor Name: David Pugh

ARCHBOLD

FARMLAND NEWS

Street Address: 104 Depot St
City: Archbold
State: OH
ZIP Code: 43502
General Phone: (419) 445-9456
General Email: ads@farmlandnews.com
Publication Website: http://www.farmlandnews.com/

ASHLAND

THE LOUDONVILLE TIMES

Street Address: 40 E. Second St
City: Ashland
State: OH
ZIP Code: 44805
General Phone: (419) 281-0581
General Email: abass@gatehousemedia.com
Publication Website: https://www.times-gazette.com/news/loudonville
Publisher Name: Bill Albrecht
Publisher Email: balbrecht@gatehousemedia.com
Publisher Phone: (330) 996-3782
Editor Name: Rick Armon
Editor Email: rarmon@times-gazette.com

ATHENS

ATHENS NEWS

Street Address: P.O. Box 543
City: Athens
State: OH
ZIP Code: 45701
General Phone: (740) 594-8219
General Email: classifieds@athensnews.com
Publication Website: https://www.athensnews.com/
Parent Company: Adams Publishing Group
Publisher Name: Terry Smith
Publisher Email: news@athensnews.com
Editor Name: Terry Smith
Editor Email: news@athensnews.com

ATTICA

ATTICA HUB

Street Address: 202 N Main St
City: Attica
State: OH
ZIP Code: 44807-9484
General Phone: (419) 426-3491
General Email: sales@atticahub.com
Publication Website: https://www.atticahub.com/

BARBERTON

THE BARBERTON HERALD

Street Address: 70 4th St NW
City: Barberton
State: OH
ZIP Code: 44203
General Phone: (330) 753-1068
General Email: ads@barbertonherald.com
Publication Website: https://www.barbertonherald.com/
Parent Company: The Vespoint Publishing Company Inc
Publisher Name: Cheryl L. Vespoint
Publisher Email: publisher@barbertonherald.com

Editor Name: Karla Tipton
Editor Email: karla@barbertonherald.com

BATAVIA

THE CLERMONT SUN

Street Address: 465 E Main St
City: Batavia
State: OH
ZIP Code: 45103
General Phone: (513) 732-2511
General Email: info@clermontsun.com
Publication Website: https://www.clermontsun.com/
Parent Company: Champion Media
Editor Name: Brett Milam
Editor Email: bmilam@clermontsun.com

BELLVILLE

BELLVILLE STAR & TRI-FORKS PRESS

Street Address: 107 Main St
City: Bellville
State: OH
ZIP Code: 44813
General Phone: (419) 886-2291
General Email: aallonas@aimmediamidwest.com
Publication Website: https://www.thebellvillestar.com/
Parent Company: AIM Media Midwest
Editor Name: Russ Kent
Editor Email: rkent@aimmediamidwest.com

BLUFFTON

THE BLUFFTON NEWS

Street Address: 101 N Main St
City: Bluffton
State: OH
ZIP Code: 45817-1245
General Phone: (419) 358-8010
General Email: kim@blufftonnews.com
Publication Website: http://www.blufftonnews.com/

BOARDMAN

BOARDMAN NEWS

Street Address: 8302 Southern Blvd. Suite 2A
City: Boardman
State: OH
ZIP Code: 44512
General Phone: (330) 758-6397
General Email: bnews@zoominternet.net
Publication Website: https://boardmannews.net/

BROOKVILLE

BROOKVILLE STAR

Street Address: 694 W. National Road
City: Brookville
State: OH
ZIP Code: 45377
General Phone: (937) 236-4990
General Email: rnunnari@aimmediamidwest.com
Publication Website: https://www.englewoodindependent.com/
Parent Company: AIM Media Midwest
Editor Name: Ron Nunnari
Editor Email: rnunnari@aimmediamidwest.com

BUCKEYE LAKE

THE BUCKEYE LAKE BEACON

Street Address: 4675 Walnut Rd
City: Buckeye Lake
State: OH
ZIP Code: 43008
General Phone: (740) 928-5541
General Email: charlesprince@buckeyelakebeacon.net
Publication Website: https://www.buckeyelakebeacon.net/
Publisher Name: Charles Prince
Publisher Email: charlesprince@buckeyelakebeacon.net
Editor Name: Charles Prince
Editor Email: charlesprince@buckeyelakebeacon.net

CADIZ

HARRISON NEWS-HERALD

Street Address: 144 S Main St
City: Cadiz
State: OH
ZIP Code: 43907
General Phone: (740) 942-2118
General Email: info@harrisonnewsherald.com
Publication Website: https://www.harrisonnewsherald.com/
Parent Company: Schloss Media, Inc.

CALDWELL

THE JOURNAL & NOBLE COUNTY LEADER

Street Address: 309 Main St
City: Caldwell
State: OH
ZIP Code: 43724
General Phone: (740) 732-2341
General Email: news@journal-leader.com
Publication Website: https://www.journal-leader.com/
Editor Name: Anne Chlovechok
Editor Email: news@journal-leader.com

CAMBRIDGE

BARNESVILLE ENTERPRISE

Street Address: 831 Wheeling Ave
City: Cambridge
State: OH
ZIP Code: 43725
General Phone: (740) 439-3531
General Email: shanning@daily-jeff.com
Publication Website: http://www.barnesville-enterprise.com/
Parent Company: Gannett
Publisher Name: John Kridelbaugh
Publisher Email: jkridelbaugh@daily-jeff.com
Publisher Phone: (740) 439-3531, ext : 1240
Editor Name: Beth Bailey
Editor Email: bbailey@daily-jeff.com

CAMBRIDGE

NEW CONCORD AREA LEADER

Street Address: 831 Wheeling Ave
City: Cambridge
State: OH
ZIP Code: 43725
General Phone: (740) 439-3531
General Email: lynn@daily-jeff.com
Publication Website: https://www.daily-jeff.com/news/20170324/new-concord-area-man-rebuilds-bridge-for-village
Publisher Name: John Kridelbaugh
Publisher Email: jkridelbaugh@daily-jeff.com
Publisher Phone: (740) 439-3531, ext : 1240
Editor Name: Beth Bailey
Editor Email: bbailey@daily-jeff.com

CANTON

THE SUBURBANITE

Street Address: 500 Market Ave. S., Ste. B
City: Canton
State: OH
ZIP Code: 44702
General Phone: (330) 580-8300
General Email: andy.harris@thesuburbanite.com
Publication Website: https://www.thesuburbanite.com/
Parent Company: Gannett
Editor Name: Greg Kohntopp
Editor Email: greg.kohntopp@thesuburbanite.com

CAREY

THE MOHAWK LEADER

Street Address: 1198 E Findlay St
City: Carey
State: OH
ZIP Code: 43316
General Phone: (419) 396-7567
General Email: ads@theprogressortimes.com
Publication Website: https://www.theprogressortimes.com/
Publisher Name: Steve Zender
Publisher Email: steve@theprogressortimes.com
Editor Name: Steve Zender
Editor Email: steve@theprogressortimes.com

CAREY

THE PROGRESSOR TIMES

Street Address: 1198 E Findlay St
City: Carey
State: OH
ZIP Code: 43316
General Phone: (419) 396-7567
General Email: ads@theprogressortimes.com
Publication Website: https://www.theprogressortimes.com/
Publisher Name: Steve Zender
Publisher Email: steve@theprogressortimes.com
Editor Name: Steve Zender
Editor Email: steve@theprogressortimes.com

CARROLLTON

THE FREE PRESS STANDARD

Street Address: 43 E Main St
City: Carrollton
State: OH
ZIP Code: 44615-1221
General Phone: (330) 627-5591
General Email: adfps44615@yahoo.com
Publication Website: https://freepressstandard.com/
Editor Email: fps44615@yahoo.com

CHARDON

GEAUGA COUNTY MAPLE LEAF

Street Address: 101 South St
City: Chardon
State: OH
ZIP Code: 44024
General Phone: (440) 285-2013
General Email: info@geaugamapleleaf.com
Publication Website: https://www.geaugamapleleaf.com/
Publisher Name: Jeffrey B. Karlovec
Publisher Email: jbkarlovec@dln.com
Editor Name: John D. Karlovec

Editor Email: editor@geaugamapleleaf.com

CLEVELAND

CLEVELAND SCENE

Street Address: 737 Bolivar Rd
City: Cleveland
State: OH
ZIP Code: 44115
General Phone: (216) 241-7550
General Email: scene@clevescene.com
Publication Website: https://www.clevescene.com/
Publisher Name: Andrew Zelman
Publisher Email: azelman@clevescene.com
Publisher Phone: (216) 802-7218
Editor Name: Vince Grzegorek
Editor Email: vgrzegorek@clevescene.com

COLUMBIA STATION

THE RURAL-URBAN RECORD

Street Address: 24487 Squire Rd
City: Columbia Station
State: OH
ZIP Code: 44028-9672
General Phone: (440) 236-8982
General Email: news@rural-urbanrecord.com
Publication Website: https://rural-urbanrecord.com/
Publisher Name: Lee Boise

COLUMBUS

COLUMBUS BUSINESS FIRST

Street Address: 300 Marconi Blvd.
City: Columbus
State: OH
ZIP Code: 43215
General Phone: (614) 461-4040
General Email: columbus@bizjournals.com
Publication Website: https://www.bizjournals.com/columbus/
Parent Company: American City Business Journals
Publisher Name: Nick Fortine
Publisher Email: nfortine@bizjournals.com
Publisher Phone: (614) 220-5416
Editor Name: Mark Somerson
Editor Email: msomerson@bizjournals.com

COLUMBUS

EASTSIDE MESSENGER

Street Address: 3500 Sullivant Ave
City: Columbus
State: OH
ZIP Code: 43204
General Phone: (614) 272-5422
General Email: phildaubel@columbusmessenger.com
Publication Website: https://www.columbusmessenger.com/
Parent Company: Columbus Messenger Newspapers
Publisher Name: Philip F. Daubel
Publisher Email: phildaubel@columbusmessenger.com
Editor Name: Rick Palsgrove

COLUMBUS

SOUTHEAST MESSENGER

Street Address: 3500 Sullivant Ave
City: Columbus
State: OH
ZIP Code: 43204
General Phone: (614) 272-5422
General Email: phildaubel@columbusmessenger.com
Publication Website: https://www.columbusmessenger.com/
Parent Company: Columbus Messenger Newspapers
Publisher Name: Philip F. Daubel
Publisher Email: phildaubel@columbusmessenger.com
Editor Name: Rick Palsgrove

COLUMBUS

SOUTHWEST MESSENGER

Street Address: 3500 Sullivant Ave
City: Columbus
State: OH
ZIP Code: 43204
General Phone: (614) 272-5422
General Email: phildaubel@columbusmessenger.com
Publication Website: https://www.columbusmessenger.com/
Parent Company: Columbus Messenger Newspapers
Publisher Name: Philip F. Daubel
Publisher Email: phildaubel@columbusmessenger.com
Editor Name: Rick Palsgrove

COLUMBUS

WESTSIDE MESSENGER

Street Address: 3500 Sullivant Ave
City: Columbus
State: OH
ZIP Code: 43204
General Phone: (614) 272-5422
General Email: phildaubel@columbusmessenger.com
Publication Website: https://www.columbusmessenger.com/
Parent Company: Columbus Messenger Newspapers
Publisher Name: Philip F. Daubel
Publisher Email: phildaubel@columbusmessenger.com
Editor Name: Rick Palsgrove

DALTON

THE DALTON GAZETTE & KIDRON NEWS

Street Address: 28 W. Main Street
City: Dalton
State: OH
ZIP Code: 44618
General Phone: (330) 760-0720
General Email: thedaltongazette@gmail.com
Publication Website: https://www.daltonkidronnews.com/

DAYTON

THE OAKWOOD REGISTER

Street Address: 435 Patterson Rd
City: Dayton
State: OH
ZIP Code: 45419
General Phone: (937) 294-2662
General Email: editor@oakwoodregister.com
Publication Website: https://www.oakwoodregister.com/
Parent Company: Winkler Publishing
Publisher Name: Brian Barr
Editor Email: editor@oakwoodregister.com

EATON

THE REGISTER-HERALD

Street Address: 532 N Barron St
City: Eaton
State: OH
ZIP Code: 45320
General Phone: (937) 456-5553
General Email: kkimbler@aimmediamidwest.com
Publication Website: https://www.registerherald.com/
Parent Company: AIM Media Midwest
Publisher Name: Ron Clausen
Publisher Email: rclausen@aimmediamidwest.com
Publisher Phone: (937) 335-5634, ext : 1631
Editor Name: Eddie Mowen
Editor Email: emowen@aimmediamidwest.com

EDGERTON

THE EDGERTON EARTH

Street Address: 178 N. Michigan Ave
City: Edgerton
State: OH
ZIP Code: 43517
General Phone: (419) 298-2369
General Email: edgertonearth@edgertonearth.com
Publication Website: https://www.edgertonearth.com/
Editor Name: Cindy Thiel

GALION

GALION INQUIRER

Street Address: 129 Harding Way E
City: Galion
State: OH
ZIP Code: 44833
General Phone: (419) 468-1117
General Email: mmcknight@aimmediamidwest.com
Publication Website: https://www.galioninquirer.com/
Parent Company: AIM Media
Publisher Name: Vicki Taylor
Publisher Email: vtaylor@aimmediamidwest.com
Publisher Phone: (567) 393-6220, ext : 2042
Editor Name: Russ Kent
Editor Email: rkent@aimmediamidwest.com

GALLIPOLIS

SUNDAY TIMES-SENTINEL

Street Address: 825 3rd Ave
City: Gallipolis
State: OH
ZIP Code: 45631
General Phone: (740) 446-2342
General Email: bsergent@aimmediamidwest.com
Publication Website: https://www.mydailytribune.com/about-us
Parent Company: AIM Media Midwest
Editor Name: Beth Sergent
Editor Email: bsergent@aimmediamidwest.com

GEORGETOWN

THE RIPLEY BEE

Street Address: 111 E State St
City: Georgetown
State: OH
ZIP Code: 45121
General Phone: (937) 444-3441
General Email: info@ripleybee.com
Publication Website: https://www.ripleybee.com/
Parent Company: Champion Media

GREENVILLE

THE EARLY BIRD

Street Address: 100 Washington Ave.
City: Greenville
State: OH
ZIP Code: 45331
General Phone: (937) 548-3330
General Email: editor@earlybirdpaper.com
Publication Website: https://www.earlybirdpaper.com/
Parent Company: AIM Media Midwest
Publisher Name: Keith L. Foutz
Publisher Email: kfoutz@aimmediamidwest.com
Editor Name: Ryan Berry
Editor Email: rberry@aimmediamidwest.com

HARTVILLE

THE HARTVILLE NEWS

Street Address: 316 E Maple St
City: Hartville
State: OH
ZIP Code: 44632
General Phone: (330) 877-9345
General Email: knowlespress@sbcglobal.net
Publication Website: http://knowlespress.com/

HICKSVILLE

THE NEWS-TRIBUNE

Street Address: 147 E High St
City: Hicksville
State: OH
ZIP Code: 43526
General Phone: (419) 542-7764
General Email: news@hicksvillenewstribune.com
Publication Website: https://www.hicksvillenewstribune.com/

JACKSON

THE TELEGRAM

Street Address: 295 East Main Street, PO Box 667
City: Jackson
State: OH
ZIP Code: 45640
General Phone: (740) 286-3023
General Email: acrabtree@yourtotalmedia.com
Publication Website: https://thetelegramnews.com/
Publisher Name: Amanda Crabtree
Publisher Email: acrabtree@yourtotalmedia.com
Publisher Phone: (740) 286-3023
Editor Name: Pete Wilson
Editor Email: jpelletier@yourtotalmedia.com

JEFFERSON

LAKE COUNTY TRIBUNE

Street Address: 46 W Jefferson St
City: Jefferson
State: OH
ZIP Code: 44047
General Phone: (440) 576-9125
General Email: tribune@gazettenews.com
Publication Website: http://www.gazettenews.com/~gazetten/index.php?option=com_content&view=category&layout=theme2090:category&id=46&Itemid=222
Parent Company: Gazette Newspapers, Inc.
Publisher Name: William Creed
Publisher Email: bcreed@gazettenews.com

Community Newspapers in the U.S.

Publisher Phone: (440) 576-9125, ext : 103
Editor Name: Katherine Wnoroski
Editor Email: kwnoroski@gazettenews.com

JEFFERSON

THE GAZETTE

Street Address: 46 W Jefferson St
City: Jefferson
State: OH
ZIP Code: 44047
General Phone: (440) 576-9125
General Email: beckecreed@gazettenews.com
Publication Website: http://www.gazettenews.com/~gazetten/index.php?option=com_content&view=category&layout=theme2090:category&id=41&Itemid=219
Parent Company: Adams Publishing Group
Publisher Name: William Creed
Publisher Email: bcreed@gazettenews.com
Publisher Phone: (440) 576-9125, ext : 103
Editor Name: Stefanie Wessell
Editor Email: swessell@gazettenews.com

JEFFERSON

THE NEWS

Street Address: 46 W Jefferson St
City: Jefferson
State: OH
ZIP Code: 44047-1028
General Phone: (440) 576-9125
General Email: beckecreed@gazettenews.com
Publication Website: http://www.gazettenews.com/~gazetten/index.php?option=com_content&view=category&layout=theme2090:category&id=42&Itemid=220
Parent Company: Paxton Media Group
Publisher Name: William Creed
Publisher Email: bcreed@gazettenews.com
Publisher Phone: (440) 576-9125, ext : 103
Editor Name: Stefanie Wessell
Editor Email: pymatuningnews@gazettenews.com

JEFFERSON

THE SHORES NEWS

Street Address: 46 W Jefferson St
City: Jefferson
State: OH
ZIP Code: 44047-1028
General Phone: (440) 576-9125
General Email: beckecreed@gazettenews.com
Publication Website: http://www.gazettenews.com/~gazetten/index.php?option=com_content&view=category&layout=theme2090:category&id=42&Itemid=220
Parent Company: Gazette Newspapers, Inc.
Publisher Name: William Creed
Publisher Email: bcreed@gazettenews.com
Publisher Phone: (440) 576-9125, ext : 103

KENT

AURORA ADVOCATE

Street Address: 1050 W Main St
City: Kent
State: OH
ZIP Code: 44240
General Phone: (330) 541-9400
General Email: ads@recordpub.com
Publication Website: http://auroraadvocate.thrivehive.com/
Parent Company: Gannett
Editor Name: Ken Lahmers

KENT

CUYAHOGA FALLS NEWS-PRESS

Street Address: 1050 W Main St
City: Kent
State: OH
ZIP Code: 44240
General Phone: (330) 541-9400
General Email: jwilliams@recordpub.com
Publication Website: https://www.mytownneo.com/fallsnewspress
Parent Company: Gannett Co., Inc.
Publisher Name: Jim Williams
Publisher Email: jwilliams@recordpub.com
Publisher Phone: (330) 298-2012
Editor Name: Heather Rainone
Editor Email: hrainone@recordpub.com

KENT

HUDSON HUB-TIMES

Street Address: 1050 W Main St
City: Kent
State: OH
ZIP Code: 44240
General Phone: (330) 541-9400
General Email: jwilliams@recordpub.com
Publication Website: https://www.mytownneo.com/hudsonhubtimes
Parent Company: Gannett
Publisher Name: Jim Williams
Publisher Email: jwilliams@recordpub.com
Publisher Phone: (330) 298-2012
Editor Name: Heather Rainone
Editor Email: hrainone@recordpub.com

KENT

NORDONIA HILLS NEWS LEADER

Street Address: 1050 W Main St
City: Kent
State: OH
ZIP Code: 44240
General Phone: (330) 541-9400
General Email: jwilliams@recordpub.com
Publication Website: https://www.mytownneo.com/about-mytownneo
Publisher Name: Jim Williams
Publisher Email: jwilliams@recordpub.com
Publisher Phone: (330) 298-2012
Editor Name: Heather Rainone
Editor Email: hrainone@recordpub.com

KENT

STOW SENTRY

Street Address: 1050 W Main St
City: Kent
State: OH
ZIP Code: 44240
General Phone: (330) 541-9400
General Email: jwilliams@recordpub.com
Publication Website: https://www.mytownneo.com/stowsentry
Parent Company: Gannett
Publisher Name: Jim Williams
Publisher Email: jwilliams@recordpub.com
Publisher Phone: (330) 298-2012
Editor Name: Heather Rainone
Editor Email: hrainone@recordpub.com

KENT

TALLMADGE EXPRESS

Street Address: 1050 W Main St
City: Kent
State: OH
ZIP Code: 44240
General Phone: (330) 541-9400
General Email: jwilliams@recordpub.com
Publication Website: https://www.mytownneo.com/tallmadgeexpress
Parent Company: Gannett
Publisher Name: Jim Williams
Publisher Email: jwilliams@recordpub.com
Publisher Phone: (330) 298-2012
Editor Name: Heather Rainone
Editor Email: hrainone@recordpub.com

KENT

TWINSBURG BULLETIN

Street Address: 1050 W Main St
City: Kent
State: OH
ZIP Code: 44240
General Phone: (330) 541-9400
General Email: jwilliams@recordpub.com
Publication Website: https://www.mytownneo.com/twinsburgbulletin
Parent Company: Gannett
Publisher Name: Jim Williams
Publisher Email: jwilliams@recordpub.com
Publisher Phone: (330) 298-2012
Editor Name: Heather Rainone
Editor Email: hrainone@recordpub.com

LONDON

MADISON MESSENGER

Street Address: 78 South Main Street
City: London
State: OH
ZIP Code: 43140
General Phone: (740) 852-0809
General Email: phildaubel@columbusmessenger.com
Publication Website: https://www.columbusmessenger.com/
Parent Company: Columbus Messenger Newspapers
Publisher Name: Philip F. Daubel
Publisher Email: phildaubel@columbusmessenger.com
Editor Name: Rick Palsgrove

LOUISVILLE

THE LOUISVILLE HERALD

Street Address: 308 S Mill St
City: Louisville
State: OH
ZIP Code: 44641
General Phone: (330) 875-5610
Publication Website: https://www.louisvilleherald.com/

LOVELAND

INDIAN HILL JOURNAL

Street Address: 394 Wards Corner Rd
City: Loveland
State: OH
ZIP Code: 45140-8333
General Phone: (513) 248-8600
General Email: acumby@communitypress.com
Publication Website: http://www.ci.indian-hill.oh.us/bulletins/bulletins-view.aspx

MARYSVILLE

THE RICHWOOD GAZETTE

Street Address: PO Box 226
City: Marysville
State: OH
ZIP Code: 43040-0226
General Phone: (740) 943-2214
General Email: editor@rgnews.biz
Publication Website: http://www.rgnews.biz/
Editor Email: editor@rgnews.biz

MC ARTHUR

THE VINTON COUNTY COURIER

Street Address: 103 S Market St
City: Mc Arthur
State: OH
ZIP Code: 45651
General Phone: (740) 596-5393
General Email: info@vintonjacksoncourier.com
Publication Website: https://www.vintonjacksoncourier.com/
Parent Company: Adams Publishing Group
Editor Name: Sydney Dawes
Editor Email: sdawes@vintoncourier.com;

MCCONNELSVILLE

MORGAN COUNTY HERALD

Street Address: 89 W Main St
City: McConnelsville
State: OH
ZIP Code: 43756
General Phone: (740) 962-3377
General Email: advertising@mchnews.com
Publication Website: http://www.mchnews.com/

MEDINA

THE POST NEWSPAPERS - BRUNSWICK

Street Address: 5164 Normandy Park Drive, Suite 100
City: Medina
State: OH
ZIP Code: 44256
General Phone: (330) 721-7678
General Email: sales@thepostnewspapers.com
Publication Website: http://www.thepostnewspapers.com/brunswick/
Parent Company: Trogdon Publishing, Inc.
Publisher Name: Michael Trogdon
Publisher Email: mtrogdon@thepostnewspapers.com
Editor Name: Melissa Martin
Editor Email: mmartin@thepostnewspapers.com

MEDINA

THE POST NEWSPAPERS - EASTERN MEDINA

Street Address: 5164 Normandy Park Drive, Suite 100
City: Medina
State: OH
ZIP Code: 44256
General Phone: (330) 721-7678
General Email: sales@thepostnewspapers.com
Publication Website: http://www.thepostnewspapers.com/eastern_medina/
Parent Company: Trogdon Publishing, Inc.
Publisher Name: Michael Trogdon
Publisher Email: mtrogdon@thepostnewspapers.com

MEDINA

THE POST NEWSPAPERS - MEDINA

Street Address: 5164 Normandy Park Drive, Suite 100

City: Medina
State: OH
ZIP Code: 44256
General Phone: (330) 721-7678
General Email: sales@thepostnewspapers.com
Publication Website: http://www.thepostnewspapers.com/medina/
Parent Company: Trogdon Publishing, Inc.
Publisher Name: Michael Trogdon
Publisher Email: mtrogdon@thepostnewspapers.com

MEDINA

THE POST NEWSPAPERS - NORTHERN WAYNE

Street Address: 5164 Normandy Park Drive, Suite 100
City: Medina
State: OH
ZIP Code: 44256
General Phone: (330) 721-7678
General Email: btrogdon@thepostnewspapers.com
Publication Website: http://www.thepostnewspapers.com/northern_wayne/
Parent Company: Trogdon Publishing, Inc.
Publisher Name: Michael Trogdon
Publisher Email: mtrogdon@thepostnewspapers.com

MEDINA

THE POST NEWSPAPERS - NORTON

Street Address: 5164 Normandy Park Drive, Suite 100
City: Medina
State: OH
ZIP Code: 44256
General Phone: (330) 721-7678
General Email: sales@thepostnewspapers.com
Publication Website: http://www.thepostnewspapers.com/norton/
Parent Company: Trogdon Publishing, Inc.
Publisher Name: Michael Trogdon
Publisher Email: mtrogdon@thepostnewspapers.com

MEDINA

THE POST NEWSPAPERS - SOUTHERN MEDINA

Street Address: 5164 Normandy Park Drive, Suite 100
City: Medina
State: OH
ZIP Code: 44256
General Phone: (330) 721-7678
General Email: sales@thepostnewspapers.com
Publication Website: http://www.thepostnewspapers.com/southern_medina/
Parent Company: Trogdon Publishing, Inc.
Publisher Name: Michael Trogdon
Publisher Email: mtrogdon@thepostnewspapers.com

MEDINA

THE POST NEWSPAPERS - STRONGSVILLE

Street Address: 5164 Normandy Park Drive, Suite 100
City: Medina
State: OH
ZIP Code: 44256
General Phone: (330) 721-7678
General Email: sales@thepostnewspapers.com
Publication Website: http://www.thepostnewspapers.com/strongsville/
Parent Company: Trogdon Publishing, Inc.
Publisher Name: Michael Trogdon
Publisher Email: mtrogdon@thepostnewspapers.com

MEDINA

THE POST NEWSPAPERS - WADSWORTH

Street Address: 5164 Normandy Park Drive, Suite 100
City: Medina
State: OH
ZIP Code: 44256
General Phone: (330) 721-7678
General Email: sales@thepostnewspapers.com
Publication Website: http://www.thepostnewspapers.com/wadsworth/
Parent Company: Trogdon Publishing, Inc.
Publisher Name: Michael Trogdon
Publisher Email: mtrogdon@thepostnewspapers.com

MIAMISBURG

FRANKLIN CHRONICLE

Street Address: 230 S 2nd St
City: Miamisburg
State: OH
ZIP Code: 45342
General Phone: (937) 866-3331
General Email: news@miamivalleynewspapers.com
Publication Website: http://www.miamivalleynewspapers.com/
Parent Company: Miami Valley Newspapers
Editor Email: skip.weaver@miamivalleynewspapers.com

MIAMISBURG

MIAMISBURG NEWS

Street Address: 230 S 2nd St
City: Miamisburg
State: OH
ZIP Code: 45342
General Phone: (937) 866-3331
General Email: news@miamivalleynewspapers.com
Publication Website: http://www.miamivalleynewspapers.com/
Parent Company: Miami Valley Newspapers
Editor Email: skip.weaver@miamivalleynewspapers.com

MIAMISBURG

THE GERMANTOWN PRESS

Street Address: 230 S 2nd St
City: Miamisburg
State: OH
ZIP Code: 45342
General Phone: (937) 866-3331
General Email: ads@miamivalleynewspapers.com
Publication Website: http://www.miamivalleynewspapers.com/
Parent Company: Miami Valley Newspapers
Editor Email: skip.weaver@miamivalleynewspapers.com

MILLERSBURG

HOLMES COUNTY JOURNAL

Street Address: 7368 County Road 623
City: Millersburg
State: OH
ZIP Code: 44654
General Phone: (330) 674-2300
Publication Website: https://thebargainhunter.com/
Parent Company: AloNovus Corp.

MILLERSBURG

WOOSTER WEEKLY NEWS

Street Address: 7368 County Road 623
City: Millersburg
State: OH
ZIP Code: 44654
General Phone: (330) 674-2300
Publication Website: https://thebargainhunter.com/
Parent Company: AloNovus Corp.

MINSTER

THE COMMUNITY POST

Street Address: 326 N Main St Ste 200
City: Minster
State: OH
ZIP Code: 45865
General Phone: (419) 628-2369
General Email: publisher@nktelco.net
Publication Website: https://www.minstercommunitypost.com/
Parent Company: Horizon Publications Inc.
Publisher Email: publisher@nktelco.net

MONTPELIER

THE LEADER-ENTERPRISE

Street Address: 319 W Main St
City: Montpelier
State: OH
ZIP Code: 43543
General Phone: (419) 485-3113
General Email: leaderenterprise@frontier.com
Publication Website: http://myplace.frontier.com/~leaderenterprise/
Editor Name: Jamie Ward
Editor Email: jward.leaderenterprise@frontier.com

MOUNT GILEAD

THE MORROW COUNTY SENTINEL

Street Address: 46 S Main St
City: Mount Gilead
State: OH
ZIP Code: 43338
General Phone: (419) 946-3010
General Email: vtaylor@aimmediamidwest.com
Publication Website: https://www.morrowcountysentinel.com/
Parent Company: AIM Media Midwest
Publisher Name: Vicki Taylor
Publisher Email: vtaylor@aimmediamidwest.com
Publisher Phone: (567) 393-6220, ext : 2042
Editor Name: Anthony Conchel
Editor Email: aconchel@aimmediamidwest.com

MOUNT ORAB

THE BROWN COUNTY PRESS

Street Address: 219 S High St
City: Mount Orab
State: OH
ZIP Code: 45154-9039
General Phone: (937) 444-3441
General Email: info@browncountypress.com
Publication Website: https://browncountypress.com/
Parent Company: Champion Media

NEW LEXINGTON

PERRY COUNTY TRIBUNE

Street Address: 116 S Main St
City: New Lexington
State: OH
ZIP Code: 43764-1376
General Phone: (740) 342-4121
General Email: pdennis@perrytribune.com
Publication Website: https://www.perrytribune.com/
Parent Company: Adams Publishing Group
Editor Name: Debra Tobin
Editor Email: dtobin@perrytribune.com

NEW LONDON

FIRELANDS FARMER

Street Address: 43 E Main St
City: New London
State: OH
ZIP Code: 44851
General Phone: (419) 929-8043
General Email: globe@sdgnewsgroup.com
Publication Website: http://www.sdgnewsgroup.com/story4.html
Parent Company: SDGNewsgroup
Editor Name: Janet Kehres

NEW LONDON

NEW LONDON RECORD

Street Address: 43 E Main St
City: New London
State: OH
ZIP Code: 44851-1213
General Phone: (419) 929-3411
General Email: record@sdgnewsgroup.com
Publication Website: http://www.sdgnewsgroup.com/story4.html
Parent Company: SDGNewsgroup
Editor Name: Lynne Phillips

NEW WASHINGTON

THE NEW WASHINGTON HERALD

Street Address: 625 S Kibler St
City: New Washington
State: OH
ZIP Code: 44854-9541
General Phone: (419) 492-2133
General Email: nwherald@theheraldinc.com
Publication Website: https://www.theheraldinc.com/

NEWARK

THE GRANVILLE SENTINEL

Street Address: 22 N 1st St
City: Newark
State: OH
ZIP Code: 43055-5608
General Phone: (740) 345-4053
General Email: atrabitz@newarkadvocate.com
Publication Website: https://www.newarkadvocate.com/news/granville-sentinel/
Editor Name: Craig McDonald
Editor Email: blanka@newarkadvocate.com

NEWARK

THE PATASKALA STANDARD

Community Newspapers in the U.S.

Street Address: 22 N 1st St
City: Newark
State: OH
ZIP Code: 43055-5608
General Phone: (740) 345-4053
General Email: atrabitz@newarkadvocate.com
Publication Website: http://www.newarkadvocate.com/news/pataskala-standard/
Editor Name: Craig McDonald
Editor Email: blanka@newarkadvocate.com

NEWCOMERSTOWN

NEWCOMERSTOWN NEWS

Street Address: 140 W Main St
City: Newcomerstown
State: OH
ZIP Code: 43832-1041
General Phone: (740) 498-7117
General Email: dkeating@newcomerstown-news.com
Publication Website: https://www.newcomerstown-news.com/
Parent Company: Gannett
Publisher Name: John Kridelbaugh
Publisher Email: jkridelbaugh@daily-jeff.com
Publisher Phone: (740) 498-3531, ext : 1240
Editor Name: Beth Bailey
Editor Email: bbailey@daily-jeff.com

OBERLIN

OBERLIN NEWS-TRIBUNE

Street Address: 42 S Main St
City: Oberlin
State: OH
ZIP Code: 44074-1627
General Phone: (440) 084-8639
General Email: news@lcnewspapers.com
Publication Website: https://www.lcnewspapers.com/category/oberlin/
Parent Company: Lorain County Printing & Publishing Co.

ONTARIO

TRIBUNE COURIER & MADISON TRIBUNE

Street Address: 347 Allen Dr
City: Ontario
State: OH
ZIP Code: 44906-1001
General Phone: (419) 529-2847
General Email: kim@tribune-courier.com
Publication Website: http://www.tribune-courier.com/
Parent Company: Stumbo Publishing Co.
Publisher Name: Marc A. Stumbo
Editor Name: Jenna M. Wolford

PERRYSBURG

HOLLAND-SPRINGFIELD JOURNAL

Street Address: 130 Louisiana Ave
City: Perrysburg
State: OH
ZIP Code: 43551-1457
General Phone: (419) 874-4491
General Email: editor@hollandsfj.us
Publication Website: https://www.hollandsfj.us/holland-springfield-journal
Parent Company: Welch Publishing Company
Editor Name: Jane Maiolo
Editor Email: editor@hollandsfj.us

PERRYSBURG

PERRYSBURG MESSENGER JOURNAL

Street Address: 117 E 2nd St
City: Perrysburg
State: OH
ZIP Code: 43551-2172
General Phone: (419) 874-4491
General Email: editor@perrysburg.com
Publication Website: https://www.hollandsfj.us/perrysburg-messenger-journal
Parent Company: Welch Publishing Company
Editor Name: Kate Oatis
Editor Email: editor@perrysburg.com

PERRYSBURG

POINT & SHORELAND JOURNAL

Street Address: 130 Louisiana Ave.
City: Perrysburg
State: OH
ZIP Code: 43551
General Phone: (419) 874-4491
General Email: debb@perrysburg.com
Publication Website: https://www.hollandsfj.us/point-and-shoreland-journal
Parent Company: Welch Publishing Company
Editor Name: Deb Brungard
Editor Email: debb@perrysburg.com

PORT CLINTON

NORTH COAST BUSINESS JOURNAL

Street Address: 205 SE Catawba Rd
City: Port Clinton
State: OH
ZIP Code: 43452
General Phone: (419) 732-2154
General Email: kwilloughby@ncbj.net
Publication Website: https://ncbj.net/
Parent Company: Schaffner Publications, Inc.
Publisher Name: John Schaffner
Publisher Email: john@thebeacon.net
Editor Name: Angie Zam
Editor Email: editor@ncbj.net

PORT CLINTON

THE BEACON

Street Address: 205 SE Catawba Rd # G
City: Port Clinton
State: OH
ZIP Code: 43452-2669
General Phone: (419) 732-2154
General Email: john@thebeacon.net
Publication Website: https://www.thebeacon.net/
Parent Company: Gannett
Publisher Name: Chris Dixon
Publisher Email: chris@thebeacon.net

PORTSMOUTH

THE COMMUNITY COMMON

Street Address: 637 6th St
City: Portsmouth
State: OH
ZIP Code: 45662-3924
General Phone: (740) 353-1151
General Email: cwilliams@civitasmedia.com
Publication Website: https://www.communitycommon.com/
Parent Company: AIM Media Midwest
Publisher Name: Hope Comer
Publisher Phone: (740) 353-3101, ext : 1911
Editor Name: Fred Pace

ROSSFORD

ROSSFORD RECORD JOURNAL

Street Address: 215 Osborne St
City: Rossford
State: OH
ZIP Code: 43460-1238
General Phone: (419) 874-4491
General Email: editor@rossford.com
Publication Website: https://www.hollandsfj.us/rossford-record-journal
Parent Company: Welch Publishing Company
Editor Name: Beth Church
Editor Email: editor@rossford.com

SPENCERVILLE

THE JOURNAL NEWS

Street Address: PO Box 8
City: Spencerville
State: OH
ZIP Code: 45887-0008
General Phone: (419) 733-0855
General Email: news@spencervillenews.com
Publication Website: https://the-journal-news.business.site/

STRUTHERS

HOMETOWN JOURNAL

Street Address: 32 State St
City: Struthers
State: OH
ZIP Code: 44471-1952
General Phone: (330) 755-2155
General Email: news@hometownjournal.biz
Publication Website: http://www.hometownjournal.biz/
Publisher Name: Nancy Johngrass
Editor Name: Nancy Johngrass

SUGARCREEK

THE BUDGET

Street Address: 134 N Factory St, PO Box 249
City: Sugarcreek
State: OH
ZIP Code: 44681
General Phone: (330) 852-4634
General Email: information@thebudgetnewspaper.com
Publication Website: http://www.thebudgetnewspaper.com/

TROY

MIAMI COUNTY ADVOCATE

Street Address: 224 S Market St
City: Troy
State: OH
ZIP Code: 45373
General Phone: (937) 335-5634
General Email: bsmith@aimmediamidwest.com
Publication Website: https://www.tdn-net.com/
Parent Company: AIM Media Midwest
Publisher Name: Ron Clausen
Publisher Email: ron@aimmediamidwest.com
Publisher Phone: (937) 552-2121
Editor Name: Melody Vallieu
Editor Email: mvallieu@aimmediamidwest.com

TROY

WEEKLY RECORD HERALD

Street Address: 224 S Market St
City: Troy
State: OH
ZIP Code: 45373-3327
General Phone: (937) 440-5275
General Email: cfox@aimmediamidwest.com
Publication Website: https://www.weeklyrecordherald.com/
Parent Company: Ohio Community Media
Editor Name: Cecilia Fox
Editor Email: cfox@aimmediamidwest.com

URBANA

THE MECHANICSBURG TELEGRAM

Street Address: 1637 E US Highway 36
City: Urbana
State: OH
ZIP Code: 43078-9156
General Phone: (937) 652-1331
General Email: lmoon@aimmediamidwest.com
Publication Website: https://www.burgtelegram.com/
Parent Company: AIM Media Midwest
Publisher Name: Lane Moon
Publisher Email: lmoon@aimmediamidwest.com
Editor Name: Brenda Burns
Editor Email: bburns@aimmediamidwest.com

UTICA

THE UTICA HERALD

Street Address: 60 N Main St
City: Utica
State: OH
ZIP Code: 43080-7704
General Phone: (740) 892-2771
General Email: theuticaherald@aol.com
Publication Website: https://www.heartlandcommunications.biz/utica-herald
Parent Company: Heartland Communications

VANDALIA

ENGLEWOOD INDEPENDENT

Street Address: 694 W National Rd
City: Vandalia
State: OH
ZIP Code: 45377-1032
General Phone: (937) 236-4990
General Email: tpatrick@aimmediamidwest.com
Publication Website: https://www.englewoodindependent.com/
Parent Company: AIM Media Midwest
Editor Name: Ron Nunnari
Editor Email: rnunnari@aimmediamidwest.coma

VANDALIA

HUBER HEIGHTS COURIER

Street Address: 694 W National Rd
City: Vandalia
State: OH
ZIP Code: 45377-1032
General Phone: (937) 236-4990
General Email: jryan@aimmediamidwest.com
Publication Website: https://www.hhcourier.com/
Parent Company: AIM Media Midwest
Editor Name: Darrell Wacker
Editor Email: dwacker@aimmediamidwest.com

VANDALIA

VANDALIA DRUMMER NEWS

Street Address: 694 W National Rd
City: Vandalia
State: OH
ZIP Code: 45377-1032
General Phone: (937) 236-4990
General Email: jryan@aimmediamidwest.com
Publication Website: https://www.vandaliadrummernews.com/
Parent Company: AIM Media Midwest
Editor Name: Darrell Wacker
Editor Email: dwacker@aimmediamidwest.com

VERSAILLES

VERSAILLES POLICY

Street Address: 308 N West St
City: Versailles
State: OH
ZIP Code: 45380-1360
General Phone: (937) 526-9131
General Email: vpolicy@roadrunner.com
Publication Website: https://www.versaillespolicy.com/

WAPAKONETA

AUGLAIZE MERCHANDISER

Street Address: 520 Industrial Dr
City: Wapakoneta
State: OH
ZIP Code: 45895-9200
General Phone: (419) 738-2128
General Email: marketingetc@wapakwdn.com
Publication Website: https://www.wapakdailynews.com/
Parent Company: The Wapakoneta Daily News
Publisher Name: Deb Zwez
Publisher Email: publisher@wapakwdn.com
Publisher Phone: (419) 739-3504
Editor Name: Deb Zwez

WARREN

AUSTINTOWN TOWN CRIER

Street Address: 240 Franklin St SE
City: Warren
State: OH
ZIP Code: 44483-5711
General Phone: (330) 629-6200
Publication Website: http://www.towncrieronline.com/page/category.detail/nav/5021/Austintown.html
Parent Company: Ogden Newspapers Inc.

WARREN

BOARDMAN TOWN CRIER

Street Address: 240 Franklin St SE
City: Warren
State: OH
ZIP Code: 44483-5711
General Phone: (330) 629-6200
Publication Website: http://www.towncrieronline.com/page/category.detail/nav/5003/Boardman.html
Parent Company: Ogden Newspapers Inc.

WARREN

CANFIELD TOWN CRIER

Street Address: 240 Franklin St SE
City: Warren
State: OH
ZIP Code: 44483-5711
General Phone: (330) 629-6200
Publication Website: http://www.towncrieronline.com/page/category.detail/nav/5004/Canfield.html
Parent Company: Ogden Newspapers Inc.

WARREN

POLAND TOWN CRIER

Street Address: 240 Franklin St SE
City: Warren
State: OH
ZIP Code: 44483-5711
General Phone: (330) 629-6200
Publication Website: http://www.towncrieronline.com/page/category.detail/nav/5008/Poland.html
Parent Company: Ogden Newspapers Inc.

WAUSEON

FULTON COUNTY EXPOSITOR

Street Address: 1270 N Shoop Ave
City: Wauseon
State: OH
ZIP Code: 43567-2211
General Phone: (419) 335-2010
General Email: jmay@aimmediamidwest.com
Publication Website: https://www.fcnews.org/
Parent Company: AIM Media Midwest
Editor Name: Drew Stambaugh

WAVERLY

THE PIKE COUNTY NEWS WATCHMAN

Street Address: PO Box 151 - 860 W. Emmitt Ave., Ste. 5
City: Waverly
State: OH
ZIP Code: 45690-8011
General Phone: (740) 947-2149
General Email: webeditor@newswatchman.com
Publication Website: https://www.newswatchman.com/
Parent Company: Adams Publishing Group
Editor Name: Matt Lucas
Editor Email: mlucas@newswatchman.com

WELLINGTON

WELLINGTON ENTERPRISE

Street Address: 119 W Herrick Ave
City: Wellington
State: OH
ZIP Code: 44090
General Phone: (440) 647-3171
General Email: news@lcnewspapers.com
Publication Website: https://www.lcnewspapers.com/category/wellington/
Parent Company: Lorain County Printing & Publishing Co.

WEST ALEXANDRIA

THE ADVERTISER

Street Address: 10 S Main St
City: West Alexandria
State: OH
ZIP Code: 45381-1216
General Phone: (937) 839-4733
General Email: twinvpub@infinet.com
Publication Website: https://www.twinvalleypublications.com/
Parent Company: Shaw Media
Publisher Name: Sam Shortes

WEST ALEXANDRIA

THE LEWISBURG LEADER

Street Address: 10 S Main St
City: West Alexandria
State: OH
ZIP Code: 45381-1216
General Phone: (937) 839-4733
General Email: twinvpub@infinet.com
Publication Website: https://www.twinvalleypublications.com/
Parent Company: Twin Valley Publications
Publisher Name: Sam Shortes

WEST ALEXANDRIA

THE TWIN VALLEY NEWS

Street Address: 10 S Main St
City: West Alexandria
State: OH
ZIP Code: 45381-1293
General Phone: (937) 839-4733
General Email: twinvpub@infinet.com
Publication Website: https://www.twinvalleypublications.com/
Parent Company: Twin Valley Publications
Publisher Name: Sam Shortes

WEST UNION

THE PEOPLE'S DEFENDER

Street Address: PO Box 308, 229 N Cross St
City: West Union
State: OH
ZIP Code: 45693-0308
General Phone: (937) 544-2391
General Email: pniswander@peoplesdefender.com
Publication Website: https://www.peoplesdefender.com/
Parent Company: Champion Media
Editor Name: Mark Carpenter
Editor Email: mcarpenter@peoplesdefender.com

WHEELERSBURG

THE SCIOTO VOICE

Street Address: 8366 Downtown Hayport Rd
City: Wheelersburg
State: OH
ZIP Code: 45694
General Phone: (740) 574-8494
General Email: info@thesciotovoice.com
Publication Website: https://www.thesciotovoice.com/
Publisher Name: Debbie Allard
Publisher Email: debbie@thesciotovoice.com
Editor Name: Debbie Allard
Editor Email: debbie@thesciotovoice.com

WILLARD

THE WILLARD TIMES-JUNCTION

Street Address: 211 S Myrtle Ave
City: Willard
State: OH
ZIP Code: 44890-1407
General Phone: (419) 935-0184
General Email: globe@sdgnewsgroup.com
Publication Website: http://www.sdgnewsgroup.com/story4.html
Parent Company: SDGNewsgroup
Publisher Name: Carla Souslin
Editor Name: Jane Ernsberger

WILMINGTON

NEWS JOURNAL STAR

Street Address: 761 S Nelson Ave
City: Wilmington
State: OH
ZIP Code: 45177-2517
General Phone: (937) 382-2574
General Email: emattingly@wnewsj.com
Publication Website: https://www.wnewsj.com/
Parent Company: AIM Media Midwest
Publisher Name: Lane Moon
Publisher Email: lmoon@aimmediamidwest.com
Publisher Phone: (937) 652-1331
Editor Name: Tom Barr
Editor Email: tbarr@wnewsj.com

WOOSTER

THE HOLMES COUNTY HUB SHOPPER

Street Address: 212 E. Liberty St.
City: Wooster
State: OH
ZIP Code: 44691
General Phone: (330) 264-1125
General Email: anixon@the-daily-record.com
Publication Website: http://www.the-daily-record.com/
Publisher Name: Bill Albrecht
Publisher Email: balbrecht@gatehousemedia.com
Publisher Phone: (330) 996-3782
Editor Name: Rick Armon
Editor Email: rarmon@the-daily-record.com

XENIA

BEAVERCREEK NEWS-CURRENT

Street Address: 1836 W Park Sq
City: Xenia
State: OH
ZIP Code: 45385-2668
General Phone: (937) 372-4444
Publication Website: https://www.beavercreeknewscurrent.com/
Parent Company: AIM Media Midwest
Editor Name: Merrilee Embs

XENIA

SUGARCREEK BELLBROOK TIMES

Street Address: 1836 W Park Sq
City: Xenia
State: OH
ZIP Code: 45385-2668
General Phone: (937) 294-7000
General Email: jmilburn@tcnewsnet.com
Publication Website: http://www.bellbrooktimes.com/?fbclid=IwAR0CvX1pM4f_7z0ZHdiJdRUYSWy2_oQEWYyqID_dDaNxXbpxT5oBceENvIY
Parent Company: Ohio Community Media

YELLOW SPRINGS

THE YELLOW SPRINGS NEWS

Street Address: Post Office Box 187
City: Yellow Springs
State: OH
ZIP Code: 45387-0187
General Phone: (937) 767-7373
General Email: ysnews@ysnews.com
Publication Website: https://ysnews.com/
Editor Name: Megan Bachman

OKLAHOMA

ALLEN

THE ALLEN ADVOCATE

Street Address: 101 S. Easton
City: Allen
State: OK
ZIP Code: 74825
General Phone: (580) 857-2687
General Email: allennews@aol.com
Publication Website: https://www.allennewspaper.com/
Editor Name: Dianna Brannan

ANTLERS

ANTLERS AMERICAN

Street Address: 110 East Main, P.O. Box 578
City: Antlers
State: OK
ZIP Code: 74523-3254
General Phone: (580) 298-3314
General Email: comp.antlers.amer@sbcglobal.net
Publication Website: https://www.theantlersamerican.com/
Parent Company: Heritage Publications (2003) Inc.; Horizon Publications Inc.
Publisher Email: ed.antlers.amer@sbcglobal.net

ATOKA

ATOKA COUNTY TIMES

Street Address: 894 W 13th St
City: Atoka
State: OK
ZIP Code: 74525-3426
General Phone: (580) 889-3319
General Email: rlinscott@atokaspeedynet.net
Publication Website: http://atokacountytimes.com/
Publisher Name: Louise Cain
Publisher Phone: (580) 889-3319, ext : 228
Editor Name: Deanna Stuart

BEAVER

THE HERALD-DEMOCRAT

Street Address: 108 Douglas Ave
City: Beaver
State: OK
ZIP Code: 73932-9620
General Phone: (580) 625-3241
General Email: bvrnews@gmail.com
Publication Website: http://www.bvrcowchipnews.com/
Publisher Name: Joe Lansden

BETHANY

THE BETHANY TRIBUNE

Street Address: 6728 NW 38th St
City: Bethany
State: OK
ZIP Code: 73008-3360
General Phone: (405) 789-1962
General Email: phillip@phillipreid.net
Publication Website: https://www.reidnewspapers.com/bethanytribune
Parent Company: Reid Newspaper Group

BLACKWELL

BLACKWELL JOURNAL-TRIBUNE

Street Address: 523 South Main St
City: Blackwell
State: OK
ZIP Code: 74631
General Phone: (580) 363-3370
General Email: classifieds@blackwelljournaltribune.net
Publication Website: https://www.blackwelljournaltribune.net/
Parent Company: West End Holdings LLC
Publisher Name: Tina Anderson
Publisher Email: composing@blackwelljournaltribune.net

CARNEGIE

CARNEGIE HERALD

Street Address: 14 W Main
City: Carnegie
State: OK
ZIP Code: 73015
General Phone: (580) 654-1443
General Email: news@carnegieherald.com
Publication Website: http://www.thecarnegieherald.com/
Publisher Name: Lori Cooper

CHEROKEE

THE CHEROKEE MESSENGER & REPUBLICAN

Street Address: 216 S Grand Ave
City: Cherokee
State: OK
ZIP Code: 73728-2030
General Phone: (580) 596-3344
General Email: ads@cherokeenewspaper.com
Publication Website: https://www.cherokeemessengerrepublican.com/
Publisher Name: Hoby Hammer
Editor Name: Kyle Spade

CHICKASHA

CHICKASHA NEWS

Street Address: 411 W Chickasha Ave
City: Chickasha
State: OK
ZIP Code: 73018-2505
General Phone: (405) 224-2600
General Email: lindsey@chickashanews.com
Publication Website: https://www.edmondsun.com/
Parent Company: CNHI, LLC
Publisher Name: Mark Millsap
Publisher Email: mark@normantranscript.com
Editor Name: Jessica Lane
Editor Email: jlane@chickashanews.com

CLEVELAND

THE CLEVELAND AMERICAN

Street Address: 212 S Broadway St
City: Cleveland
State: OK
ZIP Code: 74020-4617
General Phone: (918) 358-2553
General Email: news@theclevelandamerican.com
Publication Website: http://www.theclevelandamerican.com/
Publisher Name: Rusty Ferguson
Publisher Email: rusty@theclevelandamerican.com
Editor Name: Brandi Ball
Editor Email: brandiball.ok@gmail.com

COALGATE

THE COALGATE RECORD-REGISTER

Street Address: 602 E Lafayette Ave
City: Coalgate
State: OK
ZIP Code: 74538-4018
General Phone: (580) 927-2355
General Email: helen@coalgaterecordregister.com
Publication Website: https://www.coalgaterecordregister.com/
Parent Company: Robinson Publishing Company
Publisher Name: Dayna Robinson
Publisher Email: robpublishing@sbcglobal.net
Publisher Phone: (405) 379-5184
Editor Name: Wanda Utterbackq

COMANCHE

COMANCHE TIMES

Street Address: 513 Hillery, Suite A
City: Comanche
State: OK
ZIP Code: 73529-1200
General Phone: (580) 439-6500
General Email: comanchetimes@pldi.net
Publication Website: https://www.comancheok.net/
Publisher Name: Steve Bolton
Editor Name: Steve Bolton

CORDELL

THE CORDELL BEACON

Street Address: 115 E Main St
City: Cordell
State: OK
ZIP Code: 73632-4897
General Phone: (580) 832-3333
General Email: editor@cordellbeacon.com
Publication Website: https://www.cordellbeacon.com/
Editor Name: Bob Henline
Editor Email: editor@cordellbeacon.com

CUSHING

CUSHING CITIZEN

Street Address: 202 N Harrison Ave
City: Cushing
State: OK
ZIP Code: 74023-3302
General Phone: (918) 285-5555
General Email: publisher@cushingcitizen.com
Publication Website: http://www.cushingcitizen.com/
Publisher Name: J.D. Meisner
Publisher Email: publisher@cushingcitizen.com
Editor Email: editor@cushingcitizen.com

DAVIS

THE DAVIS NEWS

Street Address: 400 E Main St
City: Davis
State: OK
ZIP Code: 73030-1908
General Phone: (580) 369-2807
General Email: davispaper@sbcglobal.net
Publication Website: https://www.davisnewspaper.net/
Publisher Name: Alisha Thompson
Editor Name: Alisha Thompson

EDMOND

THE EDMOND SUN

Street Address: 123 S Broadway
City: Edmond
State: OK
ZIP Code: 73034-3899
General Phone: (405) 341-2121
General Email: news@edmondsun.com
Publication Website: https://www.edmondsun.com/
Parent Company: CNHI, LLC
Publisher Name: Lance Moler
Publisher Email: lmoler@edmondsun.com
Editor Name: Mark Codner
Editor Email: mcodner@edmondsun.com

EL RENO

EL RENO TRIBUNE

Street Address: 102 E Wade St
City: El Reno
State: OK
ZIP Code: 73036-2742
General Phone: (405) 262-5180
General Email: webmaster@elrenotribune.com
Publication Website: https://www.elrenotribune.com/

EUFAULA

INDIAN JOURNAL

Street Address: 109 S Main St
City: Eufaula
State: OK
ZIP Code: 74432-2875
General Phone: (918) 689-2191
General Email: ijdemolegals@bigbasinllc.com
Publication Website: https://www.eufaulaindianjournal.com/

FAIRLAND

THE AMERICAN

Street Address: P.O. Box 339
City: Fairland
State: OK
ZIP Code: 74343-4744
General Phone: (918) 676-3484
General Email: vdj@cableone.net
Publication Website: https://www.reidnewspapers.com/copy-of-nowata-star
Parent Company: Reid Newspaper Group

FAIRVIEW

FAIRVIEW REPUBLICAN

Street Address: 112 N Main St
City: Fairview
State: OK
ZIP Code: 73737
General Phone: (580) 227-4439
General Email: news@fairviewrepublican.com
Publication Website: https://www.fairviewrepublican.com/

FREDERICK

FREDERICK PRESS-LEADER

Street Address: 102 S Main St
City: Frederick
State: OK
ZIP Code: 73542
General Phone: (580) 379-0588

General Email: customerservice@durantdemocrat.com
Publication Website: https://www.press-leader.com/
Editor Name: Kathleen Guill
Editor Email: kathleen@press-leader.com

GEARY

GEARY STAR

Street Address: 116 S Broadway
City: Geary
State: OK
ZIP Code: 73040
General Phone: (580) 623-4922
General Email: ads@thegearystar.com
Publication Website: https://www.thegearystar.com/
Publisher Name: Kimberly Jenkins
Editor Email: editor@thegearystar.com

GROVE

DELAWARE COUNTY JOURNAL

Street Address: 16 W 3rd St
City: Grove
State: OK
ZIP Code: 74344
General Phone: (918) 786-2228
General Email: khutchison@grovesun.com
Publication Website: https://www.grandlakenews.com/news/20180620/delaware-county-journal-earns-honors-at-opa
Parent Company: Gannett
Publisher Name: Joe Leong
Publisher Email: jleong@gatehousemedia.com
Publisher Phone: (620) 231-2600, ext : 140
Editor Name: Patrick Richardson
Editor Email: prichardson@morningsun.net

GROVE

GROVE SUN

Street Address: 16 W 3rd St
City: Grove
State: OK
ZIP Code: 74344
General Phone: (918) 786-2228
General Email: khutchison@grovesun.com
Publication Website: https://www.grandlakenews.com/
Parent Company: Gannett
Publisher Name: Joe Leong
Publisher Email: jleong@gatehousemedia.com
Publisher Phone: (620) 231-2600, ext : 140
Editor Name: Patrick Richardson
Editor Email: prichardson@morningsun.net

GUTHRIE

GUTHRIE NEWS LEADER

Street Address: 212 W Oklahoma Ave.
City: Guthrie
State: OK
ZIP Code: 73044-0879
General Phone: (405) 282-2222
General Email: publisher@guthrienewsleader.net
Publication Website: https://www.guthrienewsleader.net/
Parent Company: West End Holdings LLC
Publisher Name: Karan Ediger
Publisher Email: publisher@guthrienewsleader.net
Publisher Phone: (405) 282-2222
Editor Name: Parker Burnett
Editor Email: gnlsports@yahoo.com

HEAVENER

THE HEAVENER LEDGER

Street Address: 507 E 1st St, P.O. Box 38
City: Heavener
State: OK
ZIP Code: 74937-3203
General Phone: (918) 653-2425
General Email: heavenerledger@windstream.net
Publication Website: https://www.ledgerlcj.com/
Parent Company: Heavener Ledger, Inc.

HENNESSEY

THE HENNESSEY CLIPPER

Street Address: PO Box 664
City: Hennessey
State: OK
ZIP Code: 73763
General Phone: (580) 822-4401
General Email: clippernews@trailmiller.com
Publication Website: https://www.hennesseyclipper.com/
Publisher Name: Paul Laubauch
Publisher Email: clippernews@trailmiller.com
Publisher Phone: (580) 822-4401

HENRYETTA

HENRYETTA FREE-LANCE

Street Address: 302 W Main St
City: Henryetta
State: OK
ZIP Code: 74437
General Phone: (918) 652-3311
General Email: advertising@henryettanewspaper.com
Publication Website: https://www.henryettafree-lance.com/

HINTON

HINTON RECORD

Street Address: P.O. Box 959
City: Hinton
State: OK
ZIP Code: 73047
General Phone: (405) 542-6644
General Email: ads@hintonrecord.com
Publication Website: https://www.hintonrecord.com/
Publisher Name: Kimberly Jenkins
Editor Email: editor@hintonrecord.com

HOLDENVILLE

HOLDENVILLE TRIBUNE

Street Address: 114 N Broadway St
City: Holdenville
State: OK
ZIP Code: 74848
General Phone: (405) 379-5184
General Email: robpublishing@sbcglobal.net
Publication Website: https://www.hughescountytribune.com/
Parent Company: Robinson Publishing Company
Publisher Name: Dayna Robinson
Publisher Email: robpublishing@sbcglobal.net
Editor Name: Jade Robinson

HUGO

HUGO NEWS

Street Address: 128 E Jackson St
City: Hugo
State: OK
ZIP Code: 74743-4082
General Phone: (580) 326-3311
General Email: linda@hugonews.com
Publication Website: http://www.hugonews.com
Parent Company: Hugo Publishing Co.
Publisher Name: Stan Stamper
Publisher Email: stan@hugonews.com
Editor Name: Krystle Taylor
Editor Email: linda@hugonews.com

KINGFISHER

THE KINGFISHER TIMES & FREE PRESS

Street Address: P.O. Box 209
City: Kingfisher
State: OK
ZIP Code: 73750
General Phone: (405) 375-3220
General Email: kfrtimesgary@pldi.net
Publication Website: https://www.kingfisherpress.net/
Publisher Name: Barry Reid
Publisher Email: bkreid59@gmail.com
Editor Name: Michael Swisher
Editor Email: ktfpsports@gmail.com

KONAWA

KONAWA LEADER

Street Address: PO Box 157
City: Konawa
State: OK
ZIP Code: 74849
General Phone: (405) 382-1100
General Email: support@etypeservices.com
Publication Website: https://www.konawaleader.com/

LINDSAY

LINDSAY NEWS

Street Address: 117 S Main St
City: Lindsay
State: OK
ZIP Code: 73052
General Phone: (405) 756-4045
General Email: darrell@cableprinting.com
Publication Website: http://www.cableprinting.com/lindsay_news.html
Editor Name: Gina Cable
Editor Email: gina@cableprinting.com

MADILL

MADILL RECORD

Street Address: 211 Plaza
City: Madill
State: OK
ZIP Code: 73446-2250
General Phone: (580) 795-3355
General Email: advertising@madillrecord.net
Publication Website: https://www.madillrecord.net/
Parent Company: Cordell Beacon Co. Inc.
Editor Name: Shalene White
Editor Email: shalene@madillrecord.net

MANGUM

THE MANGUM STAR-NEWS

Street Address: 121 S Oklahoma Ave
City: Mangum
State: OK
ZIP Code: 73554
General Phone: (580) 782-3321
General Email: mangumstarnews@sbcglobal.net
Publication Website: http://mangumstaronline.com

MARLOW

THE MARLOW REVIEW

Street Address: 316 W Main St
City: Marlow
State: OK
ZIP Code: 73055
General Phone: (580) 658-6657
General Email: news@marlowreview.com
Publication Website: https://www.marlowreview.com/
Publisher Name: Candace Hammond
Publisher Email: publisher@marlowreview.com
Editor Name: Elizabeth Pitts-Hibbard
Editor Email: news@marlowreview.com

MAYSVILLE

THE GARVIN COUNTY NEWS STAR

Street Address: 402 Williams
City: Maysville
State: OK
ZIP Code: 73057
General Phone: (405) 867-4457
General Email: news@gcnews-star.com
Publication Website: http://gcns.flywheelsites.com/
Publisher Name: Jeff Shultz
Publisher Email: publisher@gcnews-star.com
Editor Name: Jeff Shultz

MIDWEST CITY

MIDWEST CITY BEACON

Street Address: 1500 S Midwest Blvd
City: Midwest City
State: OK
ZIP Code: 73110-4944
General Phone: (405) 455-1110
General Email: mustangtimesnews@sbcglobal.net
Publication Website: https://www.centraloklahomaweeklies.com
Parent Company: Choctaw Times LLC

MOORELAND

MOORELAND LEADER

Street Address: 202 N Main St
City: Mooreland
State: OK
ZIP Code: 73852
General Phone: (580) 994-5410
General Email: leader2@pldi.net
Publication Website: https://www.moorelandleader.com/

MUSTANG

THE MUSTANG NEWS

Street Address: 120 E Trade Center Ter
City: Mustang
State: OK
ZIP Code: 73064-4410
General Phone: (405) 376-4571
General Email: pvenable@theyukonreview.com
Publication Website: https://www.theyukonreview.com/mustang-news/
Parent Company: Chisholm Trail, LLC
Editor Name: Terry Groover
Editor Email: tgroover@theyukonreview.com

Community Newspapers in the U.S.

MUSTANG

THE TUTTLE TIMES

Street Address: P.O. Box 180
City: Mustang
State: OK
ZIP Code: 73064-7002
General Phone: (405) 376-6688
General Email: editor@tuttletimes.com
Publication Website: http://www.tuttletimes.com
Parent Company: Choctaw Times LLC
Editor Email: editor@tuttletimes.com

NEWCASTLE

NEWCASTLE PACER

Street Address: 120 NE 2nd St
City: Newcastle
State: OK
ZIP Code: 73065
General Phone: (405) 387-5277
General Email: news@newcastlepacer.com
Publication Website: https://www.newcastlepacer.com/

NEWKIRK

THE NEWKIRK HERALD JOURNAL

Street Address: 121 N Main St
City: Newkirk
State: OK
ZIP Code: 74647
General Phone: (580) 362-2140
General Email: news@newkirkherald.com
Publication Website: https://www.newkirkherald.com/
Publisher Name: Scott Cloud
Publisher Email: news@newkirkherald.com
Editor Name: Scott Cloud
Editor Email: news@newkirkherald.com

NORMAN

MOORE AMERICAN

Street Address: 215 E Comanche St
City: Norman
State: OK
ZIP Code: 73069-6007
General Phone: (405) 321-1800
General Email: cityeditor@mooreamerican.com
Publication Website: https://www.edmondsun.com
Parent Company: CNHI, LLC
Publisher Name: Mark Millsap
Publisher Email: publisher@normantranscript.com
Publisher Phone: (405) 366-3590
Editor Name: Shana Adkisson
Editor Email: editor@normantranscript.com

NOWATA

THE NOWATA STAR

Street Address: PO Box 429
City: Nowata
State: OK
ZIP Code: 74048
General Phone: (918) 273-2446
General Email: nowatastar@sbcglobal.net
Publication Website: https://www.reidnewspapers.com/nowatastar
Parent Company: Reid Newspaper Group

OKEENE

OKEENE RECORD

Street Address: 211 N Main St
City: Okeene
State: OK
ZIP Code: 73763-9447
General Phone: (580) 822-4401
General Email: okeenenews@trailmiller.com
Publication Website: https://www.okeenerecord.com/
Parent Company: Trail Miller Co., LLC

OKEMAH

OKEMAH NEWS LEADER

Street Address: P.O. Box 191
City: Okemah
State: OK
ZIP Code: 74859
General Phone: (918) 623-0123
General Email: kay@okemahnewsleader.com
Publication Website: https://www.okemahnewsleader.com/

OKLAHOMA CITY

OKLAHOMA CITY FRIDAY

Street Address: PO Box 20340
City: Oklahoma City
State: OK
ZIP Code: 73156
General Phone: (405) 755-3311
General Email: lovina@okcfriday.com
Publication Website: https://okcfriday.com/

OKLAHOMA CITY

THE CITY SENTINEL

Street Address: PO Box 60876
City: Oklahoma City
State: OK
ZIP Code: 73146
General Phone: (405) 740-8687
General Email: sales@city-sentinel.com
Publication Website: http://city-sentinel.com/
Publisher Name: Pat McGuigan
Publisher Email: news@city-sentinel.com
Editor Name: Pat McGuigan
Editor Email: news@city-sentinel.com

OOLOGAH

OOLOGAH LAKE LEADER

Street Address: 109 S Maple St
City: Oologah
State: OK
ZIP Code: 74053-3299
General Phone: (918) 443-2428
General Email: carolyn.estes@sbcglobal.net
Publication Website: https://www.oologahonline.com/
Parent Company: Oologah Lake Leader LLC

OWASSO

OWASSO REPORTER

Street Address: 202 E 2nd Ave
City: Owasso
State: OK
ZIP Code: 74055-3131
General Phone: (918) 272-1155
General Email: annette.riherd@tulsaworld.com
Publication Website: https://www.tulsaworld.com/communities/owasso/
Publisher Name: Gloria Fletcher
Publisher Email: gloria.fletcher@tulsaworld.com
Publisher Phone: (918) 581-8512
Editor Name: Art Haddaway
Editor Email: art.haddaway@owassoreporter.com

PAULS VALLEY

PAULS VALLEY DEMOCRAT

Street Address: 108 S Willow St
City: Pauls Valley
State: OK
ZIP Code: 73075-3834
General Phone: (405) 238-6464
General Email: jdavenport@pvdemocrat.com
Publication Website: https://www.edmondsun.com/
Parent Company: CNHI, LLC
Publisher Name: Sara Fisher
Publisher Email: sfisher@pvdemocrat.com
Editor Name: Mike Arie
Editor Email: marie@pvdemocrat.com

PAWHUSKA

PAWHUSKA JOURNAL-CAPITAL

Street Address: 1020 Lynn Ave
City: Pawhuska
State: OK
ZIP Code: 74056
General Phone: (918) 335-8200
General Email: mtranquill@examiner-enterprise.com
Publication Website: https://www.pawhuskajournalcapital.com/
Parent Company: Gannett
Publisher Name: Matt Tranquill
Publisher Email: mtranquill@examiner-enterprise.com
Publisher Phone: (918) 335-8200
Editor Name: Robert Smith
Editor Email: rsmith@pawhuskajournalcapital.com

PERKINS

PERKINS JOURNAL

Street Address: 222 N Main St
City: Perkins
State: OK
ZIP Code: 74059
General Phone: (405) 547-2411
General Email: publisher@journalok.com
Publication Website: http://journalok.com/
Publisher Name: W. David Sasser
Publisher Email: publisher@journalok.com

PRYOR

THE PAPER

Street Address: 3 N Adair St
City: Pryor
State: OK
ZIP Code: 74361
General Phone: (918) 825-2860
General Email: thepaper@mayescounty.com
Publication Website: http://mayescounty.com/tp-welcome/

PURCELL

THE PURCELL REGISTER

Street Address: 225 W Main St
City: Purcell
State: OK
ZIP Code: 73080
General Phone: (405) 527-2126
General Email: purcellregister@gmail.com
Publication Website: http://www.purcellregister.com/
Publisher Name: John D. Montgomery
Editor Name: John D. Montgomery

RINGLING

THE RINGLING EAGLE

Street Address: 103 E Main St
City: Ringling
State: OK
ZIP Code: 73456
General Phone: (580) 662-2221
General Email: ringlingeagle@sbcglobal.net
Publication Website: http://ringlingeagle.com/The_Ringling_Eagle/Home.html
Publisher Name: Jay Grace
Editor Name: Melissa Grace

SAYRE

THE BECKHAM COUNTY RECORD

Street Address: 112 E Main St
City: Sayre
State: OK
ZIP Code: 73662
General Phone: (580) 928-5540
General Email: sayrerecord@cableone.net
Publication Website: https://www.sayrerecord.com/
Publisher Name: Brad Spitzer
Publisher Email: sayrerecord@cableone.net
Publisher Phone: (580) 928-5540
Editor Name: Connie Ferrero
Editor Email: sayrerecord@cableone.net

SEILING

THE DEWEY COUNTY RECORD

Street Address: 207 N Main St
City: Seiling
State: OK
ZIP Code: 73663-6676
General Phone: (580) 922-4296
General Email: seilingnews@trailmiller.com
Publication Website: https://www.deweycountyrecord.com/
Parent Company: Trail Miller Co. LLC

SENTINEL

SENTINEL LEADER

Street Address: 307 E Main St
City: Sentinel
State: OK
ZIP Code: 73664
General Phone: (580) 393-4348
General Email: sleader@pldi.net
Publication Website: http://www.thesentinelleader.com/
Publisher Name: Jolene Wolfenbarger
Editor Name: Jolene Wolfenbarger

SHATTUCK

NORTHWEST OKLAHOMAN

Street Address: 329 S Main St
City: Shattuck
State: OK
ZIP Code: 73858
General Phone: (580) 938-2533
General Email: nwopaper@pldi.net
Publication Website: https://www.northwestoklahoman.com/

SKIATOOK

SKIATOOK JOURNAL

Street Address: 500 W Rogers Blvd
City: Skiatook
State: OK
ZIP Code: 74070-1081
General Phone: (918) 272-1155
General Email: annette.riherd@tulsaworld.com
Publication Website: https://www.tulsaworld.com/communities/skiatook/
Publisher Name: Gloria Fletcher
Publisher Email: gloria.fletcher@tulsaworld.com
Publisher Phone: (918) 581-8512
Editor Name: Lindsey Chastain
Editor Email: lindsey.chastain@skiatookjournal.com

STIGLER

STIGLER NEWS-SENTINEL

Street Address: 204 S Broadway St
City: Stigler
State: OK
ZIP Code: 74462
General Phone: (918) 967-4655
General Email: summer@stiglernews.com
Publication Website: https://www.stiglernews.com
Publisher Name: Linus Williams
Publisher Email: linus@stiglerprinting.com
Publisher Phone: (918) 967-4655, ext : 224
Editor Name: Anita Reding
Editor Email: editor@stiglernews.com

STILWELL

STILWELL DEMOCRAT JOURNAL

Street Address: 118 N 2nd St
City: Stilwell
State: OK
ZIP Code: 74960-3028
General Phone: (918) 696-2228
General Email: stilwelldj@windstream.net
Publication Website: https://www.edmondsun.com/
Parent Company: CNHI, LLC

STILWELL

WESTVILLE REPORTER

Street Address: 118 N 2nd St
City: Stilwell
State: OK
ZIP Code: 74960
General Phone: (918) 696-2228
General Email: stilwelldj@windstream.net
Publication Website: https://www.edmondsun.com/
Parent Company: CNHI, LLC

SULPHUR

SULPHUR TIMES-DEMOCRAT

Street Address: 115 W Muskogee Ave
City: Sulphur
State: OK
ZIP Code: 73086
General Phone: (580) 622-2102
General Email: jcjohn@sulphurtimes.com
Publication Website: https://www.sulphurtimes.com/

TECUMSEH

COUNTYWIDE & SUN

Street Address: PO Box 38
City: Tecumseh
State: OK
ZIP Code: 74873
General Phone: (405) 598-3793
General Email: info@countywidenews.com
Publication Website: https://www.countywidenews.com/

THOMAS

THE THOMAS TRIBUNE

Street Address: 115 W Orient
City: Thomas
State: OK
ZIP Code: 73669
General Phone: (580) 661-3524
General Email: thethomastribune@yahoo.com
Publication Website: https://www.thomastribune.com/

TISHOMINGO

JOHNSTON COUNTY CAPITAL-DEMOCRAT

Street Address: 103 N Neshoba St
City: Tishomingo
State: OK
ZIP Code: 73460-1739
General Phone: (405) 371-2356
Publication Website: http://johnstoncountycapital-democrat.com/

TONKAWA

THE TONKAWA NEWS

Street Address: 126 East Grand
City: Tonkawa
State: OK
ZIP Code: 74653
General Phone: (580) 628-2532
General Email: news@tonkawanews.com
Publication Website: https://www.tonkawanews.com/

TULSA

OWASSO RAMBLER

Street Address: 5401 S. Sheridan Rd., Ste. 302
City: Tulsa
State: OK
ZIP Code: 74145
General Phone: (918) 254-1515
General Email: fcameron@gtrnews.com
Publication Website: https://gtrnews.com/
Parent Company: Greater Tulsa Reporter Newspapers; Union Boundry Inc.

TULSA

SAND SPRINGS LEADER

Street Address: PO Box 1770
City: Tulsa
State: OK
ZIP Code: 74102-1770
General Phone: (918) 245-6634
General Email: bernie.heller@tulsaworld.com
Publication Website: https://www.tulsaworld.com/communities/sandsprings/
Publisher Name: Gloria Fletcher
Publisher Email: gloria.fletcher@tulsaworld.com
Publisher Phone: (918) 581-8512
Editor Name: Kirk McCracken
Editor Email: kirk.mccracken@sandspringsleader.com

TULSA

TULSA BEACON

Street Address: PO Box 35099
City: Tulsa
State: OK
ZIP Code: 74153
General Phone: (918) 523-4425
General Email: orders@tulsabeacon.com
Publication Website: http://tulsabeacon.com/

TULSA

TULSA COUNTY NEWS

Street Address: 315 S Boulder Ave
City: Tulsa
State: OK
ZIP Code: 74103-3401
General Phone: (918) 582-0921
General Email: stephanie.knight@tulsaworld.com
Publication Website: https://www.tulsaworld.com/
Publisher Name: Gloria Fletcher
Publisher Email: gloria.fletcher@tulsaworld.com
Publisher Phone: (918) 581-8450
Editor Name: Susan Ellerbach
Editor Email: susan.ellerbach@tulsaworld.com

WAGONER

NEIGHBOR NEWS

Street Address: 221 E. Cherokee
City: Wagoner
State: OK
ZIP Code: 74467
General Phone: (918) 485-5505
General Email: circulation@wagonercountyat.com
Publication Website: https://www.tulsaworld.com/
Parent Company: Lee Enterprises
Publisher Name: Mike Brown
Editor Name: Christy Wheeland
Editor Email: christy.wheeland@wagonercountyat.com
Editor Phone: (918) 485-5505

WAGONER

WAGONER TRIBUNE

Street Address: 221 E Cherokee St
City: Wagoner
State: OK
ZIP Code: 74467-4703
General Phone: (918) 485-5505
General Email: bernie.heller@tulsaworld.com
Publication Website: https://www.tulsaworld.com/communities/wagoner/
Publisher Name: Gloria Fletcher
Publisher Email: gloria.fletcher@tulsaworld.com
Publisher Phone: (918) 581-8512
Editor Name: Christy Wheeland
Editor Email: christy.wheeland@wagonercountyat.com

WALTERS

WALTERS HERALD

Street Address: 112 S Broadway St
City: Walters
State: OK
ZIP Code: 73572
General Phone: (580) 875-3326
General Email: waltersheraldads@gmail.com
Publication Website: https://www.waltersherald.com/
Publisher Name: Beth Davis
Publisher Email: waltersheraldads@gmail.com
Publisher Phone: (580) 875-3326
Editor Name: Beth Davis
Editor Email: waltersheraldads@gmail.com

WATONGA

THE WATONGA REPUBLICAN

Street Address: 104 E Main St
City: Watonga
State: OK
ZIP Code: 73772-3831
General Phone: (580) 623-4922
General Email: ian@watongarepublican.com
Publication Website: https://www.thewatongarepublican.com/
Parent Company: Central Oklahoma Publishing
Publisher Name: Kimberly Jenkins
Publisher Email: kim@watongarepublican.com
Publisher Phone: (580) 623-4922
Editor Name: Connie Burcham
Editor Email: editor@watongarepublican.com

WETUMKA

THE HUGHES COUNTY TIMES

Street Address: 501 E Highway 9
City: Wetumka
State: OK
ZIP Code: 74883-6048
General Phone: (405) 452-3294
General Email: hughescountytimes@sbcglobal.net
Publication Website: https://www.hughescountytribune.com/
Parent Company: Robinson Publishing Company
Publisher Name: Dayna Robinson
Editor Name: Jade Robinson

WEWOKA

WEWOKA TIMES

Street Address: 210 S Wewoka Ave
City: Wewoka
State: OK
ZIP Code: 74884
General Phone: (405) 257-3341
General Email: support@etypeservices.com
Publication Website: https://www.thewewokatimes.com/

WYNNEWOOD

WYNNEWOOD GAZETTE

Street Address: 210 S Dean A McGee Ave
City: Wynnewood
State: OK
ZIP Code: 73098-7810
General Phone: (405) 665-4333
General Email: info@wwgazette.news
Publication Website: https://thewynnewoodgazette.com/
Parent Company: Victory Publishing LLC

YUKON

PIEDMONT SURREY GAZETTE

Street Address: 508 W. Vandament Avenue
City: Yukon
State: OK
ZIP Code: 73078-8521
General Phone: (405) 577-6208
General Email: editor@piedmontnewsonline.com
Publication Website: https://piedmontnewsonline.com/

Community Newspapers in the U.S.

Publisher Name: Randy K. Anderson
Publisher Email: randyk.anderson@sbcglobal.net
Editor Name: Conrad Dudderar
Editor Email: editor@piedmontnewsonline.com

YUKON

THE YUKON REVIEW

Street Address: 110 S 5th St
City: Yukon
State: OK
ZIP Code: 73099-2601
General Phone: (405) 354-5264
General Email: tgroover@theyukonreview.com
Publication Website: https://www.theyukonreview.com/
Parent Company: Chisholm Trail, LLC
Editor Name: Terry Groover
Editor Email: tgroover@theyukonreview.com

OREGON

BANDON

BANDON WESTERN WORLD

Street Address: 1185 BALTIMORE AVE SE
City: Bandon
State: OR
ZIP Code: 97411
General Phone: (541) 347-2423
General Email: amanda.carlton@theworldlink.com
Publication Website: https://theworldlink.com/community/bandon/
Parent Company: Southwestern Oregon Publishing Company
Publisher Name: Steven Hungerford
Publisher Email: worldpublisher@countrymedia.net
Editor Name: Amy Moss-Strong
Editor Email: amy.moss-strong@theworldlink.com
Editor Phone: (541) 266-6051
Advertising Executive Name: Amanda Carlton
Advertising Executive Email: amanda.carlton@theworldlink.com
Advertising Executive Phone: (541) 266-6002
Delivery Methods: Mail`Newsstand`Racks
Year Established: 1912
Mechanical specifications: Type page 13 x 21; E - 6 cols, 2 1/2, 1/6 between; A - 6 cols, 2 1/2, 1/6 between; C - 8 cols, 1 1/3, 1/4 between.
Published Days: Wed`Thur
Avg. Paid Circ.: 1059
Audit Company: Sworn/Estimate/Non-Audited
Audit Date: 43626

BEND

SOURCE WEEKLY

Street Address: 704 NW Georgia Ave
City: Bend
State: OR
ZIP Code: 97703-3243
General Phone: (541) 383-0800
General Email: amanda@bendsource.com
Publication Website: https://www.bendsource.com/
Publisher Name: Aaron Switzer
Publisher Email: aaron@bendsource.com
Editor Name: Nicole Vulcan
Editor Email: editor@bendsource.com
Advertising Executive Name: Amanda Klingman

Advertising Executive Email: amanda@bendsource.com
Year Established: 1997
Published Days: Wed
Avg. Paid Circ.: 325
Audit Company: Sworn/Estimate/Non-Audited
Audit Date: 43626

BROOKINGS

CURRY COASTAL PILOT

Street Address: 15957 Highway 101 S STE 1
City: Brookings
State: OR
ZIP Code: 97415
General Phone: (541) 813-1717
General Email: pilotclassifieds@countrymedia.net
Publication Website: https://www.currypilot.com/
Parent Company: Country Media Inc.
Publisher Name: Carol Hungerford
Publisher Email: carol@countrymedia.net
Editor Email: piloteditor@countrymedia.net
Advertising Executive Email: pilotclassifieds@countrymedia.net
Delivery Methods: Mail`Newsstand`Carrier`Racks
Year Established: 1946
Own Printing Facility?: Y
Commercial printers?: Y
Mechanical specifications: Type page 10 1/2 x 21 1/2; E - 6 cols
Published Days: Wed`Sat
Avg. Paid Circ.: 4759
Avg. Free Circ.: 87
Audit Company: CVC
Audit Date: 43260

BROWNSVILLE

THE TIMES

Street Address: 343 N MAIN ST
City: Brownsville
State: OR
ZIP Code: 97327
General Phone: (541) 466-5311
General Email: thetimes@peak.org
Publication Website: https://thebrownsvilletimes.com/
Parent Company: Gannett
Delivery Methods: Mail`Newsstand
Year Established: 1888
Mechanical specifications: Type page 11 3/4 x 17 1/2; E - 5 cols, 1/6, between; C - 6 cols, 1/12 between.
Published Days: Wed
Avg. Paid Circ.: 1200
Avg. Free Circ.: 62
Audit Company: Sworn/Estimate/Non-Audited
Audit Date: 43626

BURNS

BURNS TIMES-HERALD

Street Address: 355 N Broadway Ave
City: Burns
State: OR
ZIP Code: 97720-1704
General Phone: (541) 573-2022
General Email: addrop@btimesherald.com
Publication Website: http://btimesherald.com/
Parent Company: Survival Media LLC
Editor Name: Randy Parks
Editor Email: editor@btimesherald.com
Advertising Executive Name: Nolan Graham
Advertising Executive Email: ngraham@btimesherald.com
Year Established: 1887
Mechanical specifications: Type page 11 5/6 x 20 1/2; E - 6 cols, 1 5/6, 1/6 between; A - 6 cols, 1 5/6, 1/6 between; C - 8 cols, 1 1/3, 1/6 between.
Published Days: Wed
Avg. Paid Circ.: 3008
Avg. Free Circ.: 46
Audit Company: Sworn/Estimate/Non-Audited
Audit Date: 43626

COOS BAY

THE UMPQUA POST

Street Address: 350 Commercial Ave
City: Coos Bay
State: OR
ZIP Code: 97420-2269
General Phone: (541) 271-7474
General Email: amanda.carlton@theworldlink.com
Publication Website: https://theworldlink.com/community/reedsport/
Parent Company: Southwestern Oregon Publishing Company
Publisher Name: Steven Hungerford
Publisher Email: worldpublisher@countrymedia.net
Editor Name: Amy Moss-Strong
Editor Email: amy.moss-strong@theworldlink.com
Editor Phone: (541) 266-6051
Advertising Executive Name: Amanda Carlton
Advertising Executive Email: amanda.carlton@theworldlink.com
Advertising Executive Phone: (541) 266-6002
Delivery Methods: Mail`Newsstand`Racks
Year Established: 1996
Published Days: Wed
Avg. Paid Circ.: 750
Audit Company: Sworn/Estimate/Non-Audited
Audit Date: 43626

COOS BAY

THE WORLD

Street Address: 350 Commercial Ave
City: Coos Bay
State: OR
ZIP Code: 97420
General Phone: (541) 269-1222
General Email: amanda.carlton@theworldlink.com
Publication Website: https://theworldlink.com/
Parent Company: Lee Enterprises, Incorporated
Publisher Name: Steven Hungerford
Publisher Email: worldpublisher@countrymedia.net
Editor Name: Amy Moss-Strong
Editor Email: amy.moss-strong@theworldlink.com
Editor Phone: (541) 266-6051
Advertising Executive Name: Amanda Carlton
Advertising Executive Email: amanda.carlton@theworldlink.com
Advertising Executive Phone: (541) 266-6002
Year Established: 1889
Mechanical specifications: Type page 13 x 21; E - 6 cols, 2 1/12, 1/6 between; A - 6 cols, 2 1/12, 1/16 between; C - 6 cols, 2 1/12, 1/6 between.
Published Days: Thur
Avg. Paid Circ.: 2100
Audit Company: AAM
Audit Date: 43504

CORVALLIS

THE PHILOMATH EXPRESS

Street Address: 1835 NW Circle Blvd
City: Corvallis
State: OR
ZIP Code: 97330-1310

General Phone: (541) 753-2641
General Email: monica.hampton@lee.net
Publication Website: https://www.gazettetimes.com/community/philomathexpress/
Publisher Name: Jeff Precourt
Publisher Email: jeff.precourt@lee.net
Publisher Phone: (541) 812-6125
Advertising Executive Name: Monica Hampton
Advertising Executive Email: monica.hampton@lee.net
Advertising Executive Phone: (541) 812-6062
Published Days: Wed
Audit Company: Sworn/Estimate/Non-Audited
Audit Date: 43626

COTTAGE GROVE

COTTAGE GROVE SENTINEL

Street Address: 116 N 6th St
City: Cottage Grove
State: OR
ZIP Code: 97424-1601
General Phone: (541) 942-3325
General Email: gmanly@cgsentinel.com
Publication Website: https://www.cgsentinel.com/
Parent Company: News Media Grouip
Publisher Name: Gary Manly
Publisher Email: gmanly@cgsentinel.com
Publisher Phone: (541) 942-3325, ext : 1207
Editor Name: Ned Hickson
Editor Email: nhickson@cgsentinel.com
Advertising Executive Name: Gary Manly
Advertising Executive Email: gmanly@cgsentinel.com
Advertising Executive Phone: (541) 942-3325, ext : 1207
Delivery Methods: Mail`Racks
Year Established: 1889
Own Printing Facility?: Y
Published Days: Wed
Avg. Paid Circ.: 2500
Avg. Free Circ.: 225
Audit Company: Sworn/Estimate/Non-Audited
Audit Date: 43626

CRESWELL

THE CRESWELL CHRONICLE

Street Address: 34 W Oregon Ave
City: Creswell
State: OR
ZIP Code: 97426-9259
General Phone: (541) 895-2197
General Email: noel@chronicle1909.com
Publication Website: https://www.chronicle1909.com/
Parent Company: Nash Publishing Group
Publisher Name: Denise Nash
Editor Name: Erin Tierney
Advertising Executive Name: Noel Nash
Advertising Executive Email: noel@chronicle1909.com
Advertising Executive Phone: (541) 895-2197
Delivery Methods: Mail`Newsstand`Racks
Year Established: 1965
Published Days: Thur
Avg. Paid Circ.: 1050
Avg. Free Circ.: 50
Audit Company: Sworn/Estimate/Non-Audited
Audit Date: 43626

FLORENCE

SIUSLAW NEWS

Street Address: 148 Maple St
City: Florence
State: OR
ZIP Code: 97439-9656
General Phone: (541) 997-3441

General Email: jbartlett@thesiuslawnews.com
Publication Website: https://thesiuslawnews.com/
Parent Company: News Media Grouip
Publisher Name: Jenna Bartlett
Publisher Email: jbartlett@thesiuslawnews.com
Publisher Phone: (541) 902-3524
Editor Name: Ned Hickson
Editor Email: nhickson@thesiuslawnews.com
Editor Phone: (541) 902-3520
Delivery Methods: Mail`Newsstand`Racks
Year Established: 1890
Mechanical specifications: Type page 13 1/4 x 21; E - 6 cols, 2 1/12, 1/6 between; A - 6 cols, 2 1/12, 1/6 between; C - 8 cols, 1 1/2, 1/6 between.
Published Days: Wed`Sat
Avg. Paid Circ.: 6
Avg. Free Circ.: 125
Audit Company: Sworn/Estimate/Non-Audited
Audit Date: 43626

GOLD BEACH

CURRY COUNTY REPORTER

Street Address: 29822 ELLENSBURG AVE
City: Gold Beach
State: OR
ZIP Code: 97444
General Phone: (541) 247-6643
General Email: micki@currycountyreporter.com
Publication Website: https://www.currycountyreporter.com/
Delivery Methods: Mail`Racks
Year Established: 1914
Commercial printers?: Y
Mechanical specifications: Type page 13 x 21 1/2.
Published Days: Wed
Avg. Paid Circ.: 2748
Audit Company: Sworn/Estimate/Non-Audited
Audit Date: 43626

GRANTS PASS

ROGUE RIVER PRESS

Street Address: 8991 Rogue River Hwy
City: Grants Pass
State: OR
ZIP Code: 97527
General Phone: (541) 582-1707
General Email: rrpress@rogueriverpress.com
Publication Website: http://www.rogueriverpress.com/
Parent Company: Valley Pride Publications, Llc
Publisher Name: Teresa Pearson
Publisher Email: rrpress@rogueriverpress.com
Editor Email: editor@rogueriverpress.com
Advertising Executive Email: marketing@rogueriverpress.com
Delivery Methods: Mail`Newsstand`Racks
Year Established: 1915
Commercial printers?: Y
Mechanical specifications: Type page 10 1/4 x 13 1/2; E - 4 cols, 2 1/2, 1/8 between; A - 4 cols, 2 1/2, between; C - 6 cols, 1 3/20, between.
Published Days: Wed
Avg. Paid Circ.: 2000
Audit Company: Sworn/Estimate/Non-Audited
Audit Date: 43626

GRESHAM

BOOM! BOOMERS AND BEYOND

Street Address: 1190 NE Division St
City: Gresham
State: OR
ZIP Code: 97030-5727
General Phone: (503) 665-2181
General Email: aapplegate@theoutlookonline.com
Publication Website: https://pamplinmedia.com/obits-papers/
Parent Company: Pamplin Media Group
Publisher Name: Steve Brown
Publisher Email: sbrown@theoutlookonline.com
Publisher Phone: (503) 492-5119
Editor Name: Anne Endicott
Editor Email: aendicott@theoutlookonline.com
Editor Phone: (503) 492-5118
Advertising Executive Name: Alisa Applegate
Advertising Executive Email: aapplegate@theoutlookonline.com
Advertising Executive Phone: (503) 492-5111
Published Days: Wed`Mthly
Audit Company: Sworn/Estimate/Non-Audited
Audit Date: 43626

GRESHAM

THE OUTLOOK

Street Address: 1190 NE Division St
City: Gresham
State: OR
ZIP Code: 97030-5727
General Phone: (503) 665-2181
General Email: aapplegate@theoutlookonline.com
Publication Website: https://pamplinmedia.com/gresham-outlook-home/
Parent Company: Pamplin Media Group
Publisher Name: Steve Brown
Publisher Email: sbrown@theoutlookonline.com
Publisher Phone: (503) 492-5119
Editor Name: Anne Endicott
Editor Email: aendicott@theoutlookonline.com
Editor Phone: (503) 492-5118
Advertising Executive Name: Alisa Applegate
Advertising Executive Email: aapplegate@theoutlookonline.com
Advertising Executive Phone: (503) 492-5111
Year Established: 1911
Published Days: Tues`Fri
Audit Company: Sworn/Estimate/Non-Audited
Audit Date: 43626

HEPPNER

HEPPNER GAZETTE-TIMES

Street Address: 188 W Willow St
City: Heppner
State: OR
ZIP Code: 97836-2070
General Phone: (541) 676-9228
General Email: david@rapidserve.net
Publication Website: http://www.heppner.net/heppner-gazette-times/
Parent Company: Sykes Publishing, LLC
Publisher Name: David Sykes
Publisher Email: david@rapidserve.net
Editor Name: Bobbi gordon
Editor Email: editor@rapidserve.net
Advertising Executive Email: megan@rapidserve.net
Year Established: 1883
Published Days: Wed
Avg. Paid Circ.: 2000
Audit Company: Sworn/Estimate/Non-Audited
Audit Date: 43626

HERMISTON

THE HERMISTON HERALD

Street Address: 333 E Main St
City: Hermiston
State: OR
ZIP Code: 97838-1869
General Phone: (541) 567-6457
General Email: crush@eomediagroup.com
Publication Website: https://www.hermistonherald.com/
Parent Company: EO Media Group
Publisher Name: Christopher Rush
Publisher Email: crush@eomediagroup.com
Publisher Phone: (541) 278-2669
Editor Name: Jade McDowell
Editor Email: jmcdowell@eastoregonian.com
Editor Phone: (541) 564-4536
Delivery Methods: Mail`Newsstand
Year Established: 1906
Own Printing Facility?: Y
Mechanical specifications: Type page 13 x 21 1/2; E - 6 cols, 2, 1/6 between; A - 6 cols, 2, 1/6 between; C - 7 cols, 1 1/3, 1/6 between.
Published Days: Wed
Avg. Paid Circ.: 10000
Avg. Free Circ.: 156
Audit Company: Sworn/Estimate/Non-Audited
Audit Date: 43626

JUNCTION CITY

TRI-COUNTY NEWS

Street Address: 225 W 6th Ave
City: Junction City
State: OR
ZIP Code: 97448-1605
General Phone: (541) 234-2111
General Email: ads@tctrib.com
Publication Website: https://tricountynews.mn/
Delivery Methods: Mail`Newsstand
Year Established: 1977
Published Days: Wed
Avg. Paid Circ.: 2000
Audit Company: Sworn/Estimate/Non-Audited
Audit Date: 43626

KEIZER

KEIZERTIMES

Street Address: 142 Chemawa Rd N
City: Keizer
State: OR
ZIP Code: 97303-5356
General Phone: (503) 390-1051
General Email: advertising@keizertimes.com; publisher@keizertimes.com
Publication Website: https://www.keizertimes.com/
Parent Company: Wheatland Publishing Corp.
Advertising Executive Name: Lyndon Zaitz
Delivery Methods: Mail`Racks
Year Established: 1979
Commercial printers?: Y
Mechanical specifications: 1 column = 1.667 inches 2 columns = 3.45 inches 3 columns = 5.25 inches 4 columns = 7.04 inches 5 columns = 8.83 inches 6 columns = 10.62 inches 21.25 inches tall
Published Days: Fri
Avg. Paid Circ.: 1900
Audit Company: Sworn/Estimate/Non-Audited
Audit Date: 43626
Note: Two issues each are total market coverage: Iris Festival Guide in May; Holiday Guide in November

LAKEVIEW

LAKE COUNTY EXAMINER

Street Address: 739 N 2nd St
City: Lakeview
State: OR
ZIP Code: 97630-1512
General Phone: (541) 947-3378
General Email: ads@lakecountyexam.com
Publication Website: http://www.lakecountyexam.com/
Parent Company: Adams Publishing Group
Advertising Executive Name: Tillie Flynn
Advertising Executive Email: tflynn@lakecountyexam.com
Advertising Executive Phone: (541) 947-3378
Delivery Methods: Mail
Year Established: 1880
Own Printing Facility?: Y
Mechanical specifications: Type page 10.5 x 20.25; E - 6 cols, 1 5/6, 3/16 between; A - 6 cols, 1.6458, 3/16 between; C - 6 cols, 1.6458, 3/16 between.
Published Days: Wed
Avg. Paid Circ.: 2150
Avg. Free Circ.: 4300
Audit Company: Sworn/Estimate/Non-Audited
Audit Date: 43626

LEBANON

LEBANON EXPRESS

Street Address: 90 E Grant St
City: Lebanon
State: OR
ZIP Code: 97355-3201
General Phone: (541) 258-3151
General Email: crystal.harris@lee.net
Publication Website: https://lebanon-express.com/
Parent Company: Lee Enterprises
Publisher Name: Jeff Precourt
Publisher Email: jeff.precourt@lee.net
Publisher Phone: (541) 812-6125
Editor Name: Les Gehrett
Editor Email: les.gehrett@lee.net
Editor Phone: (541) 812-6092
Advertising Executive Name: Crystal Harris
Advertising Executive Email: crystal.harris@lee.net
Advertising Executive Phone: (541) 812-6275
Year Established: 1887
Published Days: Wed
Avg. Paid Circ.: 2664
Audit Company: Sworn/Estimate/Non-Audited
Audit Date: 43626

MCKENZIE BRIDGE

MCKENZIE RIVER REFLECTIONS

Street Address: 59059 Old McKenzie Hwy
City: McKenzie Bridge
State: OR
ZIP Code: 97413-9615
General Phone: (541) 822-3358
General Email: rivref@aol.com
Publication Website: http://mckenzieriverreflectionsnewspaper.com/
Publisher Name: Ken Engelman
Editor Name: Louise Engelman
Delivery Methods: Mail`Newsstand
Year Established: 1978
Mechanical specifications: 10.25"w X 16.5"h - 5 columns
Published Days: Thur
Avg. Paid Circ.: 850
Avg. Free Circ.: 80
Audit Company: Sworn/Estimate/Non-Audited
Audit Date: 43626

MCMINNVILLE

NEWS-REGISTER

Street Address: 611 NE 3rd St
City: McMinnville
State: OR
ZIP Code: 97128-4518

Community Newspapers in the U.S.

General Phone: (503) 472-5114
General Email: rsudeith@oregonlitho.com
Publication Website: https://newsregister.com/
Parent Company: Bladine Family
Delivery Methods: Mail`Newsstand`Racks
Year Established: 1866
Own Printing Facility?: Y
Commercial printers?: Y
Mechanical specifications: Type page 11 5/8 x 21 1/2; A - 6 cols, 1 3/4, 1/3 between; C - 6 cols, 1 3/4, 1/3 between.
Published Days: Tues`Fri
Avg. Paid Circ.: 8291
Avg. Free Circ.: 300
Audit Company: Sworn/Estimate/Non-Audited
Audit Date: 43626

MILTON FREEWATER

VALLEY HERALD

Street Address: 408 N Main St
City: Milton Freewater
State: OR
ZIP Code: 97862-1724
General Phone: (541) 938-6688
General Email: valleyherald@gmail.com
Publication Website: http://www.mfvalleyherald.net/
Publisher Name: Sherrie Widmer
Publisher Email: s.widmer.valleyherald@gmail.com
Year Established: 2001
Published Days: Fri
Avg. Paid Circ.: 2500
Audit Company: Sworn/Estimate/Non-Audited
Audit Date: 43626

MYRTLE CREEK

THE DOUGLAS COUNTY MAIL

Street Address: 325 NE 1st Ave
City: Myrtle Creek
State: OR
ZIP Code: 97457-9063
General Phone: (541) 863-5233
General Email: amberj@nrtoday.com
Publication Website: https://www.nrtoday.com/marketplace/industry_manufacturing/paper_cardboard_boxes/douglas-county-mail/business_2f81c24e-3c8b-5180-b786-cdae9e3ba2a9.html
Parent Company: Myrtle Tree Press, Inc.
Publisher Name: Rachelle Carter
Publisher Email: rachellec@nrtoday.com
Publisher Phone: (541) 733-5123
Editor Name: Ian Campbell
Editor Email: ian@nrtoday.com
Editor Phone: (541) 957-4209
Advertising Executive Name: Amber Johnson
Advertising Executive Email: amberj@nrtoday.com
Advertising Executive Phone: (541) 229-4323
Year Established: 1902
Mechanical specifications: Type page 13 x 21 1/2; E - 6 cols, 2, 1/6 between; A - 6 cols, 2, 1/6 between; C - 6 cols, 2, 1/6 between.
Published Days: Thur
Avg. Paid Circ.: 2000
Avg. Free Circ.: 20
Audit Company: Sworn/Estimate/Non-Audited
Audit Date: 43626

NEWPORT

NEWS-TIMES

Street Address: 831 NE Avery St
City: Newport
State: OR
ZIP Code: 97365-3033
General Phone: (541) 265-8571
General Email: bmoore@newportnewstimes.com
Publication Website: https://newportnewstimes.com/
Parent Company: News Media Corporation
Publisher Name: Jeremy Burke
Publisher Email: jburke@newportnewstimes.com
Publisher Phone: (541) 265-8571, ext : 220
Editor Name: Steve Card
Editor Email: scard@newportnewstimes.com
Editor Phone: (541) 265-8571, ext : 224
Advertising Executive Name: Barbara Moore
Advertising Executive Email: bmoore@newportnewstimes.com
Advertising Executive Phone: (541) 265-8571, ext : 213
Year Established: 1882
Own Printing Facility?: Y
Commercial printers?: Y
Mechanical specifications: Type page 12 x 21 1/2; E - 6 cols, 1 7/8, 3/20 between; A - 6 cols, 1 7/8, 3/20 between; C - 9 cols, 1 1/4, 3/20 between.
Published Days: Wed`Fri
Avg. Paid Circ.: 10100
Avg. Free Circ.: 301
Audit Company: Sworn/Estimate/Non-Audited
Audit Date: 43626

PORTLAND

BUSINESS JOURNAL OF PORTLAND

Street Address: 851 SW 6th Ave
City: Portland
State: OR
ZIP Code: 97204
General Phone: (503) 274-8733
General Email: portland@bizjournals.com
Publication Website: https://www.bizjournals.com/portland/
Parent Company: American City Business Journals
Publisher Name: Craig Wessel
Publisher Email: cwessel@bizjournals.com
Publisher Phone: (503) 219-3401
Editor Name: Andy Giegerich
Editor Email: agiegerich@bizjournals.com
Editor Phone: (503) 219-3419
Advertising Executive Name: Krista Tappan
Advertising Executive Email: ktappan@bizjournals.com
Advertising Executive Phone: (503) 219-3430
Delivery Methods: Mail`Newsstand`Racks
Year Established: 1984
Published Days: Fri
Audit Company: Sworn/Estimate/Non-Audited
Audit Date: 43626

PORTLAND

DAILY JOURNAL OF COMMERCE

Street Address: 921 S.W. Washington St., Suite 210
City: Portland
State: OR
ZIP Code: 97205
General Phone: (503) 226-1311
General Email: bbeyer@djcoregon.com
Publication Website: https://djcoregon.com/
Parent Company: Gannett
Publisher Name: Nick Bjork
Publisher Email: nbjork@djcoregon.com
Publisher Phone: (503) 802-7214
Editor Name: Joe Yovino
Editor Email: jyovino@djcoregon.com
Editor Phone: (414) 225-1829
Advertising Executive Name: Bill Beyer
Advertising Executive Email: bbeyer@djcoregon.com
Advertising Executive Phone: (503) 802-7232
Delivery Methods: Mail
Year Established: 1872
Own Printing Facility?: N
Commercial printers?: N
Mechanical specifications: 10" x 16" full page
Published Days: Mon`Wed`Fri
Weekday Frequency: m
Audit Company: Sworn/Estimate/Non-Audited
Audit Date: 43626
Classified Software: Mk.

PORTLAND

PORTLAND MERCURY

Street Address: 115 SW Ash St
City: Portland
State: OR
ZIP Code: 97204
General Phone: (503) 294-0840
General Email: salesinfo@portlandmercury.com
Publication Website: https://www.portlandmercury.com/
Parent Company: Index Newspapers LLC
Publisher Name: Rob Thompson
Editor Name: Steven Humphrey
Advertising Executive Name: Rob Thompson
Year Established: 2001
Published Days: Thur
Avg. Paid Circ.: 8
Avg. Free Circ.: 35645
Audit Company: Sworn/Estimate/Non-Audited
Audit Date: 43626

PORTLAND

REGAL COURIER

Street Address: 6605 SE Lake Rd
City: Portland
State: OR
ZIP Code: 97222
General Phone: (503) 684-0360
General Email: circulation@commnewspapers.com
Publication Website: https://pamplinmedia.com/regal-courier-home/
Parent Company: Pamplin Media Group
Publisher Name: Christine Moore
Publisher Email: cmoore@commnewspapers.com
Publisher Phone: (503) 546-0771
Editor Name: Mark Miller
Editor Email: mmiller@pamplinmedia.com
Editor Phone: (503) 913-0450
Advertising Executive Name: Christine Moore
Advertising Executive Email: cmoore@commnewspapers.com
Advertising Executive Phone: (503) 546-0771
Delivery Methods: Mail`Newsstand`Racks
Year Established: 1977
Published Days: Thur`Mthly
Avg. Free Circ.: 4800
Audit Company: Sworn/Estimate/Non-Audited
Audit Date: 43626

PORTLAND

SUSTAINABLE LIFE

Street Address: 6605 SE Lake Rd
City: Portland
State: OR
ZIP Code: 97222
General Phone: (503) 684-0360
General Email: circulation@commnewspapers.com
Publication Website: https://pamplinmedia.com/portland-tribune-sustainable-life
Parent Company: Pamplin Media Group
Editor Name: Steve Law
Editor Email: stevelaw@portlandtribune.com
Editor Phone: (503) 546-5139
Delivery Methods: Mail`Racks
Year Established: 2006
Published Days: Thur`Mthly
Avg. Paid Circ.: 80000
Avg. Free Circ.: 97000
Audit Company: Sworn/Estimate/Non-Audited
Audit Date: 43626

PORTLAND

THE SOUTHEAST EXAMINER

Street Address: 1020 SE 7th Avenue #14313
City: Portland
State: OR
ZIP Code: 97293
General Phone: (503) 254-7550
General Email: examiner@seportland.news
Publication Website: https://www.southeastexaminer.com/
Publisher Name: Kris McDowell
Publisher Email: examiner@seportland.news
Publisher Phone: (503) 254-7550
Delivery Methods: Mail`Racks
Year Established: 1988
Published Days: Sat
Avg. Free Circ.: 25975
Audit Company: Sworn/Estimate/Non-Audited
Audit Date: 43626

SAINT HELENS

THE CHRONICLE

Street Address: 1805 Columbia Blvd
City: Saint Helens
State: OR
ZIP Code: 97051
General Phone: (503) 397-0116
General Email: chronicleads@countrymedia.net
Publication Website: https://www.thechronicleonline.com/
Parent Company: Gannett
Publisher Name: Frank Perea
Publisher Email: frankperea@countrymedia.net
Editor Name: Jeremy Ruark
Editor Email: frankperea@countrymedia.net
Advertising Executive Name: Amy Trull
Advertising Executive Email: atrull@countrymedia.net
Delivery Methods: Mail
Year Established: 1881
Mechanical specifications: Type page 11 5/8 x 21; E - 6 cols, 1 5/6, between; A - 6 cols, 1 5/6, between; C - 8 cols, 1 1/3, between.
Published Days: Wed
Avg. Paid Circ.: 3100
Avg. Free Circ.: 7349
Audit Company: Sworn/Estimate/Non-Audited
Audit Date: 43626

SALEM

APPEAL TRIBUNE

Street Address: 340 Vista Ave SE
City: Salem
State: OR
ZIP Code: 97302-4546
General Phone: (503) 399-6611
General Email: golocal@statesmanjournal.com
Publication Website: https://www.statesmanjournal.com/news/silverton/
Delivery Methods: Carrier
Year Established: 1880
Own Printing Facility?: Y
Commercial printers?: Y
Published Days: Wed
Avg. Paid Circ.: 1009
Audit Company: Sworn/Estimate/Non-Audited
Audit Date: 43626

SALEM

STAYTON MAIL

Street Address: 340 Vista Ave SE
City: Salem
State: OR
ZIP Code: 97302-4546
General Phone: (503) 399-6611
General Email: golocal@statesmanjournal.com
Publication Website: https://www.statesmanjournal.com/news/stayton/
Delivery Methods: Carrier
Year Established: 1894
Mechanical specifications: Type page 13 x 21 1/2; E - 6 cols, 2, between; A - 6 cols, 2, between; C - 9 cols, 1 5/16, between.
Published Days: Wed
Avg. Paid Circ.: 765
Audit Company: AAM
Audit Date: 43649

SWEET HOME

THE NEW ERA

Street Address: 1313 Main St
City: Sweet Home
State: OR
ZIP Code: 97386
General Phone: (541) 367-2135
General Email: news@sweethomenews.com
Publication Website: https://www.sweethomenews.com
Parent Company: ScottMiriam, Inc.
Advertising Executive Email: adrep@sweethomenews.com
Delivery Methods: Mail`Racks
Year Established: 1929
Commercial printers?: Y
Mechanical specifications: 1.95/ 1 column 4.05 / 2 column 6.16 / 3 column 8.27 / 4 column 10.38 / 5 colum maximum height of ad 16.5"
Published Days: Wed
Avg. Paid Circ.: 2000
Avg. Free Circ.: 6625
Audit Company: Sworn/Estimate/Non-Audited
Audit Date: 43626

TILLAMOOK

HEADLIGHT-HERALD

Street Address: 1908 2nd St
City: Tillamook
State: OR
ZIP Code: 97141
General Phone: (503) 842-7535
General Email: circulation@countrymedia.net
Publication Website: https://www.tillamookheadlighthearld.com/
Parent Company: Country Media Inc.
Publisher Name: Joe Warren
Publisher Email: jwarren@countrymedia.net
Editor Name: Joe Warren
Editor Email: jwarren@countrymedia.net
Advertising Executive Name: Katherine Mace
Advertising Executive Email: headlightads@countrymedia.net
Year Established: 1888
Own Printing Facility?: Y
Commercial printers?: Y
Mechanical specifications: Type page 11 5/8 x 21 1/2; E - 6 cols, 1 5/6, 1/8 between; A - 6 cols, 1 5/6, 1/8 between; C - 9 cols, 1 3/16, 1/8 between.
Published Days: Wed
Avg. Paid Circ.: 8500
Avg. Free Circ.: 86
Audit Company: Sworn/Estimate/Non-Audited
Audit Date: 43626

VALE

MALHEUR ENTERPRISE

Street Address: 293 Washington St
City: Vale
State: OR
ZIP Code: 97918
General Phone: (541) 473-3377
General Email: info@malheurenterprise.com
Publication Website: https://www.malheurenterprise.com
Publisher Name: Les Zaitz
Publisher Email: les@malheurenterprise.com
Editor Name: Les Zaitz
Editor Email: les@malheurenterprise.com
Advertising Executive Name: Rose Zueger
Advertising Executive Email: rose@malheurenterprise.com
Delivery Methods: Mail`Racks
Year Established: 1909
Own Printing Facility?: N
Commercial printers?: Y
Published Days: Wed
Avg. Paid Circ.: 1300
Avg. Free Circ.: 40
Audit Company: Sworn/Estimate/Non-Audited
Audit Date: 43626

WARRENTON

THE COLUMBIA PRESS

Street Address: 5 N HIGHWAY 101
City: Warrenton
State: OR
ZIP Code: 97146
General Phone: (503) 861-3331
General Email: ads@thecolumbiapress.com
Publication Website: https://thecolumbiapress.com/
Parent Company: Clatsop County Media Services LLC
Editor Name: Cindy Yingst
Advertising Executive Name: Peggy Yingst
Delivery Methods: Mail`Newsstand`Racks
Year Established: 1922
Own Printing Facility?: N
Commercial printers?: N
Mechanical specifications: Type page 10.3x10.5
Published Days: Fri
Avg. Paid Circ.: 850
Avg. Free Circ.: 20
Audit Company: Sworn/Estimate/Non-Audited
Audit Date: 43626

PENNSYLVANIA

ALLENTOWN

BETHLEHEM PRESS

Street Address: 1633 N 26th St
City: Allentown
State: PA
ZIP Code: 18104
General Phone: (610) 625-2121
General Email: gtaylor@tnonline.com
Publication Website: http://bethlehem.thelehighvalleypress.com/
Parent Company: Pencor Services Inc.
Editor Name: George Taylor
Editor Email: gtaylor@tnonline.com
Editor Phone: 610-625-2121, ext 3112
Delivery Methods: Mail`Newsstand`Carrier`Racks
Year Established: 2005
Published Days: Wed
Avg. Paid Circ.: 5046
Audit Company: Sworn/Estimate/Non-Audited
Audit Date: 43626
Note: Bethlehem Press is part of a group of 8 weeklies called The PRESS. Ads are sold by zone. Bethlehem Press is a zone.

ALLENTOWN

CATASAUQUA PRESS

Street Address: 1633 N 26th St
City: Allentown
State: PA
ZIP Code: 18104
General Phone: (610) 740-0944
General Email: lwojciechowski@tnonline.com
Publication Website: http://catasauqua.thelehighvalleypress.com/
Parent Company: Pencor Services Inc.
Editor Name: Linda Wojciechowski
Editor Email: lwojciechowski@tnonline.com
Editor Phone: 610-740-0944, ext 3712
Delivery Methods: Mail`Newsstand`Carrier`Racks
Year Established: 2003
Published Days: Thur
Avg. Paid Circ.: 1380
Audit Company: Sworn/Estimate/Non-Audited
Audit Date: 43626
Note: Catasauqua Press is part of a group of 8 weeklies called The PRESS. Ads run by zone. The Whitehall-Coplay Press zone includes Catasauqua Press and Northampton Press.

ALLENTOWN

NORTHAMPTON PRESS

Street Address: 1633 N 26th St
City: Allentown
State: PA
ZIP Code: 18104-1805
General Phone: (610) 740-0944
General Email: nhsocialmedia@tnonline.com
Publication Website: http://northampton.thelehighvalleypress.com/
Parent Company: Pencor Services Inc.
Delivery Methods: Mail`Newsstand`Carrier`Racks
Year Established: 1998
Own Printing Facility?: Y
Commercial printers?: Y
Published Days: Thur
Avg. Paid Circ.: 2770
Audit Company: Sworn/Estimate/Non-Audited
Audit Date: 43626
Note: Northampton Press is part of a group of 8 weeklies called The PRESS. Ads run by zone. The Whitehall-Coplay Press zone includes Northampton Press and Catasauqua Press.

ALLENTOWN

NORTHWESTERN PRESS

Street Address: 1633 N 26th St
City: Allentown
State: PA
ZIP Code: 18104-1805
General Phone: (610) 740-0944
General Email: nwsocialmedia@tnonline.com
Publication Website: http://northwestern.thelehighvalleypress.com/
Parent Company: Pencor Services Inc.
Delivery Methods: Mail`Newsstand`Carrier`Racks
Year Established: 1994
Own Printing Facility?: Y
Published Days: Thur
Avg. Paid Circ.: 2344
Audit Company: Sworn/Estimate/Non-Audited
Audit Date: 43626
Note: Northwestern Press is part of a group of newspapers called The PRESS. Ads are sold by zone. Parkland Press zone includes Northwestern Press.

ALLENTOWN

PARKLAND PRESS

Street Address: 1633 N 26th St
City: Allentown
State: PA
ZIP Code: 18104-1805
General Phone: (610) 740-0944
General Email: ppsocialmedia@tnonline.com
Publication Website: http://parkland.thelehighvalleypress.com/
Parent Company: Pencor Services Inc.
Delivery Methods: Mail`Newsstand`Carrier`Racks
Year Established: 1989
Own Printing Facility?: Y
Published Days: Thur
Avg. Paid Circ.: 4174
Audit Company: Sworn/Estimate/Non-Audited
Audit Date: 43626
Note: Parkland Press is part of a group of 8 weeklies called The PRESS. Pricing is by zone. Ads in the Parkland Press zone include the Northwestern Press.

ALLENTOWN

SALISBURY PRESS

Street Address: 1633 N 26th St
City: Allentown
State: PA
ZIP Code: 18104-1805
General Phone: (610) 740-0944
General Email: spsocialmedia@tnonline.com
Publication Website: http://salisbury.thelehighvalleypress.com/
Parent Company: Pencor Services Inc.
Delivery Methods: Mail`Newsstand`Carrier`Racks
Year Established: 2000
Published Days: Wed
Avg. Paid Circ.: 1868
Audit Company: Sworn/Estimate/Non-Audited
Audit Date: 43626
Note: Salisbury Press is part of a group of 8 weeklies called The PRESS. Ads run by zone. East Penn Press zone includes Salisbury Press

ALLENTOWN

WHITEHALL-COPLAY PRESS

Street Address: 1633 N 26th St
City: Allentown
State: PA
ZIP Code: 18104
General Phone: (610) 740-0944
General Email: klutterschmidt@tnonline.com
Publication Website: http://whitehallcoplay.thelehighvalleypress.com/
Parent Company: Pencor Services Inc.
Editor Name: Kelly Lutterschmidt
Editor Email: klutterschmidt@tnonline.com
Editor Phone: 610-740-0944 x3725
Delivery Methods: Mail`Newsstand`Carrier`Racks
Year Established: 1992
Own Printing Facility?: Y
Commercial printers?: Y
Mechanical specifications: Type page 13 x 21; E - 6 cols, 2 1/12, 1/8 between; A - 6 cols, 2 1/12, 1/8 between; C - 9 cols, 1 1/3, 1/8 between.
Published Days: Thur
Avg. Paid Circ.: 3014
Audit Company: Sworn/Estimate/Non-Audited
Audit Date: 43626
Note: Whitehall-Coplay Press is part of a group of 8 weeklies called The PRESS. Ads are sold by zones. Whitehall-Coplay Press zone includes Northampton Press and Catasauqua Press.

BEDFORD

Community Newspapers in the U.S.

BEDFORD GAZETTE

Street Address: 424 W Penn St
City: Bedford
State: PA
ZIP Code: 15522-1230
General Phone: (814) 623-1151
General Email: pprice@bedfordgazette.com
Publication Website: https://www.bedfordgazette.com/
Parent Company: Sample News Group LLC
Publisher Name: Joseph A. Beegle
Publisher Email: jbeegle@bedfordgazette.com
Editor Name: Paul Rowan
Editor Email: prowan@bedfordgazette.com
Advertising Executive Name: Kathy Arnold
Advertising Executive Email: karnold@bedfordgazette.com
Advertising Executive Phone: (814) 623-1151, ext : 220
Delivery Methods: Mail`Newsstand`Carrier`Racks
Year Established: 1805
Own Printing Facility?: Y
Commercial printers?: Y
Published Days: Fri
Avg. Paid Circ.: 200
Audit Company: Sworn/Estimate/Non-Audited
Audit Date: 43626

BENSALEM

THE MIDWEEK WIRE

Street Address: 3412 Progress Dr
City: Bensalem
State: PA
ZIP Code: 19020
General Phone: (215) 354-3148
General Email: pawirenews@bsmphilly.com
Publication Website: https://midweekwire.wordpress.com/
Parent Company: Broad Street Media
Editor Name: Jack Firneno
Editor Email: jfirneno@bsmphilly.com
Editor Phone: 215.354.3148
Delivery Methods: Mail
Year Established: 1987
Own Printing Facility?: N
Commercial printers?: N
Mechanical specifications: Type page 10 5/16 x 13; E - 6 cols, 1 9/16, between; A - 6 cols, 1 9/16, between; C - 8 cols, 1 1/4, between.
Published Days: Wed
Avg. Free Circ.: 178628
Audit Company: Sworn/Estimate/Non-Audited
Audit Date: 43626

BETHLEHEM

LEHIGH VALLEY BUSINESS

Street Address: 65 E Elizabeth Ave, Suite 400
City: Bethlehem
State: PA
ZIP Code: 18018-6515
General Phone: (610) 807-9619
General Email: johnc@lvb.com
Publication Website: https://www.lvb.com/
Parent Company: Gannett
Publisher Name: Suzanne Fischer-Huettner
Publisher Email: shuettner@bridgetowermedia.com
Editor Name: Garry Lenton
Editor Email: glenton@bridgetowermedia.com
Editor Phone: (610) 807-9619, ext : 4115
Advertising Executive Name: Anthony Falduto
Advertising Executive Email: afalduto@bridgetowermedia.com
Advertising Executive Phone: (610) 807-9619, ext : 4112
Delivery Methods: Mail
Year Established: 2012
Published Days: Mon

Avg. Paid Circ.: 2425
Avg. Free Circ.: 4244
Audit Company: Sworn/Estimate/Non-Audited
Audit Date: 43626

BRADFORD

BRADFORD JOURNAL-MINER

Street Address: 69 Garlock Holw
City: Bradford
State: PA
ZIP Code: 16701-3420
General Phone: (814) 465-3468
General Email: bradfordjournal@bradfordjournalonline.com
Publication Website: https://www.bradfordjournal.com/
Delivery Methods: Mail`Newsstand`Racks
Year Established: 1940
Mechanical specifications: Type page 10 1/4 x 16; E - 6 cols, 1 9/16, 1/6 between; A - 6 cols, 1 9/16, 1/6 between; C - 6 cols, 1 9/16, 1/6 between.
Published Days: Thur
Avg. Paid Circ.: 5500
Audit Company: Sworn/Estimate/Non-Audited
Audit Date: 43626

BROOKVILLE

JEFFERSONIAN DEMOCRAT

Street Address: 301 Main St
City: Brookville
State: PA
ZIP Code: 15825-1204
General Phone: (814) 849-5339
General Email: jeffdem@windstream.net
Publication Website: http://www.thecourierexpress.com/jeffersonian_democrat/
Parent Company: Community Media Group
Advertising Executive Email: lstephens@thecourierexpress.com
Delivery Methods: Mail`Newsstand`Carrier
Year Established: 1873
Mechanical specifications: Type page 12 x 21 1/2; E - 6 cols, 1 13/16, 3/16 between; A - 6 cols, 1 13/16, 3/16 between; C - 8 cols, 1 7/16, 1/16 between.
Published Days: Wed
Avg. Paid Circ.: 3342
Audit Company: Sworn/Estimate/Non-Audited
Audit Date: 43626

CANTON

THE CANTON INDEPENDENT SENTINEL

Street Address: 10 W Main St, PO Box 128
City: Canton
State: PA
ZIP Code: 17724-1503
General Phone: (570) 673-5151
General Email: advertise@myweeklysentinel.com
Publication Website: https://www.myweeklysentinel.com/
Parent Company: Troy Gazette-Register
Editor Name: John Shaffer
Editor Email: editor@myweeklysentinel.com
Delivery Methods: Mail`Newsstand`Carrier`Racks
Year Established: 1941
Commercial printers?: Y
Published Days: Thur
Avg. Paid Circ.: 3700
Audit Company: Sworn/Estimate/Non-Audited
Audit Date: 43626

CLARION

CLARION NEWS

Street Address: 860 S 5th Ave
City: Clarion
State: PA
ZIP Code: 16214
General Phone: (814) 226-7000
General Email: rsherman.theclarionnews@gmail.com
Publication Website: https://www.theclarionnews.com/
Editor Name: Rodney L. Sherman
Editor Email: rsherman.theclarionnews@gmail.com
Editor Phone: (814) 226-7000
Advertising Executive Name: Rob Greggs
Advertising Executive Email: robgreggs@gmail.com
Advertising Executive Phone: (814) 226-7000
Delivery Methods: Mail`Newsstand`Carrier`Racks
Year Established: 1840
Commercial printers?: Y
Mechanical specifications: Type page 13 x 21; E - 6 cols, 2 1/16, 3/8 between; A - 6 cols, 2 1/16, 3/8 between; C - 9 cols, 1 3/8, 1/8 between.
Published Days: Tues`Thur
Avg. Paid Circ.: 7000
Avg. Free Circ.: 64
Audit Company: Sworn/Estimate/Non-Audited
Audit Date: 43626

COUDERSPORT

POTTER LEADER-ENTERPRISE

Street Address: 6 W 2nd St
City: Coudersport
State: PA
ZIP Code: 16915-1131
General Phone: (814) 274-8044
General Email: leader@tiogapublishing.com
Publication Website: http://www.tiogapublishing.com/potter_leader_enterprise/
Parent Company: Community Media Group
Publisher Name: Philip Husick
Editor Name: Walter Taylor
Delivery Methods: Mail`Newsstand`Racks
Year Established: 1874
Published Days: Wed
Avg. Paid Circ.: 7000
Avg. Free Circ.: 200
Audit Company: Sworn/Estimate/Non-Audited
Audit Date: 43626

CRANBERRY TOWNSHIP

THE CRANBERRY EAGLE

Street Address: 20701 Route 19
City: Cranberry Township
State: PA
ZIP Code: 16066-6009
General Phone: (724) 776-4270
General Email: jpaschl@butlereagle.com
Publication Website: http://www.thecranberryeagle.com/
Parent Company: Eagle Publications, Inc.
Editor Name: Andie Hannon
Editor Email: ahannon@butlereagle.com
Editor Phone: (724) 282-8002
Advertising Executive Name: Jill Paschl
Advertising Executive Email: jpaschl@butlereagle.com
Advertising Executive Phone: (724) 776-4270, ext : 120
Delivery Methods: Mail`Newsstand
Year Established: 1987
Published Days: Wed`Sun
Avg. Free Circ.: 21625
Audit Company: AAM
Audit Date: 44015

DILLSBURG

DILLSBURG BANNER

Street Address: 31 S Baltimore St
City: Dillsburg
State: PA
ZIP Code: 17019
General Phone: (717) 432-3456
General Email: dillsburgbanner@dillsburgbanner.net
Publication Website: http://dillsburgbanner.net/
Publisher Name: Marie Chomicki
Publisher Email: dillsburgbanner@dillsburgbanner.net
Delivery Methods: Mail`Newsstand
Year Established: 1987
Published Days: Thur
Avg. Paid Circ.: 3900
Audit Company: Sworn/Estimate/Non-Audited
Audit Date: 43626

DREXEL HILL

RIDLEY PRESS

Street Address: 3245 Garrett Rd
City: Drexel Hill
State: PA
ZIP Code: 19026-2338
General Phone: (610) 259-4141
General Email: mail@presspublishing.org
Publication Website: http://www.press-publishing.com/
Parent Company: Press Publishing Co.
Delivery Methods: Mail`Newsstand
Year Established: 1963
Own Printing Facility?: Y
Commercial printers?: Y
Mechanical specifications: Type page 10 x 15 3/4; E - 5 cols, 1 5/6, 1/6 between; A - 5 cols, 1 5/6, 1/6 between; C - 5 cols, 1 5/6, 1/6 between.
Published Days: Thur
Avg. Free Circ.: 7000
Audit Company: Sworn/Estimate/Non-Audited
Audit Date: 43626

DREXEL HILL

UPPER DARBY PRESS

Street Address: 3245 Garrett Rd
City: Drexel Hill
State: PA
ZIP Code: 19026-2338
General Phone: (610) 259-4141
General Email: mail@presspublishing.org
Publication Website: http://www.sentinelnow.com/
Parent Company: Press Publishing Co.
Delivery Methods: Mail`Newsstand
Year Established: 1926
Own Printing Facility?: Y
Commercial printers?: Y
Mechanical specifications: Type page 10 x 15 3/4; E - 5 cols, 1 5/6, 1/6 between; A - 5 cols, 1 5/6, 1/6 between; C - 5 cols, 1 5/6, 1/6 between.
Published Days: Thur
Avg. Free Circ.: 4100
Audit Company: Sworn/Estimate/Non-Audited
Audit Date: 43626

DU BOIS

TRI-COUNTY SUNDAY

Street Address: 500 Jeffers St
City: Du Bois
State: PA
ZIP Code: 15801
General Phone: (814) 371-4200
General Email: ppatterson@thecourierexpress.com
Publication Website: http://www.

thecourierexpress.com/tri_county_sunday/
Publisher Name: Pat Patterson
Publisher Email: ppatterson@thecourierexpress.com
Publisher Phone: (814) 503-8860
Editor Name: David Sullens
Editor Email: jnorwood@thecourierexpress.com
Editor Phone: (814) 503-8863
Advertising Executive Email: classified@thecourierexpress.com
Advertising Executive Phone: (814) 503-8878
Delivery Methods: Mail`Newsstand`Carrier`Racks
Year Established: 1993
Published Days: Sun
Audit Company: Sworn/Estimate/Non-Audited
Audit Date: 43626

DUSHORE

THE SULLIVAN REVIEW

Street Address: 211 Water St
City: Dushore
State: PA
ZIP Code: 18614
General Phone: (570) 928-8403
General Email: news@thesullivanreview.com
Publication Website: http://thesullivanreview.com/
Editor Name: Derek Davis
Delivery Methods: Mail`Newsstand
Year Established: 1878
Mechanical specifications: Type page 13 x 21 1/2; E - 6 cols, 2 1/12, 1/8 between; A - 6 cols, 2 1/12, 1/8 between; C - 8 cols, 1 7/12, 1/12 between.
Published Days: Wed
Avg. Paid Circ.: 6727
Avg. Free Circ.: 63
Audit Company: Sworn/Estimate/Non-Audited
Audit Date: 43626

EASTON

LE HIGH VALLEY LIVE

Street Address: 18 Centre Sq
City: Easton
State: PA
ZIP Code: 18042
General Phone: (610) 258-7171
General Email: nfalsone@lehighvalleylive.com
Publication Website: https://www.lehighvalleylive.com/
Parent Company: Advance Local Media
Advertising Executive Name: Kurt Bresswein
Advertising Executive Email: kbresswein@lehighvalleylive.com
Advertising Executive Phone: (610) 553-3307
Delivery Methods: Carrier`Racks
Year Established: 1980
Own Printing Facility?: Y
Mechanical specifications: 9.046"x10.875" 5 columns
Published Days: Wed
Avg. Free Circ.: 21000
Audit Company: Sworn/Estimate/Non-Audited
Audit Date: 43626

EIGHTY FOUR

THE WEEKLY RECORDER

Street Address: 1056 Route 519
City: Eighty Four
State: PA
ZIP Code: 15330-2812
General Phone: (724) 884-1498
General Email: recorderads01@gmail.com
Publication Website: http://www.theweeklyrecorder.com/
Delivery Methods: Mail`Newsstand

Year Established: 1888
Commercial printers?: Y
Mechanical specifications: Type page 10 x 13; E - 4 cols, 2 5/12, 1/6 between; A - 4 cols, 2 5/12, 1/6 between; C - 4 cols, 2 5/12, 1/6 between.
Published Days: Fri
Avg. Paid Circ.: 3000
Avg. Free Circ.: 10
Audit Company: Sworn/Estimate/Non-Audited
Audit Date: 43626

EMPORIUM

CAMERON COUNTY ECHO

Street Address: 300 S Broad St
City: Emporium
State: PA
ZIP Code: 15834
General Phone: (814) 486-3711
Publication Website: https://cameroncountyecho.net/
Delivery Methods: Mail`Newsstand
Published Days: Wed
Avg. Paid Circ.: 3761
Avg. Free Circ.: 48
Audit Company: Sworn/Estimate/Non-Audited
Audit Date: 43626

EPHRATA

THE SHOPPING NEWS OF LANCASTER COUNTY

Street Address: 615 E Main St
City: Ephrata
State: PA
ZIP Code: 17522
General Phone: (717) 738-1151
General Email: snews@ptd.net
Publication Website: https://www.snews.com/
Parent Company: Hocking Printing Co., Inc.
Publisher Name: Julie A. Hocking
Delivery Methods: Carrier
Year Established: 1965
Published Days: Wed
Avg. Paid Circ.: 2
Avg. Free Circ.: 37941
Audit Company: CVC
Audit Date: 43649

EXTON

AVON GROVE SUN

Street Address: 390 Eagleview Blvd.
City: Exton
State: PA
ZIP Code: 19341
General Phone: (610) 696-1775
General Email: bdouglas@21st-centurymedia.com
Publication Website: https://www.southernchestercountyweeklies.com/site/subscribe_avon_grove_sun.html
Publisher Name: Edward S. Condra
Publisher Email: econdra@21st-centurymedia.com
Editor Name: Fran Maye
Editor Email: fmaye@21st-centurymedia.com
Advertising Executive Name: Beth Douglas
Advertising Executive Email: bdouglas@21st-centurymedia.com
Advertising Executive Phone: (610) 696-1775, ext : 3
Delivery Methods: Mail`Newsstand`Carrier`Racks
Published Days: Thur
Avg. Paid Circ.: 2428
Audit Company: Sworn/Estimate/Non-Audited
Audit Date: 43626

EXTON

KING OF PRUSSIA COURIER

Street Address: 390 Eagleview Blvd.
City: Exton
State: PA
ZIP Code: 19341
General Phone: (610) 642-4300
General Email: paadvertising@medianewsgroup.com
Publication Website: https://www.mainlinemedianews.com/kingofprussiacourier/
Publisher Name: Edward S. Condra
Publisher Email: econdra@21st-centurymedia.com
Editor Name: Cheryl Rodgers
Editor Email: crodgers@timesherald.com
Advertising Executive Name: Beth Douglas
Advertising Executive Email: bdouglas@21st-centurymedia.com
Delivery Methods: Mail`Newsstand`Carrier`Racks
Mechanical specifications: Type page 12 x 21 1/2; E - 6 cols, 2 1/16, 1/6 between; A - 6 cols, 2 1/16, 1/6 between; C - 8 cols, 1 1/2, 1/6 between.
Published Days: Sun
Avg. Paid Circ.: 21
Avg. Free Circ.: 6446
Audit Company: Sworn/Estimate/Non-Audited
Audit Date: 43626

EXTON

MERCURY SAMPLER

Street Address: 390 Eagleview Blvd
City: Exton
State: PA
ZIP Code: 19341
General Phone: (610) 970-4455
General Email: sbatten@pottsmerc.com
Publication Website: https://www.pottsmerc.com/
Publisher Name: Edward S. Condra
Publisher Email: econdra@21st-centurymedia.com
Editor Name: Tony Phyrillas
Editor Email: tphyrillas@pottsmerc.com
Advertising Executive Name: Steve Batten
Advertising Executive Email: sbatten@pottsmerc.com
Delivery Methods: Mail`Newsstand`Racks
Own Printing Facility?: Y
Mechanical specifications: Type page 13 x 22; E - 6 cols, 2 1/16, between; A - 6 cols, 2 1/16, between.
Published Days: Wed`Sat
Avg. Free Circ.: 24244
Audit Company: Sworn/Estimate/Non-Audited
Audit Date: 43626

FOREST CITY

THE FOREST CITY NEWS

Street Address: 636 Main St
City: Forest City
State: PA
ZIP Code: 18421-1430
General Phone: (570) 785-3800
General Email: jennifer@forestcitynews.com
Publication Website: http://forestcitynews.com/
Publisher Name: Patricia M. Kameen
Delivery Methods: Mail`Newsstand
Year Established: 1887
Own Printing Facility?: Y
Mechanical specifications: Type page 13 x 21; E - 7 cols, 1 3/4, 1 1/2 between; A - 7 cols, 1 3/4, between; C - 7 cols, 1 3/4, between.
Published Days: Wed
Avg. Paid Circ.: 3500
Avg. Free Circ.: 140

Audit Company: Sworn/Estimate/Non-Audited
Audit Date: 43626

FORT WASHINGTON

THE COLONIAL

Street Address: 290 Commerce Dr
City: Fort Washington
State: PA
ZIP Code: 19034-2400
General Phone: (215) 542-0200
General Email: sanderer@montgomerynews.com
Publication Website: https://www.montgomerynews.com/thecolonial/
Parent Company: MediaNews Group, Inc.
Publisher Name: Edward S. Condra
Publisher Email: econdra@21st-centurymedia.com
Editor Name: Nancy March
Editor Email: nmarch@thereporteronline.com
Advertising Executive Name: Beth Douglas
Advertising Executive Email: bdouglas@21st-centurymedia.com
Delivery Methods: Mail`Newsstand`Carrier`Racks
Own Printing Facility?: Y
Commercial printers?: Y
Mechanical specifications: Type page 12 3/4 x 21 1/2; E - 6 cols, 2, 1/6 between; A - 6 cols, 2, 1/6 between; C - 10 cols, 1 1/3, 1/6 between.
Published Days: Sun
Avg. Paid Circ.: 791
Avg. Free Circ.: 125
Audit Company: CAC
Audit Date: 43622

GREENCASTLE

THE ECHO-PILOT

Street Address: 24 E. Baltimore St.
City: Greencastle
State: PA
ZIP Code: 17225
General Phone: (717) 597-2164
General Email: dfriedman@therecordherald.com
Publication Website: https://www.echo-pilot.com/
Editor Name: Dustin Haluska
Editor Email: dhaluska@therecordherald.com
Advertising Executive Name: Dawn Friedman
Advertising Executive Email: dfriedman@therecordherald.com
Delivery Methods: Mail`Newsstand
Year Established: 1849
Published Days: Wed
Avg. Paid Circ.: 2700
Audit Company: Sworn/Estimate/Non-Audited
Audit Date: 43626

GROVE CITY

ALLIED NEWS

Street Address: 201 Erie St
City: Grove City
State: PA
ZIP Code: 16127
General Phone: (724) 458-5010
General Email: news@alliednews.com
Publication Website: https://www.alliednews.com/
Parent Company: CNHI, LLC
Publisher Name: Sharon Sorg
Publisher Email: ssorg@sharonherald.com
Editor Name: Renee Carey
Editor Email: rcarey@sharonherald.com
Advertising Executive Name: Chris Guarnieri
Advertising Executive Email: chrisg@alliednews.com
Delivery Methods:

Community Newspapers in the U.S.

III-367

Mail`Newsstand`Carrier`Racks
Year Established: 1872
Published Days: Wed`Sat
Avg. Paid Circ.: 1929
Avg. Free Circ.: 7665
Audit Company: Sworn/Estimate/Non-Audited
Audit Date: 43626

HANOVER

THE EVENING SUN

Street Address: 135 Baltimore St
City: Hanover
State: PA
ZIP Code: 17331-3142
General Phone: (717) 637-3736
General Email: news@eveningsun.com
Publication Website: https://www.eveningsun.com/
Mechanical specifications: Type page 13 x 21 1/2; E - 6 cols, 2 1/16, 1/8 between; A - 6 cols, 2 1/16, 1/8 between; C - 6 cols, 2 1/16, 1/8 between.
Published Days: Tues`Thur`Sun
Weekday Frequency: e
Saturday Frequency: e
Avg. Paid Circ.: 5730
Avg. Free Circ.: 1064
Audit Company: AAM
Audit Date: 43988
Pressroom Equipment: Lines -- 8-G/Unitubular; Folders -- 1-G/2:1; Registration System -- Duarte/Pin Register.
Mailroom Equipment: Tying Machines -- 1/MLN; Address Machine -- 2-/Am;
Editorial Equipment: Hardware -- Software ÃƒÂ£Ã†Â'Ã‚Â£ÃƒÂ¢Ã¢â€šÂ¬Ã…Â¡Ãƒâ€šÃ‚Â£ÃƒÂ£Ã¢â‚¬Å¡Ã‚Â¥ÃƒÂ£Ã†Â'Ã‚Â£ÃƒÂ¢Ã¢â€šÂ¬Ã‚Â Baseview/NewsEdit.
Production Equipment: Hardware -- Offset, V/5100, Pre Press/Panther Pro, V/5300E
Production Software: QPS/QuarkXPress.

HARRISBURG

CENTRAL PENN BUSINESS JOURNAL

Street Address: 1500 Paxton St
City: Harrisburg
State: PA
ZIP Code: 17104
General Phone: (717) 236-4300
General Email: editorial@cpbj.com
Publication Website: https://www.cpbj.com/
Parent Company: Gannett
Publisher Name: Suzanne Fischer-Huettner
Publisher Email: shuettner@bridgetowermedia.com
Editor Name: Garry Lenton
Editor Email: glenton@bridgetowermedia.com
Advertising Executive Name: Anthony Falduto
Advertising Executive Email: afalduto@bridgetowermedia.com
Advertising Executive Phone: (717) 236-4300
Delivery Methods: Mail`Carrier
Year Established: 1984
Published Days: Fri
Avg. Paid Circ.: 3340
Avg. Free Circ.: 4561
Audit Company: CVC
Audit Date: 43443

HONESDALE

CARBONDALE NEWS

Street Address: 220 8th St
City: Honesdale
State: PA
ZIP Code: 18431
General Phone: (570) 253-3055
Publication Website: http://thecarbondalenews.thrivehive.com/
Delivery Methods: Mail`Newsstand`Racks
Year Established: 1851
Own Printing Facility?: N
Commercial printers?: N
Mechanical specifications: Type page 13 x 21 1/4; E - 6 cols, 2 1/24, 5/36 between; A - 6 cols, 2 1/24, 5/36 between; C - 8 cols, 1 1/2, 11/72 between.
Published Days: Fri
Avg. Paid Circ.: 1315
Audit Company: Sworn/Estimate/Non-Audited
Audit Date: 43626

HONESDALE

THE MOSCOW VILLAGER

Street Address: 220 8th St
City: Honesdale
State: PA
ZIP Code: 18431
General Phone: (570) 253-3055
General Email: mfleece@wayneindependent.com
Publication Website: http://moscowvillager.thrivehive.com/
Delivery Methods: Mail`Racks
Year Established: 1961
Mechanical specifications: Type page 10.333" x 21"; E - 6 cols, 1.583" each; A - 4 cols, standard SAU format; C - 6 cols, 1.583" each.
Published Days: Fri
Avg. Paid Circ.: 500
Audit Company: Sworn/Estimate/Non-Audited
Audit Date: 43626

HONESDALE

THE NEWS EAGLE

Street Address: 220 8th Street
City: Honesdale
State: PA
ZIP Code: 18431
General Phone: (570) 253-3055
General Email: mfleece@tricountyindependent.com
Publication Website: http://neagle.com/
Publisher Name: Michelle R. Fleece
Publisher Email: mfleece@tricountyindependent.com
Publisher Phone: (570) 253-3055, ext : 301
Editor Name: Melissa Lee
Editor Email: mlee@tricountyindependent.com
Editor Phone: 570-253-3055 ext. 329
Advertising Executive Name: Peggy Jordan
Advertising Executive Email: pjordan@tricountyindependent.com
Advertising Executive Phone: (570) 253-6666
Delivery Methods: Mail`Newsstand`Racks
Year Established: 1950
Own Printing Facility?: Y
Commercial printers?: Y
Mechanical specifications: Type page 13 1/4 x 21; E - 6 cols, 1 3/4, 1/6 between; A - 6 cols, 1 3/4, 1/6 between; C - 8 cols, 1 1/2, 1/6 between.
Published Days: Wed`Sat
Avg. Paid Circ.: 1294
Audit Company: Sworn/Estimate/Non-Audited
Audit Date: 43626

HUGHESVILLE

THE LUMINARY

Street Address: 1025 Route 405 Hwy
City: Hughesville
State: PA
ZIP Code: 17737-9069
General Phone: (570) 584-0111
General Email: advertising@muncyluminary.com
Publication Website: http://www.muncyluminary.com/
Parent Company: Ogden Newspapers Inc.
Publisher Name: Bob Rolley
Publisher Email: brolley@lockhaven.com
Editor Name: Cindy Knier
Editor Email: ckinier@muncyluminary.com
Advertising Executive Email: advertising@muncyluminary.com
Delivery Methods: Mail`Newsstand`Racks
Mechanical specifications: Type page 13 x 21 1/2; E - 6 cols, 2 1/12, 1/6 between; A - 6 cols, 2 1/12, 1/6 between; C - 9 cols, 1 5/12, between.
Published Days: Wed
Avg. Paid Circ.: 1300
Avg. Free Circ.: 12
Audit Company: Sworn/Estimate/Non-Audited
Audit Date: 43626

HUNTINGDON

THE VALLEY LOG

Street Address: PO Box 384
City: Huntingdon
State: PA
ZIP Code: 16652
General Phone: (814) 643-4040
General Email: circ@huntingdondailynews.com
Publication Website: https://www.huntingdondailynews.com/
Parent Company: Joseph F. Biddle Publishing Co.
Advertising Executive Email: dnewsads@huntingdondailynews.com
Delivery Methods: Mail`Newsstand`Racks
Year Established: 1980
Published Days: Wed
Avg. Paid Circ.: 2716
Avg. Free Circ.: 78
Audit Company: Sworn/Estimate/Non-Audited
Audit Date: 43626

LAHASKA

BUCKS COUNTY HERALD

Street Address: PO Box 685
City: Lahaska
State: PA
ZIP Code: 18931
General Phone: (215) 794-1096
General Email: herald@buckscountyherald.com
Publication Website: http://buckscountyherald.com/
Publisher Name: Joseph G. Wingert
Publisher Email: jgwingert@buckscountyherald.com
Editor Name: Bridget Wingert
Editor Email: bridget@buckscountyherald.com
Advertising Executive Name: Marc Mucelli
Advertising Executive Email: mmucelli@buckscountyherald.com
Delivery Methods: Mail`Newsstand`Racks
Year Established: 2002
Own Printing Facility?: N
Commercial printers?: N
Published Days: Thur
Weekday Frequency: m
Avg. Free Circ.: 25000
Audit Company: Sworn/Estimate/Non-Audited
Audit Date: 43626

LEBANON

LEBANON VALLEY REVIEW

Street Address: 718 Poplar St
City: Lebanon
State: PA
ZIP Code: 17042-6755
General Phone: (717) 272-5611
General Email: eweidman@mediaonepa.com
Publication Website: https://www.ldnews.com
Advertising Executive Name: Ethan Weidman
Advertising Executive Email: eweidman@mediaonepa.com
Advertising Executive Phone: (717) 675-5034
Delivery Methods: Mail`Newsstand`Carrier
Year Established: 1872
Published Days: Sun
Avg. Free Circ.: 22300
Audit Company: Sworn/Estimate/Non-Audited
Audit Date: 43626

MARTINSBURG

MORRISONS COVE HERALD

Street Address: 113 N Market St
City: Martinsburg
State: PA
ZIP Code: 16662-1207
General Phone: (814) 793-2144
General Email: news@mcheraldonline.com
Publication Website: https://www.mcheraldonline.com/
Delivery Methods: Mail`Newsstand
Year Established: 1885
Commercial printers?: Y
Mechanical specifications: Type page 13 x 21 1/2; E - 6 cols, 2 1/12, 1/6 between; A - 6 cols, 2 1/12, 1/6 between; C - 6 cols, 2 1/12, 1/6 between.
Published Days: Thur
Avg. Paid Circ.: 7609
Avg. Free Circ.: 114
Audit Company: Sworn/Estimate/Non-Audited
Audit Date: 43626

MC CONNELLSBURG

FULTON COUNTY NEWS

Street Address: PO Box 635
City: Mc Connellsburg
State: PA
ZIP Code: 17233
General Phone: (717) 485-3811
General Email: fultoncountynews@comcast.net
Publication Website: https://www.fultoncountynews.com/
Publisher Name: Jamie Greathead
Publisher Email: fultoncountynews@comcast.net
Advertising Executive Name: Trudy Gelvin
Advertising Executive Email: tgelvin@comcast.net
Delivery Methods: Mail`Newsstand`Racks
Year Established: 1899
Own Printing Facility?: Y
Commercial printers?: Y
Mechanical specifications: Type page 10 1/2 x 21; 1 1/2 inch columns with 1/8 between; 6 columns = 10 1/4
Published Days: Thur
Avg. Paid Circ.: 4850
Avg. Free Circ.: 15
Audit Company: Sworn/Estimate/Non-Audited
Audit Date: 43626

MECHANICSBURG

THE PATRIOT-NEWS

Street Address: 2020 Technology Pkwy
City: Mechanicsburg
State: PA
ZIP Code: 17050
General Phone: (717) 255-8190
General Email: listen@pennlive.com
Publication Website: http://pennlive.com/
Parent Company: Advance Newspapers
Delivery Methods:

Mail`Newsstand`Carrier`Racks
Year Established: 1852
Own Printing Facility?: Y
Commercial printers?: N
Mechanical specifications: Type page 11 5/8 x 21; E - 6 cols, 1 13/16, 1/6 between; A - 6 cols, 1 13/16, 1/6 between; C - 10 cols, 1 1/32, 1/8 between.
Published Days: Tues`Thur`Sun
Weekday Frequency: m
Avg. Paid Circ.: 50107
Avg. Free Circ.: 7666
Audit Company: Sworn/Estimate/Non-Audited
Audit Date: 43626
Pressroom Equipment: Lines -- 7-G/ Colorline double width; 56 couples; Folders -- 1-G/Double 3:2, Allen-Bradley/1336; Pasters --Enkel/Auto 2001; Registration System -- 2001, Printe.
Mailroom Equipment: Counter Stackers -- 6-QWI/350; Inserters & Stuffers -- 2-GMA/SLS 2000 28:2; Tying Machines -- 9-Dynaric/NP2, 5-AP/2, 4-NP/3; Wrapping Singles -- 1/Dynaric; Control System -- Motion Systems; Address Machine -- 1-/Ch;
Business Equipment: 2-DEC/Alpha 2100, Dell/4100, 3-Sun/V880
Business Software: CJ, Mactive- Adv., AR, Epicor - AP GL- PO 7.2
Classified Equipment: Hardware -- SII/Tandem, 3-Sun/V880; 40-Dell/Optiplex;
Classified Software: Mactive AdBase.
Editorial Equipment: Hardware -- Sun/26-HI/NMP, 101-HI/NME, 150-Dell/Optiplex, 20-Dell/Latitude, APP/Mac G3, APP/Mac G4; Printers -- 3-HP/LaserJet 5M, 6-HP/LaserJet 6
Editorial Software: HI/XP21 Newsmaker.
Production Equipment: Hardware -- 2-Newslink Pro 28/G&J, 3-Kk/2035, 1-Kk/ Dye Sublimation XLS 8600, 1-Kk/3570; Scanners -- 2-Eskofat
Production Software: 2-AU/3850 Wide.

MERCERSBURG

MERCERSBURG JOURNAL

Street Address: 120 N Main St
City: Mercersburg
State: PA
ZIP Code: 17236-1724
General Phone: (717) 307-2430
General Email: ads@mercersburgjournal.com
Publication Website: http://mercersburgjournal.com/
Delivery Methods: Mail`Newsstand
Year Established: 1843
Published Days: Wed
Avg. Paid Circ.: 2700
Avg. Free Circ.: 5950
Audit Company: Sworn/Estimate/Non-Audited
Audit Date: 43626

MEYERSDALE

THE NEW REPUBLIC

Street Address: 145 Center St
City: Meyersdale
State: PA
ZIP Code: 15552
General Phone: (814) 634-8321
General Email: sports@tnrnewspaper.com
Publication Website: http://www.tnrnewspaper.com/
Parent Company: The New Republuc
Publisher Name: Linda Gindlesperger
Publisher Email: billing@tnrnewspaper.com
Editor Name: Ashley Boarman
Editor Email: aboarman@tnrnewspaper.com
Advertising Executive Name: George Menser
Advertising Executive Email: ads@tnrnewspaper.com
Delivery Methods: Mail`Newsstand`Racks
Year Established: 1900

Own Printing Facility?: Y
Commercial printers?: Y
Mechanical specifications: Type page 15 x 22; E - 8 cols, 1 5/8, 3/16 between; A - 8 cols, 1 5/8, 3/16 between; C - 8 cols, 1 5/8, 3/16 between.
Published Days: Thur
Avg. Paid Circ.: 5000
Audit Company: Sworn/Estimate/Non-Audited
Audit Date: 43626

MIDDLEBURG

SNYDER COUNTY TIMES

Street Address: 405 E Main St
City: Middleburg
State: PA
ZIP Code: 17842-1215
General Phone: (570) 837-6065
General Email: scuc@ptd.net
Publication Website: http://www.thesnydercountytimes.com/
Parent Company: Snyder County Times, Inc.
Publisher Name: Susan Weaver
Delivery Methods: Mail`Newsstand
Year Established: 1997
Mechanical specifications: Type page 13 x 21 1/2; E - 6 cols, 2 1/16, 1/8 between; A - 6 cols, 2 1/16, 1/8 between; C - 8 cols, 1 1/2, 1/8 between.
Published Days: Sat
Avg. Paid Circ.: 26000
Audit Company: Sworn/Estimate/Non-Audited
Audit Date: 43626

MIDDLETOWN

PRESS AND JOURNAL

Street Address: 20 S Union St
City: Middletown
State: PA
ZIP Code: 17057-1466
General Phone: (717) 944-4628
General Email: juliannasukle@pressandjournal.com
Publication Website: http://pressandjournal.com/
Publisher Name: Louise Sukle
Publisher Email: louisesukle@pressandjournal.com
Editor Name: Jason Maddux
Editor Email: jasonmaddux@pressandjournal.com
Advertising Executive Name: Julianna Sukle
Advertising Executive Email: juliannasukle@pressandjournal.com
Delivery Methods: Mail`Newsstand`Racks
Year Established: 1854
Own Printing Facility?: Y
Commercial printers?: Y
Published Days: Tues`Wed
Avg. Paid Circ.: 8000
Avg. Free Circ.: 1000
Audit Company: Sworn/Estimate/Non-Audited
Audit Date: 43626

MIFFLINBURG

MIFFLINBURG TELEGRAPH

Street Address: 358 Walnut St
City: Mifflinburg
State: PA
ZIP Code: 17844-1123
General Phone: (570) 966-2255
General Email: sales@mifflinburgtelegraph.com
Publication Website: https://mifflinburgtelegraph.com/
Parent Company: Mifflinburg Telegraph, Inc.
Delivery Methods: Mail`Newsstand
Year Established: 1862
Own Printing Facility?: Y

Commercial printers?: Y
Mechanical specifications: Type page 9 5/8 x 12 7/16; E - 5 cols, 1 3/4, 3/16 between; A - 5 cols, 1 3/4, 3/16 between.
Published Days: Thur
Avg. Paid Circ.: 500
Audit Company: Sworn/Estimate/Non-Audited
Audit Date: 43626

MIFFLINTOWN

JUNIATA SENTINEL

Street Address: 1806 WILLIAM PENN HWY
City: Mifflintown
State: PA
ZIP Code: 17059
General Phone: (717) 436-8206
General Email: csmith@juniata-sentinel.com
Publication Website: http://juniata-sentinel.com/
Parent Company: Advance Publications, Inc.
Delivery Methods: Mail`Newsstand`Racks
Year Established: 1846
Mechanical specifications: Type page 11 5/8 x 21; E - 6 cols, 1 5/6, 1/8 between; A - 6 cols, 1 5/6, 1/8 between; C - 8 cols, 1 3/8, 1/8 between.
Published Days: Wed
Avg. Paid Circ.: 3617
Avg. Free Circ.: 49
Audit Company: Sworn/Estimate/Non-Audited
Audit Date: 43626

MILFORD

PIKE COUNTY DISPATCH

Street Address: 105 W Catherine St
City: Milford
State: PA
ZIP Code: 18337-1417
General Phone: (570) 296-6641
General Email: ads@pikedispatch.com
Publication Website: http://www.pikedispatch.com/
Editor Name: Chris Jones
Editor Email: editor@pikedispatch.com
Advertising Executive Email: ads@pikedispatch.com
Delivery Methods: Mail`Newsstand
Year Established: 1826
Own Printing Facility?: N
Commercial printers?: N
Mechanical specifications: Type page 13 x 21; E - 6 cols, 1 3/4, 1/8 between; A - 6 cols, 2 1/16, 1/8 between; C - 9 cols, 1 5/16, 1/8 between.
Published Days: Thur
Avg. Paid Circ.: 6500
Avg. Free Circ.: 21174
Audit Company: Sworn/Estimate/Non-Audited
Audit Date: 43626

MILLERSBURG

UPPER DAUPHIN SENTINEL

Street Address: 510 Union St
City: Millersburg
State: PA
ZIP Code: 17061
General Phone: (717) 692-4737
General Email: dgood@sentinelnow.com
Publication Website: http://sentinelnow.com/
Editor Email: news@sentinelnow.com
Advertising Executive Name: Sue King
Advertising Executive Email: ads@sentinelnow.com
Advertising Executive Phone: (717) 692-4737, ext : 113
Delivery Methods: Mail`Newsstand
Commercial printers?: Y
Published Days: Tues
Avg. Paid Circ.: 8683

Audit Company: Sworn/Estimate/Non-Audited
Audit Date: 43626

MONTROSE

THE SUSQUEHANNA COUNTY INDEPENDENT

Street Address: 231 Church St
City: Montrose
State: PA
ZIP Code: 18801
General Phone: (570) 278-6397
General Email: indynews@independentweekender.com
Publication Website: http://www.susqcoindy.com/PS/
Editor Name: Staci Wilson
Editor Email: indynews@independentweekender.com
Advertising Executive Name: Dan Tompkins
Advertising Executive Email: dtompkins@independentweekender.com
Advertising Executive Phone: (570) 278-6397
Delivery Methods: Mail`Newsstand
Year Established: 1816
Mechanical specifications: Type page 10 3/8 x 15 1/2.
Published Days: Wed
Avg. Paid Circ.: 3700
Avg. Free Circ.: 173
Audit Company: Sworn/Estimate/Non-Audited
Audit Date: 43626

MOUNTAIN TOP

MOUNTAINTOP EAGLE

Street Address: 85 S Main St
City: Mountain Top
State: PA
ZIP Code: 18707-1962
General Phone: (570) 474-6397
General Email: news@mteagle.com
Publication Website: http://www.mteagle.com/
Publisher Name: Stephanie Grubert
Delivery Methods: Mail`Newsstand
Year Established: 1970
Published Days: Wed
Avg. Paid Circ.: 2500
Avg. Free Circ.: 3
Audit Company: Sworn/Estimate/Non-Audited
Audit Date: 43626

MUNHALL

THE VALLEY MIRROR

Street Address: 3315 Main St Ste A
City: Munhall
State: PA
ZIP Code: 15120
General Phone: (412) 462-0626
General Email: valleymirror@comcast.net
Publication Website: valleymirror.com
Parent Company: Laughing Dog Media LLC
Delivery Methods: Mail`Racks
Year Established: 1981
Commercial printers?: Y
Mechanical specifications: Type page 10 1/4 x 13 3/4; E - 5 cols, 2, between; A - 5 cols, 2, between; C - 6 cols, 1 9/16, between.
Published Days: Thur
Avg. Paid Circ.: 5000
Audit Company: Sworn/Estimate/Non-Audited
Audit Date: 43626

MURRYSVILLE

PENN FRANKLIN NEWS

Community Newspapers in the U.S.

Street Address: 4021 Old William Penn Hwy
City: Murrysville
State: PA
ZIP Code: 15668-1846
General Phone: (724) 327-3471
General Email: admanager@penn-franklin.com
Publication Website: http://www.penn-franklin.com/wp/
Parent Company: Penn Franklin Publishing Co.
Delivery Methods: Mail`Newsstand`Carrier
Year Established: 1947
Published Days: Mon`Wed
Audit Company: Sworn/Estimate/Non-Audited
Audit Date: 43626

NEW BETHLEHEM

THE LEADER-VINDICATOR

Street Address: 435 Broad St
City: New Bethlehem
State: PA
ZIP Code: 16242
General Phone: (814) 275-3131
General Email: ppatterson@thecourierexpress.com
Publication Website: http://www.thecourierexpress.com/the_leader_vindicator/
Publisher Name: Pat Patterson
Publisher Email: ppatterson@thecourierexpress.com
Publisher Phone: (814) 503-8860
Editor Name: Josh Walzak
Editor Email: jwalzak@thecourierexpress.com
Editor Phone: 814-275-3131 ext 225
Advertising Executive Name: Christine Nichols
Advertising Executive Email: cnichols@thecourierexpress.com
Advertising Executive Phone: (814) 275-3131, ext : 224
Delivery Methods: Mail`Newsstand`Carrier`Racks
Year Established: 1873
Own Printing Facility?: Y
Commercial printers?: Y
Mechanical specifications: Type page 12 x 21; E - 6 cols, 1 13/16, 1/7 between; A - 6 cols, 1 13/16, 1/7 between; C - 6 cols, 1 13/16, 1/7 between.
Published Days: Wed
Avg. Paid Circ.: 4899
Avg. Free Circ.: 46
Audit Company: Sworn/Estimate/Non-Audited
Audit Date: 43626

NEW BLOOMFIELD

PERRY COUNTY TIMES

Street Address: 51 Church St
City: New Bloomfield
State: PA
ZIP Code: 17068-9683
General Phone: (717) 582-4305
General Email: advertising@perrycountytimes.com
Publication Website: https://www.pennlive.com/perry-county-times/
Parent Company: Advance Local Media
Editor Name: Gary Thomas
Editor Email: editor@perrycountytimes.com
Advertising Executive Email: advertising@perrycountytimes.com
Delivery Methods: Mail`Newsstand
Year Established: 1886
Own Printing Facility?: N
Commercial printers?: N
Mechanical specifications: Type page 11 5/8 x 21; E - 6 cols, 1 5/6, 1/8 between; A - 6 cols, 1 5/6, 1/8 between; C - 8 cols, 1 3/8, 1/8 between.
Published Days: Thur
Weekday Frequency: m
Avg. Paid Circ.: 3590
Avg. Free Circ.: 39
Audit Company: Sworn/Estimate/Non-Audited
Audit Date: 43626

NEW WILMINGTON

THE GLOBE LEADER

Street Address: 129 W Neshannock Ave
City: New Wilmington
State: PA
ZIP Code: 16142-1183
General Phone: (724) 946-8098
General Email: globepaper@aol.com
Publication Website: http://globe-leader.com/
Delivery Methods: Mail`Newsstand`Racks
Year Established: 1880
Own Printing Facility?: N
Commercial printers?: N
Published Days: Thur
Avg. Paid Circ.: 2000
Audit Company: Sworn/Estimate/Non-Audited
Audit Date: 43626

PENNSBURG

TOWN AND COUNTRY

Street Address: 2508 Kutztown Rd
City: Pennsburg
State: PA
ZIP Code: 18073
General Phone: (215) 679-5060
General Email: townandcountry@upvnews.com
Publication Website: http://www.upvnews.com/
Publisher Name: Larry J. Roeder
Publisher Email: lroeder.ljrpublishing@gmail.com
Editor Name: Robert M. Esposito
Editor Email: townandcountry@upvnews.com
Advertising Executive Name: Miranda Koder
Advertising Executive Email: mkoder.ljrpublishing@gmail.com
Delivery Methods: Mail`Newsstand
Year Established: 1899
Mechanical specifications: 5 col. tab. 10" x 12 1/4" .167 gutter.
Published Days: Thur
Avg. Paid Circ.: 5900
Avg. Free Circ.: 100
Audit Company: Sworn/Estimate/Non-Audited
Audit Date: 43626

PHILADELPHIA

JUNIATA NEWS

Street Address: P.O. Box 15336
City: Philadelphia
State: PA
ZIP Code: 19111
General Phone: (215) 435-3909
General Email: juniatanews@comcast.net
Publication Website: https://juniatanewsphilly.com/
Delivery Methods: Mail`Newsstand
Year Established: 1934
Published Days: Tues
Audit Company: Sworn/Estimate/Non-Audited
Audit Date: 43626

PHILADELPHIA

PHILADELPHIA BUSINESS JOURNAL

Street Address: 400 Market St
City: Philadelphia
State: PA
ZIP Code: 19106-2501
General Phone: (215) 238-1450
General Email: acornelius@bizjournals.com
Publication Website: https://www.bizjournals.com/philadelphia/
Parent Company: American City Business Journals
Publisher Name: Sandy Smith
Publisher Email: ssmith@bizjournals.com
Editor Name: Ryan Sharrow
Editor Email: rsharrow@bizjournals.com
Editor Phone: (215) 238-5134
Advertising Executive Name: Alex Cornelius
Advertising Executive Email: acornelius@bizjournals.com
Advertising Executive Phone: (215) 238-5123
Delivery Methods: Mail`Newsstand`Carrier
Year Established: 1982
Published Days: Fri
Audit Company: Sworn/Estimate/Non-Audited
Audit Date: 43626

PHILADELPHIA

PHILADELPHIA FREE PRESS

Street Address: 218 S 45th St
City: Philadelphia
State: PA
ZIP Code: 19104-2919
General Phone: (215) 222-2846
General Email: cchristian@pressreview.net
Publication Website: http://philadelphiafreepress.com/
Parent Company: University City Review, Inc.
Publisher Name: Robert Christian
Editor Name: Robert Christian
Delivery Methods: Mail`Carrier`Racks
Year Established: 1988
Published Days: Wed
Avg. Free Circ.: 15000
Audit Company: Sworn/Estimate/Non-Audited
Audit Date: 43626

PHILADELPHIA

THE PHILADELPHIA PUBLIC RECORD

Street Address: 21 S. 11th Street
City: Philadelphia
State: PA
ZIP Code: 19107
General Phone: (215) 755-2000
General Email: editor@phillyrecord.com
Publication Website: http://www.phillyrecord.com/
Parent Company: City & State PA
Editor Email: editor@phillyrecord.com
Advertising Executive Name: Melissa Barrett
Advertising Executive Email: mbarrett@phillyrecord.com
Delivery Methods: Mail`Carrier`Racks
Year Established: 1999
Mechanical specifications: Full page= Width 9.12" Height: 9.87".
Published Days: Thur
Avg. Paid Circ.: 4000
Avg. Free Circ.: 25000
Audit Company: Sworn/Estimate/Non-Audited
Audit Date: 43626

PHILADELPHIA

UNIVERSITY CITY REVIEW

Street Address: 218 S 45th St
City: Philadelphia
State: PA
ZIP Code: 19104
General Phone: (215) 222-2846
General Email: cchristian@pressreview.net
Publication Website: http://ucreview.com/
Publisher Name: Robert Christian
Editor Name: Robert Christian
Delivery Methods: Mail`Newsstand
Published Days: Wed
Avg. Free Circ.: 29467
Audit Company: CVC
Audit Date: 43649

PITTSBURGH

PITTSBURGH BUSINESS TIMES

Street Address: 45 S. 23rd Street
City: Pittsburgh
State: PA
ZIP Code: 15203
General Phone: (412) 481-6397
General Email: smalyszka@bizjournals.com
Publication Website: https://www.bizjournals.com/pittsburgh/
Parent Company: American City Business Journals
Publisher Name: Evan Rosenberg
Publisher Email: erosenberg@bizjournals.com
Publisher Phone: (412) 208-3810
Editor Name: Jennifer Beahm
Editor Email: jbeahm@bizjournals.com
Editor Phone: (412) 208-3820
Advertising Executive Name: Stanley Malyszka
Advertising Executive Email: smalyszka@bizjournals.com
Delivery Methods: Mail`Newsstand`Carrier
Year Established: 1981
Published Days: Fri
Audit Company: Sworn/Estimate/Non-Audited
Audit Date: 43626

SCHUYLKILL HAVEN

SOUTH SCHUYLKILL NEWS

Street Address: 960 E Main St
City: Schuylkill Haven
State: PA
ZIP Code: 17972-9752
General Phone: (570) 385-3120
General Email: printing@southschuylkill.net
Publication Website: http://www.southschuylkill.net/
Delivery Methods: Mail`Newsstand
Year Established: 1891
Commercial printers?: Y
Mechanical specifications: Type page 9.875 x 21; E - 6 cols, 2 1/16, 1/6 between; A - 6 cols, 2 1/16, 1/6 between.
Published Days: Thur
Avg. Paid Circ.: 3140
Avg. Free Circ.: 8
Audit Company: Sworn/Estimate/Non-Audited
Audit Date: 43626

SCRANTON

NORTHEAST PENNSYLVANIA BUSINESS JOURNAL

Street Address: 149 Penn Ave
City: Scranton
State: PA
ZIP Code: 18503-2056
General Phone: (570) 207-9001
General Email: biz570@timesshamrock.com
Publication Website: https://biz570.com/
Parent Company: Times-Shamrock Communications
Advertising Executive Phone: (570) 207-9001
Delivery Methods: Mail`Carrier`Racks
Published Days: Wed`Mthly
Audit Company: Sworn/Estimate/Non-Audited
Audit Date: 43626

SHIPPENSBURG

THE VALLEY TIMES-STAR

Street Address: 22 E King St
City: Shippensburg
State: PA
ZIP Code: 17257
General Phone: (717) 532-4101
General Email: editor@shipnc.com
Publication Website: http://www.shipnc.com/valley_times_star/
Parent Company: Sample News Group LLC
Delivery Methods: Mail`Racks
Published Days: Wed
Avg. Paid Circ.: 3017
Avg. Free Circ.: 75
Audit Company: Sworn/Estimate/Non-Audited
Audit Date: 43626

SOUTH WILLIAMSPORT

WEBB WEEKLY

Street Address: 280 Kane St
City: South Williamsport
State: PA
ZIP Code: 17702
General Phone: (570) 326-9322
General Email: webbnews@webbweekly.com
Publication Website: https://webbweekly.com/
Publisher Name: James A. Webb
Publisher Email: jwebb@webbweekly.com
Publisher Phone: (570) 337-0755
Editor Name: Steph Nordstrom
Editor Email: webbnews@webbweekly.com
Editor Phone: 570-326-9322
Delivery Methods: Mail`Newsstand
Published Days: Wed
Avg. Free Circ.: 57940
Audit Company: CVC
Audit Date: 43649

SUSQUEHANNA

SUSQUEHANNA COUNTY TRANSCRIPT

Street Address: 36 Exchange St
City: Susquehanna
State: PA
ZIP Code: 18847-2610
General Phone: (570) 853-3134
General Email: susqtran@gmail.com
Publication Website: http://susquehannatranscript.com/
Delivery Methods: Mail`Newsstand
Own Printing Facility?: Y
Commercial printers?: Y
Mechanical specifications: Type page 10 1/4 x 15 1/4; A - 6 cols, 1 5/16, 1/8 between.
Published Days: Wed
Avg. Paid Circ.: 6257
Avg. Free Circ.: 251
Audit Company: Sworn/Estimate/Non-Audited
Audit Date: 43626

SWARTHMORE

SPRINGFIELD PRESS

Street Address: 639 S Chester Ave
City: Swarthmore
State: PA
ZIP Code: 19081-2315
General Phone: (610) 583-4432
General Email: rcrowe@21st-centurymedia.com
Publication Website: https://www.delconewsnetwork.com/springfieldpress/
Publisher Name: Edward S. Condra
Publisher Email: econdra@21st-centurymedia.com
Editor Name: Peg DeGrassa
Editor Email: pdegrassa@delconewsnetwork.com
Advertising Executive Name: Richard Crowe
Advertising Executive Email: rcrowe@21st-centurymedia.com
Advertising Executive Phone: (610) 915-2223
Delivery Methods: Mail`Newsstand
Year Established: 1931
Own Printing Facility?: Y
Commercial printers?: N
Mechanical specifications: Type page 10 1/4 x 16; E - 6 cols, 1 5/8, 3/16 between; A - 6 cols, 1 5/8, 3/16 between; C - 6 cols, 1 5/8, 3/16 between.
Published Days: Wed
Avg. Paid Circ.: 4700
Avg. Free Circ.: 525
Audit Company: Sworn/Estimate/Non-Audited
Audit Date: 43626

SWARTHMORE

THE SWARTHMOREAN

Street Address: 117 South Chester Road
City: Swarthmore
State: PA
ZIP Code: 19081
General Phone: (610) 543-0900
General Email: editor@swarthmorean.com
Publication Website: https://www.swarthmorean.com/
Editor Name: Chris Reynolds
Editor Email: editor@swarthmorean.com
Delivery Methods: Mail`Newsstand
Year Established: 1893
Commercial printers?: Y
Published Days: Fri
Avg. Paid Circ.: 2200
Audit Company: Sworn/Estimate/Non-Audited
Audit Date: 43626

SWARTHMORE

TOWN TALK NEWSPAPERS

Street Address: 639 S Chester Rd
City: Swarthmore
State: PA
ZIP Code: 19081
General Phone: (610) 915-2223
General Email: pdegrassa@delconewsnetwork.com
Publication Website: https://www.delconewsnetwork.com/
Publisher Name: Edward S. Condra
Publisher Email: econdra@21st-centurymedia.com
Editor Name: Peg DeGrassa
Editor Email: pdegrassa@delconewsnetwork.com
Advertising Executive Name: Richard Crowe
Advertising Executive Email: rcrowe@21st-centurymedia.com
Delivery Methods: Carrier`Racks
Year Established: 1961
Own Printing Facility?: N
Commercial printers?: N
Published Days: Wed
Avg. Free Circ.: 28500
Audit Company: Sworn/Estimate/Non-Audited
Audit Date: 43626

TITUSVILLE

FOREST PRESS

Street Address: 209 W. Spring Street
City: Titusville
State: PA
ZIP Code: 16354
General Phone: (814) 827-3634
General Email: advertising@titusvilleherald.com
Publication Website: https://www.titusvilleherald.com/eedition_myforestpress/
Publisher Name: Michael Sample
Publisher Email: msample@titusvilleherald.com
Editor Name: Lorri Drumm
Editor Email: news@titusvilleherald.com
Advertising Executive Name: Libby Jones
Advertising Executive Email: advertising@titusvilleherald.com
Delivery Methods: Mail`Newsstand`Carrier`Racks
Year Established: 1867
Mechanical specifications: Type page 10 x 13.
Published Days: Wed
Avg. Paid Circ.: 3800
Audit Company: Sworn/Estimate/Non-Audited
Audit Date: 43626

VALLEY VIEW

THE CITIZEN-STANDARD

Street Address: 104 W Main St
City: Valley View
State: PA
ZIP Code: 17983-9423
General Phone: (570) 682-9081
General Email: ads@citizenstandard.com
Publication Website: https://citizenstandard.com/
Parent Company: Times-Shamrock Communications
Publisher Name: Amy Moyer
Publisher Email: amym@standard-journal.com
Editor Name: Rebecca Zemencik
Editor Email: rebecca-z@citizenstandard.com
Delivery Methods: Mail`Newsstand`Racks
Year Established: 1929
Own Printing Facility?: Y
Commercial printers?: Y
Mechanical specifications: Type page 13 x 21 1/2; E - 6 cols, 2, between; A - 6 cols, 2, between.
Published Days: Thur
Avg. Paid Circ.: 4800
Audit Company: Sworn/Estimate/Non-Audited
Audit Date: 43626

WALNUTPORT

THE HOME NEWS

Street Address: 255 E South Best Ave.
City: Walnutport
State: PA
ZIP Code: 18088-9574
General Phone: (610) 923-0382
General Email: askus@homenewspa.com
Publication Website: https://homenewspa.com/
Parent Company: Innovative Designs & Publishing
Delivery Methods: Mail`Newsstand`Racks
Year Established: 1942
Own Printing Facility?: N
Commercial printers?: Y
Mechanical specifications: Type page 10 1/2 x 14; E - 5 cols, 2 1/20, 1/6 between; A - 5 cols, 2 1/20, 1/6 between; C - 5 cols, 2 1/20, 1/6 between.
Published Days: Thur
Avg. Paid Circ.: 3500
Audit Company: Sworn/Estimate/Non-Audited
Audit Date: 43626

WASHINGTON

THE ALMANAC

Street Address: 122 S. Main St
City: Washington
State: PA
ZIP Code: 15301
General Phone: (724) 941-7725
General Email: aanews@thealmanac.net
Publication Website: https://thealmanac.net/
Parent Company: The Observer Publishing Company
Delivery Methods: Carrier`Racks
Year Established: 1965
Mechanical specifications: Type page 13 x 21; E - 6 cols, 2, 1/8 between; A - 6 cols, 2, 1/8 between; C - 6 cols, 2, 1/8 between.
Published Days: Wed
Avg. Paid Circ.: 36
Avg. Free Circ.: 32162
Audit Company: AAM
Audit Date: 43348

WAYNESBURG

GREENE COUNTY MESSENGER

Street Address: 32 Church Street
City: Waynesburg
State: PA
ZIP Code: 15370
General Phone: (724) 852-2251
General Email: info@greenecountymessenger.com
Publication Website: https://www.heraldstandard.com/gcm/
Parent Company: Ogden Newspapers Inc.
Editor Name: Samantha Karam
Editor Email: steve@greenecountymessenger.com
Advertising Executive Name: Michael Pasqua
Advertising Executive Email: mpasqua@greenecountymessenger.com
Delivery Methods: Mail`Newsstand`Carrier`Racks
Year Established: 1990
Mechanical specifications: Type page 12 1/2 x 21 1/2; E - 6 cols, 2, 1/6 between; A - 6 cols, 2, 1/6 between; C - 6 cols, 2, 1/6 between.
Published Days: Fri
Avg. Paid Circ.: 7000
Avg. Free Circ.: 150
Audit Company: Sworn/Estimate/Non-Audited
Audit Date: 43626

WAYNESBURG

GREENESPEAK

Street Address: PO Box 1003
City: Waynesburg
State: PA
ZIP Code: 15370
General Phone: (724) 344-7980
General Email: cinswind1290@fairpoint.net
Publication Website: http://greenespeak.com/
Parent Company: GreeneSpeak Publications, LLC
Publisher Name: Cindy Bailey
Publisher Email: cinswind1290@fairpoint.net
Publisher Phone: (724) 344-7980
Editor Name: Cindy Bailey
Editor Email: cinswind1290@fairpoint.net
Editor Phone: 724-344-7980
Delivery Methods: Newsstand`Racks
Year Established: 2004
Published Days: Thur`Mthly
Avg. Free Circ.: 4000
Audit Company: Sworn/Estimate/Non-Audited
Audit Date: 43626

WEST CHESTER

THE KENNETT PAPER

Street Address: 250 N Bradford Ave
City: West Chester
State: PA
ZIP Code: 19382-1912
General Phone: (610) 430-6590
Publication Website: http://kennettpaper.

Community Newspapers in the U.S.

III-371

com/
Delivery Methods: Mail`Newsstand`Carrier`Racks
Mechanical specifications: Type page 11 x 17; E - 6 cols, 1 7/8, 1/6 between; A - 6 cols, 1 7/8, 1/6 between; C - 9 cols, 1 1/4, 1/12 between.
Published Days: Thur
Avg. Paid Circ.: 5000
Audit Company: Sworn/Estimate/Non-Audited
Audit Date: 43626

WEST GROVE

CHESTER COUNTY PRESS

Street Address: 144 S Jennersville Rd
City: West Grove
State: PA
ZIP Code: 19390
General Phone: (610) 869-5533
General Email: info@chestercounty.com
Publication Website: http://www.chestercounty.com/
Parent Company: Ad Pro Inc.
Delivery Methods: Mail`Newsstand`Carrier`Racks
Year Established: 1866
Mechanical specifications: Type page 13 x 21 1/2; E - 6 cols, 2 1/4, 1/4 between; A - 6 cols, 2 1/4, 1/4 between; C - 9 cols, 1 3/8, 1/4 between.
Published Days: Wed
Avg. Paid Circ.: 13125
Avg. Free Circ.: 1441
Audit Company: Sworn/Estimate/Non-Audited
Audit Date: 43626

WHITE HAVEN

JOURNAL OF THE POCONO PLATEAU

Street Address: 211 Main Street
City: White Haven
State: PA
ZIP Code: 18661
General Phone: (570) 215-0204
General Email: journalnews@pa.metrocast.net
Publication Website: https://pocononewspapers.com/
Delivery Methods: Mail`Racks
Year Established: 1995
Own Printing Facility?: N
Mechanical specifications: 9.98"w x 12.9"h
Published Days: Mon
Avg. Paid Circ.: 35
Avg. Free Circ.: 9465
Audit Company: CVC
Audit Date: 43081

WHITE HAVEN

THE JOURNAL-HERALD

Street Address: 211 Main St
City: White Haven
State: PA
ZIP Code: 18661
General Phone: (570) 215-0204
General Email: journalads@pa.metrocast.net
Publication Website: https://pocononewspapers.com/
Delivery Methods: Mail`Newsstand
Year Established: 1878
Own Printing Facility?: N
Commercial printers?: N
Mechanical specifications: Type page 10 x 12; E - 5 cols, 1.865", 1/8 between; A - 5 cols, 1.865", 1/8 between; C - 7 cols, 1 3/4, 1/8 between.
Published Days: Thur
Avg. Paid Circ.: 845
Avg. Free Circ.: 36
Audit Company: Sworn/Estimate/Non-Audited
Audit Date: 43626
Note: affliated with affiliated with Journal of the Pocono Plateau weekly, Journal of Penn Forest monthly, and Journal Valley Views semi-monthly

WILKES-BARRE

ABINGTON JOURNAL

Street Address: 90 E. Market St
City: Wilkes-Barre
State: PA
ZIP Code: 18701
General Phone: (570) 991-6405
General Email: bjackson@timesleader.com
Publication Website: https://www.theabingtonjournal.com/
Parent Company: Civitas Media
Delivery Methods: Mail`Newsstand`Carrier
Year Established: 1947
Mechanical specifications: Type page 13 x 21; E - 6 cols, 2, between; A - 6 cols, 2, between; C - 9 cols, 1 3/8, between.
Published Days: Wed
Avg. Paid Circ.: 494
Avg. Free Circ.: 1
Audit Company: Sworn/Estimate/Non-Audited
Audit Date: 43626

WILKES-BARRE

SUNDAY DISPATCH

Street Address: 90 E. Market St.
City: Wilkes-Barre
State: PA
ZIP Code: 18640
General Phone: (570) 829-5000
General Email: mmurray@timesleader.com
Publication Website: https://www.psdispatch.com/
Parent Company: Civitas Media
Publisher Name: Mike Murray
Publisher Email: mmurray@timesleader.com
Publisher Phone: (570) 704-3986
Editor Name: Dotty Martin
Editor Email: dmartin@timesleader.com
Editor Phone: (570) 704-3982
Advertising Executive Name: Kerry Miscavage
Advertising Executive Email: kmiscavage@timesleader.com
Advertising Executive Phone: (570) 704-3953
Delivery Methods: Mail`Newsstand`Carrier`Racks
Own Printing Facility?: Y
Commercial printers?: Y
Published Days: Sun
Avg. Paid Circ.: 2179
Audit Company: AAM
Audit Date: 44380

WILKES-BARRE

THE DALLAS POST

Street Address: 90 E. Market St.
City: Wilkes-Barre
State: PA
ZIP Code: 18640
General Phone: (570) 829-5000
General Email: mmurray@timesleader.com
Publication Website: https://www.mydallaspost.com/
Parent Company:
Publisher Name: Mike Murray
Publisher Email: mmurray@timesleader.com
Publisher Phone: (570) 704-3986
Editor Name: Dotty Martin
Editor Email: dmartin@timesleader.com
Editor Phone: (570) 704-3982
Advertising Executive Name: Kerry Miscavage
Advertising Executive Email: kmiscavage@timesleader.com
Advertising Executive Phone: (570) 704-3953
Delivery Methods: Mail`Newsstand`Carrier
Year Established: 1889
Mechanical specifications: Type page 11 5/8 x 20 3/4; E - 6 cols, 1 13/16 between; A - 6 cols, 1 13/16 between; C - 10 cols, 1 1/16 between.
Published Days: Sun
Avg. Paid Circ.: 4665
Avg. Free Circ.: 20
Audit Company: Sworn/Estimate/Non-Audited
Audit Date: 43626

WILKES-BARRE

TIMES LEADER COMMUNITY NEWSPAPERS

Street Address: 90 E. Market St.
City: Wilkes-Barre
State: PA
ZIP Code: 18701
General Phone: 570-829-7100
Publication Website: www.timesleader.com
Parent Company: Avant Publications
Publisher Name: Mike Murray
Publisher Email: mmurray@timesleader.com
Publisher Phone: 570-704-3986
Editor Name: Joe Soprano
Editor Email: jsoprano@timesleader.com
Editor Phone: 570-991-6393
Advertising Executive Name: Diane McGee
Advertising Executive Email: dmcgee@timesleader.com
Advertising Executive Phone: 570-704-3955

WYALUSING

THE ROCKET-COURIER

Street Address: 302 State St
City: Wyalusing
State: PA
ZIP Code: 18853
General Phone: (570) 746-1217
General Email: rocket@epix.net
Publication Website: https://www.rocket-courier.com/
Publisher Name: W. David Keeler
Editor Name: W. David Keeler
Advertising Executive Name: Danielle Lambert
Delivery Methods: Mail`Newsstand`Racks
Year Established: 1887
Published Days: Thur
Avg. Paid Circ.: 4000
Avg. Free Circ.: 100
Audit Company: Sworn/Estimate/Non-Audited
Audit Date: 43626

RED OAK

RED OAK EXPRESS

Street Address: 2012 Commerce Drive , P.O. Box 377
State: Red Oak
ZIP Code: IA
General Phone: 51566-0377
General Email: (712) 623-2566
Publication Website: http://www.redoakexpress.com/
Parent Company: Landmark Community Newspapers
Publisher Email: Tess Nelson
Editor Name: Tess Nelson
Delivery Methods: Mail`Newsstand`Racks
Year Established: 1868
Own Printing Facility?: Y
Commercial printers?: Y
Mechanical specifications: Type page 11 5/8 x 21 1/2; E - 6 cols, 1 5/6, between; A - 6 cols, 1 5/6, between; C - 8 cols, 8 1/6, between.
Published Days: Tues
Avg. Paid Circ.: 3500
Audit Company: Sworn/Estimate/Non-Audited
Audit Date: 43626

RHODE ISLAND

BLOCK ISLAND

THE BLOCK ISLAND TIMES

Street Address: PO Box 278
City: Block Island
State: RI
ZIP Code: 02807-0278
General Phone: (401) 466-2222
General Email: mail@blockislandtimes.com
Publication Website: blockislandtimes.com
Parent Company: Central Connecticut Communications LLC
Publisher Name: Michael E. Schroeder
Publisher Email: mschroeder@blockislandtimes.com
Editor Name: Lars Trodson
Editor Email: ltrodson@blockislandtimes.com
Advertising Executive Name: Shane Howrigan
Advertising Executive Email: showrigan@blockislandtimes.com
Delivery Methods: Mail`Newsstand
Year Established: 1970
Commercial printers?: Y
Mechanical specifications: Type page 11 x 17; E - 4 cols, 2 5/16, 1/4 between; A - 4 cols, 2 5/16, 1/4 between; C - 4 cols, 2 5/16, 1/4 between.
Published Days: Fri
Avg. Paid Circ.: 4000
Audit Company: Sworn/Estimate/Non-Audited
Audit Date: 43626

BRISTOL

EAST PROVIDENCE POST

Street Address: 1 Bradford St
City: Bristol
State: RI
ZIP Code: 02809-1906
General Phone: (401) 253-6000
General Email: info@eastbaynewspapers.com
Publication Website: https://www.eastbayri.com/east-providence/
Parent Company: East Bay Newspapers
Editor Name: Mike Rego
Editor Email: mrego@eastbaymediagroup.com
Advertising Executive Name: Scott Pickering
Advertising Executive Email: spickering@eastbaymediagroup.com
Advertising Executive Phone: (401) 424-9144
Year Established: 1837
Published Days: Thur
Avg. Free Circ.: 7981
Audit Company: CVC
Audit Date: 43988

JAMESTOWN

THE JAMESTOWN PRESS

Street Address: 45 Narragansett Ave
City: Jamestown
State: RI
ZIP Code: 02835-1150
General Phone: (401) 423-3200
General Email: tim@jamestownpress.com
Publication Website: jamestownpress.com
Parent Company: Write Way Media
Publisher Name: Robert Berczuk
Publisher Email: robert@jamestownpress.com
Editor Name: Tim Riel

Editor Email: tim@jamestownpress.com
Delivery Methods: Mail`Racks
Year Established: 1989
Own Printing Facility?: N
Commercial printers?: N
Mechanical specifications: Type page 10 1/4 x 16; E - 5 cols, 1 11/12, between; A - 5 cols, between; C - 5 cols, between.
Published Days: Thur
Avg. Free Circ.: 5076
Audit Company: CVC
Audit Date: 43652

LINCOLN

THE NORTH PROVIDENCE BREEZE

Street Address: 6 Blackstone Valley Pl
City: Lincoln
State: RI
ZIP Code: 02865-1112
General Phone: (401) 334-9555
General Email: news@valleybreeze.com
Publication Website: https://www.valleybreeze.com/northprovidence
Parent Company: Breeze Publications Inc.
Publisher Name: Tom Ward
Publisher Email: tward@valleybreeze.com
Publisher Phone: (401) 334-9555, ext : 123
Editor Name: Ethan Shorey
Editor Email: ethan@valleybreeze.com
Editor Phone: (401) 334-9555, ext : 130
Advertising Executive Name: Cindy Hersom
Advertising Executive Email: cindy@valleybreeze.com
Advertising Executive Phone: (401) 334-9555, ext : 153
Delivery Methods: Newsstand
Published Days: Wed
Avg. Paid Circ.: 2
Avg. Free Circ.: 7749
Audit Company: CVC
Audit Date: 43622

LINCOLN

THE VALLEY BREEZE - CUMBERLAND/LINCOLN

Street Address: 6 Blackstone Valley Pl
City: Lincoln
State: RI
ZIP Code: 02865-1112
General Phone: (401) 334-9555
General Email: news@valleybreeze.com
Publication Website: https://www.valleybreeze.com/town/cumberland
Parent Company: Breeze Publications Inc.
Publisher Name: Tom Ward
Publisher Email: tward@valleybreeze.com
Publisher Phone: (401) 334-9555, ext : 123
Editor Name: Ethan Shorey
Editor Email: ethan@valleybreeze.com
Editor Phone: (401) 334-9555, ext : 130
Advertising Executive Name: Tammy Austin
Advertising Executive Email: tammy@valleybreeze.com
Advertising Executive Phone: (401) 334-9555, ext : 121
Delivery Methods: Mail`Racks
Year Established: 1996
Published Days: Thur
Avg. Paid Circ.: 9
Avg. Free Circ.: 17014
Audit Company: VAC
Audit Date: 43625

LINCOLN

THE VALLEY BREEZE - PAWTUCKET

Street Address: 6 Blackstone Valley Pl
City: Lincoln
State: RI
ZIP Code: 02865-1112
General Phone: (401) 334-9555
General Email: news@valleybreeze.com
Publication Website: https://www.valleybreeze.com/town/pawtucket
Parent Company: Breeze Publications Inc.
Publisher Name: Tom Ward
Publisher Email: tward@valleybreeze.com
Publisher Phone: (401) 334-9555, ext : 123
Editor Name: Ethan Shorey
Editor Email: ethan@valleybreeze.com
Editor Phone: (401) 334-9555, ext : 130
Advertising Executive Name: Cindy Hersom
Advertising Executive Email: cindy@valleybreeze.com
Advertising Executive Phone: (401) 334-9555, ext : 153
Delivery Methods: Newsstand
Published Days: Wed
Avg. Paid Circ.: 3
Avg. Free Circ.: 9083
Audit Company: VAC
Audit Date: 43622

LINCOLN

THE VALLEY BREEZE - WOONSOCKET/NORTH SMITHFIELD

Street Address: 6 Blackstone Valley Pl
City: Lincoln
State: RI
ZIP Code: 02865-1112
General Phone: (401) 334-9555
General Email: news@valleybreeze.com
Publication Website: https://www.valleybreeze.com/town/woonsocket
Parent Company: Breeze Publications Inc.
Publisher Name: Tom Ward
Publisher Email: tward@valleybreeze.com
Publisher Phone: (401) 334-9555, ext : 123
Editor Name: Ethan Shorey
Editor Email: ethan@valleybreeze.com
Editor Phone: (401) 334-9555, ext : 130
Advertising Executive Name: Diane McCarthy
Advertising Executive Email: diane@valleybreeze.com
Advertising Executive Phone: (401) 334-9555, ext : 142
Delivery Methods: Newsstand
Published Days: Thur
Avg. Paid Circ.: 7
Avg. Free Circ.: 16421
Audit Company: VAC
Audit Date: 43622

LINCOLN

THE VALLEY BREEZE & OBSERVER

Street Address: 6 Blackstone Valley Pl
City: Lincoln
State: RI
ZIP Code: 02865-1112
General Phone: (401) 334-9555
General Email: news@valleybreeze.com
Publication Website: https://www.valleybreeze.com/specialsection
Parent Company: Breeze Publications Inc.
Publisher Name: Tom Ward
Publisher Email: tward@valleybreeze.com
Publisher Phone: (401) 334-9555, ext : 123
Editor Name: Ethan Shorey
Editor Email: ethan@valleybreeze.com
Editor Phone: (401) 334-9555, ext : 130
Delivery Methods: Newsstand
Published Days: Thur
Avg. Paid Circ.: 4
Avg. Free Circ.: 10657
Audit Company: VAC
Audit Date: 43622

MIDDLETOWN

NEWPORT MERCURY

Street Address: 272 Valley Road
City: Middletown
State: RI
ZIP Code: 2842
General Phone: (401) 849-3300
General Email: nduffy@newportri.com
Publication Website: https://www.newportri.com/newport-mercury
Editor Name: Will Richmond
Editor Email: wrichmond@newportri.com
Editor Phone: (401) 380-2351
Advertising Executive Name: Nancy Duffy
Advertising Executive Email: nduffy@newportri.com
Advertising Executive Phone: (401) 380-2386
Delivery Methods: Mail`Newsstand
Year Established: 1758
Published Days: Fri
Audit Company: Sworn/Estimate/Non-Audited
Audit Date: 43626

NEWPORT

NEWPORT NAVALOG

Street Address: 101 Malbone Rd
City: Newport
State: RI
ZIP Code: 02840-1340
General Phone: (401) 849-3300
General Email: brisson@newportri.com
Publication Website: https://www.newportri.com/
Delivery Methods: Mail`Newsstand
Year Established: 1901
Published Days: Wed
Audit Company: Sworn/Estimate/Non-Audited
Audit Date: 43626

NEWPORT

NEWPORT THIS WEEK

Street Address: 86 Broadway
City: Newport
State: RI
ZIP Code: 02840-2750
General Phone: (401) 847-7766
General Email: news@newportthisweek.net
Publication Website: newportthisweek.com
Publisher Name: Lynne Tungett
Editor Name: Rob Duca
Advertising Executive Name: Kirby Varacalli
Advertising Executive Email: kirby@newportthisweek.net
Delivery Methods: Mail`Racks
Year Established: 1973
Mechanical specifications: Type page 10 3/4 x 16 3/4.
Published Days: Thur
Avg. Free Circ.: 14762
Audit Company: CVC
Audit Date: 43988

PROVIDENCE

PROVIDENCE BUSINESS NEWS

Street Address: 400 Westminster St
City: Providence
State: RI
ZIP Code: 02903-3222
General Phone: (401) 273-2201
General Email: advertising@pbn.com
Publication Website: pbn.com
Publisher Name: Roger Bergenheim
Publisher Email: publisher@pbn.com
Publisher Phone: (401) 680-4848
Editor Name: William Hamilton
Editor Email: hamilton@pbn.com
Editor Phone: (401) 680-4826
Advertising Executive Name: Joyce Rylander
Advertising Executive Email: production@pbn.com
Advertising Executive Phone: (401) 680-4810
Delivery Methods: Mail
Year Established: 1986
Published Days: Fri
Avg. Paid Circ.: 4410
Avg. Free Circ.: 2137
Audit Company: CVC
Audit Date: 43385

WAKEFIELD

THE INDEPENDENT

Street Address: P.O. Box 232
City: Wakefield
State: RI
ZIP Code: 2880
General Phone: (401) 360-2056
General Email: newsroom@independentri.com
Publication Website: independentri.com
Parent Company: Gannett
Editor Email: editorial@independentri.com
Advertising Executive Name: Carol Palmer
Advertising Executive Email: cpalmer@independentri.com
Advertising Executive Phone: (401) 440-2610
Delivery Methods: Mail`Newsstand`Racks
Year Established: 1997
Published Days: Thur
Avg. Paid Circ.: 5907
Avg. Free Circ.: 510
Audit Company: CVC
Audit Date: 43622

SOUTH CAROLINA

ABBEVILLE

THE PRESS & BANNER

Street Address: 107 W Pickens St
City: Abbeville
State: SC
ZIP Code: 29620-2415
General Phone: (864) 366-5461
General Email: pb@bannercorp.net
Publication Website: thepressandbanner.business.site
Publisher Name: John R. West
Editor Name: Henry E. Green
Editor Email: henry@bannercorp.net
Delivery Methods: Mail`Newsstand`Racks
Year Established: 1844
Own Printing Facility?: Y
Commercial printers?: Y

BAMBERG

THE ADVERTIZER-HERALD

Street Address: 369 McGee St
City: Bamberg
State: SC
ZIP Code: 29003-1338
General Phone: (803) 245-5204
General Email: ahpublisher@bellsouth.net
Publication Website: advertizerherald.com
Parent Company: Trib Publications
Delivery Methods: Mail`Newsstand
Own Printing Facility?: Y

BARNWELL

THE PEOPLE-SENTINEL

Street Address: 10481 DUNBARTON BLVD
City: Barnwell
State: SC
ZIP Code: 29812
General Phone: (803) 259-3501
General Email: advertise@chroniclemedia.com
Publication Website: thepeoplesentinel.com
Parent Company: Gannett
Publisher Name: Laura McKenzie
Publisher Email: lmckenzie@

Community Newspapers in the U.S.

thepeoplesentinel.com
Publisher Phone: 803.259.3501
Editor Name: Jonathan Vickery
Editor Email: jvickery@thepeoplesentinel.com
Editor Phone: 803.259.3501
Delivery Methods: Mail`Newsstand`Racks
Year Established: 1852
Own Printing Facility?: Y
Commercial printers?: Y

BATESBURG LEESVILLE

THE TWIN-CITY NEWS

Street Address: 114 E Columbia Ave
City: Batesburg Leesville
State: SC
ZIP Code: 29006-2130
General Phone: (803) 532-6203
General Email: bltwincitynews@gmail.com
Publication Website: twin-citynews.com
Publisher Name: Trey Bruner
Publisher Email: brunerfinancialgroup@gmail.com
Editor Name: Tony Baughman
Editor Email: Editor@twin-citynews.com
Delivery Methods: Mail`Newsstand`Racks
Year Established: 1925
Own Printing Facility?: N
Commercial printers?: Y

BELTON

THE BELTON & HONEA PATH NEWS-CHRONICLE

Street Address: 310 City Sq
City: Belton
State: SC
ZIP Code: 29627-1435
General Phone: (864) 338-6124
General Email: elaine@bhpnc.net
Publication Website: bhpnc.com
Editor Name: Elaine Ellison-Rider
Editor Email: elaine@bhpnc.net
Delivery Methods: Mail`Newsstand`Racks
Year Established: 1894
Commercial printers?: Y

BENNETTSVILLE

HERALD-ADVOCATE

Street Address: 100 Fayetteville Ave
City: Bennettsville
State: SC
ZIP Code: 29512-4022
General Phone: (843) 479-3815
General Email: ads@heraldadvocate.com
Publication Website: heraldadvocate.com
Parent Company: Marlboro Publishing Co.
Editor Name: Daniel McNeil
Editor Email: news@heraldadvocate.com
Delivery Methods: Mail`Newsstand
Year Established: 1874

BLUFFTON

BLUFFTON TODAY

Street Address: 6 Promenade St
City: Bluffton
State: SC
ZIP Code: 29910-7051
General Phone: (843) 815-0800
General Email: Kathryn.goodman@blufftontoday.com
Publication Website: blufftontoday.com
Parent Company: Gannett
Publisher Name: Michael Traynor
Publisher Email: mtraynor@blufftontoday.com
Editor Name: Susan Catron
Editor Email: scatron@savannahnow.com
Editor Phone: 912-652-0327

Advertising Executive Name: William Ginter
Advertising Executive Email: wginter@blufftontoday.com
Advertising Executive Phone: 843-253-0662
Delivery Methods: Mail`Newsstand`Carrier
Year Established: 2005

CAMDEN

CHRONICLE-INDEPENDENT

Street Address: 909 W Dekalb St
City: Camden
State: SC
ZIP Code: 29020-4259
General Phone: (803) 432-6157
General Email: bgreenway@ci-camden.com
Publication Website: chronicle-independent.com
Parent Company: Morris Multimedia, Inc.
Publisher Name: Mike Mischner
Publisher Email: mmischner@chronicle-independent.com
Publisher Phone: (803) 432-6157 x-128
Editor Name: Martin L Cahn
Editor Email: mcahn@chronicle-independent.com
Editor Phone: (803) 432-6157 x-115
Delivery Methods: Mail`Racks
Year Established: 1889
Commercial printers?: Y

CAMDEN

WEST WATEREE CHRONICLE

Street Address: 909 W Dekalb St
City: Camden
State: SC
ZIP Code: 29020-4259
General Phone: (803) 432-6157
General Email: bgreenway@ci-camden.com
Publication Website: chronicle-independent.com
Publisher Name: Mike Mischner
Publisher Email: mmischner@chronicle-independent.com
Publisher Phone: (803) 432-6157 x-128
Editor Name: Martin L Cahn
Editor Email: mcahn@chronicle-independent.com
Editor Phone: (803) 432-6157 x-115
Delivery Methods: Mail`Racks
Year Established: 1889

CHARLESTON

THE CHARLESTON CHRONICLE

Street Address: 1111 King St
City: Charleston
State: SC
ZIP Code: 29403-3761
General Phone: (843) 723-2785
General Email: sales@charlestonchronicle.net
Publication Website: charlestonchronicle.net
Editor Name: Jim French
Editor Email: news@charlestonchronicle.net
Delivery Methods: Mail`Newsstand`Racks
Year Established: 1971

CHESTER

CHESTER NEWS & REPORTER

Street Address: 104 York St
City: Chester
State: SC
ZIP Code: 29706-1427
General Phone: (803) 385-3177
General Email: addepartment@onlinechester.com
Publication Website: onlinechester.com
Editor Name: Travis Jenkins
Delivery Methods: Mail`Newsstand

Year Established: 1869

CLINTON

THE CLINTON CHRONICLE

Street Address: 513 N Broad St
City: Clinton
State: SC
ZIP Code: 29325-1705
General Phone: (864)833-1900
General Email: sales1@clintonchronicle.net
Publication Website: clintonchronicle.com
Publisher Name: Brian Whitmore
Publisher Email: publisher@clintonchronicle.net
Editor Name: Vic MacDonald
Editor Email: news@clintonchronicle.net
Advertising Executive Name: Debbie Ray
Advertising Executive Email: sales2@clintonchronicle.net
Delivery Methods: Mail`Racks
Year Established: 1900
Own Printing Facility?: Y
Commercial printers?: N

COLUMBIA

THE COLUMBIA STAR

Street Address: 723 Queen St
City: Columbia
State: SC
ZIP Code: 29205-1723
General Phone: (803) 771-0219
General Email: Gail@TheColumbiaStar.com
Publication Website: thecolumbiastar.com
Parent Company: Star Reporter Corporation
Publisher Name: Mike Maddock
Publisher Email: mikem@thecolumbiastar.com
Editor Name: Pam Staples
Editor Email: pams@thecolumbiastar.com
Advertising Executive Name: Gail Trebuchon
Advertising Executive Email: gailt@thecolumbiastar.com
Delivery Methods: Racks
Year Established: 1963
Commercial printers?: Y

CONWAY

THE HORRY INDEPENDENT

Street Address: 2510 Main St
City: Conway
State: SC
ZIP Code: 29526-3365
General Phone: (843) 248-6671
General Email: shari.harms@myhorrynews.com
Publication Website: myhorrynews.com
Parent Company: Waccamaw Publishers Inc.
Editor Name: Kathy Ropp
Editor Email: kathy.ropp@myhorrynews.com
Editor Phone: 843-488-7241
Delivery Methods: Mail`Newsstand`Racks
Year Established: 1980

CONWAY

THE LORIS SCENE

Street Address: 2510 Main St
City: Conway
State: SC
ZIP Code: 29526-3365
General Phone: (843) 248-6671
General Email: shari.harms@myhorrynews.com
Publication Website: myhorrynews.com
Parent Company: Waccamaw Publishers Inc.
Editor Name: Annette Norris
Editor Email: annette.norris@myhorrynews.com
Editor Phone: 843-488-7250

Delivery Methods: Mail`Newsstand`Racks
Year Established: 190
Own Printing Facility?: Y
Commercial printers?: N

DARLINGTON

THE NEWS & PRESS

Street Address: 1175 S MAIN ST
City: Darlington
State: SC
ZIP Code: 29532
General Phone: (843)393-3811
General Email: ads@newsandpress.net
Publication Website: www.newsandpress.net
Editor Name: Bobby Bryant
Editor Email: editor@newsandpress.net
Advertising Executive Name: Stephan Drew
Advertising Executive Email: sales@newsandpress.net
Delivery Methods: Mail`Newsstand`Racks
Year Established: 1874
Own Printing Facility?: Y
Commercial printers?: Y

DILLON

THE DILLON HERALD

Street Address: 505 Highway 301 N
City: Dillon
State: SC
ZIP Code: 29536-2957
General Phone: (843)774-3311
General Email: jd@thedillonherald.com
Publication Website: thedillonherald.com
Editor Name: Betsy Finklea
Editor Email: bf@thedillonherald.com
Advertising Executive Name: Johnie Daniels
Advertising Executive Email: jd@thedillonherald.com
Delivery Methods: Mail`Newsstand`Carrier`Racks
Year Established: 1894

EASLEY

THE EASLEY PROGRESS

Street Address: 201 W Main St
City: Easley
State: SC
ZIP Code: 29640-2040
General Phone: (864) 855-0355
General Email: cwyatt@civitasmedia.com
Publication Website: theeasleyprogress.com
Parent Company: Champion Media
Publisher Name: Denny Koenders
Publisher Phone: 803-768-3117
Editor Name: Kasie Strickland
Editor Email: kstrickland@championcarolinas.com
Editor Phone: 864-855-0355
Delivery Methods: Mail`Newsstand
Year Established: 1902
Own Printing Facility?: Y
Commercial printers?: Y

EASLEY

THE PICKENS SENTINEL

Street Address: 714-D S PENDLETON ST
City: Easley
State: SC
ZIP Code: 29640-3526
General Phone: (864) 855-0355
General Email: cwyatt@civitasmedia.com
Publication Website: pickenssentinel.com
Parent Company: Champion Media
Publisher Name: Denny Koenders
Publisher Phone: 803-768-3117
Editor Name: Kasie Strickland
Editor Email: kstrickland@championcarolinas.com

Editor Phone: 864-855-0355
Delivery Methods: Mail`Newsstand`Racks
Year Established: 1871
Commercial printers?: Y

EDGEFIELD

THE EDGEFIELD ADVERTISER

Street Address: 117 Courthouse Sq
City: Edgefield
State: SC
ZIP Code: 29824-1319
General Phone: (803) 637-3540
General Email: sharon@edgefieldadvertiser.com
Publication Website: edgefieldadvertiser.com
Editor Name: Suzanne Gile Mims Derrick
Editor Email: suzanne@edgefieldadvertiser.com
Advertising Executive Name: Sharon Nunamaker
Advertising Executive Email: sharon@edgefieldadvertiser.com
Delivery Methods: Mail`Newsstand`Racks
Year Established: 1836
Own Printing Facility?: Y
Commercial printers?: Y

FLORENCE

LAKE CITY NEWS & POST

Street Address: 310 S Dargan St
City: Florence
State: SC
ZIP Code: 29506-2537
General Phone: (843) 317-6397
General Email: news@scnow.com
Publication Website: scnow.com/newsandpost
Publisher Name: Bailey Dabney
Publisher Email: bdabney@florencenews.com
Publisher Phone: 843-317-7200
Editor Name: Don Kausler Jr.
Editor Email: dkausler@florencenews.com
Editor Phone: 843-317-7250
Advertising Executive Name: Jane Comfort
Advertising Executive Email: jcomfort@florencenews.com
Advertising Executive Phone: 843-317-7232

FLORENCE

MARION STAR & MULLINS ENTERPRISE

Street Address: 310 S Dargan St
City: Florence
State: SC
ZIP Code: 29506-2537
General Phone: (843) 317-6397
General Email: starandenterprise@scnow.com
Publication Website: scnow.com/starandenterprise
Editor Name: Naeem McFadden
Editor Email: nmcfadden@florencenews.com
Editor Phone: 843-423-2050
"Advertising Executive Name: Kathy Sawyer "
Advertising Executive Email: ksawyer@florencenews.com
Advertising Executive Phone: 843-423-2050
Delivery Methods: Mail`Newsstand`Racks
Year Established: 1846
Own Printing Facility?: Y
Commercial printers?: Y

FLORENCE

PEE DEE WEEKLY

Street Address: 310 S Dargan St
City: Florence
State: SC
ZIP Code: 29506-2537
General Phone: (843) 558-3323
General Email: jcomfort@florencenews.com
Publication Website: scnow.com
Publisher Name: Bailey Dabney
Publisher Email: bdabney@florencenews.com
Publisher Phone: 843-317-7200
Editor Name: Don Kausler Jr.
Editor Email: dkausler@florencenews.com
Editor Phone: 843-317-7250
Advertising Executive Name: Jane Comfort
Advertising Executive Email: jcomfort@florencenews.com
Advertising Executive Phone: 843-317-7232
Delivery Methods: Mail`Newsstand
Year Established: 1973
Own Printing Facility?: Y

GAFFNEY

THE GAFFNEY LEDGER

Street Address: 1604 W Floyd Baker Blvd
City: Gaffney
State: SC
ZIP Code: 29341-1206
General Phone: (864) 489-1131
General Email: greg@gaffneyledger.com
Publication Website: gaffneyledger.com
Publisher Name: Cody Sossamon
Publisher Email: cody@gaffneyledger.com
Editor Name: Klonie Jordan
Editor Email: editor@gaffneyledger.com
Advertising Executive Name: Andy Clary
Advertising Executive Email: andy@gaffneyledger.com
Delivery Methods: Mail`Newsstand`Carrier`Racks
Year Established: 1894
Own Printing Facility?: Y
Commercial printers?: Y

GREENVILLE

TRIBUNE-TIMES

Street Address: 305 S Main St
City: Greenville
State: SC
ZIP Code: 29601-2605
General Phone: (864) 298-4100
General Email: dfoster3@gannett.com
Publication Website: greenvilleonline.com
Editor Name: Katrice Hardy
Editor Email: khardy1@greenvillenews.com
Editor Phone: 864-298-4165
Advertising Executive Name: David Foster
Advertising Executive Email: dfoster3@gannett.com
Advertising Executive Phone: 864-298-4342
Delivery Methods: Mail`Newsstand
Commercial printers?: Y

GREER

THE GREER CITIZEN

Street Address: 317 Trade St
City: Greer
State: SC
ZIP Code: 29651-3431
General Phone: (864) 877-2076
General Email: sblackwell@greercitizen.com
Publication Website: greercitizen.com
Publisher Name: BLACKWELL, STEVE
Publisher Email: sblackwell@greercitizen.com
Publisher Phone: 864-877-2076 ext. 100
Editor Name: CANNADA, BILLY
Editor Email: billy@greercitizen.com
Editor Phone: 864-877-2076 ext. 103
Advertising Executive Name: MOSS, SHAUN
Advertising Executive Email: shaun@greercitizen.com
Advertising Executive Phone: 864-877-2076 ext. 112
Delivery Methods: Mail`Newsstand
Year Established: 1918
Own Printing Facility?: Y
Commercial printers?: Y

HAMPTON

HAMPTON COUNTY GUARDIAN

Street Address: 306 Lee Ave
City: Hampton
State: SC
ZIP Code: 29924-3442
General Phone: (803) 943-4645
General Email: ads@hamptoncountyguardian.com
Publication Website: hamptoncountyguardian.com
Parent Company: Gannett
Editor Name: Michael DeWitt Jr
Editor Email: michael.dewitt@hamptoncountyguardian.com
Editor Phone: (803) 943-4645
Advertising Executive Name: Catina Gadson
Advertising Executive Email: cgadson@jaspercountysun.com
Advertising Executive Phone: (803) 943-4645
Delivery Methods: Mail`Newsstand
Year Established: 1879
Commercial printers?: Y

HARTSVILLE

THE HARTSVILLE MESSENGER

Street Address: 212 Swift Creek Rd
City: Hartsville
State: SC
ZIP Code: 29550-4383
General Phone: (843) 332-6545
General Email: dwiggins@hartsvillemessenger.com
Publication Website: scnow.com
Publisher Name: Bailey Dabney
Publisher Email: bdabney@florencenews.com
Publisher Phone: 843-317-7200
Editor Name: Don Kausler Jr.
Editor Email: dkausler@florencenews.com
Editor Phone: 843-317-7250
Advertising Executive Name: Jane Comfort
Advertising Executive Email: jcomfort@florencenews.com
Advertising Executive Phone: 843-317-7232
Delivery Methods: Mail`Carrier`Racks
Year Established: 1893
Own Printing Facility?: Y

IRMO

THE LAKE MURRAY NEWS

Street Address: PO Box 175
City: Irmo
State: SC
ZIP Code: 29063-0175
General Phone: (803) 772-5584
General Email: lakemurraynews@aol.com
Publication Website: thelakemurraynews.net
Editor Name: John Griggs
Editor Email: john@thelakemurraynews.net
Delivery Methods: Mail`Newsstand
Commercial printers?: Y

LAKE CITY

NEWS & POST

Street Address: 107 N Acline St
City: Lake City
State: SC
ZIP Code: 29560-2129
General Phone: (843) 394-3571
General Email: newsandpost@florencenews.com
Publication Website: scnow.com
Publisher Name: Bailey Dabney
Publisher Email: bdabney@florencenews.com
Publisher Phone: 843-317-7200
Editor Name: Don Kausler Jr.
Editor Email: dkausler@florencenews.com
Editor Phone: 843-317-7250
Advertising Executive Name: Jane Comfort
Advertising Executive Email: jcomfort@florencenews.com
Advertising Executive Phone: 843-317-7232
Delivery Methods: Mail`Carrier`Racks
Own Printing Facility?: Y

LANCASTER

LANCASTER NEWS

Street Address: 701 N White St
City: Lancaster
State: SC
ZIP Code: 29720-2174
General Phone: (803) 283-1133
General Email: news@thelancasternews.com
Publication Website: thelancasternews.com
Parent Company: Landmark Community Newspapers
Editor Name: Brian Melton
Delivery Methods: Mail`Newsstand`Racks
Year Established: 1852
Own Printing Facility?: Y
Commercial printers?: Y

LAURENS

LAURENS COUNTY ADVERTISER

Street Address: 226 W Laurens St
City: Laurens
State: SC
ZIP Code: 29360-2960
General Phone: (864) 984-2586
General Email: advertising@lcadvertiser.com
Publication Website: laurenscountyadvertiser.net
Editor Name: John Clayton
Editor Email: news@lcadvertiser.com
Delivery Methods: Mail`Newsstand
Own Printing Facility?: Y
Commercial printers?: Y

LEXINGTON

LEXINGTON COUNTY CHRONICLE & THE DISPATCH-NEWS

Street Address: 131 Swartz Rd
City: Lexington
State: SC
ZIP Code: 29072-3623
General Phone: (803) 359-7633
General Email: lexingtonchronicle@gmail.com
Publication Website: lexingtonchronicle.com
Parent Company: Lexington Publishing Co, Inc.
Publisher Name: MacLeod Bellune
Publisher Email: lexingtonchronicle@gmail.com
Publisher Phone: 803-359-5626
Editor Name: Jerry Bellune
Editor Email: jerrybellune@yahoo.com
Editor Phone: 803-331-6695
Advertising Executive Name: Linda Sauls
Advertising Executive Email: lindasauls11@yahoo.com
Advertising Executive Phone: 803-359-2203
Delivery Methods: Mail`Newsstand`Racks
Year Established: 1870

MANNING

THE MANNING TIMES

Street Address: 230 E Boyce St

Community Newspapers in the U.S.

City: Manning
State: SC
ZIP Code: 29102-3441
General Phone: (803) 435-8422
General Email: manningsctimes@gmail.com
Publication Website: manninglive.com
Editor Name: Jake McElveen
Delivery Methods: Mail`Newsstand`Racks
Year Established: 1882

MC CORMICK

MCCORMICK MESSENGER

Street Address: 120 S Main St
City: Mc Cormick
State: SC
ZIP Code: 29835-8345
General Phone: (864) 852-3311
General Email: mccmess@wctel.net
Publication Website: themccormickmessenger.com
Editor Name: Vicki Dorn
Advertising Executive Name: Ashley Creswell
Delivery Methods: Mail`Newsstand
Year Established: 1902

MYRTLE BEACH

CAROLINA FOREST CHRONICLE

Street Address: 4761 Highway 501
City: Myrtle Beach
State: SC
ZIP Code: 29579-9457
General Phone: (843) 236-4810
General Email: shari.harms@myhorrynews.com
Publication Website: myhorrynews.com
Parent Company: Waccamaw Publishers Inc.
Editor Name: Charles Perry
Editor Email: charles.perry@myhorrynews.com
Editor Phone: 843-488-7259
Delivery Methods: Mail`Newsstand`Racks
Year Established: 2007
Own Printing Facility?: Y
Commercial printers?: N

MYRTLE BEACH

MYRTLE BEACH HERALD

Street Address: 4761 Highway 501
City: Myrtle Beach
State: SC
ZIP Code: 29579-9457
General Phone: (843) 236-4810
General Email: shari.harms@myhorrynews.com
Publication Website: myhorrynews.com
Parent Company: Waccamaw Publishers Inc.
Editor Name: Janet Morgan
Editor Email: janet.morgan@myhorrynews.com
Editor Phone: 843-488-7258
Delivery Methods: Mail`Newsstand`Racks
Year Established: 2009
Own Printing Facility?: Y
Commercial printers?: N

NEWBERRY

THE NEWBERRY OBSERVER

Street Address: 1716 Main St
City: Newberry
State: SC
ZIP Code: 29108-3548
General Phone: (803) 276-0625
General Email: news@newberryobserver.com
Publication Website: newberryobserver.com
Parent Company: Champion Media
Publisher Name: Denny Koenders
Publisher Email: dkoenders@championcarolinas.com
Publisher Phone: 803-768-3117
Editor Name: Andrew Wigger
Editor Email: awigger@championcarolinas.com
Editor Phone: 803-768-3122
Delivery Methods: Mail`Newsstand
Year Established: 1883
Own Printing Facility?: Y
Commercial printers?: Y

NORTH MYRTLE BEACH

NORTH MYRTLE BEACH TIMES

Street Address: 203 Highay 17 North
City: North Myrtle Beach
State: SC
ZIP Code: 29582
General Phone: (843) 249-3525
General Email: nmbtimes@sc.rr.com
Publication Website: nmbtimes.com
Editor Name: Polly Lowman
Delivery Methods: Mail`Newsstand
Year Established: 1971

PAGELAND

PAGELAND PROGRESSIVE-JOURNAL

Street Address: P.O. Box 218
City: Pageland
State: SC
ZIP Code: 29728-0218
General Phone: (843) 672-2358
General Email: dstokes@thelancasternews.com
Publication Website: pagelandprogressive.com
Parent Company: Landmark Community Newspapers
Editor Name: Gary Phillips
Editor Email: editor@pagelandprogressive.com
Delivery Methods: Mail`Newsstand`Racks

PAWLEYS ISLAND

COASTAL OBSERVER

Street Address: 97 Commerce Dr
City: Pawleys Island
State: SC
ZIP Code: 29585-6011
General Phone: (843) 237-8438
General Email: coastalobserverads@gmail.com
Publication Website: coastalobserver.com
Editor Name: Charles Swenson
Editor Email: editor@coastalobserver.com
Delivery Methods: Mail`Newsstand
Year Established: 1982
Commercial printers?: Y

RIDGELAND

JASPER COUNTY SUN

Street Address: 138 S RAILROAD AVE
City: Ridgeland
State: SC
ZIP Code: 29936
General Phone: (843) 726-6161
General Email: news@jaspercountysun.com
Publication Website: jaspercountysun.com
Publisher Name: Michael Traynor
Publisher Email: mtraynor@blufftontoday.com
Editor Name: Susan Catron
Editor Email: scatron@savannahnow.com
Editor Phone: 912-652-0327
Advertising Executive Name: William Ginter
Advertising Executive Email: wginter@blufftontoday.com
Advertising Executive Phone: 843-253-0662
Delivery Methods: Mail`Racks
Commercial printers?: Y

ROCK HILL

FORT MILL TIMES

Street Address: 132 W Main St
City: Rock Hill
State: SC
ZIP Code: 29730-4430
General Phone: (803) 326-4315
General Email: gkerosetz@heraldonline.com
Publication Website: fortmilltimes.com
Editor Name: Cliff Harrington
Editor Email: charrington@heraldonline.com
Editor Phone: (803) 326-4303
Advertising Executive Name: Morgenstern, Dan
Advertising Executive Email: dmorgenstern@mcclatchy.com
Advertising Executive Phone: 704-358-5333
Delivery Methods: Mail`Newsstand`Carrier`Racks
Year Established: 1892
Own Printing Facility?: Y

SAINT GEORGE

THE EAGLE-RECORD

Street Address: 5549 Memorial Blvd
City: Saint George
State: SC
ZIP Code: 29477-2473
General Phone: (843) 563-3121
General Email: eaglerecord@lowcountry.com
Publication Website: theeaglerecord.com
Editor Name: Andrew Gentry
Advertising Executive Name: Victoria M. Owens
Delivery Methods: Mail`Newsstand
Year Established: 1899

SAINT MATTHEWS

THE CALHOUN TIMES

Street Address: 1632 Bridge St
City: Saint Matthews
State: SC
ZIP Code: 29135-1373
General Phone: (803) 874-3137
General Email: thecalhountimes@windstream.net
Publication Website: https://www.northwestgeorgianews.com/calhoun_times/
Parent Company: Rome News-Tribune
Editor Name: Edwin Morris, Jr.
Delivery Methods: Mail`Newsstand
Year Established: 1929
Commercial printers?: Y

SALUDA

STANDARD SENTINEL

Street Address: 302 N Main St
City: Saluda
State: SC
ZIP Code: 29138-1353
General Phone: (864) 445-2527
General Email: sentinel@saludasc.com
Publication Website: saludastandard-sentinel.com
Editor Name: Ralph Shealy
Delivery Methods: Mail`Newsstand

WALHALLA

KEOWEE COURIER

Street Address: 118 S College St
City: Walhalla
State: SC
ZIP Code: 29691-2258
General Phone: (864) 638-5856
General Email: keoweecourier@bellsouth.net
Publication Website: laserbuddy.com/news/kc.htm
Parent Company: Trib Publications
Editor Name: Candi Phillips
Delivery Methods: Mail`Newsstand
Year Established: 1849
Commercial printers?: Y

WALTERBORO

THE PRESS AND STANDARD

Street Address: 1025 Bells Hwy
City: Walterboro
State: SC
ZIP Code: 29488-2507
General Phone: (843) 549-2586
General Email: pressadvertisiing@lowcountry.com
Publication Website: walterborolive.com
Publisher Name: Carol Haun
Publisher Email: publisher@lowcountry.com
Publisher Phone: 843-549-2586, ext 124
Editor Name: Katrena McCall
Editor Email: editor@lowcountry.com
Editor Phone: 843-549-2586, ext 114
Advertising Executive Name: Ashley Ramsey
Advertising Executive Email: ashleyramsey@lowcountry.com
Advertising Executive Phone: 843-549-2586, ext 102
Delivery Methods: Mail`Newsstand`Racks
Year Established: 1877

WESTMINSTER

THE WESTMINSTER NEWS

Street Address: 100 E Main St
City: Westminster
State: SC
ZIP Code: 29693-1715
General Phone: (864) 647-5404
General Email: westnews@bellsouth.net
Publication Website: westminstersc.com
Parent Company: Trib Publications
Editor Name: Candi Phillips
Advertising Executive Name: Angie Wheeler
Delivery Methods: Mail`Newsstand
Year Established: 1954
Own Printing Facility?: Y
Commercial printers?: Y

WILLIAMSTON

THE JOURNAL

Street Address: 106 W Main St
City: Williamston
State: SC
ZIP Code: 29697-1404
General Phone: (864) 847-7361
General Email: tina@thejournalonline.com
Publication Website: thejournalonline.com
Editor Name: David Meade
Editor Email: editor@thejournalonline.com
Delivery Methods: Mail`Newsstand`Racks
Year Established: 1955
Own Printing Facility?: Y
Commercial printers?: Y

TENNESSEE

ALAMO

THE CROCKETT COUNTY TIMES

Street Address: 46 W Main St
City: Alamo
State: TN
ZIP Code: 38001-1614
General Phone: (731) 696-4558
Publication Website: https://crockettcountytimes.com/
Parent Company: Magic Valley Publishing Co. Inc.

BARTLETT

SHELBY SUN TIMES

Street Address: 2850 Stage Village Cv
City: Bartlett
State: TN
ZIP Code: 38134
General Phone: (901) 433-9138
Publication Website: http://shelbysuntimes.wpengine.com/
Parent Company: Magic Valley Publishing Co. Inc.

BARTLETT

THE BARTLETT EXPRESS

Street Address: 2850 Stage Village Cv
City: Bartlett
State: TN
ZIP Code: 38134
General Phone: (901) 433-9138
Publication Website: https://bartlett-express.com/
Parent Company: Magic Valley Publishing Co. Inc.

BEAN STATION

GRAINGER TODAY

Street Address: 691 Main St
City: Bean Station
State: TN
ZIP Code: 37708
General Phone: (865) 993-0713
Publication Website: http://www.graingertoday.com/

BOLIVAR

BULLETIN-TIMES

Street Address: PO Box 438
City: Bolivar
State: TN
ZIP Code: 38008-0438
General Phone: (731) 658-3691
Publication Website: https://www.bulletintimesnews.com/
Parent Company: Delphos Herald, Inc.

CARTHAGE

CARTHAGE COURIER

Street Address: 509 Main St N
City: Carthage
State: TN
ZIP Code: 37030
General Phone: (615) 735-1110
Publication Website: https://www.carthagecourier.com/

CHATTANOOGA

HAMILTON COUNTY HERALD

Street Address: 735 Broad St., Suite 406
City: Chattanooga
State: TN
ZIP Code: 37402
General Phone: (800) 420-5103
Publication Website: http://hamiltoncountyherald.com/
Parent Company: The Daily News Publishing Co., Inc

CROSSVILLE

CROSSVILLE CHRONICLE

Street Address: 125 West Ave
City: Crossville
State: TN
ZIP Code: 38555
General Phone: (931) 484-5145
Publication Website: https://www.crossville-chronicle.com/
Parent Company: CNHI, LLC

DAYTON

THE HERALD-NEWS

Street Address: 916 Market Street
City: Dayton
State: TN
ZIP Code: 37321-5819
General Phone: (423) 775-6111
Publication Website: http://www.rheaheraldnews.com/
Parent Company: Adams Publishing Group

DUNLAP

THE DUNLAP TRIBUNE

Street Address: 15331 Rankin Ave
City: Dunlap
State: TN
ZIP Code: 37327
General Phone: (423) 949-2505
Publication Website: https://www.thedunlap-tribune.com/
Parent Company: Valley Publishing Company, Inc

ERWIN

THE ERWIN RECORD

Street Address: 218 Gay St
City: Erwin
State: TN
ZIP Code: 37650
General Phone: (423) 743-4112
Publication Website: https://www.erwinrecord.net/
Parent Company: Ogden Newspapers Inc.

FARRAGUT

FARRAGUT PRESS

Street Address: 11863 Kingston Pike
City: Farragut
State: TN
ZIP Code: 37934-3833
General Phone: (865) 675-6397
Publication Website: https://www.farragutpress.com/
Parent Company: Republic Newspapers, Inc.

HARTSVILLE

THE HARTSVILLE VIDETTE

Street Address: 206 River St
City: Hartsville
State: TN
ZIP Code: 37074
General Phone: (615) 374-3556
Publication Website: https://www.hartsvillevidette.com/
Parent Company: Lebanon Publishing Company

HOHENWALD

LEWIS COUNTY HERALD

Street Address: 31 E Linden Ave
City: Hohenwald
State: TN
ZIP Code: 38462
General Phone: (931) 796-3191
Publication Website: http://lewisherald.com/

HUMBOLDT

THE HUMBOLDT CHRONICLE

Street Address: 2606 Eastend Dr
City: Humboldt
State: TN
ZIP Code: 38343
General Phone: (731) 784-2531
Publication Website: https://www.milanmirrorexchange.com/
Parent Company: Milan Mirror Exchange

HUNTINGDON

CARROLL COUNTY NEWS-LEADER

Street Address: 165 Court Sq
City: Huntingdon
State: TN
ZIP Code: 38344
General Phone: (731) 986-2253
Publication Website: https://www.newsleaderonline.com/
Parent Company: Magic Valley Publishing Co. Inc.

JEFFERSON CITY

THE STANDARD BANNER

Street Address: 122 W Old Andrew Johnson Hwy
City: Jefferson City
State: TN
ZIP Code: 37760
General Phone: (865) 475-2081
Publication Website: http://www.standardbanner.com/

JOHNSON CITY

JOHNSON CITY NEWS & NEIGHBOR

Street Address: 1114 Sunset Dr
City: Johnson City
State: TN
ZIP Code: 37604
General Phone: (423) 979-1300
Publication Website: http://jcnewsandneighbor.com/
Parent Company: Johnson City News & Neighbor

JONESBOROUGH

HERALD & TRIBUNE

Street Address: 702 W Jackson Blvd
City: Jonesborough
State: TN
ZIP Code: 37659
General Phone: (423) 753-3136
Publication Website: https://www.heraldandtribune.com/
Parent Company: Sandusky Newspapers, Inc.

KINGSTON

ROANE COUNTY NEWS

Street Address: 204 Franklin St
City: Kingston
State: TN
ZIP Code: 37763
General Phone: (865) 376-3481
Publication Website: https://www.roanecounty.com/
Parent Company: Landmark Community Newspapers

LA FOLLETTE

LA FOLLETTE PRESS

Street Address: 225 N 1st St
City: La Follette
State: TN
ZIP Code: 37766
General Phone: (423) 562-8468
Publication Website: https://www.lafollettepress.com/

LAFAYETTE

MACON COUNTY TIMES

Street Address: 1100A Scottsville Rd.
City: Lafayette
State: TN
ZIP Code: 37083
General Phone: (615) 561-1031
Publication Website: https://maconcountytimes.com/
Parent Company: AIM Media Indiana

LAWRENCEBURG

LAWRENCE COUNTY ADVOCATE

Street Address: 121 N Military Ave
City: Lawrenceburg
State: TN
ZIP Code: 38464
General Phone: (931) 762-1726
Publication Website: https://www.lawrencecountyadvocate.net/

LAWRENCEBURG

THE DEMOCRAT-UNION

Street Address: 238 Hughes St
City: Lawrenceburg
State: TN
ZIP Code: 38464-3364
General Phone: (931) 762-2222
Publication Website: http://www.thedemocratunion.net/

LEBANON

MT. JULIET NEWS

Street Address: 402 N Cumberland St
City: Lebanon
State: TN

Community Newspapers in the U.S.

ZIP Code: 37087
General Phone: (615) 444-3952
Publication Website: https://www.mtjulietnews.com/
Parent Company: Lebanon Publishing Company

LEBANON

THE WILSON POST

Street Address: 223 N Cumberland St
City: Lebanon
State: TN
ZIP Code: 37087
General Phone: (615) 444-6008
Publication Website: https://www.wilsonpost.com/
Parent Company: Main Street Media of Tennessee

LENOIR CITY

NEWS-HERALD

Street Address: 201 Simpson Rd
City: Lenoir City
State: TN
ZIP Code: 37771
General Phone: (865) 986-6581
Publication Website: http://www.news-herald.net/
Parent Company: Media News Group

LENOIR CITY

THE CONNECTION

Street Address: 201 Simpson Rd
City: Lenoir City
State: TN
ZIP Code: 37771
General Phone: (865) 986-6581
Publication Website: http://www.news-herald.net/
Parent Company: Adams Publishing Group

LEWISBURG

MARSHALL COUNTY TRIBUNE

Street Address: 111 W Commerce St
City: Lewisburg
State: TN
ZIP Code: 37091
General Phone: (931) 359-1188
Publication Website: https://www.marshalltribune.com/
Parent Company: Paxton Media Group

LEXINGTON

LEXINGTON PROGRESS

Street Address: 508 S Broad St
City: Lexington
State: TN
ZIP Code: 38351
General Phone: (731) 968-6397
Publication Website: https://www.lexingtonprogress.com/

LINDEN

BUFFALO RIVER REVIEW

Street Address: P.O. Box 914 – 115 South Mill Street
City: Linden
State: TN
ZIP Code: 37096
General Phone: (931) 589-2169

Publication Website: https://www.buffaloriverreview.com/
Parent Company: Kennedy Newspapers

LIVINGSTON

OVERTON COUNTY NEWS

Street Address: 415 W Main St
City: Livingston
State: TN
ZIP Code: 38570
General Phone: (931) 403-6397
Publication Website: https://www.overtoncountynews.com/

MARTIN

WEAKLEY COUNTY PRESS

Street Address: P.O. Box 410
City: Martin
State: TN
ZIP Code: 38237
General Phone: (731) 587-3144
Publication Website: http://www.nwtntoday.com/the-weakley-county-press/
Parent Company: NWTN Today

MAYNARDVILLE

THE UNION NEWS LEADER

Street Address: 3755 Maynardville Hwy
City: Maynardville
State: TN
ZIP Code: 37807
General Phone: (865) 992-3392
Publication Website: https://www.ucnewsleader.com/

MC KENZIE

MCKENZIE BANNER

Street Address: 3 Banner Row
City: Mc Kenzie
State: TN
ZIP Code: 38201
General Phone: (731) 352-3323
Publication Website: https://www.mckenziebanner.com/
Parent Company: Tri-County Publishing, Inc.

MCMINNVILLE

SOUTHERN STANDARD

Street Address: 105 College St
City: McMinnville
State: TN
ZIP Code: 37110
General Phone: (931) 473-2191
Publication Website: https://www.southernstandard.com/
Parent Company: Morris Multimedia, Inc.

MEMPHIS

MEMPHIS BUSINESS JOURNAL

Street Address: 651 Oakleaf Office Lane
City: Memphis
State: TN
ZIP Code: 38117
General Phone: (901) 523-1000
Publication Website: https://www.bizjournals.com/memphis
Parent Company: American City Business Journals

MEMPHIS

THE MEMPHIS NEWS

Street Address: 193 Jefferson Ave
City: Memphis
State: TN
ZIP Code: 38103
General Phone: (901) 523-1561
Publication Website: https://www.memphisdailynews.com/
Parent Company: The Daily News Publishing Co.

MEMPHIS

THE MILLINGTON STAR

Street Address: 2850 Stage Village Cv
City: Memphis
State: TN
ZIP Code: 38134
General Phone: (901) 872-2286
Publication Website: http://www.millington-news.com/
Parent Company: Magic Valley Publishing Co. Inc.

MILAN

MILAN MIRROR-EXCHANGE

Street Address: 1104 S Main St
City: Milan
State: TN
ZIP Code: 38358
General Phone: (731) 686-1632
Publication Website: https://www.milanmirrorexchange.com/
Parent Company: Milan Mirror Exchange

MOUNT JULIET

THE CHRONICLE OF MT. JULIET

Street Address: 1400 N. Mt. Juliet Road, Suite 201
City: Mount Juliet
State: TN
ZIP Code: 37122
General Phone: (615) 754-6111
Publication Website: https://www.thechronicleofmtjuliet.com/

MURFREESBORO

THE MURFREESBORO POST

Street Address: 814 S. Church Street, Suite 202
City: Murfreesboro
State: TN
ZIP Code: 37130
General Phone: (615) 869-0800
Publication Website: https://www.murfreesboropost.com/
Parent Company: Main Street Media of Tennessee

NASHVILLE

LEDGER - KNOXVILLE EDITION

Street Address: 222 2nd Ave N.
City: Nashville
State: TN
ZIP Code: 37201
General Phone: (615) 254-5522
Publication Website: https://www.tnledger.com/
Parent Company: The Daily News Publishing Co.

NASHVILLE

NASHVILLE BUSINESS JOURNAL

Street Address: 1800 Church St
City: Nashville
State: TN
ZIP Code: 37203
General Phone: (615) 248-2222
Publication Website: https://www.bizjournals.com/nashville
Parent Company: American City Business Journals

NASHVILLE

NASHVILLE LEDGER

Street Address: 222 2nd Ave N
City: Nashville
State: TN
ZIP Code: 37201
General Phone: (615) 254-5522
Publication Website: https://www.tnledger.com/
Parent Company: The Daily News Publishing Co.

PIKEVILLE

THE BLEDSONIAN-BANNER

Street Address: 399 Spring St
City: Pikeville
State: TN
ZIP Code: 37367
General Phone: (423) 447-2996
Publication Website: http://www.thebledsonian-banner.com/
Parent Company: Valley Publishing Company, Inc

PULASKI

PULASKI CITIZEN

Street Address: 955 W College St
City: Pulaski
State: TN
ZIP Code: 38478-3600
General Phone: (931) 363-3544
Publication Website: http://www.pulaskicitizen.com/

SMITHVILLE

SMITHVILLE REVIEW

Street Address: 106 S 1st St
City: Smithville
State: TN
ZIP Code: 37166
General Phone: (615) 597-5485
Publication Website: https://www.smithvillereview.com/

SOUTH PITTSBURG

MARION COUNTY NEWS

Street Address: 307 Elm Ave
City: South Pittsburg
State: TN
ZIP Code: 37380-1337
General Phone: (423) 837-6312
Publication Website: https://www.mcnewstn.com/

SPARTA

THE EXPOSITOR

Street Address: 34 W Bockman Way
City: Sparta
State: TN
ZIP Code: 38583
General Phone: (931) 836-3284
Publication Website: http://spartalive.com/
Parent Company: Smith Newspaper, Inc.

SWEETWATER

THE ADVOCATE & DEMOCRAT

Street Address: PO Box 389
City: Sweetwater
State: TN
ZIP Code: 37874
General Phone: (423) 337-7101
Publication Website: http://www.advocateanddemocrat.com/
Parent Company: Adams Publishing Group

TAZEWELL

CLAIBORNE PROGRESS

Street Address: 1705 Main St
City: Tazewell
State: TN
ZIP Code: 37879-3413
General Phone: (423) 254-5588
Publication Website: https://www.claiborneprogress.net/
Parent Company: Boone Newspapers, Inc.

TIPTONVILLE

THE LAKE COUNTY BANNER

Street Address: 315 Church St
City: Tiptonville
State: TN
ZIP Code: 38079-1147
General Phone: (731) 253-6666
Publication Website: https://lakecountybanner.com/
Parent Company: Magic Valley Publishing Co. Inc.

WARTBURG

MORGAN COUNTY NEWS

Street Address: 202 N MAIDEN ST
City: Wartburg
State: TN
ZIP Code: 37887
General Phone: (423) 346-6225
Publication Website: https://www.morgancountynews.net/
Parent Company: Landmark Community Newspapers

WAVERLY

THE NEWS-DEMOCRAT

Street Address: 302A W Main St
City: Waverly
State: TN
ZIP Code: 37185
General Phone: (931) 296-2426
Publication Website: http://www.thenews-democrat.com/
Parent Company: Kennedy Newspapers Co., Inc

TEXAS

ALBANY

ALBANY NEWS

Street Address: PO Box 2139
City: Albany
State: TX
ZIP Code: 76430
General Phone: (325) 762-2201
General Email: social@thealbanynews.net
Publication Website: https://www.thealbanynews.net/
Delivery Methods: Mail`Racks
Year Established: 1875
Published Days: Thur
Avg. Paid Circ.: 1350
Audit Company: Sworn/Estimate/Non-Audited
Audit Date: 43626

ALEDO

THE COMMUNITY NEWS

Street Address: 203 Pecan Dr
City: Aledo
State: TX
ZIP Code: 76008
General Phone: (817) 441-7661
General Email: news@community-news.com
Publication Website: https://www.community-news.com/
Parent Company: Media News Group
Publisher Name: Randy Keck
Editor Name: Randy Keck
Advertising Executive Name: Rachel Noble
Delivery Methods: Mail`Newsstand`Racks
Year Established: 1995
Published Days: Fri
Avg. Paid Circ.: 2244
Audit Company: Sworn/Estimate/Non-Audited
Audit Date: 43626

ALICE

ALICE ECHO-NEWS JOURNAL

Street Address: 405 E Main St
City: Alice
State: TX
ZIP Code: 78332
General Phone: (361) 664-6588
General Email: rgruber@gatehousemedia.com
Publication Website: https://www.alicetx.com/
Parent Company: Gannett
Publisher Name: Russel Gruber
Publisher Email: rgruber@gatehousemedia.com
Publisher Phone: (361) 664-6588
Editor Name: Melissa Trevino
Editor Email: mtrevino@gatehousemedia.com
Editor Phone: (361) 664-6588
Advertising Executive Name: Nancy Ramirez
Advertising Executive Email: nancy.ramirez@aliceechonews.com
Advertising Executive Phone: (361) 664-6588
Delivery Methods: Mail`Newsstand`Carrier`Racks
Year Established: 1894
Own Printing Facility?: Y
Commercial printers?: Y
Mechanical specifications: Type page 10.5 x 16 ; E - 6 cols, 2 1/16, 1/8 between; A - 6 cols, 2 1/16, 1/8 between; C - 8 cols, 1 1/2, 1/8 between.
Published Days: Wed`Sun
Weekday Frequency: m
Avg. Paid Circ.: 3107
Avg. Free Circ.: 500
Audit Company: Sworn/Estimate/Non-Audited
Audit Date: 43626
Mailroom Equipment: Tying Machines -- Ca; Address Machine -- Am.;
Business Equipment: Onyx
Classified Equipment: Hardware -- APP/Mac;
Classified Software: BrainWorks
Editorial Equipment: Hardware -- APP/Mac/Microtek/Scanner; Printers -- APP/Mac LaserWriters
Editorial Software: Claris/MacWrite Pro, QPS/QuarkXPress.
Production Equipment: Hardware -- APP/Mac; Cameras -- R.

ALICE

NUECES COUNTY RECORD-STAR

Street Address: 405 E Main St
City: Alice
State: TX
ZIP Code: 78332
General Phone: (361) 664-6588
General Email: rgruber@gatehousemedia.com
Publication Website: https://www.recordstar.com/
Publisher Name: Russel Gruber
Publisher Email: rgruber@gatehousemedia.com
Publisher Phone: (361) 664-6588
Editor Name: Melissa Trevino
Editor Email: mtrevino@gatehousemedia.com
Editor Phone: (361) 664-6588
Advertising Executive Name: Nancy Ramirez
Advertising Executive Email: nancy.ramirez@aliceechonews.com
Advertising Executive Phone: (361) 664-6588
Delivery Methods: Mail`Newsstand`Carrier
Year Established: 1910
Mechanical specifications: Type page 13 x 21; E - 6 cols, 2, 1/6 between; A - 6 cols, 2, 1/6 between; C - 6 cols, 2, 1/6 between.
Published Days: Thur
Avg. Paid Circ.: 3100
Audit Company: Sworn/Estimate/Non-Audited
Audit Date: 43626

ALPINE

ALPINE AVALANCHE

Street Address: 118 N 5th St
City: Alpine
State: TX
ZIP Code: 79831
General Phone: (432) 837-3334
General Email: publisher@alpineavalanche.com
Publication Website: http://www.alpineavalanche.com/
Publisher Name: J. T. Maroney
Publisher Email: publisher@alpineavalanche.com
Editor Name: Gail D. Yovanovich
Editor Email: editor@alpineavalanche.com
Advertising Executive Name: J. T. Maroney
Delivery Methods: Mail`Newsstand`Racks
Year Established: 1891
Mechanical specifications: Type page 13 x 21 3/4; E - 6 cols, 2, 1/6 between; A - 6 cols, 2, 1/6 between; C - 6 cols, 2, 1/6 between.
Published Days: Thur
Avg. Paid Circ.: 1930
Avg. Free Circ.: 373
Audit Company: Sworn/Estimate/Non-Audited
Audit Date: 43626

ALVIN

ALVIN SUN-ADVERTISER

Street Address: 570 Dula St
City: Alvin
State: TX
ZIP Code: 77511
General Phone: (281) 331-4421
General Email: ads@alvinsun.net
Publication Website: http://www.alvinsun.net/
Parent Company: Hartman Newspapers, L.P.
Publisher Name: David Rupkalvis
Publisher Email: publisher@alvinsun.net
Editor Name: David Rupkalvis
Editor Email: editor@alvinsun.net
Advertising Executive Name: Brenda Groves
Advertising Executive Email: ads@alvinsun.net
Delivery Methods: Mail`Newsstand`Carrier`Racks
Year Established: 1892
Published Days: Wed`Sun
Avg. Paid Circ.: 500
Avg. Free Circ.: 14500
Audit Company: Sworn/Estimate/Non-Audited
Audit Date: 43626

ANAHUAC

THE ANAHUAC PROGRESS

Street Address: 306 Willcox St
City: Anahuac
State: TX
ZIP Code: 77514
General Phone: (409) 267-6131
General Email: theprogress@theanahuacprogress.com
Publication Website: https://www.theanahuacprogress.com/
Parent Company: Granite Publishing Partners LLC
Editor Name: theprogress@theanahuacprogress.com
Delivery Methods: Mail`Newsstand`Racks
Year Established: 1908
Mechanical specifications: Type page 10.25 x 21; E - 6 cols, 1.625", 1.250" between; A - 6 cols, 1.625", 1.25" between; C - 9 cols, 9.000", 1.250" between.
Published Days: Wed
Avg. Paid Circ.: 647
Audit Company: Sworn/Estimate/Non-Audited
Audit Date: 43626

ANDREWS

ANDREWS COUNTY NEWS

Street Address: 210 E Broadway St
City: Andrews
State: TX
ZIP Code: 79714
General Phone: (432) 523-2085
General Email: publisher@andrewscountynews.com
Publication Website: https://www.andrewscountynews.com/
Parent Company: M. Roberts Media
Publisher Name: Blake Roberts
Publisher Email: publisher@andrewscountynews.com
Advertising Executive Name: Marice Escobar
Advertising Executive Email: ads@andrewscountynews.com
Delivery Methods: Mail`Newsstand`Carrier`Racks
Year Established: 1934
Own Printing Facility?: Y
Published Days: Thur`Sun
Avg. Paid Circ.: 3100
Avg. Free Circ.: 135
Audit Company: Sworn/Estimate/Non-Audited
Audit Date: 43626

ANGLETON

Community Newspapers in the U.S.

THE BULLETIN

Street Address: PO Box 2426
City: Angleton
State: TX
ZIP Code: 77516-2426
General Phone: (979) 849-5407
General Email: sharon.bulletin@gmail.com
Publication Website: http://www.mybulletinnewspaper.com/
Parent Company: Gannett
Publisher Name: Sharon Toth
Publisher Email: sharon.bulletin@gmail.com
Editor Name: John Toth
Editor Email: john.bulletin@gmail.com
Advertising Executive Name: Stephanie Gizella Johnson
Advertising Executive Email: stephanie.bulletin@gmail.com
Delivery Methods: Racks
Year Established: 1994
Mechanical specifications: Type page 10 1/2 x 12 3/4; E - 5 cols, 2, 1/8 between; A - 5 cols, 2, 1/8 between; C - 5 cols, 2, 1/8 between.
Published Days: Tues
Avg. Free Circ.: 6000
Audit Company: Sworn/Estimate/Non-Audited
Audit Date: 43626

ARANSAS PASS

ARANSAS PASS PROGRESS

Street Address: 346 S Houston St
City: Aransas Pass
State: TX
ZIP Code: 78336
General Phone: (361) 758-5391
General Email: advertising@aransaspassprogress.com
Publication Website: https://www.aransaspassprogress.com/
Parent Company: Granite Publications
Publisher Name: John Bowers
Publisher Email: publisher@aransaspassprogress.com
Editor Name: Norma Martinez
Editor Email: editor@aransaspassprogress.com
Advertising Executive Name: John Bowers
Advertising Executive Email: advertising@aransaspassprogress.com
Delivery Methods: Mail Newsstand Racks
Year Established: 1909
Published Days: Wed
Avg. Paid Circ.: 1854
Audit Company: Sworn/Estimate/Non-Audited
Audit Date: 43626

ARANSAS PASS

THE INGLESIDE INDEX

Street Address: 346 S Houston St
City: Aransas Pass
State: TX
ZIP Code: 78336
General Phone: (361) 758-5391
General Email: advertising@aransaspassprogress.com
Publication Website: https://www.inglesideindex.com/
Parent Company: Granite Publications
Publisher Name: John Bowers
Publisher Email: publisher@aransaspassprogress.com
Editor Name: Norma Martinez
Editor Email: editor@aransaspassprogress.com
Advertising Executive Name: John Bowers
Advertising Executive Email: advertising@aransaspassprogress.com
Delivery Methods: Mail Newsstand
Year Established: 1953
Mechanical specifications: Type page 13 x 21; E - 6 cols, 2 1/16, 1/6 between; A - 6 cols, 2 1/16, 1/6 between; C - 9 cols, 1 1/2, between.
Published Days: Wed
Avg. Paid Circ.: 1500
Avg. Free Circ.: 46
Audit Company: Sworn/Estimate/Non-Audited
Audit Date: 43626

ARCHER CITY

ARCHER COUNTY NEWS

Street Address: 104 E Walnut
City: Archer City
State: TX
ZIP Code: 76351
General Phone: (940) 574-4569
General Email: archercountynews@gmail.com
Publication Website: http://www.archercountynews.com/
Delivery Methods: Mail Racks
Year Established: 1908
Published Days: Thur
Avg. Paid Circ.: 1300
Audit Company: Sworn/Estimate/Non-Audited
Audit Date: 43626

ASPERMONT

STONEWALL COUNTY COURIER

Street Address: PO Box 808
City: Aspermont
State: TX
ZIP Code: 76371
General Phone: (877) 308-9684
General Email: courier@westex.net
Publication Website: http://scc.stparchive.com/
Delivery Methods: Mail
Year Established: 1985
Published Days: Thur
Avg. Paid Circ.: 900
Avg. Free Circ.: 60
Audit Company: Sworn/Estimate/Non-Audited
Audit Date: 43626

ATLANTA

ATLANTA CITITZENS JOURNAL

Street Address: 306 W Main St
City: Atlanta
State: TX
ZIP Code: 75551
General Phone: (903) 796-7133
General Email: shawn@casscountynow.com
Publication Website: https://www.casscountynow.com/
Parent Company: Moser Community Media, LLC
Delivery Methods: Mail Newsstand Racks
Year Established: 1879
Own Printing Facility?: Y
Published Days: Wed Sun
Avg. Paid Circ.: 3100
Avg. Free Circ.: 51
Audit Company: Sworn/Estimate/Non-Audited
Audit Date: 43626

AUSTIN

AUSTIN BUSINESS JOURNAL

Street Address: 504 Lavaca, Suite 1008
City: Austin
State: TX
ZIP Code: 78701
General Phone: (512) 494-2500
General Email: austin@bizjournals.com
Publication Website: https://www.bizjournals.com/austin/
Parent Company: American City Business Journals
Publisher Name: Heather Ladage
Publisher Email: hladage@bizjournals.com
Publisher Phone: (512) 494-2511
Editor Name: Will Anderson
Editor Email: wanderson@bizjournals.com
Editor Phone: (512) 494-2528
Advertising Executive Name: Robert Nusbaum
Advertising Executive Email: rnusbaum@bizjournals.com
Advertising Executive Phone: (512) 494-2509
Delivery Methods: Mail Racks
Year Established: 1981
Published Days: Fri
Audit Company: Sworn/Estimate/Non-Audited
Audit Date: 43626

AUSTIN

LAKE TRAVIS VIEW

Street Address: 305 S Congress Ave
City: Austin
State: TX
ZIP Code: 78704
General Phone: (512) 912-2502
General Email: publisher@statesman.com
Publication Website: http://laketravisview.com/
Parent Company: Gannett
Publisher Name: Patrick Dorsey
Publisher Email: publisher@statesman.com
Publisher Phone: (512) 445-3555
Editor Name: Eileen Flynn
Editor Email: eflynn@statesman.com
Editor Phone: (512) 912-2502
Advertising Executive Name: Scott Pompe
Advertising Executive Email: spompe@statesman.com
Advertising Executive Phone: (512) 445-3715
Delivery Methods: Mail Newsstand Racks
Year Established: 1985
Mechanical specifications: Type page 10 x 11 1/2; E - 5 cols, 1 15/16, 1/8 between; A - 5 cols, 1 15/16, 1/8 between.
Published Days: Thur
Avg. Paid Circ.: 438
Avg. Free Circ.: 1476
Audit Company: AAM
Audit Date: 43293

AUSTIN

THE PFLUGERVILLE PFLAG

Street Address: 305 S Congress Ave
City: Austin
State: TX
ZIP Code: 78704
General Phone: (512) 255-5827
General Email: publisher@statesman.com
Publication Website: https://www.statesman.com/community/Pflugerville
Parent Company: Gannett
Publisher Name: Patrick Dorsey
Publisher Email: publisher@statesman.com
Publisher Phone: (512) 445-3555
Editor Name: Mike Parker
Editor Email: mparker@statesman.com
Editor Phone: (512) 255-5827
Advertising Executive Name: Scott Pompe
Advertising Executive Email: spompe@statesman.com
Advertising Executive Phone: (512) 445-3715
Delivery Methods: Mail Racks
Year Established: 1980
Mechanical specifications: Type page 10 x 11 1/2; E - 5 cols, 1 7/8, 1/6 between; A - 5 cols, 1 7/8, 1/6 between; C - 5 cols, 1 7/8, 1/6 between.
Published Days: Wed
Avg. Free Circ.: 8547
Audit Company: Sworn/Estimate/Non-Audited
Audit Date: 43626

AUSTIN

WEST AUSTIN NEWS

Street Address: 5511 Parkcrest Drive
City: Austin
State: TX
ZIP Code: 78731
General Phone: (512) 459-4070
General Email: adsales@westaustinnews.com
Publication Website: https://westaustinnews.com/
Editor Email: editor@westaustinnews.com
Advertising Executive Name: Katy Byther
Advertising Executive Email: ads@westaustinnews.com
Delivery Methods: Mail Newsstand Racks
Year Established: 1986
Published Days: Thur
Avg. Paid Circ.: 1880
Audit Company: Sworn/Estimate/Non-Audited
Audit Date: 43626

AUSTIN

WESTLAKE PICAYUNE

Street Address: 305 S Congress Ave
City: Austin
State: TX
ZIP Code: 78704
General Phone: (512) 912-2502
General Email: publisher@statesman.com
Publication Website: https://www.statesman.com/community/Westlake
Parent Company: Gannett
Publisher Name: Patrick Dorsey
Publisher Email: publisher@statesman.com
Publisher Phone: (512) 445-3555
Editor Name: Eileen Flynn
Editor Email: eflynn@statesman.com
Editor Phone: (512) 912-2502
Advertising Executive Name: Scott Pompe
Advertising Executive Email: spompe@statesman.com
Advertising Executive Phone: (512) 445-3715
Delivery Methods: Mail Newsstand
Year Established: 1976
Published Days: Thur
Avg. Paid Circ.: 463
Avg. Free Circ.: 3415
Audit Company: Sworn/Estimate/Non-Audited
Audit Date: 43626

AZLE

AZLE NEWS

Street Address: 321 W Main St
City: Azle
State: TX
ZIP Code: 76020
General Phone: (817) 270-3340
General Email: info@azlenews.net
Publication Website: https://www.azlenews.net/
Publisher Name: Kim Ware
Publisher Email: publisher@azlenews.net
Editor Name: Michael Acosta
Editor Email: michaelacosta@azlenews.net
Advertising Executive Name: Johnna Bridges
Advertising Executive Email: johnna@azlenews.net
Delivery Methods: Mail Newsstand Racks
Year Established: 1959
Own Printing Facility?: Y
Commercial printers?: N
Mechanical specifications: Type page 13 x 21; E - 5 cols, 2 1/2, 1/6 between; A - 6 cols, 2, 1/6 between; C - 6 cols, 2, 1/6 between.
Published Days: Wed
Avg. Paid Circ.: 3000
Avg. Free Circ.: 112
Audit Company: Sworn/Estimate/Non-

Audited
Audit Date: 43626

BALLINGER

THE BALLINGER LEDGER

Street Address: 709 Hutchins Ave
City: Ballinger
State: TX
ZIP Code: 76821
General Phone: (325) 365-3501
General Email: bhancock@gatehousemedia.com
Publication Website: https://www.runnelscountyregister.com/
Publisher Name: Melissa Horton
Publisher Email: mhorton@gatehousemedia.com
Publisher Phone: (325) 641-3130
Editor Name: Derrick Stuckly
Editor Email: dstuckly@brownwoodbulletin.com
Editor Phone: (325) 641-3112
Advertising Executive Name: Kendra Chism
Advertising Executive Email: kchism@brownwoodbulletin.com
Advertising Executive Phone: (325) 641-3119
Delivery Methods: Mail`Racks
Year Established: 1886
Mechanical specifications: Type page 11 7/8 x 21 1/2; E - 6 cols, 1 7/8, 1/6 between; A - 6 cols, 1 7/8, 1/6 between; C - 9 cols, 1 1/4, 1/6 between.
Published Days: Thur
Avg. Paid Circ.: 2500
Avg. Free Circ.: 13
Audit Company: Sworn/Estimate/Non-Audited
Audit Date: 43626

BALLINGER

WINTERS ENTERPRISE

Street Address: 709 Hutchins Ave
City: Ballinger
State: TX
ZIP Code: 76821
General Phone: (325) 365-3501
General Email: bhancock@gatehousemedia.com
Publication Website: https://www.runnelscountyregister.com/
Publisher Name: Melissa Horton
Publisher Email: mhorton@gatehousemedia.com
Publisher Phone: (325) 641-3130
Editor Name: Derrick Stuckly
Editor Email: dstuckly@brownwoodbulletin.com
Editor Phone: (325) 641-3112
Advertising Executive Name: Kendra Chism
Advertising Executive Email: kchism@brownwoodbulletin.com
Advertising Executive Phone: (325) 641-3119
Delivery Methods: Mail
Year Established: 1905
Published Days: Thur
Avg. Paid Circ.: 714
Avg. Free Circ.: 48
Audit Company: Sworn/Estimate/Non-Audited
Audit Date: 43626

BANDERA

BANDERA COUNTY COURIER

Street Address: 302 Dallas St
City: Bandera
State: TX
ZIP Code: 78003
General Phone: (830) 796-9799
General Email: bccourier@sbcglobal.net
Publication Website: https://www.bccourier.com/
Delivery Methods: Mail`Newsstand
Year Established: 2004
Published Days: Thur
Avg. Paid Circ.: 2000
Audit Company: Sworn/Estimate/Non-Audited
Audit Date: 43626

BARTLETT

TRIBUNE-PROGRESS

Street Address: 108 W Clark St
City: Bartlett
State: TX
ZIP Code: 76511-4371
General Phone: (254) 527-4424
General Email: newslady01@sbcglobal.net
Delivery Methods: Mail`Newsstand
Year Established: 1886
Published Days: Wed
Avg. Paid Circ.: 1259
Audit Company: Sworn/Estimate/Non-Audited
Audit Date: 43626

BASTROP

THE BASTROP ADVERTISER

Street Address: 1106 College St
City: Bastrop
State: TX
ZIP Code: 78602-3948
General Phone: (512) 321-2557
General Email: publisher@statesman.com
Publication Website: https://www.statesman.com/community/Bastrop
Publisher Name: Patrick Dorsey
Publisher Email: publisher@statesman.com
Publisher Phone: (512) 445-3555
Editor Name: Andy Sevilla
Editor Email: asevilla@statesman.com
Editor Phone: (512) 321-2557
Advertising Executive Name: Scott Pompe
Advertising Executive Email: spompe@statesman.com
Advertising Executive Phone: (512) 445-3715
Delivery Methods: Mail`Newsstand`Racks
Year Established: 1853
Own Printing Facility?: Y
Commercial printers?: Y
Mechanical specifications: Type page 11 5/8 x 20 1/2; E - 6 cols, 1 13/16, 1/8 between; A - 6 cols, 1 5/6, 1/8 between; C - 10 cols, 1 13/16, 1/9 between.
Published Days: Thur`Sat
Avg. Free Circ.: 3091
Audit Company: Sworn/Estimate/Non-Audited
Audit Date: 43626

BASTROP

THE SMITHVILLE TIMES

Street Address: PO Box 459
City: Bastrop
State: TX
ZIP Code: 78602-0459
General Phone: (512) 237-4655
General Email: publisher@statesman.com
Publication Website: https://www.statesman.com/community/Smithville
Parent Company: Gannett
Publisher Name: Patrick Dorsey
Publisher Email: publisher@statesman.com
Publisher Phone: (512) 445-3555
Editor Name: Andy Sevilla
Editor Email: asevilla@statesman.com
Editor Phone: (512) 321-2557
Advertising Executive Name: Scott Pompe
Advertising Executive Email: spompe@statesman.com
Advertising Executive Phone: (512) 445-3715
Delivery Methods: Mail`Newsstand
Year Established: 1895
Mechanical specifications: Type page 11 5/8 x 20 1/2; E - 6 cols, 2, 1/6 between; A - 6 cols, 1 5/6, 1/8 between; C - 10 cols, 2, 1/9 between.
Published Days: Thur
Avg. Paid Circ.: 1359
Audit Company: Sworn/Estimate/Non-Audited
Audit Date: 43626

BEAUMONT

THE HARDIN COUNTY NEWS

Street Address: 380 Main St
City: Beaumont
State: TX
ZIP Code: 77701
General Phone: (409) 833-3311
General Email: feedback@hearst.com
Publication Website: https://www.hearst.com/newspapers/beaumont-enterprise
Parent Company: Hearst Corp.
Publisher Name: Clarice Touhey
Publisher Email: clarice.touhey@hearst.com
Publisher Phone: (409) 838-2805
Editor Name: Ronnie Crocker
Editor Email: ronnie.crocker@chron.com
Editor Phone: (409) 838-2801
Advertising Executive Name: Payshunz Burnham
Advertising Executive Email: pburnham@beaumontenterprise.com
Advertising Executive Phone: (409) 838-2880
Delivery Methods: Mail`Racks
Year Established: 1970
Mechanical specifications: Type page 13 x 21 1/2; E - 6 cols, 2 1/16, 1/8 between; A - 6 cols, 2 1/16, 1/8 between; C - 9 cols, 1 3/8, 1/8 between.
Published Days: Wed
Avg. Free Circ.: 19000
Audit Company: Sworn/Estimate/Non-Audited
Audit Date: 43626

BEEVILLE

BEEVILLE BEE-PICAYUNE

Street Address: 111 N Washington St
City: Beeville
State: TX
ZIP Code: 78102
General Phone: (361) 358-2550
General Email: news@mysoutex.com
Publication Website: https://www.mysoutex.com/beeville_bee_picayune/
Parent Company: Mysoutx.com
Delivery Methods: Mail`Newsstand
Year Established: 1886
Published Days: Wed`Sat
Avg. Paid Circ.: 4158
Audit Company: Sworn/Estimate/Non-Audited
Audit Date: 43626

BELLVILLE

THE BELLVILLE TIMES

Street Address: 106 E Palm St
City: Bellville
State: TX
ZIP Code: 77418
General Phone: (979) 865-3131
General Email: bvtimes@sbcglobal.net
Publication Website: https://www.bellvilletimes.com/
Delivery Methods: Mail`Newsstand
Year Established: 1879
Published Days: Thur
Avg. Paid Circ.: 4100
Avg. Free Circ.: 44
Audit Company: Sworn/Estimate/Non-Audited
Audit Date: 43626

BELTON

THE BELTON JOURNAL

Street Address: 210 N Penelope St
City: Belton
State: TX
ZIP Code: 76513
General Phone: (254) 939-5754
General Email: news@beltonjournal.com
Publication Website: http://beltonjournal.com/
Advertising Executive Name: Darci Gillespey
Advertising Executive Email: darci@beltonjournal.com
Delivery Methods: Mail`Newsstand`Racks
Year Established: 1866
Published Days: Thur
Avg. Paid Circ.: 4090
Audit Company: Sworn/Estimate/Non-Audited
Audit Date: 43626

BIG LAKE

BIG LAKE WILDCAT

Street Address: 707 N. Florida Street
City: Big Lake
State: TX
ZIP Code: 76932
General Phone: (325) 884-2215
General Email: editor@mybiglake.com
Publication Website: https://mybiglake.com/
Editor Name: J.L. Mankin
Editor Email: editor@mybiglake.com
Delivery Methods: Mail`Newsstand`Racks
Year Established: 1925
Published Days: Thur
Avg. Paid Circ.: 890
Audit Company: Sworn/Estimate/Non-Audited
Audit Date: 43626

BIG SANDY

BIG SANDY-HAWKINS JOURNAL

Street Address: 100 S. Tyler St
City: Big Sandy
State: TX
ZIP Code: 75755
General Phone: (903) 636-4351
General Email: bshjournal@aol.com
Publication Website: https://bshjournal.com/
Parent Company: M. Roberts Media
Delivery Methods: Mail`Newsstand
Year Established: 1949
Published Days: Wed
Avg. Paid Circ.: 1153
Audit Company: Sworn/Estimate/Non-Audited
Audit Date: 43626

BLANCO

BLANCO COUNTY NEWS

Street Address: 714 4th St
City: Blanco
State: TX
ZIP Code: 78606
General Phone: (830) 833-4812
General Email: editor@blanconews.com
Publication Website: https://www.hillcountrypassport.com/blanco/
Parent Company: Wesner Media Publication
Editor Email: editor@blanconews.com
Advertising Executive Email: news@blanconews.com
Delivery Methods: Mail`Newsstand
Year Established: 1883
Mechanical specifications: Type page 11 5/8 x 21; E - 6 cols, 1 7/8, 1/6 between; A - 6 cols, 1 7/8, 1/6 between; C - 6 cols, 1 7/8, 1/6 between.
Published Days: Wed
Avg. Paid Circ.: 3200
Avg. Free Circ.: 35
Audit Company: Sworn/Estimate/Non-

Community Newspapers in the U.S.

Audited
Audit Date: 43626

BOOKER

BOOKER NEWS

Street Address: 204 S. Main
City: Booker
State: TX
ZIP Code: 79005
General Phone: (806) 658-4732
General Email: bnews@ptsi.net
Publication Website: https://www.bookernews.com/
Delivery Methods: Mail`Newsstand
Year Established: 1927
Published Days: Thur
Avg. Paid Circ.: 758
Audit Company: Sworn/Estimate/Non-Audited
Audit Date: 43626

BOWIE

THE BOWIE NEWS

Street Address: 201 Walnut Street
City: Bowie
State: TX
ZIP Code: 76230
General Phone: (940) 872-2247
General Email: ads@bowienewsonline.com
Publication Website: http://bowienewsonline.com/
Editor Email: editor@bowienewsonline.com
Advertising Executive Email: ads@bowienewsonline.com
Delivery Methods: Mail`Racks
Year Established: 1922
Own Printing Facility?: Y
Published Days: Wed`Sat
Avg. Paid Circ.: 4700
Avg. Free Circ.: 550
Audit Company: Sworn/Estimate/Non-Audited
Audit Date: 43626

BRADY

BRADY STANDARD-HERALD

Street Address: 201 S Bridge St
City: Brady
State: TX
ZIP Code: 76825
General Phone: (325) 597-2959
General Email: publisher@bradystandard.com
Publication Website: https://www.bradystandard.com/
Publisher Name: James Stewart
Publisher Email: publisher@bradystandard.com
Editor Name: James Stewart
Advertising Executive Name: Holly Stewart
Advertising Executive Email: advertise@bradystandard.com
Delivery Methods: Mail`Newsstand`Racks
Year Established: 1909
Own Printing Facility?: Y
Commercial printers?: Y
Published Days: Wed
Avg. Paid Circ.: 3800
Avg. Free Circ.: 68
Audit Company: Sworn/Estimate/Non-Audited
Audit Date: 43626

BRECKENRIDGE

BRECKENRIDGE AMERICAN

Street Address: 114 E Elm St
City: Breckenridge
State: TX
ZIP Code: 76424
General Phone: (254) 559-5412
General Email: admgr@breckenridgeamerican.com
Publication Website: https://www.breckenridgeamerican.com/
Parent Company: Moser Community Media, LLC
Publisher Name: Timothy O'Malley
Editor Email: editor@breckenridgeamerican.com
Advertising Executive Email: admgr@breckenridgeamerican.com
Delivery Methods: Mail`Newsstand`Racks
Year Established: 1920
Own Printing Facility?: Y
Commercial printers?: Y
Mechanical specifications: Page size: 12.5 inches by 22.5 inches Columns: 6 1 col = 1.75 inches 2 col = 3.75 inches 3 col = 5.6875 inches 4 col = 7.635 inches 5 col = 9.5625 inches 6 col = 11.50 inches Full Page charged at 6 cols x 20.5 inches
Published Days: Wed
Avg. Paid Circ.: 1504
Avg. Free Circ.: 25
Audit Company: Sworn/Estimate/Non-Audited
Audit Date: 43626

BRIDGEPORT

BRIDGEPORT INDEX

Street Address: 916 Halsell St
City: Bridgeport
State: TX
ZIP Code: 76426
General Phone: (940) 683-4021
General Email: bridwellk@bridgeportindex.com
Publication Website: http://bridgeportindex.com/
Publisher Name: Keith Bridwell
Publisher Email: bridwellk@bridgeportindex.com
Delivery Methods: Mail`Newsstand
Year Established: 1894
Published Days: Thur
Avg. Paid Circ.: 2690
Avg. Free Circ.: 30
Audit Company: Sworn/Estimate/Non-Audited
Audit Date: 43626

BRIDGEPORT

CHICO TEXAN

Street Address: 916 Halsell St
City: Bridgeport
State: TX
ZIP Code: 76426-3028
General Phone: (940) 683-4021
General Email: bridwellk@bridgeportindex.com
Publication Website: http://chicotexan.com/
Publisher Name: Keith Bridwell
Publisher Email: bridwellk@bridgeportindex.com
Delivery Methods: Mail`Newsstand
Year Established: 1894
Commercial printers?: Y
Mechanical specifications: Type page 13 x 21 1/2; E - 6 cols, 2 1/2, 1/6 between; A - 6 cols, 2 1/2, 1/6 between; C - 6 cols, 2 1/2, 1/6 between.
Published Days: Thur
Avg. Paid Circ.: 700
Audit Company: Sworn/Estimate/Non-Audited
Audit Date: 43626

BROOKSHIRE

THE TIMES TRIBUNE

Street Address: P.O. Box 1549
City: Brookshire
State: TX
ZIP Code: 77423
General Phone: (281) 934-4949
General Email: news.trib@timestribune.com
Publication Website: https://www.timestribune.com/
Parent Company: CNHI, LLC
Delivery Methods: Mail`Newsstand
Year Established: 1993
Published Days: Thur
Avg. Paid Circ.: 1100
Audit Company: Sworn/Estimate/Non-Audited
Audit Date: 43626

BROWNFIELD

BROWNFIELD NEWS

Street Address: 409 W Hill St
City: Brownfield
State: TX
ZIP Code: 79316
General Phone: (806) 637-4535
General Email: advertising@brownfieldonline.com
Publication Website: https://www.brownfieldonline.com/
Publisher Name: Christy Hawkins
Publisher Email: publisher@brownfieldonline.com
Publisher Phone: (806) 637-4535
Editor Name: Gina Kelly
Editor Email: news@brownfieldonline.com
Editor Phone: (806) 637-4535
Advertising Executive Name: Mattie Garcia
Advertising Executive Email: advertising@brownfieldonline.com
Advertising Executive Phone: (806) 637-4535
Delivery Methods: Mail`Racks
Year Established: 1904
Published Days: Wed`Sun
Avg. Paid Circ.: 3100
Avg. Free Circ.: 60
Audit Company: Sworn/Estimate/Non-Audited
Audit Date: 43626

BROWNWOOD

BROWNWOOD BULLETIN

Street Address: 700 Carnegie St
City: Brownwood
State: TX
ZIP Code: 76801
General Phone: (325) 646-2541
General Email: mhorton@gatehousemedia.com
Publication Website: https://www.brownwoodtx.com/
Parent Company: Gannett
Publisher Name: Melissa Horton
Publisher Email: mhorton@gatehousemedia.com
Publisher Phone: (325) 641-3122
Editor Name: Derrick Stuckly
Editor Email: derrick.stuckly@brownwoodbulletin.com
Editor Phone: (325) 641-3112
Advertising Executive Name: Chelsea Fulce
Advertising Executive Email: cfulce@brownwoodbulletin.com
Advertising Executive Phone: (325) 641-3124
Year Established: 1900
Own Printing Facility?: Y
Commercial printers?: Y
Mechanical specifications: Type page 12 x 21 1/2; E - 6 cols, 1 5/6, 1/8 between; A - 6 cols, 1 5/6, 1/8 between; C - 10 cols, 1 1/25, 1/8 between.
Published Days: Wed`Fri`Sun
Weekday Frequency: m
Avg. Paid Circ.: 3000
Audit Company: Sworn/Estimate/Non-Audited
Audit Date: 43626
Pressroom Equipment: Lines -- 7-G/Community; Folders -- 1-G/SC 240.;
Mailroom Equipment: Tying Machines -- 1-MLN/7CD 700; Address Machine -- 1/El.;
Business Equipment: Compaq/486, Dell/486, 2-ALR/386
Classified Equipment: Hardware -- APP/Power Mac;
Classified Software: Baseview.
Editorial Equipment: Hardware -- 1-APP/Power Mac, 1-APP/Mac G3
Editorial Software: Baseview.
Production Equipment: Hardware -- 1-APP/Mac LaserWriter II, 2-HP/LaserJet 4MV, Pre Press/Panther Pro Imagesetter; Cameras -- 1-C/Spartan II Automatic; Scanners -- LaCie/Silverscanner II.

BUFFALO

BUFFALO EXPRESS

Street Address: 912 E Commerce
City: Buffalo
State: TX
ZIP Code: 75831
General Phone: (903) 322-6009
General Email: buffaloexpress@windstream.net
Publication Website: http://www.buffaloexpressnews.com/
Publisher Name: Mary Ann Vaughn
Advertising Executive Name: Mary Ann Vaughn
Delivery Methods: Mail`Racks
Year Established: 2000
Published Days: Tues
Avg. Paid Circ.: 1695
Audit Company: Sworn/Estimate/Non-Audited
Audit Date: 43626

BUFFALO

THE BUFFALO PRESS

Street Address: 924 W Commerce
City: Buffalo
State: TX
ZIP Code: 75831
General Phone: (903) 322-4248
General Email: buffalopress@gmail.com
Publication Website: https://www.leoncountytoday.com/
Publisher Name: Mac Shadix
Delivery Methods: Mail`Newsstand
Year Established: 1931
Published Days: Wed
Avg. Paid Circ.: 3000
Avg. Free Circ.: 2500
Audit Company: Sworn/Estimate/Non-Audited
Audit Date: 43626

BUNA

THE BUNA BEACON

Street Address: 566 TX State Highway 62
City: Buna
State: TX
ZIP Code: 77612-6472
General Phone: (409) 994-2218
General Email: publisher@bunabeacon.com
Publication Website: https://bunabeacon.com/
Publisher Name: Barbara Davis
Publisher Email: publisher@bunabeacon.com
Editor Name: Barbara Davis
Delivery Methods: Mail`Newsstand`Racks
Year Established: 1990
Published Days: Wed
Avg. Paid Circ.: 1601
Audit Company: Sworn/Estimate/Non-Audited
Audit Date: 43626

BURKBURNETT

BURKBURNETT INFORMER STAR

Street Address: 417 Avenue C
City: Burkburnett
State: TX
ZIP Code: 76354-3424
General Phone: (940) 569-2191
General Email: jeff@burknews.com
Publication Website: http://burknews.com/
Editor Email: jeff@burknews.com
Delivery Methods: Mail`Racks
Year Established: 1908
Published Days: Thur
Avg. Paid Circ.: 2850
Audit Company: Sworn/Estimate/Non-Audited
Audit Date: 43626

BURLESON

BURLESON STAR

Street Address: 327 NW Renfro St
City: Burleson
State: TX
ZIP Code: 76028-3421
General Phone: (817) 295-0486
General Email: ads@thestargroup.com
Publication Website: http://www.burlesonstar.net/
Parent Company: Moser Community Media, LLC
Delivery Methods: Mail`Newsstand`Racks
Year Established: 1964
Own Printing Facility?: Y
Commercial printers?: Y
Published Days: Wed`Sun
Avg. Paid Circ.: 3328
Avg. Free Circ.: 259
Audit Company: Sworn/Estimate/Non-Audited
Audit Date: 43626

BURNET

BURNET BULLETIN

Street Address: 220 S Main St
City: Burnet
State: TX
ZIP Code: 78611
General Phone: (512) 756-6136
General Email: publisher@burnetbulletin.com
Publication Website: https://www.burnetbulletin.com/
Parent Company: Highland Lakes Newspapers
Publisher Name: Jeff Shabram
Publisher Email: jeff@highlandernews.com
Publisher Phone: (830) 693-4367, ext : 224
Editor Name: Jeff Shabram
Editor Email: jeff@highlandernews.com
Editor Phone: (830) 693-4367, ext : 224
Advertising Executive Name: Kari Sardo
Advertising Executive Email: kari@highlandernews.com
Advertising Executive Phone: (512) 756-6136
Delivery Methods: Mail`Newsstand`Racks
Year Established: 1873
Own Printing Facility?: Y
Commercial printers?: Y
Published Days: Wed
Avg. Paid Circ.: 5115
Audit Company: Sworn/Estimate/Non-Audited
Audit Date: 43626
Note: Lake Country Life, a weekly full-color dining, entertainment and realty section is distributed weekly with the Bulletin. Minimum 16 pages color.

BURNET

CITIZENS GAZETTE

Street Address: 106 Linsey Cv
City: Burnet
State: TX
ZIP Code: 78611-5886
General Phone: (512) 756-6640
General Email: cgazette@tstar.net
Delivery Methods: Mail`Newsstand
Year Established: 1991
Published Days: Wed
Avg. Paid Circ.: 1000
Audit Company: Sworn/Estimate/Non-Audited
Audit Date: 43626

CALDWELL

BURLESON COUNTY TRIBUNE

Street Address: 306 W Highway 21
City: Caldwell
State: TX
ZIP Code: 77836
General Phone: (979) 567-3286
General Email: ads@bctribune.com
Publication Website: https://www.bctribune.com/
Editor Name: Roy Sanders
Editor Email: news@bctribune.com
Advertising Executive Name: Amber Campise
Advertising Executive Email: amber@bctribune.com
Delivery Methods: Mail`Newsstand
Year Established: 1884
Mechanical specifications: Type page 13 x 21; E - 6 cols, 2 1/16, 1/8 between; A - 6 cols, 2 1/16, 1/8 between; C - 8 cols, 1 1/2, 1/8 between.
Published Days: Thur
Avg. Paid Circ.: 4300
Avg. Free Circ.: 40
Audit Company: Sworn/Estimate/Non-Audited
Audit Date: 43626

CAMERON

THE CAMERON HERALD

Street Address: P.O. Box 1230
City: Cameron
State: TX
ZIP Code: 76520-3341
General Phone: (254) 697-6671
General Email: advertising@cameronherald.com
Publication Website: https://www.cameronherald.com/
Publisher Name: Lindsey Vaculi
Publisher Email: publisher@cameronherald.com
Advertising Executive Name: Deborah Hail
Advertising Executive Email: advertising@cameronherald.com
Delivery Methods: Mail`Newsstand
Year Established: 1860
Mechanical specifications: Type page 11 5/8 x 21 1/2; E - 6 cols, 1 5/6, 1/8 between; A - 6 cols, 1 5/6, 1/8 between; C - 9 cols, 1 1/8, 1/8 between.
Published Days: Thur
Avg. Paid Circ.: 1943
Avg. Free Circ.: 123
Audit Company: Sworn/Estimate/Non-Audited
Audit Date: 43626

CAMERON

THORNDALE CHAMPION

Street Address: 108 E 1st St
City: Cameron
State: TX
ZIP Code: 76520-3341
General Phone: (254) 455-0144
General Email: tdchamp@cameronherald.com
Publication Website: https://www.cameronherald.com/
Publisher Name: Lindsey Vaculin

Publisher Email: publisher@cameronherald.com
Advertising Executive Name: Deborah Hail
Advertising Executive Email: advertising@cameronherald.com
Delivery Methods: Mail
Year Established: 1898
Published Days: Thur
Avg. Paid Circ.: 490
Audit Company: Sworn/Estimate/Non-Audited
Audit Date: 43626

CANADIAN

THE CANADIAN RECORD

Street Address: 211 Main St
City: Canadian
State: TX
ZIP Code: 79014-2212
General Phone: (806) 323-6461
General Email: news@canadianrecord.com
Publication Website: https://www.canadianrecord.com/
Publisher Name: Laurie Ezzell Brown
Editor Name: Laurie Ezzell Brown
Editor Email: editor@canadianrecord.com
Advertising Executive Name: Ray Weeks
Advertising Executive Email: advertising@canadianrecord.com
Delivery Methods: Mail`Newsstand
Year Established: 1893
Mechanical specifications: Type page 9 5/8 x 13 1/2; E - 4 cols, 2 1/2, 1/6 between; A - 4 cols, 2 1/2, 1/6 between; C - 4 cols, 2 1/2, 1/6 between.
Published Days: Thur
Avg. Paid Circ.: 1750
Avg. Free Circ.: 35
Audit Company: Sworn/Estimate/Non-Audited
Audit Date: 43626

CANTON

THE QUINLAN-TAWAKONI NEWS

Street Address: 103 E Tyler St
City: Canton
State: TX
ZIP Code: 75103
General Phone: (903) 567-4000
General Email: editor@vanzandtnews.com
Publication Website: https://www.quinlan-tawakoninews.com/
Parent Company: Van Zandt Newspapers LLC
Publisher Name: Brad Blakemore
Publisher Email: brad@vanzandtnews.com
Publisher Phone: (903) 567-4000
Editor Name: Britne Hammons
Editor Email: editor@vanzandtnews.com
Editor Phone: (903) 567-4000
Advertising Executive Name: David Barber
Advertising Executive Email: sales@vanzandtnews.com
Advertising Executive Phone: (903) 567-4000
Delivery Methods: Mail`Newsstand
Year Established: 1963
Published Days: Fri
Avg. Paid Circ.: 3000
Audit Company: Sworn/Estimate/Non-Audited
Audit Date: 43626

CANYON

THE CANYON NEWS

Street Address: 1500 5th Ave
City: Canyon
State: TX
ZIP Code: 79015-3830
General Phone: (806) 655-7121
General Email: marketing@canyonnews.com
Publication Website: http://www.canyonnews.com/

Parent Company: Hearst Corp.
Publisher Name: Jeff Shabram
Publisher Email: jshabram@hearstnp.com
Editor Name: Tim Ritter
Editor Email: reporter@canyonnews.com
Advertising Executive Name: Becky Lindmark
Advertising Executive Email: becky@canyonnews.com
Delivery Methods: Mail`Newsstand
Year Established: 1896
Mechanical specifications: Type page 13 x 21; E - 6 cols, 1/6 between; A - 6 cols, 1/6 between; C - 8 cols, 1/6 between.
Published Days: Thur`Sun
Avg. Paid Circ.: 3900
Avg. Free Circ.: 300
Audit Company: Sworn/Estimate/Non-Audited
Audit Date: 43626

CARRIZO SPRINGS

CARRIZO SPRINGS JAVELIN

Street Address: 604 N 1st St
City: Carrizo Springs
State: TX
ZIP Code: 78834-2602
General Phone: (830) 876-2318
General Email: csjavelin@yahoo.com
Publication Website: http://carrizospringsjavelin.com/
Delivery Methods: Mail`Newsstand
Year Established: 1884
Published Days: Wed
Published Other: weekly
Avg. Paid Circ.: 2100
Avg. Free Circ.: 100
Audit Company: Sworn/Estimate/Non-Audited
Audit Date: 43626

CARTHAGE

THE PANOLA WATCHMAN

Street Address: 109 W Panola St
City: Carthage
State: TX
ZIP Code: 75633-2631
General Phone: (903) 693-7888
General Email: news@panolawatchman.com
Publication Website: https://www.panolawatchman.com/
Publisher Name: Jerry Pye
Publisher Email: jpye@panolawatchman.com
Publisher Phone: (903) 927-5977
Editor Name: Meredith Shamburger
Editor Email: mshamburger@panolawatchman.com
Editor Phone: (903) 232-7261
Advertising Executive Name: Melissa Douglas
Advertising Executive Email: mdouglas@panolawatchman.com
Advertising Executive Phone: (903) 232-7220
Delivery Methods: Mail`Newsstand`Racks
Year Established: 1873
Own Printing Facility?: Y
Commercial printers?: Y
Mechanical specifications: Type page 13 x 21 1/2; E - 6 cols, 2, 1/6 between; A - 6 cols, 2, 1/6 between; C - 6 cols, 2, 1/6 between.
Published Days: Wed`Sat
Avg. Paid Circ.: 4826
Avg. Free Circ.: 80
Audit Company: Sworn/Estimate/Non-Audited
Audit Date: 43626

CASTROVILLE

CASTROVILLE NEWS BULLETIN

Street Address: 1105 Fiorella St
City: Castroville

State: TX
ZIP Code: 78009-4577
General Phone: (830) 931-9698
General Email: cornerstonenews@sbcglobal.net
Publication Website: http://cornerstonenewspapers.com/news-bulletin.html
Parent Company: Cornerstone Publication, Inc
Publisher Name: Natalie Spencer
Publisher Email: spencernatalie@sbcglobal.net
Editor Name: Gabriel Romero
Advertising Executive Name: Tony Felan
Delivery Methods: Mail`Newsstand
Year Established: 1958
Published Days: Thur
Avg. Paid Circ.: 1991
Avg. Free Circ.: 9
Audit Company: Sworn/Estimate/Non-Audited
Audit Date: 43626

CASTROVILLE

LEADER NEWS

Street Address: 1105 Fiorella St
City: Castroville
State: TX
ZIP Code: 78009-4577
General Phone: (830) 931-9698
General Email: cornerstonenews@sbcglobal.net
Publication Website: http://cornerstonenewspapers.com/leader-news.html
Parent Company: Cornerstone Publication, Inc
Publisher Name: Natalie Spencer
Publisher Email: spencernatalie@sbcglobal.net
Editor Name: Gabriel Romero
Advertising Executive Name: Tony Felan
Delivery Methods: Mail`Racks
Year Established: 1999
Mechanical specifications: Type page 13 x 21; E - 6 cols, 2, 5/16 between; A - 6 cols, 2, 5/16 between; C - 6 cols, 2, 5/16 between.
Published Days: Thur
Avg. Paid Circ.: 2300
Audit Company: Sworn/Estimate/Non-Audited
Audit Date: 43626

CASTROVILLE

MEDINA VALLEY TIMES

Street Address: 1105 Fiorella St
City: Castroville
State: TX
ZIP Code: 78009-4577
General Phone: (830) 931-9698
General Email: cornerstoneads@sbcglobal.net
Publication Website: http://cornerstonenewspapers.com/medina-valley-times.html
Parent Company: Cornerstone Publication, Inc
Publisher Name: Natalie Spencer
Publisher Email: spencernatalie@sbcglobal.net
Editor Name: Gabriel Romero
Advertising Executive Name: Tony Felan
Delivery Methods: Mail`Newsstand
Year Established: 1977
Mechanical specifications: Type page 13 x 21; E - 6 cols, 2 1/16, 1/8 between; A - 6 cols, 2 1/16, 1/8 between; C - 6 cols, 2 1/16, 1/8 between.
Published Days: Thur
Avg. Paid Circ.: 3255
Avg. Free Circ.: 44
Audit Company: Sworn/Estimate/Non-Audited
Audit Date: 43626

CLARENDON

CLARENDON ENTERPRISE

Street Address: 105 Kearney St
City: Clarendon
State: TX
ZIP Code: 79226-6051
General Phone: (806) 874-2259
General Email: news@clarendononline.com
Publication Website: https://www.clarendonlive.com/
Publisher Name: Roger A. Estlack
Editor Name: Roger A. Estlack
Delivery Methods: Mail`Newsstand`Racks
Year Established: 1878
Mechanical specifications: Type page 13 x 20; E - 6 cols, between; A - 6 cols, between; C - 6 cols, between.
Published Days: Thur
Avg. Paid Circ.: 1125
Audit Company: Sworn/Estimate/Non-Audited
Audit Date: 43626

CLARKSVILLE

CLARKSVILLE TIMES

Street Address: 109 South Locust St.
City: Clarksville
State: TX
ZIP Code: 75426
General Phone: (903) 427-0002
General Email: theclarksvilletimes@gmail.com
Publication Website: https://theclarksvilletimes.blogspot.com/
Parent Company: New Clarksville Times Publishing LLC
Publisher Name: Patricia Antonelli
Editor Name: Lou Antonelli
Delivery Methods: Mail`Newsstand`Racks
Year Established: 1873
Published Days: Thur
Avg. Paid Circ.: 1842
Avg. Free Circ.: 52
Audit Company: Sworn/Estimate/Non-Audited
Audit Date: 43626

CLAUDE

THE CLAUDE NEWS

Street Address: 119 N Trice St
City: Claude
State: TX
ZIP Code: 79019
General Phone: (806) 226-4500
General Email: editor@claudenews.com
Publication Website: https://claudenewstx.com/
Publisher Name: Christiana Mustion
Editor Name: Christiana Mustion
Delivery Methods: Mail`Racks
Year Established: 1890
Own Printing Facility?: Y
Commercial printers?: Y
Published Days: Fri
Avg. Paid Circ.: 700
Audit Company: Sworn/Estimate/Non-Audited
Audit Date: 43626

CLEVELAND

CLEVELAND ADVOCATE

Street Address: 106 W. Hanson Street
City: Cleveland
State: TX
ZIP Code: 77328
General Phone: (281) 592-2626
General Email: cadvocate@hcnonline.com
Publication Website: https://www.chron.com/neighborhood/cleveland/
Parent Company: Hearst Corp.
Editor Name: Vanesa Brashier
Editor Email: cadvocate@hcnonline.com
Advertising Executive Name: Dianne Brady
Advertising Executive Email: dbrady@hcnonline.com
Delivery Methods: Mail`Newsstand`Carrier`Racks
Year Established: 1917
Mechanical specifications: 10.388â x 20.5â
Published Days: Wed
Avg. Paid Circ.: 4152
Audit Company: Sworn/Estimate/Non-Audited
Audit Date: 43626

CLEVELAND

DAYTON NEWS

Street Address: 106 W. Hanson Street
City: Cleveland
State: TX
ZIP Code: 77328
General Phone: (281) 592-2626
General Email: dnewseditor@hcnonline.com
Publication Website: https://www.chron.com/
Parent Company: Hearst Corp.
Editor Name: Mike George
Editor Email: dnewseditor@hcnonline.com
Delivery Methods: Carrier`Racks
Year Established: 2004
Published Days: Wed
Avg. Free Circ.: 6177
Audit Company: Sworn/Estimate/Non-Audited
Audit Date: 43626

CLEVELAND

EASTEX ADVOCATE

Street Address: 106 W Hanson St
City: Cleveland
State: TX
ZIP Code: 77327-4406
General Phone: (281) 592-2626
General Email: dbrady@hcnonline.com
Publication Website: http://www.eastexadvocate.com/
Parent Company: Hearst Corp.
Publisher Name: Brenda Miller-Fergerson
Editor Name: Vanesa Brashier
Editor Email: eadvocate@hcnonline.com
Advertising Executive Name: Dianne Brady
Advertising Executive Email: dbrady@hcnonline.com
Delivery Methods: Carrier`Racks
Year Established: 1917
Mechanical specifications: 10.388â x 20.5â
Published Days: Wed
Avg. Paid Circ.: 10523
Audit Company: Sworn/Estimate/Non-Audited
Audit Date: 43626

CLIFTON

THE CLIFTON RECORD

Street Address: 310 W 5th St
City: Clifton
State: TX
ZIP Code: 76634-1611
General Phone: (254) 675-3336
General Email: bvoss@cliftonrecord.com
Publication Website: https://www.cliftonrecord.com/
Publisher Name: Ed Gambardella
Publisher Email: bvoss@cliftonrecord.com
Editor Name: Cynthia D. Davis
Editor Email: news@cliftonrecord.com
Advertising Executive Name: Jessica Brown
Advertising Executive Email: ads@meridiantribune.com
Delivery Methods: Mail`Newsstand
Year Established: 1895
Published Days: Wed
Avg. Paid Circ.: 2303
Audit Company: Sworn/Estimate/Non-Audited
Audit Date: 43626

COLUMBUS

THE BANNER PRESS NEWSPAPER

Street Address: 1217 Bowie St
City: Columbus
State: TX
ZIP Code: 78934-2343
General Phone: (979) 732-6243
General Email: banneroffice@sbcglobal.net
Publication Website: https://www.bannerpresspaper.com/
Delivery Methods: Mail`Newsstand`Racks
Year Established: 1985
Commercial printers?: Y
Mechanical specifications: Type page 13 3/4 x 21; E - 7 cols, 1 3/4, between; A - 7 cols, 1 3/4, between; C - 7 cols, 1 3/4, between.
Published Days: Thur
Avg. Paid Circ.: 4250
Avg. Free Circ.: 50
Audit Company: Sworn/Estimate/Non-Audited
Audit Date: 43626

COMANCHE

THE COMANCHE CHIEF

Street Address: 203 W Grand Ave
City: Comanche
State: TX
ZIP Code: 76442-2316
General Phone: (325) 356-2636
General Email: editor@thecomanchechief.com
Publication Website: https://www.thecomanchechief.com/
Editor Email: editor@thecomanchechief.com
Delivery Methods: Mail`Newsstand`Racks
Year Established: 1873
Own Printing Facility?: N
Commercial printers?: Y
Published Days: Thur
Avg. Paid Circ.: 3000
Audit Company: Sworn/Estimate/Non-Audited
Audit Date: 43626

COMFORT

THE COMFORT NEWS

Street Address: 636 Second Street
City: Comfort
State: TX
ZIP Code: 78013-2318
General Phone: (830) 995-3634
General Email: dukecomfort@hctc.net
Publication Website: https://www.thecomfortnews.com/
Parent Company: The Comfort News & Print, Inc.
Publisher Name: V.J. McAteer
Editor Name: Michael Hawkins
Delivery Methods: Mail`Newsstand`Racks
Year Established: 1904
Published Days: Thur
Avg. Paid Circ.: 1146
Audit Company: Sworn/Estimate/Non-Audited
Audit Date: 43626

CONROE

ATASCOCITA OBSERVER

Street Address: 100 Avenue A
City: Conroe
State: TX
ZIP Code: 77301-2946
General Phone: (713) 362-1570
General Email: cturner@hcnonline.com
Publication Website: https://www.chron.com/neighborhood/atascocita/
Parent Company: Hearst Corp.
Publisher Name: Jim Fredricks
Publisher Email: jfredricks@hcnonline.com
Publisher Phone: (936) 521-3400
Editor Name: Andy DuBois
Editor Email: adubois@hcnonline.com
Editor Phone: (936) 521-3418
Advertising Executive Name: Karen Mauermann
Advertising Executive Email: kmauermann@hcnonline.com
Advertising Executive Phone: (936) 521-3439
Delivery Methods: Carrier`Racks
Year Established: 2003
Mechanical specifications: 10.388″ x 20.5″
Published Days: Wed
Avg. Free Circ.: 17998
Audit Company: Sworn/Estimate/Non-Audited
Audit Date: 43626

CONROE

HUMBLE OBSERVER

Street Address: 100 Avenue A
City: Conroe
State: TX
ZIP Code: 77301-2946
General Phone: (281) 378-1060
General Email: news@chron.com
Publication Website: https://www.chron.com/neighborhood/humble/
Parent Company: Hearst Corp.
Delivery Methods: Mail`Newsstand`Racks
Year Established: 1975
Mechanical specifications: 10.388″ x 20.5″
Published Days: Wed
Avg. Free Circ.: 11977
Audit Company: Sworn/Estimate/Non-Audited
Audit Date: 43626

CONROE

LAKE HOUSTON OBSERVER

Street Address: 100 Avenue A
City: Conroe
State: TX
ZIP Code: 77301-2946
General Phone: (281) 378-1060
General Email: news@chron.com
Publication Website: https://www.chron.com/neighborhood/lakehouston/
Parent Company: Hearst Corp.
Delivery Methods: Carrier`Racks
Year Established: 1981
Mechanical specifications: 10.388″ x 20.5″
Published Days: Wed
Avg. Free Circ.: 7270
Audit Company: Sworn/Estimate/Non-Audited
Audit Date: 43626

CONROE

THE RANCHER

Street Address: 100 Avenue A
City: Conroe
State: TX
ZIP Code: 77301-2946
General Phone: (281) 378-1900
General Email: news@chron.com
Publication Website: https://www.chron.com/neighborhood/katy/

Parent Company: Hearst Corp.
Delivery Methods: Mail`Newsstand`Racks
Year Established: 1953
Published Days: Thur
Avg. Free Circ.: 26985
Audit Company: Sworn/Estimate/Non-Audited
Audit Date: 43626

CONROE

THE WOODLANDS VILLAGER

Street Address: 100 Avenue A
City: Conroe
State: TX
ZIP Code: 77301-2946
General Phone: (281) 378-1040
General Email: news@chron.com
Publication Website: https://www.chron.com/neighborhood/woodlands/
Parent Company: Hearst Corp.
Delivery Methods: Mail`Newsstand`Carrier`Racks
Year Established: 1977
Mechanical specifications: 6 columns (10.388″) x 20.5″
Published Days: Thur
Avg. Free Circ.: 44200
Audit Company: Sworn/Estimate/Non-Audited
Audit Date: 43626

CONROE

TOMBALL POTPOURRI

Street Address: 100 Avenue A
City: Conroe
State: TX
ZIP Code: 77301-2946
General Phone: (281) 378-1080
General Email: news@chron.com
Publication Website: https://www.chron.com/neighborhood/tomball/
Parent Company: Hearst Corp.
Delivery Methods: Mail`Newsstand`Racks
Year Established: 1986
Mechanical specifications: Type page 10 x 13; E - 6 cols, 1 1/2, 1/8 between; A - 6 cols, 1 1/2, 1/8 between; C - 6 cols, 1 1/2, 1/8 between.
Published Days: Wed
Avg. Free Circ.: 17490
Audit Company: Sworn/Estimate/Non-Audited
Audit Date: 43626

COOPER

COOPER REVIEW

Street Address: P.O. Box 430
City: Cooper
State: TX
ZIP Code: 75432-0430
General Phone: (903) 395-2175
General Email: ads@cooperreview.com
Publication Website: http://cooperreview.com/
Publisher Name: Jim Butler
Publisher Email: jimb@cooperreview.com
Editor Name: Janis Thomas
Editor Email: jthomas@cooperreview.com
Advertising Executive Email: ads@cooperreview.com
Delivery Methods: Mail`Racks
Year Established: 1880
Mechanical specifications: Type page 12 x 21 1/2; E - 6 cols, 2 1/16, 1/8 between; A - 6 cols, 2 1/16, 1/8 between; C - 6 cols, 2 1/16, 1/8 between.
Published Days: Thur
Avg. Paid Circ.: 1550
Avg. Free Circ.: 100
Audit Company: Sworn/Estimate/Non-Audited
Audit Date: 43626

COPPELL

CITIZENS' ADVOCATE

Street Address: P.O. Box 557
City: Coppell
State: TX
ZIP Code: 75019-4481
General Phone: (972) 462-8192
General Email: citizensadvocate2000@yahoo.com
Publication Website: http://www.coppellcitizensadvocate.com/
Delivery Methods: Mail`Racks
Year Established: 1984
Published Days: Fri
Avg. Paid Circ.: 5000
Audit Company: Sworn/Estimate/Non-Audited
Audit Date: 43626

COPPERAS COVE

COPPERAS COVE LEADER-PRESS

Street Address: 2210 E Business 190
City: Copperas Cove
State: TX
ZIP Code: 76522-2523
General Phone: (254) 547-4207
General Email: advertising@coveleaderpress.com
Publication Website: https://www.coveleaderpress.com/
Parent Company: Copperas Cove Newspapers Inc.
Delivery Methods: Mail`Newsstand`Carrier`Racks
Year Established: 1894
Published Days: Tues`Fri
Avg. Paid Circ.: 3650
Avg. Free Circ.: 56
Audit Company: Sworn/Estimate/Non-Audited
Audit Date: 43626

CRYSTAL CITY

ZAVALA COUNTY SENTINEL

Street Address: 202 E Nueces St
City: Crystal City
State: TX
ZIP Code: 78839-3325
General Phone: (830) 374-3465
General Email: zcsentinel@sbcglobal.net
Publication Website: https://www.zcsentinel.com/
Parent Company: Winter Garden Publishing Co., Inc.
Editor Name: Annie Lee
Delivery Methods: Mail`Racks
Year Established: 1911
Published Days: Thur
Avg. Paid Circ.: 2300
Avg. Free Circ.: 50
Audit Company: Sworn/Estimate/Non-Audited
Audit Date: 43626

CUERO

THE CUERO RECORD

Street Address: 119 E Main St
City: Cuero
State: TX
ZIP Code: 77954-3021
General Phone: (361) 275-3464
General Email: cuerorecord@cuerorecord.com
Publication Website: https://www.cuerorecord.com/
Parent Company: Moser Community Media
Publisher Name: Sonya Timpone

Advertising Executive Name: Sonya Timpone
Delivery Methods: Mail`Newsstand`Racks
Year Established: 1894
Published Days: Wed
Avg. Paid Circ.: 2445
Avg. Free Circ.: 2685
Audit Company: Sworn/Estimate/Non-Audited
Audit Date: 43626

DALHART

DALHART TEXAN

Street Address: 410 Denrock Ave
City: Dalhart
State: TX
ZIP Code: 79022-2628
General Phone: (806) 244-4511
General Email: sales@thedalharttexan.com
Publication Website: http://thedalharttexan.com/
Parent Company: Wesner Media Publication
Publisher Email: publisher@thedalharttexan.com
Editor Name: Nixie Sanderson
Advertising Executive Name: Rhonda Butters
Advertising Executive Email: sales@thedalharttexan.com
Delivery Methods: Mail`Newsstand`Racks
Year Established: 1901
Mechanical specifications: Type page 15 x 21; E - 6 cols, 2 1/16, 1/8 between; A - 6 cols, 2 1/16, 1/8 between; C - 6 cols, 2 1/16, 1/8 between.
Published Days: Tues`Fri
Avg. Paid Circ.: 2300
Audit Company: Sworn/Estimate/Non-Audited
Audit Date: 43626

DALLAS

DALLAS BUSINESS JOURNAL

Street Address: 2515 McKinney Ave
City: Dallas
State: TX
ZIP Code: 75201-7675
General Phone: (214) 696-5959
General Email: dallas@bizjournals.com
Publication Website: https://www.bizjournals.com/dallas/
Parent Company: American City Business Journals
Publisher Name: Ollie Chandhok
Publisher Email: ochandhok@bizjournals.com
Publisher Phone: (214) 706-7147
Editor Name: Anna Butler
Editor Email: abutler@bizjournals.com
Editor Phone: (214) 706-7113
Advertising Executive Name: Cheryl Hood
Advertising Executive Email: chood@bizjournals.com
Advertising Executive Phone: (214) 706-7140
Delivery Methods: Mail`Racks
Year Established: 1977
Published Days: Fri
Avg. Paid Circ.: 11847
Audit Company: Sworn/Estimate/Non-Audited
Audit Date: 43626

DALLAS

LONE STAR OUTDOOR NEWS

Street Address: PO Box 551695
City: Dallas
State: TX
ZIP Code: 75355-1695
General Phone: (214) 361-2276
General Email: cnyhus@lonestaroutdoornews.com
Publication Website: https://www.lsonews.

com/
Editor Name: Lili Sams
Editor Email: editor@lonestaroutdoornews.com
Delivery Methods: Mail`Newsstand`Racks
Year Established: 2004
Published Days: Fri
Avg. Paid Circ.: 5242
Avg. Free Circ.: 35519
Audit Company: VAC
Audit Date: 43293

DALLAS

PARK CITIES NEWS

Street Address: 4136 Greenbrier Dr
City: Dallas
State: TX
ZIP Code: 75225-6635
General Phone: (214) 369-7570
General Email: advertising@peoplenewspapers.com
Publication Website: http://www.parkcitiesnews.com/
Delivery Methods: Mail
Year Established: 1938
Own Printing Facility?: N
Commercial printers?: N
Mechanical specifications: Type page 13 x 21; E - 6 cols, 2, between; A - 6 cols, 2, between; C - 5 cols, 2 1/2, between.
Published Days: Thur
Avg. Paid Circ.: 5000
Avg. Free Circ.: 250
Audit Company: Sworn/Estimate/Non-Audited
Audit Date: 43626

DALLAS

PARK CITIES PEOPLE

Street Address: 750 North Saint Paul St. Suite 2100
City: Dallas
State: TX
ZIP Code: 75201-3214
General Phone: (214) 739-2244
General Email: pat.martin@peoplenewspapers.com
Publication Website: https://www.peoplenewspapers.com/category/park-cities/
Parent Company: People Newspapers
Publisher Name: Patricia Martin
Publisher Email: pat.martin@peoplenewspapers.com
Editor Name: William Taylor
Editor Email: william.taylor@peoplenewspapers.com
Delivery Methods: Mail`Newsstand`Racks
Year Established: 1981
Mechanical specifications: 5 column x 14" page size 1 column 1.85" 2 column 3.88" 3 column 5.92" 4 column 7.96" 5 column 10.00"
Published Days: Mthly
Published Other: Monthly - Last week of Month
Avg. Paid Circ.: 275
Avg. Free Circ.: 21536
Audit Company: CVC
Audit Date: 43658
Note: Second newspaper Preston Hollow People Circ = 26,900

DALLAS

PRESTON HOLLOW PEOPLE

Street Address: 750 N Saint Paul St
City: Dallas
State: TX
ZIP Code: 75201-3214
General Phone: (214) 739-2244
General Email: pat.martin@peoplenewspapers.com

Publication Website: https://www.peoplenewspapers.com/category/preston-hollow/
Parent Company: People Newspapers
Publisher Name: Patricia Martin
Publisher Email: pat.martin@peoplenewspapers.com
Editor Name: William Taylor
Editor Email: william.taylor@peoplenewspapers.com
Delivery Methods: Mail`Newsstand`Racks
Year Established: 1981
Mechanical specifications: 5 column x 14" page size 1 column 1.85" 2 column 3.88" 3 column 5.92" 4 column 7.96" 5 column 10.00"
Published Days: Mthly
Published Other: Monthly - last week of the month
Avg. Paid Circ.: 125
Avg. Free Circ.: 25963
Audit Company: CVC
Audit Date: 43658

DALLAS

TEXAS JEWISH POST

Street Address: 7920 Belt Line Rd., Suite #680
City: Dallas
State: TX
ZIP Code: 75254-8150
General Phone: (972) 458-7283
General Email: susanw@tjpnews.com
Publication Website: http://tjpnews.com/
Parent Company: Joseph Jacobs Organization
Advertising Executive Name: Amy Doty
Advertising Executive Email: amyd@tjpnews.com
Delivery Methods: Mail`Newsstand`Racks
Year Established: 1947
Mechanical specifications: Type page 10 1/8 x 12 1/2; E - 6 cols, between; A - 6 cols, between.
Published Days: Thur
Avg. Paid Circ.: 3569
Avg. Free Circ.: 455
Audit Company: Sworn/Estimate/Non-Audited
Audit Date: 43626

DALLAS

TEXAS LAWYER

Street Address: 1412 Main St
City: Dallas
State: TX
ZIP Code: 75202-4014
General Phone: (214) 744-9300
General Email: ccollins@alm.com
Publication Website: https://www.law.com/texaslawyer/
Parent Company: AIM Media Texas
Delivery Methods: Mail`Racks
Year Established: 1985
Published Days: Mon
Avg. Paid Circ.: 3694
Audit Company: Sworn/Estimate/Non-Audited
Audit Date: 43626

DE LEON

DE LEON FREE PRESS

Street Address: 324 S. Texas Street
City: De Leon
State: TX
ZIP Code: 76444
General Phone: (254) 893-6868
General Email: ads@deleonfreepress.com
Publication Website: http://deleonfreepress.com/
Publisher Name: Jon Awbrey
Editor Name: Laura Kestner

Advertising Executive Name: Betty Wofford
Delivery Methods: Mail`Newsstand
Year Established: 1890
Published Days: Thur
Avg. Paid Circ.: 2000
Audit Company: Sworn/Estimate/Non-Audited

DECATUR

WISE COUNTY MESSENGER

Street Address: PO Box 149, 115 South Trinity
City: Decatur
State: TX
ZIP Code: 76234-1819
General Phone: (940) 627-5987
General Email: webmaster@wcmessenger.com
Publication Website: https://www.wcmessenger.com/
Publisher Name: Kristen Tribe
Editor Name: Richard Greene
Advertising Executive Name: Lisa Davis
Delivery Methods: Mail`Racks
Year Established: 1880
Published Days: Wed`Sat
Avg. Paid Circ.: 7745
Avg. Free Circ.: 34
Audit Company: Sworn/Estimate/Non-Audited
Audit Date: 43626

DEVINE

DEVINE NEWS

Street Address: 216 S Bright Dr
City: Devine
State: TX
ZIP Code: 78016-3202
General Phone: (830) 665-2211
General Email: news@devinenews.com
Publication Website: https://devinenews.com/
Advertising Executive Name: Kayleen Holder
Advertising Executive Phone: (830) 665-2211
Delivery Methods: Mail`Newsstand`Racks
Year Established: 1897
Published Days: Thur
Audit Company: Sworn/Estimate/Non-Audited
Audit Date: 43626

DIMMITT

THE CASTRO COUNTY NEWS

Street Address: 108 W Bedford St
City: Dimmitt
State: TX
ZIP Code: 79027-2504
General Phone: (806) 647-1234
General Email: thecastrocountynews@yahoo.com
Publication Website: https://www.thecastrocountynews.com/
Delivery Methods: Mail
Year Established: 1924
Mechanical specifications: Type page 11 11/16 x 21; E - 6 cols, 1 13/16, 3/16 between; A - 6 cols, 1 13/16, 3/16 between; C - 6 cols, 1 13/16, 3/16 between.
Published Days: Thur
Avg. Paid Circ.: 1500
Avg. Free Circ.: 62
Audit Company: Sworn/Estimate/Non-Audited
Audit Date: 43626

DUBLIN

THE DUBLIN CITIZEN

Street Address: 938 N Patrick St
City: Dublin
State: TX
ZIP Code: 76446-1128
General Phone: (254) 445-2515
General Email: publisher@dublincitizen.com
Publication Website: https://www.dublincitizen.com/
Publisher Name: Scott Dykowski
Publisher Email: publisher@dublincitizen.com
Advertising Executive Name: Sarah Dykowski
Advertising Executive Email: composing@dublincitizen.com
Delivery Methods: Mail`Newsstand`Racks
Year Established: 1990
Mechanical specifications: 11.625 x 21
Published Days: Thur
Avg. Paid Circ.: 2400
Audit Company: Sworn/Estimate/Non-Audited
Audit Date: 43626

DUMAS

THE MOORE COUNTY NEWS-PRESS

Street Address: 702 S Meredith P.O. Box 757
City: Dumas
State: TX
ZIP Code: 79029-4444
General Phone: (806) 935-4111
General Email: advertising@moorenews.com
Publication Website: https://www.moorenews.com/
Parent Company: Lancaster Management, Inc.
Publisher Name: Michael Wright
Publisher Email: mwright@moorenews.com
Editor Name: Michael Wright
Editor Email: editor@moorenews.com
Advertising Executive Name: Shane Austin
Advertising Executive Email: advertising@moorenews.com
Delivery Methods: Mail`Newsstand`Carrier`Racks
Year Established: 1927
Own Printing Facility?: N
Commercial printers?: N
Mechanical specifications: Type page 12 1/2 x 20; E - 6 cols, 1 15/16, 1/8 between; A - 6 cols, 1 15/16, 1/8 between; C - 8 cols, 1 1/2, 1/8 between.
Published Days: Thur`Sun
Weekday Frequency: m
Saturday Frequency: m
Avg. Paid Circ.: 3480
Audit Company: Sworn/Estimate/Non-Audited
Audit Date: 43626

EAGLE LAKE

EAGLE LAKE HEADLIGHT

Street Address: 220 E Main St
City: Eagle Lake
State: TX
ZIP Code: 77434-2426
General Phone: (979) 234-5521
General Email: eaglelakeheadlight@sbcglobal.net
Publication Website: http://www.theeaglelakeheadlight.com/
Delivery Methods: Mail`Racks
Year Established: 1903
Published Days: Thur
Avg. Paid Circ.: 2057
Audit Company: Sworn/Estimate/Non-Audited
Audit Date: 43626

EASTLAND

CALLAHAN COUNTY STAR

Street Address: 215 S Seaman St

City: Eastland
State: TX
ZIP Code: 76448-2745
General Phone: (254) 629-1707
General Email: ecn@att.net
Delivery Methods: Mail
Year Established: 1887
Published Days: Thur
Avg. Paid Circ.: 579
Audit Company: Sworn/Estimate/Non-Audited
Audit Date: 43626

EDEN

THE EDEN ECHO

Street Address: 131 Market St, PO Box 1069
City: Eden
State: TX
ZIP Code: 76837
General Phone: (325) 869-5717
General Email: edenecho@wcc.net
Publication Website: https://www.edenecho.net/
Parent Company: EDEN APPLE TREE ENTERPRISES LLC
Delivery Methods: Mail`Racks
Year Established: 1906
Own Printing Facility?: N
Commercial printers?: Y
Published Days: Thur
Avg. Paid Circ.: 610
Avg. Free Circ.: 30
Audit Company: Sworn/Estimate/Non-Audited
Audit Date: 43626
Pressroom Equipment: 2 computers
Pressroom Software: Adobe InDesign cs4
Mailroom Software: interlink
Note: none

EDNA

JACKSON COUNTY HERALD-TRIBUNE

Street Address: 306 N Wells St
City: Edna
State: TX
ZIP Code: 77957-2729
General Phone: (361) 782-3547
General Email: advertising@jacksonconews.com
Publication Website: https://www.jacksonconews.com/
Parent Company: Moser Community Media, LLC
Publisher Name: Chris Lundstrom
Publisher Email: clundstrom@jacksonconews.com
Publisher Phone: (361) 782-3547
Editor Name: Chris Lundstrom
Editor Email: clundstrom@jacksonconews.com
Editor Phone: (361) 782-3547
Advertising Executive Name: Aldric Edwards
Advertising Executive Email: advertising@jacksonconews.com
Advertising Executive Phone: (361) 782-3547
Delivery Methods: Mail`Newsstand
Year Established: 1906
Published Days: Wed
Avg. Paid Circ.: 2700
Avg. Free Circ.: 410
Audit Company: Sworn/Estimate/Non-Audited
Audit Date: 43626

ELDORADO

ELDORADO SUCCESS

Street Address: 204 SW Main St
City: Eldorado
State: TX
ZIP Code: 76936
General Phone: (325) 853-3125
General Email: kathy@myeldorado.net
Publication Website: https://myeldorado.net/
Parent Company: Masked Rider Publishing
Publisher Name: Randy Mankin
Publisher Email: publisher@myeldorado.net
Delivery Methods: Mail`Newsstand`Racks
Year Established: 1901
Published Days: Thur
Avg. Paid Circ.: 1100
Audit Company: Sworn/Estimate/Non-Audited
Audit Date: 43626

EMORY

RAINS COUNTY LEADER

Street Address: 239 N Texas St
City: Emory
State: TX
ZIP Code: 75440-2405
General Phone: (903) 473-2653
General Email: rainsleader@earthlink.net
Publication Website: http://www.rainscountyleader.com/
Delivery Methods: Mail`Newsstand`Racks
Year Established: 1887
Mechanical specifications: Type page 13 x 21; E - 6 cols, 2, 1/4 between; A - 6 cols, 2, 1/4 between; C - 6 cols, 2, 1/4 between.
Published Days: Tues
Avg. Paid Circ.: 2400
Avg. Free Circ.: 79
Audit Company: Sworn/Estimate/Non-Audited
Audit Date: 43626
Note: E-edition password protected.

FAIRFIELD

FREESTONE COUNTY TIMES

Street Address: 401 E Commerce St
City: Fairfield
State: TX
ZIP Code: 75840-1603
General Phone: (903) 389-6397
General Email: ads2@freestonecountytimes.com
Publication Website: https://freestonecountytimesonline.com/
Publisher Name: Scott Watson Marsters
Publisher Email: news@freestonecountytimes.com
Editor Name: Karen Elizabeth Leidy
Editor Email: news@freestonecountytimes.com
Advertising Executive Name: SHERRY FAGAN
Advertising Executive Email: ads2@freestonecountytimes.com
Delivery Methods: Mail`Newsstand
Year Established: 2002
Own Printing Facility?: N
Commercial printers?: N
Published Days: Wed
Weekday Frequency: All day
Avg. Paid Circ.: 2615
Avg. Free Circ.: 52
Audit Company: Sworn/Estimate/Non-Audited
Audit Date: 43626
Note: new community mobile app Go Fairfield Texas available for download at the App Store or get it on Google Play.

FAIRFIELD

THE FAIRFIELD RECORDER

Street Address: 101 E Commerce St
City: Fairfield
State: TX
ZIP Code: 75840-1507
General Phone: (903) 389-3334
General Email: news@fairfield-recorder.com
Publication Website: https://www.fairfield-recorder.com/
Parent Company: Freestone County Publishing LP
Delivery Methods: Mail`Newsstand`Racks
Year Established: 1876
Mechanical specifications: Type page 13 x 21; E - 6 cols, between.
Published Days: Thur
Avg. Paid Circ.: 2000
Audit Company: Sworn/Estimate/Non-Audited
Audit Date: 43626

FALFURRIAS

FALFURRIAS FACTS

Street Address: 219 E Rice St
City: Falfurrias
State: TX
ZIP Code: 78355-3621
General Phone: (361) 325-2200
General Email: falfacts@yahoo.com
Publication Website: https://falfacts.wixsite.com/falfacts/about
Publisher Name: Marcelo Silva
Editor Name: Yvonne Silva
Advertising Executive Name: San Juanita Olivárez
Delivery Methods: Mail`Newsstand
Year Established: 1906
Mechanical specifications: 1 col. = 1.6111" 2 col. = 3.3889" 3 col. = 5.1667" 4 col. = 6.9444" 5 col. = 8.7222" 6 col. = 10.5"
Published Days: Thur
Avg. Paid Circ.: 3000
Audit Company: Sworn/Estimate/Non-Audited
Audit Date: 43626

FARMERSVILLE

FARMERSVILLE TIMES

Street Address: 101 S Main St
City: Farmersville
State: TX
ZIP Code: 75442-2207
General Phone: (972) 784-6397
General Email: advertising@csmediatexas.com
Publication Website: https://farmersvilletimes.com/
Parent Company: C&S Media, Inc.
Publisher Name: Chad Engbrock
Publisher Email: cengbrock@csmediatexas.com
Delivery Methods: Mail`Newsstand`Carrier`Racks
Year Established: 1885
Published Days: Thur
Avg. Paid Circ.: 3500
Audit Company: Sworn/Estimate/Non-Audited
Audit Date: 43626

FARMERSVILLE

PRINCETON HERALD

Street Address: 101 S Main St
City: Farmersville
State: TX
ZIP Code: 75442-2207
General Phone: (972) 784-6397
General Email: advertising@csmediatexas.com
Publication Website: https://princetonherald.com/
Parent Company: C&S Media, Inc.
Delivery Methods: Mail`Newsstand`Racks
Year Established: 1970
Own Printing Facility?: Y
Commercial printers?: Y
Mechanical specifications: Type page 11.5 x 21; E - 6 cols, 1.778 between; A & B sections - 6 cols C section - 8 cols, 1 3/4, 1/6 between.
Published Days: Thur
Avg. Paid Circ.: 1799
Avg. Free Circ.: 27
Audit Company: Sworn/Estimate/Non-Audited
Audit Date: 43626

FARWELL

THE STATE LINE TRIBUNE

Street Address: 404 3rd St
City: Farwell
State: TX
ZIP Code: 79325-4670
General Phone: (806) 481-3681
General Email: tribune@plateautel.net
Publication Website: http://www.statelinetribune.com/
Delivery Methods: Mail`Racks
Year Established: 1911
Published Days: Fri
Avg. Paid Circ.: 1500
Audit Company: Sworn/Estimate/Non-Audited
Audit Date: 43626

FERRIS

THE ELLIS COUNTY PRESS

Street Address: 208 S Central St
City: Ferris
State: TX
ZIP Code: 75125-2622
General Phone: (972) 544-2369
General Email: charles@elliscountypress.com
Publication Website: http://www.elliscountypress.com/
Parent Company: Hatfield & Associates
Publisher Name: Charles Hatfield
Publisher Email: charles@elliscountypress.com
Delivery Methods: Mail`Newsstand`Racks
Year Established: 1992
Own Printing Facility?: Y
Commercial printers?: N
Mechanical specifications: Type page 11 1/2 x 21 1/2; E - 6 cols, 1 7/8, 1/8 between; A - 6 cols, 1 7/8, 1/8 between; C - 9 cols, 1 1/4, 1/8 between.
Published Days: Thur
Avg. Paid Circ.: 2500
Avg. Free Circ.: 500
Audit Company: Sworn/Estimate/Non-Audited
Audit Date: 43626

FLATONIA

THE FLATONIA ARGUS

Street Address: 212 S Penn Ave
City: Flatonia
State: TX
ZIP Code: 78941
General Phone: (361) 865-3510
General Email: admanager@flatoniaargus.com
Publication Website: http://www.flatoniaargus.com/
Publisher Name: Paul Prause
Editor Name: Paul Prause
Advertising Executive Name: Paul Prause
Delivery Methods: Mail`Newsstand
Year Established: 1875
Mechanical specifications: Type page 16 x 20 1/2; E - 8 cols, 1 5/6, 1/3 between; A - 8 cols, 1 5/6, 1/3 between; C - 8 cols, 1 5/6, 1/3 between.
Published Days: Thur
Avg. Paid Circ.: 940
Avg. Free Circ.: 38
Audit Company: Sworn/Estimate/Non-Audited
Audit Date: 43626

Community Newspapers in the U.S.

FLORESVILLE

WILSON COUNTY NEWS

Street Address: 1012 C St
City: Floresville
State: TX
ZIP Code: 78114
General Phone: (830) 216-4519
General Email: reader@wcn-online.com
Publication Website: https://www.wilsoncountynews.com/
Parent Company: WCN, Inc.
Publisher Name: Elaine Kolodziej
Publisher Email: elaine@wcn-online.com
Editor Name: Nannette Kilbey-Smith
Editor Email: nkilbey-smith@wcn-online.com
Advertising Executive Name: Sandy Hiraga
Advertising Executive Email: shiraga@wcn-online.com
Delivery Methods: Mail`Newsstand
Year Established: 1973
Mechanical specifications: 9.94" x 20.75"
Published Days: Wed
Avg. Paid Circ.: 8190
Avg. Free Circ.: 1074
Audit Company: Sworn/Estimate/Non-Audited
Audit Date: 43626

FLOYDADA

FLOYD COUNTY HESPERIAN-BEACON

Street Address: 201 W California St
City: Floydada
State: TX
ZIP Code: 79235
General Phone: (806) 983-3737
General Email: fchb.editor@yahoo.com
Publication Website: http://www.hesperianbeacononline.com/
Editor Name: Barbra Anderson
Editor Email: fchb.editor@yahoo.com
Delivery Methods: Mail`Racks
Year Established: 1896
Published Days: Thur
Avg. Paid Circ.: 2600
Avg. Free Circ.: 23
Audit Company: Sworn/Estimate/Non-Audited
Audit Date: 43626

FORNEY

FORNEY MESSENGER

Street Address: 201 W Broad St
City: Forney
State: TX
ZIP Code: 75126
General Phone: (972) 564-3121
General Email: ads@forneymessenger.com
Publication Website: https://www.yourforneymessenger.com/
Publisher Name: Darrell Grooms
Publisher Email: news@forneymessenger.com
Publisher Phone: (972) 564-3121
Editor Name: Darrell Grooms
Editor Email: news@forneymessenger.com
Editor Phone: (972) 564-3121
Advertising Executive Name: Jeff Cannon
Advertising Executive Email: ads@forneymessenger.com
Advertising Executive Phone: (972) 564-3121
Delivery Methods: Mail`Newsstand
Year Established: 1896
Own Printing Facility?: N
Commercial printers?: N
Published Days: Thur
Avg. Paid Circ.: 3600
Audit Company: Sworn/Estimate/Non-Audited
Audit Date: 43626
Editorial Equipment: iMac
Editorial Software: Creatve Office Suite

FORT DAVIS

JEFF DAVIS COUNTY MT. DISPATCH

Street Address: 205 W. Court Avenue
City: Fort Davis
State: TX
ZIP Code: 79734
General Phone: (432) 426-3077
General Email: news@mountaindispatchnow.com
Publication Website: https://www.mountaindispatchnow.com/
Advertising Executive Phone: (432) 426-3077
Delivery Methods: Mail`Newsstand
Year Established: 1983
Published Days: Thur
Avg. Paid Circ.: 1500
Audit Company: Sworn/Estimate/Non-Audited
Audit Date: 43626

FORT HANCOCK

HUDSPETH COUNTY HERALD

Street Address: P.O. Box 128
City: Fort Hancock
State: TX
ZIP Code: 79837
General Phone: (915) 964-2426
General Email: hcherald@dellcity.com
Publication Website: https://hudspethcountyherald.com/
Delivery Methods: Mail`Newsstand
Year Established: 1956
Published Days: Fri
Avg. Paid Circ.: 602
Audit Company: Sworn/Estimate/Non-Audited
Audit Date: 43626

FORT SAM HOUSTON

FORT SAM NEWS LEADER

Street Address: 1212 Stanley Road, Building 124, Suite 4
City: Fort Sam Houston
State: TX
ZIP Code: 78234-5004
General Phone: (210) 221-0615
General Email: news.leader@conus.army.mil
Publication Website: https://www.mysanantonio.com/community/article/Fort-Sam-Houston-News-Leader-856098.php
Parent Company: Hearst Corp.
Advertising Executive Name: Robert Caplan
Advertising Executive Email: rcaplan@express-news.net
Advertising Executive Phone: (210) 453-3325
Delivery Methods: Mail`Newsstand
Mechanical specifications: Type page 11 5/8 x 21; E - 6 cols, 2 1/16, 1/8 between; A - 6 cols, 2 1/16, 1/8 between; C - 10 cols, 1 5/16, 1/16 between.
Published Days: Thur
Audit Company: VAC
Audit Date: 43651

FORT WORTH

FORT WORTH BUSINESS PRESS

Street Address: 3509 Hulen St.
City: Fort Worth
State: TX
ZIP Code: 76107
General Phone: (817) 336-8300
General Email: thernandez@bizpress.net
Publication Website: http://www.fortworthbusiness.com/
Advertising Executive Email: adelatorre@bizpress.net
Delivery Methods: Mail`Newsstand`Racks
Year Established: 1988
Published Days: Mon
Avg. Paid Circ.: 631
Avg. Free Circ.: 3446
Audit Company: Sworn/Estimate/Non-Audited
Audit Date: 43626

FRANKSTON

FRANKSTON CITIZEN

Street Address: 142 W Main St
City: Frankston
State: TX
ZIP Code: 75763
General Phone: (903) 876-2218
General Email: sales@frankstoncitizen.com
Publication Website: http://www.frankstoncitizen.com/
Delivery Methods: Mail`Racks
Year Established: 1910
Mechanical specifications: Type page 11 3/8 x 21 1/2; E - 6 cols, 1 3/4, 1/8 between; A - 6 cols, 1 3/4, 1/8 between; C - 8 cols, 1 5/16, 3/32 between.
Published Days: Thur
Avg. Paid Circ.: 1901
Avg. Free Circ.: 88
Audit Company: Sworn/Estimate/Non-Audited
Audit Date: 43626

FREDERICKSBURG

FREDERICKSBURG STANDARD-RADIO POST

Street Address: 712 W Main St
City: Fredericksburg
State: TX
ZIP Code: 78624
General Phone: (830) 997-2155
General Email: fbgads@fredericksburgstandard.com
Publication Website: https://www.fredericksburgstandard.com/
Parent Company: Moser Community Media, LLC
Publisher Name: Ken Esten Cooke
Publisher Email: ken@fredericksburgstandard.com
Editor Name: Ken Esten Cooke
Editor Email: ken@fredericksburgstandard.com
Advertising Executive Name: Kim Jung
Advertising Executive Email: kim@fredericksburgstandard.com
Delivery Methods: Mail`Newsstand`Carrier`Racks
Year Established: 1907
Own Printing Facility?: N
Commercial printers?: N
Published Days: Wed
Avg. Paid Circ.: 7999
Audit Company: Sworn/Estimate/Non-Audited
Audit Date: 43626
Pressroom Equipment: PCs
Pressroom Software: Adobe Creative Microsoft Office
Mailroom Equipment: PC
Mailroom Software: Interlink

FRIONA

THE FRIONA STAR

Street Address: 208 E. 11th
City: Friona
State: TX
ZIP Code: 79035
General Phone: (806) 250-2211
General Email: frionastar@wtrt.net
Publication Website: http://www.frionaonline.com/
Delivery Methods: Mail`Newsstand
Year Established: 1925
Published Days: Thur
Avg. Paid Circ.: 1350
Audit Company: Sworn/Estimate/Non-Audited
Audit Date: 43626

GATESVILLE

GATESVILLE MESSENGER AND STAR FORUM

Street Address: 116 S 6th St
City: Gatesville
State: TX
ZIP Code: 76528
General Phone: (254) 865-5212
General Email: news2@gatesvillemessenger.com
Publication Website: https://www.gatesvillemessenger.com/
Publisher Name: Debbie Day
Advertising Executive Email: advertising@gatesvillemessenger.com
Delivery Methods: Mail`Newsstand`Racks
Year Established: 1881
Mechanical specifications: 11.625" X 21" 6 col. format
Published Days: Wed`Sat
Avg. Paid Circ.: 3400
Audit Company: Sworn/Estimate/Non-Audited
Audit Date: 43626

GEORGETOWN

SUNDAY SUN

Street Address: 707 S Main St
City: Georgetown
State: TX
ZIP Code: 78626
General Phone: (512) 930-4824
General Email: ads@wilcosun.com
Publication Website: http://wilcosun.com/
Publisher Name: Clark Thurmond
Publisher Email: clark@wilcosun.com
Publisher Phone: (512) 930-4824, ext : 210
Editor Name: Lorraine Brady
Editor Email: editor@wilcosun.com
Editor Phone: (512) 930-4824, ext : 217
Advertising Executive Name: Dawn Steele
Advertising Executive Email: ads@wilcosun.com
Advertising Executive Phone: (512) 930-4824, ext : 202
Delivery Methods: Mail`Racks
Year Established: 1974
Published Days: Sun
Avg. Paid Circ.: 9000
Audit Company: Sworn/Estimate/Non-Audited
Audit Date: 43626

GEORGETOWN

THE WILLIAMSON COUNTY SUN

Street Address: 707 S Main St
City: Georgetown
State: TX
ZIP Code: 78626
General Phone: (512) 930-4824
General Email: ads@wilcosun.com
Publication Website: http://wilcosun.com/
Publisher Name: Clark Thurmond
Publisher Email: clark@wilcosun.com
Publisher Phone: (512) 930-4824, ext : 210
Editor Name: Lorraine Brady
Editor Email: editor@wilcosun.com
Editor Phone: (512) 930-4824, ext : 217
Advertising Executive Name: Dawn Steele
Advertising Executive Email: ads@wilcosun.com
Advertising Executive Phone: (512) 930-4824, ext : 202
Delivery Methods: Mail`Racks
Year Established: 1877
Own Printing Facility?: Y
Mechanical specifications: Type page 11 x 21; E - 6 cols, 2 1/16, 1/6 between; A - 6

cols, 2 1/16, 1/6 between; C - 8 cols, 1 1/2, 1/6 between.
Published Days: Wed
Avg. Paid Circ.: 9000
Audit Company: Sworn/Estimate/Non-Audited
Audit Date: 43626

GIDDINGS

GIDDINGS TIMES & NEWS

Street Address: 170 N Knox Ave
City: Giddings
State: TX
ZIP Code: 78942
General Phone: (979) 542-2222
General Email: news@giddingstimes.com
Publication Website: https://www.giddingstimes.com/
Delivery Methods: Mail`Newsstand`Racks
Year Established: 1888
Published Days: Thur
Audit Company: Sworn/Estimate/Non-Audited
Audit Date: 43626

GILMER

GILMER MIRROR

Street Address: 214 E Marshall St
City: Gilmer
State: TX
ZIP Code: 75644-2228
General Phone: (903) 843-2503
General Email: gilmermirrorclassifieds@yahoo.com
Publication Website: http://www.gilmermirror.com/
Parent Company: Greeneway Enterprises, Inc.
Advertising Executive Email: gilmermirrorclassifieds@yahoo.com
Delivery Methods: Mail`Racks
Year Established: 1877
Published Days: Thur
Avg. Paid Circ.: 3500
Avg. Free Circ.: 23
Audit Company: Sworn/Estimate/Non-Audited
Audit Date: 43626

GLADEWATER

GLADEWATER MIRROR

Street Address: 211 N Main St
City: Gladewater
State: TX
ZIP Code: 75647-2335
General Phone: (903) 845-2235
General Email: jbardwell@gladewatermirror.com
Publication Website: https://www.gladewatermirror.com/
Parent Company: Bardwell Ink LLC
Publisher Name: Jim Bardwell
Publisher Email: jbardwell@gladewatermirror.com
Editor Name: Jim Bardwell
Editor Email: jbardwell@gladewatermirror.com
Delivery Methods: Mail`Newsstand`Racks
Year Established: 1928
Own Printing Facility?: Y
Commercial printers?: Y
Published Days: Wed
Avg. Paid Circ.: 1750
Audit Company: Sworn/Estimate/Non-Audited
Audit Date: 43626

GLEN ROSE

GLEN ROSE REPORTER

Street Address: PO Box 2009
City: Glen Rose
State: TX
ZIP Code: 76043
General Phone: (254) 965-3124
General Email: advertising@theglenrosereporter.com
Publication Website: https://www.yourglenrosetx.com/
Parent Company: Gannett
Publisher Name: Melissa Horton
Publisher Email: mhorton@gatehousemedia.com
Publisher Phone: (254) 965-3124
Editor Name: Sara Vanden Berge
Editor Email: svandenberge@theglenrosereporter.com
Editor Phone: (254) 965-3124
Advertising Executive Name: Chris Wood
Advertising Executive Email: cwood@theglenrosereporter.com
Advertising Executive Phone: (225) 323-4383
Delivery Methods: Mail`Newsstand`Racks
Year Established: 1887
Published Days: Fri
Avg. Paid Circ.: 3000
Audit Company: Sworn/Estimate/Non-Audited
Audit Date: 43626

GOLDTHWAITE

GOLDTHWAITE EAGLE

Street Address: 1002 Fisher St
City: Goldthwaite
State: TX
ZIP Code: 76844
General Phone: (325) 648-2244
General Email: goldnews@centex.net
Publication Website: https://www.goldthwaiteeagle.com/
Editor Name: James Taylor
Editor Email: jamest@centex.net
Delivery Methods: Mail`Newsstand`Racks
Year Established: 1894
Published Days: Wed
Avg. Paid Circ.: 1975
Audit Company: Sworn/Estimate/Non-Audited
Audit Date: 43626

GOLIAD

GOLIAD ADVANCE-GUARD

Street Address: 202 S Commercial St
City: Goliad
State: TX
ZIP Code: 77963-4189
General Phone: (361) 645-2330
General Email: goliadoffice@mysoutex.com
Publication Website: https://www.mysoutex.com/goliad_advance_guard/
Parent Company: MYSoutx.com
Advertising Executive Email: ads@mysoutex.com
Delivery Methods: Mail`Racks
Year Established: 1913
Own Printing Facility?: Y
Commercial printers?: N
Published Days: Thur
Avg. Paid Circ.: 2000
Audit Company: Sworn/Estimate/Non-Audited
Audit Date: 43626

GONZALES

THE GONZALES CANNON

Street Address: 901 N Saint Joseph St
City: Gonzales
State: TX
ZIP Code: 78629-3566
General Phone: (830) 672-7100
General Email: advertising@gonzalescannon.com

Delivery Methods: Mail`Newsstand`Racks
Year Established: 2009
Mechanical specifications: 9.875x21
Published Days: Thur
Avg. Paid Circ.: 2500
Avg. Free Circ.: 500
Audit Company: Sworn/Estimate/Non-Audited
Audit Date: 43626

GRAHAM

THE GRAHAM LEADER

Street Address: 620 Oak St
City: Graham
State: TX
ZIP Code: 76450
General Phone: (940) 549-7800
General Email: advmgr@grahamleader.com
Publication Website: http://www.grahamleader.com/
Parent Company: Moser Community Media, LLC
Publisher Name: Timothy J. O'Malley
Publisher Email: publisher@grahamleader.com
Editor Name: Thomas Wallner
Editor Email: editor@grahamleader.com
Advertising Executive Name: Tonya Ball
Advertising Executive Email: admgr@grahamleader.com
Delivery Methods: Mail`Newsstand`Racks
Year Established: 1876
Published Days: Wed`Sun
Avg. Paid Circ.: 2700
Avg. Free Circ.: 50
Audit Company: Sworn/Estimate/Non-Audited
Audit Date: 43626

GRANBURY

HOOD COUNTY NEWS

Street Address: 1501 S Morgan St
City: Granbury
State: TX
ZIP Code: 76048
General Phone: (817) 573-7066
General Email: advertising@hcnews.com
Publication Website: https://www.hcnews.com/
Publisher Name: Jerry Tidwell
Publisher Email: jtidwell@hcnews.com
Publisher Phone: (817) 573-7066, ext : 260
Editor Name: Roger Enlow
Editor Email: editor@hcnews.com
Editor Phone: (817) 573-7066, ext : 245
Advertising Executive Name: Bonnie Espin
Advertising Executive Email: advertising@hcnews.com
Advertising Executive Phone: (817) 573-7066, ext : 227
Delivery Methods: Mail`Newsstand`Racks
Year Established: 1886
Published Days: Wed`Sat
Avg. Paid Circ.: 8959
Audit Company: Sworn/Estimate/Non-Audited
Audit Date: 43626

GRAND SALINE

GRAND SALINE SUN

Street Address: 116 N Main St
City: Grand Saline
State: TX
ZIP Code: 75140-1844
General Phone: (903) 962-4275
General Email: michelle@grandsalinesun.net
Publication Website: https://www.grandsalinesun.com/
Parent Company: Lake Country Media, LLC
Publisher Name: Bert R. Fite
Publisher Email: br@grandsalinesun.net
Advertising Executive Name: Michelle Fite

Advertising Executive Email: michelle@grandsalinesun.net
Delivery Methods: Mail`Newsstand`Racks
Year Established: 1893
Mechanical specifications: 1 Column 1.58 inches 2 Column 3.343 inches 3 Column 5.121 inches 4 Column 6.922 inches 5 Column 8.716 inches 6 Column 10.507 inches
Published Days: Thur
Avg. Paid Circ.: 1200
Avg. Free Circ.: 54
Audit Company: Sworn/Estimate/Non-Audited
Audit Date: 43626

GRAPELAND

THE MESSENGER

Street Address: 202 S Main St
City: Grapeland
State: TX
ZIP Code: 75844
General Phone: (936) 687-2424
General Email: news@messenger-news.com
Publication Website: https://messenger-news.com/
Parent Company: Paxton Media Group
Editor Name: Kelly Nicol
Editor Email: kellytnicol@yahoo.com
Delivery Methods: Mail`Newsstand`Racks
Year Established: 1899
Published Days: Thur`Sun
Avg. Paid Circ.: 2376
Audit Company: Sworn/Estimate/Non-Audited
Audit Date: 43626

GREENVILLE

COMMERCE JOURNAL

Street Address: 2305 King St
City: Greenville
State: TX
ZIP Code: 75401-3257
General Phone: (903) 455-4220
General Email: advertising@heraldbanner.com
Publication Website: https://www.commercejournal.com/
Parent Company: CNHI LLC
Publisher Name: Lisa Chappell
Publisher Email: publisher@heraldbanner.com
Publisher Phone: (903) 455-4220, ext : 345
Editor Name: Dale Gosser
Editor Email: dgosser@heraldbanner.com
Editor Phone: (903) 455-4220, ext : 324
Advertising Executive Name: Kerri Gibbs
Advertising Executive Email: addirector@heraldbanner.com
Advertising Executive Phone: (903) 455-4220, ext : 310
Delivery Methods: Mail`Newsstand
Year Established: 1889
Published Days: Thur
Avg. Paid Circ.: 2000
Avg. Free Circ.: 67
Audit Company: Sworn/Estimate/Non-Audited
Audit Date: 43626

GREENVILLE

ROCKWALL COUNTY HERALD BANNER

Street Address: 2305 King St
City: Greenville
State: TX
ZIP Code: 75401-3257
General Phone: (903) 455-4220
General Email: advertising@heraldbanner.com
Publication Website: https://www.rockwallheraldbanner.com/

Community Newspapers in the U.S.

Parent Company: CNHI LLC
Publisher Name: Lisa Chappell
Publisher Email: publisher@heraldbanner.com
Publisher Phone: (903) 455-4220, ext : 345
Editor Name: Dale Gosser
Editor Email: dgosser@heraldbanner.com
Editor Phone: (903) 455-4220, ext : 324
Advertising Executive Name: Kerri Gibbs
Advertising Executive Email: addirector@heraldbanner.com
Advertising Executive Phone: (903) 455-4220, ext : 310
Published Days: Fri
Audit Company: Sworn/Estimate/Non-Audited
Audit Date: 43626

GREENVILLE

ROYSE CITY HERALD BANNER

Street Address: 2305 King St
City: Greenville
State: TX
ZIP Code: 75401-3257
General Phone: (903) 455-4220
General Email: advertising@heraldbanner.com
Publication Website: https://www.roysecityheraldbanner.com/
Parent Company: CNHI LLC
Publisher Name: Lisa Chappell
Publisher Email: publisher@heraldbanner.com
Publisher Phone: (903) 455-4220, ext : 345
Editor Name: Dale Gosser
Editor Email: dgosser@heraldbanner.com
Editor Phone: (903) 455-4220, ext : 324
Advertising Executive Name: Kerri Gibbs
Advertising Executive Email: addirector@heraldbanner.com
Advertising Executive Phone: (903) 455-4220, ext : 310
Published Days: Wed
Audit Company: Sworn/Estimate/Non-Audited
Audit Date: 43626

GROESBECK

GROESBECK JOURNAL

Street Address: P.O. Box 440
City: Groesbeck
State: TX
ZIP Code: 76642
General Phone: (254) 729-5103
General Email: news@groesbeckjournal.com
Publication Website: https://www.groesbeckjournal.com/
Parent Company: Moser Community Media, LLC
Delivery Methods: Mail`Newsstand
Year Established: 1892
Published Days: Thur
Avg. Paid Circ.: 2550
Avg. Free Circ.: 50
Audit Company: Sworn/Estimate/Non-Audited
Audit Date: 43626

HALLETTSVILLE

HALLETTSVILLE TRIBUNE-HERALD

Street Address: 108 S Texana St
City: Hallettsville
State: TX
ZIP Code: 77964-2847
General Phone: (361) 798-2481
General Email: tribuneherald@sbcglobal.net
Publication Website: https://www.lavacacountytoday.com/
Delivery Methods: Mail`Newsstand
Year Established: 1875
Published Days: Wed
Avg. Paid Circ.: 2800
Audit Company: Sworn/Estimate/Non-Audited
Audit Date: 43626

HALLETTSVILLE

YOAKUM HERALD-TIMES

Street Address: 108 S. Texana
City: Hallettsville
State: TX
ZIP Code: 77964
General Phone: (361) 798-2481
General Email: heraldtimes@sbcglobal.net
Publication Website: https://www.lavacacountytoday.com/
Delivery Methods: Mail`Racks
Year Established: 1892
Mechanical specifications: Type page 13 x 21; E - 6 cols, 2, 1/6 between; A - 6 cols, 2, 1/6 between; C - 6 cols, 2, 1/6 between.
Published Days: Wed
Avg. Paid Circ.: 3200
Audit Company: Sworn/Estimate/Non-Audited
Audit Date: 43626

HAMILTON

HAMILTON HERALD-NEWS

Street Address: 101 North Rice
City: Hamilton
State: TX
ZIP Code: 76531-1954
General Phone: (254) 386-3145
General Email: lthompson@thehamiltonherald-news.com
Publication Website: https://www.thehamiltonherald-news.com/
Publisher Name: Maria Weaver
Publisher Email: maria@hhnpaper.com
Editor Name: Maria Weaver
Editor Email: maria@hhnpaper.com
Delivery Methods: Mail`Newsstand
Year Established: 1875
Published Days: Thur
Avg. Paid Circ.: 3200
Audit Company: Sworn/Estimate/Non-Audited
Audit Date: 43626

HAMLIN

HAMLIN HERALD

Street Address: 350 S Central Ave
City: Hamlin
State: TX
ZIP Code: 79520-4832
General Phone: (325) 576-3606
General Email: pipernews@sbcglobal.net
Publication Website: https://hamlinherald.com/
Delivery Methods: Mail`Newsstand`Racks
Year Established: 1905
Published Days: Thur
Avg. Paid Circ.: 1200
Audit Company: Sworn/Estimate/Non-Audited
Audit Date: 43626

HEARNE

FRANKLIN ADVOCATE

Street Address: 114 W 4th St
City: Hearne
State: TX
ZIP Code: 77859-2506
General Phone: (979) 279-3411
General Email: ads@robconews.com
Publication Website: https://www.franklin-advocate.com/
Parent Company: Keane Media, Inc.
Publisher Name: Dennis Phillips
Publisher Email: publisher@robconews.com
Editor Name: Margaret Salvaggio
Editor Email: editorial@robconews.com
Advertising Executive Name: Teresa Phillips
Advertising Executive Email: ads@robconews.com
Delivery Methods: Mail`Newsstand`Racks
Year Established: 1982 - Reestablished 2014
Published Days: Thur
Avg. Paid Circ.: 494
Avg. Free Circ.: 6
Audit Company: Sworn/Estimate/Non-Audited
Audit Date: 43626

HEARNE

ROBERTSON COUNTY NEWS

Street Address: 114 W 4th St
City: Hearne
State: TX
ZIP Code: 77859-2506
General Phone: (979) 279-3411
General Email: ads@robconews.com
Publication Website: https://www.robconews.com/
Parent Company: Moser Community Media, LLC
Publisher Name: Dennis Phillips
Publisher Email: publisher@robconews.com
Editor Name: Margaret Salvaggio
Editor Email: editorial@robconews.com
Advertising Executive Name: Teresa Phillips
Advertising Executive Email: ads@robconews.com
Delivery Methods: Mail`Newsstand`Racks
Year Established: 1889
Published Days: Thur
Avg. Paid Circ.: 2146
Avg. Free Circ.: 92
Audit Company: Sworn/Estimate/Non-Audited
Audit Date: 43626

HEBBRONVILLE

JIM HOGG COUNTY ENTERPRISE

Street Address: 304 E Galbraith St
City: Hebbronville
State: TX
ZIP Code: 78361-3402
General Phone: (361) 527-3261
General Email: enterprise78361@aol.com
Publication Website: http://www.enterprisenews.info/
Delivery Methods: Mail`Newsstand
Year Established: 1926
Published Days: Wed
Audit Company: Sworn/Estimate/Non-Audited
Audit Date: 43626

HEMPHILL

THE SABINE COUNTY REPORTER

Street Address: 610 Worth St
City: Hemphill
State: TX
ZIP Code: 75948-7258
General Phone: (409) 787-2172
General Email: screporter@yahoo.com
Publication Website: https://www.sabinecountyreporter.com/
Delivery Methods: Mail`Newsstand`Racks
Year Established: 1883
Published Days: Wed
Avg. Paid Circ.: 2100
Audit Company: Sworn/Estimate/Non-Audited
Audit Date: 43626

HENDERSON

OVERTON NEWS

Street Address: P.O. Box 30
City: Henderson
State: TX
ZIP Code: 75654-4509
General Phone: (903) 657-2501
General Email: leslinebarger@hendersondailynews.com
Publication Website: http://www.thehendersonnews.com
Publisher Name: Dan Moore
Publisher Email: publisher@thehendersonnews.com
Editor Name: Kent Mahoney
Editor Email: managingeditor@thehendersonnews.com
Advertising Executive Name: Valerie Reese
Advertising Executive Email: marketing@thehendersonnews.com
Delivery Methods: Mail`Newsstand`Carrier`Racks
Year Established: 1930
Own Printing Facility?: Y
Commercial printers?: Y
Mechanical specifications: Type page 13 x 21 1/2; E - 6 cols, 2 1/16, between; A - 6 cols, 2 1/16, between; C - 8 cols, 1 1/2, between.
Published Days: Wed
Avg. Paid Circ.: 7000
Avg. Free Circ.: 6400
Audit Company: Sworn/Estimate/Non-Audited
Audit Date: 43626

HENRIETTA

CLAY COUNTY LEADER

Street Address: 114 W Ikard St
City: Henrietta
State: TX
ZIP Code: 76365-2827
General Phone: (940) 538-4333
General Email: ads@claycountyleader.com
Publication Website: http://claycountyleader.com/
Editor Email: editor@claycountyleader.com
Advertising Executive Email: ads@claycountyleader.com
Delivery Methods: Mail`Newsstand
Year Established: 1932
Published Days: Thur
Audit Company: Sworn/Estimate/Non-Audited
Audit Date: 43626

HEREFORD

THE HEREFORD BRAND

Street Address: PO Box 673
City: Hereford
State: TX
ZIP Code: 79045
General Phone: (806) 364-2030
General Email: retail@herefordbrand.com
Publication Website: https://www.herefordbrand.com/
Parent Company: M. Roberts Media
Publisher Name: Jeff Blackmon
Publisher Email: publisher@herefordbrand.com
Publisher Phone: (806) 360-2030
Delivery Methods: Mail`Newsstand`Carrier`Racks
Year Established: 1901
Own Printing Facility?: Y
Commercial printers?: Y
Mechanical specifications: Type page 13 x 21; E - 6 cols, 2 1/16, 1/8 between; A - 6 cols, 2 1/16, 1/8 between; C - 6 cols, 2 1/16, 1/8 between.
Published Days: Wed`Sun
Weekday Frequency: e
Saturday Frequency: e
Avg. Paid Circ.: 2100
Audit Company: Sworn/Estimate/Non-Audited

Audit Date: 43626
Pressroom Equipment: Lines -- 4-HI/V-15 1981.;
Mailroom Equipment: Counter Stackers -- 1-BG/Count-O-Veyor; Tying Machines -- 1/Bu, 1-/Bu; Address Machine -- 1-/Elliot Dynamic/3101.;
Business Equipment: 1-Wyse/386
Business Software: SBT
Classified Equipment: Hardware -- 1-Wyse/3225, VGA Monitor; Printers -- QMS/PS-810;
Classified Software: WordPerfect.
Editorial Equipment: Hardware -- 1-Wyse/3225, 6-VGA Monitor; Printers -- QMS/PS-810
Editorial Software: WordPerfect.
Production Equipment: Hardware -- 1-Nat/A-340; Cameras -- 1-R, 1-Argyle/18-Process G18; Scanners -- CK Optical/SQU-7.

HICO

HICO NEWS REVIEW

Street Address: 110 E Second St
City: Hico
State: TX
ZIP Code: 76457-6433
General Phone: (254) 796-4325
General Email: hiconews@gmail.com
Publication Website: https://www.thehiconewsreview.com/
Publisher Name: Jerry McAdams
Editor Name: Traci Till
Delivery Methods: Mail`Racks
Year Established: 1895
Published Days: Thur
Avg. Paid Circ.: 1550
Audit Company: Sworn/Estimate/Non-Audited
Audit Date: 43626

HILLSBORO

HILLSBORO REPORTER

Street Address: 335 Country Club Rd
City: Hillsboro
State: TX
ZIP Code: 76645-2318
General Phone: (254) 582-3431
General Email: ads@hillsbororeporter.com
Publication Website: http://hillsbororeporter.com/
Delivery Methods: Mail`Newsstand`Racks
Year Established: 1963
Published Days: Mon`Thur
Avg. Paid Circ.: 4250
Audit Company: Sworn/Estimate/Non-Audited
Audit Date: 43626

HONDO

HONDO ANVIL HERALD

Street Address: 1601 Avenue K
City: Hondo
State: TX
ZIP Code: 78861-1838
General Phone: (830) 426-3346
General Email: anvil1@hondo.net
Publication Website: https://www.hondoanvilherald.com/
Publisher Name: Jeff Berger
Editor Name: Diane Cosgrove
Advertising Executive Name: Lois Davis
Delivery Methods: Mail`Newsstand
Year Established: 1886
Own Printing Facility?: Y
Commercial printers?: Y
Mechanical specifications: Type page 13 x 21 1/2; E - 6 cols, 2, 1/4 between; A - 6 cols, 2, 1/4 between; C - 9 cols, 1 1/2, 1/4 between.
Published Days: Thur

Avg. Paid Circ.: 4521
Avg. Free Circ.: 10
Audit Company: Sworn/Estimate/Non-Audited
Audit Date: 43626

HORIZON CITY

WEST TEXAS COUNTY COURIER

Street Address: 15344 Werling Ct
City: Horizon City
State: TX
ZIP Code: 79928-7012
General Phone: (915) 852-3235
General Email: wtxcc@wtxcc.com
Publication Website: http://www.wtxcc.com/
Publisher Name: Rick Shrum
Delivery Methods: Mail`Newsstand`Racks
Year Established: 1973
Mechanical specifications: Type page 10 1/2 x 15 3/4; E - 5 cols, 2, 1/8 between; A - 5 cols, 2, 1/8 between; C - 6 cols, 1 3/5, 1/8 between.
Published Days: Thur
Avg. Free Circ.: 11000
Audit Company: Sworn/Estimate/Non-Audited
Audit Date: 43626

HOUSTON

BELLAIRE EXAMINER

Street Address: 4635 Southwest Freeway #320
City: Houston
State: TX
ZIP Code: 77024-2007
General Phone: (281) 674-1360
General Email: brubio@hcnonline.com
Publication Website: https://www.chron.com/neighborhood/bellaire/
Parent Company: Hearst Corp.
Editor Name: Charlotte Aguilar
Editor Email: bellaireeditor@hcnonline.com
Advertising Executive Name: Ben Rubio
Advertising Executive Email: brubio@hcnonline.com
Delivery Methods: Mail`Newsstand`Racks
Published Days: Thur
Avg. Free Circ.: 13998
Audit Company: Sworn/Estimate/Non-Audited
Audit Date: 43626

HOUSTON

CYPRESS CREEK MIRROR

Street Address: 21901 State Highway 249
City: Houston
State: TX
ZIP Code: 77070-1545
General Phone: (281) 378-1080
General Email: rdavis@hcnonline.com
Publication Website: https://www.chron.com/neighborhood/champions-klein/
Parent Company: Hearst Corp.
Advertising Executive Phone: (713) 362-3731
Delivery Methods: Mail`Newsstand`Racks
Year Established: 2003
Published Days: Wed
Avg. Free Circ.: 6750
Audit Company: AAM
Audit Date: 43991

HOUSTON

HIGHLANDS STAR / CROSBY COURIER

Street Address: P.O. Box 405
City: Houston
State: TX
ZIP Code: 77057-7118

General Phone: (281) 328-9605
General Email: grafikstar@aol.com
Publication Website: https://www.starcouriernews.com/
Parent Company: Grafikpress Corp.
Delivery Methods: Mail`Newsstand`Carrier`Racks
Year Established: 1955
Mechanical specifications: Broadsheet 12.5 x 22.75 Column width 1.833 inches 6 col x 21 = 11.62 x 21
Published Days: Thur
Avg. Paid Circ.: 4400
Avg. Free Circ.: 3400
Audit Company: Sworn/Estimate/Non-Audited
Audit Date: 43626
Note: Additional Circulation 2200

HOUSTON

HOUSTON BUSINESS JOURNAL

Street Address: 5444 Westheimer Rd
City: Houston
State: TX
ZIP Code: 77056-5349
General Phone: (713) 688-8811
General Email: houston@bizjournals.com
Publication Website: https://www.bizjournals.com/houston/
Parent Company: American City Business Journals
Publisher Name: Bob Charlet
Publisher Email: bcharlet@bizjournals.com
Editor Name: Jonathan Adams
Editor Email: jadams@bizjournals.com
Editor Phone: (713) 395-9617
Advertising Executive Name: Guy Biermann
Advertising Executive Email: gbiermann@bizjournals.com
Advertising Executive Phone: (713) 395-9621
Delivery Methods: Mail`Newsstand
Year Established: 1971
Published Days: Fri
Published Other: Daily breaking news on web for subscribers only
Avg. Paid Circ.: 17000
Avg. Free Circ.: 3500
Audit Company: Sworn/Estimate/Non-Audited
Audit Date: 43626

HOUSTON

HOUSTON FORWARD TIMES

Street Address: 4411 Almeda Rd
City: Houston
State: TX
ZIP Code: 77004-4999
General Phone: (713) 526-4727
General Email: forwardtimes@forwardtimes.com
Publication Website: http://forwardtimes.com/
Parent Company: Houston Forward Times Publishing Co.
Publisher Name: Karen Carter Richards
Advertising Executive Email: forwardtimes@forwardtimes.com
Delivery Methods: Mail`Newsstand`Carrier`Racks
Year Established: 1960
Published Days: Wed
Avg. Paid Circ.: 35089
Audit Company: Sworn/Estimate/Non-Audited
Audit Date: 43626

HOUSTON

JEWISH HERALD-VOICE

Street Address: 3403 Audley St
City: Houston
State: TX
ZIP Code: 77098-1923

General Phone: (713) 630-0391
General Email: advertising@jhvonline.com
Publication Website: https://jhvonline.com/
Editor Name: Jeanne F. Samuels
Editor Email: jeannes@jhvonline.com
Advertising Executive Name: Lew Sampson
Advertising Executive Email: lews@jhvonline.com
Delivery Methods: Mail`Newsstand
Year Established: 1908
Mechanical specifications: 9.79" X 15.5" FULL PAGE
Published Days: Thur
Published Other: 5 separate magazines annually
Avg. Paid Circ.: 5000
Audit Company: Sworn/Estimate/Non-Audited
Audit Date: 43626

HOUSTON

MEMORIAL EXAMINER

Street Address: 4635 Southwest Freeway #320
City: Houston
State: TX
ZIP Code: 77027
General Phone: (218) 674-1360
General Email: brubio@hcnonline.com
Publication Website: https://www.chron.com/neighborhood/memorial/
Parent Company: Hearst Corp.
Editor Name: Charlotte Aguilar
Editor Email: memorialeditor@hcnonline.com
Advertising Executive Name: Ben Rubio
Advertising Executive Email: brubio@hcnonline.com
Delivery Methods: Mail`Newsstand`Racks
Year Established: 2004
Published Days: Thur
Avg. Free Circ.: 27451
Audit Company: Sworn/Estimate/Non-Audited
Audit Date: 43626

HOUSTON

NORTHEAST NEWS

Street Address: 5906 Star Ln
City: Houston
State: TX
ZIP Code: 77057-7118
General Phone: (281) 449-9945
General Email: nenewsroom@aol.com
Publication Website: https://www.nenewsroom.com/
Parent Company: Grafikpress Corp.
Delivery Methods: Mail`Newsstand`Carrier`Racks
Year Established: 1977
Mechanical specifications: Type page 13 x 21; E - 7 cols, 1 3/4, 1/8 between; A - 7 cols, 1 3/4, 1/8 between; C - 9 cols, 1 3/8, 1/8 between.
Published Days: Tues
Avg. Free Circ.: 30000
Audit Company: Sworn/Estimate/Non-Audited
Audit Date: 43626

HOUSTON

THE EXAMINERS

Street Address: 4635 Southwest Freeway #320
City: Houston
State: TX
ZIP Code: 77027
General Phone: (281) 674-1360
General Email: rdavis@hcnonline.com
Publication Website: https://www.chron.com/neighborhood/bellaire/
Parent Company: Hearst Corp.
Editor Name: Charlotte Aguilar

Community Newspapers in the U.S.

Editor Email: memorialeditor@hcnonline.com
Advertising Executive Name: Ben Rubio
Advertising Executive Email: brubio@hcnonline.com
Delivery Methods: Mail`Newsstand`Racks
Year Established: 2001
Published Days: Thur
Avg. Free Circ.: 33286
Audit Company: Sworn/Estimate/Non-Audited
Audit Date: 43626

HOUSTON

THE LEADER

Street Address: 2020 North Loop West, Suite 220
City: Houston
State: TX
ZIP Code: 77018
General Phone: (713) 686-8494
General Email: ads@theleadernews.com
Publication Website: https://theleadernews.com/
Parent Company: Adams Publishing Group
Publisher Name: Jonathan McElvy
Publisher Email: jonathan@theleadernews.com
Editor Name: Landan Kuhlman
Editor Email: landan@theleadernews.com
Delivery Methods: Mail`Newsstand`Racks
Year Established: 1954
Mechanical specifications: Type page 10 1/8 x 14; E - 6 cols, 1 1/2, 1/6 between; A - 6 cols, 1 1/2, 1/6 between; C - 7 cols, 1 1/2, 1/12 between.
Published Days: Sat
Avg. Paid Circ.: 17
Avg. Free Circ.: 33935
Audit Company: Sworn/Estimate/Non-Audited
Audit Date: 43626
Note: 2 total - The Leader (50,950); North Freeway Leader (34,950);

HOUSTON

WEST UNIVERSITY EXAMINER

Street Address: 21901 State Highway 249
City: Houston
State: TX
ZIP Code: 77070-1545
General Phone: (281) 378-1900
General Email: kkonter@hcnonline.com
Publication Website: https://www.chron.com/neighborhood/bellaire/
Parent Company: Hearst Corp.
Published Days: Thur
Avg. Paid Circ.: 5362
Audit Company: AAM
Audit Date: 43991

HUMBLE

EAST MONTGOMERY COUNTY OBSERVER

Street Address: 907 E Main St
City: Humble
State: TX
ZIP Code: 77338-4749
General Phone: (281) 378-1060
General Email: cturner@hcnonline.com
Publication Website: https://www.chron.com/neighborhood/east-montgomery/
Parent Company: Hearst Corp.
Delivery Methods: Carrier`Racks
Year Established: 1982
Mechanical specifications: 10.388â x 20.5â
Published Days: Wed
Avg. Free Circ.: 10498
Audit Company: Sworn/Estimate/Non-Audited
Audit Date: 43626

HUMBLE

KINGWOOD OBSERVER

Street Address: 907 E Main St.
City: Humble
State: TX
ZIP Code: 77338
General Phone: (281) 446-4438
General Email: cturner@hcnonline.com
Publication Website: https://www.chron.com/neighborhood/kingwood/
Parent Company: Hearst Corp.
Delivery Methods: Carrier`Racks
Year Established: 1977
Mechanical specifications: 10.388â x 20.5â
Published Days: Wed
Avg. Free Circ.: 20580
Audit Company: Sworn/Estimate/Non-Audited
Audit Date: 43626

HUMBLE

SPRING OBSERVER

Street Address: 907 (B) E. Main Street
City: Humble
State: TX
ZIP Code: 77338
General Phone: (281) 446-1071
General Email: tlegg@hcnonline.com
Publication Website: https://www.chron.com/neighborhood/spring/
Parent Company: Hearst Corp.
Editor Name: Ryan Hickman
Editor Email: observereditor@hcnonline.com
Advertising Executive Name: Trish Oliva
Advertising Executive Email: toliva@hcnonline.com
Delivery Methods: Mail`Newsstand`Carrier`Racks
Year Established: 2004
Mechanical specifications: 6 columns (10.388") x 20.5"
Published Days: Thur
Avg. Free Circ.: 18167
Audit Company: Sworn/Estimate/Non-Audited
Audit Date: 43626

INGRAM

WEST KERR CURRENT

Street Address: 107 Highway 39
City: Ingram
State: TX
ZIP Code: 78025-3286
General Phone: (830) 367-3501
General Email: wkcurrent@classicnet.net
Publication Website: https://wkcurrent.com/
Delivery Methods: Mail`Newsstand`Racks
Year Established: 2003
Published Days: Thur
Avg. Paid Circ.: 1400
Avg. Free Circ.: 25
Audit Company: Sworn/Estimate/Non-Audited
Audit Date: 43626

IOWA PARK

IOWA PARK LEADER

Street Address: 112 W Cash St
City: Iowa Park
State: TX
ZIP Code: 76367-2824
General Phone: (940) 592-4431
General Email: kcollins@iowaparkleader.com
Publication Website: https://www.iowaparkleader.com/
Publisher Name: Dolores Hamilton
Publisher Email: dhamilton@iowaparkleader.com
Editor Name: Kevin Hamilton
Editor Email: khamilton@iowaparkleader.com
Advertising Executive Name: Kari Collins
Advertising Executive Email: kcollins@iowaparkleader.com
Delivery Methods: Mail`Newsstand
Year Established: 1969
Published Days: Thur
Avg. Paid Circ.: 2700
Audit Company: Sworn/Estimate/Non-Audited
Audit Date: 43626

IRVING

THE IRVING RAMBLER

Street Address: 627 S Rogers Rd
City: Irving
State: TX
ZIP Code: 75060
General Phone: (972) 870-1992
General Email: johns@ramblernewspapers.net
Publication Website: https://ramblernewspapers.net/
Parent Company: Rambler Newspapers
Publisher Name: John Starkey
Publisher Email: johns@ramblernewspapers.net
Editor Name: Stacey Starkey
Editor Email: staceys@ramblernewspapers.net
Delivery Methods: Mail`Newsstand`Carrier`Racks
Year Established: 2003
Published Days: Sat
Avg. Paid Circ.: 4400
Avg. Free Circ.: 1900
Audit Company: Sworn/Estimate/Non-Audited
Audit Date: 43626

JACKSBORO

JACKSBORO HERALD-GAZETTE

Street Address: 212 N Church St
City: Jacksboro
State: TX
ZIP Code: 76458-1800
General Phone: (940) 567-2616
General Email: ads@jacksboronewspapers.com
Publication Website: https://www.jacksboronewspapers.com
Parent Company: Moser Community Media
Publisher Name: Timothy O'Malley
Publisher Email: publisher@grahamleader.com
Advertising Executive Name: Mary Jo Watson
Advertising Executive Email: ads@jacksboronewspapers.com
Delivery Methods: Mail`Racks
Year Established: 1880
Mechanical specifications: Type page 12 1/2 x 20 1/2; E - 6 cols, 1 15/16, 1/6 between; A - 6 cols, 1 15/16, 1/6 between; C - 6 cols, 1 15/16, 1/6 between.
Published Days: Fri
Avg. Paid Circ.: 1500
Avg. Free Circ.: 11
Audit Company: Sworn/Estimate/Non-Audited
Audit Date: 43626

JACKSONVILLE

JACKSONVILLE DAILY PROGRESS

Street Address: 525 E Commerce St
City: Jacksonville
State: TX
ZIP Code: 75766-4909
General Phone: (903) 586-2236
General Email: publisher@jacksonvilleprogress.com
Publication Website: https://www.jacksonvilleprogress.com
Parent Company: CNHI, LLC
Publisher Name: Lange Svehlak
Publisher Email: publisher@jacksonvilleprogress.com
Publisher Phone: (903) 586-2236
Editor Name: April Barbe
Editor Email: editor@jacksonvilleprogress.com
Editor Phone: (903) 586-2236
Advertising Executive Name: Sharon Claxton
Advertising Executive Email: sclaxton@jacksonvilleprogress.com
Advertising Executive Phone: (903) 586-2236
Delivery Methods: Mail`Carrier
Year Established: 1910
Own Printing Facility?: Y
Commercial printers?: Y
Mechanical specifications: Type page 12 1/2 x 21 1/2; E - 6 cols, 1 5/6, 1/8 between; A - 6 cols, 1 5/6, 1/8 between; C - 9 cols, 1 3/16, 1/8 between.
Published Days: Tues`Thur`Sat
Weekday Frequency: All day
Saturday Frequency: All day
Avg. Paid Circ.: 3000
Audit Company: Sworn/Estimate/Non-Audited
Audit Date: 43626
Pressroom Equipment: Lines -- 6-HI/V-15A 1986.;
Mailroom Equipment: Tying Machines -- 1/MLN.;
Business Equipment: PC
Business Software: Brainworks
Classified Equipment: Hardware -- APP/Power Mac; Zip Drive; Printers -- NewGen/Design Express;
Classified Software: Baseview.
Editorial Equipment: Hardware -- APP/Power Mac/Epson/Scanner, Nikon/Coolscan; Printers -- NewGen/Design Express 1200
Editorial Software: Baseview, QPS/QuarkXPress, Adobe/Photoshop.
Production Equipment: Hardware -- 1-Nu/Flip Top FT400P; Cameras -- 1-Acti/CL240.

JASPER

JASPER NEWSBOY

Street Address: 702 S Wheeler St
City: Jasper
State: TX
ZIP Code: 75951-4544
General Phone: (409) 384-3441
General Email: plinares@hearstnp.com
Publication Website: https://www.beaumontenterprise.com/jasper/
Parent Company: Hearst Corp.
Editor Name: Andrea Whitney
Editor Email: awhitney@jaspernewsboy.com
Editor Phone: (409) 384-3441
Delivery Methods: Mail`Newsstand
Year Established: 1865
Published Days: Wed
Avg. Paid Circ.: 6100
Audit Company: Sworn/Estimate/Non-Audited
Audit Date: 43626

JBSA-RANDOLPH AFB

RANDOLPH WINGSPREAD

Street Address: 1150 5th Street East
City: JBSA-Randolph AFB
State: TX
ZIP Code: 78150
General Phone: (210) 652-4410
General Email: randolphpublicaffairs@us.af.mil
Publication Website: https://www.mysanantonio.com/news/local/communities/article/Randolph-Wingspread-4752528.php
Parent Company: Hearst Corp.
Advertising Executive Name: Robert Caplan
Advertising Executive Email: rcaplan@

express-news.net
Advertising Executive Phone: (210) 250-2444
Delivery Methods: Mail`Newsstand
Mechanical specifications: Type page 11 5/8 x 21; E - 6 cols, 2 1/16, 1/8 between; A - 6 cols, 2 1/16, 1/8 between; C - 10 cols, 1 5/16, 1/16 between.
Published Days: Fri
Audit Company: VAC
Audit Date: 43651

JEFFERSON

JEFFERSON JIMPLECUTE

Street Address: 120 N Vale St
City: Jefferson
State: TX
ZIP Code: 75657
General Phone: (903) 665-2462
General Email: ads@jimplecute.com
Publication Website: https://jimplecute1848.com/
Parent Company: Red River Media
Delivery Methods: Mail`Newsstand`Carrier`Racks
Year Established: 1848
Published Days: Thur
Avg. Paid Circ.: 2000
Avg. Free Circ.: 75
Audit Company: Sworn/Estimate/Non-Audited
Audit Date: 43626

JEWETT

JEWETT MESSENGER

Street Address: 224 North Main Street
City: Jewett
State: TX
ZIP Code: 75846-4612
General Phone: (903) 626-4296
General Email: messenger3100@sbcglobal.net
Publication Website: https://www.jewettmessengeronline.com/
Publisher Name: David Clute
Editor Name: David Clute
Advertising Executive Name: Linda Chapman
Advertising Executive Email: messengeradvertising@yahoo.com
Delivery Methods: Mail`Newsstand
Year Established: 1885
Published Days: Wed
Avg. Paid Circ.: 1500
Avg. Free Circ.: 24
Audit Company: Sworn/Estimate/Non-Audited
Audit Date: 43626

JOHNSON CITY

JOHNSON CITY RECORD-COURIER

Street Address: 207 S US Hwy. 281 / P.O. Box 205
City: Johnson City
State: TX
ZIP Code: 78636
General Phone: (830) 868-7181
General Email: editor@jcrecordcourier.com
Publication Website: https://www.hillcountrypassport.com/jcrc
Parent Company: Wesner Media Publication
Editor Email: editor@jcrecordcourier.com
Delivery Methods: Mail`Newsstand
Year Established: 1880
Published Days: Thur
Avg. Paid Circ.: 1600
Avg. Free Circ.: 200
Audit Company: Sworn/Estimate/Non-Audited
Audit Date: 43626

JUNCTION

THE JUNCTION EAGLE

Street Address: 215 N 6th St
City: Junction
State: TX
ZIP Code: 76849
General Phone: (325) 446-2610
General Email: editor@junctioneagle.com
Publication Website: http://junctioneagle.com/
Parent Company: Junction Publishing Company, LLC
Editor Name: Debbie Cooper Kistler
Editor Email: editor@junctioneagle.com
Delivery Methods: Mail`Newsstand`Racks
Year Established: 1882
Published Days: Wed
Avg. Paid Circ.: 2000
Audit Company: Sworn/Estimate/Non-Audited
Audit Date: 43626

KARNES CITY

THE KARNES COUNTYWIDE

Street Address: 106 N Esplanade St
City: Karnes City
State: TX
ZIP Code: 78377
General Phone: (830) 254-8088
General Email: karnesoffice@mysoutex.com
Publication Website: https://www.mysoutex.com/karnes_countywide/
Parent Company: MYSoutx.com
Editor Email: media@mysoutex.com
Advertising Executive Email: ads@mysoutex.com
Delivery Methods: Mail`Newsstand
Year Established: 1891
Published Days: Wed
Avg. Paid Circ.: 4000
Audit Company: Sworn/Estimate/Non-Audited
Audit Date: 43626

KERRVILLE

HILL COUNTRY COMMUNITY JOURNAL

Street Address: 303 Earl Garrett St
City: Kerrville
State: TX
ZIP Code: 78028
General Phone: (830) 257-2828
General Email: web@hccommunityjournal.com
Publication Website: http://www.hccommunityjournal.com/
Publisher Name: Tammy Prout
Editor Name: Stuart Cunyus
Advertising Executive Name: Lynn Hurtado
Delivery Methods: Mail`Newsstand
Year Established: 2005
Published Days: Wed
Audit Company: Sworn/Estimate/Non-Audited
Audit Date: 43626

KILGORE

BULLARD BANNER NEWS

Street Address: 610 E Main St
City: Kilgore
State: TX
ZIP Code: 75662-2612
General Phone: (903) 894-9306
General Email: advertising@bullardnews.com
Publication Website: http://www.bullardnews.com/
Parent Company: Bluebonnet Publishing, LLC
Delivery Methods: Mail`Racks
Year Established: 1996
Published Days: Wed
Avg. Paid Circ.: 1800
Audit Company: Sworn/Estimate/Non-Audited
Audit Date: 43626

KILGORE

KILGORE NEWS HERALD

Street Address: 207 N. Kilgore St.
City: Kilgore
State: TX
ZIP Code: 75662
General Phone: (903) 984-2593
General Email: news1@kilgorenewsherald.com
Publication Website: https://www.kilgorenewsherald.com/
Parent Company: M. Roberts Media
Publisher Name: Jerry Pye
Publisher Email: jpye@kilgorenewsherald.com
Delivery Methods: Mail`Newsstand`Carrier`Racks
Year Established: 1935
Own Printing Facility?: Y
Commercial printers?: Y
Mechanical specifications: Type page 11 1/2 x 21 1/2; E - 6 cols, 2 1/16, 1/8 between; A - 6 cols, 2 1/16, 1/8 between; C - 8 cols, 1 1/2, 1/8 between.
Published Days: Wed`Sat
Weekday Frequency: m
Saturday Frequency: m
Avg. Paid Circ.: 2770
Avg. Free Circ.: 1200
Audit Company: Sworn/Estimate/Non-Audited
Audit Date: 43626
Pressroom Equipment: Lines -- 5-G/Community;
Business Equipment: PC
Business Software: Fake Brains/Account Scout
Classified Equipment: PC
Classified Software: Fake Brains/Account Scout
Editorial Equipment: PC
Editorial Software: InDesign, MS Office

KINGSVILLE

KINGSVILLE RECORD & BISHOP NEWS

Street Address: P.O. Box 951
City: Kingsville
State: TX
ZIP Code: 78364
General Phone: (361) 592-4304
General Email: editor@kingsvillerecord.com
Publication Website: http://www.kingsvillerecord.com/
Publisher Name: Christopher Maher
Publisher Email: cjmaher@king-ranch.com
Publisher Phone: (361) 221-0242
Editor Email: editor@kingsvillerecord.com
Delivery Methods: Mail`Newsstand
Year Established: 1906
Published Days: Wed`Sun
Audit Company: Sworn/Estimate/Non-Audited
Audit Date: 43626

KYLE

HAYS FREE PRESS

Street Address: 113 W Center St
City: Kyle
State: TX
ZIP Code: 78640
General Phone: (512) 268-7862
General Email: mosess@haysfreepress.com
Publication Website: https://haysfreepress.com/
Parent Company: Barton Publications, Inc.
Publisher Name: Cyndy Slovak-Barton
Publisher Email: csb@haysfreepress.com
Editor Name: Anita Miller
Editor Email: moses@haysfreepress.com
Advertising Executive Name: Tracy Mack
Advertising Executive Email: tracy@haysfreepress.com
Delivery Methods: Mail`Newsstand`Racks
Year Established: 1903
Own Printing Facility?: N
Commercial printers?: N
Published Days: Wed
Avg. Paid Circ.: 3205
Avg. Free Circ.: 454
Audit Company: Sworn/Estimate/Non-Audited
Audit Date: 43626

LA FERIA

LA FERIA NEWS

Street Address: 102 S Main St
City: La Feria
State: TX
ZIP Code: 78559-5005
General Phone: (956) 797-9920
General Email: davefavila@gmail.com
Publication Website: https://laferianews.net/
Publisher Name: Landon Jennings
Publisher Email: landon217@gmail.com
Editor Name: Dave Favila
Editor Email: davefavila@gmail.com
Advertising Executive Email: nbriones.lfn@yahoo.com
Delivery Methods: Mail`Newsstand
Year Established: 1923
Published Days: Wed
Avg. Paid Circ.: 5000
Audit Company: Sworn/Estimate/Non-Audited
Audit Date: 43626

LA GRANGE

THE FAYETTE COUNTY RECORD

Street Address: 127 S Washington St
City: La Grange
State: TX
ZIP Code: 78945
General Phone: (979) 968-3155
General Email: regina@fayettecountyrecord.com
Publication Website: https://www.fayettecountyrecord.com/
Parent Company: Fayette County Record, Inc.
Publisher Name: Regina Barton Keilers
Publisher Email: regina@fayettecountyrecord.com
Editor Name: Jeff Wick
Editor Email: jeff@fayettecountyrecord.com
Advertising Executive Name: Becky Weise
Advertising Executive Email: becky@fayettecountyrecord.com
Delivery Methods: Mail`Newsstand`Racks
Year Established: 1922
Own Printing Facility?: Y
Commercial printers?: N
Mechanical specifications: Type page 13 1/2 x 21.
Published Days: Tues`Fri
Avg. Paid Circ.: 5477
Avg. Free Circ.: 51
Audit Company: Sworn/Estimate/Non-Audited
Audit Date: 43626

LA VERNIA

LA VERNIA NEWS

Street Address: 112 E Chihuahua St
City: La Vernia
State: TX
ZIP Code: 78121
General Phone: (830) 779-3751
General Email: reader@lavernianews.com
Publication Website: https://www.

Community Newspapers in the U.S.

lavernianews.com/
Parent Company: WCN, Inc.
Publisher Name: Elaine Kolodziej
Editor Name: Nannette Kilbey-Smith
Delivery Methods: Mail`Newsstand
Year Established: 1969
Published Days: Thur
Avg. Paid Circ.: 1284
Avg. Free Circ.: 529
Audit Company: Sworn/Estimate/Non-Audited
Audit Date: 43626

LAMESA

LAMESA PRESS REPORTER

Street Address: P.O. Box 710
City: Lamesa
State: TX
ZIP Code: 79331
General Phone: (806) 872-2177
General Email: publisher@pressreporter.com
Publication Website: https://www.pressreporter.com/
Publisher Name: Russel Skiles
Publisher Email: publisher@pressreporter.com
Editor Name: Herrel Hallmark
Editor Email: editor@pressreporter.com
Advertising Executive Name: Katherine Rendon
Advertising Executive Email: adsales@pressreporter.com
Delivery Methods: Mail`Newsstand`Carrier
Year Established: 1905
Own Printing Facility?: Y
Commercial printers?: N
Mechanical specifications: Type page 12.625 x 21; E - 6 cols, 1.83, 1/8 between; A - 6 cols, 1.83, 1/8 between; C - 6 cols, 1.83, 1/8 between.
Published Days: Wed`Sun
Avg. Paid Circ.: 1970
Avg. Free Circ.: 83
Audit Company: Sworn/Estimate/Non-Audited
Audit Date: 43626

LAMPASAS

LAMPASAS DISPATCH RECORD

Street Address: 416 S Live Oak St
City: Lampasas
State: TX
ZIP Code: 76550
General Phone: (512) 556-6262
General Email: teresa@lampasas.com
Publication Website: https://www.lampasasdispatchrecord.com/
Advertising Executive Name: Teresa Thornton
Advertising Executive Email: teresa@lampasas.com
Advertising Executive Phone: (512) 556-6262
Delivery Methods: Mail`Newsstand`Racks
Year Established: 1955
Own Printing Facility?: N
Commercial printers?: N
Mechanical specifications: Type page 13 x 21; E - 6 cols, 2 1/16, 3/16 between; A - 6 cols, 2 1/16, 3/16 between; C - 6 cols, 2 1/16, 3/16 between.
Published Days: Tues`Fri
Avg. Paid Circ.: 2941
Avg. Free Circ.: 37
Audit Company: Sworn/Estimate/Non-Audited
Audit Date: 43626

LEONARD

LEONARD GRAPHIC

Street Address: 100 E Collin St
City: Leonard
State: TX
ZIP Code: 75452
General Phone: (903) 587-2850
General Email: ads@theleonardgraphic.com
Publication Website: http://theleonardgraphic.com
Editor Email: editor@theleonardgraphic.com
Advertising Executive Email: ads@theleonardgraphic.com
Delivery Methods: Mail`Newsstand`Racks
Year Established: 1890
Published Days: Thur
Avg. Paid Circ.: 724
Audit Company: Sworn/Estimate/Non-Audited
Audit Date: 43626

LEVELLAND

LEVELLAND & HOCKLEY COUNTY NEWS-PRESS

Street Address: 711 Austin St
City: Levelland
State: TX
ZIP Code: 79336
General Phone: (806) 894-3121
General Email: levellandads@valornet.com
Publication Website: http://levellandnews.net/
Parent Company: Stephen & Pat Enterprises
Advertising Executive Email: levellandads@valornet.com
Delivery Methods: Mail`Newsstand`Carrier`Racks
Year Established: 1928
Own Printing Facility?: N
Commercial printers?: N
Mechanical specifications: Type page PASS
Published Days: Wed`Sun
Avg. Paid Circ.: 4000
Avg. Free Circ.: 50
Audit Company: Sworn/Estimate/Non-Audited
Audit Date: 43626

LEXINGTON

LEXINGTON LEADER

Street Address: 612 Wheatley St
City: Lexington
State: TX
ZIP Code: 78947
General Phone: (979) 773-3022
General Email: editor@lexingtonleader.com
Publication Website: http://lexingtonleader.com/
Publisher Name: Rita J. Owen
Editor Name: Cindy Terrell
Editor Email: editor@lexingtonleader.com
Delivery Methods: Mail`Newsstand`Carrier`Racks
Year Established: 1997
Published Days: Thur
Avg. Paid Circ.: 1500
Audit Company: Sworn/Estimate/Non-Audited
Audit Date: 43626

LIBERTY HILL

THE LIBERTY HILL INDEPENDENT

Street Address: 14251 W State Highway 29
City: Liberty Hill
State: TX
ZIP Code: 78642-5843
General Phone: (512) 778-5577
General Email: info@lhindependent.com
Publication Website: http://lhindependent.com/
Parent Company: Free State Media Group
Publisher Name: Shelly Wilkison
Publisher Email: news@lhindependent.com
Publisher Phone: (512) 778-5577
Delivery Methods: Mail`Newsstand`Racks
Year Established: 1987
Published Days: Thur
Avg. Paid Circ.: 1850
Audit Company: Sworn/Estimate/Non-Audited
Audit Date: 43626

LINDALE

THE LINDALE NEWS & TIMES

Street Address: 104 N Main St
City: Lindale
State: TX
ZIP Code: 75771
General Phone: (903) 882-8880
General Email: news@lindalenewsandtimes.com
Publication Website: https://lindalenewsandtimes.com/
Parent Company: Bluebonnet Publishing, LLC
Publisher Name: Jim Bardwell
Editor Name: Terry Cannon
Editor Email: news@lindalenews-times.com
Advertising Executive Name: Holly Rand
Advertising Executive Email: advertising@lindalenews-times.com
Delivery Methods: Mail`Newsstand`Racks
Year Established: 1900
Published Days: Thur
Avg. Paid Circ.: 2127
Audit Company: Sworn/Estimate/Non-Audited
Audit Date: 43626

LINDEN

THE CASS COUNTY SUN

Street Address: 122 W Houston St
City: Linden
State: TX
ZIP Code: 75563
General Phone: (903) 756-7396
General Email: aguillory@casscountynow.com
Publication Website: https://www.casscountynow.com/
Parent Company: Northeast Texas Publishing
Delivery Methods: Mail`Newsstand`Racks
Year Established: 1876
Published Days: Wed
Avg. Paid Circ.: 1100
Avg. Free Circ.: 1075
Audit Company: Sworn/Estimate/Non-Audited
Audit Date: 43626

LINDSAY

LINDSAY LETTER

Street Address: 117 E Main St
City: Lindsay
State: TX
ZIP Code: 76250
General Phone: (940) 668-8788
General Email: news@lindsayletter.net
Publication Website: http://lindsayletter.net/
Publisher Name: Scott Wood
Editor Name: Kathy Floyd
Delivery Methods: Mail`Newsstand
Year Established: 2007
Published Days: Fri
Audit Company: Sworn/Estimate/Non-Audited
Audit Date: 43626

LITTLEFIELD

LAMB COUNTY LEADER-NEWS

Street Address: P.O. Box 310
City: Littlefield
State: TX
ZIP Code: 79339
General Phone: (806) 385-4481
General Email: ads@lambcountyleadernews.com
Publication Website: https://www.lambcountyleadernews.com/
Advertising Executive Email: ads@lambcountyleadernews.com
Delivery Methods: Mail`Newsstand`Carrier
Year Established: 1918
Published Days: Wed`Sun
Audit Company: Sworn/Estimate/Non-Audited
Audit Date: 43626

LLANO

THE LLANO NEWS

Street Address: 813 Berry St
City: Llano
State: TX
ZIP Code: 78643
General Phone: (325) 247-4433
General Email: ads@llanonews.com
Publication Website: https://www.hillcountrypassport.com/llano/
Parent Company: Wesner Media Publication
Editor Email: editor@llanonews.com
Advertising Executive Email: ads@llanonews.com
Delivery Methods: Mail`Newsstand
Year Established: 1889
Published Days: Wed
Audit Company: Sworn/Estimate/Non-Audited
Audit Date: 43626

LOCKHART

LOCKHART POST-REGISTER

Street Address: 111 S Church St
City: Lockhart
State: TX
ZIP Code: 78644
General Phone: (512) 398-4886
General Email: news@post-register.com
Publication Website: http://post-register.com/
Delivery Methods: Mail`Newsstand
Year Established: 1872
Own Printing Facility?: N
Commercial printers?: N
Mechanical specifications: Type page 10x 21; E - 6 cols, 1.562, 1/8 between
Published Days: Thur
Avg. Paid Circ.: 3086
Avg. Free Circ.: 177
Audit Company: Sworn/Estimate/Non-Audited
Audit Date: 43626

LULING

THE LULING NEWSBOY AND SIGNAL

Street Address: 415 E Davis St
City: Luling
State: TX
ZIP Code: 78648
General Phone: (830) 875-2116
General Email: slulingnewsboy@austin.rr.com
Publication Website: https://www.lulingnewsboy.com/
Parent Company: Luling Publishing Co., Inc.
Delivery Methods: Mail`Newsstand
Year Established: 1878
Own Printing Facility?: Y
Commercial printers?: N
Mechanical specifications: 5-6 columns news 7 columns classy
Published Days: Thur
Avg. Paid Circ.: 1300
Avg. Free Circ.: 39
Audit Company: Sworn/Estimate/Non-Audited
Audit Date: 43626

MALAKOFF

THE MALAKOFF NEWS

Street Address: 815 E Royall Blvd
City: Malakoff
State: TX
ZIP Code: 75148
General Phone: (903) 887-4511
General Email: thenews.hendersonco@yahoo.com
Publication Website: http://mln.stparchive.com/
Delivery Methods: Mail`Newsstand
Year Established: 1903
Own Printing Facility?: N
Commercial printers?: N
Published Days: Fri
Avg. Paid Circ.: 2000
Avg. Free Circ.: 200
Audit Company: Sworn/Estimate/Non-Audited
Audit Date: 43626

MANSFIELD

MANSFIELD NEWS-MIRROR

Street Address: PO Box 337
City: Mansfield
State: TX
ZIP Code: 76063-0337
General Phone: (817) 473-4451
General Email: kmordecai@star-telegram.com
Publication Website: https://www.star-telegram.com/news/local/community/mansfield-news-mirror/
Publisher Name: Ryan Mote
Publisher Email: rmote@star-telegram.com
Publisher Phone: (817) 390-7454
Editor Name: Tom Johanningmeier
Editor Email: tjohanningmeier@star-telegram.com
Editor Phone: (817) 390-7383
Advertising Executive Name: Stephanie Boggins
Advertising Executive Email: sboggins@star-telegram.com
Advertising Executive Phone: (817) 390-7877
Delivery Methods: Mail`Racks
Published Days: Wed
Avg. Free Circ.: 32158
Audit Company: Sworn/Estimate/Non-Audited
Audit Date: 43626

MARBLE FALLS

THE HIGHLANDER

Street Address: 304-A Highlander Circle
City: Marble Falls
State: TX
ZIP Code: 78654
General Phone: (830) 693-4367
General Email: advertising@highlandernews.com
Publication Website: https://www.highlandernews.com/
Parent Company: Highland Lakes Newspapers
Publisher Name: Jeff Shabram
Publisher Email: jeff@highlandernews.com
Publisher Phone: (830) 693-4367
Editor Name: Lew K. Cohn
Editor Email: lew@highlandernews.com
Editor Phone: (830) 693-4367, ext : 226
Advertising Executive Name: Kari Sardo
Advertising Executive Email: kari@highlandernews.com
Advertising Executive Phone: (817) 390-7877
Delivery Methods: Mail`Newsstand`Racks
Year Established: 1959
Own Printing Facility?: Y
Commercial printers?: N
Published Days: Tues`Fri

Avg. Paid Circ.: 6159
Audit Company: Sworn/Estimate/Non-Audited
Audit Date: 43626
Note: Also includes a full-color weekly dining and entertainment section. Min 16 pages tab. Package advertising available with sister papers in Llano and Burnet, Tx. to cover both Llano and Burnet Counties in Texas.

MARFA

THE BIG BEND SENTINEL

Street Address: 209 1/2 W. El Paso St
City: Marfa
State: TX
ZIP Code: 79843
General Phone: (432) 729-4342
General Email: editor@bigbendsentinel.com
Publication Website: https://bigbendsentinel.com/
Parent Company: West Texan Media Group LLC
Editor Email: editor@bigbendsentinel.com
Delivery Methods: Mail`Newsstand`Racks
Year Established: 1926
Mechanical specifications: Type page 13 x 21.
Published Days: Thur
Avg. Paid Circ.: 2658
Avg. Free Circ.: 25
Audit Company: Sworn/Estimate/Non-Audited
Audit Date: 43626

MARFA

THE PRESIDIO INTERNATIONAL

Street Address: 209 1/2 W. El Paso St
City: Marfa
State: TX
ZIP Code: 79843
General Phone: (432) 729-4342
General Email: editor@bigbendsentinel.com
Publication Website: https://bigbendsentinel.com/
Parent Company: West Texan Media Group LLC
Editor Email: editor@bigbendsentinel.com
Delivery Methods: Mail`Newsstand`Racks
Year Established: 1986
Mechanical specifications: Type page 13 x 21; E - 6 cols, 2, 1/6 between; A - 6 cols, 2, 1/6 between; C - 6 cols, 2, 1/6 between.
Published Days: Thur
Avg. Paid Circ.: 900
Audit Company: Sworn/Estimate/Non-Audited
Audit Date: 43626

MARLIN

THE MARLIN DEMOCRAT

Street Address: 211 Fortune St
City: Marlin
State: TX
ZIP Code: 76661
General Phone: (254) 883-2554
General Email: publisher@marlindemocrat.com
Publication Website: https://www.marlindemocrat.com/
Parent Company: Moser Community Media, LLC
Publisher Name: Lindsey Vaculin
Publisher Email: publisher@marlindemocrat.com
Advertising Executive Name: Mark Pelzel
Advertising Executive Email: advertising@marlindemocrat.com
Delivery Methods: Mail`Newsstand`Racks
Year Established: 1890
Mechanical specifications: 6x21.5 on 1.53-inch column width

Published Days: Wed
Avg. Paid Circ.: 2300
Avg. Free Circ.: 70
Audit Company: Sworn/Estimate/Non-Audited
Audit Date: 43626

MARLIN

THE ROSEBUD NEWS

Street Address: 251 Live Oak Street
City: Marlin
State: TX
ZIP Code: 76661
General Phone: (254) 883-2554
General Email: publisher@marlindemocrat.com
Publication Website: https://www.rosebudnews.net/
Publisher Name: Lindsey Vaculin
Publisher Email: publisher@marlindemocrat.com
Advertising Executive Name: Mark Pelzel
Advertising Executive Email: advertising@marlindemocrat.com
Delivery Methods: Mail`Newsstand`Racks
Year Established: 1893
Mechanical specifications: Type page 15 3/16 x 21; E - 7 cols, 2 1/16, 1/8 between; A - 7 cols, 2 1/16, 1/8 between; C - 8 cols, 1 13/16, 1/8 between.
Published Days: Thur
Avg. Paid Circ.: 1800
Avg. Free Circ.: 15
Audit Company: Sworn/Estimate/Non-Audited
Audit Date: 43626

MASON

MASON COUNTY NEWS

Street Address: 122 S Live Oak
City: Mason
State: TX
ZIP Code: 76856
General Phone: (325) 347-5757
General Email: mcnnews@hctc.net
Publication Website: https://www.hillcountrypassport.com/mason/
Parent Company: Wesner Media Publication
Delivery Methods: Mail`Newsstand
Year Established: 1877
Published Days: Wed
Avg. Paid Circ.: 2188
Audit Company: Sworn/Estimate/Non-Audited
Audit Date: 43626

MC GREGOR

MCGREGOR MIRROR & CRAWFORD SUN

Street Address: 311 S Main St
City: Mc Gregor
State: TX
ZIP Code: 76657
General Phone: (254) 840-2091
General Email: bonnie@mcgregormirror.com
Publication Website: https://www.mcgregormirror.com/
Publisher Name: Charles Mooney
Publisher Email: charles@mcgregormirror.com
Publisher Phone: (254) 840-2091
Editor Name: Bonnie Mullens
Editor Email: bonnie@mcgregormirror.com
Editor Phone: (254) 840-2091
Advertising Executive Name: Bonnie Mullens
Advertising Executive Email: bonnie@mcgregormirror.com
Advertising Executive Phone: (254) 840-2091
Delivery Methods: Mail`Newsstand
Year Established: 1892
Published Days: Thur
Avg. Paid Circ.: 1700

Avg. Free Circ.: 7
Audit Company: Sworn/Estimate/Non-Audited
Audit Date: 43626

MCALLEN

EDINBURG REVIEW

Street Address: 4500 N. 10th Street, Ste. 155
City: McAllen
State: TX
ZIP Code: 78504
General Phone: (956) 682-2423
General Email: ygomez@gatehousemedia.com
Publication Website: http://www.edinburgreview.com/
Publisher Name: Yvonne Gomez
Publisher Email: ygomez@gatehousemedia.com
Publisher Phone: (956) 682-2423, ext : 3983
Editor Name: Illiana Luna
Editor Email: iluna@valleytowncrier.com
Editor Phone: (956) 682-2423, ext : 3984
Advertising Executive Name: Ludmila Garcia
Advertising Executive Email: lggarcia@gatehousemedia.com
Advertising Executive Phone: (956) 682-2423, ext : 2477
Delivery Methods: Carrier`Racks
Year Established: 1914
Own Printing Facility?: N
Commercial printers?: Y
Mechanical specifications: Type page 13 x 21 1/2; E - 6 cols, 2 1/16, 1/8 between; A - 6 cols, 2 1/16, 1/8 between; C - 9 cols, 1 3/8, 1/16 between.
Published Days: Wed
Avg. Free Circ.: 24041
Audit Company: Sworn/Estimate/Non-Audited
Audit Date: 43626

MCALLEN

VALLEY TOWN CRIER

Street Address: 4500 N. 10th Street, Ste. 155
City: McAllen
State: TX
ZIP Code: 78504
General Phone: (956) 682-2423
General Email: iluna@valleytowncrier.com
Publication Website: https://www.yourvalleyvoice.com/
Publisher Name: Yvonne Gomez
Publisher Email: ygomez@gatehousemedia.com
Publisher Phone: (956) 682-2423, ext : 3983
Editor Name: Illiana Luna
Editor Email: iluna@valleytowncrier.com
Editor Phone: (956) 682-2423, ext : 3984
Advertising Executive Name: Ludmila Garcia
Advertising Executive Email: lggarcia@gatehousemedia.com
Advertising Executive Phone: (956) 682-2423, ext : 2477
Delivery Methods: Carrier`Racks
Year Established: 1964
Mechanical specifications: Type page 10.5" x 16"; E - 6 cols, 1.68", A - 6 cols,1.68"
Published Days: Wed
Avg. Free Circ.: 15000
Audit Company: VAC
Audit Date: 43293

MCKINNEY

COLLIN COUNTY COMMERCIAL RECORD

Street Address: 202 W Louisiana St
City: McKinney
State: TX
ZIP Code: 75069-4459
General Phone: (972) 562-0606
General Email: cccr@

Community Newspapers in the U.S.

collincountycommercialrecord.com
Publication Website: https://collincountycommercialrecord.com/
Delivery Methods: Newsstand
Year Established: 1982
Published Days: Tues
Audit Company: Sworn/Estimate/Non-Audited
Audit Date: 43626

MERIDIAN

MERIDIAN TRIBUNE

Street Address: 114 N MAIN
City: Meridian
State: TX
ZIP Code: 76665
General Phone: (254) 435-6333
General Email: brett@meridiantribune.com
Publication Website: https://www.cliftonrecord.com
Publisher Name: Ed Gambardella
Publisher Email: publisher@cliftonrecord.com
Editor Name: Cynthia D. Davis
Editor Email: editor@cliftonrecord.com
Advertising Executive Name: Jessica Brown
Advertising Executive Email: ads@cliftonrecord.com
Delivery Methods: Mail`Newsstand`Racks
Year Established: 1893
Published Days: Wed
Avg. Paid Circ.: 1780
Audit Company: Sworn/Estimate/Non-Audited
Audit Date: 43626

MEXIA

THE MEXIA NEWS

Street Address: 214 N Railroad St
City: Mexia
State: TX
ZIP Code: 76667
General Phone: (254) 562-2868
General Email: news@themexianews.com
Publication Website: https://www.mexiadailynews.com/
Parent Company: Moser Community Media, LLC
Publisher Name: Richard Nelson
Publisher Email: publisher@themexianews.com
Advertising Executive Name: Jennifer Bynum
Advertising Executive Email: jbynum@themexianews.com
Delivery Methods: Mail`Newsstand`Carrier`Racks
Year Established: 1899
Own Printing Facility?: Y
Commercial printers?: Y
Mechanical specifications: One col. 1.637
Published Days: Tues`Thur`Sat
Published Other: TMC product, The Bi-Stone EXTRA
Weekday Frequency: m
Saturday Frequency: m
Avg. Paid Circ.: 2350
Audit Company: Sworn/Estimate/Non-Audited
Audit Date: 43626
Pressroom Equipment: Lines -- 8 units Goss Community;
Mailroom Equipment: Tying Machines -- Bu; Address Machine -- Wm.;
Classified Equipment: Hardware -- APP/Mac; Printers -- APP/Mac LaserWriter;
Classified Software: AdPro
Editorial Equipment: Hardware -- APP/Mac/HP/Scanner IIp; Printers -- APP/Mac LaserWriter
Production Equipment: Hardware -- APP/Mac LaserWriter; Cameras -- SCREEN/Companica Screen.

MINEOLA

WOOD COUNTY MONITOR

Street Address: 715 Mimosa Dr
City: Mineola
State: TX
ZIP Code: 75773
General Phone: (903) 569-2442
General Email: editor@wood.cm
Publication Website: http://woodcountymonitor.com/
Parent Company: Bluebonnet Publishing, LLC
Publisher Name: Phil Major
Publisher Email: publisher@woodcountymonitor.com
Editor Name: Larry Tucker
Editor Email: editor@wood.cm
Advertising Executive Name: Brandi Box
Advertising Executive Email: ads@wood.cm
Delivery Methods: Mail`Racks
Year Established: 1876
Own Printing Facility?: N
Commercial printers?: Y
Published Days: Wed
Avg. Paid Circ.: 3800
Audit Company: Sworn/Estimate/Non-Audited
Audit Date: 43626

MISSION

PROGRESS TIMES

Street Address: 1217 N Conway Ave
City: Mission
State: TX
ZIP Code: 78572
General Phone: (956) 585-4893
General Email: info@progresstimes.net
Publication Website: http://www.progresstimes.net/
Parent Company: Mission Publishing Co
Delivery Methods: Mail`Newsstand`Carrier`Racks
Year Established: 1972
Own Printing Facility?: N
Commercial printers?: N
Mechanical specifications: 10.5" x 19.75" Full Page Dimension 1 Column - 1.61" 2 Column - 3.39" 3 Column - 5.17" 4 Column - 6.94" 5 Column - 8.72" 6 Column - 10.5"
Published Days: Fri
Avg. Paid Circ.: 2905
Avg. Free Circ.: 7095
Audit Company: Sworn/Estimate/Non-Audited
Audit Date: 43626

MONAHANS

THE MONAHANS NEWS

Street Address: 107 W 2nd St
City: Monahans
State: TX
ZIP Code: 79756
General Phone: (432) 943-4313
General Email: smokey@pecos.net
Publication Website: https://www.themonahansnews.com/
Publisher Name: Smokey Briggs
Publisher Email: smokey@pecos.net
Editor Name: Paul Scifres
Editor Email: editor@monahansnews.net
Advertising Executive Email: advertising@monahansnews.net
Delivery Methods: Mail`Newsstand
Year Established: 1931
Published Days: Mon`Thur
Audit Company: Sworn/Estimate/Non-Audited
Audit Date: 43626

MOUNT VERNON

MOUNT VERNON OPTIC-HERALD

Street Address: 108 Kaufman St S
City: Mount Vernon
State: TX
ZIP Code: 75457
General Phone: (903) 537-2228
General Email: optic@mt-vernon.com
Publication Website: http://www.mt-vernon.com/
Publisher Name: Susan Reeves
Publisher Phone: (903) 537-2228
Editor Name: Lillie Bush-Reves
Editor Phone: (903) 537-2228
Advertising Executive Name: Bonnie McAllister
Advertising Executive Phone: (903) 537-2228
Delivery Methods: Mail`Racks
Year Established: 1874
Published Days: Thur
Avg. Paid Circ.: 2500
Audit Company: Sworn/Estimate/Non-Audited
Audit Date: 43626

MULESHOE

MULESHOE JOURNAL

Street Address: 201 W Avenue C
City: Muleshoe
State: TX
ZIP Code: 79347
General Phone: (806) 272-4536
General Email: adsales@muleshoejournal.com
Publication Website: http://www.muleshoejournal.com/
Parent Company: Hearst Corp.
Advertising Executive Name: Rhea Gonzales
Advertising Executive Email: adsales@muleshoejournal.com
Delivery Methods: Mail`Newsstand`Carrier`Racks
Year Established: 1924
Mechanical specifications: 6 column broadsheet 10" x 21.5"
Published Days: Thur
Avg. Paid Circ.: 1600
Avg. Free Circ.: 50
Audit Company: Sworn/Estimate/Non-Audited
Audit Date: 43626

MUNDAY

KNOX COUNTY NEWS-COURIER

Street Address: 121 East B St
City: Munday
State: TX
ZIP Code: 76371
General Phone: (888) 400-1083
General Email: kcnewscourier@gmail.com
Publication Website: http://knoxcountynewsonline.com/
Parent Company: LK Media Group, LLC
Delivery Methods: Mail`Racks
Year Established: 2011
Published Days: Thur
Avg. Paid Circ.: 934
Audit Company: Sworn/Estimate/Non-Audited
Audit Date: 43626

MUNDAY

TWIN CITIES NEWS

Street Address: PO BOX 130
City: Munday
State: TX
ZIP Code: 76371
General Phone: (940) 422-4314
General Email: mcourier@westex.net
Publication Website: http://tcn.stparchive.com/
Publisher Email: mcourier@westex.net
Publisher Phone: (940) 422-4314
Delivery Methods: Mail
Own Printing Facility?: Y
Commercial printers?: Y
Published Days: Thur
Avg. Paid Circ.: 772
Avg. Free Circ.: 17
Audit Company: Sworn/Estimate/Non-Audited
Audit Date: 43626

NEEDVILLE

THE GULF COAST TRIBUNE

Street Address: 3115 School St
City: Needville
State: TX
ZIP Code: 77461-8446
General Phone: (979) 793-6560
General Email: advertising@consolidated.net
Publication Website: http://gctribune.com/
Delivery Methods: Mail`Newsstand
Year Established: 1962
Mechanical specifications: Type page 6X21; E - 6 cols, 1.833", between; C - 9 cols, between.
Published Days: Thur
Avg. Paid Circ.: 1200
Avg. Free Circ.: 67
Audit Company: Sworn/Estimate/Non-Audited
Audit Date: 43626

NEW BOSTON

BOWIE COUNTY CITIZEN TRIBUNE

Street Address: 139 E.N. Front Street
City: New Boston
State: TX
ZIP Code: 75570
General Phone: (903) 628-5801
General Email: alewter@bowiecountynow.com
Publication Website: https://www.bowiecountynow.com/
Parent Company: Northeast Texas Publishing
Publisher Name: Kenny Mitchell
Publisher Email: kmitchell@bowiecountynow.com
Delivery Methods: Mail`Newsstand
Year Established: 1885
Own Printing Facility?: Y
Commercial printers?: Y
Mechanical specifications: Type page 11 7/8 x 21; E - 6 cols, 1 7/8, 1/16 between; A - 6 cols, 1 7/8, 1/16 between; C - 6 cols, 1 7/8, 1/16 between.
Published Days: Wed
Avg. Paid Circ.: 5700
Audit Company: Sworn/Estimate/Non-Audited
Audit Date: 43626

NEWTON

NEWTON COUNTY NEWS

Street Address: 112 GLOVER DR
City: Newton
State: TX
ZIP Code: 75966
General Phone: (409) 379-2416
General Email: newtonnews@valornet.com
Publication Website: https://www.newtoncountynews.net/
Publisher Name: Shawn Wilkerson
Editor Name: Shawn Wilkerson
Advertising Executive Name: Shawn Wilkerson
Delivery Methods: Mail`Newsstand`Racks
Year Established: 1969
Published Days: Wed
Avg. Paid Circ.: 1500
Audit Company: Sworn/Estimate/Non-Audited
Audit Date: 43626

NOCONA

NOCONA NEWS

Street Address: P.O. Box 539
City: Nocona
State: TX
ZIP Code: 76255
General Phone: (940) 825-3201
General Email: advertising@noconanews.net
Publication Website: https://www.noconanews.net/
Advertising Executive Email: advertising@noconanews.net
Delivery Methods: Mail`Newsstand`Racks
Year Established: 1905
Published Days: Thur
Audit Company: Sworn/Estimate/Non-Audited
Audit Date: 43626

NORMANGEE

THE NORMANGEE STAR

Street Address: 122 Taft St.
City: Normangee
State: TX
ZIP Code: 77871
General Phone: (936) 396-3391
Publication Website: https://www.normangeestar.com/
Delivery Methods: Mail`Newsstand
Year Established: 1912
Mechanical specifications: Type page 11 5/8 x 21; E - 6 cols, 1 5/6, 1/8 between; A - 6 cols, 1 5/6, 1/8 between; C - 6 cols, 1 5/6, 1/8 between.
Published Days: Wed
Avg. Paid Circ.: 1400
Avg. Free Circ.: 50
Audit Company: Sworn/Estimate/Non-Audited
Audit Date: 43626

OLNEY

THE OLNEY ENTERPRISE

Street Address: 213 E Main St
City: Olney
State: TX
ZIP Code: 76374-1923
General Phone: (940) 564-5558
General Email: advertising@olneyenterprise.com
Publication Website: https://www.olneyenterprise.com/
Editor Email: editor@olneyenterprise.com
Delivery Methods: Mail`Newsstand`Racks
Year Established: 1908
Mechanical specifications: Page size: 12.5 inches by 22.5 inches Columns: 6 1 col = 1.75 inches 2 col = 3.75 inches 3 col = 5.6875 inches 4 col = 7.635 inches 5 col = 9.5625 inches 6 col = 11.50 inches Full Page charged at 6 cols x 20.5 inches
Published Days: Thur
Avg. Paid Circ.: 1218
Avg. Free Circ.: 15
Audit Company: Sworn/Estimate/Non-Audited
Audit Date: 43626

OLTON

THE OLTON ENTERPRISE

Street Address: 520 Eighth St
City: Olton
State: TX
ZIP Code: 79064
General Phone: (806) 285-7766
General Email: oltonenterprise@hotmail.com
Publication Website: https://oltonline.com/
Parent Company: Triple S Media
Delivery Methods: Mail`Newsstand`Racks
Year Established: 1926
Mechanical specifications: 25-inch web 6 col = 11.625 inch
Published Days: Fri
Avg. Paid Circ.: 1000
Avg. Free Circ.: 20
Audit Company: Sworn/Estimate/Non-Audited
Audit Date: 43626

ORANGE

THE ORANGE LEADER

Street Address: 841B Dal Sasso Dr
City: Orange
State: TX
ZIP Code: 77630-4825
General Phone: (409) 883-3571
General Email: candice.trahan@orangeleader.com
Publication Website: https://www.orangeleader.com/
Parent Company: Boone Newspapers
Publisher Name: Dawn Burleigh
Publisher Email: dawn.burleigh@orangeleader.com
Editor Name: Dawn Burleigh
Editor Email: dawn.burleigh@orangeleader.com
Advertising Executive Name: Candice Trahan
Advertising Executive Email: candice.trahan@orangeleader.com
Delivery Methods: Mail`Newsstand`Racks
Year Established: 1875
Mechanical specifications: Type page 11 5/8 x 21 1/2; E - 6 cols, 1 13/16, 1/8 between; A - 6 cols, 1 13/16, 1/8 between; C - 9 cols, 1 13/16, 1/8 between.
Published Days: Wed`Sat
Weekday Frequency: m
Saturday Frequency: m
Avg. Paid Circ.: 2967
Audit Company: Sworn/Estimate/Non-Audited
Audit Date: 43626

OZONA

OZONA STOCKMAN

Street Address: 1000 Avenue E
City: Ozona
State: TX
ZIP Code: 76943
General Phone: (325) 392-2551
General Email: susan@ozonastockman.com
Publication Website: https://www.ozonastockman.com/
Publisher Name: Melissa Perner
Publisher Email: publisher@ozonastockman.com
Advertising Executive Name: Susan
Advertising Executive Email: susan@ozonastockman.com
Delivery Methods: Mail`Newsstand`Racks
Year Established: 1913
Own Printing Facility?: Y
Commercial printers?: Y
Published Days: Wed
Avg. Paid Circ.: 1755
Avg. Free Circ.: 20
Audit Company: Sworn/Estimate/Non-Audited
Audit Date: 43626

PALACIOS

PALACIOS BEACON

Street Address: 310 5th St
City: Palacios
State: TX
ZIP Code: 77465-4702
General Phone: (361) 972-3009
General Email: brandi.palaciosbeacon@gmail.com
Publication Website: https://palaciosbeacon.com/
Parent Company: City by the Sea Publishing, LLC
Publisher Name: Ryan West
Publisher Email: ryan.palaciosbeacon@gmail.com
Editor Name: Ryan West
Editor Email: ryan.palaciosbeacon@gmail.com
Advertising Executive Name: Brandi West
Advertising Executive Email: brandi.palaciosbeacon@gmail.com
Delivery Methods: Mail`Newsstand
Year Established: 1907
Own Printing Facility?: N
Commercial printers?: N
Mechanical specifications: Type page 11.5 x 21 1/2; E - 6 cols, 1.75 between; A - 6 cols, 2, 1/16 between; C - 6 cols, 2, 1/16 between.
Published Days: Wed
Avg. Paid Circ.: 1600
Audit Company: Sworn/Estimate/Non-Audited
Audit Date: 43626

PANHANDLE

PANHANDLE HERALD / WHITE DEER NEWS

Street Address: 319 Main
City: Panhandle
State: TX
ZIP Code: 79068
General Phone: (806) 537-3634
General Email: shaun@panhandleherald.com
Publication Website: https://www.panhandleherald.com/
Editor Name: Shaun Wink
Advertising Executive Name: Traci McMinn
Delivery Methods: Mail`Racks
Year Established: 1887
Mechanical specifications: Type page Tabloid=10.35 inches x 11.75 inches; E - 6 cols; 1 column=1.6 inches; 2 column=3.35 inches (with .15 inch (gutter) between); 3 column=5.1 inches (with .30 inch between); 4 column=6.85 inches (with .45 inch between); 5 column=8.6 inches (with .60 inch between); 6 columns=10.35 (with .75 inch between)
Published Days: Thur
Published Other: weekly; 51 weeks of the year; closed the week of Christmas
Avg. Paid Circ.: 1251
Avg. Free Circ.: 19
Audit Company: Sworn/Estimate/Non-Audited
Audit Date: 43626
Note: White Deer News is a section of the Panhandle Herald

PASADENA

DEER PARK BROADCASTER

Street Address: 102 Shaver Street
City: Pasadena
State: TX
ZIP Code: 77506
General Phone: (713) 477-0221
General Email: tcurtis@hcnonline.com
Publication Website: https://www.chron.com/neighborhood/deerpark/
Parent Company: Hearst Corp.
Editor Name: Roy Kent
Editor Email: dpeditor@hcnonline.com
Advertising Executive Name: Tom Curtis
Advertising Executive Email: tcurtis@hcnonline.com
Delivery Methods: Carrier
Own Printing Facility?: Y
Published Days: Thur
Avg. Free Circ.: 1763
Audit Company: CVC
Audit Date: 43991

PEARLAND

FRIENDSWOOD JOURNAL

Street Address: 2206 (A) E. Broadway St.
City: Pearland
State: TX
ZIP Code: Pearland
General Phone: (281) 485-2785
General Email: mchasteen@hcnonline.com
Publication Website: https://www.chron.com/neighborhood/friendswood/
Parent Company: Hearst Corp.
Editor Name: Tom Jacobs
Editor Email: pfjournals@hcnonline.com
Advertising Executive Name: Margarette Chasteen
Advertising Executive Email: mchasteen@hcnonline.com
Delivery Methods: Mail`Newsstand`Carrier`Racks
Year Established: 1975
Mechanical specifications: 10.388â€ x 20.5â€
Published Days: Wed
Avg. Paid Circ.: 724
Avg. Free Circ.: 7995
Audit Company: Sworn/Estimate/Non-Audited
Audit Date: 43626

PEARLAND

PEARLAND JOURNAL

Street Address: 2206 E. Broadway St.
City: Pearland
State: TX
ZIP Code: 77581
General Phone: (281) 485-2785
General Email: mchasteen@hcnonline.com
Publication Website: https://www.chron.com/neighborhood/pearland/
Parent Company: Hearst Corp.
Editor Name: Tom Jacobs
Editor Email: pfjournals@hcnonline.com
Advertising Executive Name: Margarette Chasteen
Advertising Executive Email: mchasteen@hcnonline.com
Delivery Methods: Mail`Newsstand`Carrier`Racks
Year Established: 1975
Published Days: Thur
Avg. Paid Circ.: 1125
Avg. Free Circ.: 19330
Audit Company: Sworn/Estimate/Non-Audited
Audit Date: 43626

PEARLAND

PEARLAND REPORTER NEWS

Street Address: 2404 Park Ave
City: Pearland
State: TX
ZIP Code: 77581-4234
General Phone: (281) 485-7501
General Email: laurae3009@yahoo.com
Publication Website: https://myreporternews.com/category/pearland/
Parent Company: My Reporter News
Delivery Methods: Mail`Newsstand`Racks
Year Established: 1971
Published Days: Wed
Avg. Paid Circ.: 28000
Audit Company: Sworn/Estimate/Non-Audited
Audit Date: 43626

PEARSALL

FRIO-NUECES CURRENT

Street Address: 321 E San Marcos St
City: Pearsall

Community Newspapers in the U.S.

III-397

State: TX
ZIP Code: 78061-3223
General Phone: (830) 334-3644
General Email: currentads@att.net
Publication Website: https://www.frio-nuecescurrent.com/
Delivery Methods: Mail`Newsstand
Year Established: 1896
Published Days: Thur
Avg. Paid Circ.: 3453
Avg. Free Circ.: 75
Audit Company: Sworn/Estimate/Non-Audited
Audit Date: 43626

PECOS

PECOS ENTERPRISE

Street Address: 324 S Cedar St
City: Pecos
State: TX
ZIP Code: 79772-3211
General Phone: (432) 445-5475
General Email: smokey@pecos.net
Publication Website: http://www.pecos.net/news/daily/pecosent.htm
Publisher Name: York M. Briggs
Publisher Email: smokey@pecos.net
Editor Name: Jon Fulbright
Editor Email: jon@pecos.net
Delivery Methods: Mail`Newsstand
Year Established: 1887
Mechanical specifications: Type page 13 x 21 1/2; E - 6 cols, 2 1/16, 1/8 between; A - 6 cols, 2 1/16, 1/8 between; C - 6 cols, 2 1/16, 1/8 between.
Published Days: Tues`Fri
Avg. Paid Circ.: 1700
Audit Company: Sworn/Estimate/Non-Audited
Audit Date: 43626

PERRYTON

PERRYTON HERALD

Street Address: 401 S. Amherst
City: Perryton
State: TX
ZIP Code: 79070-3012
General Phone: (806) 435-3631
General Email: dclardy@ptsi.net
Publication Website: https://www.perrytonherald.com/
Delivery Methods: Mail`Newsstand
Year Established: 1917
Published Days: Thur`Sun
Avg. Paid Circ.: 3500
Audit Company: Sworn/Estimate/Non-Audited
Audit Date: 43626

PHARR

ADVANCE NEWS JOURNAL

Street Address: 217 W Newcombe Ave
City: Pharr
State: TX
ZIP Code: 78577-4742
General Phone: (956) 783-0036
General Email: gwendorf@aol.com
Publication Website: https://www.anjournal.com/
Publisher Name: Gregg Wendorf
Publisher Email: gwendorf@aol.com
Delivery Methods: Mail`Newsstand`Racks
Year Established: 1978
Published Days: Wed
Audit Company: Sworn/Estimate/Non-Audited
Audit Date: 43626

PILOT POINT

PILOT POINT POST SIGNAL

Street Address: 111 E Main St
City: Pilot Point
State: TX
ZIP Code: 76258-4532
General Phone: (940) 686-2169
General Email: kfleming@postsignal.com
Publication Website: https://www.postsignal.com/
Publisher Name: David Lewis
Publisher Email: editor@postsignal.com
Editor Name: David Lewis
Editor Email: editor@postsignal.com
Advertising Executive Name: Kim Fleming
Advertising Executive Email: kfleming@postsignal.com
Delivery Methods: Mail`Newsstand`Racks
Year Established: 1878
Published Days: Fri
Avg. Paid Circ.: 2030
Audit Company: Sworn/Estimate/Non-Audited
Audit Date: 43626

PITTSBURG

PITTSBURG GAZETTE

Street Address: 112 Quitman St
City: Pittsburg
State: TX
ZIP Code: 75686-1322
General Phone: (903) 856-6629
General Email: advertising@campcountynow.com
Publication Website: http://campcountynow.com/
Parent Company: Northeast Texas Publishing
Publisher Name: Toni Rowan
Publisher Email: trowan@tribnow.com
Advertising Executive Name: Madlen Krause
Advertising Executive Email: advertising@campcountynow.com
Delivery Methods: Mail`Newsstand`Racks
Year Established: 1884
Published Days: Thur
Avg. Paid Circ.: 3100
Avg. Free Circ.: 33
Audit Company: Sworn/Estimate/Non-Audited
Audit Date: 43626

PITTSBURG

THE BEE

Street Address: 112 Quitman
City: Pittsburg
State: TX
ZIP Code: 75686
General Phone: (903) 645-3948
General Email: thebee@etcnonline.com
Publication Website: http://www.thedaingerfieldbee.com/
Parent Company: Northeast Texas Publishing
Publisher Name: Toni Rowan
Publisher Email: trowan@tribnow.com
Editor Name: Toni Walker
Editor Email: news@steelcountrybee.com
Advertising Executive Name: Trisha Carey
Advertising Executive Email: advertising@campcountynow.com
Delivery Methods: Mail`Newsstand`Racks
Year Established: 1965
Published Days: Wed
Avg. Paid Circ.: 3100
Avg. Free Circ.: 3068
Audit Company: Sworn/Estimate/Non-Audited
Audit Date: 43626

PLANO

COLONY-COURIER LEADER

Street Address: 3501 E Plano Parkway #200
City: Plano
State: TX
ZIP Code: 75074-8304
General Phone: (972) 398-4200
General Email: llibby@starlocalmedia.com
Publication Website: https://starlocalmedia.com/thecolonycourierleader/
Parent Company: Star Local Media
Publisher Name: Scott Wright
Publisher Email: swright@starlocalmedia.com
Publisher Phone: (972) 398-4476
Editor Name: Chris Roark
Editor Email: croark@starlocalmedia.com
Editor Phone: (972) 398-4462
Advertising Executive Name: Joani Dittrich
Advertising Executive Email: jdittrich@starlocalmedia.com
Advertising Executive Phone: (972) 398-4472
Published Days: Sun
Audit Company: Sworn/Estimate/Non-Audited
Audit Date: 43626

PLEASANTON

PLEASANTON EXPRESS

Street Address: P.O. Box 880
City: Pleasanton
State: TX
ZIP Code: 78064
General Phone: (830) 281-2341
General Email: news@pleasantonexpress.com
Publication Website: https://www.pleasantonexpress.com/
Publisher Name: Noel Wilkerson Holmes
Publisher Email: nwilkersonholmes@pleasantonexpress.com
Publisher Phone: (512) 965-6876
Editor Name: Noel Wilkerson Holmes
Editor Email: nwilkersonholmes@pleasantonexpress.com
Editor Phone: (512) 965-6876
Advertising Executive Name: Rhonda Chancellor
Advertising Executive Email: rchancellor@pleasantonexpress.com
Advertising Executive Phone: (830) 569-6130
Delivery Methods: Mail`Newsstand`Racks
Year Established: 1909
Published Days: Wed
Avg. Free Circ.: 8400
Audit Company: Sworn/Estimate/Non-Audited
Audit Date: 43626

PORT ARANSAS

PORT ARANSAS SOUTH JETTY

Street Address: 141 W Cotter Ave
City: Port Aransas
State: TX
ZIP Code: 78373-4034
General Phone: (361) 749-5131
General Email: ads@portasouthjetty.com
Publication Website: https://www.portasouthjetty.com/
Publisher Name: Murray W. Judson
Publisher Email: murray@portasouthjetty.com
Editor Name: Dan Parker
Editor Email: dan@portasouthjetty.com
Advertising Executive Name: Keith Petrus
Advertising Executive Email: ads@portasouthjetty.com
Delivery Methods: Mail`Newsstand`Racks
Year Established: 1971
Mechanical specifications: 1 column = 1.5 inches 2 columns = 3.2 inches 3 columns = 4.9 inches 4 columns = 6.6 inches 5 columns = 8.25 inches 6 columns = 9.91 inches
Published Days: Thur
Avg. Paid Circ.: 3730
Avg. Free Circ.: 56
Audit Company: Sworn/Estimate/Non-Audited
Audit Date: 43626
Note: Southern Publishing, Inc. - company name

PORT ISABEL

PORT ISABEL-SOUTH PADRE PRESS

Street Address: 101 E Maxan St
City: Port Isabel
State: TX
ZIP Code: 78578-4504
General Phone: (956) 943-5545
General Email: editor@portisabelsouthpadre.com
Publication Website: https://www.portisabelsouthpadre.com/
Editor Email: editor@portisabelsouthpadre.com
Delivery Methods: Mail`Newsstand`Racks
Year Established: 1952
Published Days: Thur
Avg. Paid Circ.: 30000
Audit Company: Sworn/Estimate/Non-Audited
Audit Date: 43626

POST

THE POST DISPATCH

Street Address: 123 E Main St
City: Post
State: TX
ZIP Code: 79356-3229
General Phone: (888) 400-1083
General Email: thepostcitydispatch@gmail.com
Publication Website: https://www.thepostdispatchonline.com/
Delivery Methods: Mail`Newsstand
Year Established: 1926
Published Days: Fri
Avg. Paid Circ.: 1550
Audit Company: Sworn/Estimate/Non-Audited
Audit Date: 43626

QUANAH

QUANAH TRIBUNE-CHIEF

Street Address: PO Box 481
City: Quanah
State: TX
ZIP Code: 79252-0481
General Phone: (940) 663-5333
General Email: editor@quanahtribunechief.com
Publication Website: https://www.quanahtribunechief.com/
Delivery Methods: Mail`Newsstand`Racks
Year Established: 1889
Mechanical specifications: Type page 13 x 21; E - 6 cols, 2 1/16, 1/8 between; A - 6 cols, 2 1/16, 1/8 between; C - 6 cols, 2 1/16, 1/8 between.
Published Days: Fri
Avg. Paid Circ.: 1500
Avg. Free Circ.: 19
Audit Company: Sworn/Estimate/Non-Audited
Audit Date: 43626

QUITAQUE

THE VALLEY TRIBUNE

Street Address: 205 Cypress
City: Quitaque
State: TX
ZIP Code: 79255
General Phone: (806) 455-1101
General Email: thevalleytribune@yahoo.com
Publication Website: https://www.thevalleytribune.com/

Publisher Name: Luke Taylor
Editor Name: Brandei Taylor
Delivery Methods: Mail`Newsstand
Year Established: 1926
Mechanical specifications: Type page 13 x 21.
Published Days: Wed
Avg. Paid Circ.: 1000
Audit Company: Sworn/Estimate/Non-Audited
Audit Date: 43626

RAYMONDVILLE

RAYMONDVILLE CHRONICLE & WILLACY COUNTY NEWS

Street Address: PO Box 369
City: Raymondville
State: TX
ZIP Code: 78580-0369
General Phone: (956) 689-2421
General Email: chroniclenews@msn.com
Publication Website: https://www.raymondville-chronicle.com/
Publisher Name: Diana Whitworth Nelson
Publisher Email: diana@raymondville-chronicle.com
Publisher Phone: (956) 689-2421
Delivery Methods: Mail`Newsstand`Racks
Year Established: 1920
Own Printing Facility?: Y
Commercial printers?: N
Mechanical specifications: SAU 6 cols. x 20 inches
Published Days: Wed
Published Other: Weekly
Avg. Paid Circ.: 2500
Audit Company: Sworn/Estimate/Non-Audited
Audit Date: 43626

REFUGIO

REFUGIO COUNTY PRESS

Street Address: 412 N Alamo St
City: Refugio
State: TX
ZIP Code: 78377-
General Phone: (361) 526-2397
General Email: goliadoffice@mysoutex.com
Publication Website: https://www.mysoutex.com/refugio_county_press/
Parent Company: Mysoutx.com
Delivery Methods: Mail`Newsstand`Racks
Year Established: 1959
Published Days: Thur
Avg. Paid Circ.: 2200
Audit Company: Sworn/Estimate/Non-Audited
Audit Date: 43626

ROBERT LEE

THE OBSERVER/ENTERPRISE

Street Address: P.O. Box 1329
City: Robert Lee
State: TX
ZIP Code: 76945
General Phone: (325) 453-2433
General Email: o-e@wcc.net
Publication Website: http://www.observerenterprise.com/
Publisher Name: Melinda McCutchen
Editor Name: Morgan Brigham
Delivery Methods: Mail`Newsstand
Year Established: 1898
Mechanical specifications: Type page 10 x 16; E - 5 cols, 1 11/12, between; A - 5 cols, 1 11/12, between; C - 5 cols, 1 11/12, between.
Published Days: Fri
Avg. Paid Circ.: 1553
Avg. Free Circ.: 32
Audit Company: Sworn/Estimate/Non-Audited

Audit Date: 43626

ROCKDALE

ROCKDALE REPORTER

Street Address: 221 E. Cameron Ave
City: Rockdale
State: TX
ZIP Code: 76567-2972
General Phone: (512) 446-5838
General Email: kathy@rockdalereporter.com
Publication Website: https://www.rockdalereporter.com/
Publisher Name: Ken E. Cooke
Publisher Email: kencooke@rockdalereporter.com
Editor Name: Mike Brown
Editor Email: mike@rockdalereporter.com
Advertising Executive Name: Cassidy Paschall
Advertising Executive Email: cassidy@rockdalereporter.com
Delivery Methods: Mail`Newsstand
Year Established: 1893
Published Days: Thur
Audit Company: Sworn/Estimate/Non-Audited
Audit Date: 43626

ROCKSPRINGS

TEXAS MOHAIR WEEKLY

Street Address: P.O. Box 287
City: Rocksprings
State: TX
ZIP Code: 78880
General Phone: (830) 683-3130
General Email: tmw@swtexas.net
Publication Website: https://www.rockspringsrecord.com/
Delivery Methods: Mail`Newsstand
Year Established: 1893
Published Days: Thur
Avg. Paid Circ.: 1100
Audit Company: Sworn/Estimate/Non-Audited
Audit Date: 43626

ROTAN

DOUBLE MOUNTAIN CHRONICLE

Street Address: 114 E Sammy Baugh Ave
City: Rotan
State: TX
ZIP Code: 79546-4522
General Phone: (325) 735-2562
General Email: advertising@dmchronicle.com
Publication Website: https://www.fishercountychronicle.com/
Publisher Name: Patricia Hurt
Publisher Email: publisher@dmchronicle.com
Editor Name: Jeff Hurt
Editor Email: editor@dmchronicle.com
Advertising Executive Email: advertising@dmchronicle.com
Delivery Methods: Mail`Newsstand
Year Established: 1907
Published Days: Fri
Avg. Paid Circ.: 1038
Audit Company: Sworn/Estimate/Non-Audited
Audit Date: 43626

RUSK

CHEROKEEAN HERALD

Street Address: 595 N Main St
City: Rusk
State: TX
ZIP Code: 75785-1326
General Phone: (903) 683-2257

General Email: advertising@mediactr.com
Publication Website: https://www.thecherokeean.com/
Parent Company: Cherokeean Herald KTLU LLC
Publisher Name: Josie Fox
Publisher Email: josie@thecherokeean.com
Editor Name: Cristin Parker
Editor Email: cristin@thecherokeean.com
Delivery Methods: Mail`Newsstand`Racks
Year Established: 1850
Own Printing Facility?: N
Mechanical specifications: 6 col-11.1528 inches 1 col - 1.7778 gutter.125
Published Days: Wed
Avg. Paid Circ.: 4500
Avg. Free Circ.: 200
Audit Company: Sworn/Estimate/Non-Audited
Audit Date: 43626
Note: We also own two radio stations, KTLU-AM, KWRW-FM, and the time and temperature channel on the local cable service.

SALADO

SALADO VILLAGE VOICE

Street Address: 213 Mill Creek Dr
City: Salado
State: TX
ZIP Code: 76571-4939
General Phone: (254) 947-5321
General Email: advertising@saladovillagevoice.com
Publication Website: http://saladovillagevoice.com/
Parent Company: Salado Village Voice Inc.
Publisher Name: Tim Fleischer
Editor Name: Marilyn Fleischer
Advertising Executive Name: Marilyn Fleischer
Delivery Methods: Mail`Newsstand`Racks
Year Established: 1979
Mechanical specifications: 6 Columns/Print area 10" x 21.5"
Published Days: Thur
Avg. Paid Circ.: 1500
Audit Company: Sworn/Estimate/Non-Audited
Audit Date: 43626

SAN ANTONIO

KELLY OBSERVER

Street Address: P.O. Box 2171
City: San Antonio
State: TX
ZIP Code: 78297
General Phone: (210) 250-3385
General Email: pdavis@primetimenewspapers.com
Publication Website: https://www.mysanantonio.com/community/article/Kelly-USA-Observer-856161.php
Parent Company: Hearst Corp.
Editor Name: Richard Erickson
Editor Email: rerickson@primetimenewspapers.com
Editor Phone: (210) 250-3385
Advertising Executive Name: Paul Davis
Advertising Executive Email: pdavis@primetimenewspapers.com
Advertising Executive Phone: (210) 534-8848
Delivery Methods: Mail`Newsstand
Mechanical specifications: Type page 11 5/8 x 21; E - 6 cols, 2 1/16, 1/8 between; A - 6 cols, 2 1/16, 1/8 between; C - 10 cols, 1 5/16, 1/16 between.
Published Days: Thur
Avg. Paid Circ.: 10
Avg. Free Circ.: 6934
Audit Company: Sworn/Estimate/Non-Audited
Audit Date: 43626

SAN ANTONIO

MEDICAL PATRIOT

Street Address: P.O. Box 2171
City: San Antonio
State: TX
ZIP Code: 78297
General Phone: (210) 250-3385
General Email: pdavis@primetimenewspapers.com
Publication Website: https://www.mysanantonio.com/community/article/Medical-Patriot-856189.php
Parent Company: Hearst Corp.
Editor Name: Richard Erickson
Editor Email: rerickson@primetimenewspapers.com
Editor Phone: (210) 250-3385
Advertising Executive Name: Paul Davis
Advertising Executive Email: pdavis@primetimenewspapers.com
Advertising Executive Phone: (210) 534-8848
Delivery Methods: Mail`Newsstand
Mechanical specifications: Type page 11 5/8 x 21; E - 6 cols, 2 1/16, 1/8 between; A - 6 cols, 2 1/16, 1/8 between; C - 10 cols, 1 5/16, 1/16 between.
Published Days: Thur
Avg. Paid Circ.: 10
Avg. Free Circ.: 4898
Audit Company: Sworn/Estimate/Non-Audited
Audit Date: 43626

SAN ANTONIO

NORTH CENTRAL NEWS

Street Address: 301 Avenue E
City: San Antonio
State: TX
ZIP Code: 78205-2006
General Phone: (210) 250-3711
General Email: communitysupport@express-news.net
Publication Website: https://www.mysanantonio.com
Parent Company: Hearst Corp.
Editor Name: Edmond Ortiz
Delivery Methods: Mail`Newsstand
Mechanical specifications: Type page 11 5/8 x 21; E - 6 cols, 2 1/16, 1/8 between; A - 6 cols, 2 1/16, 1/8 between; C - 10 cols, 1 5/16, 1/16 between.
Published Days: Thur
Avg. Paid Circ.: 10
Avg. Free Circ.: 28141
Audit Company: Sworn/Estimate/Non-Audited
Audit Date: 43626

SAN ANTONIO

NORTHEAST HERALD

Street Address: 301 Avenue E
City: San Antonio
State: TX
ZIP Code: 78205-2006
General Phone: (210) 250-3711
General Email: jflinn@express-news.net
Publication Website: https://www.mysanantonio.com/news/local/communities/northeast/
Parent Company: Hearst Corp.
Delivery Methods: Mail`Newsstand
Mechanical specifications: Type page 11 5/8 x 21; E - 6 cols, 2 1/16, 1/8 between; A - 6 cols, 2 1/16, 1/8 between; C - 10 cols, 1 5/16, 1/16 between.
Published Days: Thur
Avg. Free Circ.: 15428
Audit Company: AAM
Audit Date: 43658

SAN ANTONIO

SAN ANTONIO BUSINESS JOURNAL

Community Newspapers in the U.S.

Street Address: 200 E Grayson St, Ste 110
City: San Antonio
State: TX
ZIP Code: 78215
General Phone: (210) 341-3202
General Email: sanantonio@bizjournals.com
Publication Website: https://www.bizjournals.com/sanantonio/
Parent Company: American City Business Journals
Publisher Name: Jimmy Holmes
Publisher Email: jholmes@bizjournals.com
Publisher Phone: (210) 477-0840
Editor Name: Ed Arnold
Editor Email: earnold@bizjournals.com
Editor Phone: (210) 477-0849
Advertising Executive Name: Liz English
Advertising Executive Email: lenglish@bizjournals.com
Advertising Executive Phone: (210) 477-0854
Delivery Methods: Mail`Newsstand`Racks
Year Established: 1987
Published Days: Fri
Audit Company: Sworn/Estimate/Non-Audited
Audit Date: 43626

SAN ANTONIO

SOUTHSIDE REPORTER

Street Address: 301 Avenue E
City: San Antonio
State: TX
ZIP Code: 78205-2006
General Phone: (210) 250-3000
General Email: mrenteria@express-news.net
Publication Website: https://www.mysanantonio.com/news/local/communities/southside/
Parent Company: Hearst Corp.
Delivery Methods: Mail`Carrier`Racks
Year Established: 1935
Own Printing Facility?: Y
Commercial printers?: Y
Mechanical specifications: 1 column 1.54" 2 column 3.22", 3 column 4.90" 4 column 6.58", 5 column 8.26" 6 column 9.94"
Published Days: Wed
Avg. Free Circ.: 16352
Audit Company: Sworn/Estimate/Non-Audited
Audit Date: 43626

SAN AUGUSTINE

SAN AUGUSTINE TRIBUNE

Street Address: 807 E Columbia St
City: San Augustine
State: TX
ZIP Code: 75972-2213
General Phone: (936) 275-2181
General Email: mail@sanaugustinetribune.com
Publication Website: http://www.sanaugustinetribune.com/
Delivery Methods: Mail`Racks
Year Established: 1916
Mechanical specifications: Type page 13 x 21 1/2; E - 6 cols, 2 1/16, 1/8 between; A - 6 cols, 2 1/16, 1/8 between; C - 8 cols, 1 1/6, between.
Published Days: Thur
Avg. Paid Circ.: 3000
Avg. Free Circ.: 300
Audit Company: Sworn/Estimate/Non-Audited
Audit Date: 43626

SAN BENITO

SAN BENITO NEWS

Street Address: PO Box 1791
City: San Benito
State: TX
ZIP Code: 78586-0017
General Phone: (956) 399-2436
General Email: publisher@sbnewspaper.com
Publication Website: https://www.sbnewspaper.com/
Publisher Name: Ray Quiroga
Publisher Email: publisher@sbnewspaper.com
Editor Name: David Lopez
Editor Email: editor@sbnewspaper.com
Delivery Methods: Mail`Newsstand
Year Established: 1929
Own Printing Facility?: Y
Commercial printers?: Y
Mechanical specifications: Type page 13 1/8 x 21 1/4; E - 6 cols, 2 1/16, between; A - 6 cols, 2 1/16, between; C - 6 cols, 2 1/16, between.
Published Days: Sun
Avg. Paid Circ.: 3933
Avg. Free Circ.: 231
Audit Company: Sworn/Estimate/Non-Audited
Audit Date: 43626

SAN SABA

SAN SABA NEWS & STAR

Street Address: 505 E Wallace St
City: San Saba
State: TX
ZIP Code: 76877-3603
General Phone: (325) 372-5115
General Email: sabanews@centex.net
Publication Website: https://www.sansabanews.com/
Editor Name: Karen Faught
Editor Email: sabanews@centex.net
Delivery Methods: Mail`Newsstand
Year Established: 1873
Published Days: Thur
Avg. Paid Circ.: 2394
Avg. Free Circ.: 70
Audit Company: Sworn/Estimate/Non-Audited
Audit Date: 43626

SANGER

SANGER NEWS

Street Address: 412 Bolivar St
City: Sanger
State: TX
ZIP Code: 76266-8961
General Phone: (940) 458-8515
General Email: sanger@lemonspublications.com
Publication Website: https://www.lemonspublications.com/
Parent Company: Lemons Publications
Publisher Name: Blake Lemons
Publisher Email: blake@lemonspublications.com
Advertising Executive Name: Lindsey Reindal
Advertising Executive Email: lindsey@lemonspublications.com
Delivery Methods: Mail`Racks
Year Established: 2012
Published Days: Thur
Avg. Paid Circ.: 1513
Audit Company: Sworn/Estimate/Non-Audited
Audit Date: 43626

SCHULENBURG

THE SCHULENBURG STICKER

Street Address: 405 N Main St
City: Schulenburg
State: TX
ZIP Code: 78956-1561
General Phone: (979) 743-3450
General Email: ads@schulenburgsticker.com
Publication Website: https://www.schulenburgsticker.com/
Publisher Name: Maxine Vyvjala
Editor Name: Darrell Vyvjala
Delivery Methods: Mail`Newsstand
Year Established: 1894
Mechanical specifications: Type page 13 x 21; E - 6 cols, 2 1/16, 1/8 between; A - 6 cols, 2 1/16, 1/8 between; C - 6 cols, 2 1/16, 1/8 between.
Published Days: Thur
Avg. Paid Circ.: 2823
Avg. Free Circ.: 34
Audit Company: Sworn/Estimate/Non-Audited
Audit Date: 43626

SEMINOLE

SEMINOLE SENTINEL

Street Address: 406 S Main St
City: Seminole
State: TX
ZIP Code: 79360-5058
General Phone: (432) 758-3667
General Email: ads@seminolesentinel.com
Publication Website: https://www.seminolesentinel.com/
Parent Company: Roberts Publishing
Publisher Name: Christy Hawkins
Publisher Email: publisher@seminolesentinel.com
Advertising Executive Name: Misty Ramirez
Advertising Executive Email: ads@seminolesentinel.com
Delivery Methods: Mail`Newsstand`Carrier
Year Established: 1907
Mechanical specifications: Type page 13 x 21; E - 4 cols, 3, 1/8 between; A - 6 cols, 2 1/16, between; C - 6 cols, 2 1/16, between.
Published Days: Wed`Sun
Avg. Paid Circ.: 2100
Audit Company: Sworn/Estimate/Non-Audited
Audit Date: 43626

SEYMOUR

BAYLOR COUNTY BANNER

Street Address: 109 E Morris St
City: Seymour
State: TX
ZIP Code: 76380-2140
General Phone: (940) 889-2616
General Email: banner@srcaccess.net
Publication Website: https://www.baylorbanner.com/
Delivery Methods: Mail`Racks
Year Established: 1895
Mechanical specifications: Type page 11 5/8 x 21; E - 6 cols, 1 5/6, 1/8 between; A - 6 cols, 1 5/6, 1/8 between; C - 6 cols, 1 5/6, 1/8 between.
Published Days: Thur
Avg. Paid Circ.: 2500
Avg. Free Circ.: 26
Audit Company: Sworn/Estimate/Non-Audited
Audit Date: 43626

SHAMROCK

COUNTY STAR NEWS

Street Address: 212 N Main St
City: Shamrock
State: TX
ZIP Code: 79079-2228
General Phone: (806) 256-2070
General Email: jeff@countystarnews.com
Publication Website: https://www.countystarnews.com/
Delivery Methods: Mail`Racks
Year Established: 1993
Published Days: Thur
Avg. Paid Circ.: 2400
Audit Company: Sworn/Estimate/Non-Audited
Audit Date: 43626

SHERMAN

THE VAN ALSTYNE LEADER

Street Address: 603 S Sam Rayburn Fwy
City: Sherman
State: TX
ZIP Code: 75090-7258
General Phone: (903) 893-8181
General Email: tyoung@heralddemocrat.com
Publication Website: https://www.vanalstyneleader.com/
Publisher Name: Nate Rodriguez
Publisher Email: nrodriguez@heralddemocrat.com
Publisher Phone: (903) 893-8181, ext : 1100
Editor Name: William C. Wadsack
Editor Email: wwadsack@heralddemocrat.com
Editor Phone: (903) 893-8181, ext : 1138
Advertising Executive Name: Teresa Young
Advertising Executive Email: tyoung@heralddemocrat.com
Advertising Executive Phone: (903) 893-8181, ext : 1120
Delivery Methods: Mail`Newsstand`Racks
Year Established: 1892
Published Days: Fri
Avg. Paid Circ.: 969
Audit Company: Sworn/Estimate/Non-Audited
Audit Date: 43626

SHERMAN

THE ANNA-MELISSA TRIBUNE

Street Address: 603 S Sam Rayburn Fwy
City: Sherman
State: TX
ZIP Code: 75090-7258
General Phone: (903) 893-8181
General Email: tyoung@heralddemocrat.com
Publication Website: https://www.amtrib.com/
Publisher Name: Nate Rodriguez
Publisher Email: nrodriguez@heralddemocrat.com
Publisher Phone: (903) 893-8181, ext : 1100
Editor Name: William C. Wadsack
Editor Email: wwadsack@heralddemocrat.com
Editor Phone: (903) 893-8181, ext : 1138
Advertising Executive Name: Teresa Young
Advertising Executive Email: tyoung@heralddemocrat.com
Advertising Executive Phone: (903) 893-8181, ext : 1120
Delivery Methods: Newsstand`Carrier`Racks
Year Established: 2002
Published Days: Thur
Avg. Free Circ.: 9000
Audit Company: Sworn/Estimate/Non-Audited
Audit Date: 43626

SHINER

THE SHINER GAZETTE

Street Address: 1509 North Ave E.
City: Shiner
State: TX
ZIP Code: 77984-5210
General Phone: (361) 594-3346
General Email: shinergazette@sbcglobal.net
Publication Website: http://www.baercom.com/gazette/
Publisher Name: L.M. Preuss
Delivery Methods: Mail`Newsstand
Year Established: 1892
Mechanical specifications: Type page 13 x 21; E - 6 cols, 2, 3/16 between; A - 6 cols, 2, 3/16 between; C - 6 cols, 2, 3/16 between.
Published Days: Thur

Avg. Paid Circ.: 1750
Audit Company: Sworn/Estimate/Non-Audited
Audit Date: 43626

SILSBEE

SILSBEE BEE

Street Address: P.O. Box 547
City: Silsbee
State: TX
ZIP Code: 77656-4810
General Phone: (409) 385-5278
General Email: publisher@silsbeebee.com
Publication Website: https://www.silsbeebee.com/
Parent Company: Reneau
Publisher Name: Danny Reneau
Publisher Email: publisher@silsbeebee.com
Editor Name: Dannie Oliveaux
Editor Email: editor@silsbeebee.com
Delivery Methods: Mail`Newsstand
Year Established: 1919
Published Days: Wed
Avg. Paid Circ.: 4709
Avg. Free Circ.: 25
Audit Company: Sworn/Estimate/Non-Audited
Audit Date: 43626

SLATON

THE SLATONITE

Street Address: P.O. Box 667
City: Slaton
State: TX
ZIP Code: 79364-4121
General Phone: (806) 828-6201
General Email: slatonite@sbcglobal.net
Publication Website: https://www.slatonitenews.com/
Parent Company: Slaton Media, LLC
Publisher Name: Melissa McCaghren
Publisher Email: melissa@slatonitenews.com
Advertising Executive Name: Shannon Fox
Advertising Executive Email: shannon@slatonitenews.com
Delivery Methods: Mail`Racks
Year Established: 1911
Mechanical specifications: New SAU
Published Days: Thur
Avg. Paid Circ.: 1900
Avg. Free Circ.: 25
Audit Company: Sworn/Estimate/Non-Audited
Audit Date: 43626

SONORA

DEVIL'S RIVER NEWS

Street Address: 224 E Main St
City: Sonora
State: TX
ZIP Code: 76950-2605
General Phone: (325) 387-2507
General Email: publisher@devilsriver.news
Publication Website: https://devilsriver.news/
Parent Company: Masked Rider Publishing, Inc.
Publisher Name: Randy Mankin
Publisher Email: publisher@devilsriver.news
Editor Name: Kimberley Meyer
Editor Email: editor@devilsriver.news
Delivery Methods: Mail`Newsstand
Year Established: 1890
Published Days: Thur
Audit Company: Sworn/Estimate/Non-Audited
Audit Date: 43626

SPEARMAN

THE HANSFORD COUNTY REPORTER-STATESMAN

Street Address: 310 Barkley Street
City: Spearman
State: TX
ZIP Code: 79081-2065
General Phone: (806) 659-3434
General Email: cami.peepaw@gmail.com
Publication Website: https://reporterstatesman.com/
Delivery Methods: Mail`Newsstand`Racks
Year Established: 1901
Own Printing Facility?: N
Commercial printers?: N
Published Days: Thur
Avg. Paid Circ.: 1400
Avg. Free Circ.: 300
Audit Company: Sworn/Estimate/Non-Audited
Audit Date: 43626

SPRINGTOWN

SPRINGTOWN EPIGRAPH

Street Address: 109 E 1ST ST
City: Springtown
State: TX
ZIP Code: 76082
General Phone: (817) 220-7217
General Email: johnna@azlenews.net
Publication Website: https://www.springtown-epigraph.net/
Publisher Name: Kim Ware
Publisher Email: publisher@azlenews.net
Editor Name: Michael Acosta
Editor Email: michaelacosta@azlenews.net
Advertising Executive Name: Johnna Bridges
Advertising Executive Email: johnna@azlenews.net
Delivery Methods: Mail`Newsstand`Racks
Year Established: 1964
Published Days: Thur
Avg. Paid Circ.: 1600
Audit Company: Sworn/Estimate/Non-Audited
Audit Date: 43626

SPUR

THE TEXAS SPUR

Street Address: PO Box 430
City: Spur
State: TX
ZIP Code: 79370-0430
General Phone: (806) 271-3381
General Email: classified@thetexasspur.com
Publication Website: https://www.thetexasspur.com/
Publisher Name: Kay Ellington
Publisher Email: kay.ellington@thetexasspur.com
Editor Name: Michelle Newby Lancaster
Editor Email: michelle.lancaster@thetexasspur.com
Advertising Executive Email: classified@thetexasspur.com
Delivery Methods: Mail`Newsstand
Year Established: 1909
Published Days: Thur
Avg. Paid Circ.: 1200
Audit Company: Sworn/Estimate/Non-Audited
Audit Date: 43626

STAFFORD

FORT BEND STAR

Street Address: 3944 Bluebonnet Dr
City: Stafford
State: TX
ZIP Code: 77477-3952
General Phone: (281) 690-4200
General Email: jsazma@fortbendstar.com
Publication Website: http://www.fortbendstar.com/
Publisher Name: Frank Vasquez
Editor Name: Joe Southern
Editor Email: editor@fortbendstar.com
Advertising Executive Email: jsazma@fortbendstar.com
Delivery Methods: Mail`Newsstand`Racks
Mechanical specifications: Type page 13 x 21 1/2; E - 6 cols, 2 1/16, between; A - 6 cols, 2 1/16, between; C - 10 cols, 1 1/6, 1/12 between.
Published Days: Wed
Avg. Paid Circ.: 200
Avg. Free Circ.: 34775
Audit Company: Sworn/Estimate/Non-Audited
Audit Date: 43626

STAMFORD

THE NEW STAMFORD AMERICAN

Street Address: 102 S Swenson St
City: Stamford
State: TX
ZIP Code: 79553-4624
General Phone: (325) 773-5550
General Email: ads@stamfordamerican.net
Publication Website: https://www.americannewspapers.net/
Publisher Name: Callie Metler-Smith
Publisher Email: callie@americannewspapers.net
Editor Name: Kay Spears
Editor Email: kay@americannewspapers.net
Advertising Executive Name: Callie Metler-Smith
Advertising Executive Email: ads@stamfordamerican.net
Delivery Methods: Mail`Newsstand
Year Established: 2009
Published Days: Fri
Avg. Paid Circ.: 526
Audit Company: Sworn/Estimate/Non-Audited
Audit Date: 43626

STAMFORD

THE STAMFORD STAR

Street Address: 202 E Hamilton St
City: Stamford
State: TX
ZIP Code: 79553-4730
General Phone: (325) 773-5100
General Email: audra@thestamfordstar.com
Publication Website: https://www.thestamfordstar.com/
Parent Company: The Stamford Star
Publisher Name: Audra Arendall
Publisher Email: audra@thestamfordstar.com
Publisher Phone: (325) 733-8895
Editor Name: Amber Agraz
Advertising Executive Name: Audra Arendall
Advertising Executive Email: audra@thestamfordstar.com
Advertising Executive Phone: (325) 733-8895
Delivery Methods: Mail`Newsstand`Racks
Year Established: 2006
Published Days: Fri
Avg. Paid Circ.: 1500
Avg. Free Circ.: 200
Audit Company: Sworn/Estimate/Non-Audited
Audit Date: 43626

STANTON

MARTIN COUNTY MESSENGER

Street Address: 210 Saint Peter
City: Stanton
State: TX
ZIP Code: 79782
General Phone: (432) 756-2090
General Email: mcmessenger@crcom.net
Publication Website: https://www.martincountymessenger.com/
Publisher Name: Bob Dillard
Delivery Methods: Mail`Newsstand
Year Established: 1925
Published Days: Thur
Avg. Paid Circ.: 1500
Audit Company: Sworn/Estimate/Non-Audited
Audit Date: 43626

TEAGUE

TEAGUE CHRONICLE

Street Address: 319 Main Street • P.O. Box 631
City: Teague
State: TX
ZIP Code: 75860-1621
General Phone: (254) 739-2141
General Email: teaguechronicle@sbcglobal.net
Publication Website: https://www.teaguechronicle.com/
Delivery Methods: Mail`Newsstand`Racks
Year Established: 1906
Mechanical specifications: Type page 13 x 21; E - 6 cols, 2 1/16, 1/8 between; A - 6 cols, 2 1/16, 1/8 between; C - 6 cols, 2 1/16, 1/8 between.
Published Days: Thur
Avg. Paid Circ.: 2500
Audit Company: Sworn/Estimate/Non-Audited
Audit Date: 43626

TERRELL

THE TERRELL TRIBUNE

Street Address: 150 9th St, P.O. Box 669
City: Terrell
State: TX
ZIP Code: 75160-3061
General Phone: (972) 563-6476
General Email: pbarringer@terrelltribune.com
Publication Website: http://www.terrelltribune.com/
Parent Company: Van Zandt Newspapers LLC
Publisher Name: Brad Blakemore
Publisher Email: brad@vanzandtnews.com
Editor Name: Travis Detherage
Advertising Executive Name: Patty Barringer
Advertising Executive Email: pbarringer@terrelltribune.com
Delivery Methods: Mail`Newsstand`Carrier`Racks
Year Established: 1898
Mechanical specifications: Type page 11.625 x 21, 6 cols.
Published Days: Wed`Sat
Weekday Frequency: e
Avg. Paid Circ.: 2300
Audit Company: Sworn/Estimate/Non-Audited
Audit Date: 43626
Note: We also publish a free distribution TMC on Wednesdays with 11,500 circulation. Carrier and mail delivered.

THREE RIVERS

THE PROGRESS

Street Address: 501 N Harborth Ave.
City: Three Rivers
State: TX
ZIP Code: 78071
General Phone: (361) 786-3022
General Email: theprogress@mysoutex.com
Publication Website: https://www.mysoutex.com/the_progress/
Parent Company: MYSoutx.com
Editor Email: media@mysoutex.com
Advertising Executive Email: ads@mysoutex.com

Community Newspapers in the U.S.

Delivery Methods: Mail`Newsstand`Racks
Year Established: 1928
Mechanical specifications: Type page 13 x 21 1/4; E - 6 cols, 2, 1/4 between; A - 6 cols, 2, 1/4 between; C - 6 cols, 2, 1/4 between.
Published Days: Wed
Avg. Paid Circ.: 3173
Avg. Free Circ.: 13
Audit Company: Sworn/Estimate/Non-Audited
Audit Date: 43626

THROCKMORTON

THROCKMORTON TRIBUNE

Street Address: 140 N Minter Ave
City: Throckmorton
State: TX
ZIP Code: 76483-5344
General Phone: (940) 849-0147
General Email: throckmortontribune@gmail.com
Publication Website: http://www.throcktribune.com/
Delivery Methods: Mail
Year Established: 1886
Mechanical specifications: Type page 13 1/4 x 21; E - 6 cols, 2, between.
Published Days: Thur
Avg. Paid Circ.: 1051
Avg. Free Circ.: 214
Audit Company: Sworn/Estimate/Non-Audited
Audit Date: 43626

TIMPSON

TIMPSON & TENAHA NEWS

Street Address: PO Box 740
City: Timpson
State: TX
ZIP Code: 75975
General Phone: (936) 254-3618
General Email: ttnews@ttnewsinc.com
Publication Website: https://www.easttexaspress.com/timpson
Publisher Name: Chad Pate
Publisher Phone: (936) 254-5050
Editor Name: Carol Rhodes
Editor Phone: (936) 572-1248
Delivery Methods: Mail`Racks
Year Established: 1885
Published Days: Thur
Avg. Paid Circ.: 2001
Avg. Free Circ.: 6
Audit Company: Sworn/Estimate/Non-Audited
Audit Date: 43626

TOMBALL

MAGNOLIA POTPOURRI

Street Address: 825 Village Square
City: Tomball
State: TX
ZIP Code: 77375
General Phone: (281) 357-0882
General Email: cblanchard@hcnonline.com
Publication Website: https://www.chron.com/neighborhood/magnolia/
Parent Company: Hearst Corp.
Editor Name: Allen Jones
Editor Email: potpourrieditor@hcnonline.com
Advertising Executive Name: Cora Blanchard
Advertising Executive Email: cblanchard@hcnonline.com
Delivery Methods: Mail`Newsstand`Racks
Year Established: 1986
Published Days: Wed
Avg. Free Circ.: 13545
Audit Company: Sworn/Estimate/Non-Audited
Audit Date: 43626

TULIA

SWISHER COUNTY NEWS

Street Address: 107 S Austin Ave
City: Tulia
State: TX
ZIP Code: 79088-2802
General Phone: (806) 995-0052
General Email: swishercountynews1@gmail.com
Publication Website: https://www.swishernews.com/
Delivery Methods: Mail`Racks
Year Established: 2009
Own Printing Facility?: N
Commercial printers?: N
Published Days: Thur
Avg. Paid Circ.: 1184
Audit Company: Sworn/Estimate/Non-Audited
Audit Date: 43626

TURKEY

MOTLEY COUNTY TRIBUNE

Street Address: 904 Childress Ave
City: Turkey
State: TX
ZIP Code: 79261-2022
General Phone: (806) 620-5244
General Email: caprockcourier@gmail.com
Publication Website: https://www.caprockcourier.com/motley-county-matador-news/
Publisher Name: Tori Leigh Minick
Delivery Methods: Mail`Newsstand
Year Established: 1891
Published Days: Thur
Avg. Paid Circ.: 669
Audit Company: Sworn/Estimate/Non-Audited
Audit Date: 43626

UVALDE

UVALDE LEADER-NEWS

Street Address: 110 N East St
City: Uvalde
State: TX
ZIP Code: 78801-5312
General Phone: (830) 278-3335
General Email: sbalke@uvaldeleadernews.com
Publication Website: http://uvaldeleadernews.com/
Publisher Name: Craig Garnett
Publisher Email: cgarnett@ulnnow.com
Editor Name: Meghann Garcia
Editor Email: mgarcia@ulnnow.com
Advertising Executive Name: Steve Balke
Advertising Executive Email: sbalke@ulnnow.com
Delivery Methods: Mail`Newsstand`Racks
Year Established: 1879
Published Days: Thur`Sun
Avg. Paid Circ.: 4741
Audit Company: Sworn/Estimate/Non-Audited
Audit Date: 43626

VAN HORN

THE VAN HORN ADVOCATE

Street Address: 701 W Broadway
City: Van Horn
State: TX
ZIP Code: 79855
General Phone: (432) 283-2003
General Email: lmorton@thevanhornadvocate.com
Publication Website: https://vhtx.news/
Publisher Name: Gilda Morales
Editor Name: Gilda Morales
Editor Email: editor@thevanhornadvocate.com
Advertising Executive Name: Lisa Morton
Advertising Executive Email: lmorton@thevanhornadvocate.com
Delivery Methods: Mail`Racks
Year Established: 1910
Published Days: Thur
Avg. Paid Circ.: 985
Audit Company: Sworn/Estimate/Non-Audited
Audit Date: 43626

VIDOR

VIDOR VIDORIAN

Street Address: P.O. Box 1236
City: Vidor
State: TX
ZIP Code: 77662
General Phone: (409) 769-5428
General Email: info@thevidorian.com
Publication Website: https://www.thevidorian.com/
Delivery Methods: Mail`Racks
Year Established: 1959
Own Printing Facility?: Y
Commercial printers?: Y
Mechanical specifications: Type page 13 x 21; E - 6 cols, 1 13/16, 1/8 between; A - 6 cols, 1 13/16, 1/8 between; C - 9 cols, 1, 1/8 between.
Published Days: Thur
Avg. Paid Circ.: 1502
Avg. Free Circ.: 11275
Audit Company: Sworn/Estimate/Non-Audited
Audit Date: 43626

WALLIS

WALLIS NEWS-REVIEW

Street Address: 256 Cedar St
City: Wallis
State: TX
ZIP Code: 77485
General Phone: (979) 478-6412
General Email: joanie@wallisnews.com
Publication Website: http://wallisnews.com/
Publisher Name: Joanie Griffin
Publisher Email: joanie@wallisnews.com
Editor Name: Johnny Griffin
Editor Email: johnny@wallisnews.com
Delivery Methods: Mail`Newsstand
Year Established: 1974
Mechanical specifications: Type page 13 x 21; E - 6 cols, 2 1/8, between; A - 6 cols, 2 1/8, between.
Published Days: Thur
Avg. Paid Circ.: 800
Avg. Free Circ.: 25
Audit Company: Sworn/Estimate/Non-Audited
Audit Date: 43626

WAXAHACHIE

THE MIDLOTHIAN MIRROR

Street Address: 200 W Marvin Ave
City: Waxahachie
State: TX
ZIP Code: 75165
General Phone: (972) 937-3310
General Email: advertising@waxahachietx.com
Publication Website: https://www.midlothianmirror.com/
Parent Company: Gannett
Editor Name: Rebecca Jones
Editor Email: rjones1@gatehousemedia.com
Editor Phone: (469) 517-1470
Advertising Executive Name: Colten Crist
Advertising Executive Email: ccrist@waxahachietx.com
Advertising Executive Phone: (469) 517-1440
Delivery Methods: Mail`Racks
Year Established: 1882
Own Printing Facility?: Y
Commercial printers?: Y
Mechanical specifications: Type page 13 x 21; E - 6 cols, 1 5/6, between; A - 10 cols, 1 2/25, between; C - 6 cols, 1 5/6, between.
Published Days: Wed
Avg. Paid Circ.: 6000
Audit Company: Sworn/Estimate/Non-Audited
Audit Date: 43626

WEBSTER

BAY AREA CITIZEN

Street Address: 100 E. NASA Parkway
City: Webster
State: TX
ZIP Code: 77598
General Phone: (281) 488-1108
General Email: citizen@hcnonline.com
Publication Website: https://www.chron.com/neighborhood/bayarea/
Parent Company: Hearst Corp.
Editor Name: Dana Burke
Editor Email: citizen@hcnonline.com
Advertising Executive Name: Margarette Chasteen
Advertising Executive Email: mchasteen@hcnonline.com
Delivery Methods: Carrier`Racks
Year Established: 1961
Mechanical specifications: 10.388â◻ x 20.5â◻
Published Days: Thur
Avg. Free Circ.: 28523
Audit Company: Sworn/Estimate/Non-Audited
Audit Date: 43626

WESLACO

THE MID-VALLEY TOWN CRIER

Street Address: 401 S Kansas Ave
City: Weslaco
State: TX
ZIP Code: 78596
General Phone: (956) 969-2543
Publication Website: https://www.midvalleytowncrier.com/
Parent Company: AIM Media Texas
Delivery Methods: Mail`Racks
Year Established: 1967
Published Days: Thur`Sun
Avg. Free Circ.: 21750
Audit Company: Sworn/Estimate/Non-Audited
Audit Date: 43626

WEST COLUMBIA

THE BRAZORIA COUNTY NEWS

Street Address: 113 E Bernard St
City: West Columbia
State: TX
ZIP Code: 77486
General Phone: (979) 345-3127
Publication Website: http://www.brazoriacountynews.com/
Delivery Methods: Mail`Racks
Year Established: 1962
Mechanical specifications: Type page 11 5/8 x 21; E - 6 cols, 1 5/6, 1/8 between; A - 6 cols, 1 5/6, 1/8 between; C - 9 cols, 1 3/16, 1/8 between.
Published Days: Thur
Avg. Free Circ.: 11000
Audit Company: Sworn/Estimate/Non-Audited
Audit Date: 43626

WHEELER

THE WHEELER TIMES

Street Address: 110 E Texas Ave
City: Wheeler
State: TX
ZIP Code: 79096
General Phone: (806) 826-3123
General Email: times@windstream.net
Publication Website: https://www.thewheelertimes.com/
Delivery Methods: Mail
Year Established: 1933
Published Days: Thur
Avg. Paid Circ.: 973
Audit Company: Sworn/Estimate/Non-Audited
Audit Date: 43626

WHITESBORO

WHITESBORO NEWS-RECORD

Street Address: 130 E Main St
City: Whitesboro
State: TX
ZIP Code: 76273
General Phone: (903) 564-3565
General Email: news@whitesboronews.com
Publication Website: http://whitesboronews.com/Whitesboro_News-Record/Home.html
Publisher Name: Austin Lewter
Publisher Email: news@whitesboronews.com
Editor Name: Austin Lewter
Editor Email: news@whitesboronews.com
Advertising Executive Name: Delaney Pierce
Advertising Executive Email: ads@whitesboronews.com
Delivery Methods: Mail`Newsstand`Racks
Year Established: 1877
Mechanical specifications: Type page 11 1/2 x 21 1/2; E - 6 cols, 1 13/16, 1/4 between; A - 6 cols, 1 13/16, 1/4 between; C - 6 cols, 1 13/16, 1/4 between.
Published Days: Thur
Avg. Paid Circ.: 3000
Avg. Free Circ.: 38
Audit Company: Sworn/Estimate/Non-Audited
Audit Date: 43626

WHITEWRIGHT

WHITEWRIGHT SUN

Street Address: PO Box 218
City: Whitewright
State: TX
ZIP Code: 75491-0218
General Phone: (903) 965-3890
General Email: news@whitewrightsun.com
Publication Website: https://whitewrightsun.com/
Publisher Name: Sarah Beth Owen
Publisher Email: news@whitewrightsun.com
Editor Name: Sarah Beth Owen
Editor Email: news@whitewrightsun.com
Delivery Methods: Mail`Newsstand`Racks
Year Established: 1884
Own Printing Facility?: N
Commercial printers?: N
Published Days: Thur
Avg. Paid Circ.: 1100
Avg. Free Circ.: 50
Audit Company: Sworn/Estimate/Non-Audited
Audit Date: 43626

WIMBERLEY

WIMBERLEY VIEW

Street Address: PO Box 49
City: Wimberley
State: TX
ZIP Code: 78676
General Phone: (512) 847-2202
General Email: wimberleyview@gmail.com
Publication Website: https://www.wimberleyview.com/
Parent Company: San Marcos Publishing
Publisher Name: Dalton Sweat
Publisher Email: dsweat@wimberleyview.com
Publisher Phone: (512) 644-9785
Advertising Executive Name: Susan K. Sisson
Advertising Executive Email: ssisson@wimberleyview.com
Advertising Executive Phone: (512) 847-2202
Delivery Methods: Mail`Racks
Year Established: 1976
Own Printing Facility?: Y
Published Days: Thur
Avg. Paid Circ.: 2100
Audit Company: Sworn/Estimate/Non-Audited
Audit Date: 43626

WINNIE

HOMETOWN PRESS

Street Address: 336 Broadway
City: Winnie
State: TX
ZIP Code: 77665-7829
General Phone: (409) 296-9988
General Email: htpress99@windstream.net
Publication Website: http://myhometownpress.com/
Delivery Methods: Mail`Newsstand`Racks
Year Established: 1991
Published Days: Thur
Avg. Paid Circ.: 2000
Audit Company: Sworn/Estimate/Non-Audited
Audit Date: 43626

WYLIE

MURPHY MONITOR

Street Address: 110 N Ballard Ave
City: Wylie
State: TX
ZIP Code: 75098
General Phone: (972) 442-5515
General Email: news@murphymonitor.com
Publication Website: https://murphymonitor.com/
Parent Company: C&S Media, Inc.
Delivery Methods: Mail`Newsstand`Carrier`Racks
Year Established: 2005
Mechanical specifications: 11.5 x 21
Published Days: Thur
Avg. Paid Circ.: 2568
Audit Company: Sworn/Estimate/Non-Audited
Audit Date: 43626
Note: None

WYLIE

SACHSE NEWS

Street Address: 110 N Ballard Ave
City: Wylie
State: TX
ZIP Code: 75098
General Phone: (972) 442-5515
General Email: news@sachsenews.com
Publication Website: https://sachsenews.com/
Parent Company: C&S Media, Inc.
Delivery Methods: Mail`Newsstand`Racks
Year Established: 2005
Published Days: Thur
Avg. Paid Circ.: 1533
Audit Company: Sworn/Estimate/Non-Audited
Audit Date: 43626

WYLIE

THE WYLIE NEWS

Street Address: 110 N Ballard Ave
City: Wylie
State: TX
ZIP Code: 75098
General Phone: (972) 442-5515
General Email: news@wylienews.com
Publication Website: https://wylienews.com/
Parent Company: C&S Media, Inc.
Delivery Methods: Mail`Newsstand`Racks
Year Established: 1948
Published Days: Wed
Avg. Paid Circ.: 6548
Audit Company: Sworn/Estimate/Non-Audited
Audit Date: 43626

YORKTOWN

YORKTOWN NEWS-VIEW

Street Address: 133 E MAIN ST
City: Yorktown
State: TX
ZIP Code: 78164
General Phone: (361) 564-2242
General Email: yorktownnews@sbcglobal.net
Publication Website: https://www.dewittcountytoday.com/
Publisher Name: Sonya Timpone
Advertising Executive Name: Sonya Timpone
Delivery Methods: Mail`Racks
Year Established: 1895
Published Days: Wed
Avg. Paid Circ.: 2700
Avg. Free Circ.: 75
Audit Company: Sworn/Estimate/Non-Audited
Audit Date: 43626

UTAH

BOUNTIFUL

THE DAVIS CLIPPER

Street Address: 1370 S. 500 West
City: Bountiful
State: UT
ZIP Code: 84010
General Phone: (801) 295-2251
General Email: gstahle@davisclipper.com
Publication Website: http://davisclipper.com/
Parent Company: R. Gail Stahle
Publisher Name: Gail Stahle
Publisher Email: gstahle@davisclipper.com
Publisher Phone: (801) 295-2251, ext : 114

BRIGHAM CITY

BOX ELDER NEWS JOURNAL

Street Address: 55 S 100 W
City: Brigham City
State: UT
ZIP Code: 84302
General Phone: (435) 723-3471
General Email: casey@benewsjournal.com
Publication Website: https://www.benewsjournal.com/
Publisher Name: Casey Claybaugh
Publisher Email: casey@benewsjournal.com

DELTA

MILLARD COUNTY CHRONICLE PROGRESS

Street Address: 40 N 300 W
City: Delta
State: UT
ZIP Code: 84624
General Phone: (435) 864-2400
General Email: debbie@millardccp.com
Publication Website: http://millardccp.com/home/
Parent Company: DuMor Publishing

HEBER CITY

THE WASATCH WAVE

Street Address: 165 S 100 W
City: Heber City
State: UT
ZIP Code: 84032
General Phone: (435) 654-1471
General Email: editor@wasatchwave.com
Publication Website: http://www.wasatchwave.com/
Parent Company: Wave Publishing, Inc.

MANTI

SANPETE MESSENGER

Street Address: 35 S Main St
City: Manti
State: UT
ZIP Code: 84642
General Phone: (435) 835-4241
General Email: news@sanpetemessenger.com
Publication Website: http://sanpetemessenger.com/
Parent Company: Sanpete News Company
Publisher Name: Suzanne Dean
Publisher Email: suzanne@sanpetemessenger.com

NEPHI

THE TIMES-NEWS

Street Address: 96 S Main St
City: Nephi
State: UT
ZIP Code: 84648
General Phone: (435) 623-0525
General Email: publisher@nephitimesnews.com
Publication Website: http://www.nephitimesnews.com/
Parent Company: Gannett
Publisher Name: Allan R. Gibson
Publisher Email: publisher@nephitimesnews.com

PARK CITY

PARK RECORD

Street Address: 1670 Bonanza Dr
City: Park City
State: UT
ZIP Code: 84060
General Phone: (435) 649-9014
General Email: editor@parkrecord.com
Publication Website: https://www.parkrecord.com/
Parent Company: Swift Communications
Publisher Name: Andy Bernhard

PAYSON

THE PAYSON CHRONICLE

Street Address: 145 E Utah Ave
City: Payson

Community Newspapers in the U.S.

State: UT
ZIP Code: 84651
General Phone: (801) 465-9221
General Email: thepaysonchronicle@msn.com
Publication Website: http://www.paysonads.com/

RICHFIELD

RICHFIELD REAPER

Street Address: 65 W Center St
City: Richfield
State: UT
ZIP Code: 84701
General Phone: (435) 896-5476
General Email: reaperad@richfieldreaper.com
Publication Website: http://www.richfieldreaper.com/
Parent Company: Brehm Communications Inc.
Publisher Name: Chuck Hawley
Publisher Email: reaperpub@richfieldreaper.com
Publisher Phone: (435) 896-5476, ext : 315

SALINA

SALINA SUN

Street Address: PO Box 85
City: Salina
State: UT
ZIP Code: 84654-0085
General Phone: (435) 529-6397
General Email: news@salinasunonline.com
Publication Website: http://salinasunonline.com/

TREMONTON

THE LEADER

Street Address: 2 East Main
City: Tremonton
State: UT
ZIP Code: 84337-1645
General Phone: (435) 257-5182
General Email: mstaheli@tremontonleader.com
Publication Website: https://www.hjnews.com/tremonton/
Parent Company: Adams Publishing Group

VIRGINIA

AMELIA COURT HOUSE

THE AMELIA BULLETIN MONITOR

Street Address: 16311 Goodes Bridge Rd
City: Amelia Court House
State: VA
ZIP Code: 23002-4837
General Phone: (804) 561-3655
General Email: contactus@ameliamonitor.com
Publication Website: http://www.ameliamonitor.com/
Parent Company: ABM Enterprises Inc.
Publisher Name: Ann B. Salster
Delivery Methods: Mail`Newsstand
Year Established: 1972
Own Printing Facility?: Y
Commercial printers?: Y
Mechanical specifications: Type page 10 3/8 x 16; A - 6 cols, 1 2/3, 1/6 between; C - 6 cols, 1 2/3, 1/6 between.
Published Days: Thur
Avg. Paid Circ.: 2000
Avg. Free Circ: 8500
Audit Company: Sworn/Estimate/Non-Audited
Audit Date: 43656

AMHERST

AMHERST NEW ERA-PROGRESS

Street Address: 134 2nd St
City: Amherst
State: VA
ZIP Code: 24521-2710
General Phone: (434) 385-5440
General Email: circulation@newsadvance.com
Publication Website: https://www.newsadvance.com/
Publisher Name: Kelly E. Mirt
Publisher Email: kmirt@newsadvance.com
Publisher Phone: (434) 385-5570
Editor Name: Caroline Glickman
Editor Email: cglickman@newsadvance.com
Editor Phone: 434-385-5552
Advertising Executive Name: Kevin Smith
Advertising Executive Email: ksmith@newsadvance.com
Advertising Executive Phone: (434) 385-5462
Delivery Methods: Mail`Newsstand
Published Days: Thur
Avg. Paid Circ.: 3943
Audit Company: Sworn/Estimate/Non-Audited
Audit Date: 43626

AMHERST

NELSON COUNTY TIMES

Street Address: 134 2nd St
City: Amherst
State: VA
ZIP Code: 24521-2710
General Phone: (434) 385-5450
General Email: circulation@newsadvance.com
Publication Website: https://www.newsadvance.com/nelson_county_times/
Publisher Name: Kelly E. Mirt
Publisher Email: kmirt@newsadvance.com
Publisher Phone: (434) 385-5570
Editor Name: Justin Faulconer
Editor Email: jfaulconer@newsadvance.com
Editor Phone: (434) 385-5551
Advertising Executive Name: Kevin Smith
Advertising Executive Email: ksmith@newsadvance.com
Advertising Executive Phone: (434) 385-5462
Delivery Methods: Mail`Newsstand
Published Days: Thur
Audit Company: Sworn/Estimate/Non-Audited
Audit Date: 43626

ARLINGTON

WASHINGTON BUSINESS JOURNAL

Street Address: 1100 Wilson Blvd., Suite 800
City: Arlington
State: VA
ZIP Code: 22209-2405
General Phone: (703) 258-0800
General Email: washington@bizjournals.com
Publication Website: https://www.bizjournals.com/washington
Parent Company: American City Business Journals
Publisher Name: Peter Abrahams
Publisher Email: pabrahams@bizjournals.com
Publisher Phone: (703) 258-0887
Editor Name: Michael Neibauer
Editor Email: mneibauer@bizjournals.com
Editor Phone: (703) 258-0835
Advertising Executive Name: Caroline Rountree
Advertising Executive Email: crountree@bizjournals.com
Advertising Executive Phone: (703) 258-0855
Delivery Methods: Mail`Racks
Year Established: 1982
Published Days: Fri
Audit Company: Sworn/Estimate/Non-Audited
Audit Date: 43626

BEDFORD

BEDFORD BULLETIN

Street Address: 233 W Depot St
City: Bedford
State: VA
ZIP Code: 24523-1935
General Phone: (540) 586-8612
General Email: circulation papersales@bedfordbulletin.com
Publication Website: https://www.bedfordbulletin.com/
Parent Company: Landmark Community Newspapers
Publisher Name: Jay Bondurant
Publisher Email: jaybondurant@bedfordbulletin.com
Editor Name: Tom Wilmot
Editor Email: news@bedfordbulletin.com
Advertising Executive Name: Jay Bondurant
Advertising Executive Email: jaybondurant@bedfordbulletin.com
Delivery Methods: Mail`Newsstand`Racks
Year Established: 1857
Commercial printers?: Y
Mechanical specifications: 6 column X 20.5" 1 coulmn 1.778"
Published Days: Wed
Avg. Paid Circ.: 4202
Audit Company: Sworn/Estimate/Non-Audited
Audit Date: 43626

BLACKSTONE

COURIER-RECORD

Street Address: 111 W Maple St
City: Blackstone
State: VA
ZIP Code: 23824-1707
General Phone: (434) 292-3019
General Email: frontoffice@courier-record.com
Publication Website: https://www.courier-record.com/
Parent Company: Nottoway Publishing Company
Delivery Methods: Mail`Newsstand
Year Established: 1890
Mechanical specifications: Type page 13 x 20; 5 column format
Published Days: Wed
Avg. Paid Circ.: 5219
Audit Company: Sworn/Estimate/Non-Audited
Audit Date: 43626

BRISTOL

WASHINGTON COUNTY NEWS

Street Address: 320 Bob Morrison Blvd.
City: Bristol
State: VA
ZIP Code: 24201
General Phone: (276) 628-7101
General Email: dlombardo@bristolnews.com
Publication Website: https://www.swvatoday.com/washington_county/news/
Parent Company: Gannett
Editor Name: Susan Cameron
Editor Email: scameron@bristolnews.com
Editor Phone: (276) 645-2514
Advertising Executive Name: David Lombardo
Advertising Executive Email: dlombardo@bristolnews.com
Advertising Executive Phone: (276) 645-2521
Delivery Methods: Mail`Newsstand`Racks
Mechanical specifications: Type page 13 x 21 1/2; E - 6 cols, 2 1/16, 1/9 between; A - 6 cols, 2 1/16, 1/9 between; C - 8 cols, 1 1/2, 1/9 between.
Published Days: Wed
Avg. Paid Circ.: 4255
Avg. Free Circ.: 287
Audit Company: Sworn/Estimate/Non-Audited
Audit Date: 43626

CHARLOTTESVILLE

RURAL VIRGINIAN

Street Address: 685 Rio Rd W
City: Charlottesville
State: VA
ZIP Code: 22901-1413
General Phone: (434) 978-7216
General Email: srhodes@dailyprogress.com
Publication Website: https://www.dailyprogress.com/ruralvirginian/
Publisher Name: Peter S. Yates
Publisher Email: pyates@dailyprogress.com
Publisher Phone: (434) 978-7203
Editor Name: Aaron Richardson
Editor Email: arichardson@dailyprogress.com
Editor Phone: (434) 978-7283
Advertising Executive Name: Dave Massey
Advertising Executive Email: dmassey@dailyprogress.com
Advertising Executive Phone: (434) 978-7237
Delivery Methods: Mail`Racks
Year Established: 1971
Commercial printers?: Y
Published Days: Wed
Avg. Free Circ.: 12000
Audit Company: Sworn/Estimate/Non-Audited
Audit Date: 43626

CHESTER

VILLAGE NEWS

Street Address: 11801 Centre St
City: Chester
State: VA
ZIP Code: 23831-1781
General Phone: (804) 751-0421
General Email: news@villagenewsonline.com
Publication Website: http://villagenewsonline.com/
Parent Company: Gannett
Published Days: Wed
Audit Company: Sworn/Estimate/Non-Audited
Audit Date: 43626

CHRISTIANSBURG

THE RADFORD NEWS JOURNAL

Street Address: 302 West Main Street, Suite B
City: Christiansburg
State: VA
ZIP Code: 24073-2981
General Phone: (540) 382-6171
General Email: lward@ourvalley.org
Publication Website: https://radfordnewsjournal.com/
Parent Company: Mountain Media
Delivery Methods: Mail`Newsstand`Racks
Year Established: 1884
Mechanical specifications: Type page 11 5/8 x 21; E - 6 cols, 1 5/6, 1/8 between; A - 6 cols, 1 5/6, 1/8 between; C - 8 cols, 1 5/6, 1/8 between.
Published Days: Wed`Sat
Avg. Paid Circ.: 3250
Audit Company: Sworn/Estimate/Non-Audited
Audit Date: 43626

CLINTWOOD

THE DICKENSON STAR

Street Address: 250 Main St
City: Clintwood
State: VA
ZIP Code: 24228
General Phone: (276) 926-8816
General Email: csutherland@coalfield.com
Publication Website: https://www.dickensonstar.com/
Parent Company: American Hometown Publishing
Delivery Methods: Mail`Racks
Year Established: 1982
Own Printing Facility?: Y
Commercial printers?: Y
Mechanical specifications: Type page 13 x 21; E - 6 cols, 2 1/16, between; A - 6 cols, 2 1/16, between; C - 8 cols, 1 1/2, between.
Published Days: Wed
Avg. Paid Circ.: 4000
Avg. Free Circ.: 125
Audit Company: Sworn/Estimate/Non-Audited
Audit Date: 43626

COVINGTON

VIRGINIAN REVIEW

Street Address: 201 West Locust St.
City: Covington
State: VA
ZIP Code: 24426
General Phone: (540) 962-2121
General Email: website@thevirginianreview.com
Publication Website: https://thevirginianreview.com/
Publisher Name: David Crosier
Publisher Phone: (540) 962-2121, ext : 313
Advertising Executive Email: advertising@thevirginianreview.com
Delivery Methods: Mail`Newsstand`Carrier`Racks
Year Established: 1914
Own Printing Facility?: Y
Commercial printers?: N
Mechanical specifications: Type page 11 5/8 x 21; E - 6 cols, 1 13/16, 3 1/14 between; A - 6 cols, 1 13/16, 3/16 between; C - 8 cols, 1 3/8, 1/8 between.
Published Days: Tues`Thur`Sat
Weekday Frequency: m
Saturday Frequency: m
Avg. Paid Circ.: 7119
Audit Company: Sworn/Estimate/Non-Audited
Audit Date: 43626
Pressroom Equipment: Lines -- 5-G/Community single width 1973;
Mailroom Equipment: Address Machine -- Ch/515.;
Business Equipment: IBM
Business Software: Novell, dBase
Classified Equipment: Hardware -- IBM; Printers -- Konica/Imagesetter, HP; LaserJet
Classified Software: NewsCraft/Classified.
Editorial Equipment: Hardware -- IBM; Printers -- Konica/Imagesetter, HP/LaserJet
Editorial Software: NewsCraft/Editorial System.
Production Equipment: Hardware -- Nu/Flip Top Ultra Plus; Cameras -- B.

CULPEPER

CULPEPER TIMES

Street Address: 206 S Main St
City: Culpeper
State: VA
ZIP Code: 22701-3138
General Phone: (540) 812-2282
General Email: tspargur@culpepertimes.com
Publication Website: https://www.insidenova.com/culpeper/
Parent Company: Times Community Media
Publisher Name: Tom Spargur
Publisher Email: tspargur@culpepertimes.com
Publisher Phone: (540) 422-3421
Editor Name: Jeff Say
Editor Email: jsay@culpepertimes.com
Editor Phone: (540) 812-2282
Advertising Executive Name: Audra Dickey
Advertising Executive Email: audra@piedmontpub.com
Advertising Executive Phone: (540) 812-2282
Delivery Methods: Mail`Newsstand`Racks
Year Established: 2006
Published Days: Thur
Avg. Free Circ.: 11000
Audit Company: Sworn/Estimate/Non-Audited
Audit Date: 43626

DRAKES BRANCH

THE CHARLOTTE GAZETTE

Street Address: 4789 Drakes Main St
City: Drakes Branch
State: VA
ZIP Code: 23937
General Phone: (434) 568-3341
General Email: jackie.newman@thecharlottegazette.com
Publication Website: https://www.thecharlottegazette.com/
Parent Company: Farmville Newsmedia, LLC
Publisher Name: Betty J Ramsey
Publisher Email: betty.ramsey@thecharlottegazette.com
Publisher Phone: (434) 808-0636
Editor Name: Roger Watson
Editor Email: roger.watson@thecharlottegazette.com
Editor Phone: (434) 808-0622
Advertising Executive Name: Jackie Newman
Advertising Executive Email: jackie.newman@thecharlottegazette.com
Advertising Executive Phone: (434) 808-0614
Published Days: Wed
Audit Company: Sworn/Estimate/Non-Audited
Audit Date: 43626

EMPORIA

DINWIDDIE MONITOR

Street Address: 111 Baker Street
City: Emporia
State: VA
ZIP Code: 23847
General Phone: (434) 634-4153
General Email: ads@brunswicktimes-gazette.com
Publication Website: http://www.thedinwiddiemonitor.com/
Editor Name: Michael Campbell
Editor Email: mcampbell89@icloud.com
Advertising Executive Name: Randy Velvin
Advertising Executive Phone: (434) 917-3203
Delivery Methods: Mail`Racks
Own Printing Facility?: Y
Commercial printers?: Y
Mechanical specifications: Type page 13 x 21 1/2; E - 6 cols, 2 1/16, 1/8 between; A - 6 cols, 2 1/16, 1/8 between; C - 6 cols, 2 1/16, 1/8 between.
Published Days: Wed
Avg. Paid Circ.: 5200
Avg. Free Circ.: 4100
Audit Company: Sworn/Estimate/Non-Audited
Audit Date: 43626

EMPORIA

THE PRINCE GEORGE JOURNAL

Street Address: 111 Baker Street
City: Emporia
State: VA
ZIP Code: 23847
General Phone: 434-634-4153
Publication Website: www.theprincegeorgejournal.com
Editor Name: Michael Campbell
Editor Email: mcampbell89@icloud.com
Advertising Executive Name: Amy Elliott
Advertising Executive Email: ads@imnewspaper.com
Published Days: Wed
Audit Company: Sworn/Estimate/Non-Audited
Audit Date: 43626

FALLS CHURCH

FALLS CHURCH NEWS-PRESS

Street Address: 200 Little Falls St
City: Falls Church
State: VA
ZIP Code: 22046-4302
General Phone: (703) 532-3267
General Email: fcnp@fcnp.com
Publication Website: https://fcnp.com/
Parent Company: Benton Communications Inc.
Advertising Executive Name: Nick Gatz
Advertising Executive Email: ngatz@fcnp.com
Advertising Executive Phone: (703) 532-3267, ext : 060
Delivery Methods: Mail`Newsstand`Carrier`Racks
Year Established: 1991
Own Printing Facility?: N
Commercial printers?: Y
Mechanical specifications: Type page 10 1/4 x 13 1/2; E - 5 cols, 1 7/8, 1/8 between; A - 5 cols, 1 7/8, 1/8 between; C - 5 cols, 1 7/8, 1/8 between.
Published Days: Thur
Avg. Free Circ.: 15000
Audit Company: Sworn/Estimate/Non-Audited
Audit Date: 43626

FARMVILLE

THE FARMVILLE HERALD

Street Address: 114 North St
City: Farmville
State: VA
ZIP Code: 23901-1312
General Phone: (434) 392-4151
General Email: jackie.newman@farmvilleherald.com
Publication Website: https://www.farmvilleherald.com
Parent Company: Farmville Newsmedia, LLC
Publisher Name: Betty J Ramsey
Publisher Email: betty.ramsey@thecharlottegazette.com
Publisher Phone: (434) 808-0636
Editor Name: Roger Watson
Editor Email: roger.watson@thecharlottegazette.com
Editor Phone: (434) 808-0622
Advertising Executive Name: Jackie Newman
Advertising Executive Email: jackie.newman@thecharlottegazette.com
Advertising Executive Phone: (434) 808-0614
Year Established: 1890
Published Days: Wed`Fri
Audit Company: Sworn/Estimate/Non-Audited
Audit Date: 43626

FINCASTLE

THE FINCASTLE HERALD

Street Address: 7 S. Roanoke St
City: Fincastle
State: VA
ZIP Code: 24090
General Phone: (540) 473-2741
General Email: fincastle@ourvalley.org
Publication Website: https://fincastleherald.com/
Parent Company: Virginia Media Inc.
Delivery Methods: Mail`Newsstand`Racks
Year Established: 1866
Own Printing Facility?: Y
Mechanical specifications: Type page 11 5/8 x 21; E - 6 cols, 1 5/6, 1/8 between; A - 6 cols, 1 5/6, 1/8 between; C - 8 cols, 1 1/3, 1/8 between.
Published Days: Wed
Avg. Paid Circ.: 5500
Audit Company: Sworn/Estimate/Non-Audited
Audit Date: 43626

FLOYD

THE FLOYD PRESS

Street Address: 710 E Main St
City: Floyd
State: VA
ZIP Code: 24091
General Phone: (540) 745-2127
General Email: news@floydpress.com
Publication Website: https://www.swvatoday.com/floyd/news/
Editor Name: Ashley Spinks
Editor Email: aspinks@wythenews.com
Editor Phone: (540) 745-2127, ext : 5
Advertising Executive Name: Curtis Hawkins
Advertising Executive Email: chawkins@wythenews.com
Advertising Executive Phone: (276) 228-6611, ext : 34
Delivery Methods: Mail`Newsstand`Racks
Mechanical specifications: Type page 13 x 21 1/2; E - 6 cols, 2, 1/4 between; A - 6 cols, 2, 1/4 between; C - 6 cols, 2, 1/4 between.
Published Days: Thur
Avg. Paid Circ.: 5200
Avg. Free Circ.: 63
Audit Company: Sworn/Estimate/Non-Audited
Audit Date: 43626

FRANKLIN

THE TIDEWATER NEWS

Street Address: 1000 Armory Dr
City: Franklin
State: VA
ZIP Code: 23851-1852
General Phone: (757) 562-3187
General Email: mitzi.lusk@tidewaternews.com
Publication Website: http://www.thetidewaternews.com/
Parent Company: Boone Newspapers, Inc.
Publisher Name: Tony Clark
Advertising Executive Name: Tony Clark
Delivery Methods: Mail`Newsstand`Racks
Year Established: 1905
Own Printing Facility?: Y
Commercial printers?: Y
Mechanical specifications: Type page 10.5" x 21.5; E - 6 cols, 1.6167 , 1/8 between; A - 6 cols, 1.6167, 1/8 between; C - 6 cols, 1.6167, 1/8 between.
Published Days: Wed`Fri`Sun
Avg. Paid Circ.: 5058
Avg. Free Circ.: 1500
Audit Company: Sworn/Estimate/Non-Audited
Audit Date: 43626
Note: Quarterly magazines - Western Tidewater Living Bi-annual magazine - VA.-Carolina Boomers

FRONT ROYAL

Community Newspapers in the U.S.

THE WARREN SENTINEL

Street Address: 429 N Royal Ave
City: Front Royal
State: VA
ZIP Code: 22630-2619
General Phone: (540) 635-4174
General Email: linda@thewarrensentinel.com
Publication Website: https://www.dnronline.com/the_warren_sentinel/
Parent Company: Ogden Newspapers Inc.
Publisher Name: Craig Bartoldson
Publisher Email: cbartoldson@dnronline.com
Publisher Phone: 540-574-6298
Editor Name: Sacco
Editor Email: jsacco@dnronline.com
Editor Phone: 540-574-6281
Advertising Executive Name: Rhonda McNeal
Advertising Executive Email: rmcneal@dnronline.com
Advertising Executive Phone: 540-574-6223
Delivery Methods: Mail`Newsstand`Carrier`Racks
Year Established: 1869
Commercial printers?: Y
Published Days: Thur
Avg. Paid Circ.: 3638
Audit Company: Sworn/Estimate/Non-Audited
Audit Date: 43626

GALAX

GALAX GAZETTE

Street Address: 108 W Stuart Dr
City: Galax
State: VA
ZIP Code: 24333-2114
General Phone: (276) 236-5178
General Email: ads@galaxgazette.com
Publication Website: https://www.galaxgazette.com/
Delivery Methods: Mail
Year Established: 1876
Own Printing Facility?: Y
Commercial printers?: Y
Published Days: Mon`Wed`Fri
Avg. Paid Circ.: 7170
Audit Company: Sworn/Estimate/Non-Audited
Audit Date: 43626

GATE CITY

SCOTT COUNTY VIRGINIA STAR

Street Address: 255 W Jackson St
City: Gate City
State: VA
ZIP Code: 24251-4129
General Phone: (276) 386-6300
General Email: info@virginiastar.org
Publication Website: http://www.virginiastar.net/
Parent Company: Scott County Herald-Virginia Inc.
Publisher Name: Lisa Watson McCarty
Advertising Executive Name: Daniel Barnette
Delivery Methods: Mail
Year Established: 1903
Own Printing Facility?: Y
Commercial printers?: Y
Published Days: Wed
Avg. Paid Circ.: 6500
Avg. Free Circ.: 103
Audit Company: Sworn/Estimate/Non-Audited
Audit Date: 43626

GRUNDY

THE VIRGINIA MOUNTAINEER

Street Address: 1122 Grundy Plaza Dr
City: Grundy
State: VA
ZIP Code: 24614
General Phone: (276) 935-2123
General Email: virginiamountaineer@gmail.com
Publication Website: http://www.virginiamountaineer.com/
Delivery Methods: Mail`Newsstand
Year Established: 1922
Commercial printers?: Y
Mechanical specifications: Type page 13 x 21 1/2; E - 6 cols, 2, 1/6 between; A - 6 cols, 2, 1/6 between; C - 8 cols, 1 1/2, 1/6 between.
Published Days: Wed
Avg. Paid Circ.: 6300
Avg. Free Circ.: 100
Audit Company: Sworn/Estimate/Non-Audited
Audit Date: 43626

HILLSVILLE

THE CARROLL NEWS

Street Address: 804 N MAIN ST
City: Hillsville
State: VA
ZIP Code: 24343
General Phone: (276) 728-7311
General Email: sstanley@civitasmedia.com
Publication Website: https://www.thecarrollnews.com/
Parent Company: Adams Publishing Group
Editor Name: Allen Worrell
Editor Phone: (276) 779-4062
Advertising Executive Name: Sherry Stanley
Advertising Executive Phone: (336) 415-4684
Delivery Methods: Mail`Racks
Year Established: 1920
Commercial printers?: Y
Mechanical specifications: Type page 11 1/2 x 21 1/2; E - 6 cols, 1 3/4, between; A - 6 cols, 1 3/4, between.
Published Days: Wed
Avg. Paid Circ.: 6700
Avg. Free Circ.: 10
Audit Company: Sworn/Estimate/Non-Audited
Audit Date: 43626

LEESBURG

PRINCE WILLIAM TIMES

Street Address: 9 E Market St
City: Leesburg
State: VA
ZIP Code: 20176-3013
General Phone: (703) 777-1111
General Email: skeyes@virginianewsgroup.com
Publication Website: https://www.princewilliamtimes.com/
Parent Company: Piedmont Media LLC
Publisher Name: Catherine M. Nelson
Publisher Email: cnelson@fauquier.com
Editor Name: Jill Palermo
Editor Email: jpalermo@fauquier.com
Advertising Executive Name: Kathy Godfrey
Advertising Executive Email: kgodfrey@fauquier.com
Year Established: 1963
Published Days: Wed
Audit Company: Sworn/Estimate/Non-Audited
Audit Date: 43626

LEXINGTON

THE NEWS-GAZETTE

Street Address: 20 W Nelson St
City: Lexington
State: VA
ZIP Code: 24450-2034
General Phone: (540) 463-3113
General Email: advertising@thenews-gazette.com
Publication Website: https://www.thenews-gazette.com/
Parent Company: Community Media Group
Editor Email: editor@the-news-gazette.com
Delivery Methods: Mail`Newsstand`Racks
Year Established: 1801
Own Printing Facility?: Y
Commercial printers?: N
Mechanical specifications: Type page 11.00 x 19.75; E - 6 cols, 1.66, .18 between; A - 6 cols, 1.66, .18 between; C - 6 cols, 1.66, .18 between.
Published Days: Wed
Avg. Paid Circ.: 6796
Avg. Free Circ.: 115
Audit Company: Sworn/Estimate/Non-Audited
Audit Date: 43626

LOUISA

THE CENTRAL VIRGINIAN

Street Address: 89 Rescue Ln
City: Louisa
State: VA
ZIP Code: 23093-4105
General Phone: (540) 967-0368
General Email: info@thecentralvirginian.com
Publication Website: https://www.thecentralvirginian.com/
Parent Company: Lakeway Publishers, Inc.
Publisher Name: Kelly Drumheller
Editor Name: David Holtzman
Editor Email: dholtzman@thecentralvirginian.com
Advertising Executive Name: Tommy Nelson
Advertising Executive Email: swhaley@tullahomanews.com
Advertising Executive Phone: (540) 223-1614
Delivery Methods: Mail`Newsstand`Racks
Year Established: 1912
Commercial printers?: Y
Mechanical specifications: Type page 13 x 21 1/2; E - 6 cols, 2, 1/6 between; A - 6 cols, 2, 1/6 between; C - 8 cols, 1 1/2, 1/12 between.
Published Days: Thur
Avg. Paid Circ.: 7655
Avg. Free Circ.: 205
Audit Company: Sworn/Estimate/Non-Audited
Audit Date: 43626

LURAY

PAGE NEWS & COURIER

Street Address: 17 S Broad St
City: Luray
State: VA
ZIP Code: 22835-1904
General Phone: (540) 743-5123
General Email: pncads@gmail.com
Publication Website: https://www.dnronline.com/page_news_and_courier/
Parent Company: Ogden Newspapers Inc.
Editor Name: Randy Arrington
Delivery Methods: Mail`Racks
Year Established: 1867
Own Printing Facility?: Y
Commercial printers?: N
Published Days: Thur
Avg. Paid Circ.: 6746
Audit Company: Sworn/Estimate/Non-Audited
Audit Date: 43626

MADISON

MADISON COUNTY EAGLE

Street Address: 201 N Main St
City: Madison
State: VA
ZIP Code: 22727-3053
General Phone: (540) 948-5121
General Email: tburruss@madison-news.com
Publication Website: https://www.dailyprogress.com/madisonnews/
Editor Name: Jeff Poole
Editor Email: jpoole@orangenews.com
Editor Phone: (540) 672-1266, ext. 23
Advertising Executive Name: Jennifer Jenkins
Advertising Executive Email: jjenkins@orangenews.com
Advertising Executive Phone: (540) 223-2461
Delivery Methods: Mail`Racks
Year Established: 1910
Published Days: Thur
Avg. Paid Circ.: 4500
Avg. Free Circ.: 10
Audit Company: Sworn/Estimate/Non-Audited
Audit Date: 43626

MARION

SMYTH COUNTY NEWS & MESSENGER

Street Address: 119 S Sheffey St
City: Marion
State: VA
ZIP Code: 24354-2523
General Phone: (276) 783-5121
General Email: lcorpus@bristolnews.com
Publication Website: https://www.swvatoday.com/smyth_county/
Editor Name: Stephanie Porter-Nichols
Editor Email: sporternichols@wythenews.com
Editor Phone: 800.655.1411, ext 13
Advertising Executive Name: Curtis Hawkins
Advertising Executive Email: chawkins@wythenews.com
Advertising Executive Phone: (276) 228-6611, ext : 34
Delivery Methods: Mail`Newsstand`Carrier`Racks
Year Established: 1884
Own Printing Facility?: Y
Published Days: Wed`Sat
Avg. Paid Circ.: 2652
Audit Company: Sworn/Estimate/Non-Audited
Audit Date: 43626

MECHANICSVILLE

GOOCHLAND GAZETTE

Street Address: 8460 Times Dispatch Blvd
City: Mechanicsville
State: VA
ZIP Code: 23116-2029
General Phone: (804) 775-4614
General Email: director@goochlandchamber.org
Publication Website: http://www.goochlandgazette.com
Parent Company: Lee Enterprises
Editor Name: Mike Szvetitz
Editor Email: mszvetitz@timesdispatch.com
Editor Phone: (804) 649-6456
Delivery Methods: Mail`Racks
Year Established: 1955
Published Days: Thur
Avg. Paid Circ.: 38
Avg. Free Circ.: 6854
Audit Company: AAM
Audit Date: 44175

MECHANICSVILLE

MECHANICSVILLE LOCAL

Street Address: 8460 Times Dispatch Blvd
City: Mechanicsville
State: VA
ZIP Code: 23116-2029
General Phone: (804) 649-6000
General Email: jmonopoli@rsnva.com
Publication Website: https://www.richmond.

com/news/local/hanover/mechanicsville-local/
Parent Company: Lee Enterprises
Editor Name: Mike Szvetitz
Editor Email: mszvetitz@timesdispatch.com
Editor Phone: (800) 649-6456
Delivery Methods: Mail`Racks
Year Established: 1984
Own Printing Facility?: Y
Commercial printers?: Y
Published Days: Wed
Avg. Paid Circ.: 31
Avg. Free Circ.: 22340
Audit Company: AAM
Audit Date: 44296

MIDDLEBURG

MIDDLEBURG LIFE

Street Address: 112 W Washington St
City: Middleburg
State: VA
ZIP Code: 20118
General Phone: (540) 687-6059
General Email: info@middleburglife.com
Publication Website: https://middleburglife.com/
Parent Company: Greenhill Media
Editor Name: Jennifer Gray
Editor Email: editor@middleburglife.com
Advertising Executive Name: Christian Bentley
Advertising Executive Email: christian@middleburglife.com
Published Days: Mthly
Audit Company: Sworn/Estimate/Non-Audited
Audit Date: 43626

NORFOLK

INSIDE BUSINESS, THE HAMPTON ROADS BUSINESS JOURNAL

Street Address: 150 W Brambleton Ave
City: Norfolk
State: VA
ZIP Code: 23510-2018
General Phone: (757) 222-5353
General Email: tips@pilotonline.com
Publication Website: https://www.pilotonline.com/inside-business/
Editor Name: Ryan Gilchrest
Editor Email: rgilchrest@dailypress.com
Editor Phone: 757-446-2385
Delivery Methods: Mail`Newsstand
Year Established: 1996
Mechanical specifications: Full page - 9.6" x 13.25"
Published Days: Mon
Avg. Paid Circ.: 4048
Avg. Free Circ.: 3468
Audit Company: VAC
Audit Date: 43293

NORTON

THE COALFIELD PROGRESS

Street Address: 725 Park Ave NE
City: Norton
State: VA
ZIP Code: 24273-1007
General Phone: (276) 679-1101
General Email: ktate@coalfield.com
Publication Website: https://www.thecoalfieldprogress.com/
Editor Name: Jeffery C. Lester
Editor Email: jlester@coalfield.com
Advertising Executive Name: April Bevins
Advertising Executive Email: abevins@coalfield.com
Published Days: Tues`Fri
Audit Company: Sworn/Estimate/Non-Audited
Audit Date: 43626

ORANGE

ORANGE COUNTY REVIEW

Street Address: 146 Byrd St
City: Orange
State: VA
ZIP Code: 22960-1631
General Phone: (540) 672-1266
General Email: news@orangenews.com
Publication Website: https://www.dailyprogress.com/orangenews/
Publisher Name: Peter S. Yates
Publisher Email: pyates@dailyprogress.com
Publisher Phone: (434) 978-7203
Editor Name: Aaron Richardson
Editor Email: arichardson@dailyprogress.com
Editor Phone: (434) 978-7283
Advertising Executive Name: Dave Massey
Advertising Executive Email: dmassey@dailyprogress.com
Advertising Executive Phone: (434) 978-7237
Delivery Methods: Mail`Racks
Own Printing Facility?: Y
Published Days: Thur
Avg. Paid Circ.: 7000
Avg. Free Circ.: 18
Audit Company: Sworn/Estimate/Non-Audited
Audit Date: 43626

PALMYRA

FLUVANNA REVIEW

Street Address: Crofton Plaza Building 106
City: Palmyra
State: VA
ZIP Code: 22963
General Phone: (434) 591-1000
General Email: sales@fluvannareview.com
Publication Website: https://fluvannareview.com/
Parent Company: Valley Publishing
Editor Name: Carlos Santos
Editor Email: editor@fluvannareview.com
Editor Phone: 434-591-1000
Advertising Executive Name: Judi Price
Advertising Executive Email: sales@fluvannareview.com
Advertising Executive Phone: (434) 207-0223
Delivery Methods: Mail`Carrier`Racks
Year Established: 1979
Published Days: Thur
Avg. Paid Circ.: 15
Avg. Free Circ.: 6200
Audit Company: CVC
Audit Date: 43991

POWHATAN

POWHATAN TODAY

Street Address: 3229 Anderson Hwy
City: Powhatan
State: VA
ZIP Code: 23139-7340
General Phone: (804) 598-4305
General Email: sales@powhatantoday.com
Publication Website: https://www.richmond.com/news/local/central-virginia/powhatan/powhatan-today/
Parent Company: Lee Enterprises
Publisher Name: Joy Monopoli
Publisher Email: jmonopoli@worldmediaenterprise.com
Publisher Phone: (804) 746-1235, ext : 14
Editor Name: Melody Kinser
Editor Email: mkinser@mechlocal.com
Editor Phone: (804) 746-1235 x 22
Delivery Methods: Mail`Racks
Year Established: 1986
Published Days: Wed
Avg. Paid Circ.: 72
Avg. Free Circ.: 11167
Audit Company: AAM
Audit Date: 43476

RICHLANDS

RICHLANDS NEWS-PRESS

Street Address: 1945 2nd St
City: Richlands
State: VA
ZIP Code: 24641-2303
General Phone: (276) 963-1081
General Email: bsewell@wythennews.com
Publication Website: https://www.swvatoday.com/eedition/richlands/
Editor Name: Rob Walters
Editor Email: rwalters@bristolnews.com
Editor Phone: 276.645.2513
Advertising Executive Name: Curtis Hawkins
Advertising Executive Email: chawkins@wythenews.com
Advertising Executive Phone: (276) 228-6611, ext : 34
Delivery Methods: Mail`Newsstand`Racks
Published Days: Wed
Avg. Paid Circ.: 7000
Avg. Free Circ.: 172
Audit Company: Sworn/Estimate/Non-Audited
Audit Date: 43626

ROCKY MOUNT

THE FRANKLIN NEWS-POST

Street Address: 310 S Main St
City: Rocky Mount
State: VA
ZIP Code: 24151-1711
General Phone: (540) 483-5113
General Email: info@thefranklinnewspost.com
Publication Website: https://www.thefranklinnewspost.com/
Parent Company: Lee Enterprises
Editor Name: Briana Barker
Editor Email: briana.barker@thefranklinnewspost.com
Advertising Executive Name: Susan Gauldin
Advertising Executive Email: susan.gauldin@thefranklinnewspost.com
Delivery Methods: Mail`Carrier`Racks
Year Established: 1905
Own Printing Facility?: Y
Commercial printers?: Y
Published Days: Wed`Fri
Avg. Paid Circ.: 4500
Avg. Free Circ.: 6
Audit Company: Sworn/Estimate/Non-Audited
Audit Date: 43626

SALEM

SALEM TIMES-REGISTER

Street Address: 1633 W Main St
City: Salem
State: VA
ZIP Code: 24153-3115
General Phone: (540) 389-9355
General Email: wendicraig@gmail.com
Publication Website: https://salemtimes-register.com/
Parent Company: Virginia Media, LLC
Delivery Methods: Mail`Racks
Year Established: 1884
Commercial printers?: Y
Mechanical specifications: Type page 11 5/8 x 21; E - 6 cols, 1 5/6, 1/8 between; A - 6 cols, 1 5/6, 1/8 between; C - 6 cols, 1 5/6, 1/8 between.
Published Days: Thur
Avg. Paid Circ.: 2800
Audit Company: Sworn/Estimate/Non-Audited
Audit Date: 43626

SOUTH BOSTON

THE GAZETTE-VIRGINIAN

Street Address: 3201 Halifax Rd
City: South Boston
State: VA
ZIP Code: 24592-4907
General Phone: (434) 572-3945
General Email: news@gazettevirginian.com
Publication Website: http://www.yourgv.com/
Publisher Name: Linda Shelton
Editor Name: Ashley Hodge
Editor Email: ahodge@gazettevirginian.com
Advertising Executive Name: Patricia Seat
Advertising Executive Email: pseat@gazettevirginian.com
Delivery Methods: Mail`Newsstand`Carrier`Racks
Own Printing Facility?: Y
Mechanical specifications: Type page 13 x 21 1/2; E - 6 cols, 2, between; A - 6 cols, 2, between; C - 6 cols, 2, between.
Published Days: Mon`Wed`Fri
Avg. Paid Circ.: 9100
Audit Company: Sworn/Estimate/Non-Audited
Audit Date: 43626

SOUTH HILL

MECKLENBURG REPORTER

Street Address: PO Box 60
City: South Hill
State: VA
ZIP Code: 23970-0060
General Phone: (434) 447-3178
General Email: tbrowder@womackpublishing.com
Publication Website: http://www.mecklenburgreporter.com/local-news/page/16/
Published Days: Sun
Audit Company: Sworn/Estimate/Non-Audited
Audit Date: 43626

STANARDSVILLE

THE GREENE COUNTY RECORD

Street Address: 113 Main Street
City: Stanardsville
State: VA
ZIP Code: 22973-2970
General Phone: (434) 985-2315
General Email: news@greene-news.com
Publication Website: https://www.dailyprogress.com/greenenews/
Publisher Name: Peter S. Yates
Publisher Email: pyates@dailyprogress.com
Publisher Phone: (434) 978-7203
Editor Name: Jeff Poole
Editor Email: jpoole@orangenews.com
Advertising Executive Name: Jennifer Jenkins
Advertising Executive Email: jjenkins@orangenews.com
Advertising Executive Phone: (540) 223-2461
Delivery Methods: Mail`Racks
Year Established: 1895
Commercial printers?: Y
Mechanical specifications: Type page 13 x 21 1/2; E - 6 cols, 2, 1/6 between; A - 6 cols, 2, 1/6 between; C - 9 cols, 1 1/3, between.
Published Days: Thur
Avg. Paid Circ.: 3000
Audit Company: Sworn/Estimate/Non-Audited
Audit Date: 43626

STERLING

FAIRFAX COUNTY TIMES

Street Address: 20 Pidgeon Hill Dr
City: Sterling

Community Newspapers in the U.S.

State: VA
ZIP Code: 20165-6134
General Phone: (703) 437-5400
General Email: kwashburn@fairfaxtimes.com
Publication Website: http://www.fairfaxtimes.com/
Parent Company: Whip It Media
Editor Name: Gregg MacDonald
Editor Email: gmacdonald@fairfaxtimes.com
Editor Phone: 571-323-6224
Advertising Executive Name: Karen Washburn
Advertising Executive Email: kwashburn@fairfaxtimes.com
Advertising Executive Phone: (703) 994-4940
Delivery Methods: Newsstand`Carrier`Racks
Year Established: 1964
Own Printing Facility?: N
Commercial printers?: N
Published Days: Fri
Avg. Free Circ.: 102157
Audit Company: Sworn/Estimate/Non-Audited
Audit Date: 43626

URBANNA

SOUTHSIDE SENTINEL

Street Address: 276 Virginia St
City: Urbanna
State: VA
ZIP Code: 23175-2041
General Phone: (804) 758-2328
General Email: editor@ssentinel.com
Publication Website: http://www.ssentinel.com/
Publisher Name: Fred Gaskins
Publisher Email: fred@rapprecord.com
Publisher Phone: (804) 758-2328, ext : 113
Editor Name: Tom Hardin
Editor Email: editor@ssentinel.com
Editor Phone: 804-758-2328, ext.109
Advertising Executive Name: Hannah Abbott
Advertising Executive Email: hannah@ssentinel.com
Advertising Executive Phone: (804) 758-2328, ext : 103
Delivery Methods: Mail`Newsstand
Year Established: 1896
Mechanical specifications: Type page 10.955 inch x 19.8 inch; 6 cols, 1.7217 inch, 0.125 inch gutters.
Published Days: Thur
Avg. Paid Circ.: 4394
Avg. Free Circ.: 141
Audit Company: Sworn/Estimate/Non-Audited
Audit Date: 43626

VICTORIA

THE KENBRIDGE-VICTORIA DISPATCH

Street Address: 1404 Nottoway Boulevard
City: Victoria
State: VA
ZIP Code: 23974
General Phone: (434) 696-5550
General Email: jackie.newman@kenbridgevictoriadispatch.com
Publication Website: https://www.kenbridgevictoriadispatch.com/
Publisher Name: Betty J Ramsey
Publisher Email: betty.ramsey@kenbridgevictoriadispatch.com
Publisher Phone: (434) 808-0636
Editor Name: Roger Watson
Editor Email: roger.watson@kenbridgevictoriadispatch.com
Editor Phone: (434) 808-0622
Advertising Executive Name: jackie Newman
Advertising Executive Email: jackie.newman@kenbridgevictoriadispatch.com
Advertising Executive Phone: (434) 808-0614
Published Days: Wed
Audit Company: Sworn/Estimate/Non-Audited
Audit Date: 43626

WARRENTON

FAUQUIER TIMES

Street Address: 41 Culpeper St
City: Warrenton
State: VA
ZIP Code: 20186-3319
General Phone: (540) 347-4222
General Email: news@fauquier.com
Publication Website: https://www.fauquier.com/
Parent Company: Times Community Media
Publisher Name: Catherine Nelson
Publisher Email: cnelson@fauquier.com
Editor Name: Robin Earl
Editor Email: rearl@fauquier.com
Delivery Methods: Mail`Newsstand`Racks
Year Established: 1905
Own Printing Facility?: Y
Commercial printers?: Y
Published Days: Wed
Avg. Paid Circ.: 9447
Audit Company: Sworn/Estimate/Non-Audited
Audit Date: 43626

WARSAW

NORTHERN NECK NEWS

Street Address: 132 COURT CIR
City: Warsaw
State: VA
ZIP Code: 22572
General Phone: (804) 333-6937
General Email: nnnclassifieds@lcs.net
Publication Website: https://www.northernnecknews.com/
Parent Company: Lakeway Publishers, Inc.
Publisher Name: Cathy Gerring
Editor Name: Brittlynn Powell
Editor Email: nnneditor@lcs.net
Advertising Executive Name: Amber Wilson
Advertising Executive Email: awilson@northernnecknews.com
Delivery Methods: Mail`Racks
Own Printing Facility?: Y
Commercial printers?: Y
Published Days: Wed
Avg. Paid Circ.: 8300
Audit Company: Sworn/Estimate/Non-Audited
Audit Date: 43626

WARSAW

NORTHUMBERLAND ECHO

Street Address: 132 COURT CIR
City: Warsaw
State: VA
ZIP Code: 22572
General Phone: (804) 333-6937
General Email: nnnclassifieds@lcs.net
Publication Website: https://www.northumberlandecho.com/
Parent Company: Lakeway Publishers, Inc.
Publisher Name: Cathy Gerring
Editor Name: Brittlynn Powell
Editor Email: nnneditor@lcs.net
Advertising Executive Name: Amber Wilson
Advertising Executive Email: awilson@northernnecknews.com
Delivery Methods: Mail`Racks
Year Established: 1902
Commercial printers?: Y
Published Days: Wed
Avg. Paid Circ.: 2500
Audit Company: Sworn/Estimate/Non-Audited
Audit Date: 43626

WARSAW

WESTMORELAND NEWS

Street Address: 132 Court Circle
City: Warsaw
State: VA
ZIP Code: 22572
General Phone: (804) 333-6397
General Email: wmneditor@lcs.net
Publication Website: https://www.westmorelandnews.net/
Parent Company: Lakeway Publishers, Inc.
Publisher Name: Cathy Gerring
Publisher Email: nnncirc@lcs.net
Editor Name: Brittlynn Powell
Editor Email: wmneditor@lcs.net
Delivery Methods: Mail`Newsstand`Racks
Year Established: 1948
Own Printing Facility?: Y
Mechanical specifications: Type page 13 x 21 1/2; E - 6 cols, 2, between; A - 6 cols, 2, between; C - 9 cols, 1 1/3, between.
Published Days: Wed
Avg. Paid Circ.: 7608
Audit Company: Sworn/Estimate/Non-Audited
Audit Date: 43626

WEST POINT

THE TIDEWATER REVIEW

Street Address: 425 12th St
City: West Point
State: VA
ZIP Code: 23181
General Phone: (804) 843-2282
General Email: jhaynes@tidewaterreview.com
Publication Website: https://www.dailypress.com/tidewater-review/
Editor Name: Ryan Gilchrest
Delivery Methods: Mail`Racks
Published Days: Wed
Avg. Paid Circ.: 5000
Avg. Free Circ.: 121
Audit Company: Sworn/Estimate/Non-Audited
Audit Date: 43626

WIRTZ

SMITH MOUNTAIN EAGLE

Street Address: 1650 Scruggs Road
City: Wirtz
State: VA
ZIP Code: 24184
General Phone: 540-719-5100
General Email: news@smithmountaineagle.com
Publication Website: www.smithmountaineagle.com
Editor Name: Chad Adams
Editor Email: reporter@smithmountaineagle.com
Advertising Executive Name: Tommie Jo Walker
Advertising Executive Email: advertising@smithmountaineagle.com

WOODBRIDGE

INSIDENOVA/NORTH STAFFORD

Street Address: 1372 Old Bridge Rd
City: Woodbridge
State: VA
ZIP Code: 22192-2755
General Phone: (571) 208-8059
General Email: cfields@insidenova.com
Publication Website: https://www.insidenova.com/
Parent Company: Rappahannock Media LLC
Delivery Methods: Mail`Carrier`Racks
Year Established: 1987
Own Printing Facility?: Y
Commercial printers?: Y
Mechanical specifications: Type page 12 x 20 1/2; E - 5 cols, 2 1/2, between; A - 6 cols, 2, between; C - 10 cols, 1 1/6, between.
Published Days: Fri
Avg. Paid Circ.: 516
Avg. Free Circ.: 14500
Audit Company: CVC
Audit Date: 43991

WOODBRIDGE

INSIDENOVA/PRINCE WILLIAM

Street Address: 1372 Old Bridge Rd
City: Woodbridge
State: VA
ZIP Code: 22192-2755
General Phone: (571) 208-8059
General Email: cfields@insidenova.com
Publication Website: https://www.insidenova.com/
Parent Company: Rappahannock Media LLC
Editor Name: Greg Hambrick
Editor Email: ghambrick@insidenova.com
Advertising Executive Name: Tonya Fields
Advertising Executive Email: tfields@insidenova.com
Advertising Executive Phone: (703) 771-8831
Delivery Methods: Mail`Racks
Year Established: 1987
Published Days: Fri
Avg. Paid Circ.: 1841
Avg. Free Circ.: 23211
Audit Company: CVC
Audit Date: 43991

WOODSTOCK

THE SHENANDOAH VALLEY-HERALD

Street Address: 136 W Court St
City: Woodstock
State: VA
ZIP Code: 22664-1490
General Phone: (540) 459-4078
General Email: circulation@dnronline.com
Publication Website: https://www.dnronline.com/news/shenandoah_county/
Parent Company: Ogden Newspapers Inc.
Publisher Name: Craig Bartoldson
Publisher Email: cbartoldson@dnronline.com
Publisher Phone: (540) 574-6298
Advertising Executive Name: Kimela Boyd
Advertising Executive Email: kboyd@dnronline.com
Delivery Methods: Mail`Newsstand`Carrier`Racks
Year Established: 1806
Mechanical specifications: Type page 13 x 21 1/2.
Published Days: Fri
Avg. Paid Circ.: 2503
Audit Company: Sworn/Estimate/Non-Audited
Audit Date: 43626

WYTHEVILLE

BLAND COUNTY MESSENGER

Street Address: 460 W Main St
City: Wytheville
State: VA
ZIP Code: 24382-2207
General Phone: (276) 228-6611
General Email: bsewell@wythenews.com
Publication Website: https://www.swvatoday.com/bland_county/
Editor Name: Jeff Simmons
Editor Email: jsimmons@wythenews.com
Editor Phone: 800.655.1406, ext. 19
Advertising Executive Name: Curtis Hawkins
Advertising Executive Email: chawkins@wythenews.com
Advertising Executive Phone: (276) 228-6611, ext : 34
Delivery Methods: Mail`Racks
Published Days: Wed

Avg. Paid Circ.: 2500
Avg. Free Circ.: 64
Audit Company: Sworn/Estimate/Non-Audited
Audit Date: 43626

WYTHEVILLE

WYTHEVILLE ENTERPRISE

Street Address: 460 W Main St
City: Wytheville
State: VA
ZIP Code: 24382-2207
General Phone: (276) 228-6611
General Email: chawkins@wythenews.com
Publication Website: https://www.swvatoday.com/wytheville/
Editor Name: Jeff Simmons
Editor Phone: (800) 655-1406
Advertising Executive Name: Curtis Hawkins
Advertising Executive Email: chawkins@wythenews.com
Advertising Executive Phone: (276) 228-6611, ext : 34
Delivery Methods: Mail`Newsstand`Racks
Published Days: Wed`Sat
Avg. Paid Circ.: 6700
Audit Company: Sworn/Estimate/Non-Audited
Audit Date: 43626

YORKTOWN

YORK TOWN CRIER/THE POQUOSON POST

Street Address: P.O. Box 978
City: Yorktown
State: VA
ZIP Code: 23692
General Phone: (757) 766-1776
General Email: rob@yorktowncrier.com
Publication Website: http://www.yorktowncrier.com/
Editor Name: Nancy E. Sheppard
Editor Email: nancy@yorktowncrier.com
Delivery Methods: Mail`Racks
Year Established: 1978
Commercial printers?: Y
Mechanical specifications: Type page 13 x 21 1/2; E - 6 cols, 2 1/16, 1/6 between; A - 6 cols, 2 1/16, 1/6 between; C - 6 cols, 2 1/16, 1/6 between.
Published Days: Thur
Avg. Paid Circ.: 4000
Audit Company: Sworn/Estimate/Non-Audited
Audit Date: 43626

VERMONT

BARRE

THE WORLD

Street Address: 403 US Rt 302-Berlin
City: Barre
State: VT
ZIP Code: 5641
General Phone: (802) 479-2582
General Email: sales@vt-world.com
Publication Website: https://www.vt-world.com/
Parent Company: WORLD Publications, Inc.
Delivery Methods: Mail`Newsstand`Racks
Year Established: 1972
Own Printing Facility?: N
Commercial printers?: N
Mechanical specifications: Type page 10 1/4 x 16; E - 6 cols, 1 5/8, 1/6 between; A - 6 cols, 1 5/8, 1/6 between; C - 6 cols, 1 5/8, 1/6 between.

Published Days: Wed
Weekday Frequency: All day
Avg. Paid Circ.: 28
Avg. Free Circ.: 15332
Audit Company: CVC

BARRE

TIMES ARGUS EXTRA

Street Address: 47 North Main Street, Suite 200
City: Barre
State: VT
ZIP Code: 5641
General Phone: (802) 479-0191
General Email: customerservices@timesargus.com
Publication Website: https://www.timesargus.com/
Parent Company: Brunswick Publishing
Publisher Name: Shawn Stabell
Publisher Email: shawn.stabell@timesargus.com
Publisher Phone: (802) 477-4023
Advertising Executive Phone: (802) 479-4040
Delivery Methods: Mail`Newsstand
Published Days: Sun
Audit Company: Sworn/Estimate/Non-Audited
Audit Date: 43626

BARTON

THE CHRONICLE

Street Address: 133 WATER ST
City: Barton
State: VT
ZIP Code: 5822
General Phone: (802) 525-3531
General Email: ads@bartonchronicle.com
Publication Website: https://bartonchronicle.com/
Parent Company: Gannett
Publisher Name: Tracy Davis Pierce
Publisher Email: thechronicleinc@gmail.com
Editor Name: Tena Starr
Editor Email: tenas@bartonchronicle.com
Advertising Executive Name: Kjya DeToma
Advertising Executive Email: kdetoma@hotmail.com
Delivery Methods: Mail`Racks
Year Established: 1974
Mechanical specifications: Type page 10.25 x 15 1/2; E - 3 cols, 3 1/4, 1/4 between; A - 3 cols, 3 1/4, 1/8 between; C - 4 cols, 2 1/2, 1/4 between.
Published Days: Wed
Avg. Paid Circ.: 8000
Avg. Free Circ.: 173
Audit Company: Sworn/Estimate/Non-Audited
Audit Date: 43626

BRADFORD

JOURNAL OPINION

Street Address: PO Box 378
City: Bradford
State: VT
ZIP Code: 5033
General Phone: (802) 222-5281
General Email: advertising@jonews.com
Publication Website: http://www.jonews.com/
Publisher Name: Connie Sanville
Publisher Email: publisher@jonews.com
Editor Name: Alex Nuti-de Biasi
Editor Email: editor@jonews.com
Advertising Executive Name: Michelle Sherburne
Advertising Executive Email: advertising@jonews.com
Delivery Methods: Mail`Newsstand
Year Established: 1865
Own Printing Facility?: Y

Mechanical specifications: Type page 12 x 21; E - 6 cols, 2, 1/12 between; A - 6 cols, 2, 1/12 between; C - 6 cols, 2, 1/12 between.
Published Days: Wed
Avg. Paid Circ.: 4000
Avg. Free Circ.: 200
Audit Company: Sworn/Estimate/Non-Audited

BRATTLEBORO

THE COMMONS

Street Address: 139 Main St
City: Brattleboro
State: VT
ZIP Code: 05301-2871
General Phone: (802) 246-6397
General Email: ads@commonsnews.org
Publication Website: http://www.commonsnews.org/
Parent Company: Vermont Independent Media, Inc.
Advertising Executive Email: ads@commonsnews.org
Delivery Methods: Mail`Newsstand`Racks
Year Established: 2006
Mechanical specifications: PDF with fonts embedded, continuous tones 150 pixels per inch, line art 600 pixels per inch.
Published Days: Wed
Avg. Paid Circ.: 500
Avg. Free Circ.: 10500
Audit Company: Sworn/Estimate/Non-Audited

ELIZABETHTOWN

THE EAGLE

Street Address: 14 Hand Avenue
City: Elizabethtown
State: VT
ZIP Code: 12932
General Phone: (518) 873-6368
General Email: Cyndi@addison-eagle.com
Publication Website: https://www.suncommunitynews.com/
Parent Company: Lee Enterprises
Delivery Methods: Mail`Newsstand
Year Established: 2000
Mechanical specifications: Type page 10 x 16; 6 col
Published Days: Sat
Avg. Paid Circ.: 176
Avg. Free Circ.: 12239
Audit Company: Sworn/Estimate/Non-Audited
Audit Date: 43626

ENOSBURG FALLS

COUNTY COURIER

Street Address: 349 Main St
City: Enosburg Falls
State: VT
ZIP Code: 5450
General Phone: (802) 933-4375
General Email: courierads@gmail.com
Publication Website: http://countycourier.net/
Delivery Methods: Mail
Year Established: 1878
Own Printing Facility?: N
Commercial printers?: N
Mechanical specifications: Type page 10 3/16 x 16; E - 5 cols, 11 1/2, 1/6 between; A - 5 cols, 1/6 between; C - 5 cols, 1/6 between.
Published Days: Thur
Avg. Paid Circ.: 3000
Avg. Free Circ.: 76
Audit Company: Sworn/Estimate/Non-Audited

HARDWICK

THE HARDWICK GAZETTE

Street Address: 42 S MAIN ST
City: Hardwick
State: VT
ZIP Code: 5843
General Phone: (802) 472-6521
General Email: news@hardwickgazette.com
Publication Website: https://hardwickgazette.com/
Parent Company: The Hardwick Journalism Co., Inc.
Editor Name: Ray Small
Editor Email: ray@hardwickgazette.com
Advertising Executive Name: Erica Baker
Advertising Executive Email: bythepondesign@gmail.com
Delivery Methods: Mail`Newsstand
Year Established: 1889
Own Printing Facility?: Y
Commercial printers?: N
Mechanical specifications: Type page 15 1/8 x 21 1/8; E - 7 cols, 2 1/16, between; A - 7 cols, 2 1/16, between; C - 7 cols, 2 1/16, between.
Published Days: Wed
Avg. Paid Circ.: 2300
Avg. Free Circ.: 35
Audit Company: Sworn/Estimate/Non-Audited
Audit Date: 43626

KILLINGTON

THE MOUNTAIN TIMES

Street Address: 5465 Route 4. Sherburne Flats
City: Killington
State: VT
ZIP Code: 5751
General Phone: (802) 422-2399
General Email: jason@mountaintimes.info
Publication Website: https://www.mountaintimes.info/
Parent Company: Adams Publishing Group
Publisher Name: Jason Mikula
Editor Name: Polly Lynn
Delivery Methods: Mail`Racks
Mechanical specifications: Type page 10 5/16 x 16; E - 6 cols, 1 7/12, 1/6 between; A - 6 cols, 1 7/12, 1/6 between; C - 6 cols, 1 7/12, 1/6 between.
Published Days: Wed
Avg. Free Circ.: 10000
Audit Company: Sworn/Estimate/Non-Audited
Audit Date: 43626

MANCHESTER

MANCHESTER JOURNAL

Street Address: 3624 Main Street, Room 204
City: Manchester
State: VT
ZIP Code: 5254
General Phone: (802) 855-7861
General Email: news@manchesterjournal.com
Publication Website: https://www.manchesterjournal.com/
Parent Company: New England Newspapers, Inc.
Publisher Name: Fredric D. Rutberg
Publisher Email: frutberg@berkshireeagle.com
Publisher Phone: (413) 496-6380
Editor Name: Greg Sukiennik
Editor Email: gsukiennik@manchesterjournal.com
Editor Phone: (802) 490-6000
Advertising Executive Name: Susan Plaisance
Advertising Executive Email: splaisance@manchesterjournal.com
Advertising Executive Phone: (802) 733-8827

Community Newspapers in the U.S.

Delivery Methods: Mail`Newsstand`Racks
Year Established: 1861
Published Days: Fri
Avg. Free Circ.: 15000
Audit Company: Sworn/Estimate/Non-Audited
Audit Date: 43626

MANCHESTER CENTER

VERMONT NEWS GUIDE

Street Address: 4858 Main Street
City: Manchester Center
State: VT
ZIP Code: 5255
General Phone: (802) 362-3535
General Email: jen@oldmillroadmedia.com
Publication Website: https://vermontnews-guide.com/
Parent Company: Old Mill Road Media
Publisher Name: Angie Leonard
Publisher Email: angie@oldmillroadmedia.com
Advertising Executive Email: jen@oldmillroadmedia.com
Delivery Methods: Mail`Newsstand`Racks
Year Established: 1972
Mechanical specifications: Type page 7 1/2 x 9 3/4; E - 4 cols, 1 3/4, 1/6 between; A - 4 cols, 1 3/4, 1/6 between; C - 4 cols, 1 3/4, between.
Published Days: Wed
Avg. Free Circ.: 15419
Audit Company: Sworn/Estimate/Non-Audited
Audit Date: 43626

MIDDLEBURY

ADDISON COUNTY INDEPENDENT

Street Address: 58 Maple St
City: Middlebury
State: VT
ZIP Code: 05753-1276
General Phone: (802) 388-4944
General Email: ads@addisonindependent.com
Publication Website: https://addisonindependent.com/
Parent Company: Addison County Independent
Publisher Name: Angelo S. Lynn
Publisher Email: angelo@addisonindependent.com
Advertising Executive Name: Christy Lynn
Advertising Executive Email: christy@addisonindependent.com
Delivery Methods: Mail`Newsstand
Year Established: 1946
Mechanical specifications: Type page 14 x 21; E - 6 cols, 2, 1/8 between.
Published Days: Mon`Thur
Avg. Paid Circ.: 7425
Audit Company: Sworn/Estimate/Non-Audited
Audit Date: 43625

MORRISVILLE

THE TRANSCRIPT

Street Address: 92 Lower Main St., P.O. Box 369
City: Morrisville
State: VT
ZIP Code: 05661-8510
General Phone: (802) 888-2212
General Email: community@newsandcitizen.com
Publication Website: https://www.vtcng.com/news_and_citizen/
Parent Company: Vermont Community Newspaper Group LLC
Publisher Name: Greg Popa
Publisher Phone: (802) 253-2101, ext : 29
Editor Name: Tom Kearney

Editor Phone: (802) 253-2101, ext : 18
Advertising Executive Name: Lisa Stearns
Advertising Executive Phone: (802) 888-2212
Delivery Methods: Mail`Newsstand`Racks
Published Days: Thur
Avg. Free Circ.: 15559
Audit Company: Sworn/Estimate/Non-Audited

NORTHFIELD

THE NORTHFIELD NEWS

Street Address: PO Box 43
City: Northfield
State: VT
ZIP Code: 05663-0043
General Phone: (802) 485-6397
General Email: northfieldnewsads@gmail.com
Publication Website: http://www.thenorthfieldnews.com/
Parent Company: Adams Publishing Group
Delivery Methods: Mail`Racks
Year Established: 1878
Mechanical specifications: Type page 9 3/4 x 15; E - 5 cols, 1 5/6, 1/6 between; A - 5 cols, 1 5/6, 1/6 between; C - 5 cols, 1 5/6, 1/6 between.
Published Days: Thur
Avg. Paid Circ.: 1600
Audit Company: Sworn/Estimate/Non-Audited
Audit Date: 43626

RANDOLPH

THE HERALD OF RANDOLPH

Street Address: 30 Pleasant St
City: Randolph
State: VT
ZIP Code: 05060-1156
General Phone: (802) 728-3232
General Email: ads@ourherald.com
Publication Website: https://www.ourherald.com/
Parent Company: Tim Calabro
Publisher Name: Tim Calabro
Editor Name: Tim Calabro
Advertising Executive Name: Brandi Comette
Delivery Methods: Mail`Newsstand
Year Established: 1874
Own Printing Facility?: Y
Mechanical specifications: Type page 13 x 20 1/2; E - 6 cols, 2 1/16, between; A - 6 cols, 2 1/16, between; C - 6 cols, 2 1/16, between.
Published Days: Thur
Avg. Paid Circ.: 5000
Audit Company: Sworn/Estimate/Non-Audited
Audit Date: 43626

SAINT ALBANS

MILTON INDEPENDENT

Street Address: 281 North Main Street
City: Saint Albans
State: VT
ZIP Code: 5478
General Phone: (802) 893-2028
General Email: news@miltonindependent.com
Publication Website: https://www.miltonindependent.com/
Parent Company: Champlain Valley Newspaper Group.
Publisher Name: Jim O'Rourke
Publisher Email: jorourke@samessenger.com
Publisher Phone: (802) 524-9771, ext.108
Editor Name: Michelle Monroe
Editor Email: michelle@colchestersun.com
Editor Phone: (802) 524-9771, ext : 111
Advertising Executive Name: Taylor Walters
Advertising Executive Email: taylor.walters@

essexreporter.com
Advertising Executive Phone: (802) 524-9771, ext : 105
Delivery Methods: Mail`Racks
Year Established: 1993
Published Days: Thur
Audit Company: Sworn/Estimate/Non-Audited
Audit Date: 43626

SAINT ALBANS

THE ESSEX REPORTER

Street Address: 281 N Main St
City: Saint Albans
State: VT
ZIP Code: 5478
General Phone: (802) 524-9771
General Email: news@essexreporter.com
Publication Website: https://www.essexreporter.com/
Parent Company: O'Rourke Media Group
Publisher Name: Jim O'Rourke
Publisher Email: jorourke@samessenger.com
Publisher Phone: (802) 524-9771, ext : 108
Editor Name: Michelle Monroe
Editor Email: michelle@colchestersun.com
Editor Phone: (802) 524-9771, ext : 111
Advertising Executive Name: Taylor Walters
Advertising Executive Email: taylor.walters@essexreporter.com
Advertising Executive Phone: (802) 524-9771, ext : 105
Delivery Methods: Mail`Carrier`Racks
Published Days: Thur
Avg. Free Circ.: 8800
Audit Company: Sworn/Estimate/Non-Audited
Audit Date: 43626

SOUTH BURLINGTON,

SHELBURNE NEWS

Street Address: 1340 Williston Road
City: South Burlington,
State: VT
ZIP Code: 5403
General Phone: (802) 985-3091
General Email: news@shelburnenews.com
Publication Website: https://www.vtcng.com/shelburnenews/
Parent Company: Vermont Community Newspaper Group LLC
Publisher Name: Greg Popa
Publisher Phone: (802) 253-2101, ext : 29
Editor Name: Tom Kearney
Editor Phone: (802) 253-2101, ext : 18
Advertising Executive Name: Wendy Ewing
Advertising Executive Email: wendy@shelburnenews.com
Advertising Executive Phone: (802) 985-3091
Delivery Methods: Mail`Racks
Year Established: 1982
Mechanical specifications: Type page 10 1/4 x 15 3/4; E - 5 cols, between; A - 4 cols, 2 7/16, 1/5 between; C - 6 cols, 1 9/10, 1/4 between.
Published Days: Thur
Avg. Free Circ.: 5000
Audit Company: Sworn/Estimate/Non-Audited
Audit Date: 43626

SOUTH BURLINGTON,

THE OTHER PAPER

Street Address: 1340 Williston Road
City: South Burlington,
State: VT
ZIP Code: 5403
General Phone: (802) 864-6670
General Email: news@otherpapersbvt.com
Publication Website: https://www.vtcng.com/otherpapersbvt/
Parent Company: Vermont Community

Newspaper Group LLC
Publisher Name: Greg Popa
Publisher Phone: (802) 253-2101, ext : 29
Editor Name: Tom Kearney
Editor Phone: (802) 253-2101, ext : 18
Advertising Executive Name: Judy Kearns
Advertising Executive Email: judy@otherpapersbvt.com
Advertising Executive Phone: (802) 864-6670, ext : 21
Delivery Methods: Mail`Racks
Year Established: 1977
Published Days: Thur
Audit Company: Sworn/Estimate/Non-Audited

ST ALBANS

THE COLCHESTER SUN

Street Address: 281 North Main Street
City: St Albans
State: VT
ZIP Code: 5478
General Phone: (802) 524-9771
General Email: news@colchestersun.com
Publication Website: https://www.colchestersun.com/
Parent Company: O'Rourke Media Group
Publisher Name: Jim O'Rourke
Publisher Email: jorourke@samessenger.com
Publisher Phone: (802) 524-9771, ext : 108
Editor Name: Michelle Monroe
Editor Email: michelle@colchestersun.com
Editor Phone: (802) 524-9771, ext : 111
Advertising Executive Name: Taylor Walters
Advertising Executive Email: taylor.walters@essexreporter.com
Advertising Executive Phone: (802) 524-9771, ext : 105
Delivery Methods: Mail`Racks
Published Days: Thur
Audit Company: Sworn/Estimate/Non-Audited
Audit Date: 43626

STOWE

STOWE REPORTER

Street Address: 49 School St
City: Stowe
State: VT
ZIP Code: 05672-4447
General Phone: (802) 253-2101
General Email: ads@stowereporter.com
Publication Website: https://www.vtcng.com/stowe_reporter/
Parent Company: Vermont Community Newspaper Group LLC
Publisher Name: Greg Popa
Publisher Phone: (802) 253-2101, ext : 29
Editor Name: Tom Kearney
Editor Phone: (802) 253-2101, ext : 18
Advertising Executive Name: Irene Nuzzo
Advertising Executive Phone: (802) 760-9673
Delivery Methods: Mail`Newsstand
Year Established: 1958
Published Days: Thur
Avg. Paid Circ.: 4700
Audit Company: Sworn/Estimate/Non-Audited
Audit Date: 43626

STOWE

STOWE TODAY

Street Address: P.O. Box 489
City: Stowe
State: VT
ZIP Code: 5672
General Phone: (802) 253-2101
General Email: news@stowereporter.com
Publication Website: https://www.vtcng.com/stowetoday/
Parent Company: Vermont Community Newspaper Group LLC

Publisher Name: Greg Popa
Publisher Phone: (802) 253-2101, ext : 29
Editor Name: Tom Kearney
Editor Phone: (802) 253-2101, ext : 18
Advertising Executive Name: Irene Nuzzo
Advertising Executive Phone: (802) 760-9673
Delivery Methods: Mail`Newsstand`Racks
Year Established: 1881
Own Printing Facility?: Y
Commercial printers?: Y
Published Days: Tues
Avg. Paid Circ.: 2700
Avg. Free Circ.: 28
Audit Company: Sworn/Estimate/Non-Audited

STOWE

WATERBURY RECORD

Street Address: 49 School St
City: Stowe
State: VT
ZIP Code: 05672-4447
General Phone: (802) 253-2101
General Email: sales@stowereporter.com
Publication Website: https://www.vtcng.com/waterbury_record/
Parent Company: Vermont Community Newspaper Group LLC
Publisher Name: Greg Popa
Publisher Phone: (802) 253-2101, ext : 29
Editor Name: Tom Kearney
Editor Phone: (802) 253-2101, ext : 18
Advertising Executive Name: Leslie LaFountain
Advertising Executive Phone: (802) 253-2101, ext : 26
Delivery Methods: Mail`Newsstand
Year Established: 2007
Own Printing Facility?: N
Commercial printers?: N
Published Days: Thur
Avg. Free Circ.: 4500
Audit Company: Sworn/Estimate/Non-Audited

WAITSFIELD

THE VALLEY REPORTER

Street Address: P.O. Box 119
City: Waitsfield
State: VT
ZIP Code: 05673-4445
General Phone: (802) 496-3928
General Email: ads@valleyreporter.com
Publication Website: https://www.valleyreporter.com/
Parent Company: Burlington Area Newspaper Group
Editor Name: Lisa Loomis
Delivery Methods: Mail`Newsstand`Racks
Year Established: 1971
Published Days: Thur
Avg. Paid Circ.: 3200
Avg. Free Circ.: 98
Audit Company: Sworn/Estimate/Non-Audited
Audit Date: 43626

WILLISTON

WILLISTON OBSERVER

Street Address: 300 Cornerstone Drive, Suite 330,
City: Williston
State: VT
ZIP Code: 05495-4045
General Phone: (802) 872-9000
General Email: marianne@willistonobserver.com
Publication Website: http://www.willistonobserver.com/
Parent Company: Williston Publishing & Promotions
Editor Name: Jason Starr

Editor Email: editor@willistonobserver.com
Editor Phone: (802) 872-9000, ext : 117
Advertising Executive Name: Kevin Lewis
Advertising Executive Email: advertising@willistonobserver.com
Advertising Executive Phone: (802) 872-9000, ext : 115
Delivery Methods: Mail`Racks
Year Established: 1985
Mechanical specifications: Type page 10 1/4 x 16; E - 5 cols, 2, between; A - 5 cols, 2, between.
Published Days: Thur
Avg. Free Circ.: 7000
Audit Company: Sworn/Estimate/Non-Audited

WOODSTOCK

THE VERMONT STANDARD

Street Address: PO Box 88
City: Woodstock
State: VT
ZIP Code: 05091-0088
General Phone: (802) 457-1313
General Email: mbusby@thevermontstandard.com
Publication Website: https://thevermontstandard.com
Parent Company: The Vermont Standard
Publisher Name: Dan Cotter
Publisher Email: dcotter@thevermontstandard.com
Editor Name: Neil Allen
Editor Email: vdean@thevermontstandard.com
Advertising Executive Name: Cynthia Martell
Advertising Executive Email: cmartell@thevermontstandard.com
Delivery Methods: Mail`Newsstand`Racks
Year Established: 1853
Published Days: Wed
Avg. Paid Circ.: 5400
Audit Company: Sworn/Estimate/Non-Audited
Audit Date: 43626
Note: We also have an eEdition with free downloadable app

WASHINGTON

ABERDEEN

THE DAILY WORLD

Street Address: 315 S Michigan St
City: Aberdeen
State: WA
ZIP Code: 98520
General Phone: (360) 532-4000
General Email: publisher@thedailyworld.com
Publication Website: https://www.thedailyworld.com/
Parent Company: Gannett
Publisher Name: Michael Hrycko
Publisher Email: publisher@thedailyworld.com
Editor Name: Doug Barker
Editor Email: dbarker@thedailyworld.com
Advertising Executive Email: ads@thedailyworld.com
Mechanical specifications: Type page 13 x 21 1/2; E - 6 cols, 2 1/16, 1/8 between; A - 6 cols, 2 1/16, 1/8 between; C - 9 cols, 1 3/8, 1/16 between.
Published Days: Tues`Thur`Sat
Weekday Frequency: m
Saturday Frequency: m
Avg. Paid Circ.: 5422
Avg. Free Circ.: 222
Audit Company: AAM

ANACORTES

ANACORTES AMERICAN

Street Address: 901 6th St
City: Anacortes
State: WA
ZIP Code: 98221
General Phone: (360) 293-3122
General Email: news@goanacortes.com
Publication Website: https://www.goskagit.com/anacortes/
Parent Company: Adams Publishing Group
Publisher Name: Colette Weeks
Publisher Email: cweeks@goanacortes.com
Publisher Phone: (360) 293-3122, ext : 1040
Editor Name: Colette Weeks
Editor Email: cweeks@goanacortes.com
Editor Phone: (360) 293-3122, ext : 1040
Advertising Executive Name: Deb Davis Bundy
Advertising Executive Email: dbundy@skagitpublishing.com
Advertising Executive Phone: (360) 416-2126
Delivery Methods: Carrier`Racks
Year Established: 1890
Published Days: Wed
Avg. Paid Circ.: 2355
Avg. Free Circ.: 46
Audit Company: AAM

BATTLE GROUND

THE REFLECTOR

Street Address: 208 SE 1ST ST
City: Battle Ground
State: WA
ZIP Code: 98604
General Phone: (360) 687-5151
General Email: cs2@thereflector.com
Publication Website: http://www.thereflector.com/
Parent Company: Lafromboise Communications, Inc.
Editor Name: Eric Schwartz
Editor Email: eric@thereflector.com
Editor Phone: (360) 723-5704
Advertising Executive Name: Cortina Keel
Advertising Executive Email: cortina@thereflector.com
Advertising Executive Phone: (360) 723-5706
Delivery Methods: Mail`Newsstand`Carrier`Racks
Year Established: 1909
Mechanical specifications: 9.98" x 20.43" 5 column retail 7 column classified.
Published Days: Wed
Avg. Paid Circ.: 816
Avg. Free Circ.: 28206
Audit Company: Sworn/Estimate/Non-Audited

BLAINE

THE NORTHERN LIGHT

Street Address: 225 Marine Dr
City: Blaine
State: WA
ZIP Code: 98230-4052
General Phone: (360) 332-1777
General Email: sales@thenorthernlight.com
Publication Website: https://www.thenorthernlight.com/
Parent Company: Point Roberts Press, Inc.
Publisher Name: Patrick J. Grubb
Publisher Email: publisher@thenorthernlight.com
Editor Name: Patrick J. Grubb
Editor Email: editor@thenorthernlight.com
Advertising Executive Name: Louise H. Mugar
Advertising Executive Email: lmugar@thenorthernlight.com
Delivery Methods: Mail`Racks
Year Established: 1995
Mechanical specifications: Type page 10 1/4 x 15 1/4; E - 5 cols, 2, 1/6 between; A - 5 cols, 2, 1/6 between; C - 6 cols, 1 1/2, 1/6 between.
Published Days: Thur

Avg. Paid Circ.: 15
Avg. Free Circ.: 10460
Audit Company: CVC

BURIEN

HIGHLINE TIMES

Street Address: 14006 1st Ave S
City: Burien
State: WA
ZIP Code: 98168-3402
General Phone: (425) 238-4616
General Email: donao@robinsonnews.com
Publication Website: https://www.westsideseattle.com/highline-times
Parent Company: Robinson Communications, Inc.
Publisher Name: T. C. Robinson
Publisher Email: timr@robinsonnews.com
Editor Name: Kenneth Robinson
Editor Email: kenr@robinsonnews.com
Advertising Executive Name: Dick Sherman
Advertising Executive Email: richards@robinsonnews.com
Advertising Executive Phone: (206) 356-7288
Delivery Methods: Mail`Newsstand`Racks
Year Established: 1945
Own Printing Facility?: Y
Published Days: Fri
Avg. Paid Circ.: 15000
Audit Company: Sworn/Estimate/Non-Audited

CAMAS

CAMAS-WASHOUGAL POST RECORD

Street Address: 425 NE 4th Ave
City: Camas
State: WA
ZIP Code: 98607-2129
General Phone: (360) 834-2141
General Email: shelly.atwell@camaspostrecord.com
Publication Website: http://www.camaspostrecord.com
Editor Name: Kelly Moyer
Editor Email: kelly.moyer@camaspostrecord.com
Editor Phone: (360) 735-4674
Advertising Executive Name: Shelly Atwell
Advertising Executive Email: shelly.atwell@camaspostrecord.com
Advertising Executive Phone: (360) 735-4671
Delivery Methods: Mail`Racks
Own Printing Facility?: Y
Commercial printers?: Y
Mechanical specifications: Type page 13 x 21; E - 6 cols, 2 1/16, 1/8 between; A - 6 cols, 2 1/16, 1/8 between; C - 9 cols, 1 1/4, 1/8 between.
Published Days: Tues
Avg. Paid Circ.: 10000
Audit Company: Sworn/Estimate/Non-Audited

CASHMERE

CASHMERE VALLEY RECORD

Street Address: 201 Cottage Ave
City: Cashmere
State: WA
ZIP Code: 98815
General Phone: (509) 782-3781
General Email: publisher@leavenworthecho.com
Publication Website: https://www.cashmerevalleyrecord.com/
Parent Company: NCW Media, Inc.
Publisher Name: Bill Forhan
Publisher Email: publisher@leavenworthecho.com
Publisher Phone: (509) 548-5286
Editor Name: Gary Begin
Editor Email: gary@ncwmedia.net

Community Newspapers in the U.S.

Advertising Executive Name: Carol Forhan
Advertising Executive Email: echoads@leavenworthecho.com
Advertising Executive Phone: (509) 548-5286
Delivery Methods: Mail`Newsstand`Racks
Year Established: 1905
Own Printing Facility?: Y
Commercial printers?: Y
Mechanical specifications: Super Tab - 11 5/8" X 17" 6 col. print 10 1/4" X 16"
Published Days: Wed
Avg. Paid Circ.: 1000
Audit Company: Sworn/Estimate/Non-Audited

CASHMERE

WENATCHEE BUSINESS JOURNAL

Street Address: 201 Cottage Ave
City: Cashmere
State: WA
ZIP Code: 98815
General Phone: (509) 548-5286
General Email: carol@leavenworthecho.com
Publication Website: https://www.ncwbusiness.com/
Parent Company: NCW Media, Inc.
Publisher Name: Bill Forhan
Publisher Email: publisher@leavenworthecho.com
Editor Name: Gary Begin
Editor Email: gary@ncwmedia.net
Editor Phone: (509) 571-5302
Advertising Executive Name: Carol L. Forhan
Advertising Executive Email: carol@leavenworthecho.com
Advertising Executive Phone: (509) 548-5286, ext : 6513
Delivery Methods: Mail`Newsstand
Year Established: 1987
Published Days: Mon`Mthly
Published Other: First Monday of every month
Avg. Paid Circ.: 2100
Avg. Free Circ.: 2200
Audit Company: Sworn/Estimate/Non-Audited

CATHLAMET

WAHKIAKUM COUNTY EAGLE

Street Address: P.O. Box 368
City: Cathlamet
State: WA
ZIP Code: 98612
General Phone: (360) 795-3391
Publication Website: www.waheagle.com
Publisher Name: Rick Nelson
Publisher Email: ernelson@teleport.com
Publisher Phone: (360) 795-3391
Advertising Executive Name: Kathi Howell
Advertising Executive Email: kathi@waheagle.com
Delivery Methods: Mail`Newsstand
Year Established: 1891
Mechanical specifications: Type page 10 1/2 x 21; E - 6 cols, 1 7/8, 1/8 between; A - 6 cols, 1 7/8, 1/8 between; C - 6 cols, 1 7/8, 1/8 between.
Published Days: Thur
Avg. Paid Circ.: 1660
Avg. Free Circ.: 33
Audit Company: Sworn/Estimate/Non-Audited

CENTRALIA

THE CHRONICLE

Street Address: 321 N Pearl St
City: Centralia
State: WA
ZIP Code: 98531
General Phone: (360) 736-3311
General Email: bwatson@chronline.com
Publication Website: http://www.chronline.com/
Parent Company: Gannett
Editor Name: Natalie Johnson
Editor Email: njohnson@chronline.com
Editor Phone: (360) 807-8235
Advertising Executive Name: Lindy Waring
Advertising Executive Email: lwaring@chronline.com
Advertising Executive Phone: (360) 807-8219
Delivery Methods: Mail`Newsstand`Carrier`Racks
Year Established: 1966
Own Printing Facility?: Y
Commercial printers?: Y
Mechanical specifications: Type page 9.98"x20.43" 5 column, classifieds 7 column
Published Days: Tues`Thur`Sat
Weekday Frequency: e
Saturday Frequency: m
Avg. Paid Circ.: 10200
Audit Company: Sworn/Estimate/Non-Audited

CHELAN

LAKE CHELAN MIRROR

Street Address: 310 E Johnson Ave
City: Chelan
State: WA
ZIP Code: 98816
General Phone: (509) 682-2213
General Email: publisher@leavenworthecho.com
Publication Website: https://www.lakechelanmirror.com/
Parent Company: NCW Media, Inc.
Publisher Name: Bill Forhan
Publisher Email: publisher@leavenworthecho.com
Publisher Phone: (509) 548-5286
Editor Name: Gary Begin
Editor Email: gary@ncwmedia.net
Advertising Executive Name: Carol Forhan
Advertising Executive Email: echoads@leavenworthecho.com
Advertising Executive Phone: (509) 548-5286
Delivery Methods: Mail`Newsstand`Racks
Year Established: 1891
Published Days: Wed
Avg. Paid Circ.: 1800
Audit Company: Sworn/Estimate/Non-Audited

CHELAN

QUAD CITY HERALD

Street Address: 310 E Johnson Ave
City: Chelan
State: WA
ZIP Code: 98816
General Phone: (509) 682-2213
General Email: publisher@leavenworthecho.com
Publication Website: https://www.qcherald.com/
Parent Company: NCW Media, Inc.
Publisher Name: Bill Forhan
Publisher Email: publisher@leavenworthecho.com
Editor Name: Gary Begin
Editor Email: gary@ncwmedia.net
Editor Phone: (509) 571-5302
Advertising Executive Name: Ruth Keys
Advertising Executive Email: ruthk@lakechelanmirror.com
Advertising Executive Phone: (509) 682-2213
Delivery Methods: Mail`Newsstand`Racks
Year Established: 1907
Published Days: Thur
Avg. Paid Circ.: 1000
Audit Company: Sworn/Estimate/Non-Audited

CHENEY

CHENEY FREE PRESS

Street Address: 1616 W 1st St
City: Cheney
State: WA
ZIP Code: 99004
General Phone: (509) 235-6184
General Email: info@cheneyfreepress.com
Publication Website: https://www.cheneyfreepress.com/
Parent Company: Free Press Publishing Inc.
Delivery Methods: Mail`Racks
Year Established: 1896
Published Days: Thur
Audit Company: Sworn/Estimate/Non-Audited

CHEWELAH

THE INDEPENDENT

Street Address: 401 S Park St
City: Chewelah
State: WA
ZIP Code: 99109-9337
General Phone: (509) 935-8422
General Email: theindependent@centurytel.net
Publication Website: http://www.chewelahindependent.com/
Parent Company: Gannett
Publisher Name: Jared Arnold
Publisher Email: publisher@chewelahindependent.com
Publisher Phone: (509) 935-8422
Editor Name: Brandon Hansen
Editor Email: brandon@chewelahindependent.com
Editor Phone: (509) 935-8422
Advertising Executive Name: Andrea Arnold
Advertising Executive Email: theindependent@centurytel.net
Advertising Executive Phone: (509) 935-8422
Delivery Methods: Mail`Racks
Year Established: 1903
Published Days: Thur
Avg. Paid Circ.: 2100
Avg. Free Circ.: 500
Audit Company: Sworn/Estimate/Non-Audited

CLE ELUM

NORTHERN KITTITAS COUNTY TRIBUNE

Street Address: 807 W Davis St
City: Cle Elum
State: WA
ZIP Code: 98922
General Phone: (509) 674-2511
General Email: casey@nkctribune.com
Publication Website: https://nkctribune.com/
Parent Company: Oahe Publishing Corporation
Publisher Name: Jana Stoner
Publisher Email: jana@nkctribune.com
Publisher Phone: (509) 674-2511
Delivery Methods: Mail`Newsstand`Racks
Year Established: 1953
Published Days: Thur
Avg. Paid Circ.: 3000
Audit Company: Sworn/Estimate/Non-Audited

COLFAX

WHITMAN COUNTY GAZETTE

Street Address: 211 N Main St
City: Colfax
State: WA
ZIP Code: 99111
General Phone: (509) 397-4333
General Email: wcgazette@gmail.com
Publication Website: https://www.wcgazette.com/
Parent Company: Gazette Publishing Co.

Publisher Name: Gordon Forgey
Editor Name: Gordon Forgey
Delivery Methods: Mail
Year Established: 1877
Published Days: Thur
Audit Company: Sworn/Estimate/Non-Audited

COLVILLE

STATESMAN-EXAMINER

Street Address: 220 S Main St
City: Colville
State: WA
ZIP Code: 99114
General Phone: (509) 684-4567
General Email: shannon@statesmanexaminer.com
Publication Website: https://www.statesmanexaminer.com/
Parent Company: Horizon Publications Inc.
Publisher Name: Shannon Chapman
Publisher Email: shannon@statesmanexaminer.com
Delivery Methods: Mail`Newsstand`Racks
Year Established: 1948
Published Days: Wed
Avg. Paid Circ.: 3000
Avg. Free Circ.: 100
Audit Company: Sworn/Estimate/Non-Audited

COVINGTON

VOICE OF THE VALLEY

Street Address: 26909 206th Ave SE
City: Covington
State: WA
ZIP Code: 98042
General Phone: (425) 432-9696
General Email: advertising@voiceofthevall.wpengine.com
Publication Website: https://voiceofthevalley.com/
Publisher Name: Donna Hayes
Publisher Email: donna@voiceofthevalley.com
Editor Name: Donna Hayes
Editor Email: donna@voiceofthevalley.com
Advertising Executive Name: Traci Hipple
Advertising Executive Email: traci@voiceofthevalley.com
Delivery Methods: Newsstand`Racks
Year Established: 1969
Published Days: Tues
Audit Company: Sworn/Estimate/Non-Audited

DAYTON

DAYTON CHRONICLE

Street Address: 163 E Main St
City: Dayton
State: WA
ZIP Code: 99328
General Phone: (509) 382-2221
General Email: legals@daytonchronicle.com
Publication Website: https://www.daytonchronicle.com/
Parent Company: 2Over Publishing, LLC
Editor Email: cbaker@daytonchronicle.com
Advertising Executive Email: lbaker@daytonchronicle.com
Delivery Methods: Mail
Year Established: 1878
Own Printing Facility?: Y
Commercial printers?: Y
Published Days: Wed
Avg. Paid Circ.: 1700
Audit Company: Sworn/Estimate/Non-Audited

DEER PARK

DEER PARK

DEER PARK TRIBUNE

Street Address: 104 N Main St
City: Deer Park
State: WA
ZIP Code: 99006
General Phone: (509) 276-5043
General Email: sales@dptribune.com
Publication Website: https://www.dptribune.com/
Parent Company: Horizon Publications Inc.
Advertising Executive Email: sales@dptribune.com
Delivery Methods: Mail`Racks
Year Established: 1906
Published Days: Wed
Audit Company: Sworn/Estimate/Non-Audited

EAST WENATCHEE

DOUGLAS COUNTY EMPIRE PRESS

Street Address: 2290 Grand Ave
City: East Wenatchee
State: WA
ZIP Code: 98802-8253
General Phone: (509) 886-8668
General Email: weekly@empire-press.com
Publication Website: https://empire-press.com/
Publisher Name: Sean flaherty
Advertising Executive Email: legals@empire-press.com
Delivery Methods: Mail`Racks
Year Established: 1888
Published Days: Thur
Avg. Paid Circ.: 925
Avg. Free Circ.: 10
Audit Company: Sworn/Estimate/Non-Audited

EATONVILLE

THE EATONVILLE DISPATCH

Street Address: P.O. Box 248
City: Eatonville
State: WA
ZIP Code: 98328
General Phone: (360) 832-4411
General Email: dispatch@nwlink.com
Publication Website: https://dispatchnews.com/
Parent Company: Pacific Publishing Co. Inc.
Editor Email: dispatcheditor@nwlink.com
Delivery Methods: Mail`Racks
Year Established: 1893
Published Days: Thur
Audit Company: Sworn/Estimate/Non-Audited

FERNDALE

FERNDALE RECORD

Street Address: 2008 B Main St
City: Ferndale
State: WA
ZIP Code: 98248
General Phone: (360) 384-1411
General Email: news@ferndalerecord.com
Publication Website: https://www.ferndalerecord.com/
Parent Company: Lewis Publishing Co., Inc.
Editor Name: Brent Lindquist
Editor Email: news@ferndalerecord.com
Editor Phone: (360) 384-1411
Advertising Executive Name: Jan Brown
Advertising Executive Email: jan@ferndalerecord.com
Advertising Executive Phone: (360) 384-1411
Delivery Methods: Mail`Newsstand`Racks
Year Established: 1885
Mechanical specifications: Page size 11" wide x 21" tall. Column width is 1.694" w/ .167" gutters.
Published Days: Wed

Avg. Paid Circ.: 1000
Avg. Free Circ.: 4700
Audit Company: Sworn/Estimate/Non-Audited

GOLDENDALE

GOLDENDALE SENTINEL

Street Address: 117 W Main St
City: Goldendale
State: WA
ZIP Code: 98620-9526
General Phone: (509) 773-3777
General Email: ads@goldendalesentinel.com
Publication Website: https://www.goldendalesentinel.com/
Parent Company: Tartan Publications, Inc.
Publisher Name: Lou Marzeles
Editor Name: Lou Marzeles
Advertising Executive Email: ads@goldendalesentinel.com
Advertising Executive Phone: (509) 773-3777
Delivery Methods: Mail`Newsstand`Carrier`Racks
Year Established: 1879
Own Printing Facility?: N
Commercial printers?: Y
Published Days: Wed
Avg. Paid Circ.: 3200
Audit Company: Sworn/Estimate/Non-Audited

GRAND COULEE

THE STAR

Street Address: 3 MIDWAY AVE
City: Grand Coulee
State: WA
ZIP Code: 99133
General Phone: (509) 633-1350
General Email: star@grandcoulee.com
Publication Website: https://www.grandcoulee.com/
Parent Company: Gannett
Publisher Name: Scott Hunter
Publisher Email: scott@grandcoulee.com
Editor Name: Scott Hunter
Editor Email: scott@grandcoulee.com
Advertising Executive Email: star@grandcoulee.com
Advertising Executive Phone: (509) 633-1350
Delivery Methods: Mail`Racks
Year Established: 1945
Own Printing Facility?: N
Commercial printers?: Y
Mechanical specifications: Type page 13.75 x 21.5; E - 6 cols, 2.152, 1/6 between; A - 6 cols, 2 1/4, 1/6 between; C - 6 cols, 2 1/4, 1/6 between.
Published Days: Wed
Avg. Paid Circ.: 1720
Avg. Free Circ.: 3000
Audit Company: Sworn/Estimate/Non-Audited

LA CONNER

LA CONNER WEEKLY NEWS

Street Address: 119 N 3rd St
City: La Conner
State: WA
ZIP Code: 98257
General Phone: (360) 466-3315
General Email: production@laconnernews.com
Publication Website: https://laconnerweeklynews.com/
Parent Company: La Conner News LLC
Publisher Name: Ken Stern
Editor Name: Ken Stern
Editor Email: editor@laconnernews.com
Advertising Executive Email: production@laconnernews.com
Delivery Methods: Mail`Racks
Year Established: 2006

Mechanical specifications: 20.75" page height 1 col 1.83" 2 col 3.8" 3 col 5.75" 4 col 7.71" 5 col 9.66" and 6 col 11.63" wide
Published Days: Wed
Published Other: Website updated daily
Avg. Paid Circ.: 1500
Avg. Free Circ.: 50
Audit Company: Sworn/Estimate/Non-Audited

LEAVENWORTH

THE LEAVENWORTH ECHO

Street Address: 215 14th St
City: Leavenworth
State: WA
ZIP Code: 98826-1411
General Phone: (509) 548-5286
General Email: carol@leavenworthecho.com
Publication Website: https://www.leavenworthecho.com/
Parent Company: NCW Media, Inc.
Publisher Name: Bill Forhan
Publisher Email: publisher@leavenworthecho.com
Publisher Phone: (509) 548-5286
Editor Email: editor@leavenworthecho.com
Advertising Executive Name: Carol Forhan
Advertising Executive Email: carol@leavenworthecho.com
Advertising Executive Phone: (509) 548-5286, ext : 6513
Delivery Methods: Mail`Newsstand`Racks
Year Established: 1904
Own Printing Facility?: N
Commercial printers?: N
Mechanical specifications: Super tab - 11 5/8" X 17 " Print specs - 6 col. format prints over 10 1/4" X 16" Quarter forlded
Published Days: Wed
Avg. Paid Circ.: 1600
Audit Company: Sworn/Estimate/Non-Audited

LIBERTY LAKE

LIBERTY LAKE SPLASH

Street Address: PO Box 363
City: Liberty Lake
State: WA
ZIP Code: 99019-8630
General Phone: (509) 242-7752
General Email: advertise@libertylakesplash.com
Publication Website: http://www.libertylakesplash.com/
Editor Email: editor@libertylakesplash.com
Advertising Executive Email: advertise@libertylakesplash.com
Delivery Methods: Mail`Racks
Year Established: 1999
Published Days: Thur`Mthly
Avg. Paid Circ.: 100
Avg. Free Circ.: 6900
Audit Company: Sworn/Estimate/Non-Audited

LONG BEACH

CHINOOK OBSERVER

Street Address: 205 Bolstad Ave E
City: Long Beach
State: WA
ZIP Code: 98631-9200
General Phone: (360) 642-8181
General Email: arenwick@chinookobserver.com
Publication Website: https://www.chinookobserver.com/
Parent Company: EO Media Group
Publisher Name: Matt Winters
Publisher Email: mwinters@chinookobserver.com
Publisher Phone: (360) 642-8181
Editor Name: Matt Winters

Editor Email: mwinters@chinookobserver.com
Editor Phone: (360) 642-8181
Advertising Executive Name: Andrew Renwick
Advertising Executive Email: arenwick@chinookobserver.com
Advertising Executive Phone: (360) 642-8181
Delivery Methods: Mail`Newsstand`Racks
Year Established: 1900
Published Days: Wed
Avg. Paid Circ.: 6800
Audit Company: Sworn/Estimate/Non-Audited

LYNDEN

LYNDEN TRIBUNE

Street Address: 113 6th St
City: Lynden
State: WA
ZIP Code: 98264-1901
General Phone: (360) 354-4444
General Email: mitze@lyndentribune.com
Publication Website: https://www.lyndentribune.com/
Parent Company: Lewis Publishing Co., Inc.
Publisher Name: Michael D. Lewis
Publisher Email: mdlewis@lyndentribune.com
Publisher Phone: (360) 354-4444, ext : 12
Editor Name: Calvin Bratt
Editor Email: editor@lyndentribune.com
Editor Phone: (360) 354-4444, ext : 22
Advertising Executive Name: Mitze Kester
Advertising Executive Email: mitze@lyndentribune.com
Advertising Executive Phone: (360) 510-6464
Delivery Methods: Mail`Newsstand`Carrier`Racks
Year Established: 1888
Published Days: Wed
Avg. Paid Circ.: 5000
Avg. Free Circ.: 7100
Audit Company: Sworn/Estimate/Non-Audited

MARYSVILLE

NORTH COUNTY OUTLOOK

Street Address: 1331 State Ave
City: Marysville
State: WA
ZIP Code: 98270-3604
General Phone: (360) 659-1100
General Email: sue@northcountyoutlook.com
Publication Website: https://www.northcountyoutlook.com/
Delivery Methods: Mail`Newsstand`Racks
Year Established: 2007
Published Days: Tues
Avg. Free Circ.: 21337
Audit Company: Sworn/Estimate/Non-Audited

MORTON

THE EAST COUNTY JOURNAL

Street Address: 278 W MAIN ST
City: Morton
State: WA
ZIP Code: 98356
General Phone: (360) 496-5993
General Email: ecjeditor@devaulpublishing.com
Publication Website: http://www.devaulpublishing.com/eastcounty
Parent Company: DeVaul Publishing, Inc
Publisher Name: Tammy Armstrong
Delivery Methods: Mail
Year Established: 1936
Mechanical specifications: Type page 13 x 21 1/2; E - 6 cols, 2, 1/6 between; A - 6 cols, 2, 1/6 between; C - 6 cols, 2, 1/6 between.

Community Newspapers in the U.S.

Published Days: Wed
Avg. Free Circ.: 7979
Audit Company: AAM

MOSES LAKE

BASIN BUSINESS JOURNAL FARM NEWS

Street Address: 815 W 3rd Ave
City: Moses Lake
State: WA
ZIP Code: 98837-2008
General Phone: (509) 765-8549
General Email: bbjagnews@basinbusinessjournal.com
Publication Website: http://www.basinbusinessjournal.com/
Parent Company: Hagadone Corp.
Publisher Name: Bob Richardson
Published Days: Thur
Audit Company: Sworn/Estimate/Non-Audited

MUKILTEO

EDMONDS BEACON

Street Address: 806 5th St
City: Mukilteo
State: WA
ZIP Code: 98275-1628
General Phone: (425) 347-1711
General Email: edmondssales@yourbeacon.net
Publication Website: https://www.edmondsbeacon.com/
Parent Company: Beacon Publishing Inc.
Publisher Name: Paul Archipley
Editor Name: Brian Soergel
Editor Email: edmondseditor@yourbeacon.net
Advertising Executive Name: Joy Baudart
Delivery Methods: Carrier`Racks
Year Established: 1986
Own Printing Facility?: N
Commercial printers?: N
Mechanical specifications: print size: 10"x16" 1 col: 1.875" (11 picas) 2 col: 3.875" (23 picas) 3 col: 5.875" (35 picas) 4 col: 7.875" (47 picas) 5 col: 10" (60 picas)
Published Days: Thur
Avg. Paid Circ.: 100
Avg. Free Circ.: 10000
Audit Company: Sworn/Estimate/Non-Audited

MUKILTEO

MUKILTEO BEACON

Street Address: 806 5th St
City: Mukilteo
State: WA
ZIP Code: 98275-1628
General Phone: (425) 347-5634
General Email: mukilteosales@yourbeacon.net
Publication Website: https://www.mukilteobeacon.com/
Parent Company: Beacon Publishing Inc.
Publisher Name: Paul Archipley
Editor Name: Paul Archipley
Editor Email: mukilteoeditor@yourbeacon.net
Delivery Methods: Carrier`Racks
Year Established: 1991
Own Printing Facility?: N
Commercial printers?: N
Mechanical specifications: print size: 10"x16" 1 col: 1.875" (11 picas) 2 col: 3.875" (23 picas) 3 col: 5.875" (35 picas) 4 col: 7.875" (47 picas) 5 col: 10" (60 picas)
Published Days: Wed
Avg. Paid Circ.: 166
Avg. Free Circ.: 10000
Audit Company: Sworn/Estimate/Non-Audited

NEWPORT

NEWPORT MINER

Street Address: 421 S. Spokane Ave
City: Newport
State: WA
ZIP Code: 99156-7039
General Phone: (509) 447-2433
General Email: mineradvertising@povn.com
Publication Website: https://pendoreillerivervalley.com/
Publisher Name: Michelle Nedved
Editor Name: Don Gronning
Advertising Executive Name: Micki Brass
Delivery Methods: Mail`Newsstand
Year Established: 1891
Own Printing Facility?: Y
Published Days: Wed
Avg. Paid Circ.: 6000
Avg. Free Circ.: 11000
Audit Company: Sworn/Estimate/Non-Audited

OCEAN SHORES

NORTH COAST NEWS

Street Address: 668 Ocean Shores Blvd NW
City: Ocean Shores
State: WA
ZIP Code: 98569-9346
General Phone: (360) 289-2441
General Email: editor@northcoastnews.com
Publication Website: https://www.northcoastnews.com/
Parent Company: Sound Publishing, Inc.
Publisher Name: Michael Hrycko
Publisher Email: publisher@thedailyworld.com
Editor Name: Angelo Bruscas
Editor Email: editor@northcoastnews.com
Editor Phone: (360) 289-3968
Advertising Executive Name: Doug Ames
Advertising Executive Email: dames@soundpublishing.com
Delivery Methods: Mail
Year Established: 1989
Published Days: Thur
Avg. Paid Circ.: 1224
Avg. Free Circ.: 21
Audit Company: Sworn/Estimate/Non-Audited

ODESSA

THE ODESSA RECORD

Street Address: 1 W 1st Ave
City: Odessa
State: WA
ZIP Code: 99159-7004
General Phone: (509) 982-2632
General Email: therecord@odessaoffice.com
Publication Website: https://www.odessarecord.com/
Parent Company: Free Press Publishing Inc.
Advertising Executive Phone: (509) 982-2632
Delivery Methods: Mail
Year Established: 1901
Commercial printers?: Y
Published Days: Thur
Avg. Paid Circ.: 1250
Audit Company: Sworn/Estimate/Non-Audited

OMAK

OMAK-OKANOGAN COUNTY CHRONICLE

Street Address: PO Box 553
City: Omak
State: WA
ZIP Code: 98841-0553
General Phone: (509) 826-1110
General Email: news@omakchronicle.com
Publication Website: https://www.omakchronicle.com/
Parent Company: Eagle Newspapers, Inc.
Publisher Name: Teresa Myers
Editor Name: Brock Hires
Advertising Executive Name: Teresa Myers
Delivery Methods: Mail`Newsstand`Carrier`Racks
Year Established: 1910
Published Days: Wed`Sun
Published Other: E-edition available
Avg. Paid Circ.: 6600
Avg. Free Circ.: 300
Audit Company: Sworn/Estimate/Non-Audited

OTHELLO

THE SUN TRIBUNE

Street Address: 705 E Hemlock St
City: Othello
State: WA
ZIP Code: 99344-1425
General Phone: (509) 765-4561
General Email: advertising@suntribunenews.com
Publication Website: https://suntribunenews.com/
Parent Company: Hagadone Corp.
Publisher Name: Bob Richardson
Publisher Email: publisher@suntribunenews.com
Publisher Phone: (509) 760-7870
Editor Name: Richard Byrd
Editor Email: editor@suntribunenews.com
Editor Phone: (509) 765-4561
Advertising Executive Email: advertising@suntribunenews.com
Delivery Methods: Mail`Newsstand`Racks
Year Established: 2012
Published Days: Wed
Avg. Paid Circ.: 1250
Audit Company: Sworn/Estimate/Non-Audited

POMEROY

EAST WASHINGTONIAN

Street Address: P.O. Box 70
City: Pomeroy
State: WA
ZIP Code: 99347
General Phone: (509) 843-1313
General Email: lbaker@eastwashingtonian.com
Publication Website: https://www.eastwashingtonian.com/
Parent Company: 2Over Publishing, LLC
Publisher Name: C. Baker
Publisher Email: cbaker@eastwashingtonian.com
Editor Name: C. Baker
Editor Email: cbaker@eastwashingtonian.com
Advertising Executive Name: Loyal Baker
Advertising Executive Email: lbaker@eastwashingtonian.com
Advertising Executive Phone: (509) 843-1313
Delivery Methods: Mail
Year Established: 1882
Published Days: Thur
Audit Company: Sworn/Estimate/Non-Audited

PORT TOWNSEND

PORT TOWNSEND & JEFFERSON COUNTY LEADER

Street Address: 226 Adams St
City: Port Townsend
State: WA
ZIP Code: 98368-5706
General Phone: (360) 385-2900
General Email: cbrewer@ptleader.com
Publication Website: https://www.ptleader.com/
Delivery Methods: Mail`Racks
Year Established: 1889
Published Days: Wed
Avg. Paid Circ.: 6504
Avg. Free Circ.: 561
Audit Company: Sworn/Estimate/Non-Audited

PROSSER

PROSSER RECORD-BULLETIN

Street Address: 613 7th St
City: Prosser
State: WA
ZIP Code: 99350-1459
General Phone: (509) 786-1711
General Email: ads@recordbulletin.com
Publication Website: http://www.thenewsatvalleypublishing.com/
Parent Company: Valley Publishing Company
Delivery Methods: Mail`Racks
Year Established: 1920
Published Days: Wed
Audit Company: Sworn/Estimate/Non-Audited

PUYALLUP

THE PUYALLUP HERALD

Street Address: 510 E Main
City: Puyallup
State: WA
ZIP Code: 98372-5698
General Phone: (253) 841-2481
General Email: rebecca.poynter@thenewstribune.com
Publication Website: https://www.thenewstribune.com/news/local/community/puyallup-herald/
Publisher Name: Rebecca Poynter
Publisher Email: rebecca.poynter@thenewstribune.com
Publisher Phone: (253) 597-8554
Editor Name: Adam Lynn
Editor Email: adam.lynn@thenewstribune.com
Editor Phone: (253) 597-8644
Delivery Methods: Mail`Racks
Commercial printers?: Y
Published Days: Thur
Avg. Paid Circ.: 27000
Audit Company: Sworn/Estimate/Non-Audited

QUINCY

THE QUINCY VALLEY POST-REGISTER

Street Address: 305 Central Ave S
City: Quincy
State: WA
ZIP Code: 98848-1227
General Phone: (509) 787-4511
General Email: ads@qvpr.com
Publication Website: https://www.qvpr.com/
Editor Name: Miles King
Editor Email: news@qvpr.com
Editor Phone: (509) 787-4511
Advertising Executive Name: Janette Morris
Advertising Executive Email: ads@qvpr.com
Advertising Executive Phone: (509) 787-4511
Delivery Methods: Mail`Newsstand`Carrier`Racks
Year Established: 1949
Published Days: Thur
Audit Company: Sworn/Estimate/Non-Audited

RITZVILLE

THE RITZVILLE ADAMS COUNTY JOURNAL

Street Address: 216 W Railroad Ave
City: Ritzville
State: WA
ZIP Code: 99169-2309
General Phone: (509) 659-1020
General Email: advertising@ritzvillejournal.com
Publication Website: https://www.ritzvillejournal.com
Parent Company: Free Press Publishing Inc.
Advertising Executive Name: Kim Pearson
Advertising Executive Email: advertising@ritzvillejournal.com
Advertising Executive Phone: (509) 235-6184
Delivery Methods: Mail
Year Established: 1886
Commercial printers?: Y
Mechanical specifications: Type page 12 3/4 x 21 1/4; E - 6 cols, 2, 1/6 between; A - 6 cols, 2, 1/6 between; C - 6 cols, 2, 1/6 between.
Published Days: Thur
Avg. Paid Circ.: 2100
Avg. Free Circ.: 46
Audit Company: Sworn/Estimate/Non-Audited

SEATTLE

BALLARD NEWS-TRIBUNE

Street Address: PO Box 66769
City: Seattle
State: WA
ZIP Code: 98166-0769
General Phone: (425) 238-4616
General Email: donao@robinsonnews.com
Publication Website: https://www.westsideseattle.com/ballard-news-tribune
Parent Company: Robinson Communications, Inc.
Publisher Name: T. C. Robinson
Publisher Email: timr@robinsonnews.com
Editor Name: Kenneth Robinson
Editor Email: kenr@robinsonnews.com
Advertising Executive Name: Dick Sherman
Advertising Executive Email: richards@robinsonnews.com
Advertising Executive Phone: (206) 356-7288
Delivery Methods: Mail`Newsstand`Racks
Year Established: 1898
Own Printing Facility?: Y
Published Days: Wed`Fri
Avg. Paid Circ.: 10351
Audit Company: Sworn/Estimate/Non-Audited

SEATTLE

CITY LIVING SEATTLE

Street Address: 636 S Alaska St
City: Seattle
State: WA
ZIP Code: 98108-1727
General Phone: (206) 461-1300
General Email: ppcadmanager@nwlink.com
Publication Website: https://citylivingseattle.com/
Parent Company: Pacific Publishing Co. Inc.
Publisher Name: Robert Munford
Publisher Email: ppcprint@nwlink.com
Publisher Phone: (206) 461-1304
Editor Email: citylivingeditor@nwlink.com
Editor Phone: (206) 461-1305
Advertising Executive Name: Tammy Greenaway
Advertising Executive Email: ppcadmanager@nwlink.com
Advertising Executive Phone: (206) 461-1322
Delivery Methods: Mail`Newsstand`Carrier`Racks
Own Printing Facility?: N
Commercial printers?: Y
Published Days: Thur`Mthly
Avg. Paid Circ.: 3500
Avg. Free Circ.: 18000
Audit Company: Sworn/Estimate/Non-Audited

SEATTLE

PUGET SOUND BUSINESS JOURNAL

Street Address: 801 2nd Ave
City: Seattle
State: WA
ZIP Code: 98104-1528
General Phone: (206) 876-5500
General Email: mgeoghegan@bizjournals.com
Publication Website: https://www.bizjournals.com/seattle
Parent Company: American City Business Journals
Publisher Name: Emily Parkhurst
Publisher Email: eparkhurst@bizjournals.com
Publisher Phone: (206) 876-5441
Editor Name: Ryan Lambert
Editor Email: rlambert@bizjournals.com
Editor Phone: (206) 876-5420
Advertising Executive Name: Marijane Milton
Advertising Executive Email: mmilton@bizjournals.com
Advertising Executive Phone: (206) 876-5447
Delivery Methods: Mail`Newsstand`Racks
Year Established: 1980
Published Days: Fri
Audit Company: Sworn/Estimate/Non-Audited

SEATTLE

QUEEN ANNE & MAGNOLIA NEWS

Street Address: 636 S Alaska St
City: Seattle
State: WA
ZIP Code: 98108-1727
General Phone: (206) 461-1300
General Email: ppclegalads@nwlink.com
Publication Website: https://queenannenews.com/
Parent Company: Pacific Publishing Co. Inc.
Publisher Name: Robert Munford
Publisher Email: ppcprint@nwlink.com
Publisher Phone: (206) 461-1304
Advertising Executive Name: Jody Vinson
Advertising Executive Email: ppclegalads@nwlink.com
Advertising Executive Phone: (206) 461-1323
Delivery Methods: Newsstand`Carrier`Racks
Year Established: 1919
Own Printing Facility?: Y
Commercial printers?: Y
Mechanical specifications: Type page 10 3/4 x 16; E - 5 cols, 2 1/16, between; A - 5 cols, 2 1/16, between; C - 7 cols, 1 1/3, between.
Published Days: Wed
Avg. Paid Circ.: 1898
Avg. Free Circ.: 5102
Audit Company: Sworn/Estimate/Non-Audited

SEATTLE

THE CAPITOL HILL TIMES

Street Address: 4000 Aurora Ave N
City: Seattle
State: WA
ZIP Code: 98103-7853
General Phone: (425) 213-5579
General Email: ppcadmanager@nwlink.com
Publication Website: https://www.capitolhilltimes.com/
Parent Company: RIM Publications
Editor Email: editor@capitolhilltimes.com
Advertising Executive Name: Tammy Greenaway
Advertising Executive Email: ppcadmanager@nwlink.com
Advertising Executive Phone: (206) 461-1322
Delivery Methods: Mail`Newsstand`Racks
Year Established: 1926
Published Days: Thur
Audit Company: Sworn/Estimate/Non-Audited

SEATTLE

THE MONROE MONITOR & VALLEY NEWS

Street Address: PO Box 80156
City: Seattle
State: WA
ZIP Code: 98108-0156
General Phone: (360) 794-7116
General Email: editor@monroemonitor.com
Publication Website: http://www.monroemonitor.com/
Parent Company: Pacific Publishing Co. Inc.
Editor Email: editor@monroemonitor.com
Delivery Methods: Mail`Newsstand
Year Established: 1899
Commercial printers?: Y
Published Days: Tues
Avg. Paid Circ.: 4000
Audit Company: Sworn/Estimate/Non-Audited

SEATTLE

WESTSIDE SEATTLE

Street Address: PO Box 66769
City: Seattle
State: WA
ZIP Code: 98166-0769
General Phone: (206) 251-3220
General Email: donao@robinsonnews.com
Publication Website: https://www.westsideseattle.com/
Parent Company: Robinson Communications, Inc.
Publisher Name: T. C. Robinson
Publisher Email: timr@robinsonnews.com
Editor Name: Kenneth Robinson
Editor Email: kenr@robinsonnews.com
Advertising Executive Name: Dick Sherman
Advertising Executive Email: richards@robinsonnews.com
Advertising Executive Phone: (206) 356-7288
Delivery Methods: Mail`Newsstand`Racks
Year Established: 1923
Commercial printers?: N
Mechanical specifications: Type page 10 7/8 x 16; E - 5 cols, 2 1/6, between; A - 5 cols, 2 1/6, between; C - 8 cols, between.
Published Days: Fri
Audit Company: Sworn/Estimate/Non-Audited

SHELTON

SHELTON-MASON COUNTY JOURNAL

Street Address: 227 W Cota St
City: Shelton
State: WA
ZIP Code: 98584-2263
General Phone: (360) 426-4412
General Email: ads@masoncounty.com
Publication Website: http://www.masoncounty.com/
Publisher Name: Tom Mullen
Publisher Email: publisher@masoncounty.com
Editor Name: Adam Rudnick
Editor Email: adam@masoncounty.com
Advertising Executive Name: Theresa Murray
Advertising Executive Email: theresa@masoncounty.com
Delivery Methods: Mail`Newsstand`Racks
Year Established: 1887
Published Days: Thur
Avg. Paid Circ.: 7100
Avg. Free Circ.: 100
Audit Company: Sworn/Estimate/Non-Audited

SNOHOMISH

EVERETT NEW TRIBUNE

Street Address: 127 Ave C Suite B
City: Snohomish
State: WA
ZIP Code: 98290-2768
General Phone: (360) 568-4121
General Email: becky@snoho.com
Publication Website: http://www.snoho.com/
Parent Company: Mach Publishing
Publisher Name: Becky Reed
Publisher Email: becky@snoho.com
Editor Name: Michael Whitney
Editor Email: michael@snoho.com
Advertising Executive Name: Becky Reed
Advertising Executive Email: becky@snoho.com
Delivery Methods: Mail`Newsstand
Year Established: 1892
Mechanical specifications: Type page 10 7/8 x 16 1/2; E - 5 cols, 2 1/16, between; A - 5 cols, 2 1/16, between; C - 7 cols, 1 3/8, between.
Published Days: Wed
Avg. Paid Circ.: 15000
Avg. Free Circ.: 3500
Audit Company: Sworn/Estimate/Non-Audited

SNOHOMISH

SNOHOMISH COUNTY TRIBUNE

Street Address: 127 Ave C Suite B
City: Snohomish
State: WA
ZIP Code: 98290-2768
General Phone: (360) 568-4121
General Email: becky@snoho.com
Publication Website: http://www.snoho.com/
Parent Company: Mach Publishing
Publisher Name: Becky Reed
Publisher Email: becky@snoho.com
Editor Name: Michael Whitney
Editor Email: michael@snoho.com
Advertising Executive Name: Becky Reed
Advertising Executive Email: becky@snoho.com
Delivery Methods: Mail`Newsstand
Year Established: 1892
Published Days: Wed
Avg. Paid Circ.: 8500
Avg. Free Circ.: 8000
Audit Company: Sworn/Estimate/Non-Audited

SPOKANE

SPOKANE JOURNAL OF BUSINESS

Street Address: 429 E. Third Ave.
City: Spokane
State: WA
ZIP Code: 99202-1414
General Phone: (509) 456-5257
General Email: jenniferz@spokanejournal.com
Publication Website: https://www.spokanejournal.com/
Parent Company: Northwest Business Press Inc.
Publisher Name: Paul Read
Publisher Email: publisher@spokanejournal.com
Publisher Phone: (509) 344-1262
Editor Name: Linn Parish
Editor Email: linnp@spokanejournal.com
Editor Phone: (509) 344-1265
Advertising Executive Name: Jennifer Zurlini
Advertising Executive Email: jenniferz@spokanejournal.com
Advertising Executive Phone: (509) 344-1279
Delivery Methods: Mail`Newsstand
Year Established: 1986
Published Days: Thur
Published Other: Biweekly
Avg. Paid Circ.: 5999
Avg. Free Circ.: 5232
Audit Company: CVC

Community Newspapers in the U.S.

SPOKANE VALLEY

SPOKANE VALLEY NEWS HERALD

Street Address: 1212 N Argonne Rd
City: Spokane Valley
State: WA
ZIP Code: 99212-2799
General Phone: (509) 924-2440
General Email: vnh@onemain.com
Publication Website: https://www.spokanevalleyonline.com/
Parent Company: Free Press Publishing Inc.
Advertising Executive Name: DeeAnn Gibb
Advertising Executive Email: vnh@onemain.com
Advertising Executive Phone: (509) 235-6184
Delivery Methods: Mail
Own Printing Facility?: Y
Published Days: Fri
Avg. Paid Circ.: 5500
Audit Company: Sworn/Estimate/Non-Audited

STANWOOD

STANWOOD CAMANO NEWS

Street Address: 9005 271st St NW
City: Stanwood
State: WA
ZIP Code: 98292
General Phone: (360) 629-2155
General Email: newsroom@scnews.com
Publication Website: https://www.goskagit.com/
Parent Company: Adams Publishing Group
Publisher Name: Kathy Boyd
Publisher Email: kboyd@scnews.com
Publisher Phone: (360) 629-2155, ext : 2217
Editor Name: Kathy Boyd
Editor Email: kboyd@scnews.com
Editor Phone: (360) 629-2155, ext : 2217
Advertising Executive Name: Jenny Baehm
Advertising Executive Email: jbaehm@scnews.com
Advertising Executive Phone: (360) 629-2155, ext : 2134
Year Established: 1895
Published Days: Tues
Avg. Paid Circ.: 2247
Audit Company: AAM

STEVENSON

SKAMANIA COUNTY PIONEER

Street Address: 74 SW Russell Avenue
City: Stevenson
State: WA
ZIP Code: 98648
General Phone: (509) 427-8444
General Email: scpioneerads@gorge.net
Publication Website: https://web.skamania.org/Newspaper/Skamania-County-Pioneer-688
Parent Company: DeVaul Publishing, Inc
Publisher Name: Frank DeVaul
Editor Name: Philip Watness
Editor Phone: (509) 427-8444
Delivery Methods: Mail`Newsstand
Year Established: 1898
Own Printing Facility?: Y
Commercial printers?: Y
Published Days: Wed
Avg. Paid Circ.: 2600
Audit Company: Sworn/Estimate/Non-Audited

TACOMA

SOUTH SOUND BUSINESS

Street Address: 2112 North 30th St
City: Tacoma
State: WA
ZIP Code: 98403
General Phone: (253) 588-5340
General Email: aubrey@premiermedia.net
Publication Website: https://southsoundbiz.com/
Parent Company: Premier Media Group.
Editor Name: Shelby Rowe Moyer
Editor Email: shelby@premiermedia.net
Advertising Executive Name: Lander Martinson
Advertising Executive Email: lander@premiermedia.net
Advertising Executive Phone: (253) 588-5340
Delivery Methods: Mail
Year Established: 1985
Published Days: Mthly
Avg. Paid Circ.: 954
Avg. Free Circ.: 6127
Audit Company: CVC

TENINO

THE TENINO INDEPENDENT

Street Address: 297 Sussex Ave W
City: Tenino
State: WA
ZIP Code: 98589-9360
General Phone: (360) 264-2500
General Email: independent@devaulpublishing.com
Publication Website: https://devaulpublishing.com/Tenino%20Rochester/index.html
Parent Company: DeVaul Publishing, Inc
Editor Name: Dan Fisher
Editor Email: independent@devaulpublishing.com
Advertising Executive Email: reception@devaulpublishing.com
Delivery Methods: Mail`Newsstand`Racks
Year Established: 1922
Own Printing Facility?: N
Commercial printers?: N
Mechanical specifications: Type page 10 1/2 x 16; E - 5 cols, 1 5/6, 1/6 between; A - 5 cols, 1 5/6, 1/6 between; C - 5 cols, 1 5/6, 1/6 between.
Published Days: Wed
Avg. Paid Circ.: 1200
Audit Company: Sworn/Estimate/Non-Audited

TWISP

METHOW VALLEY NEWS

Street Address: 502 Glover St S
City: Twisp
State: WA
ZIP Code: 98856-5818
General Phone: (509) 997-7011
General Email: advertising@methowvalleynews.com
Publication Website: https://methowvalleynews.com/
Parent Company: MVN Publishing LLC
Publisher Name: Don Nelson
Editor Name: Don Nelson
Editor Email: editor@methowvalleynews.com
Advertising Executive Name: Sheila Ward
Advertising Executive Email: sheila@methowvalleynews.com
Delivery Methods: Mail`Newsstand
Year Established: 1903
Commercial printers?: Y
Mechanical specifications: Type page 12 x 21; E - 6 cols, 2, 1/4 between; A - 6 cols, 2, 1/4 between; C - 6 cols, 2, 1/4 between.
Published Days: Wed
Avg. Paid Circ.: 3000
Avg. Free Circ.: 35
Audit Company: Sworn/Estimate/Non-Audited

UNIVERSITY PLACE

TACOMA WEEKLY

Street Address: 6812 27th St. West
City: University Place
State: WA
ZIP Code: 98466
General Phone: (253) 922-5317
General Email: lisa@tacomaweekly.com
Publication Website: https://tacomaweekly.com/
Parent Company: Pierce County Community Newspaper Group
Advertising Executive Name: John Weymer
Advertising Executive Email: jweymer@tacomaweekly.com
Delivery Methods: Mail`Newsstand`Racks
Year Established: 1986
Published Days: Thur
Audit Company: Sworn/Estimate/Non-Audited

WAITSBURG

THE TIMES

Street Address: PO Box 97
City: Waitsburg
State: WA
ZIP Code: 99361-0097
General Phone: (509) 337-6631
General Email: advertising@waitsburgtimes.com
Publication Website: https://www.waitsburgtimes.com/
Parent Company: Gannett
Publisher Name: Lane Gwinn
Publisher Email: lane@waitsburgtimes.com
Publisher Phone: (206) 817-8794
Editor Name: Tracy Thompson
Editor Email: editor@waitsburgtimes.com
Editor Phone: (509) 540-5956
Advertising Executive Name: Teeny McMunn
Advertising Executive Email: advertising@waitsburgtimes.com
Advertising Executive Phone: (509) 386-5287
Delivery Methods: Mail`Racks
Year Established: 1877
Published Days: Thur
Audit Company: Sworn/Estimate/Non-Audited

WESTPORT

SOUTH BEACH BULLETIN

Street Address: 114 W Pacific Ave
City: Westport
State: WA
ZIP Code: 98595-1395
General Phone: (360) 268-0156
General Email: dames@soundpublishing.com
Publication Website: https://www.thedailyworld.com/life/south-beach-bulletin-board-16/
Parent Company: Sound Publishing, Inc.
Publisher Name: Michael Hrycko
Publisher Email: publisher@thedailyworld.com
Editor Name: Doug Barker
Editor Email: dbarker@thedailyworld.com
Advertising Executive Email: ads@thedailyworld.com
Delivery Methods: Racks
Year Established: 1993
Mechanical specifications: Standard Broadsheet
Published Days: Thur
Avg. Paid Circ.: 208
Avg. Free Circ.: 4243
Audit Company: AAM

WHITE SALMON

THE ENTERPRISE

Street Address: 220 E Jewett Blvd
City: White Salmon
State: WA
ZIP Code: 98672-3000
General Phone: (509) 493-2112
General Email: ebakke@whitesalmonenterprise.com
Publication Website: https://www.whitesalmonenterprise.com/
Parent Company: Gannett
Publisher Name: Elaine Bakke
Publisher Email: ebakke@whitesalmonenterprise.com
Publisher Phone: (509) 493-2112
Editor Name: Elaine Bakke
Editor Email: ebakke@whitesalmonenterprise.com
Editor Phone: (509) 493-2112
Advertising Executive Name: Janet Barnes
Advertising Executive Phone: (509) 493-2112
Delivery Methods: Mail`Newsstand
Year Established: 1903
Published Days: Thur
Audit Company: Sworn/Estimate/Non-Audited

WOODINVILLE

THE WOODINVILLE WEEKLY

Street Address: 16932 Wdnvl Red Rd NE
City: Woodinville
State: WA
ZIP Code: 98072-6980
General Phone: (425) 483-0606
General Email: sales@woodinville.com
Publication Website: http://www.nwnews.com/
Parent Company: Eastside Media Corp
Publisher Name: Eric LaFontaine
Editor Name: Bob Kirkpatrick
Editor Email: editor@woodinville.com
Advertising Executive Email: sales@woodinville.com
Delivery Methods: Mail`Racks
Year Established: 1976
Own Printing Facility?: N
Commercial printers?: N
Mechanical specifications: Type page 10 1/4 x 16; 6 cols, 1 1/2, 1/4 between
Published Days: Mon
Avg. Free Circ.: 17700
Audit Company: Sworn/Estimate/Non-Audited

YAKIMA

YAKIMA VALLEY BUSINESS TIMES

Street Address: 416 S 3rd St
City: Yakima
State: WA
ZIP Code: 98901-2834
General Phone: (509) 457-4886
General Email: sales@yvpub.com
Publication Website: https://www.yvpub.com/
Parent Company: Yakima Valley Newspapers LLC
Advertising Executive Email: sales@yvpub.com
Delivery Methods: Mail`Racks
Year Established: 1997
Published Days: Fri
Audit Company: Sworn/Estimate/Non-Audited

YELM

NISQUALLY VALLEY NEWS

Street Address: 106 Plaza Dr SE
City: Yelm
State: WA
ZIP Code: 98597-8841
General Phone: (360) 458-2681
General Email: advertise@yelmonline.com
Publication Website: http://www.yelmonline.com/
Parent Company: Lafromboise Communications, Inc.
Publisher Name: Kim Proffit

Publisher Email: kproffit@yelmonline.com
Editor Name: Eric Rosane
Editor Email: erosane@yelmonline.com
Editor Phone: (360) 960-1503
Advertising Executive Name: Brad Brewer
Advertising Executive Email: bbrewer@yelmonline.com
Advertising Executive Phone: (360) 888-0626
Delivery Methods: Mail`Newsstand`Racks
Year Established: 1922
Own Printing Facility?: Y
Mechanical specifications: Type page 11 3/5 x ; E - 6 cols, 2, between; A - 6 cols, 3 3/4, between; C - 8 cols, 1 1/3, between.
Published Days: Fri
Avg. Paid Circ.: 4000
Audit Company: Sworn/Estimate/Non-Audited

WISCONSIN

204 MORAVIAN VALLEY RD., SUITE F

WAUNAKEE TRIBUNE

Street Address: 105 South St
City: 204 Moravian Valley Rd., Suite F
State: WI
ZIP Code: 53597-1343
General Phone: (608) 849-5227
General Email: dmcguigan@hngnews.com
Publication Website: http://www.hngnews.com/waunakee_tribune/
Parent Company: Adams Publishing Group
Editor Name: Roberta Baumann
Editor Email: tribnews@hngnews.com
Editor Phone: (608) 729-3697
Advertising Executive Name: Dan McGuigan
Advertising Executive Email: dmcguigan@hngnews.com
Advertising Executive Phone: (608) 467-1945
Delivery Methods: Mail`Newsstand`Racks
Year Established: 1920
Own Printing Facility?: Y
Commercial printers?: Y
Published Days: Thur
Avg. Paid Circ.: 3550
Audit Company: Sworn/Estimate/Non-Audited

AMERY

AMERY FREE PRESS

Street Address: 215 Keller Ave. S.
City: Amery
State: WI
ZIP Code: 54001
General Phone: 715-268-8101
Publication Website: www.theameryfreepress.com
Publisher Name: Tom Stangl
Publisher Email: tstangl@theameryfreepress.com
Publisher Phone: 715-268-8101
Editor Name: April Ziemer
Editor Email: editor@theameryfreepress.com
Editor Phone: 715-268-8101
Advertising Executive Name: Pam Humpal
Advertising Executive Email: phumpal@theameryfreepress.com
Advertising Executive Phone: 715-268-8101
Delivery Methods: Mail`Newsstand
Year Established: 1895
Mechanical specifications: Type page 16 1/2 x 23.
Published Days: Tues
Avg. Paid Circ.: 5000
Audit Company: Sworn/Estimate/Non-Audited

APPLETON

INSIGHT ON BUSINESS

Street Address: 400 N. Richmond St.
City: Appleton
State: WI
ZIP Code: 54911
General Phone: (920) 882-0491
General Email: wgilbert@insightonbusiness.com
Publication Website: https://insightonbusiness.com/
Parent Company: Insight Publications LLC
Publisher Name: Brian Rasmussen
Publisher Email: brasmussen@insightonbusiness.com
Publisher Phone: (920) 882-0491
Editor Name: MaryBeth Matzek
Editor Email: dverhagen@insightonbusiness.com
Editor Phone: (920) 560-3783
Advertising Executive Name: Diane Verhagen
Advertising Executive Email: dverhagen@insightonbusiness.com
Advertising Executive Phone: (920) 560-3784
Year Established: 2008
Published Days: Mthly
Avg. Paid Circ.: 1
Avg. Free Circ.: 11231
Audit Company: CVC

ASHLAND

BAYFIELD COUNTY JOURNAL

Street Address: 122 3rd St W
City: Ashland
State: WI
ZIP Code: 54806
General Phone: (715) 682-2313
General Email: pressclass@ashlanddailypress.net
Publication Website: https://www.apg-wi.com/bayfield_county_journal/
Published Days: Thur
Audit Company: Sworn/Estimate/Non-Audited

ASHLAND

THE DAILY PRESS: COUNTY JOURNAL

Street Address: 122 3rd St W
City: Ashland
State: WI
ZIP Code: 54806
General Phone: (715) 682-2313
General Email: ar@adamspg.com
Publication Website: https://www.apg-wi.com/ashland_daily_press/
Publisher Name: Jim Moran
Publisher Email: jmoran@ashlanddailypress.net
Publisher Phone: (715) 718-6401
Editor Name: Pete Wasson
Editor Email: pwasson@ashlanddailypress.net
Editor Phone: (715) 718-6241
Advertising Executive Name: Teri Hoffman
Advertising Executive Email: thoffman@ashlanddailypress.net
Advertising Executive Phone: (906) 364-9256
Delivery Methods: Mail
Mechanical specifications: Type page 13 x 21 1/2; E - 6 cols, 2 1/16, 1/8 between; A - 6 cols, 2 1/16, 1/8 between; C - 6 cols, 2 1/16, 1/8 between.
Published Days: Thur
Avg. Paid Circ.: 3950
Avg. Free Circ.: 25
Audit Company: Sworn/Estimate/Non-Audited

BALDWIN

THE BALDWIN BULLETIN

Street Address: 805 MAIN ST
City: Baldwin
State: WI
ZIP Code: 54002
General Phone: (715) 684-2484
General Email: editor@baldwin-bulletin.com
Publication Website: https://www.baldwin-bulletin.com/
Parent Company: Tom and Peter Hawley
Publisher Name: Tom Stangl
Publisher Email: tstangl@theameryfreepress.com
Publisher Phone: (715) 268-8101
Editor Name: Jason Schulte
Editor Email: editor@baldwin-bulletin.com
Editor Phone: (715) 684-2484
Delivery Methods: Mail`Newsstand
Year Established: 1873
Own Printing Facility?: Y
Published Days: Tues
Avg. Paid Circ.: 2050
Audit Company: Sworn/Estimate/Non-Audited

BARRON

BARRON NEWS-SHIELD

Street Address: 219 E La Salle Ave
City: Barron
State: WI
ZIP Code: 54812
General Phone: (715) 537-3117
General Email: newsshield@chibardun.net
Publication Website: https://www.news-shield.com/
Publisher Name: Mark Bell
Publisher Email: sports.bns@mosaictelecom.net
Editor Name: Robert Zientara
Editor Email: editor.barron@chibardun.net
Advertising Executive Name: Mary Goetsch
Advertising Executive Email: ads.newsshield@chibardun.net
Delivery Methods: Mail`Newsstand`Racks
Published Days: Wed
Avg. Paid Circ.: 4250
Audit Company: Sworn/Estimate/Non-Audited

BERLIN

BERLIN JOURNAL

Street Address: 301 June St
City: Berlin
State: WI
ZIP Code: 54923
General Phone: (920) 361-1515
General Email: ads@theberlinjournal.com
Publication Website: https://theberlinjournal.com/
Parent Company: Berlin Journal Company Inc
Advertising Executive Email: ads@theberlinjournal.com
Delivery Methods: Mail
Year Established: 1870
Own Printing Facility?: Y
Commercial printers?: Y
Mechanical specifications: Type page 10 x 16.
Published Days: Thur
Avg. Paid Circ.: 3500
Audit Company: Sworn/Estimate/Non-Audited
Note: The Billboard is a shopper and "Discover US" is a visitor's guide.

BERLIN

GREEN LAKE REPORTER

Street Address: 301 June St
City: Berlin
State: WI
ZIP Code: 54923
General Phone: (920) 361-1515
General Email: ads@theberlinjournal.com
Publication Website: https://theberlinjournal.com/
Parent Company: Berlin Journal Company Inc
Advertising Executive Email: ads@theberlinjournal.com
Delivery Methods: Mail
Year Established: 1870
Mechanical specifications: Type page 10 x 16.
Published Days: Thur
Avg. Paid Circ.: 3500
Audit Company: Sworn/Estimate/Non-Audited
Note: The Billboard is a shopper and "Discover US" is a visitor's guide.

BERLIN

MARKESAN REGIONAL REPORTER

Street Address: 301 June St
City: Berlin
State: WI
ZIP Code: 54923
General Phone: (920) 361-1515
General Email: ads@theberlinjournal.com
Publication Website: https://theberlinjournal.com/
Parent Company: Berlin Journal Company Inc
Advertising Executive Email: ads@theberlinjournal.com
Delivery Methods: Mail
Year Established: 1870
Mechanical specifications: Type page 10 x 16.
Published Days: Thur
Avg. Paid Circ.: 3500
Audit Company: Sworn/Estimate/Non-Audited
Note: The Billboard is a shopper and "Discover US" is a visitor's guide.

BERLIN

OMRO HERALD

Street Address: 301 June St
City: Berlin
State: WI
ZIP Code: 54923
General Phone: (920) 361-1515
General Email: ads@theberlinjournal.com
Publication Website: https://theberlinjournal.com/
Parent Company: Berlin Journal Company Inc
Advertising Executive Email: ads@theberlinjournal.com
Delivery Methods: Mail
Year Established: 1870
Mechanical specifications: Type page 10 x 16.
Published Days: Thur
Avg. Paid Circ.: 3500
Audit Company: Sworn/Estimate/Non-Audited
Note: The Billboard is a shopper and "Discover US" is a visitor's guide.

BERLIN

PRINCETON TIMES-REPUBLIC

Street Address: 301 June St
City: Berlin
State: WI
ZIP Code: 54923
General Phone: (920) 361-1515
General Email: ads@theberlinjournal.com
Publication Website: https://theberlinjournal.com/
Parent Company: Berlin Journal Company Inc
Advertising Executive Email: ads@theberlinjournal.com
Delivery Methods: Mail

Community Newspapers in the U.S.

Year Established: 1870
Mechanical specifications: Type page 10 x 16.
Published Days: Thur
Avg. Paid Circ.: 3500
Audit Company: Sworn/Estimate/Non-Audited
Note: The Billboard is a shopper and "Discover US" is a visitor's guide.

BERLIN

THE FOX LAKE REPRESENTATIVE

Street Address: 301 June St
City: Berlin
State: WI
ZIP Code: 54923
General Phone: (920) 361-1515
General Email: ads@theberlinjournal.com
Publication Website: https://theberlinjournal.com/
Parent Company: Berlin Journal Company Inc
Advertising Executive Email: ads@theberlinjournal.com
Delivery Methods: Mail
Year Established: 1870
Mechanical specifications: Type page 10 x 16.
Published Days: Thur
Avg. Paid Circ.: 3500
Audit Company: Sworn/Estimate/Non-Audited
Note: The Billboard is a shopper and "Discover US" is a visitor's guide.

BLOOMER

BLOOMER ADVANCE

Street Address: 1210 15th Ave
City: Bloomer
State: WI
ZIP Code: 54724
General Phone: (715) 568-3100
General Email: badvance@bloomer.net
Publication Website: https://www.bloomeradvance.com/
Parent Company: Jim Bell
Publisher Name: Barry Hoff
Editor Name: Barry Hoff
Delivery Methods: Mail`Newsstand`Racks
Year Established: 1886
Published Days: Wed
Avg. Paid Circ.: 2310
Avg. Free Circ.: 29
Audit Company: Sworn/Estimate/Non-Audited

BOSCOBEL

THE BOSCOBEL DIAL

Street Address: 901 Wisconsin Ave
City: Boscobel
State: WI
ZIP Code: 53805
General Phone: (608) 375-4458
General Email: dialads@boscobeldial.net
Publication Website: https://www.swnews4u.com/contact-us/boscobel-dial/
Parent Company: Morris Multimedia, Inc.
Editor Name: David Krier
Editor Email: dialeditor@boscobeldial.net
Advertising Executive Name: Lacy Bussan
Advertising Executive Email: advertising@boscobeldial.net
Delivery Methods: Mail`Newsstand`Racks
Year Established: 1872
Published Days: Thur
Avg. Paid Circ.: 5100
Audit Company: Sworn/Estimate/Non-Audited

BRILLION

THE BRILLION NEWS

Street Address: 425 W Ryan St
City: Brillion
State: WI
ZIP Code: 54110
General Phone: (920) 756-2222
General Email: kris@zanderpressinc.com
Publication Website: https://www.thebrillionnews.com/
Parent Company: Zander Press Inc.
Editor Name: David Nordby
Advertising Executive Name: Kris Bastian
Advertising Executive Email: kris@zanderpressinc.com
Delivery Methods: Mail`Newsstand
Year Established: 1894
Commercial printers?: Y
Published Days: Thur
Avg. Paid Circ.: 2100
Avg. Free Circ.: 5
Audit Company: Sworn/Estimate/Non-Audited

BRODHEAD

THE INDEPENDENT REGISTER

Street Address: 917 W. Exchange St
City: Brodhead
State: WI
ZIP Code: 53520
General Phone: (608) 897-2193
General Email: ads2@indreg.com
Publication Website: http://indreg.com/
Editor Name: Tony Carton
Editor Email: scoopshopper@rvpublishing.com
Advertising Executive Name: Jim Bruce
Advertising Executive Email: ads2@indreg.com
Delivery Methods: Mail`Newsstand
Year Established: 1860
Own Printing Facility?: Y
Commercial printers?: Y
Mechanical specifications: Type page 9 7/8 x 16; E - 5 cols, 1 5/6, 1/6 between; A - 5 cols, 1 5/6, 1/6 between; C - 5 cols, 1 5/6, 1/6 between.
Published Days: Thur
Avg. Free Circ.: 5166
Audit Company: Sworn/Estimate/Non-Audited

BROWN DEER

GERMANTOWN EXPRESS NEWS

Street Address: 8990 N 51st St
City: Brown Deer
State: WI
ZIP Code: 53223
General Phone: (262) 238-6397
General Email: info@discoverhometown.com
Publication Website: https://discoverhometown.com/category/newspaper-archive/germantown-newspaper-archive
Parent Company: Hometown News Group
Editor Name: Thomas McKillen
Editor Email: thomasj@discoverhometown.com
Advertising Executive Name: Kathy Hans
Advertising Executive Email: khans@discoverhometown.com
Delivery Methods: Mail`Racks
Year Established: 1994
Published Days: Sat
Avg. Free Circ.: 11006
Audit Company: VAC

BROWN DEER

HARTFORD EXPRESS NEWS

Street Address: 8990 N 51st St
City: Brown Deer
State: WI
ZIP Code: 53223
General Phone: (262) 238-6397
General Email: info@discoverhometown.com
Publication Website: https://discoverhometown.com/category/hartford
Parent Company: Hometown Publications, Inc.
Editor Name: Thomas McKillen
Editor Email: thomasj@discoverhometown.com
Advertising Executive Name: Kathy Hans
Advertising Executive Email: khans@discoverhometown.com
Delivery Methods: Mail`Racks
Year Established: 1994
Published Days: Thur`Sat
Avg. Free Circ.: 3909
Audit Company: VAC

BROWN DEER

JACKSON EXPRESS NEWS

Street Address: 8990 N 51st St
City: Brown Deer
State: WI
ZIP Code: 53223
General Phone: (262) 238-6397
General Email: info@discoverhometown.com
Publication Website: https://discoverhometown.com/category/jackson?filter_by=popular
Parent Company: Hometown Publications, Inc.
Editor Name: Thomas McKillen
Editor Email: thomasj@discoverhometown.com
Advertising Executive Name: Kathy Hans
Advertising Executive Email: khans@discoverhometown.com
Delivery Methods: Mail`Racks
Year Established: 1994
Published Days: Thur`Sat
Avg. Free Circ.: 4878
Audit Company: Sworn/Estimate/Non-Audited

BROWN DEER

MENOMONEE FALLS EXPRESS NEWS

Street Address: 8990 N 51st St
City: Brown Deer
State: WI
ZIP Code: 53223
General Phone: (262) 238-6397
General Email: info@discoverhometown.com
Publication Website: https://discoverhometown.com/category/menomonee-falls
Parent Company: Hometown Publications, Inc.
Editor Name: Thomas McKillen
Editor Email: thomasj@discoverhometown.com
Advertising Executive Name: Kathy Hans
Advertising Executive Email: khans@discoverhometown.com
Delivery Methods: Mail`Racks
Year Established: 1994
Published Days: Sat
Avg. Free Circ.: 12496
Audit Company: VAC

BROWN DEER

MILWAUKEE EXPRESS NEWS

Street Address: 8990 N 51st St
City: Brown Deer
State: WI
ZIP Code: 53223
General Phone: (262) 238-6397
General Email: info@discoverhometown.com
Publication Website: https://discoverhometown.com/category/newspaper-archive/milwaukee-west-news
Parent Company: Hometown Publications, Inc.
Editor Name: Thomas McKillen
Editor Email: thomasj@discoverhometown.com
Advertising Executive Name: Kathy Hans
Advertising Executive Email: khans@discoverhometown.com
Delivery Methods: Mail`Racks
Year Established: 1994
Published Days: Thur`Sat
Avg. Free Circ.: 4878
Audit Company: Sworn/Estimate/Non-Audited

BROWN DEER

SLINGER EXPRESS NEWS

Street Address: 8990 N 51st St
City: Brown Deer
State: WI
ZIP Code: 53223
General Phone: (262) 238-6397
General Email: info@discoverhometown.com
Publication Website: https://discoverhometown.com/category/slinger
Parent Company: Hometown Publications, Inc.
Editor Name: Thomas McKillen
Editor Email: thomasj@discoverhometown.com
Advertising Executive Name: Kathy Hans
Advertising Executive Email: khans@discoverhometown.com
Delivery Methods: Mail`Racks
Year Established: 1994
Published Days: Thur`Sat
Avg. Free Circ.: 3909
Audit Company: VAC

BROWN DEER

SUSSEX EXPRESS NEWS

Street Address: 8990 N 51st St
City: Brown Deer
State: WI
ZIP Code: 53223
General Phone: (262) 238-6397
General Email: info@discoverhometown.com
Publication Website: https://discoverhometown.com/category/newspaper-archive/sussex-newspaper-archive
Parent Company: Hometown Publications, Inc.
Editor Name: Thomas McKillen
Editor Email: thomasj@discoverhometown.com
Advertising Executive Name: Kathy Hans
Advertising Executive Email: khans@discoverhometown.com
Delivery Methods: Mail`Racks
Year Established: 1994
Published Days: Sat
Avg. Free Circ.: 12496
Audit Company: VAC

BROWN DEER

WAUWATOSA EXPRESS NEWS

Street Address: 8990 N 51st St
City: Brown Deer
State: WI
ZIP Code: 53223
General Phone: (262) 238-6397
General Email: info@discoverhometown.com
Publication Website: https://discoverhometown.com/category/newspaper-archive/wauwatosa-news
Parent Company: Hometown Publications, Inc.
Editor Name: Thomas McKillen
Editor Email: thomasj@discoverhometown.com
Advertising Executive Name: Kathy Hans

BROWN DEER

WEST ALLIS EXPRESS NEWS

Street Address: 8990 N 51st St
City: Brown Deer
State: WI
ZIP Code: 53223
General Phone: (262) 238-6397
General Email: info@discoverhometown.com
Publication Website: https://discoverhometown.com/category/newspaper-archive/west-allis-news
Parent Company: Hometown Publications, Inc.
Editor Name: Thomas McKillen
Editor Email: thomasj@discoverhometown.com
Advertising Executive Name: Kathy Hans
Advertising Executive Email: khans@discoverhometown.com
Delivery Methods: Mail`Racks
Year Established: 1994
Published Days: Thur`Sat
Avg. Free Circ.: 4878
Audit Company: Sworn/Estimate/Non-Audited

BROWN DEER

WEST BEND EXPRESS NEWS

Street Address: 8990 N 51st St
City: Brown Deer
State: WI
ZIP Code: 53223
General Phone: (262) 238-6397
General Email: info@discoverhometown.com
Publication Website: https://discoverhometown.com/category/west-bend
Parent Company: Hometown Publications, Inc.
Editor Name: Thomas McKillen
Editor Email: thomasj@discoverhometown.com
Advertising Executive Name: Kathy Hans
Advertising Executive Email: khans@discoverhometown.com
Delivery Methods: Mail`Racks
Year Established: 1994
Published Days: Sat
Avg. Free Circ.: 4433
Audit Company: VAC

CAMPBELLSPORT

CAMPBELLSPORT NEWS

Street Address: 101 N Fond Du Lac Ave
City: Campbellsport
State: WI
ZIP Code: 53010
General Phone: (920) 533-8338
General Email: sales@thecampbellsportnews.com
Publication Website: https://www.thecampbellsportnews.com/
Parent Company: Wisconsin Free Press, Inc.
Publisher Name: Andrew Johnson
Publisher Email: johnson@dodgecountypionier.com
Publisher Phone: (920) 387-2211
Editor Name: Andrea Hansen Abler
Editor Email: editor@thecampbellsportnews.com
Editor Phone: (920) 533-8338
Advertising Executive Name: Kathy Marin-Kopping
Advertising Executive Email: sales@thecampbellsportnews.com
Advertising Executive Phone: (920) 533-8338
Delivery Methods: Mail`Newsstand
Year Established: 1906
Published Days: Thur
Avg. Paid Circ.: 2000
Avg. Free Circ.: 11
Audit Company: Sworn/Estimate/Non-Audited

CASHTON

THE CASHTON RECORD

Street Address: 713 Broadway St
City: Cashton
State: WI
ZIP Code: 54619
General Phone: (608) 654-7330
General Email: cashtonrecord@mwt.net
Publication Website: https://www.cashtonrecord.com/
Parent Company: Paul and Kim Fanning
Advertising Executive Phone: (608) 654-7330
Delivery Methods: Mail
Year Established: 1896
Mechanical specifications: Type page 10 x 15; E - 5 cols, 2, 1/6 between; A - 5 cols, 2, 1/6 between; C - 5 cols, 2, 1/6 between.
Published Days: Wed
Avg. Paid Circ.: 1600
Audit Company: Sworn/Estimate/Non-Audited

CHETEK

THE CHETEK ALERT

Street Address: 312 Knapp St
City: Chetek
State: WI
ZIP Code: 54728
General Phone: (715) 924-4118
General Email: alert@thechetekalert.com
Publication Website: https://www.chetekalert.com/
Parent Company: Jim Bell
Publisher Name: Jim Bell
Publisher Email: jim@thechetekalert.com
Editor Name: Jim Bell
Editor Email: jim@thechetekalert.com
Delivery Methods: Mail`Newsstand
Year Established: 1882
Own Printing Facility?: N
Published Days: Wed
Avg. Paid Circ.: 3000
Avg. Free Circ.: 20
Audit Company: Sworn/Estimate/Non-Audited

CHIPPEWA FALLS

THE DUNN COUNTY NEWS

Street Address: 321 Frenette Dr
City: Chippewa Falls
State: WI
ZIP Code: 54729-3372
General Phone: (715) 738-1619
General Email: paul.pehler@lee.net
Publication Website: https://chippewa.com/community/dunnconnect/
Publisher Name: Sean Burke
Publisher Email: sean.burke@lee.net
Publisher Phone: (608) 791-8237
Advertising Executive Name: Erin Brunke
Advertising Executive Email: erin.brunke@lee.net
Advertising Executive Phone: (715) 738-1615
Delivery Methods: Mail`Newsstand`Racks
Year Established: 1860
Own Printing Facility?: Y
Mechanical specifications: Type page 12 x 21 1/2; E - 6 cols, 2, between; A - 6 cols, 2, between.
Published Days: Wed`Sat
Avg. Paid Circ.: 2047

COLFAX

THE COLFAX MESSENGER

Street Address: 511 E Railroad Ave
City: Colfax
State: WI
ZIP Code: 54730
General Phone: (715) 962-3535
General Email: messenger@dewittmedia.com
Publication Website: https://www.dewittmedia.com/colfax-messenger/
Parent Company: DeWitt Media Inc.
Publisher Name: Carlton DeWitt
Publisher Email: publisher@dewittmedia.com
Publisher Phone: (715) 265-4646
Editor Name: Shawn DeWitt
Editor Email: ads@dewittmedia.com
Editor Phone: (715) 265-4646
Advertising Executive Name: Shawn DeWitt
Advertising Executive Email: ads@dewittmedia.com
Advertising Executive Phone: (715) 265-4646
Delivery Methods: Mail`Newsstand
Year Established: 1897
Published Days: Wed
Avg. Paid Circ.: 1100
Avg. Free Circ.: 15
Audit Company: Sworn/Estimate/Non-Audited

CORNELL

COURIER SENTINEL

Street Address: 121 Main St
City: Cornell
State: WI
ZIP Code: 54732-8386
General Phone: (715) 861-4414
General Email: cornellcourier@gmail.com
Publication Website: https://centralwinews.com/courier-sentinel
Parent Company: Trygg J. Hansen Publications Inc.
Advertising Executive Email: cornellcourier@gmail.com
Advertising Executive Phone: (715) 861-4414
Delivery Methods: Mail`Racks
Year Established: 1958
Own Printing Facility?: Y
Commercial printers?: Y
Mechanical specifications: Type page 13 x 21; E - 6 cols, 2 1/16, between; A - 6 cols, 2 1/16, between; C - 6 cols, 2 1/16, between.
Published Days: Thur
Avg. Paid Circ.: 3200
Avg. Free Circ.: 59
Audit Company: Sworn/Estimate/Non-Audited

CRANDON

FLORENCE MINING NEWS

Street Address: P.O. Box 79
City: Crandon
State: WI
ZIP Code: 54121
General Phone: (715) 528-3276
General Email: upnorth2@borderlandnet.net
Publication Website: https://www.florence-forestnews.com/
Parent Company: Northeast WI Publishing Inc.
Editor Name: Sarah Giddings
Editor Email: upnorth2@borderlandnet.net
Advertising Executive Name: Deb Simons
Advertising Executive Email: deb.simons@wildriversnews.com
Published Days: Thur
Audit Company: Sworn/Estimate/Non-Audited

CRANDON

THE FOREST REPUBLICAN

Street Address: 103 S Hazeldell Ave
City: Crandon
State: WI
ZIP Code: 54520
General Phone: (715) 478-3315
General Email: news@forestrepublican.com
Publication Website: https://www.florence-forestnews.com/
Parent Company: Northeast WI Publishing Inc.
Publisher Name: Deb Sivertsen
Editor Name: Sarah Giddings
Editor Email: upnorth2@borderlandnet.net
Advertising Executive Name: Deb Simons
Advertising Executive Email: deb.simons@wildriversnews.com
Delivery Methods: Mail`Newsstand`Carrier
Year Established: 1886
Published Days: Thur
Avg. Paid Circ.: 2500
Avg. Free Circ.: 50
Audit Company: Sworn/Estimate/Non-Audited

CUBA CITY

TRI-COUNTY PRESS

Street Address: 223 S Main St
City: Cuba City
State: WI
ZIP Code: 53807
General Phone: (608) 744-2107
General Email: jinge@tds.net
Publication Website: https://www.swnews4u.com/contact-us/tri-county-press/
Parent Company: Shaw Media
Publisher Name: John Ingebritsen
Publisher Email: jinge@tds.net
Editor Name: Dan Burke
Editor Email: tcpnews@yousq.net
Delivery Methods: Mail`Newsstand
Year Established: 1894
Mechanical specifications: Type page 11 x 17; E - 6 cols, 1 5/8, 3/16 between; A - 6 cols, 1 5/8, 3/16 between; C - 6 cols, 1 5/8, 3/16 between.
Published Days: Thur
Avg. Paid Circ.: 2667
Avg. Free Circ.: 17
Audit Company: Sworn/Estimate/Non-Audited

CUMBERLAND

CUMBERLAND ADVOCATE

Street Address: 1375 2nd Ave
City: Cumberland
State: WI
ZIP Code: 54829
General Phone: (715)822-4429
General Email: ads@cumberland-advocate.com
Publication Website: http://www.cumberland-advocate.com/
Parent Company: B&H Publishing, Inc.
Advertising Executive Name: Paul Bucher
Advertising Executive Email: ads@cumberland-advocate.com
Advertising Executive Phone: (715) 822-4469
Year Established: 1882
Published Days: Wed
Avg. Paid Circ.: 2550
Audit Company: Sworn/Estimate/Non-Audited

DARLINGTON

REPUBLICAN JOURNAL

Street Address: 316 Main St

Community Newspapers in the U.S.

City: Darlington
State: WI
ZIP Code: 53530
General Phone: (608) 776-4425
General Email: ads@myrjonline.com
Publication Website: https://www.swnews4u.com/contact-us/republican-journal/
Parent Company: Morris Multimedia, Inc.
Publisher Name: Brian Lund
Publisher Email: publisher@myrjonline.com
Editor Name: Kayla Barnes
Editor Email: editor@myrjonline.com
Advertising Executive Name: Adam Ploessl
Advertising Executive Email: ads@myrjonline.com
Delivery Methods: Mail`Racks
Year Established: 1861
Mechanical specifications: 10 5/8" x16 full
Published Days: Thur
Avg. Paid Circ.: 2907
Audit Company: Sworn/Estimate/Non-Audited

DENMARK

THE DENMARK NEWS

Street Address: 116 Main St
City: Denmark
State: WI
ZIP Code: 54208
General Phone: (920) 863-2700
General Email: jc@thedenmarknews.com
Publication Website: https://thedenmarknews.com/
Parent Company: Denmark Publications, LLC
Editor Name: J.C. Marquez
Delivery Methods: Mail`Racks
Year Established: 2009
Own Printing Facility?: Y
Mechanical specifications: Type page 11 1/2 x 21 1/2; E - 6 cols, 1 13/16, 1/8 between; A - 6 cols, 1 13/16, 1/8 between; C - 9 cols, 1 1/16, 1/8 between.
Published Days: Thur
Avg. Paid Circ.: 2900
Avg. Free Circ.: 43
Audit Company: Sworn/Estimate/Non-Audited

DODGEVILLE

THE DODGEVILLE CHRONICLE

Street Address: 106 W Merrimac St
City: Dodgeville
State: WI
ZIP Code: 53533
General Phone: (608) 935-2331
General Email: ad@thedodgevillechronicle.com
Publication Website: https://thedodgevillechronicle.com/
Publisher Name: Mike Reilly
Publisher Email: mreilly@thedodgevillechronicle.com
Publisher Phone: (608) 935-2331, ext : 26
Advertising Executive Name: Shelly Roh
Advertising Executive Email: ad@thedodgevillechronicle.com
Advertising Executive Phone: (608) 935-2331, ext : 20
Delivery Methods: Mail`Newsstand`Racks
Year Established: 1862
Published Days: Thur
Avg. Paid Circ.: 4700
Avg. Free Circ.: 75
Audit Company: Sworn/Estimate/Non-Audited

DURAND

THE COURIER-WEDGE

Street Address: 103 W Main St
City: Durand

State: WI
ZIP Code: 54736-1144
General Phone: (715) 672-4252
Publication Website: https://gmdmedia.net/courier-wedge
Parent Company: Conley Media LLC
Delivery Methods: Mail
Own Printing Facility?: Y
Commercial printers?: Y
Published Days: Thur
Avg. Paid Circ.: 4300
Avg. Free Circ.: 36
Audit Company: Sworn/Estimate/Non-Audited

EAGLE RIVER

THREE LAKES NEWS

Street Address: 425 W Mill St
City: Eagle River
State: WI
ZIP Code: 54521-8002
General Phone: (715) 479-4421
General Email: kurtk@vcnewsreview.com
Publication Website: https://vcnewsreview.com/Content/Default/Three-Lakes/-3/1211
Parent Company: DHI Media
Publisher Name: Kurt Krueger
Publisher Email: kurtk@vcnewsreview.com
Editor Name: Gary Ridderbusch
Editor Email: garyr@vcnewsreview.com
Advertising Executive Name: Jo Daniel
Advertising Executive Email: jod@vcnewsreview.com
Delivery Methods: Mail`Newsstand
Year Established: 1881
Own Printing Facility?: Y
Commercial printers?: Y
Published Days: Wed
Avg. Paid Circ.: 8000
Audit Company: Sworn/Estimate/Non-Audited

EAGLE RIVER

VILAS COUNTY NEWS-REVIEW

Street Address: 425 W Mill St
City: Eagle River
State: WI
ZIP Code: 54521-8002
General Phone: (715) 479-4421
General Email: kurtk@vcnewsreview.com
Publication Website: https://vcnewsreview.com/Content/Default/Three-Lakes/-3/1211
Parent Company: DHI Media
Publisher Name: Kurt Krueger
Publisher Email: kurtk@vcnewsreview.com
Editor Name: Gary Ridderbusch
Editor Email: garyr@vcnewsreview.com
Advertising Executive Name: Jo Daniel
Advertising Executive Email: jod@vcnewsreview.com
Delivery Methods: Mail`Newsstand
Year Established: 1881
Own Printing Facility?: Y
Commercial printers?: Y
Published Days: Wed
Avg. Paid Circ.: 8000
Audit Company: Sworn/Estimate/Non-Audited

EAU CLAIRE

THE COUNTRY TODAY

Street Address: 701 S Farwell St
City: Eau Claire
State: WI
ZIP Code: 54701
General Phone: (715) 833-9270
General Email: sue.bauer@ecpc.com
Publication Website: https://www.leadertelegram.com/country-today/
Parent Company: Adams Publishing Group
Publisher Name: Randy Rickman
Publisher Email: randy.rickman@ecpc.com

Publisher Phone: (715) 833-7429
Editor Name: Gary Johnson
Editor Email: gary.johnson@ecpc.com
Editor Phone: (715) 833-9211
Advertising Executive Name: Mary Brownell
Advertising Executive Email: mary.brownell@ecpc.com
Advertising Executive Phone: (715) 830-5876
Delivery Methods: Mail`Newsstand`Racks
Published Days: Wed
Avg. Paid Circ.: 25000
Avg. Free Circ.: 1124
Audit Company: Sworn/Estimate/Non-Audited

EDGERTON

EDGERTON REPORTER

Street Address: 21 N Henry St
City: Edgerton
State: WI
ZIP Code: 53534
General Phone: (608) 884-3367
General Email: info@edgertonreporter.com
Publication Website: http://www.edgertonreporter.com/
Publisher Name: Diane Everson
Publisher Email: publisher@edgertonreporter.com
Delivery Methods: Mail
Year Established: 1874
Own Printing Facility?: Y
Published Days: Wed
Avg. Paid Circ.: 3000
Avg. Free Circ.: 2122
Audit Company: Sworn/Estimate/Non-Audited

ELKHORN

JANESVILLE MESSENGER

Street Address: 220B Commerce Ct.
City: Elkhorn
State: WI
ZIP Code: 53121
General Phone: (262) 728-3424
General Email: ewood@communityshoppers.com
Publication Website: https://www.communityshoppers.com/circulation-info
Delivery Methods: Mail`Newsstand
Year Established: 1983
Mechanical specifications: Type page: 10.375 x 16; 7 col
Published Days: Wed`Sun
Avg. Free Circ.: 64640
Audit Company: CVC

ELKHORN

WALWORTH COUNTY SUNDAY

Street Address: 220B E. Commerce Ct.
City: Elkhorn
State: WI
ZIP Code: 53121
General Phone: (262) 728-3424
General Email: kbliss@gazetteextra.com
Publication Website: https://www.communityshoppers.com/walworth-county-sunday
Delivery Methods: Mail`Newsstand
Year Established: 1926
Mechanical specifications: Type page: 10.375 x 16; 7 col
Published Days: Sun
Avg. Free Circ.: 39009
Audit Company: CVC

FENNIMORE

FENNIMORE TIMES

Street Address: 1150 Lincoln Ave

City: Fennimore
State: WI
ZIP Code: 53809
General Phone: (608) 822-3912
General Email: fennimoretimes@tds.net
Publication Website: https://www.swnews4u.com/contact-us/fennimore-times/
Parent Company: Morris Multimedia, Inc.
Publisher Name: John Ingebritsen
Publisher Email: jinge@tds.net
Editor Name: Emily Schendel
Editor Email: timeseditor@tds.net
Advertising Executive Name: Jodi White
Advertising Executive Email: jwhite@swnews4u.com
Delivery Methods: Mail`Newsstand
Year Established: 1889
Mechanical specifications: Type page 14 x 21 1/4; E - 6 cols, 2 1/8, betwoon; A - 6 cols, 2 1/8, between; C - 8 cols, 1 1/2, between.
Published Days: Thur
Avg. Paid Circ.: 1600
Avg. Free Circ.: 20
Audit Company: Sworn/Estimate/Non-Audited

FOND DU LAC

ACTION ADVERTISER

Street Address: N6637 Rolling Meadows Dr
City: Fond Du Lac
State: WI
ZIP Code: 54937-9471
General Phone: (920) 922-4600
General Email: news@actionadvertiser.com
Publication Website: https://www.fdlreporter.com/news/action-advertiser/
Delivery Methods: Carrier`Racks
Year Established: 1970
Mechanical specifications: Type page: 10.375 x 16; 6 col
Published Days: Wed
Avg. Free Circ.: 33752
Audit Company: Sworn/Estimate/Non-Audited

FOND DU LAC

ACTION SUNDAY

Street Address: N6637 Rolling Meadows Dr
City: Fond Du Lac
State: WI
ZIP Code: 54937-9471
General Phone: (920) 922-4600
General Email: jkramer2@gannett.com
Delivery Methods: Carrier`Racks
Year Established: 1988
Mechanical specifications: Type page: 10.375 x 16; 6 col
Published Days: Sun
Avg. Free Circ.: 41784
Audit Company: Sworn/Estimate/Non-Audited

FREDERIC

INTER-COUNTY LEADER

Street Address: 303 Wisconsin Ave N
City: Frederic
State: WI
ZIP Code: 54837
General Phone: (715) 327-4236
General Email: iccpaonline@centurytel.net
Publication Website: http://www.iccpaonline.com/
Parent Company: Inter-County Cooperative Publishing Association
Delivery Methods: Mail`Newsstand
Year Established: 1933
Own Printing Facility?: Y
Commercial printers?: Y
Published Days: Wed
Avg. Paid Circ.: 6870

Audit Company: Sworn/Estimate/Non-Audited

GAYS MILLS

CRAWFORD COUNTY INDEPENDENT & KICKAPOO SCOUT

Street Address: 320 Main St
City: Gays Mills
State: WI
ZIP Code: 54631
General Phone: (608) 735-4413
General Email: jinge@tds.net
Publication Website: https://www.swnews4u.com/contact-us/crawford-county-independent/
Parent Company: Morris Multimedia, Inc.
Publisher Name: John Ingebritsen
Publisher Email: jinge@tds.net
Editor Name: Charley Preusser
Editor Email: indnews@mwt.net
Published Days: Thur
Audit Company: Sworn/Estimate/Non-Audited

GLENWOOD CITY

TRIBUNE PRESS REPORTER

Street Address: 105 Misty Ct
City: Glenwood City
State: WI
ZIP Code: 54013
General Phone: (715) 265-4646
General Email: tribune@dewittmedia.com
Publication Website: https://www.dewittmedia.com/tribune-press-reporter/
Parent Company: DeWitt Media Inc.
Publisher Name: Carlton DeWitt
Publisher Email: publisher@dewittmedia.com
Publisher Phone: (715) 265-4646
Editor Name: Carlton DeWitt
Editor Phone: (715) 265-4646
Advertising Executive Name: Shawn DeWitt
Advertising Executive Email: ads@dewittmedia.com
Advertising Executive Phone: (715) 265-4646
Delivery Methods: Mail`Newsstand
Year Established: 1889
Published Days: Wed
Avg. Paid Circ.: 2785
Avg. Free Circ.: 37
Audit Company: Sworn/Estimate/Non-Audited

GRANTSBURG

BURNETT COUNTY SENTINEL

Street Address: 114 W Madison Ave
City: Grantsburg
State: WI
ZIP Code: 54840
General Phone: (715) 463-2341
General Email: editor@burnettcountysentinel.com
Publication Website: http://www.burnettcountysentinel.com/
Parent Company: Eugene Johnson
Publisher Name: Tom Stangl
Publisher Email: tstangl@theameryfreepress.com
Editor Email: tstangl@theameryfreepress.com
Delivery Methods: Mail`Racks
Year Established: 1875
Own Printing Facility?: Y
Commercial printers?: Y
Mechanical specifications: Type page 13 1/8 x 21 1/2; E - 6 cols, 2, between; A - 6 cols, 2, between; C - 6 cols, 2, between.
Published Days: Wed
Avg. Paid Circ.: 2425
Audit Company: Sworn/Estimate/Non-Audited

GREEN BAY

FARMERS ADVANCE

Street Address: 435 E. Walnut Street, PO Box 23430
City: Green Bay
State: WI
ZIP Code: 54305
General Phone: (800) 764-5635
General Email: erobinstine@gannett.com
Publication Website: https://www.farmersadvance.com/
Delivery Methods: Mail`Newsstand
Published Days: Wed
Avg. Paid Circ.: 12000
Audit Company: Sworn/Estimate/Non-Audited

HAYWARD

SAWYER COUNTY RECORD

Street Address: 15464 County Highway B
City: Hayward
State: WI
ZIP Code: 54843
General Phone: (715) 634-4881
General Email: news@sawyercountyrecord.net
Publication Website: https://www.apg-wi.com/sawyer_county_record/
Parent Company: Adams Publishing Group
Publisher Name: Mitchell Paul
Publisher Email: pmitchell@sawyercountyrecord.net
Publisher Phone: (715) 718-6445
Editor Name: Mitchell Paul
Editor Email: pmitchell@sawyercountyrecord.net
Editor Phone: (715) 718-6445
Advertising Executive Name: White Darrin
Advertising Executive Email: dwhite@sawyercountyrecord.net
Advertising Executive Phone: (715) 558-6657
Delivery Methods: Mail`Newsstand`Racks
Year Established: 1893
Own Printing Facility?: N
Commercial printers?: N
Mechanical specifications: Type page 11 1/16 x 21; E - 6 cols, 1 5/6, 1/8 between; A - 6 cols, 1 5/6, 1/8 between; C - 6 cols, 1 5/6, 1/8 between.
Published Days: Wed
Avg. Paid Circ.: 4000
Avg. Free Circ.: 44
Audit Company: Sworn/Estimate/Non-Audited

HILLSBORO

HILLSBORO SENTRY-ENTERPRISE

Street Address: 839 Water Ave
City: Hillsboro
State: WI
ZIP Code: 54634
General Phone: (608) 489-2264
General Email: office@hillsborose.com
Publication Website: https://www.morrismultimedia.com/publishing/
Parent Company: Evans Print Media Group
Editor Name: Nicolette Nauman
Editor Email: editor@hillsborose.com
Editor Phone: (608) 633-4642
Advertising Executive Name: Sue Feala
Advertising Executive Email: sue@hillsborose.com
Advertising Executive Phone: (608) 487-0151
Delivery Methods: Mail`Newsstand
Year Established: 1885
Own Printing Facility?: Y
Commercial printers?: Y
Mechanical specifications: Type page 11 x 16; E - 5 cols, 2, 1/4 between; A - 5 cols, 2, 1/4 between; C - 5 cols, 2, 1/4 between.
Published Days: Thur
Avg. Paid Circ.: 1694
Avg. Free Circ.: 108

Audit Company: Sworn/Estimate/Non-Audited

HURLEY

IRON COUNTY MINER

Street Address: 216 Copper St
City: Hurley
State: WI
ZIP Code: 54534
General Phone: (715) 561-3405
General Email: ironcountyminer@yahoo.com
Publication Website: http://ironcountyminer.com/
Delivery Methods: Mail`Newsstand
Year Established: 1884
Published Days: Thur
Avg. Paid Circ.: 2430
Avg. Free Circ.: 114
Audit Company: Sworn/Estimate/Non-Audited

KAUKAUNA

THE TIMES-VILLAGER

Street Address: 1900 Crooks Ave
City: Kaukauna
State: WI
ZIP Code: 54130
General Phone: (920) 759-2000
General Email: editor@timesvillager.com
Publication Website: http://wrightstownspirit.com/
Parent Company: News Publishing Inc.
Publisher Name: Dan Witte
Editor Name: Brian Roebke
Editor Email: editor@timesvillager.com
Advertising Executive Name: Kim Reynebeau
Advertising Executive Email: sales@timesvillager.com
Delivery Methods: Mail
Year Established: 1880
Own Printing Facility?: Y
Commercial printers?: N
Mechanical specifications: Type page 9 3/4 x 13 3/4; E - 4 cols, between; A - 4 cols, between; C - 8 cols, between.
Published Days: Wed`Sat
Avg. Paid Circ.: 5000
Avg. Free Circ.: 500
Audit Company: Sworn/Estimate/Non-Audited

KEWAUNEE

KEWAUNEE COUNTY STAR-NEWS

Street Address: 203 Ellis St
City: Kewaunee
State: WI
ZIP Code: 54216
General Phone: (920)388-3175
General Email: pharkema@gokewauneecounty.com
Publication Website: https://www.greenbaypressgazette.com/news/kewaunee-county-star-news/
Editor Name: Karl Ebert
Editor Email: karl.ebert@gannettwisconsin.com
Editor Phone: (920) 431-8302
Delivery Methods: Carrier
Year Established: 1859
Mechanical specifications: Type page 11 5/8 x 20 3/16; E - 6 cols, 1 13/16, 1/6 between; A - 6 cols, 1 13/16, 1/6 between; C - 9 cols, 1 1/16, 1/12 between.
Published Days: Sat
Avg. Free Circ.: 11060
Audit Company: Sworn/Estimate/Non-Audited

LA CROSSE

COULEE NEWS

Street Address: 401 3rd St N
City: La Crosse
State: WI
ZIP Code: 54601
General Phone: (608)782-9710
General Email: sean.burke@lee.net
Publication Website: https://lacrossetribune.com/community/couleecourier/
Publisher Name: Sean Burke
Publisher Email: sean.burke@lee.net
Publisher Phone: (608) 791-8237
Editor Name: Rusty Cunningham
Editor Email: rusty.cunningham@lee.net
Editor Phone: (608) 791-8285
Advertising Executive Name: Paul Pehler
Advertising Executive Email: paul.pehler@lee.net
Advertising Executive Phone: (608) 791-8300
Delivery Methods: Mail`Newsstand
Own Printing Facility?: Y
Commercial printers?: Y
Mechanical specifications: Type page 11 2/3 x 21 1/2; E - 6 cols, 1 1/4, 1/6 between; A - 6 cols, 1 1/4, 1/6 between; C - 6 cols, 1 1/4, 1/6 between.
Published Days: Thur
Avg. Paid Circ.: 1743
Avg. Free Circ.: 4
Audit Company: Sworn/Estimate/Non-Audited

LA CROSSE

HOUSTON COUNTY NEWS

Street Address: 401 3rd St N
City: La Crosse
State: WI
ZIP Code: 54601
General Phone: (608)782-9710
General Email: sean.burke@lee.net
Publication Website: https://www.winonadailynews.com/community/houstonconews/
Publisher Name: Sean Burke
Publisher Email: sean.burke@lee.net
Publisher Phone: (608) 791-8237
Editor Name: Rusty Cunningham
Editor Email: rusty.cunningham@lee.net
Editor Phone: (608) 791-8285
Advertising Executive Name: Paul Pehler
Advertising Executive Email: paul.pehler@lee.net
Advertising Executive Phone: (608) 791-8300
Delivery Methods: Mail`Newsstand
Year Established: 1968
Mechanical specifications: Type page 6 x 21 1/2; E - 3 cols, 3 1/4, 1/4 between; A - 3 cols, 3 1/4, 1/4 between.
Published Days: Thur
Avg. Paid Circ.: 1953
Avg. Free Circ.: 36
Audit Company: Sworn/Estimate/Non-Audited

LA CROSSE

ONALASKA HOLMEN COURIER-LIFE

Street Address: 401 3rd St N
City: La Crosse
State: WI
ZIP Code: 54601
General Phone: (608)782-9710
General Email: sean.burke@lee.net
Publication Website: https://lacrossetribune.com/
Publisher Name: Sean Burke
Publisher Email: sean.burke@lee.net
Publisher Phone: (608) 791-8237
Editor Name: Rusty Cunningham
Editor Email: rusty.cunningham@lee.net
Editor Phone: (608) 791-8285
Advertising Executive Name: Paul Pehler
Advertising Executive Email: paul.pehler@lee.net
Advertising Executive Phone: (608) 791-8300
Delivery Methods: Mail`Newsstand

Community Newspapers in the U.S.

Year Established: 2008
Own Printing Facility?: Y
Commercial printers?: Y
Mechanical specifications: Type page 11 5/8 x 21 1/2; E - 6 cols, 1/8 between; A - 6 cols, 1 5/6, 1/8 between; C - 9 cols, 1 15/16, 3/20 between.
Published Days: Fri
Avg. Paid Circ.: 3026
Audit Company: Sworn/Estimate/Non-Audited

LA CROSSE

THE WESTBY TIMES

Street Address: 401 N. Third Street
City: La Crosse
State: WI
ZIP Code: 54601
General Phone: (608) 634-4317
General Email: paul.pehler@lee.net
Publication Website: https://lacrossetribune.com/community/westbytimes/
Publisher Name: Sean Burke
Publisher Email: sean.burke@lee.net
Publisher Phone: (608) 791-8237
Editor Name: Rusty Cunningham
Editor Email: rusty.cunningham@lee.net
Editor Phone: (608) 791-8285
Advertising Executive Name: Paul Pehler
Advertising Executive Email: paul.pehler@lee.net
Advertising Executive Phone: (608) 791-8300
Delivery Methods: Mail`Racks
Mechanical specifications: Type page 15 3/4 x 21.
Published Days: Thur
Avg. Paid Circ.: 2000
Audit Company: Sworn/Estimate/Non-Audited

LADYSMITH

LADYSMITH NEWS

Street Address: 120 W 3rd St S
City: Ladysmith
State: WI
ZIP Code: 54848
General Phone: (715) 532-5591
General Email: editor@ladysmithnews.com
Publication Website: https://www.ladysmithnews.com/
Parent Company: Jim Bell
Publisher Name: Leslie Harmon
Publisher Email: manager@ladysmithnews.com
Editor Name: Luke Klink
Editor Email: editor@ladysmithnews.com
Advertising Executive Name: Brian Joles
Advertising Executive Email: adsales@ladysmithnews.com
Delivery Methods: Mail`Newsstand`Carrier`Racks
Year Established: 1895
Own Printing Facility?: Y
Commercial printers?: Y
Mechanical specifications: Type page 13 x 21 1/4; E - 6 cols, 2, 3/16 between; A - 6 cols, 2, 3/16 between; C - 6 cols, 2, 3/16 between.
Published Days: Thur
Avg. Paid Circ.: 5050
Audit Company: Sworn/Estimate/Non-Audited

LAKE GENEVA

LAKE GENEVA REGIONAL NEWS

Street Address: 315 Broad St
City: Lake Geneva
State: WI
ZIP Code: 53147
General Phone: (262) 248-4444
General Email: rireland@lakegenevanews.net
Publication Website: https://www.lakegenevanews.net/
Advertising Executive Phone: (262) 248-4444
Delivery Methods: Mail`Newsstand
Year Established: 1872
Own Printing Facility?: Y
Commercial printers?: Y
Mechanical specifications: Type page 11.125 x 19.75; E - 6 cols, 2 1/16, 1/8 between; A - 6 cols, 2 1/16, 1/8 between; C - 6 cols, 2 1/16, 1/8 between.
Published Days: Thur
Avg. Paid Circ.: 4000
Audit Company: Sworn/Estimate/Non-Audited

LAKE MILLS

LAKE MILLS LEADER

Street Address: 320 N Main St
City: Lake Mills
State: WI
ZIP Code: 53551
General Phone: (920) 648-2334
General Email: lakemillsleader@hngnews.com
Publication Website: http://www.hngnews.com/lake_mills_leader/
Parent Company: Adams Publishing Group
Editor Name: Sarah Weihert
Editor Email: leadereditor@hngnews.com
Editor Phone: (920) 297-2343
Delivery Methods: Mail`Newsstand`Racks
Year Established: 1878
Mechanical specifications: Type page 14 1/2 x 21; E - 6 cols, 2 1/16, 1/6 between; A - 6 cols, 2 1/16, 1/6 between; C - 6 cols, 2 1/16, 1/6 between.
Published Days: Thur
Avg. Paid Circ.: 2150
Audit Company: Sworn/Estimate/Non-Audited

LAKE MILLS

THE CAMBRIDGE NEWS & THE INDEPENDENT

Street Address: 320 N. Main St.
City: Lake Mills
State: WI
ZIP Code: 53551
General Phone: (608) 423-3213
General Email: cambridge.deerfield@hngnews.com
Publication Website: http://www.hngnews.com/cambridge_deerfield/
Parent Company: Hometown News Group
Editor Name: Karyn Saemann
Editor Email: cambridge.deerfield@hngnews.com
Editor Phone: (608) 423-6297
Advertising Executive Name: Mary Jo Currie
Advertising Executive Email: classifieds@hngnews.com
Advertising Executive Phone: (608) 478-2509
Delivery Methods: Mail`Racks
Year Established: 1894
Own Printing Facility?: Y
Mechanical specifications: Type page 6 x 21; E - 6 cols, 2 1/2, 1/6 between; A - 6 cols, 2 1/2, 1/6 between; C - 8 cols, 1 1/2, 1/6 between.
Published Days: Thur
Avg. Paid Circ.: 1443
Avg. Free Circ.: 17
Audit Company: Sworn/Estimate/Non-Audited

LAKE MILLS

THE WATERLOO/MARSHALL COURIER

Street Address: 320 N. Main St.
City: Lake Mills
State: WI
ZIP Code: 53551
General Phone: (920) 478-2188
General Email: wmcourier@hngnews.com
Publication Website: http://www.hngnews.com/waterloo_marshall/
Parent Company: Hometown News Group
Editor Name: Amber Gerber
Editor Email: agerber@hngnews.com
Editor Phone: (920) 478-2188
Advertising Executive Name: Mary Jo Currie
Advertising Executive Email: classifieds@hngnews.com
Advertising Executive Phone: (608) 478-2509
Delivery Methods: Mail`Newsstand`Racks
Year Established: 1871
Published Days: Thur
Avg. Paid Circ.: 1500
Audit Company: Sworn/Estimate/Non-Audited

LANCASTER

GRANT COUNTY HERALD INDEPENDENT

Street Address: Box 310
City: Lancaster
State: WI
ZIP Code: 53813
General Phone: (608) 723-2151
General Email: jinge@tds.net
Publication Website: http://www.swnews4u.com/
Parent Company: SWNew4u.com
Publisher Name: John Ingebritsen
Publisher Email: jinge@tds.net
Editor Name: David Timmerman
Editor Email: newseditor@tds.net
Advertising Executive Name: Kevin Kelly
Advertising Executive Email: kkads@tds.net
Delivery Methods: Mail`Newsstand
Year Established: 1843
Published Days: Thur
Avg. Paid Circ.: 3400
Audit Company: Sworn/Estimate/Non-Audited

LODI

POYNETTE PRESS

Street Address: 204 Moravian Valley Rd., Suite F
City: Lodi
State: WI
ZIP Code: 53555
General Phone: (606) 592-3261
General Email: lpedit@hngnews.com
Publication Website: http://www.lodienews.com/
Parent Company: Hometown News Group
Editor Name: Brian Sheridan
Editor Email: lpedit@hngnews.com
Editor Phone: (608) 729-3366
Delivery Methods: Mail`Newsstand`Racks
Year Established: 1896
Published Days: Thur
Avg. Paid Circ.: 2600
Audit Company: Sworn/Estimate/Non-Audited

LOYAL

THE TRIBUNE RECORD-GLEANER

Street Address: 318 N Main St
City: Loyal
State: WI
ZIP Code: 54446
General Phone: (715)255-8531
General Email: news@trgnews.com
Publication Website: https://centralwinews.com/tribune-record-gleaner
Parent Company: CW Media
Advertising Executive Email: classsub@tpprinting.com
Advertising Executive Phone: (715) 223-2342
Delivery Methods: Mail
Year Established: 1969
Published Days: Wed
Avg. Paid Circ.: 3100
Audit Company: Sworn/Estimate/Non-Audited

LOYAL

THE TRIBUNE-PHONOGRAPH

Street Address: 318 N Main St
City: Loyal
State: WI
ZIP Code: 54446
General Phone: (715) 223-2342
General Email: tp@tpprinting.com
Publication Website: https://www.centralwinews.com/tribune-phonograph
Parent Company: CW Media
Advertising Executive Email: classsub@tpprinting.com
Advertising Executive Phone: (715) 223-2342
Delivery Methods: Mail
Year Established: 1969
Published Days: Wed
Avg. Paid Circ.: 3100
Audit Company: Sworn/Estimate/Non-Audited

MADISON

THE CAPITAL TIMES

Street Address: 1901 Fish Hatchery Rd
City: Madison
State: WI
ZIP Code: 53713
General Phone: (608) 252-6400
General Email: cfrink@madison.com
Publication Website: http://host.madison.com/ct/
Publisher Name: Paul Fanlund
Publisher Email: pfanlund@madison.com
Publisher Phone: (608) 252-6210
Editor Name: Paul Fanlund
Editor Email: pfanlund@madison.com
Editor Phone: (608) 252-6210
Delivery Methods: Mail`Carrier`Racks
Year Established: 1917
Own Printing Facility?: Y
Published Days: Wed
Weekday Frequency: All day
Saturday Frequency: All day
Avg. Paid Circ.: 61000
Avg. Free Circ.: 8000
Audit Company: Sworn/Estimate/Non-Audited
Note: Joint owner with Lee Enterprises of Capital Newspapers

MADISON

THE CHEESE REPORTER

Street Address: 2810 Crossroads Dr
City: Madison
State: WI
ZIP Code: 53718
General Phone: (608)246-8430
General Email: info@cheesereporter.com
Publication Website: http://www.cheesereporter.com/
Publisher Name: Dick Groves
Publisher Email: dgroves@cheesereporter.com
Publisher Phone: (608) 316-3791
Editor Name: Dick Groves
Editor Email: dgroves@cheesereporter.com
Editor Phone: (608) 316-3791
Advertising Executive Name: Kevin Thome
Advertising Executive Email: marketing@cheesereporter.com
Advertising Executive Phone: (608) 316-3792
Published Days: Wed
Audit Company: Sworn/Estimate/Non-Audited

MADISON

THE MADISON TIMES

Street Address: 313 W Beltline Hwy
City: Madison
State: WI
ZIP Code: 53713
General Phone: (608)270-9470
General Email: news@madtimes.com
Publication Website: https://themadisontimes.themadent.com/
Publisher Name: Ernest Jones
Editor Name: Ernest Jones
Advertising Executive Email: sales@madtimes.com
Advertising Executive Phone: (608) 270-9470
Year Established: 1991
Published Days: Fri
Avg. Paid Circ.: 250
Avg. Free Circ.: 8750
Audit Company: Sworn/Estimate/Non-Audited

MAYVILLE

THE DODGE COUNTY PIONEER

Street Address: 126 Bridge St
City: Mayville
State: WI
ZIP Code: 53050
General Phone: (920) 387-2211
General Email: mayville@dodgecountypionier.com
Publication Website: http://www.dodgecountypionier.com/
Publisher Name: Andrew Johnson
Publisher Email: johnson@dodgecountypionier.com
Editor Name: Karen Rouse
Editor Email: mayville@dodgecountypionier.com
Delivery Methods: Mail
Year Established: 1892
Mechanical specifications: Type page 13 7/8 x 12 1/2; E - 8 cols, 1 2/3, 1/12 between; A - 8 cols, 1 2/3, 1/12 between; C - 8 cols, 1 2/3, 1/12 between.
Published Days: Thur
Avg. Paid Circ.: 3221
Audit Company: Sworn/Estimate/Non-Audited

MILTON

MILTON COURIER

Street Address: 513 Vernal Ave
City: Milton
State: WI
ZIP Code: 53563-1144
General Phone: (608) 868-2442
General Email: courierads@hngnews.com
Publication Website: http://www.hngnews.com/milton_courier/
Parent Company: Adams Publishing Group
Editor Name: Rebecca Kanable
Editor Email: couriernews@hngnews.com
Editor Phone: 608-208-1681
Delivery Methods: Mail`Newsstand
Year Established: 1878
Own Printing Facility?: Y
Mechanical specifications: 12 inch. x 21 inch.
Published Days: Thur
Avg. Paid Circ.: 2165
Avg. Free Circ.: 49
Audit Company: Sworn/Estimate/Non-Audited

MILWAUKEE

MILWAUKEE BUSINESS JOURNAL

Street Address: 825 N Jefferson St
City: Milwaukee
State: WI
ZIP Code: 53202
General Phone: (414) 278-7788
General Email: milwaukee@bizjournals.com
Publication Website: http://www.milwaukeebusinessjournal.com/
Parent Company: American City Business Journals
Publisher Name: Kira Lafond
Publisher Email: klafond@bizjournals.com
Publisher Phone: (414) 908-0584
Editor Name: Mark Kass
Editor Email: mkass@bizjournals.com
Editor Phone: (414) 908-0566
Advertising Executive Name: Steve Broas
Advertising Executive Email: sbroas@bizjournals.com
Advertising Executive Phone: (414) 908-0555
Delivery Methods: Mail`Newsstand`Racks
Year Established: 1995
Published Days: Fri
Avg. Paid Circ.: 413
Avg. Free Circ.: 11258
Audit Company: Sworn/Estimate/Non-Audited

MINOCQUA

LAKELAND TIMES

Street Address: 510 Chippewa St
City: Minocqua
State: WI
ZIP Code: 54548
General Phone: (715) 356-5236
General Email: accounting@lakelandtimes.com
Publication Website: http://www.lakelandtimes.com/
Parent Company: Lakeland Times
Publisher Name: Gregg Walker
Publisher Email: gwalker@lakelandtimes.com
Publisher Phone: (715) 356-5236
Editor Email: editor@lakelandtimes.com
Advertising Executive Name: Laura Larson
Advertising Executive Email: llarson@lakelandtimes.com
Advertising Executive Phone: (715) 356-5236
Delivery Methods: Mail`Racks
Year Established: 1891
Own Printing Facility?: Y
Mechanical specifications: Type page 10 1/2 x 16; E - 6 cols, 1 7/12, 1/6 between; A - 6 cols, 1 7/12, 1/6 between; C - 6 cols, 1 7/12, 1/6 between.
Published Days: Tues`Fri
Avg. Paid Circ.: 9873
Audit Company: Sworn/Estimate/Non-Audited

MONTELLO

THE MARQUETTE COUNTY TRIBUNE

Street Address: 120 Underwood Ave
City: Montello
State: WI
ZIP Code: 53949
General Phone: (608) 297-2424
General Email: marquettetribune@newspubinc.com
Publication Website: https://www.marquettecountytribune.com/
Parent Company: News Publishing, Co., Inc.
Delivery Methods: Mail`Newsstand
Own Printing Facility?: Y
Commercial printers?: Y
Mechanical specifications: Type page 10 x 16; E - 6 cols, 1.569, 1/8 between; A - 6 cols, 1.569, 1/8 between; C - 6 cols, 1.569, 1/8 between.
Published Days: Thur
Weekday Frequency: All day
Avg. Paid Circ.: 3203
Avg. Free Circ.: 12
Audit Company: Sworn/Estimate/Non-Audited

OCONTO

OCONTO COUNTY REPORTER

Street Address: PO Box 200
City: Oconto
State: WI
ZIP Code: 54153
General Phone: (920)834-4242
General Email: editorial@goocontocounty.com
Publication Website: http://greatnorthernconn.com/papers/oforest.html
Delivery Methods: Mail`Racks
Year Established: 1871
Own Printing Facility?: Y
Commercial printers?: N
Mechanical specifications: Type page 10 x 20; E - 6 cols, 1 1/2, between; A - 6 cols, 1 1/2, between; C - 6 cols, 1 1/2, between.
Published Days: Wed
Avg. Paid Circ.: 5000
Avg. Free Circ.: 50
Audit Company: Sworn/Estimate/Non-Audited

ONTARIO

THE COUNTY LINE

Street Address: 207 N Garden St
City: Ontario
State: WI
ZIP Code: 54651
General Phone: (608) 337-4232
General Email: sales@thecountyline.net
Publication Website: http://thecountyline.net/
Editor Email: opinion@thecountyline.net
Published Days: Thur
Audit Company: Sworn/Estimate/Non-Audited

OREGON

OREGON OBSERVER

Street Address: 156 N. Main St.
City: Oregon
State: WI
ZIP Code: 53575
General Phone: (608) 835-6677
General Email: ungeditor@wcinet.com
Publication Website: http://www.unifiednewsgroup.com/oregon_observer/
Parent Company: United News Group Publications
Publisher Name: Lee Borkowski
Publisher Email: lborkowski@wcinet.com
Editor Name: Jim Ferolie
Editor Email: ungeditor@wcinet.com
Advertising Executive Name: Kathy Neumeister
Advertising Executive Email: kathy.neumeister@wcinet.com
Delivery Methods: Mail`Racks
Year Established: 1880
Own Printing Facility?: Y
Mechanical specifications: Type page 10 5/8 x 16; E - 6 cols, 1 5/8, 1/8 between; A - 6 cols, 1 5/8, 1/8 between; C - 6 cols, 1 5/8, 1/8 between.
Published Days: Thur
Avg. Paid Circ.: 1987
Audit Company: Sworn/Estimate/Non-Audited

OSCEOLA

THE SUN

Street Address: 108 N Cascade St
City: Osceola
State: WI
ZIP Code: 54020
General Phone: (715) 294-2314
General Email: editor@osceolasun.com
Publication Website: http://www.osceolasun.com/
Parent Company: Paxton Media Group
Editor Name: Matt Anderson
Editor Email: editor@osceolasun.com
Editor Phone: (715) 294-2314
Advertising Executive Name: Elise Bourne
Advertising Executive Email: sales@osceolasun.com
Advertising Executive Phone: (715) 294-2314
Delivery Methods: Mail`Newsstand
Year Established: 1897
Published Days: Wed
Avg. Paid Circ.: 1800
Audit Company: Sworn/Estimate/Non-Audited

OSHKOSH

OSHKOSH HERALD

Street Address: 923 S Main St.
City: Oshkosh
State: WI
ZIP Code: 54902
General Phone: (920) 508-9000
General Email: karen@oshkoshherald.com
Publication Website: https://oshkoshherald.com/
Publisher Name: Karen Schneider
Publisher Email: karen@oshkoshherald.com
Publisher Phone: (920) 858-6407
Editor Name: Dan Roherty
Editor Email: editor@oshkoshherald.com
Editor Phone: (920) 508-0027
Advertising Executive Name: Andrea Toms
Advertising Executive Email: advertise@oshkoshherald.com
Advertising Executive Phone: (920) 508-0030
Year Established: 2017
Published Days: Wed
Avg. Free Circ.: 27535
Audit Company: CVC

OSSEO

TRI-COUNTY NEWS

Street Address: P.O. Box 460
City: Osseo
State: WI
ZIP Code: 54758
General Phone: (715) 597-3313
General Email: erika@media-md.net
Publication Website: https://www.gmdmedia.net/tri-county-news
Parent Company: Conley Media LLC
Delivery Methods: Mail`Racks
Own Printing Facility?: Y
Commercial printers?: Y
Mechanical specifications: Type page 13 x 21 1/2; E - 6 cols, 2, between; A - 6 cols, 2, between; C - 6 cols, 2, between.
Published Days: Thur
Avg. Paid Circ.: 1418
Avg. Free Circ.: 10
Audit Company: Sworn/Estimate/Non-Audited

PHILLIPS

PARK FALLS HERALD

Street Address: 105 N. Lake Avenue
City: Phillips
State: WI
ZIP Code: 54555
General Phone: (715) 339-3036
General Email: news@pricecountyreview.com
Publication Website: https://www.apg-wi.com/
Delivery Methods: Mail`Racks
Year Established: 1900
Published Days: Thur
Avg. Paid Circ.: 4367
Avg. Free Circ.: 6200
Audit Company: Sworn/Estimate/Non-Audited

Community Newspapers in the U.S.

PHILLIPS

PRICE COUNTY REVIEW

Street Address: 105 N. Lake Avenue
City: Phillips
State: WI
ZIP Code: 54555
General Phone: (715) 339-3036
General Email: news@pricecountyreview.com
Publication Website: https://www.apg-wi.com/
Parent Company: Adams Publishing Group
Advertising Executive Name: Jessica Sufak
Advertising Executive Email: jsufak@pricecountyreview.com
Advertising Executive Phone: (715) 718-4690
Published Days: Thur
Avg. Paid Circ.: 100
Audit Company: Sworn/Estimate/Non-Audited

PLATTEVILLE

THE PLATTEVILLE JOURNAL

Street Address: 25 E Main St
City: Platteville
State: WI
ZIP Code: 53818-3216
General Phone: (608) 348-3006
General Email: ads@theplattevillejournal.com
Publication Website: https://www.swnews4u.com
Parent Company: Morris Multimedia, Inc.
Delivery Methods: Mail`Newsstand`Racks
Year Established: 1899
Own Printing Facility?: Y
Commercial printers?: Y
Mechanical specifications: Type page 15 3/4 x 21 1/2; E - 8 cols, 1 5/6, 1/6 between; A - 8 cols, 1 5/6, 1/6 between; C - 8 cols, 1 5/6, 1/6 between.
Published Days: Wed
Avg. Paid Circ.: 4300
Avg. Free Circ.: 17665
Audit Company: Sworn/Estimate/Non-Audited

PLYMOUTH

THE REVIEW

Street Address: 113 E Mill St
City: Plymouth
State: WI
ZIP Code: 53073-1703
General Phone: (920) 893-6411
General Email: displayads@plymouth-review.com
Publication Website: https://www.plymouth-review.com/
Parent Company: Shaw Media
Publisher Name: Barry Johanson
Publisher Email: reply@plymouth-review.com
Publisher Phone: (920) 893-6411, ext : 25
Advertising Executive Name: Jori Kapla
Advertising Executive Email: reviewclassified@gmail.com
Advertising Executive Phone: (920) 893-6411, ext : 10
Delivery Methods: Mail`Newsstand
Year Established: 1895
Own Printing Facility?: Y
Commercial printers?: Y
Mechanical specifications: Type page 10 1/2 x 15 3/16; E - 5 cols, 2 1/16, 1/8 between; A - 5 cols, 2 1/16, 1/8 between; C - 5 cols, 2 1/16, 1/8 between.
Published Days: Tues`Thur
Avg. Paid Circ.: 5308
Avg. Free Circ.: 33
Audit Company: Sworn/Estimate/Non-Audited

PLYMOUTH

THE SHEBOYGAN FALLS NEWS

Street Address: 113 E Mill St
City: Plymouth
State: WI
ZIP Code: 53073-1703
General Phone: (920) 893-6411
General Email: displayads@plymouth-review.com
Publication Website: https://www.plymouth-review.com/
Publisher Name: Barry Johanson
Publisher Email: reply@plymouth-review.com
Publisher Phone: (920) 893-6411, ext : 25
Delivery Methods: Mail`Newsstand
Year Established: 1895
Own Printing Facility?: Y
Commercial printers?: Y
Mechanical specifications: Type page 10 1/4 x 15; E - 5 cols, 2, 1/8 between; A - 5 cols, 2, 1/8 between; C - 7 cols, 2, 1/8 between.
Published Days: Fri
Avg. Paid Circ.: 2133
Audit Company: Sworn/Estimate/Non-Audited

PORT WASHINGTON

OZAUKEE PRESS

Street Address: 125 E Main St
City: Port Washington
State: WI
ZIP Code: 53074
General Phone: (262) 284-3494
General Email: editor@ozaukeepress.com
Publication Website: http://www.ozaukeepress.com/
Parent Company: Ozaukee Press
Publisher Name: William F. Schanen
Editor Name: Bill Schanen
Editor Email: editor@ozaukeepress.com
Editor Phone: (262) 284-3494, ext : 1110
Advertising Executive Name: Holly Ostermann
Advertising Executive Email: holly@ozaukeepress.com
Delivery Methods: Mail`Newsstand`Racks
Year Established: 1940
Own Printing Facility?: Y
Commercial printers?: Y
Published Days: Tues`Thur
Avg. Paid Circ.: 6295
Avg. Free Circ.: 215
Audit Company: CVC

RANDOM LAKE

THE SOUNDER

Street Address: 405 2nd St
City: Random Lake
State: WI
ZIP Code: 53075
General Phone: (920) 994-9244
General Email: editor@thesounder.com
Publication Website: http://www.thesounder.com/
Editor Name: Gary J. Feider
Editor Email: editor@thesounder.com
Delivery Methods: Mail
Year Established: 1918
Own Printing Facility?: N
Commercial printers?: N
Published Days: Thur
Avg. Paid Circ.: 2122
Audit Company: Sworn/Estimate/Non-Audited

RHINELANDER

STAR JOURNAL

Street Address: 24 W Rives St
City: Rhinelander
State: WI
ZIP Code: 54501-3164
General Phone: (715) 369-3331
General Email: hodagads@mmclocal.com
Publication Website: https://starjournalnow.com/
Parent Company: Multi Media Channels, LLC
Editor Email: starjournal@mmclocal.com
Delivery Methods: Newsstand`Carrier`Racks
Year Established: 1977
Mechanical specifications: Type page: 9.75 x 11; 6 col
Published Days: Sun
Avg. Paid Circ.: 5
Avg. Free Circ.: 15940
Audit Company: Sworn/Estimate/Non-Audited

RICE LAKE

RICE LAKE CHRONOTYPE

Street Address: 28 S Main St
City: Rice Lake
State: WI
ZIP Code: 54868-2232
General Phone: (715) 234-2121
General Email: ppage@chronotype.com
Publication Website: https://www.apg-wi.com/rice_lake_chronotype/
Editor Name: Ryan Urban
Editor Email: citynews@chronotype.com
Editor Phone: (715) 790-1331
Advertising Executive Name: Pam Page
Advertising Executive Email: ppage@chronotype.com
Advertising Executive Phone: (715) 790-1555
Year Established: 1874
Published Days: Wed
Avg. Paid Circ.: 7176
Audit Company: Sworn/Estimate/Non-Audited

RICHLAND CENTER

THE RICHLAND OBSERVER

Street Address: 172 E Court St
City: Richland Center
State: WI
ZIP Code: 53581-2339
General Phone: (608) 647-6141
General Email: ads@richlandobserver.net
Publication Website: https://www.swnews4u.com/contact-us/richland-observer/
Parent Company: Morris Multimedia, Inc.
Publisher Name: John Ingebritsen
Publisher Email: jinge@tds.net
Editor Name: Dawn Kiefer
Editor Email: editor@richlandobserver.net
Advertising Executive Name: Dave McGowan
Advertising Executive Email: ads@richlandobserver.net
Year Established: 1864
Published Days: Thur
Audit Company: Sworn/Estimate/Non-Audited

RIPON

RIPON COMMONWEALTH PRESS

Street Address: 656 S Douglas St
City: Ripon
State: WI
ZIP Code: 54971
General Phone: (920) 748-3017
General Email: news@riponpress.com
Publication Website: http://www.riponpress.com/
Publisher Name: Jim O'Rourke
Editor Name: Ian Stepleton
Editor Email: istepleton@riponpress.com
Advertising Executive Name: Todd Sharp
Advertising Executive Email: tsharp@riponpress.com
Delivery Methods: Mail`Racks
Year Established: 1864
Own Printing Facility?: Y
Commercial printers?: Y
Published Days: Wed
Avg. Free Circ.: 3400
Audit Company: Sworn/Estimate/Non-Audited

RIPON

THE COMMONWEALTH EXPRESS

Street Address: 656 S Douglas St
City: Ripon
State: WI
ZIP Code: 54971
General Phone: (920) 748-3017
General Email: news@riponpress.com
Publication Website: http://www.riponpress.com/
Publisher Name: Jim O'Rourke
Editor Name: Ian Stepleton
Editor Email: istepleton@riponpress.com
Advertising Executive Name: Todd Sharp
Advertising Executive Email: tsharp@riponpress.com
Published Days: Tues
Avg. Free Circ.: 17540
Audit Company: Sworn/Estimate/Non-Audited

SEYMOUR

ADVERTISER COMMUNITY NEWS

Street Address: 530 E Wisconsin St.
City: Seymour
State: WI
ZIP Code: 54165
General Phone: (920) 833-0420
General Email: ken.h@adcommnews.com
Publication Website: http://advertisercommunitynews.com/
Parent Company:
Publisher Name: Ken Hodgden
Publisher Email: ken.h@adcommnews.com
Editor Name: Keith Skenandore
Editor Email: keith.s@adcommnews.com
Delivery Methods: Mail`Newsstand`Carrier
Year Established: 2009
Mechanical specifications: 6 Col 9.75" wide by 13.75 " Tab
Published Days: Mon
Avg. Paid Circ.: 103
Avg. Free Circ.: 8853
Audit Company: VAC

SPARTA

MONROE COUNTY HERALD

Street Address: 1302 River Rd
City: Sparta
State: WI
ZIP Code: 54656-0252
General Phone: (608) 269-3186
General Email: news@monroecountyherald.com
Publication Website: http://www.monroecountyherald.com
Parent Company: Evans Print & Media Group
Editor Name: Pat Mulvaney
Editor Email: pat@monroecountyherald.com
Editor Phone: (608) 269-3186
Advertising Executive Name: Kyle Evans
Advertising Executive Email: kyle@monroecountyherald.com
Advertising Executive Phone: (608) 269-3186
Delivery Methods: Mail`Newsstand`Racks
Year Established: 1857
Own Printing Facility?: Y
Commercial printers?: Y
Mechanical specifications: Type page 13 x 21 1/2; E - 6 cols, 2 1/16, 3/16 between; A - 6 cols, 2 1/16, 3/16 between; C - 9 cols, 1 5/16, 3/16 between.
Published Days: Mon`Thur
Avg. Paid Circ.: 5000
Avg. Free Circ.: 35
Audit Company: Sworn/Estimate/Non-

SPARTA

THE MONROE COUNTY HERALD

Street Address: 1302 River Rd
City: Sparta
State: WI
ZIP Code: 54656-0252
General Phone: (608) 269-3186
General Email: news@monroecountyherald.com
Publication Website: https://evansprinting.com/
Parent Company: Evans Print & Media Group
Editor Name: Pat Mulvaney
Editor Email: pat@monroecountyherald.com
Editor Phone: (608) 269-3186
Advertising Executive Name: Kyle Evans
Advertising Executive Email: kyle@monroecountyherald.com
Advertising Executive Phone: (608) 269-3186
Delivery Methods: Mail`Racks
Own Printing Facility?: Y
Commercial printers?: Y
Mechanical specifications: Type page 13 x 21 1/2; E - 6 cols, 2 1/16, 3/8 between; A - 6 cols, 2 1/16, 3/8 between; C - 9 cols, 1 5/16, 3/8 between.
Published Days: Mon
Avg. Paid Circ.: 4650
Avg. Free Circ.: 35
Audit Company: Sworn/Estimate/Non-Audited

SPOONER

SPOONER ADVOCATE

Street Address: 251 E Maple St
City: Spooner
State: WI
ZIP Code: 54801
General Phone: (715) 635-2181
General Email: ads@spooneradvocate.com
Publication Website: http://www.spooneradvocate.com/
Parent Company: Adams Publishing Group
Advertising Executive Name: Michelle Carlson
Advertising Executive Email: mcarlson@spooneradvocate.com
Advertising Executive Phone: (715) 939-9036
Delivery Methods: Mail
Year Established: 1901
Commercial printers?: Y
Mechanical specifications: Type page 11 5/8 x 21 1/2; E - 6 cols, 11 5/8, 1/8 between; A - 6 cols, 11 5/8, 1/8 between; C - 6 cols, 11 5/8, 1/8 between.
Published Days: Thur
Avg. Paid Circ.: 3000
Audit Company: Sworn/Estimate/Non-Audited

SPRING VALLEY

SUN-ARGUS

Street Address: W2855 730th Ave
City: Spring Valley
State: WI
ZIP Code: 54767-8512
General Phone: (715) 778-4990
General Email: admins@mygateway.news
Publication Website: https://mygateway.news/
Parent Company: Gateway Publishing, Inc.
Publisher Name: Paul Seeling
Editor Name: Paul Seeling
Editor Email: editor@mygateway.news
Advertising Executive Email: admins@mygateway.news
Advertising Executive Phone: (715) 778-4990
Delivery Methods: Mail`Newsstand
Year Established: 1892
Own Printing Facility?: N

Commercial printers?: Y
Mechanical specifications: Broadsheet. 6 column wide (2" column width) x 21" tall
Published Days: Thur
Avg. Paid Circ.: 800
Avg. Free Circ.: 2
Audit Company: Sworn/Estimate/Non-Audited

SPRING VALLEY

WOODVILLE LEADER

Street Address: W2855 730th Ave
City: Spring Valley
State: WI
ZIP Code: 54767-8512
General Phone: (715) 778-4990
General Email: admins@mygateway.news
Publication Website: https://mygateway.news/category/news/woodville-news/
Parent Company: Gateway Publishing, Inc.
Publisher Name: Paul Seeling
Editor Name: Paul Seeling
Editor Email: editor@mygateway.news
Advertising Executive Email: admins@mygateway.news
Advertising Executive Phone: (715) 778-4990
Delivery Methods: Mail`Newsstand
Year Established: 1929
Mechanical specifications: Broadsheet. 6 columns wide x 21" tall with 2" wide columns
Published Days: Thur
Avg. Paid Circ.: 196
Avg. Free Circ.: 2
Audit Company: Sworn/Estimate/Non-Audited

STEVENS POINT

THE PORTAGE COUNTY GAZETTE

Street Address: 1024 Main St
City: Stevens Point
State: WI
ZIP Code: 54481-2859
General Phone: (715)343-8045
General Email: bderezinski@mmclocal.com
Publication Website: https://stevenspoint.news/
Parent Company: Multi Media Channels, LLC
Editor Name: Kris Leonhardt
Editor Email: kleonhardt@mmclocal.com
Editor Phone: (715) 316-4617
Delivery Methods: Newsstand`Racks
Year Established: 1878
Published Days: Fri
Audit Company: Sworn/Estimate/Non-Audited

STURGEON BAY

DOOR COUNTY ADVOCATE

Street Address: 235 N 3rd Ave
City: Sturgeon Bay
State: WI
ZIP Code: 54235-2417
General Phone: (920) 615-9592
General Email: kvitela@doorcountyadvocate.com
Publication Website: http://content.doorcountyadvocate.com/door-county/
Editor Name: Christoper Clough
Editor Email: cclough@doorcountyadvocate.com
Editor Phone: (920) 741-7952
Advertising Executive Name: Katie Vitela
Advertising Executive Email: kvitela@doorcountyadvocate.com
Advertising Executive Phone: (920) 741-7957
Delivery Methods: Mail`Newsstand`Racks
Year Established: 1862
Own Printing Facility?: Y
Mechanical specifications: Type page 10 x 20 1/4; 6 col
Published Days: Wed`Sat

Avg. Paid Circ.: 5897
Avg. Free Circ.: 279
Audit Company: CVC

SUN PRAIRIE

MCFARLAND THISTLE

Street Address: 804 Liberty Blvd, Suite 201
City: Sun Prairie
State: WI
ZIP Code: 53590
General Phone: (608) 839-1544
General Email: mcfarland@hngnews.com
Publication Website: http://www.hngnews.com/mcfarland_thistle/
Parent Company: Hometown News Group
Editor Name: Kevin Passon
Editor Email: kpasson@hngnews.com
Editor Phone: (608) 839-7352
Advertising Executive Name: Mary Jo Currie
Advertising Executive Email: classifieds@hngnews.com
Advertising Executive Phone: (608) 478-2509
Published Days: Tues`Thur
Audit Company: Sworn/Estimate/Non-Audited

SUN PRAIRIE

THE STAR

Street Address: 804 Liberty Blvd, Suite 201
City: Sun Prairie
State: WI
ZIP Code: 53590-4643
General Phone: (608) 837-2521
General Email: spstar@hngnews.com
Publication Website: http://www.hngnews.com/site/contact.html
Parent Company: Gannett
Publisher Name: Robb Grindstaff
Publisher Email: rgrindstaff@dailyunion.com
Publisher Phone: (920) 563-5553
Editor Name: Chris Mertes
Editor Email: spedit@hngnews.com
Editor Phone: (608) 478-2521
Advertising Executive Name: Missy Feiler
Advertising Executive Email: mfeiler@hngnews.com
Advertising Executive Phone: (608) 478-2517
Delivery Methods: Mail`Newsstand`Racks
Year Established: 1877
Commercial printers?: Y
Mechanical specifications: Type page 13 x 21.
Published Days: Tues`Fri
Avg. Paid Circ.: 3750
Audit Company: Sworn/Estimate/Non-Audited

TOMAH

THE TOMAH JOURNAL

Street Address: 903 Superior Ave
City: Tomah
State: WI
ZIP Code: 54660-2060
General Phone: (608) 372-4123
General Email: paul.pehler@lee.net
Publication Website: https://lacrossetribune.com/community/tomahjournal/
Publisher Name: Sean Burke
Publisher Email: sean.burke@lee.net
Publisher Phone: (608) 791-8237
Editor Name: Steve Rundio
Editor Email: steve.rundio@lee.net
Editor Phone: (608) 374-7785
Advertising Executive Name: Paul Pehler
Advertising Executive Email: paul.pehler@lee.net
Advertising Executive Phone: (608) 791-8300
Delivery Methods: Mail`Racks
Published Days: Mon`Thur
Avg. Paid Circ.: 5200
Audit Company: Sworn/Estimate/Non-Audited

TOMAHAWK

TOMAHAWK LEADER

Street Address: 315 W Wisconsin Ave, PO Box 345
City: Tomahawk
State: WI
ZIP Code: 54487-1133
General Phone: (715) 453-2151
General Email: smercier@mmclocal.com
Publication Website: https://www.tomahawkleader.com/
Parent Company: Multi Media Channels, LLC
Publisher Name: Patrick J. Wood
Publisher Email: publisher@mmclocal.com
Advertising Executive Name: Sunnie Mercier
Advertising Executive Email: smercier@mmclocal.com
Delivery Methods: Mail`Newsstand
Year Established: 1887
Own Printing Facility?: Y
Mechanical specifications: Type page 11 x 21; E - 6 cols, 1.65", 1/8 between.
Published Days: Tues
Avg. Paid Circ.: 3200
Avg. Free Circ.: 5300
Audit Company: Sworn/Estimate/Non-Audited
Note: Many special sections published, including the Official Guide to the Tomahawk Fall Ride for MDA.

VERONA

STOUGHTON COURIER HUB

Street Address: 133 Enterprise Drive
City: Verona
State: WI
ZIP Code: 53593
General Phone: (608) 845-9559
General Email: kathy.neumeister@wcinet.com
Publication Website: http://www.unifiednewsgroup.com/stoughton_courier_hub/
Parent Company: Unified Newspaper Group
Publisher Name: Lee Borkowski
Publisher Email: lborkowski@wcinet.com
Editor Name: Jim Ferolie
Editor Email: ungeditor@wcinet.com
Advertising Executive Name: Kathy Neumeister
Advertising Executive Email: kathy.neumeister@wcinet.com
Delivery Methods: Mail`Racks
Year Established: 1879
Own Printing Facility?: Y
Commercial printers?: N
Mechanical specifications: Type page 10 5/8 x 16; E - 6 cols, 1 5/8, 1/8 between; A - 6 cols, 1 5/8, 1/8 between; C - 6 cols, 1 5/8, 1/8 between.
Published Days: Thur
Avg. Paid Circ.: 2458
Audit Company: Sworn/Estimate/Non-Audited

VERONA

THE FITCHBURG STAR

Street Address: 133 Enterprise Drive
City: Verona
State: WI
ZIP Code: 53593-0427
General Phone: (608) 845-9559
General Email: fitchburgstar@wcinet.com
Publication Website: http://www.unifiednewsgroup.com/fitchburg_star/
Parent Company: Unified Newspaper Group
Publisher Name: Lee Borkowski
Publisher Email: lborkowski@wcinet.com
Editor Name: Jim Ferolie
Editor Email: ungeditor@wcinet.com
Advertising Executive Name: Kathy

Community Newspapers in the U.S.

Neumeister
Advertising Executive Email: kathy.neumeister@wcinet.com
Delivery Methods: Mail
Published Days: Mthly
Avg. Free Circ.: 13277
Audit Company: Sworn/Estimate/Non-Audited

VERONA

THE VERONA PRESS

Street Address: 133 Enterprise Dr
City: Verona
State: WI
ZIP Code: 53593-9122
General Phone: (608) 845-9559
General Email: veronapress@wcinet.com
Publication Website: http://www.unifiednewsgroup.com/verona_press/
Parent Company: Unified Newspaper Group
Publisher Name: Lee Borkowski
Publisher Email: lborkowski@wcinet.com
Editor Name: Jim Ferolie
Editor Email: ungeditor@wcinet.com
Advertising Executive Name: Kathy Neumeister
Advertising Executive Email: kathy.neumeister@wcinet.com
Delivery Methods: Mail`Racks
Year Established: 1965
Own Printing Facility?: Y
Commercial printers?: Y
Mechanical specifications: Type page 10 5/8 x 16; E - 6 cols, 1 5/8, 1/8 between; A - 6 cols, 1 5/8, 1/8 between; C - 6 cols, 1 5/8, 1/8 between.
Published Days: Thur
Avg. Paid Circ.: 2100
Audit Company: Sworn/Estimate/Non-Audited

VIROQUA

VERNON COUNTY BROADCASTER

Street Address: 124 W Court St, P.O. Box 472
City: Viroqua
State: WI
ZIP Code: 54665-1505
General Phone: (608) 637-3137
General Email: vcb.news@lee.net
Publication Website: https://lacrossetribune.com/community/vernonbroadcaster/
Publisher Name: Sean Burke
Publisher Email: sean.burke@lee.net
Publisher Phone: (608) 791-8237
Editor Name: Angie Cina
Editor Email: angie.cina@lee.net
Editor Phone: (608) 637-5616
Advertising Executive Name: Paul Pehler
Advertising Executive Email: paul.pehler@lee.net
Advertising Executive Phone: (608) 791-8300
Delivery Methods: Mail`Racks
Year Established: 1854
Mechanical specifications: Type page 15 3/4 x 21 1/2; E - 6 cols, 1 3/4, 3/8 between; A - 6 cols, 1 3/4, 3/8 between; C - 6 cols, 1 3/4, 3/8 between.
Published Days: Thur
Avg. Paid Circ.: 5336
Avg. Free Circ.: 23
Audit Company: Sworn/Estimate/Non-Audited

WASHINGTON ISLAND

WASHINGTON ISLAND OBSERVER

Street Address: 1253 Main Rd
City: Washington Island
State: WI
ZIP Code: 54246-9009
General Phone: (920) 847-2661
General Email: ads@washingtonislandobserver.com
Publication Website: https://washingtonislandobserver.com/
Editor Name: Heidi Hodges
Editor Email: editor@washingtonislandobserver.com
Editor Phone: (920) 495-0629
Advertising Executive Name: Zuzka Krueger
Advertising Executive Email: ads@washingtonislandobserver.com
Advertising Executive Phone: (920) 847-2661
Published Days: Wed
Audit Company: Sworn/Estimate/Non-Audited

WAUKESHA

BAY VIEW NOW

Street Address: 1741 Dolphin Drive, Suite A
City: Waukesha
State: WI
ZIP Code: 53186-1493
General Phone: (414) 224-2100
General Email: class@journalsentinel.com
Publication Website: https://www.jsonline.com/communities/south-crime/
Editor Name: George Stanley
Editor Email: george.stanley@jrn.com
Editor Phone: (414) 224-2248
Advertising Executive Email: class@journalsentinel.com
Advertising Executive Phone: (414) 224-2121
Delivery Methods: Carrier
Year Established: 1956
Mechanical specifications: 1.729" width, 11" depth. 5 columns, full page image 5x11. Ads over 9" deep will be billed at full page depth of 11"
Published Days: Thur
Audit Company: Sworn/Estimate/Non-Audited

WAUKESHA

BROOKFIELD-ELM GROVE NOW

Street Address: 1741 Dolphin Drive, Suite A
City: Waukesha
State: WI
ZIP Code: 53186-1493
General Phone: (414) 224-2100
General Email: class@journalsentinel.com
Publication Website: http://www.jsonline.com/communities/west/
Editor Name: George Stanley
Editor Email: george.stanley@jrn.com
Editor Phone: (414) 224-2248
Advertising Executive Email: class@journalsentinel.com
Advertising Executive Phone: (414) 224-2121
Delivery Methods: Carrier
Year Established: 1956
Mechanical specifications: 1.729" width, 11" depth. 5 columns, full page image 5x11. Ads over 9" deep will be billed at full page depth of 11"
Published Days: Thur
Audit Company: Sworn/Estimate/Non-Audited

WAUKESHA

CUDAHY NOW

Street Address: 1741 Dolphin Drive, Suite A
City: Waukesha
State: WI
ZIP Code: 53186-1493
General Phone: (414) 224-2100
General Email: class@journalsentinel.com
Publication Website: http://www.jsonline.com/communities/south/
Editor Name: George Stanley
Editor Email: george.stanley@jrn.com
Editor Phone: (414) 224-2248
Advertising Executive Email: class@journalsentinel.com
Advertising Executive Phone: (414) 224-2121
Delivery Methods: Carrier
Year Established: 1956
Mechanical specifications: 1.729" width, 11" depth. 5 columns, full page image 5x11. Ads over 9" deep will be billed at full page depth of 11"
Published Days: Thur
Audit Company: Sworn/Estimate/Non-Audited

WAUKESHA

ELM GROVE NOW

Street Address: 1741 Dolphin Drive, Suite A
City: Waukesha
State: WI
ZIP Code: 53186-1493
General Phone: (414) 224-2100
General Email: class@journalsentinel.com
Publication Website: http://www.jsonline.com/communities/west/
Editor Name: George Stanley
Editor Email: george.stanley@jrn.com
Editor Phone: (414) 224-2248
Advertising Executive Email: class@journalsentinel.com
Advertising Executive Phone: (414) 224-2121
Delivery Methods: Carrier
Year Established: 1956
Mechanical specifications: 1.729" width, 11" depth. 5 columns, full page image 5x11. Ads over 9" deep will be billed at full page depth of 11"
Published Days: Thur
Audit Company: Sworn/Estimate/Non-Audited

WAUKESHA

FOX POINT NOW

Street Address: 1741 Dolphin Drive, Suite A
City: Waukesha
State: WI
ZIP Code: 53186-1493
General Phone: (414) 224-2100
General Email: class@journalsentinel.com
Publication Website: http://www.jsonline.com/communities/northshore/
Editor Name: George Stanley
Editor Email: george.stanley@jrn.com
Editor Phone: (414) 224-2248
Advertising Executive Email: class@journalsentinel.com
Advertising Executive Phone: (414) 224-2121
Delivery Methods: Carrier
Year Established: 1956
Mechanical specifications: 1.729" width, 11" depth. 5 columns, full page image 5x11. Ads over 9" deep will be billed at full page depth of 11"
Published Days: Thur
Audit Company: Sworn/Estimate/Non-Audited

WAUKESHA

GERMANTOWN NOW

Street Address: 1741 Dolphin Drive, Suite A
City: Waukesha
State: WI
ZIP Code: 53186-1493
General Phone: (414) 224-2100
General Email: class@journalsentinel.com
Publication Website: http://www.jsonline.com/communities/northwest/
Editor Name: George Stanley
Editor Email: george.stanley@jrn.com
Editor Phone: (414) 224-2248
Advertising Executive Email: class@journalsentinel.com
Advertising Executive Phone: (414) 224-2121
Delivery Methods: Carrier
Year Established: 1956
Mechanical specifications: 1.729" width, 11" depth. 5 columns, full page image 5x11. Ads over 9" deep will be billed at full page depth of 11"
Published Days: Thur
Audit Company: Sworn/Estimate/Non-Audited

WAUKESHA

GLENDALE NOW

Street Address: 1741 Dolphin Drive, Suite A
City: Waukesha
State: WI
ZIP Code: 53186-1493
General Phone: (414) 224-2100
General Email: class@journalsentinel.com
Publication Website: http://www.jsonline.com/communities/northshore/
Editor Name: George Stanley
Editor Email: george.stanley@jrn.com
Editor Phone: (414) 224-2248
Advertising Executive Email: class@journalsentinel.com
Advertising Executive Phone: (414) 224-2121
Delivery Methods: Carrier
Year Established: 1956
Mechanical specifications: 1.729" width, 11" depth. 5 columns, full page image 5x11. Ads over 9" deep will be billed at full page depth of 11"
Published Days: Thur
Audit Company: Sworn/Estimate/Non-Audited

WAUKESHA

GREENFIELD-WEST ALLIS NOW

Street Address: 1741 Dolphin Drive, Suite A
City: Waukesha
State: WI
ZIP Code: 53186-1493
General Phone: (414) 224-2100
General Email: class@journalsentinel.com
Publication Website: http://www.jsonline.com/communities/southwest/
Editor Name: George Stanley
Editor Email: george.stanley@jrn.com
Editor Phone: (414) 224-2248
Advertising Executive Email: class@journalsentinel.com
Advertising Executive Phone: (414) 224-2121
Delivery Methods: Carrier
Year Established: 1956
Mechanical specifications: 1.729" width, 11" depth. 5 columns, full page image 5x11. Ads over 9" deep will be billed at full page depth of 11"
Published Days: Thur
Audit Company: Sworn/Estimate/Non-Audited

WAUKESHA

HALES CORNERS NOW

Street Address: 1741 Dolphin Drive, Suite A
City: Waukesha
State: WI
ZIP Code: 53186-1493
General Phone: (414) 224-2100
General Email: class@journalsentinel.com
Publication Website: http://www.jsonline.com/communities/southwest/
Editor Name: George Stanley
Editor Email: george.stanley@jrn.com
Editor Phone: (414) 224-2248
Advertising Executive Email: class@journalsentinel.com
Advertising Executive Phone: (414) 224-2121
Delivery Methods: Carrier
Year Established: 1956
Mechanical specifications: 1.729" width, 11" depth. 5 columns, full page image 5x11. Ads over 9" deep will be billed at full page depth of 11"
Published Days: Thur

WAUKESHA

MENOMONEE FALLS-GERMANTOWN NOW

Street Address: 1741 Dolphin Drive, Suite A
City: Waukesha
State: WI
ZIP Code: 53186-1493
General Phone: (414) 224-2100
General Email: class@journalsentinel.com
Publication Website: http://www.jsonline.com/communities/northwest/
Editor Name: George Stanley
Editor Email: george.stanley@jrn.com
Editor Phone: (414) 224-2248
Advertising Executive Email: class@journalsentinel.com
Advertising Executive Phone: (414) 224-2121
Delivery Methods: Carrier
Year Established: 1956
Mechanical specifications: 1.729" width, 11" depth. 5 columns, full page image 5x11. Ads over 9" deep will be billed at full page depth of 11"
Published Days: Thur
Audit Company: Sworn/Estimate/Non-Audited

WAUKESHA

MEQUON NOW

Street Address: 1741 Dolphin Drive, Suite A
City: Waukesha
State: WI
ZIP Code: 53186-1493
General Phone: (414) 224-2100
General Email: class@journalsentinel.com
Publication Website: http://www.jsonline.com/communities/northshore/
Editor Name: George Stanley
Editor Email: george.stanley@jrn.com
Editor Phone: (414) 224-2248
Advertising Executive Email: class@journalsentinel.com
Advertising Executive Phone: (414) 224-2121
Delivery Methods: Carrier
Year Established: 1956
Mechanical specifications: 1.729" width, 11" depth. 5 columns, full page image 5x11. Ads over 9" deep will be billed at full page depth of 11"
Published Days: Thur
Audit Company: Sworn/Estimate/Non-Audited

WAUKESHA

MUSKEGO-NEW BERLIN NOW

Street Address: 1741 Dolphin Drive, Suite A
City: Waukesha
State: WI
ZIP Code: 53186-1493
General Phone: (414) 224-2100
General Email: class@journalsentinel.com
Publication Website: http://www.jsonline.com/communities/waukesha/
Editor Name: George Stanley
Editor Email: george.stanley@jrn.com
Editor Phone: (414) 224-2248
Advertising Executive Email: class@journalsentinel.com
Advertising Executive Phone: (414) 224-2121
Delivery Methods: Carrier
Year Established: 1956
Mechanical specifications: 1.729" width, 11" depth. 5 columns, full page image 5x11. Ads over 9" deep will be billed at full page depth of 11"
Published Days: Thur
Audit Company: Sworn/Estimate/Non-Audited

WAUKESHA

NEW BERLIN NOW

Street Address: 1741 Dolphin Drive, Suite A
City: Waukesha
State: WI
ZIP Code: 53186-1493
General Phone: (414) 224-2100
General Email: class@journalsentinel.com
Publication Website: http://www.jsonline.com/communities/waukesha/
Editor Name: George Stanley
Editor Email: george.stanley@jrn.com
Editor Phone: (414) 224-2248
Advertising Executive Email: class@journalsentinel.com
Advertising Executive Phone: (414) 224-2121
Delivery Methods: Carrier
Year Established: 1956
Mechanical specifications: 1.729" width, 11" depth. 5 columns, full page image 5x11. Ads over 9" deep will be billed at full page depth of 11"
Published Days: Thur
Audit Company: Sworn/Estimate/Non-Audited

WAUKESHA

NORTH SHORE NOW

Street Address: 1741 Dolphin Drive, Suite A
City: Waukesha
State: WI
ZIP Code: 53186-1493
General Phone: (414) 224-2100
General Email: class@journalsentinel.com
Publication Website: https://www.jsonline.com/communities/northshore/
Editor Name: George Stanley
Editor Email: george.stanley@jrn.com
Editor Phone: (414) 224-2248
Advertising Executive Email: class@journalsentinel.com
Advertising Executive Phone: (414) 224-2121
Delivery Methods: Newsstand Racks
Year Established: 1956
Published Days: Thur
Audit Company: Sworn/Estimate/Non-Audited

WAUKESHA

OAK CREEK NOW

Street Address: 1741 Dolphin Drive, Suite A
City: Waukesha
State: WI
ZIP Code: 53186-1493
General Phone: (414) 224-2100
General Email: class@journalsentinel.com
Publication Website: http://www.jsonline.com/communities/south/
Editor Name: George Stanley
Editor Email: george.stanley@jrn.com
Editor Phone: (414) 224-2248
Advertising Executive Email: class@journalsentinel.com
Advertising Executive Phone: (414) 224-2121
Delivery Methods: Carrier
Year Established: 1956
Mechanical specifications: 1.729" width, 11" depth. 5 columns, full page image 5x11. Ads over 9" deep will be billed at full page depth of 11"
Published Days: Thur
Audit Company: Sworn/Estimate/Non-Audited

WAUKESHA

OAK CREEK-FRANKLIN-GREENDALE-HALES CORNERS NOW

Street Address: 1741 Dolphin Drive, Suite A
City: Waukesha
State: WI
ZIP Code: 53186-1493
General Phone: (414) 224-2100
General Email: class@journalsentinel.com
Publication Website: http://www.jsonline.com/communities/south/
Editor Name: George Stanley
Editor Email: george.stanley@jrn.com
Editor Phone: (414) 224-2248
Advertising Executive Email: class@journalsentinel.com
Advertising Executive Phone: (414) 224-2121
Delivery Methods: Carrier
Year Established: 1956
Mechanical specifications: 1.729" width, 11" depth. 5 columns, full page image 5x11. Ads over 9" deep will be billed at full page depth of 11"
Published Days: Thur
Audit Company: Sworn/Estimate/Non-Audited

WAUKESHA

SOUTH MILWAUKEE NOW

Street Address: 1741 Dolphin Drive, Suite A
City: Waukesha
State: WI
ZIP Code: 53186-1493
General Phone: (414) 224-2100
General Email: class@journalsentinel.com
Publication Website: http://www.jsonline.com/communities/south/
Editor Name: George Stanley
Editor Email: george.stanley@jrn.com
Editor Phone: (414) 224-2248
Advertising Executive Email: class@journalsentinel.com
Advertising Executive Phone: (414) 224-2121
Delivery Methods: Carrier
Year Established: 1956
Mechanical specifications: 1.729" width, 11" depth. 5 columns, full page image 5x11. Ads over 9" deep will be billed at full page depth of 11"
Published Days: Thur
Audit Company: Sworn/Estimate/Non-Audited

WAUKESHA

ST. FRANCIS NOW

Street Address: 1741 Dolphin Drive, Suite A
City: Waukesha
State: WI
ZIP Code: 53186-1493
General Phone: (414) 224-2100
General Email: class@journalsentinel.com
Publication Website: http://www.jsonline.com/communities/south/
Editor Name: George Stanley
Editor Email: george.stanley@jrn.com
Editor Phone: (414) 224-2248
Advertising Executive Email: class@journalsentinel.com
Advertising Executive Phone: (414) 224-2121
Delivery Methods: Carrier
Year Established: 1956
Mechanical specifications: 1.729" width, 11" depth. 5 columns, full page image 5x11. Ads over 9" deep will be billed at full page depth of 11"
Published Days: Thur
Audit Company: Sworn/Estimate/Non-Audited

WAUKESHA

WAUWATOSA NOW

Street Address: 1741 Dolphin Drive, Suite A
City: Waukesha
State: WI
ZIP Code: 53186-1493
General Phone: (414) 224-2100
General Email: class@journalsentinel.com
Publication Website: http://www.jsonline.com/communities/west/
Editor Name: George Stanley
Editor Email: george.stanley@jrn.com
Editor Phone: (414) 224-2248
Advertising Executive Email: class@journalsentinel.com
Advertising Executive Phone: (414) 224-2121
Delivery Methods: Carrier
Year Established: 1956
Mechanical specifications: 1.729" width, 11" depth. 5 columns, full page image 5x11. Ads over 9" deep will be billed at full page depth of 11"
Published Days: Thur
Audit Company: Sworn/Estimate/Non-Audited

WAUKESHA

WEST ALLIS NOW

Street Address: 1741 Dolphin Drive, Suite A
City: Waukesha
State: WI
ZIP Code: 53186-1493
General Phone: (414) 224-2100
General Email: class@journalsentinel.com
Publication Website: http://www.jsonline.com/communities/southwest/
Editor Name: George Stanley
Editor Email: george.stanley@jrn.com
Editor Phone: (414) 224-2248
Advertising Executive Email: class@journalsentinel.com
Advertising Executive Phone: (414) 224-2121
Delivery Methods: Carrier
Year Established: 1956
Mechanical specifications: 1.729" width, 11" depth. 5 columns, full page image 5x11. Ads over 9" deep will be billed at full page depth of 11"
Published Days: Thur
Audit Company: Sworn/Estimate/Non-Audited

WAUNAKEE

DEFOREST TIMES-TRIBUNE

Street Address: 204 Moravian Valley Rd., Suite F
City: Waunakee
State: WI
ZIP Code: 53597
General Phone: (608) 846-5576
General Email: lkanderson@hngnews.com
Publication Website: http://www.hngnews.com/deforest_times/
Parent Company: Adams Publishing Group
Editor Name: Peter Lindblad
Editor Email: deforestedit@hngnews.com
Editor Phone: (608) 467-1557
Advertising Executive Name: Mary Jo Currie
Advertising Executive Email: classifieds@hngnews.com
Advertising Executive Phone: (608) 478-2509
Delivery Methods: Mail Newsstand Racks
Year Established: 1895
Published Days: Thur
Avg. Paid Circ.: 2825
Audit Company: Sworn/Estimate/Non-Audited

WAUPACA

WAUPACA COUNTY POST

Street Address: 1990 Godfrey Dr
City: Waupaca
State: WI
ZIP Code: 54981-7908
General Phone: (920) 217-3309
General Email: bcloud@mmlocal.com
Publication Website: https://waupacanow.com/
Parent Company: Multi Media Channels, LLC
Editor Name: Robert Cloud

Community Newspapers in the U.S.

Editor Email: bcloud@mmlocal.com
Editor Phone: (715) 258-4345
Advertising Executive Name: Bernice Fuhrmann
Advertising Executive Email: bcloud@mmlocal.com
Delivery Methods: Mail`Newsstand
Year Established: 2009
Own Printing Facility?: Y
Commercial printers?: Y
Mechanical specifications: Type page: 9.5 x 11.5; 5 col
Published Days: Wed
Avg. Paid Circ.: 5054
Avg. Free Circ.: 16828
Audit Company: CVC

WAUPACA

WISCONSIN STATE FARMER

Street Address: 600 Industrial Dr
City: Waupaca
State: WI
ZIP Code: 54981-8814
General Phone: (715)258-5546
General Email: wisfarmerclassifieds@gannett.com
Publication Website: https://static.wisfarmer.com/
Editor Name: Colleen Kottke
Editor Email: colleen.kottke@jrn.com
Editor Phone: (920) 517-2653
Advertising Executive Name: Kristin Magruder
Advertising Executive Email: kmagrude@gannett.com
Advertising Executive Phone: (920) 228-1494
Delivery Methods: Mail`Newsstand
Year Established: 1956
Own Printing Facility?: Y
Commercial printers?: Y
Published Days: Fri
Avg. Paid Circ.: 16669
Avg. Free Circ.: 511
Audit Company: Sworn/Estimate/Non-Audited

WINNECONNE

THE WINNECONNE NEWS

Street Address: 908 E Main St
City: Winneconne
State: WI
ZIP Code: 54986-9672
General Phone: (920) 582-4541
General Email: ads@winneconnenews.com
Publication Website: http://www.winneconnenews.com/
Parent Company: Rogers Printing Solutions
Publisher Name: John Rogers
Publisher Email: johnrogers@rogerspublishing.com
Editor Name: Becky LaDue
Editor Email: beckyladue@winneconnenews.com
Advertising Executive Email: ads@winneconnenews.com
Year Established: 1953
Published Days: Wed
Audit Company: Sworn/Estimate/Non-Audited

WEST VIRGINIA

BERKELEY SPRINGS

THE MORGAN MESSENGER

Street Address: 16 N Mercer St
City: Berkeley Springs
State: WV
ZIP Code: 25411-1587
General Phone: (304) 258-1800
General Email: todd@morganmessenger.com
Publication Website: morganmessenger.com
Editor Name: Sandy Buzzerd
Editor Email: news@morganmessenger.com
Editor Phone: (304) 258-1800
Advertising Executive Name: Jody Crouse
Advertising Executive Email: ads@morganmessenger.com
Delivery Methods: Mail`Newsstand
Year Established: 1893
Own Printing Facility?: Y
Commercial printers?: Y
Mechanical specifications: Type page 12 1/2 x 21; E - 6 cols, 1 3/4, 3/16 between; A - 6 cols, 1 3/4, 3/16 between; C - 8 cols, 1 1/4, 3/16 between.
Published Days: Wed
Avg. Paid Circ.: 4800
Audit Company: Sworn/Estimate/Non-Audited

BUCKHANNON

THE RECORD DELTA

Street Address: 2B Clarksburg Rd
City: Buckhannon
State: WV
ZIP Code: 26201-8461
General Phone: (304) 472-2800
General Email: news@therecorddelta.com
Publication Website: https://therecorddelta.com/
Parent Company: News Media Groiup
Publisher Name: James Austin
Publisher Email: jaustin@therecorddelta.com
Publisher Phone: (304) 472-2800
Editor Name: Tara Kennedy
Editor Email: tkennedy@therecorddelta.com
Delivery Methods: Mail`Newsstand
Own Printing Facility?: Y
Commercial printers?: Y
Published Days: Mon`Wed`Fri
Avg. Paid Circ.: 4304
Audit Company: Sworn/Estimate/Non-Audited

CHARLES TOWN

SPIRIT OF JEFFERSON

Street Address: 114 N Charles St
City: Charles Town
State: WV
ZIP Code: 25414-1508
General Phone: (304) 725-2046
General Email: editor@spiritofjefferson.com
Publication Website: spiritofjefferson.com
Parent Company: Jefferson Publishing Co.
Publisher Name: Robert Snyder
Publisher Email: rob@spiritofjefferson.com
Publisher Phone: (304) 725-2046, ext : 223
Editor Name: Justin Griffin
Editor Email: editor@spiritofjefferson.com
Editor Phone: (304) 725-2046, ext : 226
Delivery Methods: Mail`Newsstand`Carrier`Racks
Year Established: 1844
Own Printing Facility?: Y
Commercial printers?: N
Published Days: Wed
Avg. Paid Circ.: 5000
Avg. Free Circ.: 63
Audit Company: Sworn/Estimate/Non-Audited

CLARKSBURG

THE PRESTON COUNTY JOURNAL

Street Address: 324 Hewes Avenue PO Box 2000
City: Clarksburg
State: WV
ZIP Code: 26301
General Phone: (800) 982-6034
General Email: support@wvnews.com
Publication Website: https://www.wvnews.com/prestoncountynews/obits/
Parent Company: WVNews
Delivery Methods: Mail`Newsstand
Year Established: 1866
Published Days: Wed
Avg. Paid Circ.: 4700
Audit Company: Sworn/Estimate/Non-Audited

CLAY

CLAY COUNTY FREE PRESS

Street Address: 136 MAIN ST
City: Clay
State: WV
ZIP Code: 25043
General Phone: (304) 587-4250
General Email: news@claycountyfreepress.com
Publication Website: claycountyfreepress.com
Parent Company: Mountain Media
Delivery Methods: Mail`Newsstand
Mechanical specifications: Type page 13 x 21; E - 6 cols, 2, between; A - 6 cols, 2, between; C - 7 cols, 1 3/4, between.
Published Days: Wed
Avg. Paid Circ.: 3500
Audit Company: Sworn/Estimate/Non-Audited

ELIZABETH

WIRT COUNTY JOURNAL

Street Address: 1 Midway Plaza
City: Elizabeth
State: WV
ZIP Code: 26143
General Phone: (304) 275-8981
General Email: news@wirtjournal.com
Publication Website: wirtjournal.com
Delivery Methods: Mail`Newsstand
Year Established: 1907
Own Printing Facility?: Y
Commercial printers?: Y
Mechanical specifications: 13"x21/5"
Published Days: Wed
Avg. Paid Circ.: 2600
Avg. Free Circ.: 60
Audit Company: Sworn/Estimate/Non-Audited

GLENVILLE

THE GLENVILLE DEMOCRAT/PATHFINDER

Street Address: 108 North Court St
City: Glenville
State: WV
ZIP Code: 26351-0458
General Phone: (304) 462-7309
General Email: glenvillenews@gmail.com
Publication Website: glenvillenews.com
Publisher Name: David H. Corcoran
Publisher Email: glenvillenews@gmail.com
Delivery Methods: Mail`Newsstand`Carrier
Year Established: 1892
Own Printing Facility?: Y
Commercial printers?: N
Mechanical specifications: Type page 13 x 21 1/2; E - 5 cols, 2 3/8, 1/6 between; A - 6 cols, 2, 1/6 between; C - 6 cols, 2, 1/6 between.
Published Days: Thur
Avg. Paid Circ.: 3200
Avg. Free Circ.: 500
Audit Company: Sworn/Estimate/Non-Audited

GLENVILLE

THE GLENVILLE PATHFINDER

Street Address: 108 N Court St
City: Glenville
State: WV
ZIP Code: 26351-1215
General Phone: (304) 462-7309
General Email: glenvillenews@gmail.com
Publication Website: glenvillenews.com
Publisher Name: David H. Corcoran
Publisher Email: glenvillenews@gmail.com
Delivery Methods: Mail`Newsstand`Carrier
Year Established: 1892
Mechanical specifications: Type page 13 1/2 x 21 1/2; E - 5 cols, 2 3/8, 1/6 between; A - 6 cols, 2, 1/6 between; C - 6 cols, 2, 1/6 between.
Published Days: Thur
Avg. Paid Circ.: 1500
Avg. Free Circ.: 300
Audit Company: Sworn/Estimate/Non-Audited
Note: This is the Republican Party persuasion paper in Gilmer County, WV

GRAFTON

MOUNTAIN STATESMAN

Street Address: 914 W Main St
City: Grafton
State: WV
ZIP Code: 26354-1028
General Phone: (304) 265-3333
General Email: ads@mountainstatesman.com
Publication Website: mountainstatesman.com
Parent Company: News Media Groiup
Editor Name: Nicki Skinner
Editor Email: nskinner@mountainstatesman.com
Editor Phone: (304) 265-3333, ext : 11
Advertising Executive Name: Angela Reed
Advertising Executive Email: areed@mountainstatesman.com
Advertising Executive Phone: (304) 265-3333
Delivery Methods: Mail`Newsstand
Own Printing Facility?: Y
Commercial printers?: Y
Mechanical specifications: Type page 13 x 21 1/2; E - 6 cols, 2 1/10, between; A - 6 cols, 2 1/10, between; C - 8 cols, 1 1/2, between.
Published Days: Mon`Wed`Fri
Avg. Paid Circ.: 3300
Avg. Free Circ.: 20
Audit Company: Sworn/Estimate/Non-Audited

GRANTSVILLE

THE CALHOUN CHRONICLE

Street Address: PO Box 400
City: Grantsville
State: WV
ZIP Code: 26147-0400
General Phone: (304) 354-6917
General Email: office@calhounchronicle.com
Publication Website: https://www.calhounchronicle.com/
Parent Company: Calhoun County Publishing
Publisher Name: Helen Morris
Publisher Phone: (304) 354-6672
Editor Name: Newton Nichols
Editor Email: contact@calhounchronicle.com
Editor Phone: (304) 354-6917
Advertising Executive Name: Bill Bailey
Advertising Executive Phone: (304) 354-6917
Delivery Methods: Mail`Racks
Year Established: 1883
Published Days: Thur
Avg. Paid Circ.: 2800
Audit Company: Sworn/Estimate/Non-Audited

HAMLIN

THE LINCOLN JOURNAL

Street Address: 328 Walnut St
City: Hamlin
State: WV
ZIP Code: 25523-1403
General Phone: (304) 824-5101
General Email: advertising@lincolnjournal.com
Publication Website: http://lincolnjournalinc.com/
Parent Company: The Lincoln Journal, Inc.
Publisher Name: Thomas A. Robinson
Editor Name: Seán O'Donoghue
Delivery Methods: Mail`Newsstand
Year Established: 1903
Own Printing Facility?: Y
Mechanical specifications: Type page 12 x 21 1/2; E - 6 cols, between; A - 6 cols, between; C - 9 cols, between.
Published Days: Wed
Avg. Paid Circ.: 5625
Avg. Free Circ.: 12875
Audit Company: Sworn/Estimate/Non-Audited

HAMLIN

THE LINCOLN NEWS SENTINEL

Street Address: 328 Walnut St
City: Hamlin
State: WV
ZIP Code: 25523-1403
General Phone: (304) 824-5101
General Email: advertising@lincolnnewssentinel.com
Publication Website: http://lincolnjournalinc.com/
Parent Company: The Lincoln Journal, Inc.
Publisher Name: Thomas A. Robinson
Editor Name: Seán O'Donoghue
Delivery Methods: Mail`Newsstand
Own Printing Facility?: Y
Commercial printers?: Y
Published Days: Wed
Avg. Paid Circ.: 1350
Audit Company: Sworn/Estimate/Non-Audited

HAMLIN

THE LINCOLN TIMES

Street Address: 328 Walnut St
City: Hamlin
State: WV
ZIP Code: 25523-1403
General Phone: (304) 824-5101
General Email: advertising@lincolnjournal.com
Publication Website: http://lincolnjournalinc.com/
Parent Company: The Lincoln Journal, Inc.
Publisher Name: Thomas A. Robinson
Editor Name: Seán O'Donoghue
Delivery Methods: Mail`Newsstand
Year Established: 1901
Own Printing Facility?: Y
Commercial printers?: Y
Mechanical specifications: Type page 13 1/4 x 21 1/2; E - 6 cols, between; A - 6 cols, between; C - 10 cols, between.
Published Days: Sat
Avg. Paid Circ.: 5461
Avg. Free Circ.: 12638
Audit Company: Sworn/Estimate/Non-Audited

HARRISVILLE

THE PENNSBORO NEWS

Street Address: 103 N Spring St
City: Harrisville
State: WV
ZIP Code: 26362-1274
General Phone: (304) 643-4947
General Email: news@ritchiecountynews.com
Publication Website: ritchiecountynews.com
Delivery Methods: Mail`Newsstand
Year Established: 1892
Own Printing Facility?: Y
Commercial printers?: Y
Mechanical specifications: 6 cols. (13) x 21.5 SAU
Published Days: Wed
Avg. Paid Circ.: 4800
Avg. Free Circ.: 32
Audit Company: Sworn/Estimate/Non-Audited

HUNTINGTON

HERALD & DISPATCH

Street Address: 946 5th Ave
City: Huntington
State: WV
ZIP Code: 25701-2004
General Phone: (304) 526-2753
General Email: hdnews@hdmediallc.com
Publication Website: herald-dispatch.com
Parent Company: HD Media Company LLC
Editor Name: Les Smith
Editor Email: lessmith@hdmediallc.com
Editor Phone: (304) 526-2779
Advertising Executive Name: Jerry Briggs
Advertising Executive Email: jwbriggs@hdmediallc.com
Advertising Executive Phone: (304) 526-2820
Own Printing Facility?: Y
Commercial printers?: Y
Mechanical specifications: Type page 13 x 20 1/2; E - 6 cols, 1 1/4, 1/6 between; A - 6 cols, 2, 1/6 between; C - 10 cols, 1 1/4, 1/12 between.
Published Days: Sat
Avg. Paid Circ.: 1044
Avg. Free Circ.: 6
Audit Company: Sworn/Estimate/Non-Audited

LOGAN

THE LOGAN BANNER

Street Address: 218 Dingess Street
City: Logan
State: WV
ZIP Code: 25601-3913
General Phone: (304) 752-6950
General Email: dvidovich@hdmediallc.com
Publication Website: https://www.loganbanner.com/
Parent Company: HD Media
Publisher Name: NA
Editor Name: NA
Advertising Executive Name: Melissa Blair
Advertising Executive Email: mblair@hdmediallc.com
Advertising Executive Phone: (304) 236-3543
Year Established: 1888
Mechanical specifications: Type page 13 3/4 x 21 1/2; E - 6 cols, 2 1/16, 1/8 between; A - 6 cols, 2 1/16, 1/8 between; C - 9 cols, 1 3/8, 1/16 between.
Published Days: Mon`Tues`Wed`Thur`Fri`Sun
Weekday Frequency: e
Avg. Paid Circ.: 9579
Audit Company: Sworn/Estimate/Non-Audited
Mailroom Equipment: Counter Stackers -- 1/Fg; Inserters & Stuffers -- 3-/DG; Tying Machines -- 1-Ty-Tech/Tyer; Address Machine -- 2-/Am.;
Classified Equipment: Printers -- APP/Mac LaserWriter Pro 600;
Classified Software: QPS/QuarkXPress.
Editorial Equipment: Hardware -- 5-APP/Mac Quadra 610; Printers -- APP/Mac LaserWriter Pro 600
Editorial Software: QPS/QuarkXPress.
Production Equipment: Hardware -- 2-APP/Mac LaserWriter Pro 600, AG/Arcus Plus Scanner; Cameras -- R/500.

MARLINTON

THE POCAHONTAS TIMES

Street Address: 206 8th St
City: Marlinton
State: WV
ZIP Code: 24954-1031
General Phone: (304) 799-4973
General Email: jnh@pocahontastimes.com
Publication Website: pocahontastimes.com
Parent Company: Mountain Media
Editor Name: Jaynell Graham
Advertising Executive Name: Sunny Given
Delivery Methods: Mail`Racks
Year Established: 1883
Own Printing Facility?: Y
Commercial printers?: N
Mechanical specifications: Type page 13 x 21 1/2; E - 6 cols, 2, 1/5 between; A - 6 cols, 2, 1/5 between; C - 6 cols, 2, 1/5 between.
Published Days: Thur
Avg. Paid Circ.: 4500
Audit Company: Sworn/Estimate/Non-Audited

OAK HILL

MONTGOMERY HERALD

Street Address: 417 Main St.
City: Oak Hill
State: WV
ZIP Code: 25901
General Phone: (304) 442-4156
General Email: mhnews@register-herald.com
Publication Website: montgomery-herald.com
Parent Company: CNHI, LLC
Advertising Executive Name: Debbie Maxwell
Advertising Executive Email: dmaxwell@register-herald.com
Advertising Executive Phone: (304) 469-3373
Delivery Methods: Mail`Newsstand
Own Printing Facility?: Y
Commercial printers?: Y
Published Days: Wed
Avg. Paid Circ.: 1500
Avg. Free Circ.: 184
Audit Company: Sworn/Estimate/Non-Audited

OAK HILL

THE FAYETTE TRIBUNE

Street Address: 417 Main St
City: Oak Hill
State: WV
ZIP Code: 25901
General Phone: (304) 469-3373
General Email: ckeenan@register-herald.com
Publication Website: fayettetribune.com
Parent Company: CNHI, LLC
Delivery Methods: Mail`Newsstand
Own Printing Facility?: Y
Commercial printers?: Y
Published Days: Mon`Thur
Avg. Paid Circ.: 2200
Audit Company: Sworn/Estimate/Non-Audited

PETERSBURG

GRANT COUNTY PRESS

Street Address: P.O. Box 39
City: Petersburg
State: WV
ZIP Code: 26847-1766
General Phone: (304) 257-1844
General Email: ads@grantcountypress.com
Publication Website: https://www.grantcountypress.com/
Editor Name: Camille Howard
Advertising Executive Name: Tara Warner Pratt
Delivery Methods: Mail`Racks
Year Established: 1896
Own Printing Facility?: Y
Commercial printers?: Y
Mechanical specifications: Type page 13 x 21 1/2; E - 6 cols, 2 1/8, between; A - 6 cols, 2 1/8, between; C - 9 cols, 1 1/4, between.
Published Days: Tues`Sat
Avg. Paid Circ.: 3700
Avg. Free Circ.: 6200
Audit Company: Sworn/Estimate/Non-Audited

PHILIPPI

THE BARBOUR DEMOCRAT

Street Address: 113 CHURCH ST
City: Philippi
State: WV
ZIP Code: 26416
General Phone: (304) 457-2222
General Email: news@barbourdemocratwv.com
Publication Website: http://www.barbourdemocratwv.com/
Editor Name: J. Eric Cutright
Delivery Methods: Mail`Newsstand
Year Established: 1893
Published Days: Wed
Avg. Paid Circ.: 5301
Avg. Free Circ.: 300
Audit Company: Sworn/Estimate/Non-Audited

PRINCETON

PRINCETON TIMES

Street Address: 928 Bluefield Avenue
City: Princeton
State: WV
ZIP Code: 24740-2746
General Phone: (304) 425-8191
General Email: lmcvey@bdtonline.com
Publication Website: https://www.ptonline.net/
Parent Company: CNHI, LLC
Publisher Name: Randy Mooney
Publisher Email: rmooney@bdtonline.com
Publisher Phone: (304) 327-2840
Editor Name: Samantha Perry
Editor Email: sperry@bdtonline.com
Delivery Methods: Mail`Newsstand
Published Days: Fri
Avg. Paid Circ.: 4900
Audit Company: Sworn/Estimate/Non-Audited

RAVENSWOOD

JACKSON HERALD

Street Address: PO Box 38
City: Ravenswood
State: WV
ZIP Code: 26164-0038
General Phone: (304) 372-4222
General Email: tmandrake@jacksonnewspapers.com
Publication Website: https://www.mainstreetnews.com/jackson/?fbclid=IwAR2VtleER05GPW-SNPz7DBBL8mRmRDBm8dMatDsJOZriEdGksd1MUOECTho
Parent Company: Gannett
Delivery Methods: Mail`Carrier`Racks
Year Established: March 1, 1876
Published Days: Tues`Thur`Sat
Avg. Paid Circ.: 6500
Audit Company: Sworn/Estimate/Non-Audited

RAVENSWOOD

Community Newspapers in the U.S.

THE JACKSON STAR NEWS

Street Address: 410 Race Street
City: Ravenswood
State: WV
ZIP Code: 26164
General Phone: (304) 372-4222
General Email: ads@jacksonnewspapers.com
Publication Website: https://www.jacksonnewspapers.com/
Parent Company: Gannett
Advertising Executive Name: Tina Kocher
Advertising Executive Email: ads@jacksonnewspapers.com
Delivery Methods: Mail`Carrier`Racks
Year Established: January 1, 1868
Own Printing Facility?: Y
Commercial printers?: Y
Published Days: Thur`Sat
Avg. Paid Circ.: 6000
Avg. Free Circ.: 50
Audit Company: Sworn/Estimate/Non-Audited

SAINT MARYS

PLEASANTS COUNTY LEADER

Street Address: 206 George St
City: Saint Marys
State: WV
ZIP Code: 26170-1024
General Phone: (304) 684-2424
General Email: news@oracleandleader.com
Publication Website: http://ple.stparchive.com/
Delivery Methods: Mail`Newsstand
Year Established: 1899
Own Printing Facility?: Y
Commercial printers?: Y
Mechanical specifications: Type page 13 x 21 1/2; E - 6 cols, 2, 1/6 between; A - 6 cols, 2, 1/6 between; C - 6 cols, 2, 1/6 between.
Published Days: Sat
Avg. Paid Circ.: 2100
Audit Company: Sworn/Estimate/Non-Audited

SHINNSTON

SHINNSTON NEWS & HARRISON COUNTY JOURNAL

Street Address: 223 Pike St
City: Shinnston
State: WV
ZIP Code: 26431
General Phone: (304) 592-1030
General Email: debra@mountainmedianews.com
Publication Website: https://shinnstonnews.com/
Parent Company: Harrison County Publishing Co
Delivery Methods: Mail`Newsstand
Published Days: Thur
Avg. Paid Circ.: 2000
Audit Company: Sworn/Estimate/Non-Audited

SPENCER

ROANE COUNTY REPORTER

Street Address: 210 E Main St
City: Spencer
State: WV
ZIP Code: 25276-1602
General Phone: (304) 927-2360
General Email: dhedges@thetimesrecord.net
Publication Website: http://www.thetimesrecord.net/
Parent Company: HD Media Company LLC
Delivery Methods: Mail`Newsstand
Year Established: 1915
Own Printing Facility?: Y
Commercial printers?: Y
Mechanical specifications: 6 col (SAU) 13 inches by 21-1/2 inches
Published Days: Thur
Avg. Paid Circ.: 3145
Avg. Free Circ.: 100
Audit Company: Sworn/Estimate/Non-Audited
Note: Combo with The Times Record, 6,300 total circulation

SPENCER

THE TIMES RECORD

Street Address: 210 E Main St
City: Spencer
State: WV
ZIP Code: 25276-1602
General Phone: (304) 927-2360
General Email: family@thetimesrecord.net
Publication Website: https://www.thetimesrecord.net/
Parent Company: Gannett
Delivery Methods: Mail`Newsstand
Year Established: 1888
Own Printing Facility?: Y
Commercial printers?: Y
Mechanical specifications: Type page 13 x 21 1/2; E - 6 cols, 2 1/16, 1/8 between; A - 6 cols, 2 1/16, 1/8 between; C - 6 cols, 2 1/16, 1/8 between.
Published Days: Thur
Avg. Paid Circ.: 2075
Avg. Free Circ.: 25
Audit Company: Sworn/Estimate/Non-Audited

SUTTON

BRAXTON CITIZENS' NEWS

Street Address: 501 Main St
City: Sutton
State: WV
ZIP Code: 26601-1320
General Phone: (304) 765-5193
General Email: allison@bcn-news.com
Publication Website: http://www.bcn-news.com/
Editor Email: editor@bcn-news.com
Advertising Executive Email: stevie@bcn-news.com
Delivery Methods: Mail`Newsstand
Year Established: 1976
Published Days: Tues
Avg. Paid Circ.: 6150
Audit Company: Sworn/Estimate/Non-Audited

WELCH

THE WELCH NEWS

Street Address: 125 Wyoming St
City: Welch
State: WV
ZIP Code: 24801
General Phone: (304) 436-3144
General Email: welchnews@frontiernet.net
Publication Website: https://www.welchnews.com/
Delivery Methods: Mail`Newsstand
Mechanical specifications: Type page 13 x 21 1/2; E - 6 cols, 2 1/16, 1/8 between; A - 6 cols, 2 1/16, 1/8 between; C - 9 cols, 1 3/8, 1/16 between.
Published Days: Mon`Wed`Fri
Avg. Paid Circ.: 4764
Audit Company: Sworn/Estimate/Non-Audited

WESTON

WESTON DEMOCRAT

Street Address: 306 Main Ave
City: Weston
State: WV
ZIP Code: 26452-2046
General Phone: (304) 269-1600
General Email: ads@westondemocrat.com
Publication Website: https://www.wvnews.com/westondemocrat
Parent Company: Clarksburg Publishing Company
Advertising Executive Email: advertising@westondemocrat.com
Delivery Methods: Mail`Newsstand`Racks
Year Established: 1867
Mechanical specifications: Type page 13 5/8 x 20 1/2; E - 6 cols, 2 1/8, between; A - 6 cols, 2 1/8, between; C - 6 cols, 2 1/8, between.
Published Days: Wed
Avg. Paid Circ.: 7000
Avg. Free Circ.: 88
Audit Company: Sworn/Estimate/Non-Audited

WYOMING

AFTON

STAR VALLEY INDEPENDENT

Street Address: 360 S Washington St
City: Afton
State: WY
ZIP Code: 83110
General Phone: (307) 885-5727
General Email: dahle@svinews.com
Publication Website: https://svinews.com/
Publisher Name: Dan Dockstader
Editor Name: Sarah Hale
Advertising Executive Name: Duke Dance
Advertising Executive Email: duked@svinews.com
Delivery Methods: Mail`Racks
Year Established: 1902
Commercial printers?: Y
Published Days: Thur
Avg. Paid Circ.: 4000
Audit Company: Sworn/Estimate/Non-Audited

BUFFALO

BUFFALO BULLETIN

Street Address: 58 N Lobban Ave
City: Buffalo
State: WY
ZIP Code: 82834
General Phone: (307) 684-2223
General Email: publisher@buffalobulletin.com
Publication Website: http://www.buffalobulletin.com/
Publisher Name: Robb Hicks
Publisher Email: robb@buffalobulletin.com
Editor Name: Jen Sieve-Hicks
Editor Email: jen@buffalobulletin.com
Advertising Executive Name: Ashley Hughes
Advertising Executive Email: ashley@buffalobulletin.com
Delivery Methods: Mail
Commercial printers?: Y
Published Days: Thur
Avg. Paid Circ.: 3800
Audit Company: Sworn/Estimate/Non-Audited

CASPER

CASPER JOURNAL

Street Address: 170 Star Ln
City: Casper
State: WY
ZIP Code: 82604-2883
General Phone: (307) 265-3870
General Email: dale.bohren@trib.com
Publication Website: https://trib.com/casperjournal/
Publisher Name: Dale Bohren
Publisher Email: dale.bohren@trib.com
Publisher Phone: (307) 266-0516
Editor Name: Brandon Foster
Editor Email: brandon.foster@trib.com
Editor Phone: (314) 922-3744
Advertising Executive Name: Sean Johnson
Advertising Executive Email: sean.johnson@trib.com
Advertising Executive Phone: (307) 266-0569
Delivery Methods: Mail`Carrier`Racks
Year Established: 1978
Own Printing Facility?: Y
Commercial printers?: Y
Mechanical specifications: Type page 10 1/2 x 16 2/3; E - 5 cols, 2, 1/16 between; A - 5 cols, 2, 1/16 between; C - 9 cols, 1 1/16, 1/16 between.
Published Days: Wed
Avg. Paid Circ.: 600
Avg. Free Circ.: 25000
Audit Company: Sworn/Estimate/Non-Audited

CODY

THE CODY ENTERPRISE

Street Address: 3101 Big Horn Ave
City: Cody
State: WY
ZIP Code: 82414-9250
General Phone: (307) 587-2231
General Email: zac@codyenterprise.com
Publication Website: http://www.codyenterprise.com/
Parent Company: Sage Publishing Co.
Publisher Name: JT Malmberg
Publisher Email: jt@codyenterprise.com
Editor Name: Amber Peabody
Editor Email: amber@codyenterprise.com
Advertising Executive Name: Megan Barton
Advertising Executive Email: megan@codyenterprise.com
Delivery Methods: Mail`Newsstand`Racks
Year Established: 1899
Own Printing Facility?: Y
Commercial printers?: Y
Mechanical specifications: Type page 11 1/2 x 21; E - 6 cols, 1 3/4, 1/6 between; A - 6 cols, 1 3/4, 1/6 between; C - 6 cols, 1 3/4, 1/6 between.
Published Days: Tues`Thur
Avg. Paid Circ.: 7050
Audit Company: Sworn/Estimate/Non-Audited

DOUGLAS

THE DOUGLAS BUDGET

Street Address: 310 E Center St
City: Douglas
State: WY
ZIP Code: 82633
General Phone: (307) 358-2965
General Email: publisher@douglas-budget.com
Publication Website: http://www.douglas-budget.com/
Parent Company: Sage Publishing and Matt Adelman
Publisher Name: Matt Adelman
Publisher Email: publisher@douglas-budget.com
Editor Name: Matt Adelman
Editor Email: publisher@douglas-budget.com
Advertising Executive Name: Carrie Calliham
Advertising Executive Email: advertising1@douglas-budget.com
Delivery Methods: Mail`Newsstand`Carrier`Racks
Year Established: 1886

DUBOIS

DUBOIS FRONTIER

Street Address: 8 C St
City: Dubois
State: WY
ZIP Code: 82513
General Phone: (307) 455-2525
General Email: frontierads@wyoming.com
Publication Website: http://duboisfrontier.com/
Publisher Name: Christine Smith
Editor Name: Christine Smith
Advertising Executive Name: Tylyn Hust
Advertising Executive Email: frontierads@wyoming.com
Delivery Methods: Mail`Racks
Year Established: 1927
Published Days: Thur
Avg. Paid Circ.: 1200
Audit Company: Sworn/Estimate/Non-Audited

EVANSTON

UINTA COUNTY HERALD

Street Address: 849 Front St
City: Evanston
State: WY
ZIP Code: 82930
General Phone: (307) 789-6560
General Email: bglathar@uintacountyherald.com
Publication Website: https://uintacountyherald.com/
Parent Company: News Media Grouip
Publisher Name: Mark Tesoro
Publisher Email: mtesoro@uintacountyherald.com
Publisher Phone: (307) 789-6560
Editor Name: Bryon Glathar
Editor Email: bglathar@uintacountyherald.com
Editor Phone: (307) 789-6560, ext : 110
Advertising Executive Name: Brian Liechty
Advertising Executive Email: bliechty@uintacountyherald.com
Advertising Executive Phone: (307) 789-6560, ext : 102
Delivery Methods: Mail`Newsstand`Racks
Year Established: 1937
Mechanical specifications: Type page 13 x 21 1/2; E - 6 cols, 2, 1/6 between; A - 6 cols, 2, 1/6 between; C - 6 cols, 2, 1/6 between.
Published Days: Tues`Fri
Avg. Paid Circ.: 3250
Avg. Free Circ.: 73
Audit Company: Sworn/Estimate/Non-Audited

GREEN RIVER

GREEN RIVER STAR

Street Address: 445 Uinta Dr
City: Green River
State: WY
ZIP Code: 82935
General Phone: (307) 875-3103
General Email: ads@greenriverstar.com
Publication Website: https://www.greenriverstar.com/
Editor Email: editor@greenriverstar.com

Own Printing Facility?: Y
Commercial printers?: Y
Mechanical specifications: Type page 11 1/2 x 21; E - 6 cols, 1 3/4, 1/6 between; A - 6 cols, 1 3/4, 1/6 between; C - 6 cols, 1 3/4, 1/6 between.
Published Days: Wed
Avg. Paid Circ.: 3908
Avg. Free Circ.: 20
Audit Company: Sworn/Estimate/Non-Audited

Advertising Executive Name: Ronda Hefner
Advertising Executive Email: sales1@greenriverstar.com
Advertising Executive Phone: (307) 875-3103
Year Established: 1890
Published Days: Wed
Avg. Paid Circ.: 3200
Audit Company: Sworn/Estimate/Non-Audited

GUERNSEY

GUERNSEY GAZETTE

Street Address: 40 S Wyoming St
City: Guernsey
State: WY
ZIP Code: 82214
General Phone: (307) 836-2021
General Email: vhood@guernseygazette.com
Publication Website: https://www.guernseygazette.com/
Parent Company: News Media Grouip
Publisher Name: Rob Mortimore
Publisher Email: rmort@guernseygazette.com
Publisher Phone: (307) 632-5666
Editor Name: Andrew Brosig
Editor Email: abrosig@guernseygazette.com
Editor Phone: (307) 836-2021
Advertising Executive Name: Hannah Haffner
Advertising Executive Email: hhaffner@torringtontelegram.com
Advertising Executive Phone: (307) 532-2184
Delivery Methods: Mail`Newsstand`Racks
Own Printing Facility?: Y
Mechanical specifications: 6 columns, 1.5" per column, 1 pica gutter. 9.75" x 13" printed area
Published Days: Tues
Avg. Paid Circ.: 550
Audit Company: Sworn/Estimate/Non-Audited

JACKSON

JACKSON HOLE NEWS&GUIDE

Street Address: 1225 Maple Way
City: Jackson
State: WY
ZIP Code: 83001
General Phone: (307) 733-2047
General Email: adsales@jhnewsandguide.com
Publication Website: https://www.jhnewsandguide.com/
Parent Company: Teton Media Works, Inc.
Publisher Name: Kevin Olson
Publisher Email: kevin@jhnewsandguide.com
Publisher Phone: (307) 732-7060
Editor Name: Rebecca Huntington
Editor Email: rebecca@jhnewsandguide.com
Editor Phone: (307) 732-7078
Advertising Executive Name: Karen Brennan
Advertising Executive Email: karen@jhnewsandguide.com
Advertising Executive Phone: (307) 739-9541
Delivery Methods: Mail`Newsstand`Racks
Year Established: 1970
Own Printing Facility?: Y
Mechanical specifications: Type page 10 1/6 x 15 5/6; E - 4 cols, 2 2/5, 1/6 between; A - 4 cols, 2 2/5, 1/6 between; C - 7 cols, between.
Published Days: Wed
Avg. Paid Circ.: 6835
Audit Company: Sworn/Estimate/Non-Audited

KEMMERER

THE KEMMERER GAZETTE

Street Address: 708 J C Penney Dr
City: Kemmerer
State: WY

ZIP Code: 83101-2936
General Phone: (307) 877-3347
General Email: tdavis@kemmerergazette.com
Publication Website: https://www.kemmerergazette.com/
Parent Company: News Media Grouip
Publisher Name: Mark Tesoro
Publisher Email: mtesoro@uintacountyherald.com
Publisher Phone: (307) 789-6560
Editor Name: Nathanael Himes
Editor Email: nhimes@kemmerergazette.com
Editor Phone: (307) 466-3177
Advertising Executive Name: Cortney Reed
Advertising Executive Email: creed@kemmerergazette.com
Advertising Executive Phone: (307) 679-5278
Delivery Methods: Mail`Racks
Own Printing Facility?: Y
Mechanical specifications: Type page 13 x 21 1/4; E - 6 cols, 2, 1/8 between; A - 6 cols, 2, 1/8 between; C - 6 cols, 2, 1/8 between.
Published Days: Thur
Avg. Paid Circ.: 1650
Audit Company: Sworn/Estimate/Non-Audited

LANDER

LANDER JOURNAL

Street Address: 332 Main St
City: Lander
State: WY
ZIP Code: 82520
General Phone: (307) 332-2323
General Email: fremontnews@wyoming.com
Publication Website: https://thelanderjournal.com/
Parent Company: Riverton Ranger, Inc.
Publisher Name: Steve Peck
Editor Name: Kelli Ameling
Advertising Executive Name: Cathleen Cline
Delivery Methods: Mail`Racks
Own Printing Facility?: Y
Commercial printers?: Y
Published Days: Wed`Sun
Avg. Paid Circ.: 4475
Avg. Free Circ.: 2600
Audit Company: Sworn/Estimate/Non-Audited

LINGLE

THE LINGLE GUIDE

Street Address: 228 Main St
City: Lingle
State: WY
ZIP Code: 82223
General Phone: (307) 837-2255
General Email: calbers@lingleguide.com
Publication Website: https://www.lingleguide.com/
Parent Company: News Media Grouip
Publisher Name: Rob Mortimore
Publisher Email: rmort@lingleguide.com
Publisher Phone: (307) 532-2184
Editor Name: Andrew Brosig
Editor Email: abrosig@lingleguide.com
Editor Phone: (307) 532-2184
Advertising Executive Name: Hannah Haffner
Advertising Executive Email: hhaffner@torringtontelegram.com
Advertising Executive Phone: (307) 532-2184
Published Days: Mon
Audit Company: Sworn/Estimate/Non-Audited

LUSK

THE LUSK HERALD

Street Address: 1000 Main St
City: Lusk

State: WY
ZIP Code: 82225
General Phone: (307) 334-2867
General Email: hgoddard@luskherald.com
Publication Website: https://www.luskherald.com/
Parent Company: News Media Grouip
Publisher Name: Rob Mortimore
Publisher Email: rmort@luskherald.com
Publisher Phone: (307) 532-2184
Editor Name: Andrew Brosig
Editor Email: abrosig@luskherald.com
Editor Phone: (307) 334-2867
Advertising Executive Name: Hannah Haffner
Advertising Executive Email: hhaffner@torringtontelegram.com
Advertising Executive Phone: (307) 532-2184
Delivery Methods: Mail`Newsstand`Racks
Year Established: 1886
Own Printing Facility?: Y
Mechanical specifications: Type page 9 3/4 x 13; E - 6 cols, 1 1/2, 1/6 between; A - 6 cols, 1 1/2, 1/6 between; C - 6 cols, 1 1/2, 1/6 between.
Published Days: Wed
Avg. Paid Circ.: 1300
Audit Company: Sworn/Estimate/Non-Audited

LYMAN

BRIDGER VALLEY PIONEER

Street Address: 317 Bradshaw St # 2
City: Lyman
State: WY
ZIP Code: 82937
General Phone: (307) 787-3229
General Email: vgiorgis@bridgervalleypioneer.com
Publication Website: https://bridgervalleypioneer.com/
Parent Company: News Media Grouip
Publisher Name: Mark Tesoro
Publisher Email: mtesoro@uintacountyherald.com
Publisher Phone: (307) 789-6560
Editor Name: Virginia Giorgis
Editor Email: vgiorgis@bridgervalleypioneer.com
Editor Phone: (307) 787-3229
Advertising Executive Name: Randi Singleton
Advertising Executive Email: rsingleton@bridgervalleypioneer.com
Advertising Executive Phone: (307) 787-3229
Delivery Methods: Mail`Racks
Published Days: Fri
Avg. Paid Circ.: 1800
Audit Company: Sworn/Estimate/Non-Audited

MOORCROFT

MOORCROFT LEADER

Street Address: 304 N Riley Ave
City: Moorcroft
State: WY
ZIP Code: 82721
General Phone: (307) 756-3371
General Email: moorcroftleader@gmail.com
Publication Website: https://www.moorcroftleader.com/
Parent Company: Sundance Times, Inc.
Advertising Executive Email: thesundancetimes@gmail.com
Delivery Methods: Mail`Newsstand
Year Established: 1909
Commercial printers?: Y
Mechanical specifications: Type page 10 x 13; E - 6 cols, 1 7/12, 1/6 between; A - 6 cols, 1 7/12, 1/6 between; C - 6 cols, 1 7/12, 1/6 between.
Published Days: Thur
Avg. Paid Circ.: 1200
Avg. Free Circ.: 135
Audit Company: Sworn/Estimate/Non-Audited

Community Newspapers in the U.S.

NEWCASTLE

NEWS LETTER JOURNAL

Street Address: 14 W Main St
City: Newcastle
State: WY
ZIP Code: 82701
General Phone: (307) 746-2777
General Email: sales@newslj.com
Publication Website: https://newslj.com/
Publisher Name: Bob Bonnar
Editor Name: Bob Bonnar
Editor Email: editor@newslj.com
Advertising Executive Name: Stephanie Bonnar
Advertising Executive Email: ads@newslj.com
Advertising Executive Phone: (307) 746-2777
Delivery Methods: Mail`Newsstand`Racks
Year Established: 1890
Own Printing Facility?: Y
Commercial printers?: Y
Mechanical specifications: Type page 13 1/4 x 21; A - 6 cols, 2 1/16, 1/6 between; C - 6 cols, 2 1/16, 1/6 between.
Published Days: Thur
Avg. Paid Circ.: 2500
Avg. Free Circ.: 50
Audit Company: Sworn/Estimate/Non-Audited

PINE BLUFFS

PINE BLUFFS POST

Street Address: 201 E 2nd St
City: Pine Bluffs
State: WY
ZIP Code: 82082
General Phone: (307) 245-3763
General Email: pinebluffseditor@rtconnect.net
Publication Website: https://www.pinebluffspost.com/
Parent Company: Stevenson Newspapers
Advertising Executive Email: pinebluffsads@rtconnect.net
Advertising Executive Phone: (307) 245-3763
Delivery Methods: Mail`Newsstand`Racks
Year Established: 1908
Own Printing Facility?: Y
Published Days: Thur
Avg. Paid Circ.: 1100
Audit Company: Sworn/Estimate/Non-Audited

PINEDALE

SUBLETTE EXAMINER

Street Address: 41 S. Lake Ave., PO Box 1539
City: Pinedale
State: WY
ZIP Code: 82941
General Phone: (307) 367-3203
General Email: hdabb@subletteexaminer.com
Publication Website: https://subletteexaminer.com/
Parent Company: News Media Grouip
Publisher Name: Mark Tesoro
Publisher Email: mtesoro@uintacountyherald.com
Publisher Phone: (307) 789-6560
Editor Name: Holly Dabb
Editor Email: hdabb@subletteexaminer.com
Editor Phone: (307) 367-3203
Advertising Executive Name: Cortney Reed
Advertising Executive Email: creed@subletteexaminer.com
Advertising Executive Phone: (307) 367-3203
Published Days: Thur
Audit Company: Sworn/Estimate/Non-Audited

PINEDALE

THE PINEDALE ROUNDUP

Street Address: 41 S. Lake Ave., Suite 2
City: Pinedale
State: WY
ZIP Code: 82941
General Phone: (307) 367-2123
General Email: office@pinedaleroundup.com
Publication Website: https://pinedaleroundup.com/
Parent Company: News Media Grouip
Publisher Name: Mark Tesoro
Publisher Email: mtesoro@uintacountyherald.com
Publisher Phone: (307) 789-6560
Editor Name: Holly Dabb
Editor Email: hdabb@pinedaleroundup.com
Editor Phone: (307) 367-2123
Advertising Executive Name: Cortney Reed
Advertising Executive Email: creed@pinedaleroundup.com
Advertising Executive Phone: (307) 367-2123
Delivery Methods: Mail`Newsstand`Racks
Year Established: 1904
Commercial printers?: Y
Mechanical specifications: Type page 11 x 17; E - 4 cols, 2 5/12, 1/6 between; A - 4 cols, 2 5/12, 1/6 between; C - 6 cols, 1 7/12, 1/6 between.
Published Days: Fri
Avg. Paid Circ.: 4000
Audit Company: Sworn/Estimate/Non-Audited

POWELL

THE POWELL TRIBUNE

Street Address: 128 S Bent St
City: Powell
State: WY
ZIP Code: 82435
General Phone: (307) 754-2221
General Email: toby@powelltribune.com
Publication Website: https://www.powelltribune.com/
Publisher Name: Dave Bonner
Publisher Email: dave@powelltribune.com
Editor Name: CJ Baker
Editor Email: cj@powelltribune.com
Advertising Executive Name: Toby Bonner
Advertising Executive Email: toby@powelltribune.com
Delivery Methods: Mail`Racks
Year Established: 1908
Own Printing Facility?: Y
Published Days: Tues`Thur
Avg. Paid Circ.: 4000
Audit Company: Sworn/Estimate/Non-Audited

RAWLINS

RAWLINS TIMES

Street Address: 522 W Buffalo St
City: Rawlins
State: WY
ZIP Code: 82301
General Phone: (307) 324-3411
General Email: knicholson@rawlinstimes.com
Publication Website: https://www.rawlinstimes.com/
Editor Name: Ray Erku
Editor Email: rerku@rawlinstimes.com
Editor Phone: (307) 324-3411
Advertising Executive Name: Kellie Kemp
Advertising Executive Email: kkemp@rawlinstimes.com
Advertising Executive Phone: (307) 324-3411
Year Established: 1889
Own Printing Facility?: Y
Mechanical specifications: Type page 10 1/2 x 14; E - 5 cols, 2 1/16, 1/8 between; A - 5 cols, 2 1/16, 1/8 between; C - 5 cols, 2 1/16, 1/8 between.
Published Days: Wed`Sat
Weekday Frequency: m
Saturday Frequency: m
Avg. Paid Circ.: 1600
Audit Company: Sworn/Estimate/Non-Audited
Pressroom Equipment: Lines -- 6-HI/Cotrell V-15A;
Mailroom Equipment: Address Machine -- 1-Data/Star 486-335X, Microsoft/Wordperfect Labels 6.0.;
Business Equipment: MaxTech, Synaptic/Micro Solutions
Business Software: Synaptic/Micro Solutions 4.06
Classified Equipment: Hardware -- Synaptic/Micro Solutions;
Classified Software: Synaptic/Micro Solutions, SunType.
Editorial Equipment: Hardware -- Synaptic/Micro Solution; Printers -- 2-APP/Mac LaserWriter II NTX, APP/Mac LaserWriter Pro 2-640, APP/Mac LaserWriter Pro 600
Editorial Software: Synaptic/Micro Solutions, SunType.
Production Equipment: Hardware -- APP/Mac LaserWriter Pro 600, 2-APP/Mac LaserWriter II; Cameras -- 1-Argyle/23; Scanners -- APP/Mac, 2-Nikon/ScanTouch, 2-Nikon/Coolscan
Production Software: QPS/QuarkXPress 3.31, QPS/QuarkXPress 4.0.

SARATOGA

THE SARATOGA SUN

Street Address: 116 E Bridge St
City: Saratoga
State: WY
ZIP Code: 82331
General Phone: (307) 326-8311
General Email: saratogasun@union-tel.com
Publication Website: https://www.saratogasun.com/
Parent Company: Stevenson Newspapers
Publisher Name: Joshua Wood
Publisher Email: saratogasun@union-tel.com
Publisher Phone: (307) 326-8311
Editor Name: Joshua Wood
Editor Email: saratogasun@union-tel.com
Editor Phone: (307) 326-8311
Advertising Executive Email: sunads@union-tel.com
Delivery Methods: Mail`Racks
Year Established: 1888
Commercial printers?: Y
Mechanical specifications: Type page 10 1/2 x 14; E - 5 cols, 2, 1/8 between; A - 5 cols, 2, 1/8 between; C - 6 cols, 1 5/8, 1/8 between.
Published Days: Wed
Avg. Paid Circ.: 1800
Avg. Free Circ.: 20
Audit Company: Sworn/Estimate/Non-Audited

SUNDANCE

THE SUNDANCE TIMES

Street Address: 311 E Main St
City: Sundance
State: WY
ZIP Code: 82729
General Phone: (307) 283-3411
General Email: thesundancetimes@gmail.com
Publication Website: https://www.sundancetimes.com/
Parent Company: Sundance Times, Inc.
Advertising Executive Email: thesundancetimes@gmail.com
Delivery Methods: Mail`Racks
Year Established: 1884
Own Printing Facility?: Y
Mechanical specifications: Type page 13 x 21.
Published Days: Thur
Avg. Paid Circ.: 1800
Avg. Free Circ.: 35
Audit Company: Sworn/Estimate/Non-Audited

THERMOPOLIS

THERMOPOLIS INDEPENDENT RECORD

Street Address: 431 Broadway St
City: Thermopolis
State: WY
ZIP Code: 82443
General Phone: (307) 864-2328
General Email: news@thermopir.com
Publication Website: https://www.thermopir.com/
Advertising Executive Name: Amber Geis
Advertising Executive Email: ads@thermopir.com
Delivery Methods: Mail`Newsstand`Racks
Year Established: 1901
Published Days: Thur
Avg. Paid Circ.: 2280
Audit Company: Sworn/Estimate/Non-Audited

TORRINGTON

THE TORRINGTON TELEGRAM

Street Address: 2025 Main St
City: Torrington
State: WY
ZIP Code: 82240
General Phone: (307) 532-2184
General Email: rmort@torringtontelegram.com
Publication Website: https://www.torringtontelegram.com/
Parent Company: News Media Grouip
Publisher Name: Rob Mortimore
Publisher Email: rmort@torringtontelegram.com
Publisher Phone: (307) 532-2184
Editor Name: Andrew Brosig
Editor Email: abrosig@torringtontelegram.com
Editor Phone: (307) 532-2184
Advertising Executive Name: Hannah Haffner
Advertising Executive Email: hhaffner@torringtontelegram.com
Advertising Executive Phone: (307) 532-2184
Delivery Methods: Mail`Newsstand`Carrier`Racks
Year Established: 1907
Own Printing Facility?: Y
Commercial printers?: Y
Mechanical specifications: 8 columns, 1.5" per column, 1 pica gutter, 13" x 21.5" page dimension
Published Days: Wed`Fri
Avg. Paid Circ.: 2600
Avg. Free Circ.: 70
Audit Company: Sworn/Estimate/Non-Audited

WHEATLAND

THE PLATTE COUNTY RECORD-TIMES

Street Address: 1007 8th St
City: Wheatland
State: WY
ZIP Code: 82201
General Phone: (307) 322-2627
General Email: rmort@pcrecordtimes.com
Publication Website: https://pcrecordtimes.com/
Parent Company: News Media Corporation
Publisher Name: Rob Mortimore
Publisher Email: rmort@pcrecordtimes.com
Publisher Phone: (307) 322-2627
Editor Name: Andrew Brosig
Editor Email: abrosig@pcrecordtimes.com
Editor Phone: (307) 322-2627

Advertising Executive Name: Hannah Haffner
Advertising Executive Email: hhaffner@torringtontelegram.com
Advertising Executive Phone: (307) 532-2184
Delivery Methods: Mail`Newsstand`Racks
Year Established: 1960
Own Printing Facility?: Y
Commercial printers?: Y
Mechanical specifications: Type page 13 x 21; E - 8 cols, 1 1/2, between; A - 8 cols, 1 1/2, between; C - 8 cols, 1 1/2, between.
Published Days: Wed
Avg. Paid Circ.: 1900
Audit Company: Sworn/Estimate/Non-Audited

DELTA WAVERLY COMMUNITY NEWS

General Email: lsj-digital@lsj.com
Publication Website: http://www.deltawaverlycommunitynews.com/
Delivery Methods: Mail
Year Established: 1856
Mechanical specifications: Type page: 10 x 10; 6 col
Published Days: Sun
Avg. Free Circ.: 4344
Audit Company: Sworn/Estimate/Non-Audited

SHORE NEWS TODAY

Publication Website: http://www.shorenewstoday.com

SUBURBAN NEWS

Publication Website: https://www.nj.com/suburbannews/

THE NEWS DEMOCRAT

General Phone: (937) 444-3441

General Email: info@newsdemocrat.com
Publication Website: https://www.newsdemocrat.com/
Parent Company: Champion Media

THE SENTINEL OF GLOUCESTER COUNTY

Publication Website: http://thenjsentinel.com/
Parent Company: The Merckx Family of Malaga
Publisher Name: Cindy Merckx
Editor Name: Cindy Merckx

NON-DAILY NEWSPAPERS IN CANADA

100 MILE HOUSE

100 MILE HOUSE FREE PRESS

Street Address: 3-536 Horse Lake Rd. , Uptown Plaza
Province: BC
Postal: V0K 2E0
Country: Canada
Mailing address: PO Box 459
Mailing city: 100 Mile House
Province: BC
Postal: V0K 2E0
General Phone: (250) 395-2219
General Fax: (250) 395-3939
General/National Adv. E-mail: publisher@100milefreepress.net
Display Adv. E-mail: publisher@100milefreepress.net
Classified Adv. e-mail: classifieds@100milefreepress.net
Editorial e-mail: newsroom@100milefreepress.net
Primary Website: www.100milefreepress.net
Year Established: 1960
Delivery Methods: Mail`Newsstand`Carrier`Racks
Areas Served - City/County or Portion Thereof, or Zip codes: South Cariboo
Commercial printers?: Y
Published: Thur
Avg Paid Circ: 2517
Avg Free Circ: 4115
Audit By: VAC
Audit Date: 31.07.2016
Personnel: Martina Dopf (Publisher); Chris Nickless (Sales); Kerri Mingo (Advertising Creative); Debbie Theoret (Creative); Carole Rooney (Reporter); Lori Brodie (Reception/Circulation); Max Winkelman (Ed.); Evan Fentiman (Creative)
Parent company (for newspapers): Black Press Group Ltd.

ABBOTSFORD

THE ABBOTSFORD NEWS

Street Address: 34375 Gladys Ave. ,
Province: BC
Postal: V2S 2H5
Country: Canada
Mailing address: 34375 Gladys Ave.
Mailing city: Abbotsford
Province: BC
Postal: V2S 2H5
General Phone: (604) 853-1144
General Fax: (604) 852-1641
General/National Adv. E-mail: publisher@abbynews.com
Display Adv. E-mail: donb@abbynews.com

Editorial e-mail: newsroom@abbynews.com
Primary Website: abbynews.com
Year Established: 1922
Areas Served - City/County or Portion Thereof, or Zip codes: Canada
Own Printing Facility?: Y
Commercial printers?: Y
Mechanical specifications: Type page 12 1/2 x 21; E - 7 cols, 1 11/16, 11/12 between; A - 7 cols, 1 11/16, 11/12 between; C - 7 cols, 1 11/16, 11/12 between.
Published: Tues`Thur`Sat
Avg Paid Circ: 45
Avg Free Circ: 38814
Audit By: AAM
Audit Date: 31.12.2018
Personnel: Kevin Hemery (Circ. Mgr.); Andrew Holota (Mng. Ed.); Carly Ferguson (Pub); Don Barbeau (Adv Mgr)
Parent company (for newspapers): Black Press Group Ltd.

ACTON VALE

LA PENSEE DE BAGOT

Street Address: 800 Roxton St. ,
Province: QC
Postal: J0H 1A0
Country: Canada
Mailing address: 800 Roxton St.
Mailing city: Acton Vale
Province: QC
Postal: J0H 1A0
General Phone: (450) 546-3271
General Fax: (450) 546-3491
General/National Adv. E-mail: mdorais@lapensee.qc.ca
Primary Website: www.lapensee.qc.ca
Year Established: 1951
Areas Served - City/County or Portion Thereof, or Zip codes: Canada
Mechanical specifications: Type page 11 1/2 x 15; E - 8 cols, 1 1/4, 1/6 between; A - 8 cols, 1 1/4, 1/6 between; C - 8 cols, 1 1/4, 1/6 between.
Published: Wed
Avg Paid Circ: 0
Avg Free Circ: 0
Audit By: CCAB
Audit Date: 30.09.2015
Personnel: Michel Dorais (Adv. Mgr.); Robert Beauchemin (Adv. Rep.); Jean-Francois Dorais (Adv. Rep.); Benoit Chartier (Ed.)

AGASSIZ

THE AGASSIZ-HARRISON OBSERVER

Street Address: 7167 Pioneer Ave ,

Province: BC
Postal: V0M 1A0
Country: Canada
Mailing address: PO Box 129
Mailing city: Agassiz
Province: BC
Postal: V0M 1A0
General Phone: (604) 796-4300
General Fax: (604) 796-2081
General/National Adv. E-mail: publisher@abbynews.com
Display Adv. E-mail: ads@ahobserver.com
Classified Adv. e-mail: tanya@blackpressused.ca
Editorial e-mail: news@ahobserver.com
Primary Website: www.agassizharrisonobserver.com
Year Established: 1999
Areas Served - City/County or Portion Thereof, or Zip codes: Agassiz, Harrison
Published: Thur
Avg Paid Circ: 590
Avg Free Circ: 2815
Audit By: VAC
Audit Date: 30.06.2016
Personnel: Carly Ferguson (Pub.); Erin Knutson (Ed); Tanya Jeyachandran (Class. Adv); Christine Douglas (Adv, Rep)
Parent company (for newspapers): Black Press Group Ltd.

AILSA CRAIG

THE MIDDLESEX BANNER

Street Address: 175 Main St. ,
Province: ON
Postal: N0M 1A0
Country: Canada
Mailing address: PO Box 433
Mailing city: Ailsa Craig
Province: ON
Postal: N0M 1A0
General Phone: (519) 293-1095
General Fax: (519) 293-1095
General/National Adv. E-mail: editor@banner.on.ca
Primary Website: www.banner.on.ca
Year Established: 1996
Areas Served - City/County or Portion Thereof, or Zip codes: Canada
Published: Wed
Avg Paid Circ: 736
Avg Free Circ: 708
Audit By: CMCA
Audit Date: 31.12.2015
Personnel: Brad Harness (Pub./Ed.)

AIRDRIE

AIRDRIE CITY VIEW

Street Address: #403-2903 Kingsview Blvd. ,
Province: AB
Postal: T4A 0C4
Country: Canada
Mailing address: #403-2903 Kingsview Blvd.
Mailing city: Airdrie
Province: AB
Postal: T4A 0C4
General Phone: (403) 948-1885
General Fax: (403) 948-2554
Display Adv. E-mail: rsonghurst@airdrie.greatwest.ca
Classified Adv. e-mail: classifieds@airdrie.greatwest.ca
Editorial e-mail: achorney@airdrie.greatwest.ca
Primary Website: http://www.airdriecityview.com
Year Established: 2002
Areas Served - City/County or Portion Thereof, or Zip codes: Airdrie/Canada
Published: Thur
Avg Paid Circ: 557
Avg Free Circ: 18336
Audit By: VAC
Audit Date: 31.05.2016
Personnel: Cam Christianson (Pub.); Allison Chorney (Ed)
Parent company (for newspapers): Great West Newspapers LP

AIRDRIE ECHO

Street Address: 112 - 1 Ave Ne ,
Province: AB
Postal: T4B 0R6
Country: Canada
Mailing address: 112 - 1 Ave NE
Mailing city: Airdrie
Province: AB
Postal: T4B 0R6
General Phone: (403) 948-7280
General Fax: (403) 912-2341
General/National Adv. E-mail: airdrie.echo@shaw.ca
Display Adv. E-mail: rmackintosh@postmedia.com
Editorial e-mail: jchalmers@postmedia.com
Primary Website: www.airdrieecho.com
Year Established: 1975
Delivery Methods: Carrier
Areas Served - City/County or Portion Thereof, or Zip codes: Canada
Mechanical specifications: Type page 10 1/4 x 14; E - 6 cols, 1 1/2, 1/4 between; A - 6 cols, 1 1/2, 1/4 between; C - 6 cols, 1 1/2, 1/4 between.
Published: Wed

Non-Daily Newspapers in Canada

Avg Free Circ: 18330
Audit By: VAC
Audit Date: 31.03.2016
Personnel: Ed Huculak (Pub.); John Chalmers (Ed.); Roxanne Mackintosh (Adv. Dir)
Parent company (for newspapers): Postmedia Network Inc.; Quebecor Communications, Inc.

ROCKY VIEW WEEKLY

Street Address: #403 2903 Kingsview Blvd. ,
Province: AB
Postal: T4A 0C4
Country: Canada
Mailing address: #403 2903 Kingsview Blvd.
Mailing city: Airdrie
Province: AB
Postal: T4A 0C4
General Phone: (403) 948-1885
General Fax: (403) 948-2554
General/National Adv. E-mail: sales@airdrie.greatwest.ca
Display Adv. E-mail: rsonghurst@airdrie.greatwest.ca
Classified Adv. e-mail: rvwclassifieds@airdrie.greatwest.ca
Editorial e-mail: achorney@airdrie.greatwest.ca
Primary Website: www.rockyviewweekly.com
Year Established: 1970
Delivery Methods: Mail`Newsstand`Racks
Areas Served - City/County or Portion Thereof, or Zip codes: Canada
Commercial printers?: Y
Mechanical specifications: Type page 10 1/4 x 15 1/2; E - 6 cols, 1 7/12, 1/6 between; A - 6 cols, 1 7/12, 1/6 between; C - 6 cols, 1 7/12, 1/6 between.
Published: Tues
Avg Paid Circ: 457
Avg Free Circ: 12910
Audit By: VAC
Audit Date: 30.06.2016
Personnel: Cameron Christianson (Pub.); Lisa Gebruck (Circ. Mgr.); Allison Chorney (Ed)
Parent company (for newspapers): Glacier Media Group; Great West Newspapers LP; Rocky View Publishing

ALBERTON

WEST PRINCE GRAPHIC

Street Address: 4 Railway St. ,
Province: PE
Postal: C0B 1B0
Country: Canada
Mailing address: PO Box 339
Mailing city: Alberton
Province: PE
Postal: C0B 1B0
General Phone: (902) 853-3320
General Fax: (902) 853-3071
General/National Adv. E-mail: westgraphic@islandpress.pe.ca
Editorial e-mail: cindy@peicanada.com
Primary Website: www.peicanada.com
Year Established: 1980
Own Printing Facility?: Y
Mechanical specifications: Type page 13 x 21 1/3.
Published: Wed
Avg Paid Circ: 121
Avg Free Circ: 5733
Audit By: CMCA
Audit Date: 31.03.2014
Personnel: Paul MacNeill (Pub.); Jan MacNeill (Adv. Mgr.); Nicole Ford (Circ. Mgr.); Cindy Chant (Ed.)

ALDERGROVE

THE ALDERGROVE STAR

Street Address: 27118 Fraser Hwy. ,
Province: BC
Postal: V4W 3P6
Country: Canada
Mailing address: 27118 Fraser Hwy.
Mailing city: Aldergrove
Province: BC
Postal: V4W 3P6
General Phone: (604) 514-6770
General Fax: (604) 856-5212
General/National Adv. E-mail: publisher@aldergrovestar.com
Display Adv. E-mail: sales@aldergrovestar.com
Editorial e-mail: newsroom@aldergrovestar.com
Primary Website: www.aldergrovestar.com
Year Established: 1957
Delivery Methods: Carrier`Racks
Areas Served - City/County or Portion Thereof, or Zip codes: Canada
Own Printing Facility?: Y
Published: Thur
Avg Paid Circ: 728
Avg Free Circ: 6469
Audit By: VAC
Audit Date: 30.06.2016
Personnel: Janice Reid (Adv. Sales Mgr.); Kurt Langmann (Ed.); Lisa Farquharson (Pub)
Parent company (for newspapers): Black Press Group Ltd.

ALEXANDRIA

THE GLENGARRY NEWS

Street Address: 3 Main St. ,
Province: ON
Postal: K0C 1A0
Country: Canada
Mailing address: PO Box 10
Mailing city: Alexandria
Province: ON
Postal: K0C 1A0
General Phone: (613) 525-2020
General Fax: (613) 525-3824
General/National Adv. E-mail: gnews@glengarrynews.ca
Primary Website: www.glengarrynews.ca
Year Established: 1892
Delivery Methods: Mail`Newsstand
Areas Served - City/County or Portion Thereof, or Zip codes: Canada
Commercial printers?: Y
Mechanical specifications: Type page 12 7/8 x 21; E - 7 cols, 1/6 between; A - 7 cols, 1/6 between; C - 7 cols, 1/6 between.
Published: Wed
Avg Paid Circ: 1075
Avg Free Circ: 86
Audit By: VAC
Audit Date: 30.09.2016
Personnel: Bonnie MacDonald (Adv. Mgr.); Steven Warburton (Mng. Ed.); Sean Bray (Sports Ed.); JT Grossmith

ALLISTON

THE ALLISTON HERALD

Street Address: 169 Dufferin St. S , Unit 22
Province: ON
Postal: L9R 1E6
Country: Canada
General Phone: (705) 435-6228
General Fax: (705) 435-3342
Editorial e-mail: herald@simcoe.com
Primary Website: simcoe.com
Delivery Methods: Carrier
Areas Served - City/County or Portion Thereof, or Zip codes: L9R, L0G, L0N, L0L, L0M
Published: Thur
Avg Free Circ: 22860
Audit By: CCAB
Audit Date: 31.03.2017
Personnel: Angela Makaroff (Sales Mgr.)
Parent company (for newspapers): Metroland Media Group Ltd.

ALMA

LE LAC ST. JEAN

Street Address: 100 St. Joseph St., Locale 01 ,
Province: QC
Postal: G8B 7A6
Country: Canada
Mailing address: 100 St. Joseph St., Locale 01
Mailing city: Alma
Province: QC
Postal: G8B 7A6
General Phone: (418) 668-4545
General Fax: (418) 668-8522
General/National Adv. E-mail: redaction_alma@tc.tc
Primary Website: www.lelacstjean.com
Areas Served - City/County or Portion Thereof, or Zip codes: Canada
Published: Wed
Avg Paid Circ: 80
Avg Free Circ: 23534
Audit By: CCAB
Audit Date: 31.03.2014
Personnel: Michelle Dupont (Gen. Mgr.)
Parent company (for newspapers): Transcontinental Media

ALTONA

THE RED RIVER VALLEY ECHO

Street Address: 67 2nd St. ,
Province: MB
Postal: R0G 0B0
Country: Canada
Mailing address: PO Box 700
Mailing city: Altona
Province: MB
Postal: R0G 0B0
General Phone: (204) 324-5001
General Fax: (204) 324-1402
General/National Adv. E-mail: altona.news@sunmedia.ca
Display Adv. E-mail: Darcie.Morris@sunmedia.ca
Editorial e-mail: winkler.news@sunmedia.ca
Primary Website: www.altonaecho.com
Year Established: 1941
Delivery Methods: Carrier`Racks
Areas Served - City/County or Portion Thereof, or Zip codes: Altona
Commercial printers?: Y
Mechanical specifications: Type page 10 1/4 x 14; E - 6 cols, 1 3/5, between; A - 6 cols, 1 3/5, between; C - 8 cols, 1 7/12, between.
Published: Thur
Avg Paid Circ: 27
Avg Free Circ: 4427
Audit By: VAC
Audit Date: 30.06.2016
Personnel: Greg Vandermeulen (Ed.); Darcie Morris (Adv Dir.)
Parent company (for newspapers): Postmedia Network Inc.; Quebecor Communications, Inc.

AMHERST

AMHERST DAILY NEWS

Street Address: 147 S. Albion St. ,
Province: NS
Postal: B4H 2X2
Country: Canada
Mailing address: PO Box 280
Mailing city: Amherst
Province: NS
Postal: B4H 2X2
General Phone: (902) 667-5102
General Fax: (902) 667-0419
Editorial Phone: (902) 661-5426
General/National Adv. E-mail: dcole@amherstdaily.com
Display Adv. E-mail: gcoish@amherstdaily.com
Editorial e-mail: darrell.cole@tc.tc
Primary Website: www.cumberlandnewsnow.com
Year Established: 1893
Areas Served - City/County or Portion Thereof, or Zip codes: Amherst, Nova Scotia
Mechanical specifications: Type page 10.25 x 14; E - 6 cols, 2 1/16, 1/8 between; A - 6 cols, 2 1/16, 1/8 between; C - 6 cols, 2 1/16, 1/8 between.
Published: Fri
Weekday Frequency: m
Avg Paid Circ: 4057
Avg Free Circ: 349
Audit By: VAC
Audit Date: 31.12.2015
Personnel: Richard Russell (Pub.); Greg Landry (Ops. Mgr.); Gladys Coish (Adv. Mgr.); Chuck MacInnes (Circ. Mgr.); Darrell Cole (Sr. Ed.)
Parent company (for newspapers): Transcontinental Media

THE CITIZEN-RECORD

Street Address: 147 South Albion St. ,
Province: NS
Postal: B4H 2X2
Country: Canada
Mailing address: 147 South Albion St.
Mailing city: Amherst
Province: NS
Postal: B4H 2X2
General Phone: (902) 667-5102
General Fax: (902) 667-0419
General/National Adv. E-mail: chris.gooding@tc.tc
Display Adv. E-mail: gcoish@amherstdaily.com
Editorial e-mail: darrell.cole@tc.tc
Primary Website: www.cumberlandnewsnow.com
Delivery Methods: Mail`Newsstand`Carrier
Areas Served - City/County or Portion Thereof, or Zip codes: B0H
Own Printing Facility?: N
Commercial printers?: Y
Published: Wed
Avg Paid Circ: 4892
Avg Free Circ: 504
Audit By: VAC
Audit Date: 31.10.2014
Personnel: Richard Russell (Pub.); Gladys Coish (Adv. Mgr.); Darrell Cole (Ed)
Parent company (for newspapers): Transcontinental Media

AMHERSTBURG

RIVER TOWN TIMES

Street Address: 67 Richmond Street ,
Province: ON
Postal: N9V 1G1
Country: Canada
General Phone: (519) 736-4175
General Fax: (519) 736-5420
Display Adv. E-mail: sales@rivertowntimes.com
Editorial e-mail: mail@rivertowntimes.com
Primary Website: www.rivertowntimes.com
Year Established: 1995
Delivery Methods: Carrier
Areas Served - City/County or Portion Thereof, or Zip codes: Canada
Mechanical specifications: 10.25x14.75
Published: Wed
Avg Free Circ: 9183
Audit By: CMCA
Audit Date: 31.08.2016
Personnel: Ron Giofu (Ed.)

AMOS

CITOYEN DE L'HARRICANA

Street Address: 92 Rue Principale Sud ,
Province: QC
Postal: J9T 2J6
Country: Canada
Mailing address: 92 rue Principale Sud
Mailing city: Amos
Province: QC
Postal: J9T 2J6
General Phone: (819)732-6531
General Fax: (819) 732-3764
General/National Adv. E-mail: philippe.delachevrotiere@quebecormedia.com
Display Adv. E-mail: manon.poirier@quebecormedia.com
Editorial e-mail: caroline.couture@quebecormedia.com
Primary Website: www.lechoabitibien.ca
Areas Served - City/County or Portion Thereof, or Zip codes: Canada
Published: Wed
Avg Paid Circ: 19

Avg Free Circ: 11238
Audit By: CCAB
Audit Date: 31.03.2014
Personnel: Caroline Couture

AMQUI

L'AVANT-POSTE GASPESIEN

Street Address: 217 Leonidas Ave. ,
Province: QC
Postal: G5J 2B8
Country: Canada
Mailing address: 49 St-Benoit Est, Bureau 6
Mailing city: Amqui
Province: QC
Postal: G5J 2B8
General Phone: (418) 629-3443
General Fax: (418)562-4607
General/National Adv. E-mail: avant-poste@hebdosquebecor.com
Display Adv. E-mail: gaby.veilleux@hebdosquebecor.com
Editorial e-mail: lucie-rose.levesque@hebdosquebecor.com
Primary Website: lavantposte.ca
Areas Served - City/County or Portion Thereof, or Zip codes: Canada
Published: Wed
Avg Paid Circ: 22
Avg Free Circ: 16881
Audit By: CCAB
Audit Date: 30.09.2012
Personnel: Alain St-Amand (Regl. Dir. Gen.); Francis Desrosiers (Dir. Gen.); Lucy-Rose Levesque (Ed.)
Parent company (for newspapers): Quebecor Communications, Inc.

ANTIGONISH

THE CASKET

Street Address: 88 College St. ,
Province: NS
Postal: B2G 1X7
Country: Canada
Mailing address: 88 College St.
Mailing city: Antigonish
Province: NS
Postal: B2G 1X7
General Phone: (902) 863-4370
General Fax: (902) 863-1943
General/National Adv. E-mail: info@thecasket.ca
Display Adv. E-mail: brianlazzuri@thecasket.ca
Classified Adv. e-mail: brianlazzuri@thecasket.ca
Editorial e-mail: editor@thecasket.ca
Primary Website: www.thecasket.ca
Year Established: 1852
Delivery Methods: Mail`Carrier`Racks
Areas Served - City/County or Portion Thereof, or Zip codes: Canada
Own Printing Facility?: Y
Mechanical specifications: Type page 10 x 20; E - 6 cols, 2, between; A - 6 cols, 2, between; C - 6 cols, 2, between.
Published: Wed
Avg Free Circ: 27000
Audit By: Sworn/Estimate/Non-Audited
Audit Date: 12.07.2019
Personnel: Brian Lazzuri (Gen Mgr/Mng Ed/Adv Mgr)
Parent company (for newspapers): SaltWire

ARMSTRONG

OKANAGAN ADVERTISER

Street Address: 3400 Okanagan St. ,
Province: BC
Postal: V0E 1B0
Country: Canada
Mailing address: PO Box 610
Mailing city: Armstrong
Province: BC
Postal: V0E 1B0
General Phone: (250) 546-3121
General Fax: (250) 546-3636
General/National Adv. E-mail: info@okadvertiser.com
Primary Website: OkanaganAdvertiser.com
Year Established: 1902
Delivery Methods: Mail`Newsstand`Racks
Areas Served - City/County or Portion Thereof, or Zip codes: Canada
Own Printing Facility?: Y
Commercial printers?: Y
Mechanical specifications: Tabloid 1/4 Fold
Published: Thur
Avg Free Circ: 4000
Audit By: Sworn/Estimate/Non-Audited
Audit Date: 12.07.2019
Personnel: Will Hansma (Pub)
Parent company (for newspapers): Okanagan Valley Newspaper Group

ARNPRIOR

ARNPRIOR CHRONICLE GUIDE EMC

Street Address: 8 Mcgonigal St. ,
Province: ON
Postal: K7S 1L8
Country: Canada
Mailing address: 8 McGonigal St.
Mailing city: Arnprior
Province: ON
Postal: K7S 1L8
General Phone: (613) 623-6571
Display Adv. E-mail: leslie.osborne@metroland.com
Classified Adv. e-mail: christine.jarrett@metroland.com
Editorial e-mail: theresa.fritz@metroland.com
Primary Website: www.insideottawavalley.com
Areas Served - City/County or Portion Thereof, or Zip codes: Canada
Published: Thur
Avg Free Circ: 8213
Audit By: CMCA
Audit Date: 30.06.2016
Personnel: Mike Tracy (Pub); Theresa Fritz (Ed)

WEST CARLETON REVIEW

Street Address: 8 Mcgonigal St. ,
Province: ON
Postal: K7S 1L8
Country: Canada
Mailing address: 8 McGonigal St.
Mailing city: Arnprior
Province: ON
Postal: K7S 1L8
General Phone: (613) 623-6571
Display Adv. E-mail: leslie.osborne@metroland.com
Primary Website: www.insideottawavalley.com
Published: Thur
Avg Free Circ: 7099
Audit By: CMCA
Audit Date: 30.06.2014
Personnel: Theresa Fritz; Mike Tracy
Parent company (for newspapers): Metroland Media Group Ltd.

ASBESTOS

LES ACTUALITES

Street Address: 572 1st Ave. ,
Province: QC
Postal: J1T 4R4
Country: Canada
Mailing address: 572 1st Ave.
Mailing city: Asbestos
Province: QC
Postal: J1T 4R4
General Phone: (819) 879-6681
General Fax: (819) 879-2355
General/National Adv. E-mail: carole.pellerin@quebecormedia.com
Editorial e-mail: nathalie.hurdle@quebecormedia.com
Primary Website: journallesactualites.ca
Areas Served - City/County or Portion Thereof, or Zip codes: Canada
Mechanical specifications: Type page 10 1/8 x 11 13/16; E - 10 cols, 5/8 between; A - 10 cols, 5/8 between; C - 10 cols, 5/8 between.
Published: Wed
Avg Paid Circ: 4
Avg Free Circ: 13160
Audit By: CCAB
Audit Date: 31.03.2014
Personnel: Carole Pellerin (Éf©ditrice)
Parent company (for newspapers): Reseau Select/Select Network; Quebecor Communications, Inc.

ASHCROFT

THE ASHCROFT-CACHE CREEK JOURNAL

Street Address: 120 4th Street ,
Province: BC
Postal: V0K 1A0
Country: Canada
Mailing address: PO Box 190
Mailing city: Ashcroft
Province: BC
Postal: V0K 1A0
General Phone: (250) 453-2261
General Fax: (250) 453-9625
Editorial Phone: (250) 453-2261
General/National Adv. E-mail: sales@accjournal.ca
Display Adv. E-mail: publisher@accjournal.ca
Editorial e-mail: editorial@accjournal.ca
Primary Website: https://www.ashcroftcachecreekjournal.com/
Year Established: 1895
Delivery Methods: Mail`Newsstand`Carrier
Areas Served - City/County or Portion Thereof, or Zip codes: Ashcroft, Cache Creek, Clinton, Spences Bridge
Commercial printers?: Y
Mechanical specifications: Type page 10 5/16 x 14 1/2; E - 6 cols, 1 7/12, between; A - 6 cols, 1 7/12, between; C - 6 cols, 1 7/12, between.
Published: Thur
Avg Paid Circ: 850
Avg Free Circ: 87
Audit By: CMCA
Audit Date: 23.09.2018
Personnel: Barbara Roden (Editor); Christopher Roden (Salesperson); Martina Dopf (Publisher)
Parent company (for newspapers): Black Press Group Ltd.

ASSINIBOIA

ASSINIBOIA TIMES

Street Address: 410 1st Ave. E. ,
Province: SK
Postal: S0H 0B0
Country: Canada
Mailing address: PO Box 910
Mailing city: Assiniboia
Province: SK
Postal: S0H 0B0
General Phone: (306) 642-5901
General Fax: (306) 642-4519
General/National Adv. E-mail: heather@assiniboiatimes.ca
Editorial e-mail: joyce@assiniboiatimes.ca
Areas Served - City/County or Portion Thereof, or Zip codes: Canada
Commercial printers?: Y
Mechanical specifications: Type page 10 1/2 x 15; E - 6 cols, 1 7/12, between; A - 6 cols, 1 7/12, between; C - 6 cols, 1 7/12, between.
Published: Fri
Avg Paid Circ: 212
Avg Free Circ: 2937
Audit By: CMCA
Audit Date: 29.02.2016
Personnel: Joyce Simard (Editor); Kevin Rasmussen (General Manager)
Parent company (for newspapers): Prairie Newspaper Group; Glacier Media Group

ASTRA

WING COMMANDER

Street Address: Po Box 1000, Sta. Forces ,
Province: ON
Postal: K0K 3W0
Country: Canada
Mailing address: PO Box 1000, Sta. Forces
Mailing city: Astra
Province: ON
Postal: K0K 3W0
General Phone: (613) 965-7248
General Fax: (613) 965-7490
Advertising Phone: (613) 392-2811
Editorial Phone: (613) 392-2811
General/National Adv. E-mail: christopher.daniel@forces.gc.ca
Primary Website: www.forces.gc.ca
Mechanical specifications: Type page 10 1/4 x 14 1/2; E - 6 cols, 1 57/100, between; A - 6 cols, 1 57/100, between; C - 6 cols, between.
Published: Fri
Avg Free Circ: 3000
Audit By: Sworn/Estimate/Non-Audited
Audit Date: 12.07.2019
Personnel: Mark Peebles (Ed. in Chief); Andrea Steiner (Mng. Ed.); Amber Gooding (Asst. Ed.)

ATHABASCA

THE ATHABASCA ADVOCATE

Street Address: 4917b 49th Street ,
Province: AB
Postal: T9S 1C5
Country: Canada
General Phone: (780) 675-9222
General Fax: (780) 675-3143
Advertising Phone: (780) 675-9222 ext. 24
Editorial Phone: (780) 675-9222
Display Adv. E-mail: production@athabasca.greatwest.ca
Editorial e-mail: advocate@athabasca.greatwest.ca
Primary Website: www.athabascaadvocate.com
Year Established: 1981
Areas Served - City/County or Portion Thereof, or Zip codes: Athabasca County
Published: Tues
Avg Paid Circ: 41
Avg Free Circ: 106
Audit By: VAC
Audit Date: 31.03.2016
Personnel: Vanessa Annand (Ed.); Meghan McIvor (Prod. Mgr.); Mona Muzyka (Circ. Mgr.); Allendria Brunjes (Pub.)
Parent company (for newspapers): Great West Newspapers LP

ATIKOKAN

ATIKOKAN PROGRESS

Street Address: 109 Main St. E. ,
Province: ON
Postal: P0T 1C0
Country: Canada
Mailing address: PO Box 220
Mailing city: Atikokan
Province: ON
Postal: P0T 1C0
General Phone: (807) 597-2731
General Fax: (807) 597-6103
General/National Adv. E-mail: progress@nwon.com
Editorial e-mail: progress@nwon.com
Primary Website: www.atikokanprogress.ca
Year Established: 1950
Delivery Methods: Mail`Newsstand`Carrier
Areas Served - City/County or Portion Thereof, or Zip codes: P0T1C0
Mechanical specifications: Type page 10 1/2 x 15; E - 5 cols, 1 11/12, 1/6 between; A - 5 cols, 1 11/12, 1/6 between; C - 5 cols, 1 1/2, 1/6 between.
Published: Mon
Avg Paid Circ: 1173
Avg Free Circ: 38
Audit By: VAC

Non-Daily Newspapers in Canada

Audit Date: 30.04.2016
Personnel: Eve Shine (Circ. Mgr.); Michael McKinnon (Ed.)

AURORA

THE AURORA BANNER

Street Address: 250 Industrial Parkway N. ,
Province: ON
Postal: L4G 4C3
Country: Canada
Mailing address: 250 Industrial Parkway N.
Mailing city: Aurora
Province: ON
Postal: L4G 4C3
General Phone: (905) 727-0819
General Fax: (905) 727-2909
Display Adv. E-mail: lmcdonald@yrmg.com
Editorial e-mail: tmcfadden@yrmg.com
Primary Website: yorkregion.com
Areas Served - City/County or Portion Thereof, or Zip codes: Canada
Published: Thur`Sun
Avg Free Circ: 15943
Audit By: CCAB
Audit Date: 30.09.2018
Personnel: Ted McFadden (Managing Ed.)
Parent company (for newspapers): Metroland Media Group Ltd.

THE AURORAN

Street Address: 15213 Yonge St Ste 8 ,
Province: ON
Postal: L4G 1L8
Country: Canada
General Phone: (905) 727-3300
General Fax: (905) 727-2620
Advertising Phone: (416) 803-9940
General/National Adv. E-mail: bob@auroran.com
Display Adv. E-mail: zach@lpcmedia.ca
Classified Adv. e-mail: cynthia@auroran.com
Editorial e-mail: brock@auroran.com
Primary Website: www.newspapers-online.com/auroran
Year Established: 2000
Delivery Methods: Mail`Carrier`Racks
Areas Served - City/County or Portion Thereof, or Zip codes: Canada
Published: Thur
Avg Paid Circ: 15
Avg Free Circ: 20000
Audit By: CMCA
Audit Date: 2/31/2017
Personnel: Brock Weir (Ed.); Cynthia Proctor (Prod. Mgr.); Diane Buchanan (Adv. Sales); Zach Shoub (Adv. Sales)
Parent company (for newspapers): London Publishing

AYLMER

THE AYLMER EXPRESS

Street Address: 390 Talbot St. E. ,
Province: ON
Postal: N5H 2R9
Country: Canada
Mailing address: PO Box 160
Mailing city: Aylmer
Province: ON
Postal: N5H 2R9
General Phone: (519) 773-3126
General Fax: (519) 773-3147
General/National Adv. E-mail: info@aylmerexpress.ca
Display Adv. E-mail: advertise@aylmerexpress.ca
Primary Website: www.aylmerexpress.ca
Areas Served - City/County or Portion Thereof, or Zip codes: Aylmer
Mechanical specifications: Type page 15 3/4 x 21.
Published: Wed
Avg Paid Circ: 13
Avg Free Circ: 14
Audit By: VAC
Audit Date: 31.03.2016

Personnel: Pam Morton (Adv. Mgr.); Wanda Kapogines (Circ. Mgr.); John Hueston (Ed.); Karen Hueston (Prodn. Mgr.)

AYR

AYR NEWS

Street Address: 40 Piper St. ,
Province: ON
Postal: N0B 1E0
Country: Canada
Mailing address: PO Box 1173
Mailing city: Ayr
Province: ON
Postal: N0B 1E0
General Phone: (519) 632-7432
General Fax: (519) 632-7743
General/National Adv. E-mail: ayrnews@golden.net
Display Adv. E-mail: hall.ayrnews@gmail.com
Primary Website: www.ayrnews.ca
Year Established: 1854
Delivery Methods: Mail`Newsstand
Areas Served - City/County or Portion Thereof, or Zip codes: N0B 1E0
Mechanical specifications: Type page 13 x 21 1/2; E - 6 cols, 1 7/8, 1/8 between; A - 6 cols, 1 7/8, 1/8 between; C - 6 cols, 1 7/8, 1/8 between.
Published: Wed
Avg Free Circ: 0
Audit By: VAC
Audit Date: 31.07.2017
Personnel: Heidi E. Ostner (Circ. Mgr.)

BAIE COMEAU

MANIC

Street Address: Rue De Bretagne ,
Province: QC
Postal: G5C 1X5
Country: Canada
Mailing address: Rue de Bretagne
Mailing city: Baie Comeau
Province: QC
Postal: G5C 1X5
General Phone: (418) 589-9990
Areas Served - City/County or Portion Thereof, or Zip codes: Canada
Published: Wed
Avg Paid Circ: 4
Avg Free Circ: 14765
Audit By: CCAB
Audit Date: 30.09.2012
Personnel: Paul Brisson

OBJECTIF PLEIN JOUR

Street Address: 625 Bvd., Lafleche, Ste. 309 ,
Province: QC
Postal: G5C 1C5
Country: Canada
Mailing address: 625 Bvd., Lafleche, Ste. 309
Mailing city: Baie Comeau
Province: QC
Postal: G5C 1C5
General Phone: (418) 589-5900
General Fax: (418) 589-8216
General/National Adv. E-mail: sebastien.rouillard@quebecormedia.com
Primary Website: www.pleinjourdebaiecomeau.ca
Own Printing Facility?: Y
Commercial printers?: Y
Published: Wed
Avg Free Circ: 16435
Audit By: Sworn/Estimate/Non-Audited
Audit Date: 12.07.2019
Personnel: Sebastien Rouillard
Parent company (for newspapers): Quebecor Communications, Inc.

PLEIN JOUR DE BAIE COMEAU

Street Address: 625 Bvd., Lafleche, Ste. 309 ,

Province: QC
Postal: G5C 1C5
Country: Canada
Mailing address: 625 Bvd., Lafleche, Ste. 309
Mailing city: Baie Comeau
Province: QC
Postal: G5C 1C5
General/National Adv. E-mail: sebastien.rouillard@quebecormedia.com
Areas Served - City/County or Portion Thereof, or Zip codes: Canada
Published: Wed
Avg Paid Circ: 4
Avg Free Circ: 20578
Audit By: CCAB
Audit Date: 31.03.2014
Personnel: Sebastien Rouillard

PLEIN JOUR SUR MANICOUAGAN

Street Address: 625 Bvd., Lafleche, Ste. 309 ,
Province: QC
Postal: G5C 1C5
Country: Canada
Mailing address: 625 Bvd., Lafleche, Ste. 309
Mailing city: Baie Comeau
Province: QC
Postal: G5C 1C5
General Phone: (418) 589-5900
General Fax: (418) 589-8216
General/National Adv. E-mail: sebastien.rouillard@quebecormedia.com
Display Adv. E-mail: atelier.baiecomeau@hebdosquebecor.com
Editorial e-mail: raphael.hovington@hebdosquebecor.com
Primary Website: www.pleinjourdebaiecomeau.ca
Areas Served - City/County or Portion Thereof, or Zip codes: Canada
Own Printing Facility?: Y
Commercial printers?: Y
Published: Wed
Avg Paid Circ: 7
Avg Free Circ: 15628
Audit By: BPA
Audit Date: 01.03.2012
Personnel: Sebastien Rouillard
Parent company (for newspapers): Quebecor Communications, Inc.

BANCROFT

BANCROFT THIS WEEK

Street Address: 254 Hastings St. ,
Province: ON
Postal: K0L 1C0
Country: Canada
Mailing address: PO Box 1254
Mailing city: Bancroft
Province: ON
Postal: K0L 1C0
General Phone: (613) 332-2002
General Fax: (613) 332-1710
General/National Adv. E-mail: curtis.armstrong@sunmedia.ca
Display Adv. E-mail: david.zilstra@gmail.com
Classified Adv. e-mail: melissa@haliburtonpress.com
Editorial e-mail: jenn@haliburtonpress.com
Primary Website: www.bancroftthisweek.com
Areas Served - City/County or Portion Thereof, or Zip codes: Canada
Published: Fri
Avg Free Circ: 8962
Audit By: CMCA
Audit Date: 31.12.2015
Personnel: David Zilstra (Pub/Adv Dir); Jenn Watt (Mng. Ed); Melissa Armstong (Sales Rep)

THE BANCROFT TIMES

Street Address: 93 Hastings St. N. ,
Province: ON
Postal: K0L 1C0
Country: Canada

Mailing address: 93 Hastings St. N.
Mailing city: Bancroft
Province: ON
Postal: K0L 1C0
General Phone: (613) 332-2300
General Fax: (613) 332-1894
General/National Adv. E-mail: bancroft-times@sympatico.ca
Primary Website: www.thebancrofttimes.ca
Areas Served - City/County or Portion Thereof, or Zip codes: ontario & provinces
Published: Thur
Audit By: VAC
Audit Date: 30.04.2016
Personnel: Dean Walker (Owner); Jenn Watt (Managing Ed.)

BANFF

BOW VALLEY CRAG & CANYON

Street Address: 201 Bear St., 2nd Fl. ,
Province: AB
Postal: T1L 1H2
Country: Canada
Mailing address: PO Box 129
Mailing city: Banff
Province: AB
Postal: T1L 1H2
General Phone: (403) 762-2453
General Fax: (403) 762-5274
General/National Adv. E-mail: editor@thecrag.ca
Display Adv. E-mail: rmackintosh@postmedia.com
Editorial e-mail: russ.ullyot@sunmedia.ca
Primary Website: www.thecragandcanyon.ca
Year Established: 1900
Delivery Methods: Mail`Newsstand`Carrier`Racks
Areas Served - City/County or Portion Thereof, or Zip codes: Canada
Commercial printers?: Y
Mechanical specifications: Type page 10 1/4 x 14; E - 6 cols, 1 7/12, between; A - 6 cols, 1 7/12, between; C - 6 cols, 1 7/12, between.
Published: Wed
Avg Paid Circ: 0
Avg Free Circ: 8537
Audit By: CMCA
Audit Date: 28.02.2014
Personnel: Shawn Cornell (Pub); Russ Ullyot (Ed); Roxanne Mackintosh (Adv. Dir.)
Parent company (for newspapers): Postmedia Network Inc.; Quebecor Communications, Inc.

BARRHEAD

BARRHEAD LEADER

Street Address: 5015 51st St. ,
Province: AB
Postal: T7N 1A4
Country: Canada
Mailing address: P.O. Box 4520
Mailing city: Barrhead
Province: AB
Postal: T7N 1A4
General Phone: (780) 674-3823
General Fax: (780) 674-6337
General/National Adv. E-mail: leader@barrhead.greatwest.ca
Display Adv. E-mail: sales@barrhead.greatwest.ca
Editorial e-mail: lleng@barrhead.greatwest.ca
Primary Website: www.barrheadleader.com
Year Established: 1927
Delivery Methods: Mail`Newsstand
Areas Served - City/County or Portion Thereof, or Zip codes: Barrhead
Own Printing Facility?: Y
Commercial printers?: Y
Mechanical specifications: Type page 10 1/3 x 15 1/3; E - 6 cols, 1 9/16, 1/6 between; A - 6 cols, 1 9/16, 1/6 between; C - 7 cols, 1 1/3, 1/6 between.
Published: Tues
Avg Paid Circ: 3114
Avg Free Circ: 3
Audit By: VAC
Audit Date: 31.03.2016

Personnel: Lynda Leng (Pub)
Parent company (for newspapers): Glacier Media Group; Great West Newspapers LP

BARRIE

INNISFIL JOURNAL

Street Address: 21 Patterson Rd. ,
Province: ON
Postal: L4N 7W6
Country: Canada
General Phone: (705) 726-0573
General Fax: (705) 726-9350
General/National Adv. E-mail: eallain@simcoe.com
Editorial e-mail: rvanderlinde@simcoe.com
Primary Website: simcoe.com
Areas Served - City/County or Portion Thereof, or Zip codes: Canada
Published: Thur
Avg Free Circ: 10791
Audit By: CCAB
Audit Date: 31.03.2017
Personnel: Elise Allaine (Gen. Mgr.)
Parent company (for newspapers): Metroland Media Group Ltd.

THE BARRIE ADVANCE

Street Address: 21 Patterson Rd. ,
Province: ON
Postal: L4N 7W6
Country: Canada
Mailing address: 21 Patterson Rd.
Mailing city: Barrie
Province: ON
Postal: L4N 7W6
General Phone: (705) 726-0573
General Fax: (705) 726-9350
Editorial e-mail: bareditor@simcoe.com
Primary Website: simcoe.com
Areas Served - City/County or Portion Thereof, or Zip codes: Barrie
Published: Thur
Avg Free Circ: 50827
Audit By: CCAB
Audit Date: 31.12.2017
Personnel: Shaun Sauve (Adv. Dir.); Heather Harris (Distr. Mgr.); Ian Proudfoot
Parent company (for newspapers): Metroland Media Group Ltd.

BARRIERE

BARRIERE STAR JOURNAL

Street Address: 1-4353 Conner Road ,
Province: BC
Postal: V0E 1E0
Country: Canada
Mailing address: PO Box 1020
Mailing city: Barriere
Province: BC
Postal: V0E 1E0
General Phone: (250) 672-5611
General Fax: (250) 672-9900
General/National Adv. E-mail: office@starjournal.net
Display Adv. E-mail: advertising@starjournal.net
Classified Adv. e-mail: advertising@starjournal.net
Editorial e-mail: news@starjournal.net
Primary Website: www.starjournal.net
Year Established: 1999
Delivery Methods: Carrier
Areas Served - City/County or Portion Thereof, or Zip codes: Canada
Commercial printers?: Y
Published: Thur
Avg Paid Circ: 2043
Avg Free Circ: 37
Audit By: VAC
Audit Date: 12.12.2017
Personnel: Jill Hayward (Ed.); Lisa Quiding (Adv./Office/Production)
Parent company (for newspapers): Black Press Group Ltd.

BARRY'S BAY

BARRY'S BAY THIS WEEK

Street Address: 19574 Opeongo Line ,
Province: ON
Postal: K0J 1B0
Country: Canada
Mailing address: PO Box 375
Mailing city: Barry's Bay
Province: ON
Postal: K0J 1B0
General Phone: (613) 756-2944
General Fax: (613) 756-2994
General/National Adv. E-mail: newsroom@barrysbaythisweek.com
Display Adv. E-mail: michel@thevalleygazette.ca
Classified Adv. e-mail: classified@thevalleygazette.ca
Editorial e-mail: christine@thevalleygazette.ca
Primary Website: http://www.thevalleygazette.ca/node/3
Areas Served - City/County or Portion Thereof, or Zip codes: Canada
Published: Wed
Avg Paid Circ: 1292
Avg Free Circ: 0
Audit By: CMCA
Audit Date: 31.12.2012
Personnel: Pete Lapinskie (Gen. Mgr.); Michel Lavigne (Owner/Pub/Adv); Christine Hudder (Ed)
Parent company (for newspapers): Quebecor Communications, Inc.

BASS RIVER

THE SHORELINE JOURNAL

Street Address: Box 41 ,
Province: NS
Postal: B0M 1B0
Country: Canada
Mailing address: Box 41
Mailing city: Bass River
Province: NS
Postal: B0M 1B0
General Phone: (902) 647-2968
General Fax: (902) 647-2194
Advertising Phone: (902)647-2968
Advertising Fax: (902) 647-2194
Editorial Phone: (902) 647-2968
General/National Adv. E-mail: maurice@theshorelinejournal.com
Display Adv. E-mail: maurice@theshorelinejournal.com
Editorial e-mail: maurice@theshorelinejournal.com
Primary Website: www.theshorelinejournal.com
Year Established: 1994
Delivery Methods: Mail`Newsstand
Areas Served - City/County or Portion Thereof, or Zip codes: Muncipality of County of Colchester
Mechanical specifications: The Shoreline Journal is an offset tabloid. Image area is 10-1/4ÃcÂ€Âx 15-5/8ÃcÂ€Â. Column width is 1.5ÃcÂ€Â with 6 columns per page. Line Screens. B&W 100, Colour 100 lines per inch.
Published: Wed`Mthly
Avg Paid Circ: 1363
Avg Free Circ: 0
Audit By: CMCA
Audit Date: 31.12.2013
Personnel: Maurice Rees

BASSANO

THE BASSANO TIMES

Street Address: 402 First Ave. ,
Province: AB
Postal: T0J 0B0
Country: Canada
Mailing address: PO Box 780
Mailing city: Bassano
Province: AB
Postal: T0J 0B0
General Phone: (403) 641-3636
General Fax: (403) 641-3952
Advertising Phone: (403) 641-3636
General/National Adv. E-mail: btimes@telusplanet.net
Year Established: 1915
Delivery Methods: Mail`Newsstand
Areas Served - City/County or Portion Thereof, or Zip codes: Canada
Mechanical specifications: Type page 10 x 16; E - 6 cols, 1 1/2, 1/8 between; A - 6 cols, 1 1/2, 1/8 between; C - 6 cols, 1 1/2, 1/8 between.
Published: Tues
Avg Paid Circ: 503
Audit By: CMCA
Audit Date: 30.06.2017
Personnel: Mary Lou Brooks (Publisher/Advertising Manager)

BATHURST

THE NORTHERN LIGHT

Street Address: 355 King Ave. ,
Province: NB
Postal: E2A 1P4
Country: Canada
Mailing address: 355 King Ave.
Mailing city: Bathurst
Province: NB
Postal: E2A 1P4
General Phone: (506) 546-4491
General Fax: (506) 546-1491
Editorial e-mail: mulock.greg@thenorthernlight.ca
Primary Website: https://www.telegraphjournal.com/northern-light/
Areas Served - City/County or Portion Thereof, or Zip codes: Canada
Own Printing Facility?: Y
Mechanical specifications: Type page 13 x 21 1/2; E - 6 cols, 2 1/12, 1/6 between; A - 6 cols, 2 1/12, 1/6 between; C - 9 cols, 1 1/3, 1/6 between.
Published: Tues
Avg Paid Circ: 2890
Avg Free Circ: 12
Audit By: VAC
Audit Date: 31.12.2015
Personnel: Greg Mulock (Ed.)
Parent company (for newspapers): Brunswick News, Inc.

BEAUMONT

LA NOUVELLE BEAUMONT NEWS

Street Address: 5021b 52 Ave. ,
Province: AB
Postal: T4X 1E5
Country: Canada
Mailing address: 5021B 52 Ave.
Mailing city: Beaumont
Province: AB
Postal: T4X 1E5
General Phone: (780) 929-6632
General Fax: (780) 929-6634
Display Adv. E-mail: jfigeat@postmedia.com
Editorial e-mail: bobby.roy@sunmedia.ca
Primary Website: www.thebeaumontnews.ca
Year Established: 1987
Areas Served - City/County or Portion Thereof, or Zip codes: Beaumont
Published: Fri
Avg Paid Circ: 11
Avg Free Circ: 7221
Audit By: VAC
Audit Date: 31.12.2015
Personnel: Jean Figeat (Adv. Dir.); Bobby Roy (Ed)
Parent company (for newspapers): Sun Media Corporation; Post Media

BEAUPORT

BEAUPORT EXPRESS

Street Address: 710 Bouvier, Suite 107 ,
Province: QC
Postal: G2J 1C2
Country: Canada
Mailing address: 710 Bouvier, Suite 107
Mailing city: Beauport
Province: QC
Postal: G2J 1C2
General Phone: (418) 628-7460
General Fax: (418) 622-1511
General/National Adv. E-mail: redaction_quebec@tc.tc
Primary Website: www.beauportexpress.com
Areas Served - City/County or Portion Thereof, or Zip codes: Canada
Own Printing Facility?: Y
Mechanical specifications: Type page 10 x 11 3/4; C - 2 cols, 2, between.
Published: Fri
Avg Paid Circ: 11
Avg Free Circ: 28463
Audit By: CCAB
Audit Date: 31.03.2014
Personnel: Yvan Rancourt (Pub.); Paul Lessard (Ed.); Gilles Brault (Prodn. Mgr.)

BEAUPRE

AUTRE VOIX

Street Address: Boulevard Ste-anne Bureau 101 , Bureau 101
Province: QC
Postal: G0A 1E0
Country: Canada
Mailing address: boulevard Ste-Anne Bureau 101
Mailing city: Beaupre
Province: QC
Postal: G0A 1E0
General Phone: (418) 827-1511
Areas Served - City/County or Portion Thereof, or Zip codes: Canada
Published: Wed
Avg Paid Circ: 3
Avg Free Circ: 13297
Audit By: CCAB
Audit Date: 31.03.2014
Personnel: Lilianne Laprise

BEAUSEJOUR

THE CLIPPER WEEKLY & LAC DU BONNET CLIPPER

Street Address: 27a-3rd Street South ,
Province: MB
Postal: R0E 0C0
Country: Canada
Mailing address: P.O. Box 2033
Mailing city: Beausejour
Province: MB
Postal: R0E 0C0
General Phone: (204) 268-4700
General Fax: (204) 268-3858
General/National Adv. E-mail: mail@clipper.mb.ca
Primary Website: www.clipper.mb.ca
Delivery Methods: Mail`Newsstand`Racks
Areas Served - City/County or Portion Thereof, or Zip codes: R0E 0A0 R0E 0C0 R0E 1M0 R0E 0K0 R0E 0Z0 R0E 0R0 R0E 0T0 R0E 1A0 R0E 1Z0 R0E 0X0 R0E 0Y0 R0E 1A0 R0E 1J0 R0E 1L0 R0E 1M0 R0E 1R0 R0E 1T0 R0E 1V0 R0E 1X0 R0E 1Y0 R0E 1Z0 R0E 2A0 R0E 2B0 R0E 2G0
Published: Thur
Avg Paid Circ: 46
Avg Free Circ: 12340
Audit By: VAC
Audit Date: 31.03.2016
Personnel: Kim MacAulay (Publisher); Mark Buss (Editor)
Parent company (for newspapers): Clipper Publishing Corp.

BEAVERLODGE

TOWN & COUNTRY NEWS

Street Address: 916 2nd Avenue ,
Province: AB
Postal: T0H 0C0
Country: Canada
General Phone: (780) 354-2980
General Fax: (780) 354-2460

Non-Daily Newspapers in Canada   III-437

General/National Adv. E-mail: beaverlodge.
   advertiser@gmail.com
Display Adv. E-mail: rebecca@
   nextchapterpublishing.ca
Primary Website: facebook.com/
   westcountynews
Year Established: 1956
Delivery Methods: Mail`Newsstand`Carrier
Areas Served - City/County or Portion Thereof, or Zip
   codes: Canada
Published: Thur
Avg Paid Circ: 1857
Avg Free Circ: 20
Audit By: CMCA
Audit Date: 12.12.2017
Personnel: Rebecca Dika (Pub.)
Parent company (for newspapers): Next Chapter
   Printing & Publishing

BEETON
THE SCOPE OF INNISFIL

Street Address: 34 Main St. W ,
Province: ON
Postal: L0G 1A0
Country: Canada
Mailing address: P.O. Box 310
Mailing city: Beeton
Province: ON
Postal: L0G 1A0
General Phone: (905) 729-2287
General Fax: (905) 729-2541
General/National Adv. E-mail: admin@
   innisfilscope.com
Display Adv. E-mail: sales@innisfilscope.com
Editorial e-mail: editor@innisfilscope.com
Primary Website: www.innisfilscope.com
Year Established: 1968
Areas Served - City/County or Portion Thereof, or Zip
   codes: Canada
Mechanical specifications: Type page 10 1/2
   x 15; E - 6 cols, 1 2/3, 1/6 between; A - 6
   cols, 1 2/3, 1/6 between; C - 6 cols, 1 2/3,
   1/6 between.
Published: Wed
Avg Paid Circ: 100
Avg Free Circ: 12433
Audit By: CMCA
Audit Date: 30.04.2013
Personnel: Alex Pozdrowski (Adv.); Wendy
   Soloduik (Ed.)
Parent company (for newspapers): Simcoe-York
   Group

THE TIMES OF NEW TECUMSETH

Street Address: 34 Main St. W. ,
Province: ON
Postal: L0G 1A0
Country: Canada
Mailing address: PO Box 310
Mailing city: Beeton
Province: ON
Postal: L0G 1A0
General Phone: (905) 729-2287
General Fax: (905) 729-2541
General/National Adv. E-mail: admin.syp@rogers.
   com
Editorial e-mail: editor.syp@rogers.com
Primary Website: www.newtectimes.com
Year Established: 1974
Areas Served - City/County or Portion Thereof, or Zip
   codes: L0G1A0, L0G1L0, L9R, L0G 1B0
Commercial printers?: Y
Mechanical specifications: Type page 10 1/2
   x 15; E - 6 cols, 1 2/3, 1/6 between; A - 6
   cols, 1 2/3, 1/6 between; C - 6 cols, 1 2/3,
   1/6 between.
Published: Thur
Avg Paid Circ: 2230
Avg Free Circ: 100
Audit By: VAC
Audit Date: 30.04.2015
Personnel: Wendy Soloduik (Ed.); John Speziali
   (Production Mgr.); Annette Derraugh
Parent company (for newspapers): Simcoe-York
   Group

BEETON
TOTTENHAM TIMES

Street Address: 34 Main St. W. ,
Province: ON
Postal: L0G 1A0
Country: Canada
Mailing address: PO Box 310
Mailing city: Beeton
Province: ON
Postal: L0G 1A0
General Phone: (905) 729-2287
General Fax: (905) 729-2541
General/National Adv. E-mail: admin.syp@rogers.
   com
Editorial e-mail: editor.syp@rogers.com
Primary Website: www.newtectimes.com
Year Established: 1978
Areas Served - City/County or Portion Thereof, or Zip
   codes: Canada
Mechanical specifications: Type page 10 1/2
   x 15; E - 6 cols, 1 2/3, 1/6 between; A - 6
   cols, 1 2/3, 1/6 between; C - 6 cols, 1 2/3,
   1/6 between.
Published: Wed
Avg Paid Circ: 2125
Avg Free Circ: 75
Audit By: Sworn/Estimate/Non-Audited
Audit Date: 12.07.2019
Personnel: John Archibald (Adv. Mgr.); Kristen
   Haire (Prodn. Mgr.)
Parent company (for newspapers): Simcoe-York
   Group

BELLEVILLE
BELLEVILLE NEWS

Street Address: 250 Sidney St. ,
Province: ON
Postal: K8P 5E0
Country: Canada
Mailing address: PO Box 25009
Mailing city: Belleville
Province: ON
Postal: K8P 5E0
General Phone: (613) 966-2034
Advertising Phone: (613) 966-2034 ext. 504
Display Adv. E-mail: mhudgins@metroland.com
Classified Adv. e-mail: slacroix@perfprint.ca
Editorial e-mail: chris.malette@metroland.com
Primary Website: http://www.insidebelleville.
   com/belleville-on/
Published: Thur
Personnel: Paul Mitchell (Circ Mgr); Chris
   Malette (Ed); Melissa Hudgin (Adv)
Parent company (for newspapers): Metroland
   Media Group Ltd.

BELLEVILLE NEWS EMC

Street Address: 244 Ashley St ,
Province: ON
Postal: K0K 2B0
Country: Canada
Mailing address: PO Box 155
Mailing city: Belleville
Province: ON
Postal: K0K 2B0
General Phone: (613) 966-2034
General/National Adv. E-mail: jkearns@theemc.ca
Display Adv. E-mail: leslie.osborne@metroland.
   com
Classified Adv. e-mail: abarr@metroland.com
Editorial e-mail: theresa.fritz@metroland.com
Primary Website: www.insideottawavalley.com
Year Established: 2010
Delivery Methods: Mail
Areas Served - City/County or Portion Thereof, or Zip
   codes: Canada
Published: Thur
Avg Free Circ: 22549
Audit By: CMCA
Audit Date: 30.06.2016
Personnel: John Kearns (Pub.); Chris Paveley
   (Circ Mgr); Theresa Fritz (Ed); Leslie
   Osborne (Adv. Sales)
Parent company (for newspapers): Metroland
   Media Group Ltd.

CAMPBELLFORD/NORTHWEST NEWS EMC

Street Address: 244 Ashley St ,
Province: ON
Postal: K0K 2B0
Country: Canada
Mailing address: PO Box 155
Mailing city: Belleville
Province: ON
Postal: K0K 2B0
General Phone: (613) 966-2034
Advertising Phone: (613) 966-2034
Editorial Phone: (613) 966-2034 ext. 510
General/National Adv. E-mail: jkearns@theemc.ca
Display Adv. E-mail: jkearns@theemc.ca
Editorial e-mail: tbush@theemc.ca
Primary Website: www.insideottawavalley.com
Year Established: 2010
Delivery Methods: Mail
Areas Served - City/County or Portion Thereof, or Zip
   codes: Canada
Published: Thur
Avg Free Circ: 11630
Audit By: CMCA
Audit Date: 31.12.2012
Personnel: John Kearns (Pub.); Terry Bush
   (Mng. Ed.)

QUINTE WEST EMC

Street Address: 250 Sidney St. ,
Province: ON
Postal: K8P 5E0
Country: Canada
Mailing address: PO Box 25009
Mailing city: Belleville
Province: ON
Postal: K8P 5E0
General Phone: (613) 966-2034
General/National Adv. E-mail: jkearns@theemc.ca
Primary Website: www.insideottawavalley.com
Areas Served - City/County or Portion Thereof, or Zip
   codes: Canada
Published: Thur
Avg Free Circ: 23089
Audit By: CMCA
Audit Date: 31.12.2012
Personnel: John Kearns (Pub.); Sharon
   LaCroix (Community)
Parent company (for newspapers): Metroland
   Media Group Ltd.

STIRLING/NORTHEAST NEWS EMC

Street Address: 244 Ashley St. ,
Province: ON
Postal: K0K 2B0
Country: Canada
Mailing address: PO Box 155
Mailing city: Belleville
Province: ON
Postal: K0K 2B0
General Phone: (613) 966-2034
Advertising Phone: (613) 966-2034
Editorial Phone: (613) 966-2034 ext. 510
General/National Adv. E-mail: jkearns@theemc.ca
Display Adv. E-mail: jkearns@theemc.ca
Editorial e-mail: tbush@theemc.ca
Primary Website: www.insideottawavalley.com
Year Established: 2010
Delivery Methods: Mail
Areas Served - City/County or Portion Thereof, or Zip
   codes: Canada
Published: Thur
Avg Free Circ: 11564
Audit By: CMCA
Audit Date: 31.12.2012
Personnel: John Kearns (Pub.); Terry Bush
   (Mng. Ed.)

THE COMMUNITY PRESS

Street Address: 199 Front St. , Suite 118
Province: ON
Postal: K8N 5H5
Country: Canada

Mailing address: 199 Front St. Suite 118
Mailing city: Belleville
Province: ON
Postal: K8N 5H5
General Phone: (613) 395-3015
General Fax: (613) 395-2992
Editorial Phone: (613) 392-6501
Editorial Fax: (613) 392-0505
General/National Adv. E-mail: compress@redden.
   on.ca; general@communitypress-online.
   com
Display Adv. E-mail: gerry.drage@sunmedia.ca
Classified Adv. e-mail: intelligencer.classifieds@
   sunmedia.ca
Editorial e-mail: brice.mcvicar@sunmedia.ca
Primary Website: www.communitypress-online.
   com
Areas Served - City/County or Portion Thereof, or Zip
   codes: Canada
Mechanical specifications: Type page 10 1/4 x
   15 1/4; E - 9 cols, 1 1/36, 1/8 between; A
   - 9 cols, 1 1/36, 1/8 between; C - 6 cols, 1
   7/12, 1/8 between.
Published: Thur
Avg Free Circ: 46476
Audit By: CMCA
Audit Date: 30.06.2016
Personnel: Brice McVicar (Ed); Gerry Drage
   (Adv. Dir.); Jason Hawley (Circ Mgr)

BELOEIL
L'OEIL REGIONAL

Street Address: 393 Laurier Blvd. ,
Province: QC
Postal: J3G 4H6
Country: Canada
Mailing address: 393 Laurier Blvd.
Mailing city: Beloeil
Province: QC
Postal: J3G 4H6
General Phone: (450) 467-1821
General Fax: (450) 467-3087
General/National Adv. E-mail: redaction@
   oeilregional.com
Display Adv. E-mail: publicite@oeilregional.com
Editorial e-mail: redaction@oeilregional.com
Primary Website: www.oeilregional.com
Areas Served - City/County or Portion Thereof, or Zip
   codes: Canada
Mechanical specifications: Type page 10 1/4 x
   16 1/2; E - 8 cols, 1 1/6, 1/6 between; A - 8
   cols, 1 1/6, 1/6 between; C - 8 cols, 1 1/6,
   1/6 between.
Published: Sat
Avg Paid Circ: 8
Avg Free Circ: 34637
Audit By: CCAB
Audit Date: 31.03.2014
Personnel: Serge Landry
Parent company (for newspapers): Reseau Select/
   Select Network; Les Hebdos Monteregiens-
   OOB

BERTHIERVILLE
PUBLIQUIP

Street Address: Rue Gilles Villeneuve ,
Province: QC
Postal: J0K 1A0
Country: Canada
Mailing address: rue Gilles Villeneuve
Mailing city: Berthierville
Province: QC
Postal: J0K 1A0
General Phone: (450) 836-3666
Published: Sun
Avg Paid Circ: 701
Avg Free Circ: 50494
Audit By: ODC
Audit Date: 14.12.2011
Personnel: Francoise Trepanier

BIGGAR
THE INDEPENDENT

Street Address: 102 3 Ave W ,
Province: SK

Postal: S0K 0M0
Country: Canada
Mailing address: PO Box 40
Mailing city: Biggar
Province: SK
Postal: S0K 0M0
General Phone: (306) 948-3344
General Fax: (306) 948-2133
General/National Adv. E-mail: tip@sasktel.net
Areas Served - City/County or Portion Thereof, or Zip codes: Canada
Mechanical specifications: Type page 11 x 17; E - 6 cols, 1 1/2, 1/6 between; A - 6 cols, 1 1/2, 1/6 between; C - 6 cols, 1 1/2, 1/6 between.
Published: Thur
Avg Paid Circ: 1310
Avg Free Circ: 538
Audit By: CMCA
Audit Date: 30.04.2016
Personnel: Margaret Hasein (Pub.); Daryl Hasein (Gen. Mgr.); Urla Tyler (Adv. Mgr.); Kevin Bratigan (Ed.)

BLAIRMORE

CROWSNEST PASS HERALD

Street Address: 12925 20th Ave. ,
Province: AB
Postal: T0K 0E0
Country: Canada
Mailing address: PO Box 960
Mailing city: Blairmore
Province: AB
Postal: T0K 0E0
General Phone: (403) 562-2248
General Fax: (403) 562-8379
General/National Adv. E-mail: news@passherald.ca
Editorial e-mail: news@passherald.ca
Primary Website: www.passherald.ca
Year Established: 1930
Delivery Methods: Mail`Racks
Areas Served - City/County or Portion Thereof, or Zip codes: Canada
Commercial printers?: Y
Mechanical specifications: Type page 10 1/4 x 16; E - 5 cols, 2, between; A - 5 cols, 2, between.
Published: Wed
Avg Paid Circ: 1361
Avg Free Circ: 235
Audit By: Sworn/Estimate/Non-Audited
Audit Date: 12.07.2019
Personnel: Lisa Sygutek (Pub.)

BLENHEIM

BLENHEIM NEWS-TRIBUNE

Street Address: 62 Talbot St. W. ,
Province: ON
Postal: N0P 1A0
Country: Canada
Mailing address: PO Box 160
Mailing city: Blenheim
Province: ON
Postal: N0P 1A0
General Phone: (519) 676-3291
General Fax: (519) 676-3454
Advertising Phone: (519) 676-5023
Advertising Fax: (519) 676-3454
Editorial Phone: (519) 676-3321
General/National Adv. E-mail: tribune@southkent.net
Editorial e-mail: pl.tribune@southkent.net
Primary Website: facebook.com/blehheimnewstribune
Year Established: 1884
Delivery Methods: Mail
Areas Served - City/County or Portion Thereof, or Zip codes: Canada
Mechanical specifications: Type page 10 1/4 x 16; E - 6 cols, 1 7/12, between.
Published: Wed
Avg Paid Circ: 1609
Avg Free Circ: 78
Audit By: AAM
Audit Date: 31.03.2019
Personnel: Pete Laurie (Ed.); Dave Stepniak

(Prod Mgr)

BLYTH

NORTH HURON PUBLISHING INC.

Street Address: 413 Queen St. , Po Box 429
Province: ON
Postal: N0M 1H0
Country: Canada
Mailing address: PO Box 429
Mailing city: Blyth
Province: ON
Postal: N0M 1H0
General Phone: (519) 523-4792
General Fax: (519) 523-9140
General/National Adv. E-mail: info@northhuron.on.ca
Display Adv. E-mail: deb@northhuron.on.ca
Classified Adv. e-mail: deb@northhuron.on.ca
Editorial e-mail: deb@northhuron.on.ca
Primary Website: www.northhuron.on.ca
Delivery Methods: Mail`Racks
Areas Served - City/County or Portion Thereof, or Zip codes: Canada
Published: Thur
Avg Paid Circ: 1772
Avg Free Circ: 26
Audit By: CMCA
Audit Date: 28.11.2018
Personnel: Deb Sholdice (Pub.)

BOISSEVAIN

THE BOISSEVAIN RECORDER

Street Address: 425 South Railway Street ,
Province: MB
Postal: R0K 0E0
Country: Canada
Mailing address: PO Box 220
Mailing city: Boissevain
Province: MB
Postal: R0K 0E0
General Phone: (204) 534-6479
General Fax: (204) 534-2977
General/National Adv. E-mail: mail@therecorder.ca
Display Adv. E-mail: ads@therecorder.ca
Classified Adv. E-mail: mail@therecorder.ca
Editorial e-mail: editor@therecorder.ca
Primary Website: www.therecorder.ca
Year Established: 1899
Delivery Methods: Mail`Newsstand
Areas Served - City/County or Portion Thereof, or Zip codes: Canada
Mechanical specifications: Type page 10 x 14; E - 6 cols, 1 3/5, 1/6 between; A - 6 cols, 1 3/5, 1/6 between; C - 6 cols, 1 3/5, 1/6 between.
Published: Fri
Avg Paid Circ: 3863
Avg Free Circ: 44
Audit By: VAC
Audit Date: 31.01.2016
Personnel: Lorraine E. Houston (Ed.)

BOLTON

CALEDON CITIZEN

Street Address: 30 Martha St., Suite 205 ,
Province: ON
Postal: L7E 5V1
Country: Canada
Mailing address: 30 Martha St Suite 205
Mailing city: Bolton
Province: ON
Postal: L7E 5V1
General Phone: (905) 857-6626
General Fax: (905) 857-6363
General/National Adv. E-mail: admin@caledoncitizen.com
Display Adv. E-mail: erin@lpcmedia.ca
Classified Adv. e-mail: heather@caledoncitizen.com
Editorial e-mail: editor@caledoncitizen.com
Primary Website: www.caledoncitizen.com
Year Established: 1983

Delivery Methods: Mail`Carrier
Areas Served - City/County or Portion Thereof, or Zip codes: Canada
Mechanical specifications: Type page 10 7/16 x 15; E - 6 cols, 1 5/8, between.
Published: Thur
Avg Free Circ: 12240
Audit By: Sworn/Estimate/Non-Audited
Audit Date: 12.07.2019
Personnel: Alan Claridge (Pub); Mary Speck (Office Mgr); Joshua Santos
Parent company (for newspapers): Simcoe-York Group

CALEDON ENTERPRISE

Street Address: 12612 Hwy. 50 N. ,
Province: ON
Postal: L7E 5T1
Country: Canada
Mailing address: PO Box 99
Mailing city: Bolton
Province: ON
Postal: L7E 5T1
General Phone: (905) 857-3433
General Fax: (905) 857-5002
Display Adv. E-mail: mcrake@caledonenterprise.com
Classified Adv. e-mail: classifieds@metroland.com
Editorial e-mail: rwilkinson@caledonenterprise.com
Primary Website: caledonenterprise.com
Areas Served - City/County or Portion Thereof, or Zip codes: Canada
Published: Tues`Thur
Avg Paid Circ: 0
Avg Free Circ: 19199
Audit By: CCAB
Audit Date: 30.09.2017
Personnel: Sheila Ogram (Circ Mgr); Robyn Wilkinson (Ed); Melinda Crake (Adv. Rep)
Parent company (for newspapers): Metroland Media Group Ltd.; Torstar

KING WEEKLY SENTINEL

Street Address: 30 Martha Streeet, Suite 205 ,
Province: ON
Postal: L7E 5V1
Country: Canada
General Phone: (905) 857-6626
General Fax: (905) 857-6363
General/National Adv. E-mail: admin.syp@rogers.com
Display Adv. E-mail: zach@lpcmedia.ca
Classified Adv. e-mail: admin@caledoncitizen.com
Editorial e-mail: editor@kingsentinel.com
Primary Website: www.kingsentinel.com
Year Established: 1980
Delivery Methods: Newsstand`Carrier`Racks
Areas Served - City/County or Portion Thereof, or Zip codes: Caledon
Mechanical specifications: Type page 10 1/2 x 15; E - 6 cols, 1 13/20, 1/6 between; A - 6 cols, 1 13/20, 1/6 between; C - 6 cols, 1 13/20, 1/6 between.
Published: Thur
Avg Paid Circ: 30
Avg Free Circ: 10200
Audit By: Sworn/Estimate/Non-Audited
Audit Date: 12.07.2019
Personnel: Mark Pavilons (Editor)

BONNYVILLE

BONNYVILLE NOUVELLE

Street Address: 5304 50th Ave. ,
Province: AB
Postal: T9N 1Y4
Country: Canada
Mailing address: 5304 50th Ave.
Mailing city: Bonnyville
Province: AB
Postal: T9N 1Y4
General Phone: (780) 826-3876
General Fax: (780) 826-7062
Advertising Phone: (780) 826-3876

Display Adv. E-mail: aclarke@bonnyville.greatwest.ca
Editorial e-mail: koelschlagel@bonnyville.greatwest.ca
Primary Website: www.bonnyvillenouvelle.ca
Year Established: 1967
Areas Served - City/County or Portion Thereof, or Zip codes: Canada
Own Printing Facility?: Y
Commercial printers?: Y
Mechanical specifications: Type page 14 x 15 1/2; E - 7 cols, 1 3/5, 1/6 between; A - 6 cols, 1 1/3, 1/6 between; C - 6 cols, 1 1/3, 1/6 between.
Published: Tues
Avg Paid Circ: 626
Avg Free Circ: 681
Audit By: VAC
Audit Date: 31.03.2016
Personnel: Cindy Coates (Circ. Mgr.); Kristen Oelschlagel (Ed); Angie Hampshire (Pub)
Parent company (for newspapers): Glacier Media Group; Great West Newspapers LP

BOTHWELL

OLD AUTOS

Street Address: 348 Main St. ,
Province: ON
Postal: N0P 1C0
Country: Canada
Mailing address: 348 Main St, PO Box 250
Mailing city: Bothwell
Province: ON
Postal: N0P 1C0
General Phone: (800) 461-3457
General/National Adv. E-mail: info@oldautos.ca
Display Adv. E-mail: ads@oldautos.ca
Classified Adv. e-mail: classifieds@oldautos.ca
Editorial e-mail: maryjo@oldautos.ca
Primary Website: oldautos.ca
Year Established: 1987
Delivery Methods: Mail`Newsstand
Areas Served - City/County or Portion Thereof, or Zip codes: Canada
Published: Mon
Avg Paid Circ: 14045
Avg Free Circ: 285
Audit By: AAM
Audit Date: 31.03.2019
Personnel: Mary Jo DePelsmaeker (Publisher)

BOUCHERVILLE

LA RELEVE

Street Address: 528 St. Charles St. ,
Province: QC
Postal: J4B 3M5
Country: Canada
Mailing address: 528 St. Charles St.
Mailing city: Boucherville
Province: QC
Postal: J4B 3M5
General Phone: (450) 641-4844
General Fax: (450) 641-4849
Advertising Phone: (514) 926-2354
General/National Adv. E-mail: lareleve@lareleve.qc.ca
Display Adv. E-mail: c.desmarteau@videotron.ca
Classified Adv. e-mail: classees@lareleve.qc.ca
Editorial e-mail: lareleve@lareleve.qc.ca
Primary Website: www.lareleve.qc.ca
Year Established: 1987
Areas Served - City/County or Portion Thereof, or Zip codes: J4B, J4M, J4N, J4G, J3E, J0L 2S0, J3X, J0L 1N0, J0L 2R0, J0L 1A0
Commercial printers?: Y
Mechanical specifications: Type page 10 1/4" x 14 1/4".
Published: Tues
Avg Paid Circ: 0
Avg Free Circ: 59100
Audit By: Sworn/Estimate/Non-Audited
Audit Date: 12.07.2019
Personnel: Charles Desmarteau (Ed. & Gen. Mgr.)
Parent company (for newspapers): Groupe Messier

Non-Daily Newspapers in Canada

LA SEIGNEURIE
Street Address: 391 Boul. De Mortagne ,
Province: QC
Postal: J4B 3M5
Country: Canada
Mailing address: 528, St-Charles
Mailing city: Boucherville
Province: QC
Postal: J4B 1B7
General Phone: (450) 641-4844
General Fax: (450) 641-4849
General/National Adv. E-mail: info@la-seigneurie.qc.ca
Display Adv. E-mail: lareleve@lareleve.qc.ca
Editorial e-mail: redaction@la-seigneurie.qc.ca
Primary Website: www.la-seigneurie.qc.ca
Areas Served - City/County or Portion Thereof, or Zip codes: Quebec
Mechanical specifications: Type page 10 1/4 x 17; E - 8 cols, between; A - 8 cols, between; C - 8 cols, between.
Published: Wed
Avg Free Circ: 33856
Audit By: Sworn/Estimate/Non-Audited
Audit Date: 12.07.2019
Personnel: Charles Desmarteau (Pub.)
Parent company (for newspapers): La Releve

BOW ISLAND

THE 40-MILE COUNTY COMMENTATOR
Street Address: 147-5 Ave. W. ,
Province: AB
Postal: T0K 0G0
Country: Canada
Mailing address: P.O. Box 580
Mailing city: Bow Island
Province: AB
Postal: T0K 0G0
General Phone: (403) 545-2258
General Fax: (403) 545-6886
General/National Adv. E-mail: tabads@tabertimes.com
Display Adv. E-mail: editor@bowislandcommentator.com
Primary Website: www.bowislandcommentator.com
Year Established: 1971
Delivery Methods: Mail`Newsstand
Areas Served - City/County or Portion Thereof, or Zip codes: County of Forty Mile No. 8
Commercial printers?: Y
Published: Tues
Avg Paid Circ: 426
Avg Free Circ: 45
Audit By: VAC
Audit Date: 30.09.2016
Personnel: Coleen Campbell (Pub.); Tom Conquergood (Adv. Mgr.); Jamie Rieger (Ed.)

BOWEN ISLAND

BOWEN ISLAND UNDERCURRENT
Street Address: 102-495 Bowen Trunk Rd. ,
Province: BC
Postal: V0N 1V0
Country: Canada
Mailing address: PO Box 130
Mailing city: Bowen Island
Province: BC
Postal: V0N 1G0
General Phone: (604) 947-2442
General Fax: (604) 947-0148
Advertising Phone: (604) 947-2442
Editorial Phone: (604) 947-2442
General/National Adv. E-mail: publisher@bowenislandundercurrent.com
Display Adv. E-mail: ads@bowenislandundercurrent.com
Classified Adv. e-mail: ads@bowenislandundercurrent.com
Editorial e-mail: editor@bowenislandundercurrent.com
Primary Website: www.bowenislandundercurrent.com
Year Established: 1972
Areas Served - City/County or Portion Thereof, or Zip codes: Canada
Mechanical specifications: Type page 10 3/8 x 12 1/2; E - 6 cols, 1 11/18, between.
Published: Fri
Avg Free Circ: 73
Audit By: VAC
Audit Date: 31.05.2016
Personnel: Martha Perkins (Ed.); Kaana Bjork (Prodn. Mgr.); Maureen Sawasy (Adv. Sales); Peter Kvarnstrom (Pub.)
Parent company (for newspapers): Glacier Media Group

BRACEBRIDGE

BRACEBRIDGE EXAMINER
Street Address: 34 Ep Lee Dr. ,
Province: ON
Postal: P1L 1P9
Country: Canada
Mailing address: PO Box 1049
Mailing city: Bracebridge
Province: ON
Postal: P1L 1V2
General Phone: (705) 645-8771
General Fax: (705) 645-1718
General/National Adv. E-mail: examiner@muskoka.com
Display Adv. E-mail: mbradley@metroland.com
Classified Adv. e-mail: classifieds@metroland.com
Editorial e-mail: psteel@metrolandnorthmedia.com
Primary Website: www.bracebridgeexaminer.com
Areas Served - City/County or Portion Thereof, or Zip codes: Canada
Mechanical specifications: Type page 11 1/2 x 21 1/2; E - 6 cols, between; A - 6 cols, between; C - 6 cols, between.
Published: Thur
Avg Paid Circ: 83
Avg Free Circ: 8171
Audit By: CMCA
Audit Date: 30.04.2016
Personnel: Meriel Bradley (Adv. Mgr); Pamela Steel (Ed); Andrew Allen (Circ Mgr)
Parent company (for newspapers): Metroland Media Group Ltd.; Torstar

MUSKOKA DISTRICT WEEKENDER
Street Address: 34 E. P. Lee Drive ,
Province: ON
Postal: P1L 1V2
Country: Canada
Mailing address: PO Box 1049
Mailing city: Bracebridge on
Province: ON
Postal: P1L 1V2
General Phone: (705) 645-8771
General Fax: (705) 645-1718
General/National Adv. E-mail: ccunningham@metrolandnorthmedia.com
Display Adv. E-mail: ddickson@metrolandnorthmedia.com
Primary Website: www.muskokaregion.com
Areas Served - City/County or Portion Thereof, or Zip codes: Canada
Published: Fri
Avg Free Circ: 26430
Audit By: CMCA
Audit Date: 30.04.2013
Personnel: Coral Brush (Sales Coordinator)

THE MUSKOKAN
Street Address: 34 Ep Lee Dr. ,
Province: ON
Postal: P1L 1P9
Country: Canada
Mailing address: PO Box 1049
Mailing city: Bracebridge
Province: ON
Postal: P1L 1V2
General Phone: (705) 645-8771
General Fax: (705) 645-1718
General/National Adv. E-mail: muskokan@muskoka.com
Primary Website: www.muskokan.com
Own Printing Facility?: Y
Published: Thur
Avg Free Circ: 24000
Audit By: Sworn/Estimate/Non-Audited
Audit Date: 12.07.2019
Personnel: Paul Drummond (Adv. Sales Mgr.); Jake Good (Editorial Coord.); Marianne Dawson (Prodn. Coord.)
Parent company (for newspapers): Metroland Media Group Ltd.; Torstar

WHAT'S UP MUSKOKA
Street Address: Unit 12-440 Eccleston Drive ,
Province: ON
Postal: P1L 1Z6
Country: Canada
Mailing address: PO Box 180
Mailing city: Bracebridge
Province: ON
Postal: P1L 1T6
General Phone: (705) 646-1314
General Fax: (705) 645-6424
General/National Adv. E-mail: mm.info@sunmedia.ca
Primary Website: www.whatsupmuskoka.com
Year Established: 2008
Delivery Methods: Mail`Racks
Areas Served - City/County or Portion Thereof, or Zip codes: Muskoka
Own Printing Facility?: Y
Mechanical specifications: Type page 10 1/3 x 12 1/2; E - 6 cols, 1 1/2, between; A - 6 cols, 1 1/2, between; C - 6 cols, 1 1/2, between.
Published: Wed
Avg Paid Circ: 0
Avg Free Circ: 26000
Audit By: CMCA
Audit Date: 31.07.2013
Parent company (for newspapers): Postmedia Network Inc.; Quebecor Communications, Inc.

BRAMPTON

ACTION LONDON SARNIA
Street Address: Professor's Lake Parkway ,
Province: ON
Postal: L6S 4P8
Country: Canada
Mailing address: Professor's Lake Parkway
Mailing city: Brampton
Province: ON
Postal: L6S 4P8
General Phone: (800) 525-6752
Editorial e-mail: info@lemetropolitain.com
Primary Website: www.laction.ca
Published: Tues
Avg Paid Circ: 1907
Avg Free Circ: 1106
Audit By: ODC
Audit Date: 13.11.2011
Personnel: Denis Poirier (Ed); Richard Caumartin (Sales Dir)

LE REGIONAL
Street Address: 99 Professors Lake Parkway ,
Province: ON
Postal: L6S 4P8
Country: Canada
Mailing address: 99 Professors Park Way
Mailing city: Brampton
Province: ON
Postal: L6S 4P8
General Phone: (905) 732-9666
General Fax: (905) 790-9127
General/National Adv. E-mail: info@leregional.com
Display Adv. E-mail: marketing@leregional.com
Classified Adv. e-mail: marketing@leregional.com
Editorial e-mail: info@leregional.com
Primary Website: www.leregional.com
Year Established: 2000
Delivery Methods: Mail`Racks
Areas Served - City/County or Portion Thereof, or Zip codes: Canada
Published: Wed
Avg Paid Circ: 76
Avg Free Circ: 4164
Audit By: CMCA
Audit Date: 31.12.2012
Personnel: Christiane Beaupre

METROPOLITAIN (LE)
Street Address: 99 Professors Lake Pkwy ,
Province: ON
Postal: L6S 4P8
Country: Canada
Mailing address: 99 Professors Lake Pkwy
Mailing city: Brampton
Province: ON
Postal: L6S 4P8
General Phone: (905) 790-3229
General Fax: (905) 790-9127
General/National Adv. E-mail: info@lemetropolitain.com
Primary Website: www.lemetropolitain.com
Areas Served - City/County or Portion Thereof, or Zip codes: Canada
Published: Wed
Avg Paid Circ: 329
Avg Free Circ: 8028
Audit By: CMCA
Audit Date: 31.12.2012
Personnel: Denis Poirier (Ed.)

BRANDON

WESTMAN JOURNAL
Street Address: 315 College Avenue , Unit D
Province: MB
Postal: R7A 1E7
Country: Canada
Mailing address: 315 College Avenue
Mailing city: Brandon
Province: MB
Postal: R7A 1E7
General Phone: (204) 725-0209
General Fax: (204) 725-3021
General/National Adv. E-mail: info@wheatcityjournal.ca
Display Adv. E-mail: rthomson@wheatcityjournal.ca
Classified Adv. e-mail: agrelowshi@wheatcityjournal.ca
Editorial e-mail: newsroom@wheatcityjournal.ca
Primary Website: www.westmanjournal.com
Year Established: 2002
Delivery Methods: Carrier`Racks
Areas Served - City/County or Portion Thereof, or Zip codes: Brandon, MB
Published: Thur
Avg Free Circ: 13500
Audit By: VAC
Audit Date: 25.11.2017
Personnel: Rick Thomson; Alida Grelowski; Adam Wilken; Jamie Polmateer; Wade Branston; Brian Aitkinson; Judy Cluff (Admin Asst.)
Parent company (for newspapers): Glacier Media Group

BRANTFORD

BRANT NEWS
Street Address: 111 Easton Rd. ,
Province: ON
Postal: N3P 1J4
Country: Canada
Mailing address: 111 Easton Rd.
Mailing city: Brantford
Province: ON
Postal: N3P 1J4
General Phone: (519) 758-1157
General Fax: (519) 753-3567
General/National Adv. E-mail: loffless@brantnews.com
Display Adv. E-mail: lbutler@brantnews.com

Classified Adv. e-mail: classified@metrolandwest.com
Editorial e-mail: sallen@brantnews.com
Primary Website: www.brantnews.com
Year Established: 2009
Areas Served - City/County or Portion Thereof, or Zip codes: Canada
Published: Thur
Avg Paid Circ: 0
Avg Free Circ: 48716
Audit By: CCAB
Audit Date: 30.09.2017
Personnel: Linda Hill (Circ Mgr); Sean Allen (Ed); Loren Butlet (Adv Mgr)
Parent company (for newspapers): Metroland Media Group Ltd.; Metroland Media

PARIS STAR

Street Address: 195 Henry St , Building 4, Unit 1
Province: ON
Postal: N3S 5C9
Country: Canada
Mailing address: 195 Henry St, Building 4, Unit 1
Mailing city: Brantford
Province: ON
Postal: N3S 5C9
General Phone: (519) 756-2020
General Fax: (519) 756-9470
General/National Adv. E-mail: parisstar.editorial@sunmedia.ca
Editorial e-mail: parisstar.editorial@sunmedia.ca
Primary Website: parisstaronline.com
Year Established: 1850
Areas Served - City/County or Portion Thereof, or Zip codes: Canada
Own Printing Facility?: Y
Mechanical specifications: Type page 10 x 16; E - 5 cols, 2, 1/8 between; A - 5 cols, 2, 1/8 between; C - 6 cols, 1 3/4, 1/8 between.
Published: Thur
Avg Free Circ: 4877
Audit By: CMCA
Audit Date: 30.04.2019
Personnel: Ken Koyama (Pub.); Michael Peeling (Ed.)
Parent company (for newspapers): Postmedia Network Inc.; Quebecor Communications, Inc.

BRIDGEWATER

LIGHTHOUSE NOW

Street Address: 353 York St. ,
Province: NS
Postal: B4V 3K2
Country: Canada
Mailing address: 353 York St.
Mailing city: Bridgewater
Province: NS
Postal: B4V 3K2
General Phone: (902) 543-2457
General Fax: (902) 543-2228
Advertising Phone: (902) 543-1569
General/National Adv. E-mail: mail@southshorenow.ca
Display Adv. E-mail: daveda.savory@lighthousenow.ca
Classified Adv. e-mail: tracy.williams@lighthousenow.ca
Editorial e-mail: editorial@southshorenow.ca
Primary Website: https://lighthousenow.ca/
Areas Served - City/County or Portion Thereof, or Zip codes: Bridgewater
Own Printing Facility?: Y
Mechanical specifications: Type page 10 5/16 x 16; E - 6 cols, 1 5/8, 1/6 between; A - 6 cols, 1 5/8, 1/6 between; C - 6 cols, 1 5/8, 1/6 between.
Published: Thur
Avg Paid Circ: 6573
Avg Free Circ: 26963
Audit By: VAC
Audit Date: 31.10.2015
Personnel: Lynn Hennigar (Pub); Laurenda Reeves (Circ. Mgr.); Emma Smith (Ed.)

THE BULLETIN

Street Address: 353 York St. ,
Province: NS
Postal: B4V 3K2
Country: Canada
Mailing address: 353 York St.
Mailing city: Bridgewater
Province: NS
Postal: B4V 3K2
General Phone: (902) 543-2457
General Fax: (902) 543-2228
General/National Adv. E-mail: editorial@southshorenow.ca
Editorial e-mail: editorial@southshorenow.ca
Primary Website: https://lighthousenow.ca
Year Established: 1888
Areas Served - City/County or Portion Thereof, or Zip codes: Canada
Commercial printers?: Y
Mechanical specifications: Type page 10 5/16 x 16; E - 6 cols, 1 5/8, 1/6 between; A - 6 cols, 1 5/8, 1/6 between; C - 6 cols, 1 5/8, 1/6 between.
Published: Tues
Avg Paid Circ: 7030
Avg Free Circ: 127
Audit By: Sworn/Estimate/Non-Audited
Audit Date: 12.07.2019
Personnel: Lynn Hennigar (Pub); Laurenda Reeves (Circ. Mgr.); Emma Smith (Ed.)

BROCKVILLE

ST. LAWRENCE NEWS

Street Address: 7712 Kent Blvd. ,
Province: ON
Postal: K6V 7H6
Country: Canada
General Phone: (613) 498-0305
General Fax: (613) 498-0307
Primary Website: www.emcstlawrence.ca
Areas Served - City/County or Portion Thereof, or Zip codes: Canada
Published: Thur
Avg Free Circ: 29325
Audit By: CMCA
Audit Date: 30.06.2016
Parent company (for newspapers): Metroland Media Group Ltd.

THE RECORDER & TIMES

Street Address: 2479 Parkedale Avenue ,
Province: ON
Postal: K6V 3H2
Country: Canada
Mailing address: 2479 Parkedale Avenue
Mailing city: Brockville
Province: ON
Postal: K6V 3H2
General Phone: (613) 342-4441
General Fax: (613) 342-4456
Advertising Phone: (613) 342-4441 Ext. 500267
Editorial Phone: (613) 342-4441 Ext. 500107
General/National Adv. E-mail: newsroom@indynews.ca
Display Adv. E-mail: ksammon@postmedia.com
Editorial e-mail: dgordanier@postmedia.com
Primary Website: www.recorder.ca
Year Established: 1997
Delivery Methods: Newsstand`Carrier
Areas Served - City/County or Portion Thereof, or Zip codes: Leeds & Grenville Counties
Commercial printers?: Y
Mechanical specifications: Type page 10 1/4 x 14 1/4; E - 6 cols, 1 5/8, 1/8 between; A - 6 cols, 1 5/8, 1/8 between; C - 7 cols, 1 1/3, 1/8 between.
Published: Wed`Thur
Avg Free Circ: 29300
Audit By: CMCA
Audit Date: 30.09.2016
Personnel: Kerry Sammon (Med. Sales Dir.)
Parent company (for newspapers): Post Media

BROOKS

THE BROOKS BULLETIN

Street Address: 124-3 St. W. ,
Province: AB
Postal: T1R 0S3
Country: Canada
Mailing address: PO Box 1450
Mailing city: Brooks
Province: AB
Postal: T1R 1C3
General Phone: (403) 362-5571
General Fax: (403) 362-5080
Display Adv. E-mail: diane@brooksbulletin.com
Classified Adv. e-mail: diane@brooksbulletin.com
Editorial e-mail: editor@brooksbulletin.com
Primary Website: www.brooksbulletin.com
Year Established: 1910
Delivery Methods: Mail`Newsstand`Racks
Areas Served - City/County or Portion Thereof, or Zip codes: Brooks and County of Newell, Canada
Own Printing Facility?: Y
Commercial printers?: Y
Mechanical specifications: Type page 11.5 x 21.
Published: Tues
Avg Paid Circ: 2800
Avg Free Circ: 188
Audit By: Sworn/Estimate/Non-Audited
Audit Date: 12.07.2019
Personnel: Jamie Nesbitt (Ed./Pub.)
Parent company (for newspapers): Brooks Bulletin

BURKS FALLS

ALMAGUIN NEWS

Street Address: 59 Ontario St. ,
Province: ON
Postal: P0A 1C0
Country: Canada
Mailing address: PO Box 518
Mailing city: Burks Falls
Province: ON
Postal: P0A 1C0
General Phone: (705)382-9996
General Fax: (705) 382-9997
General/National Adv. E-mail: news@almaguinnews.com
Display Adv. E-mail: advertising@almaguinnews.com
Editorial e-mail: editor@almaguinnews.com
Primary Website: www.almaguinnews.com
Year Established: 1889
Delivery Methods: Mail`Newsstand
Areas Served - City/County or Portion Thereof, or Zip codes: Canada
Commercial printers?: Y
Mechanical specifications: Type page 10 x 21 1/2"; E - 9 cols, 1 1/16, between; A - 9 cols, 1 3/8, between; C - 9 cols, 1 3/8, between.
Published: Thur
Avg Paid Circ: 2230
Avg Free Circ: 150
Audit By: CMCA
Audit Date: 31.12.2015
Personnel: Bill Allen (Gen. Mgr.); Twila Armstrong (Adv. Rep.); Rob Learn (News Ed.)
Parent company (for newspapers): Metroland Media Group Ltd.

BURLINGTON

THE BURLINGTON POST

Street Address: 5040 Mainway, Unit 1 ,
Province: ON
Postal: L7L 7G5
Country: Canada
Mailing address: 5040 Mainway, Unit 1
Mailing city: Burlington
Province: ON
Postal: L7L 7G5
General Phone: (905) 632-4444
General Fax: (905) 632-9162
Editorial e-mail: letters@burlingtonpost.com
Primary Website: burlingtonpost.com
Year Established: 1965
Delivery Methods: Carrier
Areas Served - City/County or Portion Thereof, or Zip codes: Canada
Own Printing Facility?: Y
Commercial printers?: Y
Published: Thur`Fri
Avg Paid Circ: 27
Avg Free Circ: 28355
Audit By: CCAB
Audit Date: 30.09.2017
Personnel: Jill Davis (Ed. in Chief); Don Ford (Mng. Ed.); Kevin Nagel (Sports Ed.); Debbi Koppejan (Advertising Director)
Parent company (for newspapers): Metroland Media Group Ltd.; Torstar

BURNABY

BURNABY NOW

Street Address: 3430 Brighton Ave. , Ste. 201a
Province: BC
Postal: V5A 3H4
Country: Canada
General Phone: (604) 444-3451
General Fax: (604) 444-3460
Advertising Phone: (604) 444-3030
Editorial Phone: (604) 444-3007
General/National Adv. E-mail: editorial@burnabynow.com
Display Adv. E-mail: chendrix@burnabynow.com
Editorial e-mail: ptracy@royalcityrecord.com
Primary Website: burnabynow.com
Year Established: 1983
Areas Served - City/County or Portion Thereof, or Zip codes: Canada
Own Printing Facility?: Y
Mechanical specifications: Type page 10 1/4 x 14; E - 6 cols, 1 9/16, 1/6 between; A - 6 cols, 1 9/16, 1/6 between; C - 7 cols, 1 3/8, 1/12 between.
Published: Wed`Fri
Avg Paid Circ: 0
Avg Free Circ: 43521
Audit By: CCAB
Audit Date: 23.11.2017
Personnel: Lara Graham (Pub.); Pat Tracy (Ed.); Cynthia Hendrix (Adv.); Dan Olson (Sports Ed.)
Parent company (for newspapers): Glacier Media Group

BURNABY

THE RECORD

Street Address: 201a 3430 Brighton Ave. ,
Province: BC
Postal: V5A 3H4
Country: Canada
Mailing address: 201A 3430 Brighton Ave.
Mailing city: Burnaby
Province: BC
Postal: V5A 3H4
General Phone: (604) 444-3451
General Fax: (604) 444-3460
Advertising Phone: (604)444-3030
Editorial Phone: (604) 444-3007
Display Adv. E-mail: kgilmour@newwestrecord.ca
Editorial e-mail: ptracy@newwestrecord.com
Primary Website: royalcityrecord.com
Year Established: 1981
Areas Served - City/County or Portion Thereof, or Zip codes: Canada
Own Printing Facility?: Y
Published: Wed`Fri
Avg Paid Circ: 0
Avg Free Circ: 16966
Audit By: CCAB
Audit Date: 23.11.2017
Personnel: Lara Graham (Pub); Pat Tracy (Ed.); Dale Dorsett (Circ. Mgr)
Parent company (for newspapers): CanWest MediaWorks Publications, Inc.

Non-Daily Newspapers in Canada

III-441

BURNS LAKE

BURNS LAKES DISTRICT NEWS

Street Address: 23 3rd Ave. ,
Province: BC
Postal: V0J 1E0
Country: Canada
Mailing address: PO Box 309
Mailing city: Burns Lake
Province: BC
Postal: V0J 1E0
General Phone: (250) 692-7526
General Fax: (250) 692-3685
General/National Adv. E-mail: newsroom@ldnews.net; advertising@ldnews.net
Display Adv. E-mail: advertising@ldnews.net
Classified Adv. e-mail: advertising@ldnews.net
Editorial e-mail: newsroom@ldnews.net
Primary Website: www.ldnews.net
Year Established: 1986
Delivery Methods: Mail`Newsstand`Racks
Areas Served - City/County or Portion Thereof, or Zip codes:
Own Printing Facility?: Y
Published: Wed
Avg Paid Circ: 1181
Avg Free Circ: 117
Audit By: VAC
Audit Date: 30.06.2017
Personnel: Laura Blackwell (Adv. Mgr./Pub.); Annamarie Douglas (Prod. Mgr.); Kim Piper (front office); Flavio Nienow (Editor)
Parent company (for newspapers): Black Press Group Ltd.

CALEDONIA

GLANBROOK GAZETTE

Street Address: 3 Sutherland St. W. ,
Province: ON
Postal: N3W 1C1
Country: Canada
General Phone: (905) 765-4441
General Fax: (905) 765-3651
General/National Adv. E-mail: news@sachem.ca
Display Adv. E-mail: advertising@sachem.ca
Primary Website: www.sachem.ca
Areas Served - City/County or Portion Thereof, or Zip codes: Canada
Published: Thur
Avg Free Circ: 9194
Audit By: CMCA
Audit Date: 31.12.2015
Parent company (for newspapers): Metroland Media Group Ltd.

THE GRAND RIVER SACHEM

Street Address: 3 Sutherland St. W. ,
Province: ON
Postal: N3W 1C1
Country: Canada
Mailing address: 3 Sutherland St. W.
Mailing city: Caledonia
Province: ON
Postal: N3W 1C1
General Phone: (905) 765-4441
General Fax: (905) 765-3651
General/National Adv. E-mail: news@sachem.ca; sachem@sachem.ca
Display Adv. E-mail: advertising@sachem.ca
Primary Website: www.sachem.ca
Areas Served - City/County or Portion Thereof, or Zip codes: Canada
Mechanical specifications: Type page 10 1/3 x 14; E - 6 cols, 1 3/5, between; A - 6 cols, 1 1/3, between.
Published: Thur
Avg Paid Circ: 77
Avg Free Circ: 21137
Audit By: CMCA
Audit Date: 30.06.2013
Personnel: Nancy Plank (Adv. Mgr.); Georgia Mete (Adv. Mgr., Classified); Neil Dring (Ed.)
Parent company (for newspapers): Metroland Media Group Ltd.

CAMBRIDGE

CAMBRIDGE TIMES

Street Address: 475 Thompson Dr. Units 1-4 ,
Province: ON
Postal: N1T 2K7
Country: Canada
Mailing address: 475 Thompson Dr. Units 1-4
Mailing city: Cambridge
Province: ON
Postal: N1T 2K7
General Phone: (519) 623-7395
General Fax: (519) 623-9155
Display Adv. E-mail: tanderson@cambridgetimes.ca
Classified Adv. e-mail: classified@metrolandwest.com
Editorial e-mail: rvivian@cambridgetimes.ca
Primary Website: www.cambridgetimes.ca
Delivery Methods: Carrier
Areas Served - City/County or Portion Thereof, or Zip codes: Canada
Commercial printers?: Y
Mechanical specifications: Type page 11 x 17; E - 6 cols, 2 1/20, between; A - 6 cols, 2 1/20, between; C - 6 cols, 2 1/20, between.
Published: Tues`Thur
Avg Free Circ: 31628
Audit By: CMCA
Audit Date: 30.06.2016
Personnel: Donna Luelo (Pub); Richard Vivian (Ed); Carron Woods (Prod/Circ. Mgr.); Ted Anderson (Adv. Mgr.)
Parent company (for newspapers): Metroland Media Group Ltd.; Torstar

CAMPBELL RIVER

THE CAMPBELL RIVER COURIER-ISLANDER

Street Address: 104 - 250 Dogwood St ,
Province: BC
Postal: V9W 5Z5
Country: Canada
Mailing address: 104 - 250 Dogwood St
Mailing city: Campbell River
Province: BC
Postal: V9W 5Z5
General Phone: (250) 287-9227
General Fax: (250) 287-8891
Display Adv. E-mail: jacquie.duns@campbellrivermirror.com
Classified Adv. e-mail: darceyw@campbellrivermirror.com
Editorial e-mail: editor@campbellrivermirror.com
Primary Website: www.courierislander.com
Year Established: 1945
Delivery Methods: Mail`Newsstand`Carrier`Racks
Areas Served - City/County or Portion Thereof, or Zip codes: Campbell River
Own Printing Facility?: Y
Commercial printers?: N
Mechanical specifications: Type page 11 3/5 x 21 1/2; E - 10 cols, 1 1/10, 1/12 between; A - 10 cols, 1 1/10, 1/12 between; C - 10 cols, 1 1/10, 1/12 between.
Published: Wed`Fri
Avg Paid Circ: 0
Avg Free Circ: 16561
Audit By: AAM
Audit Date: 30.09.2015
Personnel: David Hamilton (Pub) Alistair Taylor (Ed) Kevin McKinnon (Circ. Mgr)

THE CAMPBELL RIVER MIRROR

Street Address: 104-250 Dogwood St. ,
Province: BC
Postal: V9W 2X9
Country: Canada
Mailing address: 104-250 Dogwood St.
Mailing city: Campbell River
Province: BC
Postal: V9W 2X9
General Phone: (250) 287-9227
General Fax: (250) 287-3238
Editorial Phone: (250) 287-9227
General/National Adv. E-mail: publisher@campbellrivermirror.com
Editorial e-mail: editor@campbellrivermirror.com
Primary Website: campbellrivermirror.com
Year Established: 1971
Delivery Methods: Mail`Newsstand`Carrier
Areas Served - City/County or Portion Thereof, or Zip codes: Canada
Own Printing Facility?: Y
Published: Wed`Fri
Avg Paid Circ: 30
Avg Free Circ: 16442
Audit By: AAM
Audit Date: 31.03.2019
Personnel: Alistair Taylor (Ed.); David Hamilton (Pub.); Michelle Hueller (Prod.); Kevin McKinnon (Circ. Mgr.); Zena Williams (Publisher); Artur Ciastkowski (Publisher)
Parent company (for newspapers): Black Press Group Ltd.

CAMPBELLTON

THE TRIBUNE

Street Address: 6 Shannon St. ,
Province: NB
Postal: E3N 3G9
Country: Canada
Mailing address: PO Box 486
Mailing city: Campbellton
Province: NB
Postal: E3N 3G9
General Phone: (506) 753-4413
General Fax: (506) 759-9595
General/National Adv. E-mail: tribune@tribunenb.ca
Editorial e-mail: tribune@tribunenb.ca
Primary Website: http://www.telegraphjournal.com/tribune/
Areas Served - City/County or Portion Thereof, or Zip codes: Campbellton
Mechanical specifications: Type page 12 7/8 x 21; E - 6 cols, 1/6 between; A - 6 cols, 1/6 between; C - 6 cols, 1/6 between.
Published: Fri
Avg Free Circ: 2
Audit By: VAC
Audit Date: 31.12.2015
Personnel: Peter Makintosh (Pub./Ed)

CAMROSE

THE CAMROSE CANADIAN

Street Address: 4610 49th Ave. ,
Province: AB
Postal: T4V 0M6
Country: Canada
General Phone: (780) 672-4421
General Fax: (780) 672-5323
Advertising Phone: (877) 786-8227
General/National Adv. E-mail: production@camrosecanadian.com
Display Adv. E-mail: ngoetz@postmedia.com
Primary Website: www.camrosecanadian.com
Year Established: 1908
Areas Served - City/County or Portion Thereof, or Zip codes: Camrose County
Commercial printers?: Y
Mechanical specifications: Type page 10 1/4 x 12 1/2; E - 8 cols, 1 3/16, 1/6 between; A - 8 cols, 1 3/16, 1/6 between; C - 8 cols, 1 1/4, 1/6 between.
Published: Thur
Avg Paid Circ: 3673
Avg Free Circ: 15292
Audit By: VAC
Audit Date: 31.12.2015
Personnel: Dan Macpherson (Adv. Mgr.); Nick Goetz (Publisher); Trent Wilkie (Editor); Vince Burke (Editor(online)); Jim Clark (Publisher(online))
Parent company (for newspapers): Postmedia Network Inc.

CANMORE

ROCKY MOUNTAIN OUTLOOK

Street Address: Box 8610 , Suite 201 - 1001. 6th Avenue
Province: AB
Postal: T1W 2V3
Country: Canada
Mailing address: Box 8610 Suite 201 - 1001. 6th Ave
Mailing city: Canmore
Province: AB
Postal: T1W 2V3
General Phone: (403) 609-0220
General Fax: (403)609-0221
Display Adv. E-mail: clacroix@outlook.greatwest.ca
Classified Adv. e-mail: jlyon@outlook.greatwest.ca
Editorial e-mail: dwhitfield@rmoutlook.com
Primary Website: www.rmoutlook.com
Year Established: 2001
Published: Thur
Avg Paid Circ: 0
Avg Free Circ: 9395
Audit By: VAC
Audit Date: 31.01.2016
Personnel: Jason Lyon (Pub/Adv. Mgr); Donna Browne (Circ. Mgr); Dave Whitfield (Ed)
Parent company (for newspapers): Glacier Media Group; Great West Newspapers LP

CANNINGTON

BROCK CITIZEN

Street Address: 2d Cameron St. E. ,
Province: ON
Postal: L0E 1E0
Country: Canada
Mailing address: 2D Cameron St. E.
Mailing city: Cannington
Province: ON
Postal: L0E 1E0
General Phone: (705) 432-8842
General Fax: (705) 432-2942
General/National Adv. E-mail: bdanford@mykawartha.com
Display Adv. E-mail: btrickett@mykawartha.com
Classified Adv. e-mail: lmunro@mykawartha.com
Editorial e-mail: ltuffin@mykawartha.com
Primary Website: http://www.mykawartha.com/brocktownship-on/
Published: Thur
Avg Free Circ: 5497
Audit By: Sworn/Estimate/Non-Audited
Audit Date: 12.07.2019
Personnel: Peter Bishop (Ed); Mary Babcock (Gen. Mgr.); Lois Tuffin (Mng. Ed.); Kim Riel (Office Mgr)
Parent company (for newspapers): Metroland Media Group Ltd.; Torstar

CANORA

CANORA COURIER

Street Address: 123 First Ave. E. ,
Province: SK
Postal: S0A 0L0
Country: Canada
Mailing address: P.O. Box 746
Mailing city: Canora
Province: SK
Postal: S0A 0L0
General Phone: (306) 563-5131
General Fax: (306) 563-6144
General/National Adv. E-mail: canoracourier@sasktel.net
Display Adv. E-mail: sales.canoracourier@sasktel.net
Classified Adv. e-mail: office.canoracourier@sasktel.net
Editorial e-mail: canoracourier@sasktel.net
Primary Website: canoracourier.com
Delivery Methods: Mail`Newsstand
Areas Served - City/County or Portion Thereof, or Zip codes: Canada
Own Printing Facility?: Y
Commercial printers?: Y
Mechanical specifications: Type page 10 1/4 x 15

1/2; E - 6 cols, 1 2/3, between; A - 6 cols, 1 2/3, between; C - 6 cols, 1 2/3, between.
Published: Wed
Avg Paid Circ: 1136
Avg Free Circ: 9
Audit By: CMCA
Audit Date: 30.09.2016
Personnel: Ken Lewchuk (Pub)
Parent company (for newspapers): Glacier Media Group

PREECEVILLE PROGRESS
Street Address: 123 First Ave. E. ,
Province: SK
Postal: S0A 0L0
Country: Canada
Mailing address: P.O. Box 319
Mailing city: Canora
Province: SK
Postal: S0A 0L0
General Phone: (306) 563-5131
General Fax: (306) 563-6144
General/National Adv. E-mail: canoracourier@sasktel.net
Display Adv. E-mail: sales.canoracourier@sasktel.net
Classified Adv. e-mail: office.canoracourier@sasktel.net
Editorial e-mail: canoracourier@sasktel.net
Primary Website: http://www.preeceviIleprogress.com/
Areas Served - City/County or Portion Thereof, or Zip codes: Canada
Own Printing Facility?: Y
Commercial printers?: Y
Mechanical specifications: Type page 10 1/4 x 15 1/2; E - 6 cols, 1 2/3, between; A - 6 cols, 1 2/3, between; C - 6 cols, 1 2/3, between.
Published: Thur
Avg Paid Circ: 971
Avg Free Circ: 4
Audit By: CMCA
Audit Date: 15.09.2014
Personnel: Ken Lewchuk
Parent company (for newspapers): Canora Courier; Glacier Media Group

THE KAMSACK TIMES
Street Address: 123 First Ave. E. ,
Province: SK
Postal: S0A 0L0
Country: Canada
Mailing address: P.O. Box 850
Mailing city: Kamsack
Province: SK
Postal: S0A 1S0
General Phone: (306) 563-5131
General Fax: (306) 563-6144
Advertising Phone: (306) 563-5131
Editorial Phone: (306) 542-2626
General/National Adv. E-mail: canoracourier@sasktel.net
Display Adv. E-mail: k.lewchuk@sasktel.net
Classified Adv. e-mail: office.canoracourier@sasktel.net
Editorial e-mail: kamsacktimes@sasktel.net
Primary Website: kamsacktimes.com
Delivery Methods: Mail`Newsstand
Areas Served - City/County or Portion Thereof, or Zip codes: Canada
Own Printing Facility?: Y
Commercial printers?: Y
Mechanical specifications: Type page 10 1/4 x 15 1/2; E - 6 cols, 1 2/3, between; A - 6 cols, 1 2/3, between; C - 6 cols, 1 2/3, between.
Published: Thur
Avg Paid Circ: 1100
Avg Free Circ: 5
Audit By: CMCA
Audit Date: 30.03.2017
Personnel: Ken Lewchuk (Publisher)
Parent company (for newspapers): Canora Courier; Glacier Media Group

CAP-AUX-MEULES
LE RADAR
Street Address: 110 Chemin Gros Cap, CP 8183 ,
Province: QC
Postal: G4T 1R3
Country: Canada
Mailing address: 110 Chemin Gros Cap, CP 8183
Mailing city: Cap-aux-Meules
Province: QC
Postal: G4T 1R3
General Phone: (418) 986-234
General Fax: (418)986-6358
General/National Adv. E-mail: secretaire@leradar.qc.ca
Display Adv. E-mail: direction@leradar.qc.ca
Classified Adv. e-mail: direction@leradar.qc.ca
Editorial e-mail: redacteur@leradar.qc.ca
Primary Website: leradar.qc.ca
Areas Served - City/County or Portion Thereof, or Zip codes: Canada
Published: Fri
Avg Paid Circ: 1512
Avg Free Circ: 1523
Audit By: AAM
Audit Date: 31.03.2019
Personnel: Hugo Miousse (Pub.); Achilles Hubert (Ed.); Lucille Tremblay (Adv. Mgr.); Francoise Decoste (Circ. Mgr.)
Parent company (for newspapers): Reseau Select/Select Network

CARBERRY
CARBERRY NEWS EXPRESS
Street Address: 34 Main St. W. ,
Province: MB
Postal: R0K 0H0
Country: Canada
Mailing address: PO Box 220
Mailing city: Carberry
Province: MB
Postal: R0K 0H0
General Phone: (204) 834-2153
General Fax: (204) 834-2714
General/National Adv. E-mail: info@carberrynews.ca
Display Adv. E-mail: ads@carberrynews.ca
Editorial e-mail: kathy@carberrynews.ca
Primary Website: www.carberrynews.ca
Year Established: 1910
Delivery Methods: Mail`Newsstand`Racks
Areas Served - City/County or Portion Thereof, or Zip codes: Carberry, Mun. of North Cypress-Langford, Manitoba, Saskatchewan, Alberta, British Columbia, Ontario, New Brunswick
Own Printing Facility?: Y
Commercial printers?: Y
Mechanical specifications: Type page 11 1/2 x 17; E - 5 cols, 1 7/8, 1/8 between; A - 6 cols, 1 5/8, 1/8 between; C - 6 cols, 1 5/8, 1/8 between.
Published: Mon
Avg Paid Circ: 593
Avg Free Circ: 34
Audit By: VAC
Audit Date: 30.09.2018
Personnel: Kathy Carr (Gen. Mgr.); Eva Rutz
Parent company (for newspapers): FP Newspapers Inc.

CARBONEAR
THE COMPASS
Street Address: 176 Water St. ,
Province: NL
Postal: A1Y 1C3
Country: Canada
Mailing address: PO Box 760
Mailing city: Carbonear
Province: NL
Postal: A1Y 1C3
General Phone: (709) 596-6458
General Fax: (709) 596-1700
General/National Adv. E-mail: editor@cbncompass.ca
Editorial e-mail: editor@cbncompass.ca
Primary Website: www.cbncompass.ca
Areas Served - City/County or Portion Thereof, or Zip codes: Carbonear
Own Printing Facility?: Y
Commercial printers?: Y
Mechanical specifications: Type page 12 x 22 1/2; E - 6 cols, 2, between; A - 6 cols, 2, between; C - 8 cols, 1 1/2, between.
Published: Tues
Avg Paid Circ: 2376
Avg Free Circ: 0
Audit By: VAC
Audit Date: 31.12.2015
Personnel: Bill Bowman (Ed)
Parent company (for newspapers): Transcontinental Media

CARDSTON
TEMPLE CITY STAR
Street Address: 30-b 3rd Ave. West ,
Province: AB
Postal: T0K 0K0
Country: Canada
Mailing address: PO Box 2060
Mailing city: Cardston
Province: AB
Postal: T0K 0K0
General Phone: (403) 653-4664
General Fax: (403) 653-3162
Advertising Phone: (403) 653-4664
General/National Adv. E-mail: info@templecitystar.net
Display Adv. E-mail: news@templecitystar.net
Editorial e-mail: news@templecitystar.net
Primary Website: www.templecitystar.net
Year Established: 1980
Delivery Methods: Mail`Newsstand
Areas Served - City/County or Portion Thereof, or Zip codes: Canada
Published: Thur
Avg Paid Circ: 650
Avg Free Circ: 50
Audit By: Sworn/Estimate/Non-Audited
Audit Date: 12.07.2019
Personnel: Robert Smith (Owner/Pub.); Dan Burt (Office Mgr.)

CARLYLE
CARLYLE OBSERVER
Street Address: 132 Main St. ,
Province: SK
Postal: S0C 0R0
Country: Canada
Mailing address: PO Box 160
Mailing city: Carlyle
Province: SK
Postal: S0C 0R0
General Phone: (306) 453-2525
General Fax: (306) 453-2938
General/National Adv. E-mail: observer@sasktel.net
Primary Website: www.carlyleobserver.com
Year Established: 1936
Areas Served - City/County or Portion Thereof, or Zip codes: Canada
Commercial printers?: Y
Mechanical specifications: Type page 11 x 17; E - 5 cols, 2, between; A - 5 cols, 2, between; C - 6 cols, 1 1/2, between.
Published: Fri
Avg Paid Circ: 113
Avg Free Circ: 2877
Audit By: CMCA
Audit Date: 30.06.2016
Personnel: Cindy Moffett (Pub.)
Parent company (for newspapers): Glacier Media Group

CARMAN
THE VALLEY LEADER
Street Address: 4 - 1st St Sw ,
Province: MB
Postal: R0G 0J0
Country: Canada
Mailing address: 4 - 1st St SW
Mailing city: Carman
Province: MB
Postal: R0G 0J0
General Phone: (204) 745-2051
General Fax: (204) 745-3976
General/National Adv. E-mail: carmenvl@mts.net
Display Adv. E-mail: Darcie.Morris@sunmedia.ca
Editorial e-mail: winkler.news@sunmedia.ca
Primary Website: http://www.pembinatoday.ca/carmanvalleyleader
Year Established: 1896
Areas Served - City/County or Portion Thereof, or Zip codes: Canada
Own Printing Facility?: Y
Mechanical specifications: Type page 11 1/2 x 15; E - 6 cols, 1 1/2, 1/8 between; A - 6 cols, 1 1/2, 1/8 between; C - 8 cols, 1 3/16, 1/8 between.
Published: Thur
Avg Paid Circ: 955
Avg Free Circ: 3872
Audit By: VAC
Audit Date: 30.06.2016
Personnel: Darcie Morris (Adv Dir); Greg Vandermeulen (Ed)
Parent company (for newspapers): Postmedia Network Inc.; Quebecor Communications, Inc.

CARNDUFF
GAZETTE-POST NEWS
Street Address: 106 Broadway ,
Province: SK
Postal: S0C 0S0
Country: Canada
Mailing address: PO Box 220
Mailing city: Carnduff
Province: SK
Postal: S0C 0S0
General Phone: (306) 482-3252
General Fax: (306) 482-3373
General/National Adv. E-mail: gazettepost.news@sasktel.net; gazette_postnews@awnet.net
Year Established: 1899
Areas Served - City/County or Portion Thereof, or Zip codes: Canada
Commercial printers?: Y
Mechanical specifications: Type page 10 x 21; E - 6 cols, 1 1/2, between; A - 6 cols, 1 1/2, between; C - 6 cols, 1 1/2, between.
Published: Fri
Avg Paid Circ: 1006
Audit By: CMCA
Audit Date: 30.06.2015
Personnel: Bruce Shwanke (Pub.)

CARTWRIGHT
SOUTHERN MANITOBA REVIEW
Street Address: B-635 Bowles St. ,
Province: MB
Postal: R0K 0L0
Country: Canada
Mailing address: PO Box 249
Mailing city: Cartwright
Province: MB
Postal: R0K 0L0
General Phone: (204) 529-2342
General Fax: (204) 529-2029
General/National Adv. E-mail: cartnews@mts.net
Editorial e-mail: cartnews@mts.net
Primary Website: www.southernmanitobareview.com
Year Established: 1899
Delivery Methods: Mail
Areas Served - City/County or Portion Thereof, or Zip codes: Canada
Mechanical specifications: Type page 11 1/2 x 15 1/2; E - 6 cols, 1.6", 1/6 between; A - 6 cols, 1.6", 1/6 between; C - 6 cols, 1.6", 1/6 between.
Published: Thur
Avg Paid Circ: 790
Avg Free Circ: 10
Audit By: CMCA

Non-Daily Newspapers in Canada

CASTLEGAR

ROSSLAND NEWS
Street Address: 1810 8th Avenue , Unit 2
Province: BC
Postal: V1N 2Y2
Country: Canada
Mailing address: 1810 8th Avenue, Unit 2
Mailing city: Castlegar
Province: BC
Postal: V1N 2Y2
General Phone: (250) 365 6497
General/National Adv. E-mail: publisher@rosslandnews.com
Display Adv. E-mail: sales@rosslandnews.com
Editorial e-mail: newsroom@castlegarnews.com
Primary Website: www.rosslandnews.com
Delivery Methods: Racks
Areas Served - City/County or Portion Thereof, or Zip codes: Rossland
Published: Thur
Avg Paid Circ: 7
Avg Free Circ: 1063
Audit By: VAC
Audit Date: 30.04.2017
Personnel: Eric Lawson (Pub.); Jennifer Cowan (Ed)
Parent company (for newspapers): Black Press Group Ltd.

THE CASTLEGAR NEWS
Street Address: Unit 2, 1810 8th Avenue ,
Province: BC
Postal: V1N 2y2
Country: Canada
General Phone: (250) 365-6397
General/National Adv. E-mail: newsroom@castlegarnews.com
Display Adv. E-mail: sales@castlegarnews.com
Classified Adv. e-mail: sales@castlegarnews.com
Editorial e-mail: newsroom@castlegarnews.com
Primary Website: www.castlegarnews.com
Year Established: 2004
Delivery Methods: Newsstand`Carrier`Racks
Areas Served - City/County or Portion Thereof, or Zip codes: Castlegar
Published: Thur
Avg Paid Circ: 0
Avg Free Circ: 6442
Audit By: VAC
Audit Date: 30.04.2017
Personnel: Eric Lawson (Pub.)
Parent company (for newspapers): Black Press Group Ltd.

CASTOR

CASTOR ADVANCE
Street Address: 5012 50 Ave. ,
Province: AB
Postal: T0C 0X0
Country: Canada
Mailing address: 5012 50 Ave.
Mailing city: Castor
Province: AB
Postal: T0C 0X0
General Phone: (403) 882-4044
Display Adv. E-mail: admin@castoradvance.com
Editorial e-mail: editor@castoradvance.com
Areas Served - City/County or Portion Thereof, or Zip codes: Canada
Published: Thur
Avg Paid Circ: 79
Avg Free Circ: 22
Audit By: VAC
Audit Date: 12.12.2017
Personnel: Mustafa Eric (Ed.)
Parent company (for newspapers): Black Press Group Ltd.

CHAMBLY

CHAMBLY EXPRESS
Street Address: C-1691, Boul Perigny ,
Province: QC
Postal: J3L 1X1
Country: Canada
Mailing address: C-1691, boul Perigny
Mailing city: Chambly
Province: QC
Postal: J3L 1X1
General Phone: (450) 658-5559
General Fax: (450) 658-1620
General/National Adv. E-mail: chamblyexpress@tc.tc
Primary Website: www.chamblyexpress.ca
Areas Served - City/County or Portion Thereof, or Zip codes: Canada
Published: Tues
Avg Free Circ: 27037
Audit By: CCAB
Audit Date: 31.03.2014

JOURNAL DE CHAMBLY
Street Address: 1685 Bourgogne Ave. ,
Province: QC
Postal: J3L 4B3
Country: Canada
Mailing address: PO Box 475
Mailing city: Chambly
Province: QC
Postal: J3L 4B3
General Phone: (450) 658-6516
General Fax: (450) 658-3785
General/National Adv. E-mail: info@journaldechambly.com
Primary Website: www.journaldechambly.com
Areas Served - City/County or Portion Thereof, or Zip codes: Canada
Mechanical specifications: Type page 10 1/4 x 17.
Published: Wed
Avg Paid Circ: 5
Avg Free Circ: 27471
Audit By: CCAB
Audit Date: 31.03.2014
Personnel: Daniel Noiseux (Mng. Ed.)
Parent company (for newspapers): Reseau Select/Select Network; Les Hebdos Monteregiens-OOB

CHATEAUGUAY

CHATEAUGUAY EXPRESS
Street Address: 69, Boul St-jean-baptiste, 2nd Floor ,
Province: QC
Postal: J6J 3H6
Country: Canada
Mailing address: 69, boul St-Jean-Baptiste, 2nd Floor
Mailing city: Chateauguay
Province: QC
Postal: J6J 3H6`
General Phone: (450) 692-9111
General Fax: (450) 692-9192
General/National Adv. E-mail: redaction_chateauguayexpress@tc.tc
Primary Website: www.chateauguayexpress.ca
Areas Served - City/County or Portion Thereof, or Zip codes: Canada
Published: Wed
Avg Free Circ: 40468
Audit By: CCAB
Audit Date: 31.03.2014

LE SOLEIL DE CHATEAUGUAY
Street Address: 101 boulevard Saint-Jean-Baptiste , Suite 215
Province: QC
Postal: J6J 3H9
Country: Canada
Mailing address: 101 boulevard Saint-Jean-Baptiste, Suite 215
Mailing city: Chateauguay
Province: QC
Postal: J6J 3H9
General Phone: (450) 692-8552
General/National Adv. E-mail: info@gravitemedia.com
Primary Website: www.monteregieweb.com
Areas Served - City/County or Portion Thereof, or Zip codes: Canada
Published: Wed`Sat
Avg Paid Circ: 11
Avg Free Circ: 34473
Audit By: CCAB
Audit Date: 31.03.2019
Personnel: Julie Voyer (Pres.); Pierre Montreuil (Mktg. Strat. Mgr.); Michel Thibault (Content Mgr.); Valerie Lessard (Asst. Content Mgr.); Sophie Bayard (Sales Coor.)
Parent company (for newspapers): Les Hebdos Monteregiens-OOB

LE SOLEIL DU ST-LAURENT
Street Address: 82 Salaberry St. S. ,
Province: QC
Postal: J6J 4J6
Country: Canada
Mailing address: 82 Salaberry St. S.
Mailing city: Chateauguay
Province: QC
Postal: J6J 4J6
General Phone: (450) 692-8552
General Fax: (450) 692-3460
General/National Adv. E-mail: info@cybersoleil.com
Display Adv. E-mail: publicite@cybersoleil.com
Editorial e-mail: redaction@cybersoleil.com
Primary Website: www.cybersoleil.com
Mechanical specifications: Type page 11 x 17; E - 5 cols, 2, between; A - 8 cols, 2 1/2, between; C - 8 cols, between.
Published: Wed`Sat
Avg Free Circ: 32750
Audit By: Sworn/Estimate/Non-Audited
Audit Date: 12.07.2019
Personnel: Diane Cadieux (Adv. Rep.); Guylaine Mercier (Adv. Rep.); Yolaine Dorais (Adv. Rep.); Michel Thibault (Ed.); Carole Gagne (Ed.)
Parent company (for newspapers): Les Hebdos Monteregiens-OOB

SOLEIL DU SAMEDI
Street Address: Rue Salaberry Sud ,
Province: QC
Postal: J6J 4J6
Country: Canada
Mailing address: rue Salaberry Sud
Mailing city: Chateauguay
Province: QC
Postal: J6J 4J6
General Phone: (450) 692-8552
Areas Served - City/County or Portion Thereof, or Zip codes: Canada
Published: Sat
Avg Paid Circ: 34
Avg Free Circ: 31092
Audit By: CCAB
Audit Date: 30.09.2012
Personnel: Jeanne-d'Arc Germain

CHATHAM

CHATHAM-KENT THIS WEEK
Street Address: 138 King Street West ,
Province: ON
Postal: N7M 1ES
Country: Canada
Mailing address: 138 King Street West
Mailing city: Chatham
Province: ON
Postal: N7M 1ES
General Phone: (519) 351-7331
General Fax: (519) 351-7774
Editorial e-mail: peter.epp@sunmedia.ca
Primary Website: www.chathamthisweek.com
Areas Served - City/County or Portion Thereof, or Zip codes: Southwestern Ontario
Published: Wed
Avg Free Circ: 19760
Audit By: CMCA
Audit Date: 31.12.2015
Personnel: Dean Muharrem; Aaron Rodrigues (Media Sales Mgr.); Peter Epp (Managing Ed.); Rachel Blain (Office Mgr.)
Parent company (for newspapers): Postmedia Network Inc.

WALLACEBURG COURIER PRESS
Street Address: 138 King Street West ,
Province: ON
Postal: N7M 1E3
Country: Canada
Mailing address: 138 King Ste West
Mailing city: Chatham
Province: ON
Postal: N7M 1E3
General Phone: (519) 354 2000
General Fax: (519) 351 7774
General/National Adv. E-mail: couriernews@kent.net
Primary Website: www.wallaceburgcourierpress.com
Year Established: 1967
Delivery Methods: Carrier
Areas Served - City/County or Portion Thereof, or Zip codes: Chatham Kent
Published: Thur
Avg Free Circ: 8914
Audit By: CMCA
Audit Date: 30.06.2015
Personnel: Dean Muharrem (Pub.); Mary Dixon (Circ. Mgr.)
Parent company (for newspapers): Postmedia Network Inc.; Sun Media

CHESTERMERE

THE CHESTERMERE ANCHOR CITY NEWS
Street Address: P.o. Box 127 ,
Province: AB
Postal: T1X 1K8
Country: Canada
Mailing address: P.O. Box 127
Mailing city: Chestermere
Province: AB
Postal: T1X 1K8
General Phone: (403) 774-1352
General Fax: (866) 552-0976
Editorial Phone: (403) 774-1322
General/National Adv. E-mail: jenn@theanchor.ca
Display Adv. E-mail: ads@theanchor.ca
Classified Adv. e-mail: classifed@theanchor.ca
Editorial e-mail: news@theanchor.ca
Primary Website: www.theanchor.ca
Year Established: 2001
Delivery Methods: Newsstand`Carrier`Racks
Areas Served - City/County or Portion Thereof, or Zip codes: Rocky View
Mechanical specifications: 10.34" Wide by 11.5" deep
Published: Thur
Avg Paid Circ: 9
Avg Free Circ: 7923
Audit By: VAC
Audit Date: 28.02.2016

CHESTERVILLE

THE CHESTERVILLE RECORD
Street Address: 7 King St. ,
Province: ON
Postal: K0C 1H0
Country: Canada
Mailing address: PO Box 368
Mailing city: Chesterville
Province: ON
Postal: K0C 1H0
General Phone: (613) 448-2321
General Fax: (613) 448-3260
General/National Adv. E-mail: rm@agrinewsinteractive.com
Display Adv. E-mail: news@chestervillerecord.com
Editorial e-mail: editor@chestervillerecord.com
Primary Website: www.agrinewsinteractive.com

Year Established: 1894
Areas Served - City/County or Portion Thereof, or Zip codes: Canada
Mechanical specifications: Type page 13 x 21 1/2; E - 6 cols, 2, 1/6 between; A - 6 cols, 2, 1/6 between; C - 6 cols, 2, 1/6 between.
Published: Wed
Avg Paid Circ: 1456
Avg Free Circ: 2
Audit By: CMCA
Audit Date: 30.06.2016
Personnel: Robin R. Morris (Pub.); Nelson Zandbergen (Ed.)

THE CHESTERVILLE RECORD/THE VILLAGER

Street Address: 7 King St. ,
Province: ON
Postal: K0C 1H0
Country: Canada
Mailing address: PO Box 368
Mailing city: Chesterville
Province: ON
Postal: K0C 1H0
General Phone: (613) 448-2321
General Fax: (613) 448-3260
General/National Adv. E-mail: thevillager.editor@gmail.com
Primary Website: www.chestervillerecord.com; russellvillager.com
Year Established: 1984
Areas Served - City/County or Portion Thereof, or Zip codes: Canada
Own Printing Facility?: Y
Mechanical specifications: Type page 10 3/8 x 13 7/8; E - 6 cols, 1 5/8, 3/16 between; A - 6 cols, 1 5/8, 3/16 between; C - 6 cols, 1 5/8, 3/16 between.
Published: Wed
Avg Paid Circ: 2600
Audit By: CMCA
Audit Date: 30.06.2013
Personnel: Muriel Carruthers (Editor)

CHILLIWACK

CHILLIWACK TIMES

Street Address: 45951 Trethewey Ave. ,
Province: BC
Postal: V2P 1K4
Country: Canada
Mailing address: 102-45951 Trethewey Ave.
Mailing city: Chilliwack
Province: BC
Postal: V2P 1K4
General Phone: (604) 792-9117
General Fax: (604) 792-9300
General/National Adv. E-mail: editor@chilliwacktimes.com
Display Adv. E-mail: nbastaja@chilliwacktimes.com
Editorial e-mail: kgoudswaard@chilliwacktimes.com
Primary Website: www.chilliwacktimes.com
Year Established: 1984
Delivery Methods: Carrier`Racks
Areas Served - City/County or Portion Thereof, or Zip codes: Canada
Own Printing Facility?: Y
Mechanical specifications: Type page 10 1/4 x 14; E - 6 cols, 1 9/16, 1/6 between; A - 6 cols, 1 9/16, 1/6 between; C - 7 cols, 1 5/16, between.
Published: Thur
Avg Free Circ: 27605
Audit By: AAM
Audit Date: 30.09.2016
Personnel: Ken Goudswaard (Ed.); Jean Hincks (Pub.)

THE CHILLIWACK PROGRESS

Street Address: 45860 Spadina Ave. ,
Province: BC
Postal: V2P 6H9
Country: Canada

Mailing address: 45860 Spadina Ave.
Mailing city: Chilliwack
Province: BC
Postal: V2P 6H9
General Phone: (604) 792-1931
General Fax: (604) 792-4936
General/National Adv. E-mail: publisher@ththeprogress.com
Display Adv. E-mail: advertising@theprogress.com
Editorial e-mail: editor@theprogress.com
Primary Website: theprogress.com
Year Established: 1891
Delivery Methods: Carrier
Areas Served - City/County or Portion Thereof, or Zip codes: Canada
Commercial printers?: Y
Mechanical specifications: Type page 12 1/2 x 21 1/4; E - 7 cols, 1 11/16, 1/8 between; A - 7 cols, 1 11/16, 1/8 between; C - 7 cols, 1 11/16, 1/8 between.
Published: Wed`Fri
Avg Paid Circ: 28
Avg Free Circ: 27657
Audit By: AAM
Audit Date: 31.12.2018
Personnel: Kyle Williams (Adv. Mgr.); Louise Meger (Circ. Mgr.); Greg Knill (Ed.); Carly Ferguson (Pub.)
Parent company (for newspapers): Black Press Group Ltd.

CLARENCE CREEK

AGRICOM

Street Address: 2474 Rue Champlain ,
Province: ON
Postal: K0A1N0
Country: Canada
Mailing address: 2474 Rue Champlain
Mailing city: Clarence Creek
Province: ON
Postal: K0A1N0
General Phone: (613) 488-2651
General Fax: (613) 488-2541
General/National Adv. E-mail: info@journalagricom.ca
Display Adv. E-mail: pub@journalagricom.ca
Editorial e-mail: redaction@journalagricom.ca
Primary Website: www.journalagricom.ca
Year Established: 1983
Delivery Methods: Mail
Areas Served - City/County or Portion Thereof, or Zip codes: Province of Ontario
Published: Fri`Bi-Mthly
Published Other: bimonthly
Avg Paid Circ: 900
Avg Free Circ: 1100
Audit By: Sworn/Estimate/Non-Audited
Audit Date: 12.07.2019
Personnel: Isabelle Lessard (Ed)

CLARENVILLE

THE PACKET

Street Address: 8 B Thomson St. ,
Province: NL
Postal: A5A 1Y9
Country: Canada
Mailing address: 8 B Thomson St.
Mailing city: Clarenville
Province: NL
Postal: A5A 1Y9
General Phone: (709) 466-2243
General Fax: (709) 466-2717
General/National Adv. E-mail: editor@thepacket.ca
Editorial e-mail: editor@thepacket.ca
Primary Website: www.thepacket.ca
Areas Served - City/County or Portion Thereof, or Zip codes: Canada
Own Printing Facility?: Y
Commercial printers?: Y
Mechanical specifications: Type page 11 x 21; E - 6 cols, 1 11/16, 3/16 between; A - 6 cols, 1 11/16, 3/16 between; C - 8 cols, 1 1/4, 3/16 between.

Published: Thur
Avg Paid Circ: 1109
Avg Free Circ: 0
Audit By: VAC
Audit Date: 31.12.2015
Personnel: Barbara Dean-Simmons (Ed.)
Parent company (for newspapers): Transcontinental Media

CLARESHOLM

CLARESHOLM LOCAL PRESS

Street Address: 4913 2nd St. W. ,
Province: AB
Postal: T0L 0T0
Country: Canada
Mailing address: PO Box 520
Mailing city: Claresholm
Province: AB
Postal: T0L 0T0
General Phone: (403) 625-4474
General Fax: (403) 625-2828
General/National Adv. E-mail: clpress@telusplanet.net, clpsales@telus.net
Display Adv. E-mail: sales@claresholmlocalpress.ca
Classified Adv. e-mail: sales@claresholmlocalpress.ca
Editorial e-mail: rob@claresholmlocalpress.ca
Primary Website: www.claresholmlocalpress.ca
Year Established: 1926
Delivery Methods: Mail`Newsstand`Racks
Areas Served - City/County or Portion Thereof, or Zip codes: Claresholm, Stavely, Granum, Alberta
Commercial printers?: Y
Published: Wed
Avg Paid Circ: 1429
Avg Free Circ: 19
Audit By: CMCA
Audit Date: 31.05.2018
Personnel: Roxanne Thompson (Owner/Pub.); Rob Vogt (Ed.); Amanda Zimmer (Prod. Mgr.); Brandy McLean (Sales contact); Jill Cook (Graphic Designer)
Parent company (for newspapers): EMS Press Ltd.

CLEARWATER

NORTH THOMPSON TIMES

Street Address: 74 Young Rd , Unit 14
Province: BC
Postal: V0E 1N2
Country: Canada
Mailing address: 14-74 Young Rd.
Mailing city: Clearwater
Province: BC
Postal: V0E 1N2
General Phone: (250) 674-3343
General Fax: (250) 674-3410
General/National Adv. E-mail: newsroom@clearwatertimes.com
Display Adv. E-mail: classifieds@clearwatertimes.com
Editorial e-mail: newsroom@clearwatertimes.com
Primary Website: www.clearwatertimes.com
Year Established: 1964
Delivery Methods: Mail
Areas Served - City/County or Portion Thereof, or Zip codes: Canada
Commercial printers?: Y
Mechanical specifications: Type page10x13.75"; E - 7 cols, 1 5/16, 1/8 between; A - 7 cols, 1 5/16, 1/8 between; C - 7cols, 1 5/16, 1/8 between.
Published: Thur
Avg Paid Circ: 751
Avg Free Circ: 20
Audit By: CMCA
Audit Date: 30.03.2017
Personnel: Keith McNeill (Ed.); Yevonne Cline (Admin Coord./Sales Rep); Lorie Williston (Pub)
Parent company (for newspapers): Black Press Group Ltd.

CLINTON

CLINTON NEWS-RECORD

Street Address: 53 Albert St. ,
Province: ON
Postal: N0M 1L0
Country: Canada
Mailing address: PO Box 39
Mailing city: Clinton
Province: ON
Postal: N0M 1L0
General Phone: (519) 482-3443
General Fax: (519) 482-7341
Display Adv. E-mail: clinton.ads@bowesnet.com
Editorial e-mail: clinton.news@bowesnet.com
Primary Website: www.clintonnewsrecord.com
Areas Served - City/County or Portion Thereof, or Zip codes: Canada
Mechanical specifications: Type page 11 1/2 x 17; E - 6 cols, 1 3/4, between; A - 6 cols, 1 3/4, between; C - 6 cols, 1 3/4, between.
Published: Wed
Avg Paid Circ: 1029
Avg Free Circ: 22
Audit By: CMCA
Audit Date: 30.06.2016
Personnel: Neil Clifford (Pub.); John Bauman (Adv. Mgr.); Cheryl Heath (Ed.)
Parent company (for newspapers): Postmedia Network Inc.; Quebecor Communications, Inc.

COALDALE

THE SUNNY SOUTH NEWS

Street Address: 1802 20th Ave. ,
Province: AB
Postal: T1M 1M2
Country: Canada
Mailing address: PO Box 30
Mailing city: Coaldale
Province: AB
Postal: T1M 1M2
General Phone: (403) 345-3081
General Fax: (403) 223-5408
General/National Adv. E-mail: office@sunnysouthnews.com
Display Adv. E-mail: office@sunnysouthnews.com
Primary Website: www.sunnysouthnews.com
Delivery Methods: Mail`Newsstand
Areas Served - City/County or Portion Thereof, or Zip codes: T1M, T0K 2H0, T0K 1V0, T0L 0V0, T0L 1M0, T0K 2A0, T0K 1G0, T0K 0T0
Own Printing Facility?: Y
Commercial printers?: Y
Mechanical specifications: Page size 11.25" wide x 16.75" deep 6 col. tab - 1 col. = 9p6
Published: Tues
Avg Paid Circ: 2263
Avg Free Circ: 48
Audit By: VAC
Audit Date: 30.09.2016
Personnel: Valorie Wiebe (Pub)

COATICOOK

LE PROGRES DE COATICOOK

Street Address: 72 Rue Child ,
Province: QC
Postal: J1A 2B1
Country: Canada
General Phone: (819) 849-9846
General Fax: (819) 849-1041
General/National Adv. E-mail: dany.jacques@tc.tc
Primary Website: www.leprogres.net
Areas Served - City/County or Portion Thereof, or Zip codes: Canada
Published: Wed
Avg Paid Circ: 77
Avg Free Circ: 8782
Audit By: CCAB
Audit Date: 31.03.2014
Personnel: Monique Cote (Ed.)
Parent company (for newspapers): Reseau Select/Select Network

Non-Daily Newspapers in Canada

COBOURG

NORTHUMBERLAND NEWS

Street Address: 884 Division St., Bldg. 2, Unit 212 ,
Province: ON
Postal: K9A 5V6
Country: Canada
Mailing address: 884 Division St., Bldg. 2, Unit 212
Mailing city: Cobourg
Province: ON
Postal: K9A 5V6
General Phone: (905) 373-7355
General Fax: (905) 373-4719
Primary Website: northumberlandnews.com
Areas Served - City/County or Portion Thereof, or Zip codes: Canada
Own Printing Facility?: Y
Published: Thur
Avg Paid Circ: 0
Avg Free Circ: 22338
Audit By: CCAB
Audit Date: 30.09.2017
Personnel: Timothy J. Whittaker (Pub.); Lillian Hook (Office Mgr.); Abe Fakhourie (Circ. Mgr.); Joanne Burghardt (Ed. in Chief); Dwight Irwin (Mng. Ed.)
Parent company (for newspapers): Metroland Media Group Ltd.; Torstar

COCHRANE

COCHRANE EAGLE

Street Address: #2, 124 River Ave ,
Province: AB
Postal: T4C 2C2
Country: Canada
Mailing address: #2, 124 River Ave
Mailing city: Cochrane
Province: AB
Postal: T4C 2C2
General Phone: (403) 932-6588
General Fax: (403) 851-6520
Display Adv. E-mail: btennant@cochrane.greatwest.ca
Classified Adv. e-mail: classifieds@cochrane.greatwest.ca
Editorial e-mail: cpuglia@cochrane.greatwest.ca
Primary Website: www.cochraneeagle.com
Year Established: 2001
Delivery Methods: Mail`Newsstand`Carrier`Racks
Areas Served - City/County or Portion Thereof, or Zip codes: Cochrane/Rocky View County/ Alberta/ T4C 2C2
Published: Thur
Avg Free Circ: 11631
Audit By: VAC
Audit Date: 31.05.2016
Personnel: Brenda Tennant (Pub./Adv. Mgr); Chris Puglia (Ed)
Parent company (for newspapers): Great West Newspapers LP

COCHRANE TIMES

Street Address: Bay 8, 206 Fifth Ave. W. ,
Province: AB
Postal: T4C 1X3
Country: Canada
Mailing address: Bay 8, 206 Fifth Ave. W.
Mailing city: Cochrane
Province: AB
Postal: T4C 1X3
General Phone: (403) 932-3500
General Fax: (403) 932-3935
Display Adv. E-mail: roxanne.mackintosh@sunmedia.ca
Classified Adv. e-mail: roxanne.mackintosh@sunmedia.ca
Editorial e-mail: editor@cochranetimes.com
Primary Website: www.cochranetimes.com
Year Established: 1985
Areas Served - City/County or Portion Thereof, or Zip codes: Canada
Commercial printers?: Y
Mechanical specifications: Type page 10 1/4 x 12 1/4; E - 8 cols, 1 1/8, 3/16 between; A - 8 cols, 1 1/8, between; C - 8 cols, 1 1/8, between.
Published: Wed
Avg Paid Circ: 1374
Avg Free Circ: 12378
Audit By: VAC
Audit Date: 31.12.2015
Personnel: Shawn Cornell (Pub); Noel Edey (Ed); Roxanne MacKintosh (Adv Dir)
Parent company (for newspapers): Postmedia Network Inc.; Quebecor Communications, Inc.

COCHRANE TIMES-POST

Street Address: 143, Sixth Avenue ,
Province: ON
Postal: P0L 1C0
Country: Canada
Mailing address: 143, Sixth Avenue
Mailing city: Cochrane
Province: ON
Postal: P0L 1C0
General Phone: (705) 272-3344
General Fax: (705) 272-3434
General/National Adv. E-mail: wayne.major@sunmedia.ca
Display Adv. E-mail: wayne.major@sunmedia.ca
Editorial e-mail: kevin.anderson@sunmedia.ca
Primary Website: www.cochranetimespost.ca
Year Established: 1904
Delivery Methods: Mail`Newsstand`Carrier
Areas Served - City/County or Portion Thereof, or Zip codes: Canada
Published: Thur
Avg Paid Circ: 1254
Audit By: CMCA
Audit Date: 30.06.2016
Personnel: Wayne Major (Pub.); Chantal Carriere (Sales Representative, print & digital); Ashley Lewis (Reporter)
Parent company (for newspapers): Postmedia Network Inc.

COLD LAKE

BEAVER RIVER BANNER

Street Address: 4110 51 Ave ,
Province: AB
Postal: t9m 2a1
Country: Canada
Mailing address: 4110 51 ave
Mailing city: cold lake
Province: AB
Postal: t9m 2a1
General Phone: (780) 201-0623
General/National Adv. E-mail: br.banner@sasktel.net
Primary Website: www.beaverriverbanner.com
Year Established: 1990
Delivery Methods: Mail
Areas Served - City/County or Portion Thereof, or Zip codes: Canada
Own Printing Facility?: Y
Commercial printers?: Y
Mechanical specifications: Type page 10 1/4 x 15 1/2; E - 6 cols, 1 3/5, 3/16 between; A - 6 cols, 1 3/5, 3/16 between; C - 6 cols, 1 3/5, 3/16 between.
Published: Wed
Avg Free Circ: 2300
Audit By: Sworn/Estimate/Non-Audited
Audit Date: 12.07.2019
Personnel: Dan Brisebois (Ed.)

COLD LAKE

COLD LAKE SUN

Street Address: 5121 50 Ave ,
Province: AB
Postal: T9M 1P1
Country: Canada
Mailing address: Box 268
Mailing city: Cold Lake
Province: AB
Postal: T9M 1P1
General Phone: (780) 594-5881
General Fax: (780) 594-2120
Display Adv. E-mail: ljohnston@postmedia.com
Editorial e-mail: plozinski@postmedia.com
Primary Website: www.coldlakesun.com
Year Established: 1977
Areas Served - City/County or Portion Thereof, or Zip codes: Cold Lake, Alberta T9M 1P1
Published: Tues
Avg Paid Circ: 71
Avg Free Circ: 7179
Audit By: VAC
Audit Date: 31.12.2015
Personnel: Mary-Ann Kostiuk (Pub); Leanne Johnson (Adv Mgr); Peter Lozinski (Ed)
Parent company (for newspapers): Postmedia Network Inc.

THE COURIER

Street Address: Bldg. 67 Centennial Bldg., Kingsway ,
Province: AB
Postal: T9M 2C5
Country: Canada
Mailing address: PO Box 6190 Stn. Forces
Mailing city: Cold Lake
Province: AB
Postal: T9M 2C5
General Phone: (780) 594-5206
General Fax: (780) 594-2139
Editorial Phone: (780) 840-8000 ext. 7854
General/National Adv. E-mail: thecourier@telus.net
Editorial e-mail: Jeff.Gaye@forces.gc.ca
Primary Website: www.thecouriernewspaper.ca
Delivery Methods: Mail`Newsstand`Carrier
Areas Served - City/County or Portion Thereof, or Zip codes: Cold Lake
Mechanical specifications: Type page 10 1/4 x 15.5; E - 6 cols, 1 1/2, between; A - 6 cols, 1 1/2, between; C - 6 cols, 1 1/2, between.
Published: Tues
Avg Paid Circ: 32
Avg Free Circ: 1995
Audit By: VAC
Audit Date: 28.02.2016
Personnel: Connie Lavigne (Mgr); Jeff Gaye (Ed); Angela Hetherington (Admin); Alina Mallais (Produc Coord)

COLLINGWOOD

COLLINGWOOD CONNECTION

Street Address: 11 Ronell Crescent, Unit B ,
Province: ON
Postal: L9Y 4J6
Country: Canada
Mailing address: 11 Ronell Crescent, Unit B
Mailing city: Collingwood
Province: ON
Postal: L9Y 4J6
General Phone: (705) 444-1875
General Fax: (705) 444-1876
Advertising Phone: (800) 387-0668
General/National Adv. E-mail: connection@simcoe.com
Editorial e-mail: editor@simcoe.com
Primary Website: simcoe.com
Delivery Methods: Carrier
Areas Served - City/County or Portion Thereof, or Zip codes: Canada
Published: Fri
Avg Free Circ: 11479
Audit By: CCAB
Audit Date: 29.09.2017
Personnel: Scott Woodhouse (Ed.); Stephen Hall (Prod. Mgr.); Kent Feagan (Prodn. Dir.); Carol Lamb (General Mgr.); Patsy McCarthy (Sales Mgr.)
Parent company (for newspapers): Metroland Media Group Ltd.; Torstar

THE ENTERPRISE-BULLETIN

Street Address: 77 Simcoe St. ,
Province: ON
Postal: L9Y 3Z4
Country: Canada
Mailing address: PO Box 98
Mailing city: Collingwood
Province: ON
Postal: L9Y 3Z4
General Phone: (705) 445-4611
General Fax: (705) 444-6477
Editorial e-mail: editorial@theenterprisebulletin.com
Primary Website: www.theenterprisebulletin.com
Areas Served - City/County or Portion Thereof, or Zip codes: Canada
Commercial printers?: Y
Mechanical specifications: Type page 11 1/2 x 21 1/2; E - 5 cols, 2 1/2, between; A - 10 cols, 1 1/6, between; C - 8 cols, 1 1/3, between.
Published: Fri
Avg Paid Circ: 295
Avg Free Circ: 18858
Audit By: CMCA
Audit Date: 30.06.2014
Personnel: Doreen Sykes (Pub.); April MacLean (Circ. Mgr.); J.T. McVeigh (Ed.)
Parent company (for newspapers): Postmedia Network Inc.; Sunmedia; Quebecor Communications, Inc.

COMEAUVILLE

LE COURRIER DE LA NOUVELLE-ECOSSE

Street Address: 795 Route 1 ,
Province: NS
Postal: B0W 2Z0
Country: Canada
Mailing address: 795 Route 1
Mailing city: Comeauville
Province: NS
Postal: B0W 2Z0
General Phone: (902) 769-3078
General Fax: (902) 769-3869
General/National Adv. E-mail: publicite@lecourrier.com
Editorial e-mail: administration@lecourrier.com,
Primary Website: www.lecourrier.com
Year Established: 1937
Areas Served - City/County or Portion Thereof, or Zip codes: Canada
Mechanical specifications: Type page 11 x 13; E - 5 cols, 2, between; A - 5 cols, 2, between.
Published: Fri
Avg Paid Circ: 1302
Avg Free Circ: 5
Audit By: ODC
Audit Date: 13.12.2011
Personnel: Stephanie LeBlanc (Prod. Mgr.); Francis Robichaud (Ed)

CONSORT

THE CONSORT ENTERPRISE

Street Address: 5012 - 52st. ,
Province: AB
Postal: T0C 1B0
Country: Canada
Mailing address: PO Box 129
Mailing city: Consort
Province: AB
Postal: T0C 1B0
General Phone: (403) 577-3337
General Fax: (403) 577-3611
Advertising Phone: (403) 577-3337
Editorial Phone: (403) 577-3337
General/National Adv. E-mail: consort_enterprise@awna.com
Display Adv. E-mail: ads@consortenterprise.com
Classified Adv. e-mail: ads@consortenterprise.com
Editorial e-mail: editor@consortenterprise.com
Primary Website: www.consortenterprise.awna.com
Year Established: 1912
Delivery Methods: Mail`Newsstand
Areas Served - City/County or Portion Thereof, or Zip codes: Canada
Mechanical specifications: Type page 10 x 16; E - 6 cols, 2, between; A - 6 cols, 2, between.
Published: Wed

Avg Paid Circ: 2935
Audit By: CMCA
Audit Date: 12.12.2017
Personnel: Carol Bruha (Circ. Mgr./Adv. Mgr.); David Bruha (Ed.)

CORNWALL
SEAWAY NEWS
Street Address: 501 Campbell Street, Unit 6
Province: ON
Postal: K6H 6X5
Country: Canada
Mailing address: 501 Campbell Street, Unit 6
Mailing city: Cornwall
Province: ON
Postal: K6H 6X5
General Phone: (613) 933-0014
General Fax: (613) 933-0024
General/National Adv. E-mail: info@cornwallseawaynews.com
Display Adv. E-mail: patrick.larose@tc.tc
Classified Adv. e-mail: diane.merpaw@tc.tc
Editorial e-mail: nicholas.seebruch@tc.tc
Primary Website: www.cornwallseawaynews.com
Year Established: 1985
Delivery Methods: Newsstand`Carrier
Areas Served - City/County or Portion Thereof, or Zip codes: Cornwall and SD&G
Own Printing Facility?: Y
Commercial printers?: Y
Mechanical specifications: Type page 10 3/8 x 16; E - 9 cols, 1 1/16, 1/10 between; A - 9 cols, 1 1/16, 1/10 between; C - 8 cols, 1 1/16, 1/10 between.
Published: Thur
Avg Free Circ: 36541
Audit By: CMCA
Audit Date: 31.12.2015
Personnel: Rick Shaver (General Manager/Publisher); Colleen Parette (Production Coordinator); Patrick Larose (Media Strategy Manager)
Parent company (for newspapers): Transcontinental Media

CORONACH
TRIANGLE NEWS
Street Address: 118 Centre St.,
Province: SK
Postal: S0H 0Z0
Country: Canada
Mailing address: Box 689
Mailing city: Coronach
Province: SK
Postal: S0H 0Z0
General Phone: (306) 267-3381
General/National Adv. E-mail: trianglenews@sasktel.net
Primary Website: www.trianglenews.sk.ca
Delivery Methods: Mail`Newsstand
Areas Served - City/County or Portion Thereof, or Zip codes: S0H - 0B0, 0Z0, 1B0, 2J0, 2W0, 3R0, 4K0, 4Lo, S0C 0Ko
Published: Mon
Avg Paid Circ: 339
Avg Free Circ: 336
Audit By: CMCA
Audit Date: 31.10.2015
Parent company (for newspapers): Transcontinental

CORONATION
EAST CENTRAL ALBERTA REVIEW
Street Address: 4923 Victoria Ave.,
Province: AB
Postal: T0C 1C0
Country: Canada
Mailing address: PO Box 70
Mailing city: Coronation
Province: AB
Postal: T0C 1C0
General Phone: (403) 578-4111
General Fax: (403) 578-2088
Advertising Phone: (403) 578-7120

General/National Adv. E-mail: publisher@ecareview.com
Display Adv. E-mail: advertise@ECAreview.com
Classified Adv. e-mail: admin@ECAreview.com
Editorial e-mail: publisher@ECAreview.com
Primary Website: www.ecareview.com
Year Established: 1911
Delivery Methods: Mail`Newsstand
Areas Served - City/County or Portion Thereof, or Zip codes: Canada
Own Printing Facility?: Y
Commercial printers?: Y
Mechanical specifications: Type page 10 1/4 x 15 1/2; E - 6 cols, 1 1/2, between; A - 6 cols, 1 1/2, between; C - 6 cols, 1 1/2, between.
Published: Thur
Avg Paid Circ: 90
Avg Free Circ: 27075
Audit By: CMCA
Audit Date: 31.03.2017
Personnel: Joyce Webster (Pub); Yvonne Thulien (Office Mgr.); Gayle Jaraway (Adv. Rep); Lisa Joy (Marketing Rep/Reporter Photographer); Lisa Myers-Sortland (Graphic Artist)

COURTENAY
COMOX VALLEY ECHO
Street Address: 407-e Fifth Street,
Province: BC
Postal: V9N 1J7
Country: Canada
Mailing address: 407-E Fifth St.
Mailing city: Courtenay
Province: BC
Postal: V9N 1J7
General Phone: (250) 334-4722
General Fax: (250) 334-3172
General/National Adv. E-mail: echo@comoxvalleyecho.com
Display Adv. E-mail: keith.currie@comoxvalleyecho.com
Classified Adv. e-mail: debra.fowler@comoxvalleyecho.com
Editorial e-mail: echo@comoxvalleyecho.com
Primary Website: www.comoxvalleyecho.com
Year Established: 1994
Delivery Methods: Mail`Newsstand`Carrier`Racks
Areas Served - City/County or Portion Thereof, or Zip codes: Canada
Commercial printers?: Y
Mechanical specifications: Type page 10.5 x 21.5; E - 10 cols, 1 1/12, between; A - 10 cols, 1 1/12, between; C - 8 cols, 1 7/23, between.
Published: Fri
Avg Paid Circ: 50
Avg Free Circ: 23000
Audit By: CCAB
Audit Date: 17.03.2013
Personnel: Keith Currie (Publisher); Debra Martin (Mng. Ed.); Ryan Getz (Prodn. Mgr.)

COMOX VALLEY RECORD
Street Address: 407D Fifth Street,
Province: BC
Postal: V9N 1J7
Country: Canada
Mailing address: 407D Fifth Street
Mailing city: Courtenay
Province: BC
Postal: V9N 1J7
General Phone: (250) 338-5811
General/National Adv. E-mail: publisher@comoxvalleyrecord.com
Display Adv. E-mail: keith.currie@comoxvalleyrecord.com
Classified Adv. e-mail: keith.currie@comoxvalleyrecord.com
Editorial e-mail: terry.farrell@comoxvalleyrecord.com
Primary Website: comoxvalleyrecord.com
Year Established: 1986
Delivery Methods: Mail`Newsstand`Carrier`Racks
Areas Served - City/County or Portion Thereof, or Zip codes: Canada

Own Printing Facility?: Y
Mechanical specifications: Type page 10 1/4 x 14 1/2; E - 6 cols, 1 7/12, 1/6 between; A - 6 cols, 1 7/12, 1/6 between; C - 7 cols, 1 7/12, 1/6 between.
Published: Tues`Thur
Avg Paid Circ: 53
Avg Free Circ: 21566
Audit By: AAM
Audit Date: 31.03.2019
Personnel: Terry Marshall (Circ. Mgr.); Terry Farrell (Ed.); Susan Granberg (Prodn. Mgr.); Keith Currie (Pub.)
Parent company (for newspapers): Black Press Group Ltd.

NORTH ISLAND MIDWEEK
Street Address: 765 Mcphee Ave,
Province: BC
Postal: V9N 2Z7
Country: Canada
Mailing address: 765 McPhee Ave
Mailing city: Courtenay
Province: BC
Postal: V9N 2Z7
General Phone: (250) 287-9227
General Fax: (250) 287-3238
General/National Adv. E-mail: publisher@comoxvalleyrecord.com
Display Adv. E-mail: sueb@blackpress.ca
Editorial e-mail: editor@comoxvalleyrecord.com
Primary Website: www.northislandmidweek.com
Year Established: 1994
Delivery Methods: Mail`Newsstand`Carrier
Areas Served - City/County or Portion Thereof, or Zip codes: Canada
Own Printing Facility?: Y
Published: Wed
Avg Paid Circ: 40
Avg Free Circ: 37030
Audit By: CMCA
Audit Date: 31.08.2014
Personnel: Chrissie Bowker (Pub); Terry Farrell (Ed); Susan Granberg (Prod. Mgr.); Terry Marshall (Circ Mgr)
Parent company (for newspapers): Black Press Group Ltd.

COWANSVILLE
LE GUIDE DE COWANSVILLE
Street Address: 121 Rue Principale,
Province: QC
Postal: J2K 1J3
Country: Canada
Mailing address: 121 Rue Principale
Mailing city: Cowansville
Province: QC
Postal: J2K 1J3
General Phone: (450) 263-5288
General Fax: (450) 263-9435
General/National Adv. E-mail: leguide@tc.tc
Primary Website: http://www.journalleguide.com
Areas Served - City/County or Portion Thereof, or Zip codes: Canada
Commercial printers?: Y
Mechanical specifications: Type page 11 1/4 x 15; C - 8 cols, 1 1/8, 1/8 between.
Published: Wed
Avg Paid Circ: 6
Avg Free Circ: 18340
Audit By: CCAB
Audit Date: 31.03.2014
Personnel: Cathy Bernard (Pub.); Louise Denicourt (Sec.); Caroline Rioux (Reg'l Ed.)

CRAIK
CRAIK WEEKLY NEWS
Street Address: 221 Third St., Box 360
Province: SK
Postal: S0G 0V0
Country: Canada

Mailing address: PO Box 360
Mailing city: Craik
Province: SK
Postal: S0G 0V0
General Phone: (306) 734-2313
General Fax: (306) 734-2789
General/National Adv. E-mail: craiknews@sasktel.net
Display Adv. E-mail: craiknews@sasktel.net
Year Established: 1908
Delivery Methods: Mail
Areas Served - City/County or Portion Thereof, or Zip codes: R.M. of Craik No. 222
Own Printing Facility?: Y
Mechanical specifications: Type page 10 1/4 x 15; E - 6 cols, 1 17/30, 1/6 between; A - 6 cols, 1 17/30, 1/6 between; C - 6 cols, 1 17/30, 1/6 between.
Published: Mon
Avg Paid Circ: 880
Audit By: Sworn/Estimate/Non-Audited
Audit Date: 12.07.2019
Personnel: Harve Friedel (Ed.)

CRANBROOK
CRANBROOK DAILY TOWNSMAN
Street Address: 822 Cranbrook St. N.,
Province: BC
Postal: V1C 3R9
Country: Canada
Mailing address: 822 Cranbrook St. N.
Mailing city: Cranbrook
Province: BC
Postal: V1C 3R9
General Phone: (250) 426-5201
General Fax: (250) 426-5003
Advertising Phone: (250) 426-5201
Advertising Fax: (250) 426-5003
Editorial Phone: (250) 426-5201
Editorial Fax: (250) 426-5003
General/National Adv. E-mail: sueb@blackpress.ca
Display Adv. E-mail: zena.williams@blackpress.ca
Classified Adv. e-mail: zena.williams@blackpress.ca
Editorial e-mail: barry.coulter@cranbrooktownsman.com
Primary Website: www.cranbrooktownsman.com
Year Established: 1956
Delivery Methods: Mail`Newsstand`Carrier`Racks
Areas Served - City/County or Portion Thereof, or Zip codes: Cranbrook, Kimberley and surrounding areas
Own Printing Facility?: Y
Commercial printers?: Y
Mechanical specifications: Type page 10.25 x 14.00
Published: Wed`Thur`Fri
Weekday Frequency: e
Avg Paid Circ: 3500
Audit By: CMCA
Audit Date: 31.12.2015
Personnel: Zena Williams (Pub.); Barry Coulter (Ed.); Nicole Koran (Adv. Sales Mgr.); Jennifer Leiman (Office Mgr.)
Parent company (for newspapers): Black Press Group Ltd.

CREEMORE
CREEMORE ECHO
Street Address: 3 Caroline St. W.,
Province: ON
Postal: L0M 1G0
Country: Canada
Mailing address: 3 Caroline St. W.
Mailing city: Creemore
Province: ON
Postal: L0M 1G0
General Phone: (705) 466-9906
General Fax: (705) 466-9908
General/National Adv. E-mail: info@creemore.com
Primary Website: www.creemore.com
Areas Served - City/County or Portion Thereof, or Zip

Non-Daily Newspapers in Canada

III-447

codes: Canada
Commercial printers?: Y
Published: Fri
Avg Paid Circ: 450
Avg Free Circ: 3396
Audit By: CMCA
Audit Date: 31.12.2015
Personnel: Sara Hershoff (Pub.); Georgi Denison (Office Mgr.); Trina Berlo (Ed.)

CRESTON

CRESTON VALLEY ADVANCE

Street Address: 1018 Canyon St. ,
Province: BC
Postal: V0B 1G0
Country: Canada
Mailing address: PO Box 1279
Mailing city: Creston
Province: BC
Postal: V0B 1G0
General Phone: (250) 428-2266
General Fax: (250) 483-1909
Display Adv. E-mail: advertising@crestonvalleyadvance.ca
Editorial e-mail: editor@crestonvalleyadvance.ca
Primary Website: www.crestonvalleyadvance.ca
Year Established: 1948
Areas Served - City/County or Portion Thereof, or Zip codes: Canada
Own Printing Facility?: Y
Mechanical specifications: Type page 10 1/4 x 16; E - 5 cols, 1 15/16, 1/8 between; A - 5 cols, 1 15/16, 1/8 between; C - 5 cols, 1 15/16, 1/8 between.
Published: Thur
Avg Paid Circ: 2
Avg Free Circ: 9
Audit By: VAC
Audit Date: 31.07.2016
Personnel: Lorne Eckersley (Pub.); Diane Audette (Circ. Mgr.); Brian Lorns (Ed.); Anita Horton (Sales Coord.); Brian Lawrence (Ed.); Jacky Smith (Prod. Department)
Parent company (for newspapers): Torstar

CUT KNIFE

HIGHWAY 40 COURIER

Street Address: 200 Steele St. ,
Province: SK
Postal: S0M 0N0
Country: Canada
Mailing address: PO Box 639
Mailing city: Cut Knife
Province: SK
Postal: S0M 0N0
General Phone: (306) 398-4901
General Fax: (306) 398-4909
General/National Adv. E-mail: ckcouriernews@sasktel.net
Year Established: 1959
Delivery Methods: Mail`Newsstand
Areas Served - City/County or Portion Thereof, or Zip codes: Canada
Commercial printers?: N
Mechanical specifications: Type page 10 1/2 x 15 1/2; E - 6 cols, 1 5/8, 3/16 between; A - 6 cols, 1 5/8, 3/16 between; C - 6 cols, 1 5/8, 3/16 between.
Published: Wed
Avg Paid Circ: 440
Avg Free Circ: 13
Audit By: CMCA
Audit Date: 31.03.2016
Personnel: Lorie Gibson (Publisher/Editor)

DAUPHIN

DAUPHIN HERALD

Street Address: 120 1st Ave. Ne ,
Province: MB
Postal: R7N 1A5
Country: Canada
Mailing address: PO Box 548
Mailing city: Dauphin
Province: MB
Postal: R7N 2V3
General Phone: (204) 638-4420
General Fax: (204) 638-8760
General/National Adv. E-mail: dherald@mts.net
Display Adv. E-mail: bwright@mymts.net
Classified Adv. e-mail: classifieds@dauphinherald.com
Editorial e-mail: psbailey@mymts.net
Primary Website: www.dauphinherald.com
Year Established: 1916
Delivery Methods: Mail`Newsstand`Carrier`Racks
Areas Served - City/County or Portion Thereof, or Zip codes: Canada
Own Printing Facility?: Y
Commercial printers?: Y
Mechanical specifications: Type page 10 1/4 x 16, E - 6 cols, 1 7/12, 1/8 between; A - 6 cols, 1 7/12, 1/8 between; C - 6 cols, 1 7/12, 1/8 between.
Published: Tues
Avg Paid Circ: 1189
Avg Free Circ: 59
Audit By: VAC
Audit Date: 30.06.2016
Personnel: Robert F. Gilroy (Pub./Owner); Brent Wright (Adv. Mgr.); Mandy Carderry (Circ. Mgr.); Shawn Bailey (Ed.)

DAVIDSON

DAVIDSON LEADER

Street Address: 205 Washington St. ,
Province: SK
Postal: S0G 1A0
Country: Canada
Mailing address: PO Box 786
Mailing city: Davidson
Province: SK
Postal: S0G 1A0
General Phone: (306) 567-2047
General Fax: (306) 567-2900
General/National Adv. E-mail: davidsonleader@sasktel.net; theleaderonline@gmail.com
Primary Website: www.leaderonline.ca
Year Established: 1904
Delivery Methods: Mail`Newsstand
Areas Served - City/County or Portion Thereof, or Zip codes: Canada
Mechanical specifications: Type page 10 1/4 x 15 3/4; E - 5 cols, 1 29/30, 1/6 between; A - 5 cols, 1 29/30, 1/6 between; C - 5 cols, 1 29/30, 1/6 between.
Published: Mon
Avg Paid Circ: 1238
Avg Free Circ: 44
Audit By: CMCA
Audit Date: 31.03.2017
Personnel: Tara De Ryk (Publisher)
Parent company (for newspapers): Davidson Publishing Ltd.

DAWSON CREEK

THE MIRROR

Street Address: 901-100th Ave. ,
Province: BC
Postal: V1G 1W2
Country: Canada
Mailing address: 901-100th Ave.
Mailing city: Dawson Creek
Province: BC
Postal: V1G 1W2
General Phone: (250) 782-4888
General Fax: (250) 782-6300
General/National Adv. E-mail: editor@dcdn.ca
Display Adv. E-mail: jkmet@dcdn.ca
Editorial e-mail: editor@dcdn.ca
Primary Website: http://www.dawsoncreekmirror.ca/
Year Established: 1980
Areas Served - City/County or Portion Thereof, or Zip codes: Canada
Own Printing Facility?: Y
Mechanical specifications: Type page 10 3/20 x 11 1/2; E - 6 cols, 1 1/2, 1/6 between; A - 6 cols, 1 1/2, 1/6 between; C - 7 cols, 1 3/10, between.
Published: Fri
Avg Paid Circ: 0
Avg Free Circ: 7457
Audit By: Sworn/Estimate/Non-Audited
Audit Date: 12.07.2019
Personnel: William Julian (Reg. Mgr.); Nicole Palfy (Assoc. Pub.); Rob Brown (Ed); Margot Owens (Circ Mgr)

THE NORTHERN HORIZON

Street Address: 901 - 100th Ave ,
Province: BC
Postal: V1G 1W2
Country: Canada
Mailing address: 901 - 100th Ave
Mailing city: Dawson Creek
Province: BC
Postal: V1G 1W2
General Phone: (250) 782-4888
General Fax: (250) 782-6300
Display Adv. E-mail: jkmet@dcdn.ca
Editorial e-mail: editor@dcdn.ca
Primary Website: http://www.northernhorizon.ca/
Published: Fri
Personnel: William Julian (Pub); Nicole Palfy (Assoc. Pub.); Rob Brown (Ed); Margot Owens (Circ. Mgr)
Parent company (for newspapers): Glacier Media Group

DEEP RIVER

THE NORTH RENFREW TIMES

Street Address: 21 Champlain St. ,
Province: ON
Postal: K0J 1P0
Country: Canada
Mailing address: PO Box 310
Mailing city: Deep River
Province: ON
Postal: K0J 1P0
General Phone: (613) 584-4161
Advertising Phone: (613) 584-4161
Editorial Phone: (613) 584-4161
General/National Adv. E-mail: drcanrt@magma.ca; NRT@magma.ca
Display Adv. E-mail: NRT@magma.ca
Classified Adv. e-mail: NRT@magma.ca
Editorial e-mail: NRT@magma.ca
Primary Website: www.northrenfrewtimes.net
Year Established: 1956
Delivery Methods: Mail`Newsstand
Areas Served - City/County or Portion Thereof, or Zip codes: Canada
Mechanical specifications: Type page 10 3/8 x 14; A - 9 cols, 1, 0.167 between
Published: Wed
Avg Paid Circ: 1661
Audit By: CMCA
Audit Date: 30.09.2016
Personnel: Kelly Lapping (Pub); Terry Myers (Editor)

DELHI

DELHI NEWS-RECORD

Street Address: 237 Main St. ,
Province: ON
Postal: N4B 2M4
Country: Canada
Mailing address: 237 Main St.
Mailing city: Delhi
Province: ON
Postal: N4B 2M4
General Phone: (519) 582-2510
General Fax: (519) 582-0627
Editorial e-mail: deleditorial@bowesnet.com
Primary Website: www.delhinewsrecord.com
Areas Served - City/County or Portion Thereof, or Zip codes: Canada
Own Printing Facility?: Y
Commercial printers?: Y
Published: Wed
Avg Paid Circ: 506
Audit By: CMCA
Audit Date: 31.12.2013
Personnel: Walter Keleer (Adv. Mgr.); Kim Novak (Ed.); Wayne Ward (Prodn. Mgr.); Ken Koyoma (Pub.)
Parent company (for newspapers): Postmedia Network Inc.; Quebecor Communications, Inc.

DELORAINE

THE DELORAINE TIMES AND STAR

Street Address: 122 Broadway, N. ,
Province: MB
Postal: R0M 0M0
Country: Canada
Mailing address: PO Box 407
Mailing city: Deloraine
Province: MB
Postal: R0M 0M0
General Phone: (204) 747-2249
General Fax: (204) 747-3999
General/National Adv. E-mail: deltimes@mts.net
Display Adv. E-mail: ads.cpocket@mts.net
Editorial e-mail: cpocket@mts.net
Primary Website: http://www.delorainetimes.ca
Year Established: 1887
Delivery Methods: Mail`Racks
Areas Served - City/County or Portion Thereof, or Zip codes: R0M IL0, R0K 0E0, R0M 0M0, R0M 0X0, R0M IK0, R0M 2E0
Own Printing Facility?: N
Commercial printers?: Y
Published: Fri
Avg Paid Circ: 770
Avg Free Circ: 57
Audit By: Sworn/Estimate/Non-Audited
Audit Date: 12.07.2019
Personnel: Judy Wells (Office Mgr.)
Parent company (for newspapers): Corner Pocket Publishing Ltd.; Glacier Media Group

DELSON

LE REFLET

Street Address: 11 Rt. 132 ,
Province: QC
Postal: J5B 1G9
Country: Canada
Mailing address: 11 Rt. 132
Mailing city: Delson
Province: QC
Postal: J5B 1G9
General Phone: (450) 635-9146
General Fax: (450) 635-4619
General/National Adv. E-mail: robert.fichaud@quebecormedia.com
Display Adv. E-mail: publicite@lereflet.qc.ca
Primary Website: www.lereflet.qc.ca
Areas Served - City/County or Portion Thereof, or Zip codes: Canada
Published: Wed
Avg Free Circ: 49427
Audit By: CCAB
Audit Date: 31.03.2014
Personnel: Robert Fichaud (Pub./Dir.); Sandy Roy (Sales Dir.); Helene Gingras (Ed.)
Parent company (for newspapers): Les Hebdos Monteregiens-OOB

DELTA

DELTA OPTIMIST

Street Address: 5008-47a Avenue ,
Province: BC
Postal: V4K 1T8
Country: Canada
Mailing address: 5008-47A Avenue
Mailing city: Delta
Province: BC
Postal: V4K 1T8
General Phone: (604) 946-4451
General Fax: (604) 946-5680
General/National Adv. E-mail: tsiba@delta-optimist.com
Display Adv. E-mail: dhamilton@delta-optimist.com
Editorial e-mail: editor@delta-optimist.com
Primary Website: delta-optimist.com

Year Established: 1922
Delivery Methods: Carrier
Areas Served - City/County or Portion Thereof, or Zip codes: Canada
Mechanical specifications: Type page 10 1/4 x 14; E - 6 cols, 1 9/16, 1/6 between; A - 6 cols, 1 9/16, 1/6 between; C - 7 cols, 1 1/3, 1/12 between.
Published: Wed`Fri
Avg Paid Circ: 0
Avg Free Circ: 17029
Audit By: CCAB
Audit Date: 22.11.2017
Personnel: Dave Hamilton (Gen Mgr); Ted Murphy (Ed.); Alvin Brouwer (Pub)
Parent company (for newspapers): Glacier Media Group

DEVON

DEVON DISPATCH NEWS

Street Address: 4b Saskatchewan Drive ,
Province: AB
Postal: T9G 1E7
Country: Canada
Mailing address: 4B Saskatchewan Drive
Mailing city: Devon
Province: AB
Postal: T9G 1E7
General Phone: (780) 987-3488
General Fax: (780) 987-4431
Display Adv. E-mail: jfigeat@postmedia.com
Editorial e-mail: bobby.roy@sunmedia.ca
Primary Website: www.devondispatch.ca
Year Established: 1976
Areas Served - City/County or Portion Thereof, or Zip codes: Devon, AB T9G 1E7, Canada
Published: Fri
Avg Paid Circ: 2021
Avg Free Circ: 5072
Audit By: VAC
Audit Date: 31.12.2015
Personnel: Susanne Holmlund (Pub.); Bobby Roy (Ed); Jean Figeat (Adv. Dir)
Parent company (for newspapers): Postmedia Network Inc.

DIGBY

THE DIGBY COUNTY COURIER

Street Address: 124 Water St. ,
Province: NS
Postal: B0V 1A0
Country: Canada
Mailing address: Box 670
Mailing city: Digby
Province: NS
Postal: B0V 1A0
General Phone: (902) 245-4715
General Fax: (902) 245-6136
General/National Adv. E-mail: info@digbycourier.ca
Display Adv. E-mail: info@digbycourier.ca
Editorial e-mail: editor@digbycourier.ca
Primary Website: www.digbycourier.ca
Year Established: 1874
Delivery Methods: Mail`Newsstand
Areas Served - City/County or Portion Thereof, or Zip codes: Canada
Commercial printers?: Y
Mechanical specifications: Type page 12 1/2 x 21; E - 7 cols, 1/8 between; A - 7 cols, 1/8 between; C - 7 cols, 1/8 between.
Published: Thur
Avg Paid Circ: 1192
Avg Free Circ: 0
Audit By: CMCA
Audit Date: 30.06.2014
Personnel: Dave Glenen (Ed)
Parent company (for newspapers): Transcontinental Media

DOLBEAU-MISTASSINI

LE NOUVELLES HEBDO

Street Address: 1741 Rue Des Pins ,
Province: QC
Postal: G8L 1J7
Country: Canada
General Phone: (418) 276-6211
General Fax: (418)276-6166
Advertising Phone: (418) 276-6211
General/National Adv. E-mail: redaction.dolbeau@tc.tc
Primary Website: http://www.nouvelleshebdo.com/
Areas Served - City/County or Portion Thereof, or Zip codes: Canada
Published: Wed
Avg Paid Circ: 55
Avg Free Circ: 12594
Audit By: CCAB
Audit Date: 31.03.2014
Personnel: Michel Aub

DONNACONA

COURRIER DE PORTNEUF

Street Address: 276,rue Notre-dame ,
Province: QC
Postal: G3M 1G7
Country: Canada
Mailing address: 276,rue Notre-Dame
Mailing city: Donnacona
Province: QC
Postal: G3M 1G7
General Phone: (418) 285-0211
General Fax: (418) 285-2441
General/National Adv. E-mail: josee-anne.fiset@courrierdeportneuf.com
Editorial e-mail: denise.paquin@courrierdeportneuf.com
Primary Website: www.courrierdeportneuf.com
Year Established: 1982
Delivery Methods: Carrier
Areas Served - City/County or Portion Thereof, or Zip codes: Canada
Published: Wed
Avg Paid Circ: 31
Avg Free Circ: 34944
Audit By: CCAB
Audit Date: 30.09.2012
Personnel: Louise Latulippe (adjointe administrative)

DORCHESTER

THE SIGNPOST

Street Address: 15 Bridge St. ,
Province: ON
Postal: N0L 1G2
Country: Canada
Mailing address: 15 Bridge St.
Mailing city: Dorchester
Province: ON
Postal: N0L 1G2
General Phone: (519) 268-7337
General Fax: (519) 268-3260
Advertising Phone: (519) 268-7337
Advertising Fax: (519) 268-3260
Editorial Phone: (519) 268-7337
Editorial Fax: (519) 268-3260
General/National Adv. E-mail: signpost@on.aibn.com
Display Adv. E-mail: advertising@dorchestersignpost.com
Classified Adv. e-mail: classifieds@dorchestersignpost.com
Editorial e-mail: w.spence@on.aibn.com
Primary Website: www.dorchestersignpost.com
Year Established: 1959
Delivery Methods: Mail`Newsstand`Carrier
Areas Served - City/County or Portion Thereof, or Zip codes: Thames Centre, Middlesex County
Published: Wed
Avg Paid Circ: 1468
Audit By: CMCA
Audit Date: 31.12.2015
Personnel: Fred Huxley (Pub.); Lyndsay Huxley (Gen. Mgr.); Wendy Spence (Ed.)

DORVAL

CITES NOUVELLES

Street Address: 455 Boulevard Fenelon , Bureau 303
Province: QC
Postal: H9S 5T8
Country: Canada
Mailing address: 455 Boulevard Fenelon
Mailing city: Dorval
Province: QC
Postal: H9S 5T8
General Phone: (514) 636-7314
General Fax: (514) 636-7317
General/National Adv. E-mail: cites.nouvelles@tc.tc
Primary Website: www.citesnouvelles.com
Year Established: 1974
Delivery Methods: Carrier`Racks
Areas Served - City/County or Portion Thereof, or Zip codes: Canada
Published: Wed
Avg Paid Circ: 4
Avg Free Circ: 44286
Audit By: CCAB
Audit Date: 31.03.2014
Personnel: Denis Therrien (Publisher); Joy-Ann Dempsey (Sales Support Supervisor); Robert Bourcier (Production manager); Jean Nicolas AubÃ© (News Director)
Parent company (for newspapers): Transcontinental Media

LACHINE MESSENGER

Street Address: 455 Boulevard Fenelon, Suite 303 ,
Province: QC
Postal: H9S 5T8
Country: Canada
Mailing address: 455 Boulevard Fenelon, suite 303
Mailing city: Dorval
Province: QC
Postal: H9S 5T8
General Phone: (514) 636-7314
General Fax: (514) 363-7315
General/National Adv. E-mail: redaction_lachine-dorval@tc.tc
Primary Website: www.messagerlachine.com
Published: Thur
Avg Free Circ: 20000
Audit By: Sworn/Estimate/Non-Audited
Audit Date: 12.07.2019
Personnel: Patricia Ann Beaulieu (Pub.); Tina Lemelin (Adv. Mgr.); Robert Leduc (Ed.)

MAGAZINE DE L'ILE-DES-SOEURS

Street Address: 455 Boulevard Fenelon ,
Province: QC
Postal: H9S 5T8
Country: Canada
Mailing address: 455 Boulevard Fenelon
Mailing city: Dorval
Province: QC
Postal: H9S 5T8
General Phone: (514) 636-7314
Areas Served - City/County or Portion Thereof, or Zip codes: Canada
Published: Wed
Avg Paid Circ: 2
Avg Free Circ: 8226
Audit By: CCAB
Audit Date: 31.03.2014
Personnel: Patricia Ann Beaulieu

MESSAGER DE LACHINE / DORVAL

Street Address: 455 Boulevard Fenelon, Suite 303 ,
Province: QC
Postal: H9S 5T8
Country: Canada
Mailing address: 455 Boulevard Fenelon, suite 303
Mailing city: Dorval
Province: QC
Postal: H9S 5T8
General Phone: (514) 636-7314
General Fax: (514) 636-7315
General/National Adv. E-mail: redaction_lachine-dorval@tc.tc
Primary Website: http://www.messagerlachine.com
Areas Served - City/County or Portion Thereof, or Zip codes: Canada
Published: Thur
Avg Paid Circ: 0
Avg Free Circ: 24993
Audit By: CCAB
Audit Date: 31.03.2014
Personnel: Patria Ann Beaulieu

MESSAGER DE VERDUN

Street Address: 455 Fenelon Suite 303 , 303
Province: QC
Postal: H9S 5T8
Country: Canada
Mailing address: 455 Fenelon Suite 303
Mailing city: Dorval
Province: QC
Postal: H9S 5T8
General Phone: (514) 636-7314
General Fax: (514) 636-7317
General/National Adv. E-mail: redaction_verdun@tc.tc
Primary Website: www.messagerverdun.com
Areas Served - City/County or Portion Thereof, or Zip codes: Canada
Published: Thur
Avg Paid Circ: 0
Avg Free Circ: 23936
Audit By: CCAB
Audit Date: 30.09.2012
Personnel: Patricia Ann Beaulieu

THE CHRONICLE

Street Address: 455 Boulevard Fenelon , Suite 303
Province: QC
Postal: H9S 5T8
Country: Canada
Mailing address: 455 Boulevard Fenelon
Mailing city: Dorval
Province: QC
Postal: H9S 5T8
General Phone: (514) 636-7314
General Fax: (514) 636-7317
Advertising Fax: (514) 636-7317
Editorial Fax: (514) 636-7317
General/National Adv. E-mail: info.chronicle@tc.tc
Primary Website: www.westislandchronicle.com
Year Established: 1925
Delivery Methods: Carrier`Racks
Areas Served - City/County or Portion Thereof, or Zip codes: Canada
Mechanical specifications: Type page 11 1/2 x 21 1/4; E - 5 cols, 2 3/16, 1/8 between; A - 10 cols, 1 1/16, 1/8 between; C - 10 cols, 1 1/16, 1/8 between.
Published: Wed
Avg Paid Circ: 5
Avg Free Circ: 43393
Audit By: CMCA
Audit Date: 31.08.2013
Personnel: Denis Therrien (General Manager); Joy-Ann Dempsey (Sales Support Supervisor); Robert Bourcier (Production Manager); Jean Nicolas AubÃ© (News Director)
Parent company (for newspapers): Transcontinental Media

DRAYTON

THE COMMUNITY NEWS

Street Address: 41 Wellington St. N. ,
Province: ON
Postal: N0G 1P0
Country: Canada
Mailing address: PO Box 189
Mailing city: Drayton
Province: ON
Postal: N0G 1P0

Non-Daily Newspapers in Canada

General Phone: (519) 638-3066
General Fax: (519) 843-7606
General/National Adv. E-mail: drayton@wellingtonadvertiser.com
Editorial e-mail: editor@wellingtonadvertiser.com
Primary Website: www.wellingtonadvertiser.com
Areas Served - City/County or Portion Thereof, or Zip codes: Canada
Mechanical specifications: Type page 10.25 x 15; E - 6 cols, 1 4/7, between; A - 6 cols, 1 4/7, between; C - 6 cols, 1 4/7, between.
Published: Fri
Avg Paid Circ: 5
Avg Free Circ: 5152
Audit By: CMCA
Audit Date: 31.03.2016
Personnel: William Adsett (Pub.); Dave Adsett (Ed.)

DRAYTON VALLEY

DRAYTON VALLEY WESTERN REVIEW

Street Address: 4905 52nd Ave. ,
Province: AB
Postal: T7A 1S3
Country: Canada
Mailing address: PO Box 6960
Mailing city: Drayton Valley
Province: AB
Postal: T7A 1S3
General Phone: (780) 542-5380
General Fax: (780) 542-9200
General/National Adv. E-mail: dvwr@bowesnet.com
Display Adv. E-mail: theresa.hunt@sunmedia.ca
Editorial e-mail: cweetman@postmedia.com
Primary Website: www.draytonvalleywesternreview.com
Year Established: 1966
Areas Served - City/County or Portion Thereof, or Zip codes: Canada
Published: Tues
Avg Paid Circ: 1132
Avg Free Circ: 5
Audit By: VAC
Audit Date: 31.12.2015
Personnel: Susanne Holmlund (Pub.); Pamela Allain (Adv. Dir) Cathy Weetman (Ed)
Parent company (for newspapers): Postmedia Network Inc.; Quebecor Communications, Inc.

DRUMHELLER

DRUMHELLER MAIL

Street Address: 515 Hwy 10 East ,
Province: AB
Postal: T0J 0Y0
Country: Canada
Mailing address: PO Box 1629
Mailing city: Drumheller
Province: AB
Postal: T0J 0Y0
General Phone: (403) 823-2580
General Fax: (403) 823-3864
General/National Adv. E-mail: information@drumhellermail.com
Display Adv. E-mail: information@drumhellermail.com
Editorial e-mail: bob@drumhellermail.com
Primary Website: www.drumhellermail.com
Year Established: 1911
Delivery Methods: Mail`Newsstand`Carrier`Racks
Areas Served - City/County or Portion Thereof, or Zip codes: Canada
Own Printing Facility?: Y
Commercial printers?: Y
Mechanical specifications: Type page 12.4 x 21; E - 6 cols, 2 1/4, between; A - 6 cols, 2 1/4, between; C - 6 cols, 2 1/4, between.
Published: Wed
Avg Paid Circ: 4400
Avg Free Circ: 0

Audit By: CMCA
Audit Date: 30.06.2017
Personnel: Ossie Sheddy (Pub.); Bob Sheddy (Mng. Ed)

DRUMMONDVILLE

JOURNAL L'IMPACT DE DRUMMONDVILLE

Street Address: 2345, Rue St-pierre ,
Province: QC
Postal: J2C 5A7
Country: Canada
Mailing address: 2345, rue St-Pierre
Mailing city: Drummondville
Province: QC
Postal: J2C 5A7
General Phone: (819) 445-7000
General Fax: (819) 445-7001
General/National Adv. E-mail: guy.levasseur@quebecormedia.com
Primary Website: www.limpact.ca
Areas Served - City/County or Portion Thereof, or Zip codes: Canada
Published: Thur
Avg Paid Circ: 4
Avg Free Circ: 46173
Audit By: CCAB
Audit Date: 31.03.2014
Personnel: Jean Crepeau (Ed.)

LA PAROLE

Street Address: 1050 Rue Cormier ,
Province: QC
Postal: J2C 2N6
Country: Canada
Mailing address: 1050 Rue Cormier
Mailing city: Drummondville
Province: QC
Postal: J2C 2N6
General Phone: (819) 478-8171
General Fax: (819) 393-0741
General/National Adv. E-mail: redaction@transcontinental.ca
Primary Website: www.journalexpress.ca
Year Established: 1929
Areas Served - City/County or Portion Thereof, or Zip codes: Canada
Published: Wed
Avg Free Circ: 46000
Audit By: Sworn/Estimate/Non-Audited
Audit Date: 12.07.2019
Personnel: Eyves Shabot (Adv. Dir.); Johanne Marceau (Ed.).
Parent company (for newspapers): Reseau Select/ Select Network

L'EXPRESS

Street Address: 1050 Cormier St. ,
Province: QC
Postal: J2C 2N6
Country: Canada
Mailing address: 1050 Cormier St.
Mailing city: Drummondville
Province: QC
Postal: J2C 2N6
General Phone: (819) 478-8171
General Fax: (819) 478-4306
General/National Adv. E-mail: redaction_dr@tc.tc
Primary Website: www.journalexpress.ca
Areas Served - City/County or Portion Thereof, or Zip codes: Canada
Published: Wed`Sun
Avg Paid Circ: 11
Avg Free Circ: 48116
Audit By: CCAB
Audit Date: 31.03.2014
Personnel: Johanne Marceau (Ed.)
Parent company (for newspapers): Transcontinental Media

DRYDEN

DRYDEN OBSERVER

Street Address: 32 Colonization Ave. ,
Province: ON
Postal: P8N 2Y9
Country: Canada
Mailing address: 32 Colonization Ave
Mailing city: Dryden
Province: ON
Postal: P8N 2Y9
General Phone: (807) 223-2390
General Fax: (807) 223-2907
Advertising Phone: (807) 223-2390 ext. 35
Advertising Fax: (807) 223-2907
Editorial Phone: (807) 223-2390 ext. 34
Display Adv. E-mail: lorie@drydenobserver.ca
Editorial e-mail: chrism@drydenobserver.ca
Primary Website: www.drydenobserver.ca
Year Established: 1897
Delivery Methods: Mail`Carrier
Areas Served - City/County or Portion Thereof, or Zip codes: Canada
Commercial printers?: Y
Mechanical specifications: Type page 11 1/2 x 21 1/2; E - 6 cols, 1 3/4, between; A - 6 cols, 1 3/4, between; C - 6 cols, 1 3/4, between.
Published: Wed
Avg Paid Circ: 2023
Avg Free Circ: 7
Audit By: CMCA
Audit Date: 19.12.2017
Personnel: LORIE LUNDY (Adv. Mgr.); Sean Clarke (Circ. Mgr.); CHRIS MARCHAND (Ed.); Michael Christianson (Reporter); Brian Kasaboski (Prod.); Laurie Fisher (Office manager)
Parent company (for newspapers): Norwest Printing

DUNCAN

COWICHAN VALLEY CITIZEN

Street Address: 251 Jubilee Street ,
Province: BC
Postal: V9L 1W8
Country: Canada
General Phone: (250) 748-2666
General/National Adv. E-mail: news@cowichanvalleycitizen.com
Display Adv. E-mail: warren.goulding@blackpress.ca
Classified Adv. e-mail: bcclassifieds@blackpress.ca
Editorial e-mail: editor@cowichanvalleycitizen.com
Primary Website: cowichanvalleycitizen.com
Year Established: 1986
Areas Served - City/County or Portion Thereof, or Zip codes: Canada
Commercial printers?: Y
Mechanical specifications: Type page 10 1/4 x 13; A - 9 cols, 1 1/16, between; C - 7 cols, 1 5/8, between.
Published: Wed`Fri
Avg Free Circ: 20910
Audit By: AAM
Audit Date: 31.03.2019
Personnel: Warren Goulding (Pub./Adv. Mgr.)
Parent company (for newspapers): Torstar

THE COWICHAN NEWS LEADER

Street Address: 251 Jubilee St ,
Province: BC
Postal: V9L 1W8
Country: Canada
Mailing address: 251 Jubilee St
Mailing city: Duncan
Province: BC
Postal: V9L1W8
General Phone: (250) 748-2666
General Fax: (250) 746-8529
General/National Adv. E-mail: publisher@cowichannewsleader.com
Editorial e-mail: editor@cowichannewsleader.com
Primary Website: www.cowichannewsleader.com

Year Established: 1905
Delivery Methods: Mail`Newsstand`Carrier`Racks
Areas Served - City/County or Portion Thereof, or Zip codes: Canada
Own Printing Facility?: Y
Mechanical specifications: Type page 12 x 21 1/2; E - 7 cols, 1 1/4, between; A - 7 cols, 1 1/4, between; C - 8 cols, 1 1/4, between.
Published: Wed`Fri
Avg Paid Circ: 0
Avg Free Circ: 22430
Audit By: CMCA
Audit Date: 30.04.2013
Personnel: Lara Stuart (Circ. Mgr.); John McKinley (Ed.); Shirley Skolos (Pub)

THE LAKE COWICHAN GAZETTE

Street Address: 251 Jubilee Street ,
Province: BC
Postal: V9L 1W8
Country: Canada
Mailing address: 251 Jubilee Street
Mailing city: Duncan
Province: BC
Postal: V9L 1W8
General Phone: (250) 748-2666
Advertising Phone: (250) 748-2666
General/National Adv. E-mail: office@lakecowichangazette.com
Display Adv. E-mail: warren.goulding@blackpress.ca
Editorial e-mail: editor@lakecowichangazette.com
Primary Website: www.lakecowichangazette.com
Year Established: 1995
Delivery Methods: Mail
Areas Served - City/County or Portion Thereof, or Zip codes: Lake Cowichan
Published: Wed
Avg Paid Circ: 430
Avg Free Circ: 26
Audit By: VAC
Audit Date: 30.09.2017
Personnel: Waren Goulding (Pub.); Classified Ads (Classifieds); Drew McLachlan (Ed)
Parent company (for newspapers): Black Press Group Ltd.

DUNDALK

ADVANCE

Street Address: 260 Main St. E. ,
Province: ON
Postal: N0C 1B0
Country: Canada
Mailing address: P.O. Box 280
Mailing city: Dundalk
Province: ON
Postal: N0C 1B0
General Phone: (519) 923-2203
General Fax: (519) 923-2747
Display Adv. E-mail: dundalk.herald@gmail.com
Editorial e-mail: dundalk.heraldnews@gmail.com
Year Established: 1881
Delivery Methods: Mail`Newsstand
Areas Served - City/County or Portion Thereof, or Zip codes: Southgate
Own Printing Facility?: Y
Commercial printers?: Y
Published: Wed
Avg Paid Circ: 1299
Audit By: Sworn/Estimate/Non-Audited
Audit Date: 12.07.2019
Personnel: Matthew Walls (Pub.)
Parent company (for newspapers): herald newspaper corp

HERALD

Street Address: 260 Main St. E. ,
Province: ON
Postal: N0C 1B0
Country: Canada
Mailing address: PO Box 280
Mailing city: Dundalk

Province: ON
Postal: N0C 1B0
General Phone: (519) 923-2203
General Fax: (519) 923-2747
Display Adv. E-mail: dundalk.herald@gmail.com
Editorial e-mail: dundalk.heraldnews@gmail.com
Primary Website: www.dundalkherald.ca
Year Established: 1881
Areas Served - City/County or Portion Thereof, or Zip codes: Canada
Own Printing Facility?: Y
Commercial printers?: Y
Published: Wed
Avg Paid Circ: 1443
Audit By: CMCA
Audit Date: 30.06.2016
Personnel: Matthew Walls (Pub.); Cathy Walls (Adv. Mgr.)

DURHAM

THE DURHAM CHRONICLE

Street Address: 190 Elizabeth St. E.,
Province: ON
Postal: N0G 1R0
Country: Canada
Mailing address: PO Box 230
Mailing city: Durham
Province: ON
Postal: N0G 1R0
General Phone: (519) 369-2504
General Fax: (519) 369-3560
General/National Adv. E-mail: themarkdalestandard@bmts.com
Areas Served - City/County or Portion Thereof, or Zip codes: Canada
Mechanical specifications: Type page 11 1/4 x 16 3/4; E - 5 cols, 2 1/5, between; A - 5 cols, 2 1/5, between; C - 9 cols, between.
Published: Wed
Avg Paid Circ: 1196
Avg Free Circ: 21
Audit By: Sworn/Estimate/Non-Audited
Audit Date: 12.07.2019
Personnel: Marie David (Pub.); Bev Stoddart (Gen. Mgr.); Christine Meingast (Ed.)

EDMONTON

EDMONTON EXAMINER

Street Address: 10006 101 St.,
Province: AB
Postal: T5J 0S1
Country: Canada
Mailing address: 10006 101 St
Mailing city: Edmonton
Province: AB
Postal: T5J 0S1
General Phone: (780) 453-9001
General Fax: (780) 447-7333
Advertising Phone: (780) 444-5450
Display Adv. E-mail: rpaterson@postmedia.com
Classified Adv. e-mail: bob.paterson@sunmedia.ca
Editorial e-mail: dave.breakenridge@sunmedia.ca
Primary Website: www.edmontonexaminer.com
Year Established: 1979
Delivery Methods: Carrier`Racks
Areas Served - City/County or Portion Thereof, or Zip codes: Canada
Mechanical specifications: Type page 10 1/4 x 12 1/2; E - 10 cols, between; A - 10 cols, between; C - 10 cols, between.
Published: Wed
Avg Paid Circ: 0
Avg Free Circ: 131000
Audit By: CCAB
Audit Date: 24.12.2017
Personnel: John Caputo (Pub); Ted Dakin (Adv. Dir); Dave Breakenridge (Ed)
Parent company (for newspapers): Postmedia Network Inc.; Quebecor Communications, Inc.

LE FRANCO

Street Address: 8627-91 St., Rm 312
Province: AB
Postal: T6C 3N1
Country: Canada
Mailing address: 8627-91 St.
Mailing city: Edmonton
Province: AB
Postal: T6C 3N1
General Phone: (780) 465-6581
General Fax: (780) 469-1129
General/National Adv. E-mail: journal@lefranco.ab.ca
Display Adv. E-mail: commercial@lefranco.ab.ca
Editorial e-mail: direction@lefranco.ab.ca
Primary Website: http://www.lefranco.ab.ca
Year Established: 1928
Delivery Methods: Mail
Areas Served - City/County or Portion Thereof, or Zip codes: Alberta
Published: Thur
Avg Paid Circ: 3206
Avg Free Circ: 302
Audit By: Sworn/Estimate/Non-Audited
Audit Date: 12.07.2019
Personnel: Emma Hautecoeur (Ed.)

EDMUNDSTON

INFO WEEK-END

Street Address: 322 Victoria St.,
Province: QC
Postal: E3V 2H9
Country: Canada
Mailing address: 322 Victoria St.
Mailing city: Edmundston
Province: NB
Postal: E3V 2H9
General Phone: (506) 739-5083
Display Adv. E-mail: pub@infoweekend.ca
Primary Website: journaux.apf.ca/infoweekend
Areas Served - City/County or Portion Thereof, or Zip codes: Canada
Published: Wed
Avg Free Circ: 21550
Audit By: CCAB
Audit Date: 30.09.2013
Personnel: Michel Chalifour

LE MADAWASKA

Street Address: 20 Rue Saint Francois,
Province: NB
Postal: E3V 1E3
Country: Canada
Mailing address: 20 Rue Saint Francois
Mailing city: Edmundston
Province: NB
Postal: E3V 1E3
General Phone: (506) 735-5575
General Fax: (506) 735-8086
General/National Adv. E-mail: madproduction@brunswicknews.com
Editorial e-mail: madproduction@brunswicknews.com
Primary Website: https://www.telegraphjournal.com/le-madawaska/
Areas Served - City/County or Portion Thereof, or Zip codes: Edmundston
Mechanical specifications: Type page 13 x 21; E - 6 cols, 2 1/8, between; A - 6 cols, 2 1/8, between.
Published: Sat
Avg Paid Circ: 2561
Avg Free Circ: 20
Audit By: VAC
Audit Date: 31.12.2015
Personnel: Hermel Volpe (Pub.)
Parent company (for newspapers): Brunswick News, Inc.

EDSON

EDSON LEADER

Street Address: 4820 3rd Ave.,
Province: AB

Postal: T7E 1T8
Country: Canada
Mailing address: 4820-3 Ave
Mailing city: Edson
Province: AB
Postal: T7E 1T8
General Phone: (780) 723-3301
General Fax: (780) 723-5171
General/National Adv. E-mail: leadernews@telusplanet.net
Display Adv. E-mail: pam.thesen@sunmedia.ca
Editorial e-mail: ian.mcinnes@sunmedia.ca
Primary Website: www.edsonleader.com
Year Established: 1989
Areas Served - City/County or Portion Thereof, or Zip codes: Canada
Published: Mon
Avg Paid Circ: 3
Avg Free Circ: 3468
Audit By: VAC
Audit Date: 31.12.2015
Personnel: Pamela Thesen (Adv. Dir); Janice Foisy (Pub.); Ian McInnes (Ed.)
Parent company (for newspapers): Postmedia Network Inc.; Quebecor Communications, Inc.

THE WEEKLY ANCHOR

Street Address: 5040 3rd Ave.,
Province: AB
Postal: T7E 1V2
Country: Canada
Mailing address: PO Box 6870
Mailing city: Edson
Province: AB
Postal: T7E 1V2
General Phone: (780) 723-5787
General Fax: (780) 723-5725
General/National Adv. E-mail: anchorwk@telusplanet.net
Display Adv. E-mail: anchorwk@telusplanet.net
Classified Adv. e-mail: anchorwk@telusplanet.net
Editorial e-mail: anchorwk@telusplanet.net
Primary Website: www.weeklyanchor.com
Year Established: 1988
Delivery Methods: Mail`Newsstand`Racks
Areas Served - City/County or Portion Thereof, or Zip codes: Canada
Mechanical specifications: Type page 15 1/2 x 15 5/9; E - 6 cols, between; A - 6 cols, between.
Published: Mon
Avg Paid Circ: 50
Avg Free Circ: 6025
Audit By: CMCA
Audit Date: 31.12.2016
Personnel: Dana McArthur (Pub./Adv. Dir.)

EGAN SOUTH

LE GATINEAU

Street Address: 135-b, Highway 105,
Province: QC
Postal: J9E 3A9
Country: Canada
General Phone: (819) 449-1725
General Fax: (819) 449-5108
General/National Adv. E-mail: direction@lagatineau.com
Editorial e-mail: redaction@lagatineau.com
Primary Website: www.lagatineau.com
Year Established: 1955
Delivery Methods: Carrier`Racks
Areas Served - City/County or Portion Thereof, or Zip codes: Canada
Mechanical specifications: Type page 10 3/4 x 14 5/16.
Published: Thur
Avg Free Circ: 11210
Audit By: CCAB
Audit Date: 31.03.2014
Personnel: Denise LacourciÃ¨re (Executive Director)

EGANVILLE

THE EGANVILLE LEADER

Street Address: 150 John St., P.o. Box 310
Province: ON
Postal: K0J 1T0
Country: Canada
Mailing address: PO Box 310
Mailing city: Eganville
Province: ON
Postal: K0J 1T0
General Phone: (613) 628-2332
General Fax: (613) 628-3291
General/National Adv. E-mail: leader@nrtco.net
Display Adv. E-mail: leaderads@nrtco.net
Editorial e-mail: leader@nrtco.net
Primary Website: www.eganvilleleader.com
Year Established: 1902
Delivery Methods: Mail`Newsstand`Racks
Areas Served - City/County or Portion Thereof, or Zip codes: Canada
Mechanical specifications: Type page 13 1/2 x 21; E - 8 cols, 1 3/5, between; A - 8 cols, 1 3/5, between; C - 8 cols, 1 3/5, between.
Published: Wed
Avg Paid Circ: 6096
Audit By: CMCA
Audit Date: 29.02.2016
Personnel: Carol Kutschke (Circ. Mgr.); Gerald J. Tracey (Ed.)

ELK POINT

ELK POINT REVIEW

Street Address: 5022 - 49 Ave,
Province: AB
Postal: T0A 1A0
Country: Canada
Mailing address: PO Box 309
Mailing city: Elk Point
Province: AB
Postal: T0A 1A0
General Phone: (780) 724-4087
General Fax: (780) 645-2346
General/National Adv. E-mail: production@stpaul.greatwest.ca; aglaser@greatwest.ca
Display Adv. E-mail: cgauvreau@greatwest.ca
Editorial e-mail: vbrooker@stpaul.greatwest.ca
Primary Website: www.greatwest.ca
Year Established: 1963
Areas Served - City/County or Portion Thereof, or Zip codes: Canada
Published: Tues
Avg Paid Circ: 2950
Avg Free Circ: 0
Audit By: VAC
Audit Date: 31.12.2015
Personnel: Clare Gauvreau (Pub./Adv. Mgr.); Vicki Brooker (Ed.); Marg Smith (Prod.)
Parent company (for newspapers): Glacier Media Group; Great West Newspapers LP

ELLIOT LAKE

THE MID-NORTH MONITOR

Street Address: 14 Hillside Drive South,
Province: ON
Postal: P5A 1M6
Country: Canada
Mailing address: 14 Hillside Drive South
Mailing city: Elliot Lake
Province: ON
Postal: P0M 3E0
General Phone: 7058661801
General Fax: (705) 869-0587
Advertising Phone: (705) 848 - 7195
General/National Adv. E-mail: mnm@sunmedia.ca
Display Adv. E-mail: kjohansen@postmedia.com
Classified Adv. e-mail: kjohansen@postmedia.com
Editorial e-mail: kjohansen@postmedia.com
Primary Website: www.midnorthmonitor.com
Year Established: 1978
Delivery Methods: Mail`Newsstand
Areas Served - City/County or Portion Thereof, or Zip codes: Canada
Mechanical specifications: Type page 10 1/4

Non-Daily Newspapers in Canada

III-451

x 15 ; E - 9 cols, 1", 1/8" between; A - 9 cols, 1", 1/8" between; C - 9 cols, 1", 1/8" between.
Published: Thur
Avg Paid Circ: 849
Audit By: Sworn/Estimate/Non-Audited
Audit Date: 12.07.2019
Personnel: Lolene Patterson (Circ. Mgr.); Kevin McSheffrey (Managing Editor)
Parent company (for newspapers): 1954; Postmedia Network Inc.

ELMVALE

SPRINGWATER NEWS

Street Address: 9 Glenview Ave. ,
Province: ON
Postal: L0L 1P0
Country: Canada
Mailing address: 9 Glenview Ave.
Mailing city: Elmvale
Province: ON
Postal: L0L 1P0
General Phone: (705) 322-2249
General Fax: (705) 322-8393
Advertising Phone: (705) 322-2249
Advertising Fax: (705) 322-8393
Editorial Phone: (705) 321-2653
General/National Adv. E-mail: springwaternews@rogers.com
Display Adv. E-mail: springwaternews@rogers.com
Classified Adv. e-mail: springwaternews@rogers.com
Editorial e-mail: springwaternews@rogers.com
Primary Website: www.springwaternews.ca
Year Established: 1998
Delivery Methods: Mail`Newsstand`Carrier`Racks
Areas Served - City/County or Portion Thereof, or Zip codes: L0L in North Simcoe County L9M near Penetanguishene L4R around Midland L0K Wyebridge L4M and L4n around Barrie
Mechanical specifications: Tabloid 11x17 24 pages - 12 in colour
Published: Thur`Other
Published Other: Bi-weekly
Avg Paid Circ: 140
Avg Free Circ: 18750
Audit By: Sworn/Estimate/Non-Audited
Audit Date: 12.07.2019
Personnel: Michael Jacobs (Ed./Pub./Owner)

EMBRUN

JOURNAL LE REFLET

Street Address: 793 Rue Notre Dame Rr 3 # 3, ,
Province: ON
Postal: K0A 1W1
Country: Canada
Mailing address: 793 Rue Notre Dame Rr 3 # 3,
Mailing city: Embrun
Province: ON
Postal: K0A 1W1
General Phone: (613) 443-2741
Primary Website: www.lereflet.qc.ca
Areas Served - City/County or Portion Thereof, or Zip codes: Embrun, ON
Published: Mon
Avg Paid Circ: 29
Avg Free Circ: 18102
Audit By: ODC
Audit Date: 14.12.2011
Personnel: Roger Duplantie (Gen. Dir.)

EMERSON

THE SOUTHEAST JOURNAL

Street Address: 108 Church Street ,
Province: MB
Postal: R0A 0L0
Country: Canada
Mailing address: Box 68
Mailing city: Emerson
Province: MB
Postal: R0A0L0

General Phone: (204) 373-2493
General Fax: (204)-272-3492
Advertising Phone: (204) 373-2493
Editorial Phone: (204) 373-2493
General/National Adv. E-mail: sej@mts.net
Display Adv. E-mail: sej@mts.net
Classified Adv. e-mail: sej@mts.net
Editorial e-mail: sej@mts.net
Primary Website: www.southeastjournal.ca
Delivery Methods: Mail
Areas Served - City/County or Portion Thereof, or Zip codes: Manitoba
Published: Thur
Avg Paid Circ: 14
Avg Free Circ: 3500
Audit By: VAC
Audit Date: 31.08.2015

ENFIELD

ENFIELD WEEKLY PRESS

Street Address: 287 Highway 2 ,
Province: NS
Postal: B2T 1C9
Country: Canada
Mailing address: 287 Highway 2
Mailing city: Enfield
Province: NS
Postal: B2T 1C9
General Phone: (902) 883-3181
General Fax: (902) 883-3180
General/National Adv. E-mail: editor@enfieldweeklypress.com
Display Adv. E-mail: michelewhite@enfieldweeklypress.com
Classified Adv. e-mail: admin@enfieldweeklypress.com
Editorial e-mail: editor@enfieldweeklypress.com
Primary Website: www.enfieldweeklypress.com
Areas Served - City/County or Portion Thereof, or Zip codes: Enfield
Published: Wed
Avg Free Circ: 10914
Audit By: VAC
Audit Date: 30.06.2016
Personnel: Leith Orr (Pub); Michele White (Adv. Rep)

FALL RIVER LAKER

Street Address: 287 Highway 2 ,
Province: NS
Postal: B2T 1C9
General Phone: (902) 883-3181, Ext. 3
General Fax: (902) 883-3180
Display Adv. E-mail: michelewhite@enfieldweeklypress.com
Classified Adv. e-mail: admin@enfieldweeklypress.com
Editorial e-mail: editor@enfieldweeklypress.com
Primary Website: www.thelaker.ca
Areas Served - City/County or Portion Thereof, or Zip codes: Enfield
Published: Thur
Avg Paid Circ: 2247
Avg Free Circ: 7703
Audit By: VAC
Audit Date: 30.04.2016
Personnel: Leith Orr (Pub); Michele White (Adv. Rep)

ERIN

THE ERIN ADVOCATE

Street Address: 8 Thompson Crescent ,
Province: ON
Postal: N0B 1T0
Country: Canada
Mailing address: 8 Thompson Crescent
Mailing city: Erin
Province: ON
Postal: N0B 1T0
General Phone: (519) 833-9603
General Fax: (519) 833-9605
General/National Adv. E-mail: esales@erinadvocate.com

Year Established: 1880
Areas Served - City/County or Portion Thereof, or Zip codes: Canada
Commercial printers?: Y
Mechanical specifications: Type page 10 3/8 x 14; E - 6 cols, 1 5/8, between; A - 6 cols, 1 5/8, between; C - 6 cols, 1 5/8, between.
Published: Wed
Avg Paid Circ: 1054
Audit By: CMCA
Audit Date: 30.06.2016
Personnel: Ken Nugent (Pub.); Bill Anderson (Adv. Mgr.); Joan Murray (Ed.)
Parent company (for newspapers): Metroland Media Group Ltd.; Torstar

ESSEX

ESSEX FREE PRESS

Street Address: 16 Centre St. ,
Province: ON
Postal: N8M 1N9
Country: Canada
Mailing address: PO Box 115
Mailing city: Essex
Province: ON
Postal: N8M 2Y1
General Phone: (519) 776-4268
General Fax: (519) 776-4014
General/National Adv. E-mail: essexfreepress@on.aibn.com
Primary Website: www.sxfreepress.com
Year Established: 1896
Areas Served - City/County or Portion Thereof, or Zip codes: Canada
Own Printing Facility?: Y
Commercial printers?: Y
Mechanical specifications: Type page 10 x 15; E - 5 cols, 2, 1/6 between.
Published: Thur
Avg Free Circ: 9925
Audit By: CMCA
Audit Date: 30.09.2016
Personnel: Lauri Brett (Pub.)

ESTERHAZY

THE ESTERHAZY MINER-JOURNAL

Street Address: 606 Veterans Ave. ,
Province: SK
Postal: S0A 0X0
Country: Canada
Mailing address: PO Box 1000
Mailing city: Esterhazy
Province: SK
Postal: S0A 0X0
General Phone: (306) 745-6669
General Fax: (306) 745-2699
General/National Adv. E-mail: miner.journal@sasktel.net
Primary Website: www.minerjournal.com
Year Established: 1907
Areas Served - City/County or Portion Thereof, or Zip codes: Canada
Commercial printers?: Y
Mechanical specifications: Type page 10 1/4 x 16; E - 5 cols, 1 11/12, between; A - 5 cols, 1 11/12, between; C - 5 cols, 1 11/12, between.
Published: Mon
Avg Paid Circ: 1334
Avg Free Circ: 0
Audit By: CMCA
Audit Date: 30.11.2013
Personnel: Brenda Matchett (Adv. Mgr.); Helen Solmes (Ed.)

ESTEVAN

ESTEVAN MERCURY

Street Address: 68 Souris Ave N. ,
Province: SK
Postal: S4A 2M3
Country: Canada
Mailing address: PO Box 730
Mailing city: Estevan
Province: SK

Postal: S4A 2A6
General Phone: (306) 634-2654
General Fax: (306) 634-3934
General/National Adv. E-mail: classifieds@estevanmercury.ca
Display Adv. E-mail: adsales@estevanmercury.ca
Editorial e-mail: editor@estevanmercury.ca
Primary Website: estevanmercury.ca
Year Established: 1903
Delivery Methods: Mail`Newsstand`Carrier`Racks
Areas Served - City/County or Portion Thereof, or Zip codes: Canada
Commercial printers?: Y
Mechanical specifications: Please call
Published: Wed
Avg Paid Circ: 252
Avg Free Circ: 4981
Audit By: AAM
Audit Date: 31.03.2019
Personnel: Rick Sadick (Pub.); Jihyun Choi (Prod. Mgr.); Norm Park (Ed.)
Parent company (for newspapers): Glacier Media Group

SOUTHEAST LIFESTYLES

Street Address: 300 Kensington Avenue ,
Province: SK
Postal: S4A 2A7
Country: Canada
Mailing address: Box 816
Mailing city: Estevan
Province: SK
Postal: S4A 2A6
General Phone: (306) 634-5112
General Fax: (306) 634-2588
General/National Adv. E-mail: lifestyles@sasktel.net
Primary Website: http://www.sasklifestyles.com/
Year Established: 1999
Delivery Methods: Mail`Newsstand`Carrier`Racks
Areas Served - City/County or Portion Thereof, or Zip codes: Canada
Mechanical specifications: Please Call
Published: Thur
Avg Paid Circ: 18
Avg Free Circ: 6585
Audit By: CMCA
Audit Date: 28.02.2014
Personnel: Rick Sadick (Pub.); Norm Park (Ed.)
Parent company (for newspapers): Glacier Media Group

ESTON

ESTON-ELROSE PRESS REVIEW

Street Address: 108 W. Main St. ,
Province: SK
Postal: S0L 1A0
Country: Canada
Mailing address: PO Box 787
Mailing city: Eston
Province: SK
Postal: S0L 1A0
General Phone: (306) 962-3221
General Fax: (306) 962-4445
General/National Adv. E-mail: estonpress@gmail.com
Areas Served - City/County or Portion Thereof, or Zip codes: Canada
Published: Tues
Avg Paid Circ: 753
Audit By: CMCA
Audit Date: 30.06.2016
Personnel: Stewart Crump (Pub.); Barry Malindine (Adv. Mgr.); Tim Crump (Ed.)
Parent company (for newspapers): Jamac Publishing

ETOBICOKE

ETOBICOKE GUARDIAN

Street Address: 307 Humberline Dr. ,
Province: ON

Postal: M9W 5V1
Country: Canada
Mailing address: 307 Humberline Dr.
Mailing city: Etobicoke
Province: ON
Postal: M9W 5V1
General Phone: (416) 675-4390
General Fax: (416) 675-9296
General/National Adv. E-mail: etg@mirror-guardian.com
Primary Website: insidetoronto.ca
Year Established: 1917
Areas Served - City/County or Portion Thereof, or Zip codes: Canada
Own Printing Facility?: Y
Commercial printers?: Y
Published: Thur
Avg Paid Circ: 0
Avg Free Circ: 67927
Audit By: CCAB
Audit Date: 30.09.2017
Personnel: Marg Middleton (Gen. Mgr.); Betty Carr (Pub.); Cor Coran (Adv. Mgr.); Lesley Duff (Asst. Dir., Dist.); Grace Peacock (Mng. Ed.); Dave Barnett (Dir., Prodn.); Katherine Bernal (Prodn. Mgr.)
Parent company (for newspapers): Metroland Media Group Ltd.; Torstar

EXETER

TIMES ADVOCATE

Street Address: 356 Main St. S. ,
Province: ON
Postal: N0M 1S6
Country: Canada
Mailing address: PO Box 850
Mailing city: Exeter
Province: ON
Postal: N0M 1S6
General Phone: (519) 235-1331
Advertising Fax: (519) 235-0766
General/National Adv. E-mail: ads@southhuron.com
Display Adv. E-mail: sales@southhuron.com
Editorial e-mail: snixon@southhuron.com
Primary Website: www.southhuron.com
Year Established: 1873
Delivery Methods: Mail
Areas Served - City/County or Portion Thereof, or Zip codes: N0M
Own Printing Facility?: N
Commercial printers?: Y
Mechanical specifications: Type page 10 1/2 x 16; E - 6 cols, 1 9/16, 3/16 between; A - 6 cols, 1 9/16, 3/16 between; C - 6 cols, 1 9/16, 3/16 between.
Published: Wed
Avg Paid Circ: 2158
Avg Free Circ: 84
Audit By: CMCA
Audit Date: 30.09.2016
Personnel: Deb Lord (Manager); Scott Nixon (Editor); Deborah Schillemore (Sales)
Parent company (for newspapers): Metroland Media Group Ltd.; Torstar

FAIRVIEW

FAIRVIEW POST

Street Address: 10118-110 St. ,
Province: AB
Postal: T0H 1L0
Country: Canada
Mailing address: PO Box 1900
Mailing city: Fairview
Province: AB
Postal: T0H 1L0
General Phone: (780) 835-4925
General Fax: (780) 835-4227
General/National Adv. E-mail: info@fairviewpost.com
Display Adv. E-mail: peter.meyerhoffer@sunmedia.ca
Editorial e-mail: chris.eakin@sunmedia.ca
Primary Website: www.fairviewpost.com
Year Established: 1940
Delivery Methods: Mail`Newsstand
Areas Served - City/County or Portion Thereof, or Zip codes: T0H
Commercial printers?: Y
Mechanical specifications: 160 Lines 10 Columns Page size: 10.33x11.43
Published: Wed
Avg Paid Circ: 119
Avg Free Circ: 8
Audit By: VAC
Audit Date: 31.12.2015
Personnel: Peter Meyerhoffer (Adv. Dir); Chris Eakin (Ed.)
Parent company (for newspapers): Postmedia Network Inc.; Quebecor Communications, Inc.

FARNHAM

JOURNAL L'AVENIR & DES RIVIERES

Street Address: 221 Main St. ,
Province: QC
Postal: J2N 1L5
Country: Canada
Mailing address: 221 Main St.
Mailing city: Farnham
Province: QC
Postal: J2N 1L5
General Phone: (450) 293-3138
General Fax: (450) 293-2093
General/National Adv. E-mail: caroline.dolce@tc.tc
Primary Website: www.laveniretdesrivieres.com
Areas Served - City/County or Portion Thereof, or Zip codes: Canada
Published: Wed
Avg Paid Circ: 3
Avg Free Circ: 11442
Audit By: CCAB
Audit Date: 31.03.2014
Personnel: Renel Bouchard (Gen. Mgr.); Elrsa Fournyer (Pub.); Charles Couture (Circ. Mgr.)

L'AVENIR DE BROME MISSISQUOI, INC.

Street Address: 221 Rue Principale Est. ,
Province: QC
Postal: J2N 1L5
Country: Canada
Mailing address: 221 Rue Principale Est.
Mailing city: Farnham
Province: QC
Postal: J2N 1L5
General Phone: (450) 293-3138
General Fax: (450) 293-2093
General/National Adv. E-mail: lavenir@canadafrancais.com
Editorial e-mail: cassandra.deblois@tc.tc
Primary Website: www.laveniretdesrivieres.com
Published: Wed
Avg Paid Circ: 34
Avg Free Circ: 8554
Audit By: Sworn/Estimate/Non-Audited
Audit Date: 12.07.2019
Personnel: Group le Canada Francais (Pub.)

FERGUS

THE FERGUS-ELORA NEWS EXPRESS

Street Address: 204 St. Andrew St. W ,
Province: ON
Postal: N1M 1M7
Country: Canada
Mailing address: PO Box 130
Mailing city: Fergus
Province: ON
Postal: N1M 1M7
General Phone: (519) 843-1310
General Fax: (519) 323-4548
Display Adv. E-mail: ads@centrewellington.com
Editorial e-mail: editor@centrewellington.com
Primary Website: www.southwesternontario.ca/ferguselora-on
Year Established: 1852
Areas Served - City/County or Portion Thereof, or Zip codes: Canada
Published: Wed
Avg Paid Circ: 100
Avg Free Circ: 7850
Audit By: CMCA
Audit Date: 31.08.2014
Personnel: Shannon Burrows (Ed.)
Parent company (for newspapers): Metroland Media Group Ltd.; Torstar

THE WELLINGTON ADVERTISER

Street Address: 905 Gartshore St. ,
Province: ON
Postal: N1M 2W8
Country: Canada
Mailing address: PO Box 252
Mailing city: Fergus
Province: ON
Postal: N1M 2W8
General Phone: (519) 843-5410
General Fax: (519) 843-7607
General/National Adv. E-mail: news@wellingtonadvertiser.com
Display Adv. E-mail: advertising@wellingtonadvertiser.com
Editorial e-mail: editor@wellingtonadvertiser.com
Primary Website: www.wellingtonadvertiser.com
Year Established: 1967
Delivery Methods: Mail`Newsstand`Carrier`Racks
Areas Served - City/County or Portion Thereof, or Zip codes: Fergus
Own Printing Facility?: Y
Mechanical specifications: E - 6 cols, 1 1/2, 1 2/3 between; A - 6 cols, 1 1/2, 1 2/3 between; C - 6 cols, 1 1/2, 1 2/3 between.
Published: Fri
Avg Paid Circ: 235
Avg Free Circ: 39898
Audit By: VAC
Audit Date: 31.03.2016
Personnel: William Adsett (Pub.); Catherine Goss (Circ. Mgr.); Dave Adsett (Ed.)

FERMONT

LE TRAIT D'UNION DU NORD

Street Address: 850 Place Daviault ,
Province: QC
Postal: G0G 1J0
Country: Canada
Mailing address: PO Box 561
Mailing city: Fermont
Province: QC
Postal: G0G 1J0
General Phone: (418) 287-3655
General Fax: (418) 287-3874
General/National Adv. E-mail: info.journaltdn@gmail.com
Display Adv. E-mail: publicite@journaltdn.ca
Classified Adv. e-mail: publicite@journaltdn.ca
Editorial e-mail: redaction@journaltdn.ca
Primary Website: www.journaltdn.ca
Year Established: 1983
Published: Mon
Published Other: Every other mon
Avg Free Circ: 1700
Audit By: Sworn/Estimate/Non-Audited
Audit Date: 12.07.2019
Personnel: Eric Cyr (Ed.); Lynda Raiche (Graphic & Adv. Consultant)

FERNIE

THE FREE PRESS

Street Address: 342 2nd Ave. ,
Province: BC
Postal: V0B 1M0
Country: Canada
Mailing address: PO Box 2350
Mailing city: Fernie
Province: BC
Postal: V0B 1M0
General Phone: (250) 423-4666
General/National Adv. E-mail: publisher@thefreepress.ca
Display Adv. E-mail: advertising@thefreepress.ca
Editorial e-mail: editor@thefreepress.ca
Primary Website: www.thefreepress.ca
Year Established: 1898
Delivery Methods: Carrier`Racks
Areas Served - City/County or Portion Thereof, or Zip codes: V0B 1M0 V0B 1M2 V0B 1H0 V0B 2G0 V0B 1T0 V0B 1T4
Own Printing Facility?: N
Commercial printers?: Y
Mechanical specifications: Type page 11 1/2 x 21 1/2; E - 10 cols, 1 1/6, between.
Published: Thur
Avg Paid Circ: 234
Avg Free Circ: 5643
Audit By: VAC
Audit Date: 30.11.2015
Personnel: Andrea Horton (Pub); Katie Smith (Ed); Jennifer Cronin (Adv); Bonny McLardy (Prod Mgr.)
Parent company (for newspapers): Black Press Group Ltd.

FLIN FLON

FLIN FLON REMINDER

Street Address: 14 North Ave. ,
Province: MB
Postal: R8A 0T2
Country: Canada
Mailing address: 14 North Ave.
Mailing city: Flin Flon
Province: MB
Postal: R8A 0T2
General Phone: (204) 687-3454
General Fax: (204) 687-4473
General/National Adv. E-mail: reminder@mb.sympatico.ca
Display Adv. E-mail: ads@thereminder.ca
Classified Adv. e-mail: sales@thereminder.ca
Editorial e-mail: news@thereminder.ca
Primary Website: www.thereminder.ca
Year Established: 1946
Areas Served - City/County or Portion Thereof, or Zip codes: Flin Flon
Published: Wed`Fri
Weekday Frequency: e
Avg Paid Circ: 12
Avg Free Circ: 38
Audit By: VAC
Audit Date: 30.06.2016
Personnel: Valerie Durnin (Pub); Jonathon Naylor (Ed); Shannon Thompson (Office Admin)
Parent company (for newspapers): Glacier Media Group

FOAM LAKE

FOAM LAKE REVIEW

Street Address: 325 Main St. ,
Province: SK
Postal: S0A 1A0
Country: Canada
Mailing address: PO Box 550
Mailing city: Foam Lake
Province: SK
Postal: S0A 1A0
General Phone: (306) 272-3262
General Fax: (306) 272-4521
General/National Adv. E-mail: review.foamlake@sasktel.net
Primary Website: www.foamlakereview.com
Areas Served - City/County or Portion Thereof, or Zip codes: Canada
Own Printing Facility?: Y
Commercial printers?: Y
Published: Mon
Avg Paid Circ: 1123
Avg Free Circ: 3
Audit By: CMCA
Audit Date: 31.12.2015
Personnel: Bob Johnson (Ed.)

Non-Daily Newspapers in Canada

FONTHILL

FONTHILL VOICE OF PELHAM

Street Address: 8-209 Highway 20 East ,
Province: ON
Postal: L0S 1E0
Country: Canada
Mailing address: PO Box 40
Mailing city: Fonthill
Province: ON
Postal: L0S 1E0
General Phone: (905) 892-8690
General Fax: (905) 892-0823
General/National Adv. E-mail: office@thevoiceofpelham.ca
Display Adv. E-mail: advertising@thevoiceofpelham.ca
Editorial e-mail: editor@thevoiceofpelham.ca
Primary Website: www.thevoiceofpelham.ca
Year Established: 1997
Areas Served - City/County or Portion Thereof, or Zip codes: Canada
Mechanical specifications: Type page 10 1/4 x 15 2/3; E - 6 cols, 1 1/2, 1/8 between; A - 6 cols, 1 1/2, 1/8 between; C - 6 cols, 1 1/2, 1/8 between.
Published: Wed
Avg Free Circ: 6782
Audit By: CMCA
Audit Date: 30.09.2015
Personnel: Leslie Chiapetta (Office Mgr.); Nate Smelle (Ed.); Dave Burket (Pub.).

FOREST

FOREST STANDARD

Street Address: 1 King St. W. ,
Province: ON
Postal: N0N 1J0
Country: Canada
Mailing address: PO Box 220
Mailing city: Forest
Province: ON
Postal: N0N 1J0
General Phone: (519) 786-5242
General Fax: (519) 786-4884
General/National Adv. E-mail: standard@xcelco.on.ca
Areas Served - City/County or Portion Thereof, or Zip codes: Canada
Commercial printers?: Y
Mechanical specifications: Type page 11 1/4 x 16; E - 6 cols, 1 1/2, 1/4 between; A - 6 cols, 1 1/2, 1/4 between.
Published: Thur
Avg Paid Circ: 1848
Audit By: CMCA
Audit Date: 30.06.2014
Personnel: Dale Hayter (Pub.); Gil De Schutter (Adv. Mgr.); Mavis Sanger (Circ. Mgr.); Gord Whitehead (Ed.).

FORESTVILLE

JOURNAL HAUTE COTE-NORD

Street Address: 100-31 Rte. 138 ,
Province: QC
Postal: G0T 1E0
Country: Canada
Mailing address: 100-31 Rte. 138
Mailing city: Forestville
Province: QC
Postal: G0T 1E0
General Phone: (418) 587-2090
General Fax: (418) 587-6407
General/National Adv. E-mail: journalhcn@globetrotter.net
Primary Website: www.journalhautecotenord.com
Areas Served - City/County or Portion Thereof, or Zip codes: Canada
Mechanical specifications: Type page 11 x 17; E - 8 cols, between; A - 8 cols, between.
Published: Wed
Avg Paid Circ: 20
Avg Free Circ: 5510
Audit By: CCAB
Audit Date: 30.09.2012
Personnel: Luc Brisson (Pub.); Guylaine Boulianne (Sec.); Shirley Kennedy (Mng. Ed.).

FORT ERIE

THE FORT ERIE TIMES

Street Address: 450 Garrison Rd., Unit 1 ,
Province: ON
Postal: L2A 1N2
Country: Canada
Mailing address: 450 Garrison Rd., Unit 1
Mailing city: Fort Erie
Province: ON
Postal: L2A 1N2
General Phone: (905) 871-3100
General Fax: (905) 871-5243
Advertising Phone: (905) 871-3100 x202
Advertising Fax: (905) 871-5243
Editorial Phone: (905) 871-3100 x207
Editorial Fax: (905) 871-5243
General/National Adv. E-mail: myra.robertson@sunmedia.ca
Display Adv. E-mail: myra.robertson@sunmedia.ca
Editorial e-mail: kris.dube@sunmedia.com
Primary Website: www.forterietimes.com
Delivery Methods: Carrier
Areas Served - City/County or Portion Thereof, or Zip codes: Canada
Own Printing Facility?: Y
Commercial printers?: Y
Mechanical specifications: Tabloid 10.4" W x 11.5" H
Published: Thur
Avg Paid Circ: 9
Avg Free Circ: 12454
Audit By: CMCA
Audit Date: 31.05.2016
Personnel: Sarag Ferguson (Ed.)
Parent company (for newspapers): Postmedia Network Inc.; Quebecor Communications, Inc.

FORT FRANCES

FORT FRANCES TIMES

Street Address: 116 First St. ,
Province: ON
Postal: P9A 3M7
Country: Canada
Mailing address: PO Box 339
Mailing city: Fort Frances
Province: ON
Postal: P9A 3M7
General Phone: (807) 274-5373
General Fax: (807) 274-7286
General/National Adv. E-mail: fort_frances_times@ocna.org
Display Adv. E-mail: ads@fortfrances.com
Primary Website: www.fortfrances.com
Areas Served - City/County or Portion Thereof, or Zip codes: Canada
Own Printing Facility?: Y
Commercial printers?: Y
Mechanical specifications: Type page 12 x 21 1/2; E - 6 cols, 2, 1/6 between; A - 6 cols, 2, 1/6 between.
Published: Wed
Avg Paid Circ: 3134
Avg Free Circ: 130
Audit By: CMCA
Audit Date: 31.03.2016
Personnel: James R. Cumming (Pub.); Linda Plumridge (Office Mgr.); Debbie Ballare (Adv. Mgr.); Michael Behan (Ed.); Don Cumming (Prod. Mgr.).

FORT MACLEOD

THE MACLEOD GAZETTE

Street Address: 310 24th St. ,
Province: AB
Postal: T0L 0Z0
Country: Canada
Mailing address: PO Box 720
Mailing city: Fort Macleod
Province: AB
Postal: T0L 0Z0
General Phone: (403) 553-3391
General Fax: (403) 553-2961
General/National Adv. E-mail: ftmgazet@telusplanet.net
Display Adv. E-mail: tmgsales@telus.net
Classified Adv. e-mail: tmgsales@telus.net
Editorial e-mail: tmgedit@telus.net
Primary Website: www.fortmacleodgazette.com
Year Established: 1882
Delivery Methods: Mail`Newsstand
Areas Served - City/County or Portion Thereof, or Zip codes: Municipal District of Willow Creek
Own Printing Facility?: Y
Commercial printers?: Y
Mechanical specifications: Type page 10.25 x 15.5; E - 6 cols, 1 3/4, 1/6 between; A - 6 cols, 1 3/4, 1/6 between; C - 6 cols, 1.5, 1/6 between.
Published: Wed
Avg Paid Circ: 1150
Avg Free Circ: 0
Audit By: CMCA
Audit Date: 28.02.2017
Personnel: Emily McTighe (Adv. Mgr.); Sharon Monical (Circ. Mgr.); Frank McTighe (Pub./Ed.)

FORT MCMURRAY

CONNECT

Street Address: 208, 9715 Main Street ,
Province: AB
Postal: T9H 1T5
Country: Canada
Mailing address: 208, 9715 Main Street
Mailing city: Fort McMurray
Province: AB
Postal: T9H 1T5
General Phone: (780) 790-6627
General Fax: (780) 714-6485
General/National Adv. E-mail: info@macmedia.ca
Display Adv. E-mail: tim@starnews.ca
Classified Adv. e-mail: tim@starnews.ca
Editorial e-mail: dawn@starnews.ca
Primary Website: www.fortmacconnect.ca
Year Established: 2002
Delivery Methods: Mail`Newsstand`Racks
Areas Served - City/County or Portion Thereof, or Zip codes: Fort McMurray/Regional Municipality of Wood Buffalo/Alberta/T9H 2C8
Published: Fri
Avg Free Circ: 19992
Audit By: VAC
Audit Date: 28.02.2015
Personnel: Tim O'Rourke (Publisher/Sales Manager)
Parent company (for newspapers): Star News Publishing Inc.

FORT NELSON

THE FORT NELSON NEWS

Street Address: 4448 50th Ave., Ste. 3 , P.o. Box 600
Province: BC
Postal: V0C 1R0
Country: Canada
Mailing address: PO Box 600
Mailing city: Fort Nelson
Province: BC
Postal: V0C 1R0
General Phone: (250) 774-2357
General Fax: (250) 774-3612
General/National Adv. E-mail: editorial@fnnews.ca
Display Adv. E-mail: ads@fnnews.ca
Classified Adv. e-mail: ads@fnnews.ca
Editorial e-mail: editorial@fortnelsonnews.ca
Primary Website: www.fortnelsonnews.ca
Year Established: 1959
Delivery Methods: Mail`Newsstand`Carrier`Racks
Areas Served - City/County or Portion Thereof, or Zip codes: Northern Rockies Regional District
Commercial printers?: Y
Mechanical specifications: Type page 11 1/2 x 21 3/8; E - 10 cols, 1 1/16, between; A - 10 cols, between; C - 10 cols, between.
Published: Wed
Avg Paid Circ: 439
Avg Free Circ: 665
Audit By: VAC
Audit Date: 12.12.2017
Personnel: Judith A. Kenyon (Ed & Pub); Alexandra Kenyon (Mng. Ed.); Kathy Smith (reporter and photographer); Abigail Neville (Mgr)

FORT QU'APPELLE

FORT QU'APPELLE TIMES

Street Address: 141 Broadway St. W. ,
Province: SK
Postal: S0G 1S0
Country: Canada
Mailing address: PO Box 940
Mailing city: Fort Qu'Appelle
Province: SK
Postal: S0G 1S0
General Phone: (306) 332-5526
General Fax: (306) 332-5414
General/National Adv. E-mail: forttimes@sasktel.net
Year Established: 1951
Delivery Methods: Mail`Newsstand
Areas Served - City/County or Portion Thereof, or Zip codes: Canada
Commercial printers?: Y
Mechanical specifications: Type page 10 1/4 x 16; E - 6 cols, 2, between; A - 6 cols, 2, between; C - 6 cols, 2, between.
Published: Tues
Avg Paid Circ: 837
Audit By: CMCA
Audit Date: 30.09.2016
Personnel: Sandra Huber (Pub.); Cassandra Archer (Adv. Mgr.); Linda Aspinall (Ed.)

FORT SAINT JOHN

NORTH PEACE EXPRESS

Street Address: 9916 98th St. ,
Province: BC
Postal: V1J 3T8
Country: Canada
Mailing address: 9916 98th St.
Mailing city: Fort Saint John
Province: BC
Postal: V1J 3T8
General Phone: (250) 785-5631
General Fax: (250) 785-3522
General/National Adv. E-mail: ahnews@awink.com
Display Adv. E-mail: wj@ahnfsj.ca
Editorial e-mail: editor@ahnfsj.ca
Year Established: 1942
Commercial printers?: Y
Mechanical specifications: Type page 10 1/4 x 13; E - 5 cols, 2 1/12, 1/3 between; A - 5 cols, 2 1/12, 1/3 between; C - 5 cols, 2 1/12, 1/3 between.
Published: Sun
Avg Free Circ: 10200
Audit By: Sworn/Estimate/Non-Audited
Audit Date: 12.07.2019
Personnel: William Julian (Pub); Debbie Oberlin (Circ. Mgr.)

THE NORTHERNER

Street Address: 9916 98th St. ,
Province: BC
Postal: V1J 3T8
Country: Canada
Mailing address: 9916 98th St.
Mailing city: Fort Saint John
Province: BC
Postal: V1J 3T8
General Phone: (250) 785-5631
General Fax: (250) 785-3522
General/National Adv. E-mail: ahnews@awink.com
Display Adv. E-mail: mhill@ahnfsj.ca
Classified Adv. e-mail: rwallace@ahnfsj.ca
Editorial e-mail: editor@ahnfsj.ca
Primary Website: www.thenortherner.ca
Year Established: 1988

Areas Served - City/County or Portion Thereof, or Zip codes: V1J 2B2
Mechanical specifications: Type page 10 1/4 x 12 3/4; E - 5 cols, 1 15/16, 3/16 between; A - 5 cols, 1 15/16, 3/16 between; C - 5 cols, 1 15/16, 3/16 between.
Published: Fri
Avg Paid Circ: 0
Avg Free Circ: 8657
Audit By: Sworn/Estimate/Non-Audited
Audit Date: 12.07.2019
Personnel: Melody Hill (Sales); William Julian (Pub.); Ryan Wallace (Sales); Debbie Oberlin (Circ.)

FORT SASKATCHEWAN

THE FORT SASKATCHEWAN RECORD

Street Address: 10404 99 Ave , 168A
Province: AB
Postal: T8L 3W2
Country: Canada
Mailing address: 10404 99 Ave, 168A
Mailing city: Fort Saskatchewan
Province: AB
Postal: T8L 3W2
General Phone: (780) 998-7070 Ext 724227
General Fax: (780) 998-5515
Editorial e-mail: agreen@postmedia.com
Primary Website: fortsaskatchewanrecord.com
Year Established: 1922
Delivery Methods: Mail`Carrier`Racks
Areas Served - City/County or Portion Thereof, or Zip codes: Strathcona County
Own Printing Facility?: N
Commercial printers?: Y
Mechanical specifications: specs available on website
Published: Thur
Avg Paid Circ: 9
Avg Free Circ: 8806
Audit By: Sworn/Estimate/Non-Audited
Audit Date: 12.07.2019
Personnel: A Green
Parent company (for newspapers): Postmedia Network Inc.

FORT SMITH

NORTHERN JOURNAL

Street Address: 207 Mcdougal Rd. ,
Province: NT
Postal: X0E 0P0
Country: Canada
Mailing address: PO Box 990
Mailing city: Fort Smith
Province: NT
Postal: X0E 0P0
General Phone: (867) 872-3000
General Fax: (867) 872-2754
General/National Adv. E-mail: don@srj.ca
Display Adv. E-mail: admin@norj.ca
Editorial e-mail: don@norj.ca
Primary Website: http://norj.ca/
Year Established: 1978
Delivery Methods: Carrier
Areas Served - City/County or Portion Thereof, or Zip codes: Canada
Mechanical specifications: Type page 11 x 17; E - 5 cols, 1 7/8, 1/6 between; A - 6 cols, 1 7/12, 1/6 between; C - 6 cols, 1 7/12, 1/6 between.
Published: Other
Avg Paid Circ: 3660
Avg Free Circ: 4065
Audit By: Sworn/Estimate/Non-Audited
Audit Date: 12.07.2019
Personnel: Sandra Jaque (Mgr) Don Jaque (Ed.)
Parent company (for newspapers): Cascade Publishing Ltd.

FORT ST. JAMES

CALEDONIA COURIER

Street Address: Box 1298 ,
Province: BC
Postal: V0J 3A0
Country: Canada
General Phone: (250) 567-9258
General Fax: (250) 567-2070
General/National Adv. E-mail: newsroom@ominecaexpress.com
Display Adv. E-mail: advertising@ominecaexpress.com
Primary Website: www.caledoniacourier.com
Year Established: 1972
Mechanical specifications: Type page 10 5/16 x 14 1/2; E - 6 cols, 1 9/16, 3/16 between; A - 6 cols, 1 9/16, 3/16 between; C - 6 cols, 1 9/16, 3/16 between.
Published: Wed
Avg Paid Circ: 562
Avg Free Circ: 31
Audit By: VAC
Audit Date: 30.06.2016
Personnel: Pam Berger (Pub./Sales Mgr.); Ruth Lloyd (Ed.); Julia Beal (Prod.); Wendy Haslam (Prod.); Mariella Drogomatz (Circ.)
Parent company (for newspapers): Black Press Group Ltd.

FRASERVILLE

MILLBROOK TIMES

Street Address: 1287 Larmer Line ,
Province: ON
Postal: K0L 1V0
Country: Canada
Mailing address: PO Box 266
Mailing city: Millbrook
Province: ON
Postal: L0A 1G0
General Phone: (705) 932-3001
General Fax: (705) 932-8816
General/National Adv. E-mail: thetimes@nixicom.net
Display Adv. E-mail: kgraham@nexicom.net
Classified Adv. E-mail: thetimes@nexicom.net
Editorial e-mail: thetimes@nexicom.net
Primary Website: http://themillbrooktimes.ca
Year Established: 1987
Delivery Methods: Mail`Newsstand
Areas Served - City/County or Portion Thereof, or Zip codes: Cavan Monaghan Twp, Peterborough County
Mechanical specifications: Type page 10 x ; E - 5 cols, 2, between; A - 5 cols, 2, between; C - 5 cols, 2, between.
Published: Thur`Mthly
Avg Paid Circ: 100
Avg Free Circ: 4000
Audit By: Sworn/Estimate/Non-Audited
Audit Date: 12.07.2019
Personnel: Karen Graham (Pub.)

FREDERICTON

NORTHSIDE THIS WEEK

Street Address: 984 Prospect St. ,
Province: NB
Postal: E3B 5A2
Country: Canada
Mailing address: 984 Prospect St.
Mailing city: Fredericton
Province: NB
Postal: E3B 5A2
General Phone: (506) 452-6671
General Fax: (506) 452-7405
General/National Adv. E-mail: northside@brunswicknews.com
Editorial e-mail: shelley.wood@brunswicknews.com
Published: Sat
Avg Free Circ: 9950
Audit By: Sworn/Estimate/Non-Audited
Audit Date: 12.07.2019
Personnel: Shelly Wood (Pub./Ed)
Parent company (for newspapers): Brunswick News, Inc.

GABRIOLA ISLAND

GABRIOLA SOUNDER

Street Address: 510 North Rd , Unit 1
Province: BC
Postal: V0R 1X0
Country: Canada
Mailing address: PO Box 62
Mailing city: Gabriola Island
Province: BC
Postal: V0R 1X0
General Phone: (250) 247-9337
General Fax: (250) 247-8147
Advertising Phone: (250) 247-9337
Editorial Phone: (250) 247-9337
General/National Adv. E-mail: derek@soundernews.com
Display Adv. E-mail: sarah@soundernew.com
Classified Adv. e-mail: derek@soundernews.com
Editorial e-mail: derek@soundernews.com
Primary Website: www.soundernews.com
Year Established: 1989
Delivery Methods: Mail`Newsstand`Racks
Areas Served - City/County or Portion Thereof, or Zip codes: Gabriola, and Mudge Island
Published: Tues
Avg Paid Circ: 50
Avg Free Circ: 2750
Audit By: Sworn/Estimate/Non-Audited
Audit Date: 12.07.2019
Personnel: Sarah Holmes (Pub.); Derek Kilbourn (Ed./Sales/Prod. Mgr.)
Parent company (for newspapers): Gabriola Sounder Media Inc.

GANDER

THE GANDER BEACON

Street Address: 61 Elizabeth Dr. ,
Province: NL
Postal: A1V 1W8
Country: Canada
Mailing address: PO Box 420
Mailing city: Gander
Province: NL
Postal: A1V 1W8
General Phone: (709) 256-4371
General Fax: (709) 256-3826
General/National Adv. E-mail: info@ganderbeacon.ca
Primary Website: www.ganderbeacon.ca
Areas Served - City/County or Portion Thereof, or Zip codes: Gander
Mechanical specifications: Type page 12 x 21; E - 6 cols, 1 1/16, 1/6 between; A - 6 cols, 1 1/16, 1/6 between; C - 8 cols, 1 3/16, 1/6 between.
Published: Thur
Avg Paid Circ: 929
Avg Free Circ: 0
Audit By: VAC
Audit Date: 31.12.2015
Personnel: Kevin Higgins (Gen. Mgr.)
Parent company (for newspapers): Transcontinental Media

GASPE

HAVRE

Street Address: Rue Jacques Cartier ,
Province: QC
Postal: G4X 1M9
Country: Canada
Mailing address: rue Jacques Cartier
Mailing city: Gaspe
Province: QC
Postal: G4X 1M9
General Phone: (418) 368-3242
Areas Served - City/County or Portion Thereof, or Zip codes: Canada
Published: Wed
Avg Paid Circ: 6
Avg Free Circ: 8207
Audit By: CCAB
Audit Date: 31.03.2014
Personnel: Bernard Johnson

LE PHARILLON

Street Address: 144 Rue De Jacques-cartier ,
Province: QC
Postal: G4X 1M9
Country: Canada
Mailing address: 144 Rue de Jacques-Cartier
Mailing city: Gaspe
Province: QC
Postal: G4X 1M9
General Phone: (418) 368-3242
General Fax: (418) 368-1705
General/National Adv. E-mail: pharillon@hebdosquebecor.com
Display Adv. E-mail: gas.redaction@tc.tc
Classified Adv. e-mail: gas.redaction@tc.tc
Editorial e-mail: gas.redaction@tc.tc
Primary Website: www.lepharillon.ca
Areas Served - City/County or Portion Thereof, or Zip codes: Canada
Mechanical specifications: Type page 12 1/2 x 11 1/2.
Published: Wed
Avg Paid Circ: 10
Avg Free Circ: 8720
Audit By: CCAB
Audit Date: 31.03.2014
Personnel: Alain St-Amand (Gen. Mgr.); Bernard Johnson (Mng. Ed.)
Parent company (for newspapers): Reseau Select/Select Network; Quebecor Communications, Inc.

GATINEAU

LA REVUE DE GATINEAU

Street Address: 160 Hospital Rd., Ste. 30 ,
Province: QC
Postal: J8T 8J1
Country: Canada
Mailing address: 160 Hospital Rd., Ste. 30
Mailing city: Gatineau
Province: QC
Postal: J8T 8J1
General Phone: (819) 568-7736
General Fax: (819) 568-8728
Editorial e-mail: pascal.laplante@tc.tc
Primary Website: www.info07.com
Areas Served - City/County or Portion Thereof, or Zip codes: Canada
Mechanical specifications: Type page 10 3/8 x 14 1/4; E - 8 cols, 1 1/8, between; A - 8 cols, 1 1/8, between; C - 8 cols, 1 1/8, between.
Published: Wed
Avg Paid Circ: 8
Avg Free Circ: 91029
Audit By: CCAB
Audit Date: 31.03.2014
Personnel: Jacques Blais (Gen. Mgr.); Martin Godcher (Ed.)
Parent company (for newspapers): Transcontinental Media

LE BULLETIN

Street Address: 435 Blvd Rue Principale ,
Province: QC
Postal: J8L 2G8
Country: Canada
Mailing address: 435 Blvd Rue Principale
Mailing city: Gatineau
Province: QC
Postal: J8L 2G8
General Phone: (819) 986-5089
General Fax: (819) 986-2073
Advertising Phone: (819) 986-5089
Advertising Fax: (819) 986-2073
Editorial Phone: (819) 986-5089
Editorial Fax: (819) 986-2073
General/National Adv. E-mail: yannick.boursier@tc.tc
Display Adv. E-mail: yannick.boursier@tc.tc
Editorial e-mail: yannick.boursier@tc.tc
Primary Website: www.lebulletin.net
Delivery Methods: Mail`Racks
Areas Served - City/County or Portion Thereof, or Zip codes: Canada
Published: Wed
Avg Paid Circ: 20

Non-Daily Newspapers in Canada

Avg Free Circ: 14308
Audit By: CCAB
Audit Date: 31.03.2014
Personnel: Yannick Boursier (Pub./Ed.)

LE BULLETIN D'AYLMER

Street Address: C-10 181 Principale St., (secteur Aylmer) ,
Province: QC
Postal: J9H 6A6
Country: Canada
Mailing address: C-10 181 Principale St., (Secteur Aylmer)
Mailing city: Gatineau
Province: QC
Postal: J9H 6A6
General Phone: (819) 684-4755
General Fax: (819) 684-6428
General/National Adv. E-mail: abawqp@videotron.ca
Display Adv. E-mail: ventes.sales@bulletinaylmer.com
Editorial e-mail: abawqp@videotron.ca
Primary Website: www.bulletinaylmer.com
Year Established: 1971
Delivery Methods: Carrier
Areas Served - City/County or Portion Thereof, or Zip codes: Canada
Own Printing Facility?: N
Commercial printers?: N
Mechanical specifications: Type page 10 1/4 x 11; E - 6 cols, 1 5/8, between; A - 6 cols, 1 5/8, between; C - 9 cols, 1 1/5, between.
Published: Wed
Avg Paid Circ: 181
Avg Free Circ: 23009
Audit By: Sworn/Estimate/Non-Audited
Audit Date: 12.07.2019
Personnel: Lily Ryan (Ed.); Lynne Lavery; Sophia Ryan (Manager operations)

LE REGIONAL DE HULL

Street Address: 160, Boul. Hospital, Office 30 ,
Province: QC
Postal: J8T 8J1
Country: Canada
Mailing address: 160, boul. hospital, office 30
Mailing city: Gatineau
Province: QC
Postal: J8T 8J1
General Phone: (819) 776-1063
General Fax: (819) 568-7544
General/National Adv. E-mail: boursiery@transcontinental.ca
Primary Website: www.info07.com
Areas Served - City/County or Portion Thereof, or Zip codes: Canada
Published: Wed
Avg Free Circ: 11000
Audit By: Sworn/Estimate/Non-Audited
Audit Date: 12.07.2019
Personnel: Dino Roberges (Adv. Mgr.); Jacques Blais (Ed.)

THE WEST-QUEBEC POST

Street Address: C-10 181 Principale St., Secteur Aylmer ,
Province: QC
Postal: J9H 6A6
Country: Canada
Mailing address: C-10 181 Principale St., Secteur Aylmer
Mailing city: Gatineau
Province: QC
Postal: J9H 6A6
General Phone: (819) 684-4755
General Fax: (819) 684-6428
General/National Adv. E-mail: l.lavery@bulletinaylmer.com
Display Adv. E-mail: ventes.sales@bulletinaylmer.com
Editorial e-mail: abawqp@videotron.ca
Year Established: 1895
Delivery Methods: Mail`Newsstand`Carrier`Racks
Areas Served - City/County or Portion Thereof, or Zip codes: Pontiac
Own Printing Facility?: N
Commercial printers?: Y
Mechanical specifications: Type page 10 2/5 x 11; E - 6 cols, 1 5/8, between; A - 6 cols, 1 5/8, between; Classifieds - 9 cols, 1 1/5, between.
Published: Fri
Avg Paid Circ: 761
Avg Free Circ: 5214
Audit By: CMCA
Audit Date: 29.02.2016
Personnel: Fred Ryan (Publisher); Lynne Lavery (General Manager); Lily Ryan (Editor); Sophia Ryan (sales manager); Nadia Paradis (Classified and subscription manager)
Parent company (for newspapers): 9040-9681 Quebec Inc.

WEEK-END OUTAOUAIS

Street Address: 160 Hospital Blvd., Ste. 30 ,
Province: QC
Postal: J8T 8J1
Country: Canada
Mailing address: 160 Hospital Blvd., Ste. 30
Mailing city: Gatineau
Province: QC
Postal: J8T 8J1
General Phone: (819) 568-7736
General Fax: (819) 568-7038
Primary Website: www.info07.com
Mechanical specifications: Type page 10 3/8 x 14 1/4; E - 8 cols, 1 1/8, between; A - 8 cols, 1 1/8, between; C - 8 cols, 1 1/8, between.
Published: Sat
Avg Free Circ: 90000
Audit By: Sworn/Estimate/Non-Audited
Audit Date: 12.07.2019
Personnel: Jacques Blais (Pub./Gen. Mgr.)

GEORGETOWN

INDEPENDENT & FREE PRESS

Street Address: 280 Guelph St., Unit 29 ,
Province: ON
Postal: L7G 4B1
Mailing address: 280 Guelph St., Unit 29
Mailing city: Georgetown
Province: ON
Postal: L7G 4B1
General Phone: (905) 873-0301
General Fax: (905) 873-0398
General/National Adv. E-mail: production@independentfreepress.com
Primary Website: independentfreepress.com
Areas Served - City/County or Portion Thereof, or Zip codes: Canada
Own Printing Facility?: Y
Commercial printers?: Y
Mechanical specifications: Type page 11 1/2 x 14 3/4; E - 9 cols, between; A - 9 cols, between.
Published: Thur
Avg Free Circ: 23045
Audit By: CCAB
Audit Date: 30.09.2017
Personnel: Steve Foreman (Gen. Mgr.); Cindi Campbell (Circ. Mgr.); Nancy Geissler (Circ. Mgr.); John McGhie (Mng. Ed.); Dana Robbins (Publisher)
Parent company (for newspapers): Metroland Media Group Ltd.; Torstar

GERALDTON

GERALDTON-LONGLAC TIMES STAR

Street Address: 401 Main St. ,
Province: ON
Postal: P0T 1M0
Country: Canada
Mailing address: PO Box 490
Mailing city: Geraldton
Province: ON
Postal: P0T 1M0
General Phone: (807) 854-1919
General Fax: (807) 854-1682
General/National Adv. E-mail: tstar@astrocom-on.com
Editorial e-mail: editor@thetimesstar.ca
Primary Website: www.thetimesstar.ca
Year Established: 1945
Areas Served - City/County or Portion Thereof, or Zip codes: Canada
Own Printing Facility?: Y
Commercial printers?: Y
Mechanical specifications: Type page 11 x 17; E - 5 cols, 1 14/15, 1/5 between; A - 5 cols, 1 14/15, 1/5 between; C - 5 cols, 1 14/15, 1/5 between.
Published: Wed
Avg Paid Circ: 642
Avg Free Circ: 19
Audit By: CMCA
Audit Date: 31.07.2016
Personnel: Mike Goulet (Prodn. Mgr.); Justin Saindon; Eric Pietsch (Ed.)

GLENBORO

GAZETTE

Street Address: 702 Railway Ave. ,
Province: MB
Postal: R0K 0X0
Country: Canada
Mailing address: PO Box 10
Mailing city: Glenboro
Province: MB
Postal: R0K 0X0
General Phone: (204) 827-2343
General Fax: (204) 827-2207
General/National Adv. E-mail: gazette@mts.net
Display Adv. E-mail: gazette2@mts.net
Editorial e-mail: gazette@mts.net
Primary Website: http://www.baldur-glenborogazette.ca/
Areas Served - City/County or Portion Thereof, or Zip codes: Canada
Commercial printers?: Y
Mechanical specifications: Type page 12 x 15 1/2; E - 5 cols, 1 3/4, 1/4 between; A - 5 cols, 1 3/4, 1/4 between; C - 5 cols, 1 3/4, 1/4 between.
Published: Tues
Avg Paid Circ: 1557
Avg Free Circ: 0
Audit By: CMCA
Audit Date: 31.05.2014
Personnel: Mike Johnson (Ed./Pub/Adv); Travis Johnson (Ed./Pub/Adv)

GLENCOE

TRANSCRIPT & FREE PRESS

Street Address: 243 Main St. ,
Province: ON
Postal: N0L 1M0
Country: Canada
Mailing address: PO Box 400
Mailing city: Glencoe
Province: ON
Postal: N0L 1M0
General Phone: (519) 287-2615
General Fax: (519) 287-2408
General/National Adv. E-mail: tranfree@xcelco.on.ca
Published: Thur
Avg Paid Circ: 1033
Audit By: CMCA
Audit Date: 30.06.2014
Personnel: Dale Hayder (Circ. Mgr.)

GLOUCESTER

EXPRESS D'ORLEANS

Street Address: Canotek Road Unit 30 , Unit 30
Province: ON
Postal: K1J 8R7
Country: Canada
Mailing address: Canotek Road Unit 30
Mailing city: Gloucester
Province: ON
Postal: K1J 8R7
General Phone: (613) 744-4800
Areas Served - City/County or Portion Thereof, or Zip codes: Gloucester, Ottawa, Ontario.
Published: Wed
Avg Paid Circ: 10742
Avg Free Circ: 200
Audit By: ODC
Audit Date: 14.12.2011
Personnel: Madeleine Joanisse

ORLEANS STAR

Street Address: Po Box 46009 ,
Province: ON
Postal: K1J 9H7
Country: Canada
Mailing address: PO Box 46009
Mailing city: Gloucester
Province: ON
Postal: K1J 9H7
General Phone: (613) 323-2801
Advertising Phone: (613) 744-4800
General/National Adv. E-mail: orleansstar@transcontinental.ca
Primary Website: www.orleansstar.ca
Areas Served - City/County or Portion Thereof, or Zip codes: Canada
Published: Thur
Avg Paid Circ: 11
Avg Free Circ: 42989
Audit By: CCAB
Audit Date: 31.03.2014

GODERICH

GODERICH SIGNAL-STAR

Street Address: 120 Huckins St. Industrial Park ,
Province: ON
Postal: N7A 3X8
Country: Canada
Mailing address: PO Box 220
Mailing city: Goderich
Province: ON
Postal: N7A 3X8
General Phone: (519) 524-2614
General Fax: (519) 524-9175
General/National Adv. E-mail: john.bauman@sunmedia.ca
Primary Website: www.goderichsignalstar.com
Year Established: 1848
Areas Served - City/County or Portion Thereof, or Zip codes: Canada
Own Printing Facility?: Y
Commercial printers?: Y
Mechanical specifications: Type page 11 1/4 x 21 1/4; E - 6 cols, 1 7/12, 1/6 between; A - 6 cols, 1 7/12, 1/6 between; C - 6 cols, 1 7/12, 1/6 between.
Published: Wed
Avg Paid Circ: 3150
Avg Free Circ: 18
Audit By: CMCA
Audit Date: 30.06.2017
Personnel: John Bauman (Sales Mgr.)
Parent company (for newspapers): Postmedia Network Inc.

GOLDEN

GOLDEN STAR

Street Address: 413a N. Ninth Ave. ,
Province: BC
Postal: V0H 1H0
Country: Canada
Mailing address: PO Box 149
Mailing city: Golden
Province: BC
Postal: V0H 1H0
General Phone: (250) 344-5251
General Fax: (250) 344-7344
General/National Adv. E-mail: publisher@thegoldenstar.net
Display Adv. E-mail: advertising@thegoldenstar.net
Classified Adv. e-mail: advertising@thegoldenstar.net
Editorial e-mail: editor@thegoldenstar.net
Primary Website: www.thegoldenstar.net
Year Established: 1891
Areas Served - City/County or Portion Thereof, or Zip

codes: Golden
Own Printing Facility?: Y
Commercial printers?: N
Mechanical specifications: Type page 10 1/3 x 15 1/2; E - 6 cols, 1 1/2, 1/6 between; A - 6 cols, 1 1/2, 1/6 between; C - 6 cols, 1 1/2, 1/6 between.
Published: Wed
Avg Paid Circ: 502
Avg Free Circ: 32
Audit By: VAC
Audit Date: 30.06.2016
Personnel: Sue Hein (Classified Mgr.); Michele Lapointe (Pub.); Jessica Schwitek (Ed.)
Parent company (for newspapers): Black Press Group Ltd.

GORE BAY

MANITOULIN RECORDER

Street Address: 37 D Meredith St. ,
Province: ON
Postal: P0P 1H0
Country: Canada
Mailing address: PO Box 235
Mailing city: Gore Bay
Province: ON
Postal: P0P 1H0
General Phone: (705) 282-2003
General Fax: (705) 282-2432
General/National Adv. E-mail: recorder@bellnet.ca
Year Established: 1908
Areas Served - City/County or Portion Thereof, or Zip codes: Canada
Published: Fri
Avg Paid Circ: 997
Avg Free Circ: 72
Audit By: AAM
Audit Date: 31.03.2018
Personnel: R.L. McCutcheon (Pub.); Tom Sasvari (Ed.); Al Ryan (Prodn. Mgr.)

GRANBY

GRANBY EXPRESS

Street Address: 398 Main St., Ste 5 ,
Province: QC
Postal: J2G 2W6
Country: Canada
Mailing address: 398 Main St., Ste 5
Mailing city: Granby
Province: QC
Postal: J2G 2W6
General Phone: (450) 777-4515
General Fax: (450) 777-4516
General/National Adv. E-mail: nancy.corriveau@monjournalexpress.com
Primary Website: www.granbyexpress.com
Areas Served - City/County or Portion Thereof, or Zip codes: Canada
Mechanical specifications: Type page 10 1/4 x 12 1/2; E - 8 cols, between; A - 8 cols, between; C - 8 cols, between.
Published: Wed
Avg Paid Circ: 3
Avg Free Circ: 41995
Audit By: CCAB
Audit Date: 31.03.2014
Personnel: Nancy Corriveau (Sales Coord.); Maritime Chagnon (Mng. Ed.); Caroline Rioux (Reg'l Ed.)

LA VOIX DE L'EST PLUS

Street Address: 76 Dufferin St. ,
Province: QC
Postal: J2G 9L4
Country: Canada
Mailing address: 76 Dufferin St.
Mailing city: Granby
Province: QC
Postal: J2G 9L4
General Phone: (450) 375-4555
General Fax: (450) 372-1308
Editorial Fax: (450) 777-4865
General/National Adv. E-mail: redaction@lavoixdelest.qc.ca
Display Adv. E-mail: pub@lapresse.ca

Editorial e-mail: redaction@lavoixdelest.qc.ca
Primary Website: www.cyberpresse.ca
Year Established: 1935
Areas Served - City/County or Portion Thereof, or Zip codes: Canada
Mechanical specifications: Type page 10 1/4 x ; E - 10 cols, 1, 1/8 between; A - 10 cols, 1, 1/8 between; C - 10 cols, 1, 1/8 between.
Published: Wed
Weekday Frequency: m
Saturday Frequency: m
Avg Paid Circ: 8965
Avg Free Circ: 128
Sat. Circulation Paid: 12703
Sat. Circulation Free: 712
Audit By: AAM
Audit Date: 31.03.2017
Personnel: Francois Beaudoin (Mng. Ed.); Daniel Touchette (Adv. Mgr.); Gilbert Arl (Dir., Finance/Admin.); Daniel Touchet (Adv. Mgr., Sales); Christian Malo (Circ. Dir.); Guy Granger (Ed.); Haswa Budway (News Ed.); Andre Bilodeau (Sports Ed.); Claudette Ospiguy (Prodn. Mgr., Pre Press); Louisse Boisvert (Pub.); Marc Gendron (Info. Mgr.); Martyne Lessard (Adv. Mgr.)
Parent company (for newspapers): Gesca Ltd.; Reseau Select/Select Network

GRAND BEND

LAKESHORE ADVANCE

Street Address: 58 Ontario St. North ,
Province: ON
Postal: N0M 1T0
Country: Canada
Mailing address: 58 ONTARIO STREET NORTH, P.O. Box 1195
Mailing city: Grand Bend
Province: ON
Postal: N0M 1T0
General Phone: (519) 238-5383
General Fax: (519) 238-5131
General/National Adv. E-mail: lakeshore.advance@sunmedia.ca
Display Adv. E-mail: lakeshore.ads@sunmedia.ca
Editorial e-mail: lakeshore.advance@sunmedia.ca
Primary Website: www.lakeshoreadvance.com
Delivery Methods: Mail
Areas Served - City/County or Portion Thereof, or Zip codes: Canada
Mechanical specifications: Page Size: 10.25" wide x 11.42" high 9 col x 160 ag
Published: Wed
Avg Paid Circ: 979
Avg Free Circ: 13
Audit By: CMCA
Audit Date: 30.06.2014
Personnel: Neil Clifford (Adv. Dir.)
Parent company (for newspapers): Quebecor

GRAND FALLS

L' ETOILE CATARACTE

Street Address: 229 Broadway Blvd. ,
Province: NB
Postal: E3Z 2K1
Country: Canada
Mailing address: PO Box 7363
Mailing city: Grand Falls
Province: NB
Postal: E3Z 2K1
General Phone: (506) 473-3083
General Fax: (506) 473-3105
General/National Adv. E-mail: cataract@nb.aibn.com
Editorial e-mail: rickard.mark@victoriastar.ca
Primary Website: https://www.telegraphjournal.com/letoile/
Areas Served - City/County or Portion Thereof, or Zip codes: Canada
Mechanical specifications: Type page 13 x 21 1/2; E - 6 cols, 2 1/16, 1/6 between; A - 6 cols, 2 1/16, 1/6 between; C - 6 cols, 2 1/16, 1/6 between.
Published: Thur
Avg Paid Circ: 0

Avg Free Circ: 6296
Audit By: CMCA
Audit Date: 30.09.2013
Personnel: Mark Rickard (Ed. English); Madeleine Leclerc (Ed., French)
Parent company (for newspapers): Brunswick News, Inc.

THE ADVERTISER

Street Address: Po Box 129 ,
Province: NL
Postal: A2A 2J4
Country: Canada
Mailing address: PO Box 129
Mailing city: Grand Falls
Province: NL
Postal: A2A 2J4
General Phone: (709) 489-2162
General Fax: (709) 489-4817
General/National Adv. E-mail: editor@advertisernl.ca
Editorial e-mail: editor@advertisernl.ca
Primary Website: www.gfwadvertiser.ca
Areas Served - City/County or Portion Thereof, or Zip codes: Grand Falls
Own Printing Facility?: Y
Commercial printers?: Y
Published: Thur
Avg Paid Circ: 1600
Avg Free Circ: 0
Audit By: VAC
Audit Date: 31.12.2015
Personnel: Ron Ennis (Ed.)
Parent company (for newspapers): Transcontinental Media

VICTORIA COUNTY STAR

Street Address: 229 Broadway Blvd. ,
Province: NB
Postal: E3Z 2K1
Country: Canada
Mailing address: PO Box 7363
Mailing city: Grand Falls
Province: NB
Postal: E3Z 2K1
General Phone: (506) 473-3083
General Fax: (506) 473-3105
Editorial e-mail: rickard.mark@victoriastar.ca
Primary Website: https://www.telegraphjournal.com/victoria-star/
Year Established: 2003
Areas Served - City/County or Portion Thereof, or Zip codes: Grand Falls
Own Printing Facility?: Y
Commercial printers?: Y
Mechanical specifications: Type page 11 1/2 x 21 1/2; E - 10 cols, 1/8 between; A - 10 cols, 1/8 between; C - 10 cols, 1/8 between.
Published: Wed
Avg Paid Circ: 2175
Avg Free Circ: 2
Audit By: VAC
Audit Date: 31.12.2015
Personnel: Mark Rickard (Ed., English); Madeleine Leclerc (Ed., French)
Parent company (for newspapers): Brunswick News, Inc.

GRAND FORKS

THE GRAND FORKS GAZETTE

Street Address: 7255 Riverside Dr. ,
Province: BC
Postal: V0H 1H0
Country: Canada
Mailing address: PO Box 700
Mailing city: Grand Forks
Province: BC
Postal: V0H 1H0
General Phone: (250) 442-2191
General Fax: (250) 442-3336
General/National Adv. E-mail: publisher@grandforksgazette.ca
Display Adv. E-mail: advertising@grandforksgazette.ca
Editorial e-mail: editor@grandforksgazette.ca

Primary Website: grandforksgazette.ca
Year Established: 1897
Delivery Methods: Mail`Newsstand`Carrier
Areas Served - City/County or Portion Thereof, or Zip codes: Canada
Commercial printers?: Y
Mechanical specifications: Type page 10 x 15 1/2.
Published: Wed
Avg Paid Circ: 2399
Avg Free Circ: 12
Audit By: VAC
Audit Date: 30.06.2017
Personnel: Della Mallette (Prodn. Mgr.); Dyan Stoochnoff (Advertising); Kathleen Saylors (Reporter); Dustin LaCroix (Graphic Artist); Darlainea Redlack (Circulation)
Parent company (for newspapers): Black Press Group Ltd.

GRANDE CACHE

GRANDE CACHE MOUNTAINEER

Street Address: 1800 Pine Plaza ,
Province: AB
Postal: T0E 0Y0
Country: Canada
Mailing address: PO Box 660
Mailing city: Grande Cache
Province: AB
Postal: T0E 0Y0
General Phone: (780) 827-3539
General/National Adv. E-mail: gcnews@telus.net
Display Adv. E-mail: gcnews@telus.net
Editorial e-mail: pamnews@telus.net
Primary Website: http://www.grandecachemountaineer.canic.ws/
Year Established: 1970
Delivery Methods: Mail`Newsstand
Areas Served - City/County or Portion Thereof, or Zip codes: Grande Cache Alberta
Published: Thur
Avg Paid Circ: 1060
Avg Free Circ: 36
Audit By: Sworn/Estimate/Non-Audited
Audit Date: 12.07.2019
Personnel: Pamela Brown (Pub./Ed./GM); Lisa Gould (Sales)

GRANDVIEW

THE EXPONENT

Street Address: 414 Main St. ,
Province: MB
Postal: R0L 0Y0
Country: Canada
Mailing address: PO Box 39
Mailing city: Grandview
Province: MB
Postal: R0L 0Y0
General Phone: (204) 546-2555
General Fax: (204) 546-3081
General/National Adv. E-mail: expos@mts.net
Editorial e-mail: expos@mts.net
Primary Website: www.grandviewexponent.com
Year Established: 1901
Delivery Methods: Mail`Newsstand
Areas Served - City/County or Portion Thereof, or Zip codes: Rol oyo R0L 0X0 and others
Own Printing Facility?: Y
Commercial printers?: N
Mechanical specifications: Type page 10 1/4 x 14 1/4; E - 6 cols, 1 7/12, 1/6 between; A - 6 cols, 1 7/12, 1/6 between; C - 6 cols, 1 7/12, 1/6 between.
Published: Tues
Avg Paid Circ: 1687
Avg Free Circ: 27
Audit By: VAC
Audit Date: 31.01.2016
Personnel: Clayton Chaloner (Ed.)

GRAVELBOURG

GRAVELBOURG TRIBUNE

Street Address: 611 Main St. ,

Non-Daily Newspapers in Canada

Province: SK
Postal: S0H 1X0
Country: Canada
Mailing address: PO Box 1017
Mailing city: Gravelbourg
Province: SK
Postal: S0H 1X0
General Phone: (306) 648-3479
General Fax: (306) 648-2520
Advertising Phone: (306) 648-3479
Advertising Fax: (306) 648-2520
Editorial Phone: (306) 648-3479
General/National Adv. E-mail: trib.editorial@sasktel.net
Display Adv. E-mail: trib.ads@sasktel.net
Classified Adv. e-mail: (306) 648-3479
Editorial e-mail: trib.editorial@sasktel.net
Primary Website: http://gravelbourgtribune.wixsite.com/tribune
Year Established: 1986
Delivery Methods: Mail`Newsstand
Areas Served - City/County or Portion Thereof, or Zip codes: R.M of Gravelbourg
Own Printing Facility?: Y
Commercial printers?: Y
Mechanical specifications: Type page 10 1/4 x 15 1/2; E - 5 cols, 1 7/8, between; A - 5 cols, 1 7/8, between; C - 5 cols, 1 7/8, between.
Published: Mon
Avg Paid Circ: 875
Avg Free Circ: 30
Audit By: CMCA
Audit Date: 27.11.2018
Personnel: Paul Boisvert (Ed)

GRAVENHURST

THE GRAVENHURST BANNER

Street Address: 140 Muskoka Rd. S. ,
Province: ON
Postal: P1P 1X2
Country: Canada
Mailing address: PO Box 849
Mailing city: Gravenhurst
Province: ON
Postal: P1P 1X2
General Phone: (705) 687-6674
General Fax: (705) 687-7213
General/National Adv. E-mail: banner@muskoka.com
Primary Website: www.muskokaregion.com/gravenhurst-on
Areas Served - City/County or Portion Thereof, or Zip codes: Canada
Published: Thur
Avg Paid Circ: 96
Avg Free Circ: 5237
Audit By: CMCA
Audit Date: 30.04.2016
Personnel: Bill Allen (Gen. Mgr.); Jack Tynan (Adv.)
Parent company (for newspapers): Metroland Media Group Ltd.; Torstar

GREENWOOD

THE AURORA

Street Address: Po Box 99 ,
Province: NS
Postal: B0P 1N0
Country: Canada
Mailing address: PO Box 99
Mailing city: Greenwood
Province: NS
Postal: B0P 1N0
General Phone: (902) 765-1494
General Fax: (902) 765-1717
General/National Adv. E-mail: aurora@auroranewspaper.com
Display Adv. E-mail: auroramarketing@ns.aliantzinc.ca
Editorial e-mail: auroraeditor@ns.aliantzinc.ca
Primary Website: www.auroranewspaper.com
Delivery Methods: Mail`Newsstand`Carrier`Racks
Areas Served - City/County or Portion Thereof, or Zip codes: Canada
Mechanical specifications: Type page 11 x 13; E - 6 cols, 1 5/8, 3/20 between; A - 6 cols, 1 5/8, 3/20 between.

Published: Mon
Avg Free Circ: 5900
Audit By: Sworn/Estimate/Non-Audited
Audit Date: 12.07.2019
Personnel: Sara Keddy (Mgr. Ed.); Dejah Roulston-Wilde (Admin Clerk); Christianne Robichaud (Adv); Brian Graves (Graphics designer)

THE BOUNDARY CREEK TIMES

Street Address: 318 Copper St. ,
Province: BC
Postal: V0H 1J0
Country: Canada
Mailing address: PO Box 99
Mailing city: Greenwood
Province: BC
Postal: V0H 1J0
General Phone: (250) 445-2233
General/National Adv. E-mail: bctimes@shaw.ca
Display Adv. E-mail: dyan.stoochnoff@boundarycreektimes.com
Primary Website: boundarycreektimes.ca
Delivery Methods: Mail`Newsstand
Areas Served - City/County or Portion Thereof, or Zip codes: Canada
Mechanical specifications: Type page 10 3/16 x 14 1/8; E - 5 cols, 1 7/16, 3/16 between; A - 5 cols, 1 7/16, 3/16 between; C - 5 cols, 1 7/16, 3/16 between.
Published: Thur
Avg Paid Circ: 471
Avg Free Circ: 1
Audit By: CMCA
Audit Date: 30.09.2017
Personnel: Dyan Stoochnoff (Associate Publisher); Darlainea Redlack (Circulation); Kathleen Saylors (Reporter)
Parent company (for newspapers): Black Press Group Ltd.

GRENFELL

BROADVIEW EXPRESS

Street Address: 813 Desmond St. ,
Province: SK
Postal: S0G 2B0
Country: Canada
Mailing address: PO Box 189
Mailing city: Grenfell
Province: SK
Postal: S0G 2B0
General Phone: (306) 697-2722
General Fax: (306) 697-2689
Advertising Phone: (306) 697-2722
Advertising Fax: (306) 697-2689
General/National Adv. E-mail: sunnews@sasktel.net
Display Adv. E-mail: sunnews@sasktel.net
Editorial e-mail: sunnews@sasktel.net
Primary Website: www.grenfellsun.sk.ca
Year Established: 1965
Delivery Methods: Mail`Newsstand
Areas Served - City/County or Portion Thereof, or Zip codes: Canada
Mechanical specifications: Type page 10 1/8 x 15 1/2; E - 6 cols, 1 1/2, between; A - 6 cols, 1 1/2, between; C - 6 cols, 1 1/2, between.
Published: Mon
Avg Paid Circ: 266
Avg Free Circ: 158
Audit By: CMCA
Audit Date: 31.03.2013
Personnel: Suzette Stone (Circ. Mgr.); Mariann Hughes (Sales Associate)
Parent company (for newspapers): Transcontinental Media

GRENFELL SUN

Street Address: 813 Desmond St. ,
Province: SK
Postal: S0G 2B0
Country: Canada
Mailing address: PO Box 189
Mailing city: Grenfell
Province: SK
Postal: S0G 2B0

General Phone: (306) 697-2722
General Fax: (306) 697-2689
General/National Adv. E-mail: sunnews@sasktel.net
Display Adv. E-mail: sunnews@sasktel.net
Editorial e-mail: sunnews@sasktel.net
Primary Website: grenfellsun.sk.ca
Year Established: 1892
Delivery Methods: Mail`Newsstand
Areas Served - City/County or Portion Thereof, or Zip codes: Canada
Commercial printers?: Y
Mechanical specifications: Type page 10 1/8 x 15 1/2; E - 6 cols, 1 1/2, between; A - 6 cols, 1 1/2, between; C - 6 cols, 1 1/2, between.
Published: Mon
Avg Paid Circ: 710
Avg Free Circ: 128
Audit By: CMCA
Audit Date: 30.09.2013
Personnel: Sarah Pacio (Office Manager)
Parent company (for newspapers): Transcontinental Media

GRIMSBY

THE GRIMSBY LINCOLN NEWS

Street Address: 32 Main St. W. ,
Province: ON
Postal: L3M 1R4
Country: Canada
Mailing address: 32 Main St. W.
Mailing city: Grimsby
Province: ON
Postal: L3M 1R4
General Phone: (905) 945-8392
General Fax: (905) 945-3916
General/National Adv. E-mail: info@thegrimsbylincolnnews.com
Primary Website: www.thegrimsbylincolnnews.com
Published: Wed
Avg Free Circ: 23800
Audit By: Sworn/Estimate/Non-Audited
Audit Date: 12.07.2019
Personnel: Mike Williscraft (Editorial Mgr.); Scott Rosts (Ed.)
Parent company (for newspapers): Metroland Media Group Ltd.; Torstar

GRIMSHAW

BANNER POST

Street Address: Po Box 686 , Po Box 1010
Province: AB
Postal: T0H 1W0
Country: Canada
Mailing address: PO Box 686
Mailing city: Manning
Province: AB
Postal: T0H 2M0
General Phone: (780) 836-3588
General Fax: (780) 836-2820
Advertising Phone: (780) 332-2215
General/National Adv. E-mail: bannerpost@mackreport.ab.ca
Display Adv. E-mail: bannerpost@mrnews.ca
Editorial e-mail: publisher@mrnews.ca
Primary Website: mrnews.ca
Year Established: 1965
Areas Served - City/County or Portion Thereof, or Zip codes: Canada
Own Printing Facility?: Y
Published: Wed
Avg Paid Circ: 0
Avg Free Circ: 45404
Audit By: CCAB
Audit Date: 31.10.2018
Personnel: Tom Mihaly (Pub/Ed); Kristin Dyck (Ed); Jillian Vandemark-Chomiak (Office/Adv. Mgr)
Parent company (for newspapers): Metroland Media Group Ltd.

GUELPH

GUELPH TRIBUNE

Street Address: 367 Woodlawn Rd. W., Unit 1 ,
Province: ON
Postal: N1H 7K9
Country: Canada
Mailing address: 367 Woodlawn Rd. W., Unit 1
Mailing city: Guelph
Province: ON
Postal: N1H 1G8
General Phone: (519) 763-3333
General Fax: (519) 763-4814
General/National Adv. E-mail: cclark@guelphtribune.ca
Primary Website: www.guelphtribune.ca
Areas Served - City/County or Portion Thereof, or Zip codes: Canada
Published: Tues`Thur
Avg Free Circ: 41612
Audit By: VAC
Audit Date: 30.06.2016
Personnel: Peter Winkler (Pub.); Heather Dunbar (Sales Mgr.); Doug Coxson (Ed.)
Parent company (for newspapers): Metroland Media Group Ltd.; Torstar

GULL LAKE

ADVANCE SOUTHWEST (FORMERLY GULL LAKE ADVANCE)

Street Address: 1462 Conrad Ave. ,
Province: SK
Postal: S0N 1A0
Country: Canada
Mailing address: PO Box 628
Mailing city: Gull Lake
Province: SK
Postal: S0N 1A0
General Phone: (306) 672-3373
Advertising Phone: (306) 741-2448
General/National Adv. E-mail: glad12@sasktel.net
Display Adv. E-mail: sales@advancesouthwest.com
Editorial e-mail: kate@advancesouthwest.com
Primary Website: www.advancesouthwest.com
Year Established: 1909
Delivery Methods: Mail`Carrier
Areas Served - City/County or Portion Thereof, or Zip codes: Southwest Saskatchewan Postal Codes: S0N, S9H, S0G
Own Printing Facility?: Y
Commercial printers?: Y
Published: Mon
Avg Paid Circ: 600
Avg Free Circ: 7900
Audit By: Sworn/Estimate/Non-Audited
Audit Date: 12.07.2019
Personnel: Kate Winquist (Pub)
Parent company (for newspapers): Winquist Ventures Ltd.

GUYSBOROUGH

GUYSBOROUGH JOURNAL

Street Address: P.O. Box 210 ,
Province: NS
Postal: B0H 1N0
Country: Canada
Mailing address: P.O. Box 210
Mailing city: Guysborough
Province: NS
Postal: B0H 1N0
General Phone: (902) 533-2851
General Fax: (902) 533-2750
General/National Adv. E-mail: news@guysboroughjournal.ca
Display Adv. E-mail: advertising@guysboroughjournal.ca
Editorial e-mail: news@guysboroughjournal.ca
Primary Website: www.guysboroughjournal.com
Areas Served - City/County or Portion Thereof, or Zip codes: Guysborough
Published: Wed
Avg Paid Circ: 6890
Avg Free Circ: 13

Audit By: VAC
Audit Date: 30.06.2016
Personnel: Allan Murphy (Pub); Hellen Murphy (Ed/Mgr/Pub); Sharon Heighton (Office/Circ. Mgr)

HAGERSVILLE

THE HALDIMAND PRESS

Street Address: 6 Parkview Rd. ,
Province: ON
Postal: N0A 1H0
Country: Canada
Mailing address: PO Box 369
Mailing city: Hagersvillel
Province: ON
Postal: N0A 1H0
General Phone: (905) 768-3111
General/National Adv. E-mail: press.h@news-net.ca
Display Adv. E-mail: alana@haldimandpress.com
Classified Adv. e-mail: design@haldimandpress.com
Editorial e-mail: kaitlyn@haldimandpress.com
Primary Website: www.haldimandpress.com
Year Established: 1868
Delivery Methods: Mail`Newsstand
Areas Served - City/County or Portion Thereof, or Zip codes: Canada
Published: Thur
Avg Paid Circ: 3073
Audit By: Sworn/Estimate/Non-Audited
Audit Date: 12.07.2019
Personnel: Jillian Zynomirski (Pub.); Kaitlyn Clark (Publisher)

HALIBURTON

THE HIGHLANDER

Street Address: 195 Highland Street , The Village Barn
Province: ON
Postal: K0M 1S0
Country: Canada
Mailing address: P.O. BOX 1024
Mailing city: Haliburton
Province: ON
Postal: K0M 1S0
General Phone: (705) 457-2900
Display Adv. E-mail: walt@haliburtonhighlander.ca
Primary Website: www.haliburtonhighlander.ca
Year Established: 2011
Delivery Methods: Newsstand`Racks
Areas Served - City/County or Portion Thereof, or Zip codes: Canada
Published: Thur
Avg Free Circ: 8062
Audit By: CMCA
Audit Date: 30.06.2016
Personnel: Bram Lebo (Pub.)

HALIFAX

BEDFORD - SACKVILLE WEEKLY NEWS

Street Address: 211 Horseshoe Lake Dr ,
Province: NS
Postal: B3S 0B9
Country: Canada
Mailing address: 211 Horseshoe lake Dr
Mailing city: Halifax
Province: NS
Postal: B3S 0B9
General Phone: (902) 426-2811
General Fax: (902) 426-1170
General/National Adv. E-mail: reception@herald.ca
Display Adv. E-mail: sales@herald.ca
Classified Adv. e-mail: classified@herald.ca
Editorial e-mail: newsroom@herald.ca
Primary Website: http://thechronicleherald.ca/community/bedfordsackvilleobserver
Delivery Methods: Mail`Newsstand
Areas Served - City/County or Portion Thereof, or Zip codes: Canada
Published: Thur
Avg Free Circ: 29302
Audit By: CMCA
Audit Date: 28.02.2013
Personnel: Sheryl Grant (Adv. Media Dir.); Kim Moar (Mng. Ed.)

COLE HARBOUR WEEKLY

Street Address: 211 Horseshoe Lake Dr,
Province: NS
Postal: B3S 0B9
Country: Canada
Mailing address: 211 Horseshoe lake Dr
Mailing city: Halifax
Province: NS
Postal: B3S 0B9
General Phone: (902) 426-2811
General Fax: (902) 426-1170
General/National Adv. E-mail: reception@herald.ca
Display Adv. E-mail: sales@herald.ca
Classified Adv. e-mail: classifieds@herald.ca
Editorial e-mail: newsroom@herald.ca
Primary Website: www.thechronicleherald.ca
Delivery Methods: Mail`Newsstand
Areas Served - City/County or Portion Thereof, or Zip codes: Canada
Published: Thur
Avg Free Circ: 37643
Audit By: CMCA
Audit Date: 28.02.2013
Personnel: Fred Fiander (Pub.); Sheryl Grant (Adv. Media Dir.)

HALIFAX WEST-CLAYTON PARK WEEKLY NEWS

Street Address: 211 Horseshoe Lake Dr ,
Province: NS
Postal: B3S 0B9
Country: Canada
Mailing address: 211 Horseshoe lake Dr
Mailing city: Halifax
Province: NS
Postal: B3S 0B9
General Phone: (902) 421-5888
General/National Adv. E-mail: reception@herald.ca
Display Adv. E-mail: sgrant@herald.ca
Classified Adv. e-mail: classified@herald.ca
Editorial e-mail: newsroom@herald.ca
Primary Website: www.thechronicleherald.ca
Delivery Methods: Mail`Newsstand
Areas Served - City/County or Portion Thereof, or Zip codes: Canada
Published: Thur
Avg Free Circ: 37145
Audit By: CMCA
Audit Date: 28.02.2013
Personnel: Sheryl Grant (Adv. Media Dir.); Kim Moar (Mng. Ed.)

HAMILTON

THE BAY OBSERVER

Street Address: 140 King Street East ,
Province: ON
Postal: L8N 1B2
Country: USA
Mailing address: 140 King Street East
Mailing city: Hamilton
Province: ON
Postal: L8N 1B2
General Phone: (905) 522-6000
General Fax: (905) 522-5838
General/National Adv. E-mail: contact@bayobserver.ca
Primary Website: www.bayobserver.ca
Areas Served - City/County or Portion Thereof, or Zip codes: Canada
Published: Thur
Avg Paid Circ: 0
Avg Free Circ: 28246
Audit By: CMCA
Audit Date: 31.01.2012
Personnel: John Best (Pub.)

HANNA

HANNA HERALD

Street Address: 113 - 1st Ave West ,
Province: AB
Postal: T0J 1P0
Country: Canada
Mailing address: PO Box 790
Mailing city: Hanna
Province: AB
Postal: T0J 1P0
General Phone: (403) 854-3366
General Fax: (403) 854-3256
Display Adv. E-mail: rmackintosh@postmedia.com
Classified Adv. e-mail: deanne.cornell@sunmedia.ca
Editorial e-mail: jackie.gold@sunmedia.ca
Primary Website: www.hannaherald.com
Year Established: 1912
Delivery Methods: Mail`Newsstand
Areas Served - City/County or Portion Thereof, or Zip codes: Canada
Published: Wed
Avg Paid Circ: 900
Avg Free Circ: 0
Audit By: CMCA
Audit Date: 30.06.2014
Personnel: Shawn Cornell (Pub); Deanne Cornell (Adv. Sales Rep.); Krista Avery (Office Mgr.); Jackie Gold (Mng. Ed.)
Parent company (for newspapers): Postmedia Network Inc.; Quebecor Communications, Inc.

HANOVER

THE POST (HANOVER)

Street Address: 413 18th Ave. ,
Province: ON
Postal: N4N 3S5
Country: Canada
General Phone: (519) 364-2001
General Fax: (519) 364-6950
General/National Adv. E-mail: marie.david@sunmedia.ca
Display Adv. E-mail: janie.harrison@sunmedia.ca
Classified Adv. e-mail: han.classifieds@sunmedia.ca
Editorial e-mail: patrick.bales@sunmedia.ca
Primary Website: www.thepost.on.ca
Year Established: 1880
Delivery Methods: Carrier
Areas Served - City/County or Portion Thereof, or Zip codes: Canada
Own Printing Facility?: Y
Commercial printers?: Y
Mechanical specifications: Tabloid 9 col x 160 lines
Published: Thur
Avg Paid Circ: 84
Avg Free Circ: 15393
Audit By: CMCA
Audit Date: 30.06.2016
Personnel: Marie David (Gen. Mgr.); Rod Currie (Circ. Mgr.); Patrick Bales (Ed.); Kiera Merriam (Adv. Mgr.)
Parent company (for newspapers): Postmedia Network Inc.; Quebecor Communications, Inc.

HAPPY VALLEY

THE LABRADORIAN

Street Address: 2 Hillcrest Rd. ,
Province: NL
Postal: A0P 1E0
Country: Canada
Mailing address: PO Box 39
Mailing city: Happy Valley-Goose Bay
Province: NL
Postal: A0P 1E0
General Phone: (709) 896-3341
General Fax: (709) 896-8781
Advertising Phone: (709) 896-3341
General/National Adv. E-mail: sgallant@thelabradorian.ca
Display Adv. E-mail: sgallant@thelabradorian.ca
Editorial e-mail: editor@thelabradorian.ca
Primary Website: www.thelabradorian.ca
Areas Served - City/County or Portion Thereof, or Zip codes: Happy Valley, Goose Bay
Mechanical specifications: Type page 11 x 21 1/2; E - 6 cols, 1 3/4, 1/8 between; A - 6 cols, 1 3/4, 1/8 between; C - 8 cols, 1 1/2, between.
Published: Mon
Avg Paid Circ: 2009
Avg Free Circ: 0
Audit By: VAC
Audit Date: 31.12.2015
Personnel: Sharon Gallant (Adv)
Parent company (for newspapers): Transcontinental Media

HARBOUR BRETON

HARBOUR BRETON COASTER

Street Address: 30-42 Canada Drive ,
Province: NL
Postal: A0H 1P0
Country: Canada
Mailing address: PO Box 298
Mailing city: Harbour Breton
Province: NL
Postal: A0H 1P0
General Phone: (709) 885-2378
General Fax: (709) 885-2393
Editorial e-mail: editor@thecoasterr.ca
Primary Website: www.thecoasterr.ca
Areas Served - City/County or Portion Thereof, or Zip codes: Canada
Published: Tues
Avg Paid Circ: 1283
Avg Free Circ: 0
Audit By: CMCA
Audit Date: 30.06.2013
Personnel: Clayton Hunt (Ed.)
Parent company (for newspapers): Transcontinental Media

HARROW

HARROW NEWS

Street Address: 5 King St. , P.o. Box 310
Province: ON
Postal: N0R 1G0
Country: Canada
Mailing address: PO Box 310
Mailing city: Harrow
Province: ON
Postal: N0R 1G0
General Phone: (519) 738-2542
General Fax: (519) 738-3874
General/National Adv. E-mail: harnews@mnsi.net
Display Adv. E-mail: harnews@mnsi.net
Classified Adv. e-mail: harnews@mnsi.net
Editorial e-mail: natalie@mdirect.net
Year Established: 1930
Delivery Methods: Mail`Newsstand
Areas Served - City/County or Portion Thereof, or Zip codes: Canada
Mechanical specifications: Type page 10 1/4 x 15; E - 6 cols, 1 1/2, 3/8 between; A - 6 cols, 1 1/2, 3/8 between; C - 6 cols, 1 1/2, 3/8 between.
Published: Tues
Avg Paid Circ: 1221
Avg Free Circ: 3
Audit By: CMCA
Audit Date: 2/29/2017
Personnel: Natalie Koziana (Circ. Mgr.)

HARTLAND

THE OBSERVER

Street Address: 941 Industrial Dr. ,
Province: NB
Postal: E7P 2G8
Country: Canada
Mailing address: 941 Industrial Dr.
Mailing city: Hartland

Non-Daily Newspapers in Canada

Province: NB
Postal: E7P 2G8
General Phone: (506) 375-4458
General Fax: (506) 375-4281
General/National Adv. E-mail: theobserver@nb.aibn.com
Year Established: 1909
Areas Served - City/County or Portion Thereof, or Zip codes: Canada
Own Printing Facility?: Y
Commercial printers?: Y
Mechanical specifications: Type page 12 x 21; E - 6 cols, 1 7/8, 1/8 between; A - 6 cols, 1 7/8, 1/8 between; C - 6 cols, 1 7/8, 1/8 between.
Published: Wed
Avg Paid Circ: 2569
Audit By: Sworn/Estimate/Non-Audited
Audit Date: 12.07.2019
Personnel: Stewart Fairgrieve (Gen. Mgr.)

HAWKESBURY

LE CARILLON

Street Address: 1100 Aberdeen St. ,
Province: ON
Postal: K6A 1K7
Country: Canada
Mailing address: 1100 Aberdeen St.
Mailing city: Hawkesbury
Province: ON
Postal: K6A 3H1
General Phone: (613) 632-4155
General Fax: (613) 632-6122
Advertising Phone: (613) 632-4155
Advertising Fax: (613) 632-6383
Editorial Phone: (613) 632-4155
Editorial Fax: (613) 632-6383
General/National Adv. E-mail: nouvelles@eap.on.ca
Display Adv. E-mail: yvan.joly@eap.on.ca; nicole.pilon@eap.on.ca
Editorial e-mail: nouvelles@eap.on.ca
Primary Website: www.lecarillon.ca
Year Established: 1948
Delivery Methods: Carrier
Areas Served - City/County or Portion Thereof, or Zip codes: Canada
Own Printing Facility?: Y
Commercial printers?: Y
Mechanical specifications: Type page 10 1/2 x 14 1/4; E - 8 cols, 1/6 between; A - 8 cols, 1/6 between; C - 8 cols, 1/6 between.
Published: Thur
Avg Paid Circ: 30
Avg Free Circ: 15000
Audit By: Sworn/Estimate/Non-Audited
Audit Date: 12.07.2019
Personnel: Bertrand Castonguay (Pres.); Gilles Normand (Circ. Mgr.); FranÃ§ois Legault (Chief Ed.)
Parent company (for newspapers): Cie d'Edition Andre Paquette, Inc.

LE/THE REGIONAL

Street Address: 124 Rue Principale E. ,
Province: ON
Postal: K6A 1A3
Country: Canada
Mailing address: 124 rue Principale E.
Mailing city: Hawkesbury
Province: ON
Postal: K6A 1A3
General Phone: (613) 632-0112
General Fax: (613) 632-0277
General/National Adv. E-mail: pub@le-regional.ca
Display Adv. E-mail: pub@le-regional.ca
Editorial e-mail: news@le-regional.ca
Primary Website: www.le-regional.ca
Year Established: 1995
Delivery Methods: Mail`Newsstand`Carrier`Racks
Areas Served - City/County or Portion Thereof, or Zip codes: K6A 1A3
Own Printing Facility?: N
Commercial printers?: Y
Mechanical specifications: Type page 11.317" x 15"; E - 8 cols, 0.1292" between;
Published: Thur
Avg Free Circ: 34484
Audit By: Sworn/Estimate/Non-Audited
Audit Date: 12.07.2019
Personnel: Sylvain Roy (Owner)

TRIBUNE EXPRESS

Street Address: 1100 Aberdeen ,
Province: ON
Postal: K6A 1K7
Country: Canada
Mailing address: PO Box 1000
Mailing city: Hawkesbury
Province: ON
Postal: K6A 3H1
General Phone: (613) 632-4155
General Fax: (613) 632-6122
Advertising Phone: (613) 632-4155
Advertising Fax: (613) 632-6383
Editorial Phone: (613) 632-4155
Editorial Fax: (613) 632-6383
General/National Adv. E-mail: nouvelles@eap.on.ca
Display Adv. E-mail: yvan.joly@eap.on.ca; nicole.pilon@eap.on.ca
Editorial e-mail: nouvelles@eap.on.ca
Primary Website: www.tribune-express.ca
Year Established: 1984
Delivery Methods: Carrier
Areas Served - City/County or Portion Thereof, or Zip codes: Canada
Own Printing Facility?: Y
Commercial printers?: Y
Mechanical specifications: Type page 10 1/2 x 14 1/4; E - 8 cols, 1/6 between; A - 8 cols, 1/6 between; C - 8 cols, 1/6 between.
Published: Wed
Avg Paid Circ: 11
Avg Free Circ: 26430
Audit By: Sworn/Estimate/Non-Audited
Audit Date: 12.07.2019
Personnel: Bertrand Castonguay (President); Gilles Normand (Circ. Mgr.); Yvan Joly (Newspaper manager); Nicole Pilon (sales secretary, national, display)
Parent company (for newspapers): Cie d'Edition Andre Paquette, Inc.

HAY RIVER

THE HUB

Street Address: 8-4 Courtoreille St. ,
Province: NT
Postal: X0E 1G2
Country: Canada
Mailing address: 8-4 Courtoreille St.
Mailing city: Hay River
Province: NT
Postal: X0E 1G2
General Phone: (867) 874-6577
General Fax: (867) 874-2679
General/National Adv. E-mail: hub@hayriverhub.com
Display Adv. E-mail: ads@hayriverhub.com
Editorial e-mail: web@hayriverhub.com
Primary Website: www.hayriverhub.com
Year Established: 1973
Areas Served - City/County or Portion Thereof, or Zip codes: X0E 1G2, X0E 0P0, X0E 0M0, X0E 0N0, X1A 2P2, X0E 0L0
Commercial printers?: Y
Mechanical specifications: Type page 10 1/4 x 15 1/2; E - 6 cols, 1 3/5, 1/6 between; A - 6 cols, 1 3/5, 1/6 between; C - 6 cols, 1 3/5, 1/6 between.
Published: Wed
Avg Paid Circ: 1996
Avg Free Circ: 182
Audit By: VAC
Audit Date: 31.01.2016
Personnel: Chris Brodeur (Pub.); Lehaina Andrews (Adv. Mgr.); Lorna Desilets (Circ. Mgr.)

HEARST

LE NORD

Street Address: 1004, Rue Prince. ,
Province: ON
Postal: P0L 1N0
Country: Canada
Mailing address: PO Box 2320
Mailing city: Hearst
Province: ON
Postal: P0L 1N0
General Phone: (705) 372-1233
General Fax: (705) 362-5954
General/National Adv. E-mail: lenord@lenord.on.ca; ocantin@lenord.on.ca
Display Adv. E-mail: lenordjournalpub@gmail.com
Classified Adv. e-mail: lenordjournalpub@gmail.com
Editorial e-mail: journalistenord@gmail.com
Primary Website: www.lenord.on.ca
Year Established: 1976
Delivery Methods: Mail`Newsstand`Carrier
Areas Served - City/County or Portion Thereof, or Zip codes: Hearst
Commercial printers?: Y
Mechanical specifications: Type page 5col. X 175 MAL
Published: Wed
Avg Paid Circ: 1409
Avg Free Circ: 65
Audit By: CMCA
Audit Date: 30.06.2014
Personnel: Omer Cantin (Ed.); Steve McInnis (Gen. Mgr.); Karine Hebert (Graphic Designer)
Parent company (for newspapers): Lignes Agates Marketing

HERBERT

THE HERALD

Street Address: 716 Herbert Ave. ,
Province: SK
Postal: S0H 2A0
Country: Canada
Mailing address: PO Box 399
Mailing city: Herbert
Province: SK
Postal: S0H 2A0
General Phone: (306) 784-2422
General Fax: (306) 784-3246
General/National Adv. E-mail: herbertherald@sasktel.net
Display Adv. E-mail: herbertherald@sasktel.net
Classified Adv. e-mail: herbertherald@sasktel.net
Editorial e-mail: herbertherald@sasktel.net
Year Established: 1911
Delivery Methods: Mail`Newsstand
Areas Served - City/County or Portion Thereof, or Zip codes: Canada
Commercial printers?: Y
Mechanical specifications: Type page 10 1/4 x 15; E - 6 cols, 1 5/8, 1/4 between; A - 6 cols, 1 5/8, 1/4 between; C - 6 cols, 1 5/8, 1/4 between.
Published: Tues
Avg Paid Circ: 1442
Avg Free Circ: 5
Audit By: CMCA
Audit Date: 31.03.2017
Personnel: Rhonda J. Ens (Ed.)

HIGH LEVEL

THE ECHO-PIONEER

Street Address: 10006 - 97th St. ,
Province: AB
Postal: T0H 1Z0
Country: Canada
Mailing address: PO Box 1018
Mailing city: High Level
Province: AB
Postal: T0H 1Z0
General Phone: (780) 926-2000
General Fax: (780) 926-2001
General/National Adv. E-mail: pioneer@mackreport.ab.ca
Display Adv. E-mail: echoads1@mrnews.ca
Classified Adv. e-mail: echoads1@mrnews.ca
Editorial e-mail: echonews2@mrnews.ca
Primary Website: www.mrnews.ca
Year Established: 1976
Areas Served - City/County or Portion Thereof, or Zip codes: Canada
Own Printing Facility?: Y
Published: Wed
Audit By: Sworn/Estimate/Non-Audited
Audit Date: 12.07.2019
Personnel: Nikki Coles (Advertising); Tom Mihaly (Pub./Mng. Ed.); Ann Bassett (Office/Adv.); Matt Marcone (Ed); Lacey Reid (Advertising)
Parent company (for newspapers): Mackenzie Report Inc.

THE MILE ZERO NEWS

Street Address: 10006-97 St. ,
Province: AB
Postal: T0H 1Z0
Country: Canada
General Phone: (780) 332-2215
General Fax: (780) 926-2001
General/National Adv. E-mail: milezeronews@mrnews.ca
Display Adv. E-mail: echo@mrnews.ca
Primary Website: www.mrnews.ca
Year Established: 1977
Published: Wed
Avg Paid Circ: 0
Avg Free Circ: 1575
Audit By: VAC
Audit Date: 31.10.2016
Personnel: Carmen Kratky (Office/Advertising); Tom Mihaly (Pub.); Ann Bassett (Circ. Mgr.); Kristen Feddema (Ed.); Barb Schofield (Adv. Sales)
Parent company (for newspapers): Mackenzie Report Inc.

HIGH PRAIRIE

SOUTH PEACE NEWS

Street Address: 4902 51st Ave. ,
Province: AB
Postal: T0G 1E0
Country: Canada
Mailing address: PO Box 1000
Mailing city: High Prairie
Province: AB
Postal: T0G 1E0
General Phone: (780) 523-4484
General Fax: (780) 523-3039
General/National Adv. E-mail: spn@cablecomet.com
Display Adv. E-mail: southpeacenews@hotmail.com
Classified Adv. e-mail: southpeacenews@hotmail.com
Editorial e-mail: spn@cablecomet.com
Primary Website: www.southpeacenews.com
Delivery Methods: Mail`Newsstand
Areas Served - City/County or Portion Thereof, or Zip codes: Canada
Commercial printers?: Y
Mechanical specifications: Type page 10 1/4 x 15 3/4.
Published: Wed
Avg Paid Circ: 1257
Avg Free Circ: 0
Audit By: CMCA
Audit Date: 30.01.2017
Personnel: Mary Burgar (Pub.); Chris Clegg (Ed.)

HIGH RIVER

THE HIGH RIVER TIMES

Street Address: 618 Centre St. S. ,
Province: AB
Postal: T1V 1E9
Country: Canada
Mailing address: 104 - 701 Centre St. SW
Mailing city: High River
Province: AB
Postal: T1V 1Y1
General Phone: (403) 652-2034
General/National Adv. E-mail: info@highrivertimes.com

Display Adv. E-mail: hmorgan@postmedia.com
Classified Adv. e-mail: hmorgan@postmedia.com
Editorial e-mail: krushworth@postmedia.com
Primary Website: www.highrivertimes.com
Year Established: 1905
Delivery Methods: Mail`Newsstand`Carrier
Areas Served - City/County or Portion Thereof, or Zip codes: Canada
Commercial printers?: Y
Published: Tues`Fri
Avg Paid Circ: 0
Avg Free Circ: 6406
Audit By: VAC
Audit Date: 31.03.2017
Personnel: Kaire Davis (Admin./Office Mgr.); Kevin Rushworth (Multimedia. Ed.); Roxanne Mackintosh (Reg. Adv. Dir.); Heather Morgan (Advertising Manager)
Parent company (for newspapers): Postmedia Network Inc.

HINTON

THE HINTON PARKLANDER

Street Address: 387 Drinnan Way ,
Province: AB
Postal: T7V 2A3
Country: Canada
General Phone: (780) 865-3115
General Fax: (780) 865-1252
General/National Adv. E-mail: news@hintonparklander.com
Classified Adv. e-mail: hintonparklander.classifieds@sunmedia.ca
Editorial e-mail: eric.plummer@sunmedia.ca
Primary Website: www.hintonparklander.com
Year Established: 1955
Delivery Methods: Mail`Newsstand`Carrier`Racks
Areas Served - City/County or Portion Thereof, or Zip codes: Canada
Mechanical specifications: Type page 10 1/4 x 12 1/2; E - 8 cols, 1 13/16, 1/6 between; A - 8 cols, 1 13/16, 1/6 between; C - 8 cols, 1 13/16, 1/6 between.
Published: Mon
Avg Paid Circ: 7
Avg Free Circ: 3720
Audit By: VAC
Audit Date: 31.12.2015
Personnel: Eric Plummer (Ed.); Terry Thachuk (Pub.); Nathalie Lovoie-Murray (Nationals & Classified Booking)
Parent company (for newspapers): Postmedia Network Inc.

THE HINTON VOICE

Street Address: 187 Pembina Ave. ,
Province: AB
Postal: T7V 2B2
Country: Canada
General Phone: (890) 865-5688
General Fax: (780) 865-5699
General/National Adv. E-mail: news@hintonvoice.ca
Display Adv. E-mail: sales@hintonvoice.ca
Primary Website: www.hintonvoice.com
Areas Served - City/County or Portion Thereof, or Zip codes: Hinton
Published: Thur
Avg Free Circ: 445
Audit By: VAC
Audit Date: 31.08.2016
Personnel: Tyler Waugh (Pub.); Sarah Burns (Mktg. Specialist); Robin Garreck (Prodn./Distrib. Mgr.); Angie Still (Accounting)

HOPE

HOPE STANDARD

Street Address: 540 Wallace St. ,
Province: BC
Postal: V0X 1L0
Country: Canada
Mailing address: PO Box 1090
Mailing city: Hope
Province: BC
Postal: V0X 1L0
General Phone: (604) 869-2421
General Fax: (604) 869-7351
General/National Adv. E-mail: news@hopestandard.com
Display Adv. E-mail: sales@hopestandard.com
Classified Adv. e-mail: classifieds@hopestandard.com
Primary Website: www.hopestandard.com
Year Established: 1959
Areas Served - City/County or Portion Thereof, or Zip codes: Canada
Commercial printers?: Y
Mechanical specifications: Type page 10 3/8 x 14; E - 6 cols, 1 5/8, 1/8 between; A - 6 cols, 1 5/8, 1/8 between; C - 6 cols, 1 5/8, 1/8 between.
Published: Thur
Avg Paid Circ: 346
Avg Free Circ: 0
Audit By: VAC
Audit Date: 30.06.2016
Personnel: Patti Desjardins (Adv. Mgr.); Janice McDonald (Circ. Mgr.); Carly Ferguson (Pub.); X.Y. Zeng (Ed.)
Parent company (for newspapers): Torstar

HORNEPAYNE

JACKFISH JOURNAL

Street Address: 113 Herbert Ave. ,
Province: ON
Postal: P0M 1Z0
Mailing address: PO Box 487
Mailing city: Hornepayne
Province: ON
Postal: P0M 1Z0
General Phone: (807) 868-2381
General Fax: (807) 868-2673
General/National Adv. E-mail: Jjournal@bell.net
Primary Website: www.hornepayne.com
Areas Served - City/County or Portion Thereof, or Zip codes: Canada
Published: Wed
Avg Paid Circ: 200
Avg Free Circ: 30
Audit By: CMCA
Audit Date: 30.04.2016
Personnel: Lisa Stewart (Pub./Ed.)

HOUSTON

HOUSTON TODAY

Street Address: 3232 Hwy 16 W. ,
Province: BC
Postal: V0J 1Z1
Country: Canada
Mailing address: PO Box 899
Mailing city: Houston
Province: BC
Postal: V0J 1Z0
General Phone: (250) 845-2890
General Fax: (250) 847-2995
General/National Adv. E-mail: editor@houston-today.com
Display Adv. E-mail: advertising@houston-today.com
Primary Website: www.houston-today.com
Areas Served - City/County or Portion Thereof, or Zip codes: Canada
Own Printing Facility?: Y
Published: Wed
Avg Paid Circ: 983
Avg Free Circ: 305
Audit By: VAC
Audit Date: 30.06.2016
Personnel: Mary Ann Ruiter (Ed.); Todd Hamilton (Mng. Ed.); Jackie Lieuwen (Reporter)
Parent company (for newspapers): Torstar

HUDSON

HUDSON GAZETTE

Street Address: 397 Main Rd. ,
Province: QC
Postal: J0P 1H0
Country: Canada
Mailing address: 397 Main Rd.
Mailing city: Hudson
Province: QC
Postal: J0P 1H0
General Phone: (450) 458-5482
General Fax: (450) 458-3337
General/National Adv. E-mail: hudsongazette@videotron.ca
Primary Website: www.hudsongazette.com
Year Established: 1950
Areas Served - City/County or Portion Thereof, or Zip codes: Canada
Commercial printers?: Y
Mechanical specifications: Type page 10 7/8 x 14 1/8; E - 8 cols, 1 1/16, 1/6 between; A - 8 cols, 1 1/16, 1/6 between; C - 8 cols, 1 1/16, 1/6 between.
Published: Wed
Avg Free Circ: 21000
Audit By: Sworn/Estimate/Non-Audited
Audit Date: 12.07.2019
Personnel: Greg Jones (Pub.); Louise Craig (Circ. Mgr.); Jim Duff (Ed.)

HUDSON BAY

HUDSON BAY POST-REVIEW

Street Address: 20 Railway Ave. ,
Province: SK
Postal: S0E 0Y0
Country: Canada
Mailing address: PO Box 10
Mailing city: Hudson Bay
Province: SK
Postal: S0E 0Y0
General Phone: (306) 865-2771
General Fax: (306) 865-2340
General/National Adv. E-mail: post.review@sasktel.net
Display Adv. E-mail: postreview3@sasktel.net
Year Established: 1950
Delivery Methods: Mail`Newsstand
Areas Served - City/County or Portion Thereof, or Zip codes: Canada
Own Printing Facility?: Y
Commercial printers?: Y
Mechanical specifications: Type page 10.25 x 15 1/2; E - 6 cols, 1 1/2, 1/3 between; A - 6 cols, 1 1/2, 1/3 between; C - 6 cols, 1 1/2, 1/3 between.
Published: Thur
Avg Paid Circ: 910
Avg Free Circ: 27
Audit By: CMCA
Audit Date: 31.03.2014
Personnel: Sherry Pilon (Mgr.)

HUMBOLDT

EAST CENTRAL TRADER

Street Address: 535 Main Street ,
Province: SK
Postal: S0K 2A0
Country: Canada
Mailing address: PO Box 970
Mailing city: Humboldt
Province: SK
Postal: S0K 2A0
General Phone: (306) 682-2561
General Fax: (306) 682-3322
Display Adv. E-mail: sford@humboldtjournal.ca
Editorial e-mail: cmcrae@humboldtjournal.ca
Primary Website: www.humboldtjournal.ca
Areas Served - City/County or Portion Thereof, or Zip codes: Canada
Published: Fri
Avg Paid Circ: 5
Avg Free Circ: 5443
Audit By: CMCA
Audit Date: 30.04.2016
Personnel: Becky Zimmer (Ed.); Brent Fitzpatrick (Group Publisher)

THE HUMBOLDT JOURNAL

Street Address: 535 Main St. ,
Province: SK
Postal: S0K 2A0
Country: Canada
Mailing address: PO Box 970
Mailing city: Humboldt
Province: SK
Postal: S0K 2A0
General Phone: (306) 682-2561
General Fax: (306) 682-3322
General/National Adv. E-mail: humboldt.journal@sasktel.net
Display Adv. E-mail: sford@humboldtjournal.ca
Editorial e-mail: cmcrae@humboldtjournal.ca
Primary Website: www.humboldtjournal.ca
Year Established: 1905
Delivery Methods: Mail`Newsstand`Carrier`Racks
Areas Served - City/County or Portion Thereof, or Zip codes: Canada
Mechanical specifications: Type page Tabloid 11x17 Column size 1.583 inches
Published: Wed
Avg Paid Circ: 1765
Avg Free Circ: 29
Audit By: CMCA
Audit Date: 30.11.2016
Personnel: Becky Zimmer (Ed.)
Parent company (for newspapers): Glacier Media Group

HUNTINGDON

LES HEBDOS MONTEREGIENS

Street Address: 66 Chateauguay St. ,
Province: QC
Postal: J0S 1H0
Country: Canada
Mailing address: 66 Chateauguay St.
Mailing city: Huntingdon
Province: QC
Postal: J0S 1H0
General Phone: (450) 264-5364
General Fax: (450) 264-9521
General/National Adv. E-mail: info@gleaner-source.com; direction@gleaner-source.com
Display Adv. E-mail: petitesannonces@gleaner-source.com; pub@gleaner-source.com
Editorial e-mail: redaction@gleaner-source.com
Primary Website: www.monteregieweb.com
Mechanical specifications: Type page 10 1/4 x 16; E - 8 cols, 1 1/8, 1/8 between; A - 8 cols, 1 1/8, 1/8 between; C - 8 cols, 1 1/8, 1/8 between.
Published: Wed
Avg Paid Circ: 5000
Avg Free Circ: 91
Audit By: Sworn/Estimate/Non-Audited
Audit Date: 12.07.2019
Personnel: Andre Castagnier (Gen. Mgr.); Susanne J. Brown (Ed.)
Parent company (for newspapers): Hebdos Quebec

HUNTSVILLE

HUNTSVILLE FORESTER

Street Address: 11 Main St. W. ,
Province: ON
Postal: P1H 2C5
Country: Canada
Mailing address: 11 Main St. W.
Mailing city: Huntsville
Province: ON
Postal: P1H 2C5
General Phone: (705) 789-5541
General Fax: (705) 789-9381
General/National Adv. E-mail: production@metrolandnorthmedia.com
Editorial e-mail: news@metrolandnorthmedia.com
Primary Website: www.huntsvilleforester.com
Year Established: 1877
Delivery Methods: Mail`Newsstand`Racks
Areas Served - City/County or Portion Thereof, or Zip codes: Canada
Own Printing Facility?: Y

Non-Daily Newspapers in Canada

Commercial printers?: Y
Mechanical specifications: Type page 10 1/4 x 15; E - 6 cols, 1 11/20, between; A - 6 cols, 1 11/20, between; C - 6 cols, 1 11/20, between.
Published: Thur
Avg Paid Circ: 161
Avg Free Circ: 9177
Audit By: CMCA
Audit Date: 31.03.2016
Personnel: Bill Allen (Pub./Gen. Mgr.); Andrew Allen (Adv. Mgr.); Tamara De la Vega (News Ed.); Jack Tynan
Parent company (for newspapers): Metroland Media Group Ltd.; Torstar

HUNTSVILLE/MUSKOKA ADVANCE

Street Address: 11 Main St. W ,
Province: ON
Postal: P1H 2C5
Country: Canada
Mailing address: 11 Main St. W
Mailing city: Huntsville
Province: ON
Postal: P1H 2C5
General Phone: (705) 789-5541
General Fax: (705) 789-9381
General/National Adv. E-mail: production@huntsvilleforester.com; news@huntsvilleforester.com
Primary Website: www.huntsvilleforester.com
Commercial printers?: Y
Mechanical specifications: Type page 10 1/4 x 15; E - 6 cols, 1 11/20, between; A - 6 cols, 1 11/20, between.
Published: Sun
Avg Paid Circ: 7100
Avg Free Circ: 23038
Audit By: Sworn/Estimate/Non-Audited
Audit Date: 12.07.2019
Personnel: Joe Anderson (Regl. Pub.); Micheal Hill (Adv. Mgr.); Brenda McGary (Circ. Mgr.); Bruce Hickey (Ed.); Paula Ashby (Prodn. Mgr.)

IGNACE
DRIFTWOOD ENTERPRISES

Street Address: 153 Balsam ,
Province: ON
Postal: P0T 1T0
Country: Canada
Mailing address: 153 Balsam
Mailing city: Ignace
Province: ON
Postal: P0T 1T0
General Phone: (807) 934-6482
Year Established: 1978
Areas Served - City/County or Portion Thereof, or Zip codes: Canada
Published: Wed
Avg Paid Circ: 303
Audit By: CMCA
Audit Date: 31.12.2015

INDIAN HEAD
INDIAN HEAD-WOLSELEY NEWS

Street Address: 508 Grand Ave. ,
Province: SK
Postal: S0G 2K0
Country: Canada
Mailing address: PO Box 70
Mailing city: Indian Head
Province: SK
Postal: S0G 2K0
General Phone: (306) 695-3565
General Fax: (306) 695-3448
General/National Adv. E-mail: ihwnews@sasktel.net
Areas Served - City/County or Portion Thereof, or Zip codes: Canada
Commercial printers?: Y
Mechanical specifications: Type page 10 1/4 x 15.
Published: Thur
Avg Paid Circ: 938
Avg Free Circ: 20
Audit By: CMCA
Audit Date: 29.02.2016
Personnel: Jodi Gendron (Pub.); Kerri McCabe (Circ. Mgr.); Marcel Gendron (Ed.)

INNISFAIL
INNISFAIL PROVINCE

Street Address: 5036 - 48th St. ,
Province: AB
Postal: T4G 1M2
Country: Canada
Mailing address: 5036 - 48th St.
Mailing city: Innisfail
Province: AB
Postal: T4G 1M2
General Phone: (403) 227-3477
General Fax: (403) 227-3330
Display Adv. E-mail: ddemers@innisfail.greatwest.ca
Editorial e-mail: jbachusky@innisfail.greatwest.ca
Primary Website: www.innisfailprovince.ca
Year Established: 1905
Delivery Methods: Mail`Carrier
Areas Served - City/County or Portion Thereof, or Zip codes: Innisfail Alberta Canada
Published: Tues
Avg Paid Circ: 7
Avg Free Circ: 8240
Audit By: VAC
Audit Date: 31.08.2018
Personnel: Brent Spilak (Pub/Adv. Mgr.); Johnnie Bachusky (Ed)
Parent company (for newspapers): Glacier Media Group; Great West Newspapers LP

INVERMERE
INVERMERE VALLEY ECHO

Street Address: 1008-8th Avenue , #8
Province: BC
Postal: V0A 1K0
Country: Canada
Mailing address: PO Box 70
Mailing city: Invermere
Province: BC
Postal: V0A 1K0
General Phone: (250) 341-6299
General/National Adv. E-mail: general@invermerevalleyecho.com
Display Adv. E-mail: advertising@invermerevalleyecho.com
Editorial e-mail: editor@invermerevalleyecho.com
Primary Website: www.invermerevalleyecho.com
Year Established: 1956
Delivery Methods: Mail`Newsstand
Areas Served - City/County or Portion Thereof, or Zip codes: n/a
Published: Wed
Avg Free Circ: 488
Audit By: VAC
Audit Date: 30.06.2016
Personnel: Dean Midyette (Pub.); Nicole Trigg (Ed.); Amanda Nason (Adv. Sales)
Parent company (for newspapers): Torstar

THE COLUMBIA VALLEY PIONEER

Street Address: #8, 1008-8th Avenue ,
Province: BC
Postal: V0A 1K0
Country: Canada
Mailing address: PO Box 868
Mailing city: Invermere
Province: BC
Postal: V0A 1K0
General Phone: (250) 341-6299
General Fax: (855) 377-0312
General/National Adv. E-mail: info@cv-pioneer.com
Display Adv. E-mail: ads@columbiavalleypioneer.com
Classified Adv. e-mail: info@columbiavalleypioneer.com
Editorial e-mail: news@columbiavalleypioneer.com
Primary Website: www.columbiavalleypioneer.com
Year Established: 2004
Delivery Methods: Newsstand`Racks
Areas Served - City/County or Portion Thereof, or Zip codes: Spillimacheen, Edgewater, Radium Hot Springs, Invermere, Panorama, Windermere, Fairmont Hot Springs, Canal Flats
Published: Fri
Avg Paid Circ: 499
Avg Free Circ: 6238
Audit By: VAC
Audit Date: 31.03.2016
Personnel: Steve Hubrecht (Reporter); Dean Midyette (Advertising Sales); Emily Rawbon (Graphic design); Nicole Trigg (Ed.); Amanda Murray (Admin.); Eric Elliott (Reporter)
Parent company (for newspapers): Misko Publishing

INVERNESS
THE INVERNESS ORAN

Street Address: 15767 Central Avenue ,
Province: NS
Postal: B0E 1N0
Country: USA
Mailing address: PO Box 100
Mailing city: Inverness
Province: NS
Postal: B0E 1N0
General Phone: (902) 258-2253
General Fax: (902) 258-2632
Editorial e-mail: editor@oran.ca
Primary Website: www.oran.ca
Year Established: 1976
Areas Served - City/County or Portion Thereof, or Zip codes: Inverness
Published: Wed
Avg Paid Circ: 16
Avg Free Circ: 54
Audit By: VAC
Audit Date: 30.09.2016
Personnel: Rankin MacDonald (Ed.)

IQALUIT
NUNATSIAQ NEWS

Street Address: Po Box 8 ,
Province: NU
Postal: X0A 0H0
Country: Canada
Mailing address: PO Box 8
Mailing city: Iqaluit
Province: NU
Postal: X0A 0H0
General Phone: (867) 979-5357
General Fax: (867) 979-4763
Advertising Phone: (800) 263-1452
Advertising Fax: (800) 417-2474
General/National Adv. E-mail: adsnunatsiaqonline.ca
Display Adv. E-mail: ads@nunatsiaqonline.ca
Editorial e-mail: editor@nunatsiaq.com
Primary Website: www.nunatsiaq.com
Year Established: 1973
Areas Served - City/County or Portion Thereof, or Zip codes: Nunavut
Mechanical specifications: Type page 10 5/16 x 13 3/4; E - 6 cols, 1 7/12, between; A - 6 cols, 1 7/12, between; C - 6 cols, 1 7/12, between.
Published: Fri
Avg Free Circ: 5388
Audit By: VAC
Audit Date: 30.06.2016
Personnel: Steven Roberts (Pub.); Bill McConkey (Adv. Mgr.); Jim Bell (Ed.)

IROQUOIS FALLS A
THE ENTERPRISE

Street Address: 441 Main Street ,
Province: ON
Postal: P0K 1G0
Country: Canada
Mailing address: P.O. Box 834
Mailing city: Iroquois Falls A
Province: ON
Postal: P0K 1G0
General Phone: (705) 232-4081
General Fax: (705) 232-4235
General/National Adv. E-mail: irofalls@ntl.sympatico.ca
Display Adv. E-mail: news@theenterprise.ca
Classified Adv. e-mail: news@theenterprise.ca
Editorial e-mail: editor@theenterprise.ca
Year Established: 1963
Delivery Methods: Mail
Areas Served - City/County or Portion Thereof, or Zip codes: Canada
Published: Thur
Avg Paid Circ: 1491
Avg Free Circ: 107
Audit By: CMCA
Audit Date: 31.03.2018
Personnel: William C. Cavell (Pub); Tory Delaurier (Adv. Mgr.)

ITUNA
THE ITUNA NEWS

Street Address: 214 1st Avenue N.e. ,
Province: SK
Postal: S0A 1N0
Country: Canada
Mailing address: PO Box 413
Mailing city: Ituna
Province: SK
Postal: S0A 1N0
General Phone: (306) 795-2412
General Fax: (306) 795-3621
General/National Adv. E-mail: news.ituna@sasktel.net
Primary Website: www.ituna.ca
Areas Served - City/County or Portion Thereof, or Zip codes: Canada
Published: Mon
Avg Paid Circ: 578
Avg Free Circ: 1
Audit By: CMCA
Audit Date: 31.12.2015
Personnel: Bob Johnson (Prodn. Mgr.); Heidi Spilchuk (Ed)

JASPER
THE FITZHUGH

Street Address: 626 Connaught Dr. ,
Province: AB
Postal: T0E 1E0
Country: Canada
Mailing address: PO Box 428
Mailing city: Jasper
Province: AB
Postal: T0E 1E0
General Phone: (780) 852-4888
General Fax: (780) 852-4858
Display Adv. E-mail: advertising@fitzhugh.ca
Classified Adv. e-mail: advertising@fitzhugh.ca
Editorial e-mail: editor@fitzhugh.ca
Primary Website: www.fitzhugh.ca
Year Established: 2005
Areas Served - City/County or Portion Thereof, or Zip codes: Jasper
Published: Thur
Avg Paid Circ: 1156
Avg Free Circ: 3359
Audit By: VAC
Audit Date: 31.07.2016
Personnel: Matt Figueira (Sales); Jeremy Derksen (Pub.); Mishelle Menzies (Prod.); Nicole Veerman (Ed.)
Parent company (for newspapers): Jasper Media Group

JOHNSTOWN

MANOTICK MESSENGER

Street Address: 3201 County Road 2.,
Province: ON
Postal: ON K0E 1T0
Country: Canada
Mailing address: Box 567
Mailing city: Manotick
Province: ON
Postal: K4M 1A5
General Phone: (613) 692-6000
General Fax: (616) 692-3758
Display Adv. E-mail: advert@bellnet.ca
Editorial e-mail: newsfile@bellnet.ca
Primary Website: www.manotickmessenger.on.ca
Areas Served - City/County or Portion Thereof, or Zip codes: Canada
Published: Thur
Avg Free Circ: 9503
Audit By: CMCA
Audit Date: 31.03.2016
Personnel: Jeff Morris (Pub.); Gary Coulombe (Adv. Rep.)

JOLIETTE

ACTION MERCREDI

Street Address: 342, Beaudry Nord,
Province: QC
Postal: J6E 6A6
Country: Canada
Mailing address: rue Beaudry Nord
Mailing city: Joliette
Province: QC
Postal: J6E 6A6
General Phone: (450) 759-3664
General Fax: (450) 759-3190
General/National Adv. E-mail: infolanaudiere@tc.tc
Primary Website: www.laction.com
Areas Served - City/County or Portion Thereof, or Zip codes: Canada
Published: Wed`Sun
Avg Paid Circ: 9
Avg Free Circ: 51680
Audit By: CCAB
Audit Date: 30.09.2012
Personnel: Benoit Bazinet; Benoit Bazinet

L'ACTION

Street Address: 342 Beaudry N.,
Province: QC
Postal: J6E 6A6
Country: Canada
Mailing address: 342 Beaudry N.
Mailing city: Joliette
Province: QC
Postal: J6E 6A6
General Phone: (450) 759-3664
Advertising Phone: (450) 752-0447
Advertising Fax: (450) 759-3190
Editorial Phone: (450) 759-3664
Editorial Fax: (450) 759-3190
General/National Adv. E-mail: infolanaudiere@tc.tc
Display Adv. E-mail: infolanaudiere@tc.tc
Primary Website: www.laction.com
Year Established: 1973
Areas Served - City/County or Portion Thereof, or Zip codes: Canada
Mechanical specifications: Type page 10 1/2 x 14 1/2; E - 8 cols, between.
Published: Wed
Avg Free Circ: 19450
Audit By: CCAB
Audit Date: 31.03.2014
Personnel: Norman Harvey (Sales Rep.); Benoit Bazinet (Pub.); Chantal Proulx (Prodn. Mgr.); Natalie Lariviere (Pres.); Carole Bonin (Mgr.); Sebastien Nadeau (Regl. Dir.); Harvey Norman (Sales Mgr.); Andre Lafreniere (Ed.); Francine Rainville (Ed.); Chantal Troulx (Prodn. Mgr.)
Parent company (for newspapers): Transcontinental Media

LE JOURNAL DE JOLIETTE

Street Address: 1075 Blvd Firestone 5e Etage,
Province: QC
Postal: J6E 6X6
Country: Canada
Mailing address: 1075 Blvd Firestone 5E Etage
Mailing city: Joliette
Province: QC
Postal: J6E 6X6
General Phone: (450) 960-2424
General Fax: (450) 960-2626
Advertising Phone: (450) 960-2424
Advertising Fax: (450) 960-2626
Editorial Phone: (450) 960-2424
Editorial Fax: (450) 960-2626
General/National Adv. E-mail: janique.duguay@quebecormedia.com
Display Adv. E-mail: johanne.roussy2@quebecormedia.com
Editorial e-mail: janique.duguay@quebecormedia.com
Primary Website: www.lejournaldejoliette.ca
Year Established: 1992
Delivery Methods: Mail`Racks
Areas Served - City/County or Portion Thereof, or Zip codes: Canada
Mechanical specifications: Type page 14 1/4 x 10 1/4; E - 8 cols, 1 1/4, between; A - 8 cols, 1 1/4, between; C - 8 cols, 1 1/4, between.
Published: Wed
Avg Free Circ: 60740
Audit By: CCAB
Audit Date: 30.09.2012
Personnel: Janique Duguay (Ed.); Patricia Beaulieu (Regional Director)
Parent company (for newspapers): Quebecor Communications, Inc.

LE REGIONAL

Street Address: 342 Beaugry N. St.,
Province: QC
Postal: J6E 6A6
Country: Canada
Mailing address: 342 Beaugry N. St.
Mailing city: Joliette
Province: QC
Postal: J6E 6A6
General Phone: (450) 759-3664
General Fax: (450) 759-9828
Primary Website: http://www.le-regional.ca/
Published: Wed
Avg Free Circ: 64096
Audit By: ODC
Audit Date: 13.12.2011
Personnel: Benoit Bazinet (Pub.)

KAHNAWAKE

THE EASTERN DOOR

Street Address: P.o. Box 1170,
Province: QC
Postal: J0L 1B0
Country: Canada
Mailing address: P.O. Box 1170
Mailing city: Kahnawake
Province: QC
Postal: J0L 1B0
General Phone: (450) 635-3050
General Fax: (450) 635-8479
General/National Adv. E-mail: reception@easterndoor.com
Primary Website: www.easterndoor.com
Areas Served - City/County or Portion Thereof, or Zip codes: Canada
Published: Fri
Avg Paid Circ: 1020
Avg Free Circ: 81
Audit By: CMCA
Audit Date: 30.06.2016
Personnel: Steve Bonspiel (Ed./Pub.)

KAMLOOPS

KAMLOOPS THIS WEEK

Street Address: 1365b Dalhousie Dr.,
Province: BC
Postal: V2C 5P6
Country: Canada
Mailing address: 1365B Dalhousie Dr.
Mailing city: Kamloops
Province: BC
Postal: V2C 5P6
General Phone: (250) 374-7467
General Fax: (250) 374-1033
Editorial Phone: (250) 374-7467
General/National Adv. E-mail: editor@kamloopsthisweek.com; ktw@kamloopsthisweek.com
Display Adv. E-mail: sales@kamloopsthisweek.com
Editorial e-mail: editor@kamloopsthisweek.com
Primary Website: kamloopsthisweek.com
Year Established: 1988
Delivery Methods: Mail`Newsstand`Carrier`Racks
Areas Served - City/County or Portion Thereof, or Zip codes: Canada
Own Printing Facility?: Y
Published: Tues`Thur`Fri
Avg Paid Circ: 0
Avg Free Circ: 30602
Audit By: CCAB
Audit Date: 23.11.2017
Personnel: Kelly Hall; Chris Foulds (Pub & Ed)
Parent company (for newspapers): Thompson River Publications

KAPUSKASING

THE NORTHERN TIMES

Street Address: 51 Riverside Dr,
Province: ON
Postal: P5N 1A7
Country: Canada
Mailing address: 51 Riverside Dr
Mailing city: Kapuskasing
Province: ON
Postal: P5N 1A7
General Phone: (705) 335-2283 ext. 222
General Fax: (705) 337-1222
Advertising Phone: (705) 335-2283 ext. 230
Advertising Fax: (705) 337-1222
Editorial Phone: (705)-335-2283 ext. 223
Editorial Fax: (705) 337-1222
General/National Adv. E-mail: wayne.major@sunmedia.ca
Display Adv. E-mail: wayne.major@sunmedia.ca
Editorial e-mail: kevin.anderson@sunmedia.ca
Primary Website: www.kapuskasingtimes.com
Year Established: 1961
Delivery Methods: Mail`Newsstand`Carrier
Areas Served - City/County or Portion Thereof, or Zip codes: Canada
Own Printing Facility?: Y
Commercial printers?: Y
Mechanical specifications: Type page 9 x 12.25; E - 9 cols, 1 1/5, 1/8 between; A - 9 cols, 1 1/5, 1/8 between; C - 9 cols, 1 1/5, 1/8 between.
Published: Wed
Avg Paid Circ: 1784
Audit By: CMCA
Audit Date: 28.02.2014
Personnel: Wayne Major (Pub.); Sylvie Genier (Senior Sales Representative); Kevin Anderson (Managing Ed.)
Parent company (for newspapers): Postmedia Network Inc.; Quebecor Communications, Inc.

THE WEEKENDER

Street Address: 51 Riverside Dr,
Province: ON
Postal: P5N 1A7
Country: Canada
Mailing address: 51 Riverside Dr
Mailing city: Kapuskasing
Province: ON
Postal: P5N 1A7
General Phone: (705) 335-2283 ext. 222
General Fax: (705) 337-1222
Advertising Phone: (705) 335-2283 ext. 230
Advertising Fax: (705) 337-1222
Editorial Phone: (705) 335-2283 ext. 223
Editorial Fax: (705) 337-1222
General/National Adv. E-mail: wayne.major@sunmedia.ca
Display Adv. E-mail: wayne.major@sunmedia.ca
Editorial e-mail: kevin.anderson@sunmedia.ca
Primary Website: www.kapuskasingtimes.com
Year Established: 1961
Delivery Methods: Mail`Newsstand`Carrier
Areas Served - City/County or Portion Thereof, or Zip codes: P5N, POL
Mechanical specifications: Type page 9 x 12.25; E - 9 cols, 1 1/5, 1/8 between; A - 9 cols, 1 1/5, 1/8 between; C - 9 cols, 1 1/5, 1/8 between.
Published: Thur
Avg Free Circ: 8486
Audit By: CMCA
Audit Date: 30.06.2016
Personnel: Wayne Major (Pub.); Sylvie Genier (Senior Sales Representative); Kevin Anderson (Managing Ed.)
Parent company (for newspapers): Postmedia Network Inc.; Quebecor Communications, Inc.

KELOWNA

KELOWNA CAPITAL NEWS

Street Address: 2495 Enterprise Way,
Province: BC
Postal: V1X 7K2
Country: Canada
Mailing address: 2495 Enterprise Way
Mailing city: Kelowna
Province: BC
Postal: V1X 7K2
General Phone: (250) 763-3212
General Fax: (250) 862-5275
General/National Adv. E-mail: candy@blackpress.ca
Display Adv. E-mail: karen.hill@blackpress.ca
Classified Adv. e-mail: karen.hill@blackpress.ca
Editorial e-mail: karen.hill@blackpress.ca
Primary Website: kelownacapnews.com
Year Established: 1930
Delivery Methods: Mail`Newsstand`Carrier`Racks
Areas Served - City/County or Portion Thereof, or Zip codes: Canada
Own Printing Facility?: Y
Commercial printers?: Y
Mechanical specifications: Type page 10 x 15; E - 6 cols, 1 31/60, 1/6 between; A - 6 cols, 1 31/60, 1/6 between; C - 6 cols, 1 31/60, 1/6 between.
Published: Tues`Thur`Fri
Avg Free Circ: 42292
Audit By: AAM
Audit Date: 31.03.2019
Personnel: Karen Hill (Pub.); Nigel Lark (Adv. Mgr.); Gary Jhonston (Sales Mgr.); Glenn Beaudry (Circ. Mgr.); Tessa Ringness (Prodn. Mgr.); Kevin Parnell (Mng. Ed.)
Parent company (for newspapers): Black Press Group Ltd.

LAKE COUNTRY CALENDAR

Street Address: 2495 Enterprise Way,
Province: BC
Postal: V1X 7K2
Country: Canada
General Phone: (250) 763-3212
General Fax: (250) 386-2624
Display Adv. E-mail: ads4web@blackpress.ca
Editorial e-mail: newsroom@lakecountrynews.net
Primary Website: www.lakecountrycalendar.net
Year Established: 2001
Areas Served - City/County or Portion Thereof, or Zip codes: Lake Country
Published: Wed
Avg Paid Circ: 306
Avg Free Circ: 3779
Audit By: Sworn/Estimate/Non-Audited
Audit Date: 12.07.2019
Personnel: Barry Gerding (Ed.); Jonathan Lawson (Trafficking Coordinator); Kolby Solinsky (Online Editor); Mark Walker (Director of Sales and Marketing)

Non-Daily Newspapers in Canada

Parent company (for newspapers): Torstar

KENORA

LAKE OF THE WOODS ENTERPRISE

Street Address: 33 Main St. ,
Province: ON
Postal: P9N 3X7
Country: Canada
Mailing address: PO Box 1620
Mailing city: Kenora
Province: ON
Postal: P9N 3X7
General Phone: (807) 468-5555
General Fax: (807) 468-4318
General/National Adv. E-mail: lotwenterprise@bowes.com
Primary Website: www.lotwenterprise.com
Year Established: 2003
Areas Served - City/County or Portion Thereof, or Zip codes: Canada
Own Printing Facility?: Y
Commercial printers?: N
Mechanical specifications: Type page 10 1/4 x 14 1/4; E - 6 cols, 1 9/16, 1/6 between; A - 6 cols, 1 9/16, 1/6 between; C - 6 cols, 1 9/16, 1/6 between.
Published: Thur
Avg Paid Circ: 122
Avg Free Circ: 7771
Audit By: CMCA
Audit Date: 31.08.2015
Personnel: Ted Weiss (Adv. Mgr.); Reg Clayton (Reg. Managing Ed.)
Parent company (for newspapers): Postmedia Network Inc.

KENTVILLE

REGISTER

Street Address: 28 Aberdeen St , Suite 6
Province: NS
Postal: B4N 2N1
Country: Canada
Mailing address: Box 430
Mailing city: Kentville
Province: NS
Postal: B4N 3X4
General Phone: (902) 538-3189
General Fax: (902) 681-0923
Display Adv. E-mail: events@kentvilleadvertiser.ca
Primary Website: http://www.kingscountynews.ca/
Areas Served - City/County or Portion Thereof, or Zip codes: Canada
Own Printing Facility?: Y
Commercial printers?: Y
Mechanical specifications: Type page 12 1/2 x 21; E - 7 cols, 1/8 between; A - 7 cols, 1/8 between; C - 7 cols, 1/8 between.
Published: Thur
Avg Paid Circ: 3392
Avg Free Circ: 47
Audit By: CMCA
Audit Date: 31.07.2014
Personnel: Fred Fiander (Pub.)
Parent company (for newspapers): Transcontinental Media

THE ADVERTISER

Street Address: 28 Aberdeen St , Suite 6
Province: NS
Postal: B4N 2N1
Country: Canada
Mailing address: Box 430
Mailing city: Kentville
Province: NS
Postal: B4N 3X4
General Phone: (902) 681-2121
General Fax: (902) 681-0830
General/National Adv. E-mail: ffiander@thevanguard.ca
Display Adv. E-mail: events@kentvilleadvertiser.ca
Editorial e-mail: ffiander@thevanguard.ca
Primary Website: http://www.kingscountynews.ca/
Areas Served - City/County or Portion Thereof, or Zip codes: Canada
Commercial printers?: Y
Mechanical specifications: Type page 10 1/2 x 15 3/4; E - 6 cols, 1/4, 1/8 between; A - 6 cols, 1/8 between; C - 6 cols, 1/8 between.
Published: Tues
Avg Paid Circ: 3189
Avg Free Circ: 49
Audit By: CMCA
Audit Date: 31.03.2014
Personnel: Fred Fiander (Pub.)
Parent company (for newspapers): Transcontinental Media

KEREMEOS

KEREMEOS REVIEW

Street Address: 605 7th Avenue ,
Province: BC
Postal: V0X 1N0
Country: Canada
Mailing address: Box 130
Mailing city: Keremeos
Province: BC
Postal: V0X 1N0
General Phone: (250) 499-2653
General Fax: (250) 499-2645
General/National Adv. E-mail: dkendall@blackpress.ca
Display Adv. E-mail: publisher@keremeosreview.com
Classified Adv. E-mail: publisher@keremeosreview.com
Primary Website: www.keremeosreview.com
Year Established: 1998
Areas Served - City/County or Portion Thereof, or Zip codes: Keremeos
Published: Thur
Avg Paid Circ: 889
Avg Free Circ: 51
Audit By: VAC
Audit Date: 31.03.2016
Personnel: Don Kendall (Pub.); Tara Bowie (Ed.); Andrea DeMeer (Assoc. Pub.); Sandi Nolan (Adv. Rep.)
Parent company (for newspapers): Torstar

KESWICK

THE GEORGINA ADVOCATE

Street Address: 184 Simcoe Ave. ,
Province: ON
Postal: L4P 2H7
Country: Canada
Mailing address: 184 Simcoe Ave.
Mailing city: Keswick
Province: ON
Postal: L4P 2H7
General Phone: (905) 476-7753
General Fax: (905) 476-5785
General/National Adv. E-mail: admin@georginaadvocate.com
Primary Website: yorkregion.com
Areas Served - City/County or Portion Thereof, or Zip codes: Canada
Own Printing Facility?: Y
Commercial printers?: Y
Mechanical specifications: Type page 10 3/8 x 14; E - 9 cols, 1 1/16, 1/8 between; A - 9 cols, 1 1/16, 1/8 between; C - 9 cols, 1 1/16, 1/8 between.
Published: Thur
Avg Free Circ: 16800
Audit By: CCAB
Audit Date: 31.12.2017
Personnel: Ian Proudfoot (Pub.); Robert Lazurko (Bus. Mgr.); Neil Moore (Adv. Mgr.); Debora Kelly (Ed. in Chief); Tracy Kibble (Ed.)
Parent company (for newspapers): Metroland Media Group Ltd.

KILLAM

THE COMMUNITY PRESS

Street Address: 4919 - 50 St., ,
Province: AB
Postal: T0B 2L0
Country: Canada
Mailing address: PO Box 178
Mailing city: Killam
Province: AB
Postal: T0B 2L0
General Phone: (780) 385-6693
General Fax: (780) 385-3107
Advertising Phone: (780) 385-6693
Display Adv. E-mail: ads@thecommunitypress.com
Classified Adv. e-mail: ads@thecommunitypress.com
Editorial e-mail: news@thecommunitypress.com
Primary Website: www.thecommunitypress.com
Year Established: 1908
Delivery Methods: Mail`Newsstand`Racks
Areas Served - City/County or Portion Thereof, or Zip codes: All of Flagstaff County, Alberta: Total municipalities covered: Bawlf, Daysland, Strome, Killam, Sedgewick, Lougheed, Hardisty, Amisk, Hughenden, Czar, Forestburg, Galahad, Heisler, Alliance
Published: Wed
Avg Paid Circ: 2000
Avg Free Circ: 500
Audit By: CMCA
Audit Date: 31.12.2016
Personnel: Leslie Cholowsky (Editor); Eric Anderson (Publisher/Sales/Production Manager); Jae Robbins (Sales); Ally Anderson (Production Manager)
Parent company (for newspapers): Caribou Publishing

KILLARNEY

KILLARNEY GUIDE

Street Address: 336 Park St. ,
Province: MB
Postal: R0K 1G0
Country: Canada
Mailing address: PO Box 670
Mailing city: Killarney
Province: MB
Postal: R0K 1G0
General Phone: (204) 523-4611
General Fax: (204) 523-4445
General/National Adv. E-mail: news@killarneyguide.ca
Display Adv. E-mail: ads@killarneyguide.ca
Editorial e-mail: news@killarneyguide.ca
Primary Website: http://new.killarneyguide.ca/
Areas Served - City/County or Portion Thereof, or Zip codes: R0K 1G0 and many more
Own Printing Facility?: Y
Commercial printers?: Y
Mechanical specifications: Type page 15 x 14 1/2; E - 6 cols, 1 7/12, 3/4 between; A - 6 cols, 1 7/12, 3/4 between; C - 6 cols, 1 7/12, 3/4 between.
Published: Fri
Avg Paid Circ: 56
Avg Free Circ: 134
Audit By: VAC
Audit Date: 30.06.2016
Personnel: Jay Struth (Ed.); Wendy Johnston (Adv. Mgr.); Iris Krahn (Circ Mgr)

KIMBERLEY

THE KIMBERLEY DAILY BULLETIN

Street Address: 335 Spokane St. ,
Province: BC
Postal: V1A 1Y9
Country: Canada
Province: BC
General Phone: (250) 427-5333
General Fax: (250) 427-5336
Advertising Phone: (250) 427-5333
Advertising Fax: (250) 427-5336
Editorial Phone: (250) 427-5333
Editorial Fax: (250) 427-5336
General/National Adv. E-mail: sueb@blackpress.ca
Editorial e-mail: carolyn.grant@kimberleybulletin.com
Primary Website: www.kimberleybulletin.com
Year Established: 1936
Delivery Methods: Mail`Newsstand`Carrier
Areas Served - City/County or Portion Thereof, or Zip codes: Cranbrook, Kimberley and surrounding areas
Own Printing Facility?: Y
Mechanical specifications: Type page 10.25 x 14.00; E - 6 cols, 2 1/16, 1/8 between; A - 6 cols, 2 1/16, 1/8 between; C - 6 cols, 2 1/16, 1/8 between.
Published: Wed`Thur`Fri
Weekday Frequency: e
Avg Paid Circ: 3350
Avg Free Circ: 3350
Audit By: CMCA
Audit Date: 31.12.2015
Personnel: Zena Williams (Pub.); Carolyn Grant (Ed.); Nicole Koran
Parent company (for newspapers): Black Press Group Ltd.

KINCARDINE

THE INDEPENDENT

Street Address: 840 Queen St. ,
Province: ON
Postal: N2Z 2Z4
Country: Canada
Mailing address: P.O. Box 1240
Mailing city: Kincardine
Province: ON
Postal: N2Z 2Z4
General Phone: (519) 396-3111
General Fax: (519) 396-3899
General/National Adv. E-mail: indepen@bmts.com
Primary Website: www.independent.on.ca
Year Established: 1975
Delivery Methods: Mail`Newsstand
Areas Served - City/County or Portion Thereof, or Zip codes: Canada
Own Printing Facility?: N
Commercial printers?: N
Mechanical specifications: Type page 10 1/4 x 15 1/2; E - 6 cols, 1 9/16, 1/6 between; A - 6 cols, 1 3/4, 1/6 between; C - 6 cols, 1 3/4, 1/6 between.
Published: Wed
Avg Paid Circ: 1906
Avg Free Circ: 82
Audit By: CMCA
Audit Date: 31.12.2015
Personnel: Eric Howald (Ed.)

KINCARDINE

THE KINCARDINE NEWS

Street Address: 719 Queen St. ,
Province: ON
Postal: N2Z 1Z9
Country: Canada
Mailing address: 719 Queen St.
Mailing city: Kincardine
Province: ON
Postal: N2Z 1Z9
General Phone: (519) 396-2963
General Fax: (519) 396-6865
General/National Adv. E-mail: kincardine.sales@sunmedia.ca
Display Adv. E-mail: kincardine.sales@sunmedia.ca
Editorial e-mail: kincardine.news@sunmedia.ca
Primary Website: www.kincardinenews.com
Delivery Methods: Mail`Newsstand`Carrier`Racks
Areas Served - City/County or Portion Thereof, or Zip codes: Canada
Own Printing Facility?: Y
Mechanical specifications: Tabloid 10.333 x 11.4288
Published: Thur
Avg Paid Circ: 59
Avg Free Circ: 5787
Audit By: Sworn/Estimate/Non-Audited

Audit Date: 12.07.2019
Personnel: Troy Patterson (Ed.)
Parent company (for newspapers): Postmedia Network Inc.

KINDERSLEY

KINDERSLEY CLARION

Street Address: 919 Main St. ,
Province: SK
Postal: S0L 1S0
Country: Canada
Mailing address: PO Box 1150
Mailing city: Kindersley
Province: SK
Postal: S0L 1S0
General Phone: (306) 463-4611
General Fax: (306) 463-6505
General/National Adv. E-mail: editor.jamac@gmail.com
Display Adv. E-Mail: ads.jamac@gmail.com
Classified Adv. e-mail: classifieds.jamac@gmail.com
Editorial e-mail: editor.jamac@gmail.com
Primary Website: theclarion.ca
Areas Served - City/County or Portion Thereof, or Zip codes: Kindersley
Own Printing Facility?: Y
Commercial printers?: Y
Mechanical specifications: Type page 13 4/5 x 21 2/5; E - 7 cols, between; A - 7 cols, between; C - 8 cols, between.
Published: Wed
Avg Paid Circ: 1238
Audit By: Sworn/Estimate/Non-Audited
Audit Date: 12.07.2019
Personnel: Stewart Crump (Pub.); Kevin Mcbain (Ed.); Laurie Kelly (Salesperson)
Parent company (for newspapers): Jamac Publishing

LEADER NEWS

Street Address: 919 Main St. ,
Province: SK
Postal: S0L 1S0
Country: Canada
Mailing address: PO Box 1150
Mailing city: Kindersley
Province: SK
Postal: S0L 1S0
General Phone: (306) 463-4611
General Fax: (306) 463-6505
Display Adv. E-mail: editor.jamac@gmail.com
Areas Served - City/County or Portion Thereof, or Zip codes: Canada
Own Printing Facility?: Y
Published: Wed
Avg Paid Circ: 710
Audit By: CMCA
Audit Date: 28.02.2014
Personnel: Stewart Crump (Pub.); Barry Malindine (Adv. Mgr.); Kevin McBain (Ed.)
Parent company (for newspapers): Jamac Publishing

WEST CENTRAL CROSSROADS

Street Address: 919 Main St. ,
Province: SK
Postal: S0L 1S0
Country: Canada
Mailing address: PO Box 1150
Mailing city: Kindersley
Province: SK
Postal: S0L 1S0
General Phone: (306) 463-4611
General Fax: (306) 463-6505
General/National Adv. E-mail: news_jamac@sasktel.net
Own Printing Facility?: Y
Commercial printers?: Y
Published: Fri
Avg Free Circ: 15160
Audit By: CMCA
Audit Date: 30.09.2016
Personnel: Stewart Crump (Pub.); Tim Crump (Ed.)

Parent company (for newspapers): Jamac Publishing

KINGSTON

FRONTENAC EMC

Street Address: 375 Select Drive Unit 14 ,
Province: ON
Postal: K7M 8R1
Country: Canada
General Phone: (613) 546-8884
General Fax: (613) 546-3607
Primary Website: www.emcfrontenac.ca
Areas Served - City/County or Portion Thereof, or Zip codes: Canada
Published: Thur
Avg Free Circ: 8639
Audit By: CMCA
Audit Date: 28.02.2013
Personnel: Duncan Weir (Pub.)

KINGSTON HERITAGE EMC

Street Address: 375 Select Dr. ,
Province: ON
Postal: K7M 8R1
Country: Canada
Mailing address: 375 Select Dr.
Mailing city: Kingston
Province: ON
Postal: K7M 8R1
General Phone: (613) 546-8885
Display Adv. E-mail: kdillon@theheritageemc.ca
Primary Website: www.insideottawavalley.com
Areas Served - City/County or Portion Thereof, or Zip codes: Canada
Published: Thur
Avg Free Circ: 45862
Audit By: CMCA
Audit Date: 30.06.2016
Personnel: Donna Glasspoole (Gen. Mgr.); Kate Lawrenence (Sales Coordinator)
Parent company (for newspapers): Metroland Media Group Ltd.

KINGSTON THIS WEEK

Street Address: 18 St. Remy Place ,
Province: ON
Postal: K7M 6C4
Country: Canada
Mailing address: 18 St. Remy Place
Mailing city: Kingston
Province: ON
Postal: K7M 6C4
General Phone: (613) 389-7400
General Fax: (613) 389-7507
General/National Adv. E-mail: news@kingstonthisweek.com
Primary Website: www.kingstonthisweek.com
Areas Served - City/County or Portion Thereof, or Zip codes: Canada
Mechanical specifications: Type page 10 3/8 x 12 4/7; E - 9 cols, 1 1/16, between; A - 9 cols, 1 1/16, between; C - 9 cols, 1 1/16, between.
Published: Thur
Avg Free Circ: 48840
Audit By: CMCA
Audit Date: 31.03.2016
Personnel: Ron Drillen (Gen. Mgr.); Tracy Weaver (Mng. Ed.); Lynn Rees Lambert (News Ed.); Rob Mooy (Photo Ed.); Liza Nelson
Parent company (for newspapers): Quebecor Communications, Inc.

THE FRONTENAC GAZETTE

Street Address: 375 Select Dr., Ste. 14 ,
Province: ON
Postal: K7M 8R1
Country: Canada
Mailing address: 375 Select Dr., Ste. 14
Mailing city: Kingston
Province: ON
Postal: K7M 8R1
General Phone: (613) 546-8885

General Fax: (613) 546-3607
General/National Adv. E-mail: kingston@theritageemc.ca
Primary Website: www.whatsonkingston.com
Areas Served - City/County or Portion Thereof, or Zip codes: Canada
Published: Thur
Avg Free Circ: 8220
Audit By: CMCA
Audit Date: 30.06.2016
Personnel: Darryl Cembal (Pub.)
Parent company (for newspapers): Metroland Media Group Ltd.

THE HERITAGE

Street Address: 375 Select Dr., Unit 14 ,
Province: ON
Postal: K7M 8R1
Country: Canada
Mailing address: 375 Select Dr., Unit 14
Mailing city: Kingston
Province: ON
Postal: K7M 8R1
General Phone: (613) 546-8885
General Fax: (613) 546-3607
General/National Adv. E-mail: kingston@theheritageemc.ca
Primary Website: www.kingstonregion.com/kingstonregion
Areas Served - City/County or Portion Thereof, or Zip codes: Canada
Mechanical specifications: Type page 10 1/4 x 15; E - 6 cols, 1 9/16, 1/6 between; A - 6 cols, 1 9/16, 1/6 between; C - 6 cols, 1 9/16, 1/6 between.
Published: Thur
Avg Paid Circ: 12
Avg Free Circ: 38833
Audit By: Sworn/Estimate/Non-Audited
Audit Date: 12.07.2019
Personnel: Darryl Cembal (Ed.)

KINGSVILLE

THE KINGSVILLE REPORTER

Street Address: 17 Chestnut St. ,
Province: ON
Postal: N9Y 1J9
Country: Canada
Mailing address: 17 Chestnut St.
Mailing city: Kingsville
Province: ON
Postal: N9Y 1J9
General Phone: (519) 733-2211
General Fax: (519) 733-6464
General/National Adv. E-mail: kingsvillereporter@canwest.com
Display Adv. E-mail: rsims@postmedia.com
Delivery Methods: Mail`Newsstand
Areas Served - City/County or Portion Thereof, or Zip codes: Canada
Own Printing Facility?: Y
Commercial printers?: Y
Mechanical specifications: Type page 10 1/4 x 15; E - 6 cols, 1 5/9, between; A - 6 cols, 1 5/9, between; C - 6 cols, 1 5/9, between.
Published: Tues
Avg Paid Circ: 1107
Avg Free Circ: 7
Audit By: CMCA
Audit Date: 30.06.2016
Personnel: Rita Sims (Adv. Mgr.); Nelson Santos (News Ed.); Joyce Pearce (Reception); Steve l'Anson (Associate News Editor)
Parent company (for newspapers): Postmedia Network Inc.

KIPLING

KIPLING CITIZEN

Street Address: #4 - 207 - 6th Avenue ,
Province: SK
Postal: S0G 2S0
Country: Canada
Mailing address: PO Box 329
Mailing city: Kipling
Province: SK

Postal: S0G 2S0
General Phone: (306) 736-2535
General Fax: (306) 736-8445
Advertising Phone: (306) 736-2535
Advertising Fax: (306) 736-8445
Editorial Phone: (306) 736-2535
Editorial Fax: (306) 736-8445
General/National Adv. E-mail: thecitizen@sasktel.net
Display Adv. E-mail: thecitizen@sasktel.net
Classified Adv. e-mail: thecitizen@sasktel.net
Editorial e-mail: thecitizen@sasktel.net
Year Established: 1936
Delivery Methods: Mail`Newsstand
Areas Served - City/County or Portion Thereof, or Zip codes: Canada
Own Printing Facility?: N
Commercial printers?: N
Mechanical specifications: Type page 9.83 x 15.7; 6 cols, .15 between columns
Published: Fri
Avg Paid Circ: 730
Avg Free Circ: 13
Audit By: CMCA
Audit Date: 03.11.2017
Personnel: Laura Kish (Gen. Mgr.); Connie Schwalm (Reporter); Sean Choo-Foo (Sales Representative)
Parent company (for newspapers): Glacier Media Group

KIRKLAND LAKE

NORTHERN NEWS THIS WEEK (KIRKLAND LAKE)

Street Address: Eight Duncan Ave. ,
Province: ON
Postal: P2N 3L4
Country: Canada
Mailing address: PO Box 1030
Mailing city: Kirkland Lake
Province: ON
Postal: P2N 3L4
General Phone: (705) 567-5321
General Fax: (705) 567-6162
Advertising Fax: (705) 567-5377
Editorial Fax: (705) 567-6162
General/National Adv. E-mail: news@northernnews.ca
Display Adv. E-mail: display@northernnews.ca
Primary Website: www.northernnews.ca
Mechanical specifications: Type page 13 x 21 1/2; E - 6 cols, 2 1/16, 1/8 between; A - 6 cols, 2 1/16, 1/8 between; C - 9 cols, 1 1/2, 1/8 between.
Published: Mon`Wed`Fri
Weekday Frequency: e
Saturday Frequency: e
Avg Paid Circ: 3122
Audit By: Sworn/Estimate/Non-Audited
Audit Date: 12.07.2019
Personnel: Tony Howell (Circ. Mgr.); Joe O'Grady (Managing Ed.); Jeff Wilkinson (Sports Ed.); Lisa Wilson (Adv. Dir.)
Parent company (for newspapers): Postmedia Network Inc.; Quebecor Communications, Inc.

KITCHENER

KITCHENER POST

Street Address: 630 Riverbend Dr Unit 104 , Unit 104
Province: ON
Postal: N2K 3S2
Mailing address: 630 Riverbend Dr Unit 104
Mailing city: Kitchener
Province: ON
Postal: N2K 3S2
General Phone: (519) 579-7166
General Fax: (519) 579-2029
Primary Website: www.kitchenerpost.ca
Areas Served - City/County or Portion Thereof, or Zip codes: Canada
Published: Fri
Avg Free Circ: 58770
Audit By: CMCA
Audit Date: 30.06.2016
Personnel: Bob Vrbanac (Managing Ed.)

Non-Daily Newspapers in Canada

KITIMAT

NORTHERN SENTINEL - KITIMAT

Street Address: 626 Enterprise Ave. ,
Province: BC
Postal: V8C 2E4
Country: Canada
Mailing address: 626 Enterprise Ave.
Mailing city: Kitimat
Province: BC
Postal: V8C 2E4
General Phone: (250) 632-6144
General Fax: (250) 639-9373
General/National Adv. E-mail: publisher@northernsentinel.com
Display Adv. E-mail: advertising@northernsentinel.com
Primary Website: www.northernsentinel.com
Year Established: 1954
Delivery Methods: Mail`Newsstand`Carrier`Racks
Areas Served - City/County or Portion Thereof, or Zip codes: Canada
Own Printing Facility?: Y
Commercial printers?: Y
Mechanical specifications: Type page 10 1/4 x 14 1/2; E - 7 cols, 1 7/12, between; A - 7 cols, 1 7/12, between; C - 7 cols, 1 7/12, between.
Published: Wed
Avg Paid Circ: 439
Avg Free Circ: 248
Audit By: VAC
Audit Date: 31.03.2016
Personnel: Louisa Genzale (Publisher); Sarah Campbell; Devyn Ens (Editor/Reporter); Johnsen Misty (Circulation)
Parent company (for newspapers): Black Press Group Ltd.

KNOWLTON

BROME COUNTY NEWS

Street Address: 5 B Rue Victoria ,
Province: QC
Postal: J0E 1V0
Country: Canada
Mailing address: 5 B Rue Victoria
Mailing city: Knowlton
Province: QC
Postal: J0E 1V0
General Phone: (450) 242-1188
General Fax: (450) 243-5155
General/National Adv. E-mail: newsroom@sherbrookerecord.com
Areas Served - City/County or Portion Thereof, or Zip codes: J0E 1V0
Own Printing Facility?: Y
Published: Tues
Avg Free Circ: 10000
Audit By: Sworn/Estimate/Non-Audited
Audit Date: 12.07.2019
Personnel: Ken Wells (Pub.); Sharon McCully (Ed.); Richard Lessard (Prodn. Mgr.)

LA MALBAIE

HEBDO CHARLEVOISIEN

Street Address: 53, Rue John-nairne Ste. 100 ,
Province: QC
Postal: G5A 1L8
Country: Canada
Mailing address: 53, rue John-Nairne
Mailing city: La Malbaie
Province: QC
Postal: G5A 1L8
General Phone: (418) 665-1299
General Fax: (418) 453-3249
General/National Adv. E-mail: journal@hebdocharlevoisien.ca
Display Adv. E-mail: hebdo@charlevoix.net
Primary Website: www.charlevoixendirect.com
Areas Served - City/County or Portion Thereof, or Zip codes: La Malbaie

Parent company (for newspapers): Metroland Media Group Ltd.
Published: Wed
Avg Paid Circ: 30
Avg Free Circ: 14487
Audit By: CCAB
Audit Date: 30.09.2012
Personnel: Charles Warren

PLEIN JOUR DE CHARLEVOIX

Street Address: 249 Rue John Nairne ,
Province: QC
Postal: G5B 1M4
Country: Canada
Mailing address: 249 rue John Nairne
Mailing city: La Malbaie
Province: QC
Postal: G5B 1M4
General Phone: (418) 665-6121
General Fax: (418) 665-3105
General/National Adv. E-mail: redaction.pjc@hebdosquebecor.com
Own Printing Facility?: Y
Commercial printers?: Y
Published: Fri
Avg Free Circ: 15438
Audit By: Sworn/Estimate/Non-Audited
Audit Date: 12.07.2019
Personnel: Richard Harley (Mng. Ed.)
Parent company (for newspapers): Quebecor Communications, Inc.

LA RONGE

THE NORTHERNER

Street Address: 715 La Ronge Ave. ,
Province: SK
Postal: S0J 1L0
Country: Canada
Mailing address: PO Box 1350
Mailing city: La Ronge
Province: SK
Postal: S0J 1L0
General Phone: (306) 425-3344
General Fax: (306) 425-2827
General/National Adv. E-mail: ads.northerner@sasktel.net
Display Adv. E-mail: ads.northerner@sasktel.net
Classified Adv. e-mail: ads.northerner@sasktel.net
Editorial e-mail: northerner@sasktel.net
Year Established: 1975
Delivery Methods: Mail`Newsstand
Areas Served - City/County or Portion Thereof, or Zip codes: Canada
Own Printing Facility?: N
Commercial printers?: N
Mechanical specifications: Type page 10.25 x 15.75; E - 6 cols, 1 11/12, 1/6 between; A - 6 cols, 1 11/12, 1/6 between; C - 6 cols, 1 11/12, 1/6 between.
Published: Thur
Avg Paid Circ: 198
Avg Free Circ: 136
Audit By: CMCA
Audit Date: 31.07.2014
Personnel: Debra Parkinson (Office Mgr./Circ.)

LA TUQUE

L'ECHO DE LA TUQUE

Street Address: 324 St. Joseph St. ,
Province: QC
Postal: G9X 1L2
Country: Canada
Mailing address: 324 St. Joseph St.
Mailing city: La Tuque
Province: QC
Postal: G9X 1L2
General Phone: (819) 523-6141
General Fax: (819) 523-6143
General/National Adv. E-mail: redaction_latuque@tc.tc
Editorial e-mail: redaction_latuque@tc.tc
Primary Website: www.lechodelatuque.com
Areas Served - City/County or Portion Thereof, or Zip codes: Canada
Published: Wed
Avg Paid Circ: 0

Avg Free Circ: 6406
Audit By: CCAB
Audit Date: 31.03.2014
Personnel: Michele Scarpeno (Dir.)
Parent company (for newspapers): Reseau Select/ Select Network; Transcontinental Media

LABRADOR CITY

THE AURORA

Street Address: 500 Vanier Ave. ,
Province: NL
Postal: A2V 2K7
Mailing address: PO Box 423
Mailing city: Labrador City
Province: NL
Postal: A2V 2K7
General Phone: (709) 944-2957
General Fax: (709) 944-2958
General/National Adv. E-mail: editor@theaurora.ca
Editorial e-mail: mmurphy@optipress.ca
Primary Website: www.theaurora.ca
Year Established: 1969
Areas Served - City/County or Portion Thereof, or Zip codes: Canada
Own Printing Facility?: Y
Commercial printers?: Y
Mechanical specifications: Type page 10 1/4 x 16; E - 9 cols, 1 7/8, 1/8 between; A - 10 cols, 1/8 between; C - 8 cols, 1 1/8, 1/8 between.
Published: Mon
Avg Paid Circ: 1001
Audit By: VAC
Audit Date: 30.06.2016
Personnel: Shawn Woodford (Pub.); Michelle Stewart (Ed.)
Parent company (for newspapers): Transcontinental Media

LAC ETCHEMIN

LA VOIX DU SUD

Street Address: 1516 A. Rt. 277 ,
Province: QC
Postal: G0R 1S0
Country: Canada
Mailing address: 1516 A. Rt. 277
Mailing city: Lac Etchemin
Province: QC
Postal: G0R 1S0
General Phone: (418) 625-7471
General Fax: (418) 625-5200
General/National Adv. E-mail: caroline.gilbert@tc.tc
Display Adv. E-mail: caroline.gilbert@tc.tc
Classified Adv. e-mail: caroline.gilbert@tc.tc
Editorial e-mail: caroline.gilbert@tc.tc
Primary Website: www.lavoixdusud.com
Areas Served - City/County or Portion Thereof, or Zip codes: Canada
Published: Wed
Avg Paid Circ: 14
Avg Free Circ: 27758
Audit By: CCAB
Audit Date: 31.03.2014
Personnel: Caroline Gilbert (Ed.); Rock Bizier (Prodn. Mgr.)
Parent company (for newspapers): Transcontinental Media

LAC LA BICHE

LAC LA BICHE POST

Street Address: 10211 101st St. ,
Province: AB
Postal: T0A 2C0
Country: Canada
Mailing address: PO Box 508
Mailing city: Lac La Biche
Province: AB
Postal: T0A 2C0
General Phone: (780) 623-4221
General Fax: (780) 623-4230
General/National Adv. E-mail: post@llb.greatwest.ca

Display Adv. E-mail: iwolstenholme@llb.greatwest.ca
Editorial e-mail: rmckinley@llb.greatwest.ca
Primary Website: www.laclabichepost.com
Year Established: 1966
Delivery Methods: Mail`Newsstand
Areas Served - City/County or Portion Thereof, or Zip codes: T0A 2C0 T0A 2C1 T0A 2T0 T0A 1Z0 Edmonton, Calgary numerous
Own Printing Facility?: Y
Commercial printers?: Y
Mechanical specifications: all inserts must be folded to a letter -sized final size.
Published: Tues
Avg Paid Circ: 1123
Avg Free Circ: 1
Audit By: VAC
Audit Date: 31.03.2016
Personnel: Robert McKinley (Pub.); Iona Wolstenholme (Sales Mgr.)
Parent company (for newspapers): Glacier Media Group; Great West Newspapers LP

LAC MEGANTIC

L'ECHO DE FRONTENAC

Street Address: 5040 Blvd. Des Veterans ,
Province: QC
Postal: G6B 2G5
Country: Canada
Mailing address: 5040 Blvd. des Veterans
Mailing city: Lac Megantic
Province: QC
Postal: G6B 2G5
General Phone: (819) 583-1630
General Fax: (819) 583-1124
General/National Adv. E-mail: hebdo@echodefrontenac.com
Primary Website: echodefrontenac.com
Areas Served - City/County or Portion Thereof, or Zip codes: Canada
Mechanical specifications: Type page 14 1/4 x 10 1/8; E - 5 cols, between; A - 8 cols, between; C - 8 cols, between.
Published: Fri
Avg Paid Circ: 3904
Avg Free Circ: 3707
Audit By: CCAB
Audit Date: 31.12.2018
Personnel: Michel Pilotte (Sales Dir.); Gaetan Poulin (Ed.); Suzanne Poulin (Asst. Ed.); Remi Tremblay (Mng. Ed.)
Parent company (for newspapers): Reseau Select/ Select Network

LACHUTE

L'ARGENTEUIL

Street Address: 52 Main St. ,
Province: QC
Postal: J8H 3A8
Country: Canada
Mailing address: PO Box 220
Mailing city: Lachute
Province: QC
Postal: J8H 3A8
General Phone: (450) 562-2494
General Fax: (450) 562-1434
General/National Adv. E-mail: argenteuil@eap.on.ca
Display Adv. E-mail: francois.leblanc@eap.on.ca
Primary Website: www.largenteuil.ca
Areas Served - City/County or Portion Thereof, or Zip codes: Canada
Own Printing Facility?: Y
Commercial printers?: Y
Published: Wed
Avg Paid Circ: 39
Avg Free Circ: 16540
Audit By: ODC
Audit Date: 13.12.2011
Personnel: Bertrand Castonguay (Pres.); Roger Duplantie (Dir. Gen.); Francois Leblanc (Dir., Adv.); Alain Morris (Circ. Mgr.); Robert Savard (Ed.)
Parent company (for newspapers): Reseau Select/Select Network; Cie d'Edition Andre Paquette, Inc.

LACOMBE

LACOMBE GLOBE

Street Address: 5019-50 St. ,
Province: AB
Postal: T4L 1W8
Country: Canada
Mailing address: 5019-50 St.
Mailing city: Lacombe
Province: AB
Postal: T4L 1W8
General Phone: (403) 782-3498
General Fax: (403) 782-5850
Display Adv. E-mail: ngoetz@postmedia.com
Editorial e-mail: ssswenson@postmedia.com
Primary Website: www.lacombeglobe.com
Year Established: 1900
Areas Served - City/County or Portion Thereof, or Zip codes: Canada
Commercial printers?: Y
Mechanical specifications: Type page 13 x 21; E - 6 cols, 2 1/12, 1/6 between; A - 6 cols, 2 1/12, 1/6 between; C - 6 cols, 2 1/12, 1/6 between.
Published: Thur
Avg Paid Circ: 1507
Avg Free Circ: 8604
Audit By: VAC
Audit Date: 31.12.2015
Personnel: Nick Goetz (Adv. Dir); Sarah Swenson (Ed)
Parent company (for newspapers): Postmedia Network Inc.; Quebecor Communications, Inc.

LADNER

SOUTH DELTA LEADER

Street Address: 5008 47a Ave ,
Province: BC
Postal: V4K 1T8
Mailing address: 5008 47A Ave
Mailing city: Ladner
Province: BC
Postal: V4K 1T8
General Phone: (604) 948-3640
General Fax: (604) 943-8619
General/National Adv. E-mail: publisher@southdeltaleader.com
Display Adv. E-mail: dhamilton@delta-optimist.com
Classified Adv. e-mail: classifieds@van.net
Editorial e-mail: tmurphy@delta-optimist.com
Primary Website: www.southdeltaleader.com
Year Established: 1999
Delivery Methods: Carrier`Racks
Areas Served - City/County or Portion Thereof, or Zip codes: Canada
Published: Fri
Published Other: Delta Leader, 30,000 - all of Delta, Monthly - last Friday of each monthly
Avg Paid Circ: 0
Avg Free Circ: 14313
Audit By: CCAB
Audit Date: 30.09.2012
Personnel: Alvin Brouwer (Pub); Ted Murphy (Ed); Dave Hamilton (Gen Mgr/Adv. Sales)

LADYSMITH

THE LADYSMITH CHRONICLE

Street Address: 940 Oyster Bay Drive ,
Province: BC
Postal: V9G 1A3
Country: Canada
Mailing address: PO Box 400
Mailing city: Ladysmith
Province: BC
Postal: V9G 1A3
General Phone: (250) 245-2277
General Fax: (250) 245-2230
Advertising Phone: (250) 245-2277
Editorial Phone: (250) 245-2277
General/National Adv. E-mail: editor@ladysmithchronicle.com
Display Adv. E-mail: publisher@ladysmithchronicle.com
Editorial e-mail: editor@ladysmithchronicle.com
Primary Website: www.ladysmithchronicle.com
Year Established: 1908
Delivery Methods: Mail`Newsstand`Carrier`Racks
Areas Served - City/County or Portion Thereof, or Zip codes: Canada
Own Printing Facility?: Y
Mechanical specifications: Type page 10 1/4 x 14 1/2; E - 6 cols, 1 5/8, 3/16 between; A - 6 cols, 1 5/8, 3/16 between; C - 6 cols, 1 5/8, 3/16 between.
Published: Tues
Avg Paid Circ: 1348
Avg Free Circ: 3678
Audit By: VAC
Audit Date: 30.09.2016
Personnel: Douglas Kent (Prodn. Mgr.); Teresa McKinley (Pub); Craig Spence (Ed)
Parent company (for newspapers): Black Press Group Ltd.

LAKEFIELD

LAKEFIELD HERALD

Street Address: 74 Bridge St. ,
Province: ON
Postal: K0L 2H0
Country: Canada
Mailing address: PO Box 1000
Mailing city: Lakefield
Province: ON
Postal: K0L 2H0
General Phone: (705) 652-6594
General Fax: (705) 652-6912
General/National Adv. E-mail: info@lakefieldherald.com
Display Adv. E-mail: ads@lakefieldherald.com
Editorial e-mail: editor@lakefieldherald.com
Primary Website: www.lakefieldherald.com
Areas Served - City/County or Portion Thereof, or Zip codes: Canada
Published: Fri
Avg Paid Circ: 937
Avg Free Circ: 39
Audit By: Sworn/Estimate/Non-Audited
Audit Date: 12.07.2019
Personnel: Terry McQuitty (Owner)

LAMONT

THE LAMONT LEADER

Street Address: 5038 50 Ave. ,
Province: AB
Postal: T0B 2R0
Country: Canada
Mailing address: PO Box 1079
Mailing city: Lamont
Province: AB
Postal: T0B 2R0
General Phone: (780) 895-2780
General Fax: (780) 895-2705
Display Adv. E-mail: lmtleader@gmail.com
Editorial e-mail: lamontnews@gmail.com
Primary Website: lamontleader.com
Year Established: 2005
Areas Served - City/County or Portion Thereof, or Zip codes: Lamont, AB.
Published: Tues
Avg Paid Circ: 0
Avg Free Circ: 2606
Audit By: VAC
Audit Date: 30.06.2016
Personnel: Kerry Anderson (Pub.); Michelle Pinon (Ed.)
Parent company (for newspapers): Caribou Pub.

LANARK

THE LANARK ERA

Street Address: 66 George St. ,
Province: ON
Postal: K0G 1K0
Country: Canada
Mailing address: PO Box 40
Mailing city: Lanark
Province: ON
Postal: K0G 1K0
General Phone: (613) 259-2220
General/National Adv. E-mail: lanarkera@primus.ca
Display Adv. E-mail: kristy.gibson@lanarkera.com
Classified Adv. e-mail: lanarkera@primus.ca
Editorial e-mail: gena.gibson@lanarkera.com
Primary Website: www.lanarkera.com
Year Established: 1895
Delivery Methods: Mail`Newsstand
Areas Served - City/County or Portion Thereof, or Zip codes: Lanark Highlands Township
Commercial printers?: N
Published: Tues
Avg Paid Circ: 888
Avg Free Circ: 27
Audit By: CMCA
Audit Date: 31.08.2016
Personnel: Gena Gibson (Ed./Owner)

LANGENBURG

LANGENBURG FOUR-TOWN JOURNAL

Street Address: 102 Carl Ave. ,
Province: SK
Postal: S0A 2A0
Country: Canada
Mailing address: PO Box 68
Mailing city: Langenburg
Province: SK
Postal: S0A 2A0
General Phone: (306) 743-2617
General Fax: (316) 743-2299
General/National Adv. E-mail: fourtown@sasktel.net
Areas Served - City/County or Portion Thereof, or Zip codes: Canada
Published: Wed
Avg Paid Circ: 1199
Audit By: CMCA
Audit Date: 31.03.2016
Personnel: Bill Johnston (Editor/Publisher)

LANGLEY

LANGLEY ADVANCE

Street Address: 6375 202 St. , Suite 112
Province: BC
Postal: V2Y 1N1
Country: Canada
Mailing address: 6375 202 St., Ste. 112
Mailing city: Langley
Province: BC
Postal: V2Y 1N1
General Phone: (604) 534-8641
General Fax: (604) 534-3383
General/National Adv. E-mail: rmcadams@langleyadvance.com
Display Adv. E-mail: peggy.obrien@langleyadvance.com
Editorial e-mail: rhooper@langleyadvance.com
Primary Website: www.langleyadvance.com
Year Established: 1931
Delivery Methods: Carrier
Areas Served - City/County or Portion Thereof, or Zip codes: Canada
Own Printing Facility?: Y
Commercial printers?: Y
Mechanical specifications: Type page 11 x 14; E - 6 cols, 1 9/16, between; A - 6 cols, 1 9/16, between; C - 7 cols, 1 3/8, between.
Published: Tues`Thur
Avg Paid Circ: 0
Avg Free Circ: 27538
Audit By: AAM
Audit Date: 31.03.2019
Personnel: Lisa Farquharson (Pub); Peggy O'Brien (Sales Mgr.); Roxanne Hooper (Ed)
Parent company (for newspapers): Black Press Group Ltd.

LANGLEY TIMES

Street Address: 20258 Fraser Hwy. ,
Province: BC
Postal: V3A 4E6
Country: Canada
Mailing address: 20258 Fraser Hwy.
Mailing city: Langley
Province: BC
Postal: V3A 4E6
General Phone: (604) 533-4157
General Fax: (604) 533-4623
General/National Adv. E-mail: newsroom@langleytimes.com
Display Adv. E-mail: admanager@langleytimes.com
Editorial e-mail: newsroom@langleytimes.com
Primary Website: www.langleytimes.com
Year Established: 1982
Delivery Methods: Carrier
Areas Served - City/County or Portion Thereof, or Zip codes: Canada
Own Printing Facility?: N
Commercial printers?: N
Published: Tues`Thur
Avg Free Circ: 28417
Audit By: AAM
Audit Date: 31.03.2019
Personnel: Kelly Myers (Sales Mgr); Lisa Farquharson (Pub); Brenda Anderson (Ed)
Parent company (for newspapers): Black Press Group Ltd.

LANIGAN

LANIGAN ADVISOR

Street Address: 42 Main Street ,
Province: SK
Postal: S0K 2M0
Country: Canada
Mailing address: P.O. Box 1029
Mailing city: Lanigan
Province: SK
Postal: S0K 2M0
General Phone: (306) 365-2010
General Fax: (306) 365-3388
General/National Adv. E-mail: laniganadvisor@sasktel.net
Areas Served - City/County or Portion Thereof, or Zip codes: Canada
Published: Mon
Avg Paid Circ: 828
Avg Free Circ: 15
Audit By: CMCA
Audit Date: 31.01.2016
Personnel: Linda Mallett (Publisher/Editor)

LASALLE

LA VOIX POPULAIRE

Street Address: 420 La Fleur St. ,
Province: QC
Postal: H8R 3H6
Country: Canada
Mailing address: 420 La Fleur St.
Mailing city: Lasalle
Province: QC
Postal: H8R 3H6
General Phone: (514) 363-5656
General Fax: (514) 363-3895
General/National Adv. E-mail: patriciaan.beaulieu@transcontinental.ca
Primary Website: www.lavoixpopulaire.com
Areas Served - City/County or Portion Thereof, or Zip codes: Canada
Published: Thur
Avg Paid Circ: 4
Avg Free Circ: 29159
Audit By: CCAB
Audit Date: 31.03.2014
Personnel: Louis Mercier (Ed.); Yannick Pinel (Ed. In Chief.)
Parent company (for newspapers): Transcontinental Media

MESSAGER DE LASALLE

Street Address: 420 Lafleur Ave , Suite 303
Province: QC
Postal: H9S 5T8

Non-Daily Newspapers in Canada

III-467

Country: Canada
Mailing address: 420 Lafleur Ave
Mailing city: Lasalle
Province: QC
Postal: H9S 5T8
General Phone: (514) 636-7314
Areas Served - City/County or Portion Thereof, or Zip codes: Canada
Published: Thur
Avg Paid Circ: 3
Avg Free Circ: 32736
Audit By: CCAB
Audit Date: 31.03.2014
Personnel: Patricia Ann Beaulieu

LAVAL

COURRIER-LAVAL

Street Address: 2700 Francis Hughes Ave., Ste. 200 ,
Province: QC
Postal: H7S 2B9
Country: Canada
Mailing address: 2700 Francis Hughes Ave., Ste. 200
Mailing city: Laval
Province: QC
Postal: H7S 2B9
General Phone: (450) 667-4360
General Fax: (450) 667-0845
General/National Adv. E-mail: redactionlaval@tc.tc
Primary Website: www.courrierlaval.com
Year Established: 1945
Areas Served - City/County or Portion Thereof, or Zip codes: Canada
Mechanical specifications: Type page 11 3/8 x 15; E - 8 cols, between; A - 8 cols, between.
Published: Wed`Sat
Avg Paid Circ: 8
Avg Free Circ: 12788
Audit By: CCAB
Audit Date: 30.09.2012
Personnel: Janique Duguay (Sales Dir.); Rejean Monette (Regl. Dir.); Claude Labelle (Ed.); Martine Cotton (Prodn. Mgr.)
Parent company (for newspapers): Transcontinental Media

L'HEBDO DE LAVAL

Street Address: 3221 Hwy. 440 W., Ste. 209 ,
Province: QC
Postal: H7P 5P2
Country: Canada
Mailing address: 3221 Hwy. 440 W., Ste. 209
Mailing city: Laval
Province: QC
Postal: H7P 5P2
General Phone: (450) 681-4948
General Fax: (450) 681-2824
Published: Fri
Avg Free Circ: 84860
Audit By: Sworn/Estimate/Non-Audited
Audit Date: 12.07.2019
Personnel: Marc Ouellette (Gen. Mgr.); Francois Forget (Mng. Ed.)

MISSIONS ETRANGERES

Street Address: Place Juge-desnoyers ,
Province: QC
Postal: H7G 1A5
Country: Canada
Mailing address: place Juge-Desnoyers
Mailing city: Laval
Province: QC
Postal: H7G 1A5
General Phone: (450) 667-4190
Published: Wed
Avg Paid Circ: 6585
Avg Free Circ: 5647
Audit By: ODC
Audit Date: 14.12.2011
Personnel: Bertrand Roy

NOUVELLES PARC EXTENSION

NEWS

Street Address: 3860 Notre-dame Blvd. , Suite 304
Province: QC
Postal: H7V 1S1
Country: Canada
Mailing address: 3860 Notre-Dame Blvd.
Mailing city: Laval
Province: QC
Postal: H7V 1S1
General Phone: (450) 978-9999
General Fax: (450) 687-6330
Display Adv. E-mail: sales@the-news.ca
Editorial e-mail: editor@the-news.ca
Primary Website: www.px-news.com
Year Established: 1993
Delivery Methods: Carrier`Racks
Areas Served - City/County or Portion Thereof, or Zip codes: H3N
Mechanical specifications: Type page 10 1/4 x 14 1/4; E - 8 cols, 1 1/6, 1/6 between; A - 8 cols, 1 1/6, 1/6 between; C - 8 cols, 1 1/6, 1/6 between.
Published: Fri
Published Other: Every other sat
Avg Paid Circ: 0
Avg Free Circ: 9403
Audit By: Sworn/Estimate/Non-Audited
Audit Date: 12.07.2019
Personnel: George S. Guzmas (Co-Publisher); George Bakoyannis (Prodn. Mgr.)

THE LAVAL NEWS

Street Address: 3860 Notre-dame Blvd. , Suite 304
Province: QC
Postal: H7V 1S1
Country: Canada
Mailing address: 3860 Notre-Dame Blvd.
Mailing city: Laval
Province: QC
Postal: H7V 1S1
General Phone: (450) 978-9999
General Fax: (450) 687-6330
General/National Adv. E-mail: editor@the-news.ca
Display Adv. E-mail: sales@the-news.ca
Editorial e-mail: editor@the-news.ca
Primary Website: www.lavalnews.com
Year Established: 1993
Delivery Methods: Carrier`Racks
Areas Served - City/County or Portion Thereof, or Zip codes: Canada
Mechanical specifications: Type page 10 3/10 x 14 1/4; E - 8 cols, 1 1/6, 1/6 between; A - 8 cols, 1 1/6, 1/6 between; C - 8 cols, 1 1/6, 1/6 between.
Published: Sat
Published Other: Every other Saturday
Avg Free Circ: 27982
Audit By: CMCA
Audit Date: 30.06.2016
Personnel: George S. Guzmas (Co-Publisher); George Bakoyannis (Prodn. Mgr.)
Parent company (for newspapers): Newsfirst Multi-Media

THE NORTH SHORE NEWS

Street Address: 3860 Notre-dame Blvd. , Suite 304
Province: QC
Postal: H7V 1S1
Country: Canada
Mailing address: 3860 Notre-Dame Blvd.Suite 304
Mailing city: Laval
Province: QC
Postal: H7V 1S1
General Phone: (450) 978-9999
General Fax: (450) 678-6330
General/National Adv. E-mail: editor@the-news.ca
Display Adv. E-mail: gg@newsfirst.ca
Editorial e-mail: editor@newsfirst.ca
Primary Website: www.ns-news.com
Year Established: 2005
Delivery Methods: Newsstand`Racks
Areas Served - City/County or Portion Thereof, or Zip codes: Canada
Mechanical specifications: Tabloid
Published: Sat
Published Other: Every 2nd week (24 per year)
Avg Paid Circ: 0
Avg Free Circ: 16353
Audit By: CMCA
Audit Date: 31.01.2017
Personnel: George Guzmas (Co-Pub)
Parent company (for newspapers): Newsfirst Multimedia

LEAMINGTON

WHEATLEY JOURNAL

Street Address: 194 Talbot Street E. , Unit #5
Province: ON
Postal: N8H 1M2
Country: Canada
General Phone: (519) 398-9098
General Fax: (519) 398-8561
General/National Adv. E-mail: journal@mnsi.net
Year Established: 1895
Delivery Methods: Mail`Newsstand
Areas Served - City/County or Portion Thereof, or Zip codes: Chatham-Kent
Own Printing Facility?: Y
Commercial printers?: Y
Published: Wed
Avg Paid Circ: 586
Avg Free Circ: 11
Audit By: CMCA
Audit Date: 30.04.2016
Personnel: Jim Heyens (Pub.)
Parent company (for newspapers): Southpoint Publishing Inc.

LEDUC

LEDUC REPRESENTATIVE

Street Address: 4504 61st Ave. ,
Province: AB
Postal: T9E 3Z1
Country: Canada
Mailing address: 4504 61st Ave.
Mailing city: Leduc
Province: AB
Postal: T9E 3Z1
General Phone: (780) 986-2271
General Fax: (780) 986-6397
Display Adv. E-mail: ngoetz@postmedia.com
Editorial e-mail: bobby.roy@sunmedia.ca
Primary Website: www.leducrep.com
Year Established: 1905
Delivery Methods: Mail`Newsstand`Carrier`Racks
Areas Served - City/County or Portion Thereof, or Zip codes: Canada
Own Printing Facility?: Y
Commercial printers?: Y
Mechanical specifications: Type page 10 1/4 x 15 3/4; E - 8 cols, 1/6 between; A - 8 cols, 1/6 between; C - 8 cols, 1/6 between.
Published: Fri
Avg Paid Circ: 3069
Avg Free Circ: 16449
Audit By: VAC
Audit Date: 31.12.2015
Personnel: Susanne Holmlund (Pub.); Jan Eyre (Circ. Mgr.); Nick Goetz (Adv. Dir.); Bobby Roy (Ed)
Parent company (for newspapers): Postmedia Network Inc.; Quebecor Communications, Inc.

LETHRBIDGE

LETHBRIDGE SUN TIMES

Street Address: 504 - 7th Street S ,
Province: AB
Postal: T1J 2G8
Country: Canada
Mailing address: 504 - 7th Street S
Mailing city: Lethbridge
Province: AB
Postal: T1J 2G8
General Phone: (403) 328-4433
General Fax: (403) 329-9355
General/National Adv. E-mail: suntimes@lethbridgeherald.com
Editorial e-mail: ccampbell@abnewsgroup.com
Primary Website: www.lethsuntimes.com
Delivery Methods: Carrier
Areas Served - City/County or Portion Thereof, or Zip codes: City of Lethbridge
Published: Mon`Tues`Wed`Thur`Fri`Sat`Sun
Weekday Frequency: m
Saturday Frequency: m
Avg Paid Circ: 19864
Sat. Circulation Paid: 10520
Sun. Circulation Paid: 12753
Audit By: AAM
Audit Date: 30.09.2017
Personnel: Coleen Campbell (Pub.)
Parent company (for newspapers): Alberta Newspaper Group LP

LEVIS

JOURNAL DE LEVIS

Street Address: 580, Boul. Alphonse-desjardins ,
Province: QC
Postal: G6V 6R8
Country: Canada
Mailing address: 515,Boul the south shore
Mailing city: Levis
Province: QC
Postal: G6V 6R8
General Phone: (418) 833-3113
General Fax: (418) 833-0890
General/National Adv. E-mail: jdl@journaldelevis.com
Primary Website: www.journaldelevis.com
Areas Served - City/County or Portion Thereof, or Zip codes: Canada
Published: Wed
Avg Paid Circ: 5
Avg Free Circ: 68595
Audit By: CCAB
Audit Date: 30.09.2015
Personnel: Sandra Fontaine

JOURNAL LE PEUPLE

Street Address: 421 Dorimene Desjardins Rue ,
Province: QC
Postal: G6V 8V6
Country: Canada
Mailing address: 421 Dorimene Desjardins Rue
Mailing city: Levis
Province: QC
Postal: G6V 8V6
General Phone: (418) 833-9398
General Fax: (418) 833-8177
General/National Adv. E-mail: paul.lessard@quebecormedia.com
Primary Website: http://www.hebdosregionaux.ca/chaudiere-appalaches/le-peuple-levis/
Year Established: 1936
Areas Served - City/County or Portion Thereof, or Zip codes: Canada
Mechanical specifications: Type page 10 x 11 3/4; E - 5 cols, 2, between; A - 10 cols, 1, between; C - 5 cols, 2, between.
Published: Wed
Avg Paid Circ: 3
Avg Free Circ: 68451
Audit By: CCAB
Audit Date: 31.03.2014
Personnel: Paul Lessard
Parent company (for newspapers): Quebecor Communications, Inc.

PEUPLE DE LOTBINIERE

Street Address: 5790, Boul. Etienne-dallaire, Suite 103 B ,
Province: QC
Postal: G6V 8V6
Country: Canada
Mailing address: 5790 Boul. Etienne-Dallaire, Suite 103 B
Mailing city: Levis
Province: QC

Postal: G6V 8V6
General Phone: (418) 728-2131
General Fax: (418) 728-4819
General/National Adv. E-mail: peuple.lotbiniere@hebdosquebecor.com
Display Adv. E-mail: ventes.lotbiniere@hebdosquebecor.com
Editorial e-mail: redaction.lotbiniere@hebdosquebecor.com
Primary Website: www.lepeuplelotbiniere.canoe.ca
Areas Served - City/County or Portion Thereof, or Zip codes: Canada
Published: Wed
Avg Paid Circ: 1
Avg Free Circ: 15029
Audit By: CCAB
Audit Date: 31.03.2014
Personnel: Lise Racette (Adv. Rep.); Paul Lessard
Parent company (for newspapers): Quebecor Communications, Inc.

LEWISPORTE

THE PILOT

Street Address: P151 Main St ,
Province: NL
Postal: A0G 3A0
Country: Canada
Mailing address: PO Box 1210
Mailing city: Lewisporte
Province: NL
Postal: A0G 3A0
General Phone: (709) 535-6910
General Fax: (709) 535-8640
General/National Adv. E-mail: editor@pilotnl.ca
Display Adv. E-mail: pilotsales@optipress.ca
Editorial e-mail: editor@pilotnl.ca
Primary Website: http://www.lportepilot.ca/
Areas Served - City/County or Portion Thereof, or Zip codes: Canada
Own Printing Facility?: Y
Commercial printers?: Y
Mechanical specifications: Type page 13 x 21; E - 6 cols, 2, 1/2 between; A - 6 cols, 2, 1/2 between; C - 9 cols, 1 3/4, 1/4 between.
Published: Wed
Avg Paid Circ: 312
Avg Free Circ: 0
Audit By: VAC
Audit Date: 31.12.2015
Personnel: Joanne Chaffey (Adv. Mgr.); Karen Wells (Ed.)
Parent company (for newspapers): Transcontinental Media

LILLOOET

BRIDGE RIVER LILLOOET NEWS

Street Address: 979 Main St. ,
Province: BC
Postal: V0K 1V0
Country: Canada
Mailing address: PO Box 709
Mailing city: Lillooet
Province: BC
Postal: V0K 1V0
General Phone: (250) 256-4219
General Fax: (250) 256-4210
Advertising Phone: (778) 773-4797
Advertising Fax: (877) 765-6483
General/National Adv. E-mail: pub@lillooetnews.net
Display Adv. E-mail: sales@lillooetnews.net
Editorial e-mail: editor@lillooetnews.net
Primary Website: www.lillooetnews.net
Year Established: 1934
Areas Served - City/County or Portion Thereof, or Zip codes: Canada
Own Printing Facility?: Y
Commercial printers?: Y
Mechanical specifications: Type page 10 1/3 x 14; E - 6 cols, 1 3/5, between; A - 6 cols, 1 3/5, between.
Published: Wed
Avg Paid Circ: 1709
Avg Free Circ: 16
Audit By: VAC

Audit Date: 28.02.2016
Personnel: Wendy Fraser (Ed.); Bruce MacLennan (Publisher); Eliza Payne (Sales Associate)
Parent company (for newspapers): Glacier Media Group

LINDSAY

KAWARTHA LAKES THIS WEEK

Street Address: 192 St. David St. ,
Province: ON
Postal: K9V 4Z4
Country: Canada
Mailing address: 192 St. David St.
Mailing city: Lindsay
Province: ON
Postal: K9V 4Z4
General Phone: (705) 324-8600
General Fax: (705) 324-5694
General/National Adv. E-mail: mtully@mykawartha.com
Display Adv. E-mail: mbabcock@mykawartha.com
Editorial e-mail: mtully@mykawartha.com
Primary Website: www.mykawartha.com
Areas Served - City/County or Portion Thereof, or Zip codes: Canada
Mechanical specifications: Type page 10 3/8 x 14; E - 9 cols, 1 1/18, 3/15 between; A - 9 cols, 1 1/18, 3/15 between; C - 9 cols, 1 1/18, 3/15 between.
Published: Tues`Thur
Avg Paid Circ: 0
Avg Free Circ: 21867
Audit By: CCAB
Audit Date: 30.09.2012
Personnel: Bruce Danford (Pub.); Linda Suddes (Bus. Admin./Opns.); Kim Riel (Office Mgr.); Shane Lockyer (Adv. Mgr.); Lois Tuffin (Ed. in Chief); Marcus Tully (News Ed.); Scott Prikker (Prodn. Mgr.); Jeff Braund (Regl. Dist. Mgr.); Tracy Magee-Graham (Dir., Distr.)
Parent company (for newspapers): Metroland Media Group Ltd.; Torstar

LISTOWEL

THE LISTOWEL BANNER

Street Address: 185 Wallace Ave. N. ,
Province: ON
Postal: N4W 1K8
Country: Canada
Mailing address: PO Box 97
Mailing city: Listowel
Province: ON
Postal: N4W 3H2
General Phone: (519) 291-1660
General Fax: (519) 291-3771
Display Adv. E-mail: ads@northperth.com
Editorial e-mail: editor@northperth.com
Primary Website: www.northperth.com
Year Established: 1866
Areas Served - City/County or Portion Thereof, or Zip codes: Canada
Published: Wed
Avg Paid Circ: 1881
Avg Free Circ: 22
Audit By: CMCA
Audit Date: 30.06.2016
Personnel: Bill Huether (Gen. Mgr.); Alicia Hunter (Adv. Mgr.); Peggy Haasnoot (Circ. Mgr.); Pauline Kerr (Ed.); Terry Bridge (Sports Ed.); Marie McKertcher (Prodn. Mgr.)
Parent company (for newspapers): Metroland Media Group Ltd.; Torstar

LITTLE CURRENT

MANITOULIN EXPOSITOR

Street Address: 1 Manitowaning Rd. ,
Province: ON
Postal: P0P 1K0
Country: Canada
Mailing address: PO Box 369
Mailing city: Little Current

Province: ON
Postal: P0P 1K0
General Phone: (705) 368-2744
General Fax: (705) 368-3822
General/National Adv. E-mail: expositor@manitoulin.ca
Display Adv. E-mail: sales@manitoulin.ca
Editorial e-mail: editor@manitoulin.ca
Primary Website: www.manitoulin.ca
Year Established: 1879
Delivery Methods: Mail`Newsstand
Areas Served - City/County or Portion Thereof, or Zip codes: Canada
Commercial printers?: Y
Mechanical specifications: Type page 10 1/4 x 16; E - 6 cols, 1 1/2, 1/8 between; A - 6 cols, 1 1/2, 1/8 between; C - 6 cols, 1 1/2, 1/8 between.
Published: Wed
Avg Paid Circ: 4181
Avg Free Circ: 178
Audit By: AAM
Audit Date: 31.03.2019
Personnel: Rick L. McCutcheon (Pub.); Kerrene Tilson (Gen. Mgr.); Greg Lloyd (Sales Mgr.); David Patterson (Production Manager); Alicia McCutcheon
Parent company (for newspapers): Manitoulin Publishing Co., Ltd.

LIVERPOOL

THE ADVANCE

Street Address: 271 Main St. ,
Province: NS
Postal: B0T 1K0
Country: Canada
Mailing address: PO Box 10
Mailing city: Liverpool
Province: NS
Postal: B0T 1K0
General Phone: (902) 354-3441
General Fax: (902) 354-2455
General/National Adv. E-mail: info@advance.ca
Editorial e-mail: ffayander@thevanguard.ca
Primary Website: http://www.theadvance.ca/
Areas Served - City/County or Portion Thereof, or Zip codes: Canada
Commercial printers?: Y
Published: Tues
Avg Paid Circ: 1573
Audit By: CMCA
Audit Date: 31.03.2013
Personnel: Fred Fayander (Pub)
Parent company (for newspapers): Transcontinental Media

LLOYDMINSTER

LLOYDMINSTER MERIDIAN BOOSTER

Street Address: 5714 44th St. ,
Province: AB
Postal: T9V 0B6
Country: Canada
Mailing address: 5714 44th St.
Mailing city: Lloydminster
Province: AB
Postal: T9V 0B6
General Phone: (780) 875-3362
General Fax: (780) 875-3423
Advertising Phone: (877) 786-8227
General/National Adv. E-mail: lisa.lamoureux@sunmedia.ca
Display Adv. E-mail: ljohnston@postmedia.com
Classified Adv. e-mail: meridianbooster.classifieds@sunmedia.ca
Editorial e-mail: tweaver@postmedia.com
Primary Website: www.meridianbooster.com
Year Established: 1954
Areas Served - City/County or Portion Thereof, or Zip codes: Canada
Own Printing Facility?: Y
Mechanical specifications: Type page 11 1/2 x 16; E - 6 cols, 1 9/16, between; A - 6 cols, 1 9/16, between; C - 6 cols, 1 9/16, between.
Published: Wed
Avg Paid Circ: 2653

Avg Free Circ: 14879
Audit By: VAC
Audit Date: 31.12.2015
Personnel: Mary-Ann Kostiuk (Pub); Leanne Johnson (Adv. Dir.); Taylor Weaver (Ed)
Parent company (for newspapers): Postmedia Network Inc.; Quebecor Communications, Inc.

LLOYDMINSTER SOURCE

Street Address: 5921-50th Ave ,
Province: SK
Postal: S9V 1W5
Country: Canada
Mailing address: PO Box 2454
Mailing city: Lloydminster
Province: SK
Postal: S9V 1W5
General Phone: (306) 825-5111
General Fax: (306) 825-5147
Editorial e-mail: colin@lloydminstersource.com
Areas Served - City/County or Portion Thereof, or Zip codes: Canada
Published: Tues`Thur
Avg Free Circ: 13889
Audit By: CMCA
Audit Date: 31.08.2016
Personnel: Reid Keebaugh (Publisher); Mike D'Armour (Mng. Ed.); Karrie Chang (Prod. Mgr.)

LONDON

ACTION (L')

Street Address: 920 Huron St. ,
Province: ON
Postal: N5Y 4K4
Country: Canada
Mailing address: 920 Huron St.
Mailing city: London
Province: ON
Postal: N5Y 4K4
General Phone: (519) 433-4130
General Fax: (905) 790-9127
General/National Adv. E-mail: journaliste@laction.ca
Display Adv. E-mail: marketing@laction.ca
Editorial e-mail: info@lemetropolitain.com
Primary Website: www.laction.ca
Areas Served - City/County or Portion Thereof, or Zip codes: Canada
Published: Wed
Avg Paid Circ: 1648
Avg Free Circ: 812
Audit By: CMCA
Audit Date: 31.12.2012
Personnel: Denis Poirier (Ed); Richard Caumartin (Sales Dir)

LONDONER

Street Address: 1147 Gainsborough Road ,
Province: ON
Postal: N6H 5L5
Country: Canada
Mailing address: 1147 Gainsborough Road
Mailing city: London
Province: ON
Postal: N6H 5L5
General Phone: (519) 673-5005
General Fax: (519) 673-4624
General/National Adv. E-mail: linda.leblanc@sunmedia.ca
Display Adv. E-mail: linda.leblanc@sunmedia.ca
Editorial e-mail: don.biggs@sunmedia.ca
Primary Website: www.thelondoner.ca
Delivery Methods: Carrier
Areas Served - City/County or Portion Thereof, or Zip codes: Canada
Published: Thur
Avg Free Circ: 140111
Audit By: CMCA
Audit Date: 31.12.2015
Personnel: Linda LeBlanc (Publisher)
Parent company (for newspapers): Postmedia Network Inc.

Non-Daily Newspapers in Canada

III-469

LONGUEUIL

BROSSARD ECLAIR
Street Address: 267 St. Charles Ouest ,
Province: QC
Postal: J4H 1E3
Country: Canada
Mailing address: 267 St. Charles Ouest
Mailing city: Longueuil
Province: QC
Postal: J4H 1E3
General Phone: (450) 646-3333
General Fax: (450) 674-0205
General/National Adv. E-mail: lucie.masse@quebecormedia.com
Primary Website: http://www.brossardeclair.ca/
Areas Served - City/County or Portion Thereof, or Zip codes: Canada
Mechanical specifications: Type page 10 1/2 x 14 1/2; E - 8 cols, between; C - 1 cols, between.
Published: Wed
Avg Free Circ: 32482
Audit By: CCAB
Audit Date: 31.03.2014
Personnel: Lucie Masse (Ed.)
Parent company (for newspapers): Reseau Select/Select Network; Quebecor Communications, Inc.

LE COURRIER DU SUD/SOUTH SHORE COURIER
Street Address: 267 Saint Charles W ,
Province: QC
Postal: J4H 1E3
Country: Canada
Mailing address: 267 Saint Charles W
Mailing city: Longueuil
Province: QC
Postal: J4H 1E3
General Phone: (450) 646-3333
General Fax: (450) 674-0205
Advertising Phone: (450) 646-3333
General/National Adv. E-mail: direction@courrierdusud.com
Display Adv. E-mail: journal@courrierdusud.com
Editorial e-mail: editeur@courrierdusud.com
Primary Website: http://www.lecourrierdusud.ca/
Year Established: 1947
Delivery Methods: Mail Racks
Areas Served - City/County or Portion Thereof, or Zip codes: Canada
Published: Wed
Avg Free Circ: 145800
Audit By: CCAB
Audit Date: 31.03.2014
Personnel: Lucie Masse (Pub.); Jinette Claude Teron (Ed.)
Parent company (for newspapers): Quebecor Communications, Inc.

MAGAZINE DE SAINT LAMBERT
Street Address: St Charles Ouest ,
Province: QC
Postal: J4H 1E3
Country: Canada
Mailing address: St Charles ouest
Mailing city: Longueuil
Province: QC
Postal: J4H 1E3
Areas Served - City/County or Portion Thereof, or Zip codes: Canada
Published: Wed
Avg Paid Circ: 0
Avg Free Circ: 14164
Audit By: CCAB
Audit Date: 30.09.2012
Personnel: Lucie Masse (Gen. Mgr.)

REVUE DE LA MACHINERIE AGRICOLE
Street Address: 468 Boul. Roland-therrien ,
Province: QC
Postal: J4H 4E3
Country: Canada
Mailing address: 468 Boul. Roland-Therrien
Mailing city: Longueuil
Province: QC
Postal: J4H 4E3
General Phone: (450) 677-2556
General Fax: (450) 677-4099
General/National Adv. E-mail: info@marevueagricole.com
Primary Website: http://www.marevueagricole.com
Published: Tues
Avg Paid Circ: 1300

Avg Free Circ: 33200
Audit By: ODC
Audit Date: 14.12.2011
Personnel: Martyne Simard

LOUISEVILLE

L'ECHO DE MASKINONGE
Street Address: 43 Saint Louis ,
Province: QC
Postal: J5V 2C7
Country: Canada
Mailing address: 43 Saint Louis
Mailing city: Louiseville
Province: QC
Postal: J5V 2C7
General Phone: (819) 228-5532
General Fax: (819) 228-9379
Advertising Fax: (819) 228-5532
General/National Adv. E-mail: redaction_em@transcontinental.ca
Primary Website: www.lechodemaskinonge.com
Year Established: 1921
Areas Served - City/County or Portion Thereof, or Zip codes: Canada
Published: Wed
Avg Paid Circ: 28
Avg Free Circ: 13907
Audit By: CCAB
Audit Date: 31.03.2014
Personnel: AndrÃƒÂƒ£££ Lamy (Dir.); Diane Beland (Sales Coord.)
Parent company (for newspapers): Transcontinental Media

LUCKNOW

THE LUCKNOW SENTINEL
Street Address: 619 Campbell St. ,
Province: ON
Postal: N0G 2H0
Country: Canada
Mailing address: PO Box 400
Mailing city: Lucknow
Province: ON
Postal: N0G 2H0
General Phone: (519) 528-2822
General Fax: (519) 528-3529
Advertising Phone: (519) 528-2822
Advertising Fax: (519) 528-3529
Editorial Phone: (519) 528-2822
Editorial Fax: (519) 528-3529
General/National Adv. E-mail: lucksent@bowesnet.com
Display Adv. E-mail: lucksentads@bowesnet.com
Editorial e-mail: lucksented@bowesnet.com
Primary Website: www.lucknowsentinel.com
Year Established: 1873
Delivery Methods: Mail Newsstand
Areas Served - City/County or Portion Thereof, or Zip codes: Canada
Commercial printers?: N
Mechanical specifications: Type page 10 .25 x 11.422; E - 9 cols, 1/16 " between columns
Published: Wed
Avg Paid Circ: 1037
Avg Free Circ: 44
Audit By: CMCA
Audit Date: 30.06.2014
Personnel: Troy Patterson (Ed.)
Parent company (for newspapers): Postmedia Network Inc.; Quebecor Communications, Inc.

LUMSDEN

WATERFRONT PRESS
Street Address: 635 James St. N. ,
Province: SK
Postal: S0G 3C0
Country: Canada
Mailing address: PO Box 507
Mailing city: Lumsden
Province: SK
Postal: S0G 3C0
General Phone: (306) 731-3143
General Fax: (306) 731-2277
General/National Adv. E-mail: watpress@sasktel.net
Areas Served - City/County or Portion Thereof, or Zip codes: S0G 0H0, S0G 0W0, S0G 3C0, S0G 3C0, S0G 4L0, S0G 4P0
Own Printing Facility?: Y
Commercial printers?: Y

Mechanical specifications: Type page 10 x 15 1/4; E - 5 cols, 2, between; A - 5 cols, 2, between; C - 5 cols, 2, between.
Published: Thur
Avg Paid Circ: 167
Avg Free Circ: 3993
Audit By: CMCA
Audit Date: 30.06.2014
Personnel: Jacqueline Chouinard (Ed.); Lucien Chouinard (Ed.)

MACKENZIE

THE TIMES
Street Address: 125-403 Mackenzie Blvd. ,
Province: BC
Postal: V0J 2C0
Country: Canada
Mailing address: PO Box 609
Mailing city: Mackenzie
Province: BC
Postal: V0J 2C0
General Phone: (250) 997-6675
General Fax: (250) 997-4747
Advertising Phone: (250) 997-6675
Advertising Fax: (250) 997-4747
Editorial Phone: (250) 997-6675
Editorial Fax: (250) 997-4747
General/National Adv. E-mail: news@mackenzietimes.com
Display Adv. E-mail: ads@mackenzietimes.com
Editorial e-mail: news@mackenzietimes.com
Primary Website: www.sterlingnews.com/Mackenzie
Year Established: 1999
Delivery Methods: Mail Newsstand Carrier
Areas Served - City/County or Portion Thereof, or Zip codes: V0J 2C0
Commercial printers?: Y
Published: Wed
Avg Paid Circ: 1000
Audit By: Sworn/Estimate/Non-Audited
Audit Date: 12.07.2019
Personnel: Jackie Benton (Pub/Ed); Andrea Massicotte (Adv Mgr)

MACKLIN

MACKLIN MIRROR
Street Address: 4701 Herald St. ,
Province: SK
Postal: S0L 2C0
Country: Canada
Mailing address: PO Box 100
Mailing city: Macklin
Province: SK
Postal: S0L 2C0
General Phone: (306) 753-2424
General Fax: (306) 753-2432
General/National Adv. E-mail: macklin.jamac@gmail.com
Display Adv. E-mail: macklin.jamac@gmail.com
Editorial e-mail: stacey.jamac@gmail.com
Year Established: 1977
Delivery Methods: Mail Newsstand Racks
Areas Served - City/County or Portion Thereof, or Zip codes: Canada
Mechanical specifications: 10.25" X 16" high
Published: Wed
Avg Paid Circ: 638
Avg Free Circ: 33
Audit By: CMCA
Audit Date: 30.04.2016
Personnel: Delilah Reschny (Editor/Publisher); Stacey Lavallie (Reporter)
Parent company (for newspapers): Jamac Publishing

MAGOG

REFLET DU LAC
Street Address: 53 Rue Centre , Bureau 300
Province: QC
Postal: J1X 5B6
Country: Canada
General Phone: (819) 843-3500
General Fax: (819) 843-3085
General/National Adv. E-mail: dany.jacques@tc.tc
Areas Served - City/County or Portion Thereof, or Zip codes: Canada
Published: Wed
Avg Paid Circ: 0
Avg Free Circ: 24662
Audit By: CCAB
Audit Date: 30.09.2012

Personnel: Monique Cote (CEO)

MAGRATH

WESTWIND WEEKLY NEWS

Street Address: 74a South - 1st Street West, Box 9
Province: AB
Postal: T0K 1J0
Country: Canada
General Phone: (403) 758-6911
General Fax: (403) 758-3661
Display Adv. E-mail: sales@westwindweekly.com
Primary Website: www.westwindweekly.com
Delivery Methods: Mail
Areas Served - City/County or Portion Thereof, or Zip codes: towns of Magrath, Raymond and Stirling
Published: Thur
Avg Paid Circ: 0
Avg Free Circ: 51
Audit By: VAC
Audit Date: 31.12.2015
Personnel: Valorie Wiebe (Pub.); Maggie Belisle (Adv. Sales Consult.); Joan Bly (Office Admin.); J.W Schnarr (Ed.)

MANITOU

THE WESTERN CANADIAN

Street Address: 424 Ellis Ave. E.,
Province: MB
Postal: R0G 1G0
Country: Canada
Mailing address: PO Box 190
Mailing city: Manitou
Province: MB
Postal: R0G 1G0
General Phone: (204) 242-2555
General Fax: (204) 242-3137
General/National Adv. E-mail: westerncanadian@goinet.ca
Editorial e-mail: thewesterncanadian@gmail.com
Primary Website: http://www.thewesterncanadian.ca/
Areas Served - City/County or Portion Thereof, or Zip codes: Canada
Own Printing Facility?: Y
Commercial printers?: Y
Mechanical specifications: Type page 10 1/4 x 14; E - 5 cols, 2, 1/8 between; A - 5 cols, 2, 1/8 between; C - 5 cols, 2, 1/8 between.
Published: Tues
Avg Paid Circ: 1057
Avg Free Circ: 0
Audit By: VAC
Audit Date: 31.05.2016
Personnel: Grant Howett (Ed.)

MANITOUWADGE

THE ECHO

Street Address: 105 Warbler,
Province: ON
Postal: P0T 2C0
Country: Canada
Mailing address: PO Box 850
Mailing city: Manitouwadge
Province: ON
Postal: P0T 2C0
General Phone: (807) 228-2333
Advertising Phone: (807) 228-2317
General/National Adv. E-mail: info@theecho.ca
Display Adv. E-mail: manitouwadgeecho@gmail.com
Editorial e-mail: news@theecho.ca
Primary Website: www.theecho.ca
Year Established: 1964
Delivery Methods: Mail`Newsstand
Areas Served - City/County or Portion Thereof, or Zip codes: Canada
Own Printing Facility?: N
Commercial printers?: Y
Mechanical specifications: Type page 10 x 15 3/4; E - 5 cols, 1 3/4, 1/4 between; A - 5 cols, 1 3/4, 1/4 between.
Published: Wed
Avg Paid Circ: 346
Audit By: CMCA
Audit Date: 30.04.2014
Personnel: B.J. Schermann (Pub.); Scott Schermann (Prodn. Mgr.)

MANSFIELD

JOURNAL OF PONTIAC

Street Address: Unit 5, 289, Rue Principale
Province: QC
Postal: J0X 1R0
Country: Canada
Mailing address: #5-289, rue Principale
Mailing city: Mansfield
Province: QC
Postal: J0X 1R0
General Phone: (819) 683-3582
General Fax: (819) 683-2977
General/National Adv. E-mail: info@journalpontiac.com
Display Adv. E-mail: journal@journalpontiac.com
Classified Adv. e-mail: notice@journalpontiac.com
Editorial e-mail: editor@journalpontiac.com
Primary Website: www.pontiacjournal.com
Year Established: 1987
Delivery Methods: Mail`Newsstand`Carrier
Areas Served - City/County or Portion Thereof, or Zip codes: Mansfield-et-Pontefract
Published: Other
Avg Paid Circ: 70
Avg Free Circ: 9302
Audit By: Sworn/Estimate/Non-Audited
Audit Date: 12.07.2019
Personnel: Lynne Lavery (Gen. Mgr.)
Parent company (for newspapers): 155106 Canada Inc.

MAPLE CREEK

MAPLE CREEK & SOUTHWEST ADVANCE TIMES

Street Address: 116 Harder Street,
Province: SK
Postal: S0N 1N0
Country: Canada
Mailing address: PO Box 1328
Mailing city: Maple Creek
Province: SK
Postal: S0N 1N0
General Phone: (306) 662-2100
General Fax: (306) 662-5005
General/National Adv. E-mail: classifieds@maplecreeknews.com
Display Adv. E-mail: ads@maplecreeknews.com
Editorial e-mail: editorial@maplecreeknews.com
Primary Website: www.maplecreeknews.com
Areas Served - City/County or Portion Thereof, or Zip codes: Canada
Published: Tues
Avg Paid Circ: 1506
Avg Free Circ: 76
Audit By: CMCA
Audit Date: 30.04.2016
Personnel: Angela Litke (Manager); Della Fournier (Advertising Sales)

THE MAPLE CREEK NEWS

Street Address: 116 Harder St.,
Province: SK
Postal: S0N 1N0
Country: Canada
Mailing address: PO Box 1328
Mailing city: Maple Creek
Province: SK
Postal: S0N 1N0
General Phone: (306) 662-2133
General Fax: (306) 662-5005
General/National Adv. E-mail: classifieds@maplecreeknews.com
Display Adv. E-mail: ads@maplecreeknews.com
Classified Adv. e-mail: classifieds@maplecreeknews.com
Editorial e-mail: editorial@maplecreeknews.com
Primary Website: www.maplecreeknews.com
Year Established: 1902
Delivery Methods: Mail`Newsstand
Areas Served - City/County or Portion Thereof, or Zip codes: Canada
Commercial printers?: Y
Mechanical specifications: Type page 13 x 21 1/2; E - 6 cols, 2, 1/6 between; A - 6 cols, 2, 1/6 between; C - 6 cols, 2, 1/6 between.
Published: Thur
Avg Paid Circ: 1406
Audit By: Sworn/Estimate/Non-Audited
Audit Date: 12.07.2019
Personnel: Editorial Team (Ed.); Advertising Team (Adv.); Classifieds Team (Classifieds)
Parent company (for newspapers): Southern Alberta Newspapers

MAPLE RIDGE

THE MAPLE RIDGE NEWS

Street Address: 22611 Dewdney Trunk Road,
Province: BC
Postal: V2X 3K1
Country: Canada
Mailing address: 22611 Dewdney Trunk Road
Mailing city: Maple Ridge
Province: BC
Postal: V2X 3K1
General Phone: (604) 467-1122
General Fax: (604) 463-4741
Advertising Phone: (604) 476-2728
General/National Adv. E-mail: publisher@mapleridgenews.com
Display Adv. E-mail: ads@mapleridgenews.com
Editorial e-mail: editor@mapleridgenews.com
Primary Website: www.mapleridgenews.com
Year Established: 1978
Delivery Methods: Carrier
Areas Served - City/County or Portion Thereof, or Zip codes: Canada
Commercial printers?: Y
Mechanical specifications: Type page 10 3/8 x 12 1/2; E - 6 cols, 1 5/8, 1/6 between; A - 6 cols, 1 5/8, 1/6 between; C - 6 cols, 1 5/8, 1/6 between.
Published: Wed`Fri
Avg Free Circ: 30223
Audit By: AAM
Audit Date: 31.03.2019
Personnel: Michael Hall (Ed.); Lisa Prophet (Pub); Brian Yip (Circ Mgr)
Parent company (for newspapers): Black Press Group Ltd.

MARATHON

THE MARATHON MERCURY

Street Address: 91 Peninsula Rd.,
Province: ON
Postal: P0T 2E0
Country: Canada
Mailing address: PO Box 369
Mailing city: Marathon
Province: ON
Postal: P0T 2E0
General Phone: (805) 229-1520
General Fax: (805) 229-1595
General/National Adv. E-mail: mmpl@onlink.net
Year Established: 1948
Areas Served - City/County or Portion Thereof, or Zip codes: Canada
Mechanical specifications: Type page 10 1/4 x 15 7/8; E - 5 cols, 2, between; A - 5 cols, 2, between; C - 5 cols, 2, between.
Published: Tues
Avg Paid Circ: 689
Avg Free Circ: 13
Audit By: CMCA
Audit Date: 31.05.2016
Personnel: Garry R. McInnes (Adv. Mgr.); P. Douglas Gale (Ed.)

MARKHAM

MARKHAM ECONOMIST & SUN

Street Address: 50 Mcintosh Drive Unit 115,
Province: ON
Postal: L3R-9T3
Country: Canada
Mailing address: 50 McIntosh Drive Unit 115
Mailing city: Markham
Province: ON
Postal: L3R-9T3
General Phone: (905) 943-6100
General Fax: (905) 943-6129
Advertising Phone: (905) 943-6100
Advertising Fax: (905) 943-6129
Editorial Phone: (905) 943-6100
Editorial Fax: (905) 943-6129
General/National Adv. E-mail: admin@econsun.com
Display Adv. E-mail: abeswick@yrmg.com
Editorial e-mail: boneill@yrmg.com
Primary Website: yorkregion.com
Year Established: 1881
Areas Served - City/County or Portion Thereof, or Zip codes: Canada
Own Printing Facility?: Y
Published: Thur
Avg Free Circ: 68613
Audit By: CMCA
Audit Date: 31.12.2015
Personnel: Ian Proudfoot (Pub.); Bernie O'Neill (Ed.); John Willems (Gen. Mgr.); Meriel Bradley (Online Adv.)
Parent company (for newspapers): Metroland Media Group Ltd.; Torstar

THE RICHMOND HILL LIBERAL

Street Address: 50 Mcintosh Drive Unit 115,
Province: ON
Postal: L3R 9T3
Country: Canada
Mailing address: 50 McIntosh Drive Unit 115
Mailing city: Markham
Province: ON
Postal: L3R 9T3
General Phone: (905) 943-6100
General Fax: (905) 943-6129
Advertising Phone: (905) 943-6095
Advertising Fax: (905) 943-6129
General/National Adv. E-mail: admin@theliberal.com
Display Adv. E-mail: abeswick@yrmg.com
Classified Adv. e-mail: jkopacz@yrmg.com
Editorial e-mail: mbeck@yrmg.com
Primary Website: yorkregion.com
Year Established: 1878
Areas Served - City/County or Portion Thereof, or Zip codes: Canada
Own Printing Facility?: Y
Commercial printers?: Y
Published: Thur
Avg Paid Circ: 0
Avg Free Circ: 47438
Audit By: CCAB
Audit Date: 20.12.2017
Personnel: Ian Proudfoot (Pub.); Robert Lazurko (Bus. Mgr.); Anne Beswick (Retail Adv. Mgr.); Debora Kelly (Ed. in Chief); Marney Beck (Ed.); John Willems (General Manager)
Parent company (for newspapers): Metroland Media Group Ltd.; Torstar

MARMORA

HAVELOCK CITIZEN

Street Address: Po Box 239,
Province: ON
Postal: K0K 2M0
Country: Canada
Mailing address: PO Box 239
Mailing city: Marmora
Province: ON
Postal: K0K 2M0
General Phone: (613) 962-2360
General Fax: (613) 472-5026
Areas Served - City/County or Portion Thereof, or Zip

Non-Daily Newspapers in Canada

codes: KOL 1ZO, KOL 2ZO
Own Printing Facility?: Y
Mechanical specifications: Type page 10 1/4 x 15 3/4; E - 6 cols, 1 5/8, between; A - 6 cols, 1 5/8, between; C - 6 cols, 1 5/8, between.
Published: Fri
Avg Paid Circ: 35000
Avg Free Circ: 2321
Audit By: Sworn/Estimate/Non-Audited
Audit Date: 12.07.2019
Personnel: Nancy Derrer (Ed.)
Parent company (for newspapers): Shield Media

MARYSTOWN

THE SOUTHERN GAZETTE

Street Address: Po Box 1116 ,
Province: NL
Postal: A0E 2M0
Country: Canada
Mailing address: PO Box 1116
Mailing city: Marystown
Province: NL
Postal: A0E 2M0
General Phone: (709) 279-3188
General Fax: (709) 279-2628
General/National Adv. E-mail: editor@southerngazette.ca
Editorial e-mail: editor@southerngazette.ca
Primary Website: www.southerngazette.ca
Areas Served - City/County or Portion Thereof, or Zip codes: Canada
Own Printing Facility?: Y
Commercial printers?: Y
Mechanical specifications: Type page 13 x 21 1/2; E - 6 cols, 2 1/12, between; A - 6 cols, 2 1/12, between; C - 9 cols, 1 1/12, between.
Published: Tues
Avg Paid Circ: 2231
Avg Free Circ: 0
Audit By: VAC
Audit Date: 31.12.2015
Personnel: George MacVicar (Ed.)
Parent company (for newspapers): Transcontinental Media

MATANE

AVANT POSTE

Street Address: 305, Rue De La Gare, Following 107 ,
Province: QC
Postal: G4W 3J2
Country: Canada
Mailing address: 305, rue de la Gare, following 107
Mailing city: Matane
Province: QC
Postal: G4W 3J2
General Phone: (418) 629-3443
General Fax: (418) 562-4607
General/National Adv. E-mail: jean.gagnon@quebecormedia.com
Primary Website: www.lavantposte.ca
Areas Served - City/County or Portion Thereof, or Zip codes: Canada
Published: Wed
Avg Paid Circ: 6
Avg Free Circ: 8609
Audit By: CCAB
Audit Date: 31.03.2014
Personnel: Jean Gagnon

LA VOIX GASPESIENNE

Street Address: 305 De La Gare St., Ste. 107 ,
Province: QC
Postal: G4W 3J2
Country: Canada
Mailing address: 305 de la Gare St., Ste. 107
Mailing city: Matane
Province: QC
Postal: G4W 3J2
General Phone: (418) 562-4040
General Fax: (418) 562-4607
Advertising Phone: (418) 562-0666
Editorial Phone: (418) 562-0666
Primary Website: http://www.lavantagegaspesien.com
Areas Served - City/County or Portion Thereof, or Zip codes: Canada
Published: Wed
Avg Paid Circ: 13
Avg Free Circ: 17247
Audit By: CCAB
Audit Date: 31.03.2014
Personnel: Jean Gagnon ((Ed.))
Parent company (for newspapers): Quebecor Communications, Inc.

VOIX DE LA MATANIE

Street Address: Rue De La Gare ,
Province: QC
Postal: G4W 3J2
Country: Canada
Mailing address: rue de la Gare
Mailing city: Matane
Province: QC
Postal: G4W 3J2
General Phone: (418) 562-4040
General Fax: (418) 562-4607
Areas Served - City/County or Portion Thereof, or Zip codes: Canada
Published: Wed
Avg Paid Circ: 11
Avg Free Circ: 17402
Audit By: CCAB
Audit Date: 31.03.2014
Personnel: Jean Gagnon

MATTAWA

THE MATTAWA RECORDER

Street Address: 341 Mcconnell St. ,
Province: ON
Postal: P0H 1V0
Country: Canada
Mailing address: PO Box 67
Mailing city: Mattawa
Province: ON
Postal: P0H 1V0
General Phone: (705) 744-5361
General Fax: (866) 831-6626
General/National Adv. E-mail: recorder@bellnet.ca
Display Adv. E-mail: recorder@bellnet.ca
Delivery Methods: Mail`Newsstand
Areas Served - City/County or Portion Thereof, or Zip codes: P0H 1V0
Mechanical specifications: Type page 10 x 14; E - 5 cols, 2, 1/4 between; A - 5 cols, 2, 1/4 between.
Published: Sun
Avg Paid Circ: 1100
Audit By: Sworn/Estimate/Non-Audited
Audit Date: 12.07.2019
Personnel: Tom Edwards (Pub.); Heather Edwards (Adv. Mgr.)

MEADOW LAKE

NORTHERN PRIDE

Street Address: 219 Centre Street ,
Province: SK
Postal: S9X 1Z4
Country: Canada
Mailing address: Box 2049
Mailing city: Meadow Lake
Province: SK
Postal: S9X 1Z4
General Phone: (306) 236-5353
Display Adv. E-mail: pride.terry@sasktel.net
Classified Adv. e-mail: pride.terry@sasktel.net
Editorial e-mail: pride.terry@sasktel.net
Primary Website: www.northernprideml.com
Year Established: 1993
Delivery Methods: Mail`Newsstand`Carrier Racks
Areas Served - City/County or Portion Thereof, or Zip codes: Canada
Published: Thur
Avg Paid Circ: 1638
Avg Free Circ: 4283
Audit By: CMCA
Audit Date: 31.12.2015
Personnel: Terry Villeneuve (Pub)

MEAFORD

BLUE MOUNTAINS COURIER-HERALD

Street Address: 24 Trowbridge St. West , Unit 6
Province: ON
Postal: N4L 1Y1
Country: Canada
Mailing address: 24 Trowbridge St. West Unit 6
Mailing city: Meaford
Province: ON
Postal: N4L 1Y1
General Phone: (519) 538-1421
General Fax: (519) 538-5028
General/National Adv. E-mail: clamb@simcoe.com
Display Adv. E-mail: pamero@simcoe.com
Editorial e-mail: lmartin@simcoe.com
Primary Website: www.simcoe.com
Areas Served - City/County or Portion Thereof, or Zip codes: Canada
Published: Wed
Avg Paid Circ: 505
Audit By: CMCA
Audit Date: 30.06.2013
Personnel: Lori Martin (Ed); Heather Harris (Circ Mgr); Pamela Amero (Adv Mgr)

EXPRESS

Street Address: 24 Trowbridge St. W Unit 6 ,
Province: ON
Postal: N4L 1Y1
Country: Canada
Mailing address: 24 Trowbridge St. W. Unit 6
Mailing city: Meaford
Province: ON
Postal: N4L 1Y1
General Phone: (519) 538-1421
General Fax: (519) 538-5028
General/National Adv. E-mail: meafordexpress@simcoe.com
Primary Website: www.meafordexpress.com
Year Established: 1906
Areas Served - City/County or Portion Thereof, or Zip codes: Canada
Commercial printers?: Y
Mechanical specifications: Type page 12 3/4 x 21; E - 6 cols, 2, 1/6 between; A - 6 cols, 2, 1/6 between; C - 6 cols, 2, 1/6 between.
Published: Wed
Avg Paid Circ: 544
Avg Free Circ: 96
Audit By: CMCA
Audit Date: 30.06.2016
Personnel: Scott Woodhouse (Ed.); Pamela Amero (Adv.); Chris Fell (Community Events)
Parent company (for newspapers): Metroland Media; Metroland Media Group Ltd.

MEDICINE HAT

PRAIRIE POST

Street Address: 3256 Dunmore Rd Se ,
Province: AB
Postal: T1B 3R2
Country: Canada
Mailing address: 3256 Dunmore Rd SE
Mailing city: Medicine Hat
Province: AB
Postal: T1B 3R2
General Phone: (403) 528-5769
General Fax: (403) 528-2276
General/National Adv. E-mail: rdahlman@prairiepost.com
Editorial e-mail: rdahlman@prairiepost.com
Primary Website: www.prairiepost.com
Areas Served - City/County or Portion Thereof, or Zip codes: County of Newell, Cypress County, County of 40-Mile, Special Areas, City of Brooks, southwest Saskatchewan, City of Swift Current, M.D. of Acadia Valley
Published: Fri
Avg Paid Circ: 0
Avg Free Circ: 12562
Audit By: VAC
Audit Date: 30.09.2015
Personnel: Ryan Dahlman (Mng Ed.)
Parent company (for newspapers): Alberta Newspaper Group LP

MELFORT

MELFORT JOURNAL

Street Address: 901 Main St. ,
Province: SK
Postal: S0E 1A0
Country: Canada
Mailing address: PO Box 1300
Mailing city: Melfort
Province: SK
Postal: S0E 1A0
General Phone: (306) 752-5737
General Fax: (306) 752-5358
General/National Adv. E-mail: ads@melfortjournal.com
Primary Website: www.melfortjournal.com
Areas Served - City/County or Portion Thereof, or Zip codes: Canada
Own Printing Facility?: Y
Commercial printers?: Y
Published: Tues
Avg Paid Circ: 1132
Audit By: CMCA
Audit Date: 30.06.2016
Personnel: Ken Sorensen (Pub.)
Parent company (for newspapers): Postmedia Network Inc.; Quebecor Communications, Inc.

NORTH EAST SUN

Street Address: 901 Main St. ,
Province: SK
Postal: S0E 1A0
Country: Canada
Mailing address: PO Box 1300
Mailing city: Melfort
Province: SK
Postal: S0E 1A0
General Phone: (306) 752-5737
General Fax: (306) 752-5358
General/National Adv. E-mail: shirley.sorensen@sunmedia.ca
Display Adv. E-mail: cassie.johnson@sunmedia.ca
Editorial e-mail: greg.wiseman@sunmedia.ca
Primary Website: www.melfortjournal.com
Areas Served - City/County or Portion Thereof, or Zip codes: Canada
Published: Fri
Avg Free Circ: 21761
Audit By: CMCA
Audit Date: 30.06.2016
Personnel: Ken Sorensen

MELITA

MELITA NEW ERA

Street Address: 128 Main St. ,
Province: MB
Postal: R0M 1L0
Country: Canada
Mailing address: 128 Main St.
Mailing city: Melita
Province: MB
Postal: R0M 1L0
General Phone: (204) 522-3491
General Fax: (204) 522-3648
General/National Adv. E-mail: newera@cpocket.mts.net
Display Adv. E-mail: ads.cpocket@mts.net
Editorial e-mail: cpocket@mts.net
Primary Website: http://www.melitanewera.ca/
Year Established: 1916
Areas Served - City/County or Portion Thereof, or Zip codes: Canada
Own Printing Facility?: Y
Commercial printers?: Y

Mechanical specifications: Type page 10 1/4 x 14; E - 6 cols, 1 3/5, 1/16 between; A - 6 cols, 1 3/5, 1/16 between; C - 6 cols, 1 3/5, 1/16 between.
Published: Fri
Avg Paid Circ: 1104
Avg Free Circ: 0
Audit By: CMCA
Audit Date: 28.02.2014
Personnel: Patty Lewis (Ed.)
Parent company (for newspapers): Glacier Media Group

MELVILLE

THE MELVILLE ADVANCE

Street Address: 218 3rd Ave. W. ,
Province: SK
Postal: S0A 2P0
Country: Canada
Mailing address: PO Box 1420
Mailing city: Melville
Province: SK
Postal: S0A 2P0
General Phone: (306) 728-5448
General Fax: (306) 728-4004
General/National Adv. E-mail: melvilleadvance@sasktel.net
Display Adv. E-mail: sales@grasslandsnews.ca
Classified Adv. e-mail: contact@grasslandsnews.ca
Editorial e-mail: editor@grasslandsnews.ca
Primary Website: www.melvilleadvance.com
Year Established: 1928
Delivery Methods: Mail`Newsstand
Areas Served - City/County or Portion Thereof, or Zip codes: Stanley
Own Printing Facility?: Y
Commercial printers?: Y
Mechanical specifications: Type page 10 1/8 x 15 3/4; E - 6 cols, 2 1/4, 1/4 between; A - 6 cols, 2 1/4, 1/4 between; C - 6 cols, 2 1/4, 1/4 between.
Published: Fri
Avg Paid Circ: 1679
Avg Free Circ: 17
Audit By: CMCA
Audit Date: 31.05.2016
Personnel: George Brown; Chris Ashfield (Group Publisher)
Parent company (for newspapers): Grasslands News Group

MERRITT

MERRITT HERALD

Street Address: 2090 Granite Ave. ,
Province: BC
Postal: V1K 1B8
Country: Canada
Mailing address: Box 9 â€“ 2090 Granite Ave
Mailing city: Merritt
Province: BC
Postal: V1K 1B8
General Phone: (250) 378-4241
General Fax: (250) 378-6818
General/National Adv. E-mail: newsroom@merrittherald.com
Display Adv. E-mail: sales2@merrittherald.com
Classified Adv. e-mail: classifieds@merrittherald.com
Editorial e-mail: newsroom@merrittherald.com
Primary Website: www.merrittherald.com
Year Established: 1999
Areas Served - City/County or Portion Thereof, or Zip codes: Merritt
Own Printing Facility?: Y
Mechanical specifications: Type page 10 5/16 x 14 1/2; E - 6 cols, 1 7/12, 1/6 between; A - 6 cols, 1 7/12, 1/6 between; C - 6 cols, 1 7/12, 1/6 between.
Published: Thur
Avg Paid Circ: 1092
Avg Free Circ: 5589
Audit By: VAC
Audit Date: 30.06.2016
Personnel: Theresa Arnold (Pub.); Cole Wagner (Ed); Kenneth Couture (Office Mgr)
Parent company (for newspapers): Aberdeen Publishing; Merrit Newspapers

MIDDLETON

MIRROR-EXAMINER

Street Address: 87 Commercial St. ,
Province: NS
Postal: B0S 1P0
Country: Canada
Mailing address: PO Box 880
Mailing city: Middleton
Province: NS
Postal: B0S 1P0
General Phone: (902) 825-3457
General Fax: (902) 825-6707
General/National Adv. E-mail: kentpub.ads@ns.sympatico.ca
Display Adv. E-mail: kentpub.ads@ns.sympatico.ca
Own Printing Facility?: Y
Commercial printers?: Y
Mechanical specifications: Type page 12 1/2 x 21; E - 7 cols, 1/8 between; A - 7 cols, 1/8 between; C - 7 cols, 1/8 between.
Published: Wed
Avg Paid Circ: 3101
Audit By: Sworn/Estimate/Non-Audited
Audit Date: 12.07.2019
Personnel: Garnet Austen (Pub.); Wayne Smith (Adv. Mgr.); Lori Errington (Ed.)

THE SPECTATOR

Street Address: 87 Commercial St. ,
Province: NS
Postal: B0S 1P0
Country: Canada
Mailing address: 87 Commercial St.
Mailing city: Middleton
Province: NS
Postal: B0S 1P0
General Phone: (902) 532-2219
General Fax: (902) 825-6707
General/National Adv. E-mail: info@annapolisspectator.ca
Display Adv. E-mail: info@annapolisspectator.ca
Editorial e-mail: editor@annapolisspectator.ca
Primary Website: www.annapoliscountyspectator.ca
Own Printing Facility?: Y
Commercial printers?: Y
Mechanical specifications: Type page 10 1/2 x 13; E - 6 cols, 1/8 between; A - 6 cols, 1/8 between; C - 6 cols, 1/8 between.
Published: Thur
Avg Paid Circ: 2048
Avg Free Circ: 0
Audit By: CMCA
Audit Date: 31.01.2013
Personnel: Fred Fiander (Pub.); Lawrence Powell (Ed.)
Parent company (for newspapers): Transcontinental Media

MIDLAND

THE MIRROR

Street Address: 488 Dominion Ave. ,
Province: ON
Postal: L4R 1P6
Country: Canada
Mailing address: 488 Dominion Ave.
Mailing city: Midland
Province: ON
Postal: L4R 1P6
General Phone: (705) 527-5500
General Fax: (705) 527-5467
General/National Adv. E-mail: themirror@simcoe.com
Primary Website: simcoe.com
Areas Served - City/County or Portion Thereof, or Zip codes: Canada
Own Printing Facility?: Y
Commercial printers?: Y
Mechanical specifications: Type page 10 3/8 x 14; E - 9 cols, 1 1/16, 3/16 between; A - 9 cols, 1 1/16, 3/16 between; C - 9 cols, 1 1/16, 3/16 between.
Published: Thur
Avg Paid Circ: 0
Avg Free Circ: 21435
Audit By: CCAB
Audit Date: 30.09.2017
Personnel: Joe Anderson (Pub.); Leigh Gate (Gen. Mgr.); Leigh Rourke (Adv. Mgr.); Kyla Mosley (Circ. Mgr.); Travis Mealing (Ed.); Lori Martin (Mng. Ed.)
Parent company (for newspapers): Metroland Media Group Ltd.; Torstar

MILDMAY

TOWN AND COUNTRY CRIER

Street Address: 100 Elora St. ,
Province: ON
Postal: N0G 2J0
Country: Canada
Mailing address: PO Box 190
Mailing city: Mildmay
Province: ON
Postal: N0G 2J0
General Phone: (519) 367-2681
General Fax: (519) 367-5417
General/National Adv. E-mail: thecrier@wightman.ca
Mechanical specifications: Type page 10 x 15 1/2; E - 5 cols, 2, 1/4 between; C - 4 cols, 2 1/2, 1/4 between.
Published: Thur
Avg Paid Circ: 1211
Avg Free Circ: 169
Audit By: CMCA
Audit Date: 30.06.2016
Personnel: John H. Hafermehl (Pub.); Susan Bross (Ed.)

MILLET

LEDUC-WETASKIWIN PIPESTONE FLYER

Street Address: 5025 - 50 Street ,
Province: AB
Postal: T0C 1Z0
Country: Canada
Mailing address: PO BOX 402
Mailing city: Millet
Province: AB
Postal: T0C 1Z0
General Phone: (780) 387-5797
General Fax: (780) 387-4397
Display Adv. E-mail: sales1@pipestoneflyer.ca
Editorial e-mail: editor@pipestoneflyer.ca
Primary Website: www.pipestoneflyer.ca
Year Established: 1997
Delivery Methods: Mail`Newsstand`Racks
Areas Served - City/County or Portion Thereof, or Zip codes: City of Leduc, Leduc County, City of Wetaskiwin, Wetaskiwin County, Town of Millet, Pigeon Lake, Calmar, Thorsby, New Sarepta, Warburg, Winfield, Mulhurst Bay, Ma-Me-O Beach
Published: Thur
Avg Paid Circ: 0
Avg Free Circ: 16935
Audit By: VAC
Audit Date: 31.07.2016
Personnel: Michele Rosenthal (Pub); Stu Salkeld (Ed)
Parent company (for newspapers): Black Press Group Ltd.; Black Press, Prairie Division

MILTON

THE MILTON CANADIAN CHAMPION

Street Address: 555 Industrial Dr. ,
Province: ON
Postal: L9T 5E1
Country: Canada
Mailing address: 555 Industrial Dr.
Mailing city: Milton
Province: ON
Postal: L9T 5E1
General Phone: (905) 878-2341
General Fax: (905) 876-2364
Editorial e-mail: editorial@miltoncanadianchampion.com
Primary Website: miltoncanadianchampion.com
Year Established: 1860
Delivery Methods: Carrier
Areas Served - City/County or Portion Thereof, or Zip codes: Canada
Own Printing Facility?: Y
Commercial printers?: Y
Published: Tues`Thur
Avg Paid Circ: 19
Avg Free Circ: 16276
Audit By: CCAB
Audit Date: 30.09.2017
Personnel: Neil Oliver (Pub.); Karen Miceli (Ed.); Steve LeBlanc (News/Sports Ed.); Tim Coles (Prodn. Mgr.); David Harvey (Regional General Manager); Katy Letourneau (Director of Advertising); Sarah McSweeney (Circ. Manager)
Parent company (for newspapers): Metroland Media Group Ltd.; Torstar

MINDEN

THE MINDEN TIMES

Street Address: 2 Iga Rd., Unit 2 ,
Province: ON
Postal: K0M 2K0
Country: Canada
Mailing address: PO Box 97
Mailing city: Minden
Province: ON
Postal: K0M 2K0
General Phone: (705) 286-1288
General Fax: (705) 286-4768
Display Adv. E-mail: jenniferm@haliburtonpress.com
Classified Adv. e-mail: classifieds@mindentimes.ca
Editorial e-mail: editor@mindentimes.ca
Primary Website: www.mindentimes.ca
Year Established: 1980
Delivery Methods: Mail`Newsstand
Areas Served - City/County or Portion Thereof, or Zip codes: Minden
Commercial printers?: Y
Published: Thur
Avg Paid Circ: 1076
Avg Free Circ: 259
Audit By: CMCA
Audit Date: 30.06.2016
Personnel: Jenn Watt (Ed.); Jennifer McEathron (Sales); Debbie Comer (Circ., Classified)
Parent company (for newspapers): White Pine Media

MINNEDOSA

MINNEDOSA TRIBUNE

Street Address: 14 3rd Ave. Sw ,
Province: MB
Postal: R0J 1E0
Country: Canada
Mailing address: PO Box 930
Mailing city: Minnedosa
Province: MB
Postal: R0J 1E0
General Phone: (204) 867-3816
General Fax: (204) 867-5171
General/National Adv. E-mail: editor@minnedosatribune.com
Display Adv. E-mail: adsales@minnedosatribune.com
Classified Adv. e-mail: class@minnedosatribune.com
Editorial e-mail: editor@minnedosatribune.com
Primary Website: www.minnedosatribune.com
Year Established: 1883
Areas Served - City/County or Portion Thereof, or Zip codes: Minnedosa
Mechanical specifications: Type page 10 1/2 x 16; E - 6 cols, between; A - 6 cols, between; C - 6 cols, between.
Published: Fri
Avg Paid Circ: 456
Avg Free Circ: 258
Audit By: VAC
Audit Date: 30.06.2016
Personnel: Darryl Holyk (Pub./Ed); Heather Horner (Adv); Georgia Kerluke (Office Mgr/

MIRAMICHI

MIRAMICHI LEADER

Street Address: 175 General Manson Way ,
Province: NB
Postal: E1N 6K7
Country: Canada
Mailing address: PO Box 500
Mailing city: Miramichi
Province: NB
Postal: E1V 3M6
General Phone: (506) 622-2600
General Fax: (506) 622-6506
General/National Adv. E-mail: news@miramichileader.com
Editorial e-mail: cook.nancy@miramichileader.com
Primary Website: https://www.telegraphjournal.com/miramichi-leader/
Areas Served - City/County or Portion Thereof, or Zip codes: Canada
Mechanical specifications: Type page 10 9/16 x 16; E - 6 cols, 1 2/3, 1/8 between; A - 6 cols, 1 2/3, 1/8 between; C - 6 cols, 1 2/3, 1/4 between.
Published: Mon`Wed
Avg Paid Circ: 3768
Avg Free Circ: 13
Audit By: CMCA
Audit Date: 31.12.2013
Personnel: Nancy Cook (Pub.); Christine Savoy (Circ. Mgr.)
Parent company (for newspapers): Brunswick News, Inc.

MISSION

MISSION CITY RECORD

Street Address: 33047 1st Ave. ,
Province: BC
Postal: V2V 1G2
Country: Canada
Mailing address: 33047 1st Ave.
Mailing city: Mission
Province: BC
Postal: V2V 1G2
General Phone: (604) 826-6221
General Fax: (604) 826-8266
Advertising Phone: (800) 363-2232
General/National Adv. E-mail: news@missioncityrecord.com
Display Adv. E-mail: karen.murtagh@missioncityrecord.com
Classified Adv. e-mail: adcontrol@missioncityrecord.com
Editorial e-mail: kevin.mills@missioncityrecord.com
Primary Website: www.missioncityrecord.com
Year Established: 1908
Areas Served - City/County or Portion Thereof, or Zip codes: Mission - Abbotsford
Commercial printers?: Y
Mechanical specifications: Type page 10 3/8 x 12 7/8; E - 6 cols, 1 5/8, between; A - 6 cols, 1 5/8, between; C - 6 cols, 1 5/8, between.
Published: Fri
Avg Paid Circ: 21
Avg Free Circ: 10968
Audit By: AAM
Audit Date: 31.12.2018
Personnel: Carly Ferguson (Pub); Kevin Mills (Ed); Krista Stobbe (Office Mgr.)
Parent company (for newspapers): Black Press Group Ltd.

MISSISSAUGA

AWAAZ PUNJABI

Street Address: 7015 Tranmere Dr. Suite #16 ,
Province: ON
Postal: L5S 1T7
Country: Canada
Mailing address: 7015 Tranmere Dr. Suite #16
Mailing city: Mississauga
Province: ON
Postal: L5S 1T7
General Phone: (905)795-8282
General Fax: (905) 795-9801
Advertising Phone: (416) 899 8140
Editorial Phone: (905) 795-0639
General/National Adv. E-mail: info@weeklyvoice.com
Display Adv. E-mail: marketing@weeklyvoice.com
Classified Adv. e-mail: admin@weeklyvoice.com
Editorial e-mail: pnews@weeklyvoice.com
Primary Website: www.awaazpunjabi.com
Year Established: 2000
Delivery Methods: Mail`Newsstand`Racks
Areas Served - City/County or Portion Thereof, or Zip codes: Canada
Published: Wed
Avg Free Circ: 9900
Audit By: CMCA
Audit Date: 29.02.2016
Personnel: Sudhir Anand

BRAMPTON GUARDIAN

Street Address: 3145 Wolfedale Rd. ,
Province: ON
Postal: L5C 3A9
Country: Canada
Mailing address: 3145 Wolfedale Rd.
Mailing city: Mississauga
Province: ON
Postal: L5C 3A9
General Phone: (905) 273-8111
General Fax: (905) 454-4385
General/National Adv. E-mail: letters@thebramptonguardian.com
Display Adv. E-mail: scotthartman@thebramptonguardian.com
Classified Adv. e-mail: classified@thebramptonguardian.com
Editorial e-mail: plonergan@metroland.com
Primary Website: thebramptonguardian.com
Delivery Methods: Carrier
Areas Served - City/County or Portion Thereof, or Zip codes: Canada
Own Printing Facility?: Y
Commercial printers?: Y
Mechanical specifications: Type page 13 x 22 1/2; E - 10 cols, 1 1/16, between; A - 10 cols, 1 1/16, between; C - 10 cols, 1 1/16, between.
Published: Thur`Fri
Avg Paid Circ: 0
Avg Free Circ: 137132
Audit By: CCAB
Audit Date: 9/31/2017
Personnel: Dave Coleman (Circ. Mgr.); Dana Robbins (Pub); Bill Anderson (Gen Mgr); Patricia Lonergan (Ed)
Parent company (for newspapers): Metroland Media Group Ltd.

MISSISSAUGA NEWS

Street Address: 3145 Wolfedale Road ,
Province: ON
Postal: L5C 3A9
Country: Canada`
Mailing address: 3145 Wolfedale Road
Mailing city: Mississauga
Province: ON
Postal: L5C 3A9
General Phone: (905) 273-8230
General Fax: (905) 568-0181
General/National Adv. E-mail: www.mississauga.com
Editorial e-mail: tlanks@mississauga.net
Primary Website: mississauga.com
Areas Served - City/County or Portion Thereof, or Zip codes: Canada
Published: Thur`Fri
Avg Paid Circ: 0
Avg Free Circ: 153598
Audit By: CCAB
Audit Date: 30.09.2017
Personnel: Dana Robbins (Pub.); Clark Kim (Community News/Ed.)
Parent company (for newspapers): Metroland Media Group Ltd.

MITCHELL

THE MITCHELL ADVOCATE

Street Address: 42 Montreal St. ,
Province: ON
Postal: N0K 1N0
Country: Canada
Mailing address: P.O. Box 669
Mailing city: Mitchell
Province: ON
Postal: N0K 1N0
General Phone: (519) 348-8431
General Fax: (519) 348-8836
General/National Adv. E-mail: abader@bowesnet.com
Primary Website: www.mitchelladvocate.com
Areas Served - City/County or Portion Thereof, or Zip codes: Canada
Mechanical specifications: Type page 11 3/8 x 21 1/4; E - 6 cols, 1 3/4, between; A - 6 cols, 1 3/4, between; C - 6 cols, 1 3/4, between.
Published: Wed
Avg Paid Circ: 1790
Avg Free Circ: 22
Audit By: CMCA
Audit Date: 30.06.2016
Personnel: Andy Bader (Ed.); Juanita Belfour (Adv. Mgr.)
Parent company (for newspapers): Postmedia Network Inc.; Quebecor Communications, Inc.

MONT TREMBLANT

INFORMATION DU NORD SAINTE-AGATHE

Street Address: 1107 Rue De Saint Jovite ,
Province: QC
Postal: J8E 3J9
Country: Canada
Mailing address: 1107 rue de Saint Jovite
Mailing city: Mont Tremblant
Province: QC
Postal: J8E 3J9
General Phone: (819) 425-8658
General Fax: (819) 425-7713
General/National Adv. E-mail: johanne.regimbald@quebecormedia.com
Primary Website: www.linformationdunordsainteagathe.ca
Commercial printers?: Y
Mechanical specifications: Type page 10 x 11 1/2; E - 10 cols, between.
Published: Thur
Avg Paid Circ: 15474
Avg Free Circ: 26
Audit By: Sworn/Estimate/Non-Audited
Audit Date: 12.07.2019
Personnel: Johanne Regimbald
Parent company (for newspapers): Quebecor Communications, Inc.

MONTAGUE

ATLANTIC POST CALLS

Street Address: 567 Main Street ,
Province: PE
Postal: C0A 1R0
Country: Canada
Mailing address: PO Box 790
Mailing city: Montague
Province: PE
Postal: C0A 1R0
General Phone: (902) 838-2515
General Fax: (902) 838-4392
Advertising Phone: (902) 838-4392 Ext. 203
Advertising Fax: (902) 838-4392
Editorial Phone: (902) 838-2515 x 201
Editorial Fax: (902) 838-4392
General/National Adv. E-mail: subscribe@peicanada.com
Display Adv. E-mail: jan@peicanada.com
Editorial e-mail: paul@peicanada.com
Primary Website: www.peicanada.com
Year Established: 1979
Areas Served - City/County or Portion Thereof, or Zip codes: Canada
Published: Fri
Avg Paid Circ: 752
Avg Free Circ: 625
Audit By: CMCA
Audit Date: 28.02.2014
Personnel: Paul MacNeill; Jan MacNeill

THE EASTERN GRAPHIC

Street Address: 567 Main St. ,
Province: PE
Postal: C0A 1R0
Country: Canada
Mailing address: PO Box 790
Mailing city: Montague
Province: PE
Postal: C0A 1R0
General Phone: (902) 838-2515
General Fax: (902) 838-4392
General/National Adv. E-mail: subscribo@peicanada.com
Editorial e-mail: editor@peicanada.com
Primary Website: www.peicanada.com
Areas Served - City/County or Portion Thereof, or Zip codes: Canada
Commercial printers?: Y
Mechanical specifications: Type page 13 x 21 1/2; E - 6 cols, 2, between; A - 6 cols, 2, between; C - 6 cols, 2, between.
Published: Wed
Avg Paid Circ: 4743
Avg Free Circ: 196
Audit By: CMCA
Audit Date: 30.06.2014
Personnel: Paul MacNeill (Pub.); Jan MacNeill (Adv. Mgr.); Heather Moore (Ed.); Kim Madigan (Prodn. Coord.)

MONT-JOLI

LE INFORMATION

Street Address: Rue Doucet ,
Province: QC
Postal: G5H 1R6
Country: Canada
Mailing address: rue Doucet
Mailing city: Mont-Joli
Province: QC
Postal: G5H 1R6
General Phone: (418) 775-4381
Areas Served - City/County or Portion Thereof, or Zip codes: Canada
Published: Wed
Avg Paid Circ: 33
Avg Free Circ: 9867
Audit By: CCAB
Audit Date: 31.03.2014
Personnel: Francis Desrosiers

MONT-LAURIER

JOURNAL LE CHOIX D'ANTOINE LABELLE

Street Address: Boulevard A.-paquette ,
Province: QC
Postal: J9L1K5
Country: Canada
Mailing address: boulevard A.-Paquette
Mailing city: Mont-Laurier
Province: QC
Postal: J9L1K5
General Phone: (819) 623-3112
Areas Served - City/County or Portion Thereof, or Zip codes: Canada
Published: Wed
Avg Paid Circ: 0
Avg Free Circ: 17000
Audit By: CCAB
Audit Date: 30.09.2012
Personnel: Andre Guillemette

JOURNAL LE COURANT DES HAUTES-LAURENTIDES

Street Address: 534, De La Madone ,
Province: QC

Postal: J9L 1S5
Country: Canada
Mailing address: 534, de la Madone
Mailing city: Mont-Laurier
Province: QC
Postal: J9L 1S5
General Phone: (819) 623-7374
General Fax: (819) 623-7375
Primary Website: www.lecourant.ca
Published: Thur
Avg Free Circ: 18400
Audit By: ODC
Audit Date: 14.12.2010
Personnel: Sylvie Vaillancourt

MONTMAGNY

LE PEUPLE COTE-SUD

Street Address: 80 Boul. Tache E. ,
Province: QC
Postal: G5V 3S7
Country: Canada
Mailing address: PO Box 430
Mailing city: Montmagny
Province: QC
Postal: G5V 3S7
General Phone: (418) 248-0415
General Fax: (418) 248-2377
General/National Adv. E-mail: peuple-cote-sud@globetrotter.net; vemtes.cote.sud@gmail.com
Primary Website: www.camoe.ca
Year Established: 1900
Areas Served - City/County or Portion Thereof, or Zip codes: Canada
Mechanical specifications: Type page 10 1/4 x 11 3/4.
Published: Wed
Avg Paid Circ: 27
Avg Free Circ: 20852
Audit By: CCAB
Audit Date: 30.09.2012
Personnel: Clauettne Tardis (Pub.)
Parent company (for newspapers): Quebecor Communications, Inc.

L'OIE BLANCHE

Street Address: 70 Rue De L'anse ,
Province: QC
Postal: G5V 1G8
Country: Canada
Mailing address: 70 Rue de L'Anse
Mailing city: Montmagny
Province: QC
Postal: G5V 1G8
General Phone: (418) 248-8820
General Fax: (418) 248-4033
General/National Adv. E-mail: oieblanc@globetrotter.net
Primary Website: www.oieblanc.com
Areas Served - City/County or Portion Thereof, or Zip codes: Canada
Mechanical specifications: Type page 11 3/4 x 15.
Published: Wed
Avg Paid Circ: 17
Avg Free Circ: 22533
Audit By: CCAB
Audit Date: 30.09.2015
Personnel: Yannick Patelli (Pub.)
Parent company (for newspapers): Reseau Select/Select Network

MONTREAL

ECHOS VEDETTES

Street Address: 465 Mcgill Ave. ,
Province: QC
Postal: H2W 2H1
Country: Canada
Mailing address: 465 McGill Ave.
Mailing city: Montreal
Province: QC
Postal: H2W 2H1
General Phone: (514) 528-7111
General Fax: (514) 528-7115
General/National Adv. E-mail: redaction@echosvedettes.ca
Areas Served - City/County or Portion Thereof, or Zip codes: Canada
Published: Sat
Avg Paid Circ: 54193
Avg Free Circ: 875
Audit By: Sworn/Estimate/Non-Audited
Audit Date: 12.07.2019
Personnel: Sylvie Bourgeault (Gen. Mgr.)

FLAMBEAU

Street Address: Boulevard Langelier Bureau 210 , Bureau 210
Province: QC
Postal: H1P 3C6
Country: Canada
Mailing address: boulevard Langelier Bureau 210
Mailing city: Montreal
Province: QC
Postal: H1P 3C6
General Phone: (514) 899-5888
Areas Served - City/County or Portion Thereof, or Zip codes: Canada
Published: Tues
Avg Paid Circ: 0
Avg Free Circ: 56194
Audit By: CCAB
Audit Date: 31.03.2014
Personnel: Stephane Desjardins

GUIDE DE MONTREAL-NORD

Street Address: Boulevard Langelier Bureau 210 , Bureau 210
Province: QC
Postal: H1P 3C6
Country: Canada
Mailing address: boulevard Langelier Bureau 210
Mailing city: Montreal
Province: QC
Postal: H1P 3C6
General Phone: (514) 899-5888
Areas Served - City/County or Portion Thereof, or Zip codes: Canada
Published: Tues
Avg Paid Circ: 0
Avg Free Circ: 34440
Audit By: CCAB
Audit Date: 31.03.2014
Personnel: Yannick Pinel

INFORMATEUR DE RIVIERE DES PRAIRIES

Street Address: Boulevard Langelier Bureau 210 , Bureau 210
Province: QC
Postal: H1P 3C6
Country: Canada
Mailing address: boulevard Langelier Bureau 210
Mailing city: Montreal
Province: QC
Postal: H1P 3C6
General Phone: (514) 899-5888
Areas Served - City/County or Portion Thereof, or Zip codes: Canada
Published: Tues
Avg Free Circ: 20917
Audit By: CCAB
Audit Date: 31.03.2014
Personnel: Yannick Pinel

JOURNAL DE ROSEMONT / PETITE PATRIE

Street Address: 8770 Langelier Boulevard Bureau 210 ,
Province: QC
Postal: H1P 3C6
Country: Canada
Mailing address: 8770 Langelier Boulevard Bureau 210
Mailing city: Montreal
Province: QC
Postal: H1P 3C6
General Phone: (514) 899-5888
General Fax: (514) 899-5001
General/National Adv. E-mail: rosepatrie@tc.tc
Primary Website: www.journalderosemont.com
Areas Served - City/County or Portion Thereof, or Zip codes: Canada
Published: Tues
Avg Paid Circ: 0
Avg Free Circ: 59344
Audit By: CCAB
Audit Date: 31.03.2014
Personnel: Stephane Desjardins

JOURNAL DE ST MICHEL

Street Address: Cp 50, Succ. St-michel ,
Province: QC
Postal: H2A 3L8
Country: Canada
Mailing address: CP 50, succ. St-Michel
Mailing city: Montreal
Province: QC
Postal: H2A 3L8
General Phone: (514) 721-4911
General Fax: (514) 374-4171
General/National Adv. E-mail: admin@journaldestmichel.com
Primary Website: www.journaldestmichel.com
Published: Sat
Avg Paid Circ: 20
Avg Free Circ: 24035
Audit By: ODC
Audit Date: 14.12.2011
Personnel: Claude Bricault

JOURNAL L'AVENIR DE L'EST

Street Address: 8770, Boulevard Langelier Bureau 210 ,
Province: QC
Postal: H1P 3C6
Country: Canada
Mailing address: 8770, boulevard Langelier Bureau 210
Mailing city: MontrÃƒÂ‚Â©al
Province: QC
Postal: H1P 3C6
General Phone: (514) 899-5888
General Fax: (514) 899-5001
General/National Adv. E-mail: redaction_est@tc.tc
Primary Website: http://www.avenirdelest.com
Areas Served - City/County or Portion Thereof, or Zip codes: Canada
Published: Tues
Avg Paid Circ: 0
Avg Free Circ: 27818
Audit By: CCAB
Audit Date: 31.03.2014
Personnel: Paul Sauve (Ed.)

NOUVELLES HOCHELAGA MAISONNEUVE

Street Address: Boulevard Langelier Bureau 210 , Bureau 210
Province: QC
Postal: H1P 3C6
Country: Canada
Mailing address: boulevard Langelier Bureau 210
Mailing city: Montreal
Province: QC
Postal: H1P 3C6
General Phone: (514) 899-5888
General/National Adv. E-mail: redactioncentre@tc.tc
Primary Website: www.nouvelleshochelagamaisonneuve.com
Areas Served - City/County or Portion Thereof, or Zip codes: Canada
Published: Tues
Avg Free Circ: 22615
Audit By: CCAB
Audit Date: 31.03.2014
Personnel: Stephane Desjardins

ORATOIRE

Street Address: Chemin Queen Mary ,
Province: QC
Postal: H3V 1H6
Country: Canada
Mailing address: chemin Queen Mary
Mailing city: Montreal
Province: QC
Postal: H3V 1H6
General Phone: (514) 733-8211
Published: Sat
Avg Paid Circ: 25131
Avg Free Circ: 4346
Audit By: ODC
Audit Date: 14.12.2011
Personnel: Claude Grou

PLATEAU

Street Address: 8770 Langelier Boulevard Bureau 210 ,
Province: QC
Postal: H1P 3C6
Country: Canada
Mailing address: 8770 Langelier boulevard Bureau 210
Mailing city: Montreal
Province: QC
Postal: H1P 3C6
General Phone: (514) 899-5888
General Fax: (514) 899-5001
General/National Adv. E-mail: redactioncentre@tc.tc
Primary Website: www.leplateau.com
Areas Served - City/County or Portion Thereof, or Zip codes: Canada
Published: Thur
Avg Free Circ: 34869
Audit By: CCAB
Audit Date: 31.03.2014
Personnel: Stephane Desjardins

THE SUBURBAN WEST ISLAND

Street Address: 7575 Trans Canada Hwy, Suite 105 ,
Province: QC
Postal: H4T 1V6
Mailing address: 7575 Trans Canada Hwy. Suite 105
Mailing city: Montreal
Province: QC
Postal: H4T 1V6
General Phone: (514) 484-1107
General Fax: (514) 484-9616
General/National Adv. E-mail: suburban@thesuburban.com
Display Adv. E-mail: amanda@thesuburban.com
Editorial e-mail: editor@thesuburban.com
Primary Website: www.westislandgazette.com
Published: Wed
Avg Free Circ: 40239
Audit By: CMCA
Audit Date: 31.12.2013
Personnel: Beryl Wajsman (Editor-in-chief); Amanda Lavigne (Director of sales)

TOURISME PLUS

Street Address: B.p. 7 Succ Ahuntsic , Succ. Ahuntsic
Province: QC
Postal: H3L 3N5
Country: Canada
Mailing address: B.P. 7 Succ Ahuntsic
Mailing city: Montreal
Province: QC
Postal: H3L 3N5
General Phone: (514) 881-8583
Published: Wed
Avg Paid Circ: 123
Avg Free Circ: 1266
Audit By: ODC
Audit Date: 14.12.2011
Personnel: Michel Villeneuve

TRANSCONTINENTAL MEDIAS

Street Address: 8770 Langelier , Suite 210

Province: QC
Postal: H1P 3C6
Country: Canada
Mailing address: 8770 Langelier
Mailing city: Montreal
Province: QC
Postal: H1P 3C6
General Phone: (514) 899-5888
Advertising Fax: (514) 899-5001
General/National Adv. E-mail: sdesjardins@transcontinental.ca
Primary Website: www.journalderosemont.com
Delivery Methods: Carrier`Racks
Mechanical specifications: Type page 10 x 14; E - 8 cols, 1 1/4, 1/8 between; A - 8 cols, 1 1/4, 1/8 between; C - 8 cols, 1 1/4, 1/8 between.
Published: Tues
Avg Free Circ: 36024
Audit By: Sworn/Estimate/Non-Audited
Audit Date: 12.07.2019
Personnel: Stephane Desjardins (publisher)
Parent company (for newspapers): Transcontinental Media

VERDUN MESSENGER
Street Address: 6239 Monk Blvd. ,
Province: QC
Postal: H4E 3H8
Country: Canada
Mailing address: 6239 Monk Blvd.
Mailing city: Montreal
Province: QC
Postal: H4E 3H8
General Phone: (514) 768-1920
General Fax: (514) 768-3306
General/National Adv. E-mail: lussierp@transcontinental.ca
Areas Served - City/County or Portion Thereof, or Zip codes: Canada
Published: Thur
Avg Paid Circ: 3
Avg Free Circ: 24364
Audit By: CCAB
Audit Date: 31.03.2014
Personnel: Lou Mercaer (Pub.); Pierre Lussier (Ed.)

MONT-TREMBLANT

INFORMATION DU NORD L'ANNONCIATION
Street Address: 1107, Rue De St-jovite ,
Province: QC
Postal: J8E 3J9
Country: Canada
Mailing address: 1107, Rue De St-Jovite
Mailing city: Mont-Tremblant
Province: QC
Postal: J8E 3J9
General Phone: (819) 425-8658
General Fax: (819) 425-7713
General/National Adv. E-mail: infonord.journal@quebecormedia.com
Primary Website: www.hebdosquebecor.com
Year Established: 1980
Commercial printers?: Y
Mechanical specifications: Type page 10 x 11 1/2.
Published: Thur
Avg Paid Circ: 7974
Avg Free Circ: 15500
Audit By: Sworn/Estimate/Non-Audited
Audit Date: 12.07.2019
Personnel: Josee Gauvin (Ed.); Johanne Regimbald (ÃƒÂƒÂ££££ditrice)
Parent company (for newspapers): Quebecor Communications, Inc.

INFORMATION DU NORD MONT TREMBLANT
Street Address: 1107 Rue De St. Jovite ,
Province: QC
Postal: J8E 3J9
Country: Canada
Mailing address: 1107 rue de St. Jovite
Mailing city: Mont-Tremblant
Province: QC
Postal: J8E 3J9
General Phone: (819) 425-8658
General Fax: (819) 425-7713
General/National Adv. E-mail: info.nord@hebdosquebecor.com
Primary Website: www.hebdosquebecor.com
Areas Served - City/County or Portion Thereof, or Zip codes: Canada
Commercial printers?: Y
Mechanical specifications: Type page 10 x .
Published: Wed
Avg Paid Circ: 4
Avg Free Circ: 15029
Audit By: CCAB
Audit Date: 31.03.2014
Personnel: Michel Gareau (Adv. Mgr.); Johanne Regimbald
Parent company (for newspapers): Quebecor Communications, Inc.

INFORMATION DU NORD VALLEE DE LA ROUGE
Street Address: Rue De St-jovite ,
Province: QC
Postal: J8E 3J9
Country: Canada
Mailing address: rue de St-Jovite
Mailing city: Mont-Tremblant
Province: QC
Postal: J8E 3J9
General Phone: (819) 425-8658
Areas Served - City/County or Portion Thereof, or Zip codes: Canada
Published: Wed
Avg Paid Circ: 2
Avg Free Circ: 15487
Audit By: CCAB
Audit Date: 31.03.2014
Personnel: Johanne Regimbald

POINT DE VUE LAURENTIDES
Street Address: 580 Rue De Saint Jovite Ste 201 ,
Province: QC
Postal: J8E 2Z9
Country: Canada
Mailing address: 580 Rue de Saint Jovite Ste 201
Mailing city: Mont-Tremblant
Province: QC
Postal: J8E 2Z9
General Phone: (819) 425-7666
General Fax: (819) 425-9111
Advertising Phone: (819) 425-7666
Advertising Fax: (819) 425-9111
Editorial Phone: (819) 425-7666
Editorial Fax: (819) 425-9111
General/National Adv. E-mail: infolaurentides@transcontinental.ca
Display Adv. E-mail: infolaurentides@transcontinental.ca
Editorial e-mail: infolaurentides@transcontinental.ca
Primary Website: www.pointdevuemonttremblant.com
Delivery Methods: Mail`Racks
Areas Served - City/County or Portion Thereof, or Zip codes: Canada
Published: Wed
Avg Free Circ: 31760
Audit By: CCAB
Audit Date: 31.03.2014

MOOSE JAW

FYI
Street Address: 44 Fairford St W. ,
Province: SK
Postal: S6H 1V1
Country: Canada
Mailing address: 44 Fairford St. W.
Mailing city: Moose Jaw
Province: SK
Postal: S6H 1V1
General Phone: (306) 692-6441
General/National Adv. E-mail: editorial@mjtimes.sk.ca
Editorial e-mail: editorial@mjtimes.sk.ca
Primary Website: www.mjtimes.sk.ca
Areas Served - City/County or Portion Thereof, or Zip codes: Canada
Published: Wed
Avg Free Circ: 24086
Audit By: CMCA
Audit Date: 31.12.2013

MOOSOMIN

WORLD-SPECTATOR
Street Address: 714 Main Street ,
Province: SK
Postal: S0G 3N0
Country: Canada
Mailing address: PO Box 250
Mailing city: Moosomin
Province: SK
Postal: S0G 3N0
General Phone: (306) 435-2445
General Fax: (306) 435-3969
General/National Adv. E-mail: world_spectator@sasktel.net
Primary Website: www.world-spectator.com
Year Established: 1884
Delivery Methods: Mail`Newsstand
Areas Served - City/County or Portion Thereof, or Zip codes: Moosomin, Rocanville, Wapella, Wawota, Redvers, Maryfield, Spy Hill, Tantallon, Elkhorn, St Lazare
Own Printing Facility?: Y
Commercial printers?: Y
Mechanical specifications: Type page 10 x 16 1/2; E - 6 cols, 1/6 between; A - 6 cols, 1/6 between; C - 6 cols, 1/6 between.
Published: Mon
Avg Paid Circ: 3609
Audit By: CMCA
Audit Date: 31.12.2015
Personnel: Kevin Weedmark (Ed.)

MORINVILLE

THE FREE PRESS
Street Address: 10126 100 Ave. ,
Province: AB
Postal: T8R 1R9
Country: Canada
Mailing address: PO Box 3005
Mailing city: Morinville
Province: AB
Postal: T8R 1R9
General Phone: (780) 939-3309
General Fax: (780) 939-3093
Advertising Phone: (780) 939-3309
General/National Adv. E-mail: redwater@shaw.ca
Display Adv. E-mail: morinville@shaw.ca
Primary Website: www.cowleynewspapers.com
Year Established: 1995
Areas Served - City/County or Portion Thereof, or Zip codes: Sturgeon County
Mechanical specifications: Type page 10 1/4 x 15 1/2; E - 6 cols, 1 1/2, 1/12 between; A - 6 cols, 1 1/2, 1/12 between; C - 6 cols, 1 1/2, 1/12 between.
Published: Tues
Avg Paid Circ: 55
Avg Free Circ: 11996
Audit By: VAC
Audit Date: 31.07.2016
Personnel: Ed Cowley (Pub.)
Parent company (for newspapers): W & E Cowley Publishing Ltd.

MORRISBURG

THE MORRISBURG LEADER
Street Address: Hwy. 2, 31 Shopping Centre, 41 Main St. ,
Province: ON
Postal: K0C 1X0
Country: Canada
Mailing address: PO Box 891
Mailing city: Morrisburg
Province: ON
Postal: K0C 1X0
General Phone: (613) 543-2987
General Fax: (613) 543-3643
General/National Adv. E-mail: info@morrisburgleader.ca
Display Adv. E-mail: leaderads@vianet.ca
Primary Website: www.morrisburgleader.ca
Year Established: 1976
Areas Served - City/County or Portion Thereof, or Zip codes: Canada
Own Printing Facility?: Y
Commercial printers?: Y
Mechanical specifications: Type page 12 3/8 x 21 1/2; E - 6 cols, 1/6 between; A - 6 cols, 1/6 between; C - 6 cols, 1/6 between.
Published: Wed
Avg Paid Circ: 1774
Avg Free Circ: 54
Audit By: CMCA
Audit Date: 30.09.2016
Personnel: Mike Laurin (Adv. Mgr.); Wanda Dawley (Circ. Mgr.); Sam Laurin (Ed.); Bonnie McNairn (Mng. Ed.); Terry Laurin (Prodn. Mgr.)

MOUNT FOREST

ARTHUR ENTERPRISE NEWS
Street Address: 277 Main St. S. ,
Province: ON
Postal: N0G 2L0
Country: Canada
Mailing address: PO Box 130
Mailing city: Mount Forest
Province: ON
Postal: N0G 2L0
General Phone: (519) 323-1550
General Fax: (519) 323-4548
General/National Adv. E-mail: editor@mountforest.com
Display Adv. E-mail: phaasnoot@northperth.com
Classified Adv. e-mail: classifieds@metroland.com
Editorial e-mail: sburrows@metroland.com
Primary Website: http://www.southwesternontario.ca/arthur-on/
Year Established: 1862
Delivery Methods: Mail`Newsstand`Racks
Areas Served - City/County or Portion Thereof, or Zip codes: North Wellington
Own Printing Facility?: Y
Mechanical specifications: Page 10.375"x11.5"
Published: Wed
Avg Paid Circ: 2699
Avg Free Circ: 0
Audit By: VAC
Audit Date: 31.12.2015
Personnel: Shannon Burrows (Ed); Peggy Haasnoot (Adv)
Parent company (for newspapers): Metroland Media Group Ltd.; Torstar

THE MOUNT FOREST CONFEDERATE
Street Address: 277 Main St. S. ,
Province: ON
Postal: N0G 2L0
Country: Canada
Mailing address: PO Box 130
Mailing city: Mount Forest
Province: ON
Postal: N0G 2L0
General Phone: (519) 323-1550
General Fax: (519) 323-4548
General/National Adv. E-mail: editor@mountforest.com
Display Adv. E-mail: klucas@mountforest.com
Editorial e-mail: editor@mountforest.com
Primary Website: www.mountforest.com
Year Established: 1865
Delivery Methods: Mail`Newsstand
Areas Served - City/County or Portion Thereof, or Zip codes: Wellington County/ Grey County
Mechanical specifications: Type page 12 3/4 x 21 1/4; E - 6 cols, 1 1/2, 1/6 between; A - 6

cols, 1 1/2, 1/6 between; C - 6 cols, 1 1/2, 1/6 between.
Published: Wed
Avg Paid Circ: 1108
Audit By: CMCA
Audit Date: 30.06.2016
Personnel: Cathy Higdon (Circ. Mgr.); Lynne Turner (Ed.); Cornelia Svela (Prodn. Mgr.); Kim Lucas (Sales)
Parent company (for newspapers): Metroland Media Group Ltd.

MUENSTER

ORDER OF ST. BENEDICT

Street Address: 100 College Dr. ,
Province: SK
Postal: S0K 2Y0
Country: Canada
Mailing address: PO Box 190
Mailing city: Muenster
Province: SK
Postal: S0K 2Y0
General Phone: (306) 682-1772
General Fax: (306) 682-5285
General/National Adv. E-mail: pm@stpeterspress.ca
Display Adv. E-mail: pm.ads@stpeterspress.ca
Editorial e-mail: pm.canadian@stpeterspress.ca
Primary Website: www.prairiemessenger.ca
Year Established: 1904
Delivery Methods: Mail
Areas Served - City/County or Portion Thereof, or Zip codes: Canada
Own Printing Facility?: Y
Commercial printers?: Y
Mechanical specifications: Type page 10 1/8 x 15; E - 5 cols, 2, 1/6 between; A - 5 cols, 2, 1/6 between; C - 5 cols, 2, 1/6 between.
Published: Wed
Avg Paid Circ: 4300
Audit By: CMCA
Audit Date: 02.09.2016
Personnel: Gail Kleefeld (Adv. Mgr.); Peter Novecosky (Ed.); Maureen Weber (Assoc. Ed.); Don Ward (Assoc. Ed.); Lucille Stewart (Layout Artist)

NAKUSP

ARROW LAKES NEWS

Street Address: 89 1st Avenue Northwest ,
Province: BC
Postal: V0G 1R0
Country: Canada
Mailing address: PO Box 189
Mailing city: Nakusp
Province: BC
Postal: V0G 1R0
General Phone: (250) 265-3841
General/National Adv. E-mail: newsroom@arrowlakesnews.com; sales@arrowlakesnews.com
Display Adv. E-mail: sales@arrowlakesnews.com
Editorial e-mail: newsroom@arrowlakesnews.com
Primary Website: www.arrowlakenews.com
Year Established: 1999
Delivery Methods: Mail`Newsstand
Areas Served - City/County or Portion Thereof, or Zip codes: Canada
Mechanical specifications: Type page 10 1/4 x 14 1/4; E - 6 cols, 1 1/2, between; A - 6 cols, 1 1/2, between; C - 6 cols, 1 1/2, between.
Published: Wed
Avg Paid Circ: 585
Avg Free Circ: 10
Audit By: VAC
Audit Date: 30.06.2017
Personnel: Eric Lawson (Pub.)
Parent company (for newspapers): Black Press Group Ltd.

NANAIMO

NANAIMO NEWS BULLETIN

Street Address: 777 Poplar St. ,
Province: BC
Postal: V9S 2H7
Country: Canada
Mailing address: 777 Poplar St.
Mailing city: Nanaimo
Province: BC
Postal: V9S 2H7
General Phone: (250) 753-3707
General Fax: (250) 753-0788
Editorial Phone: (250) 734-4621
Display Adv. E-mail: sueb@blackpress.ca
Editorial e-mail: editor@nanaimobulletin.com
Primary Website: www.nanaimobulletin.com
Year Established: 1988
Areas Served - City/County or Portion Thereof, or Zip codes: Canada
Own Printing Facility?: Y
Mechanical specifications: Type page 10 1/4 x 14 1/2; A - 6 cols, 1 7/8, 1/8 between; C - 7 cols, 1 7/8, 1/8 between.
Published: Mon`Fri`Sat
Avg Free Circ: 31789
Audit By: AAM
Audit Date: 31.03.2019
Personnel: Sean McCue (Pub); Melissa Fryer (Ed.); Darrell Summerfelt (Prodn. Mgr.)
Parent company (for newspapers): Black Press Group Ltd.

NANTON

THE NANTON NEWS

Street Address: 2019 20th Avenue ,
Province: AB
Postal: T0L 1R0
Country: Canada
Mailing address: PO Box 429
Mailing city: Nanton
Province: AB
Postal: T0L 1R0
General Phone: (403) 646-2023
General Fax: (403) 646-2848
General/National Adv. E-mail: info@highrivertimes.com
Editorial e-mail: sheena.read@sunmedia.ca
Primary Website: www.nantonnews.com
Year Established: 1903
Areas Served - City/County or Portion Thereof, or Zip codes: Canada
Commercial printers?: Y
Published: Wed
Avg Paid Circ: 592
Avg Free Circ: 8
Audit By: CMCA
Audit Date: 30.06.2014
Personnel: Nancy Middleton (Pub.); Donna Knowles (Circ. Mgr.); Shawn Cornell (Group Pub.); Lorelei Doell (Circ. Mgr.); Sheena Reed (Ed.); Roxanne Mackintosh (Reg. Adv. Dir.); Stephen Tipper (Ed.)
Parent company (for newspapers): Postmedia Network Inc.

NAPANEE

NAPANEE GUIDE

Street Address: 2 Dairy Ave., Unit 11 ,
Province: ON
Postal: K7R 3T1
Country: Canada
Mailing address: 2 Dairy Ave., Unit 11
Mailing city: Napanee
Province: ON
Postal: K7R 3T1
General Phone: (613) 354-6648
General Fax: (613) 354-6708
General/National Adv. E-mail: news@napaneeguide.com
Display Adv. E-mail: david@napaneeguide.com
Primary Website: www.napaneeguide.com
Areas Served - City/County or Portion Thereof, or Zip codes: Canada
Published: Thur
Avg Free Circ: 14962
Audit By: CMCA
Audit Date: 30.06.2016
Personnel: Liza Nelson (Group Adv. Dir.); Rob McLellan (Distribution Supervisor)
Parent company (for newspapers): Postmedia Network Inc.; Quebecor Communications, Inc.

THE NAPANEE BEAVER

Street Address: 72 Dundas St. E. ,
Province: ON
Postal: K7R 1H9
Country: Canada
Mailing address: 72 Dundas St. E.
Mailing city: Napanee
Province: ON
Postal: K7R 1H9
General Phone: (613) 354-6641
General Fax: (613) 354-2622
General/National Adv. E-mail: beaver@bellnet.ca
Primary Website: www.napaneebeaver.com
Year Established: 1870
Delivery Methods: Carrier
Areas Served - City/County or Portion Thereof, or Zip codes: Canada
Mechanical specifications: Type page 12 x 21 1/4.
Published: Thur
Avg Free Circ: 15698
Audit By: CMCA
Audit Date: 30.06.2016
Personnel: Jean M. Morrison (Pub.); Deb Mccann (Bus. Mgr.); Seth Duchene (Ed.); Michelle Bowes (Prodn. Mgr.); Scott Johnston

NAPIERVILLE

JOURNAL LE COUP D'OEIL

Street Address: 350 Saint Jacques St. ,
Province: QC
Postal: J0J 1L0
Country: Canada
Mailing address: 350 Saint Jacques St.
Mailing city: Napierville
Province: QC
Postal: J0J 1L0
General Phone: (450) 245-3344
General Fax: (450) 245-7419
General/National Adv. E-mail: coupdoeil@tc.tc
Primary Website: www.coupdoeil.info
Year Established: 1978
Areas Served - City/County or Portion Thereof, or Zip codes: Canada
Commercial printers?: Y
Published: Wed
Avg Paid Circ: 9
Avg Free Circ: 15602
Audit By: CCAB
Audit Date: 31.03.2014
Personnel: Charles Couture (Circ. Mgr.); Claude Trahan (Mng. Ed.); Jacques LaRochelle (Journalist)

NATASHQUAN

LE PORTAGEUR

Street Address: 50, Chemin D'en-haut ,
Province: QC
Postal: G0G 2E0
Country: Canada
Mailing address: CP 40
Mailing city: Natashquan
Province: QC
Postal: G0G 2E0
General Phone: (418) 726-3736
General Fax: (418) 726-3714
General/National Adv. E-mail: secom@quebectel.com
Mechanical specifications: Type page 8 1/2 x 11; E - 3 cols, 2 1/2, 1/8 between; C - 3 cols, 2 1/2, 1/8 between.
Published: Wed
Avg Free Circ: 490
Audit By: Sworn/Estimate/Non-Audited
Audit Date: 12.07.2019
Personnel: Cindy Carbonneau (Adv. Mgr.); Michel Richard (Ed.)

NEEPAWA

NEEPAWA BANNER

Street Address: 243 Hamilton St. ,
Province: MB
Postal: R0J 1H0
Country: Canada
Mailing address: PO Box 699
Mailing city: Neepawa
Province: MB
Postal: R0J 1H0
General Phone: (204) 476-3401
General Fax: (204) 476-5073
General/National Adv. E-mail: print@neepawabanner.com
Editorial e-mail: nekwaddell@neepawabanner.com
Primary Website: www.neepawabanner.com
Year Established: 1989
Areas Served - City/County or Portion Thereof, or Zip codes: Neepawa
Mechanical specifications: Type page 7 x 14; E - 8 cols, 1 7/8, 3/8 between; A - 6 cols, 1 5/8, 3/8 between; C - 6 cols, 1 5/8, 3/8 between.
Published: Fri
Avg Paid Circ: 92
Avg Free Circ: 8179
Audit By: VAC
Audit Date: 30.06.2017
Personnel: Ken Waddell (Pub/Ed.)

THE NEEPAWA BANNER AND PRESS

Street Address: 423 Hamilton St. ,
Province: MB
Postal: R0J 1H0
Country: Canada
Mailing address: PO Box 699
Mailing city: Neepawa
Province: MB
Postal: R0J 1H0
General Phone: (204) 476-3401
General Fax: (204) 476-5073
General/National Adv. E-mail: office@neepawapress.com
Display Adv. E-mail: ads@neepawabanner.com
Classified Adv. e-mail: print@neepawabanner.com
Editorial e-mail: news@neepawabanner.com
Primary Website: www.neepawabanner.com
Year Established: 1896
Delivery Methods: Mail`Newsstand`Racks
Areas Served - City/County or Portion Thereof, or Zip codes: R0J
Mechanical specifications: Type page 10 3/8 x 16; E - 6 cols, 1 9/16, 1/8 between; A - 6 cols, 1 9/16, 1/8 between; C - 6 cols, 1 9/16, 1/6 between.
Published: Fri
Avg Paid Circ: 100
Avg Free Circ: 8200
Audit By: VAC
Audit Date: 15.02.2018
Personnel: Kate Atkinson (Ed)
Parent company (for newspapers): Neepawa Banner

NELSON

NELSON STAR

Street Address: 91 Baker Street, Suite B ,
Province: BC
Postal: V1L 4G8
Country: Canada
Mailing address: 91 Baker Street, Suite B
Mailing city: Nelson
Province: BC
Postal: V1L 4G8
General Phone: (877) 365-6397
Display Adv. E-mail: advertising@nelsonstar.com
Editorial e-mail: editor@nelsonstar.com
Primary Website: www.nelsonstar.com
Year Established: 2008
Delivery Methods: Newsstand`Carrier`Racks

Non-Daily Newspapers in Canada

Areas Served - City/County or Portion Thereof, or Zip codes: Nelson and surrounding areas, British Columbia
Published: Wed`Fri
Avg Paid Circ: 0
Avg Free Circ: 8448
Audit By: VAC
Audit Date: 31.08.2016
Personnel: Eric Lawson (Publisher)
Parent company (for newspapers): Black Press Group Ltd.

NEW CARLISLE

SEA-COAST PUBLICATIONS INC./ THE GASPE SPEC

Street Address: 128 Gerard D. Levesque ,
Province: QC
Postal: G0C 1Z0
Country: Canada
Mailing address: PO Box 99
Mailing city: New Carlisle
Province: QC
Postal: G0C 1Z0
General Phone: (418) 752-5400
General Fax: (418) 752-6932
Editorial Phone: (418)752-5070
General/National Adv. E-mail: specs@globetrotter.net
Primary Website: www.gaspespec.com
Year Established: 1975
Delivery Methods: Mail`Newsstand
Areas Served - City/County or Portion Thereof, or Zip codes: Canada
Own Printing Facility?: N
Commercial printers?: Y
Mechanical specifications: Type page 10 1/4 x 15 1/2; E - 5 cols, 1 15/16, 1/8 between; A - 5 cols, 1 15/16, 1/8 between; C - 5 cols, 1 15/16, 1/8 between.
Published: Wed
Avg Paid Circ: 2309
Audit By: CMCA
Audit Date: 31.12.2015
Personnel: Sharon Renouf-Farrell (Pub.); Joan Sawyer Imhoff (Gen. Mgr.); Robert Bradbury (Adv. Mgr.); Gilles Gagne (News Ed.)

NEW HAMBURG

NEW HAMBURG INDEPENDENT

Street Address: 77 Peel St. ,
Province: ON
Postal: N3A 1E7
Country: Canada
General Phone: (519) 662-1240
General Fax: (519) 662-3521
General/National Adv. E-mail: editor@newhamburgindependent.ca
Display Adv. E-mail: kschattner@newhamburgindependent.ca
Classified Adv. e-mail: classified@metrolandwest.com
Editorial e-mail: editor@newhamburgindependent.ca
Primary Website: www.newhamburgindependent.ca
Year Established: 1878
Delivery Methods: Mail`Newsstand`Carrier
Areas Served - City/County or Portion Thereof, or Zip codes: Township of Wilmot
Own Printing Facility?: Y
Commercial printers?: N
Published: Wed
Avg Paid Circ: 1770
Audit By: CMCA
Audit Date: 30.06.2016
Personnel: Donna Luelo (Pub.); Heather Dunbar (Adv. Mgr.); Kyle Schattner (Adv. Rep.); Scott Miller Cressman (Ed); Leta Gastle (Admin/Circulation); Chris Thomson (Reporter/photographer)
Parent company (for newspapers): Metroland Media Group Ltd.; Torstar

NEW LISKEARD

SPEAKER WEEKENDER

Street Address: 18 Wellington St. ,
Province: ON
Postal: P0J 1P0
Country: Canada
Mailing address: PO Box 580
Mailing city: New Liskeard
Province: ON
Postal: P0J 1P0
General Phone: (705) 647-6791
General Fax: (705) 647-9669
General/National Adv. E-mail: loisperry@northontario.ca
Primary Website: www.facebook.com/pages/Temiskaming-Speaker-Weekender/884448971667310
Areas Served - City/County or Portion Thereof, or Zip codes: Canada
Published: Fri
Avg Free Circ: 10450
Audit By: CMCA
Audit Date: 31.03.2016
Personnel: Lois Perry (Gen. Mgr.)

TEMISKAMING SPEAKER

Street Address: 18 Wellington St. S. ,
Province: ON
Postal: P0J 1P0
Country: Canada
Mailing address: PO Box 580
Mailing city: New Liskeard
Province: ON
Postal: P0J 1P0
General Phone: (705) 647-6791
General Fax: (705) 647-9669
Advertising Fax: (705) 647-9669
General/National Adv. E-mail: ads@northernontario.ca
Editorial e-mail: editorial@northernontario.ca
Primary Website: www.northernontario.ca
Year Established: 1906
Delivery Methods: Mail`Newsstand`Carrier`Racks
Areas Served - City/County or Portion Thereof, or Zip codes: Canada
Own Printing Facility?: Y
Commercial printers?: Y
Mechanical specifications: Type page 13 x 21 1/4; E - 6 cols, 2 1/8, 1/8 between; A - 6 cols, 2 1/8, 1/8 between; C - 6 cols, 2 1/8, 1/8 between.
Published: Wed
Avg Paid Circ: 3021
Avg Free Circ: 138
Audit By: CMCA
Audit Date: 31.08.2015
Personnel: Lois Perry (Gen. Mgr.); Gordon Brock (Ed.)

NEW RICHMOND

L'ECHO DE LA BAIE

Street Address: 143 Boulevard Perron E ,
Province: QC
Postal: G0C 2B0
Country: Canada
Mailing address: 144, rue jacques cartier
Mailing city: Gaspe
Province: QC
Postal: G4X 1M9
General Phone: (418) 392-5083
General Fax: (418) 392-6605
General/National Adv. E-mail: bernard.johnson@quebecormedia.com
Editorial e-mail: redaction_latuque@tc.tc
Primary Website: lechodelabaie.canoe.ca
Areas Served - City/County or Portion Thereof, or Zip codes: Canada
Published: Wed
Avg Paid Circ: 7
Avg Free Circ: 18364
Audit By: CCAB
Audit Date: 31.03.2014
Personnel: Bernard Johnson (Pub.)
Parent company (for newspapers): Quebecor Communications, Inc.

NEW WESTMINSTER

NEW WESTMINSTER RECORD

Street Address: 201a-3430 Brighton Ave ,
Province: BC
Postal: V5A 3H4
Country: Canada
Mailing address: #201A â€" 3430 Brighton Ave.
Mailing city: Burnaby
Province: BC
Postal: V5A 3H4
General Phone: (604) 444-6451
Display Adv. E-mail: kgilmour@newwestrecord.ca
Classified Adv. e-mail: mmacleod@newwestrecord.ca
Editorial e-mail: ptracy@newwestrecord.ca
Primary Website: http://www.newwestrecord.ca/
Areas Served - City/County or Portion Thereof, or Zip codes: Canada
Published: Wed
Avg Paid Circ: 0
Avg Free Circ: 16290
Audit By: CCAB
Audit Date: 30.09.2015
Personnel: Lara Graham (Pub); Pat Tracy (Ed); Dale Dorsett (Circ Mgr)
Parent company (for newspapers): Glacier Media Group

NEWMARKET

BRADFORD & WEST GWILLIMBURY TOPIC

Street Address: 580b Steven Crt. ,
Province: ON
Postal: L3Y 4X1
Country: Canada
Mailing address: 580B Steven Crt.
Mailing city: Newmarket
Province: ON
Postal: L3Y 4X1
General Phone: (905) 775-1188
Display Adv. E-mail: asmug@metroland.com
Editorial e-mail: tmcfadden@yrmg.com
Primary Website: simcoe.com
Areas Served - City/County or Portion Thereof, or Zip codes: Canada
Published: Thur
Avg Free Circ: 10538
Audit By: CCAB
Audit Date: 31.12.2017
Personnel: Amanda Sung (Adv Mgr); Ted McFadden (Ed)
Parent company (for newspapers): Metroland Media Group Ltd.

THE NEWMARKET ERA-BANNER

Street Address: 580b Steven Ct ,
Province: ON
Postal: L3Y 4X1
Country: Canada
Mailing address: PO Box 236
Mailing city: Newmarket
Province: ON
Postal: L3Y 4X1
General Phone: (905) 773-7627
General Fax: (905) 853-5379
Advertising Phone: (416) 798-7284
Advertising Fax: (905) 853-5379
Editorial Fax: (905) 853-5379
General/National Adv. E-mail: admin@erabanner.com
Display Adv. E-mail: admin@erabanner.com
Editorial e-mail: newsroom@erabanner.com
Primary Website: yorkregion.com
Areas Served - City/County or Portion Thereof, or Zip codes: Newmarket, Aurora, East Gwillimbury, and York region
Published: Thur
Avg Paid Circ: 0
Avg Free Circ: 24371
Audit By: CCAB
Audit Date: 31.12.2017
Personnel: Ian Proudfoot (Pub.); Gord Paolucci (Dir., Adv./Prodn./Distribution); Dave Williams (Retail Sales Mgr.); Darlene Baker (Adv. Coord.); Megan Pike (Circ. Mgr.); Teresa Mathison (Distribution Coord.); Debora Kelly (Ed. in Chief); Ted McFadden (Ed.)
Parent company (for newspapers): Metroland Media Group Ltd.; Torstar

NICOLET

COURRIER-SUD

Street Address: 3255 Rte Marie-victorin ,
Province: QC
Postal: J3T 1X5
Country: Canada
Mailing address: 3255 Rte Marie-Victorin
Mailing city: Nicolet
Province: QC
Postal: J3T 1X5
General Phone: (819) 293-4551
General Fax: (819) 293-8758
General/National Adv. E-mail: redaction_cs@tc.tc
Editorial e-mail: redaction_cs@transcontinental.ca
Primary Website: www.lecourriersud.com
Areas Served - City/County or Portion Thereof, or Zip codes: Canada
Mechanical specifications: Type page 10 x 12 3/4.
Published: Wed
Avg Paid Circ: 52
Avg Free Circ: 20758
Audit By: CCAB
Audit Date: 31.03.2014
Personnel: Claire Knight (Sales Coord.); Nancy Allaire (Ed.)
Parent company (for newspapers): Transcontinental Media

NIPAWIN

NIPAWIN JOURNAL

Street Address: 117 1st Ave. ,
Province: SK
Postal: S0E 1E0
Country: Canada
Mailing address: PO Box 2014
Mailing city: Nipawin
Province: SK
Postal: S0E 1E0
General Phone: (306) 862-4618
General Fax: (306) 862-4566
Editorial e-mail: greg.wiseman@sunmedia.ca
Primary Website: www.nipawinjournal.com
Areas Served - City/County or Portion Thereof, or Zip codes: Canada
Commercial printers?: Y
Mechanical specifications: Type page 10 5/8 x 14 3/4; E - 6 cols, 1 1/2, 1/4 between; A - 6 cols, 1 1/2, 1/4 between; C - 6 cols, 1 1/2, 1/4 between.
Published: Wed
Avg Paid Circ: 1093
Audit By: CMCA
Audit Date: 31.08.2014
Personnel: Ken Sorenson (Gen. Mgr.); Greg Wiseman (Managing Ed.)
Parent company (for newspapers): Postmedia Network Inc.; Quebecor Communications, Inc.

NIPIGON

NIPIGON-RED ROCK GAZETTE

Street Address: 155b Railway Street ,
Province: ON
Postal: P0T 2J0
Country: Canada
Mailing address: Box 1057
Mailing city: Nipigon
Province: ON
Postal: P0T 2J0
General Phone: (807) 887-3583
General Fax: (807) 887-3720
General/National Adv. E-mail: nipigongazette@shaw.ca
Delivery Methods: Mail
Areas Served - City/County or Portion Thereof, or Zip

codes: Canada
Commercial printers?: Y
Published: Tues
Avg Paid Circ: 486
Avg Free Circ: 17
Audit By: CMCA
Audit Date: 30.06.2017
Personnel: Pamela Behun (Circ. Mgr./Ed.);
Blair Oborne (Pub.)

NOKOMIS

LAST MOUNTAIN TIMES

Street Address: 103 1st Ave. W. ,
Province: SK
Postal: S0G 3R0
Country: Canada
Mailing address: PO Box 340
Mailing city: Nokomis
Province: SK
Postal: S0G 3R0
General Phone: (306) 528-2020
General Fax: (306) 528-2090
Advertising Phone: (306) 528-2020
Editorial Phone: (306) 528-2020
General/National Adv. E-mail: inbox@lastmountaintimes.ca
Display Adv. E-mail: editor@lastmountaintimes.ca
Classified Adv. e-mail: editor@lastmountaintimes.ca
Editorial e-mail: editor@lastmountaintimes.ca
Primary Website: editor@lastmountaintimes.ca
Year Established: 1908
Delivery Methods: Mail
Areas Served - City/County or Portion Thereof, or Zip codes: S0G3R0, S0G4V0, S0G1Z0, S0A3J0, S0GOLO, S0G1J0, S0A3S0, S0G4P0, S0G0W0, S0G3C0, S2V1A1, S0G0H0, S0G4C0, S0G4L0,
Own Printing Facility?: Y
Commercial printers?: Y
Mechanical specifications: Type page 10 1/4 x 15 3/4; E - 5 cols, 1 29/30, 1/6 between; A - 5 cols, 1 29/30, 1/6 between; C - 5 cols, 1 29/30, 1/6 between.
Published: Mon
Avg Paid Circ: 250
Avg Free Circ: 4500
Audit By: Sworn/Estimate/Non-Audited
Audit Date: 12.07.2019
Personnel: Dave Degenstien (Owner/Publisher / Editor)
Parent company (for newspapers): Last Mountain Times

NORTH BATTLEFORD

BATTLEFORDS NEWS-OPTIMIST

Street Address: 892 104th St. ,
Province: SK
Postal: S9A 1M9
Country: Canada
Mailing address: 892 104th St
Mailing city: North Battleford
Province: SK
Postal: S9A 1M9
General Phone: (306) 445-7261
General Fax: (306) 445-3223
General/National Adv. E-mail: battlefords.publishing@sasktel.net
Editorial e-mail: newsoptimist.news@sasktel.net
Primary Website: www.newsoptimist.ca
Delivery Methods: Mail`Newsstand`Carrier`Racks
Areas Served - City/County or Portion Thereof, or Zip codes: Battlefords Region of Saskatchewan
Own Printing Facility?: Y
Commercial printers?: Y
Mechanical specifications: Type page 11 1/4 x 15 2/3; E - 6 cols, 1 1/2, 1/6 between; A - 6 cols, 1 1/2, 1/6 between; C - 6 cols, 1 7/12, 1/6 between.
Published: Thur
Avg Paid Circ: 228
Avg Free Circ: 14000
Audit By: CMCA
Audit Date: 31.03.2018

Personnel: Becky Doig (Ed.)
Parent company (for newspapers): Glacier Media Group

REGIONAL OPTIMIST

Street Address: 892-104th Street ,
Province: SK
Postal: S9A 3E6
Country: Canada
Mailing address: PO Box 1029
Mailing city: North Battleford
Province: SK
Postal: S9A 3E6
General Phone: (306) 445-7261
General Fax: (306) 445-3223
General/National Adv. E-mail: battlefords.publishing@sasktel.net
Editorial e-mail: newsoptimist.news@sasktel.net
Primary Website: www.newsoptimist.ca
Areas Served - City/County or Portion Thereof, or Zip codes: Canada
Published: Thur
Avg Free Circ: 13514
Audit By: CMCA
Audit Date: 30.11.2016
Personnel: Becky Doig (Ed)

NORTH VANCOUVER

NORTH SHORE NEWS

Street Address: 980 1st St. West, Unit 116 ,
Province: BC
Postal: V7P 3N4
Country: Canada
Mailing address: 980 1st St. West, Unit 116
Mailing city: North Vancouver
Province: BC
Postal: V7P 3N4
General Phone: (604) 985-2131
Advertising Phone: (604) 985-2131
Editorial Phone: (604) 985-2131
General/National Adv. E-mail: dfoot@nsnews.com
Display Adv. E-mail: display@nsnews.com
Classified Adv. e-mail: classifieds@van.net
Editorial e-mail: editor@nsnews.com
Primary Website: nsnews.com
Year Established: 1969
Areas Served - City/County or Portion Thereof, or Zip codes: Canada
Published: Wed`Fri`Sun
Avg Paid Circ: 0
Avg Free Circ: 57636
Audit By: CCAB
Audit Date: 23.11.2017
Personnel: Peter Kvarnstrom (Pub); Layne Christensen (Ed); Vicki Magnison (Dir, Sales & Marketing)
Parent company (for newspapers): Glacier Media Group

NORTH/WEST SHORE OUTLOOK

Street Address: 116-980 West 1st Street ,
Province: BC
Postal: V7P 3N4
Country: Canada
Mailing address: 116-980 West 1st St.
Mailing city: North Vancouver
Province: BC
Postal: V7P 3N4
General Phone: (604) 903-1000
General/National Adv. E-mail: publisher@northshoreoutlook.com
Display Adv. E-mail: vmagnison@nsnews.com
Classified Adv. e-mail: classifieds@van.net
Editorial e-mail: lchristensen@nsnews.com
Primary Website: www.northshoreoutlook.com
Areas Served - City/County or Portion Thereof, or Zip codes: Canada
Published: Thur
Avg Free Circ: 28038
Audit By: CMCA
Audit Date: 31.12.2012
Personnel: Vicki Magnison (Sales & Mktg. Dir.); Peter Kvarnstrom (Pub); Dale Dorsett (Circ. Mgr.); Layne Christensen (Ed)

OAKVILLE

OAKVILLE BEAVER

Street Address: 467 Speers Rd. ,
Province: ON
Postal: L6K 3S4
Country: Canada
Mailing address: 467 Speers Rd.
Mailing city: Oakville
Province: ON
Postal: L6K 3S4
General Phone: (905) 845-3824
General Fax: (905) 337-5568
Editorial e-mail: editor@oakvillebeaver.com
Primary Website: oakvillebeaver.com
Year Established: 1962
Delivery Methods: Carrier
Areas Served - City/County or Portion Thereof, or Zip codes: Canada
Own Printing Facility?: Y
Commercial printers?: Y
Published: Thur`Fri
Avg Paid Circ: 84
Avg Free Circ: 53165
Audit By: CCAB
Audit Date: 30.09.2017
Personnel: Neil Oliver (Pub.); Daniel Baird (Dir., Adv.); Sarah McSweeney (Circ. Mgr.); Jill Davis (Ed. in Chief); Jon Kuiperij (Sports Ed.); Manuel Garcia (Prodn. Mgr.); Angela Blackburn (Ed.)
Parent company (for newspapers): Metroland Media Group Ltd.; Torstar

OHSWEKEN

TURTLE ISLAND NEWS

Street Address: Box 329 ,
Province: ON
Postal: N0A 1M0
Country: Canada
Mailing address: Box 329
Mailing city: Ohsweken
Province: ON
Postal: N0A 1M0
General Phone: (519)445-0868
General Fax: (519) 445-0865
General/National Adv. E-mail: lynda@theturtleislandnews.com
Display Adv. E-mail: sales@theturtleislandnews.com
Primary Website: www.theturtleislandnews.com
Published: Wed
Avg Free Circ: 5000
Audit By: Sworn/Estimate/Non-Audited
Audit Date: 12.07.2019

OKOTOKS

OKOTOKS WESTERN WHEEL

Street Address: 9 Mcrae St. ,
Province: AB
Postal: T1S 2A2
Country: Canada
Mailing address: P.O. Box 150
Mailing city: Okotoks
Province: AB
Postal: T1S 2A2
General Phone: (403) 938-6397
General Fax: (403) 938-2518
General/National Adv. E-mail: westernwheel@okotoks.greatwest.ca
Display Adv. E-mail: lplathan@okotoks.greatwest.ca
Editorial e-mail: dpatterson@okotoks.greatwest.ca
Primary Website: www.westernwheel.com
Year Established: 1976
Delivery Methods: Mail`Newsstand`Carrier`Racks
Areas Served - City/County or Portion Thereof, or Zip codes: T0L 0A0,T0L 0H0, T0L 0J0,T0L 0K0,T0L 0P0,T0L 0X0,T0L 1H0,T0L 1K0,T0L 1R0,T0L 1W0,T0L 2A0,T0L 2T9,T0L 5G5,T1V and T1S.
Own Printing Facility?: Y
Commercial printers?: Y
Mechanical specifications: Type page 10 1/4 x 15 1/4; E - 6 cols, 1 7/12, between; A - 6 cols, 1 7/12, between; C - 6 cols, 1 7/12, between.
Published: Wed
Avg Paid Circ: 91
Avg Free Circ: 13879
Audit By: VAC
Audit Date: 30.04.2016
Personnel: Don Patterson (Ed); Matt Rockley (Pub)
Parent company (for newspapers): Glacier Media Group; Great West Newspapers LP

OLDS

CARSTAIRS COURIER

Street Address: 5013 - 51 Street ,
Province: AB
Postal: T4H 1P6
Country: Canada
Mailing address: PO Box 114
Mailing city: Carstairs
Province: AB
Postal: T0M 0N0
General Phone: (403) 337-2806
General Fax: (403) 556-7515
Advertising Phone: (403) 337-2806
General/National Adv. E-mail: courier@carstairs.greatwest.ca
Editorial e-mail: dsingleton@olds.greatwest.ca
Primary Website: www.carstairscourier.ca
Year Established: 1982
Areas Served - City/County or Portion Thereof, or Zip codes: Canada
Commercial printers?: Y
Published: Tues
Avg Paid Circ: 12
Avg Free Circ: 3289
Audit By: CMCA
Audit Date: 30.06.2014
Personnel: Dan Singleton (Ed)
Parent company (for newspapers): Glacier Media Group; Great West Newspapers LP

MOUNTAIN VIEW GAZETTE

Street Address: 5013 - 51 St ,
Province: AB
Postal: T4H 1P6
Country: Canada
Mailing address: PO Box 3910
Mailing city: Olds
Province: AB
Postal: T4H 1P6
General Phone: (403) 556-7510
General Fax: (403) 556-7515
General/National Adv. E-mail: gazette@olds.greatwest.ca
Editorial e-mail: dsingleton@olds.greatwest.ca
Primary Website: www.mountainviewgazette.ca/
Published: Tues
Avg Free Circ: 20000
Audit By: Sworn/Estimate/Non-Audited
Audit Date: 12.07.2019
Personnel: Murray Elliott (Grp. Pub./Gen. Mgr.); Dan Singleton (Ed)
Parent company (for newspapers): Great West Newspapers LP

OLDS ALBERTAN

Street Address: 5013 51st St. ,
Province: AB
Postal: T4H 1P6
Country: Canada
Mailing address: PO Box 3910
Mailing city: Olds
Province: AB
Postal: T4H 1P6
General Phone: (403) 556-7510
General Fax: (403) 556-7515
General/National Adv. E-mail: albertan@olds.greatwest.ca
Display Adv. E-mail: melliott@olds.greatwest.ca
Editorial e-mail: dcollie@olds.greatwest.ca
Primary Website: www.oldsalbertan.ca
Year Established: 1993
Published: Tues

Non-Daily Newspapers in Canada

III-479

Avg Paid Circ: 5
Avg Free Circ: 6933
Audit By: VAC
Audit Date: 28.02.2016
Personnel: Murray Elliott (Pub); Doug Collie (Ed)
Parent company (for newspapers): Glacier Media Group; Great West Newspapers LP

OLIVER

OLIVER CHRONICLE

Street Address: 6379 Main Street ,
Province: BC
Postal: V0H 1T0
Country: Canada
Mailing address: PO Box 880
Mailing city: Oliver
Province: BC
Postal: V0H 1T0
General Phone: (250) 498-3711
General Fax: (250) 498-3966
General/National Adv. E-mail: office@oliverchronicle.com
Display Adv. E-mail: sales@oliverchronicle.com
Editorial e-mail: editor@oliverchronicle.com
Primary Website: www.oliverchronicle.com
Year Established: 1937
Delivery Methods: Mail`Newsstand`Racks
Areas Served - City/County or Portion Thereof, or Zip codes: Canada
Own Printing Facility?: Y
Commercial printers?: Y
Mechanical specifications: Type page 14 1/4 x 21 1/2; E - 6 cols, 2 1/4, 3/16 between; A - 6 cols, 2 1/4, 3/16 between; C - 6 cols, 2 1/4, 3/16 between.
Published: Wed
Avg Paid Circ: 1723
Avg Free Circ: 0
Audit By: VAC
Audit Date: 6/31/2015
Personnel: Lyonel Doherty (Ed.); Robert Doull; Linda Bolton (Pub.)

ORANGEVILLE

ORANGEVILLE CITIZEN

Street Address: 10 First St. ,
Province: ON
Postal: L9W 2C4
Country: Canada
Mailing address: 10 First St.
Mailing city: Orangeville
Province: ON
Postal: L9W 2C4
General Phone: (519) 941-2230
General Fax: (519) 941-9361
General/National Adv. E-mail: mail@citizen.on.ca
Primary Website: www.citizen.on.ca
Delivery Methods: Mail`Newsstand`Carrier
Areas Served - City/County or Portion Thereof, or Zip codes: Canada
Own Printing Facility?: Y
Published: Thur
Avg Free Circ: 17967
Audit By: CMCA
Audit Date: 29.02.2016
Personnel: Alan M. Claridge (Pub.); Thomas M. Claridge (Ed.); Carolyn Dennis (Classifieds)

THE ORANGEVILLE BANNER

Street Address: 37 Mill St. ,
Province: ON
Postal: L9W 2M4
Country: Canada
Mailing address: 37 Mill St.
Mailing city: Orangeville
Province: ON
Postal: L9W 2M4
General Phone: (519) 941-1350
General Fax: (519) 941-9600
General/National Adv. E-mail: banner@orangevillebanner.com; info@orangevillebanner.com
Primary Website: www.orangevillebanner.com

Year Established: 1893
Areas Served - City/County or Portion Thereof, or Zip codes: Canada
Mechanical specifications: Type page 10 3/8 x 12 1/2; E - 10 cols, 1, 1/8 between; A - 10 cols, 1, 1/8 between; C - 10 cols, 1, 1/8 between.
Published: Tues`Thur
Avg Paid Circ: 85
Avg Free Circ: 20303
Audit By: CCAB
Audit Date: 31.03.2014
Personnel: Gordon Brewerton (Gen. Mgr.); Janine Taylor (Prodn. Mgr.)
Parent company (for newspapers): Metroland Media Group Ltd.; Torstar

ORILLIA

ORILLIA TODAY

Street Address: 25 Ontario St. ,
Province: ON
Postal: L3V 6H1
Country: Canada
Mailing address: 25 Ontario St.
Mailing city: Orillia
Province: ON
Postal: L3V 6H1
General Phone: (705) 329-2058
General Fax: (705) 329-2059
General/National Adv. E-mail: orillia@simcoe.com
Primary Website: orilliatoday.com
Year Established: 1991
Areas Served - City/County or Portion Thereof, or Zip codes: Canada
Published: Thur
Avg Free Circ: 24164
Audit By: CCAB
Audit Date: 31.03.2017
Personnel: Joe Anderson (Pub.); Leigh Gate (Gen. Mgr.); Leigh Rourke (Adv. Mgr.); Lori Martin (Mng. Ed.); Martin Melbourne (Community/News.); Kyla Mosley (Distr. Mgr.)
Parent company (for newspapers): Metroland Media Group Ltd.; Torstar

ORLEANS

WEEKLY JOURNAL

Street Address: 5300 Canotek Rd., Unit 30 ,
Province: ON
Postal: K1J 8R7
Country: Canada
Mailing address: 5300 Canotek Rd., Unit 30
Mailing city: Orleans
Province: ON
Postal: K1J 8R7
General Phone: (613) 744-4800
General Fax: (613) 744-0866
General/National Adv. E-mail: theweeklyjournal@transcontinental.ca
Mechanical specifications: Type page 10 1/2 x 12 1/2; E - 8 cols, 1 1/6, 1/6 between; A - 8 cols, 1 1/6, 1/6 between; C - 8 cols, 1 1/6, 1/6 between.
Published: Thur
Avg Free Circ: 47000
Audit By: Sworn/Estimate/Non-Audited
Audit Date: 12.07.2019
Personnel: Terry Tyo (Adv. Mgr.); Patricia Lonergan (Ed.); Sylvie Parsier (Prodn. Mgr.)

OROMOCTO

THE OROMOCTO POST-GAZETTE

Street Address: 291 Restigouche Rd. ,
Province: NB
Postal: E2V 2H2
Country: Canada
Mailing address: 291 Restigouche Rd.
Mailing city: Oromocto
Province: NB
Postal: E2V 2H2
General Phone: (506) 357-9813
General Fax: (506) 452-7405
General/National Adv. E-mail: allen.shari@dailygleaner.com
Display Adv. E-mail: shelley.wood@

brunswicknews.com
Editorial e-mail: williams.kimberly@dailygleaner.com
Primary Website: www.brunswicknews.com
Areas Served - City/County or Portion Thereof, or Zip codes: Canada
Mechanical specifications: Type page 10 1/4 x 11 1/2; E - 6 cols, 1 3/5, 1/6 between; A - 9 cols, 1, between; C - 8 cols, 1, between.
Published: Thur
Avg Paid Circ: 0
Avg Free Circ: 12844
Audit By: CMCA
Audit Date: 30.09.2013
Personnel: Shelly Wood (Adv. Mgr.); Kimberly Williams (Pub/Ed.)
Parent company (for newspapers): Brunswick News, Inc.

ORONO

ORONO WEEKLY TIMES

Street Address: 5310 Main St. ,
Province: ON
Postal: L0B 1M0
Country: Canada
Mailing address: PO Box 209
Mailing city: Orono
Province: ON
Postal: L0B 1M0
General Phone: (905) 983-5301
Advertising Phone: (905) 983-5301
Editorial Phone: (905) 983-5301
General/National Adv. E-mail: oronotimes@rogers.com
Display Adv. E-mail: oronotimes@rogers.com
Classified Adv. e-mail: oronotimes@rogers.com
Editorial e-mail: oronotimes@rogers.com
Primary Website: www.oronoweeklytimes.com
Year Established: 1937
Delivery Methods: Mail`Newsstand
Areas Served - City/County or Portion Thereof, or Zip codes: Municipality of Clarington, ON
Own Printing Facility?: Y
Commercial printers?: Y
Mechanical specifications: Type page 10 1/8 x 15 1/2; E - 2 cols, 3 15/16, 1/4 between.
Published: Wed
Avg Paid Circ: 1040
Audit By: CMCA
Audit Date: 30.06.2018
Personnel: Julie Cashin-Oster (Ed./Pub.)
Parent company (for newspapers): Orono Publications Inc.

OSHAWA

AJAX-PICKERING NEWS ADVERTISER

Street Address: 865 Farewell Ave. ,
Province: ON
Postal: L1H 7L5
Country: Canada
Mailing address: 865 Farewell Ave.
Mailing city: Oshawa
Province: ON
Postal: L1H 7L5
General Phone: (905) 579-4400
General Fax: (905) 579-2238
General/National Adv. E-mail: newsroom@durhamregion.com
Display Adv. E-mail: dfletcher@durhamregion.com
Editorial e-mail: jburghardt@durhamregion.com
Primary Website: durhamregion.com
Areas Served - City/County or Portion Thereof, or Zip codes: Canada
Own Printing Facility?: Y
Mechanical specifications: Type page 10 3/8 x 14; E - 9 cols, 1 1/16, between; A - 9 cols, 1 1/16, between; C - 9 cols, 1 1/16, between.
Published: Wed`Thur
Avg Paid Circ: 0
Avg Free Circ: 50016
Audit By: CCAB
Audit Date: 30.09.2017
Personnel: Timothy J. Whittaker (Pub.); Duncan Fletcher (Adv. Mgr.); Abe Fackhourie (Circ.

Mgr.); Joanne Burghardt (Ed.)
Parent company (for newspapers): Metroland Media Group Ltd.; Torstar

CANADIAN STATESMAN

Street Address: 865 Farewell St. ,
Province: ON
Postal: L1H 7L5
Country: Canada
Mailing address: 865 Farewell Ave.
Mailing city: Oshawa
Province: ON
Postal: L1H 7L5
General Phone: (905) 579-4400
General Fax: (416) 523-6161
Advertising Phone: (905) 215-0440
Editorial Phone: (905) 215 0162
General/National Adv. E-mail: newsroom@durhamregion.com
Editorial e-mail: mjohnston@durhamregion.com
Primary Website: www.durhamregion.com
Areas Served - City/County or Portion Thereof, or Zip codes: Ontario
Published: Wed`Thur`Fri
Avg Paid Circ: 104250
Audit By: Sworn/Estimate/Non-Audited
Audit Date: 12.07.2019
Personnel: Timothy J. Whittaker (Pub.); Fred Eismont (Dir. Adv.); Mike Johnston (Managing Ed.)

CLARINGTON THIS WEEK

Street Address: 865 Farewell St. ,
Province: ON
Postal: L1H 7L5
Country: Canada
Mailing address: 865 Farewell St.
Mailing city: Oshawa
Province: ON
Postal: L1H 7L5
General Phone: (905) 579-4400
General Fax: (905) 579-2238
General/National Adv. E-mail: newsroom@durhamregion.com
Primary Website: newsdurhamregion.com
Areas Served - City/County or Portion Thereof, or Zip codes: Oshawa, Ontario, L1H 7L5
Own Printing Facility?: Y
Commercial printers?: Y
Published: Wed
Avg Free Circ: 24150
Audit By: Sworn/Estimate/Non-Audited
Audit Date: 12.07.2019
Personnel: Tim Whittaker (Pub.); Lillian Hook (Office Mgr.); Fred Eismont (Adv. Dir.); Joanne Burghardt (Ed. in Chief); Mike Johnston (Mng. Ed.)
Parent company (for newspapers): Metroland Media Group Ltd.; Torstar

OSHAWA-WHITBY THIS WEEK

Street Address: 865 Farewell St. ,
Province: ON
Postal: L1H 7L5
Country: Canada
Mailing address: PO Box 481
Mailing city: Oshawa
Province: ON
Postal: L1H 7L5
General Phone: (905) 579-4400
General Fax: (905) 579-2238
Advertising Fax: (905) 579-6851
Editorial Fax: (905) 579-1809
General/National Adv. E-mail: newsroom@durhamregion.com
Primary Website: durhamregion.com
Areas Served - City/County or Portion Thereof, or Zip codes: Canada
Mechanical specifications: Type page 10 3/8 x 14; E - 9 cols, 1 1/16, between; A - 9 cols, 1 1/16, between; C - 9 cols, 1 1/16, between.
Published: Wed`Thur
Avg Paid Circ: 0
Avg Free Circ: 100554
Audit By: CCAB
Audit Date: 06.12.2017

Personnel: Timothy J. Whittaker (Pub.); Lillian Hook (Office Mgr.); Fred Eismont (Adv. Mgr.); Tina Jennings (Adv. Coord.); Abe Fakhourie (Circ. Mgr.); Joanne Burghardt (Ed. in Chief); Mike Johnston (Mng. Ed.); Tim Kelly (Copy Ed.); Christy Chase (Entertainment Ed.); Walter Passarella (Photo Ed.); Judi Bobbitt (Regl. Ed.); Brian Legree (Sports Ed.); Janice O'Neil (Prodn. Mgr.)
Parent company (for newspapers): Metroland Media Group Ltd.; Torstar

OSHWEKEN

TEKAWENNAKE
Street Address: Po Box 130 ,
Province: ON
Postal: N0A 1M0
Country: Canada
Mailing address: PO Box 130
Mailing city: Oshweken
Province: ON
Postal: N0A 1M0
General Phone: (519) 753-0077
General Fax: (519) 753-0011
General/National Adv. E-mail: teka@tekanews.com
Delivery Methods: Mail`Newsstand
Own Printing Facility?: Y
Commercial printers?: Y
Mechanical specifications: Type page 10.25 x 13.25; E - 6 cols, 2, 1/8 between; A - 5 cols, 2, 1/8 between; C - 5 cols, 2, 1/8 between.
Published: Wed
Avg Paid Circ: 2500
Audit By: Sworn/Estimate/Non-Audited
Audit Date: 12.07.2019
Personnel: G. Scott Smith (Pub.)

OSOYOOS

OSOYOOS TIMES
Street Address: 8712 Main St. ,
Province: BC
Postal: V0H 1V0
Country: Canada
Mailing address: PO Box 359
Mailing city: Osoyoos
Province: BC
Postal: V0H 1V0
General Phone: (250) 495-7225
General Fax: (250) 495-6616
General/National Adv. E-mail: admin@osoyoostimes.com
Display Adv. E-mail: sales@osoyoostimes.com
Editorial e-mail: editor@osoyoostimes.com
Primary Website: www.osoyoostimes.com
Year Established: 1947
Delivery Methods: Mail`Newsstand
Areas Served - City/County or Portion Thereof, or Zip codes: Osoyoos
Commercial printers?: Y
Mechanical specifications: Type page 10 1/4 x 14; E - 6 cols
Published: Wed
Avg Paid Circ: 1783
Avg Free Circ: 0
Audit By: VAC
Audit Date: 31.12.2015
Personnel: Jocelyn Merit (Office Mgr.); Ken Baker (Adv. Mgr.); Keith Lacey (Ed); Linda Bolton (Mng. Dir.)

OTTAWA

KANATA KOURIER-STANDARD EMC
Street Address: 57 Auriga Dr. Unit 103 ,
Province: ON
Postal: K2E 8B2
Country: Canada
Mailing address: 57 Auriga Dr. Unit 103
Mailing city: Ottawa
Province: ON
Postal: K2E 8B2
General Phone: (613) 723-5970
General Fax: (613)224-2265
General/National Adv. E-mail: mtracy@perfprint.ca
Primary Website: www.insideottawavalley.com
Areas Served - City/County or Portion Thereof, or Zip codes: Canada
Own Printing Facility?: Y
Commercial printers?: Y
Mechanical specifications: Type page 10 x 13 1/2; E - 6 cols, 1 9/16, 1/6 between; A - 6 cols, 1 9/16, 1/6 between; C - 6 cols, 1 9/16, 1/6 between.
Published: Thur
Avg Free Circ: 28642
Audit By: CMCA
Audit Date: 30.06.2014
Personnel: Mike Tracy (Pub.); Theresa Fritz (Ed.)
Parent company (for newspapers): Metroland Media Group Ltd.; Runge Newspapers, Inc.

MANOTICK NEWS EMC
Street Address: 57 Auriga Drive Unit 103 ,
Province: ON
Postal: K2E 8B2
Country: Canada
Mailing address: 57 Auriga Drive, Unit 103
Mailing city: Ottawa
Province: ON
Postal: K2E 8B2
General Phone: (613) 723-5970
General Fax: (613) 224-2265
Display Adv. E-mail: mstoodley@theemc.ca
Editorial e-mail: joe.morin@metroland.com
Primary Website: www.insideottawavalley.com
Areas Served - City/County or Portion Thereof, or Zip codes: Canada
Published: Thur
Avg Free Circ: 11392
Audit By: CMCA
Audit Date: 30.06.2014
Personnel: Mike Tracy (Pub.); Theresa Fritz (Ed.)
Parent company (for newspapers): Metroland Media Group Ltd.

NEPEAN-BARRHAVEN NEWS EMC
Street Address: 57 Auriga Drive Unit 103 ,
Province: ON
Postal: K2E 8B2
Country: Canada
Mailing address: 57 Auriga Drive, Unit 103
Mailing city: Ottawa
Province: ON
Postal: K2E 8B2
General Phone: (613) 723-5970
General Fax: (613) 224-2265
Editorial e-mail: Nevil.hunt@metroland.com
Primary Website: www.insideottawavalley.com
Areas Served - City/County or Portion Thereof, or Zip codes: Canada
Published: Thur
Avg Free Circ: 50401
Audit By: CMCA
Audit Date: 30.06.2014
Personnel: Mike Tracy (Pub.); Theresa Fritz (Ed.)
Parent company (for newspapers): Metroland Media Group Ltd.

ORLEANS NEWS EMC
Street Address: 57 Auriga Drive Unit 103 ,
Province: ON
Postal: K2E 8B2
Country: Canada
Mailing address: 57 Auriga Drive, Unit 103
Mailing city: Ottawa
Province: ON
Postal: K2E 8B2
General Phone: (613) 723-5970
Display Adv. E-mail: dave.badham@metroland.com
Primary Website: www.insideottawavalley.com
Areas Served - City/County or Portion Thereof, or Zip codes: Canada
Published: Thur
Avg Free Circ: 42273
Audit By: CMCA
Audit Date: 30.06.2014
Personnel: Mike Tracy (Pub.); Theresa Fritz (Ed.)
Parent company (for newspapers): Metroland Media Group Ltd.

OTTAWA EAST EMC
Street Address: 57 Auriga Drive Unit 103 ,
Province: ON
Postal: K2E 8B2
Country: Canada
Mailing address: 57 Auriga Drive, Unit 103
Mailing city: Ottawa
Province: ON
Postal: K2E 8B2
General Phone: (613) 723-5970
General Fax: (613) 224-2265
Display Adv. E-mail: ghamilton@thenewsemc.ca
Editorial e-mail: matthew.jay@metroland.com
Primary Website: www.insideottawavalley.com
Areas Served - City/County or Portion Thereof, or Zip codes: Canada
Published: Thur
Avg Free Circ: 36519
Audit By: CMCA
Audit Date: 30.06.2014
Personnel: Theresa Fritz (Ed.); Mike Tracy (Pub.)
Parent company (for newspapers): Metroland Media Group Ltd.

OTTAWA SOUTH EMC
Street Address: 57 Auriga Drive Unit 103 ,
Province: ON
Postal: K2E 8B2
Country: Canada
Mailing address: 57 Auriga Drive, Unit 103
Mailing city: Ottawa
Province: ON
Postal: K2E 8B2
General Phone: (613) 723-5970
General Fax: (613) 224-2265
Display Adv. E-mail: cmanor@theemc.ca
Editorial e-mail: blair.edwards@metroland.com
Primary Website: www.insideottawavalley.com
Areas Served - City/County or Portion Thereof, or Zip codes: Canada
Published: Thur
Avg Free Circ: 41820
Audit By: CMCA
Audit Date: 30.06.2014
Personnel: Mike Tracy (Pub.); Theresa Fritz (Ed.)
Parent company (for newspapers): Metroland Media Group Ltd.

OTTAWA WEST EMC
Street Address: 57 Auriga Drive Unit 103 ,
Province: ON
Postal: K2E 8B2
Country: Canada
Mailing address: 57 Auriga Drive, Unit 103
Mailing city: Ottawa
Province: ON
Postal: K2E 8B2
General Phone: (613)723-5970
Display Adv. E-mail: dave.pennett@metroland.com
Primary Website: www.insideottawavalley.com
Areas Served - City/County or Portion Thereof, or Zip codes: Canada
Published: Thur
Avg Free Circ: 35247
Audit By: CMCA
Audit Date: 30.06.2014
Personnel: Mike Tracy (Pub.); Theresa Fritz (Ed.)
Parent company (for newspapers): Metroland Media Group Ltd.

THE HILL TIMES
Street Address: 69 Sparks St. ,
Province: ON
Postal: K1P 5A5
Country: Canada
Mailing address: 69 Sparks St.
Mailing city: Ottawa
Province: ON
Postal: K1P 5A5
General Phone: (613) 232-5952
General Fax: (613) 232-9055
General/National Adv. E-mail: news@hilltimes.com; circulation@hilltimes.com
Display Adv. E-mail: production@hilltimes.com; classified@hilltimes.com
Primary Website: www.hilltimes.com
Year Established: 1989
Delivery Methods: Mail`Newsstand`Carrier`Racks
Areas Served - City/County or Portion Thereof, or Zip codes: Canada
Mechanical specifications: Type page 10 3/8 x 13 1/2; E - 4 cols
Published: Mon`Wed
Avg Paid Circ: 3614
Avg Free Circ: 9555
Audit By: CMCA
Audit Date: 29.02.2016
Personnel: Jim Creskey (Pub.); Ross Dickson (Pub.); Andrew Morrow (Gen. Mgr.); Kate Malloy (Ed.); Benoit Deneault (Prod. Mgr.); Anne Marie Creskey (Pub.)

THE STAR
Street Address: 5300 Canotek Rd., Unit 30 ,
Province: ON
Postal: K1J 8R7
Country: Canada
Mailing address: 5300 Canotek Rd., Unit 30
Mailing city: Ottawa
Province: ON
Postal: K1J 8R7
General Phone: (613) 744-4800
General Fax: (613) 744-0866
General/National Adv. E-mail: star@freenet.carlton.ca
Primary Website: www.eastottawa.ca
Published: Thur
Avg Free Circ: 45439
Audit By: CMCA
Audit Date: 30.04.2012
Personnel: Michael Curram (Pub.); Terry Tyo (Pub.); Patricia Lonergan (Ed.)
Parent company (for newspapers): Transcontinental Media

THE STITTSVILLE NEWS
Street Address: 57 Auriga Drive Unit 103 ,
Province: ON
Postal: K2E 8B2
Country: Canada
Mailing address: PO Box 610
Mailing city: Stittsville
Province: ON
Postal: K2E 8B2
General Phone: (613) 723-5970
Display Adv. E-mail: jillmartin@theemc.ca
Editorial e-mail: theresa.fritz@metroland.com
Primary Website: www.insideottawavalley.com
Published: Thur
Avg Free Circ: 13217
Audit By: CMCA
Audit Date: 30.06.2014
Personnel: Mike Tracy (Publisher)
Parent company (for newspapers): Metroland Media Group Ltd.; Runge Newspapers, Inc.

OUTLOOK

THE OUTLOOK
Street Address: 108 Saskatchewan Ave. E ,
Province: SK
Postal: S0L 2N0
Country: Canada
Mailing address: PO Box 1717
Mailing city: Outlook
Province: SK
Postal: S0L 2N0
General Phone: (306) 867-8262
General Fax: (306) 867-9556
General/National Adv. E-mail: theoutlook@sasktel.net

Non-Daily Newspapers in Canada

III-481

Year Established: 1909
Delivery Methods: Mail`Newsstand
Areas Served - City/County or Portion Thereof, or Zip codes: Canada
Own Printing Facility?: Y
Mechanical specifications: Type page 10 1/4 x 14 1/2; E - 5 cols, 1/6 between; A - 6 cols, 1/6 between;
Published: Thur
Avg Paid Circ: 1208
Avg Free Circ: 49
Audit By: CMCA
Audit Date: 30.09.2016
Personnel: Delwyn Luedtke (General Manager)
Parent company (for newspapers): Glacier Media Group

OXBOW

THE OXBOW HERALD

Street Address: Po Box 420 ,
Province: SK
Postal: S0C 2B0
Country: Canada
Mailing address: PO Box 420
Mailing city: Oxbow
Province: SK
Postal: S0C 2B0
General Phone: (306) 483-2323
General Fax: (306) 483-5258
General/National Adv. E-mail: oxbow.herald@sasktel.net
Display Adv. E-mail: lorena@oxbowherald.sk.ca
Editorial e-mail: liz@oxbowherald.sk.ca
Primary Website: www.SaskNewsNow.com
Delivery Methods: Mail`Racks
Areas Served - City/County or Portion Thereof, or Zip codes: Canada
Own Printing Facility?: Y
Commercial printers?: Y
Mechanical specifications: Type page 10 1/2 x 14 1/2; E - 5 cols, 2, 1/6 between; A - 5 cols, 2, 1/6 between; C - 5 cols, 2, 1/6 between.
Published: Mon
Avg Paid Circ: 908
Audit By: CMCA
Audit Date: 30.06.2015
Personnel: Lorena Wolensky (Advertising Manger); Lizz Bottrell (Editor); Marilyn Johnson (Reporter)
Parent company (for newspapers): Transcontinental Media

OYEN

OYEN ECHO

Street Address: 109 Sixth Ave. E. ,
Province: AB
Postal: T0J 2J0
Country: Canada
Mailing address: P.O. Box 420
Mailing city: Oyen
Province: AB
Postal: T0J 2J0
General Phone: (403) 664-3622
General Fax: (403) 664-3622
General/National Adv. E-mail: oyenecho@telusplanet.net
Display Adv. E-mail: oyenecho@telusplanet.net
Classified Adv. e-mail: 88
Editorial e-mail: oyenecho@telusplanet.net
Primary Website: www.oyenecho.ca
Year Established: 1974
Delivery Methods: Mail`Newsstand
Areas Served - City/County or Portion Thereof, or Zip codes: Special Area #3
Own Printing Facility?: Y
Commercial printers?: Y
Mechanical specifications: Type page 10 1/4 x 16; E - 6 cols, 1 3/5, 1/6 between; A - 6 cols, 1 3/5, 1/6 between.
Published: Tues
Avg Paid Circ: 986
Avg Free Circ: 22
Audit By: VAC
Audit Date: 30.06.2017
Personnel: Ronald E. Holmes (Pub.); Diana Walker (Ed.)
Parent company (for newspapers): Holmes Publishing Co. Ltd.-OOB

PALMERSTON

MINTO EXPRESS

Street Address: 171 William St. ,
Province: ON
Postal: N0G 2P0
Country: Canada
Mailing address: PO Box 757
Mailing city: Palmerston
Province: ON
Postal: N0G 2P0
General Phone: (519) 343-2440
General Fax: (519) 343-2267
General/National Adv. E-mail: editor@mintoexpress.com
Primary Website: www.mintoexpress.com
Delivery Methods: Mail`Newsstand`Racks
Areas Served - City/County or Portion Thereof, or Zip codes: Town of Minto
Published: Wed
Avg Paid Circ: 476
Avg Free Circ: 5
Audit By: CMCA
Audit Date: 30.06.2016
Personnel: Bill Heuther (Gen. Mgr.); Shannon Burrows
Parent company (for newspapers): Metroland Media Group Ltd.; Torstar

PARKHILL

THE PARKHILL GAZETTE

Street Address: 165 King St. ,
Province: ON
Postal: N0M 2K0
Country: Canada
Mailing address: PO Box 400
Mailing city: Parkhill
Province: ON
Postal: N0M 2K0
General Phone: (519) 294-6264
General Fax: (519) 294-6391
General/National Adv. E-mail: gazette@execulink.com
Areas Served - City/County or Portion Thereof, or Zip codes: Canada
Published: Thur
Avg Paid Circ: 860
Audit By: CMCA
Audit Date: 31.03.2014
Personnel: Melaime Carter (Adv. Mgr.); Dale Hayter (Circ. Mgr.); Gord Whitehead (Ed.)

PARKSVILLE

PARKSVILLE QUALICUM BEACH NEWS

Street Address: 1b/2a 1209 East Island Highway Parksville Heritage Centre ,
Province: BC
Postal: V9P 1R5
Country: Canada
Mailing address: 1B/2A 1209 East Island Highway Parksville Heritage Centre
Mailing city: Parksville
Province: BC
Postal: V9P 1R5
General Phone: (250) 248-4341
General Fax: (250) 248-4655
General/National Adv. E-mail: publisher@pqbnews.com
Display Adv. E-mail: bboyd@pqbnews.com
Classified Adv. e-mail: viads@bcclassified.com
Editorial e-mail: editor@pqbnews.com
Primary Website: www.pqbnews.com
Year Established: 1982
Areas Served - City/County or Portion Thereof, or Zip codes: Canada
Own Printing Facility?: Y
Commercial printers?: Y
Mechanical specifications: Type page 10 1/4 x 14 1/2; E - 6 cols, 1 1/2, 1/4 between; A - 6 cols, 1 1/2, 1/4 between; C - 7 cols, 1 1/4, 3/8 between.
Published: Tues`Fri
Avg Paid Circ: 6
Avg Free Circ: 16476
Audit By: AAM
Audit Date: 31.03.2019
Personnel: Peter McCully (Pub.); John Harding (Ed.); Brenda Boyd (Sales Mgr.); Michele Graham (Circ. Mgr.)
Parent company (for newspapers): Black Press Group Ltd.

THE OCEANSIDE STAR

Street Address: 166 E. Island Hwy. ,
Province: BC
Postal: V9P 2G3
Country: Canada
Mailing address: PO Box 45
Mailing city: Parksville
Province: BC
Postal: V9P 2G3
General Phone: (250) 954-0600
General Fax: (250) 954-0601
General/National Adv. E-mail: hnicholson@glaciermedia.com
Display Adv. E-mail: ads@oceansidestar.com
Editorial e-mail: bwilford@oceansidestar.com
Primary Website: www2.canada.com/oceansidestar/index.html
Areas Served - City/County or Portion Thereof, or Zip codes: Canada
Own Printing Facility?: Y
Mechanical specifications: Type page 10 7/16 x 12 1/2; E - 9 cols, 1 1/10, 1/12 between; A - 9 cols, 1 1/10, 1/12 between; C - 9 cols, 1 1/10, 1/12 between.
Published: Thur
Avg Paid Circ: 0
Avg Free Circ: 16243
Audit By: CMCA
Audit Date: 31.12.2013
Personnel: Coreen Greene (Adv. Mgr.); Michael Kelly (Circ. Mgr.); Brian Wilford (Ed.); Hugh Nicholson (Pub.)
Parent company (for newspapers): CanWest MediaWorks Publications, Inc.

PARRY SOUND

PARRY SOUND BEACON STAR

Street Address: 67 James Street ,
Province: ON
Postal: P2A 2X4
Country: Canada
Mailing address: PO Box 370
Mailing city: Parry Sound
Province: ON
Postal: P2A 2X4
General Phone: (705) 746-2104
General Fax: (705) 746-8369
General/National Adv. E-mail: jheidman@metrolandnorthmedia.com
Display Adv. E-mail: cbarnes@metrolandnorthmedia.com
Editorial e-mail: cpeck@metrolandnorthmedia.com
Primary Website: www.parrysound.com
Areas Served - City/County or Portion Thereof, or Zip codes: Canada
Published: Fri
Avg Free Circ: 7433
Audit By: CMCA
Audit Date: 31.12.2015
Personnel: Shaun Sauve (Regional Gen. Mgr.)
Parent company (for newspapers): Metroland Media Group Ltd.

PARRY SOUND NORTH STAR

Street Address: 67 James St. ,
Province: ON
Postal: P2A 2X4
Country: Canada
Mailing address: PO Box 370
Mailing city: Parry Sound
Province: ON
Postal: P2A 2X4
General Phone: (705) 746-2104
General Fax: (705) 746-8369
Display Adv. E-mail: jheidman@metrolandnorthmedia.com
Editorial e-mail: jtynan@metrolandnorthmedia.com
Primary Website: www.parrysound.com
Year Established: 1874
Areas Served - City/County or Portion Thereof, or Zip codes: Canada
Published: Wed
Avg Paid Circ: 2081
Avg Free Circ: 125
Audit By: CMCA
Audit Date: 31.12.2015
Personnel: Bill Allen (Reg'l Gen. Mgr.); Janice Heidman Louch (Adv. Sales Mgr.); Jack Tynan (Mng. Ed.)
Parent company (for newspapers): Metroland Media Group Ltd.

PEACE RIVER

THE PEACE RIVER RECORD-GAZETTE

Street Address: 10002 100th St. ,
Province: AB
Postal: T8S 1S6
Country: Canada
Mailing address: PO Box 6870
Mailing city: Peace River
Province: AB
Postal: T8S 1S6
General Phone: (780) 624-2591
General Fax: (780) 624-8600
Advertising Phone: (877) 786-8227
General/National Adv. E-mail: news@prrecordgazette.com
Display Adv. E-mail: adsales@prrecordgazette.com
Editorial e-mail: erin.steele@sunmedia.ca
Primary Website: www.prrecordgazette.com
Year Established: 1914
Areas Served - City/County or Portion Thereof, or Zip codes: Canada
Own Printing Facility?: Y
Mechanical specifications: Type page 13 x 21 1/4; E - 6 cols, 2 1/12, between; A - 6 cols, 2 1/12, between; C - 7 cols, 1 5/6, between.
Published: Wed
Avg Paid Circ: 0
Avg Free Circ: 3
Audit By: VAC
Audit Date: 31.12.2015
Personnel: Kristjanna Grimmelt (Mng. Ed.); Peter Meyerhoffer (reg. Adv. Dir.); Lori Czoba (Sales (online)); Fred Rinne (City Ed.)
Parent company (for newspapers): Postmedia Network Inc.

PENETANGUISHENE

GOUT DE VIVRE

Street Address: 343 Lafontaine St. W. ,
Province: ON
Postal: L9M 1R3
Country: Canada
Mailing address: 343 Lafontaine St. W.
Mailing city: Penetanguishene
Province: ON
Postal: L9M 1R3
General Phone: (705) 533-3349
General/National Adv. E-mail: legoutdevivre@bellnet.ca
Primary Website: www.legoutdevivre.com
Areas Served - City/County or Portion Thereof, or Zip codes: Canada
Published: Thur
Avg Paid Circ: 912
Avg Free Circ: 0
Audit By: CMCA
Audit Date: 30.04.2013
Personnel: Therese Maheux

PENTICTON

PENTICTON WESTERN NEWS

Street Address: 2250 Camrose St. ,

Province: BC
Postal: V2A 8R1
Country: Canada
Mailing address: 2250 Camrose St.
Mailing city: Penticton
Province: BC
Postal: V2A 8R1
General Phone: (250) 492-3636
General Fax: (250) 492-9843
General/National Adv. E-mail: ads@pentictonwesternnews.com
Display Adv. E-mail: larry@pentictonwesternnews.com
Classified Adv. e-mail: classifieds@pentictonwesternnews.com
Editorial e-mail: kpatton@pentictonwesternnews.com
Primary Website: www.pentictonwesternnews.com
Delivery Methods: Newsstand`Carrier
Areas Served - City/County or Portion Thereof, or Zip codes: Canada
Own Printing Facility?: Y
Commercial printers?: Y
Mechanical specifications: Type page 10 1/3 x 14 1/2; E - 6 cols, 1 1/2, 1/6 between; A - 6 cols, 1 1/2, 1/6 between; C - 6 cols, 1 1/2, 1/6 between.
Published: Wed`Fri
Avg Free Circ: 23010
Audit By: AAM
Audit Date: 31.03.2019
Personnel: Sue Kovacs (Circ. Mgr.); Shannon Simpson (Pub); Larry Mercier (Sales Mgr.); Kristi Patton (Ed)
Parent company (for newspapers): Black Press Group Ltd.

PETERBOROUGH

PETERBOROUGH THIS WEEK

Street Address: 884 Ford St. ,
Province: ON
Postal: K9J 5V4
Country: Canada
Mailing address: 884 Ford St.
Mailing city: Peterborough
Province: ON
Postal: K9J 5V4
General Phone: (705) 749-3383
General Fax: (705) 749-0074
General/National Adv. E-mail: bdanford@mykawartha.com
Editorial e-mail: prellinger@mykawartha.com
Primary Website: mykawartha.com
Areas Served - City/County or Portion Thereof, or Zip codes: Canada
Own Printing Facility?: Y
Commercial printers?: Y
Mechanical specifications: Type page 11 1/2 x 21 1/2; E - 10 cols, 1, between; A - 10 cols, 1, between.
Published: Wed`Fri
Avg Free Circ: 32354
Audit By: CCAB
Audit Date: 26.10.2017
Personnel: Bruce Danford (Pub.); Linda Sudes (Gen. Mgr.); Adam Milligan (Adv. Mgr.); Mary Babcock (Reg'l Dir., Adv.); Tracy Magee (Circ. Mgr.); Lois Tuffin (Ed. in Chief); Paul Relinger (Special Pjcts. Ed.); Mike Lacey (News Ed.); Scott Prikker (Prodn. Mgr.)
Parent company (for newspapers): Metroland Media Group Ltd.; Torstar

PICTON

THE COUNTY WEEKLY NEWS

Street Address: 3-252 Main St. ,
Province: ON
Postal: K0K 2T0
Country: Canada
Mailing address: 3-252 Main St.
Mailing city: Picton
Province: ON
Postal: K0K 2T0
General Phone: (613) 476-4714
General Fax: (613) 476-1281
General/National Adv. E-mail: bill.glisky@sunmedia.ca
Editorial e-mail: chris.malette@sunmedia.ca
Primary Website: www.countyweeklynews.ca
Areas Served - City/County or Portion Thereof, or Zip codes: Canada
Published: Thur
Avg Free Circ: 11591
Audit By: CMCA
Audit Date: 30.06.2013
Personnel: Dave Vachon (News Ed.)
Parent company (for newspapers): Postmedia Network Inc.

THE PICTON GAZETTE

Street Address: 267 Main St. ,
Province: ON
Postal: K0K 2T0
Country: Canada
Mailing address: 267 Main St.
Mailing city: Picton
Province: ON
Postal: K0K 2T0
General Phone: (613) 476-3201
General Fax: (613) 476-3464
Advertising Phone: (613) 476-3201 ext. 105
Editorial Phone: (613) 476-3201 ext. 110
General/National Adv. E-mail: gazette@bellnet.ca
Display Adv. E-mail: advertise@pictongazette.com, gazetteclass@bellnet.ca
Editorial e-mail: gazette@bellnet.ca
Primary Website: www.pictongazette.com
Year Established: 1830
Delivery Methods: Carrier
Areas Served - City/County or Portion Thereof, or Zip codes: Canada
Mechanical specifications: Tabloid pages, 6 columns, 212 agates deep
Published: Thur
Avg Free Circ: 11450
Audit By: CMCA
Audit Date: 30.06.2016
Personnel: Jean M. Morrison (Pub.); Adam Bramburger (Ed.); Michelle Bowes (Prodn. Mgr.)

THE PICTOU ADVOCATE

Street Address: 21 George St. ,
Province: NS
Postal: B0K 1H0
Country: Canada
Mailing address: 21 George St.
Mailing city: Pictou
Province: NS
Postal: B0K 1H0
General Phone: (902) 485-8014
General Fax: (902) 752-4816
Advertising Phone: (902) 759-0716
General/National Adv. E-mail: pictou.advocate@ns.sympatico.ca
Display Adv. E-mail: mark@pictouadvocate.com
Editorial e-mail: editor@pictouadvocate.com
Primary Website: www.pictouadvocate.com
Year Established: 1893
Delivery Methods: Mail
Areas Served - City/County or Portion Thereof, or Zip codes: Canada
Own Printing Facility?: Y
Published: Wed
Avg Paid Circ: 732
Avg Free Circ: 4
Audit By: VAC
Audit Date: 30.06.2016
Personnel: Jackie Jardine (Ed); Leith Orr (Pub.)

PIEDMONT

JOURNAL ACCES

Street Address: Rue Principale ,
Province: QC
Postal: J0R 1K0
Country: Canada
Mailing address: rue Principale
Mailing city: Piedmont
Province: QC
Postal: J0R 1K0
General Phone: (450) 227-7999
Primary Website: http://www.journalacces.ca/

Published: Sat
Avg Free Circ: 25720
Audit By: ODC
Audit Date: 14.12.2011
Personnel: Josee Pilotte

PILOT MOUND

THE SENTINEL COURIER

Street Address: 13 Railway St. ,
Province: MB
Postal: R0G 1P0
Country: Canada
Mailing address: PO Box 179
Mailing city: Pilot Mound
Province: MB
Postal: R0G 1P0
General Phone: (204) 825-2772
General Fax: (204) 825-2439
General/National Adv. E-mail: sentinel@sentinelcourier.com
Editorial e-mail: sentinel@mymts.net
Primary Website: www.sentinelcourier.com
Areas Served - City/County or Portion Thereof, or Zip codes: Pilot Mound
Mechanical specifications: Type page 10 1/2 x 14; E - 5 cols, 2, 1/4 between; A - 5 cols, 2, 1/4 between.
Published: Tues
Avg Paid Circ: 1273
Avg Free Circ: 31
Audit By: VAC
Audit Date: 31.05.2016
Personnel: Susan Peterson (Ed.)

PINCHER CREEK

PINCHER CREEK ECHO

Street Address: 714 Main St. ,
Province: AB
Postal: T0K 1W0
Country: Canada
Mailing address: PO Box 1000
Mailing city: Pincher Creek
Province: AB
Postal: T0K 1W0
General Phone: (403) 627-3252
General Fax: (403) 627-3949
General/National Adv. E-mail: pcecho@awna.com
Display Adv. E-mail: rmackintosh@postmedia.com
Editorial e-mail: cclow@postmedia.com
Primary Website: www.pinchercreekecho.com
Year Established: 1900
Areas Served - City/County or Portion Thereof, or Zip codes: Canada
Commercial printers?: Y
Mechanical specifications: Type page 10 1/4 x 15; E - 5 cols, 1 11/12, between; A - 6 cols, 1 1/2, between; C - 6 cols, 1 2/3, between.
Published: Wed
Avg Paid Circ: 1077
Avg Free Circ: 14
Audit By: CMCA
Audit Date: 30.06.2014
Personnel: Nancy Middleton (Pub); Martha Goforth (Office Mgr); Caitlin Clow (Ed); Roxanne Mackintoch (Adv. Dir)
Parent company (for newspapers): Postmedia Network Inc.; Quebecor Communications, Inc.

PLESSISVILLE

L'AVENIR DE L'ERABLE

Street Address: 1620 Saint-calixte St. ,
Province: QC
Postal: G6L 1P9
Country: Canada
Mailing address: 1620 Saint-Calixte St.
Mailing city: Plessisville
Province: QC
Postal: G6L 1P9
General Phone: (819) 362-7049
General Fax: (819) 362-2216
General/National Adv. E-mail: cotes2@transcontinental.ca

Primary Website: www.lavenirdelerable.com
Areas Served - City/County or Portion Thereof, or Zip codes: Canada
Own Printing Facility?: Y
Published: Wed
Avg Paid Circ: 9
Avg Free Circ: 10779
Audit By: CCAB
Audit Date: 31.03.2014
Personnel: Pierre Gaudet (Dir., Sales); Sylvia Cote (Ed.); Ghislain Chauvette (Ed.)
Parent company (for newspapers): Transcontinental Media

PONOKA

PONOKA NEWS

Street Address: 5019-a 50th Ave. ,
Province: AB
Postal: T4J 1R6
Country: Canada
Mailing address: PO Box 4217
Mailing city: Ponoka
Province: AB
Postal: T4J 1R6
General Phone: (403) 783-3311
General Fax: (403) 783-6300
Display Adv. E-mail: judy.dick@ponokanews.com
Classified Adv. E-mail: judy.dick@ponokanews.com
Editorial e-mail: jeff.heyden-kaye@ponokanews.com
Primary Website: www.ponokanews.com
Year Established: 1954
Delivery Methods: Mail`Newsstand`Carrier`Racks
Areas Served - City/County or Portion Thereof, or Zip codes: Ponoka
Own Printing Facility?: Y
Commercial printers?: Y
Mechanical specifications: Type page 10.12" x 13"; 7 cols, column width 1.3" wide
Published: Wed
Avg Paid Circ: 16
Avg Free Circ: 5856
Audit By: CMCA
Audit Date: 30.04.2018
Personnel: Mary Kemmis (Pres.)
Parent company (for newspapers): Black Press Group Ltd.

PORT ALBERNI

ALBERNI VALLEY NEWS

Street Address: 4656 Margaret Street ,
Province: BC
Postal: V9Y 6H2
Country: Canada
General Phone: (250) 723-6399
General Fax: (250) 723-6395
Display Adv. E-mail: publisher@albernivalleynews.com
Editorial e-mail: editor@albernivalleynews.com
Primary Website: albernivalleynews.com
Year Established: 2006
Delivery Methods: Carrier`Racks
Areas Served - City/County or Portion Thereof, or Zip codes: Canada
Published: Wed
Avg Free Circ: 9302
Audit By: AAM
Audit Date: 31.03.2019
Personnel: Teresa Bird (Publisher); Susan Quinn (Ed.)
Parent company (for newspapers): Black Press Group Ltd.

PORT AUX BASQUES

THE GULF NEWS

Street Address: Po Box 1090 ,
Province: NL
Postal: A0M 1C0
Country: Canada
Mailing address: PO Box 1090
Mailing city: Port aux Basques

Non-Daily Newspapers in Canada

Province: NL
Postal: A0M 1C0
General Phone: (709) 695-3671
General Fax: (709) 695-7901
Advertising Phone: (709) 279-3188
Advertising Fax: (709) 279-2628
General/National Adv. E-mail: editor@gulfnews.ca
Display Adv. E-mail: wrose@thewesternstar.com
Editorial e-mail: chantelle.macisaac@gulfnews.ca
Primary Website: www.gulfnews.ca
Areas Served - City/County or Portion Thereof, or Zip codes: Canada
Own Printing Facility?: Y
Commercial printers?: Y
Published: Mon
Avg Paid Circ: 2912
Avg Free Circ: 0
Audit By: VAC
Audit Date: 31.12.2015
Personnel: Chantelle Macisaac (Ed); Wendy Rose (Adv.)
Parent company (for newspapers): Transcontinental Media

PORT COLBORNE

IN PORT NEWS

Street Address: 228 E. Main St. ,
Province: ON
Postal: L3K 1S4
Country: Canada
Mailing address: 228 E. Main St.
Mailing city: Port Colborne
Province: ON
Postal: L3K 1S4
General Phone: (905) 732-2411
General/National Adv. E-mail: john.tobon@sunmedia.ca
Primary Website: www.inportnews.ca
Areas Served - City/County or Portion Thereof, or Zip codes: Canada
Published: Wed
Avg Free Circ: 9849
Audit By: CMCA
Audit Date: 31.03.2016
Personnel: John Tobon; Julia Coles
Parent company (for newspapers): Postmedia Network Inc.

PORT COQUITLAM

TRI CITY NEWS

Street Address: 118 - 1680 Broadway Street ,
Province: BC
Postal: V3C 2M8
Country: Canada
Mailing address: 118 - 1680 Broadway Street
Mailing city: Port Coquitlam
Province: BC
Postal: V3C 2M8
General Phone: (604) 525-6397
Advertising Phone: (604) 472-3020
Editorial Phone: (604) 472-3030
Display Adv. E-mail: admanager@tricitynews.com
Primary Website: tricitynews.com
Delivery Methods: Carrier
Areas Served - City/County or Portion Thereof, or Zip codes: Port Moody, Belcarra, Anmore, Port Coquitlam, Coquitlam
Published: Wed`Fri
Avg Paid Circ: 0
Avg Free Circ: 52297
Audit By: Sworn/Estimate/Non-Audited
Audit Date: 12.07.2019
Parent company (for newspapers): Glacier Media

TRI-CITY NEWS

Street Address: 1680 Broadway Street , Unit 118
Province: BC
Postal: V3C 2M8
Country: Canada
Mailing address: 1680 Broadway St Unit 118
Mailing city: Port Coquitlam
Province: BC
Postal: V3C 2M8
General Phone: (604) 525-6397
General/National Adv. E-mail: publisher@tricitynews.com
Display Adv. E-mail: smitchell@tricitynews.com
Editorial e-mail: newsroom@tricitynews.com
Primary Website: tricitynews.com
Year Established: 1985
Delivery Methods: Carrier
Areas Served - City/County or Portion Thereof, or Zip codes: Tri-Cities
Published: Wed`Fri
Avg Paid Circ: 0
Avg Free Circ: 51702
Audit By: CCAB
Audit Date: 23.11.2017
Personnel: Richard Dal Monte (Ed.); Shannon Mitchell (Pub); Kim Yorston (Circ Mgr)
Parent company (for newspapers): Black Press Group Ltd.; Glacier Media Group

PORT DOVER

PORT DOVER MAPLE LEAF

Street Address: 351 Main St. ,
Province: ON
Postal: N0A 1N0
Country: Canada
Mailing address: PO Box 70
Mailing city: Port Dover
Province: ON
Postal: N0A 1N0
General Phone: (519) 583-0112
General/National Adv. E-mail: info@portdovermapleleaf.com
Display Adv. E-mail: ads@portdovermapleleaf.com
Editorial e-mail: news@portdovermapleleaf.com
Primary Website: www.portdovermapleleaf.com
Year Established: 1873
Delivery Methods: Mail`Newsstand`Racks
Areas Served - City/County or Portion Thereof, or Zip codes: Norfolk County
Commercial printers?: Y
Mechanical specifications: Type page 10 1/2 x 16; E - 5 cols, 2, 1/8 between; A - 10 cols, 1, 1/8 between; C - 10 cols, 1, 1/8 between.
Published: Wed
Avg Paid Circ: 2904
Avg Free Circ: 15
Audit By: Sworn/Estimate/Non-Audited
Audit Date: 12.07.2019
Personnel: Paul Morris (Ed.); Stan Morris (Ed.)

PORT ELGIN

SHORELINE BEACON

Street Address: 694 Goderich St. ,
Province: ON
Postal: N0H 2C0
Country: Canada
Mailing address: PO Box 580
Mailing city: Port Elgin
Province: ON
Postal: N0H 2C0
General Phone: (519) 832-9001
General Fax: (519) 389-4793
General/National Adv. E-mail: shoreline@bmts.com
Primary Website: www.shorelinebeacon.com
Year Established: unknown
Areas Served - City/County or Portion Thereof, or Zip codes: Canada
Own Printing Facility?: Y
Commercial printers?: Y
Mechanical specifications: 10.33"w x 160 agates
Published: Tues
Avg Paid Circ: 2102
Avg Free Circ: 15
Audit By: CMCA
Audit Date: 30.06.2016
Personnel: Kiera Merriam (Gen. Mgr.)
Parent company (for newspapers): Postmedia Network Inc.; Quebecor Communications, Inc.

PORT HARDY

NORTH ISLAND GAZETTE

Street Address: #3-7053 Market St. ,
Province: BC
Postal: V0N 2P0
Country: Canada
Mailing address: Box 458
Mailing city: Port Hardy
Province: BC
Postal: V0N 2P0
General Phone: (250) 949-6225
General/National Adv. E-mail: production@northislandgazette.com
Display Adv. E-mail: sales@northislandgazette.com
Classified Adv. e-mail: viado@bcclassified.com
Editorial e-mail: publisher@northislandgazette.com
Primary Website: www.northislandgazette.com
Year Established: 1965
Delivery Methods: Mail`Newsstand`Carrier`Racks
Areas Served - City/County or Portion Thereof, or Zip codes: Canada
Own Printing Facility?: Y
Mechanical specifications: Type page 10 3/8 x 14.
Published: Wed
Avg Paid Circ: 1065
Avg Free Circ: 500
Audit By: CMCA
Audit Date: 30.11.2018
Personnel: Lilian Meerveld; Tyson Whitney; Thomas Kervin (Reporter); Natasha Griffiths (Advertising Sale Rep)
Parent company (for newspapers): Black Press Group Ltd.

PORT HAWKESBURY

THE REPORTER

Street Address: 2 Maclean Court ,
Province: NS
Postal: B9A 3K2
Country: Canada
Mailing address: 2 Maclean Court
Mailing city: Port Hawkesbury
Province: NS
Postal: B9A 3K2
General Phone: (902) 625-3300
General Fax: (902) 625-1701
Display Adv. E-mail: nicolefawcett@porthawkesburyreporter.com
Editorial e-mail: jake@porthawkesburyreporter.com
Primary Website: www.porthawkesburyreporter.com
Areas Served - City/County or Portion Thereof, or Zip codes: Port Hawkesbury
Published: Wed
Avg Paid Circ: 87
Audit By: VAC
Audit Date: 30.09.2016
Personnel: Rick Cluett (Pub); Nicole Fawcett (Adv)

PORT PERRY

THE PORT PERRY STAR

Street Address: 180 Mary St. , Unit 11
Province: ON
Postal: L9L 1C4
Country: Canada
Mailing address: 180 Mary St. Unit 11
Mailing city: Port Perry
Province: ON
Postal: L9L 1C4
General Phone: (905) 985-7383
General Fax: (905) 985-3708
Advertising Phone: (905) 215-0440
Editorial Phone: (905) 215-0462
General/National Adv. E-mail: chall@durhamregion.com
Display Adv. E-mail: feismont@durhamregion.com
Classified Adv. e-mail: classified@thespec.com
Editorial e-mail: chall@durhamregion.com
Primary Website: www.durhamregion.com
Year Established: 1866
Delivery Methods: Newsstand`Carrier
Areas Served - City/County or Portion Thereof, or Zip codes: Scugog Township, plus select areas in Brock/Sunderland, Little Britain, Pontypool
Own Printing Facility?: Y
Commercial printers?: Y
Published: Thur
Avg Paid Circ: 12000
Avg Free Circ: 125
Audit By: Sworn/Estimate/Non-Audited
Audit Date: 12.07.2019
Personnel: Tim Whittaker (Pub); Lisa Burgess (Sales Mgr.); Laurie Abel (Circ. Coordinator); Mike Johnston (Mng. Ed.)
Parent company (for newspapers): Metroland Media Group Ltd.

THE STANDARD NEWSPAPER

Street Address: 94a Water St. ,
Province: ON
Postal: L9L 1J2
Country: Canada
Mailing address: 94A Water St.
Mailing city: Port Perry
Province: ON
Postal: L9L 1J2
General Phone: (905) 985-6985
General Fax: (905) 985-9253
General/National Adv. E-mail: production-standard@powergate.ca
Display Adv. E-mail: standardnancy@powergate.ca
Classified Adv. e-mail: office-standard@powergate.ca
Editorial e-mail: standarddarryl@powergate.ca
Primary Website: www.thestandardnewspaper.ca
Year Established: 2004
Delivery Methods: Mail`Newsstand`Carrier`Racks
Areas Served - City/County or Portion Thereof, or Zip codes: Durham Region
Published: Thur
Avg Free Circ: 11868
Audit By: CMCA
Audit Date: 31.12.2014
Personnel: Colleen Green (Gen. Mgr.); Darryl Knight (Ed.); Nancy Lister (Adv. Rep.); Dan Cearns (Reporter)
Parent company (for newspapers): Skyline Media

PORT STANLEY

LAKE ERIE BEACON (OOB)

Street Address: 204 A Carlow Road ,
Province: ON
Postal: N5L 1C5
Country: Canada
Mailing address: 204 Carlow Rd
Mailing city: Port Stanley
Postal: N5L 1C5
General Phone: (519) 782-4563
General Fax: (519) 782-4563
Advertising Phone: (519) 782-4563
Advertising Fax: (519) 782-4563
Editorial Phone: (519) 782-4563
Editorial Fax: (519) 782-4563
General/National Adv. E-mail: beacon@lebeacon.ca
Display Adv. E-mail: linda@lebeacon.ca
Classified Adv. e-mail: linda@lebeacon.ca
Editorial e-mail: andrew@lebeacon.ca
Primary Website: www.lebeacon.ca
Year Established: 2004
Delivery Methods: Mail`Newsstand
Areas Served - City/County or Portion Thereof, or Zip codes: Central Elgin
Mechanical specifications: TIFF, JPEG, PDF, MS Word, Quark Express
Published: Fri`Bi-Mthly
Published Other: Every second week
Avg Free Circ: 7000
Audit By: CMCA
Audit Date: 31.12.2013
Parent company (for newspapers): Kettle Creek Publishing Ltd.

PORTAGE LA PRAIRIE
CENTRAL PLAINS HERALD LEADER
Street Address: 1941 Saskatchewan Ave. W.,
Province: MB
Postal: R1N 0R7
Country: Canada
Mailing address: PO Box 130
Mailing city: Portage La Prairie
Province: MB
Postal: R1N 3B4
General Phone: (204) 857-3427
General Fax: (204) 239-1270
General/National Adv. E-mail: news.dailygraphic@shawcable.com
Display Adv. E-mail: daria.zmiyiwsky@sunmedia.ca
Editorial e-mail: mickey.dumont@sunmedia.ca
Primary Website: http://www.portagedailygraphic.com/
Areas Served - City/County or Portion Thereof, or Zip codes: Central Plains
Own Printing Facility?: Y
Commercial printers?: Y
Mechanical specifications: Type page 14 x 22 3/4; E - 6 cols, 2 1/8, 1/8 between; A - 6 cols, 2 1/8, 1/8 between; C - 6 cols, 2 1/8, 1/8 between.
Published: Thur
Avg Paid Circ: 4551
Avg Free Circ: 9595
Audit By: VAC
Audit Date: 30.06.2016
Personnel: Guey Fiset (Class./Circ. Mgr.); Daria Zmiyiwsky (Adv. Dir); Mickey Dumont (Ed)
Parent company (for newspapers): Postmedia Network Inc.; Quebecor Communications, Inc.

POWELL RIVER
POWELL RIVER PEAK
Street Address: 4400 Marine Ave.,
Province: BC
Postal: V8A 2K1
Country: Canada
Mailing address: 4400 Marine Ave.
Mailing city: Powell River
Province: BC
Postal: V8A 2K1
General Phone: (604) 485-5313
General Fax: (604) 485-5007
General/National Adv. E-mail: publisher@prpeak.com
Display Adv. E-mail: sales@prpeak.com
Classified Adv. e-mail: cindy@prpeak.com
Editorial e-mail: publisher@prpeak.com
Primary Website: www.prpeak.com
Year Established: 1995
Delivery Methods: Mail`Newsstand`Carrier
Areas Served - City/County or Portion Thereof, or Zip codes: Powell River Regional District
Commercial printers?: Y
Mechanical specifications: Type page 10 1/4 x 13.8; E - 6 cols, 1 1/2, 1/8 between; A - 6 cols, 1 1/2, 1/8 between; C - 6 cols, 1 1/2, 1/8 between.
Published: Wed
Avg Paid Circ: 2084
Avg Free Circ: 48
Audit By: VAC
Audit Date: 31.12.2016
Personnel: Michele Stewart (Circ. Dir.); Jason Schreuers (Pub/Ed); Dot Campbell (Sales)
Parent company (for newspapers): Glacier Media Group

PRESCOTT
THE PRESCOTT JOURNAL
Street Address: 3201 County Rd. 2,
Province: ON
Postal: K0E 1T0
Country: Canada
Mailing address: PO Box 549
Mailing city: Prescott
Province: ON
Postal: K0E 1T0
General Phone: (613) 925-4265
General Fax: (613) 925-2837
Display Adv. E-mail: adsales@prescottjournal.com
Editorial e-mail: journal@stlawrenceprinting.on.ca
Primary Website: www.prescottjournal.com
Year Established: 1891
Delivery Methods: Mail`Newsstand`Carrier
Areas Served - City/County or Portion Thereof, or Zip codes: Canada
Own Printing Facility?: N
Commercial printers?: Y
Mechanical specifications: Type page 10.325" x 16"; 6 columns 1.125" wide x 220 agates
Published: Wed
Avg Paid Circ: 1123
Avg Free Circ: 99
Audit By: CMCA
Audit Date: 30.06.2016
Personnel: Beth Morris (Pub.); Dave Flinn (Prodn. Mgr.); Jamie Nurse

PRINCETON
PRINCETON SIMILKAMEEN SPOTLIGHT
Street Address: 282 Bridge St.,
Province: BC
Postal: V0X 1W0
Country: Canada
Mailing address: PO Box 340
Mailing city: Princeton
Province: BC
Postal: V0X 1W0
General Phone: (250) 295-3535
General Fax: (250) 295-7322
Display Adv. E-mail: advertising@similkameenspotlight.com
Editorial e-mail: editor@similkameenspotlight.com
Primary Website: www.similkameenspotlight.com
Year Established: 1948
Delivery Methods: Mail`Racks
Mechanical specifications: Type page 10 1/3 x 14; E - 6 cols, 1 9/16, between; A - 6 cols, 1 9/16, between; C - 6 cols, 1 9/16, between.
Published: Wed
Avg Paid Circ: 2227
Avg Free Circ: 43
Audit By: VAC
Audit Date: 30.06.2016
Personnel: Andrea Demeer; Andrea DeMeer (Ed/Assist. Pub); Don Kendall (Pub); Sandi Nolan (Adv Mgr.)
Parent company (for newspapers): Black Press Group Ltd.

PROVOST
THE PROVOST NEWS
Street Address: 5111 50th St.,
Province: AB
Postal: T0B 3S0
Country: Canada
Mailing address: PO Box 180, 5111-50 St.
Mailing city: Provost
Province: AB
Postal: T0B 3S0
General Phone: (780) 753-2564
General Fax: (780) 753-6117
General/National Adv. E-mail: advertising@provostnews.ca
Display Adv. E-mail: advertising@provostnews.ca
Editorial e-mail: rcholmes@agt.net
Primary Website: www.provostnews.ca
Year Established: 1910
Delivery Methods: Mail`Newsstand
Areas Served - City/County or Portion Thereof, or Zip codes: Provost M.D. No. 52
Commercial printers?: Y
Published: Wed
Avg Paid Circ: 1300
Avg Free Circ: 54
Audit By: VAC
Audit Date: 30.06.2017
Personnel: Richard C. Holmes (Ed.)

Parent company (for newspapers): Holmes Publishing Co. Ltd.-OOB

QUEBEC
CHARLESBOURG EXPRESS
Street Address: 710 Bouvier, Suite 107,
Province: QC
Postal: G2J 1C2
Country: Canada
Mailing address: 710 Bouvier, Suite 107
Mailing city: Quebec
Province: QC
Postal: G2J 1C2
General Phone: (418) 628-7460
General Fax: (418) 840-1207
General/National Adv. E-mail: redaction_quebec@tc.tc
Primary Website: www.quebechebdo.com
Areas Served - City/County or Portion Thereof, or Zip codes: Canada
Published: Fri
Avg Paid Circ: 9
Avg Free Circ: 27178
Audit By: CCAB
Audit Date: 31.03.2014
Personnel: Alain LePage (Gen. Mgr.); Lilianne Laprise (Ed.)
Parent company (for newspapers): Reseau Select/Select Network; Transcontinental Media

JOURNAL L'ACTUEL
Street Address: 710 Bouvier, Suite 107,
Province: QC
Postal: G2J 1C2
Country: Canada
Mailing address: 710 Bouvier, Suite 107
Mailing city: Quebec
Province: QC
Postal: G2J 1C2
General Phone: (418) 628-7460
General Fax: (418) 622-1511
General/National Adv. E-mail: redaction_quebec@tc.tc
Primary Website: www.lactuel.com
Areas Served - City/County or Portion Thereof, or Zip codes: Canada
Commercial printers?: Y
Published: Fri
Avg Paid Circ: 5
Avg Free Circ: 57753
Audit By: CCAB
Audit Date: 31.03.2014
Personnel: Lilianne Laprese (Ed.); Alain LePage (Dir.); Lilianne Laprise (Ed.)
Parent company (for newspapers): Transcontinental Media

L'APPEL
Street Address: 710 Rue Bouvier Bureau 107,
Province: QC
Postal: G2J 1C2
Country: Canada
Mailing address: 710 Rue Bouvier Bureau 107
Mailing city: Quebec
Province: QC
Postal: G2J 1C2
General Phone: (418) 628-7460
General Fax: (418) 622-1511
Advertising Phone: (418) 628-7460
Advertising Fax: (418) 622-1511
Editorial Phone: (418) 628-7460
Editorial Fax: (418) 622-1511
General/National Adv. E-mail: redaction_quebec@tc.tc
Display Adv. E-mail: redaction_quebec@tc.tc
Editorial e-mail: redaction_quebec@tc.tc
Primary Website: www.lappel.com
Year Established: 1945
Delivery Methods: Mail`Racks
Areas Served - City/County or Portion Thereof, or Zip codes: Canada
Published: Fri
Avg Paid Circ: 10
Avg Free Circ: 44099

Audit By: CCAB
Audit Date: 31.03.2014
Personnel: Michel Chalifour (Reg. Gen. Mgr.)

QUEBEC CHRONICLE-TELEGRAPH
Street Address: 1040 Belvedere, Suite 218,
Province: QC
Postal: G1S 3G3
Country: Canada
Mailing address: 1040 Belbedere., Ste 218
Mailing city: Quebec
Province: QC
Postal: G1S 3G3
General Phone: (418) 650-1764
General Fax: (418) 650-5172
General/National Adv. E-mail: info@qctonline.com;
Display Adv. E-mail: production@qctonline.com
Editorial e-mail: editor@qctonline.com
Primary Website: www.qctonline.com
Year Established: 1764
Delivery Methods: Mail`Newsstand
Areas Served - City/County or Portion Thereof, or Zip codes: Canada
Own Printing Facility?: N
Commercial printers?: Y
Mechanical specifications: Type page 10 1/3 x 13 7/8; E - 6 cols, 1 5/8, 3/16 between; A - 6 cols, 1 5/8, 3/16 between; C - 5 cols, 1 5/8, 3/16 between.
Published: Wed
Avg Paid Circ: 907
Avg Free Circ: 24
Audit By: CMCA
Audit Date: 30.09.2015
Personnel: Wendy Little (Circulation Manager); Stacie Stanton (Editor and Publisher)

QUEBEC EXPRESS
Street Address: 710 Bouvier, Suite 107, Bureau 900
Province: QC
Postal: G2J 1C2
Country: Canada
Mailing address: Boulevard Charest Ouest Bureau 900
Mailing city: Quebec
Province: QC
Postal: G2J 1C2
General Phone: (418) 628-7460
General Fax: (418) 622-1511
General/National Adv. E-mail: redaction_quebec@tc.tc
Areas Served - City/County or Portion Thereof, or Zip codes: Canada
Published: Fri
Avg Paid Circ: 7
Avg Free Circ: 28899
Audit By: CCAB
Audit Date: 31.03.2014
Personnel: Lilianne Laprise (Pub./Ed.)

QUEEN CHARLOTTE
HAIDA GWAII OBSERVER
Street Address: 623 7th St.,
Province: BC
Postal: V0T 1S0
Country: Canada
Mailing address: PO Box 205
Mailing city: Queen Charlotte
Province: BC
Postal: V0T 1S0
General Phone: (250) 559-4680
General Fax: (250) 559-8433
Advertising Phone: (250) 559-4680
Advertising Fax: (250) 559-4680
Editorial Phone: (250) 559-4680
Editorial Fax: (250) 559-4680
General/National Adv. E-mail: observer@haidagwaii.ca
Display Adv. E-mail: chris.williams@haidagwaiiobserver.com
Editorial e-mail: observer@haidagwaii.ca
Primary Website: www.haidagwaiiobserver.com
Year Established: 1969
Delivery Methods: Mail`Newsstand

Non-Daily Newspapers in Canada

Areas Served - City/County or Portion Thereof, or Zip codes: V0T 1S0, V0T 1T0, V0T 1R0, V0T 1Y0, V0T 1M0
Own Printing Facility?: Y
Commercial printers?: N
Mechanical specifications: Type page 7 1/2 x 10; E - 3 cols, 2 1/2, between; A - 3 cols, 2 1/2, between.
Published: Fri
Avg Paid Circ: 963
Avg Free Circ: 2
Audit By: VAC
Audit Date: 31.08.2016
Personnel: Todd Hamilton (Pub./Ed.); Chris Williams (Sales Mgr.)

QUESNEL

QUESNEL CARIBOO OBSERVER

Street Address: 188 Carson Ave. ,
Province: BC
Postal: V2J 2A8
Country: Canada
Mailing address: 188 Carson Ave.
Mailing city: Quesnel
Province: BC
Postal: V2J 2A8
General Phone: (250) 992-2121
General Fax: (250) 992-5229
General/National Adv. E-mail: newsroom@quesnelobserver.com
Display Adv. E-mail: advertising@quesnelobserver.com
Classified Adv. e-mail: publisher@quesnelobserver.com
Editorial e-mail: editor@quesnelobserver.com
Primary Website: www.quesnelobserver.com
Delivery Methods: Mail Racks
Areas Served - City/County or Portion Thereof, or Zip codes: V2J
Commercial printers?: Y
Published: Wed Fri
Avg Paid Circ: 984
Avg Free Circ: 2487
Audit By: VAC
Audit Date: 30.06.2016
Personnel: Autumn McDonald (Ed.); Tracey Roberts (Pub/Sales Mgr.)
Parent company (for newspapers): Black Press Group Ltd.

RADVILLE

RADVILLE DEEP SOUTH STAR

Street Address: #1-420 Floren St. ,
Province: SK
Postal: S0C 2G0
Country: Canada
Mailing address: PO Box 370
Mailing city: Radville
Province: SK
Postal: S0C 2G0
General Phone: (306) 869-2202
General Fax: (306) 869-2533
General/National Adv. E-mail: rstar@sasktel.net
Display Adv. E-mail: circulation@rdstar.sk.ca
Primary Website: www.rdstar.sk.ca
Areas Served - City/County or Portion Thereof, or Zip codes: Canada
Commercial printers?: Y
Published: Thur
Avg Paid Circ: 624
Audit By: CMCA
Audit Date: 31.01.2016
Personnel: Roger Holmes (Pub.)
Parent company (for newspapers): Transcontinental Media

RAINY RIVER

RAINY RIVER RECORD

Street Address: 312 Third St. ,
Province: ON
Postal: P0W 1L0
Country: Canada
Mailing address: PO Box 280
Mailing city: Rainy River
Province: ON
Postal: P0W 1L0
General Phone: (807) 852-3366
General Fax: (807) 852-4434
Editorial Phone: (807) 852-3337
General/National Adv. E-mail: info@rainyriverrecord.com
Display Adv. E-mail: advertising@rainyriverrecord.com
Editorial e-mail: editorial@rainyriverrecord.com
Primary Website: www.rainyriverrecord.com
Year Established: 1919
Areas Served - City/County or Portion Thereof, or Zip codes: Canada
Mechanical specifications: Type page 10 1/2 x 15; E - 5 cols, 1 4/5, 2/9 between; A - 5 cols, 1 4/5, 2/9 between; C - 5 cols, 1 4/5, 2/9 between.
Published: Tues
Avg Paid Circ: 609
Audit By: CMCA
Audit Date: 31.03.2014
Personnel: Anne Mailloux (Circ. Mgr.); Melissa Hudgin (Sales); Sharon LaCroix (Ed.)

RED DEER

CENTRAL ALBERTA LIFE

Street Address: 2950 Bremner Ave. ,
Province: AB
Postal: T4R 1M9
Country: Canada
Mailing address: 2950 Bremner Ave.
Mailing city: Red Deer
Province: AB
Postal: T4R 1M9
General Phone: (403) 314-4373
General Fax: (403) 342-4051
Display Adv. E-mail: advertising@reddeeradvocate.com
Classified Adv. e-mail: prausch@reddeeradvocate.com
Editorial e-mail: editorial@reddeeradvocate.com
Primary Website: www.reddeeradvocate.com
Year Established: 1995
Areas Served - City/County or Portion Thereof, or Zip codes: Canada
Own Printing Facility?: Y
Commercial printers?: Y
Mechanical specifications: Type page 10 x 12 7/8; A - 6 cols, 1 5/8, 1/6 between; C - 7 cols, 1 1/4, between.
Published: Thur
Avg Free Circ: 33301
Audit By: Sworn/Estimate/Non-Audited
Audit Date: 12.07.2019
Personnel: Mary Kemmis (Pub); Crystal Rhyno (Mng Ed); Wendy Moore (Adv. Mgr.); Deb Reitmeie (Circ. Mgr.)
Parent company (for newspapers): Red Deer Advocate

FRIDAY FORWARD

Street Address: 2950 Bremner Ave. ,
Province: AB
Postal: T4R 1M9
Country: Canada
Mailing address: 2950 Bremner Ave.
Mailing city: Red Deer
Province: AB
Postal: T4N 5G3
General Phone: (403) 343-2400
General Fax: (403) 342-4051
Advertising Phone: (403) 314-4343
Advertising Fax: (403) 342-4051
Editorial Phone: (403) 314-4325
Editorial Fax: (403) 341-6560
Display Adv. E-mail: advertising@reddeeradvocate.com
Classified Adv. e-mail: classified@reddeeradvocate.com
Editorial e-mail: editorial@reddeeradvocate.com
Primary Website: www.reddeeradvocate.com
Year Established: 1907
Delivery Methods: Newsstand Carrier
Areas Served - City/County or Portion Thereof, or Zip codes: Canada
Own Printing Facility?: Y
Commercial printers?: Y
Mechanical specifications: Type page 10 x 12 7/8; A - 6 cols, 1 9/16, 1/6 between; C - 7 cols, 1 15/16, between.
Published: Fri
Avg Paid Circ: 8500
Audit By: AAM
Audit Date: 30.06.2018
Personnel: Mary Kemmis (Pub Red Deer Advocate; Pres Prarie/ East Kootenay Division Black Press); Wendy Moore (Advt Mgr); Patricia Rausch (National Rep & Major Acct Asst); Debbie Reitmeier (Circulation Mgr); David Marsden (Managing Editor)
Parent company (for newspapers): Black Press Group Ltd.

RED DEER EXPRESS

Street Address: 121 5301-43 St. ,
Province: AB
Postal: T4N 1C8
Country: Canada
Mailing address: 121 5301-43 St.
Mailing city: Red Deer
Province: AB
Postal: T4N 1C8
General Phone: (403) 346-3356
General Fax: (403) 347-6620
Advertising Phone: (403) 625-4474
General/National Adv. E-mail: express@reddeer.greatwest.ca
Display Adv. E-mail: publisher@reddeerexpress.com
Classified Adv. e-mail: publisher@reddeerexpress.com
Editorial e-mail: editor@reddeerexpress.com
Primary Website: www.reddeerexpress.com
Year Established: 1946
Areas Served - City/County or Portion Thereof, or Zip codes: Canada
Own Printing Facility?: Y
Commercial printers?: Y
Published: Wed
Avg Paid Circ: 0
Avg Free Circ: 24718
Audit By: VAC
Audit Date: 31.08.2016
Personnel: Tracey Scheveers (Pub); Mark Weber (Ed)
Parent company (for newspapers): Black Press Group Ltd.

RED LAKE

THE NORTHERN SUN NEWS

Street Address: 200 Howey Street ,
Province: ON
Postal: P0V 2M0
Country: Canada
Mailing address: PO Box 1540
Mailing city: Red Lake
Province: ON
Postal: P0V 2M0
General Phone: (807) 727-2888
General Fax: (807) 727-3961
Display Adv. E-mail: pamela@thenorthernsun.com
Editorial e-mail: lindsay@thenorthernsun.com
Primary Website: www.thenorthernsun.com
Areas Served - City/County or Portion Thereof, or Zip codes: Canada
Published: Wed
Avg Paid Circ: 780
Audit By: CMCA
Audit Date: 31.03.2016
Personnel: Kathy Coutts (Gen Mgr.); Pamela O'Neill (Adv. Sales & Mrktg.)

REDWATER

FARM 'N' FRIENDS

Street Address: 4720 50 Ave ,
Province: AB
Postal: T0A 2W0
Country: Canada
Mailing address: PO Box 800
Mailing city: Lamont
Province: AB
Postal: T0B 2R0
General Phone: (780) 421-9715
General Fax: (780) 942-2515
General/National Adv. E-mail: redwater@shaw.ca
Display Adv. E-mail: redwater@shaw.ca
Classified Adv. e-mail: redwater@shaw.ca
Editorial e-mail: redwater@shaw.ca
Primary Website: www.cowleynewspapers.com/farm-n-friends/
Year Established: 1999
Areas Served - City/County or Portion Thereof, or Zip codes: Sturgeon
Published: Fri
Avg Free Circ: 17759
Audit By: CMCA
Audit Date: 30.04.2014
Personnel: Ed Cowley (Pub./Owner/Adv. Mgr./Ed.)
Parent company (for newspapers): W & E Cowley Pub. Ltd.

THE REVIEW

Street Address: 4720 50th Ave. ,
Province: AB
Postal: T0A 2W0
Country: Canada
Mailing address: PO Box 850
Mailing city: Redwater
Province: AB
Postal: T0A 2W0
General Phone: (780) 942-2023
General Fax: (780) 942-2515
General/National Adv. E-mail: redwater@shaw.ca
Display Adv. E-mail: redwater@shaw.ca
Primary Website: www.cowleynewspapers.com
Year Established: 1989
Commercial printers?: Y
Mechanical specifications: Type page 10 1/3 x 15 2/5; E - 6 cols, 1 1/2, 1/6 between; A - 6 cols, 1 1/2, 1/6 between; C - 6 cols, 1 1/2, 1/6 between.
Published: Tues
Avg Free Circ: 4405
Audit By: VAC
Audit Date: 30.06.2016
Personnel: Ed Cowley (Pub./Adv. Mgr./Owner)
Parent company (for newspapers): W & E Cowley Publishing Ltd.

REGINA

EAU VIVE (L')

Street Address: 210-1440 9th Ave N ,
Province: SK
Postal: S4R 8B1
Country: Canada
Mailing address: 210-1440, 9th Ave
Mailing city: Regina
Province: SK
Postal: S4R 8B1
General Phone: (306) 347-0481
General Fax: (306) 565-3450
General/National Adv. E-mail: direction@accesscomm.ca
Primary Website: http://nonprofits.accesscomm.ca/leauvive/web/
Areas Served - City/County or Portion Thereof, or Zip codes: Canada
Published: Thur
Avg Paid Circ: 1046
Audit By: CMCA
Audit Date: 30.04.2014
Personnel: Jean-Pierre Picard (Publisher); Angeline Feumba (Administrative Assistant)

RENFREW

THE RENFREW MERCURY EMC

Street Address: 35 Opeongo Rd. W. ,
Province: ON
Postal: K7V 2T2
Country: Canada
Mailing address: 35 Opeongo Rd.
Mailing city: Renfrew

Province: ON
Postal: K7V 4A8
General Phone: (613) 432-3655
General Fax: (613) 432-6689
General/National Adv. E-mail: mercury@renc.igs.net
Editorial e-mail: rmedit@runge.net
Primary Website: www.insideottawavalley.com/renfrew-on
Year Established: 1871
Areas Served - City/County or Portion Thereof, or Zip codes: Canada
Own Printing Facility?: Y
Published: Thur
Avg Free Circ: 13309
Audit By: CMCA
Audit Date: 30.06.2016
Personnel: Mike Tracy (Pub.); Theresa Fritz (Ed.)
Parent company (for newspapers): Metroland Media Group Ltd.; Runge Newspapers, Inc.

REPENTIGNY

ECHO DE REPENTIGNY

Street Address: Notre-dame Apt A , Apt. A
Province: QC
Postal: J6A 2T8
Country: Canada
Mailing address: Notre-Dame Apt A
Mailing city: Repentigny
Province: QC
Postal: J6A 2T8
General Phone: (450) 932-4782
General Fax: (450) 932-4794
General/National Adv. E-mail: martin.gravel@quebecormedia.com
Primary Website: www.lechoderepentigny.ca
Areas Served - City/County or Portion Thereof, or Zip codes: Canada
Published: Wed
Avg Free Circ: 59248
Audit By: CCAB
Audit Date: 31.03.2014
Personnel: Martin Gravel

HEBDO RIVE NORD

Street Address: 1004 Rue Notre-dame ,
Province: QC
Postal: J5Y 1S9
Country: Canada
Mailing address: 1004 Rue Notre-Dame
Mailing city: Repentigny
Province: QC
Postal: J5Y 1S9
General Phone: (450) 581-5120
General Fax: (450) 581-4515
General/National Adv. E-mail: equiperedaction@transcontinental.ca
Primary Website: www.hebdorivenord.com
Areas Served - City/County or Portion Thereof, or Zip codes: Canada
Published: Tues`Fri
Avg Paid Circ: 6
Avg Free Circ: 53954
Audit By: CCAB
Audit Date: 30.09.2012
Personnel: Yannick Boulanger (Chief Ed.); Sebastien Nadeau (Regl. Mgr.); Stephane Joseph (Sales Mgr.); Chantal Proulx (Prodn. Mgr.)
Parent company (for newspapers): Transcontinental Media

L'ARTISAN

Street Address: 1004 Rue Nortre-dame ,
Province: QC
Postal: J5Y 1S9
Country: Canada
Mailing address: 1004 Rue Nortre-Dame
Mailing city: Repentigny
Province: QC
Postal: J5Y 1S9
General Phone: (450) 581-5120
General Fax: (450) 581-4515
Primary Website: www.journallartisan.com

Published: Tues
Avg Free Circ: 45212
Audit By: Sworn/Estimate/Non-Audited
Audit Date: 12.07.2019
Personnel: Stephane Joseph (Adv. Mgr.); Yannick Boulanger (Ed.); Chantal Proulx (Prodn. Mgr.)
Parent company (for newspapers): Transcontinental Media

RESTON

THE RESTON RECORDER

Street Address: 330 4th St. ,
Province: MB
Postal: R0M 1X0
Country: Canada
Mailing address: PO Box 10
Mailing city: Reston
Province: MB
Postal: R0M 1X0
General Phone: (204) 877-3321
General Fax: (204) 522-3648
General/National Adv. E-mail: recorder@mts.net
Editorial e-mail: recorder@mts.net
Primary Website: http://www.restonrecorder.ca/
Areas Served - City/County or Portion Thereof, or Zip codes: Canada
Mechanical specifications: Type page 10 1/2 x 14; E - 6 cols, 1 3/5, 1/6 between; A - 6 cols, 1 3/5, 1/6 between; C - 6 cols, 1 3/5, 1/6 between.
Published: Fri
Avg Paid Circ: 116
Avg Free Circ: 59
Audit By: VAC
Audit Date: 31.12.2015
Personnel: Dolores Caldwell (Office Mgr.); Patty Lewis (Pub/Ed.)
Parent company (for newspapers): Glacier Media Group

REVELSTOKE

REVELSTOKE REVIEW

Street Address: 518 2nd St. ,
Province: BC
Postal: V0E 2S0
Country: Canada
Mailing address: PO Box 20
Mailing city: Revelstoke
Province: BC
Postal: V0E 2S0
General Phone: (250) 837-4667
General Fax: (250) 837-2003
General/National Adv. E-mail: editor@revelstoktimesreview.com
Display Adv. E-mail: mavis@revelstoketimesreview.com
Editorial e-mail: editor@revelstoketimesreview.com
Primary Website: www.revelstoketimesreview.com
Year Established: 1898
Delivery Methods: Mail`Newsstand`Carrier
Areas Served - City/County or Portion Thereof, or Zip codes: Canada
Published: Wed
Avg Paid Circ: 770
Avg Free Circ: 216
Audit By: VAC
Audit Date: 30.06.2016
Personnel: Mavis Cann (Pub./Adv Mgr); Fran Carlson (Office Mgr.); Alex Cooper (Ed)
Parent company (for newspapers): Black Press Group Ltd.

RICHMOND

RICHMOND NEWS

Street Address: #200-8211 Ackroyd Road ,
Province: BC
Postal: V6X 2C9
Country: Canada
Mailing address: #200-8211 Ackroyd Road
Mailing city: Richmond

Province: BC
Postal: V6X 2C9
General Phone: (604) 270-8031
General Fax: (604) 270-2248
General/National Adv. E-mail: editor@richmond-news.com
Display Adv. E-mail: rakimow@richmond-news.com
Classified Adv. E-mail: classifieds@van.net
Editorial e-mail: eedmonds@richmond-news.com
Primary Website: richmond-news.com
Year Established: 1979
Delivery Methods: Carrier
Areas Served - City/County or Portion Thereof, or Zip codes: Canada
Mechanical specifications: Type page 10 1/4 x 14; E - 6 cols, 1 9/16, between; A - 6 cols, 1 9/16, between; C - 7 cols, 1 5/16, between.
Published: Thur
Avg Paid Circ: 0
Avg Free Circ: 46113
Audit By: CCAB
Audit Date: 22.11.2017
Personnel: Pierre Pelletier (Pub); Rob Akimow (Adv Dir); Eve Edmonds (Ed); Kristene Murray (Circ Mgr)
Parent company (for newspapers): Glacier Media Group; CanWest MediaWorks Publications, Inc.

RIDGETOWN

THE RIDGETOWN INDEPENDENT NEWS

Street Address: 1 Main St. W. ,
Province: ON
Postal: N0P 2C0
Mailing address: P.O. Box 609
Mailing city: Ridgetown
Province: ON
Postal: N0P 2C0
General Phone: (519) 674-5205
General Fax: (519) 674-2573
Areas Served - City/County or Portion Thereof, or Zip codes: Canada
Published: Wed
Avg Paid Circ: 1674
Audit By: CMCA
Audit Date: 30.04.2016
Personnel: Shelia Mcbrayne (Editor in Chief); Gordon Brown (Managing Editor)

RIMBEY

RIMBEY REVIEW

Street Address: 5001-50 Ave. Main St. ,
Province: AB
Postal: T0C 2J0
Country: Canada
Mailing address: PO Box 244
Mailing city: Rimbey
Province: AB
Postal: T0C 2J0
General Phone: (403) 843-4909
General Fax: (403) 843-4907
General/National Adv. E-mail: admin@rimbeyreview.com
Display Adv. E-mail: sales@rimbeyreview.com
Editorial e-mail: editor@rimbeyreview.com
Primary Website: www.rimbeyreview.com
Year Established: 1997
Delivery Methods: Mail
Areas Served - City/County or Portion Thereof, or Zip codes: t0c
Commercial printers?: Y
Published: Tues
Avg Paid Circ: 7
Avg Free Circ: 5136
Audit By: VAC
Audit Date: 31.05.2016
Personnel: Michele Rosenthal (Pub); Connie Johnson (Sales); Treena Mielke (Ed)
Parent company (for newspapers): Black Press Group Ltd.

RIMOUSKI

AVANTAGE VOTRE JOURNAL

Street Address: 183 St-germain Ouest ,
Province: QC
Postal: G5L 4B8
Country: Canada
Mailing address: St-Germain Ouest
Mailing city: Rimouski
Province: QC
Postal: G5L 4B8
General Phone: (418) 722-0205
Primary Website: http://www.lavantage.qc.ca/
Areas Served - City/County or Portion Thereof, or Zip codes: Canada
Published: Wed
Avg Paid Circ: 64
Avg Free Circ: 43009
Audit By: CCAB
Audit Date: 31.03.2014
Personnel: Lucie Moisan

LE PROGRES-ECHO

Street Address: 217, Avenue LÃ£Â©onidas Sud, Bureau 6-d ,
Province: QC
Postal: G5L 2T5
Country: Canada
Mailing address: PO Box 3217, Branch A
Mailing city: Rimouski
Province: QC
Postal: G5L 9G6
General Phone: (418) 721-1212
Advertising Fax: (418) 723-1855
Editorial Fax: (418) 722-4078
General/National Adv. E-mail: marc.pitre@quebecormedia.com
Primary Website: www.rimouskois.ca
Areas Served - City/County or Portion Thereof, or Zip codes: Canada
Mechanical specifications: Type page 12 1/2 x 11 1/2; E - 10 cols, between; A - 10 cols, between; C - 10 cols, between.
Published: Sun
Avg Paid Circ: 4
Avg Free Circ: 29084
Audit By: CCAB
Audit Date: 31.03.2014
Personnel: Alain St. Amand (Pub.); Ernie Wells (Ed.)
Parent company (for newspapers): Quebecor Communications, Inc.

LE RIMOUSKOIS

Street Address: 217 Leonidas Ave, Po Box 3217, Branch A ,
Province: QC
Postal: G5L 9G6
Country: Canada
Mailing address: 217 Leonidas Ave, PO Box 3217, Branch A
Mailing city: Rimouski
Province: QC
Postal: G5L 9G6
General Phone: (418) 721-1212
General Fax: (418) 723-1855
Advertising Fax: (418) 723-1855
Editorial Fax: (418) 723-4078
General/National Adv. E-mail: marc.pitre@quebecormedia.com
Primary Website: www.rimouskois.ca
Areas Served - City/County or Portion Thereof, or Zip codes: Canada
Mechanical specifications: Type page 12 1/2 x 11 1/2; E - 10 cols, between; A - 10 cols, between.
Published: Wed
Avg Paid Circ: 4
Avg Free Circ: 29084
Audit By: CCAB
Audit Date: 31.03.2014
Personnel: Alain St. Amand (Pub.); Ernie Wells (Ed.)
Parent company (for newspapers): Quebecor Communications, Inc.

Non-Daily Newspapers in Canada

RIVERS

RIVERS BANNER GAZETTE-REPORTER
Street Address: 529 2nd Ave. ,
Province: MB
Postal: R0K 1X0
Country: Canada
Mailing address: PO Box 70
Mailing city: Rivers
Province: MB
Postal: R0K 1X0
General Phone: (204) 328-7494
General Fax: (204) 328-5212
General/National Adv. E-mail: info@riversbanner.com
Editorial e-mail: kwaddell@neepawabanner.com
Primary Website: www.riversbanner.com
Year Established: 1993
Delivery Methods: Mail
Areas Served - City/County or Portion Thereof, or Zip codes: Riverdale
Own Printing Facility?: Y
Commercial printers?: N
Mechanical specifications: Type page 10 x 14; E - 2 cols, 3 1/4, 1/4 between; A - 6 cols, 1 5/8, 1/4 between; C - 8 cols, 1 5/8, 1/4 between.
Published: Fri
Avg Paid Circ: 93
Avg Free Circ: 1668
Audit By: VAC
Audit Date: 30.06.2017
Personnel: Ken Waddell (Pub/Ed.); Sheila Runions (Gen. Mgr.)
Parent company (for newspapers): Neepawa Banner

RIVIERE-DU-LOUP

INFO DIMANCHE
Street Address: Rue Fraser ,
Province: QC
Postal: G5R 1C6
Country: Canada
Mailing address: rue Fraser
Mailing city: Riviere-du-Loup
Province: QC
Postal: G5R 1C6
General Phone: (418) 862-1911
General Fax: (418) 862-6165
Primary Website: www.infodimanche.com
Areas Served - City/County or Portion Thereof, or Zip codes: Canada
Published: Sun
Avg Paid Circ: 106
Avg Free Circ: 31754
Audit By: CCAB
Audit Date: 30.09.2013
Personnel: Michel Chalifour

LE SAINT-LAURENT PORTAGE
Street Address: 55-a, Rue De L'hotel De Ville ,
Province: QC
Postal: G5R 1L4
Country: Canada
Mailing address: 55-A, rue de l'Hotel de Ville
Mailing city: Riviere-du-Loup
Province: QC
Postal: G5R 1L4
General Phone: (418) 862-1774
General Fax: (418) 862-4387
General/National Adv. E-mail: francis.desrosiers@quebecormedia.com
Primary Website: www.lesaintlaurentportage.com
Areas Served - City/County or Portion Thereof, or Zip codes: Canada
Own Printing Facility?: Y
Mechanical specifications: Type page 10 1/4 x 12.
Published: Wed
Avg Paid Circ: 11
Avg Free Circ: 34286
Audit By: CCAB
Audit Date: 31.03.2014

Personnel: Gilles LeBel (Mng. Ed.); Pierre Levesque (Ed.)
Parent company (for newspapers): Quebecor Communications, Inc.

L'INFORMATION
Street Address: 55-a Rue De L'hotel De Ville ,
Province: QC
Postal: G5R 1L4
Country: Canada
Mailing address: 55-A rue de l'hotel de ville
Mailing city: Riviere-du-Loup
Province: QC
Postal: G5R 1L4
General Phone: (418) 775-4381
General Fax: (418) 862-4387
General/National Adv. E-mail: journalinformation@globetrotter.net; nsomontjoli@dosquadecoi.com
Primary Website: www.linformation.ca
Areas Served - City/County or Portion Thereof, or Zip codes: Canada
Published: Wed
Avg Paid Circ: 30
Avg Free Circ: 9311
Audit By: BPA
Audit Date: 01.03.2012
Personnel: Francis Desrosiers (Ed.)
Parent company (for newspapers): Quebecor Communications, Inc.

ROBERVAL

L'ETOILE DU LAC
Street Address: 797 Blvd. Saint Joseph, Ste. 101 , Bureau 101
Province: QC
Postal: G8H 2L4
Country: Canada
Mailing address: 797 Blvd. Saint Joseph, Ste. 101
Mailing city: Roberval
Province: QC
Postal: G8H 2L4
General Phone: (418) 275-2911
General Fax: (418) 275-2834
General/National Adv. E-mail: redaccion_roberval@transcontinental.ca
Primary Website: www.letoiledulac.com
Year Established: 1915
Areas Served - City/County or Portion Thereof, or Zip codes: Canada
Published: Wed
Avg Paid Circ: 95
Avg Free Circ: 14602
Audit By: CCAB
Audit Date: 31.03.2014
Personnel: Michel Dupont (Regional Publisher); Daniel Migneault (Ed. in Chief); Claudia Turcotte (Sales manager); Michel Aub (Publisher)
Parent company (for newspapers): Transcontinental Media

ROBLIN

THE ROBLIN REVIEW
Street Address: 119 First Ave. Nw ,
Province: MB
Postal: R0L 1P0
Country: Canada
Mailing address: PO Box 938
Mailing city: Roblin
Province: MB
Postal: R0L 1P0
General Phone: (204) 937-8377
General Fax: (204) 937-8212
General/National Adv. E-mail: roblinreview@mts.net
Display Adv. E-mail: reviewads@mts.net
Classified Adv. e-mail: reviewads@mts.net
Editorial e-mail: rreview@mts.net
Primary Website: theroblinreview.com
Year Established: 1913
Delivery Methods: Mail`Racks
Areas Served - City/County or Portion Thereof, or Zip codes: Roblin, MB
Commercial printers?: Y

Mechanical specifications: Type page 11 1/4 x 17; E - 6 cols, 1 5/8, 2/16 between; A - 6 cols, 1 5/8, 2/16 between; C - 6 cols, 1 5/8, 1/8 between.
Published: Tues
Avg Paid Circ: 50
Avg Free Circ: 26
Audit By: VAC
Audit Date: 30.06.2016
Personnel: Patricia Liske (Circ. Mgr.); Ed Doering (Ed.); Brent Wright (Production Mgr.); Jackie Edel (Ad. consultant)

ROCKLAND

ROCKLAND VISION
Street Address: 1315 Laurier St. ,
Province: ON
Postal: K4K 1L5
Country: Canada
Mailing address: PO Box 897
Mailing city: Rockland
Province: ON
Postal: K4K 1L5
General Phone: (613) 446-6456
General Fax: (613) 446-1381
General/National Adv. E-mail: vision@eap.on.ca
Display Adv. E-mail: paulo.casimiro@eap.on.ca
Primary Website: www.facebook.com/pg/Le-journal-Vision-newspaper-199878750108078/about/?ref=page_internal
Year Established: 1994
Own Printing Facility?: Y
Mechanical specifications: Type page 10 1/2 x 14; E - 8 cols, 1 5/16, between; A - 8 cols, between; C - 8 cols, between.
Published: Fri
Avg Paid Circ: 23297
Avg Free Circ: 39
Audit By: ODC
Audit Date: 13.12.2011
Personnel: Paulo Casimiro (Prodn. Mgr.)

ROCKY MOUNTAIN HOUSE

THE MOUNTAINEER
Street Address: 4814 49th St. ,
Province: AB
Postal: T4T 1S8
Country: Canada
Mailing address: 4814 49th St.
Mailing city: Rocky Mountain House
Province: AB
Postal: T4T 1S8
General Phone: (403) 845-3334
General Fax: (403) 845-5570
General/National Adv. E-mail: rocky_mountain_house@awna.com
Display Adv. E-mail: advertising@mountaineer.bz
Classified Adv. e-mail: advertising@mountaineer.bz
Editorial e-mail: editor@mountaineer.bz
Primary Website: www.mountaineer.bz
Year Established: 1923
Mechanical specifications: Type page 11 5/8 x 21 1/4; E - 6 cols, 1 5/6, 1/6 between; A - 6 cols, 1 5/6, 1/6 between; C - 6 cols, 1 5/6, 1/6 between.
Published: Tues
Avg Paid Circ: 2264
Avg Free Circ: 53
Audit By: VAC
Audit Date: 31.03.2016
Personnel: Gail Krabben (Prodn. Mgr.); Glen Mazza (Pub.); Penny Allen (Adv. Mgr.); Laura Button (Ed.); Bernie Visotto (Office Mgr.)
Parent company (for newspapers): Mountaineer Publishing Co.

ROSETOWN

THE ROSETOWN EAGLE
Street Address: 114 2nd Ave. W. ,
Province: SK
Postal: S0L 2V0

Country: Canada
Mailing address: PO Box 130
Mailing city: Rosetown
Province: SK
Postal: S0L 2V0
General Phone: (306) 882-4348
General Fax: (306) 882-4204
Advertising Phone: (306) 882-4348
Editorial Phone: (306) 882-4348
General/National Adv. E-mail: frontdesk.eagle@gmail.com
Display Adv. E-mail: ads.eagle@gmail.com
Classified Adv. e-mail: frontdesk.eagle@gmail.com
Editorial e-mail: editor.eagle@gmail.com
Year Established: 1909
Delivery Methods: Mail`Newsstand
Areas Served - City/County or Portion Thereof, or Zip codes: Canada
Own Printing Facility?: Y
Commercial printers?: Y
Mechanical specifications: Type page 12 x 20 1/2; E - 6 cols, 1 5/8, 1/4 between; A - 6 cols, 1 5/8, 1/4 between; C - 6 cols, 1 5/8, 1/4 between.
Published: Mon
Avg Paid Circ: 1562
Avg Free Circ: 57
Audit By: CMCA
Audit Date: 30.04.2017
Personnel: Stewart Crump (Owner/publisher); Simone Gaudet; Loretta Torrence (Ads); David McIver

ROUYN-NORANDA

ABITIBI EXPRESS ROUYN
Street Address: 438 Ave. Lariviere ,
Province: QC
Postal: J9X 4J1
Country: Canada
Mailing address: 438 Ave. Lariviere
Mailing city: Rouyn-Noranda
Province: QC
Postal: J9X 4J1
General Phone: (819) 797-6776
General Fax: (819) 797-4725
Editorial Phone: (819) 767-6776
Editorial Fax: (819) 797-4725
General/National Adv. E-mail: redaction.abitibi@transcontinental.ca
Primary Website: http://www.abitibiouestrouynnoranda.ca
Areas Served - City/County or Portion Thereof, or Zip codes: Canada
Published: Tues
Avg Paid Circ: 18
Avg Free Circ: 29398
Audit By: CCAB
Audit Date: 31.03.2014

CITOYEN ROUYN NORANDA
Street Address: 1 Rue Du Terminus ,
Province: QC
Postal: J9X 3B5
Country: Canada
Mailing address: 1 rue du Terminus
Mailing city: Rouyn-Noranda
Province: QC
Postal: J9X 3B5
General Phone: (819) 762-4361 x 221
General Fax: (819) 797-2450
Advertising Phone: (819) 762-4361
Editorial Phone: (819) 279-7032
Display Adv. E-mail: stefan.baillargeon@tc.tc or marie-eve.bouchard@tc.tc
Classified Adv. e-mail: vicky.aumond@tc.tc
Editorial e-mail: joel.caya@tc.tc
Primary Website: lafrontiere.ca
Year Established: 1937
Delivery Methods: Mail`Newsstand`Carrier`Racks
Areas Served - City/County or Portion Thereof, or.Zip codes: Canada
Published: Wed
Avg Paid Circ: 17
Avg Free Circ: 19749
Audit By: CCAB
Audit Date: 31.03.2014

Personnel: Joel Caya (General manager)

RUSSELL

BANNER

Street Address: 455 Main St. ,
Province: MB
Postal: R0J 1W0
Country: Canada
Mailing address: PO Box 100
Mailing city: Russell
Province: MB
Postal: R0J 1W0
General Phone: (204) 773-2069
General Fax: (204) 773-2645
General/National Adv. E-mail: rbanner@mts.net
Display Adv. E-mail: russellbannerads@mymts.net
Editorial e-mail: editor@russellbanner.com
Primary Website: russellbanner.com
Areas Served - City/County or Portion Thereof, or Zip codes: Russell and area
Own Printing Facility?: Y
Mechanical specifications: Type page 11 1/2 x 17; E - 5 cols, 2, between; A - 5 cols, 2, between; C - 5 cols, 2, between.
Published: Tues
Avg Paid Circ: 1300
Avg Free Circ: 19
Audit By: CCAB
Audit Date: 30.11.2018
Personnel: Chantelle Senchuk (Adv); Jessica Ludvig
Parent company (for newspapers): Dauphin Herald

RYCROFT

RYCROFT CENTRAL PEACE SIGNAL

Street Address: 47011 50th St. ,
Province: AB
Postal: T0H 3A0
Country: Canada
Mailing address: PO Box 250
Mailing city: Rycroft
Province: AB
Postal: T0H 3A0
General Phone: (780) 765-3604
General Fax: (780) 785-2188
General/National Adv. E-mail: admin@cpsignal.com
Display Adv. E-mail: signalads@telus.net
Classified Adv. e-mail: signalads@telus.net
Editorial e-mail: signalnews@telus.net
Year Established: 1980
Delivery Methods: Mail Newsstand
Areas Served - City/County or Portion Thereof, or Zip codes: Canada
Commercial printers?: Y
Mechanical specifications: Type page 10 15/16 x 13; E - 6 cols, 1 7/12, 1/6 between; A - 6 cols, 1 7/12, 1/6 between; C - 6 cols, 1 7/12, 1/6 between.
Published: Tues
Avg Paid Circ: 2633
Avg Free Circ: 5
Audit By: CMCA
Audit Date: 30.03.2017
Personnel: Dan Zahara (Pub/Advt Mgr); Carol Grover (Circ. Mgr.); Morgan Zahara
Parent company (for newspapers): 847562 Alberta Ltd.

SACKVILLE

THE SACKVILLE TRIBUNE-POST

Street Address: 80 Main St. ,
Province: NB
Postal: E4L 4A7
Country: Canada
Mailing address: 80 Main St.
Mailing city: Sackville
Province: NB
Postal: E4L 4A7
General Phone: (506) 536-2500
General Fax: (506) 536-4024
Editorial Fax: (506) 536-4024
General/National Adv. E-mail: sdoherty@sackvilletribunepost.com
Editorial e-mail: sdoherty@sackvilletribunepost.com
Primary Website: www.sackvilletribunepost.com
Year Established: 1902
Delivery Methods: Mail Newsstand
Areas Served - City/County or Portion Thereof, or Zip codes: Sackville
Mechanical specifications: Type page 12 x 21; E - 10 cols, 2, 1/4 between; A - 10 cols, 2, 1/4 between; C - 10 cols, 2, 1/4 between.
Published: Wed
Avg Paid Circ: 2150
Avg Free Circ: 4
Audit By: VAC
Audit Date: 31.10.2015
Personnel: Richard Russell (Pub.); Scott Doherty (Ed.); Tanya Austin (Circ/Class. Mgr)
Parent company (for newspapers): Transcontinental Media

SAGUENAY

LE COURRIER DU SAGUENAY

Street Address: 3635 Blvd Harvey Ste 201 ,
Province: QC
Postal: G7X 3B2
Country: Canada
Mailing address: 3635 Blvd Harvey Ste 201
Mailing city: Saguenay
Province: QC
Postal: G7X 3B2
General Phone: (418) 542-2442
General Fax: (418) 542-5225
Advertising Phone: (418) 542-2442
Advertising Fax: (418) 542-5225
Editorial Phone: (418) 542-2442
Editorial Fax: (418) 542-5225
General/National Adv. E-mail: redaction.saguenay@tc.tc
Display Adv. E-mail: redaction.saguenay@tc.tc
Editorial e-mail: redaction.saguenay@tc.tc
Primary Website: www.courrierdusaguenay.com
Delivery Methods: Mail Racks
Areas Served - City/County or Portion Thereof, or Zip codes: Canada
Published: Wed
Avg Paid Circ: 16
Avg Free Circ: 72964
Audit By: CCAB
Audit Date: 31.03.2014
Personnel: Joan Sullivan (Ed.)

SAINT ANDRE-AVELLIN

LA PETITE NATION

Street Address: 3 Ste.10, Principale St. ,
Province: QC
Postal: J0V 1W0
Country: Canada
Mailing address: 3 Ste.10, Principale St.
Mailing city: Saint Andre-Avellin
Province: QC
Postal: J0V 1W0
General Phone: (819) 983-2725
General Fax: (819) 983-6844
General/National Adv. E-mail: gessi.laslamme@transcontinental.ca
Editorial e-mail: pascal.laplante@tc.tc
Primary Website: http://www.lapetitenation.com
Areas Served - City/County or Portion Thereof, or Zip codes: Canada
Published: Wed
Avg Paid Circ: 19
Avg Free Circ: 10108
Audit By: CCAB
Audit Date: 31.03.2014
Personnel: Eric Bernard (Ed.)
Parent company (for newspapers): Transcontinental Media

SAINT ANTHONY

NORTHERN PEN

Street Address: 10-12 North St. ,
Province: NL
Postal: A0K 4S0
Country: Canada
Mailing address: PO Box 520
Mailing city: Saint Anthony
Province: NL
Postal: A0K 4S0
General Phone: (709) 454-2191
General Fax: (709) 454-3718
General/National Adv. E-mail: info@northernpen.ca
Display Adv. E-mail: kparsons@northernpen.ca
Editorial e-mail: arandell@nothernpen.ca
Primary Website: www.northernpen.ca
Year Established: 1980
Areas Served - City/County or Portion Thereof, or Zip codes: Canada
Mechanical specifications: Type page 11 x 21 1/2; E - 6 cols, 1 3/4, between; A - 6 cols, 1 3/4, between; C - 8 cols, 1 1/2, between.
Published: Mon
Avg Paid Circ: 1085
Avg Free Circ: 0
Audit By: VAC
Audit Date: 31.12.2015
Personnel: Kathy Parsons (Adv. Mgr.); Frances Reardon (Office/Circ Mgr); Adam Randell (Ed)
Parent company (for newspapers): Transcontinental Media

SAINT AUGUSTIN DE DESMAURES

NIC

Street Address: Route 138 Ste 100 , Suite 100
Province: QC
Postal: G3A 2C6
Country: Canada
Mailing address: route 138 Ste 100
Mailing city: Saint Augustin de Desmaures
Province: QC
Postal: G3A 2C6
General Phone: (418) 908-3438
Published: Wed
Avg Paid Circ: 2863
Avg Free Circ: 268
Audit By: ODC
Audit Date: 14.12.2011
Personnel: Sophie Bouchard

SAINT BONIFACE

LA LIBERTE

Street Address: Po Box 190 ,
Province: MB
Postal: R2H 3B4
Country: Canada
Mailing address: PO Box 190
Mailing city: Saint Boniface
Province: MB
Postal: R2H 3B4
General Phone: (204) 237-4823
General Fax: (204) 231-1998
General/National Adv. E-mail: la_liberte@la-liberte.mb.ca
Editorial e-mail: la-liberte@la-liberte.mb.ca
Primary Website: http://la-liberte.mb.ca/tag/saint-boniface
Year Established: 1913
Delivery Methods: Mail Carrier
Areas Served - City/County or Portion Thereof, or Zip codes: Winnipeg/Manitoba/CAnada/ R2H Manitoba Canada
Mechanical specifications: Type page 10 3/8 x 15 3/8; E - 5 cols, 1 15/16, 1/6 between; A - 5 cols, 1 15/16, 1/6 between; C - 5 cols, 1 15/16, 1/6 between.
Published: Wed
Avg Paid Circ: 0
Avg Free Circ: 12
Audit By: VAC
Audit Date: 30.06.2016
Personnel: Sophie Gaulin (Dir/Ed); Bernard Bocquel (Assoc. Ed); Roxanne Bouchard (Office Admin)

SAINT BRUNO

LE JOURNAL DE ST-BRUNO

Street Address: 1507 Roberval ,
Province: QC
Postal: J3V 3P8
Country: Canada
Mailing address: 1507 Roberval
Mailing city: Saint Bruno
Province: QC
Postal: J3V 3P8
General Phone: (450) 653-3685
General Fax: (450) 653-6967
General/National Adv. E-mail: redaction@journaldest-bruno.qc.ca
Editorial e-mail: pclair@versants.com
Primary Website: http://www.journaldest-bruno.qc.ca/
Areas Served - City/County or Portion Thereof, or Zip codes: Canada
Mechanical specifications: Type page 11 1/2 x 17.
Published: Fri
Avg Paid Circ: 4
Avg Free Circ: 18900
Audit By: CCAB
Audit Date: 31.03.2014
Personnel: Philippe Clair (Ed.); Stéphanie Lambert (Prod. Mgr.)
Parent company (for newspapers): Les Hebdos Monteregiens-OOB

SAINT CATHARINE'S

THOROLD NIAGARA NEWS

Street Address: 10-1 St. Paul St. ,
Province: ON
Postal: L2R 7L4
Country: Canada
Mailing address: 10-1 St. Paul St.
Mailing city: Saint Catharine's
Province: ON
Postal: L2R 7L4
General Phone: (905) 688-4332
General Fax: (905) 688-6313
Display Adv. E-mail: lauren.krause@sunmedia.ca
Primary Website: www.tholoredition.ca
Published: Thur
Published Other: 1
Avg Free Circ: 7225
Audit By: CMCA
Audit Date: 31.05.2016
Personnel: Jeff Blay (Reporter); Lauren Krause (Advertising)
Parent company (for newspapers): Postmedia Network Inc.

SAINT EUSTACHE

EVEIL

Street Address: Rue St-eustache ,
Province: QC
Postal: J7R 2L2
Country: Canada
Mailing address: rue St-Eustache
Mailing city: Saint Eustache
Province: QC
Postal: J7R 2L2
Areas Served - City/County or Portion Thereof, or Zip codes: Canada
Published: Sat
Avg Paid Circ: 0
Avg Free Circ: 55993
Audit By: CCAB
Audit Date: 31.03.2014
Personnel: Serge Langlois

LA CONCORDE

Street Address: 53 Rue St. Eustache ,
Province: QC
Postal: J7R 2L2
Country: Canada

Non-Daily Newspapers in Canada

Mailing address: 53 Rue St. Eustache
Mailing city: Saint Eustache
Province: QC
Postal: J7R 2L2
General Phone: (450) 472-3440
General Fax: (450) 473-1629
Areas Served - City/County or Portion Thereof, or Zip codes: Canada
Published: Wed
Avg Free Circ: 52172
Audit By: CCAB
Audit Date: 31.03.2014
Personnel: Jean-Claude Langlois (Ed.)

LE GROUPE JCL INC.

Street Address: 53, Rue Saint-eustache ,
Province: QC
Postal: J7R 2L2
Country: Canada
Mailing address: 53, rue Saint-Eustache
Mailing city: Saint Eustache
Province: QC
Postal: J7R 2L2
General Phone: (450) 472-3440
Advertising Fax: (450) 435-7968
Editorial Fax: (450) 435-0588
General/National Adv. E-mail: leveil@groupejcl.com
Display Adv. E-mail: infojournaux@groupejcl.com
Classified Adv. e-mail: infojournaux@groupejcl.com
Editorial e-mail: infojournaux@groupejcl.com
Primary Website: www.leveil.com
Published: Sat
Avg Free Circ: 60000
Audit By: Sworn/Estimate/Non-Audited
Audit Date: 12.07.2019
Personnel: Louis Kemp (Dir., Sales); Norman Langlois (Circ. Mgr.); Claude Desjardins (Ed. in Chief); Jean Claude Langlois (Ed.); Marco Brunelle (Sports Ed.); Yves Bourbonnais (Dir., Prodn.); Serge Langlois (Dir., Dist.)

SAINT GEORGES

JOURNAL DE LA BEAUCE

Street Address: 11720 1re Rue , Bureau 2
Province: QC
Postal: G5Y 2C8
Country: Canada
Mailing address: 11720 1re Rue
Mailing city: Saint Georges
Province: QC
Postal: G5Y 2C8
General Phone: (418) 220-0222
Published: Fri
Avg Free Circ: 32653
Audit By: ODC
Audit Date: 13.12.2011
Personnel: Lyne Genest

L'ECLAIREUR-PROGRES/BEAUCE NOUVELLES

Street Address: 12625 1st Ave. E. ,
Province: QC
Postal: G5Y 2E4
Country: Canada
Mailing address: 12625 1st Ave. E.
Mailing city: Saint Georges
Province: QC
Postal: G5Y 2E4
General Phone: (418) 228-8858
General Fax: (418) 228-0268
Primary Website: leclaireurprogres.canoe.ca
Areas Served - City/County or Portion Thereof, or Zip codes: Canada
Published: Wed
Avg Paid Circ: 13
Avg Free Circ: 38115
Audit By: CCAB
Audit Date: 31.03.2014
Personnel: Gilbert Bernier (Gen. Mgr.)
Parent company (for newspapers): Quebecor Communications, Inc.

PROGRES DE BELLECHASSE

Street Address: 98e Rue ,
Province: QC
Postal: G5Y 8G1
Country: Canada
Mailing address: 98e Rue
Mailing city: Saint Georges
Province: QC
Postal: G5Y 8G1
General Phone: (418) 228-8858
Areas Served - City/County or Portion Thereof, or Zip codes: Canada
Published: Wed
Avg Paid Circ: 0
Avg Free Circ: 19789
Audit By: CCAB
Audit Date: 30.09.2012
Personnel: Gilbert Bernier

SAINT HUBERT

VALLEE DU RICHELIEU EXPRESS

Street Address: 4480 Chemin Chambly, Bureau 204 ,
Province: QC
Postal: J3Y 3M8
Country: Canada
Mailing address: 4480 Chemin Chambly, Bureau 204
Mailing city: Saint Hubert
Province: QC
Postal: J3Y 3M8
General Phone: (450) 678-6187
Advertising Phone: (450) 678-6187
Editorial Phone: (450) 678-6187
General/National Adv. E-mail: valleedurichelieu@tc.tc
Display Adv. E-mail: valleedurichelieu@tc.tc
Editorial e-mail: valleedurichelieu@tc.tc
Primary Website: www.valleedurichelieuexpress.ca
Delivery Methods: Mail`Racks
Areas Served - City/County or Portion Thereof, or Zip codes: Canada
Published: Wed
Avg Paid Circ: 1
Avg Free Circ: 34751
Audit By: CCAB
Audit Date: 31.03.2014

SAINT HYACINTHE

LE COURRIER DE SAINT-HYACINTHE

Street Address: 655 Rue St. Anne ,
Province: QC
Postal: J2S 5G4
Country: Canada
Mailing address: 655 Rue St. Anne
Mailing city: Saint Hyacinthe
Province: QC
Postal: J2S 5G4
General Phone: (450) 773-6028
General Fax: (450) 773-3115
Advertising Phone: (450) 771-0677
General/National Adv. E-mail: redaction@leclairon.qc.ca
Display Adv. E-mail: gbedard@courrierclairon.qc.ca
Classified Adv. e-mail: gbedard@courrierclairon.qc.ca
Primary Website: lecourrier.qc.ca/accueil
Year Established: 1912
Areas Served - City/County or Portion Thereof, or Zip codes: Canada
Published: Tues
Avg Paid Circ: 9352
Avg Free Circ: 142
Audit By: AAM
Audit Date: 30.09.2018
Personnel: Guillaume Bedard (Adv. Mgr.)

SAINT JEROME

JOURNAL LE NORD

Street Address: 393 Laurentides Blvd. ,
Province: QC
Postal: J7Z 4L9
Country: Canada
Mailing address: 393 Laurentides Blvd.
Mailing city: Saint Jerome
Province: QC
Postal: J7Z 4L9
General Phone: (450) 438-8383
General Fax: (450) 438-4174
Editorial e-mail: editeur@journallenord.com
Primary Website: www.journallenord.com
Year Established: 1986
Areas Served - City/County or Portion Thereof, or Zip codes: Canada
Commercial printers?: Y
Mechanical specifications: Type page 10 1/4 x 14 1/4; E - 8 cols, 1 1/6, 1/6 between.
Published: Wed
Avg Paid Circ: 9
Avg Free Circ: 55388
Audit By: CCAB
Audit Date: 31.03.2014
Personnel: Francois LaFerriere (Pub.); Mychel Lapointe (Ed.)

LE MIRABEL

Street Address: 179 Rue St. Georges ,
Province: QC
Postal: J7Z 4Z8
Country: Canada
Mailing address: 179 rue St. Georges
Mailing city: Saint Jerome
Province: QC
Postal: J7Z 4Z8
General Phone: (450) 436-8200
General Fax: (450) 436-8912
General/National Adv. E-mail: atelier.mirabel@hebdosquebecor.com; redaction.mirabel@hebdosquebecor.com
Primary Website: www.lemirabel.com
Year Established: 1974
Areas Served - City/County or Portion Thereof, or Zip codes: Canada
Own Printing Facility?: Y
Published: Sat
Avg Free Circ: 51862
Audit By: CCAB
Audit Date: 31.03.2014
Personnel: Marc Fradellin (Pub.); Andre Guillemette (Gen. Mgr.); Christine Leonard (Prodn. Dir.)
Parent company (for newspapers): Quebecor Communications, Inc.

L'ECHO DU NORD

Street Address: 179 St. George St. ,
Province: QC
Postal: J7Z 4Z8
Country: Canada
Mailing address: 179 St. George St.
Mailing city: Saint Jerome
Province: QC
Postal: J7Z 4Z8
General Phone: (450) 436-5381
General Fax: (450) 436-5904
General/National Adv. E-mail: atelier.echo@hebdosquebecor.com; redaction.echo@hebdosquebecor.com
Primary Website: http://echosdunord.com/
Areas Served - City/County or Portion Thereof, or Zip codes: Canada
Published: Wed
Avg Paid Circ: 391
Avg Free Circ: 53385
Audit By: CCAB
Audit Date: 31.03.2014
Personnel: Andre Guillemette (Ed.); Jean-Paul Sauriol (Prodn. Mgr.)
Parent company (for newspapers): Quebecor Communications, Inc.

SAINT JOHN

THE NEW FREEMAN

Street Address: One Bayard Dr. ,
Province: NB
Postal: E2L 3L5
Country: Canada
Mailing address: 1 Bayard Dr.
Mailing city: Saint John
Province: NB
Postal: E2L 3L5
General Phone: (506) 653-6806
General Fax: (506) 653-6818
General/National Adv. E-mail: tnf@nbnet.nb.ca
Editorial e-mail: tnf@nb.aibn.com
Primary Website: http://www.dioceseofsaintjohn.org/TNF.aspx
Year Established: 1900
Areas Served - City/County or Portion Thereof, or Zip codes: Canada
Mechanical specifications: Type page 12 x ; E - 5 cols, 2, 1/4 between; A - 5 cols, 2, 1/4 between.
Published: Fri
Avg Paid Circ: 7000
Audit By: Sworn/Estimate/Non-Audited
Audit Date: 12.07.2019
Personnel: Margie Trafton (Mng. Ed.)

SAINT JULIE

INFORMATION DE STE JULIE

Street Address: Rue Jules Choquet Local 2 , Local 2
Province: QC
Postal: J3E 1W6
Country: Canada
Mailing address: rue Jules Choquet Local 2
Mailing city: Saint Julie
Province: QC
Postal: J3E 1W6
General Phone: (450) 649-0719
Areas Served - City/County or Portion Thereof, or Zip codes: Canada
Published: Wed
Avg Paid Circ: 3
Avg Free Circ: 19435
Audit By: CCAB
Audit Date: 30.09.2012
Personnel: Serge Landry

SAINT LAURENT

COURRIER-AHUNTSIC

Street Address: 1500 Jules Poitras Blvd. ,
Province: QC
Postal: H4N 1X7
Country: Canada
Mailing address: 1500 Jules Poitras Blvd.
Mailing city: Saint Laurent
Province: QC
Postal: H4N 1X7
General Phone: (514) 855-1292
General Fax: (514) 855-9916
Primary Website: www.courrierahuntsic.com; www.transcontinentalmedia.com
Areas Served - City/County or Portion Thereof, or Zip codes: Canada
Published: Fri
Avg Paid Circ: 0
Avg Free Circ: 32391
Audit By: CCAB
Audit Date: 31.03.2014
Personnel: Alain De Choiniere (Gen. Mgr.); Marilaine Bolduc-Jacob (Information Dir.)
Parent company (for newspapers): Transcontinental Media

EXPRESS D'OUTREMONT

Street Address: Jules-poitras ,
Province: QC
Postal: H4N 1X7
Country: Canada
Mailing address: 24e Ã©tage
Mailing city: MontrÃ©al
Province: QC
Postal: H3B 4X9
General Phone: (514) 286-1066
General Fax: (514) 286-9310
Primary Website: www.expressoutremont.com
Areas Served - City/County or Portion Thereof, or Zip codes: Canada
Published: Thur

Avg Paid Circ: 2
Avg Free Circ: 19654
Audit By: CCAB
Audit Date: 31.03.2014
Personnel: Jean Aube

LE COURRIER BORDEAUX/ CARTIERVILLE

Street Address: 1500 Jules Poitras Blvd. ,
Province: QC
Postal: H4N 1X7
Country: Canada
Mailing address: 1500 Jules Poitras Blvd.
Mailing city: Saint Laurent
Province: QC
Postal: H4N 1X7
General Phone: (514) 855-1292
General Fax: (514) 855-9916
Primary Website: www.transcontinental.com; www.courrierbc.com
Areas Served - City/County or Portion Thereof, or Zip codes: Canada
Mechanical specifications: Type page 11 3/8 x 15; E - 8 cols, between; A - 8 cols, between.
Published: Fri
Avg Paid Circ: 4
Avg Free Circ: 17925
Audit By: CCAB
Audit Date: 31.03.2014
Personnel: Alain De Choinire (Ed.)
Parent company (for newspapers): Transcontinental Media

PROGRES VILLERAY/ PARC EXTENSION

Street Address: Jules-poitras ,
Province: QC
Postal: H4N 1X7
Country: Canada
Mailing address: Jules-Poitras
Mailing city: Saint Laurent
Province: QC
Postal: H4N 1X7
General Phone: (514) 270-8088
Areas Served - City/County or Portion Thereof, or Zip codes: Canada
Published: Tues
Avg Free Circ: 20276
Audit By: CCAB
Audit Date: 31.03.2014
Personnel: Jean Aube

SAINT-LAURENT NEWS

Street Address: 1500 Blvd. Jules Poitras ,
Province: QC
Postal: H4N 1X7
Country: Canada
Mailing address: 1500 blvd. Jules Poitras
Mailing city: Saint Laurent
Province: QC
Postal: H4N 1X7
General Phone: (514) 855-1292
General Fax: (514) 855-1855
General/National Adv. E-mail: hebdo.redaction@transcontinental.ca
Display Adv. E-mail: petitesannonces@journalmetro.com
Classified Adv. e-mail: petitesannonces@journalmetro.com
Primary Website: www.nouvellessaint-laurent.com
Mechanical specifications: Type page 10 x 14 1/4; E - 4 cols, between; C - 8 cols, between.
Published: Sun
Avg Free Circ: 29317
Audit By: Sworn/Estimate/Non-Audited
Audit Date: 12.07.2019
Personnel: Yannick Pinel (Ed.)
Parent company (for newspapers): Transcontinental Media

THE SUBURBAN EAST END EDITION

Street Address: 7575 Trans Canada Highway, Suite 105 ,
Province: QC
Postal: H4T 1V6
Country: Canada
Mailing address: 7575 Trans Canada Highway, Suite 105
Mailing city: Saint Laurent
Province: QC
Postal: H4T 1V6
General Phone: (514) 484-1107
General Fax: (514) 484-9616
General/National Adv. E-mail: suburban@thesuburban.com
Display Adv. E-mail: amanda@thesuburban.com
Editorial e-mail: editor@thesuburban.com
Primary Website: www.thesuburban.com
Published: Thur
Avg Free Circ: 26746
Audit By: CMCA
Audit Date: 31.12.2013
Personnel: Beryl Wajsman

SAINT LEONARD

PROGRES SAINT-LEONARD

Street Address: 8770 Langelier Blvd. Ste. 210 , Bureau 210
Province: QC
Postal: H1P 3C6
Country: Canada
Mailing address: 8770 Langelier Blvd. Ste. 210
Mailing city: Saint Leonard
Province: QC
Postal: H1P 3C6
General Phone: (514) 899-5888
General Fax: (514) 899-5001
General/National Adv. E-mail: redaction_est@tc.tc
Primary Website: www.progresstleonard.com
Published: Wed
Avg Free Circ: 31355
Audit By: Sworn/Estimate/Non-Audited
Audit Date: 12.07.2019
Personnel: Yannick Pinel; Lucy Lecoures (Ed.)
Parent company (for newspapers): Transcontinental Media

SAINT LIN LAURENTIDES

EXPRESS MONTCALM

Street Address: Rue Saint-isidore ,
Province: QC
Postal: J5M 2V4
Country: Canada
Mailing address: rue Saint-Isidore
Mailing city: Saint Lin Laurentides
Province: QC
Postal: J5M 2V4
General Phone: (450) 439-2525
Areas Served - City/County or Portion Thereof, or Zip codes: Canada
Published: Wed
Avg Free Circ: 20004
Audit By: CCAB
Audit Date: 31.03.2014
Personnel: Benoit Bazinet

SAINT PASCAL

LE PLACOTEUX

Street Address: 491 Ave. D'anjou ,
Province: QC
Postal: G0L 3Y0
Country: Canada
Mailing address: CP 490
Mailing city: Saint Pascal
Province: QC
Postal: G0L 3Y0
General Phone: (418) 492-2706
General Fax: (418) 492-9706
General/National Adv. E-mail: montage@leplacoteux.com
Primary Website: www.leplacoteux.com
Areas Served - City/County or Portion Thereof, or Zip codes: Canada
Published: Wed

Avg Paid Circ: 75
Avg Free Circ: 18315
Audit By: CCAB
Audit Date: 31.03.2014
Personnel: Maurice Gagnon (Ed.); Raymond Freve (Adv. Mgr.)
Parent company (for newspapers): Reseau Select/ Select Network

SAINT PAUL

ST. PAUL JOURNAL

Street Address: 4813 50th Ave. ,
Province: AB
Postal: T0A 3A0
Country: Canada
Mailing address: PO Box 159
Mailing city: Saint Paul
Province: AB
Postal: T0A 3A0
General Phone: (780) 645-3342
General Fax: (780) 645-2346
General/National Adv. E-mail: production@stpaul.greatwest.ca; journal@stpaul.greatwest.ca
Display Adv. E-mail: rberlinguette@stpaul.greatwest.ca
Editorial e-mail: jhuser@stpaul.greatwest.ca
Primary Website: www.spjournal.com
Year Established: 1924
Delivery Methods: Mail`Newsstand
Areas Served - City/County or Portion Thereof, or Zip codes: Canada
Own Printing Facility?: Y
Commercial printers?: Y
Published: Tues
Avg Paid Circ: 21
Avg Free Circ: 460
Audit By: VAC
Audit Date: 31.12.2015
Personnel: Janice Huser (Ed); Janani Whitfield (Pub)
Parent company (for newspapers): Glacier Media Group; Great West Newspapers LP

SAINT SAUVEUR-DES-MONTS

JOURNAL LE PAYS D'EN HAUT LA VALLEE

Street Address: Rue De La Gare Bureau 104 , Bureau 104
Province: QC
Postal: J0R 1R6
Country: Canada
Mailing address: rue de la Gare Bureau 104
Mailing city: Saint Sauveur-des-Monts
Province: QC
Postal: J0R 1R6
General Phone: (450) 227-4646
Published: Fri
Avg Paid Circ: 50
Avg Free Circ: 29756
Audit By: ODC
Audit Date: 14.12.2011
Personnel: Andre Guillemette

SAINT STEPHEN

ST. CROIX COURIER

Street Address: P.O. Box 250 , 47 Milltown Boulevard
Province: NB
Postal: E3L 2X2
Country: Canada
Mailing address: P.O. Box 250
Mailing city: Saint Stephen
Province: NB
Postal: E3L 2X2
General Phone: (506) 466-3220
General Fax: (506) 466-9950
General/National Adv. E-mail: courier@nb.aibn.com
Display Adv. E-mail: cairns@stcroixcourier.ca
Editorial e-mail: editor@stcroixcourier.ca
Primary Website: www.stcroixcourier.com

Year Established: 1865
Areas Served - City/County or Portion Thereof, or Zip codes: Canada
Mechanical specifications: Type page 13 1/4 x 21; E - 6 cols, 2 1/16, 3/16 between; A - 6 cols, 2 1/16, 3/16 between; C - 6 cols, 2 1/16, 3/16 between.
Published: Tues
Avg Paid Circ: 1075
Avg Free Circ: 40
Audit By: VAC
Audit Date: 31.01.2016
Personnel: Leith Orr (Pub.); Shelley McKeeman (Gen. Mgr.); Krisi Marples (Ed)

SAINT THOMAS

ST. THOMAS/ELGIN WEEKLY NEWS

Street Address: 15 St. Catharine Street ,
Province: ON
Postal: N5P 2V7
Country: Canada
Mailing address: 15 St. Catharine St.
Mailing city: Saint Thomas
Province: ON
Postal: N5P 2V7
General Phone: (519) 633-1640
General Fax: (519) 633-0558
Display Adv. E-mail: geoff@theweeklynews.ca
Editorial e-mail: editor@theweeklynews.ca
Primary Website: www.theweeklynews.ca
Delivery Methods: Carrier
Areas Served - City/County or Portion Thereof, or Zip codes: Canada
Published: Thur
Avg Free Circ: 30393
Audit By: CMCA
Audit Date: 31.10.2017
Personnel: Geoff Rae (Office/Sales Manager)
Parent company (for newspapers): Metroland Media Group Ltd.

SAINT TITE

HEBDO MEKINAC DESCHENAUX

Street Address: C.p. 4057 ,
Province: QC
Postal: G0X 3H0
Country: Canada
Mailing address: C.P. 4057
Mailing city: Saint Tite
Province: QC
Postal: G0X 3H0
General Phone: (819) 537-5111
Published: Sat
Avg Free Circ: 13540
Audit By: ODC
Audit Date: 14.12.2011
Personnel: Lena Sauvageau

SAINTE ADELE

LE JOURNAL DES PAYS D'EN HAUT LE VALLEE

Street Address: 94 De La Gare St-saviour ,
Province: QC
Postal: J8B 2P7
Country: Canada
Mailing address: 94 De La Gare St-saviour
Mailing city: Sainte Adele
Province: QC
Postal: J8B 2P7
General Phone: (450) 229-6664
General Fax: (450) 227-8144
General/National Adv. E-mail: jpdh@hebdosquebecor.com
Primary Website: http://www.lejournaldespaysdenhautlavallee.ca/
Areas Served - City/County or Portion Thereof, or Zip codes: Canada
Mechanical specifications: Type page 11 1/2 x 12 3/4.
Published: Wed
Avg Free Circ: 30057
Audit By: CCAB
Audit Date: 31.03.2014

Non-Daily Newspapers in Canada

Personnel: Mario Marois (Pub.)
Parent company (for newspapers): Quebecor Communications, Inc.

SAINTE JEAN SUR RICHELIEU

JOURNAL LE RICHELIEU

Street Address: Rue Richelieu ,
Province: QC
Postal: J3B 6X3
Country: Canada
Mailing address: rue Richelieu
Mailing city: Sainte Jean sur Richelieu
Province: QC
Postal: J3B 6X3
General Phone: (450) 347-0323
Areas Served - City/County or Portion Thereof, or Zip codes: Canada
Published: Tues
Avg Paid Circ: 4
Avg Free Circ: 42273
Audit By: CCAB
Audit Date: 31.03.2014
Personnel: Renel Bouchard

LE CANADA FRANCAIS

Street Address: 84 Rue Richelieu ,
Province: QC
Postal: J3B 6X3
Country: Canada
Mailing address: 84 Rue Richelieu
Mailing city: Sainte Jean sur Richelieu
Province: QC
Postal: J3B 6X3
General Phone: (450) 347-0323
General Fax: (450) 347-4539
Editorial e-mail: web@tc.tc
Primary Website: www.canadafrancais.com
Areas Served - City/County or Portion Thereof, or Zip codes: Canada
Commercial printers?: Y
Mechanical specifications: Type page 11 1/2 x 15; E - 8 cols, 1 1/16, 1/6 between; A - 8 cols, 1 1/6, 1/6 between; C - 8 cols, 1 1/6, 1/6 between.
Published: Thur
Avg Paid Circ: 7708
Avg Free Circ: 7848
Audit By: AAM
Audit Date: 31.12.2018
Personnel: Renel Bouchard (Pres.); Charles Coutre (Adv. Mgr.); Christian Marleau (Circ. Mgr.); Robert Paradis (Ed.)

L'ECHO DE ST-JEAN-SUR-RICHELIEU

Street Address: 81 Rue Richelieu Bureau 102 B,
Province: QC
Postal: J3B 6X2
Country: Canada
Mailing address: 81 Rue Richelieu Bureau 102 B
Mailing city: Sainte Jean sur Richelieu
Province: QC
Postal: J3B 6X2
General Phone: (450) 376-4646
General Fax: (450) 376-4666
Advertising Phone: (450) 376-4646
Advertising Fax: (450) 376-4666
Editorial Phone: (450) 376-4646
Editorial Fax: (450) 376-4666
General/National Adv. E-mail: daniel.noiseux@quebecormedia.com
Display Adv. E-mail: henri-paul.raymond@quebecormedia.com
Editorial e-mail: daniel.noiseux@quebecormedia.com
Primary Website: www.lechodesaintjean.ca
Delivery Methods: Mail Racks
Areas Served - City/County or Portion Thereof, or Zip codes: Canada
Published: Wed
Avg Free Circ: 55426
Audit By: CCAB
Audit Date: 31.03.2014
Personnel: Daniel Noiseux (Ed.)

SAINTE JULIE

L'INFORMATION

Street Address: 566 Jules Choquet St., Local 2 ,
Province: QC
Postal: J3E 1W6
Country: Canada
Mailing address: 566 Jules Choquet St., Local 2
Mailing city: Sainte Julie
Province: QC
Postal: J3E 1W6
General Phone: (450) 649-0719
General Fax: (450) 649-7748
Display Adv. E-mail: l.bourdua@ infodeste-julie.qc.ca; ni.beausejour@ infodeste-julie.qc.ca
Editorial e-mail: redaction@infodeste-julie.qc.ca
Primary Website: www.monsaintejulie.ca
Areas Served - City/County or Portion Thereof, or Zip codes: Canada
Mechanical specifications: Type page 10 x 15; E - 8 cols, between; A - 8 cols, between; C - 8 cols, between.
Published: Wed
Avg Paid Circ: 1
Avg Free Circ: 20563
Audit By: CCAB
Audit Date: 31.03.2014
Personnel: Serge Landry (Ed.); Ariane Desrochers (Ed.)

SAINTE MARIE-DE-BEAUCE

BEAUCE MEDIA

Street Address: 1147 Blvd. Vachon N. ,
Province: QC
Postal: G6E 3B6
Country: Canada
Mailing address: PO Box 400
Mailing city: Sainte Marie-de-Beauce
Province: QC
Postal: G6E 3B6
General Phone: (418) 387-8000
General Fax: (418) 387-4495
General/National Adv. E-mail: smb.redaction@quebecormedia.com
Primary Website: www.beaucemedia.ca
Areas Served - City/County or Portion Thereof, or Zip codes: Canada
Published: Wed
Avg Paid Circ: 3
Avg Free Circ: 25092
Audit By: CCAB
Audit Date: 31.03.2014
Personnel: Gilbert Bernier
Parent company (for newspapers): Quebecor Communications, Inc.

EDITION BEAUCE NORD

Street Address: 691, Boul. Vachon Nord ,
Province: QC
Postal: G6E 1M3
Country: Canada
Mailing address: rue Baronet
Mailing city: Sainte Marie-de-Beauce
Province: QC
Postal: G6E 2R1
General Phone: (418) 387-1205
Areas Served - City/County or Portion Thereof, or Zip codes: Canada
Published: Wed
Avg Paid Circ: 2
Avg Free Circ: 24833
Audit By: CCAB
Audit Date: 31.03.2014
Personnel: Claude Grondin

SAINTE THERESE

LE COURRIER

Street Address: 190 Cure-labelle Blvd., Rm. 204 ,
Province: QC
Postal: J7E 2X5
Country: Canada
Mailing address: 190 Cure-Labelle Blvd., Rm. 204
Mailing city: Sainte Therese
Province: QC
Postal: J7E 2X5
General Phone: (450) 434-4144
General Fax: (450) 434-3142
Advertising Phone: (866) 637-5236
Primary Website: www.journallecourrier.com
Year Established: 1973
Areas Served - City/County or Portion Thereof, or Zip codes: Canada
Own Printing Facility?: Y
Mechanical specifications: Type page 10 1/4 x 14 1/4; E - 8 cols, between; A - 8 cols, between.
Published: Wed
Avg Free Circ: 55014
Audit By: CCAB
Audit Date: 31.03.2014
Personnel: Louis Sauvageau (Pub./Ed.)

LE NORD-INFO

Street Address: 50 B Rue Turgeon ,
Province: QC
Postal: J7E 3H4
Country: Canada
Mailing address: 50 B Rue Turgeon
Mailing city: Sainte Therese
Province: QC
Postal: J7E 3H4
General Phone: (450) 435-6537
General Fax: (450) 435-0588
General/National Adv. E-mail: nordinfo@groupgcl.com
Areas Served - City/County or Portion Thereof, or Zip codes: Canada
Published: Sat
Avg Free Circ: 60079
Audit By: CCAB
Audit Date: 31.03.2014
Personnel: Serge Langlois (Gen. Mgr.); Norman Langlois (Circ. Mgr.); Jean Claude Langlois (Ed.)

L'ECHO DE ST EUSTACHE

Street Address: 204 Blvd Labelle Ste 208 ,
Province: QC
Postal: J7E 2X7
Country: Canada
Mailing address: 204 Blvd Labelle Ste 208
Mailing city: Sainte Therese
Province: QC
Postal: J7E 2X7
General Phone: (450) 818-7575
General Fax: (450) 818-7582
Advertising Phone: (450) 818-7575
Advertising Fax: (450) 818-7582
Editorial Phone: (450) 818-7575
Editorial Fax: (450) 818-7582
Areas Served - City/County or Portion Thereof, or Zip codes: Canada
Published: Wed
Avg Free Circ: 57641
Audit By: CCAB
Audit Date: 31.03.2014

VOIX DES MILLE ILES

Street Address: Rue Turgeon ,
Province: QC
Postal: J7E 3H4
Country: Canada
Mailing address: rue Turgeon
Mailing city: Sainte Therese
Province: QC
Postal: J7E 3H4
General Phone: (450) 435-6537

Primary Website: http://www.nordinfo.com/
Areas Served - City/County or Portion Thereof, or Zip codes: Canada
Published: Wed
Avg Free Circ: 65177
Audit By: CCAB
Audit Date: 31.03.2014
Personnel: Serge Langlois

SAINT-GEORGES

LE POINT

Street Address: 9085, Boul. Lacroix ,
Province: QC
Postal: G5Y 2B4
Country: Canada
Mailing address: 1, rue Mont Sainte-Claire
Mailing city: Chicoutlmi
Province: QC
Postal: G7H 5G3
General Phone: (418) 695-2601
General Fax: (418) 695-1391
General/National Adv. E-mail: ralph.pilote@quebecormedia.com
Primary Website: www.lepoint.ca
Areas Served - City/County or Portion Thereof, or Zip codes: Canada
Own Printing Facility?: Y
Mechanical specifications: Type page 11 1/2 x 12 1/2; E - 5 cols, 1 7/8, 1/8 between; A - 5 cols, 1 7/8, 1/8 between; C - 5 cols, 1 7/8, 1/8 between.
Published: Tues
Avg Free Circ: 47878
Audit By: CCAB
Audit Date: 31.03.2014
Personnel: Claude Poulin (Pres.)
Parent company (for newspapers): Quebecor Communications, Inc.

LE REVEIL

Street Address: 9085, Boul. Lacroix ,
Province: QC
Postal: G5Y 2B4
Country: Canada
Mailing address: PO Box 520
Mailing city: Jonquiere
Province: QC
Postal: G7X 7W4
General Phone: (418) 695-2601
General Fax: (418) 695-1391
General/National Adv. E-mail: lereveil@videotron.ca
Primary Website: lereveil.canoe.ca
Areas Served - City/County or Portion Thereof, or Zip codes: Canada
Own Printing Facility?: Y
Commercial printers?: Y
Mechanical specifications: Type page 10 1/4 x 11 3/4; E - 5 cols, 2, 1/8 between; A - 5 cols, 2, 1/8 between; C - 5 cols, 2, 1/8 between.
Published: Tues
Avg Paid Circ: 0
Avg Free Circ: 73191
Audit By: CCAB
Audit Date: 30.09.2012
Personnel: Diane Audet (Pub.); Andre Rousseau (Prodn. Mgr.)
Parent company (for newspapers): Quebecor Communications, Inc.

SALABERRY-DE-VALLEYFIELD

LE JOURNAL SAINT-FRANCOIS

Street Address: 61 Jacques-cartier St. ,
Province: QC
Postal: J6T 4R4
Country: Canada
Mailing address: 55 Jacques-Cartier St.
Mailing city: Salaberry-de-Valleyfield
Province: QC
Postal: J6T 4R4
General Phone: (450) 371-6222
General Fax: (450) 371-7254

General/National Adv. E-mail: info@st-francois.com
Primary Website: www.st-francois.com
Areas Served - City/County or Portion Thereof, or Zip codes: Canada
Commercial printers?: Y
Mechanical specifications: Type page 11 1/2 x 15; E - 4 cols, 2 1/2, 1/6 between; C - 8 cols, 1 1/4, 1/6 between.
Published: Wed
Avg Paid Circ: 36
Avg Free Circ: 34817
Audit By: CCAB
Audit Date: 31.03.2014
Personnel: Diane Dumont (Pub./Dir.); Stephane Brais (Sales Dir.); Denis Bourbonnais (Ed. in Chief)
Parent company (for newspapers): Les Hebdos Monteregiens-OOB

LE SOLEIL DU ST-LAURENT

Street Address: 20 Academy St. ,
Province: QC
Postal: J6T 6M9
Country: Canada
Mailing address: 20 Academy St.
Mailing city: Salaberry-de-Valleyfield
Province: QC
Postal: J6T 6M9
General Phone: (450) 373-8555
General Fax: (450) 373-8666
General/National Adv. E-mail: info@lesoleil.qc.ca
Display Adv. E-mail: publicite@lesoleil.qc.ca
Editorial e-mail: redaction@lesoleil.qc.ca
Primary Website: www.lesoleil.qc.ca
Commercial printers?: Y
Mechanical specifications: Type page 10 1/4 x 17.
Published: Sat
Avg Free Circ: 32750
Audit By: Sworn/Estimate/Non-Audited
Audit Date: 12.07.2019
Personnel: Andre Mooney (Dir.); Pierre Montreuil (Sales Dir.); Diane Mayer (Adv. Rep.); Serge Proulx (Adv. Rep.); Jean-Pierre Tessier (Adv. Rep.); Peter Rozon (Adv. Rep.); Mario Pitre (Ed.)
Parent company (for newspapers): Les Hebdos Monteregiens-OOB

SOLEIL DE VALLEYFIELD

Street Address: 20 Rue De L'academie ,
Province: QC
Postal: J6T 2H8
Country: Canada
Mailing address: 20 Rue de l'Academie
Mailing city: Salaberry-de-Valleyfield
Province: QC
Postal: J6T 2H8
General Phone: (450) 373-8555
Advertising Phone: (450) 373-8555
Editorial Phone: (450) 373-8555
General/National Adv. E-mail: diane.dumont@quebecormedia.com
Editorial e-mail: diane.dumont@quebecormedia.com
Primary Website: http://www.journalsaint-francois.ca
Delivery Methods: Mail`Racks
Areas Served - City/County or Portion Thereof, or Zip codes: Canada
Published: Sat
Avg Paid Circ: 23
Avg Free Circ: 35953
Audit By: CCAB
Audit Date: 31.03.2014
Personnel: Andre Mooney (Pub.)

VALLEYFIELD EXPRESS

Street Address: 720 Blvd Monseigneur-langlois Ste 100 ,
Province: QC
Postal: J6S 5H7
Country: Canada
Mailing address: 720 Blvd Monseigneur-Langlois Ste 100
Mailing city: Salaberry-de-Valleyfield
Province: QC
Postal: J6S 5H7
General Phone: (450) 371-7117
General Fax: (450) 371-7611
Advertising Phone: (450) 371-7117
Advertising Fax: (450) 371-7611
Editorial Phone: (450) 371-7117
Editorial Fax: (450) 371-7611
General/National Adv. E-mail: redactionvalleyfieldexpress@tc.tc
Display Adv. E-mail: redactionvalleyfieldexpress@tc.tc
Editorial e-mail: redactionvalleyfieldexpress@tc.tc
Primary Website: www.valleyfieldexpress.ca
Delivery Methods: Mail`Racks
Areas Served - City/County or Portion Thereof, or Zip codes: Canada
Published: Thur
Avg Free Circ: 43310
Audit By: CCAB
Audit Date: 31.03.2014
Personnel: RÃƒÂ©seau MontÃƒÂ©rÃƒÂ©gie (Pub.)

SALMON ARM

EAGLE VALLEY NEWS

Street Address: 171 Shuswap St. Nw ,
Province: BC
Postal: V1E 4N7
Country: Canada
Mailing address: PO Box 550
Mailing city: Salmon Arm
Province: BC
Postal: V1E 4N7
General Phone: (250) 832-2131
General Fax: (250) 832-5140
General/National Adv. E-mail: publisher@saobverver.net
Display Adv. E-mail: advertising@saobserver.net
Classified Adv. e-mail: classifieds@eaglevalleynews.com
Editorial e-mail: newsroom@saobserver.net
Primary Website: www.eaglevalleynews.com
Delivery Methods: Mail`Newsstand
Areas Served - City/County or Portion Thereof, or Zip codes: Canada
Mechanical specifications: Type page 10 1/4 x 14 1/2; E - 6 cols, 1 7/12, 1/6 between; A - 6 cols, 1 7/12, 1/6 between; C - 7 cols, 1 5/8, 1/6 between.
Published: Wed
Avg Paid Circ: 376
Avg Free Circ: 12
Audit By: CMCA
Audit Date: 31.05.2017
Personnel: Rick Proznick (Adv. Mgr); Tracy Hughes (Ed.); Laura Lavigne (Sales); Lachlan Labere (Reporter/Columnist)
Parent company (for newspapers): Black Press Group Ltd.

SALMON ARM OBSERVER

Street Address: 171 Shuswap St., Nw ,
Province: BC
Postal: V1E 4N7
Country: Canada
Mailing address: P.O. Box 550
Mailing city: Salmon Arm
Province: BC
Postal: V1E 4N7
General Phone: (250) 832-2131
General Fax: (250) 832-5140
General/National Adv. E-mail: advertising@saobserver.net
Display Adv. E-mail: advertising@saobserver.net
Classified Adv. e-mail: classifieds@saobserver.net
Editorial e-mail: newsroom@saobserver.net
Primary Website: www.saobserver.net
Year Established: 1907
Delivery Methods: Mail`Newsstand
Areas Served - City/County or Portion Thereof, or Zip codes: Canada
Own Printing Facility?: N
Commercial printers?: N
Mechanical specifications: Type page 10 5/16 x 14; E - 7 cols, 1 5/16, 3/16 between; A - 7 cols, 1 5/16, 3/16 between.
Published: Wed
Avg Paid Circ: 1951
Avg Free Circ: 50
Audit By: CMCA
Audit Date: 30.04.2017
Personnel: Rick Proznick (Pub.); Tracy Hughes (Senior Ed.)
Parent company (for newspapers): Black Press Group Ltd.

SHUSWAP MARKET NEWS

Street Address: 171 Shuswap St. Nw ,
Province: BC
Postal: V1E 4N7
Country: Canada
Mailing address: P.O. Box 550
Mailing city: Salmon Arm
Province: BC
Postal: V1E 4N7
General Phone: (250) 832-2131
General Fax: (250) 832-5140
Display Adv. E-mail: advertising@saoberver.net
Classified Adv. e-mail: classifieds@saobserver.net
Editorial e-mail: newsroom@saobserver.net
Primary Website: www.saobserver.net
Year Established: 1907
Delivery Methods: Carrier`Racks
Areas Served - City/County or Portion Thereof, or Zip codes: Canada
Own Printing Facility?: N
Commercial printers?: N
Mechanical specifications: Type page 10 5/16 x 14; E - 7 cols, 1 9/16, 3/16 between; A - 7 cols, 1 9/16, 3/16 between; C - 7 cols, 1 9/16, 3/16 between.
Published: Fri
Avg Paid Circ: 0
Avg Free Circ: 12732
Audit By: CMCA
Audit Date: 30.06.2017
Personnel: Rick Proznick (Pub.); Tracy Hughes (Ed.)
Parent company (for newspapers): Black Press Group Ltd.

SALT SPRING ISLAND

GULF ISLANDS DRIFTWOOD

Street Address: 328 Lower Ganges Rd. ,
Province: BC
Postal: V8K 2V3
Country: Canada
Mailing address: 328 Lower Ganges Rd.
Mailing city: Salt Spring Island
Province: BC
Postal: V8K 2V3
General Phone: (250) 537-9933
General Fax: (250) 537-2613
General/National Adv. E-mail: inquiries@driftwoodgulfislandsmedia.com
Display Adv. E-mail: sales@driftwoodgimedia.com
Editorial e-mail: news@driftwoodgimedia.com
Primary Website: www.driftwoodgulfislandsmedia.com
Year Established: 1960
Delivery Methods: Mail`Newsstand
Areas Served - City/County or Portion Thereof, or Zip codes: Canada
Commercial printers?: Y
Published: Wed
Avg Paid Circ: 2300
Avg Free Circ: 2200
Audit By: Sworn/Estimate/Non-Audited
Audit Date: 12.07.2019
Personnel: Gail Sjuberg (Mng. Ed.); Lorraine Sullivan (Prodn. Mgr.); Amber Ogilvie (Publisher)
Parent company (for newspapers): Driftwood Publishing Ltd.

SARNIA

SARNIA & LAMBTON COUNTY THIS WEEK

Street Address: 140 Front St S ,
Province: ON
Postal: N7t2M6
Country: Canada
Mailing address: 140 Front St S
Mailing city: Sarnia
Province: ON
Postal: N7S 5P1
General Phone: (519) 336-1100
General Fax: (519) 336-1833
Advertising Phone: (519) 336-1100
Advertising Fax: (519) 336-1833
Editorial Phone: (519) 336-1100
Editorial Fax: (519) 336-1833
General/National Adv. E-mail: chris.courtis@sunmedia.ca
Display Adv. E-mail: stw.sales@sunmedia.ca
Editorial e-mail: stw.sales@sunmedia.ca
Primary Website: Www.sarniathisweek.ca
Year Established: 1993
Delivery Methods: Carrier`Racks
Areas Served - City/County or Portion Thereof, or Zip codes: N7S 5P1
Own Printing Facility?: Y
Mechanical specifications: Type page 10 1/2 x 13 1/4; A - 9 cols, 1 1/6, 1/6 between; C - 9 cols, 1 1/6, 1/6 between.
Published: Wed
Avg Free Circ: 41300
Audit By: Sworn/Estimate/Non-Audited
Audit Date: 12.07.2019
Personnel: Chris Courtis (Marketing Manager)
Parent company (for newspapers): Postmedia Network Inc.

SARNIA THIS WEEK

Street Address: 140 Front St. S ,
Province: ON
Postal: N7T 7M8
Country: Canada
Mailing address: 140 Front St. S
Mailing city: Sarnia
Province: ON
Postal: N7T 7M8
General Phone: (519) 336-1100
General Fax: (519) 336-1833
General/National Adv. E-mail: news@sarniamedia.com
Editorial e-mail: production@sarniamedia.com
Primary Website: www.sarniathisweek.com
Areas Served - City/County or Portion Thereof, or Zip codes: Canada
Published: Thur
Avg Free Circ: 39476
Audit By: CMCA
Audit Date: 30.06.2016
Personnel: Linda LeBlanc (Pub.); Penny Churchill (Distribution Mgr.)
Parent company (for newspapers): Quebecor Communications, Inc.

THE PETROLIA TOPIC

Street Address: 140 Front St. S ,
Province: ON
Postal: N7T 7M8
Country: Canada
Mailing address: 140 Front St. S
Mailing city: Sarnia
Province: ON
Postal: N7T 7M8
General Phone: (519) 336-1100 x2230
General Fax: (519) 336-1833
Advertising Phone: (519) 882-4798
Advertising Fax: (519) 882-4635
Editorial Phone: (519) 336-1100 x2230
Editorial Fax: (519) 336-1833
Editorial e-mail: reporter@petroliatopic.com
Primary Website: www.petroliatopic.com
Year Established: 1866
Delivery Methods: Mail`Newsstand
Areas Served - City/County or Portion Thereof, or Zip codes: Canada
Own Printing Facility?: N
Commercial printers?: N
Published: Wed
Avg Paid Circ: 1309

Non-Daily Newspapers in Canada

III-493

Audit By: CMCA
Audit Date: 31.12.2012
Personnel: Linda LeBlanc (Pub.)
Parent company (for newspapers): Postmedia Network Inc.; Quebecor Communications, Inc.

SAULT SAINTE MARIE

SAULT STE. MARIE THIS WEEK

Street Address: 2 Towers St. ,
Province: ON
Postal: P6A 2T9
Country: Canada
Mailing address: PO Box 188
Mailing city: Sault Sainte Marie
Province: ON
Postal: P6A 2T9
General Phone: (705) 949-6111
General Fax: (705) 942-8596
Editorial Phone: (705) 759-5825
General/National Adv. E-mail: lou.maulucci@sunmedia.ca
Display Adv. E-mail: sste.advertising@sunmedia.ca
Editorial e-mail: sandra.paul@sunmedia.ca
Primary Website: www.saultthisweek.com
Year Established: 1967
Delivery Methods: Newsstand Carrier Racks
Areas Served - City/County or Portion Thereof, or Zip codes: Canada
Own Printing Facility?: Y
Commercial printers?: N
Mechanical specifications: Type page 10 1/4 x 11 1/2; E - various, between; A - 9 cols, between; C - 9 cols, between.
Published: Thur
Avg Free Circ: 31122
Audit By: CMCA
Audit Date: 30.06.2015
Personnel: Lou Maulucci (Pub.); Sandra Paul (Ed.)
Parent company (for newspapers): Postmedia Network Inc.; Quebecor Communications, Inc.

SEAFORTH

SEAFORTH HURON EXPOSITOR

Street Address: 8 Main St. S. ,
Province: ON
Postal: N0K 1W0
Country: Canada
Mailing address: PO Box 69
Mailing city: Seaforth
Province: ON
Postal: N0K 1W0
General Phone: (519) 527-0240
General Fax: (519) 527-2858
General/National Adv. E-mail: seaforth@bowesnet.com
Display Adv. E-mail: max.bickford@sunmedia.ca
Classified Adv. e-mail: seaforth.classifieds@sunmedia.ca
Editorial e-mail: seaforth.news@sunmedia.ca
Primary Website: www.seaforthhuronexpositor.com
Year Established: 1860
Delivery Methods: Mail Newsstand
Areas Served - City/County or Portion Thereof, or Zip codes: Canada
Own Printing Facility?: Y
Mechanical specifications: Type page 11 1/4 x 11 3/8; E - 9 cols, 1 3/4, 1/8 between;
Published: Wed
Avg Paid Circ: 1160
Avg Free Circ: 22
Audit By: CMCA
Audit Date: 30.06.2016
Personnel: Neil Clifford (Pub.); Whitney South (Multi Media Journalist)
Parent company (for newspapers): Postmedia Network Inc.; Quebecor Communications, Inc.

SECHELT

COAST REPORTER

Street Address: 5485 Wharf Road ,
Province: BC
Postal: V0N 3A0
Country: Canada
Mailing address: PO Box 1388
Mailing city: Sechelt
Province: BC
Postal: V0N 3A0
General Phone: (604) 885-4811
General Fax: (604) 885-4818
General/National Adv. E-mail: pkvarnstrom@coastreporter.net
Display Adv. E-mail: pat@coastreporter.net
Classified Adv. e-mail: classified@coastreporter.net
Editorial e-mail: editor@coastreporter.net
Primary Website: www.coastreporter.net
Areas Served - City/County or Portion Thereof, or Zip codes: Sechelt, Gibsons
Published: Fri
Avg Paid Circ: 31
Avg Free Circ: 11639
Audit By: VAC
Audit Date: 30.06.2016
Personnel: Peter Kvarnstrom (Pub.); Christine Wood (Circ. Mgr.); John Gleeson (Ed./Assoc. Pub.); Pat Paproski (Sales Mgr.); Shelley Alleyne (Class. Supv.)
Parent company (for newspapers): Glacier Media Group

SELKIRK

SELKIRK JOURNAL

Street Address: 366 Main St , Unit 300
Province: MB
Postal: R1A 2J7
Country: Canada
Mailing address: 366 Main St Unit 300
Mailing city: Selkirk
Province: MB
Postal: R1A 2J7
General Phone: (204) 482-7402
General Fax: (204) 482-3336
General/National Adv. E-mail: sjournal@mts.net
Display Adv. E-mail: jbilsky@postmedia.com
Editorial e-mail: bjones@postmedia.com
Primary Website: http://www.interlaketoday.ca/selkirkjournal
Areas Served - City/County or Portion Thereof, or Zip codes: Selkirk
Own Printing Facility?: Y
Commercial printers?: Y
Mechanical specifications: Type page 10 1/8 x 14; E - 6 cols, 1 7/12, 1/6 between; A - 6 cols, 1 7/12, 1/6 between; C - 6 cols, 1 7/12, 1/6 between.
Published: Thur
Avg Free Circ: 14334
Audit By: VAC
Audit Date: 30.06.2016
Personnel: Jenifer Bilsky (Adv Dir); Brook Jones (Ed)
Parent company (for newspapers): Postmedia Network Inc.; Quebecor Communications, Inc.

SEPT-ILES

LE PORT CARTOIS

Street Address: 365 Laure Blvd. ,
Province: QC
Postal: G4R 1X2
Country: Canada
Mailing address: 365 Laure Blvd.
Mailing city: Sept-Iles
Province: QC
Postal: G4R 1X2
General Phone: (418) 962-4100
General Fax: (418) 962-0439
General/National Adv. E-mail: administration.sett-iles@hebdosquebecor.com
Primary Website: www.hebdosquebecor.com
Areas Served - City/County or Portion Thereof, or Zip codes: Canada
Published: Wed
Avg Paid Circ: 6
Avg Free Circ: 19072
Audit By: CCAB
Audit Date: 31.03.2014
Personnel: Isabelle Chiasson (Adv. Mgr.); Catherine Martin (Ed.)
Parent company (for newspapers): Quebecor Communications, Inc.

NORD COTIER

Street Address: Boulevard Laure ,
Province: QC
Postal: G4R 1Y2
Country: Canada
Mailing address: boulevard Laure
Mailing city: Sept-Iles
Province: QC
Postal: G4R 1Y2
General Phone: (418) 960-2090
Areas Served - City/County or Portion Thereof, or Zip codes: Canada
Published: Wed
Avg Paid Circ: 23
Avg Free Circ: 19095
Audit By: CCAB
Audit Date: 30.09.2012
Personnel: Gino Levesque

NORDEST PLUS

Street Address: 365 Boul. Laure ,
Province: QC
Postal: G4R 1X2
Country: Canada
Mailing address: 365 Boul. Laure
Mailing city: Sept-Iles
Province: QC
Postal: G4R 1X2
General Phone: (418) 962-4100
General Fax: (418) 962-0439
General/National Adv. E-mail: nordest@hebdosquebecor.com
Display Adv. E-mail: atelier.septiles@hebdosquebecor.com
Editorial e-mail: redaction.septiles@hebdosquebecor.com
Primary Website: www.hebdosquebecor.com
Own Printing Facility?: Y
Commercial printers?: Y
Published: Wed
Avg Free Circ: 13999
Audit By: Sworn/Estimate/Non-Audited
Audit Date: 12.07.2019
Personnel: Isabelle Chiasson (Dir.); Mario Thibeault (Mng. Ed.)

SHARBOT LAKE

THE FRONTENAC NEWS

Street Address: 1095 Garrett St. , Rear
Province: ON
Postal: K0H 2P0
Country: Canada
Mailing address: P.O. Box 229
Mailing city: Sharbot Lake
Province: ON
Postal: K0H 2P0
General Phone: (613) 279-3150
General Fax: (613) 279-3172
General/National Adv. E-mail: nfnews@frontenac.net
Display Adv. E-mail: info@frontenacnews.ca
Classified Adv. e-mail: info@frontenacnews.ca
Editorial e-mail: info@frontenacnews.ca
Primary Website: Frontenacnews.ca
Year Established: 1973
Delivery Methods: Mail
Areas Served - City/County or Portion Thereof, or Zip codes: Central Frontenac
Published: Thur
Avg Free Circ: 9135
Audit By: Sworn/Estimate/Non-Audited
Audit Date: 12.07.2019
Personnel: Jeff Green (Publisher/Editor); Scott Cox (Designer/bookeeper)

SHAUNAVON

THE SHAUNAVON STANDARD

Street Address: 346 Centre St. ,
Province: SK
Postal: S0N 2M0
Country: Canada
Mailing address: PO Box 729
Mailing city: Shaunavon
Province: SK
Postal: S0N 2M0
General Phone: (306) 297-4144
General Fax: (306) 297-3357
Display Adv. E-mail: jgregoire@theshaunavonstandard.com
Editorial e-mail: standard@theshaunavonstandard.com
Year Established: 1913
Areas Served - City/County or Portion Thereof, or Zip codes: Canada
Mechanical specifications: Type page 11 1/2 x 17; E - 5 cols, 2, 1/4 between; A - 5 cols, 2, 1/4 between; C - 5 cols, 2, 1/4 between.
Published: Tues
Avg Paid Circ: 916
Audit By: CMCA
Audit Date: 30.06.2016
Personnel: Paul MacNeil (Ed.); Joanne Gregoire (Adv. Sales)

SHAWINIGAN

HEBDO DU ST. MAURICE

Street Address: 2102 Champlain Ave. ,
Province: QC
Postal: G9N 6T8
Country: Canada
Mailing address: PO Box 10
Mailing city: Shawinigan
Province: QC
Postal: G9N 6T8
General Phone: (819) 537-5111
General Fax: (819) 537-5471
Advertising Phone: (866) 637-5236
General/National Adv. E-mail: redaction_shawinigan@transcontinental.ca
Primary Website: www.lhebdodustmaurice.com
Areas Served - City/County or Portion Thereof, or Zip codes: Canada
Mechanical specifications: Type page 11 1/4 x 13 1/2; E - 10 cols, 1, 1/6 between; A - 10 cols, 1, 1/6 between; C - 10 cols, 1, 1/6 between.
Published: Wed
Avg Paid Circ: 24
Avg Free Circ: 36640
Audit By: CCAB
Audit Date: 31.03.2014
Personnel: Michel Matteau (Pub.); Lena Sauvageau; Gilles Guay (Adv. Mgr.); Bernard Lepage (Ed./Dir., Information)
Parent company (for newspapers): Transcontinental Media

L'ECHO DE SHAWINIGAN

Street Address: 795 Blvd 5e Rue Local 101 ,
Province: QC
Postal: G9N 1G2
Country: Canada
Mailing address: 795 Blvd 5E Rue Local 101
Mailing city: Shawinigan
Province: QC
Postal: G9N 1G2
General Phone: (819) 731-0327
General Fax: (819) 731-0328
Advertising Phone: (819) 731-0327
Advertising Fax: (819) 731-0328
Editorial Phone: (819) 731-0327
Editorial Fax: (819) 731-0328
General/National Adv. E-mail: jocelyn.ouellet@quebecormedia.com
Display Adv. E-mail: serge.buchanan@quebecormedia.com
Editorial e-mail: hugues.carpentier@quebecormedia.com
Primary Website: www.lechodeshawinigan.ca
Delivery Methods: Mail Racks
Areas Served - City/County or Portion Thereof, or Zip codes: Canada

Published: Wed
Avg Free Circ: 37369
Audit By: CCAB
Audit Date: 31.03.2014
Personnel: Hugues Carpentier (Ed.)

L'HEBDO MEKINAC/DES CHENAUX

Street Address: Cp 490 ,
Province: QC
Postal: G9N 6T8
Country: Canada
Mailing address: PO Box 4057
Mailing city: Shawinigan
Province: QC
Postal: G9N 6T8
General Phone: (819) 537-5111
General Fax: (819) 537-5471
General/National Adv. E-mail: redaction_shawinigan@transcontinental.ca
Primary Website: www.lhebdomekinacdeschenaux.com
Mechanical specifications: Type page 11 1/4 x 13 1/2; E - 10 cols, 1, 1/8 between; A - 10 cols, 1, 1/8 between; C - 10 cols, 1, 1/8 between.
Published: Wed
Avg Paid Circ: 13540
Avg Free Circ: 0
Audit By: Sworn/Estimate/Non-Audited
Audit Date: 12.07.2019
Personnel: Michel Matteau (Pub.); Bernard Lepage (Dir., Information); Gilles Guay (Ed.)
Parent company (for newspapers): Transcontinental Media

SHAWVILLE

THE EQUITY

Street Address: 133 Center St. ,
Province: QC
Postal: J0X 2Y0
Country: Canada
Mailing address: 133 Center St.
Mailing city: Shawville
Province: QC
Postal: J0X 2Y0
General Phone: (819) 647-2204
General Fax: (819) 647-2206
General/National Adv. E-mail: prepress@theequity.ca
Display Adv. E-mail: kathy@theequity.ca
Classified Adv. e-mail: news@theequity.ca
Editorial e-mail: news@theequity.ca
Primary Website: www.theequity.ca
Year Established: 1883
Delivery Methods: Mail`Newsstand
Areas Served - City/County or Portion Thereof, or Zip codes: Canada
Mechanical specifications: Type page 13 1/2 x 21; E - 5 cols, 2 3/8, 1/8 between; A - 8 cols, 1 1/2, 1/8 between; C - 8 cols, 1 1/2, 1/8 between.
Published: Wed
Avg Paid Circ: 2835
Audit By: CMCA
Audit Date: 31.12.2015
Personnel: Charles Dickson (Pub)
Parent company (for newspapers): Pontiac Printshop Ltd.

SHEDIAC

LE MONITEUR ACADIEN

Street Address: Cp 5191 817, West Boudreau ,
Province: NB
Postal: E4P 8T9
Country: Canada
Mailing address: CP 5191 817, Western Boudreau
Mailing city: Shediac
Province: NB
Postal: E4P 8T9
General Phone: (506) 532-6680
General Fax: (506) 532-6681
General/National Adv. E-mail: moniteur@rogers.com
Primary Website: www.moniteuracadien.com
Delivery Methods: Mail`Newsstand`Carrier

Areas Served - City/County or Portion Thereof, or Zip codes: Westmorland county, Shediac, Dieppe, Cap-Pele, Memramcook
Mechanical specifications: Type page 10 2/5 x 13 1/4; E - 5 cols, between; A - 5 cols, between; C - 5 cols, between.
Published: Wed
Avg Paid Circ: 3500
Avg Free Circ: 500
Audit By: Sworn/Estimate/Non-Audited
Audit Date: 12.07.2019
Personnel: Gilles Hache (Ed.)

SHELBURNE

THE COAST GUARD

Street Address: 164 Water St. ,
Province: NS
Postal: B0T 1W0
Country: Canada
Mailing address: 164 Water St.
Mailing city: Shelburne
Province: NS
Postal: B0T 1W0
General Phone: (902) 875-3244
General Fax: (902) 875-3454
General/National Adv. E-mail: info@thecoastguard.ca
Display Adv. E-mail: info@thecoastguard.ca
Editorial e-mail: ffaynder@transcontinental.ca
Primary Website: www.thecoastguard.ca
Areas Served - City/County or Portion Thereof, or Zip codes: Canada
Mechanical specifications: Type page 13 x 21; E - 6 cols, 2, between; A - 6 cols, 2, between; C - 6 cols, 2, between.
Published: Tues
Avg Paid Circ: 2290
Avg Free Circ: 0
Audit By: CMCA
Audit Date: 28.02.2014
Personnel: Fred Fayander (Pub.)
Parent company (for newspapers): Transcontinental Media

SHELLBROOK

SHELLBROOK CHRONICLE

Street Address: 46 Main St. ,
Province: SK
Postal: S0J 2E0
Country: Canada
Mailing address: PO Box 10
Mailing city: Shellbrook
Province: SK
Postal: S0J 2E0
General Phone: (306) 747-2442
General Fax: (306) 747-3000
General/National Adv. E-mail: chnews@shelbrookchronicle.com
Display Adv. E-mail: chads@sbchron.com
Primary Website: http://shellbrookchronicle.com/
Year Established: 1912
Areas Served - City/County or Portion Thereof, or Zip codes: Canada
Commercial printers?: Y
Mechanical specifications: Type page 10 1/4 x 15; E - 6 cols, 1 7/12, 1/6 between; A - 6 cols, 1 7/12, 1/6 between; C - 6 cols, 1 7/12, 1/6 between.
Published: Fri
Avg Paid Circ: 155
Avg Free Circ: 3484
Audit By: CMCA
Audit Date: 30.12.2015
Personnel: C.J. Pepper (Pub.)

SPIRITWOOD HERALD

Street Address: 46 Main St. ,
Province: SK
Postal: S0J 2E0
Country: Canada
Mailing address: PO Box 10
Mailing city: Shellbrook
Province: SK

Postal: S0J 2E0
General Phone: (306) 747-2442
General Fax: (306) 747-3000
General/National Adv. E-mail: chnews@shopperchronicle.com
Display Adv. E-mail: chads@sbchron.com
Primary Website: www.spiritwoodherald.com
Delivery Methods: Mail`Newsstand`Racks
Areas Served - City/County or Portion Thereof, or Zip codes: S0J 0L0, S0M 0Y0, S0M 0Z0, S0J 1N0, S0M 1S0, S0M 1W0, S0J 1V0, S0J 2G0, S0J 2M0
Mechanical specifications: Type page 10 1/4 x 15; E - 6 cols, 1 7/12, 1/6 between; A - 6 cols, 1 7/12, 1/6 between; C - 6 cols, 1 7/12, 1/6 between.
Published: Fri
Avg Paid Circ: 52
Avg Free Circ: 2435
Audit By: Sworn/Estimate/Non-Audited
Audit Date: 12.07.2019
Personnel: Clark J Pepper (Publisher)

SHERBROOKE

JOURNAL DE MAGOG

Street Address: Galt Ouest ,
Province: QC
Postal: J1K 2V8
Country: Canada
Mailing address: Galt Ouest
Mailing city: Sherbrooke
Province: QC
Postal: J1K 2V8
General Phone: (819) 575-7575
Areas Served - City/County or Portion Thereof, or Zip codes: Canada
Published: Wed
Avg Free Circ: 28000
Audit By: CCAB
Audit Date: 31.03.2014
Personnel: Sarah Beaulieu

JOURNAL DE SHERBROOKE

Street Address: Rue Galt Ouest ,
Province: QC
Postal: J1K 2V8
Country: Canada
Mailing address: rue Galt Ouest
Mailing city: Sherbrooke
Province: QC
Postal: J1K 2V8
General Phone: (819) 575-7575
Areas Served - City/County or Portion Thereof, or Zip codes: Canada
Published: Wed
Avg Free Circ: 63500
Audit By: CCAB
Audit Date: 31.03.2014
Personnel: Sarah Beaulieu

NOUVELLE DE SHERBROOKE

Street Address: Rue Roy ,
Province: QC
Postal: J1K 2X8
Country: Canada
Mailing address: rue Roy
Mailing city: Sherbrooke
Province: QC
Postal: J1K 2X8
General Phone: (819) 566-8022
Published: Sun
Avg Free Circ: 51200
Audit By: ODC
Audit Date: 14.12.2011
Personnel: Andre Custeau

SHERWOOD PARK

SHERWOOD PARK/STRATHCONA COUNTY NEWS

Street Address: 168 Kaska Rd. , 168 Kaska Road

Province: AB
Postal: T8A 4G7
Country: Canada
Mailing address: 168 Kaska Rd.
Mailing city: Sherwood Park
Province: AB
Postal: T8A 4G7
General Phone: (780) 464-0033
General Fax: (780) 464-8512
Advertising Phone: (780) 464-0033 Ext 239
Editorial Phone: 780 464-0033
General/National Adv. E-mail: shelagh.pastoor@sunmedia.ca
Display Adv. E-mail: jfigeat@postmedia.com
Editorial e-mail: bproulx@postmedia.com
Primary Website: www.sherwoodparknews.com
Year Established: 1976
Delivery Methods: Carrier`Racks
Areas Served - City/County or Portion Thereof, or Zip codes: Strathcona
Own Printing Facility?: N
Commercial printers?: N
Mechanical specifications: Type page 10.3125" x 11.5"; E & C - 10 cols, 1";
Published: Fri
Avg Paid Circ: 1702
Avg Free Circ: 30851
Audit By: VAC
Audit Date: 31.12.2015
Personnel: Jean Figeat (Adv. Dir.); Dawn Zapatoski (Circ.); Ben Proulx (Ed)
Parent company (for newspapers): Postmedia Network Inc.; Division of Post Media

SHOAL LAKE

CROSSROADS THIS WEEK

Street Address: 353 Station Road ,
Province: MB
Postal: R0J 1Z0
Country: Canada
Mailing address: P.O. Box 160
Mailing city: Shoal Lake
Province: MB
Postal: R0J 1Z0
General Phone: (204) 759-2644
General Fax: (204) 759-2521
Advertising Phone: (204) 759-2644
Advertising Fax: (204) 759-2521
Editorial Phone: (204) 759-2644
Editorial Fax: (204) 759-2521
General/National Adv. E-mail: gnesbitt@mts.net
Display Adv. E-mail: ctwdisplay@mymts.net
Classified Adv. e-mail: ctwclassified@mymts.net
Editorial e-mail: ctwnews@mymts.net
Primary Website: www.crossroadsthisweek.com
Year Established: 1977
Delivery Methods: Mail`Newsstand
Areas Served - City/County or Portion Thereof, or Zip codes: Canada
Commercial printers?: Y
Mechanical specifications: Type page 10 5/16 x 14 1/4; E - 6 cols, 1 9/16, 1/6 between; A - 6 cols, 1 9/16, 1/6 between; C - 6 cols, 1 9/16, 1/6 between.
Published: Fri
Avg Paid Circ: 2294
Avg Free Circ: 25
Audit By: Sworn/Estimate/Non-Audited
Audit Date: 12.07.2019
Personnel: Connie Kay (Advertising Manager); Michelle Genslorek (Classified/Accounting); Darrell Nesbitt (News Reporter); Ryan Nesbitt (Publisher); Marcie Harrison (News Reporter)
Parent company (for newspapers): Nesbitt Publishing Ltd.

SOUTH MOUNTAIN PRESS

Street Address: 353 Station Road ,
Province: MB
Postal: R0J 1Z0
Country: Canada
Mailing address: Box 160
Mailing city: Shoal Lake
Province: MB
Postal: R0J 1Z0
General Phone: (204) 759-2644

Non-Daily Newspapers in Canada

General Fax: (204) 759-2521
Advertising Phone: (204) 759-2644
Advertising Fax: (204) 759-2521
Editorial Phone: (204) 759-2644
Editorial Fax: (204) 759-2521
Display Adv. E-mail: smpdisplay@mymts.net
Classified Adv. e-mail: smpclassified@mymts.net
Editorial e-mail: smpnews@mymts.net
Year Established: 2005
Delivery Methods: Racks
Areas Served - City/County or Portion Thereof, or Zip codes: Yellowhead
Published: Fri
Avg Paid Circ: 46
Avg Free Circ: 1492
Audit By: VAC
Audit Date: 19.12.2017
Personnel: Connie Kay (Advertising); Marcie Harrison (Editor); Michelle Gensiorek (Classified/Accounting); Ryan Nesbitt (Publisher); Darrell Nesbitt (Reporter/Photographer)
Parent company (for newspapers): Nesbitt Publishing Ltd.

SIDNEY

GOLDSTREAM GAZETTE

Street Address: 103-9843 Second Street ,
Province: BC
Postal: V8L 3C6
Country: Canada
Mailing address: 103-9843 Second Street
Mailing city: Sidney
Province: BC
Postal: V8L 3C6
General Phone: (250) 656-1151
General Fax: 250) 656-5526
Display Adv. E-mail: publisher@peninsulanewsreview.com
Editorial e-mail: editor@goldstreamgazette.com
Primary Website: goldstreamgazette.com
Year Established: 1976
Delivery Methods: Carrier
Areas Served - City/County or Portion Thereof, or Zip codes: Langford
Commercial printers?: Y
Published: Wed`Fri
Avg Free Circ: 17257
Audit By: AAM
Audit Date: 31.03.2019
Personnel: Mellissa Mitchell (Circ. Mgr.); Michelle Cabana (Pub.); Dale Naftel (Pub.)
Parent company (for newspapers): Black Press Group Ltd.

THE PENINSULA NEWS REVIEW

Street Address: 102-9830 Second Street ,
Province: BC
Postal: V8L 3C6
Country: Canada
Mailing address: 103-9830 Second St.
Mailing city: Sidney
Province: BC
Postal: V8L 3C6
General Phone: (250) 656-1151
General Fax: (250) 656-5526
Editorial Phone: (250) 656-1151
Display Adv. E-mail: sales@peninsulanewsreview.com
Editorial e-mail: editor@peninsulanewsreview.com
Primary Website: www.peninsulanewsreview.com
Year Established: 1905
Delivery Methods: Carrier
Areas Served - City/County or Portion Thereof, or Zip codes: Canada
Own Printing Facility?: Y
Published: Wed`Fri
Avg Free Circ: 14556
Audit By: AAM
Audit Date: 31.03.2019
Personnel: Steven Heywood; Dale Naftel; Chris R Cook; Hugo Wong; Rosemarie Bandura
Parent company (for newspapers): Black Press Group Ltd.

SIMCOE

TIMES-REFORMER

Street Address: 50 Gilbertson Dr. ,
Province: ON
Postal: N3Y 4L2
Country: Canada
Mailing address: 50 Gilbertson Dr.
Mailing city: Simcoe
Province: ON
Postal: N3Y 4L2
General Phone: (519) 426-3528
General Fax: (519) 426-9255
General/National Adv. E-mail: sdowns@bowesnet.com
Primary Website: www.simcoereformer.ca
Areas Served - City/County or Portion Thereof, or Zip codes: Canada
Published: Tues
Avg Paid Circ: 1411
Avg Free Circ: 17315
Audit By: CMCA
Audit Date: 31.12.2013
Personnel: Sue Downs (Adv. Mgr.); Kim Novak (Ed.)
Parent company (for newspapers): Postmedia Network Inc.; Quebecor Communications, Inc.

SIOUX LOOKOUT

THE BULLETIN

Street Address: 40 Front St. ,
Province: ON
Postal: P8T 1B9
Country: Canada
Mailing address: PO Box 1389
Mailing city: Sioux Lookout
Province: ON
Postal: P8T 1B9
General Phone: (807) 737-3209
General Fax: (807) 737-3084
Advertising Phone: (807) 737-4207
General/National Adv. E-mail: bulletin@siouxbulletin.com
Primary Website: www.soiuxbulletin.com
Areas Served - City/County or Portion Thereof, or Zip codes: Canada
Mechanical specifications: Type page 10 x 14.
Published: Wed
Avg Free Circ: 4472
Audit By: CMCA
Audit Date: 30.04.2016
Personnel: Dick MacKenzie (Ed.)

WAWATAY NEWS

Street Address: 16 5th Ave. ,
Province: ON
Postal: P8T 1B7
Country: Canada
Mailing address: PO Box 1180
Mailing city: Sioux Lookout
Province: ON
Postal: P8T 1B7
General Phone: (807) 737-2951
General Fax: (807) 737-3224
General/National Adv. E-mail: editor@wawatay.on.ca
Primary Website: www.wawataynews.ca
Year Established: 1974
Mechanical specifications: Type page 10 1/4 x 15 3/4; E - 6 cols, 1 9/16, 1/16 between; A - 6 cols, 1 9/16, 1/16 between; C - 6 cols, 1 9/16, 1/16 between.
Published: Thur
Published Other: Every other thur
Avg Paid Circ: 399
Avg Free Circ: 5618
Audit By: CMCA
Audit Date: 31.03.2014
Personnel: Rick Garrick (Reporter)

SLAVE LAKE

LAKESIDE LEADER

Street Address: 103 Third Ave. Ne ,
Province: AB
Postal: T0G 2A0
Country: Canada
Mailing address: PO Box 849
Mailing city: Slave Lake
Province: AB
Postal: T0G 2A0
General Phone: (780) 849-4380
General Fax: (780) 849-3903
Advertising Phone: (780) 849-4380
General/National Adv. E-mail: lsleader@telusplanet.net
Editorial e-mail: lsleader@telusplanet.net
Primary Website: www.lakesideleader.com
Year Established: 1970
Delivery Methods: Mail`Newsstand
Areas Served - City/County or Portion Thereof, or Zip codes: Canada
Published: Wed
Avg Paid Circ: 3672
Audit By: CMCA
Audit Date: 31.12.2016
Personnel: Mary Burgar (Pub); Joe McWilliams (Ed); Tammy Leslie (Circulation Mgr/Primary Ad Contact)
Parent company (for newspapers): South Peace News(High Prairie)

SMITH FALLS

THE CARLETON PLACE-ALMONTE CANADIAN GAZETTE EMC

Street Address: 65 Lorne St. ,
Province: ON
Postal: K7A 4T1
Country: Canada
Mailing address: PO Box 158
Mailing city: Smith Falls
Province: ON
Postal: K7A 4T1
General Phone: (613) 283-3182
Display Adv. E-mail: ssinfield@perfprint.ca
Editorial e-mail: akulp@perfprint.ca
Primary Website: www.insideottawavalley.com
Areas Served - City/County or Portion Thereof, or Zip codes: Canada
Own Printing Facility?: Y
Commercial printers?: Y
Published: Thur
Avg Free Circ: 12071
Audit By: CMCA
Audit Date: 30.06.2016
Personnel: Duncan Weir (Group Pub.l); Ryland Coyne (Reg. Ed.)
Parent company (for newspapers): Metroland Media Group Ltd.

THE PERTH COURIER EMC

Street Address: 65 Lorne St. ,
Province: ON
Postal: K7A 4T1
Country: Canada
Mailing address: PO Box 158
Mailing city: Smith Falls
Province: ON
Postal: K7A 4T1
General Phone: (613) 283-3180
Editorial e-mail: editor@perthcourier.com
Primary Website: www.insideottawavalley.com
Year Established: 1834
Areas Served - City/County or Portion Thereof, or Zip codes: Canada
Mechanical specifications: Type page 13 1/4 x 21; E - 8 cols, 1 1/2, 1 7/8 between; A - 8 cols, 1 1/2, 1 7/8 between; C - 11 cols, 1 1/2, 1 1/6 between.
Published: Thur
Avg Free Circ: 11641
Audit By: CMCA
Audit Date: 30.06.2016
Personnel: Duncan Weir (Pub.); Ryland Coyne
Parent company (for newspapers): Metroland Media Group Ltd.

SMITHERS

THE SMITHERS INTERIOR NEWS

Street Address: 3764 Broadway ,
Province: BC
Postal: V0J 2N0
Country: Canada
Mailing address: PO Box 2560
Mailing city: Smithers
Province: BC
Postal: V0J 2N0
General Phone: (250) 847-3266
General Fax: (250) 847-2995
General/National Adv. E-mail: publisher@interior-news.com
Display Adv. E-mail: publisher@interior-news.com
Editorial e-mail: editor@interior-news.com
Primary Website: www.interior-news.com
Year Established: 1907
Areas Served - City/County or Portion Thereof, or Zip codes: Canada
Own Printing Facility?: Y
Mechanical specifications: Type page 12 1/8 x 21; E - 7 cols, 1 3/5, 1/6 between; A - 7 cols, 1 3/5, 1/6 between; C - 7 cols, 1 3/5, 1/6 between.
Published: Wed
Avg Paid Circ: 13
Avg Free Circ: 152
Audit By: VAC
Audit Date: 30.06.2016
Personnel: Grant Harris (Pub/Sales Mgr); Chris Gareau (Ed)
Parent company (for newspapers): Black Press Group Ltd.

SMITHS FALLS

KEMPTVILLE ADVANCE EMC

Street Address: 65 Lorne St. ,
Province: ON
Postal: K7A 4T1
Country: Canada
Mailing address: PO Box 158
Mailing city: Smiths Falls
Province: ON
Postal: K7A 4T1
General Phone: (613) 283-3181
Display Adv. E-mail: liz.gray@metroland.com
Editorial e-mail: joe.morin@metroland.com
Primary Website: www.insideottawavalley.com
Areas Served - City/County or Portion Thereof, or Zip codes: Canada
Published: Thur
Avg Free Circ: 10707
Audit By: CMCA
Audit Date: 30.06.2016
Personnel: Duncan Weir (Group Pub.); Kerry Sammon (Ed.)
Parent company (for newspapers): Metroland Media Group Ltd.

SMITHS FALLS RECORD NEWS EMC

Street Address: 65 Lorne St. ,
Province: ON
Postal: K7A 4T1
Country: Canada
Mailing address: PO Box 158
Mailing city: Smiths Falls
Province: ON
Postal: K7A 4T1
General Phone: (613) 283-3182
General Fax: (613) 283-7480
General/National Adv. E-mail: emc@perfprint.ca
Primary Website: www.insideottawavalley.com/smithsfalls-on
Areas Served - City/County or Portion Thereof, or Zip codes: Canada
Own Printing Facility?: Y
Commercial printers?: Y
Published: Thur
Avg Free Circ: 11455
Audit By: CMCA
Audit Date: 30.06.2016
Personnel: Duncan Weir (Pub.); Jason Beck (Circ. Mgr); Ryland Coyne (Ed.)
Parent company (for newspapers): Metroland

SMOKY LAKE

SMOKY LAKE SIGNAL

Street Address: 4924 50th St ,
Province: AB
Postal: T0A 3C0
Country: Canada
Mailing address: Box 328
Mailing city: Smoky Lake
Province: AB
Postal: T0A 3C0
General Phone: (780) 656-6530
Advertising Phone: (780) 656-4114
Editorial Phone: (780) 656-6530
General/National Adv. E-mail: signal@mcsnet.ca
Display Adv. E-mail: lorne_taylor@smokylake.com
Classified Adv. e-mail: lornetaylor@smokylake.com
Editorial e-mail: lornetaylor@smokylake.com
Year Established: 1978
Delivery Methods: Mail`Newsstand
Areas Served - City/County or Portion Thereof, or Zip codes: T0A 3C0
Published: Tues`Wed
Avg Paid Circ: 855
Avg Free Circ: 20
Audit By: Sworn/Estimate/Non-Audited
Audit Date: 12.07.2019
Personnel: Lorne Taylor (Ed/Pub/Owner)
Parent company (for newspapers): Smoky Lake Signal Press Ltd.

SOOKE

THE SOOKE NEWS MIRROR

Street Address: #4 6631 Sooke Road ,
Province: BC
Postal: V9Z 0A3
Country: Canada
Mailing address: #4-6631 Sooke Rd.
Mailing city: Sooke
Province: BC
Postal: V9Z 0A3
General Phone: (250) 642-5752
General Fax: (250) 642-4767
Advertising Phone: (250) 642-5752
Display Adv. E-mail: sales@sookenewsmirror.com
Editorial e-mail: editor@sookenewsmirror.com
Primary Website: www.sookenewsmirror.com
Delivery Methods: Mail`Newsstand`Carrier
Areas Served - City/County or Portion Thereof, or Zip codes: District of Sooke
Commercial printers?: N
Published: Wed
Avg Paid Circ: 63
Avg Free Circ: 5713
Audit By: AAM
Audit Date: 31.03.2019
Personnel: Rod Sluggett (publisher); Laird Kevin (editor); Kelvin Phair (Advertising Sales)
Parent company (for newspapers): Black Press Group Ltd.

SOREL

JOURNAL LA VOIX

Street Address: 58 Charlotte St. ,
Province: QC
Postal: J3P 1G3
Country: Canada
Mailing address: 58 Charlotte St.
Mailing city: Sorel
Province: QC
Postal: J3P 1G3
General Phone: (450) 743-8466
General Fax: (450) 742-8567
General/National Adv. E-mail: info@journallavoix.net
Display Adv. E-mail: publicite@journallavoix.net
Editorial e-mail: redaction@journallavoix.net
Primary Website: www.journallavoix.net;
monteregieweb.com
Year Established: 1960
Areas Served - City/County or Portion Thereof, or Zip codes: Canada
Mechanical specifications: Type page 15 x 17.
Published: Fri
Avg Free Circ: 29562
Audit By: CCAB
Audit Date: 31.03.2014
Personnel: Parise Bergeron (Adv. Rep.); Anne-Marie Nadeau (Adv. Rep.); Joey Olivier (Ed.); Johanne Berthiaume (Ed.)
Parent company (for newspapers): Les Hebdos Monteregiens-OOB

SOREL-TRACY

LES 2 RIVES

Street Address: 77 George St. ,
Province: QC
Postal: J3P 1C2
Country: Canada
Mailing address: 77 George St.
Mailing city: Sorel-Tracy
Province: QC
Postal: J3P 1C2
General Phone: (450) 742-9408
General Fax: (450) 742-2493
General/National Adv. E-mail: pco2rives@biz.videotran.ca; info@les2rives.com
Primary Website: www.les2rives.com
Areas Served - City/County or Portion Thereof, or Zip codes: Canada
Commercial printers?: Y
Mechanical specifications: Type page 10 3/4 x 17.
Published: Tues
Avg Paid Circ: 1
Avg Free Circ: 29562
Audit By: CCAB
Audit Date: 31.03.2014
Personnel: Marcel Rainville (Gen. Mgr.); Louise Gregoire Racicot (Ed.)
Parent company (for newspapers): Les Hebdos Monteregiens-OOB

SOREL-TRACY EXPRESS

Street Address: 100 Rue Plante ,
Province: QC
Postal: J3P 7P5
Country: Canada
Mailing address: 100 Rue Plante
Mailing city: Sorel-Tracy
Province: QC
Postal: J3P 7P5
General Phone: (450) 746-0886
General Fax: (450) 746-0801
Advertising Phone: (450) 746-0886
Advertising Fax: (450) 746-0801
Editorial Phone: (450) 746-0886
Editorial Fax: (450) 746-0801
General/National Adv. E-mail: sorel-tracyexpress@tc.tc
Display Adv. E-mail: sorel-tracyexpress@tc.tc
Editorial e-mail: sorel-tracyexpress@tc.tc
Primary Website: www.sorel-tracyexpress.ca
Delivery Methods: Mail`Racks
Areas Served - City/County or Portion Thereof, or Zip codes: Canada
Published: Tues
Avg Free Circ: 31018
Audit By: CCAB
Audit Date: 31.03.2014
Personnel: Claude Poulin (Pres.)

SOURIS

SOURIS PLAINDEALER

Street Address: 53 Crescent Ave. W. ,
Province: MB
Postal: R0K 2C0
Country: Canada
Mailing address: PO Box 488
Mailing city: Souris
Province: MB
Postal: R0K 2C0
General Phone: (204) 483-2070
General Fax: (204) 522-3648
Editorial e-mail: spdealer@mts.net
Primary Website: http://www.sourisplaindealer.ca/
Areas Served - City/County or Portion Thereof, or Zip codes: Canada
Mechanical specifications: Type page 10 x 14; E - 6 cols, 1 7/12, 1/6 between; A - 6 cols, 1 7/12, 1/6 between; C - 6 cols, 1 7/12, 1/6 between.
Published: Fri
Avg Free Circ: 54
Audit By: VAC
Audit Date: 31.12.2015
Personnel: Darcy Semeschuk (Office Mgr.); Patti Lewis (Pub/Ed.)
Parent company (for newspapers): Glacier Media Group

SPRINGDALE

THE NOR'WESTER

Street Address: Po Box 28 ,
Province: NL
Postal: A0J 1T0
Country: Canada
Mailing address: PO Box 28
Mailing city: Springdale
Province: NL
Postal: A0J 1T0
General Phone: (709) 673-3721
General Fax: (709) 673-4171
Editorial e-mail: editor@thenorwester.ca
Primary Website: www.thenorwester.ca
Areas Served - City/County or Portion Thereof, or Zip codes: Canada
Published: Thur
Avg Paid Circ: 1730
Avg Free Circ: 0
Audit By: VAC
Audit Date: 31.12.2015
Personnel: Rudy Norman (Ed.)
Parent company (for newspapers): Transcontinental Media

SPRUCE GROVE

THE GROVE EXAMINER

Street Address: 420 King Street , #1
Province: AB
Postal: T7X 3B4
Country: Canada
General Phone: (780) 962-4257
General Fax: (780) 962-0658
Advertising Phone: (877) 786-8227
Display Adv. E-mail: matthew.maceachen@sunmedia.ca
Classified Adv. e-mail: matthew.maceachen@sunmedia.ca
Editorial e-mail: carsonm@bowesnet.com
Primary Website: www.sprucegroveexaminer.com
Year Established: 1970
Areas Served - City/County or Portion Thereof, or Zip codes: Canada
Own Printing Facility?: Y
Published: Fri
Avg Paid Circ: 1273
Avg Free Circ: 11471
Audit By: VAC
Audit Date: 31.12.2015
Personnel: Mary Ann Kostiuk (Reg. Sales Mgr.); Janet Stace (Prodn. Mgr.); Pamela Allain (Pub.); Matthew MacEachen (Adv. Mgr.); Carson Mills (Ed.)
Parent company (for newspapers): Postmedia Network Inc.

THE STONY PLAIN REPORTER

Street Address: 420 King Street , #1
Province: AB
Postal: T7X 3B4
Country: Canada
General Phone: (780) 962-4257
General Fax: (780) 962-0658
Advertising Phone: (877) 786-8227
General/National Adv. E-mail: ex.repoffice1@bowesnet.com
Display Adv. E-mail: matthew.maceachen@sunmedia.ca
Classified Adv. e-mail: matthew.maceachen@sunmedia.ca
Editorial e-mail: thomas.miller@sunmedia.ca
Primary Website: www.stonyplainreporter.com
Year Established: 1945
Areas Served - City/County or Portion Thereof, or Zip codes: Canada
Mechanical specifications: Type page 10 1/4 x 15 3/4; E - 6 cols, 1 7/12, between; A - 6 cols, 1 7/12, between; C - 6 cols, 1 7/12, between.
Published: Fri
Avg Paid Circ: 1643
Avg Free Circ: 10513
Audit By: VAC
Audit Date: 31.12.2015
Personnel: Mary-Ann Kostiuk (Circ. Mgr.); Carson Mills (Adv.); Jim Myers (Prodn. Mgr.); Pamela Allain (Pub.); Thomas Miller (CARDonline(10/31/14))
Parent company (for newspapers): Postmedia Network Inc.

SQUAMISH

SQUAMISH CHIEF

Street Address: 38117 Second Avenue ,
Province: BC
Postal: V8B 0B9
Country: Canada
Mailing address: PO BOX 3500
Mailing city: Squamish
Province: BC
Postal: V8B 0B9
General Phone: (604) 892-9161
General Fax: (604) 892-8483
Display Adv. E-mail: ads@squamishchief.com
Classified Adv. e-mail: jgibson@squamishchief.com
Editorial e-mail: michaela@squamishchief.com
Primary Website: www.squamishchief.com
Areas Served - City/County or Portion Thereof, or Zip codes: Squamish
Published: Thur
Avg Free Circ: 794
Audit By: VAC
Audit Date: 30.04.2016
Personnel: Darren Roberts (Pub); Michaela Garstin (Ed); Tina Pisch (Mktg Coord.); Jennifer Gibson (Sales & Mktg. Mgr); Denise Conway (Circ. Mgr.)
Parent company (for newspapers): Glacier Media Group

ST MARYS

ST. MARY'S JOURNAL ARGUS

Street Address: 11 Wellington St. N. ,
Province: ON
Postal: N4X 1B7
Country: Canada
Mailing address: PO Box 103
Mailing city: St Marys
Province: ON
Postal: N4X 1B7
General Phone: (519) 284-2440
General Fax: (519) 284-3650
General/National Adv. E-mail: drowe@southwesternontario.ca
Display Adv. E-mail: ksteven@stmarys.com
Classified Adv. e-mail: csmith@stmarys.com
Editorial e-mail: sslater@stmarys.com
Primary Website: www.southwesternontario.ca
Delivery Methods: Mail
Areas Served - City/County or Portion Thereof, or Zip codes: Canada
Published: Wed
Avg Paid Circ: 1354
Avg Free Circ: 110
Audit By: CMCA
Audit Date: 31.03.2016
Personnel: Anita McDonald (Business Manager); Stevens Kara (Sales Supervisor); Colleen Smith (Advertising/Circulation)
Parent company (for newspapers): Metroland

ST. ALBERT

ST. ALBERT GAZETTE

Street Address: 340 Carelton Drive ,
Province: AB
Postal: T8N 7L3
Country: Canada
Mailing address: PO Box 263
Mailing city: St. Albert
Province: AB
Postal: T8N 1N3
General Phone: (780) 460-5500
General Fax: (780) 460-8220
Editorial Phone: (780) 460-5510
General/National Adv. E-mail: gazette@stalbert.greatwest.ca
Display Adv. E-mail: advertising@stalbert.greatwest.ca
Editorial e-mail: cmartindale@stalbert.greatwest.ca
Primary Website: www.stalbertgazette.com
Year Established: 1961
Delivery Methods:
 Mail`Newsstand`Carrier`Racks
Areas Served - City/County or Portion Thereof, or Zip codes: Canada
Own Printing Facility?: Y
Commercial printers?: Y
Mechanical specifications: Type page 9.45" x 15"; E - 6 cols, 2, 1/6 between; A - 6 cols, 2, 1/6 between; C - 7 cols, 1 3/8, 1/6 between.
Published: Wed`Sat
Avg Paid Circ: 1652
Avg Free Circ: 24879
Audit By: VAC
Audit Date: 30.06.2016
Personnel: Al Glaser (Adv. Mgr.); Brian Bachynski (Pub); Carolyn Martindale (Ed)
Parent company (for newspapers): Glacier Media Group; Great West Newspapers LP

ST. JOHN'S

LE GABOTEUR

Street Address: 65 Ridge Road ,
Province: NL
Postal: A1B 4P5
Country: Canada
Mailing address: 250 - 65 Ridge Road
Mailing city: St. John's
Province: NL
Postal: A1B 4P5
General Phone: (709) 753-9585
Display Adv. E-mail: annonces@gaboteur.ca
Editorial e-mail: redaction@gaboteur.ca
Primary Website: www.gaboteur.ca
Year Established: 1984
Delivery Methods: Mail
Areas Served - City/County or Portion Thereof, or Zip codes: Canada
Published: Bi-Mthly
Avg Paid Circ: 850
Avg Free Circ: 0
Audit By: CMCA
Audit Date: 31.03.2013
Personnel: Jacinthe Tremblay (Dir/Ed)

STANSTEAD

THE STANSTEAD JOURNAL

Street Address: 620 Dufferin ,
Province: QC
Postal: J0B 3E0
Country: Canada
Mailing address: 620 Dufferin
Mailing city: Stanstead
Province: QC
Postal: J0B 3E0
General Phone: (819) 876-7514
General/National Adv. E-mail: journal@stanstead-journal.com
Display Adv. E-mail: ads@stanstead-journal.com
Editorial e-mail: communique@stanstead-journal.com
Primary Website: www.stanstead-journal.com
Year Established: 1845
Delivery Methods:
 Mail`Newsstand`Carrier`Racks
Areas Served - City/County or Portion Thereof, or Zip codes: Memphremagog
Published: Wed
Avg Paid Circ: 1625
Audit By: AAM
Audit Date: 31.03.2015
Personnel: Jean-Yves Durocher (Sales Mgr.); Mylene Piche (Prodn. Mgr.)
Parent company (for newspapers): Stanstead Journal Publishing

STEINBACH

THE CARILLON

Street Address: 377 Main St. ,
Province: MB
Postal: R5G 1A5
Country: Canada
Mailing address: 377 Main St.
Mailing city: Steinbach
Province: MB
Postal: R5G 1A5
General Phone: (204) 326-3421
General Fax: (204) 326-4860
General/National Adv. E-mail: info@thecarillon.com
Display Adv. E-mail: ads@thecarillon.com
Classified Adv. e-mail: mgauthier@thecarillon.com
Editorial e-mail: gburr@thecarillon.com
Primary Website: www.thecarillon.com
Areas Served - City/County or Portion Thereof, or Zip codes: Canada
Own Printing Facility?: Y
Commercial printers?: Y
Mechanical specifications: Type page 11 1/2 x 17; E - 5 cols, 2 1/6, between; A - 5 cols, 2 1/6, between; C - 5 cols, 2 1/6, between.
Published: Thur
Avg Paid Circ: 1140
Avg Free Circ: 234
Audit By: VAC
Audit Date: 30.09.2016
Personnel: Laurie Finley (Pub/Gen. Mgr.); Grant Burr (Ed); Holly-Jaide Nickel (Circ Mgr.)

STEPHENVILLE

THE GEORGIAN

Street Address: 43 Main St. , 43 Main Street
Province: NL
Postal: A2N 2Z4
Country: Canada
Mailing address: PO Box 283
Mailing city: Stephenville
Province: NL
Postal: A2N 2Z4
General Phone: (709) 643-4531
General Fax: (709) 643-5041
Editorial e-mail: editor@thegeorgian.ca
Primary Website: www.thegeorgian.ca
Year Established: 1970
Delivery Methods:
 Mail`Newsstand`Carrier`Racks
Areas Served - City/County or Portion Thereof, or Zip codes: Canada
Own Printing Facility?: Y
Commercial printers?: Y
Published: Mon
Avg Paid Circ: 1152
Avg Free Circ: 0
Audit By: CMCA
Audit Date: 30.06.2013
Personnel: Christopher Vaughan (Ed.)
Parent company (for newspapers): Transcontinental Media

STETTLER

STETTLER INDEPENDENT

Street Address: 4810 50th St. ,
Province: AB
Postal: T0C 2L0
Country: Canada
Mailing address: P.O. Box 310
Mailing city: Stettler
Province: AB
Postal: T0C 2L0
General Phone: (403) 742-2395
General Fax: (403) 742-8050
Editorial Phone: (403) 740-4431
General/National Adv. E-mail: stetnews@telusplanet.net
Display Adv. E-mail: nicole.stratulate@stettlerindependent.com
Classified Adv. e-mail: ddoell@stettlerindependent.com
Editorial e-mail: editor@stettlerindependent.com
Primary Website: www.stettlerindependent.com
Areas Served - City/County or Portion Thereof, or Zip codes: Town of Stettler, County of Stettler, Big Valley, Erskine, Donalda, Gadsby, Botha, Buffalo Lake,
Own Printing Facility?: Y
Published: Thur
Avg Paid Circ: 34
Avg Free Circ: 33
Audit By: VAC
Audit Date: 20.03.2017
Personnel: Debbie Doell (Ad control); Karen Fischer (Graphic artist); Landin Chambers (reporter)
Parent company (for newspapers): Black Press Group Ltd.

STONEWALL

THE INTERLAKE SPECTATOR

Street Address: 3411 3rd Avenue South , Unit 3
Province: MB
Postal: R0C 2Z0
Country: Canada
Mailing address: PO Box 190
Mailing city: Stonewall
Province: MB
Postal: R0C 2Z0
General Phone: (204) 467-2421
General Fax: (204) 467-5967
General/National Adv. E-mail: ispec@mts.net
Display Adv. E-mail: jbilsky@postmedia.com
Editorial e-mail: bjones@postmedia.com
Primary Website: http://www.interlaketoday.ca/interlakespectator
Areas Served - City/County or Portion Thereof, or Zip codes: Stonewall
Published: Thur
Avg Paid Circ: 1520
Avg Free Circ: 10780
Audit By: VAC
Audit Date: 30.06.2016
Personnel: Jenifer Bilsky (Adv Dir.); Brook Jones (Ed)
Parent company (for newspapers): Postmedia Network Inc.; Quebecor Communications, Inc.

THE STONEWALL ARGUS & TEULON TIMES

Street Address: 3411 3rd Avenue South ,
Province: MB
Postal: R0C 2Z0
Country: Canada
Mailing address: PO Box 190
Mailing city: Stonewall
Province: MB
Postal: R0C 2Z0
General Phone: (204) 467-2421
General Fax: (204) 467-5967
General/National Adv. E-mail: news@stonewallteulontribune.ca
Display Adv. E-mail: jbilsky@postmedia.com
Editorial e-mail: bjones@postmedia.com
Primary Website: http://www.interlaketoday.ca/stonewallargusteulontimes
Areas Served - City/County or Portion Thereof, or Zip codes: Canada
Own Printing Facility?: Y
Commercial printers?: Y
Mechanical specifications: Type page 10 1/8 x 14; E - 6 cols, 1 7/12, 1/6 between; A - 6 cols, 1 7/12, 1/6 between; C - 6 cols, 1 7/12, 1/6 between.
Published: Thur
Avg Paid Circ: 1219
Avg Free Circ: 6467
Audit By: VAC
Audit Date: 30.06.2016
Personnel: Brook Jones (Ed); Jenifer Bilsky (Adv Dir)
Parent company (for newspapers): Postmedia Network Inc.; Quebecor Communications, Inc.

STONEY CREEK

ANCASTER NEWS

Street Address: 333 Arvin Ave. ,
Province: ON
Postal: L8E 2M6
Country: Canada
Mailing address: 333 Arvin Ave.
Mailing city: Stoney Creek
Province: ON
Postal: L8E 2M6
General Phone: (905) 523-5800
General Fax: (905) 664-3319
General/National Adv. E-mail: editor@ancasternews.com
Display Adv. E-mail: mtherrien@metroland.com
Classified Adv. e-mail: classified@thespec.com
Editorial e-mail: mpearson@hamiltonnews.com
Primary Website: www.ancasternews.com
Year Established: 1967
Delivery Methods: Carrier
Areas Served - City/County or Portion Thereof, or Zip codes: Ancaster
Own Printing Facility?: Y
Mechanical specifications: Full page is 10 columns x 161 agate lines; same as 10.375" x 11.5"
Published: Thur
Avg Paid Circ: 4
Avg Free Circ: 13355
Audit By: CMCA
Audit Date: 21.06.2018
Personnel: Kelly Montague (Pub.); Jason Pehora (Gen. Mgr.); Lorna Lester (Office Mgr.); Michael Pearson (News Ed.); Gordon Cameron (Mng Ed); Melinda Therrien (Dir of Advt)
Parent company (for newspapers): Metroland Media Group Ltd.; Torstar

DUNDAS STAR NEWS

Street Address: 333 Arvin Ave. ,
Province: ON
Postal: L8E 2M6
Country: Canada
Mailing address: 333 Arvin Ave.
Mailing city: Stoney Creek
Province: ON
Postal: L8E 2M6
General Phone: (905) 664-8800
General Fax: (905) 664-3319
General/National Adv. E-mail: editor@dundasstarnews.com
Display Adv. E-mail: mtherrien@metroland.com
Classified Adv. e-mail: classified@thespec.com
Editorial e-mail: editor@dundasstarnews.com
Primary Website: www.dundasstarnews.com
Year Established: 1883
Delivery Methods: Carrier
Areas Served - City/County or Portion Thereof, or Zip codes: Dundas & Westdale L8S (Hamilton)
Own Printing Facility?: Y
Commercial printers?: Y
Mechanical specifications: 10 columns x 161 agate lines; same as 10.375" x 11.5"
Published: Thur
Avg Paid Circ: 4
Avg Free Circ: 14302
Audit By: CMCA
Audit Date: 21.06.2018
Personnel: Montague Kelly (Pub.); Jason Pehora (Gen. Mgr.); Lorna Lester (Office Mgr.); Gord Bowes (Ed); Mike Boyle (Produ Mgr.); Gordon Cameron (Mng Ed); Holly Christofilopoulos (Dir of Advt)

Media Group Ltd.; Torstar

Parent company (for newspapers): Metroland Media Group Ltd.; Torstar

HAMILTON MOUNTAIN NEWS

Street Address: 333 Arvin Ave. ,
Province: ON
Postal: L8E 2M6
Country: Canada
Mailing address: 333 Arvin Ave.
Mailing city: Stoney Creek
Province: ON
Postal: L8E 2M6
General Phone: (905) 664-8800
General Fax: (905) 664-3319
General/National Adv. E-mail: editor@hamiltonmountainnews.com
Display Adv. E-mail: mtherrien@metroland.com
Classified Adv. e-mail: classified@thespec.com
Editorial e-mail: gordbowes@hamiltonnews.com
Primary Website: www.hamiltonnews.com
Year Established: 1968
Delivery Methods: Carrier
Areas Served - City/County or Portion Thereof, or Zip codes: Hamilton
Own Printing Facility?: N
Commercial printers?: Y
Mechanical specifications: Full page is 10 columns x 161 agate lines; same as 10.375" x 11.5"
Published: Thur
Avg Paid Circ: 5
Avg Free Circ: 49048
Audit By: CMCA
Audit Date: 21.06.2018
Personnel: Jason Pehora (Gen. Mgr.); Gordon Cameron (Managing Editor); Holly Christofilopoulos (Director of Advertising)
Parent company (for newspapers): Metroland Media Group Ltd.; Torstar Corp.

STONEY CREEK NEWS

Street Address: 333 Arvin Ave. ,
Province: ON
Postal: L8E 2M6
Country: Canada
Mailing address: 333 Arvin Ave.
Mailing city: Stoney Creek
Province: ON
Postal: L8E 2M6
General Phone: (905) 664-8800
General Fax: (905) 664-3319
Display Adv. E-mail: editor@hamiltonmountainnews.com
Classified Adv. e-mail: classified@thespec.com
Editorial e-mail: editor@stoneycreeknews.com
Primary Website: www.stoneycreeknews.com
Year Established: 1948
Delivery Methods: Carrier
Areas Served - City/County or Portion Thereof, or Zip codes: Stoney Creek
Own Printing Facility?: Y
Commercial printers?: Y
Mechanical specifications: Full page is 10 columns x 161 agate lines; same as 10.375" x 11.5"
Published: Thur
Avg Paid Circ: 4
Avg Free Circ: 30178
Audit By: CMCA
Audit Date: 21.06.2018
Personnel: Kelly Montague (Pub.); Jason Pehora (Gen. Mgr.); Michael Pearson (Ed.); Gordon Cameron (Mng Ed.); Rhonda Ridgway (Produ Mgr.); Melinda Therrien (Adv. Dir.)
Parent company (for newspapers): Metroland Media Group Ltd.

STRATFORD

STRATFORD GAZETTE

Street Address: 10 Downie St. Unit 207 ,
Province: ON
Postal: N5A 7K4
Country: Canada

Mailing address: 10 Downie St. Unit 207
Mailing city: Stratford
Province: ON
Postal: N5A 7K4
General Phone: (519) 271-8002
General Fax: (519) 271-5636
General/National Adv. E-mail: admin@stratfordgazette.com
Display Adv. E-mail: jhaefling@stratfordgazette.com
Classified Adv. e-mail: lcarter@stratfordgazette.com
Editorial e-mail: news@stratfordgazette.com
Primary Website: www.southwesternontario.ca
Delivery Methods: Mail`Carrier
Areas Served - City/County or Portion Thereof, or Zip codes: Canada
Published: Thur
Avg Free Circ: 19855
Audit By: CMCA
Audit Date: 29.02.2016
Personnel: Laura Carter (Front Office/Distribution); Julie Haefling (Sales Supervisor); Anita McDonald (Business Manager)
Parent company (for newspapers): Metroland Media Group Ltd.

STRATHMORE

STRATHMORE STANDARD

Street Address: Unit A-510 Hwy 1 ,
Province: AB
Postal: T1P 1M6
Country: Canada
Mailing address: Unit A-510 Hwy 1
Mailing city: Strathmore
Province: AB
Postal: T1P 1M6
General Phone: (403) 934-3021
General Fax: (403) 934-5011
Display Adv. E-mail: rmackintosh@postmedia.com
Editorial e-mail: josh.chalmers@sunmedia.ca
Primary Website: www.strathmorestandard.com
Year Established: 1909
Delivery Methods: Mail`Newsstand`Carrier`Racks
Areas Served - City/County or Portion Thereof, or Zip codes: Canada
Own Printing Facility?: Y
Commercial printers?: N
Published: Wed
Avg Paid Circ: 3679
Avg Free Circ: 10858
Audit By: VAC
Audit Date: 31.12.2015
Personnel: Josh Chalmers (Ed); Roxanne MacKintosh (Adv. Dir)
Parent company (for newspapers): Postmedia Network Inc.; Quebecor Communications, Inc.

STRATHMORE TIMES

Street Address: 123 2nd Avenue ,
Province: AB
Postal: T1P 1K1
Country: Canada
Mailing address: Box 2005
Mailing city: Strathmore
Province: AB
Postal: T1K 1K1
General Phone: (403) 934-5589
General Fax: (403) 934-5546
General/National Adv. E-mail: info@strathmoretimes.com
Display Adv. E-mail: rose@strathmoretimes.com
Classified Adv. e-mail: classifieds@strathmoretimes.com
Editorial e-mail: miriam@strathmoretimes.com
Primary Website: www.strathmoretimes.com
Year Established: 2009
Delivery Methods: Mail
Areas Served - City/County or Portion Thereof, or Zip codes: Strathmore and all of Wheatland County
Published: Fri
Avg Free Circ: 11001
Audit By: Sworn/Estimate/Non-Audited

Audit Date: 12.07.2019
Personnel: Mario Prusina (Pub/Ed); Rose Hamrlik (Adv Mgr); Miriam Ostermann (Associate Editor)

STRATHROY

THE STRATHROY AGE DISPATCH

Street Address: 73 Front Street West ,
Province: ON
Postal: N7G 1X6
Country: Canada
Mailing address: 73 Front Street West
Mailing city: Strathroy
Province: ON
Postal: N7G 1X6
General Phone: (519) 245-2370
General Fax: (519) 245-1647
General/National Adv. E-mail: news@strathroyonline.com
Primary Website: www.strathroyagedispatch.com
Year Established: 1861
Delivery Methods: Mail`Carrier`Racks
Areas Served - City/County or Portion Thereof, or Zip codes: N7G, NOM, NON, NOL
Own Printing Facility?: Y
Published: Thur
Avg Paid Circ: 1480
Audit By: CMCA
Audit Date: 31.01.2014
Personnel: Bev Ponton (Pub.); Don Biggs (Reg. Ed.)
Parent company (for newspapers): Postmedia Network Inc.; Quebecor Communications, Inc.

SUDBURY

JOURNAL LE VOYAGEUR

Street Address: 336 Rue Pine , Suite 302
Province: ON
Postal: P3C 1X8
Country: Canada
Mailing address: 336 rue Pine
Mailing city: Sudbury
Province: ON
Postal: P3C 1X8
General Phone: (705) 673-3377
General Fax: (705) 673-5854
General/National Adv. E-mail: administration@levoyageur.ca
Primary Website: www.lavoixdunord.ca
Delivery Methods: Mail`Carrier
Areas Served - City/County or Portion Thereof, or Zip codes: Canada
Own Printing Facility?: Y
Mechanical specifications: Type page 10 1/4 x 14; E - 5 cols, 2, 1/6 between; A - 10 cols, 1/6 between; C - 10 cols, 1/6 between.
Published: Wed
Avg Paid Circ: 7157
Avg Free Circ: 1342
Audit By: CMCA
Audit Date: 28.02.2013
Personnel: Patrick Breton (Ed. in Chief)

NORTHERN LIFE

Street Address: 158 Elgin St. ,
Province: ON
Postal: P3E 3N5
Country: Canada
Mailing address: 158 Elgin St.
Mailing city: Sudbury
Province: ON
Postal: P3E 3N5
General Phone: (705) 673-5667
General Fax: (705) 673-4652
Advertising Phone: (705) 673-5667 Ext. 313
Editorial Phone: (705) 673-5667 Ext. 337
Display Adv. E-mail: classify@northernlife.ca
Editorial e-mail: mgentili@sudbury.com
Primary Website: sudbury.com
Year Established: 1970
Areas Served - City/County or Portion Thereof, or Zip codes: Canada
Own Printing Facility?: Y

Mechanical specifications: Type page 10 3/8 x 14; E - 9 cols, between; A - 9 cols, between; C - 9 cols, between.
Published: Tues`Thur
Avg Paid Circ: 5444
Avg Free Circ: 35536
Audit By: CCAB
Audit Date: 30.09.2017
Personnel: Abbas Homayed (Pub.); Michael R. Atkins (Pres.); Mark Gentili (Managing Ed.)

SUMMERLAND

SUMMERLAND REVIEW

Street Address: 13226 Victoria Rd. N. ,
Province: BC
Postal: V0H 1Z0
Country: Canada
Mailing address: PO Box 309
Mailing city: Summerland
Province: BC
Postal: V0H 1Z0
General Phone: (250) 494-5406
General Fax: (250) 494-5453
General/National Adv. E-mail: news@summerlandreview.com
Display Adv. E-mail: rob@summerlandreview.com
Classified Adv. e-mail: class@summerlandreview.com
Editorial e-mail: news@summerlandreview.com
Primary Website: www.summerlandreview.com
Areas Served - City/County or Portion Thereof, or Zip codes: Summerland
Own Printing Facility?: Y
Published: Thur
Avg Paid Circ: 52
Avg Free Circ: 21
Audit By: VAC
Audit Date: 30.06.2016
Personnel: John Arendt (Ed.); Shannon Simpson (Pub); Rob Murphy (Sales Mgr); Nan Cogbill (Class./Circ Mgr)
Parent company (for newspapers): Black Press Group Ltd.

SUMMERSIDE

LA VOIX ACADIENNE

Street Address: 5, Ave Maris Stella ,
Province: PE
Postal: C1N 6M9
Country: Canada
Mailing address: 5, ave Maris Stella
Mailing city: Summerside
Province: PE
Postal: C1N 6M9
General Phone: (902) 436-6005
General Fax: (902) 888-3976
Display Adv. E-mail: pub@lavoixacadienne.com
Editorial e-mail: texte@lavoixacadienne.com
Primary Website: www.lavoixacadienne.com
Year Established: 1976
Areas Served - City/County or Portion Thereof, or Zip codes: all provinces of Canada
Commercial printers?: Y
Mechanical specifications: Type page 10 1/4 x 12 1/2; E - 5 cols, between; A - 5 cols, between.
Published: Wed
Avg Paid Circ: 1517
Avg Free Circ: 20
Audit By: ODC
Audit Date: 13.12.2017
Personnel: Marcia Enman (Dir. Gen.); Jacinthe Laforest (Ed.)

SUNDRE

SUNDRE ROUND-UP

Street Address: 103 2nd St. Nw ,
Province: AB
Postal: T0M 1X0
Country: Canada
Mailing address: PO Box 599
Mailing city: Sundre
Province: AB

Non-Daily Newspapers in Canada

Postal: T0M 1X0
General Phone: (403) 638-3577
General Fax: (403) 638-3077
General/National Adv. E-mail: roundup@sundre.greatwest.ca
Display Adv. E-mail: kcomfort@sundre.greatwest.ca
Editorial e-mail: dsingleton@olds.greatwest.ca
Primary Website: www.sundreroundup.ca
Year Established: 1961
Areas Served - City/County or Portion Thereof, or Zip codes: Canada
Own Printing Facility?: Y
Mechanical specifications: Type page 10 1/4 x 14 1/2; E - 6 cols, 1 11/20, between; A - 6 cols, 1 11/20, between; C - 6 cols, 1 11/20, between.
Published: Tues
Avg Paid Circ: 879
Avg Free Circ: 0
Audit By: VAC
Audit Date: 30.06.2016
Personnel: Ray Lachambre (Pub.); Dan Singleton (Ed); Kim Comfort (Sales Mgr)
Parent company (for newspapers): Glacier Media Group; Great West Newspapers LP

SURREY

CLOVERDALE REPORTER

Street Address: 17586 56a Ave. ,
Province: BC
Postal: V3S 1G3
Country: Canada
Mailing address: 17586 56A Ave.
Mailing city: Surrey
Province: BC
Postal: V3S 1G3
General Phone: (604) 575-2400
Advertising Phone: (604) 575-2423
Display Adv. E-mail: cynthia.dunsmore@cloverdalereporter.com
Classified Adv. e-mail: bcclassifieds@blackpress.com
Editorial e-mail: editor@cloverdalereporter.com
Primary Website: www.cloverdalereporter.com
Year Established: 1996
Delivery Methods: Carrier`Racks
Areas Served - City/County or Portion Thereof, or Zip codes: Surrey, B.C.
Published: Wed
Avg Free Circ: 16159
Audit By: CMCA
Audit Date: 31.03.2018
Personnel: Cynthia Dunsmore (Sales Representative); Sam Anderson (Ed.); Grace Kennedy (Reporter)
Parent company (for newspapers): Black Press Group Ltd.

SURREY NOW-LEADER

Street Address: 102-5460 152nd St. ,
Province: BC
Postal: V3S 5J9
Country: Canada
Mailing address: 102-5460 152nd St.
Mailing city: Surrey
Province: BC
Postal: V3S 5J9
General Phone: (604) 572-0064
General Fax: (604) 575-2544
Advertising Phone: (604) 572-0064
Advertising Fax: (604)572-7948
Editorial Phone: (604)543-5816
General/National Adv. E-mail: sueb@blackpress.ca
Display Adv. E-mail: sueb@blackpress.ca
Classified Adv. e-mail: sueb@blackpress.ca
Editorial e-mail: beau.simpson@surreynowleader.com
Primary Website: www.surreynowleader.com
Delivery Methods: Carrier
Areas Served - City/County or Portion Thereof, or Zip codes: Canada
Own Printing Facility?: Y
Commercial printers?: Y
Published: Wed`Fri
Avg Free Circ: 54521
Audit By: AAM
Audit Date: 31.03.2019
Parent company (for newspapers): Black Press Group Ltd.

THE NOW NEWSPAPER

Street Address: 102 - 5460 152 St ,
Province: BC
Postal: V3S 5J9
Country: Canada
Mailing address: 102 - 5460 152 St
Mailing city: Surrey
Province: BC
Postal: V3S 5J9
General Phone: (604) 572-0064
General Fax: (604) 572-6438
Display Adv. E-mail: dal.hothi@thenownewspaper.com
Classified Adv. e-mail: sarah.sigurdswon@thenownewspaper.com
Editorial e-mail: bsimpson@thenownewspaper.com
Primary Website: www.thenownewspaper.com
Year Established: 1984
Delivery Methods: Carrier
Areas Served - City/County or Portion Thereof, or Zip codes: Canada
Commercial printers?: Y
Published: Tues`Thur
Avg Free Circ: 177757
Audit By: CCAB
Audit Date: 31.03.2014
Personnel: Beau Simpson (Ed); Dwayne Weidendorf (Pub); Sarah Sigurdson (Ad Control/Admin); Dal Hothi (Sales Mgr)

THE PEACE ARCH NEWS

Street Address: 200-2411 160 Street ,
Province: BC
Postal: V3S 0C8
Country: Canada
Mailing address: 200-2411 160 Street
Mailing city: Surrey
Province: BC
Postal: V3S 0C8
General Phone: (604) 531-1711
General Fax: (604) 531-7977
Editorial e-mail: editorial@peacearchnews.com
Primary Website: www.peacearchnews.com
Delivery Methods: Carrier
Areas Served - City/County or Portion Thereof, or Zip codes: Canada
Own Printing Facility?: Y
Mechanical specifications: Type page 10 1/4 x 12 1/2; E - 6 cols, between; A - 6 cols, between; C - 6 cols, between.
Published: Wed`Fri
Avg Free Circ: 37090
Audit By: AAM
Audit Date: 31.03.2019
Personnel: Lance Peverley (Ed.)
Parent company (for newspapers): Black Press Group Ltd.

SUSSEX

THE KINGS COUNTY RECORD

Street Address: 593 Main St. ,
Province: NB
Postal: E4E 7H5
Country: Canada
Mailing address: 593 Main St.
Mailing city: Sussex
Province: NB
Postal: E4E 7H5
General Phone: (506) 433-1070
General Fax: (506) 432-3532
General/National Adv. E-mail: news@kingcorecord.com
Editorial e-mail: craig.victoria@kingsrecord.com
Primary Website: https://www.telegraphjournal.com/kings-county-record/
Areas Served - City/County or Portion Thereof, or Zip codes: Sussex
Mechanical specifications: Type page 13 x 21 1/2; E - 6 cols, 2 1/16, 3/16 between; A - 6 cols, 2 1/16, 3/16 between; C - 8 cols, 1 1/2, 3/16 between.
Published: Tues
Avg Paid Circ: 0
Avg Free Circ: 2
Audit By: VAC
Audit Date: 31.12.2015
Personnel: Victoria Craig (Pub./Ed); Teresa Perry (Circ. Mgr.)
Parent company (for newspapers): Brunswick News, Inc.

SWAN HILLS

GRIZZLY GAZETTE

Street Address: 5435 Plaza Ave. ,
Province: AB
Postal: T0G 2C0
Country: Canada
Mailing address: PO Box 1000
Mailing city: Swan Hills
Province: AB
Postal: T0G 2C0
General Phone: (780) 333-2100
General Fax: (780) 333-2111
General/National Adv. E-mail: sgazett@telusplanet.net
Display Adv. E-mail: sgazette@telusplanet.net
Classified Adv. e-mail: sgazette@telusplanet.net
Editorial e-mail: sgazette@telusplanet.net
Primary Website: thegrizzlygazette.com
Year Established: 1977
Delivery Methods: Mail`Newsstand
Areas Served - City/County or Portion Thereof, or Zip codes: Canada
Own Printing Facility?: N
Commercial printers?: Y
Mechanical specifications: Type page 10 1/4 x 12 1/2; E - 6 cols, 1 9/16, 1/8 between; A - 6 cols, 1 9/16, 1/8 between.
Published: Tues
Avg Paid Circ: 394
Avg Free Circ: 135
Audit By: Sworn/Estimate/Non-Audited
Audit Date: 12.07.2019
Personnel: Phyllis Webster (Gen. Mgr.); Carol Webster (Ed.)

SWAN RIVER

SWAN VALLEY STAR & TIMES

Street Address: 704 Main St. E. ,
Province: MB
Postal: R0L 1Z0
Country: Canada
Mailing address: PO Box 670
Mailing city: Swan River
Province: MB
Postal: R0L 1Z0
General Phone: (204) 734-3858
General Fax: (204) 734-4935
General/National Adv. E-mail: info@starandtimes.ca
Display Adv. E-mail: info@starandtimes.ca
Classified Adv. e-mail: info@starandtimes.ca
Editorial e-mail: editor@starandtimes.ca
Primary Website: www.starandtimes.ca
Year Established: 1900
Delivery Methods: Mail`Newsstand`Racks
Areas Served - City/County or Portion Thereof, or Zip codes: Canada
Own Printing Facility?: Y
Commercial printers?: Y
Mechanical specifications: Type page 12 x 21; E - 6 cols, 2, 1/6 between; A - 6 cols, between; C - 6 cols, between.
Published: Tues
Avg Paid Circ: 2700
Avg Free Circ: 0
Audit By: CMCA
Audit Date: 30.01.2017
Personnel: Brian T. Gilroy (Adv. Mgr., Publ., Gen. Mgr., Owner); Danielle Gordon-Broome (Ed.)

SWIFT CURRENT

PRAIRIE POST

Street Address: 600 Chaplin Street East ,
Province: SK
Postal: S9H 1J3
Country: Canada
Mailing address: 600 Chaplin Street East
Mailing city: Swift Current
Province: SK
Postal: S9H 1J3
General Phone: (306) 773-8260
General Fax: (306) 773-0504
Advertising Phone: (306) 773-8260
Advertising Fax: (306) 773-0504
Editorial Phone: (306) 773-8260
Editorial Fax: (306) 773-0504
General/National Adv. E-mail: ppost@prairiepost.com
Display Adv. E-mail: ktumback@prairiepost.com
Editorial e-mail: mliebenberg@prairiepost.com
Primary Website: http://www.prairiepost.com
Areas Served - City/County or Portion Thereof, or Zip codes: Canada
Published: Fri
Avg Free Circ: 17814
Audit By: CMCA
Audit Date: 31.03.2016
Personnel: Doug Evjen (Director of Sales and Marketing); Stacey Powell (Advertising)

THE SOUTHWEST BOOSTER

Street Address: 30 4th Ave. Nw ,
Province: SK
Postal: S9H 3X4
Country: Canada
Mailing address: PO Box 1330
Mailing city: Swift Current
Province: SK
Postal: S9H 3X4
General Phone: (306) 773-9321
General Fax: (306) 773-9136
General/National Adv. E-mail: msoper@swbooster.com
Display Adv. E-mail: boosterads@swbooster.com
Primary Website: www.swbooster.com
Year Established: 1969
Areas Served - City/County or Portion Thereof, or Zip codes: Canada
Own Printing Facility?: Y
Commercial printers?: Y
Mechanical specifications: Type page 10 3/8 x 15 5/8; E - 6 cols, 1 15/16, 3/16 between; A - 6 cols, 1 15/16, 3/16 between; C - 6 cols, 1 15/16, 3/16 between.
Published: Thur
Avg Free Circ: 16985
Audit By: CMCA
Audit Date: 31.10.2016
Personnel: Bob Watson (Pub.); Mark Soper (Adv. Mgr.); Ken Mattice (Circ. Mgr.); Scott Anderson (Mng. Ed.); George Driscoll (Prodn. Mgr.)
Parent company (for newspapers): Transcontinental Media

SYLVAN LAKE

ECKVILLE ECHO

Street Address: Suite 103 5020-50 A St. ,
Province: AB
Postal: T4S 1R2
Country: Canada
Mailing address: 5020-50 A St.,
Mailing city: Sylvan Lake
Province: AB
Postal: T4S 1R2
General Phone: (403) 887-2331
General Fax: (403) 887-2081
General/National Adv. E-mail: admin@sylvanlakenews.com
Display Adv. E-mail: admin@sylvanlakenews.com
Editorial e-mail: editor@sylvanlakenews.com
Year Established: 1997
Delivery Methods: Mail`Newsstand`Racks
Areas Served - City/County or Portion Thereof, or Zip

codes: t4s, t4n, rr1, rr4
Commercial printers?: Y
Mechanical specifications: 10.12 " x 13"
Published: Thur
Avg Paid Circ: 1077
Avg Free Circ: 2466
Audit By: VAC
Audit Date: 30.09.2016
Personnel: Cheryl Hyvonen (Admin); Randy Holt (Pub); Jenna Swan (Ed)
Parent company (for newspapers): Black Press Group Ltd.

SYLVAN LAKE NEWS

Street Address: Suite 103, 5020-50a St., ,
Province: AB
Postal: T4S 1R2
Country: Canada
Mailing address: 5020-50A St.,
Mailing city: Sylvan Lake
Province: AB
Postal: T4S 1R2
General Phone: (403) 887-2331
General Fax: (403) 887-2081
Advertising Phone: (403) 887-2331
General/National Adv. E-mail: admin@sylvanlakenews.com
Display Adv. E-mail: sales@sylvanlakenews.com
Editorial e-mail: editor@sylvanlakenews.com
Primary Website: www.sylvanlakenews.com
Year Established: 1935
Delivery Methods: Mail`Carrier`Racks
Areas Served - City/County or Portion Thereof, or Zip codes: Canada
Own Printing Facility?: Y
Published: Thur
Avg Paid Circ: 377
Avg Free Circ: 7715
Audit By: VAC
Audit Date: 30.09.2016
Personnel: Cheryl Hyvonen (Admin); Randy Holt (Pub); Jenna Swan (Ed)
Parent company (for newspapers): Black Press Group Ltd.

TABER

THE TABER TIMES

Street Address: 4822-53 St. ,
Province: AB
Postal: T1G 1W4
Country: Canada
General Phone: (403) 223-2266
General Fax: (403) 223-1408
General/National Adv. E-mail: gsimmons@tabertimes.com
Display Adv. E-mail: chrissales@tabertimes.com
Primary Website: www.tabertimes.com
Year Established: 1907
Delivery Methods: Mail`Newsstand`Carrier
Areas Served - City/County or Portion Thereof, or Zip codes: Canada
Commercial printers?: Y
Mechanical specifications: Type page 11 1/2 x 21; E - 6 cols, 1 3/4, 1/4 between; A - 6 cols, 1 3/4, 1/4 between; C - 6 cols, 1 3/4, 1/4 between.
Published: Wed
Avg Paid Circ: 54
Avg Free Circ: 179
Audit By: VAC
Audit Date: 30.09.2016
Personnel: Valorie Wiebe (Pub.); Christine Mykytiw (Adv. Consult.); Erin Lickiss (Adv. Consult.); Greg Price (Ed.)

TATAMAGOUCHE

THE LIGHT

Street Address: Po Box 1000 ,
Province: NS
Postal: B0K 1V0
Country: Canada
Mailing address: PO Box 1000
Mailing city: Tatamagouche
Province: NS
Postal: B0K 1V0
General Phone: (902) 956-8099
Display Adv. E-mail: kristinhirtle@tatamagouchelight.com
Editorial e-mail: raissatetanish@tatamagouchelight.com
Primary Website: www.tatamagouchelight.com
Areas Served - City/County or Portion Thereof, or Zip codes: Tatamagouche
Published: Wed
Avg Paid Circ: 2497
Avg Free Circ: 4378
Audit By: VAC
Audit Date: 30.06.2016
Personnel: Leith Orr (Pub)

TAVISTOCK

TAVISTOCK GAZETTE

Street Address: 119 Woodstock St. S. ,
Province: ON
Postal: N0B 2R0
Country: Canada
Mailing address: PO Box 70
Mailing city: Tavistock
Province: ON
Postal: N0B 2R0
General Phone: (519) 655-2341
Advertising Phone: (519) 655-2341
Editorial Phone: (519) 655-2341
General/National Adv. E-mail: gazette@tavistock.on.ca
Primary Website: www.tavistock.on.ca
Year Established: 1895
Delivery Methods: Mail`Newsstand
Areas Served - City/County or Portion Thereof, or Zip codes: Canada
Own Printing Facility?: Y
Commercial printers?: Y
Published: Wed
Avg Paid Circ: 1178
Avg Free Circ: 2
Audit By: CMCA
Audit Date: 31.10.2017
Personnel: Sheri Gladding (Circulation Manager); William J. Gladding (Ed.)

TECUMSEH

TECUMSEH SHORELINE WEEK

Street Address: 1614 Lesperance Rd. ,
Province: ON
Postal: N8N 1X2
Country: Canada
Mailing address: 1614 Lesperance Rd.
Mailing city: Tecumseh
Province: ON
Postal: N8N 1X2
General Phone: (519) 735-2080
General Fax: (519) 735-2082
General/National Adv. E-mail: shorelineweek@canwest.com
Areas Served - City/County or Portion Thereof, or Zip codes: Canada
Mechanical specifications: Type page 10 1/4 x 15 1/2; E - 6 cols, 1 1/2, 3/16 between; A - 6 cols, 1 7/10, between; C - 7 cols, 1 3/8, 1/4 between.
Published: Fri
Avg Free Circ: 17312
Audit By: CMCA
Audit Date: 31.12.2017
Personnel: Dave Calibaba (Pub.); Rusty Wright (Mgr., Sales); William England (Ed.)
Parent company (for newspapers): Postmedia Network Inc.; CanWest MediaWorks Publications, Inc.

THE LAKESHORE NEWS

Street Address: 1116 Lesperance Road ,
Province: ON
Postal: N8N 1X2
Country: Canada
Mailing address: 1116 Lesperance Road
Mailing city: Tecumseh
Province: ON
Postal: N8N 1X2
General Phone: (519) 735-2080
General Fax: (519) 735-2082
General/National Adv. E-mail: lakeshore@canwest.com
Primary Website: www.facebook.com/Lakeshore-News-285820481600683/?ref=page_internal
Year Established: 1948
Areas Served - City/County or Portion Thereof, or Zip codes: Canada
Commercial printers?: Y
Mechanical specifications: Type page 10 1/4 x 15; E - 6 cols, 1 9/16, between; A - 6 cols, 1 9/16, between; C - 6 cols, 1 5/16, between.
Published: Thur
Avg Free Circ: 9389
Audit By: VAC
Audit Date: 31.12.2015
Personnel: Dave Calibaba (Gen. Mgr.); Bill Harris (Ed.)
Parent company (for newspapers): Postmedia Network Inc.; CanWest MediaWorks Publications, Inc.

TERRACE

THE TERRACE STANDARD

Street Address: 3210 Clinton St ,
Province: BC
Postal: V8G5R2
Country: Canada
Mailing address: 3210 Clinton St.
Mailing city: Terrace
Province: BC
Postal: V8G 5R2
General Phone: (250) 638-7283
General Fax: (250) 638-8432
General/National Adv. E-mail: newsroom@terracestandard.com
Display Adv. E-mail: bwhusband@terracestandard.com
Classified Adv. e-mail: classifieds@terracestandard.com
Editorial e-mail: newsroom@terracestandard.com
Primary Website: www.terracestandard.com
Year Established: 1969
Areas Served - City/County or Portion Thereof, or Zip codes: Canada
Own Printing Facility?: Y
Mechanical specifications: Type page 12 1/16 x 21 1/2; E - 7 cols, 1 5/8, 1/8 between; A - 7 cols, 1 5/8, 1/8 between; C - 7 cols, 1 5/8, 1/8 between.
Published: Thur
Avg Free Circ: 7729
Audit By: VAC
Audit Date: 12.12.2017
Personnel: Quinn Bender (Editor); Bert Husband (Sales)
Parent company (for newspapers): Black Press Group Ltd.

TERRACE BAY

TERRACE BAY SCHREIBER NEWS

Street Address: 25 Simcoe Plaza ,
Province: ON
Postal: P0T 2W0
Country: Canada
Mailing address: PO Box 130
Mailing city: Terrace Bay
Province: ON
Postal: P0T 2W0
General Phone: (807) 825-9425
General Fax: (807) 825-9458
General/National Adv. E-mail: nipigongazette@shaw.ca
Areas Served - City/County or Portion Thereof, or Zip codes: Canada
Own Printing Facility?: Y
Commercial printers?: Y
Published: Tues
Avg Paid Circ: 287
Avg Free Circ: 21
Audit By: CMCA
Audit Date: 30.06.2016
Personnel: Karen Schaeffer (Reporter/Photographer); Blair Oborne (Pub.); Pamela Behun (Edior)

TERREBONNE

LA REVUE DE TERREBONNE

Street Address: 231 Sainte-marie St. ,
Province: QC
Postal: J6W 3E4
Country: Canada
Mailing address: larevue@larevue.qc.ca
Mailing city: Terrebonne
Province: QC
Postal: J6W 3E4
General Phone: (450) 964-4444
General Fax: (450) 471-1023
General/National Adv. E-mail: larevue@larevue.qc.ca
Display Adv. E-mail: ventes@larevue.qc.ca
Classified Adv. e-mail: petitesannonces@larevue.qc.ca
Editorial e-mail: redaction@larevue.qc.ca
Primary Website: www.larevue.qc.ca
Year Established: 1959
Areas Served - City/County or Portion Thereof, or Zip codes: Lanaudiere
Own Printing Facility?: Y
Commercial printers?: Y
Published: Wed
Avg Paid Circ: 10
Avg Free Circ: 55990
Audit By: Sworn/Estimate/Non-Audited
Audit Date: 12.07.2019
Personnel: Gilles Bordonado (Pub./Pres./CEO.); Veronick Talbot (News Dir); Daniel Soucy (Mktg Dir); Lise Bourdages (Sales Coord)
Parent company (for newspapers): Guide Rouge; Le Trait d'Union

LE TRAIT D'UNION

Street Address: 231, Rue Sainte-marie ,
Province: QC
Postal: J6W 3E4
Country: Canada
Mailing address: 231, rue Sainte-Marie
Mailing city: Terrebonne
Province: QC
Postal: J6W 3E4
General Phone: (450) 964-4444
General Fax: (450) 471-1023
General/National Adv. E-mail: letraitdunion@transcontinental.ca
Classified Adv. e-mail: petitesannonces@larevue.qc.ca
Editorial e-mail: redaction@larevue.qc.ca
Primary Website: www.letraitdunion.com
Year Established: 1976
Delivery Methods: Newsstand`Carrier`Racks
Areas Served - City/County or Portion Thereof, or Zip codes: Terrebonne Mascouche
Published: Wed
Avg Paid Circ: 10
Avg Free Circ: 49990
Audit By: ODC
Audit Date: 12.12.2017
Personnel: Gilles Bordonado (Pr®sident); V®ronick Talbot (R®dactrice en chef); Lise Bourdages (Coordonnatrice aux ventes)
Parent company (for newspapers): La Revue de Terrebonne

THAMESVILLE

HERALD

Street Address: 105 Elizabeth St , Box 580
Province: ON
Postal: N0P 2K0
Country: Canada
Mailing address: PO Box 580
Mailing city: Thamesville
Province: ON
Postal: N0P 2K0
General Phone: (519) 692-3825
General/National Adv. E-mail: thamesvilleherald@sympatico.ca
Areas Served - City/County or Portion Thereof, or Zip codes: Canada
Commercial printers?: Y
Published: Wed

Non-Daily Newspapers in Canada

Avg Paid Circ: 594
Audit By: CMCA
Audit Date: 29.02.2016
Personnel: Orval Schilbe (Ed.); May Schilbe (Mng. Ed.)

THE PAS

OPASQUIA TIMES

Street Address: 352 Fischer Avenue , Box 750
Province: MB
Postal: R9A 1K8
Country: Canada
Mailing address: Box 750
Mailing city: The Pas
Province: MB
Postal: R9A 1K8
General Phone: (204) 623-3435
General Fax: (204) 623-5601
General/National Adv. E-mail: optmies@mts.net
Display Adv. E-mail: opads@mymts.net
Classified Adv. e-mail: opclass@mymts.net
Editorial e-mail: opeditor@mymts.net
Primary Website: www.opasquiatimes.com
Year Established: 1978
Areas Served - City/County or Portion Thereof, or Zip codes: Opasquia
Published: Wed`Fri
Avg Paid Circ: 1200
Avg Free Circ: 0
Audit By: VAC
Audit Date: 31.08.2015
Personnel: Jennifer Cook (Gen. Mgr.); Trent Allen (Ed.)

THETFORD MINES

COURRIER FRONTENAC

Street Address: Boulevard Frontenac Est Cp 789 , C.p. 789
Province: QC
Postal: G6G 5V3
Country: Canada
Mailing address: boulevard Frontenac Est CP 789
Mailing city: Thetford Mines
Province: QC
Postal: G6G 5V3
General Phone: (418) 338-5181
Areas Served - City/County or Portion Thereof, or Zip codes: Canada
Published: Wed
Avg Paid Circ: 15
Avg Free Circ: 22826
Audit By: CCAB
Audit Date: 31.03.2014
Personnel: Lucyl Lachance

THOMPSON

THOMPSON CITIZEN/NICKEL BELT NEWS

Street Address: 141 Commercial Pl. ,
Province: MB
Postal: R8N 1T1
Country: Canada
Mailing address: P.O. Box 887
Mailing city: Thompson
Province: MB
Postal: R8N 1N8
General Phone: (204) 677-4534
General Fax: (204) 677-3681
Advertising Phone: (204) 677-4534 ext 1
Editorial Phone: (204) 677-4534 ext 6
General/National Adv. E-mail: generalmanager@thompsoncitizen.net
Display Adv. E-mail: ads@thompsoncitizen.net
Classified Adv. e-mail: classifieds@thompsoncitizen.net
Editorial e-mail: editor@thompsoncitizen.net
Primary Website: www.thompsoncitizen.net
Year Established: 1961
Delivery Methods: Racks
Areas Served - City/County or Portion Thereof, or Zip codes: Canada
Own Printing Facility?: Y

Commercial printers?: N
Mechanical specifications: Type page 9 1/2 x 15; A - 5 cols, 1 3/4, between; C - 1 cols, 1 3/4, between.
Published: Fri
Avg Paid Circ: 61
Avg Free Circ: 6000
Audit By: Sworn/Estimate/Non-Audited
Audit Date: 12.07.2019
Personnel: Lynn Taylor (Gen. Mgr.); Ian Graham (Ed.)
Parent company (for newspapers): Glacier Media Group

THOROLD

FORT ERIE POST

Street Address: 3300 Merrittville Hwy Unit 1b ,
Province: ON
Postal: L2V 4Y6
Country: Canada
General Phone: (905) 688-2444
Primary Website: www.niagarathisweek.com/forterie-on
Published: Thur
Personnel: Dave Hawkins (Adv.)
Parent company (for newspapers): Metroland Media Group Ltd.

NIAGARA THIS WEEK

Street Address: 3300 Merrittville Hwy, Unit 1b ,
Province: ON
Postal: L2V 4Y6
Country: Canada
Mailing address: 3300 Merrittville Hwy, Unit 1B
Mailing city: Thorold
Province: ON
Postal: L2V 4Y6
General Phone: (905) 688-2444
General Fax: (905) 688-9272
General/National Adv. E-mail: letters@niagarathisweek.com
Primary Website: niagarathisweek.com
Areas Served - City/County or Portion Thereof, or Zip codes: Canada
Published: Wed`Thur
Avg Paid Circ: 0
Avg Free Circ: 151084
Audit By: CCAB
Audit Date: 30.09.2017
Personnel: David Bos (Gen. Mgr.); Debbi Koppejan (Adv. Mgr.); Mike Williscraft (Editorial Dir.); Dave Hawkins (Newspaper/Online Adv.)
Parent company (for newspapers): Metroland Media Group Ltd.; Torstar

THREE HILLS

THE THREE HILLS CAPITAL

Street Address: 411 Main St. ,
Province: AB
Postal: T0M 2A0
Country: Canada
Mailing address: PO Box 158
Mailing city: Three Hills
Province: AB
Postal: T0M 2A0
General Phone: (403) 443-5133
General Fax: (403) 443-7331
General/National Adv. E-mail: info@threehillscapital.com
Display Adv. E-mail: info@threehillscapital.com
Classified Adv. e-mail: info@threehillscapital.com
Editorial e-mail: info@threehillscapital.com
Primary Website: threehillscapital.com
Year Established: 1916
Delivery Methods: Mail`Newsstand
Areas Served - City/County or Portion Thereof, or Zip codes: Canada
Commercial printers?: Y
Published: Wed
Avg Paid Circ: 1029
Avg Free Circ: 4
Audit By: VAC

Audit Date: 31.12.2015
Personnel: Theresa Shearlaw (Adv. Mgr.); Timothy Shearlaw (Ed.); Jay Shearlaw (Produ Mgr)

THUNDER BAY

THUNDER BAY SOURCE

Street Address: 87 N. Hill St. ,
Province: ON
Postal: P7A 5V6
Country: Canada
Mailing address: 87 N. Hill St.
Mailing city: Thunder Bay
Province: ON
Postal: P7A 5V6
General Phone: (807) 346-2650
General Fax: (807) 345-9923
Advertising Phone: (807) 346-2510
General/National Adv. E-mail: ldunick@dougallmedia.com
Primary Website: www.tbnewswatch.com
Year Established: 1976
Delivery Methods: Carrier
Areas Served - City/County or Portion Thereof, or Zip codes: P7A, P7B, P7C, P7E
Own Printing Facility?: N
Commercial printers?: Y
Published: Thur
Avg Free Circ: 43740
Audit By: CMCA
Audit Date: 30.06.2017
Personnel: Leith Dunick (Mng. Ed.); Doug Diaczuk (Reporter); Matt Vis (Reporter); Nicole Dixon (Content editor)
Parent company (for newspapers): T.Bay Post Inc

TILBURY

THE TILBURY TIMES

Street Address: 40 Queen St. S. ,
Province: ON
Postal: N0P 2L0
Country: Canada
Mailing address: P.O. Box 490
Mailing city: Tilbury
Province: ON
Postal: N0P 2L0
General Phone: (519) 682-0411
General Fax: (519) 682-3633
Editorial Phone: (519) 809-4347
Display Adv. E-mail: dbarnwell@tilburytimes.com
Classified Adv. e-mail: dbarnwell@tilburytimes.com
Editorial e-mail: gharvieux@tilburytimes.com
Year Established: 1883
Delivery Methods: Mail`Newsstand
Areas Served - City/County or Portion Thereof, or Zip codes: N0P, N0R
Mechanical specifications: Type page 10 1/4 x 15 1/2; E - 6 cols, 1 1/2, 3/16 between; A - 6 cols, 1 7/10, between; C - 7 cols, 1 3/8, 1/4 between.
Published: Tues
Avg Paid Circ: 1100
Avg Free Circ: 50
Audit By: Sworn/Estimate/Non-Audited
Audit Date: 12.07.2019
Personnel: Bob Thwaites (Pub.); Gerry Harvieux (Ed.)
Parent company (for newspapers): Postmedia Network Inc.

TILLSONBURG

THE TILLSONBURG NEWS

Street Address: 25 Townline Rd. ,
Province: ON
Postal: N4G 4H6
Country: Canada
Mailing address: PO BOX 190
Mailing city: Tillsonburg
Province: ON
Postal: N4G 4H6
General Phone: (519) 688-6397
General Fax: (519) 842-3511

Advertising Phone: (519) 688-4400
General/National Adv. E-mail: tilledit@bowesnet.com
Primary Website: www.tillsonburgnews.com
Own Printing Facility?: Y
Commercial printers?: Y
Published: Fri
Avg Paid Circ: 1173
Audit By: CMCA
Audit Date: 31.12.2015
Personnel: Michael Walsh (Pub.)
Parent company (for newspapers): Postmedia Network Inc.; Quebecor Communications, Inc.

TIMMINS

TIMMINS TIMES

Street Address: 815 Pine St. S. ,
Province: ON
Postal: P4N 8S3
Country: Canada
Mailing address: 815 Pine St. S.
Mailing city: Timmins
Province: ON
Postal: P4N 8S3
General Phone: (705) 268-6252
General Fax: (705) 268-2255
General/National Adv. E-mail: times@timminstimes.com
Primary Website: www.timminstimes.com
Areas Served - City/County or Portion Thereof, or Zip codes: Canada
Mechanical specifications: Type page 10 x 14 1/4; E - 6 cols, 1 3/4, 1/8 between; A - 6 cols, 1 3/4, 1/8 between; C - 6 cols, 1 3/4, 1/8 between.
Published: Thur
Avg Free Circ: 16325
Audit By: CMCA
Audit Date: 31.12.2013
Personnel: Wayne Major (Pub.); Len Gillis (Ed.); Kevin Anderson (Regional Managing Editor)
Parent company (for newspapers): Postmedia Network Inc.; Quebecor Communications, Inc.

TISDALE

PARKLAND REVIEW

Street Address: 1004-102 Ave. ,
Province: SK
Postal: S0E 1T0
Country: Canada
Mailing address: PO Box 1660
Mailing city: Tisdale
Province: SK
Postal: S0E 1T0
General Phone: (306) 873-4515
General Fax: (306) 873-4712
General/National Adv. E-mail: recorderoffice@sasktel.net
Display Adv. E-mail: adsrecorder@sasktel.net
Editorial e-mail: newsrecorder@sasktel.net
Delivery Methods: Mail
Areas Served - City/County or Portion Thereof, or Zip codes: Canada
Own Printing Facility?: Y
Published: Fri
Avg Free Circ: 11625
Audit By: CMCA
Audit Date: 31.03.2016
Personnel: August Grandguillar (Adv. Mgr.); Brent Fitzpatrick (Ed.); Gord Anderson (Prodn. Mgr.); Dan Sully (Adv. Mgr.)
Parent company (for newspapers): Glacier Media Group

TISDALE

THE TISDALE RECORDER

Street Address: 1004 102nd Ave. ,
Province: SK
Postal: S0E 1T0
Country: Canada
Mailing address: PO Box 1660
Mailing city: Tisdale

Province: SK
Postal: S0E 1T0
General Phone: (306) 873-4515
General Fax: (306) 873-4712
General/National Adv. E-mail: pub@sasktel.net
Display Adv. E-mail: recorder3@sasktel.net
Editorial e-mail: newsrecorder@sasktel.net
Areas Served - City/County or Portion Thereof, or Zip codes: Canada
Own Printing Facility?: Y
Commercial printers?: Y
Published: Wed
Avg Paid Circ: 669
Avg Free Circ: 25
Audit By: CMCA
Audit Date: 31.12.2015
Personnel: Brent Fitzpatrick (Pub.); James Tarrant (Ed.); August Grandguillot (Ad.)
Parent company (for newspapers): Glacier Media Group

TOBERMORY

THE BRUCE PENINSULA PRESS

Street Address: 39 Legion St. ,
Province: ON
Postal: N0H 2R0
Country: Canada
Mailing address: PO Box 89
Mailing city: Tobermory
Province: ON
Postal: N0H 2R0
General Phone: (519) 596-2658
General Fax: (519) 596-8030
General/National Adv. E-mail: info@tobermorypress.com
Primary Website: www.brucepeninsulapress.com
Areas Served - City/County or Portion Thereof, or Zip codes: Canada
Published: Tues
Avg Paid Circ: 400
Avg Free Circ: 2235
Audit By: CMCA
Audit Date: 30.06.2017
Personnel: John Francis (Pub.); Scott McFarlane (Production Mgr./Signs); Marianne Wood (Editor)

TOFIELD

TOFIELD MERCURY

Street Address: 5312 50th St. ,
Province: AB
Postal: T0B 4J0
Country: Canada
Mailing address: PO Box 150
Mailing city: Tofield
Province: AB
Postal: T0B 4J0
General Phone: (780) 662-4046
General Fax: (780) 662-3735
Advertising Phone: (780) 662-4046
General/National Adv. E-mail: adsmercury@gmail.com
Display Adv. E-mail: kamcjm@gmail.com
Classified Adv. E-mail: kamcjm@gmail.com
Editorial e-mail: tofmerc@telusplanet.net
Primary Website: www.tofieldmerc.com
Year Established: 1918
Delivery Methods: Mail`Racks
Areas Served - City/County or Portion Thereof, or Zip codes: Canada
Commercial printers?: Y
Mechanical specifications: Type page 10 x 15 1/2; E - 5 cols, 1 5/6, between; A - 5 cols, 1 5/6, between.
Published: Wed
Avg Paid Circ: 1400
Avg Free Circ: 23
Audit By: Sworn/Estimate/Non-Audited
Audit Date: 12.07.2019
Personnel: Kerry Anderson (Pub/Advt Mgr)
Parent company (for newspapers): Caribou Publishing

TORONTO

ANGLICAN JOURNAL

Street Address: 80 Hayden Street ,
Province: ON
Postal: M4Y 3G2
Country: Canada
Mailing address: 80 Hayden Street
Mailing city: Toronto
Province: ON
Postal: M4Y 3G2
General Phone: (416) 924-9199
Advertising Phone: (226) 664-0350
General/National Adv. E-mail: editor@anglicanjournal.com
Display Adv. E-mail: advertising@national.anglican.ca
Editorial e-mail: editor@anglicanjournal.com
Primary Website: www.anglicanjournal.com
Year Established: 1875
Delivery Methods: Mail
Areas Served - City/County or Portion Thereof, or Zip codes: Toronto, ON M4Y 32
Published: Mthly
Avg Paid Circ: 123352
Avg Free Circ: 1200
Audit By: Sworn/Estimate/Non-Audited
Audit Date: 12.07.2019

ANNEX GUARDIAN

Street Address: One River View Garden ,
Postal: M6S 4E4
Country: Canada
Mailing address: One River View Garden
Mailing city: Toronto
Province: ON
Postal: M6S 4E4
General Phone: (416) 493-4400
General Fax: (416) 767-4880
Display Adv. E-mail: salesinfo@insidetoronto.com
Classified Adv. e-mail: classifieds@metroland.com
Editorial e-mail: gbalogiannis@insidetoronto.com
Primary Website: www.insidetoronto.ca
Published: Fri
Avg Free Circ: 55500
Audit By: Sworn/Estimate/Non-Audited
Audit Date: 12.07.2019
Personnel: Grace Peacock (Ed); Meriel Bradley (Sales Dir)
Parent company (for newspapers): Torstar

BEACH-RIVERDALE MIRROR

Street Address: 100 Tempo Ave. ,
Province: ON
Postal: M2H 2N8
Country: Canada
Mailing address: 100 Tempo Ave.
Mailing city: Toronto
Province: ON
Postal: M2H 2N8
General Phone: (416) 493-4400
General Fax: (416) 493-6190
General/National Adv. E-mail: bsrm@insidetoronto.com
Display Adv. E-mail: salesinfo@insidetoronto.com
Classified Adv. E-mail: classifieds@metroland.com
Editorial e-mail: newsroom@insidetoronto.com
Primary Website: www.insidetoronto.com
Areas Served - City/County or Portion Thereof, or Zip codes: Canada
Published: Thur
Avg Paid Circ: 0
Avg Free Circ: 22241
Audit By: CCAB
Audit Date: 30.09.2015
Personnel: Betty Carr (Pub); Marg Middleton (Gen. Mgr.); Meriel Bradley (Adv. Rep)
Parent company (for newspapers): Metroland Media Group Ltd.; Torstar

BLOOR WEST VILLAGER

Street Address: 2323 Bloor St. W ,
Province: ON
Postal: M6S 4W1
Country: Canada
Mailing address: 2323 Bloor St. W
Mailing city: Toronto
Province: ON
Postal: M6S 4W1
General Phone: (416) 675-4390
General Fax: (416) 767-4880
General/National Adv. E-mail: metroland@insidetoronto.com
Display Adv. E-mail: mbradley@metroland.com
Editorial e-mail: gpeacock@insidetoronto.com
Primary Website: insidetoronto.com
Areas Served - City/County or Portion Thereof, or Zip codes: Canada
Published: Thur
Avg Paid Circ: 0
Avg Free Circ: 39840
Audit By: CCAB
Audit Date: 30.09.2017
Personnel: Betty Carr (Pub.); Meriel Bradley (Adv. Dir.); Grace Peacock (Ed)
Parent company (for newspapers): Metroland Media Group Ltd.; Torstar

CITY CENTRE MIRROR

Street Address: 175 Gordon Baker Rd. ,
Province: ON
Postal: M2H 2S6
Country: Canada
Mailing address: 175 Gordon Baker Rd.
Mailing city: Toronto
Province: ON
Postal: M2H 2S6
General Phone: (416) 774-2367
General Fax: (416) 493-6190
General/National Adv. E-mail: atedesco@insidetoronto.com
Display Adv. E-mail: mbradley@insidetoronto.com
Classified Adv. E-mail: classifieds@metroland.com
Editorial e-mail: newsroom@insidetoronto.com
Primary Website: insidetoronto.com
Areas Served - City/County or Portion Thereof, or Zip codes: Canada
Published: Thur
Avg Paid Circ: 0
Avg Free Circ: 22359
Audit By: CCAB
Audit Date: 20.12.2017
Personnel: Antoine Tedesco (Managing Ed.)
Parent company (for newspapers): Metroland Media Group Ltd.

L'EXPRESS

Street Address: 17 Carlaw Ave. ,
Province: ON
Postal: M4M 2R6
Country: Canada
Mailing address: 17 Carlaw Ave.
Mailing city: Toronto
Province: ON
Postal: M4M 2R6
General Phone: (416) 465-2107
General Fax: (416) 465-3778
General/National Adv. E-mail: express@lexpress.to
Primary Website: www.lexpress.to
Areas Served - City/County or Portion Thereof, or Zip codes: Toronto, ON
Published: Tues
Avg Paid Circ: 20000
Avg Free Circ: 15000
Audit By: Sworn/Estimate/Non-Audited
Audit Date: 12.07.2019
Personnel: Jean Mazare (Pub.); Akli liu (Adv. Mgr.); Marianne Santhan (Circ. Mgr.); Francois Bergeron (Ed.)

NASHA GAZETA

Street Address: 855 Alness Street , Unit #7
Province: ON
Postal: M3J 2X3
Country: Canada
Mailing address: 855 Alness Street
Mailing city: Toronto
Province: ON
Postal: M3J 2X3
General Phone: (905) 738-1109
General Fax: (416) 514-0640
Primary Website: www.rcbcanada.com/broadcasting/nasha-gazeta
Areas Served - City/County or Portion Thereof, or Zip codes: Toronto
Published: Wed
Avg Free Circ: 2600
Audit By: AAM
Audit Date: 31.12.2018
Personnel: Garry Kukuy (Pub.)
Parent company (for newspapers): Russian Canadian Broadcasting

NORTH YORK MIRROR

Street Address: 100 Tempo Ave. ,
Province: ON
Postal: M2H 2N8
Country: Canada
Mailing address: 100 Tempo Ave.
Mailing city: Toronto
Province: ON
Postal: M2H 2N8
General Phone: (416) 493-4400
General Fax: (416) 495-6629
Display Adv. E-mail: sales@insidetoronto.com
Primary Website: insidetoronto.com
Year Established: 1957
Delivery Methods: Carrier
Areas Served - City/County or Portion Thereof, or Zip codes: Canada
Own Printing Facility?: Y
Commercial printers?: Y
Mechanical specifications: Type page 10 3/8 x 14; E - 9 cols, 1 1/16, between; A - 9 cols, 1 1/16, between; C - 9 cols, 1 1/16, between.
Published: Thur
Avg Paid Circ: 0
Avg Free Circ: 92407
Audit By: CCAB
Audit Date: 30.09.2017
Personnel: Betty Carr (V.P.); Marg Middleton (Gen. Mgr.); Dmitry Borovik (Sales Rep.); Angela Carruthers (Sales Rep.); Paul Futhey (Mng. Ed.); Stacey Allen (Dir. Adv.)
Parent company (for newspapers): Metroland Media Group Ltd.; Torstar

THE BULLETIN - JOURNAL OF DOWNTOWN TORONTO

Street Address: 260 Adelaide St E Ste 121 ,
Province: ON
Postal: M5A 1N1
Country: Canada
Mailing address: 260 Adelaide St E Ste 121
Mailing city: Toronto
Province: ON
Postal: M5A 1N1
General Phone: (416) 929-0011
General Fax: (416) 929-0011
Advertising Phone: (416) 929-0011 ext. 5
Advertising Fax: (416) 929-0011
Editorial Phone: (416) 929-0011 ext. 3
Editorial Fax: (416) 929-0011 ext. 3
Display Adv. E-mail: sales@thebulletin.ca
Classified Adv. e-mail: classified@thebulletin.ca
Editorial e-mail: deareditor@thebulletin.ca
Primary Website: www.thebulletin.ca
Year Established: 1998
Delivery Methods: Mail`Newsstand`Carrier`Racks
Areas Served - City/County or Portion Thereof, or Zip codes: Canada
Mechanical specifications: Broadsheet on supercalendar glossy stock. CMYK throughout. Width x Height: 6 ea.columns with 5-3/8" gutters over 9.5" print width x 19" height Folded for mail via Canada Post to 5" x 22" In racks at 11" x 10.5"
Published: Other
Published Other: Printed 4th Monday each

Non-Daily Newspapers in Canada

III-503

month, in mail by next Thur.
Avg Free Circ: 49822
Audit By: CMCA
Audit Date: 06.09.2017
Personnel: Paulette Touby (Pub.); Frank Touby (Ed.); Anisa Lancione (Mng Ed.)
Parent company (for newspapers): Community Bulletin Newspaper Group, Inc.

THE PARKDALE VILLAGER

Street Address: 175 Gordon Baker Rd ,
Province: ON
Postal: M2H 2S6
Country: Canada
Mailing address: 175 Gordon Baker Rd
Mailing city: Toronto
Province: ON
Postal: M2H 2S6
General Phone: (416) 493-4400
General Fax: (416) 495-6629
Advertising Phone: (416) 493-4400
Advertising Fax: (416) 493-6190
Editorial Phone: (416) 774-2367
Editorial Fax: (416) 493-6190
General/National Adv. E-mail: general@insidetoronto.com
Display Adv. E-mail: atedesco@insidetoronto.com
Editorial e-mail: atedesco@insidetoronto.com
Primary Website: www.parkdaleliberty.ca
Delivery Methods: Mail`Racks
Areas Served - City/County or Portion Thereof, or Zip codes: Canada
Published: Thur
Avg Free Circ: 24917
Audit By: CCAB
Audit Date: 30.09.2015
Personnel: Ian Proudfoot (Pub.); Antoine Tedesco (Mng. Ed.)
Parent company (for newspapers): Metroland Media Group Ltd.

THE SCARBOROUGH MIRROR

Street Address: 100 Tempo Ave. ,
Province: ON
Postal: M2H 2N8
Country: Canada
Mailing address: 100 Tempo Ave.
Mailing city: Toronto
Province: ON
Postal: M2H 2N8
General Phone: (416) 493-4400
General Fax: (416) 495-6629
General/National Adv. E-mail: scm@insidetoronto.com
Primary Website: insidetoronto.com
Areas Served - City/County or Portion Thereof, or Zip codes: Canada
Own Printing Facility?: Y
Commercial printers?: Y
Mechanical specifications: Type page 10 3/8 x 14; E - 9 cols, 1 1/16, between; A - 9 cols, 1 1/16, between; C - 9 cols, 1 1/16, between.
Published: Thur`Fri
Avg Free Circ: 120479
Audit By: CCAB
Audit Date: 20.12.2017
Personnel: Betty Carr (Vice Pres./Grp. Pub.); Marg Middleton (Gen. Mgr.); Kelly Atkinson (Regl. Mgr., HR); Bruce Espey (Dir., Bus. Admin.); Tim Corcoran (Regl. Dir, Adv.); Kayland McCully (Sales Rep.); Frank Li (Sales Rep.); Shauna Paolucci (Sales Rep.); Cathie Orban (Sales Rep.); Leema Williams (Sales Rep.); Michelle King (Sales Rep.); Al Shackleton (Mng. Ed.); Dave Burnett (Dir., Prodn.); Katherine Bernal (Prodn. Mgr.)
Parent company (for newspapers): Metroland Media Group Ltd.; Torstar

THE YORK GUARDIAN

Street Address: 100 Tempo Ave. ,
Province: ON
Postal: M2H 2N8
Country: Canada
Mailing address: 100 Tempo Ave.
Mailing city: Toronto

Province: ON
Postal: M2H 2N8
General Phone: (416) 493-4400
General Fax: (416) 495-6629
General/National Adv. E-mail: etg@insidetoronto.com
Primary Website: www.insidetoronto.com
Areas Served - City/County or Portion Thereof, or Zip codes: Canada
Own Printing Facility?: Y
Commercial printers?: Y
Mechanical specifications: Type page 10 3/8 x 14; E - 9 cols, 1 1/16, between; A - 9 cols, 1 1/16, between; C - 9 cols, 1 1/16, between.
Published: Thur
Avg Free Circ: 28544
Audit By: CCAB
Audit Date: 30.09.2017
Personnel: Betty Carr (Pub.); Marg Middleton (Gen. Mgr.); Tim Corcoran (Adv. Mgr.); Jaime Munoz (Circ. Mgr.); Paul Futhey (Mng. Ed.)
Parent company (for newspapers): Metroland Media Group Ltd.; Torstar

TREHERNE

TIMES

Street Address: 194 Broadway St. ,
Province: MB
Postal: R0G 2V0
Country: Canada
Mailing address: PO Box 50
Mailing city: Treherne
Province: MB
Postal: R0G 2V0
General Phone: (204) 723-2542
General Fax: (204) 723-2754
General/National Adv. E-mail: trehernetimes@mts.net
Editorial e-mail: trehernetimes@mts.net
Primary Website: www.trehernetimes.ca
Areas Served - City/County or Portion Thereof, or Zip codes: Treherne
Published: Mon
Avg Free Circ: 842
Audit By: VAC
Audit Date: 30.06.2016
Personnel: Gary Lodwick (Ed.)

TRENTON

THE COMMUNITY PRESS

Street Address: 41 Quinte St. ,
Province: ON
Postal: K8V 5R3
Country: Canada
Mailing address: PO Box 130
Mailing city: Trenton
Province: ON
Postal: K8V 5R3
General Phone: (613) 395-3015
General Fax: (613) 392-0505
General/National Adv. E-mail: general@communitypress-online.com; news@communitypress-online.com
Editorial e-mail: editor@communitypress-online.com
Primary Website: www.communitypress.ca
Areas Served - City/County or Portion Thereof, or Zip codes: Canada
Mechanical specifications: Type page 10 1/4 x 15; E - 9 cols, 1 1/36, 1/8 between; A - 9 cols, 1 1/36, 1/8 between; C - 6 cols, 1 7/12, 1/8 between.
Published: Thur
Avg Paid Circ: 0
Avg Free Circ: 45644
Audit By: CMCA
Audit Date: 30.06.2014
Personnel: John Knowles (Pub.); Chuck Parker (Gen. Mgr); Ross Lees (Mng. Ed.); John Campbell (News Ed.)

TRENTONIAN

Street Address: 41 Quinte St. ,
Province: ON

Postal: K8V 5R3
Country: Canada
Mailing address: PO Box 130
Mailing city: Trenton
Province: ON
Postal: K8V 5R3
General Phone: (613) 392-6501
General Fax: (613) 392-0505
Display Adv. E-mail: advertising@trentonia.ca
Editorial e-mail: newsroom@trentonian.ca
Primary Website: www.trentonian.ca
Own Printing Facility?: Y
Commercial printers?: Y
Published: Thur
Avg Free Circ: 15084
Audit By: CMCA
Audit Date: 30.06.2016
Personnel: John Knowles (Pub.); Rachel Henry (Adv. Mgr.); Tim Devine (Circ. Mgr.); Ross Lees (Mng. Ed.); Sherin Tyson (Prodn. Mgr.)
Parent company (for newspapers): Postmedia Network Inc.; Quebecor Communications, Inc.

TROIS-RIVIERES

L'ECHO DE TROIS-RIVIERES

Street Address: 3625 Blvd Du Chanoine-moreau ,
Province: QC
Postal: G8Y 5N6
Country: Canada
Mailing address: 9085, boul. Lacroix
Mailing city: Saint-Georges
Province: QC
Postal: G5Y 2B4
General Phone: (819) 371-4823
General Fax: (819) 371-4804
Advertising Phone: (819) 371-4823
Advertising Fax: (819) 371-4804
Editorial Phone: (819) 371-4823
Editorial Fax: (819) 371-4804
General/National Adv. E-mail: serge.buchanan@quebecormedia.com
Display Adv. E-mail: jocelyn.ouellet@quebecormedia.com
Editorial e-mail: serge.buchanan@quebecormedia.com
Primary Website: www.lechodetroisrivieres.ca
Delivery Methods: Mail`Racks
Areas Served - City/County or Portion Thereof, or Zip codes: Canada
Published: Wed
Avg Free Circ: 68580
Audit By: CCAB
Audit Date: 31.03.2014
Personnel: Serge Buchanan (Ed.)

L'HEBDO JOURNAL

Street Address: 525 Barkoff St., Ste. 205 , Bureau 205
Province: QC
Postal: G8T 2A5
Country: Canada
Mailing address: 525 Barkoff St., Ste. 205
Mailing city: Trois-Rivieres
Province: QC
Postal: G8T 2A5
General Phone: (819) 379-1490
General Fax: (819) 379-0705
Advertising Phone: (866) 637-5236
Display Adv. E-mail: publicite.hj@transcontinental.ca
Editorial e-mail: redaction.hj@transcontinental.ca
Primary Website: www.lhebdojournal.com
Year Established: 1967
Areas Served - City/County or Portion Thereof, or Zip codes: Canada
Published: Wed
Avg Paid Circ: 30
Avg Free Circ: 60411
Audit By: CCAB
Audit Date: 31.03.2014
Personnel: Alain Bernard (Sales Mgr.); Sylviane Lussier (Pub.); Emilie Valley (Ed.)
Parent company (for newspapers): Transcontinental Media

TUMBLER RIDGE

TUMBLER RIDGE NEWS

Street Address: 230 Mains Street ,
Province: BC
Postal: V0C 2W0
Country: Canada
Mailing address: PO Box 620
Mailing city: Tumbler Ridge
Province: BC
Postal: V0C 2W0
General Phone: (250) 242-5343
General Fax: (250) 242-5340
General/National Adv. E-mail: mail@tumblerridgenews.com
Display Adv. E-mail: advertising@tumblerridgenews.com
Editorial e-mail: editor@tumblerridgenews.com
Primary Website: www.tumblerridgenews.com
Year Established: 1997
Delivery Methods: Mail`Newsstand`Carrier
Areas Served - City/County or Portion Thereof, or Zip codes: Tumbler Ridge
Mechanical specifications: 10.25" x 16" - 8 columns Please email for rate sheet. We accept pdf, jpg, tif and word.
Published: Thur
Published Other: on line on Tuesdays
Avg Paid Circ: 2
Avg Free Circ: 1179
Audit By: VAC
Audit Date: 31.12.2015
Personnel: Loraine Funk (Owner); Trent Ernst (Pub/Ed.); Lisa Allen (Sales Mgr)

TWEED

THE TWEED NEWS

Street Address: 242 Victoria St. N. ,
Province: ON
Postal: K0K 3J0
Country: Canada
Mailing address: PO Box 550
Mailing city: Tweed
Province: ON
Postal: K0K 3J0
General Phone: (613) 478-2017
General Fax: (613) 478-2749
Advertising Phone: (613) 478-2699
Advertising Fax: (613) 478-2749
Editorial Phone: (613) 478-2017
Editorial Fax: (613) 478-2749
General/National Adv. E-mail: info@thetweednews.ca
Display Adv. E-mail: info@thetweednews.ca
Classified Adv. e-mail: info@thetweednews.ca
Editorial e-mail: info@thetweednews.ca
Primary Website: www.thetweednews.ca
Year Established: 1887
Delivery Methods: Mail`Racks
Areas Served - City/County or Portion Thereof, or Zip codes: Municpality of Tweed
Own Printing Facility?: Y
Commercial printers?: Y
Mechanical specifications: Type page 12 3/4 x 21; E - 6 cols, 2, 1/4 between; A - 6 cols, 2, 1/4 between; C - 6 cols, 2, 1/4 between.
Published: Wed
Avg Paid Circ: 8722
Avg Free Circ: 42
Audit By: CMCA
Audit Date: 26.11.2018
Personnel: Roseann Trudeau (Circ. Mgr.); Rodger Hanna (Ed./Pub.)

UCLUELET

WESTERLY NEWS

Street Address: 102-1801 Bay Street ,
Province: BC
Postal: V0R 3A0
Country: Canada
Mailing address: PO Box 317
Mailing city: Ucluelet
Province: BC
Postal: V0R 3A0
General Phone: (250) 726-7029

General Fax: (250) 726-4282
General/National Adv. E-mail: office@westerlynews.ca
Display Adv. E-mail: office@westerlynews.ca
Editorial e-mail: andrew.bailey@westerlynews.ca
Primary Website: www.westerlynews.ca
Year Established: 1987
Delivery Methods: Mail`Newsstand`Racks
Areas Served - City/County or Portion Thereof, or Zip codes: V0R 3A0, V0R 2Z0
Published: Wed
Avg Paid Circ: 7
Avg Free Circ: 0
Audit By: Sworn/Estimate/Non-Audited
Audit Date: 12.07.2019
Personnel: Andrew Bailey (Ed); Peter McCully (Pub); Nora O'Malley
Parent company (for newspapers): Black Press Group Ltd.

UNITY

UNITY-WILKIE PRESS-HERALD

Street Address: 310 Main St. ,
Province: SK
Postal: S0K 4L0
Country: Canada
Mailing address: PO Box 309
Mailing city: Unity
Province: SK
Postal: S0K 4L0
General Phone: (306) 228-2267
General Fax: (306) 228-2767
General/National Adv. E-mail: northwest.herald@sasktel.net
Display Adv. E-mail: ads.northwest.herald@sasktel.net
Editorial e-mail: northwest.herald@sasktel.net
Primary Website: http://unitystories.com/press-herald/
Delivery Methods: Mail`Newsstand
Areas Served - City/County or Portion Thereof, or Zip codes: Canada
Mechanical specifications: Type page 10 1/12 x 16; E - 5 cols, 1 11/12, 1/6 between; A - 5 cols, 1 11/12, 1/6 between; C - 5 cols, 1 11/12, 1/6 between.
Published: Fri
Avg Paid Circ: 1400
Avg Free Circ: 0
Audit By: Sworn/Estimate/Non-Audited
Audit Date: 12.07.2019
Personnel: Helena Long (Ed.); Jackie Boser (Office Manager); Tim Holtorf (ad designer)
Parent company (for newspapers): Prairie Newspaper Group

UXBRIDGE

UXBRIDGE TIMES-JOURNAL

Street Address: 16 Bascom St. ,
Province: ON
Postal: L9P 1J3
Country: Canada
Mailing address: PO Box 459
Mailing city: Uxbridge
Province: ON
Postal: L9P 19
General Phone: (905) 852-9141
General Fax: (905) 852-9341
Primary Website: www.durhamregion.com
Year Established: 1869
Areas Served - City/County or Portion Thereof, or Zip codes: Canada
Own Printing Facility?: Y
Commercial printers?: Y
Published: Thur
Avg Paid Circ: 0
Avg Free Circ: 8803
Audit By: CCAB
Audit Date: 15.11.2017
Personnel: Tim Whittaker (Pub.); Judy Pirone (Adv. Mgr.); Joanne Burghardt (Ed. in Chief); Judi Bobbitt (Ed.)
Parent company (for newspapers): Metroland Media Group Ltd.; Torstar

VAL D'OR

ABITIBI EXPRESS VAL D'OR

Street Address: 1834 3rd Ave. 2nd Floor ,
Province: QC
Postal: J9P 7A9
Country: Canada
Mailing address: 1834 3rd Ave. 2nd Floor
Mailing city: Val d'Or
Province: QC
Postal: J9P 7A9
General Phone: (819) 874-2151
General/National Adv. E-mail: redaction.abitibi@tc.tc
Primary Website: www.abitibiexpress.ca
Areas Served - City/County or Portion Thereof, or Zip codes: Canada
Published: Tues
Avg Paid Circ: 22
Avg Free Circ: 31088
Audit By: CCAB
Audit Date: 31.03.2014

LE CITOYEN DE LA VALLEE DE L'OR

Street Address: 1462 Rue De La Quebecoise ,
Province: QC
Postal: J9P 5H4
Country: Canada
Mailing address: 1462 Rue de la Quebecoise
Mailing city: Val d'Or
Province: QC
Postal: J9P 5H4
General Phone: (819) 874-4545
General Fax: (819) 874-4547
General/National Adv. E-mail: citoyens@cablevision.qc.ca
Primary Website: http://www.lechoabitibien.ca/
Areas Served - City/County or Portion Thereof, or Zip codes: Canada
Published: Wed
Avg Paid Circ: 36
Avg Free Circ: 19883
Audit By: CCAB
Audit Date: 31.03.2014
Personnel: Endre Renaud (Gen. Mgr.); Carroline Couture (Adv. Mgr.); Louis Lavoie (Mng. Ed.)
Parent company (for newspapers): Quebecor Communications, Inc.

VALEMOUNT

THE VALLEY SENTINEL

Street Address: 1418 Bruce Place ,
Province: BC
Postal: V0E 2Z0
Country: Canada
Mailing address: PO Box 688
Mailing city: Valemount
Province: BC
Postal: V0E 2Z0
General Phone: (250) 566-4425
General Fax: (250) 566-4528
General/National Adv. E-mail: insertions@thevallysentinel.com
Display Adv. E-mail: ads@valley-sentinel.com
Editorial e-mail: articles@valley-sentinel.com
Primary Website: www.thevalleysentinel.com
Year Established: 1986
Delivery Methods: Mail
Areas Served - City/County or Portion Thereof, or Zip codes: V0E, V0J
Own Printing Facility?: Y
Commercial printers?: Y
Published: Thur
Avg Paid Circ: 385
Avg Free Circ: 13
Audit By: VAC
Audit Date: 31.12.2015
Personnel: Deanna Mickelow (Ad Sales); Joshua Estabroks (Pub.)
Parent company (for newspapers): Aberdeen Publishing

VANCOUVER

GEORGIA STRAIGHT

Street Address: 1635 West Broadway ,
Province: BC
Postal: V6J 1W9
Country: Canada
General Phone: (604) 730-7000
General Fax: (604) 730-7010
General/National Adv. E-mail: gs.info@straight.com
Display Adv. E-mail: sales@straight.com
Editorial e-mail: contact@straight.com
Primary Website: www.straight.com
Year Established: 1967
Delivery Methods: Mail`Newsstand`Racks
Areas Served - City/County or Portion Thereof, or Zip codes: Metro Vancouver, British Columbia
Mechanical specifications: Type page 10 3/16 x 15 1/2.
Published: Thur
Avg Paid Circ: 25
Avg Free Circ: 81544
Audit By: VAC
Audit Date: 30.06.2017
Personnel: Tara Lalanne (Sales Director); Dexter Vosper (Circulation Manager); Dennis Jangula (IT Director); Charlie Smith (Editor)
Parent company (for newspapers): Vancouver Free Press Publishing Corp.

THE FALSE CREEK NEWS

Street Address: 661 A Market Hill ,
Province: BC
Postal: V5Z 4B5
Country: Canada
Mailing address: 661 A Market Hill
Mailing city: Vancouver
Province: BC
Postal: V5Z 4B5
General Phone: (604) 875-9626
General Fax: (604) 875-0336
General/National Adv. E-mail: news@thefalsecreeknews.com
Display Adv. E-mail: adsales@thefalsecreeknews.com
Editorial e-mail: mail@thefalsecreeknews.com
Primary Website: www.thefalsecreeknews.com
Mechanical specifications: Type page 7 1/2 x 9 1/2; E - 5 cols, 1 1/2, 1/8 between; A - 5 cols, 1 1/2, 1/8 between.
Published: Fri
Avg Paid Circ: 25000
Audit By: Sworn/Estimate/Non-Audited
Audit Date: 12.07.2019
Personnel: M. Juma (Adv. Sales); Stephen Bowell (Mng. Ed.)

THE VANCOUVER COURIER

Street Address: 303 West 5th Ave ,
Province: BC
Postal: V5Y 1J6
Country: Canada
Mailing address: 303 West 5th Ave
Mailing city: Vancouver
Province: BC
Postal: V5Y 1J6
General Phone: (604) 738-1411
General Fax: (604) 731-1474
Display Adv. E-mail: mbhatti@vancourier.com
Editorial e-mail: mperkins@vancourier.com
Primary Website: vancourier.com
Areas Served - City/County or Portion Thereof, or Zip codes: Canada
Commercial printers?: Y
Mechanical specifications: Type page 10 x 15; E - 6 cols, between; A - 6 cols, between; C - 7 cols, between.
Published: Wed`Fri
Avg Paid Circ: 0
Avg Free Circ: 106402
Audit By: CCAB
Audit Date: 22.11.2017
Personnel: Alvin Brouwer (Pub); Martha Perkins (Ed); Michelle Bhatti (Mktg Dir)
Parent company (for newspapers): Glacier Media Group; CanWest MediaWorks Publications, Inc.

THE WESTENDER

Street Address: 303 West 5th Ave ,
Province: BC
Postal: V5Y 1J6
Country: Canada
Mailing address: 205-1525 West 8th Ave
Mailing city: Vancouver
Province: V5Y 1J6
Postal: V5Y 1J6
General Phone: (604) 742-8686
Display Adv. E-mail: matty@westender.com
Editorial e-mail: editor@westender.com
Primary Website: http://www.westender.com/
Areas Served - City/County or Portion Thereof, or Zip codes: Canada
Published: Thur
Avg Paid Circ: 0
Avg Free Circ: 23887
Audit By: CCAB
Audit Date: 30.09.2017
Personnel: Gail Nugent (Pub); Kelsey Klassen (Ed); Miguel Black (Circ Mgr)
Parent company (for newspapers): Glacier Media Group

WE VANCOUVER WEEKLY

Street Address: 303 West 5th Ave ,
Province: BC
Postal: V5Y 1J6
Country: Canada
Mailing address: 303 West 5th Ave
Mailing city: Vancouver
Province: BC
Postal: V5Y 1J6
General Phone: (604) 742-8686
General Fax: (604) 606-8687
Advertising Phone: (604) 742-8677
General/National Adv. E-mail: publisher@wevancouver.com
Display Adv. E-mail: matty@westender.com
Editorial e-mail: editor@westender.com
Primary Website: www.wevancouver.com
Delivery Methods: Newsstand`Carrier`Racks
Areas Served - City/County or Portion Thereof, or Zip codes: All of Vancouver
Commercial printers?: Y
Mechanical specifications: Type page 10 3/8" wide x 14" tall
Published: Thur
Avg Paid Circ: 0
Avg Free Circ: 53671
Audit By: CMCA
Audit Date: 30.11.2013
Personnel: Gail Nugent (Pub); Kelsey Klassen (Ed); Miguel Black (Circ. Mgr.)

VANDERHOOF

VANDERHOOF OMINECA EXPRESS

Street Address: 150 W. Columbia ,
Province: BC
Postal: V0J 3A0
Country: Canada
Mailing address: PO Box 1007
Mailing city: Vanderhoof
Province: BC
Postal: V0J 3A0
General Phone: (250) 567-9258
General Fax: (250) 567-2070
General/National Adv. E-mail: newsroom@ominecaexpress.com
Display Adv. E-mail: publisher@ominecaexpress.com
Editorial e-mail: newsroom@ominecaexpress.com
Primary Website: www.ominecaexpress.com
Year Established: 1978
Areas Served - City/County or Portion Thereof, or Zip codes: Vanderhoof
Commercial printers?: Y
Mechanical specifications: Type page 10 5/16 x 14 1/2; E - 6 cols, 1 9/16, 3/16 between; A - 6 cols, 1 9/16, 3/16 between; C - 6 cols, 1 9/16, 3/16 between.
Published: Wed

Non-Daily Newspapers in Canada

Avg Paid Circ: 998
Avg Free Circ: 52
Audit By: VAC
Audit Date: 30.06.2016
Personnel: Pam Berger (Pub./Sales Mgr); Vivian Chui (Ed); Denise Smith (Office/Sales/Circ)
Parent company (for newspapers): Black Press Group Ltd.

VANKLEEK HILL

THE REVIEW

Street Address: 76 Main St. E. ,
Province: ON
Postal: K0B 1R0
Country: Canada
Mailing address: PO Box 160
Mailing city: Vankleek Hill
Province: ON
Postal: K0B 1R0
General Phone: (613) 678-3327
General Fax: (613) 937-2591
Advertising Fax: (613) 937-2591
Editorial Fax: (613) 937-2591
General/National Adv. E-mail: review@thereview.ca
Display Adv. E-mail: ads@thereview.ca
Classified Adv. e-mail: classifieds@thereview.ca
Editorial e-mail: editor@thereview.ca
Primary Website: www.thereview.ca
Year Established: 1893
Delivery Methods: Mail`Newsstand
Areas Served - City/County or Portion Thereof, or Zip codes: Champlain Township
Mechanical specifications: Type page 15 x 22 3/4; E - 8 cols, 1 1/2, 3/8 between; A - 8 cols, 1 1/2, 3/8 between; C - 8 cols, 1 1/2, 3/8 between.
Published: Wed
Avg Paid Circ: 2785
Avg Free Circ: 727
Audit By: CMCA
Audit Date: 30.06.2016
Personnel: Irene Sensyzcyzn (Classified Adv. Mgr.); Louise Sproule (Ed.); Suzanne Tessier (Prodn. Mgr.); Diane Duval (Accounts); Shirley Shuberynski (Advertising Sales); Theresa Ketterling (Reporters/Photographer); Tara Kirkpatrick (Advertising Sales); Sharon Graves-McRae (Website Designer); Dorothy Hodge (Graphic Designer)

VAUDREUIL-DORION

ETOILE DE L'OUTAOUAIS ST LAURENT

Street Address: Avenue St-charles ,
Province: QC
Postal: J7V 2N4
Country: Canada
Mailing address: avenue St-Charles
Mailing city: Vaudreuil-Dorion
Province: QC
Postal: J7V 2N4
General Phone: (450) 455-6111
Published: Sat
Avg Paid Circ: 28
Avg Free Circ: 56711
Audit By: ODC
Audit Date: 14.12.2011
Personnel: Angele Marcoux Prevost

JOURNAL PREMIERE EDITION

Street Address: 469 St. Charles Ave. ,
Province: QC
Postal: J7V 2N4
Country: Canada
Mailing address: 469 St. Charles Ave.
Mailing city: Vaudreuil-Dorion
Province: QC
Postal: J7V 2N4
General Phone: (450) 455-7955
General Fax: (450) 455-3028
Advertising Phone: (450) 455-1050
Advertising Fax: (450) 455-1050

General/National Adv. E-mail: webmestre@hebdosdusuroit.com
Primary Website: www.journalpremiereedition.com
Areas Served - City/County or Portion Thereof, or Zip codes: Canada
Published: Sat
Avg Paid Circ: 7
Avg Free Circ: 61880
Audit By: CCAB
Audit Date: 30.09.2015

VAUGHAN

VAUGHAN CITIZEN

Street Address: 8611 Weston Rd Unit 29 ,
Province: ON
Postal: L4L 9P1
Country: Canada
Mailing address: 8611 Weston Rd Unit 29
Mailing city: Vaughan
Province: ON
Postal: L4L 9P1
General Phone: (905) 264-8703
General Fax: (905) 264-9453
Advertising Phone: (905) 264-8703
Advertising Fax: (905) 264-9453
Editorial Phone: (905) 264-8703
Editorial Fax: (905) 264-9453
General/National Adv. E-mail: john.willems@metroland.com
Display Adv. E-mail: gpaolucci@yrmg.com
Editorial e-mail: dkelly@yrmg.com
Primary Website: yorkregion.com
Delivery Methods: Mail`Racks
Areas Served - City/County or Portion Thereof, or Zip codes: Maple, Woodbridge, Concord, and Kleinburg
Published: Thur
Avg Free Circ: 57677
Audit By: CCAB
Audit Date: 20.12.2017
Personnel: Ian Proudfoot (Vice Pres./Reg. Pub.); Debora Kelly (Ed. in Chief); John Willems (Reg. Gen. Mgr.)
Parent company (for newspapers): Metroland Media Group Ltd.

VAUXHALL

VAUXHALL ADVANCE

Street Address: 516 2nd Ave. N. ,
Province: AB
Postal: T0K 2K0
Country: Canada
Mailing address: P.O. Box 302
Mailing city: Vauxhall
Province: AB
Postal: T0K 2K0
General Phone: (403) 654-2122
General Fax: (403) 654-4184
Display Adv. E-mail: tabads@tabertimes.com
Primary Website: www.vauxhalladvance.com
Year Established: 1978
Delivery Methods: Mail
Areas Served - City/County or Portion Thereof, or Zip codes: Town of VAuxhall and hamlets of Hays and Enchant
Mechanical specifications: Type page 10 1/4 x 14 1/2; E - 6 cols, 1 5/8, 1/8 between; A - 6 cols, 1 5/8, 1/8 between; C - 6 cols, 1 5/8, 1/8 between.
Published: Thur
Avg Paid Circ: 0
Avg Free Circ: 47
Audit By: VAC
Audit Date: 30.09.2016
Personnel: Greg Price (Ed.); Valorie Wiebe (Pub.); Shawna Wiestm (Office/Sales)

VERMILION

VERMILION STANDARD

Street Address: 4917 50th Ave. ,
Province: AB
Postal: T9X 1A6
Country: Canada

General Phone: (780) 853-5344
General Fax: (780) 853-5203
Advertising Phone: (877) 786-8227
Display Adv. E-mail: ngoetz@postmedia.com
Classified Adv. e-mail: ngoetz@postmedia.com
Editorial e-mail: thermiston@postmedia.com
Primary Website: www.vermilionstandard.com
Year Established: 1909
Delivery Methods: Mail`Newsstand`Carrier`Racks
Areas Served - City/County or Portion Thereof, or Zip codes: T9X
Published: Wed
Avg Paid Circ: 1250
Avg Free Circ: 3972
Audit By: VAC
Audit Date: 31.12.2015
Personnel: Trina de Regt (Circulation); Mary-Ann Kostiuk (Publisher); Pat Lavigne (Production and Circulation); Nicki Goetz (Dir. of Adv.); Taylor Hermiston (Reg. Mng. Ed. ext.4)
Parent company (for newspapers): Postmedia Network Inc.

VERMILION VOICE

Street Address: 5006-50th Ave. ,
Province: AB
Postal: T9X 1A2
Country: Canada
Mailing address: 5006-50th Ave
Mailing city: Vermilion
Province: AB
Postal: T9X 1A2
General Phone: 7808536305
General Fax: (780) 853-5426
General/National Adv. E-mail: vermilionvoice@gmail.com
Display Adv. E-mail: vermilionvoice@gmail.com
Classified Adv. e-mail: vermilionvoice@gmail.com
Editorial e-mail: vermilionvoice@gmail.com
Primary Website: www.vermilionvoice.com
Year Established: 2004
Delivery Methods: Newsstand`Racks
Areas Served - City/County or Portion Thereof, or Zip codes: Canada
Published: Tues
Avg Paid Circ: 5500
Audit By: CMCA
Audit Date: 30.06.2018
Personnel: Susan Chikie (Pub.); Lorna Hamilton (Sales, reporter, newspaper layout); Angela Mouley (Reporter and Sales); Amr Rezk (Graphics, website etc.)

VERNON

THE MORNING STAR

Street Address: 4407 25th Ave. ,
Province: BC
Postal: V1T 1P5
Country: Canada
Mailing address: 4407 25th Ave.
Mailing city: Vernon
Province: BC
Postal: V1T 1P5
General Phone: (250) 545-3322
General Fax: (250) 542-1510
Display Adv. E-mail: stephanie@vernonmorningstar.com
Classified Adv. E-mail: Classifieds@vernonmorningstar.com
Editorial e-mail: glenn@vernonmorningstar.com
Primary Website: www.vernonmorningstar.com
Year Established: 1988
Areas Served - City/County or Portion Thereof, or Zip codes: Canada
Own Printing Facility?: Y
Mechanical specifications: Type page 10 5/16 x 14 1/2; E - 6 cols, 1 9/16, 1/4 between; A - 6 cols, 1 9/16, 1/4 between; C - 7 cols, 1 3/8, 3/16 between.
Published: Wed`Fri`Sun
Avg Paid Circ: 29884
Audit By: AAM
Audit Date: 30.09.2016
Personnel: Tammy Stelmachowich (Circ. Mgr.); Glenn Mitchell (Mng. Ed.); Ian Jensen

(Pub.); Carol Williment (Class. Mgr.)
Parent company (for newspapers): Torstar

VERNON MORNING STAR

Street Address: 4407 25th Avenue ,
Province: BC
Postal: V1T 1P5
Country: British Columbia
Mailing address: 2495 Enterprise Way
Mailing city: Kelowna
Province: BC
Postal: V1X 7K2
General Phone: (250) 545-3322
General Fax: (250) 862-5275
Display Adv. E-mail: karen.hill@blackpress.ca
Classified Adv. e-mail: bcclassifieds@blackpress.ca
Editorial e-mail: editor@vernonmorningstar.com
Primary Website: vernonmorningstar.com
Areas Served - City/County or Portion Thereof, or Zip codes: Vernon
Published: Wed`Fri
Avg Free Circ: 28286
Audit By: AAM
Audit Date: 31.03.2019
Personnel: Dave Hamilton (Pres.); Karen Hill (Adv. Dir.)
Parent company (for newspapers): Black Press Group Ltd.

OAK BAY NEWS

Street Address: 207a-2187 Oak Bay Avenue ,
Province: BC
Postal: V8R 1G1
Country: Canada
Mailing address: 207A-2187 Oak Bay Avenue
Mailing city: Victoria
Province: BC
Postal: V8R 1G1
General Phone: (250) 480-3251
Advertising Phone: (250) 480-3251
Editorial Phone: (250) 480-3260
Display Adv. E-mail: jgairdner@blackpress.ca
Classified Adv. e-mail: bcclassifieds@blackpress.ca
Editorial e-mail: editor@oakbaynews.com
Primary Website: www.oakbaynews.com
Year Established: 1974
Delivery Methods: Carrier
Areas Served - City/County or Portion Thereof, or Zip codes: Canada
Own Printing Facility?: Y
Published: Wed`Fri
Avg Paid Circ: 0
Avg Free Circ: 5995
Audit By: AAM
Audit Date: 31.03.2019
Personnel: Janet Gairdner (Pub.); Christine van Reeuwyk (Editor); Lyn Quan (Prod.); John Stewart (Advertising Consultant); Keri Coles (Multimedia Journalist)
Parent company (for newspapers): Black Press Group Ltd.

SAANICH NEWS

Street Address: 104b-3550 Saanich Road ,
Province: BC
Postal: V8X 1X2
Country: Canada
Mailing address: 104B-3550 Saanich Road
Mailing city: Victoria
Province: BC
Postal: V8X 1X2
General Phone: (250) 381-3484
General Fax: (250) 386-2624
Display Adv. E-mail: staylor@saanichnews.com
Classified Adv. e-mail: rod.fraser@saanichnews.com
Editorial e-mail: editor@saanichnews.com
Primary Website: www.saanichnews.com
Areas Served - City/County or Portion Thereof, or Zip codes: Canada
Published: Wed`Fri
Avg Free Circ: 30360
Audit By: AAM

Audit Date: 31.03.2019
Personnel: Rod Fraser (Sales); Oliver Sommer (Pub); Dan Ebenal (Ed); Miki Speirs (Circ Mgr); Sarah Taylor (Sales)
Parent company (for newspapers): Black Press Group Ltd.

VICTORIA NEWS
Street Address: 818 Broughton St. ,
Province: BC
Postal: V8W 1E4
Country: Canada
Mailing address: 818 Broughton St.
Mailing city: Victoria
Province: BC
Postal: V8W 1E4
General Phone: (250) 381-3484
General Fax: (250) 386-2624
Display Adv. E-mail: michelle.cabana@goldstreamgazette.com
Editorial e-mail: michelle.cabana@goldstreamgazette.com
Primary Website: vicnews.com
Areas Served - City/County or Portion Thereof, or Zip codes: Canada
Own Printing Facility?: Y
Commercial printers?: Y
Mechanical specifications: Type page 10 1/4 x 14 1/2; E - 5 cols, 1 1/2, 1/6 between; A - 6 cols, 1 1/2, 1/6 between; C - 8 cols, 1 1/4, 1/6 between.
Published: Wed`Fri
Avg Free Circ: 24056
Audit By: AAM
Audit Date: 31.03.2019
Personnel: Mike Cowan (Pub); Pamela Roth (Ed); Michelle Cabana (Pub.)
Parent company (for newspapers): Black Press Group Ltd.

VICTORIAVILLE

LA NOUVELLE
Street Address: 43 Notre Dame St. E., Cp 130 ,
Province: QC
Postal: G6P 3Z4
Country: Canada
Mailing address: PO Box 130
Mailing city: Victoriaville
Province: QC
Postal: G6P 3Z4
General Phone: (819) 758-6211
General Fax: (819) 758-2759
General/National Adv. E-mail: redaction_victo@transcontinental.ca
Primary Website: www.lanouvelle.net
Own Printing Facility?: Y
Commercial printers?: Y
Published: Sun
Avg Free Circ: 44008
Audit By: Sworn/Estimate/Non-Audited
Audit Date: 12.07.2019
Personnel: Pierre Gaudet (Sales Dir.); Michel Gauthier (Pub.); Ghislain Chauvette (Director de l'information); Sylvie Cote (Mng. Ed.); Danielle Deveault (Prodn. Mgr.)
Parent company (for newspapers): Transcontinental Media

L'ECHO DE VICTORIAVILLE
Street Address: 106 Blvd Bois-francs Nord ,
Province: QC
Postal: G6P 1E7
Country: Canada
Mailing address: 106 Blvd Bois-Francs Nord
Mailing city: Victoriaville
Province: QC
Postal: G6P 1E7
General Phone: (819) 604-6286
General Fax: (819) 604-6398
Advertising Phone: (819) 604-6286
Advertising Fax: (819) 604-6398
Editorial Phone: (819) 604-6286
Editorial Fax: (819) 604-6398
General/National Adv. E-mail: jean.crepeau@quebecormedia.com
Display Adv. E-mail: alain.saint-amand@quebecormedia.com
Editorial e-mail: jean.crepeau@quebecormedia.com
Primary Website: www.lechodevictoriaville.ca
Delivery Methods: Mail`Racks
Areas Served - City/County or Portion Thereof, or Zip codes: Canada
Published: Wed
Avg Free Circ: 42844
Audit By: CCAB
Audit Date: 31.03.2014
Personnel: Jean Crepeau (Ed.)

NOUVELLE UNION
Street Address: Rue Notre-dame Est ,
Province: QC
Postal: G6P 3Z4
Country: Canada
Mailing address: rue Notre-Dame Est
Mailing city: Victoriaville
Province: QC
Postal: G6P 3Z4
General Phone: (819) 758-6211
Areas Served - City/County or Portion Thereof, or Zip codes: Canada
Published: Wed`Fri
Avg Paid Circ: 13
Avg Free Circ: 38872
Audit By: CCAB
Audit Date: 31.03.2014
Personnel: Lucie Lecours

VIKING

THE WEEKLY REVIEW
Street Address: 5208 50th Street ,
Province: AB
Postal: T0B 4N0
Country: Canada
Mailing address: PO Box 240
Mailing city: Viking
Province: AB
Postal: T0B 4N0
General Phone: (780) 336-3422
General Fax: (780) 336-3223
General/National Adv. E-mail: vikingweeklyreview@gmail.com
Display Adv. E-mail: vikingreview@gmail.com
Editorial e-mail: vikingweeklyreview@gmail.com
Primary Website: www.weeklyreview.ca
Year Established: 1977
Areas Served - City/County or Portion Thereof, or Zip codes: Beaver County, Viking, Alberta T0B 4N0
Published: Tues
Avg Paid Circ: 0
Avg Free Circ: 10
Audit By: VAC
Audit Date: 30.06.2016
Personnel: Leslie Cholowsky (Ed.); Eric Anderson (Pub.); Kerry Anderson (Owner)
Parent company (for newspapers): Caribou Publishing

VILLE-MARIE

LE JOURNAL TEMISCAMIEN
Street Address: 22 Rue Ste-anne ,
Province: QC
Postal: J9V 2B7
Country: Canada
Mailing address: 22 rue Ste-Anne
Mailing city: Ville-Marie
Province: QC
Postal: J9Z 2B7
General Phone: (819) 622-1313
General Fax: (819) 622-1333
Published: Wed
Avg Free Circ: 8500
Audit By: Sworn/Estimate/Non-Audited
Audit Date: 12.07.2019
Personnel: Lionel Lacasse (Ed.)

VIRDEN

VIRDEN EMPIRE-ADVANCE
Street Address: 305 Nelson Street West ,
Province: MB
Postal: R0M 2C0
Country: Canada
Mailing address: PO Box 250
Mailing city: Virden
Province: MB
Postal: R0M 2C0
General Phone: (204) 748-3931
General Fax: (204) 748-1816
General/National Adv. E-mail: trehernetimes@mts.net
Display Adv. E-mail: virden@empireadvance.ca
Editorial e-mail: manager@empireadvance.ca
Primary Website: http://www.empireadvance.ca/
Areas Served - City/County or Portion Thereof, or Zip codes: Canada
Own Printing Facility?: Y
Commercial printers?: Y
Mechanical specifications: Type page 10 1/4 x 15 3/4; E - 6 cols, 1 7/12, 1/6 between; A - 6 cols, 1 7/12, 1/6 between; C - 6 cols, 1 7/12, 1/6 between.
Published: Fri
Avg Free Circ: 27
Audit By: VAC
Audit Date: 30.09.2016
Personnel: Cheryl Rushing (Gen Mgr)
Parent company (for newspapers): Glacier Media Group

VIRGIL

THE NIAGARA ADVANCE
Street Address: 1501 Niagara Stone Rd. ,
Province: ON
Postal: L0S 1T0
Country: Canada
Mailing address: PO Box 430
Mailing city: Virgil
Province: ON
Postal: L0S 1T0
General Phone: (905) 468-3283
General Fax: (905) 468-3137
General/National Adv. E-mail: tim.dundas@sunmedia.ca
Primary Website: www.niagaraadvance.ca
Year Established: 1917
Delivery Methods: Carrier
Areas Served - City/County or Portion Thereof, or Zip codes: Canada
Own Printing Facility?: Y
Commercial printers?: Y
Published: Thur
Avg Paid Circ: 20
Avg Free Circ: 7610
Audit By: CMCA
Audit Date: 31.05.2016
Personnel: Tim Dundas (Pub.); Penny Coles (Ed.)
Parent company (for newspapers): Postmedia Network Inc.; Quebecor Communications, Inc.

VULCAN

VULCAN ADVOCATE
Street Address: 112 - 3rd Ave. N ,
Province: AB
Postal: T0L 2B0
Country: Canada
Mailing address: PO Box 389
Mailing city: Vulcan
Province: AB
Postal: T0L 2B0
General Phone: (403) 485-2036
General Fax: (403) 485-6938
Advertising Phone: (877) 786-8227
General/National Adv. E-mail: maureen.howard@sunmedia.ca
Display Adv. E-mail: enid.fraser@sunmedia.ca
Classified Adv. e-mail: enid.fraser@sunmedia.ca
Editorial e-mail: stephen.tipper@sunmedia.ca
Primary Website: www.vulcanadvocate.com
Year Established: 1913
Delivery Methods: Mail`Newsstand
Own Printing Facility?: N
Mechanical specifications: Type page 10 1/4 x 15 1/2; E - 6 cols, 1 7/12, between; A - 6 cols, 1 7/12, between; C - 6 cols, 1 7/12, between.
Published: Wed
Avg Paid Circ: 1032
Avg Free Circ: 11
Audit By: CMCA
Audit Date: 31.12.2014
Personnel: Shawn Cornell (Publisher); Stephen Tipper (Editor); Roxanne MacKintosh (Reg. Dir. of Adv.)
Parent company (for newspapers): Postmedia Network Inc.

WABASCA

WABASCA FEVER
Street Address: PO Box 519 ,
Province: AB
Postal: T0G 2K0
Country: Canada
Mailing address: PO Box 519
Mailing city: Wabasca
Province: AB
Postal: T0G 2K0
General Phone: (780) 891-2108
General Fax: (888) 318-555
General/National Adv. E-mail: wabascafever4@shaw.ca
Display Adv. E-mail: wabascafever@shaw.ca
Classified Adv. e-mail: wabascafever@shaw.ca
Editorial e-mail: wabascafever@shaw.ca
Primary Website: www.fevernewspaper.com
Year Established: 1998
Delivery Methods: Mail`Newsstand
Areas Served - City/County or Portion Thereof, or Zip codes: Municipal District of Opportunity No. 17
Published: Thur
Avg Paid Circ: 630
Avg Free Circ: 200
Audit By: Sworn/Estimate/Non-Audited
Audit Date: 12.07.2019
Personnel: Patricia Thomas; Bruce Thomas (Pub.)
Parent company (for newspapers): Title

WADENA

WADENA NEWS
Street Address: 102 First St Ne ,
Province: SK
Postal: S0A 4J0
Country: Canada
Mailing address: PO Box 100
Mailing city: Wadena
Province: SK
Postal: S0A 4J0
General Phone: (306) 338-2231
General Fax: (306) 338-3421
General/National Adv. E-mail: wadena.news@sasktel.net
Primary Website: http://wadenanews.ca/
Year Established: 1908
Delivery Methods: Mail`Newsstand
Areas Served - City/County or Portion Thereof, or Zip codes: Canada
Own Printing Facility?: Y
Commercial printers?: Y
Mechanical specifications: Type page 10 1/3 x 15 1/2; E - 5 cols, 1 14/15, 1/6 between; A - 5 cols, 1 14/15, 1/6 between; C - 5 cols, 1 14/15, 1/6 between.
Published: Mon
Avg Paid Circ: 1649
Avg Free Circ: 80
Audit By: Sworn/Estimate/Non-Audited
Audit Date: 12.07.2019
Personnel: Alison Squires (Pub.)

Non-Daily Newspapers in Canada

WAINWRIGHT
WAINWRIGHT STAR EDGE
Street Address: 1027 3rd Ave ,
Province: AB
Postal: T9W 1T6
Country: Canada
Mailing address: 1027 3rd Avenue
Mailing city: Wainwright
Province: AB
Postal: T9W 1T6
General Phone: (780) 842-4465
General Fax: (780) 842-2760
Advertising Phone: (780) 842-4465 ext.112
General/National Adv. E-mail: classifieds@starnews.ca
Display Adv. E-mail: patrick@starnews.ca
Classified Adv. e-mail: classifieds@starnews.ca
Editorial e-mail: zak@starnews.ca
Primary Website: www.starnews.ca
Year Established: 2002
Delivery Methods: Newsstand`Carrier`Racks
Areas Served - City/County or Portion Thereof, or Zip codes: MD of Wainwright
Mechanical specifications: 8 Columns x 15.25" (10.25" x 15.25")
Published: Fri
Avg Paid Circ: 0
Avg Free Circ: 6500
Audit By: VAC
Audit Date: 6/31/2017
Personnel: Roger Holmes (Pub.); Patrick Moroz (Adv. Sales); Sherry Shatz (Sales & Promo); Zak McLachlan (Editor); Barb Tywoniuk (Graphic Design Dept. Manager)
Parent company (for newspapers): Star News Inc.

WAKAW
THE WAKAW RECORDER
Street Address: 224 First St. S. ,
Province: SK
Postal: S0K 4P0
Country: Canada
Mailing address: PO Box 9
Mailing city: Wakaw
Province: SK
Postal: S0K 4P0
General Phone: (306) 233-4325
General Fax: (306) 233-4386
General/National Adv. E-mail: wrecorder@sasktel.net
Delivery Methods: Mail
Areas Served - City/County or Portion Thereof, or Zip codes: Canada
Published: Wed
Avg Paid Circ: 1375
Avg Free Circ: 14
Audit By: CMCA
Audit Date: 31.03.2016
Personnel: Dwayne Biccum (Ed.)

WAKEFIELD
THE LOW DOWN TO HULL AND BACK NEWS
Street Address: 815 Riverside Drive ,
Province: QC
Postal: J0X 3G0
Country: Canada
Mailing address: 815 Riverside Drive
Mailing city: Wakefield
Province: QC
Postal: J0X 3G0
General Phone: (819) 459-2222
General Fax: (819) 459-3831
Advertising Phone: (613) 241-6767
Editorial Phone: (819) 459-2222
General/National Adv. E-mail: general@lowdownonline.com
Display Adv. E-mail: lowdowndavid1@gmail.com
Classified Adv. e-mail: classifieds@lowdownonline.com
Editorial e-mail: general@lowdownonline.com
Primary Website: www.lowdownonline.com
Year Established: 1973
Delivery Methods: Mail`Newsstand`Racks
Areas Served - City/County or Portion Thereof, or Zip codes: La PÃªche, Quebec
Mechanical specifications: 5 columns 10.4" wide x 15.25" 300 dpi for ads
Published: Wed
Avg Paid Circ: 2531
Audit By: Sworn/Estimate/Non-Audited
Audit Date: 12.07.2019
Personnel: Maya Riel Lachapelle (General Manager); Heather Hopewell (Admin. Asst.); Nikki Mantell (Pub./Owner); Agnes McMillan (Circ. Mgr.); Melanie Scott (Ed.); Hunter Cresswell (Reporter); Nicole McCormick (Reporter)

WALKERTON
WALKERTON HERALD-TIMES
Street Address: 10 Victoria St. N. ,
Province: ON
Postal: N0G 2V0
Country: Canada
Mailing address: PO Box 190
Mailing city: Walkerton
Province: ON
Postal: N0G 2V0
General Phone: (519) 881-1600
General Fax: (519) 881-0276
General/National Adv. E-mail: editor@walkerton.com
Display Adv. E-mail: ads@walkerton.com
Primary Website: www.walkerton.com
Year Established: 1861
Delivery Methods: Mail`Newsstand
Areas Served - City/County or Portion Thereof, or Zip codes: Brockton
Own Printing Facility?: Y
Commercial printers?: Y
Published: Thur
Avg Paid Circ: 1296
Avg Free Circ: 3
Audit By: CMCA
Audit Date: 30.06.2016
Personnel: April Wells (Adv. Sales Mgr.); Cathy Spitzig (Circ. Mgr.); John McPhee (Ed.)
Parent company (for newspapers): Metroland Media Group Ltd.; Torstar

WARMAN
CLARK'S CROSSING GAZETTE
Street Address: 109 Klassen Street West , 109 Klassen Street West
Province: SK
Postal: S0K 4S0
Country: Canada
Mailing address: P.O. Box 1419
Mailing city: Warman
Province: SK
Postal: S0K 4S0
General Phone: (306) 668-0575
General Fax: (306) 668-3997
General/National Adv. E-mail: tjenson@ccgazette.ca
Display Adv. E-mail: ads@ccgazette.ca
Classified Adv. e-mail: ads@ccgazette.ca
Editorial e-mail: editor@ccgazette.ca
Primary Website: http://www.ccgazette.ca
Year Established: 2008
Delivery Methods: Mail`Newsstand`Carrier`Racks
Areas Served - City/County or Portion Thereof, or Zip codes: Corman Park
Mechanical specifications: 6 col. x 212 lines page Tabloid
Published: Thur
Avg Paid Circ: 15
Avg Free Circ: 16500
Audit By: Sworn/Estimate/Non-Audited
Audit Date: 12.07.2019
Personnel: Terry Jenson (Publisher)
Parent company (for newspapers): JENSON PUBLISHING

WASAGA BEACH
THE WASAGA SUN
Street Address: 1456 Mosley St. ,
Province: ON
Postal: L9Z 2B9
Country: Canada
Mailing address: 1456 Mosley St.
Mailing city: Wasaga Beach
Province: ON
Postal: L9Z 2B9
General Phone: (705) 429-1688
General Fax: (705) 422-2446
General/National Adv. E-mail: sunnews@simcoe.com
Primary Website: wasagasun.com
Areas Served - City/County or Portion Thereof, or Zip codes: Wasaga
Mechanical specifications: Type page 11 1/2 x 21 1/2; E - 6 cols, 1 3/4, 1/6 between; A - 6 cols, 1 3/4, 1/6 between; C - 6 cols, 1 3/4, 1/6 between.
Published: Thur
Avg Free Circ: 13241
Audit By: CCAB
Audit Date: 20.12.2017
Personnel: Christine Brown (Adv. Mgr.); Joe Anderson (Pub.); Catherine Haller (Gen. Mgr.); Scott Woodhouse (Ed.); Craig Widdifield (Mng. Ed.); Stephen Hall (Prodn. Mgr.)
Parent company (for newspapers): Metroland Media Group Ltd.

WATERDOWN
THE FLAMBOROUGH REVIEW
Street Address: 30 Main St. N. ,
Province: ON
Postal: L0R 2H0
Country: Canada
Mailing address: PO Box 20
Mailing city: Waterdown
Province: ON
Postal: L0R 2H0
General Phone: (905) 689-2003
General Fax: (905) 689-3110
Advertising Phone: (905) 689-2003 ext. 272
Editorial Phone: (905) 689-2003 ext. 321
General/National Adv. E-mail: classified@haltonsearch.com
Display Adv. E-mail: tlindsay@burlingtonpost.com
Editorial e-mail: editor@flamboroughreview.com
Primary Website: flamboroughreview.com
Year Established: 1918
Delivery Methods: Carrier
Areas Served - City/County or Portion Thereof, or Zip codes: Canada
Own Printing Facility?: Y
Commercial printers?: Y
Published: Thur
Avg Paid Circ: 0
Avg Free Circ: 14075
Audit By: CCAB
Audit Date: 30.09.2017
Personnel: Neil Oliver (Pub.); Ted Lindsay (Adv. Mgr.); Charlene Hall (Circ. Mgr.); Brenda Jefferies (Ed.); Debbi Koppejan (Advertising Director)
Parent company (for newspapers): Metroland Media Group Ltd.; Torstar

WATERLOO
WATERLOO CHRONICLE
Street Address: 279 Weber St. N., Ste. 20 ,
Province: ON
Postal: N2J 3H8
Country: Canada
Mailing address: 279 Weber St. N., Ste. 20
Mailing city: Waterloo
Province: ON
Postal: N2J 3H8
General Phone: (519) 886-2830
General Fax: (519) 886-9383
General/National Adv. E-mail: classified@waterloochronicle.ca
Editorial e-mail: editorial@waterloochronicle.ca
Primary Website: www.waterloochronicle.ca
Mechanical specifications: Type page 10 5/16 x 14 1/4; E - 6 cols, 1 9/16, between; A - 6 cols, 1 9/16, between; C - 8 cols, between.
Published: Thur
Avg Free Circ: 29538
Audit By: CMCA
Audit Date: 31.03.2016
Personnel: Peter Winkler (Pub.); Gerry Mattice (Adv. Mgr., Retail Sales); Bob Vrbanac (Ed.)
Parent company (for newspapers): Metroland Media Group Ltd.; Torstar

WATFORD
WATFORD GUIDE-ADVOCATE
Street Address: 5292 Nauvoo Rd. ,
Province: ON
Postal: N0M 2S0
Country: Canada
Mailing address: PO Box 99
Mailing city: Watford
Province: ON
Postal: N0M 2S0
General Phone: (519) 876-2809
General Fax: (519) 876-2322
General/National Adv. E-mail: guideadvocate@execulink.com
Year Established: 1875
Mechanical specifications: Type page 10 x 16; E - 6 cols, 1 9/16, 1/8 between; A - 6 cols, 1 9/16, 1/8 between; C - 6 cols, 1 9/16, 1/8 between.
Published: Thur
Avg Paid Circ: 1919
Audit By: CMCA
Audit Date: 29.02.2016
Personnel: Dale Hayter (Pub.); Gill Deschutter (Adv. Mgr.); Stephanie Cattryse (Ed.)

WATROUS
THE WATROUS MANITOU
Street Address: 309 Main St. ,
Province: SK
Postal: S0K 4T0
Country: Canada
Mailing address: PO Box 100
Mailing city: Watrous
Province: SK
Postal: S0K 4T0
General Phone: (306) 946-3343
General Fax: (306) 946-2026
General/National Adv. E-mail: watrous.manitou@sasktel.net
Primary Website: www.thewatrousmanitou.com
Year Established: 1933
Delivery Methods: Mail
Areas Served - City/County or Portion Thereof, or Zip codes: Canada
Mechanical specifications: Type page 10 1/4 x 15 3/4; E - 6 cols, 1 15/16, 3/16 between; A - 6 cols, 1 15/16, 3/16 between
Published: Mon
Avg Paid Circ: 1387
Avg Free Circ: 21
Audit By: CMCA
Audit Date: 30.06.2016

WATSON
NAICAM NEWS
Street Address: 100-102 Main St. ,
Province: SK
Postal: S0K 4V0
Country: Canada
Mailing address: PO Box 576
Mailing city: Watson
Province: SK
Postal: S0K 4V0
General Phone: (306) 287-4388
General Fax: (306) 287-3308
General/National Adv. E-mail: ecpress@sasktel.net
Areas Served - City/County or Portion Thereof, or Zip

codes: Canada
Mechanical specifications: Type page 10 1/4 x 15 3/4; E - 5 cols, 1 29/30, between; A - 5 cols, 1 29/30, between; C - 5 cols, 1 29/30, between.
Published: Fri
Avg Paid Circ: 396
Audit By: Sworn/Estimate/Non-Audited
Audit Date: 12.07.2019
Personnel: Karen Mitchell (Pub./Gen. Mgr.)

WAWA

THE ALGOMA NEWS REVIEW

Street Address: 33 St. Marie St. ,
Province: ON
Postal: P0S 1K0
Country: Canada
Mailing address: P.O. Box 528
Mailing city: Wawa
Province: ON
Postal: P0S 1K0
General Phone: (705) 856-2267
General Fax: (705) 856-4952
General/National Adv. E-mail: waprint2@ontera.net
Editorial e-mail: editor@thealgomanews.ca
Primary Website: www.thealgomanews.ca
Year Established: 1964
Areas Served - City/County or Portion Thereof, or Zip codes: Canada
Commercial printers?: Y
Mechanical specifications: Type page 10 1/4 x 16 1/4; E - 5 cols, 1 15/16, 3/16 between; A - 5 cols, 1 15/16, 3/16 between; C - 5 cols, 1 15/16, 3/16 between.
Published: Wed
Avg Paid Circ: 598
Avg Free Circ: 33
Audit By: CMCA
Audit Date: 31.03.2016
Personnel: Tammy Landry (Ed.); Christel Gignac (Adv. Mgr.)

WEST LORNE

CHRONICLE

Street Address: 168 Main St. ,
Province: ON
Postal: N0L 2P0
Country: Canada
Mailing address: PO Box 100
Mailing city: West Lorne
Province: ON
Postal: N0L 2P0
General Phone: (519) 768-2220
General Fax: (519) 768-2221
General/National Adv. E-mail: chronicle@bowesnet.com
Primary Website: www.thechronicle-online.com
Year Established: 1993
Areas Served - City/County or Portion Thereof, or Zip codes: Canada
Mechanical specifications: Type page 10 1/4 x 15; E - 5 cols, 2, 1/4 between; A - 5 cols, 2, 1/4 between; C - 5 cols, 2, 1/4 between.
Published: Thur
Avg Paid Circ: 100
Avg Free Circ: 5463
Audit By: CMCA
Audit Date: 30.06.2013
Personnel: Bev Ponton; Ian McCallum (Reg. Managing Ed.)
Parent company (for newspapers): Quebecor Communications, Inc.

WEST MILL

THE MONITOR

Street Address: 345 Victoria, Ste. 508 ,
Province: QC
Postal: H3Z 2M6
Country: Canada
Mailing address: 345 Victoria, Ste. 508
Mailing city: West Mill
Province: QC
Postal: H3Z 2M6
General Phone: (514) 484-5610
General Fax: (514) 484-6028
General/National Adv. E-mail: toula.foscolos@transcontinental.ca
Primary Website: www.themonitor.ca
Mechanical specifications: Type page 10 1/8 x 14 1/8; E - 8 cols, 2, 1/16 between; A - 8 cols, 2, 1/16 between; C - 8 cols, 1 1/8, 1/16 between.
Published: Thur
Avg Free Circ: 35164
Audit By: Sworn/Estimate/Non-Audited
Audit Date: 12.07.2019
Personnel: Yannick Pinel (Ed.); Toula Foscolos (Ed. in Chief)

WESTLOCK

THE WESTLOCK NEWS

Street Address: 9871 107th St. ,
Province: AB
Postal: T7P 1R9
Country: Canada
General Phone: (780) 349-3033
General Fax: (780) 349-3677
General/National Adv. E-mail: production@westlock.greatwest.ca
Display Adv. E-mail: abaxandall@westlock.greatwest.ca
Classified Adv. e-mail: abaxandall@westlock.greatwest.ca
Editorial e-mail: dneuman@westlock.greatwest.ca
Primary Website: www.westlocknews.com
Year Established: 1901
Delivery Methods: Mail`Newsstand`Carrier
Areas Served - City/County or Portion Thereof, or Zip codes: Canada
Published: Tues
Avg Paid Circ: 10
Avg Free Circ: 5
Audit By: VAC
Audit Date: 31.03.2016
Personnel: George Blais (Pub.); Louise Strehlau (Circ. Mgr.); Olivia Bako (Ed.); Connie Onyschuk (Adv.); Joyce Weber (Adv.)
Parent company (for newspapers): Glacier Media Group

WESTMOUNT

THE WESTMOUNT EXAMINER

Street Address: 245 Victoria Street , Suite 210
Province: QC
Postal: H3Z 2M6
Country: Canada
Mailing address: 245 Victoria Street
Mailing city: Westmount
Province: QC
Postal: H3Z 2M6
General Phone: (514) 484-5610
General Fax: (514) 484-6028
Advertising Phone: (514) 484-5610
Editorial Phone: 514-484-5610
General/National Adv. E-mail: examiner@tc.tc
Display Adv. E-mail: marie-france.paquette@tc.tc
Primary Website: www.westmountexaminer.com
Year Established: 1935
Delivery Methods: Newsstand`Carrier`Racks
Areas Served - City/County or Portion Thereof, or Zip codes: H3Y, H3Z
Mechanical specifications: Type page 11 3/8 x 15; E - 8 cols, 1 1/6, 1/6 between; A - 8 cols, 1 1/6, 1/6 between; C - 8 cols, 1 1/6, 1/6 between.
Published: Thur
Avg Paid Circ: 2
Avg Free Circ: 9282
Audit By: CMCA
Audit Date: 28.02.2014
Personnel: Marie-France Paquette (Assistant publisher); Patricia-Ann Beaulieu (Publisher); Harvey Aisthental (Media Consultant)
Parent company (for newspapers): Transcontinental Media

THE WESTMOUNT INDEPENDENT

Street Address: 310 Victoria Bldg. # 105 ,
Province: QC
Postal: H3Z 2M9
Country: Canada
Mailing address: 310 Victoria Ave. #105
Mailing city: Westmount
Province: QC
Postal: H3Z 2M9
General Fax: (514) 935-9241
Advertising Phone: (514) 223-3567
Editorial Phone: (514) 223-3578
General/National Adv. E-mail: office@westmountindependent.com
Display Adv. E-mail: advertising@westmountindependent.com
Primary Website: www.westmountindependent.com
Areas Served - City/County or Portion Thereof, or Zip codes: Westmount, Quebec
Published: Tues
Avg Free Circ: 15057
Audit By: CMCA
Audit Date: 31.05.2015
Personnel: David Price (Pub); Arleen Candiotti (Advt Consultant)

WESTPORT

RIDEAU VALLEY MIRROR

Street Address: 43 Bedfrod St. ,
Province: ON
Postal: K0G 1X0
Country: Canada
Mailing address: PO Box 130
Mailing city: Westport
Province: ON
Postal: K0G 1X0
General Phone: (613) 273-8000
General Fax: (613) 273-8001
General/National Adv. E-mail: info@review-mirror.com
Display Adv. E-mail: advertising@review-mirror.com
Editorial e-mail: newsroom@review-mirror.com
Primary Website: www.review-mirror.com
Areas Served - City/County or Portion Thereof, or Zip codes: Canada
Published: Thur
Avg Paid Circ: 1662
Avg Free Circ: 57
Audit By: CMCA
Audit Date: 28.02.2013
Personnel: Bill Ritchie (Adv. Mgr.); Louise Haughton (Circ. Mgr.); Howie Crichton (Ed.)

WETASKIWIN

WETASKIWIN TIMES

Street Address: 5013 51 St. ,
Province: AB
Postal: T9A 1L4
Country: Canada
Mailing address: PO Box 6900
Mailing city: Wetaskiwin
Province: AB
Postal: T9A 2G5
General Phone: (780) 352-2231
General Fax: (780) 352-4333
General/National Adv. E-mail: production@wetaskiwintimes.com
Display Adv. E-mail: pam.tremaine@sunmedia.ca
Classified Adv. e-mail: pam.tremaine@sunmedia.ca
Editorial e-mail: editor@sunmedia.ca
Primary Website: www.wetaskiwintimes.com
Year Established: 1901
Areas Served - City/County or Portion Thereof, or Zip codes: Canada
Mechanical specifications: Type page 10 1/4 x 12.5; E - 6 cols, 1 1/6, 1/8 between; A - 6 cols, 1 1/6, 1/8 between; C - 8 cols, 1 1/6, 1/8 between.
Published: Wed
Avg Free Circ: 9957
Audit By: VAC
Audit Date: 31.12.2015
Personnel: Adam Roy (Prodn. Mgr.); Nick Goetz (Pub.); Clara Mitchell (Office Mgr.); Pam Tremaine (Adv. Mgr.); Sarah Swenson (Ed.)
Parent company (for newspapers): Postmedia Network Inc.

WEYBURN

WEYBURN REVIEW

Street Address: 904 East Ave. ,
Province: SK
Postal: S4H 2Y8
Country: Canada
Mailing address: PO Box 400
Mailing city: Weyburn
Province: SK
Postal: S4H 2K4
General Phone: (306) 842-7487
General Fax: (306) 842-0282
General/National Adv. E-mail: production@weyburnreview.com
Primary Website: www.weyburnreview.com
Year Established: 1909
Delivery Methods: Mail`Newsstand`Carrier
Areas Served - City/County or Portion Thereof, or Zip codes: Canada
Own Printing Facility?: Y
Commercial printers?: Y
Mechanical specifications: 5 (9.67") column broadsheet x 278 lines deep. 11 picas per column.
Published: Wed
Avg Paid Circ: 2189
Avg Free Circ: 59
Audit By: CMCA
Audit Date: 30.06.2016
Personnel: Rick Major (Pub.); Patricia Ward (Mng. Ed.)
Parent company (for newspapers): Glacier Media Group

WEYBURN THIS WEEK

Street Address: 115 2nd St Ne ,
Province: SK
Postal: S4H0T7
Country: Canada
Mailing address: 115 2nd St NE
Mailing city: WEYBURN
Province: SK
Postal: S4H0T7
General Phone: (306) 842-3900
General Fax: (306) 842-2515
General/National Adv. E-mail: weyburnthisweek@sasktel.net
Primary Website: www.weyburnthisweek.com
Areas Served - City/County or Portion Thereof, or Zip codes: Canada
Mechanical specifications: Type page 10 1/2 x 15; E - 6 cols, 1 7/12, 1/6 between; A - 6 cols, 1 7/12, 1/6 between; C - 6 cols, 1 7/12, 1/6 between.
Published: Fri
Avg Paid Circ: 3
Avg Free Circ: 5546
Audit By: CMCA
Audit Date: 31.01.2016
Personnel: Rick Major (Pub.)
Parent company (for newspapers): Glacier Media Group

WHEATLEY

SOUTHPOINT SUN

Street Address: 14 Talbot Street West ,
Province: ON
Postal: N0P 2P0
Country: Canada
Mailing address: PO Box 10
Mailing city: Wheatley
Province: ON
Postal: N0P 2P0
General Phone: (519) 825-4541
General Fax: (519) 825-4546
General/National Adv. E-mail: sun@southpointsun.ca
Display Adv. E-mail: journal@mnsi.net

Non-Daily Newspapers in Canada

Primary Website: www.southpointsun.ca
Areas Served - City/County or Portion Thereof, or Zip codes: Canada
Published: Wed
Avg Free Circ: 10579
Audit By: CMCA
Audit Date: 28.02.2014
Personnel: Jim Heyens (Pub.); Sheila McBrayne (Ed.)

WHISTLER

PIQUE NEWSMAGAZINE

Street Address: 103-1390 Alpha Lake Rd. ,
Province: BC
Postal: V0N 1B1
Country: Canada
Mailing address: 103-1390 Alpha Lake Rd.
Mailing city: Whistler
Province: BC
Postal: V0N 1B1
General Phone: (604) 938-0202
General Fax: (604) 938-0201
General/National Adv. E-mail: sarah@piquenewsmagazine.com
Display Adv. E-mail: susan@piquenewsmagazine.com
Classified Adv. e-mail: traffic@piquenewsmagazine.com
Editorial e-mail: edit@piquenewsmagazine.com
Primary Website: www.piquenewsmagazine.com
Year Established: 1994
Own Printing Facility?: Y
Mechanical specifications: Type page 9 1/2 x 12 7/8; E - 4 cols, 2 1/4, 3/8 between; A - 4 cols, 2 1/4, 3/8 between; C - 5 cols, 1 3/4, 3/8 between.
Published: Thur
Avg Paid Circ: 41
Avg Free Circ: 10997
Audit By: VAC
Audit Date: 30.06.2017
Personnel: Clare Ogilvie (Ed.); Sarah Strother (Pub); Susan Hutchinson (Sales Mgr); Katie Bechtel (Circ Mgr); Jennifer Treptow (Sales Coord)
Parent company (for newspapers): Glacier Media Group; Pique Publishing Inc.

THE WHISTLER QUESTION

Street Address: 103-1390 Alpha Lake Rd ,
Province: BC
Postal: V0N 1B4
Country: Canada
Mailing address: 103-1390 Alpha Lake Rd
Mailing city: Whistler
Province: BC
Postal: V0N 1B4
General Phone: (604) 932-5131
General Fax: (604) 932-2862
General/National Adv. E-mail: smatches@whistlerquestion.com
Display Adv. E-mail: susan@piquenewsmagazine.com
Classified Adv. e-mail: mail@piquenewsmagazine.com
Editorial e-mail: editor@whistlerquestion.com
Primary Website: www.whistlerquestion.com
Year Established: 1976
Areas Served - City/County or Portion Thereof, or Zip codes: Canada
Own Printing Facility?: Y
Published: Tues
Avg Paid Circ: 433
Avg Free Circ: 5762
Audit By: VAC
Audit Date: 31.08.2016
Personnel: Sarah Strother (Pres., WPLP); Kathryn Bechtel (Office/Class. Mgr); Alyssa Noel (Ed); Susan Hutchinson (Sales Mgr)
Parent company (for newspapers): Glacier Media Group

WHITECOURT

THE MAYERTHORPE FREELANCER

Street Address: 4732 - 50 Ave. ,
Province: AB
Postal: T7S 1N7
Country: Canada
Mailing address: PO Box 630
Mailing city: Whitecourt
Province: AB
Postal: T7S 1N7
General Phone: (780) 778-3977
General Fax: (780) 778-6459
General/National Adv. E-mail: info@mayerthorpefreelancer.com
Display Adv. E-mail: advertising@mayerthorpefreelancer.com
Editorial e-mail: ann.harvey@sunmedia.ca
Primary Website: www.mayerthorpefreelancer.com
Year Established: 1978
Areas Served - City/County or Portion Thereof, or Zip codes: Woodlands County
Mechanical specifications: Type page 10 1/4 x 14; E - 8 cols, 1 3/16, 3/16 between; A - 8 cols, 1 3/16, 3/16 between; C - 8 cols, 1 3/16, 3/16 between.
Published: Wed
Avg Paid Circ: 589
Avg Free Circ: 7
Audit By: CMCA
Audit Date: 31.12.2013
Personnel: Pam Allain (Reg. Dir. of Adv.); Candice Daniels (Circ. Mgr.); Christopher King (Ed.)
Parent company (for newspapers): Quebecor Communications, Inc.

THE WHITECOURT STAR

Street Address: 4732 50th Ave. ,
Province: AB
Postal: T7S 1N7
Country: Canada
Mailing address: PO Box 630
Mailing city: Whitecourt
Province: AB
Postal: T7S 1N7
General Phone: (780) 778-3977
General Fax: (780) 778-6459
General/National Adv. E-mail: wcstar.general@sunmedia.ca
Display Adv. E-mail: nikki.greening@sunmedia.ca
Editorial e-mail: wcstar.editorial@sunmedia.ca
Primary Website: www.whitecourtstar.com
Year Established: 1961
Delivery Methods: Mail`Newsstand`Carrier`Racks
Areas Served - City/County or Portion Thereof, or Zip codes: T7S
Own Printing Facility?: Y
Commercial printers?: Y
Mechanical specifications: Type page 10 1/4 x 16; E - 10 cols, 1 9/16, between; A - 10 cols, 1 9/16, between; C - 10 cols, 1 9/16, between.
Published: Wed
Avg Paid Circ: 2467
Avg Free Circ: 113
Audit By: VAC
Audit Date: 31.12.2015
Personnel: Pamela Allain (Pub.); Meghan Brown (Sales); Candice Daniels (Circ.); Nikki Greening (Sales); Tracy McKinnon (Front Office Classifieds); Christopher King (Ed.)
Parent company (for newspapers): Postmedia Network Inc.

WHITEHORSE

YUKON NEWS

Street Address: 3106 Third Ave. , Ste. 200
Province: YT
Postal: Y1A 5G1
Country: Canada
Mailing address: 200-3106 Third Ave.
Mailing city: Whitehorse
Province: YT
Postal: Y1A 5G1
General Phone: (867) 667-6285
Display Adv. E-mail: stephanie.simpson@yukon-news.com
Classified Adv. e-mail: wordads@yukon-news.com
Editorial e-mail: editor@yukon-news.com
Primary Website: yukon-news.com
Year Established: 1960
Delivery Methods: Mail`Newsstand`Racks
Areas Served - City/County or Portion Thereof, or Zip codes: Canada
Own Printing Facility?: Y
Commercial printers?: Y
Mechanical specifications: Type page 11 1/2 x 15 1/2; E - 5 cols, 1 11/12, 1/6 between; A - 5 cols, 1 11/12, 1/6 between; C - 5 cols, 1 11/12, 1/6 between.
Published: Wed`Fri
Avg Paid Circ: 1686
Avg Free Circ: 2502
Audit By: AAM
Audit Date: 31.03.2019
Personnel: Stephanie Newsome (Pub.); Stephanie Simpson (Adv.); Ashley J (Ed.)
Parent company (for newspapers): Black Press Ltd.

WHITEWOOD

THE WHITEWOOD HERALD

Street Address: 708 S. Railway St. ,
Province: SK
Postal: S0G 5C0
Country: Canada
Mailing address: PO Box 160
Mailing city: Whitewood
Province: SK
Postal: S0G 5C0
General Phone: (306) 735-2230
General Fax: (306) 735-2899
General/National Adv. E-mail: herald@whitewoodherald.com
Display Adv. E-mail: ads@whitewoodherald.com
Classified Adv. e-mail: contact@whitewoodherald.com
Editorial e-mail: herald@whitewoodherald.com
Primary Website: www.whitewoodherald.sk.ca
Delivery Methods: Mail`Newsstand
Areas Served - City/County or Portion Thereof, or Zip codes: Canada
Commercial printers?: Y
Mechanical specifications: Type page 10 1/4 x 16; E - 5 cols, 1 7/8, 3/16 between; A - 5 cols, 1 7/8, 3/16 between; C - 5 cols, 1 7/8, 3/16 between.
Published: Fri
Avg Paid Circ: 667
Avg Free Circ: 88
Audit By: CMCA
Audit Date: 30.04.2016
Personnel: Chris Ashfield (Pub)

WIARTON

THE WIARTON ECHO

Street Address: 573 Berford St. ,
Province: ON
Postal: N0H 2T0
Country: Canada
Mailing address: P.O. Box 220
Mailing city: Wiarton
Province: ON
Postal: N0H 2T0
General Phone: (519) 534-1560
General Fax: (519) 534-4616
Advertising Phone: (519) 534-1563
Advertising Fax: (519) 534-4616
Editorial Phone: (519) 534-1560
Editorial Fax: (519) 534-4616
General/National Adv. E-mail: wiartonecho@bmts.com
Display Adv. E-mail: echoads@bowesnet.com
Editorial e-mail: wiartonecho@bmts.com
Primary Website: www.wiartonecho.com
Year Established: 1879

Province: YT
Postal: Y1A 5G1
Areas Served - City/County or Portion Thereof, or Zip codes: Canada
Commercial printers?: Y
Published: Tues
Avg Paid Circ: 1361
Avg Free Circ: 6
Audit By: CMCA
Audit Date: 30.06.2016
Personnel: Keith Gilbert (Ed.)
Parent company (for newspapers): Postmedia Network Inc.; Quebecor Communications, Inc.

WILLIAMS LAKE

THE WILLIAMS LAKE TRIBUNE

Street Address: 188 N. 1st Ave. ,
Province: BC
Postal: V2G 1Y8
Country: Canada
Mailing address: 188 N. 1st Ave.
Mailing city: Williams Lake
Province: BC
Postal: V2G 1Y8
General Phone: (250) 392-2331
General Fax: (250) 392-7253
General/National Adv. E-mail: classifieds@wltribune.com
Display Adv. E-mail: advertising@wltribune.com
Classified Adv. e-mail: classifieds@wltribune.com
Editorial e-mail: editor@wltribune.com
Primary Website: www.wltribune.com
Year Established: 1930
Delivery Methods: Mail`Newsstand`Carrier`Racks
Areas Served - City/County or Portion Thereof, or Zip codes: Canada
Own Printing Facility?: Y
Commercial printers?: Y
Published: Wed
Avg Paid Circ: 1109
Avg Free Circ: 9794
Audit By: VAC
Audit Date: 30.06.2016
Personnel: Kathy McLean (Pub); Angie Mindus (Ed); Lynn Bolt (Class. Mgr)
Parent company (for newspapers): Black Press Group Ltd.

WILLOWDALE

THE EAST YORK MIRROR

Street Address: 10 Tempo Ave. ,
Province: ON
Postal: M2H 3S5
Country: Canada
Mailing address: 10 Tempo Ave.
Mailing city: Willowdale
Province: ON
Postal: M2H 3S5
General Phone: (413) 493-4400
General Fax: (413) 495-6629
General/National Adv. E-mail: eym@mirror-guardian.com
Primary Website: www.metroland.com
Year Established: 1995
Areas Served - City/County or Portion Thereof, or Zip codes: Canada
Own Printing Facility?: Y
Commercial printers?: Y
Mechanical specifications: Type page 10 3/8 x 14; E - 9 cols, 1 1/16, between; A - 9 cols, 1 1/16, between; C - 9 cols, 1 1/16, between.
Published: Thur
Avg Paid Circ: 0
Avg Free Circ: 34643
Audit By: CCAB
Audit Date: 30.09.2017
Personnel: Betty Carr (Pub.); Marg Middleton (Gen. Mgr.); Stacey Allen (Adv. Dir.); Paris Quinn (Sales Rep.); Kim Buenting (Circ. Mgr.); Deborah Bodine (Ed.); Alan Shackleton (Mng. Ed.); Katherine Bernal (Prodn. Mgr.); Dave Barnett (Prodn. Dir.)
Parent company (for newspapers): Metroland Media Group Ltd.; Torstar

WINCHESTER

WINCHESTER PRESS
Street Address: 545 St. Lawrence St.,
Province: ON
Postal: K0C 2K0
Country: Canada
Mailing address: PO Box 399
Mailing city: Winchester
Province: ON
Postal: K0C 2K0
General Phone: (613) 774-2524
General Fax: (613) 774-3967
General/National Adv. E-mail: news@winchesterpress.on.ca
Display Adv. E-mail: advert@winchesterpress.on.ca
Editorial e-mail: news@winchesterpress.on.ca
Primary Website: www.winchesterpress.on.ca
Year Established: 1888
Delivery Methods: Mail`Racks
Areas Served - City/County or Portion Thereof, or Zip codes: Canada
Own Printing Facility?: Y
Commercial printers?: Y
Mechanical specifications: Type page 13 x 21 1/2; E - 6 cols, 2 1/12, 3/4 between; A - 6 cols, 2 1/12, 3/4 between; C - 6 cols, 2 1/12, 3/4 between.
Published: Wed
Avg Paid Circ: 2646
Avg Free Circ: 342
Audit By: CMCA
Audit Date: 30.06.2016
Personnel: Beth Morris (Owner/Pres.); Donna Rushford (Adv. Mgr./Co. Pub.)

WINDSOR

ETINCELLE
Street Address: 193 Rue Saint-georges,
Province: QC
Postal: J1S 1J7
Country: Canada
Mailing address: 193 rue Saint-Georges
Mailing city: Windsor
Province: QC
Postal: J1S 1J7
General Phone: (819) 845-2705
General Fax: (819) 845-5520
General/National Adv. E-mail: journal@letincelle.qc.ca
Primary Website: www.letincelle.qc.ca
Year Established: 1970
Delivery Methods: Carrier
Areas Served - City/County or Portion Thereof, or Zip codes: Canada
Own Printing Facility?: Y
Commercial printers?: Y
Mechanical specifications: Type page 10 x 15; E - 8 cols, between; C - 8 cols, between.
Published: Wed
Avg Paid Circ: 36
Avg Free Circ: 10515
Audit By: CCAB
Audit Date: 30.09.2012
Personnel: Ralph Cote (Ed. in Chief); Genevieve Gray; Claude Frenette (Ed.)

HANTS JOURNAL
Street Address: 73 Gerrish St.,
Province: NS
Postal: B0N 2T0
Country: Canada
Mailing address: PO Box 550
Mailing city: Windsor
Province: NS
Postal: B0N 2T0
General Phone: (902) 798-8371
General Fax: (902) 798-5451
General/National Adv. E-mail: info@hantsjournal.ca
Primary Website: www.hantsjournal.ca
Year Established: 1867
Areas Served - City/County or Portion Thereof, or Zip codes: Canada
Own Printing Facility?: Y

Mechanical specifications: Type page 9 2/3 x 21 1/2.
Published: Thur
Avg Paid Circ: 2233
Avg Free Circ: 15
Audit By: CMCA
Audit Date: 30.06.2014
Personnel: Ray Savage (Sales. Mgr.)
Parent company (for newspapers): Transcontinental Media

LE REMPART
Street Address: 7515 Forest Glade Dr.,
Province: ON
Postal: N8T 3P5
Country: Canada
Mailing address: 7515 Forest Glade Dr.
Mailing city: Windsor
Province: ON
Postal: N8T 3P5
General Phone: (519) 948-4139
General Fax: (519) 948-0628
General/National Adv. E-mail: info@lerempart.ca
Primary Website: www.lerempart.ca
Year Established: 1966
Areas Served - City/County or Portion Thereof, or Zip codes: Canada
Commercial printers?: Y
Mechanical specifications: Type page 10 x 15 5/8; E - 5 cols, 2, 1/6 between; A - 5 cols, 2, 1/6 between.
Published: Wed
Avg Paid Circ: 5735
Avg Free Circ: 802
Audit By: CMCA
Audit Date: 31.12.2012
Personnel: Dennis Poirier (Pub.); Christiane Beaupre (Gen. Mgr.); Richard Caumartin (Dir., sales)

WINGHAM

THE WINGHAM ADVANCE-TIMES
Street Address: 11 Veterans Rd.,
Province: ON
Postal: N0G 2W0
Country: Canada
Mailing address: PO Box 390
Mailing city: Wingham
Province: ON
Postal: N0G 2W0
General Phone: (519) 357-2320
General Fax: (519) 357-2900
General/National Adv. E-mail: advance@wcl.on.ca
Editorial e-mail: pkerr@wingham.com
Primary Website: www.wingham.com
Own Printing Facility?: Y
Commercial printers?: Y
Published: Wed
Avg Paid Circ: 862
Audit By: CMCA
Audit Date: 30.06.2016
Personnel: Sandy Woodcock (Adv. Mgr.); Bill Huether (Ed.); Dave Russell (Prodn. Mgr.)
Parent company (for newspapers): Metroland Media Group Ltd.; Torstar

WINKLER

MORDEN TIMES
Street Address: 583 Main St.,
Province: MB
Postal: R6W 4B3
Country: Canada
Mailing address: 583 Main St.
Mailing city: Winkler
Province: MB
Postal: R6W 4B3
General Phone: (204) 325-4771
General Fax: 204-325-8646
Display Adv. E-mail: jbilsky@postmedia.com
Editorial e-mail: gvandermeulen@postmedia.com
Primary Website: www.mordentimes.com
Delivery Methods: Newsstand`Carrier
Areas Served - City/County or Portion Thereof, or Zip

codes: Morden, Manitou, Miami, Darlingford, La Riviere, R.M. of Stanley,
Own Printing Facility?: Y
Commercial printers?: Y
Mechanical specifications: Type page 10 5/16 x 14; E - 6 cols, 1 7/12, 1/6 between; A - 6 cols, 1 7/12, 1/6 between; C - 8 cols, 1 1/4, 1/12 between.
Published: Thur
Avg Paid Circ: 4924
Avg Free Circ: 5418
Audit By: Sworn/Estimate/Non-Audited
Audit Date: 12.07.2019
Personnel: Greg Vandermeulen (Ed); Lauren MacGill (Reporter)
Parent company (for newspapers): Postmedia Network Inc.

WINKLER

WINKLER TIMES
Street Address: 583 Main St.,
Province: MB
Postal: R6W 4B3
Country: Canada
Mailing address: 583 Main Street
Mailing city: Winkler
Province: MB
Postal: R6W 4B3
General Phone: (204) 325-4771
General Fax: (204) 325-8646
General/National Adv. E-mail: winkler.class@sunmedia.ca
Display Adv. E-mail: Darcie.Morris@sunmedia.ca
Editorial e-mail: winkler.news@sunmedia.ca
Primary Website: http://www.pembinatoday.ca/winklertimes
Year Established: 1997
Delivery Methods: Mail`Carrier`Racks
Areas Served - City/County or Portion Thereof, or Zip codes: Canada
Own Printing Facility?: Y
Commercial printers?: Y
Mechanical specifications: Type page 10 5/6 x 14; E - 6 cols, 1 7/12, 1/6 between; A - 6 cols, 1 7/12, 1/6 between; C - 8 cols, 1 1/4, 1/12 between.
Published: Thur
Avg Paid Circ: 7459
Audit By: VAC
Audit Date: 30.09.2016
Personnel: Darcie Morris (Adv Dir); Greg Vandermeulen (Ed)
Parent company (for newspapers): Postmedia Network Inc.; Quebecor Communications, Inc.

WINNIPEG

THE HEADLINER
Street Address: 1355 Mountain Ave.,
Province: MB
Postal: R2X 3B6
Country: Canada
Mailing address: 1355 Mountain Ave.
Mailing city: Winnipeg
Province: MB
Postal: R2X 3B6
General Phone: (204) 697-7021
General Fax: (204) 953-4300
Advertising Phone: (204) 697-7021
Editorial Phone: (204) 697-7093
Display Adv. E-mail: sales@canstarnews.com
Classified Adv. e-mail: classified@canstarnews.com
Editorial e-mail: news@canstarnews.com
Primary Website: www.canstarnews.com
Year Established: 1992
Delivery Methods: Carrier`Racks
Areas Served - City/County or Portion Thereof, or Zip codes: Headingley, St. FranÃ§ois Xavier, Cartier, Macdonald, Marquette, Rosser, Fannystelle, Portage la Prairie
Published: Wed
Avg Paid Circ: 43
Avg Free Circ: 5372
Audit By: Sworn/Estimate/Non-Audited
Audit Date: 12.07.2019
Personnel: John Kendle (Managing Editor); Barb Borden (Sales Manager)

Parent company (for newspapers): Winnipeg Free Press

THE HERALD
Street Address: 1355 Mountain Ave.,
Province: MB
Postal: R2X 3B6
Country: Canada
Mailing address: 1355 Mountain Ave.
Mailing city: Winnipeg
Province: MB
Postal: R2X 3B6
General Phone: (204) 697-7009
General Fax: (204) 953-4300
Advertising Phone: (204) 697-7021
Display Adv. E-mail: sales@canstarnews.com
Editorial e-mail: letters@canstarnews.com
Primary Website: www.canstarnews.com
Delivery Methods: Carrier
Areas Served - City/County or Portion Thereof, or Zip codes: R2E, R2C, R2G, R2K, R2L, R3W
Own Printing Facility?: Y
Published: Wed
Avg Paid Circ: 984
Avg Free Circ: 43869
Audit By: VAC
Audit Date: 31.08.2016
Personnel: Linda MacKenzie (Natl. Sales Mgr.); John Kendle (Mng. Ed.); Darren Ridgley; Barb Borden (Sales Mgr)
Parent company (for newspapers): Winnipeg Free Press

THE LANCE
Street Address: 1355 Mountain Ave.,
Province: MB
Postal: R2X 3B6
Country: Canada
General Phone: (204) 697-7009
General Fax: (204) 953-4300
Advertising Phone: (204) 697-7021
Editorial Phone: (204) 697-7093
General/National Adv. E-mail: sales@canstarnews.com
Display Adv. E-mail: sales@canstarnews.com
Classified Adv. e-mail: classifieds@canstarnews.com
Editorial e-mail: news@canstarnews.com
Primary Website: www.canstarnews.com
Year Established: 1931
Delivery Methods: Carrier
Areas Served - City/County or Portion Thereof, or Zip codes: R2H, R2J, R2M, R2N, R3X
Published: Wed
Avg Free Circ: 37996
Audit By: Sworn/Estimate/Non-Audited
Audit Date: 12.07.2019
Personnel: John Kendle (Managing Editor); Darren Ridgley (Deputy Editor); Linda Mackenzie (Executive Assistant); Barb Borden (Sales Manager)
Parent company (for newspapers): Winnipeg Free Press

THE METRO
Street Address: 1355 Mountain Ave.,
Province: MB
Postal: R2X 3B6
Country: Canada
General Phone: (204) 697-7009
General Fax: (204) 953-4300
Display Adv. E-mail: sales@canstarnews.com
Editorial e-mail: letters@canstarnews.com
Primary Website: www.canstarnews.com
Year Established: 1973
Delivery Methods: Carrier
Areas Served - City/County or Portion Thereof, or Zip codes: R2Y, R3E, R3G, R3J, R3K, R3R
Published: Wed
Avg Paid Circ: 141
Avg Free Circ: 36979
Audit By: VAC
Audit Date: 31.08.2016
Personnel: John Kendle (Mng. Ed.); Darren Ridgley (Deputy Ed); Linda Mackenzie (Exec Asst); Barb Borden (Sales Mgr)

Non-Daily Newspapers in Canada

Parent company (for newspapers): Winnipeg Free Press

THE SOU'WESTER
Street Address: 1355 Mountain Ave. ,
Province: MB
Postal: R2X 3B6
Country: Canada
Mailing address: 1355 Mountain Ave.
Mailing city: Winnipeg
Province: MB
Postal: R2X 3B6
General Phone: (204) 697-7020
General Fax: (204) 953-4300
Advertising Phone: (204) 697-7021
Display Adv. E-mail: classifieds@canstarnews.com
Editorial e-mail: news@canstarnews.com
Primary Website: www.winnipegfreepress.com
Year Established: 2009
Areas Served - City/County or Portion Thereof, or Zip codes: Southwest Winnipeg
Published: Wed
Avg Paid Circ: 0
Avg Free Circ: 38583
Audit By: Sworn/Estimate/Non-Audited
Audit Date: 12.07.2019
Personnel: John Kendle (Mng. Ed.); Barb Borden (Sales Manager)
Parent company (for newspapers): Winnipeg Free Press

THE TIMES
Street Address: 1355 Mountain Ave. ,
Province: MB
Postal: R2X 3B6
Country: Canada
Mailing address: 1355 Mountain Ave.
Mailing city: Winnipeg
Province: MB
Postal: R2X 3B6
General Phone: (204) 697-7009
General Fax: (204) 953-4300
Advertising Phone: (204) 697-7021
General/National Adv. E-mail: sales@canstarnews.com
Display Adv. E-mail: sales@canstarnews.com
Editorial e-mail: letters@canstarnews.com
Primary Website: www.canstarnews.com
Delivery Methods: Carrier
Areas Served - City/County or Portion Thereof, or Zip codes: R2P, R2R, R2V, R2W, R2X
Mechanical specifications: Type page 10 1/4 x 16; E - 6 cols, 1 5/8, 3/16 between; A - 6 cols, 1 5/8, between; C - 8 cols, 1 3/16, 1/8 between.
Published: Wed
Avg Paid Circ: 20
Avg Free Circ: 37763
Audit By: VAC
Audit Date: 31.08.2016
Personnel: John Kendle (Mng. Ed.); Darren Ridgley; Barb Borden (Sales Mgr); Linda MacKenzie
Parent company (for newspapers): Winnipeg Free Press

WOODSTOCK

THE BUGLE-OBSERVER
Street Address: 110 Carleton St. ,
Province: NB
Postal: E7M 1E4
Country: Canada
Mailing address: 110 Carleton St.
Mailing city: Woodstock
Province: NB
Postal: E7M 1E4
General Phone: (506) 328-8863
General Fax: (506) 328-3208
General/National Adv. E-mail: news@thebugle.ca
Editorial e-mail: news@thebugle.ca
Primary Website: https://www.telegraphjournal.com/bugle-observer/
Year Established: 1976
Areas Served - City/County or Portion Thereof, or Zip codes: Canada
Own Printing Facility?: Y
Commercial printers?: Y
Published: Tues`Fri
Avg Paid Circ: 2693
Avg Free Circ: 56
Audit By: CMCA
Audit Date: 31.12.2013
Personnel: Peter Macingosh (Gen Mgr.); Edward Farrell (Circ. Mgr.)
Parent company (for newspapers): Brunswick News, Inc.

THE INGERSOLL TIMES
Street Address: 16 Brock Street ,
Province: ON
Postal: N4S 3B4
Country: Canada
Mailing address: 16 Brock Street
Mailing city: Woodstock
Province: ON
Postal: N4S 3B4
General Phone: (519) 537-2341
Display Adv. E-mail: cwetton@postmedia.com
Classified Adv. e-mail: hbrubacher@postmedia.com
Editorial e-mail: jvandermeer@postmedia.com
Primary Website: www.ingersolltimes.com
Year Established: 1969
Delivery Methods: Mail`Newsstand`Carrier
Areas Served - City/County or Portion Thereof, or Zip codes: Canada
Own Printing Facility?: Y
Published: Wed
Avg Paid Circ: 500
Audit By: CMCA
Audit Date: 31.12.2016
Personnel: Jennifer Vandermeer (Ed.); Ian Dowding (Group Dir., Media Sales); Claire Wetton (Media sales)
Parent company (for newspapers): Postmedia Network Inc.; Quebecor Communications, Inc.

THE NORWICH GAZETTE
Street Address: 16 Brock Street ,
Province: ON
Postal: N4S 3B4
Country: Canada
Mailing address: 16 Brock Street
Mailing city: Woodstock
Province: ON
Postal: N4S 3B4
General Phone: (519) 537-2341
General/National Adv. E-mail: norwich@bowesnet.com
Display Adv. E-mail: tleake@postmedia.com
Classified Adv. e-mail: hbrubacher@postmedia.com
Editorial e-mail: jennifer.vandermeer@sunmedia.ca
Primary Website: www.norwichgazette.ca
Year Established: 1876
Delivery Methods: Mail`Newsstand
Areas Served - City/County or Portion Thereof, or Zip codes: Canada
Own Printing Facility?: Y
Published: Wed
Avg Paid Circ: 822
Audit By: CMCA
Audit Date: 31.12.2016
Personnel: Jennifer Vandermeer (Ed.); Ian Dowding (Group Director, Media Sales); Tara Leake (Media sales); John Macintosh (Media sales); Heidi Brubacher (Classified sales); Beth Faulkner (Circ.)
Parent company (for newspapers): Postmedia Network Inc.

WYNYARD

THE ADVANCE/GAZETTE
Street Address: 301 Bosworth St. ,
Province: SK
Postal: S0A 4T0
Country: Canada
Mailing address: PO Box 10
Mailing city: Wynyard
Province: SK
Postal: S0A 4T0
General Phone: (306) 554-2224
General Fax: (306) 554-3226
General/National Adv. E-mail: w.advance@sasktel.net
Areas Served - City/County or Portion Thereof, or Zip codes: Canada
Mechanical specifications: Type page 12 x 17; E - 5 cols, 2, between; A - 5 cols, 2, between; C - 5 cols, 2, between.
Published: Mon
Avg Paid Circ: 1211
Avg Free Circ: 18
Audit By: CMCA
Audit Date: 30.12.2015
Personnel: Bob Johnson (Ed.)

YARMOUTH

THE VANGUARD
Street Address: 2 Second St. ,
Province: NS
Postal: B5A 4B1
Country: Canada
Mailing address: PO Box 128
Mailing city: Yarmouth
Province: NS
Postal: B5A 4B1
General Phone: (902) 742-7111
General Fax: (902) 742-6527
General/National Adv. E-mail: info@thevanguard.ca
Display Adv. E-mail: fred.fiander@tc.tc
Editorial e-mail: info@thevanguard.ca
Primary Website: www.thevanguard.ca
Year Established: 1966
Areas Served - City/County or Portion Thereof, or Zip codes: Canada
Commercial printers?: Y
Mechanical specifications: Type page 13 x 21; E - 6 cols, 2, between; A - 6 cols, 2, between; C - 6 cols, 2, between.
Published: Tues
Avg Paid Circ: 3485
Avg Free Circ: 52
Audit By: CMCA
Audit Date: 31.03.2014
Personnel: Fred Fiander (Pub) Fred Hatfield (Ed)
Parent company (for newspapers): Transcontinental Media

YELLOWKNIFE

DEH CHO DRUM
Street Address: 5108 50th St. ,
Province: NT
Postal: X1A 2R1
Country: Canada
Mailing address: PO Box 2820
Mailing city: Yellowknife
Province: NT
Postal: X1A 2R1
General Phone: (867) 873-4031
General Fax: (867) 873-8507
General/National Adv. E-mail: nnsl@nnsl.com
Display Adv. E-mail: advertising@nnsl.com
Editorial e-mail: editorial@nnsl.com
Primary Website: http://www.nnsl.com/dehcho/dehcho.html
Year Established: 1993
Areas Served - City/County or Portion Thereof, or Zip codes: Yellowknife
Mechanical specifications: Type page 10 5/16 x 15 3/8; E - 6 cols, 1 9/16, 1/6 between; A - 6 cols, 1 9/16, 1/6 between; C - 6 cols, 1 9/16, 1/6 between.
Published: Thur
Avg Free Circ: 708
Audit By: VAC
Audit Date: 31.05.2016
Personnel: Jack Sigvaldason (Pub.); Michael Scott (Gen. Mgr.); Petra Ehrke (Adv. Mgr.); Debra Davis (Circ. Mgr.); Bruce Valpy (Mng. Ed.)

INUVIK DRUM
Street Address: Po Box 2820 ,
Province: NT
Postal: X1A 2R1
Country: Canada
Mailing address: PO Box 2820
Mailing city: Yellowknife
Province: NT
Postal: X1A 2R1
General Phone: (867) 873-4031
General Fax: (867) 873-8507
General/National Adv. E-mail: nnsl@nnsl.com
Display Adv. E-mail: advertising@nnsl.com
Editorial e-mail: editorial@nnsl.com
Primary Website: www.nnsl.com
Areas Served - City/County or Portion Thereof, or Zip codes: Yellowknife
Commercial printers?: Y
Mechanical specifications: Type page 10 1/8 x 15 3/8; E - 6 cols, 1 7/12, 1/6 between; A - 6 cols, 1 7/12, 1/6 between; C - 6 cols, 1 7/12, 1/6 between.
Published: Thur
Avg Paid Circ: 201
Avg Free Circ: 290
Audit By: VAC
Audit Date: 31.05.2016
Personnel: Jack Sigvaldason (Pub.); Michael Scott (Gen. Mgr.); Petra Ehrke (Adv. Mgr.); Debra Davis (Circ. Mgr.); Bruce Valpy (Mng. Ed.)

KIVALLIQ NEWS
Street Address: Po Box 2820 ,
Province: NU
Postal: X1A 2R1
Country: Canada
Mailing address: PO Box 2820
Mailing city: Yellowknife
Province: NU
Postal: X1A 2R1
General Phone: (867) 873-4031
General Fax: (867) 873-8507
General/National Adv. E-mail: nnsl@nnsl.com
Display Adv. E-mail: advertising@nnsl.com
Editorial e-mail: editorial@nnsl.com
Primary Website: www.nnsl.com
Areas Served - City/County or Portion Thereof, or Zip codes: Yellowknife
Published: Wed
Avg Free Circ: 935
Audit By: VAC
Audit Date: 31.03.2016
Personnel: Jack Sigvaldason (Pub)

L'AQUILON
Street Address: 5102-51 Street, 2nd Floor ,
Province: NT
Postal: X1A 1S7
Country: Canada
Mailing address: PO Box 456
Mailing city: Yellowknife
Province: NT
Postal: X1A 2N4
General Phone: (867) 873-6603
General Fax: (867) 873-6663
General/National Adv. E-mail: direction.aquilon@northwestel.net
Display Adv. E-mail: sandra@repco-media.ca
Editorial e-mail: aquilon@internorth.com
Primary Website: www.aquilon.nt.ca
Year Established: 1986
Delivery Methods: Mail`Racks
Areas Served - City/County or Portion Thereof, or Zip codes: X1A X0E X0A
Mechanical specifications: Type page 11 x 17; E -6 cols, 2, 1/6 between
Published: Fri
Avg Free Circ: 875
Audit By: Sworn/Estimate/Non-Audited
Audit Date: 12.07.2019
Personnel: Alain Bessette (Ed.)

NEWS/NORTH

Street Address: 5108 50th St.,
Province: NT
Postal: X1A 2R1
Country: Canada
Mailing address: PO Box 2820
Mailing city: Yellowknife
Province: NT
Postal: X1A 2R1
General Phone: (867) 873-4031
General Fax: (867) 873-8507
General/National Adv. E-mail: nnsl@nnsl.com
Display Adv. E-mail: advertising@nnsl.com
Editorial e-mail: editorial@nnsl.com
Primary Website: www.nnsl.com
Areas Served - City/County or Portion Thereof, or Zip codes: Canada
Own Printing Facility?: Y
Mechanical specifications: Type page 10 5/8 x 15 3/8; E - 6 cols, 1 9/16, 1/6 between; A - 6 cols, 1 9/16, 1/6 between; C - 6 cols, 1 9/16, 1/6 between.
Published: Mon
Avg Paid Circ: 1922
Avg Free Circ: 2167
Audit By: VAC
Audit Date: 31.03.2016
Personnel: Jack Sigvaldason (Pub.); Michael Scott (Gen. Mgr.); Petra Ehrke (Adv. Mgr.); Debra Davis (Circ. Mgr.); Bruce Valpy (Ed.)

NUNAVUT NEWS/NORTH

Street Address: Po Box 2820,
Province: NU
Postal: X1A 2R1
Country: Canada
Mailing address: PO Box 2820
Mailing city: Yelloknife
Province: NU
Postal: X1A 2R1
General Phone: (867) 873-4031
General Fax: (867) 873-8507
General/National Adv. E-mail: circulation@nnsl.com
Display Adv. E-mail: advertising@nnsl.com
Editorial e-mail: editorial@nnsl.com
Primary Website: www.nnsl.com
Areas Served - City/County or Portion Thereof, or Zip codes: Nunavut
Published: Mon
Avg Free Circ: 4161
Audit By: VAC
Audit Date: 31.03.2016
Personnel: Jack Sigvaldason (Pub); Michael Scott (Gen Mgr)

YELLOWKNIFER

Street Address: 5108 50th St.,
Province: NT
Postal: X1A 2R1
Country: Canada
Mailing address: PO Box 2820
Mailing city: Yelloknife
Province: NT
Postal: X1A 2R1
General Phone: (867) 873-4031
General Fax: (867) 873-8507
General/National Adv. E-mail: nnsladmin@nnsl.com
Display Adv. E-mail: advertising@nnsl.com
Editorial e-mail: editorial@nnsl.com
Primary Website: www.nnsl.com
Areas Served - City/County or Portion Thereof, or Zip codes: Yellowknife
Own Printing Facility?: Y
Mechanical specifications: Type page 10 5/16 x 15 3/8; E - 6 cols, 1 9/16, 1/6 between; A - 6 cols, 1 9/16, 1/6 between; C - 6 cols, 1 9/16, 1/6 between.
Published: Wed`Fri
Avg Paid Circ: 2077
Avg Free Circ: 963
Audit By: VAC
Audit Date: 30.04.2016
Personnel: Jack Sigvaldason (Pub.); Michael Scott (Gen. Mgr.); Petra Ehrke (Adv.); Debra Davis (Circ. Mgr.); Bruce Valpy (Mng. Ed.)

YORKTON

YORKTON THIS WEEK

Street Address: 20 3rd Ave. N.,
Province: SK
Postal: S3N 2X3
Country: Canada
Mailing address: PO BOX 1300
Mailing city: YORKTON
Province: SK
Postal: S3N 2X3
General Phone: (306) 782-2465
General Fax: (306) 786-1898
General/National Adv. E-mail: publisher@yorktonthisweek.com
Display Adv. E-mail: classifieds@yorktonthisweek.com
Editorial e-mail: editorial@yorktonthisweek.com
Primary Website: www.yorktonthisweek.com
Delivery Methods: Newsstand`Carrier
Areas Served - City/County or Portion Thereof, or Zip codes: Canada
Commercial printers?: Y
Published: Wed
Avg Paid Circ: 2777
Avg Free Circ: 59
Audit By: Sworn/Estimate/Non-Audited
Audit Date: 12.07.2019
Personnel: Jim Ambrose (Publisher); Debbie Barr (Prodn. Mgr.)
Parent company (for newspapers): Glacier Media Group

COMMUNITY NEWSPAPERS IN CANADA

100 MILE HOUSE
PUBLICATION NAME
100 Mile House Free Press
Street Address: 3-536 Horse Lake Rd. , Uptown Plaza
Province: BC
Postal: V0K 2E0
Country: Canada
Mailing address: PO Box 459
Mailing city: 100 Mile House
Province: BC
Postal: V0K 2E0
General Phone: (250) 395-2219
General Fax: (250) 395-3939
General/National Adv. E-mail: publisher@100milefreepress.net
Display Adv. E-mail: publisher@100milefreepress.net
Classified Adv. e-mail: classifieds@100milefreepress.net
Editorial e-mail: newsroom@100milefreepress.net
Primary Website: www.100milefreepress.net
Year Established: 1960
Delivery Methods: Mail`Newsstand`Carrier`Racks
Areas Served - City/County or Portion Thereof, or Zip codes: South Cariboo
Commercial printers?: Y
Published: Thur
Avg Paid Circ: 2517
Avg Free Circ: 4115
Audit By: VAC
Audit Date: 31.07.2016
Personnel: Martina Dopf (Publisher); Chris Nickless (Sales); Kerri Mingo (Advertising Creative); Debbie Theoret (Creative); Carole Rooney (Reporter); Lori Brodie (Reception/Circulation); Max Winkelman (Ed.); Evan Fentiman (Creative)
Parent company (for newspapers): Black Press Group Ltd.

ABBOTSFORD
PUBLICATION NAME
The Abbotsford News
Street Address: 34375 Gladys Ave. ,
Province: BC
Postal: V2S 2H5
Country: Canada
Mailing address: 34375 Gladys Ave.
Mailing city: Abbotsford
Province: BC
Postal: V2S 2H5
General Phone: (604) 853-1144
General Fax: (604) 852-1641
General/National Adv. E-mail: publisher@abbynews.com
Display Adv. E-mail: donb@abbynews.com
Editorial e-mail: newsroom@abbynews.com
Primary Website: abbynews.com
Year Established: 1922
Areas Served - City/County or Portion Thereof, or Zip codes: Canada
Own Printing Facility?: Y
Commercial printers?: Y
Mechanical specifications: Type page 12 1/2 x 21; E - 7 cols, 1 11/16, 11/12 between; A - 7 cols, 1 11/16, 11/12 between; C - 7 cols, 1 11/16, 11/12 between.
Published: Tues`Thur`Sat
Avg Paid Circ: 45
Avg Free Circ: 38814
Audit By: AAM
Audit Date: 31.12.2018
Personnel: Kevin Hemery (Circ. Mgr.); Andrew Holota (Mng. Ed.); Carly Ferguson (Pub); Don Barbeau (Adv Mgr)
Parent company (for newspapers): Black Press Group Ltd.

ACTON VALE
PUBLICATION NAME
La Pensee De Bagot
Street Address: 800 Roxton St. ,
Province: QC
Postal: J0H 1A0
Country: Canada
Mailing address: 800 Roxton St.
Mailing city: Acton Vale
Province: QC
Postal: J0H 1A0
General Phone: (450) 546-3271
General Fax: (450) 546-3491
General/National Adv. E-mail: mdorais@lapensee.qc.ca
Primary Website: www.lapensee.qc.ca
Year Established: 1951
Areas Served - City/County or Portion Thereof, or Zip codes: Canada
Mechanical specifications: Type page 11 1/2 x 15; E - 8 cols, 1 1/4, 1/6 between; A - 8 cols, 1 1/4, 1/6 between; C - 8 cols, 1 1/4, 1/6 between.
Published: Wed
Avg Paid Circ: 0
Avg Free Circ: 0
Audit By: CCAB
Audit Date: 30.09.2015
Personnel: Michel Dorais (Adv. Mgr.); Robert Beauchemin (Adv. Rep.); Jean-Francois Dorais (Adv. Rep.); Benoit Chartier (Ed.)

AGASSIZ
PUBLICATION NAME
The Agassiz-harrison Observer
Street Address: 7167 Pioneer Ave ,
Province: BC
Postal: V0M 1A0
Country: Canada
Mailing address: PO Box 129
Mailing city: Agassiz
Province: BC
Postal: V0M 1A0
General Phone: (604) 796-4300
General Fax: (604) 796-2081
General/National Adv. E-mail: publisher@abbynews.com
Display Adv. E-mail: ads@ahobserver.com
Classified Adv. e-mail: tanya@blackpressused.ca
Editorial e-mail: news@ahobserver.com
Primary Website: www.agassizharrisonobserver.com
Year Established: 1999
Areas Served - City/County or Portion Thereof, or Zip codes: Agassiz, Harrison
Published: Thur
Avg Paid Circ: 590
Avg Free Circ: 2815
Audit By: VAC
Audit Date: 30.06.2016
Personnel: Carly Ferguson (Pub.); Erin Knutson (Ed); Tanya Jeyachandran (Class. Adv); Christine Douglas (Adv, Rep)
Parent company (for newspapers): Black Press Group Ltd.

AILSA CRAIG
PUBLICATION NAME
The Middlesex Banner
Street Address: 175 Main St. ,
Province: ON
Postal: N0M 1A0
Country: Canada
Mailing address: PO Box 433
Mailing city: Ailsa Craig
Province: ON
Postal: N0M 1A0
General Phone: (519) 293-1095
General Fax: (519) 293-1095
General/National Adv. E-mail: editor@banner.on.ca
Primary Website: www.banner.on.ca
Year Established: 1996
Areas Served - City/County or Portion Thereof, or Zip codes: Canada
Published: Wed
Avg Paid Circ: 736
Avg Free Circ: 708
Audit By: CMCA
Audit Date: 31.12.2015
Personnel: Brad Harness (Pub./Ed.)

AIRDRIE
PUBLICATION NAME
Airdrie City View
Street Address: #403-2903 Kingsview Blvd. ,
Province: AB
Postal: T4A 0C4
Country: Canada
Mailing address: #403-2903 Kingsview Blvd.
Mailing city: Airdrie
Province: AB
Postal: T4A 0C4
General Phone: (403) 948-1885
General Fax: (403) 948-2554
Display Adv. E-mail: rsonghurst@airdrie.greatwest.ca
Classified Adv. e-mail: classifieds@airdrie.greatwest.ca
Editorial e-mail: achorney@airdrie.greatwest.ca
Primary Website: http://www.airdriecityview.com
Year Established: 2002
Areas Served - City/County or Portion Thereof, or Zip codes: Airdrie/Canada
Published: Thur
Avg Paid Circ: 557
Avg Free Circ: 18336
Audit By: VAC
Audit Date: 31.05.2016
Personnel: Cam Christianson (Pub.); Allison Chorney (Ed)
Parent company (for newspapers): Great West Newspapers LP

AIRDRIE
PUBLICATION NAME
Airdrie Echo
Street Address: 112 - 1 Ave Ne ,
Province: AB
Postal: T4B 0R6
Country: Canada
Mailing address: 112 - 1 Ave NE
Mailing city: Airdrie
Province: AB
Postal: T4B 0R6
General Phone: (403) 948-7280
General Fax: (403) 912-2341
General/National Adv. E-mail: airdrie.echo@shaw.ca
Display Adv. E-mail: rmackintosh@postmedia.com
Editorial e-mail: jchalmers@postmedia.com
Primary Website: www.airdrieecho.com
Year Established: 1975
Delivery Methods: Carrier
Areas Served - City/County or Portion Thereof, or Zip codes: Canada
Mechanical specifications: Type page 10 1/4 x 14; E - 6 cols, 1 1/2, 1/4 between; A - 6 cols, 1 1/2, 1/4 between; C - 6 cols, 1 1/2, 1/4 between.
Published: Wed
Avg Free Circ: 18330
Audit By: VAC
Audit Date: 31.03.2016
Personnel: Ed Huculak (Pub.); John Chalmers (Ed.); Roxanne Mackintosh (Adv. Dir)
Parent company (for newspapers): Postmedia Network Inc.; Quebecor Communications, Inc.

AIRDRIE
PUBLICATION NAME
Rocky View Weekly
Street Address: #403 2903 Kingsview Blvd. ,
Province: AB
Postal: T4A 0C4
Country: Canada
Mailing address: #403 2903 Kingsview Blvd.
Mailing city: Airdrie
Province: AB
Postal: T4A 0C4
General Phone: (403) 948-1885
General Fax: (403) 948-2554
General/National Adv. E-mail: sales@airdrie.greatwest.ca
Display Adv. E-mail: rsonghurst@airdrie.greatwest.ca
Classified Adv. e-mail: rvwclassifieds@airdrie.greatwest.ca
Editorial e-mail: achorney@airdrie.greatwest.ca
Primary Website: www.rockyviewweekly.com
Year Established: 1970
Delivery Methods: Mail`Newsstand`Racks
Areas Served - City/County or Portion Thereof, or Zip codes: Canada
Commercial printers?: Y
Mechanical specifications: Type page 10 1/4 x 15 1/2; E - 6 cols, 1 7/12, 1/6 between; A - 6 cols, 1 7/12, 1/6 between; C - 6 cols, 1 7/12, 1/6 between.
Published: Tues
Avg Paid Circ: 457
Avg Free Circ: 12910
Audit By: VAC
Audit Date: 30.06.2016
Personnel: Cameron Christianson (Pub.); Lisa Gebruck (Circ. Mgr.); Allison Chorney (Ed)
Parent company (for newspapers): Glacier Media Group; Great West Newspapers LP; Rocky View Publishing

ALBERTON
PUBLICATION NAME
West Prince Graphic
Street Address: 4 Railway St. ,
Province: PE
Postal: C0B 1B0
Country: Canada
Mailing address: PO Box 339
Mailing city: Alberton
Province: PE
Postal: C0B 1B0
General Phone: (902) 853-3320
General Fax: (902) 853-3071
General/National Adv. E-mail: westgraphic@islandpress.pe.ca
Editorial e-mail: cindy@peicanada.com
Primary Website: www.peicanada.com
Year Established: 1980
Own Printing Facility?: Y
Mechanical specifications: Type page 13 x 21 1/3.
Published: Wed
Avg Paid Circ: 121
Avg Free Circ: 5733
Audit By: CMCA
Audit Date: 31.03.2014
Personnel: Paul MacNeill (Pub.); Jan MacNeill (Adv. Mgr.); Nicole Ford (Circ. Mgr.); Cindy Chant (Ed.)

ALDERGROVE

PUBLICATION NAME

The Aldergrove Star
Street Address: 27118 Fraser Hwy. ,
Province: BC
Postal: V4W 3P6
Country: Canada
Mailing address: 27118 Fraser Hwy.
Mailing city: Aldergrove
Province: BC
Postal: V4W 3P6
General Phone: (604) 514-6770
General Fax: (604) 856-5212
General/National Adv. E-mail: publisher@aldergrovestar.com
Display Adv. E-mail: sales@aldergrovestar.com
Editorial e-mail: newsroom@aldergrovestar.com
Primary Website: www.aldergrovestar.com
Year Established: 1957
Delivery Methods: Carrier`Racks
Areas Served - City/County or Portion Thereof, or Zip codes: Canada
Own Printing Facility?: Y
Published: Thur
Avg Paid Circ: 728
Avg Free Circ: 6469
Audit By: VAC
Audit Date: 30.06.2016
Personnel: Janice Reid (Adv. Sales Mgr.); Kurt Langmann (Ed.); Lisa Farquharson (Pub)
Parent company (for newspapers): Black Press Group Ltd.

ALEXANDRIA

PUBLICATION NAME

The Glengarry News
Street Address: 3 Main St. ,
Province: ON
Postal: K0C 1A0
Country: Canada
Mailing address: PO Box 10
Mailing city: Alexandria
Province: ON
Postal: K0C 1A0
General Phone: (613) 525-2020
General Fax: (613) 525-3824
General/National Adv. E-mail: gnews@glengarrynews.ca
Primary Website: www.glengarrynews.ca
Year Established: 1892
Delivery Methods: Mail`Newsstand
Areas Served - City/County or Portion Thereof, or Zip codes: Canada
Commercial printers?: Y
Mechanical specifications: Type page 12 7/8 x 21; E - 7 cols, 1/6 between; A - 7 cols, 1/6 between; C - 7 cols, 1/6 between.
Published: Wed
Avg Paid Circ: 1075
Avg Free Circ: 86
Audit By: VAC
Audit Date: 30.09.2016
Personnel: Bonnie MacDonald (Adv. Mgr.); Steven Warburton (Mng. Ed.); Sean Bray (Sports Ed.); JT Grossmith

ALLISTON

PUBLICATION NAME

The Alliston Herald
Street Address: 169 Dufferin St. S , Unit 22
Province: ON
Postal: L9R 1E6
Country: Canada
General Phone: (705) 435-6228
General Fax: (705) 435-3342
Editorial e-mail: herald@simcoe.com
Primary Website: simcoe.com
Delivery Methods: Carrier
Areas Served - City/County or Portion Thereof, or Zip codes: L9R, L0G, L0N, L0L, L0M
Published: Thur
Avg Free Circ: 22860
Audit By: CCAB

Audit Date: 31.03.2017
Personnel: Angela Makaroff (Sales Mgr.)
Parent company (for newspapers): Metroland Media Group Ltd.

ALMA

PUBLICATION NAME

Le Lac St. Jean
Street Address: 100 St. Joseph St., Locale 01 ,
Province: QC
Postal: G8B 7A6
Country: Canada
Mailing address: 100 St. Joseph St., Locale 01
Mailing city: Alma
Province: QC
Postal: G8B 7A6
General Phone: (418) 668-4545
General Fax: (418) 668-8522
General/National Adv. E-mail: redaction_alma@tc.tc
Primary Website: www.lelacstjean.com
Areas Served - City/County or Portion Thereof, or Zip codes: Canada
Published: Wed
Avg Paid Circ: 80
Avg Free Circ: 23534
Audit By: CCAB
Audit Date: 31.03.2014
Personnel: Michelle Dupont (Gen. Mgr.)
Parent company (for newspapers): Transcontinental Media

ALTONA

PUBLICATION NAME

The Red River Valley Echo
Street Address: 67 2nd St. ,
Province: MB
Postal: R0G 0B0
Country: Canada
Mailing address: PO Box 700
Mailing city: Altona
Province: MB
Postal: R0G 0B0
General Phone: (204) 324-5001
General Fax: (204) 324-1402
General/National Adv. E-mail: altona.news@sunmedia.ca
Display Adv. E-mail: Darcie.Morris@sunmedia.ca
Editorial e-mail: winkler.news@sunmedia.ca
Primary Website: www.altonaecho.com
Year Established: 1941
Delivery Methods: Carrier`Racks
Areas Served - City/County or Portion Thereof, or Zip codes: Altona
Commercial printers?: Y
Mechanical specifications: Type page 10 1/4 x 14; E - 6 cols, 1 3/5, between; A - 6 cols, 1 3/5, between; C - 8 cols, 1 7/12, between.
Published: Thur
Avg Paid Circ: 27
Avg Free Circ: 4427
Audit By: VAC
Audit Date: 30.06.2016
Personnel: Greg Vandermeulen (Ed.); Darcie Morris (Adv Dir.)
Parent company (for newspapers): Postmedia Network Inc.; Quebecor Communications, Inc.

AMHERST

PUBLICATION NAME

Amherst Daily News
Street Address: 147 S. Albion St. ,
Province: NS
Postal: B4H 2X2
Country: Canada
Mailing address: PO Box 280
Mailing city: Amherst
Province: NS
Postal: B4H 2X2
General Phone: (902) 667-5102
General Fax: (902) 667-0419
Editorial Phone: (902) 661-5426

General/National Adv. E-mail: dcole@amherstdaily.com
Display Adv. E-mail: gcoish@amherstdaily.com
Editorial e-mail: darrell.cole@tc.tc
Primary Website: www.cumberlandnewsnow.com
Year Established: 1893
Areas Served - City/County or Portion Thereof, or Zip codes: Amherst, Nova Scotia
Mechanical specifications: Type page 10.25 x 14; E - 6 cols, 2 1/16, 1/8 between; A - 6 cols, 2 1/16, 1/8 between; C - 6 cols, 2 1/16, 1/8 between.
Published: Fri
Weekday Frequency: m
Avg Paid Circ: 4057
Avg Free Circ: 349
Audit By: VAC
Audit Date: 31.12.2015
Personnel: Richard Russell (Pub.); Greg Landry (Ops. Mgr.); Gladys Coish (Adv. Mgr.); Chuck MacInnes (Circ. Mgr.); Darrell Cole (Sr. Ed.)
Parent company (for newspapers): Transcontinental Media

PUBLICATION NAME

The Citizen-record
Street Address: 147 South Albion St. ,
Province: NS
Postal: B4H 2X2
Country: Canada
Mailing address: 147 South Albion St.
Mailing city: Amherst
Province: NS
Postal: B4H 2X2
General Phone: (902) 667-5102
General Fax: (902) 667-0419
General/National Adv. E-mail: chris.gooding@tc.tc
Display Adv. E-mail: gcoish@amherstdaily.com
Editorial e-mail: darrell.cole@tc.tc
Primary Website: www.cumberlandnewsnow.com
Delivery Methods: Mail`Newsstand`Carrier
Areas Served - City/County or Portion Thereof, or Zip codes: B0H
Own Printing Facility?: N
Commercial printers?: Y
Published: Wed
Avg Paid Circ: 4892
Avg Free Circ: 504
Audit By: VAC
Audit Date: 31.10.2014
Personnel: Richard Russell (Pub.); Gladys Coish (Adv. Mgr.); Darrell Cole (Ed)
Parent company (for newspapers): Transcontinental Media

AMHERSTBURG

PUBLICATION NAME

River Town Times
Street Address: 67 Richmond Street ,
Province: ON
Postal: N9V 1G1
Country: Canada
General Phone: (519) 736-4175
General Fax: (519) 736-5420
Display Adv. E-mail: sales@rivertowntimes.com
Editorial e-mail: mail@rivertowntimes.com
Primary Website: www.rivertowntimes.com
Year Established: 1995
Delivery Methods: Carrier
Areas Served - City/County or Portion Thereof, or Zip codes: Canada
Mechanical specifications: 10.25x14.75
Published: Wed
Avg Free Circ: 9183
Audit By: CMCA
Audit Date: 31.08.2016
Personnel: Ron Giofu (Ed.)

AMOS

PUBLICATION NAME

Citoyen De L'harricana
Street Address: 92 Rue Principale Sud ,
Province: QC
Postal: J9T 2J6
Country: Canada
Mailing address: 92 rue Principale Sud
Mailing city: Amos
Province: QC
Postal: J9T 2J6
General Phone: (819)732-6531
General Fax: (819) 732-3764
General/National Adv. E-mail: philippe.delachevrotiere@quebecormedia.com
Display Adv. E-mail: manon.poirier@quebecormedia.com
Editorial e-mail: caroline.couture@quebecormedia.com
Primary Website: www.lechoabitibien.ca
Areas Served - City/County or Portion Thereof, or Zip codes: Canada
Published: Wed
Avg Paid Circ: 19
Avg Free Circ: 11238
Audit By: CCAB
Audit Date: 31.03.2014
Personnel: Caroline Couture

AMQUI

PUBLICATION NAME

L'avant-poste Gaspesien
Street Address: 217 Leonidas Ave. ,
Province: QC
Postal: G5J 2B8
Country: Canada
Mailing address: 49 St-Benoit Est, Bureau 6
Mailing city: Amqui
Province: QC
Postal: G5J 2B8
General Phone: (418) 629-3443
General Fax: (418)562-4607
General/National Adv. E-mail: avant-poste@hebdosquebecor.com
Display Adv. E-mail: gaby.veilleux@hebdosquebecor.com
Editorial e-mail: lucie-rose.levesque@hebdosquebecor.com
Primary Website: lavantposte.ca
Areas Served - City/County or Portion Thereof, or Zip codes: Canada
Published: Wed
Avg Paid Circ: 22
Avg Free Circ: 16881
Audit By: CCAB
Audit Date: 30.09.2012
Personnel: Alain St-Amand (Regl. Dir. Gen.); Francis Desrosiers (Dir. Gen.); Lucy-Rose Levesque (Ed.)
Parent company (for newspapers): Quebecor Communications, Inc.

ANTIGONISH

PUBLICATION NAME

The Casket
Street Address: 88 College St. ,
Province: NS
Postal: B2G 1X7
Country: Canada
Mailing address: 88 College St.
Mailing city: Antigonish
Province: NS
Postal: B2G 1X7
General Phone: (902) 863-4370
General Fax: (902) 863-1943
General/National Adv. E-mail: info@thecasket.ca
Display Adv. E-mail: brianlazzuri@thecasket.ca
Classified Adv. e-mail: brianlazzuri@thecasket.ca
Editorial e-mail: editor@thecasket.ca
Primary Website: www.thecasket.ca
Year Established: 1852
Delivery Methods: Mail`Carrier`Racks
Areas Served - City/County or Portion Thereof, or Zip codes: Canada

Community Newspapers in Canada

III-515

Own Printing Facility?: Y
Mechanical specifications: Type page 10 x 20; E - 6 cols, 2, between; A - 6 cols, 2, between; C - 6 cols, 2, between.
Published: Wed
Avg Free Circ: 27000
Audit By: Sworn/Estimate/Non-Audited
Audit Date: 12.07.2019
Personnel: Brian Lazzuri (Gen Mgr/Mng Ed/Adv Mgr)
Parent company (for newspapers): SaltWire

ARMSTRONG
PUBLICATION NAME
Okanagan Advertiser
Street Address: 3400 Okanagan St. ,
Province: BC
Postal: V0E 1B0
Country: Canada
Mailing address: PO Box 610
Mailing city: Armstrong
Province: BC
Postal: V0E 1B0
General Phone: (250) 546-3121
General Fax: (250) 546-3636
General/National Adv. E-mail: info@okadvertiser.com
Primary Website: OkanaganAdvertiser.com
Year Established: 1902
Delivery Methods: Mail`Newsstand`Racks
Areas Served - City/County or Portion Thereof, or Zip codes: Canada
Own Printing Facility?: Y
Commercial printers?: Y
Mechanical specifications: Tabloid 1/4 Fold
Published: Thur
Avg Free Circ: 4000
Audit By: Sworn/Estimate/Non-Audited
Audit Date: 12.07.2019
Personnel: Will Hansma (Pub)
Parent company (for newspapers): Okanagan Valley Newspaper Group

ARNPRIOR
PUBLICATION NAME
Arnprior Chronicle Guide Emc
Street Address: 8 Mcgonigal St. ,
Province: ON
Postal: K7S 1L8
Country: Canada
Mailing address: 8 McGonigal St.
Mailing city: Arnprior
Province: ON
Postal: K7S 1L8
General Phone: (613) 623-6571
Display Adv. E-mail: leslie.osborne@metroland.com
Classified Adv. e-mail: christine.jarrett@metroland.com
Editorial e-mail: theresa.fritz@metroland.com
Primary Website: www.insideottawavalley.com
Areas Served - City/County or Portion Thereof, or Zip codes: Canada
Published: Thur
Avg Free Circ: 8213
Audit By: CMCA
Audit Date: 30.06.2016
Personnel: Mike Tracy (Pub); Theresa Fritz (Ed)

PUBLICATION NAME
West Carleton Review
Street Address: 8 Mcgonigal St. ,
Province: ON
Postal: K7S 1L8
Country: Canada
Mailing address: 8 McGonigal St.
Mailing city: Arnprior
Province: ON
Postal: K7S 1L8
General Phone: (613) 623-6571
Display Adv. E-mail: leslie.osborne@metroland.com
Primary Website: www.insideottawavalley.com
Published: Thur

Avg Free Circ: 7099
Audit By: CMCA
Audit Date: 30.06.2014
Personnel: Theresa Fritz; Mike Tracy
Parent company (for newspapers): Metroland Media Group Ltd.

ASBESTOS
PUBLICATION NAME
Les Actualites
Street Address: 572 1st Ave. ,
Province: QC
Postal: J1T 4R4
Country: Canada
Mailing address: 572 1st Ave.
Mailing city: Asbestos
Province: QC
Postal: J1T 4R4
General Phone: (819) 879-6681
General Fax: (819) 879-2355
General/National Adv. E-mail: carole.pellerin@quebecormedia.com
Editorial e-mail: nathalie.hurdle@quebecormedia.com
Primary Website: journallesactualites.ca
Areas Served - City/County or Portion Thereof, or Zip codes: Canada
Mechanical specifications: Type page 10 1/8 x 11 13/16; E - 10 cols, 5/8 between; A - 10 cols, 5/8 between; C - 10 cols, 5/8 between.
Published: Wed
Avg Paid Circ: 4
Avg Free Circ: 13160
Audit By: CCAB
Audit Date: 31.03.2014
Personnel: Carole Pellerin (Ãƒ€©ditrice)
Parent company (for newspapers): Reseau Select/Select Network; Quebecor Communications, Inc.

ASHCROFT
PUBLICATION NAME
The Ashcroft-Cache Creek Journal
Street Address: 120 4th Street ,
Province: BC
Postal: V0K 1A0
Country: Canada
Mailing address: PO Box 190
Mailing city: Ashcroft
Province: BC
Postal: V0K 1A0
General Phone: (250) 453-2261
General Fax: (250) 453-9625
Editorial Phone: (250) 453-2261
General/National Adv. E-mail: sales@accjournal.ca
Display Adv. E-mail: publisher@accjournal.com
Editorial e-mail: editorial@accjournal.com
Primary Website: https://www.ashcroftcachecreekjournal.com/
Year Established: 1895
Delivery Methods: Mail`Newsstand`Carrier
Areas Served - City/County or Portion Thereof, or Zip codes: Ashcroft, Cache Creek, Clinton, Spences Bridge
Commercial printers?: Y
Mechanical specifications: Type page 10 5/16 x 14 1/2; E - 6 cols, 1 7/12, between; A - 6 cols, 1 7/12, between; C - 6 cols, 1 7/12, between.
Published: Thur
Avg Paid Circ: 850
Avg Free Circ: 87
Audit By: CMCA
Audit Date: 23.09.2018
Personnel: Barbara Roden (Editor); Christopher Roden (Salesperson); Martina Dopf (Publisher)
Parent company (for newspapers): Black Press Group Ltd.

ASSINIBOIA
PUBLICATION NAME
Assiniboia Times

Street Address: 410 1st Ave. E. ,
Province: SK
Postal: S0H 0B0
Country: Canada
Mailing address: PO Box 910
Mailing city: Assiniboia
Province: SK
Postal: S0H 0B0
General Phone: (306) 642-5901
General Fax: (306) 642-4519
General/National Adv. E-mail: heather@assiniboiatimes.ca
Editorial e-mail: joyce@assiniboiatimes.ca
Areas Served - City/County or Portion Thereof, or Zip codes: Canada
Commercial printers?: Y
Mechanical specifications: Type page 10 1/2 x 15; E - 6 cols, 1 7/12, between; A - 6 cols, 1 7/12, between; C - 6 cols, 1 7/12, between.
Published: Fri
Avg Paid Circ: 212
Avg Free Circ: 2937
Audit By: CMCA
Audit Date: 29.02.2016
Personnel: Joyce Simard (Editor); Kevin Rasmussen (General Manager)
Parent company (for newspapers): Prairie Newspaper Group; Glacier Media Group

ASTRA
PUBLICATION NAME
Wing Commander
Street Address: Po Box 1000, Sta. Forces ,
Province: ON
Postal: K0K 3W0
Country: Canada
Mailing address: PO Box 1000, Sta. Forces
Mailing city: Astra
Province: ON
Postal: K0K 3W0
General Phone: (613) 965-7248
General Fax: (613) 965-7490
Advertising Phone: (613) 392-2811
Editorial Phone: (613) 392-2811
General/National Adv. E-mail: christopher.daniel@forces.gc.ca
Primary Website: www.forces.gc.ca
Mechanical specifications: Type page 10 1/4 x 14 1/2; E - 6 cols, 1 57/100, between; A - 6 cols, 1 57/100, between; C - 6 cols, between.
Published: Fri
Avg Free Circ: 3000
Audit By: Sworn/Estimate/Non-Audited
Audit Date: 12.07.2019
Personnel: Mark Peebles (Ed. in Chief); Andrea Steiner (Mng. Ed.); Amber Gooding (Asst. Ed.)

ATHABASCA
PUBLICATION NAME
The Athabasca Advocate
Street Address: 4917b 49th Street ,
Province: AB
Postal: T9S 1C5
Country: Canada
General Phone: (780) 675-9222
General Fax: (780) 675-3143
Advertising Phone: (780) 675-9222 ext. 24
Editorial Phone: (780) 675-9222
Display Adv. E-mail: production@athabasca.greatwest.ca
Editorial e-mail: advocate@athabasca.greatwest.ca
Primary Website: www.athabascaadvocate.com
Year Established: 1981
Areas Served - City/County or Portion Thereof, or Zip codes: Athabasca County
Published: Tues
Avg Paid Circ: 41
Avg Free Circ: 106
Audit By: VAC
Audit Date: 31.03.2016
Personnel: Vanessa Annand (Ed.); Meghan McIvor (Prod. Mgr.); Mona Muzyka (Circ. Mgr.); Allendria Brunjes (Pub.)
Parent company (for newspapers): Great West Newspapers LP

ATIKOKAN
PUBLICATION NAME
Atikokan Progress
Street Address: 109 Main St. E. ,
Province: ON
Postal: P0T 1C0
Country: Canada
Mailing address: PO Box 220
Mailing city: Atikokan
Province: ON
Postal: P0T 1C0
General Phone: (807) 597-2731
General Fax: (807) 597-6103
General/National Adv. E-mail: progress@nwon.com
Editorial e-mail: progress@nwon.com
Primary Website: www.atikokanprogress.ca
Year Established: 1950
Delivery Methods: Mail`Newsstand`Carrier
Areas Served - City/County or Portion Thereof, or Zip codes: P0T1C0
Mechanical specifications: Type page 10 1/2 x 15; E - 5 cols, 1 11/12, 1/6 between; A - 5 cols, 1 11/12, 1/6 between; C - 5 cols, 1 1/2, 1/6 between.
Published: Mon
Avg Paid Circ: 1173
Avg Free Circ: 38
Audit By: VAC
Audit Date: 30.04.2016
Personnel: Eve Shine (Circ. Mgr.); Michael McKinnon (Ed.)

AURORA
PUBLICATION NAME
The Aurora Banner
Street Address: 250 Industrial Parkway N. ,
Province: ON
Postal: L4G 4C3
Country: Canada
Mailing address: 250 Industrial Parkway N.
Mailing city: Aurora
Province: ON
Postal: L4G 4C3
General Phone: (905) 727-0819
General Fax: (905) 727-2909
Display Adv. E-mail: lmcdonald@yrmg.com
Editorial e-mail: tmcfadden@yrmg.com
Primary Website: yorkregion.com
Areas Served - City/County or Portion Thereof, or Zip codes: Canada
Published: Thur`Sun
Avg Free Circ: 15943
Audit By: CCAB
Audit Date: 30.09.2018
Personnel: Ted McFadden (Managing Ed.)
Parent company (for newspapers): Metroland Media Group Ltd.

PUBLICATION NAME
The Auroran
Street Address: 15213 Yonge St Ste 8 ,
Province: ON
Postal: L4G 1L8
Country: Canada
General Phone: (905) 727-3300
General Fax: (905) 727-2620
Advertising Phone: (416) 803-9940
General/National Adv. E-mail: bob@auroran.com
Display Adv. E-mail: zach@lpcmedia.ca
Classified Adv. e-mail: cynthia@auroran.com
Editorial e-mail: brock@auroran.com
Primary Website: www.newspapers-online.com/auroran
Year Established: 2000
Delivery Methods: Mail`Carrier`Racks
Areas Served - City/County or Portion Thereof, or Zip codes: Canada
Published: Thur
Avg Paid Circ: 15
Avg Free Circ: 20000
Audit By: CMCA
Audit Date: 2/31/2017
Personnel: Brock Weir (Ed.); Cynthia Proctor (Prod. Mgr.); Diane Buchanan (Adv. Sales);

Zach Shoub (Adv. Sales)
Parent company (for newspapers): London Publishing

AYLMER

PUBLICATION NAME

The Aylmer Express
Street Address: 390 Talbot St. E. ,
Province: ON
Postal: N5H 2R9
Country: Canada
Mailing address: PO Box 160
Mailing city: Aylmer
Province: ON
Postal: N5H 2R9
General Phone: (519) 773-3126
General Fax: (519) 773-3147
General/National Adv. E-mail: info@aylmerexpress.ca
Display Adv. E-mail: advertise@aylmerexpress.ca
Primary Website: www.aylmerexpress.ca
Areas Served - City/County or Portion Thereof, or Zip codes: Aylmer
Mechanical specifications: Type page 15 3/4 x 21.
Published: Wed
Avg Paid Circ: 13
Avg Free Circ: 14
Audit By: VAC
Audit Date: 31.03.2016
Personnel: Pam Morton (Adv. Mgr.); Wanda Kapogines (Circ. Mgr.); John Hueston (Ed.); Karen Hueston (Prodn. Mgr.)

AYR

PUBLICATION NAME

Ayr News
Street Address: 40 Piper St. ,
Province: ON
Postal: N0B 1E0
Country: Canada
Mailing address: PO Box 1173
Mailing city: Ayr
Province: ON
Postal: N0B 1E0
General Phone: (519) 632-7432
General Fax: (519) 632-7743
General/National Adv. E-mail: ayrnews@golden.net
Display Adv. E-mail: hall.ayrnews@gmail.com
Primary Website: www.ayrnews.ca
Year Established: 1854
Delivery Methods: Mail`Newsstand
Areas Served - City/County or Portion Thereof, or Zip codes: N0B 1E0
Mechanical specifications: Type page 13 x 21 1/2; E - 6 cols, 1 7/8, 1/8 between; A - 6 cols, 1 7/8, 1/8 between; C - 6 cols, 1 7/8, 1/8 between.
Published: Wed
Avg Free Circ: 0
Audit By: VAC
Audit Date: 31.07.2017
Personnel: Heidi E. Ostner (Circ. Mgr.)

BAIE COMEAU

PUBLICATION NAME

Manic
Street Address: Rue De Bretagne ,
Province: QC
Postal: G5C 1X5
Country: Canada
Mailing address: Rue de Bretagne
Mailing city: Baie Comeau
Province: QC
Postal: G5C 1X5
General Phone: (418) 589-9990
Areas Served - City/County or Portion Thereof, or Zip codes: Canada
Published: Wed
Avg Paid Circ: 4
Avg Free Circ: 14765
Audit By: CCAB

Audit Date: 30.09.2012
Personnel: Paul Brisson

PUBLICATION NAME

Objectif Plein Jour
Street Address: 625 Bvd., Lafleche, Ste. 309 ,
Province: QC
Postal: G5C 1C5
Country: Canada
Mailing address: 625 Bvd., Lafleche, Ste. 309
Mailing city: Baie Comeau
Province: QC
Postal: G5C 1C5
General Phone: (418) 589-5900
General Fax: (418) 589-8216
General/National Adv. E-mail: sebastien.rouillard@quebecormedia.com
Primary Website: www.pleinjourdebaiecomeau.ca
Own Printing Facility?: Y
Commercial printers?: Y
Published: Wed
Avg Free Circ: 16435
Audit By: Sworn/Estimate/Non-Audited
Audit Date: 12.07.2019
Personnel: Sebastien Rouillard
Parent company (for newspapers): Quebecor Communications, Inc.

PUBLICATION NAME

Plein Jour De Baie Comeau
Street Address: 625 Bvd., Lafleche, Ste. 309 ,
Province: QC
Postal: G5C 1C5
Country: Canada
Mailing address: 625 Bvd., Lafleche, Ste. 309
Mailing city: Baie Comeau
Province: QC
Postal: G5C 1C5
General Phone: (418) 589-5900
General/National Adv. E-mail: sebastien.rouillard@quebecormedia.com
Areas Served - City/County or Portion Thereof, or Zip codes: Canada
Published: Wed
Avg Paid Circ: 4
Avg Free Circ: 20578
Audit By: CCAB
Audit Date: 31.03.2014
Personnel: Sebastien Rouillard

PUBLICATION NAME

Plein Jour Sur Manicouagan
Street Address: 625 Bvd., Lafleche, Ste. 309 ,
Province: QC
Postal: G5C 1C5
Country: Canada
Mailing address: 625 Bvd., Lafleche, Ste. 309
Mailing city: Baie Comeau
Province: QC
Postal: G5C 1C5
General Phone: (418) 589-5900
General Fax: (418) 589-8216
General/National Adv. E-mail: sebastien.rouillard@quebecormedia.com
Display Adv. E-mail: atelier.baiecomeau@hebdosquebecor.com
Editorial e-mail: raphael.hovington@hebdosquebecor.com
Primary Website: www.pleinjourdebaiecomeau.ca
Areas Served - City/County or Portion Thereof, or Zip codes: Canada
Own Printing Facility?: Y
Commercial printers?: Y
Published: Wed
Avg Paid Circ: 7
Avg Free Circ: 15628
Audit By: BPA
Audit Date: 01.03.2012
Personnel: Sebastien Rouillard
Parent company (for newspapers): Quebecor Communications, Inc.

BANCROFT

PUBLICATION NAME

Bancroft This Week
Street Address: 254 Hastings St. ,
Province: ON
Postal: K0L 1C0
Country: Canada
Mailing address: PO Box 1254
Mailing city: Bancroft
Province: ON
Postal: K0L 1C0
General Phone: (613) 332-2002
General Fax: (613) 332-1710
General/National Adv. E-mail: curtis.armstrong@sunmedia.ca
Display Adv. E-mail: david.zilstra@gmail.com
Classified Adv. e-mail: melissa@haliburtonpress.com
Editorial e-mail: jenn@haliburtonpress.com
Primary Website: www.bancroftthisweek.com
Areas Served - City/County or Portion Thereof, or Zip codes: Canada
Published: Fri
Avg Free Circ: 8962
Audit By: CMCA
Audit Date: 31.12.2015
Personnel: David Zilstra (Pub/Adv Dir); Jenn Watt (Mng. Ed); Melissa Armstrong (Sales Rep)

PUBLICATION NAME

The Bancroft Times
Street Address: 93 Hastings St. N. ,
Province: ON
Postal: K0L 1C0
Country: Canada
Mailing address: 93 Hastings St. N.
Mailing city: Bancroft
Province: ON
Postal: K0L 1C0
General Phone: (613) 332-2300
General Fax: (613) 332-1894
General/National Adv. E-mail: bancroft-times@sympatico.ca
Primary Website: www.thebancrofttimes.ca
Areas Served - City/County or Portion Thereof, or Zip codes: ontario & provinces
Published: Thur
Audit By: VAC
Audit Date: 30.04.2016
Personnel: Dean Walker (Owner); Jenn Watt (Managing Ed.)

BANFF

PUBLICATION NAME

Bow Valley Crag & Canyon
Street Address: 201 Bear St., 2nd Fl. ,
Province: AB
Postal: T1L 1H2
Country: Canada
Mailing address: PO Box 129
Mailing city: Banff
Province: AB
Postal: T1L 1H2
General Phone: (403) 762-2453
General Fax: (403) 762-5274
General/National Adv. E-mail: editor@thecrag.ca
Display Adv. E-mail: rmackintosh@postmedia.com
Editorial e-mail: russ.ullyot@sunmedia.ca
Primary Website: www.thecragandcanyon.ca
Year Established: 1900
Delivery Methods:
  Mail`Newsstand`Carrier`Racks
Areas Served - City/County or Portion Thereof, or Zip codes: Canada
Commercial printers?: Y
Mechanical specifications: Type page 10 1/4 x 14; E - 6 cols, 1 7/12, between; A - 6 cols, 1 7/12, between; C - 6 cols, 1 7/12, between.
Published: Wed
Avg Paid Circ: 0
Avg Free Circ: 8537
Audit By: CMCA
Audit Date: 28.02.2014
Personnel: Shawn Cornell (Pub); Russ Ullyot

(Ed); Roxanne Mackintosh (Adv. Dir.)
Parent company (for newspapers): Postmedia Network Inc.; Quebecor Communications, Inc.

BARRHEAD

PUBLICATION NAME

Barrhead Leader
Street Address: 5015 51st St. ,
Province: AB
Postal: T7N 1A4
Country: Canada
Mailing address: P.O. Box 4520
Mailing city: Barrhead
Province: AB
Postal: T7N 1A4
General Phone: (780) 674-3823
General Fax: (780) 674-6337
General/National Adv. E-mail: leader@barrhead.greatwest.ca
Display Adv. E-mail: sales@barrhead.greatwest.ca
Editorial e-mail: lleng@barrhead.greatwest.ca
Primary Website: www.barrheadleader.com
Year Established: 1927
Delivery Methods: Mail`Newsstand
Areas Served - City/County or Portion Thereof, or Zip codes: Barrhead
Own Printing Facility?: Y
Commercial printers?: Y
Mechanical specifications: Type page 10 1/3 x 15 1/3; E - 6 cols, 1 9/16, 1/6 between; A - 6 cols, 1 9/16, 1/6 between; C - 7 cols, 1 1/3, 1/6 between.
Published: Tues
Avg Paid Circ: 3114
Avg Free Circ: 3
Audit By: VAC
Audit Date: 31.03.2016
Personnel: Lynda Leng (Pub)
Parent company (for newspapers): Glacier Media Group; Great West Newspapers LP

BARRIE

PUBLICATION NAME

Innisfil Journal
Street Address: 21 Patterson Rd. ,
Province: ON
Postal: L4N 7W6
Country: Canada
General Phone: (705) 726-0573
General Fax: (705) 726-9350
General/National Adv. E-mail: eallain@simcoe.com
Editorial e-mail: rvanderlinde@simcoe.com
Primary Website: simcoe.com
Areas Served - City/County or Portion Thereof, or Zip codes: Canada
Published: Thur
Avg Free Circ: 10791
Audit By: CCAB
Audit Date: 31.03.2017
Personnel: Elise Allaine (Gen. Mgr.)
Parent company (for newspapers): Metroland Media Group Ltd.

PUBLICATION NAME

The Barrie Advance
Street Address: 21 Patterson Rd. ,
Province: ON
Postal: L4N 7W6
Country: Canada
Mailing address: 21 Patterson Rd.
Mailing city: Barrie
Province: ON
Postal: L4N 7W6
General Phone: (705) 726-0573
General Fax: (705) 726-9350
Editorial e-mail: bareditor@simcoe.com
Primary Website: simcoe.com
Areas Served - City/County or Portion Thereof, or Zip codes: Barrie
Published: Thur
Avg Free Circ: 50827
Audit By: CCAB

Community Newspapers in Canada

Audit Date: 31.12.2017
Personnel: Shaun Sauve (Adv. Dir.); Heather Harris (Distr. Mgr.); Ian Proudfoot
Parent company (for newspapers): Metroland Media Group Ltd.

BARRIERE

PUBLICATION NAME

Barriere Star Journal
Street Address: 1-4353 Conner Road ,
Province: BC
Postal: V0E 1E0
Country: Canada
Mailing address: PO Box 1020
Mailing city: Barriere
Province: BC
Postal: V0E 1E0
General Phone: (250) 672-5611
General Fax: (250) 672-9900
General/National Adv. E-Mail: office@starjournal.net
Display Adv. E-Mail: advertising@starjournal.net
Classified Adv. e-mail: advertising@starjournal.net
Editorial e-mail: news@starjournal.net
Primary Website: www.starjournal.net
Year Established: 1999
Delivery Methods: Carrier
Areas Served - City/County or Portion Thereof, or Zip codes: Canada
Commercial printers?: Y
Published: Thur
Avg Paid Circ: 2043
Avg Free Circ: 37
Audit By: VAC
Audit Date: 12.12.2017
Personnel: Jill Hayward (Ed.); Lisa Quiding (Adv./Office/Production)
Parent company (for newspapers): Black Press Group Ltd.

BARRY'S BAY

PUBLICATION NAME

Barry's Bay This Week
Street Address: 19574 Opeongo Line ,
Province: ON
Postal: K0J 1B0
Country: Canada
Mailing address: PO Box 375
Mailing city: Barry's Bay
Province: ON
Postal: K0J 1B0
General Phone: (613) 756-2944
General Fax: (613) 756-2994
General/National Adv. E-mail: newsroom@barrysbaythisweek.com
Display Adv. E-mail: michel@thevalleygazette.ca
Classified Adv. e-mail: classified@thevalleygazette.ca
Editorial e-mail: christine@thevalleygazette.ca
Primary Website: http://www.thevalleygazette.ca/node/3
Areas Served - City/County or Portion Thereof, or Zip codes: Canada
Published: Wed
Avg Paid Circ: 1292
Avg Free Circ: 0
Audit By: CMCA
Audit Date: 31.12.2012
Personnel: Pete Lapinskie (Gen. Mgr.); Michel Lavigne (Owner/Pub/Adv); Christine Hudder (Ed)
Parent company (for newspapers): Quebecor Communications, Inc.

BASS RIVER

PUBLICATION NAME

The Shoreline Journal
Street Address: Box 41 ,
Province: NS
Postal: B0M 1B0
Country: Canada
Mailing address: Box 41
Mailing city: Bass River
Province: NS
Postal: B0M 1B0
General Phone: (902) 647-2968
General Fax: (902) 647-2194
Advertising Phone: (902)647-2968
Advertising Fax: (902) 647-2194
Editorial Phone: (902) 647-2968
General/National Adv. E-mail: maurice@theshorelinejournal.com
Display Adv. E-mail: maurice@theshorelinejournal.com
Editorial e-mail: maurice@theshorelinejournal.com
Primary Website: www.theshorelinejournal.com
Year Established: 1994
Delivery Methods: Mail`Newsstand
Areas Served - City/County or Portion Thereof, or Zip codes: Muncipality of County of Colchester
Mechanical specifications: The Shoreline Journal is an offset tabloid. Image area is 10-1/4¢€® x 15-5/8¢€®. Column width is 1.5¢€® with 6 columns per page. Line Screens. B&W 100, Colour 100 lines per inch.
Published: Wed`Mthly
Avg Paid Circ: 1363
Avg Free Circ: 0
Audit By: CMCA
Audit Date: 31.12.2013
Personnel: Maurice Rees

BASSANO

PUBLICATION NAME

The Bassano Times
Street Address: 402 First Ave. ,
Province: AB
Postal: T0J 0B0
Country: Canada
Mailing address: PO Box 780
Mailing city: Bassano
Province: AB
Postal: T0J 0B0
General Phone: (403) 641-3636
General Fax: (403) 641-3952
Advertising Phone: (403) 641-3636
General/National Adv. E-mail: btimes@telusplanet.net
Year Established: 1915
Delivery Methods: Mail`Newsstand
Areas Served - City/County or Portion Thereof, or Zip codes: Canada
Mechanical specifications: Type page 10 x 16; E - 6 cols, 1 1/2, 1/8 between; A - 6 cols, 1 1/2, 1/8 between; C - 6 cols, 1 1/2, 1/8 between.
Published: Tues
Avg Paid Circ: 503
Audit By: CMCA
Audit Date: 30.06.2017
Personnel: Mary Lou Brooks (Publisher/Advertising Manager)

BATHURST

PUBLICATION NAME

The Northern Light
Street Address: 355 King Ave. ,
Province: NB
Postal: E2A 1P4
Country: Canada
Mailing address: 355 King Ave.
Mailing city: Bathurst
Province: NB
Postal: E2A 1P4
General Phone: (506) 546-4491
General Fax: (506) 546-1491
Editorial e-mail: mulock.greg@thenorthernlight.ca
Primary Website: https://www.telegraphjournal.com/northern-light/
Areas Served - City/County or Portion Thereof, or Zip codes: Canada
Own Printing Facility?: Y
Mechanical specifications: Type page 13 x 21 1/2; E - 6 cols, 2 1/12, 1/6 between; A - 6 cols, 2 1/12, 1/6 between; C - 9 cols, 1 1/3, 1/6 between.
Published: Tues
Avg Paid Circ: 2890
Avg Free Circ: 12
Audit By: VAC
Audit Date: 31.12.2015
Personnel: Greg Mulock (Ed.)
Parent company (for newspapers): Brunswick News, Inc.

BEAUMONT

PUBLICATION NAME

La Nouvelle Beaumont News
Street Address: 5021b 52 Ave. ,
Province: AB
Postal: T4X 1E5
Country: Canada
Mailing address: 5021B 52 Ave.
Mailing city: Beaumont
Province: AB
Postal: T4X 1E5
General Phone: (780) 929-6632
General Fax: (780) 929-6634
Display Adv. E-mail: jfigeat@postmedia.com
Editorial e-mail: bobby.roy@sunmedia.ca
Primary Website: www.thebeaumontnews.com
Year Established: 1987
Areas Served - City/County or Portion Thereof, or Zip codes: Beaumont
Published: Fri
Avg Paid Circ: 11
Avg Free Circ: 7221
Audit By: VAC
Audit Date: 31.12.2015
Personnel: Jean Figeat (Adv. Dir.); Bobby Roy (Ed)
Parent company (for newspapers): Sun Media Corporation; Post Media

BEAUPORT

PUBLICATION NAME

Beauport Express
Street Address: 710 Bouvier, Suite 107 ,
Province: QC
Postal: G2J 1C2
Country: Canada
Mailing address: 710 Bouvier, Suite 107
Mailing city: Beauport
Province: QC
Postal: G2J 1C2
General Phone: (418) 628-7460
General Fax: (418) 622-1511
General/National Adv. E-mail: redaction_quebec@tc.tc
Primary Website: www.beauportexpress.com
Areas Served - City/County or Portion Thereof, or Zip codes: Canada
Own Printing Facility?: Y
Mechanical specifications: Type page 10 x 11 3/4; C - 2 cols, 2, between.
Published: Fri
Avg Paid Circ: 11
Avg Free Circ: 28463
Audit By: CCAB
Audit Date: 31.03.2014
Personnel: Yvan Rancourt (Pub.); Paul Lessard (Ed.); Gilles Brault (Prodn. Mgr.)

BEAUPRE

PUBLICATION NAME

Autre Voix
Street Address: Boulevard Ste-anne Bureau 101 , Bureau 101
Province: QC
Postal: G0A 1E0
Country: Canada
Mailing address: boulevard Ste-Anne Bureau 101
Mailing city: Beaupre
Province: QC
Postal: G0A 1E0
General Phone: (418) 827-1511
Areas Served - City/County or Portion Thereof, or Zip codes: Canada
Published: Wed
Avg Paid Circ: 3

Avg Free Circ: 13297
Audit By: CCAB
Audit Date: 31.03.2014
Personnel: Lilianne Laprise

BEAUSEJOUR

PUBLICATION NAME

The Clipper Weekly & Lac Du Bonnet Clipper
Street Address: 27a-3rd Street South ,
Province: MB
Postal: R0E 0C0
Country: Canada
Mailing address: P.O. Box 2033
Mailing city: Beausejour
Province: MB
Postal: R0E 0C0
General Phone: (204) 268-4700
General Fax: (204) 268-3858
General/National Adv. E-mail: mail@clipper.mb.ca
Primary Website: www.clipper.mb.ca
Delivery Methods: Mail`Newsstand`Racks
Areas Served - City/County or Portion Thereof, or Zip codes: R0E 0A0 R0E 0C0 R0E 1M0 R0E 0K0 R0E 0Z0 R0E 0R0 R0E 0T0 R0E 1A0 R0E 1Z0 R0E 0X0 R0E 0Y0 R0E 1A0 R0E 1J0 R0E 1L0 R0E 1M0 R0E 1R0 R0E 1T0 R0E 1V0 R0E 1X0 R0E 1Y0 R0E 1Z0 R0E 2A0 R0E 2B0 R0E 2G0
Published: Thur
Avg Paid Circ: 46
Avg Free Circ: 12340
Audit By: VAC
Audit Date: 31.03.2016
Personnel: Kim MacAulay (Publisher); Mark Buss (Editor)
Parent company (for newspapers): Clipper Publishing Corp.

BEAVERLODGE

PUBLICATION NAME

Town & Country News
Street Address: 916 2nd Avenue ,
Province: AB
Postal: T0H 0C0
Country: Canada
General Phone: (780) 354-2980
General Fax: (780) 354-2460
General/National Adv. E-mail: beaverlodge.advertiser@gmail.com
Display Adv. E-mail: rebecca@nextchapterpublishing.ca
Primary Website: facebook.com/westcountynews
Year Established: 1956
Delivery Methods: Mail`Newsstand`Carrier
Areas Served - City/County or Portion Thereof, or Zip codes: Canada
Published: Thur
Avg Paid Circ: 1857
Avg Free Circ: 20
Audit By: CMCA
Audit Date: 12.12.2017
Personnel: Rebecca Dika (Pub.)
Parent company (for newspapers): Next Chapter Printing & Publishing

BEETON

PUBLICATION NAME

The Scope Of Innisfil
Street Address: 34 Main St. W ,
Province: ON
Postal: L0G 1A0
Country: Canada
Mailing address: P.O. Box 310
Mailing city: Beeton
Province: ON
Postal: L0G 1A0
General Phone: (905) 729-2287
General Fax: (905) 729-2541
General/National Adv. E-mail: admin@innisfilscope.com
Display Adv. E-mail: sales@innisfilscope.com
Editorial e-mail: editor@innisfilscope.com
Primary Website: www.innisfilscope.com
Year Established: 1968

Areas Served - City/County or Portion Thereof, or Zip codes: Canada
Mechanical specifications: Type page 10 1/2 x 15; E - 6 cols, 1 2/3, 1/6 between; A - 6 cols, 1 2/3, 1/6 between; C - 6 cols, 1 2/3, 1/6 between.
Published: Wed
Avg Paid Circ: 100
Avg Free Circ: 12433
Audit By: CMCA
Audit Date: 30.04.2013
Personnel: Alex Pozdrowski (Adv.); Wendy Soloduik (Ed.)
Parent company (for newspapers): Simcoe-York Group

PUBLICATION NAME
The Times Of New Tecumseth
Street Address: 34 Main St. W. ,
Province: ON
Postal: L0G 1A0
Country: Canada
Mailing address: PO Box 310
Mailing city: Beeton
Province: ON
Postal: L0G 1A0
General Phone: (905) 729-2287
General Fax: (905) 729-2541
General/National Adv. E-mail: admin.syp@rogers.com
Editorial e-mail: editor.syp@rogers.com
Primary Website: www.newtectimes.com
Year Established: 1974
Areas Served - City/County or Portion Thereof, or Zip codes: L0G1A0, L0G1L0, L9R, L0G 1B0
Commercial printers?: Y
Mechanical specifications: Type page 10 1/2 x 15; E - 6 cols, 1 2/3, 1/6 between; A - 6 cols, 1 2/3, 1/6 between; C - 6 cols, 1 2/3, 1/6 between.
Published: Thur
Avg Paid Circ: 2230
Avg Free Circ: 100
Audit By: VAC
Audit Date: 30.04.2015
Personnel: Wendy Soloduik (Ed.); John Speziali (Production Mgr.); Annette Derraugh
Parent company (for newspapers): Simcoe-York Group

PUBLICATION NAME
Tottenham Times
Street Address: 34 Main St. W. ,
Province: ON
Postal: L0G 1A0
Country: Canada
Mailing address: PO Box 310
Mailing city: Beeton
Province: ON
Postal: L0G 1A0
General Phone: (905) 729-2287
General Fax: (905) 729-2541
General/National Adv. E-mail: admin.syp@rogers.com
Editorial e-mail: editor.syp@rogers.com
Primary Website: www.newtectimes.com
Year Established: 1978
Areas Served - City/County or Portion Thereof, or Zip codes: Canada
Mechanical specifications: Type page 10 1/2 x 15; E - 6 cols, 1 2/3, 1/6 between; A - 6 cols, 1 2/3, 1/6 between; C - 6 cols, 1 2/3, 1/6 between.
Published: Wed
Avg Paid Circ: 2125
Avg Free Circ: 75
Audit By: Sworn/Estimate/Non-Audited
Audit Date: 12.07.2019
Personnel: John Archibald (Adv. Mgr.); Kristen Haire (Prodn. Mgr.)
Parent company (for newspapers): Simcoe-York Group

BELLEVILLE
PUBLICATION NAME
Belleville News
Street Address: 250 Sidney St. ,
Province: ON
Postal: K8P 5E0
Country: Canada
Mailing address: PO Box 25009
Mailing city: Belleville
Province: ON
Postal: K8P 5E0
General Phone: (613) 966-2034
Advertising Phone: (613) 966-2034 ext. 504
Display Adv. E-mail: mhudgins@metroland.com
Classified Adv. e-mail: slacroix@perfprint.ca
Editorial e-mail: chris.malette@metroland.com
Primary Website: http://www.insidebelleville.com/belleville-on/
Published: Thur
Personnel: Paul Mitchell (Circ Mgr); Chris Malette (Ed); Melissa Hudgin (Adv)
Parent company (for newspapers): Metroland Media Group Ltd.

PUBLICATION NAME
Belleville News Emc
Street Address: 244 Ashley St ,
Province: ON
Postal: K0K 2B0
Country: Canada
Mailing address: PO Box 155
Mailing city: Belleville
Province: ON
Postal: K0K 2B0
General Phone: (613) 966-2034
General/National Adv. E-mail: jkearns@theemc.ca
Display Adv. E-mail: leslie.osborne@metroland.com
Classified Adv. e-mail: abarr@metroland.com
Editorial e-mail: theresa.fritz@metroland.com
Primary Website: www.insideottawavalley.com
Year Established: 2010
Delivery Methods: Mail
Areas Served - City/County or Portion Thereof, or Zip codes: Canada
Published: Thur
Avg Free Circ: 22549
Audit By: CMCA
Audit Date: 30.06.2016
Personnel: John Kearns (Pub.); Chris Paveley (Circ Mgr); Theresa Fritz (Ed); Leslie Osborne (Adv. Sales)
Parent company (for newspapers): Metroland Media Group Ltd.

PUBLICATION NAME
Campbellford/northwest News Emc
Street Address: 244 Ashley St ,
Province: ON
Postal: K0K 2B0
Country: Canada
Mailing address: PO Box 155
Mailing city: Belleville
Province: ON
Postal: K0K 2B0
General Phone: (613) 966-2034
Advertising Phone: (613) 966-2034
Editorial Phone: (613) 966-2034 ext. 510
General/National Adv. E-mail: jkearns@theemc.ca
Display Adv. E-mail: jkearns@theemc.ca
Editorial e-mail: tbush@theemc.ca
Primary Website: www.insideottawavalley.com
Year Established: 2010
Delivery Methods: Mail
Areas Served - City/County or Portion Thereof, or Zip codes: Canada
Published: Thur
Avg Free Circ: 11630
Audit By: CMCA
Audit Date: 31.12.2012
Personnel: John Kearns (Pub.); Terry Bush (Mng. Ed.)

PUBLICATION NAME
Quinte West Emc
Street Address: 250 Sidney St. ,
Province: ON
Postal: K8P 5E0
Country: Canada
Mailing address: PO Box 25009
Mailing city: Belleville
Province: ON
Postal: K8P 5E0
General Phone: (613) 966-2034
General/National Adv. E-mail: jkearns@theemc.ca
Primary Website: www.insideottawavalley.com
Areas Served - City/County or Portion Thereof, or Zip codes: Canada
Published: Thur
Avg Free Circ: 23089
Audit By: CMCA
Audit Date: 31.12.2012
Personnel: John Kearns (Pub.); Sharon LaCroix (Community)
Parent company (for newspapers): Metroland Media Group Ltd.

PUBLICATION NAME
Stirling/northeast News Emc
Street Address: 244 Ashley St. ,
Province: ON
Postal: K0K 2B0
Country: Canada
Mailing address: PO Box 155
Mailing city: Belleville
Province: ON
Postal: K0K 2B0
General Phone: (613) 966-2034
Advertising Phone: (613) 966-2034
Editorial Phone: (613) 966-2034 ext. 510
General/National Adv. E-mail: jkearns@theemc.ca
Display Adv. E-mail: jkearns@theemc.ca
Editorial e-mail: tbush@theemc.ca
Primary Website: www.insideottawavalley.com
Year Established: 2010
Delivery Methods: Mail
Areas Served - City/County or Portion Thereof, or Zip codes: Canada
Published: Thur
Avg Free Circ: 11564
Audit By: CMCA
Audit Date: 31.12.2012
Personnel: John Kearns (Pub.); Terry Bush (Mng. Ed.)

BELLEVILLE
PUBLICATION NAME
The Community Press
Street Address: 199 Front St. , Suite 118
Province: ON
Postal: K8N 5H5
Country: Canada
Mailing address: 199 Front St. Suite 118
Mailing city: Belleville
Province: ON
Postal: K8N 5H5
General Phone: (613) 395-3015
General Fax: (613) 395-2992
Editorial Phone: (613) 392-6501
Editorial Fax: (613) 392-0505
General/National Adv. E-mail: compress@redden.on.ca; general@communitypress-online.com
Display Adv. E-mail: gerry.drage@sunmedia.ca
Classified Adv. e-mail: intelligencer.classifieds@sunmedia.ca
Editorial e-mail: brice.mcvicar@sunmedia.ca
Primary Website: www.communitypress-online.com
Areas Served - City/County or Portion Thereof, or Zip codes: Canada
Mechanical specifications: Type page 10 1/4 x 15 1/4; E - 9 cols, 1 1/36, 1/8 between; A - 9 cols, 1 1/36, 1/8 between; C - 6 cols, 1 7/12, 1/8 between.
Published: Thur
Avg Free Circ: 46476
Audit By: CMCA
Audit Date: 30.06.2016

Personnel: Brice McVicar (Ed); Gerry Drage (Adv. Dir.); Jason Hawley (Circ Mgr)

BELOEIL
PUBLICATION NAME
L'oeil Regional
Street Address: 393 Laurier Blvd. ,
Province: QC
Postal: J3G 4H6
Country: Canada
Mailing address: 393 Laurier Blvd.
Mailing city: Beloeil
Province: QC
Postal: J3G 4H6
General Phone: (450) 467-1821
General Fax: (450) 467-3087
General/National Adv. E-mail: redaction@oeilregional.com
Display Adv. E-mail: publicite@oeilregional.com
Editorial e-mail: redaction@oeilregional.com
Primary Website: www.oeilregional.com
Areas Served - City/County or Portion Thereof, or Zip codes: Canada
Mechanical specifications: Type page 10 1/4 x 16 1/2; E - 8 cols, 1 1/6, 1/6 between; A - 8 cols, 1 1/6, 1/6 between; C - 8 cols, 1 1/6, 1/6 between.
Published: Sat
Avg Paid Circ: 8
Avg Free Circ: 34637
Audit By: CCAB
Audit Date: 31.03.2014
Personnel: Serge Landry
Parent company (for newspapers): Reseau Select/ Select Network; Les Hebdos Monteregiens-OOB

BERTHIERVILLE
PUBLICATION NAME
Publiquip
Street Address: Rue Gilles Villeneuve ,
Province: QC
Postal: J0K 1A0
Country: Canada
Mailing address: rue Gilles Villeneuve
Mailing city: Berthierville
Province: QC
Postal: J0K 1A0
General Phone: (450) 836-3666
Published: Sun
Avg Paid Circ: 701
Avg Free Circ: 50494
Audit By: ODC
Audit Date: 14.12.2011
Personnel: Francoise Trepanier

BIGGAR
PUBLICATION NAME
The Independent
Street Address: 102 3 Ave W ,
Province: SK
Postal: S0K 0M0
Country: Canada
Mailing address: PO Box 40
Mailing city: Biggar
Province: SK
Postal: S0K 0M0
General Phone: (306) 948-3344
General Fax: (306) 948-2133
General/National Adv. E-mail: tip@sasktel.net
Areas Served - City/County or Portion Thereof, or Zip codes: Canada
Mechanical specifications: Type page 11 x 17; E - 6 cols, 1 1/2, 1/6 between; A - 6 cols, 1 1/2, 1/6 between; C - 6 cols, 1 1/2, 1/6 between.
Published: Thur
Avg Paid Circ: 1310
Avg Free Circ: 538
Audit By: CMCA
Audit Date: 30.04.2016
Personnel: Margaret Hasein (Pub.); Daryl Hasein (Gen. Mgr.); Urla Tyler (Adv. Mgr.); Kevin Bratigan (Ed.)

Community Newspapers in Canada

BLAIRMORE

PUBLICATION NAME

Crowsnest Pass Herald
Street Address: 12925 20th Ave. ,
Province: AB
Postal: T0K 0E0
Country: Canada
Mailing address: PO Box 960
Mailing city: Blairmore
Province: AB
Postal: T0K 0E0
General Phone: (403) 562-2248
General Fax: (403) 562-8379
General/National Adv. E-mail: news@passherald.ca
Editorial e-mail: news@passherald.ca
Primary Website: www.passherald.ca
Year Established: 1930
Delivery Methods: Mail`Racks
Areas Served - City/County or Portion Thereof, or Zip codes: Canada
Commercial printers?: Y
Mechanical specifications: Type page 10 1/4 x 16; E - 5 cols, 2, between; A - 5 cols, 2, between.
Published: Wed
Avg Paid Circ: 1361
Avg Free Circ: 235
Audit By: Sworn/Estimate/Non-Audited
Audit Date: 12.07.2019
Personnel: Lisa Sygutek (Pub.).

BLENHEIM

PUBLICATION NAME

Blenheim News-tribune
Street Address: 62 Talbot St. W. ,
Province: ON
Postal: N0P 1A0
Country: Canada
Mailing address: PO Box 160
Mailing city: Blenheim
Province: ON
Postal: N0P 1A0
General Phone: (519) 676-3321
General Fax: (519) 676-3454
Advertising Phone: (519) 676-5023
Advertising Fax: (519) 676-3454
Editorial Phone: (519) 676-3321
General/National Adv. E-mail: tribune@southkent.net
Editorial e-mail: pl.tribune@southkent.com
Primary Website: facebook.com/bleheimnewstribune
Year Established: 1884
Delivery Methods: Mail
Areas Served - City/County or Portion Thereof, or Zip codes: Canada
Mechanical specifications: Type page 10 1/4 x 16; E - 6 cols, 1 7/12, between.
Published: Wed
Avg Paid Circ: 1609
Avg Free Circ: 78
Audit By: AAM
Audit Date: 31.03.2019
Personnel: Pete Laurie (Ed.); Dave Stepniak (Prod Mgr)

BLYTH

PUBLICATION NAME

North Huron Publishing Inc.
Street Address: 413 Queen St. , Po Box 429
Province: ON
Postal: N0M 1H0
Country: Canada
Mailing address: PO Box 429
Mailing city: Blyth
Province: ON
Postal: N0M 1H0
General Phone: (519) 523-4792
General Fax: (519) 523-9140
General/National Adv. E-mail: info@northhuron.on.ca
Display Adv. E-mail: deb@northhuron.on.ca
Classified Adv. E-mail: deb@northhuron.on.ca
Editorial e-mail: deb@northhuron.on.ca
Primary Website: www.northhuron.on.ca
Delivery Methods: Mail`Racks
Areas Served - City/County or Portion Thereof, or Zip codes: Canada
Published: Thur
Avg Paid Circ: 1772
Avg Free Circ: 26
Audit By: CMCA
Audit Date: 28.11.2018
Personnel: Deb Sholdice (Pub.)

BOISSEVAIN

PUBLICATION NAME

The Boissevain Recorder
Street Address: 425 South Railway Street ,
Province: MB
Postal: R0K 0E0
Country: Canada
Mailing address: PO Box 220
Mailing city: Boissevain
Province: MB
Postal: R0K 0E0
General Phone: (204) 534-6479
General Fax: (204) 534-2977
General/National Adv. E-mail: mail@therecorder.ca
Display Adv. E-mail: ads@therecorder.ca
Classified Adv. e-mail: mail@therecorder.ca
Editorial e-mail: editor@therecorder.ca
Primary Website: www.therecorder.ca
Year Established: 1899
Delivery Methods: Mail`Newsstand
Areas Served - City/County or Portion Thereof, or Zip codes: Canada
Mechanical specifications: Type page 10 x 14; E - 6 cols, 1 3/5, 1/6 between; A - 6 cols, 1 3/5, 1/6 between; C - 6 cols, 1 3/5, 1/6 between.
Published: Fri
Avg Paid Circ: 3863
Avg Free Circ: 44
Audit By: VAC
Audit Date: 31.01.2016
Personnel: Lorraine E. Houston (Ed.)

BOLTON

PUBLICATION NAME

Caledon Citizen
Street Address: 30 Martha St , Suite 205
Province: ON
Postal: L7E 5V1
Country: Canada
Mailing address: 30 Martha St Suite 205
Mailing city: Bolton
Province: ON
Postal: L7E 5V1
General Phone: (905) 857-6626
General Fax: (905) 857-6363
General/National Adv. E-mail: admin@caledoncitizen.com
Display Adv. E-mail: erin@lpcmedia.ca
Classified Adv. e-mail: heather@caledoncitizen.com
Editorial e-mail: editor@caledoncitizen.com
Primary Website: www.caledoncitizen.com
Year Established: 1983
Delivery Methods: Mail`Carrier
Areas Served - City/County or Portion Thereof, or Zip codes: Canada
Mechanical specifications: Type page 10 7/16 x 15; E - 6 cols, 1 5/8, between.
Published: Thur
Avg Paid Circ: 12240
Audit By: Sworn/Estimate/Non-Audited
Audit Date: 12.07.2019
Personnel: Alan Claridge (Pub); Mary Speck (Office Mgr); Joshua Santos
Parent company (for newspapers): Simcoe-York Group

PUBLICATION NAME

Caledon Enterprise
Street Address: 12612 Hwy. 50 N. ,
Province: ON
Postal: L7E 5T1
Country: Canada
Mailing address: PO Box 99
Mailing city: Bolton
Province: ON
Postal: L7E 5T1
General Phone: (905) 857-3433
General Fax: (905) 857-5002
Display Adv. E-mail: mcrake@caledonenterprise.com
Classified Adv. e-mail: classifieds@metroland.com
Editorial e-mail: rwilkinson@caledonenterprise.com
Primary Website: caledonenterprise.com
Areas Served - City/County or Portion Thereof, or Zip codes: Canada
Published: Tues`Thur
Avg Paid Circ: 0
Avg Free Circ: 19199
Audit By: CCAB
Audit Date: 30.09.2017
Personnel: Sheila Ogram (Circ Mgr); Robyn Wilkinson (Ed); Melinda Crake (Adv. Rep)
Parent company (for newspapers): Metroland Media Group Ltd.; Torstar

PUBLICATION NAME

King Weekly Sentinel
Street Address: 30 Martha Streeet, Suite 205 ,
Province: ON
Postal: L7E 5V1
Country: Canada
General Phone: (905) 857-6626
General Fax: (905) 857-6363
General/National Adv. E-mail: admin.syp@rogers.com
Display Adv. E-mail: zach@lpcmedia.ca
Classified Adv. e-mail: admin@caledoncitizen.com
Editorial e-mail: editor@kingsentinel.com
Primary Website: www.kingsentinel.com
Year Established: 1980
Delivery Methods: Newsstand`Carrier`Racks
Areas Served - City/County or Portion Thereof, or Zip codes: Caledon
Mechanical specifications: Type page 10 1/2 x 15; E - 6 cols, 1 13/20, 1/6 between; A - 6 cols, 1 13/20, 1/6 between; C - 6 cols, 1 13/20, 1/6 between.
Published: Thur
Avg Paid Circ: 30
Avg Free Circ: 10200
Audit By: Sworn/Estimate/Non-Audited
Audit Date: 12.07.2019
Personnel: Mark Pavilons (Editor)

BONNYVILLE

PUBLICATION NAME

Bonnyville Nouvelle
Street Address: 5304 50th Ave. ,
Province: AB
Postal: T9N 1Y4
Country: Canada
Mailing address: 5304 50th Ave.
Mailing city: Bonnyville
Province: AB
Postal: T9N 1Y4
General Phone: (780) 826-3876
General Fax: (780) 826-7062
Advertising Phone: (780) 826-3876
Display Adv. E-mail: aclarke@bonnyville.greatwest.ca
Editorial e-mail: koelschlagel@bonnyville.greatwest.ca
Primary Website: www.bonnyvillenouvelle.com
Year Established: 1967
Areas Served - City/County or Portion Thereof, or Zip codes: Canada
Own Printing Facility?: Y
Commercial printers?: Y
Mechanical specifications: Type page 14 x 15 1/2; E - 7 cols, 1 3/5, 1/6 between; A - 6 cols, 1 1/3, 1/6 between; C - 6 cols, 1 1/3, 1/6 between.
Published: Tues
Avg Paid Circ: 626
Avg Free Circ: 681
Audit By: VAC
Audit Date: 31.03.2016
Personnel: Cindy Coates (Circ. Mgr.); Kristen Oelschlagel (Ed); Angie Hampshire (Pub)
Parent company (for newspapers): Glacier Media Group; Great West Newspapers LP

BOTHWELL

PUBLICATION NAME

Old Autos
Street Address: 348 Main St. ,
Province: ON
Postal: N0P 1C0
Country: Canada
Mailing address: 348 Main St, PO Box 250
Mailing city: Bothwell
Province: ON
Postal: N0P 1C0
General Phone: (800) 461-3457
General/National Adv. E-mail: info@oldautos.ca
Display Adv. E-mail: ads@oldautos.ca
Classified Adv. e-mail: classifieds@oldautos.ca
Editorial e-mail: maryjo@oldautos.ca
Primary Website: oldautos.ca
Year Established: 1987
Delivery Methods: Mail`Newsstand
Areas Served - City/County or Portion Thereof, or Zip codes: Canada
Published: Mon
Avg Paid Circ: 14045
Avg Free Circ: 285
Audit By: AAM
Audit Date: 31.03.2019
Personnel: Mary Jo DePelsmaeker (Publisher)

BOUCHERVILLE

PUBLICATION NAME

La Releve
Street Address: 528 St. Charles St. ,
Province: QC
Postal: J4B 3M5
Country: Canada
Mailing address: 528 St. Charles St.
Mailing city: Boucherville
Province: QC
Postal: J4B 3M5
General Phone: (450) 641-4844
General Fax: (450) 641-4849
Advertising Phone: (514) 926-2354
General/National Adv. E-mail: lareleve@lareleve.qc.ca
Display Adv. E-mail: c.desmarteau@videotron.ca
Classified Adv. e-mail: classees@lareleve.qc.ca
Editorial e-mail: lareleve@lareleve.qc.ca
Primary Website: www.lareleve.qc.ca
Year Established: 1987
Areas Served - City/County or Portion Thereof, or Zip codes: J4B, J4M, J4N, J4G, J3E, J0L 2S0, J3X, J0L 1N0, J0L 2R0, J0L 1A0
Commercial printers?: Y
Mechanical specifications: Type page 10 1/4" x 14 1/4".
Published: Tues
Avg Paid Circ: 0
Avg Free Circ: 59100
Audit By: Sworn/Estimate/Non-Audited
Audit Date: 12.07.2019
Personnel: Charles Desmarteau (Ed. & Gen. Mgr.)
Parent company (for newspapers): Groupe Messier

PUBLICATION NAME

La Seigneurie
Street Address: 391 Boul. De Mortagne ,
Province: QC
Postal: J4B 3M5
Country: Canada
Mailing address: 528, St-Charles
Mailing city: Boucherville
Province: QC
Postal: J4B 1B7
General Phone: (450) 641-4844
General Fax: (450) 641-4849

General/National Adv. E-mail: info@la-seigneurie.qc.ca
Display Adv. E-mail: lareleve@lareleve.qc.ca
Editorial e-mail: redaction@la-seigneurie.qc.ca
Primary Website: www.la-seigneurie.qc.ca
Areas Served - City/County or Portion Thereof, or Zip codes: Quebec
Mechanical specifications: Type page 10 1/4 x 17; E - 8 cols, between; A - 8 cols, between; C - 8 cols, between.
Published: Wed
Avg Free Circ: 33856
Audit By: Sworn/Estimate/Non-Audited
Audit Date: 12.07.2019
Personnel: Charles Desmarteau (Pub.)
Parent company (for newspapers): La Releve

BOW ISLAND

PUBLICATION NAME

The 40-mile County Commentator
Street Address: 147-5 Ave. W. ,
Province: AB
Postal: T0K 0G0
Country: Canada
Mailing address: P.O. Box 580
Mailing city: Bow Island
Province: AB
Postal: T0K 0G0
General Phone: (403) 545-2258
General Fax: (403) 545-6886
General/National Adv. E-mail: tabads@tabertimes.com
Display Adv. E-mail: editor@bowislandcommentator.com
Primary Website: www.bowislandcommentator.com
Year Established: 1971
Delivery Methods: Mail`Newsstand
Areas Served - City/County or Portion Thereof, or Zip codes: County of Forty Mile No. 8
Commercial printers?: Y
Published: Tues
Avg Paid Circ: 426
Avg Free Circ: 45
Audit By: VAC
Audit Date: 30.09.2016
Personnel: Coleen Campbell (Pub.); Tom Conquergood (Adv. Mgr.); Jamie Rieger (Ed.)

BOWEN ISLAND

PUBLICATION NAME

Bowen Island Undercurrent
Street Address: 102-495 Bowen Trunk Rd. ,
Province: BC
Postal: V0N 1V0
Country: Canada
Mailing address: PO Box 130
Mailing city: Bowen Island
Province: BC
Postal: V0N 1G0
General Phone: (604) 947-2442
General Fax: (604) 947-0148
Advertising Phone: (604) 947-2442
Editorial Phone: (604) 947-2442
General/National Adv. E-mail: publisher@bowenislandundercurrent.com
Display Adv. E-mail: ads@bowenislandundercurrent.com
Classified Adv. e-mail: ads@bowenislandundercurrent.com
Editorial e-mail: editor@bowenislandundercurrent.com
Primary Website: www.bowenislandundercurrent.com
Year Established: 1972
Areas Served - City/County or Portion Thereof, or Zip codes: Canada
Mechanical specifications: Type page 10 3/8 x 12 1/2; E - 6 cols, 1 11/18, between.
Published: Fri
Avg Free Circ: 73
Audit By: VAC
Audit Date: 31.05.2016
Personnel: Martha Perkins (Ed.); Kaana Bjork (Prodn. Mgr.); Maureen Sawasy (Adv. Sales); Peter Kvarnstrom (Pub.)

Parent company (for newspapers): Glacier Media Group

BRACEBRIDGE

PUBLICATION NAME

Bracebridge Examiner
Street Address: 34 Ep Lee Dr. ,
Province: ON
Postal: P1L 1P9
Country: Canada
Mailing address: PO Box 1049
Mailing city: Bracebridge
Province: ON
Postal: P1L 1V2
General Phone: (705) 645-8771
General Fax: (705) 645-1718
General/National Adv. E-mail: examiner@muskoka.com
Display Adv. E-mail: mbradley@metroland.com
Classified Adv. e-mail: classifieds@metroland.com
Editorial e-mail: psteel@metrolandnorthmedia.com
Primary Website: www.bracebridgeexaminer.com
Areas Served - City/County or Portion Thereof, or Zip codes: Canada
Mechanical specifications: Type page 11 1/2 x 21 1/2; E - 6 cols, between; A - 6 cols, between; C - 6 cols, between.
Published: Thur
Avg Paid Circ: 83
Avg Free Circ: 8171
Audit By: CMCA
Audit Date: 30.04.2016
Personnel: Meriel Bradley (Adv. Mgr); Pamela Steel (Ed); Andrew Allen (Circ Mgr)
Parent company (for newspapers): Metroland Media Group Ltd.; Torstar

PUBLICATION NAME

Muskoka District Weekender
Street Address: 34 E. P. Lee Drive ,
Province: ON
Postal: P1L 1V2
Country: Canada
Mailing address: PO Box 1049
Mailing city: Bracebridge on
Province: ON
Postal: P1L 1V2
General Phone: (705) 645-8771
General Fax: (705) 645-1718
General/National Adv. E-mail: ccunningham@metrolandnorthmedia.com
Display Adv. E-mail: ddickson@metrolandnorthmedia.com
Primary Website: www.muskokaregion.com
Areas Served - City/County or Portion Thereof, or Zip codes: Canada
Published: Fri
Avg Free Circ: 26430
Audit By: CMCA
Audit Date: 30.04.2013
Personnel: Coral Brush (Sales Coordinator)

PUBLICATION NAME

The Muskokan
Street Address: 34 Ep Lee Dr. ,
Province: ON
Postal: P1L 1P9
Country: Canada
Mailing address: PO Box 1049
Mailing city: Bracebridge
Province: ON
Postal: P1L 1V2
General Phone: (705) 645-8771
General Fax: (705) 645-1718
General/National Adv. E-mail: muskokan@muskoka.com
Primary Website: www.muskokan.com
Own Printing Facility?: Y
Published: Thur
Avg Free Circ: 24000
Audit By: Sworn/Estimate/Non-Audited
Audit Date: 12.07.2019

Personnel: Paul Drummond (Adv. Sales Mgr.); Jake Good (Editorial Coord.); Marianne Dawson (Prodn. Coord.)
Parent company (for newspapers): Metroland Media Group Ltd.; Torstar

PUBLICATION NAME

What's Up Muskoka
Street Address: Unit 12-440 Ecclestone Drive ,
Province: ON
Postal: P1L 1Z6
Country: Canada
Mailing address: PO Box 180
Mailing city: Bracebridge
Province: ON
Postal: P1L 1T6
General Phone: (705) 646-1314
General Fax: (705) 645-6424
General/National Adv. E-mail: mm.info@sunmedia.ca
Primary Website: www.whatsupmuskoka.com
Year Established: 2008
Delivery Methods: Mail`Racks
Areas Served - City/County or Portion Thereof, or Zip codes: Muskoka
Own Printing Facility?: Y
Mechanical specifications: Type page 10 1/3 x 12 1/2; E - 6 cols, 1 1/2, between; A - 6 cols, 1 1/2, between; C - 6 cols, 1 1/2, between.
Published: Wed
Avg Paid Circ: 0
Avg Free Circ: 26000
Audit By: CMCA
Audit Date: 31.07.2013
Parent company (for newspapers): Postmedia Network Inc.; Quebecor Communications, Inc.

BRAMPTON

PUBLICATION NAME

Action London Sarnia
Street Address: Professor's Lake Parkway ,
Province: ON
Postal: L6S 4P8
Country: Canada
Mailing address: Professor's Lake Parkway
Mailing city: Brampton
Province: ON
Postal: L6S 4P8
General Phone: (800) 525-6752
Editorial e-mail: info@lemetropolitain.com
Primary Website: www.laction.ca
Published: Tues
Avg Paid Circ: 1907
Avg Free Circ: 1106
Audit By: ODC
Audit Date: 13.11.2011
Personnel: Denis Poirier (Ed); Richard Caumartin (Sales Dir)

PUBLICATION NAME

Le Regional
Street Address: 99 Professors Lake Parkway ,
Province: ON
Postal: L6S 4P8
Country: Canada
Mailing address: 99 Professors Park Way
Mailing city: Brampton
Province: ON
Postal: L6S 4P8
General Phone: (905) 732-9666
General Fax: (905) 790-9127
General/National Adv. E-mail: info@leregional.com
Display Adv. E-mail: marketing@leregional.com
Classified Adv. e-mail: marketing@leregional.com
Editorial e-mail: info@leregional.com
Primary Website: www.leregional.com
Year Established: 2000
Delivery Methods: Mail`Racks
Areas Served - City/County or Portion Thereof, or Zip codes: Canada
Published: Wed
Avg Paid Circ: 76

Avg Free Circ: 4164
Audit By: CMCA
Audit Date: 31.12.2012
Personnel: Christiane Beaupre

PUBLICATION NAME

Metropolitain (le)
Street Address: 99 Professors Lake Pkwy ,
Province: ON
Postal: L6S 4P8
Country: Canada
Mailing address: 99 Professors Lake Pkwy
Mailing city: Brampton
Province: ON
Postal: L6S 4P8
General Phone: (905) 790-3229
General Fax: (905) 790-9127
General/National Adv. E-mail: info@lemetropolitain.com
Primary Website: www.lemetropolitain.com
Areas Served - City/County or Portion Thereof, or Zip codes: Canada
Published: Wed
Avg Paid Circ: 329
Avg Free Circ: 8028
Audit By: CMCA
Audit Date: 31.12.2012
Personnel: Denis Poirier (Ed.)

BRANDON

PUBLICATION NAME

Westman Journal
Street Address: 315 College Avenue , Unit D
Province: MB
Postal: R7A 1E7
Country: Canada
Mailing address: 315 College Avenue
Mailing city: Brandon
Province: MB
Postal: R7A 1E7
General Phone: (204) 725-0209
General Fax: (204) 725-3021
General/National Adv. E-mail: info@wheatcityjournal.ca
Display Adv. E-mail: rthomson@wheatcityjournal.ca
Classified Adv. e-mail: agrelowshi@wheatcityjournal.ca
Editorial e-mail: newsroom@wheatcityjournal.ca
Primary Website: www.westmanjournal.com
Year Established: 2002
Delivery Methods: Carrier`Racks
Areas Served - City/County or Portion Thereof, or Zip codes: Brandon, MB
Published: Thur
Avg Free Circ: 13500
Audit By: VAC
Audit Date: 25.11.2017
Personnel: Rick Thomson; Alida Grelowski; Adam Wilken; Jamie Polmateer; Wade Branston; Brian Aitkinson; Judy Cluff (Admin Asst.)
Parent company (for newspapers): Glacier Media Group

BRANTFORD

PUBLICATION NAME

Brant News
Street Address: 111 Easton Rd. ,
Province: ON
Postal: N3P 1J4
Country: Canada
Mailing address: 111 Easton Rd.
Mailing city: Brantford
Province: ON
Postal: N3P 1J4
General Phone: (519) 758-1157
General Fax: (519) 753-3567
General/National Adv. E-mail: loffless@brantnews.com
Display Adv. E-mail: lbutler@brantnews.com
Classified Adv. e-mail: classified@metrolandwest.com
Editorial e-mail: sallen@brantnews.com

Community Newspapers in Canada

Primary Website: www.brantnews.com
Year Established: 2009
Areas Served - City/County or Portion Thereof, or Zip codes: Canada
Published: Thur
Avg Paid Circ: 0
Avg Free Circ: 48716
Audit By: CCAB
Audit Date: 30.09.2017
Personnel: Linda Hill (Circ Mgr); Sean Allen (Ed); Loren Butlet (Adv Mgr)
Parent company (for newspapers): Metroland Media Group Ltd.; Metroland Media

PUBLICATION NAME

Paris Star
Street Address: 195 Henry St , Building 4, Unit 1
Province: ON
Postal: N3S 5C9
Country: Canada
Mailing address: 195 Henry St, Building 4, Unit 1
Mailing city: Brantford
Province: ON
Postal: N3S 5C9
General Phone: (519) 756-2020
General Fax: (519) 756-9470
General/National Adv. E-mail: parisstar.editorial@sunmedia.ca
Editorial e-mail: parisstar.editorial@sunmedia.ca
Primary Website: parisstaronline.com
Year Established: 1850
Areas Served - City/County or Portion Thereof, or Zip codes: Canada
Own Printing Facility?: Y
Mechanical specifications: Type page 10 x 16; E - 5 cols, 2, 1/8 between; A - 5 cols, 2, 1/8 between; C - 6 cols, 1 3/4, 1/8 between.
Published: Thur
Avg Free Circ: 4877
Audit By: CMCA
Audit Date: 30.04.2019
Personnel: Ken Koyama (Pub.); Michael Peeling (Ed.)
Parent company (for newspapers): Postmedia Network Inc.; Quebecor Communications, Inc.

BRIDGEWATER

PUBLICATION NAME

Lighthouse Now
Street Address: 353 York St. ,
Province: NS
Postal: B4V 3K2
Country: Canada
Mailing address: 353 York St.
Mailing city: Bridgewater
Province: NS
Postal: B4V 3K2
General Phone: (902) 543-2457
General Fax: (902) 543-2228
Advertising Phone: (902) 543-1569
General/National Adv. E-mail: mail@southshorenow.ca
Display Adv. E-mail: daveda.savory@lighthousenow.ca
Classified Adv. e-mail: tracy.williams@lighthousenow.ca
Editorial e-mail: editorial@southshorenow.ca
Primary Website: https://lighthousenow.ca/
Areas Served - City/County or Portion Thereof, or Zip codes: Bridgewater
Own Printing Facility?: Y
Mechanical specifications: Type page 10 5/16 x 16; E - 6 cols, 1 5/8, 1/6 between; A - 6 cols, 1 5/8, 1/6 between; C - 6 cols, 1 5/8, 1/6 between.
Published: Thur
Avg Paid Circ: 6573
Avg Free Circ: 26963
Audit By: VAC
Audit Date: 31.10.2015
Personnel: Lynn Hennigar (Pub); Laurenda Reeves (Circ. Mgr.); Emma Smith (Ed.)

PUBLICATION NAME

The Bulletin
Street Address: 353 York St. ,
Province: NS
Postal: B4V 3K2
Country: Canada
Mailing address: 353 York St.
Mailing city: Bridgewater
Province: NS
Postal: B4V 3K2
General Phone: (902) 543-2457
General Fax: (902) 543-2228
General/National Adv. E-mail: editorial@southshorenow.ca
Editorial e-mail: editorial@southshorenow.ca
Primary Website: https://lighthousenow.ca
Year Established: 1888
Areas Served - City/County or Portion Thereof, or Zip codes: Canada
Commercial printers?: Y
Mechanical specifications: Type page 10 5/16 x 16; E - 6 cols, 1 5/8, 1/6 between; A - 6 cols, 1 5/8, 1/6 between; C - 6 cols, 1 5/8, 1/6 between.
Published: Tues
Avg Paid Circ: 7030
Avg Free Circ: 127
Audit By: Sworn/Estimate/Non-Audited
Audit Date: 12.07.2019
Personnel: Lynn Hennigar (Pub); Laurenda Reeves (Circ. Mgr.); Emma Smith (Ed.)

BROCKVILLE

PUBLICATION NAME

St. Lawrence News
Street Address: 7712 Kent Blvd. ,
Province: ON
Postal: K6V 7H6
Country: Canada
General Phone: (613) 498-0305
General Fax: (613) 498-0307
Primary Website: www.emcstlawrence.ca
Areas Served - City/County or Portion Thereof, or Zip codes: Canada
Published: Thur
Avg Free Circ: 29325
Audit By: CMCA
Audit Date: 30.06.2016
Parent company (for newspapers): Metroland Media Group Ltd.

PUBLICATION NAME

The Recorder & Times
Street Address: 2479 Parkedale Avenue ,
Province: ON
Postal: K6V 3H2
Country: Canada
Mailing address: 2479 Parkedale Avenue
Mailing city: Brockville
Province: ON
Postal: K6V 3H2
General Phone: (613) 342-4441
General Fax: (613) 342-4456
Advertising Phone: (613) 342-4441 Ext. 500267
Editorial Phone: (613) 342-4441 Ext. 500107
General/National Adv. E-mail: newsroom@indynews.ca
Display Adv. E-mail: ksammon@postmedia.com
Editorial e-mail: dgordanier@postmedia.com
Primary Website: www.recorder.ca
Year Established: 1997
Delivery Methods: Newsstand`Carrier
Areas Served - City/County or Portion Thereof, or Zip codes: Leeds & Grenville Counties
Commercial printers?: Y
Mechanical specifications: Type page 10 1/4 x 14 1/4; E - 6 cols, 1 5/8, 1/8 between; A - 6 cols, 1 5/8, 1/8 between; C - 7 cols, 1 1/3, 1/8 between.
Published: Wed`Thur
Avg Free Circ: 29300
Audit By: CMCA
Audit Date: 30.09.2016
Personnel: Kerry Sammon (Med. Sales Dir.)
Parent company (for newspapers): Post Media

BROOKS

PUBLICATION NAME

The Brooks Bulletin
Street Address: 124-3 St. W. ,
Province: AB
Postal: T1R 0S3
Country: Canada
Mailing address: PO Box 1450
Mailing city: Brooks
Province: AB
Postal: T1R 1C3
General Phone: (403) 362-5571
General Fax: (403) 362-5080
Display Adv. E-mail: diane@brooksbulletin.com
Classified Adv. e-mail: diane@brooksbulletin.com
Editorial e-mail: editor@brooksbulletin.com
Primary Website: www.brooksbulletin.com
Year Established: 1910
Delivery Methods: Mail`Newsstand`Racks
Areas Served - City/County or Portion Thereof, or Zip codes: Brooks and County of Newell, Canada
Own Printing Facility?: Y
Commercial printers?: Y
Mechanical specifications: Type page 11.5 x 21.
Published: Tues
Avg Paid Circ: 2800
Avg Free Circ: 188
Audit By: Sworn/Estimate/Non-Audited
Audit Date: 12.07.2019
Personnel: Jamie Nesbitt (Ed./Pub.)
Parent company (for newspapers): Brooks Bulletin

BURKS FALLS

PUBLICATION NAME

Almaguin News
Street Address: 59 Ontario St. ,
Province: ON
Postal: P0A 1C0
Country: Canada
Mailing address: PO Box 518
Mailing city: Burks Falls
Province: ON
Postal: P0A 1C0
General Phone: (705)382-9996
General Fax: (705) 382-9997
General/National Adv. E-mail: news@almaguinnews.com
Display Adv. E-mail: advertising@almaguinnews.com
Editorial e-mail: editor@almaguinnews.com
Primary Website: www.almaguinnews.com
Year Established: 1889
Delivery Methods: Mail`Newsstand
Areas Served - City/County or Portion Thereof, or Zip codes: Canada
Commercial printers?: Y
Mechanical specifications: Type page 10 x 21 1/2"; E - 9 cols, 1 1/16, between; A - 9 cols, 1 3/8, between; C - 9 cols, 1 3/8, between.
Published: Thur
Avg Paid Circ: 2230
Avg Free Circ: 150
Audit By: CMCA
Audit Date: 31.12.2015
Personnel: Bill Allen (Gen. Mgr.); Twila Armstrong (Adv. Rep.); Rob Learn (News Ed.)
Parent company (for newspapers): Metroland Media Group Ltd.

BURLINGTON

PUBLICATION NAME

The Burlington Post
Street Address: 5040 Mainway, Unit 1 ,
Province: ON
Postal: L7L 7G5
Country: Canada
Mailing address: 5040 Mainway, Unit 1
Mailing city: Burlington
Province: ON
Postal: L7L 7G5
General Phone: (905) 632-4444
General Fax: (905) 632-9162
Editorial e-mail: letters@burlingtonpost.com
Primary Website: burlingtonpost.com
Year Established: 1965
Delivery Methods: Carrier
Areas Served - City/County or Portion Thereof, or Zip codes: Canada
Own Printing Facility?: Y
Commercial printers?: Y
Published: Thur`Fri
Avg Paid Circ: 27
Avg Free Circ: 28355
Audit By: CCAB
Audit Date: 30.09.2017
Personnel: Jill Davis (Ed. in Chief); Don Ford (Mng. Ed.); Kevin Nagel (Sports Ed.); Debbi Koppejan (Advertising Director)
Parent company (for newspapers): Metroland Media Group Ltd.; Torstar

BURNABY

PUBLICATION NAME

Burnaby Now
Street Address: 3430 Brighton Ave. , Ste. 201a
Province: BC
Postal: V5A 3H4
Country: Canada
General Phone: (604) 444-3451
General Fax: (604) 444-3460
Advertising Phone: (604) 444-3030
Editorial Phone: (604) 444-3007
General/National Adv. E-mail: editorial@burnabynow.com
Display Adv. E-mail: chendrix@burnabynow.com
Editorial e-mail: ptracy@royalcityrecord.com
Primary Website: burnabynow.com
Year Established: 1983
Areas Served - City/County or Portion Thereof, or Zip codes: Canada
Own Printing Facility?: Y
Mechanical specifications: Type page 10 1/4 x 14; E - 6 cols, 1 9/16, 1/6 between; A - 6 cols, 1 9/16, 1/6 between; C - 7 cols, 1 3/8, 1/12 between.
Published: Wed`Fri
Avg Paid Circ: 0
Avg Free Circ: 43521
Audit By: CCAB
Audit Date: 23.11.2017
Personnel: Lara Graham (Pub.); Pat Tracy (Ed.); Cynthia Hendrix (Adv.); Dan Olson (Sports Ed.)
Parent company (for newspapers): Glacier Media Group

BURNABY

PUBLICATION NAME

The Record
Street Address: 201a 3430 Brighton Ave. ,
Province: BC
Postal: V5A 3H4
Country: Canada
Mailing address: 201A 3430 Brighton Ave.
Mailing city: Burnaby
Province: BC
Postal: V5A 3H4
General Phone: (604) 444-3451
General Fax: (604) 444-3460
Advertising Phone: (604)444-3030
Editorial Phone: (604) 444-3007
Display Adv. E-mail: kgilmour@newwestrecord.ca
Editorial e-mail: ptracy@newwestrecord.ca
Primary Website: royalcityrecord.com
Year Established: 1981
Areas Served - City/County or Portion Thereof, or Zip codes: Canada
Own Printing Facility?: Y
Published: Wed`Fri
Avg Paid Circ: 0
Avg Free Circ: 16966
Audit By: CCAB
Audit Date: 23.11.2017
Personnel: Lara Graham (Pub); Pat Tracy (Ed.); Dale Dorsett (Circ. Mgr)
Parent company (for newspapers): CanWest MediaWorks Publications, Inc.

BURNS LAKE

PUBLICATION NAME

Burns Lakes District News
Street Address: 23 3rd Ave.,
Province: BC
Postal: V0J 1E0
Country: Canada
Mailing address: PO Box 309
Mailing city: Burns Lake
Province: BC
Postal: V0J 1E0
General Phone: (250) 692-7526
General Fax: (250) 692-3685
General/National Adv. E-mail: newsroom@ldnews.net; advertising@ldnews.net
Display Adv. E-mail: advertising@ldnews.net
Classified Adv. e-mail: advertising@ldnews.net
Editorial e-mail: newsroom@ldnews.net
Primary Website: www.ldnews.net
Year Established: 1986
Delivery Methods: Mail`Newsstand`Racks
Areas Served - City/County or Portion Thereof, or Zip codes:
Own Printing Facility?: Y
Published: Wed
Avg Paid Circ: 1181
Avg Free Circ: 117
Audit By: VAC
Audit Date: 30.06.2017
Personnel: Laura Blackwell (Adv. Mgr./Pub.); Annamarie Douglas (Prod. Mgr.); Kim Piper (front office); Flavio Nienow (Editor)
Parent company (for newspapers): Black Press Group Ltd.

CALEDONIA

PUBLICATION NAME

Glanbrook Gazette
Street Address: 3 Sutherland St. W.,
Province: ON
Postal: N3W 1C1
Country: Canada
General Phone: (905) 765-4441
General Fax: (905) 765-3651
General/National Adv. E-mail: news@sachem.ca
Display Adv. E-mail: advertising@sachem.ca
Primary Website: www.sachem.ca
Areas Served - City/County or Portion Thereof, or Zip codes: Canada
Published: Thur
Avg Free Circ: 9194
Audit By: CMCA
Audit Date: 31.12.2015
Parent company (for newspapers): Metroland Media Group Ltd.

PUBLICATION NAME

The Grand River Sachem
Street Address: 3 Sutherland St. W.,
Province: ON
Postal: N3W 1C1
Country: Canada
Mailing address: 3 Sutherland St. W.
Mailing city: Caledonia
Province: ON
Postal: N3W 1C1
General Phone: (905) 765-4441
General Fax: (905) 765-3651
General/National Adv. E-mail: news@sachem.ca; sachem@sachem.ca
Display Adv. E-mail: advertising@sachem.ca
Primary Website: www.sachem.ca
Areas Served - City/County or Portion Thereof, or Zip codes: Canada
Mechanical specifications: Type page 10 1/3 x 14; E - 6 cols, 1 3/5, between; A - 6 cols, 1 1/3, between.
Published: Thur
Avg Paid Circ: 77
Avg Free Circ: 21137
Audit By: CMCA
Audit Date: 30.06.2013
Personnel: Nancy Plank (Adv. Mgr.); Georgia Mete (Adv. Mgr., Classified); Neil Dring (Ed.)
Parent company (for newspapers): Metroland Media Group Ltd.

CAMBRIDGE

PUBLICATION NAME

Cambridge Times
Street Address: 475 Thompson Dr. Units 1-4,
Province: ON
Postal: N1T 2K7
Country: Canada
Mailing address: 475 Thompson Dr. Units 1-4
Mailing city: Cambridge
Province: ON
Postal: N1T 2K7
General Phone: (519) 623-7395
General Fax: (519) 623-9155
Display Adv. E-mail: tanderson@cambridgetimes.ca
Classified Adv. e-mail: classified@metrolandwest.com
Editorial e-mail: rvivian@cambridgetimes.ca
Primary Website: www.cambridgetimes.ca
Delivery Methods: Carrier
Areas Served - City/County or Portion Thereof, or Zip codes: Canada
Commercial printers?: Y
Mechanical specifications: Type page 11 x 17; E - 6 cols, 2 1/20, between; A - 6 cols, 2 1/20, between; C - 6 cols, 2 1/20, between.
Published: Tues`Thur
Avg Free Circ: 31628
Audit By: CMCA
Audit Date: 30.06.2016
Personnel: Donna Luelo (Pub); Richard Vivian (Ed); Carron Woods (Prod/Circ. Mgr.); Ted Anderson (Adv. Mgr.)
Parent company (for newspapers): Metroland Media Group Ltd.; Torstar

CAMPBELL RIVER

PUBLICATION NAME

The Campbell River Courier-islander
Street Address: 104 - 250 Dogwood St,
Province: BC
Postal: V9W 5Z5
Country: Canada
Mailing address: 104 - 250 Dogwood St
Mailing city: Campbell River
Province: BC
Postal: V9W 5Z5
General Phone: (250) 287-9227
General Fax: (250) 287-8891
Display Adv. E-mail: jacquie.duns@campbellrivermirror.com
Classified Adv. e-mail: darceyw@campbellrivermirror.com
Editorial e-mail: editor@campbellrivermirror.com
Primary Website: www.courierislander.com
Year Established: 1945
Delivery Methods: Mail`Newsstand`Carrier`Racks
Areas Served - City/County or Portion Thereof, or Zip codes: Campbell River
Own Printing Facility?: Y
Commercial printers?: N
Mechanical specifications: Type page 11 3/5 x 21 1/2; E - 10 cols, 1 1/10, 1/12 between; A - 10 cols, 1 1/10, 1/12 between; C - 10 cols, 1 1/10, 1/12 between.
Published: Wed`Fri
Avg Paid Circ: 0
Avg Free Circ: 16561
Audit By: AAM
Audit Date: 30.09.2015
Personnel: David Hamilton (Pub); Alistair Taylor (Ed); Kevin McKinnon (Circ. Mgr)

PUBLICATION NAME

The Campbell River Mirror
Street Address: 104-250 Dogwood St.,
Province: BC
Postal: V9W 2X9
Country: Canada
Mailing address: 104-250 Dogwood St.
Mailing city: Campbell River
Province: BC
Postal: V9W 2X9
General Phone: (250) 287-9227
General Fax: (250) 287-3238
Editorial Phone: (250) 287-9227
General/National Adv. E-mail: publisher@campbellrivermirror.com
Editorial e-mail: editor@campbellrivermirror.com
Primary Website: campbellrivermirror.com
Year Established: 1971
Delivery Methods: Mail`Newsstand`Carrier
Areas Served - City/County or Portion Thereof, or Zip codes: Canada
Own Printing Facility?: Y
Published: Wed`Fri
Avg Paid Circ: 30
Avg Free Circ: 16442
Audit By: AAM
Audit Date: 31.03.2019
Personnel: Alistair Taylor (Ed.); David Hamilton (Pub.); Michelle Hueller (Prod.); Kevin McKinnon (Circ. Mgr.); Zena Williams (Publisher); Artur Ciastkowski (Publisher)
Parent company (for newspapers): Black Press Group Ltd.

CAMPBELLTON

PUBLICATION NAME

The Tribune
Street Address: 6 Shannon St.,
Province: NB
Postal: E3N 3G9
Country: Canada
Mailing address: PO Box 486
Mailing city: Campbellton
Province: NB
Postal: E3N 3G9
General Phone: (506) 753-4413
General Fax: (506) 759-9595
General/National Adv. E-mail: tribune@tribunenb.ca
Editorial e-mail: tribune@tribunenb.ca
Primary Website: http://www.telegraphjournal.com/tribune/
Areas Served - City/County or Portion Thereof, or Zip codes: Campbellton
Mechanical specifications: Type page 12 7/8 x 21; E - 6 cols, 1/6 between; A - 6 cols, 1/6 between; C - 6 cols, 1/6 between.
Published: Fri
Avg Free Circ: 2
Audit By: VAC
Audit Date: 31.12.2015
Personnel: Peter Makintosh (Pub./Ed)

CAMROSE

PUBLICATION NAME

The Camrose Canadian
Street Address: 4610 49th Ave.,
Province: AB
Postal: T4V 0M6
Country: Canada
General Phone: (780) 672-4421
General Fax: (780) 672-5323
Advertising Phone: (877) 786-8227
General/National Adv. E-mail: production@camrosecanadian.com
Display Adv. E-mail: ngoetz@postmedia.com
Primary Website: www.camrosecanadian.com
Year Established: 1908
Areas Served - City/County or Portion Thereof, or Zip codes: Camrose County
Commercial printers?: Y
Mechanical specifications: Type page 10 1/4 x 12 1/2; E - 8 cols, 1 3/16, 1/6 between; A - 8 cols, 1 3/16, 1/6 between; C - 8 cols, 1 1/4, 1/6 between.
Published: Thur
Avg Paid Circ: 3673
Avg Free Circ: 15292
Audit By: VAC
Audit Date: 31.12.2015
Personnel: Dan Macpherson (Adv. Mgr.); Nick Goetz (Publisher); Trent Wilkie (Editor); Vince Burke (Editor(online)); Jim Clark (Publisher(online))
Parent company (for newspapers): Postmedia Network Inc.

CANMORE

PUBLICATION NAME

Rocky Mountain Outlook
Street Address: Box 8610 , Suite 201 - 1001. 6th Avenue
Province: AB
Postal: T1W 2V3
Country: Canada
Mailing address: Box 8610 Suite 201 - 1001. 6th Ave
Mailing city: Canmore
Province: AB
Postal: T1W 2V3
General Phone: (403) 609-0220
General Fax: (403)609-0221
Display Adv. E-mail: clacroix@outlook.greatwest.ca
Classified Adv. e-mail: jlyon@outlook.greatwest.ca
Editorial e-mail: dwhitfield@rmoutlook.com
Primary Website: www.rmoutlook.com
Year Established: 2001
Published: Thur
Avg Paid Circ: 0
Avg Free Circ: 9395
Audit By: VAC
Audit Date: 31.01.2016
Personnel: Jason Lyon (Pub/Adv. Mgr); Donna Browne (Circ. Mgr); Dave Whitfield (Ed)
Parent company (for newspapers): Glacier Media Group; Great West Newspapers LP

CANNINGTON

PUBLICATION NAME

Brock Citizen
Street Address: 2d Cameron St. E.,
Province: ON
Postal: L0E 1E0
Country: Canada
Mailing address: 2D Cameron St. E.
Mailing city: Cannington
Province: ON
Postal: L0E 1E0
General Phone: (705) 432-8842
General Fax: (705) 432-2942
General/National Adv. E-mail: bdanford@mykawartha.com
Display Adv. E-mail: btrickett@mykawartha.com
Classified Adv. e-mail: lmunro@mykawartha.com
Editorial e-mail: ltuffin@mykawartha.com
Primary Website: http://www.mykawartha.com/brocktownship-on/
Published: Thur
Avg Free Circ: 5497
Audit By: Sworn/Estimate/Non-Audited
Audit Date: 12.07.2019
Personnel: Peter Bishop (Ed); Mary Babcock (Gen. Mgr.); Lois Tuffin (Mng. Ed.); Kim Riel (Office Mgr)
Parent company (for newspapers): Metroland Media Group Ltd.; Torstar

CANORA

PUBLICATION NAME

Canora Courier
Street Address: 123 First Ave. E.,
Province: SK
Postal: S0A 0L0
Country: Canada
Mailing address: P.O. Box 746
Mailing city: Canora
Province: SK
Postal: S0A 0L0
General Phone: (306) 563-5131
General Fax: (306) 563-6144
General/National Adv. E-mail: canoracourier@sasktel.net
Display Adv. E-mail: sales.canoracourier@sasktel.net
Classified Adv. e-mail: office.canoracourier@sasktel.net
Editorial e-mail: canoracourier@sasktel.net
Primary Website: canoracourier.com

Community Newspapers in Canada

Delivery Methods: Mail`Newsstand
Areas Served - City/County or Portion Thereof, or Zip codes: Canada
Own Printing Facility?: Y
Commercial printers?: Y
Mechanical specifications: Type page 10 1/4 x 15 1/2; E - 6 cols, 1 2/3, between; A - 6 cols, 1 2/3, between; C - 6 cols, 1 2/3, between.
Published: Wed
Avg Paid Circ: 1136
Avg Free Circ: 9
Audit By: CMCA
Audit Date: 30.09.2016
Personnel: Ken Lewchuk (Pub)
Parent company (for newspapers): Glacier Media Group

PUBLICATION NAME

Preeceville Progress
Street Address: 123 First Ave. E. ,
Province: SK
Postal: S0A 0L0
Country: Canada
Mailing address: P.O. Box 319
Mailing city: Canora
Province: SK
Postal: S0A 0L0
General Phone: (306) 563-5131
General Fax: (306) 563-6144
General/National Adv. E-mail: canoracourier@sasktel.net
Display Adv. E-mail: sales.canoracourier@sasktel.net
Classified Adv. e-mail: office.canoracourier@sasktel.net
Editorial e-mail: canoracourier@sasktel.net
Primary Website: http://www.preecevilleprogress.com/
Areas Served - City/County or Portion Thereof, or Zip codes: Canada
Own Printing Facility?: Y
Commercial printers?: Y
Mechanical specifications: Type page 10 1/4 x 15 1/2; E - 6 cols, 1 2/3, between; A - 6 cols, 1 2/3, between; C - 6 cols, 1 2/3, between.
Published: Thur
Avg Paid Circ: 971
Avg Free Circ: 4
Audit By: CMCA
Audit Date: 15.09.2014
Personnel: Ken Lewchuk
Parent company (for newspapers): Canora Courier; Glacier Media Group

PUBLICATION NAME

The Kamsack Times
Street Address: 123 First Ave. E. ,
Province: SK
Postal: S0A 0L0
Country: Canada
Mailing address: P.O. Box 850
Mailing city: Kamsack
Province: SK
Postal: S0A 1S0
General Phone: (306) 563-5131
General Fax: (306) 563-6144
Advertising Phone: (306) 563-5131
Editorial Phone: (306) 542-2626
General/National Adv. E-mail: canoracourier@sasktel.net
Display Adv. E-mail: k.lewchuk@sasktel.net
Classified Adv. e-mail: office.canoracourier@sasktel.net
Editorial e-mail: kamsacktimes@sasktel.net
Primary Website: kamsacktimes.com
Delivery Methods: Mail`Newsstand
Areas Served - City/County or Portion Thereof, or Zip codes: Canada
Own Printing Facility?: Y
Commercial printers?: Y
Mechanical specifications: Type page 10 1/4 x 15 1/2; E - 6 cols, 1 2/3, between; A - 6 cols, 1 2/3, between; C - 6 cols, 1 2/3, between.
Published: Thur
Avg Paid Circ: 1100
Avg Free Circ: 5
Audit By: CMCA
Audit Date: 30.03.2017
Personnel: Ken Lewchuk (Publisher)
Parent company (for newspapers): Canora Courier; Glacier Media Group

CAP-AUX-MEULES

PUBLICATION NAME

Le Radar
Street Address: 110 Chemin Gros Cap, CP 8183 ,
Province: QC
Postal: G4T 1R3
Country: Canada
Mailing address: 110 Chemin Gros Cap, CP 8183
Mailing city: Cap-aux-Meules
Province: QC
Postal: G4T 1R3
General Phone: (418) 986-234
General Fax: (418)986-6358
General/National Adv. E-mail: secretaire@leradar.qc.ca
Display Adv. E-mail: direction@leradar.qc.ca
Classified Adv. e-mail: direction@leradar.qc.ca
Editorial e-mail: redacteur@leradar.qc.ca
Primary Website: leradar.qc.ca
Areas Served - City/County or Portion Thereof, or Zip codes: Canada
Published: Fri
Avg Paid Circ: 1512
Avg Free Circ: 1523
Audit By: AAM
Audit Date: 31.03.2019
Personnel: Hugo Miousse (Pub.); Achilles Hubert (Ed.); Lucille Tremblay (Adv. Mgr.); Francoise Decoste (Circ. Mgr.)
Parent company (for newspapers): Reseau Select/Select Network

CARBERRY

PUBLICATION NAME

Carberry News Express
Street Address: 34 Main St. W. ,
Province: MB
Postal: R0K 0H0
Country: Canada
Mailing address: PO Box 220
Mailing city: Carberry
Province: MB
Postal: R0K 0H0
General Phone: (204) 834-2153
General Fax: (204) 834-2714
General/National Adv. E-mail: info@carberrynews.ca
Display Adv. E-mail: ads@carberrynews.ca
Editorial e-mail: kathy@carberrynews.ca
Primary Website: www.carberrynews.ca
Year Established: 1910
Delivery Methods: Mail`Newsstand`Racks
Areas Served - City/County or Portion Thereof, or Zip codes: Carberry, Mun. of North Cypress-Langford, Manitoba, Saskatchewan, Alberta, British Columbia, Ontario, New Brunswick
Own Printing Facility?: Y
Commercial printers?: Y
Mechanical specifications: Type page 11 1/2 x 17; E - 5 cols, 1 7/8, 1/8 between; A - 6 cols, 1 5/8, 1/8 between; C - 6 cols, 1 5/8, 1/8 between.
Published: Mon
Avg Paid Circ: 593
Avg Free Circ: 34
Audit By: VAC
Audit Date: 30.09.2018
Personnel: Kathy Carr (Gen. Mgr.); Eva Rutz
Parent company (for newspapers): FP Newspapers Inc.

CARBONEAR

PUBLICATION NAME

The Compass
Street Address: 176 Water St. ,
Province: NL
Postal: A1Y 1C3
Country: Canada
Mailing address: PO Box 760
Mailing city: Carbonear
Province: NL
Postal: A1Y 1C3
General Phone: (709) 596-6458
General Fax: (709) 596-1700
General/National Adv. E-mail: editor@cbncompass.ca
Editorial e-mail: editor@cbncompass.ca
Primary Website: www.cbncompass.ca
Areas Served - City/County or Portion Thereof, or Zip codes: Carbonear
Own Printing Facility?: Y
Commercial printers?: Y
Mechanical specifications: Type page 12 x 22 1/2; E - 6 cols, 2, between; A - 6 cols, 2, between; C - 8 cols, 1 1/2, between.
Published: Tues
Avg Paid Circ: 2376
Avg Free Circ: 0
Audit By: VAC
Audit Date: 31.12.2015
Personnel: Bill Bowman (Ed)
Parent company (for newspapers): Transcontinental Media

CARDSTON

PUBLICATION NAME

Temple City Star
Street Address: 30-b 3rd Ave. West ,
Province: AB
Postal: T0K 0K0
Country: Canada
Mailing address: PO Box 2060
Mailing city: Cardston
Province: AB
Postal: T0K 0K0
General Phone: (403) 653-4664
General Fax: (403) 653-3162
Advertising Phone: (403) 653-4664
General/National Adv. E-mail: info@templecitystar.net
Display Adv. E-mail: news@templecitystar.net
Editorial e-mail: news@templecitystar.net
Primary Website: www.templecitystar.net
Year Established: 1980
Delivery Methods: Mail`Newsstand
Areas Served - City/County or Portion Thereof, or Zip codes: Canada
Published: Thur
Avg Paid Circ: 650
Avg Free Circ: 50
Audit By: Sworn/Estimate/Non-Audited
Audit Date: 12.07.2019
Personnel: Robert Smith (Owner/Pub.); Dan Burt (Office Mgr.)

CARLYLE

PUBLICATION NAME

Carlyle Observer
Street Address: 132 Main St. ,
Province: SK
Postal: S0C 0R0
Country: Canada
Mailing address: PO Box 160
Mailing city: Carlyle
Province: SK
Postal: S0C 0R0
General Phone: (306) 453-2525
General Fax: (306) 453-2938
General/National Adv. E-mail: observer@sasktel.net
Primary Website: www.carlyleobserver.com
Year Established: 1936
Areas Served - City/County or Portion Thereof, or Zip codes: Canada
Commercial printers?: Y
Mechanical specifications: Type page 11 x 17; E - 5 cols, 2, between; A - 5 cols, 2, between; C - 6 cols, 1 1/2, between.
Published: Fri
Avg Paid Circ: 113
Avg Free Circ: 2877
Audit By: CMCA
Audit Date: 30.06.2016
Personnel: Cindy Moffett (Pub.)

Parent company (for newspapers): Glacier Media Group

CARMAN

PUBLICATION NAME

The Valley Leader
Street Address: 4 - 1st St Sw ,
Province: MB
Postal: R0G 0J0
Country: Canada
Mailing address: 4 - 1st St SW
Mailing city: Carman
Province: MB
Postal: R0G 0J0
General Phone: (204) 745-2051
General Fax: (204) 745-3976
General/National Adv. E-mail: carmenvl@mts.net
Display Adv. E-mail: Darcie.Morris@sunmedia.ca
Editorial e-mail: winkler.news@sunmedia.ca
Primary Website: http://www.pembinatoday.ca/carmanvalleyleader
Year Established: 1896
Areas Served - City/County or Portion Thereof, or Zip codes: Canada
Own Printing Facility?: Y
Mechanical specifications: Type page 11 1/2 x 15; E - 6 cols, 1 1/2, 1/8 between; A - 6 cols, 1 1/2, 1/8 between; C - 8 cols, 1 3/16, 1/8 between.
Published: Thur
Avg Paid Circ: 955
Avg Free Circ: 3872
Audit By: VAC
Audit Date: 30.06.2016
Personnel: Darcie Morris (Adv Dir); Greg Vandermeulen (Ed)
Parent company (for newspapers): Postmedia Network Inc.; Quebecor Communications, Inc.

CARNDUFF

PUBLICATION NAME

Gazette-post News
Street Address: 106 Broadway ,
Province: SK
Postal: S0C 0S0
Country: Canada
Mailing address: PO Box 220
Mailing city: Carnduff
Province: SK
Postal: S0C 0S0
General Phone: (306) 482-3252
General Fax: (306) 482-3373
General/National Adv. E-mail: gazettepost.news@sasktel.net; gazette_postnews@awnet.net
Year Established: 1899
Areas Served - City/County or Portion Thereof, or Zip codes: Canada
Commercial printers?: Y
Mechanical specifications: Type page 10 x 21; E - 6 cols, 1 1/2, between; A - 6 cols, 1 1/2, between; C - 6 cols, 1 1/2, between.
Published: Fri
Avg Paid Circ: 1006
Audit By: CMCA
Audit Date: 30.06.2015
Personnel: Bruce Shwanke (Pub.)

CARTWRIGHT

PUBLICATION NAME

Southern Manitoba Review
Street Address: B-635 Bowles St. ,
Province: MB
Postal: R0K 0L0
Country: Canada
Mailing address: PO Box 249
Mailing city: Cartwright
Province: MB
Postal: R0K 0L0
General Phone: (204) 529-2342
General Fax: (204) 529-2029
General/National Adv. E-mail: cartnews@mts.net
Editorial e-mail: cartnews@mts.net

Primary Website: www.southernmanitobareview.com
Year Established: 1899
Delivery Methods: Mail
Areas Served - City/County or Portion Thereof, or Zip codes: Canada
Mechanical specifications: Type page 11 1/2 x 15 1/2; E - 6 cols, 1.6", 1/6 between; A - 6 cols, 1.6", 1/6 between; C - 6 cols, 1.6", 1/6 between.
Published: Thur
Avg Paid Circ: 790
Avg Free Circ: 10
Audit By: CMCA
Audit Date: 31.03.2017
Personnel: Vicki Wallace (Ed.)

CASTLEGAR

PUBLICATION NAME

Rossland News
Street Address: 1810 8th Avenue, Unit 2
Province: BC
Postal: V1N 2Y2
Country: Canada
Mailing address: 1810 8th Avenue, Unit 2
Mailing city: Castlegar
Province: BC
Postal: V1N 2Y2
General Phone: (250) 365 6497
General/National Adv. E-mail: publisher@rosslandnews.com
Display Adv. E-mail: sales@rosslandnews.com
Editorial e-mail: newsroom@castlegarnews.com
Primary Website: www.rosslandnews.com
Delivery Methods: Racks
Areas Served - City/County or Portion Thereof, or Zip codes: Rossland
Published: Thur
Avg Paid Circ: 7
Avg Free Circ: 1063
Audit By: VAC
Audit Date: 30.04.2017
Personnel: Eric Lawson (Pub.); Jennifer Cowan (Ed)
Parent company (for newspapers): Black Press Group Ltd.

PUBLICATION NAME

The Castlegar News
Street Address: Unit 2, 1810 8th Avenue,
Province: BC
Postal: V1N 2y2
Country: Canada
General Phone: (250) 365-6397
General/National Adv. E-mail: newsroom@castlegarnews.com
Display Adv. E-mail: sales@castlegarnews.com
Classified Adv. e-mail: sales@castlegarnews.com
Editorial e-mail: newsroom@castlegarnews.com
Primary Website: www.castlegarnews.com
Year Established: 2004
Delivery Methods: Newsstand`Carrier`Racks
Areas Served - City/County or Portion Thereof, or Zip codes: Castlegar
Published: Thur
Avg Paid Circ: 0
Avg Free Circ: 6442
Audit By: VAC
Audit Date: 30.04.2017
Personnel: Eric Lawson (Pub.)
Parent company (for newspapers): Black Press Group Ltd.

CASTOR

PUBLICATION NAME

Castor Advance
Street Address: 5012 50 Ave.,
Province: AB
Postal: T0C 0X0
Country: Canada
Mailing address: 5012 50 Ave.
Mailing city: Castor

Province: AB
Postal: T0C 0X0
General Phone: (403) 882-4044
Display Adv. E-mail: admin@castoradvance.com
Editorial e-mail: editor@castoradvance.com
Areas Served - City/County or Portion Thereof, or Zip codes: Canada
Published: Thur
Avg Paid Circ: 79
Avg Free Circ: 22
Audit By: VAC
Audit Date: 12.12.2017
Personnel: Mustafa Eric (Ed.)
Parent company (for newspapers): Black Press Group Ltd.

CHAMBLY

PUBLICATION NAME

Chambly Express
Street Address: C-1691, Boul Perigny,
Province: QC
Postal: J3L 1X1
Country: Canada
Mailing address: C-1691, boul Perigny
Mailing city: Chambly
Province: QC
Postal: J3L 1X1
General Phone: (450) 658-5559
General Fax: (450) 658-1620
General/National Adv. E-mail: chamblyexpress@tc.tc
Primary Website: www.chamblyexpress.ca
Areas Served - City/County or Portion Thereof, or Zip codes: Canada
Published: Tues
Avg Free Circ: 27037
Audit By: CCAB
Audit Date: 31.03.2014

PUBLICATION NAME

Journal De Chambly
Street Address: 1685 Bourgogne Ave.,
Province: QC
Postal: J3L 4B3
Country: Canada
Mailing address: PO Box 475
Mailing city: Chambly
Province: QC
Postal: J3L 4B3
General Phone: (450) 658-6516
General Fax: (450) 658-3785
General/National Adv. E-mail: info@journaldechambly.com
Primary Website: www.journaldechambly.com
Areas Served - City/County or Portion Thereof, or Zip codes: Canada
Mechanical specifications: Type page 10 1/4 x 17.
Published: Wed
Avg Paid Circ: 5
Avg Free Circ: 27471
Audit By: CCAB
Audit Date: 31.03.2014
Personnel: Daniel Noiseux (Mng. Ed.)
Parent company (for newspapers): Reseau Select/Select Network; Les Hebdos Monteregiens-OOB

CHATEAUGUAY

PUBLICATION NAME

Chateauguay Express
Street Address: 69, Boul St-jean-baptiste, 2nd Floor,
Province: QC
Postal: J6J 3H6
Country: Canada
Mailing address: 69, boul St-Jean-Baptiste, 2nd Floor
Mailing city: Chateauguay
Province: QC
Postal: J6J 3H6`
General Phone: (450) 692-9111
General Fax: (450) 692-9192
General/National Adv. E-mail: redaction_

chateauguayexpress@tc.tc
Primary Website: www.chateauguayexpress.ca
Areas Served - City/County or Portion Thereof, or Zip codes: Canada
Published: Wed
Avg Free Circ: 40468
Audit By: CCAB
Audit Date: 31.03.2014

PUBLICATION NAME

Le Soleil De Chateauguay
Street Address: 101 boulevard Saint-Jean-Baptiste, Suite 215
Province: QC
Postal: J6J 3H9
Country: Canada
Mailing address: 101 boulevard Saint-Jean-Baptiste, Suite 215
Mailing city: Chateauguay
Province: QC
Postal: J6J 3H9
General Phone: (450) 692-8552
General/National Adv. E-mail: info@gravitemedia.com
Primary Website: www.monteregieweb.com
Areas Served - City/County or Portion Thereof, or Zip codes: Canada
Published: Wed`Sat
Avg Paid Circ: 11
Avg Free Circ: 34473
Audit By: CCAB
Audit Date: 31.03.2019
Personnel: Julie Voyer (Pres.); Pierre Montreuil (Mktg. Strat. Mgr.); Michel Thibault (Content Mgr.); Valerie Lessard (Asst. Content Mgr.); Sophie Bayard (Sales Coor.)
Parent company (for newspapers): Les Hebdos Monteregiens-OOB

PUBLICATION NAME

Le Soleil Du St-laurent
Street Address: 82 Salaberry St. S.,
Province: QC
Postal: J6J 4J6
Country: Canada
Mailing address: 82 Salaberry St. S.
Mailing city: Chateauguay
Province: QC
Postal: J6J 4J6
General Phone: (450) 692-8552
General Fax: (450) 692-3460
General/National Adv. E-mail: info@cybersoleil.com
Display Adv. E-mail: publicite@cybersoleil.com
Editorial e-mail: redaction@cybersoleil.com
Primary Website: www.cybersoleil.com
Mechanical specifications: Type page 11 x 17; E - 5 cols, 2, between; A - 8 cols, 2 1/2, between; C - 8 cols, between.
Published: Wed`Sat
Avg Free Circ: 32750
Audit By: Sworn/Estimate/Non-Audited
Audit Date: 12.07.2019
Personnel: Diane Cadieux (Adv. Rep.); Guylaine Mercier (Adv. Rep.); Yolaine Dorais (Adv. Rep.); Michel Thibault (Ed.); Carole Gagne (Ed.)
Parent company (for newspapers): Les Hebdos Monteregiens-OOB

PUBLICATION NAME

Soleil Du Samedi
Street Address: Rue Salaberry Sud,
Province: QC
Postal: J6J 4J6
Country: Canada
Mailing address: rue Salaberry Sud
Mailing city: Chateauguay
Province: QC
Postal: J6J 4J6
General Phone: (450) 692-8552
Areas Served - City/County or Portion Thereof, or Zip codes: Canada
Published: Sat
Avg Paid Circ: 34
Avg Free Circ: 31092
Audit By: CCAB
Audit Date: 30.09.2012

Personnel: Jeanne-d'Arc Germain

CHATHAM

PUBLICATION NAME

Chatham-Kent This Week
Street Address: 138 King Street West,
Province: ON
Postal: N7M 1ES
Country: Canada
Mailing address: 138 King Street West
Mailing city: Chatham
Province: ON
Postal: N7M 1ES
General Phone: (519) 351-7331
General Fax: (519) 351-7774
Editorial e-mail: peter.epp@sunmedia.ca
Primary Website: www.chathamthisweek.com
Areas Served - City/County or Portion Thereof, or Zip codes: Southwestern Ontario
Published: Wed
Avg Free Circ: 19760
Audit By: CMCA
Audit Date: 31.12.2015
Personnel: Dean Muharrem; Aaron Rodrigues (Media Sales Mgr.); Peter Epp (Managing Ed.); Rachel Blain (Office Mgr.)
Parent company (for newspapers): Postmedia Network Inc.

PUBLICATION NAME

Wallaceburg Courier Press
Street Address: 138 King Street West,
Province: ON
Postal: N7M 1E3
Country: Canada
Mailing address: 138 King Ste West
Mailing city: Chatham
Province: ON
Postal: N7M 1E3
General Phone: (519) 354 2000
General Fax: (519) 351 7774
General/National Adv. E-mail: couriernews@kent.net
Primary Website: www.wallaceburgcourierpress.com
Year Established: 1967
Delivery Methods: Carrier
Areas Served - City/County or Portion Thereof, or Zip codes: Chatham Kent
Published: Thur
Avg Free Circ: 8914
Audit By: CMCA
Audit Date: 30.06.2015
Personnel: Dean Muharrem (Pub.); Mary Dixon (Circ. Mgr.)
Parent company (for newspapers): Postmedia Network Inc.; Sun Media

CHESTERMERE

PUBLICATION NAME

The Chestermere Anchor City News
Street Address: P.o. Box 127,
Province: AB
Postal: T1X 1K8
Country: Canada
Mailing address: P.O. Box 127
Mailing city: Chestermere
Province: AB
Postal: T1X 1K8
General Phone: (403) 774-1352
General Fax: (866) 552-0976
Editorial Phone: (403) 774-1322
General/National Adv. E-mail: jenn@theanchor.ca
Display Adv. E-mail: ads@theanchor.ca
Classified Adv. e-mail: classifed@theanchor.ca
Editorial e-mail: news@theanchor.ca
Primary Website: www.theanchor.ca
Year Established: 2001
Delivery Methods: Newsstand`Carrier`Racks
Areas Served - City/County or Portion Thereof, or Zip codes: Rocky View
Mechanical specifications: 10.34" Wide by 11.5" deep
Published: Thur

Community Newspapers in Canada

Avg Paid Circ: 9
Avg Free Circ: 7923
Audit By: VAC
Audit Date: 28.02.2016

CHESTERVILLE

PUBLICATION NAME

The Chesterville Record
Street Address: 7 King St.,
Province: ON
Postal: K0C 1H0
Country: Canada
Mailing address: PO Box 368
Mailing city: Chesterville
Province: ON
Postal: K0C 1H0
General Phone: (613) 448-2321
General Fax: (613) 448-3260
General/National Adv. E-mail: rm@agrinewsinteractive.com
Display Adv. E-mail: news@chestervillerecord.com
Editorial e-mail: editor@chestervillerecord.com
Primary Website: www.agrinewsinteractive.com
Year Established: 1894
Areas Served - City/County or Portion Thereof, or Zip codes: Canada
Mechanical specifications: Type page 13 x 21 1/2; E - 6 cols, 2, 1/6 between; A - 6 cols, 2, 1/6 between; C - 6 cols, 2, 1/6 between.
Published: Wed
Avg Paid Circ: 1456
Avg Free Circ: 2
Audit By: CMCA
Audit Date: 30.06.2016
Personnel: Robin R. Morris (Pub.); Nelson Zandbergen (Ed.)

PUBLICATION NAME

The Chesterville Record/the Villager
Street Address: 7 King St.,
Province: ON
Postal: K0C 1H0
Country: Canada
Mailing address: PO Box 368
Mailing city: Chesterville
Province: ON
Postal: K0C 1H0
General Phone: (613) 448-2321
General Fax: (613) 448-3260
General/National Adv. E-mail: thevillager.editor@gmail.com
Primary Website: www.chestervillerecord.com; russellvillager.com
Year Established: 1984
Areas Served - City/County or Portion Thereof, or Zip codes: Canada
Own Printing Facility?: Y
Mechanical specifications: Type page 10 3/8 x 13 7/8; E - 6 cols, 1 5/8, 3/16 between; A - 6 cols, 1 5/8, 3/16 between; C - 6 cols, 1 5/8, 3/16 between.
Published: Wed
Avg Paid Circ: 2600
Audit By: CMCA
Audit Date: 30.06.2013
Personnel: Muriel Carruthers (Editor)

CHILLIWACK

PUBLICATION NAME

Chilliwack Times
Street Address: 45951 Trethewey Ave.,
Province: BC
Postal: V2P 1K4
Country: Canada
Mailing address: 102-45951 Trethewey Ave.
Mailing city: Chilliwack
Province: BC
Postal: V2P 1K4
General Phone: (604) 792-9117
General Fax: (604) 792-9300
General/National Adv. E-mail: editor@chilliwacktimes.com
Display Adv. E-mail: nbastaja@chilliwacktimes.com
Editorial e-mail: kgoudswaard@chilliwacktimes.com
Primary Website: www.chilliwacktimes.com
Year Established: 1984
Delivery Methods: Carrier`Racks
Areas Served - City/County or Portion Thereof, or Zip codes: Canada
Own Printing Facility?: Y
Mechanical specifications: Type page 10 1/4 x 14; E - 6 cols, 1 9/16, 1/6 between; A - 6 cols, 1 9/16, 1/6 between; C - 7 cols, 1 5/16, between.
Published: Thur
Avg Free Circ: 27605
Audit By: AAM
Audit Date: 30.09.2016
Personnel: Ken Goudswaard (Ed.); Jean Hincks (Pub.)

PUBLICATION NAME

The Chilliwack Progress
Street Address: 45860 Spadina Ave.,
Province: BC
Postal: V2P 6H9
Country: Canada
Mailing address: 45860 Spadina Ave.
Mailing city: Chilliwack
Province: BC
Postal: V2P 6H9
General Phone: (604) 792-1931
General Fax: (604) 792-4936
General/National Adv. E-mail: publisher@thheprogress.com
Display Adv. E-mail: advertising@theprogress.com
Editorial e-mail: editor@theprogress.com
Primary Website: theprogress.com
Year Established: 1891
Delivery Methods: Carrier
Areas Served - City/County or Portion Thereof, or Zip codes: Canada
Commercial printers?: Y
Mechanical specifications: Type page 12 1/2 x 21 1/4; E - 7 cols, 1 11/16, 1/8 between; A - 7 cols, 1 11/16, 1/8 between; C - 7 cols, 1 11/16, 1/8 between.
Published: Wed`Fri
Avg Paid Circ: 28
Avg Free Circ: 27657
Audit By: AAM
Audit Date: 31.12.2018
Personnel: Kyle Williams (Adv. Mgr.); Louise Meger (Circ. Mgr.); Greg Knill (Ed.); Carly Ferguson (Pub.)
Parent company (for newspapers): Black Press Group Ltd.

CLARENCE CREEK

PUBLICATION NAME

Agricom
Street Address: 2474 Rue Champlain,
Province: ON
Postal: K0A1N0
Country: Canada
Mailing address: 2474 Rue Champlain
Mailing city: Clarence Creek
Province: ON
Postal: K0A1N0
General Phone: (613) 488-2651
General Fax: (613) 488-2541
General/National Adv. E-mail: info@journalagricom.ca
Display Adv. E-mail: pub@journalagricom.ca
Editorial e-mail: redaction@journalagricom.ca
Primary Website: www.journalagricom.ca
Year Established: 1983
Delivery Methods: Mail
Areas Served - City/County or Portion Thereof, or Zip codes: Province of Ontario
Published: Fri`Bi-Mthly
Published Other: bimonthly
Avg Paid Circ: 900
Avg Free Circ: 1100
Audit By: Sworn/Estimate/Non-Audited
Audit Date: 12.07.2019
Personnel: Isabelle Lessard (Ed)

CLARENVILLE

PUBLICATION NAME

The Packet
Street Address: 8 B Thomson St.,
Province: NL
Postal: A5A 1Y9
Country: Canada
Mailing address: 8 B Thomson St.
Mailing city: Clarenville
Province: NL
Postal: A5A 1Y9
General Phone: (709) 466-2243
General Fax: (709) 466-2717
General/National Adv. E-mail: editor@thepacket.ca
Editorial e-mail: editor@thepacket.ca
Primary Website: www.thepacket.ca
Areas Served - City/County or Portion Thereof, or Zip codes: Canada
Own Printing Facility?: Y
Commercial printers?: Y
Mechanical specifications: Type page 11 x 21; E - 6 cols, 1 11/16, 3/16 between; A - 6 cols, 1 11/16, 3/16 between; C - 8 cols, 1 1/4, 3/16 between.
Published: Thur
Avg Paid Circ: 1109
Avg Free Circ: 0
Audit By: VAC
Audit Date: 31.12.2015
Personnel: Barbara Dean-Simmons (Ed.)
Parent company (for newspapers): Transcontinental Media

CLARESHOLM

PUBLICATION NAME

Claresholm Local Press
Street Address: 4913 2nd St. W.,
Province: AB
Postal: T0L 0T0
Country: Canada
Mailing address: PO Box 520
Mailing city: Claresholm
Province: AB
Postal: T0L 0T0
General Phone: (403) 625-4474
General Fax: (403) 625-2828
General/National Adv. E-mail: clpress@telusplanet.net; clpsales@telus.net
Display Adv. E-mail: sales@claresholmlocalpress.ca
Classified Adv. e-mail: sales@claresholmlocalpress.ca
Editorial e-mail: rob@claresholmlocalpress.ca
Primary Website: www.claresholmlocalpress.ca
Year Established: 1926
Delivery Methods: Mail`Newsstand`Racks
Areas Served - City/County or Portion Thereof, or Zip codes: Claresholm, Stavely, Granum, Alberta
Commercial printers?: Y
Published: Wed
Avg Paid Circ: 1429
Avg Free Circ: 19
Audit By: CMCA
Audit Date: 31.05.2018
Personnel: Roxanne Thompson (Owner/Pub.); Rob Vogt (Ed.); Amanda Zimmer (Prod. Mgr.); Brandy McLean (Sales contact); Jill Cook (Graphic Designer)
Parent company (for newspapers): EMS Press Ltd.

CLEARWATER

PUBLICATION NAME

North Thompson Times
Street Address: 74 Young Rd, Unit 14
Province: BC
Postal: V0E 1N2
Country: Canada
Mailing address: 14-74 Young Rd.
Mailing city: Clearwater
Province: BC
Postal: V0E 1N2
General Phone: (250) 674-3343
General Fax: (250) 674-3410
General/National Adv. E-mail: newsroom@clearwatertimes.com
Display Adv. E-mail: classifieds@clearwatertimes.com
Editorial e-mail: newsroom@clearwatertimes.com
Primary Website: www.clearwatertimes.com
Year Established: 1964
Delivery Methods: Mail
Areas Served - City/County or Portion Thereof, or Zip codes: Canada
Commercial printers?: Y
Mechanical specifications: Type page10x13.75"; E - 7 cols, 1 5/16, 1/8 between; A - 7 cols, 1 5/16, 1/8 between; C - 7cols, 1 5/16, 1/8 between.
Published: Thur
Avg Paid Circ: 751
Avg Free Circ: 20
Audit By: CMCA
Audit Date: 30.03.2017
Personnel: Keith McNeill (Ed.); Yvonne Cline (Admin Coord./Sales Rep); Lorie Williston (Pub)
Parent company (for newspapers): Black Press Group Ltd.

CLINTON

PUBLICATION NAME

Clinton News-record
Street Address: 53 Albert St.,
Province: ON
Postal: N0M 1L0
Country: Canada
Mailing address: PO Box 39
Mailing city: Clinton
Province: ON
Postal: N0M 1L0
General Phone: (519) 482-3443
General Fax: (519) 482-7341
Display Adv. E-mail: clinton.ads@bowesnet.com
Editorial e-mail: clinton.news@bowesnet.com
Primary Website: www.clintonnewsrecord.com
Areas Served - City/County or Portion Thereof, or Zip codes: Canada
Mechanical specifications: Type page 11 1/2 x 17; E - 6 cols, 1 3/4, between; A - 6 cols, 1 3/4, between; C - 6 cols, 1 3/4, between.
Published: Wed
Avg Paid Circ: 1029
Avg Free Circ: 22
Audit By: CMCA
Audit Date: 30.06.2016
Personnel: Neil Clifford (Pub.); John Bauman (Adv. Mgr.); Cheryl Heath (Ed.)
Parent company (for newspapers): Postmedia Network Inc.; Quebecor Communications, Inc.

COALDALE

PUBLICATION NAME

The Sunny South News
Street Address: 1802 20th Ave.,
Province: AB
Postal: T1M 1M2
Country: Canada
Mailing address: PO Box 30
Mailing city: Coaldale
Province: AB
Postal: T1M 1M2
General Phone: (403) 345-3081
General Fax: (403) 223-5408
General/National Adv. E-mail: office@sunnysouthnews.com
Display Adv. E-mail: office@sunnysouthnews.com
Primary Website: www.sunnysouthnews.com
Delivery Methods: Mail`Newsstand
Areas Served - City/County or Portion Thereof, or Zip codes: T1M, T0K 2H0, T0K 1V0, T0L 0V0, T0L 1M0, T0K 2A0, T0K 1G0, T0K 0T0
Own Printing Facility?: Y
Commercial printers?: Y
Mechanical specifications: Page size 11.25" wide x 16.75" deep 6 col. tab - 1 col. = 9p6
Published: Tues

Avg Paid Circ: 2263
Avg Free Circ: 48
Audit By: VAC
Audit Date: 30.09.2016
Personnel: Valorie Wiebe (Pub)

COATICOOK

PUBLICATION NAME

Le Progres De Coaticook
Street Address: 72 Rue Child ,
Province: QC
Postal: J1A 2B1
Country: Canada
General Phone: (819) 849-9846
General Fax: (819) 849-1041
General/National Adv. E-mail: dany.jacques@tc.tc
Primary Website: www.leprogres.net
Areas Served - City/County or Portion Thereof, or Zip codes: Canada
Published: Wed
Avg Paid Circ: 77
Avg Free Circ: 8782
Audit By: CCAB
Audit Date: 31.03.2014
Personnel: Monique Cote (Ed.)
Parent company (for newspapers): Reseau Select/ Select Network

COBOURG

PUBLICATION NAME

Northumberland News
Street Address: 884 Division St., Bldg. 2, Unit 212 ,
Province: ON
Postal: K9A 5V6
Country: Canada
Mailing address: 884 Division St., Bldg. 2, Unit 212
Mailing city: Cobourg
Province: ON
Postal: K9A 5V6
General Phone: (905) 373-7355
General Fax: (905) 373-4719
Primary Website: northumberlandnews.com
Areas Served - City/County or Portion Thereof, or Zip codes: Canada
Own Printing Facility?: Y
Published: Thur
Avg Paid Circ: 0
Avg Free Circ: 22338
Audit By: CCAB
Audit Date: 30.09.2017
Personnel: Timothy J. Whittaker (Pub.); Lillian Hook (Office Mgr.); Abe Fakhourie (Circ. Mgr.); Joanne Burghardt (Ed. in Chief); Dwight Irwin (Mng. Ed.)
Parent company (for newspapers): Metroland Media Group Ltd.; Torstar

COCHRANE

PUBLICATION NAME

Cochrane Eagle
Street Address: #2, 124 River Ave ,
Province: AB
Postal: T4C 2C2
Country: Canada
Mailing address: #2, 124 River Ave
Mailing city: Cochrane
Province: AB
Postal: T4C 2C2
General Phone: (403) 932-6588
General Fax: (403) 851-6520
Display Adv. E-mail: btennant@cochrane. greatwest.ca
Classified Adv. e-mail: classifieds@cochrane. greatwest.ca
Editorial e-mail: cpuglia@cochrane.greatwest. ca
Primary Website: www.cochraneeagle.com
Year Established: 2001
Delivery Methods: Mail`Newsstand`Carrier`Racks
Areas Served - City/County or Portion Thereof, or Zip codes: Cochrane/Rocky View County/ Alberta/ T4C 2C2

Published: Thur
Avg Free Circ: 11631
Audit By: VAC
Audit Date: 31.05.2016
Personnel: Brenda Tennant (Pub./Adv. Mgr); Chris Puglia (Ed)
Parent company (for newspapers): Great West Newspapers LP

PUBLICATION NAME

Cochrane Times
Street Address: Bay 8, 206 Fifth Ave. W. ,
Province: AB
Postal: T4C 1X3
Country: Canada
Mailing address: Bay 8, 206 Fifth Ave. W.
Mailing city: Cochrane
Province: AB
Postal: T4C 1X3
General Phone: (403) 932-3500
General Fax: (403) 932-3935
Display Adv. E-mail: roxanne.mackintosh@ sunmedia.ca
Classified Adv. e-mail: roxanne.mackintosh@ sunmedia.ca
Editorial e-mail: editor@cochranetimes.com
Primary Website: www.cochranetimes.com
Year Established: 1985
Areas Served - City/County or Portion Thereof, or Zip codes: Canada
Commercial printers?: Y
Mechanical specifications: Type page 10 1/4 x 12 1/4; E - 8 cols, 1 1/8, 3/16 between; A - 8 cols, 1 1/8, between; C - 8 cols, 1 1/8, between.
Published: Wed
Avg Paid Circ: 1374
Avg Free Circ: 12378
Audit By: VAC
Audit Date: 31.12.2015
Personnel: Shawn Cornell (Pub); Noel Edey (Ed); Roxanne MacKintosh (Adv Dir)
Parent company (for newspapers): Postmedia Network Inc.; Quebecor Communications, Inc.

PUBLICATION NAME

Cochrane Times-post
Street Address: 143, Sixth Avenue ,
Province: ON
Postal: P0L 1C0
Country: Canada
Mailing address: 143, Sixth Avenue
Mailing city: Cochrane
Province: ON
Postal: P0L 1C0
General Phone: (705) 272-3344
General Fax: (705) 272-3434
General/National Adv. E-mail: wayne.major@ sunmedia.ca
Display Adv. E-mail: wayne.major@sunmedia.ca
Editorial e-mail: kevin.anderson@sunmedia.ca
Primary Website: www.cochranetimespost.ca
Year Established: 1904
Delivery Methods: Mail`Newsstand`Carrier
Areas Served - City/County or Portion Thereof, or Zip codes: Canada
Published: Thur
Avg Paid Circ: 1254
Audit By: CMCA
Audit Date: 30.06.2016
Personnel: Wayne Major (Pub.); Chantal Carriere (Sales Representative, print & digital); Ashley Lewis (Reporter)
Parent company (for newspapers): Postmedia Network Inc.

COLD LAKE

PUBLICATION NAME

Beaver River Banner
Street Address: 4110 51 Ave ,
Province: AB
Postal: t9m 2a1
Country: Canada
Mailing address: 4110 51 ave

Mailing city: cold lake
Province: AB
Postal: t9m 2a1
General Phone: (780) 201-0623
General/National Adv. E-mail: br.banner@sasktel. net
Primary Website: www.beaverriverbanner.com
Year Established: 1990
Delivery Methods: Mail
Areas Served - City/County or Portion Thereof, or Zip codes: Canada
Own Printing Facility?: Y
Commercial printers?: Y
Mechanical specifications: Type page 10 1/4 x 15 1/2; E - 6 cols, 1 3/5, 3/16 between; A - 6 cols, 1 3/5, 3/16 between; C - 6 cols, 1 3/5, 3/16 between.
Published: Wed
Avg Free Circ: 2300
Audit By: Sworn/Estimate/Non-Audited
Audit Date: 12.07.2019
Personnel: Dan Brisebois (Ed.)

COLD LAKE

PUBLICATION NAME

Cold Lake Sun
Street Address: 5121 50 Ave ,
Province: AB
Postal: T9M 1P1
Country: Canada
Mailing address: Box 268
Mailing city: Cold Lake
Province: AB
Postal: T9M 1P1
General Phone: (780) 594-5881
General Fax: (780) 594-2120
Display Adv. E-mail: ljohnston@postmedia.com
Editorial e-mail: plozinski@postmedia.com
Primary Website: www.coldlakesun.com
Year Established: 1977
Areas Served - City/County or Portion Thereof, or Zip codes: Cold Lake, Alberta T9M 1P1
Published: Tues
Avg Paid Circ: 71
Avg Free Circ: 7179
Audit By: VAC
Audit Date: 31.12.2015
Personnel: Mary-Ann Kostiuk (Pub); Leanne Johnson (Adv Mgr); Peter Lozinski (Ed)
Parent company (for newspapers): Postmedia Network Inc.

PUBLICATION NAME

The Courier
Street Address: Bldg. 67 Centennial Bldg., Kingsway ,
Province: AB
Postal: T9M 2C5
Country: Canada
Mailing address: PO Box 6190 Stn. Forces
Mailing city: Cold Lake
Province: AB
Postal: T9M 2C5
General Phone: (780) 594-5206
General Fax: (780) 594-2139
Editorial Phone: (780) 840-8000 ext. 7854
General/National Adv. E-mail: thecourier@telus. net
Editorial e-mail: Jeff.Gaye@forces.gc.ca
Primary Website: www.thecouriernewspaper.ca
Delivery Methods: Mail`Newsstand`Carrier
Areas Served - City/County or Portion Thereof, or Zip codes: Cold Lake
Mechanical specifications: Type page 10 1/4 x 15.5; E - 6 cols, 1 1/2, between; A - 6 cols, 1 1/2, between; C - 6 cols, 1 1/2, between.
Published: Tues
Avg Paid Circ: 32
Avg Free Circ: 1995
Audit By: VAC
Audit Date: 28.02.2016
Personnel: Connie Lavigne (Mgr); Jeff Gaye (Ed); Angela Hetherington (Admin); Alina Mallais (Produc Coord)

COLLINGWOOD

PUBLICATION NAME

Collingwood Connection
Street Address: 11 Ronell Crescent, Unit B ,
Province: ON
Postal: L9Y 4J6
Country: Canada
Mailing address: 11 Ronell Crescent, Unit B
Mailing city: Collingwood
Province: ON
Postal: L9Y 4J6
General Phone: (705) 444-1875
General Fax: (705) 444-1876
Advertising Phone: (800) 387-0668
General/National Adv. E-mail: connection@ simcoe.com
Editorial e-mail: editor@simcoe.com
Primary Website: simcoe.com
Delivery Methods: Carrier
Areas Served - City/County or Portion Thereof, or Zip codes: Canada
Published: Fri
Avg Free Circ: 11479
Audit By: CCAB
Audit Date: 29.09.2017
Personnel: Scott Woodhouse (Ed.); Stephen Hall (Prod. Mgr.); Kent Feagan (Prodn. Dir.); Carol Lamb (General Mgr.); Patsy McCarthy (Sales Mgr.)
Parent company (for newspapers): Metroland Media Group Ltd.; Torstar

PUBLICATION NAME

The Enterprise-bulletin
Street Address: 77 Simcoe St. ,
Province: ON
Postal: L9Y 3Z4
Country: Canada
Mailing address: PO Box 98
Mailing city: Collingwood
Province: ON
Postal: L9Y 3Z4
General Phone: (705) 445-4611
General Fax: (705) 444-6477
Editorial e-mail: editorial@theenterprisebulletin. com
Primary Website: www.theenterprisebulletin. com
Areas Served - City/County or Portion Thereof, or Zip codes: Canada
Commercial printers?: Y
Mechanical specifications: Type page 11 1/2 x 21 1/2; E - 5 cols, 2 1/2, between; A - 10 cols, 1 1/6, between; C - 8 cols, 1 1/3, between.
Published: Fri
Avg Paid Circ: 295
Avg Free Circ: 18858
Audit By: CMCA
Audit Date: 30.06.2014
Personnel: Doreen Sykes (Pub.); April MacLean (Circ. Mgr.); J.T. McVeigh (Ed.)
Parent company (for newspapers): Postmedia Network Inc.; Sunmedia; Quebecor Communications, Inc.

COMEAUVILLE

PUBLICATION NAME

Le Courrier De La Nouvelle-ecosse
Street Address: 795 Route 1 ,
Province: NS
Postal: B0W 2Z0
Country: Canada
Mailing address: 795 Route 1
Mailing city: Comeauville
Province: NS
Postal: B0W 2Z0
General Phone: (902) 769-3078
General Fax: (902) 769-3869
General/National Adv. E-mail: publicite@ lecourrier.com
Editorial e-mail: administration@lecourrier.com,
Primary Website: www.lecourrier.com
Year Established: 1937
Areas Served - City/County or Portion Thereof, or Zip codes: Canada
Mechanical specifications: Type page 11 x 13; E

Community Newspapers in Canada

- 5 cols, 2, between; A - 5 cols, 2, between.
Published: Fri
Avg Paid Circ: 1302
Avg Free Circ: 5
Audit By: ODC
Audit Date: 13.12.2011
Personnel: Stephanie LeBlanc (Prod. Mgr.); Francis Robichaud (Ed)

CONSORT

PUBLICATION NAME

The Consort Enterprise
Street Address: 5012 - 52st. ,
Province: AB
Postal: T0C 1B0
Country: Canada
Mailing address: PO Box 129
Mailing city: Consort
Province: AB
Postal: T0C 1B0
General Phone: (403) 577-3337
General Fax: (403) 577-3611
Advertising Phone: (403) 577-3337
Editorial Phone: (403) 577-3337
General/National Adv. E-mail: consort_enterprise@awna.com
Display Adv. E-mail: ads@consortenterprise.com
Classified Adv. e-mail: ads@consortenterprise.com
Editorial e-mail: editor@consortenterprise.com
Primary Website: www.consortenterprise.awna.com
Year Established: 1912
Delivery Methods: Mail`Newsstand
Areas Served - City/County or Portion Thereof, or Zip codes: Canada
Mechanical specifications: Type page 10 x 16; E - 6 cols, 2, between; A - 6 cols, 2, between.
Published: Wed
Avg Paid Circ: 2935
Audit By: CMCA
Audit Date: 12.12.2017
Personnel: Carol Bruha (Circ. Mgr./Adv. Mgr.); David Bruha (Ed.)

CORNWALL

PUBLICATION NAME

Seaway News
Street Address: 501 Campbell Street , Unit 6
Province: ON
Postal: K6H 6X5
Country: Canada
Mailing address: 501 Campbell Street, Unit 6
Mailing city: Cornwall
Province: ON
Postal: K6H 6X5
General Phone: (613) 933-0014
General Fax: (613) 933-0024
General/National Adv. E-mail: info@cornwallseawaynews.com
Display Adv. E-mail: patrick.larose@tc.tc
Classified Adv. e-mail: diane.merpaw@tc.tc
Editorial e-mail: nicholas.seebruch@tc.tc
Primary Website: www.cornwallseawaynews.com
Year Established: 1985
Delivery Methods: Newsstand`Carrier
Areas Served - City/County or Portion Thereof, or Zip codes: Cornwall and SD&G
Own Printing Facility?: Y
Commercial printers?: Y
Mechanical specifications: Type page 10 3/8 x 16; E - 9 cols, 1 1/16, 1/10 between; A - 9 cols, 1 1/16, 1/10 between; C - 8 cols, 1 1/16, 1/10 between.
Published: Thur
Avg Free Circ: 36541
Audit By: CMCA
Audit Date: 31.12.2015
Personnel: Rick Shaver (General Manager/Publisher); Colleen Parette (Production Coordinator); Patrick Larose (Media Strategy Manager)
Parent company (for newspapers): Transcontinental Media

CORONACH

PUBLICATION NAME

Triangle News
Street Address: 118 Centre St. ,
Province: SK
Postal: S0H 0Z0
Country: Canada
Mailing address: Box 689
Mailing city: Coronach
Province: SK
Postal: S0H 0Z0
General Phone: (306) 267-3381
General/National Adv. E-mail: trianglenews@sasktel.net
Primary Website: www.trianglenews.sk.ca
Delivery Methods: Mail`Newsstand
Areas Served - City/County or Portion Thereof, or Zip codes: S0H - 0B0, 0Z0, 1B0, 2J0, 2W0, 3R0, 4K0, 4Lo, S0C 0Ko
Published: Mon
Avg Paid Circ: 339
Avg Free Circ: 336
Audit By: CMCA
Audit Date: 31.10.2015
Parent company (for newspapers): Transcontinental

CORONATION

PUBLICATION NAME

East Central Alberta Review
Street Address: 4923 Victoria Ave. ,
Province: AB
Postal: T0C 1C0
Country: Canada
Mailing address: PO Box 70
Mailing city: Coronation
Province: AB
Postal: T0C 1C0
General Phone: (403) 578-4111
General Fax: (403) 578-2088
Advertising Phone: (403) 578-7120
General/National Adv. E-mail: publisher@ecareview.com
Display Adv. E-mail: advertise@ECAreview.com
Classified Adv. e-mail: admin@ECAreview.com
Editorial e-mail: publisher@ECAreview.com
Primary Website: www.ecareview.com
Year Established: 1911
Delivery Methods: Mail`Newsstand
Areas Served - City/County or Portion Thereof, or Zip codes: Canada
Own Printing Facility?: Y
Commercial printers?: Y
Mechanical specifications: Type page 10 1/4 x 15 1/2; E - 6 cols, 1 1/2, between; A - 6 cols, 1 1/2, between; C - 6 cols, 1 1/2, between.
Published: Thur
Avg Paid Circ: 90
Avg Free Circ: 27075
Audit By: CMCA
Audit Date: 31.03.2017
Personnel: Joyce Webster (Pub); Yvonne Thulien (Office Mgr.); Gayle Jaraway (Adv. Rep); Lisa Joy (Marketing Rep/Reporter Photographer); Lisa Myers-Sortland (Graphic Artist)

COURTENAY

PUBLICATION NAME

Comox Valley Echo
Street Address: 407-e Fifth Street ,
Province: BC
Postal: V9N 1J7
Country: Canada
Mailing address: 407-E Fifth St.
Mailing city: Courtenay
Province: BC
Postal: V9N 1J7
General Phone: (250) 334-4722
General Fax: (250) 334-3172
General/National Adv. E-mail: echo@comoxvalleyecho.com
Display Adv. E-mail: keith.currie@comoxvalleyecho.com
Classified Adv. e-mail: debra.fowler@comoxvalleyecho.com
Editorial e-mail: echo@comoxvalleyecho.com
Primary Website: www.comoxvalleyecho.com
Year Established: 1994
Delivery Methods: Mail`Newsstand`Carrier`Racks
Areas Served - City/County or Portion Thereof, or Zip codes: Canada
Commercial printers?: Y
Mechanical specifications: Type page 10.5 x 21.5; E - 10 cols, 1 1/12, between; A - 10 cols, 1 1/12, between; C - 8 cols, 1 7/23, between.
Published: Fri
Avg Paid Circ: 50
Avg Free Circ: 23000
Audit By: CCAB
Audit Date: 17.03.2013
Personnel: Keith Currie (Publisher); Debra Martin (Mng. Ed.); Ryan Getz (Prodn. Mgr.)

PUBLICATION NAME

Comox Valley Record
Street Address: 407D Fifth Street ,
Province: BC
Postal: V9N 1J7
Country: Canada
Mailing address: 407D Fifth Street
Mailing city: Courtenay
Province: BC
Postal: V9N 1J7
General Phone: (250) 338-5811
General/National Adv. E-mail: publisher@comoxvalleyrecord.com
Display Adv. E-mail: keith.currie@comoxvalleyrecord.com
Classified Adv. e-mail: keith.currie@comoxvalleyrecord.com
Editorial e-mail: terry.farrell@comoxvalleyrecord.com
Primary Website: comoxvalleyrecord.com
Year Established: 1986
Delivery Methods: Mail`Newsstand`Carrier`Racks
Areas Served - City/County or Portion Thereof, or Zip codes: Canada
Own Printing Facility?: Y
Mechanical specifications: Type page 10 1/4 x 14 1/2; E - 6 cols, 1 7/12, 1/6 between; A - 6 cols, 1 7/12, 1/6 between; C - 7 cols, 1 7/12, 1/6 between.
Published: Tues`Thur
Avg Paid Circ: 53
Avg Free Circ: 21566
Audit By: AAM
Audit Date: 31.03.2019
Personnel: Terry Marshall (Circ. Mgr.); Terry Farrell (Ed.); Susan Granberg (Prodn. Mgr.); Keith Currie (Pub.)
Parent company (for newspapers): Black Press Group Ltd.

PUBLICATION NAME

North Island Midweek
Street Address: 765 Mcphee Ave ,
Province: BC
Postal: V9N 2Z7
Country: Canada
Mailing address: 765 McPhee Ave
Mailing city: Courtenay
Province: BC
Postal: V9N 2Z7
General Phone: (250) 287-9227
General Fax: (250) 287-3238
General/National Adv. E-mail: publisher@comoxvalleyrecord.com
Display Adv. E-mail: sueb@blackpress.ca
Editorial e-mail: editor@comoxvalleyrecord.com
Primary Website: www.northislandmidweek.com
Year Established: 1994
Delivery Methods: Mail`Newsstand`Carrier
Areas Served - City/County or Portion Thereof, or Zip codes: Canada
Own Printing Facility?: Y
Published: Wed
Avg Paid Circ: 40
Avg Free Circ: 37030
Audit By: CMCA
Audit Date: 31.08.2014
Personnel: Chrissie Bowker (Pub); Terry Farrell (Ed); Susan Granberg (Prod. Mgr.); Terry Marshall (Circ Mgr.)
Parent company (for newspapers): Black Press Group Ltd.

COWANSVILLE

PUBLICATION NAME

Le Guide De Cowansville
Street Address: 121 Rue Principale ,
Province: QC
Postal: J2K 1J3
Country: Canada
Mailing address: 121 Rue Principale
Mailing city: Cowansville
Province: QC
Postal: J2K 1J3
General Phone: (450) 263-5288
General Fax: (450) 263-9435
General/National Adv. E-mail: leguide@tc.tc
Primary Website: http://www.journalleguide.com/
Areas Served - City/County or Portion Thereof, or Zip codes: Canada
Commercial printers?: Y
Mechanical specifications: Type page 11 1/4 x 15; C - 8 cols, 1 1/8, 1/8 between.
Published: Wed
Avg Paid Circ: 6
Avg Free Circ: 18340
Audit By: CCAB
Audit Date: 31.03.2014
Personnel: Cathy Bernard (Pub.); Louise Denicourt (Sec.); Caroline Rioux (Reg'l Ed.)

CRAIK

PUBLICATION NAME

Craik Weekly News
Street Address: 221 Third St. , Box 360
Province: SK
Postal: S0G 0V0
Country: Canada
Mailing address: PO Box 360
Mailing city: Craik
Province: SK
Postal: S0G 0V0
General Phone: (306) 734-2313
General Fax: (306) 734-2789
General/National Adv. E-mail: craiknews@sasktel.net
Display Adv. E-mail: craiknews@sasktel.net
Year Established: 1908
Delivery Methods: Mail
Areas Served - City/County or Portion Thereof, or Zip codes: R.M. of Craik No. 222
Own Printing Facility?: Y
Mechanical specifications: Type page 10 1/4 x 15; E - 6 cols, 1 17/30, 1/6 between; A - 6 cols, 1 17/30, 1/6 between; C - 6 cols, 1 17/30, 1/6 between.
Published: Mon
Avg Paid Circ: 880
Audit By: Sworn/Estimate/Non-Audited
Audit Date: 12.07.2019
Personnel: Harve Friedel (Ed.)

CRANBROOK

PUBLICATION NAME

Cranbrook Daily Townsman
Street Address: 822 Cranbrook St. N. ,
Province: BC
Postal: V1C 3R9
Country: Canada
Mailing address: 822 Cranbrook St. N.
Mailing city: Cranbrook
Province: BC
Postal: V1C 3R9
General Phone: (250) 426-5201
General Fax: (250) 426-5003
Advertising Phone: (250) 426-5201
Advertising Fax: (250) 426-5003
Editorial Phone: (250) 426-5201

Editorial Fax: (250) 426-5003
General/National Adv. E-mail: sueb@blackpress.ca
Display Adv. E-mail: zena.williams@blackpress.ca
Classified Adv. e-mail: zena.williams@blackpress.ca
Editorial e-mail: barry.coulter@cranbrooktownsman.com
Primary Website: www.cranbrooktownsman.com
Year Established: 1956
Delivery Methods: Mail`Newsstand`Carrier`Racks
Areas Served - City/County or Portion Thereof, or Zip codes: Cranbrook, Kimberley and surrounding areas
Own Printing Facility?: Y
Commercial printers?: Y
Mechanical specifications: Type page 10.25 x 14.00
Published: Wed`Thur`Fri
Weekday Frequency: e
Avg Paid Circ: 3500
Audit By: CMCA
Audit Date: 31.12.2015
Personnel: Zena Williams (Pub.); Barry Coulter (Ed.); Nicole Koran (Adv. Sales Mgr.); Jennifer Leiman (Office Mgr.)
Parent company (for newspapers): Black Press Group Ltd.

CREEMORE
PUBLICATION NAME
Creemore Echo
Street Address: 3 Caroline St. W. ,
Province: ON
Postal: L0M 1G0
Country: Canada
Mailing address: 3 Caroline St. W.
Mailing city: Creemore
Province: ON
Postal: L0M 1G0
General Phone: (705) 466-9906
General Fax: (705) 466-9908
General/National Adv. E-mail: info@creemore.com
Primary Website: www.creemore.com
Areas Served - City/County or Portion Thereof, or Zip codes: Canada
Commercial printers?: Y
Published: Fri
Avg Paid Circ: 450
Avg Free Circ: 3396
Audit By: CMCA
Audit Date: 31.12.2015
Personnel: Sara Hershoff (Pub.); Georgi Denison (Office Mgr.); Trina Berlo (Ed.)

CRESTON
PUBLICATION NAME
Creston Valley Advance
Street Address: 1018 Canyon St. ,
Province: BC
Postal: V0B 1G0
Country: Canada
Mailing address: PO Box 1279
Mailing city: Creston
Province: BC
Postal: V0B 1G0
General Phone: (250) 428-2266
General Fax: (250) 483-1909
Display Adv. E-mail: advertising@crestonvalleyadvance.ca
Editorial e-mail: editor@crestonvalleyadvance.ca
Primary Website: www.crestonvalleyadvance.ca
Year Established: 1948
Areas Served - City/County or Portion Thereof, or Zip codes: Canada
Own Printing Facility?: Y
Mechanical specifications: Type page 10 1/4 x 16; E - 5 cols, 1 15/16, 1/8 between; A - 5 cols, 1 15/16, 1/8 between; C - 5 cols, 1 15/16, 1/8 between.
Published: Thur
Avg Paid Circ: 2

Avg Free Circ: 9
Audit By: VAC
Audit Date: 31.07.2016
Personnel: Lorne Eckersley (Pub.); Diane Audette (Circ. Mgr.); Brian Lorns (Ed.); Anita Horton (Sales Coord.); Brian Lawrence (Ed.); Jacky Smith (Prod. Department)
Parent company (for newspapers): Torstar

CUT KNIFE
PUBLICATION NAME
Highway 40 Courier
Street Address: 200 Steele St. ,
Province: SK
Postal: S0M 0N0
Country: Canada
Mailing address: PO Box 639
Mailing city: Cut Knife
Province: SK
Postal: S0M 0N0
General Phone: (306) 398-4901
General Fax: (306) 398-4909
General/National Adv. E-mail: ckcouriernews@sasktel.net
Year Established: 1959
Delivery Methods: Mail`Newsstand
Areas Served - City/County or Portion Thereof, or Zip codes: Canada
Commercial printers?: N
Mechanical specifications: Type page 10 1/2 x 15 1/2; E - 6 cols, 1 5/8, 3/16 between; A - 6 cols, 1 5/8, 3/16 between; C - 6 cols, 1 5/8, 3/16 between.
Published: Wed
Avg Paid Circ: 440
Avg Free Circ: 13
Audit By: CMCA
Audit Date: 31.03.2016
Personnel: Lorie Gibson (Publisher/Editor)

DAUPHIN
PUBLICATION NAME
Dauphin Herald
Street Address: 120 1st Ave. Ne ,
Province: MB
Postal: R7N 1A5
Country: Canada
Mailing address: PO Box 548
Mailing city: Dauphin
Province: MB
Postal: R7N 2V3
General Phone: (204) 638-4420
General Fax: (204) 638-8760
General/National Adv. E-mail: dherald@mts.net
Display Adv. E-mail: bwright@mymts.net
Classified Adv. e-mail: classifieds@dauphinherald.com
Editorial e-mail: psbailey@mymts.net
Primary Website: www.dauphinherald.com
Year Established: 1916
Delivery Methods: Mail`Newsstand`Carrier`Racks
Areas Served - City/County or Portion Thereof, or Zip codes: Canada
Own Printing Facility?: Y
Commercial printers?: Y
Mechanical specifications: Type page 10 1/4 x 16; E - 6 cols, 1 7/12, 1/8 between; A - 6 cols, 1 7/12, 1/8 between; C - 6 cols, 1 7/12, 1/8 between.
Published: Tues
Avg Paid Circ: 1189
Avg Free Circ: 59
Audit By: VAC
Audit Date: 30.06.2016
Personnel: Robert F. Gilroy (Pub./Owner); Brent Wright (Adv. Mgr.); Mandy Carderry (Circ. Mgr.); Shawn Bailey (Ed.)

DAVIDSON
PUBLICATION NAME
Davidson Leader
Street Address: 205 Washington St. ,

Province: SK
Postal: S0G 1A0
Country: Canada
Mailing address: PO Box 786
Mailing city: Davidson
Province: SK
Postal: S0G 1A0
General Phone: (306) 567-2047
General Fax: (306) 567-2900
General/National Adv. E-mail: davidsonleader@sasktel.net; theleaderonline@gmail.com
Primary Website: www.leaderonline.ca
Year Established: 1904
Delivery Methods: Mail`Newsstand
Areas Served - City/County or Portion Thereof, or Zip codes: Canada
Mechanical specifications: Type page 10 1/4 x 15 3/4; E - 5 cols, 1 29/30, 1/6 between; A - 5 cols, 1 29/30, 1/6 between; C - 5 cols, 1 29/30, 1/6 between.
Published: Mon
Avg Paid Circ: 1238
Avg Free Circ: 44
Audit By: CMCA
Audit Date: 31.03.2017
Personnel: Tara De Ryk (Publisher)
Parent company (for newspapers): Davidson Publishing Ltd.

DAWSON CREEK
PUBLICATION NAME
The Mirror
Street Address: 901-100th Ave. ,
Province: BC
Postal: V1G 1W2
Country: Canada
Mailing address: 901-100th Ave.
Mailing city: Dawson Creek
Province: BC
Postal: V1G 1W2
General Phone: (250) 782-4888
General Fax: (250) 782-6300
General/National Adv. E-mail: editor@dcdn.ca
Display Adv. E-mail: jkmet@dcdn.ca
Editorial e-mail: editor@dcdn.ca
Primary Website: http://www.dawsoncreekmirror.ca/
Year Established: 1980
Areas Served - City/County or Portion Thereof, or Zip codes: Canada
Own Printing Facility?: Y
Mechanical specifications: Type page 10 3/20 x 11 1/2; E - 6 cols, 1 1/2, 1/6 between; A - 6 cols, 1 1/2, 1/6 between; C - 7 cols, 1 3/10, between.
Published: Fri
Avg Paid Circ: 0
Avg Free Circ: 7457
Audit By: Sworn/Estimate/Non-Audited
Audit Date: 12.07.2019
Personnel: William Julian (Reg. Mgr.); Nicole Palfy (Assoc. Pub.); Rob Brown (Ed); Margot Owens (Circ Mgr)

PUBLICATION NAME
The Northern Horizon
Street Address: 901 - 100th Ave ,
Province: BC
Postal: V1G 1W2
Country: Canada
Mailing address: 901 - 100th Ave
Mailing city: Dawson Creek
Province: BC
Postal: V1G 1W2
General Phone: (250) 782-4888
General Fax: (250) 782-6300
Display Adv. E-mail: jkmet@dcdn.ca
Editorial e-mail: editor@dcdn.ca
Primary Website: http://www.northernhorizon.ca/
Published: Fri
Personnel: William Julian (Pub); Nicole Palfy (Assoc. Pub.); Rob Brown (Ed); Margot Owens (Circ. Mgr)
Parent company (for newspapers): Glacier Media Group

DEEP RIVER
PUBLICATION NAME
The North Renfrew Times
Street Address: 21 Champlain St. ,
Province: ON
Postal: K0J 1P0
Country: Canada
Mailing address: PO Box 310
Mailing city: Deep River
Province: ON
Postal: K0J 1P0
General Phone: (613) 584-4161
Advertising Phone: (613) 584-4161
Editorial Phone: (613) 584-4161
General/National Adv. E-mail: drcanrt@magma.ca; NRT@magma.ca
Display Adv. E-mail: NRT@magma.ca
Classified Adv. e-mail: NRT@magma.ca
Editorial e-mail: NRT@magma.ca
Primary Website: www.northrenfrewtimes.net
Year Established: 1956
Delivery Methods: Mail`Newsstand
Areas Served - City/County or Portion Thereof, or Zip codes: Canada
Mechanical specifications: Type page 10 3/8 x 14; A - 9 cols, 1, 0.167 between
Published: Wed
Avg Paid Circ: 1661
Audit By: CMCA
Audit Date: 30.09.2016
Personnel: Kelly Lapping (Pub); Terry Myers (Editor)

DELHI
PUBLICATION NAME
Delhi News-record
Street Address: 237 Main St. ,
Province: ON
Postal: N4B 2M4
Country: Canada
Mailing address: 237 Main St.
Mailing city: Delhi
Province: ON
Postal: N4B 2M4
General Phone: (519) 582-2510
General Fax: (519) 582-0627
Editorial e-mail: deleditorial@bowesnet.com
Primary Website: www.delhinewsrecord.com
Areas Served - City/County or Portion Thereof, or Zip codes: Canada
Own Printing Facility?: Y
Commercial printers?: Y
Published: Wed
Avg Paid Circ: 506
Audit By: CMCA
Audit Date: 31.12.2013
Personnel: Walter Keleer (Adv. Mgr.); Kim Novak (Ed.); Wayne Ward (Prodn. Mgr.); Ken Koyoma (Pub.)
Parent company (for newspapers): Postmedia Network Inc.; Quebecor Communications, Inc.

DELORAINE
PUBLICATION NAME
The Deloraine Times And Star
Street Address: 122 Broadway, N. ,
Province: MB
Postal: R0M 0M0
Country: Canada
Mailing address: PO Box 407
Mailing city: Deloraine
Province: MB
Postal: R0M 0M0
General Phone: (204) 747-2249
General Fax: (204) 747-3999
General/National Adv. E-mail: deltimes@mts.net
Display Adv. E-mail: ads.cpocket@mts.net
Editorial e-mail: cpocket@mts.net
Primary Website: http://www.delorainetimes.ca
Year Established: 1887
Delivery Methods: Mail`Racks
Areas Served - City/County or Portion Thereof, or Zip codes: R0M IL0, R0K 0E0, R0M 0M0, R0M

Community Newspapers in Canada

0X0, R0M IK0, R0M 2E0
Own Printing Facility?: N
Commercial printers?: Y
Published: Fri
Avg Paid Circ: 770
Avg Free Circ: 57
Audit By: Sworn/Estimate/Non-Audited
Audit Date: 12.07.2019
Personnel: Judy Wells (Office Mgr.)
Parent company (for newspapers): Corner Pocket Publishing Ltd.; Glacier Media Group

DELSON

PUBLICATION NAME

Le Reflet
Street Address: 11 Rt. 132 ,
Province: QC
Postal: J5B 1G9
Country: Canada
Mailing address: 11 Rt. 132
Mailing city: Delson
Province: QC
Postal: J5B 1G9
General Phone: (450) 635-9146
General Fax: (450) 635-4619
General/National Adv. E-mail: robert.fichaud@quebecormedia.com
Display Adv. E-mail: publicite@lereflet.qc.ca
Primary Website: www.lereflet.qc.ca
Areas Served - City/County or Portion Thereof, or Zip codes: Canada
Published: Wed
Avg Free Circ: 49427
Audit By: CCAB
Audit Date: 31.03.2014
Personnel: Robert Fichaud (Pub./Dir.); Sandy Roy (Sales Dir.); Helene Gingras (Ed.)
Parent company (for newspapers): Les Hebdos Monteregiens-OOB

DELTA

PUBLICATION NAME

Delta Optimist
Street Address: 5008-47a Avenue ,
Province: BC
Postal: V4K 1T8
Country: Canada
Mailing address: 5008-47A Avenue
Mailing city: Delta
Province: BC
Postal: V4K 1T8
General Phone: (604) 946-4451
General Fax: (604) 946-5680
General/National Adv. E-mail: tsiba@delta-optimist.com
Display Adv. E-mail: dhamilton@delta-optimist.com
Editorial e-mail: editor@delta-optimist.com
Primary Website: delta-optimist.com
Year Established: 1922
Delivery Methods: Carrier
Areas Served - City/County or Portion Thereof, or Zip codes: Canada
Mechanical specifications: Type page 10 1/4 x 14; E - 6 cols, 1 9/16, 1/6 between; A - 6 cols, 1 9/16, 1/6 between; C - 7 cols, 1 1/3, 1/12 between.
Published: Wed`Fri
Avg Paid Circ: 0
Avg Free Circ: 17029
Audit By: CCAB
Audit Date: 22.11.2017
Personnel: Dave Hamilton (Gen Mgr); Ted Murphy (Ed.); Alvin Brouwer (Pub)
Parent company (for newspapers): Glacier Media Group

DEVON

PUBLICATION NAME

Devon Dispatch News
Street Address: 4b Saskatchewan Drive ,
Province: AB
Postal: T9G 1E7
Country: Canada
Mailing address: 4B Saskatchewan Drive
Mailing city: Devon
Province: AB
Postal: T9G 1E7
General Phone: (780) 987-3488
General Fax: (780) 987-4431
Display Adv. E-mail: jfigeat@postmedia.com
Editorial e-mail: bobby.roy@sunmedia.ca
Primary Website: www.devondispatch.ca
Year Established: 1976
Areas Served - City/County or Portion Thereof, or Zip codes: Devon, AB T9G 1E7, Canada
Published: Fri
Avg Paid Circ: 2021
Avg Free Circ: 5072
Audit By: VAC
Audit Date: 31.12.2015
Personnel: Susanne Holmlund (Pub.); Bobby Roy (Ed); Jean Figeat (Adv. Dir)
Parent company (for newspapers): Postmedia Network Inc.

DIGBY

PUBLICATION NAME

The Digby County Courier
Street Address: 124 Water St. ,
Province: NS
Postal: B0V 1A0
Country: Canada
Mailing address: Box 670
Mailing city: Digby
Province: NS
Postal: B0V 1A0
General Phone: (902) 245-4715
General Fax: (902) 245-6136
General/National Adv. E-mail: info@digbycourier.ca
Display Adv. E-mail: info@digbycourier.ca
Editorial e-mail: editor@digbycourier.ca
Primary Website: www.digbycourier.ca
Year Established: 1874
Delivery Methods: Mail`Newsstand
Areas Served - City/County or Portion Thereof, or Zip codes: Canada
Commercial printers?: Y
Mechanical specifications: Type page 12 1/2 x 21; E - 7 cols, 1/8 between; A - 7 cols, 1/8 between; C - 7 cols, 1/8 between.
Published: Thur
Avg Paid Circ: 1192
Avg Free Circ: 0
Audit By: CMCA
Audit Date: 30.06.2014
Personnel: Dave Glenen (Ed)
Parent company (for newspapers): Transcontinental Media

DOLBEAU-MISTASSINI

PUBLICATION NAME

Le Nouvelles Hebdo
Street Address: 1741 Rue Des Pins ,
Province: QC
Postal: G8L 1J7
Country: Canada
General Phone: (418) 276-6211
General Fax: (418)276-6166
Advertising Phone: (418) 276-6211
General/National Adv. E-mail: redaction.dolbeau@tc.tc
Primary Website: http://www.nouvelleshebdo.com/
Areas Served - City/County or Portion Thereof, or Zip codes: Canada
Published: Wed
Avg Paid Circ: 55
Avg Free Circ: 12594
Audit By: CCAB
Audit Date: 31.03.2014
Personnel: Michel Aub

DONNACONA

PUBLICATION NAME

Courrier De Portneuf
Street Address: 276,rue Notre-dame ,
Province: QC
Postal: G3M 1G7
Country: Canada
Mailing address: 276,rue Notre-Dame
Mailing city: Donnacona
Province: QC
Postal: G3M 1G7
General Phone: (418) 285-0211
General Fax: (418) 285-2441
General/National Adv. E-mail: josee-anne.fiset@courrierdeportneuf.com
Editorial e-mail: denise.paquin@courrierdeportneuf.com
Primary Website: www.courrierdeportneuf.com
Year Established: 1982
Delivery Methods: Carrier
Areas Served - City/County or Portion Thereof, or Zip codes: Canada
Published: Wed
Avg Paid Circ: 31
Avg Free Circ: 34944
Audit By: CCAB
Audit Date: 30.09.2012
Personnel: Louise Latulippe (adjointe administrative)

DORCHESTER

PUBLICATION NAME

The Signpost
Street Address: 15 Bridge St. ,
Province: ON
Postal: N0L 1G2
Country: Canada
Mailing address: 15 Bridge St.
Mailing city: Dorchester
Province: ON
Postal: N0L 1G2
General Phone: (519) 268-7337
General Fax: (519) 268-3260
Advertising Phone: (519) 268-7337
Advertising Fax: (519) 268-3260
Editorial Phone: (519) 268-7337
Editorial Fax: (519) 268-3260
General/National Adv. E-mail: signpost@on.aibn.com
Display Adv. E-mail: advertising@dorchestersignpost.com
Classified Adv. e-mail: classifieds@dorchestersignpost.com
Editorial e-mail: w.spence@on.aibn.com
Primary Website: www.dorchestersignpost.com
Year Established: 1959
Delivery Methods: Mail`Newsstand`Carrier
Areas Served - City/County or Portion Thereof, or Zip codes: Thames Centre, Middlesex County
Published: Wed
Avg Paid Circ: 1468
Audit By: CMCA
Audit Date: 31.12.2015
Personnel: Fred Huxley (Pub.); Lyndsay Huxley (Gen. Mgr.); Wendy Spence (Ed.)

DORVAL

PUBLICATION NAME

Cites Nouvelles
Street Address: 455 Boulevard Fenelon , Bureau 303
Province: QC
Postal: H9S 5T8
Country: Canada
Mailing address: 455 Boulevard Fenelon
Mailing city: Dorval
Province: QC
Postal: H9S 5T8
General Phone: (514) 636-7314
General Fax: (514) 636-7317
General/National Adv. E-mail: cites.nouvelles@tc.tc
Primary Website: www.citesnouvelles.com
Year Established: 1974
Delivery Methods: Carrier`Racks
Areas Served - City/County or Portion Thereof, or Zip codes: Canada
Published: Wed
Avg Paid Circ: 4
Avg Free Circ: 44286

Audit By: CCAB
Audit Date: 31.03.2014
Personnel: Denis Therrien (Publisher); Joy-Ann Dempsey (Sales Support Supervisor); Robert Bourcier (Production manager); Jean Nicolas AubÃ© (News Director)
Parent company (for newspapers): Transcontinental Media

PUBLICATION NAME

Lachine Messenger
Street Address: 455 Boulevard Fenelon, Suite 303 ,
Province: QC
Postal: H9S 5T8
Country: Canada
Mailing address: 455 Boulevard Fenelon, suite 303
Mailing city: Dorval
Province: QC
Postal: H9S 5T8
General Phone: (514) 636-7314
General Fax: (514) 363-7315
General/National Adv. E-mail: redaction_lachine-dorval@tc.tc
Primary Website: www.messagerlachine.com
Published: Thur
Avg Free Circ: 20000
Audit By: Sworn/Estimate/Non-Audited
Audit Date: 12.07.2019
Personnel: Patricia Ann Beaulieu (Pub.); Tina Lemelin (Adv. Mgr.); Robert Leduc (Ed.)

PUBLICATION NAME

Magazine De L'ile-des-soeurs
Street Address: 455 Boulevard Fenelon ,
Province: QC
Postal: H9S 5T8
Country: Canada
Mailing address: 455 Boulevard Fenelon
Mailing city: Dorval
Province: QC
Postal: H9S 5T8
General Phone: (514) 636-7314
Areas Served - City/County or Portion Thereof, or Zip codes: Canada
Published: Wed
Avg Paid Circ: 2
Avg Free Circ: 8226
Audit By: CCAB
Audit Date: 31.03.2014
Personnel: Patricia Ann Beaulieu

PUBLICATION NAME

Messager De Lachine / Dorval
Street Address: 455 Boulevard Fenelon, Suite 303 ,
Province: QC
Postal: H9S 5T8
Country: Canada
Mailing address: 455 Boulevard Fenelon, suite 303
Mailing city: Dorval
Province: QC
Postal: H9S 5T8
General Phone: (514) 636-7314
General Fax: (514) 636-7315
General/National Adv. E-mail: redaction_lachine-dorval@tc.tc
Primary Website: http://www.messagerlachine.com
Areas Served - City/County or Portion Thereof, or Zip codes: Canada
Published: Thur
Avg Paid Circ: 0
Avg Free Circ: 24993
Audit By: CCAB
Audit Date: 31.03.2014
Personnel: Patria Ann Beauliew

PUBLICATION NAME

Messager De Verdun
Street Address: 455 Fenelon Suite 303 , 303
Province: QC

Postal: H9S 5T8
Country: Canada
Mailing address: 455 Fenelon Suite 303
Mailing city: Dorval
Province: QC
Postal: H9S 5T8
General Phone: (514) 636-7314
General Fax: (514) 636-7317
General/National Adv. E-mail: redaction_verdun@tc.tc
Primary Website: www.messageverdun.com
Areas Served - City/County or Portion Thereof, or Zip codes: Canada
Published: Thur
Avg Paid Circ: 0
Avg Free Circ: 23936
Audit By: CCAB
Audit Date: 30.09.2012
Personnel: Patricia Ann Beaulieu

PUBLICATION NAME

The Chronicle
Street Address: 455 Boulevard Fenelon , Suite 303
Province: QC
Postal: H9S 5T8
Country: Canada
Mailing address: 455 Boulevard Fenelon
Mailing city: Dorval
Province: QC
Postal: H9S 5T8
General Phone: (514) 636-7314
General Fax: (514) 636-7317
Advertising Fax: (514) 636-7317
Editorial Fax: (514) 636-7317
General/National Adv. E-mail: info.chronicle@tc.tc
Primary Website: www.westislandchronicle.com
Year Established: 1925
Delivery Methods: Carrier`Racks
Areas Served - City/County or Portion Thereof, or Zip codes: Canada
Mechanical specifications: Type page 11 1/2 x 21 1/4; E - 5 cols, 2 3/16, 1/8 between; A - 10 cols, 1 1/16, 1/8 between; C - 10 cols, 1 1/16, 1/8 between.
Published: Wed
Avg Paid Circ: 5
Avg Free Circ: 43393
Audit By: CMCA
Audit Date: 31.08.2013
Personnel: Denis Therrien (General Manager); Joy-Ann Dempsey (Sales Support Supervisor); Robert Bourcier (Production Manager); Jean Nicolas AubÃ© (News Director)
Parent company (for newspapers): Transcontinental Media

DRAYTON

PUBLICATION NAME

The Community News
Street Address: 41 Wellington St. N. ,
Province: ON
Postal: N0G 1P0
Country: Canada
Mailing address: PO Box 189
Mailing city: Drayton
Province: ON
Postal: N0G 1P0
General Phone: (519) 638-3066
General Fax: (519) 843-7606
General/National Adv. E-mail: drayton@wellingtonadvertiser.com
Editorial e-mail: editor@wellingtonadvertiser.com
Primary Website: www.wellingtonadvertiser.com
Areas Served - City/County or Portion Thereof, or Zip codes: Canada
Mechanical specifications: Type page 10.25 x 15; E - 6 cols, 1 4/7, between; A - 6 cols, 1 4/7, between; C - 6 cols, 1 4/7, between.
Published: Fri
Avg Paid Circ: 5
Avg Free Circ: 5152
Audit By: CMCA
Audit Date: 31.03.2016
Personnel: William Adsett (Pub.); Dave Adsett (Ed.)

DRAYTON VALLEY

PUBLICATION NAME

Drayton Valley Western Review
Street Address: 4905 52nd Ave. ,
Province: AB
Postal: T7A 1S3
Country: Canada
Mailing address: PO Box 6960
Mailing city: Drayton Valley
Province: AB
Postal: T7A 1S3
General Phone: (780) 542-5380
General Fax: (780) 542-9200
General/National Adv. E-mail: dvwr@bowesnet.com
Display Adv. E-mail: theresa.hunt@sunmedia.com
Editorial e-mail: cweetman@postmedia.com
Primary Website: www.draytonvalleywesternreview.com
Year Established: 1966
Areas Served - City/County or Portion Thereof, or Zip codes: Canada
Published: Tues
Avg Paid Circ: 1132
Avg Free Circ: 5
Audit By: VAC
Audit Date: 31.12.2015
Personnel: Susanne Holmlund (Pub.); Pamela Allain (Adv. Dir) Cathy Weetman (Ed)
Parent company (for newspapers): Postmedia Network Inc.; Quebecor Communications, Inc.

DRUMHELLER

PUBLICATION NAME

Drumheller Mail
Street Address: 515 Hwy 10 East ,
Province: AB
Postal: T0J 0Y0
Country: Canada
Mailing address: PO Box 1629
Mailing city: Drumheller
Province: AB
Postal: T0J 0Y0
General Phone: (403) 823-2580
General Fax: (403) 823-3864
General/National Adv. E-mail: information@drumhellermail.com
Display Adv. E-mail: information@drumhellermail.com
Editorial e-mail: bob@drumhellermail.com
Primary Website: www.drumhellermail.com
Year Established: 1911
Delivery Methods: Mail`Newsstand`Carrier`Racks
Areas Served - City/County or Portion Thereof, or Zip codes: Canada
Own Printing Facility?: Y
Commercial printers?: Y
Mechanical specifications: Type page 12.4 x 21; E - 6 cols, 2 1/4, between; A - 6 cols, 2 1/4, between; C - 6 cols, 2 1/4, between.
Published: Wed
Avg Paid Circ: 4400
Avg Free Circ: 0
Audit By: CMCA
Audit Date: 30.06.2017
Personnel: Ossie Sheddy (Pub.); Bob Sheddy (Mng. Ed)

DRUMMONDVILLE

PUBLICATION NAME

Journal L'impact De Drummondville
Street Address: 2345, Rue St-pierre ,
Province: QC
Postal: J2C 5A7
Country: Canada
Mailing address: 2345, rue St-Pierre
Mailing city: Drummondville
Province: QC
Postal: J2C 5A7
General Phone: (819) 445-7000
General Fax: (819) 445-7001
General/National Adv. E-mail: guy.levasseur@quebecormedia.com
Primary Website: www.limpact.ca
Areas Served - City/County or Portion Thereof, or Zip codes: Canada
Published: Thur
Avg Paid Circ: 4
Avg Free Circ: 46173
Audit By: CCAB
Audit Date: 31.03.2014
Personnel: Jean Crepeau (Ed.)

PUBLICATION NAME

La Parole
Street Address: 1050 Rue Cormier ,
Province: QC
Postal: J2C 2N6
Country: Canada
Mailing address: 1050 Rue Cormier
Mailing city: Drummondville
Province: QC
Postal: J2C 2N6
General Phone: (819) 478-8171
General Fax: (819) 393-0741
General/National Adv. E-mail: redaction@transcontinental.ca
Primary Website: www.journalexpress.ca
Year Established: 1929
Areas Served - City/County or Portion Thereof, or Zip codes: Canada
Published: Wed
Avg Free Circ: 46000
Audit By: Sworn/Estimate/Non-Audited
Audit Date: 12.07.2019
Personnel: Eyves Shabot (Adv. Dir.); Johanne Marceau (Ed.)
Parent company (for newspapers): Reseau Select/Select Network

PUBLICATION NAME

L'express
Street Address: 1050 Cormier St. ,
Province: QC
Postal: J2C 2N6
Country: Canada
Mailing address: 1050 Cormier St.
Mailing city: Drummondville
Province: QC
Postal: J2C 2N6
General Phone: (819) 478-8171
General Fax: (819) 478-4306
General/National Adv. E-mail: redaction_dr@tc.tc
Primary Website: www.journalexpress.ca
Areas Served - City/County or Portion Thereof, or Zip codes: Canada
Published: Wed`Sun
Avg Paid Circ: 11
Avg Free Circ: 48116
Audit By: CCAB
Audit Date: 31.03.2014
Personnel: Johanne Marceau (Ed.)
Parent company (for newspapers): Transcontinental Media

DRYDEN

PUBLICATION NAME

Dryden Observer
Street Address: 32 Colonization Ave. ,
Province: ON
Postal: P8N 2Y9
Country: Canada
Mailing address: 32 Colonization Ave
Mailing city: Dryden
Province: ON
Postal: P8N 2Y9
General Phone: (807) 223-2390
General Fax: (807) 223-2907
Advertising Phone: (807) 223-2390 ext. 35
Advertising Fax: (807) 223-2907
Editorial Phone: (807) 223-2390 ext. 34
Display Adv. E-mail: lorie@drydenobserver.ca
Editorial e-mail: chrism@drydenobserver.ca
Primary Website: www.drydenobserver.ca
Year Established: 1897
Delivery Methods: Mail`Carrier
Areas Served - City/County or Portion Thereof, or Zip codes: Canada
Commercial printers?: Y
Mechanical specifications: Type page 11 1/2 x 21 1/2; E - 6 cols, 1 3/4, between; A - 6 cols, 1 3/4, between; C - 6 cols, 1 3/4, between.
Published: Wed
Avg Paid Circ: 2023
Avg Free Circ: 7
Audit By: CMCA
Audit Date: 19.12.2017
Personnel: LORIE LUNDY (Adv. Mgr.); Sean Clarke (Circ. Mgr.); CHRIS MARCHAND (Ed.); Michael Christianson (Reporter); Brian Kasaboski (Prod.); Laurie Fisher (Office manager)
Parent company (for newspapers): Norwest Printing

DUNCAN

PUBLICATION NAME

Cowichan Valley Citizen
Street Address: 251 Jubilee Street ,
Province: BC
Postal: V9L 1W8
Country: Canada
General Phone: (250) 748-2666
General/National Adv. E-mail: news@cowichanvalleycitizen.com
Display Adv. E-mail: warren.goulding@blackpress.ca
Classified Adv. e-mail: bcclassifieds@blackpress.ca
Editorial e-mail: editor@cowichanvalleycitizen.com
Primary Website: cowichanvalleycitizen.com
Year Established: 1986
Areas Served - City/County or Portion Thereof, or Zip codes: Canada
Commercial printers?: Y
Mechanical specifications: Type page 10 1/4 x 13; A - 9 cols, 1 1/16, between; C - 7 cols, 1 5/8, between.
Published: Wed`Fri
Avg Free Circ: 20910
Audit By: AAM
Audit Date: 31.03.2019
Personnel: Warren Goulding (Pub./Adv. Mgr.)
Parent company (for newspapers): Torstar

PUBLICATION NAME

The Cowichan News Leader
Street Address: 251 Jubilee St ,
Province: BC
Postal: V9L 1W8
Country: Canada
Mailing address: 251 Jubilee St
Mailing city: Duncan
Province: BC
Postal: V9L1W8
General Phone: (250) 748-2666
General Fax: (250) 746-8529
General/National Adv. E-mail: publisher@cowichannewsleader.com
Editorial e-mail: editor@cowichannewsleader.com
Primary Website: www.cowichannewsleader.com
Year Established: 1905
Delivery Methods: Mail`Newsstand`Carrier`Racks
Areas Served - City/County or Portion Thereof, or Zip codes: Canada
Own Printing Facility?: Y
Mechanical specifications: Type page 12 x 21 1/2; E - 7 cols, 1 1/4, between; A - 7 cols, 1 1/4, between; C - 8 cols, 1 1/4, between.
Published: Wed`Fri
Avg Paid Circ: 0
Avg Free Circ: 22430
Audit By: CMCA
Audit Date: 30.04.2013
Personnel: Lara Stuart (Circ. Mgr.); John McKinley (Ed.); Shirley Skolos (Pub)

PUBLICATION NAME

The Lake Cowichan Gazette

Street Address: 251 Jubilee Street ,
Province: BC
Postal: V9L 1W8
Country: Canada
Mailing address: 251 Jubilee Street
Mailing city: Duncan
Province: BC
Postal: V9L 1W8
General Phone: (250) 748-2666
Advertising Phone: (250) 748-2666
General/National Adv. E-mail: office@lakecowichangazette.com
Display Adv. E-mail: warren.goulding@blackpress.ca
Editorial e-mail: editor@lakecowichangazette.com
Primary Website: www.lakecowichangazette.com
Year Established: 1995
Delivery Methods: Mail
Areas Served - City/County or Portion Thereof, or Zip codes: Lake Cowichan
Published: Wed
Avg Paid Circ: 430
Avg Free Circ: 26
Audit By: VAC
Audit Date: 30.09.2017
Personnel: Waren Goulding (Pub.); Classified Ads (Classifieds); Drew McLachlan (Ed)
Parent company (for newspapers): Black Press Group Ltd.

DUNDALK

PUBLICATION NAME

Advance
Street Address: 260 Main St. E. ,
Province: ON
Postal: N0C 1B0
Country: Canada
Mailing address: P.O. Box 280
Mailing city: Dundalk
Province: ON
Postal: N0C 1B0
General Phone: (519) 923-2203
General Fax: (519) 923-2747
Display Adv. E-mail: dundalk.herald@gmail.com
Editorial e-mail: dundalk.heraldnews@gmail.com
Year Established: 1881
Delivery Methods: Mail`Newsstand
Areas Served - City/County or Portion Thereof, or Zip codes: Southgate
Own Printing Facility?: Y
Commercial printers?: Y
Published: Wed
Avg Paid Circ: 1299
Audit By: Sworn/Estimate/Non-Audited
Audit Date: 12.07.2019
Personnel: Matthew Walls (Pub.)
Parent company (for newspapers): herald newspaper corp

PUBLICATION NAME

Herald
Street Address: 260 Main St. E. ,
Province: ON
Postal: N0C 1B0
Country: Canada
Mailing address: PO Box 280
Mailing city: Dundalk
Province: ON
Postal: N0C 1B0
General Phone: (519) 923-2203
General Fax: (519) 923-2747
Display Adv. E-mail: dundalk.herald@gmail.com
Editorial e-mail: dundalk.heraldnews@gmail.com
Primary Website: www.dundalkherald.ca
Year Established: 1881
Areas Served - City/County or Portion Thereof, or Zip codes: Canada
Own Printing Facility?: Y
Commercial printers?: Y
Published: Wed
Avg Paid Circ: 1443
Audit By: CMCA
Audit Date: 30.06.2016
Personnel: Matthew Walls (Pub.); Cathy Walls (Adv. Mgr.)

DURHAM

PUBLICATION NAME

The Durham Chronicle
Street Address: 190 Elizabeth St. E. ,
Province: ON
Postal: N0G 1R0
Country: Canada
Mailing address: PO Box 230
Mailing city: Durham
Province: ON
Postal: N0G 1R0
General Phone: (519) 369-2504
General Fax: (519) 369-3560
General/National Adv. E-mail: themarkdalestandard@bmts.com
Areas Served - City/County or Portion Thereof, or Zip codes: Canada
Mechanical specifications: Type page 11 1/4 x 16 3/4; E - 5 cols, 2 1/5, between; A - 5 cols, 2 1/5, between; C - 9 cols, between.
Published: Wed
Avg Paid Circ: 1196
Avg Free Circ: 21
Audit By: Sworn/Estimate/Non-Audited
Audit Date: 12.07.2019
Personnel: Marie David (Pub.); Bev Stoddart (Gen. Mgr.); Christine Meingast (Ed.)

EDMONTON

PUBLICATION NAME

Edmonton Examiner
Street Address: 10006 101 St ,
Province: AB
Postal: T5J 0S1
Country: Canada
Mailing address: 10006 101 St
Mailing city: Edmonton
Province: AB
Postal: T5J 0S1
General Phone: (780) 453-9001
General Fax: (780) 447-7333
Advertising Phone: (780) 444-5450
Display Adv. E-mail: rpaterson@postmedia.com
Classified Adv. e-mail: bob.paterson@sunmedia.ca
Editorial e-mail: dave.breakenridge@sunmedia.ca
Primary Website: www.edmontonexaminer.com
Year Established: 1979
Delivery Methods: Carrier`Racks
Areas Served - City/County or Portion Thereof, or Zip codes: Canada
Mechanical specifications: Type page 10 1/4 x 12 1/2; E - 10 cols, between; A - 10 cols, between; C - 10 cols, between.
Published: Wed
Avg Paid Circ: 0
Avg Free Circ: 131000
Audit By: CCAB
Audit Date: 24.12.2017
Personnel: John Caputo (Pub); Ted Dakin (Adv. Dir); Dave Breakenridge (Ed)
Parent company (for newspapers): Postmedia Network Inc.; Quebecor Communications, Inc.

PUBLICATION NAME

Le Franco
Street Address: 8627-91 St. , Rm 312
Province: AB
Postal: T6C 3N1
Country: Canada
Mailing address: 8627-91 St.
Mailing city: Edmonton
Province: AB
Postal: T6C 3N1
General Phone: (780) 465-6581
General Fax: (780) 469-1129
General/National Adv. E-mail: journal@lefranco.ab.ca
Display Adv. E-mail: commercial@lefranco.ab.ca
Editorial e-mail: direction@lefranco.ab.ca
Primary Website: http://www.lefranco.ab.ca
Year Established: 1928
Delivery Methods: Mail
Areas Served - City/County or Portion Thereof, or Zip codes: Alberta
Published: Thur
Avg Paid Circ: 3206
Avg Free Circ: 302
Audit By: Sworn/Estimate/Non-Audited
Audit Date: 12.07.2019
Personnel: Emma Hautecoeur (Ed.)

EDMUNDSTON

PUBLICATION NAME

Info Week-end
Street Address: 322 Victoria St. ,
Province: QC
Postal: E3V 2H9
Country: Canada
Mailing address: 322 Victoria St.
Mailing city: Edmundston
Province: NB
Postal: E3V 2H9
General Phone: (506) 739-5083
Display Adv. E-mail: pub@infoweekend.ca
Primary Website: journaux.apf.ca/infoweekend
Areas Served - City/County or Portion Thereof, or Zip codes: Canada
Published: Wed
Avg Free Circ: 21550
Audit By: CCAB
Audit Date: 30.09.2013
Personnel: Michel Chalifour

PUBLICATION NAME

Le Madawaska
Street Address: 20 Rue Saint Francois ,
Province: NB
Postal: E3V 1E3
Country: Canada
Mailing address: 20 Rue Saint Francois
Mailing city: Edmundston
Province: NB
Postal: E3V 1E3
General Phone: (506) 735-5575
General Fax: (506) 735-8086
General/National Adv. E-mail: madproduction@brunswicknews.com
Editorial e-mail: madproduction@brunswicknews.com
Primary Website: https://www.telegraphjournal.com/le-madawaska/
Areas Served - City/County or Portion Thereof, or Zip codes: Edmundston
Mechanical specifications: Type page 13 x 21; E - 6 cols, 2 1/8, between; A - 6 cols, 2 1/8, between.
Published: Sat
Avg Paid Circ: 2561
Avg Free Circ: 20
Audit By: VAC
Audit Date: 31.12.2015
Personnel: Hermel Volpe (Pub.)
Parent company (for newspapers): Brunswick News, Inc.

EDSON

PUBLICATION NAME

Edson Leader
Street Address: 4820 3rd Ave. ,
Province: AB
Postal: T7E 1T8
Country: Canada
Mailing address: 4820-3 Ave
Mailing city: Edson
Province: AB
Postal: T7E 1T8
General Phone: (780) 723-3301
General Fax: (780) 723-5171
General/National Adv. E-mail: leadernews@telusplanet.net
Display Adv. E-mail: pam.thesen@sunmedia.ca
Editorial e-mail: ian.mcinnes@sunmedia.ca
Primary Website: www.edsonleader.com
Year Established: 1989
Areas Served - City/County or Portion Thereof, or Zip codes: Canada
Published: Mon
Avg Paid Circ: 3
Avg Free Circ: 3468
Audit By: VAC
Audit Date: 31.12.2015
Personnel: Pamela Thesen (Adv. Dir); Janice Foisy (Pub.); Ian McInnes (Ed.)
Parent company (for newspapers): Postmedia Network Inc.; Quebecor Communications, Inc.

PUBLICATION NAME

The Weekly Anchor
Street Address: 5040 3rd Ave. ,
Province: AB
Postal: T7E 1V2
Country: Canada
Mailing address: PO Box 6870
Mailing city: Edson
Province: AB
Postal: T7E 1V2
General Phone: (780) 723-5787
General Fax: (780) 723-5725
General/National Adv. E-mail: anchorwk@telusplanet.net
Display Adv. E-mail: anchorwk@telusplanet.net
Classified Adv. e-mail: anchorwk@telusplanet.net
Editorial e-mail: anchorwk@telusplanet.net
Primary Website: www.weeklyanchor.com
Year Established: 1988
Delivery Methods: Mail`Newsstand`Racks
Areas Served - City/County or Portion Thereof, or Zip codes: Canada
Mechanical specifications: Type page 15 1/2 x 15 5/9; E - 6 cols, between; A - 6 cols, between.
Published: Mon
Avg Paid Circ: 50
Avg Free Circ: 6025
Audit By: CMCA
Audit Date: 31.12.2016
Personnel: Dana McArthur (Pub./Adv. Dir.)

EGAN SOUTH

PUBLICATION NAME

Le Gatineau
Street Address: 135-b, Highway 105 ,
Province: QC
Postal: J9E 3A9
Country: Canada
General Phone: (819) 449-1725
General Fax: (819) 449-5108
General/National Adv. E-mail: direction@lagatineau.com
Editorial e-mail: redaction@lagatineau.com
Primary Website: www.lagatineau.com
Year Established: 1955
Delivery Methods: Carrier`Racks
Areas Served - City/County or Portion Thereof, or Zip codes: Canada
Mechanical specifications: Type page 10 3/4 x 14 5/16.
Published: Thur
Avg Free Circ: 11210
Audit By: CCAB
Audit Date: 31.03.2014
Personnel: Denise LacourciÃ¨re (Executive Director)

EGANVILLE

PUBLICATION NAME

The Eganville Leader
Street Address: 150 John St. , P.o. Box 310
Province: ON
Postal: K0J 1T0
Country: Canada
Mailing address: PO Box 310
Mailing city: Eganville
Province: ON
Postal: K0J 1T0
General Phone: (613) 628-2332
General Fax: (613) 628-3291
General/National Adv. E-mail: leader@nrtco.net

Display Adv. E-mail: leaderads@nrtco.net
Editorial e-mail: leader@nrtco.net
Primary Website: www.eganvilleleader.com
Year Established: 1902
Delivery Methods: Mail`Newsstand`Racks
Areas Served - City/County or Portion Thereof, or Zip codes: Canada
Mechanical specifications: Type page 13 1/2 x 21; E - 8 cols, 1 3/5, between; A - 8 cols, 1 3/5, between; C - 8 cols, 1 3/5, between.
Published: Wed
Avg Paid Circ: 6096
Audit By: CMCA
Audit Date: 29.02.2016
Personnel: Carol Kutschke (Circ. Mgr.); Gerald J. Tracey (Ed.)

ELK POINT
PUBLICATION NAME

Elk Point Review
Street Address: 5022 - 49 Ave ,
Province: AB
Postal: T0A 1A0
Country: Canada
Mailing address: PO Box 309
Mailing city: Elk Point
Province: AB
Postal: T0A 1A0
General Phone: (780) 724-4087
General Fax: (780) 645-2346
General/National Adv. E-mail: production@stpaul.greatwest.ca; aglaser@greatwest.ca
Display Adv. E-mail: cgauvreau@greatwest.ca
Editorial e-mail: vbrooker@stpaul.greatwest.ca
Primary Website: www.greatwest.ca
Year Established: 1963
Areas Served - City/County or Portion Thereof, or Zip codes: Canada
Published: Tues
Avg Paid Circ: 2950
Avg Free Circ: 0
Audit By: VAC
Audit Date: 31.12.2015
Personnel: Clare Gauvreau (Pub./Adv. Mgr.); Vicki Brooker (Ed.); Marg Smith (Prod.)
Parent company (for newspapers): Glacier Media Group; Great West Newspapers LP

ELLIOT LAKE
PUBLICATION NAME

The Mid-north Monitor
Street Address: 14 Hillside Drive South ,
Province: ON
Postal: P5A 1M6
Country: Canada
Mailing address: 14 Hillside Drive South
Mailing city: Elliot Lake
Province: ON
Postal: P0M 3E0
General Phone: 7058661801
General Fax: (705) 869-0587
Advertising Phone: (705) 848 - 7195
General/National Adv. E-mail: mnm@sunmedia.ca
Display Adv. E-mail: kjohansen@postmedia.com
Classified Adv. e-mail: kjohansen@postmedia.com
Editorial e-mail: kjohansen@postmedia.com
Primary Website: www.midnorthmonitor.com
Year Established: 1978
Delivery Methods: Mail`Newsstand
Areas Served - City/County or Portion Thereof, or Zip codes: Canada
Mechanical specifications: Type page 10 1/4 x 15 ; E - 9 cols, 1", 1/8" between; A - 9 cols, 1", 1/8" between; C - 9 cols, 1", 1/8" between.
Published: Thur
Avg Paid Circ: 849
Audit By: Sworn/Estimate/Non-Audited
Audit Date: 12.07.2019
Personnel: Lolene Patterson (Circ. Mgr.); Kevin McSheffrey (Managing Editor)
Parent company (for newspapers): 1954; Postmedia Network Inc.

ELMVALE
PUBLICATION NAME

Springwater News
Street Address: 9 Glenview Ave. ,
Province: ON
Postal: L0L 1P0
Country: Canada
Mailing address: 9 Glenview Ave.
Mailing city: Elmvale
Province: ON
Postal: L0L 1P0
General Phone: (705) 322-2249
General Fax: (705) 322-8393
Advertising Phone: (705) 322-2249
Advertising Fax: (705) 322-8393
Editorial Phone: (705) 321-2653
General/National Adv. E-mail: springwaternews@rogers.com
Display Adv. E-mail: springwaternews@rogers.com
Classified Adv. e-mail: springwaternews@rogers.com
Editorial e-mail: springwaternews@rogers.com
Primary Website: www.springwaternews.ca
Year Established: 1998
Delivery Methods: Mail`Newsstand`Carrier`Racks
Areas Served - City/County or Portion Thereof, or Zip codes: L0L in North Simcoe County L9M near Penetanguishene L4R around Midland L0K Wyebridge L4M and L4n around Barrie
Mechanical specifications: Tabloid 11x17 24 pages - 12 in colour
Published: Thur`Other
Published Other: Bi-weekly
Avg Paid Circ: 140
Avg Free Circ: 18750
Audit By: Sworn/Estimate/Non-Audited
Audit Date: 12.07.2019
Personnel: Michael Jacobs (Ed./Pub./Owner)

EMBRUN
PUBLICATION NAME

Journal Le Reflet
Street Address: 793 Rue Notre Dame Rr 3 # 3, ,
Province: ON
Postal: K0A 1W1
Country: Canada
Mailing address: 793 Rue Notre Dame Rr 3 # 3,
Mailing city: Embrun
Province: ON
Postal: K0A 1W1
General Phone: (613) 443-2741
Primary Website: www.lereflet.qc.ca
Areas Served - City/County or Portion Thereof, or Zip codes: Embrun, ON
Published: Mon
Avg Paid Circ: 29
Avg Free Circ: 18102
Audit By: ODC
Audit Date: 14.12.2011
Personnel: Roger Duplantie (Gen. Dir.)

EMERSON
PUBLICATION NAME

The Southeast Journal
Street Address: 108 Church Street ,
Province: MB
Postal: R0A 0L0
Country: Canada
Mailing address: Box 68
Mailing city: Emerson
Province: MB
Postal: R0A0L0
General Phone: (204) 373-2493
General Fax: (204)-272-3492
Advertising Phone: (204) 373-2493
Editorial Phone: (204) 373-2493
General/National Adv. E-mail: sej@mts.net
Display Adv. E-mail: sej@mts.net
Classified Adv. e-mail: sej@mts.net
Editorial e-mail: sej@mts.net
Primary Website: www.southeastjournal.ca
Delivery Methods: Mail
Areas Served - City/County or Portion Thereof, or Zip codes: Manitoba
Published: Thur
Avg Paid Circ: 14
Avg Free Circ: 3500
Audit By: VAC
Audit Date: 31.08.2015

ENFIELD
PUBLICATION NAME

Enfield Weekly Press
Street Address: 287 Highway 2 ,
Province: NS
Postal: B2T 1C9
Country: Canada
Mailing address: 287 Highway 2
Mailing city: Enfield
Province: NS
Postal: B2T 1C9
General Phone: (902) 883-3181
General Fax: (902) 883-3180
General/National Adv. E-mail: editor@enfieldweeklypress.com
Display Adv. E-mail: michelewhite@enfieldweeklypress.com
Classified Adv. e-mail: admin@enfieldweeklypress.com
Editorial e-mail: editor@enfieldweeklypress.com
Primary Website: www.enfieldweeklypress.com
Areas Served - City/County or Portion Thereof, or Zip codes: Enfield
Published: Wed
Avg Free Circ: 10914
Audit By: VAC
Audit Date: 30.06.2016
Personnel: Leith Orr (Pub); Michele White (Adv. Rep)

PUBLICATION NAME

Fall River Laker
Street Address: 287 Highway 2 ,
Province: NS
Postal: B2T 1C9
General Phone: (902) 883-3181, Ext. 3
General Fax: (902) 883-3180
Display Adv. E-mail: michelewhite@enfieldweeklypress.com
Classified Adv. e-mail: admin@enfieldweeklypress.com
Editorial e-mail: editor@enfieldweeklypress.com
Primary Website: www.thelaker.ca
Areas Served - City/County or Portion Thereof, or Zip codes: Enfield
Published: Thur
Avg Paid Circ: 2247
Avg Free Circ: 7703
Audit By: VAC
Audit Date: 30.04.2016
Personnel: Leith Orr (Pub); Michele White (Adv. Rep)

ERIN
PUBLICATION NAME

The Erin Advocate
Street Address: 8 Thompson Crescent ,
Province: ON
Postal: N0B 1T0
Country: Canada
Mailing address: 8 Thompson Crescent
Mailing city: Erin
Province: ON
Postal: N0B 1T0
General Phone: (519) 833-9603
General Fax: (519) 833-9605
General/National Adv. E-mail: esales@erinadvocate.com
Year Established: 1880
Areas Served - City/County or Portion Thereof, or Zip codes: Canada
Commercial printers?: Y
Mechanical specifications: Type page 10 3/8 x 14; E - 6 cols, 1 5/8, between; A - 6 cols, 1 5/8, between; C - 6 cols, 1 5/8, between.
Published: Wed
Avg Paid Circ: 1054
Audit By: CMCA
Audit Date: 30.06.2016
Personnel: Ken Nugent (Pub.); Bill Anderson (Adv. Mgr.); Joan Murray (Ed.)
Parent company (for newspapers): Metroland Media Group Ltd.; Torstar

ESSEX
PUBLICATION NAME

Essex Free Press
Street Address: 16 Centre St. ,
Province: ON
Postal: N8M 1N9
Country: Canada
Mailing address: PO Box 115
Mailing city: Essex
Province: ON
Postal: N8M 2Y1
General Phone: (519) 776-4268
General Fax: (519) 776-4014
General/National Adv. E-mail: essexfreepress@on.aibn.com
Primary Website: www.sxfreepress.com
Year Established: 1896
Areas Served - City/County or Portion Thereof, or Zip codes: Canada
Own Printing Facility?: Y
Commercial printers?: Y
Mechanical specifications: Type page 10 x 15; E - 5 cols, 2, 1/6 between.
Published: Thur
Avg Free Circ: 9925
Audit By: CMCA
Audit Date: 30.09.2016
Personnel: Lauri Brett (Pub.)

ESTERHAZY
PUBLICATION NAME

The Esterhazy Miner-journal
Street Address: 606 Veterans Ave. ,
Province: SK
Postal: S0A 0X0
Country: Canada
Mailing address: PO Box 1000
Mailing city: Esterhazy
Province: SK
Postal: S0A 0X0
General Phone: (306) 745-6669
General Fax: (306) 745-2699
General/National Adv. E-mail: miner.journal@sasktel.net
Primary Website: www.minerjournal.com
Year Established: 1907
Areas Served - City/County or Portion Thereof, or Zip codes: Canada
Commercial printers?: Y
Mechanical specifications: Type page 10 1/4 x 16; E - 5 cols, 1 11/12, between; A - 5 cols, 1 11/12, between; C - 5 cols, 1 11/12, between.
Published: Mon
Avg Paid Circ: 1334
Avg Free Circ: 0
Audit By: CMCA
Audit Date: 30.11.2013
Personnel: Brenda Matchett (Adv. Mgr.); Helen Solmes (Ed.)

ESTEVAN
PUBLICATION NAME

Estevan Mercury
Street Address: 68 Souris Ave N. ,
Province: SK
Postal: S4A 2M3
Country: Canada
Mailing address: PO Box 730
Mailing city: Estevan
Province: SK
Postal: S4A 2A6
General Phone: (306) 634-2654
General Fax: (306) 634-3934

Community Newspapers in Canada

III-533

General/National Adv. E-mail: classifieds@estevanmercury.ca
Display Adv. E-mail: adsales@estevanmercury.ca
Editorial e-mail: editor@estevanmercury.ca
Primary Website: estevanmercury.ca
Year Established: 1903
Delivery Methods: Mail`Newsstand`Carrier`Racks
Areas Served - City/County or Portion Thereof, or Zip codes: Canada
Commercial printers?: Y
Mechanical specifications: Please call
Published: Wed
Avg Paid Circ: 252
Avg Free Circ: 4981
Audit By: AAM
Audit Date: 31.03.2019
Personnel: Rick Sadick (Pub.); Jihyun Choi (Prod. Mgr.); Norm Park (Ed.)
Parent company (for newspapers): Glacier Media Group

PUBLICATION NAME

Southeast Lifestyles
Street Address: 300 Kensington Avenue ,
Province: SK
Postal: S4A 2A7
Country: Canada
Mailing address: Box 816
Mailing city: Estevan
Province: SK
Postal: S4A 2A6
General Phone: (306) 634-5112
General Fax: (306) 634-2588
General/National Adv. E-mail: lifestyles@sasktel.net
Primary Website: http://www.sasklifestyles.com/
Year Established: 1999
Delivery Methods: Mail`Newsstand`Carrier`Racks
Areas Served - City/County or Portion Thereof, or Zip codes: Canada
Mechanical specifications: Please Call
Published: Thur
Avg Paid Circ: 18
Avg Free Circ: 6585
Audit By: CMCA
Audit Date: 28.02.2014
Personnel: Rick Sadick (Pub.); Norm Park (Ed.)
Parent company (for newspapers): Glacier Media Group

ESTON

PUBLICATION NAME

Eston-elrose Press Review
Street Address: 108 W. Main St. ,
Province: SK
Postal: S0L 1A0
Country: Canada
Mailing address: PO Box 787
Mailing city: Eston
Province: SK
Postal: S0L 1A0
General Phone: (306) 962-3221
General Fax: (306) 962-4445
General/National Adv. E-mail: estonpress@gmail.com
Areas Served - City/County or Portion Thereof, or Zip codes: Canada
Published: Tues
Avg Paid Circ: 753
Audit By: CMCA
Audit Date: 30.06.2016
Personnel: Stewart Crump (Pub.); Barry Malindine (Adv. Mgr.); Tim Crump (Ed.)
Parent company (for newspapers): Jamac Publishing

ETOBICOKE

PUBLICATION NAME

Etobicoke Guardian
Street Address: 307 Humberline Dr. ,
Province: ON
Postal: M9W 5V1
Country: Canada
Mailing address: 307 Humberline Dr.
Mailing city: Etobicoke
Province: ON
Postal: M9W 5V1
General Phone: (416) 675-4390
General Fax: (416) 675-9296
General/National Adv. E-mail: etg@mirror-guardian.com
Primary Website: insidetoronto.ca
Year Established: 1917
Areas Served - City/County or Portion Thereof, or Zip codes: Canada
Own Printing Facility?: Y
Commercial printers?: Y
Published: Thur
Avg Paid Circ: 0
Avg Free Circ: 67927
Audit By: CCAB
Audit Date: 30.09.2017
Personnel: Marg Middleton (Gen. Mgr.); Betty Carr (Pub.); Cor Coran (Adv. Mgr.); Lesley Duff (Asst. Dir., Dist.); Grace Peacock (Mng. Ed.); Dave Barnett (Dir., Prodn.); Katherine Bernal (Prodn. Mgr.)
Parent company (for newspapers): Metroland Media Group Ltd.; Torstar

EXETER

PUBLICATION NAME

Times Advocate
Street Address: 356 Main St. S. ,
Province: ON
Postal: N0M 1S6
Country: Canada
Mailing address: PO Box 850
Mailing city: Exeter
Province: ON
Postal: N0M 1S6
General Phone: (519) 235-1331
Advertising Fax: (519) 235-0766
General/National Adv. E-mail: ads@southhuron.com
Display Adv. E-mail: sales@southhuron.com
Editorial e-mail: snixon@southhuron.com
Primary Website: www.southhuron.com
Year Established: 1873
Delivery Methods: Mail
Areas Served - City/County or Portion Thereof, or Zip codes: N0M
Own Printing Facility?: N
Commercial printers?: Y
Mechanical specifications: Type page 10 1/2 x 16; E - 6 cols, 1 9/16, 3/16 between; A - 6 cols, 1 9/16, 3/16 between; C - 6 cols, 1 9/16, 3/16 between.
Published: Wed
Avg Paid Circ: 2158
Avg Free Circ: 84
Audit By: CMCA
Audit Date: 30.09.2016
Personnel: Deb Lord (Manager); Scott Nixon (Editor); Deborah Schillemore (Sales)
Parent company (for newspapers): Metroland Media Group Ltd.; Torstar

FAIRVIEW

PUBLICATION NAME

Fairview Post
Street Address: 10118-110 St. ,
Province: AB
Postal: T0H 1L0
Country: Canada
Mailing address: PO Box 1900
Mailing city: Fairview
Province: AB
Postal: T0H 1L0
General Phone: (780) 835-4925
General Fax: (780) 835-4227
General/National Adv. E-mail: info@fairviewpost.com
Display Adv. E-mail: peter.meyerhoffer@sunmedia.ca
Editorial e-mail: chris.eakin@sunmedia.ca
Primary Website: www.fairviewpost.com
Year Established: 1940
Delivery Methods: Mail`Newsstand
Areas Served - City/County or Portion Thereof, or Zip codes: T0H
Commercial printers?: Y
Mechanical specifications: 160 Lines 10 Columns Page size: 10.33x11.43
Published: Wed
Avg Paid Circ: 119
Avg Free Circ: 8
Audit By: VAC
Audit Date: 31.12.2015
Personnel: Peter Meyerhoffer (Adv. Dir); Chris Eakin (Ed.)
Parent company (for newspapers): Postmedia Network Inc.; Quebecor Communications, Inc.

FARNHAM

PUBLICATION NAME

Journal L'avenir & Des Rivieres
Street Address: 221 Main St. ,
Province: QC
Postal: J2N 1L5
Country: Canada
Mailing address: 221 Main St.
Mailing city: Farnham
Province: QC
Postal: J2N 1L5
General Phone: (450) 293-3138
General Fax: (450) 293-2093
General/National Adv. E-mail: caroline.dolce@tc.tc
Primary Website: www.laveniretdesrivieres.com
Areas Served - City/County or Portion Thereof, or Zip codes: Canada
Published: Wed
Avg Paid Circ: 3
Avg Free Circ: 11442
Audit By: CCAB
Audit Date: 31.03.2014
Personnel: Renel Bouchard (Gen. Mgr.); Elrsa Fournyer (Pub.); Charles Couture (Circ. Mgr.)

PUBLICATION NAME

L'avenir De Brome Missisquoi, Inc.
Street Address: 221 Rue Principale Est. ,
Province: QC
Postal: J2N 1L5
Country: Canada
Mailing address: 221 Rue Principale Est.
Mailing city: Farnham
Province: QC
Postal: J2N 1L5
General Phone: (450) 293-3138
General Fax: (450) 293-2093
General/National Adv. E-mail: lavenir@canadafrancais.com
Editorial e-mail: cassandra.deblois@tc.tc
Primary Website: www.laveniretdesrivieres.com
Published: Wed
Avg Paid Circ: 34
Avg Free Circ: 8554
Audit By: Sworn/Estimate/Non-Audited
Audit Date: 12.07.2019
Personnel: Group le Canada Francais (Pub.)

FERGUS

PUBLICATION NAME

The Fergus-elora News Express
Street Address: 204 St. Andrew St. W ,
Province: ON
Postal: N1M 1M7
Country: Canada
Mailing address: PO Box 130
Mailing city: Fergus
Province: ON
Postal: N1M 1N7
General Phone: (519) 843-1310
General Fax: (519) 323-4548
Display Adv. E-mail: ads@centrewellington.com
Editorial e-mail: editor@centrewellington.com
Primary Website: www.southwesternontario.ca/ferguselora-on
Year Established: 1852
Areas Served - City/County or Portion Thereof, or Zip codes: Canada
Published: Wed
Avg Paid Circ: 100
Avg Free Circ: 7850
Audit By: CMCA
Audit Date: 31.08.2014
Personnel: Shannon Burrows (Ed.)
Parent company (for newspapers): Metroland Media Group Ltd.; Torstar

PUBLICATION NAME

The Wellington Advertiser
Street Address: 905 Gartshore St. ,
Province: ON
Postal: N1M 2W8
Country: Canada
Mailing address: PO Box 252
Mailing city: Fergus
Province: ON
Postal: N1M 2W8
General Phone: (519) 843-5410
General Fax: (519) 843-7607
General/National Adv. E-mail: news@wellingtonadvertiser.com
Display Adv. E-mail: advertising@wellingtonadvertiser.com
Editorial e-mail: editor@wellingtonadvertiser.com
Primary Website: www.wellingtonadvertiser.com
Year Established: 1967
Delivery Methods: Mail`Newsstand`Carrier`Racks
Areas Served - City/County or Portion Thereof, or Zip codes: Fergus
Own Printing Facility?: Y
Mechanical specifications: E - 6 cols, 1 1/2, 1 2/3 between; A - 6 cols, 1 1/2, 1 2/3 between; C - 6 cols, 1 1/2, 1 2/3 between.
Published: Fri
Avg Paid Circ: 235
Avg Free Circ: 39898
Audit By: VAC
Audit Date: 31.03.2016
Personnel: William Adsett (Pub.); Catherine Goss (Circ. Mgr.); Dave Adsett (Ed.)

FERMONT

PUBLICATION NAME

Le Trait D'union Du Nord
Street Address: 850 Place Daviault ,
Province: QC
Postal: G0G 1J0
Country: Canada
Mailing address: PO Box 561
Mailing city: Fermont
Province: QC
Postal: G0G 1J0
General Phone: (418) 287-3655
General Fax: (418) 287-3874
General/National Adv. E-mail: info.journaltdn@gmail.com
Display Adv. E-mail: publicite@journaltdn.ca
Classified Adv. e-mail: publicite@journaltdn.ca
Editorial e-mail: redaction@journaltdn.ca
Primary Website: www.journaltdn.ca
Year Established: 1983
Published: Mon
Published Other: Every other mon
Avg Free Circ: 1700
Audit By: Sworn/Estimate/Non-Audited
Audit Date: 12.07.2019
Personnel: Eric Cyr (Ed.); Lynda Raiche (Graphic & Adv. Consultant)

FERNIE

PUBLICATION NAME

The Free Press
Street Address: 342 2nd Ave. ,
Province: BC
Postal: V0B 1M0
Country: Canada
Mailing address: PO Box 2350

Mailing city: Fernie
Province: BC
Postal: V0B 1M0
General Phone: (250) 423-4666
General/National Adv. E-mail: publisher@thefreepress.ca
Display Adv. E-mail: advertising@thefreepress.ca
Editorial e-mail: editor@thefreepress.ca
Primary Website: www.thefreepress.ca
Year Established: 1898
Delivery Methods: Carrier`Racks
Areas Served - City/County or Portion Thereof, or Zip codes: V0B 1M0 V0B 1M2 V0B 1H0 V0B 2G0 V0B 1T0 V0B 1T4
Own Printing Facility?: N
Commercial printers?: Y
Mechanical specifications: Type page 11 1/2 x 21 1/2; E - 10 cols, 1 1/6, between.
Published: Thur
Avg Paid Circ: 234
Avg Free Circ: 5643
Audit By: VAC
Audit Date: 30.11.2015
Personnel: Andrea Horton (Pub); Katie Smith (Ed); Jennifer Cronin (Adv); Bonny McLardy (Prod Mgr.)
Parent company (for newspapers): Black Press Group Ltd.

FLIN FLON

PUBLICATION NAME

Flin Flon Reminder
Street Address: 14 North Ave.,
Province: MB
Postal: R8A 0T2
Country: Canada
Mailing address: 14 North Ave.
Mailing city: Flin Flon
Province: MB
Postal: R8A 0T2
General Phone: (204) 687-3454
General Fax: (204) 687-4473
General/National Adv. E-mail: reminder@mb.sympatico.ca
Display Adv. E-mail: ads@thereminder.ca
Classified Adv. e-mail: sales@thereminder.ca
Editorial e-mail: news@thereminder.ca
Primary Website: www.thereminder.ca
Year Established: 1946
Areas Served - City/County or Portion Thereof, or Zip codes: Flin Flon
Published: Wed`Fri
Weekday Frequency: e
Avg Paid Circ: 12
Avg Free Circ: 38
Audit By: VAC
Audit Date: 30.06.2016
Personnel: Valerie Durnin (Pub); Jonathon Naylor (Ed); Shannon Thompson (Office Admin)
Parent company (for newspapers): Glacier Media Group

FOAM LAKE

PUBLICATION NAME

Foam Lake Review
Street Address: 325 Main St.,
Province: SK
Postal: S0A 1A0
Country: Canada
Mailing address: PO Box 550
Mailing city: Foam Lake
Province: SK
Postal: S0A 1A0
General Phone: (306) 272-3262
General Fax: (306) 272-4521
General/National Adv. E-mail: review.foamlake@sasktel.net
Primary Website: www.foamlakereview.com
Areas Served - City/County or Portion Thereof, or Zip codes: Canada
Own Printing Facility?: Y
Commercial printers?: Y
Published: Mon
Avg Paid Circ: 1123

Avg Free Circ: 3
Audit By: CMCA
Audit Date: 31.12.2015
Personnel: Bob Johnson (Ed).

FONTHILL

PUBLICATION NAME

Fonthill Voice Of Pelham
Street Address: 8-209 Highway 20 East,
Province: ON
Postal: L0S 1E0
Country: Canada
Mailing address: PO Box 40
Mailing city: Fonthill
Province: ON
Postal: L0S 1E0
General Phone: (905) 892-8690
General Fax: (905) 892-0823
General/National Adv. E-mail: office@thevoiceofpelham.ca
Display Adv. E-mail: advertising@thevoiceofpelham.ca
Editorial e-mail: editor@thevoiceofpelham.ca
Primary Website: www.thevoiceofpelham.ca
Year Established: 1997
Areas Served - City/County or Portion Thereof, or Zip codes: Canada
Mechanical specifications: Type page 10 1/4 x 15 2/3; E - 6 cols, 1 1/2, 1/8 between; A - 6 cols, 1 1/2, 1/8 between; C - 6 cols, 1 1/2, 1/8 between.
Published: Wed
Avg Free Circ: 6782
Audit By: CMCA
Audit Date: 30.09.2015
Personnel: Leslie Chiapetta (Office Mgr.); Nate Smelle (Ed.); Dave Burket (Pub.)

FOREST

PUBLICATION NAME

Forest Standard
Street Address: 1 King St. W.,
Province: ON
Postal: N0N 1J0
Country: Canada
Mailing address: PO Box 220
Mailing city: Forest
Province: ON
Postal: N0N 1J0
General Phone: (519) 786-5242
General Fax: (519) 786-4884
General/National Adv. E-mail: standard@xcelco.on.ca
Areas Served - City/County or Portion Thereof, or Zip codes: Canada
Commercial printers?: Y
Mechanical specifications: Type page 11 1/4 x 16; E - 6 cols, 1 1/2, 1/4 between; A - 6 cols, 1 1/2, 1/4 between.
Published: Thur
Avg Paid Circ: 1848
Audit By: CMCA
Audit Date: 30.06.2014
Personnel: Dale Hayter (Pub.); Gil De Schutter (Adv. Mgr.); Mavis Sanger (Circ. Mgr.); Gord Whitehead (Ed.)

FORESTVILLE

PUBLICATION NAME

Journal Haute Cote-nord
Street Address: 100-31 Rte. 138,
Province: QC
Postal: G0T 1E0
Country: Canada
Mailing address: 100-31 Rte. 138
Mailing city: Forestville
Province: QC
Postal: G0T 1E0
General Phone: (418) 587-2090
General Fax: (418) 587-6407
General/National Adv. E-mail: journalhcn@globetrotter.net
Primary Website: www.journalhautecotenord.com

Areas Served - City/County or Portion Thereof, or Zip codes: Canada
Mechanical specifications: Type page 11 x 17; E - 8 cols, between; A - 8 cols, between.
Published: Wed
Avg Paid Circ: 20
Avg Free Circ: 5510
Audit By: CCAB
Audit Date: 30.09.2012
Personnel: Luc Brisson (Pub.); Guylaine Bouliane (Sec.); Shirley Kennedy (Mng. Ed.)

FORT ERIE

PUBLICATION NAME

The Fort Erie Times
Street Address: 450 Garrison Rd., Unit 1,
Province: ON
Postal: L2A 1N2
Country: Canada
Mailing address: 450 Garrison Rd., Unit 1
Mailing city: Fort Erie
Province: ON
Postal: L2A 1N2
General Phone: (905) 871-3100
General Fax: (905) 871-5243
Advertising Phone: (905) 871-3100 x202
Advertising Fax: (905) 871-5243
Editorial Phone: (905) 871-3100 x207
Editorial Fax: (905) 871-5243
General/National Adv. E-mail: myra.robertson@sunmedia.ca
Display Adv. E-mail: myra.robertson@sunmedia.ca
Editorial e-mail: kris.dube@sunmedia.com
Primary Website: www.forterietimes.com
Delivery Methods: Carrier
Areas Served - City/County or Portion Thereof, or Zip codes: Canada
Own Printing Facility?: Y
Commercial printers?: Y
Mechanical specifications: Tabloid 10.4" W x 11.5" H
Published: Thur
Avg Paid Circ: 9
Avg Free Circ: 12454
Audit By: CMCA
Audit Date: 31.05.2016
Personnel: Sarag Ferguson (Ed.)
Parent company (for newspapers): Postmedia Network Inc.; Quebecor Communications, Inc.

FORT FRANCES

PUBLICATION NAME

Fort Frances Times
Street Address: 116 First St.,
Province: ON
Postal: P9A 3M7
Country: Canada
Mailing address: PO Box 339
Mailing city: Fort Frances
Province: ON
Postal: P9A 3M7
General Phone: (807) 274-5373
General Fax: (807) 274-7286
General/National Adv. E-mail: fort_frances_times@ocna.org
Display Adv. E-mail: ads@fortfrances.com
Primary Website: www.fortfrances.com
Areas Served - City/County or Portion Thereof, or Zip codes: Canada
Own Printing Facility?: Y
Commercial printers?: Y
Mechanical specifications: Type page 12 x 21 1/2; E - 6 cols, 2, 1/6 between; A - 6 cols, 2, 1/6 between.
Published: Wed
Avg Paid Circ: 3134
Avg Free Circ: 130
Audit By: CMCA
Audit Date: 31.03.2016
Personnel: James R. Cumming (Pub.); Linda Plumridge (Office Mgr.); Debbie Ballare (Adv. Mgr.); Michael Behan (Ed.); Don Cumming (Prod. Mgr.)

FORT MACLEOD

PUBLICATION NAME

The Macleod Gazette
Street Address: 310 24th St.,
Province: AB
Postal: T0L 0Z0
Country: Canada
Mailing address: PO Box 720
Mailing city: Fort Macleod
Province: AB
Postal: T0L 0Z0
General Phone: (403) 553-3391
General Fax: (403) 553-2961
General/National Adv. E-mail: ftmgazet@telusplanet.net
Display Adv. E-mail: tmgsales@telus.net
Classified Adv. e-mail: tmgsales@telus.net
Editorial e-mail: tmgedit@telus.net
Primary Website: www.fortmacleodgazette.com
Year Established: 1882
Delivery Methods: Mail`Newsstand
Areas Served - City/County or Portion Thereof, or Zip codes: Municipal District of Willow Creek
Own Printing Facility?: Y
Commercial printers?: Y
Mechanical specifications: Type page 10.25 x 15.5; E - 6 cols, 1 3/4, 1/6 between; A - 6 cols, 1 3/4, 1/6 between; C - 6 cols, 1.5, 1/6 between.
Published: Wed
Avg Paid Circ: 1150
Avg Free Circ: 0
Audit By: CMCA
Audit Date: 28.02.2017
Personnel: Emily McTighe (Adv. Mgr.); Sharon Monical (Circ. Mgr.); Frank McTighe (Pub./Ed.)

FORT MCMURRAY

PUBLICATION NAME

Connect
Street Address: 208, 9715 Main Street,
Province: AB
Postal: T9H 1T5
Country: Canada
Mailing address: 208, 9715 Main Street
Mailing city: Fort McMurray
Province: AB
Postal: T9H 1T5
General Phone: (780) 790-6627
General Fax: (780) 714-6485
General/National Adv. E-mail: info@macmedia.ca
Display Adv. E-mail: tim@starnews.ca
Classified Adv. e-mail: tim@starnews.ca
Editorial e-mail: dawn@starnews.ca
Primary Website: www.fortmacconnect.ca
Year Established: 2002
Delivery Methods: Mail`Newsstand`Racks
Areas Served - City/County or Portion Thereof, or Zip codes: Fort McMurray/Regional Municipality of Wood Buffalo/Alberta/T9H 2C8
Published: Fri
Avg Free Circ: 19992
Audit By: VAC
Audit Date: 28.02.2015
Personnel: Tim O'Rourke (Publisher/Sales Manager)
Parent company (for newspapers): Star News Publishing Inc.

FORT NELSON

PUBLICATION NAME

The Fort Nelson News
Street Address: 4448 50th Ave., Ste. 3, P.o. Box 600
Province: BC
Postal: V0C 1R0
Country: Canada
Mailing address: PO Box 600
Mailing city: Fort Nelson
Province: BC
Postal: V0C 1R0
General Phone: (250) 774-2357
General Fax: (250) 774-3612

Community Newspapers in Canada

General/National Adv. E-mail: editorial@fnnews.ca
Display Adv. E-mail: ads@fnnews.ca
Classified Adv. E-mail: ads@fnnews.ca
Editorial e-mail: editorial@fortnelsonnews.ca
Primary Website: www.fortnelsonnews.ca
Year Established: 1959
Delivery Methods: Mail`Newsstand`Carrier`Racks
Areas Served - City/County or Portion Thereof, or Zip codes: Northern Rockies Regional District
Commercial printers?: Y
Mechanical specifications: Type page 11 1/2 x 21 3/8; E - 10 cols, 1 1/16, between; A - 10 cols, between; C - 10 cols, between.
Published: Wed
Avg Paid Circ: 439
Avg Free Circ: 665
Audit By: VAC
Audit Date: 12.12.2017
Personnel: Judith A. Kenyon (Ed & Pub); Alexandra Kenyon (Mng. Ed.); Kathy Smith (reporter and photographer); Abigail Neville (Mgr)

FORT QU'APPELLE

PUBLICATION NAME

Fort Qu'appelle Times
Street Address: 141 Broadway St. W. ,
Province: SK
Postal: S0G 1S0
Country: Canada
Mailing address: PO Box 940
Mailing city: Fort Qu'Appelle
Province: SK
Postal: S0G 1S0
General Phone: (306) 332-5526
General Fax: (306) 332-5414
General/National Adv. E-mail: forttimes@sasktel.net
Year Established: 1951
Delivery Methods: Mail`Newsstand
Areas Served - City/County or Portion Thereof, or Zip codes: Canada
Commercial printers?: Y
Mechanical specifications: Type page 10 1/4 x 16; E - 6 cols, 2, between; A - 6 cols, 2, between; C - 6 cols, 2, between.
Published: Tues
Avg Paid Circ: 837
Audit By: CMCA
Audit Date: 30.09.2016
Personnel: Sandra Huber (Pub.); Cassandra Archer (Adv. Mgr.); Linda Aspinall (Ed.)

FORT SAINT JOHN

PUBLICATION NAME

North Peace Express
Street Address: 9916 98th St. ,
Province: BC
Postal: V1J 3T8
Country: Canada
Mailing address: 9916 98th St.
Mailing city: Fort Saint John
Province: BC
Postal: V1J 3T8
General Phone: (250) 785-5631
General Fax: (250) 785-3522
General/National Adv. E-mail: ahnews@awink.com
Display Adv. E-mail: wj@ahnfsj.ca
Editorial e-mail: editor@ahnfsj.ca
Year Established: 1942
Commercial printers?: Y
Mechanical specifications: Type page 10 1/4 x 13; E - 5 cols, 2 1/12, 1/3 between; A - 5 cols, 2 1/12, 1/3 between; C - 5 cols, 2 1/12, 1/3 between.
Published: Sun
Avg Free Circ: 10200
Audit By: Sworn/Estimate/Non-Audited
Audit Date: 12.07.2019
Personnel: William Julian (Pub); Debbie Oberlin (Circ. Mgr.)

FORT SAINT JOHN

PUBLICATION NAME

The Northerner
Street Address: 9916 98th St. ,
Province: BC
Postal: V1J 3T8
Country: Canada
Mailing address: 9916 98th St.
Mailing city: Fort Saint John
Province: BC
Postal: V1J 3T8
General Phone: (250) 785-5631
General Fax: (250) 785-3522
General/National Adv. E-mail: ahnews@awink.com
Display Adv. E-mail: mhill@ahnfsj.ca
Classified Adv. e-mail: rwallace@ahnfsj.ca
Editorial e-mail: editor@ahnfsj.ca
Primary Website: www.thenortherner.ca
Year Established: 1988
Areas Served - City/County or Portion Thereof, or Zip codes: V1J 2B2
Mechanical specifications: Type page 10 1/4 x 12 3/4; E - 5 cols, 1 15/16, 3/16 between; A - 5 cols, 1 15/16, 3/16 between; C - 5 cols, 1 15/16, 3/16 between.
Published: Fri
Avg Paid Circ: 0
Avg Free Circ: 8657
Audit By: Sworn/Estimate/Non-Audited
Audit Date: 12.07.2019
Personnel: Melody Hill (Sales); William Julian (Pub.); Ryan Wallace (Sales); Debbie Oberlin (Circ.)

FORT SASKATCHEWAN

PUBLICATION NAME

The Fort Saskatchewan Record
Street Address: 10404 99 Ave , 168A
Province: AB
Postal: T8L 3W2
Country: Canada
Mailing address: 10404 99 Ave, 168A
Mailing city: Fort Saskatchewan
Province: AB
Postal: T8L 3W2
General Phone: (780) 998-7070 Ext 724227
General Fax: (780) 998-5515
Editorial e-mail: agreen@postmedia.com
Primary Website: fortsaskatchewanrecord.com
Year Established: 1922
Delivery Methods: Mail`Carrier`Racks
Areas Served - City/County or Portion Thereof, or Zip codes: Strathcona County
Own Printing Facility?: N
Commercial printers?: Y
Mechanical specifications: specs available on website
Published: Thur
Avg Paid Circ: 9
Avg Free Circ: 8806
Audit By: Sworn/Estimate/Non-Audited
Audit Date: 12.07.2019
Personnel: A Green
Parent company (for newspapers): Postmedia Network Inc.

FORT SMITH

PUBLICATION NAME

Northern Journal
Street Address: 207 Mcdougal Rd. ,
Province: NT
Postal: X0E 0P0
Country: Canada
Mailing address: PO Box 990
Mailing city: Fort Smith
Province: NT
Postal: X0E 0P0
General Phone: (867) 872-3000
General Fax: (867) 872-2754
General/National Adv. E-mail: don@srj.ca
Display Adv. E-mail: admin@norj.ca
Editorial e-mail: don@norj.ca
Primary Website: http://norj.ca/
Year Established: 1978
Delivery Methods: Carrier
Areas Served - City/County or Portion Thereof, or Zip codes: Canada
Mechanical specifications: Type page 11 x 17; E - 5 cols, 1 7/8, 1/6 between; A - 6 cols, 1 7/12, 1/6 between; C - 6 cols, 1 7/12, 1/6 between.
Published: Other
Avg Paid Circ: 3660
Avg Free Circ: 4065
Audit By: Sworn/Estimate/Non-Audited
Audit Date: 12.07.2019
Personnel: Sandra Jaque (Mgr); Don Jaque (Ed.)
Parent company (for newspapers): Cascade Publishing Ltd.

FORT ST. JAMES

PUBLICATION NAME

Caledonia Courier
Street Address: Box 1298 ,
Province: BC
Postal: V0J 3A0
Country: Canada
General Phone: (250) 567-9258
General Fax: (250) 567-2070
General/National Adv. E-mail: newsroom@ominecaexpress.com
Display Adv. E-mail: advertising@ominecaexpress.com
Primary Website: www.caledoniacourier.com
Year Established: 1972
Mechanical specifications: Type page 10 5/16 x 14 1/2; E - 6 cols, 1 9/16, 3/16 between; A - 6 cols, 1 9/16, 3/16 between; C - 6 cols, 1 9/16, 3/16 between.
Published: Wed
Avg Paid Circ: 562
Avg Free Circ: 31
Audit By: VAC
Audit Date: 30.06.2016
Personnel: Pam Berger (Pub./Sales Mgr.); Ruth Lloyd (Ed.); Julia Beal (Prod.); Wendy Haslam (Prod.); Mariella Drogomatz (Circ.)
Parent company (for newspapers): Black Press Group Ltd.

FRASERVILLE

PUBLICATION NAME

Millbrook Times
Street Address: 1287 Larmer Line ,
Province: ON
Postal: K0L 1V0
Country: Canada
Mailing address: PO Box 266
Mailing city: Millbrook
Province: ON
Postal: L0A 1G0
General Phone: (705) 932-3001
General Fax: (705) 932-8816
General/National Adv. E-mail: thetimes@nixicom.net
Display Adv. E-mail: kgraham@nexicom.net
Classified Adv. e-mail: thetimes@nexicom.net
Editorial e-mail: thetimes@nexicom.net
Primary Website: http://themillbrooktimes.ca
Year Established: 1987
Delivery Methods: Mail`Newsstand
Areas Served - City/County or Portion Thereof, or Zip codes: Cavan Monaghan Twp, Peterborough County
Mechanical specifications: Type page 10 x ; E - 5 cols, 2, between; A - 5 cols, 2, between; C - 5 cols, 2, between.
Published: Thur`Mthly
Avg Paid Circ: 100
Avg Free Circ: 4000
Audit By: Sworn/Estimate/Non-Audited
Audit Date: 12.07.2019
Personnel: Karen Graham (Pub.)

FREDERICTON

PUBLICATION NAME

Northside This Week
Street Address: 984 Prospect St. ,
Province: NB
Postal: E3B 5A2
Country: Canada
Mailing address: 984 Prospect St.
Mailing city: Fredericton
Province: NB
Postal: E3B 5A2
General Phone: (506) 452-6671
General Fax: (506) 452-7405
General/National Adv. E-mail: northside@brunswicknews.com
Editorial e-mail: shelley.wood@brunswicknews.com
Published: Sat
Avg Free Circ: 9950
Audit By: Sworn/Estimate/Non-Audited
Audit Date: 12.07.2019
Personnel: Shelly Wood (Pub./Ed)
Parent company (for newspapers): Brunswick News, Inc.

GABRIOLA ISLAND

PUBLICATION NAME

Gabriola Sounder
Street Address: 510 North Rd , Unit 1
Province: BC
Postal: V0R 1X0
Country: Canada
Mailing address: PO Box 62
Mailing city: Gabriola Island
Province: BC
Postal: V0R 1X0
General Phone: (250) 247-9337
General Fax: (250) 247-8147
Advertising Phone: (250) 247-9337
Editorial Phone: (250) 247-9337
General/National Adv. E-mail: derek@soundernews.com
Display Adv. E-mail: sarah@soundernew.com
Classified Adv. e-mail: derek@soundernews.com
Editorial e-mail: derek@soundernews.com
Primary Website: www.soundernews.com
Year Established: 1989
Delivery Methods: Mail`Newsstand`Racks
Areas Served - City/County or Portion Thereof, or Zip codes: Gabriola, and Mudge Island
Published: Tues
Avg Paid Circ: 50
Avg Free Circ: 2750
Audit By: Sworn/Estimate/Non-Audited
Audit Date: 12.07.2019
Personnel: Sarah Holmes (Pub.); Derek Kilbourn (Ed./Sales/Prod. Mgr.)
Parent company (for newspapers): Gabriola Sounder Media Inc.

GANDER

PUBLICATION NAME

The Gander Beacon
Street Address: 61 Elizabeth Dr. ,
Province: NL
Postal: A1V 1W8
Country: Canada
Mailing address: PO Box 420
Mailing city: Gander
Province: NL
Postal: A1V 1W8
General Phone: (709) 256-4371
General Fax: (709) 256-3826
General/National Adv. E-mail: info@ganderbeacon.ca
Primary Website: www.ganderbeacon.ca
Areas Served - City/County or Portion Thereof, or Zip codes: Gander
Mechanical specifications: Type page 12 x 21; E - 6 cols, 1 1/16, 1/6 between; A - 6 cols, 1 1/16, 1/6 between; C - 8 cols, 1 3/16, 1/6 between.
Published: Thur
Avg Paid Circ: 929
Avg Free Circ: 0

Audit By: VAC
Audit Date: 31.12.2015
Personnel: Kevin Higgins (Gen. Mgr.)
Parent company (for newspapers): Transcontinental Media

GASPE

PUBLICATION NAME

Havre
Street Address: Rue Jacques Cartier ,
Province: QC
Postal: G4X 1M9
Country: Canada
Mailing address: rue Jacques Cartier
Mailing city: Gaspe
Province: QC
Postal: G4X 1M9
General Phone: (418) 368-3242
Areas Served - City/County or Portion Thereof, or Zip codes: Canada
Published: Wed
Avg Paid Circ: 6
Avg Free Circ: 8207
Audit By: CCAB
Audit Date: 31.03.2014
Personnel: Bernard Johnson

PUBLICATION NAME

Le Pharillon
Street Address: 144 Rue De Jacques-cartier ,
Province: QC
Postal: G4X 1M9
Country: Canada
Mailing address: 144 Rue de Jacques-Cartier
Mailing city: Gaspe
Province: QC
Postal: G4X 1M9
General Phone: (418) 368-3242
General Fax: (418) 368-1705
General/National Adv. E-mail: pharillon@hebdosquebecor.com
Display Adv. E-mail: gas.redaction@tc.tc
Classified Adv. e-mail: gas.redaction@tc.tc
Editorial e-mail: gas.redaction@tc.tc
Primary Website: www.lepharillon.ca
Areas Served - City/County or Portion Thereof, or Zip codes: Canada
Mechanical specifications: Type page 12 1/2 x 11 1/2.
Published: Wed
Avg Paid Circ: 10
Avg Free Circ: 8720
Audit By: CCAB
Audit Date: 31.03.2014
Personnel: Alain St-Amand (Gen. Mgr.); Bernard Johnson (Mng. Ed.)
Parent company (for newspapers): Reseau Select/Select Network; Quebecor Communications, Inc.

GATINEAU

PUBLICATION NAME

La Revue De Gatineau
Street Address: 160 Hospital Rd., Ste. 30 ,
Province: QC
Postal: J8T 8J1
Country: Canada
Mailing address: 160 Hospital Rd., Ste. 30
Mailing city: Gatineau
Province: QC
Postal: J8T 8J1
General Phone: (819) 568-7736
General Fax: (819) 568-8728
Editorial e-mail: pascal.laplante@tc.tc
Primary Website: www.info07.com
Areas Served - City/County or Portion Thereof, or Zip codes: Canada
Mechanical specifications: Type page 10 3/8 x 14 1/4; E - 8 cols, 1 1/8, between; A - 8 cols, 1 1/8, between; C - 8 cols, 1 1/8, between.
Published: Wed
Avg Paid Circ: 8
Avg Free Circ: 91029
Audit By: CCAB

Audit Date: 31.03.2014
Personnel: Jacques Blais (Gen. Mgr.); Martin Godcher (Ed.)
Parent company (for newspapers): Transcontinental Media

PUBLICATION NAME

Le Bulletin
Street Address: 435 Blvd Rue Principale ,
Province: QC
Postal: J8L 2G8
Country: Canada
Mailing address: 435 Blvd Rue Principale
Mailing city: Gatineau
Province: QC
Postal: J8L 2G8
General Phone: (819) 986-5089
General Fax: (819) 986-2073
Advertising Phone: (819) 986-5089
Advertising Fax: (819) 986-2073
Editorial Phone: (819) 986-5089
Editorial Fax: (819) 986-2073
General/National Adv. E-mail: yannick.boursier@tc.tc
Display Adv. E-mail: yannick.boursier@tc.tc
Editorial e-mail: yannick.boursier@tc.tc
Primary Website: www.lebulletin.net
Delivery Methods: Mail`Racks
Areas Served - City/County or Portion Thereof, or Zip codes: Canada
Published: Wed
Avg Paid Circ: 20
Avg Free Circ: 14308
Audit By: CCAB
Audit Date: 31.03.2014
Personnel: Yannick Boursier (Pub./Ed.)

PUBLICATION NAME

Le Bulletin D'aylmer
Street Address: C-10 181 Principale St., (secteur Aylmer) ,
Province: QC
Postal: J9H 6A6
Country: Canada
Mailing address: C-10 181 Principale St., (Secteur Aylmer)
Mailing city: Gatineau
Province: QC
Postal: J9H 6A6
General Phone: (819) 684-4755
General Fax: (819) 684-6428
General/National Adv. E-mail: abawqp@videotron.ca
Display Adv. E-mail: ventes.sales@bulletinaylmer.com
Editorial e-mail: abawqp@videotron.ca
Primary Website: www.bulletinaylmer.com
Year Established: 1971
Delivery Methods: Carrier
Areas Served - City/County or Portion Thereof, or Zip codes: Canada
Own Printing Facility?: N
Commercial printers?: N
Mechanical specifications: Type page 10 1/4 x 11; E - 6 cols, 1 5/8, between; A - 6 cols, 1 5/8, between; C - 9 cols, 1 1/5, between.
Published: Wed
Avg Paid Circ: 181
Avg Free Circ: 23009
Audit By: Sworn/Estimate/Non-Audited
Audit Date: 12.07.2019
Personnel: Lily Ryan (Ed.); Lynne Lavery; Sophia Ryan (Manager operations)

PUBLICATION NAME

Le Regional De Hull
Street Address: 160, Boul. Hospital, Office 30 ,
Province: QC
Postal: J8T 8J1
Country: Canada
Mailing address: 160, boul. hospital, office 30
Mailing city: Gatineau
Province: QC
Postal: J8T 8J1
General Phone: (819) 776-1063
General Fax: (819) 568-7544

General/National Adv. E-mail: boursiery@transcontinental.ca
Primary Website: www.info07.com
Areas Served - City/County or Portion Thereof, or Zip codes: Canada
Published: Wed
Avg Free Circ: 11000
Audit By: Sworn/Estimate/Non-Audited
Audit Date: 12.07.2019
Personnel: Dino Roberges (Adv. Mgr.); Jacques Blais (Ed.)

PUBLICATION NAME

The West-quebec Post
Street Address: C-10 181 Principale St., Secteur Aylmer ,
Province: QC
Postal: J9H 6A6
Country: Canada
Mailing address: C-10 181 Principale St., Secteur Aylmer
Mailing city: Gatineau
Province: QC
Postal: J9H 6A6
General Phone: (819) 684-4755
General Fax: (819) 684-6428
General/National Adv. E-mail: l.lavery@bulletinaylmer.com
Display Adv. E-mail: ventes.sales@bulletinaylmer.com
Editorial e-mail: abawqp@videotron.ca
Year Established: 1895
Delivery Methods: Mail`Newsstand`Carrier`Racks
Areas Served - City/County or Portion Thereof, or Zip codes: Pontiac
Own Printing Facility?: N
Commercial printers?: Y
Mechanical specifications: Type page 10 2/5 x 11; E - 6 cols, 1 5/8, between; A - 6 cols, 1 5/8, between; Classifieds - 9 cols, 1 1/5, between.
Published: Fri
Avg Paid Circ: 761
Avg Free Circ: 5214
Audit By: CMCA
Audit Date: 29.02.2016
Personnel: Fred Ryan (Publisher); Lynne Lavery (General Manager); Lily Ryan (Editor); Sophia Ryan (sales manager); Nadia Paradis (Classified and subscription manager)
Parent company (for newspapers): 9040-9681 Quebec Inc.

PUBLICATION NAME

Week-end Outaouais
Street Address: 160 Hospital Blvd., Ste. 30 ,
Province: QC
Postal: J8T 8J1
Country: Canada
Mailing address: 160 Hospital Blvd., Ste. 30
Mailing city: Gatineau
Province: QC
Postal: J8T 8J1
General Phone: (819) 568-7736
General Fax: (819) 568-7038
Primary Website: www.info07.com
Mechanical specifications: Type page 10 3/8 x 14 1/4; E - 8 cols, 1 1/8, between; A - 8 cols, 1 1/8, between; C - 8 cols, 1 1/8, between.
Published: Sat
Avg Free Circ: 90000
Audit By: Sworn/Estimate/Non-Audited
Audit Date: 12.07.2019
Personnel: Jacques Blais (Pub./Gen. Mgr.)

GEORGETOWN

PUBLICATION NAME

Independent & Free Press
Street Address: 280 Guelph St., Unit 29 ,
Province: ON
Postal: L7G 4B1
Mailing address: 280 Guelph St., Unit 29
Mailing city: Georgetown
Province: ON
Postal: L7G 4B1

General Phone: (905) 873-0301
General Fax: (905) 873-0398
General/National Adv. E-mail: production@independentfreepress.com
Primary Website: independentfreepress.com
Areas Served - City/County or Portion Thereof, or Zip codes: Canada
Own Printing Facility?: Y
Commercial printers?: Y
Mechanical specifications: Type page 11 1/2 x 14 3/4; E - 9 cols, between; A - 9 cols, between.
Published: Thur
Avg Free Circ: 23045
Audit By: CCAB
Audit Date: 30.09.2017
Personnel: Steve Foreman (Gen. Mgr.); Cindi Campbell (Circ. Mgr.); Nancy Geissler (Circ. Mgr.); John McGhie (Mng. Ed.); Dana Robbins (Publisher)
Parent company (for newspapers): Metroland Media Group Ltd.; Torstar

GERALDTON

PUBLICATION NAME

Geraldton-longlac Times Star
Street Address: 401 Main St. ,
Province: ON
Postal: P0T 1M0
Country: Canada
Mailing address: PO Box 490
Mailing city: Geraldton
Province: ON
Postal: P0T 1M0
General Phone: (807) 854-1919
General Fax: (807) 854-1682
General/National Adv. E-mail: tstar@astrocom-on.com
Editorial e-mail: editor@thetimesstar.ca
Primary Website: www.thetimesstar.ca
Year Established: 1945
Areas Served - City/County or Portion Thereof, or Zip codes: Canada
Own Printing Facility?: Y
Commercial printers?: Y
Mechanical specifications: Type page 11 x 17; E - 5 cols, 1 14/15, 1/5 between; A - 5 cols, 1 14/15, 1/5 between; C - 5 cols, 1 14/15, 1/5 between.
Published: Wed
Avg Paid Circ: 642
Avg Free Circ: 19
Audit By: CMCA
Audit Date: 31.07.2016
Personnel: Mike Goulet (Prodn. Mgr.); Justin Saindon; Eric Pietsch (Ed.)

GLENBORO

PUBLICATION NAME

Gazette
Street Address: 702 Railway Ave. ,
Province: MB
Postal: R0K 0X0
Country: Canada
Mailing address: PO Box 10
Mailing city: Glenboro
Province: MB
Postal: R0K 0X0
General Phone: (204) 827-2343
General Fax: (204) 827-2207
General/National Adv. E-mail: gazette@mts.net
Display Adv. E-mail: gazette2@mts.net
Editorial e-mail: gazette@mts.net
Primary Website: http://www.baldur-glenborogazette.ca/
Areas Served - City/County or Portion Thereof, or Zip codes: Canada
Commercial printers?: Y
Mechanical specifications: Type page 12 x 15 1/2; E - 5 cols, 1 3/4, 1/4 between; A - 5 cols, 1 3/4, 1/4 between; C - 5 cols, 1 3/4, 1/4 between.
Published: Tues
Avg Paid Circ: 1557
Avg Free Circ: 0
Audit By: CMCA
Audit Date: 31.05.2014

Personnel: Mike Johnson (Ed./Pub/Adv); Travis Johnson (Ed./Pub/Adv)

GLENCOE

PUBLICATION NAME

Transcript & Free Press
Street Address: 243 Main St. ,
Province: ON
Postal: N0L 1M0
Country: Canada
Mailing address: PO Box 400
Mailing city: Glencoe
Province: ON
Postal: N0l 1M0
General Phone: (519) 287-2615
General Fax: (519) 287-2408
General/National Adv. E-mail: tranfree@xcelco.on.ca
Published: Thur
Avg Paid Circ: 1033
Audit By: CMCA
Audit Date: 30.06.2014
Personnel: Dale Hayder (Circ. Mgr.)

GLOUCESTER

PUBLICATION NAME

Express D'orleans
Street Address: Canotek Road Unit 30 , Unit 30
Province: ON
Postal: K1J 8R7
Country: Canada
Mailing address: Canotek Road Unit 30
Mailing city: Gloucester
Province: ON
Postal: K1J 8R7
General Phone: (613) 744-4800
Areas Served - City/County or Portion Thereof, or Zip codes: Gloucester, Ottawa, Ontario.
Published: Wed
Avg Paid Circ: 10742
Avg Free Circ: 200
Audit By: ODC
Audit Date: 14.12.2011
Personnel: Madeleine Joanisse

PUBLICATION NAME

Orleans Star
Street Address: Po Box 46009 ,
Province: ON
Postal: K1J 9H7
Country: Canada
Mailing address: PO Box 46009
Mailing city: Gloucester
Province: ON
Postal: K1J 9H7
General Phone: (613) 323-2801
Advertising Phone: (613) 744-4800
General/National Adv. E-mail: orleansstar@transcontinental.ca
Primary Website: www.orleansstar.ca
Areas Served - City/County or Portion Thereof, or Zip codes: Canada
Published: Thur
Avg Paid Circ: 11
Avg Free Circ: 42989
Audit By: CCAB
Audit Date: 31.03.2014

GODERICH

PUBLICATION NAME

Goderich Signal-star
Street Address: 120 Huckins St. Industrial Park ,
Province: ON
Postal: N7A 3X8
Country: Canada
Mailing address: PO Box 220
Mailing city: Goderich
Province: ON
Postal: N7A 3X8
General Phone: (519) 524-2614
General Fax: (519) 524-9175
General/National Adv. E-mail: john.bauman@sunmedia.ca
Primary Website: www.goderichsignalstar.com
Year Established: 1848
Areas Served - City/County or Portion Thereof, or Zip codes: Canada
Own Printing Facility?: Y
Commercial printers?: Y
Mechanical specifications: Type page 11 1/4 x 21 1/4; E - 6 cols, 1 7/12, 1/6 between; A - 6 cols, 1 7/12, 1/6 between; C - 6 cols, 1 7/12, 1/6 between.
Published: Wed
Avg Paid Circ: 3150
Avg Free Circ: 18
Audit By: CMCA
Audit Date: 30.06.2017
Personnel: John Bauman (Sales Mgr.)
Parent company (for newspapers): Postmedia Network Inc.

GOLDEN

PUBLICATION NAME

Golden Star
Street Address: 413a N. Ninth Ave. ,
Province: BC
Postal: V0H 1H0
Country: Canada
Mailing address: PO Box 149
Mailing city: Golden
Province: BC
Postal: V0H 1H0
General Phone: (250) 344-5251
General Fax: (250) 344-7344
General/National Adv. E-mail: publisher@thegoldenstar.net
Display Adv. E-mail: advertising@thegoldenstar.net
Classified Adv. e-mail: advertising@thegoldenstar.net
Editorial e-mail: editor@thegoldenstar.net
Primary Website: www.thegoldenstar.net
Year Established: 1891
Areas Served - City/County or Portion Thereof, or Zip codes: Golden
Own Printing Facility?: Y
Commercial printers?: N
Mechanical specifications: Type page 10 1/3 x 15 1/2; E - 6 cols, 1 1/2, 1/6 between; A - 6 cols, 1 1/2, 1/6 between; C - 6 cols, 1 1/2, 1/6 between.
Published: Wed
Avg Paid Circ: 502
Avg Free Circ: 32
Audit By: VAC
Audit Date: 30.06.2016
Personnel: Sue Hein (Classified Mgr.); Michele Lapointe (Pub.); Jessica Schwitek (Ed.)
Parent company (for newspapers): Black Press Group Ltd.

GORE BAY

PUBLICATION NAME

Manitoulin Recorder
Street Address: 37 D Meredith St. ,
Province: ON
Postal: P0P 1H0
Country: Canada
Mailing address: PO Box 235
Mailing city: Gore Bay
Province: ON
Postal: P0P 1H0
General Phone: (705) 282-2003
General Fax: (705) 282-2432
General/National Adv. E-mail: recorder@bellnet.ca
Year Established: 1908
Areas Served - City/County or Portion Thereof, or Zip codes: Canada
Published: Fri
Avg Paid Circ: 997
Avg Free Circ: 72
Audit By: AAM
Audit Date: 31.03.2018
Personnel: R.L. McCutcheon (Pub.); Tom Sasvari (Ed.); Al Ryan (Prodn. Mgr.)

GRANBY

PUBLICATION NAME

Granby Express
Street Address: 398 Main St. , Ste 5 ,
Province: QC
Postal: J2G 2W6
Country: Canada
Mailing address: 398 Main St., Ste 5
Mailing city: Granby
Province: QC
Postal: J2G 2W6
General Phone: (450) 777-4515
General Fax: (450) 777-4516
General/National Adv. E-mail: nancy.corriveau@monjournalexpress.com
Primary Website: www.granbyexpress.com
Areas Served - City/County or Portion Thereof, or Zip codes: Canada
Mechanical specifications: Type page 10 1/4 x 12 1/2; E - 8 cols, between; A - 8 cols, between; C - 8 cols, between.
Published: Wed
Avg Paid Circ: 3
Avg Free Circ: 41995
Audit By: CCAB
Audit Date: 31.03.2014
Personnel: Nancy Corriveau (Sales Coord.); Maritime Chagnon (Mng. Ed.); Caroline Rioux (Reg'l Ed.)

PUBLICATION NAME

La Voix De L'est Plus
Street Address: 76 Dufferin St. ,
Province: QC
Postal: J2G 9L4
Country: Canada
Mailing address: 76 Dufferin St.
Mailing city: Granby
Province: QC
Postal: J2G 9L4
General Phone: (450) 375-4555
General Fax: (450) 372-1308
Editorial Fax: (450) 777-4865
General/National Adv. E-mail: redaction@lavoixdelest.qc.ca
Display Adv. E-mail: pub@lapresse.ca
Editorial e-mail: redaction@lavoixdelest.qc.ca
Primary Website: www.cyberpresse.ca
Year Established: 1935
Areas Served - City/County or Portion Thereof, or Zip codes: Canada
Mechanical specifications: Type page 10 1/4 x ; E - 10 cols, 1, 1/8 between; A - 10 cols, 1, 1/8 between; C - 10 cols, 1, 1/8 between.
Published: Wed
Weekday Frequency: m
Saturday Frequency: m
Avg Paid Circ: 8965
Avg Free Circ: 128
Sat. Circulation Paid: 12703
Sat. Circulation Free: 712
Audit By: AAM
Audit Date: 31.03.2017
Personnel: Francois Beaudoin (Mng. Ed.); Daniel Touchette (Adv. Mgr.); Gilbert Arl (Dir., Finance/Admin.); Daniel Touchet (Adv. Mgr., Sales); Christian Malo (Circ. Dir.); Guy Granger (Ed.); Haswa Budway (News Ed.); Andre Bilodeau (Sports Ed.); Claudette Ospiguy (Prodn. Mgr., Pre Press); Louisse Boisvert (Pub.); Marc Gendron (Info. Mgr.); Martyne Lessard (Adv. Mgr.)
Parent company (for newspapers): Gesca Ltd.; Reseau Select/Select Network

GRAND BEND

PUBLICATION NAME

Lakeshore Advance
Street Address: 58 Ontario St. North ,
Province: ON
Postal: N0M 1T0
Country: Canada
Mailing address: 58 ONTARIO STREET NORTH, P.O. Box 1195
Mailing city: Grand Bend
Province: ON
Postal: N0M 1T0
General Phone: (519) 238-5383
General Fax: (519) 238-5131
General/National Adv. E-mail: lakeshore.advance@sunmedia.ca
Display Adv. E-mail: lakeshore.ads@sunmedia.ca
Editorial e-mail: lakeshore.advance@sunmedia.ca
Primary Website: www.lakeshoreadvance.com
Delivery Methods: Mail
Areas Served - City/County or Portion Thereof, or Zip codes: Canada
Mechanical specifications: Page Size: 10.25" wide x 11.42" high 9 col x 160 ag
Published: Wed
Avg Paid Circ: 979
Avg Free Circ: 13
Audit By: CMCA
Audit Date: 30.06.2014
Personnel: Neil Clifford (Adv. Dir.)
Parent company (for newspapers): Quebecor

GRAND FALLS

PUBLICATION NAME

L' Etoile Cataracte
Street Address: 229 Broadway Blvd. ,
Province: NB
Postal: E3Z 2K1
Country: Canada
Mailing address: PO Box 7363
Mailing city: Grand Falls
Province: NB
Postal: E3Z 2K1
General Phone: (506) 473-3083
General Fax: (506) 473-3105
General/National Adv. E-mail: cataract@nb.aibn.com
Editorial e-mail: rickard.mark@victoriastar.ca
Primary Website: https://www.telegraphjournal.com/letoile/
Areas Served - City/County or Portion Thereof, or Zip codes: Canada
Mechanical specifications: Type page 13 x 21 1/2; E - 6 cols, 2 1/16, 1/6 between; A - 6 cols, 2 1/16, 1/6 between; C - 6 cols, 2 1/16, 1/6 between.
Published: Thur
Avg Paid Circ: 0
Avg Free Circ: 6296
Audit By: CMCA
Audit Date: 30.09.2013
Personnel: Mark Rickard (Ed. English); Madeleine Leclerc (Ed., French)
Parent company (for newspapers): Brunswick News, Inc.

PUBLICATION NAME

The Advertiser
Street Address: Po Box 129 ,
Province: NL
Postal: A2A 2J4
Country: Canada
Mailing address: PO Box 129
Mailing city: Grand Falls
Province: NL
Postal: A2A 2J4
General Phone: (709) 489-2162
General Fax: (709) 489-4817
General/National Adv. E-mail: editor@advertisernl.com
Editorial e-mail: editor@advertisernl.ca
Primary Website: www.gfwadvertiser.ca
Areas Served - City/County or Portion Thereof, or Zip codes: Grand Falls
Own Printing Facility?: Y
Commercial printers?: Y
Published: Thur
Avg Paid Circ: 1600
Avg Free Circ: 0
Audit By: VAC
Audit Date: 31.12.2015
Personnel: Ron Ennis (Ed.)
Parent company (for newspapers): Transcontinental Media

PUBLICATION NAME

Victoria County Star
Street Address: 229 Broadway Blvd. ,
Province: NB
Postal: E3Z 2K1
Country: Canada
Mailing address: PO Box 7363
Mailing city: Grand Falls
Province: NB
Postal: E3Z 2K1
General Phone: (506) 473-3083
General Fax: (506) 473-3105
Editorial e-mail: rickard.mark@victoriastar.ca
Primary Website: https://www.telegraphjournal.com/victoria-star/
Year Established: 2003
Areas Served - City/County or Portion Thereof, or Zip codes: Grand Falls
Own Printing Facility?: Y
Commercial printers?: Y
Mechanical specifications: Type page 11 1/2 x 21 1/2; E - 10 cols, 1/8 between; A - 10 cols, 1/8 between; C - 10 cols, 1/8 between.
Published: Wed
Avg Paid Circ: 2175
Avg Free Circ: 2
Audit By: VAC
Audit Date: 31.12.2015
Personnel: Mark Rickard (Ed., English); Madeleine Leclerc (Ed., French)
Parent company (for newspapers): Brunswick News, Inc.

GRAND FORKS

PUBLICATION NAME

The Grand Forks Gazette
Street Address: 7255 Riverside Dr. ,
Province: BC
Postal: V0H 1H0
Country: Canada
Mailing address: PO Box 700
Mailing city: Grand Forks
Province: BC
Postal: V0H 1H0
General Phone: (250) 442-2191
General Fax: (250) 442-3336
General/National Adv. E-mail: publisher@grandforksgazette.ca
Display Adv. E-mail: advertising@grandforksgazette.ca
Editorial e-mail: editor@grandforkscagazette.ca
Primary Website: grandforksgazette.ca
Year Established: 1897
Delivery Methods: Mail`Newsstand`Carrier
Areas Served - City/County or Portion Thereof, or Zip codes: Canada
Commercial printers?: Y
Mechanical specifications: Type page 10 x 15 1/2.
Published: Wed
Avg Paid Circ: 2399
Avg Free Circ: 12
Audit By: VAC
Audit Date: 30.06.2017
Personnel: Della Mallette (Prodn. Mgr.); Dyan Stoochnoff (Advertising); Kathleen Saylors (Reporter); Dustin LaCroix (Graphic Artist); Darlainea Redlack (Circulation)
Parent company (for newspapers): Black Press Group Ltd.

GRANDE CACHE

PUBLICATION NAME

Grande Cache Mountaineer
Street Address: 1800 Pine Plaza ,
Province: AB
Postal: T0E 0Y0
Country: Canada
Mailing address: PO Box 660
Mailing city: Grande Cache
Province: AB
Postal: T0E 0Y0
General Phone: (780) 827-3539
General/National Adv. E-mail: gcnews@telus.net
Display Adv. E-mail: gcnews@telus.net
Editorial e-mail: pamnews@telus.net
Primary Website: http://www.grandecachemountaineer.canic.ws/
Year Established: 1970
Delivery Methods: Mail`Newsstand
Areas Served - City/County or Portion Thereof, or Zip codes: Grande Cache Alberta
Published: Thur
Avg Paid Circ: 1060
Avg Free Circ: 36
Audit By: Sworn/Estimate/Non-Audited
Audit Date: 12.07.2019
Personnel: Pamela Brown (Pub./Ed./GM); Lisa Gould (Sales)

GRANDVIEW

PUBLICATION NAME

The Exponent
Street Address: 414 Main St. ,
Province: MB
Postal: R0L 0Y0
Country: Canada
Mailing address: PO Box 39
Mailing city: Grandview
Province: MB
Postal: R0L 0Y0
General Phone: (204) 546-2555
General Fax: (204) 546-3081
General/National Adv. E-mail: expos@mts.net
Editorial e-mail: expos@mts.net
Primary Website: www.grandviewexponent.com
Year Established: 1901
Delivery Methods: Mail`Newsstand
Areas Served - City/County or Portion Thereof, or Zip codes: Rol oyo R0L 0X0 and others
Own Printing Facility?: Y
Commercial printers?: N
Mechanical specifications: Type page 10 1/4 x 14 1/4; E - 6 cols, 1 7/12, 1/6 between; A - 6 cols, 1 7/12, 1/6 between; C - 6 cols, 1 7/12, 1/6 between.
Published: Tues
Avg Paid Circ: 1687
Avg Free Circ: 27
Audit By: VAC
Audit Date: 31.01.2016
Personnel: Clayton Chaloner (Ed.)

GRAVELBOURG

PUBLICATION NAME

Gravelbourg Tribune
Street Address: 611 Main St. ,
Province: SK
Postal: S0H 1X0
Country: Canada
Mailing address: PO Box 1017
Mailing city: Gravelbourg
Province: SK
Postal: S0H 1X0
General Phone: (306) 648-3479
General Fax: (306) 648-2520
Advertising Phone: (306) 648-3479
Advertising Fax: (306) 648-2520
Editorial Phone: (306) 648-3479
General/National Adv. E-mail: trib.editorial@sasktel.net
Display Adv. E-mail: trib.ads@sasktel.net
Classified Adv. e-mail: (306) 648-3479
Editorial e-mail: trib.editorial@sasktel.net
Primary Website: http://gravelbourgtribune.wixsite.com/tribune
Year Established: 1986
Delivery Methods: Mail`Newsstand
Areas Served - City/County or Portion Thereof, or Zip codes: R.M of Gravelbourg
Own Printing Facility?: Y
Commercial printers?: Y
Mechanical specifications: Type page 10 1/4 x 15 1/2; E - 5 cols, 1 7/8, between; A - 5 cols, 1 7/8, between; C - 5 cols, 1 7/8, between.
Published: Mon
Avg Paid Circ: 875
Avg Free Circ: 30
Audit By: CMCA
Audit Date: 27.11.2018
Personnel: Paul Boisvert (Ed)

GRAVENHURST

PUBLICATION NAME

The Gravenhurst Banner
Street Address: 140 Muskoka Rd. S. ,
Province: ON
Postal: P1P 1X2
Country: Canada
Mailing address: PO Box 849
Mailing city: Gravenhurst
Province: ON
Postal: P1P 1X2
General Phone: (705) 687-6674
General Fax: (705) 687-7213
General/National Adv. E-mail: banner@muskoka.com
Primary Website: www.muskokaregion.com/gravenhurst-on
Areas Served - City/County or Portion Thereof, or Zip codes: Canada
Published: Thur
Avg Paid Circ: 96
Avg Free Circ: 5237
Audit By: CMCA
Audit Date: 30.04.2016
Personnel: Bill Allen (Gen. Mgr.); Jack Tynan (Adv.)
Parent company (for newspapers): Metroland Media Group Ltd.; Torstar

GREENWOOD

PUBLICATION NAME

The Aurora
Street Address: Po Box 99 ,
Province: NS
Postal: B0P 1N0
Country: Canada
Mailing address: PO Box 99
Mailing city: Greenwood
Province: NS
Postal: B0P 1N0
General Phone: (902) 765-1494
General Fax: (902) 765-1717
General/National Adv. E-mail: aurora@auroranewspaper.com
Display Adv. E-mail: auroramarketing@ns.aliantzinc.ca
Editorial e-mail: auroraeditor@ns.aliantzinc.ca
Primary Website: www.auroranewspaper.com
Delivery Methods: Mail`Newsstand`Carrier`Racks
Areas Served - City/County or Portion Thereof, or Zip codes: Canada
Mechanical specifications: Type page 11 x 13; E - 6 cols, 1 5/8, 3/20 between; A - 6 cols, 1 5/8, 3/20 between.
Published: Mon
Avg Free Circ: 5900
Audit By: Sworn/Estimate/Non-Audited
Audit Date: 12.07.2019
Personnel: Sara Keddy (Mgr. Ed.); Dejah Roulston-Wilde (Admin Clerk); Christianne Robichaud (Adv); Brian Graves (Graphics designer)

PUBLICATION NAME

The Boundary Creek Times
Street Address: 318 Copper St. ,
Province: BC
Postal: V0H 1J0
Country: Canada
Mailing address: PO Box 99
Mailing city: Greenwood
Province: BC
Postal: V0H 1J0
General Phone: (250) 445-2233
General/National Adv. E-mail: bctimes@shaw.ca
Display Adv. E-mail: dyan.stoochnoff@boundarycreektimes.com
Primary Website: boundarycreektimes.ca
Delivery Methods: Mail`Newsstand
Areas Served - City/County or Portion Thereof, or Zip codes: Canada
Mechanical specifications: Type page 10 3/16 x 14 1/8; E - 5 cols, 1 7/16, 3/16 between; A - 5 cols, 1 7/16, 3/16 between; C - 5 cols, 1 7/16, 3/16 between.
Published: Thur
Avg Paid Circ: 471
Avg Free Circ: 1
Audit By: CMCA
Audit Date: 30.09.2017
Personnel: Dyan Stoochnoff (Associate Publisher); Darlainea Redlack (Circulation); Kathleen Saylors (Reporter)
Parent company (for newspapers): Black Press Group Ltd.

GRENFELL

PUBLICATION NAME

Broadview Express
Street Address: 813 Desmond St. ,
Province: SK
Postal: S0G 2B0
Country: Canada
Mailing address: PO Box 189
Mailing city: Grenfell
Province: SK
Postal: S0G 2B0
General Phone: (306) 697-2722
General Fax: (306) 697-2689
Advertising Phone: (306) 697-2722
Advertising Fax: (306) 697-2689
General/National Adv. E-mail: sunnews@sasktel.net
Display Adv. E-mail: sunnews@sasktel.net
Editorial e-mail: sunnews@sasktel.net
Primary Website: www.grenfellsun.sk.ca
Year Established: 1965
Delivery Methods: Mail`Newsstand
Areas Served - City/County or Portion Thereof, or Zip codes: Canada
Mechanical specifications: Type page 10 1/8 x 15 1/2; E - 6 cols, 1 1/2, between; A - 6 cols, 1 1/2, between; C - 6 cols, 1 1/2, between.
Published: Mon
Avg Paid Circ: 266
Avg Free Circ: 158
Audit By: CMCA
Audit Date: 31.03.2013
Personnel: Suzette Stone (Circ. Mgr.); Mariann Hughes (Sales Associate)
Parent company (for newspapers): Transcontinental Media

PUBLICATION NAME

Grenfell Sun
Street Address: 813 Desmond St. ,
Province: SK
Postal: S0G 2B0
Country: Canada
Mailing address: PO Box 189
Mailing city: Grenfell
Province: SK
Postal: S0G 2B0
General Phone: (306) 697-2722
General Fax: (306) 697-2689
General/National Adv. E-mail: sunnews@sasktel.net
Display Adv. E-mail: sunnews@sasktel.net
Editorial e-mail: sunnews@sasktel.net
Primary Website: grenfellsun.sk.ca
Year Established: 1892
Delivery Methods: Mail`Newsstand
Areas Served - City/County or Portion Thereof, or Zip codes: Canada
Commercial printers?: Y
Mechanical specifications: Type page 10 1/8 x 15 1/2; E - 6 cols, 1 1/2, between; A - 6 cols, 1 1/2, between; C - 6 cols, 1 1/2, between.
Published: Mon
Avg Paid Circ: 710
Avg Free Circ: 128
Audit By: CMCA
Audit Date: 30.09.2013
Personnel: Sarah Pacio (Office Manager)
Parent company (for newspapers): Transcontinental Media

GRIMSBY

PUBLICATION NAME

The Grimsby Lincoln News

Street Address: 32 Main St. W.,
Province: ON
Postal: L3M 1R4
Country: Canada
Mailing address: 32 Main St. W.
Mailing city: Grimsby
Province: ON
Postal: L3M 1R4
General Phone: (905) 945-8392
General Fax: (905) 945-3916
General/National Adv. E-mail: info@thegrimsbylincolnnews.com
Primary Website: www.thegrimsbylincolnnews.com
Published: Wed
Avg Free Circ: 23800
Audit By: Sworn/Estimate/Non-Audited
Audit Date: 12.07.2019
Personnel: Mike Williscraft (Editorial Mgr.); Scott Rosts (Ed.)
Parent company (for newspapers): Metroland Media Group Ltd.; Torstar

GRIMSHAW

PUBLICATION NAME

Banner Post
Street Address: Po Box 686, Po Box 1010
Province: AB
Postal: T0H 1W0
Country: Canada
Mailing address: PO Box 686
Mailing city: Manning
Province: AB
Postal: T0H 2M0
General Phone: (780) 836-3588
General Fax: (780) 836-2820
Advertising Phone: (780) 332-2215
General/National Adv. E-mail: bannerpost@mackreport.ab.ca
Display Adv. E-mail: bannerpost@mrnews.ca
Editorial e-mail: publisher@mrnews.ca
Primary Website: mrnews.ca
Year Established: 1965
Areas Served - City/County or Portion Thereof, or Zip codes: Canada
Own Printing Facility?: Y
Published: Wed
Avg Paid Circ: 0
Avg Free Circ: 45404
Audit By: CCAB
Audit Date: 31.10.2018
Personnel: Tom Mihaly (Pub/Ed); Kristin Dyck (Ed); Jillian Vandemark-Chomiak (Office/Adv. Mgr)
Parent company (for newspapers): Metroland Media Group Ltd.

GUELPH

PUBLICATION NAME

Guelph Tribune
Street Address: 367 Woodlawn Rd. W., Unit 1,
Province: ON
Postal: N1H 7K9
Country: Canada
Mailing address: 367 Woodlawn Rd. W., Unit 1
Mailing city: Guelph
Province: ON
Postal: N1H 1G8
General Phone: (519) 763-3333
General Fax: (519) 763-4814
General/National Adv. E-mail: cclark@guelphtribune.ca
Primary Website: www.guelphtribune.ca
Areas Served - City/County or Portion Thereof, or Zip codes: Canada
Published: Tues`Thur
Avg Free Circ: 41612
Audit By: VAC
Audit Date: 30.06.2016
Personnel: Peter Winkler (Pub.); Heather Dunbar (Sales Mgr.); Doug Coxson (Ed.)
Parent company (for newspapers): Metroland Media Group Ltd.; Torstar

GULL LAKE

PUBLICATION NAME

Advance Southwest (formerly Gull Lake Advance)
Street Address: 1462 Conrad Ave.,
Province: SK
Postal: S0N 1A0
Country: Canada
Mailing address: PO Box 628
Mailing city: Gull Lake
Province: SK
Postal: S0N 1A0
General Phone: (306) 672-3373
Advertising Phone: (306) 741-2448
General/National Adv. E-mail: glad12@sasktel.net
Display Adv. E-mail: sales@advancesouthwest.com
Editorial e-mail: kate@advancesouthwest.com
Primary Website: www.advancesouthwest.com
Year Established: 1909
Delivery Methods: Mail`Carrier
Areas Served - City/County or Portion Thereof, or Zip codes: Southwest Saskatchewan Postal Codes: S0N, S9H, S0G
Own Printing Facility?: Y
Commercial printers?: Y
Published: Mon
Avg Paid Circ: 600
Avg Free Circ: 7900
Audit By: Sworn/Estimate/Non-Audited
Audit Date: 12.07.2019
Personnel: Kate Winquist (Pub)
Parent company (for newspapers): Winquist Ventures Ltd.

GUYSBOROUGH

PUBLICATION NAME

Guysborough Journal
Street Address: P.O. Box 210,
Province: NS
Postal: B0H 1N0
Country: Canada
Mailing address: P.O. Box 210
Mailing city: Guysborough
Province: NS
Postal: B0H 1N0
General Phone: (902) 533-2851
General Fax: (902) 533-2750
General/National Adv. E-mail: news@guysboroughjournal.ca
Display Adv. E-mail: advertising@guysboroughjournal.ca
Editorial e-mail: news@guysboroughjournal.ca
Primary Website: www.guysboroughjournal.com
Areas Served - City/County or Portion Thereof, or Zip codes: Guysborough
Published: Wed
Avg Paid Circ: 6890
Avg Free Circ: 13
Audit By: VAC
Audit Date: 30.06.2016
Personnel: Allan Murphy (Pub); Hellen Murphy (Ed/Mgr/Pub); Sharon Heighton (Office/Circ. Mgr)

HAGERSVILLE

PUBLICATION NAME

The Haldimand Press
Street Address: 6 Parkview Rd.,
Province: ON
Postal: N0A 1H0
Country: Canada
Mailing address: PO Box 369
Mailing city: Hagersvillel
Province: ON
Postal: N0A 1H0
General Phone: (905) 768-3111
General/National Adv. E-mail: press.h@news-net.ca
Display Adv. E-mail: alana@haldimandpress.com
Classified Adv. e-mail: design@haldimandpress.com
Editorial e-mail: kaitlyn@haldimandpress.com
Primary Website: www.haldimandpress.com

Year Established: 1868
Delivery Methods: Mail`Newsstand
Areas Served - City/County or Portion Thereof, or Zip codes: Canada
Published: Thur
Avg Paid Circ: 3073
Audit By: Sworn/Estimate/Non-Audited
Audit Date: 12.07.2019
Personnel: Jillian Zynomirski (Pub.); Kaitlyn Clark (Publisher)

HALIBURTON

PUBLICATION NAME

The Highlander
Street Address: 195 Highland Street, The Village Barn
Province: ON
Postal: K0M 1S0
Country: Canada
Mailing address: PO. BOX 1024
Mailing city: Haliburton
Province: ON
Postal: K0M 1S0
General Phone: (705) 457-2900
Display Adv. E-mail: walt@haliburtonhighlander.ca
Primary Website: www.haliburtonhighlander.ca
Year Established: 2011
Delivery Methods: Newsstand`Racks
Areas Served - City/County or Portion Thereof, or Zip codes: Canada
Published: Thur
Avg Free Circ: 8062
Audit By: CMCA
Audit Date: 30.06.2016
Personnel: Bram Lebo (Pub.)

HALIFAX

PUBLICATION NAME

Bedford - Sackville Weekly News
Street Address: 211 Horseshoe Lake Dr,
Province: NS
Postal: B3S 0B9
Country: Canada
Mailing address: 211 Horseshoe lake Dr
Mailing city: Halifax
Province: NS
Postal: B3S 0B9
General Phone: (902) 426-2811
General Fax: (902) 426-1170
General/National Adv. E-mail: reception@herald.ca
Display Adv. E-mail: sales@herald.ca
Classified Adv. e-mail: classified@herald.ca
Editorial e-mail: newsroom@herald.ca
Primary Website: http://thechronicleherald.ca/community/bedfordsackvilleobserver
Delivery Methods: Mail`Newsstand
Areas Served - City/County or Portion Thereof, or Zip codes: Canada
Published: Thur
Avg Free Circ: 29302
Audit By: CMCA
Audit Date: 28.02.2013
Personnel: Sheryl Grant (Adv. Media Dir.); Kim Moar (Mng. Ed.)

PUBLICATION NAME

Cole Harbour Weekly
Street Address: 211 Horseshoe Lake Dr,
Province: NS
Postal: B3S 0B9
Country: Canada
Mailing address: 211 Horseshoe lake Dr
Mailing city: Halifax
Province: NS
Postal: B3S 0B9
General Phone: (902) 426-2811
General Fax: (902) 426-1170
General/National Adv. E-mail: reception@herald.ca
Display Adv. E-mail: sales@herald.ca
Classified Adv. e-mail: classifieds@herald.ca
Editorial e-mail: newsroom@herald.ca

Primary Website: www.thechronicleherald.ca
Delivery Methods: Mail`Newsstand
Areas Served - City/County or Portion Thereof, or Zip codes: Canada
Published: Thur
Avg Free Circ: 37643
Audit By: CMCA
Audit Date: 28.02.2013
Personnel: Fred Fiander (Pub.); Sheryl Grant (Adv. Media Dir.)

PUBLICATION NAME

Halifax West-clayton Park Weekly News
Street Address: 211 Horseshoe Lake Dr,
Province: NS
Postal: B3S 0B9
Country: Canada
Mailing address: 211 Horseshoe lake Dr
Mailing city: Halifax
Province: NS
Postal: B3S 0B9
General Phone: (902) 421-5888
General/National Adv. E-mail: reception@herald.ca
Display Adv. E-mail: sgrant@herald.ca
Classified Adv. e-mail: classified@herald.ca
Editorial e-mail: newsroom@herald.ca
Primary Website: www.thechronicleherald.ca
Delivery Methods: Mail`Newsstand
Areas Served - City/County or Portion Thereof, or Zip codes: Canada
Published: Thur
Avg Free Circ: 37145
Audit By: CMCA
Audit Date: 28.02.2013
Personnel: Sheryl Grant (Adv. Media Dir.); Kim Moar (Mng. Ed.)

HAMILTON

PUBLICATION NAME

The Bay Observer
Street Address: 140 King Street East,
Province: ON
Postal: L8N 1B2
Country: USA
Mailing address: 140 King Street East
Mailing city: Hamilton
Province: ON
Postal: L8N 1B2
General Phone: (905) 522-6000
General Fax: (905) 522-5838
General/National Adv. E-mail: contact@bayobserver.ca
Primary Website: www.bayobserver.ca
Areas Served - City/County or Portion Thereof, or Zip codes: Canada
Published: Thur
Avg Paid Circ: 0
Avg Free Circ: 28246
Audit By: CMCA
Audit Date: 31.01.2012
Personnel: John Best (Pub.)

HANNA

PUBLICATION NAME

Hanna Herald
Street Address: 113 - 1st Ave West,
Province: AB
Postal: T0J 1P0
Country: Canada
Mailing address: PO Box 790
Mailing city: Hanna
Province: AB
Postal: T0J 1P0
General Phone: (403) 854-3366
General Fax: (403) 854-3256
Display Adv. E-mail: rmackintosh@postmedia.com
Classified Adv. e-mail: deanne.cornell@sunmedia.ca
Editorial e-mail: jackie.gold@sunmedia.ca
Primary Website: www.hannaherald.com
Year Established: 1912
Delivery Methods: Mail`Newsstand

HANOVER

PUBLICATION NAME

The Post (Hanover)
Street Address: 413 18th Ave.,
Province: ON
Postal: N4N 3S5
Country: Canada
General Phone: (519) 364-2001
General Fax: (519) 364-6950
General/National Adv. E-mail: marie.david@sunmedia.ca
Display Adv. E-mail: janie.harrison@sunmedia.ca
Classified Adv. e-mail: han.classifieds@sunmedia.ca
Editorial e-mail: patrick.bales@sunmedia.ca
Primary Website: www.thepost.on.ca
Year Established: 1880
Delivery Methods: Carrier
Areas Served - City/County or Portion Thereof, or Zip codes: Canada
Own Printing Facility?: Y
Commercial printers?: Y
Mechanical specifications: Tabloid 9 col x 160 lines
Published: Thur
Avg Paid Circ: 84
Avg Free Circ: 15393
Audit By: CMCA
Audit Date: 30.06.2016
Personnel: Marie David (Gen. Mgr.); Rod Currie (Circ. Mgr.); Patrick Bales (Ed.); Kiera Merriam (Adv. Mgr.)
Parent company (for newspapers): Postmedia Network Inc.; Quebecor Communications, Inc.

HAPPY VALLEY

PUBLICATION NAME

The Labradorian
Street Address: 2 Hillcrest Rd.,
Province: NL
Postal: A0P 1E0
Country: Canada
Mailing address: PO Box 39
Mailing city: Happy Valley-Goose Bay
Province: NL
Postal: A0P 1E0
General Phone: (709) 896-3341
General Fax: (709) 896-8781
Advertising Phone: (709) 896-3341
General/National Adv. E-mail: sgallant@thelabradorian.ca
Display Adv. E-mail: sgallant@thelabradorian.ca
Editorial e-mail: editor@thelabradorian.ca
Primary Website: www.thelabradorian.ca
Areas Served - City/County or Portion Thereof, or Zip codes: Happy Valley, Goose Bay
Mechanical specifications: Type page 11 x 21 1/2; E - 6 cols, 1 3/4, 1/8 between; A - 6 cols, 1 3/4, 1/8 between; C - 8 cols, 1 1/2, between.
Published: Mon
Avg Paid Circ: 2009
Avg Free Circ: 0
Audit By: VAC
Audit Date: 31.12.2015
Personnel: Sharon Gallant (Adv)
Parent company (for newspapers): Transcontinental Media

Areas Served - City/County or Portion Thereof, or Zip codes: Canada
Published: Wed
Avg Paid Circ: 900
Avg Free Circ: 0
Audit By: CMCA
Audit Date: 30.06.2014
Personnel: Shawn Cornell (Pub); Deanne Cornell (Adv. Sales Rep.); Krista Avery (Office Mgr.); Jackie Gold (Mng. Ed.)
Parent company (for newspapers): Postmedia Network Inc.; Quebecor Communications, Inc.

HARBOUR BRETON

PUBLICATION NAME

Harbour Breton Coaster
Street Address: 30-42 Canada Drive,
Province: NL
Postal: A0H 1P0
Country: Canada
Mailing address: PO Box 298
Mailing city: Harbour Breton
Province: NL
Postal: A0H 1P0
General Phone: (709) 885-2378
General Fax: (709) 885-2393
Editorial e-mail: editor@thecoasterr.ca
Primary Website: www.thecoasterr.ca
Areas Served - City/County or Portion Thereof, or Zip codes: Canada
Published: Tues
Avg Paid Circ: 1283
Avg Free Circ: 0
Audit By: CMCA
Audit Date: 30.06.2013
Personnel: Clayton Hunt (Ed.)
Parent company (for newspapers): Transcontinental Media

HARROW

PUBLICATION NAME

Harrow News
Street Address: 5 King St., P.o. Box 310
Province: ON
Postal: N0R 1G0
Country: Canada
Mailing address: PO Box 310
Mailing city: Harrow
Province: ON
Postal: N0R 1G0
General Phone: (519) 738-2542
General Fax: (519) 738-3874
General/National Adv. E-mail: harnews@mnsi.net
Display Adv. E-mail: harnews@mnsi.net
Classified Adv. e-mail: harnews@mnsi.net
Editorial e-mail: natalie@mdirect.net
Year Established: 1930
Delivery Methods: Mail`Newsstand
Areas Served - City/County or Portion Thereof, or Zip codes: Canada
Mechanical specifications: Type page 10 1/4 x 15; E - 6 cols, 1 1/2, 3/8 between; A - 6 cols, 1 1/2, 3/8 between; C - 6 cols, 1 1/2, 3/8 between.
Published: Tues
Avg Paid Circ: 1221
Avg Free Circ: 3
Audit By: CMCA
Audit Date: 2/29/2017
Personnel: Natalie Koziana (Circ. Mgr.)

HARTLAND

PUBLICATION NAME

The Observer
Street Address: 941 Industrial Dr.,
Province: NB
Postal: E7P 2G8
Country: Canada
Mailing address: 941 Industrial Dr.
Mailing city: Hartland
Province: NB
Postal: E7P 2G8
General Phone: (506) 375-4458
General Fax: (506) 375-4281
General/National Adv. E-mail: theobserver@nb.aibn.com
Year Established: 1909
Areas Served - City/County or Portion Thereof, or Zip codes: Canada
Own Printing Facility?: Y
Commercial printers?: Y
Mechanical specifications: Type page 12 x 21; E - 6 cols, 1 7/8, 1/8 between; A - 6 cols, 1 7/8, 1/8 between; C - 6 cols, 1 7/8, 1/8 between.
Published: Wed
Avg Paid Circ: 2569
Audit By: Sworn/Estimate/Non-Audited
Audit Date: 12.07.2019
Personnel: Stewart Fairgrieve (Gen. Mgr.)

HAWKESBURY

PUBLICATION NAME

Le Carillon
Street Address: 1100 Aberdeen St.,
Province: ON
Postal: K6A 1K7
Country: Canada
Mailing address: 1100 Aberdeen St.
Mailing city: Hawkesbury
Province: ON
Postal: K6A 3H1
General Phone: (613) 632-4155
General Fax: (613) 632-6122
Advertising Phone: (613) 632-4155
Advertising Fax: (613) 632-6383
Editorial Phone: (613) 632-4155
Editorial Fax: (613) 632-6383
General/National Adv. E-mail: nouvelles@eap.on.ca
Display Adv. E-mail: yvan.joly@eap.on.ca; nicole.pilon@eap.on.ca
Editorial e-mail: nouvelles@eap.on.ca
Primary Website: www.lecarillon.ca
Year Established: 1948
Delivery Methods: Carrier
Areas Served - City/County or Portion Thereof, or Zip codes: Canada
Own Printing Facility?: Y
Commercial printers?: Y
Mechanical specifications: Type page 10 1/2 x 14 1/4; E - 8 cols, 1/6 between; A - 8 cols, 1/6 between; C - 8 cols, 1/6 between.
Published: Thur
Avg Paid Circ: 30
Avg Free Circ: 15000
Audit By: Sworn/Estimate/Non-Audited
Audit Date: 12.07.2019
Personnel: Bertrand Castonguay (Pres.); Gilles Normand (Circ. Mgr.); François Legault (Chief Ed.)
Parent company (for newspapers): Cie d'Edition Andre Paquette, Inc.

PUBLICATION NAME

Le/the Regional
Street Address: 124 Rue Principale E.,
Province: ON
Postal: K6A 1A3
Country: Canada
Mailing address: 124 rue Principale E.
Mailing city: Hawkesbury
Province: ON
Postal: K6A 1A3
General Phone: (613) 632-0112
General Fax: (613) 632-0277
General/National Adv. E-mail: pub@le-regional.ca
Display Adv. E-mail: pub@le-regional.ca
Editorial e-mail: news@le-regional.ca
Primary Website: www.le-regional.ca
Year Established: 1995
Delivery Methods: Mail`Newsstand`Carrier`Racks
Areas Served - City/County or Portion Thereof, or Zip codes: K6A 1A3
Own Printing Facility?: N
Commercial printers?: Y
Mechanical specifications: Type page 11.317" x 15"; E - 8 cols, 0.1292" between;
Published: Thur
Avg Free Circ: 34484
Audit By: Sworn/Estimate/Non-Audited
Audit Date: 12.07.2019
Personnel: Sylvain Roy (Owner)

PUBLICATION NAME

Tribune Express
Street Address: 1100 Aberdeen,
Province: ON
Postal: K6A 1K7
Country: Canada
Mailing address: PO Box 1000
Mailing city: Hawkesbury
Province: ON
Postal: K6A 3H1
General Phone: (613) 632-4155
General Fax: (613) 632-6122
Advertising Phone: (613) 632-4155
Advertising Fax: (613) 632-6383
Editorial Phone: (613) 632-4155
Editorial Fax: (613) 632-6383
General/National Adv. E-mail: nouvelles@eap.on.ca
Display Adv. E-mail: yvan.joly@eap.on.ca; nicole.pilon@eap.on.ca
Editorial e-mail: nouvelles@eap.on.ca
Primary Website: www.tribune-express.ca
Year Established: 1984
Delivery Methods: Carrier
Areas Served - City/County or Portion Thereof, or Zip codes: Canada
Own Printing Facility?: Y
Commercial printers?: Y
Mechanical specifications: Type page 10 1/2 x 14 1/4; E - 8 cols, 1/6 between; A - 8 cols, 1/6 between; C - 8 cols, 1/6 between.
Published: Wed
Avg Paid Circ: 11
Avg Free Circ: 26430
Audit By: Sworn/Estimate/Non-Audited
Audit Date: 12.07.2019
Personnel: Bertrand Castonguay (President); Gilles Normand (Circ. Mgr.); Yvan Joly (Newspaper manager); Nicole Pilon (sales secretary, national, display)
Parent company (for newspapers): Cie d'Edition Andre Paquette, Inc.

HAY RIVER

PUBLICATION NAME

The Hub
Street Address: 8-4 Courtoreille St.,
Province: NT
Postal: X0E 1G2
Country: Canada
Mailing address: 8-4 Courtoreille St.
Mailing city: Hay River
Province: NT
Postal: X0E 1G2
General Phone: (867) 874-6577
General Fax: (867) 874-2679
General/National Adv. E-mail: hub@hayriverhub.com
Display Adv. E-mail: ads@hayriverhub.com
Editorial e-mail: web@hayriverhub.com
Primary Website: www.hayriverhub.com
Year Established: 1973
Areas Served - City/County or Portion Thereof, or Zip codes: X0E 1G2, X0E 0P0, X0E 0M0, X0E 0N0, X1A 2P2, X0E 0L0
Commercial printers?: Y
Mechanical specifications: Type page 10 1/4 x 15 1/2; E - 6 cols, 1 3/5, 1/6 between; A - 6 cols, 1 3/5, 1/6 between; C - 6 cols, 1 3/5, 1/6 between.
Published: Wed
Avg Paid Circ: 1996
Avg Free Circ: 182
Audit By: VAC
Audit Date: 31.01.2016
Personnel: Chris Brodeur (Pub.); Lehaina Andrews (Adv. Mgr.); Lorna Desilets (Circ. Mgr.)

HEARST

PUBLICATION NAME

Le Nord
Street Address: 1004, Rue Prince.,
Province: ON
Postal: P0L 1N0
Country: Canada
Mailing address: PO Box 2320
Mailing city: Hearst
Province: ON
Postal: P0L 1N0
General Phone: (705) 372-1233
General Fax: (705) 362-5954
General/National Adv. E-mail: lenord@lenord.on.ca; ocantin@lenord.on.ca
Display Adv. E-mail: lenordjournalpub@gmail.com

Community Newspapers in Canada

III-541

Classified Adv. e-mail: lenordjournalpub@gmail.com
Editorial e-mail: journalistenord@gmail.com
Primary Website: www.lenord.on.ca
Year Established: 1976
Delivery Methods: Mail`Newsstand`Carrier
Areas Served - City/County or Portion Thereof, or Zip codes: Hearst
Commercial printers?: Y
Mechanical specifications: Type page 5col. X 175 MAL
Published: Wed
Avg Paid Circ: 1409
Avg Free Circ: 65
Audit By: CMCA
Audit Date: 30.06.2014
Personnel: Omer Cantin (Ed.); Steve McInnis (Gen. Mgr.); Karine Hebert (Graphic Designer)
Parent company (for newspapers): Lignes Agates Marketing

HERBERT

PUBLICATION NAME

The Herald
Street Address: 716 Herbert Ave. ,
Province: SK
Postal: S0H 2A0
Country: Canada
Mailing address: PO Box 399
Mailing city: Herbert
Province: SK
Postal: S0H 2A0
General Phone: (306) 784-2422
General Fax: (306) 784-3246
General/National Adv. E-mail: herbertherald@sasktel.net
Display Adv. E-mail: herbertherald@sasktel.net
Classified Adv. e-mail: herbertherald@sasktel.net
Editorial e-mail: herbertherald@sasktel.net
Year Established: 1911
Delivery Methods: Mail`Newsstand
Areas Served - City/County or Portion Thereof, or Zip codes: Canada
Commercial printers?: Y
Mechanical specifications: Type page 10 1/4 x 15; E - 6 cols, 1 5/8, 1/4 between; A - 6 cols, 1 5/8, 1/4 between; C - 6 cols, 1 5/8, 1/4 between.
Published: Tues
Avg Paid Circ: 1442
Avg Free Circ: 5
Audit By: CMCA
Audit Date: 31.03.2017
Personnel: Rhonda J. Ens (Ed.)

HIGH LEVEL

PUBLICATION NAME

The Echo-pioneer
Street Address: 10006 - 97th St. ,
Province: AB
Postal: T0H 1Z0
Country: Canada
Mailing address: PO Box 1018
Mailing city: High Level
Province: AB
Postal: T0H 1Z0
General Phone: (780) 926-2000
General Fax: (780) 926-2001
General/National Adv. E-mail: pioneer@mackreport.ab.ca
Display Adv. E-mail: echoads1@mrnews.ca
Classified Adv. e-mail: echoads1@mrnews.ca
Editorial e-mail: echonews2@mrnews.ca
Primary Website: www.mrnews.ca
Year Established: 1976
Areas Served - City/County or Portion Thereof, or Zip codes: Canada
Own Printing Facility?: Y
Published: Wed
Audit By: Sworn/Estimate/Non-Audited
Audit Date: 12.07.2019
Personnel: Nikki Coles (Advertising); Tom Mihaly (Pub./Mng. Ed.); Ann Bassett (Office/Adv.); Matt Marcone (Ed) Lacey Reid (Advertising)
Parent company (for newspapers): Mackenzie Report Inc.

PUBLICATION NAME

The Mile Zero News
Street Address: 10006-97 St. ,
Province: AB
Postal: T0H 1Z0
Country: Canada
General Phone: (780) 332-2215
General Fax: (780) 926-2001
General/National Adv. E-mail: milezeronews@mrnews.ca
Display Adv. E-mail: echo@mrnews.ca
Primary Website: www.mrnews.ca
Year Established: 1977
Published: Wed
Avg Paid Circ: 0
Avg Free Circ: 1575
Audit By: VAC
Audit Date: 31.10.2016
Personnel: Carmen Kratky (Office/Advertising); Tom Mihaly (Pub.); Ann Bassett (Circ. Mgr.); Kristen Feddema (Ed.); Barb Schofield (Adv. Sales)
Parent company (for newspapers): Mackenzie Report Inc.

HIGH PRAIRIE

PUBLICATION NAME

South Peace News
Street Address: 4902 51st Ave. ,
Province: AB
Postal: T0G 1E0
Country: Canada
Mailing address: PO Box 1000
Mailing city: High Prairie
Province: AB
Postal: T0G 1E0
General Phone: (780) 523-4484
General Fax: (780) 523-3039
General/National Adv. E-mail: spn@cablecomet.com
Display Adv. E-mail: southpeacenews@hotmail.com
Classified Adv. e-mail: southpeacenews@hotmail.com
Editorial e-mail: spn@cablecomet.com
Primary Website: www.southpeacenews.com
Delivery Methods: Mail`Newsstand
Areas Served - City/County or Portion Thereof, or Zip codes: Canada
Commercial printers?: Y
Mechanical specifications: Type page 10 1/4 x 15 3/4.
Published: Wed
Avg Paid Circ: 1257
Avg Free Circ: 0
Audit By: CMCA
Audit Date: 30.01.2017
Personnel: Mary Burgar (Pub.); Chris Clegg (Ed.)

HIGH RIVER

PUBLICATION NAME

The High River Times
Street Address: 618 Centre St. S. ,
Province: AB
Postal: T1V 1E9
Country: Canada
Mailing address: 104 - 701 Centre St. SW
Mailing city: High River
Province: AB
Postal: T1V 1Y1
General Phone: (403) 652-2034
General/National Adv. E-mail: info@highrivertimes.com
Display Adv. E-mail: hmorgan@postmedia.com
Classified Adv. e-mail: hmorgan@postmedia.com
Editorial e-mail: krushworth@postmedia.com
Primary Website: www.highrivertimes.com
Year Established: 1905
Delivery Methods: Mail`Newsstand`Carrier
Areas Served - City/County or Portion Thereof, or Zip codes: Canada
Commercial printers?: Y
Published: Tues`Fri
Avg Paid Circ: 0
Avg Free Circ: 6406
Audit By: VAC
Audit Date: 31.03.2017
Personnel: Kaire Davis (Admin./Office Mgr.); Kevin Rushworth (Multimedia. Ed.); Roxanne Mackintosh (Reg. Adv. Dir.); Heather Morgan (Advertising Manager)
Parent company (for newspapers): Postmedia Network Inc.

HINTON

PUBLICATION NAME

The Hinton Parklander
Street Address: 387 Drinnan Way ,
Province: AB
Postal: T7V 2A3
Country: Canada
General Phone: (780) 865-3115
General Fax: (780) 865-1252
General/National Adv. E-mail: news@hintonparklander.com
Classified Adv. e-mail: hintonparklander.classifieds@sunmedia.ca
Editorial e-mail: eric.plummer@sunmedia.ca
Primary Website: www.hintonparklander.com
Year Established: 1955
Delivery Methods: Mail`Newsstand`Carrier`Racks
Areas Served - City/County or Portion Thereof, or Zip codes: Canada
Mechanical specifications: Type page 10 1/4 x 12 1/2; E - 8 cols, 1 13/16, 1/6 between; A - 8 cols, 1 13/16, 1/6 between; C - 8 cols, 1 13/16, 1/6 between.
Published: Mon
Avg Paid Circ: 7
Avg Free Circ: 3720
Audit By: VAC
Audit Date: 31.12.2015
Personnel: Eric Plummer (Ed.); Terry Thachuk (Pub.); Nathalie Lovoie-Murray (Nationals & Classified Booking)
Parent company (for newspapers): Postmedia Network Inc.

PUBLICATION NAME

The Hinton Voice
Street Address: 187 Pembina Ave. ,
Province: AB
Postal: T7V 2B2
Country: Canada
General Phone: (890) 865-5688
General Fax: (780) 865-5699
General/National Adv. E-mail: news@hintonvoice.ca
Display Adv. E-mail: sales@hintonvoice.ca
Primary Website: www.hintonvoice.ca
Areas Served - City/County or Portion Thereof, or Zip codes: Hinton
Published: Thur
Avg Free Circ: 445
Audit By: VAC
Audit Date: 31.08.2016
Personnel: Tyler Waugh (Pub.); Sarah Burns (Mktg. Specialist); Robin Garreck (Prodn./Distrib. Mgr.); Angie Still (Accounting)

HOPE

PUBLICATION NAME

Hope Standard
Street Address: 540 Wallace St. ,
Province: BC
Postal: V0X 1L0
Country: Canada
Mailing address: PO Box 1090
Mailing city: Hope
Province: BC
Postal: V0X 1L0
General Phone: (604) 869-2421
General Fax: (604) 869-7351
General/National Adv. E-mail: news@hopestandard.com
Display Adv. E-mail: sales@hopestandard.com
Classified Adv. e-mail: classifieds@hopestandard.com
Primary Website: www.hopestandard.com
Year Established: 1959
Areas Served - City/County or Portion Thereof, or Zip codes: Canada
Commercial printers?: Y
Mechanical specifications: Type page 10 3/8 x 14; E - 6 cols, 1 5/8, 1/8 between; A - 6 cols, 1 5/8, 1/8 between; C - 6 cols, 1 5/8, 1/8 between.
Published: Thur
Avg Paid Circ: 346
Avg Free Circ: 0
Audit By: VAC
Audit Date: 30.06.2016
Personnel: Patti Desjardins (Adv. Mgr.); Janice McDonald (Circ. Mgr.); Carly Ferguson (Pub.); X.Y. Zeng (Ed.)
Parent company (for newspapers): Torstar

HORNEPAYNE

PUBLICATION NAME

Jackfish Journal
Street Address: 113 Herbert Ave. ,
Province: ON
Postal: P0M 1Z0
Mailing address: PO Box 487
Mailing city: Hornepayne
Province: ON
Postal: P0M 1Z0
General Phone: (807) 868-2381
General Fax: (807) 868-2673
General/National Adv. E-mail: Jjournal@bell.net
Primary Website: www.hornepayne.com
Areas Served - City/County or Portion Thereof, or Zip codes: Canada
Published: Wed
Avg Paid Circ: 200
Avg Free Circ: 30
Audit By: CMCA
Audit Date: 30.04.2016
Personnel: Lisa Stewart (Pub./Ed.)

HOUSTON

PUBLICATION NAME

Houston Today
Street Address: 3232 Hwy 16 W. ,
Province: BC
Postal: V0J 1Z1
Country: Canada
Mailing address: PO Box 899
Mailing city: Houston
Province: BC
Postal: V0J 1Z0
General Phone: (250) 845-2890
General Fax: (250) 847-2995
General/National Adv. E-mail: editor@houston-today.com
Display Adv. E-mail: advertising@houston-today.com
Primary Website: www.houston-today.com
Areas Served - City/County or Portion Thereof, or Zip codes: Canada
Own Printing Facility?: Y
Published: Wed
Avg Paid Circ: 983
Avg Free Circ: 305
Audit By: VAC
Audit Date: 30.06.2016
Personnel: Mary Ann Ruiter (Ed.); Todd Hamilton (Mng. Ed.); Jackie Lieuwen (Reporter)
Parent company (for newspapers): Torstar

HUDSON

PUBLICATION NAME

Hudson Gazette
Street Address: 397 Main Rd. ,
Province: QC
Postal: J0P 1H0

Country: Canada
Mailing address: 397 Main Rd.
Mailing city: Hudson
Province: QC
Postal: J0P 1H0
General Phone: (450) 458-5482
General Fax: (450) 458-3337
General/National Adv. E-mail: hudsongazette@videotron.ca
Primary Website: www.hudsongazette.com
Year Established: 1950
Areas Served - City/County or Portion Thereof, or Zip codes: Canada
Commercial printers?: Y
Mechanical specifications: Type page 10 7/8 x 14 1/8; E - 8 cols, 1 1/16, 1/6 between; A - 8 cols, 1 1/16, 1/6 between; C - 8 cols, 1 1/16, 1/6 between.
Published: Wed
Avg Free Circ: 21000
Audit By: Sworn/Estimate/Non-Audited
Audit Date: 12.07.2019
Personnel: Greg Jones (Pub.); Louise Craig (Circ. Mgr.); Jim Duff (Ed.)

HUDSON BAY

PUBLICATION NAME

Hudson Bay Post-review
Street Address: 20 Railway Ave. ,
Province: SK
Postal: S0E 0Y0
Country: Canada
Mailing address: PO Box 10
Mailing city: Hudson Bay
Province: SK
Postal: S0E 0Y0
General Phone: (306) 865-2771
General Fax: (306) 865-2340
General/National Adv. E-mail: post.review@sasktel.net
Display Adv. E-mail: postreview3@sasktel.net
Year Established: 1950
Delivery Methods: Mail Newsstand
Areas Served - City/County or Portion Thereof, or Zip codes: Canada
Own Printing Facility?: Y
Commercial printers?: Y
Mechanical specifications: Type page 10.25 x 15 1/2; E - 6 cols, 1 1/2, 1/3 between; A - 6 cols, 1 1/2, 1/3 between; C - 6 cols, 1 1/2, 1/3 between.
Published: Thur
Avg Paid Circ: 910
Avg Free Circ: 27
Audit By: CMCA
Audit Date: 31.03.2014
Personnel: Sherry Pilon (Mgr.)

HUMBOLDT

PUBLICATION NAME

East Central Trader
Street Address: 535 Main Street ,
Province: SK
Postal: S0K 2A0
Country: Canada
Mailing address: PO Box 970
Mailing city: Humboldt
Province: SK
Postal: S0K 2A0
General Phone: (306) 682-2561
General Fax: (306) 682-3322
Display Adv. E-mail: sford@humboldtjournal.ca
Editorial e-mail: cmcrae@humboldtjournal.ca
Primary Website: www.humboldtjournal.ca
Areas Served - City/County or Portion Thereof, or Zip codes: Canada
Published: Fri
Avg Paid Circ: 5
Avg Free Circ: 5443
Audit By: CMCA
Audit Date: 30.04.2016
Personnel: Becky Zimmer (Ed.); Brent Fitzpatrick (Group Publisher)

PUBLICATION NAME

The Humboldt Journal
Street Address: 535 Main St. ,
Province: SK
Postal: S0K 2A0
Country: Canada
Mailing address: PO Box 970
Mailing city: Humboldt
Province: SK
Postal: S0K 2A0
General Phone: (306) 682-2561
General Fax: (306) 682-3322
General/National Adv. E-mail: humboldt.journal@sasktel.net
Display Adv. E-mail: sford@humboldtjournal.ca
Editorial e-mail: cmcrae@humboldtjournal.ca
Primary Website: www.humboldtjournal.ca
Year Established: 1905
Delivery Methods: Mail Newsstand Carrier Racks
Areas Served - City/County or Portion Thereof, or Zip codes: Canada
Mechanical specifications: Type page Tabloid 11x17 Column size 1.583 inches
Published: Wed
Avg Paid Circ: 1765
Avg Free Circ: 29
Audit By: CMCA
Audit Date: 30.11.2016
Personnel: Becky Zimmer (Ed.)
Parent company (for newspapers): Glacier Media Group

HUNTINGDON

PUBLICATION NAME

Les Hebdos Monteregiens
Street Address: 66 Chateauguay St. ,
Province: QC
Postal: J0S 1H0
Country: Canada
Mailing address: 66 Chateauguay St.
Mailing city: Huntingdon
Province: QC
Postal: J0S 1H0
General Phone: (450) 264-5364
General Fax: (450) 264-9521
General/National Adv. E-mail: info@gleaner-source.com; direction@gleaner-source.com
Display Adv. E-mail: petitesannonces@gleaner-source.com; pub@gleaner-source.com
Editorial e-mail: redaction@gleaner-source.com
Primary Website: www.monteregieweb.com
Mechanical specifications: Type page 10 1/4 x 16; E - 8 cols, 1 1/8, 1/8 between; A - 8 cols, 1 1/8, 1/8 between; C - 8 cols, 1 1/8, 1/8 between.
Published: Wed
Avg Paid Circ: 5000
Avg Free Circ: 91
Audit By: Sworn/Estimate/Non-Audited
Audit Date: 12.07.2019
Personnel: Andre Castagnier (Gen. Mgr.); Susanne J. Brown (Ed.)
Parent company (for newspapers): Hebdos Quebec

HUNTSVILLE

PUBLICATION NAME

Huntsville Forester
Street Address: 11 Main St. W. ,
Province: ON
Postal: P1H 2C5
Country: Canada
Mailing address: 11 Main St. W.
Mailing city: Huntsville
Province: ON
Postal: P1H 2C5
General Phone: (705) 789-5541
General Fax: (705) 789-9381
General/National Adv. E-mail: production@metrolandnorthmedia.com
Editorial e-mail: news@metrolandnorthmedia.com
Primary Website: www.huntsvilleforester.com
Year Established: 1877
Delivery Methods: Mail Newsstand Racks
Areas Served - City/County or Portion Thereof, or Zip codes: Canada
Own Printing Facility?: Y
Commercial printers?: Y
Mechanical specifications: Type page 10 1/4 x 15; E - 6 cols, 1 11/20, between; A - 6 cols, 1 11/20, between; C - 6 cols, 1 11/20, between.
Published: Thur
Avg Paid Circ: 161
Avg Free Circ: 9177
Audit By: CMCA
Audit Date: 31.03.2016
Personnel: Bill Allen (Pub./Gen. Mgr.); Andrew Allen (Adv. Mgr.); Tamara De la Vega (News Ed.); Jack Tynan
Parent company (for newspapers): Metroland Media Group Ltd.; Torstar

PUBLICATION NAME

Huntsville/muskoka Advance
Street Address: 11 Main St. W ,
Province: ON
Postal: P1H 2C5
Country: Canada
Mailing address: 11 Main St. W
Mailing city: Huntsville
Province: ON
Postal: P1H 2C5
General Phone: (705) 789-5541
General Fax: (705) 789-9381
General/National Adv. E-mail: production@huntsvilleforester.com; news@huntsvilleforester.com
Primary Website: www.huntsvilleforester.com
Commercial printers?: Y
Mechanical specifications: Type page 10 1/4 x 15; E - 6 cols, 1 11/20, between; A - 6 cols, 1 11/20, between.
Published: Sun
Avg Paid Circ: 7100
Avg Free Circ: 23038
Audit By: Sworn/Estimate/Non-Audited
Audit Date: 12.07.2019
Personnel: Joe Anderson (Regl. Pub.); Micheal Hill (Adv. Mgr.); Brenda McGary (Circ. Mgr.); Bruce Hickey (Ed.); Paula Ashby (Prodn. Mgr.)

IGNACE

PUBLICATION NAME

Driftwood Enterprises
Street Address: 153 Balsam ,
Province: ON
Postal: P0T 1T0
Country: Canada
Mailing address: 153 Balsam
Mailing city: Ignace
Province: ON
Postal: P0T 1T0
General Phone: (807) 934-6482
Year Established: 1978
Areas Served - City/County or Portion Thereof, or Zip codes: Canada
Published: Wed
Avg Paid Circ: 303
Audit By: CMCA
Audit Date: 31.12.2015

INDIAN HEAD

PUBLICATION NAME

Indian Head-wolseley News
Street Address: 508 Grand Ave. ,
Province: SK
Postal: S0G 2K0
Country: Canada
Mailing address: PO Box 70
Mailing city: Indian Head
Province: SK
Postal: S0G 2K0
General Phone: (306) 695-3565
General Fax: (306) 695-3448
General/National Adv. E-mail: ihwnews@sasktel.net
Areas Served - City/County or Portion Thereof, or Zip codes: Canada
Commercial printers?: Y
Mechanical specifications: Type page 10 1/4 x 15.
Published: Thur
Avg Paid Circ: 938
Avg Free Circ: 20
Audit By: CMCA
Audit Date: 29.02.2016
Personnel: Jodi Gendron (Pub.); Kerri McCabe (Circ. Mgr.); Marcel Gendron (Ed.)

INNISFAIL

PUBLICATION NAME

Innisfail Province
Street Address: 5036 - 48th St. ,
Province: AB
Postal: T4G 1M2
Country: Canada
Mailing address: 5036 - 48th St.
Mailing city: Innisfail
Province: AB
Postal: T4G 1M2
General Phone: (403) 227-3477
General Fax: (403) 227-3330
Display Adv. E-mail: ddemers@innisfail.greatwest.ca
Editorial e-mail: jbachusky@innisfail.greatwest.ca
Primary Website: www.innisfailprovince.ca
Year Established: 1905
Delivery Methods: Mail Carrier
Areas Served - City/County or Portion Thereof, or Zip codes: Innisfail Alberta Canada
Published: Tues
Avg Paid Circ: 7
Avg Free Circ: 8240
Audit By: VAC
Audit Date: 31.08.2018
Personnel: Brent Spilak (Pub/Adv. Mgr.); Johnnie Bachusky (Ed)
Parent company (for newspapers): Glacier Media Group; Great West Newspapers LP

INVERMERE

PUBLICATION NAME

Invermere Valley Echo
Street Address: 1008-8th Avenue , #8
Province: BC
Postal: V0A 1K0
Country: Canada
Mailing address: PO Box 70
Mailing city: Invermere
Province: BC
Postal: V0A 1K0
General Phone: (250) 341-6299
General/National Adv. E-mail: general@invermerevalleyecho.com
Display Adv. E-mail: advertising@invermerevalleyecho.com
Editorial e-mail: editor@invermerevalleyecho.com
Primary Website: www.invermerevalleyecho.com
Year Established: 1956
Delivery Methods: Mail Newsstand
Areas Served - City/County or Portion Thereof, or Zip codes: n/a
Published: Wed
Avg Free Circ: 488
Audit By: VAC
Audit Date: 30.06.2016
Personnel: Dean Midyette (Pub.); Nicole Trigg (Ed.); Amanda Nason (Adv. Sales)
Parent company (for newspapers): Torstar

PUBLICATION NAME

The Columbia Valley Pioneer
Street Address: #8, 1008-8th Avenue ,
Province: BC
Postal: V0A 1K0
Country: Canada
Mailing address: PO Box 868
Mailing city: Invermere
Province: BC

Community Newspapers in Canada

III-543

Postal: V0A 1K0
General Phone: (250) 341-6299
General Fax: (855) 377-0312
General/National Adv. E-mail: info@cv-pioneer.com
Display Adv. E-mail: ads@columbiavalleypioneer.com
Classified Adv. e-mail: info@columbiavalleypioneer.com
Editorial e-mail: news@columbiavalleypioneer.com
Primary Website: www.columbiavalleypioneer.com
Year Established: 2004
Delivery Methods: Newsstand Racks
Areas Served - City/County or Portion Thereof, or Zip codes: Spillimacheen, Edgewater, Radium Hot Springs, Invermere, Panorama, Windermere, Fairmont Hot Springs, Canal Flats
Published: Fri
Avg Paid Circ: 499
Avg Free Circ: 6238
Audit By: VAC
Audit Date: 31.03.2016
Personnel: Steve Hubrecht (Reporter); Dean Midyette (Advertising Sales); Emily Rawbon (Graphic design); Nicole Trigg (Ed.); Amanda Murray (Admin.); Eric Elliott (Reporter)
Parent company (for newspapers): Misko Publishing

INVERNESS

PUBLICATION NAME

The Inverness Oran
Street Address: 15767 Central Avenue ,
Province: NS
Postal: B0E 1N0
Country: USA
Mailing address: PO Box 100
Mailing city: Inverness
Province: NS
Postal: B0E 1N0
General Phone: (902) 258-2253
General Fax: (902) 258-2632
Editorial e-mail: editor@oran.ca
Primary Website: www.oran.ca
Year Established: 1976
Areas Served - City/County or Portion Thereof, or Zip codes: Inverness
Published: Wed
Avg Paid Circ: 16
Avg Free Circ: 54
Audit By: VAC
Audit Date: 30.09.2016
Personnel: Rankin MacDonald (Ed.)

IQALUIT

PUBLICATION NAME

Nunatsiaq News
Street Address: Po Box 8 ,
Province: NU
Postal: X0A 0H0
Country: Canada
Mailing address: PO Box 8
Mailing city: Iqaluit
Province: NU
Postal: X0A 0H0
General Phone: (867) 979-5357
General Fax: (867) 979-4763
Advertising Phone: (800) 263-1452
Advertising Fax: (800) 417-2474
General/National Adv. E-mail: adsnunatsiaqonline.ca
Display Adv. E-mail: ads@nunatsiaqonline.ca
Editorial e-mail: editor@nunatsiaq.com
Primary Website: www.nunatsiaq.com
Year Established: 1973
Areas Served - City/County or Portion Thereof, or Zip codes: Nunavut
Mechanical specifications: Type page 10 5/16 x 13 3/4; E - 6 cols, 1 7/12, between; A - 6 cols, 1 7/12, between; C - 6 cols, 1 7/12, between.
Published: Fri
Avg Free Circ: 5388

Audit By: VAC
Audit Date: 30.06.2016
Personnel: Steven Roberts (Pub.); Bill McConkey (Adv. Mgr.); Jim Bell (Ed.)

IROQUOIS FALLS A

PUBLICATION NAME

The Enterprise
Street Address: 441 Main Street ,
Province: ON
Postal: P0K 1G0
Country: Canada
Mailing address: P.O. Box 834
Mailing city: Iroquois Falls A
Province: ON
Postal: P0K 1G0
General Phone: (705) 232-4081
General Fax: (705) 232-4235
General/National Adv. E-mail: irofalls@ntl.sympatico.ca
Display Adv. E-mail: news@theenterprise.ca
Classified Adv. e-mail: news@theenterprise.ca
Editorial e-mail: editor@theenterprise.ca
Year Established: 1963
Delivery Methods: Mail
Areas Served - City/County or Portion Thereof, or Zip codes: Canada
Published: Thur
Avg Paid Circ: 1491
Avg Free Circ: 107
Audit By: CMCA
Audit Date: 31.03.2018
Personnel: William C. Cavell (Pub); Tory Delaurier (Adv. Mgr.)

ITUNA

PUBLICATION NAME

The Ituna News
Street Address: 214 1st Avenue N.e. ,
Province: SK
Postal: S0A 1N0
Country: Canada
Mailing address: PO Box 413
Mailing city: Ituna
Province: SK
Postal: S0A 1N0
General Phone: (306) 795-2412
General Fax: (306) 795-3621
General/National Adv. E-mail: news.ituna@sasktel.net
Primary Website: www.ituna.ca
Areas Served - City/County or Portion Thereof, or Zip codes: Canada
Published: Mon
Avg Paid Circ: 578
Avg Free Circ: 1
Audit By: CMCA
Audit Date: 31.12.2015
Personnel: Bob Johnson (Prodn. Mgr.); Heidi Spilchuk (Ed)

JASPER

PUBLICATION NAME

The Fitzhugh
Street Address: 626 Connaught Dr. ,
Province: AB
Postal: T0E 1E0
Country: Canada
Mailing address: PO Box 428
Mailing city: Jasper
Province: AB
Postal: T0E 1E0
General Phone: (780) 852-4888
General Fax: (780) 852-4858
Display Adv. E-mail: advertising@fitzhugh.ca
Classified Adv. e-mail: advertising@fitzhugh.ca
Editorial e-mail: editor@fitzhugh.ca
Primary Website: www.fitzhugh.ca
Year Established: 2005
Areas Served - City/County or Portion Thereof, or Zip codes: Jasper
Published: Thur
Avg Paid Circ: 1156

Avg Free Circ: 3359
Audit By: VAC
Audit Date: 31.07.2016
Personnel: Matt Figueira (Sales); Jeremy Derksen (Pub.); Mishelle Menzies (Prod.); Nicole Veerman (Ed.)
Parent company (for newspapers): Jasper Media Group

JOHNSTOWN

PUBLICATION NAME

Manotick Messenger
Street Address: 3201 County Road 2. ,
Province: ON
Postal: ON K0E 1T0
Country: Canada
Mailing address: Box 567
Mailing city: Manotick
Province: ON
Postal: K4M 1A5
General Phone: (613) 692-6000
General Fax: (616) 692-3758
Display Adv. E-mail: advert@bellnet.ca
Editorial e-mail: newsfile@bellnet.ca
Primary Website: www.manotickmessenger.on.ca
Areas Served - City/County or Portion Thereof, or Zip codes: Canada
Published: Thur
Avg Free Circ: 9503
Audit By: CMCA
Audit Date: 31.03.2016
Personnel: Jeff Morris (Pub.); Gary Coulombe (Adv. Rep.)

JOLIETTE

PUBLICATION NAME

Action Mercredi
Street Address: 342, Beaudry Nord ,
Province: QC
Postal: J6E 6A6
Country: Canada
Mailing address: rue Beaudry Nord
Mailing city: Joliette
Province: QC
Postal: J6E 6A6
General Phone: (450) 759-3664
General Fax: (450) 759-3190
General/National Adv. E-mail: infolanaudiere@tc.tc
Primary Website: www.laction.com
Areas Served - City/County or Portion Thereof, or Zip codes: Canada
Published: Wed`Sun
Avg Paid Circ: 9
Avg Free Circ: 51680
Audit By: CCAB
Audit Date: 30.09.2012
Personnel: Benoit Bazinet; Benoit Bazinet

PUBLICATION NAME

L'action
Street Address: 342 Beaudry N. ,
Province: QC
Postal: J6E 6A6
Country: Canada
Mailing address: 342 Beaudry N.
Mailing city: Joliette
Province: QC
Postal: J6E 6A6
General Phone: (450) 759-3664
Advertising Phone: (450) 752-0447
Advertising Fax: (450) 759-3190
Editorial Phone: (450) 759-3664
Editorial Fax: (450) 759-3190
General/National Adv. E-mail: infolanaudiere@tc.tc
Display Adv. E-mail: infolanaudiere@tc.tc
Primary Website: www.laction.com
Year Established: 1973
Areas Served - City/County or Portion Thereof, or Zip codes: Canada
Mechanical specifications: Type page 10 1/2 x 14 1/2; E - 8 cols, between.

Published: Wed
Avg Free Circ: 19450
Audit By: CCAB
Audit Date: 31.03.2014
Personnel: Norman Harvey (Sales Rep.); Benoit Bazinet (Pub.); Chantal Proulx (Prodn. Mgr.); Natalie Lariviere (Pres.); Carole Bonin (Mgr.); Sebastien Nadeau (Regl. Dir.); Harvey Norman (Sales Mgr.); Andre Lafreniere (Ed.); Francine Rainville (Ed.); Chantal Troulx (Prodn. Mgr.)
Parent company (for newspapers): Transcontinental Media

PUBLICATION NAME

Le Journal De Joliette
Street Address: 1075 Blvd Firestone 5e Etage ,
Province: QC
Postal: J6E 6X6
Country: Canada
Mailing address: 1075 Blvd Firestone 5E Etage
Mailing city: Joliette
Province: QC
Postal: J6E 6X6
General Phone: (450) 960-2424
General Fax: (450) 960-2626
Advertising Phone: (450) 960-2424
Advertising Fax: (450) 960-2626
Editorial Phone: (450) 960-2424
Editorial Fax: (450) 960-2626
General/National Adv. E-mail: janique.duguay@quebecormedia.com
Display Adv. E-mail: johanne.roussy2@quebecormedia.com
Editorial e-mail: janique.duguay@quebecormedia.com
Primary Website: www.lejournaldejoliette.ca
Year Established: 1992
Delivery Methods: Mail`Racks
Areas Served - City/County or Portion Thereof, or Zip codes: Canada
Mechanical specifications: Type page 14 1/4 x 10 1/4; E - 8 cols, 1 1/4, between; A - 8 cols, 1 1/4, between; C - 8 cols, 1 1/4, between.
Published: Wed
Avg Free Circ: 60740
Audit By: CCAB
Audit Date: 30.09.2012
Personnel: Janique Duguay (Ed.); Patricia Beaulieu (Regional Director)
Parent company (for newspapers): Quebecor Communications, Inc.

PUBLICATION NAME

Le Regional
Street Address: 342 Beaugry N. St. ,
Province: QC
Postal: J6E 6A6
Country: Canada
Mailing address: 342 Beaugry N. St.
Mailing city: Joliette
Province: QC
Postal: J6E 6A6
General Phone: (450) 759-3664
General Fax: (450) 759-9828
Primary Website: http://www.le-regional.ca/
Published: Wed
Avg Free Circ: 64096
Audit By: ODC
Audit Date: 13.12.2011
Personnel: Benoit Bazinet (Pub.)

KAHNAWAKE

PUBLICATION NAME

The Eastern Door
Street Address: P.o. Box 1170 ,
Province: QC
Postal: J0L 1B0
Country: Canada
Mailing address: P.O. Box 1170
Mailing city: Kahnawake
Province: QC
Postal: J0L 1B0
General Phone: (450) 635-3050
General Fax: (450) 635-8479
General/National Adv. E-mail: reception@

easterndoor.com
Primary Website: www.easterndoor.com
Areas Served - City/County or Portion Thereof, or Zip codes: Canada
Published: Fri
Avg Paid Circ: 1020
Avg Free Circ: 81
Audit By: CMCA
Audit Date: 30.06.2016
Personnel: Steve Bonspiel (Ed./Pub.)

KAMLOOPS

PUBLICATION NAME

Kamloops This Week
Street Address: 1365b Dalhousie Dr. ,
Province: BC
Postal: V2C 5P6
Country: Canada
Mailing address: 1365B Dalhousie Dr.
Mailing city: Kamloops
Province: BC
Postal: V2C 5P6
General Phone: (250) 374-7467
General Fax: (250) 374-1033
Editorial Phone: (250) 374-7467
General/National Adv. E-mail: editor@kamloopsthisweek.com; ktw@kamloopsthisweek.com
Display Adv. E-mail: sales@kamloopsthisweek.com
Editorial e-mail: editor@kamloopsthisweek.com
Primary Website: kamloopsthisweek.com
Year Established: 1988
Delivery Methods: Mail`Newsstand`Carrier`Racks
Areas Served - City/County or Portion Thereof, or Zip codes: Canada
Own Printing Facility?: Y
Published: Tues`Thur`Fri
Avg Paid Circ: 0
Avg Free Circ: 30602
Audit By: CCAB
Audit Date: 23.11.2017
Personnel: Kelly Hall; Chris Foulds (Pub & Ed)
Parent company (for newspapers): Thompson River Publications

KAPUSKASING

PUBLICATION NAME

The Northern Times
Street Address: 51 Riverside Dr ,
Province: ON
Postal: P5N 1A7
Country: Canada
Mailing address: 51 Riverside Dr
Mailing city: Kapuskasing
Province: ON
Postal: P5N 1A7
General Phone: (705) 335-2283 ext. 222
General Fax: (705) 337-1222
Advertising Phone: (705)-335-2283 ext. 230
Advertising Fax: (705) 337-1222
Editorial Phone: (705)-335-2283 ext. 223
Editorial Fax: (705) 337-1222
General/National Adv. E-mail: wayne.major@sunmedia.ca
Display Adv. E-mail: wayne.major@sunmedia.ca
Editorial e-mail: kevin.anderson@sunmedia.ca
Primary Website: www.kapuskasingtimes.com
Year Established: 1961
Delivery Methods: Mail`Newsstand`Carrier
Areas Served - City/County or Portion Thereof, or Zip codes: Canada
Own Printing Facility?: Y
Commercial printers?: Y
Mechanical specifications: Type page 9 x 12.25; E - 9 cols, 1 1/5, 1/8 between; A - 9 cols, 1 1/5, 1/8 between; C - 9 cols, 1 1/5, 1/8 between.
Published: Wed
Avg Paid Circ: 1784
Audit By: CMCA
Audit Date: 28.02.2014
Personnel: Wayne Major (Pub.); Sylvie Genier (Senior Sales Representative); Kevin Anderson (Managing Ed.)
Parent company (for newspapers): Postmedia Network Inc.; Quebecor Communications, Inc.

PUBLICATION NAME

The Weekender
Street Address: 51 Riverside Dr ,
Province: ON
Postal: P5N 1A7
Country: Canada
Mailing address: 51 Riverside Dr
Mailing city: Kapuskasing
Province: ON
Postal: P5N 1A7
General Phone: (705) 335-2283 ext. 222
General Fax: (705) 337-1222
Advertising Phone: (705) 335-2283 ext. 230
Advertising Fax: (705) 337-1222
Editorial Phone: (705) 335-2283 ext. 223
Editorial Fax: (705) 337-1222
General/National Adv. E-mail: wayne.major@sunmedia.ca
Display Adv. E-mail: wayne.major@sunmedia.ca
Editorial e-mail: kevin.anderson@sunmedia.ca
Primary Website: www.kapuskasingtimes.com
Year Established: 1961
Delivery Methods: Mail`Newsstand`Carrier
Areas Served - City/County or Portion Thereof, or Zip codes: P5N, POL
Mechanical specifications: Type page 9 x 12.25; E - 9 cols, 1 1/5, 1/8 between; A - 9 cols, 1 1/5, 1/8 between; C - 9 cols, 1 1/5, 1/8 between.
Published: Thur
Avg Free Circ: 8486
Audit By: CMCA
Audit Date: 30.06.2016
Personnel: Wayne Major (Pub.); Sylvie Genier (Senior Sales Representative); Kevin Anderson (Managing Ed.)
Parent company (for newspapers): Postmedia Network Inc.; Quebecor Communications, Inc.

KELOWNA

PUBLICATION NAME

Kelowna Capital News
Street Address: 2495 Enterprise Way ,
Province: BC
Postal: V1X 7K2
Country: Canada
Mailing address: 2495 Enterprise Way
Mailing city: Kelowna
Province: BC
Postal: V1X 7K2
General Phone: (250) 763-3212
General Fax: (250) 862-5275
General/National Adv. E-mail: candy@blackpress.ca
Display Adv. E-mail: karen.hill@blackpress.ca
Classified Adv. e-mail: karen.hill@blackpress.ca
Editorial e-mail: karen.hill@blackpress.ca
Primary Website: kelownacapnews.com
Year Established: 1930
Delivery Methods: Mail`Newsstand`Carrier`Racks
Areas Served - City/County or Portion Thereof, or Zip codes: Canada
Own Printing Facility?: Y
Commercial printers?: Y
Mechanical specifications: Type page 10 x 15; E - 6 cols, 1 31/60, 1/6 between; A - 6 cols, 1 31/60, 1/6 between; C - 6 cols, 1 31/60, 1/6 between.
Published: Tues`Thur`Fri
Avg Free Circ: 42292
Audit By: AAM
Audit Date: 31.03.2019
Personnel: Karen Hill (Pub.); Nigel Lark (Adv. Mgr.); Gary Jhonston (Sales Mgr.); Glenn Beaudry (Circ. Mgr.); Tessa Ringness (Prodn. Mgr.); Kevin Parnell (Mng. Ed.)
Parent company (for newspapers): Black Press Group Ltd.

PUBLICATION NAME

Lake Country Calendar
Street Address: 2495 Enterprise Way ,
Province: BC
Postal: V1X 7K2
Country: Canada
General Phone: (250) 763-3212
General Fax: (250) 386-2624
Display Adv. E-mail: ads4web@blackpress.ca
Editorial e-mail: newsroom@lakecountrynews.net
Primary Website: www.lakecountrycalendar.net
Year Established: 2001
Areas Served - City/County or Portion Thereof, or Zip codes: Lake Country
Published: Wed
Avg Paid Circ: 306
Avg Free Circ: 3779
Audit By: Sworn/Estimate/Non-Audited
Audit Date: 12.07.2019
Personnel: Barry Gerding (Ed.); Jonathan Lawson (Trafficking Coordinator); Kolby Solinsky (Online Editor); Mark Walker (Director of Sales and Marketing)
Parent company (for newspapers): Torstar

KENORA

PUBLICATION NAME

Lake Of The Woods Enterprise
Street Address: 33 Main St. ,
Province: ON
Postal: P9N 3X7
Country: Canada
Mailing address: PO Box 1620
Mailing city: Kenora
Province: ON
Postal: P9N 3X7
General Phone: (807) 468-5555
General Fax: (807) 468-4318
General/National Adv. E-mail: lotwenterprise@bowes.com
Primary Website: www.lotwenterprise.com
Year Established: 2003
Areas Served - City/County or Portion Thereof, or Zip codes: Canada
Own Printing Facility?: Y
Commercial printers?: N
Mechanical specifications: Type page 10 1/4 x 14 1/4; E - 6 cols, 1 9/16, 1/6 between; A - 6 cols, 1 9/16, 1/6 between; C - 6 cols, 1 9/16, 1/6 between.
Published: Thur
Avg Paid Circ: 122
Avg Free Circ: 7771
Audit By: CMCA
Audit Date: 31.08.2015
Personnel: Ted Weiss (Adv. Mgr.); Reg Clayton (Reg. Managing Ed.)
Parent company (for newspapers): Postmedia Network Inc.

KENTVILLE

PUBLICATION NAME

Register
Street Address: 28 Aberdeen St , Suite 6
Province: NS
Postal: B4N 2N1
Country: Canada
Mailing address: Box 430
Mailing city: Kentville
Province: NS
Postal: B4N 3X4
General Phone: (902) 538-3189
General Fax: (902) 681-0923
Display Adv. E-mail: events@kentvilleadvertiser.ca
Primary Website: http://www.kingscountynews.ca/
Areas Served - City/County or Portion Thereof, or Zip codes: Canada
Own Printing Facility?: Y
Commercial printers?: Y
Mechanical specifications: Type page 12 1/2 x 21; E - 7 cols, 1/8 between; A - 7 cols, 1/8 between; C - 7 cols, 1/8 between.
Published: Thur
Avg Paid Circ: 3392
Avg Free Circ: 47
Audit By: CMCA
Audit Date: 31.07.2014
Personnel: Fred Fiander (Pub.)
Parent company (for newspapers): Transcontinental Media

PUBLICATION NAME

The Advertiser
Street Address: 28 Aberdeen St , Suite 6
Province: NS
Postal: B4N 2N1
Country: Canada
Mailing address: Box 430
Mailing city: Kentville
Province: NS
Postal: B4N 3X4
General Phone: (902) 681-2121
General Fax: (902) 681-0830
General/National Adv. E-mail: ffiander@thevanguard.ca
Display Adv. E-mail: events@kentvilleadvertiser.ca
Editorial e-mail: ffiander@thevanguard.ca
Primary Website: http://www.kingscountynews.ca/
Areas Served - City/County or Portion Thereof, or Zip codes: Canada
Commercial printers?: Y
Mechanical specifications: Type page 10 1/2 x 15 3/4; E - 6 cols, 1/4, 1/8 between; A - 6 cols, 1/8 between; C - 6 cols, 1/8 between.
Published: Tues
Avg Paid Circ: 3189
Avg Free Circ: 49
Audit By: CMCA
Audit Date: 31.03.2014
Personnel: Fred Fiander (Pub.)
Parent company (for newspapers): Transcontinental Media

KEREMEOS

PUBLICATION NAME

Keremeos Review
Street Address: 605 7th Avenue ,
Province: BC
Postal: V0X 1N0
Country: Canada
Mailing address: Box 130
Mailing city: Keremeos
Province: BC
Postal: V0X 1N0
General Phone: (250) 499-2653
General Fax: (250) 499-2645
General/National Adv. E-mail: dkendall@blackpress.ca
Display Adv. E-mail: publisher@keremeosreview.com
Classified Adv. e-mail: publisher@keremeosreview.com
Primary Website: www.keremeosreview.com
Year Established: 1998
Areas Served - City/County or Portion Thereof, or Zip codes: Keremeos
Published: Thur
Avg Paid Circ: 889
Avg Free Circ: 51
Audit By: VAC
Audit Date: 31.03.2016
Personnel: Don Kendall (Pub.); Tara Bowie (Ed.); Andrea DeMeer (Assoc. Pub.); Sandi Nolan (Adv. Rep.)
Parent company (for newspapers): Torstar

KESWICK

PUBLICATION NAME

The Georgina Advocate
Street Address: 184 Simcoe Ave. ,
Province: ON
Postal: L4P 2H7
Country: Canada
Mailing address: 184 Simcoe Ave.
Mailing city: Keswick

Community Newspapers in Canada

III-545

Province: ON
Postal: L4P 2H7
General Phone: (905) 476-7753
General Fax: (905) 476-5785
General/National Adv. E-mail: admin@georginaadvocate.com
Primary Website: yorkregion.com
Areas Served - City/County or Portion Thereof, or Zip codes: Canada
Own Printing Facility?: Y
Commercial printers?: Y
Mechanical specifications: Type page 10 3/8 x 14; E - 9 cols, 1 1/16, 1/8 between; A - 9 cols, 1 1/16, 1/8 between; C - 9 cols, 1 1/16, 1/8 between.
Published: Thur
Avg Free Circ: 16800
Audit By: COAD
Audit Date: 31.12.2017
Personnel: Ian Proudfoot (Pub.); Robert Lazurko (Bus. Mgr.); Neil Moore (Adv. Mgr.); Debora Kelly (Ed. in Chief); Tracy Kibble (Ed.)
Parent company (for newspapers): Metroland Media Group Ltd.

KILLAM

PUBLICATION NAME

The Community Press
Street Address: 4919 - 50 St., ,
Province: AB
Postal: T0B 2L0
Country: Canada
Mailing address: PO Box 178
Mailing city: Killam
Province: AB
Postal: T0B 2L0
General Phone: (780) 385-6693
General Fax: (780) 385-3107
Advertising Phone: (780)-385-6693
Display Adv. E-mail: ads@thecommunitypress.com
Classified Adv. e-mail: ads@thecommunitypress.com
Editorial e-mail: news@thecommunitypress.com
Primary Website: www.thecommunitypress.com
Year Established: 1908
Delivery Methods: Mail`Newsstand`Racks
Areas Served - City/County or Portion Thereof, or Zip codes: All of Flagstaff County, Alberta: Total municipalities covered: Bawlf, Daysland, Strome, Killam, Sedgewick, Lougheed, Hardisty, Amisk, Hughenden, Czar, Forestburg, Galahad, Heisler, Alliance
Published: Wed
Avg Paid Circ: 2000
Avg Free Circ: 500
Audit By: CMCA
Audit Date: 31.12.2016
Personnel: Leslie Cholowsky (Editor); Eric Anderson (Publisher/Sales/Production Manager); Jae Robbins (Sales); Ally Anderson (Production Manager)
Parent company (for newspapers): Caribou Publishing

KILLARNEY

PUBLICATION NAME

Killarney Guide
Street Address: 336 Park St. ,
Province: MB
Postal: R0K 1G0
Country: Canada
Mailing address: PO Box 670
Mailing city: Killarney
Province: MB
Postal: R0K 1G0
General Phone: (204) 523-4611
General Fax: (204) 523-4445
General/National Adv. E-mail: news@killarneyguide.ca
Display Adv. E-mail: ads@killarneyguide.ca
Editorial e-mail: news@killarneyguide.ca
Primary Website: http://new.killarneyguide.ca/
Areas Served - City/County or Portion Thereof, or Zip codes: R0K 1G0 and many more
Own Printing Facility?: Y

Commercial printers?: Y
Mechanical specifications: Type page 15 x 14 1/2; E - 6 cols, 1 7/12, 3/4 between; A - 6 cols, 1 7/12, 3/4 between; C - 6 cols, 1 7/12, 3/4 between.
Published: Fri
Avg Paid Circ: 56
Avg Free Circ: 134
Audit By: VAC
Audit Date: 30.06.2016
Personnel: Jay Struth (Ed.); Wendy Johnston (Adv. Mgr.); Iris Krahn (Circ Mgr)

KIMBERLEY

PUBLICATION NAME

The Kimberley Daily Bulletin
Street Address: 335 Spokane St. ,
Province: BC
Postal: V1A 1Y9
Country: Canada
Province: BC
General Phone: (250) 427-5333
General Fax: (250) 427-5336
Advertising Phone: (250) 427-5333
Advertising Fax: (250) 427-5336
Editorial Phone: (250) 427-5333
Editorial Fax: (250) 427-5336
General/National Adv. E-mail: sueb@blackpress.ca
Editorial e-mail: carolyn.grant@kimberleybulletin.com
Primary Website: www.kimberleybulletin.com
Year Established: 1936
Delivery Methods: Mail`Newsstand`Carrier
Areas Served - City/County or Portion Thereof, or Zip codes: Cranbrook, Kimberley and surrounding areas
Own Printing Facility?: Y
Mechanical specifications: Type page 10.25 x 14.00; E - 6 cols, 2 1/16, 1/8 between; A - 6 cols, 2 1/16, 1/8 between; C - 6 cols, 2 1/16, 1/8 between.
Published: Wed`Thur`Fri
Weekday Frequency: e
Avg Paid Circ: 3350
Avg Free Circ: 3350
Audit By: CMCA
Audit Date: 31.12.2015
Personnel: Zena Williams (Pub.); Carolyn Grant (Ed.); Nicole Koran
Parent company (for newspapers): Black Press Group Ltd.

KINCARDINE

PUBLICATION NAME

The Independent
Street Address: 840 Queen St. ,
Province: ON
Postal: N2Z 2Z4
Country: Canada
Mailing address: P.O. Box 1240
Mailing city: Kincardine
Province: ON
Postal: N2Z 2Z4
General Phone: (519) 396-3111
General Fax: (519) 396-3899
General/National Adv. E-mail: indepen@bmts.com
Primary Website: www.independent.on.ca
Year Established: 1975
Delivery Methods: Mail`Newsstand
Areas Served - City/County or Portion Thereof, or Zip codes: Canada
Own Printing Facility?: N
Commercial printers?: N
Mechanical specifications: Type page 10 1/4 x 15 1/2; E - 6 cols, 1 9/16, 1/6 between; A - 6 cols, 1 3/4, 1/6 between; C - 6 cols, 1 3/4, 1/6 between.
Published: Wed
Avg Paid Circ: 1906
Avg Free Circ: 82
Audit By: CMCA
Audit Date: 31.12.2015
Personnel: Eric Howald (Ed.)

PUBLICATION NAME

The Kincardine News
Street Address: 719 Queen St. ,
Province: ON
Postal: N2Z 1Z9
Country: Canada
Mailing address: 719 Queen St.
Mailing city: Kincardine
Province: ON
Postal: N2Z 1Z9
General Phone: (519) 396-2963
General Fax: (519) 396-6865
General/National Adv. E-mail: kincardine.sales@sunmedia.ca
Display Adv. E-mail: kincardine.sales@sunmedia.ca
Editorial e-mail: kincardine.news@sunmedia.ca
Primary Website: www.kincardinenews.com
Delivery Methods: Mail`Newsstand`Carrier`Racks
Areas Served - City/County or Portion Thereof, or Zip codes: Canada
Own Printing Facility?: Y
Mechanical specifications: Tabloid 10.333 x 11.4288
Published: Thur
Avg Paid Circ: 59
Avg Free Circ: 5787
Audit By: Sworn/Estimate/Non-Audited
Audit Date: 12.07.2019
Personnel: Troy Patterson (Ed.)
Parent company (for newspapers): Postmedia Network Inc.

KINDERSLEY

PUBLICATION NAME

Kindersley Clarion
Street Address: 919 Main St. ,
Province: SK
Postal: S0L 1S0
Country: Canada
Mailing address: PO Box 1150
Mailing city: Kindersley
Province: SK
Postal: S0L 1S0
General Phone: (306) 463-4611
General Fax: (306) 463-6505
General/National Adv. E-mail: editor.jamac@gmail.com
Display Adv. E-mail: ads.jamac@gmail.com
Classified Adv. e-mail: classifieds.jamac@gmail.com
Editorial e-mail: editor.jamac@gmail.com
Primary Website: theclarion.ca
Areas Served - City/County or Portion Thereof, or Zip codes: Kindersley
Own Printing Facility?: Y
Commercial printers?: Y
Mechanical specifications: Type page 13 4/5 x 21 2/5; E - 7 cols, between; A - 7 cols, between; C - 8 cols, between.
Published: Wed
Avg Paid Circ: 1238
Audit By: Sworn/Estimate/Non-Audited
Audit Date: 12.07.2019
Personnel: Stewart Crump (Pub.); Kevin Mcbain (Ed.); Laurie Kelly (Salesperson)
Parent company (for newspapers): Jamac Publishing

PUBLICATION NAME

Leader News
Street Address: 919 Main St. ,
Province: SK
Postal: S0L 1S0
Country: Canada
Mailing address: PO Box 1150
Mailing city: Kindersley
Province: SK
Postal: S0L 1S0
General Phone: (306) 463-4611
General Fax: (306) 463-6505
Display Adv. E-mail: editor.jamac@gmail.com
Areas Served - City/County or Portion Thereof, or Zip codes: Canada
Own Printing Facility?: Y

Published: Wed
Avg Paid Circ: 710
Audit By: CMCA
Audit Date: 28.02.2014
Personnel: Stewart Crump (Pub.); Barry Malindine (Adv. Mgr.); Kevin McBain (Ed.)
Parent company (for newspapers): Jamac Publishing

PUBLICATION NAME

West Central Crossroads
Street Address: 919 Main St. ,
Province: SK
Postal: S0L 1S0
Country: Canada
Mailing address: PO Box 1150
Mailing city: Kindersley
Province: SK
Postal: S0L 1S0
General Phone: (306) 463-4611
General Fax: (306) 463-6505
General/National Adv. E-mail: news_jamac@sasktel.net
Own Printing Facility?: Y
Commercial printers?: Y
Published: Fri
Avg Free Circ: 15160
Audit By: CMCA
Audit Date: 30.09.2016
Personnel: Stewart Crump (Pub.); Tim Crump (Ed.)
Parent company (for newspapers): Jamac Publishing

KINGSTON

PUBLICATION NAME

Frontenac Emc
Street Address: 375 Select Drive Unit 14 ,
Province: ON
Postal: K7M 8R1
Country: Canada
General Phone: (613) 546-8884
General Fax: (613) 546-3607
Primary Website: www.emcfrontenac.ca
Areas Served - City/County or Portion Thereof, or Zip codes: Canada
Published: Thur
Avg Free Circ: 8639
Audit By: CMCA
Audit Date: 28.02.2013
Personnel: Duncan Weir (Pub.)

PUBLICATION NAME

Kingston Heritage Emc
Street Address: 375 Select Dr. ,
Province: ON
Postal: K7M 8R1
Country: Canada
Mailing address: 375 Select Dr.
Mailing city: Kingston
Province: ON
Postal: K7M 8R1
General Phone: (613) 546-8885
Display Adv. E-mail: kdillon@theheritageemc.ca
Primary Website: www.insideottawavalley.com
Areas Served - City/County or Portion Thereof, or Zip codes: Canada
Published: Thur
Avg Free Circ: 45862
Audit By: CMCA
Audit Date: 30.06.2016
Personnel: Donna Glasspoole (Gen. Mgr.); Kate Lawrenence (Sales Coordinator)
Parent company (for newspapers): Metroland Media Group Ltd.

PUBLICATION NAME

Kingston This Week
Street Address: 18 St. Remy Place ,
Province: ON
Postal: K7M 6C4
Country: Canada
Mailing address: 18 St. Remy Place
Mailing city: Kingston

Province: ON
Postal: K7M 6C4
General Phone: (613) 389-7400
General Fax: (613) 389-7507
General/National Adv. E-mail: news@kingstonthisweek.com
Primary Website: www.kingstonthisweek.com
Areas Served - City/County or Portion Thereof, or Zip codes: Canada
Mechanical specifications: Type page 10 3/8 x 12 4/7; E - 9 cols, 1 1/16, between; A - 9 cols, 1 1/16, between; C - 9 cols, 1 1/16, between.
Published: Thur
Avg Free Circ: 48840
Audit By: CMCA
Audit Date: 31.03.2016
Personnel: Ron Drillen (Gen. Mgr.); Tracy Weaver (Mng. Ed.); Lynn Rees Lambert (News Ed.); Rob Mooy (Photo Ed.); Liza Nelson
Parent company (for newspapers): Quebecor Communications, Inc.

PUBLICATION NAME

The Frontenac Gazette
Street Address: 375 Select Dr., Ste. 14 ,
Province: ON
Postal: K7M 8R1
Country: Canada
Mailing address: 375 Select Dr., Ste. 14
Mailing city: Kingston
Province: ON
Postal: K7M 8R1
General Phone: (613) 546-8885
General Fax: (613) 546-3607
General/National Adv. E-mail: kingston@theritageemc.ca
Primary Website: www.whatsonkingston.com
Areas Served - City/County or Portion Thereof, or Zip codes: Canada
Published: Thur
Avg Free Circ: 8220
Audit By: CMCA
Audit Date: 30.06.2016
Personnel: Darryl Cembal (Pub.)
Parent company (for newspapers): Metroland Media Group Ltd.

PUBLICATION NAME

The Heritage
Street Address: 375 Select Dr., Unit 14 ,
Province: ON
Postal: K7M 8R1
Country: Canada
Mailing address: 375 Select Dr., Unit 14
Mailing city: Kingston
Province: ON
Postal: K7M 8R1
General Phone: (613) 546-8885
General Fax: (613) 546-3607
General/National Adv. E-mail: kingston@theheritageemc.ca
Primary Website: www.kingstonregion.com/kingstonregion
Areas Served - City/County or Portion Thereof, or Zip codes: Canada
Mechanical specifications: Type page 10 1/4 x 15; E - 6 cols, 1 9/16, 1/8 between; A - 6 cols, 1 9/16, 1/6 between; C - 6 cols, 1 9/16, 1/6 between.
Published: Thur
Avg Paid Circ: 12
Avg Free Circ: 38833
Audit By: Sworn/Estimate/Non-Audited
Audit Date: 12.07.2019
Personnel: Darryl Cembal (Ed.)

KINGSVILLE

PUBLICATION NAME

The Kingsville Reporter
Street Address: 17 Chestnut St. ,
Province: ON
Postal: N9Y 1J9
Country: Canada
Mailing address: 17 Chestnut St.
Mailing city: Kingsville
Province: ON
Postal: N9Y 1J9
General Phone: (519) 733-2211
General Fax: (519) 733-6464
General/National Adv. E-mail: kingsvillereporter@canwest.com
Display Adv. E-mail: rsims@postmedia.com
Delivery Methods: Mail`Newsstand
Areas Served - City/County or Portion Thereof, or Zip codes: Canada
Own Printing Facility?: Y
Commercial printers?: Y
Mechanical specifications: Type page 10 1/4 x 15; E - 6 cols, 1 5/9, between; A - 6 cols, 1 5/9, between; C - 6 cols, 1 5/9, between.
Published: Tues
Avg Paid Circ: 1107
Avg Free Circ: 7
Audit By: CMCA
Audit Date: 30.06.2016
Personnel: Rita Sims (Adv. Mgr.); Nelson Santos (News Ed.); Joyce Pearce (Reception); Steve l'Anson (Associate News Editor)
Parent company (for newspapers): Postmedia Network Inc.

KIPLING

PUBLICATION NAME

Kipling Citizen
Street Address: #4 - 207 - 6th Avenue ,
Province: SK
Postal: S0G 2S0
Country: Canada
Mailing address: PO Box 329
Mailing city: Kipling
Province: SK
Postal: S0G 2S0
General Phone: (306) 736-2535
General Fax: (306) 736-8445
Advertising Phone: (306) 736-2535
Advertising Fax: (306) 736-8445
Editorial Phone: (306) 736-2535
Editorial Fax: (306) 736-8445
General/National Adv. E-mail: thecitizen@sasktel.net
Display Adv. E-mail: thecitizen@sasktel.net
Classified Adv. e-mail: thecitizen@sasktel.net
Editorial e-mail: thecitizen@sasktel.net
Year Established: 1936
Delivery Methods: Mail`Newsstand
Areas Served - City/County or Portion Thereof, or Zip codes: Canada
Own Printing Facility?: N
Commercial printers?: N
Mechanical specifications: Type page 9.83 x 15.7; 6 cols, .15 between columns
Published: Fri
Avg Paid Circ: 730
Avg Free Circ: 13
Audit By: CMCA
Audit Date: 03.11.2017
Personnel: Laura Kish (Gen. Mgr.); Connie Schwalm (Reporter); Sean Choo-Foo (Sales Representative)
Parent company (for newspapers): Glacier Media Group

KIRKLAND LAKE

PUBLICATION NAME

Northern News This Week (Kirkland Lake)
Street Address: Eight Duncan Ave. ,
Province: ON
Postal: P2N 3L4
Country: Canada
Mailing address: PO Box 1030
Mailing city: Kirkland Lake
Province: ON
Postal: P2N 3L4
General Phone: (705) 567-5321
General Fax: (705) 567-6162
Advertising Fax: (705) 567-5377
Editorial Fax: (705) 567-6162
General/National Adv. E-mail: news@northernnews.ca
Display Adv. E-mail: display@northernnews.ca
Primary Website: www.northernnews.ca
Mechanical specifications: Type page 13 x 21 1/2; E - 6 cols, 2 1/16, 1/8 between; A - 6 cols, 2 1/16, 1/8 between; C - 9 cols, 1 1/2, 1/8 between.
Published: Mon`Wed`Fri
Weekday Frequency: e
Saturday Frequency: e
Avg Paid Circ: 3122
Audit By: Sworn/Estimate/Non-Audited
Audit Date: 12.07.2019
Personnel: Tony Howell (Circ. Mgr.); Joe O'Grady (Managing Ed.); Jeff Wilkinson (Sports Ed.); Lisa Wilson (Adv. Dir.)
Parent company (for newspapers): Postmedia Network Inc.; Quebecor Communications, Inc.

KITCHENER

PUBLICATION NAME

Kitchener Post
Street Address: 630 Riverbend Dr Unit 104 , Unit 104
Province: ON
Postal: N2K 3S2
Mailing address: 630 Riverbend Dr Unit 104
Mailing city: Kitchener
Province: ON
Postal: N2K 3S2
General Phone: (519) 579-7166
General Fax: (519) 579-2029
Primary Website: www.kitchenerpost.ca
Areas Served - City/County or Portion Thereof, or Zip codes: Canada
Published: Fri
Avg Free Circ: 58770
Audit By: CMCA
Audit Date: 30.06.2016
Personnel: Bob Vrbanac (Managing Ed.)
Parent company (for newspapers): Metroland Media Group Ltd.

KITIMAT

PUBLICATION NAME

Northern Sentinel - Kitimat
Street Address: 626 Enterprise Ave. ,
Province: BC
Postal: V8C 2E4
Country: Canada
Mailing address: 626 Enterprise Ave.
Mailing city: Kitimat
Province: BC
Postal: V8C 2E4
General Phone: (250) 632-6144
General Fax: (250) 639-9373
General/National Adv. E-mail: publisher@northernsentinel.com
Display Adv. E-mail: advertising@northernsentinel.com
Primary Website: www.northernsentinel.com
Year Established: 1954
Delivery Methods: Mail`Newsstand`Carrier`Racks
Areas Served - City/County or Portion Thereof, or Zip codes: Canada
Own Printing Facility?: Y
Commercial printers?: Y
Mechanical specifications: Type page 10 1/4 x 14 1/2; E - 7 cols, 1 7/12, between; A - 7 cols, 1 7/12, between; C - 7 cols, 1 7/12, between.
Published: Wed
Avg Paid Circ: 439
Avg Free Circ: 248
Audit By: VAC
Audit Date: 31.03.2016
Personnel: Louisa Genzale (Publisher); Sarah Campbell; Devyn Ens (Editor/Reporter); Johnsen Misty (Circulation)
Parent company (for newspapers): Black Press Group Ltd.

KNOWLTON

PUBLICATION NAME

Brome County News
Street Address: 5 B Rue Victoria ,
Province: QC
Postal: J0E 1V0
Country: Canada
Mailing address: 5 B Rue Victoria
Mailing city: Knowlton
Province: QC
Postal: J0E 1V0
General Phone: (450) 242-1188
General Fax: (450) 243-5155
General/National Adv. E-mail: newsroom@sherbrookerecord.com
Areas Served - City/County or Portion Thereof, or Zip codes: J0E 1V0
Own Printing Facility?: Y
Published: Tues
Avg Free Circ: 10000
Audit By: Sworn/Estimate/Non-Audited
Audit Date: 12.07.2019
Personnel: Ken Wells (Pub.); Sharon McCully (Ed.); Richard Lessard (Prodn. Mgr.)

LA MALBAIE

PUBLICATION NAME

Hebdo Charlevoisien
Street Address: 53, Rue John-nairne Ste. 100 ,
Province: QC
Postal: G5A 1L8
Country: Canada
Mailing address: 53, rue John-Nairne
Mailing city: La Malbaie
Province: QC
Postal: G5A 1L8
General Phone: (418) 665-1299
General Fax: (418) 453-3349
General/National Adv. E-mail: journal@hebdocharlevoisien.ca
Display Adv. E-mail: hebdo@charlevoix.ca
Primary Website: www.charlevoixendirect.com
Areas Served - City/County or Portion Thereof, or Zip codes: La Malbaie
Published: Wed
Avg Paid Circ: 30
Avg Free Circ: 14487
Audit By: CCAB
Audit Date: 30.09.2012
Personnel: Charles Warren

PUBLICATION NAME

Plein Jour De Charlevoix
Street Address: 249 Rue John Nairne ,
Province: QC
Postal: G58 1M4
Country: Canada
Mailing address: 249 rue John Nairne
Mailing city: La Malbaie
Province: QC
Postal: G58 1M4
General Phone: (418) 665-6121
General Fax: (418) 665-3105
General/National Adv. E-mail: redaction.pjc@hebdosquebecor.com
Own Printing Facility?: Y
Commercial printers?: Y
Published: Fri
Avg Free Circ: 15438
Audit By: Sworn/Estimate/Non-Audited
Audit Date: 12.07.2019
Personnel: Richard Harley (Mng. Ed.)
Parent company (for newspapers): Quebecor Communications, Inc.

LA RONGE

PUBLICATION NAME

The Northerner
Street Address: 715 La Ronge Ave. ,
Province: SK
Postal: S0J 1L0
Country: Canada
Mailing address: PO Box 1350
Mailing city: La Ronge
Province: SK
Postal: S0J 1L0
General Phone: (306) 425-3344
General Fax: (306) 425-2827

Community Newspapers in Canada

III-547

General/National Adv. E-mail: ads.northerner@sasktel.net
Display Adv. E-mail: ads.northerner@sasktel.net
Classified Adv. e-mail: ads.northerner@sasktel.net
Editorial e-mail: northerner@sasktel.net
Year Established: 1975
Delivery Methods: Mail`Newsstand
Areas Served - City/County or Portion Thereof, or Zip codes: Canada
Own Printing Facility?: N
Commercial printers?: N
Mechanical specifications: Type page 10.25 x 15.75; E - 6 cols, 1 11/12, 1/6 between; A - 6 cols, 1 11/12, 1/6 between; C - 6 cols, 1 11/12, 1/6 between.
Published: Thur
Avg Paid Circ: 198
Avg Free Circ: 136
Audit By: CMCA
Audit Date: 31.07.2014
Personnel: Debra Parkinson (Office Mgr./Circ.)

LA TUQUE

PUBLICATION NAME

L'echo De La Tuque
Street Address: 324 St. Joseph St. ,
Province: QC
Postal: G9X 1L2
Country: Canada
Mailing address: 324 St. Joseph St.
Mailing city: La Tuque
Province: QC
Postal: G9X 1L2
General Phone: (819) 523-6141
General Fax: (819) 523-6143
General/National Adv. E-mail: redaction_latuque@tc.tc
Editorial e-mail: redaction_latuque@tc.tc
Primary Website: www.lechodelatuque.com
Areas Served - City/County or Portion Thereof, or Zip codes: Canada
Published: Wed
Avg Paid Circ: 0
Avg Free Circ: 6406
Audit By: CCAB
Audit Date: 31.03.2014
Personnel: Michele Scarpeno (Dir.)
Parent company (for newspapers): Reseau Select/Select Network; Transcontinental Media

LABRADOR CITY

PUBLICATION NAME

The Aurora
Street Address: 500 Vanier Ave. ,
Province: NL
Postal: A2V 2K7
Mailing address: PO Box 423
Mailing city: Labrador City
Province: NL
Postal: A2V 2K7
General Phone: (709) 944-2957
General Fax: (709) 944-2958
General/National Adv. E-mail: editor@theaurora.ca
Editorial e-mail: mmurphy@optipress.ca
Primary Website: www.theaurora.ca
Year Established: 1969
Areas Served - City/County or Portion Thereof, or Zip codes: Canada
Own Printing Facility?: Y
Commercial printers?: Y
Mechanical specifications: Type page 10 1/4 x 16; E - 9 cols, 1 7/8, 1/8 between; A - 10 cols, 1/8 between; C - 8 cols, 1 1/8, 1/8 between.
Published: Mon
Avg Paid Circ: 1001
Audit By: VAC
Audit Date: 30.06.2016
Personnel: Shawn Woodford (Pub.); Michelle Stewart (Ed.)
Parent company (for newspapers): Transcontinental Media

LAC ETCHEMIN

PUBLICATION NAME

La Voix Du Sud
Street Address: 1516 A. Rt. 277 ,
Province: QC
Postal: G0R 1S0
Country: Canada
Mailing address: 1516 A. Rt. 277
Mailing city: Lac Etchemin
Province: QC
Postal: G0R 1S0
General Phone: (418) 625-7471
General Fax: (418) 625-5200
General/National Adv. E-mail: caroline.gilbert@tc.tc
Display Adv. E-mail: caroline.gilbert@tc.tc
Classified Adv. e-mail: caroline.gilbert@tc.tc
Editorial e-mail: caroline.gilbert@tc.tc
Primary Website: www.lavoixdusud.com
Areas Served - City/County or Portion Thereof, or Zip codes: Canada
Published: Wed
Avg Paid Circ: 14
Avg Free Circ: 27758
Audit By: CCAB
Audit Date: 31.03.2014
Personnel: Caroline Gilbert (Ed.); Rock Bizier (Prodn. Mgr.)
Parent company (for newspapers): Transcontinental Media

LAC LA BICHE

PUBLICATION NAME

Lac La Biche Post
Street Address: 10211 101st St. ,
Province: AB
Postal: T0A 2C0
Country: Canada
Mailing address: PO Box 508
Mailing city: Lac La Biche
Province: AB
Postal: T0A 2C0
General Phone: (780) 623-4221
General Fax: (780) 623-4230
General/National Adv. E-mail: post@llb.greatwest.ca
Display Adv. E-mail: iwolstenholme@llb.greatwest.ca
Editorial e-mail: rmckinley@llb.greatwest.ca
Primary Website: www.laclabichepost.com
Year Established: 1966
Delivery Methods: Mail`Newsstand
Areas Served - City/County or Portion Thereof, or Zip codes: T0A 2C0 T0A 2C1 T0A 2T0 T0A 1Z0 Edmonton, Calgary numerous
Own Printing Facility?: Y
Commercial printers?: Y
Mechanical specifications: all inserts must be folded to a letter -sized final size.
Published: Tues
Avg Paid Circ: 1123
Avg Free Circ: 1
Audit By: VAC
Audit Date: 31.03.2016
Personnel: Robert McKinley (Pub.); Iona Wolstenholme (Sales Mgr.)
Parent company (for newspapers): Glacier Media Group; Great West Newspapers LP

LAC MEGANTIC

PUBLICATION NAME

L'echo De Frontenac
Street Address: 5040 Blvd. Des Veterans ,
Province: QC
Postal: G6B 2G5
Country: Canada
Mailing address: 5040 Blvd. des Veterans
Mailing city: Lac Megantic
Province: QC
Postal: G6B 2G5
General Phone: (819) 583-1630
General Fax: (819) 583-1124
General/National Adv. E-mail: hebdo@echodefrontenac.com
Primary Website: echodefrontenac.com
Areas Served - City/County or Portion Thereof, or Zip codes: Canada
Mechanical specifications: Type page 14 1/4 x 10 1/8; E - 5 cols, between; A - 8 cols, between; C - 8 cols, between.
Published: Fri
Avg Paid Circ: 3904
Avg Free Circ: 3707
Audit By: CCAB
Audit Date: 31.12.2018
Personnel: Michel Pilotte (Sales Dir.); Gaetan Poulin (Ed.); Suzanne Poulin (Asst. Ed.); Remi Tremblay (Mng. Ed.)
Parent company (for newspapers): Reseau Select/Select Network

LACHUTE

PUBLICATION NAME

L'argenteuil
Street Address: 52 Main St. ,
Province: QC
Postal: J8H 3A8
Country: Canada
Mailing address: PO Box 220
Mailing city: Lachute
Province: QC
Postal: J8H 3A8
General Phone: (450) 562-2494
General Fax: (450) 562-1434
General/National Adv. E-mail: argenteuil@eap.on.ca
Display Adv. E-mail: francois.leblanc@eap.on.ca
Primary Website: www.largenteuil.ca
Areas Served - City/County or Portion Thereof, or Zip codes: Canada
Own Printing Facility?: Y
Commercial printers?: Y
Published: Wed
Avg Paid Circ: 39
Avg Free Circ: 16540
Audit By: ODC
Audit Date: 13.12.2011
Personnel: Bertrand Castonguay (Pres.); Roger Duplantie (Dir. Gen.); Francois Leblanc (Dir., Adv.); Alain Morris (Circ. Mgr.); Robert Savard (Ed.)
Parent company (for newspapers): Reseau Select/Select Network; Cie d'Edition Andre Paquette, Inc.

LACOMBE

PUBLICATION NAME

Lacombe Globe
Street Address: 5019-50 St. ,
Province: AB
Postal: T4L 1W8
Country: Canada
Mailing address: 5019-50 St.
Mailing city: Lacombe
Province: AB
Postal: T4L 1W8
General Phone: (403) 782-3498
General Fax: (403) 782-5850
Display Adv. E-mail: ngoetz@postmedia.com
Editorial e-mail: sswenson@postmedia.com
Primary Website: www.lacombeglobe.com
Year Established: 1900
Areas Served - City/County or Portion Thereof, or Zip codes: Canada
Commercial printers?: Y
Mechanical specifications: Type page 13 x 21; E - 6 cols, 2 1/12, 1/6 between; A - 6 cols, 2 1/12, 1/6 between; C - 6 cols, 2 1/12, 1/6 between.
Published: Thur
Avg Paid Circ: 1507
Avg Free Circ: 8604
Audit By: VAC
Audit Date: 31.12.2015
Personnel: Nick Goetz (Adv. Dir) Sarah Swenson (Ed)
Parent company (for newspapers): Postmedia Network Inc.; Quebecor Communications, Inc.

LADNER

PUBLICATION NAME

South Delta Leader
Street Address: 5008 47a Ave ,
Province: BC
Postal: V4K 1T8
Mailing address: 5008 47A Ave
Mailing city: Ladner
Province: BC
Postal: V4K 1T8
General Phone: (604) 948-3640
General Fax: (604) 943-8619
General/National Adv. E-mail: publisher@southdeltaleader.com
Display Adv. E-mail: dhamilton@delta-optimist.com
Classified Adv. e-mail: classifieds@van.net
Editorial e-mail: tmurphy@delta-optimist.com
Primary Website: www.southdeltaleader.com
Year Established: 1999
Delivery Methods: Carrier`Racks
Areas Served - City/County or Portion Thereof, or Zip codes: Canada
Published: Fri
Published Other: Delta Leader, 30,000 - all of Delta, Monthly - last Friday of each month
Avg Paid Circ: 0
Avg Free Circ: 14313
Audit By: CCAB
Audit Date: 30.09.2012
Personnel: Alvin Brouwer (Pub); Ted Murphy (Ed); Dave Hamilton (Gen Mgr/Adv. Sales)

LADYSMITH

PUBLICATION NAME

The Ladysmith Chronicle
Street Address: 940 Oyster Bay Drive ,
Province: BC
Postal: V9G 1A3
Country: Canada
Mailing address: PO Box 400
Mailing city: Ladysmith
Province: BC
Postal: V9G 1A3
General Phone: (250) 245-2277
General Fax: (250) 245-2230
Advertising Phone: (250) 245-2277
Editorial Phone: (250) 245-2277
General/National Adv. E-mail: editor@ladysmithchronicle.com
Display Adv. E-mail: publisher@ladysmithchronicle.com
Editorial e-mail: editor@ladysmithchronicle.com
Primary Website: www.ladysmithchronicle.com
Year Established: 1908
Delivery Methods: Mail`Newsstand`Carrier`Racks
Areas Served - City/County or Portion Thereof, or Zip codes: Canada
Own Printing Facility?: Y
Mechanical specifications: Type page 10 1/4 x 14 1/2; E - 6 cols, 1 5/8, 3/16 between; A - 6 cols, 1 5/8, 3/16 between; C - 6 cols, 1 5/8, 3/16 between.
Published: Tues
Avg Paid Circ: 1348
Avg Free Circ: 3678
Audit By: VAC
Audit Date: 30.09.2016
Personnel: Douglas Kent (Prodn. Mgr.); Teresa McKinley (Pub); Craig Spence (Ed)
Parent company (for newspapers): Black Press Group Ltd.

LAKEFIELD

PUBLICATION NAME

Lakefield Herald
Street Address: 74 Bridge St. ,
Province: ON
Postal: K0L 2H0
Country: Canada
Mailing address: PO Box 1000
Mailing city: Lakefield

Province: ON
Postal: K0L 2H0
General Phone: (705) 652-6594
General Fax: (705) 652-6912
General/National Adv. E-mail: info@lakefieldherald.com
Display Adv. E-mail: ads@lakefieldherald.com
Editorial e-mail: editor@lakefieldherald.com
Primary Website: www.lakefieldherald.com
Areas Served - City/County or Portion Thereof, or Zip codes: Canada
Published: Fri
Avg Paid Circ: 937
Avg Free Circ: 39
Audit By: Sworn/Estimate/Non-Audited
Audit Date: 12.07.2019
Personnel: Terry McQuitty (Owner)

LAMONT

PUBLICATION NAME

The Lamont Leader
Street Address: 5038 50 Ave. ,
Province: AB
Postal: T0B 2R0
Country: Canada
Mailing address: PO Box 1079
Mailing city: Lamont
Province: AB
Postal: T0B 2R0
General Phone: (780) 895-2780
General Fax: (780) 895-2705
Display Adv. E-mail: lmtleader@gmail.com
Editorial e-mail: lamontnews@gmail.com
Primary Website: www.lamontleader.com
Year Established: 2005
Areas Served - City/County or Portion Thereof, or Zip codes: Lamont, AB.
Published: Tues
Avg Paid Circ: 0
Avg Free Circ: 2606
Audit By: VAC
Audit Date: 30.06.2016
Personnel: Kerry Anderson (Pub.); Michelle Pinon (Ed.)
Parent company (for newspapers): Caribou Pub.

LANARK

PUBLICATION NAME

The Lanark Era
Street Address: 66 George St. ,
Province: ON
Postal: K0G 1K0
Country: Canada
Mailing address: PO Box 40
Mailing city: Lanark
Province: ON
Postal: K0G 1K0
General Phone: (613) 259-2220
General/National Adv. E-mail: lanarkera@primus.ca
Display Adv. E-mail: kristy.gibson@lanarkera.com
Classified Adv. e-mail: lanarkera@primus.ca
Editorial e-mail: gena.gibson@lanarkera.com
Primary Website: www.lanarkera.com
Year Established: 1895
Delivery Methods: Mail`Newsstand
Areas Served - City/County or Portion Thereof, or Zip codes: Lanark Highlands Township
Commercial printers?: N
Published: Tues
Avg Paid Circ: 888
Avg Free Circ: 27
Audit By: CMCA
Audit Date: 31.08.2016
Personnel: Gena Gibson (Ed./Owner)

LANGENBURG

PUBLICATION NAME

Langenburg Four-town Journal
Street Address: 102 Carl Ave. ,
Province: SK
Postal: S0A 2A0
Country: Canada
Mailing address: PO Box 68
Mailing city: Langenburg
Province: SK
Postal: S0A 2A0
General Phone: (306) 743-2617
General Fax: (316) 743-2299
General/National Adv. E-mail: fourtown@sasktel.net
Areas Served - City/County or Portion Thereof, or Zip codes: Canada
Published: Wed
Avg Paid Circ: 1199
Audit By: CMCA
Audit Date: 31.03.2016
Personnel: Bill Johnston (Editor/Publisher)

LANGLEY

PUBLICATION NAME

Langley Advance
Street Address: 6375 202 St. , Suite 112
Province: BC
Postal: V2Y 1N1
Country: Canada
Mailing address: 6375 202 St., Ste. 112
Mailing city: Langley
Province: BC
Postal: V2Y 1N1
General Phone: (604) 534-8641
General Fax: (604) 534-3383
General/National Adv. E-mail: rmcadams@langleyadvance.com
Display Adv. E-mail: peggy.obrien@langleyadvance.com
Editorial e-mail: rhooper@langleyadvance.com
Primary Website: www.langleyadvance.com
Year Established: 1931
Delivery Methods: Carrier
Areas Served - City/County or Portion Thereof, or Zip codes: Canada
Own Printing Facility?: Y
Commercial printers?: Y
Mechanical specifications: Type page 11 x 14; E - 6 cols, 1 9/16, between; A - 6 cols, 1 9/16, between; C - 7 cols, 1 3/8, between.
Published: Tues`Thur
Avg Paid Circ: 0
Avg Free Circ: 27538
Audit By: AAM
Audit Date: 31.03.2019
Personnel: Lisa Farquharson (Pub); Peggy O'Brien (Sales Mgr.); Roxanne Hooper (Ed)
Parent company (for newspapers): Black Press Group Ltd.

PUBLICATION NAME

Langley Times
Street Address: 20258 Fraser Hwy. ,
Province: BC
Postal: V3A 4E6
Country: Canada
Mailing address: 20258 Fraser Hwy.
Mailing city: Langley
Province: BC
Postal: V3A 4E6
General Phone: (604) 533-4157
General Fax: (604) 533-4623
General/National Adv. E-mail: newsroom@langleytimes.com
Display Adv. E-mail: admanager@langleytimes.com
Editorial e-mail: newsroom@langleytimes.com
Primary Website: www.langleytimes.com
Year Established: 1982
Delivery Methods: Carrier
Areas Served - City/County or Portion Thereof, or Zip codes: Canada
Own Printing Facility?: N
Commercial printers?: N
Published: Tues`Thur
Avg Free Circ: 28417
Audit By: AAM
Audit Date: 31.03.2019
Personnel: Kelly Myers (Sales Mgr); Lisa Farquharson (Pub); Brenda Anderson (Ed)
Parent company (for newspapers): Black Press Group Ltd.

LANIGAN

PUBLICATION NAME

Lanigan Advisor
Street Address: 42 Main Street ,
Province: SK
Postal: S0K 2M0
Country: Canada
Mailing address: P.O. Box 1029
Mailing city: Lanigan
Province: SK
Postal: S0K 2M0
General Phone: (306) 365-2010
General Fax: (306) 365-3388
General/National Adv. E-mail: laniganadvisor@sasktel.net
Areas Served - City/County or Portion Thereof, or Zip codes: Canada
Published: Mon
Avg Paid Circ: 828
Avg Free Circ: 15
Audit By: CMCA
Audit Date: 31.01.2016
Personnel: Linda Mallett (Publisher/Editor)

LASALLE

PUBLICATION NAME

La Voix Populaire
Street Address: 420 La Fleur St. ,
Province: QC
Postal: H8R 3H6
Country: Canada
Mailing address: 420 La Fleur St.
Mailing city: Lasalle
Province: QC
Postal: H8R 3H6
General Phone: (514) 363-5656
General Fax: (514) 363-3895
General/National Adv. E-mail: patriciaan.beaulieu@transcontinental.ca
Primary Website: www.lavoixpopulaire.com
Areas Served - City/County or Portion Thereof, or Zip codes: Canada
Published: Thur
Avg Paid Circ: 4
Avg Free Circ: 29159
Audit By: CCAB
Audit Date: 31.03.2014
Personnel: Louis Mercier (Ed.); Yannick Pinel (Ed. In Chief.)
Parent company (for newspapers): Transcontinental Media

PUBLICATION NAME

Messager De Lasalle
Street Address: 420 Lafleur Ave , Suite 303
Province: QC
Postal: H9S 5T8
Country: Canada
Mailing address: 420 Lafleur Ave
Mailing city: Lasalle
Province: QC
Postal: H9S 5T8
General Phone: (514) 636-7314
Areas Served - City/County or Portion Thereof, or Zip codes: Canada
Published: Thur
Avg Paid Circ: 3
Avg Free Circ: 32736
Audit By: CCAB
Audit Date: 31.03.2014
Personnel: Patricia Ann Beaulieu

LAVAL

PUBLICATION NAME

Courrier-laval
Street Address: 2700 Francis Hughes Ave., Ste. 200 ,
Province: QC
Postal: H7S 2B9
Country: Canada
Mailing address: 2700 Francis Hughes Ave., Ste. 200
Mailing city: Laval
Province: QC
Postal: H7S 2B9
General Phone: (450) 667-4360
General Fax: (450) 667-0845
General/National Adv. E-mail: redactionlaval@tc.tc
Primary Website: www.courrierlaval.com
Year Established: 1945
Areas Served - City/County or Portion Thereof, or Zip codes: Canada
Mechanical specifications: Type page 11 3/8 x 15; E - 8 cols, between; A - 8 cols, between.
Published: Wed`Sat
Avg Paid Circ: 8
Avg Free Circ: 12788
Audit By: CCAB
Audit Date: 30.09.2012
Personnel: Janique Duguay (Sales Dir.); Rejean Monette (Regl. Dir.); Claude Labelle (Ed.); Martine Cotton (Prodn. Mgr.)
Parent company (for newspapers): Transcontinental Media

PUBLICATION NAME

L'hebdo De Laval
Street Address: 3221 Hwy. 440 W. , Ste. 209 ,
Province: QC
Postal: H7P 5P2
Country: Canada
Mailing address: 3221 Hwy. 440 W., Ste. 209
Mailing city: Laval
Province: QC
Postal: H7P 5P2
General Phone: (450) 681-4948
General Fax: (450) 681-2824
Published: Fri
Avg Free Circ: 84860
Audit By: Sworn/Estimate/Non-Audited
Audit Date: 12.07.2019
Personnel: Marc Ouellette (Gen. Mgr.); Francois Forget (Mng. Ed.)

PUBLICATION NAME

Missions Etrangeres
Street Address: Place Juge-desnoyers ,
Province: QC
Postal: H7G 1A5
Country: Canada
Mailing address: place Juge-Desnoyers
Mailing city: Laval
Province: QC
Postal: H7G 1A5
General Phone: (450) 667-4190
Published: Wed
Avg Paid Circ: 6585
Avg Free Circ: 5647
Audit By: ODC
Audit Date: 14.12.2011
Personnel: Bertrand Roy

PUBLICATION NAME

Nouvelles Parc Extension News
Street Address: 3860 Notre-dame Blvd. , Suite 304
Province: QC
Postal: H7V 1S1
Country: Canada
Mailing address: 3860 Notre-Dame Blvd.
Mailing city: Laval
Province: QC
Postal: H7V 1S1
General Phone: (450) 978-9999
General Fax: (450) 687-6330
Display Adv. E-mail: sales@the-news.ca
Editorial e-mail: editor@the-news.ca
Primary Website: www.px-news.com
Year Established: 1993
Delivery Methods: Carrier`Racks
Areas Served - City/County or Portion Thereof, or Zip codes: H3N
Mechanical specifications: Type page 10 1/4 x 14 1/4; E - 8 cols, 1 1/6, 1/6 between; A - 8 cols, 1 1/6, 1/6 between; C - 8 cols, 1 1/6, 1/6 between.

Community Newspapers in Canada

Published: Fri
Published Other: Every other sat
Avg Paid Circ: 0
Avg Free Circ: 9403
Audit By: Sworn/Estimate/Non-Audited
Audit Date: 12.07.2019
Personnel: George S. Guzmas (Co-Publisher); George Bakoyannis (Prodn. Mgr.)

PUBLICATION NAME

The Laval News
Street Address: 3860 Notre-dame Blvd., Suite 304
Province: QC
Postal: H7V 1S1
Country: Canada
Mailing address: 3860 Notre-Dame Blvd.
Mailing city: Laval
Province: QC
Postal: H7V 1S1
General Phone: (450) 978-9999
General Fax: (450) 687-6330
General/National Adv. E-mail: editor@the-news.ca
Display Adv. E-mail: sales@the-news.ca
Editorial e-mail: editor@the-news.ca
Primary Website: www.lavalnews.ca
Year Established: 1993
Delivery Methods: Carrier`Racks
Areas Served - City/County or Portion Thereof, or Zip codes: Canada
Mechanical specifications: Type page 10 3/10 x 14 1/4; E - 8 cols, 1 1/6, 1/6 between; A - 8 cols, 1 1/6, 1/6 between; C - 8 cols, 1 1/6, 1/6 between.
Published: Sat
Published Other: Every other Saturday
Avg Free Circ: 27982
Audit By: CMCA
Audit Date: 30.06.2016
Personnel: George S. Guzmas (Co-Publisher); George Bakoyannis (Prodn. Mgr.)
Parent company (for newspapers): Newsfirst Multi-Media

PUBLICATION NAME

The North Shore News
Street Address: 3860 Notre-dame Blvd., Suite 304
Province: QC
Postal: H7V 1S1
Country: Canada
Mailing address: 3860 Notre-Dame Blvd.Suite 304
Mailing city: Laval
Province: QC
Postal: H7V 1S1
General Phone: (450) 978-9999
General Fax: (450) 678-6330
General/National Adv. E-mail: editor@the-news.ca
Display Adv. E-mail: gg@newsfirst.ca
Editorial e-mail: editor@newsfirst.ca
Primary Website: www.ns-news.com
Year Established: 2005
Delivery Methods: Newsstand`Racks
Areas Served - City/County or Portion Thereof, or Zip codes: Canada
Mechanical specifications: Tabloid
Published: Sat
Published Other: Every 2nd week (24 per year)
Avg Paid Circ: 0
Avg Free Circ: 16353
Audit By: CMCA
Audit Date: 31.01.2017
Personnel: George Guzmas (Co-Pub)
Parent company (for newspapers): Newsfirst Multimedia

LEAMINGTON

PUBLICATION NAME

Wheatley Journal
Street Address: 194 Talbot Street E., Unit #5
Province: ON
Postal: N8H 1M2
Country: Canada
General Phone: (519) 398-9098
General Fax: (519) 398-8561
General/National Adv. E-mail: journal@mnsi.net
Year Established: 1895
Delivery Methods: Mail`Newsstand
Areas Served - City/County or Portion Thereof, or Zip codes: Chatham-Kent
Own Printing Facility?: Y
Commercial printers?: Y
Published: Wed
Avg Paid Circ: 586
Avg Free Circ: 11
Audit By: CMCA
Audit Date: 30.04.2016
Personnel: Jim Heyens (Pub.)
Parent company (for newspapers): Southpoint Publishing Inc.

LEDUC

PUBLICATION NAME

Leduc Representative
Street Address: 4504 61st Ave.,
Province: AB
Postal: T9E 3Z1
Country: Canada
Mailing address: 4504 61st Ave.
Mailing city: Leduc
Province: AB
Postal: T9E 3Z1
General Phone: (780) 986-2271
General Fax: (780) 986-6397
Display Adv. E-mail: ngoetz@postmedia.com
Editorial e-mail: bobby.roy@sunmedia.ca
Primary Website: www.leducrep.com
Year Established: 1905
Delivery Methods: Mail`Newsstand`Carrier`Racks
Areas Served - City/County or Portion Thereof, or Zip codes: Canada
Own Printing Facility?: Y
Commercial printers?: Y
Mechanical specifications: Type page 10 1/4 x 15 3/4; E - 8 cols, 1/6 between; A - 8 cols, 1/6 between; C - 8 cols, 1/6 between.
Published: Fri
Avg Paid Circ: 3069
Avg Free Circ: 16449
Audit By: VAC
Audit Date: 31.12.2015
Personnel: Susanne Holmlund (Pub.); Jan Eyre (Circ. Mgr.); Nick Goetz (Adv. Dir.); Bobby Roy (Ed)
Parent company (for newspapers): Postmedia Network Inc.; Quebecor Communications, Inc.

LETHRBRIDGE

PUBLICATION NAME

Lethbridge Sun Times
Street Address: 504 - 7th Street S,
Province: AB
Postal: T1J 2G8
Country: Canada
Mailing address: 504 - 7th Street S
Mailing city: Lethrbidge
Province: AB
Postal: T1J 2G8
General Phone: (403) 328-4433
General Fax: (403) 329-9355
General/National Adv. E-mail: suntimes@lethbridgeherald.com
Editorial e-mail: ccampbell@abnewsgroup.com
Primary Website: www.lethsuntimes.com
Delivery Methods: Carrier
Areas Served - City/County or Portion Thereof, or Zip codes: City of Lethbridge
Published: Mon`Tues`Wed`Thur`Fri`Sat`Sun
Weekday Frequency: m
Saturday Frequency: m
Avg Paid Circ: 19864
Sat. Circulation Paid: 10520
Sun. Circulation Paid: 12753
Audit By: AAM
Audit Date: 30.09.2017
Personnel: Coleen Campbell (Pub.)
Parent company (for newspapers): Alberta Newspaper Group LP

LEVIS

PUBLICATION NAME

Journal De Levis
Street Address: 580, Boul, Alphonse-desjardins,
Province: QC
Postal: G6V 6R8
Country: Canada
Mailing address: 515,Boul the south shore
Mailing city: Levis
Province: QC
Postal: G6V 6R8
General Phone: (418) 833-3113
General Fax: (418) 833-0890
General/National Adv. E-mail: jdl@journaldelevis.com
Primary Website: www.journaldelevis.com
Areas Served - City/County or Portion Thereof, or Zip codes: Canada
Published: Wed
Avg Paid Circ: 5
Avg Free Circ: 68595
Audit By: CCAB
Audit Date: 30.09.2015
Personnel: Sandra Fontaine

PUBLICATION NAME

Journal Le Peuple
Street Address: 421 Dorimene Desjardins Rue,
Province: QC
Postal: G6V 8V6
Country: Canada
Mailing address: 421 Dorimene Desjardins Rue
Mailing city: Levis
Province: QC
Postal: G6V 8V6
General Phone: (418) 833-9398
General Fax: (418) 833-8177
General/National Adv. E-mail: paul.lessard@quebecormedia.com
Primary Website: http://www.hebdosregionaux.ca/chaudiere-appalaches/le-peuple-levis/
Year Established: 1936
Areas Served - City/County or Portion Thereof, or Zip codes: Canada
Mechanical specifications: Type page 10 x 11 3/4; E - 5 cols, 2, between; A - 10 cols, 1, between; C - 5 cols, 2, between.
Published: Wed
Avg Paid Circ: 3
Avg Free Circ: 68451
Audit By: CCAB
Audit Date: 31.03.2014
Personnel: Paul Lessard
Parent company (for newspapers): Quebecor Communications, Inc.

PUBLICATION NAME

Peuple De Lotbiniere
Street Address: 5790, Boul. Etienne-dallaire, Suite 103 B,
Province: QC
Postal: G6V 8V6
Country: Canada
Mailing address: 5790 Boul. Etienne-Dallaire, Suite 103 B
Mailing city: Levis
Province: QC
Postal: G6V 8V6
General Phone: (418) 728-2131
General Fax: (418) 728-4819
General/National Adv. E-mail: peuple.lotbiniere@hebdosquebecor.com
Display Adv. E-mail: ventes.lotbiniere@hebdosquebecor.com
Editorial e-mail: redaction.lotbiniere@hebdosquebecor.com
Primary Website: www.lepeuplelotbiniere.canoe.ca
Areas Served - City/County or Portion Thereof, or Zip codes: Canada
Published: Wed
Avg Paid Circ: 1
Avg Free Circ: 15029
Audit By: CCAB
Audit Date: 31.03.2014
Personnel: Lise Racette (Adv. Rep.); Paul Lessard
Parent company (for newspapers): Quebecor Communications, Inc.

LEWISPORTE

PUBLICATION NAME

The Pilot
Street Address: P151 Main St,
Province: NL
Postal: A0G 3A0
Country: Canada
Mailing address: PO Box 1210
Mailing city: Lewisporte
Province: NL
Postal: A0G 3A0
General Phone: (709) 535-6910
General Fax: (709) 535-8640
General/National Adv. E-mail: editor@pilotnl.ca
Display Adv. E-mail: pilotsales@optipress.ca
Editorial e-mail: editor@pilotnl.ca
Primary Website: http://www.lportepilot.ca/
Areas Served - City/County or Portion Thereof, or Zip codes: Canada
Own Printing Facility?: Y
Commercial printers?: Y
Mechanical specifications: Type page 13 x 21; E - 6 cols, 2, 1/2 between; A - 6 cols, 2, 1/2 between; C - 9 cols, 1 3/4, 1/4 between.
Published: Wed
Avg Paid Circ: 312
Avg Free Circ: 0
Audit By: VAC
Audit Date: 31.12.2015
Personnel: Joanne Chaffey (Adv. Mgr.); Karen Wells (Ed.)
Parent company (for newspapers): Transcontinental Media

LILLOOET

PUBLICATION NAME

Bridge River Lillooet News
Street Address: 979 Main St.,
Province: BC
Postal: V0K 1V0
Country: Canada
Mailing address: PO Box 709
Mailing city: Lillooet
Province: BC
Postal: V0K 1V0
General Phone: (250) 256-4219
General Fax: (250) 256-4210
Advertising Phone: (778) 773-4797
Advertising Fax: (877) 765-6483
General/National Adv. E-mail: pub@lillooetnews.net
Display Adv. E-mail: sales@lillooetnews.net
Editorial e-mail: editor@lillooetnews.net
Primary Website: www.lillooetnews.net
Year Established: 1934
Areas Served - City/County or Portion Thereof, or Zip codes: Canada
Own Printing Facility?: Y
Commercial printers?: Y
Mechanical specifications: Type page 10 1/3 x 14; E - 6 cols, 1 3/5, between; A - 6 cols, 1 3/5, between.
Published: Wed
Avg Paid Circ: 1709
Avg Free Circ: 16
Audit By: VAC
Audit Date: 28.02.2016
Personnel: Wendy Fraser (Ed.); Bruce MacLennan (Publisher); Eliza Payne (Sales Associate)
Parent company (for newspapers): Glacier Media Group

LINDSAY

PUBLICATION NAME

Kawartha Lakes This Week
Street Address: 192 St. David St.,
Province: ON

Postal: K9V 4Z4
Country: Canada
Mailing address: 192 St. David St.
Mailing city: Lindsay
Province: ON
Postal: K9V 4Z4
General Phone: (705) 324-8600
General Fax: (705) 324-5694
General/National Adv. E-mail: mtully@mykawartha.com
Display Adv. E-mail: mbabcock@mykawartha.com
Editorial e-mail: mtully@mykawartha.com
Primary Website: www.mykawartha.com
Areas Served - City/County or Portion Thereof, or Zip codes: Canada
Mechanical specifications: Type page 10 3/8 x 14; E - 9 cols, 1 1/18, 3/15 between; A - 9 cols, 1 1/18, 3/15 between; C - 9 cols, 1 1/18, 3/15 between.
Published: Tues`Thur
Avg Paid Circ: 0
Avg Free Circ: 21867
Audit By: CCAB
Audit Date: 30.09.2012
Personnel: Bruce Danford (Pub.); Linda Suddes (Bus. Admin./Opns.); Kim Riel (Office Mgr.); Shane Lockyer (Adv. Mgr.); Lois Tuffin (Ed. in Chief); Marcus Tully (News Ed.); Scott Prikker (Prodn. Mgr.); Jeff Braund (Regl. Dist. Mgr.); Tracy Magee-Graham (Dir., Distr.)
Parent company (for newspapers): Metroland Media Group Ltd.; Torstar

LISTOWEL

PUBLICATION NAME

The Listowel Banner
Street Address: 185 Wallace Ave. N. ,
Province: ON
Postal: N4W 1K8
Country: Canada
Mailing address: PO Box 97
Mailing city: Listowel
Province: ON
Postal: N4W 3H2
General Phone: (519) 291-1660
General Fax: (519) 291-3771
Display Adv. E-mail: ads@northperth.com
Editorial e-mail: editor@northperth.com
Primary Website: www.northperth.com
Year Established: 1866
Areas Served - City/County or Portion Thereof, or Zip codes: Canada
Published: Wed
Avg Paid Circ: 1881
Avg Free Circ: 22
Audit By: CMCA
Audit Date: 30.06.2016
Personnel: Bill Huether (Gen. Mgr.); Alicia Hunter (Adv. Mgr.); Peggy Haasnoot (Circ. Mgr.); Pauline Kerr (Ed.); Terry Bridge (Sports Ed.); Marie McKertcher (Prodn. Mgr.)
Parent company (for newspapers): Metroland Media Group Ltd.; Torstar

LITTLE CURRENT

PUBLICATION NAME

Manitoulin Expositor
Street Address: 1 Manitowaning Rd. ,
Province: ON
Postal: P0P 1K0
Country: Canada
Mailing address: PO Box 369
Mailing city: Little Current
Province: ON
Postal: P0P 1K0
General Phone: (705) 368-2744
General Fax: (705) 368-3822
General/National Adv. E-mail: expositor@manitoulin.ca
Display Adv. E-mail: sales@manitoulin.ca
Editorial e-mail: editor@manitoulin.ca
Primary Website: www.manitoulin.ca
Year Established: 1879
Delivery Methods: Mail`Newsstand

Areas Served - City/County or Portion Thereof, or Zip codes: Canada
Commercial printers?: Y
Mechanical specifications: Type page 10 1/4 x 16; E - 6 cols, 1 1/2, 1/8 between; A - 6 cols, 1 1/2, 1/8 between; C - 6 cols, 1 1/2, 1/8 between.
Published: Wed
Avg Paid Circ: 4181
Avg Free Circ: 178
Audit By: AAM
Audit Date: 31.03.2019
Personnel: Rick L. McCutcheon (Pub.); Kerrene Tilson (Gen. Mgr.); Greg Lloyd (Sales Mgr.); David Patterson (Production Manager); Alicia McCutcheon
Parent company (for newspapers): Manitoulin Publishing Co., Ltd.

LIVERPOOL

PUBLICATION NAME

The Advance
Street Address: 271 Main St. ,
Province: NS
Postal: B0T 1K0
Country: Canada
Mailing address: PO Box 10
Mailing city: Liverpool
Province: NS
Postal: B0T 1K0
General Phone: (902) 354-3441
General Fax: (902) 354-2455
General/National Adv. E-mail: info@advance.ca
Editorial e-mail: ffayander@thevanguard.ca
Primary Website: http://www.theadvance.ca/
Areas Served - City/County or Portion Thereof, or Zip codes: Canada
Commercial printers?: Y
Published: Tues
Avg Paid Circ: 1573
Audit By: CMCA
Audit Date: 31.03.2013
Personnel: Fred Fayander (Pub)
Parent company (for newspapers): Transcontinental Media

LLOYDMINSTER

PUBLICATION NAME

Lloydminster Meridian Booster
Street Address: 5714 44th St. ,
Province: AB
Postal: T9V 0B6
Country: Canada
Mailing address: 5714 44th St.
Mailing city: Lloydminster
Province: AB
Postal: T9V 0B6
General Phone: (780) 875-3362
General Fax: (780) 875-3423
Advertising Phone: (877) 786-8227
General/National Adv. E-mail: lisa.lamoureux@sunmedia.ca
Display Adv. E-mail: ljohnston@postmedia.com
Classified Adv. e-mail: meridianbooster.classifieds@sunmedia.ca
Editorial e-mail: tweaver@postmedia.com
Primary Website: www.meridianbooster.com
Year Established: 1954
Areas Served - City/County or Portion Thereof, or Zip codes: Canada
Own Printing Facility?: Y
Mechanical specifications: Type page 11 1/2 x 16; E - 6 cols, 1 9/16, between; A - 6 cols, 1 9/16, between; C - 6 cols, 1 9/16, between.
Published: Wed
Avg Paid Circ: 2653
Avg Free Circ: 14879
Audit By: VAC
Audit Date: 31.12.2015
Personnel: Mary-Ann Kostiuk (Pub); Leanne Johnson (Adv. Dir.); Taylor Weaver (Ed)
Parent company (for newspapers): Postmedia Network Inc.; Quebecor Communications, Inc.

PUBLICATION NAME

Lloydminster Source
Street Address: 5921-50th Ave ,
Province: SK
Postal: S9V 1W5
Country: Canada
Mailing address: PO Box 2454
Mailing city: Lloydminster
Province: SK
Postal: S9V 1W5
General Phone: (306) 825-5111
General Fax: (306) 825-5147
Editorial e-mail: colin@lloydminstersource.com
Areas Served - City/County or Portion Thereof, or Zip codes: Canada
Published: Tues`Thur
Avg Free Circ: 13889
Audit By: CMCA
Audit Date: 31.08.2016
Personnel: Reid Keebaugh (Publisher); Mike D'Armour (Mng. Ed.); Karrie Chang (Prod. Mgr.)

LONDON

PUBLICATION NAME

Action (l')
Street Address: 920 Huron St. ,
Province: ON
Postal: N5Y 4K4
Country: Canada
Mailing address: 920 Huron St.
Mailing city: London
Province: ON
Postal: N5Y 4K4
General Phone: (519) 433-4130
General Fax: (905) 790-9127
General/National Adv. E-mail: journaliste@laction.ca
Display Adv. E-mail: marketing@laction.ca
Editorial e-mail: info@lemetropolitain.com
Primary Website: www.laction.ca
Areas Served - City/County or Portion Thereof, or Zip codes: Canada
Published: Wed
Avg Paid Circ: 1648
Avg Free Circ: 812
Audit By: CMCA
Audit Date: 31.12.2012
Personnel: Denis Poirier (Ed); Richard Caumartin (Sales Dir)

PUBLICATION NAME

Londoner
Street Address: 1147 Gainsborough Road ,
Province: ON
Postal: N6H 5L5
Country: Canada
Mailing address: 1147 Gainsborough Road
Mailing city: London
Province: ON
Postal: N6H 5L5
General Phone: (519) 673-5005
General Fax: (519) 673-4624
General/National Adv. E-mail: linda.leblanc@sunmedia.ca
Display Adv. E-mail: linda.leblanc@sunmedia.ca
Editorial e-mail: don.biggs@sunmedia.ca
Primary Website: www.thelondoner.ca
Delivery Methods: Carrier
Areas Served - City/County or Portion Thereof, or Zip codes: Canada
Published: Thur
Avg Free Circ: 140111
Audit By: CMCA
Audit Date: 31.12.2015
Personnel: Linda LeBlanc (Publisher)
Parent company (for newspapers): Postmedia Network Inc.

LONGUEUIL

PUBLICATION NAME

Brossard Eclair
Street Address: 267 St. Charles Ouest ,

Province: QC
Postal: J4H 1E3
Country: Canada
Mailing address: 267 St. Charles Ouest
Mailing city: Longueuil
Province: QC
Postal: J4H 1E3
General Phone: (450) 646-3333
General Fax: (450) 674-0205
General/National Adv. E-mail: lucie.masse@quebecormedia.com
Primary Website: http://www.brossardeclair.ca/
Areas Served - City/County or Portion Thereof, or Zip codes: Canada
Mechanical specifications: Type page 10 1/2 x 14 1/2; E - 8 cols, between; C - 1 cols, between.
Published: Wed
Avg Free Circ: 32482
Audit By: CCAB
Audit Date: 31.03.2014
Personnel: Lucie Masse (Ed.)
Parent company (for newspapers): Reseau Select/Select Network; Quebecor Communications, Inc.

PUBLICATION NAME

Le Courrier Du Sud/south Shore Courier
Street Address: 267 Saint Charles W ,
Province: QC
Postal: J4H 1E3
Country: Canada
Mailing address: 267 Saint Charles W
Mailing city: Longueuil
Province: QC
Postal: J4H 1E3
General Phone: (450) 646-3333
General Fax: (450) 674-0205
Advertising Phone: (450) 646-3333
General/National Adv. E-mail: direction@courrierdusud.com
Display Adv. E-mail: journal@courrierdusud.com
Editorial e-mail: editeur@courrierdusud.com
Primary Website: http://www.lecourrierdusud.ca/
Year Established: 1947
Delivery Methods: Mail`Racks
Areas Served - City/County or Portion Thereof, or Zip codes: Canada
Published: Wed
Avg Free Circ: 145800
Audit By: CCAB
Audit Date: 31.03.2014
Personnel: Lucie Masse (Pub.); Jinette Claude Teron (Ed.)
Parent company (for newspapers): Quebecor Communications, Inc.

PUBLICATION NAME

Magazine De Saint Lambert
Street Address: St Charles Ouest ,
Province: QC
Postal: J4H 1E3
Country: Canada
Mailing address: St Charles ouest
Mailing city: Longueuil
Province: QC
Postal: J4H 1E3
Areas Served - City/County or Portion Thereof, or Zip codes: Canada
Published: Wed
Avg Paid Circ: 0
Avg Free Circ: 14164
Audit By: CCAB
Audit Date: 30.09.2012
Personnel: Lucie Masse (Gen. Mgr.)

PUBLICATION NAME

Revue De La Machinerie Agricole
Street Address: 468 Boul. Roland-therrien ,
Province: QC
Postal: J4H 4E3
Country: Canada
Mailing address: 468 Boul. Roland-Therrien
Mailing city: Longueuil
Province: QC

Community Newspapers in Canada

III-551

Postal: J4H 4E3
General Phone: (450) 677-2556
General Fax: (450) 677-4099
General/National Adv. E-mail: info@marevueagricole.com
Primary Website: www.marevueagricole.com
Published: Tues
Avg Paid Circ: 1300
Avg Free Circ: 33200
Audit By: ODC
Audit Date: 14.12.2011
Personnel: Martyne Simard

LOUISEVILLE

PUBLICATION NAME

L'echo De Maskinonge
Street Address: 43 Saint Louis ,
Province: QC
Postal: J5V 2C7
Country: Canada
Mailing address: 43 Saint Louis
Mailing city: Louiseville
Province: QC
Postal: J5V 2C7
General Phone: (819) 228-5532
General Fax: (819) 228-9239
Advertising Fax: (819) 228-5532
General/National Adv. E-mail: redaction_em@transcontinental.ca
Primary Website: www.lechodemaskinonge.com
Year Established: 1921
Areas Served - City/County or Portion Thereof, or Zip codes: Canada
Published: Wed
Avg Paid Circ: 28
Avg Free Circ: 13907
Audit By: CCAB
Audit Date: 31.03.2014
Personnel: AndrÃƒÂ£ÃƒÂ¦££££ Lamy (Dir.); Diane Beland (Sales Coord.)
Parent company (for newspapers): Transcontinental Media

LUCKNOW

PUBLICATION NAME

The Lucknow Sentinel
Street Address: 619 Campbell St. ,
Province: ON
Postal: N0G 2H0
Country: Canada
Mailing address: PO Box 400
Mailing city: Lucknow
Province: ON
Postal: N0G 2H0
General Phone: (519) 528-2822
General Fax: (519) 528-3529
Advertising Phone: (519) 528-2822
Advertising Fax: (519) 528-3529
Editorial Phone: (519) 528-2822
Editorial Fax: (519) 528-3529
General/National Adv. E-mail: lucksent@bowesnet.com
Display Adv. E-mail: lucksentads@bowesnet.com
Editorial e-mail: lucksented@bowesnet.com
Primary Website: www.lucknowsentinel.com
Year Established: 1873
Delivery Methods: Mail Newsstand
Areas Served - City/County or Portion Thereof, or Zip codes: Canada
Commercial printers?: N
Mechanical specifications: Type page 10 .25 x 11.422; E - 9 cols, 1/16 " between columns
Published: Wed
Avg Paid Circ: 1037
Avg Free Circ: 44
Audit By: CMCA
Audit Date: 30.06.2014
Personnel: Troy Patterson (Ed.)
Parent company (for newspapers): Postmedia Network Inc.; Quebecor Communications, Inc.

LUMSDEN

PUBLICATION NAME

Waterfront Press
Street Address: 635 James St. N. ,
Province: SK
Postal: S0G 3C0
Country: Canada
Mailing address: PO Box 507
Mailing city: Lumsden
Province: SK
Postal: S0G 3C0
General Phone: (306) 731-3143
General Fax: (306) 731-2277
General/National Adv. E-mail: watpress@sasktel.net
Areas Served - City/County or Portion Thereof, or Zip codes: S0G 0H0, S0G 0W0, S0G 3C0, S0G 3C0, S0G 4L0, S0G 4P0
Own Printing Facility?: Y
Commercial printers?: Y
Mechanical specifications: Type page 10 x 15 1/4; E - 5 cols, 2, between; A - 5 cols, 2, between; C - 5 cols, 2, between.
Published: Thur
Avg Paid Circ: 167
Avg Free Circ: 3993
Audit By: CMCA
Audit Date: 30.06.2014
Personnel: Jaoqueline Chouinard (Ed.); Lucien Chouinard (Ed.)

MACKENZIE

PUBLICATION NAME

The Times
Street Address: 125-403 Mackenzie Blvd. ,
Province: BC
Postal: V0J 2C0
Country: Canada
Mailing address: PO Box 609
Mailing city: Mackenzie
Province: BC
Postal: V0J 2C0
General Phone: (250) 997-6675
General Fax: (250) 997-4747
Advertising Phone: (250) 997-6675
Advertising Fax: (250) 997-4747
Editorial Phone: (250) 997-6675
Editorial Fax: (250) 997-4747
General/National Adv. E-mail: news@mackenzietimes.com
Display Adv. E-mail: ads@mackenzietimes.com
Editorial e-mail: news@mackenzietimes.com
Primary Website: www.sterlingnews.com/Mackenzie
Year Established: 1999
Delivery Methods: Mail Newsstand Carrier
Areas Served - City/County or Portion Thereof, or Zip codes: V0J 2C0
Commercial printers?: Y
Published: Wed
Avg Paid Circ: 1000
Audit By: Sworn/Estimate/Non-Audited
Audit Date: 12.07.2019
Personnel: Jackie Benton (Pub/Ed); Andrea Massicotte (Adv Mgr)

MACKLIN

PUBLICATION NAME

Macklin Mirror
Street Address: 4701 Herald St. ,
Province: SK
Postal: S0L 2C0
Country: Canada
Mailing address: PO Box 100
Mailing city: Macklin
Province: SK
Postal: S0L 2C0
General Phone: (306) 753-2424
General Fax: (306) 753-2432
General/National Adv. E-mail: macklin.jamac@gmail.com
Display Adv. E-mail: macklin.jamac@gmail.com
Editorial e-mail: stacey.jamac@gmail.com
Year Established: 1977
Delivery Methods: Mail Newsstand Racks
Areas Served - City/County or Portion Thereof, or Zip codes: Canada
Mechanical specifications: 10.25" X 16" high
Published: Wed
Avg Paid Circ: 638
Avg Free Circ: 33
Audit By: CMCA
Audit Date: 30.04.2016
Personnel: Delilah Reschny (Editor/Publisher); Stacey Lavallie (Reporter)
Parent company (for newspapers): Jamac Publishing

MAGOG

PUBLICATION NAME

Reflet Du Lac

Street Address: 53 Rue Centre , Bureau 300
Province: QC
Postal: J1X 5B6
Country: Canada
General Phone: (819) 843-3500
General Fax: (819) 843-3085
General/National Adv. E-mail: dany.jacques@tc.tc
Areas Served - City/County or Portion Thereof, or Zip codes: Canada
Published: Wed
Avg Paid Circ: 0
Avg Free Circ: 24662
Audit By: CCAB
Audit Date: 30.09.2012
Personnel: Monique Cote (CEO)

MAGRATH

PUBLICATION NAME

Westwind Weekly News
Street Address: 74a South - 1st Street West , Box 9
Province: AB
Postal: T0K 1J0
Country: Canada
General Phone: (403) 758-6911
General Fax: (403) 758-3661
Display Adv. E-mail: sales@westwindweekly.com
Primary Website: www.westwindweekly.com
Delivery Methods: Mail
Areas Served - City/County or Portion Thereof, or Zip codes: towns of Magrath, Raymond and Stirling
Published: Thur
Avg Paid Circ: 0
Avg Free Circ: 51
Audit By: VAC
Audit Date: 31.12.2015
Personnel: Valorie Wiebe (Pub.); Maggie Belisle (Adv. Sales Consult.); Joan Bly (Office Admin.); J.W Schnarr (Ed.)

MANITOU

PUBLICATION NAME

The Western Canadian
Street Address: 424 Ellis Ave. E. ,
Province: MB
Postal: R0G 1G0
Country: Canada
Mailing address: PO Box 190
Mailing city: Manitou
Province: MB
Postal: R0G 1G0
General Phone: (204) 242-2555
General Fax: (204) 242-3137
General/National Adv. E-mail: westerncanadian@goinet.ca
Editorial e-mail: thewesterncanadian@gmail.com
Primary Website: http://www.thewesterncanadian.ca/
Areas Served - City/County or Portion Thereof, or Zip codes: Canada
Own Printing Facility?: Y
Commercial printers?: Y
Mechanical specifications: Type page 10 1/4 x 14; E - 5 cols, 2, 1/8 between; A - 5 cols, 2, 1/8 between; C - 5 cols, 2, 1/8 between.
Published: Tues
Avg Paid Circ: 1057
Avg Free Circ: 0
Audit By: VAC
Audit Date: 31.05.2016
Personnel: Grant Howett (Ed.)

MANITOUWADGE

PUBLICATION NAME

The Echo
Street Address: 105 Warbler ,
Province: ON
Postal: P0T 2C0
Country: Canada
Mailing address: PO Box 850
Mailing city: Manitouwadge
Province: ON
Postal: P0T 2C0
General Phone: (807) 228-2333
Advertising Phone: (807) 228-2317
General/National Adv. E-mail: info@theecho.ca
Display Adv. E-mail: manitouwadgeecho@gmail.com
Editorial e-mail: news@theecho.ca
Primary Website: www.theecho.ca
Year Established: 1964

Delivery Methods: Mail`Newsstand
Areas Served - City/County or Portion Thereof, or Zip codes: Canada
Own Printing Facility?: N
Commercial printers?: Y
Mechanical specifications: Type page 10 x 15 3/4; E - 5 cols, 1 3/4, 1/4 between; A - 5 cols, 1 3/4, 1/4 between.
Published: Wed
Avg Paid Circ: 346
Audit By: CMCA
Audit Date: 30.04.2014
Personnel: B.J. Schermann (Pub.); Scott Schermann (Prodn. Mgr.).

MANSFIELD

PUBLICATION NAME

Journal Of Pontiac
Street Address: Unit 5 , 289, Rue Principale
Province: QC
Postal: J0X 1R0
Country: Canada
Mailing address: #5-289, rue Principale
Mailing city: Mansfield
Province: QC
Postal: J0X 1R0
General Phone: (819) 683-3582
General Fax: (819) 683-2977
General/National Adv. E-mail: info@journalpontiac.com
Display Adv. E-mail: journal@journalpontiac.com
Classified Adv. e-mail: notice@journalpontiac.com
Editorial e-mail: editor@journalpontiac.com
Primary Website: www.pontiacjournal.com
Year Established: 1987
Delivery Methods: Mail`Newsstand`Carrier
Areas Served - City/County or Portion Thereof, or Zip codes: Mansfield-et-Pontefract
Published: Other
Avg Paid Circ: 70
Avg Free Circ: 9302
Audit By: Sworn/Estimate/Non-Audited
Audit Date: 12.07.2019
Personnel: Lynne Lavery (Gen. Mgr.)
Parent company (for newspapers): 155106 Canada Inc.

MAPLE CREEK

PUBLICATION NAME

Maple Creek & Southwest Advance Times
Street Address: 116 Harder Street ,
Province: SK
Postal: S0N 1N0
Country: Canada
Mailing address: PO Box 1328
Mailing city: Maple Creek
Province: SK
Postal: S0N 1N0
General Phone: (306) 662-2100
General Fax: (306) 662-5005
General/National Adv. E-mail: classifieds@maplecreeknews.com
Display Adv. E-mail: ads@maplecreeknews.com
Editorial e-mail: editorial@maplecreeknews.com
Primary Website: www.maplecreeknews.com
Areas Served - City/County or Portion Thereof, or Zip codes: Canada
Published: Tues
Avg Paid Circ: 1506
Avg Free Circ: 76
Audit By: CMCA
Audit Date: 30.04.2016
Personnel: Angela Litke (Manager); Della Fournier (Advertising Sales)

PUBLICATION NAME

The Maple Creek News
Street Address: 116 Harder St. ,
Province: SK
Postal: S0N 1N0
Country: Canada
Mailing address: PO Box 1328

Mailing city: Maple Creek
Province: SK
Postal: S0N 1N0
General Phone: (306) 662-2133
General Fax: (306) 662-5005
General/National Adv. E-mail: classifieds@maplecreeknews.com
Display Adv. E-mail: ads@maplecreeknews.com
Classified Adv. e-mail: classifieds@maplecreeknews.com
Editorial e-mail: editorial@maplecreeknews.com
Primary Website: www.maplecreeknews.com
Year Established: 1902
Delivery Methods: Mail`Newsstand
Areas Served - City/County or Portion Thereof, or Zip codes: Canada
Commercial printers?: Y
Mechanical specifications: Type page 13 x 21 1/2; E - 6 cols, 2, 1/6 between; A - 6 cols, 2, 1/6 between; C - 6 cols, 2, 1/6 between.
Published: Thur
Avg Paid Circ: 1406
Audit By: Sworn/Estimate/Non-Audited
Audit Date: 12.07.2019
Personnel: Editorial Team (Ed.); Advertising Team (Adv.); Classifieds Team (Classifieds)
Parent company (for newspapers): Southern Alberta Newspapers

MAPLE RIDGE

PUBLICATION NAME

The Maple Ridge News
Street Address: 22611 Dewdney Trunk Road ,
Province: BC
Postal: V2X 3K1
Country: Canada
Mailing address: 22611 Dewdney Trunk Road
Mailing city: Maple Ridge
Province: BC
Postal: V2X 3K1
General Phone: (604) 467-1122
General Fax: (604) 463-4741
Advertising Phone: (604) 476-2728
General/National Adv. E-mail: publisher@mapleridgenews.com
Display Adv. E-mail: ads@mapleridgenews.com
Editorial e-mail: editor@mapleridgenews.com
Primary Website: www.mapleridgenews.com
Year Established: 1978
Delivery Methods: Carrier
Areas Served - City/County or Portion Thereof, or Zip codes: Canada
Commercial printers?: Y
Mechanical specifications: Type page 10 3/8 x 12 1/2; E - 6 cols, 1 5/8, 1/6 between; A - 6 cols, 1 5/8, 1/6 between; C - 6 cols, 1 5/8, 1/6 between.
Published: Wed`Fri
Avg Free Circ: 30223
Audit By: AAM
Audit Date: 31.03.2019
Personnel: Michael Hall (Ed.); Lisa Prophet (Pub); Brian Yip (Circ Mgr)
Parent company (for newspapers): Black Press Group Ltd.

MARATHON

PUBLICATION NAME

The Marathon Mercury
Street Address: 91 Peninsula Rd. ,
Province: ON
Postal: P0T 2E0
Country: Canada
Mailing address: PO Box 369
Mailing city: Marathon
Province: ON
Postal: P0T 2E0
General Phone: (805) 229-1520
General Fax: (805) 229-1595
General/National Adv. E-mail: mmpl@onlink.net
Year Established: 1948
Areas Served - City/County or Portion Thereof, or Zip codes: Canada
Mechanical specifications: Type page 10 1/4 x 15 7/8; E - 5 cols, 2, between; A - 5 cols, 2, between; C - 5 cols, 2, between.

Published: Tues
Avg Paid Circ: 689
Avg Free Circ: 13
Audit By: CMCA
Audit Date: 31.05.2016
Personnel: Garry R. McInnes (Adv. Mgr.); P. Douglas Gale (Ed.)

MARKHAM

PUBLICATION NAME

Markham Economist & Sun
Street Address: 50 Mcintosh Drive Unit 115 ,
Province: ON
Postal: L3R-9T3
Country: Canada
Mailing address: 50 McIntosh Drive Unit 115
Mailing city: Markham
Province: ON
Postal: L3R-9T3
General Phone: (905) 943-6100
General Fax: (905) 943-6129
Advertising Phone: (905) 943-6100
Advertising Fax: (905) 943-6129
Editorial Phone: (905) 943-6100
Editorial Fax: (905) 943-6129
General/National Adv. E-mail: admin@econsun.com
Display Adv. E-mail: abeswick@yrmg.com
Editorial e-mail: boneill@yrmg.com
Primary Website: yorkregion.com
Year Established: 1881
Areas Served - City/County or Portion Thereof, or Zip codes: Canada
Own Printing Facility?: Y
Published: Thur
Avg Free Circ: 68613
Audit By: CMCA
Audit Date: 31.12.2015
Personnel: Ian Proudfoot (Pub.); Bernie O'Neill (Ed.); John Willems (Gen. Mgr.); Meriel Bradley (Online Adv.)
Parent company (for newspapers): Metroland Media Group Ltd.; Torstar

PUBLICATION NAME

The Richmond Hill Liberal
Street Address: 50 Mcintosh Drive Unit 115 ,
Province: ON
Postal: L3R 9T3
Country: Canada
Mailing address: 50 McIntosh Drive Unit 115
Mailing city: Markham
Province: ON
Postal: L3R 9T3
General Phone: (905) 943-6100
General Fax: (905) 943-6129
Advertising Phone: (905) 943-6095
Advertising Fax: (905) 943-6129
General/National Adv. E-mail: admin@theliberal.com
Display Adv. E-mail: abeswick@yrmg.com
Classified Adv. e-mail: jkopacz@yrmg.com
Editorial e-mail: mbeck@yrmg.com
Primary Website: yorkregion.com
Year Established: 1878
Areas Served - City/County or Portion Thereof, or Zip codes: Canada
Own Printing Facility?: Y
Commercial printers?: Y
Published: Thur
Avg Paid Circ: 0
Avg Free Circ: 47438
Audit By: CCAB
Audit Date: 20.12.2017
Personnel: Ian Proudfoot (Pub.); Robert Lazurko (Bus. Mgr.); Anne Beswick (Retail Adv. Mgr.); Debora Kelly (Ed. in Chief); Marney Beck (Ed.); John Willems (General Manager)
Parent company (for newspapers): Metroland Media Group Ltd.; Torstar

MARMORA

PUBLICATION NAME

Havelock Citizen
Street Address: Po Box 239 ,
Province: ON
Postal: K0K 2M0
Country: Canada
Mailing address: PO Box 239
Mailing city: Marmora
Province: ON
Postal: K0K 2M0
General Phone: (613) 962-2360
General Fax: (613) 472-5026
Areas Served - City/County or Portion Thereof, or Zip codes: K0L 1Z0, K0L 2Z0
Own Printing Facility?: Y
Mechanical specifications: Type page 10 1/4 x 15 3/4; E - 6 cols, 1 5/8, between; A - 6 cols, 1 5/8, between; C - 6 cols, 1 5/8, between.
Published: Fri
Avg Paid Circ: 35000
Avg Free Circ: 2321
Audit By: Sworn/Estimate/Non-Audited
Audit Date: 12.07.2019
Personnel: Nancy Derrer (Ed.)
Parent company (for newspapers): Shield Media

MARYSTOWN

PUBLICATION NAME

The Southern Gazette
Street Address: Po Box 1116 ,
Province: NL
Postal: A0E 2M0
Country: Canada
Mailing address: PO Box 1116
Mailing city: Marystown
Province: NL
Postal: A0E 2M0
General Phone: (709) 279-3188
General Fax: (709) 279-2628
General/National Adv. E-mail: editor@southerngazette.ca
Editorial e-mail: editor@southerngazette.ca
Primary Website: www.southerngazette.ca
Areas Served - City/County or Portion Thereof, or Zip codes: Canada
Own Printing Facility?: Y
Commercial printers?: Y
Mechanical specifications: Type page 13 x 21 1/2; E - 6 cols, 2 1/12, between; A - 6 cols, 2 1/12, between; C - 9 cols, 1 1/12, between.
Published: Tues
Avg Paid Circ: 2231
Avg Free Circ: 0
Audit By: VAC
Audit Date: 31.12.2015
Personnel: George MacVicar (Ed.)
Parent company (for newspapers): Transcontinental Media

MATANE

PUBLICATION NAME

Avant Poste
Street Address: 305, Rue De La Gare, Following 107 ,
Province: QC
Postal: G4W 3J2
Country: Canada
Mailing address: 305, rue de la Gare, following 107
Mailing city: Matane
Province: QC
Postal: G4W 3J2
General Phone: (418) 629-3443
General Fax: (418) 562-4607
General/National Adv. E-mail: jean.gagnon@quebecormedia.com
Primary Website: www.lavantposte.ca
Areas Served - City/County or Portion Thereof, or Zip codes: Canada
Published: Wed
Avg Paid Circ: 6
Avg Free Circ: 8609

Community Newspapers in Canada

III-553

Audit By: CCAB
Audit Date: 31.03.2014
Personnel: Jean Gagnon

PUBLICATION NAME

La Voix Gaspesienne
Street Address: 305 De La Gare St., Ste. 107 ,
Province: QC
Postal: G4W 3J2
Country: Canada
Mailing address: 305 de la Gare St., Ste. 107
Mailing city: Matane
Province: QC
Postal: G4W 3J2
General Phone: (418) 562-4040
General Fax: (418) 562-4607
Advertising Phone: (418) 562-0666
Editorial Phone: (418) 562-0666
Primary Website: http://www.lavantagegaspesien.com
Areas Served - City/County or Portion Thereof, or Zip codes: Canada
Published: Wed
Avg Paid Circ: 13
Avg Free Circ: 17247
Audit By: CCAB
Audit Date: 31.03.2014
Personnel: Jean Gagnon ((Ed.))
Parent company (for newspapers): Quebecor Communications, Inc.

PUBLICATION NAME

Voix De La Matanie
Street Address: Rue De La Gare ,
Province: QC
Postal: G4W 3J2
Country: Canada
Mailing address: rue de la Gare
Mailing city: Matane
Province: QC
Postal: G4W 3J2
General Phone: (418) 562-4040
General Fax: (418) 562-4607
Areas Served - City/County or Portion Thereof, or Zip codes: Canada
Published: Wed
Avg Paid Circ: 11
Avg Free Circ: 17402
Audit By: CCAB
Audit Date: 31.03.2014
Personnel: Jean Gagnon

MATTAWA

PUBLICATION NAME

The Mattawa Recorder
Street Address: 341 Mcconnell St. ,
Province: ON
Postal: P0H 1V0
Country: Canada
Mailing address: PO Box 67
Mailing city: Mattawa
Province: ON
Postal: P0H 1V0
General Phone: (705) 744-5361
General Fax: (866) 831-6626
General/National Adv. E-mail: recorder@bellnet.ca
Display Adv. E-mail: recorder@bellnet.ca
Delivery Methods: Mail`Newsstand
Areas Served - City/County or Portion Thereof, or Zip codes: P0H 1V0
Mechanical specifications: Type page 10 x 14; E - 5 cols, 2, 1/4 between; A - 5 cols, 2, 1/4 between.
Published: Sun
Avg Paid Circ: 1100
Audit By: Sworn/Estimate/Non-Audited
Audit Date: 12.07.2019
Personnel: Tom Edwards (Pub.); Heather Edwards (Adv. Mgr.)

MEADOW LAKE

PUBLICATION NAME

Northern Pride
Street Address: 219 Centre Street ,
Province: SK
Postal: S9X 1Z4
Country: Canada
Mailing address: Box 2049
Mailing city: Meadow Lake
Province: SK
Postal: S9X 1Z4
General Phone: (306) 236-5353
Display Adv. E-mail: pride.terry@sasktel.net
Classified Adv. e-mail: pride.terry@sasktel.net
Editorial e-mail: pride.terry@sasktel.net
Primary Website: www.northernprideml.com
Year Established: 1993
Delivery Methods: Mail`Newsstand`Carrier`Racks
Areas Served - City/County or Portion Thereof, or Zip codes: Canada
Published: Thur
Avg Paid Circ: 1638
Avg Free Circ: 4283
Audit By: CMCA
Audit Date: 31.12.2015
Personnel: Terry Villeneuve (Pub)

MEAFORD

PUBLICATION NAME

Blue Mountains Courier-herald
Street Address: 24 Trowbridge St. West , Unit 6
Province: ON
Postal: N4L 1Y1
Country: Canada
Mailing address: 24 Trowbridge St. West Unit 6
Mailing city: Meaford
Province: ON
Postal: N4L 1Y1
General Phone: (519) 538-1421
General Fax: (519) 538-5028
General/National Adv. E-mail: clamb@simcoe.com
Display Adv. E-mail: pamero@simcoe.com
Editorial e-mail: lmartin@simcoe.com
Primary Website: www.simcoe.com
Areas Served - City/County or Portion Thereof, or Zip codes: Canada
Published: Wed
Avg Paid Circ: 505
Audit By: CMCA
Audit Date: 30.06.2013
Personnel: Lori Martin (Ed); Heather Harris (Circ Mgr); Pamela Amero (Adv Mgr)

PUBLICATION NAME

Express
Street Address: 24 Trowbridge St. W Unit 6 ,
Province: ON
Postal: N4L 1Y1
Country: Canada
Mailing address: 24 Trowbridge St. W. Unit 6
Mailing city: Meaford
Province: ON
Postal: N4L 1Y1
General Phone: (519) 538-1421
General Fax: (519) 538-5028
General/National Adv. E-mail: meafordexpress@simcoe.com
Primary Website: www.meafordexpress.com
Year Established: 1906
Areas Served - City/County or Portion Thereof, or Zip codes: Canada
Commercial printers?: Y
Mechanical specifications: Type page 12 3/4 x 21; E - 6 cols, 2, 1/6 between; A - 6 cols, 2, 1/6 between; C - 6 cols, 2, 1/6 between.
Published: Wed
Avg Paid Circ: 544
Avg Free Circ: 96
Audit By: CMCA
Audit Date: 30.06.2016
Personnel: Scott Woodhouse (Ed.); Pamela Amero (Adv.); Chris Fell (Community Events)

Parent company (for newspapers): Metroland Media; Metroland Media Group Ltd.

MEDICINE HAT

PUBLICATION NAME

Prairie Post
Street Address: 3256 Dunmore Rd Se ,
Province: AB
Postal: T1B 3R2
Country: Canada
Mailing address: 3256 Dunmore Rd SE
Mailing city: Medicine Hat
Province: AB
Postal: T1B 3R2
General Phone: (403) 528-5769
General Fax: (403) 528-2276
General/National Adv. E-mail: rdahlman@prairiepost.com
Editorial e-mail: rdahlman@prairiepost.com
Primary Website: www.prairiepost.com
Areas Served - City/County or Portion Thereof, or Zip codes: County of Newell, Cypress County, County of 40-Mile, Special Areas, City of Brooks, southwest Saskatchewan, City of Swift Current, M.D. of Acadia Valley
Published: Fri
Avg Paid Circ: 0
Avg Free Circ: 12562
Audit By: VAC
Audit Date: 30.09.2015
Personnel: Ryan Dahlman (Mng Ed.)
Parent company (for newspapers): Alberta Newspaper Group LP

MELFORT

PUBLICATION NAME

Melfort Journal
Street Address: 901 Main St. ,
Province: SK
Postal: S0E 1A0
Country: Canada
Mailing address: PO Box 1300
Mailing city: Melfort
Province: SK
Postal: S0E 1A0
General Phone: (306) 752-5737
General Fax: (306) 752-5358
General/National Adv. E-mail: ads@melfortjournal.com
Primary Website: www.melfortjournal.com
Areas Served - City/County or Portion Thereof, or Zip codes: Canada
Own Printing Facility?: Y
Commercial printers?: Y
Published: Tues
Avg Paid Circ: 1132
Audit By: CMCA
Audit Date: 30.06.2016
Personnel: Ken Sorensen (Pub.)
Parent company (for newspapers): Postmedia Network Inc.; Quebecor Communications, Inc.

PUBLICATION NAME

North East Sun
Street Address: 901 Main St. ,
Province: SK
Postal: S0E 1A0
Country: Canada
Mailing address: PO Box 1300
Mailing city: Melfort
Province: SK
Postal: S0E 1A0
General Phone: (306) 752-5737
General Fax: (306) 752-5358
General/National Adv. E-mail: shirley.sorensen@sunmedia.ca
Display Adv. E-mail: cassie.johnson@sunmedia.ca
Editorial e-mail: greg.wiseman@sunmedia.ca
Primary Website: www.melfortjournal.com
Areas Served - City/County or Portion Thereof, or Zip codes: Canada
Published: Fri
Avg Free Circ: 21761

Audit By: CMCA
Audit Date: 30.06.2016
Personnel: Ken Sorensen

MELITA

PUBLICATION NAME

Melita New Era
Street Address: 128 Main St. ,
Province: MB
Postal: R0M 1L0
Country: Canada
Mailing address: 128 Main St.
Mailing city: Melita
Province: MB
Postal: R0M 1L0
General Phone: (204) 522-3491
General Fax: (204) 522-3648
General/National Adv. E-mail: newera@cpocket.mts.net
Display Adv. E-mail: ads.cpocket@mts.net
Editorial e-mail: cpocket@mts.net
Primary Website: http://www.melitanewera.ca/
Year Established: 1916
Areas Served - City/County or Portion Thereof, or Zip codes: Canada
Own Printing Facility?: Y
Commercial printers?: Y
Mechanical specifications: Type page 10 1/4 x 14; E - 6 cols, 1 3/5, 1/16 between; A - 6 cols, 1 3/5, 1/16 between; C - 6 cols, 1 3/5, 1/16 between.
Published: Fri
Avg Paid Circ: 1104
Avg Free Circ: 0
Audit By: CMCA
Audit Date: 28.02.2014
Personnel: Patty Lewis (Ed.)
Parent company (for newspapers): Glacier Media Group

MELVILLE

PUBLICATION NAME

The Melville Advance
Street Address: 218 3rd Ave. W. ,
Province: SK
Postal: S0A 2P0
Country: Canada
Mailing address: PO Box 1420
Mailing city: Melville
Province: SK
Postal: S0A 2P0
General Phone: (306) 728-5448
General Fax: (306) 728-4004
General/National Adv. E-mail: melvilleadvance@sasktel.net
Display Adv. E-mail: sales@grasslandsnews.ca
Classified Adv. e-mail: contact@grasslandsnews.ca
Editorial e-mail: editor@grasslandsnews.ca
Primary Website: www.melvilleadvance.com
Year Established: 1928
Delivery Methods: Mail`Newsstand
Areas Served - City/County or Portion Thereof, or Zip codes: Stanley
Own Printing Facility?: Y
Commercial printers?: Y
Mechanical specifications: Type page 10 1/8 x 15 3/4; E - 6 cols, 2 1/4, 1/4 between; A - 6 cols, 2 1/4, 1/4 between; C - 6 cols, 2 1/4, 1/4 between.
Published: Fri
Avg Paid Circ: 1679
Avg Free Circ: 17
Audit By: CMCA
Audit Date: 31.05.2016
Personnel: George Brown; Chris Ashfield (Group Publisher)
Parent company (for newspapers): Grasslands News Group

MERRITT

PUBLICATION NAME

Merritt Herald

Street Address: 2090 Granite Ave.,
Province: BC
Postal: V1K 1B8
Country: Canada
Mailing address: Box 9 – 2090 Granite Ave
Mailing city: Merritt
Province: BC
Postal: V1K 1B8
General Phone: (250) 378-4241
General Fax: (250) 378-6818
General/National Adv. E-mail: newsroom@merrittherald.com
Display Adv. E-mail: sales2@merrittherald.com
Classified Adv. e-mail: classifieds@merrittherald.com
Editorial e-mail: newsroom@merrittherald.com
Primary Website: www.merrittherald.com
Year Established: 1999
Areas Served - City/County or Portion Thereof, or Zip codes: Merritt
Own Printing Facility?: Y
Mechanical specifications: Type page 10 5/16 x 14 1/2; E - 6 cols, 1 7/12, 1/6 between; A - 6 cols, 1 7/12, 1/6 between; C - 6 cols, 1 7/12, 1/6 between.
Published: Thur
Avg Paid Circ: 1092
Avg Free Circ: 5589
Audit By: VAC
Audit Date: 30.06.2016
Personnel: Theresa Arnold (Pub.); Cole Wagner (Ed); Kenneth Couture (Office Mgr)
Parent company (for newspapers): Aberdeen Publishing; Merrit Newspapers

MIDDLETON
PUBLICATION NAME
Mirror-examiner
Street Address: 87 Commercial St.,
Province: NS
Postal: B0S 1P0
Country: Canada
Mailing address: PO Box 880
Mailing city: Middleton
Province: NS
Postal: B0S 1P0
General Phone: (902) 825-3457
General Fax: (902) 825-6707
General/National Adv. E-mail: kentpub.ads@ns.sympatico.ca
Display Adv. E-mail: kentpub.ads@ns.sympatico.ca
Own Printing Facility?: Y
Commercial printers?: Y
Mechanical specifications: Type page 12 1/2 x 21; E - 7 cols, 1/8 between; A - 7 cols, 1/8 between; C - 7 cols, 1/8 between.
Published: Wed
Avg Paid Circ: 3101
Audit By: Sworn/Estimate/Non-Audited
Audit Date: 12.07.2019
Personnel: Garnet Austen (Pub.); Wayne Smith (Adv. Mgr.); Lori Errington (Ed.)

PUBLICATION NAME
The Spectator
Street Address: 87 Commercial St.,
Province: NS
Postal: B0S 1P0
Country: Canada
Mailing address: 87 Commercial St.
Mailing city: Middleton
Province: NS
Postal: B0S 1P0
General Phone: (902) 532-2219
General Fax: (902) 825-6707
General/National Adv. E-mail: info@annapolisspectator.ca
Display Adv. E-mail: info@annapolisspectator.ca
Editorial e-mail: editor@annapolisspectator.ca
Primary Website: www.annapoliscountyspectator.com
Own Printing Facility?: Y
Commercial printers?: Y
Mechanical specifications: Type page 10 1/2 x 13; E - 6 cols, 1/8 between; A - 6 cols, 1/8 between; C - 6 cols, 1/8 between.
Published: Thur
Avg Paid Circ: 2048

Avg Free Circ: 0
Audit By: CMCA
Audit Date: 31.01.2013
Personnel: Fred Fiander (Pub.); Lawrence Powell (Ed.)
Parent company (for newspapers): Transcontinental Media

MIDLAND
PUBLICATION NAME
The Mirror
Street Address: 488 Dominion Ave.,
Province: ON
Postal: L4R 1P6
Country: Canada
Mailing address: 488 Dominion Ave.
Mailing city: Midland
Province: ON
Postal: L4R 1P6
General Phone: (705) 527-5500
General Fax: (705) 527-5467
General/National Adv. E-mail: themirror@simcoe.com
Primary Website: simcoe.com
Areas Served - City/County or Portion Thereof, or Zip codes: Canada
Own Printing Facility?: Y
Commercial printers?: Y
Mechanical specifications: Type page 10 3/8 x 14; E - 9 cols, 1 1/16, 3/16 between; A - 9 cols, 1 1/16, 3/16 between; C - 9 cols, 1 1/16, 3/16 between.
Published: Thur
Avg Paid Circ: 0
Avg Free Circ: 21435
Audit By: CCAB
Audit Date: 30.09.2017
Personnel: Joe Anderson (Pub.); Leigh Gate (Gen. Mgr.); Leigh Rourke (Adv. Mgr.); Kyla Mosley (Circ. Mgr.); Travis Mealing (Ed.); Lori Martin (Mng. Ed.)
Parent company (for newspapers): Metroland Media Group Ltd.; Torstar

MILDMAY
PUBLICATION NAME
Town And Country Crier
Street Address: 100 Elora St.,
Province: ON
Postal: N0G 2J0
Country: Canada
Mailing address: PO Box 190
Mailing city: Mildmay
Province: ON
Postal: N0G 2J0
General Phone: (519) 367-2681
General Fax: (519) 367-5417
General/National Adv. E-mail: thecrier@wightman.ca
Mechanical specifications: Type page 10 x 15 1/2; E - 5 cols, 2, 1/4 between; C - 4 cols, 2 1/2, 1/4 between.
Published: Thur
Avg Paid Circ: 1211
Avg Free Circ: 169
Audit By: CMCA
Audit Date: 30.06.2016
Personnel: John H. Hafermehl (Pub.); Susan Bross (Ed.)

MILLET
PUBLICATION NAME
Leduc-wetaskiwin Pipestone Flyer
Street Address: 5025 - 50 Street,
Province: AB
Postal: T0C 1Z0
Country: Canada
Mailing address: PO BOX 402
Mailing city: Millet
Province: AB
Postal: T0C 1Z0
General Phone: (780) 387-5797
General Fax: (780) 387-4397
Display Adv. E-mail: sales1@pipestoneflyer.ca
Editorial e-mail: editor@pipestoneflyer.ca

Primary Website: www.pipestoneflyer.ca
Year Established: 1997
Delivery Methods: Mail`Newsstand`Racks
Areas Served - City/County or Portion Thereof, or Zip codes: City of Leduc, Leduc County, City of Wetaskiwin, Wetaskiwin County, Town of Millet, Pigeon Lake, Calmar, Thorsby, New Sarepta, Warburg, Winfield, Mulhurst Bay, Ma-Me-O Beach
Published: Thur
Avg Paid Circ: 0
Avg Free Circ: 16935
Audit By: VAC
Audit Date: 31.07.2016
Personnel: Michele Rosenthal (Pub); Stu Salkeld (Ed)
Parent company (for newspapers): Black Press Group Ltd.; Black Press, Prairie Division

MILTON
PUBLICATION NAME
The Milton Canadian Champion
Street Address: 555 Industrial Dr.,
Province: ON
Postal: L9T 5E1
Country: Canada
Mailing address: 555 Industrial Dr.
Mailing city: Milton
Province: ON
Postal: L9T 5E1
General Phone: (905) 878-2341
General Fax: (905) 876-2364
Editorial e-mail: editorial@miltoncanadianchampion.com
Primary Website: miltoncanadianchampion.com
Year Established: 1860
Delivery Methods: Carrier
Areas Served - City/County or Portion Thereof, or Zip codes: Canada
Own Printing Facility?: Y
Commercial printers?: Y
Published: Tues`Thur
Avg Paid Circ: 19
Avg Free Circ: 16276
Audit By: CCAB
Audit Date: 30.09.2017
Personnel: Neil Oliver (Pub.); Karen Miceli (Ed.); Steve LeBlanc (News/Sports Ed.); Tim Coles (Prodn. Mgr.); David Harvey (Regional General Manager); Katy Letourneau (Director of Advertising); Sarah McSweeney (Circ. Manager)
Parent company (for newspapers): Metroland Media Group Ltd.; Torstar

MINDEN
PUBLICATION NAME
The Minden Times
Street Address: 2 Iga Rd., Unit 2,
Province: ON
Postal: K0M 2K0
Country: Canada
Mailing address: PO Box 97
Mailing city: Minden
Province: ON
Postal: K0M 2K0
General Phone: (705) 286-1288
General Fax: (705) 286-4768
Display Adv. E-mail: jenniferm@haliburtonpress.com
Classified Adv. e-mail: classifieds@mindentimes.ca
Editorial e-mail: editor@mindentimes.ca
Primary Website: www.mindentimes.ca
Year Established: 1980
Delivery Methods: Mail`Newsstand
Areas Served - City/County or Portion Thereof, or Zip codes: Minden
Commercial printers?: Y
Published: Thur
Avg Paid Circ: 1076
Avg Free Circ: 259
Audit By: CMCA
Audit Date: 30.06.2016
Personnel: Jenn Watt (Ed.); Jennifer McEathron (Sales); Debbie Comer (Circ., Classified)
Parent company (for newspapers): White Pine Media

MINNEDOSA
PUBLICATION NAME
Minnedosa Tribune
Street Address: 14 3rd Ave. Sw,
Province: MB
Postal: R0J 1E0
Country: Canada
Mailing address: PO Box 930
Mailing city: Minnedosa
Province: MB
Postal: R0J 1E0
General Phone: (204) 867-3816
General Fax: (204) 867-5171
General/National Adv. E-mail: editor@minnedosatribune.com
Display Adv. E-mail: adsales@minnedosatribune.com
Classified Adv. e-mail: class@minnedosatribune.com
Editorial e-mail: editor@minnedosatribune.com
Primary Website: www.minnedosatribune.com
Year Established: 1883
Areas Served - City/County or Portion Thereof, or Zip codes: Minnedosa
Mechanical specifications: Type page 10 1/2 x 16; E - 6 cols, between; A - 6 cols, between; C - 6 cols, between.
Published: Fri
Avg Paid Circ: 456
Avg Free Circ: 258
Audit By: VAC
Audit Date: 30.06.2016
Personnel: Darryl Holyk (Pub./Ed); Heather Horner (Adv); Georgia Kerluke (Office Mgr/Class.)

MIRAMICHI
PUBLICATION NAME
Miramichi Leader
Street Address: 175 General Manson Way,
Province: NB
Postal: E1N 6K7
Country: Canada
Mailing address: PO Box 500
Mailing city: Miramichi
Province: NB
Postal: E1V 3M6
General Phone: (506) 622-2600
General Fax: (506) 622-6506
General/National Adv. E-mail: news@miramichileader.com
Editorial e-mail: cook.nancy@miramichileader.com
Primary Website: https://www.telegraphjournal.com/miramichi-leader/
Areas Served - City/County or Portion Thereof, or Zip codes: Canada
Mechanical specifications: Type page 10 9/16 x 16; E - 6 cols, 1 2/3, 1/8 between; A - 6 cols, 1 2/3, 1/8 between; C - 6 cols, 1 2/3, 1/4 between.
Published: Mon`Wed
Avg Paid Circ: 3768
Avg Free Circ: 13
Audit By: CMCA
Audit Date: 31.12.2013
Personnel: Nancy Cook (Pub.); Christine Savoy (Circ. Mgr.)
Parent company (for newspapers): Brunswick News, Inc.

MISSION
PUBLICATION NAME
Mission City Record
Street Address: 33047 1st Ave.,
Province: BC
Postal: V2V 1G2
Country: Canada
Mailing address: 33047 1st Ave.
Mailing city: Mission
Province: BC
Postal: V2V 1G2
General Phone: (604) 826-6221
General Fax: (604) 826-8266
Advertising Phone: (800) 363-2232
General/National Adv. E-mail: news@

Community Newspapers in Canada

III-555

missioncityrecord.com
Display Adv. E-mail: karen.murtagh@missioncityrecord.com
Classified Adv. e-mail: adcontrol@missioncityrecord.com
Editorial e-mail: kevin.mills@missioncityrecord.com
Primary Website: www.missioncityrecord.com
Year Established: 1908
Areas Served - City/County or Portion Thereof, or Zip codes: Mission - Abbotsford
Commercial printers?: Y
Mechanical specifications: Type page 10 3/8 x 12 7/8; E - 6 cols, 1 5/8, between; A - 6 cols, 1 5/8, between; C - 6 cols, 1 5/8, between.
Published: Fri
Avg Paid Circ: 21
Avg Free Circ: 10968
Audit By: AAM
Audit Date: 31.12.2018
Personnel: Carly Ferguson (Pub); Kevin Mills (Ed); Krista Stobbe (Office Mgr.)
Parent company (for newspapers): Black Press Group Ltd.

MISSISSAUGA

PUBLICATION NAME

Awaaz Punjabi
Street Address: 7015 Tranmere Dr. Suite #16 ,
Province: ON
Postal: L5S 1T7
Country: Canada
Mailing address: 7015 Tranmere Dr. Suite #16
Mailing city: Mississauga
Province: ON
Postal: L5S 1T7
General Phone: (905)795-8282
General Fax: (905) 795-9801
Advertising Phone: (416) 899 8140
Editorial Phone: (905) 795-0639
General/National Adv. E-mail: info@weeklyvoice.com
Display Adv. E-mail: marketing@weeklyvoice.com
Classified Adv. e-mail: admin@weeklyvoice.com
Editorial e-mail: pnews@weeklyvoice.com
Primary Website: www.awaazpunjabi.com
Year Established: 2000
Delivery Methods: Mail`Newsstand`Racks
Areas Served - City/County or Portion Thereof, or Zip codes: Canada
Published: Wed
Avg Free Circ: 9900
Audit By: CMCA
Audit Date: 29.02.2016
Personnel: Sudhir Anand

PUBLICATION NAME

Brampton Guardian
Street Address: 3145 Wolfedale Rd. ,
Province: ON
Postal: L5C 3A9
Country: Canada
Mailing address: 3145 Wolfedale Rd.
Mailing city: Mississauga
Province: ON
Postal: L5C 3A9
General Phone: (905) 273-8111
General Fax: (905) 454-4385
General/National Adv. E-mail: letters@thebramptonguardian.com
Display Adv. E-mail: scotthartman@thebramptonguardian.com
Classified Adv. e-mail: classified@thebramptonguardian.com
Editorial e-mail: plonergan@metroland.com
Primary Website: thebramptonguardian.com
Delivery Methods: Carrier
Areas Served - City/County or Portion Thereof, or Zip codes: Canada
Own Printing Facility?: Y
Commercial printers?: Y
Mechanical specifications: Type page 13 x 22 1/2; E - 10 cols, 1 1/16, between; A - 10 cols, 1 1/16, between; C - 10 cols, 1 1/16, between.
Published: Thur`Fri
Avg Paid Circ: 0
Avg Free Circ: 137132
Audit By: CCAB
Audit Date: 9/31/2017
Personnel: Dave Coleman (Circ. Mgr.); Dana Robbins (Pub); Bill Anderson (Gen Mgr); Patricia Lonergan (Ed)
Parent company (for newspapers): Metroland Media Group Ltd.

PUBLICATION NAME

Mississauga News
Street Address: 3145 Wolfedale Road ,
Province: ON
Postal: L5C 3A9
Country: Canada`
Mailing address: 3145 Wolfedale Road
Mailing city: Mississauga
Province: ON
Postal: L5C 3A9
General Phone: (905) 273-8230
General Fax: (905) 568-0181
General/National Adv. E-mail: www.mississauga.com
Editorial e-mail: tlanks@mississauga.net
Primary Website: mississauga.com
Areas Served - City/County or Portion Thereof, or Zip codes: Canada
Published: Thur`Fri
Avg Paid Circ: 0
Avg Free Circ: 153598
Audit By: CCAB
Audit Date: 30.09.2017
Personnel: Dana Robbins (Pub.); Clark Kim (Community News/Ed.)
Parent company (for newspapers): Metroland Media Group Ltd.

MITCHELL

PUBLICATION NAME

The Mitchell Advocate
Street Address: 42 Montreal St. ,
Province: ON
Postal: N0K 1N0
Country: Canada
Mailing address: P.O. Box 669
Mailing city: Mitchell
Province: ON
Postal: N0K 1N0
General Phone: (519) 348-8431
General Fax: (519) 348-8836
General/National Adv. E-mail: abader@bowesnet.com
Primary Website: www.mitchelladvocate.com
Areas Served - City/County or Portion Thereof, or Zip codes: Canada
Mechanical specifications: Type page 11 3/8 x 21 1/4; E - 6 cols, 1 3/4, between; A - 6 cols, 1 3/4, between; C - 6 cols, 1 3/4, between.
Published: Wed
Avg Paid Circ: 1790
Avg Free Circ: 22
Audit By: CMCA
Audit Date: 30.06.2016
Personnel: Andy Bader (Ed.); Juanita Belfour (Adv. Mgr.)
Parent company (for newspapers): Postmedia Network Inc.; Quebecor Communications, Inc.

MONT TREMBLANT

PUBLICATION NAME

Information Du Nord Sainte-agathe
Street Address: 1107 Rue De Saint Jovite ,
Province: QC
Postal: J8E 3J9
Country: Canada
Mailing address: 1107 rue de Saint Jovite
Mailing city: Mont Tremblant
Province: QC
Postal: J8E 3J9
General Phone: (819) 425-8658
General Fax: (819) 425-7713
General/National Adv. E-mail: johanne.regimbald@quebecormedia.com
Primary Website: www.linformationdunordsainteagathe.ca
Commercial printers?: Y
Mechanical specifications: Type page 10 x 11 1/2; E - 10 cols, between.
Published: Thur
Avg Paid Circ: 15474
Avg Free Circ: 26
Audit By: Sworn/Estimate/Non-Audited
Audit Date: 12.07.2019
Personnel: Johanne Regimbald
Parent company (for newspapers): Quebecor Communications, Inc.

MONTAGUE

PUBLICATION NAME

Atlantic Post Calls
Street Address: 567 Main Street ,
Province: PE
Postal: C0A 1R0
Country: Canada
Mailing address: PO Box 790
Mailing city: Montague
Province: PE
Postal: C0A 1R0
General Phone: (902) 838-2515
General Fax: (902) 838-4392
Advertising Phone: (902) 838-4392 Ext. 203
Advertising Fax: (902) 838-4392
Editorial Phone: (902) 838-2515 x 201
Editorial Fax: (902) 838-4392
General/National Adv. E-mail: subscribe@peicanada.com
Display Adv. E-mail: jan@peicanada.com
Editorial e-mail: paul@peicanada.com
Primary Website: www.peicanada.com
Year Established: 1979
Areas Served - City/County or Portion Thereof, or Zip codes: Canada
Published: Fri
Avg Paid Circ: 752
Avg Free Circ: 625
Audit By: CMCA
Audit Date: 28.02.2014
Personnel: Paul MacNeill; Jan MacNeill

PUBLICATION NAME

The Eastern Graphic
Street Address: 567 Main St. ,
Province: PE
Postal: C0A 1R0
Country: Canada
Mailing address: PO Box 790
Mailing city: Montague
Province: PE
Postal: C0A 1R0
General Phone: (902) 838-2515
General Fax: (902) 838-4392
General/National Adv. E-mail: subscribe@peicanada.com
Editorial e-mail: editor@peicanada.com
Primary Website: www.peicanada.com
Areas Served - City/County or Portion Thereof, or Zip codes: Canada
Commercial printers?: Y
Mechanical specifications: Type page 13 x 21 1/2; E - 6 cols, 2, between; A - 6 cols, 2, between; C - 6 cols, 2, between.
Published: Wed
Avg Paid Circ: 4743
Avg Free Circ: 196
Audit By: CMCA
Audit Date: 30.06.2014
Personnel: Paul MacNeill (Pub.); Jan MacNeill (Adv. Mgr.); Heather Moore (Ed.); Kim Madigan (Prodn. Coord.)

MONT-JOLI

PUBLICATION NAME

Le Information
Street Address: Rue Doucet ,
Province: QC
Postal: G5H 1R6
Country: Canada
Mailing address: rue Doucet
Mailing city: Mont-Joli
Province: QC
Postal: G5H 1R6
General Phone: (418) 775-4381
Areas Served - City/County or Portion Thereof, or Zip codes: Canada
Published: Wed
Avg Paid Circ: 33
Avg Free Circ: 9867
Audit By: CCAB
Audit Date: 31.03.2014
Personnel: Francis Desrosiers

MONT-LAURIER

PUBLICATION NAME

Journal Le Choix D'antoine Labelle
Street Address: Boulevard A.-paquette ,
Province: QC
Postal: J9L1K5
Country: Canada
Mailing address: boulevard A.-Paquette
Mailing city: Mont-Laurier
Province: QC
Postal: J9L1K5
General Phone: (819) 623-3112
Areas Served - City/County or Portion Thereof, or Zip codes: Canada
Published: Wed
Avg Paid Circ: 0
Avg Free Circ: 17000
Audit By: CCAB
Audit Date: 30.09.2012
Personnel: Andre Guillemette

PUBLICATION NAME

Journal Le Courant Des Hautes-laurentides
Street Address: 534, De La Madone ,
Province: QC
Postal: J9L 1S5
Country: Canada
Mailing address: 534, de la Madone
Mailing city: Mont-Laurier
Province: QC
Postal: J9L 1S5
General Phone: (819) 623-7374
General Fax: (819) 623-7375
Primary Website: www.lecourant.ca
Published: Thur
Avg Free Circ: 18400
Audit By: ODC
Audit Date: 14.12.2010
Personnel: Sylvie Vaillancourt

MONTMAGNY

PUBLICATION NAME

Le Peuple Cote-sud
Street Address: 80 Boul. Tache E. ,
Province: QC
Postal: G5V 3S7
Country: Canada
Mailing address: PO Box 430
Mailing city: Montmagny
Province: QC
Postal: G5V 3S7
General Phone: (418) 248-0415
General Fax: (418) 248-2377
General/National Adv. E-mail: peuple-cote-sud@globetrotter.net; vemtes.cote.sud@gmail.com
Primary Website: www.camoe.ca
Year Established: 1900
Areas Served - City/County or Portion Thereof, or Zip codes: Canada
Mechanical specifications: Type page 10 1/4 x 11 3/4.
Published: Wed
Avg Paid Circ: 27
Avg Free Circ: 20852
Audit By: CCAB
Audit Date: 30.09.2012
Personnel: Claueettne Tardis (Pub.)
Parent company (for newspapers): Quebecor Communications, Inc.

MONTMAGNY

PUBLICATION NAME

L'oie Blanche
Street Address: 70 Rue De L'anse ,
Province: QC
Postal: G5V 1G8
Country: Canada
Mailing address: 70 Rue De L'Anse
Mailing city: Montmagny
Province: QC
Postal: G5V 1G8
General Phone: (418) 248-8820
General Fax: (418) 248-4033
General/National Adv. E-mail: oieblanc@globetrotter.net
Primary Website: www.oieblanc.com
Areas Served - City/County or Portion Thereof, or Zip codes: Canada
Mechanical specifications: Type page 11 3/4 x 15.
Published: Wed
Avg Paid Circ: 17
Avg Free Circ: 22533
Audit By: CCAB
Audit Date: 30.09.2015
Personnel: Yannick Patelli (Pub.)
Parent company (for newspapers): Reseau Select/Select Network

MONTREAL

PUBLICATION NAME

Echos Vedettes
Street Address: 465 Mcgill Ave. ,
Province: QC
Postal: H2W 2H1
Country: Canada
Mailing address: 465 McGill Ave.
Mailing city: Montreal
Province: QC
Postal: H2W 2H1
General Phone: (514) 528-7111
General Fax: (514) 528-7115
General/National Adv. E-mail: redaction@echosvedettes.ca
Areas Served - City/County or Portion Thereof, or Zip codes: Canada
Published: Sat
Avg Paid Circ: 54193
Avg Free Circ: 875
Audit By: Sworn/Estimate/Non-Audited
Audit Date: 12.07.2019
Personnel: Sylvie Bourgeault (Gen. Mgr.)

PUBLICATION NAME

Flambeau
Street Address: Boulevard Langelier Bureau 210 , Bureau 210
Province: QC
Postal: H1P 3C6
Country: Canada
Mailing address: boulevard Langelier Bureau 210
Mailing city: Montreal
Province: QC
Postal: H1P 3C6
General Phone: (514) 899-5888
Areas Served - City/County or Portion Thereof, or Zip codes: Canada
Published: Tues
Avg Paid Circ: 0
Avg Free Circ: 56194
Audit By: CCAB
Audit Date: 31.03.2014
Personnel: Stephane Desjardins

PUBLICATION NAME

Guide De Montreal-nord
Street Address: Boulevard Langelier Bureau 210 , Bureau 210
Province: QC
Postal: H1P 3C6
Country: Canada
Mailing address: boulevard Langelier Bureau 210
Mailing city: Montreal
Province: QC
Postal: H1P 3C6
General Phone: (514) 899-5888
Areas Served - City/County or Portion Thereof, or Zip codes: Canada
Published: Tues
Avg Paid Circ: 0
Avg Free Circ: 34440
Audit By: CCAB
Audit Date: 31.03.2014
Personnel: Yannick Pinel

PUBLICATION NAME

Informateur De Riviere Des Prairies
Street Address: Boulevard Langelier Bureau 210 , Bureau 210
Province: QC
Postal: H1P 3C6
Country: Canada
Mailing address: boulevard Langelier Bureau 210
Mailing city: Montreal
Province: QC
Postal: H1P 3C6
General Phone: (514) 899-5888
Areas Served - City/County or Portion Thereof, or Zip codes: Canada
Published: Tues
Avg Free Circ: 20917
Audit By: CCAB
Audit Date: 31.03.2014
Personnel: Yannick Pinel

PUBLICATION NAME

Journal De Rosemont / Petite Patrie
Street Address: 8770 Langelier Boulevard Bureau 210 ,
Province: QC
Postal: H1P 3C6
Country: Canada
Mailing address: 8770 Langelier Boulevard Bureau 210
Mailing city: Montreal
Province: QC
Postal: H1P 3C6
General Phone: (514) 899-5888
General Fax: (514) 899-5001
General/National Adv. E-mail: rosepatrie@tc.tc
Primary Website: www.journalderosemont.com
Areas Served - City/County or Portion Thereof, or Zip codes: Canada
Published: Tues
Avg Paid Circ: 0
Avg Free Circ: 59344
Audit By: CCAB
Audit Date: 31.03.2014
Personnel: Stephane Desjardins

PUBLICATION NAME

Journal De St Michel
Street Address: Cp 50, Succ. St-michel ,
Province: QC
Postal: H2A 3L8
Country: Canada
Mailing address: CP 50, succ. St-Michel
Mailing city: Montreal
Province: QC
Postal: H2A 3L8
General Phone: (514) 721-4911
General Fax: (514) 374-4171
General/National Adv. E-mail: admin@journaldestmichel.com
Primary Website: www.journaldestmichel.com
Published: Sat
Avg Paid Circ: 20
Avg Free Circ: 24035
Audit By: ODC
Audit Date: 14.12.2011
Personnel: Claude Bricault

PUBLICATION NAME

Journal L'avenir De L'est
Street Address: 8770, Boulevard Langelier Bureau 210 ,
Province: QC
Postal: H1P 3C6
Country: Canada
Mailing address: 8770, boulevard Langelier Bureau 210
Mailing city: MontrÃƒÂ©al
Province: QC
Postal: H1P 3C6
General Phone: (514) 899-5888
General Fax: (514) 899-5001
General/National Adv. E-mail: redaction_est@tc.tc
Primary Website: http://www.avenirdelest.com
Areas Served - City/County or Portion Thereof, or Zip codes: Canada
Published: Tues
Avg Paid Circ: 0
Avg Free Circ: 27818
Audit By: CCAB
Audit Date: 31.03.2014
Personnel: Paul Sauve (Ed.)

PUBLICATION NAME

Nouvelles Hochelaga Maisonneuve
Street Address: Boulevard Langelier Bureau 210 , Bureau 210
Province: QC
Postal: H1P 3C6
Country: Canada
Mailing address: boulevard Langelier Bureau 210
Mailing city: Montreal
Province: QC
Postal: H1P 3C6
General Phone: (514) 899-5888
General/National Adv. E-mail: redactioncentre@tc.tc
Primary Website: www.nouvelleshochelagamaisonneuve.com
Areas Served - City/County or Portion Thereof, or Zip codes: Canada
Published: Tues
Avg Free Circ: 22615
Audit By: CCAB
Audit Date: 31.03.2014
Personnel: Stephane Desjardins

PUBLICATION NAME

Oratoire
Street Address: Chemin Queen Mary ,
Province: QC
Postal: H3V 1H6
Country: Canada
Mailing address: chemin Queen Mary
Mailing city: Montreal
Province: QC
Postal: H3V 1H6
General Phone: (514) 733-8211
Published: Sat
Avg Paid Circ: 25131
Avg Free Circ: 4346
Audit By: ODC
Audit Date: 14.12.2011
Personnel: Claude Grou

PUBLICATION NAME

Plateau
Street Address: 8770 Langelier Boulevard Bureau 210 ,
Province: QC
Postal: H1P 3C6
Country: Canada
Mailing address: 8770 Langelier boulevard Bureau 210
Mailing city: Montreal
Province: QC
Postal: H1P 3C6
General Phone: (514) 899-5888
General Fax: (514) 899-5001
General/National Adv. E-mail: redactioncentre@tc.tc
Primary Website: www.leplateau.com
Areas Served - City/County or Portion Thereof, or Zip codes: Canada
Published: Thur
Avg Free Circ: 34869
Audit By: CCAB
Audit Date: 31.03.2014
Personnel: Stephane Desjardins

PUBLICATION NAME

The Suburban West Island
Street Address: 7575 Trans Canada Hwy, Suite 105 ,
Province: QC
Postal: H4T 1V6
Country: Canada
Mailing address: 7575 Trans Canada Hwy. Suite 105
Mailing city: Montreal
Province: QC
Postal: H4T 1V6
General Phone: (514) 484-1107
General Fax: (514) 484-9616
General/National Adv. E-mail: suburban@thesuburban.com
Display Adv. E-mail: amanda@thesuburban.com
Editorial e-mail: editor@thesuburban.com
Primary Website: www.westislandgazette.com
Published: Wed
Avg Free Circ: 40239
Audit By: CMCA
Audit Date: 31.12.2013
Personnel: Beryl Wajsman (Editor-in-chief); Amanda Lavigne (Director of sales)

PUBLICATION NAME

Tourisme Plus
Street Address: B.p. 7 Succ Ahuntsic , Succ. Ahuntsic
Province: QC
Postal: H3L 3N5
Country: Canada
Mailing address: B.P. 7 Succ Ahuntsic
Mailing city: Montreal
Province: QC
Postal: H3L 3N5
General Phone: (514) 881-8583
Published: Wed
Avg Paid Circ: 123
Avg Free Circ: 1266
Audit By: ODC
Audit Date: 14.12.2011
Personnel: Michel Villeneuve

PUBLICATION NAME

Transcontinental Medias
Street Address: 8770 Langelier , Suite 210
Province: QC
Postal: H1P 3C6
Country: Canada
Mailing address: 8770 Langelier
Mailing city: Montreal
Province: QC
Postal: H1P 3C6
General Phone: (514) 899-5888
Advertising Fax: (514) 899-5001
General/National Adv. E-mail: sdesjardins@transcontinental.ca
Primary Website: www.journalderosemont.com
Delivery Methods: Carrier Racks
Mechanical specifications: Type page 10 x 14; E - 8 cols, 1 1/4, 1/8 between; A - 8 cols, 1 1/4, 1/8 between; C - 8 cols, 1 1/4, 1/8 between.
Published: Tues
Avg Free Circ: 36024
Audit By: Sworn/Estimate/Non-Audited
Audit Date: 12.07.2019
Personnel: Stephane Desjardins (publisher)
Parent company (for newspapers): Transcontinental Media

PUBLICATION NAME

Verdun Messenger
Street Address: 6239 Monk Blvd. ,
Province: QC
Postal: H4E 3H8
Country: Canada
Mailing address: 6239 Monk Blvd.
Mailing city: Montreal
Province: QC
Postal: H4E 3H8

Community Newspapers in Canada

III-557

General Phone: (514) 768-1920
General Fax: (514) 768-3306
General/National Adv. E-mail: lussierp@transcontinental.ca
Areas Served - City/County or Portion Thereof, or Zip codes: Canada
Published: Thur
Avg Paid Circ: 3
Avg Free Circ: 24364
Audit By: CCAB
Audit Date: 31.03.2014
Personnel: Lou Mercaer (Pub.); Pierre Lussier (Ed.)

MONT-TREMBLANT

PUBLICATION NAME

Information Du Nord L'annonciation
Street Address: 1107, Rue De St-jovite ,
Province: QC
Postal: J8E 3J9
Country: Canada
Mailing address: 1107, Rue De St-Jovite
Mailing city: Mont-Tremblant
Province: QC
Postal: J8E 3J9
General Phone: (819) 425-8658
General Fax: (819) 425-7713
General/National Adv. E-mail: infonord.journal@quebecormedia.com
Primary Website: www.hebdosquebecor.com
Year Established: 1980
Commercial printers?: Y
Mechanical specifications: Type page 10 x 11 1/2.
Published: Thur
Avg Paid Circ: 7974
Avg Free Circ: 15500
Audit By: Sworn/Estimate/Non-Audited
Audit Date: 12.07.2019
Personnel: Josee Gauvin (Ed.); Johanne Regimbald (ÃƒÂf£££ditrice)
Parent company (for newspapers): Quebecor Communications, Inc.

PUBLICATION NAME

Information Du Nord Mont Tremblant
Street Address: 1107 Rue De St. Jovite ,
Province: QC
Postal: J8E 3J9
Country: Canada
Mailing address: 1107 rue de St. Jovite
Mailing city: Mont-Tremblant
Province: QC
Postal: J8E 3J9
General Phone: (819) 425-8658
General Fax: (819) 425-7713
General/National Adv. E-mail: info.nord@hebdosquebecor.com
Primary Website: www.hebdosquebecor.com
Areas Served - City/County or Portion Thereof, or Zip codes: Canada
Commercial printers?: Y
Mechanical specifications: Type page 10 x .
Published: Wed
Avg Paid Circ: 4
Avg Free Circ: 15029
Audit By: CCAB
Audit Date: 31.03.2014
Personnel: Michel Gareau (Adv. Mgr.); Johanne Regimbald
Parent company (for newspapers): Quebecor Communications, Inc.

PUBLICATION NAME

Information Du Nord Vallee De La Rouge
Street Address: Rue De St-jovite ,
Province: QC
Postal: J8E 3J9
Country: Canada
Mailing address: rue de St-Jovite
Mailing city: Mont-Tremblant
Province: QC
Postal: J8E 3J9
General Phone: (819) 425-8658
Areas Served - City/County or Portion Thereof, or Zip codes: Canada
Published: Wed
Avg Paid Circ: 2
Avg Free Circ: 15487
Audit By: CCAB
Audit Date: 31.03.2014
Personnel: Johanne Regimbald

PUBLICATION NAME

Point De Vue Laurentides
Street Address: 580 Rue De Saint Jovite Ste 201 ,
Province: QC
Postal: J8E 2Z9
Country: Canada
Mailing address: 580 Rue de Saint Jovite Ste 201
Mailing city: Mont-Tremblant
Province: QC
Postal: J8E 2Z9
General Phone: (819) 425-7666
General Fax: (819) 425-9111
Advertising Phone: (819) 425-7666
Advertising Fax: (819) 425-9111
Editorial Phone: (819) 425-7666
Editorial Fax: (819) 425-9111
General/National Adv. E-mail: infolaurentides@transcontinental.ca
Display Adv. E-mail: infolaurentides@transcontinental.ca
Editorial e-mail: infolaurentides@transcontinental.ca
Primary Website: www.pointdevuemonttremblant.com
Delivery Methods: Mail`Racks
Areas Served - City/County or Portion Thereof, or Zip codes: Canada
Published: Wed
Avg Free Circ: 31760
Audit By: CCAB
Audit Date: 31.03.2014

MOOSE JAW

PUBLICATION NAME

Fyi
Street Address: 44 Fairford St W. ,
Province: SK
Postal: S6H 1V1
Country: Canada
Mailing address: 44 Fairford St. W.
Mailing city: Moose Jaw
Province: SK
Postal: S6H 1V1
General Phone: (306) 692-6441
General/National Adv. E-mail: editorial@mjtimes.sk.ca
Editorial e-mail: editorial@mjtimes.sk.ca
Primary Website: www.mjtimes.sk.ca
Areas Served - City/County or Portion Thereof, or Zip codes: Canada
Published: Wed
Avg Free Circ: 24086
Audit By: CMCA
Audit Date: 31.12.2013

MOOSOMIN

PUBLICATION NAME

World-spectator
Street Address: 714 Main Street ,
Province: SK
Postal: S0G 3N0
Country: Canada
Mailing address: PO Box 250
Mailing city: Moosomin
Province: SK
Postal: S0G 3N0
General Phone: (306) 435-2445
General Fax: (306) 435-3969
General/National Adv. E-mail: world_spectator@sasktel.net
Primary Website: www.world-spectator.com
Year Established: 1884
Delivery Methods: Mail`Newsstand
Areas Served - City/County or Portion Thereof, or Zip codes: Moosomin, Rocanville, Wapella, Wawota, Redvers, Maryfield, Spy Hill, Tantallon, Elkhorn, St Lazare
Own Printing Facility?: Y
Commercial printers?: Y
Mechanical specifications: Type page 10 x 16 1/2; E - 6 cols, 1/6 between; A - 6 cols, 1/6 between; C - 6 cols, 1/6 between.
Published: Mon
Avg Paid Circ: 3609
Audit By: CMCA
Audit Date: 31.12.2015
Personnel: Kevin Weedmark (Ed.)

MORINVILLE

PUBLICATION NAME

The Free Press
Street Address: 10126 100 Ave. ,
Province: AB
Postal: T8R 1R9
Country: Canada
Mailing address: PO Box 3005
Mailing city: Morinville
Province: AB
Postal: T8R 1R9
General Phone: (780) 939-3309
General Fax: (780) 939-3093
Advertising Phone: (780) 939-3309
General/National Adv. E-mail: redwater@shaw.ca
Display Adv. E-mail: morinville@shaw.ca
Primary Website: www.cowleynewspapers.com
Year Established: 1995
Areas Served - City/County or Portion Thereof, or Zip codes: Sturgeon County
Mechanical specifications: Type page 10 1/4 x 15 1/2; E - 6 cols, 1 1/2, 1/12 between; A - 6 cols, 1 1/2, 1/12 between; C - 6 cols, 1 1/2, 1/12 between.
Published: Tues
Avg Paid Circ: 55
Avg Free Circ: 11996
Audit By: VAC
Audit Date: 31.07.2016
Personnel: Ed Cowley (Pub.)
Parent company (for newspapers): W & E Cowley Publishing Ltd.

MORRISBURG

PUBLICATION NAME

The Morrisburg Leader
Street Address: Hwy. 2, 31 Shopping Centre, 41 Main St. ,
Province: ON
Postal: K0C 1X0
Country: Canada
Mailing address: PO Box 891
Mailing city: Morrisburg
Province: ON
Postal: K0C 1X0
General Phone: (613) 543-2987
General Fax: (613) 543-3643
General/National Adv. E-mail: info@morrisburgleader.ca
Display Adv. E-mail: leaderads@vianet.ca
Primary Website: www.morrisburgleader.ca
Year Established: 1976
Areas Served - City/County or Portion Thereof, or Zip codes: Canada
Own Printing Facility?: Y
Commercial printers?: Y
Mechanical specifications: Type page 12 3/8 x 21 1/2; E - 6 cols, 1/6 between; A - 6 cols, 1/6 between; C - 6 cols, 1/6 between.
Published: Wed
Avg Paid Circ: 1774
Avg Free Circ: 54
Audit By: CMCA
Audit Date: 30.09.2016
Personnel: Mike Laurin (Adv. Mgr.); Wanda Dawley (Circ. Mgr.); Sam Laurin (Ed.); Bonnie McNairn (Mng. Ed.); Terry Laurin (Prodn. Mgr.)

MOUNT FOREST

PUBLICATION NAME

Arthur Enterprise News
Street Address: 277 Main St. S. ,
Province: ON
Postal: N0G 2L0
Country: Canada
Mailing address: PO Box 130
Mailing city: Mount Forest
Province: ON
Postal: N0G 2L0
General Phone: (519) 323-1550
General Fax: (519) 323-4548
General/National Adv. E-mail: editor@mountforest.com
Display Adv. E-mail: phaasnoot@northperth.com
Classified Adv. e-mail: classifieds@metroland.com
Editorial e-mail: sburrows@metroland.com
Primary Website: http://www.southwesternontario.ca/arthur-on/
Year Established: 1862
Delivery Methods: Mail`Newsstand`Racks
Areas Served - City/County or Portion Thereof, or Zip codes: North Wellington
Own Printing Facility?: Y
Mechanical specifications: Page 10.375"x11.5"
Published: Wed
Avg Paid Circ: 2699
Avg Free Circ: 0
Audit By: VAC
Audit Date: 31.12.2015
Personnel: Shannon Burrows (Ed); Peggy Haasnoot (Adv)
Parent company (for newspapers): Metroland Media Group Ltd.; Torstar

PUBLICATION NAME

The Mount Forest Confederate
Street Address: 277 Main St. S. ,
Province: ON
Postal: N0G 2L0
Country: Canada
Mailing address: PO Box 130
Mailing city: Mount Forest
Province: ON
Postal: N0G 2L0
General Phone: (519) 323-1550
General Fax: (519) 323-4548
General/National Adv. E-mail: editor@mountforest.com
Display Adv. E-mail: klucas@mountforest.com
Editorial e-mail: editor@mountforest.com
Primary Website: www.mountforest.com
Year Established: 1865
Delivery Methods: Mail`Newsstand
Areas Served - City/County or Portion Thereof, or Zip codes: Wellington County/ Grey County
Mechanical specifications: Type page 12 3/4 x 21 1/4; E - 6 cols, 1 1/2, 1/6 between; A - 6 cols, 1 1/2, 1/6 between; C - 6 cols, 1 1/2, 1/6 between.
Published: Wed
Avg Paid Circ: 1108
Audit By: CMCA
Audit Date: 30.06.2016
Personnel: Cathy Higdon (Circ. Mgr.); Lynne Turner (Ed.); Cornelia Svela (Prodn. Mgr.); Kim Lucas (Sales)
Parent company (for newspapers): Metroland Media Group Ltd.

MUENSTER

PUBLICATION NAME

Order Of St. Benedict
Street Address: 100 College Dr. ,
Province: SK
Postal: S0K 2Y0
Country: Canada
Mailing address: PO Box 190
Mailing city: Muenster
Province: SK
Postal: S0K 2Y0
General Phone: (306) 682-1772
General Fax: (306) 682-5285
General/National Adv. E-mail: pm@stpeterspress.

ca
Display Adv. E-mail: pm.ads@stpeterspress.ca
Editorial e-mail: pm.canadian@stpeterspress.ca
Primary Website: www.prairiemessenger.ca
Year Established: 1904
Delivery Methods: Mail
Areas Served - City/County or Portion Thereof, or Zip codes: Canada
Own Printing Facility?: Y
Commercial printers?: Y
Mechanical specifications: Type page 10 1/8 x 15; E - 5 cols, 2, 1/6 between; A - 5 cols, 2, 1/6 between; C - 5 cols, 2, 1/6 between.
Published: Wed
Avg Paid Circ: 4300
Audit By: CMCA
Audit Date: 02.09.2016
Personnel: Gail Kleefeld (Adv. Mgr.); Peter Novecosky (Ed.); Maureen Weber (Assoc. Ed.); Don Ward (Assoc. Ed.); Lucille Stewart (Layout Artist)

NAKUSP

PUBLICATION NAME

Arrow Lakes News
Street Address: 89 1st Avenue Northwest ,
Province: BC
Postal: V0G 1R0
Country: Canada
Mailing address: PO Box 189
Mailing city: Nakusp
Province: BC
Postal: V0G 1R0
General Phone: (250) 265-3841
General/National Adv. E-mail: newsroom@arrowlakesnews.com; sales@arrowlakesnews.com
Display Adv. E-mail: sales@arrowlakesnews.com
Editorial e-mail: newsroom@arrowlakesnews.com
Primary Website: www.arrowlakenews.com
Year Established: 1999
Delivery Methods: Mail`Newsstand
Areas Served - City/County or Portion Thereof, or Zip codes: Canada
Mechanical specifications: Type page 10 1/4 x 14 1/4; E - 6 cols, 1 1/2, between; A - 6 cols, 1 1/2, between; C - 6 cols, 1 1/2, between.
Published: Wed
Avg Paid Circ: 585
Avg Free Circ: 10
Audit By: VAC
Audit Date: 30.06.2017
Personnel: Eric Lawson (Pub.)
Parent company (for newspapers): Black Press Group Ltd.

NANAIMO

PUBLICATION NAME

Nanaimo News Bulletin
Street Address: 777 Poplar St. ,
Province: BC
Postal: V9S 2H7
Country: Canada
Mailing address: 777 Poplar St.
Mailing city: Nanaimo
Province: BC
Postal: V9S 2H7
General Phone: (250) 753-3707
General Fax: (250) 753-0788
Editorial Phone: (250) 734-4621
Display Adv. E-mail: sueb@blackpress.ca
Editorial e-mail: editor@nanaimobulletin.com
Primary Website: www.nanaimobulletin.com
Year Established: 1988
Areas Served - City/County or Portion Thereof, or Zip codes: Canada
Own Printing Facility?: Y
Mechanical specifications: Type page 10 1/4 x 14 1/2; A - 6 cols, 1 7/8, 1/8 between; C - 7 cols, 1 7/8, 1/8 between.
Published: Mon`Fri`Sat
Avg Free Circ: 31789
Audit By: AAM
Audit Date: 31.03.2019
Personnel: Sean McCue (Pub); Melissa Fryer

(Ed.); Darrell Summerfelt (Prodn. Mgr.)
Parent company (for newspapers): Black Press Group Ltd.

NANTON

PUBLICATION NAME

The Nanton News
Street Address: 2019 20th Avenue ,
Province: AB
Postal: T0L 1R0
Country: Canada
Mailing address: PO Box 429
Mailing city: Nanton
Province: AB
Postal: T0L 1R0
General Phone: (403) 646-2023
General Fax: (403) 646-2848
General/National Adv. E-mail: info@highrivertimes.com
Editorial e-mail: sheena.read@sunmedia.ca
Primary Website: www.nantonnews.com
Year Established: 1903
Areas Served - City/County or Portion Thereof, or Zip codes: Canada
Commercial printers?: Y
Published: Wed
Avg Paid Circ: 592
Avg Free Circ: 8
Audit By: CMCA
Audit Date: 30.06.2014
Personnel: Nancy Middleton (Pub.); Donna Knowles (Circ. Mgr.); Shawn Cornell (Group Pub.); Lorelei Doell (Circ. Mgr.); Sheena Reed (Ed.); Roxanne Mackintosh (Reg. Adv. Dir.); Stephen Tipper (Ed.)
Parent company (for newspapers): Postmedia Network Inc.

NAPANEE

PUBLICATION NAME

Napanee Guide
Street Address: 2 Dairy Ave., Unit 11 ,
Province: ON
Postal: K7R 3T1
Country: Canada
Mailing address: 2 Dairy Ave., Unit 11
Mailing city: Napanee
Province: ON
Postal: K7R 3T1
General Phone: (613) 354-6648
General Fax: (613) 354-6708
General/National Adv. E-mail: news@napaneeguide.com
Display Adv. E-mail: david@napaneeguide.com
Primary Website: www.napaneeguide.com
Areas Served - City/County or Portion Thereof, or Zip codes: Canada
Published: Thur
Avg Free Circ: 14962
Audit By: CMCA
Audit Date: 30.06.2016
Personnel: Liza Nelson (Group Adv. Dir.); Rob McLellan (Distribution Supervisor)
Parent company (for newspapers): Postmedia Network Inc.; Quebecor Communications, Inc.

PUBLICATION NAME

The Napanee Beaver
Street Address: 72 Dundas St. E. ,
Province: ON
Postal: K7R 1H9
Country: Canada
Mailing address: 72 Dundas St. E.
Mailing city: Napanee
Province: ON
Postal: K7R 1H9
General Phone: (613) 354-6641
General Fax: (613) 354-2622
General/National Adv. E-mail: beaver@bellnet.ca
Primary Website: www.napaneebeaver.com
Year Established: 1870
Delivery Methods: Carrier
Areas Served - City/County or Portion Thereof, or Zip codes: Canada

Mechanical specifications: Type page 12 x 21 1/4.
Published: Thur
Avg Free Circ: 15698
Audit By: CMCA
Audit Date: 30.06.2016
Personnel: Jean M. Morrison (Pub.); Deb Mccann (Bus. Mgr.); Seth Duchene (Ed.); Michelle Bowes (Prodn. Mgr.); Scott Johnston

NAPIERVILLE

PUBLICATION NAME

Journal Le Coup D'oeil
Street Address: 350 Saint Jacques St. ,
Province: QC
Postal: J0J 1L0
Country: Canada
Mailing address: 350 Saint Jacques St.
Mailing city: Napierville
Province: QC
Postal: J0J 1L0
General Phone: (450) 245-3344
General Fax: (450) 245-7419
General/National Adv. E-mail: coupdoeil@tc.tc
Primary Website: www.coupdoeil.info
Year Established: 1978
Areas Served - City/County or Portion Thereof, or Zip codes: Canada
Commercial printers?: Y
Published: Wed
Avg Paid Circ: 9
Avg Free Circ: 15602
Audit By: CCAB
Audit Date: 31.03.2014
Personnel: Charles Couture (Circ. Mgr.); Claude Trahan (Mng. Ed.); Jacques LaRochelle (Journalist)

NATASHQUAN

PUBLICATION NAME

Le Portageur
Street Address: 50, Chemin D'en-haut ,
Province: QC
Postal: G0G 2E0
Country: Canada
Mailing address: CP 40
Mailing city: Natashquan
Province: QC
Postal: G0G 2E0
General Phone: (418) 726-3736
General Fax: (418) 726-3714
General/National Adv. E-mail: secom@quebectel.com
Mechanical specifications: Type page 8 1/2 x 11; E - 3 cols, 2 1/2, 1/8 between; C - 3 cols, 2 1/2, 1/8 between.
Published: Wed
Avg Free Circ: 490
Audit By: Sworn/Estimate/Non-Audited
Audit Date: 12.07.2019
Personnel: Cindy Carbonneau (Adv. Mgr.); Michel Richard (Ed.)

NEEPAWA

PUBLICATION NAME

Neepawa Banner
Street Address: 243 Hamilton St. ,
Province: MB
Postal: R0J 1H0
Country: Canada
Mailing address: PO Box 699
Mailing city: Neepawa
Province: MB
Postal: R0J 1H0
General Phone: (204) 476-3401
General Fax: (204) 476-5073
General/National Adv. E-mail: print@neepawanabanner.com
Editorial e-mail: nekwaddell@neepawabanner.com
Primary Website: www.neepawabanner.com
Year Established: 1989
Areas Served - City/County or Portion Thereof, or Zip

codes: Neepawa
Mechanical specifications: Type page 7 x 14; E - 8 cols, 1 7/8, 3/8 between; A - 6 cols, 1 5/8, 3/8 between; C - 6 cols, 1 5/8, 3/8 between.
Published: Fri
Avg Paid Circ: 92
Avg Free Circ: 8179
Audit By: VAC
Audit Date: 30.06.2017
Personnel: Ken Waddell (Pub/Ed.)

PUBLICATION NAME

The Neepawa Banner And Press
Street Address: 423 Hamilton St. ,
Province: MB
Postal: R0J 1H0
Country: Canada
Mailing address: PO Box 699
Mailing city: Neepawa
Province: MB
Postal: R0J 1H0
General Phone: (204) 476-3401
General Fax: (204) 476-5073
General/National Adv. E-mail: office@neepawapress.com
Display Adv. E-mail: ads@neepawabanner.com
Classified Adv. e-mail: print@neepawabanner.com
Editorial e-mail: news@neepawabanner.com
Primary Website: www.neepawabanner.com
Year Established: 1896
Delivery Methods: Mail`Newsstand`Racks
Areas Served - City/County or Portion Thereof, or Zip codes: R0J
Mechanical specifications: Type page 10 3/8 x 16; E - 6 cols, 1 9/16, 1/6 between; A - 6 cols, 1 9/16, 1/6 between; C - 6 cols, 1 9/16, 1/6 between.
Published: Fri
Avg Paid Circ: 100
Avg Free Circ: 8200
Audit By: VAC
Audit Date: 15.02.2018
Personnel: Kate Atkinson (Ed)
Parent company (for newspapers): Neepawa Banner

NELSON

PUBLICATION NAME

Nelson Star
Street Address: 91 Baker Street, Suite B ,
Province: BC
Postal: V1L 4G8
Country: Canada
Mailing address: 91 Baker Street, Suite B
Mailing city: Nelson
Province: BC
Postal: V1L 4G8
General Phone: (877) 365-6397
Display Adv. E-mail: advertising@nelsonstar.com
Editorial e-mail: editor@nelsonstar.com
Primary Website: www.nelsonstar.com
Year Established: 2008
Delivery Methods: Newsstand`Carrier`Racks
Areas Served - City/County or Portion Thereof, or Zip codes: Nelson and surrounding areas, British Columbia
Published: Wed`Fri
Avg Paid Circ: 0
Avg Free Circ: 8448
Audit By: VAC
Audit Date: 31.08.2016
Personnel: Eric Lawson (Publisher)
Parent company (for newspapers): Black Press Group Ltd.

NEW CARLISLE

PUBLICATION NAME

Sea-coast Publications Inc./the Gaspe Spec
Street Address: 128 Gerard D. Levesque ,
Province: QC
Postal: G0C 1Z0
Country: Canada

Community Newspapers in Canada

Mailing address: PO Box 99
Mailing city: New Carlisle
Province: QC
Postal: G0C 1Z0
General Phone: (418) 752-5400
General Fax: (418) 752-6932
Editorial Phone: (418)752-5070
General/National Adv. E-mail: specs@globetrotter.net
Primary Website: www.gaspespec.com
Year Established: 1975
Delivery Methods: Mail`Newsstand
Areas Served - City/County or Portion Thereof, or Zip codes: Canada
Own Printing Facility?: N
Commercial printers?: Y
Mechanical specifications: Type page 10 1/4 x 15 1/2; E - 5 cols, 1 15/16, 1/8 between; A - 5 cols, 1 15/16, 1/8 between; C - 5 cols, 1 15/16, 1/8 between.
Published: Wed
Avg Paid Circ: 2309
Audit By: CMCA
Audit Date: 31.12.2015
Personnel: Sharon Renouf-Farrell (Pub.); Joan Sawyer Imhoff (Gen. Mgr.); Robert Bradbury (Adv. Mgr.); Gilles Gagne (News Ed.)

NEW HAMBURG

PUBLICATION NAME

New Hamburg Independent
Street Address: 77 Peel St. ,
Province: ON
Postal: N3A 1E7
Country: Canada
General Phone: (519) 662-1240
General Fax: (519) 662-3521
General/National Adv. E-mail: editor@newhamburgindependent.ca
Display Adv. E-mail: kschattner@newhamburgindependent.ca
Classified Adv. e-mail: classified@metrolandwest.com
Editorial e-mail: editor@newhamburgindependent.ca
Primary Website: www.newhamburgindependent.ca
Year Established: 1878
Delivery Methods: Mail`Newsstand`Carrier
Areas Served - City/County or Portion Thereof, or Zip codes: Township of Wilmot
Own Printing Facility?: Y
Commercial printers?: N
Published: Wed
Avg Paid Circ: 1770
Audit By: CMCA
Audit Date: 30.06.2016
Personnel: Donna Luelo (Pub.); Heather Dunbar (Adv. Mgr.); Kyle Schattner (Adv. Rep.); Scott Miller Cressman (Ed); Leta Gastle (Admin/Circulation); Chris Thomson (Reporter/photographer)
Parent company (for newspapers): Metroland Media Group Ltd.; Torstar

NEW LISKEARD

PUBLICATION NAME

Speaker Weekender
Street Address: 18 Wellington St. ,
Province: ON
Postal: P0J 1P0
Country: Canada
Mailing address: PO Box 580
Mailing city: New Liskeard
Province: ON
Postal: P0J 1P0
General Phone: (705) 647-6791
General Fax: (705) 647-9669
General/National Adv. E-mail: loisperry@northontario.ca
Primary Website: www.facebook.com/pages/Temiskaming-Speaker-Weekender/884448971667310
Areas Served - City/County or Portion Thereof, or Zip codes: Canada
Published: Fri
Avg Free Circ: 10450

Audit By: CMCA
Audit Date: 31.03.2016
Personnel: Lois Perry (Gen. Mgr.)

PUBLICATION NAME

Temiskaming Speaker
Street Address: 18 Wellington St. S. ,
Province: ON
Postal: P0J 1P0
Country: Canada
Mailing address: PO Box 580
Mailing city: New Liskeard
Province: ON
Postal: P0J 1P0
General Phone: (705) 647-6791
General Fax: (705) 647-9669
Advertising Fax: (705) 647-9669
General/National Adv. E-mail: ads@northernontario.ca
Editorial e-mail: editorial@northernontario.ca
Primary Website: www.northernontario.ca
Year Established: 1906
Delivery Methods: Mail`Newsstand`Carrier`Racks
Areas Served - City/County or Portion Thereof, or Zip codes: Canada
Own Printing Facility?: Y
Commercial printers?: Y
Mechanical specifications: Type page 13 x 21 1/4; E - 6 cols, 2 1/8, 1/8 between; A - 6 cols, 2 1/8, 1/8 between; C - 6 cols, 2 1/8, 1/8 between.
Published: Wed
Avg Paid Circ: 3021
Avg Free Circ: 138
Audit By: CMCA
Audit Date: 31.08.2015
Personnel: Lois Perry (Gen. Mgr.); Gordon Brock (Ed.)

NEW RICHMOND

PUBLICATION NAME

L'echo De La Baie
Street Address: 143 Boulevard Perron E ,
Province: QC
Postal: G0C 2B0
Country: Canada
Mailing address: 144, rue jacques cartier
Mailing city: Gaspe
Province: QC
Postal: G4X 1M9
General Phone: (418) 392-5083
General Fax: (418) 392-6605
General/National Adv. E-mail: bernard.johnson@quebecormedia.com
Editorial e-mail: redaction_latuque@tc.tc
Primary Website: lechodelabaie.canoe.ca
Areas Served - City/County or Portion Thereof, or Zip codes: Canada
Published: Wed
Avg Paid Circ: 7
Avg Free Circ: 18364
Audit By: CCAB
Audit Date: 31.03.2014
Personnel: Bernard Johnson (Pub.)
Parent company (for newspapers): Quebecor Communications, Inc.

NEW WESTMINSTER

PUBLICATION NAME

New Westminster Record
Street Address: 201a-3430 Brighton Ave ,
Province: BC
Postal: V5A 3H4
Country: Canada
Mailing address: #201A â€" 3430 Brighton Ave.
Mailing city: Burnaby
Province: BC
Postal: V5A 3H4
General Phone: (604) 444-6451
Display Adv. E-mail: kgilmour@newwestrecord.ca
Classified Adv. e-mail: mmacleod@newwestrecord.ca

Editorial e-mail: ptracy@newwestrecord.ca
Primary Website: http://www.newwestrecord.ca/
Areas Served - City/County or Portion Thereof, or Zip codes: Canada
Published: Wed
Avg Paid Circ: 0
Avg Free Circ: 16290
Audit By: CCAB
Audit Date: 30.09.2015
Personnel: Lara Graham (Pub); Pat Tracy (Ed); Dale Dorsett (Circ Mgr)
Parent company (for newspapers): Glacier Media Group

NEWMARKET

PUBLICATION NAME

Bradford & West Gwillimbury Topic
Street Address: 580b Steven Crt. ,
Province: ON
Postal: L3Y 4X1
Country: Canada
Mailing address: 580B Steven Crt.
Mailing city: Newmarket
Province: ON
Postal: L3Y 4X1
General Phone: (905) 775-1188
Display Adv. E-mail: asmug@metroland.com
Editorial e-mail: tmcfadden@yrmg.com
Primary Website: simcoe.com
Areas Served - City/County or Portion Thereof, or Zip codes: Canada
Published: Thur
Avg Free Circ: 10538
Audit By: CCAB
Audit Date: 31.12.2017
Personnel: Amanda Sung (Adv Mgr); Ted McFadden (Ed)
Parent company (for newspapers): Metroland Media Group Ltd.

PUBLICATION NAME

The Newmarket Era-banner
Street Address: 580b Steven Ct ,
Province: ON
Postal: L3Y 4X1
Country: Canada
Mailing address: PO Box 236
Mailing city: Newmarket
Province: ON
Postal: L3Y 4X1
General Phone: (905) 773-7627
General Fax: (905) 853-5379
Advertising Phone: (416) 798-7284
Advertising Fax: (905) 853-5379
Editorial Fax: (905) 853-5379
General/National Adv. E-mail: admin@erabanner.com
Display Adv. E-mail: admin@erabanner.com
Editorial e-mail: newsroom@erabanner.com
Primary Website: yorkregion.com
Areas Served - City/County or Portion Thereof, or Zip codes: Newmarket, Aurora, East Gwillimbury, and York region
Published: Thur
Avg Paid Circ: 0
Avg Free Circ: 24371
Audit By: CCAB
Audit Date: 31.12.2017
Personnel: Ian Proudfoot (Pub.); Gord Paolucci (Dir., Adv./Prodn./Distribution); Dave Williams (Retail Sales Mgr.); Darlene Baker (Adv. Coord.); Megan Pike (Circ. Mgr.); Teresa Mathison (Distribution Coord.); Debora Kelly (Ed. in Chief); Ted McFadden (Ed.)
Parent company (for newspapers): Metroland Media Group Ltd.; Torstar

NICOLET

PUBLICATION NAME

Courrier-sud
Street Address: 3255 Rte Marie-victorin ,
Province: QC
Postal: J3T 1X5

Country: Canada
Mailing address: 3255 Rte Marie-Victorin ,
Mailing city: Nicolet
Province: QC
Postal: J3T 1X5
General Phone: (819) 293-4551
General Fax: (819) 293-8758
General/National Adv. E-mail: redaction_cs@tc.tc
Editorial e-mail: redaction_cs@transcontinental.ca
Primary Website: www.lecourriersud.com
Areas Served - City/County or Portion Thereof, or Zip codes: Canada
Mechanical specifications: Type page 10 x 12 3/4.
Published: Wed
Avg Paid Circ: 52
Avg Free Circ: 20758
Audit By: CCAB
Audit Date: 31.03.2014
Personnel: Claire Knight (Sales Coord.); Nancy Allaire (Ed.)
Parent company (for newspapers): Transcontinental Media

NIPAWIN

PUBLICATION NAME

Nipawin Journal
Street Address: 117 1st Ave. ,
Province: SK
Postal: S0E 1E0
Country: Canada
Mailing address: PO Box 2014
Mailing city: Nipawin
Province: SK
Postal: S0E 1E0
General Phone: (306) 862-4618
General Fax: (306) 862-4566
Editorial e-mail: greg.wiseman@sunmedia.ca
Primary Website: www.nipawinjournal.com
Areas Served - City/County or Portion Thereof, or Zip codes: Canada
Commercial printers?: Y
Mechanical specifications: Type page 10 5/8 x 14 3/4; E - 6 cols, 1 1/2, 1/4 between; A - 6 cols, 1 1/2, 1/4 between; C - 6 cols, 1 1/2, 1/4 between.
Published: Wed
Avg Paid Circ: 1093
Audit By: CMCA
Audit Date: 31.08.2014
Personnel: Ken Sorenson (Gen. Mgr.); Greg Wiseman (Managing Ed.)
Parent company (for newspapers): Postmedia Network Inc.; Quebecor Communications, Inc.

NIPIGON

PUBLICATION NAME

Nipigon-red Rock Gazette
Street Address: 155b Railway Street ,
Province: ON
Postal: P0T 2J0
Country: Canada
Mailing address: Box 1057
Mailing city: Nipigon
Province: ON
Postal: P0T 2J0
General Phone: (807) 887-3583
General Fax: (807) 887-3720
General/National Adv. E-mail: nipigongazette@shaw.ca
Delivery Methods: Mail
Areas Served - City/County or Portion Thereof, or Zip codes: Canada
Commercial printers?: Y
Published: Tues
Avg Paid Circ: 486
Avg Free Circ: 17
Audit By: CMCA
Audit Date: 30.06.2017
Personnel: Pamela Behun (Circ. Mgr./Ed.); Blair Oborne (Pub.)

NOKOMIS

PUBLICATION NAME

Last Mountain Times
Street Address: 103 1st Ave. W. ,
Province: SK
Postal: S0G 3R0
Country: Canada
Mailing address: PO Box 340
Mailing city: Nokomis
Province: SK
Postal: S0G 3R0
General Phone: (306) 528-2020
General Fax: (306) 528-2090
Advertising Phone: (306) 528-2020
Editorial Phone: (306) 528-2020
General/National Adv. E-mail: inbox@lastmountaintimes.ca
Display Adv. E-mail: editor@lastmountaintimes.ca
Classified Adv. e-mail: editor@lastmountaintimes.ca
Editorial e-mail: editor@lastmountaintimes.ca
Primary Website: www.lastmountaintimes.ca
Year Established: 1908
Delivery Methods: Mail
Areas Served - City/County or Portion Thereof, or Zip codes: S0G3R0, S0G4V0, S0G1Z0, S0A3J0, S0GOLO, S0G1J0, S0A3S0, S0G4P0, S0G0W0, S0G3C0, S2V1A1, S0G0H0, S0G4C0, S0G4L0,
Own Printing Facility?: Y
Commercial printers?: Y
Mechanical specifications: Type page 10 1/4 x 15 3/4; E - 5 cols, 1 29/30, 1/6 between; A - 5 cols, 1 29/30, 1/6 between; C - 5 cols, 1 29/30, 1/6 between.
Published: Mon
Avg Paid Circ: 250
Avg Free Circ: 4500
Audit By: Sworn/Estimate/Non-Audited
Audit Date: 12.07.2019
Personnel: Dave Degenstien (Owner/Publisher / Editor)
Parent company (for newspapers): Last Mountain Times

NORTH BATTLEFORD

PUBLICATION NAME

Battlefords News-optimist
Street Address: 892 104th St. ,
Province: SK
Postal: S9A 1M9
Country: Canada
Mailing address: 892 104th St
Mailing city: North Battleford
Province: SK
Postal: S9A 1M9
General Phone: (306) 445-7261
General Fax: (306) 445-3223
General/National Adv. E-mail: battlefords.publishing@sasktel.net
Editorial e-mail: newsoptimist.news@sasktel.net
Primary Website: www.newsoptimist.ca
Delivery Methods: Mail`Newsstand`Carrier`Racks
Areas Served - City/County or Portion Thereof, or Zip codes: Battlefords Region of Saskatchewan
Own Printing Facility?: Y
Commercial printers?: Y
Mechanical specifications: Type page 11 1/4 x 15 2/3; E - 6 cols, 1 1/2, 1/6 between; A - 6 cols, 1 1/2, 1/6 between; C - 6 cols, 1 7/12, 1/6 between.
Published: Thur
Avg Paid Circ: 228
Avg Free Circ: 14000
Audit By: CMCA
Audit Date: 31.03.2018
Personnel: Becky Doig (Ed.)
Parent company (for newspapers): Glacier Media Group

PUBLICATION NAME

Regional Optimist
Street Address: 892-104th Street ,
Province: SK
Postal: S9A 3E6
Country: Canada
Mailing address: PO Box 1029
Mailing city: North Battleford
Province: SK
Postal: S9A 3E6
General Phone: (306) 445-7261
General Fax: (306) 445-3223
General/National Adv. E-mail: battlefords.publishing@sasktel.net
Editorial e-mail: newsoptimist.news@sasktel.net
Primary Website: www.newsoptimist.ca
Areas Served - City/County or Portion Thereof, or Zip codes: Canada
Published: Thur
Avg Free Circ: 13514
Audit By: CMCA
Audit Date: 30.11.2016
Personnel: Becky Doig (Ed)

NORTH VANCOUVER

PUBLICATION NAME

North Shore News
Street Address: 980 1st St. West, Unit 116 ,
Province: BC
Postal: V7P 3N4
Country: Canada
Mailing address: 980 1st St. West, Unit 116
Mailing city: North Vancouver
Province: BC
Postal: V7P 3N4
General Phone: (604) 985-2131
Advertising Phone: (604) 985-2131
Editorial Phone: (604) 985-2131
General/National Adv. E-mail: dfoot@nsnews.com
Display Adv. E-mail: display@nsnews.com
Classified Adv. e-mail: classifieds@van.net
Editorial e-mail: editor@nsnews.com
Primary Website: nsnews.com
Year Established: 1969
Areas Served - City/County or Portion Thereof, or Zip codes: Canada
Published: Wed`Fri`Sun
Avg Paid Circ: 0
Avg Free Circ: 57636
Audit By: CCAB
Audit Date: 23.11.2017
Personnel: Peter Kvarnstrom (Pub); Layne Christensen (Ed); Vicki Magnison (Dir, Sales & Marketing)
Parent company (for newspapers): Glacier Media Group

PUBLICATION NAME

North/west Shore Outlook
Street Address: 116-980 West 1st Street ,
Province: BC
Postal: V7P 3N4
Country: Canada
Mailing address: 116-980 West 1st St.
Mailing city: North Vancouver
Province: BC
Postal: V7P 3N4
General Phone: (604) 903-1000
General/National Adv. E-mail: publisher@northshoreoutlook.com
Display Adv. E-mail: vmagnison@nsnews.com
Classified Adv. e-mail: classifieds@van.net
Editorial e-mail: lchristensen@nsnews.com
Primary Website: www.northshoreoutlook.com
Areas Served - City/County or Portion Thereof, or Zip codes: Canada
Published: Thur
Avg Free Circ: 28038
Audit By: CMCA
Audit Date: 31.12.2012
Personnel: Vicki Magnison (Sales & Mktg. Dir.); Peter Kvarnstrom (Pub); Dale Dorsett (Circ. Mgr.); Layne Christensen (Ed)

OAKVILLE

PUBLICATION NAME

Oakville Beaver
Street Address: 467 Speers Rd. ,
Province: ON
Postal: L6K 3S4
Country: Canada
Mailing address: 467 Speers Rd.
Mailing city: Oakville
Province: ON
Postal: L6K 3S4
General Phone: (905) 845-3824
General Fax: (905) 337-5568
Editorial e-mail: editor@oakvillebeaver.com
Primary Website: oakvillebeaver.com
Year Established: 1962
Delivery Methods: Carrier
Areas Served - City/County or Portion Thereof, or Zip codes: Canada
Own Printing Facility?: Y
Commercial printers?: Y
Published: Thur`Fri
Avg Paid Circ: 84
Avg Free Circ: 53165
Audit By: CCAB
Audit Date: 30.09.2017
Personnel: Neil Oliver (Pub.); Daniel Baird (Dir., Adv.); Sarah McSweeney (Circ. Mgr.); Jill Davis (Ed. in Chief); Jon Kuiperij (Sports Ed.); Manuel Garcia (Prodn. Mgr.); Angela Blackburn (Ed.)
Parent company (for newspapers): Metroland Media Group Ltd.; Torstar

OHSWEKEN

PUBLICATION NAME

Turtle Island News
Street Address: Box 329 ,
Province: ON
Postal: N0A 1M0
Country: Canada
Mailing address: Box 329
Mailing city: Ohsweken
Province: ON
Postal: N0A 1M0
General Phone: (519)445-0868
General Fax: (519) 445-0865
General/National Adv. E-mail: lynda@theturtleislandnews.com
Display Adv. E-mail: sales@theturtleislandnews.com
Primary Website: www.theturtleislandnews.com
Published: Wed
Avg Free Circ: 5000
Audit By: Sworn/Estimate/Non-Audited
Audit Date: 12.07.2019

OKOTOKS

PUBLICATION NAME

Okotoks Western Wheel
Street Address: 9 Mcrae St. ,
Province: AB
Postal: T1S 2A2
Country: Canada
Mailing address: P.O. Box 150
Mailing city: Okotoks
Province: AB
Postal: T1S 2A2
General Phone: (403) 938-6397
General Fax: (403) 938-2518
General/National Adv. E-mail: westernwheel@okotoks.greatwest.ca
Display Adv. E-mail: lplathan@okotoks.greatwest.ca
Editorial e-mail: dpatterson@okotoks.greatwest.ca
Primary Website: www.westernwheel.com
Year Established: 1976
Delivery Methods: Mail`Newsstand`Carrier`Racks
Areas Served - City/County or Portion Thereof, or Zip codes: T0L 0A0,T0L 0H0, T0L 0J0,T0L 0K0,T0L 0P0,T0L 0X0,T0L 1H0,T0L 1K0,T0L 1R0,T0L 1W0,T0L 2A0,T0I 2T9,T0L 5G5,T1V and T1S.
Own Printing Facility?: Y
Commercial printers?: Y
Mechanical specifications: Type page 10 1/4 x 15 1/4; E - 6 cols, 1 7/12, between; A - 6 cols, 1 7/12, between; C - 6 cols, 1 7/12, between.
Published: Wed
Avg Paid Circ: 91
Avg Free Circ: 13879
Audit By: VAC
Audit Date: 30.04.2016
Personnel: Don Patterson (Ed); Matt Rockley (Pub)
Parent company (for newspapers): Glacier Media Group; Great West Newspapers LP

OLDS

PUBLICATION NAME

Carstairs Courier
Street Address: 5013 - 51 Street ,
Province: AB
Postal: T4H 1P6
Country: Canada
Mailing address: PO Box 114
Mailing city: Carstairs
Province: AB
Postal: T0M 0N0
General Phone: (403) 337-2806
General Fax: (403) 556-7515
Advertising Phone: (403) 337-2806
General/National Adv. E-mail: courier@carstairs.greatwest.ca
Editorial e-mail: dsingleton@olds.greatwest.ca
Primary Website: www.carstairscourier.ca
Year Established: 1982
Areas Served - City/County or Portion Thereof, or Zip codes: Canada
Commercial printers?: Y
Published: Tues
Avg Paid Circ: 12
Avg Free Circ: 3289
Audit By: CMCA
Audit Date: 30.06.2014
Personnel: Dan Singleton (Ed)
Parent company (for newspapers): Glacier Media Group; Great West Newspapers LP

PUBLICATION NAME

Mountain View Gazette
Street Address: 5013 - 51 St ,
Province: AB
Postal: T4H 1P6
Country: Canada
Mailing address: PO Box 3910
Mailing city: Olds
Province: AB
Postal: T4H 1P6
General Phone: (403) 556-7510
General Fax: (403) 556-7515
General/National Adv. E-mail: gazette@olds.greatwest.ca
Editorial e-mail: dsingleton@olds.greatwest.ca
Primary Website: www.mountainviewgazette.ca/
Published: Tues
Avg Free Circ: 20000
Audit By: Sworn/Estimate/Non-Audited
Audit Date: 12.07.2019
Personnel: Murray Elliott (Grp. Pub./Gen. Mgr.); Dan Singleton (Ed)
Parent company (for newspapers): Great West Newspapers LP

PUBLICATION NAME

Olds Albertan
Street Address: 5013 51st St. ,
Province: AB
Postal: T4H 1P6
Country: Canada
Mailing address: PO Box 3910
Mailing city: Olds
Province: AB
Postal: T4H 1P6
General Phone: (403) 556-7510
General Fax: (403) 556-7515
General/National Adv. E-mail: albertan@olds.

Community Newspapers in Canada

III-561

greatwest.ca
Display Adv. E-mail: melliott@olds.greatwest.ca
Editorial e-mail: dcollie@olds.greatwest.ca
Primary Website: www.oldsalbertan.ca
Year Established: 1993
Published: Tues
Avg Paid Circ: 5
Avg Free Circ: 6933
Audit By: VAC
Audit Date: 28.02.2016
Personnel: Murray Elliott (Pub); Doug Collie (Ed)
Parent company (for newspapers): Glacier Media Group; Great West Newspapers LP

OLIVER

PUBLICATION NAME

Oliver Chronicle
Street Address: 6379 Main Street ,
Province: BC
Postal: V0H 1T0
Country: Canada
Mailing address: PO Box 880
Mailing city: Oliver
Province: BC
Postal: V0H 1T0
General Phone: (250) 498-3711
General Fax: (250) 498-3966
General/National Adv. E-mail: office@oliverchronicle.com
Display Adv. E-mail: sales@oliverchronicle.com
Editorial e-mail: editor@oliverchronicle.com
Primary Website: www.oliverchronicle.com
Year Established: 1937
Delivery Methods: Mail`Newsstand`Racks
Areas Served - City/County or Portion Thereof, or Zip codes: Canada
Own Printing Facility?: Y
Commercial printers?: Y
Mechanical specifications: Type page 14 1/4 x 21 1/2; E - 6 cols, 2 1/4, 3/16 between; A - 6 cols, 2 1/4, 3/16 between; C - 6 cols, 2 1/4, 3/16 between.
Published: Wed
Avg Paid Circ: 1723
Avg Free Circ: 0
Audit By: VAC
Audit Date: 6/31/2015
Personnel: Lyonel Doherty (Ed.); Robert Doull; Linda Bolton (Pub.)

ORANGEVILLE

PUBLICATION NAME

Orangeville Citizen
Street Address: 10 First St. ,
Province: ON
Postal: L9W 2C4
Country: Canada
Mailing address: 10 First St.
Mailing city: Orangeville
Province: ON
Postal: L9W 2C4
General Phone: (519) 941-2230
General Fax: (519) 941-9361
General/National Adv. E-mail: mail@citizen.on.ca
Primary Website: www.citizen.on.ca
Delivery Methods: Mail`Newsstand`Carrier
Areas Served - City/County or Portion Thereof, or Zip codes: Canada
Own Printing Facility?: Y
Published: Thur
Avg Free Circ: 17967
Audit By: CMCA
Audit Date: 29.02.2016
Personnel: Alan M. Claridge (Pub.); Thomas M. Claridge (Ed.); Carolyn Dennis (Classifieds)

PUBLICATION NAME

The Orangeville Banner
Street Address: 37 Mill St. ,
Province: ON
Postal: L9W 2M4
Country: Canada
Mailing address: 37 Mill St.
Mailing city: Orangeville
Province: ON
Postal: L9W 2M4
General Phone: (519) 941-1350
General Fax: (519) 941-9600
General/National Adv. E-mail: banner@orangevillebanner.com; info@orangevillebanner.com
Primary Website: www.orangevillebanner.com
Year Established: 1893
Areas Served - City/County or Portion Thereof, or Zip codes: Canada
Mechanical specifications: Type page 10 3/8 x 12 1/2; E - 10 cols, 1, 1/8 between; A - 10 cols, 1, 1/8 between; C - 10 cols, 1, 1/8 between.
Published: Tues`Thur
Avg Paid Circ: 85
Avg Free Circ: 20303
Audit By: CCAB
Audit Date: 31.03.2014
Personnel: Gordon Brewerton (Gen. Mgr.); Janine Taylor (Prodn. Mgr.)
Parent company (for newspapers): Metroland Media Group Ltd.; Torstar

ORILLIA

PUBLICATION NAME

Orillia Today
Street Address: 25 Ontario St. ,
Province: ON
Postal: L3V 6H1
Country: Canada
Mailing address: 25 Ontario St.
Mailing city: Orillia
Province: ON
Postal: L3V 6H1
General Phone: (705) 329-2058
General Fax: (705) 329-2059
General/National Adv. E-mail: orillia@simcoe.com
Primary Website: orilliatoday.com
Year Established: 1991
Areas Served - City/County or Portion Thereof, or Zip codes: Canada
Published: Thur
Avg Free Circ: 24164
Audit By: CCAB
Audit Date: 31.03.2017
Personnel: Joe Anderson (Pub.); Leigh Gate (Gen. Mgr.); Leigh Rourke (Adv. Mgr.); Lori Martin (Mng. Ed.); Martin Melbourne (Community/News.); Kyla Mosley (Distr. Mgr.)
Parent company (for newspapers): Metroland Media Group Ltd.; Torstar

ORLEANS

PUBLICATION NAME

Weekly Journal
Street Address: 5300 Canotek Rd., Unit 30 ,
Province: ON
Postal: K1J 8R7
Country: Canada
Mailing address: 5300 Canotek Rd., Unit 30
Mailing city: Orleans
Province: ON
Postal: K1J 8R7
General Phone: (613) 744-4800
General Fax: (613) 744-0866
General/National Adv. E-mail: theweeklyjournal@transcontinental.ca
Mechanical specifications: Type page 10 1/2 x 12 1/2; E - 8 cols, 1 1/6, 1/6 between; A - 8 cols, 1 1/6, 1/6 between; C - 8 cols, 1 1/6, 1/6 between.
Published: Thur
Avg Free Circ: 47000
Audit By: Sworn/Estimate/Non-Audited
Audit Date: 12.07.2019
Personnel: Terry Tyo (Adv. Mgr.); Patricia Lonergan (Ed.); Sylvie Parsier (Prodn. Mgr.)

OROMOCTO

PUBLICATION NAME

The Oromocto Post-gazette
Street Address: 291 Restigouche Rd. ,
Province: NB
Postal: E2V 2H2
Country: Canada
Mailing address: 291 Restigouche Rd.
Mailing city: Oromocto
Province: NB
Postal: E2V 2H2
General Phone: (506) 357-9813
General Fax: (506) 452-7405
General/National Adv. E-mail: allen.shari@dailygleaner.com
Display Adv. E-mail: shelley.wood@brunswicknews.com
Editorial e-mail: williams.kimberly@dailygleaner.com
Primary Website: www.brunswicknews.com
Areas Served - City/County or Portion Thereof, or Zip codes: Canada
Mechanical specifications: Type page 10 1/4 x 11 1/2; E - 6 cols, 1 3/5, 1/6 between; A - 9 cols, 1, between; C - 8 cols, 1, between.
Published: Thur
Avg Paid Circ: 0
Avg Free Circ: 12844
Audit By: CMCA
Audit Date: 30.09.2013
Personnel: Shelly Wood (Adv. Mgr.); Kimberly Williams (Pub/Ed.)
Parent company (for newspapers): Brunswick News, Inc.

ORONO

PUBLICATION NAME

Orono Weekly Times
Street Address: 5310 Main St. ,
Province: ON
Postal: L0B 1M0
Country: Canada
Mailing address: PO Box 209
Mailing city: Orono
Province: ON
Postal: L0B 1M0
General Phone: (905) 983-5301
Advertising Phone: (905) 983-5301
Editorial Phone: (905) 983-5301
General/National Adv. E-mail: oronotimes@rogers.com
Display Adv. E-mail: oronotimes@rogers.com
Classified Adv. e-mail: oronotimes@rogers.com
Editorial e-mail: oronotimes@rogers.com
Primary Website: www.oronoweeklytimes.com
Year Established: 1937
Delivery Methods: Mail`Newsstand
Areas Served - City/County or Portion Thereof, or Zip codes: Municipality of Clarington, ON
Own Printing Facility?: Y
Commercial printers?: Y
Mechanical specifications: Type page 10 1/8 x 15 1/2; E - 2 cols, 3 15/16, 1/4 between.
Published: Wed
Avg Paid Circ: 1040
Audit By: CMCA
Audit Date: 30.06.2018
Personnel: Julie Cashin-Oster (Ed./Pub.)
Parent company (for newspapers): Orono Publications Inc.

OSHAWA

PUBLICATION NAME

Ajax-pickering News Advertiser
Street Address: 865 Farewell Ave. ,
Province: ON
Postal: L1H 7L5
Country: Canada
Mailing address: 865 Farewell Ave.
Mailing city: Oshawa
Province: ON
Postal: L1H 7L5
General Phone: (905) 579-4400
General Fax: (905) 579-2238
General/National Adv. E-mail: newsroom@durhamregion.com
Display Adv. E-mail: dfletcher@durhamregion.com
Editorial e-mail: jburghardt@durhamregion.com
Primary Website: durhamregion.com
Areas Served - City/County or Portion Thereof, or Zip codes: Canada
Own Printing Facility?: Y
Mechanical specifications: Type page 10 3/8 x 14; E - 9 cols, 1 1/16, between; A - 9 cols, 1 1/16, between; C - 9 cols, 1 1/16, between.
Published: Wed`Thur
Avg Paid Circ: 0
Avg Free Circ: 50016
Audit By: CCAB
Audit Date: 30.09.2017
Personnel: Timothy J. Whittaker (Pub.); Duncan Fletcher (Adv. Mgr.); Abe Fackhourie (Circ. Mgr.); Joanne Burghardt (Ed.)
Parent company (for newspapers): Metroland Media Group Ltd.; Torstar

PUBLICATION NAME

Canadian Statesman
Street Address: 865 Farewell St. ,
Province: ON
Postal: L1H 7L5
Country: Canada
Mailing address: 865 Farewell Ave.
Mailing city: Oshawa
Province: ON
Postal: L1H 7L5
General Phone: (905) 579-4400
General Fax: (416) 523-6161
Advertising Phone: (905) 215-0440
Editorial Phone: (905) 215-0462
General/National Adv. E-mail: newsroom@durhamregion.com
Editorial e-mail: mjohnston@durhamregion.com
Primary Website: www.durhamregion.com
Areas Served - City/County or Portion Thereof, or Zip codes: Ontario
Published: Wed`Thur`Fri
Avg Paid Circ: 104250
Audit By: Sworn/Estimate/Non-Audited
Audit Date: 12.07.2019
Personnel: Timothy J. Whittaker (Pub.); Fred Eismont (Dir. Adv.); Mike Johnston (Managing Ed.)

PUBLICATION NAME

Clarington This Week
Street Address: 865 Farewell St. ,
Province: ON
Postal: L1H 7L5
Country: Canada
Mailing address: 865 Farewell St.
Mailing city: Oshawa
Province: ON
Postal: L1H 7L5
General Phone: (905) 579-4400
General Fax: (905) 579-2238
General/National Adv. E-mail: newsroom@durhamregion.com
Primary Website: newsdurhamregion.com
Areas Served - City/County or Portion Thereof, or Zip codes: Oshawa, Ontario, L1H 7L5
Own Printing Facility?: Y
Commercial printers?: Y
Published: Wed
Avg Free Circ: 24150
Audit By: Sworn/Estimate/Non-Audited
Audit Date: 12.07.2019
Personnel: Tim Whittaker (Pub.); Lillian Hook (Office Mgr.); Fred Eismont (Adv. Dir.); Joanne Burghardt (Ed. in Chief); Mike Johnston (Mng. Ed.)
Parent company (for newspapers): Metroland Media Group Ltd.; Torstar

PUBLICATION NAME

Oshawa-whitby This Week
Street Address: 865 Farewell St. ,
Province: ON
Postal: L1H 7L5
Country: Canada
Mailing address: PO Box 481
Mailing city: Oshawa
Province: ON
Postal: L1H 7L5
General Phone: (905) 579-4400
General Fax: (905) 579-2238

Advertising Fax: (905) 579-6851
Editorial Fax: (905) 579-1809
General/National Adv. E-mail: newsroom@durhamregion.com
Primary Website: durhamregion.com
Areas Served - City/County or Portion Thereof, or Zip codes: Canada
Mechanical specifications: Type page 10 3/8 x 14; E - 9 cols, 1 1/16, between; A - 9 cols, 1 1/16, between; C - 9 cols, 1 1/16, between.
Published: Wed`Thur
Avg Paid Circ: 0
Avg Free Circ: 100554
Audit By: CCAB
Audit Date: 06.12.2017
Personnel: Timothy J. Whittaker (Pub.); Lillian Hook (Office Mgr.); Fred Eismont (Adv. Mgr.); Tina Jennings (Adv. Coord.); Abe Fakhourie (Circ. Mgr.); Joanne Burghardt (Ed. in Chief); Mike Johnston (Mng. Ed.); Tim Kelly (Copy Ed.); Christy Chase (Entertainment Ed.); Walter Passarella (Photo Ed.); Judi Bobbitt (Regl. Ed.); Brian Legree (Sports Ed.); Janice O'Neil (Prodn. Mgr.)
Parent company (for newspapers): Metroland Media Group Ltd.; Torstar

OSHWEKEN

PUBLICATION NAME

Tekawennake
Street Address: Po Box 130 ,
Province: ON
Postal: N0A 1M0
Country: Canada
Mailing address: PO Box 130
Mailing city: Oshweken
Province: ON
Postal: N0A 1M0
General Phone: (519) 753-0077
General Fax: (519) 753-0011
General/National Adv. E-mail: teka@tekanews.com
Delivery Methods: Mail`Newsstand
Own Printing Facility?: Y
Commercial printers?: Y
Mechanical specifications: Type page 10.25 x 13.25; E - 6 cols, 2, 1/8 between; A - 5 cols, 2, 1/8 between; C - 5 cols, 2, 1/8 between.
Published: Wed
Avg Paid Circ: 2500
Audit By: Sworn/Estimate/Non-Audited
Audit Date: 12.07.2019
Personnel: G. Scott Smith (Pub.)

OSOYOOS

PUBLICATION NAME

Osoyoos Times
Street Address: 8712 Main St. ,
Province: BC
Postal: V0H 1V0
Country: Canada
Mailing address: PO Box 359
Mailing city: Osoyoos
Province: BC
Postal: V0H 1V0
General Phone: (250) 495-7225
General Fax: (250) 495-6616
General/National Adv. E-mail: admin@osoyoostimes.com
Display Adv. E-mail: sales@osoyoostimes.com
Editorial e-mail: editor@osoyoostimes.com
Primary Website: www.osoyoostimes.com
Year Established: 1947
Delivery Methods: Mail`Newsstand
Areas Served - City/County or Portion Thereof, or Zip codes: Osoyoos
Commercial printers?: Y
Mechanical specifications: Type page 10 1/4 x 14; E - 6 cols
Published: Wed
Avg Paid Circ: 1783
Avg Free Circ: 0
Audit By: VAC
Audit Date: 31.12.2015
Personnel: Jocelyn Merit (Office Mgr.); Ken Baker (Adv. Mgr.); Keith Lacey (Ed); Linda Bolton (Mng. Dir.)

OTTAWA

PUBLICATION NAME

Kanata Kourier-standard Emc
Street Address: 57 Auriga Dr. Unit 103 ,
Province: ON
Postal: K2E 8B2
Country: Canada
Mailing address: 57 Auriga Dr. Unit 103
Mailing city: Ottawa
Province: ON
Postal: K2E 8B2
General Phone: (613) 723-5970
General Fax: (613)224-2265
General/National Adv. E-mail: mtracy@perfprint.ca
Primary Website: www.insideottawavalley.com
Areas Served - City/County or Portion Thereof, or Zip codes: Canada
Own Printing Facility?: Y
Commercial printers?: Y
Mechanical specifications: Type page 10 x 13 1/2; E - 6 cols, 1 9/16, 1/6 between; A - 6 cols, 1 9/16, 1/6 between; C - 6 cols, 1 9/16, 1/6 between.
Published: Thur
Avg Free Circ: 28642
Audit By: CMCA
Audit Date: 30.06.2014
Personnel: Mike Tracy (Pub.); Theresa Fritz (Ed.)
Parent company (for newspapers): Metroland Media Group Ltd.; Runge Newspapers, Inc.

PUBLICATION NAME

Manotick News Emc
Street Address: 57 Auriga Drive Unit 103 ,
Province: ON
Postal: K2E 8B2
Country: Canada
Mailing address: 57 Auriga Drive, Unit 103
Mailing city: Ottawa
Province: ON
Postal: K2E 8B2
General Phone: (613) 723-5970
General Fax: (613) 224-2265
Display Adv. E-mail: mstoodley@theemc.ca
Editorial e-mail: joe.morin@metroland.com
Primary Website: www.insideottawavalley.com
Areas Served - City/County or Portion Thereof, or Zip codes: Canada
Published: Thur
Avg Free Circ: 11392
Audit By: CMCA
Audit Date: 30.06.2014
Personnel: Mike Tracy (Pub.); Theresa Fritz (Ed.)
Parent company (for newspapers): Metroland Media Group Ltd.

PUBLICATION NAME

Nepean-barrhaven News Emc
Street Address: 57 Auriga Drive Unit 103 ,
Province: ON
Postal: K2E 8B2
Country: Canada
Mailing address: 57 Auriga Drive, Unit 103
Mailing city: Ottawa
Province: ON
Postal: K2E 8B2
General Phone: (613) 723-5970
General Fax: (613) 224-2265
Editorial e-mail: Nevil.hunt@metroland.com
Primary Website: www.insideottawavalley.com
Areas Served - City/County or Portion Thereof, or Zip codes: Canada
Published: Thur
Avg Free Circ: 50401
Audit By: CMCA
Audit Date: 30.06.2014
Personnel: Mike Tracy (Pub.); Theresa Fritz (Ed.)
Parent company (for newspapers): Metroland Media Group Ltd.

PUBLICATION NAME

Orleans News Emc
Street Address: 57 Auriga Drive Unit 103 ,
Province: ON
Postal: K2E 8B2
Country: Canada
Mailing address: 57 Auriga Drive, Unit 103
Mailing city: Ottawa
Province: ON
Postal: K2E 8B2
General Phone: (613) 723-5970
Display Adv. E-mail: dave.badham@metroland.com
Primary Website: www.insideottawavalley.com
Areas Served - City/County or Portion Thereof, or Zip codes: Canada
Published: Thur
Avg Free Circ: 42273
Audit By: CMCA
Audit Date: 30.06.2014
Personnel: Mike Tracy (Pub.); Theresa Fritz (Ed.)
Parent company (for newspapers): Metroland Media Group Ltd.

PUBLICATION NAME

Ottawa East Emc
Street Address: 57 Auriga Drive Unit 103 ,
Province: ON
Postal: K2E 8B2
Country: Canada
Mailing address: 57 Auriga Drive, Unit 103
Mailing city: Ottawa
Province: ON
Postal: K2E 8B2
General Phone: (613) 723-5970
General Fax: (613) 224-2265
Display Adv. E-mail: ghamilton@thenewsemc.ca
Editorial e-mail: matthew.jay@metroland.com
Primary Website: www.insideottawavalley.com
Areas Served - City/County or Portion Thereof, or Zip codes: Canada
Published: Thur
Avg Free Circ: 36519
Audit By: CMCA
Audit Date: 30.06.2014
Personnel: Theresa Fritz (Ed.); Mike Tracy (Pub.)
Parent company (for newspapers): Metroland Media Group Ltd.

PUBLICATION NAME

Ottawa South Emc
Street Address: 57 Auriga Drive Unit 103 ,
Province: ON
Postal: K2E 8B2
Country: Canada
Mailing address: 57 Auriga Drive, Unit 103
Mailing city: Ottawa
Province: ON
Postal: K2E 8B2
General Phone: (613) 723-5970
General Fax: (613) 224-2265
Display Adv. E-mail: cmanor@theemc.ca
Editorial e-mail: blair.edwards@metroland.com
Primary Website: www.insideottawavalley.com
Areas Served - City/County or Portion Thereof, or Zip codes: Canada
Published: Thur
Avg Free Circ: 41820
Audit By: CMCA
Audit Date: 30.06.2014
Personnel: Mike Tracy (Pub.); Theresa Fritz (Ed.)
Parent company (for newspapers): Metroland Media Group Ltd.

PUBLICATION NAME

Ottawa West Emc
Street Address: 57 Auriga Drive Unit 103 ,
Province: ON
Postal: K2E 8B2
Country: Canada
Mailing address: 57 Auriga Drive, Unit 103
Mailing city: Ottawa
Province: ON
Postal: K2E 8B2
General Phone: (613)723-5970
Display Adv. E-mail: dave.pennett@metroland.com
Primary Website: www.insideottawavalley.com
Areas Served - City/County or Portion Thereof, or Zip codes: Canada
Published: Thur
Avg Free Circ: 35247
Audit By: CMCA
Audit Date: 30.06.2014
Personnel: Mike Tracy (Pub.); Theresa Fritz (Ed.)
Parent company (for newspapers): Metroland Media Group Ltd.

PUBLICATION NAME

The Hill Times
Street Address: 69 Sparks St. ,
Province: ON
Postal: K1P 5A5
Country: Canada
Mailing address: 69 Sparks St.
Mailing city: Ottawa
Province: ON
Postal: K1P 5A5
General Phone: (613) 232-5952
General Fax: (613) 232-9055
General/National Adv. E-mail: news@hilltimes.com; circulation@hilltimes.com
Display Adv. E-mail: production@hilltimes.com; classified@hilltimes.com
Primary Website: www.hilltimes.com
Year Established: 1989
Delivery Methods:
    Mail`Newsstand`Carrier`Racks
Areas Served - City/County or Portion Thereof, or Zip codes: Canada
Mechanical specifications: Type page 10 3/8 x 13 1/2; E - 4 cols
Published: Mon`Wed
Avg Paid Circ: 3614
Avg Free Circ: 9555
Audit By: CMCA
Audit Date: 29.02.2016
Personnel: Jim Creskey (Pub.); Ross Dickson (Pub.); Andrew Morrow (Gen. Mgr.); Kate Malloy (Ed.); Benoit Deneault (Prod. Mgr.); Anne Marie Creskey (Pub.)

PUBLICATION NAME

The Star
Street Address: 5300 Canotek Rd., Unit 30 ,
Province: ON
Postal: K1J 8R7
Country: Canada
Mailing address: 5300 Canotek Rd., Unit 30
Mailing city: Ottawa
Province: ON
Postal: K1J 8R7
General Phone: (613) 744-4800
General Fax: (613) 744-0866
General/National Adv. E-mail: star@freenet.carlton.ca
Primary Website: www.eastottawa.ca
Published: Thur
Avg Free Circ: 45439
Audit By: CMCA
Audit Date: 30.04.2012
Personnel: Michael Curram (Pub.); Terry Tyo (Pub.); Patricia Lonergan (Ed.)
Parent company (for newspapers): Transcontinental Media

PUBLICATION NAME

The Stittsville News
Street Address: 57 Auriga Drive Unit 103 ,
Province: ON
Postal: K2E 8B2
Country: Canada
Mailing address: PO Box 610
Mailing city: Stittsville
Province: ON
Postal: K2E 8B2
General Phone: (613) 723-5970

Display Adv. E-mail: jillmartin@theemc.ca
Editorial e-mail: theresa.fritz@metroland.com
Primary Website: www.insideottawavalley.com
Published: Thur
Avg Free Circ: 13217
Audit By: CMCA
Audit Date: 30.06.2014
Personnel: Mike Tracy (Publisher)
Parent company (for newspapers): Metroland Media Group Ltd.; Runge Newspapers, Inc.

OUTLOOK

PUBLICATION NAME

The Outlook
Street Address: 108 Saskatchewan Ave. E ,
Province: SK
Postal: S0L 2N0
Country: Canada
Mailing address: PO Box 1717
Mailing city: Outlook
Province: SK
Postal: S0L 2N0
General Phone: (306) 867-8262
General Fax: (306) 867-9556
General/National Adv. E-mail: theoutlook@sasktel.net
Year Established: 1909
Delivery Methods: Mail`Newsstand
Areas Served - City/County or Portion Thereof, or Zip codes: Canada
Own Printing Facility?: Y
Mechanical specifications: Type page 10 1/4 x 14 1/2; E - 5 cols, 1/6 between; A - 6 cols, 1/6 between;
Published: Thur
Avg Paid Circ: 1208
Avg Free Circ: 49
Audit By: CMCA
Audit Date: 30.09.2016
Personnel: Delwyn Luedtke (General Manager)
Parent company (for newspapers): Glacier Media Group

OXBOW

PUBLICATION NAME

The Oxbow Herald
Street Address: Po Box 420 ,
Province: SK
Postal: S0C 2B0
Country: Canada
Mailing address: PO Box 420
Mailing city: Oxbow
Province: SK
Postal: S0C 2B0
General Phone: (306) 483-2323
General Fax: (306) 483-5258
General/National Adv. E-mail: oxbow.herald@sasktel.net
Display Adv. E-mail: lorena@oxbowherald.sk.ca
Editorial e-mail: liz@oxbowherald.sk.ca
Primary Website: www.SaskNewsNow.com
Delivery Methods: Mail`Racks
Areas Served - City/County or Portion Thereof, or Zip codes: Canada
Own Printing Facility?: Y
Commercial printers?: Y
Mechanical specifications: Type page 10 1/2 x 14 1/2; E - 5 cols, 2, 1/6 between; A - 5 cols, 2, 1/6 between; C - 5 cols, 2, 1/6 between.
Published: Mon
Avg Paid Circ: 908
Audit By: CMCA
Audit Date: 30.06.2015
Personnel: Lorena Wolensky (Advertising Manger); Lizz Bottrell (Editor); Marilyn Johnson (Reporter)
Parent company (for newspapers): Transcontinental Media

OYEN

PUBLICATION NAME

Oyen Echo
Street Address: 109 Sixth Ave. E. ,
Province: AB
Postal: T0J 2J0
Country: Canada
Mailing address: P.O. Box 420
Mailing city: Oyen
Province: AB
Postal: T0J 2J0
General Phone: (403) 664-3622
General Fax: (403) 664-3622
General/National Adv. E-mail: oyenecho@telusplanet.net
Display Adv. E-mail: oyenecho@telusplanet.net
Classified Adv. e-mail: 88
Editorial e-mail: oyenecho@telusplanet.net
Primary Website: www.oyenecho.ca
Year Established: 1974
Delivery Methods: Mail`Nowsstand
Areas Served - City/County or Portion Thereof, or Zip codes: Special Area #3
Own Printing Facility?: Y
Commercial printers?: Y
Mechanical specifications: Type page 10 1/4 x 16; E - 6 cols, 1 3/5, 1/6 between; A - 6 cols, 1 3/5, 1/6 between.
Published: Tues
Avg Paid Circ: 986
Avg Free Circ: 22
Audit By: VAC
Audit Date: 30.06.2017
Personnel: Ronald E. Holmes (Pub.); Diana Walker (Ed.)
Parent company (for newspapers): Holmes Publishing Co. Ltd.-OOB

PALMERSTON

PUBLICATION NAME

Minto Express
Street Address: 171 William St. ,
Province: ON
Postal: N0G 2P0
Country: Canada
Mailing address: PO Box 757
Mailing city: Palmerston
Province: ON
Postal: N0G 2P0
General Phone: (519) 343-2440
General Fax: (519) 343-2267
General/National Adv. E-mail: editor@mintoexpress.com
Primary Website: www.mintoexpress.com
Delivery Methods: Mail`Newsstand`Racks
Areas Served - City/County or Portion Thereof, or Zip codes: Town of Minto
Published: Wed
Avg Paid Circ: 476
Avg Free Circ: 5
Audit By: CMCA
Audit Date: 30.06.2016
Personnel: Bill Heuther (Gen. Mgr.); Shannon Burrows
Parent company (for newspapers): Metroland Media Group Ltd.; Torstar

PARKHILL

PUBLICATION NAME

The Parkhill Gazette
Street Address: 165 King St. ,
Province: ON
Postal: N0M 2K0
Country: Canada
Mailing address: PO Box 400
Mailing city: Parkhill
Province: ON
Postal: N0M 2K0
General Phone: (519) 294-6264
General Fax: (519) 294-6391
General/National Adv. E-mail: gazette@execulink.com
Areas Served - City/County or Portion Thereof, or Zip codes: Canada
Published: Thur
Avg Paid Circ: 860
Audit By: CMCA
Audit Date: 31.03.2014
Personnel: Melaime Carter (Adv. Mgr.); Dale Hayter (Circ. Mgr.); Gord Whitehead (Ed.)

PARKSVILLE

PUBLICATION NAME

Parksville Qualicum Beach News
Street Address: 1b/2a 1209 East Island Highway Parksville Heritage Centre ,
Province: BC
Postal: V9P 1R5
Country: Canada
Mailing address: 1B/2A 1209 East Island Highway Parksville Heritage Centre
Mailing city: Parksville
Province: BC
Postal: V9P 1R5
General Phone: (250) 248-4341
General Fax: (250) 248-4655
General/National Adv. F-mail: publisher@pqbnews.com
Display Adv. E-mail: bboyd@pqbnews.com
Classified Adv. e-mail: viads@bcclassified.com
Editorial e-mail: editor@pqbnews.com
Primary Website: www.pqbnews.com
Year Established: 1982
Areas Served - City/County or Portion Thereof, or Zip codes: Canada
Own Printing Facility?: Y
Commercial printers?: Y
Mechanical specifications: Type page 10 1/4 x 14 1/2; E - 6 cols, 1 1/2, 1/4 between; A - 6 cols, 1 1/2, 1/4 between; C - 7 cols, 1 1/4, 3/8 between.
Published: Tues`Fri
Avg Paid Circ: 6
Avg Free Circ: 16476
Audit By: AAM
Audit Date: 31.03.2019
Personnel: Peter McCully (Pub.); John Harding (Ed.); Brenda Boyd (Sales Mgr.); Michele Graham (Circ. Mgr.)
Parent company (for newspapers): Black Press Group Ltd.

PUBLICATION NAME

The Oceanside Star
Street Address: 166 E. Island Hwy. ,
Province: BC
Postal: V9P 2G3
Country: Canada
Mailing address: PO Box 45
Mailing city: Parksville
Province: BC
Postal: V9P 2G3
General Phone: (250) 954-0600
General Fax: (250) 954-0601
General/National Adv. E-mail: hnicholson@glaciermedia.com
Display Adv. E-mail: ads@oceansidestar.com
Editorial e-mail: bwilford@oceansidestar.com
Primary Website: www2.canada.com/oceansidestar/index.html
Areas Served - City/County or Portion Thereof, or Zip codes: Canada
Own Printing Facility?: Y
Mechanical specifications: Type page 10 7/16 x 12 1/2; E - 9 cols, 1 1/10, 1/12 between; A - 9 cols, 1 1/10, 1/12 between; C - 9 cols, 1 1/10, 1/12 between.
Published: Thur
Avg Paid Circ: 0
Avg Free Circ: 16243
Audit By: CMCA
Audit Date: 31.12.2013
Personnel: Coreen Greene (Adv. Mgr.); Michael Kelly (Circ. Mgr.); Brian Wilford (Ed.); Hugh Nicholson (Pub.)
Parent company (for newspapers): CanWest MediaWorks Publications, Inc.

PARRY SOUND

PUBLICATION NAME

Parry Sound Beacon Star
Street Address: 67 James Street ,
Province: ON
Postal: P2A 2X4
Country: Canada
Mailing address: PO Box 370
Mailing city: Parry Sound
Province: ON
Postal: P2A 2X4
General Phone: (705) 746-2104
General Fax: (705) 746-8369
General/National Adv. E-mail: jheidman@metrolandnorthmedia.com
Display Adv. E-mail: cbarnes@metrolandnorthmedia.com
Editorial e-mail: cpeck@metrolandnorthmedia.com
Primary Website: www.parrysound.com
Areas Served - City/County or Portion Thereof, or Zip codes: Canada
Published: Fri
Avg Free Circ: 7433
Audit By: CMCA
Audit Date: 31.12.2015
Personnel: Shaun Sauve (Regional Gen. Mgr.)
Parent company (for newspapers): Metroland Media Group Ltd.

PUBLICATION NAME

Parry Sound North Star
Street Address: 67 James St. ,
Province: ON
Postal: P2A 2X4
Country: Canada
Mailing address: PO Box 370
Mailing city: Parry Sound
Province: ON
Postal: P2A 2X4
General Phone: (705) 746-2104
General Fax: (705) 746-8369
Display Adv. E-mail: jheidman@metrolandnorthmedia.com
Editorial e-mail: jtynan@metrolandnorthmedia.com
Primary Website: www.parrysound.com
Year Established: 1874
Areas Served - City/County or Portion Thereof, or Zip codes: Canada
Published: Wed
Avg Paid Circ: 2081
Avg Free Circ: 125
Audit By: CMCA
Audit Date: 31.12.2015
Personnel: Bill Allen (Reg'l Gen. Mgr.); Janice Heidman Louch (Adv. Sales Mgr.); Jack Tynan (Mng. Ed.)
Parent company (for newspapers): Metroland Media Group Ltd.

PEACE RIVER

PUBLICATION NAME

The Peace River Record-gazette
Street Address: 10002 100th St. ,
Province: AB
Postal: T8S 1S6
Country: Canada
Mailing address: PO Box 6870
Mailing city: Peace River
Province: AB
Postal: T8S 1S6
General Phone: (780) 624-2591
General Fax: (780) 624-8600
Advertising Phone: (877) 786-8227
General/National Adv. E-mail: news@prrecordgazette.com
Display Adv. E-mail: adsales@prrecordgazette.com
Editorial e-mail: erin.steele@sunmedia.ca
Primary Website: www.prrecordgazette.com
Year Established: 1914
Areas Served - City/County or Portion Thereof, or Zip codes: Canada
Own Printing Facility?: Y
Mechanical specifications: Type page 13 x 21 1/4; E - 6 cols, 2 1/12, between; A - 6 cols, 2 1/12, between; C - 7 cols, 1 5/6, between.
Published: Wed
Avg Paid Circ: 0
Avg Free Circ: 3
Audit By: VAC
Audit Date: 31.12.2015
Personnel: Kristjanna Grimmelt (Mng. Ed.); Peter Meyerhoffer (reg. Adv. Dir.); Lori Czoba (Sales (online)); Fred Rinne (City Ed.)
Parent company (for newspapers): Postmedia

PENETANGUISHENE

PUBLICATION NAME

Gout De Vivre
Street Address: 343 Lafontaine St. W.,
Province: ON
Postal: L9M 1R3
Country: Canada
Mailing address: 343 Lafontaine St. W.
Mailing city: Penetanguishene
Province: ON
Postal: L9M 1R3
General Phone: (705) 533-3349
General/National Adv. E-mail: legoutdevivre@bellnet.ca
Primary Website: www.legoutdevivre.com
Areas Served - City/County or Portion Thereof, or Zip codes: Canada
Published: Thur
Avg Paid Circ: 912
Avg Free Circ: 0
Audit By: CMCA
Audit Date: 30.04.2013
Personnel: Therese Maheux

PENTICTON

PUBLICATION NAME

Penticton Western News
Street Address: 2250 Camrose St.,
Province: BC
Postal: V2A 8R1
Country: Canada
Mailing address: 2250 Camrose St.
Mailing city: Penticton
Province: BC
Postal: V2A 8R1
General Phone: (250) 492-3636
General Fax: (250) 492-9843
General/National Adv. E-mail: ads@pentictonwesternnews.com
Display Adv. E-mail: larry@pentictonwesternnews.com
Classified Adv. e-mail: classifieds@pentictonwesternnews.com
Editorial e-mail: kpatton@pentictonwesternnews.com
Primary Website: www.pentictonwesternnews.com
Delivery Methods: Newsstand`Carrier
Areas Served - City/County or Portion Thereof, or Zip codes: Canada
Own Printing Facility?: Y
Commercial printers?: Y
Mechanical specifications: Type page 10 1/3 x 14 1/2; E - 6 cols, 1 1/2, 1/6 between; A - 6 cols, 1 1/2, 1/6 between; C - 6 cols, 1 1/2, 1/6 between.
Published: Wed`Fri
Avg Free Circ: 23010
Audit By: AAM
Audit Date: 31.03.2019
Personnel: Sue Kovacs (Circ. Mgr.); Shannon Simpson (Pub); Larry Mercier (Sales Mgr.); Kristi Patton (Ed)
Parent company (for newspapers): Black Press Group Ltd.

PETERBOROUGH

PUBLICATION NAME

Peterborough This Week
Street Address: 884 Ford St.,
Province: ON
Postal: K9J 5V4
Country: Canada
Mailing address: 884 Ford St.
Mailing city: Peterborough
Province: ON
Postal: K9J 5V4
General Phone: (705) 749-3383
General Fax: (705) 749-0074
General/National Adv. E-mail: bdanford@mykawartha.com
Editorial e-mail: prellinger@mykawartha.com
Primary Website: mykawartha.com
Areas Served - City/County or Portion Thereof, or Zip codes: Canada
Own Printing Facility?: Y
Commercial printers?: Y
Mechanical specifications: Type page 11 1/2 x 21 1/2; E - 10 cols, 1, between; A - 10 cols, 1, between.
Published: Wed`Fri
Avg Free Circ: 32354
Audit By: CCAB
Audit Date: 26.10.2017
Personnel: Bruce Danford (Pub.); Linda Sudes (Gen. Mgr.); Adam Milligan (Adv. Mgr.); Mary Babcock (Reg'l Dir., Adv.); Tracy Magee (Circ. Mgr.); Lois Tuffin (Ed. in Chief); Paul Relinger (Special Pjcts. Ed.); Mike Lacey (News Ed.); Scott Prikker (Prodn. Mgr.)
Parent company (for newspapers): Metroland Media Group Ltd.; Torstar

PICTON

PUBLICATION NAME

The County Weekly News
Street Address: 3-252 Main St.,
Province: ON
Postal: K0K 2T0
Country: Canada
Mailing address: 3-252 Main St.
Mailing city: Picton
Province: ON
Postal: K0K 2T0
General Phone: (613) 476-4714
General Fax: (613) 476-1281
General/National Adv. E-mail: bill.glisky@sunmedia.ca
Editorial e-mail: chris.malette@sunmedia.ca
Primary Website: www.countyweeklynews.ca
Areas Served - City/County or Portion Thereof, or Zip codes: Canada
Published: Thur
Avg Free Circ: 11591
Audit By: CMCA
Audit Date: 30.06.2013
Personnel: Dave Vachon (News Ed.)
Parent company (for newspapers): Postmedia Network Inc.

PUBLICATION NAME

The Picton Gazette
Street Address: 267 Main St.,
Province: ON
Postal: K0K 2T0
Country: Canada
Mailing address: 267 Main St.
Mailing city: Picton
Province: ON
Postal: K0K 2T0
General Phone: (613) 476-3201
General Fax: (613) 476-3464
Advertising Phone: (613) 476-3201 ext. 105
Editorial Phone: (613) 476-3201 ext. 110
General/National Adv. E-mail: gazette@bellnet.ca
Display Adv. E-mail: advertise@pictongazette.com, gazetteclass@bellnet.ca
Editorial e-mail: gazette@bellnet.ca
Primary Website: www.pictongazette.com
Year Established: 1830
Delivery Methods: Carrier
Areas Served - City/County or Portion Thereof, or Zip codes: Canada
Mechanical specifications: Tabloid pages, 6 columns, 212 agates deep
Published: Thur
Avg Free Circ: 11450
Audit By: CMCA
Audit Date: 30.06.2016
Personnel: Jean M. Morrison (Pub.); Adam Bramburger (Ed.); Michelle Bowes (Prodn. Mgr.)

PUBLICATION NAME

The Pictou Advocate
Street Address: 21 George St.,
Province: NS
Postal: B0K 1H0
Country: Canada
Mailing address: 21 George St.
Mailing city: Pictou
Province: NS
Postal: B0K 1H0
General Phone: (902) 485-8014
General Fax: (902) 752-4816
Advertising Phone: (902) 759-0716
General/National Adv. E-mail: pictou.advocate@ns.sympatico.ca
Display Adv. E-mail: mark@pictouadvocate.com
Editorial e-mail: editor@pictouadvocate.com
Primary Website: www.pictouadvocate.com
Year Established: 1893
Delivery Methods: Mail
Areas Served - City/County or Portion Thereof, or Zip codes: Canada
Own Printing Facility?: Y
Published: Wed
Avg Paid Circ: 732
Avg Free Circ: 4
Audit By: VAC
Audit Date: 30.06.2016
Personnel: Jackie Jardine (Ed); Leith Orr (Pub.)

PIEDMONT

PUBLICATION NAME

Journal Acces
Street Address: Rue Principale,
Province: QC
Postal: J0R 1K0
Country: Canada
Mailing address: rue Principale
Mailing city: Piedmont
Province: QC
Postal: J0R 1K0
General Phone: (450) 227-7999
Primary Website: http://www.journalacces.ca/
Published: Sat
Avg Free Circ: 25720
Audit By: ODC
Audit Date: 14.12.2011
Personnel: Josee Pilotte

PILOT MOUND

PUBLICATION NAME

The Sentinel Courier
Street Address: 13 Railway St.,
Province: MB
Postal: R0G 1P0
Country: Canada
Mailing address: PO Box 179
Mailing city: Pilot Mound
Province: MB
Postal: R0G 1P0
General Phone: (204) 825-2772
General Fax: (204) 825-2439
General/National Adv. E-mail: sentinel@sentinelcourier.com
Editorial e-mail: sentinel@mymts.net
Primary Website: www.sentinelcourier.com
Areas Served - City/County or Portion Thereof, or Zip codes: Pilot Mound
Mechanical specifications: Type page 10 1/2 x 14; E - 5 cols, 2, 1/4 between; A - 5 cols, 2, 1/4 between.
Published: Tues
Avg Paid Circ: 1273
Avg Free Circ: 31
Audit By: VAC
Audit Date: 31.05.2016
Personnel: Susan Peterson (Ed.)

PINCHER CREEK

PUBLICATION NAME

Pincher Creek Echo
Street Address: 714 Main St.,
Province: AB
Postal: T0K 1W0
Country: Canada
Mailing address: PO Box 1000
Mailing city: Pincher Creek
Province: AB
Postal: T0K 1W0
General Phone: (403) 627-3252
General Fax: (403) 627-3949
General/National Adv. E-mail: pcecho@awna.com
Display Adv. E-mail: rmackintosh@postmedia.com
Editorial e-mail: cclow@postmedia.com
Primary Website: www.pinchercreekecho.com
Year Established: 1900
Areas Served - City/County or Portion Thereof, or Zip codes: Canada
Commercial printers?: Y
Mechanical specifications: Type page 10 1/4 x 15; E - 5 cols, 1 11/12, between; A - 6 cols, 1 1/2, between; C - 6 cols, 1 2/3, between.
Published: Wed
Avg Paid Circ: 1077
Avg Free Circ: 14
Audit By: CMCA
Audit Date: 30.06.2014
Personnel: Nancy Middleton (Pub); Martha Goforth (Office Mgr); Caitlin Clow (Ed); Roxanne Mackintosh (Adv. Dir)
Parent company (for newspapers): Postmedia Network Inc.; Quebecor Communications, Inc.

PLESSISVILLE

PUBLICATION NAME

L'avenir De L'erable
Street Address: 1620 Saint-calixte St.,
Province: QC
Postal: G6L 1P9
Country: Canada
Mailing address: 1620 Saint-Calixte St.
Mailing city: Plessisville
Province: QC
Postal: G6L 1P9
General Phone: (819) 362-7049
General Fax: (819) 362-2216
General/National Adv. E-mail: cotes2@transcontinental.ca
Primary Website: www.lavenirdelerable.com
Areas Served - City/County or Portion Thereof, or Zip codes: Canada
Own Printing Facility?: Y
Published: Wed
Avg Paid Circ: 9
Avg Free Circ: 10779
Audit By: CCAB
Audit Date: 31.03.2014
Personnel: Pierre Gaudet (Dir., Sales); Sylvia Cote (Ed.); Ghislain Chauvette (Ed.)
Parent company (for newspapers): Transcontinental Media

PONOKA

PUBLICATION NAME

Ponoka News
Street Address: 5019-a 50th Ave.,
Province: AB
Postal: T4J 1R6
Country: Canada
Mailing address: PO Box 4217
Mailing city: Ponoka
Province: AB
Postal: T4J 1R6
General Phone: (403) 783-3311
General Fax: (403) 783-6300
Display Adv. E-mail: judy.dick@ponokanews.com
Classified Adv. e-mail: judy.dick@ponokanews.com
Editorial e-mail: jeff.heyden-kaye@ponokanews.com
Primary Website: www.ponokanews.com
Year Established: 1954
Delivery Methods: Mail`Newsstand`Carrier`Racks
Areas Served - City/County or Portion Thereof, or Zip codes: Ponoka
Own Printing Facility?: Y
Commercial printers?: Y
Mechanical specifications: Type page 10.12" x 13"; 7 cols, column width 1.3" wide
Published: Wed
Avg Paid Circ: 16

Community Newspapers in Canada

Avg Free Circ: 5856
Audit By: CMCA
Audit Date: 30.04.2018
Personnel: Mary Kemmis (Pres.)
Parent company (for newspapers): Black Press Group Ltd.

PORT ALBERNI

PUBLICATION NAME

Alberni Valley News
Street Address: 4656 Margaret Street ,
Province: BC
Postal: V9Y 6H2
Country: Canada
General Phone: (250) 723-6399
General Fax: (250) 723-6395
Display Adv. E-mail: publisher@albernivalleynews.com
Editorial e-mail: editor@albernivalleynews.com
Primary Website: albernivalleynews.com
Year Established: 2006
Delivery Methods: Carrier`Racks
Areas Served - City/County or Portion Thereof, or Zip codes: Canada
Published: Wed
Avg Free Circ: 9302
Audit By: AAM
Audit Date: 31.03.2019
Personnel: Teresa Bird (Publisher); Susan Quinn (Ed.)
Parent company (for newspapers): Black Press Group Ltd.

PORT AUX BASQUES

PUBLICATION NAME

The Gulf News
Street Address: Po Box 1090 ,
Province: NL
Postal: A0M 1C0
Country: Canada
Mailing address: PO Box 1090
Mailing city: Port aux Basques
Province: NL
Postal: A0M 1C0
General Phone: (709) 695-3671
General Fax: (709) 695-7901
Advertising Phone: (709) 279-3188
Advertising Fax: (709) 279-2628
General/National Adv. E-mail: editor@gulfnews.ca
Display Adv. E-mail: wrose@thewesternstar.com
Editorial e-mail: chantelle.macisaac@gulfnews.ca
Primary Website: www.gulfnews.ca
Areas Served - City/County or Portion Thereof, or Zip codes: Canada
Own Printing Facility?: Y
Commercial printers?: Y
Published: Mon
Avg Paid Circ: 2912
Avg Free Circ: 0
Audit By: VAC
Audit Date: 31.12.2015
Personnel: Chantelle Macisaac (Ed); Wendy Rose (Adv.)
Parent company (for newspapers): Transcontinental Media

PORT COLBORNE

PUBLICATION NAME

In Port News
Street Address: 228 E. Main St. ,
Province: ON
Postal: L3K 1S4
Country: Canada
Mailing address: 228 E. Main St.
Mailing city: Port Colborne
Province: ON
Postal: L3K 1S4
General Phone: (905) 732-2411
General/National Adv. E-mail: john.tobon@sunmedia.ca
Primary Website: www.inportnews.ca
Areas Served - City/County or Portion Thereof, or Zip codes: Canada

Published: Wed
Avg Free Circ: 9849
Audit By: CMCA
Audit Date: 31.03.2016
Personnel: John Tobon; Julia Coles
Parent company (for newspapers): Postmedia Network Inc.

PORT COQUITLAM

PUBLICATION NAME

Tri City News
Street Address: 118 - 1680 Broadway Street ,
Province: BC
Postal: V3C 2M8
Country: Canada
Mailing address: 118 - 1680 Broadway Street
Mailing city: Port Coquitlam
Province: BC
Postal: V3C 2M8
General Phone: (604) 525-6397
Advertising Phone: (604) 472-3020
Advertising Fax: (604) 472-3030
Display Adv. E-mail: admanager@tricitynews.com
Primary Website: tricitynews.com
Delivery Methods: Carrier
Areas Served - City/County or Portion Thereof, or Zip codes: Port Moody, Belcarra, Anmore, Port Coquitlam, Coquitlam
Published: Wed`Fri
Avg Paid Circ: 0
Avg Free Circ: 52297
Audit By: Sworn/Estimate/Non-Audited
Audit Date: 12.07.2019
Parent company (for newspapers): Glacier Media

PORT COQUITLAM

PUBLICATION NAME

Tri-City News
Street Address: 1680 Broadway Street , Unit 118
Province: BC
Postal: V3C 2M8
Country: Canada
Mailing address: 1680 Broadway St Unit 118
Mailing city: Port Coquitlam
Province: BC
Postal: V3C 2M8
General Phone: (604) 525-6397
General/National Adv. E-mail: publisher@tricitynews.com
Display Adv. E-mail: smitchell@tricitynews.com
Editorial e-mail: newsroom@tricitynews.com
Primary Website: tricitynews.com
Year Established: 1985
Delivery Methods: Carrier
Areas Served - City/County or Portion Thereof, or Zip codes: Tri-Cities
Published: Wed`Fri
Avg Paid Circ: 0
Avg Free Circ: 51702
Audit By: CCAB
Audit Date: 23.11.2017
Personnel: Richard Dal Monte (Ed.); Shannon Mitchell (Pub); Kim Yorston (Circ Mgr)
Parent company (for newspapers): Black Press Group Ltd.; Glacier Media Group

PORT DOVER

PUBLICATION NAME

Port Dover Maple Leaf
Street Address: 351 Main St. ,
Province: ON
Postal: N0A 1N0
Country: Canada
Mailing address: PO Box 70
Mailing city: Port Dover
Province: ON
Postal: N0A 1N0
General Phone: (519) 583-0112
General/National Adv. E-mail: info@portdovermapleleaf.com
Display Adv. E-mail: ads@portdovermapleleaf.com

Editorial e-mail: news@portdovermapleleaf.com
Primary Website: www.portdovermapleleaf.com
Year Established: 1873
Delivery Methods: Mail`Newsstand`Racks
Areas Served - City/County or Portion Thereof, or Zip codes: Norfolk County
Commercial printers?: Y
Mechanical specifications: Type page 10 1/2 x 16; E - 5 cols, 2, 1/8 between; A - 10 cols, 1, 1/8 between; C - 10 cols, 1, 1/8 between.
Published: Wed
Avg Paid Circ: 2904
Avg Free Circ: 15
Audit By: Sworn/Estimate/Non-Audited
Audit Date: 12.07.2019
Personnel: Paul Morris (Ed.); Stan Morris (Ed.)

PORT ELGIN

PUBLICATION NAME

Shoreline Beacon
Street Address: 694 Goderich St. ,
Province: ON
Postal: N0H 2C0
Country: Canada
Mailing address: PO Box 580
Mailing city: Port Elgin
Province: ON
Postal: N0H 2C0
General Phone: (519) 832-9001
General Fax: (519) 389-4793
General/National Adv. E-mail: shoreline@bmts.com
Primary Website: www.shorelinebeacon.com
Year Established: unknown
Areas Served - City/County or Portion Thereof, or Zip codes: Canada
Own Printing Facility?: Y
Commercial printers?: Y
Mechanical specifications: 10.33"w x 160 agates
Published: Tues
Avg Paid Circ: 2102
Avg Free Circ: 15
Audit By: CMCA
Audit Date: 30.06.2016
Personnel: Kiera Merriam (Gen. Mgr.)
Parent company (for newspapers): Postmedia Network Inc.; Quebecor Communications, Inc.

PORT HARDY

PUBLICATION NAME

North Island Gazette
Street Address: #3-7053 Market St. ,
Province: BC
Postal: V0N 2P0
Country: Canada
Mailing address: Box 458
Mailing city: Port Hardy
Province: BC
Postal: V0N 2P0
General Phone: (250) 949-6225
General/National Adv. E-mail: production@northislandgazette.com
Display Adv. E-mail: sales@northislandgazette.com
Classified Adv. e-mail: viads@bcclassified.com
Editorial e-mail: publisher@northislandgazette.com
Primary Website: www.northislandgazette.com
Year Established: 1965
Delivery Methods: Mail`Newsstand`Carrier`Racks
Areas Served - City/County or Portion Thereof, or Zip codes: Canada
Own Printing Facility?: Y
Mechanical specifications: Type page 10 3/8 x 14.
Published: Wed
Avg Paid Circ: 1065
Avg Free Circ: 500
Audit By: CMCA
Audit Date: 30.11.2018
Personnel: Lilian Meerveld; Tyson Whitney; Thomas Kervin (Reporter); Natasha Griffiths (Advertising Sale Rep)

Parent company (for newspapers): Black Press Group Ltd.

PORT HAWKESBURY

PUBLICATION NAME

The Reporter
Street Address: 2 Maclean Court ,
Province: NS
Postal: B9A 3K2
Country: Canada
Mailing address: 2 Maclean Court
Mailing city: Port Hawkesbury
Province: NS
Postal: B9A 3K2
General Phone: (902) 625-3300
General Fax: (902) 625-1701
Display Adv. E-mail: nicolefawcett@porthawkesburyreporter.com
Editorial e-mail: jake@porthawkesburyreporter.com
Primary Website: www.porthawkesburyreporter.com
Areas Served - City/County or Portion Thereof, or Zip codes: Port Hawkesbury
Published: Wed
Avg Paid Circ: 87
Audit By: VAC
Audit Date: 30.09.2016
Personnel: Rick Cluett (Pub); Nicole Fawcett (Adv)

PORT PERRY

PUBLICATION NAME

The Port Perry Star
Street Address: 180 Mary St. , Unit 11
Province: ON
Postal: L9L 1C4
Country: Canada
Mailing address: 180 Mary St. Unit 11
Mailing city: Port Perry
Province: ON
Postal: L9L 1C4
General Phone: (905) 985-7383
General Fax: (905) 985-3708
Advertising Phone: (905) 215-0440
Editorial Phone: (905) 215-0462
General/National Adv. E-mail: chall@durhanregion.com
Display Adv. E-mail: feismont@durhamregion.com
Classified Adv. e-mail: classified@thespec.com
Editorial e-mail: chall@durhamregion.com
Primary Website: www.durhamregion.com
Year Established: 1866
Delivery Methods: Newsstand`Carrier
Areas Served - City/County or Portion Thereof, or Zip codes: Scugog Township, plus select areas in Brock/Sunderland, Little Britain, Pontypool
Own Printing Facility?: Y
Commercial printers?: Y
Published: Thur
Avg Paid Circ: 12000
Avg Free Circ: 125
Audit By: Sworn/Estimate/Non-Audited
Audit Date: 12.07.2019
Personnel: Tim Whittaker (Pub); Lisa Burgess (Sales Mgr.); Laurie Abel (Circ. Coordinator); Mike Johnston (Mng. Ed.)
Parent company (for newspapers): Metroland Media Group Ltd.

PUBLICATION NAME

The Standard Newspaper
Street Address: 94a Water St. ,
Province: ON
Postal: L9L 1J2
Country: Canada
Mailing address: 94A Water St.
Mailing city: Port Perry
Province: ON
Postal: L9L 1J2
General Phone: (905) 985-6985
General Fax: (905) 985-9253
General/National Adv. E-mail: production-

standard@powergate.ca
Display Adv. E-mail: standardnancy@powergate.ca
Classified Adv. e-mail: office-standard@powergate.ca
Editorial e-mail: standarddarryl@powergate.ca
Primary Website: www.thestandardnewspaper.ca
Year Established: 2004
Delivery Methods: Mail`Newsstand`Carrier`Racks
Areas Served - City/County or Portion Thereof, or Zip codes: Durham Region
Published: Thur
Avg Free Circ: 11868
Audit By: CMCA
Audit Date: 31.12.2014
Personnel: Colleen Green (Gen. Mgr.); Darryl Knight (Ed.); Nancy Lister (Adv. Rep.); Dan Cearns (Reporter)
Parent company (for newspapers): Skyline Media

PORT STANLEY

PUBLICATION NAME

Lake Erie Beacon (oob)
Street Address: 204 A Carlow Road ,
Province: ON
Postal: N5L 1C5
Country: Canada
Mailing address: 204 Carlow Rd
Mailing city: Port Stanley
Postal: N5L 1C5
General Phone: (519) 782-4563
General Fax: (519) 782-4563
Advertising Phone: (519) 782-4563
Advertising Fax: (519) 782-4563
Editorial Phone: (519) 782-4563
Editorial Fax: (519) 782-4563
General/National Adv. E-mail: beacon@lebeacon.ca
Display Adv. E-mail: linda@lebeacon.ca
Classified Adv. e-mail: linda@lebeacon.ca
Editorial e-mail: andrew@lebeacon.ca
Primary Website: www.lebeacon.ca
Year Established: 2004
Delivery Methods: Mail`Newsstand
Areas Served - City/County or Portion Thereof, or Zip codes: Central Elgin
Mechanical specifications: TIFF, JPEG, PDF, MS Word, Quark Express
Published: Fri`Bi-Mthly
Published Other: Every second week
Avg Free Circ: 7000
Audit By: CMCA
Audit Date: 31.12.2013
Parent company (for newspapers): Kettle Creek Publishing Ltd.

PORTAGE LA PRAIRIE

PUBLICATION NAME

Central Plains Herald Leader
Street Address: 1941 Saskatchewan Ave. W. ,
Province: MB
Postal: R1N 0R7
Country: Canada
Mailing address: PO Box 130
Mailing city: Portage La Prairie
Province: MB
Postal: R1N 3B4
General Phone: (204) 857-3427
General Fax: (204) 239-1270
General/National Adv. E-mail: news.dailygraphic@shawcable.com
Display Adv. E-mail: daria.zmiyiwsky@sunmedia.ca
Editorial e-mail: mickey.dumont@sunmedia.ca
Primary Website: http://www.portagedailygraphic.com/
Areas Served - City/County or Portion Thereof, or Zip codes: Central Plains
Own Printing Facility?: Y
Commercial printers?: Y
Mechanical specifications: Type page 14 x 22 3/4; E - 6 cols, 2 1/8, 1/8 between; A - 6 cols, 2 1/8, 1/8 between; C - 6 cols, 2 1/8, 1/8 between.
Published: Thur

Avg Paid Circ: 4551
Avg Free Circ: 9595
Audit By: VAC
Audit Date: 30.06.2016
Personnel: Guey Fiset (Class./Circ. Mgr.); Daria Zmiyiwsky (Adv. Dir); Mickey Dumont (Ed)
Parent company (for newspapers): Postmedia Network Inc.; Quebecor Communications, Inc.

POWELL RIVER

PUBLICATION NAME

Powell River Peak
Street Address: 4400 Marine Ave. ,
Province: BC
Postal: V8A 2K1
Country: Canada
Mailing address: 4400 Marine Ave.
Mailing city: Powell River
Province: BC
Postal: V8A 2K1
General Phone: (604) 485-5313
General Fax: (604) 485-5007
General/National Adv. E-mail: publisher@prpeak.com
Display Adv. E-mail: sales@prpeak.com
Classified Adv. e-mail: cindy@prpeak.com
Editorial e-mail: publisher@prpeak.com
Primary Website: www.prpeak.com
Year Established: 1995
Delivery Methods: Mail`Newsstand`Carrier
Areas Served - City/County or Portion Thereof, or Zip codes: Powell River Regional District
Commercial printers?: Y
Mechanical specifications: Type page 10 1/4 x 13.8; E - 6 cols, 1 1/2, 1/8 between; A - 6 cols, 1 1/2, 1/8 between; C - 6 cols, 1 1/2, 1/8 between.
Published: Wed
Avg Paid Circ: 2084
Avg Free Circ: 48
Audit By: VAC
Audit Date: 31.12.2016
Personnel: Michele Stewart (Circ. Dir.); Jason Schreuers (Pub/Ed); Dot Campbell (Sales)
Parent company (for newspapers): Glacier Media Group

PRESCOTT

PUBLICATION NAME

The Prescott Journal
Street Address: 3201 County Rd. 2 ,
Province: ON
Postal: K0E 1T0
Country: Canada
Mailing address: PO Box 549
Mailing city: Prescott
Province: ON
Postal: K0E 1T0
General Phone: (613) 925-4265
General Fax: (613) 925-2837
Display Adv. E-mail: adsales@prescottjournal.com
Editorial e-mail: journal@stlawrenceprinting.on.ca
Primary Website: www.prescottjournal.com
Year Established: 1891
Delivery Methods: Mail`Newsstand`Carrier
Areas Served - City/County or Portion Thereof, or Zip codes: Canada
Own Printing Facility?: N
Commercial printers?: Y
Mechanical specifications: Type page 10.325" x 16"; 6 columns 1.125" wide x 220 agates
Published: Wed
Avg Paid Circ: 1123
Avg Free Circ: 99
Audit By: CMCA
Audit Date: 30.06.2016
Personnel: Beth Morris (Pub.); Dave Flinn (Prodn. Mgr.); Jamie Nurse

PRINCETON

PUBLICATION NAME

Princeton Similkameen Spotlight
Street Address: 282 Bridge St. ,
Province: BC
Postal: V0X 1W0
Country: Canada
Mailing address: PO Box 340
Mailing city: Princeton
Province: BC
Postal: V0X 1W0
General Phone: (250) 295-3535
General Fax: (250) 295-7322
Display Adv. E-mail: advertising@similkameenspotlight.com
Editorial e-mail: editor@similkameenspotlight.com
Primary Website: www.similkameenspotlight.com
Year Established: 1948
Delivery Methods: Mail`Racks
Mechanical specifications: Type page 10 1/3 x 14; E - 6 cols, 1 9/16, between; A - 6 cols, 1 9/16, between; C - 6 cols, 1 9/16, between.
Published: Wed
Avg Paid Circ: 2227
Avg Free Circ: 43
Audit By: VAC
Audit Date: 30.06.2016
Personnel: Andrea Demeer; Andrea DeMeer (Ed/Assist. Pub); Don Kendall (Pub); Sandi Nolan (Adv Mgr.)
Parent company (for newspapers): Black Press Group Ltd.

PROVOST

PUBLICATION NAME

The Provost News
Street Address: 5111 50th St. ,
Province: AB
Postal: T0B 3S0
Country: Canada
Mailing address: PO Box 180, 5111-50 St.
Mailing city: Provost
Province: AB
Postal: T0B 3S0
General Phone: (780) 753-2564
General Fax: (780) 753-6117
General/National Adv. E-mail: advertising@provostnews.ca
Display Adv. E-mail: advertising@provostnews.ca
Editorial e-mail: rcholmes@agt.net
Primary Website: www.provostnews.ca
Year Established: 1910
Delivery Methods: Mail`Newsstand
Areas Served - City/County or Portion Thereof, or Zip codes: Provost M.D. No. 52
Commercial printers?: Y
Published: Wed
Avg Paid Circ: 1300
Avg Free Circ: 54
Audit By: VAC
Audit Date: 30.06.2017
Personnel: Richard C. Holmes (Ed.)
Parent company (for newspapers): Holmes Publishing Co. Ltd.-OOB

QUEBEC

PUBLICATION NAME

Charlesbourg Express
Street Address: 710 Bouvier, Suite 107 ,
Province: QC
Postal: G2J 1C2
Country: Canada
Mailing address: 710 Bouvier, Suite 107
Mailing city: Quebec
Province: QC
Postal: G2J 1C2
General Phone: (418) 628-7460
General Fax: (418)840-1207
General/National Adv. E-mail: redaction_quebec@tc.tc
Primary Website: www.quebechebdo.com
Areas Served - City/County or Portion Thereof, or Zip codes: Canada
Published: Fri
Avg Paid Circ: 9
Avg Free Circ: 27178
Audit By: CCAB
Audit Date: 31.03.2014
Personnel: Alain LePage (Gen. Mgr.); Lilianne Laprise (Ed.)
Parent company (for newspapers): Reseau Select/Select Network; Transcontinental Media

PUBLICATION NAME

Journal L'actuel
Street Address: 710 Bouvier, Suite 107 ,
Province: QC
Postal: G2J 1C2
Country: Canada
Mailing address: 710 Bouvier, Suite 107
Mailing city: Quebec
Province: QC
Postal: G2J 1C2
General Phone: (418) 628-7460
General Fax: (418) 622-1511
General/National Adv. E-mail: redaction_quebec@tc.tc
Primary Website: www.lactuel.com
Areas Served - City/County or Portion Thereof, or Zip codes: Canada
Commercial printers?: Y
Published: Fri
Avg Paid Circ: 5
Avg Free Circ: 57753
Audit By: CCAB
Audit Date: 31.03.2014
Personnel: Lilianne Laprese (Ed.); Alain LePage (Dir.); Lilianne Laprise (Ed.)
Parent company (for newspapers): Transcontinental Media

PUBLICATION NAME

L'appel
Street Address: 710 Rue Bouvier Bureau 107 ,
Province: QC
Postal: G2J 1C2
Country: Canada
Mailing address: 710 Rue Bouvier Bureau 107
Mailing city: Quebec
Province: QC
Postal: G2J 1C2
General Phone: (418) 628-7460
General Fax: (418) 622-1511
Advertising Phone: (418) 628-7460
Advertising Fax: (418) 622-1511
Editorial Phone: (418) 628-7460
Editorial Fax: (418) 622-1511
General/National Adv. E-mail: redaction_quebec@tc.tc
Display Adv. E-mail: redaction_quebec@tc.tc
Editorial e-mail: redaction_quebec@tc.tc
Primary Website: www.lappel.com
Year Established: 1945
Delivery Methods: Mail`Racks
Areas Served - City/County or Portion Thereof, or Zip codes: Canada
Published: Fri
Avg Paid Circ: 10
Avg Free Circ: 44099
Audit By: CCAB
Audit Date: 31.03.2014
Personnel: Michel Chalifour (Reg. Gen. Mgr.)

PUBLICATION NAME

Quebec Chronicle-telegraph
Street Address: 1040 Belvedere, Suite 218 ,
Province: QC
Postal: G1S 3G3
Country: Canada
Mailing address: 1040 Belbedere., Ste 218
Mailing city: Quebec
Province: QC
Postal: G1S 3G3
General Phone: (418) 650-1764
General Fax: (418) 650-5172
General/National Adv. E-mail: info@qctonline.com;
Display Adv. E-mail: production@qctonline.com

Community Newspapers in Canada   III-567

Editorial e-mail: editor@qctonline.com
Primary Website: www.qctonline.com
Year Established: 1764
Delivery Methods: Mail`Newsstand
Areas Served - City/County or Portion Thereof, or Zip codes: Canada
Own Printing Facility?: N
Commercial printers?: Y
Mechanical specifications: Type page 10 1/3 x 13 7/8; E - 6 cols, 1 5/8, 3/16 between; A - 6 cols, 1 5/8, 3/16 between; C - 5 cols, 1 5/8, 3/16 between.
Published: Wed
Avg Paid Circ: 907
Avg Free Circ: 24
Audit By: CMCA
Audit Date: 30.09.2015
Personnel: Wendy Little (Circulation Manager); Stacie Stanton (Editor and Publisher)

PUBLICATION NAME

Quebec Express
Street Address: 710 Bouvier, Suite 107, Bureau 900
Province: QC
Postal: G2J 1C2
Country: Canada
Mailing address: Boulevard Charest Ouest Bureau 900
Mailing city: Quebec
Province: QC
Postal: G2J 1C2
General Phone: (418) 628-7460
General Fax: (418) 622-1511
General/National Adv. E-mail: redaction_quebec@tc.tc
Areas Served - City/County or Portion Thereof, or Zip codes: Canada
Published: Fri
Avg Paid Circ: 7
Avg Free Circ: 28899
Audit By: CCAB
Audit Date: 31.03.2014
Personnel: Lilianne Laprise (Pub./Ed.)

QUEEN CHARLOTTE

PUBLICATION NAME

Haida Gwaii Observer
Street Address: 623 7th St.,
Province: BC
Postal: V0T 1S0
Country: Canada
Mailing address: PO Box 205
Mailing city: Queen Charlotte
Province: BC
Postal: V0T 1S0
General Phone: (250) 559-4680
General Fax: (250) 559-8433
Advertising Phone: (250) 559-4680
Advertising Fax: (250) 559-4680
Editorial Phone: (250) 559-4680
Editorial Fax: (250) 559-4680
General/National Adv. E-mail: observer@haidagwaii.ca
Display Adv. E-mail: chris.williams@haidagwaiiobserver.com
Editorial e-mail: observer@haidagwaii.ca
Primary Website: www.haidagwaiiobserver.com
Year Established: 1969
Delivery Methods: Mail`Newsstand
Areas Served - City/County or Portion Thereof, or Zip codes: V0T 1S0, V0T 1T0, V0T 1R0, V0T 1Y0, V0T 1M0
Own Printing Facility?: Y
Commercial printers?: N
Mechanical specifications: Type page 7 1/2 x 10; E - 3 cols, 2 1/2, between; A - 3 cols, 2 1/2, between.
Published: Fri
Avg Paid Circ: 963
Avg Free Circ: 2
Audit By: VAC
Audit Date: 31.08.2016
Personnel: Todd Hamilton (Pub./Ed.); Chris Williams (Sales Mgr.)

QUESNEL

PUBLICATION NAME

Quesnel Cariboo Observer
Street Address: 188 Carson Ave.,
Province: BC
Postal: V2J 2A8
Country: Canada
Mailing address: 188 Carson Ave.
Mailing city: Quesnel
Province: BC
Postal: V2J 2A8
General Phone: (250) 992-2121
General Fax: (250) 992-5229
General/National Adv. E-mail: newsroom@quesnelobserver.com
Display Adv. E-mail: advertising@quesnelobserver.com
Classified Adv. e-mail: publisher@quesnelobserver.com
Editorial e-mail: editor@quesnelobserver.com
Primary Website: www.quesnelobserver.com
Delivery Methods: Mail`Racks
Areas Served - City/County or Portion Thereof, or Zip codes: V2J
Commercial printers?: Y
Published: Wed`Fri
Avg Paid Circ: 984
Avg Free Circ: 2487
Audit By: VAC
Audit Date: 30.06.2016
Personnel: Autumn McDonald (Ed.); Tracey Roberts (Pub/Sales Mgr.)
Parent company (for newspapers): Black Press Group Ltd.

RADVILLE

PUBLICATION NAME

Radville Deep South Star
Street Address: #1-420 Floren St.,
Province: SK
Postal: S0C 2G0
Country: Canada
Mailing address: PO Box 370
Mailing city: Radville
Province: SK
Postal: S0C 2G0
General Phone: (306) 869-2202
General Fax: (306) 869-2533
General/National Adv. E-mail: rstar@sasktel.net
Display Adv. E-mail: circulation@rdstar.sk.ca
Primary Website: www.rdstar.sk.ca
Areas Served - City/County or Portion Thereof, or Zip codes: Canada
Commercial printers?: Y
Published: Thur
Avg Paid Circ: 624
Audit By: CMCA
Audit Date: 31.01.2016
Personnel: Roger Holmes (Pub.)
Parent company (for newspapers): Transcontinental Media

RAINY RIVER

PUBLICATION NAME

Rainy River Record
Street Address: 312 Third St.,
Province: ON
Postal: P0W 1L0
Country: Canada
Mailing address: PO Box 280
Mailing city: Rainy River
Province: ON
Postal: P0W 1L0
General Phone: (807) 852-3366
General Fax: (807) 852-4434
Editorial Phone: (807) 852-3337
General/National Adv. E-mail: info@rainyriverrecord.com
Display Adv. E-mail: advertising@rainyriverrecord.com
Editorial e-mail: editorial@rainyriverrecord.com
Primary Website: www.rainyriverrecord.com
Year Established: 1919
Areas Served - City/County or Portion Thereof, or Zip codes: Canada
Mechanical specifications: Type page 10 1/2 x 15; E - 5 cols, 1 4/5, 2/9 between; A - 5 cols, 1 4/5, 2/9 between; C - 5 cols, 1 4/5, 2/9 between.
Published: Tues
Avg Paid Circ: 609
Audit By: CMCA
Audit Date: 31.03.2014
Personnel: Anne Mailloux (Circ. Mgr.); Melissa Hudgin (Sales); Sharon LaCroix (Ed.)

RED DEER

PUBLICATION NAME

Central Alberta Life
Street Address: 2950 Bremner Ave.,
Province: AB
Postal: T4R 1M9
Country: Canada
Mailing address: 2950 Bremner Ave.
Mailing city: Red Deer
Province: AB
Postal: T4R 1M9
General Phone: (403) 314-4373
General Fax: (403) 342-4051
Display Adv. E-mail: advertising@reddeeradvocate.com
Classified Adv. e-mail: prausch@reddeeradvocate.com
Editorial e-mail: editorial@reddeeradvocate.com
Primary Website: www.reddeeradvocate.com
Year Established: 1995
Areas Served - City/County or Portion Thereof, or Zip codes: Canada
Own Printing Facility?: Y
Commercial printers?: Y
Mechanical specifications: Type page 10 x 12 7/8; A - 6 cols, 1 5/8, 1/6 between; C - 7 cols, 1 1/4, between.
Published: Thur
Avg Free Circ: 33301
Audit By: Sworn/Estimate/Non-Audited
Audit Date: 12.07.2019
Personnel: Mary Kemmis (Pub); Crystal Rhyno (Mng Ed); Wendy Moore (Adv. Mgr.); Deb Reitmeie (Circ. Mgr.)
Parent company (for newspapers): Red Deer Advocate

PUBLICATION NAME

Friday Forward
Street Address: 2950 Bremner Ave.,
Province: AB
Postal: T4R 1M9
Country: Canada
Mailing address: 2950 Bremner Ave.
Mailing city: Red Deer
Province: AB
Postal: T4N 5G3
General Phone: (403) 343-2400
General Fax: (403) 342-4051
Advertising Phone: (403) 314-4343
Advertising Fax: (403) 342-4051
Editorial Phone: (403) 314-4325
Editorial Fax: (403) 341-6560
Display Adv. E-mail: advertising@reddeeradvocate.com
Classified Adv. e-mail: classified@reddeeradvocate.com
Editorial e-mail: editorial@reddeeradvocate.com
Primary Website: www.reddeeradvocate.com
Year Established: 1907
Delivery Methods: Newsstand`Carrier
Areas Served - City/County or Portion Thereof, or Zip codes: Canada
Own Printing Facility?: Y
Commercial printers?: Y
Mechanical specifications: Type page 10 x 12 7/8; A - 6 cols, 1 9/16, 1/6 between; C - 7 cols, 1 15/16, between.
Published: Fri
Avg Paid Circ: 8500
Audit By: AAM
Audit Date: 30.06.2018
Personnel: Mary Kemmis (Pub Red Deer Advocate; Pres Prarie/ East Kootenay Division Black Press); Wendy Moore (Advt Mgr); Patricia Rausch (National Rep & Major Acct Asst); Debbie Reitmeier (Circulation Mgr); David Marsden (Managing Editor)
Parent company (for newspapers): Black Press Group Ltd.

PUBLICATION NAME

Red Deer Express
Street Address: 121 5301-43 St.,
Province: AB
Postal: T4N 1C8
Country: Canada
Mailing address: 121 5301-43 St.
Mailing city: Red Deer
Province: AB
Postal: T4N 1C8
General Phone: (403) 346-3356
General Fax: (403) 347-6620
Advertising Phone: (403) 625-4474
General/National Adv. E-mail: express@reddeer.greatwest.ca
Display Adv. E-mail: publisher@reddeerexpress.com
Classified Adv. e-mail: publisher@reddeerexpress.com
Editorial e-mail: editor@reddeerexpress.com
Primary Website: www.reddeerexpress.com
Year Established: 1946
Areas Served - City/County or Portion Thereof, or Zip codes: Canada
Own Printing Facility?: Y
Commercial printers?: Y
Published: Wed
Avg Paid Circ: 0
Avg Free Circ: 24718
Audit By: VAC
Audit Date: 31.08.2016
Personnel: Tracey Scheveers (Pub); Mark Weber (Ed)
Parent company (for newspapers): Black Press Group Ltd.

RED LAKE

PUBLICATION NAME

The Northern Sun News
Street Address: 200 Howey Street,
Province: ON
Postal: P0V 2M0
Country: Canada
Mailing address: PO Box 1540
Mailing city: Red Lake
Province: ON
Postal: P0V 2M0
General Phone: (807) 727-2888
General Fax: (807) 727-3961
Display Adv. E-mail: pamela@thenorthernsun.com
Editorial e-mail: lindsay@thenorthernsun.com
Primary Website: www.thenorthernsun.com
Areas Served - City/County or Portion Thereof, or Zip codes: Canada
Published: Wed
Avg Paid Circ: 780
Audit By: CMCA
Audit Date: 31.03.2016
Personnel: Kathy Coutts (Gen Mgr.); Pamela O'Neill (Adv. Sales & Mrktg.)

REDWATER

PUBLICATION NAME

Farm 'n' Friends
Street Address: 4720 50 Ave,
Province: AB
Postal: T0A 2W0
Country: Canada
Mailing address: PO Box 800
Mailing city: Lamont
Province: AB
Postal: T0B 2R0
General Phone: (780) 421-9715
General Fax: (780) 942-2515
General/National Adv. E-mail: redwater@shaw.ca

Display Adv. E-mail: redwater@shaw.ca
Classified Adv. e-mail: redwater@shaw.ca
Editorial e-mail: redwater@shaw.ca
Primary Website: www.cowleynewspapers.com/farm-n-friends/
Year Established: 1999
Areas Served - City/County or Portion Thereof, or Zip codes: Sturgeon
Published: Fri
Avg Free Circ: 17759
Audit By: CMCA
Audit Date: 30.04.2014
Personnel: Ed Cowley (Pub./Owner/Adv. Mgr./Ed.)
Parent company (for newspapers): W & E Cowley Pub. Ltd.

PUBLICATION NAME

The Review
Street Address: 4720 50th Ave. ,
Province: AB
Postal: T0A 2W0
Country: Canada
Mailing address: PO Box 850
Mailing city: Redwater
Province: AB
Postal: T0A 2W0
General Phone: (780) 942-2023
General Fax: (780) 942-2515
General/National Adv. E-mail: redwater@shaw.ca
Display Adv. E-mail: redwater@shaw.ca
Primary Website: www.cowleynewspapers.com
Year Established: 1989
Commercial printers?: Y
Mechanical specifications: Type page 10 1/3 x 15 2/5; E - 6 cols, 1 1/2, 1/6 between; A - 6 cols, 1 1/2, 1/6 between; C - 6 cols, 1 1/2, 1/6 between.
Published: Tues
Avg Free Circ: 4405
Audit By: VAC
Audit Date: 30.06.2016
Personnel: Ed Cowley (Pub./Adv. Mgr./Owner)
Parent company (for newspapers): W & E Cowley Publishing Ltd.

REGINA

PUBLICATION NAME

Eau Vive (l')
Street Address: 210-1440 9th Ave N ,
Province: SK
Postal: S4R 8B1
Country: Canada
Mailing address: 210-1440, 9th Ave
Mailing city: Regina
Province: SK
Postal: S4R 8B1
General Phone: (306) 347-0481
General Fax: (306) 565-3450
General/National Adv. E-mail: direction@accesscomm.ca
Primary Website: http://nonprofits.accesscomm.ca/leauvive/web/
Areas Served - City/County or Portion Thereof, or Zip codes: Canada
Published: Thur
Avg Paid Circ: 1046
Audit By: CMCA
Audit Date: 30.04.2014
Personnel: Jean-Pierre Picard (Publisher); Angeline Feumba (Administrative Assistant)

RENFREW

PUBLICATION NAME

The Renfrew Mercury Emc
Street Address: 35 Opeongo Rd. W. ,
Province: ON
Postal: K7V 2T2
Country: Canada
Mailing address: 35 Opeongo Rd.
Mailing city: Renfrew
Province: ON
Postal: K7V 4A8
General Phone: (613) 432-3655
General Fax: (613) 432-6689
General/National Adv. E-mail: mercury@renc.igs.net
Editorial e-mail: rmedit@runge.net
Primary Website: www.insideottawavalley.com/renfrew-on
Year Established: 1871
Areas Served - City/County or Portion Thereof, or Zip codes: Canada
Own Printing Facility?: Y
Published: Thur
Avg Free Circ: 13309
Audit By: CMCA
Audit Date: 30.06.2016
Personnel: Mike Tracy (Pub.); Theresa Fritz (Ed.)
Parent company (for newspapers): Metroland Media Group Ltd.; Runge Newspapers, Inc.

REPENTIGNY

PUBLICATION NAME

Echo De Repentigny
Street Address: Notre-dame Apt A , Apt. A
Province: QC
Postal: J6A 2T8
Country: Canada
Mailing address: Notre-Dame Apt A
Mailing city: Repentigny
Province: QC
Postal: J6A 2T8
General Phone: (450) 932-4782
General Fax: (450) 932-4794
General/National Adv. E-mail: martin.gravel@quebecormedia.com
Primary Website: www.lechoderepentigny.ca
Areas Served - City/County or Portion Thereof, or Zip codes: Canada
Published: Wed
Avg Free Circ: 59248
Audit By: CCAB
Audit Date: 31.03.2014
Personnel: Martin Gravel

PUBLICATION NAME

Hebdo Rive Nord
Street Address: 1004 Rue Notre-dame ,
Province: QC
Postal: J5Y 1S9
Country: Canada
Mailing address: 1004 Rue Notre-Dame
Mailing city: Repentigny
Province: QC
Postal: J5Y 1S9
General Phone: (450) 581-5120
General Fax: (450) 581-4515
General/National Adv. E-mail: equiperedaction@transcontinental.ca
Primary Website: www.hebdorivenord.com
Areas Served - City/County or Portion Thereof, or Zip codes: Canada
Published: Tues`Fri
Avg Paid Circ: 6
Avg Free Circ: 53954
Audit By: CCAB
Audit Date: 30.09.2012
Personnel: Yannick Boulanger (Chief Ed.); Sebastien Nadeau (Regl. Mgr.); Stephane Joseph (Sales Mgr.); Chantal Proulx (Prodn. Mgr.)
Parent company (for newspapers): Transcontinental Media

PUBLICATION NAME

L'artisan
Street Address: 1004 Rue Nortre-dame ,
Province: QC
Postal: J5Y 1S9
Country: Canada
Mailing address: 1004 Rue Notre-Dame
Mailing city: Repentigny
Province: QC
Postal: J5Y 1S9
General Phone: (450) 581-5120
General Fax: (450) 581-4515
Primary Website: www.journallartisan.com
Published: Tues
Avg Free Circ: 45212
Audit By: Sworn/Estimate/Non-Audited
Audit Date: 12.07.2019
Personnel: Stephane Joseph (Adv. Mgr.); Yannick Boulanger (Ed.); Chantal Proulx (Prodn. Mgr.)
Parent company (for newspapers): Transcontinental Media

RESTON

PUBLICATION NAME

The Reston Recorder
Street Address: 330 4th St. ,
Province: MB
Postal: R0M 1X0
Country: Canada
Mailing address: PO Box 10
Mailing city: Reston
Province: MB
Postal: R0M 1X0
General Phone: (204) 877-3321
General Fax: (204) 522-3648
General/National Adv. E-mail: recorder@mts.net
Editorial e-mail: recorder@mts.net
Primary Website: http://www.restonrecorder.ca/
Areas Served - City/County or Portion Thereof, or Zip codes: Canada
Mechanical specifications: Type page 10 1/2 x 14; E - 6 cols, 1 3/5, 1/6 between; A - 6 cols, 1 3/5, 1/6 between; C - 6 cols, 1 3/5, 1/6 between.
Published: Fri
Avg Paid Circ: 116
Avg Free Circ: 59
Audit By: VAC
Audit Date: 31.12.2015
Personnel: Dolores Caldwell (Office Mgr.); Patty Lewis (Pub/Ed.)
Parent company (for newspapers): Glacier Media Group

REVELSTOKE

PUBLICATION NAME

Revelstoke Review
Street Address: 518 2nd St. ,
Province: BC
Postal: V0E 2S0
Country: Canada
Mailing address: PO Box 20
Mailing city: Revelstoke
Province: BC
Postal: V0E 2S0
General Phone: (250) 837-4667
General Fax: (250) 837-2003
General/National Adv. E-mail: editor@revelstoktimesreview.com
Display Adv. E-mail: mavis@revelstoketimesreview.com
Editorial e-mail: editor@revelstoketimesreview.com
Primary Website: www.revelstoketimesreview.com
Year Established: 1898
Delivery Methods: Mail`Newsstand`Carrier
Areas Served - City/County or Portion Thereof, or Zip codes: Canada
Published: Wed
Avg Paid Circ: 770
Avg Free Circ: 216
Audit By: VAC
Audit Date: 30.06.2016
Personnel: Mavis Cann (Pub./Adv Mgr); Fran Carlson (Office Mgr.); Alex Cooper (Ed)
Parent company (for newspapers): Black Press Group Ltd.

RICHMOND

PUBLICATION NAME

Richmond News
Street Address: #200-8211 Ackroyd Road ,
Province: BC
Postal: V6X 2C9
Country: Canada
Mailing address: #200-8211 Ackroyd Road
Mailing city: Richmond
Province: BC
Postal: V6X 2C9
General Phone: (604) 270-8031
General Fax: (604) 270-2248
General/National Adv. E-mail: editor@richmond-news.com
Display Adv. E-mail: rakimow@richmond-news.com
Classified Adv. e-mail: classifieds@van.net
Editorial e-mail: eedmonds@richmond-news.com
Primary Website: richmond-news.com
Year Established: 1979
Delivery Methods: Carrier
Areas Served - City/County or Portion Thereof, or Zip codes: Canada
Mechanical specifications: Type page 10 1/4 x 14; E - 6 cols, 1 9/16, between; A - 6 cols, 1 9/16, between; C - 7 cols, 1 5/16, between.
Published: Thur
Avg Paid Circ: 0
Avg Free Circ: 46113
Audit By: CCAB
Audit Date: 22.11.2017
Personnel: Pierre Pelletier (Pub); Rob Akimow (Adv Dir); Eve Edmonds (Ed); Kristene Murray (Circ Mgr)
Parent company (for newspapers): Glacier Media Group; CanWest MediaWorks Publications, Inc.

RIDGETOWN

PUBLICATION NAME

The Ridgetown Independent News
Street Address: 1 Main St. W. ,
Province: ON
Postal: N0P 2C0
Mailing address: P.O. Box 609
Mailing city: Ridgetown
Province: ON
Postal: N0P 2C0
General Phone: (519) 674-5205
General Fax: (519) 674-2573
Areas Served - City/County or Portion Thereof, or Zip codes: Canada
Published: Wed
Avg Paid Circ: 1674
Audit By: CMCA
Audit Date: 30.04.2016
Personnel: Shelia Mcbrayne (Editor in Chief); Gordon Brown (Managing Editor)

RIMBEY

PUBLICATION NAME

Rimbey Review
Street Address: 5001-50 Ave. Main St. ,
Province: AB
Postal: T0C 2J0
Country: Canada
Mailing address: PO Box 244
Mailing city: Rimbey
Province: AB
Postal: T0C 2J0
General Phone: (403) 843-4909
General Fax: (403) 843-4907
General/National Adv. E-mail: admin@rimbeyreview.com
Display Adv. E-mail: sales@rimbeyreview.com
Editorial e-mail: editor@rimbeyreview.com
Primary Website: www.rimbeyreview.com
Year Established: 1997
Delivery Methods: Mail
Areas Served - City/County or Portion Thereof, or Zip codes: t0c
Commercial printers?: Y
Published: Tues
Avg Paid Circ: 7
Avg Free Circ: 5136
Audit By: VAC
Audit Date: 31.05.2016
Personnel: Michele Rosenthal (Pub); Connie Johnson (Sales); Treena Mielke (Ed)
Parent company (for newspapers): Black Press Group Ltd.

RIMOUSKI

PUBLICATION NAME

Avantage Votre Journal
Street Address: 183 St-germain Ouest,
Province: QC
Postal: G5L 4B8
Country: Canada
Mailing address: St-Germain Ouest
Mailing city: Rimouski
Province: QC
Postal: G5L 4B8
General Phone: (418) 722-0205
Primary Website: http://www.lavantage.qc.ca/
Areas Served - City/County or Portion Thereof, or Zip codes: Canada
Published: Wed
Avg Paid Circ: 64
Avg Free Circ: 43009
Audit By: CCAB
Audit Date: 31.03.2014
Personnel: Lucie Moisan

PUBLICATION NAME

Le Progres-echo
Street Address: 217, Avenue LÃ£Â©onidas Sud, Bureau 6-d,
Province: QC
Postal: G5L 2T5
Country: Canada
Mailing address: PO Box 3217, Branch A
Mailing city: Rimouski
Province: QC
Postal: G5L 9G6
General Phone: (418) 721-1212
Advertising Fax: (418) 723-1855
Editorial Fax: (418) 722-4078
General/National Adv. E-mail: marc.pitre@quebecormedia.com
Primary Website: www.rimouskois.ca
Areas Served - City/County or Portion Thereof, or Zip codes: Canada
Mechanical specifications: Type page 12 1/2 x 11 1/2; E - 10 cols, between; A - 10 cols, between; C - 10 cols, between.
Published: Sun
Avg Paid Circ: 4
Avg Free Circ: 29084
Audit By: CCAB
Audit Date: 31.03.2014
Personnel: Alain St. Amand (Pub.); Ernie Wells (Ed.)
Parent company (for newspapers): Quebecor Communications, Inc.

PUBLICATION NAME

Le Rimouskois
Street Address: 217 Leonidas Ave, Po Box 3217, Branch A,
Province: QC
Postal: G5L 9G6
Country: Canada
Mailing address: 217 Leonidas Ave, PO Box 3217, Branch A
Mailing city: Rimouski
Province: QC
Postal: G5L 9G6
General Phone: (418) 721-1212
General Fax: (418) 723-1855
Advertising Fax: (418) 723-1855
Editorial Fax: (418) 723-4078
General/National Adv. E-mail: marc.pitre@quebecormedia.com
Primary Website: www.rimouskois.ca
Areas Served - City/County or Portion Thereof, or Zip codes: Canada
Mechanical specifications: Type page 12 1/2 x 11 1/2; E - 10 cols, between; A - 10 cols, between.
Published: Wed
Avg Paid Circ: 4
Avg Free Circ: 29084
Audit By: CCAB
Audit Date: 31.03.2014
Personnel: Alain St. Amand (Pub.); Ernie Wells (Ed.)
Parent company (for newspapers): Quebecor Communications, Inc.

RIVERS

PUBLICATION NAME

Rivers Banner Gazette-reporter
Street Address: 529 2nd Ave.,
Province: MB
Postal: R0K 1X0
Country: Canada
Mailing address: PO Box 70
Mailing city: Rivers
Province: MB
Postal: R0K 1X0
General Phone: (204) 328-7494
General Fax: (204) 328-5212
General/National Adv. E-mail: info@riversbanner.com
Editorial e-mail: kwaddell@neepawabanner.com
Primary Website: www.riversbanner.com
Year Established: 1993
Delivery Methods: Mail
Areas Served - City/County or Portion Thereof, or Zip codes: Riverdale
Own Printing Facility?: Y
Commercial printers?: N
Mechanical specifications: Type page 10 x 14; E - 2 cols, 3 1/4, 1/4 between; A - 6 cols, 1 5/8, 1/4 between; C - 8 cols, 1 5/8, 1/4 between.
Published: Fri
Avg Paid Circ: 93
Avg Free Circ: 1668
Audit By: VAC
Audit Date: 30.06.2017
Personnel: Ken Waddell (Pub/Ed.); Sheila Runions (Gen. Mgr.)
Parent company (for newspapers): Neepawa Banner

RIVIERE-DU-LOUP

PUBLICATION NAME

Info Dimanche
Street Address: Rue Fraser,
Province: QC
Postal: G5R 1C6
Country: Canada
Mailing address: rue Fraser
Mailing city: Riviere-du-Loup
Province: QC
Postal: G5R 1C6
General Phone: (418) 862-1911
General Fax: (418) 862-6165
Primary Website: www.infodimanche.com
Areas Served - City/County or Portion Thereof, or Zip codes: Canada
Published: Sun
Avg Paid Circ: 106
Avg Free Circ: 31754
Audit By: CCAB
Audit Date: 30.09.2013
Personnel: Michel Chalifour

PUBLICATION NAME

Le Saint-laurent Portage
Street Address: 55-a, Rue De L'hotel De Ville,
Province: QC
Postal: G5R 1L4
Country: Canada
Mailing address: 55-A, rue de l'Hotel de Ville
Mailing city: Riviere-du-Loup
Province: QC
Postal: G5R 1L4
General Phone: (418) 862-1774
General Fax: (418) 862-4387
General/National Adv. E-mail: francis.desrosiers@quebecormedia.com
Primary Website: www.lesaintlaurentportage.ca
Areas Served - City/County or Portion Thereof, or Zip codes: Canada
Own Printing Facility?: Y
Mechanical specifications: Type page 10 1/4 x 12.
Published: Wed
Avg Paid Circ: 11
Avg Free Circ: 34286
Audit By: CCAB
Audit Date: 31.03.2014
Personnel: Gilles LeBel (Mng. Ed.); Pierre Levesque (Ed.)
Parent company (for newspapers): Quebecor Communications, Inc.

PUBLICATION NAME

L'information
Street Address: 55-a Rue De L'hotel De Ville,
Province: QC
Postal: G5R 1L4
Country: Canada
Mailing address: 55-A rue de l'hotel de ville
Mailing city: Riviere-du-Loup
Province: QC
Postal: G5R 1L4
General Phone: (418) 775-4381
General Fax: (418) 862-4387
General/National Adv. E-mail: journalinformation@globetrotter.net; nsomontjoli@dosquadecoi.com
Primary Website: www.linformation.ca
Areas Served - City/County or Portion Thereof, or Zip codes: Canada
Published: Wed
Avg Paid Circ: 30
Avg Free Circ: 9311
Audit By: BPA
Audit Date: 01.03.2012
Personnel: Francis Desrosiers (Ed.)
Parent company (for newspapers): Quebecor Communications, Inc.

ROBERVAL

PUBLICATION NAME

L'etoile Du Lac
Street Address: 797 Blvd. Saint Joseph, Ste. 101, Bureau 101
Province: QC
Postal: G8H 2L4
Country: Canada
Mailing address: 797 Blvd. Saint Joseph, Ste. 101
Mailing city: Roberval
Province: QC
Postal: G8H 2L4
General Phone: (418) 275-2911
General Fax: (418) 275-2834
General/National Adv. E-mail: redaccion_roberval@transcontinental.ca
Primary Website: www.letoiledulac.com
Year Established: 1915
Areas Served - City/County or Portion Thereof, or Zip codes: Canada
Published: Wed
Avg Paid Circ: 95
Avg Free Circ: 14602
Audit By: CCAB
Audit Date: 31.03.2014
Personnel: Michel Dupont (Regional Publisher); Daniel Migneault (Ed. in Chief); Claudia Turcotte (Sales manager); Michel Aub (Publisher)
Parent company (for newspapers): Transcontinental Media

ROBLIN

PUBLICATION NAME

The Roblin Review
Street Address: 119 First Ave. Nw,
Province: MB
Postal: R0L 1P0
Country: Canada
Mailing address: PO Box 938
Mailing city: Roblin
Province: MB
Postal: R0L 1P0
General Phone: (204) 937-8377
General Fax: (204) 937-8212
General/National Adv. E-mail: roblinreview@mts.net
Display Adv. E-mail: reviewads@mts.net
Classified Adv. e-mail: reviewads@mts.net
Editorial e-mail: rreview@mts.net
Primary Website: theroblinreview.com
Year Established: 1913
Delivery Methods: Mail Racks
Areas Served - City/County or Portion Thereof, or Zip codes: Roblin, MB
Commercial printers?: Y
Mechanical specifications: Type page 11 1/4 x 17; E - 6 cols, 1 5/8, 2/16 between; A - 6 cols, 1 5/8, 2/16 between; C - 6 cols, 1 5/8, 1/8 between.
Published: Tues
Avg Paid Circ: 50
Avg Free Circ: 26
Audit By: VAC
Audit Date: 30.06.2016
Personnel: Patricia Liske (Circ. Mgr.); Ed Doering (Ed.); Brent Wright (Production Mgr.); Jackie Edel (Ad. consultant)

ROCKLAND

PUBLICATION NAME

Rockland Vision
Street Address: 1315 Laurier St.,
Province: ON
Postal: K4K 1L5
Country: Canada
Mailing address: PO Box 897
Mailing city: Rockland
Province: ON
Postal: K4K 1L5
General Phone: (613) 446-6456
General Fax: (613) 446-1381
General/National Adv. E-mail: vision@eap.on.ca
Display Adv. E-mail: paulo.casimiro@eap.on.ca
Primary Website: www.facebook.com/pg/Le-journal-Vision-newspaper-199878750108078/about/?ref=page_internal
Year Established: 1994
Own Printing Facility?: Y
Mechanical specifications: Type page 10 1/2 x 14; E - 8 cols, 1 5/16, between; A - 8 cols, between; C - 8 cols, between.
Published: Fri
Avg Paid Circ: 23297
Avg Free Circ: 39
Audit By: ODC
Audit Date: 13.12.2011
Personnel: Paulo Casimiro (Prodn. Mgr.)

ROCKY MOUNTAIN HOUSE

PUBLICATION NAME

The Mountaineer
Street Address: 4814 49th St.,
Province: AB
Postal: T4T 1S8
Country: Canada
Mailing address: 4814 49th St.
Mailing city: Rocky Mountain House
Province: AB
Postal: T4T 1S8
General Phone: (403) 845-3334
General Fax: (403) 845-5570
General/National Adv. E-mail: rocky_mountain_house@awna.com
Display Adv. E-mail: advertising@mountaineer.bz
Classified Adv. e-mail: advertising@mountaineer.bz
Editorial e-mail: editor@mountaineer.bz
Primary Website: www.mountaineer.bz
Year Established: 1923
Mechanical specifications: Type page 11 5/8 x 21 1/4; E - 6 cols, 1 5/6, 1/6 between; A - 6 cols, 1 5/6, 1/6 between; C - 6 cols, 1 5/6, 1/6 between.
Published: Tues
Avg Paid Circ: 2264
Avg Free Circ: 53
Audit By: VAC
Audit Date: 31.03.2016
Personnel: Gail Krabben (Prodn. Mgr.); Glen Mazza (Pub.); Penny Allen (Adv. Mgr.); Laura Button (Ed.); Bernie Visotto (Office Mgr.)
Parent company (for newspapers): Mountaineer

ROSETOWN

PUBLICATION NAME

The Rosetown Eagle
Street Address: 114 2nd Ave. W. ,
Province: SK
Postal: S0L 2V0
Country: Canada
Mailing address: PO Box 130
Mailing city: Rosetown
Province: SK
Postal: S0L 2V0
General Phone: (306) 882-4348
General Fax: (306) 882-4204
Advertising Phone: (306) 882-4348
Editorial Phone: (306) 882-4348
General/National Adv. E-mail: frontdesk.eagle@gmail.com
Display Adv. E-mail: ads.eagle@gmail.com
Classified Adv. e-mail: frontdesk.eagle@gmail.com
Editorial e-mail: editor.eagle@gmail.com
Year Established: 1909
Delivery Methods: Mail`Newsstand
Areas Served - City/County or Portion Thereof, or Zip codes: Canada
Own Printing Facility?: Y
Commercial printers?: Y
Mechanical specifications: Type page 12 x 20 1/2; E - 6 cols, 1 5/8, 1/4 between; A - 6 cols, 1 5/8, 1/4 between; C - 6 cols, 1 5/8, 1/4 between.
Published: Mon
Avg Paid Circ: 1562
Avg Free Circ: 57
Audit By: CMCA
Audit Date: 30.04.2017
Personnel: Stewart Crump (Owner/publisher); Simone Gaudet; Loretta Torrence (Ads); David McIver

ROUYN-NORANDA

PUBLICATION NAME

Abitibi Express Rouyn
Street Address: 438 Ave. Lariviere ,
Province: QC
Postal: J9X 4J1
Country: Canada
Mailing address: 438 Ave. Lariviere
Mailing city: Rouyn-Noranda
Province: QC
Postal: J9X 4J1
General Phone: (819) 797-6776
General Fax: (819) 797-4725
Editorial Phone: (819) 767-6776
Editorial Fax: (819) 797-4725
General/National Adv. E-mail: redaction.abitibi@transcontinental.ca
Primary Website: http://www.abitibiouestrouynnoranda.ca
Areas Served - City/County or Portion Thereof, or Zip codes: Canada
Published: Tues
Avg Paid Circ: 18
Avg Free Circ: 29398
Audit By: CCAB
Audit Date: 31.03.2014

PUBLICATION NAME

Citoyen Rouyn Noranda
Street Address: 1 Rue Du Terminus ,
Province: QC
Postal: J9X 3B5
Country: Canada
Mailing address: 1 rue du Terminus
Mailing city: Rouyn-Noranda
Province: QC
Postal: J9X 3B5
General Phone: (819) 762-4361 x 221
General Fax: (819) 797-2450
Advertising Phone: (819) 762-4361
Editorial Phone: (819) 279-7032
Display Adv. E-mail: stefan.baillargeon@tc.tc or marie-eve.bouchard@tc.tc
Classified Adv. e-mail: vicky.aumond@tc.tc
Editorial e-mail: joel.caya@tc.tc
Primary Website: lafrontiere.ca
Year Established: 1937
Delivery Methods: Mail`Newsstand`Carrier`Racks
Areas Served - City/County or Portion Thereof, or Zip codes: Canada
Published: Wed
Avg Paid Circ: 17
Avg Free Circ: 19749
Audit By: CCAB
Audit Date: 31.03.2014
Personnel: Joel Caya (General manager)

RUSSELL

PUBLICATION NAME

Banner
Street Address: 455 Main St. ,
Province: MB
Postal: R0J 1W0
Country: Canada
Mailing address: PO Box 100
Mailing city: Russell
Province: MB
Postal: R0J 1W0
General Phone: (204) 773-2069
General Fax: (204) 773-2645
General/National Adv. E-mail: rbanner@mts.net
Display Adv. E-mail: russellbannerads@mymts.net
Editorial e-mail: editor@russellbanner.com
Primary Website: russellbanner.com
Areas Served - City/County or Portion Thereof, or Zip codes: Russell and area
Own Printing Facility?: Y
Mechanical specifications: Type page 11 1/2 x 17; E - 5 cols, 2, between; A - 5 cols, 2, between; C - 5 cols, 2, between.
Published: Tues
Avg Paid Circ: 1300
Avg Free Circ: 19
Audit By: CCAB
Audit Date: 30.11.2018
Personnel: Chantelle Senchuk (Adv); Jessica Ludvig
Parent company (for newspapers): Dauphin Herald

RYCROFT

PUBLICATION NAME

Rycroft Central Peace Signal
Street Address: 47011 50th St. ,
Province: AB
Postal: T0H 3A0
Country: Canada
Mailing address: PO Box 250
Mailing city: Rycroft
Province: AB
Postal: T0H 3A0
General Phone: (780) 765-3604
General Fax: (780) 785-2188
General/National Adv. E-mail: admin@cpsignal.com
Display Adv. E-mail: signalads@telus.net
Classified Adv. e-mail: signalads@telus.net
Editorial e-mail: signalnews@telus.net
Year Established: 1980
Delivery Methods: Mail`Newsstand
Areas Served - City/County or Portion Thereof, or Zip codes: Canada
Commercial printers?: Y
Mechanical specifications: Type page 10 15/16 x 13; E - 6 cols, 1 7/12, 1/6 between; A - 6 cols, 1 7/12, 1/6 between; C - 6 cols, 1 7/12, 1/6 between.
Published: Tues
Avg Paid Circ: 2633
Avg Free Circ: 5
Audit By: CMCA
Audit Date: 30.03.2017
Personnel: Dan Zahara (Pub/Advt Mgr); Carol Grover (Circ. Mgr.); Morgan Zahara
Parent company (for newspapers): 847562 Alberta Ltd.

SACKVILLE

PUBLICATION NAME

The Sackville Tribune-post
Street Address: 80 Main St. ,
Province: NB
Postal: E4L 4A7
Country: Canada
Mailing address: 80 Main St.
Mailing city: Sackville
Province: NB
Postal: E4L 4A7
General Phone: (506) 536-2500
General Fax: (506) 536-4024
Editorial Fax: (506) 536-4024
General/National Adv. E-mail: sdoherty@sackvilletribunepost.com
Editorial e-mail: sdoherty@sackvilletribunepost.com
Primary Website: www.sackvilletribunepost.com
Year Established: 1902
Delivery Methods: Mail`Newsstand
Areas Served - City/County or Portion Thereof, or Zip codes: Sackville
Mechanical specifications: Type page 12 x 21; E - 10 cols, 2, 1/4 between; A - 10 cols, 2, 1/4 between; C - 10 cols, 2, 1/4 between.
Published: Wed
Avg Paid Circ: 2150
Avg Free Circ: 4
Audit By: VAC
Audit Date: 31.10.2015
Personnel: Richard Russell (Pub.); Scott Doherty (Ed.); Tanya Austin (Circ/Class. Mgr)
Parent company (for newspapers): Transcontinental Media

SAGUENAY

PUBLICATION NAME

Le Courrier Du Saguenay
Street Address: 3635 Blvd Harvey Ste 201 ,
Province: QC
Postal: G7X 3B2
Country: Canada
Mailing address: 3635 Blvd Harvey Ste 201
Mailing city: Saguenay
Province: QC
Postal: G7X 3B2
General Phone: (418) 542-2442
General Fax: (418) 542-5225
Advertising Phone: (418) 542-2442
Advertising Fax: (418) 542-5225
Editorial Phone: (418) 542-2442
Editorial Fax: (418) 542-5225
General/National Adv. E-mail: redaction.saguenay@tc.tc
Display Adv. E-mail: redaction.saguenay@tc.tc
Editorial e-mail: redaction.saguenay@tc.tc
Primary Website: www.courrierdusaguenay.com
Delivery Methods: Mail`Racks
Areas Served - City/County or Portion Thereof, or Zip codes: Canada
Published: Wed
Avg Paid Circ: 16
Avg Free Circ: 72964
Audit By: CCAB
Audit Date: 31.03.2014
Personnel: Joan Sullivan (Ed.)

SAINT ANDRE-AVELLIN

PUBLICATION NAME

La Petite Nation
Street Address: 3 Ste.10, Principale St. ,
Province: QC
Postal: J0V 1W0
Country: Canada
Mailing address: 3 Ste.10, Principale St.
Mailing city: Saint Andre-Avellin
Province: QC
Postal: J0V 1W0
General Phone: (819) 983-2725
General Fax: (819) 983-6844
General/National Adv. E-mail: gessi.laslamme@transcontinental.ca
Editorial e-mail: pascal.laplante@tc.tc
Primary Website: http://www.lapetitenation.com
Areas Served - City/County or Portion Thereof, or Zip codes: Canada
Published: Wed
Avg Paid Circ: 19
Avg Free Circ: 10108
Audit By: CCAB
Audit Date: 31.03.2014
Personnel: Eric Bernard (Ed.)
Parent company (for newspapers): Transcontinental Media

SAINT ANTHONY

PUBLICATION NAME

Northern Pen
Street Address: 10-12 North St. ,
Province: NL
Postal: A0K 4S0
Country: Canada
Mailing address: PO Box 520
Mailing city: Saint Anthony
Province: NL
Postal: A0K 4S0
General Phone: (709) 454-2191
General Fax: (709) 454-3718
General/National Adv. E-mail: info@northernpen.ca
Display Adv. E-mail: kparsons@nothernpen.ca
Editorial e-mail: arandell@nothernpen.ca
Primary Website: www.northernpen.ca
Year Established: 1980
Areas Served - City/County or Portion Thereof, or Zip codes: Canada
Mechanical specifications: Type page 11 x 21 1/2; E - 6 cols, 1 3/4, between; A - 6 cols, 1 3/4, between; C - 8 cols, 1 1/2, between.
Published: Mon
Avg Paid Circ: 1085
Avg Free Circ: 0
Audit By: VAC
Audit Date: 31.12.2015
Personnel: Kathy Parsons (Adv. Mgr.); Frances Reardon (Office/Circ Mgr); Adam Randell (Ed)
Parent company (for newspapers): Transcontinental Media

SAINT AUGUSTIN DE DESMAURES

PUBLICATION NAME

Nic
Street Address: Route 138 Ste 100 , Suite 100
Province: QC
Postal: G3A 2C6
Country: Canada
Mailing address: route 138 Ste 100
Mailing city: Saint Augustin de Desmaures
Province: QC
Postal: G3A 2C6
General Phone: (418) 908-3438
Published: Wed
Avg Paid Circ: 2863
Avg Free Circ: 268
Audit By: ODC
Audit Date: 14.12.2011
Personnel: Sophie Bouchard

SAINT BONIFACE

PUBLICATION NAME

La Liberte
Street Address: Po Box 190 ,
Province: MB
Postal: R2H 3B4
Country: Canada
Mailing address: PO Box 190
Mailing city: Saint Boniface
Province: MB
Postal: R2H 3B4
General Phone: (204) 237-4823
General Fax: (204) 231-1998
General/National Adv. E-mail: la_liberte@la-liberte.mb.ca

Community Newspapers in Canada

III-571

Editorial e-mail: la-liberte@la-liberte.mb.ca
Primary Website: http://la-liberte.mb.ca/tag/saint-boniface
Year Established: 1913
Delivery Methods: Mail`Carrier
Areas Served - City/County or Portion Thereof, or Zip codes: Winnipeg/Manitoba/CAnada/ R2H Manitoba Canada
Mechanical specifications: Type page 10 3/8 x 15 3/8; E - 5 cols, 1 15/16, 1/6 between; A - 5 cols, 1 15/16, 1/6 between; C - 5 cols, 1 15/16, 1/6 between.
Published: Wed
Avg Paid Circ: 0
Avg Free Circ: 12
Audit By: VAC
Audit Date: 30.06.2016
Personnel: Sophie Gaulin (Dir/Ed); Bernard Bocquel (Assoc. Ed); Roxanne Bouchard (Office Admin)

SAINT BRUNO

PUBLICATION NAME

Le Journal De St-bruno
Street Address: 1507 Roberval ,
Province: QC
Postal: J3V 3P8
Country: Canada
Mailing address: 1507 Roberval
Mailing city: Saint Bruno
Province: QC
Postal: J3V 3P8
General Phone: (450) 653-3685
General Fax: (450) 653-6967
General/National Adv. E-mail: redaction@journaldest-bruno.qc.ca
Editorial e-mail: pclair@versants.com
Primary Website: http://www.journaldest-bruno.qc.ca/
Areas Served - City/County or Portion Thereof, or Zip codes: Canada
Mechanical specifications: Type page 11 1/2 x 17.
Published: Fri
Avg Paid Circ: 4
Avg Free Circ: 18900
Audit By: CCAB
Audit Date: 31.03.2014
Personnel: Philippe Clair (Ed.); StÃ©phanie Lambert (Prod. Mgr.)
Parent company (for newspapers): Les Hebdos Monteregiens-OOB

SAINT CATHARINE'S

PUBLICATION NAME

Thorold Niagara News
Street Address: 10-1 St. Paul St. ,
Province: ON
Postal: L2R 7L4
Country: Canada
Mailing address: 10-1 St. Paul St.
Mailing city: Saint Catharine's
Province: ON
Postal: L2R 7L4
General Phone: (905) 688-4332
General Fax: (905) 688-6213
Display Adv. E-mail: lauren.krause@sunmedia.ca
Primary Website: www.thoroldedition.ca
Published: Thur
Published Other: 1
Avg Free Circ: 7225
Audit By: CMCA
Audit Date: 31.05.2016
Personnel: Jeff Blay (Reporter); Lauren Krause (Advertising)
Parent company (for newspapers): Postmedia Network Inc.

SAINT EUSTACHE

PUBLICATION NAME

Eveil
Street Address: Rue St-eustache ,
Province: QC
Postal: J7R 2L2

Country: Canada
Mailing address: rue St-Eustache
Mailing city: Saint Eustache
Province: QC
Postal: J7R 2L2
Areas Served - City/County or Portion Thereof, or Zip codes: Canada
Published: Sat
Avg Paid Circ: 0
Avg Free Circ: 55993
Audit By: CCAB
Audit Date: 31.03.2014
Personnel: Serge Langlois

PUBLICATION NAME

La Concorde
Street Address: 53 Rue St. Eustache ,
Province: QC
Postal: J7R 2L2
Country: Canada
Mailing address: 53 Rue St. Eustache
Mailing city: Saint Eustache
Province: QC
Postal: J7R 2L2
General Phone: (450) 472-3440
General Fax: (450) 473-1629
Areas Served - City/County or Portion Thereof, or Zip codes: Canada
Published: Wed
Avg Free Circ: 52172
Audit By: CCAB
Audit Date: 31.03.2014
Personnel: Jean-Claude Langlois (Ed.)

PUBLICATION NAME

Le Groupe Jcl Inc.
Street Address: 53, Rue Saint-eustache ,
Province: QC
Postal: J7R 2L2
Country: Canada
Mailing address: 53, rue Saint-Eustache
Mailing city: Saint Eustache
Province: QC
Postal: J7R 2L2
General Phone: (450) 472-3440
Advertising Phone: (450) 435-7968
Editorial Fax: (450) 435-0588
General/National Adv. E-mail: leveil@groupejcl.com
Display Adv. E-mail: infojournaux@groupejcl.com
Classified Adv. e-mail: infojournaux@groupejcl.com
Editorial e-mail: infojournaux@groupejcl.com
Primary Website: www.leveil.com
Published: Sat
Avg Free Circ: 60000
Audit By: Sworn/Estimate/Non-Audited
Audit Date: 12.07.2019
Personnel: Louis Kemp (Dir., Sales); Norman Langlois (Circ. Mgr.); Claude Desjardins (Ed. in Chief); Jean Claude Langlois (Ed.); Marco Brunelle (Sports Ed.); Yves Bourbonnais (Dir., Prodn.); Serge Langlois (Dir., Dist.)

SAINT GEORGES

PUBLICATION NAME

Journal De La Beauce
Street Address: 11720 1re Rue , Bureau 2
Province: QC
Postal: G5Y 2C8
Country: Canada
Mailing address: 11720 1re Rue
Mailing city: Saint Georges
Province: QC
Postal: G5Y 2C8
General Phone: (418) 220-0222
Published: Fri
Avg Free Circ: 32653
Audit By: ODC
Audit Date: 13.12.2011
Personnel: Lyne Genest

PUBLICATION NAME

L'eclaireur-progres/beauce Nouvelles
Street Address: 12625 1st Ave. E. ,
Province: QC
Postal: G5Y 2E4
Country: Canada
Mailing address: 12625 1st Ave. E.
Mailing city: Saint Georges
Province: QC
Postal: G5Y 2E4
General Phone: (418) 228-8858
General Fax: (418) 228-0268
Primary Website: leclaireurprogres.canoe.ca
Areas Served - City/County or Portion Thereof, or Zip codes: Canada
Published: Wed
Avg Paid Circ: 13
Avg Free Circ: 38115
Audit By: CCAB
Audit Date: 31.03.2014
Personnel: Gilbert Bernier (Gen. Mgr.)
Parent company (for newspapers): Quebecor Communications, Inc.

PUBLICATION NAME

Progres De Bellechasse
Street Address: 98e Rue ,
Province: QC
Postal: G5Y 8G1
Country: Canada
Mailing address: 98e Rue
Mailing city: Saint Georges
Province: QC
Postal: G5Y 8G1
General Phone: (418) 228-8858
Areas Served - City/County or Portion Thereof, or Zip codes: Canada
Published: Wed
Avg Paid Circ: 0
Avg Free Circ: 19789
Audit By: CCAB
Audit Date: 30.09.2012
Personnel: Gilbert Bernier

SAINT HUBERT

PUBLICATION NAME

Vallee Du Richelieu Express
Street Address: 4480 Chemin Chambly, Bureau 204 ,
Province: QC
Postal: J3Y 3M8
Country: Canada
Mailing address: 4480 Chemin Chambly, Bureau 204
Mailing city: Saint Hubert
Province: QC
Postal: J3Y 3M8
General Phone: (450) 678-6187
Advertising Phone: (450) 678-6187
Editorial Phone: (450) 678-6187
General/National Adv. E-mail: valleedurichelieu@tc.tc
Display Adv. E-mail: valleedurichelieu@tc.tc
Editorial e-mail: valleedurichelieu@tc.tc
Primary Website: www.valleedurichelieuexpress.com
Delivery Methods: Mail`Racks
Areas Served - City/County or Portion Thereof, or Zip codes: Canada
Published: Wed
Avg Paid Circ: 1
Avg Free Circ: 34751
Audit By: CCAB
Audit Date: 31.03.2014

SAINT HYACINTHE

PUBLICATION NAME

Le Courrier de Saint-Hyacinthe
Street Address: 655 Rue St. Anne ,
Province: QC
Postal: J2S 5G4
Country: Canada

Mailing address: 655 Rue St. Anne
Mailing city: Saint Hyacinthe
Province: QC
Postal: J2S 5G4
General Phone: (450) 773-6028
General Fax: (450) 773-3115
Advertising Phone: (450) 771-0677
General/National Adv. E-mail: redaction@leclairon.qc.ca
Display Adv. E-mail: gbedard@courrierclairon.qc.ca
Classified Adv. e-mail: gbedard@courrierclairon.qc.ca
Primary Website: lecourrier.qc.ca/accueil
Year Established: 1912
Areas Served - City/County or Portion Thereof, or Zip codes: Canada
Published: Tues
Avg Paid Circ: 9352
Avg Free Circ: 142
Audit By: AAM
Audit Date: 30.09.2018
Personnel: Guillaume Bedard (Adv. Mgr.)

SAINT JEROME

PUBLICATION NAME

Journal Le Nord
Street Address: 393 Laurentides Blvd. ,
Province: QC
Postal: J7Z 4L9
Country: Canada
Mailing address: 393 Laurentides Blvd.
Mailing city: Saint Jerome
Province: QC
Postal: J7Z 4L9
General Phone: (450) 438-8383
General Fax: (450) 438-4174
Editorial e-mail: editeur@journallenord.com
Primary Website: www.journallenord.com
Year Established: 1986
Areas Served - City/County or Portion Thereof, or Zip codes: Canada
Commercial printers?: Y
Mechanical specifications: Type page 10 1/4 x 14 1/4; E - 8 cols, 1 1/6, 1/6 between.
Published: Wed
Avg Paid Circ: 9
Avg Free Circ: 55388
Audit By: CCAB
Audit Date: 31.03.2014
Personnel: Francois LaFerriere (Pub.); Mychel Lapointe (Ed.)

PUBLICATION NAME

Le Mirabel
Street Address: 179 Rue St. Georges ,
Province: QC
Postal: J7Z 4Z8
Country: Canada
Mailing address: 179 rue St. Georges
Mailing city: Saint Jerome
Province: QC
Postal: J7Z 4Z8
General Phone: (450) 436-8200
General Fax: (450) 436-8912
General/National Adv. E-mail: atelier.mirabel@hebdosquebecor.com; redaction.mirabel@hebdosquebecor.com
Primary Website: www.lemirabel.com
Year Established: 1974
Areas Served - City/County or Portion Thereof, or Zip codes: Canada
Own Printing Facility?: Y
Published: Sat
Avg Free Circ: 51862
Audit By: CCAB
Audit Date: 31.03.2014
Personnel: Marc Fradellin (Pub.); Andre Guillemette (Gen. Mgr.); Christine Leonard (Prodn. Dir.)
Parent company (for newspapers): Quebecor Communications, Inc.

PUBLICATION NAME

L'echo Du Nord

Street Address: 179 St. George St. ,
Province: QC
Postal: J7Z 4Z8
Country: Canada
Mailing address: 179 St. George St.
Mailing city: Saint Jerome
Province: QC
Postal: J7Z 4Z8
General Phone: (450) 436-5381
General Fax: (450) 436-5904
General/National Adv. E-mail: atelier.echo@ hebdosquebecor.com; redaction.echo@ hebdosquebecor.com
Primary Website: http://echosdunord.com/
Areas Served - City/County or Portion Thereof, or Zip codes: Canada
Published: Wed
Avg Paid Circ: 391
Avg Free Circ: 53385
Audit By: CCAB
Audit Date: 31.03.2014
Personnel: Andre Guillemette (Ed.); Jean-Paul Sauriol (Prodn. Mgr.)
Parent company (for newspapers): Quebecor Communications, Inc.

SAINT JOHN

PUBLICATION NAME

The New Freeman
Street Address: One Bayard Dr. ,
Province: NB
Postal: E2L 3L5
Country: Canada
Mailing address: 1 Bayard Dr.
Mailing city: Saint John
Province: NB
Postal: E2L 3L5
General Phone: (506) 653-6806
General Fax: (506) 653-6818
General/National Adv. E-mail: tnf@nbnet.nb.ca
Editorial e-mail: tnf@nb.aibn.com
Primary Website: http://www. dioceseofsaintjohn.org/TNF.aspx
Year Established: 1900
Areas Served - City/County or Portion Thereof, or Zip codes: Canada
Mechanical specifications: Type page 12 x ; E - 5 cols, 2, 1/4 between; A - 5 cols, 2, 1/4 between.
Published: Fri
Avg Paid Circ: 7000
Audit By: Sworn/Estimate/Non-Audited
Audit Date: 12.07.2019
Personnel: Margie Trafton (Mng. Ed.)

SAINT JULIE

PUBLICATION NAME

Information De Ste Julie
Street Address: Rue Jules Choquet Local 2 , Local 2
Province: QC
Postal: J3E 1W6
Country: Canada
Mailing address: rue Jules Choquet Local 2
Mailing city: Saint Julie
Province: QC
Postal: J3E 1W6
General Phone: (450) 649-0719
Areas Served - City/County or Portion Thereof, or Zip codes: Canada
Published: Wed
Avg Paid Circ: 3
Avg Free Circ: 19435
Audit By: CCAB
Audit Date: 30.09.2012
Personnel: Serge Landry

SAINT LAURENT

PUBLICATION NAME

Courrier-ahuntsic
Street Address: 1500 Jules Poitras Blvd. ,
Province: QC
Postal: H4N 1X7
Country: Canada
Mailing address: 1500 Jules Poitras Blvd.
Mailing city: Saint Laurent
Province: QC
Postal: H4N 1X7
General Phone: (514) 855-1292
General Fax: (514) 855-9916
Primary Website: www.courrierahuntsic.com; www.transcontinentalmedia.com
Areas Served - City/County or Portion Thereof, or Zip codes: Canada
Published: Fri
Avg Paid Circ: 0
Avg Free Circ: 32391
Audit By: CCAB
Audit Date: 31.03.2014
Personnel: Alain De Choiniere (Gen. Mgr.); Marilaine Bolduc-Jacob (Information Dir.)
Parent company (for newspapers): Transcontinental Media

PUBLICATION NAME

Express D'outremont
Street Address: Jules-poitras ,
Province: QC
Postal: H4N 1X7
Country: Canada
Mailing address: 24e étage
Mailing city: Montréal
Province: QC
Postal: H3B 4X9
General Phone: (514) 286-1066
General Fax: (514) 286-9310
Primary Website: www.expressoutremont.com
Areas Served - City/County or Portion Thereof, or Zip codes: Canada
Published: Thur
Avg Paid Circ: 2
Avg Free Circ: 19654
Audit By: CCAB
Audit Date: 31.03.2014
Personnel: Jean Aube

PUBLICATION NAME

Le Courrier Bordeaux/cartierville
Street Address: 1500 Jules Poitras Blvd. ,
Province: QC
Postal: H4N 1X7
Country: Canada
Mailing address: 1500 Jules Poitras Blvd.
Mailing city: Saint Laurent
Province: QC
Postal: H4N 1X7
General Phone: (514) 855-1292
General Fax: (514) 855-9916
Primary Website: www.transcontinental.com; www.courrierbc.com
Areas Served - City/County or Portion Thereof, or Zip codes: Canada
Mechanical specifications: Type page 11 3/8 x 15; E - 8 cols, between; A - 8 cols, between.
Published: Fri
Avg Paid Circ: 4
Avg Free Circ: 17925
Audit By: CCAB
Audit Date: 31.03.2014
Personnel: Alain De Choinire (Ed.)
Parent company (for newspapers): Transcontinental Media

PUBLICATION NAME

Progres Villeray/ Parc Extension
Street Address: Jules-poitras ,
Province: QC
Postal: H4N 1X7
Country: Canada
Mailing address: Jules-Poitras
Mailing city: Saint Laurent
Province: QC
Postal: H4N 1X7
General Phone: (514) 270-8088
Areas Served - City/County or Portion Thereof, or Zip codes: Canada
Published: Tues
Avg Free Circ: 20276
Audit By: CCAB
Audit Date: 31.03.2014
Personnel: Jean Aube

PUBLICATION NAME

Saint-laurent News
Street Address: 1500 Blvd. Jules Poitras ,
Province: QC
Postal: H4N 1X7
Country: Canada
Mailing address: 1500 blvd. Jules Poitras
Mailing city: Saint Laurent
Province: QC
Postal: H4N 1X7
General Phone: (514) 855-1292
General Fax: (514) 855-1855
General/National Adv. E-mail: hebdo.redaction@ transcontinental.ca
Display Adv. E-mail: petitesannonces@ journalmetro.com
Classified Adv. E-mail: petitesannonces@ journalmetro.com
Primary Website: www.nouvellessaint-laurent. com
Mechanical specifications: Type page 10 x 14 1/4; E - 4 cols, between; C - 8 cols, between.
Published: Sun
Avg Free Circ: 29317
Audit By: Sworn/Estimate/Non-Audited
Audit Date: 12.07.2019
Personnel: Yannick Pinel (Ed.)
Parent company (for newspapers): Transcontinental Media

PUBLICATION NAME

The Suburban East End Edition
Street Address: 7575 Trans Canada Highway, Suite 105 ,
Province: QC
Postal: H4T 1V6
Country: Canada
Mailing address: 7575 Trans Canada Highway, Suite 105
Mailing city: Saint Laurent
Province: QC
Postal: H4T 1V6
General Phone: (514) 484-1107
General Fax: (514) 484-9616
General/National Adv. E-mail: suburban@ thesuburban.com
Display Adv. E-mail: amanda@thesuburban.com
Editorial e-mail: editor@thesuburban.com
Primary Website: www.thesuburban.com
Published: Thur
Avg Free Circ: 26746
Audit By: CMCA
Audit Date: 31.12.2013
Personnel: Beryl Wajsman

SAINT LEONARD

PUBLICATION NAME

Progres Saint-leonard
Street Address: 8770 Langelier Blvd. Ste. 210 , Bureau 210
Province: QC
Postal: H1P 3C6
Country: Canada
Mailing address: 8770 Langelier Blvd. Ste. 210
Mailing city: Saint Leonard
Province: QC
Postal: H1P 3C6
General Phone: (514) 899-5888
General Fax: (514) 899-5001
General/National Adv. E-mail: redaction_est@tc.tc
Primary Website: www.progresstleonard.com
Published: Wed
Avg Free Circ: 31355
Audit By: Sworn/Estimate/Non-Audited
Audit Date: 12.07.2019
Personnel: Yannick Pinel; Lucy Lecoures (Ed.)
Parent company (for newspapers): Transcontinental Media

SAINT LIN LAURENTIDES

PUBLICATION NAME

Express Montcalm
Street Address: Rue Saint-isidore ,
Province: QC
Postal: J5M 2V4
Country: Canada
Mailing address: rue Saint-Isidore
Mailing city: Saint Lin Laurentides
Province: QC
Postal: J5M 2V4
General Phone: (450) 439-2525
Areas Served - City/County or Portion Thereof, or Zip codes: Canada
Published: Wed
Avg Free Circ: 20004
Audit By: CCAB
Audit Date: 31.03.2014
Personnel: Benoit Bazinet

SAINT PASCAL

PUBLICATION NAME

Le Placoteux
Street Address: 491 Ave. D'anjou ,
Province: QC
Postal: G0L 3Y0
Country: Canada
Mailing address: CP 490
Mailing city: Saint Pascal
Province: QC
Postal: G0L 3Y0
General Phone: (418) 492-2706
General Fax: (418) 492-9706
General/National Adv. E-mail: montage@ leplacoteux.com
Primary Website: www.leplacoteux.com
Areas Served - City/County or Portion Thereof, or Zip codes: Canada
Published: Wed
Avg Paid Circ: 75
Avg Free Circ: 18315
Audit By: CCAB
Audit Date: 31.03.2014
Personnel: Maurice Gagnon (Ed.); Raymond Freve (Adv. Mgr.)
Parent company (for newspapers): Reseau Select/ Select Network

SAINT PAUL

PUBLICATION NAME

St. Paul Journal
Street Address: 4813 50th Ave. ,
Province: AB
Postal: T0A 3A0
Country: Canada
Mailing address: PO Box 159
Mailing city: Saint Paul
Province: AB
Postal: T0A 3A0
General Phone: (780) 645-3342
General Fax: (780) 645-2346
General/National Adv. E-mail: production@stpaul. greatwest.ca; journal@stpaul.greatwest.ca
Display Adv. E-mail: rberlinguette@stpaul. greatwest.ca
Editorial e-mail: jhuser@stpaul.greatwest.ca
Primary Website: www.spjournal.com
Year Established: 1924
Delivery Methods: Mail Newsstand
Areas Served - City/County or Portion Thereof, or Zip codes: Canada
Own Printing Facility?: Y
Commercial printers?: Y
Published: Tues
Avg Paid Circ: 21
Avg Free Circ: 460
Audit By: VAC
Audit Date: 31.12.2015
Personnel: Janice Huser (Ed); Janani Whitfield (Pub)
Parent company (for newspapers): Glacier Media Group; Great West Newspapers LP

Community Newspapers in Canada

SAINT SAUVEUR-DES-MONTS

PUBLICATION NAME

Journal Le Pays D'en Haut La Vallee
Street Address: Rue De La Gare Bureau 104, Bureau 104
Province: QC
Postal: J0R 1R6
Country: Canada
Mailing address: rue de la Gare Bureau 104
Mailing city: Saint Sauveur-des-Monts
Province: QC
Postal: J0R 1R6
General Phone: (450) 227-4646
Published: Fri
Avg Paid Circ: 50
Avg Free Circ: 29756
Audit By: ODC
Audit Date: 14.12.2011
Personnel: Andre Guillemette

SAINT STEPHEN

PUBLICATION NAME

St. Croix Courier
Street Address: P.O. Box 250, 47 Milltown Boulevard
Province: NB
Postal: E3L 2X2
Country: Canada
Mailing address: P.O. Box 250
Mailing city: Saint Stephen
Province: NB
Postal: E3L 2X2
General Phone: (506) 466-3220
General Fax: (506) 466-9950
General/National Adv. E-mail: courier@nb.aibn.com
Display Adv. E-mail: cairns@stcroixcourier.ca
Editorial e-mail: editor@stcroixcourier.ca
Primary Website: www.stcroixcourier.com
Year Established: 1865
Areas Served - City/County or Portion Thereof, or Zip codes: Canada
Mechanical specifications: Type page 13 1/4 x 21; E - 6 cols, 2 1/16, 3/16 between; A - 6 cols, 1 1/16, 3/16 between; C - 6 cols, 2 1/16, 3/16 between.
Published: Tues
Avg Paid Circ: 1075
Avg Free Circ: 40
Audit By: VAC
Audit Date: 31.01.2016
Personnel: Leith Orr (Pub.); Shelley McKeeman (Gen. Mgr.); Krisi Marples (Ed)

SAINT THOMAS

PUBLICATION NAME

St. Thomas/elgin Weekly News
Street Address: 15 St. Catharine Street,
Province: ON
Postal: N5P 2V7
Country: Canada
Mailing address: 15 St. Catharine St.
Mailing city: Saint Thomas
Province: ON
Postal: N5P 2V7
General Phone: (519) 633-1640
General Fax: (519) 633-0558
Display Adv. E-mail: geoff@theweeklynews.ca
Editorial e-mail: editor@theweeklynews.ca
Primary Website: www.theweeklynews.ca
Delivery Methods: Carrier
Areas Served - City/County or Portion Thereof, or Zip codes: Canada
Published: Thur
Avg Free Circ: 30393
Audit By: CMCA
Audit Date: 31.10.2017
Personnel: Geoff Rae (Office/Sales Manager)
Parent company (for newspapers): Metroland Media Group Ltd.

SAINT TITE

PUBLICATION NAME

Hebdo Mekinac Deschenaux
Street Address: C.p. 4057,
Province: QC
Postal: G0X 3H0
Country: Canada
Mailing address: C.P. 4057
Mailing city: Saint Tite
Province: QC
Postal: G0X 3H0
General Phone: (819) 537-5111
Published: Sat
Avg Free Circ: 13540
Audit By: ODC
Audit Date: 14.12.2011
Personnel: Lena Sauvageau

SAINTE ADELE

PUBLICATION NAME

Le Journal Des Pays D'en Haut Le Vallee
Street Address: 94 De La Gare St-saviour,
Province: QC
Postal: J8B 2P7
Country: Canada
Mailing address: 94 De La Gare St-saviour
Mailing city: Sainte Adele
Province: QC
Postal: J8B 2P7
General Phone: (450) 229-6664
General Fax: (450) 227-8144
General/National Adv. E-mail: jpdh@hebdosquebecor.com
Primary Website: http://www.lejournaldespaysdenhautlavallee.ca/
Areas Served - City/County or Portion Thereof, or Zip codes: Canada
Mechanical specifications: Type page 11 1/2 x 12 3/4.
Published: Wed
Avg Free Circ: 30057
Audit By: CCAB
Audit Date: 31.03.2014
Personnel: Mario Marois (Pub.)
Parent company (for newspapers): Quebecor Communications, Inc.

SAINTE JEAN SUR RICHELIEU

PUBLICATION NAME

Journal Le Richelieu
Street Address: Rue Richelieu,
Province: QC
Postal: J3B 6X3
Country: Canada
Mailing address: rue Richelieu
Mailing city: Sainte Jean sur Richelieu
Province: QC
Postal: J3B 6X3
General Phone: (450) 347-0323
Areas Served - City/County or Portion Thereof, or Zip codes: Canada
Published: Tues
Avg Paid Circ: 4
Avg Free Circ: 42273
Audit By: CCAB
Audit Date: 31.03.2014
Personnel: Renel Bouchard

PUBLICATION NAME

Le Canada Francais
Street Address: 84 Rue Richelieu,
Province: QC
Postal: J3B 6X3
Country: Canada
Mailing address: 84 Rue Richelieu
Mailing city: Sainte Jean sur Richelieu
Province: QC
Postal: J3B 6X3
General Phone: (450) 347-0323
General Fax: (450) 347-4539
Editorial e-mail: web@tc.tc
Primary Website: www.canadafrancais.com
Areas Served - City/County or Portion Thereof, or Zip codes: Canada
Commercial printers?: Y
Mechanical specifications: Type page 11 1/2 x 15; E - 8 cols, 1 1/16, 1/6 between; A - 8 cols, 1 1/6, 1/6 between; C - 8 cols, 1 1/6, 1/6 between.
Published: Thur
Avg Paid Circ: 7708
Avg Free Circ: 7848
Audit By: AAM
Audit Date: 31.12.2018
Personnel: Renel Bouchard (Pres.); Charles Coutre (Adv. Mgr.); Christian Marleau (Circ. Mgr.); Robert Paradis (Ed.)

PUBLICATION NAME

L'echo De St-jean-sur-richelieu
Street Address: 81 Rue Richelieu Bureau 102 B,
Province: QC
Postal: J3B 6X2
Country: Canada
Mailing address: 81 Rue Richelieu Bureau 102 B
Mailing city: Sainte Jean sur Richelieu
Province: QC
Postal: J3B 6X2
General Phone: (450) 376-4646
General Fax: (450) 376-4666
Advertising Phone: (450) 376-4646
Advertising Fax: (450) 376-4666
Editorial Phone: (450) 376-4646
Editorial Fax: (450) 376-4666
General/National Adv. E-mail: daniel.noiseux@quebecormedia.com
Display Adv. E-mail: henri-paul.raymond@quebecormedia.com
Editorial e-mail: daniel.noiseux@quebecormedia.com
Primary Website: www.lechodesaintjean.com
Delivery Methods: Mail Racks
Areas Served - City/County or Portion Thereof, or Zip codes: Canada
Published: Wed
Avg Free Circ: 55426
Audit By: CCAB
Audit Date: 31.03.2014
Personnel: Daniel Noiseux (Ed.)

SAINTE JULIE

PUBLICATION NAME

L'information
Street Address: 566 Jules Choquet St., Local 2,
Province: QC
Postal: J3E 1W6
Country: Canada
Mailing address: 566 Jules Choquet St., Local 2
Mailing city: Sainte Julie
Province: QC
Postal: J3E 1W6
General Phone: (450) 649-0719
General Fax: (450) 649-7748
Display Adv. E-mail: l.bourdua@ infoeste-julie.qc.ca; ni.beausejour@ infoeste-julie.qc.ca
Editorial e-mail: redaction@infodeste-julie.qc.ca
Primary Website: www.monsaintejulie.com
Areas Served - City/County or Portion Thereof, or Zip codes: Canada
Mechanical specifications: Type page 10 x 15; E - 8 cols, between; A - 8 cols, between; C - 8 cols, between.
Published: Wed
Avg Paid Circ: 1
Avg Free Circ: 20563
Audit By: CCAB
Audit Date: 31.03.2014
Personnel: Serge Landry (Ed.); Ariane Desrochers (Ed.)

SAINTE MARIE-DE-BEAUCE

PUBLICATION NAME

Beauce Media
Street Address: 1147 Blvd. Vachon N.,
Province: QC
Postal: G6E 3B6
Country: Canada
Mailing address: PO Box 400
Mailing city: Sainte Marie-de-Beauce
Province: QC
Postal: G6E 3B6
General Phone: (418) 387-8000
General Fax: (418) 387-4495
General/National Adv. E-mail: smb.redaction@quebecormedia.com
Primary Website: www.beaucemedia.ca
Areas Served - City/County or Portion Thereof, or Zip codes: Canada
Published: Wed
Avg Paid Circ: 3
Avg Free Circ: 25092
Audit By: CCAB
Audit Date: 31.03.2014
Personnel: Gilbert Bernier
Parent company (for newspapers): Quebecor Communications, Inc.

PUBLICATION NAME

Edition Beauce Nord
Street Address: 691, Boul. Vachon Nord,
Province: QC
Postal: G6E 1M3
Country: Canada
Mailing address: rue Baronet
Mailing city: Sainte Marie-de-Beauce
Province: QC
Postal: G6E 2R1
General Phone: (418) 387-1205
Areas Served - City/County or Portion Thereof, or Zip codes: Canada
Published: Wed
Avg Paid Circ: 2
Avg Free Circ: 24833
Audit By: CCAB
Audit Date: 31.03.2014
Personnel: Claude Grondin

SAINTE THERESE

PUBLICATION NAME

Le Courrier
Street Address: 190 Cure-labelle Blvd., Rm. 204,
Province: QC
Postal: J7E 2X5
Country: Canada
Mailing address: 190 Cure-Labelle Blvd., Rm. 204
Mailing city: Sainte Therese
Province: QC
Postal: J7E 2X5
General Phone: (450) 434-4144
General Fax: (450) 434-3142
Advertising Phone: (866) 637-5236
Primary Website: www.journallecourrier.com
Year Established: 1973
Areas Served - City/County or Portion Thereof, or Zip codes: Canada
Own Printing Facility?: Y
Mechanical specifications: Type page 10 1/4 x 14 1/4; E - 8 cols, between; A - 8 cols, between.
Published: Wed
Avg Free Circ: 55014
Audit By: CCAB
Audit Date: 31.03.2014
Personnel: Louis Sauvageau (Pub./Ed.)

PUBLICATION NAME

Le Nord-info
Street Address: 50 B Rue Turgeon,
Province: QC
Postal: J7E 3H4
Country: Canada
Mailing address: 50 B Rue Turgeon
Mailing city: Sainte Therese
Province: QC
Postal: J7E 3H4
General Phone: (450) 435-6537

General Fax: (450) 435-0588
General/National Adv. E-mail: nordinfo@groupgcl.com
Areas Served - City/County or Portion Thereof, or Zip codes: Canada
Published: Sat
Avg Free Circ: 60079
Audit By: CCAB
Audit Date: 31.03.2014
Personnel: Serge Langlois (Gen. Mgr.); Norman Langlois (Circ. Mgr.); Jean Claude Langlois (Ed.)

PUBLICATION NAME

L'echo De St Eustache
Street Address: 204 Blvd Labelle Ste 208 ,
Province: QC
Postal: J7E 2X7
Country: Canada
Mailing address: 204 Blvd Labelle Ste 208
Mailing city: Sainte Therese
Province: QC
Postal: J7E 2X7
General Phone: (450) 818-7575
General Fax: (450) 818-7582
Advertising Phone: (450) 818-7575
Advertising Fax: (450) 818-7582
Editorial Phone: (450) 818-7575
Editorial Fax: (450) 818-7582
Areas Served - City/County or Portion Thereof, or Zip codes: Canada
Published: Wed
Avg Free Circ: 57641
Audit By: CCAB
Audit Date: 31.03.2014

PUBLICATION NAME

Voix Des Mille Iles
Street Address: Rue Turgeon ,
Province: QC
Postal: J7E 3H4
Country: Canada
Mailing address: rue Turgeon
Mailing city: Sainte Therese
Province: QC
Postal: J7E 3H4
General Phone: (450) 435-6537
Primary Website: http://www.nordinfo.com/
Areas Served - City/County or Portion Thereof, or Zip codes: Canada
Published: Wed
Avg Free Circ: 65177
Audit By: CCAB
Audit Date: 31.03.2014
Personnel: Serge Langlois

SAINT-GEORGES

PUBLICATION NAME

Le Point
Street Address: 9085, Boul. Lacroix ,
Province: QC
Postal: G5Y 2B4
Country: Canada
Mailing address: 1, rue Mont Sainte-Claire
Mailing city: Chicoutimi
Province: QC
Postal: G7H 5G3
General Phone: (418) 695-2601
General Fax: (418) 695-1391
General/National Adv. E-mail: ralph.pilote@quebecormedia.com
Primary Website: www.lepoint.ca
Areas Served - City/County or Portion Thereof, or Zip codes: Canada
Own Printing Facility?: Y
Mechanical specifications: Type page 11 1/2 x 12 1/2; E - 5 cols, 1 7/8, 1/8 between; A - 5 cols, 1 7/8, 1/8 between; C - 5 cols, 1 7/8, 1/8 between.
Published: Tues
Avg Free Circ: 47878
Audit By: CCAB
Audit Date: 31.03.2014
Personnel: Claude Poulin (Pres.)
Parent company (for newspapers): Quebecor Communications, Inc.

SAINT-GEORGES

PUBLICATION NAME

Le Reveil
Street Address: 9085, Boul. Lacroix ,
Province: QC
Postal: G5Y 2B4
Country: Canada
Mailing address: PO Box 520
Mailing city: Jonquiere
Province: QC
Postal: G7X 7W4
General Phone: (418) 695-2601
General Fax: (418) 695-1391
General/National Adv. E-mail: lereveil@videotron.ca
Primary Website: lereveil.canoe.ca
Areas Served - City/County or Portion Thereof, or Zip codes: Canada
Own Printing Facility?: Y
Commercial printers?: Y
Mechanical specifications: Type page 10 1/4 x 11 3/4; E - 5 cols, 2, 1/8 between; A - 5 cols, 2, 1/8 between; C - 5 cols, 2, 1/8 between.
Published: Tues
Avg Paid Circ: 0
Avg Free Circ: 73191
Audit By: CCAB
Audit Date: 30.09.2012
Personnel: Diane Audet (Pub.); Andre Rousseau (Prodn. Mgr.)
Parent company (for newspapers): Quebecor Communications, Inc.

SALABERRY-DE-VALLEYFIELD

PUBLICATION NAME

Le Journal Saint-francois
Street Address: 61 Jacques-cartier St. ,
Province: QC
Postal: J6T 4R4
Country: Canada
Mailing address: 55 Jacques-Cartier St.
Mailing city: Salaberry-de-Valleyfield
Province: QC
Postal: J6T 4R4
General Phone: (450) 371-6222
General Fax: (450) 371-7254
General/National Adv. E-mail: info@st-francois.com
Primary Website: www.st-francois.com
Areas Served - City/County or Portion Thereof, or Zip codes: Canada
Commercial printers?: Y
Mechanical specifications: Type page 11 1/2 x 15; E - 4 cols, 2 1/2, 1/6 between; C - 8 cols, 1 1/4, 1/6 between.
Published: Wed
Avg Paid Circ: 36
Avg Free Circ: 34817
Audit By: CCAB
Audit Date: 31.03.2014
Personnel: Diane Dumont (Pub./Dir.); Stephane Brais (Sales Dir.); Denis Bourbonnais (Ed. in Chief)
Parent company (for newspapers): Les Hebdos Monteregiens-OOB

PUBLICATION NAME

Le Soleil Du St-laurent
Street Address: 20 Academy St. ,
Province: QC
Postal: J6T 6M9
Country: Canada
Mailing address: 20 Academy St.
Mailing city: Salaberry-de-Valleyfield
Province: QC
Postal: J6T 6M9
General Phone: (450) 373-8555
General Fax: (450) 373-8666
General/National Adv. E-mail: info@lesoleil.qc.ca
Display Adv. E-mail: publicite@lesoleil.qc.ca
Editorial e-mail: redaction@lesoleil.qc.ca
Primary Website: www.lesoleil.qc.ca
Commercial printers?: Y
Mechanical specifications: Type page 10 1/4 x 17.
Published: Sat
Avg Free Circ: 32750
Audit By: Sworn/Estimate/Non-Audited
Audit Date: 12.07.2019
Personnel: Andre Mooney (Dir.); Pierre Montreuil (Sales Dir.); Diane Mayer (Adv. Rep.); Serge Proulx (Adv. Rep.); Jean-Pierre Tessier (Adv. Rep.); Peter Rozon (Adv. Rep.); Mario Pitre (Ed.)
Parent company (for newspapers): Les Hebdos Monteregiens-OOB

PUBLICATION NAME

Soleil De Valleyfield
Street Address: 20 Rue De L'academie ,
Province: QC
Postal: J6T 2H8
Country: Canada
Mailing address: 20 Rue de l'Academie
Mailing city: Salaberry-de-Valleyfield
Province: QC
Postal: J6T 2H8
General Phone: (450) 373-8555
Advertising Phone: (450) 373-8555
Editorial Phone: (450) 373-8555
General/National Adv. E-mail: diane.dumont@quebecmedia.com
Editorial e-mail: diane.dumont@quebecmedia.com
Primary Website: http://www.journalsaint-francois.ca
Delivery Methods: Mail`Racks
Areas Served - City/County or Portion Thereof, or Zip codes: Canada
Published: Sat
Avg Paid Circ: 23
Avg Free Circ: 35953
Audit By: CCAB
Audit Date: 31.03.2014
Personnel: Andre Mooney (Pub.)

PUBLICATION NAME

Valleyfield Express
Street Address: 720 Blvd Monseigneur-langlois Ste 100 ,
Province: QC
Postal: J6S 5H7
Country: Canada
Mailing address: 720 Blvd Monseigneur-Langlois Ste 100
Mailing city: Salaberry-de-Valleyfield
Province: QC
Postal: J6S 5H7
General Phone: (450) 371-7117
General Fax: (450) 371-7611
Advertising Phone: (450) 371-7117
Advertising Fax: (450) 371-7611
Editorial Phone: (450) 371-7117
Editorial Fax: (450) 371-7611
General/National Adv. E-mail: redactionvalleyfieldexpress@tc.tc
Display Adv. E-mail: redactionvalleyfieldexpress@tc.tc
Editorial e-mail: redactionvalleyfieldexpress@tc.tc
Primary Website: www.valleyfieldexpress.ca
Delivery Methods: Mail`Racks
Areas Served - City/County or Portion Thereof, or Zip codes: Canada
Published: Thur
Avg Free Circ: 43310
Audit By: CCAB
Audit Date: 31.03.2014
Personnel: RÃƒÂ©seau MontÃƒÂ©rÃƒÂ©gie (Pub.)

SALMON ARM

PUBLICATION NAME

Eagle Valley News
Street Address: 171 Shuswap St. Nw ,
Province: BC
Postal: V1E 4N7
Country: Canada
Mailing address: PO Box 550
Mailing city: Salmon Arm
Province: BC
Postal: V1E 4N7
General Phone: (250) 832-2131
General Fax: (250) 832-5140
General/National Adv. E-mail: publisher@saobserver.net
Display Adv. E-mail: advertising@saobserver.net
Classified Adv. e-mail: classifieds@eaglevalleynews.com
Editorial e-mail: newsroom@saobserver.net
Primary Website: www.eaglevalleynews.com
Delivery Methods: Mail`Newsstand
Areas Served - City/County or Portion Thereof, or Zip codes: Canada
Mechanical specifications: Type page 10 1/4 x 14 1/2; E - 6 cols, 1 7/12, 1/6 between; A - 6 cols, 1 7/12, 1/6 between; C - 7 cols, 1 5/8, 1/6 between.
Published: Wed
Avg Paid Circ: 376
Avg Free Circ: 12
Audit By: CMCA
Audit Date: 31.05.2017
Personnel: Rick Proznick (Adv. Mgr); Tracy Hughes (Ed.); Laura Lavigne (Sales); Lachlan Labere (Reporter/Columnist)
Parent company (for newspapers): Black Press Group Ltd.

PUBLICATION NAME

Salmon Arm Observer
Street Address: 171 Shuswap St., Nw ,
Province: BC
Postal: V1E 4N7
Country: Canada
Mailing address: P.O. Box 550
Mailing city: Salmon Arm
Province: BC
Postal: V1E 4N7
General Phone: (250) 832-2131
General Fax: (250) 832-5140
General/National Adv. E-mail: advertising@saobserver.net
Display Adv. E-mail: advertising@saobserver.net
Classified Adv. e-mail: classifieds@saobserver.net
Editorial e-mail: newsroom@saobserver.net
Primary Website: www.saobserver.net
Year Established: 1907
Delivery Methods: Mail`Newsstand
Areas Served - City/County or Portion Thereof, or Zip codes: Canada
Own Printing Facility?: N
Commercial printers?: N
Mechanical specifications: Type page 10 5/16 x 14; E - 7 cols, 1 5/16, 3/16 between; A - 7 cols, 1 5/16, 3/16 between.
Published: Wed
Avg Paid Circ: 1951
Avg Free Circ: 50
Audit By: CMCA
Audit Date: 30.04.2017
Personnel: Rick Proznick (Pub.); Tracy Hughes (Senior Ed.)
Parent company (for newspapers): Black Press Group Ltd.

PUBLICATION NAME

Shuswap Market News
Street Address: 171 Shuswap St. Nw ,
Province: BC
Postal: V1E 4N7
Country: Canada
Mailing address: P.O. Box 550
Mailing city: Salmon Arm
Province: BC
Postal: V1E 4N7
General Phone: (250) 832-2131
General Fax: (250) 832-5140
Display Adv. E-mail: advertising@saoberver.net
Classified Adv. e-mail: classifieds@saobserver.net
Editorial e-mail: newsroom@saobserver.net
Primary Website: www.saobserver.net

Community Newspapers in Canada

Year Established: 1907
Delivery Methods: Carrier`Racks
Areas Served - City/County or Portion Thereof, or Zip codes: Canada
Own Printing Facility?: N
Commercial printers?: N
Mechanical specifications: Type page 10 5/16 x 14; E - 7 cols, 1 9/16, 3/16 between; A - 7 cols, 1 9/16, 3/16 between; C - 7 cols, 1 9/16, 3/16 between.
Published: Fri
Avg Paid Circ: 0
Avg Free Circ: 12732
Audit By: CMCA
Audit Date: 30.06.2017
Personnel: Rick Proznick (Pub.); Tracy Hughes (Ed.)
Parent company (for newspapers): Black Press Group Ltd.

SALT SPRING ISLAND

PUBLICATION NAME

Gulf Islands Driftwood
Street Address: 328 Lower Ganges Rd. ,
Province: BC
Postal: V8K 2V3
Country: Canada
Mailing address: 328 Lower Ganges Rd.
Mailing city: Salt Spring Island
Province: BC
Postal: V8K 2V3
General Phone: (250) 537-9933
General Fax: (250) 537-2613
General/National Adv. E-mail: inquiries@driftwoodgulfislandsmedia.com
Display Adv. E-mail: sales@driftwoodgimedia.com
Editorial e-mail: news@driftwoodgimedia.com
Primary Website: www.driftwoodgulfislandsmedia.com
Year Established: 1960
Delivery Methods: Mail`Newsstand
Areas Served - City/County or Portion Thereof, or Zip codes: Canada
Commercial printers?: Y
Published: Wed
Avg Paid Circ: 2300
Avg Free Circ: 2200
Audit By: Sworn/Estimate/Non-Audited
Audit Date: 12.07.2019
Personnel: Gail Sjuberg (Mng. Ed.); Lorraine Sullivan (Prodn. Mgr.); Amber Ogilvie (Publisher)
Parent company (for newspapers): Driftwood Publishing Ltd.

SARNIA

PUBLICATION NAME

Sarnia & Lambton County This Week
Street Address: 140 Front St S ,
Province: ON
Postal: N7t2M6
Country: Canada
Mailing address: 140 Front St S
Mailing city: Sarnia
Province: ON
Postal: N7S 5P1
General Phone: (519) 336-1100
General Fax: (519) 336-1833
Advertising Phone: (519) 336-1100
Advertising Fax: (519) 336-1833
Editorial Phone: (519) 336-1100
Editorial Fax: (519) 336-1833
General/National Adv. E-mail: chris.courtis@sunmedia.ca
Display Adv. E-mail: stw.sales@sunmedia.ca
Editorial e-mail: stw.sales@sunmedia.ca
Primary Website: Www.sarniathisweek.ca
Year Established: 1993
Delivery Methods: Carrier`Racks
Areas Served - City/County or Portion Thereof, or Zip codes: N7S 5P1
Own Printing Facility?: Y
Mechanical specifications: Type page 10 1/2 x 13 1/4; A - 9 cols, 1 1/6, 1/6 between; C - 9 cols, 1 1/6, 1/6 between.
Published: Wed
Avg Free Circ: 41300
Audit By: Sworn/Estimate/Non-Audited
Audit Date: 12.07.2019
Personnel: Chris Courtis (Marketing Manager)
Parent company (for newspapers): Postmedia Network Inc.

PUBLICATION NAME

Sarnia This Week
Street Address: 140 Front St. S ,
Province: ON
Postal: N7T 7M8
Country: Canada
Mailing address: 140 Front St. S
Mailing city: Sarnia
Province: ON
Postal: N7T 7M8
General Phone: (519) 336-1100
General Fax: (519) 336-1833
General/National Adv. E-mail: news@sarniamedia.com
Editorial e-mail: production@sarniamedia.com
Primary Website: www.sarniathisweek.com
Areas Served - City/County or Portion Thereof, or Zip codes: Canada
Published: Thur
Avg Free Circ: 39476
Audit By: CMCA
Audit Date: 30.06.2016
Personnel: Linda LeBlanc (Pub.); Penny Churchill (Distribution Mgr.)
Parent company (for newspapers): Quebecor Communications, Inc.

PUBLICATION NAME

The Petrolia Topic
Street Address: 140 Front St. S ,
Province: ON
Postal: N7T 7M8
Country: Canada
Mailing address: 140 Front St. S
Mailing city: Sarnia
Province: ON
Postal: N7T 7M8
General Phone: (519) 336-1100 x2230
General Fax: (519) 336-1833
Advertising Phone: (519) 882-4798
Advertising Fax: (519) 882-4635
Editorial Phone: (519) 336-1100 x2230
Editorial Fax: (519) 336-1833
Editorial e-mail: reporter@petroliatopic.com
Primary Website: www.petroliatopic.com
Year Established: 1866
Delivery Methods: Mail`Newsstand
Areas Served - City/County or Portion Thereof, or Zip codes: Canada
Own Printing Facility?: Y
Commercial printers?: N
Published: Wed
Avg Paid Circ: 1309
Audit By: CMCA
Audit Date: 31.12.2012
Personnel: Linda LeBlanc (Pub.)
Parent company (for newspapers): Postmedia Network Inc.; Quebecor Communications, Inc.

SAULT SAINTE MARIE

PUBLICATION NAME

Sault Ste. Marie This Week
Street Address: 2 Towers St. ,
Province: ON
Postal: P6A 2T9
Country: Canada
Mailing address: PO Box 188
Mailing city: Sault Sainte Marie
Province: ON
Postal: P6A 2T9
General Phone: (705) 949-6111
General Fax: (705) 942-8596
Editorial Phone: (705) 759-5825
General/National Adv. E-mail: lou.maulucci@sunmedia.ca
Display Adv. E-mail: sste.advertising@sunmedia.ca
Editorial e-mail: sandra.paul@sunmedia.ca
Primary Website: www.saultthisweek.com
Year Established: 1967
Delivery Methods: Newsstand`Carrier`Racks
Areas Served - City/County or Portion Thereof, or Zip codes: Canada
Own Printing Facility?: Y
Commercial printers?: N
Mechanical specifications: Type page 10 1/4 x 11 1/2; E - various, between; A - 9 cols, between; C - 9 cols, between.
Published: Thur
Avg Free Circ: 31122
Audit By: CMCA
Audit Date: 30.06.2015
Personnel: Lou Maulucci (Pub.); Sandra Paul (Ed.)
Parent company (for newspapers): Postmedia Network Inc.; Quebecor Communications, Inc.

SEAFORTH

PUBLICATION NAME

Seaforth Huron Expositor
Street Address: 8 Main St. S. ,
Province: ON
Postal: N0K 1W0
Country: Canada
Mailing address: PO Box 69
Mailing city: Seaforth
Province: ON
Postal: N0K 1W0
General Phone: (519) 527-0240
General Fax: (519) 527-2858
General/National Adv. E-mail: seaforth@bowesnet.com
Display Adv. E-mail: max.bickford@sunmedia.ca
Classified Adv. e-mail: seaforth.classifieds@sunmedia.ca
Editorial e-mail: seaforth.news@sunmedia.ca
Primary Website: www.seaforthhuronexpositor.com
Year Established: 1860
Delivery Methods: Mail`Newsstand
Areas Served - City/County or Portion Thereof, or Zip codes: Canada
Own Printing Facility?: Y
Mechanical specifications: Type page 11 1/4 x 11 3/8; E - 9 cols, 1 3/4, 1/8 between;
Published: Wed
Avg Paid Circ: 1160
Avg Free Circ: 22
Audit By: CMCA
Audit Date: 30.06.2016
Personnel: Neil Clifford (Pub.); Whitney South (Multi Media Journalist)
Parent company (for newspapers): Postmedia Network Inc.; Quebecor Communications, Inc.

SECHELT

PUBLICATION NAME

Coast Reporter
Street Address: 5485 Wharf Road ,
Province: BC
Postal: V0N 3A0
Country: Canada
Mailing address: PO Box 1388
Mailing city: Sechelt
Province: BC
Postal: V0N 3A0
General Phone: (604) 885-4811
General Fax: (604) 885-4818
General/National Adv. E-mail: pkvarnstrom@coastreporter.net
Display Adv. E-mail: pat@coastreporter.net
Classified Adv. e-mail: classified@coastreporter.net
Editorial e-mail: editor@coastreporter.net
Primary Website: www.coastreporter.net
Areas Served - City/County or Portion Thereof, or Zip codes: Sechelt, Gibsons
Published: Fri
Avg Paid Circ: 31
Avg Free Circ: 11639
Audit By: VAC
Audit Date: 30.06.2016
Personnel: Peter Kvarnstrom (Pub.); Christine Wood (Circ. Mgr.); John Gleeson (Ed./Assoc. Pub.); Pat Paproski (Sales Mgr.); Shelley Alleyne (Class. Supv.)
Parent company (for newspapers): Glacier Media Group

SELKIRK

PUBLICATION NAME

Selkirk Journal
Street Address: 366 Main St , Unit 300
Province: MB
Postal: R1A 2J7
Country: Canada
Mailing address: 366 Main St Unit 300
Mailing city: Selkirk
Province: MB
Postal: R1A 2J7
General Phone: (204) 482-7402
General Fax: (204) 482-3336
General/National Adv. E-mail: sjournal@mts.net
Display Adv. E-mail: jbilsky@postmedia.com
Editorial e-mail: bjones@postmedia.com
Primary Website: http://www.interlaketoday.ca/selkirkjournal
Areas Served - City/County or Portion Thereof, or Zip codes: Selkirk
Own Printing Facility?: Y
Commercial printers?: Y
Mechanical specifications: Type page 10 1/8 x 14; E - 6 cols, 1 7/12, 1/6 between; A - 6 cols, 1 7/12, 1/6 between; C - 6 cols, 1 7/12, 1/6 between.
Published: Thur
Avg Free Circ: 14334
Audit By: VAC
Audit Date: 30.06.2016
Personnel: Jenifer Bilsky (Adv Dir); Brook Jones (Ed)
Parent company (for newspapers): Postmedia Network Inc.; Quebecor Communications, Inc.

SEPT-ILES

PUBLICATION NAME

Le Port Cartois
Street Address: 365 Laure Blvd. ,
Province: QC
Postal: G4R 1X2
Country: Canada
Mailing address: 365 Laure Blvd.
Mailing city: Sept-Iles
Province: QC
Postal: G4R 1X2
General Phone: (418) 962-4100
General Fax: (418) 962-0439
General/National Adv. E-mail: administration.sett-iles@hebdosquebecor.com
Primary Website: www.hebdosquebecor.com
Areas Served - City/County or Portion Thereof, or Zip codes: Canada
Published: Wed
Avg Paid Circ: 6
Avg Free Circ: 19072
Audit By: CCAB
Audit Date: 31.03.2014
Personnel: Isabelle Chiasson (Adv. Mgr.); Catherine Martin (Ed.)
Parent company (for newspapers): Quebecor Communications, Inc.

PUBLICATION NAME

Nord Cotier
Street Address: Boulevard Laure ,
Province: QC
Postal: G4R 1Y2
Country: Canada
Mailing address: boulevard Laure
Mailing city: Sept-Iles
Province: QC
Postal: G4R 1Y2
General Phone: (418) 960-2090
Areas Served - City/County or Portion Thereof, or Zip codes: Canada
Published: Wed

Avg Paid Circ: 23
Avg Free Circ: 19095
Audit By: CCAB
Audit Date: 30.09.2012
Personnel: Gino Levesque

PUBLICATION NAME

Nordest Plus
Street Address: 365 Boul. Laure ,
Province: QC
Postal: G4R 1X2
Country: Canada
Mailing address: 365 Boul. Laure
Mailing city: Sept-Iles
Province: QC
Postal: G4R 1X2
General Phone: (418) 962-4100
General Fax: (418) 962-0439
General/National Adv. E-mail: nordest@hebdosquebecor.com
Display Adv. E-mail: atelier.septiles@hebdosquebecor.com
Editorial e-mail: redaction.septiles@hebdosquebecor.com
Primary Website: www.hebdosquebecor.com
Own Printing Facility?: Y
Commercial printers?: Y
Published: Wed
Avg Free Circ: 13999
Audit By: Sworn/Estimate/Non-Audited
Audit Date: 12.07.2019
Personnel: Isabelle Chiasson (Dir.); Mario Thibeault (Mng. Ed.)

SHARBOT LAKE

PUBLICATION NAME

The Frontenac News
Street Address: 1095 Garrett St. , Rear
Province: ON
Postal: K0H 2P0
Country: Canada
Mailing address: P.O. Box 229
Mailing city: Sharbot Lake
Province: ON
Postal: K0H 2P0
General Phone: (613) 279-3150
General Fax: (613) 279-3172
General/National Adv. E-mail: nfnews@frontenac.net
Display Adv. E-mail: info@frontenacnews.ca
Classified Adv. e-mail: info@frontenacnews.ca
Editorial e-mail: info@frontenacnews.ca
Primary Website: Frontenacnews.ca
Year Established: 1973
Delivery Methods: Mail
Areas Served - City/County or Portion Thereof, or Zip codes: Central Frontenac
Published: Thur
Avg Free Circ: 9135
Audit By: Sworn/Estimate/Non-Audited
Audit Date: 12.07.2019
Personnel: Jeff Green (Publisher/Editor); Scott Cox (Designer/bookeeper)

SHAUNAVON

PUBLICATION NAME

The Shaunavon Standard
Street Address: 346 Centre St. ,
Province: SK
Postal: S0N 2M0
Country: Canada
Mailing address: PO Box 729
Mailing city: Shaunavon
Province: SK
Postal: S0N 2M0
General Phone: (306) 297-4144
General Fax: (306) 297-3357
Display Adv. E-mail: jgregoire@theshaunavonstandard.com
Editorial e-mail: standard@theshaunavonstandard.com
Year Established: 1913
Areas Served - City/County or Portion Thereof, or Zip codes: Canada
Mechanical specifications: Type page 11 1/2 x 17; E - 5 cols, 2, 1/4 between; A - 5 cols, 2, 1/4 between; C - 5 cols, 2, 1/4 between.
Published: Tues
Avg Paid Circ: 916
Audit By: CMCA
Audit Date: 30.06.2016
Personnel: Paul MacNeil (Ed.); Joanne Gregoire (Adv. Sales)

SHAWINIGAN

PUBLICATION NAME

Hebdo Du St. Maurice
Street Address: 2102 Champlain Ave. ,
Province: QC
Postal: G9N 6T8
Country: Canada
Mailing address: PO Box 10
Mailing city: Shawinigan
Province: QC
Postal: G9N 6T8
General Phone: (819) 537-5111
General Fax: (819) 537-5471
Advertising Phone: (866) 637-5236
General/National Adv. E-mail: redaction_shawinigan@transcontinental.ca
Primary Website: www.lhebdodustmaurice.com
Areas Served - City/County or Portion Thereof, or Zip codes: Canada
Mechanical specifications: Type page 11 1/4 x 13 1/2; E - 10 cols, 1, 1/6 between; A - 10 cols, 1, 1/6 between; C - 10 cols, 1, 1/6 between.
Published: Wed
Avg Paid Circ: 24
Avg Free Circ: 36640
Audit By: CCAB
Audit Date: 31.03.2014
Personnel: Michel Matteau (Pub.); Lena Sauvageau; Gilles Guay (Adv. Mgr.); Bernard Lepage (Ed./Dir., Information)
Parent company (for newspapers): Transcontinental Media

PUBLICATION NAME

L'echo De Shawinigan
Street Address: 795 Blvd 5e Rue Local 101 ,
Province: QC
Postal: G9N 1G2
Country: Canada
Mailing address: 795 Blvd 5E Rue Local 101
Mailing city: Shawinigan
Province: QC
Postal: G9N 1G2
General Phone: (819) 731-0327
General Fax: (819) 731-0328
Advertising Phone: (819) 731-0327
Advertising Fax: (819) 731-0328
Editorial Phone: (819) 731-0327
Editorial Fax: (819) 731-0328
General/National Adv. E-mail: jocelyn.ouellet@quebecormedia.com
Display Adv. E-mail: serge.buchanan@quebecormedia.com
Editorial e-mail: hugues.carpentier@quebecormedia.com
Primary Website: www.lechodeshawinigan.ca
Delivery Methods: Mail`Racks
Areas Served - City/County or Portion Thereof, or Zip codes: Canada
Published: Wed
Avg Free Circ: 37369
Audit By: CCAB
Audit Date: 31.03.2014
Personnel: Hugues Carpentier (Ed.)

PUBLICATION NAME

L'hebdo Mekinac/des Chenaux
Street Address: Cp 490 ,
Province: QC
Postal: G9N 6T8
Country: Canada
Mailing address: PO Box 4057
Mailing city: Shawinigan
Province: QC
Postal: G9N 6T8
General Phone: (819) 537-5111
General Fax: (819) 537-5471
General/National Adv. E-mail: redaction_shawinigan@transcontinental.ca
Primary Website: www.lhebdomekinacdeschenaux.com
Mechanical specifications: Type page 11 1/4 x 13 1/2; E - 10 cols, 1, 1/8 between; A - 10 cols, 1, 1/8 between; C - 10 cols, 1, 1/8 between.
Published: Wed
Avg Paid Circ: 13540
Avg Free Circ: 0
Audit By: Sworn/Estimate/Non-Audited
Audit Date: 12.07.2019
Personnel: Michel Matteau (Pub.); Bernard Lepage (Dir., Information); Gilles Guay (Ed.)
Parent company (for newspapers): Transcontinental Media

SHAWVILLE

PUBLICATION NAME

The Equity
Street Address: 133 Center St. ,
Province: QC
Postal: J0X 2Y0
Country: Canada
Mailing address: 133 Center St.
Mailing city: Shawville
Province: QC
Postal: J0X 2Y0
General Phone: (819) 647-2204
General Fax: (819) 647-2206
General/National Adv. E-mail: prepress@theequity.ca
Display Adv. E-mail: kathy@theequity.ca
Classified Adv. e-mail: news@theequity.ca
Editorial e-mail: news@theequity.ca
Primary Website: www.theequity.ca
Year Established: 1883
Delivery Methods: Mail`Newsstand
Areas Served - City/County or Portion Thereof, or Zip codes: Canada
Mechanical specifications: Type page 13 1/2 x 21; E - 5 cols, 2 3/8, 1/8 between; A - 8 cols, 1 1/2, 1/8 between; C - 8 cols, 1 1/2, 1/8 between.
Published: Wed
Avg Paid Circ: 2835
Audit By: CMCA
Audit Date: 31.12.2015
Personnel: Charles Dickson (Pub)
Parent company (for newspapers): Pontiac Printshop Ltd.

SHEDIAC

PUBLICATION NAME

Le Moniteur Acadien
Street Address: Cp 5191 817, West Boudreau ,
Province: NB
Postal: E4P 8T9
Country: Canada
Mailing address: CP 5191 817, Western Boudreau
Mailing city: Shediac
Province: NB
Postal: E4P 8T9
General Phone: (506) 532-6680
General Fax: (506) 532-6681
General/National Adv. E-mail: moniteur@rogers.com
Primary Website: www.moniteuracadien.com
Delivery Methods: Mail`Newsstand`Carrier
Areas Served - City/County or Portion Thereof, or Zip codes: Westmorland county, Shediac, Dieppe, Cap-Pele, Memramcook
Mechanical specifications: Type page 10 2/5 x 13 1/4; E - 5 cols, between; A - 5 cols, between; C - 5 cols, between.
Published: Wed
Avg Paid Circ: 3500
Avg Free Circ: 500
Audit By: Sworn/Estimate/Non-Audited
Audit Date: 12.07.2019
Personnel: Gilles Hache (Ed.)

SHELBURNE

PUBLICATION NAME

The Coast Guard
Street Address: 164 Water St. ,
Province: NS
Postal: B0T 1W0
Country: Canada
Mailing address: 164 Water St.
Mailing city: Shelburne
Province: NS
Postal: B0T 1W0
General Phone: (902) 875-3244
General Fax: (902) 875-3454
General/National Adv. E-mail: info@thecoastguard.ca
Display Adv. E-mail: info@thecoastguard.ca
Editorial e-mail: ffaynder@transcontinental.ca
Primary Website: www.thecoastguard.ca
Areas Served - City/County or Portion Thereof, or Zip codes: Canada
Mechanical specifications: Type page 13 x 21; E - 6 cols, 2, between; A - 6 cols, 2, between; C - 6 cols, 2, between.
Published: Tues
Avg Paid Circ: 2290
Avg Free Circ: 0
Audit By: CMCA
Audit Date: 28.02.2014
Personnel: Fred Fayander (Pub.)
Parent company (for newspapers): Transcontinental Media

SHELLBROOK

PUBLICATION NAME

Shellbrook Chronicle
Street Address: 46 Main St. ,
Province: SK
Postal: S0J 2E0
Country: Canada
Mailing address: PO Box 10
Mailing city: Shellbrook
Province: SK
Postal: S0J 2E0
General Phone: (306) 747-2442
General Fax: (306) 747-3000
General/National Adv. E-mail: chnews@shelbrookchronicle.com
Display Adv. E-mail: chads@sbchron.com
Primary Website: http://shellbrookchronicle.com/
Year Established: 1912
Areas Served - City/County or Portion Thereof, or Zip codes: Canada
Commercial printers?: Y
Mechanical specifications: Type page 10 1/4 x 15; E - 6 cols, 1 7/12, 1/6 between; A - 6 cols, 1 7/12, 1/6 between; C - 6 cols, 1 7/12, 1/6 between.
Published: Fri
Avg Paid Circ: 155
Avg Free Circ: 3484
Audit By: CMCA
Audit Date: 30.12.2015
Personnel: C.J. Pepper (Pub.)

PUBLICATION NAME

Spiritwood Herald
Street Address: 46 Main St. ,
Province: SK
Postal: S0J 2E0
Country: Canada
Mailing address: PO Box 10
Mailing city: Shellbrook
Province: SK
Postal: S0J 2E0
General Phone: (306) 747-2442
General Fax: (306) 747-3000
General/National Adv. E-mail: chnews@shopperchronicle.com
Display Adv. E-mail: chads@sbchron.com
Primary Website: www.spiritwoodherald.com
Delivery Methods: Mail`Newsstand`Racks
Areas Served - City/County or Portion Thereof, or Zip codes: S0J 0L0, S0M 0Y0, S0M 0Z0, S0J 1N0, S0M 1S0, S0M 1W0, S0J 1V0, S0J

Community Newspapers in Canada

2G0, S0J 2M0
Mechanical specifications: Type page 10 1/4 x 15; E - 6 cols, 1 7/12, 1/6 between; A - 6 cols, 1 7/12, 1/6 between; C - 6 cols, 1 7/12, 1/6 between.
Published: Fri
Avg Paid Circ: 52
Avg Free Circ: 2435
Audit By: Sworn/Estimate/Non-Audited
Audit Date: 12.07.2019
Personnel: Clark J Pepper (Publisher)

SHERBROOKE

PUBLICATION NAME

Journal De Magog
Street Address: Galt Ouest ,
Province: QC
Postal: J1K 2V8
Country: Canada
Mailing address: Galt Ouest
Mailing city: Sherbrooke
Province: QC
Postal: J1K 2V8
General Phone: (819) 575-7575
Areas Served - City/County or Portion Thereof, or Zip codes: Canada
Published: Wed
Avg Free Circ: 28000
Audit By: CCAB
Audit Date: 31.03.2014
Personnel: Sarah Beaulieu

PUBLICATION NAME

Journal De Sherbrooke
Street Address: Rue Galt Ouest ,
Province: QC
Postal: J1K 2V8
Country: Canada
Mailing address: rue Galt Ouest
Mailing city: Sherbrooke
Province: QC
Postal: J1K 2V8
General Phone: (819) 575-7575
Areas Served - City/County or Portion Thereof, or Zip codes: Canada
Published: Wed
Avg Free Circ: 63500
Audit By: CCAB
Audit Date: 31.03.2014
Personnel: Sarah Beaulieu

PUBLICATION NAME

Nouvelle De Sherbrooke
Street Address: Rue Roy ,
Province: QC
Postal: J1K 2X8
Country: Canada
Mailing address: rue Roy
Mailing city: Sherbrooke
Province: QC
Postal: J1K 2X8
General Phone: (819) 566-8022
Published: Sun
Avg Free Circ: 51200
Audit By: ODC
Audit Date: 14.12.2011
Personnel: Andre Custeau

SHERWOOD PARK

PUBLICATION NAME

Sherwood Park/strathcona County News
Street Address: 168 Kaska Rd. , 168 Kaska Road
Province: AB
Postal: T8A 4G7
Country: Canada
Mailing address: 168 Kaska Rd.
Mailing city: Sherwood Park
Province: AB
Postal: T8A 4G7
General Phone: (780) 464-0033
General Fax: (780) 464-8512
Advertising Phone: (780) 464-0033 Ext 239
Editorial Phone: 780 464-0033
General/National Adv. E-mail: shelagh.pastoor@sunmedia.ca
Display Adv. E-mail: jfigeat@postmedia.com
Editorial e-mail: bproulx@postmedia.com
Primary Website: www.sherwoodparknews.com
Year Established: 1976
Delivery Methods: Carrier`Racks
Areas Served - City/County or Portion Thereof, or Zip codes: Strathcona
Own Printing Facility?: N
Commercial printers?: N
Mechanical specifications: Type page 10.3125" x 11.5"; E & C - 10 cols, 1 ";
Published: Fri
Avg Paid Circ: 1702
Avg Free Circ: 30851
Audit By: VAC
Audit Date: 31.12.2015
Personnel: Jean Figeat (Adv. Dir.); Dawn Zapatoski (Circ.); Ben Proulx (Ed)
Parent company (for newspapers): Postmedia Network Inc.; Division of Post Media

SHOAL LAKE

PUBLICATION NAME

Crossroads This Week
Street Address: 353 Station Road ,
Province: MB
Postal: R0J 1Z0
Country: Canada
Mailing address: P.O. Box 160
Mailing city: Shoal Lake
Province: MB
Postal: R0J 1Z0
General Phone: (204) 759-2644
General Fax: (204) 759-2521
Advertising Phone: (204) 759-2644
Advertising Fax: (204) 759-2521
Editorial Phone: (204) 759-2644
Editorial Fax: (204) 759-2521
General/National Adv. E-mail: gnesbitt@mts.net
Display Adv. E-mail: ctwdisplay@mymts.net
Classified Adv. e-mail: ctwclassified@mymts.net
Editorial e-mail: ctwnews@mymts.net
Primary Website: www.crossroadsthisweek.com
Year Established: 1977
Delivery Methods: Mail`Newsstand
Areas Served - City/County or Portion Thereof, or Zip codes: Canada
Commercial printers?: Y
Mechanical specifications: Type page 10 5/16 x 14 1/4; E - 6 cols, 1 9/16, 1/6 between; A - 6 cols, 1 9/16, 1/6 between; C - 6 cols, 1 9/16, 1/6 between.
Published: Fri
Avg Paid Circ: 2294
Avg Free Circ: 25
Audit By: Sworn/Estimate/Non-Audited
Audit Date: 12.07.2019
Personnel: Connie Kay (Advertising Manager); Michelle Genslorek (Classified/Accounting); Darrell Nesbitt (News Reporter); Ryan Nesbitt (Publisher); Marcie Harrison (News Reporter)
Parent company (for newspapers): Nesbitt Publishing Ltd.

SHOAL LAKE

PUBLICATION NAME

South Mountain Press
Street Address: 353 Station Road ,
Province: MB
Postal: R0J 1Z0
Country: Canada
Mailing address: Box 160
Mailing city: Shoal Lake
Province: MB
Postal: R0J 1Z0
General Phone: (204) 759-2644
General Fax: (204) 759-2521
Advertising Phone: (204) 759-2644
Advertising Fax: (204) 759-2521
Editorial Phone: (204) 759-2644
Editorial Fax: (204) 759-2521
Display Adv. E-mail: smpdisplay@mymts.net
Classified Adv. e-mail: smpclassified@mymts.net
Editorial e-mail: smpnews@mymts.net
Year Established: 2005
Delivery Methods: Racks
Areas Served - City/County or Portion Thereof, or Zip codes: Yellowhead
Published: Fri
Avg Paid Circ: 46
Avg Free Circ: 1492
Audit By: VAC
Audit Date: 19.12.2017
Personnel: Connie Kay (Advertising); Marcie Harrison (Editor); Michelle Gensiorek (Classified/Accounting); Ryan Nesbitt (Publisher); Darrell Nesbitt (Reporter/Photographer)
Parent company (for newspapers): Nesbitt Publishing Ltd.

SIDNEY

PUBLICATION NAME

Goldstream Gazette
Street Address: 103-9843 Second Street ,
Province: BC
Postal: V8L 3C6
Country: Canada
Mailing address: 103-9843 Second Street
Mailing city: Sidney
Province: BC
Postal: V8L 3C6
General Phone: (250) 656-1151
General Fax: (250) 656-5526
Display Adv. E-mail: publisher@peninsulanewsreview.com
Editorial e-mail: editor@goldstreamgazette.com
Primary Website: goldstreamgazette.com
Year Established: 1976
Delivery Methods: Carrier
Areas Served - City/County or Portion Thereof, or Zip codes: Langford
Commercial printers?: Y
Published: Wed`Fri
Avg Free Circ: 17257
Audit By: AAM
Audit Date: 31.03.2019
Personnel: Mellissa Mitchell (Circ. Mgr.); Michelle Cabana (Pub.); Dale Naftel (Pub.)
Parent company (for newspapers): Black Press Group Ltd.

PUBLICATION NAME

The Peninsula News Review
Street Address: 102-9830 Second Street ,
Province: BC
Postal: V8L 3C6
Country: Canada
Mailing address: 103-9830 Second St.
Mailing city: Sidney
Province: BC
Postal: V8L 3C6
General Phone: (250) 656-1151
General Fax: (250) 656-5526
Editorial Phone: (250) 656-1151
Display Adv. E-mail: sales@peninsulanewsreview.com
Editorial e-mail: editor@peninsulanewsreview.com
Primary Website: www.peninsulanewsreview.com
Year Established: 1905
Delivery Methods: Carrier
Areas Served - City/County or Portion Thereof, or Zip codes: Canada
Own Printing Facility?: Y
Published: Wed`Fri
Avg Free Circ: 14556
Audit By: AAM
Audit Date: 31.03.2019
Personnel: Steven Heywood; Dale Naftel; Chris R Cook; Hugo Wong; Rosemarie Bandura
Parent company (for newspapers): Black Press Group Ltd.

SIMCOE

PUBLICATION NAME

Times-reformer
Street Address: 50 Gilbertson Dr. ,
Province: ON
Postal: N3Y 4L2
Country: Canada
Mailing address: 50 Gilbertson Dr.
Mailing city: Simcoe
Province: ON
Postal: N3Y 4L2
General Phone: (519) 426-3528
General Fax: (519) 426-9255
General/National Adv. E-mail: sdowns@bowesnet.com
Primary Website: www.simcoereformer.ca
Areas Served - City/County or Portion Thereof, or Zip codes: Canada
Published: Tues
Avg Paid Circ: 1411
Avg Free Circ: 17315
Audit By: CMCA
Audit Date: 31.12.2013
Personnel: Sue Downs (Adv. Mgr.); Kim Novak (Ed.)
Parent company (for newspapers): Postmedia Network Inc.; Quebecor Communications, Inc.

SIOUX LOOKOUT

PUBLICATION NAME

The Bulletin
Street Address: 40 Front St. ,
Province: ON
Postal: P8T 1B9
Country: Canada
Mailing address: PO Box 1389
Mailing city: Sioux Lookout
Province: ON
Postal: P8T 1B9
General Phone: (807) 737-3209
General Fax: (807) 737-3084
Advertising Phone: (807) 737-4207
General/National Adv. E-mail: bulletin@siouxbulletin.com
Primary Website: www.soiuxbulletin.com
Areas Served - City/County or Portion Thereof, or Zip codes: Canada
Mechanical specifications: Type page 10 x 14.
Published: Wed
Avg Free Circ: 4472
Audit By: CMCA
Audit Date: 30.04.2016
Personnel: Dick MacKenzie (Ed.)

PUBLICATION NAME

Wawatay News
Street Address: 16 5th Ave. ,
Province: ON
Postal: P8T 1B7
Country: Canada
Mailing address: PO Box 1180
Mailing city: Sioux Lookout
Province: ON
Postal: P8T 1B7
General Phone: (807) 737-2951
General Fax: (807) 737-3224
General/National Adv. E-mail: editor@wawatay.on.ca
Primary Website: www.wawataynews.ca
Year Established: 1974
Mechanical specifications: Type page 10 1/4 x 15 3/4; E - 6 cols, 1 9/16, 1/16 between; A - 6 cols, 1 9/16, 1/16 between; C - 6 cols, 1 9/16, 1/16 between.
Published: Thur
Published Other: Every other thur
Avg Paid Circ: 399
Avg Free Circ: 5618
Audit By: CMCA
Audit Date: 31.03.2014
Personnel: Rick Garrick (Reporter)

SLAVE LAKE

PUBLICATION NAME

Lakeside Leader
Street Address: 103 Third Ave. Ne ,
Province: AB
Postal: T0G 2A0
Country: Canada
Mailing address: PO Box 849
Mailing city: Slave Lake
Province: AB
Postal: T0G 2A0
General Phone: (780) 849-4380
General Fax: (780) 849-3903
Advertising Phone: (780) 849-4380
General/National Adv. E-mail: lsleader@telusplanet.net
Editorial e-mail: lsleader@telusplanet.net
Primary Website: www.lakesideleader.com
Year Established: 1970
Delivery Methods: Mail`Newsstand
Areas Served - City/County or Portion Thereof, or Zip codes: Canada
Published: Wed
Avg Paid Circ: 3672
Audit By: CMCA
Audit Date: 31.12.2016
Personnel: Mary Burgar (Pub) Joe McWilliams (Ed); Tammy Leslie (Circulation Mgr/ Primary Ad Contact)
Parent company (for newspapers): South Peace News(High Prairie)

SMITH FALLS

PUBLICATION NAME

The Carleton Place-almonte Canadian Gazette Emc
Street Address: 65 Lorne St. ,
Province: ON
Postal: K7A 4T1
Country: Canada
Mailing address: PO Box 158
Mailing city: Smith Falls
Province: ON
Postal: K7A 4T1
General Phone: (613) 283-3182
Display Adv. E-mail: ssinfield@perfprint.ca
Editorial e-mail: akulp@perfprint.ca
Primary Website: www.insideottawavalley.com
Areas Served - City/County or Portion Thereof, or Zip codes: Canada
Own Printing Facility?: Y
Commercial printers?: Y
Published: Thur
Avg Free Circ: 12071
Audit By: CMCA
Audit Date: 30.06.2016
Personnel: Duncan Weir (Group Pub.l); Ryland Coyne (Reg. Ed.)
Parent company (for newspapers): Metroland Media Group Ltd.

PUBLICATION NAME

The Perth Courier Emc
Street Address: 65 Lorne St. ,
Province: ON
Postal: K7A 4T1
Country: Canada
Mailing address: PO Box 158
Mailing city: Smith Falls
Province: ON
Postal: K7A 4T1
General Phone: (613) 283-3180
Editorial e-mail: editor@perthcourier.com
Primary Website: www.insideottawavalley.com
Year Established: 1834
Areas Served - City/County or Portion Thereof, or Zip codes: Canada
Mechanical specifications: Type page 13 1/4 x 21; E - 8 cols, 1 1/2, 1 7/8 between; A - 8 cols, 1 1/2, 1 7/8 between; C - 11 cols, 1 1/2, 1 1/6 between.
Published: Thur
Avg Free Circ: 11641
Audit By: CMCA
Audit Date: 30.06.2016
Personnel: Duncan Weir (Pub.); Ryland Coyne

Parent company (for newspapers): Metroland Media Group Ltd.

SMITHERS

PUBLICATION NAME

The Smithers Interior News
Street Address: 3764 Broadway ,
Province: BC
Postal: V0J 2N0
Country: Canada
Mailing address: PO Box 2560
Mailing city: Smithers
Province: BC
Postal: V0J 2N0
General Phone: (250) 847-3266
General Fax: (250) 847-2995
General/National Adv. E-mail: publisher@interior-news.com
Display Adv. E-mail: publisher@interior-news.com
Editorial e-mail: editor@interior-news.com
Primary Website: www.interior-news.com
Year Established: 1907
Areas Served - City/County or Portion Thereof, or Zip codes: Canada
Own Printing Facility?: Y
Mechanical specifications: Type page 12 1/8 x 21; E - 7 cols, 1 3/5, 1/6 between; A - 7 cols, 1 3/5, 1/6 between; C - 7 cols, 1 3/5, 1/6 between.
Published: Wed
Avg Paid Circ: 13
Avg Free Circ: 152
Audit By: VAC
Audit Date: 30.06.2016
Personnel: Grant Harris (Pub/Sales Mgr); Chris Gareau (Ed)
Parent company (for newspapers): Black Press Group Ltd.

SMITHS FALLS

PUBLICATION NAME

Kemptville Advance Emc
Street Address: 65 Lorne St. ,
Province: ON
Postal: K7A 4T1
Country: Canada
Mailing address: PO Box 158
Mailing city: Smiths Falls
Province: ON
Postal: K7A 4T1
General Phone: (613) 283-3181
Display Adv. E-mail: liz.gray@metroland.com
Editorial e-mail: joe.morin@metroland.com
Primary Website: www.insideottawavalley.com
Areas Served - City/County or Portion Thereof, or Zip codes: Canada
Published: Thur
Avg Free Circ: 10707
Audit By: CMCA
Audit Date: 30.06.2016
Personnel: Duncan Weir (Group Pub.); Kerry Sammon (Ed.)
Parent company (for newspapers): Metroland Media Group Ltd.

PUBLICATION NAME

Smiths Falls Record News Emc
Street Address: 65 Lorne St. ,
Province: ON
Postal: K7A 4T1
Country: Canada
Mailing address: PO Box 158
Mailing city: Smiths Falls
Province: ON
Postal: K7A 4T1
General Phone: (613) 283-3182
General Fax: (613) 283-7480
General/National Adv. E-mail: emc@perfprint.ca
Primary Website: www.insideottawavalley.com/smithsfalls-on
Areas Served - City/County or Portion Thereof, or Zip codes: Canada
Own Printing Facility?: Y

Commercial printers?: Y
Published: Thur
Avg Free Circ: 11455
Audit By: CMCA
Audit Date: 30.06.2016
Personnel: Duncan Weir (Pub.); Jason Beck (Circ. Mgr); Ryland Coyne (Ed.)
Parent company (for newspapers): Metroland Media Group Ltd.

SMOKY LAKE

PUBLICATION NAME

Smoky Lake Signal
Street Address: 4924 50th St ,
Province: AB
Postal: T0A 3C0
Country: Canada
Mailing address: Box 328
Mailing city: Smoky Lake
Province: AB
Postal: T0A 3C0
General Phone: (780) 656-6530
Advertising Phone: (780) 656-4114
Editorial Phone: (780) 656-6530
General/National Adv. E-mail: signal@mcsnet.ca
Display Adv. E-mail: lorne_taylor@smokylake.com
Classified Adv. e-mail: lornetaylor@smokylake.com
Editorial e-mail: lornetaylor@smokylake.com
Year Established: 1978
Delivery Methods: Mail`Newsstand
Areas Served - City/County or Portion Thereof, or Zip codes: T0A 3C0
Published: Tues`Wed
Avg Paid Circ: 855
Avg Free Circ: 20
Audit By: Sworn/Estimate/Non-Audited
Audit Date: 12.07.2019
Personnel: Lorne Taylor (Ed/Pub/Owner)
Parent company (for newspapers): Smoky Lake Signal Press Ltd.

SOOKE

PUBLICATION NAME

The Sooke News Mirror
Street Address: #4 6631 Sooke Road ,
Province: BC
Postal: V9Z 0A3
Country: Canada
Mailing address: #4-6631 Sooke Rd.
Mailing city: Sooke
Province: BC
Postal: V9Z 0A3
General Phone: (250) 642-5752
General Fax: (250) 642-4767
Advertising Phone: (250) 642-5752
Display Adv. E-mail: sales@sookenewsmirror.com
Editorial e-mail: editor@sookenewsmirror.com
Primary Website: www.sookenewsmirror.com
Delivery Methods: Mail`Newsstand`Carrier
Areas Served - City/County or Portion Thereof, or Zip codes: District of Sooke
Commercial printers?: N
Published: Wed
Avg Paid Circ: 63
Avg Free Circ: 5713
Audit By: AAM
Audit Date: 31.03.2019
Personnel: Rod Sluggett (publisher); Laird Kevin (editor); Kelvin Phair (Advertising Sales)
Parent company (for newspapers): Black Press Group Ltd.

SOREL

PUBLICATION NAME

Journal La Voix
Street Address: 58 Charlotte St. ,
Province: QC
Postal: J3P 1G3
Country: Canada

Mailing address: 58 Charlotte St.
Mailing city: Sorel
Province: QC
Postal: J3P 1G3
General Phone: (450) 743-8466
General Fax: (450) 742-8567
General/National Adv. E-mail: info@journallavoix.net
Display Adv. E-mail: publicite@journallavoix.net
Editorial e-mail: redaction@journallavoix.net
Primary Website: www.journallavoix.net; monteregieweb.com
Year Established: 1960
Areas Served - City/County or Portion Thereof, or Zip codes: Canada
Mechanical specifications: Type page 15 x 17.
Published: Fri
Avg Free Circ: 29562
Audit By: CCAB
Audit Date: 31.03.2014
Personnel: Parise Bergeron (Adv. Rep.); Anne-Marie Nadeau (Adv. Rep.); Joey Olivier (Ed.); Johanne Berthiaume (Ed.)
Parent company (for newspapers): Les Hebdos Monteregiens-OOB

SOREL-TRACY

PUBLICATION NAME

Les 2 Rives
Street Address: 77 George St. ,
Province: QC
Postal: J3P 1C2
Country: Canada
Mailing address: 77 George St.
Mailing city: Sorel-Tracy
Province: QC
Postal: J3P 1C2
General Phone: (450) 742-9408
General Fax: (450) 742-2493
General/National Adv. E-mail: pco2rives@biz.videotran.ca; info@les2rives.com
Primary Website: www.les2rives.com
Areas Served - City/County or Portion Thereof, or Zip codes: Canada
Commercial printers?: Y
Mechanical specifications: Type page 10 1/4 x 17.
Published: Tues
Avg Paid Circ: 1
Avg Free Circ: 29562
Audit By: CCAB
Audit Date: 31.03.2014
Personnel: Marcel Rainville (Gen. Mgr.); Louise Gregoire Racicot (Ed.)
Parent company (for newspapers): Les Hebdos Monteregiens-OOB

PUBLICATION NAME

Sorel-tracy Express
Street Address: 100 Rue Plante ,
Province: QC
Postal: J3P 7P5
Country: Canada
Mailing address: 100 Rue Plante
Mailing city: Sorel-Tracy
Province: QC
Postal: J3P 7P5
General Phone: (450) 746-0886
General Fax: (450) 746-0801
Advertising Phone: (450) 746-0886
Advertising Fax: (450) 746-0801
Editorial Phone: (450) 746-0886
Editorial Fax: (450) 746-0801
General/National Adv. E-mail: sorel-tracyexpress@tc.tc
Display Adv. E-mail: sorel-tracyexpress@tc.tc
Editorial e-mail: sorel-tracyexpress@tc.tc
Primary Website: www.sorel-tracyexpress.ca
Delivery Methods: Mail`Racks
Areas Served - City/County or Portion Thereof, or Zip codes: Canada
Published: Tues
Avg Free Circ: 31018
Audit By: CCAB
Audit Date: 31.03.2014
Personnel: Claude Poulin (Pres.)

Community Newspapers in Canada

SOURIS

PUBLICATION NAME

Souris Plaindealer
Street Address: 53 Crescent Ave. W.,
Province: MB
Postal: R0K 2C0
Country: Canada
Mailing address: PO Box 488
Mailing city: Souris
Province: MB
Postal: R0K 2C0
General Phone: (204) 483-2070
General Fax: (204) 522-3648
General/National Adv. E-mail: spdealer@mts.net
Editorial e-mail: spdealer@mts.net
Primary Website: http://www.sourisplaindealer.ca/
Areas Served - City/County or Portion Thereof, or Zip codes: Canada
Mechanical specifications: Type page 10 x 14; E - 6 cols, 1 7/12, 1/6 between; A - 6 cols, 1 7/12, 1/6 between; C - 6 cols, 1 7/12, 1/6 between.
Published: Fri
Avg Free Circ: 54
Audit By: VAC
Audit Date: 31.12.2015
Personnel: Darcy Semeschuk (Office Mgr.); Patti Lewis (Pub/Ed.)
Parent company (for newspapers): Glacier Media Group

SPRINGDALE

PUBLICATION NAME

The Nor'wester
Street Address: Po Box 28,
Province: NL
Postal: A0J 1T0
Country: Canada
Mailing address: PO Box 28
Mailing city: Springdale
Province: NL
Postal: A0J 1T0
General Phone: (709) 673-3721
General Fax: (709) 673-4171
Editorial e-mail: editor@thenorwester.ca
Primary Website: www.thenorwester.ca
Areas Served - City/County or Portion Thereof, or Zip codes: Canada
Published: Thur
Avg Paid Circ: 1730
Avg Free Circ: 0
Audit By: VAC
Audit Date: 31.12.2015
Personnel: Rudy Norman (Ed.)
Parent company (for newspapers): Transcontinental Media

SPRUCE GROVE

PUBLICATION NAME

The Grove Examiner
Street Address: 420 King Street, #1
Province: AB
Postal: T7X 3B4
Country: Canada
General Phone: (780) 962-4257
General Fax: (780) 962-0658
Advertising Phone: (877) 786-8227
Display Adv. E-mail: matthew.maceachen@sunmedia.ca
Classified Adv. e-mail: matthew.maceachen@sunmedia.ca
Editorial e-mail: carsonm@bowesnet.com
Primary Website: www.sprucegroveexaminer.com
Year Established: 1970
Areas Served - City/County or Portion Thereof, or Zip codes: Canada
Own Printing Facility?: Y
Published: Fri
Avg Paid Circ: 1273
Avg Free Circ: 11471
Audit By: VAC
Audit Date: 31.12.2015
Personnel: Mary Ann Kostiuk (Reg. Sales Mgr.);
Janet Stace (Prodn. Mgr.); Pamela Allain (Pub.); Matthew MacEachen (Adv. Mgr.); Carson Mills (Ed.)
Parent company (for newspapers): Postmedia Network Inc.

PUBLICATION NAME

The Stony Plain Reporter
Street Address: 420 King Street, #1
Province: AB
Postal: T7X 3B4
Country: Canada
General Phone: (780) 962-4257
General Fax: (780) 962-0658
Advertising Phone: (877) 786-8227
General/National Adv. E-mail: ex.repoffice1@bowesnet.com
Display Adv. E-mail: matthew.maceachen@sunmedia.ca
Classified Adv. e-mail: matthew.maceachen@sunmedia.ca
Editorial e-mail: thomas.miller@sunmedia.ca
Primary Website: www.stonyplainreporter.com
Year Established: 1945
Areas Served - City/County or Portion Thereof, or Zip codes: Canada
Mechanical specifications: Type page 10 1/4 x 15 3/4; E - 6 cols, 1 7/12, between; A - 6 cols, 1 7/12, between; C - 6 cols, 1 7/12, between.
Published: Fri
Avg Paid Circ: 1643
Avg Free Circ: 10513
Audit By: VAC
Audit Date: 31.12.2015
Personnel: Mary-Ann Kostiuk (Circ. Mgr.); Carson Mills (Ed.); Jim Myers (Prodn. Mgr.); Pamela Allain (Pub.); Thomas Miller (CARDonline(10/31/14))
Parent company (for newspapers): Postmedia Network Inc.

SQUAMISH

PUBLICATION NAME

Squamish Chief
Street Address: 38117 Second Avenue,
Province: BC
Postal: V8B 0B9
Country: Canada
Mailing address: PO BOX 3500
Mailing city: Squamish
Province: BC
Postal: V8B 0B9
General Phone: (604) 892-9161
General Fax: (604) 892-8483
Display Adv. E-mail: ads@squamishchief.com
Classified Adv. e-mail: jgibson@squamishchief.com
Editorial e-mail: michaela@squamishchief.com
Primary Website: www.squamishchief.com
Areas Served - City/County or Portion Thereof, or Zip codes: Squamish
Published: Thur
Avg Free Circ: 794
Audit By: VAC
Audit Date: 30.04.2016
Personnel: Darren Roberts (Pub); Michaela Garstin (Ed); Tina Pisch (Mktg Coord.); Jennifer Gibson (Sales & Mktg. Mgr); Denise Conway (Circ. Mgr.)
Parent company (for newspapers): Glacier Media Group

ST MARYS

PUBLICATION NAME

St. Mary's Journal Argus
Street Address: 11 Wellington St. N.,
Province: ON
Postal: N4X 1B7
Country: Canada
Mailing address: PO Box 103
Mailing city: St Marys
Province: ON
Postal: N4X 1B7
General Phone: (519) 284-2440
General Fax: (519) 284-3650
General/National Adv. E-mail: drowe@southwesternontario.ca
Display Adv. E-mail: ksteven@stmarys.com
Classified Adv. e-mail: csmith@stmarys.com
Editorial e-mail: sslater@stmarys.com
Primary Website: www.southwesternontario.ca
Delivery Methods: Mail
Areas Served - City/County or Portion Thereof, or Zip codes: Canada
Published: Wed
Avg Paid Circ: 1354
Avg Free Circ: 110
Audit By: CMCA
Audit Date: 31.03.2016
Personnel: Anita McDonald (Business Manager); Stevens Kara (Sales Supervisor); Colleen Smith (Advertising/Circulation)
Parent company (for newspapers): Metroland Media Group Ltd.; Torstar

ST. ALBERT

PUBLICATION NAME

St. Albert Gazette
Street Address: 340 Carelton Drive,
Province: AB
Postal: T8N 7L3
Country: Canada
Mailing address: PO Box 263
Mailing city: St. Albert
Province: AB
Postal: T8N 1N3
General Phone: (780) 460-5500
General Fax: (780) 460-8220
Editorial Phone: (780) 460-5510
General/National Adv. E-mail: gazette@stalbert.greatwest.ca
Display Adv. E-mail: advertising@stalbert.greatwest.ca
Editorial e-mail: cmartindale@stalbert.greatwest.ca
Primary Website: www.stalbertgazette.com
Year Established: 1961
Delivery Methods: Mail`Newsstand`Carrier`Racks
Areas Served - City/County or Portion Thereof, or Zip codes: Canada
Own Printing Facility?: Y
Commercial printers?: Y
Mechanical specifications: Type page 9.45" x 15"; E - 6 cols, 2, 1/6 between; A - 6 cols, 2, 1/6 between; C - 7 cols, 1 3/8, 1/6 between.
Published: Wed`Sat
Avg Paid Circ: 1652
Avg Free Circ: 24879
Audit By: VAC
Audit Date: 30.06.2016
Personnel: Al Glaser (Adv. Mgr.); Brian Bachynski (Pub); Carolyn Martindale (Ed)
Parent company (for newspapers): Glacier Media Group; Great West Newspapers LP

ST. JOHN'S

PUBLICATION NAME

Le Gaboteur
Street Address: 65 Ridge Road,
Province: NL
Postal: A1B 4P5
Country: Canada
Mailing address: 250 - 65 Ridge Road
Mailing city: St. John's
Province: NL
Postal: A1B 4P5
General Phone: (709) 753-9585
Display Adv. E-mail: annonces@gaboteur.ca
Editorial e-mail: redaction@gaboteur.ca
Primary Website: www.gaboteur.ca
Year Established: 1984
Delivery Methods: Mail
Areas Served - City/County or Portion Thereof, or Zip codes: Canada
Published: Bi-Mthly
Avg Paid Circ: 850
Avg Free Circ: 0
Audit By: CMCA
Audit Date: 31.03.2013
Personnel: Jacinthe Tremblay (Dir/Ed)

STANSTEAD

PUBLICATION NAME

The Stanstead Journal
Street Address: 620 Dufferin,
Province: QC
Postal: J0B 3E0
Country: Canada
Mailing address: 620 Dufferin
Mailing city: Stanstead
Province: QC
Postal: J0B 3E0
General Phone: (819) 876-7514
General/National Adv. E-mail: journal@stanstead-journal.com
Display Adv. E-mail: ads@stanstead-journal.com
Editorial e-mail: communique@stanstead-journal.com
Primary Website: www.stanstead-journal.com
Year Established: 1845
Delivery Methods: Mail`Newsstand`Carrier`Racks
Areas Served - City/County or Portion Thereof, or Zip codes: Memphremagog
Published: Wed
Avg Paid Circ: 1625
Audit By: AAM
Audit Date: 31.03.2015
Personnel: Jean-Yves Durocher (Sales Mgr.); Mylene Piche (Prodn. Mgr.)
Parent company (for newspapers): Stanstead Journal Publishing

STEINBACH

PUBLICATION NAME

The Carillon
Street Address: 377 Main St.,
Province: MB
Postal: R5G 1A5
Country: Canada
Mailing address: 377 Main St.
Mailing city: Steinbach
Province: MB
Postal: R5G 1A5
General Phone: (204) 326-3421
General Fax: (204) 326-4860
General/National Adv. E-mail: info@thecarillon.com
Display Adv. E-mail: ads@thecarillon.com
Classified Adv. e-mail: mgauthier@thecarillon.com
Editorial e-mail: gburr@thecarillon.com
Primary Website: www.thecarillon.com
Areas Served - City/County or Portion Thereof, or Zip codes: Canada
Own Printing Facility?: Y
Commercial printers?: Y
Mechanical specifications: Type page 11 1/2 x 17; E - 5 cols, 2 1/6, between; A - 5 cols, 2 1/6, between; C - 5 cols, 2 1/6, between.
Published: Thur
Avg Paid Circ: 1140
Avg Free Circ: 234
Audit By: VAC
Audit Date: 30.09.2016
Personnel: Laurie Finley (Pub/Gen. Mgr.); Grant Burr (Ed); Holly-Jaide Nickel (Circ Mgr.)

STEPHENVILLE

PUBLICATION NAME

The Georgian
Street Address: 43 Main St., 43 Main Street
Province: NL
Postal: A2N 2Z4
Country: Canada
Mailing address: PO Box 283
Mailing city: Stephenville
Province: NL
Postal: A2N 2Z4
General Phone: (709) 643-4531
General Fax: (709) 643-5041
Editorial e-mail: editor@thegeorgian.ca
Primary Website: www.thegeorgian.ca
Year Established: 1970
Delivery Methods:

STETTLER

PUBLICATION NAME

Stettler Independent
Street Address: 4810 50th St. ,
Province: AB
Postal: T0C 2L0
Country: Canada
Mailing address: P.O. Box 310
Mailing city: Stettler
Province: AB
Postal: T0C 2L0
General Phone: (403) 742-2395
General Fax: (403) 742-8050
Editorial Phone: (403) 740-4431
General/National Adv. E-mail: stetnews@telusplanet.net
Display Adv. E-mail: nicole.stratulate@stettlerindependent.com
Classified Adv. e-mail: ddoell@stettlerindependent.com
Editorial e-mail: editor@stettlerindependent.com
Primary Website: www.stettlerindependent.com
Areas Served - City/County or Portion Thereof, or Zip codes: Town of Stettler, County of Stettler, Big Valley, Erskine, Donalda, Gadsby, Botha, Buffalo Lake,
Own Printing Facility?: Y
Published: Thur
Avg Paid Circ: 34
Avg Free Circ: 33
Audit By: VAC
Audit Date: 20.03.2017
Personnel: Debbie Doell (Ad control); Karen Fischer (Graphic artist); Landin Chambers (reporter)
Parent company (for newspapers): Black Press Group Ltd.

STONEWALL

PUBLICATION NAME

The Interlake Spectator
Street Address: 3411 3rd Avenue South , Unit 3
Province: MB
Postal: R0C 2Z0
Country: Canada
Mailing address: PO Box 190
Mailing city: Stonewall
Province: MB
Postal: R0C 2Z0
General Phone: (204) 467-2421
General Fax: (204) 467-5967
General/National Adv. E-mail: ispec@mts.net
Display Adv. E-mail: jbilsky@postmedia.com
Editorial e-mail: bjones@postmedia.com
Primary Website: http://www.interlaketoday.ca/interlakespectator
Areas Served - City/County or Portion Thereof, or Zip codes: Stonewall
Published: Thur
Avg Paid Circ: 1520
Avg Free Circ: 10780
Audit By: VAC
Audit Date: 30.06.2016
Personnel: Jenifer Bilsky (Adv Dir.); Brook Jones (Ed)
Parent company (for newspapers): Postmedia Network Inc.; Quebecor Communications, Inc.

PUBLICATION NAME

The Stonewall Argus & Teulon Times
Street Address: 3411 3rd Avenue South ,
Province: MB
Postal: R0C 2Z0
Country: Canada
Mailing address: PO Box 190
Mailing city: Stonewall
Province: MB
Postal: R0C 2Z0
General Phone: (204) 467-2421
General Fax: (204) 467-5967
General/National Adv. E-mail: news@stonewallteulontribune.ca
Display Adv. E-mail: jbilsky@postmedia.com
Editorial e-mail: bjones@postmedia.com
Primary Website: http://www.interlaketoday.ca/stonewallargusteulontimes
Areas Served - City/County or Portion Thereof, or Zip codes: Canada
Own Printing Facility?: Y
Commercial printers?: Y
Mechanical specifications: Type page 10 1/8 x 14; E - 6 cols, 1 7/12, 1/6 between; A - 6 cols, 1 7/12, 1/6 between; C - 6 cols, 1 7/12, 1/6 between.
Published: Thur
Avg Paid Circ: 1219
Avg Free Circ: 6467
Audit By: VAC
Audit Date: 30.06.2016
Personnel: Brook Jones (Ed); Jenifer Bilsky (Adv Dir)
Parent company (for newspapers): Postmedia Network Inc.; Quebecor Communications, Inc.

STONEY CREEK

PUBLICATION NAME

Ancaster News
Street Address: 333 Arvin Ave. ,
Province: ON
Postal: L8E 2M6
Country: Canada
Mailing address: 333 Arvin Ave.
Mailing city: Stoney Creek
Province: ON
Postal: L8E 2M6
General Phone: (905) 523-5800
General Fax: (905) 664-3319
General/National Adv. E-mail: editor@ancasternews.com
Display Adv. E-mail: mtherrien@metroland.com
Classified Adv. e-mail: classified@thespec.com
Editorial e-mail: mpearson@hamiltonnews.com
Primary Website: www.ancasternews.com
Year Established: 1967
Delivery Methods: Carrier
Areas Served - City/County or Portion Thereof, or Zip codes: Ancaster
Own Printing Facility?: Y
Mechanical specifications: Full page is 10 columns x 161 agate lines; same as 10.375" x 11.5"
Published: Thur
Avg Paid Circ: 4
Avg Free Circ: 13355
Audit By: CMCA
Audit Date: 21.06.2018
Personnel: Kelly Montague (Pub.); Jason Pehora (Gen. Mgr.); Lorna Lester (Office Mgr.); Michael Pearson (News Ed.); Gordon Cameron (Mng Ed); Melinda Therrien (Dir of Advt)
Parent company (for newspapers): Metroland Media Group Ltd.; Torstar

PUBLICATION NAME

Dundas Star News
Street Address: 333 Arvin Ave. ,
Province: ON
Postal: L8E 2M6
Country: Canada
Mailing address: 333 Arvin Ave.
Mailing city: Stoney Creek
Province: ON
Postal: L8E 2M6
General Phone: (905) 664-8800
General Fax: (905) 664-3319
General/National Adv. E-mail: editor@dundasstarnews.com
Display Adv. E-mail: mtherrien@metroland.com
Classified Adv. e-mail: classified@thespec.com
Editorial e-mail: editor@dundasstarnews.com
Primary Website: www.dundasstarnews.com
Year Established: 1883
Delivery Methods: Carrier
Areas Served - City/County or Portion Thereof, or Zip codes: Dundas & Westdale L8S (Hamilton)
Own Printing Facility?: Y
Commercial printers?: Y
Mechanical specifications: 10 columns x 161 agate lines; same as 10.375" x 11.5"
Published: Thur
Avg Paid Circ: 4
Avg Free Circ: 14302
Audit By: CMCA
Audit Date: 21.06.2018
Personnel: Montague Kelly (Pub.); Jason Pehora (Gen. Mgr.); Lorna Lester (Office Mgr.); Gord Bowes (Ed); Mike Boyle (Produ Mgr.); Gordon Cameron (Mng Ed); Holly Christofilopoulos (Dir of Advt)
Parent company (for newspapers): Metroland Media Group Ltd.; Torstar

PUBLICATION NAME

Hamilton Mountain News
Street Address: 333 Arvin Ave. ,
Province: ON
Postal: L8E 2M6
Country: Canada
Mailing address: 333 Arvin Ave.
Mailing city: Stoney Creek
Province: ON
Postal: L8E 2M6
General Phone: (905) 664-8800
General Fax: (905) 664-3319
General/National Adv. E-mail: editor@hamiltonmountainnews.com
Display Adv. E-mail: mtherrien@metroland.com
Classified Adv. e-mail: classified@thespec.com
Editorial e-mail: gordbowes@hamiltonnews.com
Primary Website: www.hamiltonnews.com
Year Established: 1968
Delivery Methods: Carrier
Areas Served - City/County or Portion Thereof, or Zip codes: Hamilton
Own Printing Facility?: N
Commercial printers?: Y
Mechanical specifications: Full page is 10 columns x 161 agate lines; same as 10.375" x 11.5"
Published: Thur
Avg Paid Circ: 5
Avg Free Circ: 49048
Audit By: CMCA
Audit Date: 21.06.2018
Personnel: Jason Pehora (Gen. Mgr.); Gordon Cameron (Managing Editor); Holly Christofilopoulos (Director of Advertising)
Parent company (for newspapers): Metroland Media Group Ltd.; Torstar Corp.

PUBLICATION NAME

Stoney Creek News
Street Address: 333 Arvin Ave. ,
Province: ON
Postal: L8E 2M6
Country: Canada
Mailing address: 333 Arvin Ave.
Mailing city: Stoney Creek
Province: ON
Postal: L8E 2M6
General Phone: (905) 664-8800
General Fax: (905) 664-3319
Display Adv. E-mail: editor@hamiltonmountainnews.com
Classified Adv. e-mail: classified@thespec.com
Editorial e-mail: editor@stoneycreeknews.com
Primary Website: www.stoneycreeknews.com
Year Established: 1948
Delivery Methods: Carrier
Areas Served - City/County or Portion Thereof, or Zip codes: Stoney Creek
Own Printing Facility?: Y
Commercial printers?: Y
Mechanical specifications: Full page is 10 columns x 161 agate lines; same as 10.375" x 11.5"
Published: Thur
Avg Paid Circ: 4
Avg Free Circ: 30178
Audit By: CMCA
Audit Date: 21.06.2018
Personnel: Kelly Montague (Pub.); Jason Pehora (Gen. Mgr.); Michael Pearson (Ed.); Gordon Cameron (Mng Ed.); Rhonda Ridgway (Produ Mgr.); Melinda Therrien (Adv. Dir.)
Parent company (for newspapers): Metroland Media Group Ltd.

STRATFORD

PUBLICATION NAME

Stratford Gazette
Street Address: 10 Downie St. Unit 207 ,
Province: ON
Postal: N5A 7K4
Country: Canada
Mailing address: 10 Downie St. Unit 207
Mailing city: Stratford
Province: ON
Postal: N5A 7K4
General Phone: (519) 271-8002
General Fax: (519) 271-5636
General/National Adv. E-mail: admin@stratfordgazette.com
Display Adv. E-mail: jhaefling@stratfordgazette.com
Classified Adv. e-mail: lcarter@stratfordgazette.com
Editorial e-mail: news@stratfordgazette.com
Primary Website: www.southwesternontario.ca
Delivery Methods: Mail`Carrier
Areas Served - City/County or Portion Thereof, or Zip codes: Canada
Published: Thur
Avg Free Circ: 19855
Audit By: CMCA
Audit Date: 29.02.2016
Personnel: Laura Carter (Front Office/Distribution); Julie Haefling (Sales Supervisor); Anita McDonald (Business Manager)
Parent company (for newspapers): Metroland Media Group Ltd.

STRATHMORE

PUBLICATION NAME

Strathmore Standard
Street Address: Unit A-510 Hwy 1 ,
Province: AB
Postal: T1P 1M6
Country: Canada
Mailing address: Unit A-510 Hwy 1
Mailing city: Strathmore
Province: AB
Postal: T1P 1M6
General Phone: (403) 934-3021
General Fax: (403) 934-5011
Display Adv. E-mail: rmackintosh@postmedia.com
Editorial e-mail: josh.chalmers@sunmedia.ca
Primary Website: www.strathmorestandard.com
Year Established: 1909
Delivery Methods: Mail`Newsstand`Carrier`Racks
Areas Served - City/County or Portion Thereof, or Zip codes: Canada
Own Printing Facility?: Y
Commercial printers?: N
Published: Wed
Avg Paid Circ: 3679
Avg Free Circ: 10858
Audit By: VAC
Audit Date: 31.12.2015
Personnel: Josh Chalmers (Ed); Roxanne MacKintosh (Adv. Dir)
Parent company (for newspapers): Postmedia Network Inc.; Quebecor Communications, Inc.

(top-left partial entry:)
Mail`Newsstand`Carrier`Racks
Areas Served - City/County or Portion Thereof, or Zip codes: Canada
Own Printing Facility?: Y
Commercial printers?: Y
Published: Mon
Avg Paid Circ: 1152
Avg Free Circ: 0
Audit By: CMCA
Audit Date: 30.06.2013
Personnel: Christopher Vaughan (Ed.)
Parent company (for newspapers): Transcontinental Media

Community Newspapers in Canada

III-581

PUBLICATION NAME

Strathmore Times
Street Address: 123 2nd Avenue ,
Province: AB
Postal: T1P 1K1
Country: Canada
Mailing address: Box 2005
Mailing city: Strathmore
Province: AB
Postal: T1K 1K1
General Phone: (403) 934-5589
General Fax: (403) 934-5546
General/National Adv. E-mail: info@strathmoretimes.com
Display Adv. E-mail: rose@strathmoretimes.com
Classified Adv. e-mail: classifieds@strathmoretimes.com
Editorial e-mail: miriam@strathmoretimes.com
Primary Website: www.strathmoretimes.com
Year Established: 2009
Delivery Methods: Mail
Areas Served - City/County or Portion Thereof, or Zip codes: Strathmore and all of Wheatland County
Published: Fri
Avg Free Circ: 11001
Audit By: Sworn/Estimate/Non-Audited
Audit Date: 12.07.2019
Personnel: Mario Prusina (Pub/Ed); Rose Hamrlik (Adv Mgr); Miriam Ostermann (Associate Editor)

STRATHROY

PUBLICATION NAME

The Strathroy Age Dispatch
Street Address: 73 Front Street West ,
Province: ON
Postal: N7G 1X6
Country: Canada
Mailing address: 73 Front Street West
Mailing city: Strathroy
Province: ON
Postal: N7G 1X6
General Phone: (519) 245-2370
General Fax: (519) 245-1647
General/National Adv. E-mail: news@strathroyonline.com
Primary Website: www.strathroyagedispatch.com
Year Established: 1861
Delivery Methods: Mail`Carrier`Racks
Areas Served - City/County or Portion Thereof, or Zip codes: N7G, NOM, NON, NOL
Own Printing Facility?: Y
Published: Thur
Avg Paid Circ: 1480
Audit By: CMCA
Audit Date: 31.01.2014
Personnel: Bev Ponton (Pub.); Don Biggs (Reg. Ed.)
Parent company (for newspapers): Postmedia Network Inc.; Quebecor Communications, Inc.

SUDBURY

PUBLICATION NAME

Journal Le Voyageur
Street Address: 336 Rue Pine , Suite 302
Province: ON
Postal: P3C 1X8
Country: Canada
Mailing address: 336 rue Pine
Mailing city: Sudbury
Province: ON
Postal: P3C 1X8
General Phone: (705) 673-3377
General Fax: (705) 673-5854
General/National Adv. E-mail: administration@levoyageur.ca
Primary Website: www.lavoixdunord.ca
Delivery Methods: Mail`Carrier
Areas Served - City/County or Portion Thereof, or Zip codes: Canada
Own Printing Facility?: Y
Mechanical specifications: Type page 10 1/4 x 14; E - 5 cols, 2, 1/6 between; A - 10 cols, 1/6 between; C - 10 cols, 1/6 between.
Published: Wed
Avg Paid Circ: 7157
Avg Free Circ: 1342
Audit By: CMCA
Audit Date: 28.02.2013
Personnel: Patrick Breton (Ed. in Chief)

PUBLICATION NAME

Northern Life
Street Address: 158 Elgin St. ,
Province: ON
Postal: P3E 3N5
Country: Canada
Mailing address: 158 Flgin St.
Mailing city: Sudbury
Province: ON
Postal: P3E 3N5
General Phone: (705) 673-5667
General Fax: (705) 673-4652
Advertising Phone: (705) 673-5667 Ext. 313
Editorial Phone: (705) 673-5667 Ext. 337
Display Adv. E-mail: classify@northernlife.ca
Editorial e-mail: mgentili@sudbury.com
Primary Website: sudbury.com
Year Established: 1970
Areas Served - City/County or Portion Thereof, or Zip codes: Canada
Own Printing Facility?: Y
Mechanical specifications: Type page 10 3/8 x 14; E - 9 cols, between; A - 9 cols, between; C - 9 cols, between.
Published: Tues`Thur
Avg Paid Circ: 5444
Avg Free Circ: 35536
Audit By: CCAB
Audit Date: 30.09.2017
Personnel: Abbas Homayed (Pub.); Michael R. Atkins (Pres.); Mark Gentili (Managing Ed.)

SUMMERLAND

PUBLICATION NAME

Summerland Review
Street Address: 13226 Victoria Rd. N. ,
Province: BC
Postal: V0H 1Z0
Country: Canada
Mailing address: PO Box 309
Mailing city: Summerland
Province: BC
Postal: V0H 1Z0
General Phone: (250) 494-5406
General Fax: (250) 494-5453
General/National Adv. E-mail: news@summerlandreview.com
Display Adv. E-mail: rob@summerlandreview.com
Classified Adv. e-mail: class@summerlandreview.com
Editorial e-mail: news@summerlandreview.com
Primary Website: www.summerlandreview.com
Areas Served - City/County or Portion Thereof, or Zip codes: Summerland
Own Printing Facility?: Y
Published: Thur
Avg Paid Circ: 52
Avg Free Circ: 21
Audit By: VAC
Audit Date: 30.06.2016
Personnel: John Arendt (Ed.); Shannon Simpson (Pub); Rob Murphy (Sales Mgr); Nan Cogbill (Class./Circ Mgr)
Parent company (for newspapers): Black Press Group Ltd.

SUMMERSIDE

PUBLICATION NAME

La Voix Acadienne
Street Address: 5, Ave Maris Stella ,
Province: PE
Postal: C1N 6M9
Country: Canada
Mailing address: 5, ave Maris Stella
Mailing city: Summerside
Province: PE
Postal: C1N 6M9
General Phone: (902) 436-6005
General Fax: (902) 888-3976
Display Adv. E-mail: pub@lavoixacadienne.com
Editorial e-mail: texte@lavoixacadienne.com
Primary Website: www.lavoixacadienne.com
Year Established: 1976
Areas Served - City/County or Portion Thereof, or Zip codes: all provinces of Canada
Commercial printers?: Y
Mechanical specifications: Type page 10 1/4 x 12 1/2; E - 5 cols, between; A - 5 cols, between.
Published: Wed
Avg Paid Circ: 1517
Avg Free Circ: 20
Audit By: ODC
Audit Date: 13.12.2017
Personnel: Marcia Enman (Dir. Gen.); Jacinthe Laforest (Ed.)

SUNDRE

PUBLICATION NAME

Sundre Round-up
Street Address: 103 2nd St. Nw ,
Province: AB
Postal: T0M 1X0
Country: Canada
Mailing address: PO Box 599
Mailing city: Sundre
Province: AB
Postal: T0M 1X0
General Phone: (403) 638-3577
General Fax: (403) 638-3077
General/National Adv. E-mail: roundup@sundre.greatwest.ca
Display Adv. E-mail: kcomfort@sundre.greatwest.ca
Editorial e-mail: dsingleton@olds.greatwest.ca
Primary Website: www.sundreroundup.ca
Year Established: 1961
Areas Served - City/County or Portion Thereof, or Zip codes: Canada
Own Printing Facility?: Y
Mechanical specifications: Type page 10 1/4 x 14 1/2; E - 6 cols, 1 11/20, between; A - 6 cols, 1 11/20, between; C - 6 cols, 1 11/20, between.
Published: Tues
Avg Paid Circ: 879
Avg Free Circ: 0
Audit By: VAC
Audit Date: 30.06.2016
Personnel: Ray Lachambre (Pub.); Dan Singleton (Ed); Kim Comfort (Sales Mgr)
Parent company (for newspapers): Glacier Media Group; Great West Newspapers LP

SURREY

PUBLICATION NAME

Cloverdale Reporter
Street Address: 17586 56a Ave. ,
Province: BC
Postal: V3S 1G3
Country: Canada
Mailing address: 17586 56A Ave.
Mailing city: Surrey
Province: BC
Postal: V3S 1G3
General Phone: (604) 575-2400
Advertising Phone: (604) 575-2423
Display Adv. E-mail: cynthia.dunsmore@cloverdalereporter.com
Classified Adv. e-mail: bcclassifieds@blackpress.com
Editorial e-mail: editor@cloverdalereporter.com
Primary Website: www.cloverdalereporter.com
Year Established: 1996
Delivery Methods: Carrier`Racks
Areas Served - City/County or Portion Thereof, or Zip codes: Surrey, B.C.
Published: Wed
Avg Free Circ: 16159
Audit By: CMCA
Audit Date: 31.03.2018
Personnel: Cynthia Dunsmore (Sales Representative); Sam Anderson (Ed.); Grace Kennedy (Reporter)
Parent company (for newspapers): Black Press Group Ltd.

PUBLICATION NAME

Surrey Now-leader
Street Address: 102-5460 152nd St. ,
Province: BC
Postal: V3S 5J9
Country: Canada
Mailing address: 102-5460 152nd St.
Mailing city: Surrey
Province: BC
Postal: V3S 5J9
General Phone: (604) 572-0064
General Fax: (604) 575-2544
Advertising Phone: (604) 572-0064
Advertising Fax: (604)572-7948
Editorial Phone: (604)543-5816
General/National Adv. E-mail: sueb@blackpress.ca
Display Adv. E-mail: sueb@blackpress.ca
Classified Adv. e-mail: sueb@blackpress.ca
Editorial e-mail: beau.simpson@surreynowleader.com
Primary Website: www.surreynowleader.com
Delivery Methods: Carrier
Areas Served - City/County or Portion Thereof, or Zip codes: Canada
Own Printing Facility?: Y
Commercial printers?: Y
Published: Wed`Fri
Avg Free Circ: 54521
Audit By: AAM
Audit Date: 31.03.2019
Parent company (for newspapers): Black Press Group Ltd.

PUBLICATION NAME

The Now Newspaper
Street Address: 102 - 5460 152 St ,
Province: BC
Postal: V3S 5J9
Country: Canada
Mailing address: 102 - 5460 152 St
Mailing city: Surrey
Province: BC
Postal: V3S 5J9
General Phone: (604) 572-0064
General Fax: (604) 572-6438
Display Adv. E-mail: dal.hothi@thenownewspaper.com
Classified Adv. e-mail: sarah.sigurdswon@thenownewspaper.com
Editorial e-mail: bsimpson@thenownewspaper.com
Primary Website: www.thenownewspaper.com
Year Established: 1984
Delivery Methods: Carrier
Areas Served - City/County or Portion Thereof, or Zip codes: Canada
Commercial printers?: Y
Published: Tues`Thur
Avg Free Circ: 177757
Audit By: CCAB
Audit Date: 31.03.2014
Personnel: Beau Simpson (Ed); Dwayne Weidendorf (Pub); Sarah Sigurdson (Ad Control/Admin); Dal Hothi (Sales Mgr)

PUBLICATION NAME

The Peace Arch News
Street Address: 200-2411 160 Street ,
Province: BC
Postal: V3S 0C8
Country: Canada
Mailing address: 200-2411 160 Street
Mailing city: Surrey
Province: BC
Postal: V3S 0C8
General Phone: (604) 531-1711
General Fax: (604) 531-7977
Editorial e-mail: editorial@peacearchnews.com
Primary Website: www.peacearchnews.com

Delivery Methods: Carrier
Areas Served - City/County or Portion Thereof, or Zip codes: Canada
Own Printing Facility?: Y
Mechanical specifications: Type page 10 1/4 x 12 1/2; E - 6 cols, between; A - 6 cols, between; C - 6 cols, between.
Published: Wed`Fri
Avg Free Circ: 37090
Audit By: AAM
Audit Date: 31.03.2019
Personnel: Lance Peverley (Ed.)
Parent company (for newspapers): Black Press Group Ltd.

SUSSEX

PUBLICATION NAME

The Kings County Record
Street Address: 593 Main St. ,
Province: NB
Postal: E4E 7H5
Country: Canada
Mailing address: 593 Main St.
Mailing city: Sussex
Province: NB
Postal: E4E 7H5
General Phone: (506) 433-1070
General Fax: (506) 432-3532
General/National Adv. E-mail: news@kingcorecord.com
Editorial e-mail: craig.victoria@kingscorecord.com
Primary Website: https://www.telegraphjournal.com/kings-county-record/
Areas Served - City/County or Portion Thereof, or Zip codes: Sussex
Mechanical specifications: Type page 13 x 21 1/2; E - 6 cols, 2 1/16, 3/16 between; A - 6 cols, 2 1/16, 3/16 between; C - 8 cols, 1 1/2, 3/16 between.
Published: Tues
Avg Paid Circ: 0
Avg Free Circ: 2
Audit By: VAC
Audit Date: 31.12.2015
Personnel: Victoria Craig (Pub./Ed); Teresa Perry (Circ. Mgr.)
Parent company (for newspapers): Brunswick News, Inc.

SWAN HILLS

PUBLICATION NAME

Grizzly Gazette
Street Address: 5435 Plaza Ave. ,
Province: AB
Postal: T0G 2C0
Country: Canada
Mailing address: PO Box 1000
Mailing city: Swan Hills
Province: AB
Postal: T0G 2C0
General Phone: (780) 333-2100
General Fax: (780) 333-2111
General/National Adv. E-mail: sgazett@telusplanet.net
Display Adv. E-mail: sgazette@telusplanet.net
Classified Adv. e-mail: sgazette@telusplanet.net
Editorial e-mail: sgazette@telusplanet.net
Primary Website: thegrizzlygazette.com
Year Established: 1977
Delivery Methods: Mail`Newsstand
Areas Served - City/County or Portion Thereof, or Zip codes: Canada
Own Printing Facility?: N
Commercial printers?: Y
Mechanical specifications: Type page 10 1/4 x 12 1/2; E - 6 cols, 1 9/16, 1/8 between; A - 6 cols, 1 9/16, 1/8 between.
Published: Tues
Avg Paid Circ: 394
Avg Free Circ: 135
Audit By: Sworn/Estimate/Non-Audited
Audit Date: 12.07.2019
Personnel: Phyllis Webster (Gen. Mgr.); Carol Webster (Ed.)

SWAN RIVER

PUBLICATION NAME

Swan Valley Star & Times
Street Address: 704 Main St. E. ,
Province: MB
Postal: R0L 1Z0
Country: Canada
Mailing address: PO Box 670
Mailing city: Swan River
Province: MB
Postal: R0L 1Z0
General Phone: (204) 734-3858
General Fax: (204) 734-4935
General/National Adv. E-mail: info@starandtimes.ca
Display Adv. E-mail: info@starandtimes.ca
Classified Adv. e-mail: info@starandtimes.ca
Editorial e-mail: editor@starandtimes.ca
Primary Website: www.starandtimes.ca
Year Established: 1900
Delivery Methods: Mail`Newsstand`Racks
Areas Served - City/County or Portion Thereof, or Zip codes: Canada
Own Printing Facility?: Y
Commercial printers?: Y
Mechanical specifications: Type page 12 x 21; E - 6 cols, 2, 1/6 between; A - 6 cols, between; C - 6 cols, between.
Published: Tues
Avg Paid Circ: 2700
Avg Free Circ: 0
Audit By: CMCA
Audit Date: 30.01.2017
Personnel: Brian T. Gilroy (Adv. Mgr., Publ., Gen. Mgr., Owner); Danielle Gordon-Broome (Ed.)

SWIFT CURRENT

PUBLICATION NAME

Prairie Post
Street Address: 600 Chaplin Street East ,
Province: SK
Postal: S9H 1J3
Country: Canada
Mailing address: 600 Chaplin Street East
Mailing city: Swift Current
Province: SK
Postal: S9H 1J3
General Phone: (306) 773-8260
General Fax: (306) 773-0504
Advertising Phone: (306) 773-8260
Advertising Fax: (306) 773-0504
Editorial Phone: (306) 773-8260
Editorial Fax: (306) 773-0504
General/National Adv. E-mail: ppost@prairiepost.com
Display Adv. E-mail: ktumback@prairiepost.com
Editorial e-mail: mliebenberg@prairiepost.com
Primary Website: http://www.prairiepost.com
Areas Served - City/County or Portion Thereof, or Zip codes: Canada
Published: Fri
Avg Free Circ: 17814
Audit By: CMCA
Audit Date: 31.03.2016
Personnel: Doug Evjen (Director of Sales and Marketing); Stacey Powell (Advertising)

PUBLICATION NAME

The Southwest Booster
Street Address: 30 4th Ave. Nw ,
Province: SK
Postal: S9H 3X4
Country: Canada
Mailing address: PO Box 1330
Mailing city: Swift Current
Province: SK
Postal: S9H 3X4
General Phone: (306) 773-9321
General Fax: (306) 773-9136
General/National Adv. E-mail: msoper@swbooster.com
Display Adv. E-mail: boosterads@swbooster.com
Primary Website: www.swbooster.com
Year Established: 1969
Areas Served - City/County or Portion Thereof, or Zip codes: Canada
Own Printing Facility?: Y
Commercial printers?: Y
Mechanical specifications: Type page 10 3/8 x 15 5/8; E - 6 cols, 1 15/16, 3/16 between; A - 6 cols, 1 15/16, 3/16 between; C - 6 cols, 1 15/16, 3/16 between.
Published: Thur
Avg Free Circ: 16985
Audit By: CMCA
Audit Date: 31.10.2016
Personnel: Bob Watson (Pub.); Mark Soper (Adv. Mgr.); Ken Mattice (Circ. Mgr.); Scott Anderson (Mng. Ed.); George Driscoll (Prodn. Mgr.)
Parent company (for newspapers): Transcontinental Media

SYLVAN LAKE

PUBLICATION NAME

Eckville Echo
Street Address: Suite 103 5020-50 A St. ,
Province: AB
Postal: T4S 1R2
Country: Canada
Mailing address: 5020-50 A St.,
Mailing city: Sylvan Lake
Province: AB
Postal: T4S 1R2
General Phone: (403) 887-2331
General Fax: (403) 887-2081
General/National Adv. E-mail: admin@sylvanlakenews.com
Display Adv. E-mail: admin@sylvanlakenews.com
Editorial e-mail: editor@sylvanlakenews.com
Year Established: 1997
Delivery Methods: Mail`Newsstand`Racks
Areas Served - City/County or Portion Thereof, or Zip codes: t4s, t4n, rr1, rr4
Commercial printers?: Y
Mechanical specifications: 10.12 " x 13"
Published: Thur
Avg Paid Circ: 1077
Avg Free Circ: 2466
Audit By: VAC
Audit Date: 30.09.2016
Personnel: Cheryl Hyvonen (Admin); Randy Holt (Pub); Jenna Swan (Ed)
Parent company (for newspapers): Black Press Group Ltd.

PUBLICATION NAME

Sylvan Lake News
Street Address: Suite 103, 5020-50a St., ,
Province: AB
Postal: T4S 1R2
Country: Canada
Mailing address: 5020-50A St.,
Mailing city: Sylvan Lake
Province: AB
Postal: T4S 1R2
General Phone: (403) 887-2331
General Fax: (403) 887-2081
Advertising Phone: (403) 887-2331
General/National Adv. E-mail: admin@sylvanlakenews.com
Display Adv. E-mail: sales@sylvanlakenews.com
Editorial e-mail: editor@sylvanlakenews.com
Primary Website: www.sylvanlakenews.com
Year Established: 1935
Delivery Methods: Mail`Carrier`Racks
Areas Served - City/County or Portion Thereof, or Zip codes: Canada
Own Printing Facility?: Y
Published: Thur
Avg Paid Circ: 377
Avg Free Circ: 7715
Audit By: VAC
Audit Date: 30.09.2016
Personnel: Cheryl Hyvonen (Admin); Randy Holt (Pub); Jenna Swan (Ed)
Parent company (for newspapers): Black Press Group Ltd.

TABER

PUBLICATION NAME

The Taber Times
Street Address: 4822-53 St. ,
Province: AB
Postal: T1G 1W4
Country: Canada
General Phone: (403) 223-2266
General Fax: (403) 223-1408
General/National Adv. E-mail: gsimmons@tabertimes.com
Display Adv. E-mail: chrissales@tabertimes.com
Primary Website: www.tabertimes.com
Year Established: 1907
Delivery Methods: Mail`Newsstand`Carrier
Areas Served - City/County or Portion Thereof, or Zip codes: Canada
Commercial printers?: Y
Mechanical specifications: Type page 11 1/2 x 21; E - 6 cols, 1 3/4, 1/4 between; A - 6 cols, 1 3/4, 1/4 between; C - 6 cols, 1 3/4, 1/4 between.
Published: Wed
Avg Paid Circ: 54
Avg Free Circ: 179
Audit By: VAC
Audit Date: 30.09.2016
Personnel: Valorie Wiebe (Pub.); Christine Mykytiw (Adv. Consult.); Erin Lickiss (Adv. Consult.); Greg Price (Ed.)

TATAMAGOUCHE

PUBLICATION NAME

The Light
Street Address: Po Box 1000 ,
Province: NS
Postal: B0K 1V0
Country: Canada
Mailing address: PO Box 1000
Mailing city: Tatamagouche
Province: NS
Postal: B0K 1V0
General Phone: (902) 956-8099
Display Adv. E-mail: kristinhirtle@tatamagouchelight.com
Editorial e-mail: raissatetanish@tatamagouchelight.com
Primary Website: www.tatamagouchelight.com
Areas Served - City/County or Portion Thereof, or Zip codes: Tatamagouche
Published: Wed
Avg Paid Circ: 2497
Avg Free Circ: 4378
Audit By: VAC
Audit Date: 30.06.2016
Personnel: Leith Orr (Pub)

TAVISTOCK

PUBLICATION NAME

Tavistock Gazette
Street Address: 119 Woodstock St. S. ,
Province: ON
Postal: N0B 2R0
Country: Canada
Mailing address: PO Box 70
Mailing city: Tavistock
Province: ON
Postal: N0B 2R0
General Phone: (519) 655-2341
Advertising Phone: (519) 655-2341
Editorial Phone: (519) 655-2341
General/National Adv. E-mail: gazette@tavistock.on.ca
Primary Website: www.tavistock.on.ca
Year Established: 1895
Delivery Methods: Mail`Newsstand
Areas Served - City/County or Portion Thereof, or Zip codes: Canada
Own Printing Facility?: Y
Commercial printers?: Y
Published: Wed
Avg Paid Circ: 1178
Avg Free Circ: 2
Audit By: CMCA
Audit Date: 31.10.2017

Community Newspapers in Canada   III-583

Personnel: Sheri Gladding (Circulation Manager); William J. Gladding (Ed.)

TECUMSEH

PUBLICATION NAME

Tecumseh Shoreline Week
Street Address: 1614 Lesperance Rd. ,
Province: ON
Postal: N8N 1X2
Country: Canada
Mailing address: 1614 Lesperance Rd.
Mailing city: Tecumseh
Province: ON
Postal: N8N 1X2
General Phone: (519) 735-2080
General Fax: (519) 735-2082
General/National Adv. E-mail: shorelineweek@canwest.com
Areas Served - City/County or Portion Thereof, or Zip codes: Canada
Mechanical specifications: Type page 10 1/4 x 15 1/2; E - 6 cols, 1 1/2, 3/16 between; A - 6 cols, 1 7/10, between; C - 7 cols, 1 3/8, 1/4 between.
Published: Fri
Avg Free Circ: 17312
Audit By: CMCA
Audit Date: 31.12.2017
Personnel: Dave Calibaba (Pub.); Rusty Wright (Mgr., Sales); William England (Ed.)
Parent company (for newspapers): Postmedia Network Inc.; CanWest MediaWorks Publications, Inc.

PUBLICATION NAME

The Lakeshore News
Street Address: 1116 Lesperance Road ,
Province: ON
Postal: N8N 1X2
Country: Canada
Mailing address: 1116 Lesperance Road
Mailing city: Tecumseh
Province: ON
Postal: N8N 1X2
General Phone: (519) 735-2080
General Fax: (519) 735-2082
General/National Adv. E-mail: lakeshore@canwest.com
Primary Website: www.facebook.com/Lakeshore-News-285820481600683/?ref=page_internal
Year Established: 1948
Areas Served - City/County or Portion Thereof, or Zip codes: Canada
Commercial printers?: Y
Mechanical specifications: Type page 10 1/4 x 15; E - 6 cols, 1 9/16, between; A - 6 cols, 1 9/16, between; C - 6 cols, 1 5/16, between.
Published: Thur
Avg Free Circ: 9389
Audit By: VAC
Audit Date: 31.12.2015
Personnel: Dave Calibaba (Gen. Mgr.); Bill Harris (Ed.)
Parent company (for newspapers): Postmedia Network Inc.; CanWest MediaWorks Publications, Inc.

TERRACE

PUBLICATION NAME

The Terrace Standard
Street Address: 3210 Clinton St ,
Province: BC
Postal: V8G5R2
Country: Canada
Mailing address: 3210 Clinton St.
Mailing city: Terrace
Province: BC
Postal: V8G 5R2
General Phone: (250) 638-7283
General Fax: (250) 638-8432
General/National Adv. E-mail: newsroom@terracestandard.com
Display Adv. E-mail: bwhusband@terracestandard.com
Classified Adv. e-mail: classifieds@terracestandard.com
Editorial e-mail: newsroom@terracestandard.com
Primary Website: www.terracestandard.com
Year Established: 1969
Areas Served - City/County or Portion Thereof, or Zip codes: Canada
Own Printing Facility?: Y
Mechanical specifications: Type page 12 1/16 x 21 1/2; E - 7 cols, 1 5/8, 1/8 between; A - 7 cols, 1 5/8, 1/8 between; C - 7 cols, 1 5/8, 1/8 between.
Published: Thur
Avg Free Circ: 7729
Audit By: VAC
Audit Date: 12.12.2017
Personnel: Quinn Bender (Editor); Bert Husband (Sales)
Parent company (for newspapers): Black Press Group Ltd.

TERRACE BAY

PUBLICATION NAME

Terrace Bay Schreiber News
Street Address: 25 Simcoe Plaza ,
Province: ON
Postal: P0T 2W0
Country: Canada
Mailing address: PO Box 130
Mailing city: Terrace Bay
Province: ON
Postal: P0T 2W0
General Phone: (807) 825-9425
General Fax: (807) 825-9458
General/National Adv. E-mail: nipigongazette@shaw.ca
Areas Served - City/County or Portion Thereof, or Zip codes: Canada
Own Printing Facility?: Y
Commercial printers?: Y
Published: Tues
Avg Paid Circ: 287
Avg Free Circ: 21
Audit By: CMCA
Audit Date: 30.06.2016
Personnel: Karen Schaeffer (Reporter/Photographer); Blair Oborne (Pub.); Pamela Behun (Edior)

TERREBONNE

PUBLICATION NAME

La Revue De Terrebonne
Street Address: 231 Sainte-marie St. ,
Province: QC
Postal: J6W 3E4
Country: Canada
Mailing address: larevue@larevue.qc.ca
Mailing city: Terrebonne
Province: QC
Postal: J6W 3E4
General Phone: (450) 964-4444
General Fax: (450) 471-1023
General/National Adv. E-mail: larevue@larevue.qc.ca
Display Adv. E-mail: ventes@larevue.qc.ca
Classified Adv. e-mail: petitesannonces@larevue.qc.ca
Editorial e-mail: redaction@larevue.qc.ca
Primary Website: www.larevue.qc.ca
Year Established: 1959
Areas Served - City/County or Portion Thereof, or Zip codes: Lanaudiere
Own Printing Facility?: Y
Commercial printers?: Y
Published: Wed
Avg Paid Circ: 10
Avg Free Circ: 55990
Audit By: Sworn/Estimate/Non-Audited
Audit Date: 12.07.2019
Personnel: Gilles Bordonado (Pub./Pres./CEO.); Veronick Talbot (News Dir); Daniel Soucy (Mktg Dir); Lise Bourdages (Sales Coord)
Parent company (for newspapers): Guide Rouge; Le Trait d'Union

PUBLICATION NAME

Le Trait D'union
Street Address: 231, Rue Sainte-marie ,
Province: QC
Postal: J6W 3E4
Country: Canada
Mailing address: 231, rue Sainte-Marie
Mailing city: Terrebonne
Province: QC
Postal: J6W 3E4
General Phone: (450) 964-4444
General Fax: (450) 471-1023
General/National Adv. E-mail: letraitdunion@transcontinental.ca
Classified Adv. e-mail: petitesannonces@larevue.qc.ca
Editorial e-mail: redaction@larevue.qc.ca
Primary Website: www.letraitdunion.com
Year Established: 1976
Delivery Methods: Newsstand`Carrier`Racks
Areas Served - City/County or Portion Thereof, or Zip codes: Terrebonne Mascouche
Published: Wed
Avg Paid Circ: 10
Avg Free Circ: 49990
Audit By: ODC
Audit Date: 12.12.2017
Personnel: Gilles Bordonado (PrÃ©sident); VÃ©ronick Talbot (RÃ©dactrice en chef); Lise Bourdages (Coordonnatrice aux ventes)
Parent company (for newspapers): La Revue de Terrebonne

THAMESVILLE

PUBLICATION NAME

Herald
Street Address: 105 Elizabeth St , Box 580
Province: ON
Postal: N0P 2K0
Country: Canada
Mailing address: PO Box 580
Mailing city: Thamesville
Province: ON
Postal: N0P 2K0
General Phone: (519) 692-3825
General/National Adv. E-mail: thamesvilleherald@sympatico.ca
Areas Served - City/County or Portion Thereof, or Zip codes: Canada
Commercial printers?: Y
Published: Wed
Avg Free Circ: 594
Audit By: CMCA
Audit Date: 29.02.2016
Personnel: Orval Schilbe (Ed.); May Schilbe (Mng. Ed.)

THE PAS

PUBLICATION NAME

Opasquia Times
Street Address: 352 Fischer Avenue , Box 750
Province: MB
Postal: R9A 1K8
Country: Canada
Mailing address: Box 750
Mailing city: The Pas
Province: MB
Postal: R9A 1K8
General Phone: (204) 623-3435
General Fax: (204) 623-5601
General/National Adv. E-mail: optmies@mts.net
Display Adv. E-mail: opads@mymts.net
Classified Adv. e-mail: opclass@mymts.net
Editorial e-mail: opeditor@mymts.net
Primary Website: www.opasquiatimes.com
Year Established: 1978
Areas Served - City/County or Portion Thereof, or Zip codes: Opasquia
Published: Wed`Fri
Avg Paid Circ: 1200
Avg Free Circ: 0
Audit By: VAC
Audit Date: 31.08.2015
Personnel: Jennifer Cook (Gen. Mgr.); Trent Allen (Ed.)

THETFORD MINES

PUBLICATION NAME

Courrier Frontenac
Street Address: Boulevard Frontenac Est Cp 789 , C.p. 789
Province: QC
Postal: G6G 5V3
Country: Canada
Mailing address: boulevard Frontenac Est CP 789
Mailing city: Thetford Mines
Province: QC
Postal: G6G 5V3
General Phone: (418) 338-5181
Areas Served - City/County or Portion Thereof, or Zip codes: Canada
Published: Wed
Avg Paid Circ: 15
Avg Free Circ: 22826
Audit By: CCAB
Audit Date: 31.03.2014
Personnel: Lucyl Lachance

THOMPSON

PUBLICATION NAME

Thompson Citizen/nickel Belt News
Street Address: 141 Commercial Pl. ,
Province: MB
Postal: R8N 1T1
Country: Canada
Mailing address: P.O. Box 887
Mailing city: Thompson
Province: MB
Postal: R8N 1N8
General Phone: (204) 677-4534
General Fax: (204) 677-3681
Advertising Phone: (204) 677-4534 ext 1
Editorial Phone: (204) 677-4534 ext 6
General/National Adv. E-mail: generalmanager@thompsoncitizen.net
Display Adv. E-mail: ads@thompsoncitizen.net
Classified Adv. e-mail: classifieds@thompsoncitizen.net
Editorial e-mail: editor@thompsoncitizen.net
Primary Website: www.thompsoncitizen.net
Year Established: 1961
Delivery Methods: Racks
Areas Served - City/County or Portion Thereof, or Zip codes: Canada
Own Printing Facility?: Y
Commercial printers?: N
Mechanical specifications: Type page 9 1/2 x 15; A - 5 cols, 1 3/4, between; C - 1 cols, 1 3/4, between.
Published: Fri
Avg Paid Circ: 61
Avg Free Circ: 6000
Audit By: Sworn/Estimate/Non-Audited
Audit Date: 12.07.2019
Personnel: Lynn Taylor (Gen. Mgr.); Ian Graham (Ed.)
Parent company (for newspapers): Glacier Media Group

THOROLD

PUBLICATION NAME

Fort Erie Post
Street Address: 3300 Merrittville Hwy Unit 1b ,
Province: ON
Postal: L2V 4Y6
Country: Canada
General Phone: (905) 688-2444
Primary Website: www.niagarathisweek.com/forterie-on
Areas Served - City/County or Portion Thereof, or Zip codes: Thorold, Ontario
Published: Thur
Personnel: Dave Hawkins (Adv.)
Parent company (for newspapers): Metroland Media Group Ltd.

PUBLICATION NAME

Niagara This Week

Street Address: 3300 Merrittville Hwy, Unit 1b ,
Province: ON
Postal: L2V 4Y6
Country: Canada
Mailing address: 3300 Merrittville Hwy, Unit 1B
Mailing city: Thorold
Province: ON
Postal: L2V 4Y6
General Phone: (905) 688-2444
General Fax: (905) 688-9272
General/National Adv. E-mail: letters@niagarathisweek.com
Primary Website: www.niagarathisweek.com
Areas Served - City/County or Portion Thereof, or Zip codes: Canada
Published: Wed`Thur
Avg Paid Circ: 0
Avg Free Circ: 151084
Audit By: CCAB
Audit Date: 30.09.2017
Personnel: David Bos (Gen. Mgr.); Debbi Koppejan (Adv. Mgr.); Mike Williscraft (Editorial Dir.); Dave Hawkins (Newspaper/Online Adv.)
Parent company (for newspapers): Metroland Media Group Ltd.; Torstar

THREE HILLS

PUBLICATION NAME

The Three Hills Capital
Street Address: 411 Main St. ,
Province: AB
Postal: T0M 2A0
Country: Canada
Mailing address: PO Box 158
Mailing city: Three Hills
Province: AB
Postal: T0M 2A0
General Phone: (403) 443-5133
General Fax: (403) 443-7331
General/National Adv. E-mail: info@threehillscapital.com
Display Adv. E-mail: info@threehillscapital.com
Classified Adv. e-mail: info@threehillscapital.com
Editorial e-mail: info@threehillscapital.com
Primary Website: threehillscapital.com
Year Established: 1916
Delivery Methods: Mail`Newsstand
Areas Served - City/County or Portion Thereof, or Zip codes: Canada
Commercial printers?: Y
Published: Wed
Avg Paid Circ: 1029
Avg Free Circ: 4
Audit By: VAC
Audit Date: 31.12.2015
Personnel: Theresa Shearlaw (Adv. Mgr.); Timothy Shearlaw (Ed.); Jay Shearlaw (Produ Mgr)

THUNDER BAY

PUBLICATION NAME

Thunder Bay Source
Street Address: 87 N. Hill St. ,
Province: ON
Postal: P7A 5V6
Country: Canada
Mailing address: 87 N. Hill St.
Mailing city: Thunder Bay
Province: ON
Postal: P7A 5V6
General Phone: (807) 346-2650
General Fax: (807) 345-9923
Advertising Phone: (807) 346-2510
General/National Adv. E-mail: ldunick@dougallmedia.com
Primary Website: www.tbnewswatch.com
Year Established: 1976
Delivery Methods: Carrier
Areas Served - City/County or Portion Thereof, or Zip codes: P7A, P7B, P7C, P7E
Own Printing Facility?: N
Commercial printers?: Y
Published: Thur
Avg Free Circ: 43740
Audit By: CMCA
Audit Date: 30.06.2017
Personnel: Leith Dunick (Mng. Ed.); Doug Diaczuk (Reporter); Matt Vis (Reporter); Nicole Dixon (Content editor)
Parent company (for newspapers): T.Bay Post Inc

TILBURY

PUBLICATION NAME

The Tilbury Times
Street Address: 40 Queen St. S. ,
Province: ON
Postal: N0P 2L0
Country: Canada
Mailing address: P.O. Box 490
Mailing city: Tilbury
Province: ON
Postal: N0P 2L0
General Phone: (519) 682-0411
General Fax: (519) 682-3633
Editorial Phone: (519) 809-4347
Display Adv. E-mail: dbarnwell@tilburytimes.com
Classified Adv. e-mail: dbarnwell@tilburytimes.com
Editorial e-mail: gharvieux@tilburytimes.com
Year Established: 1883
Delivery Methods: Mail`Newsstand
Areas Served - City/County or Portion Thereof, or Zip codes: N0P, N0R
Mechanical specifications: Type page 10 1/4 x 15 1/2; E - 6 cols, 1 1/2, 3/16 between; A - 6 cols, 1 7/10, between; C - 7 cols, 1 3/8, 1/4 between.
Published: Tues
Avg Paid Circ: 1100
Avg Free Circ: 50
Audit By: Sworn/Estimate/Non-Audited
Audit Date: 12.07.2019
Personnel: Bob Thwaites (Pub.); Gerry Harvieux (Ed.)
Parent company (for newspapers): Postmedia Network Inc.

TILLSONBURG

PUBLICATION NAME

The Tillsonburg News
Street Address: 25 Townline Rd. ,
Province: ON
Postal: N4G 4H6
Country: Canada
Mailing address: PO BOX 190
Mailing city: Tillsonburg
Province: ON
Postal: N4G 4H6
General Phone: (519) 688-6397
General Fax: (519) 842-3511
Advertising Phone: (519) 688-4400
General/National Adv. E-mail: tilledit@bowesnet.com
Primary Website: www.tillsonburgnews.com
Own Printing Facility?: Y
Commercial printers?: Y
Published: Fri
Avg Paid Circ: 1173
Audit By: CMCA
Audit Date: 31.12.2015
Personnel: Michael Walsh (Pub.)
Parent company (for newspapers): Postmedia Network Inc.; Quebecor Communications, Inc.

TIMMINS

PUBLICATION NAME

Timmins Times
Street Address: 815 Pine St. S. ,
Province: ON
Postal: P4N 8S3
Country: Canada
Mailing address: 815 Pine St. S.
Mailing city: Timmins
Province: ON
Postal: P4N 8S3
General Phone: (705) 268-6252
General Fax: (705) 268-2255
General/National Adv. E-mail: times@timminstimes.com
Primary Website: www.timminstimes.com
Areas Served - City/County or Portion Thereof, or Zip codes: Canada
Mechanical specifications: Type page 10 x 14 1/4; E - 6 cols, 1 3/4, 1/8 between; A - 6 cols, 1 3/4, 1/8 between; C - 6 cols, 1 3/4, 1/8 between.
Published: Thur
Avg Free Circ: 16325
Audit By: CMCA
Audit Date: 31.12.2013
Personnel: Wayne Major (Pub.); Len Gillis (Ed.); Kevin Anderson (Regional Managing Editor)
Parent company (for newspapers): Postmedia Network Inc.; Quebecor Communications, Inc.

TISDALE

PUBLICATION NAME

Parkland Review
Street Address: 1004-102 Ave. ,
Province: SK
Postal: S0E 1T0
Country: Canada
Mailing address: PO Box 1660
Mailing city: Tisdale
Province: SK
Postal: S0E 1T0
General Phone: (306) 873-4515
General Fax: (306) 873-4712
General/National Adv. E-mail: recorderoffice@sasktel.net
Display Adv. E-mail: adsrecorder@sakstel.net
Editorial e-mail: newsrecorder@sakstel.net
Delivery Methods: Mail
Areas Served - City/County or Portion Thereof, or Zip codes: Canada
Own Printing Facility?: Y
Published: Fri
Avg Free Circ: 11625
Audit By: CMCA
Audit Date: 31.03.2016
Personnel: August Grandguillar (Adv. Mgr.); Brent Fitzpatrick (Ed.); Gord Anderson (Prodn. Mgr.); Dan Sully (Adv. Mgr.)
Parent company (for newspapers): Glacier Media Group

PUBLICATION NAME

The Tisdale Recorder
Street Address: 1004 102nd Ave. ,
Province: SK
Postal: S0E 1T0
Country: Canada
Mailing address: PO Box 1660
Mailing city: Tisdale
Province: SK
Postal: S0E 1T0
General Phone: (306) 873-4515
General Fax: (306) 873-4712
General/National Adv. E-mail: pub@sasktel.net
Display Adv. E-mail: recorder3@sasktel.net
Editorial e-mail: newsrecorder@sasktel.net
Areas Served - City/County or Portion Thereof, or Zip codes: Canada
Own Printing Facility?: Y
Commercial printers?: Y
Published: Wed
Avg Paid Circ: 669
Avg Free Circ: 25
Audit By: CMCA
Audit Date: 31.12.2015
Personnel: Brent Fitzpatrick (Pub.); James Tarrant (Ed.); August Grandguillot (Ad.)
Parent company (for newspapers): Glacier Media Group

TOBERMORY

PUBLICATION NAME

The Bruce Peninsula Press
Street Address: 39 Legion St. ,
Province: ON
Postal: N0H 2R0
Country: Canada
Mailing address: PO Box 89
Mailing city: Tobermory
Province: ON
Postal: N0H 2R0
General Phone: (519) 596-2658
General Fax: (519) 596-8030
General/National Adv. E-mail: info@tobermorypress.com
Primary Website: www.brucepeninsulapress.com
Areas Served - City/County or Portion Thereof, or Zip codes: Canada
Published: Tues
Avg Paid Circ: 400
Avg Free Circ: 2235
Audit By: CMCA
Audit Date: 30.06.2017
Personnel: John Francis (Pub.); Scott McFarlane (Production Mgr./Signs); Marianne Wood (Editor)

TOFIELD

PUBLICATION NAME

Tofield Mercury
Street Address: 5312 50th St. ,
Province: AB
Postal: T0B 4J0
Country: Canada
Mailing address: PO Box 150
Mailing city: Tofield
Province: AB
Postal: T0B 4J0
General Phone: (780) 662-4046
General Fax: (780) 662-3735
Advertising Phone: (780) 662-4046
General/National Adv. E-mail: adsmercury@gmail.com
Display Adv. E-mail: kamcjm@gmail.com
Classified Adv. e-mail: kamcjm@gmail.com
Editorial e-mail: tofmerc@telusplanet.net
Primary Website: www.tofieldmerc.com
Year Established: 1918
Delivery Methods: Mail`Racks
Areas Served - City/County or Portion Thereof, or Zip codes: Canada
Commercial printers?: Y
Mechanical specifications: Type page 10 x 15 1/2; E - 5 cols, 1 5/6, between; A - 5 cols, 1 5/6, between.
Published: Wed
Avg Paid Circ: 1400
Avg Free Circ: 23
Audit By: Sworn/Estimate/Non-Audited
Audit Date: 12.07.2019
Personnel: Kerry Anderson (Pub/Advt Mgr)
Parent company (for newspapers): Caribou Publishing

TORONTO

PUBLICATION NAME

Anglican Journal
Street Address: 80 Hayden Street ,
Province: ON
Postal: M4Y 3G2
Country: Canada
Mailing address: 80 Hayden Street
Mailing city: Toronto
Province: ON
Postal: M4Y 3G2
General Phone: (416) 924-9199
Advertising Phone: (226) 664-0350
General/National Adv. E-mail: editor@anglicanjournal.com
Display Adv. E-mail: advertising@national.anglican.ca
Editorial e-mail: editor@anglicanjournal.com
Primary Website: www.anglicanjournal.com
Year Established: 1875
Delivery Methods: Mail
Areas Served - City/County or Portion Thereof, or Zip codes: Toronto, ON M4Y 32
Published: Mthly
Avg Paid Circ: 123352
Avg Free Circ: 1200

Community Newspapers in Canada

III-585

Audit By: Sworn/Estimate/Non-Audited
Audit Date: 12.07.2019

PUBLICATION NAME

Annex Guardian
Street Address: One River View Garden ,
Province: ON
Postal: M6S 4E4
Country: Canada
Mailing address: One River View Garden
Mailing city: Toronto
Province: ON
Postal: M6S 4E4
General Phone: (416) 493-4400
General Fax: (416) 767-4880
Display Adv. E-mail: salesinfo@insidetoronto.com
Classified Adv. e-mail: classifieds@metroland.com
Editorial e-mail: gbalogiannis@insidetoronto.com
Primary Website: www.insidetoronto.ca
Published: Fri
Avg Free Circ: 55500
Audit By: Sworn/Estimate/Non-Audited
Audit Date: 12.07.2019
Personnel: Grace Peacock (Ed); Meriel Bradley (Sales Dir)
Parent company (for newspapers): Torstar

PUBLICATION NAME

Beach-Riverdale Mirror
Street Address: 100 Tempo Ave. ,
Province: ON
Postal: M2H 2N8
Country: Canada
Mailing address: 100 Tempo Ave.
Mailing city: Toronto
Province: ON
Postal: M2H 2N8
General Phone: (416) 493-4400
General Fax: (416) 493-6190
General/National Adv. E-mail: bsrm@insidetoronto.com
Display Adv. E-mail: salesinfo@insidetoronto.com
Classified Adv. e-mail: classifieds@metroland.com
Editorial e-mail: newsroom@insidetoronto.com
Primary Website: www.insidetoronto.ca
Areas Served - City/County or Portion Thereof, or Zip codes: Canada
Published: Thur
Avg Paid Circ: 0
Avg Free Circ: 22241
Audit By: CCAB
Audit Date: 30.09.2015
Personnel: Betty Carr (Pub); Marg Middleton (Gen. Mgr.); Meriel Bradley (Adv. Rep)
Parent company (for newspapers): Metroland Media Group Ltd.; Torstar

PUBLICATION NAME

Bloor West Villager
Street Address: 2323 Bloor St. W ,
Province: ON
Postal: M6S 4W1
Country: Canada
Mailing address: 2323 Bloor St. W
Mailing city: Toronto
Province: ON
Postal: M6S 4W1
General Phone: (416) 675-4390
General Fax: (416) 767-4880
General/National Adv. E-mail: metroland@insidetoronto.com
Display Adv. E-mail: mbradley@metroland.com
Editorial e-mail: gpeacock@insidetoronto.com
Primary Website: insidetoronto.com
Areas Served - City/County or Portion Thereof, or Zip codes: Canada
Published: Thur
Avg Paid Circ: 0
Avg Free Circ: 39840
Audit By: CCAB
Audit Date: 30.09.2017
Personnel: Betty Carr (Pub.); Meriel Bradley (Adv. Dir.); Grace Peacock (Ed)
Parent company (for newspapers): Metroland Media Group Ltd.; Torstar

PUBLICATION NAME

City Centre Mirror
Street Address: 175 Gordon Baker Rd. ,
Province: ON
Postal: M2H 2S6
Country: Canada
Mailing address: 175 Gordon Baker Rd.
Mailing city: Toronto
Province: ON
Postal: M2H 2S6
General Phone: (416) 774-2367
General Fax: (416) 493-6190
General/National Adv. E-mail: atedesco@insidetoronto.com
Display Adv. E-mail: mbradley@metroland.com
Classified Adv. e-mail: classifieds@metroland.com
Editorial e-mail: newsroom@insidetoronto.com
Primary Website: insidetoronto.com
Areas Served - City/County or Portion Thereof, or Zip codes: Canada
Published: Thur
Avg Paid Circ: 0
Avg Free Circ: 22359
Audit By: CCAB
Audit Date: 20.12.2017
Personnel: Antoine Tedesco (Managing Ed.)
Parent company (for newspapers): Metroland Media Group Ltd.

PUBLICATION NAME

L'express
Street Address: 17 Carlaw Ave. ,
Province: ON
Postal: M4M 2R6
Country: Canada
Mailing address: 17 Carlaw Ave.
Mailing city: Toronto
Province: ON
Postal: M4M 2R6
General Phone: (416) 465-2107
General Fax: (416) 465-3778
General/National Adv. E-mail: express@lexpress.to
Primary Website: www.lexpress.to
Areas Served - City/County or Portion Thereof, or Zip codes: Toronto, ON
Published: Tues
Avg Paid Circ: 20000
Avg Free Circ: 15000
Audit By: Sworn/Estimate/Non-Audited
Audit Date: 12.07.2019
Personnel: Jean Mazare (Pub.); Akli liu (Adv. Mgr.); Marianne Santhan (Circ. Mgr.); Francois Bergeron (Ed.)

PUBLICATION NAME

Nasha Gazeta
Street Address: 855 Alness Street , Unit #7
Province: ON
Postal: M3J 2X3
Country: Canada
Mailing address: 855 Alness Street
Mailing city: Toronto
Province: ON
Postal: M3J 2X3
General Phone: (905) 738-1109
General Fax: (416) 514-0640
Primary Website: www.rcbcanada.com/broadcasting/nasha-gazeta
Areas Served - City/County or Portion Thereof, or Zip codes: Toronto
Published: Wed
Avg Free Circ: 2600
Audit By: AAM
Audit Date: 31.12.2018
Personnel: Garry Kukuy (Pub.)
Parent company (for newspapers): Russian Canadian Broadcasting

PUBLICATION NAME

North York Mirror
Street Address: 100 Tempo Ave. ,
Province: ON
Postal: M2H 2N8
Country: Canada
Mailing address: 100 Tempo Ave.
Mailing city: Toronto
Province: ON
Postal: M2H 2N8
General Phone: (416) 493-4400
General Fax: (416) 495-6629
Display Adv. E-mail: sales@insidetoronto.com
Primary Website: insidetoronto.com
Year Established: 1957
Delivery Methods: Carrier
Areas Served - City/County or Portion Thereof, or Zip codes: Canada
Own Printing Facility?: Y
Commercial printers?: Y
Mechanical specifications: Type page 10 3/8 x 14; E - 9 cols, 1 1/16, between; A - 9 cols, 1 1/16, between; C - 9 cols, 1 1/16, between.
Published: Thur
Avg Paid Circ: 0
Avg Free Circ: 92407
Audit By: CCAB
Audit Date: 30.09.2017
Personnel: Betty Carr (V.P.); Marg Middleton (Gen. Mgr.); Dmitry Borovik (Sales Rep.); Angela Carruthers (Sales Rep.); Paul Futhey (Mng. Ed.); Stacey Allen (Dir. Adv.)
Parent company (for newspapers): Metroland Media Group Ltd.; Torstar

PUBLICATION NAME

The Bulletin - Journal Of Downtown Toronto
Street Address: 260 Adelaide St E Ste 121 ,
Province: ON
Postal: M5A 1N1
Country: Canada
Mailing address: 260 Adelaide St E Ste 121
Mailing city: Toronto
Province: ON
Postal: M5A 1N1
General Phone: (416) 929-0011
General Fax: (416) 929-0011
Advertising Phone: (416) 929-0011 ext. 5
Advertising Fax: (416) 929-0011
Editorial Phone: (416) 929-0011 ext. 3
Editorial Fax: (416) 929-0011 ext. 3
Display Adv. E-mail: sales@thebulletinca
Classified Adv. e-mail: classified@thebulletin.ca
Editorial e-mail: deareditor@thebulletin.ca
Primary Website: www.thebulletin.ca
Year Established: 1998
Delivery Methods: Mail`Newsstand`Carrier`Racks
Areas Served - City/County or Portion Thereof, or Zip codes: Canada
Mechanical specifications: Broadsheet on supercalendar glossy stock. CMYK throughout. Width x Height: 6 ea.columns with 5-3/8" gutters over 9.5" print width x 19" height Folded for mail via Canada Post to 5" x 22" In racks at 11" x 10.5"
Published: Other
Published Other: Printed 4th Monday each month, in mail by next Thur.
Avg Free Circ: 49822
Audit By: CMCA
Audit Date: 06.09.2017
Personnel: Paulette Touby (Pub.); Frank Touby (Ed.); Anisa Lancione (Mng Ed.)
Parent company (for newspapers): Community Bulletin Newspaper Group, Inc.

PUBLICATION NAME

The Parkdale Villager
Street Address: 175 Gordon Baker Rd ,
Province: ON
Postal: M2H 2S6
Country: Canada
Mailing address: 175 Gordon Baker Rd
Mailing city: Toronto
Province: ON
Postal: M2H 2S6
General Phone: (416) 493-4400
General Fax: (416) 493-6190
Advertising Phone: (416) 493-4400
Advertising Fax: (416) 493-6190
Editorial Phone: (416) 774-2367
Editorial Fax: (416) 493-6190
General/National Adv. E-mail: general@insidetoronto.com
Display Adv. E-mail: atedesco@insidetoronto.com
Editorial e-mail: atedesco@insidetoronto.com
Primary Website: www.parkdaleliberty.ca
Delivery Methods: Mail`Racks
Areas Served - City/County or Portion Thereof, or Zip codes: Canada
Published: Thur
Avg Free Circ: 24917
Audit By: CCAB
Audit Date: 30.09.2015
Personnel: Ian Proudfoot (Pub.); Antoine Tedesco (Mng. Ed.)
Parent company (for newspapers): Metroland Media Group Ltd.

PUBLICATION NAME

The Scarborough Mirror
Street Address: 100 Tempo Ave. ,
Province: ON
Postal: M2H 2N8
Country: Canada
Mailing address: 100 Tempo Ave.
Mailing city: Toronto
Province: ON
Postal: M2H 2N8
General Phone: (416) 493-4400
General Fax: (416) 495-6629
General/National Adv. E-mail: scm@insidetoronto.com
Primary Website: insidetoronto.com
Areas Served - City/County or Portion Thereof, or Zip codes: Canada
Own Printing Facility?: Y
Commercial printers?: Y
Mechanical specifications: Type page 10 3/8 x 14; E - 9 cols, 1 1/16, between; A - 9 cols, 1 1/16, between; C - 9 cols, 1 1/16, between.
Published: Thur`Fri
Avg Free Circ: 120479
Audit By: CCAB
Audit Date: 20.12.2017
Personnel: Betty Carr (Vice Pres./Grp. Pub.); Marg Middleton (Gen. Mgr.); Kelly Atkinson (Regl. Mgr., HR); Bruce Espey (Dir., Bus. Admin.); Tim Corcoran (Regl. Dir, Adv.); Kayland McCully (Sales Rep.); Frank Li (Sales Rep.); Shauna Paolucci (Sales Rep.); Cathie Orban (Sales Rep.); Leema Williams (Sales Rep.); Michelle King (Sales Rep.); Al Shackleton (Mng. Ed.); Dave Burnett (Dir., Prodn.); Katherine Bernal (Prodn. Mgr.)
Parent company (for newspapers): Metroland Media Group Ltd.; Torstar

PUBLICATION NAME

The York Guardian
Street Address: 100 Tempo Ave. ,
Province: ON
Postal: M2H 2N8
Country: Canada
Mailing address: 100 Tempo Ave.
Mailing city: Toronto
Province: ON
Postal: M2H 2N8
General Phone: (416) 493-4400
General Fax: (416) 495-6629
General/National Adv. E-mail: etg@insidetoronto.com
Primary Website: www.insidetoronto.com
Areas Served - City/County or Portion Thereof, or Zip codes: Canada
Own Printing Facility?: Y
Commercial printers?: Y
Mechanical specifications: Type page 10 3/8 x 14; E - 9 cols, 1 1/16, between; A - 9 cols, 1 1/16, between; C - 9 cols, 1 1/16, between.
Published: Thur
Avg Free Circ: 28544
Audit By: CCAB
Audit Date: 30.09.2017
Personnel: Betty Carr (Pub.); Marg Middleton

TREHERNE

PUBLICATION NAME

Times
Street Address: 194 Broadway St. ,
Province: MB
Postal: R0G 2V0
Country: Canada
Mailing address: PO Box 50
Mailing city: Treherne
Province: MB
Postal: R0G 2V0
General Phone: (204) 723-2542
General Fax: (204) 723-2754
General/National Adv. E-mail: trehernetimes@mts.net
Editorial e-mail: trehernetimes@mts.net
Primary Website: www.trehernetimes.ca
Areas Served - City/County or Portion Thereof, or Zip codes: Treherne
Published: Mon
Avg Free Circ: 842
Audit By: VAC
Audit Date: 30.06.2016
Personnel: Gary Lodwick (Ed.)

TRENTON

PUBLICATION NAME

The Community Press
Street Address: 41 Quinte St. ,
Province: ON
Postal: K8V 5R3
Country: Canada
Mailing address: PO Box 130
Mailing city: Trenton
Province: ON
Postal: K8V 5R3
General Phone: (613) 395-3015
General Fax: (613) 392-0505
General/National Adv. E-mail: general@communitypress-online.com; news@communitypress-online.com
Editorial e-mail: editor@communitypress-online.com
Primary Website: www.communitypress.ca
Areas Served - City/County or Portion Thereof, or Zip codes: Canada
Mechanical specifications: Type page 10 1/4 x 15; E - 9 cols, 1 1/36, 1/8 between; A - 9 cols, 1 1/36, 1/8 between; C - 6 cols, 1 7/12, 1/8 between.
Published: Thur
Avg Paid Circ: 0
Avg Free Circ: 45644
Audit By: CMCA
Audit Date: 30.06.2014
Personnel: John Knowles (Pub.); Chuck Parker (Gen. Mgr); Ross Lees (Mng. Ed.); John Campbell (News Ed.)

PUBLICATION NAME

Trentonian
Street Address: 41 Quinte St. ,
Province: ON
Postal: K8V 5R3
Country: Canada
Mailing address: PO Box 130
Mailing city: Trenton
Province: ON
Postal: K8V 5R3
General Phone: (613) 392-6501
General Fax: (613) 392-0505
Display Adv. E-mail: advertising@trentonia.ca
Editorial e-mail: newsroom@trentonian.ca
Primary Website: www.trentonian.ca
Own Printing Facility?: Y
Commercial printers?: Y
Published: Thur
Avg Free Circ: 15084
Audit By: CMCA

Audit Date: 30.06.2016
Personnel: John Knowles (Pub.); Rachel Henry (Adv. Mgr.); Tim Devine (Circ. Mgr.); Ross Lees (Mng. Ed.); Sherin Tyson (Prodn. Mgr.)
Parent company (for newspapers): Postmedia Network Inc.; Quebecor Communications, Inc.

TROIS-RIVIERES

PUBLICATION NAME

L'echo De Trois-rivieres
Street Address: 3625 Blvd Du Chanoine-moreau ,
Province: QC
Postal: G8Y 5N6
Country: Canada
Mailing address: 9085, boul. Lacroix
Mailing city: Saint-Georges
Province: QC
Postal: G5Y 2B4
General Phone: (819) 371-4823
General Fax: (819) 371-4804
Advertising Phone: (819) 371-4823
Advertising Fax: (819) 371-4804
Editorial Phone: (819) 371-4823
Editorial Fax: (819) 371-4804
General/National Adv. E-mail: serge.buchanan@quebecormedia.com
Display Adv. E-mail: jocelyn.ouellet@quebecormedia.com
Editorial e-mail: serge.buchanan@quebecormedia.com
Primary Website: www.lechodetroisrivieres.ca
Delivery Methods: Mail Racks
Areas Served - City/County or Portion Thereof, or Zip codes: Canada
Published: Wed
Avg Free Circ: 68580
Audit By: CCAB
Audit Date: 31.03.2014
Personnel: Serge Buchanan (Ed.)

PUBLICATION NAME

L'hebdo Journal
Street Address: 525 Barkoff St., Ste. 205 , Bureau 205
Province: QC
Postal: G8T 2A5
Country: Canada
Mailing address: 525 Barkoff St., Ste. 205
Mailing city: Trois-Rivieres
Province: QC
Postal: G8T 2A5
General Phone: (819) 379-1490
General Fax: (819) 379-0705
Advertising Phone: (866) 637-5236
Display Adv. E-mail: publicite.hj@transcontinental.ca
Editorial e-mail: redaction.hj@transcontinental.ca
Primary Website: www.lhebdojournal.com
Year Established: 1967
Areas Served - City/County or Portion Thereof, or Zip codes: Canada
Published: Wed
Avg Paid Circ: 30
Avg Free Circ: 60411
Audit By: CCAB
Audit Date: 31.03.2014
Personnel: Alain Bernard (Sales Mgr.); Sylviane Lussier (Pub.); Emilie Valley (Ed.)
Parent company (for newspapers): Transcontinental Media

TUMBLER RIDGE

PUBLICATION NAME

Tumbler Ridge News
Street Address: 230 Mains Street ,
Province: BC
Postal: V0C 2W0
Country: Canada
Mailing address: PO Box 620
Mailing city: Tumbler Ridge
Province: BC

Postal: V0C 2W0
General Phone: (250) 242-5343
General Fax: (250) 242-5340
General/National Adv. E-mail: mail@tumblerridgenews.com
Display Adv. E-mail: advertising@tumblerridgenews.com
Editorial e-mail: editor@tumblerridgenews.com
Primary Website: www.tumblerridgenews.com
Year Established: 1997
Delivery Methods: Mail Newsstand Carrier
Areas Served - City/County or Portion Thereof, or Zip codes: Tumbler Ridge
Mechanical specifications: 10.25" x 16" - 8 columns Please email for rate sheet. We accept pdf, jpg, tif and word.
Published: Thur
Published Other: on line on Tuesdays
Avg Paid Circ: 2
Avg Free Circ: 1179
Audit By: VAC
Audit Date: 31.12.2015
Personnel: Loraine Funk (Owner); Trent Ernst (Pub/Ed.); Lisa Allen (Sales Mgr)

TWEED

PUBLICATION NAME

The Tweed News
Street Address: 242 Victoria St. N. ,
Province: ON
Postal: K0K 3J0
Country: Canada
Mailing address: PO Box 550
Mailing city: Tweed
Province: ON
Postal: K0K 3J0
General Phone: (613) 478-2017
General Fax: (613) 478-2749
Advertising Phone: (613) 478-2699
Advertising Fax: (613) 478-2749
Editorial Phone: (613) 478-2017
Editorial Fax: (613) 478-2749
General/National Adv. E-mail: info@thetweednews.ca
Display Adv. E-mail: info@thetweednews.ca
Classified Adv. e-mail: info@thetweednews.ca
Editorial e-mail: info@thetweednews.ca
Primary Website: www.thetweednews.ca
Year Established: 1887
Delivery Methods: Mail Racks
Areas Served - City/County or Portion Thereof, or Zip codes: Municpality of Tweed
Own Printing Facility?: Y
Commercial printers?: Y
Mechanical specifications: Type page 12 3/4 x 21; E - 6 cols, 2, 1/4 between; A - 6 cols, 2, 1/4 between; C - 6 cols, 2, 1/4 between.
Published: Wed
Avg Paid Circ: 8722
Avg Free Circ: 42
Audit By: CMCA
Audit Date: 26.11.2018
Personnel: Roseann Trudeau (Circ. Mgr.); Rodger Hanna (Ed./Pub.)

UCLUELET

PUBLICATION NAME

Westerly News
Street Address: 102-1801 Bay Street ,
Province: BC
Postal: V0R 3A0
Country: Canada
Mailing address: PO Box 317
Mailing city: Ucluelet
Province: BC
Postal: V0R 3A0
General Phone: (250) 726-7029
General Fax: (250) 726-4282
General/National Adv. E-mail: office@westerlynews.ca
Display Adv. E-mail: office@westerlynews.ca
Editorial e-mail: andrew.bailey@westerlynews.ca
Primary Website: www.westerlynews.ca
Year Established: 1987
Delivery Methods: Mail Newsstand Racks
Areas Served - City/County or Portion Thereof, or Zip codes: V0R 3A0, V0R 2Z0

Published: Wed
Avg Paid Circ: 7
Avg Free Circ: 0
Audit By: Sworn/Estimate/Non-Audited
Audit Date: 12.07.2019
Personnel: Andrew Bailey (Ed); Peter McCully (Pub); Nora O'Malley
Parent company (for newspapers): Black Press Group Ltd.

UNITY

PUBLICATION NAME

Unity-wilkie Press-herald
Street Address: 310 Main St. ,
Province: SK
Postal: S0K 4L0
Country: Canada
Mailing address: PO Box 309
Mailing city: Unity
Province: SK
Postal: S0K 4L0
General Phone: (306) 228-2267
General Fax: (306) 228-2767
General/National Adv. E-mail: northwest.herald@sasktel.net
Display Adv. E-mail: ads.northwest.herald@sasktel.net
Editorial e-mail: northwest.herald@sasktel.net
Primary Website: http://unitystories.com/press-herald/
Delivery Methods: Mail Newsstand
Areas Served - City/County or Portion Thereof, or Zip codes: Canada
Mechanical specifications: Type page 10 1/12 x 16; E - 5 cols, 1 11/12, 1/6 between; A - 5 cols, 1 11/12, 1/6 between; C - 5 cols, 1 11/12, 1/6 between.
Published: Fri
Avg Paid Circ: 1400
Avg Free Circ: 0
Audit By: Sworn/Estimate/Non-Audited
Audit Date: 12.07.2019
Personnel: Helena Long (Ed.); Jackie Boser (Office Manager); Tim Holtorf (ad designer)
Parent company (for newspapers): Prairie Newspaper Group

UXBRIDGE

PUBLICATION NAME

Uxbridge Times-journal
Street Address: 16 Bascom St. ,
Province: ON
Postal: L9P 1J3
Country: Canada
Mailing address: PO Box 459
Mailing city: Uxbridge
Province: ON
Postal: L9P 19
General Phone: (905) 852-9141
General Fax: (905) 852-9341
Primary Website: durhamregion.com
Year Established: 1869
Areas Served - City/County or Portion Thereof, or Zip codes: Canada
Own Printing Facility?: Y
Commercial printers?: Y
Published: Thur
Avg Paid Circ: 0
Avg Free Circ: 8803
Audit By: CCAB
Audit Date: 15.11.2017
Personnel: Tim Whittaker (Pub.); Judy Pirone (Adv. Mgr.); Joanne Burghardt (Ed. in Chief); Judi Bobbitt (Ed.)
Parent company (for newspapers): Metroland Media Group Ltd.; Torstar

VAL D'OR

PUBLICATION NAME

Abitibi Express Val D'or
Street Address: 1834 3rd Ave. 2nd Floor ,
Province: QC
Postal: J9P 7A9

(Gen. Mgr.); Tim Corcoran (Adv. Mgr.); Jaime Munoz (Circ. Mgr.); Paul Futhey (Mng. Ed.)
Parent company (for newspapers): Metroland Media Group Ltd.; Torstar

Community Newspapers in Canada

Country: Canada
Mailing address: 1834 3rd Ave. 2nd Floor
Mailing city: Val d'Or
Province: QC
Postal: J9P 7A9
General Phone: (819) 874-2151
General/National Adv. E-mail: redaction.abitibi@tc.tc
Primary Website: www.abitibiexpress.ca
Areas Served - City/County or Portion Thereof, or Zip codes: Canada
Published: Tues
Avg Paid Circ: 22
Avg Free Circ: 31088
Audit By: CCAB
Audit Date: 31.03.2014

PUBLICATION NAME

Le Citoyen De La Vallee De L'or
Street Address: 1462 Rue De La Quebecoise ,
Province: QC
Postal: J9P 5H4
Country: Canada
Mailing address: 1462 Rue de la Quebecoise
Mailing city: Val d'Or
Province: QC
Postal: J9P 5H4
General Phone: (819) 874-4545
General Fax: (819) 874-4547
General/National Adv. E-mail: citoyens@cablevision.qc.ca
Primary Website: http://www.lechoabitibien.ca/
Areas Served - City/County or Portion Thereof, or Zip codes: Canada
Published: Wed
Avg Paid Circ: 36
Avg Free Circ: 19883
Audit By: CCAB
Audit Date: 31.03.2014
Personnel: Endre Renaud (Gen. Mgr.); Carroline Couture (Adv. Mgr.); Louis Lavoie (Mng. Ed.)
Parent company (for newspapers): Quebecor Communications, Inc.

VALEMOUNT

PUBLICATION NAME

The Valley Sentinel
Street Address: 1418 Bruce Place ,
Province: BC
Postal: V0E 2Z0
Country: Canada
Mailing address: PO Box 688
Mailing city: Valemount
Province: BC
Postal: V0E 2Z0
General Phone: (250) 566-4425
General Fax: (250) 566-4528
General/National Adv. E-mail: insertions@thevallysentinel.com
Display Adv. E-mail: ads@valley-sentinel.com
Editorial e-mail: articles@valley-sentinel.com
Primary Website: www.thevalleysentinel.com
Year Established: 1986
Delivery Methods: Mail
Areas Served - City/County or Portion Thereof, or Zip codes: V0E, V0J
Own Printing Facility?: Y
Commercial printers?: Y
Published: Thur
Avg Paid Circ: 385
Avg Free Circ: 13
Audit By: VAC
Audit Date: 31.12.2015
Personnel: Deanna Mickelow (Ad Sales); Joshua Estabroks (Pub.)
Parent company (for newspapers): Aberdeen Publishing

PUBLICATION NAME

Georgia Straight
Street Address: 1635 West Broadway ,
Province: BC
Postal: V6J 1W9
Country: Canada
General Phone: (604) 730-7000
General Fax: (604) 730-7010
General/National Adv. E-mail: gs.info@straight.com
Display Adv. E-mail: sales@straight.com
Editorial e-mail: contact@straight.com
Primary Website: www.straight.com
Year Established: 1967
Delivery Methods: Mail`Newsstand`Racks
Areas Served - City/County or Portion Thereof, or Zip codes: Metro Vancouver, British Columbia
Mechanical specifications: Type page 10 3/16 x 15 1/2.
Published: Thur
Avg Paid Circ: 25
Avg Free Circ: 81544
Audit By: VAC
Audit Date: 30.06.2017
Personnel: Tara Lalanne (Sales Director); Dexter Vosper (Circulation Manager); Dennis Jangula (IT Director); Charlie Smith (Editor)
Parent company (for newspapers): Vancouver Free Press Publishing Corp.

PUBLICATION NAME

The False Creek News
Street Address: 661 A Market Hill ,
Province: BC
Postal: V5Z 4B5
Country: Canada
Mailing address: 661 A Market Hill
Mailing city: Vancouver
Province: BC
Postal: V5Z 4B5
General Phone: (604) 875-9626
General Fax: (604) 875-0336
General/National Adv. E-mail: news@thefalsecreeknews.com
Display Adv. E-mail: adsales@thefalsecreeknews.com
Editorial e-mail: mail@thefalsecreeknews.com
Primary Website: www.thefalsecreeknews.com
Mechanical specifications: Type page 7 1/2 x 9 1/2; E - 5 cols, 1 1/2, 1/8 between; A - 5 cols, 1 1/2, 1/8 between.
Published: Fri
Avg Free Circ: 25000
Audit By: Sworn/Estimate/Non-Audited
Audit Date: 12.07.2019
Personnel: M. Juma (Adv. Sales); Stephen Bowell (Mng. Ed.)

PUBLICATION NAME

The Vancouver Courier
Street Address: 303 West 5th Ave ,
Province: BC
Postal: V5Y 1J6
Country: Canada
Mailing address: 303 West 5th Ave
Mailing city: Vancouver
Province: BC
Postal: V5Y 1J6
General Phone: (604) 738-1411
General Fax: (604) 731-1474
Display Adv. E-mail: mbhatti@vancourier.com
Editorial e-mail: mperkins@vancourier.com
Primary Website: vancourier.com
Areas Served - City/County or Portion Thereof, or Zip codes: Canada
Commercial printers?: Y
Mechanical specifications: Type page 10 x 15; E - 6 cols, between; A - 6 cols, between; C - 7 cols, between.
Published: Wed`Fri
Avg Paid Circ: 0
Avg Free Circ: 106402
Audit By: CCAB
Audit Date: 22.11.2017
Personnel: Alvin Brouwer (Pub); Martha Perkins (Ed); Michelle Bhatti (Mktg Dir)
Parent company (for newspapers): Glacier Media Group; CanWest MediaWorks Publications, Inc.

PUBLICATION NAME

The Westender
Street Address: 303 West 5th Ave ,
Province: BC
Postal: V5Y 1J6
Country: Canada
Mailing address: 205-1525 West 8th Ave
Mailing city: Vancouver
Province: BC
Postal: V5Y 1J6
General Phone: (604) 742-8686
Display Adv. E-mail: matty@westender.com
Editorial e-mail: editor@westender.com
Primary Website: http://www.westender.com/
Areas Served - City/County or Portion Thereof, or Zip codes: Canada
Published: Thur
Avg Paid Circ: 0
Avg Free Circ: 23887
Audit By: CCAB
Audit Date: 30.09.2017
Personnel: Gail Nugent (Pub); Kelsey Klassen (Ed); Miguel Black (Circ Mgr)
Parent company (for newspapers): Glacier Media Group

PUBLICATION NAME

We Vancouver Weekly
Street Address: 303 West 5th Ave ,
Province: BC
Postal: V5Y 1J6
Country: Canada
Mailing address: 303 West 5th Ave
Mailing city: Vancouver
Province: BC
Postal: V5Y 1J6
General Phone: (604) 742-8686
General Fax: (604) 606-8687
Advertising Phone: (604) 742-8677
General/National Adv. E-mail: publisher@wevancouver.com
Display Adv. E-mail: matty@westender.com
Editorial e-mail: editor@westender.com
Primary Website: www.wevancouver.com
Delivery Methods: Newsstand`Carrier`Racks
Areas Served - City/County or Portion Thereof, or Zip codes: All of Vancouver
Commercial printers?: Y
Mechanical specifications: Type page 10 3/8" wide x 14" tall
Published: Thur
Avg Paid Circ: 0
Avg Free Circ: 53671
Audit By: CMCA
Audit Date: 30.11.2013
Personnel: Gail Nugent (Pub); Kelsey Klassen (Ed); Miguel Black (Circ. Mgr.)

VANDERHOOF

PUBLICATION NAME

Vanderhoof Omineca Express
Street Address: 150 W. Columbia ,
Province: BC
Postal: V0J 3A0
Country: Canada
Mailing address: PO Box 1007
Mailing city: Vanderhoof
Province: BC
Postal: V0J 3A0
General Phone: (250) 567-9258
General Fax: (250) 567-2070
General/National Adv. E-mail: newsroom@ominecaexpress.com
Display Adv. E-mail: publisher@ominecaexpress.com
Editorial e-mail: newsroom@ominecaexpress.com
Primary Website: www.ominecaexpress.com
Year Established: 1978
Areas Served - City/County or Portion Thereof, or Zip codes: Vanderhoof
Commercial printers?: Y
Mechanical specifications: Type page 10 5/16 x 14 1/2; E - 6 cols, 1 9/16, 3/16 between; A - 6 cols, 1 9/16, 3/16 between; C - 6 cols, 1 9/16, 3/16 between.
Published: Wed
Avg Paid Circ: 998
Avg Free Circ: 52
Audit By: VAC
Audit Date: 30.06.2016

Personnel: Pam Berger (Pub./Sales Mgr); Vivian Chui (Ed); Denise Smith (Office/Sales/Circ)
Parent company (for newspapers): Black Press Group Ltd.

VANKLEEK HILL

PUBLICATION NAME

The Review
Street Address: 76 Main St. E. ,
Province: ON
Postal: K0B 1R0
Country: Canada
Mailing address: PO Box 160
Mailing city: Vankleek Hill
Province: ON
Postal: K0B 1R0
General Phone: (613) 678-3327
General Fax: (613) 937-2591
Advertising Fax: (613) 937-2591
Editorial Fax: (613) 937-2591
General/National Adv. E-mail: review@thereview.ca
Display Adv. E-mail: ads@thereview.ca
Classified Adv. e-mail: classifieds@thereview.ca
Editorial e-mail: editor@thereview.ca
Primary Website: www.thereview.ca
Year Established: 1893
Delivery Methods: Mail`Newsstand
Areas Served - City/County or Portion Thereof, or Zip codes: Champlain Township
Mechanical specifications: Type page 15 x 22 3/4; E - 8 cols, 1 1/2, 3/8 between; A - 8 cols, 1 1/2, 3/8 between; C - 8 cols, 1 1/2, 3/8 between.
Published: Wed
Avg Paid Circ: 2785
Avg Free Circ: 727
Audit By: CMCA
Audit Date: 30.06.2016
Personnel: Irene Sensyzcyzn (Classified Adv. Mgr.); Louise Sproule (Ed.); Suzanne Tessier (Prodn. Mgr.); Diane Duval (Accounts); Shirley Shuberynski (Advertising Sales); Theresa Ketterling (Reporters/Photographer); Tara Kirkpatrick (Advertising Sales); Sharon Graves-McRae (Website Designer); Dorothy Hodge (Graphic Designer)

VAUDREUIL-DORION

PUBLICATION NAME

Etoile De L'outaouais St Laurent
Street Address: Avenue St-charles ,
Province: QC
Postal: J7V 2N4
Country: Canada
Mailing address: avenue St-Charles
Mailing city: Vaudreuil-Dorion
Province: QC
Postal: J7V 2N4
General Phone: (450) 455-6111
Published: Sat
Avg Paid Circ: 28
Avg Free Circ: 56711
Audit By: ODC
Audit Date: 14.12.2011
Personnel: Angele Marcoux Prevost

PUBLICATION NAME

Journal Premiere Edition
Street Address: 469 St. Charles Ave. ,
Province: QC
Postal: J7V 2N4
Country: Canada
Mailing address: 469 St. Charles Ave.
Mailing city: Vaudreuil-Dorion
Province: QC
Postal: J7V 2N4
General Phone: (450) 455-7955
General Fax: (450) 455-3028
Advertising Phone: (450) 455-1050
Advertising Fax: (450) 455-1050
General/National Adv. E-mail: webmestre@hebdosdusuroit.com

VAUGHAN

PUBLICATION NAME

Vaughan Citizen
Street Address: 8611 Weston Rd Unit 29 ,
Province: ON
Postal: L4L 9P1
Country: Canada
Mailing address: 8611 Weston Rd Unit 29
Mailing city: Vaughan
Province: ON
Postal: L4L 9P1
General Phone: (905) 264-8703
General Fax: (905) 264-9453
Advertising Phone: (905) 264-8703
Advertising Fax: (905) 264-9453
Editorial Phone: (905) 264-8703
Editorial Fax: (905) 264-9453
General/National Adv. E-mail: john.willems@metroland.com
Display Adv. E-mail: gpaolucci@yrmg.com
Editorial e-mail: dkelly@yrmg.com
Primary Website: yorkregion.com
Delivery Methods: Mail`Racks
Areas Served - City/County or Portion Thereof, or Zip codes: Maple, Woodbridge, Concord, and Kleinburg
Published: Thur
Avg Free Circ: 57677
Audit By: CCAB
Audit Date: 20.12.2017
Personnel: Ian Proudfoot (Vice Pres./Reg. Pub.); Debora Kelly (Ed. in Chief); John Willems (Reg. Gen. Mgr.)
Parent company (for newspapers): Metroland Media Group Ltd.

VAUXHALL

PUBLICATION NAME

Vauxhall Advance
Street Address: 516 2nd Ave. N. ,
Province: AB
Postal: T0K 2K0
Country: Canada
Mailing address: P.O. Box 302
Mailing city: Vauxhall
Province: AB
Postal: T0K 2K0
General Phone: (403) 654-2122
General Fax: (403) 654-4184
Display Adv. E-mail: tabads@tabertimes.com
Primary Website: www.vauxhalladvance.com
Year Established: 1978
Delivery Methods: Mail
Areas Served - City/County or Portion Thereof, or Zip codes: Town of VAuxhall and hamlets of Hays and Enchant
Mechanical specifications: Type page 10 1/4 x 14 1/2; E - 6 cols, 1 5/8, 1/8 between; A - 6 cols, 1 5/8, 1/8 between; C - 6 cols, 1 5/8, 1/8 between.
Published: Thur
Avg Paid Circ: 0
Avg Free Circ: 47
Audit By: VAC
Audit Date: 30.09.2016
Personnel: Greg Price (Ed.); Valorie Wiebe (Pub.); Shawna Wiestm (Office/Sales)

VERMILION

PUBLICATION NAME

Vermilion Standard
Street Address: 4917 50th Ave. ,
Province: AB
Postal: T9X 1A6
Country: Canada
General Phone: (780) 853-5344
General Fax: (780) 853-5203
Advertising Phone: (877) 786-8227
Display Adv. E-mail: ngoetz@postmedia.com
Classified Adv. e-mail: ngoetz@postmedia.com
Editorial e-mail: thermiston@postmedia.com
Primary Website: www.vermilionstandard.com
Year Established: 1909
Delivery Methods: Mail`Newsstand`Carrier`Racks
Areas Served - City/County or Portion Thereof, or Zip codes: T9X
Published: Wed
Avg Paid Circ: 1250
Avg Free Circ: 3972
Audit By: VAC
Audit Date: 31.12.2015
Personnel: Trina de Regt (Circulation); Mary-Ann Kostiuk (Publisher); Pat Lavigne (Production and Circulation); Nicki Goetz (Dir. of Adv.); Taylor Hermiston (Reg. Mng. Ed. ext.4)
Parent company (for newspapers): Postmedia Network Inc.

PUBLICATION NAME

Vermilion Voice
Street Address: 5006-50th Ave. ,
Province: AB
Postal: T9X 1A2
Country: Canada
Mailing address: 5006-50th Ave
Mailing city: Vermilion
Province: AB
Postal: T9X 1A2
General Phone: 7808536305
General Fax: (780) 853-5426
General/National Adv. E-mail: vermilionvoice@gmail.com
Display Adv. E-mail: vermilionvoice@gmail.com
Classified Adv. e-mail: vermilionvoice@gmail.com
Editorial e-mail: vermilionvoice@gmail.com
Primary Website: www.vermilionvoice.com
Year Established: 2004
Delivery Methods: Newsstand`Racks
Areas Served - City/County or Portion Thereof, or Zip codes: Canada
Published: Tues
Avg Free Circ: 5500
Audit By: CMCA
Audit Date: 30.06.2018
Personnel: Susan Chikie (Pub.); Lorna Hamilton (Sales, reporter, newspaper layout); Angela Mouley (Reporter and Sales); Amr Rezk (Graphics, website etc.)

VERNON

PUBLICATION NAME

The Morning Star
Street Address: 4407 25th Ave. ,
Province: BC
Postal: V1T 1P5
Country: Canada
Mailing address: 4407 25th Ave.
Mailing city: Vernon
Province: BC
Postal: V1T 1P5
General Phone: (250) 545-3322
General Fax: (250) 542-1510
Display Adv. E-mail: stephanie@vernonmorningstar.com
Classified Adv. e-mail: Classifieds@vernonmorningstar.com
Editorial e-mail: glenn@vernonmorningstar.com
Primary Website: www.vernonmorningstar.com
Year Established: 1988
Areas Served - City/County or Portion Thereof, or Zip codes: Canada
Own Printing Facility?: Y
Mechanical specifications: Type page 10 5/16 x 14 1/2; E - 6 cols, 1 9/16, 1/4 between; A - 6 cols, 1 9/16, 1/4 between; C - 7 cols, 1 3/8, 3/16 between.
Published: Wed`Fri`Sun
Avg Paid Circ: 29884
Audit By: AAM
Audit Date: 30.09.2016
Personnel: Tammy Stelmachowich (Circ. Mgr.); Glenn Mitchell (Mng. Ed.); Ian Jensen (Pub.); Carol Williment (Class. Mgr.)
Parent company (for newspapers): Torstar

PUBLICATION NAME

Vernon Morning Star
Street Address: 4407 25th Avenue ,
Province: BC
Postal: V1T 1P5
Country: British Columbia
Mailing address: 2495 Enterprise Way
Mailing city: Kelowana
Province: BC
Postal: V1X 7K2
General Phone: (250) 545-3322
General Fax: (250) 862-5275
Display Adv. E-Mail: karen.hill@blackpress.ca
Classified Adv. e-mail: bcclassifieds@blackpress.ca
Editorial e-mail: editor@vernonmorningstar.com
Primary Website: vernonmorningstar.com
Areas Served - City/County or Portion Thereof, or Zip codes: Vernon
Published: Wed`Fri
Avg Free Circ: 28286
Audit By: AAM
Audit Date: 31.03.2019
Personnel: Dave Hamilton (Pres.); Karen Hill (Adv. Dir.)
Parent company (for newspapers): Black Press Group Ltd.

VICTORIA

PUBLICATION NAME

Oak Bay News
Street Address: 207a-2187 Oak Bay Avenue ,
Province: BC
Postal: V8R 1G1
Country: Canada
Mailing address: 207A-2187 Oak Bay Avenue
Mailing city: Victoria
Province: BC
Postal: V8R 1G1
General Phone: (250) 480-3251
Advertising Phone: (250) 480-3251
Editorial Phone: (250) 480-3260
Display Adv. E-Mail: jgairdner@blackpress.ca
Classified Adv. e-mail: bcclassifieds@blackpress.ca
Editorial e-mail: editor@oakbaynews.com
Primary Website: www.oakbaynews.com
Year Established: 1974
Delivery Methods: Carrier
Areas Served - City/County or Portion Thereof, or Zip codes: Canada
Own Printing Facility?: Y
Published: Wed`Fri
Avg Paid Circ: 0
Avg Free Circ: 5995
Audit By: AAM
Audit Date: 31.03.2019
Personnel: Janet Gairdner (Pub.); Christine van Reeuwyk (Editor); Lyn Quan (Prod.); John Stewart (Advertising Consultant); Keri Coles (Multimedia Journalist)
Parent company (for newspapers): Black Press Group Ltd.

PUBLICATION NAME

Saanich News
Street Address: 104b-3550 Saanich Road ,
Province: BC
Postal: V8X 1X2
Country: Canada
Mailing address: 104B-3550 Saanich Road
Mailing city: Victoria
Province: BC
Postal: V8X 1X2
General Phone: (250) 381-3484
General Fax: (250) 386-2624
Display Adv. E-mail: staylor@saanichnews.com
Classified Adv. e-mail: rod.fraser@saanichnews.com
Editorial e-mail: editor@saanichnews.com
Primary Website: www.saanichnews.com
Areas Served - City/County or Portion Thereof, or Zip codes: Canada
Published: Wed`Fri
Avg Free Circ: 30360
Audit By: AAM
Audit Date: 31.03.2019
Personnel: Rod Fraser (Sales); Oliver Sommer (Pub); Dan Ebenal (Ed); Miki Speirs (Circ Mgr); Sarah Taylor (Sales)
Parent company (for newspapers): Black Press Group Ltd.

PUBLICATION NAME

Victoria News
Street Address: 818 Broughton St. ,
Province: BC
Postal: V8W 1E4
Country: Canada
Mailing address: 818 Broughton St.
Mailing city: Victoria
Province: BC
Postal: V8W 1E4
General Phone: (250) 381-3484
General Fax: (250) 386-2624
Display Adv. E-Mail: michelle.cabana@goldstreamgazette.com
Editorial e-mail: michelle.cabana@goldstreamgazette.com
Primary Website: vicnews.com
Areas Served - City/County or Portion Thereof, or Zip codes: Canada
Own Printing Facility?: Y
Commercial printers?: Y
Mechanical specifications: Type page 10 1/4 x 14 1/2; E - 5 cols, 1 1/2, 1/6 between; A - 6 cols, 1 1/2, 1/6 between; C - 8 cols, 1 1/4, 1/6 between.
Published: Wed`Fri
Avg Free Circ: 24056
Audit By: AAM
Audit Date: 31.03.2019
Personnel: Mike Cowan (Pub); Pamela Roth (Ed); Michelle Cabana (Pub.)
Parent company (for newspapers): Black Press Group Ltd.

VICTORIAVILLE

PUBLICATION NAME

La Nouvelle
Street Address: 43 Notre Dame St. E., Cp 130 ,
Province: QC
Postal: G6P 3Z4
Country: Canada
Mailing address: PO Box 130
Mailing city: Victoriaville
Province: QC
Postal: G6P 3Z4
General Phone: (819) 758-6211
General Fax: (819) 758-2759
General/National Adv. E-mail: redaction_victo@transcontinental.ca
Primary Website: www.lanouvelle.net
Own Printing Facility?: Y
Commercial printers?: Y
Published: Sun
Avg Free Circ: 44008
Audit By: Sworn/Estimate/Non-Audited
Audit Date: 12.07.2019
Personnel: Pierre Gaudet (Sales Dir.); Michel Gauthier (Pub.); Ghislain Chauvette (Director de l'information); Sylvie Cote (Mng. Ed.); Danielle Deveault (Prodn. Mgr.)
Parent company (for newspapers): Transcontinental Media

PUBLICATION NAME

L'echo De Victoriaville
Street Address: 106 Blvd Bois-francs Nord ,
Province: QC
Postal: G6P 1E7
Country: Canada
Mailing address: 106 Blvd Bois-Francs Nord
Mailing city: Victoriaville

Primary Website: www.journalpremiereedition.com
Areas Served - City/County or Portion Thereof, or Zip codes: Canada
Published: Sat
Avg Paid Circ: 7
Avg Free Circ: 61880
Audit By: CCAB
Audit Date: 30.09.2015

Community Newspapers in Canada

Province: QC
Postal: G6P 1E7
General Phone: (819) 604-6686
General Fax: (819) 604-6398
Advertising Phone: (819) 604-6686
Advertising Fax: (819) 604-6398
Editorial Phone: (819) 604-6686
Editorial Fax: (819) 604-6398
General/National Adv. E-mail: jean.crepeau@quebecormedia.com
Display Adv. E-mail: alain.saint-amand@quebecormedia.com
Editorial e-mail: jean.crepeau@quebecormedia.com
Primary Website: www.lechodevictoriaville.ca
Delivery Methods: Mail`Racks
Areas Served - City/County or Portion Thereof, or Zip codes: Canada
Published: Wed
Avg Free Circ: 42844
Audit By: CCAB
Audit Date: 31.03.2014
Personnel: Jean Crepeau (Ed.)

PUBLICATION NAME

Nouvelle Union
Street Address: Rue Notre-dame Est ,
Province: QC
Postal: G6P 3Z4
Country: Canada
Mailing address: rue Notre-Dame Est
Mailing city: Victoriaville
Province: QC
Postal: G6P 3Z4
General Phone: (819) 758-6211
Areas Served - City/County or Portion Thereof, or Zip codes: Canada
Published: Wed`Fri
Avg Paid Circ: 13
Avg Free Circ: 38872
Audit By: CCAB
Audit Date: 31.03.2014
Personnel: Lucie Lecours

VIKING

PUBLICATION NAME

The Weekly Review
Street Address: 5208 50th Street ,
Province: AB
Postal: T0B 4N0
Country: Canada
Mailing address: PO Box 240
Mailing city: Viking
Province: AB
Postal: T0B 4N0
General Phone: (780) 336-3422
General Fax: (780) 336-3223
General/National Adv. E-mail: vikingweeklyreview@gmail.com
Display Adv. E-mail: vikingreview@gmail.com
Editorial e-mail: vikingweeklyreview@gmail.com
Primary Website: www.weeklyreview.ca
Year Established: 1977
Areas Served - City/County or Portion Thereof, or Zip codes: Beaver County, Viking, Alberta T0B 4N0
Published: Tues
Avg Paid Circ: 0
Avg Free Circ: 10
Audit By: VAC
Audit Date: 30.06.2016
Personnel: Leslie Cholowsky (Ed.); Eric Anderson (Pub.); Kerry Anderson (Owner)
Parent company (for newspapers): Caribou Publishing

VILLE-MARIE

PUBLICATION NAME

Le Journal Temiscamien
Street Address: 22 Rue Ste-anne ,
Province: QC
Postal: J9V 2B7
Country: Canada

Mailing address: 22 rue Ste-Anne
Mailing city: Ville-Marie
Province: QC
Postal: J9Z 2B7
General Phone: (819) 622-1313
General Fax: (819) 622-1333
Published: Wed
Avg Free Circ: 8500
Audit By: Sworn/Estimate/Non-Audited
Audit Date: 12.07.2019
Personnel: Lionel Lacasse (Ed.)

VIRDEN

PUBLICATION NAME

Virden Empire-advance
Street Address: 305 Nelson Street West ,
Province: MB
Postal: R0M 2C0
Country: Canada
Mailing address: PO Box 250
Mailing city: Virden
Province: MB
Postal: R0M 2C0
General Phone: (204) 748-3931
General Fax: (204) 748-1816
General/National Adv. E-mail: trehernetimes@mts.net
Display Adv. E-mail: virden@empireadvance.ca
Editorial e-mail: manager@empireadvance.ca
Primary Website: http://www.empireadvance.ca/
Areas Served - City/County or Portion Thereof, or Zip codes: Canada
Own Printing Facility?: Y
Commercial printers?: Y
Mechanical specifications: Type page 10 1/4 x 15 3/4; E - 6 cols, 1 7/12, 1/6 between; A - 6 cols, 1 7/12, 1/6 between; C - 6 cols, 1 7/12, 1/6 between.
Published: Fri
Avg Free Circ: 27
Audit By: VAC
Audit Date: 30.09.2016
Personnel: Cheryl Rushing (Gen Mgr)
Parent company (for newspapers): Glacier Media Group

VIRGIL

PUBLICATION NAME

The Niagara Advance
Street Address: 1501 Niagara Stone Rd. ,
Province: ON
Postal: L0S 1T0
Country: Canada
Mailing address: PO Box 430
Mailing city: Virgil
Province: ON
Postal: L0S 1T0
General Phone: (905) 468-3283
General Fax: (905) 468-3137
General/National Adv. E-mail: tim.dundas@sunmedia.ca
Primary Website: www.niagaraadvance.ca
Year Established: 1917
Delivery Methods: Carrier
Areas Served - City/County or Portion Thereof, or Zip codes: Canada
Own Printing Facility?: Y
Commercial printers?: Y
Published: Thur
Avg Paid Circ: 20
Avg Free Circ: 7610
Audit By: CMCA
Audit Date: 31.05.2016
Personnel: Tim Dundas (Pub.); Penny Coles (Ed.)
Parent company (for newspapers): Postmedia Network Inc.; Quebecor Communications, Inc.

VULCAN

PUBLICATION NAME

Vulcan Advocate

Street Address: 112 - 3rd Ave. N ,
Province: AB
Postal: T0L 2B0
Country: Canada
Mailing address: PO Box 389
Mailing city: Vulcan
Province: AB
Postal: T0L 2B0
General Phone: (403) 485-2036
General Fax: (403) 485-6938
Advertising Phone: (877) 786-8227
General/National Adv. E-mail: maureen.howard@sunmedia.ca
Display Adv. E-mail: enid.fraser@sunmedia.ca
Classified Adv. e-mail: enid.fraser@sunmedia.ca
Editorial e-mail: stephen.tipper@sunmedia.ca
Primary Website: www.vulcanadvocate.com
Year Established: 1913
Delivery Methods: Mail`Newsstand
Own Printing Facility?: N
Mechanical specifications: Type page 10 1/4 x 15 1/2; E - 6 cols, 1 7/12, between; A - 6 cols, 1 7/12, between; C - 6 cols, 1 7/12, between.
Published: Wed
Avg Paid Circ: 1032
Avg Free Circ: 11
Audit By: CMCA
Audit Date: 31.12.2014
Personnel: Shawn Cornell (Publisher); Stephen Tipper (Editor); Roxanne MacKintosh (Reg. Dir. of Adv.)
Parent company (for newspapers): Postmedia Network Inc.

WABASCA

PUBLICATION NAME

Wabasca Fever
Street Address: PO Box 519 ,
Province: AB
Postal: T0G 2K0
Country: Canada
Mailing address: PO Box 519
Mailing city: Wabasca
Province: AB
Postal: T0G 2K0
General Phone: (780) 891-2108
General Fax: (888) 318-555
General/National Adv. E-mail: wabascafever4@shaw.ca
Display Adv. E-mail: wabascafever@shaw.ca
Classified Adv. e-mail: wabascafever@shaw.ca
Editorial e-mail: wabascafever@shaw.ca
Primary Website: www.fevernewspaper.com
Year Established: 1998
Delivery Methods: Mail`Newsstand
Areas Served - City/County or Portion Thereof, or Zip codes: Municipal District of Opportunity No. 17
Published: Thur
Avg Paid Circ: 630
Avg Free Circ: 200
Audit By: Sworn/Estimate/Non-Audited
Audit Date: 12.07.2019
Personnel: Patricia Thomas; Bruce Thomas (Pub.)
Parent company (for newspapers): Title

WADENA

PUBLICATION NAME

Wadena News
Street Address: 102 First St Ne ,
Province: SK
Postal: S0A 4J0
Country: Canada
Mailing address: PO Box 100
Mailing city: Wadena
Province: SK
Postal: S0A 4J0
General Phone: (306) 338-2231
General Fax: (306) 338-3421
General/National Adv. E-mail: wadena.news@sasktel.net
Primary Website: http://wadenanews.ca/
Year Established: 1908
Delivery Methods: Mail`Newsstand
Areas Served - City/County or Portion Thereof, or Zip codes: Canada
Own Printing Facility?: Y
Commercial printers?: Y
Mechanical specifications: Type page 10 1/3 x 15 1/2; E - 5 cols, 1 14/15, 1/6 between; A - 5 cols, 1 14/15, 1/6 between; C - 5 cols, 1 14/15, 1/6 between.
Published: Mon
Avg Paid Circ: 1649
Avg Free Circ: 80
Audit By: Sworn/Estimate/Non-Audited
Audit Date: 12.07.2019
Personnel: Alison Squires (Pub.)

WAINWRIGHT

PUBLICATION NAME

Wainwright Star Edge
Street Address: 1027 3rd Ave ,
Province: AB
Postal: T9W 1T6
Country: Canada
Mailing address: 1027 3rd Avenue
Mailing city: Wainwright
Province: AB
Postal: T9W 1T6
General Phone: (780) 842-4465
General Fax: (780) 842-2760
Advertising Phone: (780) 842-4465 ext.112
General/National Adv. E-mail: classifieds@starnews.ca
Display Adv. E-mail: patrick@starnews.ca
Classified Adv. e-mail: classifieds@starnews.ca
Editorial e-mail: zak@starnews.ca
Primary Website: www.starnews.ca
Year Established: 2002
Delivery Methods: Newsstand`Carrier`Racks
Areas Served - City/County or Portion Thereof, or Zip codes: MD of Wainwright
Mechanical specifications: 8 Columns x 15.25" (10.25' x 15.25")
Published: Fri
Avg Paid Circ: 0
Avg Free Circ: 6500
Audit By: VAC
Audit Date: 6/31/2017
Personnel: Roger Holmes (Pub.); Patrick Moroz (Adv. Sales); Sherry Shatz (Sales & Promo); Zak McLachlan (Editor); Barb Tywoniuk (Graphic Design Dept. Manager)
Parent company (for newspapers): Star News Inc.

WAKAW

PUBLICATION NAME

The Wakaw Recorder
Street Address: 224 First St. S. ,
Province: SK
Postal: S0K 4P0
Country: Canada
Mailing address: PO Box 9
Mailing city: Wakaw
Province: SK
Postal: S0K 4P0
General Phone: (306) 233-4325
General Fax: (306) 233-4386
General/National Adv. E-mail: wrecorder@sasktel.net
Delivery Methods: Mail
Areas Served - City/County or Portion Thereof, or Zip codes: Canada
Published: Wed
Avg Paid Circ: 1375
Avg Free Circ: 14
Audit By: CMCA
Audit Date: 31.03.2016
Personnel: Dwayne Biccum (Ed.)

WAKEFIELD

PUBLICATION NAME

The Low Down To Hull And Back News
Street Address: 815 Riverside Drive ,
Province: QC
Postal: J0X 3G0
Country: Canada

Mailing address: 815 Riverside Drive
Mailing city: Wakefield
Province: QC
Postal: J0X 3G0
General Phone: (819) 459-2222
General Fax: (819) 459-3831
Advertising Phone: (613) 241-6767
Editorial Phone: (819) 459-2222
General/National Adv. E-mail: general@lowdownonline.com
Display Adv. E-mail: lowdowndavid1@gmail.com
Classified Adv. e-mail: classifieds@lowdownonline.com
Editorial e-mail: general@lowdownonline.com
Primary Website: www.lowdownonline.com
Year Established: 1973
Delivery Methods: Mail`Newsstand`Racks
Areas Served - City/County or Portion Thereof, or Zip codes: La PÃªche, Quebec
Mechanical specifications: 5 columns 10.4" wide x 15.25" 300 dpi for ads
Published: Wed
Avg Paid Circ: 2531
Audit By: Sworn/Estimate/Non-Audited
Audit Date: 12.07.2019
Personnel: Maya Riel Lachapelle (General Manager); Heather Hopewell (Admin. Asst.); Nikki Mantell (Pub./Owner); Agnes McMillan (Circ. Mgr.); Melanie Scott (Ed.); Hunter Cresswell (Reporter); Nicole McCormick (Reporter)

WALKERTON

PUBLICATION NAME

Walkerton Herald-times
Street Address: 10 Victoria St. N. ,
Province: ON
Postal: N0G 2V0
Country: Canada
Mailing address: PO Box 190
Mailing city: Walkerton
Province: ON
Postal: N0G 2V0
General Phone: (519) 881-1600
General Fax: (519) 881-0276
General/National Adv. E-mail: editor@walkerton.com
Display Adv. E-mail: ads@walkerton.com
Primary Website: www.walkerton.com
Year Established: 1861
Delivery Methods: Mail`Newsstand
Areas Served - City/County or Portion Thereof, or Zip codes: Brockton
Own Printing Facility?: Y
Commercial printers?: Y
Published: Thur
Avg Paid Circ: 1296
Avg Free Circ: 3
Audit By: CMCA
Audit Date: 30.06.2016
Personnel: April Wells (Adv. Sales Mgr.); Cathy Spitzig (Circ. Mgr.); John McPhee (Ed.)
Parent company (for newspapers): Metroland Media Group Ltd.; Torstar

WARMAN

PUBLICATION NAME

Clark's Crossing Gazette
Street Address: 109 Klassen Street West , 109 Klassen Street West
Province: SK
Postal: S0K 4S0
Country: Canada
Mailing address: P.O. Box 1419
Mailing city: Warman
Province: SK
Postal: S0K 4S0
General Phone: (306) 668-0575
General Fax: (306) 668-3997
General/National Adv. E-mail: tjenson@ccgazette.ca
Display Adv. E-mail: ads@ccgazette.ca
Classified Adv. e-mail: ads@ccgazette.ca
Editorial e-mail: editor@ccgazette.ca
Primary Website: http://www.ccgazette.ca
Year Established: 2008
Delivery Methods:

Mail`Newsstand`Carrier`Racks
Areas Served - City/County or Portion Thereof, or Zip codes: Corman Park
Mechanical specifications: 6 col. x 212 lines page Tabloid
Published: Thur
Avg Paid Circ: 15
Avg Free Circ: 16500
Audit By: Sworn/Estimate/Non-Audited
Audit Date: 12.07.2019
Personnel: Terry Jenson (Publisher)
Parent company (for newspapers): JENSON PUBLISHING

WASAGA BEACH

PUBLICATION NAME

The Wasaga Sun
Street Address: 1456 Mosley St. ,
Province: ON
Postal: L9Z 2B9
Country: Canada
Mailing address: 1456 Mosley St.
Mailing city: Wasaga Beach
Province: ON
Postal: L9Z 2B9
General Phone: (705) 429-1688
General Fax: (705) 422-2446
General/National Adv. E-mail: sunnews@simcoe.com
Primary Website: wasagasun.ca
Areas Served - City/County or Portion Thereof, or Zip codes: Wasaga
Mechanical specifications: Type page 11 1/2 x 21 1/2; E - 6 cols, 1 3/4, 1/6 between; A - 6 cols, 1 3/4, 1/6 between; C - 6 cols, 1 3/4, 1/6 between.
Published: Thur
Avg Free Circ: 13241
Audit By: CCAB
Audit Date: 20.12.2017
Personnel: Christine Brown (Adv. Mgr.); Joe Anderson (Pub.); Catherine Haller (Gen. Mgr.); Scott Woodhouse (Ed.); Craig Widdifield (Mng. Ed.); Stephen Hall (Prodn. Mgr.)
Parent company (for newspapers): Metroland Media Group Ltd.

WATERDOWN

PUBLICATION NAME

The Flamborough Review
Street Address: 30 Main St. N. ,
Province: ON
Postal: L0R 2H0
Country: Canada
Mailing address: PO Box 20
Mailing city: Waterdown
Province: ON
Postal: L0R 2H0
General Phone: (905) 689-2003
General Fax: (905) 689-3110
Advertising Phone: (905) 689-2003 ext. 272
Editorial Phone: (905) 689-2003 ext. 321
General/National Adv. E-mail: classified@haltonsearch.com
Display Adv. E-mail: tlindsay@burlingtonpost.com
Editorial e-mail: editor@flamboroughreview.com
Primary Website: flamboroughreview.com
Year Established: 1918
Delivery Methods: Carrier
Areas Served - City/County or Portion Thereof, or Zip codes: Canada
Own Printing Facility?: Y
Commercial printers?: Y
Published: Thur
Avg Paid Circ: 0
Avg Free Circ: 14075
Audit By: CCAB
Audit Date: 30.09.2017
Personnel: Neil Oliver (Pub.); Ted Lindsay (Adv. Mgr.); Charlene Hall (Circ. Mgr.); Brenda Jefferies (Ed.); Debbi Koppejan (Advertising Director)
Parent company (for newspapers): Metroland Media Group Ltd.; Torstar

WATERLOO

PUBLICATION NAME

Waterloo Chronicle
Street Address: 279 Weber St. N., Ste. 20 ,
Province: ON
Postal: N2J 3H8
Country: Canada
Mailing address: 279 Weber St. N., Ste. 20
Mailing city: Waterloo
Province: ON
Postal: N2J 3H8
General Phone: (519) 886-2830
General Fax: (519) 886-9383
General/National Adv. E-mail: classified@waterloochronicle.ca
Editorial e-mail: editorial@waterloochronicle.ca
Primary Website: www.waterloochronicle.ca
Mechanical specifications: Type page 10 5/16 x 14 1/4; E - 6 cols, 1 9/16, between; A - 6 cols, 1 9/16, between; C - 8 cols, between.
Published: Thur
Avg Free Circ: 29538
Audit By: CMCA
Audit Date: 31.03.2016
Personnel: Peter Winkler (Pub.); Gerry Mattice (Adv. Mgr., Retail Sales); Bob Vrbanac (Ed.)
Parent company (for newspapers): Metroland Media Group Ltd.; Torstar

WATFORD

PUBLICATION NAME

Watford Guide-advocate
Street Address: 5292 Nauvoo Rd. ,
Province: ON
Postal: N0M 2S0
Country: Canada
Mailing address: PO Box 99
Mailing city: Watford
Province: ON
Postal: N0M 2S0
General Phone: (519) 876-2809
General Fax: (519) 876-2322
General/National Adv. E-mail: guideadvocate@execulink.com
Year Established: 1875
Mechanical specifications: Type page 10 x 16; E - 6 cols, 1 9/16, 1/8 between; A - 6 cols, 1 9/16, 1/8 between; C - 6 cols, 1 9/16, 1/8 between.
Published: Thur
Avg Paid Circ: 1919
Audit By: CMCA
Audit Date: 29.02.2016
Personnel: Dale Hayter (Pub.); Gill Deschutter (Adv. Mgr.); Stephanie Cattryse (Ed.)

WATROUS

PUBLICATION NAME

The Watrous Manitou
Street Address: 309 Main St. ,
Province: SK
Postal: S0K 4T0
Country: Canada
Mailing address: PO Box 100
Mailing city: Watrous
Province: SK
Postal: S0K 4T0
General Phone: (306) 946-3343
General Fax: (306) 946-2026
General/National Adv. E-mail: watrous.manitou@sasktel.net
Primary Website: www.thewatrousmanitou.com
Year Established: 1933
Delivery Methods: Mail
Areas Served - City/County or Portion Thereof, or Zip codes: Canada
Mechanical specifications: Type page 10 1/4 x 15 3/4; E - 6 cols, 1 15/16, 3/16 between; A - 6 cols, 1 15/16, 3/16 between
Published: Mon
Avg Paid Circ: 1387
Avg Free Circ: 21
Audit By: CMCA
Audit Date: 30.06.2016

WATSON

PUBLICATION NAME

Naicam News
Street Address: 100-102 Main St. ,
Province: SK
Postal: S0K 4V0
Country: Canada
Mailing address: PO Box 576
Mailing city: Watson
Province: SK
Postal: S0K 4V0
General Phone: (306) 287-4388
General Fax: (306) 287-3308
General/National Adv. E-mail: ecpress@sasktel.net
Areas Served - City/County or Portion Thereof, or Zip codes: Canada
Mechanical specifications: Type page 10 1/4 x 15 3/4; E - 5 cols, 1 29/30, between; A - 5 cols, 1 29/30, between; C - 5 cols, 1 29/30, between.
Published: Fri
Avg Paid Circ: 396
Audit By: Sworn/Estimate/Non-Audited
Audit Date: 12.07.2019
Personnel: Karen Mitchell (Pub./Gen. Mgr.)

WAWA

PUBLICATION NAME

The Algoma News Review
Street Address: 33 St. Marie St. ,
Province: ON
Postal: P0S 1K0
Country: Canada
Mailing address: P.O. Box 528
Mailing city: Wawa
Province: ON
Postal: P0S 1K0
General Phone: (705) 856-2267
General Fax: (705) 856-4952
General/National Adv. E-mail: waprint2@ontera.net
Editorial e-mail: editor@thealgomanews.ca
Primary Website: www.thealgomanews.ca
Year Established: 1964
Areas Served - City/County or Portion Thereof, or Zip codes: Canada
Commercial printers?: Y
Mechanical specifications: Type page 10 1/4 x 16 1/4; E - 5 cols, 1 15/16, 3/16 between; A - 5 cols, 1 15/16, 3/16 between; C - 5 cols, 1 15/16, 3/16 between.
Published: Wed
Avg Paid Circ: 598
Avg Free Circ: 33
Audit By: CMCA
Audit Date: 31.03.2016
Personnel: Tammy Landry (Ed.); Christel Gignac (Adv. Mgr.)

WEST LORNE

PUBLICATION NAME

Chronicle
Street Address: 168 Main St. ,
Province: ON
Postal: N0L 2P0
Country: Canada
Mailing address: PO Box 100
Mailing city: West Lorne
Province: ON
Postal: N0L 2P0
General Phone: (519) 768-2220
General Fax: (519) 768-2221
General/National Adv. E-mail: chronicle@bowesnet.com
Primary Website: www.thechronicle-online.com
Year Established: 1993
Areas Served - City/County or Portion Thereof, or Zip codes: Canada
Mechanical specifications: Type page 10 1/4 x 15; E - 5 cols, 2, 1/4 between; A - 5 cols, 2, 1/4 between; C - 5 cols, 2, 1/4 between.
Published: Thur
Avg Paid Circ: 100
Avg Free Circ: 5463

Community Newspapers in Canada   III-591

Audit By: CMCA
Audit Date: 30.06.2013
Personnel: Bev Ponton; Ian McCallum (Reg. Managing Ed.)
Parent company (for newspapers): Quebecor Communications, Inc.

WEST MILL

PUBLICATION NAME

The Monitor
Street Address: 345 Victoria, Ste. 508 ,
Province: QC
Postal: H3Z 2M6
Country: Canada
Mailing address: 345 Victoria, Ste. 508
Mailing city: West Mill
Province: QC
Postal: H3Z 2M6
General Phone: (514) 484-5610
General Fax: (514) 484-6028
General/National Adv. E-mail: toula.foscolos@transcontinental.ca
Primary Website: www.themonitor.ca
Mechanical specifications: Type page 10 1/8 x 14 1/8; E - 8 cols, 2, 1/16 between; A - 8 cols, 2, 1/16 between; C - 8 cols, 1 1/8, 1/16 between.
Published: Thur
Avg Free Circ: 35164
Audit By: Sworn/Estimate/Non-Audited
Audit Date: 12.07.2019
Personnel: Yannick Pinel (Ed.); Toula Foscolos (Ed. in Chief)

WESTLOCK

PUBLICATION NAME

The Westlock News
Street Address: 9871 107th St. ,
Province: AB
Postal: T7P 1R9
Country: Canada
General Phone: (780) 349-3033
General Fax: (780) 349-3677
General/National Adv. E-mail: production@westlock.greatwest.ca
Display Adv. E-mail: abaxandall@westlock.greatwest.ca
Classified Adv. e-mail: abaxandall@westlock.greatwest.ca
Editorial e-mail: dneuman@westlock.greatwest.ca
Primary Website: www.westlocknews.com
Year Established: 1901
Delivery Methods: Mail`Newsstand`Carrier
Areas Served - City/County or Portion Thereof, or Zip codes: Canada
Published: Tues
Avg Paid Circ: 10
Avg Free Circ: 5
Audit By: VAC
Audit Date: 31.03.2016
Personnel: George Blais (Pub.); Louise Strehlau (Circ. Mgr.); Olivia Bako (Ed.); Connie Onyschuk (Adv.); Joyce Weber (Adv.)
Parent company (for newspapers): Glacier Media Group

WESTMOUNT

PUBLICATION NAME

The Westmount Examiner
Street Address: 245 Victoria Street , Suite 210
Province: QC
Postal: H3Z 2M6
Country: Canada
Mailing address: 245 Victoria Street
Mailing city: Westmount
Province: QC
Postal: H3Z 2M6
General Phone: (514) 484-5610
General Fax: (514) 484-6028
Advertising Phone: (514) 484-5610
Editorial Phone: 514-484-5610
General/National Adv. E-mail: examiner@tc.tc
Display Adv. E-mail: marie-france.paquette@tc.tc
Primary Website: www.westmountexaminer.com
Year Established: 1935
Delivery Methods: Newsstand`Carrier`Racks
Areas Served - City/County or Portion Thereof, or Zip codes: H3Y, H3Z
Mechanical specifications: Type page 11 3/8 x 15; E - 8 cols, 1 1/6, 1/6 between; A - 8 cols, 1 1/6, 1/6 between; C - 8 cols, 1 1/6, 1/6 between.
Published: Thur
Avg Paid Circ: 2
Avg Free Circ: 9282
Audit By: CMCA
Audit Date: 28.02.2014
Personnel: Marie-France Paquette (Assistant publisher); Patricia-Ann Beaulieu (Publisher); Harvey Aisthental (Media Consultant)
Parent company (for newspapers): Transcontinental Media

PUBLICATION NAME

The Westmount Independent
Street Address: 310 Victoria Bldg. # 105 ,
Province: QC
Postal: H3Z 2M9
Country: Canada
Mailing address: 310 Victoria Ave. #105
Mailing city: Westmount
Province: QC
Postal: H3Z 2M9
General Fax: (514) 935-9241
Advertising Phone: (514) 223-3567
Editorial Phone: (514) 223-3578
General/National Adv. E-mail: office@westmountindependent.com
Display Adv. E-mail: advertising@westmountindependent.com
Primary Website: www.westmountindependent.com
Areas Served - City/County or Portion Thereof, or Zip codes: Westmount, Quebec
Published: Tues
Avg Free Circ: 15057
Audit By: CMCA
Audit Date: 31.05.2015
Personnel: David Price (Pub); Arleen Candiotti (Advt Consultant)

WESTPORT

PUBLICATION NAME

Rideau Valley Mirror
Street Address: 43 Bedfrod St. ,
Province: ON
Postal: K0G 1X0
Country: Canada
Mailing address: PO Box 130
Mailing city: Westport
Province: ON
Postal: K0G 1X0
General Phone: (613) 273-8000
General Fax: (613) 273-8001
General/National Adv. E-mail: info@review-mirror.com
Display Adv. E-mail: advertising@review-mirror.com
Editorial e-mail: newsroom@review-mirror.com
Primary Website: www.review-mirror.com
Areas Served - City/County or Portion Thereof, or Zip codes: Canada
Published: Thur
Avg Paid Circ: 1662
Avg Free Circ: 57
Audit By: CMCA
Audit Date: 28.02.2013
Personnel: Bill Ritchie (Adv. Mgr.); Louise Haughton (Circ. Mgr.); Howie Crichton (Ed.)

WETASKIWIN

PUBLICATION NAME

Wetaskiwin Times
Street Address: 5013 51 St. ,
Province: AB
Postal: T9A 1L4
Country: Canada
Mailing address: PO Box 6900
Mailing city: Wetaskiwin
Province: AB
Postal: T9A 2G5
General Phone: (780) 352-2231
General Fax: (780) 352-4333
General/National Adv. E-mail: production@wetaskiwintimes.com
Display Adv. E-mail: pam.tremaine@sunmedia.ca
Classified Adv. e-mail: pam.tremaine@sunmedia.ca
Editorial e-mail: editor@sunmedia.ca
Primary Website: www.wetaskiwintimes.com
Year Established: 1901
Areas Served - City/County or Portion Thereof, or Zip codes: Canada
Mechanical specifications: Type page 10 1/4 x 12.5; E - 6 cols, 1 1/6, 1/8 between; A - 6 cols, 1 1/6, 1/8 between; C - 8 cols, 1 1/6, 1/8 between.
Published: Wed
Avg Free Circ: 9957
Audit By: VAC
Audit Date: 31.12.2015
Personnel: Adam Roy (Prodn. Mgr.); Nick Goetz (Pub.); Clara Mitchell (Office Mgr.); Pam Tremaine (Adv. Mgr.); Sarah Swenson (Ed.)
Parent company (for newspapers): Postmedia Network Inc.

WEYBURN

PUBLICATION NAME

Weyburn Review
Street Address: 904 East Ave. ,
Province: SK
Postal: S4H 2Y8
Country: Canada
Mailing address: PO Box 400
Mailing city: Weyburn
Province: SK
Postal: S4H 2K4
General Phone: (306) 842-7487
General Fax: (306) 842-0282
General/National Adv. E-mail: production@weyburnreview.com
Primary Website: www.weyburnreview.com
Year Established: 1909
Delivery Methods: Mail`Newsstand`Carrier
Areas Served - City/County or Portion Thereof, or Zip codes: Canada
Own Printing Facility?: Y
Commercial printers?: Y
Mechanical specifications: 5 (9.67") column broadsheet x 278 lines deep. 11 picas per column.
Published: Wed
Avg Paid Circ: 2189
Avg Free Circ: 59
Audit By: CMCA
Audit Date: 30.06.2016
Personnel: Rick Major (Pub.); Patricia Ward (Mng. Ed.)
Parent company (for newspapers): Glacier Media Group

WEYBURN

PUBLICATION NAME

Weyburn This Week
Street Address: 115 2nd St Ne ,
Province: SK
Postal: S4H0T7
Country: Canada
Mailing address: 115 2nd St NE
Mailing city: WEYBURN
Province: SK
Postal: S4H0T7
General Phone: (306) 842-3900
General Fax: (306) 842-2515
General/National Adv. E-mail: weyburnthisweek@sasktel.net
Primary Website: www.weyburnthisweek.com
Areas Served - City/County or Portion Thereof, or Zip codes: Canada
Mechanical specifications: Type page 10 1/2 x 15; E - 6 cols, 1 7/12, 1/6 between; A - 6 cols, 1 7/12, 1/6 between; C - 6 cols, 1 7/12, 1/6 between.
Published: Fri
Avg Paid Circ: 3
Avg Free Circ: 5546
Audit By: CMCA
Audit Date: 31.01.2016
Personnel: Rick Major (Pub.)
Parent company (for newspapers): Glacier Media Group

WHEATLEY

PUBLICATION NAME

Southpoint Sun
Street Address: 14 Talbot Street West ,
Province: ON
Postal: N0P 2P0
Country: Canada
Mailing address: PO Box 10
Mailing city: Wheatley
Province: ON
Postal: N0P 2P0
General Phone: (519) 825-4541
General Fax: (519) 825-4546
General/National Adv. E-mail: sun@southpointsun.ca
Display Adv. E-mail: journal@mnsi.net
Primary Website: www.southpointsun.ca
Areas Served - City/County or Portion Thereof, or Zip codes: Canada
Published: Wed
Avg Free Circ: 10579
Audit By: CMCA
Audit Date: 28.02.2014
Personnel: Jim Heyens (Pub.); Sheila McBrayne (Ed.)

WHISTLER

PUBLICATION NAME

Pique Newsmagazine
Street Address: 103-1390 Alpha Lake Rd. ,
Province: BC
Postal: V0N 1B1
Country: Canada
Mailing address: 103-1390 Alpha Lake Rd.
Mailing city: Whistler
Province: BC
Postal: V0N 1B1
General Phone: (604) 938-0202
General Fax: (604) 938-0201
General/National Adv. E-mail: sarah@piquenewsmagazine.com
Display Adv. E-mail: susan@piquenewsmagazine.com
Classified Adv. e-mail: traffic@piquenewsmagazine.com
Editorial e-mail: edit@piquenewsmagazine.com
Primary Website: www.piquenewsmagazine.com
Year Established: 1994
Own Printing Facility?: Y
Mechanical specifications: Type page 9 1/2 x 12 7/8; E - 4 cols, 2 1/4, 3/8 between; A - 4 cols, 2 1/4, 3/8 between; C - 5 cols, 1 3/4, 3/8 between.
Published: Thur
Avg Paid Circ: 41
Avg Free Circ: 10997
Audit By: VAC
Audit Date: 30.06.2017
Personnel: Clare Ogilvie (Ed.); Sarah Strother (Pub); Susan Hutchinson (Sales Mgr); Katie Bechtel (Circ Mgr); Jennifer Treptow (Sales Coord)
Parent company (for newspapers): Glacier Media Group; Pique Publishing Inc.

PUBLICATION NAME

The Whistler Question
Street Address: 103-1390 Alpha Lake Rd ,
Province: BC
Postal: V0N 1B4
Country: Canada

Mailing address: 103-1390 Alpha Lake Rd
Mailing city: Whistler
Province: BC
Postal: V0N 1B4
General Phone: (604) 932-5131
General Fax: (604) 932-2862
General/National Adv. E-mail: smatches@whistlerquestion.com
Display Adv. E-mail: susan@piquenewsmagazine.com
Classified Adv. e-mail: mail@piquenewsmagazine.com
Editorial e-mail: editor@whistlerquestion.com
Primary Website: www.whistlerquestion.com
Year Established: 1976
Areas Served - City/County or Portion Thereof, or Zip codes: Canada
Own Printing Facility?: Y
Published: Tues
Avg Paid Circ: 433
Avg Free Circ: 5762
Audit By: VAC
Audit Date: 31.08.2016
Personnel: Sarah Strother (Pres., WPLP); Kathryn Bechtel (Office/Class. Mgr); Alyssa Noel (Ed); Susan Hutchinson (Sales Mgr)
Parent company (for newspapers): Glacier Media Group

WHITECOURT

PUBLICATION NAME

The Mayerthorpe Freelancer
Street Address: 4732 - 50 Ave. ,
Province: AB
Postal: T7S 1N7
Country: Canada
Mailing address: PO Box 630
Mailing city: Whitecourt
Province: AB
Postal: T7S 1N7
General Phone: (780) 778-3977
General Fax: (780) 778-6459
General/National Adv. E-mail: info@mayerthorpefreelancer.com
Display Adv. E-mail: advertising@mayerthorpefreelancer.com
Editorial e-mail: ann.harvey@sunmedia.ca
Primary Website: www.mayerthorpefreelancer.com
Year Established: 1978
Areas Served - City/County or Portion Thereof, or Zip codes: Woodlands County
Mechanical specifications: Type page 10 1/4 x 14; E - 8 cols, 1 3/16, 3/16 between; A - 8 cols, 1 3/16, 3/16 between; C - 8 cols, 1 3/16, 3/16 between.
Published: Wed
Avg Paid Circ: 589
Avg Free Circ: 7
Audit By: CMCA
Audit Date: 31.12.2013
Personnel: Pam Allain (Reg. Dir. of Adv.); Candice Daniels (Circ. Mgr.); Christopher King (Ed.)
Parent company (for newspapers): Quebecor Communications, Inc.

PUBLICATION NAME

The Whitecourt Star
Street Address: 4732 50th Ave. ,
Province: AB
Postal: T7S 1N7
Country: Canada
Mailing address: PO Box 630
Mailing city: Whitecourt
Province: AB
Postal: T7S 1N7
General Phone: (780) 778-3977
General Fax: (780) 778-6459
General/National Adv. E-mail: wcstar.general@sunmedia.ca
Display Adv. E-mail: nikki.greening@sunmedia.ca
Editorial e-mail: wcstar.editorial@sunmedia.com
Primary Website: www.whitecourtstar.com
Year Established: 1961
Delivery Methods: Mail`Newsstand`Carrier`Racks
Areas Served - City/County or Portion Thereof, or Zip codes: T7S
Own Printing Facility?: Y
Commercial printers?: Y
Mechanical specifications: Type page 10 1/4 x 16; E - 10 cols, 1 9/16, between; A - 10 cols, 1 9/16, between; C - 10 cols, 1 9/16, between.
Published: Wed
Avg Paid Circ: 2467
Avg Free Circ: 113
Audit By: VAC
Audit Date: 31.12.2015
Personnel: Pamela Allain (Pub.); Meghan Brown (Sales); Candice Daniels (Circ.); Nikki Greening (Sales); Tracy McKinnon (Front Office Classifieds); Christopher King (Ed.)
Parent company (for newspapers): Postmedia Network Inc.

WHITEHORSE

PUBLICATION NAME

Yukon News
Street Address: 3106 Third Ave. , Ste. 200
Province: YT
Postal: Y1A 5G1
Country: Canada
Mailing address: 200-3106 Third Ave.
Mailing city: Whitehorse
Province: YT
Postal: Y1A 5G1
General Phone: (867) 667-6285
Display Adv. E-mail: stephanie.simpson@yukon-news.com
Classified Adv. e-mail: wordads@yukon-news.com
Editorial e-mail: editor@yukon-news.com
Primary Website: yukon-news.com
Year Established: 1960
Delivery Methods: Mail`Newsstand`Racks
Areas Served - City/County or Portion Thereof, or Zip codes: Canada
Own Printing Facility?: Y
Commercial printers?: Y
Mechanical specifications: Type page 11 1/2 x 15 1/2; E - 5 cols, 1 11/12, 1/6 between; A - 5 cols, 1 11/12, 1/6 between; C - 5 cols, 1 11/12, 1/6 between.
Published: Wed`Fri
Avg Paid Circ: 1686
Avg Free Circ: 2502
Audit By: AAM
Audit Date: 31.03.2019
Personnel: Stephanie Newsome (Pub.); Stephanie Simpson (Adv.); Ashley J (Ed.)
Parent company (for newspapers): Black Press Ltd.

WHITEWOOD

PUBLICATION NAME

The Whitewood Herald
Street Address: 708 S. Railway St. ,
Province: SK
Postal: S0G 5C0
Country: Canada
Mailing address: PO Box 160
Mailing city: Whitewood
Province: SK
Postal: S0G 5C0
General Phone: (306) 735-2230
General Fax: (306) 735-2899
General/National Adv. E-mail: herald@whitewoodherald.com
Display Adv. E-mail: ads@whitewoodherald.com
Classified Adv. e-mail: contact@whitewoodherald.com
Editorial e-mail: herald@whitewoodherald.com
Primary Website: www.whitewoodherald.sk.ca
Delivery Methods: Mail`Newsstand
Areas Served - City/County or Portion Thereof, or Zip codes: Canada
Commercial printers?: Y
Mechanical specifications: Type page 10 1/4 x 16; E - 5 cols, 1 7/8, 3/16 between; A - 5 cols, 1 7/8, 3/16 between; C - 5 cols, 1 7/8, 3/16 between.
Published: Fri
Avg Paid Circ: 667
Avg Free Circ: 88
Audit By: CMCA
Audit Date: 30.04.2016
Personnel: Chris Ashfield (Pub)

WIARTON

PUBLICATION NAME

The Wiarton Echo
Street Address: 573 Berford St. ,
Province: ON
Postal: N0H 2T0
Country: Canada
Mailing address: P.O. Box 220
Mailing city: Wiarton
Province: ON
Postal: N0H 2T0
General Phone: (519) 534-1560
General Fax: (519) 534-4616
Advertising Phone: (519) 534-1563
Advertising Fax: (519) 534-4616
Editorial Phone: (519) 534-1560
Editorial Fax: (519) 534-4616
General/National Adv. E-mail: wiartonecho@bmts.com
Display Adv. E-mail: echoads@bowesnet.com
Editorial e-mail: wiartonecho@bmts.com
Primary Website: www.wiartonecho.com
Year Established: 1879
Areas Served - City/County or Portion Thereof, or Zip codes: Canada
Commercial printers?: Y
Published: Tues
Avg Paid Circ: 1361
Avg Free Circ: 6
Audit By: CMCA
Audit Date: 30.06.2016
Personnel: Keith Gilbert (Ed.)
Parent company (for newspapers): Postmedia Network Inc.; Quebecor Communications, Inc.

WILLIAMS LAKE

PUBLICATION NAME

The Williams Lake Tribune
Street Address: 188 N. 1st Ave. ,
Province: BC
Postal: V2G 1Y8
Country: Canada
Mailing address: 188 N. 1st Ave.
Mailing city: Williams Lake
Province: BC
Postal: V2G 1Y8
General Phone: (250) 392-2331
General Fax: (250) 392-7253
General/National Adv. E-mail: classifieds@wltribune.com
Display Adv. E-mail: advertising@wltribune.com
Classified Adv. e-mail: classifieds@wltribune.com
Editorial e-mail: editor@wltribune.com
Primary Website: www.wltribune.com
Year Established: 1930
Delivery Methods: Mail`Newsstand`Carrier`Racks
Areas Served - City/County or Portion Thereof, or Zip codes: Canada
Own Printing Facility?: Y
Commercial printers?: Y
Published: Wed
Avg Paid Circ: 1109
Avg Free Circ: 9794
Audit By: VAC
Audit Date: 30.06.2016
Personnel: Kathy McLean (Pub); Angie Mindus (Ed); Lynn Bolt (Class. Mgr)
Parent company (for newspapers): Black Press Group Ltd.

WILLOWDALE

PUBLICATION NAME

The East York Mirror
Street Address: 10 Tempo Ave. ,
Province: ON
Postal: M2H 3S5
Country: Canada
Mailing address: 10 Tempo Ave.
Mailing city: Willowdale
Province: ON
Postal: M2H 3S5
General Phone: (413) 493-4400
General Fax: (413) 495-6629
General/National Adv. E-mail: eym@mirror-guardian.com
Primary Website: www.metroland.com
Year Established: 1995
Areas Served - City/County or Portion Thereof, or Zip codes: Canada
Own Printing Facility?: Y
Commercial printers?: Y
Mechanical specifications: Type page 10 3/8 x 14; E - 9 cols, 1 1/16, between; A - 9 cols, 1 1/16, between; C - 9 cols, 1 1/16, between.
Published: Thur
Avg Paid Circ: 0
Avg Free Circ: 34643
Audit By: CCAB
Audit Date: 30.09.2017
Personnel: Betty Carr (Pub.); Marg Middleton (Gen. Mgr.); Stacey Allen (Adv. Dir.); Paris Quinn (Sales Rep.); Kim Buenting (Circ. Mgr.); Deborah Bodine (Ed.); Alan Shackleton (Mng. Ed.); Katherine Bernal (Prodn. Mgr.); Dave Barnett (Prodn. Dir.)
Parent company (for newspapers): Metroland Media Group Ltd.; Torstar

WINCHESTER

PUBLICATION NAME

Winchester Press
Street Address: 545 St. Lawrence St. ,
Province: ON
Postal: K0C 2K0
Country: Canada
Mailing address: PO Box 399
Mailing city: Winchester
Province: ON
Postal: K0C 2K0
General Phone: (613) 774-2524
General Fax: (613) 774-3967
General/National Adv. E-mail: news@winchesterpress.on.ca
Display Adv. E-mail: advert@winchesterpress.on.ca
Editorial e-mail: news@winchesterpress.on.ca
Primary Website: www.winchesterpress.on.ca
Year Established: 1888
Delivery Methods: Mail`Racks
Areas Served - City/County or Portion Thereof, or Zip codes: Canada
Own Printing Facility?: Y
Commercial printers?: Y
Mechanical specifications: Type page 13 x 21 1/2; E - 6 cols, 2 1/12, 3/4 between; A - 6 cols, 2 1/12, 3/4 between; C - 6 cols, 2 1/12, 3/4 between.
Published: Wed
Avg Paid Circ: 2646
Avg Free Circ: 342
Audit By: CMCA
Audit Date: 30.06.2016
Personnel: Beth Morris (Owner/Pres.); Donna Rushford (Adv. Mgr./Co. Pub.)

WINDSOR

PUBLICATION NAME

Etincelle
Street Address: 193 Rue Saint-georges ,
Province: QC
Postal: J1S 1J7
Country: Canada
Mailing address: 193 rue Saint-Georges
Mailing city: Windsor
Province: QC
Postal: J1S 1J7
General Phone: (819) 845-2705
General Fax: (819) 845-5520
General/National Adv. E-mail: journal@letincelle.qc.ca
Primary Website: www.letincelle.qc.ca

Community Newspapers in Canada

III-593

Year Established: 1970
Delivery Methods: Carrier
Areas Served - City/County or Portion Thereof, or Zip codes: Canada
Own Printing Facility?: Y
Commercial printers?: Y
Mechanical specifications: Type page 10 x 15; E - 8 cols, between; C - 8 cols, between.
Published: Wed
Avg Paid Circ: 36
Avg Free Circ: 10515
Audit By: CCAB
Audit Date: 30.09.2012
Personnel: Ralph Cote (Ed. in Chief); Genevieve Gray; Claude Frenette (Ed.)

PUBLICATION NAME

Hants Journal
Street Address: 73 Gerrish St.,
Province: NS
Postal: B0N 2T0
Country: Canada
Mailing address: PO Box 550
Mailing city: Windsor
Province: NS
Postal: B0N 2T0
General Phone: (902) 798-8371
General Fax: (902) 798-5451
General/National Adv. E-mail: info@hantsjournal.ca
Primary Website: www.hantsjournal.ca
Year Established: 1867
Areas Served - City/County or Portion Thereof, or Zip codes: Canada
Own Printing Facility?: Y
Mechanical specifications: Type page 9 2/3 x 21 1/2.
Published: Thur
Avg Paid Circ: 2233
Avg Free Circ: 15
Audit By: CMCA
Audit Date: 30.06.2014
Personnel: Ray Savage (Sales. Mgr.)
Parent company (for newspapers): Transcontinental Media

PUBLICATION NAME

Le Rempart
Street Address: 7515 Forest Glade Dr.,
Province: ON
Postal: N8T 3P5
Country: Canada
Mailing address: 7515 Forest Glade Dr.
Mailing city: Windsor
Province: ON
Postal: N8T 3P5
General Phone: (519) 948-4139
General Fax: (519) 948-0628
General/National Adv. E-mail: info@lerempart.ca
Primary Website: www.lerempart.ca
Year Established: 1966
Areas Served - City/County or Portion Thereof, or Zip codes: Canada
Commercial printers?: Y
Mechanical specifications: Type page 10 x 15 5/8; E - 5 cols, 2, 1/6 between; A - 5 cols, 2, 1/6 between.
Published: Wed
Avg Paid Circ: 5735
Avg Free Circ: 802
Audit By: CMCA
Audit Date: 31.12.2012
Personnel: Dennis Poirier (Pub.); Christiane Beaupre (Gen. Mgr.); Richard Caumartin (Dir., sales)

WINGHAM

PUBLICATION NAME

The Wingham Advance-times
Street Address: 11 Veterans Rd.,
Province: ON
Postal: N0G 2W0
Country: Canada
Mailing address: PO Box 390
Mailing city: Wingham

Province: ON
Postal: N0G 2W0
General Phone: (519) 357-2320
General Fax: (519) 357-2900
General/National Adv. E-mail: advance@wcl.on.ca
Editorial e-mail: pkerr@wingham.com
Primary Website: www.wingham.com
Own Printing Facility?: Y
Commercial printers?: Y
Published: Wed
Avg Paid Circ: 862
Audit By: CMCA
Audit Date: 30.06.2016
Personnel: Sandy Woodcock (Adv. Mgr.); Bill Huether (Ed.); Dave Russell (Prodn. Mgr.)
Parent company (for newspapers): Metroland Media Group Ltd.; Torstar

WINKLER

PUBLICATION NAME

Morden Times
Street Address: 583 Main St.,
Province: MB
Postal: R6W 4B3
Country: Canada
Mailing address: 583 Main St.
Mailing city: Winkler
Province: MB
Postal: R6W 4B3
General Phone: (204) 325-4771
General Fax: 204-325-8646
Display Adv. E-mail: jbilsky@postmedia.com
Editorial e-mail: gvandermeulen@postmedia.com
Primary Website: www.mordentimes.com
Delivery Methods: Newsstand`Carrier
Areas Served - City/County or Portion Thereof, or Zip codes: Morden, Manitou, Miami, Darlingford, La Riviere, R.M. of Stanley,
Own Printing Facility?: Y
Commercial printers?: Y
Mechanical specifications: Type page 10 5/16 x 14; E - 6 cols, 1 7/12, 1/6 between; A - 6 cols, 1 7/12, 1/6 between; C - 8 cols, 1 1/4, 1/12 between.
Published: Thur
Avg Paid Circ: 4924
Avg Free Circ: 5418
Audit By: Sworn/Estimate/Non-Audited
Audit Date: 12.07.2019
Personnel: Greg Vandermeulen (Ed); Lauren MacGill (Reporter)
Parent company (for newspapers): Postmedia Network Inc.

WINKLER

PUBLICATION NAME

Winkler Times
Street Address: 583 Main St.,
Province: MB
Postal: R6W 4B3
Country: Canada
Mailing address: 583 Main Street
Mailing city: Winkler
Province: MB
Postal: R6W 4B3
General Phone: (204) 325-4771
General Fax: (204) 325-8646
General/National Adv. E-mail: winkler.class@sunmedia.ca
Display Adv. E-mail: Darcie.Morris@sunmedia.ca
Editorial e-mail: winkler.news@sunmedia.ca
Primary Website: http://www.pembinatoday.ca/winklertimes
Year Established: 1997
Delivery Methods: Mail`Carrier`Racks
Areas Served - City/County or Portion Thereof, or Zip codes: Canada
Own Printing Facility?: Y
Commercial printers?: Y
Mechanical specifications: Type page 10 5/6 x 14; E - 6 cols, 1 7/12, 1/6 between; A - 6 cols, 1 7/12, 1/6 between; C - 8 cols, 1 1/4, 1/12 between.
Published: Thur
Avg Free Circ: 7459
Audit By: VAC

Audit Date: 30.09.2016
Personnel: Darcie Morris (Adv Dir); Greg Vandermeulen (Ed)
Parent company (for newspapers): Postmedia Network Inc.; Quebecor Communications, Inc.

WINNIPEG

PUBLICATION NAME

The Headliner
Street Address: 1355 Mountain Ave.,
Province: MB
Postal: R2X 3B6
Country: Canada
Mailing address: 1355 Mountain Ave.
Mailing city: Winnipeg
Province: MB
Postal: R2X 3B6
General Phone: (204) 697-7021
General Fax: (204) 953-4300
Advertising Phone: (204) 697-7021
Editorial Phone: (204) 697-7093
Display Adv. E-mail: sales@canstarnews.com
Classified Adv. e-mail: classified@canstarnews.com
Editorial e-mail: news@canstarnews.com
Primary Website: www.canstarnews.com
Year Established: 1992
Delivery Methods: Carrier`Racks
Areas Served - City/County or Portion Thereof, or Zip codes: Headingley, St. FranÃ§ois Xavier, Cartier, Macdonald, Marquette, Rosser, Fannystelle, Portage la Prairie
Published: Wed
Avg Paid Circ: 43
Avg Free Circ: 5372
Audit By: Sworn/Estimate/Non-Audited
Audit Date: 12.07.2019
Personnel: John Kendle (Managing Editor); Barb Borden (Sales Manager)
Parent company (for newspapers): Winnipeg Free Press

PUBLICATION NAME

The Herald
Street Address: 1355 Mountain Ave.,
Province: MB
Postal: R2X 3B6
Country: Canada
Mailing address: 1355 Mountain Ave.
Mailing city: Winnipeg
Province: MB
Postal: R2X 3B6
General Phone: (204) 697-7009
General Fax: (204) 953-4300
Advertising Phone: (204) 697-7021
Display Adv. E-mail: sales@canstarnews.com
Editorial e-mail: letters@canstarnews.com
Primary Website: www.canstarnews.com
Delivery Methods: Carrier
Areas Served - City/County or Portion Thereof, or Zip codes: R2E, R2C, R2G, R2K, R2L, R3W
Own Printing Facility?: Y
Published: Wed
Avg Paid Circ: 984
Avg Free Circ: 43869
Audit By: VAC
Audit Date: 31.08.2016
Personnel: Linda MacKenzie (Natl. Sales Mgr.); John Kendle (Mng. Ed.); Darren Ridgley; Barb Borden (Sales Mgr)
Parent company (for newspapers): Winnipeg Free Press

PUBLICATION NAME

The Lance
Street Address: 1355 Mountain Ave.,
Province: MB
Postal: R2X 3B6
Country: Canada
General Phone: (204) 697-7009
General Fax: (204) 953-4300
Advertising Phone: (204) 697-7021
Editorial Phone: (204) 697-7093
General/National Adv. E-mail: sales@canstarnews.com
Display Adv. E-mail: sales@canstarnews.com
Classified Adv. e-mail: classifieds@canstarnews.com
Editorial e-mail: news@canstarnews.com
Primary Website: www.canstarnews.com
Year Established: 1931
Delivery Methods: Carrier
Areas Served - City/County or Portion Thereof, or Zip codes: R2H, R2J, R2M, R2N, R3X
Published: Wed
Avg Free Circ: 37996
Audit By: Sworn/Estimate/Non-Audited
Audit Date: 12.07.2019
Personnel: John Kendle (Managing Editor); Darren Ridgley (Deputy Editor); Linda Mackenzie (Executive Assistant); Barb Borden (Sales Manager)
Parent company (for newspapers): Winnipeg Free Press

PUBLICATION NAME

The Metro
Street Address: 1355 Mountain Ave.,
Province: MB
Postal: R2X 3B6
Country: Canada
General Phone: (204) 697-7009
General Fax: (204) 953-4300
Display Adv. E-mail: sales@canstarnews.com
Editorial e-mail: letters@canstarnews.com
Primary Website: www.canstarnews.com
Year Established: 1973
Delivery Methods: Carrier
Areas Served - City/County or Portion Thereof, or Zip codes: R2Y, R3E, R3G, R3J, R3K, R3R
Published: Wed
Avg Paid Circ: 141
Avg Free Circ: 36979
Audit By: VAC
Audit Date: 31.08.2016
Personnel: John Kendle (Mng. Ed.); Darren Ridgley (Deputy Ed); Linda Mackenzie (Exec Asst); Barb Borden (Sales Mgr)
Parent company (for newspapers): Winnipeg Free Press

PUBLICATION NAME

The Sou'wester
Street Address: 1355 Mountain Ave.,
Province: MB
Postal: R2X 3B6
Country: Canada
Mailing address: 1355 Mountain Ave.
Mailing city: Winnipeg
Province: MB
Postal: R2X 3B6
General Phone: (204) 697-7020
General Fax: (204) 953-4300
Advertising Phone: (204) 697-7021
Display Adv. E-mail: classifieds@canstarnews.com
Editorial e-mail: news@canstarnews.com
Primary Website: www.winnipegfreepress.com
Year Established: 2009
Areas Served - City/County or Portion Thereof, or Zip codes: Southwest Winnipeg
Published: Wed
Avg Paid Circ: 0
Avg Free Circ: 38583
Audit By: Sworn/Estimate/Non-Audited
Audit Date: 12.07.2019
Personnel: John Kendle (Mng. Ed.); Barb Borden (Sales Manager)
Parent company (for newspapers): Winnipeg Free Press

PUBLICATION NAME

The Times
Street Address: 1355 Mountain Ave.,
Province: MB
Postal: R2X 3B6
Country: Canada
Mailing address: 1355 Mountain Ave.
Mailing city: Winnipeg
Province: MB

Postal: R2X 3B6
General Phone: (204) 697-7009
General Fax: (204) 953-4300
Advertising Phone: (204) 697-7021
General/National Adv. E-mail: sales@canstarnews.com
Display Adv. E-mail: sales@canstarnews.com
Editorial e-mail: letters@canstarnews.com
Primary Website: www.canstarnews.com
Delivery Methods: Carrier
Areas Served - City/County or Portion Thereof, or Zip codes: R2P, R2R, R2V, R2W, R2X
Mechanical specifications: Type page 10 1/4 x 16; E - 6 cols, 1 5/8, 3/16 between; A - 6 cols, 1 5/8, between; C - 8 cols, 1 3/16, 1/8 between.
Published: Wed
Avg Paid Circ: 20
Avg Free Circ: 37763
Audit By: VAC
Audit Date: 31.08.2016
Personnel: John Kendle (Mng. Ed.); Darren Ridgley; Barb Borden (Sales Mgr); Linda MacKenzie
Parent company (for newspapers): Winnipeg Free Press

WOODSTOCK

PUBLICATION NAME

The Bugle-observer
Street Address: 110 Carleton St. ,
Province: NB
Postal: E7M 1E4
Country: Canada
Mailing address: 110 Carleton St.
Mailing city: Woodstock
Province: NB
Postal: E7M 1E4
General Phone: (506) 328-8863
General Fax: (506) 328-3208
General/National Adv. E-mail: news@thebugle.ca
Editorial e-mail: news@thebugle.ca
Primary Website: https://www.telegraphjournal.com/bugle-observer/
Year Established: 1976
Areas Served - City/County or Portion Thereof, or Zip codes: Canada
Own Printing Facility?: Y
Commercial printers?: Y
Published: Tues`Fri
Avg Paid Circ: 2693
Avg Free Circ: 56
Audit By: CMCA
Audit Date: 31.12.2013
Personnel: Peter Macingosh (Gen Mgr.); Edward Farrell (Circ. Mgr.)
Parent company (for newspapers): Brunswick News, Inc.

PUBLICATION NAME

The Ingersoll Times
Street Address: 16 Brock Street ,
Province: ON
Postal: N4S 3B4
Country: Canada
Mailing address: 16 Brock Street
Mailing city: Woodstock
Province: ON
Postal: N4S 3B4
General Phone: (519) 537-2341
Display Adv. E-mail: cwetton@postmedia.com
Classified Adv. e-mail: hbrubacher@postmedia.com
Editorial e-mail: jvandermeer@postmedia.com
Primary Website: www.ingersolltimes.com
Year Established: 1969
Delivery Methods: Mail`Newsstand`Carrier
Areas Served - City/County or Portion Thereof, or Zip codes: Canada
Own Printing Facility?: Y
Published: Wed
Avg Paid Circ: 500
Audit By: CMCA
Audit Date: 31.12.2016
Personnel: Jennifer Vandermeer (Ed.); Ian Dowding (Group Dir., Media Sales); Claire Wetton (Media sales)
Parent company (for newspapers): Postmedia Network Inc.; Quebecor Communications, Inc.

PUBLICATION NAME

The Norwich Gazette
Street Address: 16 Brock Street ,
Province: ON
Postal: N4S 3B4
Country: Canada
Mailing address: 16 Brock Street
Mailing city: Woodstock
Province: ON
Postal: N4S 3B4
General Phone: (519) 537-2341
General/National Adv. E-mail: norwich@bowesnet.com
Display Adv. E-mail: tleake@postmedia.com
Classified Adv. e-mail: hbrubacher@postmedia.com
Editorial e-mail: jennifer.vandermeer@sunmedia.ca
Primary Website: www.norwichgazette.ca
Year Established: 1876
Delivery Methods: Mail`Newsstand
Areas Served - City/County or Portion Thereof, or Zip codes: Canada
Own Printing Facility?: Y
Published: Wed
Avg Paid Circ: 822
Audit By: CMCA
Audit Date: 31.12.2016
Personnel: Jennifer Vandermeer (Ed.); Ian Dowding (Group Director, Media Sales); Tara Leake (Media sales); John Macintosh (Media sales); Heidi Brubacher (Classified sales); Beth Faulkner (Circ.)
Parent company (for newspapers): Postmedia Network Inc.

WYNYARD

PUBLICATION NAME

The Advance/gazette
Street Address: 301 Bosworth St. ,
Province: SK
Postal: S0A 4T0
Country: Canada
Mailing address: PO Box 10
Mailing city: Wynyard
Province: SK
Postal: S0A 4T0
General Phone: (306) 554-2224
General Fax: (306) 554-3226
General/National Adv. E-mail: w.advance@sasktel.net
Areas Served - City/County or Portion Thereof, or Zip codes: Canada
Mechanical specifications: Type page 12 x 17; E - 5 cols, 2, between; A - 5 cols, 2, between; C - 5 cols, 2, between.
Published: Mon
Avg Paid Circ: 1211
Avg Free Circ: 18
Audit By: CMCA
Audit Date: 30.12.2015
Personnel: Bob Johnson (Ed.)

YARMOUTH

PUBLICATION NAME

The Vanguard
Street Address: 2 Second St. ,
Province: NS
Postal: B5A 4B1
Country: Canada
Mailing address: PO Box 128
Mailing city: Yarmouth
Province: NS
Postal: B5A 4B1
General Phone: (902) 742-7111
General Fax: (902) 742-6527
General/National Adv. E-mail: info@thevanguard.ca
Display Adv. E-mail: fred.fiander@tc.tc
Editorial e-mail: info@thevanguard.ca
Primary Website: www.thevanguard.ca
Year Established: 1966
Areas Served - City/County or Portion Thereof, or Zip codes: Canada
Commercial printers?: Y
Mechanical specifications: Type page 13 x 21; E - 6 cols, 2, between; A - 6 cols, 2, between; C - 6 cols, 2, between.
Published: Tues
Avg Paid Circ: 3485
Avg Free Circ: 52
Audit By: CMCA
Audit Date: 31.03.2014
Personnel: Fred Fiander (Pub); Fred Hatfield (Ed)
Parent company (for newspapers): Transcontinental Media

YELLOWKNIFE

PUBLICATION NAME

Deh Cho Drum
Street Address: 5108 50th St. ,
Province: NT
Postal: X1A 2R1
Country: Canada
Mailing address: PO Box 2820
Mailing city: Yellowknife
Province: NT
Postal: X1A 2R1
General Phone: (867) 873-4031
General Fax: (867) 873-8507
General/National Adv. E-mail: nnsl@nnsl.com
Display Adv. E-mail: advertising@nnsl.com
Editorial e-mail: editorial@nnsl.com
Primary Website: http://www.nnsl.com/dehcho/dehcho.html
Year Established: 1993
Areas Served - City/County or Portion Thereof, or Zip codes: Yellowknife
Mechanical specifications: Type page 10 5/16 x 15 3/8; E - 6 cols, 1 9/16, 1/6 between; A - 6 cols, 1 9/16, 1/6 between; C - 6 cols, 1 9/16, 1/6 between.
Published: Thur
Avg Free Circ: 708
Audit By: VAC
Audit Date: 31.05.2016
Personnel: Jack Sigvaldason (Pub.); Michael Scott (Gen. Mgr.); Petra Ehrke (Adv. Mgr.); Debra Davis (Circ. Mgr.); Bruce Valpy (Mng. Ed.)

PUBLICATION NAME

Inuvik Drum
Street Address: Po Box 2820 ,
Province: NT
Postal: X1A 2R1
Country: Canada
Mailing address: PO Box 2820
Mailing city: Yellowknife
Province: NT
Postal: X1A 2R1
General Phone: (867) 873-4031
General Fax: (867) 873-8507
General/National Adv. E-mail: nnsl@nnsl.com
Display Adv. E-mail: advertising@nnsl.com
Editorial e-mail: editorial@nnsl.com
Primary Website: www.nnsl.com
Areas Served - City/County or Portion Thereof, or Zip codes: Yellowknife
Commercial printers?: Y
Mechanical specifications: Type page 10 1/8 x 15 3/8; E - 6 cols, 1 7/12, 1/6 between; A - 6 cols, 1 7/12, 1/6 between; C - 6 cols, 1 7/12, 1/6 between.
Published: Thur
Avg Paid Circ: 201
Avg Free Circ: 290
Audit By: VAC
Audit Date: 31.05.2016
Personnel: Jack Sigvaldason (Pub.); Michael Scott (Gen. Mgr.); Petra Ehrke (Adv. Mgr.); Debra Davis (Circ. Mgr.); Bruce Valpy (Mng. Ed.)

PUBLICATION NAME

Kivalliq News
Street Address: Po Box 2820 ,
Province: NU
Postal: X1A 2R1
Country: Canada
Mailing address: PO Box 2820
Mailing city: Yellowknife
Province: NU
Postal: X1A 2R1
General Phone: (867) 873-4031
General Fax: (867) 873-8507
General/National Adv. E-mail: nnsl@nnsl.com
Display Adv. E-mail: advertising@nnsl.com
Editorial e-mail: editorial@nnsl.com
Primary Website: www.nnsl.com
Areas Served - City/County or Portion Thereof, or Zip codes: Yellowknife
Published: Wed
Avg Free Circ: 935
Audit By: VAC
Audit Date: 31.03.2016
Personnel: Jack Sigvaldason (Pub)

PUBLICATION NAME

L'aquilon
Street Address: 5102-51 Street, 2nd Floor ,
Province: NT
Postal: X1A 1S7
Country: Canada
Mailing address: PO Box 456
Mailing city: Yellowknife
Province: NT
Postal: X1A 2N4
General Phone: (867) 873-6603
General Fax: (867) 873-6663
General/National Adv. E-mail: direction.aquilon@northwestel.net
Display Adv. E-mail: sandra@repco-media.ca
Editorial e-mail: aquilon@internorth.com
Primary Website: www.aquilon.nt.ca
Year Established: 1986
Delivery Methods: Mail`Racks
Areas Served - City/County or Portion Thereof, or Zip codes: X1A X0E X0A
Mechanical specifications: Type page 11 x 17; E -6 cols, 2, 1/6 between
Published: Fri
Avg Free Circ: 875
Audit By: Sworn/Estimate/Non-Audited
Audit Date: 12.07.2019
Personnel: Alain Bessette (Ed.)

PUBLICATION NAME

News/north
Street Address: 5108 50th St. ,
Province: NT
Postal: X1A 2R1
Country: Canada
Mailing address: PO Box 2820
Mailing city: Yellowknife
Province: NT
Postal: X1A 2R1
General Phone: (867) 873-4031
General Fax: (867) 873-8507
General/National Adv. E-mail: nnsl@nnsl.com
Display Adv. E-mail: advertising@nnsl.com
Editorial e-mail: editorial@nnsl.com
Primary Website: www.nnsl.com
Areas Served - City/County or Portion Thereof, or Zip codes: Canada
Own Printing Facility?: Y
Mechanical specifications: Type page 10 5/8 x 15 3/8; E - 6 cols, 1 9/16, 1/6 between; A - 6 cols, 1 9/16, 1/6 between; C - 6 cols, 1 9/16, 1/6 between.
Published: Mon
Avg Paid Circ: 1922
Avg Free Circ: 2167
Audit By: VAC
Audit Date: 31.03.2016
Personnel: Jack Sigvaldason (Pub.); Michael Scott (Gen. Mgr.); Petra Ehrke (Adv. Mgr.); Debra Davis (Circ. Mgr.); Bruce Valpy (Ed.)

PUBLICATION NAME

Nunavut News/north
Street Address: Po Box 2820 ,
Province: NU
Postal: X1A 2R1

Community Newspapers in Canada

III-595

Country: Canada
Mailing address: PO Box 2820
Mailing city: Yellowknife
Province: NU
Postal: X1A 2R1
General Phone: (867) 873-4031
General Fax: (867) 873-8507
General/National Adv. E-mail: circulation@nnsl.com
Display Adv. E-mail: advertising@nnsl.com
Editorial e-mail: editorial@nnsl.com
Primary Website: www.nnsl.com
Areas Served - City/County or Portion Thereof, or Zip codes: Nunavut
Published: Mon
Avg Free Circ: 4161
Audit By: VAC
Audit Date: 31.03.2016
Personnel: Jack Sigvaldason (Pub); Michael Scott (Gen Mgr)

PUBLICATION NAME

Yellowknifer
Street Address: 5108 50th St.,
Province: NT
Postal: X1A 2R1
Country: Canada
Mailing address: PO Box 2820
Mailing city: Yellowknife
Province: NT
Postal: X1A 2R1
General Phone: (867) 873-4031
General Fax: (867) 873-8507
General/National Adv. E-mail: nnsladmin@nnsl.com
Display Adv. E-mail: advertising@nnsl.com
Editorial e-mail: editorial@nnsl.com
Primary Website: www.nnsl.com
Areas Served - City/County or Portion Thereof, or Zip codes: Yellowknife
Own Printing Facility?: Y
Mechanical specifications: Type page 10 5/16 x 15 3/8; E - 6 cols, 1 9/16, 1/6 between; A - 6 cols, 1 9/16, 1/6 between; C - 6 cols, 1 9/16, 1/6 between.
Published: Wed`Fri
Avg Paid Circ: 2077
Avg Free Circ: 963
Audit By: VAC

Audit Date: 30.04.2016
Personnel: Jack Sigvaldason (Pub.); Michael Scott (Gen. Mgr.); Petra Ehrke (Adv.); Debra Davis (Circ. Mgr.); Bruce Valpy (Mng. Ed.)

YORKTON

PUBLICATION NAME

Yorkton This Week
Street Address: 20 3rd Ave. N.,
Province: SK
Postal: S3N 2X3
Country: Canada
Mailing address: PO BOX 1300
Mailing city: YORKTON
Province: SK
Postal: S3N 2X3
General Phone: (306) 782-2465
General Fax: (306) 786-1898
General/National Adv. E-mail: publisher@yorktonthisweek.com
Display Adv. E-mail: classifieds@yorktonthisweek.com
Editorial e-mail: editorial@yorktonthisweek.com
Primary Website: www.yorktonthisweek.com
Delivery Methods: Newsstand`Carrier
Areas Served - City/County or Portion Thereof, or Zip codes: Canada
Commercial printers?: Y
Published: Wed
Avg Paid Circ: 2777
Avg Free Circ: 59
Audit By: Sworn/Estimate/Non-Audited
Audit Date: 12.07.2019
Personnel: Jim Ambrose (Publisher); Debbie Barr (Prodn. Mgr.)
Parent company (for newspapers): Glacier Media Group

SHOPPER PUBLICATIONS IN CANADA

BEETON

THE WOODBRIDGE ADVERTISER

Street Address1: 2 Main St. W.
Street address state: ON
Postal Code: L0G 1A0
Country: Canada
Mailing Address: PO Box 379
Mailing City: Beeton
Mailing province: ON
Mailing Postal Code: L0G 1A0
Office phone: (905) 729-4501
Office fax: (905) 729-3961
General e-mail: wa@csolve.net
Website: www.ontarioauctionpaper.com
Advertising (open inch rate): Open inch rate $11.10
Postal Codes Served: L0N 1P0
Frequency: Thur
Circulation Paid: 2000
Audit By: Sworn/Estimate/Non-Audited
Audit Date: 43008
Personnel: Karl Mallette (Ed.); Tina Dedels (Editorial Mgr.)
Main (survey) contact: Karl Mallette

BELLEVILLE

SHOPPER'S MARKET

Street Address1: 365 N. Front St.
Street address state: ON
Postal Code: K8P 5E6
Country: Canada
Mailing Address: PO Box 446
Mailing City: Belleville
Mailing province: ON
Mailing Postal Code: K8N 5A5
Office phone: (613) 962-3422
Office fax: (613) 962-0543
Advertising Phone: (866) 541-6757
Advertising Fax: (866) 757-0227
General e-mail: readerads@cogeco.net
Advertising e-mail: placeit@classifiedextra.ca; advertise@canoe.quebecor.com
Website: shoppersmarket.classifiedextra.ca
Advertising (open inch rate): Open inch rate $1.28
Mechanical Specifications: Type page 10 1/4 x 12 3/10; A - 6 cols, 1 5/8, 3/16 between.
Postal Codes Served: K8N 5A5
Frequency: Thur
Circulation Free: 50000
Audit By: Sworn/Estimate/Non-Audited
Audit Date: 43008
Personnel: Charles Parker (Adv. Mgr.); Martin Courchesne (Nat'l Dir., Sales)
Main (survey) contact: Charles Parker

BRANTFORD

BRANTFORD PENNYSAVER

Street Address1: 61 Dalkeith Dr.
Street Address2: Unit 5
Street address state: ON
Postal Code: N3P 1M1
Country: Canada
Mailing Address: 61 DalKeith Dr., Unit 5
Mailing City: Brantford
Mailing province: ON
Mailing Postal Code: N3P 1M1
Office phone: (519) 756-0076
Office fax: (519) 756-9034
General e-mail: classifieds@brantfordpennysaver.com
Website: www.brantfordpennysaver.com
Advertising (open inch rate): Open inch rate $1.26
Mechanical Specifications: Type page 10 1/4 x 11 1/4; E - 6 cols, 1 1/2, between.
Postal Codes Served: N3P 1M1
Frequency: Fri
Audit Date: 43008
Personnel: Andrea Demeer (Pub.); Alan Burns (Adv. Mgr.); Adrian Trombetta (Circ. Mgr.); Trudy Loslo (Prodn. Mgr.)
Main (survey) contact: Andrea Demeer

BRANTFORD

PARIS STAR

Street Address1: 195 Henry St
Street Address2: Building 4, Unit 1
Street address state: ON
Postal Code: N3S 5C9
Country: Canada
Mailing Address: 195 Henry St, Building 4, Unit 1
Mailing City: Brantford
Mailing province: ON
Mailing Postal Code: N3S 5C9
Office phone: (519) 756-2020
Office fax: (519) 756-9470
General e-mail: parisstar.editorial@sunmedia.ca
Editorial e-mail: parisstar.editorial@sunmedia.ca
Website: parisstaronline.com
Year publication established: 1850
Advertising (open inch rate): Open inch rate $.72
Mechanical Specifications: Type page 10 x 16; E - 5 cols, 2, 1/8 between; A - 5 cols, 2, 1/8 between; C - 6 cols, 1 3/4, 1/8 between.
Postal Codes Served: Canada
Frequency: Thur
Circulation Free: 4877
Audit By: CMCA
Audit Date: 43585
Hardware: APP/Mac
Software: QPS/QuarkXPress 3.31.
Personnel: Ken Koyama (Pub.); Michael Peeling (Ed.)
Parent company: Postmedia Network Inc.; Quebecor Communications, Inc.
Main (survey) contact: Ken Koyama

BRIGHTON

THE BRIGHTON INDEPENDENT

Street Address1: 21 Meade St
Street address state: ON
Postal Code: K0K 1H0
Rural Municipality: Canada
Country: Canada
Mailing Address: PO Box 1030
Mailing City: Brighton
Mailing province: ON
Mailing Postal Code: K0K 1H0
Office phone: (613) 475-0255
Office fax: (613) 475-4546
Advertising Phone: (613) 475-0255 X 214
Editorial Phone: (613) 966-2034
General e-mail: jkearns@metroland.com
Editorial e-mail: tbush@metroland.com
Advertising e-mail: jkearns@metroland.com
Website: www.metroland.com
Year publication established: 1973
Advertising (open inch rate): Open inch rate $1.33
Delivery Methods: Carrier`Racks
Postal Codes Served: K0k 1h0, K8v, K0k 1L0, K0l 1L0, K0k is0
Frequency: Thur
Circulation Free: 7816
Audit By: CMCA
Audit Date: 42551
Personnel: Benita Stansel (Circ. Mgr.); John Kearns (Publisher)
Parent company: Metroland Media Group Ltd.
Main (survey) contact: John Kearns

BURKS FALLS

OMEGA FORESTER

Street Address1: 59 Ontario St.
Street address state: ON
Postal Code: P0A 1C0
Country: Canada
Mailing Address: PO Box 518
Mailing City: Burks Falls
Mailing province: ON
Mailing Postal Code: P0A 1C0
Office phone: (705) 382-3943
Office fax: (705) 382-3440
General e-mail: anews@onlink.net
Website: www.almaguinnews.com
Advertising (open inch rate): Open inch rate $9.00
Postal Codes Served: P0A 1C0
Frequency: Fri
Audit Date: 43008
Personnel: Doug Pincoee (Sales Mgr.)
Main (survey) contact: Jennifer Thompson

BURNABY

BUY & SELL

Street Address1: 4664 Lougheed Hwy.
Street Address2: Ste. W020
Street address state: BC
Postal Code: V5C 5T5
Country: Canada
Mailing Address: Ste. W020 4664 Lougheed Hwy.
Mailing City: Burnaby
Mailing province: BC
Mailing Postal Code: V5C 5T5
Office phone: (604) 540-4455
Office fax: (604) 540-6451
Advertising Phone: (604) 280-1000
Website: www.buysell.com
Year publication established: 1971
Postal Codes Served: V6X 2C9
Frequency: Thur
Circulation Free: 42005
Audit By: Sworn/Estimate/Non-Audited
Audit Date: 43008
Editions Count: 3
Edition Names with circulation: 3 total Ã‚Â— BC Interior; Frazer Valley; Greater Vancouver;
Personnel: Zac Goodman (Prodn. Mgr.)
Main (survey) contact: Zac Goodman

CAMROSE

THE CAMROSE BOOSTER

Street Address1: 4925 48th St.
Street address state: AB
Postal Code: T4V 1L7
Rural Municipality: Camrose, Flagstaff and Beaver
Country: Canada
Mailing Address: 4925 48th St.
Mailing City: Camrose
Mailing province: AB
Mailing Postal Code: T4V 1L7
Office phone: (780) 672-3142
Office fax: (780) 672-2518
General e-mail: ads@camrosebooster.com
Editorial e-mail: news@camrosebooster.com
Advertising e-mail: ads@camrosebooster.com
Website: www.camrosebooster.com
Year publication established: 1952
Advertising (open inch rate): Open inch rate $14.84 (National)
Mechanical Specifications: Type page 9.45 x 15 ; 5 cols
Delivery Methods: Mail`Carrier`Racks
Postal Codes Served: All T4V postal codes plus T0B's
Frequency: Tues
Circulation Paid: 11
Circulation Free: 12910
Audit By: CVC
Audit Date: 43281
Personnel: Blain Fowler (Publisher); Don Hutchinson (Comptroller); Ronald Pilger (Associate Publisher / Sales Manager); Jeff Fowler (Sales Rep.); Mike Ploner (Sales Rep.); Leanne Taje (Circ. Mgr.); Kirby Fowler (Production Manager); Pat Horton (Art Director)
Main (survey) contact: Blain Fowler

CHATEAUGUAY

LE SOLEIL DE CHATEAUGUAY

Street Address1: 101 boulevard Saint-Jean-Baptiste
Street Address2: Suite 215
Street address state: QC
Postal Code: J6J 3H9
Country: Canada
Mailing Address: 101 boulevard Saint-Jean-Baptiste, Suite 215
Mailing City: Chateauguay
Mailing province: QC
Mailing Postal Code: J6J 3H9
Office phone: (450) 692-8552
General e-mail: info@gravitemedia.com
Website: www.monteregieweb.com
Advertising (open inch rate): Open inch rate $1.00
Postal Codes Served: Canada
Frequency: Wed`Sat
Circulation Paid: 11
Circulation Free: 34473
Audit By: CCAB
Audit Date: 43555
Personnel: Julie Voyer (Pres.); Pierre Montreuil (Mktg. Strat. Mgr.); Michel Thibault (Content Mgr.); Valerie Lessard (Asst. Content Mgr.); Sophie Bayard (Sales Coor.)
Parent company: Les Hebdos Monteregiens-OOB
Main (survey) contact: Jeanne-d'Arc Germain; Pierre Montreuil

CHATHAM

CHATHAM PENNYSAVER

Street Address1: 930 Richmond St.
Street address state: ON
Postal Code: N7M 5J5
Country: Canada
Mailing Address: 930 Richmond St.
Mailing City: Chatham
Mailing province: ON
Mailing Postal Code: N7M 5J5
Office phone: (519) 351-4362
Office fax: (519) 351-2452
Advertising Phone: (866) 541-6757
General e-mail: chathampennysaver@bowesnet.com
Advertising e-mail: placeit@classifiedextra.ca
Website: www.chathampennysaver.com
Mechanical Specifications: Type page 10 1/4 x 12; E - 7 cols, between; A - 7 cols, between; C - 7 cols, between.
Postal Codes Served: N7M 5J5
Frequency: Fri
Circulation Free: 38914
Audit By: Sworn/Estimate/Non-Audited
Audit Date: 43008
Personnel: Dean Muharrem (Pub./Gen. Mgr.); Melissa Steele (Office Mgr.); Tracey Weaver-Curran (Sales Mgr.); Martin Steele (Supervisor)
Main (survey) contact: Shawn Steveley

Shopper Publications in Canada

CORNWALL

STANDARD-FREEHOLDER COMPLIMENTARY

Street Address1: 1150 Montreal Road
Street address state: ON
Postal Code: K6H 1E2
Country: Canada
Mailing Address: 1150 Montreal Road
Mailing City: Cornwall
Mailing province: ON
Mailing Postal Code: K6H 1E2
Office phone: (613) 933-3160
Office fax: (613) 933-7521
Advertising Phone: (613) 933-3160 x246
Advertising Fax: (613) 933-7521
Editorial Phone: (613) 933-3160 X 225
General e-mail: mayerst@postmedia.com
Editorial e-mail: hrodrigues@postmedia.com
Advertising e-mail: ksammon@postmedia.com
Website: www.standard-freeholder.com
Mechanical Specifications: Type page 11 1/2 x 21 1/2; E - 10 cols, 1 1/10, between; A - 10 cols, 1 1/10, between; C - 10 cols, 1 1/10, between.
Frequency: Fri
Circulation Paid: 10739
Circulation Free: 21066
Audit By: Sworn/Estimate/Non-Audited
Audit Date: 43008
Personnel: Hugo Rodrigues; Kerry Sammon; Melissa Ayerist (Circ. Mgr.)
Parent company: Quebecor Communications, Inc.
Main (survey) contact: Hugo Rodrigues

DURHAM

THE DURHAM CHRONICLE

Street Address1: 190 Elizabeth St. E.
Street address state: ON
Postal Code: N0G 1R0
Rural Municipality: Canada
Country: Canada
Mailing Address: PO Box 230
Mailing City: Durham
Mailing province: ON
Mailing Postal Code: N0G 1R0
Office phone: (519) 369-2504
Office fax: (519) 369-3560
General e-mail: themarkdalestandard@bmts.com
Advertising (open inch rate): Open inch rate $.37
Mechanical Specifications: Type page 11 1/4 x 16 3/4; E - 5 cols, 2 1/5, between; A - 5 cols, 2 1/5, between; C - 9 cols, between.
Postal Codes Served: Canada
Frequency: Wed
Circulation Paid: 1196
Circulation Free: 21
Audit By: Sworn/Estimate/Non-Audited
Audit Date: 43658
Hardware: APP/Mac
Software: QPS/QuarkXPress 4.0.
Personnel: Marie David (Pub.); Bev Stoddart (Gen. Mgr.); Christine Meingast (Ed.)
Main (survey) contact: Greg Murphy

EDMONTON

FLYER FORCE

Street Address1: 5637 70 Street Nw
Street address state: AB
Postal Code: T6B 3P6
Country: Canada
Office phone: (780)436-8050
Frequency: Thur
Audit By: Sworn/Estimate/Non-Audited
Audit Date: 43008

ELLIOT LAKE

MARKETPLACE

Street Address1: 14 Hillside Dr. S.
Street address state: ON
Postal Code: P5A 1M6
Country: Canada
Mailing Address: 14 Hillside Dr. S.
Mailing City: Elliot Lake
Mailing province: ON
Mailing Postal Code: P0M 3E0
Office phone: (705) 866-1801
Office fax: (705) 848-0249
General e-mail: kjohansen@postmedia.com
Editorial e-mail: kjohansen@postmedia.com
Advertising e-mail: kjohansen@postmedia.com
Website: www.elliotlakestandard.ca
Year publication established: 1956
Advertising (open inch rate): Open inch rate $9.80
Mechanical Specifications: Page size - 10.25" wide X 15' tall, 9 column
Delivery Methods: Mail`Newsstand`Carrier`Racks
Frequency: Thur
Circulation Paid: 3623
Circulation Free: 8000
Audit By: Sworn/Estimate/Non-Audited
Audit Date: 43410
Personnel: Lolene Patterson (Circ. Mgr.); Kevin McSheffrey (Mng Ed.); Karsten Johansen (Gen. Mgr.)
Parent company: Sunmedia
Main (survey) contact: Karsten Johansen

ESTEVAN

TRADER EXPRESS

Street Address1: 68 Souris Ave. N.
Street address state: SK
Postal Code: S4A 2A6
Country: Canada
Mailing Address: PO Box 730
Mailing City: Estevan
Mailing province: SK
Mailing Postal Code: S4A 2A6
Office phone: (306) 634-2654
Office fax: (306) 634-3934
General e-mail: mercury_merc1@sasktel.net; classifieds@estevanmercury.ca
Editorial e-mail: editor@estevanmercury.ca; sports@estevanmercury.ca
Advertising e-mail: adsales@estevanmercury.ca
Website: www.estevanmercury.ca
Advertising (open inch rate): Open inch rate $.88
Mechanical Specifications: Type page 11 1/2 x 13; A - 5 cols, 2, between; C - 5 cols, 2, between.
Postal Codes Served: S4A 2A6
Frequency: Fri
Circulation Free: 6046
Audit By: Sworn/Estimate/Non-Audited
Audit Date: 43008
Personnel: Peter Ng (Pub.); Janice Boyle (Adv. Mgr.); Kim Schoff (Circ. Mgr.)
Main (survey) contact: Peter Ng

FALHER

SMOKY RIVER EXPRESS

Street Address1: 217 Main St. W.
Street address state: AB
Postal Code: T0H 1M0
Rural Municipality: Canada
Country: Canada
Mailing Address: PO Box 644
Mailing City: Falher
Mailing province: AB
Mailing Postal Code: T0H 1M0
Office phone: (780) 837-2585
Office fax: (780) 837-2102
General e-mail: srexpres@telus.net
Editorial e-mail: sreeditor@telus.net
Advertising e-mail: srexpres@telus.net
Website: www.smokyriverexpress.com
Year publication established: 1967
Advertising (open inch rate): Open inch rate $.88
Mechanical Specifications: Type page 10.33 x 15.5
Delivery Methods: Mail`Newsstand
Postal Codes Served: T0H 1M0
Frequency: Wed
Circulation Paid: 2021
Audit By: CMCA
Audit Date: 43081
Software: Microsoft/Windows 95.
Personnel: Mary Burgar (Circ. Mgr.)
Main (survey) contact: Mary Burgar

FORT SASKATCHEWAN

THE FORT SASKATCHEWAN RECORD

Street Address1: 10404 99 Ave
Street Address2: 168A
Street address state: AB
Postal Code: T8L 3W2
Rural Municipality: Strathcona County
Country: Canada
Mailing Address: 10404 99 Ave, 168A
Mailing City: Fort Saskatchewan
Mailing province: AB
Mailing Postal Code: T8L 3W2
Office phone: (780) 998-7070 Ext 724227
Office fax: (780) 998-5515
Editorial e-mail: agreen@postmedia.com
Website: fortsaskatchewanrecord.com
Year publication established: 1922
Advertising (open inch rate): Open inch rate $0.71
Mechanical Specifications: specs available on website
Delivery Methods: Mail`Carrier`Racks
Postal Codes Served: Strathcona County
Frequency: Thur
Circulation Paid: 9
Circulation Free: 8806
Audit By: Sworn/Estimate/Non-Audited
Audit Date: 43658
Hardware: APP/Mac
Presses: N/A
Software: Adobe Creative Suite
Personnel: A Green
Parent company: Postmedia Network Inc.
Main (survey) contact: A Green
Footnotes: Editorial e-mail: CARDonline; Year publication established: CARDonline; Advertising (open inch rate): CARDonline

GODERICH

GODERICH SIGNAL STAR

Street Address1: 120 Huckins St.
Street address state: ON
Postal Code: N7A 4B6
Country: Canada
Mailing Address: PO Box 220
Mailing City: Goderich
Mailing province: ON
Mailing Postal Code: N7A 4B6
Office phone: (519) 524-2614
Office fax: (519) 524-9175
Editorial e-mail: katsmith@postmedia.com
Website: goderichsignalstar.com
Advertising (open inch rate): Open inch rate $1.08
Mechanical Specifications: Type page 10 3/8 x 14 7/8; E - 6 cols, 1 7/12, 1/2 between; A - 6 cols, 1 7/12, 1/2 between; C - 6 cols, 1 7/12, 1/2 between.
Postal Codes Served: N7A 4B6
Frequency: Fri
Circulation Free: 20150
Audit By: Sworn/Estimate/Non-Audited
Audit Date: 43554
Personnel: Kat Smith
Main (survey) contact: Kat Smith

GRAND FORKS

WEST KOOTENAY ADVERTISER

Street Address1: 7255 Riverside Dr.
Street address state: BC
Postal Code: V0H 1H0
Rural Municipality: Boundary
Country: Canada
Mailing Address: Box 700
Mailing City: Grand Forks
Mailing province: BC
Mailing Postal Code: V0H 1H0
Office phone: (250) 442-2191
Office fax: (866) 897-0678
General e-mail: publisher@grandforksgazette.ca; classifieds@grandforksgazette.ca; circulation@grandforksgazette.ca; production@grandforksgazette.ca; accounting@grandforksgazette.ca
Editorial e-mail: editor@grandforksgazette.ca
Advertising e-mail: sales@grandforksgazette.ca
Website: www.grandforksgazette.ca
Advertising (open inch rate): Open inch rate $.88
Mechanical Specifications: Type page 10 1/4 x 15 1/2; E - 5 cols, 2, 1/16 between; A - 5 cols, 2, 1/16 between; C - 5 cols, 2, 1/16 between.
Postal Codes Served: v0h1h0-v0h1h9, V0H 1E0-v0h 1E3, v0h1j0,v0h1m0,v0h 1yo, v0h 1b0, v0h 2b0
Frequency: Thur
Circulation Free: 4000
Audit By: Sworn/Estimate/Non-Audited
Audit Date: 43008
Personnel: Darlainea Redlack (Circ. Mgr.)
Parent company: Black Press
Main (survey) contact: Darlainea Redlack

GUELPH

GUELPH MERCURY TRIBUNE

Street Address1: 367 Woodlawn Rd. W., Unit 1
Street address state: ON
Postal Code: N1H 7K9
Country: Canada
Mailing Address: 367 Woodlawn Rd. W., Unit 1
Mailing City: Guelph
Mailing province: ON
Mailing Postal Code: N1H 7K9
Office phone: (519) 763-3333
Advertising Phone: (519) 763-3333 ext. 240
General e-mail: customerservice@metroland.com
Editorial e-mail: newsroom@guelphmercurytribune.com
Advertising e-mail: ccampbell@starmetrolandmedia.com
Website: guelphmercury.com
Advertising (open inch rate): Open inch rate $1.52
Postal Codes Served: N1H 1A8
Frequency: Fri
Circulation Free: 47000
Audit By: Sworn/Estimate/Non-Audited
Audit Date: 43585
Personnel: Cindi Campbell (News/Adv.); Derek Prince-Cox (Subsc./ Circ.)
Main (survey) contact: Cindi Campbell

IRRICANA

WHEEL & DEAL

Street Address1: Po Box 40
Street address state: AB
Postal Code: T0M 1B0
Country: Canada
Mailing Address: PO Box 40
Mailing City: Irricana
Mailing province: AB
Mailing Postal Code: T0M 1B0
Office phone: (204) 954-1400
Office fax: (403) 935-4981
Editorial Phone: (403) 697-4703
General e-mail: deal@wheel-deal.com
Website: www.albertafarmexpress.ca
Year publication established: 1969
Advertising (open inch rate): Open inch rate $1.90
Mechanical Specifications: Type page 10 1/4 x 13; A - 6 cols, 1 1/2, 1/6 between; C - 7 cols, 1/6 between.
Postal Codes Served: T0M 1B0
Frequency: Mon
Circulation Paid: 281
Circulation Free: 71900
Audit By: Sworn/Estimate/Non-Audited
Audit Date: 43008

KASLO

PENNYWISE

Street Address1: Po Box 430
Street address state: BC
Postal Code: V0G 1M0
Country: Canada
Mailing Address: PO Box 430
Mailing City: Kaslo
Mailing province: BC
Mailing Postal Code: V0G 1M0
Office phone: (250) 353-2602
Office fax: (250) 353-7444
General e-mail: info@pennywiseads.com
Website: www.pennywiseads.com
Advertising (open inch rate): Open inch rate $.75
Frequency: Tues
Circulation Free: 27000
Audit By: Sworn/Estimate/Non-Audited
Audit Date: 43008
Editions Count: 4
Edition Names with circulation: 4 total Ã‚Â— Castlegar/Slocan Valley Pennywise; Kootenay Lake Pennywise; Nelson Pennywise; Trail/Beaver Valley/Salmo Pennywise;
Personnel: Patricia Axen-Rotch (Pub.); Julie Wilson (Adv. Mgr.); Tania Seafoot (Ed.)
Main (survey) contact: Patricia Axen-Rotch

KASLO

PENNYWISE - CASTLEGAR / SLOCAN VALLEY

Street Address1: Po Box 430
Street address state: BC
Postal Code: V0G 1M0
Country: Canada
Mailing Address: PO BOX 430
Mailing City: Kaslo
Mailing province: BC
Mailing Postal Code: V0G 1M0
Website: www.pennywiseads.com
Year publication established: 1975
Advertising (open inch rate): $60.12 (smallest modular rate)
Mechanical Specifications: Type page 6.75" x 9.7"; 2 cols
Delivery Methods: Racks
Postal Codes Served: Kalso BC
Frequency: Tues
Circulation Free: 8515
Audit By: CVC
Audit Date: 42185
Personnel: Patty Axenroth
Main (survey) contact: Patty Axenroth

KASLO

PENNYWISE - KOOTENAY LAKE

Street Address1: Po Box 430
Street address state: BC
Postal Code: V0G 1M0
Country: Canada
Mailing Address: PO BOX 430
Mailing City: Kaslo
Mailing province: BC
Mailing Postal Code: V0G 1M0
Website: www.pennywiseads.com
Year publication established: 1975
Advertising (open inch rate): $60.12 (smallest modular rate)
Mechanical Specifications: Type page 6.75" x 9.7"; 2 cols
Delivery Methods: Racks
Postal Codes Served: Kalso, BC
Frequency: Tues
Circulation Free: 3505
Audit By: CVC
Audit Date: 42185
Personnel: Patty Axenroth
Main (survey) contact: Patty Axenroth

KASLO

PENNYWISE - NELSON

Street Address1: Po Box 430
Street address state: BC
Postal Code: V0G 1M0
Country: Canada
Mailing Address: PO BOX 430
Mailing City: Kaslo
Mailing province: BC
Mailing Postal Code: V0G 1M0
Website: www.pennywiseads.com
Year publication established: 1975
Advertising (open inch rate): $60.12 (smallest modular rate)
Mechanical Specifications: Type page 6.75" x 9.7"; 2 cols
Delivery Methods: Racks
Postal Codes Served: Kalso, BC
Frequency: Tues
Circulation Paid: 0
Circulation Free: 5661
Audit By: CVC
Audit Date: 42185
Personnel: Patty Axenroth
Main (survey) contact: Patty Axenroth

KASLO

PENNYWISE - TRAIL / BEAVER VALLEY / SALMO

Street Address1: Po Box 43
Street address state: BC
Postal Code: V0G 1M0
Country: Canada
Mailing Address: PO BOX 430
Mailing City: Kaslo
Mailing province: BC
Mailing Postal Code: V0G 1M0
Website: www.pennywiseads.com
Year publication established: 1975
Advertising (open inch rate): $60.12 (smallest modular rate)
Mechanical Specifications: Type page 6.75" x 9.7"; 2 cols
Delivery Methods: Racks
Postal Codes Served: Kalso, BC
Frequency: Tues
Circulation Paid: 0
Circulation Free: 8607
Audit By: CVC
Audit Date: 42185
Personnel: Patty Axenroth
Main (survey) contact: Patty Axenroth

LEAMINGTON

LEAMINGTON SHOPPER

Street Address1: 75 Oak St.
Street address state: ON
Postal Code: N8H 2B2
Country: Canada
Mailing Address: 75 Oak St.
Mailing City: Leamington
Mailing province: ON
Mailing Postal Code: N8H 2B2
Office phone: (519) 326-4434
Office fax: (519) 326-2171
Advertising e-mail: shopper@wincom.net
Website: www.leamingtonpostandshopper.com
Year publication established: 1971
Advertising (open inch rate): Open inch rate $1.02
Mechanical Specifications: Type page 10 2/5 x 14; E - 9 cols, 1 1/16, 1/8 between; A - 9 cols, 1 1/16, 1/8 between.
Delivery Methods: Carrier
Postal Codes Served: N8H 2X8
Frequency: Fri
Circulation Free: 17400
Audit By: Sworn/Estimate/Non-Audited
Audit Date: 43008
Note: We recently added news content and changed the name from Leamington Shopper to Tri-Town News serving the communities of Kingsville, Leamington & Wheatley
Personnel: Donald Gage (Pub.); Linda Gage (Adv. Mgr.)
Main (survey) contact: Publisher

LETHBRIDGE

THE LETHBRIDGE SHOPPER

Street Address1: 12th Street B North
Street Address2: 234A
Street address state: AB
Postal Code: T1H 2K7
Rural Municipality: Canada
Country: Canada
Mailing Address: 234A 12th Street B North
Mailing City: Lethbridge
Mailing province: AB
Mailing Postal Code: T1H 2K7
Office phone: (403) 527-5777
Office fax: (403) 526-7352
General e-mail: ethurlbeck@shoppergroup.com
Editorial e-mail: ethurlbeck@shoppergroup.com
Advertising e-mail: ethurlbeck@shoppergroup.com
Website: www.shoppergroup.com
Year publication established: 1976
Advertising (open inch rate): $71.40 (smallest modular rate)
Mechanical Specifications: Type page 10.25 x 16; 6 cols
Delivery Methods: Carrier
Postal Codes Served: T1A, T1B, T1C
Frequency: Sat
Circulation Free: 33176
Audit By: CVC
Audit Date: 41455
Personnel: Ron Heizelman (Ed.); Edward Thurlbeck (Adv. Mgr.)
Main (survey) contact: Ed Thurlbeck

LETHBRIDGE

THE SOUTHERN SUN TIMES

Street Address1: 504 7th St., S.
Street address state: AB
Postal Code: T1J 2H1
Country: Canada
Mailing Address: 504 7th St., S.
Mailing City: Lethbridge
Mailing province: AB
Mailing Postal Code: T1J 2H1
Office phone: (403) 328-4411
Office fax: (403) 320-7539
Advertising (open inch rate): Open inch rate $.95
Postal Codes Served: T1H 2J1
Frequency: Wed
Audit Date: 43008
Personnel: Bob Carey (Gen. Mgr.)
Main (survey) contact: Val Wiebe

LONDON

PENNYSAVER

Street Address1: 369 York St.
Street address state: ON
Postal Code: N6A 4G1
Country: Canada
Mailing Address: PO Box 2280
Mailing City: London
Mailing province: ON
Mailing Postal Code: N6A 4G1
Office phone: (519) 685-2020
Office fax: (519) 649-0908
Advertising Phone: (519) 667-5472
Advertising Fax: (519) 667-4573
General e-mail: newsdesk@lfpress.com
Advertising e-mail: pennyreaderads@londonpennysaver.com
Website: www.lfpress.com; www.londonpennysaver.com
Advertising (open inch rate): Open inch rate $3.17
Postal Codes Served: N5Z 3L1
Frequency: Fri
Circulation Free: 159000
Audit By: Sworn/Estimate/Non-Audited
Audit Date: 43008
Personnel: Cathy Forster (Gen. Mgr.); Nick Hawkins (Sales Rep.); Tracey Spence (Circ. Mgr.)
Main (survey) contact: Sherry Hutchinson

MEDICINE HAT

THE MEDICINE HAT SHOPPER

Street Address1: 3257 Dunmore Rd. SE
Street address state: AB
Postal Code: T1B 3R2
Rural Municipality: Canada
Country: Canada
Mailing Address: 3257 Dunmore Rd. SE
Mailing City: Medicine Hat
Mailing province: AB
Mailing Postal Code: T1B 3R2
Office phone: (403) 527-5777
Office fax: (403) 526-7352
General e-mail: cbrown@medicinehatnews.com
Advertising e-mail: cbrown@medicinehatnews.com
Website: www.shoppergroup.com
Year publication established: 1976
Advertising (open inch rate): $71.40 (smallest modular rate)
Mechanical Specifications: Type page 10.25 x 16; 6 cols
Delivery Methods: Carrier
Postal Codes Served: T1A,T1B,T1C
Frequency: Sat
Circulation Free: 26089
Audit By: CVC
Audit Date: 43008
Personnel: Edward Thurlbeck (Sales Manager); Ron Heizelman (Ed.)
Main (survey) contact: Ed Thurlbeck

NAPANEE

FRIDAY REGIONAL BEAVER

Street Address1: 72 Dundas St. E.
Street address state: ON
Postal Code: K7R 1H9
Country: Canada
Mailing Address: 72 Dundas St. E.
Mailing City: Napanee
Mailing province: ON
Mailing Postal Code: K7R 1H9
Office phone: (613) 354-6641
Office fax: (613) 354-2622
General e-mail: info@napaneebeaver.ca
Website: napaneebeaver.ca
Year publication established: 1870
Advertising (open inch rate): Open inch rate $.70
Mechanical Specifications: Type page 10 5/16 x 15 1/4; E - 6 cols, 1 9/16, 1/6 between; A - 6 cols, 1 9/16, 1/6 between; C - 6 cols, 1 9/16, 1/6 between.
Frequency: Fri
Audit Date: 43008
Personnel: Jean Morrison (Pub.)
Main (survey) contact: Jean Morrison

NIAGARA FALLS

NIAGARA SHOPPING NEWS

Street Address1: 4949 Victoria Ave.
Street address state: ON
Postal Code: L2E 4C7
Country: Canada
Mailing Address: 4949 Victoria Ave.
Mailing City: Niagara Falls
Mailing province: ON
Mailing Postal Code: L2E 4C7
Office phone: (905) 357-2440
Office fax: (905) 357-1620
Advertising Phone: (877) 786-8227
General e-mail: niagaraclassifieds@cogeco.net

Personnel: Will Berboven (Pub.); Bob Willcox (Pub.); John Morriss (Assoc. Pub.); Donna Berting (Adv. Mgr.); Linda Tityk (Circ. Mgr.)
Parent company: Great West Newspapers LP
Main (survey) contact: Bob Willcox

Shopper Publications in Canada

Website: www.ospreymedia.ca; www.niagarashoppingnews.ca
Advertising (open inch rate): Open inch rate $.68
Postal Codes Served: L2E 4C7
Frequency: Wed'Fri
Circulation Free: 29250
Audit By: Sworn/Estimate/Non-Audited
Audit Date: 43008
Personnel: Tim Dundas (Pub.)
Parent company: Quebecor Communications, Inc.
Main (survey) contact: Michael Cressman

NORTH BATTLEFORD

ADVERTISER-POST

Street Address1: 892-104 St.
Street address state: SK
Postal Code: S9A 3E6
Country: Canada
Mailing Address: PO Box 1029
Mailing City: North Battleford
Mailing province: SK
Mailing Postal Code: S9A 3E6
Office phone: (306) 445-7261
Office fax: (306) 445-3223
General e-mail: battlefords.publishing@sasktel.net
Advertising (open inch rate): Open inch rate $1.03
Mechanical Specifications: Type page 10 1/4 x 15 2/3; E - 5 cols, 1 11/12, 1/6 between; A - 5 cols, 1 11/12, 1/6 between; C - 6 cols, 1 7/12, 1/6 between.
Postal Codes Served: S9A 3E6
Frequency: Fri
Circulation Free: 16000
Audit By: Sworn/Estimate/Non-Audited
Audit Date: 43008
Personnel: Alana Schweitzer (Pub.); Gary Wouters (Circ. Mgr.); Becky Doig (Ed.); Claude Paradis (Prodn. Mgr.)
Main (survey) contact: Alana Schweitzer

OAKVILLE

SHOPPING NEWS

Street Address1: 2526 Speers
Street Address2: Unit 11
Street address state: ON
Postal Code: L6L 5M2
Country: Canada
Mailing Address: 2526 Speers, Unit 11
Mailing City: Oakville
Mailing province: ON
Mailing Postal Code: L6L 5M2
Office phone: (905) 827-2244
Office fax: (905) 827-9950
Editorial e-mail: editorial@oakvilletoday.ca
Website: www.metroland.com
Advertising (open inch rate): Open inch rate $1.84
Mechanical Specifications: Type page 10 7/16 x 14 1/4; E - 8 cols, 1 3/16, 1/8 between; A - 8 cols, 1 3/16, 1/8 between; C - 8 cols, 1 3/16, 1/8 between.
Postal Codes Served: L6C 5T7
Frequency: Wed
Circulation Free: 49800
Audit By: Sworn/Estimate/Non-Audited
Audit Date: 43008
Personnel: Lars Melander (Gen. Mgr.); Ian Holryd (Adv. Mgr.)
Parent company: Torstar
Main (survey) contact: Lars Melander

OTTAWA

SMART SHOPPER

Street Address1: 6 Antares Dr.
Street address state: ON
Postal Code: K1G 5H7
Country: Canada
Mailing Address: 6 Antares Dr.
Mailing City: Ottawa
Mailing province: ON
Mailing Postal Code: K1G 5H7
Office phone: (613) 733-4099
Office fax: (613) 733-7107
Advertising e-mail: classads@ott.sunpub.com
Website: www.ottawasmartshopper.ca
Advertising (open inch rate): Open inch rate $2.22
Mechanical Specifications: Type page 10 1/4 x 11 1/2; A - 6 cols, 1 5/8, between.
Postal Codes Served: K2E 7J6
Frequency: Thur
Circulation Free: 166000
Audit By: Sworn/Estimate/Non-Audited
Audit Date: 43008
Personnel: Pierre Peladeau (CEO); Shane Patacairk (Adv. Mgr.); Marty Holski (Circ. Mgr.)
Main (survey) contact: Bruce Holmes

PETERBOROUGH

THE EXAMINER

Street Address1: 60 Hunter Street East
Street address state: ON
Postal Code: K9H 1G5
Country: Canada
Mailing Address: 60 Hunter Street East
Mailing City: Peterborough
Mailing province: ON
Mailing Postal Code: K9H 1G5
Office phone: (705) 745-4641
General e-mail: Circulation@peterboroughdaily.com
Editorial e-mail: stefanie.lynch@peterboroughdaily.com
Advertising e-mail: jillian.baldwin@peterboroughdaily.com
Website: www.peterboroughexaminer.com
Year publication established: 1847
Advertising (open inch rate): Open inch rate $1.35
Frequency: Fri
Circulation Free: 49000
Audit By: Sworn/Estimate/Non-Audited
Audit Date: 43585
Personnel: Kennedy Gordon (Mng. Ed.); Michael Everson (Mktg. Mgr.); Neil Oliver (Pub.)
Parent company: Quebecor Communications, Inc.
Main (survey) contact: Kennedy Gordon

PONOKA

THE BASHAW STAR

Street Address1: 5019a Chipman Ave.
Street address state: AB
Postal Code: T4J 1R6
Rural Municipality: Bashaw
Country: Canada
Mailing Address: P.O. Box 4217
Mailing City: Ponoka
Mailing province: AB
Mailing Postal Code: T4J 1R6
Office phone: (403) 783-3311
Office fax: (403) 783 6300
General e-mail: manager@bashawstar.com
Advertising (open inch rate): Open inch rate $.61
Mechanical Specifications: Type page 10 1/8 x 13; E - 7 cols, 1 1/12, 3/16 between; A - 7 cols, 1 1/12, 3/16 between; C - 8 cols, 3/16 between.
Frequency: Wed
Circulation Paid: 216
Circulation Free: 15
Audit By: CMCA
Audit Date: 41759
Hardware: APP/Mac
Software: QPS/QuarkXPress.
Personnel: Mustafa Eric (Ed.)
Parent company: Black Press Group Ltd.
Main (survey) contact: Mustafa Eric

PRINCE ALBERT

PRINCE ALBERT SHOPPER

Street Address1: Po Box 1930
Street address state: SK
Postal Code: S6V 6J9
Country: Canada
Mailing Address: PO Box 1930
Mailing City: Prince Albert
Mailing province: SK
Mailing Postal Code: S6V 6J9
Office phone: (306) 763-8461
Office fax: (306) 763-1856
General e-mail: pashopper@sasktel.net
Website: www.princealbertshopper.com
Advertising (open inch rate): Open inch rate $.76
Mechanical Specifications: Type page 10 3/4 x 16.
Postal Codes Served: 26V 6J9
Frequency: Mon
Circulation Free: 20000
Audit By: Sworn/Estimate/Non-Audited
Audit Date: 43008
Personnel: Jerry Paskiw (Adv. Mgr.)
Main (survey) contact: Jerry Paskiw

RENFREW

ARNPRIOR CHRONICLE
WEEKENDER

Street Address1: 35 Opeongo Road
Street address state: ON
Postal Code: K7V 2T2
Country: Canada
Mailing Address: 35 Opeongo Road
Mailing City: Renfrew
Mailing province: ON
Mailing Postal Code: K7V 2T2
Office phone: (800) 884-9195
General e-mail: valleyclassifieds@metroland.com
Editorial e-mail: SHaaima@metroland.com
Advertising e-mail: lesosborne@starmetrolandmedia.com
Website: insideottawavalley.com
Advertising (open inch rate): Open inch rate $7.14
Postal Codes Served: K7S 2N6
Frequency: Fri
Circulation Free: 6500
Audit By: Sworn/Estimate/Non-Audited
Audit Date: 43585
Personnel: Sherry Haaima; Leslie Osborne (Adv.)
Main (survey) contact: Sherry Haaima

SAINT JEAN

LE GROUP CANADA FRANCAIS

Street Address1: 84 Rue Richelieu
Street address state: QC
Postal Code: J3B 6X3
Country: Canada
Mailing Address: 84 rue Richelieu
Mailing City: Saint Jean
Mailing province: QC
Mailing Postal Code: J3B 6X3
Office phone: (450) 347-0323
Office fax: (450) 347-4539
Website: www.canadafrancais.com
Advertising (open inch rate): Open inch rate $1.69
Postal Codes Served: J3B 6X3
Frequency: Wed
Circulation Free: 18500
Audit By: Sworn/Estimate/Non-Audited
Audit Date: 43008
Personnel: Renel Bouchard (Circ. Mgr.); Robert Paradis (Ed.)
Main (survey) contact: Renel Bouchard

SALMON ARM

LAKESHORE NEWS

Street Address1: 161 Hudson Ave.
Street address state: BC
Postal Code: V1E 4N8
Country: Canada
Mailing Address: PO Box 699
Mailing City: Salmon Arm
Mailing province: BC
Mailing Postal Code: V1E 4N8
Office phone: (250) 832-9461
Office fax: (250) 832-5246
General e-mail: lsn@lakeshorenews.bc.ca
Website: lakeshorenews.bc.ca
Frequency: Fri
Circulation Paid: 0
Circulation Free: 13745
Audit By: Sworn/Estimate/Non-Audited
Audit Date: 43008
Parent company: Black Press Group Ltd.

SHELLBROOK

SHOPPER CHRONICLE

Street Address1: 44 Main St.
Street address state: SK
Postal Code: S0J 2E0
Country: Canada
Mailing Address: PO Box 10
Mailing City: Shellbrook
Mailing province: SK
Mailing Postal Code: S0J 2E0
Office phone: (306) 747-2442
Office fax: (306) 747-3000
General e-mail: chnews@shellbrookchronicle.com
Advertising (open inch rate): Open inch rate $13.72
Mechanical Specifications: Type page 10 1/4 x 15; E - 6 cols, 1 7/12, 1/6 between; A - 6 cols, 1 7/12, 1/6 between; C - 6 cols, 1 7/12, 1/6 between.
Frequency: Fri
Circulation Free: 4587
Audit By: Sworn/Estimate/Non-Audited
Audit Date: 43008
Personnel: C.J. Pepper (Pub.); Brad Dupuis (Ed.)
Main (survey) contact: C.J. Pepper

STRATHROY

STRATHROY AGE DISPATCH

Street Address1: 73 Front St W
Street address state: ON
Postal Code: N7G 1X6
Country: Canada
Mailing Address: 73 Front St W
Mailing City: Strathroy
Mailing province: ON
Mailing Postal Code: N7G 1X6
Office phone: (519) 245-2370
General e-mail: agedispatch@strathroyonline.com
Website: www.strathroyagedispatch.com
Year publication established: 1861
Advertising (open inch rate): Open inch rate $1.12
Mechanical Specifications: Type page 10 1/4 x 13; E - 8 cols, 1 3/16, 1/6 between; A - 9 cols, 1 3/16, 1/6 between; C - 8 cols, 1 3/16, 1/6 between.
Postal Codes Served: N7G 1Y4
Frequency: Wed
Circulation Free: 5000
Audit By: Sworn/Estimate/Non-Audited
Audit Date: 43585
Personnel: Linda Leblanc (Pub.); Denise Armstrong (Adv. Mgr.); Cheryl Klaver (Circ. Mgr.)
Parent company: Postmedia Network Inc.; Quebecor Communications, Inc.
Main (survey) contact: Linda Leblanc

SURREY

THE LINK

Street Address1: 12732 80th Avenue
Street Address2: #200
Street address state: BC
Postal Code: V3W 3A7
Rural Municipality: BC
Country: Canada
Mailing Address: #421-15380 - 102A Avenue
Mailing City: Surrey
Mailing province: BC
Mailing Postal Code: V3R 0B3
Office phone: (604) 880-3463
Office fax: (604) 591-2113
Advertising Phone: (604) 880-3463
Editorial Phone: (604) 880-3463
Other phone: (604) 880-3463
General e-mail: editorpd@hotmail.com
Editorial e-mail: editorpd@hotmail.com
Advertising e-mail: editorpd@hotmail.com
Website: www.thelinkpaper.ca
Year publication established: 1972
Advertising (open inch rate): Open inch rate $12.00
Mechanical Specifications: Type page 10 1/4 x 14 3/4; E - 6 cols, 1 7/12, 1/6 between; A - 6 cols, 1 1/3, 1/6 between.
Delivery Methods: Mail`Newsstand`Carrier`Racks
Frequency: Sat
Circulation Free: 20000
Audit By: Sworn/Estimate/Non-Audited
Audit Date: 43434
Personnel: Paul Dhillon (Ed.)
Parent company: South Asian Link Publications
Main (survey) contact: Paul Dhillon

THOROLD

FORT ERIE SHOPPING TIMES

Street Address1: 3300 Merrittville Hwy
Street Address2: Unit 1B
Street address state: ON
Postal Code: L2V 4Y6
Country: Canada
Mailing Address: 3300 Merrittville Hwy, Unit 1B
Mailing City: Thorold
Mailing province: ON
Mailing Postal Code: L2V 4Y6
Office phone: (905) 871-3100
Office fax: (905) 871-5243
General e-mail: classifieds@metroland.com
Editorial e-mail: letters@niagarathisweek.com
Advertising e-mail: dhawkins@niagarathisweek.com
Website: niagarathisweek.com
Advertising (open inch rate): Open inch rate $.44
Postal Codes Served: L2A 5Y2
Frequency: Wed
Circulation Free: 11800
Audit By: Sworn/Estimate/Non-Audited
Audit Date: 43554
Personnel: Mark Dawson; Dave Hawkins
Parent company: Postmedia Network Inc.; Quebecor Communications, Inc.
Main (survey) contact: Dave Hawkins

TILLSONBURG

LAKE SHORE SHOPPER (TILLSONBURG)

Street Address1: 25 Townline Rd.
Street address state: ON
Postal Code: N4G 4H6
Country: Canada
Mailing Address: PO Box 190
Mailing City: Tillsonburg
Mailing province: ON
Mailing Postal Code: N4G 4H6
Office phone: (519) 688-1177
Office fax: (519) 688-9353
Website: www.theshopper.ca
Advertising (open inch rate): Open inch rate $.96
Mechanical Specifications: Type page 10 3/8 x 15; A - 9 cols, 1 9/16, between.
Frequency: Fri
Circulation Free: 40434
Audit By: Sworn/Estimate/Non-Audited
Audit Date: 43008
Personnel: Michael Walsh (Pub.); David Hopkins (Adv. Mgr.); Joan Tewes (Circ. Mgr.); Sharon Craig (Prodn. Mgr.)
Parent company: Postmedia Network Inc.; Quebecor Communications, Inc.
Main (survey) contact: David Hopkins

TISDALE

PARKLAND REVIEW

Street Address1: 1004-102 Ave.
Street address state: SK
Postal Code: S0E 1T0
Country: Canada
Mailing Address: PO Box 1660
Mailing City: Tisdale
Mailing province: SK
Mailing Postal Code: S0E 1T0
Office phone: (306) 873-4515
Office fax: (306) 873-4712
General e-mail: recorderoffice@sasktel.net
Editorial e-mail: newsrecorder@sasktel.net
Advertising e-mail: adsrecorder@sasktel.net
Advertising (open inch rate): Open inch rate $1.26
Delivery Methods: Mail
Postal Codes Served: Canada
Frequency: Fri
Circulation Free: 11625
Audit By: CMCA
Audit Date: 42460
Personnel: August Grandguillar (Adv. Mgr.); Brent Fitzpatrick (Ed.); Gord Anderson (Prodn. Mgr.); Dan Sully (Adv. Mgr.)
Parent company: Glacier Media Group
Main (survey) contact: Brent Fitzpatrick

TRURO

WEEKEND READ

Street Address1: 6 Louise St.
Street address state: NS
Postal Code: B2N 5C3
Country: Canada
Mailing Address: PO Box 220
Mailing City: Truro
Mailing province: NS
Mailing Postal Code: B2N 5C3
Office phone: (902) 893-9405
Office fax: (902) 895-6104
General e-mail: news@trurodaily.com
Website: www.trurodaily.com
Advertising (open inch rate): Open inch rate $1.06
Postal Codes Served: B2N 5C3
Frequency: Fri
Circulation Free: 20479
Audit By: Sworn/Estimate/Non-Audited
Audit Date: 43008
Personnel: Richard Russell (Pub.); Carl Fleming (Ed.)
Main (survey) contact: Richard Russell

VEGREVILLE

VEGREVILLE NEWS ADVERTISER

Street Address1: 5110 50th St.
Street address state: AB
Postal Code: T9C 1R9
Country: Canada
Mailing Address: PO Box 810
Mailing City: Vegreville
Mailing province: AB
Mailing Postal Code: T9C 1R9
Office phone: (780) 632-2861
Office fax: (780) 632-7981
Editorial e-mail: editor@newsadvertiser.com
Advertising e-mail: ads@newsadvertiser.com
Website: www.newsadvertiser.com
Year publication established: 1950
Advertising (open inch rate): Open inch rate $15.26
Mechanical Specifications: Type page 10.25" x 15.5"; 6 cols
Delivery Methods: Mail`Carrier`Racks
Postal Codes Served: T9C 1R9 T0B 0C0 T0B 0K0 T0b 0P0 T0B 0R0 T0B 0W0 T0B 1C0 T0B 1S0 T0B 2B0 T0B 2C0 T0B 2G0 T0B 2R0 T0B 2S0 T0B 2W0 T0B 3B0 T0B 3H0 T0B 3K0 T0B 3T0 T0B 4A0 T0A 3C0 T0B 4B0 T0B 4J0 T0B 4K0 all of T9C T0B 4N0 T0B 4R0 T0B 4S0
Frequency: Wed
Circulation Paid: 50
Circulation Free: 11241
Audit By: Sworn/Estimate/Non-Audited
Audit Date: 43008
Presses: Digitala and small offset
Software: Adobe Creative Cloud, CorelDRAW, Windows 10, Xerox FreeFlow
Editions Count: 1
Edition Names with circulation: News Advertiser (11241), News Advertiser Insider (6000)
Personnel: Arthur Beaudette (Gen. Mgr.); Dan Beaudette (Ed.)
Main (survey) contact: Dan Beaudette

WASAGA BEACH

THE STAYNER SUN

Street Address1: 1456 Mosley St.
Street address state: ON
Postal Code: L9Z 2B9
Rural Municipality: Canada
Country: Canada
Mailing Address: 1456 Mosley St.
Mailing City: Wasaga Beach
Mailing province: ON
Mailing Postal Code: L9Z 2B9
Office phone: (705) 428-2638
Office fax: (705) 422-2446
General e-mail: sunnews@simcoe.com
Website: www.staynersun.ca
Advertising (open inch rate): Open inch rate $1.12
Mechanical Specifications: Type page 11 1/2 x 21 1/2; E - 10 cols, 1 1/16, 3/32 between; A - 10 cols, 1 1/16, 3/32 between; C - 10 cols, 1 1/16, 3/32 between.
Frequency: Thur
Circulation Free: 4088
Audit By: CMCA
Audit Date: 41820
Hardware: APP/Mac
Software: QPS/QuarkXPress 3.32.
Personnel: Joe Anderson (Pub.); Catherine Haller (Gen. Mgr.); Mary Ellis (Bus. Mgr.); Shaun Sauve (Adv. Dir.); Wendy Sherk (Adv. Mgr.); Scott Woodhouse (Ed.); Stephen Hall (Prodn. Mgr.)
Parent company: Metroland Media Group Ltd.; Torstar
Main (survey) contact: Carol Lamb

WELLAND

WELLAND SHOPPING NEWS

Street Address1: 440 Niagara St.
Street Address2: Unit 7
Street address state: ON
Postal Code: L3C 1L5
Country: Canada
Mailing Address: 440 Niagara St., Unit 7
Mailing City: Welland
Mailing province: ON
Mailing Postal Code: L3C 1L5
Office phone: (905) 735-9222
Office fax: (905) 735-9224
General e-mail: nsncirculation@niagaracommunitynewspapers.com; wsnclassified@wellandshoppingnews.com
Website: www.wellandshoppingnews.ca
Advertising (open inch rate): Open inch rate $.55
Mechanical Specifications: Type page 10 3/8 x 16 3/4; E - 6 cols, 1 5/8, 1/8 between; A - 6 cols, 1 5/8, 1/8 between.
Postal Codes Served: L3B 3W5
Frequency: Wed
Circulation Free: 22900
Audit By: Sworn/Estimate/Non-Audited
Audit Date: 43008

WEYBURN

WEYBURN & AREA BOOSTER

Street Address1: 904 East Ave.
Street address state: SK
Postal Code: S4H 2K4
Country: Canada
Mailing Address: PO Box 400
Mailing City: Weyburn
Mailing province: SK
Mailing Postal Code: S4H 2K4
Office phone: (306) 842-7487
Office fax: (306) 842-0282
General e-mail: production@weyburnreview.com
Website: www.weyburnreview.com
Advertising (open inch rate): Open inch rate $15.96
Mechanical Specifications: 5 column tabloid 9.67" x 15.75"
Delivery Methods: Newsstand`Carrier`Racks
Postal Codes Served: S4H 2K4
Frequency: Sat
Other Type of Frequency: Delivered Friday and Saturday
Circulation Free: 6280
Audit By: Sworn/Estimate/Non-Audited
Audit Date: 43008
Hardware: Mac platform
Software: Indesign, Photoshop
Editions Count: 52
Personnel: Darryl D. Ward (Pub.); Patricia A. Ward (Ed.)
Parent company: Priaire Newspaper Group
Main (survey) contact: Darryl D. Ward

WINDSOR

WINDSOR SMART SHOPPER

Street Address1: 4525 Rhodes Dr.
Street Address2: Unit 400
Street address state: ON
Postal Code: NEW 5R8
Country: Canada
Mailing Address: 4525 Rhodes Dr., Unit 400
Mailing City: Windsor
Mailing province: ON
Mailing Postal Code: NEW 5R8
Office phone: (519) 966-4500
Office fax: (519) 966-3660
General e-mail: design@windsorpennysaver.com; delivery@windsorpennysaver.com; sales@windsorpennysaver.com
Advertising e-mail: placeit@classifiedextra.cam
Website: www.windsorpennysaver.com
Advertising (open inch rate): Open inch rate $2.41
Postal Codes Served: N8T 1R1
Frequency: Thur
Circulation Free: 119000
Audit By: Sworn/Estimate/Non-Audited
Audit Date: 43008
Personnel: Shannon Ricker (Pub.); Ed Donovan (Sales Mgr)
Main (survey) contact: Shannon Ricker

YORKTON

THE MARKETPLACE

Street Address1: 20 Third Ave.
Street address state: SK
Postal Code: S3N 2X3
Country: Canada
Mailing Address: PO Box 1300
Mailing City: Yorkton
Mailing province: SK
Mailing Postal Code: S3N 2X3
Office phone: (306) 782-2465
Office fax: (306) 786-1898
General e-mail: publisher@yorktonthisweek.

com
Website: www.yorktonthisweek.com
Advertising (open inch rate): Open inch rate $13.86
Mechanical Specifications: Type page 13 1/2 x 16; E - 5 cols, 2 1/12, 1/6 between; A - 5 cols, 2 1/12, 1/6 between; C - 5 cols, 2 1/12, 1/6 between.
Delivery Methods: Newsstand`Carrier`Racks
Postal Codes Served: S3N, SOA, SOE, ROJ, SOG, ROM
Frequency: Fri
Circulation Free: 20000
Audit By: Sworn/Estimate/Non-Audited
Audit Date: 43134
Personnel: Jim Kinaschuk (Circ. Mgr.); Jim Ambrose (Publisher); Debbie Barr (Prodn. Mgr.)
Main (survey) contact: Jim Ambrose

YORKTON
YORKTON NEWS REVIEW

Street Address1: 18 1st Ave. N
Street address state: SK
Postal Code: S3N 1J4
Rural Municipality: Canada
Country: Canada
Mailing Address: 18 1st Ave. N
Mailing City: Yorkton
Mailing province: SK
Mailing Postal Code: S3N 1J4
Office phone: (306) 783-7355
Office fax: (306) 782-9138
General e-mail: web@yorktonnews.com
Editorial e-mail: web@yorktonnews.com
Advertising e-mail: web@yorktonnews.com
Website: yorktonnews.com
Year publication established: 21
Advertising (open inch rate): Open inch rate $14.70
Mechanical Specifications: Type page 9.875 x 15 1/2; E - 6 cols, 1.5, 1/6 between; A - 6 cols, 1.5, 1/6 between; C - 6 cols, 1.5, 1/6 between.
Delivery Methods: Newsstand`Carrier`Racks
Postal Codes Served: S3N
Frequency: Thur
Circulation Free: 6797
Audit By: CMCA
Audit Date: 43584
Hardware: APP/Mac
Software: Adobe, QPS/QuarkXPress. In Design
Personnel: Ken Chyz (Adv. Mgr.); Shannon Deveau (Ed.); Carol Melnechenko (Prodn. Mgr.)
Parent company: Glacier Media Group
Main (survey) contact: Ken Chyz

SHOPPER PUBLICATIONS IN THE U.S.

ALABAMA

ALBERTVILLE

THE SHOPPER

Street Address1: PO Box 1729
Street address state: AL
Postal code: 35950-0028
County: Marshall
Country: USA
Mailing address: PO Box 1729
Mailing city: Albertville
Mailing state: AL
Mailing zip: 35950-0028
Office phone: (256) 840-3000
Office fax: (256) 840-2987
Advertising (open inch rate): Open inch rate $4.10
Frequency: Tues
Circulation Free: 13600
Audit By: Sworn/Estimate/Non-Audited
Audit Date: 43658
Personnel: Ben Shurett (Pub.)
Main (survey) contact: Ben Shurett

ENTERPRISE

DALEVILLE SUN-COURIER

Street Address1: 628-A Glover Ave
Street address state: AL
Postal code: 36330-2014
County: Coffee
Country: USA
Mailing address: PO Box 311546
Mailing city: Enterprise
Mailing state: AL
Mailing zip: 36331-1546
Office phone: (334) 393-2969
Office fax: (334) 393-2987
General e-mail: news@southeastsun.com
Advertising e-mail: rquattlebaum@southeastsun.com
Website: news@southeastsun.com
Year publication established: 1986
Advertising (open inch rate): Open inch rate $15.60
Mechanical specifications: Type page 9.9"x20"; 6 cols
Delivery methods: Newsstand`Carrier`Racks
Zip Codes Served: 36322, 36362, 36352
Frequency: Wed
Circulation Paid: 37
Circulation Free: 6056
Audit By: CVC
Audit Date: 42643
Hardware: APP
Software: Indesign/CS.
Personnel: Russell Quattlebaum (Adv. Mgr.); Caroline Quattlebaum (Co-pub.); Josh Boutwell (Sports Ed.); Janet Corneil (Circ. Mgr)
Main (survey) contact: Russell Quattlebaum

QST PUBLICATIONS

Street Address1: 628-A Glover Ave
Street address state: AL
Postal code: 36330-2014
County: Coffee
Country: USA
Mailing address: PO Box 311546
Mailing city: Enterprise
Mailing state: AL
Mailing zip: 36331-1546
Office phone: (334) 393-2969
Office fax: (334) 393-2987
General e-mail: circulation@southeastsun.com
Advertising e-mail: publisher@southeastsun.com
Editorial e-mail: rquattlebaum@southeastsun.com
Website: circulation@southeastsun.com
Year publication established: 1982
Delivery methods: Mail`Carrier`Racks
Frequency: Wed
Circulation Paid: 325
Circulation Free: 20336
Audit By: CVC
Audit Date: 42979
Personnel: Russell Quattlebaum (Co-publisher); Caroline Quattlebaum (Co-publisher); Janet Corneil (Circulation Manager)
Main (survey) contact: Russell Quattlebaum

SOUTHEAST SUN

Street Address1: 628-A Glover Ave
Street address state: AL
Postal code: 36330-2014
County: Coffee
Country: USA
Mailing address: PO Box 311546
Mailing city: Enterprise
Mailing state: AL
Mailing zip: 36331-1546
Office phone: (334) 393-2969
Office fax: (334) 393-2987
General e-mail: circulation@southeastsun.com
Editorial e-mail: rquattlebaum@southeastsun.com
Website: circulation@southeastsun.com
Year publication established: 1982
Advertising (open inch rate): Open inch rate $15.60
Mechanical specifications: Type page 9.9" x 20"; 6 cols
Delivery methods: Racks
Zip Codes Served: 36331, 36330, 36351, 36318, 36316
Frequency: Wed
Circulation Paid: 294
Circulation Free: 14365
Audit By: CVC
Audit Date: 42643
Personnel: Russell Quattlebaum (Pub.); Caroline Quattlebaum (Co-Pub.); Josh Boutwell (Sports Ed.); Janet Corneil (Circ. Mgr)
Main (survey) contact: Russell Quattlebaum

FORT PAYNE

SAND MOUNTAIN SHOPPER'S GUIDE

Street Address1: 811 Greenhill Blvd NW
Street address state: AL
Postal code: 35967
County: De Kalb
Country: USA
Mailing address: P.O. Box 680349
Mailing city: Fort Payne
Mailing state: AL
Mailing zip: 35968
Office phone: (256) 845-2550
Office fax: (256) 845-7459
Advertising e-mail: advertising@times-journal.com
Editorial e-mail: news@times-journal.com
Year publication established: 1900
Advertising (open inch rate): Open inch rate $9.75
Delivery methods: Mail
Zip Codes Served: 3,59673596835971E+39
Frequency: Tues
Circulation Free: 12500
Audit By: CAC
Audit Date: 42406
Personnel: Tricia Dunne (Publisher)
Main (survey) contact: Tricia Dunne

GADSDEN

TIMES2

Street Address1: 401 Locust St
Street address state: AL
Postal code: 35901-3737
County: Etowah
Country: USA
Mailing address: PO Box 188
Mailing city: Gadsden
Mailing state: AL
Mailing zip: 35902-0188
Office phone: (256) 549-2000
Office fax: (256) 549-2013
Advertising phone: (256) 549-2077
Advertising fax: (256) 549-2013
Editorial phone: (256) 549-2049
Editorial fax: (256) 549-2105
General e-mail: glen.porter@gadsdentimes.com
Advertising e-mail: david.bragg@gadsdentimes.com
Editorial e-mail: news@gadsdentimes.com
Website: glen.porter@gadsdentimes.com
Year publication established: 2005
Advertising (open inch rate): Open inch rate $10.00
Mechanical specifications: Type page 12 x 21 1/2; E - 6 cols, 1 13/16, between; A - 6 cols, 1 13/16, between; C - 9 cols, 1 13/16, between.
Delivery methods: Mail`Carrier`Racks
Zip Codes Served: 35901, 35903, 35904, 35905, 35906, 35907, 35954, 35956
Digital Platform - Mobile: Apple`Android`Windows`Blackberry
Digital Platform - Tablet: Apple iOS`Android`Windows 7`Blackberry Tablet OS`Kindle`Nook`Kindle Fire
Frequency: Wed
Circulation Free: 19000
Audit By: Sworn/Estimate/Non-Audited
Audit Date: 43658
Software: QPS/QuarkXPress.
Personnel: Glen Porter (Pub.); John Chapman (Circ. Mgr.); David Bragg (Sales Mgr.)
Parent company: The Hays Daily News
Main (survey) contact: Glen Porter

LUVERNE

BONUS EXPRESS

Street Address1: 118 S Forest Ave
Street address state: AL
Postal code: 36049-1502
County: Crenshaw
Country: USA
Mailing address: PO Box 152
Mailing city: Luverne
Mailing state: AL
Mailing zip: 36049-0152
Office phone: (334) 335-3541
Office fax: (334) 371-7104
Advertising (open inch rate): Open inch rate $6.75
Frequency: Wed
Circulation Free: 6500
Audit By: Sworn/Estimate/Non-Audited
Audit Date: 43658
Personnel: Ed Darling (Pub.); Tammy Faulk (Bus. Mgr.)
Main (survey) contact: Tammy Faulk

MOBILE

AMERICAN CLASSIFIEDS - MOBILE

Street Address1: PO Box 91329
Street address state: AL
Postal code: 36691-1329
County: Mobile
Country: USA
Mailing address: PO Box 91329
Mailing city: Mobile
Mailing state: AL
Mailing zip: 36691-1329
Office phone: (251) 344-5454
Office fax: (251) 344-5743
General e-mail: mobile@americanclassifies.com
Website: mobile@americanclassifies.com
Year publication established: 1989
Advertising (open inch rate): Open inch rate $16.65
Mechanical specifications: Type page 10"x16"; 1 col.x 1.2"; 8 col. page
Delivery methods: Racks
Zip Codes Served: 3,6507365093652E+174
Digital Platform - Mobile: Windows
Digital Platform - Tablet: Windows 7
Frequency: Thur
Circulation Paid: 0
Circulation Free: 24330
Audit By: CVC
Audit Date: 42368
Personnel: Tom Carter (Publisher)
Main (survey) contact: Dave Wenke

MONTGOMERY

BULLETIN BOARD

Street Address1: 425 Molton St
Street address state: AL
Postal code: 36104-3523
County: Montgomery
Country: USA
Mailing address: PO Box 241207
Mailing city: Montgomery
Mailing state: AL
Mailing zip: 36124-1207
Office phone: (334) 272-1225
Office fax: (334) 271-2143
Advertising e-mail: ads@thebulletinboard.com
Advertising (open inch rate): Open inch rate $13.25
Mechanical specifications: Type page 7 1/2 x 10; A - 3 cols, 2 1/2, 1/6 between; C - 3 cols, 2 1/2, 1/6 between.
Frequency: Thur
Circulation Paid: 17250
Circulation Free: 300
Audit By: Sworn/Estimate/Non-Audited
Audit Date: 43658
Hardware: APP/Super Mac
Software: QPS/QuarkXPress 3.32.
Personnel: French Salter (Gen. Mgr.)
Parent company: Gannett
Main (survey) contact: French Salter

PELHAM

AMERICAN CLASSIFIEDS - BIRMINGHAM

Street Address1: 250 Yeager Pkwy
Street address state: AL
Postal code: 35124-1800
County: Shelby
Country: USA
Mailing address: 250 Yeager Pkwy
Mailing city: Pelham
Mailing state: AL
Mailing zip: 35124-1800
Advertising (open inch rate): Open inch rate $29.00
Mechanical specifications: Type page 10" x 16"; 8 cols
Delivery methods: Racks
Zip Codes Served: BIRMINGHAM, AL MSA

Shopper Publications in the U.S.

Frequency: Thur
Circulation Paid: 0
Circulation Free: 33538
Audit By: CVC
Audit Date: 42277
Personnel: Brian Merrill
Main (survey) contact: Brian Merrill

ARKANSAS

CROSSETT

ASHLEY COUNTY SHOPPER GUIDE

Street Address1: 106 E 2nd Ave
Street address state: AR
Postal code: 71635-2902
County: Ashley
Country: USA
Mailing address: PO Box 798
Mailing city: Crossett
Mailing state: AR
Mailing zip: 71635-0798
Office phone: (870) 364-5186
Office fax: (870) 364-2116
General e-mail: ad@ashleynewsobserver.com
Website: ad@ashleynewsobserver.com
Advertising (open inch rate): Open inch rate $6.50
Frequency: Mon
Circulation Free: 11157
Audit By: Sworn/Estimate/Non-Audited
Audit Date: 43658
Personnel: Barney White (Pub.); Pat Tullos (Adv. Mgr.)
Main (survey) contact: Barney White

DUMAS

DELTA ADVERTISER

Street Address1: 136 E Waterman St
Street address state: AR
Postal code: 71639-2227
County: Desha
Country: USA
Mailing address: PO Box 220
Mailing city: Dumas
Mailing state: AR
Mailing zip: 71639-0220
Office phone: (870) 382-4925
Office fax: (870) 382-6421
Advertising (open inch rate): Open inch rate $8.05
Frequency: Mon
Circulation Free: 5537
Audit By: Sworn/Estimate/Non-Audited
Audit Date: 43658
Presses: HI/Cottrell V-15
Software: QPS/QuarkXPress 4.1.
Personnel: Terry G. Hawkins (Pub.)
Main (survey) contact: Terry G. Hawkins

FORREST CITY

EAST ARKANSAS ADVERTISER

Street Address1: 222 N Izard St
Street address state: AR
Postal code: 72335-3324
County: Saint Francis
Country: USA
Mailing address: PO Box 1699
Mailing city: Forrest City
Mailing state: AR
Mailing zip: 72336-1699
Office phone: (870) 633-3131
Office fax: (870) 633-0599
General e-mail: fctimes@thnews.com
Advertising e-mail: addept@thnews.com
Editorial e-mail: tamjohn@thnews.com
Website: fctimes@thnews.com
Year publication established: 1978
Advertising (open inch rate): Open inch rate $13.76
Mechanical specifications: edit page 6 x 21: 1 col 1.833, 2 col 3.792, 3 col 5.75, 4 col 7.708, 5 col 9.667, 6 col 11.625; class 9x21: 1.181, 2.487, 3.793, 5.099, 6.405, 7.711, 9.017, 10.323, 11.625
Delivery methods: Mail`Newsstand`Carrier`Racks
Zip Codes Served: 72336
Frequency: Wed
Circulation Free: 16200
Audit By: Sworn/Estimate/Non-Audited
Audit Date: 43658
Hardware: Mac OS X v10.6.8, ECRM MAKO NEWS CTP
Presses: 7-G/Community
Software: QP6/QuarkXPress 6.52, Multi-Ad/Creator 7.0.6, Adobe/Photoshop cs2 v 9.0.2, Illustrator cs2 12.0.1, Adobe/Acrobat 7 Pro v 7.1.0
Personnel: Weston McCollum Lewey (Pub.); Bonner McCollum (Pub.); Ronnie Barnett (Circ. Mgr.); Tamara Johnson (Mng. Ed.); Tammy Long (ad sales)
Main (survey) contact: Weston Lewey

FORT SMITH

RIVER VALLEY ADVERTISER

Street Address1: 3600 Wheeler Ave
Street address state: AR
Postal code: 72901-6621
County: Sebastian
Country: USA
Office phone: (479) 785-7711
Frequency: Wed

HOT SPRINGS

THRIFTY NICKEL WANT ADS

Street Address1: 670 Ouachita Ave
Street address state: AR
Postal code: 71901-3920
County: Garland
Country: USA
Mailing address: PO Box 1200
Mailing city: Hot Springs
Mailing state: AR
Mailing zip: 71902-1200
Office phone: (501) 623-4404
Office fax: (501) 623-2454
General e-mail: hstn@swbell.net
Website: hstn@swbell.net
Advertising (open inch rate): Open inch rate $6.00
Zip Codes Served: 71913
Frequency: Thur
Circulation Free: 30000
Audit By: Sworn/Estimate/Non-Audited
Audit Date: 43658
Personnel: Danny Encow (Pub.)
Main (survey) contact: Danny Enlow

JASPER

THE NEWTON COUNTY TIMES

Street Address1: 101 CHURCH$8.25 Per Col Inch St
Street address state: AR
Postal code: 72641
County: Newton
Country: USA
Mailing address: PO Box 453
Mailing city: Jasper
Mailing state: AR
Mailing zip: 72641-0453
Office phone: (870) 446-2645
Office fax: (870) 446-6286
Advertising phone: (870) 741-2325
General e-mail: NewtonCoTimes <news@newtoncountycom>
Website: NewtonCoTimes <news@newtoncountytimes.com>
Year publication established: 1917
Advertising (open inch rate): $8.25 per column inch
Mechanical specifications: Type page 10.25" x 20.5"; 6 cols
Delivery methods: Racks
Digital Platform - Tablet: Apple iOS
Frequency: Wed
Circulation Paid: 1872
Circulation Free: 100
Audit By: CVC
Audit Date: 42644
Hardware: APP/Mac
Software: Adobe/PageMaker, Microsoft/Word, QPS/QuarkXPress.
Personnel: Jim Perry (Publisher); Jeff Dezort (Editor); Todd Edwards (Advertising Manager)
Parent company: Phillips Media Group LLC; Community Publishers, Inc.
Main (survey) contact: Jeff Dezort

SILOAM SPRINGS

NEIGHBOR SHOPPER

Street Address1: 151 HWY 412 E.
Street Address2: Suite B
Street address state: AR
Postal code: 72761
County: Benton
Country: USA
Mailing address: 151 HWY 412 E. Suite B
Mailing city: Siloam Springs
Mailing state: AR
Mailing zip: 72761
Office phone: (479) 202-9255
General e-mail: hleditor@nwadg.com
Advertising e-mail: lgraves@nwadg.com
Editorial e-mail: gthomas@nwadg.com
Website: hleditor@nwadg.com
Advertising (open inch rate): Open inch rate $6.53
Mechanical specifications: Type page 13 x 21 1/4; A - 6 cols, between; C - 9 cols, between.
Zip Codes Served: 72712
Frequency: Tues
Circulation Free: 11600
Audit By: Sworn/Estimate/Non-Audited
Audit Date: 43585
Hardware: APP/Mac
Presses: G
Software: Baseview.
Personnel: Graham Thomas (Mng. Ed.); Janelle Jessen (Asst. Ed.); Don Jones (Adv.); Lane Graves (Adv.)
Main (survey) contact: Graham Thomas

ARIZONA

COTTONWOOD

KUDOS

Street Address1: 116 S Main St
Street address state: AZ
Postal code: 86326-3909
County: Yavapai
Country: USA
Mailing address: PO Box 429
Mailing city: Cottonwood
Mailing state: AZ
Mailing zip: 86326-0429
Office phone: (928) 634-2241
Office fax: (928) 634-2312
General e-mail: pmiller@verdenews.com
Advertising e-mail: pmiller@verdenews.com
Website: pmiller@verdenews.com
Year publication established: 1947
Delivery methods: Mail
Zip Codes Served: Yavapai County
Frequency: Wed
Circulation Free: 11499
Audit By: VAC
Audit Date: 41455
Personnel: Pam Miller (Publisher); Dan Engler (Editor)
Parent company: Western News&Info, Inc.
Main (survey) contact: Pam Miller

SMART SHOPPER

Street Address1: 116 S Main St
Street address state: AZ
Postal code: 86326-3909
County: Yavapai
Country: USA
Mailing address: PO Box 429
Mailing city: Cottonwood
Mailing state: AZ
Mailing zip: 86326-0429
Office phone: (928) 634-2241
Office fax: (928) 634-2312
General e-mail: pmiller@verdenews.com
Advertising e-mail: pmiller@verdenews.com
Website: pmiller@verdenews.com
Year publication established: 1947
Delivery methods: Mail
Zip Codes Served: Yavapai County
Frequency: Wed
Circulation Free: 18077
Audit By: VAC
Audit Date: 41455
Personnel: Pam Miller (Publisher); Dan Engler (Editor)
Parent company: Western News&Info, Inc.
Main (survey) contact: Pam Miller

GLOBE

GILE COUNTY ADVANTAGE

Street Address1: 298 N Pine St
Street address state: AZ
Postal code: 85501-2516
County: Gila
Country: USA
Mailing address: PO Box 31
Mailing city: Globe
Mailing state: AZ
Mailing zip: 85502-0031
Office phone: (928) 425-7121
Office fax: (928) 425-7001
Advertising (open inch rate): Open inch rate $7.00
Frequency: Tues
Circulation Free: 3700
Audit By: Sworn/Estimate/Non-Audited
Audit Date: 43658
Personnel: Marc Marian (Pub.); Andrea Marcandi (Ed.)
Main (survey) contact: Marc Marian

LAKE HAVASU CITY

RIVER EXTRA

Street Address1: 2225 Acoma Blvd W
Street address state: AZ
Postal code: 86403-2907
County: Mohave
Country: USA
Office phone: (928) 453-4237
Office fax: (928) 855-2637
Advertising fax: (928) 855-9892
General e-mail: sales@havasunews.com
Advertising e-mail: ads@havasunews.com
Website: sales@havasunews.com
Advertising (open inch rate): Open inch rate $21.38
Mechanical specifications: Type page 11 5/8 x 21; E - 6 cols, 1 13/16, between; A - 6 cols, 1 13/16, between; C - 6 cols, 1 13/16, between.
Zip Codes Served: 86403, 86404, 86406
Frequency: Sun
Circulation Free: 6445
Audit By: VAC
Audit Date: 41547
Personnel: Michael E. Quinn (Pub.); Becky Maxedon (Ed.); Kelly Parks (Prodn. Mgr.)
Parent company: Western News&Info, Inc.
Main (survey) contact: Steve Stevens

SMART BUYER

Street Address1: 2225 Acoma Blvd W
Street address state: AZ
Postal code: 86403-2907
County: Mohave
Country: USA
Mailing address: 2225 W Acoma Blvd
Mailing city: Lake Havasu City
Mailing state: AZ
Mailing zip: 86403-2907
Office phone: (928) 453-4237
Office fax: (928) 855-2637
Advertising phone: (928) 855-2197
Advertising fax: (928) 855-9892
General e-mail: sales@havasunews.com
Advertising e-mail: ads@havasunews.com
Website: sales@havasunews.com
Advertising (open inch rate): Open inch rate $21.38
Mechanical specifications: Type page 11 5/8 x 21; E - 6 cols, 1 13/16, between; A - 6 cols, 1 13/16, between; C - 6 cols, 1 13/16, between.
Zip Codes Served: 86403, 86404, 86406
Frequency: Tues
Circulation Paid: 0
Circulation Free: 27044
Audit By: VAC
Audit Date: 42916
Personnel: Michael E. Quinn (Pub.); Becky Maxedon (Ed.)
Parent company: Western News&Info, Inc.
Main (survey) contact: Steve Stevens

PRESCOTT

SMART SHOPPER

Street Address1: 1958 Commerce Center Cir
Street address state: AZ
Postal code: 86301-4454
County: Yavapai
Country: USA
Mailing address: PO Box 26564
Mailing city: Prescott
Mailing state: AZ
Mailing zip: 86302-0312
Office phone: (928) 445-3333
Office fax: (928) 445-4756
Frequency: Wed
Circulation Free: 53061
Audit By: VAC
Audit Date: 41820
Personnel: Kit K. Atwell (Executive Editor); Gary Brinkman (Prodn. Dir.); Kelly Soldwedel (Publisher/CEO); Joe Mickelson (Advertising Director)
Parent company: Western News&Info, Inc.
Main (survey) contact: Tim Wiederaenders

SMART SHOPPER ASH FORK

Street Address1: 1958 Commerce Center Cir
Street address state: AZ
Postal code: 86301-4454
County: Yavapai
Country: USA
Mailing address: 1958 Commerce Center Cir
Mailing city: Prescott
Mailing state: AZ
Mailing zip: 86301-4454
Office phone: (928) 445-3333
Office fax: (928) 445-4756
Advertising phone: (928) 445-3333
Advertising fax: (928) 445-4756
Delivery methods: Mail
Zip Codes Served: Ash Fork
Frequency: Wed
Circulation Free: 1052
Audit By: VAC
Audit Date: 41455
Personnel: Kit K. Atwell (Executive Editor); Gary Brinkman (Prodn. Dir.); Kelly Soldwedel (Publisher/CEO); Joe Mickelson (Advertising Director)
Parent company: Western News&Info, Inc.
Main (survey) contact: Tim Wiederaenders

SIERRA VISTA

SIERRA VISTA HERALD - SUNDAY
BRAVO SHOPPER

Street Address1: 102 Fab Ave
Street address state: AZ
Postal code: 85635-1741
County: Cochise
Country: USA
Office phone: (520) 458-9440
Office fax: (520) 459-0120
Advertising phone: (520) 515-4630
Advertising fax: (520) 515-4610
General e-mail: becky.bjork@svherald.com
Advertising e-mail: becky.bjork@svherald.com
Editorial e-mail: eric.petermann@svherald.com
Website: becky.bjork@svherald.com
Year publication established: 1955
Advertising (open inch rate): Open inch rate $15.25
Mechanical specifications: Type page 9 89/100 x 21; E - 6 cols, 1 56/100, 5/6 between; A - 6 cols, 1 56/100, 5/6 between; C - 9 cols, 1, 58/100 between.
Delivery methods: Mail`Newsstand`Carrier`Racks
Zip Codes Served: 85635, 85650, 85615, 85616, 85636, 85603
Digital Platform - Mobile: Apple`Windows
Digital Platform - Tablet: Apple iOS`Windows 7
Frequency: Sun
Other Type of Frequency: Special Thanksgiving Day issue
Circulation Paid: 10372
Circulation Free: 8854
Audit By: VAC
Audit Date: 42886
Presses: 15-unit Goss Community
Note: Advertisements in the Sierra Vista Herald (mS) are automatically included in the Bisbee Daily Review (mS).
Personnel: Robert Wick (Co-Chrmn.); Philip Vega (Pub.); Becky Bjork (Adv. Dir.); Patricia Wick (Dir., Mktg.); Jeremy Feldman (Circ. Mgr.); Matt Hickman (Sports Ed.); Joan Hancock (Data Processing Mgr.); Don Judd (IT Mgr.); Rebecca Jackson (Prodn. Mgr., Composing); Rhett Hartgrove (Prodn. Foreman, Press/Camera); Eric Petermann (Managing Editor)
Parent company: Wick Communications
Main (survey) contact: Philip Vega

SUN CITY

GLENDALE-PEORIA TODAY

Street Address1: 10102 W Santa Fe Dr
Street address state: AZ
Postal code: 85351-3106
County: Maricopa
Country: USA
Mailing address: 10102 W Santa Fe Dr
Mailing city: Sun City
Mailing state: AZ
Mailing zip: 85351-3106
Office phone: (623) 977-8351
Office fax: (623) 876-2555
General e-mail: jjoseph@yourwestvalley.com
Website: jjoseph@yourwestvalley.com
Frequency: Fri
Circulation Paid: 8
Circulation Free: 20490
Audit By: AAM
Audit Date: 43555
Personnel: Dan McCarthy (Editor)
Parent company: Independent Newsmedia Inc. Usa
Main (survey) contact: Jason Joseph

SURPRISE TODAY

Street Address1: 10102 W Santa Fe Dr
Street address state: AZ
Postal code: 85351-3106
County: Maricopa
Country: USA
Mailing address: 10102 Santa Fe Dr.
Mailing city: Sun City
Mailing state: AZ
Mailing zip: 85351
Office phone: (623) 977-8351
Office fax: (623) 876-3698
Advertising phone: (623) 876-2572
Editorial phone: (623) 876-2534
General e-mail: pbruns@yourwestvalley.com
Editorial e-mail: dmccarthy@yourwestvalley.com
Website: pbruns@yourwestvalley.com
Year publication established: 1996
Advertising (open inch rate): Open inch rate $21.25
Mechanical specifications: Type page 10" x 12.75"; 6 cols
Delivery methods: Carrier`Racks
Zip Codes Served: 85351
Frequency: Wed
Circulation Paid: 8
Circulation Free: 26508
Audit By: CAC
Audit Date: 43555
Personnel: Marji Ranes (Pub.); Dan McCarthy (Exec. Ed.); Tom Legg (Dir, Nat'l Accts.)
Parent company: Independent Newsmedia Inc. Usa
Main (survey) contact: Dan McCarthy
Footnotes: Advertising (open inch rate): SRDS (11/12/2014)

TUCSON

BUYER'S EDGE

Street Address1: 4850 S Park Ave
Street address state: AZ
Postal code: 85714-1637
County: Pima
Country: USA
Office phone: (520) 573-4395
Frequency: Wed

DANDY DIME CLASSIFIEDS

Street Address1: 4500 E Speedway Blvd
Street Address2: Ste 72-73
Street address state: AZ
Postal code: 85712-5303
County: Pima
Country: USA
Mailing address: 4500 E Speedway Blvd Ste 52
Mailing city: Tucson
Mailing state: AZ
Mailing zip: 85712-5320
Office phone: (800) 575-4574
Office fax: (520) 327-4900
Year publication established: 1973
Advertising (open inch rate): Open inch rate $30.00
Mechanical specifications: Type page 10 1/4 x 16; A - 8 cols, 1 1/4, 1/8 between; C - 8 cols, 1 1/4, 1/8 between.
Zip Codes Served: 85732
Frequency: Fri
Circulation Free: 25000
Audit By: Sworn/Estimate/Non-Audited
Audit Date: 43658
Hardware: APP/Power Macs, HP/Vectra VL
Software: Multi-Ad/Creator, Adobe/Photoshop, SUN/Suntype, QPS/QuarkXPress, Microsoft/Windows 95.
Editions Count: 2
Edition Names with circulation: 2 total Â‚Â — Dandy Dime Classifieds-North;
Personnel: Ross Elmore (Gen. Mgr.)
Main (survey) contact: Ross Elmore

TUCSON SHOPPER - WEEK B

Street Address1: 1861 W Grant Rd
Street address state: AZ
Postal code: 85745-1223
County: Pima
Country: USA
Mailing address: PO Box 87770
Mailing city: Tucson
Mailing state: AZ
Mailing zip: 85754-7770
Year publication established: 1980
Advertising (open inch rate): $86.00 (smallest modular rate)
Mechanical specifications: Type page 7.5" x 10"; 4 cols
Delivery methods: Newsstand`Racks
Zip Codes Served: TUCSON, AZ
Frequency: Fri
Circulation Free: 30875
Audit By: CVC
Audit Date: 40633
Personnel: Dave Fredricks
Main (survey) contact: Dave Fredricks

WICKENBURG

SHOPPER NEWS

Street Address1: 179 N Washington
Street address state: AZ
Postal code: 85358
County: Maricopa
Country: USA
Office phone: (928) 684-7218
Frequency: Wed

CALIFORNIA

AUBURN

AUBURN JOURNAL

Street Address1: 1030 High St
Street address state: CA
Postal code: 95603-4707
County: Placer
Country: USA
Mailing address: 1030 High St
Mailing city: Auburn
Mailing state: CA
Mailing zip: 95603-4707
Office phone: (530) 885-5656
General e-mail: circulation@goldcountrymedia.com
Advertising e-mail: betho@goldcountrymedia.com
Editorial e-mail: ajournal@goldcountrymedia.com
Website: circulation@goldcountrymedia.com
Year publication established: 1981
Advertising (open inch rate): modular
Delivery methods: Mail`Racks
Zip Codes Served: 95603 95604
Frequency: Thur
Circulation Free: 15000
Audit By: Sworn/Estimate/Non-Audited
Audit Date: 43576
Personnel: Beth O'Brien (Adv.)
Parent company: Brehm Communications, Inc.
Main (survey) contact: Beth O'Brien

COVERSTORY

Street Address1: 1030 High St
Street address state: CA
Postal code: 95603-4707
County: Placer
Country: USA

Shopper Publications in the U.S.

Mailing address: PO Box 5910
Mailing city: Auburn
Mailing state: CA
Mailing zip: 95604-5910
Office phone: (530) 885-5656
Office fax: (530) 887-1231
General e-mail: auburnjournal@goldcountrymedia.com
Website: auburnjournal@goldcountrymedia.com
Year publication established: 1872
Advertising (open inch rate): Open inch rate $4.00
Mechanical specifications: Type page 11 1/16 x 21; E - 6 cols, 1 13/16, 1/8 between; A - 6 cols, 1 13/16, 1/8 between; C - 9 cols, 1 1/8, 1/8 between.
Zip Codes Served: 95604, 95602, 95603
Frequency: Wed
Circulation Free: 11250
Audit By: Sworn/Estimate/Non-Audited
Audit Date: 43658
Hardware: PC, APP/Mac
Presses: G
Software: APT.
Editions Count: 2
Edition Names with circulation: 2 total ÃƒÂ‚Â‚Â—Auburn Journal CoverStory (11,286); Colfax CoverStory (3,685);
Personnel: Tony Hazarian (Pub.); Jim Easterly (Gen. Mgr., Print Div.); Jim Therma (Adv. Mgr.); Kady Guyton (Internet Sales/Mktg. Mgr.); Gary John (Circ. Dir.); Deric Rothe (Exec. Ed.); Tom Taylor (Sr. Ed.); Daniel Eggen (IT Mgr.); Susan Morin (Prodn. Mgr., Adv.)
Main (survey) contact: Tony Hazarian

BLYTHE

DESERT SHOPPER

Street Address1: 153 S Broadway
Street address state: CA
Postal code: 92225-2501
County: Riverside
Country: USA
Mailing address: PO Box 1159
Mailing city: Blythe
Mailing state: CA
Mailing zip: 92226-1159
Office phone: (760) 922-3181
Office fax: (760) 922-3184
Advertising e-mail: advertising@pvvt.com
Editorial e-mail: mbachman@pvvt.com
Year publication established: 1925
Frequency: Thur
Circulation Free: 6877
Audit By: VAC
Audit Date: 41455
Personnel: Debbie Hoel (Publisher); Jill Madsen (Adv. Rep.); Jaclyn Randall (Mng. Ed.)
Parent company: Western News&Info, Inc.
Main (survey) contact: News Room

CANYON COUNTRY

SANTA CLARITA GAZETTE & FREE CLASSIFIEDS

Street Address1: 27261 Camp Plenty Rd
Street address state: CA
Postal code: 91351-2634
County: Los Angeles
Country: USA
Mailing address: 27261 Camp Plenty Rd
Mailing city: Canyon Country
Mailing state: CA
Mailing zip: 91351-2634
Year publication established: 1998
Advertising (open inch rate): $75.00 (smallest modular rate)
Mechanical specifications: Type page 10.75" x 17"; 6 cols
Delivery methods: Newsstand Racks
Zip Codes Served: LOS ANGELES--RIVERSIDE--ORANGE COUNTY, CA
Frequency: Fri

Circulation Paid: 114
Circulation Free: 8594
Audit By: CVC
Audit Date: 42003
Personnel: Doug Sutton
Main (survey) contact: Doug Sutton

EUREKA

ON THE MARKET

Street Address1: 930 6th St
Street address state: CA
Postal code: 95501-1112
County: Humboldt
Country: USA
Mailing address: PO Box 3580
Mailing city: Eureka
Mailing state: CA
Mailing zip: 95502-3580
Office phone: (707) 441-0500
Office fax: (707) 441-0568
General e-mail: realestate@times-standard.com
Website: realestate@times-standard.com
Advertising (open inch rate): Open inch rate $14.61
Mechanical specifications: Type page 9 7/8 x 11 1/2; E - 5 cols, 1 7/8, 3/16 between; A - 5 cols, 1 7/8, 3/16 between.
Zip Codes Served: 95440, 95501, 95503, 95511, 95519, 95521, 95524, 95525, 95526, 95527, 95528, 95536, 95537, 95540, 95542, 95546, 95547, 95549, 95551, 95552, 95553, 95554, 95559, 95560, 95562, 95563, 95564, 95565, 95569, 95570, 95571, 95573, 95595
Other Type of Frequency: Every other sat
Circulation Paid: 20135
Circulation Free: 270
Audit By: Sworn/Estimate/Non-Audited
Audit Date: 43658
Hardware: IBM
Presses: G/Urbanite
Software: Adobe/Photoshop 6.0, Adobe/PageMaker.
Personnel: Dianna Crow (Pub.); Shonnie Bradbury (Adv. Dir.); Ron Maloney (System Admin.); Jason Kennedy (Prodn. Mgr.)
Main (survey) contact: Dianna Crow

GALT

GALT SHOPPER

Street Address1: 604 N Lincoln Way
Street address state: CA
Postal code: 95632-8601
County: Sacramento
Country: USA
Mailing address: PO Box 307
Mailing city: Galt
Mailing state: CA
Mailing zip: 95632-0307
Office phone: (209) 745-1551
Office fax: (209) 745-4492
Advertising phone: (209) 745-1551
Advertising fax: (209) 745-4492
General e-mail: advertising@herburger.net
Advertising e-mail: classified@herburger.net
Editorial e-mail: editor_galtherald@herburger.net
Website: advertising@herburger.net
Advertising (open inch rate): Open inch rate $9.25
Delivery methods: Mail
Zip Codes Served: 95632
Frequency: Wed
Circulation Free: 6743
Audit By: VAC
Audit Date: 42004
Personnel: David Herburger (Pub.); Jim O'Donnell (Adv. Mgr.); Bonnie Rodriguez (Mng. Ed.)
Parent company: Herburger Publications, Inc.
Main (survey) contact: David Herburger

GRIDLEY

THE GRIDLEY SHOPPING NEWS

Street Address1: 650 Kentucky St
Street address state: CA
Postal code: 95948-2118
County: Butte
Country: USA
Mailing address: PO Box 68
Mailing city: Gridley
Mailing state: CA
Mailing zip: 95948-0068
Office phone: (530) 846-3661
Office fax: (530) 846-4519
General e-mail: gherald@gridleyherald.com
Editorial e-mail: publisher@gridleyherald.com
Website: gherald@gridleyherald.com
Advertising (open inch rate): Open inch rate $12.00
Mechanical specifications: Type page 13 x 21; E - 6 cols, 2, 1/8 between; A - 6 cols, 2, 1/8 between; C - 9 cols, 1/8 between.
Delivery methods: Carrier
Frequency: Wed
Circulation Free: 5500
Audit By: Sworn/Estimate/Non-Audited
Audit Date: 43658
Personnel: Lisa Van De Hey (Ed.); Rachel Marubashi (Circ. Mgr.)
Parent company: The Hays Daily News
Main (survey) contact: Lisa Van De Hey

LAKEPORT

LAKE COUNTY'S PENNY SAVER

Street Address1: 2150 S Main St
Street address state: CA
Postal code: 95453-5620
County: Lake
Country: USA
Mailing address: 2150 S Main St
Mailing city: Lakeport
Mailing state: CA
Mailing zip: 95453-5620
Office phone: (707) 263-5636
Advertising phone: (707) 263-5636
General e-mail: advertising@record-bee.com
Advertising e-mail: advertising@record-bee.com
Website: advertising@record-bee.com
Advertising (open inch rate): Open inch rate $5.38
Delivery methods: Newsstand Racks
Frequency: Wed
Circulation Free: 15500
Audit By: Sworn/Estimate/Non-Audited
Audit Date: 43658
Parent company: Digital First Media
Main (survey) contact: Kevin McConnell

LODI

SENTINEL EXPRESS

Street Address1: 125 N Church St
Street address state: CA
Postal code: 95240-2102
County: San Joaquin
Country: USA
Mailing address: PO Box 1360
Mailing city: Lodi
Mailing state: CA
Mailing zip: 95241-1360
Office phone: (209) 369-2761
Office fax: (209) 369-1084
Editorial phone: (209) 369-7035
Editorial fax: (209) 369-6706
General e-mail: news@lodinews.com
Advertising e-mail: ads@lodinews.com
Editorial e-mail: news@lodinews.com
Website: news@lodinews.com
Year publication established: 2010
Advertising (open inch rate): Open inch rate 6/47 (plus pick-up in Lodi News-Sentinel)
Mechanical specifications: Type page 13 x 21 1/2; E - 6 cols, 2 1/16, 1/8 between; A - 6 cols, 2 1/16, 1/8 between; C - 8 cols, 1 7/16, 1/8 between.

Delivery methods: Carrier
Zip Codes Served: 95240, 95242, 95258
Frequency: Wed
Circulation Free: 10014
Audit By: Sworn/Estimate/Non-Audited
Audit Date: 43658
Hardware: APP/Mac G3
Presses: 12-G/Community
Software: Multi-Ad/Creator 4.01.
Note: This is a TMC product printed in combination with the Lodi News-Sentinel.
Personnel: Marty Weybret (Pub.); Richard Hanner (Ed.); Tracy Kelley (Ad Director)
Parent company: Lodi News-Sentinel
Main (survey) contact: Marty Weybret

MANTECA

BULLETIN EXTRA

Street Address1: 531 E Yosemite Ave
Street address state: CA
Postal code: 95336-5806
County: San Joaquin
Country: USA
Mailing address: PO Box 1958
Mailing city: Manteca
Mailing state: CA
Mailing zip: 95336-1156
Office phone: (209) 249-3500
Office fax: (209) 249-3559
Advertising fax: (209) 249-3559
Advertising e-mail: ads@mantecabulletin.com
Advertising (open inch rate): Open inch rate $19.48
Delivery methods: Carrier
Zip Codes Served: 95336, 95337, 95366, 95330, 95231
Frequency: Fri
Circulation Free: 16518
Audit By: Sworn/Estimate/Non-Audited
Audit Date: 43658
Personnel: Chuck Higgs (Advertising Director)
Parent company: Morris Newspaper Group of California
Main (survey) contact: Chuck Higgs

MOUNT SHASTA

VOICE OF THE MOUNTAIN

Street Address1: 924 N Mount Shasta Blvd
Street address state: CA
Postal code: 96067-8700
County: Siskiyou
Country: USA
Mailing address: PO Box 127
Mailing city: Mount Shasta
Mailing state: CA
Mailing zip: 96067-0127
Office phone: (530) 926-5214
Office fax: (530) 926-4166
General e-mail: news@mtshatanews.com
Website: news@mtshatanews.com
Year publication established: 1954
Advertising (open inch rate): Open inch rate $11.00
Frequency: Wed
Circulation Free: 5000
Audit By: Sworn/Estimate/Non-Audited
Audit Date: 43658
Hardware: APP/Mac OS 9.2
Presses: Goss/Community
Software: QPS/QuarkXPress 4.11.
Personnel: Genny Axtman (Pub.); Linda Bonebrake (Office Mgr.); Dave Reynolds (Circ. Mgr.); Steve Gerace (Ed.)
Main (survey) contact: Genny Axtman

OJAI

OJAI VALLEY SHOPPER

Street Address1: 408 Bryant Cir
Street Address2: Ste A
Street address state: CA
Postal code: 93023-4210
County: Ventura
Country: USA

Mailing address: PO Box 277
Mailing city: Ojai
Mailing state: CA
Mailing zip: 93024-0277
Office phone: (805) 646-1476
Office fax: (805) 646-4281
Year publication established: 1891
Advertising (open inch rate): Open inch rate $11.65
Zip Codes Served: 93024
Frequency: Wed`Fri
Circulation Free: 12000
Audit By: Sworn/Estimate/Non-Audited
Audit Date: 43658
Personnel: Jodie Miller (Gen. Mgr.); Lenny Roberts (Mng. Ed.); Bret Bradigan (Ed.)
Main (survey) contact: Tim Dewar

ONTARIO

NUESTRA GENTE

Street Address1: 1511 W Holt Blvd
Street Address2: Ste J
Street address state: CA
Postal code: 91762-3658
County: San Bernardino
Country: USA
Mailing address: 1511 W Holt Blvd Ste J
Mailing city: Ontario
Mailing state: CA
Mailing zip: 91762-3658
Office phone: (909) 460-2555
Office fax: (909) 460-2558
Editorial e-mail: editor@nuestra-gente.com
Year publication established: 1996
Advertising (open inch rate): Open inch rate $36.00
Zip Codes Served: San Bernadino County
Frequency: Thur
Circulation Free: 88000
Audit By: Sworn/Estimate/Non-Audited
Audit Date: 43658
Main (survey) contact: Survey Contact

OROVILLE

THE DIGGER & SHOPPER NEWS

Street Address1: PO Box 5006
Street Address2: 2057 Mitchell Ave.
Street address state: CA
Postal code: 95966-0006
County: Butte
Country: USA
Mailing address: PO Box 5006
Mailing city: Oroville
Mailing state: CA
Mailing zip: 95966-0006
Office phone: (530) 533-2170
Office fax: (530) 533-2181
General e-mail: suzanne@diggernews.com
Advertising e-mail: dave@diggernews.com
Editorial e-mail: pat@diggernews.com
Website: suzanne@diggernews.com
Year publication established: 1977
Advertising (open inch rate): 17,15
Delivery methods: Mail`Newsstand`Racks
Zip Codes Served: 95965, 95966, 95968, 95916
Frequency: Tues
Circulation Paid: 324
Circulation Free: 15139
Audit By: CVC
Audit Date: 43008
Personnel: David Miller (Publisher)
Main (survey) contact: David Miller

PALM DESERT

WHITE SHEET

Street Address1: 73400 Highway 111
Street address state: CA
Postal code: 92260-3908
County: Riverside
Country: USA
Mailing address: 73400 Highway 111
Mailing city: Palm Desert
Mailing state: CA
Mailing zip: 92260-3911
Office phone: (760) 346-0601
Office fax: (760) 346-3597
Advertising phone: (760) 346-0601
Advertising (open inch rate): Open inch rate $12.36
Mechanical specifications: Type page 10 x 10; E - 6 cols, 1 7/12, 1/8 between; A - 6 cols, 1 7/12, 1/8 between; C - 6 cols, 1 7/12, 1/8 between.
Zip Codes Served: 92260
Frequency: Tues
Circulation Free: 40000
Audit By: Sworn/Estimate/Non-Audited
Audit Date: 43585
Hardware: PCs, Gateway
Software: Microsoft/Windows.

PALMDALE

ANTELOPE VALLEY PRESS EXPRESS

Street Address1: 37404 Sierra Hwy
Street address state: CA
Postal code: 93550-9343
County: Los Angeles
Country: USA
Mailing address: PO Box 4050
Mailing city: Palmdale
Mailing state: CA
Mailing zip: 93590-4050
Office phone: (661) 273-2700
Office fax: (661) 947-4870
General e-mail: circulation@avpress.com
Advertising e-mail: classified@avpress.com
Editorial e-mail: editor@avpress.com
Website: circulation@avpress.com
Year publication established: 1915
Advertising (open inch rate): Open inch rate $13.50
Mechanical specifications: Type page 13 x 21 1/2; E - 6 cols, 2 1/30, 1/6 between; A - 6 cols, 2 1/16, 1/6 between; C - 9 cols, 1 3/8, between.
Delivery methods: Carrier`Racks
Zip Codes Served: 9,35349353593536E+39
Frequency: Sat
Circulation Free: 35091
Audit By: Sworn/Estimate/Non-Audited
Audit Date: 43585
Hardware: MPS
Presses: Goss
Personnel: Jennifer Garcia (Ed.); Mike McMullin (Pub.); Jeanne Gomez (Circ. Mgr.)
Parent company: Antelope Valley Newspapers Inc
Main (survey) contact: Jennifer Garcia

RAMONA

RAMONA SENTINEL

Street Address1: 850 Main St
Street Address2: Ste 106
Street address state: CA
Postal code: 92065-1968
County: San Diego
Country: USA
Mailing address: 850 Main Street, suite 106
Mailing city: Ramona
Mailing state: CA
Mailing zip: 92065-3936
Office phone: (760) 789-1350
Office fax: (760) 789-4057
Advertising phone: (760) 789-1350
Advertising fax: (760) 789-4057
Editorial phone: (760) 789-1350
Editorial fax: (760) 789-4057
General e-mail: admin@ramonasentinel.com
Advertising e-mail: admin@ramonasentinel.com
Website: admin@ramonasentinel.com
Year publication established: 1862
Advertising (open inch rate): Open inch rate $19.05
Mechanical specifications: 6 Column 10.33" x 12.25"
Delivery methods: Carrier`Racks
Zip Codes Served: 92065
Digital Platform - Mobile: Apple`Android`Windows`Blackberry
Digital Platform - Tablet: Apple iOS`Android`Windows 7`Nook`Kindle Fire
Frequency: Thur
Circulation Paid: 12924
Audit By: AAM
Audit Date: 43100
Personnel: Maureen Robertson (Ed.); Tina Tamburino (Gen Mgr); Don Parks (VP of Sales)
Parent company: NantMedia Holdings, LLC
Main (survey) contact: Don Parks

REDLANDS

GREEN SHEET

Street Address1: 721 Nevada St
Street Address2: Ste 207
Street address state: CA
Postal code: 92373-8051
County: San Bernardino
Country: USA
Mailing address: 721 Nevada St Ste 207
Mailing city: Redlands
Mailing state: CA
Mailing zip: 92373
Office phone: (800) 678-4237
Office fax: (760) 346-3597
General e-mail: cch-greensheet@worldnet.att.net
Website: cch-greensheet@worldnet.att.net
Advertising (open inch rate): Open inch rate $28.01
Mechanical specifications: Type page 10 x 10; E - 6 cols, 1 7/12, 1/8 between; A - 6 cols, 1 7/12, 1/8 between; C - 6 cols, 1 7/12, 1/8 between.
Zip Codes Served: 92261
Frequency: Thur
Circulation Free: 75000
Audit By: Sworn/Estimate/Non-Audited
Audit Date: 43658
Hardware: PCs, Gateway
Software: Microsoft/Windows.
Editions Count: 4
Edition Names with circulation: 4 total ÃƒÂƒ,Ãƒ ÃƒÂ,Â,ÃƒÂƒÂ,Â,ÃƒÂ,Â,Â— Green Sheet-Redlands (18,500); Green Sheet-Riverside (16,500); Green Sheet-San Bernardino (17,500); Green Sheet-West San Bernardino (22,500);
Personnel: Hal J. Paradis (Pub.); Chuck Holcomb (Gen. Mgr.)
Main (survey) contact: Hal J. Paradis

REEDLEY

HERALD ADVERTISER

Street Address1: 1130 G St
Street address state: CA
Postal code: 93654-3004
County: Fresno
Country: USA
Mailing address: 1130 G St
Mailing city: Reedley
Mailing state: CA
Mailing zip: 93654-3004
Office phone: (559) 638-2244
Office fax: (559) 638-5021
General e-mail: reedleyexponent@yahoo.com
Website: reedleyexponent@yahoo.com
Advertising (open inch rate): Open inch rate $11.50
Zip Codes Served: 93657
Frequency: Tues
Circulation Free: 14285
Audit By: Sworn/Estimate/Non-Audited
Audit Date: 43658
Personnel: Fred Hall (Pub.); Cheri Williams (Mktg. Dir.); Cheryl Lingo (Mng. Ed.)
Main (survey) contact: Fred Hall

SAN FRANCISCO

THE ADVERTISER

Street Address1: 132 10th St
Street address state: CA
Postal code: 94103-2605
County: San Francisco
Country: USA
Mailing address: 132 10th St.
Mailing city: San Francisco
Mailing state: CA
Mailing zip: 94103-2605
Office phone: (415) 861-8370
Office fax: (415) 861-0521
General e-mail: info@sfadvertiser.com
Website: info@sfadvertiser.com
Mechanical specifications: Type page 10 1/4 x 16 1/2.
Frequency: Thur
Circulation Free: 52000
Audit By: Sworn/Estimate/Non-Audited
Audit Date: 43658
Hardware: APP/Mac, IBM/PC
Presses: WPC/Web Leader
Software: Microsoft/Word 5.1A, QPS/QuarkXPress, Adobe/Photoshop.
Personnel: Tom Lee (Pub.); Wilbur Lee (Pub.)
Main (survey) contact: Tom Lee

SANTA CLARITA

SCV EXPRESS

Street Address1: 24000 Creekside Rd
Street address state: CA
Postal code: 91355-1726
County: Los Angeles
Country: USA
Mailing address: 24000 Creekside Rd
Mailing city: Santa Clarita
Mailing state: CA
Mailing zip: 91355-1726
Office phone: (661) 259-1234
Office fax: (661) 254-8068
Advertising (open inch rate): Open inch rate $25.60
Frequency: Fri`Sun
Circulation Free: 100571
Audit By: Sworn/Estimate/Non-Audited
Audit Date: 43658
Personnel: Jay Horn (Pub.); Laila Little John (Ed.)
Main (survey) contact: Morris Thomas

SANTA CRUZ

SANTA CRUZ GOOD TIMES

Street Address1: 1205 Pacific Ave
Street Address2: Ste 301
Street address state: CA
Postal code: 95060-3936
County: Santa Cruz
Country: USA
Mailing address: 1205 Pacific Ave Ste 301
Mailing city: Santa Cruz
Mailing state: CA
Mailing zip: 95060-3936
Office phone: (831) 458-1100
Office fax: (831) 458-1295
General e-mail: letters@gtweekly.com
Website: letters@gtweekly.com
Year publication established: 1975
Advertising (open inch rate): $168.00 (smallest modular rate)
Mechanical specifications: Type page 9.4" x 11.5"; 5 cols
Delivery methods: Newsstand`Racks
Digital Platform - Mobile: Apple`Android`Windows`Blackberry`Other
Digital Platform - Tablet: Apple iOS`Android`Blackberry Tablet OS`Kindle`Kindle Fire
Frequency: Thur
Circulation Paid: 4
Circulation Free: 34777
Audit By: CVC
Audit Date: 41639
Hardware: APP/Mac
Software: QPS/QuarkXPress 3.31, Adobe/Photoshop 3.0, Adobe/Illustrator 6.0.
Personnel: Pamela Pollard (Circ. Mgr.); Greg Archer (Ed.); Josh Becker (Prodn. Mgr.); Jeff Mitchell (Publisher); Phyllis Pfeiffer (Pub. Mgr); Don Parks (Adv. Mgr); Christina

Shopper Publications in the U.S.

Clayton (Circ. Mgr)
Parent company: C-VILLE Holdings LLC; Mainstreet Media Group, LLC
Main (survey) contact: Greg Archer

TAFT

BARGAIN HUNTER

Street Address1: 800 Center St
Street address state: CA
Postal code: 93268-3129
County: Kern
Country: USA
Mailing address: PO Box 958
Mailing city: Taft
Mailing state: CA
Mailing zip: 93268-0958
Office phone: (661) 763-3171
Office fax: (661) 763-5638
General e-mail: cmainard@taftmidwaydriller.com
Advertising e-mail: cthompson@taftmidwaydriller.com
Editorial e-mail: dkeeler@taftmidwaydriller.com
Website: cmainard@taftmidwaydriller.com
Advertising (open inch rate): Open inch rate $10.00
Frequency: Tues
Circulation Free: 4000
Audit By: Sworn/Estimate/Non-Audited
Audit Date: 43585
Personnel: John Watkins (Pub.); Doug Keeler (Ed.); Cooper Mainard (Circ. Mgr.); Christine Thompson (Adv. Mgr.)
Parent company: Gatehouse Media, LLC
Main (survey) contact: Doug Keeler

TURLOCK

THE JOURNAL SHOPPING NEWS

Street Address1: 138 S Center St
Street address state: CA
Postal code: 95380-4508
County: Stanislaus
Country: USA
Mailing address: 138 S Center St
Mailing city: Turlock
Mailing state: CA
Mailing zip: 95380-4508
Office phone: (209) 634-9141
Office fax: (209) 632-8813
Advertising phone: (209) 634-9141
Advertising fax: (209) 632-8813
Editorial phone: (209) 634-9141
Editorial fax: (209) 632-8813
General e-mail: adinfo@turlockjournal.com
Advertising e-mail: classifieds@turlockjournal.com
Editorial e-mail: news@turlockjournal.com
Website: adinfo@turlockjournal.com
Year publication established: 1904
Advertising (open inch rate): Open inch rate $13.91
Mechanical specifications: Type page 13 x 21 1/2; E - 6 cols, 2 1/16, 1/8 between; A - 6 cols, 2 1/16, 1/8 between; C - 9 cols, 1 5/16, 1/8 between.
Zip Codes Served: 95380, 95381, 95382, 95315, 95324, 95316, 95326, 95328
Frequency: Sat
Circulation Paid: 6030
Circulation Free: 14500
Audit By: Sworn/Estimate/Non-Audited
Audit Date: 43658
Hardware: 2-APP/Power Mac, 1-APP/Mac IIci, APP/Mac G4
Presses: 8-G/Community
Software: Adobe/PageMaker 6.5, QPS/QuarkExpress 3.04, Adobe/Photoshop 5.0, Baseview/NewsEdit Pro, Adobe/Illustrator, Multi-Ad/Creator.
Personnel: Hank Veen (Pub.); Kristina Hacker (Ed.); Victoria Batesole (Adv. Sales); Taylor Phillips (Sales Mgr.)
Main (survey) contact: Kristina Hacker

UKIAH

HOMETOWN SHOPPER

Street Address1: 212 W Mill St
Street address state: CA
Postal code: 95482-5474
County: Mendocino
Country: USA
Mailing address: 212 W Mill St
Mailing city: Ukiah
Mailing state: CA
Mailing zip: 95482-5474
Office phone: (707) 462-1573
Office fax: (707) 462-3550
General e-mail: willbutler@hometown-shopper.com
Website: willbutler@hometown-shopper.com
Year publication established: 1989
Advertising (open inch rate): Frequency discount available
Mechanical specifications: Type Full page 8 column x 11" = 10"x11" Half page vertical 8 column x 5.458" = 10"x5.458" Half page horizontal 4 column x 11" = 4.958" x 11" Quarter page Vertical 2 column x 11" = 2.431" x 11" Quarter page horizontal 4 column x 5.458"
Delivery methods: Mail
Zip Codes Served: 95482
Digital Platform - Mobile: Apple`Android
Frequency: Tues
Circulation Free: 43357
Audit By: Sworn/Estimate/Non-Audited
Audit Date: 43658
Hardware: APP/Mac.
Software: Ad Base
Note: Printed at the Paradise Post Chico Calif. a sister paper.
Personnel: Will Butler (Gen. Mgr.); Patsy Jordan (Prodn. Mgr.)
Parent company: Media News Group; Digital First Media
Main (survey) contact: Will Butler

VICTORVILLE

REVIEW

Street Address1: 13891 Park Ave
Street address state: CA
Postal code: 92392-2435
County: San Bernardino
Country: USA
Mailing address: PO Box 1389
Mailing city: Victorville
Mailing state: CA
Mailing zip: 92393-1389
Office phone: (760) 241-7744
Office fax: (760) 241-1860
Advertising phone: (760) 951-6288
Advertising fax: (760) 955-5376
General e-mail: vvnews@link.freedom.com
Website: vvnews@link.freedom.com
Advertising (open inch rate): Open inch rate $15.02
Mechanical specifications: Type page 13 x 21 1/2; E - 6 cols, 2 1/16, 1/8 between; A - 6 cols, 2 1/16, 1/8 between; C - 9 cols, 1 1/3, 1/8 between.
Zip Codes Served: 92392
Frequency: Tues
Circulation Free: 26600
Audit By: Sworn/Estimate/Non-Audited
Audit Date: 43658
Hardware: Dewar
Presses: 10-G/Urbanite
Software: Baseview.
Editions Count: 2
Edition Names with circulation: 2 total ÃƒÂ£Ã¯Â¿Â½; Preview-Barstow (5,600); Preview-Victor Valley (34,000);
Personnel: Stephan Wingert (Pub.); Jackie Parsons (Circ. Mgr.); Don Holland (Ed.); Harry Pontius (Prodn. Mgr.)
Main (survey) contact: Janet Baldwin

VISALIA

AMERICAN CLASSIFIEDS - VISALIA

Street Address1: 1516 W Mineral King Ave
Street address state: CA
Postal code: 93291-5819
County: Tulare
Country: USA
Year publication established: 1986
Advertising (open inch rate): Open inch rate $10.00
Mechanical specifications: Type page 10.25" x 15.70"; 8 cols
Delivery methods: Newsstand`Carrier`Racks
Zip Codes Served: VISALIA--TULARE--PORTERVILLE, CA
Frequency: Thur
Circulation Paid: 0
Circulation Free: 26235
Audit By: CVC
Audit Date: 42004
Personnel: Glen Christensen
Main (survey) contact: Glen Christensen

WOODLAND HILLS

VALLEY VANTAGE

Street Address1: 23009 Ventura Blvd
Street address state: CA
Postal code: 91364-1107
County: Los Angeles
Country: USA
Mailing address: 23009 Ventura Blvd
Mailing city: Woodland Hills
Mailing state: CA
Mailing zip: 91364-1107
Office phone: (818) 223-9545
Office fax: (818) 223-9552
General e-mail: wnrcnews@instanet.com
Website: wnrcnews@instanet.com
Advertising (open inch rate): Open inch rate $25.00
Zip Codes Served: 91364, 91365, 91367, 91302, 91356
Frequency: Thur
Circulation Free: 20000
Audit By: Sworn/Estimate/Non-Audited
Audit Date: 43658
Personnel: Kathleen Sterling (Pub. /Ed.)
Main (survey) contact: Kathleen Sterling

YUCAIPA

CENTURY GROUP NEWSPAPERS

Street Address1: 35154 Yucaipa Blvd
Street address state: CA
Postal code: 92399-4339
County: San Bernardino
Country: USA
Mailing address: 35154 Yucaipa Blvd
Mailing city: Yucaipa
Mailing state: CA
Mailing zip: 92399-4339
Office phone: (909) 797-9101
Office fax: (909) 797-0502
General e-mail: tbush@centurygroup.com
Website: tbush@centurygroup.com
Frequency: Fri
Circulation Paid: 5278
Circulation Free: 65861
Audit By: CVC
Audit Date: 42643
Personnel: Toebe Bush (President / CEO / Pub.); Gerald A. Bean (Owner)
Main (survey) contact: Toebe Bush

COLORADO

BRIGHTON

BRIGHTON STANDARD BLADE

Street Address1: 143 S 2nd Place
Street address state: CO
Postal code: 80601
County: Adams
Country: USA
Mailing address: PO Box 646
Mailing city: Brighton
Mailing state: CO
Mailing zip: 80601-0646
Office phone: (303) 659-2522
Office fax: (303) 637-7955
General e-mail: subscriptions@metrowestnewspapers.com
Editorial e-mail: news@metrowestnewspapers.com
Website: subscriptions@metrowestnewspapers.com
Year publication established: 1903
Frequency: Wed
Circulation Paid: 21000
Audit By: Sworn/Estimate/Non-Audited
Audit Date: 43585
Personnel: Steve Smith
Main (survey) contact: Steve Smith

BURLINGTON

THE PLAINSDEALER

Street Address1: 202 S 14th St
Street address state: CO
Postal code: 80807-2322
County: Kit Carson
Country: USA
Mailing address: PO Box 459
Mailing city: Burlington
Mailing state: CO
Mailing zip: 80807-0459
Office phone: (719) 346-5381
Office fax: (719) 346-5514
Advertising phone: (719) 346-5381
Advertising fax: (719) 346-5514
Editorial phone: (719) 346-5381
Editorial fax: (719) 346-5514
General e-mail: brecord@plainstel.com
Advertising e-mail: brecordadverting@plainstel.com
Editorial e-mail: brecordeditor@plainstel.com
Website: brecord@plainstel.com
Advertising (open inch rate): Open inch rate $11.00
Delivery methods: Mail
Digital Platform - Mobile: Windows
Frequency: Thur
Circulation Paid: 3100
Circulation Free: 3350
Audit By: Sworn/Estimate/Non-Audited
Audit Date: 43658
Hardware: APP/Mac
Presses: 4-KP/News King
Software: QPS/QuarkXPress, Adobe/Photoshop.
Personnel: Rol Hudler (Pub.); Shannon Floyd (Advt Dir)
Main (survey) contact: Rol Hudler

ESTES PARK

ESTES INSIDE & OUT

Street Address1: 351 Moraine Ave
Street Address2: Unit B
Street address state: CO
Postal code: 80517-8056
County: Larimer
Country: USA
Mailing address: PO Box 1707
Mailing city: Estes Park
Mailing state: CO
Mailing zip: 80517-1707

Office phone: (970) 586-3356
Office fax: (970) 586-9532
General e-mail: tgcirculation@eptrail.com
Advertising e-mail: tgcirculation@eptrail.com
Editorial e-mail: srowan@eptrail.com
Website: tgcirculation@eptrail.com
Year publication established: 1921
Advertising (open inch rate): 11,5
Delivery methods: Mail`Newsstand`Racks
Digital Platform - Mobile:
  Apple`Android`Windows`Blackberry
Digital Platform - Tablet: Apple
  iOS`Android`Windows 7`Blackberry Tablet
  OS`Kindle`Nook`Kindle Fire
Frequency: Fri
Circulation Free: 2900
Audit By: Sworn/Estimate/Non-Audited
Audit Date: 43658
Parent company: Prairie Mountain Publishing
Main (survey) contact: Deborah Thelander

FORT COLLINS

AMERICAN CLASSIFIEDS - FORT COLLINS / GREELEY / DENVER

Street Address1: 1229 E Mulberry St
Street address state: CO
Postal code: 80524-3513
County: Larimer
Country: USA
Mailing address: 1229 E Mulberry St
Mailing city: Fort Collins
Mailing state: CO
Mailing zip: 80524-3513
Frequency: Thur
Circulation Paid: 0
Circulation Free: 36664
Audit By: CVC
Audit Date: 40878
Personnel: Shelia Skinner
Main (survey) contact: Shelia Skinner

COLORADO CONNECTION

Street Address1: 1300 Riverside Ave
Street address state: CO
Postal code: 80524-4353
County: Larimer
Country: USA
Mailing address: 1300 Riverside Ave
Mailing city: Fort Collins
Mailing state: CO
Mailing zip: 80524-4353
Office phone: (970) 493-6397
Office fax: (970) 224-7726
Advertising (open inch rate): Open inch rate $20.75
Mechanical specifications: Type page 11 5/8 x 21 1/2; E - 6 cols, 1 5/6, 1/8 between; A - 6 cols, 1 5/6, 1/8 between; C - 10 cols, 1 3/32, 3/32 between.
Zip Codes Served: 80524, 80521, 80525, 80526, 80528
Frequency: Wed`Sat
Circulation Free: 24500
Audit By: Sworn/Estimate/Non-Audited
Audit Date: 43658
Hardware: IBM/AS 400
Presses: G/Urbanite
Software: ACT/APT.
Personnel: Kim Roegner (Pub.); Cathy Jack-Romero (Circ. Mgr.); Bob Moore (Exec. Ed.)
Parent company: Gannett
Main (survey) contact: Joshua Awtry

GRAND JUNCTION

THE NICKEL

Street Address1: 1635 N 1st St
Street address state: CO
Postal code: 81501-2124
County: Mesa
Country: USA
Mailing address: 1635 N 1st St
Mailing city: Grand Junction

Mailing state: CO
Mailing zip: 81501-2124
Office phone: (970) 242-5555
Office fax: (970) 245-9250
General e-mail: doug.freed@nickads.com
Website: doug.freed@nickads.com
Advertising (open inch rate): Open inch rate $8.00
Mechanical specifications: Type page 10 1/8 x 11 7/8; A - 7 cols, 1 3/8, 1/6 between; C - 7 cols, 1 3/8, 1/6 between.
Zip Codes Served: 81413, 81416, 81501, 81503, 81504, 81505, 81506, 81520, 81521, 81526, 81601, 81624, 81635, 81643, 81646, 81650, 81652
Frequency: Wed
Circulation Free: 26000
Audit By: Sworn/Estimate/Non-Audited
Audit Date: 43658
Hardware: APP/Power Macs
Software: QPS/QuarkXPress, Baseview/Classflow, Adobe/Illustrator, Adobe/Photoshop.
Personnel: Doug Freed (Gen. Mgr.); Kari Fowler (Sales Mgr.); Sharon Sale (Dist. Mgr.); Randy Raisch (Prodn. Mgr.)
Parent company: Cox Media Group
Main (survey) contact: Kari Fowler

MONTE VISTA

SLV LIFESTYLES

Street Address1: 835 1st Ave
Street address state: CO
Postal code: 81144-1474
County: Rio Grande
Country: USA
Mailing address: 835 1st Ave
Mailing city: Monte Vista
Mailing state: CO
Mailing zip: 81144-1474
Office phone: (719) 852-3531
Office fax: (719) 852-3387
Advertising e-mail: jfapublisher@gmail.com
Editorial e-mail: MonteVistaNews@gmail.com
Advertising (open inch rate): Open inch rate $24.75
Frequency: Wed
Circulation Free: 18000
Audit By: Sworn/Estimate/Non-Audited
Audit Date: 43658
Personnel: Jennifer Alonzo (Pub.); Stacy Turner (Sales Mgr.); Elli Bone (Prodn. Mgr.)
Parent company: Valley Publishing, Inc.
Main (survey) contact: Jennifer Alonzo

PAONIA

HIGH COUNTRY SHOPPER

Street Address1: 231 Grand Ave
Street address state: CO
Postal code: 81428
County: Delta
Country: USA
Mailing address: PO Box 7
Mailing city: Paonia
Mailing state: CO
Mailing zip: 81428-0007
Office phone: (970) 527-4576
Office fax: (970) 527-6191
General e-mail: info@highcountryshopper.com
Advertising e-mail: display@highcountryshopper.com
Editorial e-mail: content@highcountryshopper.com
Website: info@highcountryshopper.com
Year publication established: 1978
Advertising (open inch rate): Open inch rate $6.50 black/white
Mechanical specifications: Type page 10 1/4 x 15; A - 6 cols, 1 1/2, 1/4 between; C - 6 cols, 1 1/2, 1/4 between.
Delivery methods: Mail`Racks
Zip Codes Served: 81428, 81425, 81416, 81410, 81414, 81418,81413, 81415, 81419
Digital Platform - Mobile:
  Apple`Android`Windows`Blackberry
Digital Platform - Tablet: Apple

iOS`Android`Windows 7`Blackberry Tablet OS`Kindle`Nook`Kindle Fire
Frequency: Wed
Circulation Free: 17500
Audit By: Sworn/Estimate/Non-Audited
Audit Date: 43658
Hardware: APP/Mac
Software: InDesign
Editions Count: 1
Edition Names with circulation: High Country Shopper
Note: We are a direct mail publication.
Personnel: Rita Olin (Office Manager); Tina Walker (Production Manager)
Parent company: Medrano Holdings LLC
Main (survey) contact: Rita Olin

PUEBLO

AMERICAN CLASSIFIEDS - PUEBLO

Street Address1: 811 W 4th St
Street address state: CO
Postal code: 81003-2393
County: Pueblo
Country: USA
Mailing address: 811 W 4th St.
Mailing city: Pueblo
Mailing state: CO
Mailing zip: 81003-2393
Office phone: (719) 544-4752
Year publication established: 1975
Delivery methods: Racks
Zip Codes Served: 81001, 81003, 81004, 81005, 81006, 81007, 81008, 81019, 81022, 81025, 81039, 81052, 81054, 81055, 81058, 81063, 81067, 81069, 81050, 81101, 81089, 81082, 81212, 81120, 81123, 81133, 81140, 811044, 81201, 81211, 81222, 81223, 81226, 81233, 81240, 81242, 81252, 81253
Frequency: Thur
Other Type of Frequency: Rack Display Sign
Circulation Free: 20991
Audit By: CVC
Audit Date: 40878
Personnel: Ernie Montano (Pres.)
Main (survey) contact: Ernie Montano

PUEBLO WEST

PUEBLO WEST VIEW

Street Address1: 215 S Purcell Blvd
Street address state: CO
Postal code: 81007-5083
County: Pueblo
Country: USA
Mailing address: 825 W 6th St
Mailing city: Pueblo
Mailing state: CO
Mailing zip: 81003-2313
Office phone: (719) 547-9606
Office fax: (719) 547-4380
General e-mail: comments@pueblowestview.com
Website: comments@pueblowestview.com
Year publication established: 1996
Advertising (open inch rate): Open inch rate $12.45
Mechanical specifications: Type page 13 x 21 1/2; E - 6 cols, 2 1/16, 1/8 between; A - 6 cols, 2 1/16, 1/8 between; C - 6 cols, 2 1/16, 1/8 between.
Zip Codes Served: 81007
Frequency: Thur
Circulation Free: 15000
Audit By: Sworn/Estimate/Non-Audited
Audit Date: 43658
Hardware: APP/Mac
Presses: MAN/Uniset.
Personnel: Robert H. Rawlings (Pub.); Lou Braden (Adv. Dir.)
Main (survey) contact: Robert H. Rawlings

WOODLAND PARK

COURIER EXTRA

Street Address1: 1200 Highway 24

Street address state: CO
Postal code: 80863-9229
County: Teller
Country: USA
Mailing address: PO Box 340
Mailing city: Woodland Park
Mailing state: CO
Mailing zip: 80866-0340
Office phone: (719) 687-3006
Office fax: (719) 687-3009
Advertising (open inch rate): Open inch rate $9.41
Mechanical specifications: Type page 11 1/2 x 21; E - 6 cols, between; A - 6 cols, between; C - 6 cols, between.
Frequency: Wed
Circulation Free: 10911
Audit By: CVC
Audit Date: 41729
Hardware: APP/Macs
Presses: 10-G/Community
Software: QPS/QuarkXPress.
Personnel: Asa Cole (Sales Mgr.)
Main (survey) contact: Asa Cole

CONNECTICUT

BROOKFIELD

YANKEE PENNYSAVER

Street Address1: 246 Federal Rd, Commons Ste D-15
Street address state: CT
Postal code: 06804
County: Fairfield
Country: USA
Mailing address: 246 Federal Rd., Commons Ste. D-15
Mailing city: Brookfield
Mailing state: CT
Mailing zip: 06804-2649
Office phone: (203) 775-9122
Office fax: (203) 775-9623
General e-mail: steven@ctpennysaver.com
Advertising e-mail: ads@ctpennysaver.com
Editorial e-mail: susan@ctpennysaver.com
Website: steven@ctpennysaver.com
Year publication established: 1994
Advertising (open inch rate): Open inch rate $20.10
Mechanical specifications: Type page 6 3/4 x 9 3/4; E - 2 cols, 3, between; A - 2 cols, 3, between; C - 2 cols, 3, between.
Delivery methods: Mail
Zip Codes Served: 06755, 06757, 06776, 06784, 06785, 06793, 06794, 06804, 06810, 06811, 06877, 06790, 06468, 06482, 06470
Digital Platform - Mobile: Apple`Android
Digital Platform - Tablet: Apple iOS`Android
Frequency: Thur
Circulation Free: 95397
Audit By: Sworn/Estimate/Non-Audited
Audit Date: 43658
Hardware: APP/Power Mac
Software: QPS/QuarkXPress.
Editions Count: 9
Edition Names with circulation: 9 total
  Ã‚Â— Ridgefield Paper-Ridgefield CT (10,500); Yankee Pennysaver-Bethel/Newtown (15,522); Yankee Pennysaver-Brewster/Carmel/Pawling (2,900); Yankee Pennysaver-Danbury (15,430); Yankee Pennysaver-Danbury/Brookfield (18,538); Yankee Pennysaver-Monroe/Ea
Note: We publish Legal Notices, Probate and Foreclosures. We accept tobacco & firearms ads.
Personnel: Susan K. Blumenthal (Pub.); Steven Silver (Pub.)
Main (survey) contact: Steven Silver

Shopper Publications in the U.S.   III-609

GUILFORD

SHORE LINE SHOPPER

Street Address1: PO Box 349
Street address state: CT
Postal code: 06437-0349
County: New Haven
Country: USA
Mailing address: 40 Sargent Dr
Mailing city: New Haven
Mailing state: CT
Mailing zip: 06511-6111
Office phone: (203) 453-2711
Office fax: (203) 453-4152
General e-mail: jcompton@journalregister.com
Website: jcompton@journalregister.com
Advertising (open inch rate): Open inch rate $5.23
Mechanical specifications: Type page 10 1/4 x 16; E - 4 cols, 2 1/2, 1/6 between; A - 6 cols, 1 5/8, 1/6 between; C - 6 cols, 1 5/8, 1/6 between.
Zip Codes Served: 8608
Frequency: Sat
Circulation Free: 20530
Audit By: Sworn/Estimate/Non-Audited
Audit Date: 43658
Hardware: APP/Mac
Software: Multi-Ad/Creator.
Editions Count: 2
Edition Names with circulation: 2 total ÃƒÂ,Ã,Ã— Shore Line Shopper-East (8,927); Shore Line Shopper-West (11,603);
Personnel: John Shields (Pub.); Peter Johnson (Adv. Mgr.)
Main (survey) contact: John Shields

HARTFORD

HARTFORD COURANT

Street Address1: 285 Broad Street
Street address state: CT
Postal code: 06115
Country: USA
Mailing city: Hartford
Mailing state: CT
Mailing zip: 06115
Office phone: (860) 241-6200
General e-mail: custserv@courant.com
Advertising e-mail: classifieds@courant.com
Editorial e-mail: letters@courant.com
Website: custserv@courant.com
Advertising (open inch rate): Open inch rate $6.50
Zip Codes Served: 6226
Frequency: Fri
Circulation Free: 26577
Audit By: Sworn/Estimate/Non-Audited
Audit Date: 43609
Personnel: Mary Lou Stoneburner (Adv. VP); Andrew S. Julien (Pub./ Ed. in Chief); Gary Olszewski (Dir. Circ.)
Parent company: Tribune Publishing, Inc.
Main (survey) contact: Andrew Julien

SOUTHINGTON

STEP SAVER

Street Address1: 213 Spring St
Street address state: CT
Postal code: 06489-1542
County: Hartford
Country: USA
Mailing address: 213 Spring St
Mailing city: Southington
Mailing state: CT
Mailing zip: 06489-1530
Office phone: (860) 628-9438
Office fax: (860) 621-1841
General e-mail: sales@stepsaver.com; info@stepsaver.com; circulation@stepsaver.com
Website: sales@stepsaver.com; info@stepsaver.com; circulation@stepsaver.com
Advertising (open inch rate): Open inch rate $30.30

Mechanical specifications: Type page 10 1/2 x 15; E - 6 cols, between; A - 6 cols, between.
Zip Codes Served: 6489
Frequency: Fri
Circulation Free: 43000
Audit By: Sworn/Estimate/Non-Audited
Audit Date: 43658
Hardware: 21-APP/Mac
Presses: 9-G/Community SSC, G/Community SSC 4 color
Software: QPS/QuarkXPress.
Editions Count: 4
Edition Names with circulation: 4 total Ã,Â— Step Saver-Bristol (25,226); Step Saver-Cheshire (9,754); Step Saver-Plainville/Farmington (12,372); Step Saver-Southington (16,893);
Personnel: Kevin Smalley (Prodn. Mgr.)
Main (survey) contact: Kevin Smalley

TORRINGTON

BETTER LIVING

Street Address1: 190 Water St
Street address state: CT
Postal code: 06790-5325
County: Litchfield
Country: USA
Mailing address: PO Box 58
Mailing city: Torrington
Mailing state: CT
Mailing zip: 06790-0058
Office phone: (860) 489-3121
Office fax: (860) 489-6790
Editorial e-mail: editor@registercitizen.com
Advertising (open inch rate): Open inch rate $6.19
Mechanical specifications: Type page 12 x 21 1/2; E - 6 cols, 1 7/8, between; A - 6 cols, 1 7/8, between; C - 9 cols, 1 1/4, between.
Zip Codes Served: 6790
Frequency: Fri
Circulation Free: 16000
Audit By: Sworn/Estimate/Non-Audited
Audit Date: 43658
Personnel: Wes Rowe (Pub.); Peter Robustelli (Prodn. Mgr.)
Main (survey) contact: Kevin Corrado

THE GOOD NEWS ABOUT TORRINGTON

Street Address1: PO Box 58
Street address state: CT
Postal code: 06790-0058
County: Litchfield
Country: USA
Office phone: (860) 489-3121
Office fax: (860) 489-6790

TRUMBULL

BARGAIN NEWS LLC

Street Address1: 30 Nutmeg Dr
Street address state: CT
Postal code: 06611-5453
County: Fairfield
Country: USA
Mailing address: PO Box 317
Mailing city: Trumbull
Mailing state: CT
Mailing zip: 06611-5453
Office phone: (203) 377-3000
Office fax: (203) 377-2632
Advertising (open inch rate): Open inch rate $12.75
Mechanical specifications: Type page 10 x 15; A - 5 cols, 2, between; C - 5 cols, 2, 1/6 between.
Frequency: Thur
Circulation Paid: 33000
Circulation Free: 500
Audit By: Sworn/Estimate/Non-Audited
Audit Date: 43658
Hardware: PCs, APP/Macs.

Personnel: John F. Roy (Pub.); Carol Leach (Gen. Mgr.)
Main (survey) contact: John F. Roy

WATERTOWN

TOWN TIMES

Street Address1: 449 Main St
Street address state: CT
Postal code: 06795-2628
County: Litchfield
Country: USA
Mailing address: PO Box 1
Mailing city: Watertown
Mailing state: CT
Mailing zip: 06795-0001
Office phone: (860) 274-8851
Office fax: (860) 945-3116
General e-mail: voicespub@earthlink.net; towntimes@earthlink.net
Editorial e-mail: jtaylor@towntimesnews.com
Website: voicespub@earthlink.net; towntimes@earthlink.net
Advertising (open inch rate): Open inch rate $15.35
Mechanical specifications: Type page 10 x 15; E - 5 cols, 2, 1/2 between; A - 5 cols, 2, 1/2 between; C - 5 cols, 2, 1/2 between.
Frequency: Wed`Thur`Sun
Circulation Paid: 23114
Audit By: CAC
Audit Date: 42277
Hardware: APP/Mac, PC
Software: QPS/QuarkXPress, Brainworks.
Personnel: Annette Linster (Gen. Mgr.); Rudy Mazurosky (Adv. Mgr.); Walter K. Mazurosky (Circ. Mgr.); James Taylor (Ed.); Kurt Mazurosky (Prodn. Mgr.)
Main (survey) contact: Rudy Mazurosky

DELAWARE

DOVER

INDEPENDENT NEWSMEDIA INC.

USA

Street Address1: 110 Galaxy Dr
Street address state: DE
Postal code: 19901-9262
County: Kent
Country: USA
Mailing address: 110 Galaxy Dr
Mailing city: Dover
Mailing state: DE
Mailing zip: 19901-9262
Office phone: (302) 674-3600
Office fax: (877) 377-2424
General e-mail: newsroom@newszap.com
Website: newsroom@newszap.com
Year publication established: 1953
Circulation Paid: 1580
Circulation Free: 1939
Audit By: CAC
Audit Date: 42004
Note: Independent Newspapers Inc. owns three daily newspapers and 25 weekly publications.
Personnel: Joe Smyth (Chrmn. of the Bd./CEO); Tamra Brittingham (Corp. Pres.); Ed Dulin (Pres., Opns.); Darel LaPrade (Vice Pres., Adv.); Chris Engel (Dir., Research/Devel.); Sheila Clendaniel (Exec. Asst.); Greg Tock (Pub.)
Main (survey) contact: Joe Smyth

FLORIDA

BONIFAY

HOLMES COUNTY ADVERTISER

Street Address1: 112 E Virginia Ave
Street address state: FL
Postal code: 32425-2327
County: Holmes
Country: USA
Mailing address: 112 E Virginia Ave
Mailing city: Bonifay
Mailing state: FL
Mailing zip: 32425-2327
Office phone: (850) 547-2270
Office fax: (850) 547-9200
General e-mail: holmescoadvertiser@wseca.net
Website: holmescoadvertiser@wseca.net
Advertising (open inch rate): Open inch rate $4.00
Zip Codes Served: 32425
Frequency: Wed
Circulation Free: 4200
Audit By: Sworn/Estimate/Non-Audited
Audit Date: 43658
Personnel: Gary Woodham (Pub.); Michelle Pate (Adv. Mgr.); Terri Tomkiewicz (Circ. Mgr.); Kathy Foster (Ed.); Kim McDonald (Prodn. Mgr.)
Main (survey) contact: Nicole Barefield

BUNNELL

FLAGLER PENNYSAVER

Street Address1: 2729 E Moody Blvd
Street address state: FL
Postal code: 32110-5963
County: Flagler
Country: USA
Mailing address: 2729 E Moody Blvd.
Mailing city: Bunnell
Mailing state: FL
Mailing zip: 32110
Office phone: (386) 437-5971
Office fax: (386) 437-2232
General e-mail: flagleri@psavers.com
Website: flagleri@psavers.com
Advertising (open inch rate): Open inch rate $10.80
Frequency: Wed
Circulation Free: 36966
Audit By: CVC
Audit Date: 42368
Personnel: Leonard A. Marsh (Pub.); Kelli Hull (Bus. Mgr.); Pat Waterman (Sales Supvr.); Jan Ridell (Circ. Mgr.); James Drummond (Sales Mgr)
Parent company: News-Journal Corp.
Main (survey) contact: Romaine Fine

CAPE CORAL

LEE COUNTY SHOPPER

Street Address1: 2510 Del Prado Blvd
Street address state: FL
Postal code: 33904-5750
County: Lee
Country: USA
Mailing address: PO Box 151306
Mailing city: Cape Coral
Mailing state: FL
Mailing zip: 33915
Office phone: (239) 574-1110
Office fax: (239) 573-2318
Editorial phone: 574-1110 ext. 119
Editorial e-mail: vharring@breezenewspapers.com
Year publication established: 1961
Advertising (open inch rate): Open inch rate $40.00
Mechanical specifications: Type page 10 5/16 x 15; E - 6 cols, 1 2/3, 1/6 between; A - 6 cols, 1 2/3, 1/6 between; C - 6 cols, 1 2/3,

1/6 between.
Delivery methods:
Mail`Newsstand`Carrier`Racks
Zip Codes Served: 33904, 33901, 33903, 33905, 33907, 33908,33909, 33912,33913, 33914, 33916, 33917,33919, 33920,33924, 33931, 33936,33966, 33971,33972,33974,33976, 33990, 33991, 33993
Frequency: Wed
Circulation Paid: 4
Circulation Free: 61202
Audit By: CVC
Audit Date: 42368
Hardware: APP/Macs
Presses: DGM 430 4/Cold Set Towers 1/UV Tower
Software: Multi-Ad/Creator 8.04, QPS/QuarkXPress 8
Personnel: Valarie Harring (Pub.)
Parent company: Ogden Newspapers Inc.
Main (survey) contact: Valarie Harring

SANIBEL - CAPTIVA SHOPPER'S GUIDE

Street Address1: 2510 Del Prado Blvd S
Street address state: FL
Postal code: 33904-5750
County: Lee
Country: USA
Mailing address: 2510 Del Prado Blvd S
Mailing city: Cape Coral
Mailing state: FL
Mailing zip: 33904-5750
Advertising (open inch rate): N/A
Frequency: Mthly
Circulation Paid: 1
Circulation Free: 4843
Audit By: CVC
Audit Date: 42368
Personnel: Scott Blonde
Parent company: Ogden Newspapers Inc.
Main (survey) contact: Scott Blonde

CLERMONT
SUMTER SHOPPER

Street Address1: 637 8th St
Street address state: FL
Postal code: 34711-2159
County: Lake
Country: USA
Mailing address: 637 Eighth Street
Mailing city: Clermont
Mailing state: FL
Mailing zip: 34711
Office phone: (352) 748-2424
Office fax: (352) 567-5640
Advertising (open inch rate): Open inch rate $8.86
Zip Codes Served: 34731
Frequency: Wed
Circulation Free: 22000
Audit By: Sworn/Estimate/Non-Audited
Audit Date: 43658
Personnel: Linda Briody (Pub.)
Parent company: Independent Publications Inc; Sun Publications of Fla.
Main (survey) contact: Linda Briody

DAYTONA
DAYTONA PENNYSAVER

Street Address1: 901 6th St.
Street address state: FL
Postal code: 32117
County: Volusia
Country: USA
Mailing address: 901 6th St.
Mailing city: Daytona
Mailing state: FL
Mailing zip: 32117
Office phone: (386) 681-2200
General e-mail: Romaine.Fine@PSavers.com
Website: Romaine.Fine@PSavers.com
Year publication established: 1981
Advertising (open inch rate): Open inch rate $19.65
Zip Codes Served: 32174
Frequency: Wed
Circulation Free: 66186
Audit By: Sworn/Estimate/Non-Audited
Audit Date: 43585
Personnel: Romaine Fine (GM)
Parent company: News-Journal Corp.
Main (survey) contact: Romaine Fine
Footnotes: Mailing address: Change of address from postcard sent to survey contacts 6-1-15.

DELAND
FLORIDA PENNYSAVER

Street Address1: 120 S. Woodland Boulevard
Street Address2: Suite C
Street address state: FL
Postal code: 32723
County: Palm Beach
Country: USA
Mailing address: 120 S. Woodland Boulevard Suite C
Mailing city: Deland
Mailing state: FL
Mailing zip: 32723
Office phone: (386) 736-2880
Advertising e-mail: mary.morrissey@psavers.com
Advertising (open inch rate): Open inch rate $109.78
Zip Codes Served: 33416
Frequency: Thur
Circulation Free: 36300
Audit By: Sworn/Estimate/Non-Audited
Audit Date: 43585
Editions Count: 22
Personnel: Mary Morrissey (Adv.)
Parent company: Cox Media Group
Main (survey) contact: Mary Morrisey

WEST VOLUSIA PENNYSAVER

Street Address1: 120 S. Woodland Boulevard
Street Address2: Suite C
Street address state: FL
Postal code: 32723
Country: USA
Mailing address: 120 S. Woodland Boulevard Suite C
Mailing city: Deland
Mailing state: FL
Mailing zip: 32177
Office phone: (386) 736-2880
General e-mail: Romaine.Fine@PSavers.com
Advertising e-mail: mary.morrissey@psavers.com
Website: Romaine.Fine@PSavers.com
Frequency: Thur
Circulation Free: 15426
Audit By: Sworn/Estimate/Non-Audited
Audit Date: 43585
Personnel: Romaine Fine (GM); Mary Morrissey (Adv./ Sales Mgr.)
Main (survey) contact: Romaine Fine

WEST VOLUSIA PENNYSAVER

Street Address1: 1422 N Woodland Blvd
Street address state: FL
Postal code: 32720-2260
County: Volusia
Country: USA
Mailing address: 1422 N Woodland Blvd
Mailing city: Deland
Mailing state: FL
Mailing zip: 32720-2260
Office phone: (386) 736-2880
Office fax: (386) 736-3587
Advertising phone: (800) 218-2186
General e-mail: wvpsoa@psavers.com
Website: wvpsoa@psavers.com
Year publication established: 1971
Advertising (open inch rate): Open inch rate $15.75
Mechanical specifications: Type page 9 7/8 x 11 1/2; A - 7 cols, 1 5/16, 1/6 between; C - 7 cols, 1 5/16, 1/6 between.
Delivery methods: Carrier`Racks
Zip Codes Served: 32723, 32180, 32190, 32130, 32720, 32724, 32725, 32738, 32713, 32706
Frequency: Wed
Circulation Free: 55620
Audit By: CVC
Audit Date: 42368
Hardware: APP/Power Mac, APP/Mac G4
Software: Multi-Ad Creator 6.5, Adobe/Photoshop 6, QPS/QuarkXPress 4.02, Adobe/Illustrator 9.0.
Editions Count: 2
Edition Names with circulation: 2 total ÃƒÂƒ££ West Volusia Pennysaver-North (19,000 sat. 19,000 wed.);
Personnel: Linda Sherwood (Display Sales Manager); Kelli Hull (Gen. Mgr.); Jon Riddell (Circ. Mgr.); Evan Baldwin (Circ. Suprv.)
Parent company: Halifax Media; News-Journal Corp.
Main (survey) contact: Romaine Fine

DESTIN
LOG EXTRA

Street Address1: 1225 Airport Rd
Street address state: FL
Postal code: 32541-2909
County: Okaloosa
Country: USA
Mailing address: PO Box 957
Mailing city: Destin
Mailing state: FL
Mailing zip: 32540-0957
Office phone: (850) 863-1111
Office fax: (850) 654-5982
General e-mail: thelog@link.freedom.com
Website: thelog@link.freedom.com
Advertising (open inch rate): Open inch rate $4.50
Frequency: Wed
Circulation Free: 4200
Audit By: Sworn/Estimate/Non-Audited
Audit Date: 43585
Personnel: Tim Thompson (Pub.); Carla Foster (Circ. Mgr.); Jason Blakeney (Ex. Ed.); Wendy Victoria (Mng. Ed.); Noel Shauf (IT Dir.); Jennifer Hoda (Adv. Ex.)
Parent company: Gatehouse Media, LLC
Main (survey) contact: Jason Blakeney

FORT LAUDERDALE
TEENLINK

Street Address1: 500 E Broward Blvd
Street address state: FL
Postal code: 33394-3000
County: Broward
Country: USA
Mailing address: 500 E. Broward Blvd.
Mailing city: Fort Lauderdale
Mailing state: FL
Mailing zip: 33394
Editorial phone: (954) 574-5316
Editorial e-mail: jjhon@sfteenlink.com
Frequency: Thur
Circulation Free: 66773
Audit By: CVC
Audit Date: 40878
Personnel: Lisa Goodlin
Main (survey) contact: Cheryl Amico

KISSIMMEE
OSCEOLA NEWS-GAZETTE

Street Address1: 108 Church St
Street address state: FL
Postal code: 34741-5055
County: Osceola
Country: USA
Mailing address: 108 Church St
Mailing city: Kissimmee
Mailing state: FL
Mailing zip: 34741
Office phone: (407) 846-7600
Office fax: (321) 402-2946
General e-mail: kbeckham@osceolanewsgazette.com
Advertising e-mail: jsousse@osceolanewsgazette.com
Editorial e-mail: bmcbride@osceolanewsgazette.com
Website: kbeckham@osceolanewsgazette.com
Year publication established: 1891
Advertising (open inch rate): Open inch rate $22.25
Mechanical specifications: 6 col. x 16" - 96" page 1 Column: 1.54â 2 Column: 3.23â 3 Column: 4.92â 4 Column: 6.61â 5 Column: 8.30â 6 Column: 10.00â
Delivery methods: Mail`Newsstand`Carrier`Racks
Zip Codes Served: 34741 34743 34744 34746 34758 34759 34771 34769 34772 34747
Frequency: Thur`Sat
Other Type of Frequency: 2x Wkly
Circulation Paid: 561
Circulation Free: 40126
Audit By: CVC
Audit Date: 42767
Hardware: APP/Mac
Presses: 9-G
Software: In Design, QPS/QuarkXPress 4.1, Adobe/Photoshop 6.0, Adobe/Illustrator 9.0, Macromedia/Freehand 7.0, Adobe/Acrobat 4.0.
Personnel: Tom Overton (Pub.); Brian McBride (Ed.); Jamie Sousse (Adv.); Kathy Beckham (Circ. Mgr.)
Main (survey) contact: Tom Overton

LAKELAND
POLK VOICE

Street Address1: 300 W Lime St
Street address state: FL
Postal code: 33815-4649
County: Polk
Country: USA
Office phone: (863) 802-7452

MELBOURNE
THRIFTY NICKEL - MERRITT ISLAND

Street Address1: 2525 Aurora Rd
Street Address2: Ste 102
Street address state: FL
Postal code: 32935-2833
County: Brevard
Country: USA
Mailing address: 2525 Aurora Rd Ste 102
Mailing city: Melbourne
Mailing state: FL
Mailing zip: 32935-2833
Year publication established: 1982
Advertising (open inch rate): CP
Mechanical specifications: Type page 10.5" x 15.5"; 8 cols
Delivery methods: Mail`Carrier`Racks
Frequency: Thur
Circulation Paid: 0
Circulation Free: 14975
Audit By: CVC
Audit Date: 42004
Personnel: Joey Laurino
Main (survey) contact: Joey Laurino

MIAMI
HERALD VALUES

Street Address1: 1 Herald Plz
Street address state: FL
Postal code: 33132-1609

Shopper Publications in the U.S.

County: Miami-Dade
Country: USA
Mailing address: 3511 NW 91st Ave
Mailing city: Miami
Mailing state: FL
Mailing zip: 33132-1609
Office phone: (305) 350-2111
Advertising phone: (305) 376-3315
Frequency: Thur
Circulation Paid: 0
Circulation Free: 787390
Audit By: VAC
Audit Date: 42093
Personnel: David A. Landsberg (Pres./Pub.); Greg Curling (Vice Pres., Finance/CFO); Donna Dickey (Vice Pres./Broward Bus. Mgr.); Susan A. Rosenthal (Vice Pres./CFO); Dory Trinka (Vice Pres., Targeted Publications); Elissa Vanaver (Vice Pres., HR/Asst. to Pub.); Raul Lopez (Gen. Mgr., MiamiHerald.com); Patricia Royal (Adv. Dir., Classified); David Jost (Adv. Dir., Local); Matthew Fine (Adv. Dir., Nat'l); Jackie Kaplan (Interactive Sales Mgr.); Willard Soper (Vice Pres., Mktg./Bus. Devel.); Bernie Kosanke (Circ. Vice Pres.); Aminda Marques Gonzalez (Vice Pres./Exec. Ed.); Tony Espetia (Dir., Int'l Edition); Rick Hirsch (Mng. Ed., Multimedia); Dave Wilson (Mng. Ed., News); Pat Andrews (Asst. Mng. Ed., Broward); Luis Rios (Dir., Photography)
Parent company: The McClatchy Company
Main (survey) contact: Matty Lopez; Aminda Marques

MOUNT DORA

TRIANGLE NEWS LEADER

Street Address1: 4645 N Highway 19A
Street address state: FL
Postal code: 32757-2039
County: Lake
Country: USA
Mailing address: 4645 N Highway 19A
Mailing city: Mount Dora
Mailing state: FL
Mailing zip: 32757-2039
Office phone: (352) 589-8811
Office fax: (352) 357-3202
Advertising e-mail: ayager@trianglenewsleader.com
Editorial e-mail: ayager@trianglenewsleader.com
Year publication established: 1956
Advertising (open inch rate): Open inch rate $11.81
Zip Codes Served: 32757
Frequency: Wed
Circulation Free: 28006
Audit By: CVC
Audit Date: 42916
Personnel: Ann Yager (Pub.); Marion Witt (Office Mgr.); Donna Covert (Gen. Mgr.); Randi Weeks (Circ. Mgr.); Val Neeley (Prodn. Mgr.); Dawn Hendry (Prod. Mgr)
Parent company: Independent Publications Inc; Lakeway Publishers, Inc.; Sun Publications of Fla.
Main (survey) contact: Marion Witt; Ann Yager

NEW SMYRNA BEACH

NEW SMYRNA PENNYSAVER

Street Address1: 223 Canal St
Street address state: FL
Postal code: 32168-7089
County: Volusia
Country: USA
Mailing address: 223 Canal St Ste A
Mailing city: New Smyrna Beach
Mailing state: FL
Mailing zip: 32168-7090
Advertising (open inch rate): Open inch rate $12.70
Frequency: Wed
Circulation Free: 27035
Audit By: CVC
Audit Date: 42368

Personnel: Bill Offill
Main (survey) contact: Jay Kemp

ORMOND BEACH

VOLUSIA PENNYSAVER, INC.

Street Address1: 454 S Yonge St
Street address state: FL
Postal code: 32174-7501
County: Volusia
Country: USA
Mailing address: PO Box 919422
Mailing city: Orlando
Mailing state: FL
Mailing zip: 32891-0001
Office phone: (386) 677-4262
Office fax: (386) 677-6608
General e-mail: clarissa.williams@psavers.com
Website: clarissa.williams@psavers.com
Year publication established: 1971
Advertising (open inch rate): Rate Card by Request
Delivery methods: Mail`Carrier`Racks
Frequency: Wed`Thur`Sat
Circulation Free: 112300
Audit By: Sworn/Estimate/Non-Audited
Audit Date: 43658
Personnel: Clarissa Williams (Group General Manager); Leonard A. Marsh (Pub./Gen. Mgr.); Kelli Hull (Gen. Mgr.); Toni Maddux (Gen. Sales Mgr.); Mary Morrissey (Gen. Sales Mgr.); Jon Riddell (Circ. Mgr.); Daniele Lowe (Sales Mgr)
Main (survey) contact: Jay Kemp
Footnotes: Mailing address: Address change from postcard sent to survey contacts on 6-1-15.

PANAMA CITY

THE ADVERTISER

Street Address1: 2905 E Highway 98
Street address state: FL
Postal code: 32401-5429
County: Bay
Country: USA
Mailing address: 2905 E Highway 98
Mailing city: Panama City
Mailing state: FL
Mailing zip: 32401-5429
Office phone: (850) 785-7355
Office fax: (850) 785-1509
General e-mail: pcadvertiser@bellsouth.net
Website: pcadvertiser@bellsouth.net
Year publication established: 1983
Advertising (open inch rate): Open inch rate $8.00
Mechanical specifications: Type page 10 1/4 x 15 2/5.
Frequency: Thur
Circulation Free: 20000
Audit By: Sworn/Estimate/Non-Audited
Audit Date: 43658
Hardware: 6-APP/Mac
Software: Adobe/Photoshop 3.0, Adobe/PageMaker 6.0.
Personnel: Pamela Howell (Pub.); Michelle Skipper (Adv. Mgr.)
Main (survey) contact: Rhonda Hillier

THRIFTY NICKEL - FT. WALTON BEACH

Street Address1: 1522 Chestnut Ave.
Street address state: FL
Postal code: 32405
County: Okaloosa
Country: USA
Mailing address: PO Box 5301
Mailing city: Fort Walton Beach
Mailing state: FL
Mailing zip: 32549-5301
Office phone: (850) 747-1155
Office fax: (850) 784-0677

Editorial e-mail: karenltnol@gmail.com
Year publication established: 1980
Advertising (open inch rate): Open inch rate $5.00 - $10.50
Mechanical specifications: 8 Columns x 16" = 1 page 1 column = 7,6 picas 2 columns = 15,6 picas
Delivery methods: Racks
Zip Codes Served: 32433, 32434, 32439, 32531, 32536, 32541, 32542, 32544, 32547, 32548, 32549, 32550, 32564, 32566, 32567, 32569, 32578, 32579, 36420, 35467
Digital Platform - Mobile: Apple`Android`Windows`Blackberry`Other
Digital Platform - Tablet: Apple iOS`Android`Windows 7`Blackberry Tablet OS`Kindle`Nook`Kindle Fire`Other
Frequency: Thur
Circulation Free: 11709
Audit By: Sworn/Estimate/Non-Audited
Audit Date: 43598
Hardware: IBM
Software: coreldraw ver 8, pagemaker 5
Editions Count: 1
Personnel: Karen White; Stephen White (Pub.)
Parent company: Thrifty Nickel Publications, Llc-OOB
Main (survey) contact: Karen White

PENSACOLA

THRIFTY NICKEL - PENSACOLA

Street Address1: 225 N Pace Blvd
Street address state: FL
Postal code: 32505-7915
County: Escambia
Country: USA
Mailing address: PO Box 161990
Mailing city: Pensacola
Mailing state: FL
Mailing zip: 32507-6190
Office phone: (850) 469-9712
Office fax: (850) 469-9718
General e-mail: steveroot@pensacola.com
Website: steveroot@pensacola.com
Year publication established: 1885
Advertising (open inch rate): Open inch rate $5.66 - $12.00
Mechanical specifications: Type page 10.75" x 16"; 8 cols
Delivery methods: Mail`Carrier`Racks
Zip Codes Served: 32505, 32507, 32504, 32506
Digital Platform - Mobile: Apple`Android`Windows`Blackberry`Other
Digital Platform - Tablet: Apple iOS`Android`Windows 7`Blackberry Tablet OS`Kindle`Nook`Kindle Fire`Other
Frequency: Thur
Circulation Free: 37129
Audit By: CVC
Audit Date: 42643
Hardware: IBM
Editions Count: 1
Personnel: Steve Root (General Manager)
Parent company: Thrifty Nickel Publications, Llc-OOB
Main (survey) contact: Steve Root

STUART

FLASHES SHOPPING GUIDE

Street Address1: 5675 SE Grouper Ave
Street address state: FL
Postal code: 34997-3103
County: Martin
Country: USA
Mailing address: 5675 SE Grouper Ave
Mailing city: Stuart
Mailing state: FL
Mailing zip: 34997-3103
Office phone: (772) 287-0650
Office fax: (772) 283-5090
Editorial phone: (772) 219-2741
General e-mail: flashesreceptionist@theflashes.com
Advertising e-mail: sales@theflashes.com
Editorial e-mail: classifieds@theflashes.com; goodneighbor@theflashes.com; communityevents@theflashes.com

Website: flashesreceptionist@theflashes.com
Year publication established: 1951
Advertising (open inch rate): Open inch rate $15.20
Zip Codes Served: 34944
Frequency: Wed
Circulation Free: 60000
Audit By: Sworn/Estimate/Non-Audited
Audit Date: 43658
Hardware: APP/Mac, DTI, APP/Mac LaserWriter
Software: Synaptic.
Editions Count: 3
Edition Names with circulation: 3 total Ã‚Â— Central Flashes Shopping Guide (20,000); North Flashes Shopping Guide (20,000); South Flashes Shopping Guide (20,000);
Personnel: Kevin Hawken (Pub.); Gary Dean (Adv. Mgr.)
Main (survey) contact: Kevin Hawken

TALLAHASSEE

AMERICAN CLASSIFIEDS - TALLAHASSEE

Street Address1: 2441 Monticello Dr
Street address state: FL
Postal code: 32303-4761
County: Leon
Country: USA
Mailing address: 2441 Monticello Dr
Mailing city: Tallahassee
Mailing state: FL
Mailing zip: 32303-4761
Advertising (open inch rate): Open inch rate $12.00
Mechanical specifications: Type page 10.5" x 16"; 8 cols
Delivery methods: Racks
Frequency: Thur
Circulation Paid: 0
Circulation Free: 23886
Audit By: CVC
Audit Date: 41912
Personnel: Larrie Jemison
Main (survey) contact: Larrie Jemison

TAMPA

THE FLYER, INC.

Street Address1: 201 Kelsey Ln
Street Address2: Ste A
Street address state: FL
Postal code: 33619-4310
County: Hillsborough
Country: USA
Mailing address: 201 Kelsey Ln
Mailing city: Tampa
Mailing state: FL
Mailing zip: 33619-4312
Office phone: (813) 626-9430
Advertising phone: (813) 626-9430
Year publication established: 1977
Mechanical specifications: Type page 6.25" x 9.25"; 4 cols
Delivery methods: Mail
Digital Platform - Mobile: Apple`Android`Windows
Digital Platform - Tablet: Apple iOS
Frequency: Wed
Circulation Free: 1600000
Audit By: CVC
Audit Date: 43009
Hardware: Mac, PCs, iPADs
Presses: Goss Community, Didde
Software: CS 6
Editions Count: 73
Main (survey) contact: Lee Smith

VENICE

THE SUN SHOPPER

Street Address1: 200 E Venice Ave
Street address state: FL
Postal code: 34285-1941

County: Sarasota
Country: USA
Mailing address: 200 E Venice Ave
Mailing city: Venice
Mailing state: FL
Mailing zip: 34285-1941
Office phone: (941) 207-1000
Office fax: (941) 484-8460
Advertising (open inch rate): Open inch rate $22.00
Mechanical specifications: Type page 13 x 21; E - 6 cols, 2 1/16, 5/16 between; A - 6 cols, 2 1/16, 5/16 between; C - 9 cols, 1 3/8, 1/8 between.
Zip Codes Served: 34285
Frequency: Fri
Circulation Free: 18000
Audit By: Sworn/Estimate/Non-Audited
Audit Date: 43658
Hardware: APP/Mac
Presses: HI/V-15A
Software: Multi-Ad/Creator 4.01, Baseview, QPS/QuarkXPress 3.32, Adobe/Photoshop 5.0.
Editions Count: 2
Edition Names with circulation: 2 total Ã‚Â— Englewood/West Port; Venice;
Personnel: Bob Vedder (Pub.); Lang Capasso (Adv. Mgr.); Karen Gardner (Circ. Mgr.); Bob Mudge (Ed.); James King (Prodn. Mgr.)
Main (survey) contact: Bob Mudge

WINTER HAVEN
ADVERTISER OF POLK COUNTY

Street Address1: 1122 5th St SW
Street address state: FL
Postal code: 33880-3725
County: Polk
Country: USA
Mailing address: 1122 5th St SW
Mailing city: Winter Haven
Mailing state: FL
Mailing zip: 33880-3725
Office phone: (863) 299-2201
Office fax: (863) 299-5672
General e-mail: advpaper@aol.com
Website: advpaper@aol.com
Advertising (open inch rate): Open inch rate $6.50
Mechanical specifications: Type page 10 1/4 x 17.
Zip Codes Served: 33880
Frequency: Wed
Circulation Free: 37000
Audit By: Sworn/Estimate/Non-Audited
Audit Date: 43658
Hardware: APP/Mac
Software: First Class.
Personnel: Larry A. Knowles (Pub.); Cindy Yates (Co Pub.)
Main (survey) contact: Larry A. Knowles

WINTER HAVEN
LAKE WALES SHOPPER

Street Address1: 455 6th St NW
Street address state: FL
Postal code: 33881-4061
County: Polk
Country: USA
Mailing address: 455 Sixth St. N.W.
Mailing city: Winter Haven
Mailing state: FL
Mailing zip: 33881
Office phone: (863) 401-6900
Office fax: (863) 401-6999
Advertising phone: (863) 802-7473
Editorial phone: (863) 802-7504
General e-mail: news@newschief.com
Advertising e-mail: legals@newschief.com
Editorial e-mail: lynne.maddox@theledger.com
Website: news@newschief.com
Advertising (open inch rate): Open inch rate $10.00
Mechanical specifications: Type page 10 3/16 x 16; E - 8 cols, 1 1/8, 1/8 between; A - 8 cols, 1 1/8, 1/8 between; C - 8 cols, 1 1/8,

1/8 between.
Zip Codes Served: 33853
Frequency: Wed
Circulation Free: 16710
Audit By: Sworn/Estimate/Non-Audited
Audit Date: 43658
Hardware: APP/Mac
Presses: G/Urbanite, HI/V-15D
Software: QPS/QuarkXPress.
Personnel: Joe Braddy (Mng. Ed.)
Main (survey) contact: Kevin Drake

ZEPHYRHILLS
PASCO SHOPPER

Street Address1: 5739 Gall Blvd
Street address state: FL
Postal code: 33542-3453
County: Pasco
Country: USA
Mailing address: 5739 Gall Blvd
Mailing city: Zephyrhills
Mailing state: FL
Mailing zip: 33542
Office phone: (352) 567-5639
Office fax: (352) 567-5640
General e-mail: info@pasconews.com
Website: info@pasconews.com
Advertising (open inch rate): Open inch rate $14.20
Mechanical specifications: Type page 9 5/8 x 16; E - 5 cols, 1 7/8, 1/8 between; A - 5 cols, 1 7/8, 1/8 between; C - 5 cols, 1 7/8, between.
Zip Codes Served: 33524, 33525, 33535, 33537, 33540, 33541, 33543, 33544, 33574, 33576, 34602
Frequency: Wed
Circulation Free: 31050
Audit By: Sworn/Estimate/Non-Audited
Audit Date: 43658
Hardware: APP/Power Mac
Presses: KP, 8-WPC/Web Leader
Software: Adobe/PageMaker, Adobe/Photoshop, QPS/QuarkXPress.
Editions Count: 3
Edition Names with circulation: 3 total ÃƒÂ‚Â— Pasco News (15,000); Wesley Chapel Connection (4,000); Zephyrhills Sun (19,000);
Personnel: Ann Licate (Pub.)
Parent company: Independent Publications Inc; Sun Publications of Fla.
Main (survey) contact: Tammie Rogers

GEORGIA

AMERICUS
THE AMERICUS SHOPPER

Street Address1: 1403 Felder St
Street address state: GA
Postal code: 31709-5362
County: Sumter
Country: USA
Mailing address: PO Box 6314
Mailing city: Americus
Mailing state: GA
Mailing zip: 31709-6314
Office phone: (229) 924-9000
Office fax: (229) 928-2977
Advertising (open inch rate): Open inch rate $5.00
Frequency: Tues
Circulation Free: 17000
Audit By: Sworn/Estimate/Non-Audited
Audit Date: 43658
Personnel: Joel Ward (Pub.)
Main (survey) contact: Joel Ward

BAINBRIDGE
POST-SEARCHLIGHT EXTRA

Street Address1: 301 N Crawford St
Street address state: GA
Postal code: 39817-3612
County: Decatur
Country: USA
Mailing address: PO Box 277
Mailing city: Bainbridge
Mailing state: GA
Mailing zip: 39818-0277
Office phone: (229) 246-2827
Office fax: (229) 246-7665
General e-mail: publisher@e-postprint.com
Website: publisher@e-postprint.com
Year publication established: 1907
Advertising (open inch rate): Open inch rate $13.30
Mechanical specifications: Type page 13 x 21 1/2; E - 6 cols, 2 1/3, 1/8 between; A - 6 cols, 2 1/3, 1/8 between; C - 6 cols, 2 1/3, 1/8 between.
Zip Codes Served: 31717
Frequency: Wed`Sat
Circulation Free: 34000
Audit By: Sworn/Estimate/Non-Audited
Audit Date: 43658
Hardware: APP/Mac
Presses: G/Community
Software: QPS/QuarkXPress, Adobe/Photoshop.
Personnel: Jeff Findley (Adv. Mgr.); Tameka Thomas (Asst. Adv. Mgr.); Teshiki Parrish (Circ. Mgr.); Carol Heard (Mng. Ed.); Joe Crine (Sports Ed.)
Parent company: Boone Newspapers, Inc.
Main (survey) contact: Jeff Findley

CANTON
CHEROKEE TRIBUNE PLUS

Street Address1: 521 E Main St
Street address state: GA
Postal code: 30114-2805
County: Cherokee
Country: USA
Mailing address: 521 E Main St
Mailing city: Canton
Mailing state: GA
Mailing zip: 30114-2805
Office phone: (770) 795-5000
Office fax: (770) 479-3505
Advertising (open inch rate): Open inch rate $18.00
Zip Codes Served: 30061
Frequency: Wed
Circulation Free: 10000
Audit By: CAC
Audit Date: 41182
Personnel: Otis A. Brumby (Pub.); Wade Stephens (Vice Pres. Sales/Mktg.); Kim Fowler (Adv. Mgr.); Matt Heck (Circ. Dir.); Barbara Jacoby (Ed.); John Bednarowski (Sports Ed.)
Parent company: Times-Journal, Inc.
Main (survey) contact: Otis A. Brumby

COLUMBUS
THRIFTY NICKEL - COLUMBUS

Street Address1: 4425 Holly Ave
Street address state: GA
Postal code: 31904-6525
County: Muscogee
Country: USA
Mailing address: 4425 Holly Ave
Mailing city: Columbus
Mailing state: GA
Mailing zip: 31904-6525
Office phone: (706) 571-3463
Office fax: (706) 327-8075
Advertising phone: (706) 571-3463
Advertising fax: (706) 327-8075
General e-mail: columbus@peachads.com
Advertising e-mail: charlie@peachads.com
Website: columbus@peachads.com

Year publication established: 1990
Delivery methods: Racks
Digital Platform - Mobile: Apple
Digital Platform - Tablet: Apple iOS
Frequency: Thur
Circulation Free: 32352
Audit By: CVC
Audit Date: 41182
Personnel: Randy Eiland
Main (survey) contact: Randy Eiland

CONYERS
MIKE'S SHOPPER

Street Address1: 2274 Salem Rd SE
Street Address2: Ste 106-232
Street address state: GA
Postal code: 30013-2097
County: Rockdale
Country: USA
Mailing address: 1009 Milstead Ave NE Ste 200
Mailing city: Conyers
Mailing state: GA
Mailing zip: 30012-4510
Office phone: (770) 388-0438
Office fax: (770) 922-3338
General e-mail: Info@mikeshoppers.com
Website: Info@mikesshoppers.com
Advertising (open inch rate): Open inch rate $7.50
Mechanical specifications: Type page 6 x 16; A - 6 cols, 1 1/2, between; C - 6 cols, 1 1/2, between.
Zip Codes Served: 30013
Frequency: Mthly
Circulation Free: 25450
Audit By: Sworn/Estimate/Non-Audited
Audit Date: 43658
Hardware: COM/7700-4400, APP/Mac IIsi
Software: QPS/QuarkXPress 4.0.
Personnel: Thad Doug (Pub.)
Main (survey) contact: Stephanie Stapp

CORDELE
BUYERS GUIDE

Street Address1: 306 W 13th Ave
Street address state: GA
Postal code: 31015-2348
County: Crisp
Country: USA
Mailing address: PO Box 1058
Mailing city: Cordele
Mailing state: GA
Mailing zip: 31010-1058
Office phone: (229) 273-2277
Office fax: (229) 273-0067
Advertising e-mail: chris.lewis@cordeledispatch.com
Editorial e-mail: gabe.jordan@cordeledispatch.com
Advertising (open inch rate): Open inch rate $5.42
Mechanical specifications: Type page 13 x 21 1/2; E - 6 cols, 2 1/8, between; A - 6 cols, 2 1/8, between; C - 9 cols, 2 1/8, between.
Zip Codes Served: 31015
Frequency: Tues
Circulation Free: 12500
Audit By: Sworn/Estimate/Non-Audited
Audit Date: 43658
Personnel: Gabe Jordan; Chris Lewis
Main (survey) contact: Gabe Jordan

DOUGLAS
DOUGLAS SHOPPER

Street Address1: 404 Peterson Ave N
Street address state: GA
Postal code: 31533-4916
County: Coffee
Country: USA
Mailing address: PO Box 390
Mailing city: Douglas
Mailing state: GA
Mailing zip: 31534-0390

Shopper Publications in the U.S.

Office phone: (912) 384-9112
Office fax: (912) 384-4220
Advertising phone: (912) 384-1980
General e-mail: Graphics@YourDouglasShopper.com
Advertising e-mail: Sales@YourDouglasShopper.com
Website: Graphics@YourDouglasShopper.com
Advertising (open inch rate): Open inch rate $6.25
Mechanical specifications: Type page 10 1/4 x 15; E - 6 cols, 1 1/2, between; A - 6 cols, 1 1/2, between; C - 6 cols, 1 1/2, between.
Zip Codes Served: 31533
Frequency: Tues
Circulation Free: 20760
Audit By: Sworn/Estimate/Non-Audited
Audit Date: 43658
Hardware: APP/Power Macs
Presses: 5-KP
Software: Multi-Ad/Creator, QPS/QuarkXPress.
Personnel: Sharon Mart (Office Mgr.)
Main (survey) contact: Sharon Mart

EATONTON

THE EATONTON MESSENGER

Street Address1: 100 N Jefferson Ave
Street address state: GA
Postal code: 31024-1020
County: Putnam
Country: USA
Mailing address: 100 N Jefferson Ave
Mailing city: Eatonton
Mailing state: GA
Mailing zip: 31024-1020
Office phone: (706) 485-3501
Office fax: (706) 485-4166
General e-mail: msgr@msgr.com
Editorial e-mail: editor@msgr.com
Website: msgr@msgr.com
Year publication established: 1968
Advertising (open inch rate): Open inch rate $9.
Mechanical specifications: six columns- 13x21-column-1.8 inches
Delivery methods:
  Mail`Newsstand`Carrier`Racks
Zip Codes Served: 31024, 31061
Frequency: Thur
Circulation Paid: 5500
Audit By: USPS
Audit Date: 43009
Hardware: HP/ScanJet, HP/LaserJet 5p
Presses: !8 unit Urbanite- double out- 90% color pages
Software: Microsoft/Windows 6.1.
Edition Names with circulation: Total circulation 18,500
Personnel: Lynn Hobbs (Associate Editor); Mark Smith, Sr. (Pub)
Parent company: Smith Communications, Inc
Main (survey) contact: Mark Smith Jr.

GRIFFIN

TOWN & COUNTRY SHOPPER

Street Address1: 1422 Georgia Highway 16 W
Street address state: GA
Postal code: 30223-2054
County: Spalding
Country: USA
Mailing address: PO Box 278
Mailing city: Princeton
Mailing state: MN
Mailing zip: 55371-0278
Office phone: (770) 467-8888
Office fax: (763) 389-1728
General e-mail: pueproduction@ecm-inc.com
Website: pueproduction@ecm-inc.com
Year publication established: 1976
Advertising (open inch rate): Open inch rate $8.80
Mechanical specifications: Type page 9 9/16 x 15; E - 6 cols, 1 5/6, 1/4 between; A - 5 cols, 1 5/6, 1/4 between; C - 6 cols, 1 1/2, 1/4 between.
Zip Codes Served: 55371
Frequency: Sun
Circulation Free: 16611

Audit By: CVC
Audit Date: 41274
Hardware: APP/Mac
Software: QPS/QuarkXPress 3.32.
Personnel: Julian L. Andersen (Pub.); Timothy Enger (Adv. Mgr.)
Parent company: Adams Publishing Group, LLC
Main (survey) contact: Julian L. Andersen

HINESVILLE

BARROW COUNTY NEWS

Street Address1: 125 S Main St
Street address state: GA
Postal code: 31313-3217
County: Liberty
Country: USA
Mailing address: PO Box 498
Mailing city: Hinesville
Mailing state: GA
Mailing zip: 31310-0498
Office phone: (912) 876-0156
Office fax: (912) 368-6329
General e-mail: pleon@coastalcourier.com
Advertising e-mail: cwhite@coastalcourier.com
Editorial e-mail: detheridge@coastalcourier.com
Website: pleon@coastalcourier.com
Advertising (open inch rate): Open inch rate $8.60
Mechanical specifications: Type page 10 1/4 x 13; A - 6 cols, 1 9/16, 1/6 between.
Frequency: Wed
Circulation Free: 13000
Audit By: Sworn/Estimate/Non-Audited
Audit Date: 43585
Personnel: Denise Etheridge (Ed.); Cindy White (Adv. Mgr.)
Main (survey) contact: Denise Etheridge

TRI-COUNTY PENNYSAVER

Street Address1: 123 S Main St
Street address state: GA
Postal code: 31313-3217
County: Liberty
Country: USA
Mailing address: PO Box 498
Mailing city: Hinesville
Mailing state: GA
Mailing zip: 31310-0498
Office phone: (912) 876-0156
Office fax: (912) 368-6329
Advertising (open inch rate): Open inch rate $12.30
Mechanical specifications: Type page 10 1/4 x 13; E - 6 cols, 2, between; A - 6 cols, 2, between.
Zip Codes Served: 31313
Frequency: Wed
Circulation Free: 20872
Audit By: Sworn/Estimate/Non-Audited
Audit Date: 43658
Personnel: Marshall Griffin (Pub.); Kathryn Fox (Gen. Mgr.); Lillian McKnight (Adv. Rep.); Patrick Donahue (Exec. Ed.); Pat Watkins (Mng. Ed.); Leslie Miller (Prodn. Mgr.)
Parent company: Morris Multimedia, Inc.
Main (survey) contact: Marshall Griffin

LA FAYETTE

WALKER COUNTY PLUS

Street Address1: 102 N Main St
Street address state: GA
Postal code: 30728-2418
County: Walker
Country: USA
Mailing address: 102 North Main Street
Mailing city: La Fayette
Mailing state: GA
Mailing zip: 30728-0766
Office phone: (706) 638-1859
Office fax: (706) 638-7045
General e-mail: walkercountymessenger@walkermessenger.com
Website: walkercountymessenger@walkermessenger.com
Year publication established: 1877
Advertising (open inch rate): Open inch rate $7.49
Mechanical specifications: Type page 13 x 21 1/4; E - 6 cols, 2 1/16, 1/8 between; A - 6 cols, 2 1/16, 1/8 between; C - 9 cols, 1 3/8, 1/8 between.
Zip Codes Served: 30728, 30707, 30739, 30741
Frequency: Tues
Circulation Free: 15350
Audit By: Sworn/Estimate/Non-Audited
Audit Date: 43658
Presses: 8-G/Community.
Personnel: Don Stilwell (Pub.); Rebekah Rollins (Office Mgr./Classifieds/Legals); Alycia Edgeman (Adv. Rep.); Becky McDaniel (Ed.); Scott Herpst (Sports Ed.); Kristi Sellers (Editorial Asst.)
Parent company: Rome News-Tribune
Main (survey) contact: Don Stilwell

LAGRANGE

LA GRANGE SHOPPER

Street Address1: 105 Ashton St
Street address state: GA
Postal code: 30240-3111
County: Troup
Country: USA
Mailing address: PO Box 929
Mailing city: Lagrange
Mailing state: GA
Mailing zip: 30241-0117
Office phone: (706) 884-7311
Office fax: (706) 884-8712
Year publication established: 1983
Advertising (open inch rate): Open inch rate $11.75
Mechanical specifications: Type page 11 5/8 x 21 1/2; E - 6 cols, 1 5/6, between; A - 6 cols, 1 5/6, between; C - 9 cols, 1 5/24, between.
Zip Codes Served: 30230, 30217, 30222, 31822, 31833, 36274
Frequency: Wed
Circulation Free: 14800
Audit By: Sworn/Estimate/Non-Audited
Audit Date: 43658
Hardware: APP/Mac
Presses: G
Software: Baseview.
Personnel: Lynn McLamb (Pub.); Judy Phillips (Bus./Office Mgr.); Daniel Baker (Ed.)
Parent company: Boone Newsmedia, LLC
Main (survey) contact: Lynn McLamb

MARIETTA

THRIFTY NICKEL OF METRO ATLANTA LLC

Street Address1: 4757 Canton Road
Street Address2: Suite 110
Street address state: GA
Postal code: 30066-3246
County: Cobb
Country: United States
Mailing address: 4757 Canton Road STE 110
Mailing city: Marietta
Mailing state: GA
Mailing zip: 30066-3246
Office phone: (770) 971-8333
Office fax: (678) 648-1999
General e-mail: office@atlantathriftynickel.com
Advertising e-mail: brittanytnatl@gmail.com
Editorial e-mail: cheryltnatl@gmail.com
Website: office@atlantathriftynickel.com
Year publication established: 1983
Advertising (open inch rate): Open inch rate $15.00
Mechanical specifications: Eight (8) columns x 15.5" depth
Delivery methods:
  Mail`Newsstand`Carrier`Racks
Zip Codes Served: all south metro atlanta
Digital Platform - Mobile:
Apple`Android`Windows
Digital Platform - Tablet: Apple iOS`Android`Windows 7`Kindle`Nook`Kindle Fire
Frequency: Thur
Other Type of Frequency: Online Daily
Circulation Paid: 500
Circulation Free: 17134
Audit By: Sworn/Estimate/Non-Audited
Audit Date: 43658
Presses: Offset Newspaper
Software: InDesign
Editions Count: 52
Personnel: Cheryl Baker (Publisher); Andy Baker (Sales Mgr.); Brandon Ballew (Prod.); Brittany Miles (Adv. Sales)
Main (survey) contact: Cheryl Baker

SAVANNAH

SAVANNAH PENNYSAVER

Street Address1: 1464 E Victory Dr
Street address state: GA
Postal code: 31404-4108
County: Chatham
Country: USA
Mailing address: 1464 E Victory Dr
Mailing city: Savannah
Mailing state: GA
Mailing zip: 31404-4195
Office phone: (912) 238-2040
Advertising fax: (912) 944-0010
General e-mail: classifieds@savpennysaver.com
Advertising e-mail: wleach@savpennysaver.com
Editorial e-mail: circulation@savpennysaver.com
Website: classifieds@savpennysaver.com
Advertising (open inch rate): Open inch rate $19.51
Mechanical specifications: Type page 10 1/4 x 13; E - 6 cols, 1 5/8, 1/8 between; A - 6 cols, 1 5/8, 1/8 between.
Zip Codes Served: 31401, 31404, 31405, 31406, 31407, 31408, 31410, 31411, 31412, 31419, 31302, 31322, 31324, 31326, 31328
Frequency: Wed
Circulation Free: 65411
Audit By: AAM
Audit Date: 43465
Hardware: APP/Mac
Presses: 12-G
Software: QPS/QuarkXPress 3.31.
Editions Count: 3
Personnel: Av Rocker (Pub.); Wayne Leach (Adv. Mgr.); Robert Foy (Circ. Mgr.); Joe McGlamery (Contact)
Parent company: Morris Multimedia, Inc.
Main (survey) contact: Joe McGlamery; Wayne Leach

THOMSON

DOLLAR SAVER

Street Address1: 101 Church St
Street address state: GA
Postal code: 30824-2613
County: McDuffie
Country: USA
Mailing address: PO Box 1090
Mailing city: Thomson
Mailing state: GA
Mailing zip: 30824-1090
Office phone: (706) 595-1601
Office fax: (706) 597-8974
General e-mail: composing@mcduffieprogress.com
Editorial e-mail: classifieds@mcduffieprogress.com
Website: composing@mcduffieprogress.com
Advertising (open inch rate): Open inch rate $9.00
Zip Codes Served: 30824
Frequency: Wed
Circulation Free: 15000
Audit By: Sworn/Estimate/Non-Audited
Audit Date: 43658
Hardware: APP/Mac

Presses: 10-KP
Software: QPS/QuarkXPress, Baseview.
Personnel: Dick Mitchell (Pub); Tim Phillips (Adv. Mgr.); Justin Schuver (Ed.)
Main (survey) contact: Wayne Parham

TIFTON

TIFTON SHOPPER

Street Address1: 211 Tift Ave N
Street address state: GA
Postal code: 31794-4463
County: Tift
Country: USA
Mailing address: PO Box 708
Mailing city: Tifton
Mailing state: GA
Mailing zip: 31793-0708
Office phone: (229) 382-4321
Office fax: (229) 387-7322
Advertising (open inch rate): Open inch rate $6.85
Mechanical specifications: Type page 6 x 13; E - 6 cols, 1 9/16, 1/6 between; A - 6 cols, 1 9/16, 1/6 between; C - 6 cols, 1 9/16, 1/6 between.
Zip Codes Served: 31620
Frequency: Tues
Circulation Free: 15661
Audit By: Sworn/Estimate/Non-Audited
Audit Date: 43658
Hardware: APP/Mac LC III, APP/Mac Quadra 650, APP/Mac 8500
Software: Custom Hypercard, Claris/Macdraw Pro, Adobe/PageMaker, Multi-Ad/Creator, Adobe/Illustrator, Adobe/Photoshop.
Personnel: Frank Sayles (Pub.); Lisa Beckham (Adv. Mgr.); Rachel Wainwright (Circ. Mgr.); Flo Rankin (Mng. Ed.); Kyle Dean (Sports Ed.)
Main (survey) contact: Dan Sutton

VIDALIA

ADVANTAGE

Street Address1: 205 First St
Street address state: GA
Postal code: 30474
County: Toombs
Country: USA
Mailing address: PO Box 669
Mailing city: Vidalia
Mailing state: GA
Mailing zip: 30474
Office phone: (912) 537-3131
Office fax: (912) 537-4899
General e-mail: theadvancenews@gmail.com
Website: theadvancenews@gmail.com
Advertising (open inch rate): Open inch rate $7.50
Zip Codes Served: 30474
Frequency: Mon
Circulation Free: 23000
Audit By: Sworn/Estimate/Non-Audited
Audit Date: 43585
Personnel: William F. Ledford (Ed.); Daniel Ford (Adv. Mgr.)
Parent company: Advance Publications, Inc.
Main (survey) contact: William F. Ledford

WARNER ROBINS

WARNER ROBINS BUYERS GUIDE

Street Address1: 1553 Watson Blvd
Street address state: GA
Postal code: 31093-3449
County: Houston
Country: USA
Mailing address: 1553 Watson Blvd
Mailing city: Warner Robins
Mailing state: GA
Mailing zip: 31093-3449
Office phone: (478) 744-4200
Office fax: (478) 329-1591
Advertising (open inch rate): Open inch rate $9.75

Mechanical specifications: Type page 10 1/2 x 16; E - 6 cols, 1 9/16, between; A - 6 cols, 1 9/16, between; C - 6 cols, 1 9/16, between.
Zip Codes Served: 31088
Frequency: Wed
Circulation Free: 24325
Audit By: Sworn/Estimate/Non-Audited
Audit Date: 43658
Hardware: APP/Mac
Presses: G/Rockwell, 8-G/Community
Software: Macromedia/Freehand, QPS/QuarkXPress, Adobe/Illustrator.
Personnel: T.J. Browning (Pub.); David Cranshaw (Ed.)
Main (survey) contact: T.J. Browning

WAYCROSS

WAYCROSS SHOPPER

Street Address1: 540 Plant Ave
Street address state: GA
Postal code: 31501-3510
County: Ware
Country: USA
Mailing address: PO Box 1304
Mailing city: Waycross
Mailing state: GA
Mailing zip: 31502-1304
Office phone: (912) 285-8539
Office fax: (912) 283-5231
General e-mail: info@thewaycrossshopper.com
Website: info@thewaycrossshopper.com
Year publication established: 1981
Advertising (open inch rate): Open inch rate $8.00
Mechanical specifications: Type page 10.25" x 14"; 6 cols
Delivery methods: Racks
Zip Codes Served: 31501, 31502, 31503, 31516, 31542, 31550, 31552, 31553, 31557
Frequency: Tues
Circulation Free: 28268
Audit By: CVC
Audit Date: 42643
Hardware: APP/Mac
Presses: 5-G
Software: Multi-Ad/Creator.
Personnel: Al Joiner (Pub.); Louise Carter (Adv.); Lori McGill (Circ.)
Main (survey) contact: Al Joiner

WINDER

BARROW NEWS-JOURNAL

Street Address1: 120 West Athens Street
Street Address2: Suite A
Street address state: GA
Postal code: 30680-1951
County: Barrow
Country: USA
Mailing address: PO Box 908
Mailing city: Jefferson
Mailing state: GA
Mailing zip: 30549
Office phone: (770) 867-6397
Office fax: (706) 367-8056
Advertising phone: (706) 367-5233
Advertising fax: (706) 621-4118
Editorial phone: (706) 367-5233
Editorial fax: (706) 367-8056
General e-mail: ads@mainstreetnews.com
Advertising e-mail: scott@mainstreetnews.com
Editorial e-mail: mike@mainstreetnews.com
Website: ads@mainstreetnews.com
Year publication established: 1893
Advertising (open inch rate): Open inch rate $7.00
Mechanical specifications: 6 column broadsheet format (ROP, Legal and Classified Pages)
1 column..................1.5625 inches 2
columns..................3.25 inches 3
columns..................4.9375 inches 4
columns..................6.625 inches
5columns..................8.3125 inches
6 columns..................10.0 inches Full column depth is 21 inches
Delivery methods: Mail Newsstand Racks
Zip Codes Served: 30680, 30011, 30666, 30620

Digital Platform - Mobile: Apple Android
Digital Platform - Tablet: Apple iOS Android
Frequency: Wed
Circulation Paid: 4500
Circulation Free: 0
Audit By: Sworn/Estimate/Non-Audited
Audit Date: 43658
Hardware: Mac
Presses: Goss Community
Software: Adobe Creative Suite
Personnel: Scott Buffington (Co-Pub); Mike Buffington (Co-Publisher)
Parent company: MainStreet Newspapers, Inc.
Main (survey) contact: Scott Buffington

IOWA

ALGONA

THE REMINDER

Street Address1: 14 E Nebraska St
Street address state: IA
Postal code: 50511-2630
County: Kossuth
Country: USA
Mailing address: 14 E Nebraska St
Mailing city: Algona
Mailing state: IA
Mailing zip: 50511-2630
Frequency: Tues
Circulation Free: 13300
Audit By: CVC
Audit Date: 42368
Personnel: Kate Thompson
Main (survey) contact: Kurt Dahl

AMES

STORY COUNTY ADVERTISER

Street Address1: 317 5th St
Street address state: IA
Postal code: 50010-6101
County: Story
Country: USA
Mailing address: PO Box 380
Mailing city: Ames
Mailing state: IA
Mailing zip: 50010-0380
Office phone: (515) 232-2160
Office fax: (515) 232-2364
General e-mail: results@amesadvertiser.com; news@amestrib.com
Editorial e-mail: letters@amestrib.com
Website: results@amesadvertiser.com; news@amestrib.com
Advertising (open inch rate): Open inch rate $19.41
Mechanical specifications: Type page 10 1/2 x 13; E - 8 cols, 1 3/8, between; A - 8 cols, 1 3/8, between; C - 8 cols, 1 3/8, between.
Zip Codes Served: 50010, 50014
Frequency: Wed
Circulation Free: 23558
Audit By: CVC
Audit Date: 38717
Hardware: APP/Macs
Presses: 4-G/Urbanite
Software: QPS/QuarkXPress.
Personnel: John Goossen (Pub.); John Greving (Dir., Adv.); Dan Cronin (Dir., Circ.); Don Roof (Dir., Prodn.)
Parent company: Iowa Newspapers, Inc.
Main (survey) contact: Michael Crumb

ANAMOSA

JOURNAL-EUREKA AND TOWN CRIER

Street Address1: 405 E Main St
Street Address2: P.O. Box 108
Street address state: IA

Postal code: 52205-1866
County: Jones
Country: USA
Mailing address: PO Box 108
Mailing city: Anamosa
Mailing state: IA
Mailing zip: 52205-0108
Office phone: (319) 462-3511
Office fax: (319) 462-4540
General e-mail: Admin@AnamosaJE.com
Advertising e-mail: Advertising@anamosaje.com
Editorial e-mail: Editorial@anamosaje.com
Website: Admin@AnamosaJE.com
Year publication established: 1855
Advertising (open inch rate): Open inch rate $10
Mechanical specifications: Type page 6 x 21; E - 6 cols, 1.5 inches, 1 pica between; A - 6 cols, 1.5 inches, 1 pica between.
Delivery methods: Mail
Zip Codes Served: 52205, 52212, 52214, 52252, 52305, 52306, 52310, 52312, 52320, 52321, 52323, 52219, 52336, 52362,
Frequency: Tues Thur
Circulation Paid: 2150
Circulation Free: 11218
Audit By: Sworn/Estimate/Non-Audited
Audit Date: 43658
Hardware: APP/Mac.
Software: Word, Adobe Creative Suite
Personnel: W. James Johnson (Publisher)
Parent company: Anamosa Publications

ATLANTIC

SOUTHWEST IOWA SHOPPER

Street Address1: PO Box 230
Street address state: IA
Postal code: 50022-0230
County: Cass
Country: USA
Mailing address: PO Box 230
Mailing city: Atlantic
Mailing state: IA
Mailing zip: 50022-0230
Frequency: Tues
Circulation Free: 13374
Audit By: CVC
Audit Date: 40878
Personnel: Connie Collins
Main (survey) contact: Jeff Lundquist

AUBURN

TRI-COUNTY SPECIAL

Street Address1: PO Box 106
Street address state: IA
Postal code: 51433-0106
County: Sac
Country: USA
Mailing address: P.O. Box 106
Mailing city: Auburn
Mailing state: IA
Mailing zip: 50579
Frequency: Wed
Circulation Free: 8132
Audit By: CVC
Audit Date: 41090
Personnel: Gary D. Dudley
Main (survey) contact: Gary D. Dudley

BELMOND

REMINDER

Street Address1: PO Box 263
Street address state: IA
Postal code: 50421-0263
County: Wright
Country: USA
Mailing address: PO Box 263
Mailing city: Belmond
Mailing state: IA
Mailing zip: 50421-0263
Advertising (open inch rate): Open inch rate $7.30
Frequency: Wed
Circulation Free: 9413

Shopper Publications in the U.S.

III-615

Audit By: CVC
Audit Date: 42003
Personnel: JONI WORDEN
Main (survey) contact: JONI WORDEN

BLOOMFIELD

TRI-COUNTY SHOPPER

Street Address1: PO Box 168
Street address state: IA
Postal code: 52537-0168
County: Davis
Country: USA
Mailing address: PO Box 168
Mailing city: Bloomfield
Mailing state: IA
Mailing zip: 52537-0168
Advertising (open inch rate): Open inch rate $8.00
Frequency: Wed
Circulation Paid: 0
Circulation Free: 11746
Audit By: CVC
Audit Date: 41729
Personnel: Jeri Lyn Rupe
Main (survey) contact: Jeri Rupe

BOONE

BOONE COUNTY SHOPPING NEWS

Street Address1: 2136 Mamie Eisenhower Ave
Street Address2: 2136 Mamie Eisenhower Ave
Street address state: IA
Postal code: 50036-4437
County: Boone
Country: USA
Mailing address: 2136 Mamie Eisenhower Ave
Mailing city: Boone
Mailing state: IA
Mailing zip: 50036-4437
Office phone: (515) 432-6694
General e-mail: results@newsrepublican.com
Advertising e-mail: mscott@amestrib.com
Editorial e-mail: lkahler@newsrepublican.com
Website: results@newsrepublican.com
Frequency: Wed
Circulation Free: 11318
Audit By: Sworn/Estimate/Non-Audited
Audit Date: 43585
Personnel: Logan Kahler (Ed.); Mary Beth Scott (Sales Mgr.); Randy Terwilliger (Circ. Dir.)
Parent company: Gatehouse Media, LLC
Main (survey) contact: Logan Kahler

BURLINGTON

HAWK EYE SHOPPER

Street Address1: 800 S Main St
Street address state: IA
Postal code: 52601-5870
County: Des Moines
Country: USA
Mailing address: PO Box 10
Mailing city: Burlington
Mailing state: IA
Mailing zip: 52601-0010
Office phone: (319) 754-8461
Office fax: (319) 754-6824
General e-mail: circulation@thehawkeye.com
Advertising e-mail: slewis@thehawkeye.com
Editorial e-mail: jgaines@thehawkeye.com
Website: circulation@thehawkeye.com
Advertising (open inch rate): Open inch rate $4.65
Mechanical specifications: Type page 10 3/4 x 13 1/2, A - 5 cols, 1/8 between; C - 5 cols, 1/8 between.
Zip Codes Served: 52601
Frequency: Tues
Circulation Paid: 14457
Audit By: VAC
Audit Date: 43008
Hardware: APP/Macs
Presses: G/Urbanite.
Personnel: John Gaines (Mng. Ed.); Sean Lewis (GM/ Adv. Dir.)
Main (survey) contact: John Gaines

CARROLL

CARROLL TODAY

Street Address1: PO Box 593
Street address state: IA
Postal code: 51401-0593
County: Carroll
Country: USA
Mailing address: PO Box 593
Mailing city: Carroll
Mailing state: IA
Mailing zip: 51401-0593
Office phone: (712) 792-2179
Office fax: (712) 792-2309
General e-mail: ldndesign@thewebunwired.com
Website: ldndesign@thewebunwired.com
Advertising (open inch rate): Open inch rate $4.95
Delivery methods: Mail
Frequency: Tues
Circulation Free: 19000
Audit By: Sworn/Estimate/Non-Audited
Audit Date: 43658
Personnel: Lucas Knowles (Pub.)
Main (survey) contact: Luke Knowles

SMART SHOPPER

Street Address1: 220 W 7th St
Street address state: IA
Postal code: 51401-2317
County: Carroll
Country: USA
Mailing address: PO Box 910
Mailing city: Carroll
Mailing state: IA
Mailing zip: 51401-0593
Office phone: (712) 792-2179
Office fax: (712) 792-2309
Advertising (open inch rate): Open inch rate $6.00
Frequency: Tues
Circulation Free: 13701
Audit By: CVC
Audit Date: 42368
Personnel: Lucas Knowles (Pub.)
Main (survey) contact: Lucas Knowles

TIMES HERALD ADVERTISER

Street Address1: 508 N Court St
Street address state: IA
Postal code: 51401-2747
County: Carroll
Country: USA
Mailing address: PO Box 546
Mailing city: Carroll
Mailing state: IA
Mailing zip: 51401-0546
Office phone: (712) 792-3573
Office fax: (712) 792-5218
General e-mail: general@carrollspaper.com
Editorial e-mail: newspaper@carrollspaper.com
Website: general@carrollspaper.com
Advertising (open inch rate): Open inch rate $8.00
Mechanical specifications: Type page 12 15/16 x 21; E - 8 cols, 1 1/2, 1/6 between; A - 8 cols, 1 1/2, 1/6 between; C - 8 cols, 1 1/2, 1/6 between.
Zip Codes Served: 51401
Frequency: Tues
Circulation Free: 23700
Audit By: Sworn/Estimate/Non-Audited
Audit Date: 43658
Personnel: James Wilson (Pub.); Ann Wilson (Gen. Mgr.); Tom Burns (Adv. Mgr.); Daniel Haberl (Circ. Mgr.); Beckham Miller (Prodn. Mgr.)
Main (survey) contact: Luke Knowles

CEDAR RAPIDS

PENNY SAVER

Street Address1: 500 3rd Ave SE
Street address state: IA
Postal code: 52401-1608
County: Linn
Country: USA
Mailing address: 500 3rd Ave SE
Mailing city: Cedar Rapids
Mailing state: IA
Mailing zip: 52401-1608
Office phone: (319) 398-8222
Office fax: (319) 398-5848
Advertising (open inch rate): Open inch rate $20.00
Mechanical specifications: Type page 9 1/4 x 11 5/8; E - 5 cols, 1 11/16, 1/8 between; A - 5 cols, 1 11/16, 1/8 between; C - 7 cols, 1 1/4, 1/8 between.
Zip Codes Served: 52401
Frequency: Wed
Circulation Free: 82659
Audit By: CVC
Audit Date: 38717
Hardware: APP/Mac
Presses: G/Community.
Personnel: Chris Edwards (Adv.Dir); Audrey Wheeler (Prodn. Mgr.)
Main (survey) contact: Chris Edwards

TIDBITS OF LINN COUNTY

Street Address1: 5001 1st Ave SE
Street Address2: Ste 105 PMB 162
Street address state: IA
Postal code: 52402-3251
County: Linn
Country: USA
Mailing address: 5001 1st Ave. SE
Mailing city: Cedar Rapids
Mailing state: IA
Mailing zip: 52402-3229
Office phone: (319) 360-3936
General e-mail: russ@tidbitpapers.com
Website: russ@tidbitpapers.com
Year publication established: 2005
Advertising (open inch rate): $150 (smallest modular rate)
Delivery methods: Mail`Racks
Frequency: Tues
Circulation Free: 12980
Audit By: CVC
Audit Date: 42368
Personnel: Russ Swart
Main (survey) contact: Russ Swart

CENTERVILLE

AD EXPRESS

Street Address1: 201 N 13th St
Street address state: IA
Postal code: 52544-1748
County: Appanoose
Country: USA
Mailing address: PO Box 610
Mailing city: Centerville
Mailing state: IA
Mailing zip: 52544-0610
Office phone: (641) 856-6336
Office fax: (641) 856-8118
General e-mail: sellis@dailyiowegian.com
Advertising e-mail: bmaxwell@dailyiowegian.com
Editorial e-mail: newsroom@dailyiowegian.com
Website: sellis@dailyiowegian.com
Advertising (open inch rate): Open inch rate $8.00
Mechanical specifications: Type page 13 x 21 1/2; E - 6 cols, between; A - 6 cols, between; C - 6 cols, between.
Zip Codes Served: 52544
Frequency: Wed
Circulation Paid: 580
Circulation Free: 11343

Audit By: Sworn/Estimate/Non-Audited
Audit Date: 43601
Hardware: APP/Mac
Presses: G/Community.
Personnel: Kyle Ocker (Ed.); Becky Maxwell (Pub.); Tina Long (Adv. Ex.); Sandy Ellis (Circ. Dir.)
Parent company: Community Newspaper Holdings, Inc.
Main (survey) contact: Kyle Ocker

CHARITON

CHARITON SHOPPER'S GUIDE

Street Address1: 815 Braden Ave
Street address state: IA
Postal code: 50049-1742
County: Lucas
Country: USA
Mailing address: PO Box 651
Mailing city: Chariton
Mailing state: IA
Mailing zip: 50049-0651
Office phone: (641) 774-2137
Office fax: (641) 774-2139
General e-mail: charnews@charitonleader.com
Website: charnews@charitonleader.com
Advertising (open inch rate): Open inch rate $7.20
Frequency: Tues`Thur
Circulation Free: 4000
Audit By: Sworn/Estimate/Non-Audited
Audit Date: 43658
Personnel: David A. Paxton (Ed.)
Main (survey) contact: David A. Paxton

CHARLES CITY

NORTHEAST IOWA SHOPPER

Street Address1: 801 Riverside Dr
Street address state: IA
Postal code: 50616-2248
County: Floyd
Country: USA
Mailing address: 801 Riverside Dr
Mailing city: Charles City
Mailing state: IA
Mailing zip: 50616-0397
Office phone: (641) 228-3211
Office fax: (641) 228-2641
Advertising e-mail: joelg@charlescitypress.com
Editorial e-mail: editor@charlescitypress.com
Year publication established: 1963
Advertising (open inch rate): Open inch rate $17.63
Delivery methods: Mail`Newsstand`Carrier`Racks
Zip Codes Served: 50616, 50435, 50471, 50468, 50653, 50658, 50636, 50619, 50628, 50461, 50466, 50460, 50603, 50645, 50659
Frequency: Tues
Circulation Free: 16306
Audit By: CVC
Audit Date: 42368
Hardware: APP/Mac
Presses: 13-G/Community
Software: QPS/QuarkXPress, Multi-Ad.
Personnel: Christopher Hall Hall (Pub.); Joel Gray (Adv. Mgr.)
Parent company: Enterprise Media Inc
Main (survey) contact: Christopher Hall

THE EXTRA

Street Address1: 801 Riverside Dr
Street address state: IA
Postal code: 50616-2248
County: Floyd
Country: USA
Mailing address: PO Box 28
Mailing city: Rock Rapids
Mailing state: IA
Mailing zip: 51246
Office phone: (641) 228-3211
Office fax: (641) 228-2641

Advertising e-mail: ads@charlescitypress.com
Advertising (open inch rate): Open inch rate $8.95
Frequency: Thur
Circulation Free: 2264
Audit By: CVC
Audit Date: 41728
Personnel: Gene Hall (Pub.); Joel Gray (Gen. Mgr.); Lisa Miller (Pub.); Lois Kuehl (Adv. Mgr); Tasha Lange (Circ. Mgr)
Parent company: The Hays Daily News
Main (survey) contact: Gene Hall

CHEROKEE

AREA ADVERTISER

Street Address1: 111 S 2nd St
Street address state: IA
Postal code: 51012-1839
County: Cherokee
Country: USA
Mailing address: 111 South 2nd St.
Mailing city: Cherokee
Mailing state: IA
Mailing zip: 51012-1084
Office phone: (712) 225-5111
Office fax: (712) 225-2910
General e-mail: editor@ctimes.biz
Website: editor@ctimes.biz
Advertising (open inch rate): Open inch rate $10.50
Zip Codes Served: 51012
Frequency: Tues
Circulation Free: 10000
Audit By: Sworn/Estimate/Non-Audited
Audit Date: 43658
Personnel: Paul Struck (Pub.); Troy Valentine (Adv. Mgr.); Patrice Martin (Circ. Mgr.); Ken Ross (Mng. Ed.)
Main (survey) contact: Ken Ross

CRESCO

CRESCO SHOPPER

Street Address1: 116 2nd Ave SE
Street address state: IA
Postal code: 52136-1838
County: Howard
Country: USA
Mailing address: PO Box 117
Mailing city: Cresco
Mailing state: IA
Mailing zip: 52136-0117
Office phone: (563) 547-2025
Office fax: (563) 547-3831
Advertising phone: (563) 547-2025
General e-mail: shopper@iowatelecom.net
Advertising e-mail: shopper1@iowatelecom.net
Website: shopper@iowatelecom.net
Year publication established: 1965
Advertising (open inch rate): Open inch rate $9.00
Delivery methods: Mail
Zip Codes Served: 50455, 50466, 50603, 50628, 50659, 50661, 52101, 52130, 52131, 52132, 52134, 52136, 52144, 52150, 52154, 52155, 52163, 52165, 52171, 55939, 55951, 55965, 55977
Digital Platform - Mobile: Apple
Frequency: Tues
Circulation Free: 13551
Audit By: Sworn/Estimate/Non-Audited
Audit Date: 43658
Hardware: Apple G-4's & G-5's
Presses: 2-KP/News King
Software: Adobe/PageMaker & Adobe Creative Suite/InDesign
Personnel: Peggy Loveless (Adv. Mgr./Co-Owner); John Loveless (Ed.)
Main (survey) contact: John Loveless

CRESTON

SOUTHWEST IOWA ADVERTISER

Street Address1: 503 W Adams St
Street address state: IA
Postal code: 50801-3112
County: Union
Country: USA
Mailing address: PO Box 126
Mailing city: Creston
Mailing state: IA
Mailing zip: 50801-0126
Office phone: (641) 782-2141
Office fax: (641) 782-6628
General e-mail: publisher@crestonnews.com; office@crestonnews.com; news@crestonnews.com
Website: publisher@crestonnews.com; office@crestonnews.com; news@crestonnews.com
Advertising (open inch rate): Open inch rate $11.63
Mechanical specifications: Type page 13 x 21 1/2; A - 6 cols, 2, 1/6 between; C - 9 cols, 1 5/16, 1/6 between.
Zip Codes Served: 50801
Frequency: Wed
Circulation Free: 8195
Audit By: CVC
Audit Date: 42368
Hardware: APP/Mac
Presses: 7-G/Community
Software: QPS/QuarkXPress.
Personnel: Rich Paulsen (Pub.); Craig Mittag (Adv.Mgr.); Ron Bernard (Circ. Mgr.); Stephani Finley (Mng. Ed) Kevin Lindley (Prodn. Mgr.)
Parent company: Shaw Media
Main (survey) contact: Rich Paulsen

DAVENPORT

THRIFTY NICKEL

Street Address1: 500 E 3rd St
Street address state: IA
Postal code: 52801-1708
County: Scott
Country: USA
Mailing address: 500 E 3rd St
Mailing city: Davenport
Mailing state: IA
Mailing zip: 52801-1708
Office phone: (563) 333-2601
Office fax: (563) 333-2666
General e-mail: qcnickel@qcthriftynickel.com
Website: qcnickel@qcthriftynickel.com
Year publication established: 1982
Advertising (open inch rate): Open inch rate $17.00
Mechanical specifications: Type page 10 1/4 x 16; A - 7 cols, 1 1/3, 1/6 between; C - 7 cols, 1 1/3, 1/6 between.
Zip Codes Served: 61244, 61265, 61282, 61201, 61264
Frequency: Thur
Circulation Free: 7521
Audit By: CVC
Audit Date: 42277
Hardware: APP/Power Mac, Umax/Scanners, HP/4MV Printer
Software: QPS/QuarkXPress 3.32, Adobe/Photoshop 4.0, Adobe/Illustrator, Multi-Ad/CAMS 3.32.
Personnel: Karla Pinner (Pub.)
Main (survey) contact: Karla Pinner

DENISON

CRAWFORD COUNTY ADVISOR

Street Address1: 1410 Broadway
Street address state: IA
Postal code: 51442-2053
County: Crawford
Country: USA
Mailing address: 1410 Broadway
Mailing city: Denison
Mailing state: IA
Mailing zip: 51442-2053
General e-mail: greg.wehle@bulletinreview.com
Advertising e-mail: greg.wehle@bulletinreview.com
Website: greg.wehle@bulletinreview.com
Year publication established: 1934
Advertising (open inch rate): Open inch rate $7.75
Mechanical specifications: Type page 10.25" x 21.5"; 6 cols
Delivery methods: Mail`Racks
Frequency: Wed
Circulation Free: 10807
Audit By: CVC
Audit Date: 42368
Personnel: Greg Wehle
Main (survey) contact: Greg Wehle

DUBUQUE

DUBUQUE ADVERTISER

Street Address1: 2966 John F Kennedy Rd
Street address state: IA
Postal code: 52002-1049
County: Dubuque
Country: USA
Mailing address: 2966 John F Kennedy Rd
Mailing city: Dubuque
Mailing state: IA
Mailing zip: 52002-1049
Frequency: Wed
Circulation Free: 36109
Audit By: Sworn/Estimate/Non-Audited
Audit Date: 43658
Personnel: Randall Aird; Greg Birkett (President)
Main (survey) contact: Randall Aird

DYERSVILLE

EASTERN IOWA SHOPPING NEWS

Street Address1: 223 1st Ave E
Street address state: IA
Postal code: 52040-1202
County: Dubuque
Country: USA
Mailing address: 223 1st Ave E
Mailing city: Dyersville
Mailing state: IA
Mailing zip: 52040-1202
Office phone: (563) 875-7131
Office fax: (563) 875-2279
General e-mail: easternshopnews@wcinet.com
Website: easternshopnews@wcinet.com
Year publication established: 1978
Advertising (open inch rate): 12,5
Mechanical specifications:
Delivery methods: Mail
Zip Codes Served:
Frequency: Tues
Circulation Paid: 43
Circulation Free: 20137
Audit By: CVC
Audit Date: 43080
Hardware:
Personnel: Mary Ungs-Sogaard (Pub/Gen Mgr); Beth Lutgen (Managing Editor); Kari Voss (Director of Prepress Production)
Parent company: Woodward Communications, Inc.
Main (survey) contact: Jacque Engling

EAGLE GROVE

WRIGHT COUNTY SHOPPER'S GUIDE

Street Address1: PO Box 6
Street address state: IA
Postal code: 50533-0006
County: Wright
Country: USA
Mailing address: PO Box 6
Mailing city: Eagle Grove
Mailing state: IA
Mailing zip: 50533-0006
Office phone: (515) 448-4745
Office fax: (515) 448-3182
General e-mail: egeagle@goldfieldaccess.net
Website: egeagle@goldfieldaccess.net
Advertising (open inch rate): Open inch rate $4.80
Mechanical specifications: Type page 14 x 21; E - 6 cols, 2 1/8, 1/6 between; A - 6 cols, 2 1/8, 1/6 between.
Zip Codes Served: 50533
Frequency: Wed
Circulation Free: 2800
Audit By: Sworn/Estimate/Non-Audited
Audit Date: 43658
Hardware: APP/Mac.
Software: Microsoft/Word, Adobe/PageMaker, QPS/QuarkXPress, Adobe/Photoshop.
Personnel: Ryan Harvey (Pub.); Leigh Banwell (Adv. Mgr.); Regina Lesher (Circ. Mgr.); Kim Demory (Ed.)
Main (survey) contact: Ryan Harvey; Ryan Harvey

ELDRIDGE

EASTERN IOWA BIZZZY BEE

Street Address1: 214 N 2nd St
Street address state: IA
Postal code: 52748-1208
County: Scott
Country: USA
Mailing address: PO Box 200
Mailing city: Eldridge
Mailing state: IA
Mailing zip: 52748-0200
Office phone: (563) 285-8111
Office fax: (563) 285-8114
Advertising phone: (563) 285-8111
Editorial phone: (563) 285-8111
General e-mail: btubbs@northscottpress.com
Advertising e-mail: jmartens@northscottpress.com
Website: btubbs@northscottpress.com
Year publication established: 1968
Advertising (open inch rate): Open inch rate $11.00
Mechanical specifications: Type page 10 3/8 x 16; E - 4 cols, 2 1/2, between; A - 4 cols, 2 1/2, between; C - 6 cols, 1 3/4, between.
Delivery methods: Mail`Racks
Zip Codes Served: Scott, Clinton, Jackson, Jones and Cedar counties.
Digital Platform - Mobile: Apple
Frequency: Wed
Circulation Paid: 18000
Audit By: Sworn/Estimate/Non-Audited
Audit Date: 43658
Hardware: APP/Mac
Software: Adobe/InDesign Photoshop Microsoft World
Note: The Eastern Iowa Bizzzy Bee is a common section with five newspapers: Eldridge North Scott Press, DeWitt Observer, Maquoketa Sentinel-Press, Anamosa Journal, Tipton Conservative.
Personnel: William F. Tubbs (Pub); Scott Campbell (Mng. Ed.); Jeff Martens (Advertising Mgr)
Parent company: North Scott Press, Inc.
Main (survey) contact: William F. Tubbs

FOREST CITY

THE WINNEBAGO

Street Address1: PO Box 350
Street address state: IA
Postal code: 50436-0350
County: Winnebago
Country: USA
Mailing address: PO Box 350
Mailing city: Forest City
Mailing state: IA
Mailing zip: 50436-0350
Frequency: Tues
Circulation Free: 9794
Audit By: Sworn/Estimate/Non-Audited
Audit Date: 43658
Personnel: Howard Query
Main (survey) contact: Howard Query

FORT DODGE

CONSUMER NEWS

Street Address1: 713 Central Ave
Street address state: IA
Postal code: 50501-3813

Shopper Publications in the U.S.

County: Webster
Country: USA
Office phone: (515) 576-6721
Office fax: (515) 573-2136
General e-mail: cnews@fdconsumernews.com
Website: cnews@fdconsumernews.com
Year publication established: 1970
Advertising (open inch rate): Open inch rate $13.05
Mechanical specifications: Type page 10 3/8 x 10.5; E - 6 cols, 1 5/8, 1/8 between; A - 6 cols, 1 5/8, 1/8 between; C - 6 cols, 1 5/8, 1/8 between.
Delivery methods: Mail`Carrier`Racks
Zip Codes Served: 50501, 50516,50040, 50132, 5021, 50246, 50249, 50518, 50523, 50524, 50530, 50532, 50543, 50544, 5055, 50566, 50569, 50594, 50548, 50529
Frequency: Wed
Circulation Free: 17503
Audit By: CVC
Audit Date: 42368
Hardware: APP/Mac G4
Presses: Offset
Software: Multi-Ad/Creator 4.0.4.
Editions Count: 1
Edition Names with circulation: Consumer News (17,750;
Personnel: Charlene Peterson (Adv. Mgr.)
Parent company: Ogden Newspapers Inc.
Main (survey) contact: Charlene Peterson

MESSENGER EXTRA

Street Address1: 713 Central Ave
Street address state: IA
Postal code: 50501-3813
County: Webster
Country: USA
Mailing address: PO Box 659
Mailing city: Fort Dodge
Mailing state: IA
Mailing zip: 50501-0659
Office phone: (515) 573-2141
Office fax: (515) 573-2148
Advertising phone: (515) 573-2141 ext. 416
Editorial phone: (515) 573-2141 ext 465
Advertising e-mail: cbargfrede@messengernews.net
Editorial e-mail: jcurtis@messengernews.net
Year publication established: 1856
Advertising (open inch rate): 14,7
Mechanical specifications: Type page 11 x 21 1/2; E - 6 cols, 1 3/4, 1/16 between; A - 6 cols, 1 3/4, 1/16 between; C - 9 cols, 1 1/4, 1/16 between.
Delivery methods: Mail`Carrier
Zip Codes Served: 50501, 50518, 50524, 50533, 50557, 50569, 50574
Frequency: Wed
Circulation Free: 15065
Audit By: Sworn/Estimate/Non-Audited
Audit Date: 43658
Hardware: HP LaserJet 5500n Printer, HP 5550n Printer, Epson V330 Scanner
Presses: 14-G, Press Drive - 2 Fin/100 hp
Software: Multi-Ad/Creator 8, Adobe
Personnel: Terry Christensen (Pub.); Melissa Wendland (Office Mgr.); Cory Bargfrede (Adv. Mgr.); Grant Gibbons (Circ. Mgr.); Bill Shea (City Ed)
Parent company: The Nutting Company, Inc.
Main (survey) contact: Melissa Wendland

GRINNELL

GRINNELL PENNYSAVER

Street Address1: 925 Broad St
Street address state: IA
Postal code: 50112-2047
County: Poweshiek
Country: USA
Mailing address: 925 Broad St
Mailing city: Grinnell
Mailing state: IA
Mailing zip: 50112-2047
Office phone: (515) 284-8000

Advertising (open inch rate): Open inch rate $11.0
Mechanical specifications: Type page 10 1/4 x 14; A - 6 cols, 1 1/2, 1/16 between; C - 6 cols, 1 1/2, 1/16 between.
Zip Codes Served: 50112
Frequency: Wed
Circulation Free: 14635
Audit By: Sworn/Estimate/Non-Audited
Audit Date: 43609
Hardware: APP/Mac.
Personnel: Carol Hunter (Ex. Ed.); Kevin Johnson (Reg. Dir. /GM); Allen Jones (Reg. Pres. Adv. Sales); Shannon Welch (Reg. VP Adv. Sales); Paige Windsor (News Dir.)
Parent company: Gannett
Main (survey) contact: Paige Windsor

HARLAN

PENNYSAVER

Street Address1: 1114 7th St
Street address state: IA
Postal code: 51537-1338
County: Shelby
Country: USA
Mailing address: PO Box 721
Mailing city: Harlan
Mailing state: IA
Mailing zip: 51537-0721
Office phone: (712) 755-3111
Office fax: (712) 755-3324
General e-mail: news2@harlanonline.com
Website: news2@harlanonline.com
Year publication established: 1971
Advertising (open inch rate): Open inch rate $9.00
Mechanical specifications: Type page 14 3/4 x 21 1/2; A - 6 cols, 2 1/4, 1/6 between.
Delivery methods: Mail`Newsstand`Racks
Zip Codes Served: 51442, 51446, 51454, 51521, 51527, 51530, 51531, 51536, 51537, 51543, 51553, 51559, 51562, 51565, 51570
Frequency: Tues
Other Type of Frequency: weekly
Circulation Free: 8900
Audit By: Sworn/Estimate/Non-Audited
Audit Date: 43658
Hardware: APP/Mac, APP/Mac LaserWriter II, APP/Power Mac 7500
Presses: 10-G/Community
Software: Multi-Ad/Creator 4.0, Adobe/PageMaker 6.0.
Personnel: Alan Mores (Pub.); Steven Mores (Pub.); Mike Kolbe (Adv. Mgr.); Robert Bjoin (Ed.)
Main (survey) contact: Steven Mores

HAWARDEN

AREA WIDE AD-VERTISER

Street Address1: 926 Avenue F
Street address state: IA
Postal code: 51023-2275
County: Sioux
Country: USA
Mailing address: PO Box 31
Mailing city: Hawarden
Mailing state: IA
Mailing zip: 51023-0031
Office phone: (712) 551-1051
Office fax: (712) 551-1057
General e-mail: independent@longlines.com
Website: independent@longlines.com
Year publication established: 1970
Advertising (open inch rate): Open inch rate $8.40
Mechanical specifications: 6 column full-page 10" x 14.5"
Delivery methods: Mail
Zip Codes Served: 51023, 51027, 51001, 57001, 57004, 51062, 57025
Frequency: Wed
Circulation Free: 6685
Audit By: CVC
Audit Date: 42368
Software: Creative Suite
Personnel: Bruce Odson

Main (survey) contact: Bruce Odson

IDA GROVE

REMINDER

Street Address1: 210 2nd St
Street address state: IA
Postal code: 51445-1403
County: Ida
Country: USA
Mailing address: PO Box 249
Mailing city: Ida Grove
Mailing state: IA
Mailing zip: 51445-0249
Office phone: (712) 364-3131
Office fax: (712) 364-3010
Advertising (open inch rate): Open inch rate $7.90
Mechanical specifications: Type page 11 1/2 x 21; A - 6 cols, 1 13/16, 1/8 between; C - 6 cols, 1 13/16, 1/8 between.
Frequency: Tues
Circulation Free: 6100
Audit By: Sworn/Estimate/Non-Audited
Audit Date: 43658
Hardware: APP/Mac
Software: InDesign 2.02.
Personnel: Roger D. Rector (Pub); Amy Forbes (Bus. Mgr.)
Main (survey) contact: Amy Forbes

INDIANOLA

EXTRA

Street Address1: 112 N Howard St
Street address state: IA
Postal code: 50125-2510
County: Warren
Country: USA
Mailing address: PO Box 259
Mailing city: Indianola
Mailing state: IA
Mailing zip: 50125-0259
Office phone: (515) 961-2511
Office fax: (515) 961-4833
Advertising (open inch rate): Open inch rate $13.70
Mechanical specifications: Type page 13 x 21; E - 6 cols, 2, 1/6 between; A - 6 cols, 2, 1/6 between; C - 10 cols, 1 3/16, 1/6 between.
Zip Codes Served: 50125
Frequency: Tues
Circulation Free: 10467
Audit By: Sworn/Estimate/Non-Audited
Audit Date: 43658
Personnel: Amy Duncan (Pub.); Adam Wilson (Ed.)
Parent company: Gannett
Main (survey) contact: Amy Duncan

IOWA CITY

ADD SHEET

Street Address1: 1725 N Dodge St
Street address state: IA
Postal code: 52245-9589
County: Johnson
Country: USA
Mailing address: 1725 N Dodge St
Mailing city: Iowa City
Mailing state: IA
Mailing zip: 52245-9589
Office phone: (319) 337-3181
General e-mail: customerservice@press-citizen.com
Advertising e-mail: mvitti@press-citizen.com
Editorial e-mail: zberg@press-citizen.com
Website: customerservice@press-citizen.com
Advertising (open inch rate): Open inch rate $7.95
Mechanical specifications: Type page 11 5/8 x 21 1/4; A - 6 cols, 1 4/5, 2/5 between; C - 9 cols, 1 3/5, 2/5 between.
Zip Codes Served: 52245
Frequency: Wed
Circulation Free: 24000

Audit By: Sworn/Estimate/Non-Audited
Audit Date: 43585
Personnel: Zach Berg; Michael Vitti (Sales Mgr.)
Parent company: Gannett
Main (survey) contact: Michael Vitti

IOWA FALLS

TIMES-CITIZEN

Street Address1: 406 Stevens St
Street address state: IA
Postal code: 50126-2214
County: Hardin
Country: USA
Mailing address: PO Box 640
Mailing city: Iowa Falls
Mailing state: IA
Mailing zip: 50126-0640
Office phone: (641) 648-2521
Office fax: (641) 648-4606
General e-mail: tcc@iafalls.com
Website: tcc@iafalls.com
Advertising (open inch rate): Open inch rate $6.55
Mechanical specifications: Type page 6 x 21; A - 6 cols, between; C - 6 cols, between.
Zip Codes Served: 50126
Frequency: Wed`Sat
Circulation Free: 34000
Audit By: Sworn/Estimate/Non-Audited
Audit Date: 43658
Hardware: APP/Power Macs, CD-ROMs, Scanners, Image Setter
Software: QPS/QuarkXPress 3.2, Adobe/PageMaker 6.0, Adobe/Illustrator 6.5.
Personnel: Mark H. Hamilton (Pub.); Jo Martin (Gen. Mgr.); Susan Duncan (Circ. Mgr.)
Main (survey) contact: Mark H. Hamilton

KNOXVILLE

MARION COUNTY REMINDER

Street Address1: 122 E Robinson St
Street address state: IA
Postal code: 50138-2329
County: Marion
Country: USA
Mailing address: PO Box 458
Mailing city: Knoxville
Mailing state: IA
Mailing zip: 50138-0458
Office phone: (641) 842-2155
Office fax: (641) 842-2929
General e-mail: class@journalexpress.net
Advertising e-mail: advertising@journalexpress.net
Editorial e-mail: editor@journalexpress.net
Website: class@journalexpress.net
Advertising (open inch rate): Open inch rate $10.00
Mechanical specifications: 6 Col. 1 Column 1.583â€³ - 9p6 2 Columns 3.292â€³ - 19p9 3 Columns 5â€³ - 30p 4 Columns 6.708â€³ 5 - 40p3 5 Columns 8.417â€³ - 50p6 6 Columns 10.125â€³ - 60p9 Tab Sizes Ad Lengths 1 Inch   6 picas 2 Inches   12 picas 3 Inches   18 picas 4 Inches   24 picas 5 Inches   30 picas 6 Inches   36 picas 7 Inches   42 picas 8 Inches   48 picas 9 Inches   54 picas 10 Inches   60 picas 11 Inches   66 picas 12 Inches   72 picas 13 Inches   78 picas 14 Inches   84 picas 15 Inches   90 picas 16 Inches   96 picas 17 Inches   102 picas 18 Inches   108 picas 19 Inches   114 picas 20 Inches   120 picas Full Page 60p x 58p6 (10â€³ x 9.776â€³) 1/2 Page Vertical 30p x 58p6 (5â€³ x 9.776â€³) 1/2 Page Horizontal 60p x 29p3 10â€³ x 4.888â€³ 1/4 Page 30p x 29p3 (5â€³ x 4.888â€³) 1/8 Page 30p x 14p6 (5â€³ x 2.444â€³)
Delivery methods: Mail`Carrier`Racks
Zip Codes Served: 50138 50219 50214 50232 50143 50049 50062 50163 50025 50057 50118 50170 50272 50150 50044/50016

50119 50265 50119/50265
Digital Platform - Mobile:
Apple˙Android˙Windows
Digital Platform - Tablet: Apple
iOS˙Android˙Windows 7˙Blackberry Tablet
OS˙Kindle˙Nook˙Kindle Fire
Frequency: Tues
Circulation Free: 20615
Audit By: CVC
Audit Date: 42734
Software: Adobe/Illustrator CS5, QuarkXPress
3.31, Adobe/Photoshop CS5, Adobe
InDesign CS5, Quark XPress 9.3
Personnel: Rebecca Maxwell (Pub.); Beth
Adamcik (Marketing Consultant); Susan
Martin (Marketing Consultant); Amanda
Heck (Head Expeditor); Kelly Binns
(Cashier); Becky Maxwell (Publisher)
Parent company: Community Newspaper
Holdings, Inc.
Main (survey) contact: Rebecca Maxwell

LE MARS

SHOPPERS GUIDE

Street Address1: 41 1st Ave NE
Street address state: IA
Postal code: 51031-3535
County: Plymouth
Country: USA
Mailing address: 41 1st Ave NE
Mailing city: Le Mars
Mailing state: IA
Mailing zip: 51031-3535
Office phone: (712) 546-7031
Office fax: (712) 546-7035
General e-mail: sentinel@lemarscomm.net
Website: sentinel@lemarscomm.net
Year publication established: 1857
Advertising (open inch rate): Open inch rate $14.55
Mechanical specifications: Type page 13 x 21 1/2.
Zip Codes Served: 51031
Frequency: Wed
Circulation Free: 7000
Audit By: Sworn/Estimate/Non-Audited
Audit Date: 43658
Hardware: APP/Mac
Presses: 6-G/Community
Software: Claris/Works 5.0, Multi-Ad/Creator, QPS/QuarkXPress, Microsoft/Publisher.
Personnel: Tom Stangl (Pub.); David Copenhaver (Adv.); Christine Pape (Circ. Mgr.); Monte Jost (Mktg. Dir.); Magdalene Landegent (Ed.); Don Luksan (Prodn. Mgr.)
Parent company: Rust Communications
Main (survey) contact: Joann Glamm

MAQUOKETA

THE SHOPPER

Street Address1: 108 N Main St
Street address state: IA
Postal code: 52060-2201
County: Jackson
Country: USA
Mailing address: 108 N Main St
Mailing city: Maquoketa
Mailing state: IA
Mailing zip: 52060-2201
Office phone: (563) 652-6803
Office fax: (563) 652-3406
Advertising (open inch rate): Open inch rate $4.75
Frequency: Wed
Circulation Free: 12996
Audit By: CVC
Audit Date: 43008
Personnel: Judy Van Hecke (Adv. Mgr.)
Main (survey) contact: Judy Van Hecke

MARENGO

IOWA COUNTY ADVERTISER

Street Address1: 100 W Main St
Street address state: IA
Postal code: 52301-4705
County: Iowa
Country: USA
Mailing address: PO Box 208
Mailing city: Marengo
Mailing state: IA
Mailing zip: 52301-0208
Office phone: (319) 642-5506
Office fax: (319) 642-5509
Advertising (open inch rate): Open inch rate $5.00
Mechanical specifications: Type page 6 x 14; E - 6 cols, 2 1/3, 1/6 between; A - 9 cols, 1 2/3, 1/6 between.
Frequency: Wed
Circulation Paid: 3979
Circulation Free: 6309
Audit By: CVC
Audit Date: 38717
Hardware: APP/Mac
Presses: 8-KP/News King 2000
Software: Adobe/Photoshop, Adobe/PageMaker, QPS/QuarkXPress, Microsoft.
Personnel: Diane Godlow (Pub.); John Rotter (Sales Mgr.); Audrey Yardley (Circ. Mgr.)
Main (survey) contact: Diane Godlow

MARSHALLTOWN

PENNYSAVER

Street Address1: 507 E Anson St
Street address state: IA
Postal code: 50158-3317
County: Marshall
Country: USA
Mailing address: PO Box 246
Mailing city: Marshalltown
Mailing state: IA
Mailing zip: 50158-0246
Office phone: (641) 752-6630
Office fax: (641) 752-7073
General e-mail: ps@marshalltownpennysaver.com
Website: ps@marshalltownpennysaver.com
Advertising (open inch rate): Open inch rate $13.75
Mechanical specifications: Type page 10 1/4 x 16; E - 7 cols, 1 1/4, 3/16 between; A - 7 cols, 1 1/4, 3/16 between; C - 7 cols, 1 1/4, 3/16 between.
Zip Codes Served: 50158
Frequency: Wed˙Sat
Circulation Free: 30000
Audit By: Sworn/Estimate/Non-Audited
Audit Date: 43658
Presses: G/Community
Software: Multi-Ad/Creator 4.0, Adobe/Photoshop.
Personnel: Mike Schlesinger (Pub.); Denise Kemp (Marketing Director)
Parent company: Ogden Newspapers Inc.
Main (survey) contact: Mike Schlesinger

MASON CITY

THE MASON CITY SHOPPER

Street Address1: 300 N Washington Ave
Street address state: IA
Postal code: 50401-3222
County: Cerro Gordo
Country: USA
Mailing address: PO Box 271
Mailing city: Mason City
Mailing state: IA
Mailing zip: 50402-0271
Office phone: (641) 421-0500
Office fax: (641) 421-0592
General e-mail: classads@globegazette.com
Website: classads@globegazette.com
Advertising (open inch rate): Open inch rate $10.00
Mechanical specifications: Type page 10 1/2 x 16; E - 5 cols, 1 11/12, 3/16 between; A - 5 cols, 1 15/16, 3/16 between; C - 5 cols, 1 15/16, 3/16 between.
Zip Codes Served: 50401
Frequency: Tues
Circulation Free: 23016
Audit By: CVC
Audit Date: 42003
Hardware: APP/Mac 7100
Software: Multi-Ad/Creator 3.6.2, QPS/QuarkXPress.
Personnel: Howard Query; Linda Hawk (Sales Rep.)
Main (survey) contact: Howard Query

MONTICELLO

MONTICELLO SHOPPERS' GUIDE

Street Address1: 111 E Grand St
Street address state: IA
Postal code: 52310-1688
County: Jones
Country: USA
Mailing address: PO Box 191
Mailing city: Monticello
Mailing state: IA
Mailing zip: 52310-0191
Office phone: (319) 465-3555
Office fax: (319) 465-4611
General e-mail: mexpress@n-connect.net
Website: mexpress@n-connect.net
Advertising (open inch rate): Open inch rate $9.20
Mechanical specifications: Type page 10 1/4 x 16; E - 6 cols, 1 9/16, 1/6 between; A - 6 cols, 1 9/16, 1/6 between; C - 6 cols, 1 9/16, 1/6 between.
Zip Codes Served: 52310
Frequency: Wed
Circulation Free: 10200
Audit By: Sworn/Estimate/Non-Audited
Audit Date: 43658
Hardware: 12-APP/Power Mac
Software: Microsoft/Word, Adobe/Photoshop, Adobe/PageMaker 6.5.
Personnel: Dan Goodyear (Co-Pub.); Mark Spensley (Adv. Mgr.); Jill Brokaw (Prodn. Mgr.); Kim Brooks (Ed.)
Main (survey) contact: Dan Goodyear

MOUNT VERNON

THE SUNLIGHT

Street Address1: 108 1st St SW
Street address state: IA
Postal code: 52314-4706
County: Linn
Country: USA
Mailing address: PO Box 129
Mailing city: Mount Vernon
Mailing state: IA
Mailing zip: 52314-0129
Office phone: (319) 895-6216
Office fax: (319) 895-6217
General e-mail: news@mtvernonlisbonsun.com
Advertising e-mail: advertising@mtvernonlisbonsun.com
Website: news@mtvernonlisbonsun.com
Year publication established: 1975
Advertising (open inch rate): Open inch rate $7.00
Mechanical specifications: Type page 13 x 21 1/2; E - 6 cols, 2, 1/6 between; A - 6 cols, 2, 1/6 between; C - 8 cols, 1 1/2, 1/6 between.
Zip Codes Served: 52314
Frequency: Thur
Circulation Free: 3350
Audit By: Sworn/Estimate/Non-Audited
Audit Date: 43658
Hardware: APP/Mac
Software: QPS/QuarkXPress, APP/AppleWorks, 2-Multi-Ad/Creator, Adobe/Photoshop.
Personnel: Rich Eskelsen (Adv. Mgr.); Valerie Burkhart-Fisher (Circ. Mgr.); Jake Krob (Ed.)
Main (survey) contact: Jake Krob

MT PLEASANT

MT. PLEASANT SHOPPER

Street Address1: 215 W Monroe St
Street address state: IA
Postal code: 52641-2110
County: Henry
Country: USA
Mailing address: 215 W Monroe St
Mailing city: Mt Pleasant
Mailing state: IA
Mailing zip: 52641-2110
Office phone: (319) 385-3131
Office fax: (319) 385-8048
Advertising phone: (319) 385-3131
Advertising fax: (319) 385-8048
Editorial phone: (319) 385-3131
Editorial fax: (319) 385-8048
General e-mail: adv@mpnews.net
Advertising e-mail: adv@mpnews.net
Editorial e-mail: news@mpnews.net
Website: pub@mpnews.net
Year publication established: 1890
Advertising (open inch rate): Open inch rate $9.70
Mechanical specifications: Type page 10 1/4 x 16; A - 6 cols, 1 1/2, 1/6 between; C - 6 cols, 1 1/2, 1/6 between.
Delivery methods: Carrier˙Racks
Zip Codes Served: 52641, 52644, 52645, 52646, 52647, 52648, 52649, 52651, 52652, 52653, 52654, 52656, 52659
Frequency: Tues
Circulation Free: 11622
Audit By: CVC
Audit Date: 42368
Hardware: APP/Mac
Presses: 4-G/Community
Software: Photoshop, InDesign
Personnel: Bill Gray (Publisher/Ad Director)
Parent company: Inland Media Company, Inc.
Main (survey) contact: Bill Gray

MUSCATINE

THE POST

Street Address1: 301 E 3rd St
Street address state: IA
Postal code: 52761-4116
County: Muscatine
Country: USA
Mailing address: 301 E 3rd St
Mailing city: Muscatine
Mailing state: IA
Mailing zip: 52761-4116
Office phone: (563) 263-2331
Office fax: (563) 262-8042
General e-mail: sales@muscatinepost.com
Website: sales@muscatinepost.com
Advertising (open inch rate): Open inch rate $8.00
Mechanical specifications: Type page 10 3/4 x 16; E - 7 cols, 1 5/12, 1/12 between; A - 7 cols, 1 5/12, 1/12 between; C - 7 cols, 1 5/12, 1/12 between.
Zip Codes Served: 52761
Frequency: Wed
Circulation Paid: 811
Audit By: AAM
Audit Date: 42674
Hardware: APP/Mac Quadra 650, APP/Mac Performa 6300CD
Software: QPS/QuarkXPress, Multi-Ad/Creator.
Personnel: Bob Blackman (Pub.); Jaime Bryant (Adv. Mgr.); Tom McCoy (Circ. Mgr.); Rusty Schrader (News Ed.)
Main (survey) contact: Bob Blackman

NEW HAMPTON

NEW HAMPTON SHOPPER

Street Address1: 10 N Chestnut Ave
Street address state: IA
Postal code: 50659-1349
County: Chickasaw
Country: USA
Mailing address: PO Box 380
Mailing city: New Hampton
Mailing state: IA
Mailing zip: 50659-0380
Office phone: (641) 394-2111
Office fax: (641) 394-2113
General e-mail: nhtribune@mchsi.com

Shopper Publications in the U.S.

Website: nhtribune@mchsi.com
Advertising (open inch rate): Open inch rate $3.80
Mechanical specifications: Type page 15 1/8 x 21 1/2; A - 9 cols, 1 9/16, between; C - 9 cols, 1 9/16, between.
Frequency: Tues
Circulation Free: 20000
Audit By: Sworn/Estimate/Non-Audited
Audit Date: 43658
Personnel: Matt Bryant (Pub.); Dan Feuling (Pub.); Amannda Pemble (Adv. Mgr.); Ruth Walden (Circ. Mgr.)
Main (survey) contact: Matt Bryant

NEWTON
JASPER COUNTY ADVERTISER

Street Address1: 200 1st Ave E
Street address state: IA
Postal code: 50208-3716
County: Jasper
Country: USA
Mailing address: 200 1st Ave E
Mailing city: Newton
Mailing state: IA
Mailing zip: 50208-3716
Advertising (open inch rate): Open inch rate $13.77
Frequency: Wed
Circulation Free: 15012
Audit By: CVC
Audit Date: 42643
Personnel: Dan Goetz
Parent company: Shaw Media
Main (survey) contact: Dan Goetz

OELWEIN
SHOPPER'S REMINDER

Street Address1: 25 1st St SE
Street address state: IA
Postal code: 50662-2306
County: Fayette
Country: USA
Mailing address: Box 511
Mailing city: Oelwein
Mailing state: IA
Mailing zip: 50662-0511
Office phone: (319) 283-2144
Office fax: (319) 283-3268
General e-mail: debweigel@oelweindailyregister.com
Advertising e-mail: tracy.cummings@oelweindailyregister.com
Website: debweigel@oelweindailyregister.com
Advertising (open inch rate): Open inch rate $17.84
Delivery methods: Mail
Zip Codes Served: 50662
Frequency: Mon
Circulation Free: 20280
Audit By: Sworn/Estimate/Non-Audited
Audit Date: 43658
Personnel: Tracy Cummings (Adv. Mgr.); Sue Hosto (Circ. Mgr.); Chris Baldus (Editor); Deb Weigel (Pub)
Parent company: Community Media Group
Main (survey) contact: Deb Weigel

ORANGE CITY
AD-VISOR

Street Address1: 113 Central Ave SE
Street address state: IA
Postal code: 51041-1738
County: Sioux
Country: USA
Mailing address: 113 Central Ave SE
Mailing city: Orange City
Mailing state: IA
Mailing zip: 51041-1738
Office phone: (712) 737-4266
Office fax: (712) 737-3896
Advertising phone: same
Advertising fax: same
Editorial phone: (712) 737-4266
Editorial fax: (712) 737-3896
General e-mail: pluimpub@orangecitycomm.net
Advertising e-mail: same
Editorial e-mail: same
Website: pluimpub@orangecitycomm.net
Year publication established: 1951
Advertising (open inch rate): Open inch rate $7.25
Mechanical specifications: Broadsheet page 8 col. wide x 21.5 tall
Delivery methods: Mail`Carrier
Zip Codes Served: 51041
Frequency: Tues
Circulation Free: 8878
Audit By: CVC
Audit Date: 41244
Hardware: APP/Mac
Presses: Heidelburg MOZP-Heidelburg Quick Master-# unit Harris V15 web- 2 Color AB Dick
Editions Count: 52
Edition Names with circulation: Ad-Visor
Personnel: Robert Hulstein (Pres.); Dennis Den Hartog (Adv. Mgr.); Amy Rassel (Circ. Mgr.); Doug Calsbeek (Ed.); Dale H. Pluim (Mng. Ed.); El Top (Prodn. Mgr.)
Main (survey) contact: Robert Hulstein

OSAGE
TOWN & COUNTRY SHOPPER

Street Address1: 112 N 6th St
Street address state: IA
Postal code: 50461-1202
County: Mitchell
Country: USA
Mailing address: PO Box 60
Mailing city: Osage
Mailing state: IA
Mailing zip: 50461-0060
Office phone: (641) 732-3721
Office fax: (641) 732-5689
General e-mail: mcpress@mcpress.com
Editorial e-mail: editor@mcpress.com
Website: mcpress@mcpress.com
Advertising (open inch rate): Open inch rate $7.50
Mechanical specifications: Type page 14 x 21 1/2; E - 6 cols, 2, 1/6 between; A - 6 cols, 2, 1/6 between; C - 6 cols, 2, 1/6 between.
Zip Codes Served: 50461
Frequency: Wed
Circulation Free: 6500
Audit By: Sworn/Estimate/Non-Audited
Audit Date: 43658
Hardware: APP/Power Mac
Presses: KP/News King
Software: Adobe/PageMaker.
Personnel: Dave Stanley (Pub.); Kelly Kuper (Adv. Sales Mgr.); David Namanny (Ed.)
Main (survey) contact: Howard Query

OSCEOLA
THE ADVERTISER

Street Address1: 111 E Washington St
Street address state: IA
Postal code: 50213-1244
County: Clarke
Country: USA
Mailing address: 111 E Washington St
Mailing city: Osceola
Mailing state: IA
Mailing zip: 50213-1244
Frequency: Tues
Circulation Paid: 65
Circulation Free: 11265
Audit By: CVC
Audit Date: 40878
Personnel: Rich Paulsen
Main (survey) contact: Rich Paulsen

OSKALOOSA
OSKALOOSA SHOPPER

Street Address1: 1901 A Ave W
Street address state: IA
Postal code: 52577-1962
County: Mahaska
Country: USA
Mailing address: 1901 A Ave W
Mailing city: Oskaloosa
Mailing state: IA
Mailing zip: 52577-1962
Office phone: (641) 672-2581
Office fax: (641) 672-2294
Advertising phone: (641) 672-2581 ext. 413
Advertising fax: (641) 673-8226
Editorial phone: (641) 672-2581 ext. 425
Editorial fax: (641) 672-1264
General e-mail: debve@oskyherald.com
Advertising e-mail: debve@oskyherald.com
Editorial e-mail: oskynews@oskyherald.com
Website: debve@oskyherald.com
Year publication established: 1960
Advertising (open inch rate): $11.55 pci
Mechanical specifications: 6 col. x 21 inches (10.2125" x 21")
Delivery methods: Mail`Carrier`Racks
Zip Codes Served: 52577, 50207, 50027, 52543, 52553, 52561, 50143, 52586, 52595, 50136, 52591, 50256, 52355, 50268, 50104, 52563, 52566, 50138, 50150, 50219, 50242, 50255, 52222, 50171, 50044, 50116
Digital Platform - Mobile: Android
Digital Platform - Tablet: Apple iOS`Android`Kindle`Nook`Kindle Fire
Frequency: Wed
Circulation Free: 16973
Audit By: CVC
Audit Date: 42368
Personnel: Deb Van Engelenhoven (PUblisher)
Parent company: Community Newspaper Holdings, Inc.
Main (survey) contact: Deb VanEngelenhoven

PELLA
TOWN CRIER

Street Address1: 810 E 1st St
Street address state: IA
Postal code: 50219-1529
County: Marion
Country: USA
Mailing address: 810 E 1st St
Mailing city: Pella
Mailing state: IA
Mailing zip: 50219-1585
Office phone: (641) 628-1130
Office fax: (641) 628-2826
Advertising (open inch rate): Open inch rate $5.00
Mechanical specifications: Type page 16 x 21 1/2; A - 9 cols, 1 11/16, 1/8 between; C - 9 cols, 1 11/16, 1/8 between.
Zip Codes Served: 50219
Frequency: Wed
Circulation Free: 12000
Audit By: Sworn/Estimate/Non-Audited
Audit Date: 43658
Hardware: AM/Desktop.
Personnel: Keith Aldrich (Pub.); Logan Andeweg (Pub.); Dede Doschadis (Adv. Mgr.); Wilma Brouwer (Circ. Mgr.)
Main (survey) contact: Dede Doschadis

PERRY
CHIEFLAND SHOPPER

Street Address1: 1323 2nd St
Street address state: IA
Postal code: 50220-1511
County: Dallas
Country: USA
Mailing address: PO Box 98
Mailing city: Perry
Mailing state: IA
Mailing zip: 50220-0098
Office phone: (515) 465-4666
Office fax: (515) 465-3087
General e-mail: publisher@theperrychief.com
Advertising e-mail: ads@theperrychief.com
Editorial e-mail: news@theperrychief.com
Website: publisher@theperrychief.com
Year publication established: 1874
Advertising (open inch rate): Open inch rate $9.30
Mechanical specifications: Type page 14 7/8 x 21; E - 8 cols, 1 3/4, between; A - 8 cols, 1 5/6, between; C - 8 cols, 1 5/6, between.
Delivery methods: Mail`Carrier
Zip Codes Served: 50220 50003 50026 50029 50039 50059 50063 50066 50070 50107 50109 50115 50129 50146 50156 50167 50216 50233 50235 50276 50277
Frequency: Tues
Circulation Free: 12500
Audit By: Sworn/Estimate/Non-Audited
Audit Date: 43658
Hardware: Dell Studio XPS 9100 (6)
Software: Adobe CS 5.5
Personnel: Patricia Snyder (Publisher); Linda Schumacher (Adv. Mgr.); Donald Thomas (Prodn. Mgr.); Laura Pieper (Managing Editor)
Main (survey) contact: Patricia Snyder

POCAHONTAS
POCAHONTAS COUNTY ADVERTISER

Street Address1: 218 N Main St
Street address state: IA
Postal code: 50574-1605
County: Pocahontas
Country: USA
Mailing address: 218 N Main St
Mailing city: Pocahontas
Mailing state: IA
Mailing zip: 50574-1624
Office phone: (712) 335-3553
Office fax: (712) 335-3856
General e-mail: publisher@pokyrd.com
Advertising e-mail: ads@pokyrd.com
Editorial e-mail: editor@pokyrd.com
Website: publisher@pokyrd.com
Advertising (open inch rate): Open inch rate $7.17
Delivery methods: Mail`Newsstand`Carrier`Racks
Zip Codes Served: 50574, 50581, 50510, 50515, 50527, 50540, 50541, 50546, 50554, 50562, 50563, 50565, 50568, 50571, 50576, 50575, 50593, 51366
Frequency: Tues
Circulation Free: 5820
Audit By: Sworn/Estimate/Non-Audited
Audit Date: 43658
Hardware: APP/Power Mac
Software: Adobe/InDesign, Microsoft/Word.
Personnel: Chris Vrba (Owner/Publisher/Editor)
Main (survey) contact: Chris Vrba

ROCK RAPIDS
THE NORTHWEST IOWA EXTRA

Street Address1: 310 1st Ave
Street address state: IA
Postal code: 51246-1506
County: Lyon
Country: USA
Mailing address: PO BOX 28
Mailing city: ROCK RAPIDS
Mailing state: IA
Mailing zip: 51246-0028
Office phone: (712) 472-2525
Office fax: (712) 472-3414
Advertising phone: (712) 472-2525
Advertising fax: (712) 472-3414
Editorial phone: (712) 472-2525
Editorial fax: (712) 472-3414
General e-mail: lmiller@ncppub.com
Advertising e-mail: lkuehl@ncppub.com
Editorial e-mail: jjensen@ncppub.com
Website: lmiller@ncppub.com
Advertising (open inch rate): Open inch rate $10.44
Mechanical specifications: Type page 11 5/8 x 21 1/2; E - 6 cols, 1 13/16, 1/6 between; A - 6 cols, 1 13/16, 1/6 between; C - 6 cols, 1 13/16, 1/6 between.
Delivery methods: Mail`Newsstand
Zip Codes Served: 51246

ROCKWELL CITY

CALHOUN COUNTY REMINDER

Street Address1: 515 4th St
Street address state: IA
Postal code: 50579-1901
County: Calhoun
Country: USA
Mailing address: 515 4th St
Mailing city: Rockwell City
Mailing state: IA
Mailing zip: 50579-1901
Office phone: (712) 297-8931
Office fax: (712) 297-7193
Advertising e-mail: ads@calhouncontyreminder.com
Advertising (open inch rate): Open inch rate $5.00
Mechanical specifications: Type page 6 x 16; E - 6 cols, 1 1/2, between; A - 6 cols, 1 1/2, between.
Zip Codes Served: 50579
Frequency: Tues
Circulation Free: 6061
Audit By: CVC
Audit Date: 41090
Hardware: APP/Mac
Presses: G
Software: Adobe/PageMaker
Personnel: Gary D. Dudley (Adv. Mgr.); Janet Anderson (Circ. Mgr.); Robert Johnson (Prodn. Mgr.)
Main (survey) contact: Gary D. Dudley

SHELDON

THE GOLDEN SHOPPER

Street Address1: 227 Nineth St
Street address state: IA
Postal code: 51201
County: Obrien
Country: USA
Mailing address: PO Box 160
Mailing city: Sheldon
Mailing state: IA
Mailing zip: 51201-0160
Office phone: (712) 324-5347
Office fax: (712) 324-2345
General e-mail: pww@iowainformation.com
Advertising e-mail: ads@iowainformation.com
Editorial e-mail: editor@iowainformation.com
Website: pww@iowainformation.com
Year publication established: 1962
Advertising (open inch rate): Open inch rate $8.82
Mechanical specifications: Type page 12 7/8 x 21 1/2; E - 6 cols, 2, 1/6 between; A - 6 cols, 2, 1/6 between; C - 6 cols, 2, 1/6 between.
Delivery methods: Mail`Newsstand`Carrier`Racks
Zip Codes Served: 51003, 51041, 51046, 51201, 51231, 51232, 51234, 51237, 51238, 51243, 51244, 51248, 51249, 51250, 51346, 51349, 51350, 51237, 51022, 51245
Digital Platform - Mobile: Apple
Frequency: Tues
Circulation Free: 16448
Audit By: CVC
Audit Date: 43081
Hardware: Most current Mac's, direct to plate
Presses: SIX MERCURY FOUR-HIGH

PRESSES AND SPLICERS CONNECTED TO TWO FOLDERS
Personnel: Jeff Wagner (Pres); Peter W. Wagner (Adv. Mgr.); Jeff Grant (Ed.); Dawn Groen (Prodn. Mgr.)
Parent company: Iowa Information, Inc.
Main (survey) contact: Peter W. Wagner

SHENANDOAH

WEEKLY TIMES

Street Address1: 617 W Sheridan Ave
Street address state: IA
Postal code: 51601-1707
County: Page
Country: USA
Mailing address: PO Box 369
Mailing city: Shenandoah
Mailing state: IA
Mailing zip: 51601-0369
Office phone: (712) 246-3097
Office fax: (712) 246-3099
General e-mail: ads@valleynewstoday.com
Editorial e-mail: editorial@valleynewstoday.com
Website: ads@valleynewstoday.com
Year publication established: 1882
Advertising (open inch rate): Open inch rate $22.15
Mechanical specifications: Type page 11.832" x 21"; 7 cols
Delivery methods: Mail`Racks
Frequency: Mon
Circulation Free: 22847
Audit By: CVC
Audit Date: 42368
Personnel: Barbara Trimble (Pub.); Mark Anderson (Adv.); Kimberly Kellison (Circ. Mgr.); Kevin Slater (Ed.)
Main (survey) contact: Thomas Schmitt

SIOUX CENTER

SIOUX CENTER SHOPPER

Street Address1: 67 3rd St NE
Street address state: IA
Postal code: 51250-1834
County: Sioux
Country: USA
Mailing address: 67 3rd St NE
Mailing city: Sioux Center
Mailing state: IA
Mailing zip: 51250-1834
Office phone: (712) 722-0511
Office fax: (712) 722-0507
General e-mail: ads@siouxcenternews.com
Website: ads@siouxcenternews.com
Advertising (open inch rate): Open inch rate $6.45
Zip Codes Served: 51250
Frequency: Tues
Circulation Free: 12500
Audit By: Sworn/Estimate/Non-Audited
Audit Date: 43658
Hardware: APP/Mac
Software: OSystem 9, Adobe/PageMaker 6.5, QPS/QuarkXPress 4.1, Macromedia/Freehand 9, Adobe/Illustrator 9, Adobe/Photoshop 6.0.
Personnel: Scott Beernink (Ed.); Denise VanderBroek (Prodn. Mgr.)
Main (survey) contact: Steve Hoogland

SIOUX CITY

SHOPPER'S GUIDE

Street Address1: 515 Pavonia St
Street address state: IA
Postal code: 51101-2245
County: Woodbury
Country: USA
Mailing address: PO Box 118
Mailing city: Sioux City
Mailing state: IA
Mailing zip: 51102-0118

Office phone: (712) 224-6277
Office fax: (712) 255-7301
General e-mail: steve.griffith@lee.net
Website: steve.griffith@lee.net
Year publication established: 1985
Advertising (open inch rate): Open inch rate $15.00
Mechanical specifications: Type Page 9.889" x 10" 6 column format 1 column 1.556" wide
Delivery methods: Carrier`Racks
Zip Codes Served: 51101, 51102, 51103, 51104, 51105, 51108, 51109, 51054, 51117, 51024, 51030, 51039, 68776, 68030, 68741, 57049, 57025, 57038
Frequency: Wed
Circulation Free: 49550
Audit By: Sworn/Estimate/Non-Audited
Audit Date: 43658
Hardware: Gateway
Software: APT/Falcon
Personnel: Steve Griffith (Gen. Mgr.)
Main (survey) contact: Steve Griffith

SIOUXLAND WEEKLY SHOPPER'S GUIDE

Street Address1: 515 Pavonia St.
Street address state: IA
Postal code: 51101
County: Bates
Country: USA
Mailing address: 515 Pavonia St.
Mailing city: Sioux City
Mailing state: IA
Mailing zip: 51101
Office phone: (712) 293-4253
Editorial e-mail: cpauling@siouxcityjournal.com
Advertising (open inch rate): Open inch rate $6.85
Mechanical specifications: Type page 14 x 21; E - 6 cols, 2, 1/6 between; A - 6 cols, 2, 1/6 between; C - 6 cols, 2, 1/6 between.
Zip Codes Served: 64720
Frequency: Wed
Circulation Free: 5500
Audit By: Sworn/Estimate/Non-Audited
Audit Date: 43615
Personnel: C Paulling
Main (survey) contact: C Pauling

SPENCER

THE NORTHWEST IOWA SHOPPER WEEKEND

Street Address1: 310 E Milwaukee St
Street address state: IA
Postal code: 51301-4569
County: Clay
Country: USA
Mailing address: PO Box 197
Mailing city: Spencer
Mailing state: IA
Mailing zip: 51301-0197
Office phone: (712) 262-6610
Office fax: (712) 262-3044
General e-mail: advertising@spencerdailyreporter.com
Website: advertising@spencerdailyreporter.com
Advertising (open inch rate): Open inch rate $11.75
Mechanical specifications: Type page 13 x 21 1/2; E - 6 cols, 2, between; A - 6 cols, 2, between; C - 6 cols, 2, between.
Zip Codes Served: 57301
Frequency: Sat
Circulation Free: 18000
Audit By: Sworn/Estimate/Non-Audited
Audit Date: 43658
Hardware: APP/Mac
Presses: 11-G/community.
Personnel: Paula Buenger (Pub.); Randy Cauthron (Ed.)
Main (survey) contact: Paula Buenger

STORM LAKE

ADVERTISING GUIDE

Street Address1: 527 Cayuga St
Street address state: IA
Postal code: 50588-2319
County: Buena Vista
Country: USA
Mailing address: PO Box 1187
Mailing city: Storm Lake
Mailing state: IA
Mailing zip: 50588-1187
Office phone: (712) 732-3130
Office fax: (712) 732-3152
General e-mail: info@stormlakepilottribune.com; sledt@ncn.net
Website: info@stormlakepilottribune.com; sledt@ncn.net
Advertising (open inch rate): Open inch rate $7.45
Mechanical specifications: Type page 13 4/5 x 21 1/2; E - 8 cols, 1 7/12, 1/6 between; A - 8 cols, 1 7/12, 1/6 between; C - 8 cols, 1 7/12, 1/6 between.
Zip Codes Served: 50510, 50535, 50540, 50554, 50565, 50567, 50568, 50574, 50575, 50576, 50583, 50585, 50588, 50592, 50593, 51002, 51005, 51020, 51025, 51033, 51047, 51053, 51431, 51445, 51450, 51458, 51466
Frequency: Tues
Circulation Free: 15575
Audit By: CVC
Audit Date: 42185
Hardware: APP/Mac
Presses: 4-G/Community.
Personnel: Paula Buenger (Pub.); Janelle Madison (Adv. Mgr.); Tim Marlow (Prodn. Mgr.)
Main (survey) contact: Janelle Madison

STORM LAKE PILOT TRIBUNE

Street Address1: 527 Cayuga St
Street Address2: PO Box 1187
Postal code: 50588-2319
County: Buena Vista
Country: USA
Mailing address: P.O. Box 1187
Mailing city: Storm Lake
Mailing state: IA
Mailing zip: 50588-1187
Office phone: (712) 732-3130
Office fax: (712) 732-3152
General e-mail: info@stormlakepilottribune.com
Advertising e-mail: kari@stormlakepilottribune.com
Editorial e-mail: dlarsen@stormlakepilottribune.com
Website: info@stormlakepilottribune.com
Year publication established: 1840
Advertising (open inch rate): Open inch rate $11.50
Mechanical specifications: Type page 10 x 21 1/2; E - 6 cols, 1 9/16, 2/16 between;
Delivery methods: Mail`Newsstand`Racks
Zip Codes Served: 50588, 51002, 51005, 50535, 50540, 51020, 51025, 50554, 51033, 50565, 50588, 51047, 50576, 51053, 50585, 50592, 50593,
Digital Platform - Mobile: Apple`Android`Windows
Digital Platform - Tablet: Apple iOS`Android`Windows 7`Kindle Fire
Frequency: Tues`Thur`Sat
Circulation Paid: 2000
Circulation Free: 15690
Audit By: Sworn/Estimate/Non-Audited
Audit Date: 43658
Hardware: ctp Presteligence
Presses: G/Community.
Personnel: Kari Vander Woude (Gen. Mgr.); Jason Lindsay (Adv. Mgr.); Paula Buenger (Pub.)
Main (survey) contact: Kari Vander Woude

Digital Platform - Mobile: Apple`Android`Windows`Blackberry
Digital Platform - Tablet: Apple iOS`Android`Windows 7`Blackberry Tablet OS`Kindle`Nook`Kindle Fire
Frequency: Thur
Circulation Free: 1163
Audit By: CVC
Audit Date: 43099
Software: QPS/QuarkXPress 4.0.
Personnel: Jim Hensley (Pub./COO); Jessica Jensen (Ed.); Lisa Miller (Gen. Mgr.)
Parent company: New Century Press
Main (survey) contact: Jessica Jensen; Lisa Miller

Shopper Publications in the U.S.

STUART

FOUR COUNTY BULLETIN
Street Address1: 119 NW 2nd St
Street Address2: PO Box 608
Street address state: IA
Postal code: 50250-7704
County: Guthrie
Country: USA
Mailing address: 119 NW 2nd St PO Box 608
Mailing city: Stuart
Mailing state: IA
Mailing zip: 50250-7704
Office phone: (515) 523-1010
Office fax: (515) 523-2825
General e-mail: ads@thestuartherald.com
Advertising e-mail: ads@thestuartherald.com
Editorial e-mail: news@thestuartherald.com
Website: ads@thestuartherald.com
Year publication established: 1871
Advertising (open inch rate): Open inch rate $7.75
Delivery methods: Mail`Newsstand
Zip Codes Served: 5,02505000250003E+74
Digital Platform - Mobile: Apple
Digital Platform - Tablet: Apple iOS
Frequency: Tues`Bi-Mthly
Circulation Free: 9500
Audit By: Sworn/Estimate/Non-Audited
Audit Date: 43658
Personnel: Kristy Lonsdale (Owner)
Main (survey) contact: Kristy Lonsdale

TAMA

TAMA COUNTY SHOPPER
Street Address1: 220 W 3rd St
Street address state: IA
Postal code: 52339-2308
County: Tama
Country: USA
Mailing address: PO Box 118
Mailing city: Tama
Mailing state: IA
Mailing zip: 52339-0118
Office phone: (641) 484-2841
Office fax: (641) 484-5705
Advertising e-mail: nsund@tamatoledonews.com
Editorial e-mail: editor@tamatoledonews.com
Advertising (open inch rate): Open inch rate $12.46
Mechanical specifications: Type page 10 x 21 1/2; A - 6 cols, 1 2/5, between; C - 6 cols, 1 2/5, between.
Delivery methods: Mail`Racks
Zip Codes Served: 52339, 52342, 52215, 50675, 52217, 50635, 52208, 52224, 50173, 50632
Frequency: Wed
Circulation Free: 12
Audit By: Sworn/Estimate/Non-Audited
Audit Date: 43658
Personnel: D. Michael Schlessinger (Pub.); Nancy Sund (Adv. Mgr.); John Speer (Ed.)
Parent company: Ogden Newspapers Inc.
Main (survey) contact: Nancy Sund

VINTON

VINTON LIVEWIRE
Street Address1: 108 E 5th St
Street address state: IA
Postal code: 52349-1759
County: Benton
Country: USA
Mailing address: PO Box 468
Mailing city: Vinton
Mailing state: IA
Mailing zip: 52349-0468
Office phone: (319) 472-3303
Office fax: (319) 472-4811
Advertising e-mail: ads@vintonnewspapers.com
Year publication established: 1957
Advertising (open inch rate): Open inch rate $10.25 through Dec. 2018
Mechanical specifications: Page Size 10 1/4 x 14; 6 col. format; 1 col = 1.6".
Delivery methods: Mail
Zip Codes Served: 52349, 52210, 52229, 52313, 52332, 52345, 52213, 52352, 52206, 52209, 52224, 52249, 52315, 50651, 52346
Frequency: Wed
Circulation Free: 11505
Audit By: CVC
Audit Date: 43100
Personnel: Mona Garwood (Gen. Mgr.)
Parent company: Community Media Group
Main (survey) contact: Mona Garwood

WASHINGTON

WASHINGTON COUNTY SHOPPERS GUIDE
Street Address1: 111 N Marion Ave
Street address state: IA
Postal code: 52353-1728
County: Washington
Country: USA
Mailing address: 111 N Marion Ave
Mailing city: Washington
Mailing state: IA
Mailing zip: 52353-1748
Office phone: (319) 653-2191
Office fax: (319) 653-7524
General e-mail: pub@washjrnl.com; news@washjrnl.com
Website: pub@washjrnl.com; news@washjrnl.com
Advertising (open inch rate): Open inch rate $12.34
Mechanical specifications: Type page 10 5/8 x 16; A - 6 cols, 1 7/12, 1/6 between; C - 6 cols, 1 7/12, 1/6 between.
Delivery methods: Carrier
Frequency: Tues
Circulation Free: 11451
Audit By: CVC
Audit Date: 42368
Hardware: APP/Mac
Presses: 4-HI/V-15A
Software: Adobe/PageMaker 5.2, Microsoft/Word 6.0, QPS/QuarkXPress 3.1.1, Adobe/Photoshop 3.0, Claris 4.0, Multi-Ad/Creator 3.3.7.
Personnel: Matt Bryant (Publisher); Darwin Sherman (Pres.); John Butters (News Ed.)
Parent company: Inland Media Company, Inc.; The Siebold Company, Inc. (TSC)
Main (survey) contact: Matt Bryant

WATERLOO

CEDAR VALLEY SAVER
Street Address1: 3641 Kimball Ave
Street address state: IA
Postal code: 50702-5757
County: Black Hawk
Country: USA
Mailing address: 3641 Kimball Ave Ste 8
Mailing city: Waterloo
Mailing state: IA
Mailing zip: 50702-5757
Office phone: (319) 232-4500
Office fax: (319) 232-4500
Other fax: (319) 232-4510
General e-mail: brian@cvsaver.com
Advertising e-mail: ton@cvsaver.com
Website: brian@cvsaver.com
Year publication established: 2004
Advertising (open inch rate): $21 / col. in.
Mechanical specifications: Tabloid - 11.25" x 17"
Zip Codes Served: 50701, 50702, 50703
Frequency: Thur`Bi-Mthly
Circulation Free: 37832
Audit By: Sworn/Estimate/Non-Audited
Audit Date: 43658
Hardware: Macs & PCs
Presses: N/A
Software: N/A
Personnel: Brian Lewis (Pub.)
Main (survey) contact: Brian Lewis

INSIDER
Street Address1: 501 Commercial St
Street address state: IA
Postal code: 50701-5413
County: Black Hawk
Country: USA
Mailing address: PO Box 540
Mailing city: Waterloo
Mailing state: IA
Mailing zip: 50704-0540
Office phone: (319) 291-1400
Office fax: (319) 291-2069
Advertising e-mail: woo.ads@wcfcourier.com
Advertising (open inch rate): 14
Mechanical specifications: Type page 6 x 13; E - 4 cols, 1 7/12, between; A - 4 cols, 1 7/12, between.
Zip Codes Served: 50613
Frequency: Tues
Circulation Paid: 8574
Circulation Free: 786
Audit By: Sworn/Estimate/Non-Audited
Audit Date: 43602
Hardware: APP/Mac
Presses: HI
Software: Baseview/Class Act II.
Editions Count: 3
Edition Names with circulation: 3 total Ã‚Â— Insider-Cedar Falls (21,000); Insider-E. Waterloo (21,200); Insider-W. Waterloo (19,300);
Personnel: Roy Biondi; Nancy Newhoff (Ed.); Adam Bolander (Circ. Dir.); Tara Seible (Adv. Dir.)
Parent company: Lee Enterprises, Incorporated
Main (survey) contact: Roy Biondi

WAVERLY

BREMER-BUTLER SUPER SHOPPER
Street Address1: 311 W Bremer Ave
Street address state: IA
Postal code: 50677-3144
County: Bremer
Country: USA
Mailing address: P.O. Box 858
Mailing city: Waverly
Mailing state: IA
Mailing zip: 50677-0858
Office phone: (319) 352-3334
Office fax: (319) 352-5135
General e-mail: news@waverlynewspapers.com; circ@waverlynewspapers.com
Website: news@waverlynewspapers.com; circ@waverlynewspapers.com
Advertising (open inch rate): Open inch rate $7.30
Delivery methods: Mail
Zip Codes Served: 50677 50602 50619 50622 50636 50647 50666 50668 50670 50674 50676 50658 50645 50613
Digital Platform - Mobile: Apple
Digital Platform - Tablet: Apple iOS
Frequency: Tues
Circulation Free: 7942
Audit By: Sworn/Estimate/Non-Audited
Audit Date: 43658
Personnel: Deb Weigel (Pub.); Michael Izer (Adv. Mgr.); Anelia Dimitrova; Pat Racette (Sports Ed.)
Parent company: Community Media Group
Main (survey) contact: Melaine Buzynski

WEST POINT

BONNY BUYER
Street Address1: 403 Avenue D
Street address state: IA
Postal code: 52656-9391
County: Lee
Country: USA
Mailing address: 1226 Avenue H
Mailing city: Fort Madison
Mailing state: IA
Mailing zip: 52627-4544
Office phone: (319) 837-6232
Office fax: (319) 837-6913
General e-mail: buyer@iowatelecom.net; bbclassifieds@gmail.com
Website: buyer@iowatelecom.net; bbclassifieds@gmail.com
Advertising (open inch rate): Open inch rate $9.50
Frequency: Wed
Circulation Free: 22058
Audit By: CVC
Audit Date: 43008
Personnel: Lucinda Ward (Pub.)
Parent company: Community Media Group
Main (survey) contact: Lucinda Ward

IDAHO

BLACKFOOT

BINGHAM COUNTY BARGAINS
Street Address1: 34 N Ash St
Street address state: ID
Postal code: 83221-2101
County: Bingham
Country: USA
Mailing address: PO Box 70
Mailing city: Blackfoot
Mailing state: ID
Mailing zip: 83221-0070
Office phone: (208) 785-1100
Office fax: (208) 785-4239
General e-mail: mnews@cableone.net
Website: mnews@cableone.net
Advertising (open inch rate): Open inch rate $8.00
Mechanical specifications: Type page 10.16x 21 1/2; E - 6 cols, 1.6", 1/6 between columns
Delivery methods: Newsstand`Carrier
Zip Codes Served: 83203, 83210, 83215, 83218, 83221, 83236, 83256 and 83262.
Frequency: Wed
Circulation Paid: 0
Circulation Free: 4250
Audit By: Sworn/Estimate/Non-Audited
Audit Date: 43658
Hardware: Macs
Presses: 6-KP
Software: Indesign
Personnel: Leonard C. Martin (Pub.); Wayne Ingram (Adv. Mgr.); Joe Kimbro (Circ. Mgr.); Kelly Koontz (Press Foreman)
Parent company: Horizon Publications Inc.
Main (survey) contact: Leonard C. Martin

BURLEY

WEEKLY MAILER
Street Address1: 221 W Main St
Street Address2: P.O. Box 327
Street address state: ID
Postal code: 83318-1616
County: Cassia
Country: USA
Mailing address: PO Box 327
Mailing city: Burley
Mailing state: ID
Mailing zip: 83318-2909
Office phone: 2086786643
Office fax: (208) 678-6375
Advertising phone: (208) 678-6643
Advertising fax: (208) 678-6375
General e-mail: paul@theweeklymailer.com
Advertising e-mail: paul@theweeklymailer.com
Editorial e-mail: jay@theweeklymailer.com
Website: paul@theweeklymailer.com
Year publication established: 2005
Advertising (open inch rate): Open inch rate $16.00
Mechanical specifications: 9 pica column, one pica gutter, 6 columns wide by 11 inches tall.

COEUR D ALENE

NICKELS WORTH

Street Address1: 107 N 5th St
Street address state: ID
Postal code: 83814-2708
County: Kootenai
Country: USA
Mailing address: PO Box 2048
Mailing city: Coeur D Alene
Mailing state: ID
Mailing zip: 83816-2048
Office phone: (208) 667-0651
Office fax: (208) 765-6969
General e-mail: ads@nicklesworth.com
Advertising e-mail: ads@nicklesworth.com
Editorial e-mail: time@nicklesworth.com
Website: ads@nicklesworth.com
Year publication established: 1972
Advertising (open inch rate): Open inch rate $10.70
Mechanical specifications: Type page 10 x 15; A - 6 cols, 1 7/12, 1/6 between; C - 6 cols, 1 7/12, 1/6 between.
Zip Codes Served: 83816
Frequency: Thur
Circulation Paid: 13
Circulation Free: 31471
Audit By: CVC
Audit Date: 42916
Personnel: Tim Rostkoski (Distribution Mgr.); Chrissy Johnson (Ed.)
Main (survey) contact: Tim Rostkoski

Delivery methods: Mail
Zip Codes Served: 83318, 83350, 83336, 83343, 83347, 83311, 83312, 83323, 83342, 83346, 83350,
Digital Platform - Mobile: Windows
Frequency: Tues
Circulation Paid: 0
Circulation Free: 15722
Audit By: CVC
Audit Date: 42916
Personnel: Jay Lenkersdorfer (Ed. / Pub.); Paul Lyons (Circ & Adv. Mgr.)
Parent company: Sierra Marketing
Main (survey) contact: Jay Lenkersdorfer
Footnotes: Advertising (open inch rate): SRDS (11/10/2014); Frequency: SRDS (11/10/2014)

GRANGEVILLE

THE SHOPPER

Street Address1: 900 W Main St
Street Address2: Pob 690
Street address state: ID
Postal code: 83530-5192
County: Idaho
Country: USA
Mailing address: PO Box 690
Mailing city: Grangeville
Mailing state: ID
Mailing zip: 83530-0690
Office phone: (208) 983-1200
Office fax: (208) 983-1336
Advertising e-mail: amcnab@idahocountyfreepress.com
Year publication established: 1981
Advertising (open inch rate): $12.40 (combo with Free Press)
Mechanical specifications: 10-in X 20-in; 6-cols; 1.562-col
Delivery methods: Mail`Racks
Zip Codes Served: 83530;83522;83526;83523;83548;83555;83525;83536;83539;83539;83552;83539;83543;83542;83850;83547;83549;83554
Digital Platform - Mobile: Android
Digital Platform - Tablet: Windows 7
Frequency: Tues
Circulation Free: 10425
Audit By: CVC
Audit Date: 42185
Personnel: Andrew McNab
Main (survey) contact: Andrew McNab

IDAHO FALLS

THRIFTY NICKEL WANT ADS

Street Address1: 444 E Elva St
Street Address2: P.O. Box 1705
Street address state: ID
Postal code: 83401-2652
County: Bonneville
Country: USA
Mailing address: PO Box 1705
Mailing city: Idaho Falls
Mailing state: ID
Mailing zip: 83403-1705
Office phone: (208) 529-9360
Office fax: (208) 529-9491
General e-mail: photo@tnwa.org
Website: photo@tnwa.org
Year publication established: 1978
Advertising (open inch rate): Open inch rate $12.00
Mechanical specifications: Quarter Fold
Delivery methods: Newsstand`Racks
Zip Codes Served: 83403
Digital Platform - Mobile: Apple`Android
Frequency: Thur
Circulation Free: 3995
Audit By: CVC
Audit Date: 40878
Personnel: David Marlowe (Gen. Mgr.); Sherri Griffen (Adv. Mgr.)
Parent company: WantAds of Idaho Falls, Inc.
Main (survey) contact: David Marlowe

LEWISTON

MONEYSAVER-LEWIS CLARK EDITION

Street Address1: 626 Thain Rd
Street address state: ID
Postal code: 83501-5742
County: Nez Perce
Country: USA
Mailing address: PO Box 682
Mailing city: Lewiston
Mailing state: ID
Mailing zip: 83501-0682
Office phone: (208) 746-0483
Office fax: (208) 746-8507
Advertising e-mail: ads@lcmoneysaver.com
Year publication established: 1973
Advertising (open inch rate): Open inch rate $12.65
Mechanical specifications: Type page 10 1/12 x 15 1/2; E - 7 cols, 1 5/6, 1/6 between; A - 7 cols, 1 5/6, 1/6 between.
Zip Codes Served: 83501, 83520, 83522, 83523, 83524, 83525, 83526, 83530, 83533, 83534, 83535, 83536, 83536, 83537, 83538, 83539, 83540, 83541, 83543, 83544, 83545, 83546, 83551, 83552, 83553, 83554, 83555, 83806, 83823, 83825, 83827, 83834, 83836, 83843, 83855, 83857, 838
Frequency: Thur
Circulation Free: 37274
Audit By: CVC
Audit Date: 42185
Hardware: PCs, QMS/Laser Printer
Software: QPS/QuarkXPress 5.0, Adobe/PageMaker 6.5, Archetype/Corel Draw 6.5.
Personnel: Diane Johnson (Publication Mgr.); Ron Carroll (Circ. Mgr.)
Parent company: Eagle Newspapers, Inc.
Main (survey) contact: Diane Johnson

MONEYSAVER-PALOUSE EDITION

Street Address1: 626 Thain Rd
Street address state: ID
Postal code: 83501-5742
County: Nez Perce
Country: USA
Mailing address: 626 Thain Road
Mailing city: Lewiston
Mailing state: ID
Mailing zip: 83501

Office phone: (208) 882-2595
Office fax: (208) 883-4420
General e-mail: palouse@moneysav.com
Website: palouse@moneysav.com
Advertising (open inch rate): Open inch rate $6.50
Mechanical specifications: Type page 10 1/2 x 15 1/2; A - 7 cols, 1 5/6, 1/6 between; C - 7 cols, 1 5/6, 1/6 between.
Zip Codes Served: 83843, 99163
Frequency: Thur
Circulation Free: 5834
Audit By: CVC
Audit Date: 40787
Hardware: PCs, QMS/Laser Printer, Illustrator
Software: QPS/QuarkXPress, Adobe/PageMaker, Archetype/Corel Draw.
Personnel: Diane Johnson (Mgr.)
Parent company: Eagle Newspapers, Inc.
Main (survey) contact: Diane Johnson

MOUNTAIN HOME

FAMILY LINE

Street Address1: 195 S Third East St
Street address state: ID
Postal code: 83647
County: Elmore
Country: USA
Mailing address: PO Box 1330
Mailing city: Mountain Home
Mailing state: ID
Mailing zip: 83647-1330
Office phone: (208) 587-3331
Office fax: (208) 587-9205
General e-mail: bfincher@mountainhomenews.com
Website: bfincher@mountainhomenews.com
Advertising (open inch rate): 7,35
Mechanical specifications: 10.75" x 13"
Delivery methods: Mail`Racks
Zip Codes Served: 83647
Frequency: Tues
Circulation Free: 6000
Audit By: Sworn/Estimate/Non-Audited
Audit Date: 43658
Main (survey) contact: Brenda Fincher

NAMPA

IDAHO PRESS

Street Address1: 1618 N Midland Blvd
Street address state: ID
Postal code: 83651-1751
County: Canyon
Country: USA
Mailing address: PO Box 9399
Mailing city: Nampa
Mailing state: ID
Mailing zip: 83652-9399
Office phone: (208) 467-9251
Office fax: (208) 467-1863
Editorial e-mail: op-ed@idahopress.com
Zip Codes Served: 83651
Frequency: Wed
Circulation Free: 35000
Audit By: Sworn/Estimate/Non-Audited
Audit Date: 43658
Hardware: APP/Mac, PC
Presses: G/Community
Software: QPS/QuarkXPress 4.1.
Personnel: Angela Sammons (Media Sales Rep.); Ron Tincher (Circ. Dir.); Vickie Schaffeld Holbrook (Ed.); Joe Hansen (IT Dir.); Roger Stowell (Prodn. Dir.); Matt Davison (Publisher)
Parent company: Pioneer Newspapers Inc
Main (survey) contact: Matt Davison

POCATELLO

PORTNEUF VALLEY TRADER

Street Address1: 305 S Arthur Ave
Street address state: ID
Postal code: 83204-3306
County: Bannock

Country: USA
Mailing address: PO Box 431
Mailing city: Pocatello
Mailing state: ID
Mailing zip: 83204-0431
Office phone: (208) 232-4161
Office fax: (208) 233-8007
Advertising (open inch rate): Open inch rate $6.00
Mechanical specifications: Type page 11 2/3 x 20 1/2; A - 6 cols, 1 4/5, 1/7 between; C - 9 cols, 1 1/6, 1/5 between.
Zip Codes Served: 83204
Frequency: Wed
Circulation Free: 16800
Audit By: Sworn/Estimate/Non-Audited
Audit Date: 43658
Hardware: APP/Mac
Presses: G/Urbanite
Software: QPS/QuarkXPress.
Personnel: Bill Kunerth (Pub.); Matt Petrie (Adv. Dir.); Mikkel McBride (Adv. Asst.); Nathan Slater (Circ. Dir); Ian Fennell (Mng. Ed.); Justin Smith (Dir., IT Services)
Main (survey) contact: Bill Kunerth

TWIN FALLS

SOOPER ADS

Street Address1: 453 Main Ave E
Street address state: ID
Postal code: 83301-6422
County: Twin Falls
Country: USA
Mailing address: 453 Main Ave E
Mailing city: Twin Falls
Mailing state: ID
Mailing zip: 83301-6422
Frequency: Thur
Circulation Free: 11444
Audit By: CVC
Audit Date: 40969
Personnel: Richard Borah
Main (survey) contact: Richard Borah

ILLINOIS

ALEDO

TOWN CRIER

Street Address1: PO Box 309
Street address state: IL
Postal code: 61231-0309
County: Mercer
Country: USA
Office phone: (800) 582-4373

AUBURN

SOUTH COUNTY EXPRESS

Street Address1: 110 N 5th St
Street address state: IL
Postal code: 62615-1449
County: Sangamon
Country: USA
Mailing address: PO Box 50
Mailing city: Auburn
Mailing state: IL
Mailing zip: 62615-0050
Office phone: (217) 438-6155
Office fax: (217) 438-6156
General e-mail: southco@royell.org
Website: southco@royell.org
Advertising (open inch rate): Open inch rate $6.00
Mechanical specifications: Type page 10 3/16 x 15 1/2; A - 5 cols, 1 7/8, between.
Zip Codes Served: 62615, 62530, 62558, 62629, 62536, 62661
Frequency: Thur
Circulation Free: 10073
Audit By: Sworn/Estimate/Non-Audited
Audit Date: 43658

Shopper Publications in the U.S.

Personnel: Joseph Michelich (Pub.); Connie Michelich (Adv. Mgr.)
Parent company: South County Publications
Main (survey) contact: Joseph Michelich

BEARDSTOWN

STAR-GAZETTE EXTRA

Street Address1: 1210 Wall St
Street address state: IL
Postal code: 62618-2327
County: Cass
Country: USA
Mailing address: PO Box 79
Mailing city: Beardstown
Mailing state: IL
Mailing zip: 62618
Office phone: (217) 323-1010
Office fax: (217) 323-1644
Advertising phone: (217) 323-1010
Editorial phone: (217) 323-1010
Editorial fax: (217) 323-1644
Other phone: (217) 242-8221
General e-mail: sgbusiness@casscomm.com
Advertising e-mail: melissa.clements@casscomm.com
Editorial e-mail: editor@casscomm.com
Website: sgbusiness@casscomm.com
Year publication established: 1842
Advertising (open inch rate): please inquire
Mechanical specifications: please inquire
Delivery methods: Mail`Newsstand`Racks
Zip Codes Served: 62618
Digital Platform - Mobile: Apple`Android`Windows
Digital Platform - Tablet: Apple iOS`Android`Windows 7
Frequency: Mon`Thur
Circulation Paid: 2233
Circulation Free: 10008
Audit By: Sworn/Estimate/Non-Audited
Audit Date: 43658
Personnel: Melissa Clements (General Manager)
Parent company: Delphos Herald, Inc.
Main (survey) contact: Melissa Clements

BELLEVILLE

COMMAND POST

Street Address1: 120 S Illinois St
Street address state: IL
Postal code: 62220-2130
County: Saint Clair
Country: USA
Mailing address: PO Box 427
Mailing city: Belleville
Mailing state: IL
Mailing zip: 62222-0427
Office phone: (618) 234-1000
Office fax: (618) 235-0556
Advertising e-mail: classified@bnd.com; obits@bnd.com
Editorial e-mail: newsroom@bnd.com
Year publication established: 1858
Advertising (open inch rate): Open inch rate $15.96
Mechanical specifications: Type page 10 x 11 1/2; A - 5 cols, 2 1/16, 1/8 between; C - 8 cols, 1 1/4, 1/8 between.
Delivery methods: Mail`Racks
Zip Codes Served: 62220
Frequency: Fri
Circulation Free: 44000
Audit By: Sworn/Estimate/Non-Audited
Audit Date: 43658
Hardware: DEC/VAX, APP/Macs, PCs
Presses: G/Urbanite.
Personnel: Todd Eschman (Group Manager); Melissa Mason (Adv. Dir.); Marsha Hopkins (Sales Mgr.); John Grove (Circ. Dir.); Jeffry Couch (Ed.)
Main (survey) contact: Todd Eschman; Todd Eschman

BELVIDERE

BOONE COUNTY SHOPPER

Street Address1: 112 Leonard Ct
Street address state: IL
Postal code: 61008-3613
County: Boone
Country: USA
Mailing address: 112 Leonard Ct
Mailing city: Belvidere
Mailing state: IL
Mailing zip: 61008-3694
Office phone: (815) 544-2166
Office fax: (815) 544-5558
General e-mail: info@boonecountyshopper.com
Website: info@boonecountyshopper.com
Year publication established: 1957
Advertising (open inch rate): Open inch rate $16.75
Mechanical specifications: Type page 10 3/8 x 15; A - 6 cols, 1 5/8, 1/8 between.
Delivery methods: Mail
Zip Codes Served: 61008 61011 61065 61038 61012
Frequency: Thur
Circulation Paid: 0
Circulation Free: 20639
Audit By: CVC
Audit Date: 43081
Hardware: APP/Mac G3, APP/Mac G4
Software: Multi-Ad/Creator 4.0.2, Photoshop
Personnel: Edward Branom (Pres./Gen. Mgr.); Matthew Branom (Sales Mgr.)
Main (survey) contact: Edward L. Branom

CANTON

FULTON COUNTY SHOPPER

Street Address1: 53 W Elm St
Street address state: IL
Postal code: 61520-2511
County: Fulton
Country: USA
Mailing address: PO Box 540
Mailing city: Canton
Mailing state: IL
Mailing zip: 61520-0540
Office phone: (309) 647-5100
Office fax: (309) 647-4665
Advertising e-mail: twilliams@cantondailyledger.com
Editorial e-mail: drobinson@cantondailyledger.com
Advertising (open inch rate): Open inch rate $9.30
Frequency: Mon
Circulation Free: 17000
Audit By: Sworn/Estimate/Non-Audited
Audit Date: 43609
Personnel: Deb Robinson (Ed.); Rick Bybee (Circ. Mgr.); Terri Williams (Adv.)
Parent company: Gatehouse Media, LLC
Main (survey) contact: Deb Robinson

CARBONDALE

AT HOME WITH FLIPSIDE

Street Address1: 710 N Illinois Ave
Street address state: IL
Postal code: 62901-1283
County: Jackson
Country: USA
Mailing address: PO Box 2108
Mailing city: Carbondale
Mailing state: IL
Mailing zip: 62902-2108
Office phone: (618) 529-5454
Office fax: (618) 457-2935
General e-mail: shad.hicks@thesouthern.com
Advertising e-mail: lyn.sargent@thesouthern.com
Editorial e-mail: tom.english@thesouthern.com
Website: shad.hicks@thesouthern.com
Advertising (open inch rate): Open inch rate $10.50
Zip Codes Served: 62901, 62918, 62959, 62948, 62966
Frequency: Thur
Circulation Free: 36500
Audit By: Sworn/Estimate/Non-Audited
Audit Date: 43585
Personnel: Terra Kerkemeyer (Pub.); Tom English (Ed.); Lyn Sargent (Adv. Dir.); Shad Hicks (Circ. Dir.)
Parent company: Lee Enterprises, Incorporated
Main (survey) contact: Tom English

CARLINVILLE

ENQUIRER EXPRESS

Street Address1: 125 E Main St
Street address state: IL
Postal code: 62626-1726
County: Macoupin
Country: USA
Mailing address: PO Box 200
Mailing city: Carlinville
Mailing state: IL
Mailing zip: 62626-0200
Office phone: (217) 854-2534
Office fax: (217) 854-2535
General e-mail: enquirer@dtnspeed.net
Website: enquirer@dtnspeed.net
Advertising (open inch rate): Open inch rate $6.30
Mechanical specifications: Type page 10 x 15 1/2; A - 5 cols, 2, between.
Zip Codes Served: 62626
Frequency: Mon
Circulation Free: 15000
Audit By: Sworn/Estimate/Non-Audited
Audit Date: 43658
Personnel: Eric Berlin (Cir.Mgr); Jay Hendrids (Ed.)
Main (survey) contact: Jay Hendrids

CARMI

THE MONEY STRETCHER WHITE COUNTY

Street Address1: 323 E Main St
Street address state: IL
Postal code: 62821-1810
County: White
Country: USA
Mailing address: 323 E Main St
Mailing city: Carmi
Mailing state: IL
Mailing zip: 62821-1810
Office phone: (618) 382-4176
Office fax: (618) 384-2163
General e-mail: tknox@carmitimes.com
Advertising e-mail: ctrout@carmitimes.com
Website: tknox@carmitimes.com
Year publication established: 2012
Advertising (open inch rate): Open inch rate $8.80
Delivery methods: Mail
Zip Codes Served: 62821, 62835, 62887, 62820, 62869, 62827, 62867, 62871, 62844
Frequency: Tues
Circulation Free: 8200
Audit By: Sworn/Estimate/Non-Audited
Audit Date: 43658
Personnel: Tammy Knox (General Manager, Content)
Parent company: The Hays Daily News
Main (survey) contact: Kerry Kocher

CENTRALIA

CRIER/SCHROL,RLC CLOCKTOWEER

Street Address1: 232 E Broadway
Street address state: IL
Postal code: 62801-3251
County: Marion
Country: USA
Mailing address: PO Box 627
Mailing city: Centralia
Mailing state: IL
Mailing zip: 62801-9110
Office phone: (618) 532-5604
Office fax: (618) 532-5919
Advertising phone: same
Advertising fax: same
Editorial phone: (618) 532-5604
Editorial fax: (618) 532-5919
General e-mail: dnichols@moringsentinel.com
Advertising e-mail: same
Editorial e-mail: luanne Dreoge
Website: dnichols@moringsentinel.com
Year publication established: 1965
Advertising (open inch rate): Open inch rate $10.78
Delivery methods: Mail`Newsstand
Zip Codes Served: 62801 62881
Frequency: Wed
Other Type of Frequency: weekly
Circulation Free: 8000
Audit By: Sworn/Estimate/Non-Audited
Audit Date: 43658
Hardware: 227 mueller
Presses: Urbanite
Editions Count: 3
Edition Names with circulation: Rend Lake Clock tower 2300, Crier 2400 The Schrol 2200
Note: Single buy goes into all tmc targeted publications. TMC's are addressed and mailed to non Sentinel and Salem Times Commoner customers
Personnel: John Perrine (Pub.); Julie Copple (Bus. Office Mgr.); Dan Nichols (Adv. Mgr.); Ray Albert (circulation manager); Debbie Elling (Advertising Manager); luAnn Droege (editor)
Parent company: Centralia Press Ltd.
Main (survey) contact: Dan Nichols

THE SHOPPERS WEEKLY PAPERS

Street Address1: 301 E Broadway
Street address state: IL
Postal code: 62801-3252
County: Marion
Country: USA
Mailing address: PO Box 1223
Mailing city: Centralia
Mailing state: IL
Mailing zip: 62801-9118
Office phone: (618) 533-7283
Office fax: (618) 533-7284
General e-mail: info@theshoppersweekly.com
Advertising e-mail: ads@theshoppersweekly.com
Editorial e-mail: info@theshoppersweekly.com
Website: info@theshoppersweekly.com
Year publication established: 1988
Advertising (open inch rate): Open inch rate $14.00
Mechanical specifications: Type page 10 1/4 x 14; A - 6 cols, 1 2/3".
Delivery methods: Mail`Carrier`Racks
Zip Codes Served: 62801, 62881, 62864, 62812 & 20 others
Frequency: Wed
Circulation Free: 25500
Audit By: Sworn/Estimate/Non-Audited
Audit Date: 43658
Editions Count: 2
Edition Names with circulation: 2 total ÃƒÂ‚Ã‚Â—The Shopper's Weekly Mt. Vernon / Benton Paper (10,500); The Shopper's Weekly Centralia / Salem Paper (15,000);
Personnel: John Stuehmeier (General Manager); Rhonda Hatcher (Display Adv.); Cathy Stuehmeier (Publisher); Scott Pinkowski (Prodn. Mgr.)
Main (survey) contact: John Stuehmeier

CHICAGO

INSIDE BOOSTER

Street Address1: 6221 N Clark St
Street address state: IL
Postal code: 60660-1207
County: Cook
Country: USA
Mailing address: 6221 N Clark St
Mailing city: Chicago

Mailing state: IL
Mailing zip: 60660-1207
Office phone: (773) 465-9700
Office fax: (773) 465-9800
General e-mail: insidepublicationschicago@gmail.com
Advertising e-mail: inside1958@gmail.com
Editorial e-mail: insidepublicationschicago@gmail.com
Website: insidepublicationschicago@gmail.com
Year publication established: 1906
Advertising (open inch rate): 25
Mechanical specifications: 10.25" x 15.75" / 5 Columns
Delivery methods:
 Mail`Newsstand`Carrier`Racks
Zip Codes Served: 60618, 60613, 60647, 60657, 60614, 60622, 60610, 60611, 60625, 60640
Digital Platform - Tablet: Apple iOS`Android`Windows 7`Kindle`Nook`Kindle Fire
Frequency: Wed
Circulation Paid: 18
Circulation Free: 8433
Audit By: CVC
Audit Date: 43081
Hardware: iMac
Presses: none
Software: CS4
Editions Count: 52
Edition Names with circulation: News-Star, Inside-Booster & Skyline
Personnel: Ron Roenigk (publisher)
Main (survey) contact: Ron Roenigk

INSIDE-BOOSTER

Street Address1: 6221 N Clark St
Street address state: IL
Postal code: 60660-1207
County: Cook
Country: USA
Mailing address: 6221 N Clark St
Mailing city: Chicago
Mailing state: IL
Mailing zip: 60660-1207
Office phone: (773) 465-9700
Office fax: (773) 465-9800
Advertising phone: (773) 465-9700
Advertising fax: (773) 465-9800
Editorial phone: (773) 465-9700
Editorial fax: (773) 465-9800
General e-mail: insidepublicationschicago@gmail.com
Advertising e-mail: inside1958@gmail.com
Editorial e-mail: insidepublicationschicago@gmail.com
Website: insidepublicationschicago@gmail.com
Year publication established: 1906
Advertising (open inch rate): 22
Mechanical specifications: page size 10.25" wide x 15.75" tall
Delivery methods:
 Mail`Newsstand`Carrier`Racks
Zip Codes Served: 60610, 60611, 60613, 60614, 60618, 60622, 60625, 60626, 60640, 60657, 60660
Frequency: Wed
Other Type of Frequency: Bi-weekly
Circulation Paid: 18
Circulation Free: 8081
Audit By: CVC
Audit Date: 43100
Hardware: iMac
Presses: none
Software: CS4
Edition Names with circulation: Skyline, News-Star and Inside-Booster
Note: In Jan. 2013 we purchased Skyline newspaper
Personnel: Ron Roenigk (Publisher)
Main (survey) contact: Ron Roenigk

SKYLINE

Street Address1: 6221 N Clark St
Street address state: IL
Postal code: 60660-1207
County: Cook
Country: USA
Mailing address: 6221 N Clark St
Mailing city: Chicago
Mailing state: IL
Mailing zip: 60660-1207
Office phone: (773) 465-9700
Office fax: (773) 465-9800
General e-mail: insidepublicationschicago@gmail.com
Advertising e-mail: inside1958@gmail.com
Editorial e-mail: insidepublicationschicago@gmail.com
Website: insidepublicationschicago@gmail.com
Year publication established: 1906
Advertising (open inch rate): 22
Mechanical specifications: 10.25" x 15.75" / 5 Columns
Delivery methods:
 Mail`Newsstand`Carrier`Racks
Zip Codes Served: 60602, 60603, 60604, 60605, 60607, 60610, 60611, 60614, 60654
Digital Platform - Mobile: Apple
Digital Platform - Tablet: Apple iOS`Android`Windows 7`Kindle`Nook`Kindle Fire
Frequency: Wed
Circulation Paid: 18
Circulation Free: 3007
Audit By: CVC
Audit Date: 43100
Hardware: iMac
Presses: none
Software: CS4
Editions Count: 52
Edition Names with circulation: News-Star, Inside-Booster & Skyline
Personnel: Ron Roenigk (Pub.)
Main (survey) contact: Ron Roenigk

CRYSTAL LAKE
NORTHWEST CITIZEN SHOPPER

Street Address1: 7717 S Rte 31
Street address state: IL
Postal code: 60014
County: McHenry
Country: USA
Mailing address: 7717 S. Route 31
Mailing city: Crystal Lake
Mailing state: IL
Mailing zip: 60014-8132
Office phone: (815) 459-4040
Office fax: (815) 477-4960
Advertising phone: (815) 455-4800
Advertising fax: (815) 477-8898
Editorial phone: (815) 459-4122
Advertising (open inch rate): Open inch rate $7.15
Mechanical specifications: Type page 10 5/8 x 13; A - 5 cols, 2, 1/8 between; C - 7 cols, 1 1/4, 1/8 between.
Frequency: Wed
Circulation Paid: 4500
Circulation Free: 44818
Audit By: Sworn/Estimate/Non-Audited
Audit Date: 43658
Hardware: APP/Mac G3, AU/Oman Production System
Presses: 10-G/Urbanite
Software: QPS/QuarkXPress, Adobe/Photoshop, Adobe/Illustrator.
Editions Count: 3
Edition Names with circulation: 3 total Ã‚Â— Shopper's Service-North (9,653); Shopper's Service-South (22,735); Shopper's Service-West (16,930);
Personnel: John Rung (Pub./COO); Scott Rosenburgh (Vice Pres./Adv. Dir.); Chris Rutherford (Adv. Mgr.); J.Tom Shaw (Vice Pres./Mkt. Devel.); Brent Maring (Mktg. Dir.); Kara Hansen (Circ. Dir.); Dan McCaleb (Ed.); Chris Krug (Vice Pres./Exec. Ed.); Scott Helmchen (Features Ed.); Eric Olson (Sports Ed.)
Main (survey) contact: John Rung

DECATUR
HERALD NEWS REVIEW

Street Address1: 601 E William St
Street address state: IL
Postal code: 62523-1142
County: Macon
Country: USA
Mailing address: 601 East William Street
Mailing city: Decatur
Mailing state: IL
Mailing zip: 62523
Office phone: (219) 429-5151
Other phone: (800) 437-2533
General e-mail: http://herald-review.com/
Editorial e-mail: news@thenewsdispatch.com
Website: http://herald-review.com/
Advertising (open inch rate): Open inch rate $10.00
Mechanical specifications: Broadsheet format 10.125" wide by 20.75" deep
Delivery methods: Carrier
Zip Codes Served: 46360
Frequency: Mon
Circulation Free: 20000
Audit By: Sworn/Estimate/Non-Audited
Audit Date: 43658
Personnel: Julie McKiel (Circ. Mgr.); Adam Parkhouse (Sports Ed.); Bill Hackney (Publisher); Patrick Kellar (Pub.); Isis Cains (Adv. Dir.); Chris Schable (Exec. Ed.); David Hawk (Mng. Ed.)
Main (survey) contact: Gary Sawyer

PRAIRIE SHOPPER

Street Address1: 601 E William St
Street address state: IL
Postal code: 62523-1142
County: Macon
Country: USA
Mailing address: 601 E William St
Mailing city: Decatur
Mailing state: IL
Mailing zip: 62523-1142
Office phone: (217) 421-8940
Office fax: (217) 421-6942
Advertising (open inch rate): Open inch rate $12.59
Mechanical specifications: Type page 10 x 13; E - 6 cols, 1 2/3, between; A - 6 cols, 1 2/3, between.
Zip Codes Served: 62523
Frequency: Wed
Circulation Free: 25000
Audit By: Sworn/Estimate/Non-Audited
Audit Date: 43658
Hardware: APP/Mac
Software: Adobe/PageMaker 6.0, QPS/QuarkXPress, Adobe/Photoshop, Multi-Ad/Creator.
Personnel: John Knieriem (Circ. Mgr.); Gary Sawyer (Ed.); Don Whitman (Prodn. Mgr)
Main (survey) contact: John Knieriem

DEKALB
THE MIDWEEK

Street Address1: 1586 Barber Greene Rd
Street address state: IL
Postal code: 60115-7900
County: Dekalb
Country: USA
Mailing address: PO Box 587
Mailing city: Dekalb
Mailing state: IL
Mailing zip: 60115-0587
Office phone: (815) 756-4841
Office fax: (815) 756-2079
Editorial phone: (815) 787-7861
Advertising e-mail: obits@daily-chronicle.com
Editorial e-mail: news@daily-chronicle.com
Zip Codes Served: 60115, 60178, 60135, 60112, 60145, 60146, 60150
Frequency: Wed
Circulation Free: 28500
Audit By: Sworn/Estimate/Non-Audited
Audit Date: 43658
Personnel: Don Bricker (Pub.); Karen Pletsch (Advertising Director); Dana Herra
Parent company: Shaw Media
Main (survey) contact: Don Bricker

DURAND
VOLUNTEER PLUS

Street Address1: 109 E Oak St
Street address state: IL
Postal code: 61024-8000
County: Winnebago
Country: USA
Mailing address: PO Box 369
Mailing city: Durand
Mailing state: IL
Mailing zip: 61024-0369
Office phone: (815) 248-4407
Office fax: (815) 248-9176
General e-mail: volunteer@stateline-isp.com
Website: volunteer@stateline-isp.com
Advertising (open inch rate): Open inch rate $9.50
Mechanical specifications: Type page 10 x 16; A - 6 cols, 1 7/12, between; C - 6 cols, 1 7/12, between.
Frequency: Wed
Circulation Free: 5100
Audit By: Sworn/Estimate/Non-Audited
Audit Date: 43658
Software: Microsoft/Windows 95, Adobe/PageMaker 6.5.
Personnel: Curt Stalheim (Pub.); C.J. Gregg (Adv. Mgr.); Cheryl Bradt (Circ. Mgr.)
Main (survey) contact: Curt Stalheim

EFFINGHAM
CROSSROADS SUPERSAVER

Street Address1: 201 N Banker St
Street address state: IL
Postal code: 62401-2304
County: Effingham
Country: USA
Mailing address: PO Box 370
Mailing city: Effingham
Mailing state: IL
Mailing zip: 62401-0370
Office phone: (217) 347-7151
Office fax: (217) 342-9315
Advertising phone: (217) 347-7151
Advertising fax: (217) 342-9315
General e-mail: advertising@effinghamdailynews.com
Advertising e-mail: advertising@effinghamdailynews.com
Editorial e-mail: news@effinghamdailynews.com
Website: advertising@effinghamdailynews.com
Year publication established: 1980
Delivery methods: Mail`Carrier
Zip Codes Served: 62401, 62467, 62411, 62414, 62424, 62426, 62838, 62443, 62445, 62461, 62473, 62839, 62434, 62858, 62428, 62436, 62447, 62448, 62418,62426, 62458, 62880, 62432, 62448, 62459, 62475, 62479, 62480, 62481, 62854, 62422, 62431, 62444, 62462, 62463, 62465, 61957
Frequency: Wed
Circulation Free: 10000
Audit By: Sworn/Estimate/Non-Audited
Audit Date: 43658
Hardware:
Personnel: Todd Buenker (Circ. Mgr.)
Parent company: CNHI, LLC
Main (survey) contact: Darrell Lewis

EUREKA

WOODFORD STAR

Street Address1: 1926 S Main St
Street address state: IL
Postal code: 61530-1666
County: Woodford
Country: USA
Mailing address: PO Box 36
Mailing city: Eureka
Mailing state: IL
Mailing zip: 61530-0036
Office phone: (309) 467-3314
Office fax: (309) 467-4563
Advertising phone: (309) 467-3314 Ext. 203
Editorial phone: (309) 467-3314 Ext. 209
General e-mail: mbarra@mtco.com
Advertising e-mail: hbowman@mtco.com
Editorial e-mail: mcdowell@mtco.com
Website: mbarra@mtco.com
Year publication established: 1980
Advertising (open inch rate): Open inch rate $13.31
Mechanical specifications: Type page 11 5/8 x 21; E - 6 cols, 1 3/4, between; A - 6 cols, 1 3/4, 3/16 between; C - 9 cols, 1 3/16, 1/8 between.
Delivery methods: Mail
Zip Codes Served: 61530
Frequency: Mon
Circulation Free: 16200
Audit By: Sworn/Estimate/Non-Audited
Audit Date: 43658
Hardware: APP/Mac
Software: Photoshop Indesign
Personnel: Mark Barra (Dir.); Barry Winterland (Gen. Mgr.)
Main (survey) contact: Mark Barra

FREEPORT

FREEPORT SHOPPING NEWS

Street Address1: 1705 S Galena Ave
Street address state: IL
Postal code: 61032-2519
County: Stephenson
Country: USA
Mailing address: 1705 S Galena Ave
Mailing city: Freeport
Mailing state: IL
Mailing zip: 61032-2519
Office phone: (815) 235-4106
Advertising phone: (815) 235-4106
General e-mail: freeportshopnews@themonroetimes.com
Advertising e-mail: lhughes@themonroetimes.com
Website: freeportshopnews@themonroetimes.com
Year publication established: 1970
Advertising (open inch rate): Open inch rate $26.23
Mechanical specifications: Type page 10 3/8 x 16 3/4; A - 6 cols, 1 5/8, between.
Delivery methods: Mail Carrier
Zip Codes Served: 61032, 61013, 61018, 61019, 61048, 61070, 61027, 61044, 61062, 61085, 61030, 61046, 61078, 61007, 61039, 61067
Frequency: Wed
Other Type of Frequency: Weekly
Circulation Free: 21221
Audit By: CVC
Audit Date: 42368
Personnel: Laura Hughes (Sales Mgr.); Jaimie Tran (Prodn. Mgr.); Carl Hearing (Gen. Mgr.)
Main (survey) contact: Carl Hearing

GALATIA

SI DOLLAR SAVER

Street Address1: 109 N Main Cross St.
Street address state: IL
Postal code: 62935
County: Saline
Country: USA
Mailing address: 109 N Main Cross St.
Mailing city: Galatia
Mailing state: IL
Mailing zip: 62935
Office phone: (618) 268-4027
Office fax: (618) 268-4002
Editorial e-mail: jeanettebond492012@gmail.com
Year publication established: 2012
Advertising (open inch rate): Open inch rate $15.00
Mechanical specifications: Type page 9 3/4 x 14 1/2; E - 6 cols, 1 1/2, 1/6 between; A - 6 cols, 1 1/2, 1/6 between; C - 6 cols, 1 1/2, 1/6 between.
Frequency: Tues
Circulation Free: 27844
Audit By: Sworn/Estimate/Non-Audited
Audit Date: 43585
Hardware: APP/Power Mac 7200/90, Microtek/Scanmaker E6, QMS/Laserwriter 860, APP/Mac Quadra 630
Software: Multi-Ad/Creator 4.0, Adobe/Photoshop 4.0.
Personnel: Janette Bond (Pub.); James D. Bond (Pub.).
Parent company: The Hays Daily News
Main (survey) contact: Jeanette Bond

GALVA

WROVA WEEKLY SHOPPER

Street Address1: 348 Front St
Street address state: IL
Postal code: 61434-1365
County: Henry
Country: USA
Mailing address: 348 Front St
Mailing city: Galva
Mailing state: IL
Mailing zip: 61434-1365
Office phone: (309) 932-2103
Office fax: (309) 932-3282
General e-mail: galvinnews@mchsi.com
Website: galvinnews@mchsi.com
Advertising (open inch rate): Open inch rate $3.70
Frequency: Wed
Circulation Free: 2245
Audit By: Sworn/Estimate/Non-Audited
Audit Date: 43658
Personnel: Donald Cooper (Pub.); Kelly Duke (Adv. Mgr.); Doug Boock (Ed.)
Main (survey) contact: Mindy Calrs

GREENVILLE

BOND AND FAYETTE COUNTY SHOPPER

Street Address1: 201 N 3rd St
Street address state: IL
Postal code: 62246-1003
County: Bond
Country: USA
Mailing address: PO Box 16
Mailing city: Greenville
Mailing state: IL
Mailing zip: 62246-0016
Office phone: (618) 664-4566
Office fax: (618) 664-4567
Advertising phone: (618) 664-4566
Advertising (open inch rate): Open inch rate $9.25
Mechanical specifications: Type page 9 1/2 x 16.
Zip Codes Served: 62246
Frequency: Mon
Circulation Free: 20200
Audit By: Sworn/Estimate/Non-Audited
Audit Date: 43658
Hardware: APP/Mac
Software: Adobe/PageMaker, Multi-Ad/Creator.
Personnel: Steve Holt (Gen. Mgr.); Terri Holt (Ed.)
Main (survey) contact: Jill Tompkins

HIGHLAND

SHOPPER'S REVIEW

Street Address1: 1200 12th St
Street address state: IL
Postal code: 62249-1909
County: Madison
Country: USA
Mailing address: 1200 12th St
Mailing city: Highland
Mailing state: IL
Mailing zip: 62249-1909
Office phone: (618) 654-4459
Office fax: (618) 654-9702
Advertising e-mail: shoppersreview@charter.net
Year publication established: 1984
Advertising (open inch rate): Open inch rate $9.75
Delivery methods: Mail Newsstand
Zip Codes Served: 62201, 62216, 62230, 62245, 62249, 62061, 62074, 62273, 62275, 62281, 62293
Frequency: Tues
Circulation Paid: 133
Circulation Free: 18476
Audit By: CVC
Audit Date: 42368
Personnel: Jeff Stratton (Owner/Publisher)
Main (survey) contact: Jeff Stratton

HILLSBORO

M & M JOURNAL

Street Address1: 431 S Main St
Street address state: IL
Postal code: 62049-1433
County: Montgomery
Country: USA
Mailing address: PO Box 100
Mailing city: Hillsboro
Mailing state: IL
Mailing zip: 62049-0100
Office phone: (217) 532-3933
Office fax: (217) 532-3632
General e-mail: thejournal-news@consolidated.net
Advertising e-mail: advertisejn@consolidated.net
Website: thejournal-news@consolidated.net
Year publication established: 1974
Advertising (open inch rate): Open inch rate $4.00
Mechanical specifications: Type page 13 x 21 1/2; E - 9 cols, 1 3/10, 1/6 between; A - 9 cols, 1 3/10, 1/6 between; C - 9 cols, 1 3/10, 1/6 between.
Delivery methods: Mail
Zip Codes Served: 62049 62056 62075 62560 62626 62640 62690 and others
Frequency: Mon
Circulation Free: 21350
Audit By: Sworn/Estimate/Non-Audited
Audit Date: 43658
Hardware: APP/Mac
Presses: Nine Unit News King
Software: Adobe/PageMaker, QPS/QuarkXPress, Adobe/Photoshop, Adobe/Illustrator.
Personnel: John M. Galer (Publisher)
Main (survey) contact: John M. Galer

HOFFMAN ESTATES

DOLLAR WISE

Street Address1: 2500 W Higgins Rd
Street Address2: Ste 350
Street address state: IL
Postal code: 60169-7207
County: Cook
Country: USA
Mailing address: 2500 W Higgins Rd Ste 350
Mailing city: Hoffman Estates
Mailing state: IL
Mailing zip: 60169
Office phone: (630) 894-0934
Office fax: (630) 894-0953
Advertising (open inch rate): Open inch rate $50.00
Frequency: Wed
Circulation Free: 236580
Audit By: CVC
Audit Date: 38717
Personnel: Dino Thanos (Ed.)
Main (survey) contact: Dino Thanos

HOOPESTON

THE EXTRA

Street Address1: 308 E Main St
Street address state: IL
Postal code: 60942-1505
County: Vermilion
Country: USA
Mailing address: 308 E Main St
Mailing city: Hoopeston
Mailing state: IL
Mailing zip: 60942-1505
Office phone: (217) 283-5111
Office fax: (217) 283-5846
Advertising phone: (217) 283-5111
Advertising fax: (217) 283-5846
Editorial phone: (217) 283-5111
Editorial fax: (217) 283-5846
Advertising e-mail: chronads@frontier.com
Editorial e-mail: chronreporter@frontier.com
Year publication established: 1872
Advertising (open inch rate): Open inch rate $16.00
Mechanical specifications: Type page 10 1/4 x ; E - 6 cols, between; A - 6 cols, between; C - 6 cols, between.
Delivery methods: Mail
Zip Codes Served: 60942 60924 60953 60967 60960 60932 60963 60973 61811 61814 61848 47917 60924
Frequency: Wed`Fri
Circulation Paid: 602
Circulation Free: 7588
Audit By: Sworn/Estimate/Non-Audited
Audit Date: 43658
Editions Count: 52
Personnel: Jordan Crook (Reporter)
Parent company: Community Media Group
Main (survey) contact: Roberta Kempen

LA SALLE

ILLINOIS VALLEY SHOPPER

Street Address1: 426 2nd St
Street address state: IL
Postal code: 61301-2334
County: La Salle
Country: USA
Office phone: (815) 223-3200
Office fax: (815) 223-2543
Advertising phone: (815) 220-6945
Editorial phone: (815) 220-6940
General e-mail: sales@newstrib.com; support@newstrib.com
Advertising e-mail: vpsales@newstrib.com
Editorial e-mail: ntnews@newstrib.com
Website: sales@newstrib.com; support@newstrib.com
Year publication established: 1970
Advertising (open inch rate): Open inch rate $8.00
Mechanical specifications: Type page 13 x 21 1/2; E - 6 cols, 2 1/2, 1/3 between; A - 6 cols, 2 1/2, 1/3 between; C - 9 cols, 1 1/10, 1/3 between.
Delivery methods: Carrier`Racks
Zip Codes Served: LaSalle, Bureau & Putnam counties
Frequency: Wed
Circulation Free: 15000
Audit By: Sworn/Estimate/Non-Audited
Audit Date: 43658
Hardware: APP/Mac, PC
Presses: G/Urbanite
Software: QPS/QuarkXPress, APT, Adobe/Illustrator, Adobe/Photoshop.
Personnel: Joyce McCullough (Pub.); Scott Stravrakas (Adv.); Linda Kleczewski (Ed.); Joseph Zokal (Pre Press Mgr.); Mike Miller (Circ. Mgr.); Fort Miller (Mailroom Mgr.)
Parent company: NEWSTRIBUNE
Main (survey) contact: Joyce McCullough

LANARK

PRAIRIE ADVOCATE

Street Address1: 446 S Broad St
Street address state: IL
Postal code: 61046-1245
County: Carroll
Country: USA
Mailing address: PO Box 84
Mailing city: Lanark
Mailing state: IL
Mailing zip: 61046-0084
Office phone: (815) 493-2560
Office fax: (815) 493-2561
General e-mail: pa@pacc-news.com
Website: pa@pacc-news.com
Year publication established: 1937
Advertising (open inch rate): Open inch rate $14.80
Mechanical specifications: Type page 10 1/5 x 16; E - 5 cols, 2, 1/9 between; A - 5 cols, 2, 1/9 between; C - 5 cols, 2, 1/9 between.
Zip Codes Served: 61046, 61078, 61062, 61051, 61014, 61053, 61074, 61285, 61081, 61041, 61030, 61064, 52070
Frequency: Wed
Circulation Paid: 1994
Circulation Free: 14342
Audit By: CVC
Audit Date: 40969
Personnel: Elizabeth Lang (Circ. Mgr.); Thomas Kocal (Ed.); Craig Lang (Sports Ed.); Andrew Williamson (Marketing Rep); Lynn Kocal (Executive)
Main (survey) contact: Thomas Kocal

LINCOLN

LOGAN COUNTY SHOPPER

Street Address1: 2201 Woodlawn Rd
Street Address2: Ste 350
Street address state: IL
Postal code: 62656-9645
County: Logan
Country: USA
Mailing address: PO Box 740
Mailing city: Lincoln
Mailing state: IL
Mailing zip: 62656-0740
Office phone: (217) 732-2101
Office fax: (217) 732-7039
General e-mail: courier@lincolncourier.com
Website: courier@lincolncourier.com
Advertising (open inch rate): Open inch rate $5.59
Mechanical specifications: Type page 13 x 21 1/4; E - 6 cols, 2, 1/8 between; A - 6 cols, 2, 1/8 between; C - 9 cols, 1 3/8, between.
Zip Codes Served: 62656
Frequency: Wed
Circulation Free: 6200
Audit By: Sworn/Estimate/Non-Audited
Audit Date: 43658
Hardware: Dewar
Presses: G/Community.
Personnel: Michele Long (Pub.); Jody Roberts (Adv. Mgr.); Diana Wagner (Circ. Mgr.); Dan Tackett (News Ed.); Justin Tierney (Sports Ed.); Lisa Whitson (Website Mgr.)
Parent company: The Hays Daily News
Main (survey) contact: Greg Baumer

MENDOTA

MENDOTA SHOPPING GUIDE

Street Address1: 1313 Lakewood Dr
Street address state: IL
Postal code: 61342-1097
County: La Salle
Country: USA
Mailing address: 1313 Lakewood Drive
Mailing city: Mendota
Mailing state: IL
Mailing zip: 61342-1749
Office phone: (815) 539-9800
Office fax: (815) 539-7477
General e-mail: msg1@tsf.net
Website: msg1@tsf.net
Advertising (open inch rate): Open inch rate $7.40
Zip Codes Served: 61342
Frequency: Wed
Circulation Free: 11500
Audit By: Sworn/Estimate/Non-Audited
Audit Date: 43658
Personnel: Thomas G. Merkel (Ed.)
Main (survey) contact: Thomas G. Merkel

MOLINE

AD EXTRA

Street Address1: 1720 5th Ave
Street address state: IL
Postal code: 61265-7907
County: Rock Island
Country: USA
Mailing address: 1720 5th Ave
Mailing city: Moline
Mailing state: IL
Mailing zip: 61265-7907
Office phone: (309) 764-4344
Office fax: (309) 797-0311
Advertising phone: (309) 757-5019
Advertising fax: (309) 797-0321
Editorial phone: (309) 757-4990
Editorial fax: (309) 757-4992
Editorial e-mail: mchristensen@qctimes.com
Advertising (open inch rate): Open inch rate $19.79
Mechanical specifications: Type page 10.50" x 19.50"; 6 columns 1.56"
Delivery methods: Mail
Zip Codes Served: 61230, 61231, 61412, 61413, 61232, 61233, 61234, 61235, 61236, 61238, 61239, 61241, 61240, 61241, 61242, 61244, 61284, 61250, 61434, 61254, 61256, 61257, 61258, 61259, 61260, 61442, 61443, 61453, 61261, 61262, 61263, 61264, 61344, 61265, 61462, 61272, 61465, 61468, 61273, 61274, 61275, 61276, 61277, 61278, 61279, 61201, 61476, 61281, 61282, 61283, 61284, 61486, 61490, 52722, 52801, 52802, 52803, 52804, 52806, 52807
Frequency: Wed
Circulation Paid: 0
Circulation Free: 28000
Audit By: Sworn/Estimate/Non-Audited
Audit Date: 43658
Personnel: Deb Anslem (Pub.); Matt Christensen (Ed.)
Parent company: Dispatch-Argus
Main (survey) contact: Matt Christensen

MONMOUTH

PENNYSAVER

Street Address1: 400 S Main St
Street address state: IL
Postal code: 61462-2164
County: Warren
Country: USA
Mailing address: 400 S Main St
Mailing city: Monmouth
Mailing state: IL
Mailing zip: 61462-2164
Office phone: (309) 734-3176
Office fax: (309) 734-7649
General e-mail: generalmanager@reviewatlas.com
Website: generalmanager@reviewatlas.com
Advertising (open inch rate): Open inch rate $9.25
Mechanical specifications: Type page 10 1/4 x 16; E - 6 cols, between; A - 6 cols, between; C - 6 cols, between.
Zip Codes Served: 61462, 61473, 61469, 61447, 61453
Frequency: Wed
Circulation Free: 14350
Audit By: CVC
Audit Date: 38717
Hardware: APP/Power Mac G4, APP/Power Mac G3
Presses: 7-G/Community
Software: QPS/QuarkXPress, Multi-Ad/Creator, Adobe/Photoshop.
Personnel: Tony Scott (Gen. Mgr.); Cheryl Free (Bus. Mgr.); Wendy Todd (Adv. Mgr.); Dave Spence (Circ. Mgr.); Matt Hutton (Ed.); Marty Touchette (Sports Ed.); Ken Exum (Website Mgr.)
Parent company: The Hays Daily News
Main (survey) contact: Tony Scott

ALTERNATIVE NEWSPAPERS IN CANADA

EDMONTON

VUE WEEKLY

Publication Street Address: Suite 200-11230 119 St NW
Province: AB
Postal Code: T5G 2X3
Country: Canada
General Phone: (780) 426-1996
Personnel:
General/National Adv. Email:
Display Adv. Email:
Editorial Email:
Primary Website: www.vueweekly.com
Year Established:
Delivery Methods:
Own Printing Facility?:
Commercial printers?:
Mechanical specifications:
Published:
Avg Free Circ:
Audit By:
Audit Date:

HALIFAX

THE COAST

Publication Street Address: 2309 Maynard Street
Province: NS
Postal Code: B3K 3T8
Country: Canada
General Phone: (902) 422-6278
Personnel: Kyle Shaw (Ed)
General/National Adv. Email: audram@thecoast.ca
Display Adv. Email: sales@thecoast.ca
Editorial Email: news@thecoast.ca
Primary Website: https://thecoast.ca
Year Established: 1993
Delivery Methods: Newsstand`Racks
Own Printing Facility?:
Commercial printers?:
Mechanical specifications:
Published: Thur
Avg Free Circ: 22140
Audit By: Sworn/Estimate/Non-Audited
Audit Date: 43658

MONTREAL

HOUR

Publication Street Address: 355 St. Catherine W., 7th Fl.
Province: QC
Postal Code: H3B 1A5
Country: Canada
General Phone: (514) 848-0777
Personnel: Pierre Paquet (Pub.); Hugues Mailhot (Circ. Mgr.); Jamie O'Meara (Ed. in Chief)
General/National Adv. Email: listings@hour.ca
Display Adv. Email:
Editorial Email:
Primary Website: www.hour.ca
Year Established:
Delivery Methods:
Own Printing Facility?:
Commercial printers?:
Mechanical specifications:
Published: Thur
Avg Free Circ: 51700
Audit By: VAC
Audit Date: 37894

LE JOURNAL VOIR

Publication Street Address: 355 St. Catherine W., 7th Fl.
Province: QC
Postal Code: H3B 1A5
Country: Canada
General Phone: (514) 848-0805
Personnel: Simon Jodoin (Ed.-in-Chief)
General/National Adv. Email: courier@voir.ca
Display Adv. Email:
Editorial Email:
Primary Website: www.voir.ca
Year Established:
Delivery Methods:
Own Printing Facility?:
Commercial printers?:
Mechanical specifications:
Published: Thur
Avg Free Circ: 37292
Audit By: VAC
Audit Date: 40787

TORONTO

BAYVIEW POST

Publication Street Address: 30 Lesmill Road
Province: ON
Postal Code: M3B 2T6
Country: Canada
General Phone: (416) 250-7979
Personnel: Lorne London (Publisher)
General/National Adv. Email:
Display Adv. Email: advertising@postcity.com
Editorial Email: concerns@postcity.com
Primary Website: www.postcity.com
Year Established:
Delivery Methods:
Own Printing Facility?:
Commercial printers?:
Mechanical specifications:
Published: Mthly
Avg Free Circ: 24516
Audit By: VAC
Audit Date: 41912

NORTH TORONTO POST

Publication Street Address: 30 Lesmill Road
Province: ON
Postal Code: M3B 2T6
Country: Canada
General Phone: (416) 250-7979
Personnel: Lorne London (Publisher)
General/National Adv. Email:
Display Adv. Email: advertising@postcity.com
Editorial Email: concerns@postcity.com
Primary Website: www.postcity.com
Year Established:
Delivery Methods:
Own Printing Facility?:
Commercial printers?:
Mechanical specifications:
Published: Mthly
Avg Free Circ: 29392
Audit By: VAC
Audit Date: 40787

NORTH YORK POST

Publication Street Address: 30 Lesmill Road
Province: ON
Postal Code: M3B 2T6
Country: Canada
General Phone: (416) 250-7979
Personnel: Lorne London (Publisher)
General/National Adv. Email:
Display Adv. Email: advertising@postcity.com
Editorial Email: concerns@postcity.com
Primary Website: www.postcity.com
Year Established:
Delivery Methods:
Own Printing Facility?:
Commercial printers?:
Mechanical specifications:
Published: Mthly
Avg Free Circ: 24491
Audit By: VAC
Audit Date: 41912

NOW

Publication Street Address: 192 Spadina Ave
Province: ON
Postal Code: M5T 2C2
Country: Canada
General Phone: (416) 364-1300
Personnel: Alice Klein (Ed.); Ellie Kirzner (Sr. News Ed.); Enzo Dimatteo (Editorial Dir.); Kevin Ritchie (Sr. Culture Ed.); Lulu El-Atab (Art Dir.); Michelle Da Silva (Life & Social Media Ed.); Glenn Sumi (Assoc. Enter. Ed.); Norman Wilner (Sr. Writer); Natalia Manzacco (Food Writer)
General/National Adv. Email: news@nowtoronto.com
Display Adv. Email:
Editorial Email:
Primary Website: www.nowtoronto.com
Year Established: 1981
Delivery Methods: Mail`Newsstand`Racks
Own Printing Facility?:
Commercial printers?:
Mechanical specifications: Type page 9 13/16 x 11 1/4; E - 5 cols, 1 13/16, 3/16 between; A - 5 cols, 1 13/16, 3/16 between; C - 8 cols, 1 1/6, 1/8 between.
Published: Thur
Avg Free Circ: 71000
Audit By: CCAB
Audit Date: 43373

RICHMOND HILL POST

Publication Street Address: 30 Lesmill Road
Province: ON
Postal Code: M3B 2T6
Country: Canada
General Phone: (416) 250-7979
Personnel: Lorne London (Publisher)
General/National Adv. Email:
Display Adv. Email: advertising@postcity.com
Editorial Email: concerns@postcity.com
Primary Website: www.postcity.com
Year Established:
Delivery Methods:
Own Printing Facility?:
Commercial printers?:
Mechanical specifications:
Published: Mthly
Avg Free Circ: 24970
Audit By: VAC
Audit Date: 41912

THORNHILL POST

Publication Street Address: 30 Lesmill Road
Province: ON
Postal Code: M3B 2T6
Country: Canada
General Phone: (416) 250-7979
Personnel: Lorne London (Publisher)
General/National Adv. Email:
Display Adv. Email: advertising@postcity.com
Editorial Email: concerns@postcity.com
Primary Website: www.postcity.com
Year Established:
Delivery Methods:
Own Printing Facility?:
Commercial printers?:
Mechanical specifications:
Published: Mthly
Avg Free Circ: 24591
Audit By: VAC
Audit Date: 41912

VILLAGE POST

Publication Street Address: 30 Lesmill Road
Province: ON
Postal Code: M3B 2T6
Country: Canada
General Phone: (416) 250-7979
Personnel: Lorne London (Publisher)
General/National Adv. Email:
Display Adv. Email: advertising@postcity.com
Editorial Email: concerns@postcity.com
Primary Website: www.postcity.com
Year Established:
Delivery Methods:
Own Printing Facility?:
Commercial printers?:
Mechanical specifications:
Published: Mthly
Avg Free Circ: 24620
Audit By: VAC
Audit Date: 41912

VICTORIA

MONDAY MAGAZINE

Publication Street Address: 818 Broughton St.
Province: BC
Postal Code: V8W 1E4
Country: Canada
General Phone: (250) 480-3251
Personnel: Kyle Slavin; Janet Gairdner; Ruby Della-Siega
General/National Adv. Email:
Display Adv. Email: janet@mondaymag.com
Editorial Email: editorial@mondaymag.com
Primary Website: www.mondaymag.com
Year Established: 1975
Delivery Methods: Racks
Own Printing Facility?: Y
Commercial printers?: Y
Mechanical specifications:
Published: Mthly
Avg Free Circ: 18000
Audit By: Sworn/Estimate/Non-Audited
Audit Date: 43658

ALTERNATIVE NEWSPAPERS IN THE U.S.

ALBUQUERQUE

WEEKLY ALIBI
Website: http://alibi.com/
State: NM
Publisher Name: Pat Davis
Publisher Email: pat@abq.news

ASHEVILLE

MOUNTAIN XPRESS
Website: http://mountainx.com/
State: NC
Publisher Name: Jeff Fobes
Publisher Email: publisher@mountainx.com

ATHENS

FLAGPOLE MAGAZINE
Website: http://flagpole.com/
State: GA
Publisher Name: Pete McCommons
Publisher Email: editor@flagpole.com

AURORA

AURORA SENTINEL
Website: http://sentinelcolorado.com/
State: CO
Publisher Name: James Gold
Publisher Email: jgold@sentinelcolorado.com

AUSTIN

AUSTIN CHRONICLE
Website: http://austinchronicle.com/
State: TX
Publisher Name: Nick Barbaro
Publisher Email: barbaro@austinchronicle.com

BEND

SOURCE WEEKLY
Website: http://bendsource.com/
State: OR
Publisher Name: Aaron Switzer
Publisher Email: aaron@bendsource.com

BOISE

BOISE WEEKLY
Parent Company: Idaho Press
Website: http://boiseweekly.com/
State: ID
Publisher Name: A Gordon
Publisher Email: agordon@idahopress.com

BOSTON

DIG BOSTON
Website: http://digboston.com/
State: MA
Publisher Name: John Loftus
Publisher Email: john@digboston.com

BOULDER

BOULDER WEEKLY
Website: http://boulderweekly.com/
State: CO
Publisher Name: Stewart Sallo
Publisher Email: ssallo@boulderweekly.com

BURLINGTON

SEVEN DAYS
Website: http://sevendaysvt.com/
State: VT
Publisher Name: Paula Routly
Publisher Email: paula@sevendaysvt.com

CHARLESTON

CHARLESTON CITY PAPER
Website: http://charlestoncitypaper.com/
State: SC
Publisher Name: Andy Brack
Publisher Email: brack@charlestoncitypaper.com

CHARLOTTE

QUEEN CITY NERVE
Website: https://qcnerve.com/
State: NC
Publisher Name: Justin LaFrancois
Publisher Email: jlafrancois@qcnerve.com

CHARLOTTESVILLE

C-VILLE WEEKLY
Website: http://c-ville.com/
State: VA
Publisher Name: Anna
Publisher Email: anna@c-ville.com

CHICAGO

CHICAGO READER
Website: http://chicagoreader.com/
State: IL
Publisher Name: Tracy Baim
Publisher Email: tbaim@cicagoreader.com

CHICO

CHICO NEWS & REVIEW
Parent Company: News & Review
Website: http://newsreview.com/
State: CA
Publisher Name: Jeff von Kaenel
Publisher Email: jeffv@newsreview.com

CINCINNATI

CINCINNATI CITYBEAT
Parent Company: Euclid
Website: http://citybeat.com/
State: OH
Publisher Name: Tony Frank
Publisher Email: tfrank@citybeat.com

CLEVELAND

CLEVELAND SCENE
Parent Company: Euclid
Website: http://clevscene.com/
State: OH
Publisher Name: Andrew Zelman
Publisher Email: azelman@clevescene.com

COLORADO SPRINGS

COLORADO SPRINGS INDEPENDENT
Website: https://www.csindy.com/
State: CO
Publisher Name: Amy Sweet
Publisher Email: amy.sweet@csbj.com

COLUMBIA

COLUMBIA FREE TIMES
Website: http://free-times.com/
State: SC
Publisher Name: Chase Heatherly
Publisher Email: chaseh@free-times.com

DALLAS

DALLAS OBSERVER
Parent Company: Voice Media Group
Website: http://dallasobserver.com/
State: TX
Publisher Name: Stuart Folb
Publisher Email: Stuart.Folb@dallasobserver.com

DENVER

WESTWORD
Parent Company: Voice Media Group
Website: http://westword.com/
State: CO
Publisher Name: Scott Tobias
Publisher Email: scott.tobias@westword.com

DETROIT

METROTIMES
Parent Company: Euclid
Website: http://metrotimes.com/
State: MI
Publisher Name: Chris Keating
Publisher Email: ckeating@clevescene.com

EAU CLAIRE

VOLUME ONE
Website: https://volumeone.org/home
State: WI
Publisher Name: Nick Meyer
Publisher Email: nickm@volumeone.org

ERIE

ERIE READER
Website: http://eriereader.com/
State: PA
Publisher Name: David Hunter
Publisher Email: dhunter@epicwebstudios.com

EUGENE

EUGENE WEEKLY
Website: https://www.eugeneweekly.com/
State: OR
Publisher Name: Anita Johnson
Publisher Email: anitaj1@mindspring.com

EUREKA

NORTHBAY BOHEMIAN
Parent Company: Metro Newspapers
Website: http://bohemian.com/
State: CA
Publisher Name: Rosemary Olson
Publisher Email: rolson@bohemian.com

GREENSBORO, HIGH POINT, WINSTON-SALEM

TRIAD CITY BEAT
Website: http://triad-city-beat.com/
State: NC
Publisher Name: Brian Clarey
Publisher Email: brian@triad-city-beat.com

YES! WEEKLY
Website: http://yesweekly.com/
State: NC
Publisher Name: Charles Womack
Publisher Email: publisher@yesweekly.com

HALIFAX

COAST, THE
Website: http://thecoast.ca/
State: Nova Scotia CA
Publisher Name: Christine Oreskovich
Publisher Email: christineo@thecoast.ca

HOUSTON

HOUSTON PRESS
Parent Company: Voice Media Group
Website: http://houstonpress.com/
State: TX
Publisher Name: Stuart Folb
Publisher Email: stuart.folb@houstonpress.com

HUDSON VALLEY

CHRONOGRAM
Website: http://chronogram.com/
State: NY
Publisher Name: Amara Projansky
Publisher Email: amara@chronogram.com

IOWA CITY

LITTLE VILLAGE
Website: http://littlevillagemag.com/
State: IA
Publisher Name: Matthew Steele
Publisher Email: matt@littlevillagemag.com

JACKSON

JACKSON FREE PRESS
Website: http://jacksonfreepress.com/
State: MS
Publisher Name: Todd Stauffer
Publisher Email: todd@jacksonfreepress.com

JACKSONVILLE

FOLIO
Website: http://folioweekly.com/

Alternative Newspapers in the U.S.

State: FL
Publisher Name: John M Phillips
Publisher Email: jmp@folioweekly.com

KANSAS CITY

PITCH, THE

Website: http://thepitchkc.com/
State: KS
Publisher Name: Stephanie Carey
Publisher Email: stephanie@thepitchkc.com

LANSING

CITY PULSE

Website: http://lansingcitypulse.com/
State: MI
Publisher Name: Berl Schwartz
Publisher Email: publisher@lansingcitypulse.com

LAS VEGAS

LASVEGAS WEEKLY

Website: https://lasvegasweekly.com/
State: NV
Publisher Name: Mark De Pooter
Publisher Email: mark.depooter@gmgvegas.com

LEWISTON-CLARKSON

INLAND 360

Website: https://inland360.com/
State: ID/WA
Publisher Name: Nathan Alford
Publisher Email: alford@lmtribune.com

LITTLE ROCK

ARKANSAS TIMES

Website: http://arktimes.com/
State: AR
Publisher Name: Alan Leveritt
Publisher Email: alanleveritt@arktimes.com

LONGYEARBYEN, SVALBARD

ICE PEOPLE

Website: http://icepeople.net/
State: Norway

LOUISVILLE

LEO WEEKLY

Website: http://leoweekly.com/
State: KY
Publisher Name: Laura Snyder
Publisher Email: lsnyder@leoweekly.com

MADISON

ISTHMUS

Website: http://isthmus.com/
State: WI
Publisher Name: Jeff Haupt
Publisher Email: jhaupt@isthmus.com

MARIN CO.

PACIFIC SUN

Parent Company: Metro Newspapers
Website: http://pacificsun.com/
State: CA

Publisher Name: Rosemary Olson
Publisher Email: rolson@pacificsun.com

MEMPHIS

DAILY MEMPHIAN

Website: https://dailymemphian.com/
State: TN
Publisher Name: Eric Barnes
Publisher Email: barnes@dailymemphian.com

MEMPHIS

MEMPHIS FLYER

Website: http://memphisflyer.com/
State: TN
Publisher Name: Anna Traverse
Publisher Email: anna@contemporary-media.com

MIAMI

MIAMI NEW TIMES

Parent Company: Voice Media Group
Website: http://miaminewtimes.com/
State: FL
Publisher Name: Adam Simon
Publisher Email: adam.simon@miaminewtimes.com

MILWAUKEE

SHEPHERD EXPRESS

Website: http://shepex.com/
State: WI
Publisher Name: Louis Fortis
Publisher Email: Louis@shepex.com

MOBILE

LAGNIAPPE

Website: https://lagniappemobile.com/
State: AL
Publisher Name: "Rob Holbert"
Publisher Email: rholbert@lagniappemobile.com

MONTEREY COUNTY

MONTEREY COUNTY WEEKLY

Website: http://mcweekly.com/
State: CA
Publisher Name: Erik Cushman
Publisher Email: erik@mcweekly.com

NASHVILLE

NASHVILLE SCENE

Website: http://nashvillescene.com/
State: TN
Publisher Name: Mike Smith
Publisher Email: msmith@fwpublishing.com

NATIONAL

AMERICAN PROSPECT

Website: https://prospect.org/
Publisher Name: Ellen Meany
Publisher Email: ejmeany@prospect.org

NATIONAL

RAWSTORY

Website: http://rawstory.com/
Publisher Name: Roxanne Cooper

Publisher Email: rox@rawstory.com

NEW ORLEANS

GAMBIT

Website: http://gambitweekly.com/
State: LA
Publisher Name: Jeanne Foster
Publisher Email: jeannee@gambitweekly.com

OAKLAND

EAST BAY EXPRESS

Parent Company: Metro Newspapers
Website: http://eastbayexpress.com/
State: CA
Publisher Name: Dan Pulcrano
Publisher Email: dp@metronews.com

OMAHA

READER, THE

Website: http://thereader.com/
State: NE
Publisher Name: John Heaston
Publisher Email: john@thereader.com

ORLANDO

ORLANDO WEEKLY

Parent Company: Euclid
Website: http://orlandoweekly.com/
State: FL
Publisher Name: Graham Jarrett
Publisher Email: Graham@orlandoweekly.com

PALM SPRINGS

COACHELLA VALLEY INDEPENDENT

Website: http://cvindependent.com/
State: CA
Publisher Name: Jimmy Boegle
Publisher Email: jboegle@cvindependent.com

PALO ALTO

PALO ALTO WEEKLY

Website: https://www.paloaltoonline.com/
State: CA
Publisher Name: Bill Johnson
Publisher Email: bjohnson@embarcaderopublishing.com

PHOENIX

PHOENIX NEW TIMES

Parent Company: Voice Media Group
Website: http://newtimes.com/
State: AZ
Publisher Name: Kurtis Barton
Publisher Email: kurtis.barton@newtimes.com

PITTSBURGH

PITTSBURGH CITY PAPER

Website: http://pghcitypaper.com/
State: PA
Publisher Name: Jasmine Hughes
Publisher Email: jhughes@pghcitypaper.com

PITTSBURGH

PITTSBURGH CURRENT

Website: http://pittsburghcurrent.com/
State: PA
Publisher Name: Charlie Deitch

Publisher Email: charlie@pittsburghcurrent.com

PORTLAND

WILLAMETTE WEEK

Parent Company: City of Roses
Website: http://wweek.com/
State: OR
Publisher Name: Mark Zusman
Publisher Email: mzusman@wweek.com

RALEIGH-DURHAM

INDY WEEK

Parent Company: City of Roses
Website: http://indyweek.com/
State: NC
Publisher Name: Susan Harper
Publisher Email: sharper@indyweek.com

RENO

RENO NEWS & REVIEW

Parent Company: News & Review
Website: http://newsreview.com/
State: NV
Publisher Name: Jeff von Kaenel
Publisher Email: jeffv@newsreview.com

RICHMOND

STYLE WEEKLY

Website: http://styleweekly.com/
State: VA
Publisher Name: Lori Waran
Publisher Email: lori.waran@styleweekly.com

ROCHESTER

CITY

Website: http://rochester-citynews.com/
State: NY
Publisher Name: Norm Silverstein
Publisher Email: norms@wxxi.org

SACRAMENTO

SACRAMENTO NEWS & REVIEW

Parent Company: News & Review
Website: https://www.newsreview.com/sacramento/home
State: CA
Publisher Name: Jeff von Kaenel
Publisher Email: jeffv@newsreview.com

SALT LAKE CITY

SALT LAKE CITY WEEKLY

Website: http://cityweekly.net/
State: UT
Publisher Name: Pete Saltas
Publisher Email: pete@cityweekly.net

SAN ANTONIO

SAN ANTONIO CURRENT

Parent Company: Euclid
Website: http://sacurrent.com/
State: CA
Publisher Name: Michael Wagner
Publisher Email: mwagner@sacurrent.com

SAN DIEGO

SAN DIEGO READER

Website: http://sandiegoreader.com/

State: CA
Publisher Name: Jim Holman
Publisher Email: jholman@nethere.com

SAN JOSE
METRO SILICON VALLEY
Parent Company: Metro Newspapers
Website: http://metronews.com/
State: CA
Publisher Name: Dan Pulcrano
Publisher Email: dp@metronews.com

SAN LUIS OBISPO
NEW TIMES
Website: http://newtimesslo.com/
State: CA
Publisher Name: Bob Rucker, Alex Zuniga
Publisher Email: bob@newtimesslo.com, Alex@newtimesslo.com

SAN PEDRO
RANDOM LENGTHS NEWS
Website: http://randomlengthsnews.com/
State: CA
Publisher Name: James Preston Allen
Publisher Email: james@randomlengthsnews.com

SANTA BARBARA
SANTA BARBARA INDEPENDENT
Website: http://independent.com/
State: CA
Publisher Name: Brandi Rivera
Publisher Email: brandi@independent.com

SANTA CRUZ
SANTA CRUZ GOOD TIMES
Parent Company: Metro Newspapers
Website: http://santacruz.com/
State: CA
Publisher Name: Dan Pulcrano
Publisher Email: dp@metronews.com

SANTA FE
SANTA FE REPORTER
Parent Company: City of Roses
Website: http://sfreporter.com/
State: NM
Publisher Name: Julie Ann Grimm
Publisher Email: editor@sfreporter.com

SONOMA AND NAPA CO.
NORTHCOAST JOURNAL
Parent Company: Metro Newspapers
Website: http://northcoastjournal.com/
State: CA
Publisher Name: Judy Hodgson
Publisher Email: judy@northcoastjournal.com

SPOKANE
INLANDER
Website: http://inlander.com/
State: WA
Publisher Name: Ted S. McGregor, Jr.
Publisher Email: tedm@inlander.com

SPRINGFIELD
ILLINOIS TIMES
Website: http://illinoistimes.com/
State: IL
Publisher Name: Michelle Ownbey
Publisher Email: mownbey@illinoistimes.com

ST. LOUIS
RIVERFRONT TIMES
Parent Company: Euclid
Website: https://www.riverfronttimes.com/
State: MO
Publisher Name: Chris Keating
Publisher Email: ckeating@clevescene.com

STATEWIDE
MONTANA PRESS
Website: https://www.montanapress.net/
State: MT
Publisher Name: Reilly Neill
Publisher Email: info@montanapress.net

TAMPA
CREATIVE LOAFING TAMPA
Parent Company: Euclid
Website: http://cltampa.com/
State: FL
Publisher Name: James Howard
Publisher Email: james.howard@cltampa.com

TOLEDO
TOLEDO CITY PAPER
Website: http://toledocitypaper.com/
State: OH
Publisher Name: Collette Jacobs
Publisher Email: cjacobs@toledocitypaper.com

TUCSON
TUCSON WEEKLY
Website: https://www.tucsonweekly.com/
State: AZ
Publisher Name: Jason Joseph
Publisher Email: jjoseph@azlocalmedia.com

WAILUKU
MAUI TIME
Website: http://mauitime.com/
State: HI
Publisher Name: Tommy Russo
Publisher Email: tommy@mauitjme.com

WASHINGTON
WASHINGTON CITY PAPER
Website: http://washingtoncitypaper.com/
State: DC
Publisher Name: Duc Luu
Publisher Email: dluu@washingtoncitypaper.com

WAUSAU
WAUSAU CITY PAGES
Website: http://thecitypages.com/
State: WI
Publisher Name: Tim Schreiber
Publisher Email: tschreiber@mmclocal.com

WORCESTER
WORCESTER MAGAZINE
Website: https://www.worcestermag.com/
State: MA
Publisher Name: Paul Provost
Publisher Email: paul.provost@telegram.com

BLACK NEWSPAPERS IN THE U.S.

ALBANY

ALBANY SOUTHWEST GEORGIAN
Street Address: 311 S Jackson St, Ste A
State: GA
ZIP Code: 31701-0689
County: Dougherty
Country: USA
Mailing Address: PO Box 1943
Mailing City: Albany
Mailing State: GA
Mailing ZIP: 31702-1943
General Phone: (229) 436-2156
General Fax: (229) 435-6860
General/National Adv. E-mail: aswgeorgian@gmail.com
Year Established: Year Established: 1938
Delivery Methods: Mail`Carrier`Racks
Areas Served - City/County or Portion Thereof, or ZIP Codes: 317 013 170 531 707 000 000 000 000 000 000 000 000 000 000 000 000 000 000 000
Mechanical specifications: Full page: 21x10.833, Half page: 10x10.833, 1/4 page:10x5.333
Published: Wed
Audit By: Sworn/Estimate/Non-Audited
Audit Date: 12.07.2019
Personnel: G Searles (Publisher)

ALEXANDRIA

ALEXANDRIA NEWS WEEKLY
Street Address: 1746 Mason St,
State: LA
ZIP Code: 71301-6242
County: Rapides
Country: USA
Mailing Address: 1746 Mason St
Mailing City: Alexandria
Mailing State: LA
Mailing ZIP: 71301-6242
General Phone: (318) 443-7664
Advertising Fax: (318) 487-1227
General/National Adv. E-mail: anwnews@bellsouth.net
Mechanical specifications: Type page 14 x 21; E - 6 cols, between; A - 6 cols, between; C - 9 cols, between.
Published: Thur
Avg Paid Circ: 10000
Audit By: Sworn/Estimate/Non-Audited
Audit Date: 12.07.2019
Personnel: Leon Coleman (Adv. Mgr.); Alice Coleman (Ed.)

ATLANTA

ATLANTA DAILY WORLD
Street Address: 3485 N Desert Dr, Ste 2109
State: GA
ZIP Code: 30344-8125
County: Fulton
Country: USA
Mailing Address: 100 Hartsfield Centre Pkwy Ste 500
Mailing City: Atlanta
Mailing State: GA
Mailing ZIP: 30344
General Phone: 404-761-1114
General Fax: 404-761-1164
Advertising Phone: 678-515-2053
General/National Adv. E-mail: publisher@atlantadailyworld.com; adwnews@atlantadailyworld.com
Display Adv. E-mail: advertising@atlantadailyworld.com
Editorial e-mail: adwnews@atlantadailyworld.com
Primary Website: www.atlantadailyworld.com
Year Established: Year Established: 1928

Delivery Methods: Mail`Newsstand`Carrier`Racks
Commercial printers?: Y
Mechanical specifications: Type page 10.5 X 13; E - 6 cols, 2, 1/8 between; A - 6 cols, 2, 1/8 between; C - 8 cols, 1 1/2, 1/16 between.
Published: Thur
Published Other: daily online
Avg Paid Circ: 0
Avg Free Circ: 3836
Audit By: VAC
Audit Date: 31.03.2016
Personnel: Alexis Scott (Pub.); Michelle Gipson (Adv. Dir.); Maria Odum-Hinmon (Mng. Ed.); Wendell Scott (Prodn. Mgr.)
Parent company (for newspapers): Real Times Media, Inc.

THE ATLANTA INQUIRER
Street Address: 947 Martin Luther King Jr Dr NW,
State: GA
ZIP Code: 30314-2947
County: Fulton
Country: USA
Mailing Address: 947 Martin Luther KingJr. Dr. NW
Mailing City: Atlanta
Mailing State: GA
Mailing ZIP: 30314-0367
General Phone: (404) 523-6086
General Fax: (404) 523-6088
General/National Adv. E-mail: news@atlinq.com
Display Adv. E-mail: ads@atlinq.com
Editorial e-mail: news@atlinq.com
Primary Website: www.atlinq.com
Year Established: Year Established: 1960
Areas Served - City/County or Portion Thereof, or ZIP Codes: 30001, 30181, 30265, 30333, 30453, 31208
Mechanical specifications: Type page 11 1/2 x 21 1/2; E - 6 cols, 2 1/16, between; A - 6 cols, 2 1/16, between; C - 6 cols, 2 1/16, between.
Published: Thur
Avg Paid Circ: 0
Avg Free Circ: 0
Audit By: Sworn/Estimate/Non-Audited
Audit Date: 12.07.2019
Personnel: Sallie Pope Howard (Adv. Mgr.); Herbert Linsey (Circ. Mgr.); John B. Smith (Ed.); Kimberly Bryant (Prodn. Mgr.)

THE ATLANTA VOICE
Street Address: 633 Pryor St SW,
State: GA
ZIP Code: 30312-2738
County: Fulton
Country: USA
Mailing Address: 633 Pryor St SW
Mailing City: Atlanta
Mailing State: GA
Mailing ZIP: 30312-2789
General Phone: (404) 524-6426
General Fax: (404) 523-7853
Advertising Phone: (404) 524-6426 x 15
Editorial Phone: (404) 524-6426 x 13
General/National Adv. E-mail: info@theatlantavoice.com
Display Adv. E-mail: ads@theatlantavoice.com
Primary Website: www.theatlantavoice.com
Year Established: Year Established: 1966
Delivery Methods: Mail`Newsstand`Racks
Own Printing Facility?: Y
Mechanical specifications: Type page 10 x 13 1/2; A - 6 cols, 1 1/2, 1/4 between; C - 6 cols, 1 1/2, 1/4 between.
Published: Fri
Published Other: Electronic Edition
Avg Free Circ: 17440
Audit By: AAM
Audit Date: 30.06.2018
Personnel: Janis L. Ware (Pub.); James A. Washington (Editor); April Ivey (Sales Asst.); Stan Washington (Ed. in Chief.); April

Armstrong (Adv./Circ. Mgr.)
Parent company (for newspapers): Voice News Network

AUGUSTA

THE METRO COURIER
Street Address: 314 Walton Way,
State: GA
ZIP Code: 30901-2436
County: Richmond
Country: USA
Mailing Address: PO Box 2385
Mailing City: Augusta
Mailing State: GA
Mailing ZIP: 30903-2385
General Phone: (706) 724-6556
General Fax: (706) 722-7104
General/National Adv. E-mail: metrocourier@comcast.net
Mechanical specifications: Type page 13 x 21; E - 6 cols, 2, 1/5 between; A - 6 cols, 2, 1/5 between; C - 6 cols, 2, 1/5 between.
Published: Thur
Avg Paid Circ: 29010
Audit By: Sworn/Estimate/Non-Audited
Audit Date: 12.07.2019
Personnel: Barbara A. Gordon (Ed.)

AUSTIN

THE VILLAGER
Street Address: 4132 E 12th St,
State: TX
ZIP Code: 78721-1905
County: Travis
Country: USA
Mailing Address: 4132 E 12th St
Mailing City: Austin
Mailing State: TX
Mailing ZIP: 78721-1905
General Phone: (512) 476-0082
General Fax: (512) 476-0179
General/National Adv. E-mail: vil3202@aol.com
Display Adv. E-mail: vil3202@aol.com
Editorial e-mail: vil3202@aol.com
Primary Website: N/A
Year Established: Year Established: 1973
Delivery Methods: Racks
Areas Served - City/County or Portion Thereof, or ZIP Codes: 78701, 78702, 78704, 78721, 78723, 78744, 78741, 78751, 7860
Own Printing Facility?: N
Commercial printers?: N
Mechanical specifications: Type page 11.25 x 21; E - 6 cols, 1.75 between; A - 6 cols, 2, 1/8 between; C - 6 cols, 2, 1/8 between.
Published: Fri
Avg Free Circ: 5975
Audit By: CVC
Audit Date: 31.12.2018
Personnel: T.L. Wyatt (Ed./Pub)

BAKERSFIELD

BAKERSFIELD NEWS OBSERVER
Street Address: 1219 20th St,
State: CA
ZIP Code: 93301-4611
County: Kern
Country: USA
Mailing Address: PO Box 2341
Mailing City: Bakersfield
Mailing State: CA
Mailing ZIP: 93303
General Phone: (661) 324-9466
General Fax: (661) 324-9472
General/National Adv. E-mail: observernews@gmail.com
Display Adv. E-mail: observeradvertising@

gmail.com
Editorial e-mail: jamesluckey@thenewsobserver.net
Primary Website: theobservergroup.com
Year Established: Year Established: 1977
Delivery Methods: Newsstand`Carrier`Racks
Areas Served - City/County or Portion Thereof, or ZIP Codes: 93301, 93304, 93305, 93306, 93307, 93309, 93312, 93313, 93314
Mechanical specifications: Type page 13 x 21; E - 6 cols, 2, 1/4 between; A - 6 cols, 2, 1/4 between; C - 10 cols, 1 1/2, 1/4 between.
Published: Wed
Avg Free Circ: 40000
Audit By: Sworn/Estimate/Non-Audited
Audit Date: 12.07.2019
Personnel: Ellen Coley (Owner); James Luckey (Editor); Jon Coley (Owner)

BALTIMORE

EVERY WEDNESDAY
Street Address: 2519 N Charles St,
State: MD
ZIP Code: 21218-4602
County: Baltimore City
Country: USA
Mailing Address: 2519 N Charles St
Mailing City: Baltimore
Mailing State: MD
Mailing ZIP: 21218-4602
General Phone: (410) 554-8200
General Fax: (410) 554-8150
Primary Website: www.afro.com
Published: Wed
Personnel: John J. Oliver (Pub.); Susan Warshaw (Adv. Mgr.); Dorothy Boulware (Ed.)

PRINCE GEORGE'S COUNTY TIMES
Street Address: 2513 N Charles St,
State: MD
ZIP Code: 21218-4602
County: Baltimore City
Country: USA
Mailing Address: 2513 N Charles St
Mailing City: Baltimore
Mailing State: MD
Mailing ZIP: 21218-4602
General Phone: (410) 366-3900
General Fax: (410) 243-1627
General/National Adv. E-mail: btimes@btimes.com
Primary Website: www.btimes.com
Published: Fri
Personnel: Donnie Manuel (Adv. Sales Mgr.); Joy Bramble (Mng. Ed.); Freddie Howard (Prodn. Mgr.)

THE AFRO AMERICAN NEWSPAPER-BALTIMORE
Street Address: 2519 N Charles St,
State: MD
ZIP Code: 21218-4602
County: Baltimore City
Country: USA
Mailing Address: 2519 N Charles St
Mailing City: Baltimore
Mailing State: MD
Mailing ZIP: 21218-4602
General Phone: (410) 554-8200
General Fax: (877) 570-9297
General/National Adv. E-mail: adafro@afro.com
Primary Website: www.afro.com
Mechanical specifications: Type page 13 x 21; E - 6 cols, 2, 1/8 between; A - 6 cols, 2, 1/8 between; C - 9 cols, 1 1/2, between.
Published: Sat
Avg Paid Circ: 5234
Avg Free Circ: 261
Audit By: AAM
Audit Date: 30.09.2014

Personnel: John J. Oliver (Pub.); Susan Warshaw (Adv. Mgr.); Sammy Graham (Circ. Mgr.); Tiffaney Ginyard (Mng. Ed.); Lenora Howze (Adv. Dir.)

THE AFRO AMERICAN NEWSPAPER-WASHINGTON

Street Address: 2519 N Charles St,
State: MD
ZIP Code: 21218-4602
County: Baltimore City
Country: USA
Mailing Address: 2519 N Charles St
Mailing City: Baltimore
Mailing State: MD
Mailing ZIP: 21218-4602
General Phone: (410) 554-8200
General Fax: (877) 570-9297
General/National Adv. E-mail: adafro@afro.com
Primary Website: www.afro.com
Published: Sat
Personnel: John J. Oliver (Pub.); Susan Warshaw (Adv. Mgr.)

THE ANNAPOLIS TIMES

Street Address: 2513 N Charles St,
State: MD
ZIP Code: 21218-4602
County: Baltimore City
Country: USA
Mailing Address: 2513 N Charles St
Mailing City: Baltimore
Mailing State: MD
Mailing ZIP: 21218-4602
General Phone: (410) 366-3900
General Fax: (410) 243-1627
General/National Adv. E-mail: btimes@btimes.com
Display Adv. E-mail: ads@btimes.com
Editorial e-mail: jbramble@btimes.com
Primary Website: btimes.com
Year Established: Year Established: 1986
Delivery Methods: Carrier`Racks
Own Printing Facility?: Y
Published: Fri
Avg Free Circ: 3975
Audit By: CVC
Audit Date: 30.03.2017
Personnel: Joy Bramble (Pub.); Ida Neal (Circ. Mgr)

THE BALTIMORE TIMES

Street Address: 2513 N Charles St,
State: MD
ZIP Code: 21218-4602
County: Baltimore City
Country: USA
Mailing Address: 2513 N Charles St
Mailing City: Baltimore
Mailing State: MD
Mailing ZIP: 21218-4602
General Phone: (410) 366-3900
General Fax: (410) 243-1627
General/National Adv. E-mail: ineal@btimes.com
Display Adv. E-mail: ads@btimes.com
Editorial e-mail: jbramble@btimes.com
Primary Website: baltimoretimes-online.com
Year Established: Year Established: 1986
Delivery Methods: Carrier`Racks
Own Printing Facility?: Y
Mechanical specifications: Type page 10 x 13; E - 5 cols, 1 19/20, between; A - 5 cols, 1 19/20, between; C - 5 cols, 1 19/20, between.
Published: Fri
Avg Free Circ: 19975
Audit By: CVC
Audit Date: 30.03.2017
Personnel: Joy Bramble (Pub.); Donnie Manuel (Sales Mgr.); Dena Wane (Mng. Ed.); Freddie Howard (Prodn. Mgr.); Ida Neal (Circ. Mgr)

BROOKLYN

AFRO TIMES

Street Address: 1195 Atlantic Ave,
State: NY
ZIP Code: 11216-2709
County: Kings
Country: USA
Mailing Address: 1195 Atlantic Ave
Mailing City: Brooklyn
Mailing State: NY
Mailing ZIP: 11216-2709
General Phone: (718) 636-9119
General Fax: (718) 857-9115
General/National Adv. E-mail: challengegroup@yahoo.com
Published: Thur
Avg Paid Circ: 57004
Audit By: Sworn/Estimate/Non-Audited
Audit Date: 12.07.2019
Personnel: Thomas H. Watkins (Pub.); Ariana Perez (Adv. Mgr.); Janel Gross (Mng. Ed.)

OUR TIME PRESS

Street Address: 679 Lafayette Ave,
State: NY
ZIP Code: 11216-1009
County: Kings
Country: USA
Mailing Address: 679 Lafayette Ave
Mailing City: Brooklyn
Mailing State: NY
Mailing ZIP: 11216-1009
General Phone: (718) 599-6828
General Fax: (718) 599-6825
Editorial e-mail: editors@ourtimepress.com
Primary Website: www.ourtimepress.com
Year Established: Year Established: 1995
Delivery Methods: Mail`Carrier`Racks
Areas Served - City/County or Portion Thereof, or ZIP Codes: 11201, 11205, 11207, 11212, 11213, 11216, 11217, 11221, 11225, 11233, 11238
Mechanical specifications: Type page 10 x 15; E - 4 cols, 2 3/8, 1/6 between; A - 4 cols, 2 3/8, 1/6 between; C - 5 cols, 1 7/8, 1/6 between.
Published: Thur
Avg Free Circ: 20000
Audit By: Sworn/Estimate/Non-Audited
Audit Date: 12.07.2019
Personnel: David Mark Greaves (Ed.); Bernice Elizabeth Green (Ed.)

THE NEW AMERICAN

Street Address: 1195 Atlantic Ave,
State: NY
ZIP Code: 11216-2709
County: Kings
Country: USA
Mailing Address: 1195 Atlantic Ave
Mailing City: Brooklyn
Mailing State: NY
Mailing ZIP: 11216-2709
General Phone: (718) 636-9119
General Fax: (718) 857-9115
General/National Adv. E-mail: challengegroup@yahoo.com; newamerican@hotmail.com
Published: Thur
Avg Paid Circ: 60137
Audit By: Sworn/Estimate/Non-Audited
Audit Date: 12.07.2019
Personnel: Thomas H. Watkins (Pub.); Ariana Perez (Adv. Mgr.); Tatianna Singleton (Mng. Ed.)

BUFFALO

BUFFALO CRITERION

Street Address: 623-625 William St,
State: NY
ZIP Code: 14206
County: Erie
Country: USA
Mailing Address: 623-625 William St.
Mailing City: Buffalo
Mailing State: NY
Mailing ZIP: 14206
General Phone: (716) 882-9570
General Fax: (716) 882-9570
General/National Adv. E-mail: criterion@apollo3.com
Primary Website: www.buffalocriterion.com
Mechanical specifications: Type page 10.5 x 21; E - 6 cols, 2 1/16, 1/8 between; A - 6 cols, 2 1/16, 1/8 between; C - 8 cols, between.
Published: Sat
Avg Paid Circ: 10000
Audit By: Sworn/Estimate/Non-Audited
Audit Date: 12.07.2019
Personnel: Evelyn Merriweather (Pub.); Pat Ferguson (Adv. Mgr.); Frances J. Merriweather (Ed.); Evelyn Ferguson (Prodn. Mgr.)

BUFFALO

CHALLENGER COMMUNITY NEWS CORP.

Street Address: 140 Linwood Ave, Apt C12
State: NY
ZIP Code: 14209-2022
County: Erie
Country: USA
Mailing Address: PO Box 474
Mailing City: Buffalo
Mailing State: NY
Mailing ZIP: 14209-0474
General Phone: (716) 881-1051
General Fax: (716) 881-1053
General/National Adv. E-mail: editor@thechallengernews.com
Display Adv. E-mail: advertising@thechallengernews.com
Editorial e-mail: editor@thechallengernews.com
Primary Website: www.challengercn.com
Year Established: Year Established: 1963
Special Editions: Martin Luther King -January Black History - February Black Press Month - March Salute to Barbers and Beauticians / Mother's Day- May Juneteenth & Father's Day - June Back to School - September Black Achievers Edition - October Kwanzaa & Christmas Edition - December
Delivery Methods: Mail`Newsstand`Racks
Own Printing Facility?: N
Mechanical specifications: Type page 10 x 14; E - 5 cols, between; A - 5 cols, between; C - 5 cols, between.
Published: Wed
Avg Paid Circ: 12500
Audit By: Sworn/Estimate/Non-Audited
Audit Date: 12.07.2019
Personnel: Barbara Banks (Ed.)

CHARLESTON

CHARLESTON CHRONICLE

Street Address: 1111 King St,
State: SC
ZIP Code: 29403-3761
County: Charleston
Country: USA
Mailing Address: PO Box 20548
Mailing City: Charleston
Mailing State: SC
Mailing ZIP: 29413-0548
General Phone: (843) 723-2785
General Fax: (843) 577-6099
General/National Adv. E-mail: chaschron@aol.com
Mechanical specifications: Type page 13 x 21; E - 6 cols, 2 1/16, 1/8 between; A - 6 cols, 2 1/16, 1/8 between; C - 6 cols, 2 1/16, 1/8 between.
Published: Wed
Avg Paid Circ: 6000
Audit By: Sworn/Estimate/Non-Audited
Audit Date: 12.07.2019
Personnel: Tolbert Small (Adv. Mgr.); Jim French (Ed.)

CHARLOTTE

CHARLOTTE POST

Street Address: 1531 Camden Rd,
State: NC
ZIP Code: 28203-4753
County: Mecklenburg
Country: USA
Mailing Address: PO Box 30144
Mailing City: Charlotte
Mailing State: NC
Mailing ZIP: 28230-0144
General Phone: (704) 376-0496
General Fax: (704) 342-2160
General/National Adv. E-mail: publisher@thecharlottepost.com
Primary Website: www.thecharlottepost.com
Year Established: Year Established: 1975
Mechanical specifications: Type page 13 1/4 x 22; E - 6 cols, 2, 1/4 between; A - 6 cols, 2, 1/4 between; C - 9 cols, 1 1/2, 1/8 between.
Published: Thur
Avg Paid Circ: 20400
Audit By: Sworn/Estimate/Non-Audited
Audit Date: 12.07.2019
Personnel: Gerald O. Johnson (Pub.); Bob Johnson (Gen. Mgr.); Betty Potts (Bus. Mgr.); Herb White (Ed.)

CHICAGO

CHICAGO CRUSADER

Street Address: 6429 S Martin Luther King Dr,
State: IL
ZIP Code: 60637
County: Cook
Country: USA
Mailing Address: 6429 S. Martin Luther King Dr.
Mailing City: Chicago
Mailing State: IL
Mailing ZIP: 60637
General Phone: (773) 752-2500
General Fax: (773) 752-2817
Advertising Phone: (773) 752-2500
Advertising Fax: (773) 752-2817
Editorial Phone: (773) 752-2500
Editorial Fax: (773) 752-2817
General/National Adv. E-mail: crusaderil@aol.com
Display Adv. E-mail: achicagocrusader@aol.com
Editorial e-mail: crusaderil@aol.com
Primary Website: www.chicagocrusader.com
Year Established: Year Established: 1940
Delivery Methods: Mail`Newsstand
Areas Served - City/County or Portion Thereof, or ZIP Codes: Call (773) 752-2500 for complete list
Mechanical specifications: Call (773) 752-2500
Published: Thur
Avg Paid Circ: 90661
Audit By: Sworn/Estimate/Non-Audited
Audit Date: 12.07.2019
Personnel: John L. Smith (Adv. Dir.); Dorothy R. Leavell (Ed.); Erick Johnson (Ed.)

CHICAGO DEFENDER

Street Address: 4445 S Dr Martin Luther King Dr,
State: IL
ZIP Code: 60653
County: Cook
Country: USA
Mailing Address: 4445 S. Dr. Martin Luther King Dr.
Mailing City: Chicago
Mailing State: IL
Mailing ZIP: 60653
General Phone: (312) 225-2400
General Fax: (312) 225-5659
Advertising Phone: (312) 225-2400
Advertising Fax: (312) 225-9231
Editorial Phone: (312) 225-2400
Editorial Fax: (312) 225-9231
Editorial e-mail: editorial@chicagodefender.com
Primary Website: www.chicagodefender.com
Year Established: Year Established: 1905
Special Editions: Easter Special (Apr); Back-to-School (Aug); Shopping Guide (Christmas-Kwanzaa) (Dec); African-American History Month (Feb); Dr. Martin Luther King, Jr. (Jan); Health & Fitness (Jun); Career Week (Mar); Healthcare & Wellness (Nov); Financial (Sept).
Delivery Methods: Mail`Newsstand`Racks
Commercial printers?: Y
Mechanical available: Offset; Black and 3 ROP colors.
Mechanical specifications: Type page 10 13/16

Black Newspapers in the U.S.

x 13; E - 5 cols, 2 1/16, 1/8 between; A - 5 cols, 2 1/16, 1/8 between; C - 5 cols, 2 1/16, 1/8 between.
Published: Wed
Weekday Frequency: m
Avg Paid Circ: 3178
Avg Free Circ: 7907
Audit By: VAC
Audit Date: 31.05.2017
Personnel: Michael A. House (Pres./COO); Shari Noland (Exec. Ed.); Leanne Muller-Wharton (Adv. Sr. Acct. Exec.); Kathy Chaney (Managing Editor); Carol Bell (CFO, Dir. of Fin & Bus Op)
Parent company (for newspapers): Real Times Media, Inc.

HYDE PARK CITIZEN

Street Address: 806 E 78th St,
State: IL
ZIP Code: 60619-2937
County: Cook
Country: USA
Mailing Address: 806 E 78th St
Mailing City: Chicago
Mailing State: IL
Mailing ZIP: 60619-2937
General Phone: (773) 783-1251
General Fax: (773) 783-1301
Published: Wed
Avg Free Circ: 20418
Audit By: CVC
Audit Date: 31.03.2005
Personnel: William Garth (Pub.); Janice Garth (Adv. Mgr.)

N'DIGO

Street Address: 1006 S Michigan Ave, Ste 200
State: IL
ZIP Code: 60605-2209
County: Cook
Country: USA
Mailing Address: 1006 S Michigan Ave Ste 200
Mailing City: Chicago
Mailing State: IL
Mailing ZIP: 60605-2209
General Phone: (312) 822-0202
General Fax: 312 431 8893
Advertising Phone: 312 264 6272
Advertising Fax: 312 431 8893
General/National Adv. E-mail: hhartman@ndigo.com
Display Adv. E-mail: hhartman@ndigo.com
Editorial e-mail: dsmallwood@ndigo.com
Primary Website: www.ndigo.com
Year Established: Year Established: 1989
Delivery Methods: Racks
Areas Served - City/County or Portion Thereof, or ZIP Codes: 60610, 60611, 60612, 60613, 60614, 60615, 60616, 60617, 60618, 60619, 60620, 60621, 60622, 60623, 60624, 60625, 60626, 60627, 60628, 60629, 60631, 60632, 60634, 60636, 60637, 60639, 60640, 60642, 60643, 60644, 60645, 60647, 60648, 60651, 60652, 60653, 606
Mechanical specifications: Type page 10 1/8 x 12 1/2; E - 5 cols, 2 1/4, between; A - 4 cols, 2 1/2, between; C - 5 cols, 2, between.
Published: Thur
Avg Free Circ: 130000
Audit By: Sworn/Estimate/Non-Audited
Audit Date: 12.07.2019
Personnel: Hermene D. Hartman (Pub.); David Smallwood (Editor); Sylvester Cosby (Administrator); Walter Aikens (Business Development)

SOUTH SUBURBAN CITIZEN

Street Address: 806 E 78th St,
State: IL
ZIP Code: 60619-2937
County: Cook
Country: USA
Mailing Address: 806 E 78th St
Mailing City: Chicago
Mailing State: IL
Mailing ZIP: 60619-2937
General Phone: (773) 783-1251
General Fax: (773) 783-1301
General/National Adv. E-mail: citizen_newsroom@yahoo.com
Primary Website: www.thechicagocitizen.com

Published: Wed
Avg Free Circ: 20355
Audit By: CVC
Audit Date: 31.03.2005
Personnel: William Garth (Pub.); Janice Garth (Adv. Mgr)

SOUTHEND CITIZEN

Street Address: 806 E 78th St,
State: IL
ZIP Code: 60619-2937
County: Cook
Country: USA
Mailing Address: 806 E 78th St
Mailing City: Chicago
Mailing State: IL
Mailing ZIP: 60619-2937
General Phone: (773) 783-1251
General Fax: (773) 783-1301
Primary Website: www.thechicagocitizen.com
Published: Wed
Avg Free Circ: 30130
Audit By: CVC
Audit Date: 31.03.2005
Personnel: William Garth (Pub.); Janice Garth (Adv. Mgr.)

CINCINNATI

CINCINNATI HERALD

Street Address: 354 Hearne Ave,
State: OH
ZIP Code: 45229-2818
County: Hamilton
Country: USA
Mailing Address: 354 Hearne Ave
Mailing City: Cincinnati
Mailing State: OH
Mailing ZIP: 45229-2818
General Phone: (513) 961-3331
General Fax: (513) 961-0304
General/National Adv. E-mail: jmkearney@mail.com
Primary Website: www.thecincinnatiherald.com
Mechanical specifications: Type page 13 x 21; E - 6 cols, 2 1/16, 1/8 between; A - 6 cols, 2 1/16, 1/8 between; C - 10 cols, between.
Published: Thur
Avg Paid Circ: 16000
Audit By: Sworn/Estimate/Non-Audited
Audit Date: 12.07.2019
Personnel: Jan Michele Kearney (Pub.); Walter White (Adv. Mgr.); Dan Yount (Ed. in Chief); Wade Lacey (Prodn. Mgr.)

COLUMBIA

BLACK NEWS

Street Address: 1310 Harden St,
State: SC
ZIP Code: 29204-1820
County: Richland
Country: USA
Mailing Address: PO Box 11128
Mailing City: Columbia
Mailing State: SC
Mailing ZIP: 29211-1128
General Phone: (803) 799-5252
General Fax: (803) 799-7709
General/National Adv. E-mail: scbnews@aol.com
Primary Website: www.scblacknews.com
Mechanical specifications: Type page 13 x 21 1/2; E - 6 cols, 2 1/16, 1/8 between; A - 6 cols, 2 1/16, 1/8 between; C - 9 cols, between.
Published: Thur
Avg Paid Circ: 75000
Audit By: Sworn/Estimate/Non-Audited
Audit Date: 12.07.2019
Personnel: Isaac Washington (Pres./CEO/Pub.); Clannie Washington (Gen. Mgr.); Melvin Hart (Adv. Mgr.); Benjamin Jackson (Circ. Mgr.); Wendy Brinker (Prodn.Mgr.); Ruth Carlton (Asst. Bus. Mgr.)

CAROLINA PANORAMA

Street Address: 2346 Two Notch Rd, Ste B
State: SC

ZIP Code: 29204-2279
County: Richland
Country: USA
Mailing Address: PO Box 11205
Mailing City: Columbia
Mailing State: SC
Mailing ZIP: 29211-1205
General Phone: (803) 256-4015
General Fax: (803) 256-6732
General/National Adv. E-mail: cpanorama@aol.com
Display Adv. E-mail: Ads@CarolinaPanorama.com
Editorial e-mail: News@CarolinaPanorama.com
Primary Website: www.carolinapanorama.com
Year Established: Year Established: 1986
Delivery Methods: Newsstand Racks
Areas Served - City/County or Portion Thereof, or ZIP Codes: 29016, 29033, 29044, 29052, 29053, 29063, 29072, 29115, 29118, 29130, 29135, 29169, 29172, 29180, 29201, 29203, 29204, 29205, 29209, 29210, 29212, 29223, 29229
Mechanical specifications: Type page 11 x 21 1/2; E - 6 cols, 2 1/16, 1/8 between; A - 6 cols, 2 1/16, 1/8 between; C - 10 cols, between.
Published: Thur
Avg Free Circ: 12000
Audit By: Sworn/Estimate/Non-Audited
Audit Date: 12.07.2019
Personnel: Nate Abraham Jr. (Pub.)
Parent company (for newspapers): MBD Media, LLC

COLUMBUS

KING MEDIA ENTERPRISES

Street Address: 750 E Long St, Ste 3000
State: OH
ZIP Code: 43203-1874
County: Franklin
Country: USA
Mailing Address: 750 E Long St Ste 3000
Mailing City: Columbus
Mailing State: OH
Mailing ZIP: 43203-1874
General Phone: (614) 224-8123
General Fax: (216) 451-0404
General/National Adv. E-mail: info@call-post.com
Display Adv. E-mail: advertising@call-post.com; classifieds@call-post.com
Primary Website: www.cleveland.com
Mechanical specifications: Type page 13 x 21; E - 6 cols, between; A - 6 cols, between; C - 6 cols, between.
Published: Wed
Personnel: Douglas Rice (Vice Pres., Mktg./Adv.); Carl Matthews (Circ. Mgr.); Gil Price (Mng. Ed.); Cheri Daniels (Vice Pres., Opns.)

THE COLUMBUS TIMES

Street Address: 2230 Buena Vista Rd,
State: GA
ZIP Code: 31906-3111
County: Muscogee
Country: USA
Mailing Address: 2230 Buena Vista Rd
Mailing City: Columbus
Mailing State: GA
Mailing ZIP: 31906-3111
General Phone: (706) 324-2404
General Fax: (706) 596-0657
General/National Adv. E-mail: columbustimes@knology.net
Primary Website: www.columbustimes.com
Mechanical specifications: Type page 13 x 21 1/2; E - 6 cols, 2 1/16, between; A - 6 cols, 2 1/16, between; C - 6 cols, 2 1/16, between.
Published: Wed
Avg Paid Circ: 10000
Audit By: Sworn/Estimate/Non-Audited
Audit Date: 12.07.2019
Personnel: Ophelia Devore-Mitchell (Pub.); Helmut Gertjegerdes (Mng. Ed.); Carol Gertjegerdes (News Ed.)

DALLAS

DALLAS POST TRIBUNE

Street Address: PO Box 570769,
State: TX
ZIP Code: 75357
County: Dallas
Country: USA
Mailing Address: PO Box 570769
Mailing City: Dallas
Mailing State: TX
Mailing ZIP: 75357
General Phone: (214) 946-7678
General Fax: (214) 275-3425
Display Adv. E-mail: chloe@dallasposttrib.net
Editorial e-mail: sgray@dallasposttrib.net
Primary Website: dallasposttrib.com
Year Established: Year Established: 1947
Mechanical specifications: Type page 13 x 21; E - 6 cols, 2 1/16, 1/8 between; A - 6 cols, 2 1/16, 1/8 between; C - 6 cols, 2 1/16, 1/8 between.
Published: Thur
Avg Paid Circ: 60
Avg Free Circ: 3915
Audit By: CVC
Audit Date: 30.12.2018
Personnel: Shirley Gray (Pub.); Chloe Buckley (Production Manager)
Parent company (for newspapers): Tribune Publishing, Inc.

DALLAS WEEKLY

Street Address: 3101 Martin Luther King Jr Blvd,
State: TX
ZIP Code: 75215-2415
County: Dallas
Country: USA
Mailing Address: PO Box 151789
Mailing City: Dallas
Mailing State: TX
Mailing ZIP: 75315-1789
General Phone: (214) 428-8958
General Fax: (214) 428-2807
Primary Website: www.dallasweekly.com
Mechanical specifications: Type page 9 7/8 x 12; A - 6 cols, 1 9/16, between; C - 6 cols, 1 9/16, between.
Published: Thur
Avg Paid Circ: 10
Avg Free Circ: 4890
Audit By: CAC
Audit Date: 30.06.2017
Personnel: James Washington (Pub.); Gordon Jackson (Ed. in chief)

GARLAND JOURNAL NEWS

Street Address: 320 S R L Thornton Fwy, Ste 220
State: TX
ZIP Code: 75203-1804
County: Dallas
Country: USA
Mailing Address: 320 South R L Thornton Fwy Ste 220
Mailing City: Dallas
Mailing State: TX
Mailing ZIP: 75203-1804
General Phone: (214) 941-0110
General/National Adv. E-mail: publisher@texasmetronews.com
Display Adv. E-mail: sales@texasmetronews.com
Editorial e-mail: editor@texasmetronews.com
Primary Website: texasmetronews.com
Year Established: Year Established: 1994
Delivery Methods: Mail Racks
Areas Served - City/County or Portion Thereof, or ZIP Codes: Dallas County Tarrant County Ellis County Denton County Wise County Hunt County Collin County
Published: Other
Published Other: 1st & 15th of the month
Avg Paid Circ: 15
Avg Free Circ: 2960
Audit By: CVC
Audit Date: 30.12.2018
Personnel: Cheryl Smith (Pub.); BJ Fullylove (Advertising Manger); K Davis (Circulation

Manger)

IMESSENGER
Street Address: 320 S R.L. Thornton Freeway, Suite 220
State: TX
ZIP Code: 75203
Country: USA
Mailing Address: 320 S R.L. Thornton Freeway, Ste. 220
Mailing City: Dallas
Mailing State: TX
Mailing ZIP: 75203
General Phone: (214) 941-0110
Display Adv. E-mail: sales@garlandjournal.com
Editorial e-mail: editor@texasmetronews.com
Primary Website: texasmetronews.com
Year Established: Year Established: 2011
Published: Wed
Avg Paid Circ: 34
Avg Free Circ: 7916
Audit By: CVC
Audit Date: 19.12.2018
Personnel: Cheryl Smith (Pub.); Stewart Curet (GM); Nina Garcia (Mkt/ Sales Mgr.); Lajuana Barton (Ed. Team)

TEXAS METRO NEWS
Street Address: 320 S R L Thornton Fwy, Ste 220
State: TX
ZIP Code: 75203-1804
County: Dallas
Country: USA
Mailing Address: 320 South RL Thornton Fwy Ste 220
Mailing City: Dallas
Mailing State: TX
Mailing ZIP: 75203-1804
General Phone: (214) 941-0110
Advertising Phone: (214) 941-0110
General/National Adv. E-mail: stewartcuret@myimessenger.com
Display Adv. E-mail: sales@garlandjournal.com
Editorial e-mail: penonfire2@gmail.com
Primary Website: texasmetronews.com
Year Established: Year Established: 2012
Delivery Methods: Mail`Newsstand`Carrier`Racks
Areas Served - City/County or Portion Thereof, or ZIP Codes: Dallas County Tarrant County Ellis County Denton County Wise County Hunt County Collin County
Published: Wed`Other
Published Other: Bi-Weekly (1st and 15th each month)
Avg Paid Circ: 19
Avg Free Circ: 4956
Audit By: CVC
Audit Date: 30.12.2018
Personnel: Cheryl Smith (Pub./Gen. Mgr.); K Davis (Circulation Manager); Stewart Curet (Adv.)

THE DALLAS EXAMINER
Street Address: 4510 S. Malcolm X Blvd.,
State: TX
ZIP Code: 75215
County: Dallas
Country: USA
Mailing Address: P.O. Box 3720
Mailing City: Dallas
Mailing State: TX
Mailing ZIP: 75208
General Phone: (214) 941-3100
General Fax: (214) 941-3117
General/National Adv. E-mail: jones@dallasexaminer.com
Display Adv. E-mail: advertising@dallasexaminer.com
Editorial e-mail: mbelt@dallasexaminer.com
Primary Website: dallasexaminer.com
Year Established: Year Established: 1986
Delivery Methods: Mail`Newsstand`Racks
Published: Thur
Avg Paid Circ: 919
Avg Free Circ: 9055
Audit By: CVC
Audit Date: 30.03.2018
Personnel: Mollie Belt (Publisher); James Belt (Adv.); Tina Jones (Circ.); Robyn Jimenez

(Prod.)

DAVIDSON

DENVER WEEKLY NEWS
Street Address: 209 Delburg St, Ste 209
State: NC
ZIP Code: 28036
Country: USA
Mailing Address: 209 Delburg St Ste 209
Mailing City: Davidson
Mailing State: NC
Mailing ZIP: 28036
General Phone: (704) 766-2100
General Fax: (704) 992-0801
General/National Adv. E-mail: rdiaz@lakenormanpublications.com
Display Adv. E-mail: pmoon@lakenormanpublications.com
Editorial e-mail: rdiaz@lakenormanpublications.com
Primary Website: lakenormanpublications.com
Year Established: Year Established: 2011
Published: Fri
Avg Paid Circ: 0
Avg Free Circ: 8182
Audit By: CVC
Audit Date: 30.12.2017
Personnel: Kelly Wright (Pub.); Richard Diaz (Circ.); Patty Moon (Adv.)

DECATUR

THE CHAMPION
Street Address: 114 New St, Ste E
State: GA
ZIP Code: 30030-5356
County: Dekalb
Country: USA
Mailing Address: PO Box 1347
Mailing City: Decatur
Mailing State: GA
Mailing ZIP: 30031-1347
General Phone: (404) 373-7779
General Fax: (404) 373-7721
General/National Adv. E-mail: JohnH@dekalbchamp.com
Display Adv. E-mail: JohnH@dekalbchamp.com
Editorial e-mail: Kathy@dekalbchamp.com
Primary Website: championnewspaper.com
Delivery Methods: Mail`Newsstand`Racks
Mechanical specifications: Type page 10 1/4 x 14 1/4; E - 5 cols, 2, 3/16 between; A - 5 cols, 2, 3/16 between; C - 7 cols, 1 5/16, 3/16 between.
Published: Thur
Avg Paid Circ: 443
Avg Free Circ: 97
Audit By: CVC
Audit Date: 30.09.2018
Personnel: Carolyn Glenn (Pub.); John Hewitt (COO/Gen. Mgr.); Kathy Mitchell (Ed.); Gale Horton Gay (Mng. Ed.); Kemesha Hunt (Prodn. Mgr.); Travis Hutchins (Classic/Web Designer)

DETROIT

MICHIGAN CHRONICLE
Street Address: 479 Ledyard St,
State: MI
ZIP Code: 48201-2641
County: Wayne
Country: USA
Mailing Address: 479 Ledyard St
Mailing City: Detroit
Mailing State: MI
Mailing ZIP: 48201-2687
General Phone: (313) 963-8100
General Fax: (313) 963-8788
General/National Adv. E-mail: chronicle4@aol.com
Primary Website: www.michronicleonline.com
Year Established: Year Established: 1936
Mechanical specifications: Type page 11 5/8 x 21 1/4; E - 6 cols, 1 5/6, 1/8 between; A - 6 cols, 1 5/6, 1/8 between; C - 9 cols, 1 3/16, between.

Published: Wed
Avg Paid Circ: 20910
Avg Free Circ: 1321
Audit By: CVC
Audit Date: 30.09.2016
Personnel: Karen A. Love (COO); Samuel Logan (Pub.); Cornelius Fortune (Mng. Ed.); Raymond Allen (Prodn. Mgr.)
Parent company (for newspapers): Real Times, Inc.

DORCHESTER

BAY STATE BANNER
Street Address: 1100 Washington St,
State: MA
ZIP Code: 02124-5520
County: Suffolk
Country: USA
Mailing Address: 1100 Washington St
Mailing City: Dorchester
Mailing State: WA
Mailing ZIP: 02124-5520
General Phone: (617) 261-4600
General/National Adv. E-mail: kmiller@bannerpub.com
Display Adv. E-mail: ads@bannerpub.com
Editorial e-mail: yawu@bannerpub.com
Primary Website: baystatebanner.com
Year Established: Year Established: 1965
Published: Thur
Avg Free Circ: 27400
Audit By: AAM
Audit Date: 30.06.2018
Personnel: Melvin Miller (Pub.); Yawu Miller (Ed.); Rachel Reardon (Adv. Mgr./Circ.)

DURHAM

THE CAROLINA TIMES
Street Address: 923 Old Fayetteville St,
State: NC
ZIP Code: 27701-3914
County: Durham
Country: USA
Mailing Address: P.O. Box 3825
Mailing City: Durham
Mailing State: NC
Mailing ZIP: 27702-3825
General Phone: (919) 682-2913
General Fax: (919) 688-8434
General/National Adv. E-mail: thecarolinatimes@cs.com
Display Adv. E-mail: adstct@cs.com
Editorial e-mail: thecarolinatimes@cs.com
Year Established: Year Established: 1927
Delivery Methods: Mail`Newsstand`Racks
Areas Served - City/County or Portion Thereof, or ZIP Codes: 27701, 27702, 27703, 27704, 27705, 27708, 27709, 27710, 27712, 27713, 27715, 27717, 27722, 27514, 27516, 27517;, 27601, 27601, 27603, 27604, 27605, 27606, 27607, 27608, 27610, 27611, 27612
Mechanical specifications: Type page 10.75 x 21; E - 6 cols, 2 1/16, 1/8 between; A - 6 cols, 2 1/16, 1/8 between; C - 6 cols, 2 1/16, 1/8 between.
Published: Thur
Avg Paid Circ: 6100
Audit By: USPS
Audit Date: 12.12.2017
Personnel: Kenneth W. Edmonds (Pub.)

THE TRIANGLE TRIBUNE
Street Address: 115 Market St, Ste 360G
State: NC
ZIP Code: 27701-3252
County: Durham
Country: USA
Mailing Address: 115 Market St Ste 360G
Mailing City: Durham
Mailing State: NC
Mailing ZIP: 27701-3241
General Phone: (919) 688-9408
General Fax: (919) 688-2740
Advertising Phone: (919) 688-9086
General/National Adv. E-mail: editor@triangletribune.com
Display Adv. E-mail: linda.lanel@triangletribune.

com
Primary Website: www.triangletribune.com
Year Established: Year Established: 1997
Delivery Methods: Mail`Newsstand`Carrier
Areas Served - City/County or Portion Thereof, or ZIP Codes: 27701, 27713, 27610
Own Printing Facility?: N
Commercial printers?: Y
Mechanical specifications: Type page 11 5/8 x 21; E - 6 cols, 1 5/6, between; A - 6 cols, 1 5/6, between; C - 9 cols, 1 3/20, between.
Published: Sun
Avg Free Circ: 1713
Audit By: Sworn/Estimate/Non-Audited
Audit Date: 12.07.2019
Personnel: Gerald Johnson (CEO/Pub.); Bonitta Best (Ed.)
Parent company (for newspapers): The Charlotte Post Publshing

EAST RANCHO DOMINGUEZ

COMPTON BULLETIN
Street Address: 800 E Compton Blvd,
State: CA
ZIP Code: 90221-3302
County: Los Angeles
Country: USA
Mailing Address: 800 E. Compton Blvd.
Mailing City: Compton
Mailing State: CA
Mailing ZIP: 90221
General Phone: (310) 635-6776
General Fax: (310) 635-4045
General/National Adv. E-mail: news@thecomptonbulletin.com
Display Adv. E-mail: ads@thecomptonbulletin.com
Editorial e-mail: news@thecomptonbulletin.com
Primary Website: www.thecomptonbulletin.com
Published: Wed
Avg Paid Circ: 32516
Avg Free Circ: 42484
Audit By: Sworn/Estimate/Non-Audited
Audit Date: 12.07.2019
Personnel: Lisa Grace-Kellogg (Pub.); Allison Eaton (Ed.)

EAST SAINT LOUIS

EAST ST. LOUIS MONITOR
Street Address: 1501 State St,
State: IL
ZIP Code: 62205-2011
County: Saint Clair
Country: USA
Mailing Address: PO Box 2137
Mailing City: East Saint Louis
Mailing State: IL
Mailing ZIP: 62202-2137
General Phone: (618) 271-0468
General Fax: (618) 271-8443
Mechanical specifications: Type page 12 x 21 1/2; E - 6 cols, 2, between.
Published: Thur
Avg Paid Circ: 8800
Audit By: Sworn/Estimate/Non-Audited
Audit Date: 12.07.2019
Personnel: George Laktzian (Adv. Mgr.); Ahmad Saae (Circ. Mgr.); Anne Jordan (Ed.); Frazier Garner (Prodn. Mgr.)

ECORSE

TELEGRAM
Street Address: PO Box 29085,
State: MI
ZIP Code: 48229-0085
County: Wayne
Country: USA
Mailing Address: PO Box 29085
Mailing City: Ecorse
Mailing State: MI
Mailing ZIP: 48229-0085
General Phone: (313) 928-2955
General Fax: (313) 928-3014
General/National Adv. E-mail: telegram@

Black Newspapers in the U.S.

telegramnews.net
Primary Website: www.telegramnews.net
Published: Thur
Avg Paid Circ: 35000
Audit By: Sworn/Estimate/Non-Audited
Audit Date: 12.07.2019
Personnel: Gina Wilson (Adv. Dir.)

EUTAW

GREENE COUNTY DEMOCRAT

Street Address: P. O. Box 82,
State: AL
ZIP Code: 35462
County: Greene
Country: United States
Mailing Address: P. O. Box 82
Mailing City: Eutaw
Mailing State: AL
Mailing ZIP: 35462
General Phone: (334) 372-3373
General Fax: (334) 372-3373
Advertising Phone: (334) 372-3373
Advertising Fax: (334) 372-3373
Editorial Phone: (334) 372-3373
Editorial Fax: (334) 372-3373
General/National Adv. E-mail: jzippert@aol.com
Display Adv. E-mail: jzippert@aol.com
Editorial e-mail: jzippert@aol.com
Primary Website: www.greenecodemocrat.com
Year Established: Year Established: 1890
Delivery Methods: Mail Racks
Areas Served - City/County or Portion Thereof, or ZIP Codes: 35460 to 35470
Mechanical specifications: Type page 13 x 29 1/2; E - 6 cols, 2 1/16, 1/8 between; A - 6 cols, 2 1/16, 1/8 between; C - 6 cols, 2 1/16, 1/8 between.
Published: Wed
Avg Paid Circ: 4000
Avg Free Circ: 300
Audit By: Sworn/Estimate/Non-Audited
Audit Date: 12.07.2019
Personnel: Carol Zippert (Co-Pub.); Barbara Amerson (Circ. Mgr.); John Zippert (Ed.)

FORT LAUDERDALE

SOUTH FLORIDA TIMES

Street Address: 3020 NE 32nd Ave, Ste 200
State: FL
ZIP Code: 33308-7233
County: Broward
Country: USA
Mailing Address: 3020 Northeast 32nd Avenue #200
Mailing City: Fort Lauderdale
Mailing State: FL
Mailing ZIP: 33308
General Phone: (954) 356-9360
General Fax: (954) 356-9395
Display Adv. E-mail: advertising@sfltimes.com
Primary Website: www.sfltimes.com
Mechanical specifications: Type page 13 x 21; E - 6 cols, 2 1/16, 1/8 between; A - 6 cols, 2 1/16, 1/8 between.
Published: Fri
Avg Paid Circ: 20000
Audit By: Sworn/Estimate/Non-Audited
Audit Date: 12.07.2019
Personnel: Robert Beatty, Esq. (Pub.); Brad Bennett (Ed.)

WESTSIDE GAZETTE

Street Address: 545 NW 7th Ter,
State: FL
ZIP Code: 33311-8140
County: Broward
Country: USA
Mailing Address: PO Box 5304
Mailing City: Fort Lauderdale
Mailing State: FL
Mailing ZIP: 33310-5304
General Phone: (954) 525-1489
General Fax: (954) 525-1861
General/National Adv. E-mail: wgazette@bellsouth.net
Primary Website: www.thewestsidegazette.com

Mechanical specifications: Type page 13 x 21 1/2; E - 6 cols, 2 1/16, 1/8 between; A - 6 cols, 2 1/16, 1/8 between.
Published: Thur
Avg Paid Circ: 30000
Audit By: Sworn/Estimate/Non-Audited
Audit Date: 12.07.2019
Personnel: Bobby Henry (Pub.); Charles Moseley (Adv. Mgr.); Elizabeth Miller (Circ. Mgr.); Pamela Lewis (Ed.)

FORT MYERS

COMMUNITY VOICE

Street Address: 3046 Lafayette St,
State: FL
ZIP Code: 33916-4324
County: Lee
Country: USA
Mailing Address: 3046 Lafayette St
Mailing City: Fort Myers
Mailing State: FL
Mailing ZIP: 33916-4324
General Phone: (239) 337-4444
General Fax: (239) 334-8289
General/National Adv. E-mail: commuvoice@aol.com
Year Established: Year Established: 1987
Mechanical specifications: Type page 10 5/6 x 12; E - 6 cols, 1 9/16, between; A - 6 cols, 1 9/16, between.
Published: Thur
Avg Free Circ: 12000
Audit By: Sworn/Estimate/Non-Audited
Audit Date: 12.07.2019
Personnel: Corey F. Weaver (Ed.)

FORT WAYNE

FROST ILLUSTRATED

Street Address: 3121 S Calhoun St,
State: IN
ZIP Code: 46807-1901
County: Allen
Country: USA
Mailing Address: 3121 S Calhoun St
Mailing City: Fort Wayne
Mailing State: IN
Mailing ZIP: 46807-1901
General Phone: (260) 745-0552
General/National Adv. E-mail: news@frostillustrated.com
Display Adv. E-mail: fwfrostads@gmail.com
Editorial e-mail: fwfrostnews@gmail.com
Primary Website: www.frostillustrated.com
Year Established: Year Established: 1968
Delivery Methods: Mail Newsstand Racks
Areas Served - City/County or Portion Thereof, or ZIP Codes: 46801, 46802, 46803, 46804, 45805, 46806, 46807, 46808, 46809, 46815, 46816, 46818, 46819, 46825, 46835
Mechanical specifications: Type page 10 2/5 x 16; E - 5 cols, between; A - 5 cols, between; C - 8 cols, between.
Published: Wed
Avg Paid Circ: 1380
Avg Free Circ: 39
Audit By: CVC
Audit Date: 30.06.2015
Personnel: Edward N. Smith (Pub.); Michael Patterson (Managing Ed.); Andy Kurzen (Layout & Production Manager)

GARY

GARY CRUSADER

Street Address: 1549 Broadway,
State: IN
ZIP Code: 46407-2240
County: Lake
Country: USA
Mailing Address: 1549 Broadway
Mailing City: Gary
Mailing State: IN
Mailing ZIP: 46407-2240
General Phone: (219) 885-4357
General Fax: (219) 883-3317
General/National Adv. E-mail: crusaderil@aol.com

Primary Website: www.crusaderil.com
Mechanical specifications: Type page 10 x 14; E - 5 cols, between; A - 5 cols, between; C - 6 cols, between.
Published: Thur
Avg Paid Circ: 44000
Audit By: Sworn/Estimate/Non-Audited
Audit Date: 12.07.2019
Personnel: Dorothy R. Leavell (Ed.); David Denson (Mng. Ed.); John Smith (Prodn. Mgr.)

GLENDALE

MILWAUKEE COURIER

Street Address: 6310 N Port Washington Rd,
State: WI
ZIP Code: 53217-4300
County: Milwaukee
Country: USA
Mailing Address: PO Box 6279
Mailing City: Milwaukee
Mailing State: WI
Mailing ZIP: 53206-0279
General Phone: (414) 449-4860
General Fax: (414) 906-5383
General/National Adv. E-mail: milwaukeecourier@aol.com
Primary Website: milwaukeecourieronline.com
Mechanical specifications: Type page 13 x 21; E - 6 cols, 2, 1/4 between; A - 6 cols, 2, 1/4 between; C - 9 cols, 1 1/4, between.
Published: Sat
Avg Paid Circ: 60000
Avg Free Circ: 60000
Audit By: Sworn/Estimate/Non-Audited
Audit Date: 12.07.2019
Personnel: Sandra Robinson (Gen. Mgr.); Robert Robinson (Circ. Mgr.)

GRAND RAPIDS

THE GRAND RAPIDS TIMES

Street Address: 2016 Eastern Ave SE,
State: MI
ZIP Code: 49507-3235
County: Kent
Country: USA
Mailing Address: PO Box 7258
Mailing City: Grand Rapids
Mailing State: MI
Mailing ZIP: 49510-7258
General Phone: (616) 245-8737
General Fax: (616) 245-1026
General/National Adv. E-mail: staff@grtimes.com
Primary Website: www.grtimes.com
Mechanical specifications: Type page 10 x 15; E - 5 cols, between; A - 5 cols, between.
Published: Fri
Avg Paid Circ: 6000
Audit By: Sworn/Estimate/Non-Audited
Audit Date: 12.07.2019
Personnel: Patricia Pulliam (Ed.)

GREENSBORO

CAROLINA PEACEMAKER

Street Address: 807 Summit Ave,
State: NC
ZIP Code: 27405-7833
County: Guilford
Country: USA
Mailing Address: PO Box 20853
Mailing City: Greensboro
Mailing State: NC
Mailing ZIP: 27420-0853
General Phone: (336) 274-6210
General Fax: (336) 273-5103
Display Adv. E-mail: ads@carolinapeacemaker.com
Editorial e-mail: editor@carolinapeacemaker.com
Primary Website: www.carolinapeacemaker.com
Year Established: Year Established: 1967
Delivery Methods: Mail Racks
Commercial printers?: Y
Mechanical specifications: Type page 11 x 20

3/4; E - 6 cols, 1 7/8, 1/4 between; A - 6 cols, between; C - 10 cols, between.
Published: Thur
Avg Paid Circ: 8100
Audit By: Sworn/Estimate/Non-Audited
Audit Date: 12.07.2019
Personnel: John Marshall Kilimanjaro (Pub.); C. Vickie Kilimanjaro (Adv. Mgr.); Afraque Kilimanjaro (Ed.)

HOUSTON

AFRICAN AMERICAN NEWS & ISSUES

Street Address: 6130 Wheatley St,
State: TX
ZIP Code: 77091-3947
County: Harris
Country: USA
Mailing Address: 6130 Wheatley St
Mailing City: Houston
Mailing State: TX
Mailing ZIP: 77091-3947
General Phone: (713) 692-1892
General Fax: (713) 692-1183
General/National Adv. E-mail: news@aframnews.com
Display Adv. E-mail: sales@aframnews.com
Editorial e-mail: prod@aframnews.com
Primary Website: www.aframnews.com
Year Established: Year Established: 1996
Delivery Methods: Mail Newsstand Carrier Racks
Mechanical specifications: Type page 11 5/8 x 21.
Published: Wed Sun
Avg Paid Circ: 2228
Avg Free Circ: 312818
Audit By: Sworn/Estimate/Non-Audited
Audit Date: 12.07.2019
Personnel: Roy Douglas Malonson (Pub.); Shirley Ann Malonson (Gen. Mgr.); Rebecca Jones (Ed.)

FORWARD TIMES

Street Address: 4411 Almeda Rd,
State: TX
ZIP Code: 77004-4901
County: Harris
Country: USA
Mailing Address: PO Box 8346
Mailing City: Houston
Mailing State: TX
Mailing ZIP: 77288-8346
General Phone: (713) 526-4727
General Fax: (713) 526-3170
General/National Adv. E-mail: forwardtimes@forwardtimes.com
Primary Website: www.forwardtimes.com
Own Printing Facility?: Y
Mechanical specifications: Type page 13 x 21 1/2; E - 6 cols, 2 1/16, 1/8 between; A - 6 cols, 2 1/16, 1/8 between; C - 6 cols, 2 1/16, 1/8 between.
Published: Thur
Avg Paid Circ: 64580
Audit By: Sworn/Estimate/Non-Audited
Audit Date: 12.07.2019
Personnel: Karen Carter Richards (Assoc. Pub.); Henrietta Smith (Adv. Mgr.); Lenora Carter (Ed.); Shirley Daughery (Prodn. Mgr.)

HOUSTON DEFENDER

Street Address: 12401 S Post Oak Rd,
State: TX
ZIP Code: 77045-2020
County: Harris
Country: USA
Mailing Address: PO Box 8005
Mailing City: Houston
Mailing State: TX
Mailing ZIP: 77288-8005
General Phone: (713) 663-6996
General Fax: (713) 663-7116
General/National Adv. E-mail: news@defendermediagroup.com
Display Adv. E-mail: selma@defendermediagroup.com

Editorial e-mail: news@defendermediagroup.com
Primary Website: defendernetwork.com
Year Established: Year Established: 1930
Delivery Methods: Mail`Newsstand`Racks
Areas Served - City/County or Portion Thereof, or ZIP Codes: Houston Metro
Own Printing Facility?: N
Commercial printers?: Y
Mechanical specifications: Type page Tabloid - 10.75" x 14"; Full Page: 9.75" x 13"; Half Page (h) 9.75 x 6.5"; Half Page (v) 5.78" x 11"; Qtr) 5.78" x 5.65"
Published: Thur
Avg Free Circ: 30444
Audit By: AAM
Audit Date: 30.09.2018
Personnel: Sonceria Messiah-Jiles (Pub. & CEO); Von Jiles (Ed.); Selma Dodson Tyler (Adv. & Marketing Dir.); Marilyn Marshall (Print Ed.); ReShonda Billingsley (Online Ed.); LaGloria Wheatfall (Multi-media Mgr.)

HOUSTON METRO WEEKENDER

Street Address: 4411 Almeda Rd,
State: TX
ZIP Code: 77004-4901
County: Harris
Country: USA
Mailing Address: PO Box 8346
Mailing City: Houston
Mailing State: TX
Mailing ZIP: 77288-8346
General Phone: (713) 526-4727
General Fax: (713) 526-3170
General/National Adv. E-mail: fowardtimes@forwardtimes.com
Primary Website: www.forwardtimes.com
Mechanical specifications: Type page 13 x 21 1/2; E - 6 cols, 2 1/16, 1/8 between; A - 6 cols, 2 1/16, 1/8 between; C - 6 cols, 2 1/16, 1/8 between.
Published: Fri
Avg Free Circ: 75000
Audit By: Sworn/Estimate/Non-Audited
Audit Date: 12.07.2019
Personnel: Karen Carter Richard (Assoc. Pub.); Henrietta Smith-Wilson (Adv. Dir.); Lenora Carter (Mng. Ed.); Shirley Daugherty (Prodn. Mgr.)

HOUSTON SUN

Street Address: 1520 Isabella St,
State: TX
ZIP Code: 77004-4042
County: Harris
Country: USA
Mailing Address: 1520 Isabella St
Mailing City: Houston
Mailing State: TX
Mailing ZIP: 77004-4042
Primary Website: www.houstonsun.com
Published: Fri
Avg Free Circ: 9925
Audit By: Sworn/Estimate/Non-Audited
Audit Date: 12.07.2019
Personnel: Dorris Ellis

HUNTSVILLE

SPEAKIN' OUT WEEKLY

Street Address: 101 Oakwood Ave NE,
State: AL
ZIP Code: 35811-1960
County: Madison
Country: USA
Mailing Address: PO Box 2826
Mailing City: Huntsville
Mailing State: AL
Mailing ZIP: 35804-2826
General Phone: (256) 551-1020
General Fax: (256) 551-0607
General/National Adv. E-mail: WSmoth3193@aol.com
Primary Website: www.speakinoutweeklynews.com
Year Established: Year Established: 1980
Delivery Methods: Mail`Newsstand
Areas Served - City/County or Portion Thereof, or ZIP Codes: 35810 35811 35816 35806 35601 35801 35758
Mechanical specifications: Type page 10.25" by 21"
Published: Wed
Avg Paid Circ: 26000
Avg Free Circ: 1000
Audit By: Sworn/Estimate/Non-Audited
Audit Date: 12.07.2019
Personnel: Jemeana Smothers-Roberson (Assoc. Pub.); William Smothers (Ed.)

INDIANAPOLIS

INDIANAPOLIS RECORDER

Street Address: 2901 N Tacoma Ave,
State: IN
ZIP Code: 46218-2737
County: Marion
Country: USA
Mailing Address: 2901 N Tacoma Ave
Mailing City: Indianapolis
Mailing State: IN
Mailing ZIP: 46218-2700
General Phone: (317) 924-5143
General Fax: (317) 924-5148
General/National Adv. E-mail: newsroom@indyrecorder.com
Primary Website: www.indianapolisrecorder.com
Commercial printers?: Y
Mechanical specifications: Type page 13 x 21; E - 6 cols, between; A - 6 cols, between; C - 9 cols, between.
Published: Fri
Avg Paid Circ: 6358
Avg Free Circ: 5257
Audit By: CVC
Audit Date: 31.12.2004
Personnel: William G. Mays (Owner/Chrmn.); Carolene Mays (Pub.); Angie Kuhn (Circ. Mgr.); Shannon Williams (Ed.); Jeana Lewis (Prodn. Mgr.)

JACKSON

JACKSON ADVOCATE

Street Address: 100 W Hamilton St,
State: MS
ZIP Code: 39202-3237
County: Hinds
Country: USA
Mailing Address: PO Box 3708
Mailing City: Jackson
Mailing State: MS
Mailing ZIP: 39207-3708
General Phone: (601) 948-4122
General Fax: (601) 948-4125
General/National Adv. E-mail: jadvocat@aol.com
Primary Website: www.jacksonadvocate.com
Year Established: Year Established: 1938
Mechanical specifications: Type page 13 x 21.
Published: Thur
Avg Paid Circ: 17000
Audit By: Sworn/Estimate/Non-Audited
Audit Date: 12.07.2019
Personnel: Alice Tisdale (Adv. Mgr.)

MISSISSIPPI LINK

Street Address: 2659 Livingston Rd,
State: MS
ZIP Code: 39213-6926
County: Hinds
Country: USA
Mailing Address: P.O. Box 11307
Mailing City: Jackson
Mailing State: MS
Mailing ZIP: 39283-1307
General Phone: (601) 896-0084
General Fax: (601) 896-0091
Advertising Phone: (601) 368-8481
Editorial Phone: (601) 896-0084
General/National Adv. E-mail: publisher@mississippilink.com
Display Adv. E-mail: jlinkads@bellsouth.net
Editorial e-mail: editor@mississippilink.com
Primary Website: www.mississippilink.com
Year Established: Year Established: 1993
Delivery Methods:
Mail`Newsstand`Carrier`Racks
Mechanical specifications: 6 columns (11.625") X 21"
Published: Thur
Avg Paid Circ: 17000
Avg Free Circ: 150
Audit By: Sworn/Estimate/Non-Audited
Audit Date: 12.07.2019
Personnel: Jackie Hampton (Pub.); Ayesha Mustafaa (Ed.)

JACKSONVILLE

FLORIDA STAR

Street Address: PO Box 40629,
State: FL
ZIP Code: 32203-0629
County: Duval
Country: USA
Mailing Address: PO Box 40629
Mailing City: Jacksonville
Mailing State: FL
Mailing ZIP: 32203-0629
General Phone: (904) 766-8834
General Fax: (904) 765-1673
General/National Adv. E-mail: info@thefloridastar.com
Display Adv. E-mail: ad@thefloridastar.com
Editorial e-mail: clara@thefloridastar.com
Primary Website: www.thefloridastar.com
Year Established: Year Established: 1951
Special Editions: Black History MLK Memorial Juneteenth Black Music Month Special Events related to the Black communities of Florida and Georgia At Home (Homes of FL/GA residents
Delivery Methods:
Mail`Newsstand`Carrier`Racks
Commercial printers?: Y
Mechanical specifications: Type page 13 x 21 1/2; E - 6 cols, 2 1/16, 1/8 between; A - 6 cols, 2 1/16, 1/8 between; C - 6 cols, 2 1/16, 1/8 between.
Published: Sat
Avg Paid Circ: 35000
Audit By: Sworn/Estimate/Non-Audited
Audit Date: 12.07.2019
Personnel: Clara McLaughlin (Owner/Editor-in-Chief)
Parent company (for newspapers): SCC Communications-The Florida Star Newspaper, The Georgia Star Newspaper

JACKSONVILLE FREE PRESS

Street Address: 1122 Edgewood Ave W,
State: FL
ZIP Code: 32208-3419
County: Duval
Country: USA
Mailing Address: P.O. Box 43580
Mailing City: Jacksonville
Mailing State: FL
Mailing ZIP: 32203
General Phone: (904) 634-1993
General Fax: (904) 765-3803
General/National Adv. E-mail: jfreepress@aol.com
Primary Website: www.jacksonvillefreepress.com
Year Established: Year Established: 1986
Delivery Methods: Mail`Newsstand
Areas Served - City/County or Portion Thereof, or ZIP Codes: All throughout Duval County, Florida
Mechanical specifications: Type page 13 x 21 1/2; A - 6 cols, 2 1/8, 1/8 between.
Published: Thur
Avg Paid Circ: 43500
Audit By: Sworn/Estimate/Non-Audited
Audit Date: 12.07.2019
Personnel: Brenda Burwell (Adv. Mgr.); Sylvia Perry (Ed.); Lynette Jones (Editor); Reggie Fullwood (Editorial Director); Charles Griggs (Community Relations)

KANSAS CITY

KANSAS CITY GLOBE

Street Address: 615 E 29th St,
State: MO
ZIP Code: 64109-1110
County: Jackson
Country: USA
Mailing Address: 615 E 29th St
Mailing City: Kansas City
Mailing State: MO
Mailing ZIP: 64109-1110
General Phone: (816) 531-5253
General Fax: (816) 531-5256
General/National Adv. E-mail: kcglobe@swbell.net
Primary Website: www.thekcglobe.com
Own Printing Facility?: Y
Mechanical specifications: Type page 13 x 21; E - 6 cols, 2 1/16, 1/8 between; A - 6 cols, 2 1/16, 1/8 between.
Published: Thur
Avg Paid Circ: 10500
Audit By: Sworn/Estimate/Non-Audited
Audit Date: 12.07.2019
Personnel: Marion Jordon (Ed.); Denise Jordon (Prodn. Mgr.)

THE CALL

Street Address: 1715 E 18th St,
State: MO
ZIP Code: 64108-1611
County: Jackson
Country: USA
Mailing Address: PO Box 410-477
Mailing City: Kansas City
Mailing State: MO
Mailing ZIP: 64141
General Phone: (816) 842-3804
General Fax: (816) 842-4420
Advertising Phone: (816) 842-3804
Advertising Fax: (816) 842-4420
Editorial Phone: (816) 842-3804
Editorial Fax: (816) 842-4420
General/National Adv. E-mail: kccallnews@hotmail.com
Primary Website: www.kccall.com
Delivery Methods:
Mail`Newsstand`Carrier`Racks
Mechanical specifications: Type page 13 x 21; E - 6 cols, between; A - 6 cols, between; C - 8 cols, between.
Published: Fri
Avg Paid Circ: 16456
Audit By: Sworn/Estimate/Non-Audited
Audit Date: 12.07.2019
Personnel: Donna Stewart (Pub.); Barbara Way (Circ. Mgr.); Donna F. Stewart (Mng. Ed.)

LAS VEGAS

LAS VEGAS SENTINEL-VOICE

Street Address: 900 E Charleston Blvd,
State: NV
ZIP Code: 89104-1554
County: Clark
Country: USA
Mailing Address: 900 E Charleston Blvd
Mailing City: Las Vegas
Mailing State: NV
Mailing ZIP: 89104-1554
General Phone: (702) 380-8100
General Fax: (702) 380-8102
General/National Adv. E-mail: lvsentinelvoice@earthlink.net
Mechanical specifications: Type page 10 1/4 x 14; E - 6 cols, 1 5/8, between; A - 6 cols, 1 5/8, between; C - 6 cols, 1 5/8, between.
Published: Thur
Avg Free Circ: 6500
Audit By: Sworn/Estimate/Non-Audited
Audit Date: 12.07.2019
Personnel: Kathi Overstreet (Assoc. Pub.); Ramon Savoy (Ed.)

LONGVIEW

EAST TEXAS REVIEW

Street Address: 517 S Mobberly Ave,
State: TX
ZIP Code: 75602-1827
County: Gregg
Country: USA
Mailing Address: 517 S Mobberly Ave

Black Newspapers in the U.S.

Mailing City: Longview
Mailing State: TX
Mailing ZIP: 75602-1827
Primary Website: www.easttexasreview.com
Year Established: Year Established: 1995
Published: Thur
Avg Paid Circ: 0
Avg Free Circ: 3980
Audit By: VAC
Audit Date: 30.06.2016
Personnel: Joycelyne Fadojutimi (Publisher/General Manager); LaDana Moore (Advertising Manager); Teddy LaRose (Circulation Manager); Teresa Shearer (Production Manager)

LOS ANGELES

LA WATTS TIMES

Street Address: 3540 Wilshire Blvd,
State: CA
ZIP Code: 90010-2357
County: Los Angeles
Country: USA
Mailing Address: PO Box 83847
Mailing City: Los Angeles
Mailing State: CA
Mailing ZIP: 90083-0847
General Phone: (213) 251-5700
General Fax: (213) 251-5720
General/National Adv. E-mail: LAWATTSNUS@AOL.COM
Display Adv. E-mail: advertising@lawattstimes.com
Editorial e-mail: editorial@lawattstimes.com
Primary Website: www.lawattstimes.com
Mechanical specifications: Type page 10 x 16; E - 5 cols, 2 1/8 between; A - 5 cols, 2, 1/8 between; C - 5 cols, 2, 1/8 between.
Published: Thur
Avg Paid Circ: 450
Avg Free Circ: 25000
Audit By: Sworn/Estimate/Non-Audited
Audit Date: 12.07.2019
Personnel: Melanie Polk (Pub.); Vincent Martin (Bus. Mgr.); Willa Robinson (Adv. Dir.); Sam Richard (Mng. Ed.); Issac Mctyiere (Dist. Mgr.)

LOS ANGELES SENTINEL

Street Address: 3800 S Crenshaw Blvd,
State: CA
ZIP Code: 90008-1813
County: Los Angeles
Country: USA
Mailing Address: 3800 S Crenshaw Blvd
Mailing City: Los Angeles
Mailing State: CA
Mailing ZIP: 90008-1813
General Phone: (323) 299-3800
General Fax: (323) 291-6804
General/National Adv. E-mail: angela@lasentinel.net
Display Adv. E-mail: pamela@lasentinel.net
Editorial e-mail: dannyjr@lasentinel.net
Primary Website: lasentinel.net
Year Established: Year Established: 1998
Own Printing Facility?: Y
Mechanical specifications: Type page 13 x 21 1/2; E - 6 cols, 2 1/16, 1/8 between; A - 6 cols, 2 1/16, 1/8 between; C - 10 cols, between.
Published: Thur
Avg Paid Circ: 0
Avg Free Circ: 29902
Audit By: CVC
Audit Date: 30.09.2018
Personnel: Danny Bakewell (Pub.); Ken Miller (Ed.); Pamela Blackwell (Adv.); Angela Howard (Circ.)
Parent company (for newspapers): Bakewell Media LLC

OUR WEEKLY

Street Address: 8732 S Western Ave,
State: CA
ZIP Code: 90047-3326
County: Los Angeles
Country: USA
Mailing Address: 8732 S Western Ave

Mailing City: Los Angeles
Mailing State: CA
Mailing ZIP: 90047-3326
General Phone: (323) 905-1316
General Fax: (323) 753-5985
Primary Website: www.ourweekly.com
Year Established: Year Established: 2004
Published: Thur
Avg Paid Circ: 0
Avg Free Circ: 49975
Audit By: CVC
Audit Date: 9/31/2018
Personnel: Natalie Cole (Publisher); David Miller (Adv. Mgr.); Arnold Cole (Circ. Mgr.); Brandon Norwood

WAVE COMMUNITY NEWSPAPER

Street Address: 1730 W Olympic Blvd, Ste 500,
State: CA
ZIP Code: 90015-1008
County: Los Angeles
Country: USA
Mailing Address: 3731 Wilshire Blvd Ste 840
Mailing City: Los Angeles
Mailing State: CA
Mailing ZIP: 90010-2851
General Phone: (323) 556-5720
General Fax: (213) 835-0584
Advertising Phone: 323-556-5720 ext.245
Advertising Fax: 213-835-0584
General/National Adv. E-mail: dwanlass@wavepublication.com
Display Adv. E-mail: rbush@wavepublication.com
Primary Website: www.wavenewspapers.com
Year Established: Year Established: 1912
Delivery Methods: Newsstand`Carrier`Racks
Areas Served - City/County or Portion Thereof, or ZIP Codes: Greater Los Angels
Mechanical specifications: Type page 13 x 21 1/2; E - 6 cols, 2 1/16, 1/8 between; A - 6 cols, 2 1/16, 1/8 between; C - 10 cols, between.
Published: Thur
Avg Free Circ: 150000
Audit By: AAM
Audit Date: 01.08.2012
Personnel: Pluria Marshall (Pub.); Andre Herndon (Ed.); Don Wanlass (Mng. Ed.); Robert Bush (Sr. VP Sales &Marketing)

LOUISVILLE

THE LOUISVILLE DEFENDER

Street Address: 1720 Dixie Hwy,
State: KY
ZIP Code: 40210-2314
County: Jefferson
Country: USA
Mailing Address: PO Box 2557
Mailing City: Louisville
Mailing State: KY
Mailing ZIP: 40201-2557
General Phone: (502) 772-2591
General Fax: (502) 775-8655
General/National Adv. E-mail: loudefender@aol.com
Mechanical specifications: Type page 13 x 21 1/2; E - 6 cols, between; A - 6 cols, between; C - 8 cols, between.
Published: Thur
Avg Paid Circ: 2615
Avg Free Circ: 73
Audit By: Sworn/Estimate/Non-Audited
Audit Date: 12.07.2019
Personnel: Clarence Leslie (Adv. Mgr.); Marie Brown (Circ. Mgr.); Yvonne Coleman (Ed.)

LUBBOCK

SOUTHWEST DIGEST

Street Address: 902 E 28th St,
State: TX
ZIP Code: 79404-1718
County: Lubbock
Country: USA
Mailing Address: PO Box 2553
Mailing City: Lubbock
Mailing State: TX

Mailing ZIP: 79408-2553
General Phone: (806) 762-3612
General Fax: (806) 762-4605
General/National Adv. E-mail: swdigest@sbcglobal.net
Primary Website: www.southwestdigest.com
Delivery Methods: Mail`Newsstand`Racks
Areas Served - City/County or Portion Thereof, or ZIP Codes: 79401, 79403, 79404, 79413, 79414, 79423, 79424
Mechanical specifications: Type page 13 x 21; E - 6 cols, 2 1/16, 1/8 between; A - 6 cols, 2 1/16, 1/8 between; C - 6 cols, 2 1/16, 1/8 between.
Published: Thur
Avg Paid Circ: 800
Avg Free Circ: 4000
Audit By: Sworn/Estimate/Non-Audited
Audit Date: 12.07.2019
Personnel: T.J. Patterson (Ed.)

MEMPHIS

TRI STATE DEFENDER

Street Address: 203 Beale St, Ste 200
State: TN
ZIP Code: 38103-3727
County: Shelby
Country: USA
Mailing Address: 203 Beale St Ste 200
Mailing City: Memphis
Mailing State: TN
Mailing ZIP: 38103-3727
General Phone: (901) 523-1818
General Fax: (901) 578-5037
Editorial e-mail: editorial@tri-statedefender.com
Primary Website: www.tri-statedefenderonline.com
Mechanical specifications: Type page 13 x 21; E - 6 cols, 2 1/16, 1/8 between; A - 6 cols, 2 1/16, 1/8 between; C - 9 cols, 1 5/16, between.
Published: Thur
Avg Paid Circ: 524
Avg Free Circ: 3709
Audit By: Sworn/Estimate/Non-Audited
Audit Date: 12.07.2019
Personnel: Karanja Ajanaku (Associate Publisher/Exec. Ed.)

MIAMI

THE MIAMI TIMES

Street Address: 900 NW 54th St,
State: FL
ZIP Code: 33127-1818
County: Miami-Dade
Country: USA
Mailing Address: 900 NW 54th St
Mailing City: Miami
Mailing State: FL
Mailing ZIP: 33127-1897
General Phone: 305-694-6210
General Fax: 305-757-5770
Advertising Phone: (305) 693-7093
Advertising Fax: (305) 694-6215
Display Adv. E-mail: advertising@miamitimesonline.com
Editorial e-mail: editorial@miamitimesonline.com
Primary Website: www.miamitimesonline.com
Year Established: Year Established: 1923
Delivery Methods: Mail`Newsstand
Areas Served - City/County or Portion Thereof, or ZIP Codes: 33009 33056 33010 33125 33012 33126 33013 33127 33014 33128 33015 33130 33016 33132 33018 33133 33020 33134 33021 33135 33023 33136 33024 33137 33025 33138 33026 33139 33030 33140 33031 33141 33032 33141 33033 33142 33034 33143 33050 33144 33054 33145 33055 33146 33147 33149 33150 33153 33154 33155 33156 33157 33159 33160 33161 33162 33163 33165 33166 33167 33168 33169 33170 33172 33173 33174 33175 33176 33177 33179 33180 33181 33182 33183 33184 33185 33186 33189 33193 33196 33247 33302 33309 33311 33312 33313 33314 33317

Mechanical specifications: 1 Column = 1.78" 2 Columns = 3.72" 3 Columns = 5.67" 4 Columns = 7 .61" 5 Columns = 9.56" 6 Columns = 11.50" Full Page - 6 Col (w) x 21" (h)
Published: Wed
Avg Paid Circ: 15660
Audit By: Sworn/Estimate/Non-Audited
Audit Date: 12.07.2019
Personnel: Rachel J. Reeves (Pub.); Karen Franklin (Assistant To The Publisher); Garth B. Reeves (VP Business Development); Carolyn Guniss (Executive Editor); Lorraine Cammock (Operations Manager)

MILWAUKEE

MILWAUKEE COMMUNITY JOURNAL

Street Address: 3612 N Martin Luther King Dr,
State: WI
ZIP Code: 53212-4134
County: Milwaukee
Country: USA
Mailing Address: 3612 N Dr Martin Luther King Dr
Mailing City: Milwaukee
Mailing State: WI
Mailing ZIP: 53212-4198
General Phone: (414) 265-5300
General Fax: (414) 265-6647
Display Adv. E-mail: advertising@communityjournal.net
Editorial e-mail: editorial@communityjournal.net
Primary Website: www.communityjournal.net
Commercial printers?: Y
Mechanical specifications: Type page 13 x 21 1/2; E - 6 cols, 2, 1/8 between; A - 6 cols, 2, 1/8 between; C - 8 cols, 1 2/3, 1/8 between.
Published: Wed`Fri
Avg Free Circ: 75000
Audit By: Sworn/Estimate/Non-Audited
Audit Date: 12.07.2019
Personnel: Patricia O. Pattillo (Pub.); Colleen Newsom (Adv. Mgr.); Robert Thomas (Circ. Mgr.); Thomas Mitchell (Ed.); Teretha Mallard (PRODN. MGR.)

THE MILWAUKEE COURIER

Street Address: 2003 W Capitol Dr,
State: WI
ZIP Code: 53206-1939
County: Milwaukee
Country: USA
Mailing Address: PO Box 6279
Mailing City: Milwaukee
Mailing State: WI
Mailing ZIP: 53206-0279
General Phone: (414) 449-4860
General Fax: (414) 585-9101
General/National Adv. E-mail: milwaukeecourier@aol.com
Primary Website: www.milwaukeecourier.com
Year Established: Year Established: 1964
Delivery Methods: Newsstand`Carrier`Racks
Mechanical specifications: Type page full page 10"x18", half page horizontal 10"x9" half page vertical 4.9375"x18", quarter page 4.9375"x9"
Published: Sat
Avg Free Circ: 40000
Audit By: Sworn/Estimate/Non-Audited
Audit Date: 12.07.2019
Personnel: Jerrel Jones (Pub)
Parent company (for newspapers): Milwaukee Courier Inc

MINNEAPOLIS

INSIGHT NEWS

Street Address: 1815 Bryant Ave N,
State: MN
ZIP Code: 55411-3212
County: Hennepin
Country: USA
Mailing Address: 1815 Bryant Avenue North
Mailing City: Minneapolis
Mailing State: MN
Mailing ZIP: 55411
General Phone: (612) 588-1313

General Fax: (612)588-2031
General/National Adv. E-mail: info@insightnews.com
Display Adv. E-mail: selene@insightnews.com
Editorial e-mail: al@insightnews.com
Primary Website: www.insightnews.com
Year Established: Year Established: 1976
Delivery Methods: Newsstand Racks
Areas Served - City/County or Portion Thereof, or ZIP Codes: Minneapolis and St. Paul Metro Area
Commercial printers?: Y
Mechanical available: www.insightnews.com
Published: Mon
Avg Paid Circ: 65
Avg Free Circ: 34835
Audit By: CAC
Audit Date: 31.03.2015
Personnel: Batala McFarlane (Publisher); Jamal Mohammed (Circ. Mgr.); Al McFarlane (President); Patricia Weaver (Prodn. Mgr.)
Parent company (for newspapers): McFarlane Media Interests, Inc.

MINNESOTA SPOKESMAN-RECORDER

Street Address: 3744 4th Ave S, P.O. Box 8558
State: MN
ZIP Code: 55409-1327
County: Hennepin
Country: USA
Mailing Address: 3744 4th Ave S
Mailing City: Minneapolis
Mailing State: MN
Mailing ZIP: 55409-1327
General Phone: (612) 827-4021
General Fax: (612) 827-0577
Advertising Phone: 612-827-4021
Advertising Fax: 612-827-0577
Editorial Phone: 612-827-4021
Editorial Fax: 612-827-0577
General/National Adv. E-mail: display@spokesman-recorder.com
Display Adv. E-mail: display@spokesman-recorder.com
Editorial e-mail: jfreeman@spokesman-recorder.com
Primary Website: www.spokesman-recorder.com
Year Established: Year Established: 1934
Special Editions: MLK, BHM, high school gradauation, rondo days, juneteenth, education
Delivery Methods: Mail Newsstand Carrier Racks
Mechanical specifications: Type page 6 x 21 1/4; E - 6 cols, 2 1/16, 1/8 between; A - 6 cols, 2 1/16, 1/8 between; C - 6 cols, 2 1/16, 1/8 between.
Published: Thur
Avg Paid Circ: 9800
Avg Free Circ: 50000
Audit By: Sworn/Estimate/Non-Audited
Audit Date: 12.07.2019
Personnel: Tracey Williams (CEO/Pub.); Cecelia Viel (Account rep)

MOBILE

MOBILE BEACON AND ALABAMA CITIZEN

Street Address: 2311 Costarides St,
State: AL
ZIP Code: 36617-2442
County: Mobile
Country: USA
Mailing Address: PO Box 1407
Mailing City: Mobile
Mailing State: AL
Mailing ZIP: 36633-1407
General Phone: (251) 479-0629
General Fax: (251) 479-0610
General/National Adv. E-mail: mobilebeaconinc@bellsouth.net
Own Printing Facility?: Y
Published: Wed
Avg Paid Circ: 7000
Avg Free Circ: 20
Audit By: Sworn/Estimate/Non-Audited
Audit Date: 12.07.2019

Personnel: Cleretta T. Blackmon (Ed.)

MONROE

MONROE FREE PRESS

Street Address: 216 Collier St,
State: LA
ZIP Code: 71201-7202
County: Ouachita
Country: USA
Mailing Address: PO Box 4717
Mailing City: Monroe
Mailing State: LA
Mailing ZIP: 71211-4717
General Phone: (318) 388-1310
General Fax: (318) 388-2911
General/National Adv. E-mail: rooseveltwright@prodigy.net
Primary Website: www.monroefreepress.com
Mechanical specifications: Type page 13 x 21; E - 6 cols, 2 1/16, 1/8 between; A - 6 cols, 2 1/16, 1/8 between; C - 6 cols, 2 1/16, 1/8 between.
Published: Thur
Avg Paid Circ: 15000
Audit By: Sworn/Estimate/Non-Audited
Audit Date: 12.07.2019
Personnel: Roosevelt Wright (Ed.)

MONTGOMERY

MONTGOMERY/TUSKEGEE TIMES

Street Address: 525 Augusta Ave,
State: AL
ZIP Code: 36111-1315
County: Montgomery
Country: USA
Mailing Address: PO Box 9133
Mailing City: Montgomery
Mailing State: AL
Mailing ZIP: 36108-0003
General Phone: (334) 280-2444
General Fax: (334) 280-2454
General/National Adv. E-mail: adixon711@aol.com
Published: Thur
Personnel: Almaria Dixon Smith (Gen. Mgr.); Daryl Watkins (Circ. Mgr.); Rev. Al Dixon (Ed.); Alphonso Dixon (Mng. Ed.); Alverene Butler (Prodn. Mgr.)

NASHVILLE

CHATTANOOGA COURIER

Street Address: 805 Bradford Ave,
State: TN
ZIP Code: 37204-2105
County: Davidson
Country: USA
General Phone: (615) 292-9150
General Fax: (615) 292-9056
General/National Adv. E-mail: npnews@comcast.net
Primary Website: www.pridepublishinggroup.net
Mechanical specifications: Type page 13 1/4 x 21 1/2; E - 6 cols, 2 1/8, between; A - 6 cols, 2 1/8, between; C - 6 cols, 2 1/8, between.
Published: Thur
Avg Paid Circ: 24000
Audit By: Sworn/Estimate/Non-Audited
Audit Date: 12.07.2019
Personnel: Meekahl Davis (Pub.); Scott Davies (Circ. Mgr.); Geraldine D. Heath (Ed.)

MURFREESBORO VISION

Street Address: 805 Bradford Ave,
State: TN
ZIP Code: 37204-2105
County: Davidson
Country: USA
General Phone: (615) 292-9150
General Fax: (615) 292-9056
General/National Adv. E-mail: npnews@comcast.net
Primary Website: www.pridepublishinggroup.net

Mechanical specifications: Type page 13 1/4 x 21 1/2; E - 6 cols, 2 1/8, between; A - 6 cols, 2 1/8, between; C - 6 cols, 2 1/8, between.
Published: Thur
Avg Paid Circ: 16000
Audit By: Sworn/Estimate/Non-Audited
Audit Date: 12.07.2019
Personnel: Meekahl Davis (Pub.); Scotty Davis (Circ. Mgr.); Geraldine Heath (Mng. Ed.)

NASHVILLE PRIDE

Street Address: 805 Bradford Ave,
State: TN
ZIP Code: 37204-2105
County: Davidson
Country: USA
General Phone: (615) 292-9150
General Fax: (615) 292-9056
General/National Adv. E-mail: npnews@comcast.net
Primary Website: www.pridepublishinggroup.com
Mechanical specifications: Type page 13 x 21; E - 6 cols, between; A - 6 cols, between; C - 6 cols, between.
Published: Fri
Avg Paid Circ: 42000
Audit By: Sworn/Estimate/Non-Audited
Audit Date: 12.07.2019
Personnel: Meekahl Davis (Pub.); Scott Davis (Adv. Mgr.); Geraldine Heath (Mng. Ed.); James Lewis (Prodn. Mgr.)

TENNESSEE TRIBUNE

Street Address: 1501 Jefferson St,
State: TN
ZIP Code: 37208-3016
County: Davidson
Country: USA
Mailing Address: 1501 JEFFERSON ST
Mailing City: NASHVILLE
Mailing State: TN
Mailing ZIP: 37208-3016
General Phone: (615) 321 3268
General Fax: 1-866 694 7534
Advertising Phone: (615) 321 3268
Advertising Fax: (866) 694-7534
Editorial Phone: 615 509 3181
General/National Adv. E-mail: tennesseetribunenews@aol.com
Display Adv. E-mail: sales1501@aol.com
Editorial e-mail: tennesseetribunenews@aol.com
Primary Website: www.tntribune.com
Year Established: Year Established: 1970
Delivery Methods: Mail Newsstand Carrier Racks
Areas Served - City/County or Portion Thereof, or ZIP Codes: Nashville, Jackson, Memphis, Chattanooga, Knoxville
Own Printing Facility?: Y
Commercial printers?: Y
Mechanical specifications: Type page 13 x 20 1/4; E - 6 cols, 2 1/6, between; A - 6 cols, between.
Published: Thur
Avg Paid Circ: 1200
Avg Free Circ: 24450
Audit By: CVC
Audit Date: 30.11.2017
Personnel: Rosetta Miller Perry (Pub.); William Miller III (Assoc. Pub.); Wanda Benson (Assoc. Pub.); James Artis (VP Advert.)

THE ENLIGHTENER

Street Address: 625 Main St,
State: TN
ZIP Code: 37206-3603
County: Davidson
Country: USA
Mailing Address: 625 Main St
Mailing City: Nashville
Mailing State: TN
Mailing ZIP: 37206-3603
General Phone: (615) 292-9150
General Fax: (615) 292-9056
General/National Adv. E-mail: npnews@comcast.net
Primary Website: www.pridepublishinggroup.net

Mechanical specifications: Type page 13 1/4 x 21 1/2; E - 6 cols, 2 1/8, between; A - 6 cols, 2 1/8, between; C - 6 cols, 2 1/8, between.
Published: Thur
Avg Paid Circ: 26700
Audit By: Sworn/Estimate/Non-Audited
Audit Date: 12.07.2019
Personnel: Meekahl Davis (Pub.); Lisa Pate (Mng. Ed.)

NEW HAVEN

INNER-CITY NEWS

Street Address: 50 Fitch St, Ste 2
State: CT
ZIP Code: 06515-1366
County: New Haven
Country: USA
Mailing Address: 50 FITCH ST.
Mailing City: NEW HAVEN
Mailing State: CT
Mailing ZIP: 06515
General Phone: (203) 387-0354
General Fax: (203) 387-2684
Advertising Phone: 203 387-0354
Advertising Fax: (203) 387-2684
Editorial Phone: (203) 387-0354
Editorial Fax: (203) 387-2684
General/National Adv. E-mail: jthomas@penfieldcomm.com
Display Adv. E-mail: jthomas@penfieldcomm.com
Editorial e-mail: jthomas@penfieldcomm.com
Year Established: Year Established: 1990
Delivery Methods: Newsstand Racks
Areas Served - City/County or Portion Thereof, or ZIP Codes: 6515
Mechanical specifications: Type page 9 3/4 x 13 5/8; E - 4 cols, 2 5/6, between; A - 4 cols, 2 5/6, between; C - 8 cols, 1 5/6, between.
Published: Mon
Avg Free Circ: 25000
Audit By: Sworn/Estimate/Non-Audited
Audit Date: 12.07.2019
Personnel: John Thomas (CEO)

NEW ORLEANS

LOUISIANA WEEKLY

Street Address: 2215 Pelopidas St,
State: LA
ZIP Code: 70122-4957
County: Orleans
Country: USA
Mailing Address: PO Box 8628
Mailing City: New Orleans
Mailing State: LA
Mailing ZIP: 70182-8628
General Phone: (504) 282-3705
General Fax: (504) 282-3773
General/National Adv. E-mail: info@louisianaweekly.com
Primary Website: www.louisianaweekly.com
Mechanical specifications: Type page 13 x 21 1/2; E - 6 cols, 2 1/8, between; A - 6 cols, 2 1/8, between; C - 8 cols, 1 1/2, between.
Published: Mon
Avg Paid Circ: 8300
Avg Free Circ: 1700
Audit By: Sworn/Estimate/Non-Audited
Audit Date: 12.07.2019
Personnel: Chris Hall (Mktg. Mgr.); Jim Hall (Circ. Mgr.); Renette Dejoie-Hall (Exec. Ed.); Edmund W. Lewis (Ed.); David T. Baker (Webmaster)

NEW ORLEANS DATA NEWS WEEKLY

Street Address: 3501 Napoleon Ave,
State: LA
ZIP Code: 70125-4843
County: Orleans
Country: USA
Mailing Address: 3501 Napoleon Ave
Mailing City: New Orleans
Mailing State: LA
Mailing ZIP: 70125-4843
General Phone: (504) 821-7421
General Fax: (504) 821-7622

Black Newspapers in the U.S.

General/National Adv. E-mail: datanewsad@bellsouth.net
Editorial e-mail: datanewsad@bellsouth.net
Primary Website: www.ladatanews.com
Year Established: Year Established: 1967
Delivery Methods: Racks
Mechanical specifications: Type page 10 3/4 x 14; E - 5 cols, between; A - 5 cols, between.
Published: Sat
Avg Paid Circ: 0
Avg Free Circ: 19965
Audit By: CVC
Audit Date: 31.03.2018
Personnel: Terry B. Jones (Pub.); Terrence Lee (Circ.)
Parent company (for newspapers): New Orleans Data News Weekly
Newspapers (for newspaper groups): New Orleans Data News Weekly, New Orleans

NEW YORK

BLACK STAR NEWS

Street Address: 32 Broadway, Ste 511
State: NY
ZIP Code: 10004-1665
County: New York
Country: USA
Mailing Address: PO Box 1472
Mailing City: New York
Mailing State: NY
Mailing ZIP: 10274-1472
General Phone: (646) 261-7566
Advertising Phone: (212) 422-2352
Editorial Phone: (646) 261-7566
General/National Adv. E-mail: advertise@blackstarnews.com
Display Adv. E-mail: advertise@blackstarnews.com
Editorial e-mail: Milton@blackstarnews.com
Primary Website: www.blackstarnews.com
Year Established: Year Established: 1977
Delivery Methods: Mail`Racks
Areas Served - City/County or Portion Thereof, or ZIP Codes: New York County
Published: Thur
Personnel: Milton Allimadi (Pub./Ed.-in-Chief); Neanda Salvaterra (Assistant Web Ed.)

NEW YORK AMSTERDAM NEWS

Street Address: 2340 Frederick Douglass Blvd,
State: NY
ZIP Code: 10027-3619
County: New York
Country: USA
Mailing Address: 2340 Frederick Douglass Blvd
Mailing City: New York
Mailing State: NY
Mailing ZIP: 10027-3691
General Phone: (212) 932-7400
Advertising Phone: (212) 932-7498
Advertising Fax: (212) 932-7497
Editorial Phone: (212) 932-7465
Editorial Fax: (212) 932-7467
General/National Adv. E-mail: info@amsterdamnews.com
Display Adv. E-mail: penda.howell@amsterdamnews.com
Editorial e-mail: kfm@amsterdamnews.com
Primary Website: www.amsterdamnews.com
Year Established: Year Established: 1909
Delivery Methods: Mail`Newsstand
Areas Served - City/County or Portion Thereof, or ZIP Codes: New York, NY
Mechanical specifications: 1 column......1.342" 2 columns......2.833" 3 columns......4.313" 4 columns......5.788" 6 columns......8.75" 12 columns....18.5" Gutter space vertically and horizontally is .125" Page depth is 11.5"
Published: Thur
Avg Paid Circ: 4845
Avg Free Circ: 1480
Audit By: AAM
Audit Date: 31.12.2018
Personnel: Elinor Tatum (Publisher / Editor in Chief); Penda Howell (Vice President, Advertising, Sales, Partnerships.); Nayaba Arinde (Editor); Kristin Fayne-Mulroy (Mng. Ed./ Arts/Enter. Ed.)

NEW YORK BEACON

Street Address: 237 W 37th St, Rm 201
State: NY
ZIP Code: 10018-6958
County: New York
Country: USA
Mailing Address: 237 W 37th St Rm 201
Mailing City: New York
Mailing State: NY
Mailing ZIP: 10018-6958
General Phone: (212) 213-8585
General Fax: (212) 213-6291
General/National Adv. E-mail: newyorkbeacon@yahoo.com
Primary Website: www.newyorkbeacon.net
Delivery Methods: Newsstand
Areas Served - City/County or Portion Thereof, or ZIP Codes: 212, 718, 646, 916' 915
Mechanical specifications: Type page 10 x 14; E - 2 cols, 2, between; A - 5 cols, 2, between; C - 5 cols, between.
Published: Fri
Avg Paid Circ: 71750
Avg Free Circ: 12722
Audit By: Sworn/Estimate/Non-Audited
Audit Date: 12.07.2019
Personnel: Miatta Smith (Adv. Dir.); Walter Smith (Ed. in Chief); Willie Egyir (Mng. Ed.)

NORFOLK

JOURNAL AND GUIDE

Street Address: 974 Norfolk Sq,
State: VA
ZIP Code: 23502-3212
County: Norfolk City
Country: USA
Mailing Address: PO Box 209
Mailing City: Norfolk
Mailing State: VA
Mailing ZIP: 23501-0209
General Phone: (757) 543-6531
General Fax: (757) 543-7620
General/National Adv. E-mail: njguide@gmail.com
Mechanical specifications: Type page 13 x 21; E - 6 cols, between; A - 6 cols, between.
Published: Thur
Avg Paid Circ: 15000
Audit By: Sworn/Estimate/Non-Audited
Audit Date: 12.07.2019
Personnel: Brenda H. Andrews (Pub.); Michael Brooks (Circ. Mgr.); David Todd (Prodn. Mgr.)

OKLAHOMA CITY

BLACK CHRONICLE

Street Address: 1528 NE 23rd St,
State: OK
ZIP Code: 73111-3260
County: Oklahoma
Country: USA
Mailing Address: PO Box 17498
Mailing City: Oklahoma City
Mailing State: OK
Mailing ZIP: 73136-1498
General Phone: (405) 424-4695
General Fax: (405) 424-6708
General/National Adv. E-mail: alisdsey@blackchronicle.com
Primary Website: www.blackchronicle.com
Mechanical specifications: Type page 14 1/2 x 21 1/2; E - 8 cols, 1 2/3, between; A - 8 cols, 1 2/3, between; C - 8 cols, 1 2/3, between.
Published: Thur
Avg Paid Circ: 30000
Audit By: Sworn/Estimate/Non-Audited
Audit Date: 12.07.2019
Personnel: T.C. Brown (Adv. Rep.); Russell M. Perry (Ed.); Albert J. Lindsey (Mng. Ed.)

ORLANDO

THE ORLANDO TIMES

Street Address: 4403 Vineland Rd Ste B5, Quorum Center
State: FL
ZIP Code: 32811-7362
County: Orange
Country: USA
Mailing Address: 4403 Vineland Rd. Ste B5
Mailing City: Orlando
Mailing State: FL
Mailing ZIP: 32811
General Phone: (407) 841-3052
General Fax: (407) 849-0434
Advertising Phone: (407) 849-0434
General/National Adv. E-mail: calvincollinsjr@aol.com
Display Adv. E-mail: calvincollinsjr@aol.com
Primary Website: www.orlando-times.com
Year Established: Year Established: 1976
Delivery Methods: Mail`Newsstand`Carrier`Racks
Mechanical specifications: Type page 10 x 21; E - 6 cols, between; A - 6 cols, between; C - 6 cols, between.
Published: Thur
Avg Paid Circ: 7289
Avg Free Circ: 3111
Audit By: Sworn/Estimate/Non-Audited
Audit Date: 12.07.2019
Personnel: Dr. Calvin Collins (Pres./Pub.); Kevin T. Collins (Adv. Mgr.); Lottie H. Collins (Prodn. Mgr.)

PASADENA

PASADENA JOURNAL-NEWS

Street Address: 1541 N Lake Ave, Ste A,
State: CA
ZIP Code: 91104-2375
County: Los Angeles
Country: USA
Mailing Address: 1541 N Lake Ave Ste A
Mailing City: Pasadena
Mailing State: CA
Mailing ZIP: 91104-2375
General Phone: (626) 798-3972
General Fax: (626) 798-3282
General/National Adv. E-mail: pasjour@pacbell.net
Primary Website: www.pasadenajournal.com
Areas Served - City/County or Portion Thereof, or ZIP Codes: 91001, 91101, 91105, 91105, 91107, 91107, 91109, 91706, 91730, 91184, 91342, 91745, 91765, 91770, 91775, 91792, 91104, 91103, 91106, 91102, 91108, 91702, 91710, 91737, 91201, 91740, 91763, 91766, 91773, 91790, 91801
Mechanical specifications: Type page 10 x 15; E - 5 cols, 1 3/4, between; A - 5 cols, 1 3/4, between; C - 5 cols, 1 3/4, between.
Published: Thur
Avg Paid Circ: 7500
Audit By: Sworn/Estimate/Non-Audited
Audit Date: 12.07.2019
Personnel: Joe C. Hopkins (Co-Pub.); Ruthie Hopkins (Ed.); Harmony Coburn (Webmaster)

PHILADELPHIA

PHILADELPHIA SUNDAY SUN

Street Address: 6661 Germantown Ave, Ste 63
State: PA
ZIP Code: 19119-2251
County: Philadelphia
Country: USA
Mailing Address: 6661 GERMANTOWN AVE # 63
Mailing City: PHILADELPHIA
Mailing State: PA
Mailing ZIP: 19119-2251
General Phone: (215) 848-7864
General Fax: (215) 848-7893
General/National Adv. E-mail: sundaysunads@yahoo.com
Editorial e-mail: taesun@philasun.com
Primary Website: www.philasun.com
Year Established: Year Established: 1992
Delivery Methods: Mail`Newsstand`Carrier`Racks
Areas Served - City/County or Portion Thereof, or ZIP Codes: Philadelphia County
Mechanical specifications: Type page 10 1/4 x 14; E - 5 cols, 1 7/8, 1/6 between; A - 5 cols, 1 7/8, 1/6 between; C - 5 cols, 1 7/8, 1/6 between.
Published: Sun
Avg Paid Circ: 20000
Audit By: Sworn/Estimate/Non-Audited
Audit Date: 12.07.2019
Personnel: Teresa Emerson (Mng. Ed.); Tera Moyet (Adv.)

PHILADELPHIA TRIBUNE

Street Address: 520 S 16th St, # 26
State: PA
ZIP Code: 19146-1565
County: Philadelphia
Country: USA
Mailing Address: 520 S 16th St # 26
Mailing City: Philadelphia
Mailing State: PA
Mailing ZIP: 19146-1565
General Phone: (215) 893-4050
General Fax: (215) 735-3612
General/National Adv. E-mail: info@phila-tribune.com
Display Adv. E-mail: advertising@phillytrib.com
Primary Website: phillytrib.com
Published: Tues`Fri`Sun
Avg Paid Circ: 3856
Avg Free Circ: 6207
Audit By: AAM
Audit Date: 31.03.2018
Personnel: Al Thomas (Mktg. Dir.); Michael Levere (Circ. Mgr.); Robert W. Bogle (CEO Pres.); Irv Randolph (Mng. Ed.); John Mason (Adv. Dir.)

SCOOP USA

Street Address: 1354 W. Girard Avenue, 2nd floor rear,
State: PA
ZIP Code: 19123
County: Philadelphia
Country: USA
Mailing Address: PO Box 14013
Mailing City: Philadelphia
Mailing State: PA
Mailing ZIP: 19122-0013
General Phone: 215 309-3139
General Fax: 267 534-2943
General/National Adv. E-mail: Info@scoopusamedia.com
Display Adv. E-mail: advertisements@scoopusamedia.com
Editorial e-mail: editorial@scoopusamedia.com
Primary Website: www.scoopusamedia.com
Year Established: Year Established: 1960
Delivery Methods: Mail`Newsstand`Carrier`Racks
Areas Served - City/County or Portion Thereof, or ZIP Codes: 191.. / 081.. / 190..
Mechanical specifications: Type page 10 x 16; E - 6 cols, 1 1/2, 3/16 between.
Published: Fri
Published Other: Digital Thursday
Avg Free Circ: 36000
Audit By: Sworn/Estimate/Non-Audited
Audit Date: 12.07.2019
Personnel: Sherri Darden (Publisher)
Parent company (for newspapers): Scoop USA Media

PITTSBURGH

NEW PITTSBURGH COURIER

Street Address: 315 E Carson St,
State: PA
ZIP Code: 15219-1202
County: Allegheny
Country: USA
Mailing Address: 479 Ledyard St
Mailing City: Detroit
Mailing State: MI
Mailing ZIP: 15219-1278
General Phone: (412) 481-8302
General Fax: (412) 481-1360
Advertising Phone: (313) 963-8100
General/National Adv. E-mail: webmaster@newpittsburghcourier.com
Display Adv. E-mail: ads@newpittsburghcourier.com

com
Editorial e-mail: newsroom@
   newpittsburghcourier.com
Primary Website: www.
   newpittsburghcourieronline.com
Year Established: Year Established: 1910
Delivery Methods:
   Mail`Newsstand`Carrier`Racks
Own Printing Facility?: N
Commercial printers?: Y
Mechanical specifications: Type page
   Broadsheet 10.625 x 20 1/2; E - 6 cols,
   1.667, 1/8 between
Published: Wed
Avg Paid Circ: 2014
Avg Free Circ: 593
Audit By: CVC
Audit Date: 30.09.2017
Personnel: Stephan Broadus (Asst. to Pub.);
   Eric Gaines (Adv. Mgr.); Jeff Marion (Circ.
   Mgr.); Rod Doss (Editor & Publisher); Ulish
   Carter (Managing Editor)
Parent company (for newspapers): Real Times
   Media, Inc.

PLANO

NORTH DALLAS GAZETTE

Street Address: 3401 Custer Rd, Ste 169
State: TX
ZIP Code: 75023-7546
County: Collin
Country: USA
Mailing Address: PO Box 763866
Mailing City: Dallas
Mailing State: TX
Mailing ZIP: 75376-3866
General Phone: (972) 432-5219
General Fax: (972) 509-9058
Display Adv. E-mail: marketing@
   northdallasgazette.com
Primary Website: northdallasgazette.com
Year Established: Year Established: 1991
Areas Served - City/County or Portion Thereof, or ZIP
   Codes: 75023, 75149, 75201, 75040, 75080,
   75069, 75002, 75006, 75098
Mechanical specifications: Type page 12 1/2 x
   20 1/2; E - 6 cols, 2, between; A - 6 cols, 2,
   between; C - 6 cols, 2, between.
Published: Thur
Avg Paid Circ: 8
Avg Free Circ: 9976
Audit By: VAC
Audit Date: 30.12.2014
Personnel: Thurman R. Jones (Pub.); Ruth
   Ferguson (Ed.); Ana Camacho (Sales and
   Mktg.)

PORTLAND

PORTLAND OBSERVER

Street Address: 4747 NE M L King Blvd,
State: OR
ZIP Code: 97211-3398
County: Multnomah
Country: USA
Mailing Address: PO Box 3137
Mailing City: Portland
Mailing State: OR
Mailing ZIP: 97208-3137
General Phone: (503) 288-0033
General Fax: (503) 288-0015
General/National Adv. E-mail: news@
   portlandobserver.com
Primary Website: www.portlandobserver.com
Mechanical specifications: Type page 13 x 21;
   E - 6 cols, 2 1/16, 1/8 between; A - 6 cols, 2
   1/16, 1/8 between; C - 6 cols, between.
Published: Wed
Avg Paid Circ: 7000
Avg Free Circ: 30000
Audit By: Sworn/Estimate/Non-Audited
Audit Date: 12.07.2019
Personnel: Mark Washington (Pub.); Mike
   Leighton (Ed.); Paul Newfeldt (Prodn. Mgr.)

THE SKANNER

Street Address: 415 N Killingsworth St,
State: OR
ZIP Code: 97217-2440
County: Multnomah
Country: USA
Mailing Address: PO Box 5455
Mailing City: Portland
Mailing State: OR
Mailing ZIP: 97228-5455
General Phone: (503) 285-5555
General Fax: (503) 285-3400
General/National Adv. E-mail: info@theskanner.
   com; adver@theskanner.com
Primary Website: www.theskanner.com
Own Printing Facility?: Y
Mechanical specifications: Type page 10 1/2 x
   16; E - 6 cols, 1 5/8, between; A - 6 cols, 1
   5/8, between.
Published: Thur
Published Other: Every other Thurs
Avg Paid Circ: 10500
Audit By: Sworn/Estimate/Non-Audited
Audit Date: 12.07.2019
Personnel: Bernie Foster (Pub.); Jerry Foster
   (Circ. Mgr.); Bobbie Dore Foster (Ed.); David
   Kidd (Prodn. Mgr.)

PROVIDENCE

THE PROVIDENCE AMERICAN

Street Address: PO Box 5859,
State: RI
ZIP Code: 02903-0859
County: Providence
Country: USA
Mailing Address: PO Box 5859
Mailing City: Providence
Mailing State: RI
Mailing ZIP: 02903-0859
General Phone: (401) 475-6480
General Fax: (401) 475-6254
Primary Website: The Providence American
Commercial printers?: Y
Mechanical specifications: Type page 10 x
   16; E - 4 cols, 1 1/2, between; A - 6 cols,
   between; C - 6 cols, between.
Published: Mthly
Avg Free Circ: 11000
Audit By: Sworn/Estimate/Non-Audited
Audit Date: 12.07.2019
Personnel: Peter C. Wills (Pub.)

RALEIGH

THE CAROLINIAN

Street Address: 519 S Blount St,
State: NC
ZIP Code: 27601-1827
County: Wake
Country: USA
Mailing Address: PO Box 25308
Mailing City: Raleigh
Mailing State: NC
Mailing ZIP: 27611-5308
General Phone: (919) 834-5558
General Fax: (919) 832-3243
General/National Adv. E-mail: thecarolinian@
   bellsouth.net
Primary Website: www.raleighcarolinian.info
Mechanical specifications: Type page 13 x 21;
   E - 6 cols, 2 1/16, 1/8 between; A - 6 cols,
   2 1/16, 1/8 between; C - 6 cols, 2 1/16, 1/8
   between.
Published: Thur
Published Other: Thur`Every other Mon
Avg Paid Circ: 15202
Audit By: Sworn/Estimate/Non-Audited
Audit Date: 12.07.2019
Personnel: Paul R. Jervay (Pub.); Paul Jervay
   (Adv. Mgr.); Andrew Alston (Circ. Mgr.);
   Evelyn Jervay (Ed.)

RICHMOND

RICHMOND FREE PRESS

Street Address: 422 E Franklin St, Fl 2
State: VA
ZIP Code: 23219-2226
County: Richmond City
Country: USA
Mailing Address: PO Box 27709
Mailing City: Richmond
Mailing State: VA
Mailing ZIP: 23261-7709
General Phone: (804) 644-0496
Advertising Fax: (804) 643-5436
Editorial Fax: (804) 643-7519
General/National Adv. E-mail: news@
   richmondfreepress.com
Display Adv. E-mail: advertising@
   richmondfreepress.com
Primary Website: www.richmondfreepress.com
Year Established: Year Established: 1991
Delivery Methods: Newsstand`Racks
Areas Served - City/County or Portion Thereof, or ZIP
   Codes: 23219, 23220, 23223, 23224, 23227,
   23225, 23230, 23803, 23221, 23231, 23235,
   23228, 23234, 23150, 23113, 23060, 23294,
   23229, 23005, 23233
Mechanical specifications: Printed page
   area: 11" wide x 21" deep â€¢ 126
   column inchest 6 Column Width Display
   Measurements COLUMN SIZE 1 column
   1.698" 2 columns 3.558" 3 columns 5.418"
   4 columns 7.278" 5 columns 9.138" 6
   columns 11" 8 Column Width Legal/
   Classified Measurements COLUMN SIZE 1
   column 1.223" 2 columns 2.625" 3 columns
   4.02" 4 columns 5.417" 5 columns 6.813" 6
   columns 8.2" 7 columns 9.593" 8 columns
   11"
Published: Thur
Avg Paid Circ: 69
Avg Free Circ: 31259
Audit By: VAC
Audit Date: 31.12.2016
Personnel: Jean Patterson Boone (Pres./Pub.);
   April A. Coleman (Prodn. Mgr.)
Parent company (for newspapers): Paradigm
   Communications, Inc.

THE VOICE

Street Address: 205 E Clay St,
State: VA
ZIP Code: 23219-1325
County: Richmond City
Country: USA
Mailing Address: 205 E Clay St
Mailing City: Richmond
Mailing State: VA
Mailing ZIP: 23219-1325
General Phone: (804) 644-9060
General Fax: (804) 644-5617
General/National Adv. E-mail: info@
   voicenewspaper.com
Display Adv. E-mail: ads@voicenewspaper.com
Editorial e-mail: editor@voicenewspaper.com
Primary Website: www.voicenewspaper.com
Year Established: Year Established: 1985
Delivery Methods: Racks
Areas Served - City/County or Portion Thereof, or ZIP
   Codes: 23219, 23235, 23228, 23223, 23220,
   23806, 23040, 23139, 23002, 23911, 23922,
   23930, 23824, 23901, 23942, 23966, 23944,
   23947, 23111,
Mechanical specifications: Type page 10.20 x
   11.25; E - 4 cols, 2.375" between; A - 4
   cols, 2 1/4, 1/4 between; C - 6 cols, 1 1/2,
   between.
Published: Wed
Avg Paid Circ: 100
Avg Free Circ: 25000
Audit By: CVC
Audit Date: 08.08.2014
Personnel: Algeree Johnson (Ed.); Marlene
   Jones (Executive Manager)
Parent company (for newspapers): Southside
   Voice, Inc.

RIVERSIDE

BLACK VOICE NEWS

Street Address: 4290 Brockton Ave,
State: CA
ZIP Code: 92501-3447
County: Riverside
Country: USA
Mailing Address: PO Box 1581
Mailing City: Riverside
Mailing State: CA
Mailing ZIP: 92502-1581
General Phone: (951) 682-6070
General Fax: (951) 276-0877
General/National Adv. E-mail: cherylbrown@
   blackvoicenews.com
Primary Website: www.blackvoicenews.com
Year Established: Year Established: 1972
Mechanical specifications: Type page 13 x 21;
   E - 6 cols, 2, 1/6 between; C - 8 cols, 1 3/4,
   1/6 between.
Published: Thur
Avg Paid Circ: 10000
Avg Free Circ: 1810
Audit By: CVC
Audit Date: 30.06.2005
Personnel: Cheryl R. Brown (Co-Pub.); Hardy L.
   Brown (Co-Pub.); Lee Ragin (Circ. Mgr.)

ROANOKE

THE ROANOKE TRIBUNE

Street Address: 2318 Melrose Ave NW,
State: VA
ZIP Code: 24017-3906
County: Roanoke City
Country: USA
Mailing Address: 2318 Melrose Ave NW
Mailing City: Roanoke
Mailing State: VA
Mailing ZIP: 24017-3906
General Phone: (540) 343-0326
General Fax: (540) 343-7366
General/National Adv. E-mail: trib@rt.roacoxmail.
   com
Primary Website: www.theroanoketribune.org
Mechanical specifications: Type page 13 x 21;
   E - 6 cols, 2 1/8, between; A - 6 cols, 2 1/8,
   between; C - 6 cols, 2 1/8, between.
Published: Thur
Avg Paid Circ: 6000
Audit By: Sworn/Estimate/Non-Audited
Audit Date: 12.07.2019
Personnel: Claudia A. Whitworth (Ed.); Stan
   Hale (Assoc. Ed.)

RUSK

TEXAS INFORMER

Street Address: PO Box 332, 941 Loop 343
State: TX
ZIP Code: 75785-0332
County: Cherokee
Country: USA
Mailing Address: PO Box 332
Mailing City: Rusk
Mailing State: TX
Mailing ZIP: 75785-0332
General Phone: (903) 683-5743
General Fax: (903) 683-1577
Advertising Phone: 903 721 3112
Advertising Fax: 903 683-1577
Editorial Phone: 903 721-3112
Editorial Fax: 903-683-1577
General/National Adv. E-mail: info@texasinformer.
   com
Display Adv. E-mail: info@texasinformer.com
Editorial e-mail: informernews08@aol.com
Primary Website: www.texasinformer.com
Year Established: Year Established: 1995
Delivery Methods: Mail`Racks
Areas Served - City/County or Portion Thereof, or
   ZIP Codes: Cherokee County Jacksonville,
   Tx. - 75766 Rusk, TX. - 75785 Alto,
   TX. - 75925 Anderson County Palestine
   - 75801 Houston County Crockett,
   TX. - 75835 Angelina County Lufkin,
   TX. - 75901 Rusk County Henderson,
   TX. - 75652
Mechanical specifications: Three (3) columns
   x 13-inch column depth. Full page: 10.5"
   wide x 13" depth. Local: $2,000.00
   Full page - $250.00 1/8 page National:
   $2,000.00 Full page - $250.00 1/8 page
   Insert Open Rate: $100. per thousand
   Classified Rate: 15.00 for first 10 words
   Volume, frequency, contract, color
   and other rates may be available from
   publisher.
Published: Mthly
Avg Paid Circ: 0
Avg Free Circ: 2500

Black Newspapers in the U.S.

Audit By: Sworn/Estimate/Non-Audited
Audit Date: 12.07.2019
Personnel: Maxine Session (Pub./Ed. Maxine Session - Co-Publisher/ Editor Walater Session -Co-Publisher)

SACRAMENTO

OBSERVER GROUP

Street Address: 2330 Alhambra Blvd,
State: CA
ZIP Code: 95817-1121
County: Sacramento
Country: USA
Mailing Address: PO Box 209
Mailing City: Sacramento
Mailing State: CA
Mailing ZIP: 95812-0209
General Phone: (916) 452-4781
General Fax: (916) 452-7744
General/National Adv. E-mail: circulation@sacobserver.com
Primary Website: www.sacobserver.com
Own Printing Facility?: Y
Mechanical specifications: Type page 12 15/16 x 21; E - 6 cols, between; A - 6 cols, between.
Published: Fri
Avg Paid Circ: 50000
Avg Free Circ: 100
Audit By: Sworn/Estimate/Non-Audited
Audit Date: 12.07.2019
Personnel: William H. Lee (Pub.); Joe Stinson (Circ. Mgr.); Larry Lee (Prodn. Mgr.)

SAINT LOUIS

ST. LOUIS AMERICAN

Street Address: 2315 Pine St,
State: MO
ZIP Code: 63103-2218
County: Saint Louis City
Country: United States
Mailing Address: 2315 Pine Street
Mailing City: St. Louis
Mailing State: MO
Mailing ZIP: 63103
General Phone: (314) 533-8000
General Fax: (314) 533-2332
General/National Adv. E-mail: kjones@stlamerican.com
Primary Website: www.stlamerican.com
Year Established: Year Established: 1928
Delivery Methods: Newsstand`Racks
Areas Served - City/County or Portion Thereof, or ZIP Codes: 74 different throughout St. Louis
Mechanical specifications: Type page 12 x 21; E - 6 cols, between; A - 6 cols, between; C - 10 cols, between.
Published: Thur
Avg Paid Circ: 60
Avg Free Circ: 56652
Audit By: AAM
Audit Date: 30.09.2018
Personnel: Donald Suggs (Pub.); Kevin Jones (COO/Adv. Dir.); Mike Terhaar (Prodn. Mgr.)

SAINT LOUIS

ST. LOUIS EVENING WHIRL

Street Address: PO Box 8055,
State: MO
ZIP Code: 63156-8055
County: Saint Louis City
Country: USA
Mailing Address: PO Box 8055
Mailing City: Saint Louis
Mailing State: MO
Mailing ZIP: 63156
General Phone: (678) 778-2616
General Fax: N/A
Advertising Phone: N/A
Advertising Fax: N/A
General/National Adv. E-mail: tpcwhirl@aol.com
Display Adv. E-mail: tpcwhirl@aol.com
Editorial e-mail: tpcwhirl@aol.com
Primary Website: www.thewhirlonline.com

Year Established: Year Established: 1938
Delivery Methods: Mail`Newsstand
Own Printing Facility?: N
Commercial printers?: Y
Mechanical specifications: Type page 12 1/2 x 21 1/2; E - 7 cols, 1 5/8, 3/16 between; A - 7 cols, 1 5/8, 3/16 between; C - 9 cols, 1 1/4, 1/8 between.
Published: Mon
Avg Paid Circ: 50500
Audit By: Sworn/Estimate/Non-Audited
Audit Date: 12.07.2019
Personnel: Barry R. Thomas (Pub); Anthony L. Sanders (Ed.)

SAINT PETERSBURG

WEEKLY CHALLENGER

Street Address: 2500 Martin Luther King St S, Ste F
State: FL
ZIP Code: 33705-3554
County: Pinellas
Country: USA
Mailing Address: 2500 Dr Martin Luther King Jr St S Ste F
Mailing City: Saint Petersburg
Mailing State: FL
Mailing ZIP: 33705-3554
General Phone: (727) 896-2922
General Fax: (727) 823-2568
General/National Adv. E-mail: editor@theweeklychallenger.com
Primary Website: www.theweeklychallenger.com
Mechanical specifications: Type page 13 3/4 x 21; E - 8 cols, 1 1/2, 1/4 between; A - 8 cols, 1 1/2, 1/4 between; C - 8 cols, 1 1/2, 1/4 between.
Published: Thur
Avg Paid Circ: 552
Avg Free Circ: 4511
Audit By: VAC
Audit Date: 30.03.2013
Personnel: Ephel Johnson (Pub.); Dianne Speithes (Adv. Mgr.); Lorraine Bellinger (Graphic Artist)

SAN ANTONIO

SAN ANTONIO OBSERVER

Street Address: 3427 Belgium Ln,
State: TX
ZIP Code: 78219-2501
County: Bexar
Country: USA
Mailing Address: PO Box 200226
Mailing City: San Antonio
Mailing State: TX
Mailing ZIP: 78220-0226
General Phone: (210) 212-6397
General Fax: (210) 271-0441
General/National Adv. E-mail: taylor2039@aol.com
Mechanical specifications: Type page 10 1/4 x 11 1/4; E - 4 cols, between.
Published: Wed
Avg Paid Circ: 60
Avg Free Circ: 16051
Audit By: Sworn/Estimate/Non-Audited
Audit Date: 12.07.2019
Personnel: Lanell Taylor (Pres.); Sherry Logan (Adv. Mgr.); Gus Lopez (Prodn. Mgr.)

THE SAN ANTONIO OBSERVER

Street Address: 3427 Belgium Ln,
State: TX
ZIP Code: 78219-2501
County: Bexar
Country: USA
Mailing Address: 3427 Belgium Ln
Mailing City: San Antonio
Mailing State: TX
Mailing ZIP: 78219-2501
Primary Website: www.saobserver.com
Year Established: Year Established: 1995
Published: Wed
Avg Paid Circ: 22
Avg Free Circ: 2934

Audit By: VAC
Audit Date: 30.12.2014
Personnel: Fabby Ali; Sherry Logan (Publisher); Waseem Ali (Advertising Manager); Charles Jones (Production Manager)

THE SAN ANTONIO REGISTER

Street Address: 3427 Belgium Ln,
State: TX
ZIP Code: 78219-2501
County: Bexar
Country: USA
Mailing Address: 3427 Belgium Ln
Mailing City: San Antonio
Mailing State: TX
Mailing ZIP: 78219-2501
Primary Website: www.saregister.com
Year Established: Year Established: 1931
Published: Wed
Avg Paid Circ: 0
Avg Free Circ: 9486
Audit By: CVC
Audit Date: 30.06.2014
Personnel: Sherry Logan

THE TYMES

Street Address: 3427 Belgium Ln,
State: TX
ZIP Code: 78219-2501
County: Bexar
Country: USA
Mailing Address: 3427 Belgium Ln
Mailing City: San Antonio
Mailing State: TX
Mailing ZIP: 78219-2501
General Phone: 2102229220
Advertising Phone: 2102229220
Editorial Phone: 2102229220
General/National Adv. E-mail: Wsmali@aol.com
Display Adv. E-mail: Wsmali@aol.com
Editorial e-mail: Wsmali@aol.com
Primary Website: www.tha-tymes.com
Year Established: Year Established: 2002
Delivery Methods: Mail`Newsstand`Racks
Mechanical specifications: 10.25x9.75
Published: Wed
Avg Free Circ: 10000
Audit By: CVC
Audit Date: 01.01.2012
Personnel: Waseem Ali (President/CEO)

SAN BERNARDINO

PRECINCT REPORTER

Street Address: 670 N Arrowhead Ave, Ste B, Ste B
State: CA
ZIP Code: 92401-1102
County: San Bernardino
Country: USA
Mailing Address: 670 N Arrowhead Ave Ste B
Mailing City: San Bernardino
Mailing State: CA
Mailing ZIP: 92401-1102
General Phone: (909) 889-0597
General Fax: (909) 889-1706
General/National Adv. E-mail: news@precinctreporter.com
Display Adv. E-mail: sales@precinctreporter.com
Primary Website: www.precinctreporter.com
Year Established: Year Established: 1965
Delivery Methods: Newsstand`Carrier`Racks
Mechanical specifications: 10 x 21
Published: Thur
Audit By: Sworn/Estimate/Non-Audited
Audit Date: 12.07.2019
Personnel: Brian Townsend (Ed.)

SAN DIEGO

SAN DIEGO VOICE & VIEWPOINT

Street Address: 3619 College Ave,
State: CA
ZIP Code: 92115-7041
County: San Diego

Country: USA
Mailing Address: P.O. Box 120095
Mailing City: San Diego
Mailing State: CA
Mailing ZIP: 92112
General Phone: (619) 266-2233
General Fax: (619) 266-0533
General/National Adv. E-mail: voiceandviewpoint@gmail.com
Primary Website: www.sdvoice.com
Published: Thur
Avg Paid Circ: 25000
Audit By: Sworn/Estimate/Non-Audited
Audit Date: 12.07.2019
Personnel: John Warren (Ed.); Gerri Adams-Warren (Mng. Ed.)

SAN FRANCISCO

CALIFORNIA VOICE

Street Address: 1791 Bancroft Ave,
State: CA
ZIP Code: 94124-2644
County: San Francisco
Country: USA
Mailing Address: 1791 Bancroft Ave
Mailing City: San Francisco
Mailing State: CA
Mailing ZIP: 94124-2644
General Phone: (415) 671-1000
General Fax: (415) 671-1005
General/National Adv. E-mail: sunmedia97@aol.com
Primary Website: www.sunreporter.com
Published: Sun
Avg Paid Circ: 38840
Audit By: CVC
Audit Date: 31.12.2004
Personnel: Amelia Ashley-Ward (Pub.)

METRO REPORTER

Street Address: 1791 Bancroft Ave,
State: CA
ZIP Code: 94124-2644
County: San Francisco
Country: USA
Mailing Address: 1791 Bancroft Ave
Mailing City: San Francisco
Mailing State: CA
Mailing ZIP: 94124-2644
General Phone: (415) 671-1000
General Fax: (415) 671-1005
General/National Adv. E-mail: sundoc97@aol.com; sunmedia97@aol.com
Primary Website: www.sunreporter.com
Own Printing Facility?: Y
Mechanical specifications: Type page 13 x 21; E - 6 cols, 2 1/16, between; A - 6 cols, 2 1/16, between; C - 6 cols, 2 1/16, between.
Published: Tues
Avg Free Circ: 111013
Audit By: CVC
Audit Date: 31.12.2004
Personnel: Lovie Ward (Circ. Mgr.); Amelia Ashley-Ward (Ed.)

SAN FRANCISCO BAY VIEW

Street Address: 4917 3rd St,
State: CA
ZIP Code: 94124-2309
County: San Francisco
Country: USA
Mailing Address: 4917 3rd St
Mailing City: San Francisco
Mailing State: CA
Mailing ZIP: 94124-2309
General Phone: (415) 671-0789
General Fax: (415) 671-0789
Advertising Phone: (415) 671-0789
Editorial Phone: (415) 671-0789
General/National Adv. E-mail: editor@sfbayview.com
Display Adv. E-mail: editor@sfbayview.com
Editorial e-mail: editor@sfbayview.com
Primary Website: www.sfbayview.com
Year Established: Year Established: 1976
Delivery Methods: Mail`Newsstand`Racks
Areas Served - City/County or Portion Thereof, or ZIP Codes: 94102, 94103, 94107, 94112, 94115,

94117, 94124, 94132, 94134, 94577, 94601, 94603, 94605, 94607, 94609, 94610, 94612, 94619, 94621, 94702, 94703, 94704, 94705, 94710
Own Printing Facility?: N
Commercial printers?: Y
Mechanical specifications: Type page 12.5 x 22.5; E - 6 cols, 2", 1/6 between; A - 6 cols, 2", 1/6 between; C - 6 cols, 2", 1/6 between.
Published: Mthly
Avg Paid Circ: 700
Avg Free Circ: 20000
Audit By: Sworn/Estimate/Non-Audited
Audit Date: 12.07.2019
Personnel: Willie Ratcliff (Pub.); Mary Ratcliff (Ed.)

SUN REPORTER

Street Address: 11286 Fillmore St,
State: CA
ZIP Code: 94115
County: San Francisco
Country: USA
Mailing Address: 1791 BANCROFT AVE
Mailing City: SAN FRANCISCO
Mailing State: CA
Mailing ZIP: 94124-2644
General Phone: (415) 671-1000
General Fax: (415) 671-1005
General/National Adv. E-mail: sunmedia97@aol.com
Primary Website: No Website
Year Established: Year Established: 1949
Areas Served - City/County or Portion Thereof, or ZIP Codes: 94124
Own Printing Facility?: Y
Mechanical specifications: Type page 11 x 14; E - 5 cols, 2 1/16, between; A - 5 cols, 2 1/16, between; C - 5 cols, 2 1/16, between.
Published: Thur
Avg Paid Circ: 20000
Avg Free Circ: 5000
Audit By: Sworn/Estimate/Non-Audited
Audit Date: 12.07.2019
Personnel: Amelia Ashley-Ward (Ed.); Amelia Ashley Ward (Ed.); Roslyn Gillis (Mktg./Adv. Mgr.)
footnotes: Advertising (Open Inch Rate) Weekday/Saturday: SRDS (11/13/2014)

SAVANNAH

SAVANNAH HERALD

Street Address: 2135 Rowland Ave, Ste B
State: GA
ZIP Code: 31404-4453
County: Chatham
Country: USA
Mailing Address: PO Box 486
Mailing City: Savannah
Mailing State: GA
Mailing ZIP: 31402-0486
General Phone: (912) 356-0025
General Fax: (912) 356-0028
General/National Adv. E-mail: news@savannahherald.net
Display Adv. E-mail: sales@savannahherald.net
Editorial e-mail: news@savannahherald.net
Primary Website: www.savannahherald.net
Delivery Methods: Newsstand`Racks
Mechanical specifications: Type page 10.5 x 20; E - 6 cols, between; A - 6 cols, between; C - 6 cols, between.
Published: Wed
Published Other: Weekly
Avg Free Circ: 12500
Audit By: Sworn/Estimate/Non-Audited
Audit Date: 12.07.2019
Personnel: Kenneth Adams (Publisher); Khristi Chisholm (Co-Publisher)

THE SAVANNAH TRIBUNE

Street Address: PO Box 2066,
State: GA
ZIP Code: 31402-2066
County: Chatham
Country: USA
Mailing Address: PO Box 2066

Mailing City: Savannah
Mailing State: GA
Mailing ZIP: 31402-2066
General Phone: (912) 233-6128
General Fax: (912) 233-6140
General/National Adv. E-mail: newsroom@savannahtribune.com
Display Adv. E-mail: tanyam@savannahtribune.com
Primary Website: www.savannahtribune.com
Year Established: Year Established: 1875
Delivery Methods: Carrier`Racks
Areas Served - City/County or Portion Thereof, or ZIP Codes: 31401, 31404, 31405, 31406, 31419, 31411, 31410, 31314, 31409, 31415, 31408, 31407
Mechanical specifications: Type page 11 5/8 x 21 1/2; E - 6 cols, 1 5/6, 1/8 between; A - 6 cols, 1 5/6, 1/8 between; C - 6 cols, 1 5/6, 1/8 between.
Published: Wed
Avg Free Circ: 15000
Audit By: Sworn/Estimate/Non-Audited
Audit Date: 12.07.2019
Personnel: Tanya Milton (Adv. Mgr.); Shirley James (Ed.); Tirany Reeves (Graphic Designer)

SEATTLE

FACTS NEWS

Street Address: 2765 E Cherry St,
State: WA
ZIP Code: 98122-4900
County: King
Country: USA
Mailing Address: PO Box 22015
Mailing City: Seattle
Mailing State: WA
Mailing ZIP: 98122-0015
General Phone: (206) 324-0552
General Fax: (206) 324-1007
General/National Adv. E-mail: seattlefacts@yahoo.com
Commercial printers?: Y
Mechanical specifications: Type page 9 x 17 1/2; E - 8 cols, between; A - 8 cols, between.
Published: Wed
Avg Paid Circ: 100000
Audit By: Sworn/Estimate/Non-Audited
Audit Date: 12.07.2019
Personnel: Dennis Beaver (Pub.); Marla Beaver (Adv. Mgr.); Lavonne Marla (Ed.)

SEATTLE MEDIUM

Street Address: 2600 S Jackson St,
State: WA
ZIP Code: 98144-2402
County: King
Country: USA
Mailing Address: PO Box 18205
Mailing City: Seattle
Mailing State: WA
Mailing ZIP: 98118-0205
General Phone: (206) 323-3070
General Fax: (206) 322-6518
General/National Adv. E-mail: mediumnews@aol.com
Primary Website: www.seattlemedium.com
Own Printing Facility?: Y
Published: Wed
Avg Paid Circ: 13500
Audit By: Sworn/Estimate/Non-Audited
Audit Date: 12.07.2019
Personnel: Chris B. Bennett (Co-Pub.); Joan Owens (Co-Pub.); Prisilla Hailey (Gen. Mgr.)

TACOMA TRUE-CITIZEN

Street Address: 2600 S Jackson St,
State: WA
ZIP Code: 98144-2402
County: King
Country: USA
Mailing Address: PO Box 18205
Mailing City: Seattle
Mailing State: WA
Mailing ZIP: 98118-0205
General Phone: (206) 323-3070
General Fax: (206) 322-6518
General/National Adv. E-mail: mediumnews@aol.com
Primary Website: www.seattlemedium.com
Own Printing Facility?: Y
Mechanical specifications: Type page 13 x 21; E - 6 cols, 2 1/16, 1/8 between; A - 6 cols, 2 1/16, 1/8 between; C - 10 cols, 1 1/4, between.
Published: Thur
Avg Paid Circ: 13500
Audit By: Sworn/Estimate/Non-Audited
Audit Date: 12.07.2019
Personnel: Chris B. Bennett (Co-Pub.); Joan Owens (Co-Pub.); Pricilla Hailey (Gen. Mgr.)

SHREVEPORT

SHREVEPORT SUN

Street Address: 2224 Jewella Ave,
State: LA
ZIP Code: 71109-2410
County: Caddo
Country: USA
Mailing Address: PO Box 3915
Mailing City: Shreveport
Mailing State: LA
Mailing ZIP: 71133-3915
General Phone: (318) 631-6222
General Fax: (318) 635-2822
General/National Adv. E-mail: sunweekly@aol.com
Display Adv. E-mail: sunweeklyads@aol.com
Editorial e-mail: sunweekly@aol.com
Primary Website: www.sunweeklynews.com
Year Established: Year Established: 1920
Delivery Methods: Mail`Newsstand`Racks
Mechanical specifications: Type page 13 x 21 1/2; E - 6 cols, 2 1/16, 1/8 between; A - 6 cols, 2 1/16, 1/8 between; C - 10 cols, between.
Published: Thur
Avg Paid Circ: 5000
Audit By: Sworn/Estimate/Non-Audited
Audit Date: 12.07.2019
Personnel: Sonya C. Landry (Ed.); Larry Rogers (Advt Mgr); Brenda Demming (Circulation Mgr); Ronald Collins (Reporter)

STATESVILLE

COUNTY NEWS

Street Address: 211 S Center St,
State: NC
ZIP Code: 28677-5873
County: Iredell
Country: USA
Mailing Address: PO Box 820
Mailing City: Statesville
Mailing State: NC
Mailing ZIP: 28687-0820
General Phone: (704) 873-1054
General Fax: (704) 873-1054
General/National Adv. E-mail: publisher@countynews4you.com
Mechanical specifications: Type page 13 x 21 1/2; E - 6 cols, 2 1/12, 1/8 between; A - 6 cols, 2 1/12, 1/8 between; C - 6 cols, 2 1/12, 1/8 between.
Published: Wed
Avg Paid Circ: 7500
Audit By: Sworn/Estimate/Non-Audited
Audit Date: 12.07.2019
Personnel: Fran Farrer (Pub.)

TALLAHASSEE

CAPITAL OUTLOOK

Street Address: 1363 E Tennessee St,
State: FL
ZIP Code: 32308-5107
County: Leon
Country: USA
Mailing Address: 1363 E Tennessee St
Mailing City: Tallahassee
Mailing State: FL
Mailing ZIP: 32308-5107
General Phone: (850) 877-0105
General Fax: (850) 877-5110
Advertising Phone: (850) 877-0105

Advertising Fax: (850) 877-5110
Editorial Phone: (859) 877-0105
Editorial Fax: (850) 877-5110
General/National Adv. E-mail: info@capitaloutlook.com
Display Adv. E-mail: advertising@capitaloutlook.com
Editorial e-mail: pressreleases@capitaloutlook.com
Primary Website: www.capitaloutlook.com
Year Established: Year Established: 1975
Delivery Methods: Mail`Newsstand`Racks
Areas Served - City/County or Portion Thereof, or ZIP Codes: Multiple
Mechanical specifications: Full Page: 6C (10") x 20.5" Half Page: 6C (10") x 10.25" Quarter Page: Vertical: 3C (5") x 10.25" Horizontal : 6C (10") x 5.125" Eighth Page: 3C (5") x 5.125"
Published: Thur
Avg Paid Circ: 1000
Audit By: Sworn/Estimate/Non-Audited
Audit Date: 12.07.2019
Personnel: Taralisha Sanders (Gen. Mgr.); St. Clair Murraine (Ed.); Rev. Dr. R.B. Holmes, Jr. (Pub.)
Parent company (for newspapers): LIVE Communications, Inc.

TAMPA

DAYTONA TIMES

Street Address: PO Box 48857,
State: FL
ZIP Code: 33646-0124
County: Hillsborough
Country: USA
Mailing Address: PO Box 48857
Mailing City: Tampa
Mailing State: FL
Mailing ZIP: 33646-0124
General Phone: (813) 319-0961
General Fax: (813) 628-0713
General/National Adv. E-mail: sales@flcourier.com
Display Adv. E-mail: sales@flcourier.com
Primary Website: www.daytonatimes.com
Year Established: Year Established: 1977
Delivery Methods: Mail`Newsstand`Racks
Areas Served - City/County or Portion Thereof, or ZIP Codes: 32116,32117, 32118, 32119, 32122, 32114, 32115, 32120, 32121, 32124, 32125, 32126, 32198
Mechanical specifications: 6C x 20" 1C =1.66"
Published: Thur
Published Other: on-line daily
Avg Free Circ: 15000
Audit By: Sworn/Estimate/Non-Audited
Audit Date: 12.07.2019
Personnel: Glenn Cherry (Circ. Mgr.); Charles W. Cherry (Ed.)

FLORIDA SENTINEL-BULLETIN

Street Address: 2207 E 21st Ave,
State: FL
ZIP Code: 33605-2043
County: Hillsborough
Country: USA
Mailing Address: PO Box 3363
Mailing City: Tampa
Mailing State: FL
Mailing ZIP: 33601-3363
General Phone: (813) 248-1921
General Fax: (813) 248-4507
General/National Adv. E-mail: hadams@flsentinel.com
Display Adv. E-mail: bdawkins@flsentinel.com
Editorial e-mail: publisher@flsentinel.com
Primary Website: flsentinel.com
Year Established: Year Established: 1945
Own Printing Facility?: Y
Mechanical specifications: Type page 10 x 15; E - 5 cols, 2, between; A - 5 cols, 2, between; C - 5 cols, 2, between.
Published: Tues`Fri
Avg Paid Circ: 0
Avg Free Circ: 12
Audit By: CVC
Audit Date: 30.06.2018
Personnel: S. Kay Andrews Wells (Pub.); Betty

Dawkins (Adv. Dir.); Gwen Hayes (Ed.); Harold Adams (Circ.)

TOLEDO

THE TOLEDO JOURNAL

Street Address: 3021 Douglas Rd,
State: OH
ZIP Code: 43606-3504
County: Lucas
Country: USA
Mailing Address: PO Box 12559
Mailing City: Toledo
Mailing State: OH
Mailing ZIP: 43606-0159
General Phone: (419) 472-4521
General Fax: (419) 472-1604
General/National Adv. E-mail: toledo411@aol.com; toljour@aol.com
Primary Website: www.thetoledojournal.com
Year Established: Year Established: 1975
Areas Served - City/County or Portion Thereof, or ZIP Codes: 43602, 43611, 43620, 43560
Mechanical specifications: Type page 10 1/4 x 16; E - 6 cols, 1, 1/8 between; A - 6 cols, 1, between.
Published: Wed
Avg Paid Circ: 12
Avg Free Circ: 11397
Audit By: CVC
Audit Date: 30.09.2014
Personnel: Sandra S. Stewart (Pub.); Myron A. Stewart (Circulation Manager); Jeff Willis (Production Manager)

TULSA

THE OKLAHOMA EAGLE

Street Address: 624 E Archer St,
State: OK
ZIP Code: 74120-1000
County: Tulsa
Country: USA
Mailing Address: PO Box 3267
Mailing City: Tulsa
Mailing State: OK
Mailing ZIP: 74101-3267
General Phone: (918) 582-7124
General Fax: (918) 582-8905
General/National Adv. E-mail: editor@theoklahomaeagle.net
Mechanical specifications: Type page 13 x 21; A - 6 cols, 2 1/16, between.
Published: Fri
Avg Paid Circ: 5000
Audit By: Sworn/Estimate/Non-Audited
Audit Date: 12.07.2019
Personnel: James O. Goodwin (Pub.)

UNION CITY

ATLANTA-NEWS LEADER

Street Address: 4405 Mall Blvd, Ste 521
State: GA
ZIP Code: 30291-2083
County: Fulton
Country: USA
Mailing Address: 4405 Mall Blvd Ste 521
Mailing City: Union City
Mailing State: GA
Mailing ZIP: 30291-2083
General Phone: (770) 969-7711
General Fax: (770) 969-7811
General/National Adv. E-mail: atlmet@bellsouth.net
Mechanical specifications: Type page 13 x 21 1/2; E - 6 cols, 2 1/4, between; A - 6 cols, 2 1/4, between; C - 6 cols, 2 1/4, 1/8 between.
Published: Fri
Avg Paid Circ: 5000
Avg Free Circ: 30000
Audit By: Sworn/Estimate/Non-Audited
Audit Date: 12.07.2019
Personnel: Esther Edans (Gen. Mgr.); Creed W. Pannell (Adv. Mgr.); Nicole Robinson (Ed.); Carla Harper (Assoc. Ed.)

THE ATLANTA METRO

Street Address: 4405 Mall Blvd, Ste 521
State: GA
ZIP Code: 30291-2083
County: Fulton
Country: USA
Mailing Address: 4405 Mall Blvd Ste 521
Mailing City: Union City
Mailing State: GA
Mailing ZIP: 30291-2083
General Phone: (770) 969-7711
General Fax: (770) 969-7811
General/National Adv. E-mail: atlmet@bellsouth.net
Mechanical specifications: Type page 10 3/20 x 14 1/4; E - 4 cols, 2 1/8, 3/16 between; C - 4 cols, 2 1/8, 3/16 between.
Published: Fri
Avg Paid Circ: 5000
Avg Free Circ: 30000
Audit By: Sworn/Estimate/Non-Audited
Audit Date: 12.07.2019
Personnel: Willie Robinson (Circ. Mgr.); Creed W. Pannell (Ed.); Carla Harper (Assoc. Ed.)

VICTORVILLE

THE SAN BERNARDINO AMERICAN NEWS

Street Address: 14537 Anacapa Rd, Ste 24,
State: CA
ZIP Code: 92392-2705
County: San Bernardino
Country: USA
Mailing Address: PO Box 837
Mailing City: Victorville
Mailing State: CA
Mailing ZIP: 92393-0837
General Phone: (909) 889-7677
General Fax: (909) 889-2882
Advertising Phone: (909) 889-7677
Advertising Fax: (909) 889-2882
Editorial Phone: (909) 889-7677
Editorial Fax: (909) 889-2882
General/National Adv. E-mail: msbamericannews@gmail.com
Display Adv. E-mail: sbamericannews@gmail.com
Editorial e-mail: samerisam1@earthlink.net
Primary Website: sbnews.us
Year Established: Year Established: 1969
Delivery Methods: Mail`Carrier
Areas Served - City/County or Portion Thereof, or ZIP Codes: 92405, 92410-11, 92335-6, 92346, 92324,92392-4, 92301, 92345, 92307, 92311,91730, 92570, 92552, 92521, 92392, 92395, 91737, 92572,
Published: Thur
Avg Paid Circ: 10000
Audit By: Sworn/Estimate/Non-Audited
Audit Date: 12.07.2019
Personnel: Mary Harris (Pub.); Clifton Harris (Co-Pub.)
Parent company (for newspapers): Don Roberto Group Inc

WASHINGTON

DISTRICT CHRONICLES

Street Address: 525 NW Bryant St,
State: DC
ZIP Code: 20059-1005
County: District Of Columbia
Country: USA
Mailing Address: 525 NW Bryant St
Mailing City: Washington
Mailing State: DC
Mailing ZIP: 20059-1005
General Phone: 202-806-9401
Advertising Phone: 202-806-9401
Editorial Phone: 202-806-9401
General/National Adv. E-mail: lkaggwa@howard.edu
Display Adv. E-mail: lkaggwa@howard.edu
Editorial e-mail: lkaggwa@howard.edu
Primary Website: www.districtchronicles.com
Year Established: Year Established: 2001
Mechanical specifications: 1.94"
Published: Thur
Avg Free Circ: 9975
Audit By: Sworn/Estimate/Non-Audited
Audit Date: 12.07.2019
Personnel: Lawrence Kaggwa (Publisher)

WASHINGTON AFRO-AMERICAN

Street Address: 1917 Benning Rd NE,
State: DC
ZIP Code: 20002-4723
County: District Of Columbia
Country: USA
Mailing Address: 1917 Benning Rd NE
Mailing City: Washington
Mailing State: DC
Mailing ZIP: 20002-4723
General Phone: (202) 332-0080
General Fax: (877) 570-9297
General/National Adv. E-mail: editor@afro.com
Primary Website: www.afro.com
Year Established: Year Established: 1892
Delivery Methods: Mail`Newsstand`Racks
Mechanical specifications: Type page 13 x 21; E - 6 cols, 2, 1/8 between; A - 6 cols, 2, between; C - 9 cols, 1, 1/8 between.
Published: Fri
Avg Paid Circ: 5463
Avg Free Circ: 649
Audit By: AAM
Audit Date: 30.09.2014
Personnel: John J. Oliver (Pub.); Edgar Brookins (Circ. Mgr.); Denise Dorsey (Prodn. Mgr.)

WASHINGTON INFORMER

Street Address: 3117 Martin Luther King Jr Ave SE,
State: DC
ZIP Code: 20032-1537
County: District Of Columbia
Country: USA
Mailing Address: 3117 Martin Luther King Jr Ave SE
Mailing City: Washington
Mailing State: DC
Mailing ZIP: 20032-1537
General Phone: (202) 888-6835
Editorial Phone: (202) 561-4100
General/National Adv. E-mail: news@washingtoninformer.com
Display Adv. E-mail: rburke@washingtoninformer.com
Editorial e-mail: news@washingtoninformer.com
Primary Website: www.washingtoninformer.com
Year Established: Year Established: 1964
Delivery Methods: Mail`Carrier`Racks
Areas Served - City/County or Portion Thereof, or ZIP Codes: 20001- 22314
Mechanical specifications: 1 column 1.75â€� 2 columns 3.625â€� 3 columns 5.625â€� 4 columns 7.562â€� 5 columns 9.5â€� Page Depth 12.375 Total Inches Per Page 61.875â€�
Published: Thur
Avg Paid Circ: 153
Avg Free Circ: 16341
Audit By: CVC
Audit Date: 30.03.2017
Personnel: Denise Rolark Barnes (Pub.); Ron Burke (Director of Advertising); Angie Johnson (Circ. Mgr.); Kevin McNeir (Editor)

WASHINGTON SUN

Street Address: 830 Kennedy St NW,
State: DC
ZIP Code: 20011-2948
County: District Of Columbia
Country: USA
Mailing Address: 830 Kennedy St NW Ste B2
Mailing City: Washington
Mailing State: DC
Mailing ZIP: 20011-2948
General Phone: (202) 882-1021
General Fax: (202) 882-9817
General/National Adv. E-mail: thewashingtonsun@aol.com
Mechanical specifications: Type page 13 x 21 1/2; E - 6 cols, 2 1/16, 1/8 between; A - 6 cols, 2 1/16, 1/8 between.
Published: Thur
Avg Paid Circ: 55000
Audit By: Sworn/Estimate/Non-Audited
Audit Date: 12.07.2019
Personnel: Stephen Cooke (Ed.); Mae Lynn (Mng. Ed.)

WICHITA

THE COMMUNITY VOICE

Street Address: 2918 E Douglas Ave,
State: KS
ZIP Code: 67214-4709
County: Sedgwick
Country: USA
Mailing Address: PO Box 20804
Mailing City: Wichita
Mailing State: KS
Mailing ZIP: 67208-6804
General Phone: (316) 681-1155
General/National Adv. E-mail: press@tcvpub.com
Display Adv. E-mail: adcopy@tcvpub.com
Editorial e-mail: press@tcvpub.com
Primary Website: tcvpub.com
Year Established: Year Established: 1993
Delivery Methods: Mail`Newsstand
Areas Served - City/County or Portion Thereof, or ZIP Codes: 67214, 67219, 67220, 67226, 67203, 67208, 67206 major service area
Mechanical specifications: Tabloid. 9.90"W X 10.25"H
Published: Thur
Published Other: Every other Thurs
Avg Free Circ: 10892
Audit By: CVC
Audit Date: 30.03.2016
Personnel: Bonita Gooch (Editor-in-Chief)

WILMINGTON

GREATER DIVERSITY NEWS

Street Address: 272 N Front St, Ste 406
State: NC
ZIP Code: 28401-4078
County: New Hanover
Country: USA
Mailing Address: PO Box 1679
Mailing City: Wilmington
Mailing State: NC
Mailing ZIP: 28402-1679
General Phone: (910) 762-1337
General Fax: (910) 763-6304
Primary Website: www.greaterdiversity.com
Mechanical specifications: Type page 13 x 21 1/2; E - 6 cols, 2, 1/6 between; A - 6 cols, 2, 1/6 between; C - 6 cols, 2, 1/6 between.
Published: Thur
Avg Paid Circ: 2500
Avg Free Circ: 2500
Audit By: Sworn/Estimate/Non-Audited
Audit Date: 12.07.2019
Personnel: Kathy Grear (Pub.); Peter Grear (Pub.)

WILMINGTON JOURNAL

Street Address: 412 S 7th St,
State: NC
ZIP Code: 28401-5214
County: New Hanover
Country: USA
Mailing Address: PO Box 1020
Mailing City: Wilmington
Mailing State: NC
Mailing ZIP: 28402-1020
General Phone: (910) 762-5502
General Fax: (910) 343-1334
General/National Adv. E-mail: wilmjourn@aol.com
Primary Website: www.wilmingtonjournal.com
Mechanical specifications: Type page 13 x 21; E - 6 cols, 2 1/16, 1/8 between; A - 6 cols, 2 1/16, 1/8 between.
Published: Thur
Avg Paid Circ: 10120
Avg Free Circ: 880
Audit By: Sworn/Estimate/Non-Audited
Audit Date: 12.07.2019
Personnel: Shawn Jervay Thatch (Office Mgr.);

WINSTON SALEM

THE CHRONICLE

Street Address: 1300 E. Fifth St.,
State: NC
ZIP Code: 27101
County: Forsyth
Country: USA
Mailing Address: PO Box 1636
Mailing City: Winston Salem
Mailing State: NC
Mailing ZIP: 27102-1636
General Phone: (336) 722-8624
General Fax: (336) 723-9173
General/National Adv. E-mail: news@wschronicle.com
Display Adv. E-mail: adv@wschronicle.com
Primary Website: www.wschronicle.com
Year Established: Year Established: 1974
Own Printing Facility?: Y
Mechanical specifications: Type page 13 x 21; E - 6 cols, 2 1/8, 1/8 between; A - 6 cols, 2 1/8, 1/8 between; C - 9 cols, 1 1/4, 1/8 between.
Published: Thur
Avg Paid Circ: 10000

Audit By: Sworn/Estimate/Non-Audited
Audit Date: 12.07.2019
Personnel: James Taylor Jr. (Publisher); Deanna Taylor (Office Manager)
Parent company (for newspapers): Chronicle Media Group

YOUNGSTOWN

THE BUCKEYE REVIEW

Street Address: 1201 Belmont Ave,
State: OH
ZIP Code: 44504-1101
County: Mahoning
Country: USA
Mailing Address: 1201 Belmont Ave
Mailing City: Youngstown
Mailing State: OH
Mailing ZIP: 44504-1101
General Phone: (330) 743-2250
General Fax: (330) 746-2340
General/National Adv. E-mail: buckeyereview@yahoo.com
Year Established: Year Established: 1927
Published: Tues
Avg Free Circ: 5250
Audit By: Sworn/Estimate/Non-Audited
Audit Date: 12.07.2019
Personnel: Mike McNair (Ed.)

COLLEGE AND UNIVERSITY NEWSPAPERS

ABERDEEN

GRAYS HARBOR COLLEGE

Street Address 1: 1620 Edward P Smith Dr
State: WA
Zip/Postal code: 98520-7500
Country: USA
Mailing Address: 1620 Edward P Smith Dr
Mailing City: Aberdeen
Mailing State: WA
Mailing ZIP Code: 98520-7599
General Phone: (360) 532-9020
General Fax: (360) 538-4299
Website: www.ghc.ctc.edu

NORTHERN STATE UNIV.

Street Address 1: 1200 S Jay St, Student Ctr, Rm 201
State: SD
Zip/Postal code: 57401
Country: USA
Mailing Address: 1200 S. Jay St., Student Ctr., Rm. 201
Mailing City: Aberdeen
Mailing State: SD
Mailing ZIP Code: 57401
General Phone: (605) 626-2534
General Fax: (605) 626-2559
General/National Adv. Email: stupub@northern.edu
Website: www.nsuexponent.com
Published: Mthly
Personnel: Tracy Rasmussen (Advisor)

ABILENE

ABILENE CHRISTIAN UNIV.

Street Address 1: PO Box 27892
State: TX
Country: USA
Mailing Address: PO Box 27892
Mailing City: Abilene
Mailing State: TX
Mailing ZIP Code: 79699-0001
General Fax: (325) 674-2463
Advertising Fax: (325) 674-2139
General/National Adv. Email: christi.stark@acu.edu
Website: www.acuoptimist.com
Personnel: Colter Hettich (Ed.)

HARDIN-SIMMONS UNIV.

Street Address 1: 2200 Hickory St
State: TX
Zip/Postal code: 79601-2345
Country: USA

Mailing Address: 2200 Hickory St
Mailing City: Abilene
Mailing State: TX
Mailing ZIP Code: 79601-2345
General Phone: (325) 670-1438
General Fax: (325) 677-8351
General/National Adv. Email: brand@hsutx.edu
Display Adv. Email: brandadv@hsutx.edu
Website: www.hsutx.edu
Personnel: Adriel Wong (Ed. in Chief)

MCMURRY UNIV.

Street Address 1: PO Box 277
State: TX
Zip/Postal code: 79604-0277
Country: USA
Mailing Address: Box 277, McMurry Sta.
Mailing City: Abilene
Mailing State: TX
Mailing ZIP Code: 79697
General Phone: (325) 793-3800
General Fax: (325) 793-4679

ABINGTON

PENN STATE UNIV.

Street Address 1: 1600 Woodland Rd
State: PA
Zip/Postal code: 19001-3918
Country: USA
Mailing Address: 1600 Woodland Rd
Mailing City: Abington
Mailing State: PA
Mailing ZIP Code: 19001-3990
General Phone: (215) 881-7507
General Fax: (215) 881-7660
General/National Adv. Email: fdq1@psu.edu
Website: www.abington.psu.edu
Personnel: Frank Quattrone (Ed.)

ADA

EAST CENTRAL UNIVERSITY

Street Address 1: 1100 E 14th St
State: OK
Zip/Postal code: 74820-6915
Country: USA
Mailing Address: 1100 E 14th St
Mailing City: Ada
Mailing State: OK
Mailing ZIP Code: 74820-6915
General Phone: (580) 559-5250
General Fax: (580) 559-5251
General/National Adv. Email: journal@ecok.edu; ecujournal@me.com
Website: www.ecujournal.com
Personnel: Cathie Harding (Advisor); Melissa

Hubble (Adv. Mgr.); Jonnathon Hicks (Ed. in Chief)

OHIO NORTHERN UNIV.

Street Address 1: 525 S Main St
State: OH
Zip/Postal code: 45810-6000
Country: USA
Mailing Address: 525 S Main St
Mailing City: Ada
Mailing State: OH
Mailing ZIP Code: 45810
General Phone: (419) 772-2409
General Fax: (419) 772-1880
General/National Adv. Email: northern-review@onu.edu
Website: https://nr.onu.edu
Published: Mon`Tues`Wed`Thur`Fri`Sat`Sun
Personnel: Bill O'Connell (Advisor); Nick Dutro (Ed. in Chief)

AIKEN

UNIV. OF SOUTH CAROLINA

Street Address 1: 471 University Pkwy
State: SC
Zip/Postal code: 29801-6389
Country: USA
Mailing Address: 471 University Pkwy
Mailing City: Aiken
Mailing State: SC
Mailing ZIP Code: 29801-6399
General Phone: (803) 648-6851
General Fax: (803) 641-3494
Website: www.pacertimes.com
Personnel: Israel Butler (Ed.)

AKRON

THE UNIVERSITY OF AKRON

Street Address 1: 302 Buchtel Cmn
State: OH
Zip/Postal code: 44325-0001
County: Summit
Country: USA
Mailing Address: 302 Buchtel Common
Mailing City: Akron
Mailing State: OH
Mailing ZIP Code: 44325-4206
General Phone: 330-972-7919
General Fax: 330-972-7810
Advertising Phone: 330-972-5912
Advertising Fax: 330-972-7810
Editorial Phone: 330-972-6184
Editorial Fax: 330-972-7810
General/National Adv. Email: adviser@buchtelite.com

Display Adv. Email: business-manager@buchtelite.com
Editorial Email: editor-in-chief@buchtelite.com
Website: buchtelite.com
Year Established: 1889
Delivery Methods: Newsstand
Own Printing Facility?: N
Commercial printers?: Y
Published: Tues`Thur
Avg Free Circ: 2700
Personnel: Adam Bernhard (Business Manager); Zaina Salem (Editor-in-Chief)

UNIV. OF AKRON

Street Address 1: 303 Carroll St, Student Union, Rm 51
State: OH
Zip/Postal code: 44325-0001
Country: USA
Mailing Address: 303 Carroll St Student Un Rm 51
Mailing City: Akron
Mailing State: OH
Mailing ZIP Code: 44325-0001
General Phone: (330) 972-5475
General Fax: (330) 972-7810
Advertising Phone: (330) 972-7919
Editorial Phone: (330) 972-6184
General/National Adv. Email: adviser@buchtelite.com
Editorial Email: editor@buchtelite.com
Website: www.buchtelite.com
Personnel: Maryanne Bailey-Porter (Acct. Coord.); Kevin Curwin (Ed. in Chief); Allison Strouse (News Ed.)

ALBANY

ALBANY COLLEGE OF PHARMACY

Street Address 1: 106 New Scotland Ave
State: NY
Zip/Postal code: 12208-3425
Country: USA
Mailing Address: 106 New Scotland Ave
Mailing City: Albany
Mailing State: NY
Mailing ZIP Code: 12208-3492
General Phone: (518) 445-7200
General Fax: (518) 445-7202
Personnel: Jennie O'Rourke (Ed.)

COLLEGE OF ST. ROSE

Street Address 1: 432 Western Ave
State: NY
Zip/Postal code: 12203-1400
Country: USA
Mailing Address: 432 Western Ave

College and University Newspapers

Mailing City: Albany
Mailing State: NY
Mailing ZIP Code: 12203-1490
General Phone: (518) 454-5151
General Fax: (518) 454-2001
General/National Adv. Email: chronicle@strose.edu
Website: www.strosechronicle.com
Delivery Methods: Racks
Published: Tues
Personnel: Cailin Brown (Advisor); Josh Heller (Execu Ed); Jonas Miller (Mng Ed)

DARTON COLLEGE

Street Address 1: 2400 Gillionville Rd
State: GA
Zip/Postal code: 31707-3023
Country: USA
Mailing Address: 2400 Gillionville Rd
Mailing City: Albany
Mailing State: GA
Mailing ZIP Code: 31707-3098
General Phone: (229) 317-6808
Personnel: Roger Marietta (Advisor)

LINN-BENTON CMTY. COLLEGE

Street Address 1: 6500 Pacific Blvd SW
State: OR
Zip/Postal code: 97321-3755
Country: USA
Mailing Address: 6500 Pacific Blvd SW
Mailing City: Albany
Mailing State: OR
Mailing ZIP Code: 97321-3774
General Phone: (541) 917-4451
General Fax: (541) 917-4454
Editorial Phone: (541) 917-4452
General/National Adv. Email: commuter@linnbenton.edu
Website: www.commuter.linnbenton.edu
Personnel: Rob Priewe (Advisor); Frank Warren (Adv. Mgr.); Ryan henson Henson (Ed. in Chief)

SUNY/ALBANY

Street Address 1: 353 Broadway
State: NY
Zip/Postal code: 12246-2915
Country: USA
Mailing Address: 353 Broadway
Mailing City: Albany
Mailing State: NY
Mailing ZIP Code: 12246-2915
General Phone: (518) 442-5666
General Fax: (518) 442-5664
General/National Adv. Email: asp_online@hotmail.com
Website: www.albanystudentpress.org
Personnel: Brett Longo (Bus. Mgr.); Ted Bean (Ed. in Chief); Jon Campbell (Mng. Ed.)

ALBION

ALBION COLLEGE

Street Address 1: 611 E Porter St
State: MI
Zip/Postal code: 49224-1831
Country: USA
Mailing Address: 611 E. Porter St.
Mailing City: Albion
Mailing State: MI
Mailing ZIP Code: 49224
General Phone: (517) 629-1315
General Fax: (517) 629-0509
General/National Adv. Email: pleiad@albion.edu
Display Adv. Email: pleaid@albion.edu
Editorial Email: pleiad@albion.edu
Website: www.albionpleiad.com
Year Established: 1883
Published: Mon`Wed`Fri
Personnel: Glenn Deutsch (Advisor); Steve Markowski (Mng. Ed.); Beau Brockett, Jr. (Mng. Ed.); Katie Boni (Features Editor); Andrew Wittland; Morgan Garmo (Opinions editor)

ALBUQUERQUE

NEW MEXICO DAILY LOBO

Street Address 1: 1 University of New Mexico
Street Address 2: MS 3
State: NM
Zip/Postal code: 87131-0001
County: Bernalillo
Country: USA
Mailing Address: 1 University of New Mexico MS 3
Mailing City: Albuquerque
Mailing State: NM
Mailing ZIP Code: 87131-0001
General Phone: (505) 277-7527
General Fax: (505) 277-6228
Advertising Phone: (505) 277-5656
Advertising Fax: (505) 277-7530
Editorial Phone: (505) 277-5656
Editorial Fax: (505) 277-7530
General/National Adv. Email: advertising@dailylobo.com
Display Adv. Email: advertising@dailylobo.com
Editorial Email: news@dailylobo.com
Website: www.dailylobo.com
Year Established: 1895
Delivery Methods: Mail`Newsstand
Published: Mon`Tues`Wed`Thur`Fri`Sat
Personnel: Jyllian Roach (Ed. in Chief); JR Oppenheim (Managing Ed.); Jonathan Baca (News Ed.); Daniel Montano (News Ed.); Sergio Jimenez (Photo Ed.); William Aranda (Asst. Photo Ed.); Stephen Montoya (Culture Ed.); Tomas Lujan (Asst. Culture Ed.); Thomas Romero-Salas (Sports Ed.); Jonathan Gamboa (Design Dir.); Sarah Lynas (Design Dir.); Craig Dubyk (Copy Chief); Leanne Lucero (Copy Ed.); Zach Pavlik (Ad. Mgr.); Sammy Chumpolpakdee (Sales Mgr.); Hannah Dowdy-Sue (Class. Mgr.); David Lynch (News Ed.); Nick Fojud (Photo Ed.); Veronica Munoz (Web Ed.)

UNIV. OF NEW MEXICO

Street Address 1: 1 University of New Mexico
Street Address 2: MS 3
State: NM
Zip/Postal code: 87131-0001
Country: USA
Mailing Address: 1 University of New Mexico MS 3
Mailing City: Albuquerque
Mailing State: NM
Mailing ZIP Code: 87131-0001
General Phone: (505) 277-5656
General Fax: (505) 277-7530
Advertising Phone: (505) 277-5656
Advertising Fax: (505) 277-7530
Editorial Phone: (505) 277-7527
General/National Adv. Email: advertising@dailylobo.com
Display Adv. Email: advertising@dailylobo.com
Editorial Email: editorinchief@dailylobo.com
Website: www.dailylobo.com
Year Established: 1895
News Services: AP
Delivery Methods: Mail`Racks
Commercial printers?: N
Published: Mon`Tues`Wed`Thur`Fri
Avg Free Circ: 9000
Personnel: Jim Fisher (Bus. Mgr.)

ALCORN STATE

ALCORN STATE UNIV.

Street Address 1: 1000 Asu Dr, Ste 269
State: MS
Country: USA
Mailing Address: 1000 Alcorn Dr Ste 269
Mailing City: Lorman
Mailing State: MS
Mailing ZIP Code: 39096-7500
General Phone: (601) 877-6557
General Fax: (601) 877-2213
General/National Adv. Email: tnimox@lorman.alcorn.edu
Website: www.alcornchronicle.com
Personnel: Toni Terrett (Advisor); Larry Sanders (Advisor); Erica L. Turner (Ed. in Chief)

ALEXANDRIA

LOUISIANA STATE UNIV.

Street Address 1: 1800 Hwy 71 S
State: LA
Zip/Postal code: 71302
Country: USA
Mailing Address: 1800 Hwy. 71 S.
Mailing City: Alexandria
Mailing State: LA
Mailing ZIP Code: 71302
General Phone: (318) 767-2602
General/National Adv. Email: sentrynews@lsua.edu
Personnel: Elizabeth Beard (Advisor); Nancy Borden (Advisor); Trayce Snow (Ed.)

ALFRED

ALFRED UNIV.

Street Address 1: Powell Campus Ctr
State: NY
Country: USA
Mailing Address: Powell Campus Ctr.
Mailing City: Alfred
Mailing State: NY
Mailing ZIP Code: 14802
General Phone: (607) 871-2192
General Fax: (607) 871-3797
General/National Adv. Email: fiatlux@alfred.edu
Website: www.thefiatlux.com/
Personnel: Robyn Goodman (Advisor); Nadine Titus (Adv. Mgr.); Thomas Fleming (Ed. in Chief)

ALLENDALE

GRAND VALLEY STATE UNIV.

Street Address 1: 1 Campus Dr
State: MI
Zip/Postal code: 49401-9401
Country: USA
Mailing Address: 1 Campus Dr, 0051 Kirkhof Center, Grand Valley State University
Mailing City: Allendale
Mailing State: MI
Mailing ZIP Code: 49401
General Phone: (616) 331-2460
General Fax: (616) 331-2465
Advertising Phone: (616) 331-2484
General/National Adv. Email: lanthorn@gvsu.edu
Display Adv. Email: advertising@lanthorn.com
Editorial Email: editorial@lanthorn.com
Website: www.lanthorn.com
Year Established: 1964
Published: Mon`Thur
Personnel: Shelby Carter (Business Manager); Emily Doran (Editor-and-Chief); Ian Borthwick (Advertising Manager)

ALLENTOWN

CEDAR CREST COLLEGE

Street Address 1: 100 College Dr
State: PA
Zip/Postal code: 18104-6132
Country: USA
Mailing Address: 100 College Dr
Mailing City: Allentown
Mailing State: PA
Mailing ZIP Code: 18104-6196
General Phone: (610) 437-4471
General Fax: (610) 437-5955
General/National Adv. Email: crestiad@cedarcrest.edu
Website: www.cedarcrest.edu/crestiad
Year Established: 1932
Commercial printers?: Y
Personnel: Elizabeth Ortiz (Advisor)

MUHLENBERG COLLEGE

Street Address 1: 2400 Chew St
State: PA
Zip/Postal code: 18104-5564
Country: USA
Mailing Address: 2400 W. Chew Street
Mailing City: Allentown
Mailing State: PA
Mailing ZIP Code: 18104
General Phone: (484) 664-3195
General/National Adv. Email: weeklyeditor@gmail.com
Website: www.muhlenbergweekly.com
Year Established: 1883
Published: Thur
Personnel: Gregory Kantor (Editor in Chief)

ALLIANCE

MT. UNION COLLEGE

Street Address 1: 1972 Clark Ave
State: OH
Zip/Postal code: 44601-3929
Country: USA
Mailing Address: 1972 Clark Ave
Mailing City: Alliance
Mailing State: OH
Mailing ZIP Code: 44601-3993
General Phone: (330) 823-2884
General Fax: (330) 821-0425
General/National Adv. Email: dynamo@muc.edu
Website: www.mucdynamo.com
Personnel: Len Cooper (Advisor)

ALMA

ALMA COLLEGE

Street Address 1: 614 W Superior St
State: MI
Zip/Postal code: 48801-1504
Country: USA
Mailing Address: 614 W Superior St
Mailing City: Alma
Mailing State: MI
Mailing ZIP Code: 48801-1599
General Phone: (989) 463-7161
General Fax: (989) 463-7161
General/National Adv. Email: almanian@alma.edu; almanianopinion@yahoo.com; almanian@hotmail.com
Display Adv. Email: almanianadvert@yahoo.com
Website: students.alma.edu/organizations/almanian
Personnel: Robert Vivian (Advisor); Brendan Guilford (Ed. in Chief); Olga Wrobel (News Ed.)

ALPINE

SUL ROSS STATE UNIV.

Street Address 1: PO Box C-112
State: TX
Zip/Postal code: 79832-0001
Country: USA
Mailing Address: PO Box C112
Mailing City: Alpine
Mailing State: TX
Mailing ZIP Code: 79832-0001
General Phone: (432) 837-8011
General Fax: (432) 837-8664
General/National Adv. Email: skyline@sulross.edu
Website: ^www.sulross.edu
Personnel: Cheryl Zinsmeyer (Student Publications Advisor)

ALTOONA

PENN STATE UNIV.

Street Address 1: Raymond Smith Bldg
State: PA
Zip/Postal code: 16601
Country: USA
Mailing Address: Raymond Smith Bldg.
Mailing City: Altoona
Mailing State: PA
Mailing ZIP Code: 16601
General Phone: (814) 940-4658
General Fax: (814) 949-5007

Personnel: Savannah Straub (Contact); Margaret Moses (Contact)

ALVA

NORTHWESTERN OKLAHOMA STATE UNIV.

Street Address 1: 709 Oklahoma Blvd
State: OK
Zip/Postal code: 73717-2749
Country: USA
Mailing Address: 709 Oklahoma Blvd
Mailing City: Alva
Mailing State: OK
Mailing ZIP Code: 73717-2749
General Phone: (580) 327-8479
General Fax: (580) 327-8127
Advertising Phone: (580) 327-8479
Editorial Phone: (580) 327-8479
General/National Adv. Email: nwnewsroom@hotmail.com; nwnews@nwosu.edu
Display Adv. Email: nwnewsroom@hotmail.com
Editorial Email: nwnewsroom@hotmail.com
Website: www.nwosu.edu/northwestern-news or www.rangerpulse.com
Year Established: 1897
Published: Thur
Avg Free Circ: 1400
Personnel: Melanie Wilderman (Advisor)

AMARILLO

AMARILLO COLLEGE

Street Address 1: 2201 S Washington St
State: TX
Zip/Postal code: 79109-2411
Country: USA
Mailing Address: PO Box 447
Mailing City: Amarillo
Mailing State: TX
Mailing ZIP Code: 79178-0001
General Phone: (806) 371-5283
General Fax: (806) 371-5398
General/National Adv. Email: therangereditor@gmail.com
Display Adv. Email: jlgibson@actx.edu
Editorial Email: therangereditor@gmail.com
Website: www.acranger.com
Year Established: 1930
Delivery Methods: Racks
Commercial printers?: N
Published: Thur
Published Other: biweekly
Avg Free Circ: 2500
Personnel: Jill Gibson (Student Media Adviser Matney Mass Media Program Coord); Maddisun Fowler (Student Media Coord)
Parent company (for newspapers): Amarillo College

AMERICUS

GEORGIA SOUTHWESTERN STATE UNIV.

Street Address 1: 800 Georgia Southwestern State University Dr
State: GA
Zip/Postal code: 31709
Country: USA
Mailing Address: 800 Georgia Southwestern State University Dr.
Mailing City: Americus
Mailing State: GA
Mailing ZIP Code: 31709
General Phone: (229) 931-2003
General Fax: (229) 931-2059
General/National Adv. Email: gswpaper@yahoo.com; gswpaper@canes.gsw.edu
Website: www.gsw.edu
Personnel: Josh Curtin (Advisor); Emily Immke (Bus. Mgr.); Sidney Davis (Ed. in Chief)

AMES

IOWA STATE DAILY

Street Address 1: 108 Hamilton Hall
State: IA
Zip/Postal code: 50011-1180
County: Story
Country: USA
Mailing Address: 108 Hamilton Hall
Mailing City: Ames
Mailing State: IA
Mailing ZIP Code: 50011-1181
General Phone: (515) 294-4120
General Fax: (515) 294-4119
Advertising Phone: (515) 294-2403
Advertising Fax: (515) 294-4119
Editorial Phone: (515) 294-5688
Editorial Fax: (515) 294-4119
General/National Adv. Email: ads@iowastatedaily.com
Display Adv. Email: ads@iowastatedaily.com
Editorial Email: editor@iowastatedaily.com
Website: www.iowastatedaily.com
Year Established: 1890
News Services: AP
Special Editions: Wellness Fair (Jan); Games Book (Jan); Spring Career Guide (Feb); Valentine's Section (Feb); Student Choice (Feb); Nightlife (Mar); Celebrate Summer (Jun); Unions (Jun)
Special Weekly Sections: Sports; Arts & Entertainment; Fashion; Food
Delivery Methods: Mail`Newsstand`Carrier
Own Printing Facility?: Y
Commercial printers?: Y
Published: Mon`Tues`Wed`Thur`Fri
Personnel: Laura Widmer (Gen. Mgr.); Mark Witherspoon (Ed. Advisor); Stephen Koenigsfeld (Ed.)

IOWA STATE UNIVERSITY

Street Address 1: 2420 Lincoln Way
Street Address 2: Ste 205
State: IA
Zip/Postal code: 50014-8340
Country: USA
Mailing Address: 2420 Lincoln Way, Suite 205
Mailing City: Ames
Mailing State: IA
Mailing ZIP Code: 50014
General Phone: (515) 294-4120
General Fax: (515) 294-4119
Advertising Fax: (515) 294-4119
Editorial Phone: (515) 294-4815
Editorial Fax: (515) 294-4119
General/National Adv. Email: spoon@iowastatedaily.com
Display Adv. Email: sara.brown@iowastatedaily.com
Editorial Email: news@iowastatedaily.com
Website: www.iowastatedaily.com
Year Established: 1890
Published: Mon`Tues`Wed`Thur`Fri
Avg Free Circ: 12500
Personnel: Mark Witherspoon (Advisor); Lawrence Cunningham (General Manager of the Iowa State Daily Media Group); Janey Nicholas (Business Manager); Sarah Lefebre (Operations manager); Sara Brown (Advertising manager); Emily Barske (Editor in chief)
Parent company (for newspapers): Iowa State Daily Media Group

AMHERST

AMHERST COLLEGE

Street Address 1: 31 Mead Dr
Street Address 2: Keefe Campus Center
State: MA
Zip/Postal code: 01002-1786
Country: USA
Mailing Address: AC#1912, Keefe Campus Center
Mailing City: Amherst
Mailing State: MA
Mailing ZIP Code: 01002-5000
General Phone: (413) 206-9319
General/National Adv. Email: astudent@amherst.edu
Display Adv. Email: astudent@amherst.edu
Website: www.amherststudent.amherst.edu
Published: Wed
Avg Free Circ: 1600
Personnel: Christopher Friend (Publisher)

HAMPSHIRE COLLEGE

Street Address 1: 893 West St
State: MA
Zip/Postal code: 01002-3372
Country: USA
Mailing Address: 893 West St
Mailing City: Amherst
Mailing State: MA
Mailing ZIP Code: 01002-3359
General Phone: (413) 549-4600
General Fax: (413) 559-5664
General/National Adv. Email: hampshireclimax@gmail.com
Website: climax.hampshire.edu
Personnel: Nicki Feldman (Admin. Sec.)

UNIV. OF MASSACHUSETTS

Street Address 1: 123 S Burrowes St
State: MA
Zip/Postal code: 1003
Country: USA
General Phone: (413) 545-3500
General Fax: (413) 545-3699
Editorial Email: editor@dailycollegian.com
Website: www.dailycollegian.com; www.umass.edu
Personnel: Alyssa Creamer (Ed.)

UNIVERSITY AT BUFFALO SCHOOL OF LAW

Street Address 1: 410 Obrian Hall
State: NY
Zip/Postal code: 14260-1100
Country: USA
Mailing Address: 410 O'Brian Hall
Mailing City: Amherst
Mailing State: NY
Mailing ZIP Code: 14260-1100
General Phone: (716) 645-3176
General Fax: (716) 645-5940
Editorial Phone: (716) 645-3176
General/National Adv. Email: lmueller@buffalo.edu
Editorial Email: lmueller@buffalo.edu
Website: www.law.buffalo.edu
Year Established: 2000
Published: Mthly
Avg Free Circ: 12000
Personnel: Kristina Lively (Webmaster)
Parent company (for newspapers): University at Buffalo

ANCHORAGE

ALASKA PACIFIC UNIV.

Street Address 1: 4101 University Dr
Street Address 2: Ste 19
State: AK
Zip/Postal code: 99508-4625
Country: USA
Mailing Address: 4101 University Dr Ste 19
Mailing City: Anchorage
Mailing State: AK
Mailing ZIP Code: 99508-4625
General Phone: (907) 564-8297
General Fax: (907) 564-8236
General/National Adv. Email: journal@alaskapacific.edu
Personnel: Rosanne Pagano (Advisor); Michelle Coles (Ed.)

UNIV. OF ALASKA ANCHORAGE

Street Address 1: 3211 Providence Dr, Campus Ctr 215
State: AK
Zip/Postal code: 99508
Country: USA
Mailing Address: 3211 Providence Dr., Campus Ctr. 215
Mailing City: Anchorage
Mailing State: AK
Mailing ZIP Code: 99508-4614
General Phone: (907) 786-1434
General Fax: (907) 786-1331
Advertising Phone: (907) 786-4690
Editorial Phone: (907) 786-1313
Display Adv. Email: ads@thenorthernlight.org
Editorial Email: editor@thenorthernlight.org
Website: www.thenorthernlight.org
Year Established: 1988
Special Weekly Sections: Motion (Arts & Sports)
Commercial printers?: Y
Personnel: Paola Banchero (Advisor); Mariya Proskuryakova (Adv. Mgr.); Shana Roberson (Executive Editor)

ANDERSON

ANDERSON UNIV.

Street Address 1: 1100 E 5th St
State: IN
Zip/Postal code: 46012-3462
Country: USA
Mailing Address: 1100 E 5th St
Mailing City: Anderson
Mailing State: IN
Mailing ZIP Code: 46012-3495
General Phone: (765) 641-4341
General Fax: (765) 641-3851
General/National Adv. Email: andersonian@anderson.edu
Website: www.anderson.edu/andersonian/
Personnel: David Baird (Advisor); Kayla Dunkman (Ed. in Chief); Tarah Novak (Ed.); Stacy Wood (Ed.)

ANGWIN

PACIFIC UNION COLLEGE

Street Address 1: 1 Angwin Ave
Street Address 2: Campus Ctr.
State: CA
Zip/Postal code: 94508-9713
Country: USA
Mailing Address: 1 Angwin Ave
Mailing City: Angwin
Mailing State: CA
Mailing ZIP Code: 94508-9797
General Phone: (707) 965-6747
General Fax: (707) 965-7123
General/National Adv. Email: cc@puc.edu
Website: c2.puc.edu
Personnel: Tammy McGuire (Advisor); Peter Katz (Ed.)

ANKENY

DES MOINES AREA CMTY. COLLEGE

Street Address 1: 2006 S Ankeny Blvd
Street Address 2: Bldg 2
State: IA
Zip/Postal code: 50023-8995
Country: USA
Mailing Address: 2006 S Ankeny Blvd Bldg 2
Mailing City: Ankeny
Mailing State: IA
Mailing ZIP Code: 50023-8995
General Phone: (515) 965-6425
General Fax: (515) 433-5033
General/National Adv. Email: chronicle@dmacc.edu
Website: www.campuschronicle.net
Personnel: Julie Roosa (Advisor); Julie Cahill (Adv. Mgr); Kelsey Edwards (Ed. in Chief)

ANN ARBOR

UNIV. OF MICHIGAN

Street Address 1: 420 Maynard St
State: MI
Zip/Postal code: 48109-1327

College and University Newspapers

III-647

Country: USA
Mailing Address: 420 Maynard St
Mailing City: Ann Arbor
Mailing State: MI
Mailing ZIP Code: 48109-1327
General Phone: (734) 763-2459
General Fax: (734) 764-4275
Advertising Phone: (734) 764-0554
General/National Adv. Email: news@michigandaily.com; tmdbusiness@gmail.com
Website: www.michigandaily.com
Personnel: Jacob Smilovitz (Ed. in Chief); Matt Aaronson (Mng. Ed.); Dan Newman (Bus. Mgr.)

UNIV. OF MICHIGAN BUS. SCHOOL

Street Address 1: 701 Tappan Ave
Street Address 2: Ste 766
State: MI
Zip/Postal code: 48109-1234
Country: USA
Mailing Address: 701 Tappan Ave Ste 766
Mailing City: Ann Arbor
Mailing State: MI
Mailing ZIP Code: 48109-1234
General Phone: (734) 764-2074
General Fax: (734) 763-6450
Display Adv. Email: msj.office@gmail.com
Editorial Email: msj.editor@gmail.com
Website: www.themsj.com
Personnel: Robyn Katzman (Pub.); Maggie Sadowski (Ed. In Chief)

WASHTENAW COMMUNITY COLLEGE

Street Address 1: 4800 E Huron River Dr
State: MI
Zip/Postal code: 48105-9481
Country: USA
Mailing City: Ann Arbor
Mailing State: MI
Mailing ZIP Code: 48105
General Phone: (734) 677-5125
General Fax: (734) 677-5126
Advertising Phone: (734) 973-3662
General/National Adv. Email: thewasntehawvoice@gmail.com
Display Adv. Email: ealliston@wccnet.edu
Editorial Email: kgave@wccnet.edu
Website: www.washtenawvoice.com
Year Established: 1967
Published: Bi-Mthly
Avg Free Circ: 5000
Personnel: Keith Gave (Advisor); Becky Alliston (Adv. Mgr.); Natalie Wright (Ed.)

ANNANDALE

BARD COLLEGE

Street Address 1: PO Box 5000
State: NY
Zip/Postal code: 12504-5000
Country: USA
Mailing Address: PO Box 5000
Mailing City: Annandale
Mailing State: NY
Mailing ZIP Code: 12504-5000
General Phone: (845) 758-7131
General Fax: (845) 758-4294
General/National Adv. Email: observer@bard.edu
Website: observer.bard.edu/index.shtml
Personnel: Becca Rom Frank (Ed. in Chief); Lilian Robinson (Ed.); Christine Gehringer (Mng. Ed.)

ANNAPOLIS

ST. JOHNS COLLEGE

Street Address 1: 60 College Ave
State: MD
Zip/Postal code: 21401-1687
Country: USA
Mailing Address: 60 College Ave
Mailing City: Annapolis
Mailing State: MD
Mailing ZIP Code: 21401-1655
General Phone: (410) 263-2212
Personnel: Ian McCracken (Ed.)

US NAVAL ACADEMY

Street Address 1: 121 Blake Rd
State: MD
Zip/Postal code: 21402-1300
Country: USA
Mailing Address: 121 Blake Rd
Mailing City: Annapolis
Mailing State: MD
Mailing ZIP Code: 21402-1300
General Phone: (410) 293-1536
General Fax: (410) 293-3133
Website: www.dcmilitary.com
Personnel: Jessica Clark (Ed.); Martha Thorn (Mng. Ed.)

ANNVILLE

LEBANON VALLEY COLLEGE

Street Address 1: 101 N College Ave
State: PA
Zip/Postal code: 17003-1404
Country: USA
Mailing Address: 101 N College Ave
Mailing City: Annville
Mailing State: PA
Mailing ZIP Code: 17003-1400
General Phone: (717) 867-6169
General/National Adv. Email: lavic@lvc.edu
Website: lavieonline.lvc.edu
Personnel: Bob Vicic (Advisor); Jake King (Co Ed. in Chief); Katie Zwiebel (Co Ed. in Chief)

APPLETON

LAWRENCE UNIVERSITY

Street Address 1: 711 E Boldt Way
Street Address 2: Spc 51
State: WI
Zip/Postal code: 54911-5699
Country: USA
Mailing Address: 711 E Boldt Way Spc 51
Mailing City: Appleton
Mailing State: WI
Mailing ZIP Code: 54911-5699
General Phone: (920) 832-6768
General Fax: (920) 832-7031
General/National Adv. Email: lawrentian@lawrence.edu
Website: www.lawrentian.com
Year Established: 1884
Published: Fri
Avg Free Circ: 1000
Personnel: Emily Zawacki (Editor-in-Chief); Nathan Lawrence (Copy Chief)

ARCATA

HUMBOLDT STATE UNIV.

Street Address 1: 1 Harpst St
Street Address 2: Gist Hall 227
State: CA
Zip/Postal code: 95521-8222
Country: USA
Mailing Address: 1 Harpst Street
Mailing City: Arcata
Mailing State: CA
Mailing ZIP Code: 95521-8299
General Phone: (707) 826-3271
Advertising Phone: (707) 826-5921
General/National Adv. Email: thejack@humboldt.edu
Website: www.thejackonline.org
Personnel: Marcy Burstiner (Advisor); Sara Wilmot (Ed.)

ARKADELPHIA

HENDERSON STATE UNIV.

Street Address 1: PO Box 7681
Street Address 2: 1100 Henderson St.
State: AR
Zip/Postal code: 71999-7693
Country: USA
Mailing Address: PO Box 7693
Mailing City: Arkadelphia
Mailing State: AR
Mailing ZIP Code: 71999-7693
General Phone: (870) 230-5221
General Fax: (870) 230-5549
Advertising Phone: (870) 230-5288
General/National Adv. Email: oracle@hsu.edu
Display Adv. Email: oracleads@hsu.edu
Website: www.hsuoracle.com
Year Established: 1910
Published: Wed
Avg Free Circ: 2000
Personnel: Steve Listopad (Advisor)

OUACHITA BAPTIST UNIV.

Street Address 1: Obu Box 3759
State: AR
Zip/Postal code: 71998-0001
Country: USA
Mailing Address: Obu # 3759
Mailing City: Arkadelphia
Mailing State: AR
Mailing ZIP Code: 71998-0001
General Phone: (870) 245-5210
General Fax: (870) 245-5209
General/National Adv. Email: Signal@obu.edu
Display Adv. Email: Signal@obu.edu
Editorial Email: Signal@obu.edu
Website: www.obusignal.com
Published: Thur
Personnel: Jeff Root (Advisor)

ARKANSAS CITY

COWLEY COUNTY CMTY. COLLEGE

Street Address 1: 125 S 2nd St
State: KS
Zip/Postal code: 67005-2662
Country: USA
Mailing Address: 125 S 2nd St
Mailing City: Arkansas City
Mailing State: KS
Mailing ZIP Code: 67005-2662
General Phone: (620) 441-5287
General Fax: (620) 441-5377
General/National Adv. Email: editor@cowleypress.com
Website: www.cowleypress.com
Personnel: Meg Smith (Faculty Advisor); Alyssa Campbell (Adv. Mgr.); Richard Gould (Ed.)

ARLINGTON

MARYMOUNT UNIV.

Street Address 1: 2807 N Glebe Rd
State: VA
Zip/Postal code: 22207-4224
Country: USA
Mailing Address: 2807 N Glebe Rd
Mailing City: Arlington
Mailing State: VA
Mailing ZIP Code: 22207-4299
General Phone: (703) 522-5600
General Fax: (703) 284-3817
General/National Adv. Email: banner@marymount.edu
Website: www.marymount.edu
Personnel: Paul Byers (Mass Commun. Coord.); Vincent Stovall (Dir., Student Activities); Ralph Frasca (Mass Commun. Coord.)

UNIVERSITY OF TEXAS AT ARLINGTON

Street Address 1: University Ctr, Lower Level, 300 W 1st St
Street Address 2: B100
State: TX
Zip/Postal code: 76019-0001
Country: USA
Mailing Address: P.O. Box 19038
Mailing City: Arlington
Mailing State: TX
Mailing ZIP Code: 76019-0001
General Phone: (817) 272-3188
General Fax: (817) 272-5009
Editorial Phone: (817) 272-3205
General/National Adv. Email: editor.shorthorn@uta.edu
Display Adv. Email: ads.shorthorn@uta.edu
Editorial Email: editor.shorthorn@uta.edu; calendar.shorthorn@uta.edu
Website: www.theshorthorn.com
Year Established: 1919
Delivery Methods: Racks
Published: Wed
Published Other: Daily online
Personnel: Brian Schopf (Office Mgr.); Tammy Skrehart (Adv. Mgr./Asst. Dir.); Adam Drew (Production Mgr.); Beth Francesco (Dir. of Student Pubs.); Laurie Fox (Newsroom advisor); Lori Doskocil (Bus Mgr)
Parent company (for newspapers): University of Texas at Arlington

ARNOLD

ANNE ARUNDEL CMTY. COLLEGE

CAMPUS CURRENT

Street Address 1: 101 College Pkwy
Street Address 2: Hum 206
State: MD
Zip/Postal code: 21012-1857
Country: USA
Mailing Address: 101 College Pkwy Hum 206
Mailing City: Arnold
Mailing State: MD
Mailing ZIP Code: 21012-1857
General Phone: (410) 777-2803
General Fax: (410) 777-2021
General/National Adv. Email: campuscurrent@aacc.edu
Website: www.campus-current.com
Commercial printers?: Y
Published: Bi-Mthly
Avg Free Circ: 2500
Personnel: Sheri Venema (Advisor)

ASHEVILLE

UNIV. OF NORTH CAROLINA

Street Address 1: 1 University Hts
State: NC
Zip/Postal code: 28804-3251
Country: USA
Mailing Address: 1 University Heights
Mailing City: Asheville
Mailing State: NC
Mailing ZIP Code: 28804-3251
General Fax: (828) 251-6591
Advertising Fax: (828) 232-2421
General/National Adv. Email: www.thebluebanner.net
Display Adv. Email: banner@unca.edu
Personnel: Michael Gouge (Advisor); Anna Kiser (Adv. Mgr.); Sam Hunt (Ed. in Chief)

ASHLAND

ASHLAND UNIV.

Street Address 1: 401 College Ave
State: OH
Zip/Postal code: 44805-3702
Country: USA
Mailing Address: 401 College Ave
Mailing City: Ashland
Mailing State: OH
Mailing ZIP Code: 44805-3799
General Phone: (419) 289-4142
General Fax: (419) 289-5604
General/National Adv. Email: collegian@ashland.edu
Website: www.ashland.edu/collegian
Personnel: Katie Ryder (Ed.)

College and University Newspapers

RANDOLPH-MACON COLLEGE
Street Address 1: 204 Henry St
State: VA
Zip/Postal code: 23005-1634
Country: USA
Mailing Address: PO Box 5005
Mailing City: Ashland
Mailing State: VA
Mailing ZIP Code: 23005-5505
General Phone: (804) 752-7200
General Fax: (804) 752-3748
General/National Adv. Email: yellowjacket@rmc.edu
Website: www.rmc.edu
Personnel: Robert Thomas (Bus. Mgr.); Derek Gayle (News Ed.); Lara O'Brien (Sports Ed.)

SOUTHERN OREGON UNIV.
Street Address 1: Stevenson Union, Rm 336, 1250 Siskiyou Blvd
State: OR
Zip/Postal code: 97520
Country: USA
Mailing Address: Stevenson Union, Rm. 336, 1250 Siskiyou Blvd.
Mailing City: Ashland
Mailing State: OR
Mailing ZIP Code: 97520-5001
General Phone: (541) 552-6307
General Fax: (541) 552-6440
Advertising Phone: (541) 552-6306
General/National Adv. Email: siskiyou@students.sou.edu
Website: www.sou.edu/su/siskiyou
Personnel: Karen Finnegan (Advisor); Dwight Melton (Ed.)

ASTON

THE JOUST
Street Address 1: 1 Neumann Dr
Street Address 2: Neumann University
State: PA
Zip/Postal code: 19014-1277
Country: USA
Mailing Address: 1 Neumann Dr
Mailing City: Aston
Mailing State: PA
Mailing ZIP Code: 19014
General Phone: 610-358-4570
General Fax: 610-361-5314
General/National Adv. Email: glassj@neumann.edu
Website: www.neumann.edu

ATCHISON

BENEDICTINE COLLEGE
Street Address 1: 1020 N 2nd St
State: KS
Zip/Postal code: 66002-1402
Country: USA
Mailing Address: 1020 N 2nd St
Mailing City: Atchison
Mailing State: KS
Mailing ZIP Code: 66002-1499
General Phone: (913) 360-7390
General Fax: (913) 367-6102
General/National Adv. Email: circuit@benedictine.edu
Website: www.bccircuit.com
Personnel: Kevin Page (Advisor)

ATHENS

ATHENS STATE UNIV.
Street Address 1: 300 N Beaty St
State: AL
Zip/Postal code: 35611-1902
Country: USA
Mailing Address: 300 N Beaty St
Mailing City: Athens
Mailing State: AL
Mailing ZIP Code: 35611-1999
General Phone: (256) 233-8169
General Fax: (256) 233-8128
General/National Adv. Email: the.athenian@athens.edu.
Personnel: Tena Bullington (Adv. Mgr.); Aletha Pardue (Ed.)

CONCORD COLLEGE
Street Address 1: PO Box 1000
State: WV
Zip/Postal code: 24712-1000
Country: USA
Mailing Address: PO Box 1000
Mailing City: Athens
Mailing State: WV
Mailing ZIP Code: 24712-1000
General Phone: (304) 384-5364
General/National Adv. Email: concordian@concord.edu
Website: www.cunewspaper.com
Personnel: Lindsey Mullins (Advisor); Wendy Holdren (Ed. in Chief)

OHIO UNIV.
Street Address 1: 325 Baker University Center
State: OH
Zip/Postal code: 45701
Country: USA
Mailing Address: 325 Baker University Center
Mailing City: Athens
Mailing State: OH
Mailing ZIP Code: 45701
General Phone: (740) 593-4011
General Fax: (740) 593-0561
Advertising Phone: (740) 593-4018
General/National Adv. Email: posteditorial@ohiou.edu
Website: www.thepost.ohiou.edu
Personnel: Ashley Lutz (Ed. in Chief); Dave Hendricks (Managing Ed.); Ryan Dunn (Associate Ed.); Natalie Debruin (Asst. Managing Ed.); Joe (Sports Ed.); Robert (Advertising Admin.)

TRINITY VALLEY CMTY. COLLEGE
Street Address 1: 100 Cardinal St
State: TX
Zip/Postal code: 75751-3243
Country: USA
Mailing Address: 100 Cardinal St
Mailing City: Athens
Mailing State: TX
Mailing ZIP Code: 75751-3243
General Phone: (903) 675-6302
General Fax: (903) 675-6316
General/National Adv. Email: journalstaff@tvcc.edu
Website: www.tvccnewsjournal.com
Year Established: 1972
Personnel: Danny Teague (Advisor); Judy Greenlee (Asst. Advisor); Melisa Boon (Ed.); Deidre Jones (Media Instructor/Adviser)

UNIV. OF GEORGIA
Street Address 1: 540 Baxter St
State: GA
Zip/Postal code: 30605-1106
Country: USA
Mailing Address: 540 Baxter St
Mailing City: Athens
Mailing State: GA
Mailing ZIP Code: 30605-1106
General Phone: (706) 433-3000
General Fax: (706) 433-3033
Advertising Phone: (706) 433-3012
Editorial Phone: (706) 433-3002
General/National Adv. Email: news@randb.com
Website: www.redandblack.com
Personnel: Ed Morales (Editorial Adviser); Natalie McClure (General Manager)

ATHERTON

MENLO COLLEGE
Street Address 1: 1000 El Camino Real
State: CA
Zip/Postal code: 94027-4300
County: San Mateo County
Country: USA
Mailing Address: 1000 El Camino Real
Mailing City: Atherton
Mailing State: CA
Mailing ZIP Code: 94027-4301
General Phone: (650) 543-3786
General/National Adv. Email: pr@menlo.edu
Website: www.menlo.edu
Personnel: Priscila de Souza (Dean of Enrollment Management)

ATLANTA

ATLANTA UNIVERSITY CENTER
Street Address 1: 117 Vine St SW
Street Address 2: Fl 1
State: GA
Zip/Postal code: 30314-4205
Country: USA
Mailing Address: PO Box 3191
Mailing City: Atlanta
Mailing State: GA
Mailing ZIP Code: 30302-3191
General Phone: (404) 523-6136
General/National Adv. Email: aucdigestmail@aol.com
Website: www.aucdigest.com
Year Established: 1973
Published: Thur
Personnel: Lo Jelks (Ed.)
Parent company (for newspapers): Collegiate Broadcasting Group, Inc.

CLARK ATLANTA UNIV.
Street Address 1: 223 James P Brawley Dr SW
State: GA
Zip/Postal code: 30314-4358
Country: USA
Mailing Address: PO Box 1523
Mailing City: Atlanta
Mailing State: GA
Mailing ZIP Code: 30301-1523
General Phone: (404) 880-6219
General/National Adv. Email: caunews05@yahoo.com
Delivery Methods: Mail
Personnel: James McJunkins (Advisor)

EMORY UNIV.
Street Address 1: 605 Asbury Cir
State: GA
Zip/Postal code: 30322-1006
Country: USA
Mailing Address: P.O. Box W
Mailing City: Atlanta
Mailing State: GA
Mailing ZIP Code: 30322-1006
General Phone: (404) 727-0279
Advertising Phone: (404) 727-3613
Editorial Phone: (404) 727-6178
General/National Adv. Email: emorywheelexec@gmail.com
Editorial Email: emorywheelexec@gmail.com
Website: www.emorywheel.com
Year Established: 1919
Published: Tues Fri
Personnel: Priyanka Krishnamurthy (Ed.); Sonam Vashi (Exec. Ed.); Lizzie Howell (Managing Ed.)

GEORGIA INST. OF TECHNOLOGY
Street Address 1: 353 Ferst Dr
Street Address 2: Rm 137
State: GA
Zip/Postal code: 30318-5602
Country: USA
Mailing Address: 353 Ferst Dr Rm 137
Mailing City: Atlanta
Mailing State: GA
Mailing ZIP Code: 30332-0001
General Phone: (404) 894-2830
General Fax: (404) 894-1650
General/National Adv. Email: editor@technique.gatech.edu
Website: www.nique.net
Personnel: Mac Pitts (Advisor); Emily Chambers (Ed. in Chief); Jonathan Saethang (Mng. Ed.); Hahnming Lee (Bus. Mgr.)

GEORGIA STATE UNIVERSITY
Street Address 1: 310 Student Center East
Street Address 2: 55 Gilmer St SE
State: GA
Zip/Postal code: 30303
Country: USA
Mailing Address: 310 Student Center East
Mailing City: Atlanta
Mailing State: GA
Mailing ZIP Code: 30303-3011
General Phone: (404) 413-1617(404) 413-1868
General Fax: 404-413-1868
Advertising Phone: 404-413-1869
Advertising Fax: 404-413-1868
Editorial Phone: 404-413-1617
General/National Adv. Email: editor@georgiastatesignal.com
Display Adv. Email: whenley@gsu.edu
Editorial Email: editor@georgiastatesignal.com
Website: www.georgiastatesignal.com
Year Established: 1933
Published: Tues
Published Other: (Fall & Spring with summer magazine)
Avg Free Circ: 4000
Personnel: Bryce McNeil (Director, Student Media); Daniel Varitek (Editor-in-Chief); Wakesha Henley (Business Coordinator); Zoana Price (Student Media Advisor, Perimeter College)

MOREHOUSE COLLEGE
Street Address 1: 830 Westview Dr SW
State: GA
Zip/Postal code: 30314-3773
Country: USA
Mailing Address: 830 Westview Dr SW
Mailing City: Atlanta
Mailing State: GA
Mailing ZIP Code: 30314-3776
General Phone: (404) 681-2800
General/National Adv. Email: mtiger@morehouse.edu
Website: www.morehouse.edu/themaroontiger/
Personnel: Edward T. Mitchell (Ed. in Chief); Donovan Ramsey (Mng. Ed.)

CAYUGA COMMUNITY COLLEGE
Street Address 1: 197 Franklin St
State: NY
Zip/Postal code: 13021-3011
Country: USA
Mailing Address: 197 Franklin St
Mailing City: Auburn
Mailing State: NY
Mailing ZIP Code: 13021-3011
General Phone: (315) 255-1743
General Fax: (315) 255-2117
General/National Adv. Email: cayugacollegian@gmail.com
Year Established: 1954
Delivery Methods: Newsstand
Commercial printers?: Y
Published Other: ON ANNOUNCED SCHEDULE
Avg Free Circ: 1000
Personnel: Mary Gelling Merrit (Advisor)

GREEN RIVER COMMUNITY COLLEGE
Street Address 1: 12401 SE 320th St
State: WA
Zip/Postal code: 98092-3622
Country: USA
Mailing Address: 12401 SE 320th St
Mailing City: Auburn

College and University Newspapers

Mailing State: WA
Mailing ZIP Code: 98092-3699
General Phone: (253) 833-9111 x2375
General Fax: (253) 288-3457
Advertising Phone: (253) 833-9111 x2376
Editorial Phone: (253) 833-9111 x2375
General/National Adv. Email: thecurrent@greenriver.edu
Website: www.thecurrentonline.net
Delivery Methods: Racks
Published Other: Every two weeks (approximately), excluding summer
Avg Free Circ: 1200
Personnel: Brian Schraum (Adviser)

AUBURN UNIVERSITY

AUBURN UNIV.

Street Address 1: Student Center 1111
State: AL
Zip/Postal code: 1985
Country: USA
Mailing Address: 255 Duncan Dr Ste 1111
Mailing City: Auburn University
Mailing State: AL
Mailing ZIP Code: 36849-0001
General Phone: (334) 844-9021
General Fax: (334) 844-9114
General/National Adv. Email: news@theplainsman.com
Display Adv. Email: advertising@theplainsman.com
Website: www.theplainsman.com
Personnel: Jennifer Adams (Advisor); Tom Hopf (Bus. Mgr.); Lindsey Davidson (Ed.); Rod Guajardo (Mng. Ed.)

AUBURNDALE

LASELL COLLEGE

Street Address 1: 1844 Commonwealth Ave
State: MA
Zip/Postal code: 02466-2709
Country: USA
Mailing Address: 1844 Commonwealth Ave
Mailing City: Auburndale
Mailing State: MA
Mailing ZIP Code: 02466-2716
General Phone: (617) 243-2000
General Fax: (617) 243-2468
General/National Adv. Email: newspaper@lasell.edu
Personnel: Marie C. Franklin (Advisor); Michelle McNickle (Ed. in Chief); Briana Nestor (Features Ed.)

AUGUSTA

AUGUSTA STATE UNIV.

Street Address 1: 2500 Walton Way
State: GA
Zip/Postal code: 30904-4562
Country: USA
Mailing Address: 2500 Walton Way
Mailing City: Augusta
Mailing State: GA
Mailing ZIP Code: 30904-2200
General Phone: (706) 737-1600
General Fax: (706) 729-2247
General/National Adv. Email: bellringerproduction@gmail.com
Website: www.asubellringer.com
Delivery Methods: Racks
Personnel: Matthew Bosisio (Advisor); Kara Mauldin (Ed. in Chief); Stacie Cooper (Prodn. Mgr.); Dee Taylor (Adv. Mgr.)

AUSTIN

HUSTON TILLOTSON COLLEGE

Street Address 1: 900 Chicon St
State: TX
Zip/Postal code: 78702-2753
Country: USA
Mailing Address: 900 Chicon St
Mailing City: Austin

Mailing State: TX
Mailing ZIP Code: 78702-9997
General Phone: (512) 505-3000

ST. EDWARDS UNIV.

Street Address 1: 3001 S Congress Ave
Street Address 2: Campus Mailox #964
State: TX
Zip/Postal code: 78704-6425
Country: USA
Mailing Address: PO Box 1033
Mailing City: Austin
Mailing State: TX
Mailing ZIP Code: 78767-1033
General Phone: (512) 448-8426
General Fax: (512) 428-1084
General/National Adv. Email: hilltopviewsonline@gmail.com
Display Adv. Email: hilltopviewsads@gmail.com
Editorial Email: hilltopviewseditors@gmail.com
Website: hilltopviewsonline.com
Published: Wed
Personnel: Andrea Guzman (Editor-In-Chief); Gabrielle Wilkosz (Editor-In-Chief); Amanda Gonzalez (Managing Editor)

TEXAS STUDENT MEDIA

Street Address 1: 2500 Whitis Ave
State: TX
Zip/Postal code: 78712-1502
Country: USA
Mailing Address: PO Box D
Mailing City: Austin
Mailing State: TX
Mailing ZIP Code: 78713-8904
General Phone: (512) 471-4591
General Fax: (512) 471-2952
Advertising Phone: (512) 471-1865
Editorial Phone: (512) 232-2207
Website: www.dailytexanonline.com
Year Established: 1900
Delivery Methods: Racks
Commercial printers?: N
Published: Mon`Tues`Wed`Thur`Fri
Avg Free Circ: 13000
Personnel: Doug Warren (Advisor)

UNIV. OF TEXAS COLLEGE OF BUS.

Street Address 1: Cba 3.328 A
State: TX
Zip/Postal code: 78712
Country: USA
Mailing Address: CBA 3.328 A
Mailing City: Austin
Mailing State: TX
Mailing ZIP Code: 78712
General Phone: (512) 708-9357
Personnel: Sunio Varghese (Ed.)

UNIV. OF TEXAS COLLEGE OF ENGINEERING

Street Address 1: 301 E Dean Keeton St
State: TX
Zip/Postal code: 78712-1476
Country: USA
Mailing Address: 301 E. Dean Keeton St. C2100
Mailing City: Austin
Mailing State: TX
Mailing ZIP Code: 78712-2100
General Phone: (512) 471-3003
General Fax: (512) 471-4304
General/National Adv. Email: vector.ut@gmail.com
Website: www.engr.utexas.edu
Personnel: An Nguyen (Ed.)

BABSON PARK

BABSON COLLEGE

Street Address 1: 231 Forest St
State: MA
Country: USA

Mailing Address: 231 Forest St.
Mailing City: Babson Park
Mailing State: MA
Mailing ZIP Code: 02457
General Phone: (781) 239-5541
General Fax: (781) 239-5554
General/National Adv. Email: freepress@babson.edu
Display Adv. Email: babsonfreep@babson.edu
Website: www.babsonfreep.com
Personnel: Anthony Micale (Ed.)

BAKERSFIELD

BAKERSFIELD COLLEGE

Street Address 1: 1801 Panorama Dr
State: CA
Zip/Postal code: 93305-1219
Country: USA
Mailing Address: 1801 Panorama Dr
Mailing City: Bakersfield
Mailing State: CA
Mailing ZIP Code: 93305-1299
General Phone: (661) 395-4324
General Fax: (661) 395-4027
Editorial Fax: Free
General/National Adv. Email: ripmail@bakersfieldcollege.edu
Display Adv. Email: daedward@bakersfieldcollege.edu
Website: www.therip.com
Year Established: 1929
Published Other: bi-weekly (once every two weeks on Wednesdays)
Avg Free Circ: 3000
Personnel: Danny Edwards (Advisor)

CALIFORNIA STATE UNIVERSITY, BAKERSFIELD

Street Address 1: 9001 Stockdale Hwy
State: CA
Zip/Postal code: 93311-1022
Country: USA
Mailing Address: 9001 Stockdale Hwy.
Mailing City: Bakersfield
Mailing State: CA
Mailing ZIP Code: 93311-1022
General Phone: (661) 654-2165
General/National Adv. Email: runner@csub.edu
Website: therunneronline.com
Year Established: 1974
Published: Wed
Published Other: Back-to-School issue - 1st Day of Fall
Personnel: Jennifer Burger (Lecturer and Adviser to the Runner Student Media Center)

BALDWIN CITY

BAKER UNIVERSITY

Street Address 1: PO Box 65
State: KS
Zip/Postal code: 66006-0065
Country: USA
Mailing Address: PO Box 65
Mailing City: Baldwin City
Mailing State: KS
Mailing ZIP Code: 66006-0065
General Phone: (913) 594-6451
General Fax: (913) 594-3570
General/National Adv. Email: bayha@harvey.bakeru.edu
Website: www.thebakerorange.com
Personnel: Gwyn Mellinger (Advisor); Ann Rosenthal (Chair); Dave Bostwick (Advisor); Chris Smith (Ed.)

BALTIMORE

CMTY. COLLEGE OF BALTIMORE CITY ESSEX

Street Address 1: 7201 Rossville Blvd
Street Address 2: Rm 116

State: MD
Zip/Postal code: 21237-3855
Country: USA
Mailing Address: 7201 Rossville Blvd Rm 116
Mailing City: Baltimore
Mailing State: MD
Mailing ZIP Code: 21237-3855
General Phone: (443) 840-1576
General Fax: (410) 780-6209
Personnel: Jeremy Caplan (Advisor); Corey States (Ed.)

LOYOLA COLLEGE

Street Address 1: 4501 N Charles St
Street Address 2: Bellarmine Hall 1
State: MD
Zip/Postal code: 21210-2601
Country: USA
Mailing Address: 4501 N Charles St Bellarmine Hall 1
Mailing City: Baltimore
Mailing State: MD
Mailing ZIP Code: 21210-2694
General Phone: (410) 617-2282
General Fax: (410) 617-2982
General/National Adv. Email: greyhoundads@loyola.edu
Website: www.loyolagreyhound.com
Personnel: Joe Morelli (Bus. Mgr.); Kat Kienle (Ed. in Chief)

NOTRE DAME OF MARYLAND UNIVERSITY

Street Address 1: 4701 N Charles St
State: MD
Zip/Postal code: 21210-2404
Country: USA
Mailing Address: 4701 N. Charles St.
Mailing City: Baltimore
Mailing State: MD
Mailing ZIP Code: 21210-2476
General Phone: (410) 532-5580
General Fax: (410) 532-5796
General/National Adv. Email: Columns@ndm.edu
Display Adv. Email: Columns@ndm.edu
Editorial Email: Columns@ndm.edu
Website: www.ndmcolumns.com
Personnel: Mariel Guerrero (Editor-in-Chief); Marguerite Linz (Lead Writer/ Managing Editor)

THE JOHNS HOPKINS NEWS-LETTER

Street Address 1: Levering Unit 102
State: MD
Zip/Postal code: 21218
Country: USA
Mailing Address: 3400 N Charles St
Mailing City: Baltimore
Mailing State: MD
Mailing ZIP Code: 21218-2680
General Phone: (410) 516-4228
General/National Adv. Email: chiefs@jhunewsletter.com; business@jhunewsletter.com
Display Adv. Email: business@jhunewsletter.com
Website: www.jhunewsletter.com
Year Established: 1896
Published: Thur
Personnel: Marie Cushing (Ed. in Chief); Leah Maniero (Mng. Ed.)

UNIV. OF MARYLAND BALTIMORE COUNTY

Street Address 1: Uc 214, 1000 Hilltop Cir
State: MD
Zip/Postal code: 21250-0001
Country: USA
Mailing Address: Uc 214, 1000 Hilltop Cir
Mailing City: Baltimore
Mailing State: MD
Mailing ZIP Code: 21250-0001

General Phone: (410) 455-1260
General Fax: (410) 455-1265
General/National Adv. Email: eic@retrieverweekly.com
Website: www.retrieverweekly.com
Personnel: Christopher Corbett (Advisor); Nimit Bhatt (Adv./Bus. Mgr.); Gaby Arevalo (Ed. in Chief)

BANGOR

HUSSON COLLEGE

Street Address 1: 1 College Cir
State: ME
Zip/Postal code: 04401-2929
Country: USA
Mailing Address: 1 College Cir
Mailing City: Bangor
Mailing State: ME
Mailing ZIP Code: 04401-2999
General Phone: (207) 941-7700
General Fax: (207) 941-7190
Personnel: Josh Scroggins (Ed.)

BARTLESVILLE

BARTLESVILLE WESLEYAN COLLEGE

Street Address 1: 2201 Silver Lake Rd
State: OK
Zip/Postal code: 74006-6233
Country: USA
Mailing Address: 2201 Silver Lake Rd
Mailing City: Bartlesville
Mailing State: OK
Mailing ZIP Code: 74006-6299
General Phone: (918) 335-6200
Website: www.okwu.edu

BATESVILLE

LYON COLLEGE

Street Address 1: PO Box 2317
State: AR
Zip/Postal code: 72503-2317
Country: USA
Mailing Address: PO Box 2317
Mailing City: Batesville
Mailing State: AR
Mailing ZIP Code: 72503-2317
General Phone: (870) 698-4288
General Fax: (870) 698-4622
General/National Adv. Email: highlander@lyon.edu
Personnel: Gavin Johannsen (Exec. Ed.)

BATON ROUGE

LOUISIANA STATE UNIVERSITY

Street Address 1: Office of Student Media, B-39 Hodges Hall
State: LA
Zip/Postal code: 70803-0001
Country: USA
Mailing Address: Of Student Media B-39 Hodges Hall Ofc
Mailing City: Baton Rouge
Mailing State: LA
Mailing ZIP Code: 70803-0001
General Phone: (225) 578-4810
General Fax: (225) 578-1698
Advertising Phone: (225) 578-6090
Editorial Phone: (225) 578-4811
General/National Adv. Email: editor@lsureveille.com
Display Adv. Email: national@tigers.lsu.edu
Editorial Email: editor@lsureveille.com
Website: www.lsureveille.com
Year Established: 1887
Published: Mon`Tues`Wed`Thur`Fri
Personnel: Nicholas Persac (Ed.); Kyle Whitfield (Ed.); Kodi Wilson (Adv. Mgr.); Andrea Gallo (Editor in Chief); Balkom Taylor (Editor in Chief); Chandler Rome (Editor-in-Chief)

SOUTHERN UNIV. A&M COLLEGE

Street Address 1: T H Harris Hall, Ste 1064
State: LA
Zip/Postal code: 70813-0001
Country: USA
Mailing Address: PO Box 10180
Mailing City: Baton Rouge
Mailing State: LA
Mailing ZIP Code: 70813-0180
General Phone: (225) 771-2230
General Fax: (225) 771-3253
General/National Adv. Email: editor@southerndigest.com
Website: www.southerndigest.com
Year Established: 1928
Personnel: Stephanie Cain (Bus./Adv. Mgr.); Derick Hackett (Dir., Student Media); Christopher Jones (Asst. Dir.); Fran Hoskins (Ed.)

SOUTHERN UNIVERSITY

Street Address 1: T H Harris Hall
Street Address 2: Suite 1064
State: LA
Zip/Postal code: 70813-0001
Country: USA
Mailing Address: PO Box 10180
Mailing City: Baton Rouge
Mailing State: LA
Mailing ZIP Code: 70813-0180
General Phone: (225) 771-2231
General Fax: (225) 771-5840
Advertising Phone: 225-771-5833
Advertising Fax: 225-771-5840
Editorial Phone: 225-771-5829
Editorial Fax: 225-771-5840
General/National Adv. Email: digest@subr.edu
Display Adv. Email: camelia_gardner@subr.edu
Editorial Email: fredrick_batiste@subr.edu
Website: www.southerndigest.com
Year Established: 1926
Published: Tues`Thur
Avg Free Circ: 4000
Personnel: Heather Freeman (Student Media Director); Camelia Jackson (Advertising/Business Manager); Fredrick Batiste (Publications Assistant/Advisor)

BAY MINETTE

JAMES FAULKNER STATE CMTY. COLLEGE

Street Address 1: 1900 S US Highway 31
State: AL
Zip/Postal code: 36507-2619
Country: USA
Mailing Address: 1900 S US Highway 31
Mailing City: Bay Minette
Mailing State: AL
Mailing ZIP Code: 36507-2698
General Phone: (251) 580-2100
Personnel: Margaret Strickland (Dir., College Rel.)

BAYSIDE

QUEENSBOROUGH CMTY. COLLEGE

Street Address 1: 22205 56th Ave
State: NY
Zip/Postal code: 11364-1432
Country: USA
Mailing Address: 22205 56th Ave
Mailing City: Bayside
Mailing State: NY
Mailing ZIP Code: 11364-1432
General Phone: (718) 631-6262
General Fax: (718) 631-6637
Website: www.qcc.cuny.edu
Personnel: Andrew Levy (Advisor)

BEAUMONT

LAMAR UNIV.

Street Address 1: 200 Setzer Student Ctr
State: TX
Zip/Postal code: 77710
Country: USA
Mailing Address: PO Box 10055
Mailing City: Beaumont
Mailing State: TX
Mailing ZIP Code: 77710-0055
General Phone: (409) 880-8102
General Fax: (409) 880-8735
General/National Adv. Email: advertising@lamaruniversitypress.com
Website: www.lamaruniversitypress.com
Published: Thur
Published Other: end of semester special editions, seasonal editions
Personnel: Andy Coughlan (Advisor); Linda Barrett (Adv. Mgr.)

BEAVER FALLS

GENEVA COLLEGE

Street Address 1: 3200 College Ave
State: PA
Zip/Postal code: 15010-3557
Country: USA
Mailing Address: 3200 College Ave
Mailing City: Beaver Falls
Mailing State: PA
Mailing ZIP Code: 15010-3599
General Phone: (724) 847-6605
General Fax: (724) 847-6772
General/National Adv. Email: cabinet.editor@gmail.comcabinet
Website: www.geneva.edu
Personnel: Tom Copeland (Advisor)

BEDFORD

MIDDLESEX CMTY. COLLEGE

Street Address 1: 591 Springs Rd
State: MA
Zip/Postal code: 01730-1120
Country: USA
Mailing Address: 591 Springs Rd
Mailing City: Bedford
Mailing State: MA
Mailing ZIP Code: 01730-1197
General Phone: (781) 280-3769
General Fax: (781) 275-4396
Personnel: Sarah Screaux (Ed.)

BELLEVUE

BELLEVUE CMTY. COLLEGE

Street Address 1: 3000 Landerholm Cir SE
State: WA
Zip/Postal code: 98007-6406
Country: USA
Mailing Address: 3000 Landerholm Cir SE
Mailing City: Bellevue
Mailing State: WA
Mailing ZIP Code: 98007-6484
General Phone: (425) 564-2434
General Fax: (425) 564-4152
General/National Adv. Email: ataylor@bellevuecollege.edu
Display Adv. Email: advertising@thejibsheet.com
Website: www.thejibsheet.com
Personnel: Katherine Oleson (Pub.); Janelle Gardener (Advisor); Anne Taylor (Adv. Mgr.)

BELLINGHAM

WESTERN WASHINGTON UNIV.

Street Address 1: 516 High St
Street Address 2: # CF230
State: WA
Zip/Postal code: 98225-5946
Country: USA
Mailing Address: 516 High St # CF230
Mailing City: Bellingham
Mailing State: WA
Mailing ZIP Code: 98225-5946
General Phone: (360) 650-3160
General Fax: (360) 650-7775
Advertising Phone: (360) 650-3160
General/National Adv. Email: editor@westernfrontonline.net; thewesternfronteditor@yahoo.com
Website: www.westernfrontonline.net
Year Established: 1899
Delivery Methods: Racks
Commercial printers?: N
Personnel: Carolyn Nielsen (Advisor); Aletha Macomber (Bus. Mgr.); Michele Anderson (Advertising Mgr.); Nicholas Johnson (Ed. in Chief); Katie (Managing Ed.); Alex (Online Ed.)

WHATCOM CMTY. COLLEGE

Street Address 1: Syre Student Ctr Rm 202 237 W Kellogg Rd
State: WA
Zip/Postal code: 98226
Country: USA
Mailing Address: Syre Student Ctr. Rm. 202 237 W. Kellogg Rd.
Mailing City: Bellingham
Mailing State: WA
Mailing ZIP Code: 98226
General Phone: (360) 383-3101
General Fax: (360) 676-2171
General/National Adv. Email: horizonads@hotmail.com; admanager@whatcomhorizon.com
Editorial Email: editor@whatcomhorizon.com
Website: www.whatcomhorizon.com
Year Established: 1972
Published: Bi-Mthly
Avg Free Circ: 1000
Personnel: Toby Sonneman (Faculty Advisor)

BELMONT

BELMONT ABBEY COLLEGE

Street Address 1: 100 Belmont Mount Holly Rd
State: NC
Zip/Postal code: 28012-2702
Country: USA
Mailing Address: 100 Belmont Mount Holly Rd
Mailing City: Belmont
Mailing State: NC
Mailing ZIP Code: 28012-1802
General/National Adv. Email: albenthall@bac.edu
Display Adv. Email: cathycomeau@bac.edu
Editorial Email: anthonygwyatt@abbey.bac.edu
Website: www.thecrusaderonline.com
Published: Mthly

BELMONT

NOTRE DAME DE NAMUR UNIVERSITY

Street Address 1: 1500 Ralston Ave
State: CA
Zip/Postal code: 94002-1908
Country: USA
Mailing Address: 1500 Ralston Ave
Mailing City: Belmont
Mailing State: CA
Mailing ZIP Code: 94002-1997
General Phone: (650) 508-3500
General Fax: (650) 508-3487
General/National Adv. Email: argonaut@ndnu.edu
Website: www.theargonaut.net
Personnel: Danielle Russo (Adv. Mgr.); Victor Gonzales (Ed.)

BELOIT

BELOIT COLLEGE

Street Address 1: 700 College St
State: WI
Zip/Postal code: 53511-5509
Country: USA

College and University Newspapers

Mailing Address: 700 College St
Mailing City: Beloit
Mailing State: WI
Mailing ZIP Code: 53511-5595
General Phone: (608) 363-2000
General Fax: (608) 363-2718
General/National Adv. Email: admiss@beloit.edu
Website: www.beloit.edu
Delivery Methods: Newsstand
Commercial printers?: N
Personnel: India John (Co Editor-in-Chief); Steven Jackson (Co Editor-in-Chief)

BELTON

UNIV. OF MARY HARDIN-BAYLOR

Street Address 1: 900 College St
Street Address 2: # 8012
State: TX
Zip/Postal code: 76513-2578
Country: USA
Mailing Address: 900 College St # 8012
Mailing City: Belton
Mailing State: TX
Mailing ZIP Code: 76513-2578
General Phone: (254) 295-4598
Website: thebells.umhb.edu
Personnel: Crystal Donahue (Ed.)

BEMIDJI

BEMIDJI STATE UNIV.

Street Address 1: 1500 Birchmont Dr NE
State: MN
Zip/Postal code: 56601-2600
Country: USA
Mailing Address: PO Box 58
Mailing City: Bemidji
Mailing State: MN
Mailing ZIP Code: 56619-0058
General Phone: (218) 755-2001
General Fax: (218) 755-2913
General/National Adv. Email: northernstudent@yahoo.com
Website: www.northernstudent.com
Year Established: 1926
Published: Wed
Avg Free Circ: 3000
Personnel: Robby Robinson (Advisor)

BEND

CENTRAL OREGON COMMUNITY COLLEGE

Street Address 1: 2600 NW College Way
State: OR
Zip/Postal code: 97703-5933
Country: USA
Mailing Address: 2600 NW College Way
Mailing City: Bend
Mailing State: OR
Mailing ZIP Code: 97701-5933
General Phone: (541) 383-7252
General Fax: (541) 383-7284
Editorial Fax: Free
General/National Adv. Email: broadsidemail@cocc.edu
Website: broadside.cocc.edu
Published: Bi-Mthly
Personnel: Leon Pantenburg (advisor)

BENNINGTON

BENNINGTON COLLEGE

Street Address 1: 1 College Dr
State: VT
Zip/Postal code: 05201-6003
Country: USA
Mailing Address: 1 College Dr
Mailing City: Bennington
Mailing State: VT
Mailing ZIP Code: 05201-6004
General Phone: (802) 442-5401
General Fax: (802) 442-6164
Personnel: Veronica Jorgensen (Asst.Dean of Student)

BENNINGTON SOUTHERN VERMONT COLLEGE

Street Address 1: 982 Mansion Dr
State: VT
Zip/Postal code: 05201-9269
Country: USA
Mailing Address: 982 Mansion Dr
Mailing City: Bennington
Mailing State: VT
Mailing ZIP Code: 05201-6002
General Phone: (802) 447-6347
General Fax: (802) 447-4695
General/National Adv. Email: mountainpress@svc.edu
Personnel: Peter Seward (Advisor)

BEREA

BALDWIN-WALLACE COLLEGE

Street Address 1: 275 Eastland Rd
State: OH
Zip/Postal code: 44017-2005
Country: USA
Mailing Address: 275 Eastland Rd
Mailing City: Berea
Mailing State: OH
Mailing ZIP Code: 44017-2088
General Phone: (440) 826-2900
General Fax: (440) 826-8581
General/National Adv. Email: exponent@bw.edu
Personnel: Peter Kerlin (Dir.); Gerrie

BEREA COLLEGE

Street Address 1: Cpo 2150
State: KY
Country: USA
Mailing Address: 2150 Cpo
Mailing City: Berea
Mailing State: KY
Mailing ZIP Code: 40404-0001
General Phone: (859) 985-3208
General Fax: (859) 985-3914
General/National Adv. Email: pinnacle@berea.edu
Website: www.bereacollegepinnacle.com
Personnel: Chris Lakes (Advisor); Kwadwo Juantuah (Ed.)

BERKELEY

UNIV. OF CALIFORNIA BUS. SCHOOL

Street Address 1: Cheit Hall, Rm 138
State: CA
Zip/Postal code: 94720-0001
Country: USA
Mailing Address: Cheit Hall Rm 138
Mailing City: Berkeley
Mailing State: CA
Mailing ZIP Code: 94720-0001
General Phone: (510) 642-7480
General Fax: (510) 643-8764
Personnel: Joe Moss (Ed.)

UNIV. OF CALIFORNIA, BERKELEY

Street Address 1: 2483 Hearst Ave
State: CA
Zip/Postal code: 94709-1320
Country: USA
Mailing Address: 2483 Hearst Avenue Berkeley, CA 94709
Mailing City: Berkeley
Mailing State: CA
Mailing ZIP Code: 94701-1949
General Phone: (510) 548-8300
General Fax: (510) 849-2803
General/National Adv. Email: dailycal@dailycal.org; dailycalifornian@dailycal.org
Display Adv. Email: advertising@dailycal.org
Editorial Email: editor@dailycal.org
Website: www.dailycal.org
Year Established: 1871
Published: Mon`Tues`Thur`Fri

Personnel: Karim Doumar (Editor in Chief and President)

UNIV. OF CALIFORNIA-BERKELEY LAW SCHOOL

Street Address 1: 215 Boalt Hall
State: CA
Zip/Postal code: 94720-0001
Country: USA
Mailing Address: 215 Boalt Hall
Mailing City: Berkeley
Mailing State: CA
Mailing ZIP Code: 94720-0001
General Phone: (510) 642-6483
General Fax: (510) 642-9893
Commercial printers?: N
Personnel: Joshua Rider (Ed.)

BERRIEN SPRINGS

ANDREWS UNIV.

Street Address 1: Student Ctr 05
State: MI
Country: USA
Mailing Address: 5 Student Ctr
Mailing City: Berrien Springs
Mailing State: MI
Mailing ZIP Code: 49104-0001
General Phone: (269) 471-3385
General Fax: (269) 471-3524
General/National Adv. Email: smeditor@andrews.edu
Website: www.andrews.edu/sm
Personnel: Ashleigh Burtnett (Ed. in Chief); Michele Krpalek (Ed.); Stephanie Smart (Asst. Ed.)

BETHANY

BETHANY COLLEGE

Street Address 1: 31 E Campus Dr
State: WV
Zip/Postal code: 26032-3002
Country: USA
Mailing Address: 31 E Campus Dr
Mailing City: Bethany
Mailing State: WV
Mailing ZIP Code: 26032-3002
General Phone: (304) 829-7951
General Fax: (304) 829-7950
General/National Adv. Email: tower@bethanywv.edu
Website: www2.bethanywv.edu/tower
Personnel: Mike King (Advisor)

SOUTHERN NAZARENE UNIV.

Street Address 1: 6729 NW 39th Expy
State: OK
Zip/Postal code: 73008-2605
Country: USA
Mailing Address: 6729 NW 39th Expy
Mailing City: Bethany
Mailing State: OK
Mailing ZIP Code: 73008-2694
General Phone: (405) 491-6382
General Fax: (405) 491-6378
General/National Adv. Email: echo@snu.edu
Display Adv. Email: grwillia@mail.snu.edu
Editorial Email: kirarobe@mail.snu.edu
Website: echo.snu.edu
Published: Fri
Personnel: Pam Broyles (Speech Commun. Dept.); Marcia Feisal (Yearbook); Jim Wilcox (Newspaper); Andrew Baker (Graphic Design); Les Dart (Broadcasting)

BETHLEHEM

LEHIGH UNIV.

Street Address 1: 33 Coppee Dr
State: PA
Zip/Postal code: 18015-3165
Country: USA
Mailing Address: 33 Coppee Dr
Mailing City: Bethlehem
Mailing State: PA
Mailing ZIP Code: 18015-3165
General Phone: (610) 758-4454
General Fax: (610) 758-6198
General/National Adv. Email: bw@lehigh.edu
Website: www.thebrownandwhite.com
Personnel: Wally Trimble (Head); Julie Stewart (Ed. In Chief); Jack Lule (Ed. in Chief)

MORAVIAN COLLEGE

Street Address 1: 1200 Main St
State: PA
Zip/Postal code: 18018-6614
Country: USA
Mailing Address: 1200 Main St
Mailing City: Bethlehem
Mailing State: PA
Mailing ZIP Code: 18018-6650
General Phone: (610) 625-7509
General Fax: (610) 866-1682
General/National Adv. Email: comenian@moravian.edu
Website: comenian.org
Published: Bi-Mthly
Personnel: Mark Harris (Advisor); Kaytlyn Gordon (Editor-in-Chief)

NORTHAMPTON CMTY. COLLEGE

Street Address 1: 3835 Green Pond Rd
State: PA
Zip/Postal code: 18020-7568
Country: USA
Mailing Address: 3835 Green Pond Rd
Mailing City: Bethlehem
Mailing State: PA
Mailing ZIP Code: 18020-7599
General Phone: (610) 861-5372
General Fax: (610) 332-6163
Advertising Phone: (610) 861-5372
Editorial Phone: (610) 861-5372
General/National Adv. Email: thecommuter@northampton.edu
Display Adv. Email: thecommuter@northampton.edu
Editorial Email: thecommuter@northampton.edu
Website: www.ncccommuter.org
Published: Mthly
Avg Free Circ: 2000
Personnel: Rob Hays (Advisor)

BEVERLY

ENDICOTT COLLEGE

Street Address 1: 376 Hale St, Callahan Ctr
State: MA
Zip/Postal code: 1915
Country: USA
Mailing Address: 376 Hale St., Callahan Ctr.
Mailing City: Beverly
Mailing State: MA
Mailing ZIP Code: 01915-2096
General Phone: (978) 232-2050
General Fax: (978) 232-3003
General/National Adv. Email: observer@mail.endicott.edu
Website: www.endicott.edu
Personnel: Abigail Bottome (Advisor)

BIG RAPIDS

FERRIS STATE TORCH.

Street Address 1: 401 South St
Street Address 2: Student Rec Center Room 102
State: MI
Zip/Postal code: 49307-2744
Country: USA
Mailing Address: 401 South St
Mailing City: Big Rapids
Mailing State: MI
Mailing ZIP Code: 49307-2744
General Phone: (231) 591-5946
General Fax: (231) 591-3617

Advertising Phone: 231-591-2609
General/National Adv. Email: torchads@ferris.edu
Editorial Email: torch@ferris.edu
Website: www.fsutorch.com
Year Established: 1931
Special Editions: Welcome Back Orientation Housing Guide
Delivery Methods: Newsstand Racks
Commercial printers?: N
Mechanical specifications: Tabloid 9.75 x 15.0
Published: Wed
Avg Free Circ: 4300
Personnel: Steve Fox (Advisor); Laura Anger (Bus. Mgr.)

BILLINGS

ROCKY MOUNTAIN COLLEGE

Street Address 1: 1511 Poly Dr
State: MT
Zip/Postal code: 59102-1739
Country: USA
Mailing Address: 1511 Poly Dr
Mailing City: Billings
Mailing State: MT
Mailing ZIP Code: 59102-1796
General Phone: (406) 657-1093
General Fax: (406) 259-9751
Personnel: Wilbur Wood (Advisor)

BINGHAMTON

BROOME CMTY. COLLEGE

Street Address 1: PO Box 1017
State: NY
Zip/Postal code: 13902-1017
Country: USA
Mailing Address: PO Box 1017
Mailing City: Binghamton
Mailing State: NY
Mailing ZIP Code: 13902-1017
General Phone: (607) 778-5110
Personnel: Bill Frobe (Ed.)

SUNY/BINGHAMTON

Street Address 1: University Union Rm WB03
State: NY
Zip/Postal code: 13902
Country: USA
Mailing Address: PO Box 6000
Mailing City: Binghamton
Mailing State: NY
Mailing ZIP Code: 13902-6000
General Phone: (607) 777-2515
General Fax: (607) 777-2600
Editorial Email: editor@bupipedream.com
Website: www.bupipedream.com
Personnel: Shinsuke Kawano (Bus. Mgr.); Ashley Tarr (Ed. in Chief); Chris Carpenter (Managing Ed.); Melissa Bykofsky (News Ed.); Teressa (Photo Ed.); Marina (Opinion Ed.)

BIRMINGHAM-SOUTHERN COLLEGE

Street Address 1: 900 Arkadelphia Rd
Street Address 2: # 549014
State: AL
Zip/Postal code: 35254-0002
Country: USA
Mailing Address: 900 Arkadelphia Rd # 549014
Mailing City: Birmingham
Mailing State: AL
Mailing ZIP Code: 35254-0002
General Phone: (205) 226-7706
General/National Adv. Email: hilltop@bsc.edu
Website: www.bsc.edu
Personnel: Peter Donahue (Advisor); Kimmie Farris (Ed. in Chief); Kimmie Sarris (Ed.); Yuan Gong (Bus. Mgr.); Glorious (Adv. Mgr.)

SAMFORD UNIV.

Street Address 1: 800 Lakeshore Dr
State: AL
Zip/Postal code: 35229-0001

Country: USA
Mailing Address: Su # 292269
Mailing City: Birmingham
Mailing State: AL
Mailing ZIP Code: 35229-0001
General Phone: (205) 726-2466
General Fax: (205) 726-2586
Editorial Phone: (205) 726-2998
General/National Adv. Email: crimson@samford.edu
Website: www.samfordcrimson.com
Personnel: Jon Clemmensen (Advisor)

UNIV. OF ALABAMA AT BIRMINGHAM

Street Address 1: 1110 12th St S
State: AL
Zip/Postal code: 35205-5211
Country: USA
Mailing Address: 1110 12th Street South
Mailing City: Birmingham
Mailing State: AL
Mailing ZIP Code: 35205
General Phone: (205) 934-3354
General Fax: (205) 934-8050
General/National Adv. Email: masutton@uab.edu
Display Adv. Email: ads@insideuab.com
Website: studentmedia.uab.edu
Year Established: 1967
Published: Tues
Avg Free Circ: 6000
Personnel: Amy Kilpatrick (Advisor./Adv. Mgr.); Daniel Twieg (Ed. in Chief); Bill Neville (Prodn. Mgr.); Marie Sutton (Director)

BISMARCK

BISMARCK STATE COLLEGE

Street Address 1: 1500 Edwards Ave
State: ND
Zip/Postal code: 58501-1276
Country: USA
Mailing Address: 1500 Edwards Ave
Mailing City: Bismarck
Mailing State: ND
Mailing ZIP Code: 58501-1299
General Phone: (701) 224-5467
General Fax: (701) 224-5529
Editorial Phone: (701) 224-5467
General/National Adv. Email: editor@mystician.org
Website: www.mystician.org
Year Established: 1939
Delivery Methods: Racks
Published: Mthly
Personnel: Karen Bauer (Advisor)

BLACKSBURG

VIRGINIA POLYTECHNIC INSTITUTE

Street Address 1: 365 Squires Student Ctr
State: VA
Zip/Postal code: 24061-1000
Country: USA
Mailing Address: 365 Squires Student Ctr
Mailing City: Blacksburg
Mailing State: VA
Mailing ZIP Code: 24061-1000
General Phone: (540) 231-9870
General Fax: (540) 231-9151
Advertising Phone: (540) 961-9860
Display Adv. Email: advertising@collegemedia.com
Editorial Email: campuseditor@collegiatetimes.com; editor@collegiatetimes.com
Website: www.collegiatetimes.com
Year Established: 1903
Published: Tues`Fri
Personnel: Kiley Thompson (General Manager)
Parent company (for newspapers): Educational Media Company at Virginia Tech

BLACKWOOD

CAMDEN COUNTY COLLEGE

Street Address 1: PO Box 200
State: NJ
Zip/Postal code: 08012-0200
Country: USA
Mailing Address: PO Box 200
Mailing City: Blackwood
Mailing State: NJ
Mailing ZIP Code: 08012-0200
General Phone: (856) 227-7200
General Fax: (856) 227-3541
General/National Adv. Email: campuspress@camdencc.edu
Website: www.camdencc.edu/campuspress

BLOOMINGTON

ILLINOIS WESLEYAN UNIVERSITY

Street Address 1: 104 University Ave
State: IL
Zip/Postal code: 61701-1798
Country: USA
Mailing Address: 104 University Ave
Mailing City: Bloomington
Mailing State: IL
Mailing ZIP Code: 61701-1798
General/National Adv. Email: argus@iwu.edu
Website: www.iwuargus.com
Year Established: 1894
Published: Fri
Personnel: James Plath (Advisor)

INDIANA UNIV.

Street Address 1: 940 E 7th St
Street Address 2: Rm 120
State: IN
Zip/Postal code: 47405-7108
Country: USA
Mailing Address: 940 E 7th St Rm 120
Mailing City: Bloomington
Mailing State: IN
Mailing ZIP Code: 47405-7108
General Phone: (812) 855-0763
General Fax: (812) 855-8009
General/National Adv. Email: ids@indiana.edu
Website: www.idsnews.com
Published: Mon`Tues`Wed`Thur`Fri
Personnel: Susan McGlocklin (Advisor)

INDIANA UNIV. KELLEY SCHOOL OF BUS.

Street Address 1: 1309 E 10th St
State: IN
Zip/Postal code: 47405-1701
Country: USA
Mailing Address: 1309 E 10th St
Mailing City: Bloomington
Mailing State: IN
Mailing ZIP Code: 47405-5308
General Phone: (812) 855-8100
General Fax: (812) 855-9039
Personnel: Chris Hildreth (Ed.)

NORMANDALE COMMUNITY COLLEGE

Street Address 1: 9700 France Ave S
State: MN
Zip/Postal code: 55431-4309
Country: USA
Mailing Address: 9700 France Ave S
Mailing City: Bloomington
Mailing State: MN
Mailing ZIP Code: 55431-4399
General Phone: (952) 358-8129
Advertising Phone: (952) 358-8193
General/National Adv. Email: lionsroar@normandale.edu
Website: www.lionsroar.info
Year Established: 1969
News Services: MCT Campus
Commercial printers?: N

Personnel: Mark Plenke (Advisor)

BLOOMSBURG

BLOOMSBURG UNIV.

Street Address 1: 400 E 2nd St
State: PA
Zip/Postal code: 17815-1301
Country: USA
Mailing Address: 400 E. Second St.
Mailing City: Bloomsburg
Mailing State: PA
Mailing ZIP Code: 17815
General Phone: (570) 389-4457
General Fax: (570) 389-3905
Website: www.bloomu.edu/voice/index.php
Personnel: Mary Bernath (Advisor); Zach Sands (Adv. Dir.); Joe Arleth (Ed. in Chief)

BLUE BELL

MONTGOMERY COUNTY CMTY. COLLEGE

Street Address 1: 340 Dekalb Pike
State: PA
Zip/Postal code: 19422-1412
Country: USA
Mailing Address: 340 Dekalb Pike
Mailing City: Blue Bell
Mailing State: PA
Mailing ZIP Code: 19422-1400
General Phone: (215) 619-7306
General Fax: (215) 619-7191
Personnel: Brian Brendlinger (Dir., Student Activities)

BLUEFIELD

BLUEFIELD COLLEGE

Street Address 1: 3000 College Dr
State: VA
Zip/Postal code: 24605-1737
Country: USA
Mailing Address: 3000 College Dr
Mailing City: Bluefield
Mailing State: VA
Mailing ZIP Code: 24605-1799
General Phone: (276) 326-3682
General Fax: (276) 326-4288
Website: www.bluefield.edu
Personnel: Mimi Merritt (Advisor)

BLUFFTON

BLUFFTON COLLEGE

Street Address 1: 1 University Dr
State: OH
Zip/Postal code: 45817-2104
Country: USA
Mailing Address: 1 University Dr
Mailing City: Bluffton
Mailing State: OH
Mailing ZIP Code: 45817-2104
General Phone: (419) 358-3000
General Fax: (419) 358-3356
General/National Adv. Email: witmarsum@bluffton.edu
Website: www.witmarsum.org
Personnel: Colin Lasu (Advisor); Cyrus Weigand (Bus. Mgr.); Bethany Rayle (Ed.)

BOCA RATON

FLORIDA ATLANTIC UNIV.

Street Address 1: 777 Glades Rd
State: FL
Zip/Postal code: 33431-6424
Country: USA
Mailing Address: 777 Glades Rd
Mailing City: Boca Raton
Mailing State: FL
Mailing ZIP Code: 33431-6496
General Phone: (561) 297-2960

College and University Newspapers

General Fax: (561) 297-2106
General/National Adv. Email: upress@fau.edu
Website: www.upressonline.com
Personnel: Michael Koretzky (Advisor); Devin Desjarlais (Ed. in Chief); Karla Bowsher (Mng. Ed.); Lindsey Voltoline (Art Dir.)

LYNN UNIV.

Street Address 1: 3601 N Military Trl
State: FL
Zip/Postal code: 33431-5507
Country: USA
Mailing Address: 3601 N Military Trl
Mailing City: Boca Raton
Mailing State: FL
Mailing ZIP Code: 33431-5598
General Phone: (561) 237-7463
General Fax: (561) 237-7097
General/National Adv. Email: advertise@lynnipulse.org
Website: www.lynnipulse.org
Personnel: Stefani Powers (Advisor)

BOISE

BOISE STATE UNIV.

Street Address 1: 1910 University Dr
State: ID
Zip/Postal code: 83725-0001
Country: USA
Mailing Address: 1910 University Dr
Mailing City: Boise
Mailing State: ID
Mailing ZIP Code: 83725-0002
General Phone: (208) 426-6300
General Fax: (208) 426-3884
General/National Adv. Email: mcox@boisestate.edu
Website: www.arbiteronline.com
Personnel: Brad Arendt (Gen. Mgr.); V. Marvin Cox (Chrmn.); Steve Lyons (Advisor); Dwight Murphy (Avd. Mgr.); Shannon Morgan (Ed. in Chief)

BOLIVAR

SOUTHWEST BAPTIST UNIV.

Street Address 1: 1600 University Ave
State: MO
Zip/Postal code: 65613-2578
Country: USA
Mailing Address: 1600 University Ave
Mailing City: Bolivar
Mailing State: MO
Mailing ZIP Code: 65613-2597
General Phone: (417) 328-1833
General Fax: (417) 328-1579
General/National Adv. Email: info@omnibusonline.com
Website: www.omnibusonline.com
Personnel: Jessica Oliver (Ed. in Chief); Nicole Heitman (Adv. Mgr.)

BOONE

APPALACHIAN STATE UNIV.

Street Address 1: 217 Plemmons Student Union
State: NC
Country: USA
Mailing Address: Asu # 9025
Mailing City: Boone
Mailing State: NC
Mailing ZIP Code: 28608-0002
General Phone: (828) 262-6149
General Fax: (828) 262-6502
General/National Adv. Email: theapp@appstate.edu
Website: www.theapp.appstate.edu
Personnel: Jon LaFontaine (Ed. in Chief)

BOONEVILLE

NORTHEAST MISSISSIPPI COMMUNITY COLLEGE

Street Address 1: 101 Cunningham Blvd
Street Address 2: Box 67
State: MS
Zip/Postal code: 38829-1726
Country: USA
General Phone: (662) 720-7304
General Fax: (662) 720-7216
Editorial Phone: (662) 720-7421
General/National Adv. Email: beacon@nemcc.edu
Display Adv. Email: beacon@nemcc.edu
Editorial Email: beacon@nemcc.edu
Year Established: 1949
Published: Other
Published Other: Two times each semester
Avg Free Circ: 3600
Personnel: Tony Finch (Advisor); Michael H Miller (Advisor)

BOSSIER CITY

BOSSIER PARISH CMTY. COLLEGE

Street Address 1: 6220 E Texas St
State: LA
Zip/Postal code: 71111-6922
Country: USA
Mailing Address: 6220 E Texas St
Mailing City: Bossier City
Mailing State: LA
Mailing ZIP Code: 71111-6922
General Phone: (318) 678-6000
General Fax: X
General/National Adv. Email: kaleidoscope@bpcc.edu
Website: www.bpcc.edu
Personnel: Candice Gibson (Advisor); Cathy Hammel (Advisor)

BOSTON

BOSTON UNIV.

Street Address 1: 648 Beacon St
State: MA
Zip/Postal code: 02215-2013
Country: USA
Mailing Address: 648 Beacon St
Mailing City: Boston
Mailing State: MA
Mailing ZIP Code: 02215-2013
General Phone: (617) 236-4433
General Fax: (617) 236-4414
General/National Adv. Email: editor@dailyfreepress.com
Display Adv. Email: ads@dailyfreepress.com
Website: www.dailyfreepress.com
Year Established: 1970
Published: Mon`Tues`Wed`Thur
Published Other: Online for summer, breaking content.
Avg Free Circ: 5000
Personnel: Kyle Plantz (Ed.); Felicia Gans (Managing Ed.)

EMERSON COLLEGE

Street Address 1: 150 Boylston St
State: MA
Zip/Postal code: 02116-4608
Country: USA
Mailing Address: 150 Boylston St
Mailing City: Boston
Mailing State: MA
Mailing ZIP Code: 02116-4608
General Phone: (617) 824-8687
General Fax: (617) 824-8908
General/National Adv. Email: berkeley_beacon@emerson.edu
Website: www.berkeleybeacon.com
Personnel: Ric Kahn (Advisor); Matt Byrne (Ed. in Chief); Paddy Shea (Ed. in Chief)

EMMANUEL COLLEGE

Street Address 1: 400 Fenway
State: MA
Zip/Postal code: 02115-5725
Country: USA
Mailing Address: 400 Fenway
Mailing City: Boston
Mailing State: MA
Mailing ZIP Code: 02115-5798
General Phone: (617) 735-9715
General/National Adv. Email: editors@emmanuel.edu
Personnel: Anne Tyson (Ed.)

HARVARD BUSINESS SCHOOL

Street Address 1: Gallatin Hall D Basement
State: MA
Zip/Postal code: 2163
Country: USA
General Phone: (617) 495-6528
General Fax: (617) 495-8619
General/National Adv. Email: general@harbus.org
Website: www.harbus.org
Personnel: Matthew Grayson (Gen.Mgr.); Joanne Knight (Pub.)

MASSACHUSETTS COLLEGE OF PHARMACY

Street Address 1: 179 Longwood Ave
State: MA
Zip/Postal code: 02115-5804
Country: USA
Mailing Address: 179 Longwood Ave
Mailing City: Boston
Mailing State: MA
Mailing ZIP Code: 02115-5896
General Phone: (617) 732-2800
Website: www.mcphs.edu
Personnel: Stephany Orphan (ed.)

NEW ENGLAND SCHOOL OF LAW

Street Address 1: 154 Stuart St
State: MA
Zip/Postal code: 02116-5616
Country: USA
Mailing Address: 154 Stuart St
Mailing City: Boston
Mailing State: MA
Mailing ZIP Code: 02116-5687
General Phone: (617) 451-0010
General Fax: (617) 422-7224
General/National Adv. Email: dueprocess@nesl.edu
Display Adv. Email: dueprocess@nesl.edu
Editorial Email: dueprocess@nesl.edu
Website: https://www.nesl.edu/students/stuorg_dp.cfm
Year Established: 2012
Published: Other
Published Other: Due Process publishes five (5) regular issues, and one (1) end of year commemorative yearbook.
Personnel: Rebecca Castaneda (Ed. in Chief); Tara Cho (Exec. Ed.); Kelly Lavari (Photo Ed.); Joe Sciabica (Editor-In-Chief; Emily White (Assistant Editor-In-Chief)

NORTHEASTERN UNIVERSITY

Street Address 1: 295 Huntington Ave
Street Address 2: Ste 208
State: MA
Zip/Postal code: 02115-4433
Country: USA
Mailing Address: 295 Huntington Ave Ste 208
Mailing City: Boston
Mailing State: MA
Mailing ZIP Code: 02115-4433
General Phone: (857) 362-7325
General Fax: (857) 362-7326
General/National Adv. Email: editor@huntnewsnu.com
Display Adv. Email: advertise@huntnewsnu.com
Editorial Email: editorial@huntnewsnu.com
Website: www.HuntNewsNU.com
Year Established: 1926
Published: Thur
Personnel: Colin Young (Editor in chief)
Parent company (for newspapers): World Series Way Publishing Co., Inc.

SIMMONS COLLEGE

Street Address 1: 300 Fenway
State: MA
Zip/Postal code: 02115-5820
Country: USA
Mailing Address: 300 The Fenway
Mailing City: Boston
Mailing State: MA
Mailing ZIP Code: 02115-5820
General Phone: (617) 521-2442
General Fax: (617) 521-3148
General/National Adv. Email: voice@simmons.edu
Website: www.thesimmonsvoice.com
Published: Thur
Avg Free Circ: 1500
Personnel: James Corcoran (Adviser); Sarah Kinney (Advisor Editor)

SUFFOLK UNIV.

Street Address 1: 41 Temple St
Street Address 2: Rm 428
State: MA
Zip/Postal code: 02114-4241
Country: USA
Mailing Address: 41 Temple St Rm 428
Mailing City: Boston
Mailing State: MA
Mailing ZIP Code: 02114-4241
General Phone: (617) 573-8323
General Fax: (617) 994-6400
General/National Adv. Email: suffolkjournal@gmail.com
Website: www.suffolkjournal.net; www.suffolk.edu
Year Established: 1940
Published: Wed
Personnel: Bruce Butterfield (Advisor); Melissa Hanson; Jeremy Hayes

SUFFOLK UNIV. LAW SCHOOL

Street Address 1: 120 Tremont St
State: MA
Zip/Postal code: 02108-4910
Country: USA
Mailing Address: 120 Tremont St
Mailing City: Boston
Mailing State: MA
Mailing ZIP Code: 02108-4977
General Phone: (617) 305-3011
General Fax: (617) 573-8706

UNIV. OF MASSACHUSETTS

Street Address 1: 100 William T Morrissey Blvd
State: MA
Zip/Postal code: 02125-3300
Country: USA
Mailing Address: 100 Morrissey Blvd
Mailing City: Boston
Mailing State: MA
Mailing ZIP Code: 02125-3393
General Phone: (617) 287-7992
General Fax: (617) 287-7897
General/National Adv. Email: editor@umassmedia.com
Website: www.umassmedia.com
Year Established: 1966
Delivery Methods: Newsstand
Commercial printers?: N
Personnel: Donna Neal (Advisor); Caleb Nelson (Ed.)

BOURBONNAIS

OLIVET NAZARENE UNIV.

Street Address 1: PO Box 592
State: IL
Zip/Postal code: 60914-0592
Country: USA
Mailing Address: PO Box 592
Mailing City: Bourbonnais
Mailing State: IL
Mailing ZIP Code: 60914-0592
General Phone: (815) 939-5315
General Fax: (815) 928-5549
Editorial Email: glimmerglass@olivet.edu

Year Established: 1941
Published: Tues
Personnel: Jay Martinson (Advisor)

BOWIE

BOWIE STATE UNIV.

Street Address 1: 14000 Jericho Park Rd
Street Address 2: Rm 260
State: MD
Zip/Postal code: 20715-3319
Country: USA
Mailing Address: 14000 Jericho Park Rd Rm 260
Mailing City: Bowie
Mailing State: MD
Mailing ZIP Code: 20715-3319
General Phone: (301) 860-3729
General Fax: (301) 860-3714
Personnel: Rex Martin (Advisor); Kristina Rowley (Mng. Ed.); Jocelyn Jones (Asst. Mng. Ed.)

BOWLING GREEN

BOWLING GREEN STATE UNIV.

Street Address 1: 100 Kuhlin Center
State: OH
Zip/Postal code: 43403-0001
Country: USA
Mailing Address: 100 Kuhlin Center
Mailing City: Bowling Green
Mailing State: OH
Mailing ZIP Code: 43403-0001
General Phone: (419) 372-0328
General Fax: (419) 372-0202
Advertising Phone: (419) 372-2606
Advertising Fax: (419) 372-9090
Editorial Phone: (419) 372-6966
Editorial Fax: (419) 372-9090
General/National Adv. Email: thenews@bgnews.com
Display Adv. Email: twhitma@bgsu.edu
Editorial Email: thenews@bgnews.com
Website: www.bgviews.com
Year Established: 1920
Published: Mon`Thur
Avg Free Circ: 4500
Personnel: Robert Bortel (Director of Student Media); Hannah Finnerty; Holly Shively

BOWLING GREEN STATE UNIVERSITY

Street Address 1: 204 West Hall
State: OH
Zip/Postal code: 43403-0001
Country: USA
Mailing Address: 204 W Hall
Mailing City: Bowling Green
Mailing State: OH
Mailing ZIP Code: 43403-0001
General Phone: (419) 372-2607
General/National Adv. Email: thenews@bgnews.com

WESTERN KENTUCKY UNIVERSITY

Street Address 1: 1660 Normal St
Street Address 2: Western Kentucky University
State: KY
Zip/Postal code: 42101-3536
Country: USA
Mailing Address: 1906 College Heights Blvd #11084
Mailing City: Bowling Green
Mailing State: KY
Mailing ZIP Code: 42101-1084
General Phone: (270) 745-2653
Advertising Phone: (270) 745-2653
Editorial Phone: (270) 745-2653
General/National Adv. Email: carrie.pratt@wku.edu
Display Adv. Email: william.hoagland@wku.edu
Editorial Email: herald.editor@wku.edu
Website: www.wkuherald.com

Year Established: 1925
Published: Tues`Thur
Published Other: Topper Extra sports section published on home football days
Avg Free Circ: 7000
Personnel: Sherry West (Operations Mgr); Carrie Pratt (Herald Adviser, Multiplatform News Adviser); Tracy Newton (Office Associate); Will Hoagland (Advt Adviser and Sales Mgr); Chuck Clark (Dir of Student Publications); Sam Oldenburg (Talisman adviser)
Parent company (for newspapers): WKU Student Publications

BOZEMAN

MONTANA STATE UNIV. BOZEMAN

Street Address 1: 305 Strand Union Bldg
State: MT
Zip/Postal code: 59717
Country: USA
Mailing Address: P.O. Box 174140
Mailing City: Bozeman
Mailing State: MT
Mailing ZIP Code: 59717
General Phone: (406) 994-3976
General Fax: (406) 994-2253
Personnel: Amanda Larrinaga (Ed.in.Chief)

BRADFORD

UNIV. OF PITTSBURGH AT BRADFORD

Street Address 1: 300 Campus Dr
State: PA
Zip/Postal code: 16701-2812
Country: USA
Mailing Address: 300 Campus Dr
Mailing City: Bradford
Mailing State: PA
Mailing ZIP Code: 16701-2898
General Phone: (814) 362-7682
General Fax: (814) 362-7518
General/National Adv. Email: source@pitt.edu
Display Adv. Email: tfjz@atlanticbb.net
Editorial Email: tfjz@atlanticbb.net
Personnel: Tim Ziaukas (Advisor)

BREMERTON

OLYMPIC COLLEGE

Street Address 1: 1600 Chester Ave
State: WA
Zip/Postal code: 98337-1600
Country: USA
Mailing Address: 1600 Chester Ave
Mailing City: Bremerton
Mailing State: WA
Mailing ZIP Code: 98337-1699
General Phone: (360) 792-6050
General Fax: (360) 475-7684
General/National Adv. Email: olyeditor@olympic.edu
Website: www.ocolympian.com
Personnel: Michael Prince (Advisor); Jon Miller (Ed.); Josh Nothnagle (Mng. Ed.)

BREVARD

BREVARD COLLEGE

Street Address 1: 1 Brevard Dr
State: NC
Zip/Postal code: 28712
Country: USA
Mailing Address: 1 Brevard Dr.
Mailing City: Brevard
Mailing State: NC
Mailing ZIP Code: 28712
General Phone: (828) 883-8292
General/National Adv. Email: clarion@brevard.edu
Display Adv. Email: clarion@brevard.edu
Editorial Email: clarion@brevard.edu
Website: www.brevard.edu/clarion
Year Established: 1935

Published: Fri
Published Other: August-May (no summer publication)
Avg Free Circ: 300
Personnel: John Padgett (Advisor); Althea Dunn (Editor in Chief, 2013-2014)

BRIDGEPORT

UNIV. OF BRIDGEPORT

Street Address 1: 244 University Ave
State: CT
Zip/Postal code: 06604-7775
Country: USA
Mailing Address: 244 University Ave
Mailing City: Bridgeport
Mailing State: CT
Mailing ZIP Code: 06604-7775
General Phone: (203) 576-4382
General Fax: (203) 576-4493
General/National Adv. Email: scribe@bridgeport.edu
Website: www.thescribeonline.com
Personnel: Richard Unger (Ed. in Chief); Sharon Loh (Ed.)

BRIDGEWATER

BRIDGEWATER COLLEGE

Street Address 1: 101 N 3rd St
State: VA
Zip/Postal code: 22812-1714
Country: USA
Mailing Address: PO Box 193
Mailing City: Bridgewater
Mailing State: VA
Mailing ZIP Code: 22812-0193
General Phone: (540) 828-5329
General Fax: (540) 828-5479
Advertising Phone: (540) 828-5329
Editorial Phone: (540) 828-5329
General/National Adv. Email: veritas@bridgewater.edu
Display Adv. Email: veritas@bridgewater.edu
Editorial Email: veritas@bridgewater.edu
Website: veritas.bridgewater.edu/
Special Editions: yes
Delivery Methods: Carrier`Racks
Commercial printers?: N
Published: Wed
Avg Free Circ: 1700
Personnel: Bernardo Motta (Assistant Professor of Communication Studies)

BRIDGEWATER STATE COLLEGE

Street Address 1: Rondileau Campus Ctr, Rm.103A
State: MA
Country: USA
Mailing Address: Rondileau Campus Ctr Rm 103A
Mailing City: Bridgewater
Mailing State: MA
Mailing ZIP Code: 02325-0001
General Phone: (508) 531-1719
General Fax: (508) 531-6181
General/National Adv. Email: comment@bridgew.edu
Website: www.bsccomment.com
Personnel: Justin McCauley (Advisor); Monica Monteiro (Ed. in Chief)

BRISTOL

KING COLLEGE

Street Address 1: 1350 King College Rd
State: TN
Zip/Postal code: 37620-2632
Country: USA
Mailing Address: 1350 King College Rd
Mailing City: Bristol
Mailing State: TN
Mailing ZIP Code: 37620-2649
General Phone: (423) 652-4829
General Fax: (423) 968-4456

Personnel: Katie Vandebrake (Advisor)

ROGER WILLIAMS UNIV.

Street Address 1: 1 Old Ferry Rd
State: RI
Zip/Postal code: 02809-2923
Country: USA
Mailing Address: 1 Old Ferry Rd
Mailing City: Bristol
Mailing State: RI
Mailing ZIP Code: 02809-2921
General Phone: (401) 254-3229
General Fax: (401) 254-3355
General/National Adv. Email: hawksherald@gmail.com
Website: www.hawksherald.com
Personnel: Ben Whitmore (Ed. in Chief); Adrianne Mukiria (Advisor); Adrianne Henderson (Advisor)

BROCKPORT

THE COLLEGE AT BROCKPORT, SUNY

Street Address 1: 350 New Campus Dr
State: NY
Zip/Postal code: 14420-2997
Country: USA
Mailing Address: 350 New Campus Dr
Mailing City: Brockport
Mailing State: NY
Mailing ZIP Code: 14420-2914
General Phone: (585) 395-2230
General/National Adv. Email: stylus@brockport.edu
Website: www.brockportstylus.org
Year Established: 1914
Published: Wed
Personnel: Alyssa Daley (Editor-in-Chief); Kristina Livingston (Executive Editor); Victoria Martinez (Managing Editor); Breonnah Colon (Campus Talk Editor); Lou Venditti (News Editor); Alexandra Weaver (Lifestyles Editor); Panagiotis Argitis (Sports Editor)

BRONX

BRONX CMTY. COLLEGE

Street Address 1: W 181st St & University Ave
State: NY
Zip/Postal code: 10453
Country: USA
Mailing Address: W. 181st St. & University Ave.
Mailing City: Bronx
Mailing State: NY
Mailing ZIP Code: 10453-2895
General Phone: (718) 289-5445
General Fax: (718) 289-6324
General/National Adv. Email: communicator@bcc.cuny.edu
Website: www.bcc.cuny.edu
Personnel: Andrew Rowan (Advisor)

COLLEGE OF MT. ST. VINCENT

Street Address 1: 6301 Riverdale Ave
State: NY
Zip/Postal code: 10471-1046
Country: USA
Mailing Address: The Mount Times
Mailing City: Bronx
Mailing State: NY
Mailing ZIP Code: 10471-1093
General Phone: (718) 405-3471
Editorial Phone: (516) 474-5563
General/National Adv. Email: mountimes@mountsaintvincent.edu
Editorial Email: nquaranto.student@mountsaintvincent.edu
Year Established: 1980
Published: Bi-Mthly
Personnel: Nicole Quaranto (EIC); Micheal Stephens-Emerson (Co-EIC)

College and University Newspapers

CUNY SCHOOLS

Street Address 1: 250 Bedford Park Blvd W
State: NY
Zip/Postal code: 10468-1527
Country: USA
Mailing Address: 250 Bedford Park Blvd W
Mailing City: Bronx
Mailing State: NY
Mailing ZIP Code: 10468-1527
General Phone: (718) 960-4966
General Fax: (718) 960-7848
General/National Adv. Email: lehmanmeridian@gmail.com
Personnel: Michael Sullivan (Advisor)

FORDHAM UNIV.

Street Address 1: 441 E Fordham Rd, Sta 37, Box B
State: NY
Zip/Postal code: 10458
Country: USA
Mailing Address: 441 E. Fordham Rd., Sta. 37, Box B
Mailing City: Bronx
Mailing State: NY
Mailing ZIP Code: 10458
General Phone: (718) 817-4379
General Fax: (718) 817-4319
General/National Adv. Email: theram@fordham.edu
Website: www.theramonline.com
Personnel: Beth Knobel (Faculty Advisor); Amanda Fiscina (Ed. in Chief); Abigail Forget (Mng. Ed.)

LEHMAN COLLEGE

Street Address 1: 250 Bedford Park Blvd W
Street Address 2: Rm 108
State: NY
Zip/Postal code: 10468-1527
Country: USA
Mailing Address: 250 Bedford Park Blvd W Rm 108
Mailing City: Bronx
Mailing State: NY
Mailing ZIP Code: 10468-1589
General Phone: (718) 960-4966
General Fax: (718) 960-8075
General/National Adv. Email: lehmanmeridian@gmail.com
Website: www.lcmeridian.com
Published: Mthly
Personnel: Jennifer Mackenzie (Advisor); Alisia Cordero (Ed. in Chief); Sidra Lackey (Mng. Ed.)

MANHATTAN COLLEGE

Street Address 1: 4513 Manhattan College Pkwy
State: NY
Zip/Postal code: 10471-4004
Country: USA
Mailing Address: 4513 Manhattan College Pkwy
Mailing City: Riverdale
Mailing State: NY
Mailing ZIP Code: 10471
General Phone: (718) 862-7270
Advertising Phone: (718) 862-8043
General/National Adv. Email: thequad@manhatten.edu
Website: www.mcquadrangle.org
Personnel: Jonathan Stone (Ed. in Chief); Dom Delgardo (Exec. Ed.); Brian O'Connor (Mng. Ed.)

BRONXVILLE

WADE WALLERSTEIN

Street Address 1: 1 Mead Way
State: NY
Zip/Postal code: 10708-5940
Country: USA
Mailing Address: 1 Mead Way
Mailing City: Bronxville
Mailing State: NY
Mailing ZIP Code: 10708-5999
General Phone: (973) 856-2617
General Fax: (973) 856-2617
Advertising Phone: (973) 856-2617
Advertising Fax: (973) 856-2617
Editorial Phone: (973) 856-2617
Editorial Fax: (973) 856-2617
General/National Adv. Email: phoenix@gm.slc.edu; phoenix@slc.edu
Display Adv. Email: phoenix@gm.slc.edu
Editorial Email: wwallerstein@gm.slc.edu
Website: sarahlawrencephoenix.com
Personnel: Wade Wallerstein (Editor-in-Chief)

BROOKHAVEN

OGLETHORPE UNIVERSITY

Street Address 1: 4484 Peachtree Rd NE
State: GA
Zip/Postal code: 30319-2797
Country: USA
Mailing Address: 4484 Peachtree Rd. NE
Mailing City: Atlanta
Mailing State: GA
Mailing ZIP Code: 30319
General Phone: (404) 364-8425
General Fax: (404) 364-8442
General/National Adv. Email: stormypetrel@oglethorpe.edu
Website: 3443 Somerset Trace
Published: Mthly
Personnel: Tali Schroeder (Ed.)

BROOKLYN

CUNY/BROOKLYN COLLEGE

Street Address 1: 2900 Bedford Ave
State: NY
Zip/Postal code: 11210-2850
Country: USA
Mailing Address: 2900 Bedford Ave
Mailing City: Brooklyn
Mailing State: NY
Mailing ZIP Code: 11210-2850
General Phone: (718) 951-5000
General Fax: (718) 434-0875
Editorial Phone: (516) 557-5714
General/National Adv. Email: Dylc23@gmail.com
Display Adv. Email: kingsman.buisness@
Editorial Email: Dylc23@gmail.com
Website: kingsmanbc.com
Published: Tues
Personnel: Paul Moses (Advisor)

KINGSBOROUGH CMTY. COLLEGE

Street Address 1: 2001 Oriental Blvd
Street Address 2: # M230
State: NY
Zip/Postal code: 11235-2333
Country: USA
Mailing Address: 2001 Oriental Blvd # M230
Mailing City: Brooklyn
Mailing State: NY
Mailing ZIP Code: 11235-2333
General Phone: (718) 368-5603
General Fax: (718) 368-4833
General/National Adv. Email: scepter@kingsborough.edu
Website: www.kbcc.cuny.edu/aboutKCC/Scepter
Personnel: Kim Gill (Ed.)

LONG ISLAND UNIV.

Street Address 1: 1 University Plz
Street Address 2: Rm S305
State: NY
Zip/Postal code: 11201-5301
Country: USA
Mailing Address: 1 University Plz Rm S305
Mailing City: Brooklyn
Mailing State: NY
Mailing ZIP Code: 11201-5301
General Phone: (718) 488-1591
General Fax: (718) 780-4182
General/National Adv. Email: seawanhakapress@yahoo.com
Website: seawanhakapress.blogspot.com
Personnel: Hal Bock (Advisor); Ian Smith (Ed. in Chief); Christina Long (News Ed.)

MEDGAR EVERS COLLEGE OF CUNY

Street Address 1: 1637 Bedford Ave
Street Address 2: Rm S-304
State: NY
Zip/Postal code: 11225-2001
Country: USA
Mailing Address: 1637 Bedford Ave Rm S-304
Mailing City: Brooklyn
Mailing State: NY
Mailing ZIP Code: 11225-2001
General Phone: (718) 270-6436
General/National Adv. Email: adafi@mec.cuny.edu; student-club@mec.cuny.edu
Website: www.adafi.org
Personnel: Robin Regina Ford (Advisor); Luc Josaphat (Ed. in Chief); Samantha Sylvester (Mng. Ed.)

POLYTECHNIC INSTITUTE OF NYU

Street Address 1: 6 Metrotech Ctr
State: NY
Zip/Postal code: 11201-3840
Country: USA
Mailing Address: 6 Metrotech Ctr
Mailing City: Brooklyn
Mailing State: NY
Mailing ZIP Code: 11201-3840
General Phone: (718) 260-3600
Website: www.poly.edu
Personnel: Lowell Scheiner (Advisor); Robert Griffin (Coord.); William Modeste Jr. (Ed. in Chief); Cheryl Mcnear (Business Adviser)

PRATT INSTITUTE

Street Address 1: 200 Willoughby Ave
State: NY
Zip/Postal code: 11205-3802
Country: USA
Mailing Address: 200 Willoughby Ave
Mailing City: Brooklyn
Mailing State: NY
Mailing ZIP Code: 11205
General Phone: 7186363600
General/National Adv. Email: theprattler@gmail.com
Editorial Email: theprattler@gmail.com
Website: www.prattleronline.com
Year Established: 1940
Published: Other
Personnel: Emily Oldenquist (Ed. in Cheif)

ST. FRANCIS COLLEGE

Street Address 1: 180 Remsen St
State: NY
Zip/Postal code: 11201-4305
Country: USA
Mailing Address: 180 Remsen St
Mailing City: Brooklyn
Mailing State: NY
Mailing ZIP Code: 11201-4398
General Phone: (718) 522-2300
General Fax: (718) 522-1274
General/National Adv. Email: sscvoice@gmail.com
Personnel: Emily Horowitz (Advisor); Kevin Korber (Ed.)

BROOKVILLE

LONG ISLAND UNIV./C.W.POST

Street Address 1: Hillwood Commons, Rm 199, 720 Northern Blvd (25A)
State: NY
Zip/Postal code: 11548
Country: USA
Mailing Address: Hillwood Commons, Rm. 199, 720 Northern Blvd. (25A)
Mailing City: Brookville
Mailing State: NY
Mailing ZIP Code: 11548
General Phone: (516) 299-2619
General Fax: (516) 299-2617
General/National Adv. Email: pioneer@cwpost.liu.edu
Year Established: 1954
Personnel: Valerie Kellogg (Advisor); Daniel Schrafel (Ed. in Chief); Lisa Martens (News Ed.)

BROWNSVILLE

UNIVERSITY OF TEXAS AT BROWNSVILLE

Street Address 1: 1 W University Blvd
Street Address 2: Student Union 1.16
State: TX
Zip/Postal code: 78520-4933
Country: USA
Mailing Address: 1 West University Boulevard
Mailing City: Brownsville
Mailing State: TX
Mailing ZIP Code: 78520-4956
General Phone: (956) 882-5143
General Fax: (956) 882-5176
General/National Adv. Email: collegian@utb.edu
Display Adv. Email: collegian.advertising@utb.edu
Editorial Email: collegian@utb.edu
Website: utbcollegian.com
Published: Mon
Avg Free Circ: 4000
Personnel: Azenett Cornejo (Advisor); Cleiri Quezada (Editor)

BRUNSWICK

BOWDOIN COLLEGE

Street Address 1: 6200 College Sta
State: ME
Zip/Postal code: 04011-8462
Country: USA
Mailing Address: 6200 College Sta
Mailing City: Brunswick
Mailing State: ME
Mailing ZIP Code: 04011-8462
General Phone: (207) 725-3300
General Fax: (207) 725-3975
General/National Adv. Email: orient@bowdoin.edu
Display Adv. Email: orientads@bowdoin.edu
Website: orient.bowdoin.edu/orient
Personnel: Zoe Lescaze; Lizzy Tarr (Bus. Mgr.); Will Jacob (Ed. in Chief); Gemma Leghorn (Ed. in Chief)

BRYN MAWR

BRYN MAWR-HAVERFORD COLLEGE

Street Address 1: 101 N Merion Ave
State: PA
Zip/Postal code: 19010-2859
Country: USA
Mailing Address: 101 N Merion Ave
Mailing City: Bryn Mawr
Mailing State: PA
Mailing ZIP Code: 19010-2899
General Phone: (610) 526-5000
General Fax: (610) 526-7479
General/National Adv. Email: biconews@haverford.edu
Website: www.biconews.com
Personnel: Eurie Kim (Bus. Mgr.); Sam Kaplan (Ed. in Chief); Dave Merrell (Ed. Emer./Web Ed.)

BUFFALO

CANISIUS COLLEGE

Street Address 1: 2001 Main St
State: NY
Zip/Postal code: 14208-1035
Country: USA
Mailing Address: 2001 Main St
Mailing City: Buffalo
Mailing State: NY

Mailing ZIP Code: 14208-1098
General Phone: (716) 888-2115
General Fax: (716) 888-3118
General/National Adv. Email: Irwin@canisius.edu
Personnel: Barbara Irwin (Professor of Communications); Eric Koehler (Ed.); Jennifer Gorczynski (Ed.); Marisa Loffredo (News Ed.)

MEDAILLE COLLEGE

Street Address 1: 18 Agassiz Cir
State: NY
Zip/Postal code: 14214-2601
Country: USA
Mailing Address: 18 Agassiz Cir
Mailing City: Buffalo
Mailing State: NY
Mailing ZIP Code: 14214-2695
General Phone: (716) 884-3281
General Fax: (716) 884-0291
Website: www.medailleperspective.com
Personnel: Lisa Murphy (Advisor); Megan Fitzgerald (Ed.)

SUNY COLLEGE/BUFFALO

Street Address 1: 1300 Elmwood Ave, Student Union 414
State: NY
Zip/Postal code: 14222
Country: USA
Mailing Address: 1300 Elmwood Ave., Student Union 414
Mailing City: Buffalo
Mailing State: NY
Mailing ZIP Code: 14222
General Phone: (716) 878-4531
General Fax: (716) 878-4532
General/National Adv. Email: bscrecord@gmail.com
Display Adv. Email: pignatelli.record@live.com
Editorial Email: bscrecord@gmail.com
Website: www.bscrecord.com
Year Established: 1913
Published: Wed
Avg Free Circ: 1500
Personnel: Brandon Schlager (Managing Editor); Mike Meiler (Executive Editor); Brian Alexander (Opinion Editor); Michael Canfield (News Editor); Tom Gallagher (Sports Editor); Jennifer Waters (Culture Editor)

SUNY/BUFFALO

Street Address 1: 132 Student Un
State: NY
Zip/Postal code: 14260-2100
Country: USA
Mailing Address: 132 Student Un
Mailing City: Buffalo
Mailing State: NY
Mailing ZIP Code: 14260-2100
General Phone: (716) 645-2152
General Fax: (716) 645-2766
General/National Adv. Email: spectrum@buffalo.edu
Website: www.ubspectrum.com
Personnel: Debbie Smith (Bus. Mgr.); Steven Marth (Ed. in Chief)

BUIES CREEK

CAMPBELL UNIV.

Street Address 1: PO Box 130
Street Address 2: 165 Dr. McKoy Drive
State: NC
Zip/Postal code: 27506-0130
Country: USA
Mailing Address: PO Box 130
Mailing City: Buies Creek
Mailing State: NC
Mailing ZIP Code: 27506-0130
General Phone: (910) 893-1200
General Fax: (910) 893-1924
Website: www.campbell.edu
Published: Bi-Mthly

Personnel: Michael Smith (Advisor); Courtney Schultz (editor)

BURLINGTON

UNIVERSITY OF VERMONT

Street Address 1: Uvm Student Life
Street Address 2: 590 Main St. #310
State: VT
Zip/Postal code: 05405-0001
Country: USA
Mailing Address: UVM Student Life
Mailing City: Burlington
Mailing State: VT
Mailing ZIP Code: 05405
General Phone: (802) 656-4412
General Fax: (802) 656-8482
General/National Adv. Email: crevans@uvm.edu
Display Adv. Email: crevans@uvm.edu
Editorial Email: crevans@uvm.edu
Website: https://vtcynic.com/
Year Established: 1883
Published: Wed
Avg Free Circ: 5000
Personnel: Chris Evans (Adv.)

BUTLER

BUTLER COUNTY CMTY. COLLEGE

Street Address 1: 107 College Dr
State: PA
Zip/Postal code: 16002-3807
Country: USA
Mailing Address: PO Box 1203
Mailing City: Butler
Mailing State: PA
Mailing ZIP Code: 16003-1203
General Phone: (724) 287-8711
General Fax: (724) 285-6047
General/National Adv. Email: cube.stass@bc3.edu
Website: www.bc3.edu
Personnel: David Moser (Advisor); Patrick Reddick (Ed.)

BUTTE

MONTANA TECH. UNIV.

Street Address 1: 1300 W Park St
State: MT
Zip/Postal code: 59701-8932
Country: USA
Mailing Address: 1300 W Park St
Mailing City: Butte
Mailing State: MT
Mailing ZIP Code: 59701-8932
General Phone: (406) 496-4241
General Fax: (406) 496-4702
General/National Adv. Email: technocrat@mtech.edu
Personnel: Patrick Munday (Advisor)

CALDWELL

COLLEGE OF IDAHO

Street Address 1: 2112 Cleveland Blvd
State: ID
Zip/Postal code: 83605-4432
Country: USA
Mailing Address: PO Box 52
Mailing City: Caldwell
Mailing State: ID
Mailing ZIP Code: 83606-0052
General Phone: (208) 459-5509
General Fax: (208) 459-5849
Website: www.collegeofidaho.edu/media/phonebooks/default.asp?dpt=COYN
Delivery Methods: Carrier
Commercial printers?: N
Personnel: Danielle Blenker (Pres.); Nicole Watson (Vice Pres.); Debbie Swanson (Administrative Asst.); Colleen Smith (Ed.)

CAMBRIDGE

HARVARD LAW SCHOOL

Street Address 1: Harvard Law Record, Harvard Law School
State: MA
Zip/Postal code: 2138
Country: USA
Mailing Address: Harvard Law Record, Harvard Law School
Mailing City: Cambridge
Mailing State: MA
Mailing ZIP Code: 02138-9984
General Phone: (617) 297-3590
General Fax: (617) 495-8547
General/National Adv. Email: record@law.harvard.edu
Website: www.hlrecord.org
Personnel: Matt Hutchins (Ed. in Chief); Chris Szabla (Ed. in Chief); Rebecca Agule (News Ed.); Mark Samburg (Sports Ed.)

HARVARD UNIV.

Street Address 1: 14 Plympton St
State: MA
Zip/Postal code: 02138-6606
Country: USA
Mailing Address: 14 Plympton St
Mailing City: Cambridge
Mailing State: MA
Mailing ZIP Code: 02138-6606
General Phone: (617) 576-6600
General Fax: (617) 576-7860
General/National Adv. Email: ads@thecrimson.com
Website: www.thecrimson.com
Personnel: Peter F. Zhu (Pres.); Julian L. Bouma (Bus. Mgr)

HARVARD UNIV./JFK SCHOOL OF GOV'T

Street Address 1: 30 Jfk St
State: MA
Zip/Postal code: 02138-4902
Country: USA
Mailing Address: 30 Jfk St
Mailing City: Cambridge
Mailing State: MA
Mailing ZIP Code: 02138-4902
General Phone: (617) 495-5969
Personnel: Stephanie Geosits (Ed.)

LESLEY UNIVERSITY

Street Address 1: 47 Oxford St
State: MA
Zip/Postal code: 02138-1902
Country: USA
Mailing Address: 47 Oxford St
Mailing City: Cambridge
Mailing State: MA
Mailing ZIP Code: 02138-1972
General Phone: (617) 349-8501
General Fax: (617) 349-8558
Website: www.chronicle.com
Personnel: Gabriella Montell (Assoc. Ed.)

MASSACHUSETTS INST. OF TECHNOLOGY

Street Address 1: 84 Massachusetts Ave
Street Address 2: Ste 483
State: MA
Zip/Postal code: 02139-4300
Country: USA
Mailing Address: 84 Massachusetts Ave Ste 483
Mailing City: Cambridge
Mailing State: MA
Mailing ZIP Code: 02139-4300
General Phone: (617) 253 1541
General Fax: (617) 258-8226
General/National Adv. Email: general@tech.mit.edu; letters@the-tech.mit.edu

Display Adv. Email: ads@tech.mit.edu
Website: thetech.com
Year Established: 1881
Commercial printers?: Y
Published: Thur
Avg Free Circ: 8100
Personnel: Aislyn Schalck (Chrmn.); Jessica Pourian (Ed. in Chief); Karleigh Moore (Chairman)

CAMDEN

RUTGERS UNIV.

Street Address 1: 326 Penn St
State: NJ
Zip/Postal code: 08102-1410
Country: USA
Mailing Address: 326 Penn St
Mailing City: Camden
Mailing State: NJ
Mailing ZIP Code: 08102-1412
General Phone: (856) 225-6304
General Fax: (856) 225-6579
General/National Adv. Email: gleaner@camden.rutgers.edu
Website: gleaner.camden.rutgers.edu
Personnel: Joe Capuzzo (Advisor)

CAMPBELLSVILLE

CAMPBELLSVILLE UNIVERSITY

Street Address 1: Up 897 Campbellsville University
State: KY
Zip/Postal code: 42718
County: Taylor
Country: USA
Mailing Address: 1 University Dr.
Mailing City: Campbellsville
Mailing State: KY
Mailing ZIP Code: 42718
General Phone: (270) 789-5035
General Fax: (270)789-5145
Website: www.campbellsville.edu/campus-times
Published Other: Monthly when school is in session
Avg Free Circ: 2000

CANTON

CULVER-STOCKTON COLLEGE

Street Address 1: 1 College Hl
State: MO
Zip/Postal code: 63435-1257
Country: USA
Mailing Address: 1 College Hl
Mailing City: Canton
Mailing State: MO
Mailing ZIP Code: 63435-1299
General Phone: (573) 231-6371
General Fax: (573) 231-6611
General/National Adv. Email: swiegenstein@culver.edu
Website: www.culver.edu
Year Established: 1853
Personnel: Fred Berger (Asst. Prof Comm.); Tyler Tomlinson (Lecturer in Comm.)

MALONE COLLEGE

Street Address 1: 2600 Cleveland Ave NW
State: OH
Zip/Postal code: 44709-3308
Country: USA
Mailing Address: 2600 Cleveland Ave NW
Mailing City: Canton
Mailing State: OH
Mailing ZIP Code: 44709-3308
General Phone: (330) 471-8212
General Fax: (330) 454-6977
Website: www.theaviso.org
Year Established: 1958
Personnel: David Dixon (Advisor)

College and University Newspapers

MALONE UNIVERSITY
Street Address 1: 2600 Cleveland Ave NW
State: OH
Zip/Postal code: 44709-3308
Country: USA
Mailing Address: 2600 Cleveland Ave NW
Mailing City: Canton
Mailing State: OH
Mailing ZIP Code: 44709-3897
General Phone: 330-471-8277
Website: theaviso.org/

ST. LAWRENCE UNIV.
Street Address 1: 23 Romoda Dr
State: NY
Zip/Postal code: 13617-1423
Country: USA
Mailing Address: 23 Romoda Dr
Mailing City: Canton
Mailing State: NY
Mailing ZIP Code: 13617-1501
General Phone: (315) 229-5139
General/National Adv. Email: hillnews@stlawu.edu
Website: www.blogs.stlawu.edu/thehillnews
Personnel: Juri Kittler (Advisor); Rachel Barman (Ed.)

SUNY COLLEGE OF TECHNOLOGY/CANTON
Street Address 1: 34 Cornell Dr
Street Address 2: Ofc
State: NY
Zip/Postal code: 13617-1037
Country: USA
Mailing Address: 34 Cornell Dr Ofc
Mailing City: Canton
Mailing State: NY
Mailing ZIP Code: 13617-1037
General Phone: (315) 386-7315
General Fax: (315) 386-7962
General/National Adv. Email: quinells@canton.edu
Personnel: Scott Quinell (Advisor)

WEST TEXAS A&M UNIV.
Street Address 1: PO Box 60747
State: TX
Zip/Postal code: 79016-0001
Country: USA
Mailing Address: PO Box 60747
Mailing City: Canyon
Mailing State: TX
Mailing ZIP Code: 79016-0001
General Phone: (806) 651-2410
General Fax: (806) 651-2818
Advertising Phone: (806) 651-2413
General/National Adv. Email: bleschper@mail.wtamu.edu; theprairiemail@yahoo.com
Website: www.theprairieonline.com; www.theprairienews.com
Personnel: Christaan Eayrs (Advisor); Joe Dowd (Bus. Mgr.); Kayla Goodman (Ed.)

CAPE GIRARDEAU

SOUTHEAST MISSOURI STATE UNIV.
Street Address 1: 1 University Plz
Street Address 2: MS 2225
State: MO
Zip/Postal code: 63701-4710
Country: USA
Mailing Address: 1 University Plz MS 2225
Mailing City: Cape Girardeau
Mailing State: MO
Mailing ZIP Code: 63701-4710
General Phone: (573) 651-2540
General Fax: (573) 651-2825
Editorial Email: thearrow.news@gmail.com
Website: www.capahaarrow.com
Personnel: Sam Blackwell (Advisor); Erin Mustain (Ed. in Chief); Ben Marxer (Arts/Entertainment Ed.)

CARBONDALE

SOUTHERN ILLINOIS UNIV.
Street Address 1: 1100 Lincoln Dr
State: IL
Zip/Postal code: 62901-4306
Country: USA
Mailing Address: Communications Bldg, 1100 Lincoln Dr
Mailing City: Carbondale
Mailing State: IL
Mailing ZIP Code: 62901
General Phone: (618) 536-3311
General Fax: (618) 453-3248
General/National Adv. Email: deadvert@siu.edu
Website: www.siude.com
Year Established: 1916
Personnel: Eric J. Fidler (Advisor/Mng. Ed.); Jerry Bush (Bus./Adv. Dir.); Sherri Killion (Classified Mgr.); Andrea Zimmerman (Ed. in Chief); Diana (Ed. in Chief); Derek (Features Ed.); Edyta (Photo Ed.); Stile (Sports Ed.); Ashley (Webmaster)

CARLISLE

DICKINSON COLLEGE
Street Address 1: PO Box 1773
State: PA
Zip/Postal code: 17013-2896
Country: USA
Mailing Address: PO Box 1773
Mailing City: Carlisle
Mailing State: PA
Mailing ZIP Code: 17013-2896
General Phone: (717) 254-8434
General Fax: (717) 254-8430
General/National Adv. Email: dsonian@dickinson.edu
Website: www.dickinson.edu/dickinsonian
Personnel: Alec Johnson (Ed. in Chief); Eddie Small (Mng. Ed.)

CARROLLTON

STATE UNIV. OF WEST GEORGIA
Street Address 1: 1601 Maple St
State: GA
Zip/Postal code: 30118-0001
Country: USA
Mailing Address: 1601 Maple St
Mailing City: Carrollton
Mailing State: GA
Mailing ZIP Code: 30118-0002
General Phone: (678) 839-5000
Website: www.westga.edu
Personnel: Stephanie Smith (Adv. Mgr.)

CARSON

CALIFORNIA STATE UNIV. DOMINGUEZ
Street Address 1: 1000 E Victoria St
Street Address 2: Dept Sac
State: CA
Zip/Postal code: 90747-0001
Country: USA
Mailing Address: 1000 E Victoria St Dept Sac
Mailing City: Carson
Mailing State: CA
Mailing ZIP Code: 90747-0001
General Phone: (310) 243-2312
General Fax: (310) 217-6935
General/National Adv. Email: bulletin@csudh.edu
Display Adv. Email: Advertise@csudh.edu
Website: www.csudh.edu/bulletin
Published: Wed
Published Other: Bi-Weekly
Personnel: Catherine Risling (Advisor); Marjan Khorashadi-Zadeh (Adv. Mgr.); Karen Mossiah (Prodn. Mgr.)

CARTERVILLE

JOHN A. LOGAN COLLEGE
Street Address 1: 700 Logan College Dr
State: IL
Zip/Postal code: 62918-2500
Country: USA
Mailing Address: 700 Logan College Dr
Mailing City: Carterville
Mailing State: IL
Mailing ZIP Code: 62918-2501
General Phone: (618) 985-2828
General Fax: (618) 985-4654
General/National Adv. Email: volunteernews@jalc.edu
Personnel: Matt Garrison (Advisor); Tara Fasol (Ed.)

CARTHAGE

PANOLA COLLEGE
Street Address 1: 1109 W Panola St
State: TX
Zip/Postal code: 75633-2341
Country: USA
Mailing Address: 1109 W Panola St
Mailing City: Carthage
Mailing State: TX
Mailing ZIP Code: 75633-2397
General Phone: (903) 693-2079
General Fax: (903) 693-5588
Website: www.panola.edu
Personnel: Teresa Beasley (Advisor)

CASPER

CASPER COLLEGE
Street Address 1: 125 College Dr
Street Address 2: # CE-109
State: WY
Zip/Postal code: 82601-4612
Country: USA
Mailing Address: 125 College Dr # CE-109
Mailing City: Casper
Mailing State: WY
Mailing ZIP Code: 82601-4699
General Phone: (307) 268-2100
General Fax: (307) 268-2203
Personnel: Pete Vanhouten (Advisor); Derek Schroder (Ed.)

CEDAR CITY

SOUTHERN UTAH UNIV.
Street Address 1: 351 W University Blvd
Street Address 2: University Journal
State: UT
Zip/Postal code: 84720-2415
Country: USA
Mailing Address: 351 W University Blvd
Mailing City: Cedar City
Mailing State: UT
Mailing ZIP Code: 84720-2415
General Phone: (435) 865-8226
Advertising Phone: 435-704-4733
Editorial Phone: 435-865-8226
General/National Adv. Email: journal@suu.edu
Display Adv. Email: Gholdston@suuews.com
Editorial Email: journal@suu.edu
Website: www.suunews.com
Year Established: 1937
News Services: TMS
Special Editions: Graduation Edition
Delivery Methods: Newsstand`Racks
Commercial printers?: Y
Published: Mon`Thur
Avg Free Circ: 2000
Personnel: John Gholdston (Advisor)
Parent company (for newspapers): Southern Utah University

CEDAR FALLS

UNIV. OF NORTHERN IOWA
Street Address 1: L011 Maucker Union
State: IA
Zip/Postal code: 50614-0001
Country: USA
Mailing Address: L011 Maucker Un
Mailing City: Cedar Falls
Mailing State: IA
Mailing ZIP Code: 50614-0001
General Phone: (319) 273-2157
General Fax: (319) 273-5931
General/National Adv. Email: northern-iowan@uni.edu
Website: www.northerniowan.com
Published: Mon`Thur
Avg Free Circ: 5000
Personnel: Michele Smith (Mgr.); Dana Klesner (Office Asst.); Seth Hadenfelt (Sales); Alex Johansen (Circ.); Jeremy (Circ.); Nikki (Exec. Ed.); Larissa (News Ed.); Anna (Prodn.)

CEDAR RAPIDS

COE COLLEGE
Street Address 1: 1220 1st Ave NE
State: IA
Zip/Postal code: 52402-5008
Country: USA
Mailing Address: 1220 1st Ave NE # 1
Mailing City: Cedar Rapids
Mailing State: IA
Mailing ZIP Code: 52402-5092
General Phone: (319) 399-8646
General Fax: (319) 399-8667
General/National Adv. Email: cosmos@coe.edu
Website: www.coe.edu
Year Established: 1889
Published: Fri
Personnel: Susanne Gubanc (Advisor)

KIRKWOOD COMMUNITY COLLEGE
Street Address 1: 6301 Kirkwood Blvd SW
State: IA
Zip/Postal code: 52404-5260
Country: USA
Mailing Address: 6301 Kirkwood Blvd. SW
Mailing City: Cedar Rapids
Mailing State: IA
Mailing ZIP Code: 52404
General Phone: (319) 398-5444
General Fax: (319) 398-7141
General/National Adv. Email: communique@kirkwood edu.
Website: www.kirkwoodstudentmedia.com
Published Other: six times each semester
Personnel: Sarah Baker (Advisor); Rose Kodet (Publisher)

MT. MERCY COLLEGE
Street Address 1: 1330 Elmhurst Dr NE
State: IA
Zip/Postal code: 52402-4763
Country: USA
Mailing Address: 1330 Elmhurst Dr NE
Mailing City: Cedar Rapids
Mailing State: IA
Mailing ZIP Code: 52402-4797
General Phone: (319) 363-1323
General Fax: (319) 366-0893
General/National Adv. Email: mmctimes@mtmercy.edu
Website: times.mtmercy.edu
Personnel: Joe Sheller (Advisor); Mellette Maurice (Bus. Mgr.); Brian Heinemann (Ed.)

CEDARVILLE

CEDARVILLE UNIV.
Street Address 1: 251 N Main St
State: OH
Zip/Postal code: 45314-8501
Country: USA

Mailing Address: 251 N Main St
Mailing City: Cedarville
Mailing State: OH
Mailing ZIP Code: 45314-8564
General Phone: (937) 766-3298
General Fax: (937) 766-3456
General/National Adv. Email: cedars@cedarville.edu
Display Adv. Email: jgilbert@cedarville.edu
Website: cedars.cedarville.edu/
Published: Mthly
Avg Free Circ: 1200
Personnel: Jeff Gilbert (Faculty adviser)

CENTER VALLEY

DESALES UNIV.

Street Address 1: 2755 Station Ave
State: PA
Zip/Postal code: 18034-9565
Country: USA
Mailing Address: 2755 Station Ave
Mailing City: Center Valley
Mailing State: PA
Mailing ZIP Code: 18034-9568
General Phone: (610) 282-1100
General Fax: (610) 282-3798
General/National Adv. Email: minstrel.desales@gmail.com
Website: www.desalesminstrel.org
Published: Bi-Mthly
Personnel: Kellie Dietrich (Editor-in-Chief)

CENTRAL ISLIP

TOURO COLLEGE JACOB D. FUCHSBERG LAW CENTER

Street Address 1: 225 Eastview Dr
State: NY
Zip/Postal code: 11722-4539
Country: USA
Mailing Address: 225 Eastview Dr
Mailing City: Central Islip
Mailing State: NY
Mailing ZIP Code: 11722-4539
General Phone: (631) 761-7000
General Fax: (631) 761-7009
Website: www.tourolaw.edu
Personnel: Patti Desrochers (Dir. Comm.)

CENTRALIA

KASKASKIA COLLEGE

Street Address 1: 27210 College Rd
State: IL
Zip/Postal code: 62801-7800
Country: USA
Mailing Address: 27210 College Rd
Mailing City: Centralia
Mailing State: IL
Mailing ZIP Code: 62801-7878
General Phone: (618) 545-3000
General Fax: (618) 532-2365
Website: scroll.kaskaskia.edu
Personnel: Dale Hill (Advisor); Nathan Wilkins (Advisor); Sue Hardebeck (Advisor)

CHADRON

CHADRON STATE COLLEGE

Street Address 1: 1000 Main St
Street Address 2: # 235
State: NE
Zip/Postal code: 69337-2667
Country: USA
Mailing Address: 1000 Main St # 235
Mailing City: Chadron
Mailing State: NE
Mailing ZIP Code: 69337-2690
General Phone: (308) 432-6303
Advertising Phone: (308) 432-6304
General/National Adv. Email: editor@csceagle.com
Display Adv. Email: ads@csceagle.com
Editorial Email: opinion@csceagle.com
Website: www.csceagle.com
Year Established: 1920
Published: Thur
Avg Free Circ: 4000
Personnel: Michael D. Kennedy (Advisor); Jordyn Hulinsky (Mgr Ed); Janelle Kesterson (Opinion Ed); Angie Webb (Advt Dir); Preston Goehring (Sports Ed); Justine Stone (Lifestyles Ed); Melanie Nelson (News Ed)

CHAMBERSBURG

WILSON COLLEGE

Street Address 1: 1015 Philadelphia Ave
State: PA
Zip/Postal code: 17201-1279
Country: USA
Mailing Address: 1015 Philadelphia Ave
Mailing City: Chambersburg
Mailing State: PA
Mailing ZIP Code: 17201-1285
General Phone: (717) 264-4141
General Fax: (717) 264-1578
Personnel: Aimee-Marie Dorsten (Advisor)

CHAMPAIGN

PARKLAND COLLEGE

Street Address 1: 2400 W Bradley Ave
Street Address 2: Rm X-155
State: IL
Zip/Postal code: 61821-1806
Country: USA
Mailing Address: 2400 W Bradley Ave Rm X-155
Mailing City: Champaign
Mailing State: IL
Mailing ZIP Code: 61821-1899
General Phone: (217) 351-2216
Advertising Phone: 217 351-2206
General/National Adv. Email: prospectus@parkland.edu
Display Adv. Email: prospectusads@parkland.edu
Editorial Email: prospectus.editor@gmail.com
Website: www.prospectusnews.com
Year Established: 1969
Published: Wed
Avg Free Circ: 1000
Personnel: John Eby (Advisor); Sean Herman (Ed. in Chief)

UNIV. OF ILLINOIS

Street Address 1: 512 E Green St
State: IL
Zip/Postal code: 61820-6483
Country: USA
Mailing Address: 512 E Green St
Mailing City: Champaign
Mailing State: IL
Mailing ZIP Code: 61820-5720
General Phone: (217) 337-8300
General Fax: (217) 337-8303
Advertising Phone: 2173378382
Advertising Fax: 2173378303
Editorial Phone: 2173378350
Editorial Fax: 2173378328
Display Adv. Email: adsales@illinimedia.com
Editorial Email: news@illinimedia.com
Website: www.dailyillini.com
Year Established: 1871
Published: Mon`Tues`Wed`Thur
Avg Free Circ: 10000
Personnel: Lilyan Levant (Advisor); Nancy Elliott (Adv. Dir.); Darshan Patel (Ed. in Chief); Travis Truitt (Ad Director)
Parent company (for newspapers): Illini Media Company

CHAPEL HILL

THE DAILY TAR HEEL

Street Address 1: 151 E Rosemary St
State: NC
Zip/Postal code: 27514-3539
County: Orange
Country: USA
Mailing Address: 151 E Rosemary St
Mailing City: Chapel Hill
Mailing State: NC
Mailing ZIP Code: 27514-3539
General Phone: (919) 962-1163
Advertising Phone: 919.962.1163
Editorial Phone: 919.962.0245
General/National Adv. Email: sales@dailytarheel.com
Display Adv. Email: sales@dailytarheel.com
Editorial Email: dth@dailytarheel.com
Website: dailytarheel.com
Year Established: 1893
Personnel: Elise Young (Managing Ed.)

UNIV. OF NORTH CAROLINA - THE DAILY TAR HEEL

Street Address 1: 151 E Rosemary St
State: NC
Zip/Postal code: 27514-3539
Country: USA
Mailing Address: 151 E Rosemary St
Mailing City: Chapel Hill
Mailing State: NC
Mailing ZIP Code: 27514-3539
General Phone: (919) 962-1163
General Fax: (919) 962-1609
Editorial Phone: 919=962-0245
Display Adv. Email: ads@unc.edu
Editorial Email: dth@dailytarheel.com
Website: www.dailytarheel.com
Year Established: 1893
Delivery Methods: Newsstand
Commercial printers?: N
Published: Mon`Tues`Wed`Thur`Fri
Avg Free Circ: 17000
Personnel: Erica Perel (Advisor); Megan Mcginity (Adv. Mgr.)

UNIV. OF NORTH CAROLINA LAW SCHOOL

Street Address 1: Cb #3380, Vanhecke-Wettach Hall
State: NC
Zip/Postal code: 27599-0001
Country: USA
Mailing Address: 3380 Vanhecke-Wettach Hall
Mailing City: Chapel Hill
Mailing State: NC
Mailing ZIP Code: 27599-0001
General Phone: (919) 962-6200

CHARLESTON

COLLEGE OF CHARLESTON

Street Address 1: 66 George St
State: SC
Zip/Postal code: 29424-0001
Country: USA
Mailing Address: 66 George St
Mailing City: Charleston
Mailing State: SC
Mailing ZIP Code: 29424-0001
General Phone: (843) 953-7017
General Fax: (843) 953-7037
General/National Adv. Email: mcgeeb@cofc.edu
Website: www.cofc.edu/communication
Personnel: Brian McGee (Chair); Katie Orlando (Ed. in Chief)

EASTERN ILLINOIS UNIV.

Street Address 1: 600 Lincoln Ave
State: IL
Zip/Postal code: 61920-3011
Country: USA
Mailing Address: 600 Lincoln Ave.
Mailing City: Charleston
Mailing State: IL
Mailing ZIP Code: 61920
General Phone: (217) 581-2812
General Fax: (217) 581-2923
General/National Adv. Email: DENeic@gmail.com; DENnewsdesk@gmail.com; DENNews.com@gmail.com
Website: www.dailyeasternnews.com/
Personnel: Taylor Angelo (Ed. In chief); Lola Burnham (Advisor); Emily Steele (News Ed.); Chris Lee (Mng.Ed.); Collin (Mng. Ed.)

MEDICAL UNIV. OF SOUTH CAROLINA

Street Address 1: PO Box 12110
State: SC
Zip/Postal code: 29422-2110
Country: USA
Mailing Address: PO Box 12110
Mailing City: Charleston
Mailing State: SC
Mailing ZIP Code: 29422-2110
General Phone: (843) 792-4107
General Fax: (843) 849-0214
General/National Adv. Email: catalyst@musc.edu
Website: www.musc.edu/catalyst
Personnel: Kim Draughn (Ed.)

UNIV. OF CHARLESTON

Street Address 1: 2300 Maccorkle Ave SE
State: WV
Zip/Postal code: 25304-1045
Country: USA
Mailing Address: 2300 Maccorkle Ave SE
Mailing City: Charleston
Mailing State: WV
Mailing ZIP Code: 25304-1099
General Phone: (304) 357-4716
General Fax: (304) 357-4988
Personnel: Andy Spradling (Advisor); Ginny Bennett Helmick (Ed.)

CHARLOTTE

QUEENS UNIVERSITY OF CHARLOTTE

Street Address 1: 1900 Selwyn Ave
State: NC
Zip/Postal code: 28207-2450
Country: USA
Mailing Address: Msc # 892
Mailing City: Charlotte
Mailing State: NC
Mailing ZIP Code: 28274-0001
General Phone: (704) 337-2220
General Fax: (704) 337-2503
General/National Adv. Email: quoc.chronicle@gmail.com
Website: www.queens-chronicle.com
Published: Bi-Mthly
Personnel: Dustin Saunders (Editor-in-Chief)

UNIV. OF NORTH CAROLINA AT CHARLOTTE

Street Address 1: 9201 University City Blvd
State: NC
Zip/Postal code: 28223-0001
Country: USA
Mailing Address: 9201 University City Blvd
Mailing City: Charlotte
Mailing State: NC
Mailing ZIP Code: 28223-1000
General Phone: (704) 687-3253
Advertising Phone: (704) 687-7145
Advertising Fax: (704) 687-7139
Editorial Phone: (704) 687-7148
General/National Adv. Email: www.nineronline.com
Display Adv. Email: smpads@uncc.edu
Editorial Email: editor@ninertimes.com
Website: www.ninertimes.com
Published: Tues
Avg Free Circ: 7000
Personnel: Christine Litchfield (Ed. in Chief); Hunter Heilman (EIC)

College and University Newspapers

CHARLOTTESVILLE

COLGATE DARDEN GRAD. SCHOOL OF BUS.
Street Address 1: 100 Darden Blvd
State: VA
Zip/Postal code: 22903-1760
Country: USA
Mailing Address: 100 Darden Blvd
Mailing City: Charlottesville
Mailing State: VA
Mailing ZIP Code: 22903-1760
General Phone: (434) 982-2395
General/National Adv. Email: cchronicle@darden.virginia.edu
Website: coldcallchronicle.com
Personnel: Sarah Yoder (Pub.); Laura Dart (Adv. Mgr.); Tyler Lifton (Ed.)

UNIV. OF VIRGINIA
Street Address 1: PO Box 400703
State: VA
Zip/Postal code: 22904-4703
Country: USA
Mailing Address: PO Box 400703
Mailing City: Charlottesville
Mailing State: VA
Mailing ZIP Code: 22904-4703
General Fax: (434) 924-7290
General/National Adv. Email: editor@cavalierdaily.com
Website: www.cavalierdaily.com
Year Established: 1890
Published: Mon`Thur
Avg Free Circ: 10000
Personnel: Karoline Komolafe (Editor-in-chief)

UNIV. OF VIRGINIA SCHOOL OF LAW
Street Address 1: 580 Massie Rd
State: VA
Zip/Postal code: 22903-1738
Country: USA
Mailing Address: 580 Massie Rd
Mailing City: Charlottesville
Mailing State: VA
Mailing ZIP Code: 22903-1789
General Phone: (434) 924-3070
General Fax: (434) 924-7536
General/National Adv. Email: editor@lawweekly.org
Website: www.lawweekly.org
Year Established: 1948
Published: Wed
Personnel: Jenna Goldman (Editor-in-Chief)

CHATTANOOGA

CHATTANOOGA STATE TECH. CMTY. COLLEGE
Street Address 1: Paul Starnes Ctr, Rm S-260, 4501 Amnicola Hwy
State: TN
Country: USA
Mailing Address: Paul Starnes Ctr., Rm. S-260, 4501 Amnicola Hwy.
Mailing City: Chattanooga
Mailing State: TN
Mailing ZIP Code: 37406
General Phone: (423) 697-2471
General Fax: (423) 697-4758
General/National Adv. Email: communicator.editor@gmail.com
Personnel: Betty A. Proctor (Advisor); Keith Burkhalter (Ed.)

UNIV. OF TENNESSEE CHATTANOOGA
Street Address 1: 615 McCallie Ave
State: TN
Zip/Postal code: 37403-2504
Country: USA
Mailing Address: 615 McCallie Ave
Mailing City: Chattanooga
Mailing State: TN
Mailing ZIP Code: 37403-2504
General Phone: (423) 425-4298
General Fax: (423) 425-8100
Advertising Phone: (423) 425-8101
General/National Adv. Email: echo@utcecho.com
Website: www.utcecho.com
Personnel: Holly Cowart (Advisor); Alexa Branblet (Adv. Mgr.); Paige Gabriel (Ed. in Chief); Kate Bissinger (Mng. Ed.); Hayley (Features Ed.); Rachel (News Ed.); Michael (Sports Ed.)

CHENEY

THE EASTERNER
Street Address 1: 102 Isle Hall
State: WA
Zip/Postal code: 99004-2417
Country: USA
Mailing Address: 102 Isle Hall
Mailing City: Cheney
Mailing State: WA
Mailing ZIP Code: 99004-2417
General Phone: (509) 359-6737
Advertising Phone: (509) 359-7010
Display Adv. Email: advertising@ewu.edu
Editorial Email: easterner.editor@ewu.edu
Website: www.easterneronline.com
Year Established: 1916
Delivery Methods: Carrier`Racks
Commercial printers?: Y
Published: Wed
Avg Free Circ: 2500
Personnel: Contact Us (Contact Us); Carleigh Hill (Dir.)
Parent company (for newspapers): Eastern Washington University

CHESTNUT HILL

BOSTON COLLEGE
Street Address 1: McElroy Commons 113, 140 Commonwealth Ave
State: MA
Zip/Postal code: 1919
Country: USA
Mailing Address: McElroy Commons 113, 140 Commonwealth Ave.
Mailing City: Chestnut Hill
Mailing State: MA
Mailing ZIP Code: 02467-3800
General Phone: (617) 552-2221
General Fax: (617) 552-1753
Advertising Phone: (617) 552-4823
Editorial Phone: (617) 552-2220
Editorial Fax: (617) 552-2223
Display Adv. Email: ads@bcheights.com
Website: www.bcheights.com
Personnel: Dave Givler (Adv. Mgr.); Matt DeLuca (Ed. in chief)

CHEYENNE

LARAMIE COUNTY CMTY. COLLEGE
Street Address 1: 1400 E College Dr
State: WY
Zip/Postal code: 82007-3204
Country: USA
Mailing Address: 1400 E. College Dr.
Mailing City: Cheyenne
Mailing State: WY
Mailing ZIP Code: 82007-3204
General Phone: (307) 778-1304
General/National Adv. Email: wingspan@lccc.wy.edu
Year Established: 1976
Published: Mthly
Avg Free Circ: 1000
Personnel: J.L. O'Brien (Advisor); Jake Sherlock (Adviser)

CHEYNEY

CHEYNEY UNIV. OF PENNSYLVANIA
Street Address 1: 1837 University Cir
Street Address 2: PO Box 200
State: PA
Zip/Postal code: 19319-1019
Country: USA
Mailing Address: 1837 University Cir
Mailing City: Cheyney
Mailing State: PA
Mailing ZIP Code: 19319-1019
General Phone: (610) 399-2121
Personnel: Owens Gwen (Advisor)

CHICAGO

CHICAGO KENT COLLEGE OF LAW
Street Address 1: 565 W Adams St
Street Address 2: Rm C86
State: IL
Zip/Postal code: 60661-3652
Country: USA
Mailing Address: 565 W Adams St Fl 2
Mailing City: Chicago
Mailing State: IL
Mailing ZIP Code: 60661-3652
General Phone: (312) 906-5016
General Fax: (312) 906-5280
General/National Adv. Email: comment@kentlaw.edu
Website: www.kentlaw.edu/student_orgs/commentator

COLUMBIA COLLEGE
Street Address 1: 33 E Congress Pkwy
State: IL
Zip/Postal code: 60605-1218
Country: USA
Mailing Address: 600 S Michigan Ave Fl 5
Mailing City: Chicago
Mailing State: IL
Mailing ZIP Code: 60605-1996
General Phone: 312-369-8903
Advertising Phone: 312-369-8984
Editorial Phone: 312-369-8999
Editorial Fax: 312-369-8430
Editorial Email: jlyon@colum.edu
Website: www.columbiachronicle.com
Year Established: 1965
News Services: AP, MCT
Special Editions: Yes
Special Weekly Sections: Yes
Delivery Methods: Racks
Commercial printers?: Y
Personnel: Jeff Lyon (Faculty advisor)

COLUMBIA COLLEGE CHICAGO
Street Address 1: 33 E Congress Pkwy
Street Address 2: Ste 224
State: IL
Zip/Postal code: 60605-1237
Country: USA
Mailing Address: 33 E Congress Pkwy Ste 224
Mailing City: Chicago
Mailing State: IL
Mailing ZIP Code: 60605-1237
General Phone: 312-369-8955
General Fax: (312)369-8430
Advertising Phone: 312-369-8955
Editorial Phone: (312) 369-8999
General/National Adv. Email: chronicle@colum.edu
Display Adv. Email: crichert@colum.edu
Editorial Email: chronicle@colum.edu
Website: www.columbiachronicle.com
Year Established: 1978
Published: Mon
Avg Free Circ: 6000
Personnel: Chris Richert (General Manager)

DEPAUL UNIVERSITY
Street Address 1: 14 E Jackson Blvd
Street Address 2: Fl 11
State: IL
Zip/Postal code: 60604-2259
Country: USA
Mailing Address: 14 E. Jackson Blvd.
Mailing City: Chicago
Mailing State: IL
Mailing ZIP Code: 60604
General Phone: (312) 362-7644
General/National Adv. Email: eic@depauliaonline.com
Display Adv. Email: business@depauliaonline.com
Editorial Email: eic@depauliaonline.com
Website: www.depauliaonline.com
Year Established: 1923
News Services: AP
Delivery Methods: Newsstand
Commercial printers?: Y
Published: Mon
Avg Free Circ: 5000
Personnel: Marla Krause (Advisor)

DEVRY UNIVERSITY
Street Address 1: 3300 N Campbell Ave, Campus Life Ctr
State: IL
Zip/Postal code: 60618
Country: USA
Mailing Address: 3300 N. Campbell Ave., Campus Life Ctr.
Mailing City: Chicago
Mailing State: IL
Mailing ZIP Code: 60618
General Phone: (773) 697-2089
General Fax: (773) 697-2706
General/National Adv. Email: dvu.chi.hardcopy@gmail.com
Personnel: Joe Onorio (Assoc. Dean, Campus Life/ Advisor); Marvin Cespedes (Ed.)

HAROLD WASHINGTON COLLEGE
Street Address 1: 30 E Lake St
Street Address 2: Rm 635
State: IL
Zip/Postal code: 60601-2408
Country: USA
Mailing Address: 30 E Lake St Rm 635
Mailing City: Chicago
Mailing State: IL
Mailing ZIP Code: 60601-2449
General Phone: (312) 553-3141
General Fax: (312) 553-5647
Advertising Phone: 312-553-5631
Editorial Phone: 312-553-5630
General/National Adv. Email: hwc_heraldnews@ccc.edu
Website: www.theheraldhwc.com
Year Established: 1979
News Services: none
Delivery Methods: Mail`Newsstand`Racks
Commercial printers?: Y
Personnel: Molly Turner (Faculty Advisor)

ILLINOIS INST. OF TECHNOLOGY
Street Address 1: Herman Union Bldg State St
Street Address 2: Rm 3201221
State: IL
Zip/Postal code: 60616
Country: USA
Mailing Address: Herman Union Bldg., 3201 S. State St., Rm. 221
Mailing City: Chicago
Mailing State: IL
Mailing ZIP Code: 60616
General Phone: (312) 567-3085
General/National Adv. Email: technews@iit.edu
Personnel: Aanchal Taneja (Bus. Mgr.); Brian Wolber (Adv. Mgr.); Lory Mishra (Ed. in Chief)

KENNEDY-KING COLLEGE
Street Address 1: 1751 W 47th St
Street Address 2: Fl 2
State: IL

III-659

Zip/Postal code: 60609-3825
Country: USA
Mailing City: Chicago
Mailing State: IL
Mailing ZIP Code: 60621
General Phone: (773) 602-5179
General Fax: (773) 602-5521
General/National Adv. Email: editor@thegatenewpaper.com
Display Adv. Email: editor@thegatenewpaper.com
Website: www.thegatenewspaper.com
Year Established: 2010
Published: Bi-Mthly
Avg Free Circ: 13000
Personnel: Adriana Maria Cardona-Maguigad (Editor)

LOYOLA UNIV.

Street Address 1: 6525 N Sheridan Rd
State: IL
Zip/Postal code: 60626-5761
Country: USA
Mailing Address: 6525 N Sheridan Rd Ste 1
Mailing City: Chicago
Mailing State: IL
Mailing ZIP Code: 60626-5386
General Phone: (773) 508-7120
General Fax: (773) 508-7121
General/National Adv. Email: phoenixbusiness@luc.edu
Website: www.loyolaphoenix.com
Personnel: Kimberly Boonjathai (Bus.Mgr.); Leeann Maton (Ed. in chief)

LOYOLA UNIV. LAW SCHOOL

Street Address 1: 33 N Dearborn St
State: IL
Zip/Postal code: 60602-3102
Country: USA
Mailing Address: 33 N Dearborn St
Mailing City: Chicago
Mailing State: IL
Mailing ZIP Code: 60602-3102
General Phone: (312) 346-3191
General Fax: (312) 915-7201
Personnel: Sam Puleo (Ed.)

MALCOLM X COLLEGE

Street Address 1: 1900 W Van Buren St
Street Address 2: Rm 2519
State: IL
Zip/Postal code: 60612-3145
Country: USA
Mailing Address: 1900 W Van Buren St Rm 2218
Mailing City: Chicago
Mailing State: IL
Mailing ZIP Code: 60612-3145
General Phone: (312) 850-7462
General Fax: (312) 850-7323
Editorial Phone: (312) 850-7462
Delivery Methods: Racks
Commercial printers?: Y
Personnel: Cynthia-Val Chapman (Advisor); Beth Lewis (Adv. Mgr.)

NORTH PARK UNIV.

Street Address 1: 3225 W Foster Ave
State: IL
Zip/Postal code: 60625-4823
Country: USA
Mailing Address: 3225 W Foster Ave
Mailing City: Chicago
Mailing State: IL
Mailing ZIP Code: 60625-4895
General Phone: (773) 649-2816
General/National Adv. Email: northparkpress@gmail.com
Website: www.northparkpress.com
Delivery Methods: Racks
Personnel: Casey Smagala (Adv. Dir.); Erin Hegarty (Editor-In-Chief); Kristie Vuocolo (Staff Advisory); Hannah Williams (Online Editor)

NORTHEASTERN ILLINOIS UNIVERSITY

Street Address 1: 5500 N Saint Louis Ave
Street Address 2: Rm E049
State: IL
Zip/Postal code: 60625-4625
Country: USA
Mailing Address: 5500 N Saint Louis Ave Rm E049
Mailing City: Chicago
Mailing State: IL
Mailing ZIP Code: 60625-4699
General Phone: (773) 442-4577
General Fax: (773) 442-4579
General/National Adv. Email: neiuadindependent@gmail.com
Display Adv. Email: neiuadvertising@yahoo.com
Website: www.neiuindependent.org
Year Established: 1961
Published: Tues`Bi-Mthly
Personnel: Jacklyn Nowotnik (Editor-in-Chief); Matthew Greenberg (Managing Editor)

NORTHWESTERN UNIV. SCHOOL OF LAW

Street Address 1: 357 E Chicago Ave
State: IL
Zip/Postal code: 60611-3059
Country: USA
Mailing Address: 357 E Chicago Ave
Mailing City: Chicago
Mailing State: IL
Mailing ZIP Code: 60611-3069
General Phone: (312) 503-4714
Personnel: Unknown Unknown (Advisor)

ROBERT MORRIS COLLEGE

Street Address 1: 401 S State St
State: IL
Zip/Postal code: 60605-1229
Country: USA
Mailing Address: 401 S State St Fl 2
Mailing City: Chicago
Mailing State: IL
Mailing ZIP Code: 60605-1225
General Phone: (312) 935-6876
General Fax: (312) 935-6880
General/National Adv. Email: eaglenews@robertmorris.edu; eagle@robertmorris.edu
Personnel: Cherie Meador (Advisor); Matt Kirouac (Ed.)

ROOSEVELT UNIV.

Street Address 1: 430 S Michigan Ave
State: IL
Zip/Postal code: 60605-1315
Country: USA
Mailing Address: 430 S Michigan Ave
Mailing City: Chicago
Mailing State: IL
Mailing ZIP Code: 60605-1394
General Phone: (312) 281-3246
General Fax: (312) 341-3732
General/National Adv. Email: torchcu@roosevelt.edu
Website: www.roosevelttorch.com
Personnel: Billy Montgomery (Advisor); Mallory Blazetic (Mng. Ed.)

SAINT XAVIER UNIVERSITY

Street Address 1: 3700 W 103rd St
State: IL
Zip/Postal code: 60655-3105
Country: USA
Mailing Address: 3700 W 103rd St
Mailing City: Chicago
Mailing State: IL
Mailing ZIP Code: 60655-3199
General Phone: (773) 298-3380
General Fax: (773) 298-3381
General/National Adv. Email: thexavierite@yahoo.com
Display Adv. Email: thexavierite@yahoo.com

Editorial Email: thexavierite@yahoo.com
Website: www.thexavierite.com
Year Established: 1935
Commercial printers?: Y
Personnel: Peter Kreten (Asst. Dir)

SCHOOL OF THE ART INSTITUTE

Street Address 1: 112 S Michigan Ave
State: IL
Zip/Postal code: 60603-6105
Country: USA
Mailing Address: 112 S Michigan Ave
Mailing City: Chicago
Mailing State: IL
Mailing ZIP Code: 60603-6105
General Phone: (312) 345-3838
General Fax: (312) 345-3839
General/National Adv. Email: fadvertising@saic.edu
Editorial Email: editors@fnewsmagazine.com
Website: www.fnewsmagazine.com
Personnel: Paul Elitzik (Advisor); Rachel Oginni (Adv. Mgr.); Natalie Edwards (Ed. in Chief)

UNIV. OF CHICAGO

Street Address 1: 1212 E 59th St
Street Address 2: Lowr Level
State: IL
Zip/Postal code: 60637-1604
Country: USA
Mailing Address: 1212 E 59th St Lowr Level
Mailing City: Chicago
Mailing State: IL
Mailing ZIP Code: 60637-1604
General Phone: (773) 702-1403
General Fax: (773) 702-3032
General/National Adv. Email: editor@chicagomaroon.com
Display Adv. Email: ads@chicagomaroon.com
Website: www.chicagomaroon.com
Year Established: 1892
Published: Tues`Fri
Personnel: Rebecca Guterman (Editor-in-Chief); Sam Levine (Editor-in-Chief); Emily Wang (Managing Editor)

UNIV. OF CHICAGO LAW SCHOOL

Street Address 1: 1111 E 60th St
State: IL
Zip/Postal code: 60637-2776
Country: USA
Mailing Address: 1111 E 60th St
Mailing City: Chicago
Mailing State: IL
Mailing ZIP Code: 60637-2786
General Phone: (773) 702-3164
General Fax: (773) 834-4332
General/National Adv. Email: phoenix@law.uchicago.edu
Website: www.ÃƒÂ°law.ÃƒÂ°uchicago.ÃƒÂ°edu
Year Established: 1901
Personnel: William Weaver (Ed.); Lisa Alvarez (Contact)

UNIV. OF ILLINOIS AT CHICAGO

Street Address 1: 1212 E 59th St
Street Address 2: Ida Noyes Hall
State: IL
Zip/Postal code: 60637-1604
Country: USA
Mailing Address: 1001 W Van Buren St
Mailing City: Chicago
Mailing State: IL
Mailing ZIP Code: 60607-2900
General Phone: (312) 421-0480
General Fax: (312) 421-0491
Editorial Phone: (312) 996-5421
General/National Adv. Email: chicagomaroon@gmail.com
Website: www.chicagoflame.com
Year Established: 1988
Personnel: Darryl Brehm (Bus. Mgr.); Kate Lee (Ed.)

UNIVERSITY OF CHICAGO BOOTH SCHOOL OF BUSINESS

Street Address 1: 5807 S Woodlawn Ave
Street Address 2: # C26A
State: IL
Zip/Postal code: 60637-1610
Country: USA
Mailing Address: 5807 S Woodlawn Ave # C26A
Mailing City: Chicago
Mailing State: IL
Mailing ZIP Code: 60637-1610
General Phone: (773) 702-1234
General Fax: (773) 834-0628
General/National Adv. Email: chibusmag@gmail.com
Display Adv. Email: chibusmag@gmail.com
Editorial Email: chibusmag@gmail.com
Website: www.chibus.com
Published Other: Biweekly
Avg Free Circ: 1000
Personnel: Christopher Laws (Editor in Chief); Elizabeth Oates (Editor in Chief)

WILBUR WRIGHT COLLEGE

Street Address 1: 4300 N Narragansett Ave
State: IL
Zip/Postal code: 60634-1591
Country: USA
Mailing Address: 4300 N Narragansett Ave
Mailing City: Chicago
Mailing State: IL
Mailing ZIP Code: 60634-1500
General Phone: (773) 481-8555
General Fax: (773) 481-8555
Editorial Phone: (773) 481-8444
General/National Adv. Email: web.wrighttimes@yahoo.com
Website: www.wrighttimes.net; wright.ccc.edu
Personnel: Terrence Doherty (Advisor); Juan Pintor (Ed. in Chief)

CHICAGO HEIGHTS

PRAIRIE STATE COLLEGE

Street Address 1: 202 S Halsted St
Street Address 2: Rm 1260
State: IL
Zip/Postal code: 60411-8200
Country: USA
Mailing Address: 202 S Halsted St Rm 1260
Mailing City: Chicago Heights
Mailing State: IL
Mailing ZIP Code: 60411-8226
General Phone: (708) 709-3910
General Fax: (708) 755-2587
Editorial Phone: (708) 709-3535
General/National Adv. Email: psc_student_review@yahoo.com
Website: www.prairiestate.edu/studentreview
Personnel: Helen Manley (Advisor); Nike Atewologun (Adv. Mgr.); Sam Williams (Ed. in Chief)

CHICKASHA

UNIV. OF SCIENCE & ARTS OF OKLAHOMA

Street Address 1: 1727 W Alabama Ave
State: OK
Zip/Postal code: 73018-5322
Country: USA
Mailing Address: 1727 W Alabama Ave
Mailing City: Chickasha
Mailing State: OK
Mailing ZIP Code: 73018-5371
General Phone: (405) 224-3140
General Fax: (405) 521-6244
Website: www.trend.usao.edu
Published: Other
Published Other: Ongoing (post several times a week)
Personnel: J. C. Casey (Faculty Advisor & Professor of Communication)
Parent company (for newspapers): University of Science & Arts of Oklahoma

College and University Newspapers

CHICO

CALIFORNIA STATE UNIV.
Street Address 1: Chico Dept. of Journalism
Street Address 2: Zip 600 Chico
State: CA
Zip/Postal code: 95926
Country: USA
Mailing Address: Chico Dept. of Journalism
Mailing City: Chico
Mailing State: CA
Mailing ZIP Code: 95926
General Phone: (530) 898-4237
General Fax: (530) 898-4799
Editorial Fax: (530) 898-4033
Display Adv. Email: advertising@theorion.com
Website: www.theorion.com
Personnel: David Waddell (Advisor); Gillian Leeds (Bus. Mgr.); Jennifer Siino (Mng. Ed.); Mike North (News Ed.)

CHICOPEE

ELMS COLLEGE
Street Address 1: 291 Springfield St
State: MA
Zip/Postal code: 01013-2837
Country: USA
Mailing Address: 291 Springfield St
Mailing City: Chicopee
Mailing State: MA
Mailing ZIP Code: 01013-2839
General Phone: (413) 594-2761
Website: www.elms.edu
Personnel: James Gallant (Advisor)

CHULA VISTA

SOUTHWESTERN COLLEGE
Street Address 1: 900 Otay Lakes Rd
State: CA
Zip/Postal code: 91910-7223
Country: USA
Mailing Address: 900 Otay Lakes Rd
Mailing City: Chula Vista
Mailing State: CA
Mailing ZIP Code: 91910-7297
General Phone: (619) 482-6368
General Fax: (619) 482-6513
General/National Adv. Email: southwestern_sun@yahoo.com
Website: www.southwesterncollegesun.com
Personnel: Max Branfcomb (Advisor)

CICERO

MORTON COLLEGE
Street Address 1: 3801 S Central Ave
Street Address 2: Rm 328-C
State: IL
Zip/Postal code: 60804-4300
Country: USA
Mailing Address: 3801 S Central Ave Rm 328-C
Mailing City: Cicero
Mailing State: IL
Mailing ZIP Code: 60804-4398
General Phone: (708) 656-8000
General Fax: (708) 656-3924
General/National Adv. Email: collegian@morton.edu
Website: www.morton.edu
Personnel: Rose Dimesio (Advisor)

CINCINNATI

MOUNT ST. JOSEPH UNIVERSITY
Street Address 1: 5701 Delhi Rd
State: OH
Zip/Postal code: 45233-1669
Country: USA
Mailing Address: 5701 Delhi Rd
Mailing City: Cincinnati
Mailing State: OH
Mailing ZIP Code: 45233-1670
General Phone: (513) 244-4200
Website: www.msj.edu
Published: Mthly
Personnel: Elizabeth Barkley (Faculty Advisor)

THE NEWS RECORD
Street Address 1: Swift Hall, Ste 510
State: OH
Zip/Postal code: 45221-0001
Country: USA
Mailing Address: PO Box 210135
Mailing City: Cincinnati
Mailing State: OH
Mailing ZIP Code: 45221-0135
General Phone: (513) 556-5900
General Fax: (513) 556-5922
General/National Adv. Email: newsrecordbiz@gmail.com; chief.newsrecord@gmail.com
Editorial Email: chief.newsrecord@gmail.com
Website: www.newsrecord.org
Year Established: 1880
Special Weekly Sections: TNR Extra
Delivery Methods: Newsstand Racks
Personnel: Ariel Cheung (Editor-in-chief); Kristy Conlin (Ed. in Chief)

UNIVERSITY OF CINCINNATI
Street Address 1: PO Box 210135
State: OH
Zip/Postal code: 45221-0135
Country: USA
Mailing Address: PO Box 210135
Mailing City: Cincinnati
Mailing State: OH
Mailing ZIP Code: 45221-0135
General Phone: (513) 556-5912
General Fax: (513) 556Â-5922
Website: www.newsrecord.org

XAVIER UNIV.
Street Address 1: 3800 Victory Pkwy
State: OH
Zip/Postal code: 45207-1035
Country: USA
Mailing Address: 3800 Victory Pkwy Dept 156
Mailing City: Cincinnati
Mailing State: OH
Mailing ZIP Code: 45207-8010
General Phone: (513) 745-3607
General Fax: (513) 745-2898
Advertising Phone: (513) 745-3561
Website: www.xavier.edu/newswire
Personnel: Kathryn Rosenbaum (Ed. in Chief); Andrew Chestnut (Mng. Ed.); Meghan Berneking (News Ed.)

CLAREMONT

CLAREMONT COLLEGES
Street Address 1: 175 E 8th St
State: CA
Zip/Postal code: 91711-3956
Country: USA
Mailing Address: 175 E 8th St
Mailing City: Claremont
Mailing State: CA
Mailing ZIP Code: 91711-3956
General Phone: (909) 621-8000
General Fax: (909) 607-7825
Personnel: Keith Koyano (Ed.)

CLAREMONT MCKENNA COLLEGE
Street Address 1: Heggblade Ctr, 500 E 9th St
State: CA
Zip/Postal code: 91711
Country: USA
Mailing Address: Heggblade Ctr., 500 E. 9th St.
Mailing City: Claremont
Mailing State: CA
Mailing ZIP Code: 91711
General Phone: (909) 607-6709
General Fax: (909) 607-9489
Personnel: Adam Sivitz (Ed.)

POMONA COLLEGE
Street Address 1: Smith Campus Ctr.
Street Address 2: Pomona College
State: CA
Zip/Postal code: 91711
Country: USA
Mailing Address: Smith Campus Ctr.
Mailing City: Claremont
Mailing State: CA
Mailing ZIP Code: 91711-7003
General Phone: (909) 607-6709
General/National Adv. Email: info@tsl.pomona.edu
Display Adv. Email: business@tsl.pomona.edu
Editorial Email: editor@tsl.pomona.edu
Website: www.tsl.pomona.edu
Year Established: 1889
Delivery Methods: Mail Racks
Commercial printers?: Y
Published: Fri
Avg Free Circ: 2000
Personnel: Ian Gallogly; Adam Belzberg (Business Manager); Jeff Zalesin (Editor-in-Chief)

CLARION

CLARION UNIV. OF PENNSYLVANIA
Street Address 1: 270 Gemmell Student Ctr
State: PA
Zip/Postal code: 16214
Country: USA
Mailing Address: 270 Gemmell Student Ctr.
Mailing City: Clarion
Mailing State: PA
Mailing ZIP Code: 16214
General Phone: (814) 393-2000
General Fax: (814) 393-2557
General/National Adv. Email: call@clarion.edu
Website: www.clarioncallnews.com
Personnel: Laurie Miller (Advisor); Elizabeth Presutti (Adv. Mgr.); Luke Hampton (Ed. in Chief)

CLARKSTON

GEORGIA PERIMETER COLLEGE
Street Address 1: 555 N Indian Creek Dr
State: GA
Zip/Postal code: 30021-2361
Country: USA
Mailing Address: 555 N Indian Creek Dr
Mailing City: Clarkston
Mailing State: GA
Mailing ZIP Code: 30021-2361
General Phone: (678)-891-3381
General Fax: (404) 298-3882
General/National Adv. Email: gpccollegian@gmail.com
Website: www.gpc.edu
Year Established: 1986
Personnel: Alice Murray (Bus. Mgr.); Nathan Guest (Ed. in Chief)

CLAYTON

FONTBONNE COLLEGE
Street Address 1: 6800 Wydown Blvd
State: MO
Zip/Postal code: 63105-3043
Country: USA
Mailing Address: 6800 Wydown Blvd
Mailing City: Clayton
Mailing State: MO
Mailing ZIP Code: 63105-3098
General Phone: (314) 889-1477
General Fax: (314) 889-1451
Personnel: Jason Sommer (Prof.); Sara Lubbes (Ed.)

CLEMSON

CLEMSON UNIV.
Street Address 1: 315 Hendrix Ctr
State: SC
Zip/Postal code: 29634-0001
Country: USA
Mailing Address: 315 Hendrix Ctr
Mailing City: Clemson
Mailing State: SC
Mailing ZIP Code: 29634-0001
General Phone: (864) 656-2150
General Fax: (864) 656-4772
Website: www.thetigernews.com
Personnel: Patrick Neal (Advisor); Cory Bowers (Bus. Mgr.); Ashley Chris (Ed.)

CLEVELAND

CASE WESTERN RESERVE UNIV.
Street Address 1: 11111 Euclid Ave
Street Address 2: Rm A09
State: OH
Zip/Postal code: 44106-1715
Country: USA
Mailing Address: 11111 Euclid Ave Rm A09
Mailing City: Cleveland
Mailing State: OH
Mailing ZIP Code: 44106-1715
General Phone: (216) 368-6949
General Fax: (216) 368-2914
Website: www.cwruobserver.com
Personnel: Tricia Schellenbach (Advisor); Bruce Douglas (Adv. Mgr.); Bryan Bourgeois (Ed. in Chief)

CLEVELAND STATE CMTY. COLLEGE
Street Address 1: 3535 Adkisson Dr NW
State: TN
Zip/Postal code: 37312-2813
Country: USA
Mailing Address: PO Box 3570
Mailing City: Cleveland
Mailing State: TN
Mailing ZIP Code: 37320-3570
General Phone: (423) 472-7141
General Fax: (423) 478-6255
General/National Adv. Email: tbartolo@clevelandstatecc.edu
Website: www.clevelandstatecc.edu
Personnel: Tony Bartolo (Adv. Mgr.); Priscilla Simms (Ed.)

CLEVELAND STATE UNIV.
Street Address 1: 2121 Euclid Ave
Street Address 2: Student Center, Room 319
State: OH
Zip/Postal code: 44115-2214
Country: USA
Mailing Address: 2121 Euclid Ave
Mailing City: Cleveland
Mailing State: OH
Mailing ZIP Code: 44115-2226
General Phone: (216) 687-2270
General Fax: (216) 687-5155
General/National Adv. Email: cauldroneditors@gmail.com
Display Adv. Email: cauldronadverts@gmail.com
Website: www.csucauldron.com
Published: Tues
Personnel: Dan Lenhart (Advisor); Samah Assad (Editor-in-Chief)

DELTA STATE UNIV.
Street Address 1: 1003 W Sunflower Rd
State: MS
Zip/Postal code: 38733-0001
Country: USA
Mailing Address: 1003 W Sunflower Rd
Mailing City: Cleveland
Mailing State: MS
Mailing ZIP Code: 38733-0002
General Phone: (662) 846-4715
General Fax: (662) 846-4737
General/National Adv. Email: statemnt@deltastate.edu
Website: www.deltastate.edu
Personnel: Patricia Roberts (Advisor); Kaitlyn Mize (Bus. Mgr.); Ashley Robertson (Ed. in Chief)

LEE UNIV.

Street Address 1: 1120 N Ocoee St
State: TN
Zip/Postal code: 37311-4458
Country: USA
Mailing Address: 1120 N Ocoee St
Mailing City: Cleveland
Mailing State: TN
Mailing ZIP Code: 37311-4475
General Phone: (423) 614-8489
General Fax: (423) 614-8341
General/National Adv. Email: news@leeclarion.com
Website: www.leeclarion.com
Personnel: Kevin Trowbridge (Advisor); Michelle Bouman (Ed.)

CLINTON

HAMILTON COLLEGE

Street Address 1: 198 College Hill Rd
State: NY
Zip/Postal code: 13323-1218
Country: USA
Mailing Address: 198 College Hill Rd
Mailing City: Clinton
Mailing State: NY
Mailing ZIP Code: 13323-1295
General Phone: (315) 859-4011
General Fax: (315) 859-4563
Personnel: Erin W. Hoener (Ed. in Chief)

MISSISSIPPI COLLEGE

Street Address 1: 200 S Capitol St
State: MS
Zip/Postal code: 39056-4026
Country: USA
Mailing Address: 200 W College St
Mailing City: Clinton
Mailing State: MS
Mailing ZIP Code: 39058-0001
General Phone: (601) 925-3462
General Fax: (601) 925-3804
Website: news.mc.edu/~collegian/
Personnel: Tim Nicholas (Faculty Advisor); Gabriel Winston (Adv. Mgr.); Terra Kirkland (Co. Ed.)

PRESBYTERIAN COLLEGE

Street Address 1: 503 S Broad St
State: SC
Zip/Postal code: 29325-2865
Country: USA
Mailing Address: 503 S Broad St
Mailing City: Clinton
Mailing State: SC
Mailing ZIP Code: 29325-2998
General Phone: (864) 833-8488
General/National Adv. Email: pcbluestocking@gmail.com
Year Established: 1927
Published: Mthly
Personnel: Justin Brent (Advisor); Rachel Miles (Co-Editor); Ashleigh Bethea (Co-Editor)

COEUR D ALENE

NORTH IDAHO COLLEGE

Street Address 1: 1000 W Garden Ave
State: ID
Zip/Postal code: 83814-2161
Country: USA
Mailing Address: North Idaho College Receiving Department (c/o Geoff Carr)
Mailing City: Coeur D Alene
Mailing State: ID
Mailing ZIP Code: 83814-2199
General Phone: (208) 769-3388
General Fax: (208) 769-3361
General/National Adv. Email: sentinel@nic.edu
Website: www.nicsentinel.com
Published Other: Tri-weekly
Avg Free Circ: 3000
Personnel: Geoff Carr (Advisor)

COFFEYVILLE

COFFEYVILLE CMTY. COLLEGE

Street Address 1: 400 W 11th St
State: KS
Zip/Postal code: 67337-5065
Country: USA
Mailing Address: 400 W. 11th
Mailing City: Coffeyville
Mailing State: KS
Mailing ZIP Code: 67337
General Phone: (316) 252-7137

COLBY

COLBY CMTY. COLLEGE

Street Address 1: 1255 S Range Ave
State: KS
Zip/Postal code: 67701-4007
Country: USA
Mailing Address: 1255 S Range Ave
Mailing City: Colby
Mailing State: KS
Mailing ZIP Code: 67701-4099
General Phone: (785) 462-3984
General Fax: (785) 460-4699
Website: www.freewebs.com/trojanexpress
Personnel: Trent Rose (Advisor)

COLCHESTER

ST. MICHAEL'S COLLEGE

Street Address 1: 1 Winooski Park
State: VT
Zip/Postal code: 05439-1000
Country: USA
Mailing Address: 1 Winooski Park
Mailing City: Colchester
Mailing State: VT
Mailing ZIP Code: 05439-1000
General Phone: (802) 654-2421
Advertising Phone: (802) 654-2560
General/National Adv. Email: defender@smcvt.edu
Personnel: Paul Beique; Andrew Dennett (Ed.)

COLLEGE PARK

UNIVERSITY OF MARYLAND

Street Address 1: 3136 S Campus Dining Hall
State: MD
Zip/Postal code: 20742-8401
Country: USA
Mailing Address: 3136 S Campus Dining Hall
Mailing City: College Park
Mailing State: MD
Mailing ZIP Code: 20742-8401
General Phone: (301) 314-8000
General Fax: (301) 314-8358
Advertising Phone: (301) 314-8000
Editorial Phone: (301) 314-8000
General/National Adv. Email: diamondbackeditor@gmail.com
Display Adv. Email: dbkadvertising@gmail.com
Editorial Email: newsumdbk@gmail.com
Website: dbknews.com
Year Established: 1909
Published: Thur
Personnel: Mina Haq (Ed. in chief)

COLLEGE PLACE

WALLA WALLA COLLEGE

Street Address 1: 204 S College Ave
State: WA
Zip/Postal code: 99324-1139
Country: USA
Mailing Address: 204 S College Ave
Mailing City: College Place
Mailing State: WA
Mailing ZIP Code: 99324-1198
General Phone: (509) 527-2971
General Fax: (509) 527-2674
General/National Adv. Email: comm@wwc.edu
Personnel: Ross Brown (Ed.); Pamela Harris (Chair)

COLLEGE STATION

TEXAS A&M UNIV.

Street Address 1: the Grove Bldg 8901, 215 Limar St
State: TX
Zip/Postal code: 77843-0001
Country: USA
Mailing Address: the Grove Bldg 8901, 215 Limar St
Mailing City: College Station
Mailing State: TX
Mailing ZIP Code: 77843-0001
General Phone: (979) 845-3313
General Fax: (979) 845-2647
Advertising Phone: (979) 845-0569
Advertising Fax: (979) 845-2678
Editorial Phone: (979) 845-3315
General/National Adv. Email: editor@thebatt.com
Display Adv. Email: battads@thebatt.com
Website: www.thebatt.com
Personnel: Cheri Shipman (News Advisor); Amanda Casanova (Ed. in Chief)

TEXAS A&M UNIVERSITY

Street Address 1: 4234 Tamu
State: TX
Zip/Postal code: 77843-0001
Country: USA
Mailing Address: 4234 Tamu
Mailing City: College Station
Mailing State: TX
Mailing ZIP Code: 77843-0001
General Phone: (979) 458-1802
General Fax: (979) 845-6594
General/National Adv. Email: r-sumpter@tamu.edu; jourminor@tamu.edu
Personnel: Randall S. Sumpter (Dir., Journ. Studies/Assoc. Prof., Commun.); Roberto Farias (Program Asst.); Edward L. Walraven (Sr. Lectr.); Dale A. Rice (Lectr.)

TEXAS A&M UNIVERSITY

Street Address 1: 107 Scoates Hall
State: TX
Zip/Postal code: 77843-0001
Country: USA
Mailing Address: 107 Scoates Hall
Mailing City: College Station
Mailing State: TX
Mailing ZIP Code: 77843-0001
General Phone: (979) 862-3003
General Fax: (979) 845-6296
General/National Adv. Email: dj-king@tamu.edu
Personnel: Deborah Dunsford (Program Coord.)

THE BATTALION

Street Address 1: Grove 215 Lamar St Bldg 8901
State: TX
Zip/Postal code: 77843-0001
County: Brazos
Country: USA
Mailing Address: 1111 Tamu
Mailing City: College Station
Mailing State: TX
Mailing ZIP Code: 77843-0001
General Phone: 979-845-3313
General Fax: 979-845-2647
General/National Adv. Email: editor@thebatt.com
Website: thebatt.com/
Year Established: 1893
Published: Mon`Tues`Wed`Thur`Fri

COLLEGEVILLE

ST. JOHNS UNIV.

Street Address 1: PO Box 2000
State: MN
Zip/Postal code: 56321-2000
Country: USA
Mailing Address: PO Box 2000
Mailing City: Collegeville
Mailing State: MN
Mailing ZIP Code: 56321-2000
General Phone: (320) 363-2540
General Fax: (320) 363-2061
General/National Adv. Email: record@csbsju.edu
Website: www.users.csbsju.edu/record
Personnel: Kate Kompas (Advisor)

URSINUS COLLEGE

Street Address 1: 601 E Main St
State: PA
Zip/Postal code: 19426-2509
Country: USA
Mailing Address: PO Box 1000
Mailing City: Collegeville
Mailing State: PA
Mailing ZIP Code: 19426-1000
General Phone: (610) 409-2448
General/National Adv. Email: grizzly@ursinus.edu
Personnel: Rebecca Jaroff (Advisor)

COLORADO SPGS

US AIR FORCE ACADEMY

Street Address 1: 2304 Cadet Dr, Ste 3100
State: CO
Zip/Postal code: 80904
Country: USA
Mailing Address: 2304 Cadet Dr., Ste. 3100
Mailing City: Colorado Springs
Mailing State: CO
Mailing ZIP Code: 80904-5016
General Phone: (719) 333-7731
General Fax: (719) 333-4094
Personnel: Kim Karda (Ed. In Chief)

COLORADO SPRINGS

COLORADO COLLEGE

Street Address 1: 1028 N Weber St
State: CO
Zip/Postal code: 80903-2422
Country: USA
Mailing Address: 1028 N. Weber St.
Mailing City: Colorado Springs
Mailing State: CO
Mailing ZIP Code: 80903
General Phone: (719) 389-6000
General Fax: (719) 389-6962
General/National Adv. Email: catalyst@coloradocollege.edu
Website: www.coloradocollege.edu
Personnel: Jackson Solway (Ed.); Alex Kronman (Ed.)

PIKES PEAK CMTY. COLLEGE

Street Address 1: 5675 S Academy Blvd
Street Address 2: # C12
State: CO
Zip/Postal code: 80906-5422
Country: USA
Mailing Address: 5675 S Academy Blvd # C12
Mailing City: Colorado Springs
Mailing State: CO
Mailing ZIP Code: 80906-5422
General Phone: (719) 502-2000
General Fax: (719) 579-3015
Website: www.ppcc.edu
Personnel: Linda McGowan (Advisor); Sonia Gonzales (Ed.)

UNIV. OF COLORADO

Street Address 1: 1420 Austin Bluffs Pkwy
State: CO
Zip/Postal code: 80918-3733
Country: USA
Mailing Address: 1420 Austin Bluffs Pkwy
Mailing City: Colorado Springs
Mailing State: CO
Mailing ZIP Code: 80918-3908
General Phone: (719) 262-3658
General Fax: (719) 262-3600

College and University Newspapers

General/National Adv. Email: scribe@uccs.edu
Website: www.uccs.edu/scribe
Personnel: Paul Fair (Ed.)

COLUMBIA

BENEDICT COLLEGE

Street Address 1: 1600 Harden St
State: SC
Zip/Postal code: 29204-1058
Country: USA
Mailing Address: 1600 Harden St
Mailing City: Columbia
Mailing State: SC
Mailing ZIP Code: 29204-1086
General Phone: (803) 705-4645
General Fax: (803) 253-5065
Website: www.benedict.edu
Personnel: Carolyn Drakeford (Chair); Momo Rogers (Ed.)

HOWARD CMTY. COLLEGE

Street Address 1: 10901 Little Patuxent Pkwy
State: MD
Zip/Postal code: 21044-3110
Country: USA
Mailing Address: 10901 Little Patuxent Pkwy
Mailing City: Columbia
Mailing State: MD
Mailing ZIP Code: 21044-3197
General Phone: (410) 772-4937
General Fax: (410) 772-4280
General/National Adv. Email: newspaper@howardcc.edu
Website: www.howardcc.edu
Published: Bi-Mthly
Personnel: Michelle Plummer (Advertising Manager)

STEPHENS COLLEGE

Street Address 1: 1200 E Broadway, Campus Box 2014
State: MO
Zip/Postal code: 65215-0001
Country: USA
Mailing Address: 1200 E Broadway, Campus Box 2014
Mailing City: Columbia
Mailing State: MO
Mailing ZIP Code: 65215-0001
General Phone: (573) 876-7133
General/National Adv. Email: stephenslifemagazine@gmail.com
Website: www.stephens.edu/stephenslife
Personnel: Kathy Vogt (Bus. Mgr.); Josh Nichol-Caddy (Stephens Life Adviser)

UNIV. OF MISSOURI

Street Address 1: G210 Mu Student Center
State: MO
Zip/Postal code: 65211-0001
Country: USA
Mailing Address: G210 MU Student Center
Mailing City: Columbia
Mailing State: MO
Mailing ZIP Code: 65211
General Phone: (573) 882-5500
Display Adv. Email: advertising@themaneater.com
Editorial Email: editors@themaneater.com
Website: www.themaneater.com
Year Established: 1955
Delivery Methods: Racks
Commercial printers?: N
Published: Wed
Avg Free Circ: 5000
Personnel: Becky Diehl (Advisor)

UNIV. OF SOUTH CAROLINA

Street Address 1: 1400 Greene St
State: SC
Zip/Postal code: 29225-4002
Country: USA
Mailing Address: 1400 Greene St
Mailing City: Columbia
Mailing State: SC
Mailing ZIP Code: 29225-4002
General Phone: (803) 777-5064
General Fax: (803) 777-6482
Advertising Phone: (803) 777-3888
Editorial Phone: (803) 777-7182
Editorial Email: gamecockeditor@sc.edu
Website: www.dailygamecock.com
Personnel: Scott Lindenberg (Dir., Student Media); Erik Collins (Advisor); Amanda Davis (Ed. in Chief); Calli Burnett (Mng. Ed.)

COLUMBUS

CAPITAL UNIV.

Street Address 1: 1 College and Main
State: OH
Zip/Postal code: 43209-7812
Country: USA
Mailing Address: 1 College and Main
Mailing City: Columbus
Mailing State: OH
Mailing ZIP Code: 43209-2394
General Phone: (614) 236-6567
General Fax: (614) 236-6948
General/National Adv. Email: chimes@capital.edu
Website: cuchimes.com
Year Established: 1926
Special Editions: freshmen orientation
Published: Thur
Avg Free Circ: 1200
Personnel: Kelly Messinger (Advisor)

CAPITAL UNIV. LAW SCHOOL

Street Address 1: 303 E Broad St
State: OH
Zip/Postal code: 43215-3201
Country: USA
Mailing Address: 303 E Broad St
Mailing City: Columbus
Mailing State: OH
Mailing ZIP Code: 43215-3200
General Phone: (614) 236-6011
General Fax: (614) 445-7125
General/National Adv. Email: resipsa@law.capital.edu
Personnel: Susan Gilles (Advisor); Sharon Simpson (Ed. in Chief); Amanda Tuttle (Ed.)

COLUMBUS STATE UNIV.

Street Address 1: 4225 University Ave
State: GA
Zip/Postal code: 31907-5679
Country: USA
Mailing Address: 4225 University Ave
Mailing City: Columbus
Mailing State: GA
Mailing ZIP Code: 31907-5645
General Phone: (706) 562-1494
General Fax: (706) 568-2434
General/National Adv. Email: csusaber@yahoo.com; csusaber@gmail.com; saber@colstate.edu
Website: thesaber.wixsite.com/thesaber
Year Established: 1958
Published: Other
Personnel: Linda Reynold (Advisor)

FRANKLIN UNIVERSITY

Street Address 1: 201 S Grant Ave
State: OH
Zip/Postal code: 43215-5301
Country: USA
Mailing Address: 201 S Grant Ave
Mailing City: Columbus
Mailing State: OH
Mailing ZIP Code: 43215-5399
General Phone: (614) 797-4700
General Fax: (614) 224-4025
Advertising Phone: N/A
Advertising Fax: N/A
Editorial Phone: N/A
Editorial Fax: N/A
Display Adv. Email:
Editorial Email:
Website: www.franklin.edu
Year Established: 1902
Commercial printers?: N
Personnel: Sherry Mercurio (Ed.)

MISSISSIPPI UNIV. FOR WOMEN

Street Address 1: 1100 College St
State: MS
Zip/Postal code: 39701-5821
Country: USA
Mailing Address: 1100 College St
Mailing City: Columbus
Mailing State: MS
Mailing ZIP Code: 39701-5802
General Phone: (662) 329-7268
General Fax: (662) 329-7269
General/National Adv. Email: spectator@muw.edu
Website: www.muw.edu/spectator
Personnel: Sarah Wilson (Ed. in Chief); Juna'uh Allgood (Ed.)

OHIO STATE UNIV.

Street Address 1: 242 W 18th Ave
Street Address 2: Rm 211
State: OH
Zip/Postal code: 43210-1107
Country: USA
Mailing Address: 242 W 18th Ave Rm 211
Mailing City: Columbus
Mailing State: OH
Mailing ZIP Code: 43210-1107
General Phone: (614) 292-2031
General Fax: (614) 292-5240
Editorial Phone: (614) 292-5721
General/National Adv. Email: lantern@osu.edu
Editorial Email: lanternnewsroom@gmail.com
Website: www.thelantern.com
Year Established: 1881
Personnel: Tom O'Hara (Advisor); John Milliken (Mgr.); Kevin Bruffy (Mgr., Display Adv.)

OHIO STATE UNIV. COLLEGE OF ENGINEERING

Street Address 1: 2070 Neil Ave
State: OH
Zip/Postal code: 43210-1226
Country: USA
Mailing Address: 2070 Neil Ave
Mailing City: Columbus
Mailing State: OH
Mailing ZIP Code: 43210-1278
General Phone: (614) 292-7931
General Fax: (614) 688-3805
Website: www.engineering.osu.edu
Personnel: Edward McCaul (Advisor)

OHIO STATE UNIV. COLLEGE OF LAW

Street Address 1: 55 W 12th Ave
State: OH
Zip/Postal code: 43210-1338
Country: USA
Mailing Address: 55 W 12th Ave
Mailing City: Columbus
Mailing State: OH
Mailing ZIP Code: 43210-1391
General Phone: (614) 292-2631
Advertising Phone: (614) 292-3202

OHIO STATE UNIVERSITY

Street Address 1: 242 W 18th Ave
State: OH
Zip/Postal code: 43210-1107
Country: USA
Mailing Address: 242 W 18th Ave
Mailing City: Columbus
Mailing State: OH
Mailing ZIP Code: 43210-1107
General Phone: 614-292-5721
General Fax: 614-292-3722
Website: www.thelantern.com

COMMERCE

TEXAS A&M UNIV. COMMERCE

Street Address 1: PO Box 4104
State: TX
Zip/Postal code: 75429-4104
Country: USA
Mailing Address: PO Box 4104
Mailing City: Commerce
Mailing State: TX
Mailing ZIP Code: 75429-4104
General Phone: (903) 886-5985
General Fax: (903) 468-3128
Advertising Phone: (903) 886-5231
General/National Adv. Email: theeasttexan@gmail.com
Website: www.theeasttexan.com
Year Established: 1915
Published: Bi-Mthly
Avg Free Circ: 1000
Personnel: Fred Stewart (Fac. Advisor)

CONWAY

COASTAL CAROLINA UNIV.

Street Address 1: PO Box 261954
State: SC
Zip/Postal code: 29528-6054
Country: USA
Mailing Address: PO Box 261954
Mailing City: Conway
Mailing State: SC
Mailing ZIP Code: 29528-6054
General Phone: (843) 349-2330
General Fax: (843) 349-2743
General/National Adv. Email: chanticleer@coastal.edu
Website: www.coastal.edu/chanticleer
Personnel: Issac Bailey (Advisor); Kyle Drapeau (Bus. Mgr.); Clarie Arambulla (Ed.)

HENDRIX COLLEGE

Street Address 1: 1600 Washington Ave
State: AR
Zip/Postal code: 72032-4115
Country: USA
Mailing Address: 1600 Washington Ave.
Mailing City: Conway
Mailing State: AR
Mailing ZIP Code: 72032
General Phone: (501) 329-6811
General/National Adv. Email: proed@hendrix.edu
Website: www.theprofileonline.com
Personnel: Alice Hines (Advisor)

UNIVERSITY OF CENTRAL ARKANSAS

Street Address 1: 201 Donaghey Ave
Street Address 2: Stanley Russ Hall 124
State: AR
Zip/Postal code: 72035-5001
Country: USA
Mailing Address: PO Box 5038
Mailing City: Conway
Mailing State: AR
Mailing ZIP Code: 72035-0001
General Phone: 501-499-9822
Advertising Phone: 501-499-9822
Advertising Fax: 501-852-2375
General/National Adv. Email: ucaechoeditor@gmail.com
Display Adv. Email: echonewspaperads@gmail.com
Website: www.ucaecho.net
Published: Wed
Avg Free Circ: 2500
Personnel: David Keith (Advisor); Jordan Johnson (editor); Hayley Trejo (business manager)

COOKEVILLE

TENNESSEE TECHNOLOGICAL UNIV.

Street Address 1: 1000 N Dixie Ave

Street Address 2: Ruc 376
State: TN
Zip/Postal code: 38505-0001
Country: USA
Mailing Address: PO Box 5072
Mailing City: Cookeville
Mailing State: TN
Mailing ZIP Code: 38505-0001
General Phone: (931) 372-3060
General Fax: (931) 372-6225
Advertising Phone: (931) 372-3031
Advertising Fax: (931) 372-6225
Editorial Phone: (931) 372-3285
Editorial Fax: (931) 372-6225
General/National Adv. Email: oracle@tntech.edu
Display Adv. Email: ttuoracleads@gmail.com
Editorial Email: oracle@tntech.edu
Website: www.tntechoracle.com
Year Established: 1924
Published: Fri
Published Other: Weekly during Fall and Spring semesters
Avg Free Circ: 3000
Personnel: Jon Ezell (Advisor / Assistant Professor)
Parent company (for newspapers): Tennessee Technological University

COOS BAY

SOUTHWESTERN OREGON CMTY. COLLEGE

Street Address 1: 1988 Newman Ave
State: OR
Zip/Postal code: 97420
Country: USA
Mailing Address: 1988 Newman Ave.
Mailing City: Coos Bay
Mailing State: OR
Mailing ZIP Code: 97420-2956
General Phone: (541) 888-7442
Personnel: Bridget Hildreth (Advisor)

CORAL GABLES

UNIV. OF MIAMI

Street Address 1: 1330 Miller Rd
Street Address 2: Ste 200
State: FL
Zip/Postal code: 33146-2322
Country: USA
Mailing Address: 1330 Miller Road, Suite 200
Mailing City: Coral Gables
Mailing State: FL
Mailing ZIP Code: 33146-2322
General Phone: (305) 284-4401
General Fax: (305) 284-4404
Advertising Phone: same
Advertising Fax: same
Editorial Phone: (305) 284-2016
Editorial Fax: (305) 284-4406
General/National Adv. Email: editor@themiamihurricane.com
Display Adv. Email: tara@themiamihurricane.com
Editorial Email: editor@themiamihurricane.com
Website: www.themiamihurricane.com
Year Established: 1929
Delivery Methods: Mail`Racks
Commercial printers?: Y
Published: Mon`Thur
Avg Free Circ: 10000
Personnel: Bob Radziewicz (Sr. Advisor)
Parent company (for newspapers): University of Miami

UNIV. OF MIAMI SCHOOL OF LAW

Street Address 1: 1311 Miller Rd
State: FL
Zip/Postal code: 33146-2300
Country: USA
Mailing Address: 1311 Miller Rd
Mailing City: Coral Gables
Mailing State: FL
Mailing ZIP Code: 33146-2300
General Phone: (305) 284-2339
General Fax: (305) 284-3554
General/National Adv. Email: resipsa@law.miami.edu
Website: www.law.miami.edu
Personnel: Jennifer C. Pratt-Garces (Ed. in Chief); Alex Britell (Mng. Ed.)

CORNING

CORNING CMTY. COLLEGE

Street Address 1: 1 Academic Dr
State: NY
Zip/Postal code: 14830-3297
Country: USA
Mailing Address: 1 Academic Dr
Mailing City: Corning
Mailing State: NY
Mailing ZIP Code: 14830-3299
General Phone: (607) 962-9339
General Fax: (607) 962-9008
General/National Adv. Email: criernewspaper@yahoo.com
Personnel: Paul McNaney (Advisor)

CORPUS CHRISTI

DEL MAR COLLEGE FOGHORN

Street Address 1: 101 Baldwin Blvd
Street Address 2: # HC210
State: TX
Zip/Postal code: 78404-3805
Country: USA
Mailing Address: 101 Baldwin Blvd # HC210
Mailing City: Corpus Christi
Mailing State: TX
Mailing ZIP Code: 78404-3805
General Phone: 361/698-1390
General Fax: (361/698-2153
Advertising Phone: 361/698-1246
Advertising Fax: 361/698-2153
Editorial Phone: 361/698-1390
Editorial Fax: 361/698-2153
General/National Adv. Email: editor@delmar.edu
Display Adv. Email: rmuilenburg@delmar.edu
Editorial Email: editor@delmar.edu
Website: www.foghornnews.com
Year Established: 1935
Delivery Methods: Newsstand`Racks
Commercial printers?: Y
Mechanical specifications: Broadsheet - 11.625 in. (6 col) X 20.5 in Column widths 1 col - 1.833 2 col - 3.792 3 col - 5.75 4 col - 7.708 5 col - 9.667 6 col - 11.625
Published: Tues`Bi-Mthly
Published Other: Tuesday every two weeks; no issues in summer
Avg Free Circ: 2500
Personnel: Robert Muilenburg (Advisor); Donna Strong (Adv. Mgr.)

TEXAS A&M UNIV. CORPUS CHRISTI

Street Address 1: 6300 Ocean Dr
State: TX
Zip/Postal code: 78412-5503
Country: USA
Mailing Address: 6300 Ocean Dr
Mailing City: Corpus Christi
Mailing State: TX
Mailing ZIP Code: 78412-5599
General Phone: (361) 825-7024
General Fax: (361) 825-3931
Display Adv. Email: islandwaves.ads@tamucc.edu
Editorial Email: editor-in-chief.islandwaves@tamucc.edu
Website: islandwaves.tamucc.edu; www.tamucc.edu
Personnel: Rob Boscamp (Advisor); Brittnye Screws (Adv. Mgr.)

CORTLAND

SUNY COLLEGE/CORTLAND

Street Address 1: PO Box 2000
State: NY
Zip/Postal code: 13045-0900
Country: USA
Mailing Address: PO Box 2000
Mailing City: Cortland
Mailing State: NY
Mailing ZIP Code: 13045-0900
General Phone: (607) 753-2803
General/National Adv. Email: dragonchronicle@cortland.edu
Website: www.cortland.edu

CORVALLIS

OREGON STATE UNIV.

Street Address 1: 118 Memorial Un E
State: OR
Zip/Postal code: 97331-8592
Country: USA
Mailing Address: 118 Memorial Un E
Mailing City: Corvallis
Mailing State: OR
Mailing ZIP Code: 97331-8592
General Phone: (541) 737-3374
General Fax: (541) 737-4999
Website: www.dailybarometer.com
Personnel: Brandon Southward (Ed. in chief); Taryn Luna (Ed.); Gail Cole (Ed. in Chief); Candice Ruud (Mng. Ed.)

COSTA MESA

ORANGE COAST COLLEGE

Street Address 1: 2701 Fairview Rd
State: CA
Zip/Postal code: 92626-5563
Country: USA
Mailing Address: 2701 Fairview Rd
Mailing City: Costa Mesa
Mailing State: CA
Mailing ZIP Code: 92626-5561
General Phone: (714) 432-5561
General Fax: (714) 432-5978
Advertising Phone: 714-432-5978
Advertising Fax: 714-432-5673
Editorial Phone: 714-432-5561
Editorial Fax: 714-432-5673
Display Adv. Email: coastreportads@yahoo.com
Editorial Email: editor@coastreportonline.com; coastreport@yahoo.com
Website: www.coastreportonline.com
Year Established: 1948
Personnel: Cathy Werblin (Advisor)

VANGUARD UNIV.

Street Address 1: 55 Fair Dr
State: CA
Zip/Postal code: 92626-6520
Country: USA
Mailing Address: 55 Fair Dr
Mailing City: Costa Mesa
Mailing State: CA
Mailing ZIP Code: 92626-6597
General Phone: (714) 662-5203
General Fax: (714) 966-5482
General/National Adv. Email: thevoice@vanguard.edu
Website: www.vanguard.edu
Personnel: Kristy Eudy (Advisor); Hannah Petrak (Ed.)

COUNCIL BLUFFS

IOWA WESTERN CMTY. COLLEGE

Street Address 1: 2700 College Rd
State: IA
Zip/Postal code: 51503-1057
Country: USA
Mailing Address: 2700 College Rd
Mailing City: Council Bluffs
Mailing State: IA
Mailing ZIP Code: 51503-1057
General Phone: (712) 325-3200
Website: iwccrover.wordpress.com
Personnel: Camille Steed (Advisor)

CRANFORD

UNION COUNTY COLLEGE

Street Address 1: 1033 Springfield Ave
State: NJ
Zip/Postal code: 07016-1528
Country: USA
Mailing Address: 1033 Springfield Ave
Mailing City: Cranford
Mailing State: NJ
Mailing ZIP Code: 07016-1598
General Phone: (908) 709-7000
Website: www.ucc.edu
Personnel: John R. Farrell (Vice Pres.)

CRETE

DOANE COLLEGE

Street Address 1: 1014 Boswell Ave
State: NE
Zip/Postal code: 68333-2426
Country: USA
Mailing Address: 1014 Boswell Ave Ste 289
Mailing City: Crete
Mailing State: NE
Mailing ZIP Code: 68333-2440
General Fax: (402) 826-8269
Advertising Fax: (402) 826-8600
General/National Adv. Email: www.doaneline.com
Display Adv. Email: owl@doane.edu
Personnel: David Swartzlander (Advisor); Bob Kenny (Ed.)

CRYSTAL LAKE

MCHENRY COUNTY COLLEGE

Street Address 1: 8900 US Highway 14
State: IL
Zip/Postal code: 60012-2738
Country: USA
Mailing Address: 8900 US Highway 14
Mailing City: Crystal Lake
Mailing State: IL
Mailing ZIP Code: 60012-2761
General Phone: (815) 455-8571
General Fax:
General/National Adv. Email: tartan@mchenry.edu
Website: www.mchenry.edu; www.mcctartan.net
Published: Mthly
Avg Free Circ: 2000
Personnel: Toni Countryman (Advisor)

CULLOWHEE

WESTERN CAROLINA UNIV.

Street Address 1: 109A Old Student Union
State: NC
Zip/Postal code: 28723
Country: USA
Mailing Address: 109A Old Student Union
Mailing City: Cullowhee
Mailing State: NC
Mailing ZIP Code: 28723
General Phone: (828) 227-2694
General Fax: (828) 227-7201
General/National Adv. Email: jcaudell@westerncarolinian.com
Display Adv. Email: jcaudell@westerncarolinian.com
Editorial Email: amenz@westerncarolinian.com
Website: www.westerncarolinian.com
Year Established: 1933
Delivery Methods: Mail`Newsstand`Racks
Published: Bi-Mthly
Avg Free Circ: 5000
Personnel: Justin Caudell (Ed. in Chief); Alexa Menz (Editor-in-Chief)

CUPERTINO

DE ANZA COLLEGE

Street Address 1: 21250 Stevens Creek Blvd
Street Address 2: Rm L-41
State: CA

College and University Newspapers

Zip/Postal code: 95014-5702
Country: USA
Mailing Address: 21250 Stevens Creek Blvd Rm L-41
Mailing City: Cupertino
Mailing State: CA
Mailing ZIP Code: 95014-5797
General Phone: (408) 864-5626
Advertising Phone: (408) 864-5626
Editorial Fax: Free
General/National Adv. Email: lavoz@fhda.edu
Display Adv. Email: lavozadvertising@gmail.com
Editorial Email: lavoz@fhda.edu
Website: www.lavozdeanza.com
Year Established: 1967
Published: Mon`Bi-Mthly
Published Other: 16 issues from late September to mid-June
Avg Free Circ: 2200
Personnel: Cecilia Deck (Journalism Chair)

CYPRESS

CYPRESS COLLEGE CHRONICLE

Street Address 1: 9200 Valley View St
State: CA
Zip/Postal code: 90630-5805
Country: USA
Mailing Address: 9200 Valley View St.
Mailing City: Cypress
Mailing State: CA
Mailing ZIP Code: 90630-5805
General Phone: 714-484-7267
General Fax: (714) 484-7466
Advertising Phone: 714-484-7268
Editorial Phone: 714-484-7269
General/National Adv. Email: rmercer@cypresscollege.edu
Website: www.cychron.com
Year Established: 1966
Delivery Methods: Newsstand
Commercial printers?: N
Published: Mthly
Avg Free Circ: 4000
Personnel: Robert Mercer (Advisor)

DAHLONEGA

NORTH GEORGIA COLLEGE

Street Address 1: PO Box 5432
State: GA
Zip/Postal code: 30597-0001
Country: USA
Mailing Address: PO Box 5432
Mailing City: Dahlonega
Mailing State: GA
Mailing ZIP Code: 30597-0001
General Phone: (706) 864-1468
General Fax: (706) 864-1485
General/National Adv. Email: voice@ngcsu.edu
Website: www.ngcsu.edu/voice
Personnel: Debbie Martin (Ed.)

DALLAS

MISERICORDIA UNIVERSITY

Street Address 1: 301 Lake St
State: PA
Zip/Postal code: 18612-7752
Country: USA
Mailing Address: 301 Lake St
Mailing City: Dallas
Mailing State: PA
Mailing ZIP Code: 18612-7752
General Phone: (570) 674-6737
General Fax: (570) 674-6751
General/National Adv. Email: highland@misericordia.edu
Website: www.highlandernews.net
Published Other: Bi-Monthly

PAUL QUINN COLLEGE

Street Address 1: 3837 Simpson Stuart Rd
State: TX
Zip/Postal code: 75241-4331
Country: USA
Mailing Address: 3837 Simpson Stuart Rd
Mailing City: Dallas
Mailing State: TX
Mailing ZIP Code: 75241-4398
General Phone: (214) 302-3600

RICHLAND COLLEGE

Street Address 1: 12800 Abrams Rd
State: TX
Zip/Postal code: 75243-2104
Country: USA
Mailing Address: 12800 Abrams Rd.
Mailing City: Dallas
Mailing State: TX
Mailing ZIP Code: 75243-2199
General Phone: (972) 238-6079
General Fax: (972) 238-6037
Advertising Phone: (972) 238-6068
Display Adv. Email: advertise@dcccd.edu
Website: www.richlandchronicle.com
Delivery Methods: Racks
Commercial printers?: Y
Published: Tues
Published Other: Weekly on Tuesday
Avg Free Circ: 3000

SOUTHERN METHODIST UNIV.

Street Address 1: 3140 Dyer St
Street Address 2: Ste 315
State: TX
Zip/Postal code: 75205-1977
Country: USA
Mailing Address: 3140 Dyer St Ste 315
Mailing City: Dallas
Mailing State: TX
Mailing ZIP Code: 75205-1977
General Phone: (214) 768-4555
General Fax: (214) 768-4573
Advertising Phone: (214) 768-4111
Advertising Fax: (214) 768-4573
Editorial Phone: (214) 768-4111
Display Adv. Email: dcads@smu.edu
Website: www.smudailycampus.com
Year Established: 1915
News Services: AP, MCT
Delivery Methods: Mail`Racks
Commercial printers?: N
Published: Thur
Avg Free Circ: 3000
Personnel: Jay Miller (Exec. Dir./Editorial Advisor); Dyann Slosar (Assoc. Dir.); Candace Barnhill (Int. Exec. Dir.)
Parent company (for newspapers): Student Media Company, Inc

DANBURY

WESTERN CONNECTICUT STATE UNIV.

Street Address 1: 181 White St
State: CT
Zip/Postal code: 06810-6826
Country: USA
Mailing Address: 181 White St
Mailing City: Danbury
Mailing State: CT
Mailing ZIP Code: 06810-6855
General Phone: (203) 837-8706
General Fax: (203) 837-8709
General/National Adv. Email: wcsuecho@gmail.com
Display Adv. Email: wcsuechoads@gmail.com
Website: wcsuecho.com/news/
Personnel: John Birks (Advisor); Todd Passan (Bus. Mgr.); Sarah Menichelli (Adv. Mgr.); Jessylyn Foley (Ed. in Chief)

DANVILLE

CENTRE COLLEGE

Street Address 1: 600 W Walnut St
State: KY
Zip/Postal code: 40422-1309
Country: USA
Mailing Address: 600 W Walnut St
Mailing City: Danville
Mailing State: KY
Mailing ZIP Code: 40422-1394
General Phone: (859) 238-5350
General/National Adv. Email: cento@centre.edu
Display Adv. Email: business@centre.edu
Editorial Email: ed-in-chief@centre.edu
Year Established: 1888
Personnel: Tess Simon (Ed.); Katy Meyer; Amy Senders

DAVENPORT

PALMER COLLEGE OF CHIROPRACTIC

Street Address 1: 1000 Brady St
State: IA
Zip/Postal code: 52803-5214
Country: USA
Mailing Address: 1000 Brady St.
Mailing City: Davenport
Mailing State: IA
Mailing ZIP Code: 52803
General Phone: (563) 884-5686
General Fax: (563) 884-5719
General/National Adv. Email: beacon@palmer.edu
Website: www.palmerbeacon.com
Personnel: Ramneek Bhogal (Advisor); Stephanie O'Neill (Advisor); Stewart McMillan (Ed.)

DAVIDSON

DAVIDSON COLLEGE

Street Address 1: PO Box 7182
State: NC
Zip/Postal code: 28035-7182
Country: USA
Mailing Address: PO Box 7182
Mailing City: Davidson
Mailing State: NC
Mailing ZIP Code: 28035-7182
General/National Adv. Email: davidsonian@davidson.edu
Display Adv. Email: davidsonian@davidson.edu
Website: www.davidsonian.com
Year Established: 1914
Delivery Methods: Mail`Newsstand`Racks
Published: Wed
Personnel: Laura Chuckray; Caroline Queen; Lyla Halsted

DAVIE

NOVA SOUTHEASTERN UNIV.

Street Address 1: 3301 College Ave
Street Address 2: Modular 4
State: FL
Zip/Postal code: 33314-7721
Country: USA
Mailing Address: 3301 College Ave Modular 4
Mailing City: Davie
Mailing State: FL
Mailing ZIP Code: 33314-7721
General Phone: (954) 262-8455
General Fax: (954) 262-8456
General/National Adv. Email: thecurrent@nova.edu; nsnews@nova.edu
Display Adv. Email: thecurrentad@nova.edu
Website: www.nsucurrent.com
Personnel: Fiona Banton

UNIV. OF CALIFORNIA SCHOOL OF LAW

Street Address 1: 400 Mrak Hall Dr
State: CA
Zip/Postal code: 95616-5203
Country: USA
Mailing Address: 400 Mrak Hall Dr
Mailing City: Davis
Mailing State: CA
Mailing ZIP Code: 95616-5203
General Phone: (530) 752-0243
Personnel: Heather Melton (Prodn. Ed.)

UNIVERSITY OF CALIFORNIA, DAVIS

Street Address 1: 1 Shields Avenue
Street Address 2: 25 Lower Freeborn Hall
State: CA
Zip/Postal code: 95616-5270
Country: USA
Mailing Address: 25 Lower Freeborn Hall
Mailing City: Davis
Mailing State: CA
Mailing ZIP Code: 95616-5270
General Phone: (530) 752-9887
Advertising Phone: (530) 752-6851
Editorial Phone: (530) 752-9887
General/National Adv. Email: editor@theaggie.org
Display Adv. Email: admanager@theaggie.org
Editorial Email: editor@theaggie.org
Website: www.theaggie.org
Year Established: 1915
Published: Thur
Personnel: Emily Stack (Editor-in-Chief); Olivia Rockeman (Managing Editor); Hannah Holzer (Campus News Editor); Kaelyn Tuermer-Lee (City News Editor); Liz Jacobson (Arts and Culture Editor); Dominic Faria (Sports Editor); Harnoor Gill (Science and Technology Editor); Olivia Luchini (Features Editor); Taryn DeOilers (Opinion Editor); Brian Landry (Photo Director); Trevor Goodman (Video Production Manager); Sydney Odman (New Media Manager); Zoe Reinhardt (Website Manager); Hali Zweigoron (Social Media Manager); Grace Simmons (Newsletter Manager); Shaelin Green (Distribution Manager); Jonathan Chen (Layout Director); Olivia Kotlarek (Design Director); Laurie Pederson (Business Development Manager); Hanna Baublitz (Copy Chief); Cecilia Morales (Copy Chief)

DAYTON

BRYAN COLLEGE

Street Address 1: 721 Bryan Dr
State: TN
Zip/Postal code: 37321-6275
Country: USA
Mailing Address: Box 7807
Mailing City: Dayton
Mailing State: TN
Mailing ZIP Code: 37321
General Phone: (423) 775-7285
General Fax: (423) 775-7330
General/National Adv. Email: triangle@bryan.edu; info@bryan.edu
Website: www.bryan.edu/7229; www.bryan.edu
Personnel: John Carpenter (Advisor); Allison McLean (Ed. in Chief)

SINCLAIR COMMUNITY COLLEGE

Street Address 1: 444 W 3rd St
Street Address 2: Rm 6314
State: OH
Zip/Postal code: 45402-1421
Country: USA
Mailing Address: 444 W 3rd St Rm 6314
Mailing City: Dayton
Mailing State: OH
Mailing ZIP Code: 45402-1421
General Phone: (937) 512-2744
General Fax: (937) 512-4590
Advertising Phone: (937) 512-2744
Advertising Fax: (937) 512-4590
Editorial Phone: (937) 512-2958
Editorial Fax: (937) 512-4590
General/National Adv. Email: clarion@sinclair.edu
Display Adv. Email: clarion@sinclair.edu
Editorial Email: clarion@sinclair.edu
Website: www.sinclairclarion.com
Year Established: 1977
Delivery Methods: Racks
Commercial printers?: Y
Published: Tues

Avg Free Circ: 4000
Personnel: Gabrielle Sharp (Exec Ed); Barton Kleen (Mng Ed); Laina Yost (Associate Ed); Susan Day (Advt Rep)

UNIV. OF DAYTON

Street Address 1: 232 Kennedy Union
Street Address 2: 300 College Park
State: OH
Zip/Postal code: 45469-0001
Country: USA
Mailing Address: 232 Kennedy Union
Mailing City: Dayton
Mailing State: OH
Mailing ZIP Code: 45469-0626
General Phone: (937) 229-3226
General Fax: (937) 229-3893
Advertising Phone: (937) 229-3813
Editorial Phone: (937) 229-3878
General/National Adv. Email: news@flyernews.com
Display Adv. Email: advertising@flyernews.com
Editorial Email: fn.editor@udayton.edu
Website: www.flyernews.com
Published: Tues
Published Other: B-Weekly (Daily online)
Avg Free Circ: 3000
Personnel: Frazier Smith (Advisor); Amy Lopez-Matthews (Co-Advisor); CC Hutten (Ed.); Matthew Worsham (Mng. Ed.); Meredith Whelchel (Mng. Ed.); Julia Hall (Print-Ed.)

UNIV. OF DAYTON LAW SCHOOL

Street Address 1: 300 College Park
State: OH
Zip/Postal code: 45469-0001
Country: USA
Mailing Address: 300 College Park
Mailing City: Dayton
Mailing State: OH
Mailing ZIP Code: 45469-0002
General Phone: (937) 229-3211
Personnel: Jennifer Tate (Ed.)

WRIGHT STATE UNIV.

Street Address 1: 014 Student Union, 3640 Colonel Glenn Hwy
State: OH
Zip/Postal code: 45435-0001
Country: USA
Mailing Address: 14 Stud Ent Union 3640 Colonel Glenn Hwy
Mailing City: Dayton
Mailing State: OH
Mailing ZIP Code: 45435-0001
General Phone: (937) 775-5534
General Fax: (937) 775-5535
Display Adv. Email: advertising@theguardianonline.com
Editorial Email: editorial@theguardianonline.com
Website: www.theguardianonline.com
Personnel: Tiffany Johnson (Ed. in chief)

DAYTONA BEACH

BETHUNE-COOKMAN COLLEGE

Street Address 1: 640 Dr Mary McLeod Bethune Blvd
State: FL
Zip/Postal code: 32114-3012
Country: USA
Mailing Address: 640 Dr. Mary McLeod Bethune Blvd.
Mailing City: Daytona Beach
Mailing State: FL
Mailing ZIP Code: 32114
General Phone: (386) 481-2000
General Fax: (386) 481-2701
General/National Adv. Email: voiceofthewildcats@gmail.com
Display Adv. Email: voiceofthewildcats@gmail.com
Editorial Email: voiceofthewildcats@gmail.com
Website: voiceofthewildcats.wordpress.com; www.cookman.edu
Year Established: 1904
Delivery Methods: Newsstand
Commercial printers?: Y
Published: Mthly
Published Other: UniverCity Magazine
Avg Free Circ: 1000
Personnel: Petra Merrick (Ed); Jamie Cobb (Layout/Paginator); Timothy White (Sports Ed); Augustinas Navickas (Columnist); Andres Whipple Girbes (Technology Writer)
Parent company (for newspapers): Bethune-Cookman University

DAYTONA STATE COLLEGE

Street Address 1: 1200 W International Speedway Blvd
State: FL
Zip/Postal code: 32114-2817
Country: USA
Mailing Address: 1200 W International Speedway Blvd
Mailing City: Daytona Beach
Mailing State: FL
Mailing ZIP Code: 32114-2817
General Phone: (386) 506-3268
General Fax: (386) 506-3155
Editorial Phone: (386) 506-3686
General/National Adv. Email: inmotion@daytonastate.edu
Display Adv. Email: inmotion@daytonastate.edu
Editorial Email: inmotion@daytonastate.edu
Website: www.daytonastateinmotion.com
Year Established: 1991
Published: Mthly
Avg Free Circ: 10002000
Personnel: Elena Jarvis (Advisor)
Parent company (for newspapers): Daytona State College

EMBRY-RIDDLE AERONAUTICAL UNIVERSITY

Street Address 1: 600 S Clyde Morris Blvd
State: FL
Zip/Postal code: 32114-3966
Country: USA
Mailing Address: 600 S Clyde Morris Blvd
Mailing City: Daytona Beach
Mailing State: FL
Mailing ZIP Code: 32114-3900
General Phone: (386) 226-6049
Advertising Phone: (386) 226-6727
Advertising Fax: (386) 226-7697
Editorial Phone: (386) 226-6079
General/National Adv. Email: theavion@gmail.com
Display Adv. Email: avionadvertising@gmail.com
Website: www.theavion.com
Year Established: 1969
Published: Tues
Avg Free Circ: 2000
Personnel: Jessica Searcy (Advisor)

DE PERE

ST. NORBERT COLLEGE

Street Address 1: 100 Grant St
Street Address 2: Ste 320
State: WI
Zip/Postal code: 54115-2002
Country: USA
Mailing Address: 100 Grant St Ste 320
Mailing City: De Pere
Mailing State: WI
Mailing ZIP Code: 54115-2002
General Phone: (920) 403-3268
General Fax: (920) 403-4092
General/National Adv. Email: times@snc.edu
Personnel: John Pennington (Advisor); Samantha Christian (Ed. in Chief)

DEARBORN

HENRY FORD CMTY. COLLEGE

Street Address 1: 5101 Evergreen Rd
Street Address 2: # C-117
State: MI
Zip/Postal code: 48128-2407
Country: USA
Mailing Address: 5101 Evergreen Rd # C-117
Mailing City: Dearborn
Mailing State: MI
Mailing ZIP Code: 48128-2407
General Phone: (313) 845-9639
General Fax: (313) 845-9876
General/National Adv. Email: mirrorbm@hfcc.edu
Website: www.hfccmirror.com
Personnel: Cassandra Fluker (Advisor); Joshua Gillis (Ed.)

UNIVERSITY OF MICHIGAN-DEARBORN

Street Address 1: 4901 Evergreen Rd
Street Address 2: Ste 2130
State: MI
Zip/Postal code: 48128-2406
Country: USA
Mailing Address: 4901 Evergreen Rd Ste 2130
Mailing City: Dearborn
Mailing State: MI
Mailing ZIP Code: 48128-2406
General Phone: (313) 593-5428
General Fax: (313) 593-5594
Advertising Phone: (313) 593-3097
General/National Adv. Email: themichiganj@gmail.com
Website: www.michiganjournal.org
Year Established: 1971
Published: Tues
Personnel: Tim Kiska (Adviser); Ricky Lindsay (Editor-in-Chief); Kaitlynn Riley (Advertising Manager)

DECATUR

AGNES SCOTT COLLEGE

Street Address 1: 141 E College Ave
State: GA
Zip/Postal code: 30030-3770
Country: USA
Mailing Address: 141 E College Ave
Mailing City: Decatur
Mailing State: GA
Mailing ZIP Code: 30030-3797
General Phone: (404) 471-6000
Personnel: Jeniffer Owen (Dir. Commun.); Josie Hoilman (Ed.)

JOHN C. CALHOUN STATE CMTY. COLLEGE

Street Address 1: PO Box 2216
State: AL
Zip/Postal code: 35609-2216
Country: USA
Mailing Address: PO Box 2216
Mailing City: Decatur
Mailing State: AL
Mailing ZIP Code: 35609-2216
General Phone: (256) 306-2500
Personnel: Robin Philip (Sec.)

MILLIKIN UNIV.

Street Address 1: 1184 W Main St
State: IL
Zip/Postal code: 62522-2039
Country: USA
Mailing Address: 1184 W Main St
Mailing City: Decatur
Mailing State: IL
Mailing ZIP Code: 62522-2084
General Phone: (217) 425-4626
General Fax: (217) 425-1687
General/National Adv. Email: decaturian@millikin.edu
Website: www.thedeconline.com
Personnel: Priscilla Marie Meddaugh (Faculty Advisor); Caitlin Hennessy (Co-Ed. in Chief); Lauren Krage (Co-Ed. in Chief)

RICHLAND CMTY. COLLEGE

Street Address 1: 1 College Park
State: IL
Zip/Postal code: 62521-8512
Country: USA
Mailing Address: 1 College Park
Mailing City: Decatur
Mailing State: IL
Mailing ZIP Code: 62521-8513
General Phone: (217) 875-7211
General Fax: (217) 875-6961
General/National Adv. Email: comm@richland.edu; communicatur@richland.edu
Website: www.richland.edu
Personnel: Marlise McDaniel (Ed. in Chief); Todd Houser (Ed.); Tina Cooper (Copy Ed.)

DEERFIELD

TRINITY INTERNATIONAL UNIV.

Street Address 1: 2065 Half Day Rd
State: IL
Zip/Postal code: 60015-1241
Country: USA
Mailing Address: 2065 Half Day Rd # T-2922
Mailing City: Deerfield
Mailing State: IL
Mailing ZIP Code: 60015-1241
General Phone: (847) 317-8155
General Fax: (847) 317-8142
Personnel: Erika Sjogren (Ed.)

DEKALB

NORTHERN ILLINOIS UNIV.

Street Address 1: Northern Illinois University, Campus Life Building, Suite 130
State: IL
Zip/Postal code: 60115
Country: USA
Mailing Address: Northern Illinois University, Campus Life Building, Suite 130
Mailing City: Dekalb
Mailing State: IL
Mailing ZIP Code: 60115
General Phone: (815) 753-4239
General Fax: (815) 753-0708
General/National Adv. Email: editor@northernstar.info
Display Adv. Email: ads@northernstar.info
Editorial Email: editor@northernstar.info
Website: www.northernstar.info
Year Established: 1899
News Services: AP
Commercial printers?: N
Personnel: Jim Killam (Advisor); Maria Krull (Bus. Advisor); Justin Weaver (Ed.)

DELAND

STETSON UNIV.

Street Address 1: 421 N Woodland Blvd
State: FL
Zip/Postal code: 32723-8300
Country: USA
Mailing Address: 421 N Woodland Blvd
Mailing City: Deland
Mailing State: FL
Mailing ZIP Code: 32720
General Phone: (386)-822-7100
General Fax: (904) 822-7233
Display Adv. Email: advertising@stetson.edu
Editorial Email: reporter@stetson.edu
Website: www.stetsonreporter.com
Personnel: Andrew Davis (Commun. Coord.); Joseph O'Brien (Ed. in Chief); Jason Rickner (Mng. Ed.)

College and University Newspapers

DELAWARE

OHIO WESLEYAN UNIVERSITY

Street Address 1: 61 S Sandusky St
Street Address 2: Rm 106
State: OH
Zip/Postal code: 43015-2333
Country: USA
Mailing Address: 61 S Sandusky St Rm 106
Mailing City: Delaware
Mailing State: OH
Mailing ZIP Code: 43015-2398
General Phone: (740) 368-2911
General Fax: (740) 368-3649
General/National Adv. Email: owunews@owu.edu
Display Adv. Email: owunews@owu.edu
Editorial Email: owunews@owu.edu
Website: transcript.owu.edu
Year Established: 1867
Delivery Methods: Newsstand
Commercial printers?: Y
Published: Thur
Avg Free Circ: 1000
Personnel: Jo Ingles (Media Adviser)

DELHI

SUNY COLLEGE OF TECHNOLOGY/DELHI

Street Address 1: 454 Delhi Dr
Street Address 2: 222 Farrell Center
State: NY
Zip/Postal code: 13753-4454
Country: USA
Mailing Address: 222 Farrell Center
Mailing City: Delhi
Mailing State: NY
Mailing ZIP Code: 13753
General Phone: (607) 746-4270
General Fax: (607) 746-4323
Advertising Phone: (607) 746-4573
Advertising Fax: (607) 746-4323
Editorial Phone: (607) 746-4573
Editorial Fax: (607) 746-4323
General/National Adv. Email: campusvoice@delhi.edu
Display Adv. Email: campusvoice@delhi.edu
Editorial Email: campusvoice@delhi.edu
Website: www.delhi.edu/campus-life/activities/campus-voice/index.php
Published: Mthly
Personnel: Christina Viafore (Advisor)

DENTON

TEXAS WOMAN'S UNIV.

Street Address 1: PO Box 425828
State: TX
Zip/Postal code: 76204-5828
Country: USA
Mailing Address: PO Box 425828
Mailing City: Denton
Mailing State: TX
Mailing ZIP Code: 76204-5828
General Phone: (940) 898-2191
General Fax: (940) 898-2188
Advertising Phone: (940) 898-2183
General/National Adv. Email: twu_lasso@yahoo.com
Website: www.twu.edu/lasso
Personnel: Alejandro Barrientos (Bus. Mgr.); Luis Rendon (Ed. in Chief); Rhonda Ross (Advisor)

UNIV. OF NORTH TEXAS

Street Address 1: 225 S Ave B, Gab Room 117
State: TX
Zip/Postal code: 76201
Country: USA
Mailing Address: 225 S Ave B, GAB Room 117
Mailing City: Denton
Mailing State: TX
Mailing ZIP Code: 76201
General Phone: (940) 565-2851
General Fax: (940) 565-3573
Advertising Phone: (940) 565-3989
Editorial Phone: (940) 565-2353
General/National Adv. Email: editor@ntdaily.com
Website: www.ntdaily.com
Personnel: Allie Durham (Adv. Mgr.); Kerry Solan (Ed. in Chief); Courtney Roberts (Mng. Ed.)

DENVER

METROPOLITAN STATE COLLEGE

Street Address 1: PO Box 173362
State: CO
Zip/Postal code: 80217-3362
Country: USA
Mailing Address: PO Box 173362
Mailing City: Denver
Mailing State: CO
Mailing ZIP Code: 80217-3362
General Phone: (303) 556-2507
General Fax: (303) 556-3421
Website: themet.metrostudentmedia.com; www.mscd.edu/themet
Year Established: 1979
Personnel: Dianne Harrison Miller (Dir.); Dominic Graziano (Ed.)

REGIS UNIV.

Street Address 1: 3333 Regis Blvd
State: CO
Zip/Postal code: 80221-1154
Country: USA
Mailing Address: 3333 Regis Blvd
Mailing City: Denver
Mailing State: CO
Mailing ZIP Code: 80221-1099
General Phone: (303) 964-5391
General Fax: (303) 964-5530
Website: www.regishighlander.com
Personnel: Mary Beth Callie (Advisor); Maricor Coquia (Ed. in Chief)

UNIV. OF COLORADO

Street Address 1: PO Box 173364
State: CO
Zip/Postal code: 80217-3364
Country: USA
Mailing Address: PO Box 173364
Mailing City: Denver
Mailing State: CO
Mailing ZIP Code: 80217-3364
General Phone: (303) 556-2535
General Fax: (303) 556-3679
Display Adv. Email: advertising@ucdadvocate.com
Editorial Email: editorinchief@ucdadvocate.com
Website: www.ucdadvocate.com
Year Established: 1984
Published: Wed
Personnel: Madilyn Bates (Editor in Chief); Isra Yousif (Office Coordinator)

UNIV. OF DENVER

Street Address 1: 2199 S University Blvd
State: CO
Zip/Postal code: 80210-4711
Country: USA
Mailing Address: 2199 S University Blvd
Mailing City: Denver
Mailing State: CO
Mailing ZIP Code: 80210-4700
General Phone: (303) 871-3131
General Fax: (303) 871-2568
General/National Adv. Email: duclarion@du.edu
Website: www.duclarion.com
Personnel: Arianna Ranahosseini (Ed. in Chief)

DES MOINES

DRAKE UNIV.

Street Address 1: 2507 Univ, Ave 124N Meredith Hall
State: IA
Zip/Postal code: 50311
Country: USA
Mailing Address: 2507 Univ., Ave. 124N Meredith Hall
Mailing City: Des Moines
Mailing State: IA
Mailing ZIP Code: 50311-4516
General Phone: (515) 271-3867
General Fax: (515) 271-2798
General/National Adv. Email: times.delphic@drake.edu
Website: www.timesdelphic.com
Personnel: Jill Van Wyke (Advisor); Caleb Bailey (Adv. Mgr.); Matt Vasilogambros (Ed. in Chief)

GRAND VIEW UNIVERSITY

Street Address 1: Cowles Communication Ctr, 1331 Grandview Ave
State: IA
Zip/Postal code: 50316
Country: USA
Mailing Address: Cowles Communication Ctr., 1331 Grandview Ave.
Mailing City: Des Moines
Mailing State: IA
Mailing ZIP Code: 50316-1453
General Phone: (515) 263-2806
General Fax: (515) 263-2990
General/National Adv. Email: grandviews@grandview.edu
Website: www.thegrandviews.com; www.grandview.edu
Year Established: 1949
Published: Fri
Personnel: Mark Siebert (Advisor); Stephanie Ivankovich (Editor)

HIGHLINE COLLEGE

Street Address 1: 2400 S 240th St
State: WA
Zip/Postal code: 98198-2714
Country: USA
Mailing Address: PO Box 98000
Mailing City: Des Moines
Mailing State: WA
Mailing ZIP Code: 98198-9800
General Phone: (206) 592-3291
General Fax: (206) 870-3771
Advertising Phone: (206) 592-3292
Editorial Phone: (206) 592-3317
General/National Adv. Email: tword@highline.edu; thunderword@highline.edu
Display Adv. Email: thunderword@highline.edu
Website: https://thunderword.highline.edu/
Year Established: 1961
Delivery Methods: Carrier
Commercial printers?: N
Published: Thur
Avg Free Circ: 2000
Personnel: T.M. Sell (Advisor)

DES PLAINES

OAKTON CMTY. COLLEGE

Street Address 1: 1600 E Golf Rd
State: IL
Zip/Postal code: 60016-1234
Country: USA
Mailing Address: 1600 E Golf Rd
Mailing City: Des Plaines
Mailing State: IL
Mailing ZIP Code: 60016-1268
General Phone: (847) 635-1678
General Fax: (847) 635-2610
General/National Adv. Email: occurrence@oakton.edu
Personnel: Sue Fox (Advisor)

DETROIT

WAYNE STATE UNIV.

Street Address 1: 5221 Gullen Mall
Street Address 2: Ste 101
State: MI
Zip/Postal code: 48202-3919
Country: USA
Mailing Address: 5221 Gullen Mall, Student Center Bldg., Ste. 101
Mailing City: Detroit
Mailing State: MI
Mailing ZIP Code: 48202
General Phone: (313) 577-8067
General Fax: (313) 993-8108
Advertising Phone: (313) 577-8666
General/National Adv. Email: dv7262@wayne.edu
Editorial Email: tseletters@gmail.com
Website: www.thesouthendnews.com
Personnel: Carolyn Chin (Mng. Ed.)

DOBBS FERRY

MERCY COLLEGE

Street Address 1: 555 Broadway
State: NY
Zip/Postal code: 10522-1186
Country: USA
Mailing Address: 555 Broadway Frnt
Mailing City: Dobbs Ferry
Mailing State: NY
Mailing ZIP Code: 10522-1189
General Phone: (914) 674-7422
General Fax: (914) 674-7433
General/National Adv. Email: mercyimpactnews@hotmail.com
Website: www.theimpactnews.com
Personnel: Michael Perrota (Advisor)

DOVER

DELAWARE STATE UNIV.

Street Address 1: 1200 N Dupont Hwy
State: DE
Zip/Postal code: 19901-2202
Country: USA
Mailing Address: 1200 N Dupont Hwy
Mailing City: Dover
Mailing State: DE
Mailing ZIP Code: 19901-2276
General Phone: (302) 857-6290
Website: www.desu.edu
Published: Mthly
Personnel: Marcia Taylor (Advisor); Synquette Wilks (EIC)

DOWAGIAC

SOUTHWESTERN MICHIGAN COLLEGE

Street Address 1: 58900 Cherry Grove Rd
State: MI
Zip/Postal code: 49047-9726
Country: USA
Mailing Address: 58900 Cherry Grove Rd
Mailing City: Dowagiac
Mailing State: MI
Mailing ZIP Code: 49047-9726
General Phone: (269) 782-1457
General Fax: (269) 782-1446
Editorial Phone: (269) 782-1457
Editorial Fax: (269) 782-1446
General/National Adv. Email: swester@swmich.edu
Editorial Email: swester@swmich.edu
Website: southwester.swmich.edu/
Year Established: 1968
Personnel: John Eby (Senior Writer and Coordinator of Media Relations)

DOYLESTOWN

DELAWARE VALLEY COLLEGE

Street Address 1: 700 E Butler Ave
State: PA
Zip/Postal code: 18901-2607
Country: USA
Mailing Address: 700 E Butler Ave
Mailing City: Doylestown
Mailing State: PA

Mailing ZIP Code: 18901-2698
General Phone: (215) 489-2345
General Fax: (215) 230-2966
General/National Adv. Email: rampages@delval.edu
Website: www.delvalrampages.com
Personnel: James O'Connor (Advisor)

DUBUQUE

CLARKE UNIVERSITY

Street Address 1: 1550 Clarke Dr
State: IA
Zip/Postal code: 52001-3117
Country: USA
Mailing Address: 1550 Clarke Dr
Mailing City: Dubuque
Mailing State: IA
Mailing ZIP Code: 52001-3198
General Phone: (563) 588-6335
General Fax: (563) 588-6789
General/National Adv. Email: abdul.sinno@clarke.edu
Website: clarke.edu
Personnel: Diana Russo (Advisor); Abdul Karim Sinno (Chair); Sarah Bradford (Ed.); David Deifell, Ph.D. (Assoc. Prof. Comm.)

LORAS COLLEGE

Street Address 1: 1450 Alta Vista St
State: IA
Zip/Postal code: 52001-4327
Country: USA
Mailing Address: 1450 Alta Vista St
Mailing City: Dubuque
Mailing State: IA
Mailing ZIP Code: 52001-4399
General Phone: (563) 588-7954
General Fax: (563) 588-7339
Advertising Phone: (563) 588-7828
Editorial Phone: (563) 588-7954
General/National Adv. Email: lorian@loras.edu
Display Adv. Email: lorian@loras.edu
Editorial Email: lorian@loras.edu
Website: myduhawk.com
Year Established: 1913
Published: Thur
Avg Free Circ: 1600
Personnel: Timothy Manning (Advisor); Anna Sweeney (Adv. Mgr.); Cassandra Busch (Co-Exec. Ed.)
Parent company (for newspapers): Loras College

UNIV. OF DUBUQUE

Street Address 1: 2000 University Ave
Street Address 2: # 6
State: IA
Zip/Postal code: 52001-5050
Country: USA
Mailing Address: 2000 University Ave # 6
Mailing City: Dubuque
Mailing State: IA
Mailing ZIP Code: 52001-5050
General Phone: (563) 589-3369
General Fax: (319) 589-3419
Personnel: Laura Steinbeck (Ed.)

DUDLEY

NICHOLS COLLEGE

Street Address 1: 124 Center Rd
State: MA
Zip/Postal code: 01571-6310
Country: USA
Mailing Address: PO Box 5000
Mailing City: Dudley
Mailing State: MA
Mailing ZIP Code: 01571-5000
General Phone: (508) 213-1560
General Fax: (508) 943-5354
General/National Adv. Email: admissions@nichols.edu
Website: http://www.nichols.edu/
Year Established: 1815
Commercial printers?: N

Personnel: Emily Reardon (Assistant Director of Admissions / International Students Counselor)

DULUTH

COLLEGE OF ST. SCHOLASTICA

Street Address 1: 1200 Kenwood Ave
State: MN
Zip/Postal code: 55811-4199
Country: USA
Mailing Address: 1200 Kenwood Ave
Mailing City: Duluth
Mailing State: MN
Mailing ZIP Code: 55811-4199
General Phone: (218) 723-6187
General Fax: (218) 723-6290
General/National Adv. Email: cable1@css.edu
Website: www.css.edu
Personnel: Joe Wicklund (Advisor); Print Corp (Pub.); Kirby Montgomery (Ed. in Chief)

DULUTH

UNIV. OF MINNESOTA DULUTH

Street Address 1: 118 Kirby Ctr, 10 University Dr
State: MN
Zip/Postal code: 55812
Country: USA
Mailing Address: 118 Kirby Ctr., 10 University Dr.
Mailing City: Duluth
Mailing State: MN
Mailing ZIP Code: 55812-2403
General Phone: (218) 726-8154
General Fax: (218) 726-8276
General/National Adv. Email: statesman@d.umn.edu
Website: www.umdstatesman.com
Personnel: Lisa Hansen (Advisor)

DURANGO

FT. LEWIS COLLEGE

Street Address 1: 1000 Rim Dr
Street Address 2: # 252
State: CO
Zip/Postal code: 81301-3911
Country: USA
Mailing Address: 1000 Rim Dr # 252
Mailing City: Durango
Mailing State: CO
Mailing ZIP Code: 81301-3911
General Phone: (970) 247-7405
General Fax: (970) 247-7487
General/National Adv. Email: independent@fortlewis.edu
Website: www.flcindependent.com
Personnel: Leslie Blood (Advisor); Kayala Andersen (News Ed.)

DURANT

SOUTHEASTERN OKLAHOMA STATE UNIV.

Street Address 1: 425 W University Blvd
State: OK
Zip/Postal code: 74701-3347
Country: USA
Mailing Address: 425 W University Blvd.
Mailing City: Durant
Mailing State: OK
Mailing ZIP Code: 74701-0609
General Phone: (580) 745-2944
General Fax: (580) 745-7475
General/National Adv. Email: campuspages@gmail.com
Website: www.thesoutheastern.com
Published: Mthly
Published Other: Website updated weekly. Newspaper published monthly. Magazine released once a year.
Personnel: Tascha Bond (Adviser); Kourtney Kaufman (Managing Editor)
Parent company (for newspapers): Southeastern

Oklahoma State University

DURHAM

DUKE UNIV. FUQUA BUS. SCHOOL

Street Address 1: PO Box 90120
State: NC
Zip/Postal code: 27708-0120
Country: USA
Mailing Address: PO Box 90120
Mailing City: Durham
Mailing State: NC
Mailing ZIP Code: 27708-0120
General Phone: (919) 660-7700
General Fax: (919) 684-2818
General/National Adv. Email: fuquatimes@gmail.com
Website: www.axml.net/fuquatimes
Personnel: Mary Murphy (Ed.)

DUKE UNIVERSITY

Street Address 1: 101 W Union
State: NC
Zip/Postal code: 27708-9980
Country: USA
Mailing Address: PO Box 90858
Mailing City: Durham
Mailing State: NC
Mailing ZIP Code: 27708-0858
General Phone: (919) 684-8111
General Fax: (919) 668-1247
Advertising Phone: (919) 684-3811
Editorial Phone: (919) 684-2663
Website: dukechronicle.com
Published: Mon`Tues`Wed`Thur`Fri
Avg Free Circ: 12000
Personnel: Yeshwanth Kandamalla (Editor)

NORTH CAROLINA CENTRAL UNIV.

Street Address 1: 1801 Fayetteville St
State: NC
Zip/Postal code: 27707-3129
Country: USA
Mailing Address: 1801 Fayetteville St
Mailing City: Durham
Mailing State: NC
Mailing ZIP Code: 27707-3129
General Phone: (919) 530-7116
General Fax: (919) 530-7991
General/National Adv. Email: campusecho@nccu.edu
Website: www.campusecho.com
Personnel: Dr. Bruce DePyssler (Advisor); Thomas Evans (Associate Professor); Carlton Koonce (Ed. in Chief)

THE DUKE CHRONICLE

Street Address 1: 301 Flowers
State: NC
Zip/Postal code: 27708-0001
County: Durham
Country: USA
Mailing Address: 301 Flowers
Mailing City: Durham
Mailing State: NC
Mailing ZIP Code: 27708-0001
General Phone: 919-684-2663
General Fax: 919-684-4696
Advertising Phone: 919-684-3811
Advertising Fax: 919-668-1247
Editorial Phone: 919-684-2663
Editorial Fax: 919-684-4696
General/National Adv. Email: advertising@chronicle.duke.edu
Display Adv. Email: advertising@chronicle.duke.edu
Editorial Email: chronicleletters@duke.edu
Website: www.dukechronicle.com
Year Established: 1905

THE NEW HAMPSHIRE

Street Address 1: Memorial Union Bldg, Rm

132, 83 Main St
State: NH
Zip/Postal code: 3824
Country: USA
Mailing Address: Memorial Union Bldg., Rm. 132, 83 Main St.
Mailing City: Durham
Mailing State: NH
Mailing ZIP Code: 03824-2538
General Phone: (603) 862-1323
General Fax: (603) 862-1920
General/National Adv. Email: tnh.news@unh.edu
Display Adv. Email: tnh.advertising@unh.edu
Editorial Email: tnh.editor@unh.edu
Website: www.tnhdigital.com
Year Established: 1911
Special Weekly Sections: Arts on Fridays
Delivery Methods: Racks
Commercial printers?: N
Published: Mon`Thur
Avg Free Circ: 4000
Personnel: Julie Pond (Advisor)
Parent company (for newspapers): University of New Hampshire

UNIVERSITY OF NEW HAMPSHIRE

Street Address 1: 104 Hamilton Smith Hall
State: NH
Zip/Postal code: 3824
Country: USA
Mailing Address: 104 Hamilton Smith Hall
Mailing City: Durham
Mailing State: NH
Mailing ZIP Code: 3824
General Phone: (603) 862-0251
General Fax: (603) 862-3563
General/National Adv. Email: lcm@cisunix.unh.edu
Personnel: Lisa Miller (Dir.)

EAST LANSING

THE STATE NEWS/MICHIGAN STATE UNIVERSITY

Street Address 1: 435 E Grand River Ave
Street Address 2: Fl 2
State: MI
Zip/Postal code: 48823-4456
Country: USA
Mailing Address: 435 E Grand River Ave
Mailing City: East Lansing
Mailing State: MI
Mailing ZIP Code: 48823-4456
General Phone: (517) 295-1680
Advertising Phone: (517) 295-1680
Editorial Phone: (517) 295-1680
General/National Adv. Email: feedback@statenews.com
Display Adv. Email: advertising@statenews.com
Editorial Email: editorinchief@statenews.com
Website: www.statenews.com
Year Established: 1909
Special Editions: Welcome week, housing guide, new students mail-home, international students, finals week
Delivery Methods: Mail`Newsstand`Carrier`Racks
Published: Thur
Published Other: Digital-only during summer semester at MSU
Avg Free Circ: 7500
Personnel: Omar Sofradzija (Advisor); Marty Sturgeon (Gen. Mgr.); Mike Joseph (Webmaster); Travis Ricks (Creative Adviser)
Parent company (for newspapers): State News, Inc.

EAST STROUDSBURG

EAST STROUDSBURG UNIV.

Street Address 1: University Ctr
State: PA
Zip/Postal code: 18301
Country: USA
Mailing Address: 200 Prospect Street
Mailing City: East Stroudsburg

College and University Newspapers

Mailing State: PA
Mailing ZIP Code: 18301
General Phone: (570) 422-3295
General Fax: (570) 422-3053
General/National Adv. Email: stroudcourier@yahoo.com
Website: www.stroudcourier.com
Personnel: Ryan Doyle (Adv. Mgr.); Stephanie Snyder (Ed. in Chief)

EASTON

LAFAYETTE COLLEGE

Street Address 1: 111 Quad Dr
State: PA
Zip/Postal code: 18042-1768
Country: USA
Mailing Address: Farinon Center Box 9470
Mailing City: Easton
Mailing State: PA
Mailing ZIP Code: 18042
General Phone: (610) 330-5354
General Fax: (610) 330-5724
General/National Adv. Email: thelafayette@gmail.com
Website: www.lafayettestudentnews.com
Personnel: William Gordon (EIC); Ian Morse (Mgr Ed)

EAU CLAIRE

UNIV. OF WISCONSIN EAU CLAIRE

Street Address 1: 105 Garfield Ave
State: WI
Zip/Postal code: 54701-4811
Country: USA
Mailing Address: 104B Hibbard Hall, 105 Garfield Ave
Mailing City: Eau Claire
Mailing State: WI
Mailing ZIP Code: 54701
General Phone: (715) 836-5618
General Fax: (715) 836-3829
Advertising Phone: (715) 836-4366
Editorial Phone: (715) 836-4416
General/National Adv. Email: spectator@uwec.edu
Website: www.spectatornews.com
Personnel: John Cayer (Adv. Mgr.); Scott Hansen (Ed. in Cheif); Breann Schossow (Mng. Ed.); Frank Pellegrino (News Ed.)

EDINBORO

EDINBORO UNIV. OF PENNSYLVANIA

Street Address 1: 119 San Antonio Hall
State: PA
Zip/Postal code: 16444-0001
Country: USA
Mailing Address: 119 San Antonio Hall
Mailing City: Edinboro
Mailing State: PA
Mailing ZIP Code: 16444-0001
General Phone: (814) 732-2266
General Fax: (814) 732-2270
General/National Adv. Email: eupspectator1@yahoo.com
Website: www.eupspectator.com
Personnel: Josh Tysiachney (Advisor); Carli Hoehn (Adv. Mgr.); Britney Kemp (Ed. in Chief); Canuron Ferranti (Mng. Ed.)

EDINBURG

UNIV. OF TEXAS PAN AMERICAN

Street Address 1: 1201 W University Dr
State: TX
Zip/Postal code: 78539-2909
Country: USA
Mailing Address: 1201 W. University Dr.
Mailing City: Edinburg
Mailing State: TX
Mailing ZIP Code: 78539
General Phone: (956) 381-2541
General Fax: (956) 316-7122
General/National Adv. Email: spubs@utpa.edu
Website: www.panamericanonline.com
Personnel: Gregory M. Selber (Advisor); Mariel Cantu (Adv. Mgr.); Brian Silva (Ed. in chief)

EDISON

MIDDLESEX COUNTY COLLEGE

Street Address 1: 2600 Woodbridge Ave
State: NJ
Zip/Postal code: 08837-3604
Country: USA
Mailing Address: 2600 Woodbridge Ave
Mailing City: Edison
Mailing State: NJ
Mailing ZIP Code: 08837-3675
General Phone: (732) 548-6000
General Fax: (732) 906-4167
General/National Adv. Email: quovadis_newspaper@hotmail.com
Personnel: Melissa Edwards (Ed.)

EDMOND

THE VISTA

Street Address 1: 100 N University Dr
State: OK
Zip/Postal code: 73034-5207
Country: USA
Mailing Address: 100 N University Dr
Mailing City: Edmond
Mailing State: OK
Mailing ZIP Code: 73034-5207
General Phone: (405) 974-5123
General Fax: (405) 974-3839
Editorial Phone: (405) 974-5549
General/National Adv. Email: vistamedia@yahoo.com
Editorial Email: vista1903@gmail.com
Website: www.uco360.com
Year Established: 1903
Personnel: Teddy Burch (Advisor); Nelson Solomon (Ed. in Chief)

EDWARDSVILLE

SOUTHERN ILLINOIS UNIVERSITY EDWARDSVILLE

Street Address 1: One Hairpin Drive, Morris University Ctr, Rm 2022
State: IL
Zip/Postal code: 6202
Country: USA
Mailing Address: One Hairpin Drive, Morris University Ctr, Rm 2022
Mailing City: Edwardsville
Mailing State: IL
Mailing ZIP Code: 62026
General Phone: (618) 650-3528
General Fax: (618) 650-3514
Display Adv. Email: advertising@alestlelive.com
Editorial Email: editor@alestlelive.com
Website: www.alestlelive.com
Year Established: 1959
Published: Tues`Thur
Published Other: Tuesdays online exclusively
Avg Free Circ: 3500
Personnel: Tammy Merrett (Advisor)
Parent company (for newspapers): Southern Illinois University Edwardsville

EL CAJON

CUYAMACA COLLEGE

Street Address 1: 900 Rancho San Diego Pkwy
Street Address 2: Bldg G-109
State: CA
Zip/Postal code: 92019-4369
Country: USA
Mailing Address: 900 Rancho San Diego Pkwy Bldg G-109
Mailing City: El Cajon
Mailing State: CA
Mailing ZIP Code: 92019-4369
General Phone: (619) 660-4000
General Fax: (619) 660-4399
Website: www.cuyamaca.edu/coyoteexpress
Year Established: 1977
Personnel: Seth Slater (Contact); Mary Graham (Contact)

GROSSMONT COLLEGE

Street Address 1: 8800 Grossmont College Dr
State: CA
Zip/Postal code: 92020-1765
Country: USA
Mailing Address: 8800 Grossmont College Dr
Mailing City: El Cajon
Mailing State: CA
Mailing ZIP Code: 92020-1798
Advertising Phone: (619) 644-7271
Advertising Fax: (619) 644-7914
Editorial Phone: (619) 644-1730
General/National Adv. Email: summit@gcccd.edu
Website: gcsummit.com
Published: Mthly

EL DORADO

BUTLER COUNTY CMTY. COLLEGE

Street Address 1: 901 S Haverhill Rd
State: KS
Zip/Postal code: 67042-3225
Country: USA
Mailing Address: 901 S Haverhill Rd
Mailing City: El Dorado
Mailing State: KS
Mailing ZIP Code: 67042-3225
General Phone: (316) 322-3170
General Fax: (316) 322-3109
General/National Adv. Email: lantern@butlercc.edu
Website: www.lanternonline.com; www.butlercc.edu
Personnel: Melissa Roberts (Bus. Mgr.)

EL PASO

EL PASO CMTY. COLLEGE

Street Address 1: PO Box 20500
State: TX
Zip/Postal code: 79998-0500
Country: USA
Mailing Address: PO Box 20500
Mailing City: El Paso
Mailing State: TX
Mailing ZIP Code: 79998-0500
General Phone: (915) 831-2500
General Fax: (915) 831-2155
General/National Adv. Email: tejanotribune@eppcc.edu
Personnel: Steve Escajeda (Contact); Joe Old (Advisor)

EL PASO

UNIV. OF TEXAS EL PASO

Street Address 1: 105 Union East
Street Address 2: 500 W. University Ave.
State: TX
Zip/Postal code: 79968-0001
Country: USA
Mailing Address: 105 Union East
Mailing City: El Paso
Mailing State: TX
Mailing ZIP Code: 79968-0622
General Phone: (915) 747-5161
General Fax: (915) 747-8031
Advertising Phone: (915) 747-7434
Editorial Phone: (915) 747-7446
General/National Adv. Email: studentpublications@utep.edu
Display Adv. Email: prospectorads@utep.edu
Editorial Email: theprospector1@gmail.com
Website: www.theprospectordaily.com
Year Established: 1914
Published: Tues
Published Other: www.theprospectordaily.com
Avg Free Circ: 5000
Personnel: Kathleen Flores (Dir); Veronica Gonzalez (Asst. Adv. Dir.)

ELGIN

ELGIN COMMUNITY COLLEGE

Street Address 1: 1700 Spartan Dr
State: IL
Zip/Postal code: 60123-7189
Country: USA
Mailing Address: 1700 Spartan Dr
Mailing City: Elgin
Mailing State: IL
Mailing ZIP Code: 60123-7193
General Phone: (847) 697-1000
General Fax: (847) 888-7352
General/National Adv. Email: elgincollegeobserver@yahoo.com
Display Adv. Email: elgincollegeobserver@yahoo.com
Editorial Email: observereditorinchief@gmail.com
Website: www.elgin.edu
Year Established: 1951
Delivery Methods: Racks
Published Other: Bi-weekly
Personnel: Lori Clark (Faculty Advisor); Michelle Pain (Editor-in-Chief); Fernando Chang (Managing Editor)

ELIZABETH CITY

ELIZABETH CITY STATE UNIV.

Street Address 1: 1704 Weeksville Rd
State: NC
Zip/Postal code: 27909-7977
Country: USA
Mailing Address: 1704 Weeksville Rd
Mailing City: Elizabeth City
Mailing State: NC
Mailing ZIP Code: 27909
General Phone: (252) 335-3343
General Fax: (252) 335-3795
Personnel: Kip Branch (Advisor)

ELIZABETHTOWN

ELIZABETHTOWN COLLEGE

Street Address 1: 1 Alpha Dr
State: PA
Zip/Postal code: 17022-2298
Country: USA
Mailing Address: 1 Alpha Dr
Mailing City: Elizabethtown
Mailing State: PA
Mailing ZIP Code: 17022-2297
General Phone: (717) 361-1132
General/National Adv. Email: editor@etown.edu
Display Adv. Email: etownianads@etown.edu
Editorial Email: editor@etown.edu
Website: www.etownian.com
Year Established: 1904
Published: Thur
Avg Free Circ: 700
Personnel: Aileen Ida (EIC); Katie Weiler (Asst. EIC); Amanda Jobes (Mng. Ed.)

ELLENSBURG

CENTRAL WASHINGTON UNIV.

Street Address 1: 400 E University Way
Street Address 2: Mail Stop 7435, Bouillon 222
State: WA
Zip/Postal code: 98926-7502
Country: USA
Mailing Address: 400 E University Way Rm 222
Mailing City: Ellensburg
Mailing State: WA
Mailing ZIP Code: 98926-7502
General Phone: (509) 963-1026
General Fax: (509) 963-1027
Advertising Phone: 509-963-1095
Advertising Fax: 509-963-1027
Editorial Phone: (509) 963-1073
Editorial Fax: Free
General/National Adv. Email: cwuobserver@gmail.com
Display Adv. Email: gaskillk@cwu.edu
Editorial Email: cwuobserver@gmail.com
Website: www.cwuobserver.com

Special Editions: Orientation/Back to School
Delivery Methods: Newsstand`Racks
Commercial printers?: N
Published: Thur
Avg Free Circ: 6000

ELLISVILLE

JONES COUNTY JUNIOR COLLEGE

Street Address 1: 900 S Court St
State: MS
Zip/Postal code: 39437-3901
Country: USA
Mailing Address: 900 S Court St
Mailing City: Ellisville
Mailing State: MS
Mailing ZIP Code: 39437-3999
General Phone: (601) 477-4084
General Fax: (601) 477-4191
General/National Adv. Email: radionian@jcjc.edu
Display Adv. Email: radionian@jcjc.edu
Editorial Email: radionian@jcjc.edu
Website: www.jcjc.edu
Year Established: 1927
Published: Mthly
Personnel: Kelly Atwood (Newspaper Adviser)

ELMHURST

ELMHURST COLLEGE

Street Address 1: 190 S Prospect Ave
State: IL
Zip/Postal code: 60126-3271
Country: USA
Mailing Address: 190 S Prospect Ave
Mailing City: Elmhurst
Mailing State: IL
Mailing ZIP Code: 60126-3296
General Phone: (630)617-3320
Advertising Phone: (630) 617-3321
General/National Adv. Email: leadernewsec@gmail.com
Display Adv. Email: advertising@ecleader.org
Editorial Email: leadernewsec@gmail.com
Website: ecleader.org
Published: Tues
Published Other: Published bi-weekly
Personnel: Ron Wiginton (Advisor); Aaron Schroeder (Bus. Mgr.); Eric Lutz (Ed. in Chief); Haleema Shah (Editor-in-Chief)

ELMIRA

ELMIRA COLLEGE

Street Address 1: 1 Park Pl
State: NY
Zip/Postal code: 14901-2085
Country: USA
Mailing Address: 1 Park Pl
Mailing City: Elmira
Mailing State: NY
Mailing ZIP Code: 14901-2099
General Phone: (607) 735-1800
Advertising Phone: (607) 735-1758
General/National Adv. Email: octagon@elmira.edu; admissions@elmira.edu
Website: www.elmira.edu
Personnel: David Williams (Advisor); Jolene Carr (Ed.)

ELON

ELON UNIVERSITY

Street Address 1: 130 N Williamson Ave
State: NC
Zip/Postal code: 27244
Country: USA
Mailing Address: 7012 Campus Box
Mailing City: Elon
Mailing State: NC
Mailing ZIP Code: 27244-2062
General Phone: (336) 278-7247
General Fax: (336) 278-7426
General/National Adv. Email: pendulum@elon.edu
Display Adv. Email: pendulum@elon.edu

Website: elonpendulum.com
Personnel: Colin Donohue (Advisor); Andie Diemer (Ed. in Chief); Pam Richter (Sports Ed.); Anna Johnson

ELSAH

PRINCIPIA COLLEGE

Street Address 1: 1 Maybeck Pl
State: IL
Zip/Postal code: 62028-9720
Country: USA
Mailing Address: 1 Maybeck Pl
Mailing City: Elsah
Mailing State: IL
Mailing ZIP Code: 62028-9799
General Phone: (618) 374-5415
General Fax: (618) 374-5122
General/National Adv. Email: principia.pilot@gmail.com
Website: www.prin.edu; www.principiapilot.org
Year Established: 1944
Personnel: Craig Savoye (Advisor); David Miller (Ed. in Chief); Katie Ward (Ed. in Chief); Ben Chernivsky (Photo Ed.)

ELYRIA

LORAIN COUNTY CMTY. COLLEGE

Street Address 1: 1005 Abbe Rd N
State: OH
Zip/Postal code: 44035-1613
Country: USA
Mailing Address: 1005 Abbe Rd N
Mailing City: Elyria
Mailing State: OH
Mailing ZIP Code: 44035-1692
General Phone: (440) 366-4037
General Fax: (440) 365-6519
Editorial Phone: (440) 366-7729
General/National Adv. Email: lcccstories@lorainccc.edu; colegian@lorainccc.edu
Website: www.collegianonline.org
Published: Bi-Mthly
Personnel: Cliff Anthony (Advisor)
Parent company (for newspapers): Lorain County Community College

EMMITSBURG

MOUNT ST. MARY'S UNIV.

Street Address 1: 16300 Old Emmitsburg Rd
State: MD
Zip/Postal code: 21727-7700
Country: USA
Mailing Address: 16300 Old Emmitsburg Rd
Mailing City: Emmitsburg
Mailing State: MD
Mailing ZIP Code: 21727-7700
General Phone: (301) 447-5246
General Fax: (301) 447-5755
General/National Adv. Email: echo@msmary.edu
Website: www.themountainecho.com
Personnel: Sheldon Shealer (Advisor); Allison Doherty (Mng. Ed.)

EMORY

EMORY & HENRY COLLEGE

Street Address 1: PO Box 947
State: VA
Zip/Postal code: 24327-0947
Country: USA
Mailing Address: PO Box 947
Mailing City: Emory
Mailing State: VA
Mailing ZIP Code: 24327-0947
General Phone: (276) 944-6870
Advertising Phone: (276) 944-6934
General/National Adv. Email: ehcwhitetopper@ehc.edu
Personnel: Kathy Borterfield (Advisor)

EPHRAIM

SNOW COLLEGE

Street Address 1: 150 College Ave
State: UT
Zip/Postal code: 84627-1550
Country: USA
Mailing Address: 150 College Ave
Mailing City: Ephraim
Mailing State: UT
Mailing ZIP Code: 84627-1299
General Phone: (435) 283-7385
General/National Adv. Email: snowdrift@snow.edu
Website: www.snow.edu/snowdrift
Personnel: Greg Dart (Advisor); Justin Albee (Bus. Mgr.); Kelly Peterson (Ed. in Chief)

ERIE

GANNON UNIV.

Street Address 1: 109 University Sq
Street Address 2: # 2142
State: PA
Zip/Postal code: 16541-0002
Country: USA
Mailing Address: 109 University Sq # 2142
Mailing City: Erie
Mailing State: PA
Mailing ZIP Code: 16541-0002
General Phone: (814) 871-7294
General Fax: (814) 871-7208
General/National Adv. Email: gannonknight@gannon.edu
Website: www.gannon.edu
Personnel: Frank Garland (Advisor)

MERCYHURST UNIVERSITY

Street Address 1: 501 E 38th St
State: PA
Zip/Postal code: 16546-0002
Country: USA
Mailing Address: 501 E 38th St
Mailing City: Erie
Mailing State: PA
Mailing ZIP Code: 16546-0002
General Phone: (814) 824-2376
General Fax:
General/National Adv. Email: editormerciad@mercyhurst.edu
Display Adv. Email: admerciad@mercyhurst.edu
Editorial Email: opinionmerciad@mercyhurst.edu
Website: merciad.mercyhurst.edu
Year Established: 1929
Delivery Methods: Racks
Commercial printers?: Y
Published: Wed
Avg Free Circ: 1200
Personnel: Bill Welch (Advisor)

PENN STATE UNIV.

Street Address 1: 4701 College Dr
State: PA
Zip/Postal code: 16563-4117
Country: USA
Mailing Address: 4701 College Dr
Mailing City: Erie
Mailing State: PA
Mailing ZIP Code: 16563-4117
General Phone: (814) 898-6488
General Fax: (814) 898-6019
General/National Adv. Email: www.pserie.psu.edu
Published: Tues
Personnel: Sarah Veslany (Editor in Chief)

THE BEHREND BEACON

Street Address 1: Penn State University-Erie the Behrend College
Street Address 2: 0171 Irvin Kochel Center
State: PA
Zip/Postal code: 16563-0001
Country: USA
Mailing Address: Penn State University-Erie

the Behrend College
Mailing City: Erie
Mailing State: PA
Mailing ZIP Code: 16563
General Phone: 814-898-6488
General/National Adv. Email: editor@psu.edu
Website: www.thebehrendbeacon.com

ESTHERVILLE

IOWA LAKES CMTY. COLLEGE

Street Address 1: 300 S 18th St
State: IA
Zip/Postal code: 51334-2721
Country: USA
Mailing Address: 300 S 18th St
Mailing City: Estherville
Mailing State: IA
Mailing ZIP Code: 51334-2721
General Phone: (712) 362-2604
General Fax: (712) 362-8363
General/National Adv. Email: pbuchholz@iowalakes.edu; info@iowalakes.edu
Website: www.iowalakes.edu
Personnel: Pam Bushholz (Journalism Instructor/Advisor)

EUGENE

LANE CMTY. COLLEGE

Street Address 1: 4000 E 30th Ave
Street Address 2: Rm 008
State: OR
Zip/Postal code: 97405-0640
Country: USA
Mailing Address: 4000 East 30th Ave. Center Building, Room 008
Mailing City: Eugene
Mailing State: OR
Mailing ZIP Code: 97405-0640
General Phone: (541) 463-5881
General Fax: (541) 463-3993
General/National Adv. Email: torch@lanecc.edu
Website: www.lcctorch.com
Personnel: Dorothy Wearne (Advisor); Lana Boles (Ed. in Cheif); James Anderson (Ed.)

UNIV. OF OREGON

Street Address 1: 1395 University St
State: OR
Zip/Postal code: 97403-2572
Country: USA
Mailing Address: PO Box 3159
Mailing City: Eugene
Mailing State: OR
Mailing ZIP Code: 97403-0159
General Phone: (541) 346-5511
General Fax: (541) 346-5821
General/National Adv. Email: news@dailyemerald.com
Editorial Email: editor@dailyemerald.com
Website: www.dailyemerald.com
Personnel: Allie Grasgreen (Ed. in chief); Emily E. Smith (Mng. Ed.); Ivar Vong (Photo Ed.)

EVANSTON

KELLOGG GRAD. SCHOOL OF MGMT.

Street Address 1: 2001 Sheridan Rd
State: IL
Zip/Postal code: 60208-0814
Country: USA
Mailing Address: 2001 Sheridan Rd
Mailing City: Evanston
Mailing State: IL
Mailing ZIP Code: 60208-0814
General Phone: (847) 491-3924
General Fax: (847) 467-6173
Personnel: Nick Slater (Ed.)

NORTHWESTERN UNIVERSITY

Street Address 1: 1845 Sheridan Rd
State: IL
Zip/Postal code: 60208-0815

College and University Newspapers

Country: USA
Mailing Address: 1845 Sheridan Rd
Mailing City: Evanston
Mailing State: IL
Mailing ZIP Code: 60208-0815
General Phone: (847) 467-1882
General Fax: (847) 491-5565
Personnel: John Lavine (Dean); David Abrahamson (Prof.); Martin Block (Prof.); Jack Doppelt (Prof.); Loren Ghiglione (Prof.); Alec Klein (Prof.); Donna Leff (Prof.); Frank Mulhern (Prof.); Jon Petrovich (Prof.); David Protess (Prof.); Don Schultz (Prof.); Ellen Shearer (Prof.); Clarke Caywood (Assoc. Prof.); Mary Coffman (Assoc. Prof.); Tom Collinger (Assoc. Prof.); Doug Foster (Assoc. Prof.); Jeremy Gilbert (Assoc. Prof.); Rich Gordon (Assoc. Prof.); John Greening (Assoc. Prof.); Ava Greenwell (Assoc. Prof.)

NORTHWESTERN UNIVERSITY

Street Address 1: 1999 Campus Dr
State: IL
Zip/Postal code: 60208-0825
Country: USA
Mailing Address: 1999 Campus Dr
Mailing City: Evanston
Mailing State: IL
Mailing ZIP Code: 60208-2532
General Phone: (847) 491-3222
General Fax: (847) 491-9905
Editorial Phone: (847) 491-7206
General/National Adv. Email: eic@dailynorthwestern.com
Display Adv. Email: spc-compshop@northwestern.edu
Website: www.dailynorthwestern.com
Year Established: 1881
Published: Mon`Tues`Wed`Thur`Fri
Parent company (for newspapers): Students Publishing Company

EVANSVILLE

UNIV. OF EVANSVILLE

Street Address 1: 1800 Lincoln Ave
State: IN
Zip/Postal code: 47722-1000
Country: USA
Mailing Address: 1800 Lincoln Ave
Mailing City: Evansville
Mailing State: IN
Mailing ZIP Code: 47714-1506
General Phone: (812) 488-2846
General Fax: (812) 488-2224
Advertising Phone: 812-488-2221
Advertising Fax: (812) 488-2224
Editorial Phone: (812) 488-2846
Editorial Fax: (812) 488-2224
General/National Adv. Email: crescentmagazine@evansville.edu
Display Adv. Email: crescentadvertising@evansville.edu
Editorial Email: crescentmagazine@evansville.edu
Year Established: 2009
Published: Thur`Mthly
Avg Free Circ: 1700
Personnel: Amy Reinhart (Writing Director); Rebecca Kish (Marketing & Sales Director)

UNIV. OF SOUTHERN INDIANA

Street Address 1: 8600 University Blvd
State: IN
Zip/Postal code: 47712-3534
Country: USA
Mailing Address: 8600 University Blvd
Mailing City: Evansville
Mailing State: IN
Mailing ZIP Code: 47712-3590
General Phone: (812) 464 8600
General Fax: (812) 465-1632
Advertising Phone: (812) 464-1870
General/National Adv. Email: sheild@usi.edu
Display Adv. Email: shieldads@gmail.com
Editorial Email: shieldpix@gmail.com
Website: www.usishield.com; www.usi.edu

Personnel: Jon Webb (Ed. in Chief)

EVERETT

EVERETT COMMUNITY COLLEGE

Street Address 1: 2000 Tower St
Street Address 2: Whitehorse Hall 265-268
State: WA
Zip/Postal code: 98201-1352
Country: USA
Mailing Address: 2000 Tower St.
Mailing City: Everett
Mailing State: WA
Mailing ZIP Code: 98201-1390
General Phone: (425) 388-9522
General/National Adv. Email: clipper@everettcc.edu
Website: www.everettclipper.com
Year Established: 1943
Special Weekly Sections: Arts and Entertainment
Delivery Methods: Mail`Racks
Commercial printers?: Y
Published: Other
Published Other: Every three weeks
Avg Free Circ: 2500
Personnel: T. Andrew Wahl (Adviser); Terresa King (Business & Circulation Director); Nataya Foss (Editor-in-chief)

EWING

THE COLLEGE OF NEW JERSEY

Street Address 1: PO Box 7718
State: NJ
Zip/Postal code: 08628-0718
Country: USA
Mailing Address: PO Box 7718
Mailing City: Ewing
Mailing State: NJ
Mailing ZIP Code: 08628-0718
General Phone: (609) 771-2499
General Fax: (609) 771-3433
Advertising Phone: (609) 771-3433
Editorial Phone: (609) 771-2424
General/National Adv. Email: signal@tcnj.edu
Display Adv. Email: signalad@tcnj.edu
Website: tcnjsignal.net
Year Established: 1885
Published: Wed
Personnel: Emilie Lounsberry (Advisor)

FAIRBANKS

UNIV. OF ALASKA FAIRBANKS

Street Address 1: PO Box 756640
State: AK
Zip/Postal code: 99775-6640
Country: USA
Mailing Address: PO Box 756640
Mailing City: Fairbanks
Mailing State: AK
Mailing ZIP Code: 99775-6640
General Phone: (907) 474-6039
General Fax: (907) 474-5508
General/National Adv. Email: fystar@uaf.edu
Website: www.uafsunstar.com
Published: Tues
Personnel: Chavis Lakeidra (Editor-in-Chief); Manager Advertising

FAIRFAX

GEORGE MASON UNIVERSITY

Street Address 1: 4400 University Dr
Street Address 2: MS 2C5
State: VA
Zip/Postal code: 22030-4422
Country: USA
Mailing Address: 4400 University Dr MS 2C5
Mailing City: Fairfax
Mailing State: VA
Mailing ZIP Code: 22030-4444
General Phone: (703) 993-2947
General Fax: (703) 993-2948
Advertising Phone: (703) 993-2942

Editorial Phone: (703) 993-2944
General/National Adv. Email: cwilso12@gmu.edu
Website: gmufourthestate.com
Published: Mon
Avg Free Circ: 6000
Personnel: Kathryn Mangus (Advisor)

FAIRFIELD

FAIRFIELD UNIV.

Street Address 1: 1073 N Benson Rd
State: CT
Zip/Postal code: 06824-5171
Country: USA
Mailing Address: PO Box AA
Mailing City: Fairfield
Mailing State: CT
Mailing ZIP Code: 06824
General Phone: (203) 254-4000
General Fax: (203) 254-4162
Display Adv. Email: advertising@fairfieldmirror.com
Website: www.fairfieldmirror.com
Published: Wed
Avg Free Circ: 3500
Personnel: Lei Xie (Faculty adviser)

MAHARISHI UNIV. OF MGMT.

Street Address 1: 1000 N 4th St
State: IA
Zip/Postal code: 52557
Country: USA
Mailing Address: 1000 N 4th St # 694
Mailing City: Fairfield
Mailing State: IA
Mailing ZIP Code: 52557
General Phone: (641) 472-0778
Advertising Phone: (641) 472-0778
Editorial Phone: (641) 472-0778
General/National Adv. Email: jkarpen@mum.edu
Display Adv. Email: jkarpen@mum.edu
Editorial Email: jkarpen@mum.edu
Website: https://www.mum.edu/the-review/recent-issues/
Year Established: 1985
Published: Other
Published Other: every two weeks
Avg Free Circ: 1000
Personnel: Jim Karpen (Ed.)

SACRED HEART UNIV.

Street Address 1: 5151 Park Ave
State: CT
Zip/Postal code: 06825-1090
Country: USA
Mailing Address: 5151 Park Ave
Mailing City: Fairfield
Mailing State: CT
Mailing ZIP Code: 06825-1000
General Phone: (203) 371-7966
General Fax: (203) 371-7828
Advertising Phone: (203) 371-7963
General/National Adv. Email: spectrum@sacredheart.edu
Display Adv. Email: spectrum-advertising@sacredheart.edu
Website: www.shuspectrum.wordpress.com
Personnel: Joanne Kabak (Advisor); Lauren Sampson (Adv. Mgr.); Carli-Rae Panny (Ed. in Chief); Kate Poole (Mng. Ed.)

SOLANO COMMUNITY COLLEGE

Street Address 1: 4000 Suisun Valley Rd
State: CA
Zip/Postal code: 94534-4017
Country: USA
Mailing Address: 4000 Suisun Valley Rd
Mailing City: Fairfield
Mailing State: CA
Mailing ZIP Code: 94534-3197
General Phone: (707) 864-7000
General Fax: (707) 864-0361
General/National Adv. Email: tempest@solano.edu
Display Adv. Email: samanda.dorger@solano.

edu
Editorial Email: tempest@solano.edu
Website: www.solanotempest.net
Published: Bi-Mthly
Avg Free Circ: 1500
Personnel: Samanda Dorger (Journalism Adviser)

FALL RIVER

BRISTOL CMTY. COLLEGE

Street Address 1: 777 Elsbree St
State: MA
Zip/Postal code: 02720-7307
Country: USA
Mailing Address: 777 Elsbree St
Mailing City: Fall River
Mailing State: MA
Mailing ZIP Code: 02720-7399
General Phone: (508) 678-2811
General Fax: (508) 676-7146
General/National Adv. Email: observer@bristolcc.edu
Website: www.bristolcc.edu/Students/observer/index.cfm
Personnel: Alex Potter (Ed. in Chief)

FARGO

NORTH DAKOTA STATE UNIV.

Street Address 1: 254 Memorial Union
State: ND
Zip/Postal code: 58102
Country: USA
Mailing Address: P.O. Box 6050
Mailing City: Fargo
Mailing State: ND
Mailing ZIP Code: 58108-6050
General Phone: (701) 231-8929
General Fax: (701) 231-9402
Advertising Phone: (701) 231-8994
Editorial Phone: (701) 231-8629
General/National Adv. Email: ad.manager@ndsuspectrum.com
Display Adv. Email: ad.manager@ndsuspectrum.com
Editorial Email: editor@ndsuspectrum.com
Website: www.ndsuspectrum.com
Year Established: 1896
News Services: AP
Delivery Methods: Racks
Commercial printers?: Y
Published: Mon`Thur
Avg Free Circ: 7000
Personnel: Andrew Pritchard (Advisor)

FARMERS BRANCH

BROOKHAVEN COLLEGE

Street Address 1: 3939 Valley View Ln
State: TX
Zip/Postal code: 75244-4906
Country: USA
Mailing Address: 3939 Valley View Ln
Mailing City: Farmers Branch
Mailing State: TX
Mailing ZIP Code: 75244-4997
General Phone: (972) 860-4700
General Fax: (972) 860-4142
General/National Adv. Email: bhc2110@dcccd.edu
Website: www.brookhavencourier.com; www.brookhavencollege.edu
Personnel: Wendy Moore (Advisor); Daniel Rodrigue (Advisor)

FARMINGDALE

SUNY COLLEGE OF TECHNOLOGY/FARMINGDALE

Street Address 1: Melville Rd, Roosevelt Hall
State: NY
Zip/Postal code: 11735
Country: USA

Mailing Address: Melville Rd., Roosevelt Hall
Mailing City: Farmingdale
Mailing State: NY
Mailing ZIP Code: 11735
General Phone: (631) 420-2611
General Fax: (631) 420-2692
General/National Adv. Email: rambler@farmingdale.edu
Personnel: Jeff Borga (Ed. in Chief)

FARMVILLE

LONGWOOD COLLEGE

Street Address 1: PO Box 2901
State: VA
Zip/Postal code: 23909-0001
Country: USA
Mailing Address: PO Box 2901
Mailing City: Farmville
Mailing State: VA
Mailing ZIP Code: 23909-0001
General Phone: (434) 395-2120
General Fax: (434) 395-2237
General/National Adv. Email: rotunda@longwood.edu
Personnel: Ramesh Rao (Advisor); Emily Grove (Ed. in Chief); Benjamin Byrnes (Mng. Ed.)

FAYETTEVILLE

ARKANSAS TRAVELER

Street Address 1: 119 Kimpel Hall
State: AR
Zip/Postal code: 72701
Country: USA
Mailing Address: 119 Kimpel Hall
Mailing City: Fayetteville
Mailing State: AR
Mailing ZIP Code: 72701
General Phone: (479) 575-3406
General Fax: (479) 575-3306
General/National Adv. Email: traveler@uark.edu
Website: www.uatrav.com/
Personnel: Saba Naseem (Editor-in-Chief)

FAYETTEVILLE STATE UNIV.

Street Address 1: 1200 Murchison Rd
State: NC
Zip/Postal code: 28301-4252
Country: USA
Mailing Address: 1200 Murchison Rd
Mailing City: Fayetteville
Mailing State: NC
Mailing ZIP Code: 28301-4298
General Phone: (910) 672-2210
General Fax: (910) 672-1964
Website: www.fsuvoice.com
Personnel: Valonda Calloway (Advisor); Nathalie Rivera (Bus. Mgr.); L'Asia Brown (Ed. in Chief)

METHODIST UNIVERSITY

Street Address 1: 5400 Ramsey St
State: NC
Zip/Postal code: 28311-1420
Country: USA
Mailing Address: 5400 Ramsey St
Mailing City: Fayetteville
Mailing State: NC
Mailing ZIP Code: 28311-1420
General Phone: (910) 630-7292
General Fax: (910) 630-7253
General/National Adv. Email: dmunoz@methodist.edu
Website: www.smalltalkmu.com
Published: Bi-Mthly
Avg Free Circ: 2400
Personnel: Doris Munoz (Director of Student Life)

FENNIMORE

SOUTHWEST WISCONSIN TECH. COLLEGE

Street Address 1: 1800 Bronson Blvd
State: WI
Zip/Postal code: 53809-9778
Country: USA
Mailing Address: 1800 Bronson Blvd
Mailing City: Fennimore
Mailing State: WI
Mailing ZIP Code: 53809-9778
General Phone: (608) 822-3262
General Fax: (608) 822-6019
General/National Adv. Email: jcullen@swtc.edu
Website: www.swtc.edu
Personnel: Jackie Cullen (Advisor)

FERGUS FALLS

FERGUS FALLS CMTY. COLLEGE

Street Address 1: 1414 College Way
State: MN
Zip/Postal code: 56537-1009
Country: USA
Mailing Address: 1414 College Way
Mailing City: Fergus Falls
Mailing State: MN
Mailing ZIP Code: 56537-1009
General Phone: (877) 450-3322
General Fax: (218) 736-1510
Personnel: Angela Schroeder (Ed.)

FERRUM

FERRUM COLLEGE

Street Address 1: PO Box 1000
State: VA
Zip/Postal code: 24088-9001
Country: USA
Mailing Address: PO Box 1000
Mailing City: Ferrum
Mailing State: VA
Mailing ZIP Code: 24088-9001
General Phone: (540) 365-4334
General Fax: (540) 365-4203
Website: www.ferrum.edu/ironblade
Personnel: Dr. Lana Whited (Advisor)

FINDLAY

THE UNIVERSITY OF FINDLAY

Street Address 1: 1000 N Main St
State: OH
Zip/Postal code: 45840-3653
Country: USA
Mailing Address: 1000 N Main St
Mailing City: Findlay
Mailing State: OH
Mailing ZIP Code: 45840-3653
General Phone: (419) 434-5892
Advertising Phone: (419) 434-5892
Editorial Phone: (419) 434-5892
General/National Adv. Email: pulse@findlay.edu
Display Adv. Email: pulse@findlay.edu
Editorial Email: pulse@findlay.edu
Website: www.findlay.edu/pulse
Year Established: 1986 (as the Pulse)
Published: Fri
Avg Free Circ: 1000
Personnel: Olivia Wile (Pulse Editor)

FITCHBURG

FITCHBURG STATE COLLEGE

Street Address 1: 160 Pearl St
State: MA
Zip/Postal code: 01420-2631
Country: USA
Mailing Address: 160 Pearl St
Mailing City: Fitchburg
Mailing State: MA
Mailing ZIP Code: 01420-2697
General Phone: (978) 665-3647
Advertising Phone: (978) 665-3650
General/National Adv. Email: pointstorybudget@yahoo.com
Website: www.thepointfsc.com; www.fsc.edu
Personnel: Doris Schmidt (Advisor); John McGinn (Ed.)

FLAGSTAFF

NORTHERN ARIZONA UNIV.

Street Address 1: PO Box 6000
State: AZ
Zip/Postal code: 86011-0180
Country: USA
Mailing Address: PO Box 6000
Mailing City: Flagstaff
Mailing State: AZ
Mailing ZIP Code: 86011-0180
General Phone: (928) 523-4921
General Fax: (928) 523-9313
General/National Adv. Email: lumberjack@nau.edu
Website: www.jackcentral.com
Personnel: Ace Mcmillin (Ed. In Cheif); Gary Sundt (Gen. Mgr.); Joshua Garcia (Adv. Dir.); Jesica Demarco (Adv. Dir.)

FLINT

MOTT CMTY. COLLEGE

Street Address 1: 1401 E Court St
State: MI
Zip/Postal code: 48503-6208
Country: USA
Mailing Address: 1401 E Court St
Mailing City: Flint
Mailing State: MI
Mailing ZIP Code: 48503-2090
General Phone: (810) 762-5616
General Fax: (810) 762-5646
Personnel: Steve Bossey (Ed.)

FLINT

UNIV. OF MICHIGAN

Street Address 1: 303 E Kearsley St
State: MI
Zip/Postal code: 48502-1907
Country: USA
Mailing Address: 303 E Kearsley St
Mailing City: Flint
Mailing State: MI
Mailing ZIP Code: 48502-1907
General Phone: (810) 762-3475
General Fax: (810) 762-3023
Advertising Phone: (810) 762-0919
General/National Adv. Email: mtimes@hotmail.com
Website: www.themichigantimes.com
Personnel: Joseph Patterson (Adv. Mgr.); Jennifer Profitt (Ed. in Chief)

FLORENCE

FRANCIS MARION UNIVERSITY

Street Address 1: Rm 201 University Center
State: SC
Zip/Postal code: 29506
Country: USA
Mailing Address: PO Box 100547
Mailing City: Florence
Mailing State: SC
Mailing ZIP Code: 29502-0547
General Phone: (843) 661-1350
General Fax: (843) 661-1373
General/National Adv. Email: patriotnews@hotmail.com
Display Adv. Email: patriotads@hotmail.com
Website: www.patriotnewsonline.com
Delivery Methods: Carrier
Commercial printers?: N
Published: Bi-Mthly
Personnel: David Sacash (Faculty Advisor)

UNIV. OF NORTH ALABAMA

Street Address 1: 1 Harrison Plz
Street Address 2: # 5300
State: AL
Zip/Postal code: 35632-0002
Country: USA
Mailing Address: One Harrison Plaza, UNA Box 5300
Mailing City: Florence
Mailing State: AL
Mailing ZIP Code: 35632
General Phone: (256) 765-4364
Advertising Phone: (256) 765-4427
General/National Adv. Email: editor@florala.net
Website: www.florala.net
Year Established: 1830
Published: Thur`Other
Published Other: biweekly
Personnel: Scott Morris (Student Media Advisor)

FLUSHING

QUEENS COLLEGE/CUNY

Street Address 1: 6530 Kissena Blvd
Street Address 2: Student Union Rm. LL-34
State: NY
Zip/Postal code: 11367-1575
Country: USA
Mailing Address: 6530 Kissena Blvd
Mailing City: Flushing
Mailing State: NY
Mailing ZIP Code: 11367-1597
General Phone: (718) 997-5000
Advertising Fax: (718) 997-3755
General/National Adv. Email: info@theknightnews.com
Website: www.theknightnews.com
Published: Tues
Personnel: Gerry Solomon (Advisor); Will Sammon (Editor-in-Chief); Andrea Hardalo (Editor-In-Chief)

FOND DU LAC

MARIAN UNIVERSITY

Street Address 1: 45 S National Ave
State: WI
Zip/Postal code: 54935-4621
Country: USA
Mailing Address: 45 S National Ave
Mailing City: Fond Du Lac
Mailing State: WI
Mailing ZIP Code: 54935-4621
General Phone: (920) 923-8776
General Fax: (920) 923-8158
Website: www.marianuniversitysabre.com
Personnel: Vicky Hildebrandt (Advisor); Katie Leist (Ed.)

FOREST CITY

WALDORF COLLEGE

Street Address 1: 206 John K Hanson Dr
State: IA
Zip/Postal code: 50436
Country: USA
Mailing Address: 106 S 6th St
Mailing City: Forest City
Mailing State: IA
Mailing ZIP Code: 50436-1797
General Phone: (641) 585-2450
General Fax: (641) 582-8194
General/National Adv. Email: lobbyist@waldorf.edu
Website: lobbyist.waldorf.edu
Personnel: David Damm (Advisor); Sarah Soy (Mng. Ed.); Caitlin Leitzen (Mng. Ed.); Matt Knutson (Web Ed.)

FOREST GROVE

PACIFIC UNIV.

Street Address 1: 2043 College Way
State: OR
Zip/Postal code: 97116-1756
Country: USA
Mailing Address: 2043 College Way

College and University Newspapers

Mailing City: Forest Grove
Mailing State: OR
Mailing ZIP Code: 97116
General Phone: (503) 352-2855
Advertising Phone: 503 352 2855
Advertising Fax: (503) 352-3130
Editorial Phone: 503 352 2855
General/National Adv. Email: index@pacificu.edu
Editorial Email: karissa@pacindex.com
Website: www.pacindex.com
Year Established: 1897
Delivery Methods: Newsstand
Published: Bi-Mthly
Avg Free Circ: 1200
Personnel: Dave Cassady (Adviser); Karrisa George (Managing editor); Kathleen Rohde (Web edition editor)

FORT COLLINS

COLORADO STATE UNIV.

Street Address 1: PO Box 13
State: CO
Zip/Postal code: 80522-0013
Country: USA
Mailing Address: PO Box 13
Mailing City: Fort Collins
Mailing State: CO
Mailing ZIP Code: 80522-0013
General Phone: (970) 491-1146
General Fax: (970) 491-1690
General/National Adv. Email: editor@collegian.com
Website: www.collegian.com
Personnel: Holly Wolcott (Advisor); Virginia Singarayar (Ed. in Chief); Madeline Novey (News Mng. Ed.); Matt Minich (News Ed.); Matt L. (Sports Ed.); Kim (Adv. Mgr.)

COLORADO STATE UNIV. ENGINEERING COLLEGE

Street Address 1: PO Box 13
State: CO
Zip/Postal code: 80522-0013
Country: USA
Mailing Address: PO Box 13
Mailing City: Fort Collins
Mailing State: CO
Mailing ZIP Code: 80522-0013
General Phone: (970) 491-1686
General Fax: (970) 491-1690
Website: www.collegian.com
Personnel: Brandon Lowrey (Ed. in Chief)

FORT DODGE

IOWA CENTRAL CMTY. COLLEGE

Street Address 1: 330 Avenue M
State: IA
Zip/Postal code: 50501-5739
Country: USA
Mailing Address: 330 Avenue M
Mailing City: Fort Dodge
Mailing State: IA
Mailing ZIP Code: 50501-5739
General Phone: (515) 576-0099
General Fax: (515) 576-7724
General/National Adv. Email: mcintyre@iowacentral.com
Website: www.iccc.cc.ia.us/collegian/staff.htm
Personnel: Bill McIntyre (Advisor); Ian Schmit (Ed.)

FORT MORGAN

MORGAN CMTY. COLLEGE

Street Address 1: 920 Barlow Rd
State: CO
Zip/Postal code: 80701-4371
Country: USA
Mailing Address: 920 Barlow Rd
Mailing City: Fort Morgan
Mailing State: CO
Mailing ZIP Code: 80701-4371
General Phone: (970) 542-3170

General Fax: (970) 867-3084
Personnel: Jennifer Lankford (Ed.)

FORT SMITH

WESTARK CMTY. COLLEGE

Street Address 1: PO Box 3649
State: AR
Zip/Postal code: 72913-3649
Country: USA
Mailing Address: PO Box 3649
Mailing City: Fort Smith
Mailing State: AR
Mailing ZIP Code: 72913-3649
General Phone: (501) 788-7261

FORT VALLEY

FT. VALLEY STATE UNIV.

Street Address 1: 1005 State University Dr
State: GA
Zip/Postal code: 31030-4313
Country: USA
Mailing Address: 121 Huntington Chase Cir
Mailing City: Warner Robins
Mailing State: GA
Mailing ZIP Code: 31088-2675
General Phone: (478) 825-6910
General Fax: (478) 825-6140
General/National Adv. Email: peachite@fvsu.edu.
Personnel: Valerie White (Advisor); Mick-Aela Nobles (Ed.).

FORT WAYNE

INDIANA-PURDUE UNIV.

Street Address 1: 2101 E Coliseum Blvd
Street Address 2: Walb 215
State: IN
Zip/Postal code: 46805-1445
Country: USA
Mailing Address: 2101 E Coliseum Blvd Ste 100
Mailing City: Fort Wayne
Mailing State: IN
Mailing ZIP Code: 46805-1499
General Phone: (260) 481-6583
General Fax: (260) 481-6045
General/National Adv. Email: publisher@ipfwcommunicator.org
Display Adv. Email: ads@ipfwcommunicator.org
Website: www.ipfwcommunicator.org
Personnel: Matt cClure (Pub.); Kristin Conley (Adv. Mgr.); Aaron Greene (Ed. in Chief)

FORT WORTH

TEXAS CHRISTIAN UNIVERSITY

Street Address 1: 2805 S University Dr
Street Address 2: Moudy South Rm. 215
State: TX
Zip/Postal code: 76129-0001
Country: USA
Mailing Address: TCU Box 298050
Mailing City: Fort Worth
Mailing State: TX
Mailing ZIP Code: 76129-0001
General Phone: (817) 257-7428
General Fax: (817) 257-7133
Advertising Phone: (817) 257-7426
Advertising Fax: 8172577133
Editorial Phone: 8172573600
Editorial Fax: 8172577133
General/National Adv. Email: 360@tcu360.com
Display Adv. Email: ads@tcu360.com
Editorial Email: 360@tcu360.com
Website: www.tcu360.com
Year Established: 1902
Published: Thur
Published Other: IMAGE Magazine
Avg Free Circ: 2000
Personnel: Leah Griffin (Manager of Student Media Sales and Marketing); Jean Marie Brown (Assistant Professor of Professional Practice)

THE RAMBLER

Street Address 1: 1201 Wesleyan St
State: TX
Zip/Postal code: 76105-1536
Country: USA
Mailing Address: 1201 Wesleyan St
Mailing City: Fort Worth
Mailing State: TX
Mailing ZIP Code: 76105-1536
General Phone: (817) 531-7552
General Fax: (817) 531-4878
Advertising Phone: (817) 531-6525
Advertising Fax: 817-531-4878
Editorial Phone: 817-531-7552
Editorial Fax: 817-531-4878
General/National Adv. Email: twurambler@yahoo.com
Display Adv. Email: rambleradvertising@yahoo.com
Editorial Email: twurambler@yahoo.com
Website: www.therambler.org
Year Established: 1917
Commercial printers?: Y
Published Other: Biweekly print; weekly online
Avg Free Circ: 1200
Personnel: Kelli Lamers (Advisor); Ashely Oldham (Adv. Mgr.); Tiara Nugent (Ed. in Chief); Martin Garcia (News Ed.); Kay Colley (Student Media Director)

FRAMINGHAM

FRAMINGHAM STATE UNIVERSITY - THE GATEPOST

Street Address 1: 100 State St
Street Address 2: Rm 410
State: MA
Zip/Postal code: 01702-2499
Country: USA
Mailing Address: McCarthy Center 410
Mailing City: Framingham
Mailing State: MA
Mailing ZIP Code: 01702-2499
General Phone: (508) 626-4605
General Fax: (508) 626-4097
Advertising Phone: (508) 626-4605
Advertising Fax: (508) 626-4097
Editorial Phone: (508) 626-4605
Editorial Fax: (508) 626-4097
General/National Adv. Email: gatepost@framingham.edu
Display Adv. Email: gatepost@framingham.edu
Editorial Email: gatepost@framingham.edu
Website: www.fsugatepost.com
Year Established: 1930
Delivery Methods: Mail Racks
Published: Fri
Personnel: Desmond McCarthy (Advisor); Meredith O'Brien-Weiss (Advisor); Robin KurKomelis (Administrative Assistant); Kerrin Murray (Editor-in-Chief); Joe Kourieh (Associate Editor); Karin Radoc (Associate Editor)

FRANKFORT

KENTUCKY STATE UNIV.

Street Address 1: 400 E Main St
State: KY
Zip/Postal code: 40601-2334
Country: USA
Mailing Address: 400 E Main St
Mailing City: Frankfort
Mailing State: KY
Mailing ZIP Code: 40601-2355
General Phone: (502) 597-5915
General Fax: (502) 597-5927
Website: www.ksuthorobreds.com/
Personnel: Sepricia White (Ed. in Chief); Terri McCray (Features Ed.); Cornell Ferrill (Sports Ed.)

FRANKLIN

DEAN COLLEGE

Street Address 1: 99 Main St

State: MA
Zip/Postal code: 02038-1941
Country: USA
Mailing Address: 99 Main St
Mailing City: Franklin
Mailing State: MA
Mailing ZIP Code: 02038-1994
General Phone: (508) 541-1630
General Fax: (508) 541-1946

FRANKLIN COLLEGE

Street Address 1: 101 Branigin Blvd
State: IN
Zip/Postal code: 46131-2598
Country: USA
Mailing Address: 101 Branigin Blvd
Mailing City: Franklin
Mailing State: IN
Mailing ZIP Code: 46131-2623
General Phone: (317) 738-8191
General Fax: (317) 738-8234
General/National Adv. Email: thefranklin@franklincollege.edu
Website: www.thefranklinonline.com
Personnel: Katie Coffin (Ed.)

FREDERICK

HOOD COLLEGE

Street Address 1: 401 Rosemont Ave
State: MD
Zip/Postal code: 21701-8524
Country: USA
Mailing Address: 401 Rosemont Ave
Mailing City: Frederick
Mailing State: MD
Mailing ZIP Code: 21701-8575
General Phone: (301) 696-3641
General Fax: (301) 696-3578
General/National Adv. Email: weinberg@hood.edu
Personnel: Rita Davis (Ed.); Al Weinberg (Dir./Prof. of Journalism)

FREDERICKSBURG

UNIVERSITY OF MARY WASHINGTON

Street Address 1: 1301 College Ave
State: VA
Zip/Postal code: 22401-5300
Country: USA
Mailing Address: 1301 College Ave
Mailing City: Fredericksburg
Mailing State: VA
Mailing ZIP Code: 22401-5300
General Phone: (540) 654-1536
Display Adv. Email: blueandgray.eic@gmail.com
Website: blueandgraypress.com
Delivery Methods: Carrier
Commercial printers?: Y
Personnel: Michael McCarthy (Advisor)

FREEPORT

HIGHLAND CMTY. COLLEGE

Street Address 1: 2998 W Pearl City Rd
State: IL
Zip/Postal code: 61032-9338
Country: USA
Mailing Address: 2998 W Pearl City Rd
Mailing City: Freeport
Mailing State: IL
Mailing ZIP Code: 61032-9341
General Phone: (815) 235-6121
General Fax: (815) 235-6130
General/National Adv. Email: highland.chronicle@highland.edu
Personnel: Sam Tucibat (Advisor)

FREMONT

OHLONE COLLEGE

Street Address 1: 43600 Mission Blvd

State: CA
Zip/Postal code: 94539-5847
Country: USA
Mailing Address: PO Box 3909
Mailing City: Fremont
Mailing State: CA
Mailing ZIP Code: 94539-0390
General Phone: (510) 659-6074
General Fax: (510) 659-6076
General/National Adv. Email: monitor@ohlone.edu; monitor@ohlone.cc.ca.us
Website: www.ohlonemonitoronline.com
Published Other: Nine times per semester
Personnel: Rob Dennis (Adviser)

FRESNO

ALLIANT INTERNATIONAL UNIV.

Street Address 1: 5130 E Clinton Way
State: CA
Zip/Postal code: 93727-2014
Country: USA
Mailing Address: 5130 E Clinton Way
Mailing City: Fresno
Mailing State: CA
Mailing ZIP Code: 93727-2014
General Phone: (559) 456-2777
General Fax: (858) 635-4853
Editorial Phone: (858) 635-4540
General/National Adv. Email: envoy@alliant.edu; envoy.alliant@gmail.com
Personnel: Miles Beauchamp (Advisor); Alexandria Proff (Ed.)

CALIFORNIA STATE UNIV.

Street Address 1: 5201 N Maple Ave
Street Address 2: MS SA42
State: CA
Zip/Postal code: 93740-0001
Country: USA
Mailing Address: 5201 N Maple Ave MS SA42
Mailing City: Fresno
Mailing State: CA
Mailing ZIP Code: 93740-0001
General Phone: (559) 278-5735
General Fax: (559) 278-2679
Editorial Phone: (559) 278-5732
General/National Adv. Email: collegian@csufresno.edu
Website: www.csufresno.edu/collegian
Personnel: Jefferson Beavers (Advisor); Virginia Sellars-Erxleben (Bus. Mgr.); Brian Maxey (Ed. in Chief)

FRESNO CITY COLLEGE

Street Address 1: 1101 E University Ave
State: CA
Zip/Postal code: 93741-0001
Country: USA
Mailing Address: 1101 E University Ave
Mailing City: Fresno
Mailing State: CA
Mailing ZIP Code: 93741-0002
General Phone: (559) 442-8262
General Fax: (559) 265-5783
General/National Adv. Email: rampage-news@fresnocitycollege.edu
Website: www.fresnocitycollegerampage.com
Personnel: Dynpna Ugwu-Oju (Advisor); Leah Edward (Adv. Mgr.); Ramiro Gudino (Prodn. Mgr.)

FROSTBURG

THE BOTTOM LINE

Street Address 1: 101 Braddock Rd
Street Address 2: Lane Center 217
State: MD
Zip/Postal code: 21532-2303
Country: USA
Mailing Address: Lane Center 217
Mailing City: Frostburg
Mailing State: MD
Mailing ZIP Code: 21532-2303
General Phone: (301) 687-4326
General Fax: (301) 687-3054
General/National Adv. Email: thebottomline@frostburg.edu; tblonline@gmail.comthebottomline
Website: www.thebottomlineonline.org
Year Established: 1948
Delivery Methods: Newsstand
Commercial printers?: Y
Personnel: Dustin Davis (Advisor); Marina Byerly (Editor-in-Chief); Michelle Giambruno (Manging Editor); Marissa Nedved (Business Manager)

FULLERTON

CALIFORNIA STATE UNIV., FULLERTON

Street Address 1: College Park Bldg Nutwood Ave
Street Address 2: Ste 2600660
State: CA
Zip/Postal code: 1960
Country: USA
Mailing Address: College Park Bldg., 2600 E. Nutwood Ave., Ste. 660
Mailing City: Fullerton
Mailing State: CA
Mailing ZIP Code: 92831-3110
General Phone: (657) 278-4411
General Fax: (657) 278-2702
Editorial Phone: (657) 278-5815
Display Adv. Email: ads@dailytitan.com
Editorial Email: editorinchief@dailytitan.com
Website: www.dailytitan.com
Year Established: 1960
News Services: MCT
Delivery Methods: Newsstand`Racks
Commercial printers?: Y
Published: Mon`Tues`Wed`Thur
Avg Free Circ: 6000
Personnel: Robert Sage (Bus. Mgr.)

FULLERTON COLLEGE

Street Address 1: 321 E Chapman Ave
State: CA
Zip/Postal code: 92832-2011
Country: USA
Mailing Address: 321 E Chapman Ave
Mailing City: Fullerton
Mailing State: CA
Mailing ZIP Code: 92832-2095
General Phone: (714) 992-7154
General Fax: (714) 447-4097
General/National Adv. Email: hornet@fullcoll.edu
Website: www.fullcoll.edu
Year Established: 1922
Published: Wed
Personnel: Jay Seidel (Advisor)

FULTON

ITAWAMBA CMTY. COLLEGE

Street Address 1: 602 W Hill St
State: MS
Zip/Postal code: 38843-1022
Country: USA
Mailing Address: 602 W. Hill St.
Mailing City: Fulton
Mailing State: MS
Mailing ZIP Code: 38843-1022
General Phone: (662) 862-8244
General/National Adv. Email: dsthomas@iccms.edu
Editorial Email: dsthomas@iccms.edu
Website: www.iccms.edu
Delivery Methods: Racks
Published Other: Three times each semester
Personnel: Donna Thomas (Dir., PR)

WESTMINSTER COLLEGE

Street Address 1: 501 Westminster Ave
State: MO
Zip/Postal code: 65251-1230
Country: USA
Mailing Address: 501 Westminster Ave
Mailing City: Fulton
Mailing State: MO
Mailing ZIP Code: 65251-1299
General Phone: (573) 592-5000
General Fax: (573) 642-2699
Website: www.westminster-mo.edu
Personnel: Debra Brenegan (Advisor); Sarah Blackmon (Ed. in Chief); Aassan Sipra (Ed. in Chief)

GAINESVILLE

BRENAU UNIV.

Street Address 1: 500 Washington St SE
State: GA
Zip/Postal code: 30501-3628
Country: USA
Mailing Address: 500 Washington St SE
Mailing City: Gainesville
Mailing State: GA
Mailing ZIP Code: 30501-3628
General Phone: (770) 538-4762
General Fax: (770) 538-4558
General/National Adv. Email: alchemist@brenau.edu
Personnel: Nathan R. Goss (Coord., Admissions)

UNIV. OF FLORIDA

Street Address 1: PO Box 14257
State: FL
Zip/Postal code: 32604-2257
Country: USA
Mailing Address: PO Box 14257
Mailing City: Gainesville
Mailing State: FL
Mailing ZIP Code: 32604-2257
General Phone: (352) 376-4458
General Fax: (352) 376-4556
General/National Adv. Email: advertising@alligator.org
Editorial Email: editor@alligator.org
Website: www.alligator.org
Personnel: Chelsea Keenan (Ed. in Chief)

GALESBURG

CARL SANDBURG COLLEGE

Street Address 1: 140 S Prairie St
State: IL
Zip/Postal code: 61401-4605
Country: USA
Mailing Address: 140 S Prairie St
Mailing City: Galesburg
Mailing State: IL
Mailing ZIP Code: 61401-4605
General Phone: (309) 344-2518
General Fax: (309) 342-5171

KNOX COLLEGE

Street Address 1: 2 E South St
Street Address 2: Knox College K-240
State: IL
Zip/Postal code: 61401-4938
Country: USA
Mailing Address: 2 E South St Knox College K-240
Mailing City: Galesburg
Mailing State: IL
Mailing ZIP Code: 61401-4999
General Phone: (646) 784-4367
General Fax: (309) 341-7081
General/National Adv. Email: tks@knox.edu
Display Adv. Email: tksmarketing@knox.edu
Website: KNOX COLLEGE BOX 2 E SOUTH ST
Year Established: 1878
Published: Thur
Personnel: Tom Martin (Advisor); Jonathan Schrag (Co-Editor-in-Chief); Lillie Chamberlin (Co-Editor-in-Chief)

GALLATIN

VOLUNTEER STATE CMTY. COLLEGE

Street Address 1: 1480 Nashville Pike
State: TN
Zip/Postal code: 37066-3148
Country: USA
Mailing Address: 1480 Nashville Pike
Mailing City: Gallatin
Mailing State: TN
Mailing ZIP Code: 37066-3148
General Phone: (615) 452-8600
General Fax: (615) 230-3481
General/National Adv. Email: thesettler@allstate.edu
Website: www.settleronline.com
Personnel: Clay Scott (Advisor); Amy Webb (Ed.)

GALLOWAY

RICHARD STOCKTON COLLEGE

Street Address 1: 101 Vera King Farris Dr
State: NJ
Zip/Postal code: 08205-9441
Country: USA
Mailing Address: 101 Vera King Farris Dr
Mailing City: Galloway
Mailing State: NJ
Mailing ZIP Code: 08205-9441
General Phone: (609) 652-4296
General Fax: (609) 748-5565
Display Adv. Email: argoadvertising@yahoo.com
Personnel: Craig Stambaugh (Advisor); Lina Wayman (Ed.)

GALVESTON

TEXAS A&M UNIV. GALVESTON

Street Address 1: PO Box 1675
State: TX
Zip/Postal code: 77553-1675
Country: USA
Mailing Address: PO Box 1675
Mailing City: Galveston
Mailing State: TX
Mailing ZIP Code: 77553-1675
General Phone: (409) 740-4420
General Fax: (409) 740-4775
General/National Adv. Email: nautilus@tamug.edu
Website: www.tamug.edu/stuact/Nautilusmain.htm
Personnel: Kayce Peirce (Ed. in Chief)

GAMBIER

KENYON COLLEGE

Street Address 1: Student Affairs Ctr, 100 Gaskin Ave
State: OH
Zip/Postal code: 43022
Country: USA
Mailing Address: PO Box 832
Mailing City: Gambier
Mailing State: OH
Mailing ZIP Code: 43022-0832
General Phone: (740) 427-5338
General Fax: (740) 427-5339
General/National Adv. Email: collegian@kenyon.edu
Website: www. kenyoncollegian.com
Personnel: Sarah Queller (Ed.)

GARDEN CITY

NASSAU CMTY. COLLEGE

Street Address 1: College Ctr, 1 Education Dr
State: NY
Zip/Postal code: 11530
Country: USA
Mailing Address: College Ctr., 1 Education Dr.
Mailing City: Garden City
Mailing State: NY
Mailing ZIP Code: 11530-6793
General Phone: (516) 222-7071

College and University Newspapers

General Fax: (516) 572-3566
General/National Adv. Email: informationservices@ncc.edu; vignetters@yahoo.com
Personnel: Richard Conway (Advisor)

GARY

INDIANA UNIV. NORTHWEST

Street Address 1: 3400 Broadway, Moraine 110
State: IN
Zip/Postal code: 46408
Country: USA
Mailing Address: 3400 Broadway, Moraine 110
Mailing City: Gary
Mailing State: IN
Mailing ZIP Code: 46408-1101
General Phone: (219) 980-6795
General Fax: (219) 980-6948
General/National Adv. Email: phoenixn@iun.edu
Website: www.iun.edu/~phoenixn
Personnel: Scott Fulk (Coordinator); Don Sjoerdsma (Ed. in Chief)

GENESEO

SUNY COLLEGE AT GENESEO

Street Address 1: 10 Macvittie Cir
Street Address 2: # 42
State: NY
Zip/Postal code: 14454-1427
Country: USA
Mailing Address: 10 Macvittie Cir # 42
Mailing City: Geneseo
Mailing State: NY
Mailing ZIP Code: 14454-1427
General Phone: (585) 245-5896
General Fax: (585) 245-5284
Advertising Phone: (585) 245-5890
General/National Adv. Email: lamron@geneseo.edu
Display Adv. Email: lamronad@geneseo.edu
Website: www.thelamron.com
Year Established: 1922
Published: Thur
Avg Free Circ: 3000
Personnel: Maddy Smith (Advisor); Maria Lima (Advisor); Tom Wilder (Ed. in Chief)

GENEVA

HOBART & WILLIAM SMITH COLLEGE

Street Address 1: 300 Pulteney St
State: NY
Zip/Postal code: 14456-3304
Country: USA
Mailing Address: 300 Pulteney St
Mailing City: Geneva
Mailing State: NY
Mailing ZIP Code: 14456-3382
General Phone: (315) 781-3857
General/National Adv. Email: herald@hws.edu
Personnel: Charlie Wilson (Advisor); Belinda Littlefield (Ed.)

GEORGETOWN

GEORGETOWN COLLEGE

Street Address 1: 400 E College St
Street Address 2: # 280
State: KY
Zip/Postal code: 40324-1628
Country: USA
Mailing Address: 400 E College St Ste 1 # 280
Mailing City: Georgetown
Mailing State: KY
Mailing ZIP Code: 40324-1628
General Fax: (502) 863-8150
Personnel: Whitley Arens (ed.)

GERMANTOWN

MONTGOMERY COLLEGE

Street Address 1: 20200 Observation Dr
State: MD
Zip/Postal code: 20876-4067
Country: USA
Mailing Address: 20200 Observation Dr
Mailing City: Germantown
Mailing State: MD
Mailing ZIP Code: 20876-4098
General Phone: (240) 567-7840
General Fax: (240) 567-7843
General/National Adv. Email: theglobe@montgomerycollege.edu
Website: www.montgomerycollege.edu
Personnel: Dave Anthony (Advisor)

GETTYSBURG

GETTYSBURG COLLEGE

Street Address 1: PO Box 434
State: PA
Zip/Postal code: 17325
Country: USA
Mailing Address: PO Box 434
Mailing City: Gettysburg
Mailing State: PA
Mailing ZIP Code: 17325
General Phone: (717) 337-6449
General Fax: (717) 337-6463
Website: www.thegettysburgian.com
Personnel: Joel Berg (Advisor); Sean Parke (Ed.)

GILROY

GAVILAN COLLEGE

Street Address 1: 5055 Santa Teresa Blvd
State: CA
Zip/Postal code: 95020-9578
Country: USA
Mailing Address: 5055 Santa Teresa Blvd
Mailing City: Gilroy
Mailing State: CA
Mailing ZIP Code: 95020-9599
General Phone: (408) 848-4837
General Fax: (408) 848-4801
Editorial Fax: Free
Published: Bi-Mthly
Avg Free Circ: 0
Personnel: Esmeralda Montenegro (Faculty Advisor)

GLASSBORO

ROWAN UNIV.

Street Address 1: 201 Mullica Hill Rd
State: NJ
Zip/Postal code: 08028-1700
Country: USA
Mailing Address: 201 Mullica Hill Rd
Mailing City: Glassboro
Mailing State: NJ
Mailing ZIP Code: 08028-1702
General Phone: (856) 256-4713
General Fax: (856) 256-4929
General/National Adv. Email: communication@rowan.edu
Website: www.thewhitonline.com
Personnel: Don Bagin (Prof.); Kathryn Quigley (Advisor); R. Michael Donovan (Prof.); Anthony Fulginiti (Prof.); Richard Grupenhoff (Prof.); Kenneth Kaleta (Prof.); Janice Rowan (Prof.); Edward Streb (Prof.); Julia Chang (Assoc. Prof.); Cynthia Corison (Assoc. Prof.); Edgar Eckhardt (Assoc. Prof.); Suzanne Fitzgerald (Assoc. Prof.); Carl Hausman (Assoc. Prof.); Martin Itzkowitz (Assoc. Prof.); Frances Johnson (Assoc. Prof.); Diane Penrod (Assoc. Prof.); Donald Stoll (Assoc. Prof.); Sanford Tweedie (Assoc. Prof.); Kenneth Albone (Asst. Prof.); Lorin Arnold (Asst. Prof.)

GLEN ELLYN

COLLEGE OF DUPAGE

Street Address 1: 425 Fawell Blvd
State: IL
Zip/Postal code: 60137-6708
Country: USA
Mailing Address: 425 Fawell Blvd.
Mailing City: Glen Ellyn
Mailing State: IL
Mailing ZIP Code: 60137-6599
General Phone: (630) 942-2113
General Fax: (630) 942-3747
Editorial Email: editor@cod.edu
Website: www.codcourier.org
Year Established: 1967
Delivery Methods: Newsstand
Commercial printers?: Y
Published: Wed
Personnel: Nick Davison (Editor-in-chief)

GLENDALE

GLENDALE CMTY. COLLEGE

Street Address 1: 6000 W Olive Ave
State: AZ
Zip/Postal code: 85302-3006
Country: USA
Mailing Address: 6000 W Olive Ave
Mailing City: Glendale
Mailing State: AZ
Mailing ZIP Code: 85302-3090
General Phone: (623) 845-3820
General Fax: (623) 845-3072
General/National Adv. Email: ads@gccvoice.com
Website: www.gccvoice.com
Personnel: Mike Mullins (Advisor); Eric Carroll (Adv. Mgr.); Michelle Tabatabai-Shab (Ed. in chief)

GLENDALE CMTY. COLLEGE

Street Address 1: 1500 N Verdugo Rd
Street Address 2: Rm AD212
State: CA
Zip/Postal code: 91208-2809
Country: USA
Mailing Address: 1500 N Verdugo Rd Rm AD212
Mailing City: Glendale
Mailing State: CA
Mailing ZIP Code: 91208-2809
General Phone: (818) 551-5214
General Fax: (818) 551-5278
Website: www.elvaq.com
Personnel: Michael Moreau (Advisor); Jeff Smith (Classified Mgr.)

THUNDERBIRD SCHOOL OF GLOBAL MGMT.

Street Address 1: 1 Global Pl
State: AZ
Zip/Postal code: 85306-3216
Country: USA
Mailing Address: 1 Global Pl
Mailing City: Glendale
Mailing State: AZ
Mailing ZIP Code: 85306-3216
General Phone: (602) 978-7000
General Fax: (602) 978-7971
General/National Adv. Email: dastor@thunderbird.edu
Website: www.thunderbird.edu
Personnel: Sailaja Kattubadi (Ed. in Chief)

WEST NEWS

Street Address 1: 4701 W Thunderbird Rd
Street Address 2: # 117
State: AZ
Zip/Postal code: 85306-4900
Country: USA
Mailing Address: 4701 W Thunderbird Rd # 117
Mailing City: Glendale
Mailing State: AZ
Mailing ZIP Code: 85306-4900
General Phone: 602-543-8575

Editorial Fax: Free
Year Established: 2010
Personnel: Robert Gehl (Editor-in-chief)

GLENDORA

CITRUS COLLEGE

Street Address 1: 1000 W Foothill Blvd
State: CA
Zip/Postal code: 91741-1885
Country: USA
Mailing Address: 1000 W Foothill Blvd
Mailing City: Glendora
Mailing State: CA
Mailing ZIP Code: 91741-1899
General Phone: (626) 914-8586
General Fax: (626) 914-8797
General/National Adv. Email: ccclarion@hotmail.com
Website: www.theclariononline.com
Personnel: Margaret O'Neill (Advisor); Emily Rios (Ed.)

GLENSIDE

ARCADIA UNIV.

Street Address 1: 450 S Easton Rd
State: PA
Zip/Postal code: 19038-3215
Country: USA
Mailing Address: 450 S Easton Rd
Mailing City: Glenside
Mailing State: PA
Mailing ZIP Code: 19038-3295
General Phone: (215) 572-4082
General Fax: (215) 881-8781
Website: www.arcadia.edu; www.thetoweronline.com
Personnel: Michele Cain (Sec)

GLENVILLE

GLENVILLE STATE COLLEGE

Street Address 1: 200 High St
State: WV
Zip/Postal code: 26351-1200
Country: USA
General Phone: (304) 462-4133
General Fax: (304) 462-4407
General/National Adv. Email: news.paper@glenville.edu
Website: www.glenville.edu/life/phoenix.php
Published: Thur
Published Other: Print edition twice a semester
Personnel: Marjorie Stewart (Assistant Professor of English)

GODFREY

LEWIS AND CLARK CMTY. COLLEGE

Street Address 1: 5800 Godfrey Rd
State: IL
Zip/Postal code: 62035-2426
Country: USA
Mailing Address: 5800 Godfrey Rd
Mailing City: Godfrey
Mailing State: IL
Mailing ZIP Code: 62035-2466
General Phone: (618) 468-6042
General Fax: (618) 468-6055
Editorial Phone: (618) 468-6044
General/National Adv. Email: bridge@lc.edu
Personnel: Lori Artis (Advisor); Anthony Lanham (Ed.)

GOLDEN

COLORADO SCHOOL OF MINES

Street Address 1: 1600 Maple St
State: CO
Zip/Postal code: 80401-6114
Country: USA
Mailing Address: 1600 Maple St
Mailing City: Golden

Mailing State: CO
Mailing ZIP Code: 80401-6114
General Phone: (303) 384-2188
General Fax: (303) 273-3931
General/National Adv. Email: oredig@mines.edu
Website: www.oredigger.net
Delivery Methods: Racks
Commercial printers?: Y
Published: Mon
Personnel: Emily McNair (Managing Editor); Lucy Orsi (Editor-in-Chief); Taylor Polodna (Design Editor); Connor McDonald (Webmaster); Arnaud Filliat (Copy Editor); Karen Gilbert (Faculty Advisor); Deborah Good (Editor-in-Chief)

GOODMAN

HOLMES CMTY. COLLEGE

Street Address 1: No 1, Hill St
State: MS
Zip/Postal code: 39079
Country: USA
Mailing Address: PO Box 369
Mailing City: Goodman
Mailing State: MS
Mailing ZIP Code: 39079-0369
General Phone: (662) 472-2312
General Fax: (662) 472-0012
Website: www.holmescc.edu
Published Other: Twice a senester
Personnel: Steve Diffey (District Director of Communications)

GOODWELL

OKLAHOMA PANHANDLE STATE UNIV.

Street Address 1: PO Box 430
State: OK
Zip/Postal code: 73939-0430
Country: USA
Mailing Address: PO Box 430
Mailing City: Goodwell
Mailing State: OK
Mailing ZIP Code: 73939-0430
General Phone: (580) 349-2611
General Fax: (580) 349-1350
General/National Adv. Email: collegian@opsu.edu
Website: www.opsu.edu
Personnel: Lora Hays (Advisor); Samuel Moore (Ed.)

GOSHEN

GOSHEN COLLEGE

Street Address 1: 1700 S Main St
State: IN
Zip/Postal code: 46526-4724
Country: USA
Mailing Address: 1700 S Main St
Mailing City: Goshen
Mailing State: IN
Mailing ZIP Code: 46526-4794
General Phone: (574) 535-7745
General Fax: (574) 535-7660
General/National Adv. Email: record@goshen.edu
Website: record.goshen.edu
Personnel: Duane Stoltzfus; Marlys Weaver (Ed. in Chief)

GRAMBLING

GRAMBLING STATE UNIVERSITY

Street Address 1: 403 Main St
State: LA
Zip/Postal code: 71245-2715
Country: USA
Mailing Address: 403 Main St
Mailing City: Grambling
Mailing State: LA
Mailing ZIP Code: 71245-2761
General Phone: (318) 247-3331
General Fax: (318) 274-3194
Editorial Phone: (318) 274-2866
General/National Adv. Email: mediarelations@gram.edu
Website: www.thegramblinite.com
Published: Thur
Personnel: Mitzi LaSalle (Interim Director of University Communications, Marketing, and Media Relations)

GRAND FORKS

UNIV. OF NORTH DAKOTA

Street Address 1: 2901 University Ave Stop 8385
Street Address 2: University of North Dakota Memorial Union
State: ND
Zip/Postal code: 58202-8385
Country: USA
Mailing Address: University of North Dakota Memorial Union
Mailing City: Grand Forks
Mailing State: ND
Mailing ZIP Code: 58201
General Phone: (701) 777-2677
General Fax: (701) 777-3137
Advertising Phone: (701) 777-2677
General/National Adv. Email: dakotastudentmedia@gmail.com
Display Adv. Email: und.dakotastudent@email.und.edu
Website: www.dakotastudent.com
Year Established: 1888
Published: Tues`Fri
Personnel: Carrie Sandstrom (Editor-in-Chief); Melissa Bakke (Sales and Marketing Coordinator); Adam Christianson (Managing/Opinion Editor); Kelsi Ward (Features Editor); Larry Philbin (News Editor); Elizabeth Erickson (Sports Editor); Jaye Millspaugh (Multimedia Editor); Keisuke Yoshimura (Photo Editor)

GRAND JUNCTION

COLORADO MESA UNIVERSITY

Street Address 1: 1100 North Ave
State: CO
Zip/Postal code: 81501-3122
Country: USA
Mailing Address: PO Box 2647
Mailing City: Grand Junction
Mailing State: CO
Mailing ZIP Code: 81502-2647
General Phone: (970) 248-1570
General Fax: (970) 248-1708
Website: www.thecrite.com
Year Established: 1934
Commercial printers?: Y
Personnel: Eric Sandstrom (Advisor); Jamie Banks (Ed.)

GRAND RAPIDS

AQUINAS COLLEGE

Street Address 1: 1700 Fulton St E
State: MI
Zip/Postal code: 49506-1801
Country: USA
Mailing Address: 1607 Robinson Rd SE
Mailing City: Grand Rapids
Mailing State: MI
Mailing ZIP Code: 49506-1799
General Phone: (616) 632-2975
General Fax: (616) 732-4487
Advertising Phone: (616) 632-2975
Editorial Phone: (616) 632-2975
General/National Adv. Email: saint.editors@aquinas.edu
Display Adv. Email: saint.business@aquinas.edu
Editorial Email: saint.editors@aquinas.edu
Website: www.aquinas.edu/thesaint
Year Established: 1980
Published: Bi-Mthly
Avg Free Circ: 1000
Personnel: Dan Brooks (Advisor); Matt Kuczynski (Editor in Chief)

CALVIN COLLEGE

Street Address 1: 3201 Burton St, Student Commons
State: MI
Zip/Postal code: 49546
Country: USA
Mailing Address: 3201 Burton St., Student Commons
Mailing City: Grand Rapids
Mailing State: MI
Mailing ZIP Code: 49546-4301
General Phone: (616) 819-0011
General Fax: (616) 957-8551
General/National Adv. Email: chimes@calvin.edu
Website: clubs.calvin.edu/chimes
Published: Fri
Personnel: Lauren DeHaan (Ed.); Emma Slager (Ed. in Chief)

GRAND RAPIDS CMTY. COLLEGE

Street Address 1: 143 Bostwick Ave NE
State: MI
Zip/Postal code: 49503-3201
Country: USA
Mailing Address: 143 Bostwick Ave NE
Mailing City: Grand Rapids
Mailing State: MI
Mailing ZIP Code: 49503-3201
General Phone: (616) 234-4157
General Fax: (616) 234-4158
General/National Adv. Email: grcc_collegiate@yahoo.com
Website: www.thecollegiatelive.com

GRANVILLE

DENISON UNIV.

Street Address 1: 100 W College St
State: OH
Zip/Postal code: 43023-1100
Country: USA
Mailing Address: 100 W College St
Mailing City: Granville
Mailing State: OH
Mailing ZIP Code: 43023
General Phone: (740) 587-6378
General Fax: (740) 587-6767
General/National Adv. Email: denisonian@denison.edu
Website: www.denisonian.com
Personnel: Alan Miller (Advisor)

GRAYSLAKE

COLLEGE OF LAKE COUNTY

Street Address 1: 19351 W Washington St
State: IL
Zip/Postal code: 60030-1148
Country: USA
Mailing Address: 19351 W Washington St
Mailing City: Grayslake
Mailing State: IL
Mailing ZIP Code: 60030-1198
General Phone: (847) 543-2057
Advertising Phone: (847) 543-2362
Website: www.clcillinois.edu/activities/chronicle.asp
Personnel: John Kupetz (Faculty Advisor); Nathan Caldwell (Ed. in Chief)

GREAT BEND

BARTON COUNTY CMTY. COLLEGE

Street Address 1: 245 NE 30 Rd
State: KS
Zip/Postal code: 67530-9251
Country: USA
Mailing Address: 245 NE 30 Rd
Mailing City: Great Bend
Mailing State: KS
Mailing ZIP Code: 67530-9107
General Phone: (620) 792-9239
General Fax: 6207861157
Website: www.bartonccc.edu
Year Established: 1969

Delivery Methods: Mail`Newsstand`Racks
Commercial printers?: N
Published Other: Bi-weekly Print; Weekly Online
Personnel: Yvonda Acker (Advisor)

GREAT FALLS

UNIV. OF GREAT FALLS

Street Address 1: 1301 20th St S
State: MT
Zip/Postal code: 59405-4934
Country: USA
Mailing Address: 1301 20th St S
Mailing City: Great Falls
Mailing State: MT
Mailing ZIP Code: 59405-4996
General Phone: (406) 791-5231
General Fax: (406) 791-5220
Personnel: Jerry Habets (Ed.)

GREELEY

UNIV. OF NORTHERN COLORADO

Street Address 1: 823 16th St
State: CO
Zip/Postal code: 80631-5617
Country: USA
Mailing Address: 823 16th St
Mailing City: Greeley
Mailing State: CO
Mailing ZIP Code: 80631-5617
General Phone: (970) 392-9270
General Fax: (970) 392-9025
Advertising Phone: (970) 392-9270
Editorial Phone: (970) 392-9270
General/National Adv. Email: info@uncmirror.com
Display Adv. Email: ads@uncmirror.com
Editorial Email: editor@uncmirror.com
Website: www.uncmirror.com
Year Established: 1919
Delivery Methods: Newsstand`Racks
Commercial printers?: N
Published: Mon
Avg Free Circ: 4000
Personnel: Kurt Hinkle (Gen. Mgr.); Josh Espinoza (Ed. in Chief); Eric Heinz (News Ed.); Jordan Freemyer (Sports Ed.); Corey (Adv. Mgr.); Lauren (Adv. Prodn. Mgr.)

GREEN BAY

UNIV. OF WISCONSIN GREEN BAY

Street Address 1: 2420 Nicolet Dr
State: WI
Zip/Postal code: 54311-7003
Country: USA
Mailing Address: 2420 Nicolet Dr
Mailing City: Green Bay
Mailing State: WI
Mailing ZIP Code: 54311-7003
General Phone: (920) 465-2719
General Fax: (920) 465-2895
Advertising Phone: (920) 465-2719
Advertising Fax: (920) 465-2895
Editorial Phone: (920) 465-2719
Editorial Fax: (920) 465-2895
General/National Adv. Email: 4e@uwgb.edu
Display Adv. Email: 4e@uwgb.edu
Editorial Email: 4e@uwgb.edu
Website: www.fourthestatenewspaper.com
Published: Thur
Avg Free Circ: 6600
Personnel: Victoria Goff (Advisor); Nicole Angelucci (Adv. Mgr.); Maureen Malone (Ed. in chief)

GREENCASTLE

DEPAUW UNIV.

Street Address 1: 609 S Locust St
State: IN
Zip/Postal code: 46135-2047
Country: USA
Mailing Address: 609 S Locust St

College and University Newspapers

Mailing City: Greencastle
Mailing State: IN
Mailing ZIP Code: 46135-2047
General Phone: (765) 658-5972
General Fax: (765) 658-5991
Website: www.thedepauw.com
Personnel: Lili Wright (Advisor); Samuel Autman (Advisor); Jonathan Batuello (Ed. in Chief); Alex Turco (Exec. Ed.); Macy Ayers (Mng. Ed.)

GREENEVILLE

TUSCULUM COLLEGE

Street Address 1: 60 Shiloh Rd
State: TN
Zip/Postal code: 37745-0595
Country: USA
Mailing Address: PO Box 5098
Mailing City: Greeneville
Mailing State: TN
Mailing ZIP Code: 37743-0001
General Phone: (423) 636-7300
General Fax: (423) 638-7166
Website: www.tusculum.edu
Personnel: Barth Cox (Advisor)

GREENSBORO

BENNETT COLLEGE

Street Address 1: 900 E Washington St
State: NC
Zip/Postal code: 27401-3239
Country: USA
Mailing Address: 900 E Washington St
Mailing City: Greensboro
Mailing State: NC
Mailing ZIP Code: 27401-3298
General Phone: (336) 517-2305
General Fax: (336) 517-2303
General/National Adv. Email: banner@bennett.edu
Website: www.bennettbanner.com
Personnel: Yvonne Welbon (Advisor)

GREENSBORO COLLEGE

Street Address 1: 815 W Market St
State: NC
Zip/Postal code: 27401-1823
Country: USA
Mailing Address: 815 W Market St
Mailing City: Greensboro
Mailing State: NC
Mailing ZIP Code: 27401-1875
General Phone: (336) 272-7102
General Fax: (336) 271-6634
Personnel: L. Wayne Johns (Advisor)

GUILFORD COLLEGE

Street Address 1: 5800 W Friendly Ave
State: NC
Zip/Postal code: 27410-4108
Country: USA
Mailing Address: 5800 W Friendly Ave
Mailing City: Greensboro
Mailing State: NC
Mailing ZIP Code: 27410-4173
General Phone: (336) 316-2306
Advertising Phone: (336) 316-2306
Website: www.guilfordian.com
Commercial printers?: Y
Personnel: Jeff Jeske (Advisor)

NORTH CAROLINA A&T STATE UNIV.

Street Address 1: 1601 E Market St
State: NC
Zip/Postal code: 27411-0002
Country: USA
Mailing Address: PO Box E25
Mailing City: Greensboro
Mailing State: NC
Mailing ZIP Code: 27411-0001
General Phone: (336) 334-7700
General Fax: (336) 334-7173

General/National Adv. Email: theatregister@gmail.com
Website: www.ncatregister.com
Personnel: Emiley Burch Harris (Advisor); Dexter R. Mullins (Ed. in Chief)

UNIV. OF NORTH CAROLINA

Street Address 1: Uncg, Box N1, Euc
State: NC
Zip/Postal code: 27412-0001
Country: USA
Mailing Address: Uncg # N1
Mailing City: Greensboro
Mailing State: NC
Mailing ZIP Code: 27412-0001
General Phone: (336) 334-5752
General Fax: (336) 334-3518
General/National Adv. Email: the_carolinian@hotmail.com
Website: www.carolinianonline.com
Personnel: Y-Phuc Ayun (Bus. Mgr.); Casey Mann (Pub.); John Boschini (Ed. in Chief)

GREENSBURG

SETON HILL UNIVERSITY

Street Address 1: 1 Seton Hill Dr
Street Address 2: PO Box 343K
State: PA
Zip/Postal code: 15601-1548
Country: USA
Mailing Address: PO Box 343K
Mailing City: Greensburg
Mailing State: PA
Mailing ZIP Code: 15601-1599
General Phone: (724) 830-4791
General Fax: (724) 830-4611
General/National Adv. Email: setonian@gmail.com
Website: www.setonhill.edu
Published: Mthly
Personnel: Olivia Goudy (Editor-in-Chief)

UNIV. OF PITTSBURGH/GREENSBURG

Street Address 1: 150 Finoli Dr
Street Address 2: 122 Village Hall
State: PA
Zip/Postal code: 15601-5804
Country: USA
General Phone: (724) 836-7481
General Fax: (724) 836-9888
General/National Adv. Email: upginsider@gmail.com
Website: www.upginsider.com
Personnel: Lori Jakiela (Advisor)

GREENVILLE

BOB JONES UNIVERSITY

Street Address 1: 1700 Wade Hampton Blvd
State: SC
Zip/Postal code: 29614-1000
Country: USA
Mailing Address: 1700 Wade Hampton Blvd
Mailing City: Greenville
Mailing State: SC
Mailing ZIP Code: 29614-0001
General Phone: (864) 370-1800
General Fax: (864) 770-1307
Advertising Phone: 864-370-1800
Advertising Fax: 864-770-1307
General/National Adv. Email: bsolomon@bju.edu
Editorial Email: editor@bju.edu
Website: www.collegianonline.com/
Year Established: 1987
Published: Fri
Personnel: David Lovegrove (Advisor); Betty Solomon (Advisor); Joanne Kappel (Adv. Coord.); Larry Stofer (Campus Media Supervisor)

FURMAN UNIV.

Street Address 1: 3300 Poinsett Hwy
State: SC
Zip/Postal code: 29613-0002
Country: USA
Mailing Address: PO Box 28584
Mailing City: Greenville
Mailing State: SC
Mailing ZIP Code: 29613-0001
General/National Adv. Email: paladin@furman.edu
Website: www.furmannewsaper.com
Published: Bi-Mthly
Personnel: Tyler Sines (Circ. Mgr.); Evan Bohnenblust (Ed. in Chief); Jessica Lopez (Ed.)

GREENVILLE COLLEGE

Street Address 1: 315 E College Ave
State: IL
Zip/Postal code: 62246-1145
Country: USA
Mailing Address: 315 E College Ave
Mailing City: Greenville
Mailing State: IL
Mailing ZIP Code: 62246-1145
General Phone: (618) 664-2800
General Fax: (618) 664-1373
General/National Adv. Email: papyrus@greenville.edu
Website: www.greenville.edu
Personnel: Susan Chism (Advisor)

THE EAST CAROLINIAN

Street Address 1: Self Help Bldg Ecu
State: NC
Zip/Postal code: 27858
Country: USA
Mailing Address: Self Help Bldg. ECU
Mailing City: Greenville
Mailing State: NC
Mailing ZIP Code: 27858
General Phone: (252) 328-9238
General Fax: (252) 328-9143
Advertising Phone: (252) 328-9245
Advertising Fax: (252) 328-9143
Editorial Phone: (205) 328-9249
Editorial Fax: (252) 328-9143
Display Adv. Email: ads@theeastcarolinian.com
Editorial Email: editor@theeastcarolinian.com
Website: www.theeastcarolinian.com
Year Established: 1925
News Services: AP, MCT
Special Editions: Housing guide
Delivery Methods: Newsstand`Carrier`Racks
Commercial printers?: Y
Personnel: Paul Isom (Advisor); Caitlin Hale (Editor); Katelyn Crouse (Ed. in Chief)
Parent company (for newspapers): ECU Media Board

THIEL COLLEGE

Street Address 1: 75 College Ave
State: PA
Zip/Postal code: 16125-2186
Country: USA
Mailing Address: 75 College Ave
Mailing City: Greenville
Mailing State: PA
Mailing ZIP Code: 16125-2181
General Phone: (724) 589-2416
General/National Adv. Email: newspaper@thiel.edu
Website: www.thiel.edu/thielensian
Personnel: James Raykie (Advisor); Alivia Lapcevich (Ed. in Chief)

GREENWICH

NEW YORK METRO COMMUNITY COLLEGES

Street Address 1: 39 County Route 70
State: NY
Zip/Postal code: 12834-6300

Country: USA
Mailing Address: 39 County Route 70
Mailing City: Greenwich
Mailing State: NY
Mailing ZIP Code: 12834
General Phone: (518) 879 0965
General Fax: (518) 507 6782
Advertising Phone: (518) 879 0965
Advertising Fax: (518) 507 6782
General/National Adv. Email: editor@campus-news.org
Display Adv. Email: advertising@campus-news.org
Editorial Email: editor@campus-news.org
Website: www.campus-news.org
Year Established: 2010
Published: Mthly`Bi-Mthly
Avg Free Circ: 10000
Personnel: Darren Johnson (Advisor)

GREENWOOD

LANDER UNIV.

Street Address 1: 320 Stanley Ave
State: SC
Zip/Postal code: 29649-2056
Country: USA
Mailing Address: 320 Stanley Ave
Mailing City: Greenwood
Mailing State: SC
Mailing ZIP Code: 29649-2099
General Phone: (864) 388-8000
General Fax: (864) 388-8890
Website: www.lander.edu
Personnel: Robert Stevenson (Advisor)

GRESHAM

MT. HOOD CMTY. COLLEGE

Street Address 1: 26000 SE Stark St
State: OR
Zip/Postal code: 97030-3300
Country: USA
Mailing Address: 26000 SE Stark St
Mailing City: Gresham
Mailing State: OR
Mailing ZIP Code: 97030-3300
General Phone: (503) 491-7250
General Fax: (503) 491-6064
General/National Adv. Email: advocatt@mhcc.edu
Published: Fri
Personnel: Ivy Davis (EIC); Dan Ernst (Advisor)

GRINNELL

GRINNELL COLLEGE

Street Address 1: 1115 8th Ave
State: IA
Zip/Postal code: 50112-1553
Country: USA
Mailing Address: P.O. Box 5886
Mailing City: Grinnell
Mailing State: IA
Mailing ZIP Code: 50112-3128
General Phone: (641) 269-3325
General Fax: (641) 269-4888
General/National Adv. Email: newspapr@grinnell.edu
Website: www.thesandb.com
Published: Fri

GROVE CITY

GROVE CITY COLLEGE

Street Address 1: 100 Campus Dr
State: PA
Zip/Postal code: 16127-2101
Country: USA
Mailing Address: 100 Campus Dr
Mailing City: Grove City
Mailing State: PA
Mailing ZIP Code: 16127-2104
General Phone: (724) 458-2193
General Fax: (724) 458-2167
General/National Adv. Email: collegian@gcc.edu
Year Established: 1891

Published: Fri
Avg Free Circ: 1500
Personnel: Nick Hildebrand (Adviser); Karen Postupac (Editor-in_Chief); James Sutherland (Managing Editor)

GUNNISON

WESTERN STATE COLLEGE

Street Address 1: 600 N Adams St
State: CO
Zip/Postal code: 81231-7000
Country: USA
Mailing Address: 103 College Ctr
Mailing City: Gunnison
Mailing State: CO
Mailing ZIP Code: 81231-0001
General Phone: 970-943-2138
General Fax: 970-943-2702
General/National Adv. Email: top@western.edu
Display Adv. Email: topworld.ads@gmail.com
Website: www.western.edu/academics/communicationtheatre/top-o-the-world
Year Established: 1921

HACKETTSTOWN

CENTENARY COLLEGE

Street Address 1: 400 Jefferson St
State: NJ
Zip/Postal code: 07840-2184
Country: USA
Mailing Address: 400 Jefferson St Ste 1
Mailing City: Hackettstown
Mailing State: NJ
Mailing ZIP Code: 07840-2184
General Phone: (908) 852-1400 x2243
Advertising Phone: (908) 852-1400x2243
General/National Adv. Email: levd@centenarycollege.edu
Display Adv. Email: levd@centenarycollege.edu
Website: www.centenarycollege.edu
Year Established: 1991
Published: Mthly
Avg Free Circ: 1600
Personnel: Deborah Lev (Advisor)

HAMBURG

HILBERT COLLEGE

Street Address 1: 5200 S Park Ave
State: NY
Zip/Postal code: 14075-1519
Country: USA
Mailing Address: 5200 S Park Ave
Mailing City: Hamburg
Mailing State: NY
Mailing ZIP Code: 14075-1597
General Phone: (716) 649-7900
General Fax: (716) 649-0702
General/National Adv. Email: info@hilbert.edu
Website: www.hilbert.edu
Published Other: 3 months in fall & spring
Personnel: Charles A. S. Ernst (Advisor)

HAMDEN

QUINNIPIAC COLLEGE SCHOOL OF LAW

Street Address 1: 275 Mount Carmel Ave
State: CT
Zip/Postal code: 06518-1905
Country: USA
Mailing Address: 275 Mount Carmel Ave
Mailing City: Hamden
Mailing State: CT
Mailing ZIP Code: 06518-1908
General Phone: (203) 582-8358
General Fax: (203) 582-5203
General/National Adv. Email: thequchronicle@gmail.com
Website: www.quchronicle.com
Personnel: Andrew Fletcher (Ed. in Chief); Joe Pelletier (Mng. Ed.)

QUINNIPIAC UNIVERSITY

Street Address 1: 275 Mount Carmel Ave
State: CT
Zip/Postal code: 06518-1905
Country: USA
Mailing Address: 275 Mount Carmel Ave
Mailing City: Hamden
Mailing State: CT
Mailing ZIP Code: 06518-1908
General Phone: 8608301017
General/National Adv. Email: editor@quchronicle.com
Website: www.quinnipiac.edu; quchronicle.com
Personnel: David Friedlander (Editor-in-Chief)

HAMILTON

COLGATE UNIV.

Street Address 1: 13 Oak Dr
Street Address 2: Student Union
State: NY
Zip/Postal code: 13346-1338
Country: USA
Mailing Address: Student Union
Mailing City: Hamilton
Mailing State: NY
Mailing ZIP Code: 13346
General Phone: (315) 228-7744
General Fax: (315) 228-6839
General/National Adv. Email: maroonnews@colgate.edu
Display Adv. Email: ads.maroonnews@gmail.com
Editorial Email: colgatemaroonnews@gmail.com
Website: thecolgatemaroonnews.com
Year Established: 1868
Published: Thur
Avg Free Circ: 1600
Personnel: Matthew Knowles (Ed.); Luke Currim (Ed.); Amanda Golden (Exec. Ed.)

HAMMOND

PURDUE UNIVERSITY CALUMET

Street Address 1: 2200 169th St
State: IN
Zip/Postal code: 46323-2068
Country: USA
Mailing Address: 2200 169th St
Mailing City: Hammond
Mailing State: IN
Mailing ZIP Code: 46323-2068
General Phone: (219) 989-2547
General Fax: (219) 989-2770
General/National Adv. Email: pucchronicle@gmail.com
Display Adv. Email: chronicle.businessmanager@gmail.com
Editorial Email: pucchronicle@gmail.com
Website: pucchronicle.com
Year Established: 1982
Published: Mon
Personnel: Jessica Gerlich (Editor-in-Chief); William Koester (Sports Editor); Michelle Mullins (Entertainment Editor); Dante Vidal Silguero (Business Manager); Morgan Walker (Photo Editor); Samantha Gonzalez (Production Manager)

SOUTHEASTERN LOUISIANA UNIV.

Street Address 1: 303 Texas Ave, Student Union, Rm 211D
State: LA
Zip/Postal code: 70402-0001
Country: USA
Mailing Address: Slu 10877
Mailing City: Hammond
Mailing State: LA
Mailing ZIP Code: 70402-0001
General Phone: (985) 549-3731
General Fax: (985) 549-3842
General/National Adv. Email: lionsroar@selu.edu
Website: www.selu.edu/lionsroar
Year Established: 1929
Personnel: Lee Lind (Dir., Student Pub.); Don Aime (Ed. in Chief)

HAMPDEN SYDNEY

HAMPDEN-SYDNEY COLLEGE

Street Address 1: 1 College Rd
State: VA
Zip/Postal code: 23943
Country: USA
Mailing Address: PO Box 127
Mailing City: Hampden Sydney
Mailing State: VA
Mailing ZIP Code: 23943-0127
General Phone: (434) 223-6000
General Fax: (434) 223-6345
General/National Adv. Email: newspaper@hsc.edu
Year Established: 1920
Published: Bi-Mthly
Personnel: Max Dash (Editor-in-Chief)

HANOVER

DARTMOUTH COLLEGE

Street Address 1: 6175 Robinson Hall
State: NH
Zip/Postal code: 03755-3507
Country: USA
Mailing Address: 6175 Robinson Hall
Mailing City: Hanover
Mailing State: NH
Mailing ZIP Code: 03755-3507
General Phone: (603) 646-2600
General Fax: (603) 646-3443
General/National Adv. Email: publisher@dartmouth.com; thedartmouth@dartmouth.edu
Website: www.thedartmouth.com
Year Established: 1799
Personnel: Ray Lu (Ed. in chief); Phil Rasansky (Pub.)

HANOVER COLLEGE

Street Address 1: PO Box 890
State: IN
Zip/Postal code: 47243-0890
Country: USA
Mailing Address: PO Box 890
Mailing City: Hanover
Mailing State: IN
Mailing ZIP Code: 47243-0890
General Phone: (812) 866-7073
General Fax: (812) 866-7077
General/National Adv. Email: triangle@hanover.edu
Website: www.hanovertriangle.com
Personnel: Kay Stokes (Fac. Advisor); Melisa Cole (Mng. Ed.)

HARRISBURG

THE FOURTH ESTATE

Street Address 1: 1 Hacc Dr Cooper 110
Street Address 2: Harrisburg Area Community College
State: PA
Zip/Postal code: 17110-2903
Country: USA
Mailing Address: Harrisburg Area Community College
Mailing City: Harrisburg
Mailing State: PA
Mailing ZIP Code: 17110
General Phone: 717-780-2582
General/National Adv. Email: 4estate@hacc.edu

HARRISONBURG

JAMES MADISON UNIVERSITY

Street Address 1: 1598 S Main St
State: VA
Zip/Postal code: 22807-1025
Country: USA
Mailing Address: 1598 South Main Street
Mailing City: Harrisonburg
Mailing State: VA
Mailing ZIP Code: 22807
General Phone: (540) 568-6127
General Fax: (540) 568-6736
Advertising Phone: (540) 568-6127
Editorial Phone: (540) 568-6127
General/National Adv. Email: breezeeditor@gmail.com
Display Adv. Email: thebreezeads@gmail.com
Editorial Email: breezeeditor@gmail.com
Website: www.breezejmu.org
Year Established: 1922
Syndicated Publications: Port & Main
Delivery Methods: Racks
Commercial printers?: N
Published: Thur
Avg Free Circ: 5000
Personnel: Brad Jenkins (General Manager); Blake Shepherd (Advertising and Marketing Coordinator)

HARTFORD

TRINITY COLLEGE

Street Address 1: 300 Summit St
State: CT
Zip/Postal code: 06106-3100
Country: USA
Mailing Address: 300 Summit St Ste 1
Mailing City: Hartford
Mailing State: CT
Mailing ZIP Code: 06106-3186
General Phone: (860) 297-2584
General Fax: (860) 297-5361
General/National Adv. Email: tripod@trincoll.edu
Website: https://commons.trincoll.edu/tripod/
Year Established: 1904
Delivery Methods: Newsstand
Published: Tues

HARTSVILLE

COKER COLLEGE

Street Address 1: 300 E College Ave
State: SC
Zip/Postal code: 29550-3742
Country: USA
Mailing Address: 300 E College Ave
Mailing City: Hartsville
Mailing State: SC
Mailing ZIP Code: 29550-3797
General Phone: (843) 383-8000
General Fax: (843) 383-8047
Personnel: Dick Puffer (Advisor); Lance Player (Ed.)

HASTINGS

HASTINGS COLLEGE

Street Address 1: 710 N Turner Ave
State: NE
Zip/Postal code: 68901-7621
Country: USA
Mailing Address: 710 N Turner Ave
Mailing City: Hastings
Mailing State: NE
Mailing ZIP Code: 68901-7696
General Phone: (402) 461-7399
General Fax: (402) 461-7442
Personnel: Alicia O'Donnell (Advisor); Lauren Lee (Ed.)

HATTIESBURG

UNIV. OF SOUTHERN MISSISSIPPI

Street Address 1: 118 College Dr
Street Address 2: # 5121
State: MS
Zip/Postal code: 39406-0002
Country: USA
Mailing Address: PO Box 5121
Mailing City: Hattiesburg
Mailing State: MS
Mailing ZIP Code: 39406-0001
General Phone: (601) 266-4288

College and University Newspapers

General Fax: (601) 266-6473
Advertising Phone: (601) 266-5188
General/National Adv. Email: printz@usm.edu
Editorial Email: printzeditors@gmail.com
Website: www.studentprintz.com
Year Established: 1927
News Services: MC-T
Commercial printers?: N
Published: Wed
Avg Free Circ: 1700
Personnel: Chuck Cook (News Content Adviser)

HAVERHILL

NORTHERN ESSEX COMMUNITY COLLEGE

Street Address 1: 100 Elliott St
State: MA
Zip/Postal code: 01830-2306
Country: USA
Mailing Address: 100 Elliott St.
Mailing City: Haverhill
Mailing State: MA
Mailing ZIP Code: 01830-2399
General Phone: (978) 556-3633
General/National Adv. Email: observer@necc.mass.edu
Website: 100 Elliott Street
Year Established: 1962
Published: Bi-Mthly
Personnel: Amy Callahan (Professor)

HAVRE

MONTANA STATE UNIV. NORTHERN

Street Address 1: 300 11th St W
State: MT
Zip/Postal code: 59501-4917
Country: USA
Mailing Address: PO Box 7751
Mailing City: Havre
Mailing State: MT
Mailing ZIP Code: 59501-7751
General Phone: (406) 265-4112
General Fax: (406) 265-3777
Website: www.msun.edu
Personnel: Lori Renfeld (Ed.)

HAYS

FT. HAYS STATE UNIV.

Street Address 1: 600 Park St
Street Address 2: Picken 104
State: KS
Zip/Postal code: 67601-4009
Country: USA
Mailing Address: 600 Park St Picken 104
Mailing City: Hays
Mailing State: KS
Mailing ZIP Code: 67601-4009
General Phone: (785) 628-3478
General Fax: (785) 628-4004
Website: www.fhsu.edu
Personnel: Gretchen Fields (Advisor)

HAYWARD

CALIFORNIA STATE UNIVERSITY, EAST BAY.

Street Address 1: 25800 Carlos Bee Blvd
State: CA
Zip/Postal code: 94542-3000
Country: USA
Mailing Address: 25800 Carlos Bee Blvd
Mailing City: Hayward
Mailing State: CA
Mailing ZIP Code: 94542-3001
General Phone: (510) 885-3292
General Fax: (510) 885-4099
Advertising Phone: (510) 885-3526
Advertising Fax: (510) 885-2584
Editorial Phone: (510) 885-3176
Editorial Fax: (510) 885-2584

Display Adv. Email: pioneer.advertising@csueastbay.edu
Editorial Email: pioneernewspaper@sueastbay.edu
Website: thepioneeronline.com/
Published: Thur
Avg Free Circ: 10000

CHABOT COLLEGE

Street Address 1: 25555 Hesperian Blvd
Street Address 2: Ste 1635
State: CA
Zip/Postal code: 94545-2447
Country: USA
Mailing Address: 25555 Hesperian Blvd Ste 1635
Mailing City: Hayward
Mailing State: CA
Mailing ZIP Code: 94545-2400
General Phone: (510) 723-7082
General Fax: (510) 723-6919
General/National Adv. Email: chabot_spectator@hotmail.com
Website: www.chabotspectator.com
Personnel: Jeannie Wakeland (Advisor)

HAZLETON

PENN STATE UNIV.

Street Address 1: 76 University Dr
State: PA
Zip/Postal code: 18202-8025
Country: USA
Mailing Address: 76 University Dr
Mailing City: Hazleton
Mailing State: PA
Mailing ZIP Code: 18202-1291
General Phone: (570) 450-3131
General Fax: (570) 450-3182
Personnel: April Snyder (Advisor)

HELENA

CARROLL COLLEGE

Street Address 1: 1601 N Benton Ave
State: MT
Zip/Postal code: 59625-0001
Country: USA
Mailing Address: 1601 N Benton Ave
Mailing City: Helena
Mailing State: MT
Mailing ZIP Code: 59625-2826
General Phone: (406) 447-4300
General Fax: (406) 447-4533
Website: www.carroll.edu
Personnel: Brent Northup (Advisor)

HEMPSTEAD

HOFSTRA UNIV.

Street Address 1: 200 Hofstra Univ, Rm 203 Student Ctr
State: NY
Zip/Postal code: 11550
Country: USA
Mailing Address: 200 Hofstra Univ., Rm. 203 Student Ctr.
Mailing City: Hempstead
Mailing State: NY
Mailing ZIP Code: 11550-1022
General Phone: (516) 463-6965
General Fax: (516) 463-6977
Website: www.hofstrachronicle.com
Published: Tues
Personnel: Peter Goodman (Advisor)

HOFSTRA UNIVERSITY

Street Address 1: 200 Hofstra University, Student Ctr, Room 203
State: NY
Zip/Postal code: 48202
Country: USA
Mailing Address: 200 Hofstra University, Student Ctr., Room 203

Mailing City: Hempstead
Mailing State: NY
Mailing ZIP Code: 11550
General Phone: (516) 463-6921
General/National Adv. Email: hofstrachronicle@gmail.com
Display Adv. Email: thechronicle.business@gmail.com
Website: www.thehofstrachronicle.com
Year Established: 1935
Published: Thur
Avg Free Circ: 3000
Personnel: Jake Nussbaum (Business Manager)

HENDERSON

FREED-HARDEMAN UNIV.

Street Address 1: 158 E Main St
State: TN
Zip/Postal code: 38340-2306
Country: USA
Mailing Address: 158 E Main St
Mailing City: Henderson
Mailing State: TN
Mailing ZIP Code: 38340-2398
General Fax: (731) 989-6000
General/National Adv. Email: belltower@fhu.edu
Website: www.fhu.edu
Personnel: Derrick Spradlin (Advisor); Eddie Eaton (Ed.)

HENDERSON CMTY. COLLEGE

Street Address 1: 2660 S Green St
State: KY
Zip/Postal code: 42420-4623
Country: USA
Mailing Address: 2660 S Green St
Mailing City: Henderson
Mailing State: KY
Mailing ZIP Code: 42420-4699
General Phone: (270) 827-1867
Advertising Phone: 270-831-9770
Year Established: 1978
Personnel: Scott Taylor (Ed.)

HENNIKER

NEW ENGLAND COLLEGE

Street Address 1: 98 Bridge St
State: NH
Zip/Postal code: 03242-3292
Country: USA
Mailing Address: 98 Bridge St
Mailing City: Henniker
Mailing State: NH
Mailing ZIP Code: 03242-3292
General Phone: (603) 428-2000
General Fax: (603) 428-7230
Website: www.nec.edu
Personnel: William Homestead (Advisor)

HICKORY

LENOIR-RHYNE UNIVERSITY

Street Address 1: 625 7th Ave NE
State: NC
Zip/Postal code: 28601-3984
Country: USA
Mailing Address: P.O. 7341
Mailing City: Hickory
Mailing State: NC
Mailing ZIP Code: 28603
General Phone: (828) 328-7176
General/National Adv. Email: harrisl@lr.edu
Display Adv. Email: harrisl@lr.edu
Editorial Email: richard.gould@lr.edu
Website: therhynean.wordpress.com/
Delivery Methods: Newsstand
Published: Mthly

HIGH POINT

HIGH POINT UNIV.

Street Address 1: 1 University Pkwy
State: NC
Zip/Postal code: 27268-0002
Country: USA
Mailing Address: 833 Montlieu Ave
Mailing City: High Point
Mailing State: NC
Mailing ZIP Code: 27262-4260
General Phone: (800) 345-6993
General Fax: (336) 841-4513
General/National Adv. Email: news@highpoint.edu
Website: www.highpoint.edu
Personnel: Bobby Hayes (Advisor); Wilfrid Tremblay (Dir./Prof.); Kate Fowkes (Prof.); Judy Isaksen (Assoc. Prof.); John Luecke (Assoc. Prof.); Nahed Eltantawy (Asst. Prof.); Jim Goodman (Asst. Prof.); Brad Lambert (Asst. Prof.); Jim Trammell (Asst. Prof.); Gerald Voorhees (Asst. Prof.); Kristina Bell (Lectr.); Don Moore (Opns. Mgr.); Martin Yount (Video Producer); Michelle Devlin (Admin. Asst.)

HILLSBORO

TABOR COLLEGE

Street Address 1: 400 S Jefferson St
State: KS
Zip/Postal code: 67063-1753
Country: USA
Mailing Address: 400 S. Jefferson St.
Mailing City: Hillsboro
Mailing State: KS
Mailing ZIP Code: 67063-1753
General Phone: (620) 947-3121
General Fax: (620) 947-2607
General/National Adv. Email: theview@tabor.edu
Display Adv. Email: theview@tabor.edu
Editorial Email: theview@tabor.edu
Website: https://www.facebook.com/TaborView?ref=hl
Published: Mthly
Personnel: Sara Jo Waldron (Advisor); Jared Janzen (Editor-in-Chief); Sara Sigley (Advisor); Heather Deckert (Ed.)

HILLSDALE

HILLSDALE COLLEGE

Street Address 1: 33 E College St
State: MI
Zip/Postal code: 49242-1205
Country: USA
Mailing Address: 33 E College St
Mailing City: Hillsdale
Mailing State: MI
Mailing ZIP Code: 49242-1298
General Phone: (517) 437-7341
General Fax: (517) 437-3293
General/National Adv. Email: collegian@hillsdale.edu
Website: www.hillsdale.edu
Personnel: Ingrid Jacques (Advisor)

HILO

UNIV. OF HAWAII HILO

Street Address 1: 200 W Kawili St, Campus Ctr 215
State: HI
Zip/Postal code: 96720
Country: USA
Mailing Address: 200 W. Kawili St., Campus Ctr. 215
Mailing City: Hilo
Mailing State: HI
Mailing ZIP Code: 96720-4091
General Phone: (808) 974-7504
General Fax: (808) 974-7782
General/National Adv. Email: kalahea@hawaii.edu
Website: www.uhh.hawaii.edu/news/kekalahea
Personnel: Marc Burba (Advisor); Roxanne Yamane (Bus. Mgr.)

HIRAM

HIRAM COLLEGE
Street Address 1: PO Box 67
State: OH
Zip/Postal code: 44234-0067
Country: USA
Mailing Address: PO Box 67
Mailing City: Hiram
Mailing State: OH
Mailing ZIP Code: 44234-0067
General Phone: (330) 569-5203
General Fax: (330) 569-5479
General/National Adv. Email: advance@hiram.edu
Personnel: Christopher Benek (Ed. in Chief)

HOBOKEN

STEVENS INSTITUTE OF TECHNOLOGY
Street Address 1: Stevens Institute of Technology
Street Address 2: Castle Point on Hudson
State: NJ
Zip/Postal code: 7030
Country: USA
General Phone: (201) 216-3404
General/National Adv. Email: stute@stevens.edu
Display Adv. Email: stuteads@stevens.edu
Editorial Email: eboard@thestute.com
Website: www.thestute.com
Year Established: 1904
Published: Fri
Personnel: Joseph Brosnan (Ed.)

HOLLAND

HOPE COLLEGE
Street Address 1: 141 E 12th St
State: MI
Zip/Postal code: 49423-3663
Country: USA
Mailing Address: P.O. Box 9000
Mailing City: Holland
Mailing State: MI
Mailing ZIP Code: 49422-9000
General Phone: (616) 395-7877
General Fax: (616) 395-7183
General/National Adv. Email: anchor@hope.edu
Display Adv. Email: anchorads@hope.edu
Website: anchor.hope.edu
Year Established: 1887
Personnel: Rosie Jahng (Advisor); Amanda Long (Co-Editor-in-Chief); James Champane (Co-Editor-in-Chief); Patterson (Co-Ed. in chief); Emily West (Co-Ed. in chief)

HOLLY SPRINGS

RUST COLLEGE
Street Address 1: 150 Rust Ave
State: MS
Zip/Postal code: 38635-2330
Country: USA
Mailing Address: 150 Rust Ave
Mailing City: Holly Springs
Mailing State: MS
Mailing ZIP Code: 38635-2328
General Phone: (662) 252-8000 ext. 4553
General Fax: (662) 252-8869
General/National Adv. Email: rustorian_@hotmail.com
Display Adv. Email: rustorian_@hotmail.com
Website: www.rustorian.com
Delivery Methods: Racks
Published: Mthly
Personnel: Debayo Moyo (Advisor)

HOLYOKE

HOLYOKE CMTY. COLLEGE
Street Address 1: 303 Homestead Ave
State: MA
Zip/Postal code: 01040-1091
Country: USA
Mailing Address: 303 Homestead Ave
Mailing City: Holyoke
Mailing State: MA
Mailing ZIP Code: 01040-1099
General Phone: (413) 538-7000
General Fax: (413) 552-2045
Personnel: Fred Cooksey (Advisor)

HONOLULU

CHAMINADE UNIV.
Street Address 1: 3140 Waialae Ave
State: HI
Zip/Postal code: 96816-1510
Country: USA
Mailing Address: 3140 Waialae Ave
Mailing City: Honolulu
Mailing State: HI
Mailing ZIP Code: 96816-1578
General Phone: (808) 739-4636
General Fax: (808) 735-4891
General/National Adv. Email: cuhpress@chaminade.edu
Website: www.cuhnews.com; www.chaminade.edu
Personnel: Ashlee Duenas (Ed.)

HAWAII PACIFIC UNIVERSITY
Street Address 1: 1154 Fort Street Mall
Street Address 2: Ste 312
State: HI
Zip/Postal code: 96813-2712
Country: USA
Mailing Address: 1154 Fort Street Mall Ste 312
Mailing City: Honolulu
Mailing State: HI
Mailing ZIP Code: 96813-2712
General Phone: (808) 544-9379
General Fax: (808) 566-2418
Editorial Phone: (808)687-7030
General/National Adv. Email: kalamalama@hpu.edu
Website: www.hpu.edu/kalamalamaonline/index.html
Year Established: 1992
Personnel: Dayna Kalakau (Bus. Mgr.); Susanne Haala (Student Editor); Nicole Kato (Copy Editor); Kara Jernigan (Associate Editor); John Windrow (Faculty Editor); Riana Stellburg (Photo Editor); Emily Tall (Sports Editor); David Chow (Social Media Tech)

HONOLULU CMTY. COLLEGE UNIV. OF HAWAII
Street Address 1: 874 Dillingham Blvd
State: HI
Zip/Postal code: 96817-4505
Country: USA
Mailing Address: 874 Dillingham Blvd
Mailing City: Honolulu
Mailing State: HI
Mailing ZIP Code: 96817-4598
General Phone: (808) 845-9211
General Fax: (808) 847-9876
Editorial Phone: 808-227-5922
General/National Adv. Email: hcckala@gmail.com
Website: www.thekala.net
Year Established: 1963
Published: Mthly
Avg Free Circ: 900
Personnel: Michael Leidemann (Adviser, Asst Professor of Journalism)

KAPIOLANI CMTY. COLLEGE
Street Address 1: 4303 Diamond Head Rd
State: HI
Zip/Postal code: 96816-4421
Country: USA
Mailing Address: 4303 Diamond Head Rd
Mailing City: Honolulu
Mailing State: HI
Mailing ZIP Code: 96816-4496
General Phone: (808) 734-9166
General Fax: (808) 734-9287
General/National Adv. Email: kapio@hawaii.edu
Website: www.kapiolani.hawaii.edu/
Personnel: Catherine E. Toth (Advisor); Janell Nakahara (Adv. Mgr.)

UNIVERSITY OF HAWAII MANOA
Street Address 1: 2445 Campus Rd
Street Address 2: Hemenway 107
State: HI
Zip/Postal code: 96822-2216
Country: USA
Mailing Address: 2445 Campus Rd.
Mailing City: Honolulu
Mailing State: HI
Mailing ZIP Code: 96822-2216
General Phone: (808) 956-7043
General Fax: (808) 956-9962
Advertising Phone: (808) 956-7043
Editorial Phone: (808) 956-7043
General/National Adv. Email: editor@kaleo.org
Display Adv. Email: advertising@kaleo.org
Editorial Email: editor@kaleo.org
Website: www.kaleo.org
Year Established: 1922
Delivery Methods: Racks
Commercial printers?: N
Published: Mon
Published Other: every two weeks
Avg Free Circ: 10000
Personnel: Jay Hartwell (Ed. Advisor); Sandy Matsui (Dir)
Parent company (for newspapers): Student Media Board, University of Hawaii at Manoa

HOUGHTON

HOUGHTON COLLEGE
Street Address 1: 1 Willard Ave
Street Address 2: Cpo 378
State: NY
Zip/Postal code: 14744-8732
Country: USA
Mailing Address: 1 Willard Ave Cpo 378
Mailing City: Houghton
Mailing State: NY
Mailing ZIP Code: 14744-8732
General Phone: (585) 567-9500
General Fax: (585) 567-9570
General/National Adv. Email: star@houghton.edu
Website: www.houghtonstar.com
Personnel: Joel Vanderweele (Ed. in Chief)

MICHIGAN TECHNOLOGICAL UNIV.
Street Address 1: 1400 Townsend Dr
Street Address 2: Mub 106
State: MI
Zip/Postal code: 49931-1200
Country: USA
Mailing Address: MUB 106 1400 Townsend Dr
Mailing City: Houghton
Mailing State: MI
Mailing ZIP Code: 49931
General Phone: (906) 487-2404
General Fax: (906) 487-3125
Website: www.mtulode.com
Personnel: Kara W. Sokol (Advisor); Kayla R. Herrera (Ed. in chief)

HOUSTON

HOUSTON BAPTIST UNIV.
Street Address 1: 7502 Fondren Rd
State: TX
Zip/Postal code: 77074-3200
Country: USA
Mailing Address: 7502 Fondren Rd
Mailing City: Houston
Mailing State: TX
Mailing ZIP Code: 77074-3298
General Phone: (281) 649-3670
General Fax: (281) 649-3246
Advertising Phone: (281) 649-3668
Editorial Phone: (281) 649-3670
General/National Adv. Email: thecollegian@hbucollegian.com
Display Adv. Email: ads@hbucollegian.com
Website: www.hbucollegian.com
Year Established: 1963
Published: Bi-Mthly
Personnel: Jeffrey Wilkinson (Faculty Adviser); Katie Brown (Editor in Chief); Tabatha Trapp (Advertising Manager)

RICE UNIV.
Street Address 1: 6100 Main St
Street Address 2: Fl 2MS-524
State: TX
Zip/Postal code: 77005-1827
Country: USA
Mailing Address: 6100 Main St., MS-524
Mailing City: Houston
Mailing State: TX
Mailing ZIP Code: 77251-1892
General Phone: (713) 348-4801
General/National Adv. Email: thresher@rice.edu
Website: www.ricethresher.org
Personnel: Kelley Callaway (Advisor)

TEXAS SOUTHERN UNIV.
Street Address 1: 3100 Cleburne Ave, Student Ctr
State: TX
Zip/Postal code: 77004
Country: USA
Mailing Address: 3100 Cleburne Ave., Student Ctr.
Mailing City: Houston
Mailing State: TX
Mailing ZIP Code: 77004-4501
General Phone: (713) 313-1976
General Fax: (713) 313-4453
Website: www.tsu.edu
Personnel: Alice Rogers (Advisor)

UNIV. OF HOUSTON
Street Address 1: Rm 7, Uc Satellite, Student Publications
State: TX
Zip/Postal code: 77204-0001
Country: USA
Mailing Address: 7 Uc Satellite Student Publications
Mailing City: Houston
Mailing State: TX
Mailing ZIP Code: 77204-0001
General Phone: (713) 743-5350
General Fax: (713) 743-5384
Editorial Phone: (713) 743-5360
General/National Adv. Email: news@thedailycougar.com
Display Adv. Email: ads@thedailycougar.com
Website: www.thedailycougar.com
Personnel: Ronnie Turner (Ed. in Chief); Matthew Keever (Managing Ed.); Hiba Adi (News Ed.); Patricia Estrada (News Ed.); Alan (Opinion Ed.)

UNIV. OF HOUSTON CLEAR LAKE
Street Address 1: 2700 Bay Area Blvd
State: TX
Zip/Postal code: 77058-1002
Country: USA
Mailing Address: 2700 Bay Area Blvd
Mailing City: Houston
Mailing State: TX
Mailing ZIP Code: 77058-1002
General Phone: (281) 283-2569
General Fax: (281) 283-2569
Advertising Phone: (281) 283-3975
Editorial Phone: (281) 283-2570
General/National Adv. Email: thesignal@uhcl.edu
Website: uhclthesignal.com/wordpress; prtl.uhcl.edu/thesignal
Personnel: Taleen Washington (Advisor); Lindsay Humphrey (Adv. Mgr./Prodn. Asst.); Matt Griesmyer (Ed.)

College and University Newspapers

UNIV. OF HOUSTON DOWNTOWN
Street Address 1: 1 Main St
Street Address 2: S-260
State: TX
Zip/Postal code: 77002-1014
Country: USA
Mailing Address: 1 Main St
Mailing City: Houston
Mailing State: TX
Mailing ZIP Code: 77002-1014
General Phone: (713) 221-8569
General Fax: (713) 221-8119
Advertising Phone: (832) 533-7659
Editorial Phone: (832) 495-5381
General/National Adv. Email: datelinedowntownhtx@gmail.com
Display Adv. Email: editor@dateline-downtown.com
Editorial Email: editor@dateline-downtown.com
Website: 2103 Hickory Trail Place
Year Established: 1973
Delivery Methods: Newsstand`Racks
Commercial printers?: Y
Published: Mon
Published Other: bi-weekly
Personnel: Joe Sample (Associate Prof.)

UNIV. OF ST. THOMAS
Street Address 1: 3800 Montrose Blvd
State: TX
Zip/Postal code: 77006-4626
Country: USA
Mailing Address: 3800 Montrose Blvd
Mailing City: Houston
Mailing State: TX
Mailing ZIP Code: 77006-4626
General Phone: (713) 525-3579
General Fax: (713) 525-2159
Personnel: Michelle Gautreau (Ed.)

HUNTINGDON

JUNIATA COLLEGE
Street Address 1: 1700 Moore St
State: PA
Zip/Postal code: 16652-2119
Country: USA
Mailing Address: 1700 Moore St
Mailing City: Huntingdon
Mailing State: PA
Mailing ZIP Code: 16652-2196
General Phone: (814) 641-3000
Advertising Fax: (814) 643-3620
Editorial Phone: (814) 641-3132
Website: www.juniatian.com
Delivery Methods: Racks
Commercial printers?: Y
Published: Bi-Mthly

MARSHALL UNIVERSITY
Street Address 1: 109 Communications Bldg
Street Address 2: 1 John Marshall Dr.
State: WV
Zip/Postal code: 25755-0001
Country: USA
Mailing Address: 109 Communications Building
Mailing City: Huntington
Mailing State: WV
Mailing ZIP Code: 25755-0001
General Phone: (304) 696-6696
General Fax: (304) 696-2732
Advertising Phone: (304) 526-2836
Editorial Phone: (304) 696-6696
Editorial Fax: (304) 696-2732
General/National Adv. Email: parthenon@marshall.edu
Display Adv. Email: parthenon@marshall.edu
Editorial Email: parthenon@marshall.edu
Website: www.marshallparthenon.com
Year Established: 1898
Delivery Methods: Racks
Commercial printers?: N
Published: Tues`Fri
Published Other: Print Tuesday and Friday, online 24-7.
Avg Free Circ: 6000

Personnel: Sandy York (Adviser)

HUNTINGTON BEACH

GOLDEN WEST COLLEGE
Street Address 1: 15744 Goldenwest St
Street Address 2: Rm 138
State: CA
Zip/Postal code: 92647-3103
Country: USA
Mailing Address: 15744 Goldenwest St Rm 138
Mailing City: Huntington Beach
Mailing State: CA
Mailing ZIP Code: 92647-3103
General Phone: (714) 895-8786
General Fax: (714) 895-8795
Advertising Phone: 714-315-9450
Advertising Fax: (714) 895-8795
General/National Adv. Email: twsatgwc@aol.com
Display Adv. Email: gwckcumper@yahoo.com
Website: www.westernsun.us; www.goldenwestcollege.edu/westernsun
Year Established: 1966
Published: Bi-Mthly
Avg Free Circ: 15000
Personnel: Jim Tortolano (Advisor); Katie Cumper (Adv. Dir.); Lanace Tonelli (Exec. Ed.); Opal McClain (Opinion Ed.); Fernando (Sports Ed.)

HUNTSVILLE

OAKWOOD COLLEGE
Street Address 1: 7000 Adventist Blvd NW
State: AL
Zip/Postal code: 35896-0001
Country: USA
Mailing Address: 7000 Adventist Blvd NW
Mailing City: Huntsville
Mailing State: AL
Mailing ZIP Code: 35896-0003
General Phone: (256) 726-7000
General/National Adv. Email: oakspread@yahoo.com
Website: www.oakwood.edu
Personnel: Michael Vance (Ed.)

SAM HOUSTON STATE UNIVERSITY
Street Address 1: 1804 Ave J, Dan Rather Communications Bldg, Ste 210
State: TX
Zip/Postal code: 77341-0001
Country: USA
Mailing Address: PO Box 2178
Mailing City: Huntsville
Mailing State: TX
Mailing ZIP Code: 77341-0001
General Phone: (936) 294-1505
General Fax: (936) 294-1888
Advertising Phone: (936) 294-1500
Advertising Fax: (936) 294-1888
Editorial Phone: (936) 294-1505
Editorial Fax: (936) 294-1888
General/National Adv. Email: pcm009@shsu.edu
Display Adv. Email: advertise@houstonianonline.com
Editorial Email: eic@houstonianonline.com
Website: www.houstonianonline.com
Year Established: 1913
Published: Wed
Published Other: Orientation Edition, Student Guide
Avg Free Circ: 2500
Personnel: Paty Mason (Business Manager); Dr. Marcus Funk (Faculty Advisor); Carlos Medina (Advertising Manager)

SAM HOUSTON STATE UNIVERSITY
Street Address 1: 1804 Ave J
State: TX
Zip/Postal code: 77341-0001
Country: USA
Mailing Address: PO Box 2207SHSU
Mailing City: Huntsville
Mailing State: TX

Mailing ZIP Code: 77341-0001
General Phone: (936) 294-1341
General Fax: (936) 294-1888
Personnel: Janet A. Bridges (Chair/Prof.); Michael L. Blackman (Philip J. Warner Chair in Journ.); Mickey Herskowitz (Philip J. Warner Chair in Journ.); Tony R. DeMars (Assoc. Prof.); Anthony Friedmann (Assoc. Prof.); Hugh S. Fullerton (Assoc. Prof.); Christopher White (Assoc. Prof.); Rene Qun Chen (Asst. Prof.); Wanda Reyes Velazquez (Asst. Prof.); Ruth M. Pate (Instr.); Richard O. Kosuowei (Lectr.); Mel Strait (Lectr.); Patsy K. Ziegler (Lectr.)

UNIV. OF ALABAMA HUNTSVILLE
Street Address 1: 301 Sparkman Dr
Street Address 2: Charger Union 201
State: AL
Zip/Postal code: 35805-1911
Country: USA
Mailing Address: 301 Sparkman Drive
Mailing City: Huntsville
Mailing State: AL
Mailing ZIP Code: 35899-0001
General/National Adv. Email: chargertimes@uah.edu
Display Adv. Email: ctlayout@uah.edu
Editorial Email: cteditor@uah.edu
Website: chargertimes.com ; chargertimes.net ; chargertimes.uah.edu
Published: Tues`Fri
Personnel: Morgan Blair (Editor-in-Chief); Amy Dunham (Managing Editor)

HURST

TARRANT COUNTY COLLEGE
Street Address 1: 828 W Harwood Rd
Street Address 2: Cab 1124A
State: TX
Zip/Postal code: 76054-3219
Country: USA
Mailing Address: 828 W Harwood Rd Cab 1124A
Mailing City: Hurst
Mailing State: TX
Mailing ZIP Code: 76054-3219
General Phone: (817) 515-6391
General Fax: (817) 515-6767
Editorial Phone: (817) 515-6392
Editorial Email: tccdeditor@lycos.com
Website: www.tccd.net/collegian
Personnel: Eddye Gallagher (Dir.); Chris Webb (Ed. in Chief)

HYDE PARK

CULINARY INSTITUTE OF AMERICA
Street Address 1: 1946 Campus Dr
State: NY
Zip/Postal code: 12538-1430
Country: USA
Mailing Address: 1946 Campus Dr
Mailing City: Hyde Park
Mailing State: NY
Mailing ZIP Code: 12538-1499
General Phone: (845) 452-1412
General Fax: (845) 451-1093
General/National Adv. Email: lapapillote@culinary.edu
Website: www.ciachef.edu
Year Established: 1979
Published: Fri`Mthly
Personnel: David Whalen (Advisor)

INA

REND LAKE COLLEGE
Street Address 1: 468 N Ken Gray Pkwy
State: IL
Zip/Postal code: 62846-2408
Country: USA
Mailing Address: 468 N Ken Gray Pkwy
Mailing City: Ina
Mailing State: IL
Mailing ZIP Code: 62846-2408

General Phone: (618) 437-5321
Personnel: Michael Peeples (Ed.)

INDIANA

INDIANA UNIV. OF PENNSYLVANIA
Street Address 1: 319 Pratt Dr
State: PA
Zip/Postal code: 15701-2954
Country: USA
Mailing Address: 319 Pratt Dr
Mailing City: Indiana
Mailing State: PA
Mailing ZIP Code: 15701-2954
General Phone: (724) 357-1306
General Fax: (724) 357-0127
Advertising Phone: (724) 357-0127
Editorial Phone: (724) 357-1306
Display Adv. Email: the-penn@iup.edu
Website: www.thepenn.org
Personnel: Joe Lawley (Advisor); Heather Blake (Ed. in Chief); Branden Oakes (Photo Ed.)

INDIANAPOLIS

BUTLER UNIV.
Street Address 1: 4600 Sunset Ave
State: IN
Zip/Postal code: 46208-3443
Country: USA
Mailing Address: 4600 Sunset Ave # 112
Mailing City: Indianapolis
Mailing State: IN
Mailing ZIP Code: 46208-3487
General Phone: (317) 940-9358
General Fax: (317) 940-9713
General/National Adv. Email: mweiteka@butler.edu
Display Adv. Email: advertising@butler.edu
Website: dawgnet.butler.edu
Personnel: Kwadwo Anokwa (Dir.); Charles St. Cyr (Advisor); Lauren Fisher (Adv. Mgr); Meg Shaw (Ed.)

MARIAN COLLEGE
Street Address 1: 3200 Cold Spring Rd
State: IN
Zip/Postal code: 46222-1960
Country: USA
Mailing Address: 3200 Cold Spring Rd
Mailing City: Indianapolis
Mailing State: IN
Mailing ZIP Code: 46222-1997
General Phone: (317) 955-6397
General Fax: (317) 955-6448
Website: www.marian.edu
Personnel: Gay Lynn Crossley (Faculty Supvr.); Sarah Kreicker (Ed.)

UNIV. OF INDIANAPOLIS
Street Address 1: 1400 E Hanna Ave
State: IN
Zip/Postal code: 46227-3630
Country: USA
Mailing Address: 1400 E Hanna Ave
Mailing City: Indianapolis
Mailing State: IN
Mailing ZIP Code: 46227-3697
General Phone: (317) 788-3269
General Fax: (317) 788-3490
General/National Adv. Email: reflector@uindy.edu
Website: www.reflector.uindy.edu
Personnel: Jeanne Criswell (Advisor.); JP Sinclair (Bus. Mgr.); Adrian Kendrick (Ed. in Chief); Samantha Cotten (Ed.)

INDIANOLA

SIMPSON COLLEGE
Street Address 1: 701 N C St
State: IA
Zip/Postal code: 50125-1201
Country: USA
Mailing Address: 701 N C St

Mailing City: Indianola
Mailing State: IA
Mailing ZIP Code: 50125-1202
General Phone: (515) 961-1738
General Fax: (515) 961-1350
General/National Adv. Email: thesimp@simpson.edu
Website: www.thesimpsonian.com
Personnel: Emily Schettler (Ed)

INSTITUTE

WEST VIRGINIA STATE UNIV.

Street Address 1: 214 Wilson Student Union
State: WV
Zip/Postal code: 25112
Country: USA
Mailing Address: 214 Wilson Student Union
Mailing City: Institute
Mailing State: WV
Mailing ZIP Code: 25112-1000
General Phone: (304) 766-3212
General Fax: (304) 766-3309
Website: www.wvstateu.edu/~yellowjacket
Personnel: Robin Broughton (Advisor); Mary Casto (Ed. in Chief); Patrick Felton (Ed. in Chief)

INVER GROVE HEIGHTS

INVER HILLS CMTY. COLLEGE

Street Address 1: 2500 80th St E
Street Address 2: Ste A
State: MN
Zip/Postal code: 55076-3224
Country: USA
Mailing Address: 2500 80th St E Ste A
Mailing City: Inver Grove Heights
Mailing State: MN
Mailing ZIP Code: 55076-3224
General Phone: (651) 450-8563
General Fax: (651) 450-8679
Personnel: Dave Page (Advisor)

IOWA CITY

UNIV. OF IOWA

Street Address 1: 104 West Washington St
State: IA
Zip/Postal code: 52240
Country: USA
Mailing Address: 104 West Washington St
Mailing City: Iowa City
Mailing State: IA
Mailing ZIP Code: 52240
General Phone: (319) 335-5791
General Fax: (319) 335-6297
General/National Adv. Email: daily-iowan@uiowa.edu
Website: www.dailyiowan.com
Personnel: William Casey (Pub.); Debra Plath (Bus. Mgr.); Pete Recker (Adv./Circ. Mgr)

IRVINE

UNIV. OF CALIFORNIA IRVINE

Street Address 1: 3100 Gateway Commons, 3rd Fl
State: CA
Zip/Postal code: 92697-0001
Country: USA
Mailing Address: 3100 Gateway Cmns Fl 3
Mailing City: Irvine
Mailing State: CA
Mailing ZIP Code: 92697-0001
General Phone: (949) 824-8788
General Fax: (949) 824-4828
Advertising Phone: (949) 824-4284
Editorial Phone: (949) 824-8788
General/National Adv. Email: eic@newuniversity.org
Display Adv. Email: admanager@newu.uci.edu
Editorial Email: eic@newuniversity.org
Website: www.newuniversity.org
Avg Free Circ: 8000
Personnel: David Lumb (Ed. in Chief); Sandy Rose (Mng. Ed.)

IRVING

NORTH LAKE COLLEGE

Street Address 1: 5001 N MacArthur Blvd
Street Address 2: Rm A-234
State: TX
Zip/Postal code: 75038-3804
Country: USA
Mailing Address: 5001 N MacArthur Blvd Rm A-234
Mailing City: Irving
Mailing State: TX
Mailing ZIP Code: 75038-3804
General Phone: (972) 273-3057
General Fax: (972) 273-3441
Advertising Phone: 972-273-3498
General/National Adv. Email: nnr7420@dcccd.edu
Website: www.newsregisteronline.com
Published: Mthly
Personnel: Kathleen Stockmier (Advisor); Grant V. Ziegler (Editor-in-Chief); Joanna Mikolajczak (Photography Editor)

UNIV. OF DALLAS

Street Address 1: 1845 E Northgate Dr
Street Address 2: # 732
State: TX
Zip/Postal code: 75062-4736
Country: USA
Mailing Address: 1845 E Northgate Dr # 732
Mailing City: Irving
Mailing State: TX
Mailing ZIP Code: 75062-4736
General Phone: (972) 721-4070
General Fax: (972) 721-4136
Advertising Phone: (972) 721-5142
Editorial Phone: 972-721-5089
General/National Adv. Email: udnews1@yahoo.com
Website: www.udallasnews.com
Year Established: 1993
News Services: none
Delivery Methods: Mail Racks
Personnel: Raymond Wilkerson (Fac. Adviser)

ITHACA

CORNELL LAW SCHOOL

Street Address 1: Myron Taylor Hall
State: NY
Zip/Postal code: 14853
Country: USA
Mailing Address: Myron Taylor Hall
Mailing City: Ithaca
Mailing State: NY
Mailing ZIP Code: 14853
General Phone: (607) 255-0565
Personnel: Rick Silverman (Ed.)

CORNELL UNIV. ECONOMICS SCHOOL

Street Address 1: Cornell Dept of Economics, Uris Hall, 4th Fl
State: NY
Zip/Postal code: 14850
Country: USA
Mailing Address: Cornell Dept. of Economics, Uris Hall, 4th Fl.
Mailing City: Ithaca
Mailing State: NY
Mailing ZIP Code: 14850
General Phone: (607) 255-8501
Website: www.rso.cornell.edu/ces
Personnel: Rabia Muqaddam (Ed. in Chief)

ITHACA COLLEGE

Street Address 1: 269 Park Hall
State: NY
Zip/Postal code: 14850-7258
Country: USA
Mailing Address: 269 Park Hall
Mailing City: Ithaca
Mailing State: NY
Mailing ZIP Code: 14850-7258
General Phone: (607) 274-3208
General Fax: (607) 274-1376
Advertising Phone: (607) 274-1618
General/National Adv. Email: ithacan@ithaca.edu
Display Adv. Email: ithacanads@ithaca.edu
Website: www.theithacan.org
Published: Thur
Avg Free Circ: 4000
Personnel: Michael Serino (Advisor); Kira Maddox (Ed. in Chief); Rachel Wolfgang (Mng. Ed.); Lawrence Hamacher (Advertising Sales Manager)

THE CORNELL DAILY SUN

Street Address 1: 139 W State St
State: NY
Zip/Postal code: 14850-5427
Country: USA
Mailing Address: 139 W State St
Mailing City: Ithaca
Mailing State: NY
Mailing ZIP Code: 14850-5427
General Phone: (607) 273-3606
General Fax: (607) 273-0746
General/National Adv. Email: letters@cornelldailysun.com
Website: www.cornellsun.com
Year Established: 1880
Personnel: Ben Gitlin (Editor in Chief); Michael Linhorst (Managing Editor); Dani Neuharth-Keusch (Associate Editor); Rahul Kishore (Web Editor); Chloe Gatta (Business Manager); Helene Beauchemin (Advertising Manager); Justin wheeler (Bus. Mgr.); Keenan Weatherford (Ed. in Chief); Michael J. Stratford (Managing Ed.); Sophia Qasir (Advertising Mgr.)

ITTA BENA

MISSISSIPPI VALLEY STATE UNIV.

Street Address 1: 14000 Highway 82 W
State: MS
Zip/Postal code: 38941-1400
County: Leflore
Country: USA
Mailing Address: 14000 Highway 82 W
Mailing City: Itta Bena
Mailing State: MS
Mailing ZIP Code: 38941-1401
General Phone: (662) 254-3458
General Fax: (622) 254-6704
Advertising Phone: (662) 254-3458
Advertising Fax: (662) 254-3458
Editorial Phone: (662) 254-3458
General/National Adv. Email: deltadevilsgazettefacad@gmail.com
Display Adv. Email: ehmcclary@mvsu.edu
Editorial Email: deltadevilsgazettefacad@gmail.com
Website: deltadevilsgazette.com
Published Other: three per semester
Avg Free Circ: 2000
Personnel: Esin C. Turk (Asst. Prof.); Samuel Osunde (Asst. Prof./Dir., Forensics); Carolyn Gordon; Zainul Abedin (Mr.)

JACKSON

BELHAVEN COLLEGE

Street Address 1: 1500 Peachtree St
State: MS
Zip/Postal code: 39202-1754
Country: USA
Mailing Address: 1500 Peachtree St
Mailing City: Jackson
Mailing State: MS
Mailing ZIP Code: 39202-1789
General Phone: (601) 968-8702
Personnel: Don Hubele (Advisor)

JACKSON CMTY. COLLEGE

Street Address 1: 2111 Emmons Rd
State: MI
Zip/Postal code: 49201-8395
Country: USA
Mailing Address: 2111 Emmons Rd
Mailing City: Jackson
Mailing State: MI
Mailing ZIP Code: 49201-8399
General Phone: (517) 787-0800
General Fax: (517) 787-8663
General/National Adv. Email: phoenix@jccmi.edu
Website: www.jccmi.edu
Personnel: Karessa E. Weir (Advisor)

JACKSON STATE UNIVERSITY

Street Address 1: 1400 J R Lynch St
Street Address 2: Blackburn Language Arts Building, Room 208
State: MS
Zip/Postal code: 39217-0002
Country: USA
Mailing Address: PO Box 18449
Mailing City: Jackson
Mailing State: MS
Mailing ZIP Code: 39217-0001
General Phone: (601) 979-2167
General Fax: (601) 979-2876
Advertising Phone: (601) 979-2167
Advertising Fax: (601) 979-2876
Editorial Phone: (601) 979-2167
Editorial Fax: (601) 979-2876
General/National Adv. Email: theflash@jsums.edu
Display Adv. Email: shannon.d.tatum@jsums.edu
Editorial Email: theflash@jsums.edu
Website: www.thejsuflash.com
Published: Thur
Avg Free Circ: 3000
Personnel: Shannon Tatum (Publications Coordinator/Ad Manager)

MILLSAPS COLLEGE

Street Address 1: Box 150847
State: MS
Zip/Postal code: 39210-0001
Country: USA
Mailing Address: PO Box 150847
Mailing City: Jackson
Mailing State: MS
Mailing ZIP Code: 39210-0001
General Phone: (601) 974-1211
General Fax: (601) 974-1229
Personnel: Woody Woodrick (Advisor); Kate Royals (Ed, in Chief); Kathleen Morrison (Copy Ed.)

UNION UNIV.

Street Address 1: 1050 Union University Dr
Street Address 2: Dept Jenningshall
State: TN
Zip/Postal code: 38305-3656
Country: USA
Mailing Address: 1050 Union University Dr Dept Jenningshall
Mailing City: Jackson
Mailing State: TN
Mailing ZIP Code: 38305-3656
General Phone: (731) 668-1818
General Fax: (731) 661-5243
Website: www.cardinalandcream.info
Personnel: Michael Chute (Advisor); Gray Coyner (Adv. Mgr.); Andrea Turner (Ed. in Chief)

JACKSONVILLE

FLORIDA STATE COLLEGE AT JACKSONVILLE

Street Address 1: 101 State St W
Street Address 2: Rm C103
State: FL
Zip/Postal code: 32202-3099
Country: USA
Mailing Address: 101 State St W Rm C103
Mailing City: Jacksonville

College and University Newspapers

Mailing State: FL
Mailing ZIP Code: 32202-3099
General Phone: (904) 633-8283
General Fax: (904) 632-3279
General/National Adv. Email: campusvoice@fscj.edu
Website: www.campusvoiceonline.com
Published: Bi-Mthly
Personnel: Zak Gragg (Adv. Mgr.); Jocelyn Rhoten (Editor-in-Chief)

ILLINOIS COLLEGE

Street Address 1: 1101 W College Ave
State: IL
Zip/Postal code: 62650-2212
Country: USA
Mailing Address: 1101 W College Ave
Mailing City: Jacksonville
Mailing State: IL
Mailing ZIP Code: 62650-2299
General Phone: (217) 245-3030
General Fax: (217) 245-3056
General/National Adv. Email: rambler@ic.edu
Website: www.ic.edu
Personnel: John S. Rush (Advisor); Laurel Berkel (Ed.)

JACKSONVILLE STATE UNIV.

Street Address 1: 700 Pelham Rd N
Street Address 2: Rm 180
State: AL
Zip/Postal code: 36265-1602
Country: USA
Mailing Address: 700 Pelham Rd N Rm 180
Mailing City: Jacksonville
Mailing State: AL
Mailing ZIP Code: 36265-1602
General Phone: (256) 782-8192
General Fax: (256) 782-5645
Advertising Phone: (256) 782-5932
Editorial Phone: (256) 782-8191
General/National Adv. Email: chantyeditor@gmail.com
Website: www.thechanticleeronline.com
Personnel: Mike Stedham (Advisor); Zach Childree (Ed. in Chief); Ryan Rutledge (Staff Writer)

JACKSONVILLE UNIV.

Street Address 1: 2800 University Blvd N
State: FL
Zip/Postal code: 32211-3321
Country: USA
Mailing Address: 2800 University Blvd N
Mailing City: Jacksonville
Mailing State: FL
Mailing ZIP Code: 32211-3394
General Phone: (904) 256-7526
General Fax: (904) 256-7684
General/National Adv. Email: navigator@jacksonville.edu
Website: navigator.ju.edu
Personnel: Peter Moberg (Advisor); Jean Sils (Adv. Mgr); Renae Ingram (Ed. in Chief)

UNIV. OF NORTH FLORIDA

Street Address 1: 1 U N F Dr
State: FL
Zip/Postal code: 32224-7699
Country: USA
Mailing Address: 1 U N F Drive
Mailing City: Jacksonville
Mailing State: FL
Mailing ZIP Code: 32224
General Phone: (904) 620-2727
General Fax: (904) 620-3924
General/National Adv. Email: spinsads@unf.edu
Website: www.espinnaker.com
Year Established: 1977
Personnel: Adina Daar (Bus. Mgr.)

JAMAICA

ST. JOHN'S UNIVERSITY

Street Address 1: 8000 Utopia Pkwy
State: NY
Zip/Postal code: 11439-9000
Country: USA
Mailing Address: 8000 Utopia Pkwy
Mailing City: Jamaica
Mailing State: NY
Mailing ZIP Code: 11439-9000
General Phone: (718) 990-6756
General Fax: (718) 990-5849
Display Adv. Email: torchads@gmail.com
Editorial Email: torchnews@gmail.com
Website: www.torchonline.com
Published: Wed
Avg Free Circ: 3000
Personnel: Michael Cunniff (Editor-in-Chief)

YORK COLLEGE OF CUNY

Street Address 1: 9420 Guy R Brewer Blvd
State: NY
Zip/Postal code: 11451-0001
Country: USA
Mailing Address: 9420 Guy R Brewer Blvd
Mailing City: Jamaica
Mailing State: NY
Mailing ZIP Code: 11451-0002
General Phone: (718) 262-2529
General Fax: (718) 262-5234
General/National Adv. Email: pandora@york.cuny.edu
Display Adv. Email: pandora@york.cuny.edu
Editorial Email: pandora@york.cuny.edu
Website: pbwire.cunycampuswire.com/
Year Established: 1967
Published: Mthly
Avg Free Circ: 3000
Personnel: William Hughes (Advisor)

JAMESTOWN

JAMESTOWN COLLEGE

Street Address 1: 6086 College Ln
State: ND
Zip/Postal code: 58405-0001
Country: USA
Mailing Address: 6086 College Ln
Mailing City: Jamestown
Mailing State: ND
Mailing ZIP Code: 58405-0001
General Phone: (701) 252-3467
General Fax: (701) 253-4318
Website: www.jc.edu
Personnel: Steve Listopad (Advisor); Richard Schmit (Ed. in Cheif)

JANESVILLE

BLACKHAWK TECHNICAL COLLEGE

Street Address 1: 6004 Prairie Rd
State: WI
Country: USA
Mailing Address: PO Box 5009
Mailing City: Janesville
Mailing State: WI
Mailing ZIP Code: 53547-5009
General Phone: (608) 757-7702
General Fax: (608) 743-4407
Personnel: Amber Feibel (Advisor)

JEFFERSON CITY

CARSON-NEWMAN UNIVERSITY

Street Address 1: 1646 Russell Ave
State: TN
Zip/Postal code: 37760-2204
Country: USA
Mailing Address: 1646 Russell Ave
Mailing City: Jefferson City
Mailing State: TN
Mailing ZIP Code: 37760
General Phone: (865) 471-3434

General Fax: (865) 471-3416
General/National Adv. Email: oandb@cn.edu
Website: www.orangeandblueonline.com; www.cn.edu
Personnel: Glenn Cragwall (Advisor)

LINCOLN UNIV.

Street Address 1: Elliff Hall, Rm 208
State: MO
Zip/Postal code: 65102
Country: USA
Mailing Address: Elliff Hall, Rm. 208
Mailing City: Jefferson City
Mailing State: MO
Mailing ZIP Code: 65102
General Phone: (573) 681-5446
General Fax: (573) 681-5438
Website: www.lincolnu.edu
Personnel: Yusuf Kalyango (Advisor)

JERSEY CITY

NEW JERSEY CITY UNIV.

Street Address 1: 2039 Kennedy Blvd, Gsub 305
State: NJ
Zip/Postal code: 7305
Country: USA
Mailing Address: 2039 Kennedy Blvd., GSUB 305
Mailing City: Jersey City
Mailing State: NJ
Mailing ZIP Code: 07305-1596
General Phone: (201) 200-3575
Website: www.njcu.edu
Personnel: James Broderick (Advisor); Erica Molina (Ed.); Marlen Gonzalez (Mng. Ed.)

ST. PETERS COLLEGE

Street Address 1: 2641 John F Kennedy Blvd
State: NJ
Zip/Postal code: 07306-5943
Country: USA
Mailing Address: 2641 John F Kennedy Blvd
Mailing City: Jersey City
Mailing State: NJ
Mailing ZIP Code: 07306-5997
General Phone: (201) 938-1254
General Fax: (201) 938-1254
Advertising Phone: (201) 761-7378
General/National Adv. Email: pauwwow@hotmail.com
Display Adv. Email: ads@pauwwow.com
Website: pauwwow.com
Personnel: Paul Almonte (Advisor); Frank DeMichele (Ed. in Chief); Rozen Pradhan (Mng. Ed.)

JOHNSON

JOHNSON STATE COLLEGE

Street Address 1: 337 College Hl
State: VT
Zip/Postal code: 05656-9741
Country: USA
Mailing Address: 337 College Hl
Mailing City: Johnson
Mailing State: VT
Mailing ZIP Code: 05656-9898
General Phone: (802) 635-1357
Website: www.jsc.edu
Personnel: Nathan Burgess (Ed.)

JOHNSON CITY

EAST TENNESSEE STATE UNIV.

Street Address 1: Culp Ctr, Jl Seehorn Jr Rd
State: TN
Zip/Postal code: 37614
Country: USA
Mailing Address: PO Box 70688
Mailing City: Johnson City
Mailing State: TN
Mailing ZIP Code: 37614-1709
General Phone: (423) 439-6170

General Fax: (423) 439-8407
Editorial Phone: (423) 439-4677
General/National Adv. Email: etnews@etsu.edu
Website: www.easttennessean.com
Personnel: Martha Milner (Advisor); Candy Naff (Office Supvr.)

JOHNSTOWN

UNIV. OF PITTSBURGH

Street Address 1: 147 Student Union, 450 School House Rd
State: PA
Zip/Postal code: 15904
Country: USA
Mailing Address: 147 Student Union, 450 School House Rd.
Mailing City: Johnstown
Mailing State: PA
Mailing ZIP Code: 15904-1200
General Phone: (814) 269-7470
General/National Adv. Email: joo10@pitt.edu
Website: www.upjadvocate.com
Personnel: Leland Wood (Staff Advisor); Michael Cuccaro (Adv. Mgr.); Jon O' Connel (Ed. in Chief); Ryan Brown (News Ed.)

JOLIET

JOLIET JUNIOR COLLEGE

Street Address 1: 1215 Houbolt Rd
State: IL
Zip/Postal code: 60431-8938
Country: USA
Mailing Address: 1215 Houbolt Rd
Mailing City: Joliet
Mailing State: IL
Mailing ZIP Code: 60431-8800
General Phone: (815) 280-2313
General Fax: (815) 280-6730
Advertising Phone: (815) 280-2313
Advertising Fax: (815) 280-6730
Editorial Phone: (815) 280-2313
Editorial Fax: (815) 280-2313
General/National Adv. Email: blazermail@jjc.edu
Display Adv. Email: blazermail@jjc.edu
Editorial Email: blazermail@jjc.edu
Website: www.jjc.edu/blazer
News Services: None
Special Editions: None
Special Weekly Sections: None
Delivery Methods: Racks
Published: Other
Published Other: Our frequency is tri-weekly, or 5 times per semester.
Avg Free Circ: 2000
Personnel: Robert Marcink (Advisor)

UNIV. OF ST. FRANCIS

Street Address 1: 500 Wilcox St
State: IL
Zip/Postal code: 60435-6169
Country: USA
Mailing Address: 500 Wilcox St
Mailing City: Joliet
Mailing State: IL
Mailing ZIP Code: 60435-6188
General Phone: (815) 740-3816
General Fax: (815) 740-4285
General/National Adv. Email: encounter@stfrancis.edu
Website: usfencounter.stfrancis.edu
Published: Mthly
Avg Free Circ: 500
Personnel: Brien McHugh (Advisor); Mike Clinton (Editor in Chief); Thaschara VanDyke (Asst. Editor in Chief)

JOPLIN

MISSOURI SOUTHERN UNIVERSITY

Street Address 1: 3950 Newman Rd
State: MO

Zip/Postal code: 64801-1512
Country: USA
Mailing Address: 3950 Newman Rd
Mailing City: Joplin
Mailing State: MO
Mailing ZIP Code: 64801-1595
General Phone: (417) 625-9823
General Fax: (417) 625-9585
General/National Adv. Email: chart@mssu.edu
Website: www.thechartonline.com
Year Established: 1939
Personnel: J.R. Moorman (Head); Chad Stebbins (Advisor); T.R. Hanrahan (Publications Mgr.); Alexandra Nicolas (Ed. in Chief)

JUNEAU

UNIV. OF ALASKA SOUTHEAST

Street Address 1: 11120 Glacier Hwy
State: AK
Zip/Postal code: 99801-86
Country: USA
Mailing Address: 11120 Glacier Hwy
Mailing City: Juneau
Mailing State: AK
Mailing ZIP Code: 99801-8699
General Phone: (907) 796-6434
General Fax: (907) 796-6399
General/National Adv. Email: uas.whalesong@gmail.com; whalesong@uas.alaska.edu
Website: www.uas.alaska.edu/whalesong
Year Established: 1981
Personnel: Jeremy Hsieh (Advisor); Taylor Murph (Adv. Mgr.); Randi Spary (Ed.); Hollis Kitchin (Prodn. Mgr.)

KALAMAZOO

KALAMAZOO COLLEGE

Street Address 1: 1200 Academy St
State: MI
Zip/Postal code: 49006-3268
Country: USA
Mailing Address: 1200 Academy St Ofc
Mailing City: Kalamazoo
Mailing State: MI
Mailing ZIP Code: 49006-3295
General Phone: (269) 337-7000
General Fax: (269) 337-7216
Website: www.kzoo.edu
Personnel: Brian Ditez (Advisor)

WESTERN MICHIGAN UNIV.

Street Address 1: 1903 W Michigan Ave
Street Address 2: 1517 Faunce Student Servs. Bldg.
State: MI
Zip/Postal code: 49008-5200
Country: USA
Mailing Address: 1517 Faunce Student Servs. Bldg.
Mailing City: Kalamazoo
Mailing State: MI
Mailing ZIP Code: 49008-5363
General Phone: (269) 387-2110
General Fax: (269) 387-3820
Advertising Phone: 269-387-2107
Advertising Fax: 269-387-3820
Editorial Phone: 269-323-2101
Editorial Fax: 269-387-3820
General/National Adv. Email: herald-general-manager@wmich.edu
Display Adv. Email: herald-advertising@wmich.edu
Editorial Email: herald-editor@wmich.edu
Website: www.westernherald.com
Year Established: 1916
Published: Bi-Mthly
Avg Free Circ: 10000
Personnel: Meghan Chandler (Editor-in-chief); Richard Junger (General Manager)

KANSAS CITY

AVILA UNIVERSITY

Street Address 1: 11901 Wornall Rd
State: MO
Zip/Postal code: 64145-1007
Country: USA
Mailing Address: 11901 Wornall Rd
Mailing City: Kansas City
Mailing State: MO
Mailing ZIP Code: 64145-1007
General Phone: (816) 942-8400
General Fax: (816) 501-2459
General/National Adv. Email: talon@mail.avila.edu
Website: www.thetalon-online.com
Personnel: Joe Snorgrass (Advisor)

KANSAS CITY CMTY. COLLEGE

Street Address 1: 7250 State Ave
State: KS
Zip/Postal code: 66112-3003
Country: USA
Mailing Address: 7250 State Ave
Mailing City: Kansas City
Mailing State: KS
Mailing ZIP Code: 66112-3003
General Phone: (913) 334-1100
General Fax: (913) 288-7617
Website: kckcc.edu
Personnel: Bryan Whitehead (Faculty Advisor)

ROCKHURST UNIV.

Street Address 1: 1100 Rockhurst Rd
State: MO
Zip/Postal code: 64110-2508
Country: USA
Mailing Address: 1100 Rockhurst Rd
Mailing City: Kansas City
Mailing State: MO
Mailing ZIP Code: 64110-2561
General Phone: (816) 501-4051
General Fax: (816) 501-4290
General/National Adv. Email: sentinel@rockhurst.edu
Website: www.rockhurstsentinel.com
Personnel: Brian Roewe (Ed. in Chief)

UNIV. OF MISSOURI

Street Address 1: 5327 Holmes St
State: MO
Zip/Postal code: 64110-2437
Country: USA
Mailing Address: 5327 Holmes St
Mailing City: Kansas City
Mailing State: MO
Mailing ZIP Code: 64110-2437
General Phone: (816) 235-1393
General Fax: (816) 235-6514
Website: www.unews.com
Personnel: BJ Allen (Bus. Mgr.); Stefanie Crabtree (Adv. Mgr.); Hilary Hedges (Ed. in Chief)

KEARNEY

UNIV. OF NEBRASKA

Street Address 1: Mitchel Ctr 156
State: NE
Zip/Postal code: 68847
Country: USA
Mailing Address: Mitchel Ctr. 156
Mailing City: Kearney
Mailing State: NE
Mailing ZIP Code: 68847
General Phone: (308) 865-8487
General Fax: (308) 865-1537
Display Adv. Email: antelopeads@unk.edu
Personnel: Tereca M Diffenderfer (Advisor)

KEENE

SOUTHWESTERN ADVENTIST UNIV.

Street Address 1: 100 W Hillcrest St

State: TX
Zip/Postal code: 76059-1922
Country: USA
Mailing Address: 100 W Hillcrest St
Mailing City: Keene
Mailing State: TX
Mailing ZIP Code: 76059-1922
General Phone: (817) 645-3921
General Fax: (817) 202-6790
General/National Adv. Email: southwesterner@swau.edu
Website: southwesterner.swau.edu
Year Established: 1958
Personnel: Glen Robinson (Ed.); Julena Allen (Associate Editor); Sierra Hernandez

KENNESAW

KENNESAW STATE UNIVERSITY

Street Address 1: 395 Cobb Ave NW
Street Address 2: Ste 274 # 501
State: GA
Zip/Postal code: 30144-5660
Country: USA
Mailing Address: 395 Cobb Ave NW
Mailing City: Kennesaw
Mailing State: GA
Mailing ZIP Code: 30144-5588
General Phone: (470) 578-5470
General Fax: (470) 578-9165
General/National Adv. Email: sentinel@ksumedia.com
Display Adv. Email: marketingmgr@ksumedia.com
Editorial Email: eic@ksusentinel.com
Website: www.ksusentinel.com
Year Established: 1967
Published: Tues
Avg Free Circ: 5000
Personnel: Ed Bonza (Advisor)

KENOSHA

CARTHAGE COLLEGE

Street Address 1: 2001 Alford Park Dr
State: WI
Zip/Postal code: 53140-1929
Country: USA
Mailing Address: 2001 Alford Park Dr
Mailing City: Kenosha
Mailing State: WI
Mailing ZIP Code: 53140-1994
General Phone: (262) 551-5800
General Fax: (262) 551-6629
Website: current.carthage.edu
Personnel: Meg Durbin (Ed. in Chief); Carmelo Chimera (Mng. Ed.); Lauren Hansen (Bus. Mng.)

UNIV. OF WISCONSIN PARKSIDE

Street Address 1: 900 Wood Rd
State: WI
Zip/Postal code: 53144-1133
Country: USA
Mailing Address: PO Box 2000
Mailing City: Kenosha
Mailing State: WI
Mailing ZIP Code: 53141-2000
General Phone: (262) 595-2287
General Fax: (262) 595-2295
General/National Adv. Email: rangernews@uwp.edu
Display Adv. Email: advertising@therangernews.com
Website: www.therangernews.com
Personnel: Jo Kirst (Ed.)

KENT

KENT STATE UNIV.

Street Address 1: 201 Franklin Hall, Rm 205
State: OH
Zip/Postal code: 44242-0001
Country: USA
Mailing Address: 201 Franklin Hall Rm 205
Mailing City: Kent

Mailing State: OH
Mailing ZIP Code: 44242-0001
General Phone: (330) 672-0887
General Fax: (330) 672-4880
General/National Adv. Email: dksads@gmail.com
Website: www.kent.edu
Personnel: Carl Schierhorn (Advisor); Lori Cantor (Mgr.); Tami Bongiorni (Adv. Mgr.)

KENTFIELD

COLLEGE OF MARIN

Street Address 1: 835 College Ave
State: CA
Zip/Postal code: 94904-2551
Country: USA
Mailing Address: 835 College Ave
Mailing City: Kentfield
Mailing State: CA
Mailing ZIP Code: 94904-2590
General Phone: (415) 485-9690
General Fax: (415) 485-0135
General/National Adv. Email: echotimes@marin.cc.ca.us
Website: www.theechotimes.com
Personnel: Elisa Forsgren (Adv. Mgr.); William Kennedy (Ed. in Chief); Yukie Sano (Mng. Ed.)

KEUKA PARK

KEUKA COLLEGE

Street Address 1: Office of Commun
State: NY
Zip/Postal code: 14478
Country: USA
Mailing Address: Office of Commun.
Mailing City: Keuka Park
Mailing State: NY
Mailing ZIP Code: 14478
General Phone: (315) 279-5231
General Fax: (315) 279-5281
Website: www.keukonian.keuka.edu
Personnel: Christen Smith (Advisor); Kilee Brown (Ed.); Chelsea DeGroote (Asst. Ed.)

KILGORE

KILGORE COLLEGE

Street Address 1: 1100 Broadway Blvd
State: TX
Zip/Postal code: 75662-3204
Country: USA
Mailing Address: 1100 Broadway Blvd
Mailing City: Kilgore
Mailing State: TX
Mailing ZIP Code: 75662-3299
General Phone: (903) 983-8194
General Fax: (903) 983-8193
General/National Adv. Email: kc_flare@yahoo.com
Website: www.theflareonline.com
Personnel: Betty Craddock (Advisor); christian Keit (Ed. in Chief)

KILLEEN

CENTRAL TEXAS COLLEGE

Street Address 1: 6200 W Central Texas Expy
State: TX
Zip/Postal code: 76549-1272
Country: USA
Mailing Address: 6200 W Central Texas Expy
Mailing City: Killeen
Mailing State: TX
Mailing ZIP Code: 76549-1272
General Phone: (254) 526-1755
General Fax: (254) 526-1126

KINGSTON

UNIV. OF RHODE ISLAND

Street Address 1: 125 Memorial Union, 50 Lower College Rd
State: RI

College and University Newspapers

Zip/Postal code: 2881
Country: USA
Mailing Address: 125 Memorial Union, 50 Lower College Rd.
Mailing City: Kingston
Mailing State: RI
Mailing ZIP Code: 02881
General Phone: (401) 874-2914
General Fax: (401) 874-5607
General/National Adv. Email: uricigar@gmail.com
Website: www.ramcigar.com
Personnel: Lindsay Lorenz (Ed. in Chief)

KINGSVILLE

TEXAS A&M UNIV. KINGSVILLE

Street Address 1: 700 N University Blvd
State: TX
Zip/Postal code: 78363-8202
Country: USA
Mailing Address: MSC 123
Mailing City: TX
Mailing ZIP Code: 78363
General Phone: (361) 593-2111
General Fax: (361) 593-4046
General/National Adv. Email: thesouthtexan@yahoo.com
Website: www.tamek.edu/southtexan
Personnel: Manuel Flores (Advisor); Jaime Gonzalez (Mng. Ed.); Amanda Marcum (Ed. in Chief)

KIRKSVILLE

TRUMAN STATE UNIV.

Street Address 1: Barnett Hall News Ctr 1200, 100 E Normal St
State: MO
Zip/Postal code: 63501
Country: USA
Mailing Address: Barnett Hall News Ctr. 1200, 100 E. Normal St.
Mailing City: Kirksville
Mailing State: MO
Mailing ZIP Code: 63501-4200
General Phone: (660) 785-4449
General Fax: (660) 785-7601
Advertising Phone: (660) 785-4319
General/National Adv. Email: indexads@truman.edu
Website: www.trumanindex.com
Personnel: Don Krause (Advisor); Blake Toppmeyer (Ed. in Chief); Jessica Rapp (Mng. Ed.); Stephanie Hall (News Ed.)

KIRKWOOD

ST. LOUIS CMTY. COLLEGE

MERAMEC

Street Address 1: 11333 Big Bend Rd
State: MO
Zip/Postal code: 63122-5720
Country: USA
Mailing Address: 11333 Big Bend Rd
Mailing City: Kirkwood
Mailing State: MO
Mailing ZIP Code: 63122-5799
General Phone: (314) 984-7955
General Fax: (314) 984-7947
Editorial Phone: 314-984-7857
General/National Adv. Email: meramecmontage@gmail.com
Website: www.meramecmontage.com
Year Established: 1962
Published: Other
Published Other: bi-weekly
Personnel: Shannon Philpott-Sanders (Advisor)

KIRTLAND

LAKELAND CMTY. COLLEGE

Street Address 1: 7700 Clocktower Dr
State: OH
Zip/Postal code: 44094-5198
Country: USA
Mailing Address: 7700 Clocktower Dr
Mailing City: Kirtland
Mailing State: OH
Mailing ZIP Code: 44094-5198
General Phone: (440) 953-7264
General/National Adv. Email: lakelander@lakelandcc.edu
Website: www.lakelandcc.edu
Personnel: Susan Zimmerman (Advisor)

KLAMATH FALLS

OREGON INSTITUTE OF TECHNOLOGY

Street Address 1: 3201 Campus Dr
Street Address 2: # CU111C
State: OR
Zip/Postal code: 97601-8801
Country: USA
Mailing Address: 3201 Campus Dr # CU111C
Mailing City: Klamath Falls
Mailing State: OR
Mailing ZIP Code: 97601-8801
General Phone: (541) 885-1371
General Fax: (541) 885-1024
General/National Adv. Email: edge@oit.edu
Personnel: Steve Matthies (Advisor)

KNOXVILLE

UT DAILY BEACON (UNIVERSITY OF TENNESSEE)

Street Address 1: 11 Communications Bldg
Street Address 2: 1345 Circle Park Dr.
State: TN
Zip/Postal code: 37996-0001
Country: USA
Mailing Address: 11 Communications Bldg.
Mailing City: Knoxville
Mailing State: TN
Mailing ZIP Code: 37996-0314
General Phone: (865) 974-5206
General Fax: (865) 974-5569
Editorial Phone: (865) 974-3226
General/National Adv. Email: editorinchief@utdailybeacon.com
Display Adv. Email: beaconads@utk.edu
Editorial Email: letters@utdailybeacon.com
Website: utdailybeacon.com
Year Established: 1906
Special Editions: Special Editions Information available online in Ratecard, Page 8: http://media.utdailybeacon.com/advertising/ratecards/dailybeacon-ad-ratecard-2011-6.pdf For more information, contact Advertising Office: 865-974-5206 Special Editions/Sections: Welcome Back (August) Contact in June for Section Deadlines in July Football Preview (First Home Game) Contact in August Basketball Preview (November) Contact in early November Student Appreciation Day (February) Contact in early February Orientation (June/July) Contact in April
Delivery Methods: Mail`Racks
Commercial printers?: Y
Published: Mon`Thur
Published Other: Special issues (See Rate Card above)
Avg Free Circ: 6000
Personnel: Jerry Bush (Dir. of Student Media)

KOKOMO

INDIANA UNIV.

Street Address 1: 2300 S Washington St
State: IN
Zip/Postal code: 46902-3557
Country: USA
Mailing Address: PO Box 9003
Mailing City: Kokomo
Mailing State: IN
Mailing ZIP Code: 46904-9003
General Phone: (765) 455-9280
General Fax: (765) 455-9537
General/National Adv. Email: paper@iuk.edu
Website: www.kokomocorrespondent.com
Personnel: David Brewster (Advisor); Alyx Arnett (Entertainment Ed.); Johnathan Grant (Ed. in Chief)

LA CROSSE

UNIV. OF WISCONSIN LA CROSSE

Street Address 1: 1725 State St
State: WI
Zip/Postal code: 54601-3742
Country: USA
Mailing Address: 1725 State St
Mailing City: La Crosse
Mailing State: WI
Mailing ZIP Code: 54601-3788
General Phone: (608) 785-8378
General Fax: (608) 785-6575
General/National Adv. Email: racquet@uwlax.edu
Website: www.theracquet.net
Personnel: Chris Rochester (Ed in Chief); Mary Beth Valhalla (Advisor)

VITERBO COLLEGE

Street Address 1: 900 Viterbo Dr
State: WI
Zip/Postal code: 54601-8804
Country: USA
Mailing Address: 900 Viterbo Dr
Mailing City: La Crosse
Mailing State: WI
Mailing ZIP Code: 54601-8804
General Phone: (608) 796-3046
General Fax: (608) 796-3050
Advertising Phone: (608) 796-3041
General/National Adv. Email: communication@viterbo.edu
Website: www.viterbolumen.com
Personnel: Pat Kerrigan (Vice Pres., Commun.); Jessica Weber (Ed.)

LA GRANDE

EASTERN OREGON UNIV.

Street Address 1: 1 University Blvd
Street Address 2: Hoke 320
State: OR
Zip/Postal code: 97850-2807
Country: USA
Mailing Address: 1 University Blvd Hoke 320
Mailing City: La Grande
Mailing State: OR
Mailing ZIP Code: 97850-2807
General Phone: (541) 962-3386
General Fax: (541) 962-3706
General/National Adv. Email: thevoice@eou.edu
Website: www.eou.edu/thevoice
Personnel: Kyle Janssen (Ed. in Chief); Taylor Stanely Pawley (Adv. Mgr.)

LA JOLLA

UNIVERSITY OF CALIFORNIA SAN DIEGO

Street Address 1: 9500 Gilman Dr
Street Address 2: Dept 316
State: CA
Zip/Postal code: 92093-0316
Country: USA
Mailing Address: 9500 Gilman Dr Dept 316
Mailing City: La Jolla
Mailing State: CA
Mailing ZIP Code: 92093-0316
General Phone: (858) 534-3466
General Fax: (858) 534-7691
Display Adv. Email: ads@ucsdguardian.org
Editorial Email: managing@ucsdguardian.org
Website: www.ucsdguardian.org
Year Established: 1967
Special Editions: Back to school, restaurant guide, Best of San Diego, Sun God Festival, local music, holiday and Valentine's gift guides
Delivery Methods: Mail`Racks
Commercial printers?: Y

Published: Mon`Thur
Personnel: Laira Martin (Editor in Chief)

LA MIRADA

BIOLA UNIVERSITY

Street Address 1: 13800 Biola Ave
State: CA
Zip/Postal code: 90639-0002
Country: USA
Mailing Address: 13800 Biola Ave
Mailing City: La Mirada
Mailing State: CA
Mailing ZIP Code: 90639-0001
General Phone: (562) 906-4569
General Fax: (562) 906-4515
Advertising Phone: (562) 587-7339
General/National Adv. Email: lily.park@biola.edu
Display Adv. Email: chimes.advertising@biola.edu
Website: chimes.biola.edu
Published: Thur
Personnel: Michael A. Longinow (Chair/Prof.); Sarah Sjoberg (Advertising Manager); J. Douglas Tarpley (Prof.); Michael Bower (Assoc. Prof.); Tamara Welter (Asst. Prof.); James Hirsen (Instr.); Chi-Chung Keung (Instr.); Mark Landsbaum (Instr.); Greg Schneider (Instr.); Melissa Nunnally (Instr.)

LA PLATA

COLLEGE OF SOUTHERN MARYLAND

Street Address 1: PO Box 910
State: MD
Zip/Postal code: 20646-0910
Country: USA
Mailing Address: PO Box 910
Mailing City: La Plata
Mailing State: MD
Mailing ZIP Code: 20646-0910
General Phone: (301) 934-2251
General Fax: (301) 934-7680
General/National Adv. Email: hawkeye@csmd.edu
Personnel: Karen Smith-Hupp (Ed.)

LA PLUME

THE KEY

Street Address 1: 1 College Grn
Street Address 2: Keystone College
State: PA
Zip/Postal code: 18440-1000
Country: USA
Mailing Address: Keystone College
Mailing City: La Plume
Mailing State: PA
Mailing ZIP Code: 18440
General Phone: 570-945-8449

LA VERNE

UNIVERSITY OF LA VERNE

Street Address 1: 1950 3rd St
State: CA
Zip/Postal code: 91750-4401
Country: USA
Mailing Address: 1950 3rd St
Mailing City: La Verne
Mailing State: CA
Mailing ZIP Code: 91750-4401
General Phone: (909) 593-3511
General Fax: (909) 392-2706
Advertising Phone: 909-392-2712
General/National Adv. Email: ctimes@laverne.edu
Display Adv. Email: ctimesad@laverne.edu
Editorial Email: ctimes@laverne.edu
Website: www.laverne.edu/campus-times
Year Established: 1919
Published: Fri
Avg Free Circ: 2000
Personnel: Elizabeth Zwerling (Faculty Advisor); Jennifer Lemus Fernandez (Adv. Mgr.); Kevin Garrity (Ed. in Chief); Eric Borer

(Layout Asst.)

LAFAYETTE

UNIV. OF LOUISIANA AT LAFAYETTE

THE VERMILION

Street Address 1: PO Box 44813
State: LA
Zip/Postal code: 70504-0001
Country: USA
Mailing Address: PO Box 44813
Mailing City: Lafayette
Mailing State: LA
Mailing ZIP Code: 70504-0001
General Phone: (337) 482-6110
General Fax: (337) 482-6959
Advertising Phone: (337) 482-6960
Advertising Fax: (337) 472-6959
Editorial Phone: (337) 482-6110
Editorial Fax: (337) 482-6959
General/National Adv. Email: vermadvertising@gmail.com
Display Adv. Email: vermadvertising@gmail.com
Editorial Email: hollyhoooot@gmail.com
Website: thevermilion.com
Year Established: 1904
Delivery Methods: Newsstand`Carrier`Racks
Commercial printers?: Y
Published: Wed
Published Other: Aug, Sept, Oct, Nov
Personnel: Thomas Schumacher (Business Manager)
Parent company (for newspapers): Vermilion Communication Committee of UL Lafayette

LAGRANGE

LAGRANGE COLLEGE

Street Address 1: 601 Broad St
Street Address 2: # 1165
State: GA
Zip/Postal code: 30240-2955
Country: USA
Mailing Address: 601 Broad St # 1165
Mailing City: Lagrange
Mailing State: GA
Mailing ZIP Code: 30240-2955
General Phone: (706) 880-8020
General Fax: (706) 880-8920
General/National Adv. Email: hilltopnews@laagrange.edu
Personnel: John Tures (Advisor); Kate Bush (Co-Ed.); Chris Nylund (Co-Ed.)

LAIE

BRIGHAM YOUNG UNIV.

Street Address 1: 55-220 Kulanui St
State: HI
Zip/Postal code: 96762-1266
Country: USA
Mailing Address: 55-220 Kulanui St Ste 1
Mailing City: Laie
Mailing State: HI
Mailing ZIP Code: 96762-1266
General Phone: (808) 675-3696
General Fax: (808) 675-3491
Website: kealakai.byuh.edu
Personnel: Leeann Lambert (Advisor); Karen Hemenway (Copy Ed.)

LAKE CHARLES

MCNEESE STATE UNIV.

Street Address 1: PO Box 91375
State: LA
Zip/Postal code: 70609-0001
Country: USA
Mailing Address: PO Box 91375
Mailing City: Lake Charles
Mailing State: LA
Mailing ZIP Code: 70609-0001
General Phone: (337) 475-5646
General Fax: (337) 475-5259
General/National Adv. Email: contraband@mcneese.edu; msucontraband@gmail.com
Website: www.msucontraband.com
Personnel: Candace Townsend (Advisor); Robert Teal (Ed. in Chief); Sarah Puckett (Ed.)

LAKE FOREST

LAKE FOREST COLLEGE

Street Address 1: 555 N Sheridan Rd
State: IL
Zip/Postal code: 60045-2338
Country: USA
Mailing Address: 555 N Sheridan Rd
Mailing City: Lake Forest
Mailing State: IL
Mailing ZIP Code: 60045-2399
General Phone: (847) 735-5215
General Fax: (847) 735-6298
General/National Adv. Email: stentor@lakeforest.edu
Website: www.thestentor.com
Personnel: Heather Brown (Advisor); Annie Cooper (Ed. in Chief); Nate Butala (Mng. Ed.)

LAKE WORTH

PALM BEACH CMTY. COLLEGE

Street Address 1: 4200 S Congress Ave
State: FL
Zip/Postal code: 33461-4705
Country: USA
Mailing Address: 4200 S Congress Ave
Mailing City: Lake Worth
Mailing State: FL
Mailing ZIP Code: 33461-4796
General Phone: (561) 862-4327
General Fax: (561) 439-8210
General/National Adv. Email: beachcomber@pbcc.edu.campus
Personnel: Pam Jarret (Pub.)

LAKELAND

FLORIDA SOUTHERN COLLEGE

Street Address 1: 111 Lake Hollingsworth Dr
State: FL
Zip/Postal code: 33801-5607
Country: USA
Mailing Address: 111 Lake Hollingsworth Dr
Mailing City: Lakeland
Mailing State: FL
Mailing ZIP Code: 33801-5698
General Phone: (863) 680-4155
General Fax: (863) 680-6244
Display Adv. Email: mtrice@flsouthern.edu
Editorial Email: fscsouthern@gmail.com
Website: www.fscsouthern.com
Published: Fri`Other
Published Other: every other week
Avg Free Circ: 1200
Personnel: Michael Trice (Advisor)

SOUTHEASTERN UNIVERSITY

Street Address 1: 1000 Longfellow Blvd
State: FL
Zip/Postal code: 33801-6034
Country: USA
Mailing Address: 1000 Longfellow Blvd
Mailing City: Lakeland
Mailing State: FL
Mailing ZIP Code: 33801-6034
General Phone: (863) 667-5000
General Fax: (863) 667-5200
General/National Adv. Email: thetimes@seuniversity.edu
Website: www.seuniversity.edu
Personnel: Chad Neuman (Advisor)

SOUTHEASTERN UNIVERSRITY

Street Address 1: 1000 Longfellow Blvd
State: FL
Zip/Postal code: 33801-6034
Country: USA
Mailing Address: 1000 Longfellow Blvd
Mailing City: Lakeland
Mailing State: FL
Mailing ZIP Code: 33801-6034
General Phone: 8005008760
Website: www.seu.edu
Published: Mthly

LAKEWOOD

COLORADO CHRISTIAN UNIV.

Street Address 1: 8787 W Alameda Ave
State: CO
Zip/Postal code: 80226-2824
Country: USA
Mailing Address: 8787 W Alameda Ave
Mailing City: Lakewood
Mailing State: CO
Mailing ZIP Code: 80226-2824
General Phone: (303) 202-0100
General Fax: (303) 963-3001
General/National Adv. Email: cougartrax@ccu.edu
Website: luke.ccu.edu/; www.ccu.edu
Personnel: Jim McCormick (Advisor); Daniel Cohrs (Bus. Mgr.)

PIERCE COLLEGE

Street Address 1: 9401 Farwest Dr SW
State: WA
Zip/Postal code: 98498-1919
Country: USA
Mailing Address: 9401 Farwest Dr SW
Mailing City: Lakewood
Mailing State: WA
Mailing ZIP Code: 98498-1999
General Phone: (253) 964-6604
General Fax: (253) 964-6764
General/National Adv. Email: pioneer@pierce.ctc.edu
Website: www.piercecollege.edu/
Personnel: Michael Parks (Advisor); Blake York (Ed. in chief)

LAMONI

GRACELAND COLLEGE

Street Address 1: 1 University Pl
State: IA
Zip/Postal code: 50140-1641
Country: USA
Mailing Address: 1 University Pl
Mailing City: Lamoni
Mailing State: IA
Mailing ZIP Code: 50140-1684
General Phone: (641) 784-5000
General Fax: (641) 784-5480
General/National Adv. Email: tower@graceland.edu
Website: www.graceland.edu
Personnel: Nicky Kerr (Ed. in Chief)

LANCASTER

ANTELOPE VALLEY COLLEGE

Street Address 1: 3041 W Avenue K
State: CA
Zip/Postal code: 93536-5402
Country: USA
Mailing Address: 3041 W Avenue K
Mailing City: Lancaster
Mailing State: CA
Mailing ZIP Code: 93536-5426
General Phone: (661) 722-6496
General Fax: (661) 943-5573
Website: www.avc.edu
Personnel: Charles Hood (Advisor)

FRANKLIN & MARSHALL COLLEGE

Street Address 1: PO Box 3003
State: PA
Zip/Postal code: 17604-3003
Country: USA
Mailing Address: PO Box 3003
Mailing City: Lancaster
Mailing State: PA
Mailing ZIP Code: 17604-3003
General Phone: (717) 291-4095
General Fax: (717) 291-3886
Display Adv. Email: reporterads@fandm.edu
Editorial Email: reporter@fandm.edu
Website: thediplomat.fandm.edu
Personnel: Justin Quinn (Advisor); Patrick Bernard (Advisor); Christian Wedekind (Ed.)

LANGSTON

LANGSTON UNIV.

Street Address 1: Sanford Hall Rm 308W
State: OK
Zip/Postal code: 73050
Country: USA
Mailing Address: Sanford Hall Rm. 308W
Mailing City: Langston
Mailing State: OK
Mailing ZIP Code: 73050
General Phone: (405) 466-3245
General/National Adv. Email: lugazette@yahoo.com
Website: www.lugazette.com
Personnel: Chaz Kyser (Advisor)

LANSING

LANSING CMTY. COLLEGE

Street Address 1: 411 N Grand Ave
Street Address 2: Rm 351
State: MI
Zip/Postal code: 48933-1215
Country: USA
Mailing Address: Mail Code 1170
Mailing City: Lansing
Mailing State: MI
Mailing ZIP Code: 48933
General Phone: (517) 483-1291
General Fax: (517) 483-1290
Advertising Phone: (517) 483-1295
Advertising Fax: (517) 483-1290
Editorial Phone: (517) 483-1288
Editorial Fax: (517) 483-1290
General/National Adv. Email: hookl@lcc.edu
Display Adv. Email: hookl@lcc.edu
Editorial Email: hookl@lcc.edu
Website: www.lcc.edu/lookout
Year Established: 1959
Published: Bi-Mthly
Personnel: Larry Hook (Advisor)

LARAMIE

UNIV. OF WYOMING

Street Address 1: 1000 E University Ave
Street Address 2: Dept 3625
State: WY
Zip/Postal code: 82071-2000
Country: USA
Mailing Address: 1000 E University Ave Dept 3625
Mailing City: Laramie
Mailing State: WY
Mailing ZIP Code: 82071-2000
General Phone: (307) 766-6190
General Fax: (307) 766-4027
Advertising Phone: (307) 766-6336
General/National Adv. Email: bi@uwyo.edu
Editorial Email: letters@brandingironline.info
Website: www.brandingironline.info
Personnel: Carry Berry-Smith (Advisor); Sasha Fahrenkops (Ed. in Chief)

LARGO

PRINCE GEORGES CMTY. COLLEGE

Street Address 1: 301 Largo Rd
State: MD
Zip/Postal code: 20774-2109
Country: USA

College and University Newspapers

Mailing Address: 301 Largo Rd
Mailing City: Largo
Mailing State: MD
Mailing ZIP Code: 20774-2109
General Phone: (301) 336-6000
General Fax: (301) 808-0960
General/National Adv. Email: theowlnewspaper@hotmail.com
Website: www.pgcc.edu
Personnel: Patrick Peterson (Bus. Mgr.); Malcolm Beech (Advisor); Abelaja Obajimi (Ed. in Chief)

LAS CRUCES

NEW MEXICO STATE UNIV.

Street Address 1: PO Box 30001
State: NM
Zip/Postal code: 88003-8001
Country: USA
Mailing Address: PO Box 30001
Mailing City: Las Cruces
Mailing State: NM
Mailing ZIP Code: 88003-8001
General Phone: (575) 646-6397
General Fax: (575) 646-5557
General/National Adv. Email: roundup@nmsu.edu
Website: www.roundupnews.com
Personnel: Jeff Hand (Advisor); Jon Blazak (Ed. in Chief)

LAS VEGAS

UNIVERSITY OF NEVADA, LAS VEGAS

Street Address 1: 4505 S Maryland Pkwy
Street Address 2: # 2011
State: NV
Zip/Postal code: 89154-9900
Country: USA
Mailing Address: 4505 S Maryland Pkwy
Mailing City: Las Vegas
Mailing State: NV
Mailing ZIP Code: 89154-9900
General Phone: (702) 895-2028
General Fax: (702) 895-1515
Editorial Fax: Free
General/National Adv. Email: chief.freepress@unlv.edu
Display Adv. Email: marketing.freepress@unlv.edu
Editorial Email: managing.freepress@unlv.edu
Website: www.unlvfreepress.com
Year Established: 1955
Published: Mon
Avg Free Circ: 3800
Personnel: Rick Velotta (Adviser); Bianca Cseke (Editor-in-Chief); Blaze Lovell (Managing Editor); Nicole Gallego (Director of Marketing & Sales)

UNIVERSITY OF NEVADA, LAS VEGAS

Street Address 1: 4505 S Maryland Pkwy
State: NV
Zip/Postal code: 89154-9900
Country: USA
Mailing Address: PO Box 2011
Mailing City: Las Vegas
Mailing State: NV
Mailing ZIP Code: 89125-2011
Advertising Phone: (702) 895-3878
General/National Adv. Email: chief.freepress@unlv.edu
Display Adv. Email: marketing.freepress@unlv.edu
Editorial Email: managing.freepress@unlv.edu
Website: www.unlvfreepress.com
Year Established: 1955
Published: Mon
Avg Free Circ: 3800
Personnel: Bianca Cseke (Editor-in-Chief); Kathy Schreiber (Business Manager); Rick Velotta (Adviser); Blaze Lovell (Managing Editor); Nicole Gallego (Director of Marketing & Sales)

LATROBE

SAINT VINCENT COLLEGE

Street Address 1: 300 Fraser Purchase Rd
State: PA
Zip/Postal code: 15650-2667
Country: USA
Mailing Address: 300 Fraser Purchase Rd
Mailing City: Latrobe
Mailing State: PA
Mailing ZIP Code: 15650-2690
General Phone: (724) 539-9761
Advertising Phone: (717)669-0703
Editorial Phone: (717)669-0703
General/National Adv. Email: review.stvincent@gmail.com
Editorial Email: bridget.fertal@stvincent.edu
Website: www.stvincentreview.com/
Published: Wed
Personnel: Dennis McDaniel (Advisor); Bridget Fertal (Editor-in-Chief); Cheyenne Dunbar (Business Manager)

LAWRENCE

THE UNIVERSITY DAILY KANSAN

Street Address 1: 1000 Sunnyside Ave
State: KS
Zip/Postal code: 66045-7599
Country: USA
Mailing Address: 1000 Sunnyside Ave
Mailing City: Lawrence
Mailing State: KS
Mailing ZIP Code: 66045-7599
General Phone: (785) 864-4724
General Fax: (785) 864-5261
Advertising Phone: (785) 864-4358
Editorial Phone: (785) 864-4812
General/National Adv. Email: editor@kansan.com
Display Adv. Email: adsales@kansan.com
Editorial Email: editor@kansan.com
Website: www.kansan.com
Year Established: 1904
Special Editions: Sex on the Hill; Jayhawker magazine; football and basketball special editions
Special Weekly Sections: Jayplay (weekly entertainment)
Delivery Methods: Newsstand`Racks
Published: Mon`Tues`Wed`Thur
Published Other: Weekly in summer (June/July)
Personnel: Malcolm Gibson (Gen. Mgr./News Advisor); Jon Schlitt (Sales and Marketing Adviser)

UNIV. OF KANSAS ENGINEERING SCHOOL

Street Address 1: 4010 Learned Hall
State: KS
Zip/Postal code: 66045-7526
Country: USA
Mailing Address: 4010 Learned Hall
Mailing City: Lawrence
Mailing State: KS
Mailing ZIP Code: 66045-7526
General Phone: (785) 864-8853
Personnel: Mary Jane Dunlap (News Ed.); Jill Hummels (PR Dir.)

LAWRENCEVILLE

THE RIDER NEWS / RIDER UNIVERSITY

Street Address 1: 2083 Lawrenceville Rd
State: NJ
Zip/Postal code: 08648-3099
Country: USA
Mailing Address: 2083 Lawrenceville Rd
Mailing City: Lawrenceville
Mailing State: NJ
Mailing ZIP Code: 08648-3099
General Phone: (609) 896-5256
General Fax: (609) 895-5696
General/National Adv. Email: ridernews@rider.edu
Website: www.theridernews.com
Year Established: 1930
Commercial printers?: Y
Personnel: Dianne Garyantes (Co-Adviser)

LAWTON

CAMERON UNIV.

Street Address 1: 2800 W Gore Blvd
State: OK
Zip/Postal code: 73505-6320
Country: USA
Mailing Address: 2800 W Gore Blvd
Mailing City: Lawton
Mailing State: OK
Mailing ZIP Code: 73505-6377
General Phone: (580) 581-2259
Advertising Phone: (580) 581-2897
General/National Adv. Email: collegian@cameron.edu
Personnel: Christopher Keller (Advisor)

LEBANON

CUMBERLAND UNIV.

Street Address 1: 1 Cumberland Sq
State: TN
Zip/Postal code: 37087-3408
Country: USA
Mailing Address: 1 Cumberland Sq.
Mailing City: Lebanon
Mailing State: TN
Mailing ZIP Code: 37087-3408
General Phone: (615) 444-2562
General Fax: (615) 444-2569
General/National Adv. Email: cumberlandchronicle@gmail.com
Website: www.cumberland.edu
Published: Mon`Bi-Mthly
Personnel: Michael Rex (Advisor)

MCKENDREE UNIVERSITY

Street Address 1: 701 College Rd
State: IL
Zip/Postal code: 62254-1291
Country: USA
Mailing Address: 701 College Rd
Mailing City: Lebanon
Mailing State: IL
Mailing ZIP Code: 62254-1291
General Phone: (618) 537-6821
General Fax: (618) 537-2377
General/National Adv. Email: mckreview@mckendree.edu
Website: lance.mckendree.edu/review/
Personnel: Gabe Shapiro (Faculty Advisor); Sarah Adams (Editor in Chief); Chris Moore (Associate Editor); Kevin Schaefer (Web/Design Editor); Theresa Schmidt (Ed. in Chief)

LEES SUMMIT

LONGVIEW CMTY. COLLEGE

Street Address 1: 500 SW Longview Rd
State: MO
Zip/Postal code: 64081-2105
Country: USA
Mailing Address: 500 SW Longview Rd
Mailing City: Lees Summit
Mailing State: MO
Mailing ZIP Code: 64081-2100
General Phone: (816) 672-2308
General Fax: (816) 672-2025
General/National Adv. Email: current@mcckc.edu
Website: www.longviewcurrent.com
Personnel: Pat Sparks (Advisor)

LEESBURG

LAKE SUMTER CMTY. COLLEGE

Street Address 1: 9501 US Highway 441
State: FL
Zip/Postal code: 34788-3950
Country: USA
Mailing Address: 9501 US Highway 441
Mailing City: Leesburg
Mailing State: FL
Mailing ZIP Code: 34788-3950
General Phone: (352) 323-3629
General Fax: (352) 435-5023
General/National Adv. Email: anglern@lscc.edu; angler4always@yahoo.com
Website: www.lscc.edu
Delivery Methods: Racks
Commercial printers?: Y
Personnel: Heather Elmatti (Advisor); Gina Mussatti (Ed.)

LEVELLAND

SOUTH PLAINS COLLEGE

Street Address 1: 1401 College Ave
State: TX
Zip/Postal code: 79336-6503
Country: USA
Mailing Address: PO Box 46
Mailing City: Levelland
Mailing State: TX
Mailing ZIP Code: 79336-0046
General Phone: (806) 894-9611
General Fax: (806) 894-5274
General/National Adv. Email: ppress@southplainscollege.edu
Website: www.southplainscollege.edu/ppress/News.html
Published Other: Bi-weekly
Personnel: Charles Ehrenfeld (Advisor); Jayme Wheeler

LEWISBURG

BUCKNELL UNIV.

Street Address 1: PO Box C-3952
State: PA
Zip/Postal code: 17837
Country: USA
Mailing Address: PO Box C-3952
Mailing City: Lewisburg
Mailing State: PA
Mailing ZIP Code: 17837-9988
General Phone: (570) 577-1520
General Fax: (570) 577-1176
Editorial Phone: (570) 577-1085
Display Adv. Email: bucknellianads@bucknell.edu
Website: bucknellian.blogs.bucknell.edu/
Year Established: 1896
Published: Fri
Avg Free Circ: 4000
Personnel: James F. Lee (Advisor); Winnie Warner (Ed. in Chief); Ben Kaufman (Editor in Chief)

BUCKNELL UNIV. COLLEGE OF ENGINEERING

Street Address 1: 701 Moore Ave
State: PA
Zip/Postal code: 17837-2010
Country: USA
Mailing Address: 701 Moore Ave
Mailing City: Lewisburg
Mailing State: PA
Mailing ZIP Code: 17837-2010
General Phone: (570) 577-1520
General/National Adv. Email: bucknellian@bucknell.edu
Website: www.bucknell.edu/bucknellian
Personnel: James Lee (Advisor); Lily Beauvilliers (Ed. in Chief)

LEWISTON

BATES COLLEGE

Street Address 1: 2 Andrews Rd
State: ME
Zip/Postal code: 04240-6020
Country: USA
Mailing Address: 2 Andrews Rd

Mailing City: Lewiston
Mailing State: ME
Mailing ZIP Code: 04240-6028
General Phone: (207) 795-7494
Advertising Phone: (207) 786-6035
General/National Adv. Email: thebatesstudent@hotmail.com
Website: www.batesstudent.com
Personnel: Regina Tavani (Ed. in Chief); Zoe Rosenthal (Deputy Ed. in Chief)

LEWIS-CLARK STATE COLLEGE

Street Address 1: 500 8th Ave
Street Address 2: Student Union Building Room 201
State: ID
Zip/Postal code: 83501-2691
Country: USA
Mailing Address: 500 8th Avenue
Mailing City: Lewiston
Mailing State: ID
Mailing ZIP Code: 83501
General Phone: (208) 792-2470
General Fax: (208) 792-2082
General/National Adv. Email: thepathfinder@lcmail.lcsc.edu
Display Adv. Email: pathfinderbusmgr@lcmail.lcsc.edu
Website: www.lcsc.edu/pathfinder/
Published: Wed
Avg Free Circ: 1000
Personnel: Bryce Kammers (Advisor); Kaylee Brewster (Ed.); Aaron Waits (Asst. Ed.); Ryan Grether (Business Manager)

LEXINGTON

UNIV. OF KENTUCKY

Street Address 1: Grehan Journalism Bldg, Rm 026
State: KY
Zip/Postal code: 40506-0001
Country: USA
Mailing Address: Grehan Journalism Bldg Rm 26
Mailing City: Lexington
Mailing State: KY
Mailing ZIP Code: 40506-0001
General Phone: (859) 257-2872
General Fax: (859) 323-1906
General/National Adv. Email: features@kykernel.com
Display Adv. Email: news@kykernel.com
Website: www.kykernel.com
Personnel: Chris Poore (Advisor); Kenny Colston (Ed. in Chief)

VIRGINIA MILITARY INSTITUTE

Street Address 1: PO Box 7
State: VA
Zip/Postal code: 24450-0007
Country: USA
Mailing Address: PO Box 7
Mailing City: Lexington
Mailing State: VA
Mailing ZIP Code: 24450-0007
General Phone: (540) 464-7326
General Fax: (540) 463-5679
General/National Adv. Email: vmicadet@vmi.edu
Website: www.vmicadetpublication.com
Personnel: Captain Christopher Perry (Advisor); Nick Weishar (Ed. in Chief)

WASHINGTON AND LEE UNIV.

Street Address 1: 204 W Washington St
State: VA
Zip/Postal code: 24450-2116
Country: USA
Mailing Address: 204 West Washington Street
Mailing City: Lexington
Mailing State: VA
Mailing ZIP Code: 24450
General Phone: (540) 458-4060
General Fax: (540) 458-4059
General/National Adv. Email: phi-business@wlu.edu; phi@wlu.edu

Personnel: David Seifert (Bus. Mgr.)

LIBERTY

WILLIAM JEWELL COLLEGE

Street Address 1: 500 College Hl
Street Address 2: # 1016
State: MO
Zip/Postal code: 64068-1843
Country: USA
Mailing Address: 500 College Hl # 1016
Mailing City: Liberty
Mailing State: MO
Mailing ZIP Code: 64068-1896
General Phone: (816) 781-7700
General/National Adv. Email: monitor@william.jewell.edu
Website: www.thehilltopmonitor.com
Personnel: Samantha Sanders (Adv. Mgr.); Jessie Newman (Ed. in Chief); Trista Turley (Mng. Ed.)

LINCOLN

NEBRASKA WESLEYAN UNIV.

Street Address 1: 5000 Saint Paul Ave
Street Address 2: Smb 1221
State: NE
Zip/Postal code: 68504-2760
Country: USA
Mailing Address: 5000 Saint Paul Ave Smb 1221
Mailing City: Lincoln
Mailing State: NE
Mailing ZIP Code: 68504-2760
General Phone: (402) 465-2352
General Fax: (402) 465-2179
General/National Adv. Email: reveille@nebrwesleyan.edu
Website: www.thereveillenwu.com
Published: Bi-Mthly
Personnel: Jim Schaffer (Advisor); Hannah Tangeman (Editor)

UNIV. OF NEBRASKA-LINCOLN

Street Address 1: 1400 R St
Street Address 2: 20 Nebraska Union
State: NE
Zip/Postal code: 68588-0007
Country: USA
Mailing Address: P.O. Box 880448
Mailing City: Lincoln
Mailing State: NE
Mailing ZIP Code: 68588-0448
General Phone: (402) 472-2588
Advertising Phone: (402) 472-2589
General/National Adv. Email: dn@unl.edu
Display Adv. Email: dn@unl.edu
Editorial Email: news@dailynebraskan.com
Website: DailyNebraskan.com
Year Established: 1901
Delivery Methods: Racks
Commercial printers?: N
Published: Mthly
Avg Free Circ: 4500
Personnel: Daniel Shattil (Gen. Mgr.); David Thiemann (Director of Sales and Marketing)

LINCOLN UNIVERSITY

LINCOLN UNIV.

Street Address 1: 1570 Baltimore Pike
State: PA
Zip/Postal code: 19352-9141
Country: USA
Mailing Address: 1570 Baltimore Pike
Mailing City: Lincoln University
Mailing State: PA
Mailing ZIP Code: 19352-9141
General Phone: (484) 365-7524
General Fax: (610) 932-1256
Website: www.thelincolnianonline.com
Personnel: Eric Watson (Advisor)

LINCROFT

BROOKDALE CMTY. COLLEGE

Street Address 1: 765 Newman Springs Rd
State: NJ
Zip/Postal code: 07738-1543
Country: USA
Mailing Address: 765 Newman Springs Rd
Mailing City: Lincroft
Mailing State: NJ
Mailing ZIP Code: 07738-1599
General Phone: (732) 224-2266
General Fax: (732) 450-1591
General/National Adv. Email: stallbcc@gmail.com
Editorial Email: stall@brookdalecc.edu
Published: Mon`Other
Published Other: six times a semester
Personnel: Debbie Mura (Advisor)

LINDSBORG

BETHANY COLLEGE

Street Address 1: PO Box 184
State: KS
Zip/Postal code: 67456-0184
Country: USA
Mailing Address: PO Box 184
Mailing City: Lindsborg
Mailing State: KS
Mailing ZIP Code: 67456-0184
General Phone: (785) 227-8234
General Fax: (785) 227-2004
Personnel: Joel Wiede (Ed.)

LISLE

BENEDICTINE UNIV.

Street Address 1: 5700 College Rd
State: IL
Zip/Postal code: 60532-2851
Country: USA
Mailing Address: 5700 College Rd
Mailing City: Lisle
Mailing State: IL
Mailing ZIP Code: 60532-0900
General Phone: (630) 829-6252
General Fax: (630) 960-1126
General/National Adv. Email: thecandor@yahoo.com
Website: www.thecandor.com
Year Established: 1982
Published: Wed
Avg Free Circ: 2000
Personnel: Chris Birks (Advisor)

LITTLE ROCK

PHILANDER SMITH COLLEGE

Street Address 1: 900 W Daisy L Gatson Bates Dr
State: AR
Zip/Postal code: 72202-3726
Country: USA
Mailing Address: 900 W Daisy L Gatson Bates Dr
Mailing City: Little Rock
Mailing State: AR
Mailing ZIP Code: 72202-3717
General Phone: (501) 370-5354
General/National Adv. Email: jcheffen@philander.edu
Personnel: Jimmy Cheffen (Advisor)

THE FORUM, UNIVERSITY OF ARKANSAS AT LITTLE ROCK

Street Address 1: 2801 S University Ave
Street Address 2: Ste 116
State: AR
Zip/Postal code: 72204-1000
Country: USA
Mailing Address: 2801 S University Ave Dsc 201J
Mailing City: Little Rock
Mailing State: AR

Mailing ZIP Code: 72204-1000
General Phone: (501) 569-3319
General Fax: (501) 569-3209
Display Adv. Email: adman@ualr.edu
Editorial Email: editor@ualr.edu
Website: ualr.edu/forum
Published: Bi-Mthly
Avg Free Circ: 2500
Personnel: Sonny Rhodes (Advisor); Jacob Ellerbee (Exec. Ed.)

LITTLETON

ARAPAHOE CMTY. COLLEGE

Street Address 1: 5900 S Santa Fe Dr
State: CO
Zip/Postal code: 80120-1801
Country: USA
Mailing Address: 5900 S Santa Fe Dr
Mailing City: Littleton
Mailing State: CO
Mailing ZIP Code: 80120-1801
General Phone: (303) 797-5666
General Fax: (303) 797-5650
Personnel: Chris Ransick (Advisor); Reem Al-Omari (Ed.)

LIVINGSTON

UNIV. OF WEST ALABAMA

Street Address 1: 100 US-11
State: AL
Zip/Postal code: 35470
Country: USA
Mailing Address: 100 US-11
Mailing City: Livingston
Mailing State: AL
Mailing ZIP Code: 35470
General Phone: (205) 652-3892
General Fax: (205) 652-3586
Website: www.uwa.edu/thelife
Personnel: Betsy Compton (Advisor)

LIVONIA

SCHOOLCRAFT COLLEGE

Street Address 1: 18600 Haggerty Rd
Street Address 2: Rm W169
State: MI
Zip/Postal code: 48152-3932
Country: USA
Mailing Address: 18600 Haggerty Rd Rm W169
Mailing City: Livonia
Mailing State: MI
Mailing ZIP Code: 48152-2696
General Phone: (734) 462-4422
General Fax: (734) 462-4554
General/National Adv. Email: sao@schoolcraft.edu
Website: www.schoolcraft.edu; sao.schoolcraft.edu
Personnel: Jeffrey Petts (Advisor); Kathy Hansen (Adv. Mgr.); Ryan Russell (Ed.)

LOCH SHELDRAKE

SUNY SULLIVAN

Street Address 1: 112 College Rd
State: NY
Zip/Postal code: 12759-5721
Country: USA
Mailing Address: 112 College Rd
Mailing City: Loch Sheldrake
Mailing State: NY
Mailing ZIP Code: 12759-5721
General Phone: (845) 434-5750
General Fax: (914) 434-4806
Website: www.sunysullivan.edu
Published: Mon
Personnel: Kathleen Birkett (Admin. Asst.)

LOCK HAVEN

LOCK HAVEN UNIV. OF

College and University Newspapers

PENNSYLVANIA

Street Address 1: 401 N Fairview St
Street Address 2: Parsons Union Bldg.
State: PA
Zip/Postal code: 17745-2342
Country: USA
General Phone: (570) 484-2334
General/National Adv. Email: lhueagleye@yahoo.com
Website: www.lhueagleye.com
Personnel: Joe Stender (Ed. in Chief); Jamie Kessinger (Mng. Ed.)

LOGAN

UTAH STATE UNIV.

Street Address 1: Taggart Ctr 105
State: UT
Zip/Postal code: 84322-0001
Country: USA
Mailing Address: PO Box 1249
Mailing City: Logan
Mailing State: UT
Mailing ZIP Code: 84322-0001
General Phone: (435) 797-6397
General Fax: (435) 797-1760
General/National Adv. Email: statesmanoffice@aggiemail.com
Website: www.utahstatesman.com
Year Established: 1902
Personnel: Jay Wamsley (Advisor)

LOMA LINDA

LOMA LINDA UNIV.

Street Address 1: 11041 Anderson St
State: CA
Zip/Postal code: 92350-1737
Country: USA
Mailing Address: Anderson St Burden Hall 11041
Mailing City: Loma Linda
Mailing State: CA
Mailing ZIP Code: 92350-0001
General Phone: (909) 558-4526
General Fax: (909) 558-4181
Website: www.llu.edu/news/today

LOMBARD

NATIONAL COLLEGE OF CHIROPRACTIC

Street Address 1: 200 E Roosevelt Rd
State: IL
Zip/Postal code: 60148-4539
Country: USA
Mailing Address: 200 E. Roosevelt Rd
Mailing City: Lombard
Mailing State: IL
Mailing ZIP Code: 60148-4539
General Phone: (630) 889-6628
General Fax: (630) 889-6554
Published: Mthly
Avg Free Circ: 5000
Personnel: Frank Sutter (Ed.)

LONG BEACH

CALIFORNIA STATE UNIV. LONG BEACH

Street Address 1: 1250 Bellflower Blvd
Street Address 2: Sppa 010B
State: CA
Zip/Postal code: 90840-0004
Country: USA
Mailing Address: 1250 Bellflower Blvd
Mailing City: Long Beach
Mailing State: CA
Mailing ZIP Code: 90840-4601
General Phone: (562) 985-8001
General Fax: (562) 985-1740
Advertising Phone: (562)985-5736
Editorial Phone: (562)985-8000
Display Adv. Email: beverly.munson@csulb.edu
Editorial Email: eicd49er@gmail.com
Website: www.daily49er.com
Year Established: 1949
Published: Mon`Tues`Wed`Thur
Avg Free Circ: 6000
Personnel: Beverly Munson (Gen. Mgr.); Barbara Kingsley-Wilson (Advisor)

LONG BEACH CITY COLLEGE

Street Address 1: 4901 E Carson St
Street Address 2: Mail Drop Y-16
State: CA
Zip/Postal code: 90808-1706
Country: USA
Mailing Address: 4901 E Carson St Mail Drop Y-16
Mailing City: Long Beach
Mailing State: CA
Mailing ZIP Code: 90808-1780
General Phone: (562) 938-4284
General Fax: (562) 938-4948
General/National Adv. Email: vikingnews@lbcc.edu
Website: www.lbccvikingnews.com
Year Established: 1927
Personnel: Patrick McKean (Advisor); Kori Filipek (Adv. Mgr.); Michel Simmons (Co-Ed. in Chief)

LONG ISLAND CITY

CUNY SCHOOL OF LAW

Street Address 1: 2 Court Sq
State: NY
Zip/Postal code: 11101-4356
Country: USA
Mailing Address: 2 Court Sq
Mailing City: Long Island City
Mailing State: NY
Mailing ZIP Code: 11101-4356
General Phone: (718) 340-4222
Website: www.law.cuny.edu
Parent company (for newspapers): City University of New York

LONGVIEW

LETOURNEAU UNIV.

Street Address 1: 2100 S Mobberly Ave
State: TX
Zip/Postal code: 75602-3564
Country: USA
Mailing Address: PO Box 7001
Mailing City: Longview
Mailing State: TX
Mailing ZIP Code: 75607-7001
General Phone: (800) 759-8811
General Fax: (903) 236-3129

LOWER COLUMBIA COLLEGE

Street Address 1: 1600 Maple St
State: WA
Zip/Postal code: 98632-3907
Country: USA
Mailing Address: PO Box 3010
Mailing City: Longview
Mailing State: WA
Mailing ZIP Code: 98632-0310
General Phone: (360) 442-2311
General Fax: (360) 442-2120
Website: www.lowercolumbia.edu
Personnel: Jill Homme (Ed.)

LOOKOUT MOUNTAIN

COVENANT COLLEGE

Street Address 1: 14049 Scenic Hwy
State: GA
Zip/Postal code: 30750-4100
Country: USA
Mailing Address: 14049 Scenic Hwy
Mailing City: Lookout Mountain
Mailing State: GA
Mailing ZIP Code: 30750-4100
General Phone: (706) 820-1560
General Fax: (706) 820-0672
General/National Adv. Email: bagpipe@covenant.edu
Website: www.bagpipeonline.com
Personnel: Cliff Foreman (Faculty Advisor); Kaitlin Fender (Ed. in Chief)

LORETTO

ST. FRANCIS UNIV.

Street Address 1: PO Box 600
State: PA
Zip/Postal code: 15940-0600
Country: USA
Mailing Address: PO Box 600
Mailing City: Loretto
Mailing State: PA
Mailing ZIP Code: 15940-0600
General Phone: (814) 472-3038
General Fax: (814) 472-3358
Personnel: Dean Allison (Advisor); Andrew Maloney (Ed.)

LOS ALTOS HILLS

FOOTHILL COLLEGE

Street Address 1: 12345 S El Monte Rd
State: CA
Zip/Postal code: 94022-4504
Country: USA
Mailing Address: 12345 S El Monte Rd
Mailing City: Los Altos Hills
Mailing State: CA
Mailing ZIP Code: 94022-4597
General Phone: (650) 949-7372
General Fax: (650) 949-7375
Website: www.foothillsentinel.org
Personnel: Drew Dara Abrams (Ed.)

LOS ANGELES

CALIFORNIA STATE UNIV.

Street Address 1: 5151 State University Dr
Street Address 2: # KH-C3098
State: CA
Zip/Postal code: 90032-4226
Country: USA
Mailing Address: 5151 State University Dr # KH-C3098
Mailing City: Los Angeles
Mailing State: CA
Mailing ZIP Code: 90032-4226
General Phone: (323) 343-4215
General Fax: (323) 343-5337
Editorial Fax: Free
General/National Adv. Email: universitytimes@yahoo.com
Display Adv. Email: jmunson@cslanet.calstatela.edu
Editorial Email: universitytimes@yahoo.com
Website: www.calstatela.edu
Year Established: 1947
News Services: AP, Uwire, United Features
Syndicated Publications: NA
Delivery Methods: Racks
Commercial printers?: Y
Mechanical specifications: 11X16; RGB
Personnel: Jim Munson (Business, Advt. Mgr.)
Parent company (for newspapers): California State University, Los Angeles

LOS ANGELES CITY COLLEGE

Street Address 1: 855 N Vermont Ave
State: CA
Zip/Postal code: 90029-3516
Country: USA
Mailing Address: 855 N Vermont Ave
Mailing City: Los Angeles
Mailing State: CA
Mailing ZIP Code: 90029-3588
General Phone: (323) 953-4000
Website: wwwa.lacitycollege.edu
Personnel: Rhonda Guess (Advisor)

LOYOLA MARYMOUNT UNIV.

Street Address 1: 1 Lmu Dr
Street Address 2: Ste 8470
State: CA
Zip/Postal code: 90045-2682
Country: USA
Mailing Address: 1 Lmu Dr Ste 8470
Mailing City: Los Angeles
Mailing State: CA
Mailing ZIP Code: 90045-2682
General Phone: (310) 338-7509
General Fax: (310) 338-7887
General/National Adv. Email: loyolan@lmu.edu; editor@theloyolan.com
Website: www.laloyolan.com
Personnel: Tom Nelson (Advisor); Gil Searano (Ed.); Samantha Eisner (Adv. Sales Mgr.); Jose Martinez (Ed. in Chief); Heather Chong (Managing Ed.); Emily (Mng. Ed.); Laura (News Ed.)

OCCIDENTAL COLLEGE

Street Address 1: 1600 Campus Rd
Street Address 2: # M-40
State: CA
Zip/Postal code: 90041-3314
Country: USA
Mailing Address: 1600 Campus Rd # M-40
Mailing City: Los Angeles
Mailing State: CA
Mailing ZIP Code: 90041-3314
General Phone: (323) 259-2886
General Fax: (323) 341-4982
General/National Adv. Email: weekly@oxy.edu
Website: www.oxyweekly.com
Year Established: 1893
Personnel: Riley Hooper (Ed. in Chief); Ben Dalgetty (Ed. in Chief); Ashly Burch (Mng. Ed.); Marty Cramer (Asst. Opinion Ed.); Elana (Bus. Mgr.); Tucker (Adv. Mgr.)

UNIV. OF CALIFORNIA GRAD. SCHOOL OF MGMT.

Street Address 1: 110 Westwood Plz, Rm D216
State: CA
Zip/Postal code: 90095-0001
Country: USA
Mailing Address: 110 Westwood Plz, Rm D216
Mailing City: Los Angeles
Mailing State: CA
Mailing ZIP Code: 90095-0001
General Phone: (310) 825-6488
General Fax: (310) 206-3981
General/National Adv. Email: exchange@anderson.ucla.edu
Website: andersonexchange.collegepublisher.com
Personnel: Steve Gilison (Ed. in Chief); Daniel Gelsi (Ed. in Chief); Julie Lacouture (Ed. in Chief)

UNIV. OF SOUTHERN CALIFORNIA

Street Address 1: Student Union 404
State: CA
Zip/Postal code: 90089-0001
Country: USA
Mailing Address: 404 Student Un
Mailing City: Los Angeles
Mailing State: CA
Mailing ZIP Code: 90089-0001
General Phone: (213) 740-2707
General Fax: (213) 740-5666
General/National Adv. Email: dtrojan@usc.edu
Editorial Email: editor@dailytorjan.com
Website: www.dailytrojan.com
Personnel: Mona Cravens (Dir., of Student Publication); Scott A. Smith (Assoc. Dir); David Khalaf (Adv. Mgr.); Sheri Brundage (Adv. Mgr.)

UNIVERSITY OF CALIFORNIA, LOS

ANGELES

Street Address 1: 308 Westwood Plz
State: CA
Zip/Postal code: 90095-8355
Country: USA
Mailing Address: 308 Westwood Plaza
Mailing City: Los Angeles
Mailing State: CA
Mailing ZIP Code: 90095-8355
General Phone: (310) 825-9898
General Fax: (310) 206-0906
Advertising Phone: (310) 825-2221
Display Adv. Email: ads@media.ucla.edu
Editorial Email: editor@media.ucla.edu
Website: www.dailybruin.com
Year Established: 1919
Delivery Methods: Newsstand
Published: Mon`Tues`Wed`Thur`Fri
Personnel: Jeremy Wildman (Bus. Mgr.); Abigail Goldman (Media Advisor); Doria Deen (Student Media Dir); Mackenzie Possee (Editor in chief)

LOUDONVILLE

SIENA COLLEGE

Street Address 1: 515 Loudon Rd, Student Union
State: NY
Zip/Postal code: 12211
Country: USA
Mailing Address: 515 Loudon Rd., Student Union
Mailing City: Loudonville
Mailing State: NY
Mailing ZIP Code: 12211-1459
General Phone: (518) 783-2330
General Fax: (518) 786-5053
General/National Adv. Email: newspaper@siena.edu
Display Adv. Email: newspaper@siena.edu
Editorial Email: newspaper@siena.edu
Website: www.siena.edu
Year Established: 1937
Published: Fri
Published Other: Published biweekly
Avg Free Circ: 500
Personnel: Emily Radigan (Editor-in-Chief)

LOUISVILLE

BELLARMINE COLLEGE

Street Address 1: 2001 Newburg Rd
State: KY
Zip/Postal code: 40205-1863
Country: USA
Mailing Address: 2001 Newburg Rd
Mailing City: Louisville
Mailing State: KY
Mailing ZIP Code: 40205-0671
General Phone: (502) 452-8157
Advertising Phone: (502) 452-8050
Editorial Phone: (502) 452-8157
General/National Adv. Email: theconcard@bellarmine.edu
Website: www.theconcordonline.com
Personnel: Erika Osborne (Ed. in Chief)

UNIVERSITY OF LOUISVILLE

Street Address 1: Houehens Bldg, Ste LL07
State: KY
Zip/Postal code: 40292-0001
Country: USA
Mailing Address: Houehens Bldg, Ste LL07
Mailing City: Louisville
Mailing State: KY
Mailing ZIP Code: 40292-0001
General Fax: (502) 852-0700
Advertising Phone: (502) 852-0701
Editorial Phone: (502) 852-0667
Display Adv. Email: advertising@louisvillecardinal.com
Editorial Email: editor@louisvillecardinal.com
Website: www.louisvillecardinal.com
Year Established: 1926
Published: Tues
Avg Free Circ: 8000

Personnel: Simon Isham (Editor-in-Chief); Ralph Merkel (Adviser)

LOWELL

UNIV. OF MASSACHUSETTS LOWELL CONNECTOR

Street Address 1: 71 Wilder St
Street Address 2: Ste 6
State: MA
Zip/Postal code: 01854-3096
Country: USA
Mailing Address: 71 Wilder St Ste 6
Mailing City: Lowell
Mailing State: MA
Mailing ZIP Code: 01854-3096
General Phone: (978) 934-5001
General Fax: (978) 934-3072
General/National Adv. Email: connector@uml.edu
Website: www.uml.edu/connector
Year Established: 1924
Personnel: Ruben Sanca (Office Mgr.)

LUBBOCK

TEXAS TECH UNIVERSITY

Street Address 1: 3003 15th St
Street Address 2: Media & Comm. Bldg., Room 180
State: TX
Zip/Postal code: 79409-9816
Country: USA
Mailing Address: Box 43081
Mailing City: Lubbock
Mailing State: TX
Mailing ZIP Code: 79409-3081
General Phone: (806) 742-3388
General Fax: (806) 742-2434
General/National Adv. Email: dailytoreador@ttu.edu
Display Adv. Email: dawn.zuerker@ttu.edu
Editorial Email: editor@dailytoreador.com
Website: www.dailytoreador.com
Year Established: 1925
Delivery Methods: Mail`Carrier`Racks
Commercial printers?: Y
Published: Mon`Thur
Published Other: Summer semesters: once per week
Personnel: Susan Peterson (Student Media Dir.); Dawn Zuerker (Asst. Dir./Adv. Mgr.); Sheri Lewis (Asst. Dir./Editorial/Broadcasting Advisor); Andrea Watson (Asst Dir/Media Advisor); Kristi Deitiker; Amie Ward

LUFKIN

ANGELINA COLLEGE

Street Address 1: 3500 S 1st St
State: TX
Zip/Postal code: 75901-7328
Country: USA
Mailing Address: PO Box 1768
Mailing City: Lufkin
Mailing State: TX
Mailing ZIP Code: 75902-1768
General Phone: (936) 633-5288
General/National Adv. Email: lstapleton@angelina.edu
Year Established: 1968
Delivery Methods: Mail`Racks
Commercial printers?: N
Published: Bi-Mthly
Avg Free Circ: 1500
Personnel: Libby Stapleton (Advisor)

LYNCHBURG

LIBERTY UNIV.

Street Address 1: 1971 University Blvd
State: VA
Zip/Postal code: 24515-0002
Country: USA
Mailing Address: 1971 University Blvd

Mailing City: Lynchburg
Mailing State: VA
Mailing ZIP Code: 24515-0002
General Phone: (434) 582-2128
General Fax: (434) 582-2420
Editorial Phone: (434) 582-2128
General/National Adv. Email: advertising@liberty.edu
Website: www.liberty.edu/champion
Year Established: 1971
Personnel: William Gribbin (Dean, School of Commun.); Debra Huff (Advisor); Cecil V. Kramer (Jr. Assoc. Dean); Benjamin Lesley (Adv. Dir.); William Mullen (Chrmn.); Amanda Sullivan (Ed. in Chief)

LYNCHBURG COLLEGE

Street Address 1: 1501 Lakeside Dr
State: VA
Zip/Postal code: 24501-3113
Country: USA
Mailing Address: 1501 Lakeside Dr
Mailing City: Lynchburg
Mailing State: VA
Mailing ZIP Code: 24501-3113
General Phone: (434) 544-8301
General Fax: (804) 544-8661
General/National Adv. Email: critograph@lynchburg.edu
Display Adv. Email: critograph@lynchburg.edu
Editorial Email: critograph@lynchburg.edu
Website: www.critograph.com
Published: Tues
Personnel: Rachad Davis (Editor-in-Chief); Heywood Greenberg (Dena/Prof., Journ.); Wayne Garret (Copy Desk Chief)

RANDOLPH-MACON WOMAN'S COLLEGE

Street Address 1: 2500 Rivermont Ave
State: VA
Zip/Postal code: 24503-1555
Country: USA
Mailing Address: 2500 Rivermont Ave
Mailing City: Lynchburg
Mailing State: VA
Mailing ZIP Code: 24503-1526
General Phone: (434) 947-8000
General Fax: (434) 947-8298
Website: www.randolphcollege.edu
Personnel: Dawn Linsner (Ed.)

LYNDONVILLE

NORTHERN VERMONT UNIVERSITY-LYNDON

Street Address 1: 1001 College Rd
State: VT
Zip/Postal code: 5851
Country: USA
Mailing Address: PO Box 919
Mailing City: Lyndonville
Mailing State: VT
Mailing ZIP Code: 05851-0919
General Phone: (802) 626-6413
General/National Adv. Email: thecritic@northernvermont.edu
Website: https://www.facebook.com/NVULyndonCritic/
Year Established: 1965
Personnel: Bryanna Smith (Editor-in-Chief for 2018-2019 Academic Year.)

LYNNWOOD

EDMONDS CMTY. COLLEGE

Street Address 1: 20000 68th Ave W
State: WA
Zip/Postal code: 98036-5912
Country: USA
Mailing Address: 20000 68th Ave W
Mailing City: Lynnwood
Mailing State: WA
Mailing ZIP Code: 98036-5999

General Phone: (425) 640-1315
General/National Adv. Email: revedic@edcc.edu
Website: thetritonreview.com
Published: Other
Published Other: Twice per quarter during the academic year.
Personnel: Rob Harrill (Advisor); Madeleine Jenness (Editor in Chief)

MACOMB

WESTERN ILLINOIS UNIVERSITY

Street Address 1: 1 University Cir
Street Address 2: Western Illinois University
State: IL
Zip/Postal code: 61455-1367
Country: USA
Mailing Address: 1 University Cir
Mailing City: Macomb
Mailing State: IL
Mailing ZIP Code: 61455-1390
General Phone: (309) 298-1876
General Fax: (309) 298-2309
Advertising Phone: (309) 298-1876
Advertising Fax: (309) 298-2309
Editorial Phone: (309) 298-1876
Editorial Fax: (309) 298-2309
General/National Adv. Email: westerncourier@wiu.edu; micour@wiu.edu
Display Adv. Email: westerncourier@gmail.com
Editorial Email: wj-buss@wiu.edu
Website: www.westerncourier.com
Year Established: 1905
Delivery Methods: Carrier
Commercial printers?: N
Published: Mon`Wed`Fri
Avg Free Circ: 4000
Personnel: Devon Greene (Editor-In-Chief); Nick Ebelhack (Editor-in-Chief); Rachel Nelson (Advertising Manager); Will Buss (Advisor)

MACON

MACON STATE COLLEGE

Street Address 1: 100 University Pkwy
State: GA
Zip/Postal code: 31206-5100
Country: USA
Mailing Address: 100 College Station Dr
Mailing City: Macon
Mailing State: GA
Mailing ZIP Code: 31206-5145
General Phone: (478) 471-2700
General Fax: (478) 757-2626
General/National Adv. Email: mscmatrix@maconstate.edu; statement@maconstate.edu
Website: www.maconstatement.com
Personnel: Ray Lightner (Advisor); Glen Stone (Ed. in Chief)

MERCER UNIV.

Street Address 1: PO Box 72728
State: GA
Zip/Postal code: 31207-5272
Country: USA
Mailing Address: PO Box 72728
Mailing City: Macon
Mailing State: GA
Mailing ZIP Code: 31207-5272
General Phone: (478) 301-2871
General Fax: (478) 301-2977
Personnel: Lee Greenway (Advisor)

WESLEYAN COLLEGE

Street Address 1: 4760 Forsyth Rd
State: GA
Zip/Postal code: 31210-4407
Country: USA
Mailing Address: 4760 Forsyth Rd
Mailing City: Macon
Mailing State: GA
Mailing ZIP Code: 31210-4462
General Phone: (478) 757-5100

College and University Newspapers

General Fax: (478) 757-4027
General/National Adv. Email: pioneer@wesleyancollege.edu
Website: www.wesleyancollege.edu
Personnel: Dana Amihere (Ed.)

MADISON

DAKOTA STATE UNIV.

Street Address 1: 820 N Washington Ave
State: SD
Zip/Postal code: 57042-1735
Country: USA
Mailing Address: 820 N Washington Ave
Mailing City: Madison
Mailing State: SD
Mailing ZIP Code: 57042-1799
General Phone: (605) 256-5278
General Fax: (605) 256-5021
General/National Adv. Email: times@dsu.edu
Website: www.clubs.dsu.edu/trojantimes
Personnel: Justin Blessinger (Advisor); Jenny Grabinger (Adv. Mgr.); Samantha Moulton (Ed. in Chief)

DREW UNIV.

Street Address 1: PO Box 802
State: NJ
Zip/Postal code: 07940-0802
Country: USA
Mailing Address: PO Box 802
Mailing City: Madison
Mailing State: NJ
Mailing ZIP Code: 07940-0802
General Phone: (973) 408-4207
General Fax: (973) 408-3887
General/National Adv. Email: acorn@drew.edu
Website: www.drewacorn.com
Personnel: David A.M. Wilensky (Ed. in Chief); Sheryl Mccabe (Mng. Ed.)

MADISON AREA TECHNICAL COLLEGE

Street Address 1: 3550 Anderson St
State: WI
Zip/Postal code: 53704-2520
Country: USA
Mailing Address: 1701 Wright St
Mailing City: Madison
Mailing State: WI
Mailing ZIP Code: 53704-2599
General Phone: (608) 243-4809
General Fax: (608) 246-6488
General/National Adv. Email: clarioned@matcmadison.edu
Website: www.matc-clarion.com
Personnel: Doug Kirchberg (Advisor); Vishmaa Ramsaroop Briggs (Ed.)

UNIVERSITY OF WISCONSIN MADISON

Street Address 1: 152 W Johnson St
Street Address 2: Ste 202
State: WI
Zip/Postal code: 53703-2296
Country: USA
Mailing Address: 152 West Johnson Street
Mailing City: Madison
Mailing State: WI
Mailing ZIP Code: 53703-2017
General Phone: (608) 257-4712
General Fax: (608) 258-3029
Advertising Phone: (608) 257-4712
Editorial Phone: (608) 257-4712
General/National Adv. Email: publisher@badgerherald.com
Display Adv. Email: addirector@badgerherald.com
Editorial Email: editor@badgerherald.com
Website: www.badgerherald.com
Year Established: 1969
Published: Tues
Personnel: Alice Vagun (Editor-in-Chief)

WISCONSIN ENGINEER MAGAZINE

Street Address 1: Room M1066, Engineering Centers Bldg
State: WI
Zip/Postal code: 53706
Country: USA
Mailing Address: 1550 Engineering Dr.
Mailing City: Madison
Mailing State: WI
Mailing ZIP Code: 53706
General Phone: (608) 262-3494
General Fax: (608) 262-3494
General/National Adv. Email: wiscengr@cae.wisc.edu
Website: www.wisconsinengineer.com
Year Established: 1912
Special Editions: Published 4x a year
Commercial printers?: N
Personnel: Steven Zwickel (Advisor)

MAGNOLIA

SOUTHERN ARKANSAS UNIV.

Street Address 1: PO Box 1400
State: AR
Zip/Postal code: 71753
Country: USA
Mailing Address: P.O. Box 1400
Mailing City: Magnolia
Mailing State: AR
Mailing ZIP Code: 71753-71753
General Phone: (870) 235-4269
General Fax: (870) 235-5005
General/National Adv. Email: saubrayeditors@yahoo.com
Editorial Email: brayeditor@yahoo.com
Website: www.saumag.edu
Personnel: John Cary (Advisor); Wes Dowdy (Ed. in Chief); Terri Richardson (Asst. Ed.); Jamal Brown (Sports Ed.)

MALIBU

PEPPERDINE UNIV.

Street Address 1: 24255 Pacific Coast Hwy
State: CA
Zip/Postal code: 90263-0001
Country: USA
Mailing Address: 24255 Pacific Coast Hwy
Mailing City: Malibu
Mailing State: CA
Mailing ZIP Code: 90263-3999
General Phone: (310) 506-4318
General Fax: (310) 506-4411
Display Adv. Email: graphicadvertising@pepperdine.edu
Website: www.pepperdine-graphic.com
Personnel: Elizabeth Smith (Advisor); Amanda Gordon (Adv. Dir.); Ryan Hagen (Ed. in Chief)

MALTA

KISHWAUKEE COLLEGE

Street Address 1: 21193 Malta Rd
State: IL
Zip/Postal code: 60150-9600
Country: USA
Mailing Address: 21193 Malta Rd
Mailing City: Malta
Mailing State: IL
Mailing ZIP Code: 60150-9699
General Phone: (815) 825-2086
General Fax: (815) 825-2072
General/National Adv. Email: kscope@kishwaukeecollege.edu
Website: www.kishkscope.com
Personnel: Melissa Blake (Advisor); John Myers (Adv. Mgr.); Andrew Hallgren (Ed. in Chief); Nelle Smith (Ed.); John (Instructor); Marissa Skonie (Ed. In Chief)

MANCHESTER

MANCHESTER COMMUNITY COLLEGE

Street Address 1: 60 Bidwell St
State: CT
Zip/Postal code: 06040-6449
Country: USA
Mailing Address: 60 Bidwell Street
Mailing City: Manchester
Mailing State: CT
Mailing ZIP Code: 06045-1046
General Phone: (860) 512-3290
Editorial Phone: (860) 512-3289
General/National Adv. Email: livewire@manchestercc.edu
Website: www.livewiremcc.org
Year Established: 1979
Published Other: Every six weeks
Avg Free Circ: 4000
Personnel: Stephania Davis (Advisor)

SOUTHERN NEW HAMPSHIRE UNIV.

Street Address 1: 2500 N River Rd
Street Address 2: # 1084
State: NH
Zip/Postal code: 03106-1018
Country: USA
Mailing Address: 2500 N River Rd # 1084
Mailing City: Manchester
Mailing State: NH
Mailing ZIP Code: 03106-1018
General/National Adv. Email: Penmenpress@snhu.edu
Display Adv. Email: Penmenpress@snhu.edu
Website: PenmenPress.com
Published: Bi-Mthly
Personnel: Jon Boroshok (Advisor)

ST. ANSELM COLLEGE

Street Address 1: 100 Saint Anselm Dr
State: NH
Zip/Postal code: 03102-1308
Country: USA
Mailing Address: PO Box 1719
Mailing City: Manchester
Mailing State: NH
Mailing ZIP Code: 03102
General Phone: (603) 641-7016
General Fax: (603) 222-4289
General/National Adv. Email: crier@anslem.edu
Website: www.saintanselmcrier.com
Personnel: Jerome Day (Advisor)

MANHATTAN

STUDENT PUBLICATIONS INC.

Street Address 1: 103 Kedzie Hall
State: KS
Zip/Postal code: 66506-1500
Country: USA
Mailing Address: 103 Kedzie Hall
Mailing City: Manhattan
Mailing State: KS
Mailing ZIP Code: 66506-1505
General Phone: (785) 532-6555
General Fax: (785) 532-6236
General/National Adv. Email: news@spub.ksu.edu
Display Adv. Email: adsales@spub.ksu.edu; classifieds@spub.ksu.edu
Website: www.kstatecollegian.com
Year Established: 1896
Personnel: Steve Wolgast (Advisor); Tim Schrag (Ed.)

MANITOWOC

UNIV. OF WISCONSIN CENTER

Street Address 1: 705 Viebahn St
State: WI
Zip/Postal code: 54220-6601
Country: USA
Mailing Address: 705 Viebahn St
Mailing City: Manitowoc
Mailing State: WI
Mailing ZIP Code: 54220-6601
General Phone: (920) 683-4731
General Fax: (920) 683-4776
Personnel: Larry Desch (Advisor)

MANKATO

MINNESOTA STATE UNIV. MANKATO

Street Address 1: 293 Centennial Student Un
Street Address 2: Minnesota State University, Mankato
State: MN
Zip/Postal code: 56001-6051
Country: USA
Mailing Address: Centennial Student Union 293
Mailing City: Mankato
Mailing State: MN
Mailing ZIP Code: 56001
General Phone: (507) 389-1776
General Fax: (507) 389-5812
Advertising Phone: (507)389-1079
Advertising Fax: (507)389-1595
General/National Adv. Email: reporter-editor@mnsu.edu
Display Adv. Email: reporter-ad@mnsu.edu
Website: www.msureporter.com
Delivery Methods: Newsstand Racks
Personnel: Anne Schuelke (Adv.Mgr.); Nicole Smith (Ed. in Chief); Higginbotham (News Ed.); Shelly Christ (Advertising Sales Manager)

MANSFIELD

MANSFIELD UNIV. OF PENNSYLVANIA

Street Address 1: 202M Alumni Hall
State: PA
Zip/Postal code: 16933
Country: USA
Mailing Address: PO Box 1
Mailing City: Mansfield
Mailing State: PA
Mailing ZIP Code: 16933-0001
General Phone: (570) 662-4986
General Fax: (570) 662-4386
General/National Adv. Email: flashlit@mnsfld.edu
Personnel: Daniel Mason (Advisor)

MARIETTA

MARIETTA COLLEGE

Street Address 1: 215 5th St
State: OH
Zip/Postal code: 45750-4033
Country: USA
Mailing Address: 215 5th St Dept 32
Mailing City: Marietta
Mailing State: OH
Mailing ZIP Code: 45750-4071
General Phone: (740) 376-4848
General Fax: (740) 376-4807
General/National Adv. Email: mac@Marietta.edu
Website: www.marcolian.com/
Personnel: Jack L. Hillwig (Chair)

MARIETTA COLLEGE

Street Address 1: 215 5th St
Street Address 2: # A-20
State: OH
Zip/Postal code: 45750-4033
Country: USA
Mailing Address: 215 5th St Dept 32
Mailing City: Marietta
Mailing State: OH
Mailing ZIP Code: 45750-4071
General Phone: (740) 376-4555
General Fax: (740) 376-4807
General/National Adv. Email: marc@marietta.edu
Website: www.marcolian.com
Personnel: Jessie Schmac (Ed. in Chief); Jamie Tidd (Mng. Ed.); Amy Bitely (Viewpoints Ed.)

MARION

INDIANA WESLEYAN UNIVERSITY

Street Address 1: 4201 S Washington St
State: IN
Zip/Postal code: 46953-4974
Country: USA
Mailing Address: 4201 S Washington St
Mailing City: Marion
Mailing State: IN
Mailing ZIP Code: 46953-4974
General Phone: (765) 677-1818
General Fax: (765) 677-1755
General/National Adv. Email: amy.smelser@indwes.edu
Website: https://www.indwes.edu/undergraduate/majors/division-of-communication-and-theatre/
Personnel: Amy Smelser (Ed.); Amy Smelser (Instructor)

MARQUETTE

NORTHERN MICHIGAN UNIVIVERSITY

Street Address 1: 1401 Presque Isle Ave
Street Address 2: 2310 University Center
State: MI
Zip/Postal code: 49855-2818
Country: USA
Mailing Address: 1401 Presque Isle Ave
Mailing City: Marquette
Mailing State: MI
Mailing ZIP Code: 49855-5301
General Phone: (906) 227-2545
General Fax: (906) 227-2449
General/National Adv. Email: northwind@gmail.com
Display Adv. Email: hkasberg@nmu.edu
Website: www.thenorthwindonline.com
Year Established: 1972
Delivery Methods: Mail Racks
Commercial printers?: N
Published: Thur
Personnel: Kristy Basolo (Advisor)

MARSHALL

MISSOURI VALLEY COLLEGE

Street Address 1: 500 E College St
State: MO
Zip/Postal code: 65340-3109
Country: USA
Mailing Address: 500 E. College St.
Mailing City: Marshall
Mailing State: MO
Mailing ZIP Code: 65340-3109
General Phone: (660) 831-4214
General/National Adv. Email: postc@moval.edu
Display Adv. Email: postc@moval.edu
Website: www.mvcdelta.com
Personnel: Chris Post

SOUTHWEST STATE UNIV.

Street Address 1: 1501 State St
Street Address 2: Bellows Academic 246
State: MN
Zip/Postal code: 56258-3306
Country: USA
Mailing Address: Bellows Academic 246
Mailing City: Marshall
Mailing State: MN
Mailing ZIP Code: 56258
General Phone: (507) 537-6228
General Fax: (507) 537-7359
General/National Adv. Email: smsuspur@yahoo.com; smsuspur@gmail.com
Website: www.smsuspur.net
Personnel: Jessica Boeve (Bus. Mgr.); Jason Zahn (Ed. in Chief); McMellan Legaspi (Mng. Ed.)

WILEY COLLEGE

Street Address 1: 711 Wiley Ave
State: TX
Zip/Postal code: 75670-5151
Country: USA
Mailing Address: 711 Wiley Ave
Mailing City: Marshall
Mailing State: TX
Mailing ZIP Code: 75670-5151
General Phone: (903) 923-2400

MARSHFIELD

UNIV. OF WISCONSIN MARSHFIELD

Street Address 1: 2000 W 5th St
State: WI
Zip/Postal code: 54449-3310
Country: USA
Mailing City: Marshfield
Mailing State: WI
Mailing ZIP Code: 54449
General Phone: (715) 389-6545
General Fax: (715) 389-6517
General/National Adv. Email: msfur@uwc.edu
Editorial Email: insight@uwc.edu
Website: www.marshfield.uwc.edu
Personnel: Stacey Oelrich (Contact)

MARTIN

UNIV. OF TENNESSEE MARTIN

Street Address 1: 314 Gooch Hall
State: TN
Zip/Postal code: 38238-0001
Country: USA
Mailing Address: 314 Gooch Hall
Mailing City: Martin
Mailing State: TN
Mailing ZIP Code: 38238-0001
General Phone: (731) 881-7780
General Fax: (731) 881-7791
General/National Adv. Email: pacer@ut.utm.edu
Website: www.utmpacer.com
Personnel: Tomi McCutchen Parrish (Advisor); Josh Lemons (Ed.); Spencer Taylor (Mgr./News Ed.)

MARYVILLE

MARYVILLE COLLEGE

Street Address 1: 502 E Lamar Alexander Pkwy
State: TN
Zip/Postal code: 37804-5907
Country: USA
Mailing Address: 502 E Lamar Alexander Pkwy
Mailing City: Maryville
Mailing State: TN
Mailing ZIP Code: 37804-5919
General Phone: (865) 981-8241
General/National Adv. Email: highland.echo@gmail.com
Website: echo.maryvillecollege.edu
Personnel: Kim Trevathan (Advisor)

MARYVILLE

NORTHWEST MISSOURI STATE UNIV.

Street Address 1: 800 University Dr, Wells 4
State: MO
Zip/Postal code: 64468
Country: USA
Mailing Address: 800 University Dr., Wells 4
Mailing City: Maryville
Mailing State: MO
Mailing ZIP Code: 64468-6001
General Phone: (660) 562-1635
General Fax: (660) 562-1521
Editorial Phone: (816) 516-7030
General/National Adv. Email: northwestmissourian@gmail.com
Website: www.nwmissourinews.com
Year Established: 1914
Published: Thur
Personnel: Steven Chappell (Advisor); Brandon Zenner (Editor-in-Chief)

MASON CITY

NORTH IOWA AREA CMTY. COLLEGE

Street Address 1: 500 College Dr
State: IA
Zip/Postal code: 50401-7213
Country: USA
Mailing Address: 500 College Drive
Mailing City: Mason City
Mailing State: IA
Mailing ZIP Code: 50401
General Phone: (641) 422-4304
General Fax: (641) 422-4280
General/National Adv. Email: peterpau@niacc.edu
Website: www.niacc.edu/logos
Personnel: Paul Peterson (Advisor); Emily Knoop (Adv. Mgr.); Collie Wood (Ed.)

MATHISTON

WOOD COLLEGE

Street Address 1: Weber Dr
State: MS
Zip/Postal code: 39752
Country: USA
Mailing Address: Weber Dr.
Mailing City: Mathiston
Mailing State: MS
Mailing ZIP Code: 39752
General Phone: (662) 263-5352
Personnel: Jeanna Graves (Ed.)

MATTOON

LAKE LAND COLLEGE

Street Address 1: 5001 Lake Land Blvd
State: IL
Zip/Postal code: 61938-9366
Country: USA
Mailing Address: 5001 Lake Land Blvd
Mailing City: Mattoon
Mailing State: IL
Mailing ZIP Code: 61938-9366
General Phone: (217) 234-5269
General Fax: (217) 234-5390
General/National Adv. Email: studentpublications@lakeland.cc.il.us
Website: www.navigatornews.org
Published: Mthly
Personnel: Valerie Lynch (Dir of Student Life)

MAYS LANDING

ATLANTIC CAPE CMTY. COLLEGE

Street Address 1: 5100 Black Horse Pike
State: NJ
Zip/Postal code: 08330-2623
Country: USA
Mailing Address: 5100 Black Horse Pike
Mailing City: Mays Landing
Mailing State: NJ
Mailing ZIP Code: 08330-2699
General Phone: (609) 343-5109
General Fax: (609) 343-5030
Editorial Email: atlanticcapereview9@gmail.com
Personnel: Marge Nocito (Advisor); Jerry Carcache (Dir., Adv.); Anne Kemp (Ed. in Chief)

MCKEESPORT

PENN STATE UNIV.

Street Address 1: 4000 University Dr
State: PA
Zip/Postal code: 15131-7644
Country: USA
Mailing Address: 4000 University Dr
Mailing City: White Oak
Mailing State: PA
Mailing ZIP Code: 15131-7644
General Phone: (412) 675-9143
Personnel: Kathleen Taylor Brown (Advisor); Monica Michna (Ed. in Chief)

MCMINNVILLE

LINFIELD COLLEGE

Street Address 1: 900 SE Baker St
Street Address 2: Ste A518
State: OR
Zip/Postal code: 97128-6808
Country: USA
Mailing Address: 900 SE Baker St Ste A518
Mailing City: McMinnville
Mailing State: OR
Mailing ZIP Code: 97128-6894
General Phone: (503) 883-2200
General/National Adv. Email: review@linfield.edu
Website: www.linfield.edu/linfield-review
Personnel: William Lingle (Advisor); Dominic Baez (Ed. in Chief)

MCPHERSON

MCPHERSON COLLEGE

Street Address 1: 1600 E Euclid St
State: KS
Zip/Postal code: 67460-3847
Country: USA
Mailing Address: PO Box 1402
Mailing City: McPherson
Mailing State: KS
Mailing ZIP Code: 67460-1402
General Phone: (620) 242-0449
General Fax: (620) 241-8443
Website: spectator.mcpherson.edu
Personnel: Adam Pracht (Adviser); Shannon Williams (Editor-in-Chief)

MEADVILLE

ALLEGHENY COLLEGE

Street Address 1: PO Box 12
State: PA
Zip/Postal code: 16335-0012
Country: USA
Mailing Address: PO Box 12
Mailing City: Meadville
Mailing State: PA
Mailing ZIP Code: 16335-0012
General Phone: (814) 332-2754
General Fax: (814) 724-6834
General/National Adv. Email: thecampus1@gmail.com
Website: www.alleghenycampus.com
Personnel: Penny Schaefer (Advisor); Kristin Baldwin (Ed. in Chief)

MECHANICSBURG

MESSIAH COLLEGE

Street Address 1: 1 College Ave
Street Address 2: Ste 3058
State: PA
Zip/Postal code: 17055-6806
Country: USA
Mailing Address: PO Box 3043
Mailing City: Mechanicsburg
Mailing State: PA
Mailing ZIP Code: 17055
General Phone: (717) 796-5095
General Fax: (717) 796-5249
General/National Adv. Email: theswingingbridge@messiah.edu
Display Adv. Email: theswingingbridge@messiah.edu
Editorial Email: theswingingbridge@messiah.edu
Website: www.messiahsb.com
Delivery Methods: Newsstand
Commercial printers?: Y
Personnel: Ed Arke (Professor of Communications)

MEDFORD

TUFTS UNIV.

Street Address 1: PO Box 53018
State: MA

College and University Newspapers

Zip/Postal code: 02153-0018
Country: USA
Mailing Address: PO Box 53018
Mailing City: Medford
Mailing State: MA
Mailing ZIP Code: 02153-0018
General Phone: (617) 627-3090
General Fax: (617) 627-3910
Website: www.tuftsdaily.com
Personnel: Giovanni Russonello (Ed.)

MEDIA

PENN STATE UNIV. DELAWARE COUNTY

Street Address 1: 25 Yearsley Mill Rd
State: PA
Zip/Postal code: 19063-5522
Country: USA
Mailing Address: 25 Yearsley Mill Rd
Mailing City: Media
Mailing State: PA
Mailing ZIP Code: 19063-5596
General Phone: (610) 892-1200
General Fax: (610) 892-1357
General/National Adv. Email: kab4@psu.edu
Personnel: Karrie Bowen (Ed./Advisor)

MELBOURNE

FLORIDA INSTITUTE OF TECHNOLOGY

Street Address 1: 150 W University Blvd
State: FL
Zip/Postal code: 32901-6982
Country: USA
Mailing Address: 150 W University Blvd Ofc
Mailing City: Melbourne
Mailing State: FL
Mailing ZIP Code: 32901-6975
General Phone: (321) 674-8024
General Fax: (321) 674-8017
General/National Adv. Email: crimson@fit.edu
Editorial Email: crimson@fit.edu
Website: crimson@fit.edu
Year Established: 1967
Delivery Methods: Racks
Personnel: Ted Petersen (Adviser); Drew Lacy (Editor-in-Chief)

MEMPHIS

LEMOYNE-OWEN COLLEGE

Street Address 1: 807 Walker Ave
State: TN
Zip/Postal code: 38126-6510
Country: USA
Mailing Address: 807 Walker Ave
Mailing City: Memphis
Mailing State: TN
Mailing ZIP Code: 38126-6595
General Phone: (901) 435-1309
General Fax: (901) 435-1349
Editorial Phone: (901) 435-1318
General/National Adv. Email: magican@loc.edu
Website: www.locmagicianonline.com
Personnel: Lydia Lay (Instructor)

RHODES COLLEGE

Street Address 1: 2000 N Parkway
State: TN
Zip/Postal code: 38112-1624
Country: USA
Mailing Address: PO Box 3010
Mailing City: Memphis
Mailing State: TN
Mailing ZIP Code: 38173-0010
General Phone: (901) 843-3885
General Fax: (901) 843-3576
General/National Adv. Email: Souwester souwester@rhodes.edu
Website: www.thesouwester.org
Personnel: John Blaisdell

SOUTHWEST TENNESSEE CMTY. COLLEGE

Street Address 1: 5983 Macon Cv
State: TN
Zip/Postal code: 38134-7642
Country: USA
Mailing Address: 5983 Macon Cv
Mailing City: Memphis
Mailing State: TN
Mailing ZIP Code: 38134-7693
General Phone: (901) 333-4196
General Fax: (901) 333-4995
General/National Adv. Email: pworthy@southwest.tn.edu
Display Adv. Email: cherron@southwest.tn.edu
Website: southwest.tn.edu/clubs
Year Established: 2000
Personnel: Phoenix Worthy (Advisor); Connie Herron (Coorindator)

UNIV. OF MEMPHIS

Street Address 1: 113 Meeman Journalism Bldg
State: TN
Zip/Postal code: 38152-3290
Country: USA
Mailing Address: 113 Meeman Journalism Bldg
Mailing City: Memphis
Mailing State: TN
Mailing ZIP Code: 38152-3290
General Phone: (901) 678-5474
General Fax: (901) 678-0882
Display Adv. Email: rlwillis@memphis.edu
Website: www.dailyhelmsman.com
Delivery Methods: Racks
Commercial printers?: Y
Published: Tues`Wed`Thur`Fri
Avg Free Circ: 6500
Personnel: Bob Willis (Bus. Mgr.)

MENASHA

UNIVERSITY OF WISCONSIN, FOX VALLEY

Street Address 1: 1478 Midway Rd
State: WI
Zip/Postal code: 54952-1224
Country: USA
Mailing Address: 1478 Midway Rd
Mailing City: Menasha
Mailing State: WI
Mailing ZIP Code: 54952-1224
General Phone: (920) 832-2810
General Fax: (920) 832-2674
General/National Adv. Email: foxjournal@uwc.edu
Website: www.uwfox.uwc.edu/foxjournal
Personnel: Paula Lovell (Advisor)

MENOMONIE

UNIVERSITY OF WISCONSIN-STOUT

Street Address 1: 712 Broadway St S
Street Address 2: Memorial Student Center
State: WI
Zip/Postal code: 54751-2458
Country: USA
Mailing Address: 712 Broadway St S
Mailing City: Menomonie
Mailing State: WI
Mailing ZIP Code: 54751
General Phone: (715) 232-1141
General/National Adv. Email: stoutonia@uwstout.edu
Display Adv. Email: stoutoniaads@uwstout.edu
Editorial Email: stoutonia@uwstout.edu
Website: www.stoutonia.com
Year Established: 1915
Published Other: Every two weeks (7 issues per semester). Not published during the summer.
Avg Free Circ: 2700
Personnel: Kate Edenborg (Advisor); Shaun Dudek

MEQUON

CONCORDIA UNIV. OF WISCONSIN

Street Address 1: 12800 N Lake Shore Dr
State: WI
Zip/Postal code: 53097-2418
Country: USA
Mailing Address: 12800 N Lake Shore Dr
Mailing City: Mequon
Mailing State: WI
Mailing ZIP Code: 53097-2402
General Phone: (262) 243-5700
General Fax: (262) 243-4351
Personnel: Sarah Holtan (Faculty Advisor); Alax Tomter (Exec. Ed.)

MESA

MESA COMMUNITY COLLEGE

Street Address 1: 1833 W Southern Ave
State: AZ
Zip/Postal code: 85202-4822
Country: USA
Mailing Address: 1833 W Southern Ave
Mailing City: Mesa
Mailing State: AZ
Mailing ZIP Code: 85202-4866
General Phone: (480) 461-7270
General Fax: (480) 461-7334
General/National Adv. Email: jackm@mesacc.edu
Website: www.mesalegend.com
Year Established: 1962
Published: Bi-Mthly
Avg Free Circ: 5000
Personnel: Jack Mullins (Advisor)

MESQUITE

EASTFIELD COLLEGE

Street Address 1: 3737 Motley Dr
State: TX
Zip/Postal code: 75150-2033
Country: USA
Mailing Address: 3737 Motley Dr
Mailing City: Mesquite
Mailing State: TX
Mailing ZIP Code: 75150-2099
General Phone: (972) 860-7130
General Fax: (972) 860-7040
General/National Adv. Email: etc4640@dcccd.edu
Website: www.eastfieldnews.com
Year Established: 1970
Personnel: Sabine Winter (Faculty)

MIAMI

FLORIDA INTERNATIONAL UNIV.

Street Address 1: University Park Campus, 11200 SW 8th St, Graham Ctr, Ste 210
State: FL
Zip/Postal code: 33174-
Country: USA
Mailing Address: University Park Campus, 11200 SW 8th St., Graham Ctr., Ste. 210
Mailing City: Miami
Mailing State: FL
Mailing ZIP Code: 33174-2516
General Phone: (305) 348-6993
General Fax: (305) 348-2712
General/National Adv. Email: beacon@fiu.edu
Website: fiusm.com
Personnel: Robert jaross (Advisor); Tatiana Cantillo (Bus. Mgr.); Chris Necuze (Ed. in Chief); Jessica Maya (Prodn. Mgr.)

MIAMI DADE COLLEGE

Street Address 1: 11380 NW 27th Ave
Street Address 2: Rm 4209
State: FL
Zip/Postal code: 33167-3418
Country: USA
Mailing Address: 11380 NW 27th Ave., Rm. 4209
Mailing City: Miami
Mailing State: FL
Mailing ZIP Code: 33167
General Phone: (305) 237-1255
General/National Adv. Email: mbarco@mdc.edu
Display Adv. Email: thereporteradvertising@gmail.com
Website: www.mdc.edu/main/thereporter/archive/vol02-02/
Year Established: 2010
Published: Bi-Mthly
Avg Free Circ: 10250
Personnel: Manolo Barco (Advisor)

NORTHEASTERN OKLAHOMA A&M COLLEGE

Street Address 1: 206 I St NW
State: OK
Zip/Postal code: 74354-5630
Country: USA
Mailing Address: PO Box 3988
Mailing City: Miami
Mailing State: OK
Mailing ZIP Code: 74354
General Phone: (918) 542-8441
Personnel: Rebecca Kirk (Advisor)

MIAMI GARDENS

FLORIDA MEMORIAL COLLEGE

Street Address 1: 15800 NW 42nd Ave
State: FL
Zip/Postal code: 33054-6155
Country: USA
Mailing Address: 15800 NW 42nd Ave.
Mailing City: Miami Gardens
Mailing State: FL
Mailing ZIP Code: 33054
General Phone: (305) 626-3103
General Fax: (305) 626-3102
General/National Adv. Email: lionstal@fmuniv.edu
Website: www.fmuniv.edu
Personnel: Nathanael Paul (Ed.)

MIAMI SHORES

BARRY UNIV.

Street Address 1: 11300 NE 2nd Ave
State: FL
Zip/Postal code: 33161-6628
Country: USA
Mailing Address: 11300 NE 2nd Ave
Mailing City: Miami Shores
Mailing State: FL
Mailing ZIP Code: 33161-6695
General Phone: (305) 899-3093
General Fax: (305) 899-4744
General/National Adv. Email: buccaneer@mail.barry.edu
Website: student.barry.edu/buccaneer
Personnel: Susannah Nesmith (Advisor); Amor Tagan (Adv. Dir.); Samantha Stanton (Ed. in Chief)

MIDDLEBURY

MIDDLEBURY COLLEGE

Street Address 1: PO Box 30
State: VT
Zip/Postal code: 05753-0030
Country: USA
Mailing Address: PO Box 30
Mailing City: Middlebury
Mailing State: VT
Mailing ZIP Code: 05753-0030
General Phone: (802) 443-4827
General Fax: (802) 443-2068
General/National Adv. Email: campus@middlebury.edu
Website: www.middleburycampus.com
Personnel: Zachary Karst (Bus. Mgr.); Brian Fung (Ed. in Chief); Tess Russell (Mng. Ed.)

MIDDLETOWN

MIAMI UNIV.
Street Address 1: 4200 N University Blvd
State: OH
Zip/Postal code: 45042-3458
Country: USA
Mailing Address: 4200 N University Blvd
Mailing City: Middletown
Mailing State: OH
Mailing ZIP Code: 45042-3497
General Phone: (513) 727-3200
General Fax: (513) 727-3223
General/National Adv. Email: miamistudent@gmail.com; miamistudent@muohio.edu
Website: www.mid.muohio.edu/orgs/hawkseye/
Personnel: Catherine Couretas (Ed.); John Heyda (Advisor)

ORANGE COUNTY CMTY. COLLEGE
Street Address 1: 115 South St
State: NY
Zip/Postal code: 10940-6404
Country: USA
Mailing Address: 115 South St
Mailing City: Middletown
Mailing State: NY
Mailing ZIP Code: 10940-6404
General Phone: (845) 341-4240
General Fax: (845) 341-4238

PENN STATE UNIV. HARRISBURG
Street Address 1: 777 W Harrisburg Pike
Street Address 2: # E-126
State: PA
Zip/Postal code: 17057-4846
Country: USA
Mailing Address: 777 W Harrisburg Pike # E-126
Mailing City: Middletown
Mailing State: PA
Mailing ZIP Code: 17057-4846
General Phone: (717) 948-6440
General Fax: (717) 948-6724
General/National Adv. Email: captimes@psu.edu
Personnel: Patrick Burrows (Advisor); James Speed (Adv. Mgr.); Jenna Denoyelles (Ed. in Chief)

WESLEYAN UNIVERSITY
Street Address 1: 45 Wyllys Ave
State: CT
Zip/Postal code: 06459-3211
Country: USA
Mailing Address: 45 Wyllys Ave
Mailing City: Middletown
Mailing State: CT
Mailing ZIP Code: 06459-3211
General Phone: (860) 685-6902
General Fax: (860) 685-3411
General/National Adv. Email: argus@wesleyan.edu
Display Adv. Email: argusads@wesleyan.edu
Website: www.wesleyanargus.com
Published: Tues`Fri
Personnel: Natasha Nurjadin (Editor-in-Chief); Aaron Stagoff-Belfort (Editor-in-Chief)

MIDLAND

MIDLAND COLLEGE
Street Address 1: 3600 N Garfield St
State: TX
Zip/Postal code: 79705-6329
Country: USA
Mailing Address: 3600 N Garfield St
Mailing City: Midland
Mailing State: TX
Mailing ZIP Code: 79705-6397
General Phone: (432) 685-4768
General Fax: (432) 685-4769
General/National Adv. Email: studentpublications@midland.edu
Website: www.midland.edu; www.midlandcollegepress.com
Personnel: Karen Lenier (Instructor)

MILLEDGEVILLE

GEORGIA COLLEGE & STATE UNIV.
Street Address 1: 231 W Hancock St
State: GA
Zip/Postal code: 31061-3375
Country: USA
Mailing Address: 231 W. Hancock St.
Mailing City: Milledgeville
Mailing State: GA
Mailing ZIP Code: 31061
General Phone: (478) 445-4511
General Fax: (478) 445-2559
General/National Adv. Email: colonnade@gcsu.edu
Website: www.gcsunade.com
Personnel: Macon McGinley (Advisor); Claire Dykes (Ed. in Chief); Amanda Boddy (News Ed.); Elise Colcord (Adv. Mgr.)

MILLERSVILLE

MILLERSVILLE UNIV. OF PENNSYLVANIA
Street Address 1: 1 South George St, Rm.18
State: PA
Zip/Postal code: 17551
Country: USA
Mailing Address: PO Box 1002
Mailing City: Millersville
Mailing State: PA
Mailing ZIP Code: 17551-0302
General Phone: (717) 871-2102
General Fax: (717) 872-3515
Editorial Phone: (717) 871-2102
Editorial Fax: (717) 872-3516
General/National Adv. Email: snapper@marauder.millersville.edu
Website: thesnapper.com
Personnel: Gene Ellis (Advisor); Bradley Giuranna (Ed. in Chief); Ashley Palm (News Ed.)

MILLIGAN COLLEGE

MILLIGAN COLLEGE
Street Address 1: 1 Blowers Blvd
State: TN
Zip/Postal code: 37682
Country: USA
Mailing Address: PO Box 500
Mailing City: Milligan College
Mailing State: TN
Mailing ZIP Code: 37682-0500
General Phone: (423) 461-8995
General Fax: (423) 461-8965
General/National Adv. Email: stampede@milligan.edu
Website: www.milliganstampede.com
Year Established: 1866
Personnel: Jim Dahlman (Advisor); Kalee Nagel (Ed.)

MILWAUKEE

CARDINAL STRITCH UNIV.
Street Address 1: 6801 N Yates Rd
State: WI
Zip/Postal code: 53217-3945
Country: USA
Mailing Address: 6801 N Yates Rd
Mailing City: Milwaukee
Mailing State: WI
Mailing ZIP Code: 53217-3985
General Phone: (414) 410-4173
General Fax: (414) 410-4111
Personnel: Mary Carson (Advisor)

MARQUETTE UNIV.
Street Address 1: 1131 W Wisconsin Ave
State: WI
Zip/Postal code: 53233-2313
Country: USA
Mailing Address: 1131 W Wisconsin Ave
Mailing City: Milwaukee
Mailing State: WI
Mailing ZIP Code: 53233-2313
General Phone: (414) 288-1739
General Fax: (414) 288-5896
General/National Adv. Email: student.media@mu.edu; viewpoints@marquettetribune.org
Website: marquettetribune.org
Personnel: Kim Zawada (Advisor); Lauren Frey (Adv. Dir.); Jim McLaughlin (Ed. in Chief)

MILWAUKEE AREA TECH. COLLEGE
Street Address 1: 700 W State St
Street Address 2: Rm S220
State: WI
Zip/Postal code: 53233-1419
Country: USA
Mailing Address: 700 W State St Rm S220
Mailing City: Milwaukee
Mailing State: WI
Mailing ZIP Code: 53233-1419
General Phone: (414) 297-6250
General Fax: (414) 297-7925
General/National Adv. Email: matctimes@gmail.com
Website: www.matctimes.com
Year Established: 1959
Delivery Methods: Newsstand
Commercial printers?: N
Published Other: bi-weekly
Avg Free Circ: 2500
Personnel: Bob Hanson (Faculty Adviser)

MILWAUKEE SCHOOL OF ENGINEERING
Street Address 1: 1025 N Milwaukee St
State: WI
Zip/Postal code: 53202
Country: USA
Mailing Address: 1025 N. Milwaukee St.
Mailing City: Milwaukee
Mailing State: WI
Mailing ZIP Code: 53202-3109
General Phone: (414) 277-7255
General Fax: (414) 277-7248
Personnel: Nicholas Petrovits (Ed.)

MOUNT MARY COLLEGE
Street Address 1: 2900 N Menomonee River Pkwy
State: WI
Zip/Postal code: 53222-4545
Country: USA
Mailing Address: 2900 N Menomonee River Pkwy
Mailing City: Milwaukee
Mailing State: WI
Mailing ZIP Code: 53222-4597
General Phone: (414) 258-4810
General Fax: (414) 443-3602
Website: www.mtmary.edu
Personnel: Heather Schroeder (Advisor); Laura Otto (Ed. in Chief); Elaina Meier (Ed.)

UNIV. OF WISCONSIN MILWAUKEE
Street Address 1: 2200 E Kenwood Blvd
Street Address 2: Ste EG80
State: WI
Zip/Postal code: 53211-3361
Country: USA
Mailing Address: PO Box 413
Mailing City: Milwaukee
Mailing State: WI
Mailing ZIP Code: 53201-0413
General Phone: (414) 229-4578
General Fax: (414) 229-4579
Advertising Phone: (414) 229-5969
General/National Adv. Email: post@uwm.edu; post@uwmpost.com
Website: www.uwmpost.com
Personnel: Simon Bouwman (Bus. Mgr.); Kurt Raether (Adv. Mgr.); Kevin Lessmiller (Ed. in Chief)

MINNEAPOLIS

AUGSBURG COLLEGE
Street Address 1: 2211 Riverside Ave
State: MN
Zip/Postal code: 55454-1350
Country: USA
Mailing Address: 2211 Riverside Ave
Mailing City: Minneapolis
Mailing State: MN
Mailing ZIP Code: 55454-1351
General Phone: (612) 330-1018
General Fax: (612) 330-1649
Display Adv. Email: echo@augsburg.edu
Website: www.augsburg.edu/organizations/descriptions/echo.html
Personnel: Boyd Koehler (Adviser); Jenny Pinther (Editor-in-chief)

MINNEAPOLIS CMTY. & TECH. COLLEGE
Street Address 1: 1501 Hennepin Ave
State: MN
Zip/Postal code: 55403-1710
Country: USA
Mailing Address: 1501 Hennepin Ave
Mailing City: Minneapolis
Mailing State: MN
Mailing ZIP Code: 55403-1710
General Phone: (612) 659-6796
General Fax: (612) 659-6825
Website: www.citycollegenews.com
Personnel: Ben Lathrop (Advisor); Andrea Johnson (Mng. Ed.)

NORTH CENTRAL UNIV.
Street Address 1: 910 Elliot Ave
State: MN
Zip/Postal code: 55404-1322
Country: USA
Mailing Address: 910 Elliot Ave
Mailing City: Minneapolis
Mailing State: MN
Mailing ZIP Code: 55404-1391
General Phone: (612) 343-4495
General Fax: (612) 343-4780
Website: www.ncunortherner.com
Personnel: Reuben David (Advisor)

UNIV. OF MINNESOTA
Street Address 1: 2221 University Ave SE
Street Address 2: Ste 450
State: MN
Zip/Postal code: 55414-3077
Country: USA
Mailing Address: 2221 University Ave SE Ste 450
Mailing City: Minneapolis
Mailing State: MN
Mailing ZIP Code: 55414-3077
General Phone: (612) 627-4080
General Fax: (612) 435-5865
General/National Adv. Email: news@mndaily.com
Website: www.mndaily.com
Personnel: Holly Miller (Ed. in Chief)

UNIV. OF MINNESOTA INST. OF TECH
Street Address 1: 207 Church St SE
Street Address 2: Lind Hall 5
State: MN
Zip/Postal code: 55455-0134
Country: USA
Mailing Address: 207 Church St SE Lind Hall 5
Mailing City: Minneapolis
Mailing State: MN
Mailing ZIP Code: 55455-0134
General Phone: (612) 624-9816
General Fax: (612) 626-0261
General/National Adv. Email: technolog@itdean.

College and University Newspapers

umn.edu
Website: technolog.it.umn.edu/technolog
Personnel: Paul Sorenson (Advisor); Nate Johnson (Ed.); Michelle Walter (Ed,)

MINOT

MINOT STATE UNIV.

Street Address 1: 500 University Ave W
State: ND
Zip/Postal code: 58707-0001
Country: USA
Mailing Address: 500 University Ave W
Mailing City: Minot
Mailing State: ND
Mailing ZIP Code: 58707-0002
General Phone: (701) 858-3000
General/National Adv. Email: redgreen@minotstateu.edu
Website: www.minotstateu.edu
Personnel: Bryce Berginski (Ed.)

MISENHEIMER

PFEIFFER UNIV.

Street Address 1: PO Box 960
State: NC
Zip/Postal code: 28109-0960
Country: USA
Mailing Address: PO Box 960
Mailing City: Misenheimer
Mailing State: NC
Mailing ZIP Code: 28109-0960
General Phone: (704) 463-1360
General Fax: (704) 463-1363
Website: www.pfeiffer.edu
Personnel: Charisse Levine (Advisor)

MISHAWAKA

BETHEL COLLEGE

Street Address 1: 1001 Bethel Cir
State: IN
Zip/Postal code: 46545-2232
Country: USA
Mailing Address: 1001 Bethel Cir
Mailing City: Mishawaka
Mailing State: IN
Mailing ZIP Code: 46545-5591
General Phone: (574) 257-2672
General Fax: (574) 257-2583
General/National Adv. Email: beacon@bethelcollege.edu
Website: www.bethelcollege.edu/studentlife/media/beacon/
Personnel: Tim Ceravolo (Dir., Student Media); Amanda Armstrong (Ed. in Chief)

MISSION VIEJO

SADDLEBACK COLLEGE

Street Address 1: 28000 Marguerite Pkwy
State: CA
Zip/Postal code: 92692-3635
Country: USA
General Phone: (626) 815-6000
Advertising Phone: (863) 604-9250
Editorial Phone: (863) 604-9460
Editorial Fax: (863) 604-9460
General/National Adv. Email: clause@apu.edu
Display Adv. Email: tim.posada@gmail.com
Editorial Email: tim.posada@gmail.com
Website: www.lariatnews.com
Year Established: 1967
Published: Wed
Personnel: Tim Posada (Advisor)

MISSISSIPPI STATE

MISSISSIPPI STATE UNIV.

Street Address 1: Henry F Meyer Student Media Ctr
State: MS
Zip/Postal code: 39759
Country: USA
Mailing Address: PO Box 5407
Mailing City: Mississippi State
Mailing State: MS
Mailing ZIP Code: 39762-5407
General Phone: (662) 325-2374
General Fax: (662) 325-8985
Advertising Phone: (662) 325-7907
General/National Adv. Email: editor@reflector.msstate.edu
Display Adv. Email: advertise@reflector.msstate.edu
Website: www.reflector-online.com
Year Established: 1884
Published: Tues`Fri
Avg Free Circ: 10000
Personnel: Julia Langford (Adv. Mgr.)

MISSOULA

UNIVERSITY OF MONTANA

Street Address 1: 32 Campus Dr
State: MT
Zip/Postal code: 59812-0003
Country: USA
Mailing Address: Don Anderson Hall Ste 207
Mailing City: Missoula
Mailing State: MT
Mailing ZIP Code: 59812-0001
General Phone: (406) 243-6541
General Fax: (406) 243-5475
Advertising Phone: (406) 243-6541
Advertising Fax: (406) 243-5475
Editorial Phone: 406-243-4101
Editorial Fax: 406-243-5475
General/National Adv. Email: kaiminads@gmail.com
Display Adv. Email: kaiminads@gmail.com
Editorial Email: editor@montanakaimin.com
Website: www.montanakaimin.com
Year Established: 1898
News Services: AP
Special Editions: Football specials sections for home games
Delivery Methods: Mail`Racks
Commercial printers?: N
Published: Tues`Wed`Thur`Fri
Published Other: Published online daily, updated as news breaks
Avg Free Circ: 4000
Personnel: Ruth Johnson (Office manager); Nadia White (Advisor); Amy Sisk (Editor); Nick McKinney (Business manager)

MOBILE

SPRING HILL COLLEGE

Street Address 1: 4000 Dauphin St
State: AL
Zip/Postal code: 36608-1780
County: Mobile
Country: USA
Mailing Address: 4000 Dauphin St
Mailing City: Mobile
Mailing State: AL
Mailing ZIP Code: 36608-1791
General Phone: (251) 380-3850
General Fax: (251) 460-2185
General/National Adv. Email: shcmedia@shc.edu; sbabington@shc.edu
Display Adv. Email: hillian@stumail.shc.edu
Editorial Email: hillian@stumail.shc.edu
Website: newswire.shc.edu/
Delivery Methods: Racks
Commercial printers?: Y
Published: Thur
Personnel: Stuart Babington (Advisor); J.L. Stevens II (Integrated Multimedia Center (IMC) Operations Mgr and Student Media adviser)

UNIVERSITY OF SOUTH ALABAMA

Street Address 1: 336 Alpha Hall South
State: AL
Zip/Postal code: 36688-0001
Country: USA
Mailing Address: 336 Alpha Hall South
Mailing City: Mobile
Mailing State: AL
Mailing ZIP Code: 36688-0001
General Phone: (251)460-6442
General Fax: (251) 414-8293
Website: www.usavanguard.com
Year Established: 1963
Published: Mon
Avg Free Circ: 2000
Personnel: Cassie Fambro (Editor-in-Chief); Aucoin J (Adviser); Alanna Whitaker (Managing Editor)
Parent company (for newspapers): University of South Alabama

MODESTO

MODESTO JUNIOR COLLEGE

Street Address 1: 435 College Ave
State: CA
Zip/Postal code: 95350-5808
Country: USA
Mailing Address: 435 College Ave
Mailing City: Modesto
Mailing State: CA
Mailing ZIP Code: 95350-5800
General Phone: (209) 575-6223
General Fax: (209) 575-6612
Editorial Phone: (209) 575-6224
Website: www.pirateslog.org
Personnel: Laura Paull (Advisor)

MOLINE

BLACK HAWK COLLEGE

Street Address 1: 6600 34th Ave
Street Address 2: Bldg 4
State: IL
Zip/Postal code: 61265-5870
Country: USA
Mailing Address: 6600 34th Ave Bldg 4
Mailing City: Moline
Mailing State: IL
Mailing ZIP Code: 61265-5899
General Phone: (309) 796-5477
General Fax: (309) 792-5976
General/National Adv. Email: chieftain@bhc.edu
Personnel: Tory Becht (Advisor); Thomas Cross (Ed.); David Craig (Ed.)

MONMOUTH

MONMOUTH COLLEGE

Street Address 1: 700 E Broadway
State: IL
Zip/Postal code: 61462-1963
Country: USA
Mailing Address: 700 E Broadway
Mailing City: Monmouth
Mailing State: IL
Mailing ZIP Code: 61462-1998
General Phone: (309) 457-3456
General Fax: (309) 457-2363
General/National Adv. Email: courier@monm.edu
Website: www.monm.edu/courier
Personnel: Michelle Nutting (Adv. Mgr.); Lucas Pauley (Ed. in Chief)

WESTERN OREGON UNIV.

Street Address 1: 345 Monmouth Ave N
State: OR
Zip/Postal code: 97361-1329
Country: USA
Mailing Address: 345 Monmouth Ave N
Mailing City: Monmouth
Mailing State: OR
Mailing ZIP Code: 97361-1371
General Phone: (503) 838-9697
General Fax: (503) 838-8616
Advertising Phone: (503) 838-8836
Personnel: Marissa Hufstader (Bus./Adv. Mgr.)

MONROE

UNIV. OF LOUISIANA AT MONROE

Street Address 1: 700 University Ave
Street Address 2: Stubbs 131
State: LA
Zip/Postal code: 71209-9000
Country: USA
Mailing Address: 700 University Ave
Mailing City: Monroe
Mailing State: LA
Mailing ZIP Code: 71209
General Phone: (318) 342-5454
Advertising Phone: (318) 342-5453
Editorial Phone: 9318) 342-5450
General/National Adv. Email: ulmhawkeye@gmail.com
Display Adv. Email: ulmhawkeyead@gmail.com
Editorial Email: ulmhawkeye@gmail.com
Website: www.ulmhawkeye.com
Year Established: 1934
Published: Mon
Personnel: Ethan Dennis (Editor in Chief); Clarence Nash, Jr. (Advertising Director)
Parent company (for newspapers): University of Louisiana Monroe

MONROEVILLE

CMTY. COLLEGE OF ALLEGHENY COUNTY BOYCE

Street Address 1: 595 Beatty Rd
State: PA
Zip/Postal code: 15146-1348
Country: USA
Mailing Address: 595 Beatty Rd
Mailing City: Monroeville
Mailing State: PA
Mailing ZIP Code: 15146-1348
General Phone: (724) 325-6730
General Fax: (724) 325-6799
Personnel: Peggy Roche (Adv. Mgr.)

MONTEREY PARK

EAST LOS ANGELES COLLEGE

Street Address 1: 1301 Avenida Cesar Chavez
State: CA
Zip/Postal code: 91754-6001
Country: USA
Mailing Address: 1301 Avenida Cesar Chavez
Mailing City: Monterey Park
Mailing State: CA
Mailing ZIP Code: 91754-6001
General Phone: (323) 265-8821
General Fax: (323) 415-4190
Advertising Phone: (323) 265-8821
Advertising Fax: (323) 425-4190
Editorial Phone: (323) 265-8819
Editorial Fax: (323) 425-4190
General/National Adv. Email: Elaccampusnews@gmail.com
Display Adv. Email: jonfanie@yahoo.com
Editorial Email: elaccampusnews@gmail.com
Website: elaccampusnews.com
Year Established: 1945
Delivery Methods: Mail`Racks
Published: Wed`Other
Published Other: Not published in summer or January. Weekly during school year.
Avg Free Circ: 4800
Personnel: Jean Stapleton (Adviser); Sylvia Rico-Sanchez (Co-Adviser)

MONTEVALLO

UNIV. OF MONTEVALLO

Street Address 1: 75 College Dr
Street Address 2: Station 6222
State: AL
Zip/Postal code: 35115-3732
Country: USA
Mailing Address: 75 College Dr
Mailing City: Montevallo
Mailing State: AL

Mailing ZIP Code: 35115
General Phone: (205) 665-6222
General Fax: (205) 665-6232
General/National Adv. Email: alabamian@montevallo.edu
Website: www.thealabamian.com/
Published: Bi-Mthly
Personnel: Tiffany Bunt (Adviser); Reed Strength (Editor); Stephanie Howe (Business Manager)

MONTGOMERY

ALABAMA STATE UNIV.

Street Address 1: 915 S Jackson St
State: AL
Zip/Postal code: 36104-5716
Country: USA
Mailing Address: PO Box 271
Mailing City: Montgomery
Mailing State: AL
Mailing ZIP Code: 36101-0271
General Phone: (334) 229-4419
General Fax: (334) 229-4934
General/National Adv. Email: ayoleke@aol.com
Website: www.thehornettribune.com
Personnel: David Okeowo (Prof./Chair); Bryan Weaver (Exec. Ed.); E.K. Daufin (Prof.); Julian K. Johnson (Mng. Ed.); Tracy Banks (Assoc. Prof./Dir., Forensics); James B. Lucy (News Ed.); Elizabeth Fitts (Assoc. Prof.); Richard Emmanuel (Asst. Prof.); James Adams (Instr.); Coke Ellington (Instr.); Valerie Heard (Instr.); Jonathan Himsel (Instr.); John Moore (Instr.); Walter Murphy (Instr.); Larry Owens (Instr.)

AUBURN UNIV.

Street Address 1: 7400 East Dr
Street Address 2: Rm 326
State: AL
Zip/Postal code: 36117-7088
Country: USA
Mailing Address: PO Box 244023
Mailing City: Montgomery
Mailing State: AL
Mailing ZIP Code: 36124-4023
General Phone: (334) 244-3662
General Fax: (334) 244-3131
General/National Adv. Email: aumnibuseditor@yahoo.com
Website: aumnews.squarespace.com
Personnel: Taylor Manning (Ed. in Chief); Christine Kneidter (Exec. Ed.); Amber Acker (Mng. Ed.)

HUNTINGDON COLLEGE

Street Address 1: 1500 E Fairview Ave
State: AL
Zip/Postal code: 36106-2114
Country: USA
Mailing Address: 1500 E Fairview Ave
Mailing City: Montgomery
Mailing State: AL
Mailing ZIP Code: 36106-2148
General Phone: (314) 833-4354
General Fax: (334) 264-2951
General/National Adv. Email: gargoyle@huntingdon.edu
Personnel: Jackie Trimble (Advisor); Matthew Adams (Co-Ed.); Beth Woodfin (Co-Ed.)

WEST VIRGINIA UNIV. INST. OF TECHNOLOGY

Street Address 1: PO Box 1
State: WV
Zip/Postal code: 25136-0001
Country: USA
Mailing Address: PO Box 1
Mailing City: Montgomery
Mailing State: WV
Mailing ZIP Code: 25136-0001
General Phone: (304) 442-3180
General Fax: (304) 442-3838
General/National Adv. Email: collegianwv@hotmail.com
Website: collegian.wvutech.edu
Personnel: Jim Kerrigan (Advisor); Emily Wilkinson (Ed.)

MOON TOWNSHIP

ROBERT MORRIS UNIVERSITY : THE SENTRY

Street Address 1: 6001 University Blvd
Street Address 2: Dept of
State: PA
Zip/Postal code: 15108-2574
Country: USA
Mailing Address: 6001 University Blvd
Mailing City: Moon Township
Mailing State: PA
Mailing ZIP Code: 15108
General Phone: 412-397-6826
General Fax: 412-397-2436
Advertising Phone: (412) 397-6826
Editorial Phone: (412) 397-6826
General/National Adv. Email: sentrynews@mail.rmu.edu
Display Adv. Email: sentrynewsads@mail.rmu.edu
Editorial Email: sentrynews@mail.rmu.edu
Website: www.rmusentrymedia.com
Year Established: 2006
Published Other: Online only
Avg Free Circ: 500

MOORHEAD

CONCORDIA COLLEGE

Street Address 1: 901 8th St S
State: MN
Zip/Postal code: 56562-0001
Country: USA
Mailing Address: PO Box 104
Mailing City: Moorhead
Mailing State: MN
Mailing ZIP Code: 56561-0104
General Phone: (218) 299-3826
General Fax: (218) 299-4313
General/National Adv. Email: concord@cord.edu; cordadd@cord.edu
Display Adv. Email: cordadd@cord.edu
Editorial Email: concord@cord.edu
Website: www.theconcordian.org
Year Established: 1920
Published: Thur
Avg Free Circ: 2000
Personnel: Cathy McMullen (Advisor); Terence Tang (Bus. Mgr.); Suzanne Maanum (Adv. Mgr.)

MINNESOTA STATE UNIV. MOORHEAD

Street Address 1: 1104 7th Ave S
State: MN
Zip/Postal code: 56563-0001
Country: USA
Mailing Address: PO Box 306
Mailing City: Moorhead
Mailing State: MN
Mailing ZIP Code: 56561-0306
General Phone: (218)477-2552
General Fax: (218) 477-4662
General/National Adv. Email: advocate@mnstate.edu
Website: www.mnstate.edu/advocate
Personnel: Kristi Monson (Advisor)

MOORPARK

MOORPARK COLLEGE

Street Address 1: 7075 Campus Rd
State: CA
Zip/Postal code: 93021-1605
Country: USA
Mailing Address: 7075 Campus Rd.
Mailing City: Moorpark
Mailing State: CA

Mailing ZIP Code: 93021-1605
General Phone: (805) 378-1552
General Fax: (805) 378-1438
General/National Adv. Email: studentvoice@vcccd.edu
Website: www.studentvoiceonline.com
Personnel: Joanna Miller (Advisor)

MORAGA

SAINT MARY'S COLLEGE OF CALIFORNIA

Street Address 1: 1928 Saint Marys Rd
State: CA
Zip/Postal code: 94556-2715
Country: USA
Mailing Address: P.O. Box 4407
Mailing City: Moraga
Mailing State: CA
Mailing ZIP Code: 94575-4407
General Phone: (925) 631-4279
Advertising Phone: (925) 421-1515
Editorial Fax: Free
General/National Adv. Email: staff@stmaryscollegian.com
Display Adv. Email: collegianads@gmail.com
Website: www.stmaryscollegian.com
Year Established: 1903
Published: Tues
Avg Free Circ: 1000
Personnel: Shawny Anderson (Advisor); Charlie Guese (Co-Editor-in-Chief); Sara DeSantis (Co-Editor-in-Chief); Michael Bruer (Ed. In Chief)

MOREHEAD

MOREHEAD STATE UNIV.

Street Address 1: 150 University Blvd
State: KY
Zip/Postal code: 40351-1684
Country: USA
Mailing Address: 150 University Blvd
Mailing City: Morehead
Mailing State: KY
Mailing ZIP Code: 40351
General Phone: (606) 783-2697
General Fax: (606) 783-9113
General/National Adv. Email: editor@trailblazeronline.net
Website: www.trailblazeronline.net
Personnel: Joan Atkins

MORGANTOWN

WEST VIRGINIA UNIV.

Street Address 1: 284 Prospect St
State: WV
Zip/Postal code: 26505-5021
Country: USA
Mailing Address: PO Box 6427
Mailing City: Morgantown
Mailing State: WV
Mailing ZIP Code: 26506-6427
General Phone: (304) 293-2540
General Fax: (304) 293-6857
Editorial Phone: (304) 293-5092
General/National Adv. Email: da-mail@mail.wvu.edu
Website: www.da.wvu.edu
Personnel: Alan R. Waters (Advisor)

MORRIS

UNIV. OF MINNESOTA

Street Address 1: 600 E 4th St
State: MN
Zip/Postal code: 56267-2132
Country: USA
Mailing Address: 600 East Fourth Street
Mailing City: Morris
Mailing State: MN
Mailing ZIP Code: 56267
General Phone: (320) 589-6078
General Fax: (320) 589-6079

General/National Adv. Email: register@mrs.umn.edu
Year Established: 1987
Personnel: Ingrid Luisa AvendaÃƒÂ£Ã‚Â±o (Adv. Mgr.); Joy Heysse (Ed. in Chief); Eli Mayfield (Mng. Ed.)

MORRISTOWN

COLLEGE OF ST. ELIZABETH

Street Address 1: 2 Convent Rd
State: NJ
Zip/Postal code: 07960-6923
Country: USA
Mailing Address: 2 Convent Rd
Mailing City: Morristown
Mailing State: NJ
Mailing ZIP Code: 07960-6989
General Phone: (973) 290-4242
General Fax: (973) 290-4389
General/National Adv. Email: thestation@cse.edu
Personnel: Kristene Both (Ed. in Chief)

WALTERS STATE CMTY. COLLEGE

Street Address 1: 500 S Davy Crockett Pkwy
State: TN
Zip/Postal code: 37813-1908
Country: USA
Mailing Address: 500 S Davy Crockett Pkwy
Mailing City: Morristown
Mailing State: TN
Mailing ZIP Code: 37813-6899
General Phone: (423) 585-6816
Personnel: Dianna Pearson (Contact)

MORRISVILLE

MORRISVILLE STATE COLLEGE

Street Address 1: Journalism Dept
State: NY
Zip/Postal code: 10901
Country: USA
Mailing Address: Journalism Dept.
Mailing City: Morrisville
Mailing State: NY
Mailing ZIP Code: 13408
General Phone: (315) 684-6041
General Fax: (315) 684-6247
General/National Adv. Email: chimes@morrisville.edu
Display Adv. Email: mcdowebl@morrisville.edu
Website: thechimes.morrisville.edu
Personnel: Brian McDowell (Advisor)

MORROW

CLAYTON STATE UNIV.

Street Address 1: 2000 Clayton State Blvd
State: GA
Zip/Postal code: 30260-1250
Country: USA
Mailing Address: 2000 Clayton State Blvd
Mailing City: Morrow
Mailing State: GA
Mailing ZIP Code: 30260-1250
General Phone: (678) 466-5436
General Fax: (678) 466-5470
General/National Adv. Email: info@thebenttree.org
Website: www.thebenttree.org
Published: Mthly
Personnel: Randy Clark (Advisor); Sunitha Caton (Ed.)

MOSCOW

UNIV. OF IDAHO

Street Address 1: 301 Student Union Bldg
State: ID
Zip/Postal code: 83844-0001
Country: USA
Mailing Address: 301 Student Un
Mailing City: Moscow

College and University Newspapers

III-697

Mailing State: ID
Mailing ZIP Code: 83844-0001
General Phone: (208) 885-7825
General Fax: (208) 885-2222
General/National Adv. Email: argonaut@uidaho.edu
Website: www.uiargonaut.com
Personnel: Shawn O'Neal (Advisor); Hannah Liter (Adv. Mgr.); Greg Connolly (Ed. in Chief)

MOUNT BERRY

BERRY COLLEGE

Street Address 1: 2277 Martha Berry Hwy NW
State: GA
Zip/Postal code: 30149-9707
Country: USA
Mailing Address: 2277 Martha Berry Hwy NW
Mailing City: Mount Berry
Mailing State: GA
Mailing ZIP Code: 30149-9707
General Phone: (706) 238-7871
General Fax: (706) 238-5846
General/National Adv. Email: campus_carrier@berry.edu
Personnel: Kevin Kleine (Advisor); Jeanne Mathews (Asst. Vice Pres., PR); Rick Woodall (Dir., News/Editorial Servs.)

MOUNT PLEASANT

CENTRAL MICHIGAN UNIVERSITY

Street Address 1: 436 Moore Hall
Street Address 2: Central Michigan University
State: MI
Zip/Postal code: 48859-0001
Country: USA
Mailing Address: 436 Moore Hall
Mailing City: Mount Pleasant
Mailing State: MI
Mailing ZIP Code: 48859-0001
General Phone: (989) 774-3493
General Fax: (989) 774-7805
Advertising Phone: (989) 774-3493
Advertising Fax: (989) 774-7805
Editorial Phone: (989) 774-3493
Editorial Fax: (989) 774-7805
General/National Adv. Email: advertising@cm-life.com
Display Adv. Email: advertising@cm-life.com
Editorial Email: editor@cm-life.com
Website: www.cm-life.com
Year Established: 1919
Published: Mon`Wed`Fri
Avg Free Circ: 10000
Personnel: Kathy Simon (Advisor); David Clark (Director, Student Publications); Catey Traylor (Editor, 2013-2014); Julie Bushart (Advertising Manager, 2013-2014)

IOWA WESLEYAN COLLEGE

Street Address 1: 601 N Main St
State: IA
Zip/Postal code: 52641-1348
Country: USA
Mailing Address: 601 N Main St
Mailing City: Mount Pleasant
Mailing State: IA
Mailing ZIP Code: 52641-1398
General Phone: (319) 385-8021
General Fax: (319) 385-6363
Website: www.iwc.edu

NORTHEAST TEXAS CMTY. COLLEGE

Street Address 1: PO Box 1307
State: TX
Zip/Postal code: 75456-9991
Country: USA
Mailing Address: PO Box 1307
Mailing City: Mount Pleasant
Mailing State: TX
Mailing ZIP Code: 75456-9991
General Phone: (903) 434-8232
General Fax: (903) 572-6712

General/National Adv. Email: eagle@ntcc.edu
Website: www.ntcc.edu
Personnel: Mandy Smith (Advisor); Daniel Lockler (Mng. Ed.)

MOUNT VERNON

CORNELL COLLEGE

Street Address 1: 600 1st St SW
State: IA
Zip/Postal code: 52314-1006
Country: USA
Mailing Address: 600 First St SW
Mailing City: Mount Vernon
Mailing State: IA
Mailing ZIP Code: 52314
General Phone: (319) 895-4430
General Fax: (319) 895-5264
General/National Adv. Email: cornellian@cornellcollege.edu
Website: www.thecornellian.com
Delivery Methods: Mail
Commercial printers?: Y

SKAGIT VALLEY CMTY. COLLEGE

Street Address 1: 2405 E College Way
State: WA
Zip/Postal code: 98273-5821
Country: USA
Mailing Address: 2405 E College Way
Mailing City: Mount Vernon
Mailing State: WA
Mailing ZIP Code: 98273-5899
General Phone: (360) 416-7710
General Fax: (360) 416-7822
General/National Adv. Email: cardinal.news@skagit.edu
Personnel: Beverly Saxon (Advisor)

MUNCIE

BALL STATE UNIVERSITY

Street Address 1: Aj 278
Street Address 2: Ball State University
State: IN
Zip/Postal code: 47306-0001
Country: USA
Mailing Address: AJ 276
Mailing City: Muncie
Mailing State: IN
Mailing ZIP Code: 47306-0001
General Phone: (765) 285-8218
General/National Adv. Email: editor@bsudailynews.com
Website: www.bsudailynews.com
Year Established: 1922
Published: Wed
Avg Free Circ: 10000
Personnel: Lisa Renze-Rhodes (Publications Adviser)

MURFREESBORO

MIDDLE TENNESSEE STATE UNIV.

Street Address 1: 1301 E Main St
State: TN
Zip/Postal code: 37132-0002
Country: USA
Mailing Address: 1301 East Main Street, Box 36
Mailing City: Murfreesboro
Mailing State: TN
Mailing ZIP Code: 37132-0001
General Phone: (615) 904-8357
General Fax: (615) 494-7648
Editorial Phone: 6156924488
General/National Adv. Email: editor@mtsusidelines.com
Display Adv. Email: editor@mtsusidelines.com
Editorial Email: editor@mtsusidelines.com
Website: www.mtsusidelines.com
Year Established: 1925
Published: Mthly
Avg Free Circ: 4000
Personnel: Meagan White (Editor-in-chief); Dylan Aycock (Managing Editor); Sarah Taylor (News Editor); Rhiannon Gilbert

(Lifestyles Editor); Ethan Clark (Assistant Lifestyles Editor); Michael Ward (Sports Editor); Connor Ulrey (Assistant Sports Editor); Grant Massey (Multimedia Editor); Darian Lindsay (Chief Videographer); Austin Lewis (Photography Editor); Anna Claire Farmer (Design Editor); Justin Morales (Design Editor); Savannah Hazlewood (Assistant News Editor)

MURRAY

MURRAY STATE UNIV.

Street Address 1: 111 Wilson Hall
State: KY
Zip/Postal code: 42071-3311
Country: USA
Mailing Address: 111 Wilson Hall
Mailing City: Murray
Mailing State: KY
Mailing ZIP Code: 42071-3311
General Phone: (270) 809-6877
General Fax: (270) 809-3175
General/National Adv. Email: news@murraystate.edu
Website: www.thenews.org
Personnel: Mia Walters (Ed. in chief)

MUSCATINE

MUSCATINE CMTY. COLLEGE

Street Address 1: 152 Colorado St
State: IA
Zip/Postal code: 52761-5329
Country: USA
Mailing Address: 152 Colorado St
Mailing City: Muscatine
Mailing State: IA
Mailing ZIP Code: 52761-5396
General Phone: (563) 288-6053
General Fax: (563) 264-6074
Personnel: Kristina Koch (Advisor)

NACOGDOCHES

STEPHEN F. AUSTIN UNIV.

Street Address 1: 1936 North St, Baker Center Rm 2.308
State: TX
Zip/Postal code: 75962-0001
Country: USA
Mailing Address: PO Box 13049, Sfa Station
Mailing City: Nacogdoches
Mailing State: TX
Mailing ZIP Code: 75962-0001
General Phone: (936) 468-4703
General Fax: (936) 468-1016
General/National Adv. Email: pinelog@sfasu.edu
Website: www.thepinelog.com
Year Established: 1924
Personnel: Pat Spence (Dir.); Mark Rhoudes (Editor in Cheif)

NAMPA

NORTHWEST NAZARENE UNIV.

Street Address 1: 623 Holly St
State: ID
Zip/Postal code: 83686-5487
Country: USA
Mailing Address: 623 Holly St
Mailing City: Nampa
Mailing State: ID
Mailing ZIP Code: 83686-5897
General Phone: (208) 467-8656
General Fax: (208) 467-8468
General/National Adv. Email: crusader@nnu.edu
Personnel: Amber Ford (Ed.)

NANTICOKE

LUZERNE COUNTY CMTY. COLLEGE

Street Address 1: 1333 S Prospect St
State: PA
Zip/Postal code: 18634-3814

Country: USA
Mailing Address: 1333 S Prospect St
Mailing City: Nanticoke
Mailing State: PA
Mailing ZIP Code: 18634-3899
General Phone: (570) 740-0638
General Fax: (570) 740-0605
Personnel: Brett Bonanny (Ed.)

NAPERVILLE

NORTH CENTRAL COLLEGE

Street Address 1: 31 N Loomis St
State: IL
Zip/Postal code: 60540-4756
Country: USA
Mailing Address: 31 N Loomis St
Mailing City: Naperville
Mailing State: IL
Mailing ZIP Code: 60540
General Phone: (630) 637-5422
General Fax: (630) 637-5441
General/National Adv. Email: chronicle@noctrl.edu
Website: orgs.noctrl.edu/chronicle
Personnel: Nancy Kirby (Faculty Advisor)

NASHVILLE

BELMONT UNIV.

Street Address 1: 1900 Belmont Blvd
State: TN
Zip/Postal code: 37212-3758
Country: USA
Mailing Address: 1900 Belmont Blvd
Mailing City: Nashville
Mailing State: TN
Mailing ZIP Code: 37212-3757
General Phone: (615) 460-6000
General Fax: (615) 460-5532
General/National Adv. Email: vision@mail.belmont.edu
Website: www.belmontvision.com; www.belmont.edu
Personnel: Linda Quigley (Advisor); Thom Storey (Chair); Karen Bennett (Adv. Mgr.); Bethany Brinton; Lance Conzett (Ed. in Chief)

FISK UNIV.

Street Address 1: Humanities Div, 1000 17th Ave N
State: TN
Zip/Postal code: 37208
Country: USA
Mailing Address: Humanities Div., 1000 17th Ave. N.
Mailing City: Nashville
Mailing State: TN
Mailing ZIP Code: 37208-3045
General Phone: (615) 329-8500
General Fax: (615) 329-8714
Website: www.fisk.edu
Personnel: Karen Taylor (Ed.); Keen West (Ed.)

LIPSCOMB UNIV.

Street Address 1: 3901 Granny White Pike
Street Address 2: # 4126
State: TN
Zip/Postal code: 37204-3903
Country: USA
Mailing Address: 1 University Park Dr
Mailing City: Nashville
Mailing State: TN
Mailing ZIP Code: 37204-3956
General Phone: (615) 966-6604
General Fax: (615) 966-6605
General/National Adv. Email: babbler@lipscomb.edu
Display Adv. Email: babbleradvertising@lipscomb.edu
Website: babbler.lipscomb.edu
Personnel: Jimmy McCollum (Advisor); Michael Gilbert (Adv. Mgr.); Kaitie McDermott (Ed. in Chief)

VANDERBILT UNIV.

Street Address 1: 2301 Vanderbilt Pl
Street Address 2: # 351504
State: TN
Zip/Postal code: 37235-0002
Country: USA
Mailing Address: 2301 Vanderbilt Place Vu Sta B351504
Mailing City: Nashville
Mailing State: TN
Mailing ZIP Code: 37235-0001
General Phone: (615) 322-4705
General Fax: (615) 343-4969
General/National Adv. Email: advertising@vanderbilthustler.com
Editorial Email: editor@vanderbilthustler.com
Website: www.insidevandy.com
Personnel: Chris Carroll (Advisor); George Fischer (Dir. Mktg.); Carolyn Fischer (Adv. Mgr.); Hannah Twillman (Ed.)

NATCHITOCHES

NORTHWESTERN STATE UNIVERSITY

Street Address 1: 225 Kyser Hall
Street Address 2: Northwestern State University
State: LA
Zip/Postal code: 71497-0001
Country: USA
Mailing Address: The Current Sauce
Mailing City: Natchitoches
Mailing State: LA
Mailing ZIP Code: 71497
General Phone: (318) 357-5456
Advertising Phone: (318) 357-5456
Editorial Phone: (318) 357-5456
General/National Adv. Email: thecurrentsauce@gmail.com
Display Adv. Email: thecurrentsauce@gmail.com
Editorial Email: thecurrentsauce@gmail.com
Website: www.nsulastudentmedia.com
Year Established: 1914
Published: Wed
Avg Free Circ: 1000
Personnel: Alec Horton (Editor-in-Chief); Jordan Reich (Associate Editor); Christina Arrechavala (Managing Editor); Valentina Perez (Photo Editor); Elisabeth Perez (PR Manager); Chloe' Romano (Assistant PR Manager); Julia Towry (Ad Sales Representative); Sarah Hill (Designer); Maygin Chesson (Administrative Assistant)

NEOSHO

CROWDER COLLEGE

Street Address 1: 601 Laclede Ave
State: MO
Zip/Postal code: 64850-9165
Country: USA
Mailing Address: 601 Laclede Ave
Mailing City: Neosho
Mailing State: MO
Mailing ZIP Code: 64850-9165
General Phone: (417) 451-3223
General Fax: (417) 451-4280
General/National Adv. Email: sentry@crowder.edu
Website: www.crowder.edu
Personnel: Leona Bailey (Advisor.); Fabian Oechsle (Ed.)

NEW ALBANY

INDIANA UNIV. SOUTHEAST

Street Address 1: 4201 Grant Line Rd
State: IN
Zip/Postal code: 47150-2158
Country: USA
Mailing Address: 4201 Grant Line Rd
Mailing City: New Albany
Mailing State: IN
Mailing ZIP Code: 47150-6405
General Phone: (812) 941-2253
General/National Adv. Email: horizon@ius.edu
Website: iushorizon.com

Published: Mon
Published Other: Every two weeks
Avg Free Circ: 2000
Personnel: Adam Maksl (Adviser)

NEW BRITAIN

CENTRAL CONNECTICUT STATE UNIV.

Street Address 1: 1615 Stanley St
State: CT
Zip/Postal code: 06050-2439
Country: USA
Mailing Address: 1615 Stanley St
Mailing City: New Britain
Mailing State: CT
Mailing ZIP Code: 06050-2439
General Phone: (860) 832-3744
General Fax: (860) 832-3747
General/National Adv. Email: ccsurecorder@gmail.com; ccsurecorder.ads@gmail.com
Website: www.centralrecorder.com
Personnel: Vivian B. Martin (Coord.); Melissa Traynor (Ed. in Chief); Michael Walsh (Mng. Ed.); Christopher Boulay (Sports Ed.); Christina LoBello (Opinion Ed.); Kelsey (Adv. Mgr.)

NEW BRUNSWICK

RUTGERS UNIV.

Street Address 1: 126 College Ave
Street Address 2: Ste 431
State: NJ
Zip/Postal code: 08901-1166
Country: USA
Mailing Address: 126 College Ave Ste 431
Mailing City: New Brunswick
Mailing State: NJ
Mailing ZIP Code: 08901-1166
General Phone: (732) 932-7051
General Fax: (732) 932-0079
General/National Adv. Email: news@dailytargum.com
Website: www.dailytargum.com
Personnel: John Clyde (Ed. in Cheif)

RUTGERS UNIV. SCHOOL OF ENVIRONMENTAL & BIOLOGICAL SCIENCES

Street Address 1: 88 Lipman Dr
State: NJ
Zip/Postal code: 08901-8525
Country: USA
Mailing Address: 88 Lipman Dr
Mailing City: New Brunswick
Mailing State: NJ
Mailing ZIP Code: 08901-8525
General Phone: (732) 932-3000
General Fax: (732) 932-8526
Personnel: Kathryn E. Barry (Ed. in Chief)

NEW CONCORD

MUSKINGUM COLLEGE

Street Address 1: 163 Stormont St
State: OH
Zip/Postal code: 43762-1118
Country: USA
Mailing Address: 163 Stormont St
Mailing City: New Concord
Mailing State: OH
Mailing ZIP Code: 43762
General Phone: (740) 826-8296
General Fax: (740) 826-8404
Website: www.bandmonline.com
Personnel: Vivian Wagner (Advisor); Josh Chaney (Web Ed.)

NEW HAVEN

SOUTHERN CONNECTICUT STATE UNIV.

Street Address 1: 501 Crescent St
Street Address 2: # 58
State: CT
Zip/Postal code: 06515-1330
Country: USA
Mailing Address: 501 Crescent St # 58
Mailing City: New Haven
Mailing State: CT
Mailing ZIP Code: 06515-1330
General Phone: (203) 392-5804
General Fax: (203) 392-6927
General/National Adv. Email: snews@southernct.edu
Website: snews.southernct.edu
Personnel: Frank Harris (Advisor)

YALE UNIV.

Street Address 1: 202 York St
State: CT
Zip/Postal code: 06511-4804
Country: USA
Mailing Address: PO Box 209007
Mailing City: New Haven
Mailing State: CT
Mailing ZIP Code: 06520-9007
General Phone: (203) 432-2400
General Fax: (203) 432-7425
General/National Adv. Email: ydn@yale.edu; ydn@yaledailynews.com
Display Adv. Email: business@yaledailynews.com
Website: www.yaledailynews.com
Personnel: Jason Chen (Pub.); Katherine Kavaler (Adv. Dir.); Thomas Kaplan (Ed. in Chief)

YALE UNIV. LAW SCHOOL

Street Address 1: PO Box 208215
State: CT
Zip/Postal code: 06520-8215
Country: USA
Mailing Address: PO Box 208215
Mailing City: New Haven
Mailing State: CT
Mailing ZIP Code: 06520-8215
General Fax: (203) 432-1666
Personnel: Nicola Williams (Ed.)

NEW KENSINGTON

PENN STATE NEW KENSINGTON:COMMUNICATIONS DEPT

Street Address 1: 3550 7th Street Rd
State: PA
Zip/Postal code: 15068-1765
Country: USA
Mailing Address: 3550 Seventh St rd
Mailing City: New Kensington
Mailing State: PA
Mailing ZIP Code: 15068
General Phone: 724-334-6713
General/National Adv. Email: aka11@psu.edu
Website: nk.psu.edu
Parent company (for newspapers): Tribune-Review Publishing Co.

NEW LONDON

CONNECTICUT COLLEGE

Street Address 1: 270 Mohegan Ave
State: CT
Zip/Postal code: 06320-4125
Country: USA
Mailing Address: PO Box 4970
Mailing City: New London
Mailing State: CT
Mailing ZIP Code: 06320-4196
General Phone: (860) 439-2841
General Fax: (860) 439-2843
General/National Adv. Email: ccvoice@conncoll.edu; contact@thecollegevoice.org

Website: thecollegevoice.org
Personnel: Justin O'Shea (Bus. Mgr.); Benjamin Eagle (Ed. in Chief); Claire Gould (Mng. Ed.); CR Baker

NEW ORLEANS

DELGADO COMMUNITY COLLEGE

Street Address 1: 615 City Park Ave
State: LA
Zip/Postal code: 70119-4399
Country: USA
Mailing Address: 615 City Park Ave
Mailing City: New Orleans
Mailing State: LA
Mailing ZIP Code: 70119-4399
General Phone: (504) 671-6008
General Fax: (504) 483-1953
General/National Adv. Email: thedolphin29@gmail.com
Website: www.dcc.edu
Personnel: Susan Hague (Faculty Advisor); J.C. Romero (Ed. in Chief)

DILLARD UNIV.

Street Address 1: 2601 Gentilly Blvd
State: LA
Zip/Postal code: 70122-3043
Country: USA
Mailing Address: 2601 Gentilly Blvd
Mailing City: New Orleans
Mailing State: LA
Mailing ZIP Code: 70122-3097
General Phone: (504) 283-8822
General Fax: (504) 816-4107
Website: www.dillard.edu

LOYOLA UNIVERSITY NEW ORLEANS

Street Address 1: 6363 Saint Charles Ave
Street Address 2: Campus Box 64
State: LA
Zip/Postal code: 70118-6143
Country: USA
Mailing Address: 6363 Saint Charles Ave
Mailing City: New Orleans
Mailing State: LA
Mailing ZIP Code: 70118-6195
General Phone: (504) 865-3535
General Fax: (504) 865-3534
Advertising Phone: (504) 865-3536
General/National Adv. Email: maroon@loyno.edu
Display Adv. Email: ads@loyno.edu
Website: www.loyolamaroon.com
Year Established: 1923
Published: Fri
Avg Free Circ: 2750
Personnel: Michael Giusti (Advisor)

TULANE UNIVERSITY

Street Address 1: Lavin-Bernick Center for University Life G06
State: LA
Zip/Postal code: 70118
Country: USA
Mailing Address: Lavin-Bernick Center G06
Mailing City: New Orleans
Mailing State: LA
Mailing ZIP Code: 70118
General Phone: (504) 865-5657
Advertising Phone: (504) 865-5657
General/National Adv. Email: hull@tulane.edu
Display Adv. Email: hullabaloo.advertising@gmail.com
Website: www.thehullabaloo.com
Year Established: 1902
Published: Thur
Published Other: Homecoming Magazine and Spring Magazine
Avg Free Circ: 4000
Personnel: Brooke Rhea (Senior Business Manager); Lily Milwit (Editor In-Chief)

College and University Newspapers

UNIVERSITY OF NEW ORLEANS
Street Address 1: 2000 Lakeshore Dr
Street Address 2: # Ba 250/252
State: LA
Zip/Postal code: 70148-3520
Country: USA
Mailing Address: 2000 Lakeshore Dr # UC252
Mailing City: New Orleans
Mailing State: LA
Mailing ZIP Code: 70148-0001
General Phone: (504) 280-6378
General Fax: (504) 280-6010
General/National Adv. Email: driftwood@uno.edu
Website: driftwood.uno.edu
Personnel: Edie Talley (Editor in Chief)

XAVIER UNIV. OF LOUISIANA
Street Address 1: 1 Drexel Dr
Street Address 2: # 299
State: LA
Zip/Postal code: 70125-1056
Country: USA
Mailing Address: 1 Drexel Drive, Box 299
Mailing City: New Orleans
Mailing State: LA
Mailing ZIP Code: 70125-1098
General Phone: (504) 520-5092
General Fax: (504) 520-7919
Display Adv. Email: herald@xula.edu
Website: www.xula.edu; www.xulaherald.com
Year Established: 1925
Commercial printers?: Y
Published: Bi-Mthly
Avg Free Circ: 2000
Personnel: Melinda Shelton (Advisor)

NEW PALTZ

SUNY COLLEGE/NEW PALTZ
Street Address 1: Rm 417, Student Union Bldg, 1 Hawk Dr
State: NY
Zip/Postal code: 12561
Country: USA
Mailing Address: Rm. 417, Student Union Bldg., 1 Hawk Dr.
Mailing City: New Paltz
Mailing State: NY
Mailing ZIP Code: 12561
General Phone: (845) 257-3030
General Fax: (845) 257-3031
General/National Adv. Email: oracle@hawkmail.newpaltz.edu
Website: oracle.newpaltz.edu
Published: Thur
Personnel: Melisa Goldman (Bus. Mgr.); Emma Boddors (Ed.); Andrew Wyrich (Editor-in-Chief)

NEW ROCHELLE

COLLEGE OF NEW ROCHELLE
Street Address 1: 29 Castle Pl
State: NY
Zip/Postal code: 10805-2330
Country: USA
Mailing Address: 29 Castle Pl Ste 1
Mailing City: New Rochelle
Mailing State: NY
Mailing ZIP Code: 10805-2339
General Phone: (914) 654-5207
General Fax: (914) 654-5866
General/National Adv. Email: tatler@cnr.edu
Personnel: Elizabeth Brinkman (Advisor)

IONA COLLEGE
Street Address 1: 715 North Ave, Lapenta Student Union, 2nd Fl
State: NY
Zip/Postal code: 10801
Country: USA
Mailing Address: 715 North Ave., LaPenta Student Union, 2nd Fl.
Mailing City: New Rochelle
Mailing State: NY
Mailing ZIP Code: 10801-1830
General Phone: (914) 633-2370
General/National Adv. Email: ionian@iona.edu
Website: www.iona.edu
Personnel: Hugh Short (Moderator); James Hurley (Ed. in Chief); Alana Rome (Mng. Ed.); Heather Nannery (News Ed.)

NEW WILMINGTON

WESTMINSTER COLLEGE
Street Address 1: 319 S Market St
State: PA
Zip/Postal code: 16172-0002
Country: USA
Mailing Address: 319 S Market St
Mailing City: New Wilmington
Mailing State: PA
Mailing ZIP Code: 16172-0001
General Phone: (724) 946-7224
General/National Adv. Email: holcad@westminster.edu
Website: www.theholcad.com
Personnel: Shannon Richtor (Ed.)

NEW YORK

BARNARD COLLEGE
Street Address 1: 3009 Broadway
State: NY
Zip/Postal code: 10027-6909
Country: USA
Mailing Address: 3009 Broadway Frnt 1
Mailing City: New York
Mailing State: NY
Mailing ZIP Code: 10027-6598
General Phone: (212) 854-5262
General Fax: (212) 854-6220
General/National Adv. Email: bulletinedboard@gmail.com; backcover@barnardbulletin.com
Website: barnardbulletin.com
Personnel: Iffat Kabeer (Adv. Mgr.); Alison Hodgson (Ed. Emer.); Meagan McElroy (Mng. Ed.)

BARUCH COLLEGE/CUNY
Street Address 1: 1 Bernard Baruch Way
Street Address 2: Ste 3-290
State: NY
Zip/Postal code: 10010-5585
Country: USA
Mailing Address: 1 Bernard Baruch Way Ste 3-290
Mailing City: New York
Mailing State: NY
Mailing ZIP Code: 10010-5585
General Phone: (646) 312-4712
General Fax: (646) 312-4711
Website: www.theticker.org
Personnel: Carl Aylman (Dir., Student Lant); Jhaneel Lockhart (Ed. in Chief)

BOROUGH OF MANHATTAN CMTY. COLLEGE
Street Address 1: 199 Chambers St
Street Address 2: Rm S-207
State: NY
Zip/Postal code: 10007-1044
Country: USA
Mailing Address: 199 Chambers St Rm S-207
Mailing City: New York
Mailing State: NY
Mailing ZIP Code: 10007-1044
General Phone: (212) 220-8000
Website: www.bmcc.cuny.edu
Personnel: Dr. Juliet Emanuel (Advisor)

CARDOZO SCHOOL OF LAW/YESHIVA
Street Address 1: 55 5th Ave
Street Address 2: Ste 119
State: NY
Zip/Postal code: 10003-4301
Country: USA
Mailing Address: 55 5th Ave Fl 6
Mailing City: New York
Mailing State: NY
Mailing ZIP Code: 10003-4301
General Phone: (212) 790-0283
General Fax: (212) 790-0345
General/National Adv. Email: cardozoinsider@att.net
Personnel: Heela Justin (Ed.)

CITY COLLEGE OF NEW YORK
Street Address 1: Rm 1-119, North Academic Center Bldg, 160 Convent Ave
State: NY
Zip/Postal code: 10031
Country: USA
Mailing Address: Rm. 1-119, North Academic Center Bldg., 160 Convent Ave.
Mailing City: New York
Mailing State: NY
Mailing ZIP Code: 10031
General Phone: (212) 650-8177
General Fax: (212) 650-8197
General/National Adv. Email: ccnycampus@gmail.com
Website: www.ccnycampus.com
Personnel: Linda Villarosa (Advisor); Tania Bhuiyan (Bus. Mgr.)

COLUMBIA UNIV.
Street Address 1: 2875 Broadway
Street Address 2: Ste 3
State: NY
Zip/Postal code: 10025-7847
Country: USA
Mailing Address: 2875 Broadway Ste 3
Mailing City: New York
Mailing State: NY
Mailing ZIP Code: 10025-7847
General Phone: (212) 854-9550
General Fax: (212) 854-9553
General/National Adv. Email: info@columbiaspectator.com; spectator@columbia.edu
Website: www.columbiaspectator.com
Personnel: Akhil Mehta (Pub.); Ben Cotton (Ed. in Chief); Thomas Rhiel (Managing Ed.); Andrew Hitti (Dir., Sales); Oscar (Dir., Fin); Yipeng (Dir.)

COLUMBIA UNIV. BUS. SCHOOL
Street Address 1: 3022 Broadway
Street Address 2: Rm 242
State: NY
Zip/Postal code: 10027-6945
Country: USA
Mailing Address: 3022 Broadway Rm 242
Mailing City: New York
Mailing State: NY
Mailing ZIP Code: 10027-6945
General Phone: (212) 854-8396
General Fax: (212) 854-7557
Personnel: Matt Wong (Bus. Mgr.)

COLUMBIA UNIV. LAW SCHOOL
Street Address 1: 435 W 116th St
State: NY
Zip/Postal code: 10027-7237
Country: USA
Mailing Address: 435 W 116th St
Mailing City: New York
Mailing State: NY
Mailing ZIP Code: 10027-7237
General Phone: (212) 854-5833
General Fax: (212) 854-1229
General/National Adv. Email: jar2045@columbia.edu
Personnel: Matthew Dean (Ed.)

COOPER UNION
Street Address 1: 30 Cooper Sq
State: NY
Zip/Postal code: 10003-7120
Country: USA
Mailing Address: 30 Cooper Sq Fl 3
Mailing City: New York
Mailing State: NY
Mailing ZIP Code: 10003-7120
General Phone: (212) 353-4133
General Fax: (212) 353-4343
Editorial Email: Cooperpioneer@gmail.com
Personnel: Bill McAllister (ed.)

FASHION INST. OF TECHNOLOGY
Street Address 1: 227 W 27th St
Street Address 2: Ste A727
State: NY
Zip/Postal code: 10001-5902
Country: USA
Mailing Address: 227 W 27th St Ste A727
Mailing City: New York
Mailing State: NY
Mailing ZIP Code: 10001-5902
General Phone: (212) 217-7999
General Fax: (212) 217-7144
General/National Adv. Email: w27newspaper@gmail.com
Website: www.fitnyc.edu
Personnel: Richard Baleschrino (Advisor)

FORDHAM UNIV. LINCOLN CENTER
Street Address 1: 140 W 62nd St
Street Address 2: Rm G-32
State: NY
Zip/Postal code: 10023-7407
Country: USA
Mailing Address: 140 W. 62nd St., Rm. G-32
Mailing City: New York
Mailing State: NY
Mailing ZIP Code: 10023-7414
General Phone: (212) 636-6280
General Fax: (212) 636-7047
General/National Adv. Email: fordhamobserver@gmail.com
Display Adv. Email: fordhamobserveradvertising@gmail.com
Website: www.fordhamobserver.com
Published: Other
Personnel: Elizabeth Stone (Advisor); Ashley WennersHerron (Ed. in Chief)

HUNTER COLLEGE/CUNY
Street Address 1: 695 Park Ave
Street Address 2: Rm 211
State: NY
Zip/Postal code: 10065-5024
Country: USA
Mailing Address: 695 Park Ave Rm 211
Mailing City: New York
Mailing State: NY
Mailing ZIP Code: 10065-5024
General Phone: (212) 772-4251
General Fax: (212) 772-5539
Website: www.thehunterenvoy.com
Personnel: Joe Ireland (Ed. in Chief)

JEWISH STUDENT PRESS SERVICE
Street Address 1: 114 W 26th St
Street Address 2: Rm 1004
State: NY
Zip/Postal code: 10001-6812
Country: USA
Mailing Address: 114 W 26th St Rm 1004
Mailing City: New York
Mailing State: NY
Mailing ZIP Code: 10001-6812
General Phone: (212) 675-1168
General Fax: (212) 929-3459
Website: www.newvoices.org
Year Established: 1970
Personnel: Ben Sales (Ed.)

JOHN JAY COLLEGE OF CRIMINAL

JUSTICE

Street Address 1: 899 10th Ave
State: NY
Zip/Postal code: 10019-1069
Country: USA
Mailing Address: 524 W 59th St
Mailing City: New York
Mailing State: NY
Mailing ZIP Code: 10019-1007
General Phone: (212) 237-8308
General Fax: (212) 237-8036
Personnel: Babafunmilayo Oke (Ed.)

NEW YORK INSTITUTE OF TECHNOLOGY

Street Address 1: 1849 Broadway
Street Address 2: Rm 212
State: NY
Zip/Postal code: 10023-7602
Country: USA
Mailing Address: 1849 Broadway Rm 212
Mailing City: New York
Mailing State: NY
Mailing ZIP Code: 10023-7602
General Phone: (212) 261-1693
General/National Adv. Email: chronicle@nyit.edu
Personnel: William Lawrence (Advisor)

NEW YORK LAW SCHOOL

Street Address 1: 57 Worth St
Street Address 2: Rm L2
State: NY
Zip/Postal code: 10013-2926
Country: USA
Mailing Address: 57 Worth St Rm L2
Mailing City: New York
Mailing State: NY
Mailing ZIP Code: 10013-2926
General Phone: (212) 431-2100
Personnel: Sally Harding (Head, Student Life)

NEW YORK UNIV.

Street Address 1: 7 E 12th St
Street Address 2: Ste 800
State: NY
Zip/Postal code: 10003-4475
Country: USA
Mailing Address: 7 E 12th St Ste 800
Mailing City: New York
Mailing State: NY
Mailing ZIP Code: 10003-4475
General Phone: (212) 998-4300
General Fax: (212) 995-3790
Website: www.nyunews.com
Personnel: David Cosgrove (Dir., Opns.); Julia McCarthy (Bus. Mgr.); Eric Platt (Ed. in Chief); Rachael Smith (Ed.)

NEW YORK UNIVERSITY SCHOOL OF LAW

Street Address 1: 240 Mercer St Bsmt
Street Address 2: Hayden Hall
State: NY
Zip/Postal code: 10012-1590
Country: USA
Mailing Address: 40 Washington Sq S Rm 110
Mailing City: New York
Mailing State: NY
Mailing ZIP Code: 10012-1005
General Phone: (212) 998-0564
General Fax: (212) 995-4032
General/National Adv. Email: Law.commentator@nyu.edu
Display Adv. Email: Law.commentator@nyu.edu
Editorial Email: Law.commentator@nyu.edu
Website: www.law.nyu.edu/studentorganizations/thecommentator
Year Established: 1966
Personnel: Naeem Crawford-Muhammad (Advisor); Andrew S. Gehring (Ed. in Chief); Robert Gerrity (Sr. Mng. Ed.); Ana Namaki
Parent company (for newspapers): New York University School of Law Student Bar Association

NYU STERN SCHOOL OF BUS.

Street Address 1: 44 W 4th St
Street Address 2: Mec 6-130
State: NY
Zip/Postal code: 10012-1106
Country: USA
Mailing Address: 44 W 4th St Mec 6-130
Mailing City: New York
Mailing State: NY
Mailing ZIP Code: 10012-1106
General Phone: (212) 995-4432
General Fax: (212) 995-4606
General/National Adv. Email: opportun@stern.nyu.edu; helpdesk@stern.nyu.edu
Website: www.sternopportunity.com
Personnel: Jeremy Carrine (Advisor); Deborah Garcia (Ed. in chief); Rakesh Duggal (Co-Ed.)

PACE UNIV.

Street Address 1: 41 Park Row
Street Address 2: Rm 902
State: NY
Zip/Postal code: 10038-1508
Country: USA
Mailing Address: 41 Park Row Rm 902
Mailing City: New York
Mailing State: NY
Mailing ZIP Code: 10038-1508
General Phone: (212) 346-1553
General Fax: (212) 346-1265
General/National Adv. Email: editor@pacepress.org
Website: www.pacepress.org
Personnel: Mark McSherry (Advisor)

SCHOOL OF VISUAL ARTS

Street Address 1: 209 E 23rd St
State: NY
Zip/Postal code: 10010-3901
Country: USA
Mailing Address: 209 E 23rd St
Mailing City: New York
Mailing State: NY
Mailing ZIP Code: 10010-3994
General Phone: (212) 592-2280
General Fax: (212) 725-3587
Personnel: Tina Crayton (Advisor); Jane Resnick (Ed.)

STERN COLLEGE FOR WOMEN

Street Address 1: 245 Lexington Ave
State: NY
Zip/Postal code: 10016-4605
Country: USA
Mailing Address: 245 Lexington Ave
Mailing City: New York
Mailing State: NY
Mailing ZIP Code: 10016-4699
General Phone: (212) 340-7715
General Fax: (212) 340-7773
General/National Adv. Email: scwobserver@gmail.com
Website: www.yuobserver.com

THE EMPIRE STATE TRIBUNE

Street Address 1: 56 Broadway
Street Address 2: Fl 5
State: NY
Zip/Postal code: 10004-1613
County: New York
Country: USA
General Phone: 212-659-0742
Advertising Phone: 212-659-0742
Editorial Phone: 212-659-0742
General/National Adv. Email: estribune@tkc.edu
Display Adv. Email: estribune@tkc.edu
Editorial Email: estribune@tkc.edu
Website: www.empirestatetribune.com
Year Established: 2005
Delivery Methods: Racks
Own Printing Facility?: Y
Commercial printers?: N
Published: Mon
Avg Free Circ: 100
Personnel: Clemente Lisi (Assistant Affiliate Professor of Journalism)

YESHIVA UNIV.

Street Address 1: 500 W 185th St
Street Address 2: Ste 416
State: NY
Zip/Postal code: 10033-3201
Country: USA
Mailing Address: 500 W 185th St Ste 416
Mailing City: New York
Mailing State: NY
Mailing ZIP Code: 10033-3201
General Phone: (212) 795-4308
General Fax: (212) 928-8637
General/National Adv. Email: news@yucommentator.com
Website: www.yucommentator.com
Personnel: Michael Cinnamon (Ed. in Chief); Simeon Botwinick (Mng. Ed.); Isaac Silverstein (Mng. Ed.)

NEWARK

ESSEX COUNTY COLLEGE

Street Address 1: 303 University Ave
State: NJ
Zip/Postal code: 07102-1719
Country: USA
Mailing Address: 303 University Ave
Mailing City: Newark
Mailing State: NJ
Mailing ZIP Code: 07102-1798
General Phone: (973) 877-3559
General Fax: (973) 877-3488
Personnel: Kyle Miller (Ed.); Nessie Hill (Advisor)

NEW JERSEY INST. OF TECHNOLOGY

Street Address 1: 150 Bleeker St
State: NJ
Zip/Postal code: 07103-3902
Country: USA
Mailing Address: 150 Bleeker St
Mailing City: Newark
Mailing State: NJ
Mailing ZIP Code: 07103-3902
General Phone: (973) 596-5416
General Fax: (973) 596-3613
General/National Adv. Email: news@njitvector.com
Display Adv. Email: ads@njitvector.com
Website: www.njitvector.com
Personnel: Melissa Silderstang (Exec. Ed.)

RUTGERS UNIV.

Street Address 1: 350 M L King Blvd
Street Address 2: Paul Robeson Campus Ctr., Rm. 237
State: NJ
Zip/Postal code: 07102-1801
Country: USA
Mailing Address: 350 Martin Luther King Jr Blvd
Mailing City: Newark
Mailing State: NJ
Mailing ZIP Code: 07102-1801
General Phone: (973) 353-5023
General Fax: (973) 353-1333
General/National Adv. Email: observercopy@gmail.com
Website: www.rutgersobserver.com
Personnel: Dina Sayedahmed (Executive Editor)

THE REVIEW

Street Address 1: 325 Academy St
Street Address 2: Rm 250
State: DE
Zip/Postal code: 19716-6186
Country: USA
Mailing Address: 325 Academy St Rm 250
Mailing City: Newark
Mailing State: DE
Mailing ZIP Code: 19716-6185
General Phone: (302) 831-1397
General Fax: (302) 831-1396
Advertising Phone: (302) 831-1398
Advertising Fax: (302) 831-1395
Editorial Phone: (302) 831-2774
General/National Adv. Email: business@udreview.com
Display Adv. Email: ads@udreview.com
Editorial Email: editor@udreview.com; thereview.editorial@gmail.com
Website: www.udreview.com
Year Established: 1882
Delivery Methods: Newsstand
Personnel: Kerry Bowden (Editor-in-Chief)

NEWBERRY

NEWBERRY COLLEGE

Street Address 1: 2100 College St
State: SC
Zip/Postal code: 29108-2126
Country: USA
Mailing Address: 2100 College St
Mailing City: Newberry
Mailing State: SC
Mailing ZIP Code: 29108-2197
General Phone: (803) 276-5010
General Fax: (803) 321-5269
Website: www.newberry.edu
Personnel: Jodie Peeler (Advisor)

MT. ST. MARY COLLEGE

Street Address 1: 330 Powell Ave
State: NY
Zip/Postal code: 12550-3412
Country: USA
Mailing Address: 330 Powell Ave
Mailing City: Newburgh
Mailing State: NY
Mailing ZIP Code: 12550-3494
General Phone: (845) 569-3100
General Fax: (845) 561-6762
Personnel: Vince Begley (Advisor); Nathan Rosenblum (Ed.)

NEWPORT

NORTHERN KENTUCKY UNIV.

Street Address 1: University Ctr, Rm 335, Nunn Dr
State: KY
Zip/Postal code: 41099-0001
Country: USA
Mailing Address: University Ctr Rm 335
Mailing City: Newport
Mailing State: KY
Mailing ZIP Code: 41099-0001
General Phone: (859) 572-5772
General Fax: (859) 572-5772
Advertising Fax: (859) 572-5232
General/National Adv. Email: northerner@nku.edu
Website: www.thenortherner.com
Personnel: Drew Laskey (Sports Ed.)

NEWPORT NEWS

CHRISTOPHER NEWPORT UNIV.

Street Address 1: 1 University Pl
State: VA
Zip/Postal code: 23606-2949
Country: USA
Mailing Address: 1 University Pl
Mailing City: Newport News
Mailing State: VA
Mailing ZIP Code: 23606-2949
General Phone: (757) 594-7196
General/National Adv. Email: desk@thecaptainslog.org
Website: www.thecaptainslog.org
Published: Wed
Personnel: Terry Lee (Faculty Advisor); Ben Leistensnider (Ed. in Chief); Nicole Emmelhainz (Faculty advisor)

College and University Newspapers

NEWTON CENTER

MOUNT IDA COLLEGE

Street Address 1: 777 Dedham St
State: MA
Zip/Postal code: 02459-3323
Country: USA
Mailing Address: 777 Dedham St
Mailing City: Newton Center
Mailing State: MA
Mailing ZIP Code: 02459-3310
General Phone: (617) 928-4754
General Fax: (617) 928-4766
Personnel: Melissa Constantine (Advisor); Matt Caldwell (Ed. in Chief); Jen Barrett (Asst. Ed.)

NEWTOWN

BUCKS COUNTY CMTY. COLLEGE

Street Address 1: 275 Swamp Rd
State: PA
Zip/Postal code: 18940-4106
Country: USA
Mailing Address: 275 Swamp Rd
Mailing City: Newtown
Mailing State: PA
Mailing ZIP Code: 18940-9677
General Phone: (215) 968-8379
General Fax: (215) 968-8271
Editorial Phone: (215) 968-8379
General/National Adv. Email: buckscenturion@gmail.com
Display Adv. Email: orders@mymediamate.com
Editorial Email: buckscenturion@gmail.com
Website: www.bucks-news.com
Year Established: 1964
Delivery Methods: Newsstand
Commercial printers?: Y
Published: Thur
Avg Free Circ: 2000
Personnel: Tony Rogers (Advisor)

NIAGARA UNIVERSITY

NIAGARA UNIV.

Street Address 1: Gallagher Ctr
State: NY
Zip/Postal code: 14109
Country: USA
Mailing Address: Gallagher Ctr.
Mailing City: Niagara University
Mailing State: NY
Mailing ZIP Code: 14109-1919
General Phone: (716) 286-8512
General Fax: (716) 286-8542
General/National Adv. Email: theniagaraindex@yahoo.com
Personnel: Bill Wolcott (Advisor); Mary Colleen Mahoney (Bus. Mgr.); Marissa Christman (Ed. in Chief)

NORFOLK

NORFOLK STATE UNIVERSITY

Street Address 1: 700 Park Ave
Street Address 2: Student Activities
State: VA
Zip/Postal code: 23504-8050
Country: USA
Mailing Address: 700 Park Ave.
Mailing City: Norfolk
Mailing State: VA
Mailing ZIP Code: 23504-8090
General Phone: (757) 823-8200
Advertising Phone: (757) 823-8200
Editorial Phone: (757) 823-8200
General/National Adv. Email: spartanecho@nsu.edu
Display Adv. Email: spartanecho@nsu.edu
Editorial Email: spartanecho@nsu.edu
Website: www.spartanecho.org
Year Established: 1952
Commercial printers?: Y
Published: Bi-Mthly
Avg Free Circ: 1000
Personnel: Tarrye Venable (Student Activities Director)
Parent company (for newspapers): Norfolk State University

NORTHEAST CMTY. COLLEGE

Street Address 1: 801 E Benjamin Ave
State: NE
Zip/Postal code: 68701-6831
Country: USA
Mailing Address: PO Box 469
Mailing City: Norfolk
Mailing State: NE
Mailing ZIP Code: 68702-0469
General Phone: (402) 844-7352
Website: www.neaccviewpoint.com
Personnel: Jason Elznic (Advisor)

OLD DOMINION UNIVERSITY

Street Address 1: 1051 Webb Center
State: VA
Zip/Postal code: 23529-0001
Country: USA
Mailing Address: 1051 Webb Center
Mailing City: Norfolk
Mailing State: VA
Mailing ZIP Code: 23529
General Phone: (757) 683-3452
Advertising Phone: (757) 683-4773
General/National Adv. Email: editorinchief@maceandcrown.com
Display Adv. Email: advertising@maceandcrown.com
Editorial Email: editorinchief@maceandcrown.com
Website: www.maceandcrown.com
Year Established: 1930
Delivery Methods: Newsstand
Published: Wed
Personnel: Adam Flores (Editor-in-Chief); Kavita Butani (Advertising & Business Manager)

NORMAL

ALABAMA A&M UNIV.

Street Address 1: 4900 Meridian St NW
State: AL
Zip/Postal code: 35762-7500
Country: USA
Mailing Address: 4900 Meridian St.
Mailing City: Normal
Mailing State: AL
Mailing ZIP Code: 35762
General Phone: (256) 372-5385
General Fax: (256) 372-8795
Personnel: Diane Anderson (Advisor)

ILLINOIS STATE UNIVERSITY

Street Address 1: Illinois State University
Street Address 2: Campus Box 0890
State: IL
Zip/Postal code: 61761
Country: USA
Mailing Address: 100 North University Street
Mailing City: Normal
Mailing State: IL
Mailing ZIP Code: 61761
General Phone: (309) 438-7685
General Fax: (309) 438-5211
Advertising Phone: (309) 438-8742
Editorial Phone: (309) 438-8745
General/National Adv. Email: vidette@ilstu.edu
Display Adv. Email: vidette@ilstu.edu
Editorial Email: vidette@ilstu.edu
Website: www.videtteonline.com
Year Established: 1888
Delivery Methods: Racks
Personnel: John Plevka (Gen. Mgr.); Brooke Goodwin (Bus. Mgr.); Amy Gorczowski (Ed.); Kristi Demonbreun (Ed.)

NORMAN

UNIV. OF OKLAHOMA

Street Address 1: 860 Van Vleet
Street Address 2: Rm 149A
State: OK
Zip/Postal code: 73019-2035
Country: USA
Mailing Address: 860 Van Vleet Rm 149A
Mailing City: Norman
Mailing State: OK
Mailing ZIP Code: 73019-2035
General Phone: (405) 325-2521
General Fax: (405) 325-5160
Advertising Fax: (405) 325-7517
General/National Adv. Email: dailynews@ou.edu; studentmedia@ou.edu
Website: www.oudaily.com; www.ou.edu
Personnel: Judy Robinson (Advisor); Jamie Hughes (Ed.); Caitlin Harrison (Mng. Ed.); Michelle Gray (Photo Ed.)

NORTH ADAMS

MASSACHUSETTS COLLEGE OF LIBERAL ARTS

Street Address 1: 375 Church St
Street Address 2: Rm 111
State: MA
Zip/Postal code: 01247-4124
Country: USA
Mailing Address: 375 Church St Rm 111
Mailing City: North Adams
Mailing State: MA
Mailing ZIP Code: 01247-4124
General Phone: (413) 662-5535
General Fax: (413) 662-5010
Editorial Phone: (413) 662-5404
General/National Adv. Email: beacon@mcla.edu
Website: www.mclabeacon.com
Published: Wed
Avg Free Circ: 1000
Personnel: Jennifer Augur (Advisor)

NORTH ANDOVER

MERRIMACK COLLEGE

Street Address 1: 315 Turnpike St
State: MA
Zip/Postal code: 01845-5806
Country: USA
Mailing Address: 315 Turnpike St
Mailing City: North Andover
Mailing State: MA
Mailing ZIP Code: 01845-5800
General Phone: (978) 837-5000
General Fax: (978) 837-5004
Website: www.merrimack.edu
Personnel: Russ Mayer (Advisor); Michael Salvucci (Ed. in Chief)

NORTH CANTON

STARK STATE COLLEGE OF TECHNOLOGY

Street Address 1: 6200 Frank Ave NW
State: OH
Zip/Postal code: 44720-7228
Country: USA
Mailing Address: 6200 Frank Ave NW
Mailing City: North Canton
Mailing State: OH
Mailing ZIP Code: 44720-7299
General Phone: (330) 494-6170
General Fax: (330) 497-6313
General/National Adv. Email: studentinformer@starkstate.edu
Website: www.starkstate.edu/studentinformer

NORTH DARTMOUTH

UNIV. OF MASSACHUSETTS

Street Address 1: 285 Old Westport Rd, Campus Ctr, 2nd Fl
State: MA
Zip/Postal code: 2747
Country: USA
Mailing Address: 285 Old Westport Rd., Campus Ctr., 2nd Fl.
Mailing City: North Dartmouth
Mailing State: MA
Mailing ZIP Code: 02747-2300
General Phone: (508) 999-8158
General Fax: (508) 999-8128
General/National Adv. Email: torch@umassd.edu
Display Adv. Email: TorchAds@umassd.edu
Website: www.umasstorch.com
Personnel: Jason Jones (Adv. Mgr.); Chris Donovan (Ed. in Chief); Megan Gauthier (Mng. Ed.)

NORTH EASTON

STONEHILL COLLEGE

Street Address 1: 320 Washington St
Street Address 2: # 1974
State: MA
Zip/Postal code: 02357-7800
Country: USA
Mailing Address: 320 Washington St # 1974
Mailing City: North Easton
Mailing State: MA
Mailing ZIP Code: 02357-0001
General Phone: (508) 565-1000
General Fax: (508) 565-1794
Personnel: Matt Gorman (News Ed.)

NORTH LAS VEGAS

CMTY. COLLEGE OF SOUTHERN NEVADA

Street Address 1: 3200 E Cheyenne Ave
Street Address 2: # J2A
State: NV
Zip/Postal code: 89030-4228
Country: USA
Mailing Address: 3200 E Cheyenne Ave # J2A
Mailing City: North Las Vegas
Mailing State: NV
Mailing ZIP Code: 89030-4228
General Phone: (702) 651-4339
General Fax: (702) 643-6427
General/National Adv. Email: coyotepressonline@yahoo.com
Personnel: Arnold Vell (Advisor)

NORTH MANCHESTER

MANCHESTER COLLEGE

Street Address 1: 604 E College Ave
Street Address 2: # 11
State: IN
Zip/Postal code: 46962-1276
Country: USA
Mailing Address: 604 E College Ave # 11
Mailing City: North Manchester
Mailing State: IN
Mailing ZIP Code: 46962-1232
General Phone: (260) 982-5317
General Fax: (260) 982-5043
Website: www.manchester.edu/OSD/OakLeaves/index.htm
Personnel: Katherine Ings (Advisor); Adam King (Ed. in Chief); Cyndel Taylor (Ed. in Chief)

NORTH NEWTON

BETHEL COLLEGE

Street Address 1: 300 E 27th St
State: KS
Zip/Postal code: 67117-8061
Country: USA
Mailing Address: 300 E 27th St
Mailing City: North Newton
Mailing State: KS
Mailing ZIP Code: 67117-1716
General Phone: (316) 284-5271

General Fax: (316) 284-5286
General/National Adv. Email: collegian@bethelks.edu
Display Adv. Email: collegian@bethelks.edu
Editorial Email: collegian@bethelks.edu
Website: www.bethelks.edu/collegian
Personnel: Christine Crouse-Dick (Advisor)

NORTHAMPTON

SMITH COLLEGE

Street Address 1: Capen Annex
State: MA
Zip/Postal code: 01063-0001
Country: USA
Mailing Address: Capen Anx
Mailing City: Northampton
Mailing State: MA
Mailing ZIP Code: 01063-0001
General Phone: (413) 585-4971
General Fax: (413) 585-2075
General/National Adv. Email: sophian@smith.edu
Website: www.smithsophian.com
Year Established: 1911
Published: Thur
Personnel: Hira Humayun (EIC)

NORTHFIELD

CARLETON COLLEGE

Street Address 1: 1 N College St
State: MN
Zip/Postal code: 55057-4001
Country: USA
Mailing Address: 1 N College St
Mailing City: Northfield
Mailing State: MN
Mailing ZIP Code: 55057-4044
General Fax: (507) 222-4000
General/National Adv. Email: carletonian@carleton.edu
Website: www.carleton.edu/carletonian
Personnel: James McMenimen (Adv. Mgr); Vivyan Tran (Ed. in Chief); Emily Howell (Ed. in Chief)

NORWICH UNIV.

Street Address 1: Communications Ctr
State: VT
Zip/Postal code: 5663
Country: USA
Mailing Address: 158 Harmon Dr
Mailing City: Northfield
Mailing State: VT
Mailing ZIP Code: 05663-1097
General Phone: (802) 485-2763
General Fax: (802) 485-2580
General/National Adv. Email: syoungwo@norwich.edu
Delivery Methods: Racks
Commercial printers?: N
Personnel: Susan Youngwood (Advisor)

ST. OLAF COLLEGE

Street Address 1: 1520 Saint Olaf Ave
State: MN
Zip/Postal code: 55057-1574
Country: USA
Mailing Address: 1520 Saint Olaf Ave
Mailing City: Northfield
Mailing State: MN
Mailing ZIP Code: 55057-1099
General Phone: (507) 786-3275
General Fax: (507) 786-3650
General/National Adv. Email: manitoumessenger@stolaf.edu.com
Display Adv. Email: mess-advertise@stolaf.edu
Editorial Email: mess-exec@stolaf.edu
Website: www.manitoumessenger.com
Personnel: Bridget Dinter (Adv. Mgr.)

NORTHRIDGE

CALIFORNIA STATE UNIVERSITY,

NORTHRIDGE

Street Address 1: 18111 Nordhoff St
State: CA
Zip/Postal code: 91330-0001
Country: USA
Mailing Address: 18111 Nordhoff St
Mailing City: Northridge
Mailing State: CA
Mailing ZIP Code: 91330-8200
General Phone: (818) 677-3135
General Fax: (818) 677-3438
Advertising Phone: 818-677-2998
Editorial Phone: (818) 677-2915
Display Adv. Email: ads@sundial.csun.edu
Editorial Email: editor@csun.edu
Website: www.csun.edu
Year Established: 1957
Delivery Methods: Racks
Published: Mon`Tues`Wed`Thur
Avg Free Circ: 6000
Personnel: Kent Kirkton (Chair/Prof.); Melissa Lalum (Pub.); Susan Henry (Prof.); Jody Holcomb (Gen. Mgr.); Maureen Rubin (Prof.); Rick Marks (Assoc. Prof.); Loren Townsley (Editor); Jose Luis Benavides (Asst. Prof.); David Blumenkrantz (Asst. Prof.); Linda Bowen (Asst. Prof.); Jim Hill (Asst. Prof.); Melissa Wall (Asst. Prof.); Lori Baker-Schena (Lectr.); Jerry Jacobs (Prof. Emer.); DeWayne Johnson (Prof. Emer.); Lawrence Schneider (Prof. Emer.); Joe Giampietro (Part-time Fac.); Henrietta Charles (Part-time Fac.); Jeffrey Duclos (Part-time Fac.); Barbara Eisenstock (Part-time Fac.); Mariel Garza (Part-time Fac.); Keith Goldstein (Part-time Fac.); Lincoln Harrison (Part-time Fac.)

NORWALK

CERRITOS COLLEGE

Street Address 1: 11110 Alondra Blvd
State: CA
Zip/Postal code: 90650-6203
Country: USA
Mailing Address: 11110 Alondra Blvd
Mailing City: Norwalk
Mailing State: CA
Mailing ZIP Code: 90650-6298
General Phone: (562) 860-2451
General Fax: (562) 467-5044
General/National Adv. Email: editor@talonmarks.com
Website: www.talonmarks.com
Personnel: Rich Cameron (Advisor); Elieth Koulzons (Ed. in Chief); Rick Gomez (Online Ed.); Joey Berumen (News Ed.); Joey (News Ed.); Megan (Arts Ed.)

NOTRE DAME

UNIV. OF NOTRE DAME

Street Address 1: 024 S Dining Hall
State: IN
Zip/Postal code: 46556
Country: USA
Mailing Address: PO Box 779
Mailing City: Notre Dame
Mailing State: IN
Mailing ZIP Code: 46556-0779
General Phone: (574) 631-7471
General Fax: (574) 631-6927
Advertising Phone: (574) 631-6900
General/National Adv. Email: observad@nd.edu
Website: www.ndsmcobserver.com
Personnel: Theresa Bea (Adv. Mgr.); Mary Claire Rodriguez (Adv. Mgr.); Jenn Metz (Ed. in Chief); Bill Brink (Mng. Ed.)

UNIV. OF NOTRE DAME
ENGINEERING SCHOOL

Street Address 1: 257 Cushing Hall
State: IN
Zip/Postal code: 46556
Country: USA
Mailing Address: 257 Cushing Hall
Mailing City: Notre Dame
Mailing State: IN
Mailing ZIP Code: 46556
General Phone: (574) 631-5530
General Fax: (574) 631-8007
General/National Adv. Email: techrev@nd.edu
Website: www.nd.edu
Personnel: Cathy Pieronek (Asst. Dean); Brandon Chynowegh (Ed.)

NYACK

NYACK COLLEGE

Street Address 1: 1 S Boulevard
State: NY
Zip/Postal code: 10960-3604
Country: USA
Mailing Address: 1 S Boulevard
Mailing City: Nyack
Mailing State: NY
Mailing ZIP Code: 10960-3698
General Phone: (845) 358-1710
General/National Adv. Email: wnyk@nyack.edu; forum@nyack.edu
Website: www.nyack.edu
Personnel: Charles Beach (Advisor)

OAKDALE

DOWLING COLLEGE

Street Address 1: 150 Idle Hour Blvd
State: NY
Zip/Postal code: 11769-1906
Country: USA
Mailing Address: 150 Idle Hour Blvd
Mailing City: Oakdale
Mailing State: NY
Mailing ZIP Code: 11769-1999
General Phone: (631) 244-3000
General Fax: (631) 244-3028
Website: lionsvoice.dowling.edu
Personnel: Laura Pope Robbins (Advisor); Derek Stevens (Ed.)

OAKLAND

LANEY COLLEGE

Street Address 1: 900 Fallon St
State: CA
Zip/Postal code: 94607-4808
Country: USA
Mailing Address: 900 Fallon St # 160
Mailing City: Oakland
Mailing State: CA
Mailing ZIP Code: 94607-4893
General Phone: (510) 464-3460
General Fax: (510) 834-3452
General/National Adv. Email: laneytower@peralta.edu
Website: www.laneytower.com
Published: Thur
Published Other: Every other week
Personnel: Burt Dragin (Advisor); Scott Strain (Sports Ed.); Felix Solomon (Technical Ed.)

MILLS COLLEGE

Street Address 1: 157 Rothwell Ctr, 5000 MacArthur Blvd
State: CA
Zip/Postal code: 94613
Country: USA
Mailing Address: 157 Rothwell Ctr., 5000 MacArthur Blvd.
Mailing City: Oakland
Mailing State: CA
Mailing ZIP Code: 94613
General Phone: (510) 430-2246
General Fax: (510) 430-3176
General/National Adv. Email: eic@thecampanil.com
Display Adv. Email: ads@thecampanil.com
Website: www.thecampanil.com
Personnel: Sarah Pollock (Advisor); Jennifer Courtney (Ed. in Chief); Rashida Harmon (Mng. Ed.); Morgan Ross (News Ed.); Nicole (Opinion Ed.); Anna Belle (Features Ed.)

OAKWOOD

GAINESVILLE COLLEGE

Street Address 1: 3820 Mundy Mill Rd
State: GA
Zip/Postal code: 30566-3414
Country: USA
Mailing Address: PO Box 1358
Mailing City: Gainesville
Mailing State: GA
Mailing ZIP Code: 30503-1358
General Phone: (678) 717-3820
General Fax: (678) 717-3832
General/National Adv. Email: compass@gsc.edu
Display Adv. Email: compass@gsc.edu
Editorial Email: compass@gsc.edu
Website: www.gsccompass.org
Published: Mthly
Avg Free Circ: 1000
Personnel: Merrill Morris (Advisor); Audrey Williams (Editor in Chief); Brent VanFleet (Associate Editor)

OBERLIN

OBERLIN COLLEGE

Street Address 1: 135 W Lorain St
Street Address 2: # 90
State: OH
Zip/Postal code: 44074-1053
Country: USA
Mailing Address: 135 W Lorain St # 90
Mailing City: Oberlin
Mailing State: OH
Mailing ZIP Code: 44074-1053
General Phone: (440) 775-8123
General Fax: (440) 775-6733
General/National Adv. Email: advertisements@oberlinreview.org
Website: www.oberlin.edu
Personnel: Daniel Dudley (Bus. Mgr.); Talia Chicherio (Adv. Mgr.); Caitlin Duke (Ed. in Chief); Piper Niehaus (Ed. in Chief)

OCALA

CENTRAL FLORIDA CMTY. COLLEGE

Street Address 1: 3001 SW College Rd
State: FL
Zip/Postal code: 34474-4415
Country: USA
Mailing Address: 3001 SW College Rd.
Mailing City: Ocala
Mailing State: FL
Mailing ZIP Code: 34474
General Phone: (352) 873-5800
General Fax: (352) 291-4450
General/National Adv. Email: patpress@cf.edu
Website: patpress.cf.edu; www.cfcc.cc.fl.us
Personnel: Rob Marino (Advisor)

OCEANSIDE

MIRACOSTA COLLEGE

Street Address 1: 1 Barnard Dr
Street Address 2: Rm 3441
State: CA
Zip/Postal code: 92056-3820
Country: USA
Mailing Address: 1 Barnard Dr Rm 3441
Mailing City: Oceanside
Mailing State: CA
Mailing ZIP Code: 92056-3820
General Phone: (760) 757-2121
General Fax: (760) 757-8209
General/National Adv. Email: www.mccechariot.com
Personnel: Meghan Sills (Staff Writer)

ODESSA

UNIV. OF TEXAS PERMIAN BASIN

Street Address 1: 4901 E University Blvd
Street Address 2: Rm MB
State: TX

College and University Newspapers

Zip/Postal code: 79762-8122
Country: USA
Mailing Address: 4901 E University Blvd Rm MB2215A
Mailing City: Odessa
Mailing State: TX
Mailing ZIP Code: 79762-8122
General Phone: (432) 552-2659
General Fax: (432) 552-3654
General/National Adv. Email: mesajournal@utpb.edu
Website: mesajournalnews.com
Year Established: 1975
Published: Mon`Tues`Wed`Thur`Sat
Avg Free Circ: 6000
Personnel: myra Salcedo (Advisor)

OGDEN

WEBER STATE UNIVERSITY

Street Address 1: 3910 W Campus Dr
Street Address 2: Dept 2110
State: UT
Zip/Postal code: 84408-2110
Country: USA
Mailing Address: 3910 West Campus Drive Dept 2110
Mailing City: Ogden
Mailing State: UT
Mailing ZIP Code: 84408-2110
General Phone: (801) 626-7526
General Fax: (801) 626-7401
Advertising Phone: (801) 626-6359
Advertising Fax: (801) 626-7401
Editorial Phone: (801) 626-7121
Editorial Fax: (801) 626-7401
General/National Adv. Email: thesignpost@weber.edu
Display Adv. Email: Kcsanders@weber.edu
Editorial Email: Kcsanders@weber.edu
Website: MyWeberMedia.com
Year Established: 1937
Published: Mon`Thur
Published Other: 8 issues (once a week) during the summer semester
Avg Free Circ: 2000
Personnel: KC Sanders (Advt Mgr); Georgia Edwards (Office Mgr); Jean Norman (Signpost Adviser)
Parent company (for newspapers): Weber State University

OKLAHOMA CITY

OKLAHOMA CHRISTIAN UNIV.

Street Address 1: PO Box 11000
State: OK
Zip/Postal code: 73136-1100
Country: USA
Mailing Address: PO Box 11000
Mailing City: Oklahoma City
Mailing State: OK
Mailing ZIP Code: 73136-1100
General Phone: (405) 425-5538
General Fax: (405) 425-5351
Editorial Email: talon.letter@oc.edu
Personnel: Philip Patterson (Faculty Advisor); Kimberlee Rhodes (Adv. Mgr.); Will Kooi (Ed. in Chief)

OKLAHOMA CITY COMMUNITY COLLEGE

Street Address 1: 7777 S May Ave
State: OK
Zip/Postal code: 73159-4419
Country: USA
Mailing Address: 7777 S May Ave
Mailing City: Oklahoma City
Mailing State: OK
Mailing ZIP Code: 73159-4499
General Phone: (405) 682-1611
General/National Adv. Email: editor@occc.edu
Display Adv. Email: matthew.s.carter@occc.edu
Editorial Email: editor@occc.edu
Website: pioineer.occc.edu
Year Established: 1978
Published: Fri
Avg Free Circ: 2500
Personnel: M Scott Carter (Advisor)
Parent company (for newspapers): Oklahoma City Community College

OKLAHOMA CITY UNIVERSITY

Street Address 1: 2501 N Blackwelder Ave
State: OK
Zip/Postal code: 73106-1402
Country: USA
Mailing Address: 2501 N Blackwelder Ave Rm 117
Mailing City: Oklahoma City
Mailing State: OK
Mailing ZIP Code: 73106-1493
General Phone: (405) 208-6068
General Fax: (405) 208-6069
Advertising Phone: (405) 208-6068
Advertising Fax: (405) 208-6069
General/National Adv. Email: stupub@okcu.edu
Website: www.mediaocu.com
Year Established: 1907
Delivery Methods: Newsstand
Commercial printers?: Y
Personnel: Kenna Griffin (Advisor)

OLATHE

MIDAMERICA NAZARENE UNIVERSITY

Street Address 1: 2030 E College Way
State: KS
Zip/Postal code: 66062-1851
Country: USA
Mailing Address: 2030 E. College Way
Mailing City: Olathe
Mailing State: KS
Mailing ZIP Code: 66062
General Phone: (913) 971-3289
General Fax: (913) 971-3421
Advertising Phone: (913) 961-8615
Editorial Phone: (913) 530-0854
Display Adv. Email: ehodgson@mnu.edu
Editorial Email: tb-edit@mnu.edu
Website: www.trailblazer.mnubox.com
Year Established: 1967
Personnel: Sarah Glass (Editor-in-Chief); Molly Farnsworth (Managing Editor); Christina Wilkins (Section Editor); Melinda Smith (Faculty Advisor)

OLD WESTBURY

NEW YORK INSTITUTE OF TECHNOLOGY

Street Address 1: PO Box 8000
State: NY
Zip/Postal code: 11568-8000
Country: USA
Mailing Address: Northern Boulevard PO Box 8000
Mailing City: Old Westbury
Mailing State: NY
Mailing ZIP Code: 11568
General Phone: (516) 686-7646
General Fax: (516) 626-1290
Editorial Phone: 516-589-1615
General/National Adv. Email: slate@nyit.edu
Display Adv. Email: slate@nyit.edu
Website: www.campusslate.com
Year Established: 1966
Personnel: John Hanc (Advisor); John Santamaria (Editor in Chief); Kyle Reitan (Managing Editor)

SUNY COLLEGE/OLD WESTBURY

Street Address 1: 223 Store Hill Rd
State: NY
Zip/Postal code: 11568-1717
Country: USA
Mailing Address: PO Box 210
Mailing City: Old Westbury
Mailing State: NY
Mailing ZIP Code: 11568-0210
General Phone: (516) 876-3000
General/National Adv. Email: owcatalyst@gmail.com
Personnel: Alicia Grant (Exec.Ed.)

OLIVET

OLIVET COLLEGE

Street Address 1: 320 S Main St
State: MI
Zip/Postal code: 49076-9406
Country: USA
Mailing Address: 320 S. Main St.
Mailing City: Olivet
Mailing State: MI
Mailing ZIP Code: 49076-9456
General Phone: (269) 749-7622
General/National Adv. Email: echo@olivetcollege.edu
Display Adv. Email: echo@olivetcollege.edu
Editorial Email: echo@olivetcollege.edu
Website: www.ocecho.com
Year Established: 1888
Delivery Methods: Newsstand
Published: Fri`Bi-Mthly
Published Other: Every other Friday during academic year
Avg Free Circ: 1100
Personnel: Joanne Williams (Advisor); Brian Freiberger (Editor)

OLYMPIA

THE EVERGREEN STATE COLLEGE

Street Address 1: 2700 Evergreen Pkwy
Street Address 2: Cab 316
State: WA
Zip/Postal code: 98505-0001
Country: USA
Mailing Address: 2700 Evergreen Pkwy Cab 316
Mailing City: Olympia
Mailing State: WA
Mailing ZIP Code: 98505-0005
General Phone: (360) 867-6213
General Fax: (360) 867-6685
General/National Adv. Email: cpj@evergreen.edu
Website: cpj.evergreen.edu
Personnel: Dianne Conrad (Advisor); Madeline Berman (Mng. Ed.); Jason Slotkin (Ed. in Chief)

OMAHA

CREIGHTON UNIV.

Street Address 1: 2500 California Plz
State: NE
Zip/Postal code: 68178-0133
Country: USA
Mailing Address: 2500 California Plz
Mailing City: Omaha
Mailing State: NE
Mailing ZIP Code: 68178-0002
General Phone: (402) 280-4058
General Fax: (402) 280-1494
General/National Adv. Email: emw@creighton.edu
Website: www.creightonian.com
Personnel: Melissa Hillebrand (Ed.); Eileen M. Wirth (Chair/Prof.); Father Don Doll (Prof./Charles and Mary Heider Endowed Jesuit Chair); Kelly Fitzgerald (Asst. Ed.); Timothy S. Guthrie (Assoc. Prof.); Jeffrey Maciejewski (Assoc. Prof.); Carol Zuegner (Assoc. Prof.); Kristoffer Boyle (Asst. Prof.); Joel Davies (Asst. Prof.); Charles Heider (Asst. Prof.); Mary Heider (Asst. Prof.); Andrew Hughes (Lectr.); Kathleen Hughes (Lectr.); Richard Janda (Lectr.); Kathryn Larson (Lectr.); Brian Norton (Lectr.); Wendy Wiseman (Lectr.); Angela Zegers (Lectr.)

OMAHA

UNIV. OF NEBRASKA AT OMAHA

Street Address 1: 6001 Dodge St
Street Address 2: Unit 116
State: NE
Zip/Postal code: 68182-1107
Country: USA
Mailing Address: 6001 Dodge St Unit 116
Mailing City: Omaha
Mailing State: NE
Mailing ZIP Code: 68182-1107
General Phone: (402) 554-2470
General Fax: (402) 554-2735
Advertising Phone: (402) 554-2494
Editorial Phone: (402) 554-2352
Editorial Email: jloza@unomaha.edu
Website: www.unogateway.com
Year Established: 1913
Published: Tues
Avg Free Circ: 2500
Personnel: Josie Loza (Advisor); Cody Willmer; Kate O'Dell

ONEONTA

HARTWICK COLLEGE

Street Address 1: PO Box 250
State: NY
Zip/Postal code: 13820-0250
Country: USA
Mailing Address: c/o Daily Star, PO Box 250
Mailing City: Oneonta
Mailing State: NY
Mailing ZIP Code: 13820
General Phone: (607) 432-1000
General Fax: (607) 432-5847
General/National Adv. Email: breeves@thedailystar.com; hilltops@hartwick.edu
Personnel: Bill Reeves (Advisor); Danielle Peloquin (Ed.)

ONEONTA

SUNY COLLEGE/ONEONTA

Street Address 1: Ravine Pkwy
State: NY
Zip/Postal code: 13820
Country: USA
Mailing Address: Ravine Pkwy.
Mailing City: Oneonta
Mailing State: NY
Mailing ZIP Code: 13820
General Phone: (607) 436-2492
General Fax: (607) 436-2002
Personnel: Janet Day (Advisor); Juliette Price (Mng. Ed.)

OPA LOCKA

ST. THOMAS UNIV.

Street Address 1: 16401 NW 37th Ave
State: FL
Zip/Postal code: 33054-6313
Country: USA
Mailing Address: 16401 NW 37th Ave
Mailing City: Opa Locka
Mailing State: FL
Mailing ZIP Code: 33054-6313
General Phone: (305) 628-6674
General Fax: (305) 443-1210
General/National Adv. Email: basic@stu.edu
Website: www.stu.edu
Personnel: Sharon Brehm (Ed.)

ORANGE

CHAPMAN UNIV.

Street Address 1: 1 University Dr
State: CA
Zip/Postal code: 92866-1005
Country: USA
Mailing Address: 1 University Dr
Mailing City: Orange
Mailing State: CA
Mailing ZIP Code: 92866-1005
General Phone: (714) 997-6870
General Fax: (714) 744-7898
General/National Adv. Email: panthernewspaper@gmail.com
Website: www.thepantheronline.com; www.chapman.edu/panthernewspaper

Personnel: Amber Gonzales (Ed. in Chief); Martin Syjuco (Mng. Ed.); Michelle Thomas (Opinions Ed.); Jillian Freitas (News Ed.); Jennifer (Business Mgr.); Kim (Dir., Art)

ORANGE CITY

NORTHWESTERN COLLEGE

Street Address 1: 101 7th St SW
State: IA
Zip/Postal code: 51041-1923
Country: USA
Mailing Address: 101 7th St SW
Mailing City: Orange City
Mailing State: IA
Mailing ZIP Code: 51041-1996
General Phone: (712) 707-7043
General Fax: (712) 707-7345
General/National Adv. Email: beacon@nwciowa.edu
Website: beacon.nwciowa.edu
Personnel: Carl Vandermeulen (Advisor); Kim Eason (Ed.)

ORANGEBURG

CLAFLIN UNIVERSITY

Street Address 1: 400 Magnolia St
State: SC
Zip/Postal code: 29115-6815
Country: USA
Mailing Address: 400 Magnolia Street
Mailing City: Orangeburg
Mailing State: SC
Mailing ZIP Code: 29115
Website: claflin.edu/the-panther
Published: Other
Published Other: print once per semester
Personnel: Lee Harter (Advisor)

SOUTH CAROLINA STATE UNIV.

Street Address 1: 300 College St NE
State: SC
Zip/Postal code: 29117-0002
Country: USA
Mailing Address: 300 College St NE
Mailing City: Orangeburg
Mailing State: SC
Mailing ZIP Code: 29117-0002
General Phone: (803) 536-7237
General Fax: (803) 536-7131
Website: www.thescsucollegian.com/
Personnel: Rolondo Davis (Advisor)

OREGON CITY

CLACKAMAS CMTY. COLLEGE

Street Address 1: 19600 Molalla Ave
State: OR
Zip/Postal code: 97045-8980
Country: USA
Mailing Address: 19600 Molalla Ave
Mailing City: Oregon City
Mailing State: OR
Mailing ZIP Code: 97045-7998
General Phone: (503) 657-6958
General Fax: (503) 650-7350
General/National Adv. Email: chiefed@clackamus.edu
Personnel: Melissa Jones (Advisor); Kayla Berge (Ed.); John Hurlburg (Ed.)

OREM

UTAH VALLEY UNIVERSITY

Street Address 1: 800 W University Pkwy
State: UT
Zip/Postal code: 84058-6703
Country: USA
Mailing Address: 800 W University Pkwy # Mt
Mailing City: Orem
Mailing State: UT
Mailing ZIP Code: 84058-6703
General Phone: (801) 863-8688

General Fax: (801) 863-8601
Display Adv. Email: robbina@uvu.edu
Website: www.uvureview.com
Delivery Methods: Newsstand
Published: Mon
Personnel: Robbin Anthony (Bus. Mgr.); Brent Sumner (Advisor)

ORLANDO

UNIV. OF CENTRAL FLORIDA

Street Address 1: 11825 High Tech Ave
Street Address 2: Ste 100
State: FL
Zip/Postal code: 32817-8474
Country: USA
Mailing Address: 11825 High Tech Ave. Ste. 100
Mailing City: Orlando
Mailing State: FL
Mailing ZIP Code: 32817
General Phone: (407) 447-4555
General Fax: (407) 447-4556
General/National Adv. Email: sales@ucfnews.com
Website: www.centralfloridafuture.com
Year Established: 1968
Personnel: Heissam Jebailey (Pub.); Brian Linden (Gen. Mgr.); Trisha Irwin (Office. Mgr.); Ray Bush (Adv. Mgr.)

VALENCIA CMTY. COLLEGE

Street Address 1: 1800 S Kirkman Rd
State: FL
Zip/Postal code: 32811-2302
Country: USA
Mailing Address: 1800 S Kirkman Rd
Mailing City: Orlando
Mailing State: FL
Mailing ZIP Code: 32811-2302
General Phone: (407) 582-1572
Personnel: Ken Carpenter (Advisor)

ORONO

UNIVERSITY OF MAINE

Street Address 1: Memorial Union, University of Maine Rm 131
Street Address 2: rm. 131
State: ME
Zip/Postal code: 04469-0001
Country: USA
Mailing Address: Memorial Union, University of Maine
Mailing City: Orono
Mailing State: ME
Mailing ZIP Code: 04469-5748
General Phone: (207) 581-1273
General/National Adv. Email: info@mainecampus.com
Display Adv. Email: ads@mainecampus.com
Editorial Email: eic@mainecampus.com
Website: www.mainecampus.com
Year Established: 1875
Published: Mon
Avg Free Circ: 1500
Personnel: Jordan Houdeshell (Ed. in Chief); Elliott Simpson (Bus. Mgr.)

OSHKOSH

UNIV. OF WISCONSIN OSHKOSH

Street Address 1: 800 Algoma Blvd
State: WI
Zip/Postal code: 54901-3551
Country: USA
Mailing Address: 800 Algoma Blvd
Mailing City: Oshkosh
Mailing State: WI
Mailing ZIP Code: 54901-8651
General Phone: (920) 424-3048
General Fax: (920) 424-0866
Website: www.advancetitan.com
Published: Thur
Personnel: Vince Filak (Advisor)

OSKALOOSA

WILLIAM PENN UNIV.

Street Address 1: 201 Trueblood Ave
State: IA
Zip/Postal code: 52577-1757
Country: USA
Mailing Address: 201 Trueblood Ave.
Mailing City: Oskaloosa
Mailing State: IA
Mailing ZIP Code: 52577
General Phone: (641) 673-2170
Display Adv. Email: chronicle@wmpenn.edu
Published: Mthly

OSWEGO

SUNY COLLEGE/OSWEGO

Street Address 1: 135 A Campus Ctr
State: NY
Zip/Postal code: 13126
Country: USA
Mailing Address: 139A Campus Ctr.
Mailing City: Oswego
Mailing State: NY
Mailing ZIP Code: 13126
General Phone: (315) 312-3600
General Fax: (315) 312-3542
General/National Adv. Email: gonian@oswego.edu; info@oswegonian.com
Display Adv. Email: advertising@oswegonian.com
Website: www.oswegonian.com
Year Established: 1935
Commercial printers?: N
Personnel: Arvin Diddi (Faculty Adviser); Adam Wolfe (Editor-in-Chief)

OVERLAND PARK

JOHNSON COUNTY CMTY. COLLEGE

Street Address 1: 12345 College Blvd
Street Address 2: # 7
State: KS
Zip/Postal code: 66210-1283
Country: USA
Mailing Address: 12345 College Blvd # 7
Mailing City: Overland Park
Mailing State: KS
Mailing ZIP Code: 66210-1283
General Phone: (913) 469-8500
General Fax: (913) 469-2577
Website: www.campusledger.com
Personnel: Anne Christiansen-Bullers (Advisor); Matt Galloway (Ed. in Chief)

OWENSBORO

KENTUCKY WESLEYAN COLLEGE

Street Address 1: 3000 Frederica St
State: KY
Zip/Postal code: 42301-6057
Country: USA
Mailing Address: 3000 Frederica St
Mailing City: Owensboro
Mailing State: KY
Mailing ZIP Code: 42301-6055
General Phone: (270) 852-3596
General Fax: (270) 852-3597
General/National Adv. Email: panogram@kwc.edu
Published: Bi-Mthly
Personnel: Randall Vogt (Advisor); Devyn Lott (General Editor)

OXFORD

THE UNIVERSITY OF MISSISSIPPI

Street Address 1: 201 Bishop Hall
State: MS
Zip/Postal code: 38677
Country: USA
Mailing Address: 201 Bishop Hall
Mailing City: Oxford
Mailing State: MS
Mailing ZIP Code: 38677

General Phone: (662) 915-5503
General Fax: (662) 915-5703
General/National Adv. Email: studentmedia@olemiss.edu
Editorial Email: dmeditor@gmail.com
Website: www.thedmonline.com
Year Established: 1911
Published: Mon`Tues`Wed`Thur`Fri
Avg Free Circ: 12000
Personnel: Lacey Russell (Ed.); Patricia Thompson (Dir. of Student Media/Faculty Adviser)

OXNARD

OXNARD COLLEGE

Street Address 1: 4000 S Rose Ave
State: CA
Zip/Postal code: 93033-6699
Country: USA
Mailing Address: 4000 S Rose Ave
Mailing City: Oxnard
Mailing State: CA
Mailing ZIP Code: 93033-6699
General Phone: (805) 986-5836
General Fax: (805) 986-5806

PALATINE

WILLIAM RAINEY HARPER COLLEGE

Street Address 1: 1200 W Algonquin Rd
State: IL
Zip/Postal code: 60067-7373
Country: USA
Mailing Address: 1200 W Algonquin Rd
Mailing City: Palatine
Mailing State: IL
Mailing ZIP Code: 60067-7398
General Phone: (847) 925-6460
General Fax: (847) 925-6033
General/National Adv. Email: harperharbinger@gmail.com
Website: www.harpercollege.edu
Personnel: Kent McDill (Advisor)

PALM DESERT

COLLEGE OF THE DESERT

Street Address 1: 43500 Monterey Ave
State: CA
Zip/Postal code: 92260-9305
Country: USA
Mailing Address: 43500 Monterey Ave
Mailing City: Palm Desert
Mailing State: CA
Mailing ZIP Code: 92260-9399
General Phone: (760) 776-7244
General Fax: (760) 862-1338
General/National Adv. Email: chaparral@collegeofthedesert.edu
Website: www.thechaparral.com
Personnel: Aaron White (Adv. Mgr.); Edward Grofer (Co-Ed.); Sarah Wilson (Co-Ed.)

PALOS HEIGHTS

TRINITY CHRISTIAN COLLEGE

Street Address 1: 6601 W College Dr
State: IL
Zip/Postal code: 60463-1768
Country: USA
Mailing Address: 6601 W College Dr
Mailing City: Palos Heights
Mailing State: IL
Mailing ZIP Code: 60463-0929
General Phone: (708) 239-4715
General Fax: (708) 385-5665
General/National Adv. Email: www.trnty.edu
Personnel: Whitney Dickison (Ed. in Chief)

PALOS HILLS

MORAINE VALLEY CMTY. COLLEGE

Street Address 1: 9000 W College Pkwy

College and University Newspapers

State: IL
Zip/Postal code: 60465-1444
Country: USA
Mailing Address: 9000 W. College Pkwy.
Mailing City: Palos Hills
Mailing State: IL
Mailing ZIP Code: 60465-0937
General Phone: (708) 608-4177
General Fax: (708) 974-0790
General/National Adv. Email: glacier@morainevalley.edu
Website: www.mvccglacier.com
Published Other: Bi-Wkly
Personnel: Stacey Reichard (Advisor); William Lukitsch; Rob Peto (Ed. in Chief); Frank Florez (News Ed.)

PARIS

PARIS JUNIOR COLLEGE

Street Address 1: 2400 Clarksville St
State: TX
Zip/Postal code: 75460-6258
Country: USA
Mailing Address: 2400 Clarksville St
Mailing City: Paris
Mailing State: TX
Mailing ZIP Code: 75460-6298
General Phone: (903) 785-7661
General Fax: (903) 782-0370
Website: www.parisjc.edu
Personnel: Sharon Dennehy (Advisor)

PARKERSBURG

WEST VIRGINIA UNIV. PARKERSBURG

Street Address 1: 300 Campus Dr
State: WV
Zip/Postal code: 26104-8647
Country: USA
Mailing Address: 300 Campus Dr
Mailing City: Parkersburg
Mailing State: WV
Mailing ZIP Code: 26104-8647
General Phone: (304) 424-8247
General Fax: (304) 424-8315
Advertising Phone: (304) 424-8247
Editorial Phone: (304) 424-8247
General/National Adv. Email: chronicle@wvup.edu
Display Adv. Email: chronicle@wvup.edu
Editorial Email: chronicle@wvup.edu
Website: issuu.com/wvuparkersburgchronicle
Year Established: 1969
Published: Thur
Avg Free Circ: 3500
Personnel: Torie Jackson (Advisor)

PARKTON

UNIV. OF MARYLAND BALTIMORE

Street Address 1: PO Box 600
State: MD
Zip/Postal code: 21120-0600
Country: USA
Mailing Address: PO Box 600
Mailing City: Parkton
Mailing State: MD
Mailing ZIP Code: 21120-0600
General Phone: (410) 706-7820
General Fax: (410) 343-3371
Personnel: Susie Flaherty (Sr. Ed.); Clare Banks (Ed.)

PASADENA

CALIFORNIA INST. OF TECHNOLOGY

Street Address 1: Caltech Msc 40-58
State: CA
Country: USA
Mailing Address: Caltech MSC 40-58
Mailing City: Pasadena
Mailing State: CA
Mailing ZIP Code: mpearson@calbaptist.edu
General Phone: (626) 395-6154
Advertising Phone: (626) 577-1294
General/National Adv. Email: business@caltech.edu
Website: tech.caltech.edu
Personnel: Vi Tran (Bus. Mgr.)

FULLER THEOLOGICAL SEMINARY

Street Address 1: 135 N Oakland Ave
State: CA
Zip/Postal code: 91182-0001
Country: USA
Mailing Address: 135 N Oakland Ave
Mailing City: Pasadena
Mailing State: CA
Mailing ZIP Code: 91182-0002
General Phone: (626) 584-5430
General Fax: (626) 304-3730
Personnel: Carmen Valdez (Advisor); Eugene Suen (Adv. Mgr.); Ben Cassil (Ed.)

PASADENA CITY COLLEGE

Street Address 1: 1570 E Colorado Blvd
Street Address 2: Rm T110-A
State: CA
Zip/Postal code: 91106-2003
Country: USA
Mailing Address: 1570 E Colorado Blvd Rm T110-A
Mailing City: Pasadena
Mailing State: CA
Mailing ZIP Code: 91106-2041
General Phone: (626) 585-7130
General Fax: (626) 585-7971
Advertising Phone: (626) 585-7979
General/National Adv. Email: pasadenacourier@yahoo.com
Display Adv. Email: courierads@yahoo.com
Website: www.pcccourier.com
Personnel: Warren Swil (Advisor); John Avery (Adv. Mgr.); Barbara Beaser (Ed. in Chief)

SAN JACINTO COLLEGE

Street Address 1: 8060 Spencer Hwy
State: TX
Zip/Postal code: 77505-5903
Country: USA
Mailing Address: 8060 Spencer Hwy
Mailing City: Pasadena
Mailing State: TX
Mailing ZIP Code: 77505-5998
General Phone: (281) 478-2752
General Fax: (281) 478-2703
General/National Adv. Email: rsaldivar88@yahoo.com
Website: www.sanjacintotimes.com
Personnel: Fred F. Faour (Advisor)

PATCHOGUE

ST. JOSEPHS COLLEGE

Street Address 1: 155 W Roe Blvd
State: NY
Zip/Postal code: 11772-2325
Country: USA
Mailing Address: 155 W Roe Blvd
Mailing City: Patchogue
Mailing State: NY
Mailing ZIP Code: 11772-2399
General Phone: (631) 447-3200
General Fax: (631) 654-1782
General/National Adv. Email: talon.li@student.sjcny.edu
Personnel: Erin Bailey (Ed.)

PEARL CITY

LEEWARD CMTY. COLLEGE

Street Address 1: 96-045 Ala Ike St
Street Address 2: # SC-216
State: HI
Zip/Postal code: 96782-3366
Country: USA
Mailing Address: 96-045 Ala Ike St # SC-216
Mailing City: Pearl City
Mailing State: HI
Mailing ZIP Code: 96782-3366
General Phone: (808) 455-0603
General Fax: (808) 455-0471
Website: emedia.leeward.hawaii.edu/kamanao/
Personnel: Margaret Yasuhara (Ed.)

PELLA

CENTRAL COLLEGE

Street Address 1: 812 University St
State: IA
Zip/Postal code: 50219-1902
Country: USA
Mailing Address: 812 University
Mailing City: Pella
Mailing State: IA
Mailing ZIP Code: 50219
General Phone: (877) 462-3687
General Fax: (515) 628-5316
General/National Adv. Email: theray@central.edu
Editorial Email: carmane@central.edu
Website: www.central.edu
Personnel: Emily Betz (Ed.)

PEMBROKE

UNIV. OF NORTH CAROLINA

Street Address 1: 1 University Rd
State: NC
Zip/Postal code: 28372-8699
Country: USA
Mailing Address: PO Box 1510
Mailing City: Pembroke
Mailing State: NC
Mailing ZIP Code: 28372-1510
General Phone: (910) 521-6204
General Fax: (910) 522-5795
General/National Adv. Email: pineneedle@uncp.edu
Website: www.uncp.edu/pineneedle
Personnel: Judy Curtis (Advisor); Jodie Johnson (Adv. Mgr.); Wade Allen (Ed.)

PENSACOLA

PENSACOLA JUNIOR COLLEGE

Street Address 1: 1000 College Blvd
Street Address 2: Bldg 96
State: FL
Zip/Postal code: 32504-8910
Country: USA
Mailing Address: 1000 College Blvd Bldg 96
Mailing City: Pensacola
Mailing State: FL
Mailing ZIP Code: 32504-8910
General Phone: (850) 484-1458
General Fax: (850) 484-1149
General/National Adv. Email: corsair@pjc.edu
Website: www.ecorsair.com
Year Established: 1949
Personnel: Christina Drain (Advisor); Audrey Davis (Adv. Mgr.); Rose Jansen (Mktg. Mgr.)

UNIV. OF WEST FLORIDA

Street Address 1: 11000 University Pkwy
Street Address 2: Comm Arts 36
State: FL
Zip/Postal code: 32514-5732
Country: USA
Mailing Address: 11000 University Pkwy Comm Arts 36
Mailing City: Pensacola
Mailing State: FL
Mailing ZIP Code: 32514-5732
General Phone: (850) 474-2193
General/National Adv. Email: mdp17@students.uwf.edu

PEORIA

BRADLEY UNIVERSITY

Street Address 1: 1501 W Bradley Ave
State: IL
Zip/Postal code: 61625-0001
Country: USA
Mailing Address: 1501 W Bradley Ave
Mailing City: Peoria
Mailing State: IL
Mailing ZIP Code: 61625-0003
General Phone: (309) 676-7611
General Fax: (309) 677-2609
Advertising Phone: (309) 676-7611
General/National Adv. Email: bradleyscout@gmail.com
Display Adv. Email: bradleyscout@gmail.com
Editorial Email: bradleyscout@gmail.com
Website: www.bradleyscout.com
Year Established: 1898
Commercial printers?: N
Published: Fri
Avg Free Circ: 4000
Personnel: Sam Pallini (Ed.); Kristin Kreher (Managing Ed.); Travis Kelso (Adv. Mgr.)

PERU

PERU STATE COLLEGE

Street Address 1: PO Box 10
State: NE
Zip/Postal code: 68421-0010
Country: USA
Mailing Address: PO Box 10
Mailing City: Peru
Mailing State: NE
Mailing ZIP Code: 68421-0010
General Phone: (402) 872-2260
General Fax: (402) 872-2302
General/National Adv. Email: psctimes@yahoo.com
Personnel: Savannah Wenzel (Adv. Mgr.)

PETERSBURG

VIRGINIA STATE UNIV.

Street Address 1: 402 Foster Hall, Box 9063
State: VA
Zip/Postal code: 23806-0001
Country: USA
Mailing Address: 402 Foster Hall # 9063
Mailing City: Petersburg
Mailing State: VA
Mailing ZIP Code: 23806-0001
General Phone: (804) 524-5991
General Fax: (804) 524-5406
Personnel: Howard Hall (Advisor); Thysha Shabazz (Ed.)

PHILADELPHIA

COMMUNITY COLLEGE OF PHILADELPHIA

Street Address 1: 1700 Spring Garden St
State: PA
Zip/Postal code: 19130-3936
Country: USA
Mailing Address: 1700 Spring Garden St.
Mailing City: Philadelphia
Mailing State: PA
Mailing ZIP Code: 19130-3936
General Phone: (215) 751-8200
General Fax: (215) 972-6201
Website: www.thestudentvanguard.com
Year Established: 1964
Delivery Methods: Newsstand Racks
Commercial printers?: Y
Published: Bi-Mthly
Personnel: Randy LoBasso (Faculty Advisor); Michael Castaneda (Editor-In-Chief); Rachel Byrd (Associate Editor); Imzadi Davis (Managing Editor); Devonte Gillespie (Business Manager)

DREXEL UNIV.

Street Address 1: 3141 Chestnut St
State: PA
Zip/Postal code: 19104-2816
Country: USA
Mailing Address: 3141 Chestnut St
Mailing City: Philadelphia
Mailing State: PA
Mailing ZIP Code: 19104-2875
General Phone: (215) 895-2585
Website: www.thetriangle.org
Year Established: 1926
Commercial printers?: Y
Published: Fri
Personnel: David Stephenson (EIC); Keith Hobin (Mng Ed); Laura DiSanto (Staff Mgr); Alexandra Jones (EIC); Gina Vitale

HOLY FAMILY COLLEGE

Street Address 1: 9801 Frankford Ave
State: PA
Zip/Postal code: 19114-2009
Country: USA
Mailing Address: 9801 Frankford Ave
Mailing City: Philadelphia
Mailing State: PA
Mailing ZIP Code: 19114
General Phone: (215) 637-5321
General Fax: (215) 824-2438
Website: www.tri-liteonline.com
Personnel: Laura Wkovitz (Ed.)

LA SALLE UNIV.

Street Address 1: 1900 W Olney Ave
Street Address 2: # 417
State: PA
Zip/Postal code: 19141-1108
Country: USA
Mailing Address: 1900 W Olney Ave # 417
Mailing City: Philadelphia
Mailing State: PA
Mailing ZIP Code: 19141-1108
General Phone: (215) 951-1000
General Fax: (215) 763-9686
General/National Adv. Email: collegian@lasalle.edu
Website: www.lasalle.edu/collegian
Personnel: Robert O'Brien (Advisor); Olivia Biagi (Mng. Ed.)

PHILADELPHIA NEIGHBORHOODS

Street Address 1: 1515 Market St
Street Address 2: Fl 1
State: PA
Zip/Postal code: 19102-1904
Country: USA
Mailing Address: 1515 Market St First Floor
Mailing City: Philadelphia
Mailing State: PA
Mailing ZIP Code: 19102
General Phone: 315-729-9020
General/National Adv. Email: charper@temple.edu
Website: www.philadelphianeighborhoods.com

ST. JOSEPHS UNIV.

Street Address 1: 5600 City Ave, 314 Campion Ctr
State: PA
Zip/Postal code: 19131
Country: USA
Mailing Address: 5600 City Ave., 314 Campion Ctr.
Mailing City: Philadelphia
Mailing State: PA
Mailing ZIP Code: 19131-1395
General Phone: (610) 660-1079
General Fax: (610) 660-1089
Advertising Phone: (610) 660-1080
General/National Adv. Email: thehawk@sju.edu
Website: www.sjuhawknews.com
Personnel: Dr. Jenny Spinner (Advisor); Karrin Randle (Ed. in Chief); Katy Yavorek (Bus. Mgr.)

TEMPLE UNIVERSITY

Street Address 1: 1755 N 13th St
Street Address 2: 304 Howard Gittis Student Center
State: PA
Zip/Postal code: 19122-6011
Country: USA
Mailing Address: 1755 N 13th St
Mailing City: Philadelphia
Mailing State: PA
Mailing ZIP Code: 19122-6011
General Phone: 215-204-6737
General Fax: 215-204-1663
Advertising Phone: 215-204-9538
Advertising Fax: 215-204-6609
General/National Adv. Email: editor@temple-news.com
Display Adv. Email: advertising@temple-news.com
Website: www.temple-news.com
Year Established: 1921
Published: Tues
Published Other: Daily online
Avg Free Circ: 5000
Personnel: John Di Carlo (Advisor)

UNIV. OF PENNSYLVANIA ENGINEERING SCHOOL

Street Address 1: 220 S 33rd St
State: PA
Zip/Postal code: 19104-6315
Country: USA
Mailing Address: 220 S 33rd St Rm 107
Mailing City: Philadelphia
Mailing State: PA
Mailing ZIP Code: 19104-6315
General Phone: (215) 898-1444
General Fax: (801) 469-4487
General/National Adv. Email: triangle@seas.upenn.edu
Website: www.seas.upenn.edu/~triangle/
Personnel: Mark Smyda (Ed. in Chief); Bezhou Feng (Ed. in Chief)

UNIV. OF PENNSYLVANIA LAW SCHOOL

Street Address 1: 3400 Chestnut St
State: PA
Zip/Postal code: 19104-6253
Country: USA
Mailing Address: 3400 Chestnut St Ste 1
Mailing City: Philadelphia
Mailing State: PA
Mailing ZIP Code: 19104-6204
General Phone: (215) 898-7483
General Fax: (215) 573-2025
Personnel: Doug Rennie (Ed.)

UNIV. OF THE SCIENCES IN PHILADELPHIA

Street Address 1: 600 S 43rd St
State: PA
Zip/Postal code: 19104-4418
Country: USA
Mailing Address: 600 S 43rd St
Mailing City: Philadelphia
Mailing State: PA
Mailing ZIP Code: 19104-4495
General Phone: (215) 596-8800
Website: www.usp.edu
Personnel: Miriam Gilbert (Advisor); Leeann Tan (Co. Ed.); Meghan Baker (Co. Ed.)

UNIVERSITY OF PENNSYLVANIA

Street Address 1: 4015 Walnut St
State: PA
Zip/Postal code: 19104-3513
Country: USA
Mailing Address: 4015 Walnut St. 2nd Fl
Mailing City: Philadelphia
Mailing State: PA
Mailing ZIP Code: 19104-6198
General Phone: (215) 422-4640
General Fax: (215) 422-4646
Advertising Phone: (215) 422-4640 x1
Advertising Fax: (215) 422-4646
Editorial Phone: (215) 422-4060 x2
Editorial Fax: (215) 422-4646
General/National Adv. Email: advertising@theDP.com
Display Adv. Email: advertising@theDP.com
Website: www.theDP.com
Year Established: 1885
Published: Mon`Thur
Avg Free Circ: 6000
Personnel: Eric Jacobs (Gen. Mgr.); Michel Liu (Assignments Ed.); Harry Trustman (Opinions Ed.)

WHARTON SCHOOL OF GRAD. BUS.

Street Address 1: 3730 Walnut St
Street Address 2: 330 Jon M. Huntsman Hall
State: PA
Zip/Postal code: 19104-3615
Country: USA
Mailing Address: 3730 Walnut St
Mailing City: Philadelphia
Mailing State: PA
Mailing ZIP Code: 19104-3615
General Phone: (215) 898-3200
General Fax: (215) 898-1200
General/National Adv. Email: journal@wharton.upenn.edu
Website: www.whartonjournal.com
Personnel: Mark Hanson (Pub.); Anix Vyas (Ed. in Chief); Gareth Keane (Mng. Ed.)

PHILIPPI

ALDERSON-BROADDUS COLLEGE

Street Address 1: 101 College Hill Dr
State: WV
Zip/Postal code: 26416-4600
Country: USA
Mailing Address: 101 College Hill Dr
Mailing City: Philippi
Mailing State: WV
Mailing ZIP Code: 26416
General Phone: (304) 457-6357
General Fax: (304) 457-6239
Website: www.ab.edu/performing_arts/battler_columns
Personnel: Jim Wilkie (Advisor); Melissa Riffle (Asst. Ed.)

PHOENIX

PARADISE VALLEY CMTY. COLLEGE

Street Address 1: 18401 N 32nd St
State: AZ
Zip/Postal code: 85032-1210
Country: USA
Mailing Address: 18401 N 32nd St
Mailing City: Phoenix
Mailing State: AZ
Mailing ZIP Code: 85032-1200
General Phone: (602) 787-6772
General Fax: (602) 787-7285
Advertising Phone: (602) 787-6772
Advertising Fax: (602) 787-7285
Editorial Phone: (602) 787-6772
General/National Adv. Email: pumapress@pvmail.maricopa.edu
Display Adv. Email: judy.galbraith@paradisevalley.edu
Editorial Email: judy.galbraith@paradisevalley.edu
Website: nevalleynews.org/
Year Established: 1991
Published: Mthly
Avg Free Circ: 2000
Personnel: Judy Galbraith (Advisor)
Parent company (for newspapers): Paradise Valley Community College

PINE BLUFF

UNIVERSITY OF ARKANSAS AT PINE BLUFF

Street Address 1: 1200 Universtiy Dr
State: AR
Zip/Postal code: 71601-2799
Country: USA
Mailing Address: 1200 N. University Dr.
Mailing City: Pine Bluff
Mailing State: AR
Mailing ZIP Code: 71601
General Phone: (870) 575-8427
Advertising Phone: (870) 575-8427
Editorial Phone: (870) 575-8427
General/National Adv. Email: arkansawyer@uapb.edu
Display Adv. Email: arkansawyer@uapb.edu
Editorial Email: arkansawyer@uapb.edu
Year Established: 1921
Published: Other
Published Other: Bi-weekly
Avg Free Circ: 1000
Personnel: Alicia Dorn (Editor)
Parent company (for newspapers): University of Arkansas at Pine Bluff

PINEVILLE

LOUISIANA COLLEGE

Street Address 1: 1140 College Dr
Street Address 2: Dept English
State: LA
Zip/Postal code: 71359-1000
Country: USA
Mailing Address: 1140 College Dr Dept English
Mailing City: Pineville
Mailing State: LA
Mailing ZIP Code: 71359-1000
General Phone: (318) 487-7011
General Fax: (318) 487-7310
General/National Adv. Email: wildcat@lacollege.edu
Personnel: Jessie Redd (Ed.)

PITTSBURG

LOS MEDANOS COLLEGE

Street Address 1: 2700 E Leland Rd
State: CA
Zip/Postal code: 94565-5107
Country: USA
Mailing Address: 2700 E Leland Rd
Mailing City: Pittsburg
Mailing State: CA
Mailing ZIP Code: 94565-5197
General Phone: (925) 439-2181
General Fax: (925) 427-1599
Website: www.losmedanos.edu
Year Established: 1974
Personnel: Cindy McGrath (Advisor)

PITTSBURGH

CARNEGIE MELLON UNIV.

Street Address 1: 5000 Forbes Ave
State: PA
Zip/Postal code: 15213-3815
Country: USA
Mailing Address: Box 119
Mailing City: Pittsburgh
Mailing State: PA
Mailing ZIP Code: 15213
General Phone: (412) 268-2111
General Fax: (412) 268-1596
General/National Adv. Email: contact@tartan.org
Display Adv. Email: advertising@thetartan.org
Website: www.thetartan.org
Published: Mon
Avg Free Circ: 6000

CMTY. COLLEGE ALLEGHENY

College and University Newspapers

COUNTY

Street Address 1: 808 Ridge Ave
State: PA
Zip/Postal code: 15212-6003
Country: USA
Mailing Address: Office of Student Life
Mailing City: Pittsburgh
Mailing State: PA
General Phone: (412) 237-2543
General Fax: (412) 237-6548
Website: www.ccac.edu
Personnel: Christine McQuaide (Advisor)

COMMUNITY COLLEGE OF ALLEGHENY: NORTH CAMPUS VOICE

Street Address 1: 8701 Perry Hwy
Street Address 2: Rm 2003
State: PA
Zip/Postal code: 15237-5353
Country: USA
Mailing Address: 8701 Perry Hwy, Rm 2003 B
Mailing City: Pittsburgh
Mailing State: PA
Mailing ZIP Code: 15237
General Phone: 412-369-4156
General/National Adv. Email: rbeighey@ccac.edu
Website: ccac.edu

DUQUESNE UNIVERSITY

Street Address 1: 600 Forbes Ave
Street Address 2: 113 College Hall
State: PA
Zip/Postal code: 15282-0001
Country: USA
Mailing Address: 600 Forbes Ave
Mailing City: Pittsburgh
Mailing State: PA
Mailing ZIP Code: 15282-0001
General Phone: (412) 396-6629
General/National Adv. Email: theduke@duq.edu
Display Adv. Email: dukeads@yahoo.com
Website: www.duqsm.com
Year Established: 1925
Published: Thur
Personnel: Bobby Kerlik (Advisor); Jess Eagle (Ed. in Chief); Brian Tierney (Associate Ed.); Matt Noonan (Managing Ed.); Shawn (News Ed.); Mickey (Advertising Mgr.)

LA ROCHE COLLEGE

Street Address 1: 9000 Babcock Blvd
State: PA
Zip/Postal code: 15237-5808
Country: USA
Mailing Address: 9000 Babcock Blvd
Mailing City: Pittsburgh
Mailing State: PA
Mailing ZIP Code: 15237-5898
General Phone: (412) 536-1147
General Fax: (412) 536-1067
General/National Adv. Email: courier@laroche.edu
Website: www.larochecourier.com
Personnel: Ed Stankowski (Advisor); Rebecca Jeskey (Ed. in Chief); Maggie Kelly (Mng. Ed.)

POINT PARK COLLEGE

Street Address 1: 201 Wood St
State: PA
Zip/Postal code: 15222-1912
Country: USA
Mailing Address: PO Box 627
Mailing City: Pittsburgh
Mailing State: PA
Mailing ZIP Code: 15222
General Phone: (412) 392-4740
General Fax: (412) 392-3902
General/National Adv. Email: theglobeadvertising@gmail.com
Editorial Email: szullo@pointpark.edu
Website: www.pointparkglobe.com
Personnel: Steve Hallock (Advisor); Sara Zullo (Ed. in Chief)

TEPPER SCHOOL OF BUSINESS AT CARNEGIE MELLON UNIVERSITY

Street Address 1: 5000 Forbes Ave
State: PA
Zip/Postal code: 15213-3815
Country: USA
Mailing Address: 5000 Forbes Ave
Mailing City: Pittsburgh
Mailing State: PA
Mailing ZIP Code: 15213-3815
General Phone: (412) 268-2269
General/National Adv. Email: jywong@tepper.cmu.edu
Display Adv. Email: robberbaronstepper@gmail.com
Website: tepper.campusgroups.com/rbp/about/
Published: Thur
Personnel: Tyson Bauer (Ed.)

UNIV. OF PITTSBURGH

Street Address 1: 434 William Pitt Un
Street Address 2: University of Pittsburgh
State: PA
Zip/Postal code: 15260-5900
Country: USA
General Phone: (412) 648-7980
General Fax: (412) 648-8491
General/National Adv. Email: pittnews@pittnews.com
Website: www.pittnews.com
Published: Mon`Tues`Wed`Thur`Fri
Personnel: Harry Kloman (Advisor); Ashwini Sivaganesh (Ed. in Chief); John Hamilton (Mng. Ed.); Victor Powell (Online Ed.)

PLAINVIEW

WAYLAND BAPTIST UNIV.

Street Address 1: 1900 W 7th St
Street Address 2: # 1272
State: TX
Zip/Postal code: 79072-6900
Country: USA
Mailing Address: 1900 W 7th St # 1272
Mailing City: Plainview
Mailing State: TX
Mailing ZIP Code: 79072-6900
General Phone: (806) 291-1088
General Fax: (806) 291-1980
General/National Adv. Email: trailblazer@wbu.edu
Website: www.wbu.edu
Year Established: 1950
Commercial printers?: N
Published: Bi-Mthly
Published Other: Bi-Weekly
Avg Free Circ: 1500
Personnel: Steven Long (Advisor)
Parent company (for newspapers): Wayland Baptist University

PLATTEVILLE

UNIV. OF WISCONSIN PLATTEVILLE

Street Address 1: 1 University Plz
Street Address 2: 618 Pioneer Tower
State: WI
Zip/Postal code: 53818-3001
Country: USA
Mailing Address: 1 University Plz Stop 1
Mailing City: Platteville
Mailing State: WI
Mailing ZIP Code: 53818-3001
General Phone: (608) 342-1471
General Fax: (608) 342-1671
General/National Adv. Email: exponent@uwplatt.edu
Website: www.uwpexponent.org
Year Established: 1889
Delivery Methods: Mail`Newsstand`Carrier
Published: Thur
Avg Free Circ: 3600
Personnel: Becky Troy (Administrative assistant); Arthur Ranney (Advisor)

PLATTSBURGH

SUNY PLATTSBURGH

Street Address 1: 101 Broad St
Street Address 2: 118 Ward Hall
State: NY
Zip/Postal code: 12901-2637
Country: USA
Mailing Address: 101 Broad St
Mailing City: Plattsburgh
Mailing State: NY
Mailing ZIP Code: 12901-2637
General Phone: (518) 564-2174
General Fax: (518) 564-6397
Advertising Phone: (518) 564-3173
Editorial Phone: (518) 564-2174
General/National Adv. Email: cp@cardinalpointsonline.com
Display Adv. Email: advertising@cardinalpointsonline.com
Editorial Email: cp@cardinalpointsonline.com
Website: www.cardinalpointsonline.com
Year Established: 1969
Published: Fri
Avg Free Circ: 1300
Personnel: Shawn Murphy (Advisor); Maureen Provost (Bus Mgr)
Parent company (for newspapers): Plattsburgh State Media Inc.

PLEASANT HILL

DIABLO VALLEY COLLEGE

Street Address 1: 321 Golf Club Rd
State: CA
Zip/Postal code: 94523-1529
Country: USA
Mailing Address: 321 Golf Club Rd
Mailing City: Pleasant Hill
Mailing State: CA
Mailing ZIP Code: 94523-1544
General Phone: (925) 685-1230
General Fax: (925) 681-3045
General/National Adv. Email: inquirer@dvc.edu
Website: www.dvc.edu/journalism
Personnel: Ann Stenmark (Adv. Mgr.); Ashley Pittson (Ed.); Catharine Ahr (Ed.); Barbara (Ed.)

JOHN F. KENNEDY UNIVERSITY

Street Address 1: 100 Ellinwood Way
State: CA
Zip/Postal code: 94523-4817
Country: USA
Mailing Address: 100 Ellinwood Way
Mailing City: Pleasant Hill
Mailing State: CA
Mailing ZIP Code: 94523-4817
General Phone: 925.969.3584
General Fax: 925.969.3136
Website: www.jfku.edu

PLEASANTVILLE

PACE UNIV.

Street Address 1: 861 Bedford Rd
State: NY
Zip/Postal code: 10570-2700
Country: USA
Mailing Address: 861 Bedford Rd.
Mailing City: Pleasantville
Mailing State: NY
Mailing ZIP Code: 10570-2799
General/National Adv. Email: pacechronicle@pace.edu
Published: Wed
Personnel: Katherine Fink

PLYMOUTH

PLYMOUTH STATE COLLEGE

Street Address 1: Hub Ste A9
State: NH
Zip/Postal code: 3264
Country: USA
Mailing Address: HUB Ste. A9
Mailing City: Plymouth
Mailing State: NH
Mailing ZIP Code: 03264
General Phone: (603) 535-2947
General Fax: (603) 535-2729
Editorial Phone: (603) 535-2279
Editorial Email: editor@clock.plymouth.edu
Website: www.theclockonline.com
Personnel: Joe Mealey (Advisor); Meghan Plumpton (Adv. Mgr.); Samantha Kenney (Ed. in Chief)

POCATELLO

IDAHO STATE UNIV.

Street Address 1: PO Box 8009
State: ID
Zip/Postal code: 83209-0001
Country: USA
Mailing Address: PO Box 8009
Mailing City: Pocatello
Mailing State: ID
Mailing ZIP Code: 83209-0001
General Phone: (208) 282-4812
General Fax: (208) 282-5301
General/National Adv. Email: bgads@isu.edu
Website: www.isubengal.com
Personnel: Jerry Miller (Dir.); Clay Nelson (Ed. in Chief)

POMONA

THE POLY POST

Street Address 1: 3801 W Temple Ave
Street Address 2: Bldg 1
State: CA
Zip/Postal code: 91768-2557
Country: USA
Mailing Address: 3801 W Temple Ave Bldg 1
Mailing City: Pomona
Mailing State: CA
Mailing ZIP Code: 91768-2557
General Phone: (909) 869-5483
General Fax: (909) 869-3533
Advertising Phone: (909) 869-5179
Advertising Fax: (909) 869-3863
Editorial Phone: (909) 869-3528
Editorial Fax: (909) 869-3530
General/National Adv. Email: advisor@thepolypost.com
Display Adv. Email: advertise@thepolypost.com
Website: www.thepolypost.com
Delivery Methods: Racks
Commercial printers?: Y
Personnel: Doug Spoon (Advisor); Amanda Newfield (Ed. in Chief); Aaron Castrejon (Mng. Ed.); Linda Perez (Mktg. Dir.)

POPLARVILLE

PEARL RIVER COMMNITY COLLEGE

Street Address 1: 101 Highway 11 N
State: MS
Zip/Postal code: 39470-2216
Country: USA
Mailing Address: 101 Highway 11 N
Mailing City: Poplarville
Mailing State: MS
Mailing ZIP Code: 39470-2201
General Phone: (601) 403-1312
Editorial Phone: (601) 403-1328
General/National Adv. Email: cabadie@prcc.edu
Display Adv. Email: cabadie@prcc.edu
Editorial Email: cabadie@prcc.edu
Website: www.prcc.edu
Year Established: 1909
Published: Mthly
Avg Free Circ: 2000
Personnel: Chuck Adadie (Ed./Advisor)

PORT HURON

ST. CLAIR COUNTY COMMUNITY

COLLEGE

Street Address 1: 323 Erie St
Street Address 2: # 5015
State: MI
Zip/Postal code: 48060-3812
Country: USA
Mailing Address: 323 Erie St # 5015
Mailing City: Port Huron
Mailing State: MI
Mailing ZIP Code: 48060-3812
General Phone: (810) 989-5733
General Fax: (810) 984-4730
General/National Adv. Email: eriesquaregazette@gmail.com
Display Adv. Email: esgadvertising@gmail.com
Website: www.esgonline.org
Year Established: 1931
Published Other: Bi-weekly
Personnel: John Lusk (Advisor); Erick Fredendall (Editor-in-Chief)

PORTALES

EASTERN NEW MEXICO UNIV.

Street Address 1: 1500 S Avenue K
Street Address 2: Department of Communication
State: NM
Zip/Postal code: 88130-7400
Country: USA
Mailing Address: Station 27
Mailing City: Portales
Mailing State: NM
Mailing ZIP Code: 88130-7400
General Phone: (575) 562-2130
General Fax: (575) 562-2847
General/National Adv. Email: janet.birkey@enmu.edu
Website: https://www.enmuthechaseonline.com/
Published: Mon
Published Other: Hard copy published every other week; online in between
Personnel: Janet Birkey (Advisor)

PORTLAND

LEWIS & CLARK COLLEGE

Street Address 1: 0615 SW Palatine Hill Rd
State: OR
Zip/Postal code: 97219-7879
Country: USA
Mailing Address: 0615 SW Palatine Hill Rd
Mailing City: Portland
Mailing State: OR
Mailing ZIP Code: 97219-7879
General Phone: (503) 768-7146
General Fax: (503) 768-7130
Editorial Fax: Free
General/National Adv. Email: piolog@lclark.edu
Display Adv. Email: ads.piolog@gmail.com
Editorial Email: piolog@gmail.com
Website: www.piolog.com
Year Established: 1947
Special Editions: New Student Orientation, April Fool's
Delivery Methods: Mail Racks
Commercial printers?: N
Published: Fri
Avg Free Circ: 1200
Personnel: Caleb Diehl (Editor-in-Chief)

PORTLAND CMTY. COLLEGE

Street Address 1: 12000 SW 49th Ave
State: OR
Zip/Postal code: 97219-7132
Country: USA
Mailing Address: PO Box 19000
Mailing City: Portland
Mailing State: OR
Mailing ZIP Code: 97280-0990
General Phone: (503) 977-4184
General Fax: (503) 977-4956
General/National Adv. Email: tsteffen@pcc.edu
Year Established: 1963

Personnel: Tami Steffenhagen (Gen. Mgr.)

PORTLAND STATE UNIV.

Street Address 1: PO Box 347
State: OR
Zip/Postal code: 97207-0347
Country: USA
Mailing Address: PO Box 751
Mailing City: Portland
Mailing State: OR
Mailing ZIP Code: 97207-0751
General Phone: (503) 725-5691
General Fax: (503) 725-5860
General/National Adv. Email: vanguardadvertising@gmail.com
Website: www.dailyvanguard.com
Year Established: 1948
Personnel: Judson Randall (Advisor); Matthew Kirtley (Adv. Mgr.); Sarah J. Christensen (Ed. in Chief)

REED COLLEGE

Street Address 1: 3203 SE Woodstock Blvd
State: OR
Zip/Postal code: 97202-8138
Country: USA
Mailing Address: 3203 SE Woodstock Blvd
Mailing City: Portland
Mailing State: OR
Mailing ZIP Code: 97202-8199
General Phone: (503) 777-7707
General Fax: (503) 788-6657
General/National Adv. Email: quest@reed.edu

THE BEACON/ UNIV. OF PORTLAND

Street Address 1: 5000 N Willamette Blvd
Street Address 2: MS 161
State: OR
Zip/Postal code: 97203-5743
Country: USA
Mailing Address: 5000 N Willamette Blvd
Mailing City: Portland
Mailing State: OR
Mailing ZIP Code: 97203-5798
General Phone: (503) 943-7376
General Fax: (503) 943-7833
General/National Adv. Email: beacon@up.edu
Display Adv. Email: beaconads@up.edu
Website: www.upbeacon.com
Year Established: 1935
Delivery Methods: Racks
Commercial printers?: Y
Published Other: We are now digital only!!!
Personnel: Nancy Copic (Advisor)

UNIVERSITY OF SOUTHERN MAINE

Street Address 1: 92 Bedford St 2nd Fl
Street Address 2:
State: ME
Zip/Postal code: 04102-2801
Country: USA
Mailing Address: PO Box 9300
Mailing City: Portland
Mailing State: ME
Mailing ZIP Code: 04104-9300
General Phone: (207) 780-4084 x2
General Fax: N/A
Advertising Phone: 207780-4084 x2
Advertising Fax: N/A
Editorial Phone: 207-780-4084 x1
Editorial Fax: N/A
General/National Adv. Email: editor@usmfreepress.org
Display Adv. Email: ads@usmfreepress.org
Editorial Email: editor@usmfreepress.org
Website: usmfreepress.org
Year Established: 1972
Delivery Methods: Newsstand Racks
Published: Mon
Published Other: 10 issues per semester plus Summer orientation issues
Avg Free Circ: 2000
Personnel: Lucille Siegler (Business Manager)

PORTSMOUTH

SHAWNEE STATE UNIV.

Street Address 1: 940 2nd St
State: OH
Zip/Postal code: 45662-4303
Country: USA
Mailing Address: 940 2nd St
Mailing City: Portsmouth
Mailing State: OH
Mailing ZIP Code: 45662-4347
General Phone: (740) 351-3278
General Fax: (740) 351-3546
Advertising Phone: (740) 351-3502
General/National Adv. Email: chronicle@shawnee.edu
Website: www.shawnee.edu/pub/chrn
Personnel: Terry Hapney (Advisor)

POTEAU

CARL ALBERT STATE COLLEGE

Street Address 1: 1507 S McKenna St
State: OK
Zip/Postal code: 74953-5207
Country: USA
Mailing Address: 1507 S McKenna St
Mailing City: Poteau
Mailing State: OK
Mailing ZIP Code: 74953-5207
General Phone: (918) 647-1200
General Fax: (918) 647-1266
Personnel: Marcus Blair (PR Dir.)

POTSDAM

CLARKSON UNIV.

Street Address 1: PO Box 8710
State: NY
Zip/Postal code: 13699-0001
Country: USA
Mailing Address: PO Box 8710
Mailing City: Potsdam
Mailing State: NY
Mailing ZIP Code: 13699-0001
General Phone: (315) 265-9050
General Fax: (315) 268-7661
General/National Adv. Email: integrat@clarkson.edu
Website: www.clarksonintegrator.com
Personnel: Mary Konecnik (Ed. in Chief); Robert Trerice (Mng. Ed.)

POUGHKEEPSIE

DUTCHESS CMTY. COLLEGE

Street Address 1: 53 Pendell Rd
State: NY
Zip/Postal code: 12601-1512
Country: USA
Mailing Address: 53 Pendell Rd
Mailing City: Poughkeepsie
Mailing State: NY
Mailing ZIP Code: 12601-1595
General Phone: (845) 431-8000
General Fax: (845) 431-8989
General/National Adv. Email: communityrelations@sunydutchess.edu; Helpdesk@sunydutchess.edu
Website: www.sunydutchess.edu
Personnel: Kevin Lang (Advisor)

MARIST COLLEGE

Street Address 1: 3399 North Rd
Street Address 2: Lowell Thomas Communications Building Room 135-MAC Lab
State: NY
Zip/Postal code: 12601-1350
Country: USA
Mailing Address: Lowell Thomas Communications Building Room 135-Mac Lab
Mailing City: Poughkeepsie
Mailing State: NY

Mailing ZIP Code: 12601-1387
General Phone: (845) 575-3000
General/National Adv. Email: writethecircle@hotmail.com
Website: www.maristcircle.com
Personnel: Margeaux Lippman (Ed. in Chief); Kaitlyn Smith (Mng. Ed.); Matthew Spillane (Mng. Ed.)

VASSAR COLLEGE

Street Address 1: 124 Raymond Ave
Street Address 2: Box 149, Vassar College
State: NY
Zip/Postal code: 12604-0001
Country: USA
Mailing Address: Box 149, Vassar College
Mailing City: Poughkeepsie
Mailing State: NY
Mailing ZIP Code: 12604
General Phone: (518) 755-2042
General/National Adv. Email: misc@vassar.edu
Website: PO Box 23
Published: Wed
Personnel: Talya Phelps (Editor-in-Chief)

POWELL

NORTHWEST COLLEGE

Street Address 1: 231 W 6th St
State: WY
Zip/Postal code: 82435-1898
Country: USA
Mailing Address: 231 W 6th St Bldg 3
Mailing City: Powell
Mailing State: WY
Mailing ZIP Code: 82435-1898
General Phone: (307) 754-6438
General Fax: (307) 754-6700
Website: www.northwesttrail.org
Personnel: Rob Breeding (Advisor); Kayla Dumas (Ed.)

PRAIRIE VIEW

PRAIRIE VIEW A&M UNIV.

Street Address 1: PO Box 519
State: TX
Zip/Postal code: 77446-0519
Country: USA
Mailing Address: PO Box 519
Mailing City: Prairie View
Mailing State: TX
Mailing ZIP Code: 77446-0519
General Phone: (936) 261-1353
General Fax: (936) 261-1365
General/National Adv. Email: panther@pvamu.edu
Website: www.pvpanther.com
Personnel: Lewis Smith (Advisor); Whitney Harris (Ed. in chief)

PRATT

PRATT CMTY. COLLEGE

Street Address 1: 348 NE Hwy 61
State: KS
Zip/Postal code: 67124
Country: USA
Mailing Address: 348 NE Hwy. 61
Mailing City: Pratt
Mailing State: KS
Mailing ZIP Code: 67124
General Phone: (316) 672-5641
General Fax: (316) 672-5641

PRESCOTT

EMBRY-RIDDLE AERO UNIV.

Street Address 1: 3700 Willow Creek Rd
State: AZ
Zip/Postal code: 86301-3721
Country: USA
Mailing Address: 3700 Willow Creek Road
Mailing City: Prescott
Mailing State: AZ

College and University Newspapers

Mailing ZIP Code: 86301
General Phone: (928) 777-3891
Advertising Phone: (928) 777-3830
General/National Adv. Email: prnews@erau.edu
Website: www.erau.edu/
Personnel: Alan Malnar (Advisor); Katie (Gen Mgr.)

YAVAPAI COLLEGE

Street Address 1: 1100 E Sheldon St
Street Address 2: Bldg 3-118
State: AZ
Zip/Postal code: 86301-3220
Country: USA
Mailing Address: 1100 E Sheldon St Bldg 3-118
Mailing City: Prescott
Mailing State: AZ
Mailing ZIP Code: 86301-3297
General Fax: (928) 717-7678
Advertising Fax: (928) 717-7742
General/National Adv. Email: roughwriter.yc.edu
Display Adv. Email: ycwriters@yahoo.com
Website: roughwriter.yc.edu/
Personnel: Colette Strassburg (Advisor); Brandon Ross (Ed.); Elizabeth Zieche (Asst. Ed.)

PRESQUE ISLE

UNIV. OF MAINE

Street Address 1: 181 Main St
State: ME
Zip/Postal code: 04769-2844
Country: USA
Mailing Address: PO Box 417
Mailing City: Presque Isle
Mailing State: ME
Mailing ZIP Code: 04769
General Phone: (207) 768-9400
General/National Adv. Email: utimes@maine.edu
Personnel: Tara White (Ed.)

PRICE

UTAH STATE UNIVERSITY EASTERN

Street Address 1: 451 N 400 E St
State: UT
Zip/Postal code: 84501
Country: USA
Mailing Address: 451 N. 400 E. St.
Mailing City: Price
Mailing State: UT
Mailing ZIP Code: 84501-3315
General Phone: (435) 613-5123
Advertising Phone: (435) 613-5213
General/National Adv. Email: Susan.polster@usu.edu
Website: Usueagle.com
Year Established: 1937
Published: Thur`Other
Avg Free Circ: 1000
Personnel: Susan Polster (Adviser)

PRINCETON

PRINCETON UNIVERSITY

Street Address 1: PO Box 469
State: NJ
Zip/Postal code: 08542-0469
Country: USA
Mailing Address: PO Box 469
Mailing City: Princeton
Mailing State: NJ
Mailing ZIP Code: 08542-0469
General Phone: (609) 258-3632
General/National Adv. Email: eic@dailyprincetonian.com
Display Adv. Email: bm@dailyprincetonian.com
Editorial Email: eic@dailyprincetonian.com
Website: www.dailyprincetonian.com
Year Established: 1876
Published: Mon`Tues`Wed`Thur`Fri
Personnel: Marcelo Rochabrun (Editor in Chief)

PROVIDENCE

BROWN UNIV./RHODE ISLAND SCHOOL OF DESIGN

Street Address 1: PO Box 1930
State: RI
Country: USA
Mailing Address: PO Box 1930
Mailing City: Providence
Mailing State: RI
Mailing ZIP Code: 02912-1930
General Phone: (401) 863-2008
General/National Adv. Email: independent@brown.edu; theindyads@gmail.com
Website: www.theindy.org
Personnel: Emily Segal (Ed.); Alex Verdolini (Mng. Ed.)

JOHNSON & WALES UNIV.

Street Address 1: 8 Abbott Park Pl
State: RI
Zip/Postal code: 02903-3703
Country: USA
Mailing Address: 8 Abbott Park Pl
Mailing City: Providence
Mailing State: RI
Mailing ZIP Code: 02903-3775
General Phone: (401) 598-1000
General Fax: (401) 598-1171
Editorial Phone: (401) 598-1489
Editorial Fax: (401) 598-2867
General/National Adv. Email: campusherald@jwu.edu
Website: www.jwu.edu
Personnel: Michael Berger (Advisor); Jessica Long (Advisor); Catlin Benoit (Ed. in Chief); Samantha Krivorit (Ed. in Cheif)

PROVIDENCE COLLEGE

Street Address 1: 549 River Ave
State: RI
Zip/Postal code: 02918-7000
Country: USA
Mailing Address: 549 River Ave
Mailing City: Providence
Mailing State: RI
Mailing ZIP Code: 02918-0001
General Phone: (401) 865-2214
General Fax: (401) 865-1202
General/National Adv. Email: cowl@providence.edu
Website: www.providence.edu
Personnel: Richard F. Kless (Advisor)

RHODE ISLAND COLLEGE

Street Address 1: Student Union Plz, 600 Mt Pleasant Ave
State: RI
Zip/Postal code: 2908
Country: USA
Mailing Address: Student Union Plz., 600 Mt. Pleasant Ave.
Mailing City: Providence
Mailing State: RI
Mailing ZIP Code: 02908-1940
General Phone: (401) 456-8544
General Fax: (401) 456-8792
General/National Adv. Email: news@anchorweb.org
Website: www.anchorweb.org
Personnel: Rudy Cheeks (Professional Advisor); Ashley Dalton (Adv. Mgr.); Kameron Stualting (Ed. in Chief)

THE BROWN DAILY HERALD

Street Address 1: 195 Angell St
State: RI
Zip/Postal code: 02906-1207
Country: USA
Mailing Address: PO Box 2538
Mailing City: Providence
Mailing State: RI
Mailing ZIP Code: 02906-0538
General Phone: (401) 351-3260

General Fax: (401) 351-9297
General/National Adv. Email: herald@browndailyherald.com
Display Adv. Email: advertising@browndailyherald.com
Website: www.browndailyherald.com
Year Established: 1891
Special Weekly Sections: Post- Magazine
Published: Mon`Tues`Wed`Thur`Fri
Personnel: Lauren Aratani

PROVO

BRIGHAM YOUNG UNIVERSITY

Street Address 1: 152 Brmb
State: UT
Zip/Postal code: 84602-3701
Country: USA
Mailing Address: 152 BRMB
Mailing City: Provo
Mailing State: UT
Mailing ZIP Code: 84602-3701
General Phone: (801) 422-2957
General/National Adv. Email: dureceptionist@gmail.com
Display Adv. Email: ellen_hernandez@byu.edu
Editorial Email: universe.ideas@gmail.com
Website: universe.byu.edu
Published: Tues
Personnel: Steve Fidel (Director)

PUEBLO

COLORADO STATE UNIVERSITY-PUEBLO

Street Address 1: 2200 Bonforte Blvd
Street Address 2: # AM110
State: CO
Zip/Postal code: 81001-4901
Country: USA
Mailing Address: 2200 Bonforte Blvd Bcc 103P
Mailing City: Pueblo
Mailing State: CO
Mailing ZIP Code: 81001-4901
General Phone: 719-549-2847
General Fax: 719-549-2977
Advertising Phone: 719-549-2812
Advertising Fax: 719-549-2977
General/National Adv. Email: leticia.steffen@csupueblo.edu
Website: www.csupueblotoday.com
Published Other: once per semester (fall and spring)
Avg Free Circ: 3000
Personnel: Leticia L. Steffen (Advisor); Savana Charter

PULLMAN

WASHINGTON STATE UNIVERSITY, DAILY EVERGREEN

Street Address 1: 455 NE Veterans Way
State: WA
Zip/Postal code: 99164-0001
Country: USA
Mailing Address: PO Box 642510
Mailing City: Pullman
Mailing State: WA
Mailing ZIP Code: 99164-2510
General Phone: (509) 335-4573
General Fax: (509) 335-7401
Advertising Phone: (509) 335-1572
Editorial Phone: (509) 335-3194
Display Adv. Email: advertise@dailyevergreen.com
Editorial Email: news@dailyevergreen.com
Website: www.dailyevergreen.com
Year Established: 1895
Delivery Methods: Carrier`Racks
Commercial printers?: N
Published: Mon`Tues`Wed`Thur`Fri
Avg Free Circ: 5945
Personnel: Tracy Milano (Program Coord.); Richard Miller (Dir of Student Media); K. Denise Boyd (Fiscal Officer); Jacob Jones (Content Adviser)

PURCHASE

MANHATTANVILLE COLLEGE

Street Address 1: 2900 Purchase St
State: NY
Zip/Postal code: 10577-2131
Country: USA
Mailing Address: 2900 Purchase St
Mailing City: Purchase
Mailing State: NY
Mailing ZIP Code: 10577-2132
General Phone: (914) 323-5498
General/National Adv. Email: touchstone@mville.edu
Website: mvilletouchstone.com/
Personnel: Dana Schildkraut (Office Mgr.)

QUINCY

EASTERN NAZARENE COLLEGE

Street Address 1: 23 E Elm Ave
State: MA
Zip/Postal code: 02170-2905
Country: USA
Mailing Address: 23 E Elm Ave
Mailing City: Quincy
Mailing State: MA
Mailing ZIP Code: 02170-2999
General Phone: (617) 745-3000
General Fax: (617) 745-3490
Website: www1.enc.edu
Personnel: Erica Scott Mcgrath (Advisor); Emily Prugh (Ed. in Chief)

QUINCY

QUINCY UNIV.

Street Address 1: 1800 College Ave
State: IL
Zip/Postal code: 62301-2670
Country: USA
Mailing Address: 1800 College Ave
Mailing City: Quincy
Mailing State: IL
Mailing ZIP Code: 62301-2699
General Phone: (217) 228-5275
General Fax: (217) 228-5473
General/National Adv. Email: qufalcon@gmail.com
Website: www.quincy.edu/information/publications-a-media/the-falcon
Year Established: 1929
Published: Mthly
Personnel: David Adam (Advisor); Barbara Schleppenbach (Chair of Fine Arts & Communication)

RADFORD

RADFORD UNIV.

Street Address 1: PO Box 6985
State: VA
Zip/Postal code: 24142-6985
Country: USA
Mailing Address: PO Box 6985
Mailing City: Radford
Mailing State: VA
Mailing ZIP Code: 24142-6985
General Phone: (540) 831-5474
General Fax: (540) 831-6725
Advertising Fax: (540) 831-6051
General/National Adv. Email: tartan@radford.edu
Website: www.thetartan.com
Personnel: Matt Labelle (Ed. in chief); Justin Ward (Mng. Ed.); Colin Daileda (News Ed.)

RADNOR

CABRINI UNIVERSITY LOQUITUR

Street Address 1: 610 King of Prussia Rd
State: PA
Zip/Postal code: 19087-3623
Country: USA
Mailing Address: 610 King of Prussia Rd
Mailing City: Radnor

Mailing State: PA
Mailing ZIP Code: 19087-3698
General Phone: (610) 902-8360
General Fax: (610) 902-8285
General/National Adv. Email: loquitur@cabrini.edu
Display Adv. Email: loquitur@cabrini.edu
Editorial Email: loquitur@cabrini.edu
Website: www.theloquitur.com
Year Established: 1959
News Services: MCT
Delivery Methods: Racks
Commercial printers?: Y
Published: Thur`Bi-Mthly
Avg Free Circ: 1400
Personnel: Jerome Zurek (Chair); Angelina Miller (EIC)

RALEIGH

MEREDITH COLLEGE

Street Address 1: 3800 Hillsborough St
State: NC
Zip/Postal code: 27607-5237
Country: USA
Mailing Address: 3800 Hillsborough St
Mailing City: Raleigh
Mailing State: NC
Mailing ZIP Code: 27607-5298
General Phone: (919) 760-8600
General/National Adv. Email: herald@meredith.edu
Personnel: Suzanne Britt (Advisor)

NORTH CAROLINA STATE UNIV.

Street Address 1: 323 Witherspoon Student Ctr, Ncsu Campus Box 7318
State: NC
Zip/Postal code: 27695-0001
Country: USA
Mailing Address: 323 Witherspoon Student Ctr Ncsu Campus Box 7318
Mailing City: Raleigh
Mailing State: NC
Mailing ZIP Code: 27695-0001
General Phone: (919) 515-2411
General Fax: (919) 515-5133
General/National Adv. Email: editor@technicianonline.com
Display Adv. Email: advertising@technicianonline.com
Website: www.technicianonline.com
Year Established: 1923
Personnel: Bradley Wilson (Advisor); Russell Witham (Ed. in Chief)

PEACE COLLEGE

Street Address 1: 15 E Peace St
State: NC
Zip/Postal code: 27604-1176
Country: USA
Mailing Address: 15 E Peace St
Mailing City: Raleigh
Mailing State: NC
Mailing ZIP Code: 27604-1194
General Phone: (919) 508-2214
General Fax: (919) 508-2326
Website: peace.edu
Personnel: John Hill (Advisor)

RANCHO CUCAMONGA

CHAFFEY COLLEGE

Street Address 1: 5885 Haven Ave
State: CA
Zip/Postal code: 91737-3002
Country: USA
Mailing Address: 5885 Haven Ave.
Mailing City: Rancho Cucamonga
Mailing State: CA
Mailing ZIP Code: 91737
General Phone: (909) 652-6934
General/National Adv. Email: thebreeze@chaffey.edu
Display Adv. Email: michelle.dowd@chaffey.edu
Website: www.thebreezeonline.com
Published: Mon`Bi-Mthly

Avg Free Circ: 3000
Personnel: Michelle Dowd (Adviser)

RANDOLPH

COUNTY COLLEGE OF MORRIS

Street Address 1: 214 Center Grove Rd
Street Address 2: Rm Scc
State: NJ
Zip/Postal code: 07869-2007
Country: USA
Mailing Address: 214 Center Grove Rd Rm Scc
Mailing City: Randolph
Mailing State: NJ
Mailing ZIP Code: 07869-2007
General Phone: (973) 328-5224
General Fax: (973) 361-4031
General/National Adv. Email: theyoungtownedition@yahoo.com
Personnel: Matthew Ayres (Advisor); Frank Blaha (Ed. in Chief)

RAPID CITY

SOUTH DAKOTA SCHOOL OF MINES & TECHNOLOGY

Street Address 1: 501 E Saint Joseph St
State: SD
Zip/Postal code: 57701-3901
Country: USA
Mailing Address: 501 E Saint Joseph St
Mailing City: Rapid City
Mailing State: SD
Mailing ZIP Code: 57701-3995
General/National Adv. Email: aurum.sdsmt@gmail.com
Display Adv. Email: aurum.sdsmt@gmail.com
Editorial Email: aurum.sdsmt@gmail.com
Year Established: 1900
Published: Mthly
Avg Free Circ: 2000
Personnel: Daniel Cerfus (Business Manager); Quinn del Val (Secretary); Robin Jerman (Cuisiner Columnist); Dan Eitreim (EIC)

RAYMOND

HINDS CMTY. COLLEGE

Street Address 1: PO Box 1100
State: MS
Zip/Postal code: 39154-1100
Country: USA
Mailing Address: PO Box 1100
Mailing City: Raymond
Mailing State: MS
Mailing ZIP Code: 39154-1100
General Phone: (601) 857-3323
Website: www.hindscc.edu
Personnel: Cathy Hayden (Advisor)

READING

ALBRIGHT COLLEGE

Street Address 1: N 13th and Bern Streets
State: PA
Zip/Postal code: 19612
Country: USA
Mailing Address: P.O. Box 15234
Mailing City: Reading
Mailing State: PA
Mailing ZIP Code: 19612
General Phone: (610) 921-7558
General/National Adv. Email: albrightian@albright.edu
Website: www.albright.edu/albrightian
Published: Bi-Mthly
Personnel: Jon Bekken (Advisor); Sarah Timmons (Editor-in-chief); Megan Homsher (Assistant Editor-in-Chief)

ALVERNIA UNIVERSITY

Street Address 1: 400 Saint Bernardine St
State: PA

Zip/Postal code: 19607-1737
Country: USA
Mailing Address: 400 Saint Bernardine St
Mailing City: Reading
Mailing State: PA
Mailing ZIP Code: 19607-1737
General Phone: (610) 568-1557
Editorial Phone: 610.796.8358
General/National Adv. Email: ryan.lange@alvernia.edu
Website: www.alvernia.edu/alvernian
Published: Mthly
Avg Free Circ: 700
Personnel: Ryan Lange (Faculty Advisor)

READING AREA CMTY. COLLEGE

Street Address 1: 10 S 2nd St
State: PA
Zip/Postal code: 19602-1014
Country: USA
Mailing Address: PO Box 1706
Mailing City: Reading
Mailing State: PA
Mailing ZIP Code: 19603-1706
General Phone: (610) 607-6212
General Fax: (610) 375-8255
Website: racc.edu
Personnel: Melissa Kushner (Mktg. PR)

SHASTA COLLEGE

Street Address 1: 11555 Old Oregon Trl
State: CA
Zip/Postal code: 96003-7692
Country: USA
Mailing Address: PO Box 496006
Mailing City: Redding
Mailing State: CA
Mailing ZIP Code: 96049-6006
General Phone: (530) 242-7729
General Fax: (530) 225-3925
General/National Adv. Email: editorial@sclance.com
Website: www.sclance.com
Personnel: Craig Harrington (Advisor)

REDLANDS

UNIV. OF REDLANDS

Street Address 1: 1200 E Colton Ave
State: CA
Zip/Postal code: 92374-3755
Country: USA
Mailing Address: PO Box 3080
Mailing City: Redlands
Mailing State: CA
Mailing ZIP Code: 92373-0999
General Phone: (909) 748-8880
Personnel: Jessie Stapleton (Advisor)

RENO

UNIV. OF NEVADA

Street Address 1: the Nevada Sagebrush, Mail Stop 058
State: NV
Zip/Postal code: 89557-0001
Country: USA
Mailing Address: Mill Stop 58
Mailing City: Reno
Mailing State: NV
Mailing ZIP Code: 89557-0001
General Phone: (775) 784-4033
General Fax: (775) 784-1952
Advertising Phone: (775) 784-7773
Editorial Email: editor@nevadasagebrush.com
Website: www.nevadasagebrush.com
Personnel: Amy Koeckes (Advisor); Jessica Fryman (Ed. in Chief)

RENSSELAER

ST. JOSEPH'S COLLEGE

Street Address 1: 231 US Highway
State: IN

Zip/Postal code: 47978
Country: USA
Mailing Address: PO Box 870
Mailing City: Rensselaer
Mailing State: IN
Mailing ZIP Code: 47978-0870
General Phone: (219) 866-6224
Personnel: Charles Kerlin (Faculty Facilitator); Mike Koscielny (Ed. in Chief)

REXBURG

BRIGHAM YOUNG UNIV. IDAHO

Street Address 1: Spori Bldg 114B
State: ID
Zip/Postal code: 1908
Country: USA
Mailing Address: Spori Bldg # 114B
Mailing City: Rexburg
Mailing State: ID
Mailing ZIP Code: 83460-0001
General Phone: (208) 496-2411
General Fax: (208) 496-2911
General/National Adv. Email: scrolleditor@byui.edu
Website: www.byui.edu/scroll; www.byuicomm.net
Personnel: Jeff Hochstrasser (Advisor); John Thompson (Advisor); Ryan Hales (Advisor)

RICHARDSON

UNIV. OF TEXAS DALLAS

Street Address 1: PO Box 830688
State: TX
Zip/Postal code: 75083-0688
Country: USA
Mailing Address: PO Box 830688
Mailing City: Richardson
Mailing State: TX
Mailing ZIP Code: 75083-0688
General Phone: (972) 883-2286
General Fax: (972) 883-2772
Editorial Phone: (972) 883-2210
General/National Adv. Email: mercury@utdallas.edu
Display Adv. Email: ads@mercury.utdallas.edu
Website: www.utdmercury.com
Year Established: 1980
Personnel: James Wooley (Adv. Mgr.); Lauren Buell (Ed.)

RICHLANDS

SOUTHWEST VIRGINIA CMTY. COLLEGE

Street Address 1: PO Box Svcc
State: VA
Zip/Postal code: 24641
Country: USA
Mailing Address: PO Box SVCC
Mailing City: Richlands
Mailing State: VA
Mailing ZIP Code: 24641
General Phone: (276) 964-2555
General/National Adv. Email: pat.bussard@sw.edu
Personnel: Pat Bussard (Advisor)

RICHMOND

EARLHAM COLLEGE

Street Address 1: PO Box 273
State: IN
Zip/Postal code: 47375-0273
Country: USA
Mailing Address: PO Box 273
Mailing City: Richmond
Mailing State: IN
Mailing ZIP Code: 47375-0273
General Phone: (765) 983-1569
General Fax: (765) 983-1641
Website: ecword.org
Personnel: Maria Salvador (Ed. in Chief); Marisa Keller (Mng. Ed.)

College and University Newspapers

EASTERN KENTUCKY UNIV.
Street Address 1: 521 Lancaster Ave
Street Address 2: Combs Bldg. 226
State: KY
Zip/Postal code: 40475-3100
Country: USA
Mailing Address: 521 Lancaster Ave
Mailing City: Richmond
Mailing State: KY
Mailing ZIP Code: 40475-3102
General Phone: (859) 622-1881
General Fax: (859) 622-2354
General/National Adv. Email: progress@eku.edu
Display Adv. Email: progressads@eku.edu
Website: www.easternprogress.com
Year Established: 1922
Published: Thur
Published Other: During semesters
Avg Free Circ: 8000
Personnel: Reggie Beehner (Advisor); Kristie Hamon (Ed.); Gina Portwood (Bus. Mgr.); Park Greer (Adv. Mgr.)

INDIANA UNIV. EAST
Street Address 1: 2325 Chester Blvd
State: IN
Zip/Postal code: 47374-1220
Country: USA
Mailing Address: 2325 Chester Blvd
Mailing City: Richmond
Mailing State: IN
Mailing ZIP Code: 47374-1289
General Phone: (765) 973-8255
General Fax: (765) 973-8388
General/National Adv. Email: howler@iue.edu
Website: www.iue.edu
Personnel: Belinda Wyss (Advisor); Rob Zinkan (Exec. Ed.)

UNIV. OF RICHMOND
Street Address 1: 40 W Hampton Way, North Ct, Rm B1
State: VA
Zip/Postal code: 23173-0001
Country: USA
Mailing Address: 40 W Hampton Way North Ct Rm B1
Mailing City: Richmond
Mailing State: VA
Mailing ZIP Code: 23173-0001
General Phone: (804) 289-8483
General Fax: (804) 287-6092
Editorial Email: collegianstories@gmail.com
Website: www.thecollegianur.com
Year Established: 1914
Published: Mon`Tues`Wed`Thur`Fri`Sat`Sun
Personnel: Claire Comey (Editor in Chief); Liza David (Managing Editor)

VIRGINIA COMMONWEALTH UNIV.
Street Address 1: 817 W Broad St
State: VA
Zip/Postal code: 23284-9104
Country: USA
Mailing Address: PO Box 842010
Mailing City: Richmond
Mailing State: VA
Mailing ZIP Code: 23284-2010
General Phone: (804) 828-1058
General Fax: (804) 828-9201
Editorial Email: editor@commonwealthtimes.com
Website: www.commonwealthtimes.com
Personnel: Greg Weatherford (Student Media Dir.); Lauren Geerdes (Bus. Mgr.)

VIRGINIA UNION UNIV.
Street Address 1: 1500 N Lombardy St
State: VA
Zip/Postal code: 23220-1711
Country: USA
Mailing Address: 1500 N Lombardy St
Mailing City: Richmond
Mailing State: VA
Mailing ZIP Code: 23220-1784
General Phone: (804) 257-5655
General Fax: (804) 257-5818
Personnel: Gloria D. Brogdon (Dept. Chair); Peter S. Tahsoh (Advisor)

RINDGE

FRANKLIN PIERCE COLLEGE
Street Address 1: 40 University Dr
State: NH
Zip/Postal code: 03461-5046
Country: USA
Mailing Address: 40 University Dr
Mailing City: Rindge
Mailing State: NH
Mailing ZIP Code: 03461-5045
General Phone: (603) 899-4170
General Fax: (603) 899-1077
Website: www.franklinpierce.edu/
Personnel: Kristen Nevious (Advisor); Tony Catinella (Ed.); Robin Michael (Mng. Ed.)

RIO GRANDE

UNIV. OF RIO GRANDE
Street Address 1: 218 N College Ave
State: OH
Zip/Postal code: 45674-3100
Country: USA
Mailing Address: 218 N College Ave
Mailing City: Rio Grande
Mailing State: OH
Mailing ZIP Code: 45674-3131
General Phone: (740) 245-7521
General Fax: (740) 245-7239
General/National Adv. Email: signals@rio.edu
Personnel: Nick Claussen (Advisor)

RIPON

RIPON COLLEGE
Street Address 1: 300 W Seward St
State: WI
Zip/Postal code: 54971-1477
Country: USA
Mailing Address: PO Box 248
Mailing City: Ripon
Mailing State: WI
Mailing ZIP Code: 54971-0248
General Phone: (920) 748-8126
General Fax: (920) 748-9262
Website: www.riponcollegedays.com
Personnel: Jonathan Bailey (Ed. in Chief); John Bailey (Asst. Ed.)

RIVER FALLS

UNIVERSITY OF WISCONSIN-RIVER FALLS
Street Address 1: 410 S 3rd St
Street Address 2: 310 North Hall
State: WI
Zip/Postal code: 54022-5010
County: Pierce
Country: USA
Mailing Address: 410 S. Third St.
Mailing City: River Falls
Mailing State: WI
Mailing ZIP Code: 54022
General Phone: (715) 425-3169
General Fax: (715) 425-0658
General/National Adv. Email: journalism@uwrf.edu
Display Adv. Email: advertising@uwrfvoice.com
Editorial Email: editor@uwrfvoice.com
Website: uwrfvoice.com
Year Established: 1916
Delivery Methods: Racks
Published: Fri
Avg Free Circ: 1000
Personnel: Andris Straumanis (Advisor); Sandra Ellis (Chair)

RIVER FOREST

CONCORDIA UNIV.
Street Address 1: 7400 Augusta St
State: IL
Zip/Postal code: 60305-1402
Country: USA
Mailing Address: 7400 Augusta Street
Mailing City: River Forest
Mailing State: IL
Mailing ZIP Code: 60305-1499
General Phone: (708) 209-3191
General Fax: (708) 209-3176
Display Adv. Email: spectator@cuchicago.edu
Website: www.cuchicago.edu/student_life/spectator
Personnel: Melissa Williams (Advisor); Benjamin Parviz (Adv. Mgr.); Kathryn Klement (Ed.)

DOMINICAN UNIV.
Street Address 1: 7900 Division St
State: IL
Zip/Postal code: 60305-1066
Country: USA
Mailing Address: 7900 Division St
Mailing City: River Forest
Mailing State: IL
Mailing ZIP Code: 60305-1066
General Phone: (708) 524-6800
General Fax: (708) 524-5900
General/National Adv. Email: domadmis@dom.edu
Personnel: Marie Simpson (Advisor)

RIVER GROVE

TRITON COLLEGE
Street Address 1: 2000 5th Ave
State: IL
Zip/Postal code: 60171-1907
Country: USA
Mailing Address: 2000 5th Ave
Mailing City: River Grove
Mailing State: IL
Mailing ZIP Code: 60171-1995
General Phone: (708) 456-0300
Website: www.triton.edu
Personnel: Dawn Unger (Ed. in Chief)

RIVERSIDE

CALIFORNIA BAPTIST COLLEGE
Street Address 1: 8432 Magnolia Ave
State: CA
Zip/Postal code: 92504-3206
Country: USA
Mailing Address: 8432 Magnolia Ave
Mailing City: Riverside
Mailing State: CA
Mailing ZIP Code: 92504-3297
General Phone: (951) 343-4401
General Fax: (951) 351-1808
General/National Adv. Email: banner@calbaptist.edu
Personnel: Mary Ann Pearson (Advisor); Amanda Tredinnick (Adv. Mgr.); Kendall Dewitt (Ed.)

RIVERSIDE CMTY. COLLEGE
Street Address 1: 4800 Magnolia Ave
State: CA
Zip/Postal code: 92506-1201
Country: USA
Mailing Address: 4800 Magnolia Ave
Mailing City: Riverside
Mailing State: CA
Mailing ZIP Code: 92506-1201
General Phone: (951) 222-8488
General Fax: (951) 328-3505
General/National Adv. Email: viewpoints@rcc.edu
Website: www.viewpointsonline.org
Personnel: Allan Lovelace (Advisor); Stephanie Holland (Ed. in Chief); Chanelle Williams (Mng. Ed.); Vanessa Soto (Adv. Mgr.); Lauren (Photo Ed.)

UNIV. OF CALIFORNIA, RIVERSIDE
Street Address 1: 101 Highlander Union Bldg
State: CA
Zip/Postal code: 92507
Country: USA
Mailing Address: 101 Highlander Union Bldg.
Mailing City: Riverside
Mailing State: CA
Mailing ZIP Code: 92521-0001
General Phone: (951) 827-3617
General Fax: (951) 827-7049
Advertising Phone: (951) 827-3457
Advertising Fax: (951) 827-7049
Editorial Phone: (951) 827-2105
General/National Adv. Email: editorinchief@highlandernews.org
Display Adv. Email: highlanderads@ucr.edu
Editorial Email: editorinchief@highlandernews.org
Website: www.highlandernews.org
Year Established: 1956
Delivery Methods: Newsstand
Published: Tues
Avg Free Circ: 4000
Personnel: Chris LoCascio (EIC); Kevin Keckeisen (Mgr Ed); Sandy Van (News Ed); Erin Mahoney (Advisor); Emily Wells (A&E Ed.); Kendall Petersen (Sports Ed.); Brian Tuttle (Photo Ed.); Myles Andrews-Duve (EIC); Andreas Rauch (EIC)

ROANOKE

HOLLINS UNIV.
Street Address 1: PO Box 9707
State: VA
Zip/Postal code: 24020-1707
Country: USA
Mailing Address: PO Box 9707
Mailing City: Roanoke
Mailing State: VA
Mailing ZIP Code: 24020-1707
General Phone: (540) 362-6000
General Fax: (540) 362-6642
General/National Adv. Email: hollinscolumns@hollins.edu
Website: www.columns.proboards.com
Personnel: Emileigh Clare (Ed. in Chief); Julie Abernethy (Ed.); KaRenda J. LaPrade (Copy Ed.)

ROCHESTER

MONROE CMTY. COLLEGE
Street Address 1: 1000 E Henrietta Rd
State: NY
Zip/Postal code: 14623-5701
Country: USA
Mailing Address: 1000 E Henrietta Rd
Mailing City: Rochester
Mailing State: NY
Mailing ZIP Code: 14623-5780
General Phone: (585) 292-2540
General/National Adv. Email: monroedoctrine@me.com
Website: www.monroedoctrine.org
Year Established: 1963
News Services: MCT campus
Delivery Methods: Racks
Commercial printers?: Y
Published: Other
Published Other: bi-weekly
Avg Free Circ: 3500
Personnel: Lori Moses (Advisor)

NAZARETH COLLEGE OF ROCHESTER
Street Address 1: 4245 East Ave
State: NY
Zip/Postal code: 14618-3703
Country: USA
Mailing Address: 4245 East Ave

Mailing City: Rochester
Mailing State: NY
Mailing ZIP Code: 14618-3790
General Phone: (585) 389-2525
General Fax: (585) 586-2452
Personnel: Halinka Spencer (Ed.)

OAKLAND UNIV.

Street Address 1: 61 Oakland Ctr
State: MI
Zip/Postal code: 48309-4409
Country: USA
Mailing Address: 61 Oakland Ctr
Mailing City: Rochester
Mailing State: MI
Mailing ZIP Code: 48309-4409
General Phone: (248) 370-4268
General Fax: (248) 370-4264
General/National Adv. Email: editor@oaklandpostonline.com
Website: www.oaklandpostonline.com
Year Established: 1957
Published: Tues
Personnel: Holly Gilbert (Advisor); Don Ritenburgh (Business Manager)
Parent company (for newspapers): Oakland Sail

ROBERTS WESLEYAN COLLEGE

Street Address 1: 2301 Westside Dr
State: NY
Zip/Postal code: 14624-1933
Country: USA
Mailing Address: 2301 Westside Dr Ofc
Mailing City: Rochester
Mailing State: NY
Mailing ZIP Code: 14624-1997
General Phone: (585) 594-6385
General Fax: (585) 594-6567
General/National Adv. Email: beacon@roberts.edu
Published: Mthly
Personnel: Taylor Plourde (Editor-In-Chief); Elisabeth Lindke (Assistant Editor); Derick Trost (Layout Editor)

ROCHESTER INST. OF TECHNOLOGY

Street Address 1: 37 Lomb Memorial Dr
State: NY
Zip/Postal code: 14623-5602
Country: USA
Mailing Address: 37 Lomb Memorial Dr
Mailing City: Rochester
Mailing State: NY
Mailing ZIP Code: 14623-5602
General Phone: (585) 475-2213
General Fax: (585) 475-2214
General/National Adv. Email: reporter@rit.edu
Website: www.reportermag.com
Personnel: Rudy Pugliese (Advisor); Andy Rees (Ed. in Chief)

ST. JOHN FISHER COLLEGE

Street Address 1: 3690 East Ave
State: NY
Zip/Postal code: 14618-3537
Country: USA
Mailing Address: 3690 East Ave
Mailing City: Rochester
Mailing State: NY
Mailing ZIP Code: 14618-3537
General Phone: (585) 385-8360
General Fax: (585) 385-7311
Advertising Phone: (585) 385-7393
General/National Adv. Email: cardinalcourier@sjfc.edu
Display Adv. Email: mvilla@sjfc.edu
Editorial Email: eem00114@sjfc.edu
Website: www.cardinalcourieronline.com
Year Established: 2002
Published: Bi-Mthly
Personnel: Lauren Vicker (Chair/Prof.); Marie Villa (Media Adviser)

UNIV. OF ROCHESTER

Street Address 1: PO Box 277086
State: NY
Zip/Postal code: 14627-7086
Country: USA
Mailing Address: CPU 277086 Campus Post Office
Mailing City: Rochester
Mailing State: NY
Mailing ZIP Code: 14627
General Phone: (585) 275-5942
General Fax: (585) 273-5303
General/National Adv. Email: ctads@mail.rochester.edu
Editorial Email: editor@campustimes.org
Website: www.campustimes.org
Personnel: Dan Wasserman (Pub.); Liz Bremer (Bus. Mgr.); Dana Hilfinger (Ed. in Chief)

WATS, SIMON GRAD. SCHOOL OF BUS.

Street Address 1: Schlegel Hall, University of Rochester
State: NY
Zip/Postal code: 14627
Country: USA
Mailing Address: Schlegel Hall, University of Rochester
Mailing City: Rochester
Mailing State: NY
Mailing ZIP Code: 14627
General Phone: (585) 275-9287
General/National Adv. Email: wats@simon.rochester.edu
Delivery Methods: Racks
Commercial printers?: Y
Personnel: Natalie Antal (Acting Managing Editor); Vincent Pelletier (Assignment Editor); Durba Ray (Ed. in Chief)

ROCHESTER HILLS

ROCHESTER COLLEGE

Street Address 1: 800 W Avon Rd
State: MI
Zip/Postal code: 48307-2704
Country: USA
Mailing Address: 800 W Avon Rd
Mailing City: Rochester Hills
Mailing State: MI
Mailing ZIP Code: 48307-2704
General Phone: (248) 218-2030
General Fax: (248) 218-2045
General/National Adv. Email: theshield@rc.edu
Website: www.rcshield.com
Commercial printers?: N
Published: Bi-Mthly
Avg Free Circ: 550
Personnel: Liz Fulton (Mng./Design Ed.); Chelsea Hackel

ROCK HILL

THE JOHNSONIAN

Street Address 1: 1808 Ebenezer Rd Apt B
Street Address 2: 1808-B Ebenezer Rd
State: SC
Zip/Postal code: 29732-1170
Country: USA
Mailing Address: 104 Digiorgio Campus Center Winthrop University
Mailing City: Rock Hill
Mailing State: SC
Mailing ZIP Code: 29733-0001
General Phone: (803) 323-3419
General Fax: (803) 323-3698
Advertising Phone: 803 984-7748
Advertising Fax: 803 984-7748
Editorial Phone: 803 984-7748
Editorial Fax: 803 984-7748
General/National Adv. Email: thejohnsonian@yahoo.com
Editorial Email: editors@mytjnow.com
Website: www.mytjnow.com
Personnel: Guy Reel (Faculty Adviser)

ROCK ISLAND

AUGUSTANA COLLEGE

Street Address 1: 639 38th St
State: IL
Zip/Postal code: 61201-2210
Country: USA
Mailing Address: 639 38th St
Mailing City: Rock Island
Mailing State: IL
Mailing ZIP Code: 61201-2296
General Phone: (309) 794-3460
General Fax: (309) 794-3460
Advertising Phone: (309) 794-7484
Editorial Phone: (309) 794-7485
General/National Adv. Email: observer@augustana.edu
Website: www.augustana.edu
Personnel: Carolyn Yaschur (Advisor); David Schwartz (Advisor)

ROCKFORD

ROCK VALLEY COLLEGE

Street Address 1: 3301 N Mulford Rd
State: IL
Zip/Postal code: 61114-5640
Country: USA
Mailing Address: 3301 N Mulford Rd
Mailing City: Rockford
Mailing State: IL
Mailing ZIP Code: 61114-5699
General Phone: (815) 921-7821
General Fax: (815) 921-3333
Personnel: Frank Coffman (Advisor)

ROCKLIN

SIERRA COLLEGE

Street Address 1: 5000 Rocklin Rd
State: CA
Zip/Postal code: 95677-3337
Country: USA
Mailing Address: 5000 Rocklin Rd
Mailing City: Rocklin
Mailing State: CA
Mailing ZIP Code: 95677-3397
General Phone: (916) 789-2699
General Fax: (916) 789-2854
Personnel: Kelly Kukis (Ed.)

ROCKVILLE

MONTGOMERY COLLEGE

Street Address 1: 51 Mannakee St
State: MD
Zip/Postal code: 20850-1101
Country: USA
Mailing Address: 51 Mannakee St
Mailing City: Rockville
Mailing State: MD
Mailing ZIP Code: 20850-1199
General Phone: (240) 567-7176
General Fax: (240) 567-5091
General/National Adv. Email: info@mcadvocate.com
Display Adv. Email: info@mcadvocate.com
Editorial Email: editor@mcadvocate.com
Website: mcadvocate.com
Year Established: 1957
Personnel: Steve Thurston (Advisor)

ROHNERT PARK

SONOMA STATE UNIVERSITY

Street Address 1: 1801 E Cotati Ave
Street Address 2: Salazar Hall 1053
State: CA
Zip/Postal code: 94928-3613
Country: USA
Mailing Address: 1801 E Cotati Ave Salazar Hall 1053
Mailing City: Rohnert Park
Mailing State: CA
Mailing ZIP Code: 94928-3613
General Phone: (707) 664-2776
General Fax: (707) 664-4262
General/National Adv. Email: star@sonoma.edu
Display Adv. Email: sonomastatestar@gmail.com
Editorial Email: star@sonoma.edu
Website: www.sonomastatestar.com
Year Established: 1979
Published: Tues
Avg Free Circ: 2000
Personnel: Dylan Sirdofsky (Editor-in-Chief); Amanda Saiki (Advertising Manager); Paul Gullixson (Faculty Advisor); Corinne Asturus

ROLLA

MISSOURI UNIV. OF SCIENCE & TECHNOLOGY

Street Address 1: Missouri S&T
Street Address 2: Altman Hall
State: MO
Zip/Postal code: 65401
Country: USA
Mailing Address: Missouri S&T
Mailing City: Rolla
Mailing State: MO
Mailing ZIP Code: 65401-0249
General Phone: (573) 341-4312
General Fax: (573) 341-4235
General/National Adv. Email: miner@mst.edu
Website: mominer.mst.edu
Personnel: Fred Ekstam (Advisor); Frank Sauer (Bus. Mgr.); Sarah Richmond (Ed. in Chief); Andrea Unnerstall (Mng. Ed.); Jacob (News Ed.)

ROME

GEORGIA HIGHLANDS COLLEGE

Street Address 1: 3175 Cedartown Hwy SE
State: GA
Zip/Postal code: 30161-3897
Country: USA
Mailing Address: 3175 Cedartown Highway
Mailing City: Rome
Mailing State: GA
Mailing ZIP Code: 30161
General Phone: (706) 295-6361
General Fax: (706) 295-6610
Editorial Fax: (678) 872-8040
General/National Adv. Email: 6mpost@highlands.edu
Display Adv. Email: ads6MP@student.highlands.edu
Website: www.sixmilepost.com
Personnel: Kristie Kemper (Advisor); Nick Godfrey (Ed.)

SHORTER COLLEGE

Street Address 1: 315 Shorter Ave SW
State: GA
Zip/Postal code: 30165-4267
Country: USA
Mailing Address: 315 Shorter Ave SW
Mailing City: Rome
Mailing State: GA
Mailing ZIP Code: 30165-4267
General Phone: (706) 233-7208
General Fax: (706) 236-1515
General/National Adv. Email: the_periscope@hotmail.com
Website: www.theperiscope.org
Personnel: Ashley Ottinger (Ed. in chief)

ROMEOVILLE

LEWIS UNIV.

Street Address 1: 1 University Pkwy
State: IL
Zip/Postal code: 60446-2200
Country: USA
Mailing Address: 1 University Pkwy
Mailing City: Romeoville
Mailing State: IL

College and University Newspapers

Mailing ZIP Code: 60446-1832
General Phone: (815) 836-5196
General/National Adv. Email: lewisflyernews@gmail.com
Website: www.thelewisflyer.com
Personnel: Lisa O'Toole (Advisor); Adam Olszeski (Ed. in Chief)

ROSEBURG

UMPQUA CMTY. COLLEGE

Street Address 1: 1140 College Rd
State: OR
Zip/Postal code: 97470
Country: USA
Mailing Address: PO Box 967
Mailing City: Roseburg
Mailing State: OR
Mailing ZIP Code: 97470-0226
General Phone: (541) 440-4687
General Fax: (541) 677-3214
General/National Adv. Email: uccmainstream@yahoo.com
Website: www.mainstreamonline.org
Personnel: Melinda Benton (Advisor)

RUSSELLVILLE

ARKANSAS TECH. UNIV.

Street Address 1: 1815 Coliseum Dr
State: AR
Zip/Postal code: 72801-8820
Country: USA
Mailing Address: 1815 Coliseum Drive
Mailing City: Russellville
Mailing State: AR
Mailing ZIP Code: 72801-7400
General Phone: (479) 968-0284
General Fax: (479) 964-0889
General/National Adv. Email: arkatech@atu.edu
Display Adv. Email: arkatech.ads@atu.edu
Website: www.arkatechnews.com
Year Established: 1923
Delivery Methods: Newsstand
Commercial printers?: N
Published: Thur
Avg Free Circ: 2100
Personnel: Tommy Mumert (Advisor)

SACRAMENTO

AMERICAN RIVER COLLEGE

Street Address 1: 4700 College Oak Dr
State: CA
Zip/Postal code: 95841-4217
Country: USA
Mailing Address: 4700 College Oak Dr
Mailing City: Sacramento
Mailing State: CA
Mailing ZIP Code: 95841-4286
General Phone: (916) 484-8653
General Fax: (916) 484-8668
General/National Adv. Email: current@arc.losrios.edu
Website: www.americanrivercurrent.com
Personnel: Jill Wagner (Advisor); Carol Hartman (Advisor); Andrew Clementi (Ed.)

COSUMNES RIVER COLLEGE

Street Address 1: 8401 Center Pkwy
State: CA
Zip/Postal code: 95823-5704
Country: USA
Mailing Address: 8401 Center Pkwy
Mailing City: Sacramento
Mailing State: CA
Mailing ZIP Code: 95823-5799
General Phone: (916) 691-7471
General Fax: (916) 688-7181
Website: www.crcconnection.com
Personnel: Yvette Lessard (Ed. in Chief); Erin Bates (Features Ed.); Bhavisha Patel (Online Ed.); Lehsee Gausi (Opinion Ed.)

SACRAMENTO CITY COLLEGE

Street Address 1: 3835 Freeport Blvd
State: CA
Zip/Postal code: 95822-1318
Country: USA
Mailing Address: 3835 Freeport Blvd
Mailing City: Sacramento
Mailing State: CA
Mailing ZIP Code: 95822-1386
General Phone: (916) 558-2562
General Fax: (916) 558-2282
General/National Adv. Email: express@scc.losrios.edu
Website: www.scc.losrios.edu/express
Personnel: Dianne Heimer (Advisor); Hannah Ucol (Adv. Mgr.); Cecilio Padilla (Ed.)

SACRAMENTO STATE

Street Address 1: 6000 J St
State: CA
Zip/Postal code: 95819-2605
Country: USA
Mailing Address: 6000 J Street
Mailing City: Sacramento
Mailing State: CA
Mailing ZIP Code: 95819
General Phone: 9162786584
Advertising Phone: 9162784092
General/National Adv. Email: editor@statehornet.com
Display Adv. Email: ads@statehornet.com
Editorial Email: editor@statehornet.com
Website: 6000 J Street
Year Established: 1949
Published: Wed
Personnel: Stu VanAirsdale (Faculty Adviser)

SAINT AUGUSTINE

FLAGLER COLLEGE

Street Address 1: PO Box 1027
State: FL
Zip/Postal code: 32085-1027
Country: USA
Mailing Address: PO Box 1027
Mailing City: Saint Augustine
Mailing State: FL
Mailing ZIP Code: 32085-1027
General Phone: (904) 819-6333
General Fax: (904) 826-3224
General/National Adv. Email: gargoyle@flagler.edu
Website: gargoyle.flagler.edu
Year Established: 1968
Personnel: Brain Thomson (Advisor)

SAINT BONAVENTURE

ST. BONAVENTURE UNIV.

Street Address 1: PO Box X
State: NY
Zip/Postal code: 14778-2303
Country: USA
Mailing Address: PO Box X
Mailing City: Saint Bonaventure
Mailing State: NY
Mailing ZIP Code: 14778-2303
General Phone: (716) 375-2227
General Fax: (716) 375-2252
Editorial Phone: (716) 375-2128
General/National Adv. Email: bonavent@sbu.edu
Website: www.thebv.org
Personnel: Carole McNall (Faculty Advisor); Samantha Berkhead (Editor in Chief); Kevin Rogers (Managing Editor)

SAINT BONIFACIUS

CROWN COLLEGE

Street Address 1: 8700 College View Dr
State: MN
Zip/Postal code: 55375-9002
Country: USA
Mailing Address: 8700 College View Dr
Mailing City: Saint Bonifacius
Mailing State: MN
Mailing ZIP Code: 55375-9001
General Phone: (952) 446-4100
General Fax: (952) 446-4149
Website: www.crown.edu
Personnel: William Allen (Advisor)

SAINT CLOUD

ST. CLOUD STATE UNIV.

Street Address 1: 720 4th Ave S
State: MN
Zip/Postal code: 56301-4442
Country: USA
Mailing Address: 720 4th Ave S
Mailing City: Saint Cloud
Mailing State: MN
Mailing ZIP Code: 56301-4498
General Phone: (320) 308-4086
Advertising Phone: (320) 308-3943
General/National Adv. Email: editor@universitychronicle.net
Display Adv. Email: advertising@universitychronicle.net
Editorial Email: editor@universitychronicle.net
Website: www.universitychronicle.net
Year Established: 1924
Special Editions: End of the year review issue, beginning of the year orientation issue
Delivery Methods: Newsstand`Carrier`Racks
Published: Mon
Personnel: Sandesh Malla (Bus. Mgr.); Ashley Kalkbrenner (Adv. Mgr.); Tiffany Krupke; Jason Tham; Kamana Karki

SAINT GEORGE

DIXIE STATE COLLEGE

Street Address 1: 225 S 700 E
State: UT
Zip/Postal code: 84770-3875
Country: USA
Mailing Address: 225 S. 700 E. JEN
Mailing City: Saint George
Mailing State: UT
Mailing ZIP Code: 84770
General Phone: (435) 652-7818
General Fax: (435) 656-4019
Advertising Phone: (435) 652-7818
Advertising Fax: (435) 656-4019
General/National Adv. Email: dixiesun@dixie.edu
Display Adv. Email: dixiesunads@dixie.edu
Editorial Email: dixiesun@dixie.edu
Website: www.dixiesunlink.com
News Services: MCT
Delivery Methods: Newsstand`Racks
Commercial printers?: Y
Personnel: Rhiannon Bent (Advisor); Taylor Forbes (Adv. Mgr.); Rachel Tanner (Ed. in Chief)

SAINT JOSEPH

MISSOURI WESTERN STATE UNIVERSITY

Street Address 1: 4525 Downs Dr
Street Address 2: Eder 221
State: MO
Zip/Postal code: 64507-2246
Country: USA
Mailing Address: 4525 Downs Dr Eder 221
Mailing City: Saint Joseph
Mailing State: MO
Mailing ZIP Code: 64507-2246
General Phone: (816) 271-4412
General Fax: (816) 271-4543
General/National Adv. Email: bergland@missouriwestern.edu
Website: www.thegriffonnews.com
Year Established: 1924
Published: Thur
Avg Free Circ: 2500
Personnel: Robert Bergland (Advisor)

SAINT LEO

SAINT LEO UNIVERSITY

Street Address 1: 33701 State Road 52
Street Address 2: Mc 2127, Dept. of English
State: FL
Zip/Postal code: 33574-9700
Country: USA
Mailing Address: 33701 State Road 52
Mailing City: Saint Leo
Mailing State: FL
Mailing ZIP Code: 33574-9701
General Phone: (352) 588-7424
General Fax: (352) 588-8300
General/National Adv. Email: thelionspridenewspaper@gmail.com
Display Adv. Email: thelionspridenewspaper@gmail.com
Editorial Email: thelionspridenewspaper@gmail.com
Website: https://prideonlinedotnet.wordpress.com/
Published: Fri
Personnel: Valerie Kasper (Advisor); Cassidy Whitaker (Editor-in-Chief)

SAINT LOUIS

ST. LOUIS CMTY. COLLEGE FLORISSANT VALLEY

Street Address 1: 3400 Pershall Rd
State: MO
Zip/Postal code: 63135-1408
Country: USA
Mailing Address: 3400 Pershall Rd
Mailing City: Saint Louis
Mailing State: MO
Mailing ZIP Code: 63135-1408
General Phone: (314) 513-4454
Advertising Phone: (314) 513-4588
General/National Adv. Email: fvfoumeditor@stlcc.edu
Editorial Email: fvforumeditor@stlcc.edu
Year Established: 1963
Published: Mthly
Personnel: Renee Thomas-Woods (Advisor); Stephan Curry (Adv. Mgr.); Joshua Schoenhoff (Ed. in Chief)

ST. LOUIS CMTY. COLLEGE FOREST PARK

Street Address 1: 5600 Oakland Ave
State: MO
Zip/Postal code: 63110-1316
Country: USA
Mailing Address: 5600 Oakland Ave
Mailing City: Saint Louis
Mailing State: MO
Mailing ZIP Code: 63110-1393
General Phone: (314) 644-9140
General/National Adv. Email: the_scene_fp@yahoo.com

ST. LOUIS UNIV.

Street Address 1: 20 N Grand Blvd
Street Address 2: Ste 354
State: MO
Zip/Postal code: 63103-2005
Country: USA
Mailing Address: 20 N Grand Blvd Ste 354
Mailing City: Saint Louis
Mailing State: MO
Mailing ZIP Code: 63103-2005
General Phone: (314) 977-2812
General Fax: (314) 977-7177
General/National Adv. Email: unews.slu@gmail.com
Website: www.unewsonline.com
Personnel: Jason L. Young (Advisor); Peter Zagotta (Gen. Mgr); Kat Patke (Ed. in Chief)

UNIV. OF MISSOURI

Street Address 1: 1 University Blvd

State: MO
Zip/Postal code: 63121-4400
Country: USA
Mailing Address: 1 University Blvd
Mailing City: Saint Louis
Mailing State: MO
Mailing ZIP Code: 63121-4400
General Phone: (314) 516-5174
General Fax: (314) 516-6811
General/National Adv. Email: thecurrent@umsl.edu
Website: www.thecurrentonline.com
Published: Mon
Avg Free Circ: 5000
Personnel: Charlotte Petty (Advisor); Dan Pryor (Bus. Mgr.); Ryan Krull (Advisor)

WASHINGTON UNIV.

Street Address 1: 1 Brookings Dr
Street Address 2: Campus Box 1039
State: MO
Zip/Postal code: 63130-4862
Country: USA
Mailing Address: 1 Brookings Dr.
Mailing City: Saint Louis
Mailing State: MO
Mailing ZIP Code: 63130-4862
General Phone: (314) 935-4240
General Fax: (314) 935-5938
Advertising Phone: (314) 935-7209
Advertising Fax: (314) 935-5938
Editorial Fax: (314) 935-5938
Display Adv. Email: advertising@studlife.com
Editorial Email: editor@studlife.com
Website: www.studlife.com
Year Established: 1878
Published: Mon`Thur
Avg Free Circ: 4000
Personnel: Raymond Bush (General Manager)
Parent company (for newspapers): Washington University Student Media, Inc.

WEBSTER UNIV.

Street Address 1: 470 E Lockwood Ave
State: MO
Zip/Postal code: 63119-3141
Country: USA
Mailing Address: 470 E Lockwood Ave
Mailing City: Saint Louis
Mailing State: MO
Mailing ZIP Code: 63119-3194
General Phone: (314) 961-2660
General Fax: (314) 968-7059
Editorial Phone: (314) 968-7088
General/National Adv. Email: wujournal@gmail.com
Editorial Email: editor@webujournal.com
Website: www.webujournal.com
Published: Wed
Personnel: Don Corrigan (Journ. Seq.); Kelly Kendall (Ed. in Chief)

SAINT MARYS CITY

ST. MARY'S COLLEGE OF MARYLAND

Street Address 1: 18952 E Fisher’S Road
State: MD
Zip/Postal code: 20686
Country: USA
Mailing Address: 18952 E Fisher’s Road
Mailing City: Saint Mary's City
Mailing State: MD
Mailing ZIP Code: 20686
General Phone: (240) 895-4213
General Fax: (240) 895-4445
General/National Adv. Email: pointnews@smcm.edu
Website: www.smcm.edu/PointNews
Personnel: Justin Perry (Ed. in Chief); Matt Molek (Mng. Ed.)

SAINT PAUL

BETHEL COLLEGE

Street Address 1: 3900 Bethel Dr
Street Address 2: Ste 1504
State: MN
Zip/Postal code: 55112-6902
Country: USA
Mailing Address: 3900 Bethel Dr Ste 1504
Mailing City: Saint Paul
Mailing State: MN
Mailing ZIP Code: 55112-6999
General Phone: (651) 635-8643
General Fax: (651) 635-8650
General/National Adv. Email: bethelclarion@gmail.com
Personnel: Marie Wisner (Advisor)

CONCORDIA UNIV. AT ST. PAUL

Street Address 1: 275 Syndicate St N
State: MN
Zip/Postal code: 55104-5436
Country: USA
Mailing Address: 275 Syndicate St N
Mailing City: Saint Paul
Mailing State: MN
Mailing ZIP Code: 55104-5436
General Phone: (651) 641-8221
General Fax: (651) 659-0207
General/National Adv. Email: sword@csp.edu
Website: www.csp.edu/sword
Personnel: Eric Dregni (Advisor); Helena Woodruff (Ed. in Chief); Rachel Kuhnle (Art Ed.)

HAMLINE UNIV.

Street Address 1: 1536 Hewitt Ave
State: MN
Zip/Postal code: 55104-1205
Country: USA
Mailing Address: 1536 Hewitt Ave
Mailing City: Saint Paul
Mailing State: MN
Mailing ZIP Code: 55104-1284
General Phone: (651) 523-2268
General Fax: (651) 523-3144
General/National Adv. Email: oracle@hamline.edu
Website: www.hamlineoracle.com
Year Established: 1888
Published: Wed
Avg Free Circ: 600
Personnel: David Hudson (Adviser); Stolz Catherine (Editor-in-Chief)

MACALESTER COLLEGE

Street Address 1: 1600 Grand Ave
State: MN
Zip/Postal code: 55105-1801
Country: USA
Mailing Address: 1600 Grand Ave
Mailing City: Saint Paul
Mailing State: MN
Mailing ZIP Code: 55105-1899
General Phone: (651) 696-6212
General Fax: (651) 696-6685
Editorial Phone: (651) 696-6684
General/National Adv. Email: macweekly@macalester.edu
Website: www.themacweekly.com
Year Established: 1914
Published: Fri
Personnel: Will Milch (Editor in Chief); Jen Katz (Editor in Cheif); Carrigan Miller (Ad Manager)

UNIVERSITY OF NORTHWESTERN

Street Address 1: 3003 Snelling Ave N
State: MN
Zip/Postal code: 55113-1501
Country: USA
Mailing Address: 3003 Snelling Ave N
Mailing City: Saint Paul
Mailing State: MN
Mailing ZIP Code: 55113
General Phone: (651) 631-5100
General Fax: (651) 651-5124
General/National Adv. Email: examiner@unwsp.edu
Display Adv. Email: examinerads@unwsp.edu
Website: www.unwexaminer.com/about/
Published: Bi-Mthly
Personnel: Doug Trouten (Advisor)

WILLIAM MITCHELL COLLEGE OF LAW

Street Address 1: 875 Summit Ave
State: MN
Zip/Postal code: 55105-3030
Country: USA
Mailing Address: 875 Summit Ave
Mailing City: Saint Paul
Mailing State: MN
Mailing ZIP Code: 55105-3076
General/National Adv. Email: theopinion@wmitchell.edu
Personnel: Lucas Hjelle

SAINT PETER

GUSTAVUS ADOLPHUS COLLEGE

Street Address 1: 800 W College Ave
State: MN
Zip/Postal code: 56082-1485
Country: USA
Mailing Address: 800 W College Ave
Mailing City: Saint Peter
Mailing State: MN
Mailing ZIP Code: 56082-1498
General Phone: (507) 933-7636
General Fax: (507) 933-7633
General/National Adv. Email: weekly@gac.edu
Website: www.gustavus.edu/weekly
Year Established: 1891
Commercial printers?: Y
Published: Fri
Personnel: David Kogler (Advisor); Victoria Clark; Jacob Seamans (Ed.); Chelsea Johnson (Editor In Chief 2013-14); Caroline Probst (Editor-in-Chief)

SAINT PETERSBURG

THE CURRENT - ECKERD COLLEGE

Street Address 1: 4200 54th Ave S
State: FL
Zip/Postal code: 33711-4744
Country: USA
Mailing Address: 4200 54th Ave S
Mailing City: Saint Petersburg
Mailing State: FL
Mailing ZIP Code: 33711-4700
General Phone: 610 4317931
General Fax: 610 4317931
Advertising Phone: 610 4317931
Advertising Fax: 610 4317931
Editorial Phone: 610 4317931
Editorial Fax: 610 4317931
General/National Adv. Email: thecurrent@eckerd.edu
Display Adv. Email: currentads@eckerd.edu
Editorial Email: danielsa1@mac.com
Website: www.theonlinecurrent.com
Year Established: 2009
Delivery Methods: Mail
Commercial printers?: Y
Personnel: Ashley Daniels (Editor-in-Chief); Max Martinez (Managing Editor)

SALEM

CHEMEKETA CMTY. COLLEGE

Street Address 1: PO Box 14007
State: OR
Zip/Postal code: 97309-7070
Country: USA
Mailing Address: PO Box 14007
Mailing City: Salem
Mailing State: OR
Mailing ZIP Code: 97309-7070
General Phone: (503) 399-5000
General Fax: (503) 399-2519
General/National Adv. Email: courier@chemeketa.edu
Display Adv. Email: careeradvertising@yahoo.com
Website: www.chemeketa.edu/collegelife/newspaper/index.html
Personnel: William Florence (Advisor); Gale Hann (Adv. Mgr.); Russell Vineyard (Mng. Ed.)

ROANOKE COLLEGE

Street Address 1: 221 College Ln
Street Address 2: Ofc Studentactivities
State: VA
Zip/Postal code: 24153-3747
Country: USA
Mailing Address: 221 College Ln Ofc Studentactivities
Mailing City: Salem
Mailing State: VA
Mailing ZIP Code: 24153-3794
General Phone: (540) 375-2327
General Fax: (540) 378-5129
General/National Adv. Email: bracketyack@roanoke.edu
Website: www.roanoke.edu
Personnel: Daniel Sarabia (Ed.)

SALEM INTERNATIONAL UNIV.

Street Address 1: 223 W Main St
State: WV
Zip/Postal code: 26426-1227
Country: USA
Mailing Address: 223 W Main St
Mailing City: Salem
Mailing State: WV
Mailing ZIP Code: 26426-1227
General Phone: (304) 326-1538
General Fax: (304) 782-1592
Personnel: Nicole Michaelas (Advisor)

SALEM STATE COLLEGE

Street Address 1: 352 Lafayette St, Ellison Campus Ctr
State: MA
Zip/Postal code: 1970
Country: USA
Mailing Address: 352 Lafayette St., Ellison Campus Ctr.
Mailing City: Salem
Mailing State: MA
Mailing ZIP Code: 01970-5348
General Phone: (978) 542-6448
General Fax: (978) 542-2077
General/National Adv. Email: thelog@ssclog.com
Website: www.salemstate.edu/log
Personnel: Peggy Dillon (Advisor)

WILLAMETTE UNIV.

Street Address 1: 900 State St
State: OR
Zip/Postal code: 97301-3922
Country: USA
Mailing Address: 900 State St
Mailing City: Salem
Mailing State: OR
Mailing ZIP Code: 97301-3931
General Phone: (503) 370-6053
General/National Adv. Email: collegian-exec@willamette.edu
Display Adv. Email: collegian-ads@willamette.edu
Website: www.willamettecollegian.com
Published: Bi-Mthly
Personnel: Avery Bento (Advisor); James Hoodecheck (Bus. Mgr.); Gianni Marabella (Ed. in Chief)

SALINA

KANSAS WESLEYAN UNIV.

Street Address 1: 100 E Claflin Ave

College and University Newspapers

Street Address 2: # 87
State: KS
Zip/Postal code: 67401-6146
Country: USA
Mailing Address: 100 E Claflin Ave Ste 87
Mailing City: Salina
Mailing State: KS
Mailing ZIP Code: 67401-6100
General Phone: (785) 827-5541
General Fax: (785) 827-0927
Personnel: Jack Morris (Advisor)

SALISBURY

CATAWBA COLLEGE

Street Address 1: 2300 W Innes St
State: NC
Zip/Postal code: 28144-2441
Country: USA
Mailing Address: 2300 W Innes St
Mailing City: Salisbury
Mailing State: NC
Mailing ZIP Code: 28144-2488
General Phone: (704) 637-4257
Website: www.catawba.edu
Personnel: Cyndy Allison (Advisor)

SALISBURY

SALISBURY UNIV.

Street Address 1: 1101 Camden Ave
State: MD
Zip/Postal code: 21801-6837
Country: USA
Mailing Address: PO Box 3183
Mailing City: Salisbury
Mailing State: MD
Mailing ZIP Code: 21802-3183
General Phone: (410) 543-6191
General Fax: (410) 677-5359
General/National Adv. Email: flyer@salisbury.edu
Website: www.suflyerblog.blogspot.com
Personnel: Leslie Pusey (Advisor.); Vanessa Junkin (Ed.)

SALT LAKE CITY

UNIV. OF UTAH

Street Address 1: 200 Central Campus Dr
Street Address 2: Rm 234
State: UT
Zip/Postal code: 84112-9110
Country: USA
Mailing Address: 200 Central Campus Dr Rm 234
Mailing City: Salt Lake City
Mailing State: UT
Mailing ZIP Code: 84112-9110
General Phone: (801) 581-2788
General Fax: (801) 581-6882
Editorial Email: news@chronicle.utah.edu; press@chronicle.utah.edu
Website: www.dailyutahchronicle.com
Personnel: Rachel Hanson (Chief Ed.); Michael Mcfall (Ed.)

WESTMINSTER COLLEGE

Street Address 1: 1840 S 1300 E
State: UT
Zip/Postal code: 84105-3617
Country: USA
Mailing Address: 1840 S 1300 E
Mailing City: Salt Lake City
Mailing State: UT
Mailing ZIP Code: 84105-3697
General Phone: (801) 832-2320
General Fax: (801) 466-6916
General/National Adv. Email: forum@wesminstercollege.edu
Editorial Email: forumeditor@westminstercollege.edu
Website: www.forumfortnightly.com
Personnel: Ann Green (Bus. Mgr.); Fred Fogo (Advisor); Kimberly Zarkin (Advisor)

SAN ANGELO

ANGELO STATE UNIV.

Street Address 1: 2601 W Avenue N
State: TX
Zip/Postal code: 76909-2601
Country: USA
Mailing Address: PO Box 10895
Mailing City: San Angelo
Mailing State: TX
Mailing ZIP Code: 76909-0001
General Phone: (325) 942-2040
General/National Adv. Email: rampage@angelo.edu
Website: www.asurampage.com
Personnel: Leah Cooper (Ed. in Chief)

OUR LADY OF THE LAKE UNIV.

Street Address 1: 411 SW 24th St
Street Address 2: Ste 105
State: TX
Zip/Postal code: 78207-4617
Country: USA
Mailing Address: 411 SW 24th St Ste 105
Mailing City: San Antonio
Mailing State: TX
Mailing ZIP Code: 78207-4617
General Phone: (210) 434-6711
General Fax: (210) 436-0824
General/National Adv. Email: lakefront@lake.ollusa.edu; lakefrontads@lake.ollusa.edu
Website: lakefront.ollusa.edu
Personnel: Kay O'Donnell (Advisor); Tessa Benavides (Ed.)

PALO ALTO COLLEGE

Street Address 1: 1400 W Villaret Blvd
State: TX
Zip/Postal code: 78224-2417
Country: USA
Mailing Address: 1400 W Villaret Blvd
Mailing City: San Antonio
Mailing State: TX
Mailing ZIP Code: 78224-2499
General Phone: (210) 486-3880
General Fax: (210) 486-9271
Editorial Phone: 210-486-3237
General/National Adv. Email: pac-info@alamo.edu
Website: alamo.edu/pac
Year Established: 1983
Special Editions: Student newsletter published 2x per semester.
Published: Bi-Mthly

SAN ANTONIO COLLEGE

Street Address 1: 1300 San Pedro Ave
State: TX
Zip/Postal code: 78212-4201
Country: USA
Mailing Address: 1300 San Pedro Ave
Mailing City: San Antonio
Mailing State: TX
Mailing ZIP Code: 78212-4299
General Phone: (210) 486-1765
General Fax: (210) 486-9239
Advertising Phone: (210) 486-1786
Advertising Fax: (210) 486-9239
Editorial Phone: (210) 486-1773
Editorial Fax: (210) 486-9292
General/National Adv. Email: sac-ranger@alamo.edu
Website: www.theranger.org
Year Established: 1926
Special Editions: Winter edition produced in November for distribution at beginning of Spring Semester Summer edition produced in May for distribution during Summer and before Fall Semester
Delivery Methods: Racks
Commercial printers?: Y
Personnel: Marianne Odom (Advisor)

ST. MARY'S UNIV. OF SAN ANTONIO

Street Address 1: 1 Camino Santa Maria St
Street Address 2: University Center Room 258
State: TX
Zip/Postal code: 78228-5433
Country: USA
Mailing Address: 1 Camino Santa Maria
Mailing City: San Antonio
Mailing State: TX
Mailing ZIP Code: 78228
General Phone: (210) 436-3401
General Fax: (210) 431-4307
General/National Adv. Email: rattlernews@stmarytx.edu
Website: www.stmurattlernews.com/home/
Personnel: Patricia R. Garcia (Advisor); Leo Reyes (Adv. Mgr.); Sarah Mills (Ed.)

TRINITY UNIV.

Street Address 1: 1 Trinity Pl
State: TX
Zip/Postal code: 78212-4674
Country: USA
Mailing Address: 1 Trinity Pl
Mailing City: San Antonio
Mailing State: TX
Mailing ZIP Code: 78212-7201
General Phone: (210) 999-8555
General Fax: (210) 999-7034
General/National Adv. Email: trinitonian-adv@trinity.edu
Website: www.trinitonian.com
Personnel: Kathryn Martin (Advisor); Jordan Krueger (Ed.)

UNIV. OF TEXAS

Street Address 1: 14545 Roadrunner Way
State: TX
Zip/Postal code: 78249-1515
Country: USA
Mailing Address: 14545 Roadrunner Way
Mailing City: San Antonio
Mailing State: TX
Mailing ZIP Code: 78249-1515
General Phone: (210) 690-9301
General Fax: (210) 690-3423
General/National Adv. Email: paisanoeditor@sbcglobal.net
Website: www.Paisano-online.com
Personnel: Rachel Hill (Ed.)

UNIVERSITY OF THE INCARNATE WORD

Street Address 1: 4301 Broadway, Cpo 494
State: TX
Zip/Postal code: 78209
Country: USA
Mailing Address: 4301 Broadway, CPO 494
Mailing City: San Antonio
Mailing State: TX
Mailing ZIP Code: 78209-6318
General Phone: (210) 829-3964
General Fax: (210) 283-5005
Advertising Phone: (210) 829-6069
Advertising Fax: (210) 283-5005
Editorial Phone: (210) 829-6069
Editorial Fax: (210) 283-5005
General/National Adv. Email: mercer@uiwtx.edu
Display Adv. Email: mercer@uiwtx.edu
Editorial Email: mercer@uiwtx.edu
Website: www.uiw.edu/logos
Year Established: 1935
Published: Mthly
Personnel: Michael L. Mercer (Advisor)

SAN BERNARDINO

CALIFORNIA STATE UNIV.

Street Address 1: 5500 University Pkwy
State: CA
Zip/Postal code: 92407-2318
Country: USA
Mailing Address: 5500 University Pkwy
Mailing City: San Bernardino
Mailing State: CA
Mailing ZIP Code: 92407-2318
General Phone: (909) 537-5289
General Fax: (909)-537-7072
Editorial Phone: (909) 537-5815
General/National Adv. Email: sbchron@csusb.edu
Website: www.coyotechronicle.com
Personnel: Jim Smart (Advisor); Linda Sand (Adv. Mgr.); Ken Dillard (Ed. in Chief)

SAN BERNARDINO VALLEY COLLEGE

Street Address 1: 701 S Mount Vernon Ave
State: CA
Zip/Postal code: 92410-2705
Country: USA
Mailing Address: 701 S Mount Vernon Ave
Mailing City: San Bernardino
Mailing State: CA
Mailing ZIP Code: 92410-2798
General Phone: (909) 888-1996
General Fax: (909) 381-4604
Website: www.sbvcarrowhead.com
Personnel: Gary Kellam (Ed.)

SAN DIEGO

POINT LOMA NAZARENE UNIV.

Street Address 1: 3900 Lomaland Dr
State: CA
Zip/Postal code: 92106-2810
Country: USA
Mailing Address: 3900 Lomaland Dr
Mailing City: San Diego
Mailing State: CA
Mailing ZIP Code: 92106-2899
General Phone: (619) 849-2444
General Fax: (619) 849-7009
General/National Adv. Email: news@pointweekly.com; sports@pointweekly.com; advertising@pointweekly.com
Website: www.pointweekly.com
Personnel: Stephanie Gant (Adv. Mgr.); Dean Nelson (Journalism Dir.); Coco Jones (Ed. in Chief); Nathan Scharn (Features Ed.)

SAN DIEGO CITY COLLEGE

Street Address 1: 1313 Park Blvd
Street Address 2: Rm T-316
State: CA
Zip/Postal code: 92101-4712
Country: USA
Mailing Address: 1313 Park Blvd Rm T-316
Mailing City: San Diego
Mailing State: CA
Mailing ZIP Code: 92101-4787
General Phone: (619) 388-4026
General Fax: (619) 388-3814
General/National Adv. Email: citytimes@gmail.com
Display Adv. Email: ads.citytimes@gmail.com
Website: www.sdcitytimes.com
Personnel: Roman Koenig (Advisor); Vanessa Gomez (Ed. in Chief)

SAN DIEGO MESA COLLEGE

Street Address 1: 7250 Mesa College Dr
State: CA
Zip/Postal code: 92111-4902
Country: USA
Mailing Address: 7250 Mesa College Dr
Mailing City: San Diego
Mailing State: CA
Mailing ZIP Code: 92111-4999
General Phone: (619) 388-2630
General Fax: (619) 388-2836
General/National Adv. Email: mesa.press@gmail.com
Website: www.mesapress.com
Year Established: 1966
Personnel: Janna Braun (Advisor)

SAN DIEGO MIRAMAR COLLEGE

Street Address 1: 10440 Black Mountain Rd
State: CA

Zip/Postal code: 92126-2910
Country: USA
Mailing Address: 10440 Black Mountain Rd
Mailing City: San Diego
Mailing State: CA
Mailing ZIP Code: 92126-2999
General Phone: (619) 388-7800
General Fax: (619)-388-7900
Website: www.sdmiramar.edu
Personnel: Leslie Klipper (Advisor); Sandy Treivasan (Advertisments)

SAN DIEGO STATE UNIV.

Street Address 1: EBA-2
State: CA
Zip/Postal code: 92182-0001
Country: USA
Mailing Address: EBA-2
Mailing City: San Diego
Mailing State: CA
Mailing ZIP Code: 92182-0001
General Phone: (619) 594-1804
General Fax: (619) 594-1804
Advertising Phone: (619) 594-6977
General/National Adv. Email: daads@mail.sdsu.edu
Website: 2259 Birds Nest
Year Established: 1913
Published: Wed
Avg Free Circ: 5000
Personnel: Andrew Dyer

UNIV. OF SAN DIEGO

Street Address 1: 5998 Alcala Park
State: CA
Zip/Postal code: 92110-8001
Country: USA
Mailing Address: 5998 Alcala Park Frnt
Mailing City: San Diego
Mailing State: CA
Mailing ZIP Code: 92110-2492
General Phone: (619) 260-4714
General Fax: (619) 260-4807
Editorial Phone: (619) 260-4584
Website: www.uofsdmedia.com
Published: Thur
Personnel: Brooklyn Dippo (EIC); Sarah Brewington (Associate Ed); Diego Luna (Mgr Ed)

UNIV. OF SAN DIEGO SCHOOL OF LAW

Street Address 1: 5998 Alcala Park
State: CA
Zip/Postal code: 92110-8001
Country: USA
Mailing Address: 5998 Alcala Park
Mailing City: San Diego
Mailing State: CA
Mailing ZIP Code: 92110-8001
General Phone: (619) 260-4600
General Fax: (619) 260-4753
General/National Adv. Email: motions@sandiego.edu
Website: www.sandiego.edu/motions
Personnel: Damien Schiff (Ed.)

SAN FRANCISCO

CITY COLLEGE OF SAN FRANCISCO

Street Address 1: 50 Phelan Ave
Street Address 2: # V67
State: CA
Zip/Postal code: 94112-1821
Country: USA
Mailing Address: 50 Phelan Ave # V67
Mailing City: San Francisco
Mailing State: CA
Mailing ZIP Code: 94112-1898
General Phone: (415) 239-3446
General Fax: (415) 239-3884
General/National Adv. Email: email@theguardsman.com
Display Adv. Email: advertising@theguardsman.com
Editorial Email: editor@theguardsman.com
Website: www.theguardsman.com
Year Established: 1935
Delivery Methods: Racks
Commercial printers?: N
Published: Wed
Published Other: Bi-Weekly
Avg Free Circ: 7000
Personnel: Juan Gonzales (Advisor)

GOLDEN GATE UNIV.

Street Address 1: 536 Mission St
State: CA
Zip/Postal code: 94105-2921
Country: USA
Mailing Address: 536 Mission St
Mailing City: San Francisco
Mailing State: CA
Mailing ZIP Code: 94105-2968
General Phone: (415) 442-7871
General Fax: (415) 442-7896
General/National Adv. Email: campuscurrent@gguol.ggu.edu
Website: www.ggu.edu
Personnel: Brian Louie (Vice Pres., PR/Mktg.); Ambrose Tse (Vice Pres., Finance/Admin.)

HASTINGS COLLEGE OF LAW

Street Address 1: 200 McAllister St
State: CA
Zip/Postal code: 94102-4707
Country: USA
Mailing Address: 200 McAllister St
Mailing City: San Francisco
Mailing State: CA
Mailing ZIP Code: 94102-4978
General Phone: (415) 565-4786
General Fax: (707) 313-0161
Personnel: John Hendrickson (Ed.)

SAN FRANCISCO STATE UNIVERSITY

Street Address 1: 1600 Holloway Ave
State: CA
Zip/Postal code: 94132-1722
Country: USA
Mailing Address: 1600 Holloway Ave # 4200
Mailing City: San Francisco
Mailing State: CA
Mailing ZIP Code: 94132-1740
General Phone: (415) 338-1689
General Fax: (415) 338-2084
General/National Adv. Email: jour@sfsu.edu
Website: www.journalism.sfsu.edu
Year Established: 1934
Personnel: Venise Wagner (Dept. Chair/Assoc. Prof.); Jon Funabiki (Assoc. Dept. Chair/Prof.); Dottie Katzeff (Adv. Mgr.); John Burks (Prof.); Barbara Landes (Prodn. Mgr.); Nathan Codd (Ed. in Chief); Yvonne Daley (Prof.); Kenneth Kobre (Prof.); Erna R. Smith (Prof.); Rachele Kanigel (Assoc. Prof.); Austin Long-Scott (Assoc. Prof.); Cristina Azocar (Asst. Prof./Dir., Ctr. for Integration/Improvement of Journalism); Yumi Wilson (Asst. Prof.); John T. Johnson (Prof. Emer.); B.H. Liebes (Prof. Emer.); Betty Medsger (Prof. Emer.); Leonard Sellers (Prof. Emer.); Jerrold Werthimer (Prof. Emer.); Harriet Chiang (Lectr.); Roland DeWolk (Lectr.); Jesse Garnier (Lectr.); David Greene (Lectr.); Sibylla Herbrich (Lectr.)

UNIV. OF SAN FRANCISCO

Street Address 1: 2130 Fulton St
State: CA
Zip/Postal code: 94117-1080
Country: USA
Mailing Address: 2130 Fulton St
Mailing City: San Francisco
Mailing State: CA
Mailing ZIP Code: 94117-1050
General Fax: (415) 422-2751
General/National Adv. Email: foghorn_ads@yahoo.com
Display Adv. Email: advertising@sffoghorn.info
Website: foghorn.usfca.edu/
Personnel: Theresa Moore (Advisor); Laura Plantholt (Ed. in Chief); Nicholas Muhkar (Mng. Ed.); Chelsea Sterling (News Ed.); Matt (Sports Ed.); Mark (Adv. Mgr.); Erika (Bus. Mgr.)

UNIV. OF SAN FRANCISCO LAW SCHOOL

Street Address 1: 2130 Fulton St
State: CA
Zip/Postal code: 94117-1080
Country: USA
Mailing Address: 2130 Fulton St
Mailing City: San Francisco
Mailing State: CA
Mailing ZIP Code: 94117-1050
General Phone: (415) 422-6586
General Fax: (415) 666-6433
General/National Adv. Email: theforumusf@gmail.com
Personnel: Andie Vallee (Ed.)

UNIVERSITY OF CALIFORNIA, SAN FRANCISCO

Street Address 1: 500 Parnassus Ave
Street Address 2: # 108W
State: CA
Zip/Postal code: 94143-2203
Country: USA
Mailing Address: 108 W Millberry Un
Mailing City: San Francisco
Mailing State: CA
Mailing ZIP Code: 94143-0001
General Phone: (415) 476-2211
General Fax: (415) 502-4537
General/National Adv. Email: synapse@ucsf.edu
Display Adv. Email: synapse@ucsf.edu
Website: synapse.ucsf.edu
Published: Thur
Personnel: Steven Chin (Managing Editor)

SAN JOSE

EVERGREEN VALLEY COLLEGE

Street Address 1: 3095 Yerba Buena Rd
State: CA
Zip/Postal code: 95135-1513
Country: USA
Mailing Address: 3095 Yerba Buena Rd
Mailing City: San Jose
Mailing State: CA
Mailing ZIP Code: 95135-1598
General Phone: (408) 274-7900

SAN JOSE CITY COLLEGE

Street Address 1: 2100 Moorpark Ave
State: CA
Zip/Postal code: 95128-2723
Country: USA
Mailing Address: 2100 Moorpark Ave
Mailing City: San Jose
Mailing State: CA
Mailing ZIP Code: 95128-2799
General Phone: (408) 298-2181
General Fax: (408) 288-6331
General/National Adv. Email: thesjcctimes@hotmail.com
Website: www.sjcc.edu

SAN JOSE STATE UNIV.

Street Address 1: 1 Washington Sq
State: CA
Zip/Postal code: 95112-3613
Country: USA
Mailing Address: 1 Washington Sq
Mailing City: San Jose
Mailing State: CA
Mailing ZIP Code: 95112-3613
General Phone: (408) 924-3281
General Fax: (408) 924-3282
Advertising Phone: (408) 924-3270
General/National Adv. Email: spartandaily@casa.sjsu.edu
Display Adv. Email: spartandailyads@casa.sjsu.edu
Website: www.thespartandaily.com
Personnel: Richard Craig (Advisor); Timothy Hendrick (Advisor); Jenny Ngo (Adv. Dir.); Joey Akeley (Exec. Ed.)

SAN LUIS OBISPO

CALIFORNIA POLYTECHNIC STATE UNIV.

Street Address 1: 1 Grand Ave
State: CA
Zip/Postal code: 93407-9000
Country: USA
Mailing Address: 1 Grand Ave
Mailing City: San Luis Obispo
Mailing State: CA
Mailing ZIP Code: 93407-9000
General Phone: (805) 756-2537
General Fax: (805) 756-6784
Advertising Phone: (805) 756-1143
Advertising Fax: (805) 756-6784
Editorial Phone: (805) 756-1796
Editorial Fax: (805) 756-6784
General/National Adv. Email: editor@mustangnews.net
Display Adv. Email: advertising@mustangnews.net
Website: www.mustangnews.net
Year Established: 1916
Special Editions: Freshman Week of Welcome Back to School Fall Graduation Best for Cal Poly Housing Fair Open House Spring Graduation Summer Orientation, Advising and Registration (SOAR)
Delivery Methods: Newsstand Racks
Commercial printers?: N
Published: Mon`Thur
Avg Free Circ: 6000
Personnel: Paul Bittick (GM)

CUESTA COLLEGE

Street Address 1: Bldg 7400, Hwy 1
State: CA
Zip/Postal code: 93403
Country: USA
Mailing Address: PO Box 8106
Mailing City: San Luis Obispo
Mailing State: CA
Mailing ZIP Code: 93403-8106
General Phone: (805) 546-3288
General Fax: (805) 546-3904
General/National Adv. Email: cuestonian@cuesta.edu
Website: www.cuestonian.cuesta.edu; www.cuesta.edu
Personnel: Patrick Howe (Advisor); Mary Mc Corkle (Advisor); Sarah Clifford (Ed.); Bethany Fraker (Ed.)

SAN MARCOS

CALIFORNIA STATE UNIVERSITY, SAN MARCOS

Street Address 1: 333 S Twin Oaks Valley Rd
State: CA
Zip/Postal code: 92096-0001
Country: USA
Mailing Address: 333 S Twin Oaks Valley Rd
Mailing City: San Marcos
Mailing State: CA
Mailing ZIP Code: 92096-0001
General Phone: (760) 750-6099
General Fax: (760) 750-3345
Advertising Phone: (760) 750-6099
Advertising Fax: (760) 750-3345
Editorial Phone: (760) 750-6099
Editorial Fax: Free
General/National Adv. Email: csusm.chronicle@gmail.com
Editorial Email: csusm.chronicle@gmail.com
Website: www.csusmchronicle.com

College and University Newspapers

Year Established: 1992
Delivery Methods: Newsstand
Published: Wed
Avg Free Circ: 1500
Personnel: Pam Kragen (Advisor); Morgan Hall (Co-Editor-in-Chief, Editor of Design); Kristin Melody (Co-Editor-in-Chief); Rogers Jaffarian (Advertising Manager)

PALOMAR COLLEGE

Street Address 1: 1140 W Mission Rd
Street Address 2: Rm CH-7
State: CA
Zip/Postal code: 92069-1415
Country: USA
Mailing Address: 1140 W Mission Rd Rm CH-7
Mailing City: San Marcos
Mailing State: CA
Mailing ZIP Code: 92069-1487
General Phone: (760) 744-1150
General Fax: (760) 744-8123
General/National Adv. Email: telescopead@palomar.edu
Website: www.the-telescope.com
Year Established: 1946
Personnel: Erin Hiro (Advisor); Sara Burbidge (Adv. Mgr.); Kelley Foyt (Co-Ed. in Chief)

TEXAS STATE UNIV.

Street Address 1: 601 University Dr Bldg Trinity
Street Address 2: 203 Pleasant Street
State: TX
Zip/Postal code: 78666-4684
Country: USA
Mailing Address: 601 University Dr Bldg Trinity
Mailing City: San Marcos
Mailing State: TX
Mailing ZIP Code: 78666-4684
General Phone: (512) 245-3487
General Fax: (512) 245-3708
Advertising Phone: (512 245-2261
Advertising Fax: (512) 245-3708
General/National Adv. Email: stareditor@txstate.edu
Display Adv. Email: starad1@txstate.edu
Editorial Email: stareditor@txstate.edu
Website: www.universitystar.com
Year Established: 1911
News Services: Tribune
Delivery Methods: Newsstand`Racks
Commercial printers?: Y
Published: Mon`Wed`Thur
Personnel: Bob Bajackson (Advisor)

SAN MATEO

COLLEGE OF SAN MATEO

Street Address 1: 94402 -3757
State: CA
Country: USA
Mailing Address: 1700 W Hillsdale Blvd
Mailing City: San Mateo
Mailing State: CA
Mailing ZIP Code: 94402-3784
General Phone: (650) 574-6330
Editorial Phone: (650) 652-6721
General/National Adv. Email: sanmatean@smccd.edu
Website: www.sanmatean.com
Year Established: 1928
Personnel: Ed Remitz (Advisor); Margeret Baum (Ed.); Sharon Ho (Mng. Ed.); Laura Babbitt (News Ed.)

SAN PABLO

CONTRA COSTA COLLEGE

Street Address 1: 2600 Mission Bell Dr
State: CA
Zip/Postal code: 94806-3166
Country: USA
Mailing Address: 2600 Mission Bell Dr
Mailing City: San Pablo
Mailing State: CA
Mailing ZIP Code: 94806-3195

General Phone: (510) 235-7800
General Fax: (510) 235-6397
General/National Adv. Email: advocate@contracosta.edu
Website: www.contracosta.edu; www.accentadvocate.com
Personnel: Paul DeBlot (Advisor); Holly Pablo (Ed. in Chief); Sam Attal (Ed.)

SAN PEDRO

LOS ANGELES HARBOR COLLEGE

Street Address 1: 1300 S Pacific Ave
State: CA
Zip/Postal code: 90731-4108
Country: USA
Mailing Address: PO Box 731
Mailing City: San Pedro
Mailing State: CA
Mailing ZIP Code: 90733-0731
General Phone: (310) 519-1016
General Fax: (310) 832-1000
Advertising Fax: 1310 832-1000
Editorial Phone: (310) 519-1442
Display Adv. Email: rlnsales@randomlengthsnews.com
Editorial Email: editor@randomlengthsnews.com
Website: www.randomlengthsnews.com
Year Established: 1979
Published: Thur`Bi-Mthly
Personnel: James Preston Allen (Pub.); Paul Rosenberg (Mng. Ed.); Terelle Jerricks (Mng Ed)

SAN RAFAEL

DOMINICAN COLLEGE

Street Address 1: 50 Acacia Ave
State: CA
Zip/Postal code: 94901-2230
Country: USA
Mailing Address: 50 Acacia Ave
Mailing City: San Rafael
Mailing State: CA
Mailing ZIP Code: 94901-2298
General Phone: (415) 485-3204
General Fax: (415) 485-3205
Website: www.dominican.edu
Personnel: Melva Bealf (Advisor)

SANBORN

NIAGARA COUNTY CMTY. COLLEGE

Street Address 1: 3111 Saunders Settlement Rd
State: NY
Zip/Postal code: 14132-9506
Country: USA
Mailing Address: 3111 Saunders Settlement Rd Ste 1
Mailing City: Sanborn
Mailing State: NY
Mailing ZIP Code: 14132-9460
General Phone: (716) 614-6259
General Fax: (716) 614-6264
General/National Adv. Email: spirit@niagaracc.suny.edu
Personnel: Amanda Pucci (Advisor)

SANTA ANA

SANTA ANA COLLEGE

Street Address 1: 1530 W 17th St
State: CA
Zip/Postal code: 92706-3398
Country: USA
Mailing Address: 1530 W 17th St
Mailing City: Santa Ana
Mailing State: CA
Mailing ZIP Code: 92706-3398
General Phone: (714) 564-5617
General Fax: (714) 564-0821
General/National Adv. Email: eldonbusiness@sac.edu
Website: www.eldononline.org
Personnel: Charles Little (Advisor); Allene

Symons (Adv. Mgr.)

SANTA BARBARA

RANDY VANDERMEY

Street Address 1: 132 Walnut Ln
State: CA
Zip/Postal code: 93111-2148
Country: USA
Mailing Address: 132 Walnut Lane
Mailing City: Santa Barbara
Mailing State: CA
Mailing ZIP Code: 93111
General Phone: (805) 683-1115
General Fax:
Advertising Phone: (805) 683-1115
Advertising Fax: (805) 683-1115
Editorial Phone: (805) 683-1115
Editorial Fax:
General/National Adv. Email: vanderme@westmont.edu
Display Adv. Email: horizon@westmont.edu
Editorial Email: horizon@westmont.edu
Website: horizon.westmont.edu/pages/contact
Year Established: c. 1945
Published: Tues
Avg Free Circ: 800
Personnel: Randy VanderMey (Advisor); M<itchell MacMahon (Editor-in-Chief)

SANTA BARBARA CITY COLLEGE

Street Address 1: 721 Cliff Dr
Street Address 2: Rm 123
State: CA
Zip/Postal code: 93109-2312
Country: USA
Mailing Address: 721 Cliff Dr Rm 123
Mailing City: Santa Barbara
Mailing State: CA
Mailing ZIP Code: 93109-2394
General Phone: (805) 965-0581
General Fax: (805) 730-3079
General/National Adv. Email: channels@sbcc.edu
Website: www.thechannelsonline.com
Personnel: Patricia Stark (Advisor)

UNIV. OF CALIFORNIA, SANTA BARBARA

Street Address 1: PO Box 13402
State: CA
Zip/Postal code: 93107-3402
Country: USA
Mailing Address: PO Box 13402
Mailing City: Santa Barbara
Mailing State: CA
Mailing ZIP Code: 93107-3402
General Phone: (805) 893-3828
Advertising Phone: (805) 893-4006
General/National Adv. Email: production@dailynexus.com
Display Adv. Email: LINDA.MEYER@SA.UCSB.EDU
Editorial Email: EIC@DAILYNEXUS.COM
Website: www.dailynexus.com
Published: Thur
Avg Free Circ: 4000
Personnel: Linda Meyer (Adv. Mgr.)

SANTA CLARA

SANTA CLARA UNIVERSITY

Street Address 1: Center for Student Leadership
State: CA
Zip/Postal code: 95053-0001
Country: USA
Mailing Address: 500 El Camino Real # 3190
Mailing City: Santa Clara
Mailing State: CA
Mailing ZIP Code: 95053-0001
General Phone: (408) 554-4849
General/National Adv. Email: news@thesantaclara.com
Display Adv. Email: advertising@thesantaclara.com

Editorial Email: editor@thesantaclara.com; letters@thesantaclara.com; news@thesantaclara.com
Website: www.thesantaclara.com
Year Established: 1922
Published: Thur
Avg Free Circ: 1100
Personnel: Sophie Mattson

SANTA CLARITA

COLLEGE OF THE CANYONS

Street Address 1: 26455 Rockwell Canyon Rd
State: CA
Zip/Postal code: 91355-1803
Country: USA
Mailing Address: 26455 Rockwell Canyon Rd
Mailing City: Santa Clarita
Mailing State: CA
Mailing ZIP Code: 91355-1899
General Phone: (661) 259-7800
General Fax: (661) 362-3043
Personnel: Jim Ruebsamen (Advisor)

SANTA MONICA

SANTA MONICA COLLEGE

Street Address 1: 1900 Pico Blvd
Street Address 2: # 303
State: CA
Zip/Postal code: 90405-1628
Country: USA
Mailing Address: 1900 Pico Blvd # 303
Mailing City: Santa Monica
Mailing State: CA
Mailing ZIP Code: 90405-1644
General Phone: (310) 434-4340
General Fax: (310) 434-3648
Editorial Fax: Free
General/National Adv. Email: corsair.editorinchief@gmail.com
Display Adv. Email: blaize_ashanti@smc.edu
Editorial Email: corsair.editorinchief@gmail.com
Website: www.thecorsaironline.com
Year Established: 1929
Delivery Methods: Mail`Newsstand`Racks
Commercial printers?: Y
Personnel: Saul Rubin (Advisor)

SANTA ROSA

SANTA ROSA JUNIOR COLLEGE

Street Address 1: 1501 Mendocino Ave
State: CA
Zip/Postal code: 95401-4332
Country: USA
Mailing Address: 1501 Mendocino Ave.
Mailing City: Santa Rosa
Mailing State: CA
Mailing ZIP Code: 95401-4332
General Phone: (707) 527-4401
Advertising Phone: (707) 527-4254
General/National Adv. Email: abelden@santarosa.edu
Display Adv. Email: oakleaf-ads@santarosa.edu
Editorial Email: abelden@santarosa.edu
Website: www.santarosa.edu
Year Established: 1928
Personnel: Ann Belden (Advisor)

SARATOGA

WEST VALLEY COLLEGE

Street Address 1: 14000 Fruitvale Ave
State: CA
Zip/Postal code: 95070-5640
Country: USA
Mailing Address: 14000 Fruitvale Ave
Mailing City: Saratoga
Mailing State: CA
Mailing ZIP Code: 95070-5698
General Phone: (408) 867-2200
General Fax: (408) 741-4040
Website: www.westvalley.edu
Personnel: Janine Gerzanics (Advisor)

SARATOGA SPRINGS

THE SKIDMORE NEWS

Street Address 1: 815 N Broadway
Street Address 2: Skidmore College
State: NY
Zip/Postal code: 12866-1632
Country: USA
Mailing Address: 815 N Broadway
Mailing City: Saratoga Springs
Mailing State: NY
Mailing ZIP Code: 12866-1632
General Phone: (518) 580-5000
General Fax: (518) 580-5188
General/National Adv. Email: skidnews@skidmore.edu
Website: www.skidmorenews.com
Year Established: 1925
Personnel: Savannah Grier (Ed. in Chief)

SAULT SAINTE MARIE

LAKE SUPERIOR STATE UNIV.

Street Address 1: 650 W Easterday Ave
Street Address 2: Cisler Center 106
State: MI
Zip/Postal code: 49783-1626
Country: USA
Mailing Address: 650 W Easterday Ave
Mailing City: Sault Sainte Marie
Mailing State: MI
Mailing ZIP Code: 49783-1626
General Phone: (906) 635-2551
General Fax: (906) 635-7510
General/National Adv. Email: compass@lssu.edu
Display Adv. Email: compass@lssu.edu
Editorial Email: compass@lssu.edu
Website: compass.lssu.edu
Year Established: 1946
Delivery Methods: Mail`Newsstand`Racks
Commercial printers?: Y
Published: Mthly
Personnel: Asher Stephenson (Editor In Chief)
Parent company (for newspapers): Lake Superior State University; LSSU Student Assembly

SAVANNAH

ARMSTRONG ATLANTIC STATE UNIV.

Street Address 1: Memorial College Ctr, 11935 Abercorn St, Rm 202
State: GA
Country: USA
Mailing Address: Memorial College Ctr., 11935 Abercorn St., Rm. 202
Mailing City: Savannah
Mailing State: GA
Mailing ZIP Code: 31419-1909
General Phone: (912) 344-3252
General Fax: (912) 344-3475
General/National Adv. Email: inkwellnews@gmail.com
Website: www.theinkwellonline.com
Personnel: Tony Morris (Advisor); Kristin Alonso (Ed. in Chief)

SAVANNAH COLLEGE OF ART/DESIGN

Street Address 1: PO Box 3146
State: GA
Zip/Postal code: 31402-3146
Country: USA
Mailing Address: PO Box 3146
Mailing City: Savannah
Mailing State: GA
Mailing ZIP Code: 31402-3146
General Phone: (912) 525-5500
General Fax: (912) 525-5506
General/National Adv. Email: district@scad.edu
Website: www.scaddistrict.com
Personnel: Aisha Michael (Circ./Classified Mgr.)

SCHENECTADY

UNION COLLEGE CONCORDIENSIS

Street Address 1: 807 Union St
State: NY
Zip/Postal code: 12308-3256
Country: USA
Mailing Address: 807 Union St.
Mailing City: Schenectady
Mailing State: NY
Mailing ZIP Code: 12308
General Phone: (518) 388-7128
General/National Adv. Email: concordy@gmail.com
Display Adv. Email: advertising@concordy.com
Website: www.concordy.com/
Year Established: 1877
Commercial printers?: N
Personnel: Ajay Major (Ed. in Chief)

SCHUYLKILL HAVEN

PENN STATE UNIV.

Street Address 1: 200 University Dr
State: PA
Zip/Postal code: 17972-2202
Country: USA
Mailing Address: 200 University Dr
Mailing City: Schuylkill Haven
Mailing State: PA
Mailing ZIP Code: 17972-2208
General Phone: (570) 385-6000
Personnel: Wes Loder (Advisor)

SCOTTSBLUFF

WESTERN NEBRASKA COMMUNITY COLLEGE

Street Address 1: 1601 E 27th St
State: NE
Zip/Postal code: 69361-1815
Country: USA
Mailing Address: 1601 E 27th St
Mailing City: Scottsbluff
Mailing State: NE
Mailing ZIP Code: 69361-1899
General Phone: (308) 635-6058
Advertising Phone: 308-636-6057
General/National Adv. Email: spectator@wncc.edu
Delivery Methods: Mail`Racks
Commercial printers?: Y
Personnel: Mark Rein (Adv. Mgr.); Jay Grote

SCRANTON

MARYWOOD UNIVERSITY

Street Address 1: 2300 Adams Ave
State: PA
Zip/Postal code: 18509-1514
Country: USA
Mailing Address: 2300 Adams Ave
Mailing City: Scranton
Mailing State: PA
Mailing ZIP Code: 18509-1598
General Phone: (570) 348-6211
General Fax: (570) 961-4768
General/National Adv. Email: thewoodword@m.marywood.edu
Website: www.thewoodword.org
Published: Mthly
Personnel: Ann Williams (Advisor); Lindsey Wotanis (Advisor)

SCRANTON

UNIV. OF SCRANTON

Street Address 1: 800 Linden St
State: PA
Zip/Postal code: 18510-2429
Country: USA
Mailing Address: 800 Linden St
Mailing City: Scranton
Mailing State: PA
Mailing ZIP Code: 18510
General Phone: (570) 941-7464
General Fax: (570) 941-4836
General/National Adv. Email: aquinas@scranton.edu
Website: academic.scranton.edu/organization/aquinas
Personnel: Scott Walsh (Advisor)

SEARCY

HARDING UNIV.

Street Address 1: PO Box 11192
State: AR
Zip/Postal code: 72149-0001
Country: USA
Mailing Address: PO Box 11192
Mailing City: Searcy
Mailing State: AR
Mailing ZIP Code: 72149-0001
General Phone: (501) 279-4139
General Fax: (501) 279-4127
General/National Adv. Email: thebison@harding.edu
Website: thebison.harding.edu
Personnel: Jermy Beauchamp (Dir., Publications); Jermy (Advisor)

SEATTLE

SEATTLE CENTRAL CMTY. COLLEGE

Street Address 1: 1701 Broadway
Street Address 2: # BE1145
State: WA
Zip/Postal code: 98122-2413
Country: USA
Mailing Address: 1701 Broadway # BE1145
Mailing City: Seattle
Mailing State: WA
Mailing ZIP Code: 98122-2413
General Phone: (206) 587-6959
General Fax: (206) 903-3235
General/National Adv. Email: editor@thecitycollegian.com
Personnel: Rachel Swedish (Ed. in Chief)

SEATTLE PACIFIC UNIV.

Street Address 1: 3307 3rd Ave W
State: WA
Zip/Postal code: 98119-1940
Country: USA
Mailing Address: 3307 3rd Ave W
Mailing City: Seattle
Mailing State: WA
Mailing ZIP Code: 98119-1997
General Phone: (206) 281-2913
General Fax: (206) 378-5003
General/National Adv. Email: falcon-ads@spu.edu
Editorial Email: falcon-online@spu.edu; falcon-news@spu.edu; falcon-sports@spu.edu; falcon-features@spu.edu; falcon-opinions@spu.edu
Website: www.thefalcononline.com
Personnel: Katie-Joy Blanksma (Ed. in Chief); Haley Libak (Layout Ed.); Madeline Tremain (Layout Ed.)

SEATTLE UNIVERSITY

Street Address 1: 901 12th Ave
State: WA
Zip/Postal code: 98122-4411
Country: USA
Mailing Address: PO Box 222000
Mailing City: Seattle
Mailing State: WA
Mailing ZIP Code: 98122-1090
General Phone: (206) 296-6470
General Fax: (206) 296-2163
Advertising Phone: (206) 296-6474
Editorial Email: editor@su-spectator.com; support@collegepublisher.com
Website: www.seattlespectator.com
Year Established: 1933
Published: Wed
Personnel: Sonora Jha (Advisor)

SOUTH SEATTLE CMTY. COLLEGE

Street Address 1: 6000 16th Ave SW
Street Address 2: Jmb 135
State: WA
Zip/Postal code: 98106-1401
Country: USA
Mailing Address: 6000 16th Ave SW Jmb 135
Mailing City: Seattle
Mailing State: WA
Mailing ZIP Code: 98106-1401
General Phone: (206) 764-5335
General Fax: (206) 764-7936
Advertising Phone: (206) 764-5335
Editorial Phone: (206) 764-5333
General/National Adv. Email: sentinelads@sccd.ctc.edu
Editorial Email: sentineleditor@sccd.ctc.edu
Website: sites.southseattle.edu/thesentinel
Personnel: Betsy Berger (Advisor)

UNIV. OF WASHINGTON

Street Address 1: 144 Communications Bldg
Street Address 2: Box 353720
State: WA
Zip/Postal code: 98195-0001
Country: USA
Mailing Address: 132 Communications
Mailing City: Seattle
Mailing State: WA
Mailing ZIP Code: 98195-0001
General Phone: (206) 543-2336
General Fax: (206) 543-2345
Advertising Phone: (206) 543-2335
Editorial Phone: 206-543-2700
Display Adv. Email: ads@dailyuw.com
Editorial Email: editor@dailyuw.com
Website: www.dailyuw.com
Year Established: 1891
Published: Mon`Tues`Wed`Thur`Fri
Avg Free Circ: 7500
Personnel: Diana Kramer (Dir., Student Publications); Andreas Redd (Editor-in-Chief)

SEGUIN

TEXAS LUTHERAN UNIV.

Street Address 1: 1000 W Court St
State: TX
Zip/Postal code: 78155-5978
Country: USA
Mailing Address: 1000 W Court St
Mailing City: Seguin
Mailing State: TX
Mailing ZIP Code: 78155-9996
General Phone: (830) 372-8073
General Fax: (830) 372-8074
General/National Adv. Email: lonestarlutheran@tlu.edu
Website: www.lslonline.net
Personnel: Robin Bisha (Advisor); Steven S. Vrooman (Chair); Kristi Quiros (Pub.); Emmalee Drummond (Ed. in Chief); Naomi Urquiza (Mng. Ed.)

SELINSGROVE

SUSQUEHANNA UNIV.

Street Address 1: 1858 Weber Way
State: PA
Zip/Postal code: 17870-1150
Country: USA
Mailing Address: CA Box 18
Mailing City: Selinsgrove
Mailing State: PA
Mailing ZIP Code: 17870
General Phone: (570) 374-4298
General Fax: (570) 372-2745
General/National Adv. Email: suquill@susqu.edu
Website: www.suquill.com
Year Established: 1896
Published: Fri
Avg Free Circ: 2200
Personnel: Catherine Hastings (Advisor)

College and University Newspapers

SENATOBIA

NORTHWEST MISSISSIPPI CMTY. COLLEGE

Street Address 1: 4975 Highway 51 N
State: MS
Zip/Postal code: 38668-1714
Country: USA
Mailing Address: PO Box 7039
Mailing City: Senatobia
Mailing State: MS
Mailing ZIP Code: 38668
General Phone: (662) 562-3276
General Fax: (662) 562-3499
General/National Adv. Email: rangerrocket1@northwestms.edu
Website: www.northwestms.edu
Year Established: 1927
Personnel: Ranate Ferreira (Advisor); Chris Creasy (Ed.)

SEWANEE

UNIV. OF THE SOUTH

Street Address 1: 735 University Ave
State: TN
Zip/Postal code: 37383-2000
Country: USA
Mailing Address: 735 University Ave
Mailing City: Sewanee
Mailing State: TN
Mailing ZIP Code: 37383-1000
General Phone: (931) 598-1204
General/National Adv. Email: spurple@sewanee.edu
Website: www.sewaneepurple.com
Personnel: Virginia Craighll (Advisor)

SEWARD

CONCORDIA UNIVERSITY-NEBRASKA

Street Address 1: 800 N Columbia Ave
State: NE
Zip/Postal code: 68434-1500
Country: USA
Mailing Address: 800 N Columbia Ave Ste 1
Mailing City: Seward
Mailing State: NE
Mailing ZIP Code: 68434-1599
General Phone: 703-434-0355
General/National Adv. Email: sower@cune.org
Website: www.cunesower.com
Delivery Methods: Carrier`Racks
Commercial printers?: N
Published: Mthly
Published Other: Website updated throughout the week
Avg Free Circ: 1300
Personnel: Ellen Beck (Adviser)

SEWELL

GLOUCESTER COUNTY COLLEGE

Street Address 1: 1400 Tanyard Rd
State: NJ
Zip/Postal code: 08080-4222
Country: USA
Mailing Address: 1400 Tanyard Rd
Mailing City: Sewell
Mailing State: NJ
Mailing ZIP Code: 08080-4249
General Phone: (856) 468-5000
General Fax: (856) 464-9153
General/National Adv. Email: gazette@gccnj.edu
Commercial printers?: Y
Personnel: Brooke Hoffman (Advisor); Keesha Patterson (Advisor)

SHAWNEE

OKLAHOMA BAPTIST UNIV.

Street Address 1: 500 W University St
Street Address 2: Ste 61704
State: OK
Zip/Postal code: 74804-2522
Country: USA
Mailing Address: 500 W University St Ste 61704
Mailing City: Shawnee
Mailing State: OK
Mailing ZIP Code: 74804-2522
General Phone: (405) 878-2128
General Fax: (405) 878-2113
General/National Adv. Email: Holly.easttom@okbu.edu
Display Adv. Email: Holly.easttom@okbu.edu
Website: www.okbu.edu
Year Established: 1942
Published: Wed
Avg Free Circ: 1800
Personnel: Holly Easttom (Advisor); Andrew Adams (Ed. in Chief)

ST. GREGORY'S COLLEGE

Street Address 1: 1900 W MacArthur St
State: OK
Zip/Postal code: 74804-2403
Country: USA
Mailing Address: 1900 W MacArthur St
Mailing City: Shawnee
Mailing State: OK
Mailing ZIP Code: 74804-2499
General Phone: (405) 878-5100
General Fax: (405) 878-5198
Personnel: Andrew Sneider (Advisor)

SHEBOYGAN

LAKELAND COLLEGE

Street Address 1: PO Box 359
State: WI
Zip/Postal code: 53082-0359
Country: USA
Mailing Address: PO Box 359
Mailing City: Sheboygan
Mailing State: WI
Mailing ZIP Code: 53082-0359
General Phone: (920) 565-1316
General Fax: (920) 565-1344
General/National Adv. Email: mirror@lakeland.edu
Website: www.lakelandmirror.com
Personnel: Becky Meyer (Author); Ashley Paulson (Adv. Mgr.)

UNIV. OF WISCONSIN SHEBOYGAN

Street Address 1: 1 University Dr
State: WI
Zip/Postal code: 53081-4760
Country: USA
Mailing Address: 1 University Dr
Mailing City: Sheboygan
Mailing State: WI
Mailing ZIP Code: 53081-4789
General Phone: (920) 459-6600
General Fax: (920) 459-6602
General/National Adv. Email: shbinfo@uwc.edu
Editorial Email: shbvoice@uwc.edu
Website: www.sheboygan.uwc.edu

SHEPHERDSTOWN

SHEPHERD UNIVERSITY

Street Address 1: PO Box 3210
State: WV
Zip/Postal code: 25443-3210
Country: USA
Mailing Address: PO Box 3210
Mailing City: Shepherdstown
Mailing State: WV
Mailing ZIP Code: 25443-3210
General Phone: (304) 876-5100
General Fax: (304) 876-5100
Advertising Phone: (304) 876-5687
Editorial Phone: (304) 876-5377
General/National Adv. Email: pickweb@shepherd.edu
Website: www.picketonline.com
Personnel: Jim Lewin (Advisor); Jeb Inge (Ed. in Chief)

SHERMAN

AUSTIN COLLEGE

Street Address 1: 900 N Grand Ave
Street Address 2: Ste 6J
State: TX
Zip/Postal code: 75090-4440
Country: USA
Mailing Address: 900 N Grand Ave Ste 6J
Mailing City: Sherman
Mailing State: TX
Mailing ZIP Code: 75090-4400
General Phone: (903) 813-2296
General Fax: (903) 813-2339
General/National Adv. Email: observer@austincollege.edu
Personnel: Felecia Garvin (Advisor); Lauren Chiodo (Ed. in Chief)

SHIPPENSBURG

SHIPPENSBURG UNIVERSITY:THE SLATE

Street Address 1: Shippensburg University
Street Address 2: Ceddia Union Bldg, Second Floor
State: PA
Zip/Postal code: 17257
Country: USA
Mailing Address: Shippensburg University
Mailing City: Shippensburg
Mailing State: PA
Mailing ZIP Code: 17257
General Phone: 717-477-1778
General Fax: 717-477-4022
General/National Adv. Email: slate@ship.edu
Website: www.theslateonline.com
Personnel: Michael Drager (Advisor)

SHORELINE

SHORELINE CMTY. COLLEGE

Street Address 1: 16101 Greenwood Ave N
Street Address 2: Rm 9101
State: WA
Zip/Postal code: 98133-5667
Country: USA
Mailing Address: 16101 Greenwood Ave N Rm 9101
Mailing City: Shoreline
Mailing State: WA
Mailing ZIP Code: 98133-5667
General Phone: (206) 546-4730
General Fax: (206) 546-5869
General/National Adv. Email: webbtide@yahoo.com
Website: www.shoreline.edu/ebbtide/
Personnel: Patti Jones (Advisor); Amelia Rivera (Ed. in Chief); Daniel Demay (Copy Ed.); Sean Sherman (Photo Ed.)

SHREVEPORT

CENTENARY COLLEGE

Street Address 1: 2911 Centenary Blvd
State: LA
Zip/Postal code: 71104-3335
Country: USA
Mailing Address: PO Box 41188
Mailing City: Shreveport
Mailing State: LA
Mailing ZIP Code: 71134-1188
General Phone: (318) 792-5136
General/National Adv. Email: paper@centenary.edu
Website: www.centenary.edu/life/congo
Personnel: Mark Gruettner (Advisor); Roxie Smith (Ed. in chief)

LOUISIANA STATE UNIV.

Street Address 1: 1 University Pl
Street Address 2: No 344
State: LA
Zip/Postal code: 71115-2301
Country: USA
Mailing Address: 1 University Pl No 344
Mailing City: Shreveport
Mailing State: LA
Mailing ZIP Code: 71115-2301
General Phone: (318) 797-5328
General Fax: (318) 797-5328
Display Adv. Email: almagest@lsus.edu
Website: www.thealmagest.com
Personnel: Rose-Marie Lillian (Advisor); Karen Wissing (Exec. Ed.)

SILOAM SPRINGS

JOHN BROWN UNIV.

Street Address 1: 2000 W University St
State: AR
Zip/Postal code: 72761-2112
Country: USA
Mailing Address: 2000 W University St
Mailing City: Siloam Springs
Mailing State: AR
Mailing ZIP Code: 72761-2121
General Phone: (479) 524-7255
General Fax: (479) 524-7394
General/National Adv. Email: advocate@jbu.edu
Website: advoacte.jbu.edu
Personnel: Candy Gregor (Assistant Professor of Communication Faculty adviser for the Threefold Advocate); KJ Roh (Executive Editor of the Threefold Advocate)

SIOUX FALLS

AUGUSTANA UNIVERSITY

Street Address 1: 2001 S Summit Ave
State: SD
Zip/Postal code: 57197-0001
Country: USA
Mailing Address: 2001 S Summit Ave
Mailing City: Sioux Falls
Mailing State: SD
Mailing ZIP Code: 57197-0002
General Phone: (605) 274-4423
General Fax: (605) 274-5288
Advertising Fax: (605) 274-5288
General/National Adv. Email: augustanamirror@gmail.com
Website: www.augiemirror.com
Year Established: 1909
Published: Fri
Avg Free Circ: 1000
Personnel: Jeffrey Miller (Advisor)

SIOUX FALLS

UNIV. OF SIOUX FALLS

Street Address 1: 1101 W 22nd St
State: SD
Zip/Postal code: 57105-1600
Country: USA
Mailing Address: 1101 W 22nd St
Mailing City: Sioux Falls
Mailing State: SD
Mailing ZIP Code: 57105-1699
General Phone: (605) 331-6776
General Fax: (605) 331-6692
Personnel: Tiffany Leach (Advisor); Janet Davison (Ed.)

SLIPPERY ROCK

SLIPPERY ROCK UNIV.

Street Address 1: 220 Eisenberg Classroom Bldg
State: PA
Zip/Postal code: 16057
Country: USA
Mailing Address: 220 Eisenberg Classroom Bldg.
Mailing City: Slipper Rock
Mailing State: PA
Mailing ZIP Code: 16057
General Phone: (724) 738-2643
General Fax: (724) 738-4896
General/National Adv. Email: rocket.letters@

sru.edu
Website: www.theonlinerocket.com
Personnel: Joseph Harry (Advisor); Josh Rizzo (Ed. in Chief)

SMITHFIELD

BRYANT COLLEGE

Street Address 1: 1150 Douglas Pike
Street Address 2: # 7
State: RI
Zip/Postal code: 02917-1291
Country: USA
Mailing Address: 1150 Douglas Pike Ste 1
Mailing City: Smithfield
Mailing State: RI
Mailing ZIP Code: 02917-1290
General Phone: (401) 232-6028
General Fax: (401) 232-6710
General/National Adv. Email: archway@bryant.edu
Website: www.bryantarchway.com
Personnel: Meagan Sage (Advisor); Tracey Gant (Adv. Mgr.); John Crisafulli (Ed. in Chief)

SOCORRO

NEW MEXICO INST. OF MINING & TECHNOLOGY

Street Address 1: 801 Leroy Pl
State: NM
Zip/Postal code: 87801-4681
Country: USA
Mailing Address: 801 Leroy Pl
Mailing City: Socorro
Mailing State: NM
Mailing ZIP Code: 87801-4750
General Phone: (575) 835-5525
General Fax: (505) 835-6364
General/National Adv. Email: paydirt@nmt.edu; paydirt-editor@nmt.edu; paydirt-ads@nmt.edu
Personnel: Roger Renteria (Ed. in Chief); Rachel Armstrong (Ed.)

SOUTH BEND

INDIANA UNIV.

Street Address 1: 1700 Mishawaka Ave
State: IN
Zip/Postal code: 46615-1408
Country: USA
Mailing Address: PO Box 7111
Mailing City: South Bend
Mailing State: IN
Mailing ZIP Code: 46634-7111
General Phone: (574) 520-4878
General Fax: (574) 237-4599
Website: www.iusb.edu
Personnel: Beth Stutsman (Ed.)

SOUTH HADLEY

MOUNT HOLYOKE COLLEGE

Street Address 1: 50 College St
Street Address 2: Blanchard Campus Center 324
State: MA
Zip/Postal code: 01075-1423
Country: USA
Mailing Address: 9007 Blanchard Campus Center
Mailing City: South Hadley
Mailing State: MA
Mailing ZIP Code: 01075-1423
General Phone: (413) 538-2269
General Fax: (413) 538-2476
General/National Adv. Email: mhnews@mtholyoke.edu
Website: mountholyokenews.org/
Year Established: 1917
Published: Thur
Personnel: Linda Valencia Xu (Publisher); Geena Molinaro (Editor-in-Chief)

SOUTH ORANGE

SETON HALL UNIVERSITY

Street Address 1: 400 S Orange Ave, Student Ctr, Rm 224
State: NJ
Zip/Postal code: 7079
Country: USA
Mailing Address: 400 S. Orange Ave., Student Ctr., Rm. 224
Mailing City: South Orange
Mailing State: NJ
Mailing ZIP Code: 07079
General Phone: (732) 925-7647
General Fax: (973) 761-7943
General/National Adv. Email: Thesetonian@gmail.com
Website: www.thesetonian.com
Year Established: 1924
Published: Thur
Personnel: Amy Nyberg (Advisor); Brian Wisowaty (Mng. Ed.)

SOUTH ROYALTON

VERMONT LAW SCHOOL

Street Address 1: PO Box 96
State: VT
Zip/Postal code: 05068-0096
Country: USA
Mailing Address: PO Box 96
Mailing City: South Royalton
Mailing State: VT
Mailing ZIP Code: 05068-0096
General Phone: (802) 831-1299
General Fax: (802) 763-7159
General/National Adv. Email: forum@vermontlaw.edu
Website: www.vermontlaw.edu/students/x8685.xml
Personnel: Sean Williams (Adv. Mgr.); Kevin Schrems (Ed. in Chief)

SOUTHAMPTON

SOUTHAMPTON COLLEGE

Street Address 1: 239 Montauk Hwy
State: NY
Zip/Postal code: 11968-4100
Country: USA
Mailing Address: 239 Montauk Hwy
Mailing City: Southampton
Mailing State: NY
Mailing ZIP Code: 11968-4198
General Phone: (631) 287-8239
General Fax: (631) 287-5147
Personnel: Diane Prescott (Ed.)

SPARKILL

ST. THOMAS AQUINAS COLLEGE

Street Address 1: 125 Route 340
State: NY
Zip/Postal code: 10976-1041
Country: USA
Mailing Address: 125 Route 340
Mailing City: Sparkill
Mailing State: NY
Mailing ZIP Code: 10976-1050
General Phone: (845) 398-4075
General Fax: (845) 359-8136
General/National Adv. Email: thoma@yahoo.com; thoma@stac.edu
Website: www.stac.edu
Personnel: Kathleen Giroux (Ed. in Chief)

SPARTANBURG

CONVERSE COLLEGE

Street Address 1: 580 E Main St
State: SC
Zip/Postal code: 29302-1931
Country: USA
Mailing Address: 580 E Main St
Mailing City: Spartanburg
Mailing State: SC
Mailing ZIP Code: 29302-0006
General Phone: (864) 596-9000
General/National Adv. Email: admissions@converse.edu
Personnel: Whitney Fisher (Advisor.)

UNIV. OF SOUTH CAROLINA

Street Address 1: 800 University Way
Street Address 2: Clc 112
State: SC
Zip/Postal code: 29303-4932
Country: USA
Mailing Address: 800 University Way Clc 112
Mailing City: Spartanburg
Mailing State: SC
Mailing ZIP Code: 29303-4932
General Phone: (864) 503-5138
General Fax: (864) 503-5100
General/National Adv. Email: carolinian@uscupstate.edu
Website: www.sc.edu/carolinian/
Personnel: Chioma Ugochukwu (Advisor); India Brown (Ed.)

SPEARFISH

BLACK HILLS STATE UNIV.

Street Address 1: 1200 University St
State: SD
Zip/Postal code: 57799-8840
Country: USA
Mailing Address: 1200 University St
Mailing City: Spearfish
Mailing State: SD
Mailing ZIP Code: 57799-0002
General Phone: (605) 642-6389
General Fax: (605) 642-6119
General/National Adv. Email: jacketjournal@bhsu.edu
Website: www.bhsu.edu/jacketjournal1
Personnel: Mary Caton-Rosser (Advisor); Shelby Cihak (Bus. Mgr.); Kendra Bertsch (Adv. Mgr.)

SPOKANE

GONZAGA UNIVERSITY

Street Address 1: 502 E Boone Ave
State: WA
Zip/Postal code: 99258-1774
Country: USA
Mailing Address: Msc # 2477
Mailing City: Spokane
Mailing State: WA
Mailing ZIP Code: 99258-0001
General Phone: (509) 313-6826
General Fax: (509) 313-5848
Advertising Phone: (509) 313-6839
Advertising Fax: (509) 313-5848
Editorial Phone: (509) 313-6826
Editorial Fax: (509) 313-5848
General/National Adv. Email: bulletin@zagmail.gonzaga.edu
Display Adv. Email: adoffice@gonzaga.edu
Editorial Email: bulletin@zagmail.gonzaga.edu
Website: www.gonzagabulletin.com
Published: Thur
Avg Free Circ: 3000
Personnel: Tom Miller (Advisor); Susan English (Adviser); John Kafentzis (Adviser); Joanne Shiosaki (Student Publications Manager); Chris Wheatley (Student Publications Assistant Manager)

SPOKANE CMTY. COLLEGE

Street Address 1: 1810 N Greene St
State: WA
Zip/Postal code: 99217-5320
Country: USA
Mailing Address: 1810 N Greene St
Mailing City: Spokane
Mailing State: WA
Mailing ZIP Code: 99217-5399
General Phone: (509) 533-7000
General Fax: (509) 533-8163

General/National Adv. Email: reporter@scc.spokane.edu
Personnel: Rob Vogel (Advisor); Danie Elle (Ed.)

SPOKANE FALLS CMTY. COLLEGE

Street Address 1: 3410 W Fort George Wright Dr
Street Address 2: MS 3180
State: WA
Zip/Postal code: 99224-5204
Country: USA
Mailing Address: 3410 W Fort George Wright Dr MS 3180
Mailing City: Spokane
Mailing State: WA
Mailing ZIP Code: 99224-5204
General Phone: (509) 533-3246
General Fax: (509) 533-3856
General/National Adv. Email: communicator@spokanefalls.edu
Website: www.spokanefalls.edu/communicator
Personnel: Jason Nix (Advisor); Sarah Radmer (Mng. Ed.); Madison Mccord (Ed.); Wendy Gaskill (Ed.)

WHITWORTH UNIVERSITY

Street Address 1: 300 W Hawthorne Rd
State: WA
Zip/Postal code: 99251-2515
Country: USA
Mailing Address: 300 W Hawthorne Rd
Mailing City: Spokane
Mailing State: WA
Mailing ZIP Code: 99251-2515
General Phone: (509) 777-3248
General Fax: (509) 777-3710
Editorial Fax: Free
Editorial Email: editor@whitworthian.com
Website: www.thewhitworthian.com
Year Established: 1905
Published: Wed
Personnel: Jim McPherson (Advisor); Rebekah Bresee (Editor-in-Chief)

SPRING ARBOR

SPRING ARBOR UNIV.

Street Address 1: 106 E Main St
Street Address 2: Ste A28
State: MI
Zip/Postal code: 49283-9701
Country: USA
Mailing Address: 106 E Main St Ste A28
Mailing City: Spring Arbor
Mailing State: MI
Mailing ZIP Code: 49283-9701
General Phone: (517) 523-3616
General Fax: (517) 750-2108
Personnel: Eric Platt (Ed.)

SPRINGFIELD

AMERICAN INTERNATIONAL COLLEGE

Street Address 1: 1000 State St
Street Address 2: # 4
State: MA
Zip/Postal code: 01109-3151
Country: USA
Mailing Address: 1000 State St # 4
Mailing City: Springfield
Mailing State: MA
Mailing ZIP Code: 01109-3151
General Phone: (413) 205-3265
General Fax: (413) 205-3955
Editorial Email: yellowjacket@aic.edu
Personnel: Will Hughes (Advisor); Brian Steele (Ed. in Chief)

DRURY COLLEGE

Street Address 1: 900 N Benton Ave
State: MO
Zip/Postal code: 65802-3712

College and University Newspapers

Country: USA
Mailing Address: 900 N Benton Ave
Mailing City: Springfield
Mailing State: MO
Mailing ZIP Code: 65802-3791
General Phone: (417) 873-7879
General Fax: (417) 873-7897
General/National Adv. Email: mirror@drurymirror.com
Website: www.drurymirror.com
Personnel: Cristina Gilstrap (Advisor); Jeromy Layman (Ed. in Chief); Mallory Noelke (Mng. Ed.)

EVANGEL UNIVERSITY

Street Address 1: 1111 N Glenstone Ave
State: MO
Zip/Postal code: 65802-2125
Country: USA
Mailing Address: 1111 N. Glenstone Ave.
Mailing City: Springfield
Mailing State: MO
Mailing ZIP Code: 65802-2125
General Phone: (417) 865-2815
Advertising Phone: (417) 865-2815, ext. 8636
Editorial Phone: (417) 865-2815, ext. 8634
General/National Adv. Email: evangellance@gmail.com
Editorial Email: evangellance@gmail.com
Website: www.evangellance.com
Year Established: 1955
Delivery Methods: Racks
Commercial printers?: Y
Published: Fri`Bi-Mthly
Avg Free Circ: 1500
Personnel: Melinda Booze (Advisor)

LINCOLN LAND CMTY. COLLEGE

Street Address 1: 5250 Shepherd Rd
State: IL
Zip/Postal code: 62703-5402
Country: USA
Mailing Address: 5250 Shepherd Rd
Mailing City: Springfield
Mailing State: IL
Mailing ZIP Code: 62703-5408
General Phone: (217) 786-2318
General Fax: (217) 786-2340
Website: www.llcc.edu
Personnel: Brenda Protz (Advisor)

MISSOURI STATE UNIV.

Street Address 1: 901 S National Ave
State: MO
Zip/Postal code: 65897-0027
Country: USA
Mailing Address: 901 S National Ave
Mailing City: Springfield
Mailing State: MO
Mailing ZIP Code: 65897-0001
General Phone: (417) 836-5272
General Fax: (417) 836-6738
Editorial Phone: (417) 836-6512
General/National Adv. Email: standard@missouristate.edu
Website: www.the-standard.org
Personnel: Jess Rollins (Ed. in Chief)

SPRINGFIELD COLLEGE

Street Address 1: 263 Alden St
State: MA
Zip/Postal code: 01109-3707
Country: USA
Mailing Address: 263 Alden St
Mailing City: Springfield
Mailing State: MA
Mailing ZIP Code: 01109-3788
General Phone: (413) 748-3000
General Fax: (413) 748-3473
General/National Adv. Email: activities@spfldcol.edu
Website: www.spsldcol.edu
Personnel: Claire Wright (Advisor); Evin Giglio (Ed. in Cheif)

UNIV. OF ILLINOIS/SPRINGFIELD

Street Address 1: 1 University Plz
Street Address 2: Sab 20
State: IL
Zip/Postal code: 62703-5497
Country: USA
Mailing Address: 1 University Plz
Mailing City: Springfield
Mailing State: IL
Mailing ZIP Code: 62703-5407
General Phone: (217) 206-6397
General Fax: (217) 206-6048
Advertising Phone: (217) 206-7717
Advertising Fax: (217) 206-6048
Editorial Phone: (217) 206-6397
Editorial Fax: (217) 206-6048
General/National Adv. Email: journal@uis.edu
Display Adv. Email: journalmgr@uis.edu
Editorial Email: journal@uis.edu
Website: www.uisjournal.com
Year Established: 1985
Published: Wed
Published Other: Back-to-school edition in July/mailed to newly enrolled students and circulated
Avg Free Circ: 3000
Personnel: Debra Landis (Faculty Advisor); Marc Cox (EIC)

WESTERN NEW ENGLAND COLLEGE

Street Address 1: 1215 Wilbraham Rd
State: MA
Zip/Postal code: 01119-2612
Country: USA
Mailing Address: 1215 Wilbraham Rd
Mailing City: Springfield
Mailing State: MA
Mailing ZIP Code: 01119-2684
General Phone: (413) 782-1580
General Fax: (413) 796-2008
Personnel: Wayne Barr (Ed.)

WITTENBERG UNIVERSITY

Street Address 1: 200 W Ward St
State: OH
Zip/Postal code: 45504-2120
Country: USA
Mailing Address: PO Box 720
Mailing City: Springfield
Mailing State: OH
Mailing ZIP Code: 45501-0720
General Phone: 512.968.4648
General/National Adv. Email: torch_editors@wittenberg.edu
Website: www.thewittenbergtorch.com
Published: Wed
Personnel: D'Arcy Fallon (Faculty Advisor); Maggie McKune (Ed. in Chief); Tara Osborne (Bus. Mgr.)

ST DAVIDS

EASTERN UNIVERSITY:THE WALTONIAN

Street Address 1: 1300 Eagle Rd
State: PA
Zip/Postal code: 19087-3617
Country: USA
Mailing Address: 1300 Eagle Rd
Mailing City: St Davids
Mailing State: PA
Mailing ZIP Code: 19087
General Phone: 610-341-1710
General Fax: 610-225-5255
General/National Adv. Email: wtonline@eastern.edu
Website: www.waltonian.com

STANFORD

STANFORD UNIV.

Street Address 1: 456 Panama Mall
Street Address 2: Lorry Lokey Stanford Daily Bldg.
State: CA
Zip/Postal code: 94305-4006
Country: USA
Mailing Address: 456 Panama Mall
Mailing City: Stanford
Mailing State: CA
Mailing ZIP Code: 94305-5294
General Phone: (650) 721-5803
General Fax: (650) 725-1329
General/National Adv. Email: eic@stanforddaily.com
Website: www.stanforddaily.com
Personnel: Jason Shen (COO & Bus Mgr.); Mary Liz McCurdy (Vice Pres., Sales); Devin Banerjee (Ed. in Chief); Kamil Dada (Ed. in Chief); Eric (Sr. Mng. Ed.)

STARKVILLE

BULLDOG BEAT

Street Address 1: 304 E Lampkin St
State: MS
Zip/Postal code: 39759-2910
County: Oktibbeha
Country: USA
Mailing Address: PO Box 1068
Mailing City: Starkville
Mailing State: MS
Mailing ZIP Code: 39760-1068
General Phone: (662) 323-1642
General Fax: (662) 323-6586
Advertising Phone: (662) 323-1642
Advertising Fax: (662) 323-6586
Editorial Phone: (662) 324-8092
Editorial Fax: (662) 323-6586
General/National Adv. Email: sdnads@bellsouth.net
Display Adv. Email: sdnads@bellsouth.net
Editorial Email: sdneditor@bellsouth.net
Website: www.starkvilledailynews.com
Year Established: 1875
News Services: AP.
Special Editions: Bulldog Weekend (Apr); Welcome Back Miss. State (Aug); Progress (Feb); Christmas Gift Guide (Nov).
Special Weekly Sections: Entertainment (Fri); Weddings (S); Religion (Sat); Agriculture (Thur); Business (Tues); Education (Wed).
Syndicated Publications: American Profile (S).
Delivery Methods: Mail`Carrier
Mechanical specifications: Type page 10 x 21 1/2; E - 6 cols, 1 9/16, 1/8 between; A - 6 cols, 1 9/16, 1/8 between; C - 9 cols, 1 1/32, 1/8 between.
Published: Mon`Tues`Wed`Thur`Fri`Sat`Sun
Personnel: Don Norman (Pub.); Mona Howell (Bus. Mgr.); Byron Norman (Circ. Mgr.); Larry Bost (Creative Dir.); Shea Staskowski (Educ. Ed.); Brian Hawkins (Online Ed.)
Parent company (for newspapers): Horizon Publications Inc.

STATE COLLEGE

PENN STATE UNIV.

Street Address 1: 123 S Burrowes St
State: PA
Zip/Postal code: 16801-3867
Country: USA
Mailing Address: 123 S Burrowes St Ste 200
Mailing City: State College
Mailing State: PA
Mailing ZIP Code: 16801-3882
General Phone: (814) 865-2531
General Fax: (814) 865-3848
General/National Adv. Email: collegian@psu.edu
Display Adv. Email: mycollegianrep@gmail.com
Website: www.collegian.psu.edu
Published: Mon`Tues`Wed`Thur`Fri
Personnel: Wayne Lowman (Opns. Mgr.)

STATE UNIVERSITY

ARKANSAS STATE UNIV.

Street Address 1: 104 Cooley Drive
Street Address 2: Journalism Department
State: AR
Zip/Postal code: 1921
Country: USA
Mailing Address: PO Box 1930
Mailing City: State University
Mailing State: AR
Mailing ZIP Code: 72467-1930
General Phone: (870) 972-3076
General Fax: (870) 972-3339
Advertising Phone: 870-972-2961
Editorial Phone: (870) 972-3076
General/National Adv. Email: herald@astate.edu
Display Adv. Email: herald@astate.edu
Editorial Email: herald@astate.edu
Website: www.asuherald.com
Year Established: 1921
Delivery Methods: Racks
Commercial printers?: N
Published: Mon`Thur
Avg Free Circ: 5000
Personnel: Bonnie Thrasher (Advisor); Lindsey Blakely (Editor); Jana Waters (Advertising Manager)

STATEN ISLAND

COLLEGE OF STATEN ISLAND

Street Address 1: 2800 Victory Blvd
State: NY
Zip/Postal code: 10314-6609
Country: USA
Mailing Address: 2800 Victory Blvd
Mailing City: Staten Island
Mailing State: NY
Mailing ZIP Code: 10314-6600
General Phone: (718) 982-3056
General Fax: (718) 982-3087
Website: www.csi.cuny.edu
Personnel: Philip Masciantonio (Gen. Mgr.)

ST. JOHNS UNIV.

Street Address 1: 300 Howard Ave
State: NY
Zip/Postal code: 10301-4450
Country: USA
Mailing Address: 300 Howard Ave
Mailing City: Staten Island
Mailing State: NY
Mailing ZIP Code: 10301-4496
General Phone: (718) 390-4500
General Fax: (718) 447-0941
General/National Adv. Email: siadmhelp@stjohns.edu
Website: www.stjohns.edu
Personnel: Crista Camerlengl (Ed.)

WAGNER COLLEGE

Street Address 1: 1 Campus Rd
State: NY
Zip/Postal code: 10301-4479
Country: USA
Mailing Address: 1 Campus Rd
Mailing City: Staten Island
Mailing State: NY
Mailing ZIP Code: 10301-4495
General Phone: (718) 390-3110
General/National Adv. Email: wagnerian@wagner.edu
Published: Wed
Published Other: Bi-Weekly

STATESBORO

GEORGIA SOUTHERN UNIV.

Street Address 1: Williams Center Rm 2023
State: GA
Zip/Postal code: 30460-0001
Country: USA
Mailing Address: PO Box 8001
Mailing City: Statesboro
Mailing State: GA
Mailing ZIP Code: 30460-1000
General Phone: (912) 478-5246
General Fax: (912) 478-7113
Editorial Phone: (912) 478-5418
General/National Adv. Email: gaeditor@georgiasouthern.edu

STAUNTON

MARY BALDWIN COLLEGE

Street Address 1: PO Box 1500
State: VA
Zip/Postal code: 24402-1500
Country: USA
Mailing Address: PO Box 1500
Mailing City: Staunton
Mailing State: VA
Mailing ZIP Code: 24402-1500
General Phone: (540) 887-7112
General Fax: (540) 887-7231
General/National Adv. Email: campuscomments@mbc.edu
Personnel: Bruce Dorries (Advisor); Dawn Medley (Advisor); Hannah Barrow (Ed. in Chief)

STEPHENVILLE

TARLETON STATE UNIVERSITY

Street Address 1: 201 St Felix
State: TX
Zip/Postal code: 76401
Country: USA
Mailing Address: Box T-0440
Mailing City: Stephenville
Mailing State: TX
Mailing ZIP Code: 76402
General Phone: (254) 968-9056
General Fax: (254) 968-9709
Advertising Phone: (254) 968-9057
Advertising Fax: (254) 968-9709
Editorial Phone: (254) 968-9058
Editorial Fax: (254) 968-9709
General/National Adv. Email: jtac@tarleton.edu
Display Adv. Email: jtac_ads@tarleton.edu
Editorial Email: jtac@tarleton.edu
Website: www.jtacnews.com
Year Established: 1919
Published: Wed
Avg Free Circ: 1000
Personnel: Caleb Chapman (Dir.)

STERLING

NORTHEASTERN JUNIOR COLLEGE

Street Address 1: 100 College Ave
State: CO
Zip/Postal code: 80751-2345
Country: USA
Mailing Address: 100 College Ave
Mailing City: Sterling
Mailing State: CO
Mailing ZIP Code: 80751-2399
General Phone: (970) 521-6796
Personnel: Ian Storey (Advisor); Patrick Kelling (Advisor)

STEUBENVILLE

FRANCISCAN UNIVERSITY OF STEUBENVILLE

Street Address 1: 1235 University Blvd
State: OH
Zip/Postal code: 43952-1792
Country: USA
Mailing Address: 1235 University Blvd
Mailing City: Steubenville
Mailing State: OH
Mailing ZIP Code: 43952-1796
General Phone: (740) 284-5014
General Fax: (740) 284-5452
General/National Adv. Email: troub@franciscan.edu
Website: www.troubonline.com
Personnel: Chris Pagano; Elizabeth Wong; Emily Lahr

STEVENS POINT

UNIV. OF WISCONSIN STEVENS POINT

Street Address 1: 1101 Reserve St
Street Address 2: # 104
State: WI
Zip/Postal code: 54481-3868
Country: USA
Mailing Address: 1101 Reserve Street 104 CAC
Mailing City: Stevens Point
Mailing State: WI
Mailing ZIP Code: 54481-3897
General Phone: (715) 346-3707
General Fax: (715) 346-4712
General/National Adv. Email: pointer@uwsp.edu
Website: pointer.uwsp.edu
Personnel: Liz Fakazis (Advisor); Steve Roeland (Ed. in Chief)

STEVENSON

STEVENSON UNIVERSITY

Street Address 1: 1525 Greenspring Valley Rd
State: MD
Zip/Postal code: 21153-0641
Country: USA
Mailing Address: 1525 Greenspring Valley Rd
Mailing City: Stevenson
Mailing State: MD
Mailing ZIP Code: 21153-0641
General Phone: (443) 394-9781
General/National Adv. Email: suvillager@gmail.com
Website: stevensonvillager.com
Year Established: 2016 online
Published: Thur
Published Other: every Thursday online
Personnel: Chip Rouse (Fac. Advisor)

STILLWATER

OKLAHOMA STATE UNIV.

Street Address 1: 106 Paul Miller
State: OK
Zip/Postal code: 74078-4050
Country: USA
Mailing Address: 106 Paul Miller
Mailing City: Stillwater
Mailing State: OK
Mailing ZIP Code: 74078-4050
General Phone: (405) 744-6365
General Fax: (405) 744-7936
Editorial Email: editor@ocolly.com
Website: www.ocolly.com
Personnel: Barbara Allen (Advisor); Emily Holman (Ed. in Chief)

STOCKTON

SAN JOAQUIN DELTA COLLEGE

Street Address 1: 5151 Pacific Ave
Street Address 2: Shima 203
State: CA
Zip/Postal code: 95207-6304
Country: USA
Mailing Address: 5151 Pacific Ave Shima 203
Mailing City: Stockton
Mailing State: CA
Mailing ZIP Code: 95207-6370
General Phone: (209) 954-5156
General Fax: (209) 954-5288
General/National Adv. Email: deltacollegian@gmail.com
Website: www.deltacollegian.com
Personnel: Bill Davis (Advisor); Junifer Mamsaang (Ed. in Chief)

UNIV. OF THE PACIFIC

Street Address 1: 3601 Pacific Ave
State: CA
Zip/Postal code: 95211-0110
Country: USA
Mailing Address: 3601 Pacific Ave
Mailing City: Stockton
Mailing State: CA
Mailing ZIP Code: 95211-0197
General Phone: (209) 946-2115
General Fax: (209) 946-2195
Advertising Phone: (209) 946-2114
Display Adv. Email: pacificanads@pacific.edu
Editorial Email: pacificannews@pacific.edu; pacificaneditors@pacific.edu; pacificanlifestyles@pacific.edu; pacificansports@pacific.edu
Website: www.thepacificanonline.com
Personnel: Dave Frederickson (Advisor); Ruben Moreno (Bus. Mgr.); Devon Blount (Ed. in Chief); Andrew Mitchell (News Ed.)

STONY BROOK

SUNY/STONY BROOK

Street Address 1: PO Box 1530
State: NY
Zip/Postal code: 11790-0609
Country: USA
Mailing Address: PO Box 1530
Mailing City: Stony Brook
Mailing State: NY
Mailing ZIP Code: 11790-0609
General Phone: (631) 632-6480
General Fax: (631) 632-9128
General/National Adv. Email: advertise@sbstatesman.org
Website: www.sbstatesman.com
Personnel: Frank D'alessandro (Bus. Mgr.); Bradley Donaldson (Ed. in Chief)

STORM LAKE

BUENA VISTA UNIV.

Street Address 1: 610 W 4th St
State: IA
Zip/Postal code: 50588-1713
Country: USA
Mailing Address: 610 W 4th St
Mailing City: Storm Lake
Mailing State: IA
Mailing ZIP Code: 50588-1798
General Phone: (712) 749-1247
General/National Adv. Email: ucbvu@bvu.edu
Personnel: Jamii Claiborne (Advisor); Carly Evans (Co Ed. in Chief); Lindsey Marean (Co Ed. in Chief)

STORRS

UNIV. OF CONNECTICUT

Street Address 1: 11 Dog Ln
State: CT
Zip/Postal code: 06268-2206
Country: USA
Mailing Address: 11 Dog Ln
Mailing City: Storrs
Mailing State: CT
Mailing ZIP Code: 06268-2206
General Phone: (860) 486-3407
General Fax: (860) 486-4388
General/National Adv. Email: advertising@dailycampus.com
Website: www.dailycampus.com
Personnel: Valerie Nezvesky (Bus. Mgr./Adv. Dir.); Christopher Duray (Ed. in Chief)

SUFFERN

ROCKLAND CMTY. COLLEGE

Street Address 1: 145 College Rd
State: NY
Zip/Postal code: 10901-3620
Country: USA
Mailing Address: 145 College Rd
Mailing City: Suffern
Mailing State: NY
Mailing ZIP Code: 10901-3699
General Phone: (845) 574-4389
General/National Adv. Email: outlookpress@gmail.com
Website: www.sunyrockland.edu

SUGAR GROVE

WAUBONSEE CMTY. COLLEGE

Street Address 1: Rt 47 at Waubonsee Dr
State: IL
Zip/Postal code: 60554
Country: USA
Mailing Address: Rt. 47 at Waubonsee Dr.
Mailing City: Sugar Grove
Mailing State: IL
Mailing ZIP Code: 60554
General Phone: (630) 466-2555
General Fax: (630) 466-9102
General/National Adv. Email: insight@waubonsee.edu
Website: www.waubonsee.edu
Personnel: Gary Clarke (Advisor); DJ Terek (Ed. in Chief)

SUPERIOR

UNIV. OF WISCONSIN SUPERIOR

Street Address 1: 1600 Catlin Ave
State: WI
Zip/Postal code: 54880-2953
Country: USA
Mailing Address: 1600 Catlin Ave
Mailing City: Superior
Mailing State: WI
Mailing ZIP Code: 54880-2954
General Phone: (715) 394-8438
General Fax: (715) 394-8454
General/National Adv. Email: stinger@uwsuper.edu
Website: www.uwsuper-stinger.com
Personnel: Joel Anderson (Advisor)

SUSANVILLE

LASSEN CMTY. COLLEGE

Street Address 1: 478-200 Hwy 139
State: CA
Zip/Postal code: 96130
Country: USA
Mailing Address: PO Box 3000
Mailing City: Susanville
Mailing State: CA
Mailing ZIP Code: 96130-3000
General Phone: (530) 251-8821
General Fax: (530) 251-8839
General/National Adv. Email: trougar@lassen.cc.ca.us
Website: www.lassencougar.com; www.lassen.cc.ca.us
Personnel: Andrew Owen (Ed. in Chief)

SWARTHMORE

SWARTHMORE COLLEGE

Street Address 1: 500 College Ave
State: PA
Zip/Postal code: 19081-1306
Country: USA
Mailing Address: 500 College Ave Ste 2
Mailing City: Swarthmore
Mailing State: PA
Mailing ZIP Code: 19081-1390
General Phone: (610) 328-8000
General Fax: (208) 439-9864
General/National Adv. Email: phoenix@swarthmore.edu
Website: www.swarthmorephoenix.com
Personnel: Mara Revkin (Ed. in Chief)

Display Adv. Email: ads1@georgiasouthern.edu
Website: Georgia Southern University GSU Student Media Box 8001
Year Established: 1927
Published: Tues`Thur
Personnel: Jozsef Papp (Exec. Ed.)
Parent company (for newspapers): Student Media at Georgia Southern

College and University Newspapers

SWEET BRIAR

SWEET BRIAR COLLEGE

Street Address 1: PO Box H
State: VA
Zip/Postal code: 24595-1058
Country: USA
Mailing Address: PO Box 1058
Mailing City: Sweet Briar
Mailing State: VA
Mailing ZIP Code: 24595-1058
General Phone: (434) 381-6100
General Fax: (434) 381-6132
General/National Adv. Email: sbvoice@sbc.edu
Website: www.voice.sbc.edu
Personnel: Katy Johnstone (Ed. in chief); Carinna Finn (Mng. Ed.)

SYRACUSE

ONONDAGA CMTY. COLLEGE

Street Address 1: Rt 173, Student Ctr G100
State: NY
Zip/Postal code: 13215
Country: USA
Mailing Address: Rt. 173, Student Ctr. G100
Mailing City: Syracuse
Mailing State: NY
Mailing ZIP Code: 13215
General Phone: (315) 498-2278
General Fax: (315) 498-2001
Personnel: Patti Orty (Ed.)

SYRACUSE UNIVERSITY

Street Address 1: 744 Ostrom Ave
State: NY
Zip/Postal code: 13244-2977
Country: USA
Mailing Address: 744 Ostrom Ave
Mailing City: Syracuse
Mailing State: NY
Mailing ZIP Code: 13210-2942
General Phone: (315) 443-2314
General Fax: (315) 443-3689
Advertising Phone: (315) 443-9794
General/National Adv. Email: ads@dailyorange.com
Display Adv. Email: ads@dailyorange.com
Editorial Email: editor@dailyorange.com
Website: www.dailyorange.com
Year Established: 1903
Delivery Methods: Mail`Newsstand`Racks
Commercial printers?: N
Published: Mon`Tues`Wed`Thur`Fri
Avg Free Circ: 6000
Personnel: Peter Waack (Advisor/Gen. Mgr.)

THE DOLPHIN

Street Address 1: 1419 Salt Springs Rd
State: NY
Zip/Postal code: 13214-1302
Country: USA
Mailing Address: 1419 Salt Springs Rd
Mailing City: Syracuse
Mailing State: NY
Mailing ZIP Code: 13214-1302
General Phone: (315) 445-4542
Advertising Phone: (607) 221-8080
Editorial Phone: (315) 445-4542
General/National Adv. Email: dolphin@lemoyne.edu
Display Adv. Email: dolphin@lemoyne.edu
Editorial Email: dolphin@lemoyne.edu
Website: www.lemoyne.edu/DOING/CLUBS/TheDolphin/tabid/1959/Default.aspx
Delivery Methods: Newsstand`Racks
Commercial printers?: N
Personnel: Ashley Casey (Co-Executive Editor); Amy Dieffenbacher

TACOMA

PACIFIC LUTHERAN UNIV.

Street Address 1: the Mooring Mast Pacific Lutheran University 1010 122nd Street
State: WA
Zip/Postal code: 98447-0001
Country: USA
Mailing Address: the Mooring Mast Pacific Lutheran University 1010 122nd Street S
Mailing City: Tacoma
Mailing State: WA
Mailing ZIP Code: 98447-0001
General Phone: (253) 535-7492
General Fax: (253) 536-5067
Advertising Phone: (425) 622-2693
General/National Adv. Email: mast@plu.edu
Display Adv. Email: mastads@plu.edu
Website: www.plu.edu/~mast
Year Established: 1924
Delivery Methods: Racks
Commercial printers?: Y
Published: Fri
Avg Free Circ: 3500
Personnel: Winston Alder (Business and Ads Manager); Jessica Trondsen (Editor-in-Chief)

TACOMA CMTY. COLLEGE

Street Address 1: 6501 S 19th St
Street Address 2: Bldg 216
State: WA
Zip/Postal code: 98466-6139
Country: USA
Mailing Address: 6501 S 19th St Bldg 216
Mailing City: Tacoma
Mailing State: WA
Mailing ZIP Code: 98466-6139
General Phone: (253) 566-6045
General Fax: (253) 566-5384
Website: www.tacomachallenge.com
Personnel: Serrell Collins (Advisor); Kathy Tavia (Ed.)

THE UNIVERSITY OF WASHINGTON TACOMA LEDGER STUDENT NEWSPAPER

Street Address 1: 1900 Commerce St
Street Address 2: Mat 151
State: WA
Zip/Postal code: 98402-3112
Country: USA
Mailing Address: 1900 Commerce St Mat 151
Mailing City: Tacoma
Mailing State: WA
Mailing ZIP Code: 98402-3112
General Phone: (253) 692-4428
General Fax: (253) 692-5602
Advertising Phone: (253) 692-4529
General/National Adv. Email: ledger@uw.edu
Display Adv. Email: ledger@u.washington.edu
Editorial Email: ledger@u.washington.edu
Website: www.thetacomaledger.com
Delivery Methods: Racks
Published: Mon
Personnel: Daniel Nash (Publications Manager); Kelsie Abram (Editor-in-Chief)

UNIV. OF PUGET SOUND

Street Address 1: 1500 N Warner St
Street Address 2: Stop 1095
State: WA
Zip/Postal code: 98416-1095
Country: USA
Mailing Address: 1500 N Warner St Stop 1095
Mailing City: Tacoma
Mailing State: WA
Mailing ZIP Code: 98416-1095
General Phone: (253) 879-3100
General Fax: (253) 879-3645
General/National Adv. Email: trail@pugetsound.edu
Website: www.pugetsound.edu
Personnel: Anna Marie Ausnes (Contact)

TAKOMA PARK

COLUMBIA UNION COLLEGE

Street Address 1: 7600 Flower Ave
State: MD
Zip/Postal code: 20912-7744
Country: USA
Mailing Address: 7600 Flower Ave
Mailing City: Takoma Park
Mailing State: MD
Mailing ZIP Code: 20912-7794
General Phone: (301) 891-4118
General/National Adv. Email: cj@cuc.edu
Personnel: Athina Lavinos (Pub.); Jaclyn Wile (Ed.); Heidi Lohr (News Ed.)

MONTGOMERY COLLEGE

Street Address 1: 7600 Takoma Ave, Commons Rm 202
State: MD
Zip/Postal code: 20912
Country: USA
Mailing Address: 7600 Takoma Ave., Commons Rm. 202
Mailing City: Takoma Park
Mailing State: MD
Mailing ZIP Code: 20912
General Phone: (240) 567-1490
General Fax: (301) 650-1334
General/National Adv. Email: excaliburnewspaper@montgomerycollege.edu
Personnel: Angela Clubb (Ed.)

TALLAHASSEE

FLORIDA A&M UNIV.

Street Address 1: 510 Orr Dr, Ste 3081
State: FL
Zip/Postal code: 32307-0001
Country: USA
Mailing Address: 510 Orr Dr Ste 3081
Mailing City: Tallahassee
Mailing State: FL
Mailing ZIP Code: 32307-0001
General Phone: (850) 599-3159
General Fax: (850) 561-2570
General/National Adv. Email: thefamuanec@gmail.com
Display Adv. Email: famuanads@hotmail.com
Website: www.thefamuan.com
Personnel: Andrew Skeritt (Advisor); Erica Butler (Ed. in Chief)

FSVIEW & FLORIDA FLAMBEAU

Street Address 1: 954 W Brevard St
State: FL
Zip/Postal code: 32304-7709
Country: USA
Mailing Address: 277 N Magnolia Dr
Mailing City: Tallahassee
Mailing State: FL
Mailing ZIP Code: 32301-2664
General Phone: 850-561-1600
General Fax: 850-574-6578
Advertising Phone: 8505611600
Advertising Fax: 8505746578
Editorial Phone: 850-561-1606
General/National Adv. Email: @tallahassee.com
Display Adv. Email: eleporin@tallahassee.com
Editorial Email: eleporin@tallahassee.com
Website: www.fsunews.com
Year Established: 1915
Special Editions: All FSU Home Games Football Previews Student Living Guides 3X a year
Delivery Methods: Mail`Newsstand`Racks
Commercial printers?: N
Personnel: Eliza LePorin (General Manager); Justin Dyke (Content Supervisor); Bailey Shertizinger (Editor-in-Chief); Chris Lewis (Gen. Mgr.); Liz Cox (Ed. In Chief); Arriale Douglas (Prodn. Mgr.)
Parent company (for newspapers): Tallahassee Democrat

TALLAHASSEE CMTY. COLLEGE

Street Address 1: 444 Appleyard Dr
State: FL
Zip/Postal code: 32304-2815
Country: USA
Mailing Address: 444 Appleyard Dr
Mailing City: Tallahassee
Mailing State: FL
Mailing ZIP Code: 32304-2895
General Phone: (850) 201-8035
General Fax: (850) 201-8427
Advertising Phone: (850) 201-8425
Editorial Phone: (850) 201-8525
General/National Adv. Email: talon@tcc.fl.edu
Display Adv. Email: talon@tcc.fl.edu
Editorial Email: talon@tcc.fl.edu
Website: www.thetcctalon.com
Year Established: 1968
Published: Bi-Mthly
Avg Free Circ: 3000
Personnel: Dana Peck (Advisor)

TAMPA

UNIV. OF SOUTH FLORIDA

Street Address 1: 4202 E Fowler Ave
Street Address 2: Svc 2
State: FL
Zip/Postal code: 33620-9951
Country: USA
Mailing Address: 4202 E Fowler Ave Svc 2
Mailing City: Tampa
Mailing State: FL
Mailing ZIP Code: 33620-9951
General Phone: (813) 974-5190
General Fax: (813) 974-4887
Advertising Phone: (813) 974-6254
Display Adv. Email: ads@usforacle.com
Editorial Email: oracleeditor@gmail.com
Website: www.usforacle.com
Year Established: 1966
Delivery Methods: Racks
Published: Mon`Thur
Avg Free Circ: 8000
Personnel: Jay Lawrence (Advisor); Anastasia Dawson (Ed. in chief); Jimmy Geurts (Mng. Ed.)

UNIV. OF TAMPA

Street Address 1: Rm 211, Vaughn Ctr, 401 W Kennedy Blvd
State: FL
Zip/Postal code: 33606-
Country: USA
Mailing Address: 401 W Kennedy Blvd
Mailing City: Tampa
Mailing State: FL
Mailing ZIP Code: 33606-1490
General Phone: (813) 257-3636
General Fax: (813) 253-6207
General/National Adv. Email: minaret@ut.edu; ut.minaret@gmail.com
Website: www.theminaretonline.com
Personnel: Stephanie Tripp (Advisor); Zoe LeCain (Adv. Mgr.); Charlie Hambos (Ed. in Chief); Kyle Bennett (Sports Ed.)

TEANECK

FAIRLEIGH DICKINSON UNIV.

Street Address 1: 1000 River Rd
State: NJ
Zip/Postal code: 07666-1914
Country: USA
Mailing Address: 1000 River Rd
Mailing City: Teaneck
Mailing State: NJ
Mailing ZIP Code: 07666-1914
General Phone: (201) 692-2046
General Fax: (201) 692-2376
General/National Adv. Email: equinoxfdu@gmail.com
Website: https://fduequinox.wordpress.com/
Published: Thur
Personnel: Bruno Battistoli (Advisor); Sarah

Latson (Faculty Adviser); Kayla Hastrup (Editor-in-Chief); Miruna Seitan (Mng. Ed.); Lorena Chouza (Exec. Ed.); Melissa Hartz (News Editor)

TEMPE

ARIZONA STATE UNIV.

Street Address 1: PO Box 871502
State: AZ
Zip/Postal code: 85287-1502
Country: USA
Mailing Address: PO Box 871502
Mailing City: Tempe
Mailing State: AZ
Mailing ZIP Code: 85287-1502
General Phone: (480) 965-7572
General Fax: (480) 965-8484
General/National Adv. Email: state.press@asu.edu
Website: www.statepress.com
Personnel: Jason Manning (Advisor); Tosh Stuart (Bus. Mgr.); Leo Gonzalez (Adv. Mgr.)

TERRE HAUTE

INDIANA STATE UNIV.

Street Address 1: 550 Chestnut St
State: IN
Zip/Postal code: 47809-1910
Country: USA
Mailing Address: 716 Hulman Memorial Student Un
Mailing City: Terre Haute
Mailing State: IN
Mailing ZIP Code: 47809-0001
General Phone: (812) 237-7629
General Fax: (812) 237-7629
Editorial Phone: (812) 237-3025
Website: www.indianastatesman.com
Personnel: Heidi Staggs (Mng. Ed.); Caitlin Hancock (Adv.Mgr.); Daniel Greenwell (Ed. in Chief)

ROSE-HULMAN INST. OF TECHNOLOGY

Street Address 1: 5500 Wabash Ave
Street Address 2: # CM5037
State: IN
Zip/Postal code: 47803-3920
Country: USA
Mailing Address: 5500 Wabash Ave # CM5037
Mailing City: Terre Haute
Mailing State: IN
Mailing ZIP Code: 47803-3920
General Phone: (812) 877-8255
Advertising Phone: (812) 877-8255
General/National Adv. Email: thorn@rose-hulman.edu
Display Adv. Email: thorn-biz@rose-hulman.edu
Website: thorn.rose-hulman.edu/
Delivery Methods: Racks
Commercial printers?: Y
Published: Fri
Avg Free Circ: 1000
Personnel: Thomas Adams (Advisor); Marcus Willerscheidt (Business Manager); Katrina Brandenburg (Editor-in-Chief)

TEXARKANA

TEXARKANA COLLEGE

Street Address 1: 2500 N Robison Rd
State: TX
Zip/Postal code: 75599-0002
Country: USA
Mailing Address: 2500 N Robison Rd
Mailing City: Texarkana
Mailing State: TX
Mailing ZIP Code: 75599-0001
General Phone: (903) 838-4541
General Fax: (903) 832-5030
Editorial Phone: (903) 838-4541
Website: www.tc.cc.tx.us; www.texarkanacollege.edu

Personnel: Jean Cotten (Advisor); Caitlin Williams (Ed.)

THIBODAUX

NICHOLLS STATE UNIV.

Street Address 1: PO Box 2010
State: LA
Zip/Postal code: 70310-0001
Country: USA
Mailing Address: PO Box 2010
Mailing City: Thibodaux
Mailing State: LA
Mailing ZIP Code: 70310-0001
General Phone: (985) 448-4259
General Fax: (985) 448-4267
Website: www.thenichollsworth.com
Personnel: Stephen Hartmann (Advisor)

THIEF RIVER FALLS

NORTHLAND CMTY. & TECH. COLLEGE

Street Address 1: 1101 Highway 1 E
State: MN
Zip/Postal code: 56701-2528
Country: USA
Mailing Address: 1101 Highway 1 E
Mailing City: Thief River Falls
Mailing State: MN
Mailing ZIP Code: 56701-2528
General Phone: (218) 683-8801
General Fax: (218) 683-8980
Website: www.northlandcollege.edu
Personnel: Adam Paulson (Contact); Elizabeth Perfecto (Ed.)

THOMASVILLE

THOMAS COLLEGE

Street Address 1: 1501 Millpond Rd
State: GA
Zip/Postal code: 31792-7478
Country: USA
Mailing Address: 1501 Millpond Rd
Mailing City: Thomasville
Mailing State: GA
Mailing ZIP Code: 31792-7636
General Phone: (229) 226-1621
General Fax: (229) 226-1653
Personnel: Charity Nixon (Ed.)

THOUSAND OAKS

CALIFORNIA LUTHERAN UNIVERSITY

Street Address 1: 60 W Olsen Rd
State: CA
Zip/Postal code: 91360-2700
Country: USA
Mailing Address: 60 W Olsen Rd # 4200
Mailing City: Thousand Oaks
Mailing State: CA
Mailing ZIP Code: 91360-2787
General Phone: (805) 493-3366
General Fax: (805) 493-3479
Advertising Phone: (805) 493-3327
General/National Adv. Email: kelley@robles.callutheran.edu
Editorial Email: echo@clunet.edu
Personnel: Colleen Cason (Advisor); Sharon Docter (Chair); Jonathan Culmer (Bus. Mgr.); Margaret Nolan (Ed. in Chief)

TIFFIN

HEIDELBERG UNIVERSITY

Street Address 1: 310 E Market St
State: OH
Zip/Postal code: 44883-2434
Country: USA
Mailing Address: 310 E. Market St.

Mailing City: Tiffin
Mailing State: OH
Mailing ZIP Code: 44883-2462
General Phone: (419) 448-2180
Year Established: 1894
Personnel: Mary Garrison (Visiting Assistant Professor of Communication)

TIFTON

ABRAHAM BALDWIN AGRI COLLEGE

Street Address 1: 2802 Moore Hwy
State: GA
Zip/Postal code: 31793-5679
Country: USA
Mailing Address: 2802 Moore Hwy
Mailing City: Tifton
Mailing State: GA
Mailing ZIP Code: 31793-5698
General Fax: (229) 391-4978
Advertising Fax: (229) 386-7158
General/National Adv. Email: stallion@stallion.abac.edu
Website: www.thestalliononline.com
Personnel: Eric Cash (Faculty Advisor)

TOCCOA FALLS

TOCCOA FALLS COLLEGE

Street Address 1: 107 Kincaid Dr
State: GA
Zip/Postal code: 30598-9602
Country: USA
Mailing Address: 107 Kincaid Dr
Mailing City: Toccoa Falls
Mailing State: GA
Mailing ZIP Code: 30598-9602
General Phone: (706) 886-7299
General Fax: (706) 886-0210
General/National Adv. Email: talon@tfc.edu
Website: www.tfc.edu
Personnel: Christine Brubaker (Ed. in Chief)

TOLEDO

UNIVERSITY OF TOLEDO

Street Address 1: 2801 W Bancroft St
Street Address 2: Mail Stop 530
State: OH
Zip/Postal code: 43606-3328
Country: USA
Mailing Address: 2801 W Bancroft St
Mailing City: Toledo
Mailing State: OH
Mailing ZIP Code: 43606-3390
General Phone: (419) 530-7788
General Fax: (419) 530-7770
Advertising Phone: (419) 530-7788
Advertising Fax: (419) 530-7770
Editorial Phone: (419) 530-7788
Editorial Fax: (419) 530-7770
General/National Adv. Email: editor@independentcollegian.com
Display Adv. Email: sales@independentcollegian.com
Editorial Email: editor@independentcollegian.com
Website: www.independentcollegian.com
Year Established: 1919
Special Editions: Back to school edition-August 22nd and August 25
Published: Wed
Avg Free Circ: 8000
Personnel: J.R. Hoppenjans (Chairman of the board of trustees); Erik Gable (Adviser); Danielle Gamble (Editor-in-Chief)
Parent company (for newspapers): Collegian Media Foundation

TOMS RIVER

OCEAN COUNTY COLLEGE

Street Address 1: PO Box 2001
State: NJ
Zip/Postal code: 08754-2001
Country: USA

Mailing Address: PO Box 2001
Mailing City: Toms River
Mailing State: NJ
Mailing ZIP Code: 08754-2001
General Phone: (732) 255-0481
General Fax: None
General/National Adv. Email: vnews@ocean.edu
Year Established: 1965
Delivery Methods: Racks
Commercial printers?: Y
Published Other: Irregularly
Personnel: Karen Bosley

TONKAWA

NORTHERN OKLAHOMA COLLEGE

Street Address 1: 1220 E Grand Ave
State: OK
Zip/Postal code: 74653-4022
Country: USA
Mailing Address: PO Box 310
Mailing City: Tonkawa
Mailing State: OK
Mailing ZIP Code: 74653-0310
General Phone: (580) 628-6444
General Fax: (580) 628-6209
Website: www.north-ok.edu
Personnel: Jeremy Stillwell (Advisor)

TOPEKA

WASHBURN UNIV.

Street Address 1: 1700 SW College Ave
State: KS
Zip/Postal code: 66621-0001
Country: USA
Mailing Address: 1700 SW College Ave
Mailing City: Topeka
Mailing State: KS
Mailing ZIP Code: 66621-1101
General Phone: (785) 670-2506
General Fax: (785) 670-1035
Advertising Phone: (785) 670-1173
General/National Adv. Email: review@washburn.edu
Website: www.washburnreview.org
Personnel: Nicole Stejskal (Ed. in Chief)

TORRANCE

EL CAMINO COLLEGE

Street Address 1: 16007 Crenshaw Blvd
Street Address 2: Rm H-113
State: CA
Zip/Postal code: 90506-0001
Country: USA
Mailing Address: 16007 Crenshaw Blvd.
Mailing City: Torrance
Mailing State: CA
Mailing ZIP Code: 90506
General Phone: (310) 660-3328
General Fax: (310) 660-6092
Advertising Phone: (310) 660-3329
Editorial Phone: (310) 660-3328
General/National Adv. Email: elcounionads000@yahoo.com
Display Adv. Email: elcounionads000@yahoo.com
Editorial Email: eccunion@gmail.com
Website: eccunion.com
Year Established: 1946
Published: Bi-Mthly
Published Other: Twice per month
Avg Free Circ: 5000
Personnel: Jack Mulkey (Adv. Mgr.); Kate McLaughlin (Adviser); Stefanie Frith (Adviser); Gary Kohatsu (Photo Adviser)

TOUGALOO

TOUGALOO COLLEGE

Street Address 1: 500 W County Line Rd
State: MS
Zip/Postal code: 39174-9700
Country: USA
Mailing Address: 500 W County Line Rd

College and University Newspapers

Mailing City: Tougaloo
Mailing State: MS
Mailing ZIP Code: 39174-9700
General Phone: (601) 977-6159
General Fax: (601) 977-6160
General/National Adv. Email: cwhite@tougaloo.edu
Personnel: Teressa Fulgham (Mng. Ed.); Colleen White (Dir. Journ. Program)

TOWSON

GOUCHER COLLEGE

Street Address 1: 1021 Dulaney Valley Rd
State: MD
Zip/Postal code: 21204-2753
Country: USA
Mailing Address: 1021 Dulaney Valley Rd
Mailing City: Towson
Mailing State: MD
Mailing ZIP Code: 21204-2780
General Phone: (410) 337-6322
General Fax: (410) 337-6434
General/National Adv. Email: quin@goucher.edu; askhd@goucher.edu
Website: www.thequindecim.com
Personnel: Matt Simon (Mng. Ed.); Lori Shull (News Ed.); Ben Spangler (Photo Ed.)

TOWSON UNIV.

Street Address 1: 8000 York Rd, University Union, Rm 309
State: MD
Zip/Postal code: 21252-0001
Country: USA
Mailing Address: 8000 York Rd University Un Rm 309
Mailing City: Towson
Mailing State: MD
Mailing ZIP Code: 21252-0001
General Phone: (410) 704-2288
General Fax: (410) 704-3862
General/National Adv. Email: towerlight@towson.edu
Display Adv. Email: towerlightads@yahoo.com
Editorial Email: towerlighteditor@gmail.com
Website: www.thetowerlight.com
Personnel: Mike Raymond (Gen. Mgr.); Ashley Rabe (Sr. Ed.); Daniel Gross (News Ed.)

TRAVERSE CITY

NORTHWESTERN MICHIGAN COLLEGE

Street Address 1: 1701 E Front St
State: MI
Zip/Postal code: 49686-3016
Country: USA
Mailing Address: 1701 E Front St
Mailing City: Traverse City
Mailing State: MI
Mailing ZIP Code: 49686-3061
General Phone: (231) 995-1173
General Fax: (231) 995-1952
General/National Adv. Email: whitepinepress@gmail.com
Website: www.whitepinepress.org
Personnel: Michael Anderson (Advisor); Nora Stone (Ed. in Chief); Jacob Bailey (Mng. Ed.)

TRINIDAD

TRINIDAD STATE JUNIOR COLLEGE

Street Address 1: 600 Prospect St
Street Address 2: # 182
State: CO
Zip/Postal code: 81082-2356
Country: USA
Mailing Address: 600 Prospect St # 182
Mailing City: Trinidad
Mailing State: CO
Mailing ZIP Code: 81082-2356
General Phone: (719) 846-5011
General Fax: (719) 846-5667

Personnel: Charlene Duran (Adv. Mgr.)

TROY

HUDSON VALLEY CMTY. COLLEGE

Street Address 1: 80 Vandenburgh Ave
State: NY
Zip/Postal code: 12180-6037
Country: USA
Mailing Address: 80 Vandenburgh Ave
Mailing City: Troy
Mailing State: NY
Mailing ZIP Code: 12180-6037
General Phone: (518) 629-7187
General Fax: (518) 629-7496
General/National Adv. Email: hudnews@yahoo.com
Website: www.hvcc.edu
Personnel: Mat Cantore (Advisor); Nicole Monsees (Mng. Ed.)

RENSSELAER POLYTECHNIC INST.

Street Address 1: 110 8th St Ste 702
Street Address 2: Rensselaer Union
State: NY
Zip/Postal code: 12180-3522
Country: USA
Mailing Address: Rensselaer Union
Mailing City: Troy
Mailing State: NY
Mailing ZIP Code: 12180-3590
General Phone: (518) 276-6000
General Fax: (518) 276-8728
General/National Adv. Email: poly@rpi.edu; business@poly.rpi.edu
Display Adv. Email: notices@poly.rpi.edu
Editorial Email: editor@poly.rpi.edu; news@poly.rpi.edu; edop@poly.rpi.edu; sports@poly.rpi.edu; photo@poly.rpi.edu; notices@poly.rpi.edu
Website: www.poly.rpi.edu
Personnel: Richard Hartt (Advisor)

RUSSELL SAGE COLLEGE

Street Address 1: 65 1st St
State: NY
Zip/Postal code: 12180-4013
Country: USA
Mailing Address: 65 1st St
Mailing City: Troy
Mailing State: NY
Mailing ZIP Code: 12180-4003
General Phone: 518-244-2016
Editorial Phone: 518-244-2016
General/National Adv. Email: perkip@sage.edu
Display Adv. Email: perkip@sage.edu
Editorial Email: perkip@sage.edu
Website: www.thequillrsc.com
Year Established: 1950s
Personnel: Penny Perkins (Advisor)

TROY UNIVERSITY

Street Address 1: Hall School of Journalism and Communication
Street Address 2: 103 Wallace Hall, Troy University
State: AL
Zip/Postal code: 36082-0001
Country: USA
Mailing Address: Hall School of Journalism and Communication
Mailing City: Troy
Mailing State: AL
Mailing ZIP Code: 36082-0001
General Phone: (334) 670-3583
General Fax: (334) 670-3707
Advertising Phone: (334) 670-3328
Advertising Fax: (334) 670-3707
Editorial Phone: (334) 670-3328
Editorial Fax: (334) 670-3707
General/National Adv. Email: sstewart71298@troy.edu
Display Adv. Email: sstewart71298@troy.edu
Editorial Email: sstewart71298@troy.edu
Website: www.tropnews.com; www.troy.edu

Delivery Methods: Mail`Racks
Commercial printers?: N
Published: Thur
Published Other: Certain home sports game days
Personnel: Steve Stewart (Advisor)

TUCSON

PIMA COMMUNITY COLLEGE

Street Address 1: 2202 W Anklam Rd
State: AZ
Zip/Postal code: 85709-0001
Country: USA
Mailing Address: 2202 W. Anklam Rd.
Mailing City: Tucson
Mailing State: AZ
Mailing ZIP Code: 85709-0001
General Phone: (520) 206-6800
General Fax: (520) 206-6834
Advertising Phone: (520) 206-6901
General/National Adv. Email: aztec_press@pima.edu
Display Adv. Email: aztecpress_ad@pima.edu
Website: aztecpressonline.com
Year Established: 1970
Published: Bi-Mthly
Avg Free Circ: 5000
Personnel: Andrew Paxton (Business manager)

UNIV. OF ARIZONA

Street Address 1: 615 N Park Ave
Street Address 2: Ste 101
State: AZ
Zip/Postal code: 85719-5096
Country: USA
Mailing Address: 615 N. Park Ave., Ste. 101
Mailing City: Tucson
Mailing State: AZ
Mailing ZIP Code: 85719-5094
General Phone: (520) 621-8659
General Fax: (520) 626-8303
Advertising Phone: (520) 621-5982
Editorial Phone: (520) 621-7879
General/National Adv. Email: display@wildcat.arizona.edu
Editorial Email: editor@wildcat.arizona.edu
Website: www.wildcat.arizona.edu
Year Established: 1899
Published: Mon`Tues`Wed`Thur`Fri
Personnel: Mark Woodhams (Dir.); Brett Fera (Asst. Dir.)

TULSA

ORAL ROBERTS UNIV.

Street Address 1: 7777 S Lewis Ave
Street Address 2: Lrc 175
State: OK
Zip/Postal code: 74171-0003
Country: USA
Mailing Address: 7777 S Lewis Ave Lrc 175
Mailing City: Tulsa
Mailing State: OK
Mailing ZIP Code: 74171-0001
General Phone: (918) 495-7080
General Fax: (918) 495-6345
Advertising Phone: (918) 495-7080
Advertising Fax: (918) 495-6345
Editorial Phone: (918) 495-7080
Editorial Fax: (918) 495-6345
General/National Adv. Email: oracle@oru.edu
Display Adv. Email: oracleads@oru.edu
Website: www.oruoracle.com
Year Established: 1965
News Services: Religion News Service
Delivery Methods: Carrier`Racks
Commercial printers?: Y
Published: Fri`Bi-Mthly
Avg Free Circ: 3500
Personnel: Kevin Armstrong (Advisor)

TULSA CMTY. COLLEGE

Street Address 1: 909 S Boston Ave

Street Address 2: Rm G-31
State: OK
Zip/Postal code: 74119-2011
Country: USA
Mailing Address: 909 S Boston Ave Rm G-31
Mailing City: Tulsa
Mailing State: OK
Mailing ZIP Code: 74119-2011
General Phone: (918) 595-7388
General Fax: (918) 595-7308
Personnel: Jerry Goodwin (Advisor); Eric Bruce (Ed.)

UNIV. OF TULSA

Street Address 1: 800 S Tucker Dr
State: OK
Zip/Postal code: 74104-9700
Country: USA
Mailing Address: 800 Tucker Dr
Mailing City: Tulsa
Mailing State: OK
Mailing ZIP Code: 74104-9700
General Phone: (918) 631-2259
General Fax: (918) 631-2885
General/National Adv. Email: collegian@utulsa.edu
Website: www.utulsa.edu/collegian/
Published: Mon
Avg Free Circ: 2500
Personnel: Kendra Blevins (Advisor); J.Christopher Proctor (Editor-in-Chief); Elizabeth Cohen (Business and Advertising Manager)

TUMWATER

SOUTH PUGET SOUND CMTY. COLLEGE

Street Address 1: 2011 Mottman Rd SW
State: WA
Zip/Postal code: 98512-6218
Country: USA
Mailing Address: 2011 Mottman Rd SW
Mailing City: Tumwater
Mailing State: WA
Mailing ZIP Code: 98512-6218
General Phone: (360) 754-7711
General Fax: (360) 596-5708
General/National Adv. Email: soundsnewspaper@spscc.ctc.edu
Website: www.spscc.ctc.edu
Personnel: Steve Valandra (Advisor); Erin Landgraf (Ed. in Chief)

TURLOCK

CALIFORNIA STATE UNIVERSITY, STANISLAUS

Street Address 1: 1 University Cir
State: CA
Zip/Postal code: 95382-3200
Country: USA
Mailing Address: 1 University Cir
Mailing City: Turlock
Mailing State: CA
Mailing ZIP Code: 95382-3200
General Phone: (209) 667-3411
General Fax: (209) 667-3868
General/National Adv. Email: sstevens2@csustan.edu
Website: www.csusignal.com

TUSCALOOSA

STILLMAN COLLEGE

Street Address 1: PO Box 1430
State: AL
Zip/Postal code: 35403-1430
Country: USA
Mailing Address: PO Box 1430
Mailing City: Tuscaloosa
Mailing State: AL
Mailing ZIP Code: 35403-1430
General Phone: (205) 349-4240

College and University Newspapers

UNIV. OF ALABAMA
Street Address 1: PO Box 870170
State: AL
Zip/Postal code: 35487-0001
Country: USA
Mailing Address: PO Box 870170
Mailing City: Tuscaloosa
Mailing State: AL
Mailing ZIP Code: 35487-0170
General Phone: (205) 348-7845
General Fax: (205) 348-8036
General/National Adv. Email: news@cw.ua.edu
Website: www.cw.ua.edu
Year Established: 1894
Personnel: Drew Gunn (Adv. Mgr.); Corey Craft (Ed. in Chief); Amanda Peterson (Ed.)

TYLER

TYLER JUNIOR COLLEGE
Street Address 1: 1400 E Devine St
Street Address 2: # 204
State: TX
Zip/Postal code: 75701-2207
Country: USA
Mailing Address: 1400 E Devine St # 204
Mailing City: Tyler
Mailing State: TX
Mailing ZIP Code: 75701-2207
General Phone: (903) 510-2335
General Fax: (903) 510-3246
Website: www.tjcnewspaper.com
Personnel: Laura Krantz (Advisor)

UNIV. OF TEXAS AT TYLER
Street Address 1: 3900 University Blvd
State: TX
Zip/Postal code: 75799-6600
Country: USA
Mailing Address: 3900 University Blvd
Mailing City: Tyler
Mailing State: TX
Mailing ZIP Code: 75799-0001
General Phone: (903) 565-7131
Advertising Phone: (903) 566-5536
Editorial Phone: (903) 566-7131
Display Adv. Email: ads@patriottalon.com
Editorial Email: editor@patriottalon.com
Website: www.patriottalon.com
Year Established: 1976
Published: Bi-Mthly
Avg Free Circ: 2000
Personnel: Lorri Allen (Adviser); Nathan Wright (Editor in Chief)

UKIAH

MENDOCINO COLLEGE
Street Address 1: 1000 Hensley Creek Rd
State: CA
Zip/Postal code: 95482-7821
Country: USA
Mailing Address: 1000 Hensley Creek Rd
Mailing City: Ukiah
Mailing State: CA
Mailing ZIP Code: 95482-3017
General Phone: (707) 468-3096
General Fax: (707) 468-3120
Personnel: Debra Wallace (Ed.)

UNION

KEAN UNIV.
Street Address 1: 1000 Morris Ave
State: NJ
Zip/Postal code: 07083-7133
Country: USA
Mailing Address: 1000 Morris Ave Ste 1
Mailing City: Union
Mailing State: NJ
Mailing ZIP Code: 07083-7131
General Phone: (908) 737-0468
General Fax: (908) 737-0465
General/National Adv. Email: thetower@kean.edu
Website: www.kean.edu/~thetower
Personnel: Pat Winters Lauro (Faculty Advisor); Eileen Ruf (Bus. Mgr.); Jillian Johnson (Ed. in Chief); Emannuel Urenea (Ed.)

UNIVERSITY CENTER

DELTA COLLEGE
Street Address 1: 1961 Delta Rd
State: MI
Zip/Postal code: 48710-1001
Country: USA
Mailing Address: 1961 Delta Rd # H
Mailing City: University Center
Mailing State: MI
Mailing ZIP Code: 48710-1002
General Phone: (989) 686-9000
General/National Adv. Email: collegiate@delta.edu; info@delta.edu
Website: www.delta.edu/collegiate
Personnel: Kathie Bachleda (Advisor); Megan Tobias (Ed in Chief)

SAGINAW VALLEY STATE UNIV.
Street Address 1: 125 Curtiss Hall, 7400 Bay Rd
State: MI
Zip/Postal code: 48710-0001
Country: USA
Mailing Address: 125 Curtiss Hall, 7400 Bay Rd
Mailing City: University Center
Mailing State: MI
Mailing ZIP Code: 48710-0001
General Phone: (989) 964-4248
General/National Adv. Email: vanguard@svsu.edu
Website: www.thevalleyvanguard.com
Personnel: Sara Kitchen (Ed. in Chief)

UNIVERSITY HEIGHTS

JOHN CARROLL UNIVERSITY
Street Address 1: 1 John Carroll Blvd
State: OH
Zip/Postal code: 44118-4538
Country: USA
Mailing Address: 1 John Carroll Blvd
Mailing City: Cleveland
Mailing State: OH
Mailing ZIP Code: 44118-4582
General Phone: (216) 397-1711
General Fax: (216) 397-1729
Advertising Phone: (216) 397-4398
Editorial Phone: (216) 397-1711
General/National Adv. Email: jcunews@gmail.com
Display Adv. Email: jcunews@gmail.com
Editorial Email: jcunews@gmail.com
Website: www.jcunews.com
Year Established: 1925
Published: Thur
Avg Free Circ: 1600
Personnel: Mary Ann Flannery (Chair/Assoc. Prof.); Robert T. Noll (Advisor); Jacqueline J. Schmidt (Prof.); Katie Sheridan (Ed. in Chief); Bob Seeholzer (Mng. Ed.); Alan Stephenson (Prof.); Mary Beadle (Assoc. Prof.); Tim Ertle (Sports Ed.); Margaret Algren (Asst. Prof.); Richard Hendrickson (Asst. Prof.); Robert Prisco (Asst. Prof.); Bob Noll (Instr.); David Reese (Instr.); Fred Buchstein (Part-time Instr.); Mark Eden (Part-time Instr.); Bill Nichols (Part-time Instr.)

UNIVERSITY PARK

GOVERNORS STATE UNIV.
Street Address 1: 1 University Pkwy
Street Address 2: E2543
State: IL
Zip/Postal code: 60484-3165
Country: USA
Mailing Address: 1 University Pkwy.
Mailing City: University Park
Mailing State: IL
Mailing ZIP Code: 60484-3165
General Phone: (708) 534-4517
General Fax: (708) 534-7895
General/National Adv. Email: phoenix@govst.edu
Website: www.gsuphoenix.com
Published: Wed
Published Other: First and third Wednesdays
Personnel: Debbie James (Faculty Advisor); Michael Purdy (Emeritus Professor)

PENN STATE UNIVERSITY: COLLEGE OF COMMUNICATIONS
Street Address 1: 201 Carnegie Bldg
State: PA
Zip/Postal code: 16802-5101
Country: USA
Mailing Address: 201 Carnegie Bldg
Mailing City: University Park
Mailing State: PA
Mailing ZIP Code: 16802
General Phone: 814-863-1484
General Fax: 814-863-8044
Website: comm.psu.edu

UPLAND

TAYLOR UNIV.
Street Address 1: 236 W Reade Ave
State: IN
Zip/Postal code: 46989-1001
Country: USA
Mailing Address: 236 W. Reade Ave
Mailing City: Upland
Mailing State: IN
Mailing ZIP Code: 46989
General Phone: (765) 998-5359
General/National Adv. Email: echo@taylor.edu
Published: Fri
Personnel: Alan Blanchard (Faculty Advisor)

TAYLOR UNIV.
Street Address 1: 236 W Reade Ave
State: IN
Zip/Postal code: 46989-1001
Country: USA
Mailing Address: 236 W. Reade Ave.
Mailing City: Upland
Mailing State: IN
Mailing ZIP Code: 46989-1001
General Phone: (765) 998-5359
General/National Adv. Email: echo@taylor.edu
Display Adv. Email: echoads@taylor.edu
Website: theechonews.com/
Year Established: 1913
Published: Fri
Personnel: Donna Downs (Ed. in Chief); Alan Blanchard (Faculty Adviser)

UPPER MONTCLAIR

MONTCLAIR STATE UNIV.
Street Address 1: Student Ctr. Annex Room 113
Street Address 2: Room 113
State: NJ
Zip/Postal code: 7043
Country: USA
General Phone: (973) 655-5230
General Fax: (973) 655-7804
General/National Adv. Email: montclarioneditor@gmail.com
Website: www.themontclarion.org
Personnel: Kristen Bryfogle (Ed. in Chief); Kulsoom Rizvi (News Editor); Nelson DePasquale (Sports Editor)

UTICA

SUNY INST. OF TECHNOLOGY

UTICA/ROME
Street Address 1: PO Box 3050
Street Address 2: Campus Ctr., Rm. 216
State: NY
Zip/Postal code: 13504-3050
Country: USA
Mailing Address: PO Box 3050
Mailing City: Utica
Mailing State: NY
Mailing ZIP Code: 13504-3050
General Phone: (315) 792-7426
General Fax: (315) 734-4198
General/National Adv. Email: factorytimes@gmail.com
Personnel: Patricia Murphy (Advisor); Mark Ziobro (Mng. Ed.)

UTICA COLLEGE
Street Address 1: 1600 Burrstone Rd
Street Address 2: Hubbard 55
State: NY
Zip/Postal code: 13502-4857
Country: USA
Mailing Address: 1600 Burrstone Rd Hubbard 55
Mailing City: Utica
Mailing State: NY
Mailing ZIP Code: 13502-4892
General Phone: (315) 792-3065
General Fax: (315) 792-3173
Website: www.uctangerine.com
Year Established: 1946
Delivery Methods: Newsstand
Commercial printers?: Y
Personnel: Christopher Cooper (Editor-in-Chief); Jonathan Monsiletto (Ed. in Chief)

UVALDE

SOUTHWEST TEXAS JUNIOR COLLEGE
Street Address 1: 2401 Garner Field Rd
State: TX
Zip/Postal code: 78801-6221
Country: USA
Mailing Address: 2401 Garner Field Rd
Mailing City: Uvalde
Mailing State: TX
Mailing ZIP Code: 78801-6221
General Phone: (830) 591-7350
General Fax: (830) 591-4185
Website: www.swtjc.net
Personnel: Terrie Wilson (Advisor/Journalism Instructor)

VALDOSTA

VALDOSTA STATE UNIV.
Street Address 1: 1500 N Patterson St
State: GA
Zip/Postal code: 31698-0100
Country: USA
Mailing Address: 1500 N Patterson St
Mailing City: Valdosta
Mailing State: GA
Mailing ZIP Code: 31698-0001
General Phone: (229) 333-5686
General Fax: (229) 249-2618
General/National Adv. Email: spec@valdosta.edu
Website: www.vsuspectator.com
Personnel: Pat Miller (Advisor); John Pickworth (Adv. Mgr.); Desiree Thompson (Editor In Chief)

VALHALLA

WESTCHESTER CMTY. COLLEGE
Street Address 1: 75 Grasslands Rd
State: NY
Zip/Postal code: 10595-1550
Country: USA
Mailing Address: 75 Grasslands Rd
Mailing City: Valhalla
Mailing State: NY
Mailing ZIP Code: 10595-1550
General Phone: (914) 606-6600
General/National Adv. Email: thevikingnewswcc@hotmail.com
Website: www.sunywcc.edu
Personnel: Craig Padawer (Advisor)

College and University Newspapers

VALLEY CITY

VALLEY CITY STATE UNIV.

Street Address 1: Box 1431, Vcsc Student Ctr
State: ND
Zip/Postal code: 58072
Country: USA
Mailing Address: Box 1431, VCSC Student Ctr.
Mailing City: Valley City
Mailing State: ND
Mailing ZIP Code: 58072
General Phone: (701) 845-7722

VALLEY GLEN

LOS ANGELES VALLEY COLLEGE

Street Address 1: 5800 Fulton Ave
State: CA
Zip/Postal code: 91401-4062
Country: USA
Mailing Address: 5800 Fulton Ave
Mailing City: Valley Glen
Mailing State: CA
Mailing ZIP Code: 91401-4062
General Phone: (818) 947-2576
General Fax: (818) 947-2610
General/National Adv. Email: valleystar@lavalleystar.com
Website: www.lavalleystar.com
Personnel: Rod Lyons (Advisor); Bill Dauber (Advisor); Sarah Knowles (Ed.); Lucas Thompson (Mng. Ed.)

VALPARAISO

VALPARAISO UNIVERSITY

Street Address 1: 1809 Chapel Dr
State: IN
Zip/Postal code: 46383-4517
Country: USA
Mailing Address: 1809 Chapel Dr
Mailing City: Valparaiso
Mailing State: IN
Mailing ZIP Code: 46383-4517
General Phone: (219) 464-5271
General Fax: (219) 464-6742
General/National Adv. Email: douglas.kocher@valpo.edu
Website: www.valpo.edu/torch
Personnel: Douglas J. Kocher (Chair); Jason Paupore (Advisor); Andy Simmons (Bus. Mgr.); Luis Fifuentes (Adv.Mgr.); Kathryn Kattalia (Ed. in chief)

VANCOUVER

CLARK COLLEGE

Street Address 1: 1933 Fort Vancouver Way
State: WA
Zip/Postal code: 98663-3529
Country: USA
Mailing Address: 1933 Fort Vancouver Way #124
Mailing City: Vancouver
Mailing State: WA
Mailing ZIP Code: 98663-3598
General Phone: (360) 992-2159
General Fax: (360) 992-2879
Website: clarkindependent.wordpress.com
Personnel: Audrey McDougal (Ed. in Chief); Nick Jensen (Mng. Ed.); Daniel Hampton (News Ed.)

VENTURA

VENTURA COLLEGE

Street Address 1: 4667 Telegraph Rd
State: CA
Zip/Postal code: 93003-3872
Country: USA
Mailing Address: 4667 Telegraph Rd
Mailing City: Ventura
Mailing State: CA
Mailing ZIP Code: 93003-3899
General Phone: (805) 654-6200
General Fax: (805) 654-6466
Website: www.venturacollegepress.com
Personnel: C. Weinstock (Advisor)

VERMILLION

UNIV. OF SOUTH DAKOTA

Street Address 1: 555 N Dakota St
State: SD
Zip/Postal code: 57069-2300
Country: USA
Mailing Address: 555 N Dakota St
Mailing City: Vermillion
Mailing State: SD
Mailing ZIP Code: 57069-2300
General Phone: (605) 677-5494
General Fax: (605) 677-5105
General/National Adv. Email: volante@usd.edu; volanteonline@gmail.com
Website: www.volanteonline.com

VIENNA

OHIO VALLEY UNIVERSITY

Street Address 1: 1 Campus View Dr
State: WV
Zip/Postal code: 26105-8000
Country: USA
Mailing Address: 1 Campus View Dr
Mailing City: Vienna
Mailing State: WV
Mailing ZIP Code: 26105-8000
General Phone: (304) 865-6151
Website: www.ovu.edu/site.cfm/newspaper.cfm
Personnel: Philip Sturm (Advisor)

VILLANOVA

VILLANOVA UNIV.

Street Address 1: 800 E Lancaster Ave
State: PA
Zip/Postal code: 19085-1603
Country: USA
Mailing Address: 800 E Lancaster Ave
Mailing City: Villanova
Mailing State: PA
Mailing ZIP Code: 19085-1478
General Phone: (610) 519-7207
General Fax: (610) 519-5666
General/National Adv. Email: business@villanovan.com
Website: www.villanovan.com
Personnel: Jessica Ramey (Bus. Mgr.); Jody Ross (Advisor); Tom Mogan (Advisor); Tim Richer (Ed. in Chief); Laura (Ed. in Chief)

VINCENNES

JOURNALISM PROGRAM, VINCENNES UNIVERSITY

Street Address 1: 1002 N 1st St
State: IN
Zip/Postal code: 47591-1504
Country: USA
Mailing Address: 1002 N 1st St
Mailing City: Vincennes
Mailing State: IN
Mailing ZIP Code: 47591-1500
General Phone: (812) 888-4551
General Fax: (812) 888-5531
General/National Adv. Email: trailblazer@vinu.edu
Website: www.vutrailblazernews.com
Year Established: 1923
Published: Other
Personnel: Emily Taylor (Journalism Asst. Professor, Department Chair of Media Production)

VISALIA

COLLEGE OF THE SEQUOIAS

Street Address 1: 915 S Mooney Blvd
State: CA
Zip/Postal code: 93277-2214
Country: USA
Mailing Address: 915 S Mooney Blvd
Mailing City: Visalia
Mailing State: CA
Mailing ZIP Code: 93277-2234
General Phone: (559) 730-3844
General Fax: (559) 730-3991
General/National Adv. Email: campusnews@cos.edu
Display Adv. Email: campusads@cos.edu
Editorial Email: campusnews@cos.edu
Website: www.coscampusonline.com
Year Established: 1933

WACO

BAYLOR UNIVERSITY

Street Address 1: 1 Bear Pl
Street Address 2: Unit 97330
State: TX
Zip/Postal code: 76798-7330
Country: USA
Mailing Address: 1 Bear Pl Unit 97330
Mailing City: Waco
Mailing State: TX
Mailing ZIP Code: 76798-7330
General Phone: (254) 710-3407
General Fax: (254) 710-1714
Advertising Phone: (254) 710-3407
Advertising Fax: (254) 710-1714
Editorial Fax: (254) 710-1714
General/National Adv. Email: lariat@baylor.edu
Display Adv. Email: Lariat_Ads@baylor.edu
Editorial Email: Lariat-Letters@baylor.edu
Website: www.baylorlariat.com
Year Established: 1900
Commercial printers?: N
Published: Tues`Wed`Thur`Fri
Avg Free Circ: 4000
Personnel: Paul Carr (Dir., Mktg. Information); Jamile Yglecias (Advertising Sales and Marketing Manager); Julie Freeman (Asst. Media Adviser)
Parent company (for newspapers): Baylor University

WACO

MCLENNAN CMTY. COLLEGE

Street Address 1: 1400 College Dr
State: TX
Zip/Postal code: 76708-1402
Country: USA
Mailing Address: 1400 College Dr
Mailing City: Waco
Mailing State: TX
Mailing ZIP Code: 76708-1499
General Phone: (254) 299-8524
General Fax: (254) 299-8568

WAHPETON

NORTH DAKOTA STATE COLLEGE OF SCIENCE

Street Address 1: PO Box 760
State: ND
Zip/Postal code: 58074-0760
Country: USA
Mailing Address: c/o Daily News, PO Box 760
Mailing City: Wahpeton
Mailing State: ND
Mailing ZIP Code: 58074-0760
General Phone: (701) 642-8585
General Fax: (701) 642-6068
Personnel: Pam Marquart (Advisor)

WALTHAM

BENTLEY UNIVERSITY

Street Address 1: 175 Forest St
State: MA
Zip/Postal code: 02452-4713
Country: USA
Mailing State: MA
General Phone: (781) 891-2921
General Fax: (781) 891-2574
Editorial Phone: (781) 891-3497
General/National Adv. Email: ga_vanguard@bentley.edu
Website: www.bentleyvanguard.com; www.bentleyvanguardonline.com
Published: Thur
Personnel: Maria Dilorenzo (Advisor); Sindhu Palaniappan (Ed. in Chief); Greg Kokino (Adv. Mgr.)

BRANDEIS UNIVERSITY

Street Address 1: 415 South St
Street Address 2: MS 214
State: MA
Zip/Postal code: 02453-2728
Country: USA
Mailing Address: 415 South St MS 214
Mailing City: Waltham
Mailing State: MA
Mailing ZIP Code: 02453-2728
General Phone: (781) 736-3750
General Fax: (781) 736-3756
Editorial Phone: (781) 736-3751
General/National Adv. Email: editor@thejustice.org
Display Adv. Email: ads@thejustice.org
Website: www.thejustice.org
Year Established: 1949
Published: Tues
Personnel: Editor (Ed.)

WARRENSBURG

UNIVERSITY OF CENTRAL MISSOURI

Street Address 1: Martin 136, University of Central Missouri
State: MO
Zip/Postal code: 64093
Country: USA
Mailing Address: Martin 136, University of Central Missouri
Mailing City: Warrensburg
Mailing State: MO
Mailing ZIP Code: 64093
General Phone: (660) 543-4050
General Fax: (660) 543-8663
Advertising Phone: (660) 543-4051
General/National Adv. Email: muleskinner@ucmo.edu
Display Adv. Email: muleskinnerads@ucmo.edu
Website: www.digitalburg.com
Year Established: 1906
News Services: Associated Press
Delivery Methods: Racks
Published: Thur
Published Other: digitalburg.com
Avg Free Circ: 3000
Personnel: Matt Bird-Meyer (Adviser); Jacque Flanagan (Managing Editor)

WASHINGTON

AMERICAN UNIV.

Street Address 1: 252 Mary Graydon Ctr
State: DC
Country: USA
Mailing Address: 4400 Massachusetts Ave NW
Mailing City: Washington
Mailing State: DC
Mailing ZIP Code: 20016-8003
General Phone: (202) 885-1414
General Fax: (202) 885-1428
Editorial Phone: (202) 885-1402
General/National Adv. Email: editor@theeagleonline.com
Website: www.theeagleonline.com
Personnel: Jen Calantone (Ed. in Chief); Charlie Szold (News Ed.); Andrew Tomlinson (Sports Ed.); Caitlin E. Moore (A&E Ed.); Kelsey (Photo Ed.)

CATHOLIC UNIV. OF AMERICA
Street Address 1: 127 Pryzbyla Ctr
State: DC
Country: USA
Mailing Address: 127 Pryzbyla Ctr
Mailing City: Washington
Mailing State: DC
Mailing ZIP Code: 20064-0001
General Phone: (202) 319-5779
General Fax: (202) 319-6675
Website: www.cuatower.com
Personnel: William McQuillen (Advisor.); Ben Newell (Ed.)

GALLAUDET UNIVERSITY
Street Address 1: 800 Florida Ave NE
State: DC
Zip/Postal code: 20002-3600
Country: USA
Mailing Address: PO Box 2334
Mailing City: Washington
Mailing State: DC
Mailing ZIP Code: 20013-2334
General Phone: (202) 651-5000
General Fax: (202) 651-5916
General/National Adv. Email: ursabuffinblue@gmail.comursabuffinblue
Website: www.gallaudet.edu
Personnel: Mary Lott (Dir.)

GEORGE WASHINGTON UNIV.
Street Address 1: 2140 G St NW
State: DC
Zip/Postal code: 20052-0072
Country: USA
Mailing Address: 2140 G St NW
Mailing City: Washington
Mailing State: DC
Mailing ZIP Code: 20052-0072
General Phone: (202) 994-7080
General Fax: (202) 994-1309
Advertising Fax: (202) 994-7550
General/National Adv. Email: news@gwhatchet.comgwhatchet
Display Adv. Email: ads@gwhatchet.comgwhatchet
Website: www.gwhatchet.com
Year Established: 1904
Personnel: Howard Marshall (Gen. Mgr.); Arron Elkins (Adv. Mgr.); Alex Byers (Ed. in Chief); Beyers

GEORGE WASHINGTON UNIV. LAW SCHOOL
Street Address 1: 2008 H St NW
Street Address 2: Bsmt
State: DC
Zip/Postal code: 20052-0026
Country: USA
Mailing Address: 2008 H St NW Bsmt
Mailing City: Washington
Mailing State: DC
Mailing ZIP Code: 20052-0026
General Phone: (202) 994-6261
General/National Adv. Email: notabene@law.gwu.edu
Website: notabene.gwsba.com
Personnel: Sarah Valerio (Pres.); Katie Earnest (Ed. in Chief)

GEORGETOWN UNIV. LAW CENTER
Street Address 1: 600 New Jersey Ave NW
State: DC
Zip/Postal code: 20001-2022
Country: USA
Mailing Address: 600 New Jersey Ave NW
Mailing City: Washington
Mailing State: DC
Mailing ZIP Code: 20001-2075
General Phone: (202) 662-9357
General Fax: (202) 662-9491
Personnel: Brett Marston (Advisor)

GEORGETOWN UNIVERSITY
Street Address 1: Leavey Ctr Rm 421, 37th & O Sts NW
State: DC
Zip/Postal code: 20057-0001
Country: USA
Mailing Address: PO Box 571065
Mailing City: Washington
Mailing State: DC
Mailing ZIP Code: 20057-1065
General Phone: (202) 687-3947
General Fax: (202) 687-2741
Advertising Phone: (202) 687-3947
Advertising Fax: (202) 687-2741
Editorial Phone: (202) 687-3415
General/National Adv. Email: gm@thehoya.com
Display Adv. Email: sales@thehoya.com
Editorial Email: editor@thehoya.com
Website: www.thehoya.com
Year Established: 1920
Published: Tues`Fri
Avg Free Circ: 6500
Personnel: Roshan Vora (Advisor); Michelle Lee (Adv. Mgr.); Kaphryn Devincenzo (Ed. in chief); Eamon O' connor (Exec. Ed.); Kathryn (Mng. Ed.); Mary Nancy Walter (General Manager)

HOWARD UNIV.
Street Address 1: 2251 Sherman Ave NW
State: DC
Zip/Postal code: 20001-4003
Country: USA
Mailing Address: 816 Easley St Apt 805
Mailing City: Silver Spring
Mailing State: MD
Mailing ZIP Code: 20910-4581
General Phone: (202) 806-4749
General Fax: (202) 328-1681
General/National Adv. Email: bussinessoffice@thehilltoponline.com
Website: www.thehilltoponline.com
Personnel: Kevin Reed (Advisor); Vanessa Rozier (Ed. in Chief)

MCDONOUGH BUS. SCHOOL/ GEORGETOWN UNIV.
Street Address 1: 3520 Prospect St NW
Street Address 2: Ste 215
State: DC
Zip/Postal code: 20007-2631
Country: USA
Mailing Address: 3520 Prospect St NW Ste 215
Mailing City: Washington
Mailing State: DC
Mailing ZIP Code: 20007-2631
General Phone: (202) 678-0268
General Fax: (202) 678-0268
General/National Adv. Email: mba-globe@msb.edu
Website: www.georgetownglobe.com
Personnel: Brenna Fleener (Ed. in Chief)

WASHINGTON & JEFFERSON COLLEGE
Street Address 1: 60 S Lincoln St
State: PA
Zip/Postal code: 15301-4812
Country: USA
Mailing Address: 60 S Lincoln St
Mailing City: Washington
Mailing State: PA
Mailing ZIP Code: 15301-4801
General Phone: (724) 222-4400
General Fax: (724) 223-6534
General/National Adv. Email: redandblackstaff@jay.washjeff.edu
Website: www.washjeff.edu
Year Established: 1909
Published: Thur
Personnel: Dale Lolley (Advisor)

WATERBURY
NAUGATUCK VALLEY COMMUNITY COLLEGE
Street Address 1: 750 Chase Pkwy
State: CT
Zip/Postal code: 06708-3011
Country: USA
Mailing Address: 750 Chase Pkwy
Mailing City: Waterbury
Mailing State: CT
Mailing ZIP Code: 06708-3089
General Phone: (203) 575-8040
General Fax: (203) 596-8721
General/National Adv. Email: nvcc@nvcc.commnet.edu
Website: www.nvcc.commnet.edu
Published: Mthly
Personnel: Steve Parlato (Faculty Advisor); Chelsea Clow (Editor-in-Chief)

WATERTOWN
JEFFERSON CMTY. COLLEGE
Street Address 1: 1220 Coffeen St
State: NY
Zip/Postal code: 13601-1822
Country: USA
Mailing Address: 1220 Coffeen St
Mailing City: Watertown
Mailing State: NY
Mailing ZIP Code: 13601-1897
General Phone: (315) 786-2200
General Fax: (315) 788-0716
Website: www.sunyjefferson.edu
Personnel: Andrea Pedrick (Advisor); Danielle Sacca (Ed.); Rachel Hunter (Ed.)

WATERVILLE
COLBY COLLEGE
Street Address 1: 4600 Mayflower Hill Dr
State: ME
Zip/Postal code: 4901
Country: USA
Mailing Address: 4600 Mayflower Hill Dr.
Mailing City: Waterville
Mailing State: ME
Mailing ZIP Code: 04901
General Phone: (207) 859-4000
General Fax: (207) 872-3555
General/National Adv. Email: echo@colbyecho.com
Website: www.colbyecho.com
Personnel: Peter Rummel (Bus. Mgr.); Kira Novak (Adv. Mgr); Elisabeth Ponsot (Ed. in Chief)

WAUKESHA
THE NEW PERSPECTIVE
Street Address 1: 100 N East Ave
State: WI
Zip/Postal code: 53186-3103
Country: USA
Mailing Address: 1111 Sentry Dr
Mailing City: Waukesha
Mailing State: WI
Mailing ZIP Code: 53186-5965
General Phone: (262) 524-7351
General/National Adv. Email: perspect@carrollu.edu
Display Adv. Email: npadvertising@gmail.com
Editorial Email: persepct@carrollu.edu
Website: www.thedigitalnp.com
Year Established: 1874
Special Editions: Welcome Week
Delivery Methods: Racks
Commercial printers?: Y

WAUSAU
UNIV. OF WISCONSIN CENTER MARATHON
Street Address 1: 518 S 7th Ave
State: WI
Zip/Postal code: 54401-5362
Country: USA
Mailing Address: 518 S 7th Ave
Mailing City: Wausau
Mailing State: WI
Mailing ZIP Code: 54401-5362
General Phone: (715) 261-6264
General Fax: (715) 261-6333
General/National Adv. Email: theforumuwmc@gmail.com
Website: www.uwmcforum.com
Personnel: Mark Parman (Advisor); Haley Zblewski (Ed. in Chief)

WAVERLY
WARTBURG COLLEGE
Street Address 1: 100 Wartburg Blvd
State: IA
Zip/Postal code: 50677-2215
Country: USA
Mailing Address: 100 Wartburg Blvd
Mailing City: Waverly
Mailing State: IA
Mailing ZIP Code: 50677-2200
General Phone: (319) 352-8289
General Fax: (319) 352-8242
General/National Adv. Email: trumpet@wartburg.edu
Website: www.wartburg.edu/trumpet
Personnel: Cliff Brockmen (Advisor); Luke Shanno (Ed. in Chief); Jackie Albrecht (News Ed.)

WAYNE
VALLEY FORGE MILITARY COLLEGE
Street Address 1: 1001 Eagle Rd
State: PA
Zip/Postal code: 19087-3613
Country: USA
Mailing Address: 1001 Eagle Rd
Mailing City: Wayne
Mailing State: PA
Mailing ZIP Code: 19087-3695
General Phone: (610) 989-1403
Personnel: Charles A. McGeorge (Pres.)

WAYNE STATE COLLEGE
Street Address 1: 1111 Main St
State: NE
Zip/Postal code: 68787-1181
Country: USA
Mailing Address: 1111 Main St
Mailing City: Wayne
Mailing State: NE
Mailing ZIP Code: 68787-1172
General Phone: (402) 375-7324
General Fax: (402) 375-7204
Advertising Phone: (402) 375-7489
General/National Adv. Email: wstater@wsc.edu
Website: wildcat.wsc.edu/stater/
Personnel: Max McElwain (Faculty Advisor); Skylar Osovski (Ed. in Chief); Katelynn Wolfe (News Ed.)

WILLIAM PATERSON UNIV.
Street Address 1: 300 Pompton Rd
Street Address 2: # SC329A
State: NJ
Zip/Postal code: 07470-2103
Country: USA
Mailing Address: 300 Pompton Rd # SC329A
Mailing City: Wayne
Mailing State: NJ
Mailing ZIP Code: 07470-2103
General Phone: (973) 720-3265
General Fax: (973) 720-2093
General/National Adv. Email: wpubeacon@hotmail.com
Website: www.wpubeacon.com
Personnel: Jeff Wakemen (Advisor); Tim

College and University Newspapers

Kauffeld (Ed. in Chief); Robin Mulder (News Ed.)

WAYNESBURG

WAYNESBURG UNIVERSITY: THE YELLOW JACKET

Street Address 1: 51 W College St
State: PA
Zip/Postal code: 15370-1258
Country: USA
Mailing Address: 51 West College St.
Mailing City: Waynesburg
Mailing State: PA
Mailing ZIP Code: 15370
General Phone: 724-627-8191
General/National Adv. Email: jacket@waynesburg.edu

WELLESLEY

WELLESLEY COLLEGE

Street Address 1: 106 Central St
Street Address 2: Fl 4
State: MA
Zip/Postal code: 02481-8203
Country: USA
Mailing Address: 106 Central St
Mailing City: Wellesley
Mailing State: MA
Mailing ZIP Code: 02481-8210
General Phone: (781) 283-2689
General Fax: (781) 431-7520
General/National Adv. Email: thewellesleynews@gmail.com
Display Adv. Email: thewellesleynews@gmail.com
Editorial Email: thewellesleynews@gmail.com
Website: www.thewellesleynews.com
Year Established: 1901
Published: Wed
Personnel: Alice Liang (Managing Editor); Stephanie Yeh (Editor-in-Chief)

WENHAM

GORDON COLLEGE

Street Address 1: 255 Grapevine Rd
State: MA
Zip/Postal code: 01984-1813
Country: USA
Mailing Address: 255 Grapevine Rd
Mailing City: Wenham
Mailing State: MA
Mailing ZIP Code: 01984-1899
General Phone: (978) 927-2306
General Fax: (978) 524-3300
General/National Adv. Email: tartan@gordon.edu
Personnel: Eric Convey (Advisor)

WESSON

COPIAH-LINCOLN CMTY. COLLEGE

Street Address 1: Hwy 51 S
State: MS
Zip/Postal code: 39191
Country: USA
Mailing Address: PO Box 649
Mailing City: Wesson
Mailing State: MS
Mailing ZIP Code: 39191-0649
General Phone: (601) 643-8354
General Fax: (601) 643-8226
Website: www.colin.edu
Personnel: Mary Warren (Advisor)

WEST BARNSTABLE

CAPE COD CMTY. COLLEGE

Street Address 1: 2240 Iyannough Rd
Street Address 2: North Building Room 206
State: MA
Zip/Postal code: 02668-1532
Country: USA
Mailing Address: 2240 Iyannough Rd
Mailing City: West Barnstable
Mailing State: MA
Mailing ZIP Code: 02668
General Phone: (508) 362-2131
General Fax: (508) 375-4116
General/National Adv. Email: info@capecod.edu
Website: www.capecod.edu
Year Established: 1961
Personnel: James Kershner (Advisor)

WEST CHESTER

WEST CHESTER UNIVERSITY

Street Address 1: 253 Sykes Union Bldg
State: PA
Zip/Postal code: 19383-0001
Country: USA
Mailing Address: 253 Sykes Union
Mailing City: West Chester
Mailing State: PA
Mailing ZIP Code: 19383-0001
General Phone: (610) 436-2375
General Fax: (610) 436-3280
Advertising Phone: (610) 436-2375
General/National Adv. Email: quad@wcupa.edu
Display Adv. Email: quadadvertising@wcupa.edu
Editorial Email: quadeic@wcupa.edu
Website: www.wcuquad.com
Year Established: 1934
News Services: MCT Campus
Delivery Methods: Racks
Published: Mon
Avg Free Circ: 2500
Personnel: Philip Thompsen (Advisor); Samantha Mineroff (EIC)

WEST HARTFORD

UNIV. OF HARTFORD

Street Address 1: 200 Bloomfield Ave
Street Address 2: Rm 158
State: CT
Zip/Postal code: 06117-1545
Country: USA
Mailing Address: 200 Bloomfield Ave Rm 158
Mailing City: West Hartford
Mailing State: CT
Mailing ZIP Code: 06117-1545
General Phone: (860) 768-4723
General Fax: (860) 768-4728
General/National Adv. Email: informer@hartford.edu
Website: www.hartfordinformer.com
Personnel: Jonathan Whitson (Bus. Mgr.); Melissa O' Brien (Ed. in Chief)

WEST HAVEN

UNIV. OF NEW HAVEN

Street Address 1: 300 Boston Post Rd
State: CT
Zip/Postal code: 06516-1916
Country: USA
Mailing Address: 300 Boston Post Rd
Mailing City: West Haven
Mailing State: CT
Mailing ZIP Code: 06516-1999
General Phone: (203) 932-7182
General Fax: (203) 931-6037
General/National Adv. Email: chargerbulletin@newhaven.edu
Website: www.chargerbulletin.com
Year Established: 1938
Published: Wed
Personnel: Zack Rosen (Ed. in Chief); Erin Ennis (Asst. Ed.); Sara McGuire (A&E Ed.); Michelle Blydenburg (Adv. Mgr.); Charles (Distribution Mgr.); Liana Teixeira; Elizabeth Field

WEST LAFAYETTE

THE PURDUE EXPONENT

Street Address 1: 460 Northwestern Ave
State: IN
Zip/Postal code: 47906-2966
Country: USA
Mailing Address: PO Box 2506
Mailing City: West Lafayette
Mailing State: IN
Mailing ZIP Code: 47996-2506
General Phone: (765) 743-1111
General Fax: (765) 743-6087
Advertising Phone: Ext. 122
Editorial Phone: Ext. 254
General/National Adv. Email: help@purdueexponent.org
Display Adv. Email: advertising@purdueexponent.org
Website: www.purdueexponent.org
Year Established: 1889
Delivery Methods: Carrier
Commercial printers?: Y
Published: Mon`Tues`Wed`Thur`Fri
Published Other: M Th during summer
Avg Free Circ: 12000
Personnel: Patirck Kuhnle (Pub.); Ingraham Vancel (Prodn. Dir.); Mindy Coddington (Advertising director)
Parent company (for newspapers): Purdue Student Publishing Foundation

WEST LIBERTY

WEST LIBERTY UNIVERSITY

Street Address 1: 208 Faculty Drive
Street Address 2: Cub 153
State: WV
Zip/Postal code: 26074
Country: USA
Mailing Address: 208 Faculty Drive
Mailing City: West Liberty
Mailing State: WV
Mailing ZIP Code: 26074
General Phone: (304) 336-8873
General Fax: (304) 336-8323
Editorial Phone: (304) 336-8213
General/National Adv. Email: wltrumpet@wlsc.edu
Website: westlibertylive.com/thetrumpet
Year Established: 1922
Published: Wed
Avg Free Circ: 1500
Personnel: Tammie Beagle (Advisor)

WEST LONG BRANCH

MONMOUTH UNIVERSITY

Street Address 1: 400 Cedar Ave
Street Address 2: Rm 260
State: NJ
Zip/Postal code: 07764-1804
Country: USA
Mailing Address: 400 Cedar Ave Rm 260
Mailing City: West Long Branch
Mailing State: NJ
Mailing ZIP Code: 07764-1804
General Phone: (732) 571-3481
Advertising Phone: (732) 263-5151
General/National Adv. Email: outlook@monmouth.edu
Display Adv. Email: outlookads@monmouth.edu
Website: outlook.monmouth.edu
Year Established: 1933
Published: Wed
Avg Free Circ: 5000
Personnel: John Morano (Professor of Journalism); Sandra Brown (Office Coordinator)

WEST MIFFLIN

CMTY. COLLEGE ALLEGHENY COUNTY SOUTH

Street Address 1: 1750 Clairton Rd
Street Address 2: # RT885
State: PA
Zip/Postal code: 15122-3029
Country: USA
Mailing Address: 1750 Clairton Rd # Rt
Mailing City: West Mifflin
Mailing State: PA
Mailing ZIP Code: 15122-3029
General Phone: (412) 469-6352
General Fax: (412) 469-4333
Website: www.ccac.edu
Personnel: Aaron Kindeall (Ed.)

WEST MIFFLIN

COMMUNITY COLLEGE OF ALLEGHENY: THE FORUM

Street Address 1: 1750 Clourton Rd Rt 885
State: PA
Zip/Postal code: 15122
Country: USA
Mailing Address: 1750 Clourton Rd Rt 885
Mailing City: West Mifflin
Mailing State: PA
Mailing ZIP Code: 15122
General Phone: 412-469-6352
General Fax: 412-469-4333
Website: www.ccac.edu

WEST PALM BEACH

PALM BEACH ATLANTIC UNIVERSITY

Street Address 1: 901 S Flagler Dr
State: FL
Zip/Postal code: 33401-6505
Country: USA
Mailing Address: PO Box 24708
Mailing City: West Palm Beach
Mailing State: FL
Mailing ZIP Code: 33416-4708
General Phone: (561) 803-2566
General Fax: (561) 803-2577
General/National Adv. Email: beacon@pba.edu
Website: readmybeacon.com
Personnel: John Sizemore (Advisor/Exec. Ed.)

WESTERVILLE

OTTERBEIN UNIVERSITY

Street Address 1: 1 S Grove St
Street Address 2: Otterbein University
State: OH
Zip/Postal code: 43081-2004
Country: USA
Mailing Address: Communication Department
Mailing City: Westerville
Mailing State: OH
Mailing ZIP Code: 43081
General Phone: (614) 823 1159
Advertising Phone: 614 823 1159
Editorial Phone: 614 823 1159
General/National Adv. Email: adviser@otterbein360.com
Display Adv. Email: sales@otterbein360.com
Website: www.otterbein360.com
Year Established: 1880
Published: Mon`Tues`Wed`Thur`Fri`Sat`Sun
Personnel: Hillary Warren (Advisor)

WESTFIELD

WESTFIELD STATE UNIVERSITY

Street Address 1: 577 Western Ave
Street Address 2: Ely Campus Center, Room 305
State: MA
Zip/Postal code: 01085-2580
Country: USA
Mailing Address: 577 Western Avenue
Mailing City: Westfield
Mailing State: MA
Mailing ZIP Code: 01085
General Phone: (413) 572-5431
General Fax: (413) 572-5477

Advertising Phone: (413) 572-5431
Editorial Phone: (413) 572-5431
General/National Adv. Email: thevoice@westfield.ma.edu
Display Adv. Email: thevoiceadvertisement@gmail.com
Year Established: 1946
Published: Fri
Personnel: Joshua Clark (Editor-in-Chief); Andrew Burke (Editor-in-Chief); Emily Hanshaw (Managing Editor); Matthew Carlin (Assistant Managing Editor)

WESTMINSTER

FRONT RANGE CMTY. COLLEGE

Street Address 1: 3645 W 112th Ave
State: CO
Zip/Postal code: 80031-2105
Country: USA
Mailing Address: 3645 W 112th Ave
Mailing City: Westminster
Mailing State: CO
Mailing ZIP Code: 80031-2199
General Phone: (303) 404-5314
General Fax: (303) 404-5199
General/National Adv. Email: frontpage@frontrange.com
Website: www.frontrange.edu
Personnel: John Heisel (Advisor); Stephanie Munger (Ed. in Chief); Jon Strungis (Ed.)

MCDANIEL COLLEGE

Street Address 1: 2 College Hl
State: MD
Zip/Postal code: 21157-4303
Country: USA
Mailing Address: 2 College Hill
Mailing City: Westminster
Mailing State: MD
Mailing ZIP Code: 21157-4390
General Phone: (410) 751-8600
General Fax: (410) 857-2729
General/National Adv. Email: freepress@mcdaniel.edu
Website: mcdanielfreepress.com
Published: Mthly
Personnel: Sarah Hull (Co-Editor-In-Chief); Daniel Valentin-Morales (Co-Editor-In-Chief)

WESTVILLE

PURDUE UNIV. NORTH CENTRAL

Street Address 1: 1401 S U S 421
State: IN
Zip/Postal code: 46391
Country: USA
Mailing Address: 1401 S. U.S. 421
Mailing City: Westville
Mailing State: IN
Mailing ZIP Code: 46391-9542
General Phone: (219) 785-5213
General Fax: (219) 785-5544
General/National Adv. Email: spectator@pnc.edu
Editorial Email: thevoice@pnc.edu
Website: www.pnc.edu
Personnel: Suzanne Webber (Ed.); Lyndsie Daikhi (Print Ed.)

WHEATON

WHEATON COLLEGE

Street Address 1: 501 College Ave
Street Address 2: Cpo W135
State: IL
Zip/Postal code: 60187-5501
Country: USA
Mailing Address: 501 College Ave.
Mailing City: Wheaton
Mailing State: IL
Mailing ZIP Code: 60187
General Phone: (630) 752-5077
General/National Adv. Email: the.record@my.wheaton.edu
Display Adv. Email: ads.wheatonrecord@gmail.com
Editorial Email: the.record@wheaton.edu
Website: www.wheatonrecord.com/
Year Established: 1876
Delivery Methods: Mail Racks
Published: Thur
Personnel: Philip Kline (Co-editor in chief); Alycia Vander Vegt (Co-editor in chief)

WHEELING

WHEELING JESUIT UNIV.

Street Address 1: 316 Washington Ave
State: WV
Zip/Postal code: 26003-6243
Country: USA
Mailing Address: 316 Washington Ave
Mailing City: Wheeling
Mailing State: WV
Mailing ZIP Code: 26003-6295
General Phone: (304) 243-2250
Editorial Email: news@wju.edu
Website: www.wju.edu/cardinal
Personnel: Becky Forney (Advisor)

WHITE PLAINS

PACE UNIV. LAW SCHOOL

Street Address 1: 78 N Broadway
State: NY
Zip/Postal code: 10603-3710
Country: USA
Mailing Address: 78 N Broadway
Mailing City: White Plains
Mailing State: NY
Mailing ZIP Code: 10603-3710
General Phone: (914) 422-4205
General/National Adv. Email: hearsay@law.case.edu
Website: www.law.pace.edu
Personnel: Angela D'agostino (Dean, Student Servs.)

WHITEWATER

UNIV. OF WISCONSIN WHITEWATER

Street Address 1: 800 W Main St
Street Address 2: 66 University Ctr.
State: WI
Zip/Postal code: 53190-1705
Country: USA
Mailing Address: 66 University Ctr.
Mailing City: Whitewater
Mailing State: WI
Mailing ZIP Code: 53190
General Phone: (262) 472-5100
General Fax: (262) 472-5101
Display Adv. Email: rpads@uww.edu
Editorial Email: rp@uww.edu
Website: www.royalpurplenews.com
Year Established: 1901
Delivery Methods: Racks
Personnel: Sam Martino (Advisor); Kyle Geissler (Adviser)

WHITING

CALUMET COLLEGE OF ST. JOSEPH

Street Address 1: 2400 New York Ave
State: IN
Zip/Postal code: 46394-2146
Country: USA
Mailing Address: 2400 New York Ave
Mailing City: Whiting
Mailing State: IN
Mailing ZIP Code: 46394-2195
General Phone: (219) 473-4322
General Fax: (219) 473-4219
Website: www.ccsj.edu
Published: Bi-Mthly
Personnel: Dawn Muhammad (PD); Daren Jasieniecki (Mktg. Mgr.); Mark Cassello

WHITTIER

RIO HONDO COLLEGE

Street Address 1: 3600 Workman Mill Rd
State: CA
Zip/Postal code: 90601-1616
Country: USA
Mailing Address: 3600 Workman Mill Rd
Mailing City: Whittier
Mailing State: CA
Mailing ZIP Code: 90601-1699
General Phone: (562) 908-3453
General Fax: (562) 463-4641
General/National Adv. Email: elpaisano@riohondo.edu
Website: www.elpaisanonewspaper.com
Personnel: John Francis (Advisor); Mary Cowan (Ed. in Chief); Salomon Baeza (Ed. in Chief); James Tapparo (Adv. Dir.); Kathy (Exec. Dir.)

SOUTHERN CALIFORNIA UNIV. OF HEALTH SCIENCES

Street Address 1: 16200 Amber Valley Dr
State: CA
Zip/Postal code: 90604-4051
Country: USA
Mailing Address: 16200 Amber Valley Dr
Mailing City: Whittier
Mailing State: CA
Mailing ZIP Code: 90604-4051
General Phone: (562) 947-8755
General Fax: (562) 902-3321
Personnel: Pam Roosevelt (Ed.)

WHITTIER COLLEGE

Street Address 1: 13406 Philadelphia St
State: CA
Zip/Postal code: 90601-4446
Country: USA
Mailing Address: PO Box 634
Mailing City: Whittier
Mailing State: CA
Mailing ZIP Code: 90608-0634
General Phone: (562) 907-4254
General Fax: (562) 945-5301
General/National Adv. Email: qc@whittier.edu
Website: www.thequakercampus.org/
Year Established: 1914
Published: Thur
Personnel: justin dennis (EIC, Mgr Ed); matther anson

WICHITA

NEWMAN UNIVERSITY - THE VANTAGE

Street Address 1: 3100 W McCormick St
State: KS
Zip/Postal code: 67213-2008
Country: USA
Mailing Address: 3100 W McCormick St
Mailing City: Wichita
Mailing State: KS
Mailing ZIP Code: 67213-2008
General Phone: (316) 942-4291
General Fax: (316) 942-4483
General/National Adv. Email: vantage@newmanu.edu
Delivery Methods: Newsstand Racks
Personnel: Kristen McCurdy (Editor)

WICHITA STATE UNIV.

Street Address 1: 1845 Fairmount St
State: KS
Zip/Postal code: 67260-9700
Country: USA
Mailing Address: 1845 Fairmount St
Mailing City: Wichita
Mailing State: KS
Mailing ZIP Code: 67260-0001
General Phone: (316) 978-3456
General Fax: (316) 978-3778
Editorial Email: editor@thesunflower.com; sports.editor@thesunflower.com
Website: www.thesunflower.com
Personnel: Ronda Voorhis (Advisor); Candice Tullis (Ed. in Chief); Scott Elpers (Mng. Ed.); Jorge M. De Hoyos (Sports Ed.)

WICHITA FALLS

MIDWESTERN STATE UNIVERSITY

Street Address 1: 3410 Taft Blvd
State: TX
Zip/Postal code: 76308-2036
Country: USA
Mailing Address: 3410 Taft Blvd
Mailing City: Wichita Falls
Mailing State: TX
Mailing ZIP Code: 76307-0014
General Phone: (940) 397-4704
Advertising Phone: (940) 397-4704
Editorial Phone: (940) 397-4704
General/National Adv. Email: wichitan@msutexas.edu
Display Adv. Email: wichitan@msutexas.edu
Editorial Email: wichitan@msutexas.edu
Website: thewichitan.com/
Year Established: 1935
Published: Wed
Avg Free Circ: 1000
Personnel: Bradley Wilson (Adviser)

WILBERFORCE

CENTRAL STATE UNIV.

Street Address 1: PO Box 1004
State: OH
Zip/Postal code: 45384-1004
Country: USA
Mailing Address: PO Box 1004
Mailing City: Wilberforce
Mailing State: OH
Mailing ZIP Code: 45384-1004
General Phone: (937) 376-6095
General Fax: (937) 376-6530
General/National Adv. Email: info@centralstate.edu
Website: www.centralstate.edu
Personnel: Mike Gormley (Advisor)

WILBERFORCE

WILBERFORCE UNIV.

Street Address 1: 1055 N Bickett Rd
State: OH
Zip/Postal code: 45384-5801
Country: USA
Mailing Address: PO Box 1001
Mailing City: Wilberforce
Mailing State: OH
Mailing ZIP Code: 45384-1001
General Phone: (937) 376-2911
General Fax: (937) 708-5793
General/National Adv. Email: tmorah@wilberforce.edu
Website: www.wilberforce.edu
Personnel: Tanya Morah (Advisor); Courtney Wiggins (Ed.)

WILKES BARRE

WILKES UNIV.

Street Address 1: 130 S River St, Conyngham Ctr, Office 101
State: PA
Zip/Postal code: 18701
Country: USA
Mailing Address: 130 S. River St., Conyngham Ctr., Office 101
Mailing City: Wilkes-Barre
Mailing State: PA
Mailing ZIP Code: 18701
General Phone: (570) 408-5903
General Fax: (570) 408-5902
Advertising Phone: (570) 408-2962
General/National Adv. Email: wilkesbeacon@wilkes.edu

College and University Newspapers

Website: www.wilkesbeacon.com
Personnel: Andrea Frantz (Advisor); Michele Flannery (Bus./Adv. Mgr.); Nicole Frail (Ed. in Chief)

WILLIAMSBURG

COLLEGE OF WILLIAM AND MARY

Street Address 1: Campus Ctr, Jamestown Rd
State: VA
Zip/Postal code: 23187
Country: USA
Mailing Address: PO Box 8795
Mailing City: Williamsburg
Mailing State: VA
Mailing ZIP Code: 23187-8795
General/National Adv. Email: flathat.editor@gmail.com
Display Adv. Email: flathatads@gmail.com
Editorial Email: fhnews@gmail.com
Website: www.flathatnews.com
Year Established: 1911
Published: Tues
Personnel: Trici Fredrick (Advisor); Tucker Higgins (Editor-in-chief)

UNIVERSITY OF THE CUMBERLANDS

Street Address 1: 6191 College Station Dr
State: KY
Zip/Postal code: 40769-1372
Country: USA
Mailing Address: 6191 College Station Dr
Mailing City: Williamsburg
Mailing State: KY
Mailing ZIP Code: 40769-1372
General Phone: 606.539.4172
General/National Adv. Email: thepatriot@ucumberlands.edu
Website: www.thepatriot.ucumberlands.ed

WILLIAMSPORT

LYCOMING COLLEGE

Street Address 1: 700 College Pl
Street Address 2: Campus Box 169
State: PA
Zip/Postal code: 17701-5157
Country: USA
Mailing Address: 700 College Place
Mailing City: Williamsport
Mailing State: PA
Mailing ZIP Code: 17701-5192
General Phone: (570) 321-4315
General/National Adv. Email: lycourier@lycoming.edu
Display Adv. Email: lycourier@lycoming.edu
Editorial Email: lycourier@lycoming.edu
Website: lycourier.lycoming.edu
Delivery Methods: Racks
Commercial printers?: Y
Published: Other
Published Other: Bl-Wkly on Thursdays
Avg Free Circ: 800
Personnel: Dave Heemer (Advisor); Jordyn Hotchkiss (Editor-in-Chief)

WILLIAMSTOWN

WILLIAMS COLLEGE

Street Address 1: 209 Paresky Center
State: MA
Zip/Postal code: 1267
Country: USA
Mailing Address: 39 Chapin Hall Dr.
Mailing City: Williamstown
Mailing State: MA
Mailing ZIP Code: 01267
General Phone: (413) 597-2289
General Fax: (413) 597-2450
General/National Adv. Email: williamsrecordeic@gmail.com
Display Adv. Email: williamsrecordadvertising@gmail.com
Editorial Email: williamsrecordeic@gmail.com
Website: www.williamsrecord.com

Year Established: 1887
Published: Wed
Avg Free Circ: 2000
Personnel: Rachel Scharf (Editor-in-Chief); Matthew Borin (Ed. In Chief)

WILLIMANTIC

EASTERN CONNECTICUT STATE UNIV.

Street Address 1: 83 Windham St, 103 Student Ctr
State: CT
Zip/Postal code: 6226
Country: USA
Mailing Address: 83 Windham St., 103 Student Ctr.
Mailing City: Willimantic
Mailing State: CT
Mailing ZIP Code: 06226-2211
General Phone: (860) 465-4445
General Fax: (860) 465-4685
General/National Adv. Email: general@campuslantern.org; lantern@stu.easternct.edu
Website: www.campuslantern.org
Personnel: Edmond Chibeau (Advisor); Daniel McCue (Ed. in Chief); Christine Smith (Mng. Ed.); Michael Rouleau (News Ed.); Andrew (A&E Ed.); Zach (Sports Ed.); Jacquelyn (Opinion Ed.)

WILLMAR

RIDGEWATER COLLEGE

Street Address 1: 2101 15th Ave NW
State: MN
Zip/Postal code: 56201-3096
Country: USA
Mailing Address: 2101 15th Ave NW
Mailing City: Willmar
Mailing State: MN
Mailing ZIP Code: 56201-3096
General Phone: (320) 222-5200
General Fax: (320) 231-6602
General/National Adv. Email: info@ridgewater.edu
Website: www.ridgewater.edu
Personnel: Gregg Aamot (Advisor)

WILMINGTON

UNIV. OF NORTH CAROLINA

Street Address 1: 601 S College Rd
State: NC
Zip/Postal code: 28403-3201
Country: USA
Mailing Address: 601 S College Rd
Mailing City: Wilmington
Mailing State: NC
Mailing ZIP Code: 28403-3201
General Phone: (910) 962-3229
Advertising Phone: (910) 962-7131
General/National Adv. Email: seahawk.news@uncw.edu
Editorial Email: seahawk.editor@gmail.com
Website: www.theseahawk.org
Year Established: 1948
Personnel: Autumn Beam (Ed. in Chief); Lisa Huynh (Mng. Ed); Bethany Bestwina (Photo Ed.)

WIDENER UNIV. SCHOOL OF LAW

Street Address 1: PO Box 7474
State: DE
Zip/Postal code: 19803-0474
Country: USA
Mailing Address: PO Box 7474
Mailing City: Wilmington
Mailing State: DE
Mailing ZIP Code: 19803-0474
General Phone: (302) 477-2100
General Fax: (302) 478-3495
General/National Adv. Email: widenerlawforum@yahoo.com
Personnel: Doretta McGinnis (Advisor); Christopher Balala (Ed. in Chief); Harry Matt Taylor (Bus. Mgr.)

WILMINGTON COLLEGE

Street Address 1: 1870 Quaker Way
State: OH
Zip/Postal code: 45177-2473
Country: USA
Mailing Address: 1870 Quaker Way
Mailing City: Wilmington
Mailing State: OH
Mailing ZIP Code: 45177-2499
General Phone: (937) 382-6661
General Fax: (937) 382-7077
Website: www2.wilmington.edu; www.wilmington.edu
Personnel: Coreen Cockerill (Advisor); Clair Green (Ed. in Chief)

WILMORE

ASBURY COLLEGE

Street Address 1: 1 Macklem Dr
State: KY
Zip/Postal code: 40390-1152
Country: USA
Mailing Address: 1 Macklem Dr
Mailing City: Wilmore
Mailing State: KY
Mailing ZIP Code: 40390-1198
General Phone: (859) 858-3511
General Fax: (859) 858-3921
General/National Adv. Email: mlonginow@asbury.edu
Website: collegian.asbury.edu
Personnel: Deanna Morono (Exec. Ed.); James R. Owens (Chair); Kayla Dubois (Mng. Ed.); Zack Klemme (News Ed.); Morgan Schutters (Web Design)

WILSON

BARTON COLLEGE

Street Address 1: PO Box 5000
State: NC
Zip/Postal code: 27893-7000
Country: USA
Mailing Address: PO Box 5000
Mailing City: Wilson
Mailing State: NC
Mailing ZIP Code: 27893-7000
General Phone: (252) 399-6370
General Fax: (252) 399-6572
Personnel: Rick Stewart (Advisor); Brittaney Rosencrance (Ed. in chief)

WINGATE

WINGATE UNIV.

Street Address 1: PO Box 2
State: NC
Zip/Postal code: 28174-0002
Country: USA
Mailing Address: PO Box 2
Mailing City: Wingate
Mailing State: NC
Mailing ZIP Code: 28174-0002
General Phone: (704) 233-8163
General Fax: (704) 233-8285
Personnel: Keith Cannon (Advisor); Brittany Ruffner (Contact)

WINONA

ST. MARYS UNIV. OF MINNESOTA

Street Address 1: 700 Terrace Hts
Street Address 2: Ste 37
State: MN
Zip/Postal code: 55987-1321
Country: USA
Mailing Address: 700 Terrace Hts Ste 37

Mailing City: Winona
Mailing State: MN
Mailing ZIP Code: 55987-1321
General Phone: (507) 457-1497
General Fax: (507) 457-6967
Website: www.smumn.edu
Commercial printers?: N
Personnel: Bob Conover (Advisor)

WINONA STATE UNIV.

Street Address 1: 175 W Mark St
State: MN
Zip/Postal code: 55987-3384
Country: USA
Mailing Address: 175 W Mark St
Mailing City: Winona
Mailing State: MN
Mailing ZIP Code: 55987
General Phone: (507) 457-5119
General/National Adv. Email: winonan@winona.edu
Website: www.winona.edu/winonan
Published: Wed
Personnel: Jenna Cameron (Adv. Mgr.); Alyx Minor (Ed. in Chief); Julia Sand (Editor-in-chief)

WINSTON SALEM

SALEM COLLEGE

Street Address 1: 601 S Church St
State: NC
Zip/Postal code: 27101-5318
Country: USA
Mailing Address: 601 S Church St
Mailing City: Winston Salem
Mailing State: NC
Mailing ZIP Code: 27101-5376
General Phone: (336) 917-5113
General Fax: (336) 917-5117
Website: www.thesalemite.com
Personnel: Sarah Boyenger (Bus. Mgr.); Susan Smith (Ed. in Chief)

WAKE FOREST UNIV.

Street Address 1: PO Box 7569
State: NC
Zip/Postal code: 27109
Country: USA
Mailing Address: PO Box 7569
Mailing City: Winston Salem
Mailing State: NC
Mailing ZIP Code: 27109-6240
General Phone: (336) 758-5279
General Fax: (336) 758-4561
General/National Adv. Email: ogb@wfu.edu
Website: www.oldgoldandblack.com
Personnel: Wayne King (Advisor); Tyler Kellner (Bus. Mgr.); Mariclaire Hicks (Ed. in Chief)

WINSTON-SALEM STATE UNIV.

Street Address 1: 103 Old Nursing
Street Address 2: 601 S. Martin Luther King Jr. Dr.
State: NC
Zip/Postal code: 27110-0001
Country: USA
Mailing Address: 103 Old Nursing
Mailing City: Winston Salem
Mailing State: NC
Mailing ZIP Code: 27110-0001
General Phone: 3367502327
General Fax: 3367508704
Advertising Phone: 3367508701
Advertising Fax: 3367508704
Editorial Phone: 3367508701
General/National Adv. Email: thenewsargus@gmail.com
Display Adv. Email: thenewsargus@gmail.com
Editorial Email: thenewsargus@gmail.com
Website: www.thenewsargus.com
Year Established: 1960
Published: Mon`Bi-Mthly
Personnel: Lona D. Cobb (Advisor)

WINTER HAVEN

POLK CMTY. COLLEGE
Street Address 1: 999 Avenue H NE
State: FL
Zip/Postal code: 33881-4256
Country: USA
Mailing Address: 999 Avenue H NE
Mailing City: Winter Haven
Mailing State: FL
Mailing ZIP Code: 33881-4256
General Phone: (863) 297-1000
General Fax: (863) 297-1037
Personnel: Patrick Jones (Advisor)

WINTER PARK

THE SANDSPUR
Street Address 1: 1000 Holt Ave
Street Address 2: # 2742
State: FL
Zip/Postal code: 32789-4499
Country: USA
Mailing Address: 1000 Holt Ave # 2742
Mailing City: Winter Park
Mailing State: FL
Mailing ZIP Code: 32789-4499
General Phone: (407) 646-2696
Advertising Phone: (407) 646-2695
Display Adv. Email: advertising@thesandspur.org
Editorial Email: staff@thesandspur.org
Website: www.thesandspur.org
Year Established: 1894
Published: Thur
Avg Free Circ: 1200

WISE

UNIV. OF VIRGINIA
Street Address 1: 1 College Ave
State: VA
Zip/Postal code: 24293-4400
Country: USA
Mailing Address: PO Box 3043
Mailing City: Wise
Mailing State: VA
Mailing ZIP Code: 24293-3043
General Fax: (276) 328-0212
General/National Adv. Email: info@uvawise.edu
Website: www.wise.virginia.edu
Personnel: Michael McGill (Adv. Mgr.)

WOODLAND HILLS

LOS ANGELES PIERCE COLLEGE
Street Address 1: 6201 Winnetka Ave
Street Address 2: # 8212
State: CA
Zip/Postal code: 91371-0001
Country: USA
Mailing Address: 6201 Winnetka Ave # 8212
Mailing City: Woodland Hills
Mailing State: CA
Mailing ZIP Code: 91371-0001
General Phone: (818) 719-6483
General Fax: (818) 719-6447
Advertising Phone: (818) 710-2960
Advertising Fax: (818) 719-6447
Editorial Phone: (818) 719-6427
Editorial Fax: (818) 719-6447
General/National Adv. Email: newsroom.roundupnews@baileyjd.piercecollege.edu
Display Adv. Email: baileyjd@piercecollege.edu
Editorial Email: newsroom.roundupnews@gmail.com
Website: www.theroundupnews.com
Year Established: 1949
Syndicated Publications: The BULL
Delivery Methods: Newsstand
Commercial printers?: Y
Mechanical specifications: Call office or email advertising
Published: Wed
Avg Free Circ: 5000
Personnel: Jill Connelly (Dept. Chrmn.); Julie Bailey (Office Mgr./Adv. Mgr.); Stefanie Frith (Adviser to the Roundup newspaper)

WOOSTER

COLLEGE OF WOOSTER
Street Address 1: 1189 Beall Ave
State: OH
Zip/Postal code: 44691-2393
Country: USA
Mailing Address: Box C-1387
Mailing City: Wooster
Mailing State: OH
Mailing ZIP Code: 44691-2393
General Phone: (330) 263-2598
General Fax: (330) 263-2596
General/National Adv. Email: voice@wooster.edu
Display Adv. Email: nisles@wooster.edu
Editorial Email: voice@wooster.edu
Website: thewoostervoice.com
Published: Tues
Personnel: Travis Marmon (Ed. in Chief); Ian Benson (Ed. in Chief)

WORCESTER

ASSUMPTION COLLEGE
Street Address 1: 500 Salisbury St
State: MA
Zip/Postal code: 01609-1265
Country: USA
Mailing Address: 500 Salisbury St
Mailing City: Worcester
Mailing State: MA
Mailing ZIP Code: 01609-1296
General Phone: (508) 767-7155
General Fax: (508) 799-4401
General/National Adv. Email: provoc@assumption.edu
Website: www.leprovoc.com
Personnel: Sara Swillo (Advisor); Greg Sebastiao (Ed. in Chief)

BECKER COLLEGE
Street Address 1: 61 Sever St
State: MA
Zip/Postal code: 01609-2165
Country: USA
Mailing Address: 61 Sever St
Mailing City: Worcester
Mailing State: MA
Mailing ZIP Code: 01609-2195
General Phone: (508) 791-9241
General Fax: (508) 831-7505
General/National Adv. Email: info@becker.edu

CLARK UNIVERSITY
Street Address 1: 950 Main St
Street Address 2: # B-13
State: MA
Zip/Postal code: 01610-1400
Country: USA
Mailing Address: 950 Main St # B-13
Mailing City: Worcester
Mailing State: MA
Mailing ZIP Code: 01610-1400
General Phone: (508) 793-7508
General Fax: (508) 793-8813
General/National Adv. Email: scarlet@clarku.edu
Website: www.clarku.edu
Published: Thur
Avg Free Circ: 700
Personnel: Jeremy Levine (Editor-In-Chief)

COLLEGE OF THE HOLY CROSS
Street Address 1: 1 College St
State: MA
Zip/Postal code: 01610-2322
County: Worcester
Country: USA
Mailing Address: 1 COLLEGE ST
Mailing City: WORCESTER
Mailing State: MA
Mailing ZIP Code: 01610-2395
General Phone: (508) 293-1283
General Fax: (508) 793-3823
General/National Adv. Email: crusader@g.holycross.edu
Display Adv. Email: crusaderadvertising@gmail.com
Website: www.thehccrusader.com
Published: Fri
Personnel: Steve Vineberg (Faculty Advisor); Sara Bovat (Co-Editor-in-Chief); Emily Vyse (Co-Editor-in-Chief)

QUINSIGAMOND CMTY. COLLEGE
Street Address 1: 670 W Boylston St
State: MA
Zip/Postal code: 01606-2064
Country: USA
Mailing Address: 670 W Boylston St
Mailing City: Worcester
Mailing State: MA
Mailing ZIP Code: 01606-2092
General Phone: (508) 854-4285
General Fax: (508) 852-6943
General/National Adv. Email: opendoor@qcc.mass.edu
Published: Mthly
Personnel: Pat Bisha-Valencia (Advisor)

WORCESTER POLYTECHNIC INSTITUTE
Street Address 1: 100 Institute Rd
State: MA
Zip/Postal code: 01609-2247
Country: USA
Mailing Address: 100 Institute Rd
Mailing City: Worcester
Mailing State: MA
Mailing ZIP Code: 01609-2280
General Phone: (508) 831-5464
General Fax: (508) 831-5721
General/National Adv. Email: technews@wpi.edu
Display Adv. Email: ads@wpi.edu
Website: www.wpi.edu/News/TechNews
Personnel: Michelle Ephraim (Advisor)

WORCESTER STATE COLLEGE
Street Address 1: 486 Chandler St
State: MA
Zip/Postal code: 01602-2861
Country: USA
Mailing Address: 486 Chandler St # G-209
Mailing City: Worcester
Mailing State: MA
Mailing ZIP Code: 01602-2861
General Phone: (508) 929-8589
General Fax: (508) 756-8210
General/National Adv. Email: studentvoice@worcester.edu
Personnel: Elizabeth Bidinger (Advisor)

YAKIMA

YAKIMA VALLEY CMTY. COLLEGE
Street Address 1: PO Box 22520
State: WA
Zip/Postal code: 98907-2520
Country: USA
Mailing Address: PO Box 22520
Mailing City: Yakima
Mailing State: WA
Mailing ZIP Code: 98907-2520
General Phone: (509) 574-4600
General Fax: (509) 574-6860
Advertising Phone: 509-574-6870
Advertising Fax: 509-574-6870
Display Adv. Email: nhopkins@yvcc.edu
Website: www.yvcc.edu
Year Established: 1928
Personnel: Niki Hopkins (Ed.)

YANKTON

MT. MARTY COLLEGE
Street Address 1: 1105 W 8th St
Street Address 2: Ste 564
State: SD
Zip/Postal code: 57078-3725
Country: USA
Mailing Address: 1105 W 8th St Ste 564
Mailing City: Yankton
Mailing State: SD
Mailing ZIP Code: 57078-3725
General Phone: (605) 668-1293
General Fax: (605) 668-1508
General/National Adv. Email: moderator@mtmc.edu
Website: www.mtmc.edu/student/moderator
Personnel: Jill Paulson (Advisor); Lauren Donlin (Adv. Mgr.); Alicia Pick (Circ. Mgr.)

YBOR CITY

HILLSBOROUGH CMTY. COLLEGE
Street Address 1: 2112 N 15th St
State: FL
Zip/Postal code: 33605-3648
Country: USA
Mailing Address: 2112 N. 15th Street
Mailing City: Ybor City
Mailing State: FL
Mailing ZIP Code: 33605
General Phone: (813) 227-7048
General Fax: (813) 253-7760
Website: www.hccfl.edu
Personnel: Valerie Zell (Advisor)

YORK

YORK COLLEGE OF PENNSYLVANIA
Street Address 1: 441 Country Club Rd
State: PA
Zip/Postal code: 17403-3614
Country: USA
Mailing Address: 441 Country Club Rd
Mailing City: York
Mailing State: PA
Mailing ZIP Code: 17403-3651
General Phone: (717) 815-1312
General/National Adv. Email: spartan@ycp.edu
Website: spartan.ycp.edu
Personnel: Steven Brikowski (Advisor)

YOUNGSTOWN

YOUNGSTOWN STATE UNIV.
Street Address 1: 1 University Plz
State: OH
Zip/Postal code: 44555-0001
Country: USA
Mailing Address: 1 University Plz
Mailing City: Youngstown
Mailing State: OH
Mailing ZIP Code: 44555-0002
General Phone: (330) 941-1991
General Fax: (330) 941-2322
General/National Adv. Email: thejambar@gmail.com
Website: www.thejambar.com
Year Established: 1931
Delivery Methods: Newsstand Racks
Personnel: Mary Beth Earnheardt (Advisor); Joshua Stipanovich (Editor in Chief); Chelsea Pflugh (Ed. in Chief); Adam Rogers (Mng. Ed.)

YOUNGSTOWN

YOUNGSTOWN STATE UNIVERSITY
Street Address 1: 1 University Plz
State: OH
Zip/Postal code: 44555-0001
Country: USA
Mailing Address: 1 University Plz
Mailing City: Youngstown
Mailing State: OH

College and University Newspapers

Mailing ZIP Code: 44555-0002
General Phone: (330) 941-3095
General Fax: (330) 941-2322
Website: www.thejambar.com

YPSILANTI

EASTERN MICHIGAN UNIVERSITY

Street Address 1: 228 King Hall
State: MI
Zip/Postal code: 48197-2239
Country: USA
Mailing Address: 228 King Hall
Mailing City: Ypsilanti
Mailing State: MI
Mailing ZIP Code: 48197-2239
General Phone: (734) 487-1026
General Fax: (734) 487-6702
Advertising Phone: (734) 748-1458
Advertising Fax: (734) 487-1241
General/National Adv. Email: editor@easternecho.com
Display Adv. Email: brian.peterson24@gmail.com
Editorial Email: editor@easternecho.com
Website: www.easternecho.com
Year Established: 1881
Published: Mon`Thur
Personnel: Sydney Smith

AUSTIN PEAY STATE UNIV.

Street Address 1: 601 College St
State: TN
Country: USA
Mailing Address: PO Box 4634
Mailing City: Clarksville
Mailing State: TN
Mailing ZIP Code: 37044-0001
General Phone: (931) 221-7376
General Fax: (931) 221-7377
Editorial Phone: (931) 221-7374
General/National Adv. Email: theallstate@apsu.edu
Display Adv. Email: allstateads@apsu.edu
Website: www.theallstate.org; www.apsu.edu
Personnel: Tabitha Gillaland (Advisor); Nicole June (Adv. Mgr.); Patrick Armstrong (Ed. in Chief)

GEORGIA HEALTH SCIENCES UNIVERSITY (FORMERLY MEDICAL COLLEGE OF GEORGIA)

State: GA
Country: USA
Mailing Address: 1120 15th St
Mailing City: Augusta
Mailing State: GA
Mailing ZIP Code: 30912-0004
General Fax: (706) 721-6397
Editorial Phone: (706) 721-4410
Editorial Email: smcgowen@georgiahealth.edu
Website: connection.georgiahealth.edu/
Delivery Methods: Racks
Commercial printers?: Y
Personnel: Stacey Hudson (Communications Coordinator Editor, The Connection (formerly the Beeper)); Sharron Walls (Ed.)

TRUE NORTH CUSTOM PUBLISHING

State: TN
Country: USA
Mailing Address: 5600 Brainerd Rd Ste 1
Mailing City: Chattanooga
Mailing State: TN
Mailing ZIP Code: 37411-5373
General Phone: 423.266.3234

Website: www.truenorthcustom.com
Personnel: Emily Young (Ed.); Tim Lale (Advisor); Katie Hammond (Managing Ed.); Alison Quiring (News Ed.); Stephanie (Opinion Ed.)

ETHNIC NEWSPAPERS IN CANADA

CALGARY

JEWISH FREE PRESS

Street Address: 8411 Elbow Dr. SW
Province: AB
Postal Code: T2V 1K8
Country: Canada
General Phone: (403) 252-9423
General Fax: (403) 255-5640
General/National Adv. E-mail: jewishfp@tellus.net
Primary Website: www.jewishfreepress.ca
Year Established: 1990
Mechanical specifications: Type page 9 x 13; E - 5 cols, 1 7/8, between; A - 5 cols, 1 7/8, between.
Published Other: 2 x Mthly
Audit By: Sworn/Estimate/Non-Audited
Audit Date: 12.07.2019

EDMONTON

EDMONTON JEWISH LIFE

Street Address: 7200 156th St. NE
Province: AB
Postal Code: T5R 1X3
Country: Canada
General Phone: (780) 487-0585
General Fax: (780) 484-4978
General/National Adv. E-mail: ejlife@shaw.ca
Primary Website: www.jewishedmonton.org
Mechanical specifications: Type page 10 1/4 x 12 .
Published: Mon`Bi-Mthly
Published Other: second and fourth Mondays of the month
Avg Paid Circ: 2100
Avg Free Circ: 70
Audit By: Sworn/Estimate/Non-Audited
Audit Date: 12.07.2019

MISSISSAUGA

EL EXPRESO

Street Address: 1233 Nigel Road Mississauga
Province: ON
Postal Code: M6E 2G8
Country: Canada
General Phone: 647-642-3260
General Fax: (416) 781-8420
General/National Adv. E-mail: expreso@interlog.com
Display Adv. E-mail: expreso-inter@uniserve.com
Primary Website: www.elexpresocanada.com
Year Established: 1992
Delivery Methods: Mail
Mechanical specifications: Type page 7 1/2 x 10; E - 5 cols, 1 3/8, 1/8 between; A - 5 cols, 1 3/8, 1/8 between.
Published: Fri
Avg Paid Circ: 2950
Avg Free Circ: 25000
Audit By: Sworn/Estimate/Non-Audited
Audit Date: 12.07.2019

KANADSKY SLOVAK / THE CANADIAN SLOVAK

Street Address: 259 Traders Bouleward East
Province: ON
Postal Code: L4Z 2E5
Country: Canada
General Phone: (905) 507 8004
Editorial e-mail: editor@kanadskyslovak.ca
Advertising Phone: (403) 933 2741
General/National Adv. E-mail: editor@kanadskyslovak.ca
Display Adv. E-mail: administrator@kanadskyslovak.ca
Primary Website: www.kanadskyslovak.ca
Year Established: 194
Special Editions: Christmas, Easter
Delivery Methods: Mail`Racks
Areas Served - City/County or Portion Thereof, or Zip codes: Globally
Commercial printers?: Y
Market Information: 65,000 strong community in Canada, more in the USA and Europe
Mechanical specifications: Type page 10 x 13 1/2.
Published: Tues`Fri`Sat
Avg Free Circ: 12000
Audit By: Sworn/Estimate/Non-Audited
Audit Date: 12.07.2019

MONTREAL

GREEK CANADIAN TRIBUNE

Street Address: 7835 Wiseman Ave.
Province: QC
Postal Code: H3N 2N8
Country: Canada
General Phone: (514) 272-6873
General Fax: (514) 272-3157
General/National Adv. E-mail: info@bhma.net
Primary Website: www.bhma.net
Published Other: 2 x Mthly
Avg Free Circ: 6000
Audit By: Sworn/Estimate/Non-Audited
Audit Date: 12.07.2019

IL CITTADINO CANADESE

Street Address: 5960 Jean Talon E., Ste. 209
Province: QC
Postal Code: H1S 1M2
Country: Canada
General Phone: (514) 253-2332
General Fax: (514) 253-6574
General/National Adv. E-mail: journal@cittadinocanadese.com
Primary Website: www.cittadinocanadese.com
Mechanical specifications: Type page 10 1/4 x 15; E - 6 cols, 1 9/16, between; A - 6 cols, 1 9/16, between.
Published: Mthly
Audit By: Sworn/Estimate/Non-Audited
Audit Date: 12.07.2019

LA VOZ DE MONTREAL

Street Address: 5960 Jean Talon E., Ste. 209
Province: QC
Postal Code: H1S 1M2
Country: Canada
General Phone: (514) 253-2332
General Fax: (514) 253-6574
General/National Adv. E-mail: journal@cittadinocanadese.com
Primary Website: www.cittadinocanadese.com
Mechanical specifications: Type page 14 x 22 1/2; E - 6 cols, 2 1/3, between; A - 6 cols, 2 1/3, between.
Published: Fri
Published Other: weekly
Avg Free Circ: 55000
Audit By: Sworn/Estimate/Non-Audited
Audit Date: 12.07.2019

L'AVENIR/AL-MOUSTAKBAL

Street Address: 1305 Rue Mazurette, Office Ste. 206
Province: QC
Postal Code: H4N 1G8
Country: Canada
General Phone: (514) 334-0909
General Fax: (514) 332-5419
General/National Adv. E-mail: journal@almustakbal.com
Primary Website: www.almustakbal.com
Mechanical specifications: Type page 10 1/2 x 13.5; E - 6 cols, between; A - 6 cols, between; C - 6 cols, between.
Published: Mon`Wed`Fri
Published Other: 3 times per week
Avg Paid Circ: 10,5
Avg Free Circ: 200
Audit By: Sworn/Estimate/Non-Audited
Audit Date: 12.07.2019

N. VANCOUVER

COMMUNITY DIGEST

Street Address: 3707 Dollarton Hwy.
Province: BC
Postal Code: V7G 1A1
Country: Canada
General Phone: (604) 987-8313
General/National Adv. E-mail: mail@communitydigest.ca;
Display Adv. E-mail: adsales@communitydigest.ca
Primary Website: www.communitydigest.ca
Year Established: 1983
Delivery Methods: Mail`Newsstand`Carrier`Racks
Areas Served - City/County or Portion Thereof, or Zip codes: Alberta, BC , Ontario
Mechanical specifications: Type page 10 x 13 3/4.
Published: Sat
Avg Paid Circ: 1000
Avg Free Circ: 13200
Audit By: Sworn/Estimate/Non-Audited
Audit Date: 12.07.2019

SAINT CATHARINE'S

CHRISTIAN COURIER

Street Address: 5 Joanna Dr.
Province: ON
Postal Code: L2N 1V1
Country: Canada
General Phone: (905) 937-3314
Editorial e-mail: editor@christiancourier.ca
General/National Adv. E-mail: admin@christiancourier.ca
Display Adv. E-mail: ads@christiancourier.ca
Primary Website: www.christiancourier.ca
Year Established: 1945
Delivery Methods: Mail
Areas Served - City/County or Portion Thereof, or Zip codes: all
Mechanical specifications: Type page 11 1/4 x 15; E - 6 cols, 1 7/12, between; A - 6 cols, 1 7/12, between.
Published: Wed
Avg Paid Circ: 20000
Audit By: Sworn/Estimate/Non-Audited
Audit Date: 12.07.2019

SCARBOROUGH

PHILIPPINE REPORTER

Street Address: 2682 Eglinton Ave. East
Province: ON
Postal Code: M1K 5K2
Country: Canada
General Phone: (416) 461-8694
General Fax: n/a
Editorial e-mail: philreporter@gmail.com
Advertising Phone: (416) 461-8694
General/National Adv. E-mail: philreporter@gmail.com
Display Adv. E-mail: ads@philreporter.com
Primary Website: www.philippinereporter.com
Year Established: 1989
Delivery Methods: Carrier
Areas Served - City/County or Portion Thereof, or Zip codes: Greater Toronto Area, Niagara Region, Peel Region, Durham Region, York Region
Mechanical specifications: Type page 10 1/8 x 15 1/4; E - 6 cols, 1 1/2, 1/8 between; A - 6 cols, 1 1/2, 1/8 between.
Published: Thur
Avg Paid Circ: 50
Avg Free Circ: 2100
Audit By: Sworn/Estimate/Non-Audited
Audit Date: 12.07.2019

STEINBACH

MENNONITISCHE POST

Street Address: 383 Main St.
Province: MB
Postal Code: R5G 1Z4
Country: Canada
General Phone: (204) 326-6790
General Fax: (204) 326-6302
Editorial e-mail: editor@mennpost.org
General/National Adv. E-mail: office@mennpost.org
Mechanical specifications: Type page 9 13/16 x 13; E - 5 cols, 1 13/16, between; A - 5 cols, 1 13/16, between; C - 5 cols, 1 13/16, between.
Published: Fri
Audit By: Sworn/Estimate/Non-Audited
Audit Date: 12.07.2019

TORONTO

DA ZHONG BAO

Street Address: 50 Weybright Ct., Unit 11
Province: ON
Postal Code: M1S 5A8
Country: Canada
General Phone: (416) 504-0761
General Fax: (416) 504-4928
General/National Adv. E-mail: cng@chinesenewsgroup.com
Primary Website: www.chinesenewsgroup.com
Published: Sat
Avg Paid Circ: 2500
Avg Free Circ: 100
Audit By: Sworn/Estimate/Non-Audited
Audit Date: 12.07.2019

DALIL AL ARAB

Street Address: 368 Queen St. E.
Province: ON
Postal Code: M5A 1T1
Country: Canada
General Phone: (416) 362-0304
General Fax: (416) 861-0238
Editorial e-mail: arabnews@yahoo.com
General/National Adv. E-mail: info@arabnews.ca
Primary Website: www.arabnews.ca
Published: Sat
Avg Paid Circ: 900
Avg Free Circ: 300
Audit By: Sworn/Estimate/Non-Audited
Audit Date: 12.07.2019

EL POPULAR

Street Address: 2413 Dundas St. W.
Province: ON
Postal Code: M6P 1X3
Country: Canada
General Phone: (416) 531-2495
General Fax: (416) 531-7187
Editorial e-mail: nixa@diarioelpopular.com
General/National Adv. E-mail: director@diarioelpopular.com
Display Adv. E-mail: ads@diarioelpopular.com
Primary Website: www.diarioelpopular.com
Year Established: 1970
Delivery Methods: Mail`Newsstand
Areas Served - City/County or Portion Thereof, or Zip codes: all GTA
Mechanical specifications: Type page 11 1/4 x 15; E - 6 cols, 1 7/12, between; A - 6 cols, 1 7/12, between.
Published: Mthly
Avg Paid Circ: 13000
Audit By: Sworn/Estimate/Non-Audited
Audit Date: 12.07.2019

LATVIJA-AMERIKA

Street Address: 4 Credit Union Dr.
Province: ON
Postal Code: M4A 2N8
Country: Canada
General Phone: (416) 466-1514
Editorial Phone: (416) 465-7902
Advertising Phone: (416) 466-1514
General/National Adv. E-mail: latvija.amerika@gmail.com
Year Established: 1951
Delivery Methods: Mail`Newsstand
Published: Sat
Avg Paid Circ: 1000
Audit By: Sworn/Estimate/Non-Audited
Audit Date: 12.07.2019

NOVY DOMOV (NEW HOMELAND)

Street Address: 450 Scarborough Golf Club Rd.
Province: ON
Postal Code: M1G 1H1
Country: Canada
General Phone: (416) 439-4354
Editorial Phone: (416) 439-4354
Editorial e-mail: office@masaryktown.ca
Advertising Phone: (416) 439-4354
General/National Adv. E-mail: office@masaryktown.ca
Display Adv. E-mail: vera.toronto@gmail.com
Primary Website: www.masaryktown.ca
Year Established: 1946
Delivery Methods: Mail`Racks
Areas Served - City/County or Portion Thereof, or Zip codes: Canada, USA
Own Printing Facility?: N
Commercial printers?: Y
Mechanical specifications: Type page 17 x 11; E - 7 cols, 1 5/16, between.
Published: Tues
Avg Paid Circ: 27875
Audit By: Sworn/Estimate/Non-Audited
Audit Date: 12.07.2019

SATELLITE 1416

Street Address: 365 St. Clarence Ave.
Province: ON
Postal Code: M6H 3W2
Country: Canada
General Phone: (416) 530-4222
General/National Adv. E-mail: abe@satellite1-416.com
Primary Website: www.satellite1-416.com
Year Established: 1991
Delivery Methods: Mail
Areas Served - City/County or Portion Thereof, or Zip codes: M6H 4E2
Mechanical specifications: Type page 10 1/4 x 15 1/2.
Published: Fri
Avg Paid Circ: 7700
Avg Free Circ: 300
Audit By: Sworn/Estimate/Non-Audited
Audit Date: 12.07.2019

SHARE

Street Address: 658 Vaughan Rd.
Province: ON
Postal Code: M6E 2Y5
Country: Canada
General Phone: (416) 656-3400
General Fax: (416) 656-3711
General/National Adv. E-mail: share@interlog.com
Primary Website: www.sharenews.com
Year Established: 1978
Delivery Methods: Carrier`Racks
Published: Other
Published Other: every 3 rd week
Avg Paid Circ: 560
Avg Free Circ: 200
Audit By: Sworn/Estimate/Non-Audited
Audit Date: 12.07.2019

VANCOUVER

JEWISH INDEPENDENT

Street Address: PO Box 47100
Province: BC
Postal Code: V5Z 4L6
Country: Canada
General Phone: (604) 689-1520
Editorial e-mail: editor@jewishindependent.ca
Display Adv. E-mail: sales@jewishindependent.ca
Primary Website: www.jewishindependent.ca
Year Established: 1930
Delivery Methods: Mail`Newsstand`Carrier`Racks
Areas Served - City/County or Portion Thereof, or Zip codes: Any
Mechanical specifications: Type page 10 1/2 x 15 3/8; E - 5 cols, 2, between; A - 5 cols, 2, between.
Published: Bi-Mthly
Published Other: 2 x Mthly
Avg Paid Circ: 10000
Avg Free Circ: 100
Audit By: Sworn/Estimate/Non-Audited
Audit Date: 12.07.2019

WILLOWDALE

AL-HILAL

Street Address: 338 Hollyberry Trail
Province: ON
Postal Code: M2H 2P6
Country: Canada
General Phone: (416) 493-4374
General Fax: (416) 493-4374
General/National Adv. E-mail: lowaisi@rogers.com
Published: Thur
Published Other: One in month
Avg Paid Circ: 300
Avg Free Circ: 300
Audit By: Sworn/Estimate/Non-Audited
Audit Date: 12.07.2019

WINNIPEG

KANADA KURIER

Street Address: 955 Alexander Ave.
Province: MB
Postal Code: R3C 2X8
Country: Canada
General Phone: (204) 774-1883
General Fax: (204) 783-5740
General/National Adv. E-mail: kanadakurier@mb.sypatico.ca
Own Printing Facility?: Y
Published: Thur
Avg Free Circ: 32400
Audit By: Sworn/Estimate/Non-Audited
Audit Date: 12.07.2019

UKRAINSKY HOLOS

Street Address: 842 Main St.
Province: MB
Postal Code: R2W 3N8
Country: Canada
General Phone: (204) 589-5871
General Fax: (204) 586-3618
Editorial Phone: (204) 589-5871
Editorial e-mail: presstr@mts.net
Advertising Phone: (204) 589-5871
General/National Adv. E-mail: presstr@mts.net
Display Adv. E-mail: presstr@mts.net
Primary Website: ukrvoice.ca
Year Established: 1910
Delivery Methods: Mail`Newsstand
Own Printing Facility?: Y
Mechanical specifications: Type page 14 1/2 x 22 3/4; E - 6 cols, 2, 1/8 between; A - 6 cols, 2, 1/8 between; C - 6 cols, 2, 1/8 between.
Published: Mon
Published Other: 2 x Mthly
Avg Paid Circ: 1890
Avg Free Circ: 42
Audit By: Sworn/Estimate/Non-Audited
Audit Date: 12.07.2019

ETHNIC NEWSPAPERS IN THE U.S.

CALGARY

JEWISH FREE PRESS
Street Address: 8411 Elbow Dr. SW
Province: AB
Postal Code: T2V 1K8
Country: Canada
General Phone: (403) 252-9423
General Fax: (403) 255-5640
General/National Adv. E-mail: jewishfp@tellus.net
Primary Website: www.jewishfreepress.ca
Year Established: 1990
Mechanical specifications: Type page 9 x 13; E - 5 cols, 1 7/8, between; A - 5 cols, 1 7/8, between.
Published Other: 2 x Mthly
Audit By: Sworn/Estimate/Non-Audited
Audit Date: 12.07.2019

EDMONTON

EDMONTON JEWISH LIFE
Street Address: 7200 156th St. NE
Province: AB
Postal Code: T5R 1X3
Country: Canada
General Phone: (780) 487-0585
General Fax: (780) 484-4978
General/National Adv. E-mail: ejlife@shaw.ca
Primary Website: www.jewishedmonton.org
Mechanical specifications: Type page 10 1/4 x 12.
Published: Mon`Bi-Mthly
Published Other: second and fourth Mondays of the month
Avg Paid Circ: 2100
Avg Free Circ: 70
Audit By: Sworn/Estimate/Non-Audited
Audit Date: 12.07.2019

MISSISSAUGA

EL EXPRESO
Street Address: 1233 Nigel Road Mississauga
Province: ON
Postal Code: M6E 2G8
Country: Canada
General Phone: 647-642-3260
General Fax: (416) 781-8420
General/National Adv. E-mail: expreso@interlog.com
Display Adv. E-mail: expreso-inter@uniserve.com
Primary Website: www.elexpresocanada.com
Year Established: 1992
Delivery Methods: Mail
Mechanical specifications: Type page 7 1/2 x 10; E - 5 cols, 1 3/8, 1/8 between; A - 5 cols, 1 3/8, 1/8 between.
Published: Fri
Avg Paid Circ: 2950
Avg Free Circ: 25000
Audit By: Sworn/Estimate/Non-Audited
Audit Date: 12.07.2019

KANADSKY SLOVAK / THE CANADIAN SLOVAK
Street Address: 259 Traders Boulevard East
Province: ON
Postal Code: L4Z 2E5
Country: Canada
General Phone: (905) 507 8004
Editorial e-mail: editor@kanadskyslovak.ca
Advertising Phone: (403) 933 2741
General/National Adv. E-mail: editor@kanadskyslovak.ca
Display Adv. E-mail: administrator@kanadskyslovak.ca
Primary Website: www.kanadskyslovak.ca
Year Established: 194
Special Editions: Christmas, Easter
Delivery Methods: Mail`Racks
Areas Served - City/County or Portion Thereof, or Zip codes: Globally
Commercial printers?: Y
Market Information: 65,000 strong community in Canada, more in the USA and Europe
Mechanical specifications: Type page 10 x 13 1/2.
Published: Tues`Fri`Sat
Avg Free Circ: 12000
Audit By: Sworn/Estimate/Non-Audited
Audit Date: 12.07.2019

MONTREAL

GREEK CANADIAN TRIBUNE
Street Address: 7835 Wiseman Ave.
Province: QC
Postal Code: H3N 2N8
Country: Canada
General Phone: (514) 272-6873
General Fax: (514) 272-3157
General/National Adv. E-mail: info@bhma.net
Primary Website: www.bhma.net
Published Other: 2 x Mthly
Avg Free Circ: 6000
Audit By: Sworn/Estimate/Non-Audited
Audit Date: 12.07.2019

IL CITTADINO CANADESE
Street Address: 5960 Jean Talon E., Ste. 209
Province: QC
Postal Code: H1S 1M2
Country: Canada
General Phone: (514) 253-2332
General Fax: (514) 253-6574
General/National Adv. E-mail: journal@cittadinocanadese.com
Primary Website: www.cittadinocanadese.com
Mechanical specifications: Type page 10 1/4 x 15; E - 6 cols, 1 9/16, between; A - 6 cols, 1 9/16, between.
Published: Mthly
Audit By: Sworn/Estimate/Non-Audited
Audit Date: 12.07.2019

LA VOZ DE MONTREAL
Street Address: 5960 Jean Talon E., Ste. 209
Province: QC
Postal Code: H1S 1M2
Country: Canada
General Phone: (514) 253-2332
General Fax: (514) 253-6574
General/National Adv. E-mail: journal@cittadinocanadese.com
Primary Website: www.cittadinocanadese.com
Mechanical specifications: Type page 14 x 22 1/2; E - 6 cols, 2 1/3, between; A - 6 cols, 2 1/3, between.
Published: Fri
Published Other: weekly
Avg Free Circ: 55000
Audit By: Sworn/Estimate/Non-Audited
Audit Date: 12.07.2019

L'AVENIR/AL-MOUSTAKBAL
Street Address: 1305 Rue Mazurette, Office Ste. 206
Province: QC
Postal Code: H4N 1G8
Country: Canada
General Phone: (514) 334-0909
General Fax: (514) 332-5419
General/National Adv. E-mail: journal@almustakbal.com
Primary Website: www.almustakbal.com
Mechanical specifications: Type page 10 1/2 x 13.5; E - 6 cols, between; A - 6 cols, between; C - 6 cols, between.
Published: Mon`Wed`Fri
Published Other: 3 times per week
Avg Paid Circ: 10,5
Avg Free Circ: 200
Audit By: Sworn/Estimate/Non-Audited
Audit Date: 12.07.2019

N. VANCOUVER

COMMUNITY DIGEST
Street Address: 3707 Dollarton Hwy.
Province: BC
Postal Code: V7G 1A1
Country: Canada
General Phone: (604) 987-8313
General/National Adv. E-mail: mail@communitydigest.ca;
Display Adv. E-mail: adsales@communitydigest.ca
Primary Website: www.communitydigest.ca
Year Established: 1983
Delivery Methods: Mail`Newsstand`Carrier`Racks
Areas Served - City/County or Portion Thereof, or Zip codes: Alberta, BC, Ontario
Mechanical specifications: Type page 10 x 13 3/4.
Published: Sat
Avg Paid Circ: 1000
Avg Free Circ: 13200
Audit By: Sworn/Estimate/Non-Audited
Audit Date: 12.07.2019

SAINT CATHARINE'S

CHRISTIAN COURIER
Street Address: 5 Joanna Dr.
Province: ON
Postal Code: L2N 1V1
Country: Canada
General Phone: (905) 937-3314
Editorial e-mail: editor@christiancourier.ca
General/National Adv. E-mail: admin@christiancourier.ca
Display Adv. E-mail: ads@christiancourier.ca
Primary Website: www.christiancourier.ca
Year Established: 1945
Delivery Methods: Mail
Areas Served - City/County or Portion Thereof, or Zip codes: all
Mechanical specifications: Type page 11 1/4 x 15; E - 6 cols, 1 7/12, between; A - 6 cols, 1 7/12, between.
Published: Wed
Avg Paid Circ: 20000
Audit By: Sworn/Estimate/Non-Audited
Audit Date: 12.07.2019

SCARBOROUGH

PHILIPPINE REPORTER
Street Address: 2682 Eglinton Ave. East
Province: ON
Postal Code: M1K 5K2
Country: Canada
General Phone: (416) 461-8694
General Fax: n/a
Editorial e-mail: philreporter@gmail.com
Advertising Phone: (416) 461-8694
General/National Adv. E-mail: philreporter@gmail.com
Display Adv. E-mail: ads@philreporter.com
Primary Website: www.philippinereporter.com
Year Established: 1989
Delivery Methods: Carrier
Areas Served - City/County or Portion Thereof, or Zip codes: Greater Toronto Area, Niagara Region, Peel Region, Durham Region, York Region
Mechanical specifications: Type page 10 1/8 x 15 1/4; E - 6 cols, 1 1/2, 1/8 between; A - 6 cols, 1 1/2, 1/8 between.
Published: Thur
Avg Paid Circ: 50
Avg Free Circ: 2100
Audit By: Sworn/Estimate/Non-Audited
Audit Date: 12.07.2019

STEINBACH

MENNONITISCHE POST
Street Address: 383 Main St.
Province: MB
Postal Code: R5G 1Z4
Country: Canada
General Phone: (204) 326-6790
General Fax: (204) 326-6302
Editorial e-mail: editor@mennpost.org
General/National Adv. E-mail: office@mennpost.org
Mechanical specifications: Type page 9 13/16 x 13; E - 5 cols, 1 13/16, between; A - 5 cols, 1 13/16, between; C - 5 cols, 1 13/16, between.
Published: Fri
Audit By: Sworn/Estimate/Non-Audited
Audit Date: 12.07.2019

TORONTO

DA ZHONG BAO
Street Address: 50 Weybright Ct., Unit 11
Province: ON
Postal Code: M1S 5A8
Country: Canada
General Phone: (416) 504-0761
General Fax: (416) 504-4928
General/National Adv. E-mail: cng@chinesenewsgroup.com
Primary Website: www.chinesenewsgroup.com
Published: Sat
Avg Paid Circ: 2500
Avg Free Circ: 100
Audit By: Sworn/Estimate/Non-Audited
Audit Date: 12.07.2019

DALIL AL ARAB
Street Address: 368 Queen St. E.
Province: ON
Postal Code: M5A 1T1
Country: Canada
General Phone: (416) 362-0304
General Fax: (416) 861-0238
Editorial e-mail: arabnews@yahoo.com
General/National Adv. E-mail: info@arabnews.ca
Primary Website: www.arabnews.ca
Published: Sat
Avg Paid Circ: 900
Avg Free Circ: 300
Audit By: Sworn/Estimate/Non-Audited
Audit Date: 12.07.2019

EL POPULAR
Street Address: 2413 Dundas St. W.
Province: ON
Postal Code: M6P 1X3
Country: Canada
General Phone: (416) 531-2495
General Fax: (416) 531-7187
Editorial e-mail: nixa@diarioelpopular.com
General/National Adv. E-mail: director@diarioelpopular.com
Display Adv. E-mail: ads@diarioelpopular.com
Primary Website: www.diarioelpopular.com
Year Established: 1970
Delivery Methods: Mail`Newsstand
Areas Served - City/County or Portion Thereof, or Zip codes: all GTA
Mechanical specifications: Type page 11 1/4 x 15; E - 6 cols, 1 7/12, between; A - 6 cols, 1 7/12, between.
Published: Mthly
Avg Paid Circ: 13000

Audit By: Sworn/Estimate/Non-Audited
Audit Date: 12.07.2019

LATVIJA-AMERIKA
Street Address: 4 Credit Union Dr.
Province: ON
Postal Code: M4A 2N8
Country: Canada
General Phone: (416) 466-1514
Editorial Phone: (416) 465-7902
Advertising Phone: (416) 466-1514
General/National Adv. E-mail: latvija.amerika@gmail.com
Year Established: 1951
Delivery Methods: Mail`Newsstand
Published: Sat
Avg Paid Circ: 1000
Audit By: Sworn/Estimate/Non-Audited
Audit Date: 12.07.2019

NOVY DOMOV (NEW HOMELAND)
Street Address: 450 Scarborough Golf Club Rd.
Province: ON
Postal Code: M1G 1H1
Country: Canada
General Phone: (416) 439-4354
Editorial Phone: (416) 439-4354
Editorial e-mail: office@masaryktown.ca
Advertising Phone: (416) 439-4354
General/National Adv. E-mail: office@masaryktown.ca
Display Adv. E-mail: vera.toronto@gmail.com
Primary Website: www.masaryktown.ca
Year Established: 1946
Delivery Methods: Mail`Racks
Areas Served - City/County or Portion Thereof, or Zip codes: Canada, USA
Own Printing Facility?: N
Commercial printers?: Y
Mechanical specifications: Type page 17 x 11; E - 7 cols, 1 5/16, between.
Published: Tues
Avg Paid Circ: 27875
Audit By: Sworn/Estimate/Non-Audited
Audit Date: 12.07.2019

SATELLITE 1416
Street Address: 365 St. Clarence Ave.
Province: ON
Postal Code: M6H 3W2
Country: Canada
General Phone: (416) 530-4222
General/National Adv. E-mail: abe@satellite1-416.com
Primary Website: www.satellite1-416.com
Year Established: 1991
Delivery Methods: Mail
Areas Served - City/County or Portion Thereof, or Zip codes: M6H 4E2
Mechanical specifications: Type page 10 1/4 x 15 1/2.
Published: Fri
Avg Paid Circ: 7700
Avg Free Circ: 300
Audit By: Sworn/Estimate/Non-Audited
Audit Date: 12.07.2019

SHARE
Street Address: 658 Vaughan Rd.
Province: ON
Postal Code: M6E 2Y5
Country: Canada
General Phone: (416) 656-3400
General Fax: (416) 656-3711
General/National Adv. E-mail: share@interlog.com
Primary Website: www.sharenews.com
Year Established: 1978
Delivery Methods: Carrier`Racks
Published: Other
Published Other: every 3 rd week
Avg Paid Circ: 560
Avg Free Circ: 200
Audit By: Sworn/Estimate/Non-Audited
Audit Date: 12.07.2019

VANCOUVER

JEWISH INDEPENDENT
Street Address: PO Box 47100
Province: BC
Postal Code: V5Z 4L6
Country: Canada
General Phone: (604) 689-1520
Editorial e-mail: editor@jewishindependent.ca
Display Adv. E-mail: sales@jewishindependent.ca
Primary Website: www.jewishindependent.ca
Year Established: 1930
Delivery Methods: Mail`Newsstand`Carrier`Racks
Areas Served - City/County or Portion Thereof, or Zip codes: Any
Mechanical specifications: Type page 10 1/2 x 15 3/8; E - 5 cols, 2, between; A - 5 cols, 2, between.
Published: Bi-Mthly
Published Other: 2 x Mthly
Avg Paid Circ: 10000
Avg Free Circ: 100
Audit By: Sworn/Estimate/Non-Audited
Audit Date: 12.07.2019

WILLOWDALE

AL-HILAL
Street Address: 338 Hollyberry Trail
Province: ON
Postal Code: M2H 2P6
Country: Canada
General Phone: (416) 493-4374
General Fax: (416) 493-4374
General/National Adv. E-mail: lowaisi@rogers.com
Published: Thur
Published Other: One in month
Avg Paid Circ: 300
Avg Free Circ: 300
Audit By: Sworn/Estimate/Non-Audited
Audit Date: 12.07.2019

WINNIPEG

KANADA KURIER
Street Address: 955 Alexander Ave.
Province: MB
Postal Code: R3C 2X8
Country: Canada
General Phone: (204) 774-1883
General Fax: (204) 783-5740
General/National Adv. E-mail: kanadakurier@mb.sypatico.ca
Own Printing Facility?: Y
Published: Thur
Avg Free Circ: 32400
Audit By: Sworn/Estimate/Non-Audited
Audit Date: 12.07.2019

UKRAINSKY HOLOS
Street Address: 842 Main St.
Province: MB
Postal Code: R2W 3N8
Country: Canada
General Phone: (204) 589-5871
General Fax: (204) 586-3618
Editorial Phone: (204) 589-5871
Editorial e-mail: presstr@mts.net
Advertising Phone: (204) 589-5871
General/National Adv. E-mail: presstr@mts.net
Display Adv. E-mail: presstr@mts.net
Primary Website: ukrvoice.ca
Year Established: 1910
Delivery Methods: Mail`Newsstand
Own Printing Facility?: Y
Mechanical specifications: Type page 14 1/2 x 22 3/4; E - 6 cols, 2, 1/8 between; A - 6 cols, 2, 1/8 between; C - 6 cols, 2, 1/8 between.
Published: Mon
Published Other: 2 x Mthly
Avg Paid Circ: 1890
Avg Free Circ: 42
Audit By: Sworn/Estimate/Non-Audited
Audit Date: 12.07.2019

GAY & LESBIAN NEWSPAPERS IN THE U.S.

BENSON

OUT IN THE MOUNTAINS
Street address 1: PO Box 287
Street address state: VT
Postal code: 05731-0287
County: Rutland
Country: USA
Mailing address: PO Box 287
Mailing city: Benson
Mailing state or province: VT
Mailing postal code: 05731
Office phone: (802) 275-5027
General e-mail: editor@oitm.org

BOSTON

BAY WINDOWS
Street address 1: 28 Damrell St
Street address 2: Ste 204
Street address state: MA
Postal code: 02127-3077
County: Suffolk
Country: USA
Mailing address: 28 Damrell St Ste 204
Mailing city: Boston
Mailing state or province: MA
Mailing postal code: 02127-3077
Office phone: 617-464-7280
Office fax: 617-464-7286

Advertising phone: 617 464 7280 x202
Advertising fax: 617 464 7286
Editorial phone: 617 464 7280 x215
Editorial fax: 617 464 7286
General e-mail: jcoakley@baywindows.com
Advertising e-mail: jcoakley@baywindows.com
Editorial e-mail: sue.baywindows@gmail.com

CHARLOTTE

Q NOTES
Street address 1: 920 Central Ave
Street address state: NC
Postal code: 28204-2028
County: Mecklenburg
Country: USA
Mailing address: PO Box 221841
Mailing city: Charlotte
Mailing state or province: NC
Mailing postal code: 28222-1841
Office phone: (704) 531-9988
Office fax: (704) 531-1361
General e-mail: info@goqnotes.com
Editorial e-mail: editor@goqnotes.com

CHICAGO

BLACK LINES
Street address 1: 5315 N Clark St
Street address 2: Ste 192

Street address state: IL
Postal code: 60640-2290
County: Cook
Country: USA
Mailing address: 5315 N Clark St Ste 192
Mailing city: Chicago
Mailing state or province: IL
Mailing postal code: 60640-2290
Office phone: (773) 871-7610
Office fax: (773) 871-7609
Editorial e-mail: editor@windycitymediagroup.com

CHICAGO

EN LA VIDA
Street address 1: 5443 N Broadway St
Street address 2: Ste 101
Street address state: IL
Postal code: 60640-1703
County: Cook
Country: USA
Mailing address: 5443 N Broadway St Ste 101
Mailing city: Chicago
Mailing state or province: IL
Mailing postal code: 60640-1703
Office phone: (773) 871-7610
Office fax: (773) 871-7609
Editorial e-mail: editor@windycitymediagroup.com

CHICAGO

NIGHTSPOTS
Street address 1: 5315 N Clark St
Street address 2: Ste 192
Street address state: IL
Postal code: 60640-2290
County: Cook
Country: USA
Mailing address: 5315 N Clark St Ste 192
Mailing city: Chicago
Mailing state or province: IL
Mailing postal code: 60640-2290
Office phone: (773) 871-7610
Office fax: (773) 871-7609
General e-mail: nightspots@windycitymediagroup.com
Advertising e-mail: advertising@windycitymediagroup.com
Editorial e-mail: nightspots@windycitymediagroup.com

CHICAGO

WINDY CITY TIMES
Street address 1: 5315 N Clark St
Street address 2: Ste 192
Street address state: IL
Postal code: 60640-2290
County: Cook

Gay & Lesbian Newspapers in the U.S.

Country: USA
Mailing address: 5315 N Clark St Ste 192
Mailing city: Chicago
Mailing state or province: IL
Mailing postal code: 60640-2290
Office phone: (773) 871-7610
Office fax: (773) 871-7609
General e-mail: publisher@windycitymediagroup.com
Advertising e-mail: advertising@windycitymediagroup.com
Editorial e-mail: editor@windycitymediagroup.com; calendar@windycitymediagroup.com; theater@windycitymediagroup.com; graphics@windycitymediagroup.com

COLUMBUS

STONEWALL COLUMBUS

Street address 1: 1160 N High St
Street address state: OH
Postal code: 43201-2411
County: Franklin
Country: USA
Mailing address: 1160 N High St
Mailing city: Columbus
Mailing state or province: OH
Mailing postal code: 43201-2411
Office phone: (614) 299-7764
Office fax: (614) 299-4408
Advertising phone: (614) 930-2262
Advertising fax: (614) 299-4408
Editorial phone: (614) 930-2264
Editorial fax: (614) 299-4408
General e-mail: info@stonewallcolumbus.org
Advertising e-mail: info@lavenderlistings.com
Editorial e-mail: info@stonewallcolumbus.org

DALLAS

DALLAS VOICE

Street address 1: 4145 Travis St
Street address 2: Fl 3
Street address state: TX
Postal code: 75204-1840
County: Dallas
Country: USA
Mailing address: 4145 Travis St Ste 300
Mailing city: Dallas
Mailing state or province: TX
Mailing postal code: 75204-1830
Office phone: (214) 754-8710
Office fax: (214) 969-7271
General e-mail: editor@dallasvoice.com; advertising@dallasvoice.com
Advertising e-mail: advertising@dallasvoice.com
Editorial e-mail: editor@dallasvoice.com; advertising@dallasvoice.com

DENVER

OUT FRONT

Street address 1: 3535 Walnut St
Street address state: CO
Postal code: 80205-2433
County: Denver
Country: USA
Office phone: (303) 477-4000
Office fax: 303-325-2642
General e-mail: info@outfrontonline.com
Advertising e-mail: advertising@outfrontonline.com
Editorial e-mail: editorial@outfrontonline.com

EDINA

LAVENDER

Street address 1: 7701 York Ave S
Street address 2: Ste 225
Street address state: MN
Postal code: 55435-5884
County: Hennepin
Country: USA
Mailing address: 7701 York Ave S, Suite 225
Mailing city: Edina
Mailing state or province: MN
Mailing postal code: 55435
Office phone: (612) 436-4660
Office fax: (612) 436-4685
General e-mail: info@lavendermagazine.com

LIVONIA

BETWEEN THE LINES

Street address 1: 11920 Farmington Rd
Street address state: MI
Postal code: 48150-1724
County: Wayne
Country: USA
Mailing address: 20222 Farmington Rd
Mailing city: Livonia
Mailing state or province: MI
Mailing postal code: 48152-1412
Office phone: (734) 293-7200
Office fax: (734) 293-7201
General e-mail: info@pridesource.com
Advertising e-mail: sales@pridesource.com
Editorial e-mail: editor@pridesource.com; editor@pridesource.com

MIDDLETOWN

CENTRAL VOICE

Street address 1: 20 S Union St
Street address state: PA
Postal code: 17057-1445
County: Dauphin
Country: USA
Mailing address: 20 S Union St
Mailing city: Middletown
Mailing state or province: PA
Mailing postal code: 17110
Office phone: (717) 839-9788
Office fax: (717) 944-2083
General e-mail: frankpizzoli@gmail.com
Advertising e-mail: frankpizzoli@gmail.com
Editorial e-mail: frankpizzoli@gmail.com

NASHVILLE

OUT & ABOUT NASHVILLE

Street address 1: 3951 Moss Rose Dr
Street address state: TN
Postal code: 37216-2925
County: Davidson
Country: USA
Mailing address: 3951 Moss Rose Dr
Mailing city: Nashville
Mailing state or province: TN
Mailing postal code: 37216-2925
Office phone: (615) 596-6210
Office fax: 615-246-2787
General e-mail: sales@outandaboutnashville.com
Advertising e-mail: sales@outandaboutnashville.com
Editorial e-mail: editor@outandaboutnashville.com

NEW YORK

GAY CITY NEWS

Street address 1: 515 Canal St
Street address state: NY
Postal code: 10013-1330
County: New York
Country: USA
Mailing address: 515 Canal St Fl 1
Mailing city: New York
Mailing state or province: NY
Mailing postal code: 10013-1330
Office phone: 212-229-1890
Office fax: 2152-229-2790
General e-mail: editor@gaycitynews.com
Advertising e-mail: ads@communitymediallc.com

ORLANDO

WATERMARK MEDIA

Street address 1: 414 N Ferncreek Ave
Street address state: FL
Postal code: 32803-5432
County: Orange
Country: USA
Mailing address: PO Box 533655
Mailing city: Orlando
Mailing state or province: FL
Mailing postal code: 32853-3655
Office phone: (407) 481-2243
Office fax: (407) 481-2246
General e-mail: editor@watermarkonline.com; sales@watermarkonline.com

PHILADELPHIA

PHILADELPHIA GAY NEWS

Street address 1: 505 S 4th St
Street address state: PA
Postal code: 19147-1506
County: Philadelphia
Country: USA
Mailing address: 505 S 4th St
Mailing city: Philadelphia
Mailing state or province: PA
Mailing postal code: 19147-1506
Office phone: (215) 625-8501 ext 200
Office fax: (215) 925-6437
Advertising phone: (215) 625-8501 ext 212
Advertising fax: (215) 925-6437
Editorial phone: (215) 625-8501 ext 206
Editorial fax: (215) 925-6437
General e-mail: pgn@epgn.com
Advertising e-mail: prab@epgn.com
Editorial e-mail: jen@epgn.com

ROCHESTER

GAY ALLIANCE

Street address 1: 100 College Ave
Street address 2: Ste 100
Street address state: NY
Postal code: 14607-1073
County: Monroe
Country: United States
Mailing address: 100 College Ave
Mailing city: Rochester
Mailing state or province: NY
Mailing postal code: 14607
Office phone: (585) 244-8640
Office fax: (585) 244-8246
Advertising phone:
Editorial phone: (585) 244-8640
Other phone: (585) 244-8640
General e-mail: jeffreym@gayalliance.org
Advertising e-mail: jeffm@gayalliance.org
Editorial e-mail: jeffm@gayalliance.org

SAN DIEGO

GAY SAN DIEGO

Street address 1: 444 Camino del Rio South #102
Street address state: CA
Postal code: 92108
County: San Diego
Country: USA
Mailing address: 444 Camino del Rio South #102
Mailing city: San Diego
Mailing state or province: CA
Mailing postal code: 92108
Office phone: (619) 519-7775
General e-mail: david@sdcnn.com
Advertising e-mail: mike@sdcnn.com
Editorial e-mail: albert@sdcnn.com

SAN FRANCISCO

BAY AREA REPORTER

Street address 1: 44 Gough St.
Street address 2: #204
Street address state: CA
Postal code: 94103
County: San Francisco
Country: USA
Mailing address: 44 Gough St. #204
Mailing city: San Francisco
Mailing state or province: CA
Mailing postal code: 94103
Office phone: (415) 861-5019
Office fax: (415) 861-8144
General e-mail: information@ebar.com

SEATTLE

SEATTLE GAY NEWS

Street address 1: 1605 12th Ave
Street address 2: Ste 31
Street address state: WA
Postal code: 98122-2487
County: King
Country: USA
Mailing address: 1605 12th Ave Ste 31
Mailing city: Seattle
Mailing state or province: WA
Mailing postal code: 98122-2487
Office phone: (206) 324-4297
Office fax: (206) 322-7188
General e-mail: sgn2@sgn.org

WASHINGTON

WASHINGTON BLADE

Street address 1: 1712 14th St NW
Street address state: DC
Postal code: 20009-5070
County: District Of Columbia
Country: USA
Office phone: (202) 747-2077
Office fax: (202) 747-2070
General e-mail: info@washblade.com
Advertising e-mail: lbrown@washblade.com
Editorial e-mail: knaff@washblade.com

WILTON MANORS

SOUTH FLORIDA GAY NEWS

Street address 1: 2520 N Dixie Hwy
Street address state: FL
Postal code: 33305-1247
County: Broward
Country: USA
Mailing address: 2520 N Dixie Hwy
Mailing city: Wilton Manors
Mailing state or province: FL
Mailing postal code: 33305-1247
Office phone: 954-530-4970
Office fax: 954-530-7943

HISPANIC NEWSPAPERS IN THE U.S.

ABILENE

ABILENE HISPANIC GUIDE

Street address 1: 122 McGlothlin Campus Center
Street address 2: Acu Box 29004
Street address state: TX
Postal code: 79699-0001
County: Taylor
Country: USA
Mailing address: ACU Box 29004
Mailing city: Abilene
Mailing state: TX
Mailing zip: 79699
Office phone: (325) 674-2067
Office fax: (325) 674-6475
Website: www.hispanicabilene.com
Year newspaper established: 1992
Advertising (open inch rate): Open inch rate $8.00
Mechanical specifications: Type page 10 1/8 x 12 1/2; E - 5 cols, 1 3/4, 1/6 between.
Zip Codes Served: 10003
Frequency: Thur
Circulation Free: 6000
Audit By: Sworn/Estimate/Non-Audited
Audit Date: 12.07.2019
Hardware: Pentium/486
Software: Microsoft/Windows 98.
Personnel: Patricia Olvera (Owner)
Main (survey) contact: Ana Arango

ACTON

ACTON-AGUA DULCE NEWS

Street address 1: 3413 Soledad Canyon Rd
Street address state: CA
Postal code: 93510-1974
County: Los Angeles
Country: USA
Mailing address: PO Box 57
Mailing city: Acton
Mailing state: CA
Mailing zip: 93510-0057
Office phone: (661) 269-1169
Office fax: (661) 269-2139
General e-mail: aadnews@joycemediainc.com; help@joycemediainc.com
Website: www.aadnews.com
Year newspaper established: 1969
Advertising (open inch rate): Open inch rate $10.97
Mechanical specifications: Type page 11 x 17.
Frequency: Mon
Circulation Paid: 1000
Circulation Free: 575
Audit By: Sworn/Estimate/Non-Audited
Audit Date: 12.07.2019
Hardware: APP/Mac, HP
Presses: RKW
Software: Adobe/PageMaker 6.5.
Personnel: John Joyce (Pub.); M. Gayle Joyce (Ed.); Micah Joyce (Mng. Ed.); Jana Miranda (Data Supvr.)
Main (survey) contact: John Joyce

ARLINGTON HEIGHTS

REFLEJOS BILINGUAL PUBLICATIONS

Street address 1: 155 E Algonquin Rd
Street address 2:
Street address state: IL
Postal code: 60005-4617
County: Cook
Country: USA
Mailing address: 155 E. Algonquin Road
Mailing city: Arlington Heights
Mailing state: IL
Mailing zip: 60005
Office phone: (847) 806-1111
Office fax: (847) 806-1112
Advertising phone: (847)806-1411
Editorial phone: (847) 806-1171
General e-mail: lsiete@reflejos.com
Advertising e-mail: lsiete@reflejos.com
Editorial e-mail: mortiz@reflejos.com
Website: www.reflejos.com
Year newspaper established: 1990
Advertising (open inch rate): N/A
Mechanical specifications: Type page 9 x 11 1/4; E - 9 cols, 1 1/12, between; A - 9 cols, 11/12, between; C - 9 cols, 1 1/12, between.
Delivery methods: Mail`Newsstand`Racks
Zip Codes Served: 8 counties out side of Chicago
Digital Platform - Mobile: Apple`Android
Digital Platform - Tablet: Apple iOS`Android
Frequency: Fri
Circulation Paid: 5
Circulation Free: 32549
Audit By: CVC
Audit Date: 30.12.2018
Hardware: APP/Mac
Software: Adobe/Acrobat, Adobe/Illustrator CS, Adobe/PageMaker, Adobe/Photoshop CS, Macromedia/Freehand, QPS/QuarkXPRess, Adobe/InDesign CS2.
Personnel: Linda Siete (Pub./Adv. Mgr.); John Janos (Circ.); Hector Gomez (Prod.)
Parent company: Paddock Publications
Main (survey) contact: Linda Siete

ATLANTA

ATLANTA LATINO

Street address 1: 2865 Amwiler Rd
Street address 2: Ste 100
Street address state: GA
Postal code: 30360-2827
County: Gwinnett
Country: USA
Mailing address: 2865 Amwiler Rd Ste 100
Mailing city: Atlanta
Mailing state: GA
Mailing zip: 30360-2827
Office phone: (770) 416-7570
Office fax: (770) 416-7991
Advertising e-mail: sales@atlantalatino.com
Editorial e-mail: editor@atlantalatino.com
Website: www.atlantalatino.com
Advertising (open inch rate): Open inch rate $20.00
Zip Codes Served: 30338, 30339, 30340, 30341, 30341, 30342, 30344, 30345, 30360, 30501, 30504, 30507, 30518, 30519, 30001, 30004, 30005, 30008, 30022, 30024, 30030, 30032, 30033, 30035, 30039, 30040, 30043, 30044, 30045, 30047, 30059, 30060, 30062, 30064, 30066, 30071, 300
Other Type of Frequency: Every other Thur
Circulation Free: 20000
Audit By: Sworn/Estimate/Non-Audited
Audit Date: 12.07.2019
Hardware: APP/Power Mac G4
Software: Adobe/InDesign CS.
Personnel: Farid Sadri (Adv. Mgr.); Judith Martinez (Ed. in Chief)
Main (survey) contact: M. Saout

ATLANTA

MUNDO HISPÁNICO NEWSPAPER

Street address 1: 5269 Buford Highway
Street address state: GA
Postal code: 30340
Country: USA
Mailing address: 5269 Buford Highway
Mailing city: Atlanta
Mailing state: GA
Mailing zip: 30340
Office phone: (404) 881-0441
Office fax: (404) 881-6085
General e-mail: mbesares@mundohispanico.com
Editorial e-mail: gdelaney@mundohispanico.com
Website: mundohispanico.com
Year newspaper established: 1979
Advertising (open inch rate): CP
Delivery methods: Racks
Digital Platform - Mobile: Apple`Android
Digital Platform - Tablet: Apple iOS`Android
Frequency: Thur
Circulation Paid: 20
Circulation Free: 70955
Audit By: CVC
Audit Date: 30.12.2018
Personnel: Melvin Besares; Gerard Delaney (Pub.); Jimmy Vega (Circ.); Marcelo Wheelock (Prod.)
Main (survey) contact: Gerard Delaney; Melvin Besares

AUSTIN

AHORA SI!

Street address 1: 305 S Congress Ave
Street address state: TX
Postal code: 78704-1200
County: Travis
Country: USA
Mailing address: 305 S Congress Ave
Mailing city: Austin
Mailing state: TX
Mailing zip: 78704-1200
Office phone: (512) 445-3500
Office fax: n/a
Advertising phone: (512) 912-2949
Editorial phone: (512) 445-3500
General e-mail: eventos@ahorasi.com
Advertising e-mail: Johnny.Flores@coxinc.com
Editorial e-mail: jcasati@ahorasi.com
Website: www.statesman.com
Year newspaper established: 2004
Advertising (open inch rate): Open inch rate $42.58
Delivery methods: Carrier`Racks
Zip Codes Served: 78701-78705, 78708-78739, 78741-78742, 78744-78769
Frequency: Thur
Other Type of Frequency: on web, daily
Circulation Free: 37535
Audit By: Sworn/Estimate/Non-Audited
Audit Date: 12.07.2019
Hardware: APP/Mac, Sim/Enterprise 4000
Presses: 9-G/Metroliner double width (5 half decks), KBA/Towers
Software: DTI/PageSpeed, DTI/SpeedPlanner.
Personnel: Josefina Villicana Casati (Ed.)
Parent company: Austin American-Statesman
Main (survey) contact: Josefina Villicana Casati

EL MUNDO - AUSTIN / SAN ANTONIO

Street address 1: 2116 E Cesar Chavez St
Street address state: TX
Postal code: 78702-4514
County: Travis
Country: USA
Mailing address: PO Box 6519
Mailing city: Austin
Mailing state: TX
Mailing zip: 78762-6519
Office phone: 512-476-8636
Office fax: 512-476-6402
Editorial phone: 512-474-8535
Editorial fax: 512-476-6402
General e-mail: info@elmundonewspaper.com
Advertising e-mail: angela@elmundonewspaper.com
Editorial e-mail: jg@elmundonewspaper.com
Website: www.elmundonewspaper.com
Year newspaper established: 1989
Advertising (open inch rate): $28 Fc and $25

B&W
Mechanical specifications: 11.98 x 21.5
Delivery methods: Racks
Digital Platform - Mobile: Apple`Android
Digital Platform - Tablet: Apple iOS`Android
Frequency: Thur
Circulation Paid: 0
Circulation Free: 45000
Audit By: CVC
Audit Date: 30.03.2013
Presses: Harris V15
Software: Indesign CS6
Personnel: Alba Angulo (Publisher)
Main (survey) contact: Angela Angulo

PERIODICO BUENA SUERTE - AUSTIN

Street address 1: 6901 N Lamar Blvd
Street address 2: Ste 139
Street address state: TX
Postal code: 78752-3532
County: Travis
Country: USA
Mailing address: 7324 Southwest Fwy Ste 1720
Mailing city: Houston
Mailing state: TX
Mailing zip: 77074-2058
Office phone: (512) 345-0101
Website: www.austin.buenasuerte.com
Year newspaper established: 1986
Advertising (open inch rate): Open inch rate $13.00
Delivery methods: Newsstand`Racks
Zip Codes Served: 78701 78702 78703 78704
Digital Platform - Mobile: Apple`Android`Windows
Digital Platform - Tablet: Apple iOS`Android`Windows 7
Frequency: Thur
Circulation Paid: 0
Circulation Free: 6180
Audit By: Sworn/Estimate/Non-Audited
Audit Date: 12.07.2019
Personnel: Emilio Martinez
Main (survey) contact: Emilio Martinez

BAKERSFIELD

EL POPULAR

Street address 1: 404 Truxtun Ave
Street address state: CA
Postal code: 93301-5316
County: Kern
Country: USA
Mailing address: 404 Truxtun Ave
Mailing city: Bakersfield
Mailing state: CA
Mailing zip: 93301-5316
Office phone: (661) 325-7725
Office fax: (661) 325-1351
Advertising phone: (661) 325-1351
Advertising fax: (661) 325-1351
Editorial phone: (661) 325-1351
Editorial fax: (661) 325-1351
General e-mail: pub@elpopularnews.com
Advertising e-mail: ads@elpopularnews.com
Editorial e-mail: news@elpopularnews.com
Website: www.elpopularnews.com
Year newspaper established: 1983
Advertising (open inch rate): Open inch rate $17.50
Mechanical specifications: Six (6) columns x 21.50-inch column dept Full page: 10.25" wide x 21.5" depth
Delivery methods: Carrier`Racks
Zip Codes Served: 93203, 93215, 93241, 93250, 93263, 93280, 93301, 93304, 93305, 93306, 93307, 93308, 93309,
Digital Platform - Mobile: Apple
Digital Platform - Tablet: Apple iOS
Frequency: Fri
Circulation Paid: 100

Hispanic Newspapers in the U.S.

Circulation Free: 23000
Audit By: CVC
Audit Date: 30.12.2015
Personnel: George Camacho (President/Publisher); Raul Camacho (Founding Publisher/Editor); Lupe Medina (Associate Editor)
Parent company: EL POPULAR, INC
Main (survey) contact: George Camacho

BLUE ASH

LA JORNADA LATINA

Street address 1: 4412 Carver Woods Dr
Street address 2: Ste 200
Street address state: OH
Postal code: 45242-5539
County: Hamilton
Country: USA
Mailing address: 4412 Carver Woods Dr Ste 200
Mailing city: Blue Ash
Mailing state: OH
Mailing zip: 45242-5539
Website: www.lajornadalatina.com
Frequency: Fri
Circulation Paid: 25
Circulation Free: 8933
Audit By: Sworn/Estimate/Non-Audited
Audit Date: 12.07.2019
Personnel: Jason Riveiro; Josh Guttman (General Adv.)
Main (survey) contact: Josh Guttman

BOSTON

EL MUNDO

Street address 1: 408 S Huntington Ave
Street address state: MA
Postal code: 02130-4814
County: Suffolk
Country: USA
Mailing address: 408 S Huntington Ave
Mailing city: Boston
Mailing state: MA
Mailing zip: 02130-4814
Office phone: (617) 522-5060
Office fax: (617) 524-5886
Advertising e-mail: sales@elmundoboston.com
Editorial e-mail: editor@elmundoboston.com
Website: www.elmundoboston.com
Year newspaper established: 1972
Advertising (open inch rate): Open inch rate $25.00
Mechanical specifications: Type page 9 3/4 x 16; E - 5 cols, 1 3/4, between; A - 5 cols, 1 3/4, between.
Delivery methods: Mail`Newsstand`Racks
Frequency: Thur
Circulation Paid: 38000
Audit By: Sworn/Estimate/Non-Audited
Audit Date: 12.07.2019
Hardware: APP/Mac
Software: Adobe/PageMaker, QPS/QuarkXPress.
Personnel: Jay Cosmopoulos (Adv. Mgr.); Alberto Vasallo (Ed.); Elvis Jocol (CMO)
Main (survey) contact: Alberto Vasallo; Bob Reichman

EL PLANETA PUBLISHING

Street address 1: 126 Brookline Ave
Street address 2: Ste 3
Street address state: MA
Postal code: 02215-3920
County: Suffolk
Country: USA
Mailing address: 126 Brookline Ave Ste 3
Mailing city: Boston
Mailing state: MA
Mailing zip: 02215-3920
Office phone: (617) 937-5900
Office fax: (617) 536-1463
Advertising e-mail: sales@elplaneta.com
Editorial e-mail: editor@elplaneta.com
Website: www.tuboston.com
Year newspaper established: 2004
Frequency: Fri

Circulation Free: 50000
Audit By: Sworn/Estimate/Non-Audited
Audit Date: 12.07.2019
Personnel: Marcela Garcia (Ed.)
Main (survey) contact: Marcela Garcia

LA SEMANA

Street address 1: 903 Albany St
Street address state: MA
Postal code: 02119-2534
County: Suffolk
Country: USA
Mailing address: 903 Albany St
Mailing city: Boston
Mailing state: MA
Mailing zip: 02119-2534
Office phone: (617) 541-2222
Office fax: (617) 427-6227
General e-mail: wcea2000@aol.com
Website: www.lasemanawceatv.com
Year newspaper established: 1978
Advertising (open inch rate): Open inch rate $28.00 Classified, $24.00 Retail display
Delivery methods: Newsstand`Racks
Frequency: Thur
Circulation Free: 10000
Audit By: Sworn/Estimate/Non-Audited
Audit Date: 12.07.2019
Hardware: Pentium IV
Software: WordPerfect.
Personnel: Nicolas Cuenca (Adv. Mgr.); Peter N. Cuenca (Ed.)
Main (survey) contact: Peter N. Cuenca

BROOKFIELD

CHICAGO DEPORTIVO

Street address 1: PO Box 411
Street address state: IL
Postal code: 60513
Country: USA
Mailing address: PO Box 411
Mailing city: Brookfield
Mailing state: IL
Mailing zip: 60513
Office phone: (312) 375-8979
Advertising phone: (312) 375-8979
Editorial phone: (312) 375-8979
General e-mail: eparrdeportivo@yahoo.com
Advertising e-mail: eparrdeportivo@yahoo.com
Editorial e-mail: eparrdeportivo@yahoo.com
Website: www.chicagodeportivo.net
Year newspaper established: 1988
Personnel: Julio Parrales (Ed./Pub.); Julie Parrales Cisneros (Office Mgr.); Chris Parrales Gonzalez (Media/Pub. Rel. Dir.); Edward Parrales (Mktg./Sales Dir.)
Main (survey) contact: Julio Parrales

BROOKLYN

EL DIARIO LA PRENSA

Street address 1: 1 Metrotech Ctr
Street address 2: Fl 18
Street address state: NY
Postal code: 11201-3948
County: Kings
Country: USA
Mailing address: 1 Metrotech Ctr Fl 18
Mailing city: Brooklyn
Mailing state: NY
Mailing zip: 11201-3949
Office phone: (212) 807-4662
Office fax: (212) 807-4746
General e-mail: editorial@eldiariolaprensa.com
Advertising e-mail: communications@impremedia.com
Website: www.eldiariony.com
Year newspaper established: 1913
Advertising (open inch rate): Open inch rate $52.08
Mechanical specifications: Type page 9 13/16 x 13 1/2; E - 6 cols, 1 1/2, 1/6 between; A - 6 cols, 1 1/2, 1/6 between; C - 7 cols, 1 1/3, 1/6 between.
Delivery methods: Mail`Newsstand
Digital Platform - Mobile: Apple`Android
Digital Platform - Tablet: Apple

iOS`Android`Windows 7
Other Type of Frequency: Daily
Circulation Paid: 134696
Audit By: Sworn/Estimate/Non-Audited
Audit Date: 12.07.2019
Hardware: Dell/PC. Apple
Personnel: Denny PeÃ±a (Circ. Dir.); Francisco Seghezzo (CEO); Ivan Adaime (General Mgr Digital); Juan Varela (Content Dir.); Jorge Ayala (VP of Adv.); Fernando Lang (Director, Ad Rev/Operations); Angel Vazquez; Lizbeth Rodriguez (Marketing Dir.)
Parent company: Impremedia
Main (survey) contact: Lizbeth Rodriguez

BROWNSVILLE

EL NUEVO HERALDO

Street address 1: 1135 E Van Buren St
Street address state: TX
Postal code: 78520-7055
County: Cameron
Country: USA
Mailing address: PO Box 351
Mailing city: Brownsville
Mailing state: TX
Mailing zip: 78522-0351
Office phone: (956) 542-4301
Office fax: (956) 504-1119
Advertising phone: (956) 982-6636
Advertising fax: (956) 982-4201
Editorial phone: (956) 982-6625
Editorial fax: (956) 430-6233
General e-mail: tbhpress@brownsvilleherald.com
Website: www.brownsvilleherald.com
Advertising (open inch rate): Open inch rate $8.95
Mechanical specifications: Type page 13 x 21 1/4; E - 6 cols, 2 1/4, 1/8 between; A - 6 cols, 2 1/16, 1/8 between; C - 10 cols, 1 1/4, 3/8 between.
Frequency: Mon`Tues`Wed`Thur`Fri`Sat`Sun
Circulation Paid: 20575
Audit By: AAM
Audit Date: 31.03.2017
Personnel: R. Daniel Cavazos (Pub.); Karen Ashanholtzer (Adv. Dir.); Abe Gonzalez (Circ. Dir.); Rachel Benavides (Ed.); Marci Ponce (Ed.); Gary Long (News Ed.); Brad Doherty (Photo Ed.); Speedy Aldape (Prodn. Mgr., Systems)
Main (survey) contact: Louisa Ferrera

CAGUAS

LA SEMANA

Street address 1: Calle Crista Bal Colafan
Street address 2: Esquina Ponce De Leafan
Street address state: PR
Postal code: 725
County: Caguas
Country: Puerto Rico
Mailing address: PO Box 6537
Mailing city: Caguas
Mailing state: PR
Mailing zip: 00726-6537
Office phone: (787) 743-5606
Office fax: (787) 743-5100
General e-mail: lasemanaelpionero@gmail.com
Editorial e-mail: redaccion@periodicolasemana.net
Website: www.lasemana.com
Frequency: Thur
Circulation Free: 80060
Audit By: AAM
Audit Date: 31.03.2015
Main (survey) contact: Dear Editor

CAMARILLO

SIGLO 21

Street address 1: 550 Paseo Camarillo
Street address state: CA
Postal code: 93010-5900
County: Ventura
Country: USA

Frequency: Wed
Circulation Free: 16361
Audit By: VAC
Audit Date: 11.03.2012

CAROLINA

PERIODICO PRESENCIA

Street address 1: PO Box 1928
Street address state: PR
Postal code: 00984-1928
County: Carolina
Country: USA
Mailing address: P.O. Box 1928
Mailing city: Carolina
Mailing state: PR
Mailing zip: 00984-1928
Office phone: (787) 946-1391
Office fax: (787) 946-1392
General e-mail: ernestoalmodovarlopez@gmail.com
Advertising e-mail: ingrid.vicente@prenciapr.com
Editorial e-mail: dcamara@presenciapr.com
Website: presenciapr.com
Year newspaper established: 2013
Delivery methods: Newsstand
Frequency: Thur
Circulation Free: 69414
Audit By: CVC
Audit Date: 30.06.2018
Personnel: Diana Camara Santiago (Pub.); Ingrid Vincente (Adv.); Ernesto Almodovar (Circ.); Hector Alvarez (Prod.)
Main (survey) contact: Diana Camara-Santiago

CARRIZO SPRINGS

THE CARRIZO SPRINGS JAVELIN

Street address 1: 610 N 1st St
Street address state: TX
Postal code: 78834-2602
County: Dimmit
Country: USA
Mailing address: PO Box 1046
Mailing city: Carrizo Springs
Mailing state: TX
Mailing zip: 78834-7046
Office phone: (830) 876-2318
Office fax: (830) 876-2620
General e-mail: csjaveline@yahoo.com
Website: www.carrizospringsjavelin.com
Advertising (open inch rate): Open inch rate $4.00
Mechanical specifications: Type page 13 x 21; E - 6 cols, 2 1/16, 1/6 between; A - 6 cols, 2 1/16, between; C - 6 cols, 2 1/16, between.
Frequency: Thur
Circulation Paid: 2000
Circulation Free: 100
Audit By: Sworn/Estimate/Non-Audited
Audit Date: 12.07.2019
Hardware: PC
Software: Adobe/PageMaker, Microsoft.
Personnel: Howard McDaniel (Pub.); Claudia McDaniel (Ed.)
Main (survey) contact: Howard McDaniel

CHARLOTTE

HOLA NOTICIAS

Street address 1: 4801 E Independence Blvd
Street address 2: Ste 815
Street address state: NC
Postal code: 28212-5490
County: Mecklenburg
Country: USA
Mailing address: 4801 E Independence Blvd Ste 815
Mailing city: Charlotte
Mailing state: NC
Mailing zip: 28212-5490
Website: www.holanoticias.com
Frequency: Tues
Audit By: Sworn/Estimate/Non-Audited
Audit Date: 12.07.2019

Personnel: Judy Galindo
Main (survey) contact: Judy Galindo

LA NOTICIA

Street address 1: 5936 Monroe Rd
Street address state: NC
Postal code: 28212-6106
County: Mecklenburg
Country: USA
Mailing address: 5936 Monroe Rd
Mailing city: Charlotte
Mailing state: NC
Mailing zip: 28212-6106
Office phone: (704) 568-6966
Office fax: (704) 568-8936
General e-mail: hgurdian@lanoticia.com
Advertising e-mail: hgurdian@lanoticia.com
Editorial e-mail: editor@lanoticia.com
Website: www.lanoticia.com
Year newspaper established: 1992
Advertising (open inch rate): N/A
Mechanical specifications: Type page 10 x 13 1/2.
Delivery methods: Racks
Digital Platform - Mobile: Apple
Digital Platform - Tablet: Apple iOS
Frequency: Wed
Circulation Free: 26000
Audit By: Sworn/Estimate/Non-Audited
Audit Date: 12.07.2019
Hardware: APP/Mac.
Personnel: Hilda Gurdian (Pub.)
Main (survey) contact: Hilda Gurdian

MI GENTE

Street address 1: 4801 E Independence Blvd
Street address 2: Ste 800
Street address state: NC
Postal code: 28212-5408
County: Mecklenburg
Country: USA
Mailing address: PO Box 12876
Mailing city: Winston Salem
Mailing state: NC
Mailing zip: 27117-2876
Office phone: (704) 319-5044
Advertising phone: (704) 449-0769
Website: www.migenteweb.com
Frequency: Tues
Circulation Free: 20873
Audit By: Sworn/Estimate/Non-Audited
Audit Date: 12.07.2019
Personnel: Rafael Prieto
Main (survey) contact: Rafael Prieto

CHICAGO

COLOMBIA HOY NEWSPAPER

Street address state: IL
Postal code: 12345
Country: USA
Mailing city: Chicago
Mailing state: IL
Office phone: (800) 344 0538
Editorial e-mail: editor@colombiahoy.net
Personnel: Margarita Mendoza (Dir.); Isabella Recio (Collaborator); Mercedes Jimenez (Collaborator)
Main (survey) contact: Margarita Mendoza

EXTRA BILINGUAL COMMUNITY NEWSPAPER

Street address 1: 3906 W North Ave
Street address state: IL
Postal code: 60647-4618
County: Cook
Country: USA
Mailing address: 3906 W North Ave
Mailing city: Chicago
Mailing state: IL
Mailing zip: 60647-4618
Office phone: (773) 252-3534
Office fax: (773) 252-4073
Advertising e-mail: sales@extranews.net
Editorial e-mail: editor@extranews.net
Website: www.extranews.net

Year newspaper established: 1980
Advertising (open inch rate): Open inch rate $46.15
Mechanical specifications: Full Page: 10.375" by 10.5", HP 10.375" by 5.166", Quarter Page 5.104" by 5.166"
Delivery methods: Newsstand`Racks
Zip Codes Served: 60804, 60632, 60623, 60647, 60639, 60629, 60608, 60618, 60625, 60609, 60641, 60617, 60622, 60402, 60651, 60601
Frequency: Fri
Circulation Free: 66
Audit By: CVC
Audit Date: 30.09.2011
Hardware: APP/Mac
Software: Adobe/Photoshop, Adobe/PageMaker, Microsoft/Excel, QPS/QuarkXPress.
Personnel: Mila Tellez (Pub.); Nile Wendorf (Assoc. Pub./Gen. Mgr.); Christina Elizabeth Rodriguez (Managing Editor)
Main (survey) contact: Jose Gonzalez

LA PRENSA DE CHICAGO

Street address 1: 4518 W. Fullerton
Street address state: IL
Postal code: 60639
Country: USA
Mailing address: 4518 W. Fullerton
Mailing city: Chicago
Mailing state: IL
Mailing zip: 60639
Office phone: (773) 521-7286
Office fax: (773) 486-9877
General e-mail: laprensaus@gmail.com
Advertising e-mail: laprensachicago@hotmail.com
Website: laprensaus.com
Personnel: Contact Us
Main (survey) contact: Contact Us; Contact Us

LA RAZA NEWSPAPER

Street address 1: 605 N Michigan Ave
Street address 2: 4th Fl
Street address state: IL
Postal code: 60611
County: Cook
Country: USA
Mailing address: 605 N Michigan Ave, 4th Fl
Mailing city: Chicago
Mailing state: IL
Mailing zip: 60611
Office phone: (312) 807-7043
Advertising e-mail: advertising@impremedia.com
Editorial e-mail: agenda@laraza.com
Website: laraza.com
Year newspaper established: 1970
Advertising (open inch rate): Open inch rate $95.00
Mechanical specifications: Display Advertising: 6 Col X 11" Classified Advertising: 8 Col X 11"
Delivery methods: Mail`Newsstand`Carrier`Racks
Zip Codes Served: 26 Zip Codes: Chicago and Suburbs
Frequency: Sun
Circulation Free: 153620
Audit By: AAM
Audit Date: 31.03.2019
Hardware: APP/Mac.
Software: Adobe/Photoshop, QPS/QuarkXPress.
Personnel: Brian Baase (Nat'l Acct. Exec.); Jimena Catarivas Corbett (Adv. Dir./Gen. Mgr.); Fabiola Pomareda (Managing d.); Tatiana Canaval (Mktg. Mgr.); Hugo Jordan (Sr. Account Mgr., Local Sales); Martha DeLuna (Nat'l Acct. Exec.); Jesus del Toro
Parent company: impreMedia LLC
Main (survey) contact: Jimena Catarivas Corbett; Jesus Del Toro

NEGOCIOS NOW

Street address 1: 70 W Madison St
Street address 2: Ste 1400
Street address state: IL
Postal code: 60602
Mailing address: 70 W Madison St, Ste 1400
Mailing city: Chicago

Mailing state: IL
Mailing zip: 60602
Office phone: (773) 942-7410
General e-mail: info@negociosnow.com
Personnel: Contact Us
Main (survey) contact: Contact Us

CHULA VISTA

EL LATINO

Street address 1: 1550 Broadway
Street address 2: Ste U
Street address state: CA
Postal code: 91911-4091
County: San Diego
Country: USA
Mailing address: PO Box 120550
Mailing city: San Diego
Mailing state: CA
Mailing zip: 92112-0550
Office phone: (619) 426-1491
Office fax: (619) 426-3206
General e-mail: fanny@ellatino.net
Website: www.ellatinoonline.com
Year newspaper established: 1988
Advertising (open inch rate): Open inch rate $53.50
Frequency: Fri
Circulation Free: 80000
Audit By: Sworn/Estimate/Non-Audited
Audit Date: 12.07.2019
Personnel: Fanny Miller (Pub./Pres.)
Main (survey) contact: Fanny Miller

CICERO

TELE GUIA DE CHICAGO

Street address 1: 3116 S Austin Blvd
Street address state: IL
Postal code: 60804-3729
County: Cook
Country: USA
Mailing address: 3116 S Austin Blvd
Mailing city: Cicero
Mailing state: IL
Mailing zip: 60804-3729
Office phone: 708-656-6666
Office fax: 866-4156776
Advertising phone: 708-656-6666 x1080
Advertising fax: 866-4156776
Editorial phone: 708-656-6666 x1074
Editorial fax: 866-4156776
Advertising e-mail: rosemontes@aol.com
Editorial e-mail: avazquez@teleguia.us
Website: www.teleguia.us
Year newspaper established: 1985
Advertising (open inch rate): 708-656-6666
Delivery methods: Mail`Newsstand`Racks
Digital Platform - Mobile: Apple`Android
Digital Platform - Tablet: Apple iOS`Android`Windows 7`Kindle Fire
Frequency: Sun
Circulation Paid: 7481
Circulation Free: 20692
Audit By: CVC
Audit Date: 19.10.2017
Personnel: Zeke Montes
Main (survey) contact: Zeke Montes

THE LAWNDALE NEWS/SU NOTICIERO BILINGUE

Street address 1: 5533 W 25th St
Street address state: IL
Postal code: 60804-3319
County: Cook
Country: USA
Mailing address: 5533 W 25th St
Mailing city: Cicero
Mailing state: IL
Mailing zip: 60804-3319
Office phone: (708) 656-6400
Office fax: (708) 656-2433
Advertising phone: (708) 656-6400
Advertising fax: (708) 656-2433
General e-mail: printing@lawndalenews.com
Advertising e-mail: pilar@lawndalenews.com

Editorial e-mail: mandou@lawndalenews.com
Website: www.lawndalenews.com
Year newspaper established: 1940
Advertising (open inch rate): Open inch rate $55.00
Mechanical specifications: Type page 10"W x 10Â½" H; E - 6 cols, 1 1/2, between; A - 6 cols, 1 1/2, between; C - 6 cols, 1 1/2, between.
Delivery methods: Newsstand`Carrier`Racks
Zip Codes Served: ZIP CODES ATTACHED
Digital Platform - Mobile: Android`Windows`Blackberry
Digital Platform - Tablet: Android`Windows 7`Kindle`Nook`Kindle Fire
Frequency: Thur`Sun
Other Type of Frequency: Twice a month
Audit By: Sworn/Estimate/Non-Audited
Audit Date: 12.07.2019
Hardware: PC
Software: Adobe, PageMaker, Microsoft.
Personnel: JamesL. Nardini (VP); Lynda Nardini (Pub.); Gary Miller (Adv. Mgr.); Robert Nardini (Gen. Mgr.); Pilar Merino (Prodn. Mgr.); Ashmar Mandou (Ed.)
Main (survey) contact: Ashmar Mandou

DALLAS

AL DIA DALLAS

Street address 1: 1954 Commerce St.
Street address 2: 3rd floor
Street address state: TX
Postal code: 75201
County: Dallas
Country: USA
Mailing address: 1954 Commerce St. 3rd floor
Mailing city: Dallas
Mailing state: TX
Mailing zip: 75201
Office phone: (469) 977-3740
General e-mail: preguntas@aldiatx.com; circulation@aldiatx.com
Website: www.aldiadallas.com
Advertising (open inch rate): Open inch rate $78.00
Delivery methods: Mail`Newsstand`Carrier`Racks
Frequency: Wed`Sat
Circulation Free: 20059
Audit By: AAM
Audit Date: 31.03.2018
Personnel: Alvin Hysong (Pub.); Alfredo Carbajal (Ed./Mktg.); Silvana Pagliuca (Ed. Entertainment); Juan F. Jaramillo (Ed. Local); Lorena Flores (Web Ed.); Yadira Gonzalez (Cliente Serv. Coord.); Alfredo Carbajal (Ed. in Chief); Anthony Trejo (Online Ed.); Mauro Diaz (Sports Ed.)
Parent company: A.H. Belo Corporation
Main (survey) contact: Alvin Hysong

EL EXTRA NEWSPAPER

Street address 1: 1214 Gardenview Dr
Street address state: TX
Postal code: 75217-4311
County: Dallas
Country: USA
Mailing address: PO Box 270432
Mailing city: Dallas
Mailing state: TX
Mailing zip: 75227-0432
Office phone: 214-309-0990
Office fax: 214-309-0204
Advertising phone: 214-309-0990
Advertising fax: 214-309-0204
Editorial phone: 214-309-0990
General e-mail: pressrelease@elextranewspaper.com
Advertising e-mail: clasificados@elextranewspaper.com
Editorial e-mail: pressrelease@elextranewspaper.com
Website: www.elextranewspaper.com
Year newspaper established: 1987
Advertising (open inch rate): Open inch rate $23.00
Mechanical specifications: Offset - PDF - CMYK
Delivery methods: Newsstand`Racks
Digital Platform - Mobile: Windows
Digital Platform - Tablet: Windows 7

Hispanic Newspapers in the U.S.

Frequency: Thur
Circulation Paid: 34095
Audit By: AAM
Audit Date: 31.12.2018
Personnel: Emmy Silva (Publisher/Editor Advertising Manager)
Main (survey) contact: Emmy Silva

EL HERALDO

Street address 1: PO Box 141354
Street address state: TX
Postal code: 75214
Country: USA
Mailing address: PO Box 141354
Mailing city: Dallas
Mailing state: TX
Mailing zip: 75214
Office phone: (214) 827-9700
Advertising phone: (214) 827-9700
Editorial phone: (214) 827-9700
General e-mail: ellie@elheraldonews.com
Website: www.elheraldonews.com
Advertising (open inch rate): Open inch rate $20.00
Mechanical specifications: Type page 10 1/4 x 16; E - 5 cols, 2 1/16, between; A - 5 cols, 2 1/16, between; C - 6 cols, 2 1/16, between.
Delivery methods: Carrier`Racks
Zip Codes Served: 60612 - multiple zip codes
Frequency: Bi-Mthly
Circulation Paid: 0
Circulation Free: 1000
Audit By: Sworn/Estimate/Non-Audited
Audit Date: 12.07.2019
Hardware: Microsoft
Software: QPS/QuarkXPress./Microsoft edition
Personnel: Marta Foster (Adv. Mgr.); Gonzalo Sanchez (Ed.)
Main (survey) contact: Marta Foster

EL HERALDO NEWS

Street address 1: 4532 Columbia Ave
Street address state: TX
Postal code: 75226-1016
County: Dallas
Country: USA
Mailing address: 4532 Columbia Ave
Mailing city: Dallas
Mailing state: TX
Mailing zip: 75226-1016
Office phone: (214) 827-9700
Office fax: (214) 827-8200
General e-mail: ellie@elheraldonews.com
Website: www.elheraldonews.com
Advertising (open inch rate): Open inch rate $25.00
Mechanical specifications: Type page 11.25 x 20.55; E - 6 cols, between; A - 6 cols, between.
Frequency: Fri
Circulation Paid: 2
Circulation Free: 17998
Audit By: CAC
Audit Date: 30.09.2013
Hardware: PC, APP/Mac
Software: QPS/QuarkXPress, Adobe/Photoshop.
Personnel: Ellie Byrd (Adv. Mgr.); Francisco Rayo (Ed.)
Main (survey) contact: Ellie Byrd

EL HISPANO NEWS

Street address 1: 2102 Empire Central
Street address state: TX
Postal code: 75235-4302
County: Dallas
Country: USA
Mailing address: 2102 Empire Central
Mailing city: Dallas
Mailing state: TX
Mailing zip: 75235
Office phone: (214) 357-2186
Office fax: (214) 357-2195
Advertising phone: (214) 357-2186 ext. 202
Editorial phone: (214) 357-2186 ext. 225
General e-mail: editor@elhispanonews.com
Advertising e-mail: lupita@elhispanonews.com
Editorial e-mail: reynaldo@elhispanonews.com
Website: www.elhispanonews.com

Year newspaper established: 1986
Advertising (open inch rate): Open inch rate $26.00
Mechanical specifications: File Format Specs Web offset on 30 pound newsprint 50 lbs white stock Ã¢Â€Â¢ Composite PDF (Postscript): Files must be created carefully to ensure that they are properly optimized for hi-res resolution output. Fonts need to be either outlined or properly embedded. Ã¢Â€Â¢ File must be process in CMYK mode, no fifth color will be accepted. Ã¢Â€Â¢ Trapping must be include in the file if is needed. Ã¢Â€Â¢ Standard trim; include bleed and center marks (cropping mark), no marks in the Ã¢Â€Â¢liveÃ¢Â€Â¢ or Ã¢Â€Â¢bleedÃ¢Â€Â¢ image area. Printing Specification 1 Column = 1.611Ã¢Â€Â 2 Column = 3.389Ã¢Â€Â 3 Column = 5.167Ã¢Â€Â 4 Column = 6.994Ã¢Â€Â 5 Column = 8.722Ã¢Â€Â 6 Column = 10.5Ã¢Â€Â 1/2 Page = 10.5Ã¢Â€Â x 10.5Ã¢Â€Â Full Page = 10.5Ã¢Â€Â x 21Ã¢Â€Â Unit Dimensions Minimum depth in inches must be equal to/or greater than the number of columns used. Bleed pages are not available.
Delivery methods: Mail`Newsstand`Carrier`Racks
Digital Platform - Mobile: Apple`Android`Windows
Digital Platform - Tablet: Apple iOS`Android`Windows 7`Kindle`Nook
Frequency: Thur
Circulation Free: 20390
Audit By: CAC
Audit Date: 31.12.2016
Software: Microsoft/Windows 95, Adobe/PageMaker 6.5, Adobe/Photoshop.
Note: El Hispano News is the oldest Hispanic newspaper in North Texas, serving the Hispanic community since 1986. With a 20,000 copies verified distribution, and our active involvement with the community, especially with issues regarding education (including financial aspects), makes El Hispano News a prefer medium of information for the Dallas Fort Worth Hispanic community.
Personnel: Lupita Colmenero (Adv. Mgr., Nat'l); Ruben Colmenero (Circ. Mgr.); Roxanna Lopez (Office Mgr); Einer Agredo (Graphics); Reynaldo Mena (Managing Ed); Beana Ramirez; Rodolfo Bustillos (Marketing Mgr)
Parent company: RBLC, Inc
Main (survey) contact: Maria Lupita Colmenero

LA SUBASTA DE DALLAS

Street address 1: 502 N Haskell ave
Street address state: TX
Postal code: 75246
County: TX
Country: United States
Mailing address: 6120 tarnef dr
Mailing city: Houston
Mailing state: TX
Mailing zip: 77074
Office phone: (713) 777-1010
Office fax: (214) 951-9400
Advertising phone: (713) 777-1010
General e-mail: sales@lasubasta.com
Advertising e-mail: cynthial@lasubasta.com
Editorial e-mail: cynthial@lasubasta.com
Website: www.lasubasta.com
Year newspaper established: 1981
Mechanical specifications: 10"X 12"
Delivery methods: Newsstand`Racks
Digital Platform - Mobile: Apple`Android
Digital Platform - Tablet: Apple iOS`Android`Windows 7`Blackberry Tablet OS`Kindle`Nook`Kindle Fire`Other
Frequency: Tues`Fri
Circulation Free: 67000
Audit By: VAC
Audit Date: 30.09.2018
Personnel: cynthia aristizabal (Sales Director)
Main (survey) contact: cynthia aristizabal

NOVEDADES NEWS

Street address 1: 121 S Zang Blvd
Street address 2: P.O. Box# 4752

Street address state: TX
Postal code: 75208-4530
County: Dallas
Country: USA
Mailing address: PO Box 4752
Mailing city: Dallas
Mailing state: TX
Mailing zip: 75208-0752
Office phone: (214) 943-2932
Office fax: (214) 943-7352
Advertising phone: (214) 943-2932
Advertising fax: (214) 943-7352
Editorial phone: (214) 943-2932
Editorial fax: (214) 943-7352
Other phone: (214) 770-6693
General e-mail: editorial@novedadesnews.com
Advertising e-mail: spuerto@novedadesnews.com
Editorial e-mail: editorial@novedadesnews.com
Website: www.novedadesnews.com
Year newspaper established: 1986
Advertising (open inch rate): Open inch rate $26.00
Mechanical specifications: Web Offset Full Color Available
Delivery methods: Newsstand`Racks
Zip Codes Served: Dallas/Fort Worth Texas
Digital Platform - Mobile: Apple`Android
Digital Platform - Tablet: Apple iOS`Android
Frequency: Wed
Circulation Paid: 0
Circulation Free: 38000
Audit By: Sworn/Estimate/Non-Audited
Audit Date: 12.07.2019
Hardware: MAC
Presses: OFFSET
Software: Adobe, InDesign and related
Editions Count: 1535
Edition Names with Circ figures: Novedades News - Circulation 38000
Note: Largest and Oldest Newspaper in the Dallas/Fort Worth Texas Area.
Personnel: Sergio Puerto (Mktg. Dir.); Sergio Puerto Sr. (Pres./CEO); Estela Ortiz (Chief Writter); Mike Garza (Marketing Director, Ass.); Angel Puerto (Distribution Manager); Miriam Puerto (Public Relations, Director); Hassel Luzanilla (Accountant)
Parent company: Novedades news, Inc.
Main (survey) contact: Sergio Puerto Sr.

PERIODICO BUENA SUERTE - DALLAS

Street address 1: 1545 W Mockingbird Ln
Street address 2: Ste 1012
Street address state: TX
Postal code: 75235-5014
County: Dallas
Country: USA
Mailing address: 7324 Southwest Fwy Ste 1720
Mailing city: Houston
Mailing state: TX
Mailing zip: 77074-2058
Office phone: (214) 575-4545
Advertising e-mail: sales@buenasuerte.com
Website: www.buenasuerte.com
Year newspaper established: 2010
Advertising (open inch rate): Open inch rate $13.00
Delivery methods: Newsstand`Racks
Zip Codes Served: 75235
Digital Platform - Mobile: Apple`Android`Windows
Digital Platform - Tablet: Apple iOS`Android`Windows 7
Frequency: Wed`Thur
Circulation Paid: 0
Circulation Free: 15051
Audit By: Sworn/Estimate/Non-Audited
Audit Date: 12.07.2019
Personnel: Emilio Martinez
Main (survey) contact: Emilio Martinez

DENVER

LA VOZ NEWSPAPER

Street address 1: 4047 Tejon St
Street address 2: # 202

Street address state: CO
Postal code: 80211-2214
County: Denver
Country: USA
Mailing address: PO Box 11398
Mailing city: Denver
Mailing state: CO
Mailing zip: 80211-0398
Office phone: (303) 936-8556
Office fax: (720) 889-2455
Advertising e-mail: advertising@lavozcolorado.com; classifieds@lavozcolorado.com
Editorial e-mail: news@lavozcolorado.com
Website: www.lavozcolorado.com
Year newspaper established: 1974
Advertising (open inch rate): Open inch rate $22.50
Mechanical specifications: Type page 10 1/3 x 14; E - 6 cols, 1 7/12, 1/6 between; A - 6 cols, 1 7/12, 1/6 between; C - 6 cols, 1 7/12, 1/6 between.
Delivery methods: Mail`Newsstand`Racks
Zip Codes Served: 80002-800011, 80202-80236, 80621-80645
Frequency: Wed
Circulation Paid: 596
Circulation Free: 25778
Audit By: CAC
Audit Date: 30.09.2012
Hardware: 4-MAC/G4
Software: Adobe/Acrobat 5.0, QPS/QuarkXPress 4.1.
Personnel: Pauline Rivera (Pub.); Romelia Ulibarri (Sales Mgr.); Emma Lynch (Entertainment Ed.); Charles Corrales (Prodn. Coord.)
Main (survey) contact: Pauline Rivera

DETROIT

EL CENTRAL

Street address 1: 4124 W Vernor Hwy
Street address state: MI
Postal code: 48209-2145
County: Wayne
Country: USA
Mailing address: 4124 W Vernor Hwy
Mailing city: Detroit
Mailing state: MI
Mailing zip: 48209-2145
Office phone: (313) 841-0100
Office fax: (313) 841-0155
General e-mail: elcentral1@aol.com
Advertising e-mail: elcentralads@aol.com
Advertising (open inch rate): Open inch rate $16.00
Mechanical specifications: Type page 10 x 16; E - 5 cols, 2, between; A - 5 cols, 2, between; C - 5 cols, 2, between.
Zip Codes Served: 48212
Frequency: Thur
Circulation Free: 14000
Audit By: Sworn/Estimate/Non-Audited
Audit Date: 12.07.2019
Hardware: IBM, PC.
Personnel: Dolores Sanchez (Ed.)
Main (survey) contact: Dolores Sanchez

LATINO PRESS

Street address 1: 6301 Michigan Ave
Street address state: MI
Postal code: 48210-2954
County: Wayne
Country: USA
Mailing address: 6301 Michigan Ave
Mailing city: Detroit
Mailing state: MI
Mailing zip: 48210-2954
Office phone: (313) 361-3000
Office fax: (313) 361-3001
Advertising phone: (313) 361-3000
Editorial phone: (313) 361-3002
General e-mail: hotline@latinodetroit.com
Advertising e-mail: marketing@latinodetroit.com
Editorial e-mail: editorial@latinodetroit.com
Website: www.latinodetroit.com
Year newspaper established: 1993
Advertising (open inch rate): Open inch rate $25.00

Mechanical specifications: AD DESIGN: Our creative staff is ready to design your ad. Basic ad design is $250 per ad which includes three proofs. Additional proof will incur additional charges. For custom design quotes, please consult your account representative. LAYOUT SPECIFICATIONS: £ All digital art files must be sized to the dimensions listed at the top of this page £ All colors must be converted to CMYK process. IMAGES: £ Effective resolution for color and grayscale images must be at least 300 dpi. £ All color images must be sent to color mode of CMYK. £ All images must be embedded correctly into the PDF file or included with the page layout file. TRANSFERRING FILES FOR PUBLICATION USE: £ File under 5 mb in size may be submitted via e-mail. £ Submit materials to production@latinodetroit.com £ Larger files sizes call for instructions.
Delivery methods: Mail`Newsstand`Racks
Zip Codes Served: 48209, 48210, 48216, 48342, 48101, 48108, 48238, 48146, 48185
Digital Platform - Mobile: Apple`Android`Blackberry
Digital Platform - Tablet: Apple iOS`Android`Blackberry Tablet OS
Frequency: Thur
Circulation Paid: 1500
Circulation Free: 20000
Audit By: Sworn/Estimate/Non-Audited
Audit Date: 12.07.2019
Personnel: Elias M. Gutierrez (President)
Main (survey) contact: Elias M. Gutierrez

DORADO

EL EXPRESSO DE PUERTO RICO

Street address 1: PO Box 465
Street address state: PR
Postal code: 00646-0465
County: Dorado
Country: Puerto Rico
Mailing address: PO Box 465
Mailing city: Dorado
Mailing state: PR
Mailing zip: 00646-0465
Office phone: 787-794-2000
Office fax: 787-794-2273
Advertising phone: 787-794-2000
Advertising fax: 787-794-2273
Editorial phone: 787-794-2006
Editorial fax: 787-794-2716
General e-mail: info@elexpresso.com
Advertising e-mail: anuncios@elexpresso.com
Editorial e-mail: redaccion@elexpresso.com
Website: www.elexpresso.com
Year newspaper established: 1995
Advertising (open inch rate): Open inch rate $35.00
Mechanical specifications: 13" Heigh 10" widht
Delivery methods: Mail`Newsstand`Racks
Digital Platform - Mobile: Android`Windows
Digital Platform - Tablet: Android`Windows 7
Frequency: Thur
Circulation Paid: 0
Circulation Free: 74900
Audit By: VAC
Audit Date: 30.03.2016
Hardware: PC
Software: Photoshop InDesign Others
Note: Delivered in 24 towns, North of Puerto Rico.
Personnel: Angel Fret (Publisher)
Main (survey) contact: Angel Fret

DORAL

EL NUEVO HERALD

Street address 1: 3511 NW 91st Ave
Street address state: FL
Postal code: 33172-1216
County: Miami-Dade
Country: USA
Mailing address: 3511 NW 91 Avenue
Mailing city: Miami
Mailing state: FL
Mailing zip: 33172
Office phone: (305) 376-3535
Office fax: (305) 376-2138
Website: www.elnuevoherald.com
Advertising (open inch rate): Open inch rate $32.10
Mechanical specifications: Type page 13 x 22 1/4; E - 6 cols, 1/6 between; C - 10 cols, between.
Other Type of Frequency: Daily
Circulation Paid: 382896
Audit By: Sworn/Estimate/Non-Audited
Audit Date: 12.07.2019
Hardware: APP/Mac, PC
Presses: Offset
Software: SII, QPS/QuarkXPress, Adobe/Photoshop, Microsoft/Windows 95, Microsoft/Windows NT.
Personnel: Aminda Marquez Gonzalez (Exec Ed); Maru AntuÃ±ano (Ed., Prod. Spec.)
Parent company: McClatchy
Main (survey) contact: Aminda Marquez Gonzalez

EAGLE PASS

THE NEWS GRAM/THE GRAM

Street address 1: 2543 Del Rio Blvd
Street address state: TX
Postal code: 78852-3627
County: Maverick
Country: USA
Mailing address: 2543 Del Rio Blvd
Mailing city: Eagle Pass
Mailing state: TX
Mailing zip: 78852-3627
Office phone: (830) 773-8610
Office fax: (830) 773-1641
General e-mail: elgram@hilconet.com
Website: thenewsgramonline.net
Advertising (open inch rate): Open inch rate $7.35
Delivery methods: Racks
Zip Codes Served: 78852, 78853, 78834, 78877
Frequency: Tues`Wed`Thur`Fri`Sun
Circulation Free: 23000
Audit By: Sworn/Estimate/Non-Audited
Audit Date: 12.07.2019
Personnel: Ruben Carrillo Mazuka (Pub.); Celina Ramos (Adv. Mgr.); Jesus Maldonado (Ed.)
Main (survey) contact: Ruben Carrillo Mazuka

EL PASO

EL PASO Y MAS

Street address 1: 500 W Overland Ave
Street address 2: Ste 150
Street address state: TX
Postal code: 79901-1108
County: El Paso
Country: USA
Mailing address: 500 W. Overland Ave.
Mailing city: El Paso
Mailing state: TX
Mailing zip: 79901
Office phone: (915) 546-6300
Office fax: (915) 546-6284
Advertising phone: (915) 542-6066
Editorial phone: (915) 546-6149
Advertising e-mail: jmolina@elpasotimes.com
Editorial e-mail: bmoore@elpasotimes.com
Website: http://www.elpasotimes.com/
Frequency: Sun
Circulation Free: 72750
Audit By: AAM
Audit Date: 30.09.2017
Personnel: Sergio H. Salinas (CEO/President & Publisher); Malena Field (Dir., HR); Cecilia Uebel (Senior VP of Advertising and Marketing); Jim Weddell (VP of Online/Digital); Phillip Cortez (Mktg. Dir.); Jim Dove (Circ. Dir.); Craig Pogorzelski (Circ. Mgr., City Home Delivery); Randy Waldrop (Circ. Mgr., Transportation); Ramon Bracamontes (Bus. Ed.); Armando V. Durazo (City/Metro Ed.); Carlita Costello (Design Ed.); Charlie Edgren (Editorial Page Ed.); Melissa Martinez (Features Ed.); Mario Ontiveros (Online Sales Mgr.); Paz Garcia (Information Technolgy Dir.); Patsy Hernandez (VP of Production); Margaret Gallardo (Sports Editor); Robert Moore (Ed.)
Parent company: Gannett - USA Today Network
Main (survey) contact: Sal Hernandez, Jr.

ELIZABETH

LA VOZ

Street address 1: PO Box 899
Street address state: NJ
Postal code: 07207-0899
County: Union
Country: USA
Mailing address: PO Box 899
Mailing city: Elizabeth
Mailing state: NJ
Mailing zip: 07207-0899
Office phone: (908) 352-6654
Office fax: (908) 352-9735
General e-mail: lavoznj@aol.com
Website: www.lavoznj.com
Advertising (open inch rate): Open inch rate $12.40
Mechanical specifications: Type page 10 1/8 x 16; E - 7 cols, 1 3/8, 1/6 between; A - 7 cols, 1 3/8, 1/6 between; C - 7 cols, 1 3/8, 1/6 between.
Other Type of Frequency: 2 x Mthly
Circulation Free: 38000
Audit By: Sworn/Estimate/Non-Audited
Audit Date: 12.07.2019
Hardware: APP/Mac
Software: Adobe/PageMaker, QPS/QuarkXPress.
Personnel: Abel Berry (Pub.); Daniel Garcia (Adv. Mgr.)
Main (survey) contact: Abel Berry

ESCONDIDO

HISPANOS UNIDOS

Street address 1: 411 W 9th Ave
Street address state: CA
Postal code: 92025-5034
County: San Diego
Country: USA
Mailing address: PO Box 462016
Mailing city: Escondido
Mailing state: CA
Mailing zip: 92046-2016
Office phone: (760) 740-9561
Office fax: (760) 737-3035
General e-mail: info@hispanosnews.com
Website: www.hispanosnews.com
Advertising (open inch rate): Open inch rate $24.00
Mechanical specifications: Type page 11 3/4 x 21; E - 6 cols, 1.828, 0.1564 between; A - 6 cols, 1.828, 0.1564 between; C - 6 cols, 1.828, 0.1564 between.
Frequency: Fri
Circulation Free: 26000
Audit By: Sworn/Estimate/Non-Audited
Audit Date: 12.07.2019
Hardware: PC
Software: QPS/QuarkXPress 4.2.
Personnel: Ana Hannagan (Pub.); Jaime A. Castaneda (Prodn. Mgr.)
Main (survey) contact: Ana Hannagan

ESPANOLA

RIO GRANDE SUN

Street address 1: 123 N Railroad Ave
Street address state: NM
Postal code: 87532-2627
County: Rio Arriba
Country: USA
Mailing address: PO Box 790
Mailing city: Espanola
Mailing state: NM
Mailing zip: 87532-0790
Office phone: (505) 753-2126
Office fax: (505) 753-2140
Advertising phone: 505-753-2126
Advertising fax: 505-753-2140
General e-mail: rgsun@cybermesa.com
Advertising e-mail: rgsunads@cybermesa.com
Editorial e-mail: rgsun@cybermesa.com
Website: www.riograndesun.com
Year newspaper established: 1956
Advertising (open inch rate): Open inch rate $10.80
Mechanical specifications: SAU
Delivery methods: Mail`Newsstand`Racks
Zip Codes Served: 87532, 87520, 87567, 87528, 87575, 87501, 87505, 87544, 87510, 87511, 87515, 87518, 87522, 87012, 87527, 87530, 87531, 87533, 87537, 87539, 87549, 87521, 87551, 87553, 87566, 87578, 87579, 87581, 87582, 87577, 87017, 87029, 87046, 87064, 87548
Digital Platform - Mobile: Apple
Digital Platform - Tablet: Apple iOS
Frequency: Thur
Circulation Paid: 10000
Audit By: Sworn/Estimate/Non-Audited
Audit Date: 12.07.2019
Personnel: Maria Garcia (General Manager); Robert Trapp (Publisher)
Main (survey) contact: Maria Garcia

EVANSTON

EL CHICAGO HISPANO

Street address 1: 701 Main St.
Street address state: IL
Postal code: 60202
Mailing address: PO Box 268722
Mailing city: Chicago
Mailing state: IL
Mailing zip: 60626
Office phone: (312) 593-2557
Advertising phone: (773) 942-7410
Editorial phone: (312) 593-2557
General e-mail: editor@elchicagohispano.com
Advertising e-mail: acano@elchicagohispano.com
Website: elchicagohispano.com
Year newspaper established: 2010
Personnel: Alejandra Cano (Sales); Kelly Yelmene (Mktg.)
Main (survey) contact: Editor Contact; Alejandra Cano

FAYETTEVILLE

LA PRENSA LIBRE

Street address 1: 212 N East Ave
Street address state: AR
Postal code: 72701-5225
County: Washington
Country: USA
Office phone: (479) 530-9313
Office fax: (479) 684-5570
Advertising fax: (479) 251-8206
General e-mail: acueva@nwaonline.com
Advertising e-mail: acueva@nwaonline.com
Editorial e-mail: lpleditor@nwaonline.com
Website: www.laprensanwa.com
Year newspaper established: 1996
Advertising (open inch rate): Open inch rate $10.50
Delivery methods: Newsstand`Racks
Zip Codes Served: 72767, 72765, 72701, 72703, 72704, 72756, 72758, 72712
Digital Platform - Mobile: Apple
Frequency: Thur
Circulation Free: 15000
Audit By: Sworn/Estimate/Non-Audited
Audit Date: 12.07.2019
Personnel: Jenser Morales (Ed.); Ariana Cisneros (Acct. Exec.); Hector Cueva (Gen. Mgr.)
Parent company: Northwest Arkansas Newspapers LLC; WEHCO Media, Inc.
Main (survey) contact: Ariana Cisneros; Jenser Morales

FORT LAUDERDALE

EL HERALDO DE BROWARD

Street address 1: 1975 E Sunrise Blvd
Street address 2: Ste 540

Hispanic Newspapers in the U.S.

Street address state: FL
Postal code: 33304-1453
County: Broward
Country: USA
Mailing address: 2600 NE 9th St
Mailing city: Fort Lauderdale
Mailing state: FL
Mailing zip: 33304-3610
Office phone: (954) 527-0627
Office fax: (954) 792-7402
General e-mail: elheralbroward@aol.com
Website: www.elheraldo.com
Advertising (open inch rate): Open inch rate $23.00
Mechanical specifications: Type page 10 1/2 x 13; E - 5 cols, 2 1/16, 1/16 between; A - 5 cols, 2 1/16, 1/16 between; C - 5 cols, 2 1/16, 1/16 between.
Audit By: Sworn/Estimate/Non-Audited
Audit Date: 12.07.2019
Hardware: APP/Power Mac 7200, APP/iMac
Software: QPS/QuarkXPress 3.2.
Personnel: Elaine Vasquez (Pub.); Elaine Miceli-Vasquez (Ed.); Lisa Micelli (Prodn. Mgr.)
Main (survey) contact: Erwin M. Vasquez

EL NOTICIERO

Street address 1: PO Box 480729
Street address state: FL
Postal code: 33348-0729
County: Broward
Country: USA
Mailing address: PO Box 480729
Mailing city: Fort Lauderdale
Mailing state: FL
Mailing zip: 33348-0729
Office phone: (954) 766-4492
Office fax: (954) 766-4492
General e-mail: elnoti2@aol.com
Advertising (open inch rate): Open inch rate $12.00
Mechanical specifications: Type page 11 x 17; E - 5 cols, 2, 3/16 between; A - 5 cols, 2, 3/16 between; C - 5 cols, 2, 3/16 between.
Delivery methods: Mail`Newsstand`Carrier`Racks
Other Type of Frequency: Every other Week
Circulation Free: 15000
Audit By: Sworn/Estimate/Non-Audited
Audit Date: 12.07.2019
Hardware: 4-APP/Mac G4, APP/Mac 7500, APP/Mac Performa 6220
Software: Adobe/PageMaker 6.5, Adobe/Photoshop 5.0.
Personnel: Lilia Mantilla (Ed.); Rodrigo Martinez (Director)
Main (survey) contact: Rodrigo Martinez

FORT WORTH

LA ESTRELLA

Street address 1: 400 W 7th St
Street address state: TX
Postal code: 76102-4701
County: Tarrant
Country: USA
Mailing address: 400 W 7th St
Mailing city: Fort Worth
Mailing state: TX
Mailing zip: 76102-4701
Office phone: (817) 390-7180
Office fax: (817) 390-7280
General e-mail: jaramos@laestrelladigital.com
Website: www.laestrelladigital.com
Advertising (open inch rate): Open inch rate $30.12
Mechanical specifications: Type page 13 1/2 x 22; E - 6 cols, 2, 1/6 between; A - 6 cols, 2, 1/6 between; C - 10 cols, 1 1/4, between.
Zip Codes Served: 76102
Frequency: Sat
Circulation Free: 123150
Audit By: AAM
Audit Date: 30.06.2015
Hardware: PC
Presses: G/Metroliner
Software: QPS/QuarkXPress 3.32.
Personnel: Baker Haymes (Adv. Mgr.); Juan Antonio Ramos (Ed.); Raul Caballero (Mng. Ed.)
Main (survey) contact: Baker Haymes

PANORAMA DE NUEVOS HORIZONTES

Street address 1: 3501 Williams Rd
Street address state: TX
Postal code: 76116-7029
County: Tarrant
Country: USA
Mailing address: 3501 Williams Rd
Mailing city: Fort Worth
Mailing state: TX
Mailing zip: 76116-7029
Website: www.panorama-news.com
Year newspaper established: 2002
Advertising (open inch rate): N/A
Frequency: Sat
Circulation Paid: 0
Circulation Free: 15450
Audit By: CVC
Audit Date: 31.12.2014
Personnel: Julia Martinez-Smit
Main (survey) contact: Julie Martinez-Smit

FRESNO

VIDA EN EL VALLE

Street address 1: 1626 E St
Street address state: CA
Postal code: 93786
County: Fresno
Country: USA
Mailing address: 1626 E St
Mailing city: Fresno
Mailing state: CA
Mailing zip: 93786
Office phone: (559) 441-6780
Office fax: (559) 441-6790
Advertising phone: (559) 441-6769
Advertising fax: (559) 441-6790
Editorial phone: (559) 441-6781
Editorial fax: (559) 441-6790
General e-mail: aguajardo@vidaenelvalle.com
Advertising e-mail: bgutierrez@vidaenelvalle.com
Editorial e-mail: jesparza@vidaenelvalle.com
Website: vidaenelvalle.com
Year newspaper established: 1990
Advertising (open inch rate): 46.90 National/36.50 Local retail
Mechanical specifications: Braodsheet
Delivery methods: Carrier`Racks
Frequency: Wed
Circulation Free: 35584
Audit By: AAM
Audit Date: 31.03.2019
Personnel: Monica Stevens (Pub.); Morgie Rice (Office Mgr.); Juan Esparza Loera (Ed.); Anna Ramseier (Prodn. Mgr.); John Coakley (Vp, Sales/Mktg)
Parent company: The McClatchy Company
Main (survey) contact: Juan Esparza Loera; John Coakley

GARDEN CITY

LA SEMANA EN EL SUROESTE DE KANSAS

Street address 1: 310 N 7th St
Street address state: KS
Postal code: 67846-5521
County: Finney
Country: USA
Mailing address: PO Box 958
Mailing city: Garden City
Mailing state: KS
Mailing zip: 67846-0958
Office phone: (620) 275-8500
Office fax: (620) 275-5165
General e-mail: lasemana@gctelegram.com
Website: www.gctelegram.com
Advertising (open inch rate): Open inch rate $5.28
Frequency: Fri
Circulation Free: 3000
Audit By: Sworn/Estimate/Non-Audited
Audit Date: 12.07.2019
Hardware: APP/Mac.
Personnel: Dena Sattler (Pub.); Charity Ochs (Adv. Mgr.); Jeremy Banwell (Circ. Mgr.); Brett Riggs (Mng. Ed.)
Main (survey) contact: Dena Sattler

GETTYSBURG

EL DAIRIO LATINO

Street address 1: 1570 Fairfield Rd
Street address state: PA
Postal code: 17325-7252
County: Adams
Country: USA
Mailing address: PO Box 3669
Mailing city: Gettysburg
Mailing state: PA
Mailing zip: 17325-0669

GOSHEN

EL PUENTE

Street address 1: 1906 W Clinton St
Street address state: IN
Postal code: 46526-1618
County: Elkhart
Country: USA
Mailing address: PO Box 553
Mailing city: Goshen
Mailing state: IN
Mailing zip: 46527-0553
Office phone: (574) 533-9082
Office fax: (574) 537-0552
Advertising phone: (574) 533-9082
Editorial phone: (574) 533-9082
General e-mail: mail@webelpuente.com
Advertising e-mail: design@webelpuente.com
Editorial e-mail: mail@webelpuente.com
Website: www.webelpuente.com
Year newspaper established: 1992
Advertising (open inch rate): Open inch rate $17.00
Mechanical specifications: Mini Tabloid format. Printable area is 9.88 W x 9.6 H. Four-column format. One-column ads are 2.35 inches wide Two-column ads are 4.85 inches wide. Three-column ads are 7.4 inches wide. Four-column ads are 9.88 inches wide. Color costs an additional $100 for Full Color.
Delivery methods: Newsstand`Racks
Zip Codes Served: 46563 - 46802 (34 Zip Codes total.)
Frequency: Tues
Other Type of Frequency: 1st & 3rd Tuesday of the month (24 yearly issues)
Circulation Free: 9000
Audit By: Sworn/Estimate/Non-Audited
Audit Date: 12.07.2019
Hardware: APP/Mac/PC
Software: Adobe/PageMaker 6.0, Adobe/Photoshop. Quarks.
Note: The First Hispanic Newspaper in Indiana.
Personnel: Yizzar Prieto (Production Director. Marketing.); Jimmer Prieto (Editor); Zulma Prieto (Editor)
Parent company: El Puente LLC
Main (survey) contact: Zulma Prieto

GUAYNABO

PERIODICO METRO PUERTO RICO

Street address 1: Carazo St
Street address state: PR
Postal code: 969
County: Guaynabo
Country: USA
Office phone: (787)705-0920
Office fax: (787)705-0926
Advertising e-mail: multimedia@metro.pr
Editorial e-mail: multimedia@metro.pr
Website: www.metro.pr
Delivery methods: Newsstand`Racks
Frequency: Mon`Tues`Wed`Thur`Fri
Circulation Free: 83793
Audit By: CAC
Audit Date: 31.12.2017

PRIMERA HORA

Street address 1: A 16 Genoa Street
Street address 2: Extension Villa Caparra
Street address state: PR
Postal code: 965
County: Guaynabo
Country: Puerto Rico
Mailing address: PO Box 2009
Mailing city: Catano
Mailing state: PR
Mailing zip: 00963-2009
Office phone: 787-641-4475
Office fax: 787-641-4473
Advertising phone: 787-641-4469
Advertising fax: 787-641-4470
Website: http://www.primerahora.com
Frequency: Mon`Tues`Wed`Thur`Fri`Sat
Circulation Paid: 152295
Audit By: AAM
Audit Date: 31.12.2018
Parent company: GFR MEDIA, LLC.
Main (survey) contact: Carlos Nido

HARTFORD

EXPRESO LATINO

Street address 1: 293 Franklin Ave
Street address state: CT
Postal code: 06114
Country: USA
Mailing address: 293 Franklin Ave
Mailing city: Hartford
Mailing state: CT
Mailing zip: 06114
Website: expresolatino.net
Advertising (open inch rate): Open inch rate $15.95
Mechanical specifications: Type page 9 3/16 x 11.
Frequency: Fri
Circulation Free: 8322
Audit By: CAC
Audit Date: 30.09.2008
Personnel: Expresso Latino (Pub.)
Main (survey) contact: Expresso Latino

HEMPSTEAD

LA TRIBUNA HISPANA-USA

Street address 1: 48 Main St
Street address 2: Fl 2
Street address state: NY
Postal code: 11550-4052
County: Nassau
Country: USA
Mailing address: PO Box 186
Mailing city: Hempstead
Mailing state: NY
Mailing zip: 11551-0186
Office phone: (516) 486-6457
Office fax: (866) 215-5982
General e-mail: editorial@tribunahispana.com
Website: www.tribunahispanausa.com
Advertising (open inch rate): Open inch rate $10.95
Mechanical specifications: Type page 13 3/4 x 13 3/4; E - 6 cols, 1 1/2, 1/4 between; A - 6 cols, 1 1/2, 1/4 between; C - 8 cols, between.
Delivery methods: Racks
Digital Platform - Mobile: Apple`Android`Windows
Digital Platform - Tablet: Apple iOS`Android`Windows 7`Blackberry Tablet OS`Kindle`Nook`Kindle Fire
Frequency: Wed
Circulation Free: 49000
Audit By: Sworn/Estimate/Non-Audited
Audit Date: 12.07.2019
Editions Count: 6
Edition Names with Circ figures: 6 total ÃƒÂ‚Â—La Tribuna Hispana-Brooklyn Edition (10,000); La Tribuna Hispana-Nassau Edition (10,000); La Tribuna Hispana-New York Edition (10,000); La Tribuna Hispana-

New Jersey Edition (10,000); La Tribuna Hispana-Queens Edition (10,000); La Tribuna Hispan
Personnel: Dora Escobar (Gen. Mgr.); Emilio A. Ruiz (Adv. Mgr.); Luis Aguilar (Ed.)
Main (survey) contact: Luis Aguilar

HOUSTON

ENFOQUE DEPORTIVO

Street address 1: 13227 Noblecrest Dr
Street address state: TX
Postal code: 77041-1871
County: Harris
Country: USA
Mailing address: 13227 Noblecrest Dr
Mailing city: Houston
Mailing state: TX
Mailing zip: 77041-1871
Office phone: (713) 785-7191
Office fax: (832) 467-9792
General e-mail: enfoque@sbcglobal.net
Website: www.enfoquedeportivo.com
Advertising (open inch rate): Open inch rate $17.00
Mechanical specifications: Type page 10 1/2 x 14; E - 5 cols, 2, 1/8 between.
Zip Codes Served: 77057
Audit By: Sworn/Estimate/Non-Audited
Audit Date: 12.07.2019
Personnel: William Jose Reyes (Pub.); Juana Reyes (Adv. Mgr.); Maritza Reyes (Ed.)
Main (survey) contact: William Jose Reyes

LA SUBASTA

Street address 1: 6120 Tarnef Dr
Street address 2: Ste 110
Street address state: TX
Postal code: 77074-3754
County: Harris
Country: USA
Mailing address: 6120 Tarnef Dr Ste 110
Mailing city: Houston
Mailing state: TX
Mailing zip: 77074-3754
Office phone: (713) 772-8900
Office fax: (713) 772-8999
Website: www.eldiausa.com
Advertising (open inch rate): Open inch rate $1.40
Audit By: Sworn/Estimate/Non-Audited
Audit Date: 12.07.2019
Personnel: German Arango (Pub.)
Main (survey) contact: German Arango

LA VOZ DE HOUSTON

Street address 1: 4747 Southwest Fwy
Street address state: TX
Postal code: 77027-6901
County: Harris
Country: USA
Mailing address: 4747 Southwest Fwy
Mailing city: Houston
Mailing state: TX
Mailing zip: 77027-6901
Office phone: (713) 362-8100
Office fax: (713) 362-8630
General e-mail: aurora.losada@chron.com
Website: www.chron.com
Advertising (open inch rate): Open inch rate $84.00
Mechanical specifications: Type page 12 x 21; E - 6 cols, 1 7/8, 1/8 between; A - 6 cols, 1 7/8, 1/8 between; C - 10 cols, 1 1/4, 1/16 between.
Frequency: Wed
Circulation Free: 271040
Audit By: AAM
Audit Date: 30.09.2018
Hardware: Software Ã‚Â— QPS/QuarkXPress 4.0.
Personnel: Loida Ruiz (Mgr.); Craig Hurluy (Adv. Sales Mgr.); Aurora Losada (Ed.)
Main (survey) contact: Aurora Losada

MERCADO LATINO

Street address 1: 5327 Aldine Mail Route Rd
Street address state: TX
Postal code: 77039-4919
County: Harris
Country: USA
Mailing address: 5327 Aldine Mail Rd
Mailing city: Houston
Mailing state: TX
Mailing zip: 77039-4919
Office phone: (281) 449-9945
Office fax: (713) 977-1188
General e-mail: nenewsroom@aol.com
Website: www.nenewsroom.com
Advertising (open inch rate): Open inch rate $10.00
Mechanical specifications: Type page 10 1/4 x 13; E - 6 cols, 2 1/8, 1/8 between; A - 7 cols, 1 3/4, 1/8 between; C - 9 cols, 1 1/8, 1/8 between.
Delivery methods: Mail`Newsstand`Carrier`Racks
Zip Codes Served: 7 703 977 093 770 600 000 000 000
Frequency: Tues
Circulation Free: 30000
Audit By: Sworn/Estimate/Non-Audited
Audit Date: 12.07.2019
Hardware: APP/Mac/PC
Presses: 5 unit King web press Two 4 color heidelberg sheet presses
Software: Adobe/PageMaker 6.5/photoshop/indesign
Personnel: Gil Hoffman (Editor/PUblisher)
Parent company: Grafikpress Corp.
Main (survey) contact: Gil Hoffman

PERIODICO BUENA SUERTE - HOUSTON

Street address 1: 7324 Southwest Fwy
Street address 2: Ste 1720
Street address state: TX
Postal code: 77074-2058
County: Harris
Country: USA
Mailing address: 7324 Southwest Fwy Ste 1720
Mailing city: Houston
Mailing state: TX
Mailing zip: 77074-2058
Office phone: 713-272-0101
Advertising e-mail: sales@buenasuerte.com
Website: www.buenasuerte.com
Year newspaper established: 1986
Advertising (open inch rate): Open inch rate $13.00
Delivery methods: Newsstand`Racks
Zip Codes Served: 77002 77036 77055 77074 77036 77055 77478
Digital Platform - Mobile: Apple`Android`Windows
Digital Platform - Tablet: Apple iOS`Android`Windows 7`Kindle Fire
Frequency: Tues`Wed`Thur`Fri
Circulation Free: 84918
Audit By: Sworn/Estimate/Non-Audited
Audit Date: 12.07.2019
Personnel: Emilio Martinez
Main (survey) contact: Emilio Martinez

HYATTSVILLE

EL PREGONERO

Street address 1: 5001 Eastern Ave
Street address state: MD
Postal code: 20782-3447
County: Prince Georges
Country: USA
Mailing address: PO Box 4464
Mailing city: Washington
Mailing state: DC
Mailing zip: 20017-0464
Office phone: (202) 281-2404
Office fax: (202) 281-2448
Advertising phone: (202) 281-2406
Editorial phone: (202) 281-2442
General e-mail: rafael@elpreg.org
Advertising e-mail: irieska@elpreg.org
Editorial e-mail: rafael@elpreg.org
Website: elpreg.org
Year newspaper established: 1977
Advertising (open inch rate): Open inch rate $19.00
Mechanical specifications: Type page 10 1/4 x 13 1/2; E - 5 cols, 1 5/6, 1/6 between; A - 5 cols, 1/6 between; C - 7 cols, 1 1/3, 1/6 between.
Delivery methods: Newsstand`Carrier
Frequency: Thur
Circulation Free: 24993
Audit By: AAM
Audit Date: 30.06.2018
Hardware: 5-APP/Mac, 3-APP/Mac LaserPrinters
Software: QPS/QuarkXPress, Adobe/Photoshop, Adobe/Illustrator, Multi-Ad/Creator, Baseview/NewsEdit Pro, Class Manager/Plus.
Personnel: Rafael Roncal (Ed.); Irieska D. Caetano (Circ. Mgr.)
Main (survey) contact: Rafael Roncal

JACKSONVILLE

LA OPINION

Street address 1: 404 College Ave
Street address state: TX
Postal code: 75766-2244
County: Cherokee
Country: USA
Mailing address: 404 College Ave
Mailing city: Jacksonville
Mailing state: TX
Mailing zip: 75766-2244
Year newspaper established: 1989
Advertising (open inch rate): Open inch rate $15.00
Frequency: Other
Other Type of Frequency: Bi-Weekly (Every Other Wednesday)
Circulation Paid: 0
Circulation Free: 0
Audit By: VAC
Audit Date: 30.09.2015
Personnel: Judith Cantua
Main (survey) contact: Judith Cantua

JAMAICA

RESUMEN NEWSPAPER

Street address 1: 13842 90th Ave
Street address 2: Apt F1
Street address state: NY
Postal code: 11435-4104
County: Queens
Country: USA
Mailing address: 13842 90th Ave Apt F1
Mailing city: Jamaica
Mailing state: NY
Mailing zip: 11435-4104
Office phone: (718) 899-8603
Advertising phone: 718-424-7976
Other phone: 347-845-0888
General e-mail: rojas123@aol.com
Advertising e-mail: rojas123@aol.com
Editorial e-mail: TRACEMYMOVES@GMAIL.COM
Website: www.resumen.8m.net
Year newspaper established: 1971
Advertising (open inch rate): Open inch rate $14.00
Mechanical specifications: Type page 13 x 10 3/4; E - 4 cols, 2 1/8, 1/3 between; A - 4 cols, 2 1/8, 1/3 between; C - 4 cols, 2 1/8, 1/3 between.
Delivery methods: Carrier
Zip Codes Served: 11102, 10034, 11201, 11201, 10451
Other Type of Frequency: Daily
Circulation Paid: 8000
Circulation Free: 32000
Audit By: Sworn/Estimate/Non-Audited
Audit Date: 12.07.2019
Hardware: APP/Power Mac
Software: Adobe/PageMaker 5.6, Adobe/Paint 2.1.
Personnel: Fernando F. Rojas (Pub.); Jasmina Abril (Gen. Mgr.); Fernando J. Rojas (Ed.)
Main (survey) contact: Fernando F. Rojas

KANSAS CITY

DOS MUNDOS

Street address 1: 1701 S 55th St
Street address state: KS
Postal code: 66106-2241
County: Wyandotte
Country: USA
Mailing address: 1701 S. 55th. Street
Mailing city: Kansas City
Mailing state: KS
Mailing zip: 66106
Office phone: (816) 221-4747
Office fax: (816) 221-4894
Advertising phone: (816)221-4747
Other phone: 9130302-6656
General e-mail: newstaff@dosmundos.com
Editorial e-mail: CREYES@DOSMUNDOS.COM
Website: www.dosmundos.com
Year newspaper established: 1981
Advertising (open inch rate): Open inch rate $14.00
Mechanical specifications: Type page 13 x 21; E - 8 cols, 1 1/2, 1/4 between; A - 8 cols, 1 1/2, 1/4 between; C - 8 cols, 1 1/2, 1/4 between.
Delivery methods: Newsstand`Carrier`Racks
Digital Platform - Mobile: Apple
Frequency: Thur
Circulation Paid: 20000
Circulation Free: 7000
Audit By: Sworn/Estimate/Non-Audited
Audit Date: 12.07.2019
Hardware: PC, APP/Mac
Software: QPS/QuarkXPress, Adobe/PageMaker.
Personnel: Manuel Reyes (Pub.); Diana Raymer (Adv. Mgr.); Clara Reyes (Ed.)
Main (survey) contact: Clara Reyes

KIRKLAND

EL MUNDO - WA

Street address 1: 11410 NE 124th St
Street address 2: # 441
Street address state: WA
Postal code: 98034-4399
County: King
Country: USA
Mailing address: 11410 NE 124th St # 441
Mailing city: Kirkland
Mailing state: WA
Mailing zip: 98034-4399
Website: www.elmundous.com
Year newspaper established: 1989
Advertising (open inch rate): Open inch rate $18.00
Mechanical specifications: Type page: 10.625 x 20; 6 columns
Frequency: Thur
Circulation Paid: 500
Circulation Free: 14113
Audit By: CVC
Audit Date: 30.06.2013
Personnel: Martha Montoya
Main (survey) contact: Martha Montoya

LAKEWOOD

FRONTERAS

Street address 1: 8312 Custer Rd SW
Street address state: WA
Postal code: 98499-2526
County: Pierce
Country: USA
Mailing address: PO Box 98801
Mailing city: Lakewood
Mailing state: WA
Mailing zip: 98496-8801
Office phone: (253) 584-1212
Office fax: (253) 581-5962
General e-mail: swarnerkm@aol.com
Year newspaper established: 2007
Advertising (open inch rate): Open inch rate $11.00
Audit By: Sworn/Estimate/Non-Audited
Audit Date: 12.07.2019

Hispanic Newspapers in the U.S.

Personnel: Bill White (Adv. Mgr.); Ken Swarner (Ed.)
Main (survey) contact: Ken Swarner

LAREDO

EL TIEMPO DE LAREDO

Street address 1: 111 Esperanza Dr
Street address state: TX
Postal code: 78041-2607
County: Webb
Country: USA
Mailing address: PO Box 2129
Mailing city: Laredo
Mailing state: TX
Mailing zip: 78044-2129
Office phone: (956) 728-2500
Office fax: (956) 724-3036
Website: www.lmtonline.com
Advertising (open inch rate): Open inch rate $30.50
Mechanical specifications: Type page 13 x 21; E - 6 cols, between; A - 6 cols, 2 1/16, between.
Audit By: Sworn/Estimate/Non-Audited
Audit Date: 12.07.2019
Hardware: APP/Mac, IBM
Software: Adobe/Photoshop, QPS/QuarkXPress.
Personnel: William B. Green (Pub.); Adriana DeVally (Gen. Mgr.); Christian Cruz (Circ. Mgr.); Melva Lavin (Ed.); Diana Fuentes (Ed.); Raul Cruz (Creative Dir.)
Parent company: Hearst Communications, Inc.
Main (survey) contact: William B. Green

LAS VEGAS

BLOQUE LATINO AMERICANO DE PRENSA EL EXITO LATIN AMERICAN PRESS

Street address 1: PO Box 12599
Street address state: NV
Postal code: 89112-0599
County: Clark
Country: USA
Mailing address: PO Box 12599
Mailing city: Las Vegas
Mailing state: NV
Mailing zip: 89112-0599
Office phone: (702) 431-1904
Office fax: (702) 431-3339
General e-mail: elexito2@cox.net
Advertising e-mail: elexito2@cox.net
Website: www.elexitolasvegas.com
Year newspaper established: 1988
Advertising (open inch rate): Open inch rate $18.00
Mechanical specifications: Page is 10"x16"; 5 cols. each col. 2" wide
Frequency: Fri
Circulation Free: 50662
Audit By: Sworn/Estimate/Non-Audited
Audit Date: 12.07.2019
Hardware: APP/Mac
Software: Adobe/PageMaker.
Personnel: Maggy Ruiz (Adv. Mgr.); Luz Delgado (Circ. Mgr.); Magaly Ruiz (Ed.); Tirso Del Pozo (Prodn. Mgr.)
Main (survey) contact: Maggy Ruiz

EL MUNDO

Street address 1: 760 N Eastern Ave
Street address 2: Ste 110
Street address state: NV
Postal code: 89101-2888
County: Clark
Country: USA
Mailing address: 760 N Eastern Ave Ste 110
Mailing city: Las Vegas
Mailing state: NV
Mailing zip: 89101-2888
Office phone: (702) 649-8553
Office fax: (702) 649-7429
General e-mail: distribution@elmundo.net
Advertising e-mail: advertising@elmundo.net
Editorial e-mail: hescobedo@elmundo.net
Website: elmundo.net
Year newspaper established: 1980
Advertising (open inch rate): Open inch rate $16.50
Mechanical specifications: Type page 10 x 16; E - 6 cols, 1 3/4, between; A - 6 cols, 1 3/4, between.
Frequency: Fri
Circulation Free: 29975
Audit By: CVC
Audit Date: 31.12.2018
Hardware: APP/Mac.
Personnel: Hilda Escobedo (Pub.); Nick Escobedo (Circ.); Flora Hernandez (Prodn. Mgr.)
Main (survey) contact: Hilda Escobedo

EL TIEMPO

Street address 1: 1111 W Bonanza Rd
Street address state: NV
Postal code: 89106-3545
County: Clark
Country: USA
Mailing address: 1111 W Bonanza Rd
Mailing city: Las Vegas
Mailing state: NV
Mailing zip: 89106-3545
Office phone: 702-383-0300
Office fax: 702-383-0402
Advertising phone: (702) 477-3846
Advertising fax: (702) 387-2981
Editorial phone: 702-387-2972
Editorial fax: 702-251-0736
Other phone: 702-387-5287
General e-mail: anahangi@reviewjournal.com
Advertising e-mail: gjurica@reviewjournal.com
Editorial e-mail: hamaya@reviewjournal.com
Website: www.eltiempov.com
Year newspaper established: 1994
Advertising (open inch rate): $71,22
Mechanical specifications: 4col (10") x 20.50"
Delivery methods: Carrier`Racks
Zip Codes Served: All
Frequency: Fri
Circulation Paid: 94128
Audit By: AAM
Audit Date: 30.06.2018
Hardware: pc and mac
Presses: Goss Newsliner
Software: Atex, NewEngin, Indesign, CS5.5
Editions Count: 50000
Personnel: Maria Cristina Matta-Caro (Pub./ Ed.); Anthony Avelleneda (Reporter); Jorge Betancourt (Graphic Des.); Eddie Corrarrubias (Sr. Account Ex.)
Main (survey) contact: Maria-Cristina Matta-Caro

EL TIEMPO

Street address 1: 1111 W Bonanza Rd
Street address state: NV
Postal code: 89106-3545
County: Clark
Country: USA
Mailing address: PO BOX 70
Mailing city: LAS VEGAS
Mailing state: NV
Mailing zip: 89125-0070
Office phone: (702) 477-3845
Advertising phone: (702) 477-3845
Editorial phone: (702) 47-3846
General e-mail: gjuricad@reviewjournal.com
Advertising e-mail: ddyer@reviewjournal.com
Editorial e-mail: mcmatta@reviewjournal.com
Website: http://www.eltiempolv.com/
Year newspaper established: 1994
Advertising (open inch rate): Full - $4,090; 1/2 - $2,105; 1/4 - $1,025; 1/8 - $525
Mechanical specifications: Full Page 10" x 20.50" 1/2 Page V 4.90" x 20.50" H 10" x 10" 1/4 page Std 4.90 x 10" 1/8 page V 4.90" x 4.875" H 10" x 2.50"
Delivery methods: Carrier`Racks
Zip Codes Served: Las Vegas Valley, Henderson, North Las Vegas,.
Digital Platform - Mobile: Apple`Android`Windows`Blackberry
Frequency: Fri
Circulation Paid: 0
Circulation Free: 51878

Audit By: CAC
Audit Date: 30.09.2014
Hardware: PC
Personnel: Maria Cristina Matta-Caro (Pub./ Ed.)
Main (survey) contact: Maria Cristina Matta-Caro

LITTLE ROCK

EL LATINO

Street address 1: 201 E Markham St
Street address 2: Fl 2
Street address state: AR
Postal code: 72201-1627
County: Pulaski
Country: USA
Mailing address: 201 East Markham, 2nd floor
Mailing city: Little Rock
Mailing state: AR
Mailing zip: 72201
Office phone: (501)-375-2985
Frequency: Thur
Circulation Paid: 7
Circulation Free: 4605
Audit By: VAC
Audit Date: 30.06.2017
Parent company: Arkansas Times Limited Partnership

LONGWOOD

LA PRENSA

Street address 1: 685 S Ronald Reagan Blvd
Street address 2: Ste 1001
Street address state: FL
Postal code: 32750-6435
County: Seminole
Country: USA
Mailing address: 685 S RONALD REAGAN BLVD STE 200
Mailing city: LONGWOOD
Mailing state: FL
Mailing zip: 32750-6435
Office phone: (407) 767-0070
Office fax: (407) 767-5478
Advertising phone: (407) 767-0070
Editorial phone: (407) 767-0070
General e-mail: dora.toro@laprensaorlando. com
Advertising e-mail: vicky.llevada@laprensaorlando.com
Editorial e-mail: jesus.deltoro@impremedia.com
Website: www.laprensafl.com
Year newspaper established: 1981
Advertising (open inch rate): 1/8 Pg $287; 1/4 Pg $575.00; 1/2 pag. $1.167.; 1 page $2,334.
Mechanical specifications: Type page 10 1/16 x 13; E - 5 cols, 1 7/8, 1/10 between; A - 5 cols, 1 7/8, 1/10 between; C - 5 cols, 1 7/8, 1/10 between.
Delivery methods: Newsstand`Carrier`Racks
Zip Codes Served: Counties in Central Florida.
Frequency: Thur
Circulation Paid: 35000
Audit By: CAC
Audit Date: 30.06.2015
Hardware: 6-APP/Mac
Software: QPS/QuarkXPress.
Personnel: Dora Casanova de Toro (Pub./CEO); Julia Torres (Office Mgr.); Adalgiza Zouain (Sales); Milly Colon (Sales); Liza Ordonez (Sales); Vicky Llevada (Calssified / Display Classifieds); Jesus del Toro (EIC)
Parent company: impreMedia LLC
Main (survey) contact: Dora Casanova de Toro
footnotes: Advertising (open inch rate): SRDS (11/19/2014)

LOS ANGELES

BELL GARDENS SUN

Street address 1: 111 S Avenue 59
Street address state: CA
Postal code: 90042-4211
County: Los Angeles
Country: USA

Office phone: (323) 341-7970
Office fax: (323) 341-7976
General e-mail: service@egpnews.com
Advertising e-mail: advertise@egpnews.com
Editorial e-mail: editorial@egpnews.com
Website: www.egpnews.com
Year newspaper established: 1945
Advertising (open inch rate): N/A
Mechanical specifications: Type page 13 x 21; 6 cols
Delivery methods: Mail`Carrier`Racks
Zip Codes Served: 90001, 90011, 90012, 90014, 90022, 90023, 90031, 90032, 90033, 90040, 90041, 90042, 90063, 90065, 91731, 91732, 91733, 91744, 91754, 91766, 91770, 91803, 91104
Frequency: Thur
Circulation Paid: 2
Circulation Free: 6973
Audit By: CVC
Audit Date: 30.09.2014
Hardware: 3-Dell/Dell Dimension 2400 Series, 5-APP/IMac 24, 4-APP/MAC G5
Software: Adobe/Illustrator CS, Adobe/InDesign CS, Microsoft/Office 2008, 4-QPS/QuarkXPress 7.0, 6-Adobe/Photoshop CS, Adobe CS3.
Personnel: Dolores Sanchez (Pub.); Jonathan M. Sanchez (Adv. Mgr.); Bianca Sanchez (Circ. Mgr.); Gloria Alvarez (Mng. Ed.); Elizabeth Chou (Prodn. Mgr.)
Main (survey) contact: Jonathan M. Sanchez

CITY TERRACE COMET

Street address 1: 111 S Avenue 59
Street address state: CA
Postal code: 90042-4211
County: Los Angeles
Country: USA
Office phone: (323) 341-7970
Office fax: (323) 341-7976
General e-mail: service@egpnews.com
Advertising e-mail: advertise@egpnews.com
Editorial e-mail: editorial@egpnews.com
Website: www.egpnews.com
Year newspaper established: 1945
Advertising (open inch rate): N/A
Mechanical specifications: Type page 13 x 21; 6 cols
Delivery methods: Mail`Carrier`Racks
Zip Codes Served: 90001, 90011, 90012, 90014, 90022, 90023, 90031, 90032, 90033, 90040, 90041, 90042, 90063, 90065, 91731, 91732, 91733, 91744, 91754, 91766, 91770, 91803, 91104
Frequency: Thur
Circulation Paid: 4
Circulation Free: 2971
Audit By: CVC
Audit Date: 30.09.2014
Hardware: 3-Dell/Dell Dimension 2400 Series, 5-APP/IMac 24, 4-APP/MAC G5
Software: Adobe/Illustrator CS, Adobe/InDesign CS, Microsoft/Office 2008, 4-QPS/QuarkXPress 7.0, 6-Adobe/Photoshop CS, Adobe CS3.
Personnel: Dolores Sanchez (Pub.); Jonathan M. Sanchez (Adv. Mgr.); Bianca Sanchez (Circ. Mgr.); Gloria Alvarez (Mng. Ed.); Elizabeth Chou (Prodn. Mgr.)
Main (survey) contact: Jonathan M. Sanchez

COMMERCE COMET

Street address 1: 111 S Avenue 59
Street address state: CA
Postal code: 90042-4211
County: Los Angeles
Country: USA
Office phone: (323) 341-7970
Office fax: (323) 341-7976
General e-mail: service@egpnews.com
Advertising e-mail: advertise@egpnews.com
Editorial e-mail: editorial@egpnews.com
Website: www.egpnews.com
Year newspaper established: 1945
Advertising (open inch rate): N/A
Mechanical specifications: Type page 13 x 21; 6 cols
Delivery methods: Carrier`Racks
Zip Codes Served: 90001, 90011, 90012, 90014, 90022, 90023, 90031, 90032, 90033, 90040, 90041, 90042, 90063, 90065, 91731, 91732,

91733, 91744, 91754, 91766, 91770, 91803, 91104
Frequency: Thur
Circulation Paid: 5
Circulation Free: 6475
Audit By: CVC
Audit Date: 30.09.2014
Hardware: 3-Dell/Dell Dimension 2400 Series, 5-APP/IMac 24, 4-APP/MAC G5
Software: Adobe/Illustrator CS, Adobe/InDesign CS, Microsoft/Office 2008, 4-QPS/QuarkXPress 7.0, 6-Adobe/Photoshop CS, Adobe CS3.
Personnel: Dolores Sanchez (Pub.); Jonathan M. Sanchez (Adv. Mgr.); Bianca Sanchez (Circ. Mgr.); Gloria Alvarez (Mng. Ed.); Elizabeth Chou (Prodn. Mgr.)
Main (survey) contact: Jonathan M. Sanchez

EASTSIDE SUN

Street address 1: 161 S Avenue 24
Street address state: CA
Postal code: 90031-2247
County: Los Angeles
Country: USA
Office phone: (323) 221-1092
Office fax: (323) 221-1096
Advertising phone: (323) 221-1090
Editorial phone: (323) 221-1092
General e-mail: service@egpnews.com
Advertising e-mail: advertise@egpnews.com
Editorial e-mail: editorial@egpnews.com
Website: www.egpnews.com
Year newspaper established: 1945
Advertising (open inch rate): N/A
Mechanical specifications: Type page 13 x 21; 6 cols
Delivery methods: Carrier`Racks
Zip Codes Served: 90001, 90011, 90012, 90014, 90022, 90023, 90031, 90032, 90033, 90040, 90041, 90042, 90063, 90065, 91731, 91732, 91733, 91744, 91754, 91766, 91770, 91803, 91104
Digital Platform - Mobile: Apple
Frequency: Thur
Circulation Paid: 131
Circulation Free: 43944
Audit By: CVC
Audit Date: 12.12.2017
Hardware: 3-Dell/Dell Dimension 2400 Series, 5-APP/IMac 24, 4-APP/MAC G5
Software: Adobe/Illustrator CS, Adobe/InDesign CS, Microsoft/Office 2008, 4-QPS/QuarkXPress 7.0, 6-Adobe/Photoshop CS, Adobe CS3.
Personnel: Dolores Sanchez (Pub.); Gloria Alvarez (Mng. Ed.); Bianca Preciado (Advertising/Office Manager)
Main (survey) contact: Dolores Sanchez

ELA BROOKLYN-BELVEDERE COMET

Street address 1: 111 S Avenue 59
Street address state: CA
Postal code: 90042-4211
County: Los Angeles
Country: USA
Office phone: (323) 341-7970
Office fax: (323) 341-7976
General e-mail: service@egpnews.com
Advertising e-mail: advertise@egpnews.com
Editorial e-mail: editorial@egpnews.com
Website: www.egpnews.com
Year newspaper established: 1945
Advertising (open inch rate): N/A
Mechanical specifications: Type page 13 x 21; 6 cols
Delivery methods: Carrier`Racks
Zip Codes Served: 90001, 90011, 90012, 90014, 90022, 90023, 90031, 90032, 90033, 90040, 90041, 90042, 90063, 90065, 91731, 91732, 91733, 91744, 91754, 91766, 91770, 91803, 91104
Frequency: Thur
Circulation Paid: 4
Circulation Free: 2971
Audit By: CVC
Audit Date: 30.09.2014
Hardware: 3-Dell/Dell Dimension 2400 Series, 5-APP/IMac 24, 4-APP/MAC G5
Software: Adobe/Illustrator CS, Adobe/InDesign CS, Microsoft/Office 2008, 4-QPS/QuarkXPress 7.0, 6-Adobe/Photoshop CS, Adobe CS3.
Personnel: Dolores Sanchez (Pub.); Jonathan M. Sanchez (Adv. Mgr.); Bianca Sanchez (Circ. Mgr.); Gloria Alvarez (Mng. Ed.); Elizabeth Chou (Prodn. Mgr.)
Main (survey) contact: Jonathan M. Sanchez

EXCELSIOR LOS ANGELES

Street address 1: 523 N Grand Ave
Street address state: CA
Postal code: 90012-2149
County: Los Angeles
Country: USA
Mailing address: 523 N GRAND AVE
Mailing city: SANTA ANA
Mailing state: CA
Mailing zip: 92701-4345
Office phone: (714) 796-4300
Office fax: (714) 796-4316
Advertising fax: (714) 796-4316
Editorial fax: (714) 796-4319
General e-mail: adesantos@ocregister.com
Advertising e-mail: excelsiorads@ocregister.com
Website: www.ocexcelsior.com
Advertising (open inch rate): Open inch rate $48.78
Zip Codes Served: Orange County
Frequency: Fri
Circulation Free: 52529
Audit By: Sworn/Estimate/Non-Audited
Audit Date: 12.07.2019
Personnel: Carlos Aviles (Pub.); Angelica De Santos; Trinidad Verduzco (Ed.)
Parent company: Southern California News Group
Main (survey) contact: Carlos Aviles

HOY FIN DE SEMANA

Street address 1: 202 W 1st St
Street address state: CA
Postal code: 90012-4299
County: Los Angeles
Country: USA
Advertising phone: (213) 237-3453
Advertising e-mail: hcabral@hoyllc.com
Website: www.vivalohoy.com
Frequency: Sat
Circulation Free: 813384
Audit By: CAC
Audit Date: 30.09.2016
Personnel: Hector Cabral (Adv. Dir.); Ronaldo Moran (Pub.); Deborah Albright (Division Mgr.)
Parent company: Tribune Publishing, Inc.
Main (survey) contact: Hector Cabral

HOY LLC

Street address 1: 145 S Spring St
Street address 2: Fl 2
Street address state: CA
Postal code: 90012-4053
County: Los Angeles
Country: USA
Office phone: (213) 237-4388
Advertising phone: (213) 237-3453
Editorial phone: (213) 237-3374
General e-mail: amaciel@hoyllc.com
Advertising e-mail: hcabral@hoyllc.com
Editorial e-mail: jmaciel@vivelohoy.com
Website: www.hoylosangeles.com
Year newspaper established: 2004
Delivery methods: Mail`Racks
Zip Codes Served: 90000
Digital Platform - Mobile: Apple`Android
Digital Platform - Tablet: Apple iOS
Frequency: Mon`Fri`Sat
Other Type of Frequency: weekly
Circulation Free: 1000400
Audit By: Sworn/Estimate/Non-Audited
Audit Date: 12.07.2019
Editions Count: 5
Edition Names with Circ figures: Hoy (Mon and Fri) and 3 Hoy Fin de Semana (Weekend edition on Saturdays)
Note: Hoy is published Mo and Fr and Hoy Fin de Semana (weekend edition) is published on Saturday.
Personnel: John Trainor (Gen. Mgr); Michael Roenna (Sales Director); Fernando Diaz (Managing Editor); Kim Benz (Director of Sales Strategy); Roaldo Moran (General Manager Hoy Los Angeles); Alejandro Maciel (Director Editorial Hoy/ Los Angeles); Javier T. Calle (Editor Adjunto Hoy/ Los Angeles)
Parent company: Tribune Media Group; Tribune Publishing, Inc.; Los Angeles Times Media Group
Main (survey) contact: Javier T. Calle

HOY LOS ANGELES

Street address 1: 202 W 1st St
Street address state: CA
Postal code: 90012-4299
County: Los Angeles
Country: USA
Advertising phone: (213) 237-3453
Advertising e-mail: hcabral@hoyllc.com
Website: http://www.hoylosangeles.com
Frequency: Mon`Fri
Circulation Free: 130813
Audit By: CAC
Audit Date: 30.09.2018
Personnel: Hector Cabral (Adv. Dir.); Deborah Albright (Division Mgr.); Ronaldo Moran (Pub.)
Parent company: Tribune Publishing, Inc.
Main (survey) contact: Hector Cabral

LA OPINION - CONTIGO

Street address 1: 700 S Flower St
Street address state: CA
Postal code: 90017-4101
County: Los Angeles
Country: USA
Frequency: Mon`Wed`Thur`Fri`Sat`Sun
Circulation Paid: 0
Circulation Free: 581129
Audit By: AAM
Audit Date: 31.03.2015
Personnel: Patricia Prieto (Adv. Dir.); Damian Mazzotta (Gen. Mgr,); Greg Hatch (Circ. Dir.)
Parent company: impreMedia LLC
Main (survey) contact: Patricia Prieto

LA PRENSA DE LOS ANGELES

Street address 1: 5554 Carlton Way
Street address 2: Apt 4
Street address state: CA
Postal code: 90028-6847
County: Los Angeles
Country: USA
Office phone: (323) 572-0106
Other phone: 323-289-5067
General e-mail: laprensa@laprensadelosangeles.com
Advertising e-mail: sales@laprensadelosangeles.com
Editorial e-mail: comentarios@laprensadelosangeles.com
Website: www.laprensadelosangeles.com
Year newspaper established: 1999
Advertising (open inch rate): $75 1/4 page black and white (not sold by the inch)
Delivery methods: Newsstand`Racks
Frequency: Sat
Other Type of Frequency: once a month
Circulation Paid: 10000
Circulation Free: 30000
Audit By: Sworn/Estimate/Non-Audited
Audit Date: 12.07.2019
Personnel: Carlos Groppa (Ed.)
Main (survey) contact: Carlos Groppa

MEXICAN AMERICAN SUN

Street address 1: 111 S Avenue 59
Street address state: CA
Postal code: 90042-4211
County: Los Angeles
Country: USA
Mailing address: 111 S Avenue 59
Mailing city: Los Angeles
Mailing state: CA
Mailing zip: 90042-4211
Office phone: (323) 341-7970
Office fax: (323) 341-7976
General e-mail: service@egpnews.com
Advertising e-mail: advertise@egpnews.com
Editorial e-mail: editorial@egpnews.com
Website: www.egpnews.com
Year newspaper established: 1945
Advertising (open inch rate): N/A
Mechanical specifications: Type page 13 x 21; 6 cols
Delivery methods: Mail`Racks
Zip Codes Served: 90001, 90011, 90012, 90014, 90022, 90023, 90031, 90032, 90033, 90040, 90041, 90042, 90063, 90065, 91731, 91732, 91733, 91744, 91754, 91766, 91770, 91803, 91104
Frequency: Thur
Circulation Paid: 186
Circulation Free: 15789
Audit By: CVC
Audit Date: 30.09.2014
Hardware: 3-Dell/Dell Dimension 2400 Series, 5-APP/IMac 24, 4-APP/MAC G5
Software: Adobe/Illustrator CS, Adobe/InDesign CS, Microsoft/Office 2008, 4-QPS/QuarkXPress 7.0, 6-Adobe/Photoshop CS, Adobe CS3.
Personnel: Dolores Sanchez (Pub.); Jonathan M. Sanchez (Adv. Mgr.); Bianca Sanchez (Circ. Mgr.); Gloria Alvarez (Mng. Ed.); Elizabeth Chou (Prodn. Mgr.)
Main (survey) contact: Jonathan M. Sanchez

MONTEBELLO COMET

Street address 1: 111 S Avenue 59
Street address state: CA
Postal code: 90042-4211
County: Los Angeles
Country: USA
Mailing address: 111 S Avenue 59
Mailing city: Los Angeles
Mailing state: CA
Mailing zip: 90042-4211
Office phone: (323) 341-7970
Office fax: (323) 341-7976
General e-mail: service@egpnews.com
Advertising e-mail: advertise@egpnews.com
Editorial e-mail: editorial@egpnews.com
Website: www.egpnews.com
Year newspaper established: 1945
Advertising (open inch rate): N/A
Mechanical specifications: Type page 13 x 21; 6 cols
Delivery methods: Mail`Carrier`Racks
Zip Codes Served: 90001, 90011, 90012, 90014, 90022, 90023, 90031, 90032, 90033, 90040, 90041, 90042, 90063, 90065, 91731, 91732, 91733, 91744, 91754, 91766, 91770, 91803, 91104
Frequency: Thur
Circulation Paid: 4
Circulation Free: 16971
Audit By: CVC
Audit Date: 30.09.2014
Hardware: 3-Dell/Dell Dimension 2400 Series, 5-APP/IMac 24, 4-APP/MAC G5
Software: Adobe/Illustrator CS, Adobe/InDesign CS, Microsoft/Office 2008, 4-QPS/QuarkXPress 7.0, 6-Adobe/Photoshop CS, Adobe CS3.
Personnel: Dolores Sanchez (Pub.); Jonathan M. Sanchez (Adv. Mgr.); Bianca Sanchez (Circ. Mgr.); Gloria Alvarez (Mng. Ed.); Elizabeth Chou (Prodn. Mgr.)
Main (survey) contact: Jonathan M. Sanchez

MONTEREY PARK COMET

Street address 1: 111 S Avenue 59
Street address state: CA
Postal code: 90042-4211
County: Los Angeles
Country: USA
Mailing address: 111 S Avenue 59
Mailing city: Los Angeles
Mailing state: CA
Mailing zip: 90042-4211
Office phone: (323) 341-7970
Office fax: (323) 341-7976
General e-mail: service@egpnews.com
Advertising e-mail: advertise@egpnews.com
Editorial e-mail: editorial@egpnews.com
Website: www.egpnews.com
Year newspaper established: 1945
Advertising (open inch rate): N/A
Mechanical specifications: Type page 13 x 21; 6 cols

Hispanic Newspapers in the U.S.

Delivery methods: Mail`Carrier`Racks
Zip Codes Served: 90001, 90011, 90012, 90014, 90022, 90023, 90031, 90032, 90033, 90040, 90041, 90042, 90063, 90065, 91731, 91732, 91733, 91744, 91754, 91766, 91770, 91803, 91104
Frequency: Thur
Circulation Paid: 4
Circulation Free: 6971
Audit By: CVC
Audit Date: 30.09.2014
Hardware: 3-Dell/Dell Dimension 2400 Series, 5-APP/IMac 24, 4-APP/MAC G5
Software: Adobe/Illustrator CS, Adobe/InDesign CS, Microsoft/Office 2008, 4-QPS/QuarkXPress 7.0, 6-Adobe/Photoshop CS, Adobe CS3.
Personnel: Dolores Sanchez (Pub.); Jonathan M. Sanchez (Adv. Mgr.); Bianca Sanchez (Circ. Mgr.); Gloria Alvarez (Mng. Ed.); Elizabeth Chou (Prodn. Mgr.)
Main (survey) contact: Jonathan M. Sanchez

NORTHEAST SUN

Street address 1: 111 S Avenue 59
Street address state: CA
Postal code: 90042-4211
County: Los Angeles
Country: USA
Office phone: (323) 341-7970
Office fax: (323) 341-7976
General e-mail: service@egpnews.com
Advertising e-mail: advertise@egpnews.com
Editorial e-mail: editorial@egpnews.com
Website: www.egpnews.com
Year newspaper established: 1945
Advertising (open inch rate): N/A
Mechanical specifications: Type page 13 x 21; 6 cols
Delivery methods: Mail`Carrier`Racks
Zip Codes Served: 90001, 90011, 90012, 90014, 90022, 90023, 90031, 90032, 90033, 90040, 90041, 90042, 90063, 90065, 91731, 91732, 91733, 91744, 91754, 91766, 91770, 91803, 91104
Frequency: Thur
Circulation Paid: 10
Circulation Free: 18465
Audit By: CVC
Audit Date: 30.09.2014
Hardware: 3-Dell/Dell Dimension 2400 Series, 5-APP/IMac 24, 4-APP/MAC G5
Software: Adobe/Illustrator CS, Adobe/InDesign CS, Microsoft/Office 2008, 4-QPS/QuarkXPress 7.0, 6-Adobe/Photoshop CS, Adobe CS3.
Personnel: Dolores Sanchez (Pub.); Jonathan M. Sanchez (Adv. Mgr.); Bianca Sanchez (Circ. Mgr.); Gloria Alvarez (Mng. Ed.); Elizabeth Chou (Prodn. Mgr.)
Parent company: Postmedia Network Inc.
Main (survey) contact: Jonathan M. Sanchez

VERNON SUN

Street address 1: 111 S Avenue 59
Street address state: CA
Postal code: 90042-4211
County: Los Angeles
Country: USA
Office phone: (323) 341-7970
Office fax: (323) 341-7976
General e-mail: service@egpnews.com
Advertising e-mail: advertise@egpnews.com
Editorial e-mail: editorial@egpnews.com
Website: www.egpnews.com
Year newspaper established: 1945
Advertising (open inch rate): N/A
Mechanical specifications: Type page 13 x 21; 6 cols
Delivery methods: Mail`Carrier`Racks
Zip Codes Served: 90001, 90011, 90012, 90014, 90022, 90023, 90031, 90032, 90033, 90040, 90041, 90042, 90063, 90065, 91731, 91732, 91733, 91744, 91754, 91766, 91770, 91803, 91104
Frequency: Thur
Circulation Paid: 4
Circulation Free: 2471
Audit By: CVC
Audit Date: 30.09.2014
Hardware: 3-Dell/Dell Dimension 2400 Series, 5-APP/IMac 24, 4-APP/MAC G5

Software: Adobe/Illustrator CS, Adobe/InDesign CS, Microsoft/Office 2008, 4-QPS/QuarkXPress 7.0, 6-Adobe/Photoshop CS, Adobe CS3.
Personnel: Dolores Sanchez (Pub.); Jonathan M. Sanchez (Adv. Mgr.); Bianca Sanchez (Circ. Mgr.); Gloria Alvarez (Mng. Ed.); Elizabeth Chou (Prodn. Mgr.)
Main (survey) contact: Jonathan M. Sanchez

WAVE PUBLICATIONS

Street address 1: 3731 W Olympic Blvd
Street address 2: Ste 840
Street address state: CA
Postal code: 90019-2030
County: Los Angeles
Country: USA
Mailing address: 3731 Wilshire Blvd Ste 840
Mailing city: Los Angeles
Mailing state: CA
Mailing zip: 90010-2851
Office phone: (323) 556-5720
Office fax: (213) 835-0584
General e-mail: newsroom@wavepublication.com
Website: www.wavenewspapers.com
Year newspaper established: 1912
Advertising (open inch rate): Open inch rate $70.00
Frequency: Thur
Circulation Free: 100000
Audit By: Sworn/Estimate/Non-Audited
Audit Date: 12.07.2019
Personnel: Pluria Marshall (Pub.)
Main (survey) contact: Don Wanlass

WYVERNWOOD CHRONICLE

Street address 1: 111 S Avenue 59
Street address state: CA
Postal code: 90042-4211
County: Los Angeles
Country: USA
Office phone: (323) 341-7970
Office fax: (323) 341-7976
General e-mail: service@egpnews.com
Advertising e-mail: advertise@egpnews.com
Editorial e-mail: editorial@egpnews.com
Website: www.egpnews.com
Year newspaper established: 1945
Advertising (open inch rate): N/A
Mechanical specifications: Type page 13 x 21; 6 cols
Delivery methods: Mail`Carrier`Racks
Zip Codes Served: 90001, 90011, 90012, 90014, 90022, 90023, 90031, 90032, 90033, 90040, 90041, 90042, 90063, 90065, 91731, 91732, 91733, 91744, 91754, 91766, 91770, 91803, 91104
Frequency: Thur
Circulation Free: 1975
Audit By: CVC
Audit Date: 30.09.2014
Hardware: 3-Dell/Dell Dimension 2400 Series, 5-APP/IMac 24, 4-APP/MAC G5
Software: Adobe/Illustrator CS, Adobe/InDesign CS, Microsoft/Office 2008, 4-QPS/QuarkXPress 7.0, 6-Adobe/Photoshop CS, Adobe CS3.
Personnel: Dolores Sanchez (Pub.); Jonathan M. Sanchez (Adv. Mgr.); Bianca Sanchez (Circ. Mgr.); Gloria Alvarez (Mng. Ed.); Elizabeth Chou (Prodn. Mgr.)
Main (survey) contact: Jonathan M. Sanchez

LUBBOCK

EL EDITOR-LUBBOCK

Street address 1: 1502 Avenue M
Street address state: TX
Postal code: 79401-4950
County: Lubbock
Country: USA
Mailing address: PO Box 11250
Mailing city: Lubbock
Mailing state: TX
Mailing zip: 79408-7250
Office phone: (806) 763-3841
Office fax: (806) 741-1110
Other phone: 806: 741-0371
General e-mail: eleditor@sbcglobal.net

Advertising e-mail: eleditorsales@sbcglobal.net
Website: www.eleditor.com
Year newspaper established: 1977
Advertising (open inch rate): Open inch rate $20.00
Mechanical specifications: Type page 13 x 21; E - 6 cols, 2 1/4, 1/8 between; A - 6 cols, 2 1/4, 1/8 between; C - 6 cols, 2 1/2, 1/8 between.
Delivery methods: Racks
Frequency: Thur
Circulation Paid: 0
Circulation Free: 4017
Audit By: VAC
Audit Date: 30.12.2015
Hardware: APP/Power Mac
Software: Adobe/PageMaker 6.9, Adobe/Illustrator 5.0.
Personnel: Olga Riojas-Aguero (Owner)
Main (survey) contact: Bidal Aguero

EL EDITOR-PERMIAN BASIN

Street address 1: 1502 Avenue M
Street address state: TX
Postal code: 79401-4950
County: Lubbock
Country: USA
Mailing address: PO Box 11250
Mailing city: Lubbock
Mailing state: TX
Mailing zip: 79408-7250
Office phone: (806) 763-3841
Office fax: (806) 741-1110
General e-mail: eleditor@sbcglobal.net
Website: www.eleditor.com
Advertising (open inch rate): Open inch rate $19.50
Mechanical specifications: Type page 13 x 21 1/2; E - 6 cols, 2 1/16, 1/8 between; A - 6 cols, 2 1/16, 1/8 between; C - 6 cols, 2 1/16, 1/8 between.
Frequency: Wed
Circulation Free: 15000
Audit By: Sworn/Estimate/Non-Audited
Audit Date: 12.07.2019
Hardware: CSI, APP/Mac.
Personnel: Gilbert Acuna (Circ. Mgr.); Bidal Aguero (Ed.); Olga Aguero (Prodn. Mgr.)
Main (survey) contact: Bidal Aguero

MCALLEN

EL PERIODICO USA

Street address 1: 801 E Fir Ave
Street address state: TX
Postal code: 78501-9320
County: Hidalgo
Country: USA
Mailing address: 801 E Fir Ave
Mailing city: McAllen
Mailing state: TX
Mailing zip: 78501-9320
Office phone: (956) 631-5628
Office fax: (956) 631-0832
Advertising phone: 956-631-5628
Advertising fax: 956-631-0832
Editorial phone: 956-631-5628
Editorial fax: 956-631-0832
Other phone: 956-631-1891
General e-mail: subscribe@elperiodicousa.com
Website: www.elperiodicousa.com
Year newspaper established: 1986
Advertising (open inch rate): Open inch rate $25.00
Mechanical specifications: Type page 10.5 x 19 3/4; E - 6 cols, 1 3/4, 1/4 between; A - 6 cols, 1 3/4, 1/4 between; C - 6 cols, 1 3/4, 1/4 between.
Delivery methods: Carrier`Racks
Zip Codes Served: 78516, 78537, 78539, 78557, 78501, 785013, 78504, 78557, 78589, 78506, 78520, 78521
Frequency: Wed
Circulation Free: 38502
Audit By: CAC
Audit Date: 30.09.2018
Hardware: APP/Mac
Software: In Design, Photoshop, Ilustrator, Office
Personnel: Jose B. Garza (Ed.); Kathy Letelier (Pub.)

Parent company: El Periodico USA
Main (survey) contact: Jose B. Garza

MERIDEN

TIEMPO

Street address 1: 11 Crown St
Street address state: CT
Postal code: 06450-5713
County: New Haven
Country: USA
Mailing address: 11 Crown St
Mailing city: Meriden
Mailing state: CT
Mailing zip: 06450-5713
Office phone: (203) 235-1661
Advertising phone: (203) 317-2337
Advertising fax: (203) 235-4048
General e-mail: tiempo@record-journal.com
Website: www.tiempo.com
Advertising (open inch rate): Open inch rate $15.50
Audit By: Sworn/Estimate/Non-Audited
Audit Date: 12.07.2019
Personnel: Eliot C. White (Pub.); Leyda Ortiz-Sanchez (Adv. Mgr.); Elizabeth Tirado (Ed.)
Main (survey) contact: Ralph Tomaselli

MIAMI

DIARIO LAS AMERICAS

Street address 1: 888 Brickell Ave
Street address 2: Fl 5
Street address state: FL
Postal code: 33131-2913
County: Miami-Dade
Country: USA
Mailing address: 888 Brickell Ave 5th
Mailing city: Miami
Mailing state: FL
Mailing zip: 33131
Office phone: (305) 633-3341
Office fax: (305) 635-7668
Advertising phone: (305) 633-3341
Advertising fax: (305) 635-4002
Editorial phone: (305) 633-3341
Editorial fax: (305) 635-7668
General e-mail: contacto@diariolasamericas.com
Advertising e-mail: advertising@diariolasamericas.com
Editorial e-mail: editorial@diariolasamericas.com
Website: www.diariolasamericas.com
Year newspaper established: 1953
Advertising (open inch rate): Open inch rate $32.25
Mechanical specifications: Type page 13 x 21; E - 6 cols, 2 1/16, 1/8 between; A - 6 cols, 2 1/16, 1/8 between; C - 10 cols, 1/8 between.
Frequency: Sun
Circulation Paid: 5692
Circulation Free: 30453
Audit By: VAC
Audit Date: 30.09.2014
Hardware: Presses ÃƒÂƒÃ‚Â¢ G/Urbanite.
Personnel: Maribel Suarez (Asst. Pub.); Victor M. Vega (Bus. Mgr./Controller); Ariel Martinez (Prodn. Mgr.); Daniel Medina (Credit Mgr.); Alejandro Aguirre (Adv. Dir.); Bertha V. Enriquez (Adv. Mgr., Nat'l); Jose A. Yuste (Adv. Mgr., Classified); Horacio Aguirre (Ed.); Alejandro J. Aguirre (Deputy Ed.); Virginia Godoy (Food Ed.); Gustavo Pena (News Ed.); Luis David Rodriguez (Society Ed.); Jesus Hernandez (Data Processing Mgr.); Gustavo De La Osa (Prod. Mgr.)
Main (survey) contact: Horacio Aguirre

EL ARGENTINO NEWSPAPER

Street address 1: PO Box 802133
Street address state: FL
Postal code: 33280-2133
County: Miami-Dade
Country: USA
Mailing address: PO Box 802133
Mailing city: Miami

Mailing state: FL
Mailing zip: 33280-2133
Office fax: (305) 371-1656
General e-mail: showmgz@gate.net; info@elargentino.com
Website: www.elargentino.com
Audit By: Sworn/Estimate/Non-Audited
Audit Date: 12.07.2019
Personnel: Grace Micheli (Adv. Mgr.); Alberto Micheli (Ed.)
Main (survey) contact: Grace Micheli

EL NUEVO HERALD

Street address 1: 1 Herald Plz
Street address state: FL
Postal code: 33132-1609
County: Miami-Dade
Country: USA
Mailing address: 1 Herald Plz
Mailing city: Miami
Mailing state: FL
Mailing zip: 33132-1609
Office phone: 1-800-843-4372
Website: http://www.elnuevoherald.com/
Frequency: Mon`Tues`Wed`Thur`Fri`Sun
Circulation Paid: 45526
Audit By: AAM
Audit Date: 30.06.2017
Parent company: The McClatchy Company

EL NUEVO PATRIA

Street address 1: 425 NW 27th Ave Ste 2
Street address 2: Jose Marti Station
Street address state: FL
Postal code: 33135-4767
County: Miami-Dade
Country: USA
Mailing address: PO Box 350002
Mailing city: Miami
Mailing state: FL
Mailing zip: 33135
Office phone: (305) 530-8787
Advertising phone: (786) 286-8787
Advertising fax: (305) 698-8787
General e-mail: patrianews@aol.com
Editorial e-mail: enpnews@aol.com
Year newspaper established: 1959
Advertising (open inch rate): Open inch rate $25.00
Mechanical specifications: Type page 10 x 16; E - 6 cols, 1 3/5, 3/20 between; A - 6 cols, 1 3/5, 3/20 between; C - 6 cols, 1 3/5, 3/20 between.
Delivery methods: Mail`Newsstand`Racks
Frequency: Wed
Circulation Paid: 7180
Circulation Free: 22820
Audit By: Sworn/Estimate/Non-Audited
Audit Date: 12.07.2019
Hardware: 4-APP/Power Mac
Software: QPS/QuarkXPress, Adobe/Photoshop, Microsoft/Word.
Personnel: Maria Laura Figueroa (Gen. Mgr.); Dr. Carlos Diaz Lujan (Ed.); Omar R. Rosa (Prodn. Mgr.); Sara P. Armesto (Associate Ed.); Eladio Jose Armesto (Publisher); Sandra Baroja (Food & Wine Editor); Ralph Garcia (Book Editor); Madeline Sandoval (Feature Editor)
Parent company: Patria Media Foundation, Inc.
Main (survey) contact: Eladio Jose Armesto

LIBRE

Street address 1: 2700 SW 8th St
Street address state: FL
Postal code: 33135-4619
County: Miami-Dade
Country: USA
Mailing address: 2700 SW 8th St
Mailing city: Miami
Mailing state: FL
Mailing zip: 33135-4619
Office phone: (305) 643-2947
Office fax: (305) 649-2767
General e-mail: main@libreonline.com
Website: www.libreonline.com
Year newspaper established: 1966
Advertising (open inch rate): Open inch rate $21.00
Mechanical specifications: Type page 10 x 12 1/4; E - 6 cols, 1 1/2, 1/8 between; A - 6 cols, 1 1/2, 1/8 between.
Frequency: Wed
Circulation Paid: 1100
Circulation Free: 3850
Audit By: Sworn/Estimate/Non-Audited
Audit Date: 12.07.2019
Hardware: Software Ã‚Â— QPS/QuarkXPress 6.5, Adobe/Photoshop CS.
Personnel: Demetrio Perez (Pub.)
Main (survey) contact: Demetrio Perez

MINNEAPOLIS

LA PRENSA DE MINNESOTA

Street address 1: 1516 E Lake St
Street address 2: Ste 200
Street address state: MN
Postal code: 55407-3579
County: Hennepin
Country: USA
Mailing address: 2909 Bryant Ave. S.
Mailing city: Minneapolis
Mailing state: MN
Mailing zip: 55408
Office phone: (612) 729-5900
Office fax: (612) 729-5999
General e-mail: marian@lcnmedia.com
Website: www.laprensademn.com
Advertising (open inch rate): Open inch rate $25.00
Frequency: Thur
Circulation Free: 15000
Audit By: Sworn/Estimate/Non-Audited
Audit Date: 12.07.2019
Personnel: Mario Duarte (Pub.); Lorena Duarte (Ed.)
Main (survey) contact: Brad Sigal

MOUNT PLEASANT

EL INFORMADOR SPANISH LANGUAGE NEWSPAPER

Street address 1: PO Box 2458
Street address state: SC
Postal code: 29465-2458
County: Charleston
Country: USA
Mailing address: PO Box 2458
Mailing city: Mount Pleasant
Mailing state: SC
Mailing zip: 29465-2458
Office phone: 843-693-1116
Office fax: 843-352-4506
Advertising phone: 843-817-2896
Advertising fax: 843-352-4506
Editorial phone: 843-693-1116
Editorial fax: 843-352-4506
General e-mail: lisa@elinformadornewspaper.com
Advertising e-mail: sales@elinformadornewspaper.com
Editorial e-mail: lisa@elinformadornewspaper.com
Website: www.elinformador.us
Year newspaper established: 2008
Delivery methods: Racks
Zip Codes Served: 29418, 29406, 29401,29403,29405,29407, 20410, 29420, 29445, 29455, 29456, 29461, 29464, 29483, 29485,29906, 29907, 29920, 29935, 29936, 29926,29928,29910,29927
Frequency: Wed
Other Type of Frequency: Biweekly
Circulation Free: 10000
Audit By: Sworn/Estimate/Non-Audited
Audit Date: 12.07.2019
Personnel: Lisa De Armas (Director); Pedro De Armas (Publisher)
Main (survey) contact: Lisa De Armas

NEW YORK

DIARIO DE MEXICO USA

Street address 1: 106 32nd Street New York
Street address 2: Suite 160
Street address state: NY
Postal code: 01001
County: New York
Country: USA
Mailing address: 106 32nd Street New York, Suite 160
Mailing city: New York
Mailing state: NY
Mailing zip: 01001
Office phone: (212) 725-1521
General e-mail: contacto@diariodemexicousa.com
Website: www.diariodemexicousa.com
Frequency: Mon`Tues`Wed`Thur`Fri
Circulation Paid: 12181
Audit By: AAM
Audit Date: 30.09.2011
Personnel: Contact Us
Main (survey) contact: Contact Us

IMPACTO LATIN NEWS

Street address 1: 225 W 35th St
Street address 2: Ste 1001
Street address state: NY
Postal code: 10001-1949
County: New York
Country: USA
Mailing address: 132 W 31st St Fl 15
Mailing city: New York
Mailing state: NY
Mailing zip: 10001-3437
Office phone: (212) 807-0400
Office fax: (212) 807-0408
General e-mail: media@impactony.com
Advertising e-mail: vsmith@impactony.com
Editorial e-mail: media@impactony.com
Website: impactolatino.com
Year newspaper established: 1967
Advertising (open inch rate): Open inch rate $49.75
Delivery methods: Newsstand`Racks
Frequency: Wed
Circulation Free: 57000
Audit By: AAM
Audit Date: 31.03.2014
Personnel: Gail M Smith (Pub.); Jason. K Smith (Ed.); Vanessa. M Smith (VP, Adv./Mktg.); Mar Verdugo (Market Research Analyst)
Parent company: Impacto Latin News Publishing
Main (survey) contact: Gail Smith

LA VOZ HISPANA NEWSPAPER

Street address 1: 159 E 116th St
Street address state: NY
Postal code: 10029-1399
County: New York
Country: USA
Mailing address: 159 E 116th St Fl 2
Mailing city: New York
Mailing state: NY
Mailing zip: 10029-1399
Office phone: (212) 348-8270
Office fax: (212) 348-4469
Advertising phone: (212) 348-8270
Editorial phone: (917) 225-8576
Editorial fax: (212) 348-4469
Other phone: (212) 348-8270
General e-mail: discomund@aol.com
Website: www.lavozhispanany.com
Year newspaper established: 1970
Advertising (open inch rate): Open inch rate $32.00
Mechanical specifications: Type page 9 3/4 x 14.
Delivery methods: Mail`Racks
Frequency: Thur
Circulation Paid: 61879
Circulation Free: 9200
Audit By: Sworn/Estimate/Non-Audited
Audit Date: 12.07.2019
Personnel: Nick Lugo (Pub.); Joaquin Del Rio (Exec. Ed.)
Parent company: Casa Publications
Main (survey) contact: Joaquin Del Rio

NUESTRO MUNDO

Street address 1: 235 W 23rd St
Street address state: NY
Postal code: 10011-2371
County: New York
Country: USA
Mailing address: 235 W 23rd St
Mailing city: New York
Mailing state: NY
Mailing zip: 10011-2302
Office phone: (212) 924-2523
Office fax: (212) 229-1713
General e-mail: pww@pww.org; contact@peoplesworld.org
Website: www.pww.org
Advertising (open inch rate): Open inch rate $20.00
Mechanical specifications: Type page 11 x 17; E - 5 cols, between; A - 5 cols, between; C - 5 cols, between.
Frequency: Sat
Circulation Paid: 15000
Circulation Free: 10000
Audit By: Sworn/Estimate/Non-Audited
Audit Date: 12.07.2019
Hardware: APP/Mac
Software: QPS/QuarkXPress.
Personnel: Jose Cruz (Ed.)
Main (survey) contact: Jose Cruz

NORTH PROVIDENCE

PROVIDENCE EN ESPANOL

Street address 1: 45 Meadow View Blvd
Street address state: RI
Postal code: 02904-2916
County: Providence
Country: USA
Office phone: 401.834.5552
Office fax: 401.233.7500
Advertising e-mail: ads@providenceenespanol.com
Editorial e-mail: news@providenceenespanol.com
Website: www.providenceenespanol.com
Year newspaper established: 1999
Digital Platform - Mobile: Apple`Android`Windows
Digital Platform - Tablet: Apple iOS`Android`Windows 7
Frequency: Mon`Tues`Wed`Thur`Fri`Sat`Sun
Other Type of Frequency: daily updates
Personnel: Arelis Pena (Ed.); Vivian Cuenca; Victor Cuenca
Main (survey) contact: Victor Cuenca

NORWALK

EL CLASIFICADO

Street address 1: 11205 Imperial Hwy
Street address state: CA
Postal code: 90650-2229
County: Los Angeles
Country: USA
Mailing address: 11205 Imperial Hwy
Mailing city: Norwalk
Mailing state: CA
Mailing zip: 90650-2229
Office phone: 1800-242-2527
Advertising phone: 866-893-0028
Editorial phone: 888-261-9772
Other phone: 888-279-3009
Website: www.elclasificado.com
Year newspaper established: 1988
Delivery methods: Racks
Zip Codes Served: 92126 92129 92131 92134 92136 92139 92624 92629 92630 92637 92651 92653 92656 92672 92673 92675 92677 92688 92691 92692 92694 93206 93215 93249 93250 93263 93280 93616 93618 93625 93631 93646 93648 93654 93657 93662 93673 93610 93636 93637 93638 92313 92316 92324 92376 92377 92501 92503 92504 92505 92506 92507 92508 92509 92521 92220 92223 92230 92320 92518 92543 92544 92545 92551 92553 92555 92557 92567 92582 92583 90033 90063 90006 90017 90019 90057 93013 93101 93103 93111 93117 93420 93433 93434 93436 93444 93445 93454 93455 93458
Digital Platform - Mobile: Apple
Digital Platform - Tablet: Apple iOS
Frequency: Tues`Wed

Hispanic Newspapers in the U.S.

Circulation Free: 486626
Audit By: CVC
Audit Date: 30.03.2018
Personnel: Martha C. De la Torre; Joe Badame
Main (survey) contact: Martha C. de la Torre; Joe Badame

OGDEN

EL ESTANDAR

Street address 1: 332 Standard Way
Street address state: UT
Postal code: 84404-1371
County: Weber
Country: USA
Mailing address: 332 Standard Way
Mailing city: Ogden
Mailing state: UT
Mailing zip: 84404-1371
Office phone: (801) 625-4400
Advertising phone: (801) 625-4333
Editorial phone: (801) 625-4225
Other phone: (800) 651-2105
Website: www.standard.net
Frequency: Wed
Circulation Free: 15625
Audit By: Sworn/Estimate/Non-Audited
Audit Date: 12.07.2019
Personnel: Jordan Carroll (Ex. Ed.); Becky Cairns (TX Section Coordinator); Patrick Carr (Sports Rep.); Ryan Christner (Print Admin.); Ryan Comer (Copy Ed.)
Main (survey) contact: Jordan Carroll

PALATINE

NUEVA SEMANA

Street address 1: 1180 E Dundee Rd
Street address state: IL
Postal code: 60074-8305
County: Cook
Country: USA
Mailing address: 1180 E Dundee Rd
Mailing city: Palatine
Mailing state: IL
Mailing zip: 60074
Office phone: (847) 239-4815
Office fax: (847) 890-6327
General e-mail: info@lanuevasemana.com
Editorial e-mail: ealegria@lanuevasemana.com
Website: www.lanuevasemana.com
Year newspaper established: 1999
Mechanical specifications: Type page 10 1/4 x 12 3/4; E - 5 cols, 2 1/8, between; A - 5 cols, 2 1/8, between; C - 5 cols, 2 1/8, between.
Delivery methods: Newsstand`Racks
Frequency: Fri
Circulation Free: 9000
Audit By: Sworn/Estimate/Non-Audited
Audit Date: 12.07.2019
Hardware: PC
Personnel: Rober Reyes (Pub.)
Main (survey) contact: Rober Reyes

PHILADELPHIA

AL DIA NEWS MEDIA

Street address 1: 1835 Market St
Street address 2: Fl 4
Street address state: PA
Postal code: 19103-2968
County: Philadelphia
Country: USA
Mailing address: 1835 Market St Ste 450
Mailing city: Philadelphia
Mailing state: PA
Mailing zip: 19103-2939
Office phone: (215) 569-4666
Office fax: (215) 569-2721
Advertising phone: (215) 789-6975
Advertising fax: (215) 569-2721
Editorial phone: (215) 789-6973
General e-mail: adsales@aldiainc.com
Advertising e-mail: ads@aldiainc.com
Editorial e-mail: editor@aldiainc.com
Website: aldianews.com
Year newspaper established: 1992

Advertising (open inch rate): Open inch rate $91.77
Mechanical specifications: Type page 11 x 12; A - 5 cols, 2 1/16, 1/8 between.
Delivery methods: Mail`Racks
Zip Codes Served: 19120, 08102
Frequency: Sun
Circulation Free: 42425
Audit By: CAC
Audit Date: 30.09.2014
Hardware: APP/Mac
Software: InDesign, Adobe/Photoshop.
Personnel: Gaby Guaracao (Strategy & Operations); Hernan Guaracao (Founder & CEO); Sabrina Vourvoulias (Managing Editor); Yesid Vargas (Art Dir.)
Main (survey) contact: Hernan Guaracao

PHOENIX

LA VOZ ARIZONA

Street address 1: 7600 N 16th St
Street address 2: Ste 150
Street address state: AZ
Postal code: 85020-4487
County: Maricopa
Country: USA
Mailing address: 7600 N 16th St Ste 150
Mailing city: Phoenix
Mailing state: AZ
Mailing zip: 85004-2238
Office phone: (602) 252-5331
Office fax: (602) 444-3894
Advertising phone: (602) 444-3800
Advertising fax: (602) 444-3999
Editorial phone: (602) 444-3800
Editorial fax: (602) 444-3893
Advertising e-mail: lisa.simpson@lavozarizona.com
Website: www.lavozarizona.com
Year newspaper established: 2000
Advertising (open inch rate): Open inch rate $27.00
Delivery methods: Carrier`Racks
Frequency: Wed
Circulation Paid: 0
Circulation Free: 58277
Audit By: VAC
Audit Date: 30.03.2015
Personnel: Elvira Diaz (Gen. Mgr.); Nadia Cantu (Ed.); Javier Arce (Dig. Prod.); Mi-Ai Parrish (Pres./Pub.)
Main (survey) contact: Elvira Diaz

PRENSA HISPANA

Street address 1: 809 E Washington St
Street address 2: Ste 209
Street address state: AZ
Postal code: 85034-1018
County: Maricopa
Country: USA
Mailing address: 809 E Washington St Ste 209
Mailing city: Phoenix
Mailing state: AZ
Mailing zip: 85034-1018
Office phone: (602) 256-2443
Office fax: (602) 256-2644
General e-mail: prensahispana@qwest.net
Website: www.prensahispanaaz.com
Frequency: Wed
Circulation Free: 65000
Audit By: Sworn/Estimate/Non-Audited
Audit Date: 12.07.2019
Personnel: Manny Garcia (Pres.); Lety Miranda-Garcia (Adv. Mgr., Classified)
Main (survey) contact: Manny Garcia

PILGRIM GARDENS

EL HISPANO

Street address 1: PO Box 396
Street address state: PA
Postal code: 19026-0396
County: Delaware
Country: USA
Mailing address: PO Box 396
Mailing city: Pilgrim Gardens

Mailing state: PA
Mailing zip: 19026-0396
Office phone: 484-472-6059
Office fax: 484-472-8153
Advertising phone: 484-472-6059
Advertising fax: 474-472-8153
General e-mail: alopez5268@aol.com
Advertising e-mail: hispads@aol.com
Editorial e-mail: alopez5268@aol.com
Website: www.el-hispano.com
Advertising (open inch rate): $31 per CI
Mechanical specifications: 10" x 12" FP - Tabloid size 10" x 6" HP
Delivery methods: Mail`Racks
Zip Codes Served: 08101-5, 08608-29, 17101-05, 18015-18, 18101-04, 19601-19606, 19101-19152
Frequency: Wed
Circulation Paid: 500
Circulation Free: 18000
Audit By: CVC
Audit Date: 30.06.2011
Hardware: Macs
Software: Indesign
Personnel: Aaron G. Lopez; Madelyn Madary
Parent company: Lopez Publicatons, Inc.
Main (survey) contact: Aaron G. Lopez

PORTLAND

EL HISPANIC NEWS

Street address 1: 6700 N New York Ave
Street address 2: Ste 212
Street address state: OR
Postal code: 97203-2836
County: Multnomah
Country: USA
Mailing address: PO Box 306
Mailing city: Portland
Mailing state: OR
Mailing zip: 97207-0306
Office phone: (503) 228-3139
Office fax: (503) 228-3384
General e-mail: info@elhispanicnews.com
Website: www.elhispanicnews.com
Advertising (open inch rate): Open inch rate $22.00
Zip Codes Served: 97214
Frequency: Thur
Circulation Free: 20000
Audit By: CVC
Audit Date: 31.12.2003
Hardware: Software Ã‚Â— Adobe/PageMaker.
Personnel: Clara Padilla Andrews (Pub.); Melanie Davis (Mng. Partner); Maria Perry Crawshaw (Adv. Mgr.); Julie Cortez (Ed.); Christopher Alvarez (Prodn. Mgr.)
Main (survey) contact: Julie Cortez

PRESIDIO

THE PRESIDIO INTERNATIONAL

Street address 1: Market @ Ralph England Streets
Street address state: TX
Postal code: 79845
County: Presidio
Country: USA
Mailing address: PO Box P
Mailing city: Marfa
Mailing state: TX
Mailing zip: 79843
Office phone: (432) 729-4342
General e-mail: editor@bigbendnow.com
Website: www.bigbendnow.com
Year newspaper established: 1986
Advertising (open inch rate): Open inch rate $9.50
Mechanical specifications: Type page 13 x 21 1/2; E - 6 cols, 2 1/16, 1/8 between; A - 6 cols, 2 1/16, 1/8 between; C - 6 cols, 2 1/16, 1/8 between.
Delivery methods: Mail`Newsstand`Racks
Digital Platform - Mobile: Apple
Digital Platform - Tablet: Apple iOS
Frequency: Thur
Circulation Paid: 900
Circulation Free: 100
Audit By: USPS

Audit Date: 16.10.2017
Hardware: Mac
Presses: Monahans News, Monahans, Texas
Software: Adobe creative suite
Personnel: Robert L. Halpern (Ed.); Rosario Salgado-Halpern (Mng. Ed.)
Main (survey) contact: Robert L. Halpern

RALEIGH

QUE PASA - RALEIGH

Street address 1: 4801 Glenwood Ave
Street address 2: Suite 200
Street address state: NC
Postal code: 27612
Country: USA
Mailing address: 4801 Glenwood Ave Ste. 200
Mailing city: Raleigh
Mailing state: NC
Mailing zip: 27612
Office phone: (919) 645-1680
Advertising phone: (336) 935-9673
General e-mail: distribution@quepasamedia.com
Advertising e-mail: sales@quepasamedia.com
Editorial e-mail: editor@quepasamedia.com
Website: quepasamedia.com
Year newspaper established: 1994
Advertising (open inch rate): Open inch rate $15.88
Mechanical specifications: Type page: 10 x 21; 6 col
Frequency: Thur
Circulation Paid: 0
Circulation Free: 11336
Audit By: CVC
Audit Date: 31.12.2018
Personnel: Jose Isasi; Amith Arrieta; Marina Aleman (Adv.); Hernando Ramirez (Ed.)
Main (survey) contact: Amith Arrieta

RENO

AHORA LATINO JOURNAL

Street address 1: 605 S Wells Ave
Street address state: NV
Postal code: 89502-1825
County: Washoe
Country: USA
Mailing address: 9584 Autumn Leaf Way
Mailing city: Reno
Mailing state: NV
Mailing zip: 89506-4502
Office phone: (775) 677-9694
Advertising phone: 775-378-7025
Editorial phone: 775-378-7025
General e-mail: marioreno@live.com
Advertising e-mail: marioreno@live.com
Editorial e-mail: adelitazapata@live.com
Website: www.ahoralatinojournal.com
Year newspaper established: 2010
Advertising (open inch rate): Open inch rate $10.00
Mechanical specifications: Type page 10 x 14; E - 5 cols, 2, 1/6 between.
Delivery methods: Racks
Zip Codes Served: 89501, 89502, 89503, 89506, 89423, 89721, etc
Digital Platform - Mobile: Android
Digital Platform - Tablet: Other
Frequency: Tues`Wed`Other
Other Type of Frequency: Bi-weekly
Circulation Free: 8000
Audit By: Sworn/Estimate/Non-Audited
Audit Date: 12.07.2019
Software: Adobe C4
Main (survey) contact: Mario Delarosa

RIVERSIDE

LA PRENSA

Street address 1: 1825 Chicago Avenue
Street address 2: Suite 100
Street address state: CA
Postal code: 92507
County: Riverside

Country: USA
Mailing address: 1825 Chicago Avenue, Ste. 100
Mailing city: Anaheim
Mailing state: CA
Mailing zip: 92507
Office phone: (909) 806-3201
General e-mail: oramirez@pe.com
Website: www.laprensaenlinea.com
Advertising (open inch rate): Open inch rate $35.70
Frequency: Fri
Circulation Free: 95478
Audit By: VAC
Audit Date: 31.03.2013
Personnel: Carlos Aviles (Mng. Ed.); Jose Fuentes (Ed.); Angelica De Santos (Local Sales); Trinidad Verduzco (Local Sales)
Parent company: Southern California News Group
Main (survey) contact: Carlos Aviles

SACRAMENTO

EL HISPANO

Street address 1: 1903 21st St
Street address state: CA
Postal code: 95811-6813
County: Sacramento
Country: USA
Mailing address: PO Box 2856
Mailing city: Sacramento
Mailing state: CA
Mailing zip: 95812-2856
Office phone: (916) 442-0267
Office fax: (916) 442-2818
General e-mail: plarenas2@yahoo.com
Advertising (open inch rate): Open inch rate $15.29
Mechanical specifications: Type page 13 1/16 x 21; E - 6 cols, 2, between; A - 6 cols, 2, between.
Frequency: Wed
Circulation Free: 15000
Audit By: Sworn/Estimate/Non-Audited
Audit Date: 12.07.2019
Hardware: APP/Mac
Software: Adobe/PageMaker, Adobe/Photoshop.
Personnel: Patrick Larenas (Ed.)
Main (survey) contact: Patrick Larenas

SALINAS

EL SOL

Street address 1: 1093 S Main St Suite 101
Street address state: CA
Postal code: 93901
County: Monterey
Country: USA
Mailing address: 1093 S Main St Suite 101
Mailing city: Salinas
Mailing state: CA
Mailing zip: 93901
Office phone: (831) 424-2221
Office fax: (831) 754-4286
Editorial phone: (831) 754-4272
General e-mail: jbrooks@usatoday.com
Advertising e-mail: tdean@gannett.com
Editorial e-mail: pgoudreau@gannett.com
Website: thecalifornian.com
Year newspaper established: 1968
Advertising (open inch rate): Open inch rate $21.68
Mechanical specifications: Type page 11 5/8 x 21; E - 6 cols, 1 3/4, between; A - 6 cols, 1 3/4, between; C - 6 cols, 1 1/8, between.
Delivery methods: Racks
Frequency: Sat
Circulation Free: 29980
Audit By: CVC
Audit Date: 30.03.2018
Hardware: PC
Presses: G/Urbanite
Software: QPS/QuarkXPress 4.1.
Personnel: Terry Feinberg (Gen. Mgr.); Silvia Sancen (Ed.); Theresa Simpson; Paula Goudreau (Pub.); Trey Dean (Adv.); John Brooks (Circ.)
Main (survey) contact: Paula Goudreau

SAN ANTONIO

PERIODICO BUENA SUERTE - SAN ANTONIO

Street address 1: 1804 NE Interstate 410 Loop
Street address 2: Suite #280A
Street address state: TX
Postal code: 78217
County: Bexar
Country: USA
Mailing address: 7324 Southwest Fwy Ste 1720
Mailing city: Houston
Mailing state: TX
Mailing zip: 77074-2058
Office phone: (210) 444-0001
Advertising e-mail: sales@BuenaSuerte.com
Website: www.buenasuerte.com
Year newspaper established: 1986
Advertising (open inch rate): Open inch rate $13.00
Delivery methods: Newsstand`Racks
Digital Platform - Mobile: Apple`Android`Windows
Digital Platform - Tablet: Apple iOS`Android`Windows 7
Frequency: Fri
Circulation Paid: 0
Circulation Free: 14004
Audit By: Sworn/Estimate/Non-Audited
Audit Date: 12.07.2019
Personnel: Emilio Martinez
Main (survey) contact: Emilio Martinez

SAN DIEGO

EL SOL DE SAN DIEGO

Street address 1: 2629 National Ave
Street address state: CA
Postal code: 92113-3617
County: San Diego
Country: USA
Mailing address: PO Box 13447
Mailing city: San Diego
Mailing state: CA
Mailing zip: 92170-3447
Office phone: (619) 233-8496
Office fax: (619) 233-5017
General e-mail: elsolsd@aol.com
Website: www.elsoldesandiego.com
Advertising (open inch rate): Open inch rate $20.00
Mechanical specifications: Type page 10 13/16 x 13; E - 5 cols, 2 1/16, 1/8 between; A - 5 cols, 2 1/16, 1/8 between; C - 5 cols, 2 1/16, 1/8 between.
Zip Codes Served: 92170
Audit By: Sworn/Estimate/Non-Audited
Audit Date: 12.07.2019
Hardware: PC.
Personnel: Lynn Johansen (Adv. Mgr.); Julie J. Rocha (Ed.)
Main (survey) contact: Julie J. Rocha

HOY SAN DIEGO - THE SAN DIEGO UNION TRIBUNE

Street address 1: 600 B St
Street address 2: Ste 1201
Street address state: CA
Postal code: 92101-4505
County: San Diego
Country: USA
Mailing address: P.O. Box 120191
Mailing city: San Diego
Mailing state: CA
Mailing zip: 92112
Office phone: 619-299-4141
Website: http://www.sandiegouniontribune.com/hoy-san-diego/
Frequency: Sat
Circulation Paid: 80920
Audit By: AAM
Audit Date: 31.12.2015
Personnel: Jeff Light (Publisher and Editor); Phyllis Pfeiffer (President and General Manager); Lora Cicalo (Managing Editor)

LA PRENSA SAN DIEGO

Street address 1: 1712 Logan Avenue
Street address state: CA
Postal code: 92113
County: San Diego
Country: USA
Mailing address: 1712 Logan Avenue
Mailing city: San Diego
Mailing state: CA
Mailing zip: 92113
Office phone: (619) 425-7400
General e-mail: laprensasd@gmail.com
Website: laprensa-sandiego.org
Year newspaper established: 1976
Advertising (open inch rate): Open inch rate $28.00
Mechanical specifications: Type page 11 1/2 x 21; E - 6 cols, 1 13/16, 1/8 between; A - 6 cols, 1 13/16, 1/8 between; C - 8 cols, 1 1/3, 3/32 between.
Delivery methods: Newsstand`Racks
Zip Codes Served: 91902; 91910; 91911; 91932; 91945; 91950; 91977; 91978; 92008; 92021; 92022; 92025; 92026; 92027; 92054; 92055; 92056; 92069; 92083; 92084; 92101; 92102; 92104; 92111; 92113; 92114; 92117; 92126; 92153; 92173
Frequency: Fri
Circulation Free: 25000
Audit By: Sworn/Estimate/Non-Audited
Audit Date: 12.07.2019
Hardware: IBM
Software: Adobe/PageMaker.
Personnel: Art Castanares (Publisher)
Main (survey) contact: Art Castanares

VIDA LATINA - THE SAN DIEGO UNION TRIBUNE

Street address 1: 600 B St
Street address 2: Ste 1201
Street address state: CA
Postal code: 92101-4505
County: San Diego
Country: USA
Mailing address: P.O. Box 120191
Mailing city: San Diego
Mailing state: CA
Mailing zip: 92112
Office phone: (619)299-4141
Website: http://www.sandiegouniontribune.com/hoy-san-diego/vida-latina/
Frequency: Fri
Circulation Paid: 30500
Audit By: AAM
Audit Date: 31.12.2015
Personnel: Jeff Light (Pub. & Ed.); Phyllis Pfeiffer (Pres. & Gen. Mgr.); Paul Ingegneri (V. Pres. Adv.)

SAN FRANCISCO

EL BOHEMIO NEWS

Street address 1: 3288 21st St
Street address 2: # 116
Street address state: CA
Postal code: 94110-2423
County: San Francisco
Country: USA
Mailing address: 3288 21st Street #116
Mailing city: San Francisco
Mailing state: CA
Mailing zip: 94110
Office phone: (415) 469-9579
Office fax: (415) 970-8853
General e-mail: bohemio@ix.netcom.com
Website: www.elbohemionews.info
Advertising (open inch rate): Open inch rate $30.00
Mechanical specifications: Type page 13 x 21; E - 6 cols, 2 1/4, 1/6 between.
Frequency: Fri
Circulation Free: 22472
Audit By: CVC
Audit Date: 31.03.2006
Hardware: APP/Mac
Software: Adobe/PageMaker, Great Works.
Personnel: Rosalina Contreras (Adv. Mgr.); Benny Velarde (Circ. Mgr.); Fernando Rosado (Ed.)
Main (survey) contact: Rosalina Contreras

EL MENSAJERO

Street address 1: 333 Valencia St
Street address 2: Ste. 410
Street address state: CA
Postal code: 94103-3500
County: San Francisco
Country: USA
Mailing address: 333 Valencia St., Ste. 400
Mailing city: LOS ANGELES
Mailing state: CA
Mailing zip: 90017
Office phone: (415) 206-7230
Office fax: (415) 206-7238
Advertising phone: (415) 206-7230
Advertising fax: (415) 206-7230
General e-mail: comentarios@elmensajero.com
Advertising e-mail: michael.howard@elmensajero.com
Editorial e-mail: comentarios@elmensajero.com
Website: www.elmensajero.com
Year newspaper established: 1987
Advertising (open inch rate): Open inch rate $58.79
Delivery methods: Carrier`Racks
Zip Codes Served: 95116, 95122, 95002, 95110, 95112. 95121, 95125, 95126, 95127, 95131, 95133, 94025, 94061, 94063, 94080, 94103, 94105, 94110, 94112, 94158, 94303, 94401, 94403, 94520, 94541, 94544, 94577, 94578, 94587, 94601, 94603, 94605, 94621, 94801, 94806
Digital Platform - Mobile: Apple`Android`Windows
Digital Platform - Tablet: Apple iOS`Android`Windows 7
Frequency: Sun
Circulation Paid: 0
Circulation Free: 103800
Audit By: CAC
Audit Date: 30.09.2014
Personnel: Gabriel Guthellez (Nat'l Sales Dir.); Madia Mejia (Ed.); Damian Mazzotta (Gen. Mgr./West, IM Corp); Greg Hatch (Circ. Dir.)
Parent company: impreMedia LLC
Main (survey) contact: Michael Howard

EL TECOLOTE

Street address 1: 2958 24th St
Street address state: CA
Postal code: 94110-4132
County: San Francisco
Country: USA
Mailing address: 2958 24th St
Mailing city: San Francisco
Mailing state: CA
Mailing zip: 94110-4132
Office phone: (415) 648-1045
Office fax: (415) 648-1046
Editorial e-mail: editor@accionlatina.org
Website: www.eltecolote.org
Year newspaper established: 1970
Advertising (open inch rate): Open inch rate $16.25
Mechanical specifications: Type page 10 1/4 x 16; E - 4 cols, 2 1/4, 1/4 between; A - 4 cols, 2 1/4, 1/4 between; C - 4 cols, 2 1/4, 1/4 between.
Other Type of Frequency: 2 x Mthly
Circulation Paid: 250
Circulation Free: 10000
Audit By: Sworn/Estimate/Non-Audited
Audit Date: 12.07.2019
Hardware: APP/Mac LC II, APP/Mac II, APP/Mac 6200, APP/iMac, APP/Mac G3
Software: Microsoft/Word 5.0.
Personnel: Roberto Daza (Ed.)
Main (survey) contact: Inaki Fernandez Retana

SAN JOSE

ALIANZA METROPOLITAN NEWS

Street address 1: 1090 Lincoln Ave
Street address 2: Ste 8
Street address state: CA
Postal code: 95125-3156
County: Santa Clara

Hispanic Newspapers in the U.S.

Country: USA
Mailing address: 3290 Cuesta Dr
Mailing city: San Jose
Mailing state: CA
Mailing zip: 95148-1601
Office phone: (408) 272-9394
Office fax: (408) 272-9395
Website: www.alianzanews.com
Advertising (open inch rate): Open inch rate $24.50
Mechanical specifications: Type page 13 x 21 1/2; E - 6 cols, 2 1/16, 1/8 between; A - 6 cols, 2 1/16, 1/8 between; C - 6 cols, 2 1/16, 1/8 between.
Zip Codes Served: 95151
Other Type of Frequency: Every other Thur
Circulation Free: 40000
Audit By: Sworn/Estimate/Non-Audited
Audit Date: 12.07.2019
Hardware: APP/Mac
Software: Adobe/PageMaker, Adobe/Photoshop.
Personnel: Rosana Drumond (Pub.); Manuel Ortiz (Ed.)
Main (survey) contact: Rosana Drumond

EL OBSERVADOR

Street address 1: 1042 W Hedding St
Street address 2: Ste 250
Street address state: CA
Postal code: 95126-1206
County: Santa Clara
Country: USA
Mailing address: 1042 W. Hedding St. #250
Mailing city: San Jose
Mailing state: CA
Mailing zip: 95126
Office phone: (408) 938-1700
Office fax: (408) 938-1705
Advertising fax: 408 938 1700
Editorial fax: 408-938-1705
Other phone: 408-718-9590
Other fax: 650-493-0924
General e-mail: angelica@el-observador.com
Advertising e-mail: angelica@el-observador.com
Editorial e-mail: arturo@el-observador.com
Website: www.el-observador.com
Year newspaper established: 1980
Advertising (open inch rate): Open inch rate $30.00
Mechanical specifications: Type page 13 x 21; E - 6 cols, 2 1/16, between; A - 6 cols, 2 1/16, between; C - 10 cols, 1 5/16, between.
Delivery methods: Mail`Newsstand`Carrier`Racks
Zip Codes Served: Santa Clara County
Digital Platform - Mobile: Apple`Android`Windows`Blackberry
Digital Platform - Tablet: Apple iOS`Android`Windows 7`Blackberry Tablet OS`Kindle`Nook`Kindle Fire
Frequency: Fri
Circulation Free: 34500
Audit By: Sworn/Estimate/Non-Audited
Audit Date: 12.07.2019
Hardware: IBM/486, APP/Power Mac 7100/66, APP/Mac IIcx, APP/Mac SE, APP/Mac Classic II, 4-APP/Mac Plus
Software: Microsoft/Word, Microsoft/Excel, QPS/QuarkXPress, Adobe/Photoshop.
Note: El Observador is a multi-media service company offering advertising (print & digital) advertising and promotions via EO's social media platforms, legal notices, classifieds, jobs board, translations, graphic design, web development & motion graphics, photography, video production.
Personnel: Angelica Rossi (Pres./Pub.); Justin Rossi (Sales); Arturo Hilario (Ed.); Leila Velasco (Graphic Des.); Erica Medrano (Office Manager); Arturo Hilario (Managing Editor); Hilbert Morales (Pub.); Monica Amador (Adv./Mktg. Dir.); Angelica Rossi (Acct. Rep.); Roberto Romo (Graphics Design)
Main (survey) contact: Angelica Rossi

LA OFERTA REVIEW

Street address 1: 1009 E. Capitol Expwy
Street address 2: # 525
Street address state: CA
Postal code: 95121
County: Santa Clara
Country: USA
Mailing address: 1009 E. Capitol Expwy # 525
Mailing city: San Jose
Mailing state: CA
Mailing zip: 95121
Office phone: (408)-436-7850
Office fax: (408) 436-7861
General e-mail: info@laoferta.com
Website: www.laoferta.com
Year newspaper established: 1978
Advertising (open inch rate): Open inch rate $29.75
Zip Codes Served: 95002, 94086, 94089, 95035, 95036, 94059, 94061, 95065, 94301, 94310, 94546, 94039, 94560, 94560, 94536, 94555, 94587, 95050, 95110, 95112, 95113, 95114, 95116, 95118, 95120, 95121, 951232, 95132, 95132, 95125, 94605, 94112, 94114
Frequency: Fri
Circulation Free: 21000
Audit By: Sworn/Estimate/Non-Audited
Audit Date: 12.07.2019
Hardware: Software Ã‚Â— Adobe/PageMaker 6.5, QPS/QuarkXPress 4.0, Microsoft/Word.
Personnel: Franklin G. Andrade (Co Pub.); Tatiana Andrade (Adv. Dir.); Mary J. Andrade (Ed.)
Main (survey) contact: Frank Andrade

NUEVO MUNDO

Street address 1: 750 Ridder Park Dr
Street address state: CA
Postal code: 95131-2432
County: Santa Clara
Country: USA
Mailing address: 750 Ridder Park Dr
Mailing city: San Jose
Mailing state: CA
Mailing zip: 95190-0001
Office phone: (408) 920-5843
Office fax: (408) 271-3732
Advertising (open inch rate): Open inch rate $55.00
Audit By: Sworn/Estimate/Non-Audited
Audit Date: 12.07.2019
Personnel: Rosaura Miramontes (Adv. Mgr., Natl' Sales); Marina Hinestrosa (Ed.)
Main (survey) contact: Marina Hinestrosa

EL NUEVO DIA

Street address 1: Cond Almirante
Street address state: PR
Postal code: 911
County: San Juan
Country: Puerto Rico
Mailing address: Cond Almirante
Mailing city: San Juan
Mailing state: PR
Mailing zip: 00911-1232
Office phone: 787-641-8000
Website: www.elnuevodia.net
Frequency: Mon`Tues`Wed`Thur`Fri`Sat`Sun
Circulation Paid: 165840
Audit By: AAM
Audit Date: 31.12.2017
Parent company: GFR MEDIA, LLC.

SAN YSIDRO

AHORA NOW

Street address 1: 378 E San Ysidro Blvd
Street address state: CA
Postal code: 92173-2722
County: San Diego
Country: USA
Mailing address: 378 E San Ysidro Blvd
Mailing city: Dan Ysidro
Mailing state: CA
Mailing zip: 92173-2722
Office phone: (619) 428-2277
Office fax: (619) 428-0871
General e-mail: ahoranow2008@hotmail.com
Advertising (open inch rate): Open inch rate $19.00
Frequency: Thur
Circulation Free: 20000
Audit By: Sworn/Estimate/Non-Audited
Audit Date: 12.07.2019

Personnel: Juan Manuel Torres (Adv. Mgr.); Bertha Alicia Gonzalez (Ed.)
Main (survey) contact: Bertha Alicia Gonzalez

SANTA ANA

AZTECA NEWS

Street address 1: 1823 E 17th St
Street address 2: Ste 312
Street address state: CA
Postal code: 92705-8630
County: Orange
Country: USA
Office phone: (714) 972-9912
Advertising phone: (714) 760-4939
General e-mail: aztecanews@aol.com
Advertising e-mail: fvelo@aztecanews.com
Editorial e-mail: rromano@aztecanews.com
Website: www.aztecanews.com
Year newspaper established: 1980
Advertising (open inch rate): Net inch rate $21.50
Delivery methods: Racks
Frequency: Wed
Other Type of Frequency: weekly
Circulation Free: 42
Audit By: Sworn/Estimate/Non-Audited
Audit Date: 12.07.2019
Personnel: Fernando Velo (Pub.); Alessandro Hernandez (Adv. Mgr.); Rosanna Romano (Mng. Ed.)
Main (survey) contact: Fernando Velo

SANTA ROSA

LA PRENSA SONOMA

Street address 1: 427 Mendocino Ave
Street address state: CA
Postal code: 95401-6313
County: Sonoma
Country: USA
Mailing address: ricardo.ibarra@pressdemocrat.com
Office phone: (707) 526-8501
Advertising phone: 707-521-5342
Advertising e-mail: jose.delcastillo@pressdemocrat.com
Editorial e-mail: ricardo.ibarra@pressdemocrat.com
Website: http://www.laprensasonoma.com/
Year newspaper established: 2016
Digital Platform - Mobile: Apple`Android
Digital Platform - Tablet: Apple iOS`Android
Frequency: Mthly
Circulation Free: 30000
Audit By: Sworn/Estimate/Non-Audited
Audit Date: 12.07.2019
Personnel: Ricardo Ibarra
Parent company: Sonoma Media Investments
Main (survey) contact: Ricardo Ibarra

LA VOZ BILINGUAL NEWSPAPER

Street address 1: PO Box 3688
Street address state: CA
Postal code: 95402
County: Berks
Country: USA
Mailing address: PO Box 3688
Mailing city: Santa Rosa
Mailing state: CA
Mailing zip: 95402
Office phone: (707) 538-1812
General e-mail: ads@lavoz.us.com
Website: lavoz.us.com
Advertising (open inch rate): Open inch rate $12.48
Mechanical specifications: Type page 9 2/3 x 11 1/2.
Frequency: Wed
Circulation Free: 3986
Audit By: Sworn/Estimate/Non-Audited
Audit Date: 12.07.2019
Personnel: Ani Weaver (Pub./Ed./Owner)
Main (survey) contact: Ani Weaver

SILVER SPRING

WASHINGTON HISPANIC

Street address 1: 8455 Colesville Rd
Street address state: MD
Postal code: 20910-7600
County: Montgomery
Country: USA
Mailing address: 8455 Colesville Rd
Mailing city: Washington
Mailing state: DC
Mailing zip: 20910
Office phone: (202) 667-8881
Office fax: (202) 667-8902
General e-mail: info@washingtonhispanic.com
Website: www.washingtonhispanic.com
Advertising (open inch rate): Open inch rate $43.00
Mechanical specifications: Type page 13 x 21 1/10; E - 6 cols, 1 7/8, 1/6 between; A - 6 cols, 1 7/8, 1/6 between; C - 6 cols, 1 7/8, 1/6 between.
Audit By: Sworn/Estimate/Non-Audited
Audit Date: 12.07.2019
Hardware: APP/Mac
Software: Adobe/Photoshop, QPS/QuarkXPress.
Personnel: Johnny Yataco (Adv. Mgr.)
Main (survey) contact: Johnny Yataco

TAMPA

LA GACETA

Street address 1: 3210 E 7th Ave
Street address state: FL
Postal code: 33605-4302
County: Hillsborough
Country: USA
Mailing address: PO Box 5536
Mailing city: Tampa
Mailing state: FL
Mailing zip: 33675-5536
Office phone: (813) 248-3921
Office fax: (813) 247-5357
General e-mail: lagaceta@tampabay.rr.com
Advertising e-mail: lagaceta@tampabay.rr.com
Editorial e-mail: lagaceta@tampabay.rr.com
Website: www.lagacetanewspaper.com
Year newspaper established: 1922
Advertising (open inch rate): Open inch rate $11.00
Mechanical specifications: Type page 10 x 16 1/2; E - 5 cols, 1 3/4, 1/4 between; A - 5 cols, 1 3/4, 1/4 between; C - 5 cols, 1 3/4, 1/4 between.
Delivery methods: Mail`Newsstand`Racks
Frequency: Fri
Circulation Paid: 18000
Audit By: Sworn/Estimate/Non-Audited
Audit Date: 12.07.2019
Hardware: Dell
Software: Adobe/Creative Suite.
Personnel: Peggy Schmechel (Adv. Mgr.); Gene Siudut (Circ. Mgr.); Patrick Manteiga (Ed.); Angela Manteiga (Mng. Ed.); Angie Manteiga (Prodn. Mgr.)
Main (survey) contact: Angie Manteiga

TAMPA

NUEVO SIGLO

Street address 1: 7137 N Armenia Ave
Street address 2: Ste B
Street address state: FL
Postal code: 33604-5263
County: Hillsborough
Country: USA
Mailing address: 100 Rose Way
Mailing city: Tullahoma
Mailing state: TN
Mailing zip: 37388-9545
Office phone: (813) 932-7181
Office fax: (813) 932-8202
General e-mail: n.siglo@verizon.net
Website: www.nuevosiglotampa.com
Advertising (open inch rate): Open inch rate $16.00
Mechanical specifications: Type page 10 1/4

x 16; E - 6 cols, 1 1/2, 1/4 between; A - 6 cols, 1 1/2, 1/4 between; C - 2 cols, 3 1/2, 1/4 between.
Frequency: Thur
Circulation Paid: 3000
Circulation Free: 24000
Audit By: Sworn/Estimate/Non-Audited
Audit Date: 12.07.2019
Hardware: PC.
Personnel: Neris Ramon Palacios (Pub.); Rosmeli Palacios (Gen. Mgr.); Griseldis Palacios (Adv. Mgr.); Ledis Palacios (Mng. Ed.)
Main (survey) contact: Neris Ramon Palacios

THORNTON

LA VOZ BILINGUE

Street address 1: 12021 Pennsylvania St Ste 201
Street address 2: #201
Street address state: CO
Postal code: 80241-3152
County: Adams
Country: USA
Office phone: (303) 936-8556
Office fax: (720) 889-2455
Advertising phone: (303) 936-8556
General e-mail: privera@lavozcolorado.com
Advertising e-mail: privera@lavozcolorado.com
Editorial e-mail: news@lavozcolorado.com
Website: lavozcolorado.com
Advertising (open inch rate): Open inch rate $18.00
Delivery methods: Mail
Frequency: Wed
Circulation Free: 32000
Audit By: AAM
Audit Date: 31.12.2018
Personnel: Pauline Rivera (Pub./Adv. Dir.); Romelia Ulibarri (Classified Mgr.); Jim Koucherik (Circ. Mgr.); Charles Corrales (Prod. Coord.)
Main (survey) contact: Pauline Rivera
footnotes: Advertising (open inch rate): SRDS (11/13/2014)

TORRANCE

IMPACTO USA

Street address 1: 21250 Hawthorne Blvd
Street address state: CA
Postal code: 90503-5506
County: Los Angeles
Country: USA
Mailing address: 21250 Hawthorne Blvd Ste 170
Mailing city: Torrance
Mailing state: CA
Mailing zip: 90503-5514
Office phone: (562) 499-1415
Office fax: (562) 499-1484
Website: www.impactousa.com
Advertising (open inch rate): Open inch rate $62.00
Zip Codes Served: 90650, 90723, 90280, 90222, 90201, 90716
Frequency: Fri
Circulation Paid: 207248
Audit By: AAM
Audit Date: 31.03.2015
Hardware: APP/Mac
Software: QPS/QuarkXPress.
Editions Count: 250000
Personnel: Raúl Martánez (Dsgn. Mgr.); Trinidad Verduzco (Ed.)
Main (survey) contact: Raúl Martánez

TUSTIN

MINIONDAS

Street address 1: 17291 Irvine Blvd
Street address 2: Ste 225
Street address state: CA
Postal code: 92780-2941
County: Orange
Country: USA

Mailing zip: 93510-005
Office phone: (714) 668-1010
Website: www.miniondas.com
Year newspaper established: 1975
Advertising (open inch rate): Open inch rate $10.97
Frequency: Thur
Personnel: Sandra Cervantes (Pub.)
Main (survey) contact: Sandra Cervantes

UNION CITY

CONTINENTAL NEWSPAPER

Street address 1: 212 48th St
Street address state: NJ
Postal code: 07087-6436
County: Hudson
Country: USA
Mailing address: 212 48th St Ste A
Mailing city: Union City
Mailing state: NJ
Mailing zip: 07087-6436
Office phone: (201) 864-9505
Office fax: (201) 864-9456
General e-mail: continews@aol.com
Advertising (open inch rate): Open inch rate $35.00
Mechanical specifications: Type page 10 x 14; E - 5 cols, 2, between; A - 5 cols, 2, between.
Frequency: Fri
Circulation Paid: 38000
Audit By: Sworn/Estimate/Non-Audited
Audit Date: 12.07.2019
Hardware: APP/Mac
Software: Adobe/PageMaker, Microsoft/Word.
Editions Count: 2
Edition Names with Circ figures: 2 total Ã‚Â— Continental Newspaper-New York (23,000);
Personnel: M. Ofelia Dones (Pres.); Mario Ciria (Exec. Dir.); Veronica Romero (Mng. Ed.)
Main (survey) contact: M. Ofelia Dones

EL ESPECIALITO

Street address 1: 3711 Hudson Ave
Street address state: NJ
Postal code: 07087-6015
County: Hudson
Country: USA
Mailing address: 3711 Hudson Ave
Mailing city: Union City
Mailing state: NJ
Mailing zip: 07087
Office phone: (201) 348-1959
Office fax: (201) 348-3385
General e-mail: anthony@elespecial.com
Advertising e-mail: anthony@elespecial.com
Editorial e-mail: jsibaja@elespecial.com
Website: www.elespecial.com
Year newspaper established: 1985
Advertising (open inch rate): Open inch rate $55.00
Mechanical specifications: Type page 10 x 11.25"; E - 4 cols, 2 3/8, between; A - 4 cols, between; C - 6 cols, between.
Delivery methods: Carrier`Racks
Zip Codes Served: New York and New Jersey
Digital Platform - Mobile: Apple`Android`Windows`Blackberry
Digital Platform - Tablet: Apple iOS`Android`Windows 7`Blackberry Tablet OS`Nook
Frequency: Fri
Other Type of Frequency: Weekly
Circulation Free: 251339
Audit By: AAM
Audit Date: 30.06.2018
Hardware: APP/Mac G3
Software: QPS/QuarkXPress, Adobe/Photoshop.
Editions Count: 13
Edition Names with Circ figures: El Especialito
Personnel: John Ibarria (VP); Anthony Ibarria (Adv. Mgr.); Jose Sibaja (Ed. Dir.)
Main (survey) contact: Elsie Miolan; Anthony Ibarria

LA TRIBUNA PUBLICATION

Street address 1: 300 36th St

Street address state: NJ
Postal code: 07087-4724
County: Hudson
Country: USA
Mailing address: PO Box 805
Mailing city: Union City
Mailing state: NJ
Mailing zip: 07087-0805
Office phone: (201) 863-3310
Office fax: (201) 617-0042
General e-mail: info@latribuna.com
Website: www.latribuna.com
Advertising (open inch rate): Open inch rate $19.80
Mechanical specifications: Type page 9 3/4 x 15; E - 6 cols, 1 1/2, 1/8 between; A - 6 cols, 1 1/2, 1/8 between; C - 6 cols, 1 1/2, 1/8 between.
Audit By: Sworn/Estimate/Non-Audited
Audit Date: 12.07.2019
Hardware: PC
Software: Adobe/PageMaker, Microsoft/Excel, Microsoft/Word, Microsoft/Office, Quicker, Aldus.
Personnel: Ruth Molenaar (Pub.); Soraya Molenaar (Adv. Mgr.); Rosario Tineo (Circ. Mgr.); Lionel Rodriquez (Ed.)
Main (survey) contact: Ruth Molenaar

UPPER DARBY

EL HISPANO

Street address 1: 8605 W Chester Pike
Street address state: PA
Postal code: 19082-1101
County: Delaware
Country: USA
Mailing address: 8605 W Chester Pike
Mailing city: Upper Darby
Mailing state: PA
Mailing zip: 19082-1101
Office phone: (610) 789-5512
Office fax: (610) 789-5524
General e-mail: alopez5268@aol.com; hispads@aol.com
Website: www.el-hispano.com
Year newspaper established: 1976
Advertising (open inch rate): Open inch rate $41.00
Mechanical specifications: Type page 10 1/8 x 12; E - 5 cols, 1 7/8, 1/8 between; A - 5 cols, 1 7/8, 1/8 between; C - 7 cols, 1 3/8, 1/6 between.
Zip Codes Served: 19102, 08101, 08625, 19601, 17101, 18015
Frequency: Wed
Circulation Paid: 100
Circulation Free: 40000
Audit By: Sworn/Estimate/Non-Audited
Audit Date: 12.07.2019
Hardware: 2-APP/Mac Quadra 650, 2-APP/Mac II, APP/Mac Power MC, 2-APP/Power Mac G3s, 2-Umax/PowerLook II Scanner, 2-Elite/XL808, 1-Epson/Stylus Color 1520, 2-APP/Mac G4
Presses: G
Software: Adobe/InDesign, Adobe/Photoshop 5.0, Microsoft/Word.
Personnel: Madelyn Madary (Adv. Mgr.); Philip Madary (Circ. Mgr.); Aaron G. Lopez (Mng. Ed.); Sara Lopez (Ed.); Aaron Galicia (Prodn. Mgr.)
Main (survey) contact: Aaron G. Lopez

WASHINGTON

EL TIEMPO LATINO

Street address 1: 1150 15th St
Street address state: DC
Postal code: 20071-0001
County: District Of Columbia
Country: USA
Mailing address: 1150 15th St NW
Mailing city: Washington
Mailing state: DC
Mailing zip: 20071-0001
Office phone: 202-334-9100
Office fax: 202-496-3599
Advertising phone: 202-334-9146

Advertising fax: 202-496-3599
Editorial phone: 202-334-9159
Editorial fax: 202-496-3599
Advertising e-mail: zulema@eltiempolatino.com
Editorial e-mail: paula@eltiempolatino.com
Website: www.eltiempolatino.com
Year newspaper established: 1991
Advertising (open inch rate): Open inch rate $38.00
Mechanical specifications: Type page 12 x 21; E - 6 cols, 1 43/50, 1/16 between; A - 6 cols, 1 43/50, 1/16 between; C - 6 cols, 1/16 between.
Delivery methods: Newsstand`Carrier`Racks
Frequency: Fri
Circulation Free: 50000
Audit By: AAM
Audit Date: 15.01.2012
Hardware: APP/Power Mac
Software: QPS/QuarkXPress 3.3, Adobe/Photoshop, Macromedia/Freehand, Adobe/Illustrator.
Personnel: Alberto Avendano (Director of Business Development); Kris Holmes (Office Mgr.); Zulema Tijero (Adv. Mgr.)
Parent company: The Washington Post
Main (survey) contact: Alberto Avendano

WEST GROVE

UNIDAD LATINA

Street address 1: 144 S Jennersville Rd
Street address state: PA
Postal code: 19390-9430
County: Chester
Country: USA
Mailing address: PO Box 150
Mailing city: Kelton
Mailing state: PA
Mailing zip: 19346-0150
Office phone: (610) 869-5553
Office fax: (610) 869-9628
General e-mail: info@chestercounty.com
Website: www.chestercounty.com/unidad/default.htm
Year newspaper established: 1995
Advertising (open inch rate): Open inch rate $10.00
Mechanical specifications: Type page 10 x 15 1/2; E - 4 cols, 2 3/4, 1/4 between; A - 4 cols, 2 3/4, 1/4 between; C - 4 cols, 2 3/4, between.
Zip Codes Served: 19363
Audit By: Sworn/Estimate/Non-Audited
Audit Date: 12.07.2019
Hardware: PC
Software: Microsoft, Adobe/Photoshop.
Personnel: Randall S. Lieberman (Pub.); Alan Turns (Adv. Mgr.); Steve Hoffman (Mng. Ed.)
Main (survey) contact: Randall S. Lieberman

WEST PALM BEACH

EL LATINO NEWSPAPER

Street address 1: 4404 Georgia Ave
Street address state: FL
Postal code: 33405-2500
County: Palm Beach
Country: USA
Mailing address: 4404 Georgia Ave.
Mailing city: West Palm Beach
Mailing state: FL
Mailing zip: 33405-2524
Office phone: (561) 835-4913
Office fax: (561) 655-5059
General e-mail: ellatino@msn.com
Website: www.ellatinosemanal.com
Advertising (open inch rate): Open inch rate $16.00
Frequency: Fri
Circulation Free: 39000
Audit By: Sworn/Estimate/Non-Audited
Audit Date: 12.07.2019
Personnel: Miguel A. Lavin (Pub.); Eduardo Monzon (Adv. Mgr.); Jose Uzal (Ed.)
Main (survey) contact: Jose Uzal

Hispanic Newspapers in the U.S.

WINSTON SALEM

QUE PASA - CHARLOTTE

Street address 1: 7520 East Independence Blvd.
Street address 2: Suite 255
Street address state: NC
Postal code: 28227
County: Forsyth
Country: USA
Mailing address: 3025 Waughtown St Ste G
Mailing city: Winston Salem
Mailing state: NC
Mailing zip: 27107-1679
Office phone: (704) 319-5044
General e-mail: distribution@quepasamedia.com
Advertising e-mail: sales@quepasamedia.com
Editorial e-mail: editor@quepasamedia.com
Website: quepasamedia.com
Year newspaper established: 1994
Advertising (open inch rate): Open inch rate $15.88
Mechanical specifications: Type page: 9.889 x 12.85; 6 col
Frequency: Thur
Circulation Paid: 0
Circulation Free: 37078
Audit By: CVC
Audit Date: 31.12.2018
Personnel: Amith Arrieta; Jose Isasi (Pub.); Marina Aleman (Adv.); Hernando Ramirez (Ed.)
Main (survey) contact: Amith Arrieta

QUE PASA - WINSTON-SALEM

Street address 1: 3067 Waughtown St
Street address state: NC
Postal code: 27107-1679
Country: USA
Mailing address: 3067 Waughtown St
Mailing city: Winston Salem
Mailing state: NC
Mailing zip: 27107
Office phone: (336) 784-9004
General e-mail: distribution@quepasamedia.com
Advertising e-mail: sales@quepasamedia.com
Editorial e-mail: editor@quepasamedia.com
Website: quepasamedia.com
Year newspaper established: 1994
Advertising (open inch rate): Open inch rate $15.88
Mechanical specifications: Type page: 10 x 21; 6 col
Frequency: Wed
Circulation Paid: 0
Circulation Free: 12698
Audit By: CVC
Audit Date: 31.12.2018
Personnel: Amith Arrieta; Jose Isasi (Pub.); Marina Aleman (Adv.)
Main (survey) contact: Amith Arrieta

YUMA

BAJO EL SOL

Street address 1: 2055 S Arizona Ave
Street address state: AZ
Postal code: 85364-6549
County: Yuma
Country: USA
Mailing address: PO BOX 271
Mailing city: YUMA
Mailing state: AZ
Mailing zip: 85366-0271
Office phone: (928) 539-6800
Office fax: (928) 343-1009
Advertising phone: (928) 539-6829
Advertising fax: (928) 343-6928
Editorial phone: (928) 539-6850
Editorial fax: (928) 782-7369
General e-mail: nationals@yumasun.com
Advertising e-mail: nationals@yumasun.com
Editorial e-mail: jvaughn@yumasun.com
Website: www.bajoelsol.com
Year newspaper established: 1991
Advertising (open inch rate): Open inch rate $17.65 gross
Mechanical specifications: Type page 9.889 x 21
Delivery methods: Carrier`Racks
Zip Codes Served: 85364, 85365, 92283, 85367, 85356, 85352, 85350, 85336, 85349
Digital Platform - Mobile: Apple`Android`Windows`Blackberry
Digital Platform - Tablet: Apple iOS`Android`Windows 7`Blackberry Tablet OS`Kindle Fire
Frequency: Fri
Circulation Free: 15002
Audit By: AAM
Audit Date: 30.06.2018
Hardware: APP/Mac
Presses: 9-G/Urbanite
Software: DTI/AdSpeed 4.1, Adobe/Illustrator 7.0, Adobe/Photoshop 5.0.
Editions Count: 15000
Personnel: Darlene Firestone (Ntl. Acct Mgr.)
Parent company: Yuma Sun, Inc.
Main (survey) contact: Darlene Firestone

JEWISH NEWSPAPERS IN THE U.S.

ALBUQUERQUE

NEW MEXICO JEWISH LINK

Street address 1: 5520 Wyoming Blvd NE
Street address state: NM
Postal code: 87109-3238
County: Bernalillo
Country: USA
Mailing address: 5520 Wyoming Blvd NE
Mailing city: Albuquerque
Mailing state: NM
Mailing zip: 87109-3238
Office phone: (505) 821-3214
Office fax: (505) 821-3351
General e-mail: news@nmjlink.org
Web address: www.jewishnewmexico.org
Mechanical specifications: Type page 10 1/16 x 14 3/4; E - 5 cols, 1 7/8, 3/16 between; A - 5 cols, 1 7/8, 3/16 between.
Zip Codes Served: 87109
Frequency: Mthly
Circulation Free: 6500
Audit By: Sworn/Estimate/Non-Audited
Audit Date: 12.07.2019
Hardware: APP/Mac IIci
Software: Microsoft/Word 7.0, Adobe/PageMaker.
Personnel: Erin Tarica (Dir.); Jen Dennis (Sr. Serv. Mgr.); Rabbi Art Flicker (Chaplain)
Main (survey) contact: Erin Tarica

ATLANTA

ATLANTA JEWISH TIMES

Street address 1: 270 Carpenter Dr
Street address 2: Ste 320
Street address state: GA
Postal code: 30328-4933
County: Fulton
Country: USA
Mailing address: 270 Carpenter Dr Ste 320
Mailing city: Atlanta
Mailing state: GA
Mailing zip: 30328
Office phone: (404) 883-2130
Office fax: (404) 883-2136
General e-mail: kaylene@atljewishtimes.com
Advertising e-mail: kaylene@atljewishtimes.com
Editorial e-mail: mjacobs@atljewishtimes.com
Web address: www.atlantajewishtimes.com
Year newspaper established: 1925
Advertising (open inch rate): Open inch rate $24.80
Mechanical specifications: Type page 10 x 13;
Delivery methods: Mail`Newsstand`Carrier`Racks
Digital Platform - Mobile: Apple`Android`Windows`Blackberry`Other
Digital Platform - Tablet: Apple iOS`Android`Windows 7`Blackberry Tablet OS`Kindle`Nook`Kindle Fire`Other
Frequency: Fri
Other Type of Frequency: weekly
Circulation Paid: 3500
Circulation Free: 11500
Audit By: Sworn/Estimate/Non-Audited
Audit Date: 12.07.2019
Hardware: APP/Mac
Personnel: Kaylene Ladinsky (Assoc. Pub.); Michael Morris (Pub.); Michael Jacobs (Ed.)
Parent company: Southern Israelite LLC
Main (survey) contact: Kaylene Ladinsky

BALTIMORE

JEWISH TIMES

Street address 1: 1040 Park Ave
Street address 2: Ste 200
Street address state: MD
Postal code: 21201-5634
County: Baltimore City
Country: USA
Mailing address: 11459 Cronhill Dr Ste A
Mailing city: Owings Mills
Mailing state: MD
Mailing zip: 21117-6280
Office phone: (410) 752-3504
General e-mail: information@jewishtimes.com
Web address: www.jewishtimes.com
Advertising (open inch rate): Open inch rate $39.06
Mechanical specifications: Type page 9 13/16 x 12; E - 4 cols, 2 5/16, between; A - 4 cols, 2 5/16, between; C - 6 cols, 1 1/2, between.
Frequency: Fri
Circulation Paid: 35000
Audit By: Sworn/Estimate/Non-Audited
Audit Date: 12.07.2019
Hardware: APP/Mac.
Personnel: Maayan Jaffe (Pub.); Claudia Meyers (Gen. Mgr.); Phil Jacobs (Ed.); Erin Clare (Prodn. Mgr.)
Main (survey) contact: Andrew Buerger

BEACHWOOD

CLEVELAND JEWISH NEWS

Street address 1: 23880 Commerce Park
Street address 2: Ste 1
Street address state: OH
Postal code: 44122-5830
County: Cuyahoga
Country: USA
Office phone: (216)454-8300
Office fax: (216)454-8100
Advertising phone: (216)342-5191
Advertising fax: (216)454-8100
Editorial phone: (216)342-5207
Editorial fax: (216)454-8200
General e-mail: info@cjn.org
Advertising e-mail: amandell@cjn.org
Editorial e-mail: editorial@cjn.org
Web address: www.cjn.org
Year newspaper established: 1964
Advertising (open inch rate): $330
Delivery methods: Mail`Newsstand
Zip Codes Served: Cleveland and suburbs
Frequency: Fri
Circulation Paid: 7036
Circulation Free: 540
Audit By: USPS
Audit Date: 28.09.2018
Personnel: Kevin Adelstein (Pres., Pub. & CEO); Adam Mandell (VP of Sales); Bob Jacob (Mng. Ed.); Tracy DiDomenico (Controller)
Parent company: Cleveland Jewish Publication Company
Main (survey) contact: Abby Royer

BOSTON

THE JEWISH ADVOCATE

Street address 1: 15 School St
Street address state: MA
Postal code: 02108-4307
County: Suffolk
Country: USA
Office phone: (617) 367-9100
Office fax: (617) 367-9310
General e-mail: sharonh@thejewishadvocate.com
Advertising e-mail: business@thejewishadvocate.com
Editorial e-mail: editorial@thejewishadvocate.com
Web address: www.thejewishadvocate.com
Year newspaper established: 1902
Advertising (open inch rate): Open inch rate $33.00
Mechanical specifications: Type page 10 1/4 x 14 1/4; E - 5 cols, 1 15/16, 1/8 between; A - 5 cols, 1 15/16, 1/8 between; C - 10 cols, 1 3/16, 1/8 between.
Delivery methods: Mail`Newsstand
Digital Platform - Mobile: Blackberry
Digital Platform - Tablet: Kindle`Kindle Fire
Frequency: Fri
Circulation Paid: 30000
Audit By: Sworn/Estimate/Non-Audited
Audit Date: 12.07.2019
Personnel: Grand Rabbi Y. A. Korff (Pub.); Michael Whalen (Ed.); Sharon Harrau (Administrator); Ian Thal
Main (survey) contact: Daniel M. Kimmel

BROOKLYN

ALGEMEINER JOURNAL

Street address 1: 508 Montgomery St
Street address state: NY
Postal code: 11225-3023
County: Kings
Country: USA
Mailing address: 508 Montgomery St
Mailing city: Brooklyn
Mailing state: NY
Mailing zip: 11225-3023
Office phone: (347) 741-7830
Office fax: (718) 771-0308
General e-mail: algemeiner@aol.com
Web address: www.algemeiner.com
Advertising (open inch rate): Open inch rate $31.50
Frequency: Wed
Circulation Paid: 30000

Circulation Free: 28000
Audit By: Sworn/Estimate/Non-Audited
Audit Date: 12.07.2019
Personnel: Simon Jacobson (Pub.); Dovid Efune (Dir.); Moshe Hecht (Adv. Mgr.); Yosef Jacobson (Ed.)
Parent company: Joseph Jacobs Organization
Main (survey) contact: Simon Jacobson

DER YID

Street address 1: 191 Rodney St
Street address state: NY
Postal code: 11211-7787
County: Kings
Country: USA
Mailing address: 191 rodney St
Mailing city: Brooklyn
Mailing state: NY
Mailing zip: 11211
Office phone: (718) 797-3900
Office fax: (718) 797-1985
General e-mail: adv@deryid.org
Web address: deryid.org
Advertising (open inch rate): Open inch rate $15.00
Mechanical specifications: Type page 10 x 15 1/2; E - 5 cols, 2, between.
Delivery methods: Mail`Newsstand`Racks
Frequency: Thur
Audit By: Sworn/Estimate/Non-Audited
Audit Date: 12.07.2019
Hardware: APP/Mac.
Personnel: Herman Friedman (Gen. Mgr.); Aron Friedman (Ed.)
Parent company: Joseph Jacobs Organization
Main (survey) contact: Herman Friedman

THE JEWISH PRESS

Street address 1: 338 3rd Ave
Street address state: NY
Postal code: 11215-1816
County: Kings
Country: USA
Mailing address: 4915 16th Ave
Mailing city: Brooklyn
Mailing state: NY
Mailing zip: 11204-1115
Office phone: (718) 330-1100
Office fax: (718) 935-1215
General e-mail: editor@jewishpress.com
Web address: www.jewishpress.com
Year newspaper established: 1955
Advertising (open inch rate): Open inch rate $77.00
Mechanical specifications: Type page 10 1/4 x 14; E - 6 cols, 1 5/8, between; A - 6 cols, 1 5/8, between.
Frequency: Fri
Circulation Paid: 67409
Circulation Free: 1875
Audit By: Sworn/Estimate/Non-Audited
Audit Date: 12.07.2019
Hardware: IBM
Software: Adobe/PageMaker 7.0, Microsoft/Word 2000, Adobe/Acrobat 6.0, Adobe/Illustrator 9.0.
Personnel: Irene Klass (Pub.); Heshy Kornblit (Display Dept. Mgr.); Joseph Hochberg (Circ. Mgr.); Jason Maoz (Sr. Ed.); Jerry Greenwald (Mng. Ed.)
Main (survey) contact: Irene Klass

BUFFALO

BUFFALO JEWISH REVIEW

Street address 1: 964 Kenmore Ave
Street address state: NY
Postal code: 14216-1450
County: Erie
Country: USA
Mailing address: 964 Kenmore Ave.
Mailing city: Buffalo
Mailing state: NY
Mailing zip: 14216
Office phone: (716) 854-2192
Office fax: (716) 854-2198
General e-mail: buffjewrev@aol.com
Web address: http://www.buffalojewishreview.com/
Advertising (open inch rate): Open inch rate $14.20
Mechanical specifications: Type page 10 1/2 x 15; E - 5 cols, 2, between; A - 5 cols, 2, between.
Frequency: Fri
Circulation Paid: 3500
Audit By: Sworn/Estimate/Non-Audited
Audit Date: 12.07.2019
Hardware: APP/Mac.
Personnel: Arnold Weiss (Pub.); Rita Weiss (Ed.)
Parent company: Joseph Jacobs Organization
Main (survey) contact: Moshe Abraham

CANTON

STARK JEWISH NEWS

Street address 1: 2631 Harvard Ave NW
Street address state: OH
Postal code: 44709-3147
County: Stark
Country: USA
Mailing address: 432 30th St NW
Mailing city: Canton
Mailing state: OH
Mailing zip: 44709-3108
Office phone: (330) 452-6444
Office fax: (330) 452-4487
General e-mail: starkjewishnews@aol.com
Web address: www.jewishcanton.org
Advertising (open inch rate): Open inch rate $7.00
Mechanical specifications: Type page 11 1/2 x 13 3/4.
Zip Codes Served: 44709
Frequency: Mthly
Circulation Paid: 500
Circulation Free: 1500
Audit By: Sworn/Estimate/Non-Audited
Audit Date: 12.07.2019
Hardware: APP/Mac
Software: Adobe/PageMaker 4.2.
Personnel: Bonnie Manello (CEO)
Parent company: Joseph Jacobs Organization
Main (survey) contact: Bonnie Manello

CHARLOTTE

CHARLOTTE JEWISH NEWS

Street address 1: 5007 Providence Rd
Street address state: NC
Postal code: 28226-5849
County: Mecklenburg
Country: USA
Mailing address: 5007 Providence Rd Ste 112
Mailing city: Charlotte
Mailing state: NC
Mailing zip: 28226-5907
Office phone: (704) 944-6757
Office fax: (704) 944-6766
General e-mail: info@jewishcharlotte.org
Editorial e-mail: amontoni@shalomcharlotte.org
Web address: www.jewishcharlotte.org
Year newspaper established: 1979
Advertising (open inch rate): Open inch rate $15.46
Frequency: Mthly
Circulation Free: 4200
Audit By: Sworn/Estimate/Non-Audited
Audit Date: 12.07.2019
Personnel: Rita Mond (Adv. Mgr.); Amy Montoni (Ed.)
Parent company: Joseph Jacobs Organization
Main (survey) contact: Amy Montoni

CHERRY HILL

JEWISH VOICE

Street address 1: 1301 Springdale Rd
Street address 2: Ste 250
Street address state: NJ
Postal code: 08003-2763
County: Camden
Country: USA
Mailing address: 1301 Springdale Road
Mailing city: Cherry Hill
Mailing state: NJ
Mailing zip: 08003-2762
Office phone: (856) 751-9500 x1217
Office fax: (856) 489-8253
Editorial phone: (856) 751-9500 x1237
General e-mail: jvoice@jfedsnj.org
Editorial e-mail: dportnoe@jfedsnj.org
Web address: jewishvoicesnj.org
Advertising (open inch rate): Open inch rate $18.50
Mechanical specifications: Type page 10 x 14; E - 5 cols, 2, between.
Zip Codes Served: 7723
Audit By: Sworn/Estimate/Non-Audited
Audit Date: 10.06.2019
Personnel: Stuart Abraham (Pub.); Howard Gases (Pub.); Judy Robinowitz (Adv. Mgr.); Lauren Silver (Ed.); Oscar Trugler (Prodn. Mgr.)
Parent company: Joseph Jacobs Organization
Main (survey) contact: David Portnoe

CHICAGO

JEWISH UNITED FUND

Street address 1: 30 S. Wells St.
Street address state: IL
Postal code: 60606
County: Cook
Country: USA
Mailing address: 30 S. Wells St.
Mailing city: Chicago
Mailing state: IL
Mailing zip: 60606
Office phone: (312) 346-6700
Office fax: (312) 855-2470
Editorial e-mail: editorial@juf.org
Web address: www.juf.org
Advertising (open inch rate): Open inch rate $31.15
Personnel: Kathleen Evans-Mazur (Gen. Mgr.); Robert Feiger (Adv. Mgr.); Aaron Cohen (Ed.)
Main (survey) contact: Aaron B. Cohen

CINCINNATI

THE AMERICAN ISRAELITE

Street address 1: 18 W 9th St
Street address 2: Ste 2
Street address state: OH
Postal code: 45202-2037
County: Hamilton
Country: USA
Mailing address: 18 W 9th St Ste 2
Mailing city: Cincinnati
Mailing state: OH
Mailing zip: 45202-2037
Office phone: (513) 621-3145
Office fax: (513) 621-3744
General e-mail: publisher@americanisraelite.com
Web address: www.americanisraelite.com
Advertising (open inch rate): Open inch rate $20.30
Mechanical specifications: Type page 10 x 13 1/4; E - 5 cols, between; A - 5 cols, between.
Frequency: Thur
Circulation Paid: 6522
Circulation Free: 461
Audit By: Sworn/Estimate/Non-Audited
Audit Date: 12.07.2019
Hardware: APP/Power Mac
Software: QPS/QuarkXPress.
Personnel: Ted Deutsch (Pub.); Sauni Lerner (Mng. Ed.)
Parent company: Joseph Jacobs Organization
Main (survey) contact: Ted Deutsch

CLEARWATER

JEWISH PRESS OF PINELLAS

COUNTY
Street address 1: 1101 S Belcher Rd, Ste H
Street address state: FL
Postal code: 33758
County: Pinellas
Country: USA
Mailing address: PO Box 6970
Mailing city: Clearwater
Mailing state: FL
Mailing zip: 33758-6970
Office phone: (727) 535-4400
Office fax: (727) 530-3039
General e-mail: jewishpress@aol.com
Year newspaper established: 1985
Advertising (open inch rate): Open inch rate $13.75
Mechanical specifications: Type page 10 1/4 x 15 3/4; E - 5 cols, 2, 1/6 between; A - 5 cols, 2, 1/6 between.
Zip Codes Served: 34664, 34689, 33701, 33728, 33729, 33789
Hardware: APP/Mac
Software: Adobe/Pagemaker 6.0, Adobe/Photoshop 5.0, QPS/QuarkXPress.
Personnel: Jim Dawkins (Adv. Mgr.); Karen Dawkins (Mng. Ed.)
Main (survey) contact: Jim Dawkins

COLUMBUS

OHIO JEWISH CHRONICLE

Street address 1: 2862 Johnstown Rd
Street address state: OH
Postal code: 43219-1793
County: Franklin
Country: USA
Mailing address: PO Box 30965
Mailing city: Columbus
Mailing state: OH
Mailing zip: 43230-0965
Office phone: (614) 337-2055
Office fax: (614) 337-2059
General e-mail: ojc@insight.rr.com
Advertising (open inch rate): Open inch rate $10.50
Mechanical specifications: Type page 10 1/4 x 14; E - 6 cols, 1 5/8, 1/3 between; A - 6 cols, 1 5/8, 1/3 between.
Frequency: Thur
Circulation Paid: 2481
Circulation Free: 322
Audit By: Sworn/Estimate/Non-Audited
Audit Date: 12.07.2019
Personnel: Angela Miller (Adv. Mgr.); Stephen Pinsky (Mng. Ed.)
Parent company: Joseph Jacobs Organization
Main (survey) contact: Stephen Pinsky

DAYTON

THE DAYTON JEWISH OBSERVER

Street address 1: 525 Versailles Dr
Street address state: OH
Postal code: 45459-6074
County: Montgomery
Country: USA
Mailing address: 525 Versailles Dr
Mailing city: Dayton
Mailing state: OH
Mailing zip: 45459-6074
Office phone: (937) 610-1555
Office fax: (937) 853-0378
General e-mail: mweiss@jfgd.net
Web address: www.jewishdayton.org
Year newspaper established: 1996
Advertising (open inch rate): Open inch rate $15.50
Mechanical specifications: Type page 10 3/16 x 12 1/4; E - 5 cols, 1 7/8, 1/8 between; A - 5 cols, 1 7/8, 1/8 between; C - 5 cols, 1 7/8, 1/8 between.
Delivery methods: Mail`Newsstand`Racks
Zip Codes Served: Southwest Ohio
Digital Platform - Mobile: Other
Digital Platform - Tablet: Other
Frequency: Mthly
Circulation Free: 3232
Audit By: Sworn/Estimate/Non-Audited
Audit Date: 12.07.2019

Hardware: PC
Presses: Web press
Software: Adobe CS
Personnel: Marshall Weiss (Ed./Pub.)
Parent company: Jewish Federation of Greater Dayton
Main (survey) contact: Marshall Weiss

DEERFILED BEACH
JEWISH JOURNAL

Street address 1: 333 SW 12th Ave.
Street address state: FL
Postal code: 33442
County: Broward
Country: USA
Mailing address: 333 SW 12th Ave.
Mailing city: Deerfield Beach
Mailing state: FL
Mailing zip: 33442
Office phone: (954) 572-2050
Editorial phone: (954) 596-5648
Other phone: (800) 548-6397
General e-mail: rdaley@tribune.com
Advertising e-mail: gbehar@tribune.com
Editorial e-mail: ctouey@tribune.com
Web address: www.sun-sentinel.com/florida-jewish-journal
Year newspaper established: 1973
Advertising (open inch rate): Open inch rate $21.00
Mechanical specifications: Type page 10 3/8 x 16.
Delivery methods: Mail`Racks
Zip Codes Served: Broward County
Digital Platform - Mobile: Apple`Android`Windows`Blackberry
Digital Platform - Tablet: Apple iOS`Android`Windows 7`Blackberry Tablet OS
Frequency: Mthly
Circulation Paid: 0
Circulation Free: 30531
Audit By: CVC
Audit Date: 31.12.2012
Personnel: Tom Adams (Pub./Gen. Mgr.); Tracy Kolody (Mng. Ed.); Ed Wilder (Circ. Mgr.); Ray Daley (Adv. Mgr.); Stewart Cady (Prodn. Mgr.)
Parent company: Sun-Sentinel Co.
Main (survey) contact: Judith Jantz

DENVER
INTERMOUNTAIN JEWISH NEWS

Street address 1: 1177 N Grant St
Street address 2: Ste 200
Street address state: CO
Postal code: 80203-2362
County: Denver
Country: USA
Mailing address: 1177 Grant St Ste 200
Mailing city: Denver
Mailing state: CO
Mailing zip: 80203-2362
Office phone: (303) 861-2234
Office fax: (303) 832-6942
General e-mail: email@ijn.com
Web address: www.ijn.com
Advertising (open inch rate): Open inch rate $46.07
Mechanical specifications: Type page 10 x 16; E - 4 cols, 2 1/4, 1/4 between; A - 5 cols, 2, 1/6 between.
Frequency: Fri
Circulation Paid: 3000
Circulation Free: 287
Audit By: Sworn/Estimate/Non-Audited
Audit Date: 12.07.2019
Hardware: APP/Mac
Software: QPS/QuarkXPress, Adobe/Illustrator.
Personnel: Rabbi Hillel Goldberg (Gen. Mgr.); Lori Aron (Adv. Mgr.); Miriam Goldberg (Ed.); Larry Hankin (Mng. Ed.); Judy Waldren (Prodn. Mgr.)
Parent company: Joseph Jacobs Organization
Main (survey) contact: Miriam Goldberg

ENCINO
JEWISH NEWS

Street address 1: 16501 Ventura Blvd
Street address 2: Ste 504
Street address state: CA
Postal code: 91436-2047
County: Los Angeles
Country: USA
Mailing address: 16501 Ventura Blvd Ste 504
Mailing city: Encino
Mailing state: CA
Mailing zip: 91436-2047
Office phone: (818) 786-4000
Office fax: (818) 380-9232
General e-mail: info@jewishlifetv.com
Web address: www.jewishlifetv.com
Advertising (open inch rate): Open inch rate $28.00
Frequency: Mthly
Circulation Paid: 106000
Audit By: Sworn/Estimate/Non-Audited
Audit Date: 12.07.2019
Personnel: Phil Blazer (Ed.)
Main (survey) contact: Phil Blazer

ENGLEWOOD
JEWISH VOICE AND OPINION

Street address 1: PO Box 8097
Street address state: NJ
Postal code: 07631-8097
County: Bergen
Country: USA
Mailing address: PO Box 8097
Mailing city: Englewood
Mailing state: NJ
Mailing zip: 07631
Office phone: (201) 569-2845
Advertising phone: (201) 569-2845
Editorial phone: (201) 569-2845
General e-mail: susan@JewishVoiceAndOpinion.com
Advertising e-mail: susan@JewishVoiceAndOpinion.com
Editorial e-mail: susan@JewishVoiceAndOpinion.com
Web address: TheJewishVoiceAndOpinion.com
Year newspaper established: 1987
Advertising (open inch rate): Open inch rate $50.00
Mechanical specifications: Type page 8 1/2 x 11; E - 4 cols, 1 1/2, 1/4 between.
Delivery methods: Mail`Racks
Zip Codes Served: 07010, 07011, 07012, 07013, 07014, 07024, 07036, 07039, 07047, 07052, 07055, 07078, 07079, 07081, 07087, 07094, 07202, 07205, 07208, 07302, 07304, 07305, 07306, 07307, 07410, 07470, 07605, 07621, 06531, 07632, 07646, 07652, 07666, 07670, 07726, 07747, 07866, 07960, 07962, 08002, 08003, 08034, 08402, 08406, 08816, 08817, 08820, 08901, 08902, 08904, 10461, 10463, 10467, 10471, 10475, 10901, 10952, 10956, 10977
Frequency: Mthly
Circulation Paid: 20000
Circulation Free: 18000
Audit By: Sworn/Estimate/Non-Audited
Audit Date: 12.07.2019
Hardware: APP/Mac
Software: Adobe/PageMaker.
Personnel: Susan L. Rosenbluth (Editor)
Parent company: The Jewish Voice and Opinion
Main (survey) contact: Susan L. Rosenbluth

FAIRWAY
THE KANSAS CITY JEWISH CHRONICLE

Street address 1: 4210 Shawnee Mission Pkwy
Street address 2: Ste 314A
Street address state: KS
Postal code: 66205-2546
County: Johnson
Country: USA
Mailing address: 4210 Shawnee Mission Parkway, Suite 314A
Mailing city: Fairway
Mailing state: KS
Mailing zip: 66205
Office phone: (913) 648-4620
Office fax: (913) 381-1402
General e-mail: chronicle@sunpublications.com
Web address: www.kcjc.com
Year newspaper established: 1920
Advertising (open inch rate): Open inch rate $25.30
Mechanical specifications: Type page 10 x 13 1/2; E - 6 cols, 1 1/2, between; A - 6 cols, 1 1/2, between.
Frequency: Fri
Circulation Paid: 4000
Audit By: Sworn/Estimate/Non-Audited
Audit Date: 12.07.2019
Hardware: APP/Mac
Software: QPS/QuarkXPress.
Personnel: David Small (Pub.); David Nevels (Circ. Mgr.); Rick Hellman (Ed.)
Main (survey) contact: David Small

FAR ROCKAWAY
JEWISH TRIBUNE OF ROCKLAND COUNTY

Street address 1: 1525 Central Ave
Street address state: NY
Postal code: 11691-4019
County: Queens
Country: USA
Mailing address: 511 Hempstead Ave Ste 1
Mailing city: West Hempstead
Mailing state: NY
Mailing zip: 11552-2737
Office phone: (516) 829-4000
Office fax: (516) 594-4900
General e-mail: lijeworld@aol.com
Advertising (open inch rate): Open inch rate $19.00
Mechanical specifications: Type page 10 7/16 x 13; E - 5 cols, 2, 1/8 between; A - 5 cols, 2, 1/8 between; C - 7 cols, 1 7/16, between.
Frequency: Fri
Circulation Paid: 7541
Circulation Free: 750
Audit By: Sworn/Estimate/Non-Audited
Audit Date: 12.07.2019
Personnel: Jerome W. Lippman (Mng. Ed.)
Main (survey) contact: Jerome W. Lippman

LONG ISLAND JEWISH WORLD

Street address 1: 1525 Central Ave
Street address state: NY
Postal code: 11691-4019
County: Queens
Country: USA
Mailing address: 511 Hempstead Ave Ste 1
Mailing city: West Hempstead
Mailing state: NY
Mailing zip: 11552-2737
Office phone: (516) 829-4000
Office fax: (516) 594-4900
General e-mail: lijeworld@aol.com
Advertising (open inch rate): Open inch rate $40.00
Mechanical specifications: Type page 10 7/16 x 13; E - 5 cols, 2, 1/8 between; A - 5 cols, 2, 1/8 between; C - 7 cols, 1 7/16, between.
Frequency: Fri
Circulation Paid: 15284
Circulation Free: 1159
Audit By: Sworn/Estimate/Non-Audited
Audit Date: 12.07.2019
Hardware: IBM.
Personnel: Jerome W. Lippman (Mng. Ed.)
Main (survey) contact: Jerome W. Lippman

MANHATTAN JEWISH SENTINEL

Street address 1: 1525 Central Ave
Street address state: NY
Postal code: 11691-4019
County: Queens
Country: USA
Mailing address: 511 Hempstead Ave Ste 1
Mailing city: West Hempstead
Mailing state: NY
Mailing zip: 11552-2737
Office phone: (516) 829-4000
Office fax: (516) 594-4900
General e-mail: lijeworld@aol.com
Advertising (open inch rate): Open inch rate $40.00
Mechanical specifications: Type page 10 7/16 x 13; E - 5 cols, 2, 1/8 between; A - 5 cols, 2, 1/8 between; C - 7 cols, 1 7/16, between.
Hardware: IBM.
Personnel: Jerome W. Lippman (Ed.)
Parent company: Joseph Jacobs Organization
Main (survey) contact: Jerome W. Lippman

FERN PARK
HERITAGE FLORIDA JEWISH NEWS

Street address 1: 207 Obrien Rd
Street address 2: Ste 101
Street address state: FL
Postal code: 32730-2838
County: Seminole
Country: USA
Mailing address: PO Box 300742
Mailing city: Fern Park
Mailing state: FL
Mailing zip: 32730-0742
Office phone: (407) 834-8787
Office fax: (407) 831-0507
General e-mail: news@orlandoheritage.com
Advertising e-mail: jeff@orlandoheritage.com
Web address: www.heritagefl.com
Year newspaper established: 1976
Advertising (open inch rate): Open inch rate $12.55
Mechanical specifications: Type page 10 5/16 x 16; E - 6 cols, 1/6 between; A - 6 cols, 1/6 between; C - 6 cols, 1/6 between.
Delivery methods: Mail`Newsstand`Racks
Frequency: Fri
Circulation Paid: 5200
Audit By: Sworn/Estimate/Non-Audited
Audit Date: 12.07.2019
Hardware: APP/Mac
Software: Adobe/PageMaker, Adobe/Photoshop, Microsoft/Word.
Personnel: Jeffrey Gaeser (Ed.)
Main (survey) contact: Jeffery Gaeser

FORT LAUDERDALE
SHALOM - BROWARD

Street address 1: 500 E Broward Blvd
Street address state: FL
Postal code: 33394-3000
County: Broward
Country: USA
Mailing address: 500 E. Broward Blvd.
Mailing city: Fort Lauderdale
Mailing state: FL
Mailing zip: 33394
Office phone: (954) 536-4000
Office fax: (954) 429-1207
Advertising phone: (954) 698-6397
Advertising fax: (954) 429-1207
Editorial phone: (954) 698-6397
Editorial fax: (954) 429-1207
General e-mail: rdaley@tribune.com
Advertising e-mail: ewilder@tribune.com
Editorial e-mail: ctouey@tribune.com
Web address: www.forumpubs.com
Year newspaper established: 1973
Advertising (open inch rate): Open inch rate $21.00
Mechanical specifications: Type page 10 3/8 x 16.
Delivery methods: Mail`Racks
Zip Codes Served: Broward County
Digital Platform - Mobile: Apple`Android`Windows`Blackberry
Digital Platform - Tablet: Apple iOS`Android`Windows 7`Blackberry Tablet OS
Frequency: Mthly
Circulation Paid: 0

Circulation Free: 25448
Audit By: CVC
Audit Date: 31.12.2012
Personnel: Tom Adams (Pub./Gen. Mgr.); Tracy Kolody (Mng. Ed.); Ed Wilder (Circ. Mgr.); Ray Daley (Adv. Mgr.); Stewart Cady (Prodn. Mgr.)
Parent company: Sun-Sentinel Co.
Main (survey) contact: Judith Jantz

FRAMINGHAM

METROWEST JEWISH REPORTER

Street address 1: 29 Upper Joclyn Ave
Street address state: MA
Postal code: 01701-4400
County: Middlesex
Country: USA
Mailing address: 126 High St Ste 1
Mailing city: Boston
Mailing state: MA
Mailing zip: 02110-2776
Office phone: (508) 879-3300
Office fax: (508) 879-5856
General e-mail: jewishreporter@aol.com
Advertising (open inch rate): Open inch rate $25.00
Frequency: Mthly
Circulation Free: 10500
Audit By: Sworn/Estimate/Non-Audited
Audit Date: 12.07.2019
Personnel: Nancy Atlas (Mng. Ed.); Wendy Davis (Asst. Mng. Ed.)
Main (survey) contact: Wendy Davis

THE JEWISH REPORTER

Street address 1: 29 Upper Joclyn Ave
Street address state: MA
Postal code: 01701-4400
County: Middlesex
Country: USA
Mailing address: 126 High St Ste 1
Mailing city: Boston
Mailing state: MA
Mailing zip: 02110-2776
Office phone: (508) 872-4808
Office fax: (508) 879-5856
General e-mail: jewishreporter@aol.com
Advertising (open inch rate): Open inch rate $25.00
Frequency: Mthly
Circulation Free: 6500
Audit By: Sworn/Estimate/Non-Audited
Audit Date: 12.07.2019
Personnel: Nancy Atlas (Ed.)
Parent company: Joseph Jacobs Organization
Main (survey) contact: Nancy Atlas

HARRISBURG

COMMUNITY REVIEW

Street address 1: 3301 N Front St
Street address state: PA
Postal code: 17110-1436
County: Dauphin
Country: USA
Mailing address: 3301 N. Front St.
Mailing city: Harrisburg
Mailing state: PA
Mailing zip: 17110
Office phone: (717) 236-9555
Office fax: (717) 236-8104
General e-mail: o.yagil@jewishfedhbg.org
Advertising e-mail: o.yagil@jewishfedhbg.org
Editorial e-mail: o.yagil@jewishfedhbg.org
Web address: www.jewishharrisburg.org
Year newspaper established: 1925
Advertising (open inch rate): Open inch rate $12.50
Mechanical specifications: Type page 9 3/4 x 12 1/2; E - 5 cols, 2 1/4, 1/6 between; A - 5 cols, 1/6 between; C - 5 cols, 1/6 between.
Zip Codes Served: 17013-17112
Frequency: Fri
Circulation Paid: 2100
Audit By: Sworn/Estimate/Non-Audited
Audit Date: 12.07.2019
Hardware: APP/Mac
Software: InDesign
Personnel: Jennifer Ross (Pres./CEO); Lorissa Delaney (COO); Adam Grobman (Mktg. Mgr.)
Parent company: Jewish Federation of Greater Harrisburg
Main (survey) contact: Jennifer Ross

HOUSTON

JEWISH HERALD-VOICE

Street address 1: 3403 Audley St
Street address state: TX
Postal code: 77098-1923
County: Harris
Country: USA
Mailing address: 3403 Audley St
Mailing city: Houston
Mailing state: TX
Mailing zip: 77098-1923
Office phone: (713) 630-0391
Office fax: (713) 630-0404
Advertising phone: (713) 630-0391
Advertising fax: (713) 630-0404
Editorial phone: (713) 630-0391
Editorial fax: (713) 630-0404
General e-mail: news@jhvonline.com
Advertising e-mail: advertising@jhvonline.com
Editorial e-mail: editor@jhvonline.com
Web address: www.jhvonline.com
Year newspaper established: 1908
Advertising (open inch rate): Open inch rate $40.00
Mechanical specifications: Type page 9 3/4 x 15 1/2; E - 4 cols, 2 1/4, 1/6 between; A - 4 cols, 2 1/4, 1/6 between.
Delivery methods: Mail
Zip Codes Served: All
Frequency: Thur
Circulation Paid: 5000
Circulation Free: 200
Audit By: Sworn/Estimate/Non-Audited
Audit Date: 12.07.2019
Hardware: MAC
Personnel: Vicki Samuels (Advertising Manager); Jeanne F. Samuels (Editor); Aaron Poscovsky (Production Manager); Levy Lawrence (Circulation)
Main (survey) contact: Vicki Samuels

INDIANAPOLIS

NATIONAL JEWISH POST & OPINION

Street address 1: 1427 W 86th St
Street address 2: # 228
Street address state: IN
Postal code: 46260-2103
County: Marion
Country: USA
Mailing address: 1427 W 86th St # 228
Mailing city: Indianapolis
Mailing state: IN
Mailing zip: 46260-2103
Office phone: (317) 405-8084
Office fax: (317) 405-8084
General e-mail: jpostopinion@gmail.com
Web address: www.jewishpostopinion.com
Year newspaper established: 1935
Mechanical specifications: Type page 8-1/2 x 11; E - 3 cols, 2, between; A - 3 cols, 2, between.
Delivery methods: Mail`Newsstand
Zip Codes Served: 46260, 46032, 46033, 47401,
Other Type of Frequency: Monthly
Circulation Paid: 10000
Audit By: Sworn/Estimate/Non-Audited
Audit Date: 12.07.2019
Hardware: APP/Mac
Software: Adobe/PageMaker 5.0.
Personnel: Jennie Cohen (Ed.)
Main (survey) contact: Jennie Cohen

THE INDIANA JEWISH POST & OPINION

Street address 1: 1427 W 86th St
Street address 2: # 228
Street address state: IN
Postal code: 46260-2103
County: Marion
Country: USA
Mailing address: 1427 W 86th St # 228
Mailing city: Indianapolis
Mailing state: IN
Mailing zip: 46260-2103
Office phone: (317) 405-8084
General e-mail: jpostopinion@gmail.com
Web address: www.jewishpostopinion.com
Year newspaper established: 1935
Advertising (open inch rate): Open inch rate $12.00
Mechanical specifications: Type page 8-1/2 x 11; E - 3 cols, 2, between; A - 3 cols, 2, between.
Zip Codes Served: 46260, 46032, 46033, 46260, 46240, 46038, 46268, and others
Frequency: Wed
Other Type of Frequency: Every other Wed
Circulation Paid: 5200
Audit By: Sworn/Estimate/Non-Audited
Audit Date: 12.07.2019
Hardware: APP/Mac
Software: Adobe/PageMaker 5.0.
Personnel: Jennie Cohen (Ed.)
Main (survey) contact: Jennie Cohen

LA MESA

SAN DIEGO JEWISH TIMES

Street address 1: 4731 Palm Ave
Street address state: CA
Postal code: 91941-5221
County: San Diego
Country: USA
Mailing address: 4731 Palm Ave
Mailing city: La Mesa
Mailing state: CA
Mailing zip: 91941-5221
Office phone: (619) 463-5515
Office fax: (619) 463-1309
General e-mail: sdjt@sdjewishtimes.com
Advertising e-mail: kgreen@sdjewishtimes.com
Editorial e-mail: msirota@sdjewishtimes.com
Web address: www.sdjewishtimes.com
Year newspaper established: 1980
Advertising (open inch rate): Open inch rate $60.00
Mechanical specifications: Type page 10 x 14.
Personnel: Michael Schwarz (Pub.); Michael Sirota (Ed.); Leslie Pebley (Prodn. Mgr.)
Main (survey) contact: Mike Schwartz

LARGO

JEWISH PRESS OF TAMPA

Street address 1: 1101 Belcher Rd S
Street address 2: Ste H
Street address state: FL
Postal code: 33771-3356
County: Pinellas
Country: USA
Mailing address: PO Box 6970
Mailing city: Clearwater
Mailing state: FL
Mailing zip: 33758-6970
Office phone: (727) 535-4400
Office fax: (727) 530-3039
General e-mail: jewishpress@aol.com
Advertising e-mail: jewishpressads@aol.com
Editorial e-mail: Jewishpressnews@aol.com
Web address: www.jewishpresstampabay.com
Year newspaper established: 1988
Advertising (open inch rate): Open inch rate $16.00
Mechanical specifications: Type page 10 1/4 x 15 3/4; E - 5 cols, 1/6 between; A - 5 cols, 2, 1/6 between.
Delivery methods: Mail
Zip Codes Served: 337s, 336s, 346s
Frequency: Bi-Mthly
Other Type of Frequency: Every other Friday
Circulation Free: 11500
Audit By: Sworn/Estimate/Non-Audited
Audit Date: 12.07.2019
Hardware: APP/Mac
Software: Adobe CS5.5
Editions Count: 2
Edition Names: Jewish Press of Tampa, Jewish Press of Pinellas Ątounty
Personnel: Jim Dawkins (Pub.); Karen Dawkins (Mng. Ed.); Harold Wolfson (Prodn. Mgr.)
Main (survey) contact: Jim Dawkins

LAS VEGAS

JEWISH REPORTER

Street address 1: 2317 Renaissance Dr
Street address state: NV
Postal code: 89119-6191
County: Clark
Country: USA
Mailing address: 2317 Renaissance Dr
Mailing city: Las Vegas
Mailing state: NV
Mailing zip: 89119-6191
Office phone: (702) 732-0556
Office fax: (702) 732-3228
General e-mail: info@jewishlasvegas.com
Advertising e-mail: ads@jewishlasvegas.com
Editorial e-mail: editor@jewishlasvegas.com
Web address: www.jewishlasvegas.com
Mechanical specifications: Type page 10 3/4 x 13; E - 4 cols, 2 1/2, 1/4 between; A - 4 cols, 2 1/2, 1/4 between.
Zip Codes Served: 89119
Hardware: APP/Power Mac
Software: Adobe/PageMaker 5.1.
Personnel: Joanne Friedland (Adv. Sales Dir.); Leah Brown (Ed.); Arthur Bloberger (Ed.); Andrew Bemson (Graphics/Layout Artist)
Parent company: Joseph Jacobs Organization
Main (survey) contact: Joanne Friedland

LONG BEACH

JEWISH COMMUNITY CHRONICLE

Street address 1: 3801 E Willow St
Street address state: CA
Postal code: 90815-1734
County: Los Angeles
Country: USA
Mailing address: 3801 E Willow St
Mailing city: Long Beach
Mailing state: CA
Mailing zip: 90815-1792
Office phone: (562) 426-7601
Office fax: (562) 424-3915
General e-mail: chronicle@jewishlongbeach.org
Web address: www.jewishlongbeach.org
Year newspaper established: 1947
Advertising (open inch rate): Open inch rate $16.00
Mechanical specifications: Type page 9.5 x 12; E - 5 cols, 1 11/12, 1/6 between; A - 5 cols, 1 11/12, 1/6 between; C - 5 cols, 1 11/12, 1/6 between.
Delivery methods: Mail`Newsstand`Racks
Digital Platform - Mobile: Apple`Android`Windows`Blackberry`Other
Digital Platform - Tablet: Apple iOS`Android`Windows 7`Blackberry Tablet OS`Kindle`Nook`Kindle Fire`Other
Frequency: Mthly
Circulation Free: 6300
Audit By: Sworn/Estimate/Non-Audited
Audit Date: 12.07.2019
Hardware: APP/Mac
Software: Adobe Creative Cloud
Editions Count: 12
Edition Names: Health, High Holy Days, Wedding/B'nai Mitzvah/Simchahs, Chanukah/Thanksgiving, Planned Giving, Seniors, Camp, Purim, Passover, Israel, Arts & Culture
Personnel: Deborah Goldfarb (CEO); Danny Levy (Director of Development)
Parent company: Jewish Federation of Greater Long Beach & West Orange County
Main (survey) contact: Deborah Goldfarb

Jewish Newspapers in the U.S.

LOS ANGELES

THE JEWISH JOURNAL OF GREATER LOS ANGELES

Street address 1: 3580 Wilshire Blvd
Street address 2: Ste 1510
Street address state: CA
Postal code: 90010-2516
County: Los Angeles
Country: USA
Mailing address: 3580 Wilshire Blvd Ste 1510
Mailing city: Los Angeles
Mailing state: CA
Mailing zip: 90010-2516
Office phone: (213) 368-1661
Office fax: (213) 368-1684
General e-mail: marketing@jewishjournal.com
Advertising e-mail: advertising@jewishjournal.com
Web address: jewishjournal.com
Year newspaper established: 1986
Advertising (open inch rate): N/A
Mechanical specifications: Type page 11 1/4 x 15; E - 5 cols, 1 11/12, 1/60 between; A - 5 cols, 1 11/12, 1/60 between; C - 6 cols, 1 3/5, 3/25 between.
Frequency: Fri
Circulation Paid: 0
Circulation Free: 49975
Audit By: CVC
Audit Date: 30.06.2015
Personnel: Matthew Tenney (Circ. Mgr.); Rob Eshman (Ed. in Chief); Adam Wills (Sr. Ed.); Susan Freudenheim (Mng. Ed.); Lionel Ochoa (Prodn. Dir.)
Main (survey) contact: Matthew Tenney

LOS GATOS

JEWISH COMMUNITY NEWS

Street address 1: 14855 Oka Rd
Street address 2: Ste 202
Street address state: CA
Postal code: 95032-1957
County: Santa Clara
Country: USA
Mailing address: PO Box 320070
Mailing city: Los Gatos
Mailing state: CA
Mailing zip: 95032-0101
Office phone: (408) 556-0600
General e-mail: jfs@jfssv.org
Web address: www.jfssv.org
Advertising (open inch rate): Open inch rate $14.00
Personnel: Lori Cinnamon (Adv. Mgr.); Amanda Glincher (Ed.)
Parent company: Joseph Jacobs Organization
Main (survey) contact: Amanda Glincher

LOUISVILLE

JEWISH LOUISVILLE COMMUNITY

Street address 1: 3600 Dutchmans Ln
Street address state: KY
Postal code: 40205-3302
County: Jefferson
Country: USA
Office phone: (502) 459-0660
Office fax: (502) 238-2724
Advertising phone: (502) 418-5845
General e-mail: lchottiner@jewishlouisville.org
Advertising e-mail: lsinger@jewishlouisville.org
Web address: www.jewishlouisville.org
Year newspaper established: 1975
Advertising (open inch rate): sold in increments from 1/16 pg at $70 to full page at $1000
Mechanical specifications: Type page 10 x 13.75; E - 4 cols, 2 1/3, 1/4 between; A - 4 cols, 2 1/3, 1/4 between; C - 5 cols, 1 11/12, 1/6 between.
Delivery methods: Mail Racks
Zip Codes Served: 40200-40299
Frequency: Mthly
Circulation Paid: 6472
Circulation Free: 515
Audit By: Sworn/Estimate/Non-Audited
Audit Date: 12.07.2019
Hardware: PC/Windows
Software: In Design CC, Adobe/Acrobat.
Note: Community is published Monthly
Personnel: Shiela Steinman Wallace (Ed.); Larry Singer (Adv Sales); Misty Hamilton (Graphic Artist)
Parent company: Jewish Community of Louisville

MEMPHIS

HEBREW WATCHMAN

Street address 1: 4646 Poplar Ave
Street address 2: Ste 232
Street address state: TN
Postal code: 38117-4426
County: Shelby
Country: USA
Mailing address: PO Box 770846
Mailing city: Memphis
Mailing state: TN
Mailing zip: 38177-0846
Office phone: (901) 763-2215
Office fax: (901) 763-2216
General e-mail: hebwat@bellsouth.net
Year newspaper established: 1925
Advertising (open inch rate): Open inch rate $9.00
Mechanical specifications: Type page 10 3/4 x 13; E - 5 cols, 2 1/16, between; A - 5 cols, 2 1/16, between.
Delivery methods: Mail
Frequency: Thur
Circulation Paid: 3000
Audit By: Sworn/Estimate/Non-Audited
Audit Date: 12.07.2019
Hardware: APP/Mac.
Personnel: Herman I. Goldberger (Ed.)
Main (survey) contact: Herman I. Goldberger

METAIRIE

JEWISH NEWS

Street address 1: 3747 W Esplanade Ave N
Street address state: LA
Postal code: 70002-3145
County: Jefferson
Country: USA
Mailing address: 3747 W Esplanade Ave N
Mailing city: Metairie
Mailing state: LA
Mailing zip: 70002-3145
Office phone: (504) 780-5600
Office fax: (504) 780-5601
General e-mail: jewishnews@jewishnola.com
Web address: www.jewishnola.com
Year newspaper established: 1995
Mechanical specifications: Type page 10 x 14.
Frequency: Mthly
Circulation Free: 4563
Audit By: CVC
Audit Date: 31.12.2004
Hardware: APP/Mac
Software: QPS/QuarkXPress 4.1, Adobe/Photoshop 5.5, Adobe/Illustrator 7.0, Adobe/Acrobat.
Personnel: Cait Muldoon (Prodn. Mgr.)
Parent company: Joseph Jacobs Organization
Main (survey) contact: Michael Weil

MILWAUKEE

THE WISCONSIN JEWISH CHRONICLE

Street address 1: 1360 N Prospect Ave
Street address state: WI
Postal code: 53202-3056
County: Milwaukee
Country: USA
Mailing address: 1360 N Prospect Ave Ste 2
Mailing city: Milwaukee
Mailing state: WI
Mailing zip: 53202-3090
Office phone: (414) 390-5770
Office fax: (414) 390-5766
Advertising phone: (414) 390-5765
General e-mail: chronicle@milwaukeejewish.org
Web address: www.jewishchronicle.org
Year newspaper established: 1921
Advertising (open inch rate): Open inch rate $13.00
Mechanical specifications: Type page 9 3/4 x 12 1/2; E - 5 cols, between; A - 5 cols, between.
Frequency: Mthly
Circulation Free: 8000
Audit By: Sworn/Estimate/Non-Audited
Audit Date: 12.07.2019
Hardware: APP/Mac
Software: QPS/QuarkXPress.
Personnel: Yvonne Chapman (Production Manager); Leon Cohen (Editor)
Parent company: Milwaukee Jewish Federation
Main (survey) contact: Leon Cohen

MINNEAPOLIS

AMERICAN JEWISH WORLD

Street address 1: 4820 Minnetonka Blvd
Street address 2: Ste 104
Street address state: MN
Postal code: 55416-2278
County: Hennepin
Country: USA
Mailing address: 4820 Minnetonka Blvd Ste 104
Mailing city: Minneapolis
Mailing state: MN
Mailing zip: 55416-2278
Office phone: (952) 259-5237
Office fax: (952) 920-6205
Advertising phone: (952) 259-5234
Advertising fax: (952) 920-6205
Editorial phone: (952) 259-5239
Editorial fax: (952) 920-6205
General e-mail: news@ajwnews.com
Advertising e-mail: editor@ajwnews.com
Editorial e-mail: community@ajwnews.com
Web address: www.ajwnews.com
Year newspaper established: 1912
Advertising (open inch rate): Open inch rate $15.00
Mechanical specifications: Type page 10 x 16; E - 5 cols, 1 7/8, 1/8 between; A - 5 cols, 1 7/8, 1/8 between; C - 5 cols, 1 7/8, 1/8 between.
Delivery methods: Mail
Zip Codes Served: 55401, 55402, 55118, 55416, 55426, 55105, 55116
Frequency: Bi-Mthly
Other Type of Frequency: Every other Fri
Circulation Paid: 3500
Audit By: Sworn/Estimate/Non-Audited
Audit Date: 12.07.2019
Hardware: APP/Mac
Software: Adobe CS, Microsoft/Word.
Personnel: Mordecai Specktor (Ed.)
Parent company: Minnesota Jewish Media, LLC
Main (survey) contact: Mordecai Specktor

MOUNTAIN BRK

SOUTHERN JEWISH LIFE

Street address 1: 14 Office Park Cir
Street address 2: Ste 104
Street address state: AL
Postal code: 35223-2792
County: Jefferson
Country: USA
Mailing address: PO Box 130052
Mailing city: Birmingham
Mailing state: AL
Mailing zip: 35213-0052
Office phone: (205) 322-9002
Office fax: (866) 392-7750
Advertising phone: (205) 870-7889
General e-mail: connect@sjlmag.com
Advertising e-mail: lee@sjlmag.com
Editorial e-mail: editor@sjlmag.com
Web address: www.sjlmag.com
Year newspaper established: 1990
Advertising (open inch rate): Open inch rate $31.67
Mechanical specifications: Glossy magazine, 8.5x11 finished. 7.75"x10" live area.
Delivery methods: Mail
Zip Codes Served: 324-325, 350-368, 386-397, 700-714
Frequency: Mthly
Circulation Free: 9500
Audit By: USPS
Audit Date: 25.06.2018
Hardware: APP/Mac
Software: Adobe Creative Cloud, MS Office
Editions Count: 2
Edition Names: Deep South, New Orleans
Note: Formerly Deep South Jewish Voice, became Southern Jewish Life in August 2009. Official publication of the New Orleans Jewish community.
Personnel: Lee Green (Adv. Mgr.); Larry Brook (Ed/Pub); Annetta Dolowitz (Advertising); Jeff Pizzo (V.P. Sales and Marketing, New Orleans)
Main (survey) contact: Larry Brook

NASHVILLE

THE JEWISH OBSERVER

Street address 1: 801 Percy Warner Blvd
Street address 2: Ste 102
Street address state: TN
Postal code: 37205-4128
County: Davidson
Country: USA
Mailing address: 801 Percy Warner Blvd Ste 102
Mailing city: Nashville
Mailing state: TN
Mailing zip: 37205-4128
Office phone: (615) 354-1653
Office fax: (615) 352-0056
Advertising phone: (615) 354-1699
Editorial phone: (615) 354-1653
General e-mail: info@jewishnashville.org
Advertising e-mail: carrie@nashvillejcc.org
Editorial e-mail: charles@jewishnashville.org
Web address: www.jewishobservernashville.org
Year newspaper established: 1937
Advertising (open inch rate): Open inch rate $12.50
Mechanical specifications: Type page 10 x 14; E - 4 cols, 2 1/4, 1/4 between; A - 4 cols, 2 1/2, between.
Delivery methods: Mail
Zip Codes Served: Nashville - Middle Tennessee
Frequency: Mthly
Circulation Free: 4000
Audit By: Sworn/Estimate/Non-Audited
Audit Date: 12.07.2019
Hardware: Windows Desktop
Presses: Web
Software: InDesign and Quark
Personnel: Carrie Mills (Adv. Mgr.); Charles Bernsen (Editor)
Parent company: Jewish Federation of Nashville and Middle Tennessee
Main (survey) contact: Mark Freedman

NEW LONDON

THE JEWISH LEADER

Street address 1: 28 Channing St
Street address state: CT
Postal code: 06320-5756
County: New London
Country: USA
Office phone: (860) 442-7395
Office fax: (860) 443-4175
General e-mail: office.jfec@gmail.com
Advertising e-mail: office.jfec@gmail.com
Editorial e-mail: office.jfec@gmail.com
Web address: www.jfec.com
Year newspaper established: 1970
Advertising (open inch rate): Open inch rate $10.00
Mechanical specifications: Type page 10 x 12; E - 5 cols, 1 13/16, 3/16 between.
Delivery methods: Mail
Zip Codes Served: 06320, 06360, 06385, 06333, 06357, 06340, 06415, 06226, 06260, 06475, 02891
Frequency: Other
Other Type of Frequency: Twice a month on

Fridays
Circulation Paid: 400
Circulation Free: 1075
Audit By: Sworn/Estimate/Non-Audited
Audit Date: 12.07.2019
Hardware: PC
Software: Adobe/InDesign2
Personnel: Mimi Perl (Ed.)
Parent company: Jewish Federation of Eastern CT
Main (survey) contact: Mimi Perl

NEW YORK

JEWISH TELEGRAPHIC AGENCY DAILY NEWS BULLETIN

Street address 1: 330 7th Ave
Street address 2: Fl 17
Street address state: NY
Postal code: 10001-5010
County: New York
Country: USA
Mailing address: 24 W 30th St Fl 4
Mailing city: New York
Mailing state: NY
Mailing zip: 10001-4443
Office phone: (212) 643-1890
Office fax: (212) 643-8499
General e-mail: info@jta.org
Web address: www.jta.org
Mechanical specifications: Type page 8 1/2 x 11; E - 2 cols, 3 5/8, 1/4 between.
Other Type of Frequency: Daily
Circulation Paid: 1200
Circulation Free: 50
Audit By: Sworn/Estimate/Non-Audited
Audit Date: 12.07.2019
Hardware: PC
Software: WordPerfect 6.0.
Personnel: Mark J. Joffe (Pub.); Lenore A. Silverstein (Gen. Mgr.); Ami Eden (Mng. Ed.)
Main (survey) contact: Mark J. Joffe

JEWISH WEEK

Street address 1: 1501 Broadway
Street address 2: Ste 505
Street address state: NY
Postal code: 10036-5501
County: New York
Country: USA
Mailing address: 1501 Broadway Ste 505
Mailing city: New York
Mailing state: NY
Mailing zip: 10036-5504
Office phone: (212) 921-7822
Office fax: (212) 921-8420
Web address: www.thejewishweek.com
Advertising (open inch rate): Open inch rate $104.00
Mechanical specifications: Type page 10 1/4 x 13; A - 6 cols, 1 2/3, 1/6 between; C - 7 cols, 1 5/12, 1/6 between.
Frequency: Thur
Circulation Paid: 74000
Audit By: Sworn/Estimate/Non-Audited
Audit Date: 12.07.2019
Hardware: APP/Mac, IBM
Software: Graphix/Adtaker, XYQUEST/XyWrite.
Personnel: Richard Waloff (Assoc. Pub.); Gershon Fastow (Adv. Coord.); Ruth Rothseid (Sales Mgr.); Paul Bukzin (Circ. Mgr.); Gary Rosenblatt (Ed.); Robert Goldblum (Mng. Ed.)
Parent company: Joseph Jacobs Organization
Main (survey) contact: Robert Goldblum

MANHATTAN/WESTCHESTER JEWISH WEEK

Street address 1: 1501 Broadway
Street address 2: Ste 505
Street address state: NY
Postal code: 10036-5501
County: New York
Country: USA
Mailing address: 1501 Broadway Ste 505
Mailing city: New York
Mailing state: NY
Mailing zip: 10036-5504
Office phone: (212) 921-7822
Office fax: (212) 921-8420
Advertising phone: (212) 921-7822 x254
Editorial phone: (212) 921-7822 x213
General e-mail: ruth@jewishweek.org
Editorial e-mail: robert@jewishweek.org
Web address: www.thejewishweek.com
Advertising (open inch rate): (Modular Rates) 1/24 page, 2.833 x 1.5 - $252 1x
Mechanical specifications: Type page 8.75 x 11.75; 6 cols, 1.354, 0.125 between
Frequency: Fri
Personnel: Robert Goldblum (Managing Ed.); Ruth Rothseid (Sales Dir.); Gary Rosenblatt (Ed. & Pub.)
Main (survey) contact: Gary Rosenblatt

THE FORWARD

Street address 1: 125 Maiden Ln
Street address 2: Fl 8
Street address state: NY
Postal code: 10038-5015
County: New York
Country: USA
Mailing address: 125 Maiden Ln Fl 8
Mailing city: New York
Mailing state: NY
Mailing zip: 10038-5015
Office phone: (212) 889-8200
Office fax: (212) 689-4255
Advertising e-mail: advertising@forward.com
Web address: www.forward.com
Advertising (open inch rate): Open inch rate $40.00
Mechanical specifications: Type page 13 x 21; E - 6 cols, 2 1/16, between; A - 6 cols, 2 1/16, between; C - 6 cols, 2 1/16, between.
Frequency: Fri
Circulation Paid: 14222
Circulation Free: 10701
Audit By: AAM
Audit Date: 31.03.2015
Hardware: APP/Mac.
Personnel: Jerry Koenig (Adv. Mgr.); Jane Eisner (Ed. in Chief); Lil Swanson (Mng. Ed.)
Main (survey) contact: Jerry Koenig

THE JEWISH WEEK

Street address 1: 1501 Broadway
Street address 2: Ste 505
Street address state: NY
Postal code: 10036-5501
County: New York
Country: USA
Mailing address: 1501 Broadway Ste 505
Mailing city: New York
Mailing state: NY
Mailing zip: 10036-5504
Office phone: (212) 921-7822
Office fax: (212) 921-8420
Advertising phone: (212) 997-2954
General e-mail: editor@jewishweek.org
Advertising e-mail: ruth@jewishweek.org
Editorial e-mail: editor@jewishweek.org
Web address: www.thejewishweek.com
Year newspaper established: 1979
Advertising (open inch rate): Open inch rate $101.00
Mechanical specifications: Live area, page size is 8.75 wide x 11. There ar 6 advertising columns per page and 3 or 4 editorial columns
Delivery methods: Mail`Newsstand`Carrier
Zip Codes Served: 10001 through 11999, primarily
Digital Platform - Mobile: Apple
Digital Platform - Tablet: Apple iOS
Frequency: Fri
Circulation Paid: 44731
Circulation Free: 6289
Audit By: AAM
Audit Date: 31.12.2004
Hardware: PC and MAC
Software: InDesign, Photoshop, etc.
Personnel: Gary Rosenblatt (Pub.); Richard Waloff (Assoc. Pub.); Robert Goldblum (Mng. Ed.); Ruth Rothseid (Sales Manager)
Main (survey) contact: Robert Goldblum

THE LONG ISLAND JEWISH WEEK

Street address 1: 1501 Broadway
Street address 2: Ste 505
Street address state: NY
Postal code: 10036-5501
County: New York
Country: USA
Mailing address: 1501 Broadway Ste 505
Mailing city: New York
Mailing state: NY
Mailing zip: 10036-5504
Office phone: (212) 921-7822
Office fax: (212) 921-8420
Web address: www.thejewishweek.com
Frequency: Fri
Circulation Paid: 90000
Circulation Free: 259
Audit By: Sworn/Estimate/Non-Audited
Audit Date: 12.07.2019
Personnel: Richard Waloff (Pub.); Robert Goldblum (Mng. Ed.); Gary Rosenblatt (Ed.)
Main (survey) contact: Robert Goldblum

THE QUEENS JEWISH WEEK

Street address 1: 1501 Broadway
Street address 2: Ste 505
Street address state: NY
Postal code: 10036-5501
County: New York
Country: USA
Mailing address: 1501 Broadway Ste 505
Mailing city: New York
Mailing state: NY
Mailing zip: 10036-5504
Office phone: (212) 921-7822
Office fax: (212) 921-8420
Web address: www.thejewishweek.com
Advertising (open inch rate): Open inch rate $92.00
Frequency: Fri
Circulation Paid: 14500
Circulation Free: 116
Audit By: Sworn/Estimate/Non-Audited
Audit Date: 12.07.2019
Personnel: Gary Rosenblatt (Pub.); Richard Waloff (Adv. Mgr.); Robert Goldblum (Mng. Ed.)
Main (survey) contact: Robert Goldblum

THE WESTCHESTER JEWISH WEEK

Street address 1: 1501 Broadway
Street address 2: Ste 505
Street address state: NY
Postal code: 10036-5501
County: New York
Country: USA
Mailing address: 1501 Broadway Ste 505
Mailing city: New York
Mailing state: NY
Mailing zip: 10036-5504
Office phone: (212) 921-7822
Office fax: (212) 921-8420
Web address: www.thejewishweek.com
Advertising (open inch rate): Open inch rate $92.00
Frequency: Fri
Circulation Paid: 15661
Circulation Free: 192
Audit By: Sworn/Estimate/Non-Audited
Audit Date: 12.07.2019
Personnel: Gary Rosenblatt (Pub.); Richard Waloff (Adv. Mgr.); Robert Goldblum (Mng. Ed.)
Main (survey) contact: Robert Goldblum

OMAHA

JEWISH PRESS

Street address 1: 333 S 132nd St
Street address state: NE
Postal code: 68154-2106
County: Douglas
Country: USA
Mailing address: 333 S 132nd St
Mailing city: Omaha
Mailing state: NE
Mailing zip: 68154-2198
Office phone: (402) 334-6448
Office fax: (402) 334-5422
General e-mail: jpress@jewishomaha.org
Web address: www.jewishomaha.org
Year newspaper established: 1920
Advertising (open inch rate): Open inch rate $13.00
Mechanical specifications: Type page 10 5/16 x 16; E - 3 cols, 3 5/16, 1/6 between; A - 6 cols, 1 9/16, 1/6 between.
Frequency: Fri
Circulation Paid: 67409
Circulation Free: 1875
Audit By: Sworn/Estimate/Non-Audited
Audit Date: 12.07.2019
Hardware: APP/Mac, PC, APP/Mac G4
Software: QPS/QuarkXPress 6.5, Adobe/ Photoshop 7.0.
Personnel: Allan Handleman (Adv. Mgr.); Carol Katzman (Ed.); Richard Busse (Mng. Ed.)
Parent company: Joseph Jacobs Organization
Main (survey) contact: Annette van de Kamp-Wright

PELHAM

WESTCHESTER JEWISH LIFE

Street address 1: 629 Fifth Ave
Street address state: NY
Postal code: 10803-1251
County: Westchester
Country: USA
Mailing address: 629 Fifth Ave
Mailing city: Pelham
Mailing state: NY
Mailing zip: 10803-1251
Office phone: (914) 738-7869
Office fax: (914) 738-7876
General e-mail: hp@shorelinepub.com
Advertising e-mail: hp@shorelinepub.com
Editorial e-mail: hp@shorelinepub.com
Web address: www.shorelinepub.com
Year newspaper established: 1996
Advertising (open inch rate): Open inch rate $8.65
Mechanical specifications: Type page 10 x 11; E - 4 cols, 2 1/4, between; A - 6 cols, 1 3/4, between; C - 6 cols, between.
Delivery methods: Newsstand
Zip Codes Served: All Westchester County
Digital Platform - Mobile: Windows
Frequency: Mthly
Circulation Paid: 500
Circulation Free: 24000
Audit By: Sworn/Estimate/Non-Audited
Audit Date: 12.07.2019
Hardware: IBM
Software: Adobe/PageMaker 6.0.
Personnel: Edward Shapiro (Adv. Mgr.); Helene Pollack (Editor and Publisher)
Parent company: Shoreline Publishing
Main (survey) contact: Helene Pollack

PHILADELPHIA

JEWISH EXPONENT

Street address 1: 2100 Arch St
Street address 2: 4th Floor
Street address state: PA
Postal code: 19103-1300
County: Philadelphia
Country: USA
Mailing address: 2100 Arch St. 4th Floor
Mailing city: Philadelphia
Mailing state: PA
Mailing zip: 19103-1300
Office phone: (215) 832-0700
Office fax: (215) 832-0785
General e-mail: production@jewishexponent.com
Web address: www.jewishexponent.com
Year newspaper established: 1887

Jewish Newspapers in the U.S.

Advertising (open inch rate): Open inch rate $57.75
Mechanical specifications: Type page 10 1/2 x 13; E - 5 cols, 2, between; A - 5 cols, 2, between; C - 7 cols, 1 3/8, between.
Frequency: Thur
Circulation Paid: 40406
Circulation Free: 4460
Audit By: Sworn/Estimate/Non-Audited
Audit Date: 12.07.2019
Hardware: APP/Mac
Software: QPS/QuarkXPress, Adobe/Photoshop, Adobe/Illustrator.
Personnel: Steve Rosenburg (Pub. Rep./Gen. Mgr.); Joshua Runyan (Ed.-In-Chief); Cheryl Lutz (Dir. Bus. Ops.); Nicole McNally (Classifieds); Andy Gotlieb (Mng. Ed.); Liz Spikol (Sr. Staff Writer); Marissa Stern (Staff Writer); Steve Burke (Art/Prod. Coor.); Sharon Schmuckler (Dir. Sales/Adv.)
Parent company: Joseph Jacobs Organization
Main (survey) contact: Steve Rosenburg

PITTSBURGH

THE JEWISH CHRONICLE

Street address 1: 5915 Beacon St
Street address 2: Fl 3
Street address state: PA
Postal code: 15217-2005
County: Allegheny
Country: USA
Mailing address: 5915 Beacon St Fl 3
Mailing city: Pittsburgh
Mailing state: PA
Mailing zip: 15217-2005
Office phone: (412) 687-1000
Office fax: (412) 521-0154
General e-mail: newsdesk@thejewishchronicle.net
Advertising e-mail: advertising@thejewishchronicle.net
Editorial e-mail: newsdesk@thejewishchronicle.net
Web address: www.thejewishchronicle.net
Year newspaper established: 1962
Advertising (open inch rate): Open inch rate $20.50
Mechanical specifications: Type page 10 1/4 x 14 1/2; E - 4 cols, 2 1/3, 3/8 between; A - 4 cols, 2 1/3, 3/8 between; C - 6 cols, 1 1/2, 1/4 between.
Delivery methods: Mail
Zip Codes Served: All
Frequency: Thur
Circulation Paid: 3800
Circulation Free: 300
Audit By: Sworn/Estimate/Non-Audited
Audit Date: 12.07.2019
Hardware: Macintosh, PC
Software: QPS/QuarkXPress 4.0, Adobe/Photoshop 6.0, Microsoft/Word 5.1A.
Personnel: Lee Chottiner (Exec. Ed.); Dawn Wanninger (Prodn. Mgr.); Jim Busis (Interim CEO)
Main (survey) contact: Jim Busis

PITTSFIELD

BERKSHIRE JEWISH VOICE

Street address 1: 196 South St
Street address state: MA
Postal code: 01201-6807
County: Berkshire
Country: USA
Mailing address: 196 South St
Mailing city: Pittsfield
Mailing state: MA
Mailing zip: 01201-6807
Office phone: (413) 442-4360
Office fax: (413) 443-6070
General e-mail: jfb.berkshirevoice@verizon.net
Advertising (open inch rate): Open inch rate $8.40
Frequency: Mthly
Circulation Free: 3000
Audit By: Sworn/Estimate/Non-Audited
Audit Date: 12.07.2019
Hardware: Presses Ã‚Â— Web press
Software: Adobe/PageMaker 6.5.
Personnel: Dara Kaufman (Exec. Dir.); Jenny Greenfield (Office Mgr.); Albert Stern (Ed.)
Parent company: Joseph Jacobs Organization
Main (survey) contact: Albert Stern

PLEASANTVILLE

JEWISH TIMES

Street address 1: 21 W Delilah Rd
Street address state: NJ
Postal code: 08232-1403
County: Atlantic
Country: USA
Mailing address: 21 W Delilah Rd
Mailing city: Pleasantville
Mailing state: NJ
Mailing zip: 08232-1403
Office phone: (609) 407-0909
Office fax: (609) 407-0999
General e-mail: jwishtimes@aol.com
Web address: www.jewishtimes-sj.com
Advertising (open inch rate): Open inch rate $13.11
Mechanical specifications: Type page 12 x 13; E - 5 cols, 2, between; A - 5 cols, 2, between.
Frequency: Fri
Circulation Paid: 4000
Circulation Free: 1000
Audit By: Sworn/Estimate/Non-Audited
Audit Date: 12.07.2019
Hardware: APP/Mac.
Personnel: Shy Kramer (Pub.); Bonnie La Roche (Adv. Mgr.); Gerald Etter (Mng. Ed.)
Parent company: Joseph Jacobs Organization
Main (survey) contact: Gerald Etter

PROVIDENCE

JEWISH VOICE OF RHODE ISLAND

Street address 1: 130 Sessions St
Street address state: RI
Postal code: 02906-3444
County: Providence
Country: USA
Mailing address: 130 Sessions St
Mailing city: Providence
Mailing state: RI
Mailing zip: 02906-3444
Office phone: (401) 421-4111
Office fax: (410) 331-7961
General e-mail: editor@jewishallianceri.org
Editorial e-mail: editor@jewishallianceri.org
Web address: www.jvhri.org
Advertising (open inch rate): Open inch rate $13.00
Mechanical specifications: Type page 10 x 13; E - 5 cols, 1 7/8, 1/4 between; A - 5 cols, 1 7/8, 1/4 between.
Delivery methods: Mail`Racks
Zip Codes Served: all Rhode Island and Southeastern Mass.
Digital Platform - Mobile: Apple
Digital Platform - Tablet: Apple iOS
Frequency: Other
Other Type of Frequency: 2 x Mthly
Circulation Free: 10000
Audit By: Sworn/Estimate/Non-Audited
Audit Date: 12.07.2019
Hardware: APP/Mac
Software: Adobe/InDesignCC
Personnel: Leah Camara (Prodn. Mgr.)
Main (survey) contact: Leah Camara; Fran Ostendorf

THE JEWISH VOICE

Street address 1: 401 Elmgrove Ave
Street address state: RI
Postal code: 02906-3451
County: Providence
Country: USA
Mailing address: 401 Elmgrove Avenue
Mailing city: Providence
Mailing state: RI
Mailing zip: 02906-3444
Office phone: (401) 421-4111
Office fax: (401) 331-7961
General e-mail: editor@jewishallianceri.org
Editorial e-mail: editor@jewishallianceri.org
Web address: www.jvhri.org
Advertising (open inch rate): Open inch rate $18
Mechanical specifications: Type page 10.25 x 13.5; C - 2 cols, 4, 1/2 between.
Digital Platform - Mobile: Apple`Android`Windows`Blackberry
Digital Platform - Tablet: Apple iOS`Android`Windows 7`Blackberry Tablet OS`Kindle`Nook`Kindle Fire
Other Type of Frequency: Every other Fri
Circulation Free: 9000
Audit By: Sworn/Estimate/Non-Audited
Audit Date: 12.07.2019
Hardware: Mac
Software: Adobe
Personnel: Chris Westerkamp (Adv. Mgr.); Fran Ostendorf (Exec. Ed)
Parent company: Jewish Alliance of Greater Rhode Island
Main (survey) contact: Adam Greenman

RICHMOND

VIRGINIA JEWISH LIFE

Street address 1: 212 N Gaskins Rd
Street address state: VA
Postal code: 23238-5526
County: Henrico
Country: USA
Mailing address: 212 N Gaskins Rd
Mailing city: Richmond
Mailing state: VA
Mailing zip: 23238-5526
Office phone: (804) 740-2000
Office fax: (804) 750-1341
Editorial e-mail: editor@virginiajewishlife.com
Web address: www.virginiajewishlife.com
Year newspaper established: 1977
Personnel: Dana Zedd (Adv. Rep.); Allie Vered (Mng. Ed.)
Main (survey) contact: Allie Vered

ROCHESTER

THE JEWISH LEDGER

Street address 1: 2535 Brighton Henrietta Tl Rd
Street address state: NY
Postal code: 14623-2711
County: Monroe
Country: USA
Mailing address: 2535 Brighton-Henrietta TL Rd.
Mailing city: Rochester
Mailing state: NY
Mailing zip: 14623
Office phone: (585) 427-2434
Office fax: (585) 427-8521
Advertising phone: (585) 427-2468
Editorial phone: 5854272434
General e-mail: info@thejewishledger.com
Advertising e-mail: info@thejewishledger.com
Editorial e-mail: info@thejewishledger.com
Web address: www.thejewishledger.com
Year newspaper established: 1924
Advertising (open inch rate): Open inch rate $35.00
Mechanical specifications: Tabloid, five columns, 10.25"wide by 15"deep
Delivery methods: Mail`Newsstand
Zip Codes Served: 146 171 461 814 620 000 000 000 000 000
Digital Platform - Mobile: Apple
Digital Platform - Tablet: Apple iOS
Frequency: Thur
Other Type of Frequency: Weekly
Circulation Paid: 6500
Circulation Free: 1000
Audit By: USPS
Audit Date: 09.11.2017
Hardware: APP/Mac
Software: InDesign
Personnel: George Morgenstern (Gen. Mgr.); Barbara G. Morgenstern (Ed.)
Main (survey) contact: Barbara G. Morgenstern

ROCKVILLE

WASHINGTON JEWISH WEEK

Street address 1: 11426 Rockville Pike
Street address 2: Ste 236
Street address state: MD
Postal code: 20852-3075
County: Montgomery
Country: USA
Mailing address: 11900 Parklawn Dr Ste 300
Mailing city: Rockville
Mailing state: MD
Mailing zip: 20852-2768
Office phone: 301-230-0474
Office fax: (301) 881-6362
General e-mail: editorial@washingtonjewishweek.com
Web address: www.washingtonjewishweek.com
Year newspaper established: 1965
Advertising (open inch rate): Open inch rate $39.05
Mechanical specifications: Type page 9 3/4 x 13; A - 5 cols, 2, between; C - 8 cols, between.
Frequency: Thur
Circulation Paid: 10000
Audit By: Sworn/Estimate/Non-Audited
Audit Date: 12.07.2019
Hardware: APP/Mac
Software: QPS/QuarkXPress.
Personnel: Larry Fishbein (Pub.); Debra Rubin (Ed.); Patrick Fisher (Prodn. Mgr.)
Parent company: Joseph Jacobs Organization
Main (survey) contact: Geoffrey W. Melada

SAINT LOUIS

SAINT LOUIS JEWISH LIGHT

Street address 1: 6 Millstone Campus Dr
Street address 2: Ste 3010
Street address state: MO
Postal code: 63146-6603
County: Saint Louis
Country: USA
Mailing address: 6 Millstone Campus Dr Ste 3010
Mailing city: Saint Louis
Mailing state: MO
Mailing zip: 63146-6603
Office phone: (314) 743-3600
Office fax: (314) 743-3690
Advertising phone: (314) 743-3677
Advertising fax: (314) 743-3690
Editorial phone: (314) 743-3669
Editorial fax: (314) 743-3690
General e-mail: office@thejewishlight.com
Advertising e-mail: jschack@thejewishlight.com
Editorial e-mail: msherwin@thejewishlight.com
Web address: www.stljewishlight.com
Year newspaper established: 1947
Advertising (open inch rate): Call 3147433663 for details
Mechanical specifications: Call 3147433663 for details
Delivery methods: Mail`Racks
Digital Platform - Mobile: Apple`Android`Blackberry
Frequency: Wed
Other Type of Frequency: Quarterly Oy! Magazine, 24/7 website, weekly e-newsletter
Circulation Paid: 5000
Circulation Free: 4000
Audit By: Sworn/Estimate/Non-Audited
Audit Date: 12.07.2019
Personnel: Robert A. Cohn (CEO/Pub.)
Main (survey) contact: Robert A. Cohn

ST. LOUIS JEWISH LIGHT

Street address 1: 6 Millstone Campus Drive
Street address 2: Ste 3010
Street address state: MO
Postal code: 63146-6603
County: Saint Louis
Country: USA
Mailing address: 6 Millstone Campus Drive, Suite 3010

Mailing city: Saint Louis
Mailing state: MO
Mailing zip: 63146-6603
Office phone: (314) 743-3660
Office fax: (314) 743-3690
Advertising phone: (314) 743-3677
Advertising fax: (314) 743-3690
Editorial phone: (314) 743-3669
Editorial fax: (314) 743-3690
General e-mail: office@thejewishlight.com
Advertising e-mail: advertising@thejewishlight.com
Editorial e-mail: news@thejewishlight.com
Web address: www.stljewishlight.com
Year newspaper established: 1963
Advertising (open inch rate): contact for details
Mechanical specifications: Type page: 10.444 x 16; 6 col
Delivery methods: Mail`Racks
Zip Codes Served: 63xxx (St. Louis Metro)
Digital Platform - Mobile: Apple`Android`Blackberry
Digital Platform - Tablet: Other
Frequency: Wed
Other Type of Frequency: Quarterly magazine, 24/7 website, weekly email blast
Circulation Paid: 4813
Circulation Free: 4097
Audit By: CVC
Audit Date: 01.06.2012
Edition Names: St. Louis Jewish Light; OY! Magazine
Note: The Jewish Light is the nonprofit news organization of the St. Louis Jewish community.
Personnel: Robert A. Cohn (Ed. in Chief); Scott Berzon (Exec. Dir.)
Main (survey) contact: Robert A. Cohn

SALEM

NORTH SHORE JEWISH PRESS

Street address 1: 27 Congress St
Street address 2: Ste 501
Street address state: MA
Postal code: 01970-5577
County: Essex
Country: USA
Mailing address: 27 Congress Street, Suite 501
Mailing city: Salem
Mailing state: MA
Mailing zip: 01970
Office phone: (978) 745-4111
Office fax: (978) 745-5333
Advertising phone: (978) 745-4111X114
Editorial phone: (978) 745-4111X140
General e-mail: business@jewishjournal.org
Web address: www.jewishjournal.org
Year newspaper established: 1976
Advertising (open inch rate): Open inch rate $23.93
Mechanical specifications: Type page 9 3/4 x 15 3/4; E - 5 cols, 1 3/4, 1/4 between; A - 5 cols, 1 3/4, 1/4 between; C - 6 cols, 1 1/4, 1/4 between.
Frequency: Thur
Circulation Free: 16000
Audit By: Sworn/Estimate/Non-Audited
Audit Date: 12.07.2019
Hardware: APP/Mac
Software: QPS/QuarkXPress 4.1.
Personnel: Barbara Schneider (Pub.); Susan Jacobs (Editor); Bette Keva (Ed.)
Main (survey) contact: Joshua Resnek

SAN ANTONIO

THE JEWISH JOURNAL OF SAN ANTONIO

Street address 1: 12500 NW Military Hwy
Street address 2: Ste 200
Street address state: TX
Postal code: 78231-1868
County: Bexar
Country: USA
Office phone: (210) 302-6960
Office fax: (210) 408-2332
General e-mail: jewishj@jfsatx.org
Advertising e-mail: advertising@jfsatx.org
Web address: www.jfsatx.org
Delivery methods: Mail`Racks
Frequency: Mthly
Circulation Free: 4000
Audit By: Sworn/Estimate/Non-Audited
Audit Date: 12.07.2019
Personnel: Leslie Ausburn (Ed.)
Parent company: Jewish Federation of San Antonio
Main (survey) contact: Leslie Ausburn

SAN FRANCISCO

J. THE JEWISH NEWS WEEKLY OF NORTHERN CALIFONIA

Street address 1: 225 Bush St
Street address 2: Ste 1480
Street address state: CA
Postal code: 94104-4216
County: San Francisco
Country: USA
Mailing address: 225 Bush St Ste 1480
Mailing city: San Francisco
Mailing state: CA
Mailing zip: 94104-4216
Office phone: (415) 263-7200
Office fax: (415) 263-7222
Advertising phone: (415) 263-7200
Advertising fax: (415) 263-7222
General e-mail: info@jweekly.com
Advertising e-mail: nora@jweekly.com
Editorial e-mail: editors@jweekly.com
Web address: www.jweekly.com
Year newspaper established: 1946
Delivery methods: Mail
Zip Codes Served: SF Bay Area
Frequency: Fri
Circulation Paid: 17000
Circulation Free: 1000
Audit By: Sworn/Estimate/Non-Audited
Audit Date: 12.07.2019
Hardware: APP/Mac
Software: Microsoft/Word 98, QPS/QuarkXPress 6.0.
Personnel: Nora Contini (Publisher); Cathleen Maclearie (Art Dir.); Sue Fishkoff (Editor)
Main (survey) contact: Sue Fishkoff

SCHENECTADY

THE JEWISH WORLD

Street address 1: 1635 Eastern Pkwy
Street address state: NY
Postal code: 12309-6011
County: Schenectady
Country: USA
Mailing address: 1635 Eastern Pkwy
Mailing city: Schenectady
Mailing state: NY
Mailing zip: 12309-6011
Office phone: (518) 344-7018
Office fax: (518) 713-2137
General e-mail: news@jewishworldnews.org
Web address: www.jewishworldnews.org
Year newspaper established: 1965
Advertising (open inch rate): Open inch rate $13.50
Mechanical specifications: Type page 10 x 15 3/4.
Delivery methods: Mail`Newsstand
Frequency: Thur`Other
Other Type of Frequency: twice a month
Circulation Paid: 8500
Audit By: Sworn/Estimate/Non-Audited
Audit Date: 12.07.2019
Hardware: APP/Mac G3, GCC/Elite 1200
Software: QPS/QuarkXPress 4.0. Word
Note: serving Albany,Schenectady, Troy,all northeastern NY, western Mass, and south Vt
Personnel: Laurie Clevenson (editor.)
Main (survey) contact: Laurie J. Clevenson

SCOTTSDALE

JEWISH NEWS

Street address 1: 12701 N. Scottsdale Rd.
Street address 2: Ste. 206
Street address state: AZ
Postal code: 85254
County: Maricopa
Country: USA
Mailing address: 12701 N. Scottsdale Rd. Ste. 206
Mailing city: Scottsdale
Mailing state: AZ
Mailing zip: 85254
Office phone: (602) 870-9470
Office fax: (602) 870-0426
General e-mail: publisher@jewishaz.com
Editorial e-mail: editor@jewishaz.com
Web address: www.jewishaz.com
Year newspaper established: 1948
Advertising (open inch rate): N/A
Mechanical specifications: Type page 10" x 10.5"; 4 cols
Delivery methods: Mail`Newsstand
Digital Platform - Mobile: Other
Digital Platform - Tablet: Other
Frequency: Fri
Other Type of Frequency: annual Community Directory, annual Best of Jewish Phoenix magazine
Circulation Free: 4870
Audit By: CVC
Audit Date: 30.06.2016
Hardware: PC, APP/Mac
Software: Adobe/PageMaker.
Editions Count: 54
Personnel: Janet Perez (Mng. Ed.); Jodi Lipson (Adv. Acc. Exec.); Sandra Goldberg (Adv. Acc. Exec.); Nick Enquist (Staff Writer)
Parent company: Jewish Community Foundation
Main (survey) contact: Janet Perez

SKOKIE

CHICAGO JEWISH NEWS

Street address 1: 5301 Dempster St
Street address 2: Ste 100
Street address state: IL
Postal code: 60077-1800
County: Cook
Country: USA
Mailing address: 5301 Dempster St., Suite 100
Mailing city: Skokie
Mailing state: IL
Mailing zip: 60077-1800
Office phone: (847) 966-0606
Office fax: (847) 966-1656
Advertising e-mail: info@chicagojewishnews.com
Web address: www.chicagojewishnews.com
Year newspaper established: 1994
Advertising (open inch rate): Open inch rate $37.50
Mechanical specifications: Type page 9 3/4 x 14; E - 5 cols, 1 7/8, 1/6 between; A - 5 cols, 1 7/8, 1/6 between; C - 5 cols, 1 7/8, 1/6 between.
Delivery methods: Mail`Racks
Frequency: Fri
Circulation Paid: 10468
Circulation Free: 2422
Audit By: Sworn/Estimate/Non-Audited
Audit Date: 12.07.2019
Hardware: APP/Mac
Software: QPS/QuarkXPress 4.1, Adobe/Photoshop 3.0.5, Adobe/Illustrator 6.0.
Personnel: Joseph Aaron (Ed. and Pub.); Denise Kus (Production Manager)
Main (survey) contact: Joseph Aaron

CHICAGO JEWISH STAR

Street address 1: PO Box 268
Street address state: IL
Postal code: 60076-0268
County: Cook
Country: USA
Mailing address: PO Box 268
Mailing city: Skokie
Mailing state: IL
Mailing zip: 60076-0268
Office phone: (847) 674-7827
Office fax: (847) 674-0014
General e-mail: chicagojewishstar@comcast.net
Advertising (open inch rate): Open inch rate $27.00
Mechanical specifications: Type page 10 1/4 x 16; E - 6 cols, 1 5/8, 1/6 between; A - 6 cols, 1 5/8, 1/6 between; C - 6 cols, 1 5/8, 1/6 between.
Other Type of Frequency: 2 x Mthly
Circulation Paid: 100
Circulation Free: 17500
Audit By: Sworn/Estimate/Non-Audited
Audit Date: 12.07.2019
Hardware: PC
Software: QPS/QuarkXPress 3.32.
Personnel: Doug Wertheimer (Ed./Pub.)
Main (survey) contact: Doug Wertheimer

SOUTHFIELD

THE DETROIT JEWISH NEWS

Street address 1: 29200 Northwestern Hwy
Street address 2: Ste 110
Street address state: MI
Postal code: 48034-1055
County: Oakland
Country: USA
Mailing address: 29200 Northwestern Hwy Ste 110
Mailing city: Southfield
Mailing state: MI
Mailing zip: 48034-1055
Office phone: (248) 354-6060
Editorial fax: (248) 304-0032
Web address: www.thejewishnews.com
Mechanical specifications: Type page 9 13/16 x 13; E - 4 cols, 1 9/16, between; A - 4 cols, 1 9/16, between; C - 6 cols, 1 7/16, between.
Frequency: Thur
Circulation Paid: 17134
Circulation Free: 54
Audit By: Sworn/Estimate/Non-Audited
Audit Date: 12.07.2019
Hardware: Software ÃƒÂ‚Â‚Â— QPS/QuarkXPress 3.0, Adobe/Photoshop, Adobe/Illustrator 6.0.
Personnel: Arthur Horwitz (Pub.); Kevin Browett (COO); Keith Farber (Adv. Mgr.); Zina Davis (Circ. Mgr.); Robert Sklar (Ed.); Alan Hitsky (Assoc. Ed.)
Parent company: Joseph Jacobs Organization
Main (survey) contact: Arthur Horwitz

SYLVANIA

TOLEDO JEWISH NEWS

Street address 1: 6465 Sylvania Ave
Street address state: OH
Postal code: 43560-3916
County: Lucas
Country: USA
Mailing address: 6465 Sylvania Ave
Mailing city: Sylvania
Mailing state: OH
Mailing zip: 43560-3916
Office phone: (419) 724-0318
Office fax: (419) 885-3207
General e-mail: paul@jewishtoledo.org
Web address: www.jewishtoledo.org
Advertising (open inch rate): Open inch rate $13.25
Delivery methods: Mail`Racks
Frequency: Mthly
Circulation Paid: 2000
Audit By: Sworn/Estimate/Non-Audited
Audit Date: 12.07.2019
Personnel: Paul Causman (Marketing Manager and Editor); Emily Gordon (Staff writer, Marketing Associate)
Parent company: Jewish Federation of Greater Toledo
Main (survey) contact: Paul Causman

Jewish Newspapers in the U.S.

SYRACUSE

THE JEWISH OBSERVER

Street address 1: 5655 Thompson Rd
Street address state: NY
Postal code: 13214-1234
County: Onondaga
Country: USA
Mailing address: 5655 Thompson Rd
Mailing city: Syracuse
Mailing state: NY
Mailing zip: 13214-1234
Office phone: (315) 445-0161
Office fax: (315) 445-1559
Advertising phone: (800) 779-7896 ext 244
Editorial phone: (315) 445-0161
Editorial fax: (315) 445-1559
General e-mail: jewishobservercny@gmail.com
Advertising e-mail: jewishobserversyr@gmail.com
Editorial e-mail: jewishobservercny@gmail.com
Web address: www.jewishfederationcnyp.org
Year newspaper established: 1976
Mechanical specifications: Type page 10 3/8 x 16; E - 3 cols, 3 3/8, 1/6 between; A - 6 cols, 1 5/8, 1/6 between.
Delivery methods: Mail
Zip Codes Served: 01701-97201
Frequency: Thur
Other Type of Frequency: bii-weekly
Circulation Paid: 3000
Audit By: Sworn/Estimate/Non-Audited
Audit Date: 12.07.2019
Personnel: Bette Siegel (Ed.)
Main (survey) contact: Bette Siegel

TEANECK

JEWISH STANDARD

Street address 1: 1086 Teaneck Rd
Street address state: NJ
Postal code: 07666-4854
County: Bergen
Country: USA
Mailing address: 1086 Teaneck Rd Ste 2F
Mailing city: Teaneck
Mailing state: NJ
Mailing zip: 07666-4839
Office phone: (201) 837-8818
Office fax: (201) 833-4959
Advertising e-mail: ads@jewishmediagroup.com
Web address: www.jstandard.com
Advertising (open inch rate): Open inch rate $42.95
Frequency: Fri
Circulation Paid: 24000
Audit By: Sworn/Estimate/Non-Audited
Audit Date: 12.07.2019
Personnel: James Janoff (Pub.); Rebecca Boroson (Ed.)
Parent company: Joseph Jacobs Organization
Main (survey) contact: James Janoff

TUCSON

ARIZONA JEWISH POST

Street address 1: 3822 E River Rd
Street address 2: Ste 300
Street address state: AZ
Postal code: 85718-6635
County: Pima
Country: USA
Office phone: (520)319-1112
Office fax: (520) 319-1118
Advertising phone: (520) 319-1112 ext. 136
Editorial phone: (520) 319-1112 ext. 135
General e-mail: office@azjewishpost.com
Advertising e-mail: berti@azjewishpost.com
Editorial e-mail: localnews@azjewishpost.com
Web address: www.azjewishpost.com
Year newspaper established: 1946
Advertising (open inch rate): Open inch rate $20.00
Mechanical specifications: Six (6) columns x 12.75Ã¢Â€Âinch column depth Full page: 10.25" wide X 12.75Â£ depth.
Delivery methods: Mail`Carrier`Racks
Zip Codes Served: 85614, 85641, 85653, 85658, 85701, 85702, 85704, 85705, 85706, 8576, 85710, 85711, 85712, 85713, 85715, 85716, 85718, 85719, 85730, 85737, 85739, 85741
Frequency: Fri
Other Type of Frequency: 24x per year
Circulation Paid: 2063
Circulation Free: 4314
Audit By: CVC
Audit Date: 30.06.2018
Personnel: Phyllis Braun (Exec. Ed.); Berti Brodsky (Pub.); Maris Finley (Account Executive); April Bauer (Circ.); Michelle Shapiro (Adv.)
Parent company: Jewish Federation of Southern Arizona
Main (survey) contact: Phyllis Braun

VALLEY STREAM

JEWISH JOURNAL

Street address 1: 11 Sunrise Plz
Street address state: NY
Postal code: 11580-6170
County: Nassau
Country: USA
Mailing address: 11 Sunrise Plz
Mailing city: Valley Stream
Mailing state: NY
Mailing zip: 11580-6170
Office phone: (516) 561-6900
Office fax: (516) 561-3529
Advertising (open inch rate): Open inch rate $1.40
Frequency: Fri
Circulation Paid: 47000
Circulation Free: 33000
Audit By: Sworn/Estimate/Non-Audited
Audit Date: 12.07.2019
Hardware: APP/Mac
Software: QPS/QuarkXPress.
Personnel: Paul Rubin (Ed.)
Parent company: Joseph Jacobs Organization
Main (survey) contact: Rob Eshman

VESTAL

THE REPORTER

Street address 1: 500 Clubhouse Rd
Street address state: NY
Postal code: 13850-4700
County: Broome
Country: USA
Mailing address: 500 Clubhouse Rd Ste 2
Mailing city: Vestal
Mailing state: NY
Mailing zip: 13850-3734
Office phone: (607) 724-2360
Office fax: (607) 724-2311
General e-mail: treporter@aol.com
Web address: www.thereportergroup.org
Year newspaper established: 1971
Advertising (open inch rate): Open inch rate $9.15
Mechanical specifications: Type page 10 3/8 x 16; E - 3 cols, 3 3/8, 1/6 between; A - 6 cols, 1 5/8, 1/6 between.
Frequency: Fri
Circulation Paid: 2400
Audit By: Sworn/Estimate/Non-Audited
Audit Date: 12.07.2019
Personnel: Bonnie Rosen (Adv. Mgr.); Diana sochor (Layout Ed.); Jenn DePersis (Prodn. Coord.)
Main (survey) contact: Bonnie Rosen

THE VOICE

Street address 1: 500 Clubhouse Rd
Street address state: NY
Postal code: 13850-4700
County: Broome
Country: USA
Mailing address: 500 Clubhouse Rd
Mailing city: Vestal
Mailing state: NY
Mailing zip: 13850-4700
Office phone: (607) 724-2360
Office fax: (607) 724-2311
General e-mail: treporter@aol.com
Web address: www.thereportergroup.org
Year newspaper established: 1989
Mechanical specifications: Type page 10 3/8 x 16; E - 3 cols, 3 3/8, 1/6 between; A - 6 cols, 1 5/8, 1/6 between.
Frequency: Mthly
Circulation Paid: 3000
Audit By: Sworn/Estimate/Non-Audited
Audit Date: 12.07.2019
Personnel: Dan Springer (Bus. Mgr.); Jenn DePersis (Prodn. Mgr.)
Main (survey) contact: Dan Springer

WEST HARTFORD

CONNECTICUT JEWISH LEDGER

Street address 1: 740 N Main St
Street address 2: Ste W
Street address state: CT
Postal code: 06117-2403
County: Hartford
Country: USA
Mailing address: 36 Woodland St Ste 1
Mailing city: Hartford
Mailing state: CT
Mailing zip: 06105-2328
Office phone: (860) 231-2424
Office fax: (860) 231-2485
Editorial fax: (860) 231-2428
Advertising e-mail: advertising@jewishledger.com
Editorial e-mail: editorial@jewishledger.com
Web address: www.jewishledger.com
Advertising (open inch rate): Open inch rate $39.00
Mechanical specifications: Type page 8 x 13; E - 5 cols, between; A - 5 cols, between.
Frequency: Fri
Circulation Paid: 35000
Audit By: Sworn/Estimate/Non-Audited
Audit Date: 12.07.2019
Hardware: IBM
Software: QPS/QuarkXPress, Adobe/PageMaker.
Personnel: N. Richard Greenfield (Pub.); Leslie Iarusso (Prodn. Mgr.); Judie Jacobson (Mng. Ed.)
Parent company: Joseph Jacobs Organization
Main (survey) contact: Judie Jacobson

WHIPPANY

NEW JERSEY JEWISH NEWS

Street address 1: 901 State Route 10
Street address state: NJ
Postal code: 07981-1105
County: Morris
Country: USA
Mailing address: 901 State Route 10
Mailing city: Whippany
Mailing state: NJ
Mailing zip: 07981-1157
Office phone: (973) 887-8500
Office fax: (973) 887-4152
Editorial fax: (973) 887-5999
General e-mail: info@njjewishnews.com
Web address: www.njjewishnews.com
Advertising (open inch rate): Open inch rate $66.00
Mechanical specifications: Type page 10 1/4 x 13 1/2; E - 5 cols, 1 7/8, 1/4 between; A - 5 cols, 1 7/8, 1/4 between; C - 6 cols, 1 9/16, 1/8 between.
Delivery methods: Mail
Frequency: Thur
Circulation Paid: 50000
Audit By: Sworn/Estimate/Non-Audited
Audit Date: 12.07.2019
Hardware: APP/Mac
Software: QPS/QuarkXPress, Microsoft/Word.
Editions Count: 3
Edition Names: 3 total Ã‚Â— New Jersey Jewish News-MetroWest Edition (27,000);
Personnel: Andrew Silow-Carroll (Editor in Chief/CEO); Rick Kestenbaum
Main (survey) contact: Andrew Silow-Carroll

WILMINGTON

THE JEWISH FEDERATION OF DELAWARE

Street address 1: 101 Garden of Eden Rd
Street address state: DE
Postal code: 19803-1511
County: New Castle
Country: USA
Mailing address: 101 Garden of Eden Rd Ste 102
Mailing city: Wilmington
Mailing state: DE
Mailing zip: 19803-1511
Office phone: (302) 427-2100
Office fax: (302) 427-2438
General e-mail: seth@shalomdel.org
Advertising e-mail: kat@shalomdel.org
Editorial e-mail: shoshana@shalomdel.org
Web address: www.shalomdelaware.org
Year newspaper established: 1951
Delivery methods: Mail
Zip Codes Served: 19801, 19803, 19806, 19809, 19810
Frequency: Mthly
Circulation Paid: 3000
Circulation Free: 500
Audit By: Sworn/Estimate/Non-Audited
Audit Date: 12.07.2019
Personnel: Shoshana Martyniak (Editor)
Main (survey) contact: Seth Katzen

WORCESTER

THE JEWISH CHRONICLE

Street address 1: 131 Lincoln St
Street address state: MA
Postal code: 01605-2408
County: Worcester
Country: USA
Mailing address: 131 Lincoln St
Mailing city: Worcester
Mailing state: MA
Mailing zip: 01605-2421
Office phone: (508) 752-2512
Office fax: (508) 752-9057
General e-mail: chronicle.sales@verizon.net
Advertising (open inch rate): Open inch rate $12.00
Mechanical specifications: Type page 10 x 16; E - 4 cols, 2 1/2, between; A - 6 cols, 1 1/2, between.
Zip Codes Served: 1605
Frequency: Thur
Circulation Paid: 1000
Circulation Free: 4000
Audit By: Sworn/Estimate/Non-Audited
Audit Date: 12.07.2019
Personnel: Sondra Shapiro (Pub.); Reva Catellari (Adv. Mgr.); Ellen Weingart (Ed.)
Main (survey) contact: Sondra Shapiro

WYOMISSING

SHALOM NEWSPAPER

Street address 1: 223 Hawthorne Ct N
Street address state: PA
Postal code: 19610-1064
County: Berks
Country: USA
Mailing address: 223 Hawthorne Ct N
Mailing city: Wyomissing
Mailing state: PA
Mailing zip: 19610-1064
Office phone: (610) 921-0624
Office fax: (610) 929-0886
General e-mail: joan@friedman.net
Web address: www.readingjewishcommunity.org
Advertising (open inch rate): Open inch rate $19.50
Frequency: Mthly
Circulation Paid: 3000
Audit By: Sworn/Estimate/Non-Audited
Audit Date: 12.07.2019

MILITARY NEWSPAPERS IN THE U.S.

ABILENE

SOUND OF FREEDOM

Street address 1: 101 Cypress St
Street address state: TX
Postal code: 79601-5816
County: Taylor
Country: USA
Mailing address: PO Box 30
Mailing city: Abilene
Mailing state: TX
Mailing zip: 79604-0030
Office phone: (325) 673-4271
Office fax: (325) 670-5222
Advertising e-mail: ads@reporternews.com
Website: www.reporternews.com
Year newspaper established: 1984
Advertising (open inch rate): Open inch rate $7.95
Mechanical specifications: Type page 9 5/8 x 11 5/8; E - 5 cols, 1 5/6, between; A - 5 cols, 1 5/6, between; C - 7 cols, 1 1/16, between.
Weekly Paper Frequency: Fri
Circulation Free: 7500
Audit By: Sworn/Estimate/Non-Audited
Audit Date: 12.07.2019
Personnel: Kim Nussbaum (Pub.); Stephanie Boggins (Adv. Mgr.); Barton Cromeens (Ed.); Mike Hall (Opns Dir.)
Main (survey) contact: Doug Williamson

BARSTOW

BARSTOW LOG

Street address 1: Marine Corps Logistics Base, Bldg 204
Street address state: CA
Postal code: 92311
County: San Bernardino
Country: USA
Mailing address: PO Box 110130
Mailing city: Barstow
Mailing state: CA
Mailing zip: 92311-5050
Office phone: (760) 577-6430
Office fax: (760) 577-6350
General e-mail: robert.l.jackson@usmc.mil
Advertising (open inch rate): Open inch rate $6.00
Mechanical specifications: Type page 10 1/4 x 13; E - 5 cols, 1 11/12, 1/8 between; A - 5 cols, 1 11/12, 1/8 between; C - 5 cols, 1 11/12, 1/8 between.
Weekly Paper Frequency: Thur
Circulation Free: 3700
Audit By: Sworn/Estimate/Non-Audited
Audit Date: 12.07.2019
Personnel: Rob L. Jackson (Pub. Affairs Officer); Quentin Grogan (Ed.)
Parent company: Brehm Communications, Inc.
Main (survey) contact: Rob L. Jackson

BELLEVUE

AIR PULSE

Street address 1: 604 Fort Crook Rd N
Street address state: NE
Postal code: 68005-4557
County: Sarpy
Country: USA
Mailing address: 604 Fort Crook Rd N
Mailing city: Bellevue
Mailing state: NE
Mailing zip: 68005-4557
Office phone: (402) 733-7300
Office fax: (402) 733-9116
Editorial e-mail: news@bellevueleader.com
Website: www.omahanewsstand.com
Year newspaper established: 1946

Advertising (open inch rate): Open inch rate $16.22
Mechanical specifications: Type page 9 3/4 x 11 1/2; E - 6 cols, 1 1/2, between; A - 6 cols, 1 1/2, between.
Weekly Paper Frequency: Thur
Circulation Free: 9500
Audit By: Sworn/Estimate/Non-Audited
Audit Date: 12.07.2019
Weeklies Equipment - Hardware: Apt, Dell.
Personnel: Shon Barenklau (Pub.); Paul Swanson (Adv. Mgr.); Mellissa Vanek (Circ. Mgr.); Amy Corrigan (Prodn. Mgr.)
Main (survey) contact: Shon Barenklau

BRUNSWICK

THE PATROLLER

Street address 1: 3 Business Pkwy
Street address state: ME
Postal code: 04011-7390
County: Cumberland
Country: USA
Mailing address: PO Box 10
Mailing city: Brunswick
Mailing state: ME
Mailing zip: 04011-1302
Office phone: (207) 729-3311
Office fax: (207) 729-5728
Advertising e-mail: adsales@timesrecord.com
Website: www.timesrecord.com
Advertising (open inch rate): Open inch rate $6.95
Mechanical specifications: Type page 10 1/8 x 15 1/4; E - 5 cols, between; A - 5 cols, between; C - 6 cols, between.
Weekly Paper Frequency: Thur
Circulation Free: 3500
Audit By: Sworn/Estimate/Non-Audited
Audit Date: 12.07.2019
Weeklies Equipment - Presses: G/Community.
Personnel: Chris Miles (Pub.); John Bamford (Adv. Dir.)
Main (survey) contact: Chris Miles

CAMDEN

THE SHAW NEWS

Street address 1: 909 W Dekalb St
Street address state: SC
Postal code: 29020-4259
County: Kershaw
Country: USA
Mailing address: 909 W Dekalb St
Mailing city: Camden
Mailing state: SC
Mailing zip: 29020-4259
Office phone: (803) 432-6157
Advertising phone: (803) 432-6157
Advertising fax: (803) 432-7609
Editorial phone: (803) 236-8425
General e-mail: mmischner@ci-camden.com
Website: www.ci-camden.com
Advertising (open inch rate): Open inch rate $13.15
Mechanical specifications: Type page 10 x 14.
Weekly Paper Frequency: Fri
Circulation Free: 7200
Audit By: Sworn/Estimate/Non-Audited
Audit Date: 12.07.2019
Weeklies Equipment - Hardware: PC.
Personnel: Michael Mischner (Pub.); Betsy Greenway (Adv. Mgr.)
Parent company: Morris Multimedia, Inc.
Main (survey) contact: Betsy Greenway

CHEYENNE

WARREN SENTINEL

Street address 1: 307 E 20th St

Street address state: WY
Postal code: 82001-3705
County: Laramie
Country: USA
Mailing address: 307 E 20th St
Mailing city: Cheyenne
Mailing state: WY
Mailing zip: 82001-3705
Office phone: (307) 632-5666
Office fax: (307) 632-1554
General e-mail: graphics@warrensentinel.com
Advertising e-mail: ads@warrensentinel.com
Website: www.warrensentinel.com
Advertising (open inch rate): Open inch rate $9.00
Mechanical specifications: Type page 9 3/4 x 13; E - 6 cols, 1 1/2, 1/6 between; A - 6 cols, 1 1/2, 1/6 between; C - 6 cols, 1 1/2, 1/6 between.
Weekly Paper Frequency: Fri
Circulation Free: 5200
Audit By: Sworn/Estimate/Non-Audited
Audit Date: 12.07.2019
Weeklies Equipment - Hardware: APP/Power Mac 7600-120
Weeklies Equipment - Presses: 5-G/Community
Weeklies Equipment - Software: Adobe/PageMaker 6.0, Adobe/Photoshop 3.0, Multi-Ad/Creator 3.8.
Personnel: Jim Wood (Pub.); Kelly Sebastian (Sales Mgr.); Barbara Coursey (Inside Adv. Sales); Monica Valdez (Prodn. Mgr./Graphics)
Main (survey) contact: Jim Wood

COLORADO SPRINGS

MOUNTAINEER

Street address 1: 31 E Platte Ave
Street address 2: Ste 300
Street address state: CO
Postal code: 80903-1246
County: El Paso
Country: USA
Mailing address: 31 E Platte Ave Ste 300
Mailing city: Colorado Springs
Mailing state: CO
Mailing zip: 80903-1246
Office phone: (719) 634-1593
Office fax: (719) 632-0265
General e-mail: advertising@gowdyprint.com
Advertising (open inch rate): Open inch rate $13.00
Mechanical specifications: Type page 10 7/8 x 15 5/8; E - 6 cols, 1 1/2, between; A - 6 cols, 1 1/2, between.
Zip Codes Served: 80903
Weekly Paper Frequency: Fri
Circulation Free: 75000
Audit By: Sworn/Estimate/Non-Audited
Audit Date: 12.07.2019
Weeklies Equipment - Hardware: IBM, APP/Mac
Weeklies Equipment - Presses: Komori/M29, HI/25
Weeklies Equipment - Software: QPS/QuarkXPress, Adobe/Photoshop, Adobe/Illustrator.
Personnel: Tex Stewart (Pub.); Barbara Hedges (Adv. Mgr.)
Main (survey) contact: Tex Stewart

COTUIT

OTIS NOTICE

Street address 1: 4507 Falmouth Rd
Street address state: MA
Postal code: 02635-2652
County: Barnstable
Country: USA
Mailing address: PO Box 571
Mailing city: Osterville
Mailing state: MA
Mailing zip: 02655-0571

Office phone: (508) 428-8700
Office fax: (508) 428-8524
General e-mail: L.printing@comcast.net
Editorial e-mail: otis@lujeanprinting.com
Website: www.lujeanprinting.com
Year newspaper established: 1963
Mechanical specifications: Type page 10 1/4 x 16; E - 6 cols, 1 5/8, 1/8 between; A - 6 cols, 1 5/8, 1/8 between.
Delivery methods: Mail Carrier Racks
Zip Codes Served: 2 536 025 590 253 200 000
Weekly Paper Frequency: Mthly
Circulation Free: 5000
Audit By: Sworn/Estimate/Non-Audited
Audit Date: 12.07.2019
Weeklies Equipment - Hardware: APP/Mac
Weeklies Equipment - Presses: HI/V-15A
Weeklies Equipment - Software: Adobe/InDesign
Personnel: Michael Lally (Pub.); Gerry Lynn Galati (Graphic Manager)
Main (survey) contact: Michael Lally

EL CENTRO

SANDPAPER

Street address 1: 1500 8th St
Street address state: CA
Postal code: 92243-5041
County: Imperial
Country: USA
Mailing address: 1500 8th St
Mailing city: El Centro
Mailing state: CA
Mailing zip: 92243-5041
Office phone: (760) 339-2519
Office fax: (760) 339-2699
General e-mail: elcnpao@navy.mil
Website: www.nafec.navy.mil
Audit By: Sworn/Estimate/Non-Audited
Audit Date: 12.07.2019
Personnel: Michelle Dee (Ed.)
Main (survey) contact: Michelle Dee

EL PASO

FORT BLISS MONITOR

Street address 1: 1420 Geronimo Dr
Street address 2: Bldg E
Street address state: TX
Postal code: 79925-1855
County: El Paso
Country: USA
Mailing address: 5959 Gateway Blvd W Ste 450
Mailing city: El Paso
Mailing state: TX
Mailing zip: 79925-3396
Office phone: (915) 772-0934
Office fax: (915) 772-1594
General e-mail: sflav@whc.net
Website: www.lavenpublishing.com
Year newspaper established: 1985
Advertising (open inch rate): Open inch rate $13.60
Mechanical specifications: Type page 10 1/8 x 16; E - 4 cols, 2 1/4, 1/2 between; A - 4 cols, 2 1/4, 1/2 between; C - 7 cols, 1 1/4, 1/4 between.
Zip Codes Served: 79906, 79924, 79925, 79936, 79902
Weekly Paper Frequency: Thur
Circulation Free: 20000
Audit By: Sworn/Estimate/Non-Audited
Audit Date: 12.07.2019
Personnel: Mike Laven (Vice Pres., Sales); Skip Laven (Adv. Mgr.); Susan Laven (Vice Pres., Prodn.)
Main (survey) contact: Skip Laven

Military Newspapers in the U.S.

FAYETTEVILLE

CAROLINA FLYER

Street address 1: PO Box 849
Street address state: NC
Postal code: 28302-0849
County: Cumberland
Country: USA
Mailing address: PO Box 849
Mailing city: Fayetteville
Mailing state: NC
Mailing zip: 28302-0849
Office phone: (910) 323-4848
Office fax: (910) 486-3544
Website: www.fayobserver.com
Advertising (open inch rate): Open inch rate $7.13
Mechanical specifications: Type page 12 1/2 x 22; E - 6 cols, 1 5/6, 1/6 between; A - 6 cols, 1 5/6, 1/6 between; C - 10 cols, 1, 1/10 between.
Weekly Paper Frequency: Fri
Circulation Free: 4019
Audit By: Sworn/Estimate/Non-Audited
Audit Date: 12.07.2019
Weeklies Equipment - Hardware: Presses Ã‚Â— 24-KBA/Colora.
Personnel: Charles W. Broadwell (Pub.); Brad Parker (Weekly Sales Mgr.); Jim Adkins (Circ. Dir.); Brian Tolley (Exec. Ed.)
Main (survey) contact: The Editor

FORT BRAGG PARAGLIDE

Street address 1: 458 Whitfield St
Street address state: NC
Postal code: 28306-1614
County: Cumberland
Country: USA
Mailing address: PO Box 849
Mailing city: Fayetteville
Mailing state: NC
Mailing zip: 28302-0849
Office phone: (910) 396-6817
Office fax: (910) 396-9629
Advertising phone: (910) 323-4848
General e-mail: paraglidebragg@gmail.com
Website: www.paraglideonline.net
Advertising (open inch rate): Open inch rate $25.00
Mechanical specifications: Type page 12 1/2 x 22; E - 6 cols, 1 5/6, 1/6 between; A - 6 cols, 1 5/6, 1/6 between; C - 10 cols, 1, 1/10 between.
Zip Codes Served: 28307
Weekly Paper Frequency: Thur
Circulation Free: 25000
Audit By: Sworn/Estimate/Non-Audited
Audit Date: 12.07.2019
Weeklies Equipment - Presses: 24-KBA/Colora.
Personnel: Charles W. Broadwell (Pub.); Brad Parker (Mgr., Adv. Sales); James Adkins (Circ. Mgr.)
Main (survey) contact: Charles W. Broadwell

FORT BENNING

THE BAYONET

Street address 1: 6460 Way Ave
Street address 2: Ste 102
Street address state: GA
Postal code: 31905-3771
County: Chattahoochee
Country: USA
Mailing address: 6460 Way St., Suite 102
Mailing city: Fort Benning
Mailing state: GA
Mailing zip: 31905-4584
Office phone: (706) 545-4622
Advertising phone: (706) 576-6239
Website: www.thebayonet.com
Advertising (open inch rate): Open inch rate $21.00
Mechanical specifications: Type page 13 x 20 1/2; E - 6 cols, 2 1/16, 1/6 between; A - 6 cols, 2 1/16, 1/6 between; C - 6 cols, 2 1/16, 1/6 between.
Delivery methods: Mail`Newsstand`Carrier`Racks
Zip Codes Served: 31905
Weekly Paper Frequency: Wed
Circulation Free: 22000
Audit By: Sworn/Estimate/Non-Audited
Audit Date: 12.07.2019
Weeklies Equipment - Hardware: APP/Mac
Weeklies Equipment - Software: QPS/QuarkXPress 3.32.
Personnel: Lori Egan (Ed.)
Main (survey) contact: Lori Egan

FORT DRUM

THE MOUNTAINEER

Street address 1: 10012 S Riva Ridge Loop
Street address state: NY
Postal code: 13602-5492
County: Jefferson
Country: USA
Mailing address: 10012 S. Riva Ridge Loop
Mailing city: Fort Drum
Mailing state: NY
Mailing zip: 13602
Office phone: (315) 772-5469
Office fax: (315) 772-8295
Weekly Paper Frequency: Thur
Circulation Free: 10000
Audit By: Sworn/Estimate/Non-Audited
Audit Date: 12.07.2019
Personnel: Lisa Albrecht (Managing editor)
Main (survey) contact: Lisa Albrecht

FORT HOOD

FORT HOOD SENTINEL

Street address 1: 761 Tank Battalion
Street address 2: Bldg W105
Street address state: TX
Postal code: 76544-4906
County: Bell
Country: USA
Office phone: (254) 287-9495
Advertising phone: (254) 634-6666
Editorial phone: (254) 287-9495
Advertising e-mail: advertise@forthoodsentinel.com
Editorial e-mail: todd.pruden@forthoodsentinel.com
Website: www.forthoodsentinel.com
Year newspaper established: 1942
Advertising (open inch rate): Open inch rate $12.50
Mechanical specifications: Type page 12 x 21 1/2; E - 6 cols, 1 4/5, 1/8 between; A - 6 cols, 1 4/5, 1/8 between; C - 9 cols, 1 1/5, 1/16 between.
Delivery methods: Mail`Newsstand`Carrier`Racks
Zip Codes Served: 76541, 76544
Weekly Paper Frequency: Thur
Circulation Free: 25000
Audit By: Sworn/Estimate/Non-Audited
Audit Date: 12.07.2019
Weeklies Equipment - Hardware: Dell
Weeklies Equipment - Presses: 10-G/Urbanite.
Weeklies Equipment - Software: InDesign
Personnel: Sue Mayborn (Pub.); Ray Reed (Gen. Mgr.)
Parent company: Frank Mayborn Enterprises, Inc.
Main (survey) contact: Todd Pruden

FORT KNOX

TURRET

Street address 1: Bldg 1109, Wing D, Sixth St
Street address state: KY
Postal code: 40121-
County: Hardin
Country: USA
Mailing address: PO Box 995
Mailing city: Fort Knox
Mailing state: KY
Mailing zip: 40121-0995
Office phone: (502) 624-6517
Office fax: (502) 624-2096
Advertising phone: (270) 769-1200
Website: www.turret.com; www.newsenterpriseonline.com
Advertising (open inch rate): Open inch rate $9.49
Mechanical specifications: Type page 13 1/2 x 21 1/2; E - 6 cols, 2 1/8, between; A - 6 cols, 2 1/8, between.
Weekly Paper Frequency: Thur
Circulation Free: 20896
Audit By: Sworn/Estimate/Non-Audited
Audit Date: 12.07.2019
Personnel: Larry Barnes (Ed.); Maureen Rose (Assoc. Ed.); Kellie Etheridge (Leisure Ed.); Ally Rogers (Sports Ed.)
Main (survey) contact: Maureen Rose

FORT LEAVENWORTH

FORT LEAVENWORTH LAMP

Street address 1: 290 Grant Ave
Street address 2: Ste 6
Street address state: KS
Postal code: 66027-1292
County: Leavenworth
Country: USA
Mailing address: 290 Grant Ave Unit 6
Mailing city: Fort Leavenworth
Mailing state: KS
Mailing zip: 66027-1292
Office phone: (913) 682-0305
Office fax: (913) 682-1089
Advertising phone: (913) 682-0305
Advertising fax: (913) 682-1089
Editorial phone: (913) 684-1728
Advertising e-mail: shattock@leavenworthtimes.com
Editorial e-mail: editor@ftleavenworthlamp.com
Website: www.ftleavenworthlamp.com
Year newspaper established: 1971
Advertising (open inch rate): Open inch rate $9.70
Mechanical specifications: Type page 10 x 16; E - 5 cols, 2, between; A - 5 cols, 2, between; C - 5 cols, 2, between.
Delivery methods: Newsstand`Carrier`Racks
Zip Codes Served: 66027, 66048, 66043
Weekly Paper Frequency: Thur
Circulation Free: 8000
Audit By: Sworn/Estimate/Non-Audited
Audit Date: 12.07.2019
Personnel: Jeffery Wingo (Public Affairs Officer); Sandy Hattock (Adv. Mgr.); Robert Kerr (Ed.)
Parent company: The Hays Daily News
Main (survey) contact: Robert Kerr

FORT MEADE

SOUNDOFF!

Street address 1: 4409 Llewellyn Avenue
Street address state: MD
Postal code: 20755
County: Anne Arundel
Country: USA
Mailing address: 4409 Llewellyn Avenue
Mailing city: Fort Meade
Mailing state: MD
Mailing zip: 20755-5025
Office phone: (301) 677-5602
Advertising phone: (410) 332-6300
Editorial phone: (301) 677-6806
Editorial fax: 301- 677-1305
Other phone: (301) 677-1438
General e-mail: soundoff@conus.army.mil
Advertising e-mail: advertise@baltsun.com
Editorial e-mail: rhirsch@tribune.com
Delivery methods: Carrier`Racks
Weekly Paper Frequency: Thur
Circulation Paid: 263
Circulation Free: 12031
Audit By: CAC
Audit Date: 30.09.2017
Personnel: Dijon Rolle (Editor)
Parent company: Tribune Publishing, Inc.
Main (survey) contact: Rona Hirsch

FORT POLK

GUARDIAN

Street address 1: 7033 Magnolia Dr
Street address state: LA
Postal code: 71459-3495
County: Vernon
Country: USA
Mailing address: 7033 Magnolia Dr.
Mailing city: Fort Polk
Mailing state: LA
Mailing zip: 71459
Office phone: (337) 462-0616
Advertising phone: (337) 462-0616
Advertising fax: (337) 463-5347
Editorial phone: (337) 531-4033
Editorial fax: (337) 531-1401
General e-mail: guardian@wnonline.net
Website: www.thefortpolkguardian.com
Advertising (open inch rate): Open inch rate $15.05
Weekly Paper Frequency: Fri
Circulation Free: 13000
Audit By: Sworn/Estimate/Non-Audited
Audit Date: 12.07.2019
Personnel: Theresa Larue (Adv. Mgr.); Kimberly Reischling (Command Info., Media Rel. Chief)
Main (survey) contact: Kimbery Reischling

FORT RUCKER

ARMY FLIER

Street address 1: 453 S Novasel St
Street address 2: Bldg 112
Street address state: AL
Postal code: 36362-5109
County: Dale
Country: USA
Mailing address: 453 S Novasel St Bldg 112
Mailing city: Fort Rucker
Mailing state: AL
Mailing zip: 36362-5109
Office phone: (334) 255-2613
Office fax: (334) 255-1004
Website: www.armyflier.com
Advertising (open inch rate): Open inch rate $10.00
Mechanical specifications: Type page 13 x 21 1/2; E - 6 cols, 2 1/8, between; A - 6 cols, 2 1/8, between; C - 9 cols, 1 9/20, between.
Weekly Paper Frequency: Thur
Circulation Free: 10000
Audit By: Sworn/Estimate/Non-Audited
Audit Date: 12.07.2019
Personnel: Marty Gatlin (Ed.)
Parent company: BH Media Group
Main (survey) contact: Jim Hughes

FORT SILL

THE CANNONEER

Street address 1: 455 McNair Hall, Ste 118
Street address state: OK
Postal code: 73503
County: Comanche
Country: USA
Mailing address: 455 McNair Hall, Ste. 118
Mailing city: Fort Sill
Mailing state: OK
Mailing zip: 73503-5100
Office phone: (580) 442-5150
Office fax: (580) 585-5103
General e-mail: cannoneersill@conus.army.mil
Website: www.woknews.com
Advertising (open inch rate): Open inch rate $7.25
Mechanical specifications: Type page 13 x 21 1/6; E - 6 cols, 2 1/16, 1/8 between; A - 6 cols, 2 1/16, 1/8 between; C - 9 cols, 1 1/4, 1/8 between.
Weekly Paper Frequency: Thur
Circulation Free: 12000
Audit By: Sworn/Estimate/Non-Audited
Audit Date: 12.07.2019
Weeklies Equipment - Hardware: APP/Mac, PC
Weeklies Equipment - Presses: HI/1660

GAITHERSBURG

ANDREWS GAZETTE
Street address 1: 9030 Comprint Ct
Street address state: MD
Postal code: 20877-1307
County: Montgomery
Country: USA
Mailing address: 9030 Comprint Ct
Mailing city: Gaithersburg
Mailing state: MD
Mailing zip: 20877-1307
Weekly Paper Frequency: Wed`Thur`Fri
Circulation Paid: 14350
Circulation Free: 5734
Audit By: Sworn/Estimate/Non-Audited
Audit Date: 12.07.2019
Main (survey) contact: Art Crofoot

CAPITAL FLYER
Street address 1: 9030 Comprint Ct
Street address state: MD
Postal code: 20877-1307
County: Montgomery
Country: USA
Mailing address: 9030 Comprint Ct
Mailing city: Gaithersburg
Mailing state: MD
Mailing zip: 20877-1307
Office phone: (301) 921-2800
Office fax: (301) 948-2787
General e-mail: jrives@gazette.net
Advertising (open inch rate): Open inch rate $18.20
Mechanical specifications: Type page 9 5/8 x 13 1/2; E - 6 cols, between; A - 6 cols, between; C - 7 cols, between.
Weekly Paper Frequency: Fri
Circulation Free: 15000
Audit By: Sworn/Estimate/Non-Audited
Audit Date: 12.07.2019
Weeklies Equipment - Hardware: APP/Mac
Weeklies Equipment - Presses: G/Urbanite, G/Community
Weeklies Equipment - Software: QPS/QuarkXPress.
Personnel: John Rives (Pub.); Matt Dunigan (Adv. Mgr.)
Main (survey) contact: John Rives

FORT DETRICK STANDARD
Street address 1: 9030 Comprint Ct
Street address state: MD
Postal code: 20877-1307
County: Montgomery
Country: USA
Mailing address: 9030 Comprint Ct
Mailing city: Gaithersburg
Mailing state: MD
Mailing zip: 20877-1307
Office phone: (301) 921-2800
Office fax: (301) 948-2787
Website: www.dcmilitary.com
Advertising (open inch rate): Open inch rate $12.85
Mechanical specifications: Type page 9 5/8 x 13 1/2; E - 6 cols, between; A - 6 cols, between; C - 7 cols, between.
Other Type of Frequency: Every other Thur
Circulation Free: 4100
Audit By: Sworn/Estimate/Non-Audited
Audit Date: 12.07.2019
Weeklies Equipment - Hardware: APP/Mac
Weeklies Equipment - Presses: G/Urbanite, G/Community
Weeklies Equipment - Software: QPS/QuarkXPress.
Personnel: John Rives (Adv. Mgr.); Jean Casey (Circ. Mgr.); Ann Duble (Ed.)
Main (survey) contact: Art Crofoot

HENDERSON HALL NEWS
Street address 1: 9030 Comprint Ct

Street address state: MD
Postal code: 20877-1307
County: Montgomery
Country: USA
Mailing address: 9030 Comprint Ct
Mailing city: Gaithersburg
Mailing state: MD
Mailing zip: 20877-1307
Office phone: (301) 921-2800
Office fax: (301) 948-2787
Website: www.dcmilitary.com
Advertising (open inch rate): Open inch rate $12.47
Mechanical specifications: Type page 9 5/8 x 13 1/2; E - 6 cols, between; A - 6 cols, between; C - 7 cols, between.
Audit By: Sworn/Estimate/Non-Audited
Audit Date: 12.07.2019
Weeklies Equipment - Hardware: APP/Mac
Weeklies Equipment - Presses: G/Urbanite, G/Community
Weeklies Equipment - Software: QPS/QuarkXPress.
Personnel: Brent Wucher (Ed.)
Main (survey) contact: Brent Wucher

JOINT BASE JOURNAL
Street address 1: 9030 Comprint Ct
Street address state: MD
Postal code: 20877-1307
County: Montgomery
Country: USA
Mailing address: 9030 Comprint Ct
Mailing city: Gaithersburg
Mailing state: MD
Mailing zip: 20877-1307
Office phone: (301) 921-2800
Office fax: (301) 948-2787
Website: www.dcmilitary.com
Advertising (open inch rate): Open inch rate $29.62
Mechanical specifications: Type page 9 5/8 x 13 1/2; E - 6 cols, between; A - 6 cols, between; C - 7 cols, between.
Weekly Paper Frequency: Wed`Thur
Circulation Free: 24000
Audit By: Sworn/Estimate/Non-Audited
Audit Date: 12.07.2019
Weeklies Equipment - Hardware: APP/Mac
Weeklies Equipment - Presses: G/Urbanite, G/Community
Weeklies Equipment - Software: QPS/QuarkXPress.
Personnel: John Rives (Adv. Mgr.)
Main (survey) contact: Art Crofoot

PENTAGRAM
Street address 1: 9030 Comprint Ct
Street address state: MD
Postal code: 20877-1307
County: Montgomery
Country: USA
Mailing address: 9030 Comprint Ct
Mailing city: Gaithersburg
Mailing state: MD
Mailing zip: 20877-1307
Office phone: (301) 921-2800
Office fax: (301) 948-2787
Website: www.dcmilitary.com
Advertising (open inch rate): Open inch rate $29.62
Mechanical specifications: Type page 9 5/8 x 13 1/2; E - 6 cols, between; A - 6 cols, between; C - 7 cols, between.
Weekly Paper Frequency: Wed`Thur
Circulation Free: 24000
Audit By: Sworn/Estimate/Non-Audited
Audit Date: 12.07.2019
Weeklies Equipment - Hardware: APP/Mac
Weeklies Equipment - Presses: G/Urbanite, G/Community
Weeklies Equipment - Software: QPS/QuarkXPress.
Personnel: John Rives (Adv. Mgr.)
Main (survey) contact: Art Crofoot

SOUTH POTOMAC PILOT
Street address 1: 9030 Comprint Ct
Street address state: MD

Postal code: 20877-1307
County: Montgomery
Country: USA
Mailing address: 9030 Comprint Ct
Mailing city: Gaithersburg
Mailing state: MD
Mailing zip: 20877-1307
Office phone: (301) 921-2800
Office fax: (301) 948-2787
Website: www.dcmilitary.com
Advertising (open inch rate): Open inch rate $29.62
Mechanical specifications: Type page 9 5/8 x 13 1/2; E - 6 cols, between; A - 6 cols, between; C - 7 cols, between.
Weekly Paper Frequency: Wed`Thur
Circulation Free: 24000
Audit By: Sworn/Estimate/Non-Audited
Audit Date: 12.07.2019
Weeklies Equipment - Hardware: APP/Mac
Weeklies Equipment - Presses: G/Urbanite, G/Community
Weeklies Equipment - Software: QPS/QuarkXPress.
Personnel: John Rives (Adv. Mgr.)
Main (survey) contact: Art Crofoot

TESTER
Street address 1: 9030 Comprint Ct
Street address state: MD
Postal code: 20877-1307
County: Montgomery
Country: USA
Mailing address: 9030 Comprint Ct
Mailing city: Gaithersburg
Mailing state: MD
Mailing zip: 20877-1307
Office phone: (301) 921-2800
Office fax: (301) 948-2787
Website: www.dcmilitary.com
Advertising (open inch rate): Open inch rate $17.17
Mechanical specifications: Type page 13 1/4 x 21; E - 8 cols, between; A - 8 cols, between; C - 9 cols, between.
Weekly Paper Frequency: Thur
Circulation Free: 15000
Audit By: Sworn/Estimate/Non-Audited
Audit Date: 12.07.2019
Weeklies Equipment - Hardware: APP/Mac
Weeklies Equipment - Presses: G/Urbanite, G/Community
Weeklies Equipment - Software: QPS/QuarkXPress.
Personnel: Matt Dunigan (Adv. Mgr.); John Rives (Ed.)
Main (survey) contact: Art Crofoot

THE NNMC JOURNAL
Street address 1: 9030 Comprint Ct
Street address state: MD
Postal code: 20877-1307
County: Montgomery
Country: USA
Mailing address: 9030 Comprint Ct
Mailing city: Gaithersburg
Mailing state: MD
Mailing zip: 20877-1307
Office phone: (301) 921-2800
Office fax: (301) 948-2787
Website: www.dcmilitary.com
Advertising (open inch rate): Open inch rate $14.37
Mechanical specifications: Type page 9 5/8 x 13 1/2; E - 4 cols, between; A - 6 cols, between; C - 7 cols, between.
Weekly Paper Frequency: Thur
Circulation Free: 7000
Audit By: Sworn/Estimate/Non-Audited
Audit Date: 12.07.2019
Weeklies Equipment - Hardware: APP/Mac
Weeklies Equipment - Presses: G/Community, G/Urbanite
Weeklies Equipment - Software: QPS/QuarkXPress.
Personnel: Matt Dunigan (Gen. Mgr.); John Rives (Adv. Mgr.)
Main (survey) contact: Art Crofoot

THE WATER LINE
Street address 1: 9030 Comprint Ct

Street address state: MD
Postal code: 20877-1307
County: Montgomery
Country: USA
Mailing address: 9030 Comprint Ct
Mailing city: Gaithersburg
Mailing state: MD
Mailing zip: 20877-1307
Office phone: (301) 921-2800
Office fax: (301) 948-2787
Website: www.dcmilitary.com
Advertising (open inch rate): Open inch rate $15.85
Mechanical specifications: Type page 9 5/8 x 13 1/2; E - 6 cols, between; A - 6 cols, between; C - 7 cols, between.
Weekly Paper Frequency: Thur
Circulation Free: 9000
Audit By: Sworn/Estimate/Non-Audited
Audit Date: 12.07.2019
Weeklies Equipment - Hardware: APP/Mac
Weeklies Equipment - Presses: G/Urbanite, G/Community
Weeklies Equipment - Software: QPS/QuarkXPress.
Personnel: John Rives (Pub.); Matt Dunigan (Adv. Mgr.); Jake Joy (Ed.)
Main (survey) contact: John Rives

THE WATERLINE
Street address 1: 9030 Comprint Ct
Street address state: MD
Postal code: 20877-1307
County: Montgomery
Country: USA
Mailing address: 9030 Comprint Ct
Mailing city: Gaithersburg
Mailing state: MD
Mailing zip: 20877-1307
Office phone: 301-921-2800
Office fax: (301) 948-2787
General e-mail: jrives@gazette.net
Website: www.dcmilitary.com
Year newspaper established: 1984
Personnel: John Rives (Publisher)
Main (survey) contact: Art Crofoot

GRAYSLAKE

LAKE COUNTY SUBURBAN LIFE
Street address 1: 1100 E Washington St
Street address 2: Ste 101
Street address state: IL
Postal code: 60030-7963
County: Lake
Country: USA
Mailing address: 1100 Washington St., Suite 101
Mailing city: Grayslake
Mailing state: IL
Mailing zip: 60030-0268
Office phone: (847) 223-8161
Office fax: (847) 223-8810
General e-mail: edit@lakelandmedia.com
Website: www.lakecountyjournals.com
Advertising (open inch rate): Open inch rate $16.00
Mechanical specifications: Type page 10 1/4 x 16; E - 5 cols, 1 11/12, 1/4 between; A - 5 cols, 1 11/12, 1/4 between; C - 7 cols, 1 1/3, 1/6 between.
Weekly Paper Frequency: Fri
Circulation Free: 22000
Audit By: Sworn/Estimate/Non-Audited
Audit Date: 12.07.2019
Weeklies Equipment - Hardware: 40-APP/Mac, Ethernet, 3-Flatbed Scanner, 2-Negative Scanner, CD-ROM 4x Burner, SyQuest/EZ135 drive, 2-1200 dpi Printer, 4-600 dpi Printer
Weeklies Equipment - Presses: G/Urbanite
Weeklies Equipment - Software: Adobe/Illustrator 6.0, QPS/QuarkXPress 3.32, Adobe/Photoshop 3.0.5, Micr
Personnel: Jill McDermott (VP of Adv.); Paul Engstrom (Ed.); Ryan Wells
Main (survey) contact: Jill McDermott; Ryan Wells

Weeklies Equipment - Software: Freedom System Integrators.
Personnel: James Brabanec; Jeff Crawley; Marie Berberea
Main (survey) contact: James Brabanec

Military Newspapers in the U.S.

GRETNA

THE CURRENTS

Street address 1: 359 Fairfield Ave
Street address state: LA
Postal code: 70056-7004
County: Jefferson
Country: USA
Mailing address: 359 Fairfield Ave
Mailing city: Gretna
Mailing state: LA
Mailing zip: 70056-7004
Office phone: (504) 363-9010
Office fax: (504) 366-4826
General e-mail: polov13@aol.com
Year newspaper established: 1989
Advertising (open inch rate): Open inch rate $15.75
Mechanical specifications: Type page 10 1/4 x 13 3/8; E - 4 cols, between; A - 6 cols, between.
Audit By: Sworn/Estimate/Non-Audited
Audit Date: 12.07.2019
Weeklies Equipment - Hardware: APP/Mac
Weeklies Equipment - Presses: WPC
Weeklies Equipment - Software: Adobe/PageMaker.
Personnel: Vicki A. Polo (Pres.); Samuel F. Polo (Pub.); Gina D. Polo (Adv. Mgr.); David P. Leger (Circ. Mgr.); Donnie R. Ryan (Ed.); Roy P. Griggs (Mng. Ed.); Carolyn R. Cuccia (Prodn. Mgr.)
Main (survey) contact: Samuel F. Polo

GROTON

THE DOLPHIN

Street address 1: PO Box 44
Street address 2: Naval Submarine Base New London
Street address state: CT
Postal code: 06349-5044
County: New London
Country: USA
Mailing address: SUBASE NLON PAO PO Box 44
Mailing city: Groton
Mailing state: CT
Mailing zip: 06349-5044
Office phone: (860) 694-3514
Office fax: (860) 694-5012
Advertising phone: (203) 680-9935
General e-mail: nhr.dolphin@hearstmediact.com
Advertising e-mail: betsy.lemkin@hearstmediact.com
Editorial e-mail: nhr.dolphin@hearstmediact.com
Website: www.dolphin-news.com
Year newspaper established: 1918
Advertising (open inch rate): Open inch rate $11.62
Mechanical specifications: Type page 12 x 21; E - 6 cols, 2, 1/6 between; A - 6 cols, 1 5/8, 1/6 between; C - 6 cols, 1 5/8, 1/6 between.
Delivery methods: Racks
Zip Codes Served: 06340
Weekly Paper Frequency: Thur
Circulation Free: 6600
Audit By: Sworn/Estimate/Non-Audited
Audit Date: 12.07.2019
Weeklies Equipment - Hardware: 2-APP/Mac G4, HP/LaserJet Scanner, HP/LaserJet 5100
Weeklies Equipment - Software: Multi-Ad/Creator, InDesign, Adobe/Photoshop 7.0, Microsoft/Word, Adobe/Acrobat.
Personnel: Sheryl Walsh (Ed.)
Parent company: Hearst Communications, Inc.
Main (survey) contact: Sheryl Walsh; Main Contact

GULFPORT

SUNHERALD

Street address 1: 205 Debuys Rd
Street address state: MS
Postal code: 39507-2838
County: Harrison
Country: USA
Mailing address: PO Box 4567
Mailing city: Biloxi
Mailing state: MS
Mailing zip: 39535-4567
Office phone: (228) 896-2100
Office fax: (228) 896-2362
Advertising phone: (228) 896-2463
Advertising fax: (228) 896-0516
Editorial phone: (228) 377-3163
General e-mail: specialpublications@sunherald.com
Advertising e-mail: cbiasi@sunherald.com
Editorial e-mail: stephen.hoffmann.ctr@us.af.mil
Website: www.sunherald.com
Year newspaper established: 1974
Advertising (open inch rate): Open inch rate $14.69
Mechanical specifications: Type page 10 x 11; A - 5 cols,
Delivery methods: Mail`Newsstand`Carrier`Racks
Zip Codes Served: 39534 39531 39532 39535
Weekly Paper Frequency: Thur
Circulation Free: 8500
Audit By: Sworn/Estimate/Non-Audited
Audit Date: 12.07.2019
Weeklies Equipment - Hardware: APP/Mac, APP/Power Mac
Weeklies Equipment - Presses: 6-G/Headliner Offset
Weeklies Equipment - Software: InDesign v 4
Note: Published weekly by Sun Herald MultiMedia for Keesler Air Force Base under contract with the Department of the Air Force
Personnel: Sandi Menendez (Adv. Mgr.); Glen Nardi (Publisher); Susan Griggs (Ed.); John McFarland (Special Publications Manager); Stephen Hoffmann (Editor)
Parent company: The McClatchy Company
Main (survey) contact: Kim Anderson

HAVELOCK

HAVELOCK NEWS

Street address 1: 230 Stonebridge Sq
Street address state: NC
Postal code: 28532-9505
County: Craven
Country: USA
Mailing address: PO Box 777
Mailing city: Havelock
Mailing state: NC
Mailing zip: 28532-0777
Office phone: (252) 444-1999
Office fax: (252) 447-0897
Website: www.havenews.com
Advertising (open inch rate): Open inch rate $12.70
Mechanical specifications: Type page 13 x 21 1/2; E - 6 cols, 2 1/16, 1/6 between; A - 6 cols, 2 1/16, 1/6 between; C - 9 cols, 1 5/16, between.
Weekly Paper Frequency: Thur
Circulation Free: 11500
Audit By: Sworn/Estimate/Non-Audited
Audit Date: 12.07.2019
Weeklies Equipment - Hardware: APP/Mac G3s
Weeklies Equipment - Software: QPS/QuarkXPress 4.0, Adobe/PageMaker.
Personnel: Taylor Shannon (Adv. Media Consult.); Roxanne Smith (Circ. Mgr.); Ken Buday (Ed.); Drew Wilson (Reporter)
Main (survey) contact: Ken Buday

HINESVILLE

THE FRONTLINE

Street address 1: 125 S Main St
Street address state: GA
Postal code: 31313-3217
County: Liberty
Country: USA
Mailing address: 125 S Main St
Mailing city: Hinesville
Mailing state: GA
Mailing zip: 31313-3217
Office phone: (912) 876-0156
Office fax: (912) 368-6329
Website: www.coastalcourier.com
Advertising (open inch rate): Open inch rate $11.10
Mechanical specifications: Type page 11 3/4 x 21 1/2; E - 6 cols, 2 1/16, between; A - 6 cols, 2 1/16, between; C - 6 cols, 2 1/16, between.
Weekly Paper Frequency: Thur
Circulation Free: 17000
Audit By: Sworn/Estimate/Non-Audited
Audit Date: 12.07.2019
Personnel: Denise Ethridge (Ed.); Patty Leon (Gen. Mgr.)
Parent company: Morris Multimedia, Inc.
Main (survey) contact: Denise Ethridge; Patty Leon

HOPKINSVILLE

FORT CAMPBELL COURIER

Street address 1: 1618 E 9th St
Street address state: KY
Postal code: 42240-4430
County: Christian
Country: USA
Mailing address: PO Box 729
Mailing city: Hopkinsville
Mailing state: KY
Mailing zip: 42241-0729
Office phone: (270) 887-3220
Office fax: (270) 887-3222
Advertising phone: (270) 887-3270
General e-mail: editor@kentuckynewera.com
Website: www.kentuckynewera.com
Advertising (open inch rate): Open inch rate $15.20
Mechanical specifications: Type page 13 x 21 1/2; E - 6 cols, 2 1/30, 1/6 between; A - 6 cols, 2 1/30, 1/6 between; C - 8 cols, 1 1/3, 1/6 between.
Weekly Paper Frequency: Thur
Circulation Free: 23000
Audit By: Sworn/Estimate/Non-Audited
Audit Date: 12.07.2019
Weeklies Equipment - Hardware: 3-PC 486
Weeklies Equipment - Presses: G/Urbanite
Weeklies Equipment - Software: QPS/QuarkXPress, Microsoft/Word, Archetype/Corel Draw.
Personnel: Taylor Wood Hayes (Pub.); Charles A. Henderson (Gen. Mgr.); Sheryl Ellis (Bus. Mgr.); Nancy Reese (Classified Mgr.); Ted Jatczak (Sales/Mktg. Dir.); George McCouch (Circ. Mgr.); Jennifer Brown (Ed.); Joe Wilson (Sports Ed.); Chris Hollis (Prodn. Mgr.)
Main (survey) contact: Charles A. Henderson

JACKSONVILLE

JAX AIR NEWS

Street address 1: PO Box 2
Street address state: FL
Postal code: 32212-0002
County: Duval
Country: USA
Mailing address: Code 00G, Box 2
Mailing city: Jacksonville
Mailing state: FL
Mailing zip: 32212-5000
Office phone: (904) 542-3531
Office fax: (904) 542-1534
Advertising phone: (904) 359-4168
General e-mail: jaxairnews@comcast.net
Website: jaxairnews.com
Year newspaper established: 1940
Advertising (open inch rate): Open inch rate $16.55
Delivery methods: Newsstand`Racks
Zip Codes Served: 32 202 322 033 220 400 000 000 000 000 000 000 000 000 000 000 000
Weekly Paper Frequency: Thur
Circulation Free: 10000
Audit By: Sworn/Estimate/Non-Audited
Audit Date: 12.07.2019
Personnel: Clark Pierce (Ed.)
Main (survey) contact: Clark Pierce

ROTOVUE

Street address 1: 149 Rea St
Street address 2: Ste 100
Street address state: NC
Postal code: 28546-5717
County: Onslow
Country: USA
Mailing address: 149 Rea St., Suite #100
Mailing city: Jacksonville
Mailing state: NC
Mailing zip: 28546
Office phone: (910) 347-9624
Office fax: (910) 347-9628
Website: www.newriverrotovue.com
Advertising (open inch rate): Open inch rate $11.59
Mechanical specifications: Type page 9 9/16 x 11 1/2; E - 5 cols, 1 25/32, between; A - 5 cols, 1 25/32, between; C - 5 cols, 1 25/32, between.
Other Type of Frequency: Every other Wed
Circulation Free: 8600
Audit By: Sworn/Estimate/Non-Audited
Audit Date: 12.07.2019
Weeklies Equipment - Hardware: 9-APP/Mac G4, 1-Agfa/Jet Sherpa, Kayak, IBM/Pentium III, 2-Agfa/Avantra 25E, HP, XU, 4-Umax/Powerlook 1100 Scanners
Weeklies Equipment - Software: QPS/QuarkXPress 4.1, Adobe/Photoshop 5.5, Adobe/PageMaker 6.5, Adobe/Illustrator 9.0.
Personnel: Jim Connors (Pub.); Heather Miller (Adv. Mgr.); Ena Sellers (Ed)
Main (survey) contact: Ena Sellers

THE MIRROR

Street address 1: Massey Avenue
Street address state: FL
Postal code: 32228
County: Duval
Country: USA
Mailing address: PO Box 280032
Mailing city: Jacksonville
Mailing state: FL
Mailing zip: 32228-0032
Office phone: (904) 270-7817
Office fax: (904) 270-5329
General e-mail: mayportmirror@comcast.net
Website: www.mayportmirror.com
Advertising (open inch rate): Open inch rate $14.00
Zip Codes Served: 32228
Weekly Paper Frequency: Thur
Circulation Free: 10000
Audit By: Sworn/Estimate/Non-Audited
Audit Date: 12.07.2019
Personnel: Ellen S. Rykert (Pub.); Paige Gnann (Adv. Mgr.)
Main (survey) contact: Paige Gnann

LAKEWOOD

NORTHWEST AIRLIFTER

Street address 1: 8312 Custer Rd SW
Street address state: WA
Postal code: 98499-2526
County: Pierce
Country: USA
Mailing address: PO Box 98801
Mailing city: Lakewood
Mailing state: WA
Mailing zip: 98496-8801
Office phone: (253) 584-1212
Office fax: (253) 581-5962
Editorial e-mail: editor@ftlewisranger.com
Website: www.ftlewisranger.com
Mechanical specifications: Type page 10 1/2 x 16; A - 7 cols, between; C - 8 cols, between.
Weekly Paper Frequency: Thur
Circulation Free: 8200
Audit By: Sworn/Estimate/Non-Audited
Audit Date: 12.07.2019
Weeklies Equipment - Hardware: APP/Mac
Weeklies Equipment - Software: Microsoft/Word, Multi-Ad/Creator, Adobe/PageMaker, QPS/QuarkXPress, Adobe/Illustrator, Microsoft/Excel, Adobe/Photoshop.

Personnel: Ken Swarner (Pub.); Bill White (Circ. Mgr.)
Main (survey) contact: Ken Swarner

LANCASTER

AEROTECH NEWS & REVIEW

Street address 1: 456 E Avenue K4
Street address 2: Ste 8
Street address state: CA
Postal code: 93535-4642
County: Los Angeles
Country: USA
Mailing address: 456 E Avenue K4 Ste 8
Mailing city: Lancaster
Mailing state: CA
Mailing zip: 93535-4642
Office phone: (661) 945-5634
Office fax: (661) 723-7757
General e-mail: aerotech@aerotechnews.com
Website: www.aerotechnews.com
Advertising (open inch rate): Open inch rate $15.70
Mechanical specifications: Type page 10 1/4 x 13; E - 5 cols, 1 11/12, 1/8 between; A - 5 cols, 1 11/12, 1/8 between; C - 5 cols, 1 11/12, 1/8 between.
Weekly Paper Frequency: Fri
Circulation Free: 15000
Audit By: Sworn/Estimate/Non-Audited
Audit Date: 12.07.2019
Weeklies Equipment - Hardware: APP/Mac
Weeklies Equipment - Software: Adobe/PageMaker 6.5, Adobe/Photoshop 4.0, Microsoft/Word 6.0.
Editions Count: 2
Edition Names: 2 total Ã‚Â— Aerotech News & Review (35,000);
Personnel: Paul J. Kinison (Pub.); Gail Ellis (Adv. Mgr.); Stewart Ibberson (Ed.)
Main (survey) contact: Paul J. Kinison

LEESBURG

QUANTICO SENTRY

Street address 1: 19 N King St
Street address state: VA
Postal code: 20176-2819
County: Loudoun
Country: USA
Mailing address: 19 N. King St.
Mailing city: Leesburg
Mailing state: VA
Mailing zip: 20176
Office phone: 703-771-8800
Office fax: (540) 659-0039
Advertising phone: (703) 771-8800
General e-mail: Jlesh@insidenova.com
Advertising e-mail: bpowell@staffordcountysun.com
Editorial e-mail: adolzenko@staffordcountysun.com
Website: http://www.quanticosentryonline.com/
Advertising (open inch rate): Open inch rate $21.50
Mechanical specifications: Type page 6 x 21; E - 6 cols, 2 1/16, 1/6 between; A - 6 cols, 2 1/16, 1/6 between.
Delivery methods: Carrier
Weekly Paper Frequency: Thur
Circulation Free: 8500
Audit By: Sworn/Estimate/Non-Audited
Audit Date: 12.07.2019
Weeklies Equipment - Hardware: 12-HP/PC
Weeklies Equipment - Software: QPS/QuarkXPress 4.1, Adobe/Illustrator 9.0, Adobe/Photoshop 6.0.
Personnel: Tom Spargur (GM/Sales mgr)
Parent company: Northern Virginia Media Services
Main (survey) contact: Brenda Powell

MACON

THE TELEGRAPH

Street address 1: 487 Cherry St
Street address state: GA
Postal code: 31201-7972
County: Bibb
Country: USA
Mailing address: P.O. Box 4167
Mailing city: Macon
Mailing state: GA
Mailing zip: 31208
Office phone: (478) 744-4200
Advertising phone: (478) 744-4245
Editorial phone: (478) 744-4411
Website: www.macon.com
Delivery methods: Newsstand`Carrier`Racks
Digital Platform - Mobile: Apple`Android
Digital Platform - Tablet: Apple iOS`Android`Other
Weekly Paper Frequency: Mon`Tues`Wed`Thur`Fri`Sat`Sun
Circulation Free: 18000
Audit By: AAM
Audit Date: 19.06.2013
Weeklies Equipment - Hardware: APP/Mac
Weeklies Equipment - Presses: G/Community (offset)
Weeklies Equipment - Software: Baseview, QPS/QuarkXPress.
Personnel: Crystal Ragan (Local Adv. Mgr.)
Parent company: The McClatchy Company
Main (survey) contact: Classified Advertising

MASCOUTAH

SCOTT FLIER

Street address 1: 314 E Church St
Street address state: IL
Postal code: 62258-2100
County: Saint Clair
Country: USA
Mailing address: PO Box C
Mailing city: Mascoutah
Mailing state: IL
Mailing zip: 62258-0189
Office phone: (618) 566-8282
Office fax: (618) 566-8283
General e-mail: heraldpubs@cbnstl.com
Website: www.heraldpubs.com
Advertising (open inch rate): Open inch rate $9.31
Weekly Paper Frequency: Thur
Circulation Free: 8000
Audit By: Sworn/Estimate/Non-Audited
Audit Date: 12.07.2019
Personnel: Greg Hoskins (Pub.); Keith Gillette (Mng. Ed.)
Main (survey) contact: Greg Hoskins

MELBOURNE

MISSILEER

Street address 1: PO Box 419000
Street address state: FL
Postal code: 32941-9000
County: Brevard
Country: USA
Mailing address: PO Box 419000
Mailing city: Melbourne
Mailing state: FL
Mailing zip: 32941-9000
Office phone: (321) 242-3500
Office fax: (321) 242-6618
Website: www.floridatoday.com
Year newspaper established: 1966
Advertising (open inch rate): Open inch rate $11.91
Mechanical specifications: Type page 9 2/3 x 11 1/2; E - 5 cols, 1 5/6, 1/8 between; A - 5 cols, 1 5/6, 1/8 between; C - 80 cols, 1 1/10, 1/16 between.
Audit By: Sworn/Estimate/Non-Audited
Audit Date: 12.07.2019
Weeklies Equipment - Hardware: APP/Mac Platinum G3
Weeklies Equipment - Presses: Offset
Weeklies Equipment - Software: Multi-Ad/Creator 4.02, Adobe/Photoshop 5.0, Adobe/Illustrator 7.0.
Personnel: Mark Mikolajczyk (Pub.); John Vizzini (Opns. Dir.); Bob Stover (Exec. Ed.); John Kelly (Mng. Ed.); Chris Wood (Adv. Dir.)
Main (survey) contact: Mark Mikolajczyk

MERIDIAN

SKYLINE

Street address 1: 814 22nd Ave
Street address state: MS
Postal code: 39301-5023
County: Lauderdale
Country: USA
Mailing address: PO Box 1591
Mailing city: Meridian
Mailing state: MS
Mailing zip: 39302-1591
Office phone: (601) 693-1551
Office fax: (601) 485-1229
General e-mail: info@themeridianstar.com
Advertising e-mail: eryan@themeridianstar.com
Website: www.meridianstar.com
Advertising (open inch rate): Open inch rate $9.18
Mechanical specifications: Type page 9 11/16 x 11 3/4; E - 5 cols, 1 13/16, between; A - 5 cols, 1 11/16, between.
Weekly Paper Frequency: Thur
Other Type of Frequency: Every other Thur
Circulation Free: 1800
Audit By: Sworn/Estimate/Non-Audited
Audit Date: 12.07.2019
Weeklies Equipment - Hardware: 1-Catra 46
Weeklies Equipment - Software: QPS/QuarkXPress 4.1.
Personnel: Timothy Holder (Publisher); Michael Stewart (Editor for The Meridian Star); Elizabeth Ryan (Skyline Advertising)
Parent company: Community Newspaper Holdings, Inc.
Main (survey) contact: Timothy Holder

MILLINGTON

THE BLUEJACKET

Street address 1: 5107 Easley Ave
Street address state: TN
Postal code: 38053-2107
County: Shelby
Country: USA
Mailing address: PO Box 305
Mailing city: Millington
Mailing state: TN
Mailing zip: 38083-0305
Office phone: (901) 872-2286
Office fax: (901) 872-2965
General e-mail: mstar@bigriver.net
Website: www.nsamidsouth.navy.mil/news-bj.htm
Advertising (open inch rate): Open inch rate $8.40
Mechanical specifications: Type page 13 x 21 1/4; E - 6 cols, 2, between; A - 6 cols, 2, between; C - 9 cols, between.
Weekly Paper Frequency: Thur
Circulation Free: 6100
Audit By: Sworn/Estimate/Non-Audited
Audit Date: 12.07.2019
Weeklies Equipment - Hardware: APP/Power Mac
Weeklies Equipment - Software: Adobe/PageMaker 6.5, Adobe/Photoshop 4.0.
Personnel: John Fee (Pub.); Julia A. Wallis (Ed.)
Main (survey) contact: John Fee

MILTON

WHITING TOWER

Street address 1: Whiting Field, 7550 USS Essex St, Ste 109
Street address state: FL
Postal code: 32570
County: Santa Rosa
Country: USA
Mailing address: Whiting Field, 7550 USS Essex St., Ste. 109
Mailing city: Milton
Mailing state: FL
Mailing zip: 32570-6155
Office phone: (850) 665-6121
Office fax: (850) 623-7601
Advertising phone: N/A
Editorial phone: (850) 665-6121
Editorial fax: (850) 623-7601
General e-mail: jay.cope@navy.mil
Advertising e-mail: N/A
Editorial e-mail: jay.cope@navy.mil
Year newspaper established: 1943
Weekly Paper Frequency: Wed
Circulation Free: 3000
Audit By: Sworn/Estimate/Non-Audited
Audit Date: 12.07.2019
Personnel: Jay Cope (Ed.)
Main (survey) contact: Jay Cope

MINOT

THE NORTHERN SENTRY

Street address 1: 15-1 Ave SE
Street address state: ND
Postal code: 58701
County: Ward
Country: USA
Mailing address: PO Box 2183
Mailing city: Minot
Mailing state: ND
Mailing zip: 58702-2183
Office phone: (701) 839-0946
Office fax: (701) 839-1867
Advertising e-mail: nsads@srt.com
Advertising (open inch rate): Open inch rate $8.00
Mechanical specifications: Type page 10 x 16; E - 5 cols, 2, between; A - 5 cols, 2, between.
Weekly Paper Frequency: Fri
Circulation Free: 6000
Audit By: Sworn/Estimate/Non-Audited
Audit Date: 12.07.2019
Personnel: Michael W. Gackle (Pub.); Sharon Olson (Adv. Mgr.)
Parent company: BHG, Inc.
Main (survey) contact: Michael W. Gackle

MOUNTAIN HOME

MOUNTAIN HOME PATRIOT

Street address 1: PO Box 1330
Street address state: ID
Postal code: 83647-1330
County: Elmore
Country: USA
Mailing address: PO Box 1330
Mailing city: Mountain Home
Mailing state: ID
Mailing zip: 83647-1330
Office phone: (208) 587-3331
Office fax: (208) 587-9205
General e-mail: bfincher@mountainhomenews.com
Website: www.mountainhomenews.com
Year newspaper established: 1888
Advertising (open inch rate): 10.55 thur 10/31/14 call for current pricing
Mechanical specifications: 13x21.5
Delivery methods: Mail`Racks
Zip Codes Served: 83648/47
Weekly Paper Frequency: Fri
Circulation Free: 4500
Audit By: Sworn/Estimate/Non-Audited
Audit Date: 12.07.2019
Weeklies Equipment - Hardware: APP/Mac
Weeklies Equipment - Presses: WPC/Leader.
Personnel: Brenda Fincher (Business Manager); Kelly Everitt (Ed.)
Main (survey) contact: Brenda Fincher

NEWPORT

NEWPORT NAVALOG

Street address 1: 101 Malbone Rd
Street address state: RI
Postal code: 02840-1340
County: Newport
Country: USA
Mailing address: PO Box 420
Mailing city: Newport
Mailing state: RI
Mailing zip: 02840-0936
Office phone: (401) 849-3300
Office fax: (401) 849-3335
General e-mail: prepress@newportri.com
Website: www.newportdailynews.com

Military Newspapers in the U.S.

Advertising (open inch rate): Open inch rate $16.50
Weekly Paper Frequency: Fri
Circulation Free: 4400
Audit By: Sworn/Estimate/Non-Audited
Audit Date: 12.07.2019
Personnel: Albert K. Sherman (Pub.); William F. Lucey (Gen. Mgr.); Ann Marie Brisson (Adv. Mgr.); Richard Alexander (Ed.); Kevin Schoen (Prodn. Mgr.)
Main (survey) contact: Albert K. Sherman

NORFOLK

FLAGSHIP

Street address 1: 150 W Brambleton Ave
Street address state: VA
Postal code: 23510-2018
County: Norfolk City
Country: USA
Mailing address: 150 W Brambleton Ave
Mailing city: Norfolk
Mailing state: VA
Mailing zip: 23510-2018
Office phone: (757) 222-3990
Office fax: (757) 622-6885
General e-mail: laura.baxter@militarynews.com
Website: www.norfolknavyflagship.com
Advertising (open inch rate): Open inch rate $20.50
Mechanical specifications: Type page 11 1/2 x 21 1/2; E - 6 cols, 1 3/4, 1/8 between; A - 6 cols, 1 3/4, 1/8 between; C - 10 cols, 1 1/10, 1/16 between.
Digital Platform - Mobile: Apple`Android`Windows`Blackberry
Digital Platform - Tablet: Apple iOS`Android`Windows 7`Blackberry Tablet OS`Kindle`Nook`Kindle Fire
Weekly Paper Frequency: Thur
Circulation Free: 35000
Audit By: Sworn/Estimate/Non-Audited
Audit Date: 12.07.2019
Weeklies Equipment - Hardware: APP/Mac
Weeklies Equipment - Presses: Metro/Offset
Weeklies Equipment - Software: QPS/QuarkXPress.
Main (survey) contact: Laura Baxter

PENINSULA WARRIOR- AIR FORCE

Street address 1: 150 W Brambleton Ave
Street address state: VA
Postal code: 23510-2018
County: Norfolk City
Country: USA
Mailing address: 150 W Brambleton Ave
Mailing city: Norfolk
Mailing state: VA
Mailing zip: 23510-2018
Office phone: (757) 222-3990
Office fax: (757) 622-6885
General e-mail: sales@militarynews.com
Website: www.militarynews.com
Advertising (open inch rate): Open rate $18.85
Mechanical specifications: Type page 9 7/8 x 14; E - 6 cols, 1 1/2, between; A - 6 cols, 1 1/2, between; C - 6 cols, 1 1/2, between.
Delivery methods: Racks
Digital Platform - Mobile: Apple`Android`Windows`Blackberry`Other
Digital Platform - Tablet: Apple iOS`Android`Windows 7`Blackberry Tablet OS`Kindle`Nook`Other
Weekly Paper Frequency: Fri
Circulation Free: 14000
Audit By: Sworn/Estimate/Non-Audited
Audit Date: 12.07.2019
Personnel: Laura Baxter (Pub.)
Main (survey) contact: Laura Baxter

SOUNDINGS

Street address 1: 10 W Brambleton Ave
Street address state: VA
Postal code: 23510
County: Norfolk City
Country: USA
Office phone: (757) 222-3990
Office fax: (757) 853-1634
General e-mail: sales@militarynews.com
Website: www.militarynews.com
Advertising (open inch rate): Open inch rate $26.97
Mechanical specifications: Type page 9 7/8 x 14; E - 6 cols, 1 1/2, between; A - 6 cols, 1 1/2, between; C - 6 cols, 1 1/2, between.
Audit By: Sworn/Estimate/Non-Audited
Audit Date: 12.07.2019
Weeklies Equipment - Hardware: 9-APP/Mac G4, 2-AG/Avantra 25E, 1-AG/Jet Sherpa, HP, Kayak, XU, 1-Pentium III, 4-Umax/Powerlook 1100 Scanners
Weeklies Equipment - Presses: 8-Perfecting Units, 1-Quadra/Color Unit
Weeklies Equipment - Software: QPS/QuarkXPress 4.1, Adobe/PageMaker 6.5, Adobe/Photoshop 5.5, Adobe/II
Personnel: Laura Baxter (Pub.); Jim Van Slyke (Ed.); Reagan Haynes
Main (survey) contact: Jim Van Slyke

THE WHEEL

Street address 1: 258 Granby St
Street address state: VA
Postal code: 23510-1812
County: Norfolk City
Country: USA
Mailing address: 150 W Brambleton Ave
Mailing city: Norfolk
Mailing state: VA
Mailing zip: 23510-2018
Office phone: (757) 222-3990
Office fax: (757) 853-1634
Website: www.militarynews.com
Year newspaper established: 1970
Advertising (open inch rate): Open inch rate $15.98
Mechanical specifications: Type page 9 7/8 x 14; E - 6 cols, 1 1/2, between; A - 6 cols, 1 1/2, between; C - 6 cols, 1 1/2, between.
Weekly Paper Frequency: Thur
Circulation Free: 10500
Audit By: Sworn/Estimate/Non-Audited
Audit Date: 12.07.2019
Weeklies Equipment - Hardware: 9-APP/Mac G4, 2-AG/Avantra 25E, 1-AG/Jet Sherpa, HP, Kayak, XU, 1-Pentium III, 4-Umax/Powerlook 1100 Scanners
Weeklies Equipment - Presses: 8-Perfecting Units, 1-Quadra/Color Unit
Weeklies Equipment - Software: QPS/QuarkXPress 4.1, Adobe/Photoshop 5.5, Adobe/PageMaker 6.5, Adobe/II
Personnel: Laura Baxter (Adv. Mgr.); Zack Shelby (Ed.)
Main (survey) contact: Laura Baxter

OGDEN

HILLTOP TIMES

Street address 1: 332 Standard Way
Street address state: UT
Postal code: 84404-1371
County: Weber
Country: USA
Mailing address: PO Box 12790
Mailing city: Ogden
Mailing state: UT
Mailing zip: 84412-2790
Office phone: (801) 625-4310
Office fax: (801) 625-4508
Advertising phone: (801) 625-4333
Advertising fax: (801) 625-4508
Editorial phone: (801) 777-3622
Editorial fax: (801) 625-4299
Other phone: (801) 625-4273
General e-mail: hilltoptimes@standard.net
Advertising e-mail: advertise@standard.net
Website: www.hilltoptimes.com
Year newspaper established: 1966
Advertising (open inch rate): Open inch rate $18.36
Mechanical specifications: 6 col. (11") x 20.5". One col. = 1.74"; gutter = .125"
Delivery methods: Newsstand`Carrier`Racks
Zip Codes Served: 84056, 84041, 84015, 84040, 84067
Weekly Paper Frequency: Thur
Circulation Free: 12000
Audit By: Sworn/Estimate/Non-Audited
Audit Date: 12.07.2019
Weeklies Equipment - Presses: KBA/Comet.
Personnel: Brad Roghaar (Adv. Dir.); Vaughn Jacobsen (Circ. Mgr.)
Parent company: Sandusky Newspapers, Inc.
Main (survey) contact: Mark Shenefelt

PANAMA CITY

GULF DEFENDER

Street address 1: 501 W 11th St
Street address state: FL
Postal code: 32401-2330
County: Bay
Country: USA
Mailing address: PO Box 1940
Mailing city: Panama City
Mailing state: FL
Mailing zip: 32402-1940
Office phone: (850) 747-5005
Office fax: (850) 763-4636
General e-mail: phgregory@pcnh.com
Website: www.newsherald.com
Advertising (open inch rate): Open inch rate $18.00
Mechanical specifications: Type page 10 1/4 x 11 1/4; E - 6 cols, 2 1/16, 1/8 between; A - 6 cols, 2 1/16, 1/8 between.
Zip Codes Served: 32403
Other Type of Frequency: 2 x Mthly
Circulation Free: 12000
Audit By: Sworn/Estimate/Non-Audited
Audit Date: 12.07.2019
Weeklies Equipment - Hardware: Advanced Publishing Technology
Weeklies Equipment - Presses: 6-G/Community
Weeklies Equipment - Software: Dewar Sys 4.
Personnel: Karen E. Hanes (Pub./Reg'l Vice Pres.); Wayne Kight (Adv. Mgr.); Pam Gregory (Adv. Dir.); Mike Miller (Reg'l Circ. Dir.); Ron Smith (Opns. Dir.)
Main (survey) contact: Karen E. Hanes

PENSACOLA

GOSPORT

Street address 1: 41 N Jefferson St
Street address state: FL
Postal code: 32502-5681
County: Escambia
Country: USA
Mailing address: 41 N Jefferson St
Mailing city: Pensacola
Mailing state: FL
Mailing zip: 32502-5681
Office phone: (850) 202-2242
Office fax: (850) 202-2248
Advertising phone: (850) 433-1166
Editorial phone: (850) 452-4466
Editorial e-mail: scott.hallford@navy.mil
Website: www.ballingerpublishing.com
Year newspaper established: 1921
Advertising (open inch rate): Open inch rate $20.30
Mechanical specifications: Type page 10 x 16; E - 5 cols, 2, 1/4 between.
Delivery methods: Mail`Racks
Zip Codes Served: 32501,02,03,04,05,06,07,08,09
Weekly Paper Frequency: Fri
Circulation Free: 25000
Audit By: Sworn/Estimate/Non-Audited
Audit Date: 12.07.2019
Weeklies Equipment - Hardware: APP/Mac, PC
Weeklies Equipment - Presses: HI/M-1000
Weeklies Equipment - Software: QPS/QuarkXPress, Adobe/Photoshop.
Personnel: Malcolm Ballinger (Pub.); Scott Hallford (Ed.); Mike O'Connor (Assoc. Ed.); Simone Sands; Janet Thomas
Parent company: U.S. Navy
Main (survey) contact: Scott Hallford

RIDGECREST

ON TARGET

Street address 1: 1 Administration Cir
Street address 2: Stop 1014
Street address state: CA
Postal code: 93555-6104
County: Kern
Country: USA
Mailing address: 1 Administration Cir Stop 1014
Mailing city: Ridgecrest
Mailing state: CA
Mailing zip: 93555-6104
Office phone: (760) 939-3354
Office fax: (760) 939-2796
Advertising (open inch rate): Open inch rate $14.60
Other Type of Frequency: Every other Thur
Circulation Free: 5000
Audit By: Sworn/Estimate/Non-Audited
Audit Date: 12.07.2019
Personnel: Dee Rorex (Ed.)
Main (survey) contact: Dee Rorex

SAINT ROBERT

GUIDON

Street address 1: 394 Old Route 66
Street address state: MO
Postal code: 65584-3829
County: Pulaski
Country: USA
Office phone: (573) 336-0061
Office fax: (573) 336-5487
General e-mail: guidon_staff@mygiidon.com
Website: www.myguidon.com
Advertising (open inch rate): Open inch rate $10.40
Mechanical specifications: Type page 13 1/2 x 21 1/2; E - 4 cols, 3 1/12, 1/6 between; A - 6 cols, 2 1/12, 1/6 between; C - 6 cols, 2 1/12, 1/6 between.
Weekly Paper Frequency: Thur
Circulation Free: 10000
Audit By: Sworn/Estimate/Non-Audited
Audit Date: 12.07.2019
Weeklies Equipment - Hardware: PC
Weeklies Equipment - Software: Adobe/PageMaker 5.0.
Personnel: Mike Bowers (Adv. Mgr.); Robert Johnson (Ed.)
Main (survey) contact: Mike Brame

SAN DIEGO

COMPASS

Street address 1: 937 N Harbor Dr
Street address state: CA
Postal code: 92132-5001
County: San Diego
Country: USA
Mailing address: 937 N Harbor Dr
Mailing city: San Diego
Mailing state: CA
Mailing zip: 92132-5001
Office phone: (619) 532-1434
Office fax: (619) 532-4537
General e-mail: johnb@navycompass.com
Website: www.navycompass.com
Advertising (open inch rate): Open inch rate $25.00
Weekly Paper Frequency: Thur
Circulation Free: 43000
Audit By: Sworn/Estimate/Non-Audited
Audit Date: 12.07.2019
Personnel: Jim Missit (Adv. Mgr.); Jess Levens (Ed.)
Main (survey) contact: Jim Missit

SPRINGFIELD

DEFENSE NEWS

Street address 1: 6883 Commercial Dr
Street address state: VA
Postal code: 22159-0002
County: Fairfax
Country: USA
Mailing address: 6883 Commercial Dr
Mailing city: Springfield
Mailing state: VA
Mailing zip: 22159-0002
Office phone: (703) 642-7330
Office fax: (703) 642-7386

General e-mail: cust-svc@atpco.com
Website: www.defensenews.com
Advertising (open inch rate): Open inch rate $200.00
Weekly Paper Frequency: Mon
Circulation Paid: 7319
Circulation Free: 30822
Audit By: Sworn/Estimate/Non-Audited
Audit Date: 12.07.2019
Personnel: Donna Peterson (Vice Pres., Adv.); Vago Muradian (Ed.)
Main (survey) contact: Donna Peterson

NAVY TIMES

Street address 1: 6883 Commercial Dr
Street address state: VA
Postal code: 22159-0002
County: Fairfax
Country: USA
Mailing address: 6883 Commercial Dr
Mailing city: Springfield
Mailing state: VA
Mailing zip: 22159-0002
Office phone: (703) 750-8636
Office fax: (703) 750-8767
General e-mail: navylet@atpco.com
Website: www.navytimes.com
Editorial e-mail: navylet@atpco.com
Advertising (open inch rate): Open inch rate $25.96
Mechanical specifications: Type page 21 1/2 x 12 1/4.
Weekly Paper Frequency: Mon
Circulation Paid: 79500
Circulation Free: 2400
Audit By: Sworn/Estimate/Non-Audited
Audit Date: 12.07.2019
Editions Count: 1
Edition Names: 1 total Ã‚Â— Navy Times-Overseas Edition (3,304);
Personnel: Elaine Howard (Pres./Pub.); Dick Howlett (Circ. Mgr.); Christopher P. Cavas (Ed.); Christopher Lawson (Mng. Ed.); Phil Rose (Prodn. Mgr.)
Main (survey) contact: Elaine Howard

STEILACOOM

THE RANGER

Street address 1: 218 Wilkes St
Street address state: WA
Postal code: 98388-2122
County: Pierce
Country: USA
Mailing address: 218 Wilkes
Mailing city: Steilacoom
Mailing state: WA
Mailing zip: 98388
Office phone: (253) 584-1212
Office fax: (253) 581-5962
Advertising e-mail: sales@northwestmilitary.com
Editorial e-mail: publisher@northwestmilitary.com
Website: www.northwestmilitary.com
Year newspaper established: 1951
Advertising (open inch rate): $85 a unit
Mechanical specifications: 24 units to the page. 4 units across by 6 units deep
Delivery methods: Mail`Racks
Zip Codes Served: Pierce & Thurston counties
Weekly Paper Frequency: Thur
Circulation Free: 23000
Audit By: VAC
Audit Date: 30.06.2017
Weeklies Equipment - Hardware: APP/Mac
Weeklies Equipment - Software: Microsoft/Word, Multi-Ad/Creator, Adobe/PageMaker, QPS/QuarkXPress, Adobe/Illustrator, Microsoft/Excel, Adobe/Photoshop.
Personnel: Bill White (Circ. Mgr.); Ken Swarner (Ed.); Diana Halstead (Prodn. Mgr.)
Main (survey) contact: Ken Swarner

VIENNA

AIR FORCE TIMES

Street address 1: 1919 Gallows Rd
Street address 2: 4th Floor
Street address state: VA
Postal code: 22182-4038
County: Fairfax
Country: USA
Mailing address: 1919 Gallows Road, 4th Floor
Mailing city: VIENNA
Mailing state: VA
Mailing zip: 22182-4038
Office phone: (703) 642-7330
Office fax: (703) 642-7386
Advertising phone: (703) 642-7330
Advertising fax: (703) 642-7386
Editorial phone: (703) 642-7330
Editorial fax: (703) 642-7386
General e-mail: Cust-svc@airforcetimes.com
Advertising e-mail: advertisingsales@sightlinemg.com
Editorial e-mail: tips@airforcetimes.com
Website: www.airforcetimes.com
Year newspaper established: 1947
Advertising (open inch rate): Open inch rate $7,680.00 (Full-Page)
Delivery methods: Mail`Newsstand`Racks
Zip Codes Served: Fairfax County
Digital Platform - Mobile: Apple`Android`Windows`Blackberry
Digital Platform - Tablet: Apple iOS`Android`Windows 7`Blackberry Tablet OS
Weekly Paper Frequency: Mon
Personnel: Kent Miller (Ed.); Andrew Tilghman (Exec. Ed.); Michelle Tan (Mng. Ed.)
Parent company: Gannett
Main (survey) contact: Kent Miller; Becky Iannotta

WAYNESBORO

THE SIGNAL

Street address 1: Nelson Hall Rm 215
Street address state: GA
Postal code: 30830
County: Burke
Country: USA
Mailing address: PO Box 948
Mailing city: Waynesboro
Mailing state: GA
Mailing zip: 30830-0948
Office phone: (706) 791-7069
Office fax: (706) 791-5463
General e-mail: thesignal@conus.army.mil
Website: www.fortgordonsignal.com
Advertising (open inch rate): Open inch rate $11.97
Mechanical specifications: Type page 13 x 21 1/2; E - 4 cols, 3 1/6, 1/6 between; A - 6 cols, 2 1/12, 1/6 between; C - 6 cols, 2 1/12, 1/6 between.
Weekly Paper Frequency: Fri
Circulation Free: 18600
Audit By: Sworn/Estimate/Non-Audited
Audit Date: 12.07.2019
Weeklies Equipment - Hardware: PC, APP/Mac
Weeklies Equipment - Presses: G/Community
Weeklies Equipment - Software: Adobe/PageMaker 6.5, QPS/QuarkXPress, Archetype/Corel Draw, Adobe/Photoshop.
Personnel: Roy F. Chalker (Pub.); Bonnie Taylor (Gen. Mgr.); Deborah Kitchens (Adv. Mgr.); Jill Dumars (Prodn. Mgr.)
Main (survey) contact: Roy Chalker

WHITE SANDS MISSILE RANGE

WHITE SANDS MISSILE RANGER

Street address 1: Public Affairs Office
Street address state: NM
Postal code: 88002
County: Dona Ana
Country: USA
Mailing address: Bldg. 1782
Mailing city: White Sands
Mailing state: NM
Mailing zip: 88002
Office phone: (575) 678-2716
Office fax: (575) 678-8814
General e-mail: wsmrranger@conus.army.mil
Website: www.missileranger.com
Advertising (open inch rate): Open inch rate $7.65
Mechanical specifications: Type page 11 x 11 3/4; E - 5 cols, 2 1/16, 1/8 between; A - 5 cols, 2 1/16, 1/8 between; C - 5 cols, 1/8 between.
Weekly Paper Frequency: Thur
Circulation Free: 6000
Audit By: Sworn/Estimate/Non-Audited
Audit Date: 12.07.2019
Personnel: Miriam U. Rodriguez (Ed.)
Main (survey) contact: Miriam U. Rodriguez

WHITEMAN AFB

WHITEMAN WARRIOR

Street address 1: 1081 Arnold Ave
Street address state: MO
Postal code: 65305-5108
County: Johnson
Country: USA
Mailing address: 509th Bomb Wing, 1081 Arnold Ave., Bldg. 59
Mailing city: Whiteman AFB
Mailing state: MO
Mailing zip: 65305
Office phone: (660) 826-1000
Office fax: (660) 826-2413
Advertising e-mail: advertising@sedaliademocrat.com
Advertising (open inch rate): Open inch rate $8.75
Mechanical specifications: Type page 10 1/4 x 14; E - 6 cols, 1 7/12, between; A - 6 cols, 1 7/12, between; C - 7 cols, 1 1/3, 1/6 between.
Delivery methods: Mail`Racks
Zip Codes Served: 65305
Weekly Paper Frequency: Fri
Circulation Free: 4800
Audit By: Sworn/Estimate/Non-Audited
Audit Date: 12.07.2019
Weeklies Equipment - Hardware: APP/Mac
Weeklies Equipment - Presses: 10-G/Urbanite.
Personnel: Will Weibert (Publisher)
Parent company: Phillips Media
Main (survey) contact: Eddie Crouch

YUCCA VALLEY

OBSERVATION POST

Street address 1: 56445 29 Palms Hwy
Street address state: CA
Postal code: 92284-2861
County: San Bernardino
Country: USA
Mailing address: PO Box 880
Mailing city: Yucca Valley
Mailing state: CA
Mailing zip: 92286-0880
Office phone: (760) 365-3315
Office fax: (760) 365-4181
Advertising e-mail: advertising@hidesertstar.com
Editorial e-mail: editor@hidesertstar.com
Website: www.hidesertstar.com
Advertising (open inch rate): Open inch rate $15.00
Mechanical specifications: Type page 10 x 21 ; E - 6 cols, 1 3/4, 1/8 between; A - 6 cols, 1 3/4, 1/8 between; C - 9 cols, 1 3/16, 1/8 between.
Delivery methods: Carrier`Racks
Zip Codes Served: 92278 and 92277
Weekly Paper Frequency: Fri
Circulation Free: 6500
Audit By: Sworn/Estimate/Non-Audited
Audit Date: 12.07.2019
Weeklies Equipment - Hardware: APP/Mac G4
Weeklies Equipment - Presses: G/Community
Weeklies Equipment - Software: In Design, Adobe/Photoshop 6.0, MultiAd 6.5.
Personnel: Cindy Melland (Pub.)
Parent company: Brehm Communications, Inc.; Hi-Desert Publishing Co., Inc.
Main (survey) contact: Cindy Melland

YUMA

DESERT WARRIOR

Street address 1: PO Box 99113
Street address state: AZ
Postal code: 85369-9113
County: Yuma
Country: USA
Mailing address: PO Box 99113
Mailing city: Yuma
Mailing state: AZ
Mailing zip: 85369-9113
Office phone: (928) 269-2275
General e-mail: shelby.shields@usmc.mil
Website: www.yuma.usmc.mil
Advertising (open inch rate): Open inch rate $15.47
Mechanical specifications: Type page 11 13/16 x 21; E - 6 cols, 1 7/8, 1/16 between; A - 6 cols, 1 7/8, 1/16 between; C - 6 cols, 1 7/8, 1/16 between.
Zip Codes Served: 85369
Weekly Paper Frequency: Thur
Circulation Free: 3300
Audit By: Sworn/Estimate/Non-Audited
Audit Date: 12.07.2019
Weeklies Equipment - Hardware: APP/Mac
Weeklies Equipment - Presses: G
Weeklies Equipment - Software: DTI/AdSpeed 4.1, Adobe/Illustrator 2.1.
Personnel: Shelby Shields (Ed.)
Main (survey) contact: Shelby Shields

PARENTING PUBLICATIONS IN THE U.S.

ALAMEDA

PARENTS' PRESS

Street address 1: 875A Island Dr
Street address 2: Ste 421
Street address city: Alameda
Street address state: CA
Postal code: 94502-6751
Country: USA
Mailing address 1: 875-A Island Dr. Ste 421
Mailing city: Alameda
Mailing state: CA
Mailing zip: 94502
Office phone: (510)-748-9122
Office fax: (510) 926-4131
General e-mail: sales@parentspress.com
Website: www.parentspress.com
Year publication established: 1980
Delivery methods: Racks
Zip Codes Served: 94710; SAN FRANCISCO–OAKLAND–SAN JOSE, CA
Frequency: Mthly
Circulation Free: 62000
Audit By: Sworn/Estimate/Non-Audited
Audit Date: 12.07.2019
Hardware: APP/Macs
Software: InDesign
Personnel: Tracy McKean (Pub.)
Main (survey) contact: Peggy Spear

ALBANY

CAPITAL DISTRICT PARENT

Street address 1: 595 New Loudon Rd
Street address 2: Ste 102
Street address city: Latham
Street address state: NY
Postal code: 12110-4063
Country: USA
Mailing address 1: 595 New Loudon Rd Ste 102
Mailing city: Latham
Mailing state: NY
Mailing zip: 12110-4063
Office phone: (518) 862-2056
Office fax: (845) 562-3681
General e-mail: publisher@excitingread.com
Advertising e-mail: sales@excitingread.com
Editorial e-mail: editor@excitingread.com
Website: www.cdparent.com
Frequency: Mthly
Personnel: Terrie Goldstein (Adv. Mgr.); Leah Black (Ed.); Lisa Jabbour (Art Dir.)
Main (survey) contact: Leah Black

ANNE ARUNDEL

CHESAPEAKE FAMILY LIFE

Street address 1: 121 Cathedral St
Street address 2: Fl 3
Street address city: Annapolis
Street address state: MD
Postal code: 21401-2777
Country: USA
Mailing address 1: 13 Southgate Ave
Mailing city: Annapolis
Mailing state: MD
Mailing zip: 21401-2709
Office phone: (410) 263-1641
Office fax: (410) 280-0255
General e-mail: dj@jecoannapolis.com
Advertising e-mail: dj@jecoannapolis.com
Editorial e-mail: editor@chesapeakefamily.com
Website: www.chesapeakefamily.com
Year publication established: 1990
Advertising (open inch rate): N/A
Delivery methods: Newsstand`Racks
Zip Codes Served: 21401, 21061, 21146, 21403, 21062, 21012, 21666, 20715, 20678, 21114
Digital Platform - Mobile:
Apple`Android`Windows
Digital Platform - Tablet: Apple iOS`Android
Frequency: Mthly
Circulation Free: 34641
Audit By: Sworn/Estimate/Non-Audited
Audit Date: 12.07.2019
Personnel: Donna Jefferson (Adv. Mgr.); Jeanne Slaughter (Mktg. Mgr.); Kristen Page-Kirby (Ed.)
Parent company: Jefferson Communications
Main (survey) contact: Donna Jefferson

BALTIMORE

BOSTON PARENT

Street address 1: 11 Dutton Ct
Street address city: Baltimore
Street address state: MD
Postal code: 21228-4922
Main (survey) contact: Robert McKean

MARYLAND FAMILY MAGAZINE

Street address 1: 409 Washington Ave
Street address 2: Ste 400
Street address city: Towson
Street address state: MD
Postal code: 21204-4919
Country: USA
Mailing address 1: 409 Washington Ave Ste 400
Mailing city: Towson
Mailing state: MD
Mailing zip: 21204-4919
Office phone: (410) 337-2400
Office fax: (410) 296-2707
Website: www.marylandfamilymagazine.com
Frequency: Bi-Mthly
Circulation Paid: 0
Circulation Free: 43645
Audit By: CAC
Audit Date: 31.03.2015
Personnel: Cheryl Clemens (Ed.); Kristine Henry (Ed.)
Main (survey) contact: Kristine Henry

BEXAR

OUR KIDS SAN ANTONIO

Street address 1: 8400 Blanco Rd
Street address 2: Ste 300
Street address city: San Antonio
Street address state: TX
Postal code: 78216-3055
Country: USA
Mailing address 1: PO Box 1809
Mailing city: Castroville
Mailing state: TX
Mailing zip: 78009
Office phone: (210) 349-6667
Office fax: (210) 349-5618
Advertising phone: (210) 305-4181 Ext. 101
General e-mail: sanantonio.parenting@parenthood.com
Advertising e-mail: pat@ourkidsmagazine.com
Website: http://www.ourkidsmagazine.com/
Zip Codes Served: 78216
Frequency: Wed
Circulation Free: 50000
Audit By: Sworn/Estimate/Non-Audited
Audit Date: 12.07.2019
Personnel: Rudy Riojas (Pub.); Cynthia Ladson (Ed.)
Main (survey) contact: Kelley Ramotowski

BIBB

GEORGIA FAMILY MAGAZINE

Street address 1: 523 Sioux Dr
Street address city: Macon
Street address state: GA
Postal code: 31210-4217
Country: USA
Mailing address 1: 523 Sioux Dr
Mailing city: Macon
Mailing state: GA
Mailing zip: 31210-4217
Office phone: (478) 471-7393
Advertising phone: (478) 471-7393
Editorial phone: 478 471-7393
General e-mail: publisher@georgiafamily.com
Advertising e-mail: publisher@georgiafamily.com
Editorial e-mail: editorial.gfm@gmail.com
Website: www.GeorgiaFamily.com
Year publication established: 1992
Advertising (open inch rate): open full-page rate $1185.00
Mechanical specifications: Type page 7 1/4 x 10. 4/C/300dpi
Delivery methods: Mail`Carrier`Racks
Zip Codes Served: Central Georgia too many to list
Frequency: Mthly
Other Type of Frequency: Monthly
Circulation Paid: 105
Circulation Free: 55000
Audit By: CVC
Audit Date: 30.06.2011
Hardware: Computers 4C Laser printers
Software: Adobe Creative Suite 6 Quickbooks TrendMicro
Editions Count: 2
Edition Names: Hard copy & digital
Personnel: Olya Fessard (Ed. in Chief); Veronique Saiya (Mng. Ed.)
Main (survey) contact: Olya Fessard

BREVARD

CINCINNATI PARENT

Street address 1: 1 Gannett Plaza
Street address city: Melbourne
Street address state: FL
Postal code: 32940
Country: USA
Mailing address 1: 9435 Waterstone Blvd Ste 140
Mailing city: Cincinnati
Mailing state: OH
Mailing zip: 45249-8229
Office phone: (513) 444-2015
Advertising phone: (317) 710-6622
Editorial phone: (317) 722-8500, ext. 164
Other phone: (317) 722-8500
General e-mail: mary@cincinnatiparent.com
Advertising e-mail: mary@cincinnatiparent.com
Editorial e-mail: susan@cincinnatiparent.com
Website: www.cincinnatiparent.com
Year publication established: 1986
Delivery methods: Mail`Newsstand`Carrier`Racks
Zip Codes Served: 46220-1039
Digital Platform - Mobile: Apple`Android`Windows`Blackberry
Digital Platform - Tablet: Apple iOS`Android`Windows 7`Blackberry Tablet OS`Kindle`Kindle Fire`Other
Frequency: Mthly
Circulation Free: 44000
Audit By: CVC
Audit Date: 01.07.2016
Hardware: 4-APP/Mac, APP/Power Mac 7200-90
Software: QPS/QuarkXPress 3.1, Adobe/Photoshop 3.0.
Personnel: Mary Wynne Cox (Publisher)
Parent company: Midwest Parenting Publications
Main (survey) contact: Mary Cox

BROWARD

FORT WORTH CHILD MAGAZINE

Street address 1: 6501 Nob Hill Rd
Street address city: Tamarac
Street address state: FL
Postal code: 33321-6422
Country: USA
Mailing address 1: 4275 Kellway Cir Ste 146
Mailing city: Addison
Mailing state: TX
Mailing zip: 75001-5731
Office phone: (972) 447-9188
Office fax: (972) 447-0633
General e-mail: support@dfwchild.com
Advertising e-mail: advertising@dfwchild.com
Editorial e-mail: editorial@dfwchild.com
Website: www.dfwchild.com/fortworth
Year publication established: 1992
Advertising (open inch rate): N/A
Delivery methods: Racks
Zip Codes Served: Fort Worth, Arlington, Hurst Euless Bedford, Grapevine, Southlake, Colleyville, Keller
Digital Platform - Mobile: Apple`Android
Digital Platform - Tablet: Apple iOS`Android
Frequency: Mthly
Other Type of Frequency: monthly
Circulation Free: 40000
Audit By: CVC
Audit Date: 30.06.2017
Personnel: Joylyn Niebes (Pub.); Susan Horn (Graphics Designer)
Parent company: Lauren Publications
Main (survey) contact: Joylyn Niebes

BUTLER

PITTSBURGH PARENT

Street address 1: 1126 Pittsburgh Rd
Street address 2: # RT8
Street address city: Valencia
Street address state: PA
Postal code: 16059-1930
Country: USA
Mailing address 1: PO Box 674
Mailing city: Valencia
Mailing state: PA
Mailing zip: 16059-0674
Office phone: (724) 898-1898
Office fax: (724) 898-1877
General e-mail: manager@pittsburghparent.com
Advertising e-mail: manager@pittsburghparent.com
Editorial e-mail: editor@pittsburghparent.com
Website: www.pittsburghparent.com
Year publication established: 1988
Delivery methods: Mail`Racks
Zip Codes Served: ti-state area of western PA
Digital Platform - Mobile: Apple
Digital Platform - Tablet: Apple iOS
Frequency: Mthly
Circulation Paid: 32
Circulation Free: 45728
Audit By: VAC
Audit Date: 30.09.2016
Personnel: Lynn Honeywill (Circ. Mgr.)
Parent company: Honey Hill Publishing
Main (survey) contact: Patricia Poshard

CALVERT

PARENT LINE

Street address 1: 11135 Beacon Way
Street address city: Lusby
Street address state: MD
Postal code: 20657-2449
Country: USA
Mailing address 1: 11135 Beacon Way

Mailing city: Lusby
Mailing state: MD
Mailing zip: 20657-2449
Office phone: (410) 326-7030
Office fax: (410) 326-0999
General e-mail: parentline@comcast.net; parentlinecalendar@comcast.net
Mechanical specifications: Type page 10 13/16 x 13.
Frequency: Mthly
Circulation Free: 25000
Audit By: Sworn/Estimate/Non-Audited
Audit Date: 12.07.2019
Personnel: Kelly Wilder (Pub.)
Main (survey) contact: Kelly Wilder

CHARLESTON
LOWCOUNTRY PARENT MAGAZINE
Street address 1: 134 Columbus St
Street address city: Charleston
Street address state: SC
Postal code: 29403-4809
Country: USA
Mailing address 1: 134 Columbus St
Mailing city: Charleston
Mailing state: SC
Mailing zip: 29403-4809
Office phone: (843) 577-7111
Office fax: (843) 937-5579
Advertising phone: (843) 958-7394
Advertising fax: (843) 937-5579
Editorial phone: (843) 958-7393
Editorial fax: (843) 937-5579
General e-mail: info@lowcountryparent.com
Advertising e-mail: dkifer@postandcourier.com
Editorial e-mail: editor@lowcountryparent.com
Website: www.lowcountryparent.com
Year publication established: 1997
Frequency: Mthly
Circulation Free: 41000
Audit By: Sworn/Estimate/Non-Audited
Audit Date: 12.07.2019
Personnel: Doug Kifer (Adv. Sales Mgr.); Shannon Brigham (Ed.)
Parent company: The Post and Courier
Main (survey) contact: Rachel Cook

COOK
CHICAGO PARENT
Street address 1: 141 S Oak Park Ave
Street address city: Oak Park
Street address state: IL
Postal code: 60302-2972
Country: USA
Mailing address 1: 141 S Oak Park Ave Ste 1
Mailing city: Oak Park
Mailing state: IL
Mailing zip: 60302-2972
Office phone: (708) 386-5555
Office fax: (708) 524-8360
General e-mail: chiparent@chicagoparent.com
Website: www.chicagoparent.com
Year publication established: 1984
Mechanical specifications: Type page 9 1/2 x 11 5/6; E - 3 cols, between; A - 4 cols, 2 3/16, 1/4 between; C - 6 cols, between.
Delivery methods: Mail`Carrier`Racks
Zip Codes Served: 60302
Digital Platform - Mobile: Apple`Android`Blackberry
Digital Platform - Tablet: Apple iOS`Android`Kindle`Kindle Fire
Frequency: Mthly
Circulation Paid: 13
Circulation Free: 125000
Audit By: Sworn/Estimate/Non-Audited
Audit Date: 12.07.2019
Editions Count: 3
Edition Names: 3 total Ã‚Â— Chicago Parent Zone A (50,000);
Personnel: Dan Haley (Pub.); Kathy Hansen (Circ. Mgr.); Tamara O'Shaughnessy (Ed.)
Main (survey) contact: Dan Haley

DALLAS
DALLASCHILD
Street address 1: 4275 Kellway Cir
Street address 2: Ste 146
Street address city: Addison
Street address state: TX
Postal code: 75001-5731
Country: USA
Mailing address 1: 4275 Kellway Circle
Mailing city: Addison
Mailing state: TX
Mailing zip: 75001
Office phone: (972) 447-9188
Advertising phone: (214) 707-6174
Editorial phone: (214) 707-6174
Other phone: (214) 707-6174
General e-mail: publishing@dfwchild.com
Advertising e-mail: advertising@dfwchild.com
Editorial e-mail: editorial@dfwchild.com
Website: dfwchild.com
Year publication established: 1984
Delivery methods: Racks
Zip Codes Served: 75001, 75002, 75019, 75006, 75007, 75010, 75023, 75024, 75093, 75204, 75205, 75209, 75219, 75220, 75225, 75218, 75214, 75243, 75248, 75252,75033, 75034, 75035, 75068, 75078, 75070. 75002, 75013, 75025.
Digital Platform - Mobile: Apple`Android
Digital Platform - Tablet: Apple iOS`Android
Frequency: Mthly
Circulation Free: 55000
Audit By: CVC
Audit Date: 18.12.2017
Hardware: APP/Mac
Software: QPS/QuarkXPress, Adobe/Photoshop, Adobe/Illustrator.
Personnel: Joylyn Niebes (Publisher); Lauren Niebes-Piccirillo (Creative & Content Director)
Parent company: Lauren Publications
Main (survey) contact: Joylyn Niebes

METROKIDS MAGAZINE
Street address 1: 4275 Kellway Cir
Street address 2: Ste 146
Street address city: Addison
Street address state: TX
Postal code: 75001-5731
Country: USA
Mailing address 1: 1414 Pine Street
Mailing city: Philadelphia
Mailing state: PA
Mailing zip: 19112-1202
Office phone: (215) 291-5560
Office fax: (215) 291-5565
General e-mail: info@metrokids.com
Advertising e-mail: sales@metrokids.com
Editorial e-mail: editor@metrokids.com
Website: www.metrokids.com
Year publication established: 1991
Delivery methods: Racks
Zip Codes Served: Greater Philadelphia MetroMarket 5 County Southeastern PA, Southern New Jersey and Delaware
Digital Platform - Mobile: Apple`Android`Windows`Blackberry`Other
Digital Platform - Tablet: Apple iOS`Android`Windows 7`Blackberry Tablet OS`Kindle`Nook`Kindle Fire`Other
Frequency: Mthly
Other Type of Frequency: Special Editions Annually, Bi Annually
Circulation Free: 90
Audit By: Sworn/Estimate/Non-Audited
Audit Date: 12.07.2019
Editions Count: 3
Edition Names: Pennsylvania, South Jersey and Delaware
Personnel: Darlene Weinmann (Publisher); Nancy Lisagor (Ed. in Chief); Sara Murphy (Managing Editor)
Main (survey) contact: Sara Murphy

QUEENS PARENT
Street address 1: 4275 Kellway Cir
Street address 2: Ste 146
Street address city: Addison

Street address state: TX
Postal code: 75001-5731
Country: USA
Mailing address 1: 498 Seventh Ave, 10th Floor
Mailing city: New York
Mailing state: NY
Mailing zip: 10018-2385
Office phone: (212) 315-0800
Website: www.nymetroparents.com
Year publication established: 1985
Advertising (open inch rate): N/A
Frequency: Mthly
Circulation Free: 54910
Audit By: CVC
Audit Date: 14.06.2014
Main (survey) contact: Christina Vercelletto

DANE
DANE COUNTY KIDS
Street address 1: 2420 Evans Rd
Street address city: Mc Farland
Street address state: WI
Postal code: 53558-9043
Country: USA
Mailing zip: 53744-505
Office phone: (608) 444-0654
Advertising phone: (608) 444-0654
Editorial phone: same
General e-mail: kerickson@ericksonpublishing.com
Advertising e-mail: same
Editorial e-mail: same
Website: tbd...revising
Year publication established: 1992
Advertising (open inch rate): $1200. per full page 7.5"H x 9.75"V
Mechanical specifications: full color available; send PDFs; inquire about full-page bleed ads and special placement and four-color vs. black and white.
Delivery methods: Mail`Racks
Zip Codes Served: throughout southcentral Wisconsin and nationwide with our special family tourism guide
Digital Platform - Mobile: Apple
Digital Platform - Tablet: Apple iOS`Android`Other
Frequency: Mthly
Circulation Free: 50000
Audit By: Sworn/Estimate/Non-Audited
Audit Date: 12.07.2019
Hardware: Macintosh
Presses: Web Press
Software: Quark, Illustrator, Photoshop
Editions Count: 1
Edition Names: tbd
Note: We need the latest, most interesting info.about parenting kids birth-18. Also info.pertaining to women 25-54. We are also in need of info.re: new books, CDs, toys, parenting equip. of all kinds, education-related materials, pampering products for mom, pregnancy products, gifts, the best the women's and parenting industries have to offer. We want to share the news.Send product samples to Kristin Erickson, Publisher, Dane County Kids, 2420 Evans Road, McFarland, WI 53558.
Personnel: Kristin Erickson (Pres./Pub.); Lynn Wittsell (Assoc. Editor)
Main (survey) contact: Kristin Erickson

DAUPHIN
CENTRAL PENN PARENT
Street address 1: 1500 Paxton St
Street address city: Harrisburg
Street address state: PA
Postal code: 17104-2615
Country: USA
Mailing address 1: 1500 Paxton St
Mailing city: Harrisburg
Mailing state: PA
Mailing zip: 17104-2615
Office phone: (717) 236-4300
Office fax: (717) 236-6803
Editorial fax: (717) 909-0538
General e-mail: annas@journalpub.com
Editorial e-mail: editor@centralpennparent.com

Website: www.centralpennparent.com
Year publication established: 1996
Mechanical specifications: Type page 10 1/8 x 13; E - 4 cols, 2 3/8, 3/16 between; C - 4 cols, 2 3/8, 3/16 between.
Frequency: Mthly
Circulation Paid: 0
Circulation Free: 40325
Audit By: CVC
Audit Date: 01.06.2012
Hardware: APP/Power Mac
Software: QPS/QuarkXPress 4.1, Adobe/Photoshop 4.0, Adobe/Illustrator 6.0.
Personnel: ShaunJude McCoach (Pub.); Carley Lucas (Adv. Acct. Exec.); Leslie Penkunas (Ed.); Tracy Bumba (Aud. Dev. Mgr.)
Main (survey) contact: ShaunJude McCoach

DAVIDSON
DAY COM MEDIA
Street address 1: 3212 West End Ave
Street address 2: #201
Street address city: Nashville
Street address state: TN
Postal code: 37203
Country: USA
Mailing address 1: 2200 Rosa L Parks Blvd
Mailing city: Nashville
Mailing state: TN
Mailing zip: 37228-1306
Office phone: (615) 256-2158
Office fax: (615) 256-2114
General e-mail: stewart@daycommedia.com
Editorial e-mail: susan@daycommedia.com
Website: www.parentworld.com
Year publication established: 1993
Advertising (open inch rate): N/A
Mechanical specifications: Type page 9 1/2 x 11.
Delivery methods: Newsstand`Carrier`Racks
Zip Codes Served: 37215, 37027, 37069, 37064, 37075, 37127, 37121,
Digital Platform - Mobile: Apple
Digital Platform - Tablet: Apple iOS
Frequency: Mthly
Circulation Paid: 10
Circulation Free: 50000
Audit By: Sworn/Estimate/Non-Audited
Audit Date: 12.07.2019
Personnel: Stewart Day (Pub.); Susan Day (Ed.); Chad Young (Mng. Ed.); Tim Henard (Prodn. Mgr.)
Parent company: Day Communications Inc
Main (survey) contact: Stewart Day

RUTHERFORD PARENT
Street address 1: 2200 Rosa L Parks Blvd
Street address city: Nashville
Street address state: TN
Postal code: 37228-1306
Country: USA
Mailing address 1: 2200 Rosa L Parks Blvd
Mailing city: Nashville
Mailing state: TN
Mailing zip: 37228-1306
Office phone: (615) 256-2158
Office fax: (615) 256-2114
General e-mail: stewart@daycommedia.com
Website: www.parentworld.com
Year publication established: 1993
Advertising (open inch rate): N/A
Frequency: Mthly
Circulation Free: 13111
Audit By: CVC
Audit Date: 30.06.2015
Personnel: Stewart Day (Adv. Mgr.); Tom Guardino (Circ. Mgr.); Susan Day (Ed. in Chief.); Chad Young (Mng. Ed.); Tim Henard (Prodn. Mgr.)
Main (survey) contact: Stewart Day

DEKALB
ATLANTA PARENT
Street address 1: 2346 Perimeter Park Dr
Street address 2: Ste 101
Street address city: Atlanta
Street address state: GA

Parenting Publications in the U.S.

Postal code: 30341-1319
Country: USA
Mailing address 1: 2346 Perimeter Park Dr Ste 101
Mailing city: Atlanta
Mailing state: GA
Mailing zip: 30341-1319
Office phone: (770) 454-7599
Office fax: (770) 454-7699
General e-mail: atlantaparent@atlantaparent.com
Advertising e-mail: calendar@atlantaparent.com; advertising@atlantaparent.com
Editorial e-mail: editor@atlantaparent.com
Website: www.atlantaparent.com
Advertising (open inch rate): N/A
Mechanical specifications: Type page 7 3/8 x 10; E - 3 cols, 2 1/4, 1/4 between; A - 3 cols, 2 1/4, 1/4 between; C - 3 cols, 2 1/4, 1/4 between.
Zip Codes Served: 30338
Frequency: Mthly
Circulation Free: 99900
Audit By: CVC
Audit Date: 30.06.2014
Software: Adobe/PageMaker 7.0.
Personnel: Michelle McGunagle (Asst. Pub.); Amy Smith (Bus. Devel. Mgr.); Liz White (Adv. Sales Dir.); Kate Parrott (Mng. Ed.); Neal Wilkes (Prodn. Mgr.)
Main (survey) contact: Laura Powell

DELAWARE

COLUMBUS PARENT

Street address 1: 7801 N Central Dr
Street address city: Lewis Center
Street address state: OH
Postal code: 43035-9407
Country: USA
Mailing address 1: 7801 N Central Dr
Mailing city: Lewis Center
Mailing state: OH
Mailing zip: 43035-9407
Office phone: (740) 888-6000
Office fax: (740) 888-6001
Advertising phone: (614) 883-1921
General e-mail: columbusparent@thisweeknews.com
Website: www.columbusparent.com
Year publication established: 1990
Mechanical specifications: Type page 10 x 13; E - 4 cols, 2 1/4, 1/8 between; A - 4 cols, 2 1/4, 1/8 between; C - 6 cols, 1 1/2, 1/8 between.
Zip Codes Served: 43017, 43016, 43123, 43220, 43229, 43081, 43212, 43068, 43082, 43235, 43204, 43222, 43223, 43228, 43201, 43211, 43215, 43224, 43209, 43213, 43227, 43232
Frequency: Mthly
Circulation Free: 40634
Audit By: AAM
Audit Date: 31.03.2019
Hardware: APP/Power Mac G3
Presses: Offset Color Press
Software: QPS/QuarkXPress 4.04.
Personnel: Rheta Gallagher (Assoc. Pub.); Ray Paprocki (Pub.); Julanne Hohbach (Ed.)
Main (survey) contact: Julanne Hohbach

DENVER

COLORADO PARENT

Street address 1: 1515 Wazee St Ste 400
Street address 2: Suite 400
Street address city: Denver
Street address state: CO
Postal code: 80202-1672
Country: USA
Office phone: (303) 320-1000
Office fax: (303) 265-9411
Website: www.coloradoparent.com
Year publication established: 1986
Advertising (open inch rate): N/A
Mechanical specifications: Type page 8 3/8 x 11 1/8; E - 4 cols, 2 1/4, 1/4 between.
Delivery methods: Newsstand`Racks
Zip Codes Served: Greater Denver/Boulder Metro
Digital Platform - Mobile: Apple`Android`Windows
Digital Platform - Tablet: Apple iOS`Android
Frequency: Mthly
Circulation Free: 45133
Audit By: CVC
Audit Date: 30.06.2015
Hardware: APP/Macs
Software: QPS/QuarkXPress.
Personnel: Deborah Mock (Ed.); Christina Cook (Assoc. Ed.); Lydia Rueger (Copy Ed.); Heather Gott (Art Dir.)
Parent company: 5280 Publishing, Inc.
Main (survey) contact: Deborah Mock

DURHAM

SOUTH FLORIDA PARENTING MAGAZINE

Street address 1: 5716 Fayetteville Rd
Street address 2: Ste 201
Street address city: Durham
Street address state: NC
Postal code: 27713-9662
Country: USA
Mailing address 1: 6501 Nob Hill Rd
Mailing city: Tamarac
Mailing state: FL
Mailing zip: 33321-6422
Office phone: (954) 747-3050
Office fax: (954) 747-3055
General e-mail: parentingsubmissions@sfparenting.com
Website: www.southflorida.com/sfparenting
Zip Codes Served: 33146
Frequency: Mthly
Circulation Free: 91546
Audit By: CVC
Audit Date: 31.12.2012
Software: QPS/QuarkXPress, Multi-Ad/Creator, Adobe/Photoshop.
Personnel: Lisa Goodlin (Pub.); Angela Bartolone (Adv. Mgr.)
Parent company: Forum Publishing Group
Main (survey) contact: Lisa Goodlin

EAST BATON ROUGE

BATON ROUGE PARENTS MAGAZINE

Street address 1: 11831 Wentling Ave
Street address city: Baton Rouge
Street address state: LA
Postal code: 70816-6055
Country: USA
Mailing address 1: 11831 Wentling Ave
Mailing city: Baton Rouge
Mailing state: LA
Mailing zip: 70816-6275
Office phone: (225) 292-0032
Office fax: (225) 292-0038
General e-mail: brpm@brparents.com; brpmcalendar@brparents.com
Advertising e-mail: sales@brparents.com
Website: www.brparents.com
Year publication established: 1990
Advertising (open inch rate): N/A
Frequency: Mthly
Circulation Paid: 31
Circulation Free: 14776
Audit By: CVC
Audit Date: 30.06.2015
Personnel: Amy Foreman-Plaisance (Pub.); Theresa Dold Payment (Sales Mgr.)
Main (survey) contact: Amy Foreman-Plaisance

ERIE

WESTERN NEW YORK FAMILY

Street address 1: 3147 Delaware Ave
Street address 2: Ste B
Street address city: Buffalo
Street address state: NY
Postal code: 14217-2002
Country: USA
Mailing address 1: 3147 Delaware Ave Ste B
Mailing city: Buffalo
Mailing state: NY
Mailing zip: 14217-2002
Office phone: (716) 836-3486
Office fax: (716) 836-3680
General e-mail: feedback@wnyfamilymagazine.com
Advertising e-mail: advertising@wnyfamilymagazine.com
Editorial e-mail: michele@wnyfamilymagazine.com
Website: www.wnyfamilymagazine.com
Year publication established: 1984
Advertising (open inch rate): Modular ad rates
Mechanical specifications: Our complete media kit with specs can be downloaded from our website.
Delivery methods: Racks
Zip Codes Served: We cover Erie and Niagara Counties of upstate New York. We are NOT a New York City publication. Call our office to receive a PDF of our complete audit report including zip codes.
Digital Platform - Mobile: Apple`Android`Windows`Blackberry`Other
Digital Platform - Tablet: Apple iOS`Android`Windows 7`Kindle`Nook`Kindle Fire`Other
Frequency: Mthly
Circulation Paid: 0
Circulation Free: 20000
Audit By: CVC
Audit Date: 30.06.2017
Hardware: Apple Computers Hewlett Packard Printers
Presses: NONE
Software: Adobe Creative Suite
Personnel: Michele Miller (Editor & Publisher)
Main (survey) contact: Michele Miller

FAYETTE

LEXINGTON FAMILY MAGAZINE

Street address 1: 138 E Reynolds Rd
Street address 2: Ste 201
Street address city: Lexington
Street address state: KY
Postal code: 40517-1259
Country: USA
Mailing address 1: 138 E Reynolds Rd Ste 201
Mailing city: Lexington
Mailing state: KY
Mailing zip: 40517-1259
Office phone: (859) 223-1765
Office fax: (859) 224-4270
Website: www.lexingtonfamily.com
Year publication established: 1996
Advertising (open inch rate): N/A
Mechanical specifications: Type page 10 x 12 1/2; E - 4 cols, 2 23/60, 1/6 between; A - 4 cols, 2 23/60, 1/6 between.
Frequency: Mthly
Circulation Free: 28539
Audit By: CVC
Audit Date: 30.06.2015
Personnel: Dana Tackett (Pub.); Karyn Potts (Adv. Rep.); John Lynch (Ed.)
Main (survey) contact: John Lynch

HARRIS

HOUSTON FAMILY MAGAZINE

Street address 1: 5131 Braesvalley Dr
Street address city: Houston
Street address state: TX
Postal code: 77096-2609
Country: USA
Mailing address 1: 5131 Braesvalley Dr
Mailing city: Houston
Mailing state: TX
Mailing zip: 77096-2609
Office phone: (713) 266-1885
Office fax: (713) 266-1915
General e-mail: dana@houstonfamilymagazine.com
Advertising e-mail: kim@houstonfamilymagazine.com
Editorial e-mail: dana@houstonfamilymagazine.com
Website: www.houstonfamilymagazine.com
Advertising (open inch rate): Open inch rate $51.00
Frequency: Mthly
Circulation Free: 60000
Audit By: Sworn/Estimate/Non-Audited
Audit Date: 12.07.2019
Personnel: Kimberly Davis-Guerra (Publisher); Wendy Jackson-Slaton (Ed. in Chief); Casey Johnson (Creative Dir.); Gayle Wheeler-Lesuer (Graphic Des.)
Main (survey) contact: Kimberly Davis-Guerra

HILLSBOROUGH

PARENTING NEW HAMPSHIRE

Street address 1: 150 Dow St
Street address city: Manchester
Street address state: NH
Postal code: 03101-1227
Country: USA
Mailing address 1: 150 Dow St Ste 202
Mailing city: Manchester
Mailing state: NH
Mailing zip: 03101-1227
Office phone: (603) 624-1310
Office fax: (603) 624-1310
Advertising phone: (603) 624-1442
Editorial phone: (603) 624-1442
Website: http://www.parentingnh.com/
Year publication established: 1993
Advertising (open inch rate): Open inch rate $22.80
Mechanical specifications: Type page 9 1/2 x 11 5/8; E - 4 cols, 2 1/8, between; A - 4 cols, 2 1/8, between; C - 4 cols, 2 1/8, between.
Frequency: Mthly
Circulation Free: 27303
Audit By: CVC
Audit Date: 30.06.2005
Hardware: PC, APP/Mac
Software: QPS/QuarkXPress 4.0.
Personnel: Sharron Mccarthy (Pub.); David Kruger (Adv. Dir.); Shannon Spiliotis (Circ. Mgr.); Melanie Hitchcock (Ed.)
Main (survey) contact: Sharron Mccarthy

HONOLULU

ISLAND FAMILY

Street address 1: 1000 Bishop St
Street address 2: Ste 405
Street address city: Honolulu
Street address state: HI
Postal code: 96813-4204
Country: USA
Mailing address 1: 1000 Bishop St.
Mailing city: Honolulu
Mailing state: HI
Mailing zip: 96813
Office phone: (808) 534-7544
Office fax: (808) 537-6455
Advertising phone: (808) 534-7501
Editorial phone: (808) 534-7105
General e-mail: chuckt@pacificbasin.net
Advertising e-mail: Donnaky@honolulumagazine.com
Editorial e-mail: Christiy@honolulufamily.com
Website: http://www.honolulufamily.com/
Frequency: Mthly
Circulation Free: 40000
Audit By: Sworn/Estimate/Non-Audited
Audit Date: 12.07.2019
Personnel: Lennie Omalza (Adv. Mgr.); Helen McNeil (Ed.)
Main (survey) contact: Christi Young

JEFFERSON

TODAY'S FAMILY

Street address 1: 9750 Ormsby Station Rd
Street address 2: Ste 307
Street address city: Louisville
Street address state: KY
Postal code: 40223-4064
Country: USA
Mailing address 1: 9750 Ormsby Station Rd

Ste 307
Mailing city: Louisville
Mailing state: KY
Mailing zip: 40223-4064
Office phone: (502) 327-8855
Advertising phone: (502) 327-8855
Editorial phone: (502) 327-8855
General e-mail: info@todaysmedianow.com
Advertising e-mail: advertising@todaysmedianow.com
Editorial e-mail: editor@todaysmedianow.com
Website: www.todaysfamilynow.com
Year publication established: 1982
Delivery methods: Racks
Digital Platform - Mobile: Apple`Android`Windows`Blackberry
Digital Platform - Tablet: Apple iOS`Android`Windows 7`Blackberry Tablet OS`Kindle`Nook`Kindle Fire
Frequency: Other
Other Type of Frequency: Semi-Annual – Spring & Fall
Circulation Free: 34975
Audit By: CVC
Audit Date: 30.06.2018
Personnel: Cathy Zion (Owner/Pub); Anita Oldham (Ed.); Susan Allen (Ad. Dir.)
Parent company: Zion Publications, LLC
Main (survey) contact: Susan Allen

JOHNSON

NEW YORK FAMILY

Street address 1: 11936 W 119th St
Street address 2: Ste 335
Street address city: Overland Park
Street address state: KS
Postal code: 66213-2216
Country: USA
Mailing address 1: 141 Halstead Ave Ste 3D
Mailing city: Mamaroneck
Mailing state: NY
Mailing zip: 10543-2607
Office phone: (914) 381-7474
Office fax: (914) 381-7672
General e-mail: mamaroneck.reception@parenthood.com
Website: www.parenthood.com
Frequency: Mthly
Personnel: Cate Sanderson (Pub.); Sherine R. Chenault-Usher (Adv. Coord.); Thomas Butcher (Circ. Mgr.); Heather Hart (Sr. Ed.); Larissa Phillips (Ed.); Carolyn Rogalsky (Calendar Ed.)
Main (survey) contact: Heather Hart

KERN

KERN COUNTY FAMILY MAGAZINE

Street address 1: 1400 Easton Dr
Street address 2: Ste 112
Street address city: Bakersfield
Street address state: CA
Postal code: 93309-9403
Country: USA
Office phone: (661) 861-4939
Office fax: (661) 861-4930
General e-mail: kerncountyfamily@earthlink.net
Website: www.kerncountyfamily.com
Year publication established: 1996
Advertising (open inch rate): N/A
Mechanical specifications: Type page 10 1/4 x 12.
Frequency: Mthly
Circulation Paid: 9
Circulation Free: 28207
Audit By: CVC
Audit Date: 31.12.2014
Hardware: APP/Mac
Presses: 4-WPC
Software: Adobe/PageMaker 6.5, Macromedia/Freehand 7.0, Adobe/Photoshop 5.0.
Personnel: L.J. Corby (Ed.)
Main (survey) contact: L.J. Corby

KING

PARENTMAP

Street address 1: 7683 SE 27th St
Street address city: Mercer Island
Street address state: WA
Postal code: 98040-2804
Country: USA
Mailing address 1: PMB #190 7683 SE 27th Street
Mailing city: Mercer Island
Mailing state: WA
Mailing zip: 98040
Office phone: (206) 709-9026
Office fax: (206) 455-7984
Advertising phone: (206) 709-9026
General e-mail: admin@parentmap.com
Advertising e-mail: jess@parentmap.com
Editorial e-mail: jody@parentmap.com
Website: https://www.parentmap.com/
Year publication established: 2003
Mechanical specifications: Type page 10 3/16 x 13 1/4.
Delivery methods: Mail`Carrier`Racks
Zip Codes Served: Over 140 zip codes
Digital Platform - Mobile: Apple`Android
Frequency: Mthly
Circulation Paid: 120
Circulation Free: 45000
Audit By: Sworn/Estimate/Non-Audited
Audit Date: 12.07.2019
Note: ParentMap is a free monthly news magazine for parents in the Puget Sound area of the Pacific Northwest. ParentMap also offers a web site with searchable online events calendar for family-related activities, as well as a family directory, where parents can search for local businesses and classes that cater to families.
Personnel: Ida Wicklund (Advertising & Partnerships, Manager); Danielle Sackett (Circ. Mgr.); Karen Matthee (Ed.); Anton Hafele (Prodn. Mgr.)
Main (survey) contact: Alayne Sulkin

KINGS

NEW YORK PARENTING - BROOKLYN FAMILY/MANHATTAN FAMILY/QUEENS FAMILY/BRONX-RIVERDALE FAMILY/WESTCHESTER FAMILY

Street address 1: 1 Metrotech Ctr N
Street address 2: Fl 10
Street address city: Brooklyn
Street address state: NY
Postal code: 11201-3875
Country: USA
Mailing address 1: 1 Metrotech Ctr N Fl 10
Mailing city: Brooklyn
Mailing state: NY
Mailing zip: 11201-3875
Office phone: (718) 260-4554
Office fax: (718) 260-2568
Advertising phone: (718) 260-4554
Editorial phone: (718) 260-2587
General e-mail: Susank@NYParenting.com
Advertising e-mail: Family@NYParenting.com
Editorial e-mail: Susan@NYParenting.com
Website: www.nyparenting.com
Year publication established: 1999
Advertising (open inch rate): N/A
Delivery methods: Mail`Carrier`Racks
Zip Codes Served: New York City and Westchester
Digital Platform - Mobile: Apple`Android`Windows`Blackberry
Digital Platform - Tablet: Apple iOS`Android`Windows 7`Blackberry Tablet OS`Kindle`Nook`Kindle Fire
Frequency: Mthly
Other Type of Frequency: Special Child magazines - Bi-Annual
Circulation Free: 167500
Audit By: CVC
Audit Date: 30.06.2017
Personnel: Susan Weiss (Publisher/Exec. Editor); Clifford Luster (Pub./Bus. Mgr.); Vincent Dimecili (Ed.)
Parent company: CNG
Main (survey) contact: Susan Weiss-Voskidis

LAKE

LAKE COUNTY KIDS

Street address 1: 7085 Mentor Ave
Street address city: Willoughby
Street address state: OH
Postal code: 44094-7948
Country: USA
Mailing address 1: 7085 Mentor Ave.
Mailing city: Willoughby
Mailing state: OH
Mailing zip: 44094
Office phone: (440) 951-0000
Office fax: (440) 951-0917
Advertising phone: 440-951-7653
Other phone: 800-947-2737
General e-mail: countykids@news-herald.com
Editorial e-mail: tambrose@news-herald.com
Website: www.news-herald.com
Frequency: Mthly
Circulation Free: 13000
Audit By: Sworn/Estimate/Non-Audited
Audit Date: 12.07.2019
Personnel: Steve Roszczyk (Pub.); Rachel DiBiasio (Gen. Mgr.); Tricia Ambrose (Ed.)
Main (survey) contact: Jeff Sudbrook

LANE

OREGON FAMILY MAGAZINE

Street address 1: PO Box 21732
Street address city: Eugene
Street address state: OR
Postal code: 97402-0411
Country: USA
Mailing address 1: PO Box 21732
Mailing city: Eugene
Mailing state: OR
Mailing zip: 97402-0411
Office phone: (541) 683-7452
Advertising phone: (541) 683-7452
General e-mail: info@oregonfamily.com
Advertising e-mail: sandy@oregonfamily.com
Editorial e-mail: info@oregonfamily.com
Website: www.oregonfamily.com
Year publication established: 1994
Mechanical specifications: Type page 10x12
Delivery methods: Newsstand`Carrier`Racks
Zip Codes Served: 97401, 97402, 97477, 97405, 97478, 97404, 97403
Digital Platform - Mobile: Apple`Android`Windows`Blackberry
Digital Platform - Tablet: Apple iOS`Android`Blackberry Tablet OS
Frequency: Mthly
Circulation Free: 20000
Audit By: Sworn/Estimate/Non-Audited
Audit Date: 12.07.2019
Hardware: PC, APP/Mac
Presses: web, cold, UV
Software: Adobe InDesign
Editions Count: 264
Edition Names: month/year
Personnel: Sandra Kauten (Owner/Pub); Christi Kessler (Advt Acct Mgr)
Parent company: Pacific Parents Publishing
Main (survey) contact: Sandra Kauten

LARIMER

DALLASCHILD

Street address 1: 825 Laporte Ave
Street address 2: STE 146
Street address city: Fort Collins
Street address state: CO
Postal code: 80521-2520
Country: USA
Mailing address 1: 4275 Kellway Cir Ste 146
Mailing city: Addison
Mailing state: TX
Mailing zip: 75001-5731
Office phone: (972) 447-9188
Office fax: (972) 447-0633
Advertising phone: (972) 447-9188
Editorial phone: (972) 447-9188
General e-mail: Joy@dfwchild.com
Advertising e-mail: advertising@dfwchild.com
Editorial e-mail: editorial@dfwchild.com
Website: www.dfwchild.com
Year publication established: 1986
Advertising (open inch rate): N/A
Delivery methods: Racks
Zip Codes Served: 75001, 75002, 75093, 75025, 75225, 75230, 75220, 75205, 75208, 75214, 75218, 75228, 75234, 75229, 75219, 7524
Digital Platform - Mobile: Apple`Android
Digital Platform - Tablet: Apple iOS`Android
Frequency: Mthly
Circulation Free: 60000
Audit By: CAC
Audit Date: 30.06.2017
Hardware: Apple
Note: Lauren Publications has 5 publications. DallasChild, FortWorthChild, NorthTexasChild, DFWBaby and DFWThrive magazines.
Personnel: Joylyn Niebes (Pub.); Susan Horn (Prodn. Mgr.); Alison Davis (Sales Director); Lauren Niebes (Creative Director)
Parent company: Lauren Publications
Main (survey) contact: Joylyn Niebes; Carrie Stiengruber

LEBANON

ABOUT FAMILIES PARENTING NEWSPAPER

Street address 1: 100 E Cumberland St
Street address city: Lebanon
Street address state: PA
Postal code: 17042-5400
Country: USA
Mailing address 1: PO Box 840
Mailing city: Lebanon
Mailing state: PA
Mailing zip: 17042-0840
Office phone: (717) 273-8127
Office fax: (717) 273-0420
Editorial e-mail: editor@aboutfamiliespa.com
Website: www.aboutfamiliespa.com
Year publication established: 1995
Advertising (open inch rate): N/A
Mechanical specifications: Type page 10 1/2 x 13; E - 4 cols, 2 1/2, 1/4 between; A - 4 cols, 2 1/2, 1/4 between; C - 4 cols, 2 1/2, 1/4 between.
Frequency: Mthly
Circulation Free: 42390
Audit By: CVC
Audit Date: 31.03.2015
Hardware: APP/Mac
Software: Microsoft/Word `97, QPS/QuarkXPress 4.0.
Personnel: Judy Fetterolf (Publication Coord.); James Snyder (Adv. Mgr.); Susan Zeller (Ed.)
Main (survey) contact: Suzan Sadler

LOS ANGELES

LA PARENT MAGAZINE

Street address 1: 5855 Topanga Canyon Blvd
Street address 2: Ste 210
Street address city: Woodland Hills
Street address state: CA
Postal code: 91367-4671
Country: USA
Mailing address 1: 5855 Topanga Canyon Blvd. Ste. 210
Mailing city: Woodland Hills
Mailing state: CA
Mailing zip: 91367
Office phone: (818) 264-2222
General e-mail: ron.epstein@laparent.com
Advertising e-mail: ron.epstein@laparent.com
Editorial e-mail: christina.elston@laparent.com
Website: www.laparent.com
Year publication established: 1980
Mechanical specifications: media kit is on our

Parenting Publications in the U.S.

website
Delivery methods: Carrier`Racks
Zip Codes Served: All of LA County, and parts of Ventura County
Digital Platform - Mobile: Apple`Android`Windows`Blackberry
Digital Platform - Tablet: Apple iOS`Android`Windows 7`Blackberry Tablet OS`Kindle`Nook
Frequency: Mthly
Circulation Free: 70000
Audit By: Sworn/Estimate/Non-Audited
Audit Date: 12.07.2019
Hardware: Mac platform
Presses: 48-page
Software: Unsure
Editions Count: 2
Edition Names: City and Valley/Ventura County
Note: We have 2 annual editions: Inclusive L.A., which is published each April for families in LA who have children with learning differences, and our Education Guide that is published in October and addresses all things education – vital to parents in LA.
Personnel: Christina Elston (Ed)
Parent company: Epstein Custom Media Inc.
Main (survey) contact: Christina Elston

LUCAS

ANN ARBOR FAMILY PRESS

Street address 1: 1120 Adams St
Street address city: Toledo
Street address state: OH
Postal code: 43604-5509
Country: USA
Mailing address 1: 1120 Adams St
Mailing city: Toledo
Mailing state: OH
Mailing zip: 43604-5509
Office phone: (419) 244-9859
Office fax: (419) 244-9871
General e-mail: cjacobs@adamsstreetpublishing.com
Advertising e-mail: sales@adamsstreetpublishing.com
Editorial e-mail: editor@adamsstreetpublishing.com
Website: www.annarborfamily.com
Year publication established: 1998
Advertising (open inch rate): N/A
Mechanical specifications: Type page 9 1/2 x 11 7/8; E - 4 cols, 2 1/8, 1/4 between; A - 4 cols, 2 1/8, 1/8 between; C - 5 cols, 1 3/4, 3/16 between.
Delivery methods: Newsstand
Zip Codes Served: 48103, 48118, 48130, 48198, 43624, 48176
Frequency: Mthly
Circulation Paid: 0
Circulation Free: 21708
Audit By: CVC
Audit Date: 16.03.2013
Hardware: APP/Mac
Software: QPS/QuarkXPress 3.30, Adobe/Photoshop 3.0, Adobe/Illustrator.
Personnel: Robin Armstrong (Accounting); Collette Jacobs (Ed. in Chief)
Parent company: Adams Street Publishing Co.
Main (survey) contact: Collette Jacobs

TOLEDO AREA PARENT NEWS

Street address 1: 1120 Adams St
Street address city: Toledo
Street address state: OH
Postal code: 43604-5509
Country: USA
Mailing address 1: 1120 Adams St
Mailing city: Toledo
Mailing state: OH
Mailing zip: 43604-5509
Office phone: (419) 244-9859
Office fax: (419) 244-9871
General e-mail: general@toledocitypaper.com
Website: www.toledocitypaper.com
Year publication established: 1992
Advertising (open inch rate): Open inch rate $60
Mechanical specifications: Type page 9 1/2 x 11 7/8; E - 4 cols, 2 1/8, 1/4 between; A - 4 cols, 2 1/8, 3/8 between; C - 5 cols, 1 3/4, 3/16 between.
Zip Codes Served: 43560, 43566, 43551, 43537, 48182, 48144, 48161, 48157, 43620, 43623, 43624, 43402, 43463, 43556, 43528, 43602, 43604, 43605, 43606, 43607, 43608, 43609, 43610, 43611, 43612, 43613, 43614, 43615, 43616, 43617, 43618, 43619
Frequency: Mthly
Circulation Free: 36000
Audit By: Sworn/Estimate/Non-Audited
Audit Date: 12.07.2019
Hardware: APP/Mac
Software: QPS/QuarkXPress 3.30, Adobe/Photoshop 3.0, Adobe/Illustrator.
Personnel: Collette Jacobs (Pub.); Robin Armstrong (Admin. Acct.); Andrew Spahr (Acct. Exec.)
Main (survey) contact: Collette Jacobs

MARICOPA

ARIZONA PARENTING

Street address 1: 4848 E Cactus Rd
Street address 2: Ste 110
Street address city: Scottsdale
Street address state: AZ
Postal code: 85254-4127
Country: USA
Mailing address 1: 4848 E Cactus Rd Ste 110
Mailing city: Scottsdale
Mailing state: AZ
Mailing zip: 85254-4127
Office phone: (602) 279-7977
Office fax: (602) 279-7978
Website: www.azparenting.com
Mechanical specifications: Type page 9 1/2 x 12 1/8.
Frequency: Mthly
Circulation Free: 60000
Audit By: Sworn/Estimate/Non-Audited
Audit Date: 12.07.2019
Hardware: APP/Mac
Software: QPS/QuarkXPress.
Personnel: Todd Fisher (Pub.); Chris Neiman (Circ. Mgr.); Kimberley Fischer (Adv. Rep.); Todd Fischer (Ed.)
Main (survey) contact: Todd Fisher

MARION

INDY'S CHILD

Street address 1: 6340 E Westfield Blvd
Street address 2: Ste 200
Street address city: Indianapolis
Street address state: IN
Postal code: 46220-1746
Country: USA
Mailing address 1: 6340 Westfield Blvd.
Mailing city: Indianapolis
Mailing state: IN
Mailing zip: 48220
Office phone: (317) 722-8500
Office fax: (317) 722-8510
General e-mail: indyschild@indyschild.com
Editorial e-mail: susan@indyschild.com
Website: www.indyschild.com
Year publication established: 1984
Advertising (open inch rate): Open inch rate $25.00
Mechanical specifications: Type page 10 x 13; E - 4 cols, 2 3/8, 1/8 between; A - 4 cols, 2 3/8, 1/8 between; C - 5 cols, 1 7/8, between.
Zip Codes Served: 46240
Frequency: Wed`Mthly
Circulation Paid: 0
Circulation Free: 45278
Audit By: Sworn/Estimate/Non-Audited
Audit Date: 12.07.2019
Hardware: APP/Mac
Software: QPS/QuarkXPress 3.3, Adobe/Photoshop 3.0.
Personnel: Mary Cox (Pub.); Roxanne Burns (Circ. Mgr.); Mike Hussey (Adv. Mgr.); Lynette Rowland (Ed.)
Parent company: Midwest Parenting Publications
Main (survey) contact: Mary Cox

MECKLENBURG

CHARLOTTE PARENT

Street address 1: 214 W Tremont Ave
Street address 2: Ste 302
Street address city: Charlotte
Street address state: NC
Postal code: 28203-5161
Country: USA
Mailing address 1: 214 W Tremont Ave Ste 302
Mailing city: Charlotte
Mailing state: NC
Mailing zip: 28203-5161
Office phone: (704) 344-1980
Office fax: (704) 344-1983
Advertising phone: (704) 248-5221
Editorial phone: (704) 248-5225
General e-mail: info@charlotteparent.com; promo@charlotteparent.com
Advertising e-mail: advertising@charlotteparent.com
Editorial e-mail: editor@charlotteparent.com
Website: www.charlotteparent.com
Year publication established: 1987
Advertising (open inch rate): N/A
Mechanical specifications: Type page 9 1/2 x 11; E - 4 cols, 2 1/4, 1/4 between.
Delivery methods: Newsstand
Zip Codes Served: 28203
Frequency: Mthly
Circulation Paid: 0
Circulation Free: 39900
Audit By: CVC
Audit Date: 30.06.2015
Hardware: APP/Mac
Presses: Offset
Software: QPS/QuarkXPress.
Personnel: Michelle Huggins (Ed.); Allison Hollins (Dig. Dir.)
Main (survey) contact: Michelle Huggins

MIAMI

ROCKY MOUNTAIN PARENT MAGAZINE

Street address 1: 224 S Market St
Street address city: Troy
Street address state: OH
Postal code: 45373-3327
Country: USA
Mailing address 1: 825 Laporte Ave
Mailing city: Fort Collins
Mailing state: CO
Mailing zip: 80521-2520
Office phone: (970) 221-9210
Office fax: (970) 221-8556
General e-mail: editor@rockymountainpub.com
Website: www.rmparentmagazine.com
Advertising (open inch rate): Open inch rate $28.00
Frequency: Mthly
Circulation Free: 20000
Audit By: Sworn/Estimate/Non-Audited
Audit Date: 12.07.2019
Personnel: Scott Titterington (Pub.); Greg Hoffman (Adv. Mgr.); Kristin Titterington (Ed.)
Main (survey) contact: Kristin Titterington

MIDDLESEX

SUBURBAN PARENT

Street address 1: 8344 Sterling Street
Street address city: Irving
Street address state: TX
Postal code: 75063
Country: USA
Mailing address 1: 8344 Sterling Street
Mailing city: Irving
Mailing state: TX
Mailing zip: 75063
Office phone: (972) 887-7779
Advertising e-mail: advertising@suburbanparent.com
Editorial e-mail: editor@suburbanparent.com
Website: www.suburbanparent.com
Frequency: Mthly
Circulation Free: 300000
Audit By: Sworn/Estimate/Non-Audited
Audit Date: 12.07.2019
Editions Count: 3
Edition Names: 3 total Suburban Parent-Zone 1 (30,000);
Personnel: Mark Chelton (Pub.); Melodie Susan Dhondt (Sr. Ed.); Matthew White (Prodn. Mgr); Mary Ellen Caldwell (Owner/CEO)
Main (survey) contact: The Editor

MILWAUKEE

METROPARENT

Street address 1: 333 W State St
Street address city: Milwaukee
Street address state: WI
Postal code: 53203-1305
Country: USA
Mailing address 1: 333 W State St
Mailing city: Milwaukee
Mailing state: WI
Mailing zip: 53203-1305
Office phone: (414) 647-2478
Office fax: (414) 224-7690
Advertising phone: 414-647-4734
Advertising fax: 414-224-7690
General e-mail: info@metroparentmagazine.com
Advertising e-mail: bsteimle@journalsentinel.com
Editorial e-mail: rchristman@metroparentmagazine.com
Website: www.jsonline.com/life/wisconsin-family
Year publication established: 1986
Advertising (open inch rate): Open inch rate $39.00
Mechanical specifications: Type page 9 x 11; E - 4 cols, 2 1/4, between; A - 4 cols, 2 1/4, between; C - 4 cols, 2 1/4, between.
Delivery methods: Newsstand`Racks
Frequency: Mthly
Circulation Free: 42233
Audit By: CVC
Audit Date: 30.06.2004
Hardware: APP/Power Mac 8500, APP/Mac Performa 600, APP/Mac Performa 638, APP/Mac Laserwriter 360/6cc, Elite XI 616, SyQuest 200mb
Presses: G/Community, G/Urbanite
Software: QPS/QuarkXPress 3.32.
Personnel: George Stanley (Ed./Sr. VP); Chuck Melvin (Asst. Mng. Ed.); Steve Jagler (Bus. Ed.)
Parent company: Journal Media Group
Main (survey) contact: George Stanley

MONTGOMERY

SOUTH JERSEY PARENTS EXPRESS

Street address 1: 290 Commerce Dr
Street address city: Fort Washington
Street address state: PA
Postal code: 19034-2400
Country: USA
Mailing address 1: 290 Commerce Dr
Mailing city: Fort Washington
Mailing state: PA
Mailing zip: 19034-2400
Office phone: (215) 542-0200
Office fax: (215) 629-4853
Editorial e-mail: dkaye@montgomerynews.com
Website: www.parents-express.net
Mechanical specifications: Type page 9 1/2 x 12 1/4; E - 3 cols, 1 7/8, between; A - 4 cols, 1 7/8, 1/8 between.
Frequency: Mthly
Hardware: Software Ã‚Â— QPS/QuarkXPress 4.11, Adobe/Photoshop 5.5.
Personnel: John Bell (Adv. Mgr.); Daniel Kaye (Ed.)
Main (survey) contact: Daniel Kaye

WASHINGTON PARENT MAGAZINE

Street address 1: 4701 Sangamore Rd
Street address 2: Ste N270
Street address city: Bethesda
Street address state: MD

Postal code: 20816-2528
Country: USA
Mailing address 1: 5825 Highland Dr
Mailing city: Chevy Chase
Mailing state: MD
Mailing zip: 20815-5231
Office phone: (301) 320-2321
Office fax: (301) 229-9187
General e-mail: contactus@washingtonparent.net
Website: www.washingtonparent.com
Year publication established: 1996
Advertising (open inch rate): $295 (smallest modular rate)
Frequency: Mthly
Circulation Paid: 36
Circulation Free: 66939
Audit By: CVC
Audit Date: 30.06.2012
Hardware: PC
Software: Adobe/PageMaker.
Personnel: Deborah Benke (Pub.); Mary Fran Gildea (Adv. Mgr.); George Benke (Circ. Mgr.); Margaret Hut (Ed.); Jane MacNealy (Prodn. Mgr.)
Main (survey) contact: Margaret Hut

NEW HAVEN

CONNECTICUT PARENT MAGAZINE

Street address 1: 420 E Main St
Street address 2: Ste 18
Street address city: Branford
Street address state: CT
Postal code: 06405-2942
Country: USA
Mailing address 1: 420 E Main St Ste 18
Mailing city: Branford
Mailing state: CT
Mailing zip: 06405-2942
Office phone: (203) 483-1700
Advertising fax: (203) 483-0522
General e-mail: joel.macclaren@ctparent.com
Advertising e-mail: joel.macclaren@ctparent.com
Editorial e-mail: editorial@ctparent.com
Website: www.ctparent.com
Year publication established: 1984
Advertising (open inch rate): N/A
Mechanical specifications: call
Delivery methods: Racks
Zip Codes Served: 06001-06999
Digital Platform - Mobile: Apple`Android
Digital Platform - Tablet: Apple iOS
Frequency: Mthly
Circulation Paid: 0
Circulation Free: 47239
Audit By: Sworn/Estimate/Non-Audited
Audit Date: 12.07.2019
Software: QPS/QuarkXPress.
Editions Count: 2
Edition Names: 2 total
 ÃƒÂ£££ÃƒÂ£££ Fairfield County (25,000); Hartford County (26,000);
Personnel: Joel MacClaren (Ed./Pub.)
Parent company: Choice Media, LLC
Main (survey) contact: Joel MacClaren

NEW YORK

NY METRO PARENTS

Street address 1: 498 Seventh Avenue, 10th Floor
Street address city: New York
Street address state: NY
Postal code: 10018
Country: USA
Mailing address 1: 498 Seventh Avenue, 10th Floor
Mailing city: New York
Mailing state: NY
Mailing zip: 10018-2385
Office phone: (212) 315-0800
Office fax: (212) 271-2239
Advertising phone: (212) 315-0800
Editorial phone: (646) 652-7516
Editorial fax: (212) 271-2239
General e-mail: info@nymetroparents.com
Advertising e-mail: info@nymetroparents.com
Editorial e-mail: dskolnik@davlermedia.com
Website: www.nymetroparents.com
Year publication established: 1985
Mechanical specifications: Full page 7.3" W x 9.6" D Full page bleed 8.9" W x 11.25" D Junior page 5.4" x 7.0" D 1.2 page (H) 7.3" W x 4.7" D 1.2 page (V) 3.55" W x 9.6" D 1.4 page (H) 7.3" W x 2.25" D 1.4 page (V) 3.55" W x 4.7" D 1.6 page (H) 3.55" W x 3.0" D 1.8 Page (H) 3.55" W x 2.25" D Digital file of ads from advertisers or their ad agencies can be e-mailed as high resolution PDF, EPS (outlined), or TIFF file at least 300 dpi. Alternatively you can send your large materials via dropbox.yousendit.com/Davler-Traffic. Camera ready art should use an 85 line screen, which will be scanned and digitized by our production department. Ads created in InDesign (Mac platform) should include: fonts (no stylized or TrueType fonts), artwork and photos (saved as TIFF or EPS files - CMYK - at least 300 dpi). INK DENSITIES FOR 3. COLOR IMAGES SHOULD NEVER EXCEED 220.
Delivery methods: Mail`Newsstand`Carrier`Racks
Zip Codes Served: All zip codes in Westchester, Rockland/Bergen, Suffolk, Nassau, Manhattan, Queens, and Brooklyn
Digital Platform - Mobile: Apple`Android`Windows`Blackberry
Digital Platform - Tablet: Apple iOS`Android`Windows 7`Blackberry Tablet OS`Kindle`Nook`Kindle Fire`Other
Frequency: Mthly
Circulation Paid: 0
Circulation Free: 335000
Audit By: CVC
Audit Date: 15.10.2017
Hardware: Mac
Presses: Outside printing companies
Software: InDesign CS6 Version 8.1
Editions Count: 84
Edition Names: Big Apple Parent; Long Island Parent - Suffolk Edition; Long Island Parent - Nassau Edition; Westchester Parent; Queens Parent, Bergen / Rockland Parent; Brooklyn Parent
Personnel: David Miller (CEO)
Parent company: Davler Media Group
Main (survey) contact: David Miller

SPACE COAST PARENT

Street address 1: 498 Seventh Ave, 10th Floor
Street address city: New York
Street address state: NY
Postal code: 10018
Country: USA
Mailing address 1: 1 Gannett Plaza
Mailing city: Melbourne
Mailing state: FL
Mailing zip: 32940
Office phone: (321) 242-3500
Office fax: (321) 242-0760
General e-mail: brevardcounty@MomsLikeMe.com
Website: brevardcounty.momslikeme.com
Mechanical specifications: Type page 9 1/2 x 11.
Frequency: Mthly
Circulation Free: 29950
Audit By: Sworn/Estimate/Non-Audited
Audit Date: 12.07.2019
Personnel: Ann Greeville (Adv. Mgr.); Kim Lyons (Adv. Mgr.); Sharon Kindred (Ed.); Corinne Ishler (Prodn. Mgr.)
Main (survey) contact: Suzy Leonard

OAKLAND

METRO PARENT MAGAZINE

Street address 1: 22041 Woodward Ave
Street address city: Ferndale
Street address state: MI
Postal code: 48220-2520
Country: USA
Mailing address 1: 22041 Woodward Ave
Mailing city: Ferndale
Mailing state: MI
Mailing zip: 48220-2520
Office phone: (248) 398-3400
Office fax: (248) 399-4215
General e-mail: metroparent@metroparent.com
Website: www.metroparent.com
Advertising (open inch rate): N/A
Mechanical specifications: Type page 9 1/2 x 11 1/4; E - 4 cols, between; A - 4 cols, between.
Zip Codes Served: 48075
Frequency: Mthly
Circulation Free: 59763
Audit By: CVC
Audit Date: 30.06.2015
Personnel: Alyssa Martina (Pub.); Alexis Bourkoulas (Gen. Mgr.); Tracy Connelly (Office Mgr.); Ruth Robbins (Assoc. Pub.); Julia Elliott (Ed.)
Main (survey) contact: Alyssa Martina

OKLAHOMA

METROFAMILY MAGAZINE

Street address 1: 318 NW 13th St
Street address 2: Ste 101
Street address city: Oklahoma City
Street address state: OK
Postal code: 73103-3709
Country: USA
Mailing address 1: 318 NW 13th Street
Mailing city: Oklahoma City
Mailing state: OK
Mailing zip: 73103-3709
Office phone: (405) 601-2081
Office fax: (405) 445-7509
General e-mail: sarah@metrofamilymagazine.com
Advertising e-mail: sarah@metrofamilymagazine.com
Editorial e-mail: hannah@metrofamilymagazine.com
Website: www.metrofamilymagazine.com
Year publication established: 1998
Advertising (open inch rate): full page open rate: $2024
Delivery methods: Racks
Zip Codes Served: 73034, 73013, 73120, 73116, 73069 (and many more)
Digital Platform - Mobile: Apple`Android
Digital Platform - Tablet: Apple iOS`Android
Frequency: Mthly
Circulation Paid: 20
Circulation Free: 30000
Audit By: CVC
Audit Date: 30.09.2018
Editions Count: 12
Personnel: Kathy Alberty (Dist. Mgr.); Sarah Taylor (Publisher); Hannah Schmitt (Editor)
Main (survey) contact: Sarah Taylor

ONONDAGA

SYRACUSE PARENT

Street address 1: 5910 Firestone Dr
Street address city: Syracuse
Street address state: NY
Postal code: 13206-1103
Country: USA
Mailing address 1: 5910 Firestone Dr
Mailing city: Syracuse
Mailing state: NY
Mailing zip: 13206-1103
Office phone: (315) 434-8889
Office fax: (315) 434-8883
General e-mail: syracuseparent@ yahoo.com
Editorial e-mail: editor@syracuseparent.net
Website: www.syracuseparent.net
Mechanical specifications: Type page 10 x 13; E - 4 cols, 2 1/4, 1/4 between; A - 4 cols, 2 1/4, 1/4 between; C - 6 cols, 1 1/4, 1/8 between.
Frequency: Mthly
Circulation Free: 26500
Audit By: Sworn/Estimate/Non-Audited
Audit Date: 12.07.2019
Hardware: PC
Presses: G/Community
Software: Adobe/PageMaker.
Personnel: Linda Tocci (Adv. Mgr.); Colleen Kompf (Adv. Sales); Rachel Gillette (Prodn. Mgr.)
Main (survey) contact: Linda Tocci

ORANGE

HUDSON VALLEY PARENT

Street address 1: 174 South St
Street address city: Newburgh
Street address state: NY
Postal code: 12550-4546
Country: USA
Mailing address 1: 174 South St
Mailing city: Newburgh
Mailing state: NY
Mailing zip: 12550-4546
Office phone: (845) 562-3606
Office fax: (845) 562-3681
General e-mail: publisher@excitingread.com
Advertising e-mail: sales@excitingread.com
Editorial e-mail: editor@excitingread.com
Website: www.hvparent.com
Year publication established: 1994

Parenting Publications in the U.S.

III-775

Delivery methods: Carrier
Frequency: Mthly
Circulation Free: 36000
Audit By: Sworn/Estimate/Non-Audited
Audit Date: 12.07.2019
Personnel: Terrie Goldstein (Pub.); Felicia Hodges (Editor)
Main (survey) contact: Felicia Hodges

ORANGE

PARENTING MAGAZINE OF ORANGE COUNTY

Street address 1: 172 N Tustin St
Street address 2: Ste 304
Street address city: Orange
Street address state: CA
Postal code: 92867-7780
Country: USA
Mailing address 1: 1100 N Tustin Ave Ste 101
Mailing city: Anaheim
Mailing state: CA
Mailing zip: 92807-1730
Office phone: (714) 771-7454
Office fax: (714) 771-5852
Website: www.parentingoc.com
Advertising (open inch rate): Open inch rate $105
Mechanical specifications: Type page 10 1/8 x 12; E - 4 cols, 2 1/4, 1/6 between; A - 4 cols, 2 1/4, 1/6 between; C - 5 cols, 1 3/4, 1/6 between.
Frequency: Mthly
Circulation Paid: 108
Circulation Free: 80000
Audit By: Sworn/Estimate/Non-Audited
Audit Date: 12.07.2019
Hardware: APP/Mac G3
Presses: WPC, G
Software: QPS/QuarkXPress 4.0.
Personnel: Randall Tierney (Ed. in Chief); Bahram Fattahinia (Art Dir.)
Main (survey) contact: Randall Tierney

PHILADELPHIA

BALTIMORE'S CHILD

Street address 1: 1414 Pine St
Street address city: Philadelphia
Street address state: PA
Postal code: 19102-4603
Country: USA
Mailing address 1: 11 Dutton Ct
Mailing city: Baltimore
Mailing state: MD
Mailing zip: 21228-4922
Office phone: (410) 542-4166
Office fax: 443-697-0212
General e-mail: info@baltimoreschild.com
Website: www.baltimoreschild.com
Year publication established: 1983
Advertising (open inch rate): Open inch rate $40.40
Mechanical specifications: Full page:7.125 x 9.4375, 1/2 page: 3.5 x 9.4375, 1/3 page: 2.25 x 9.4375, 1/4 page: 3.5 x 4.625. Other sizes available.
Delivery methods: Racks
Zip Codes Served: 20707, 20708, 20723, 20724, 20759, 20763, 20777, 20794, 21001, 21005, 21009, 21014, 21015, 21017, 21017, 21022, 21028, 21029, 21030, 21030, 21031, 21040, 21042, 21043, 21044, 21045, 21046, 21047, 21048, 21050, 21051, 21057, 21061, 21071, 21074, 21075, 21076, 21078, 21084, 21085, 21087, 21090, 21093, 21093, 21102, 21104, 21108, 21111, 21113, 21117, 21120, 21122, 21128, 21131, 21136, 21146, 21153, 21156, 21157, 21158, 21162, 21163, 21201, 21202, 21203, 21204, 21205, 21206, 21207, 21208, 21209, 21210, 21211, 21212, 21213, 21214, 21215, 21216, 21217, 21218, 21219, 21220, 21221, 21221, 21222, 21223, 21224, 21225, 21225, 21226, 21226, 21227, 21228, 21229, 21230, 21231, 21234, 21234, 21235, 21236, 21237, 21239, 21244, 21252, 21285, 21286, 21287, 21401, 21723, 21771, 21771, 21776, 21784, 21784, 21797, 21901, 21903, 21904, 21911, 21914, 21915, 21915, 21919, 21921,
21930, 21102-0408, 21229-5299
Digital Platform - Mobile: Apple`Android
Digital Platform - Tablet: Apple iOS`Android`Kindle
Frequency: Mthly
Circulation Free: 45000
Audit By: Sworn/Estimate/Non-Audited
Audit Date: 12.07.2019
Personnel: Joanne Giza (Pub.); Sharon Keech (Mng. Ed.); Jen Perkins Frantz (Prodn. Mgr.)
Main (survey) contact: Sharon Keech

METROKIDS DELAWARE

Street address 1: 1412-1414 Pine St
Street address city: Philadelphia
Street address state: PA
Postal code: 19102
Country: USA
Mailing address 1: 1412-1414 Pine St.
Mailing city: Philadelphia
Mailing state: PA
Mailing zip: 19102-4603
Office phone: (856) 667-3555
Office fax: (215) 291-5563
General e-mail: info@metrokids.com
Advertising e-mail: sales@metrokids.com
Editorial e-mail: editor@metrokids.com
Website: www.metrokids.com
Year publication established: 1990
Mechanical specifications: Type page 10 x 12 3/8; E - 4 cols, 2 3/8, 1/6 between; A - 4 cols, 2 3/8, 1/6 between; C - 4 cols, 2 3/8, 1/6 between.
Zip Codes Served: 19701, 19973, 21901, 21921
Frequency: Mthly
Hardware: APP/Macs.
Personnel: Darlene Weinmann (Adv. Mgr.); Andrea Spiegel (Circ. Mgr.); Nancy Lisagor (Ed. in Chief); Tom Livingston (Exec. Ed.); Tracie Rucker (Prod. Mgr.)
Main (survey) contact: Darlene Weinmann

METROKIDS SOUTH JERSEY

Street address 1: 1412-1414 Pine St
Street address city: Philadelphia
Street address state: PA
Postal code: 19102
Country: USA
Mailing address 1: 1412-1414 Pine St.
Mailing city: Philadelphia
Mailing state: PA
Mailing zip: 19102-4603
Office phone: (215) 291-5560
Office fax: (215) 291-5563
General e-mail: info@metrokids.com
Advertising e-mail: sales@metrokids.com
Editorial e-mail: editor@metrokids.com
Website: www.metrokids.com
Mechanical specifications: Type page 10 x 11 1/4; E - 4 cols, 2 3/8, between; A - 4 cols, 2 3/8, between; C - 5 cols, 1 5/8, between.
Zip Codes Served: 08002, 08691
Frequency: Mthly
Hardware: APP/Mac
Software: QPS/QuarkXPress.
Personnel: Darlene Weinmann (Adv. Mgr.); Andrea Miller (Circ. Mgr.); Nancy Lisagor (Ed. in Chief); Tom Livingston (Exec. Ed.); Tracie Rucker (Prod. Mgr.)
Main (survey) contact: Darlene Weinmann

PLACER

SACRAMENTO PARENT

Street address 1: 457 Grass Valley Hwy
Street address 2: Ste 5
Street address city: Auburn
Street address state: CA
Postal code: 95603-3725
Country: USA
Mailing address 1: 457 Grass Valley Hwy Ste 5
Mailing city: Auburn
Mailing state: CA
Mailing zip: 95603-3725
Office phone: (530) 888-0573
Office fax: (530) 888-1536
General e-mail: info@sacramentoparent.com
Website: www.sacramentoparent.com
Year publication established: 1992
Advertising (open inch rate): N/A
Frequency: Mthly
Circulation Free: 44975
Audit By: CVC
Audit Date: 30.06.2014
Main (survey) contact: Sue Leto Cole

PULASKI

LITTLE ROCK FAMILY

Street address 1: 114 Scott St
Street address city: Little Rock
Street address state: AR
Postal code: 72201-1514
Country: USA
Mailing address 1: PO Box 3686
Mailing city: Little Rock
Mailing state: AR
Mailing zip: 72203-3686
Office phone: (501) 372-1443
Office fax: (501) 375-7933
Advertising e-mail: rtucker@abpg.com
Editorial e-mail: mbettis@abpg.com
Website: www.littlerockfamily.com
Year publication established: 1994
Advertising (open inch rate): N/A
Delivery methods: Racks
Frequency: Mthly
Circulation Free: 19947
Audit By: CVC
Audit Date: 30.06.2015
Personnel: Robin Tucker (Sales Dir); Mitch Bettis (Pub)
Parent company: Arkansas Business Publishing Group
Main (survey) contact: Mitch Bettis

SAINT LOUIS

SAVVY FAMILY

Street address 1: 14522 S Outer 40 Rd
Street address city: Chesterfield
Street address state: MO
Postal code: 63017-5737
Country: USA
Mailing address 1: 14522 S Outer 40 Rd
Mailing city: Chesterfield
Mailing state: MO
Mailing zip: 63017-5737
Office phone: (314) 821-1110
Office fax: (314) 821-3408
Website: www.stltoday.com
Frequency: Mthly
Hardware: IBM, APP/Mac.
Personnel: Mary Ann Wagner (Pub.)
Main (survey) contact: Mary Ann Wagner

SAN DIEGO

SAN DIEGO FAMILY MAGAZINE

Street address 1: 1475 6th Ave
Street address 2: #500
Street address city: San Diego
Street address state: CA
Postal code: 92101-3245
Country: USA
Mailing address 1: 1475 6th Ave, #500
Mailing city: San Diego
Mailing state: CA
Mailing zip: 92101
Office phone: (619) 685-6970
Office fax: (619) 685-6978
General e-mail: family@sandiegofamily.com
Advertising e-mail: sharon@sandiegofamily.com
Editorial e-mail: sharon@sandiegofamily.com
Website: www.sandiegofamily.com
Year publication established: 1982
Advertising (open inch rate): N/A
Mechanical specifications: Type page 8 x 10; E - 3 cols, 2 1/4, between; A - 3 cols, 2 1/4, between; C - 4 cols, 1 3/4, between.
Delivery methods: Racks
Zip Codes Served: All of San Diego County
Digital Platform - Mobile: Apple
Digital Platform - Tablet: Apple iOS
Frequency: Mthly
Circulation Paid: 24
Circulation Free: 75000
Audit By: Sworn/Estimate/Non-Audited
Audit Date: 12.07.2019
Hardware: APP/Mac
Software: Adobe/Photoshop, Macromedia/Freehand.
Personnel: Sharon Bay (Pub); Michele Hancock (Mktg. Coord.)
Main (survey) contact: Sharon Bay

THE PARENT CONNECTION/SCRIPPS MEMORIAL HOSPITAL

Street address 1: 4275 Campus Point Ct # CP10
Street address 2: Scripps Memorial Hospital
Street address city: San Diego
Street address state: CA
Postal code: 92121-1513
Country: USA
Mailing address 1: 4275 Campus Pt. Ct. CP10
Mailing city: San Diego
Mailing state: CA
Mailing zip: 92122
Office phone: (858) 626-6944
General e-mail: info@sandiegoparent.com
Advertising e-mail: info@sandiegoparent.com
Website: www.sandiegoparent.com
Year publication established: 1980
Delivery methods: Mail
Digital Platform - Mobile: Apple`Android`Windows`Blackberry
Frequency: Mthly
Circulation Paid: 1500
Circulation Free: 1000
Audit By: Sworn/Estimate/Non-Audited
Audit Date: 12.07.2019
Hardware: APP/Mac G3
Presses: WPC, G
Software: QPS/QuarkXPress 4.0.
Personnel: Pam Nagata (Coord); Martha Stillwell (Adv. Mgr.); Alison Rob (Circ. Mgr.); Colleen McNatt (Ed.); Angel Salazar (Prodn. Mgr.)
Parent company: Parent Connection
Main (survey) contact: Pam Nagata

SANTA CLARA

BAY AREA PARENT

Street address 1: 901 Campisi Way
Street address 2: Ste 300
Street address city: Campbell
Street address state: CA
Postal code: 95008-2376
Country: USA
Mailing address 1: 901 Campisi Way #300
Mailing city: Campbell
Mailing state: CA
Mailing zip: 95008-2087
Office phone: (408) 533-4413
Office fax: (408) 963-6124
Advertising phone: (408) 533-4403
Other phone: (408) 533-4403
General e-mail: dawn.hall@parenthood.com
Advertising e-mail: dawn.hall@parenthood.com
Editorial e-mail: jill.wolfson@parenthood.com
Website: www.bayareaparent.com
Year publication established: 1983
Delivery methods: Newsstand`Racks
Zip Codes Served: 6 county bay area
Digital Platform - Mobile: Apple`Android`Windows`Other
Digital Platform - Tablet: Apple iOS`Android
Frequency: Mthly
Other Type of Frequency: Five print special editions plus 16 special digital-only magazines
Circulation Paid: 0
Circulation Free: 122000
Audit By: CVC
Audit Date: 12.12.2017
Editions Count: 3
Edition Names: 3 total Ã‚Â— East Bay Edition; San Francisco City & Peninsula Edition; Silicon Valley Edition;
Personnel: Jill Wolfson (Editor); Daniel Payomo Jr (Group Publisher)
Main (survey) contact: Daniel Payomo Jr.

SHELBY

MEMPHIS PARENT
Street address 1: 65 Union Avenue
Street address 2: 2nd Floor
Street address city: Memphis
Street address state: TN
Postal code: 38103
Country: USA
Mailing address 1: 65 Union Avenue, 2nd Floor
Mailing city: Memphis
Mailing state: TN
Mailing zip: 38103
Office phone: (901) 521-9000
Office fax: (901) 521-0129
General e-mail: mphsparent@contemporary-media.com
Website: www.memphisparent.com
Advertising (open inch rate): N/A
Mechanical specifications: Type page 9 3/4 x 12 1/2; E - 4 cols, 2 5/16, 1/4 between; A - 4 cols, 2 5/16, between; C - 4 cols, 2 5/16, between.
Frequency: Mthly
Circulation Free: 34975
Audit By: CVC
Audit Date: 30.06.2015
Personnel: Kenneth Neill (Pub./CEO); Bryan Rollins (Art Dir.); Shara Clark (Mng. Ed.); Sheryl Butler (Adv. Dir.)
Main (survey) contact: Shara Clark

SNOHOMISH

SEATTLE'S CHILD
Street address 1: 4303 198th St SW
Street address city: Lynnwood
Street address state: WA
Postal code: 98036-6777
Country: USA
Mailing address 1: 4303 198th St SW
Mailing city: Lynnwood
Mailing state: WA
Mailing zip: 98036-6725
Office phone: (206) 441-0191
Office fax: (425) 774-8622
Editorial e-mail: editor@seattleschild.com
Website: www.seattleschild.com
Mechanical specifications: Type page 10 3/16 x 13 1/4.
Zip Codes Served: 98121
Frequency: Mthly
Circulation Free: 80000
Audit By: Sworn/Estimate/Non-Audited
Audit Date: 12.07.2019
Editions Count: 1
Edition Names: 1 total Ã‚Â— Snohomish Co. (28,000);
Personnel: Mary Armstrong (Pub. Asst.); Ann Bergman (Ed.)
Main (survey) contact: Ann Bergman

SONOMA

FAMILY-LIFE MAGAZINE
Street address 1: 134 Lystra Ct
Street address city: Santa Rosa
Street address state: CA
Postal code: 95403-8076
Country: USA
Mailing address 1: PO Box 351
Mailing city: Philo
Mailing state: CA
Mailing zip: 95466-0351
Office phone: (707) 305 1539
Office fax: (707) 895-2154
Advertising phone: (707) 205-1539
Advertising fax: (707) 586-9571
Editorial phone: (707) 205-1544
Editorial fax: (707) 586-9571
Other phone: (707) 895-2223
Other fax: (707) 895-2154
General e-mail: info@family-life.us
Advertising e-mail: Sales@family-life.us
Editorial e-mail: Editor@family-life.us
Website: www.sonomafamilylife.com
Year publication established: 1989
Delivery methods: Mail`Carrier`Racks
Digital Platform - Mobile: Apple
Digital Platform - Tablet: Apple iOS
Frequency: Mthly
Other Type of Frequency: Weekly E-newsletters.
Circulation Free: 46000
Audit By: VAC
Audit Date: 27.12.2012
Editions Count: 2
Edition Names: Sonoma Family Life Magazine & Mendo Lake Family Life Magazine
Personnel: Sharon Gowan (Publisher/Editor)
Main (survey) contact: Sharon Gowan

SONOMA FAMILY-LIFE MAGAZINE
Street address 1: 100 Professional Center Dr
Street address 2: Ste 104
Street address city: Rohnert Park
Street address state: CA
Postal code: 94928-2137
Country: USA
Mailing address 1: PO Box 351
Mailing city: Philo
Mailing state: CA
Mailing zip: 95466-0351
Office phone: (707) 586-9562
Office fax: (707) 895-2154
General e-mail: info@family-life.us
Website: www.sonomafamilylife.com
Advertising (open inch rate): Open inch rate $15.00
Frequency: Mthly
Circulation Free: 23000
Audit By: Sworn/Estimate/Non-Audited
Audit Date: 12.07.2019
Personnel: Sharon Gowan (Ed.)
Main (survey) contact: Sharon Gowan

STOKES

PIEDMONT PARENT
Street address 1: PO Box 530
Street address city: King
Street address state: NC
Postal code: 27021-0530
Country: USA
Mailing address 1: PO Box 530
Mailing city: King
Mailing state: NC
Mailing zip: 27021-0530
Office phone: (336) 983-4789
Office fax: (336) 983-2378
General e-mail: info@piedmontparent.com
Website: www.piedmontparent.com
Advertising (open inch rate): N/A
Frequency: Mthly
Circulation Paid: 1
Circulation Free: 30766
Audit By: CVC
Audit Date: 30.09.2014
Personnel: Sharon Havranek (Pub.); Myra Wrigh (Ed.)
Main (survey) contact: Myra Wrigh

TRUMBULL

MAHONING VALLEY PARENT MAGAZINE
Street address 1: 240 Franklin St SE
Street address city: Warren
Street address state: OH
Postal code: 44483-5711
Country: USA
Mailing address 1: 240 Franklin St SE
Mailing city: Warren
Mailing state: OH
Mailing zip: 44483-5711
Office phone: (330) 629-6229
Advertising phone: (330) 651-5411
General e-mail: editor@mvparentmagazine.com
Advertising e-mail: advertising@forparentsonline.com
Editorial e-mail: editor@mvparentmagazine.com
Website: www.forparentsonline.com
Year publication established: 1989
Mechanical specifications: Type page 7 1/4 x 9 1/2; E - 5 cols, 2 5/16, 1/12 between; A - 5 cols, 2 5/16, 1/12 between; C - 5 cols, 2 5/16, 1/12 between.
Delivery methods: Carrier
Zip Codes Served: 44512, 44514, 44515, 44484, 44408
Frequency: Mthly
Circulation Free: 36830
Audit By: CVC
Audit Date: 30.06.2012
Edition Names: Trumbull County Parent Magazine
Personnel: Robert Kurtz (Adv. Sales); Amy Leigh Wilson (Ed.)
Parent company: Ogden Newspapers Inc.
Main (survey) contact: Amy Leigh Wilson

TULSA

TULSAKIDS
Street address 1: 1622 S Denver Ave
Street address city: Tulsa
Street address state: OK
Postal code: 74119-4233
Country: USA
Mailing address 1: 224 S Market St
Mailing city: Troy
Mailing state: OH
Mailing zip: 45373-3327
Office phone: (918) 582-8504
Office fax: (918) 583-1366
Website: www.tulsakids.com
Frequency: Mthly
Personnel: Chuck Foshee (Pub.); Betty Casey (Mng. Ed.)
Main (survey) contact: Chuck Foshee; Betty Casey

UNION

KANSAS CITY PARENT
Street address 1: 1122 US Highway 22
Street address city: Mountainside
Street address state: NJ
Postal code: 07092-2812
Country: USA
Mailing address 1: 11936 W 119th St Ste 335
Mailing city: Overland Park
Mailing state: KS
Mailing zip: 66213-2216
Office phone: (913) 782-3238
Office fax: (913) 681-5139
General e-mail: kcparent@mindspring.com
Advertising e-mail: advertising@kcparent.com
Editorial e-mail: editor@kcparent.com
Website: www.kcparent.com
Year publication established: 1985
Advertising (open inch rate): N/A
Mechanical specifications: Type page 10 1/2 x 12.
Frequency: Mthly
Circulation Free: 26200
Audit By: CVC
Audit Date: 30.06.2014
Personnel: L. Richard Bruursema (Pub.)
Main (survey) contact: L. Richard Bruursema

NEW JERSEY FAMILY
Street address 1: 480 Morris Ave
Street address city: Summit
Street address state: NJ
Postal code: 07901-1523
Country: USA
Mailing address 1: 480 Morris Ave.
Mailing city: Summit
Mailing state: NJ
Mailing zip: 07901
Office phone: 9082771919
Office fax: 9082771977
Advertising phone: 9082771919x110
Editorial phone: 9082771919
General e-mail: publisher@njfamily.com
Advertising e-mail: sales@njfamily.com
Editorial e-mail: dina@njfamily.com
Website: www.njfamily.com
Year publication established: 1990
Advertising (open inch rate): N/A
Mechanical specifications: Type page 7 7/8 x 10 1/8.
Delivery methods: Newsstand`Racks
Zip Codes Served: 07901
Digital Platform - Mobile: Apple
Digital Platform - Tablet: Apple iOS
Frequency: Mthly
Circulation Paid: 8
Circulation Free: 134221
Audit By: CVC
Audit Date: 30.06.2017
Editions Count: 5
Edition Names: Central, Essex, Morris, North, Union
Personnel: Cindy Mironovich (Co-Pub.); Mary Lucid (Bus. Mgr.); Marcy Holeton (Advertising Director); Dina El Nabli (Editorial Director)
Main (survey) contact: Dina El Nabli

WARREN

Street address 1: 9435 Waterstone Blvd
Street address 2: Ste 140
Street address city: Cincinnati
Street address state: OH
Postal code: 45249-8229

WESTCHESTER

CAROLINA PARENT
Street address 1: 5716 Fayetteville Rd.
Street address 2: Suite 201
Street address city: Durham
Street address state: NC
Postal code: 27713
Country: USA
Mailing address 1: 5716 Fayetteville Rd., Suite 201
Mailing city: Durham
Mailing state: NC
Mailing zip: 27713
Office phone: (919) 956-2430
Office fax: (919) 956-2427
General e-mail: info@carolinaparent.com
Advertising e-mail: cgriffin@carolinaparent.com
Editorial e-mail: bshugg@carolinaparent.com
Website: www.carolinaparent.com
Year publication established: 1988
Advertising (open inch rate): N/A
Mechanical specifications: Page 7.125x9.25; 1/2 page (h) 7.125 x 4.5; 1/2 page (v) 3.475 x 9.25; 1/4 page 3.475 x 4.5; 1/8 page 3.475 x 2.187
Delivery methods: Carrier`Racks
Zip Codes Served: 27701
Digital Platform - Mobile: Apple`Android`Windows`Blackberry
Digital Platform - Tablet: Apple iOS`Android`Windows 7`Blackberry Tablet OS`Kindle`Nook`Kindle Fire
Frequency: Mthly
Circulation Free: 37044
Audit By: CVC
Audit Date: 30.06.2015
Hardware: APP/Mac
Software: Adobe, CS6, Microsoft Office packages
Personnel: Julianne Clune (Adv. Serv. Coor.); Beth Shugg (Ed.); Katie Reeves (Pub.); Lauren Isaacs (Dig & Social Media Specialist); Janice Lewine (Assoc. Ed.)
Parent company: Morris Media Network/Morris Visitor Publications
Main (survey) contact: Katie Reeves

CONNECTICUT FAMILY
Street address 1: 141 Halstead Ave
Street address 2: Ste 3D
Street address city: Mamaroneck
Street address state: NY
Postal code: 10543-2607
Country: USA
Mailing address 1: 141 Halstead Ave Ste 3D
Mailing city: Mamaroneck
Mailing state: NY
Mailing zip: 10543-2607
Office phone: (203) 625-9825
Office fax: (914) 381-7672
General e-mail: mamaroneckreception@unitedad.com

Parenting Publications in the U.S.

Website: www.parenthood.com
Frequency: Mthly
Personnel: Thomas Butcher (Circ. Mgr.); Heather Hart (Ed.)
Main (survey) contact: Heather Hart

WESTCHESTER PARENT

Street address 1: 1872 Pleasantville Rd
Street address 2: Ste 173
Street address city: Briarcliff Manor
Street address state: NY
Postal code: 10510-1051
Country: USA
Mailing address 1: 901 N Broadway Ste 21
Mailing city: White Plains
Mailing state: NY
Mailing zip: 10603-2414
Office phone: (914) 397-0200
Office fax: (914) 397-1466
Website: www.nymetroparents.com
Advertising (open inch rate): N/A
Frequency: Mthly
Circulation Free: 55004
Audit By: CVC
Audit Date: 30.06.2014
Personnel: David Miller (Pub.); Phyllis Singer (Ed. Dir.); Christine Tarulli (Mng. Ed.)
Main (survey) contact: Phyllis Singer

WESTCHESTER FAMILY

Street address 1: 1872 Pleasantville Road, Suite 173
Street address city: Braircliff Manor
Street address state: NY
Postal code: 10510
Country: USA
Mailing address 1: 1872 Pleasantville Road
Mailing city: Braircliff Manor
Mailing state: NY
Mailing zip: 10510
Office phone: (914) 381-7474
Office fax: (914) 462-3311
General e-mail: jean.sheff@westchesterfamily.com
Website: http://westchesterfamily.com/

Advertising (open inch rate): N/A
Frequency: Mthly
Circulation Paid: 0
Circulation Free: 35000
Audit By: Sworn/Estimate/Non-Audited
Audit Date: 12.07.2019
Personnel: Jean Sheff (Ed./Co-Pub)
Main (survey) contact: Jean Sheff

WILLIAMSON

AUSTIN FAMILY

Street address 1: PO Box 7559
Street address city: Round Rock
Street address state: TX
Postal code: 78683-7559
Country: USA
Mailing address 1: PO Box 7559
Mailing city: Round Rock
Mailing state: TX
Mailing zip: 78683-7559
Office phone: (512) 733-0038
Advertising e-mail: kaye2003@austinfamily.com
Editorial e-mail: editor2003@austinfamily.com
Website: www.austinfamily.com
Year publication established: 1991
Mechanical specifications: Type page 10 x 13.
Frequency: Mthly
Circulation Free: 35000
Audit By: Sworn/Estimate/Non-Audited
Audit Date: 12.07.2019
Personnel: Kaye Kemper (Pub.); Melanie Dunham (Ed.); Dr. Betty Kehl Richardson (Advising Ed.); John Faranzetti (Art Dir.); Betty Kemper (Calendar Ed.)
Main (survey) contact: Kaye Kemper

MORRIS COUNTY FAMILY

Street address 1: 480 Morris Ave.
Street address city: Summit
Street address state: NJ
Postal code: 07901
Country: USA
Mailing address 1: 480 Morris Ave.

Mailing city: Summit
Mailing state: NJ
Mailing zip: 07901
Office phone: (908) 277-1919
General e-mail: publisher@njfamily.com
Editorial e-mail: editor@njfamily.com
Website: www.njfamily.com
Mechanical specifications: Type page 7 7/8 x 10 1/8.
Frequency: Mthly
Circulation Free: 30000
Audit By: Sworn/Estimate/Non-Audited
Audit Date: 12.07.2019
Personnel: Cindy Mironovich (Pub.); Mary Lucid (Bus. Mgr.); Linda Galli (Dir., Adv.); Dina El Nabli (Ed. Dir.); Angel Madison (Mng. Ed.)
Main (survey) contact: Mary Lucid

NEW JERSEY FAMILY

Street address 1: 1122 Rt. 22 W.
Street address city: Mountainside
Street address state: NJ
Postal code: 07092-2812
Country: USA
Mailing address 1: 1122 US Highway 22 Ste 204
Mailing city: Mountainside
Mailing state: NJ
Mailing zip: 07092-2813
Office phone: (908) 232-2913
Office fax: (908) 317-9518
General e-mail: publisher@njfamily.com
Editorial e-mail: editor@njfamily.com
Website: www.njfamily.com
Year publication established: 1991
Mechanical specifications: Type page 7 7/8 x 10 1/8.
Frequency: Mthly
Circulation Free: 126000
Audit By: Sworn/Estimate/Non-Audited
Audit Date: 12.07.2019
Personnel: Cindy Mironovich (Pub.); Bonnie Vohden (Assoc. Pub.); Linda Galli (Dir., Adv.); Farn Dupre (Ed.); Lucy Banta (Mng. Ed.)
Main (survey) contact: Bonnie Vohden

WASHINGTON FAMILY MAGAZINE

Street address 1: 11900 Parklawn Dr.
Street address 2: Ste. 300
Street address city: Rockville
Street address state: MD
Postal code: 20852
Country: USA
Mailing address 1: 11900 Parklawn Dr., Ste. 300
Mailing city: Rockville
Mailing state: MD
Mailing zip: 20852
Office phone: (301) 230-2222
Advertising phone: (301) 230-0819
Editorial phone: (301) 230-6696
Other phone: (301) 230-2222
General e-mail: info@washingtonfamily.com
Advertising e-mail: advertising@washingtonfamily.com
Editorial e-mail: editor@washingtonfamily.com
Website: www.washingtonfamily.com
Year publication established: 1992
Advertising (open inch rate): N/A
Mechanical specifications: Type page 8 x 11; E - 3 cols, 1 11/16, 1/2 between; A - 3 cols, 1 11/16, 1/2 between; C - 3 cols, 1 11/16, 1/2 between.
Delivery methods: Racks
Digital Platform - Mobile: Apple`Android`Windows`Blackberry
Digital Platform - Tablet: Apple iOS`Android`Windows 7`Blackberry Tablet OS`Kindle`Kindle Fire
Frequency: Mthly
Circulation Paid: 7
Circulation Free: 53500
Audit By: CVC
Audit Date: 31.03.2017
Hardware: APP/Mac
Software: Adobe/InDesign
Personnel: Craig Burke (Chief Operating Officer); Sylvia Witaschek (Assoc. Pub.)
Parent company: Northern Virginia Media Services
Main (survey) contact: Sylvia Witaschek

REAL ESTATE PUBLICATIONS IN THE U.S.

ALTA LOMA

THE HOMES MAGAZINE

Street address 1: 6683 Capitol Pl
Street address state: CA
Postal code: 91701-7784
County: San Bernardino
Country: USA
Mailing address: 6683 Capitol Pl
Mailing city: Alta Loma
Mailing state: CA
Mailing zip: 91701-7784
Office phone: (909) 948-7255
Office fax: (909) 948-7258
General e-mail: homemag@earthlink.net
Website: www.thehomesmagazine.com
Frequency: Mthly
Circulation Free: 25500
Audit By: Sworn/Estimate/Non-Audited
Audit Date: 12.07.2019
Hardware: APP/Mac G3
Software: QPS/QuarkXPress 3.3.
Personnel: Connie Endter (Pub.); Dave Endter (Gen. Mgr.)
Main (survey) contact: Dave Endter

ATASCADERO

CENTRAL COAST HOMES MAGAZINE

Street address 1: 7544 Morro Rd

Street address state: CA
Postal code: 93422-4404
County: San Luis Obispo
Country: USA
Mailing address: PO Box 657
Mailing city: Atascadero
Mailing state: CA
Mailing zip: 93423-0657
Office phone: (805) 461-7898
Office fax: (805) 466-8359
General e-mail: mraike@homesmagazine.com; sales@globalhomes.com
Website: www.globalhomes.com
Frequency: Mthly
Circulation Free: 30000
Audit By: Sworn/Estimate/Non-Audited
Audit Date: 12.07.2019
Personnel: Mike Raike (Pub.)
Main (survey) contact: Mike Raike

BOHEMIA

FSBO

Street address 1: 3140 Veterans Memorial Hwy
Street address state: NY
Postal code: 11716-1039
County: Suffolk
Country: USA
Mailing address: 3140 Veterans Memorial Hwy
Mailing city: Bohemia
Mailing state: NY
Mailing zip: 11716-1039
Office phone: (800) 584-3726
Office fax: (631) 928-1755

General e-mail: info@lifsbo.com
Year publication established: 1988
Mechanical specifications: Type page 7 x 10.
Other Type of Frequency: 17 x a year
Circulation Free: 50000
Audit By: Sworn/Estimate/Non-Audited
Audit Date: 12.07.2019
Software: QPS/QuarkXPress 3.30.
Personnel: Sean Scully (Ed.); Henry Lutz (Wine Reporter/ Copy Ed.); Barry Eberling (Napa County Reporter); Sasha Paulsen (Features Ed.)
Parent company: Dispatch-Argus
Main (survey) contact: Sean Scully

BRATTLEBORO

NEW ENGLAND SHOWCASE

Street address 1: 14 Noahs Lane
Street address 2: P.O. Box 996
Street address state: VT
Postal code: 05302-0996
County: Windham
Country: USA
Mailing address: 14 Noahs Lane, P.O. Box 996
Mailing city: Brattleboro
Mailing state: VT
Mailing zip: 05302-0996
Office phone: (802) 257-4387
Office fax: (802) 257-1453
General e-mail: info@newenglandshowcase.com
Editorial e-mail: editor@newenglandshowcase.com

Website: www.newenglandshowcase.com
Zip Codes Served: 5303
Other Type of Frequency: 3 x Mthly
Circulation Free: 20000
Audit By: Sworn/Estimate/Non-Audited
Audit Date: 12.07.2019
Edition Names: 2 total New England Showcase-Central and N. Vermont/W. New Hampshire
Personnel: Teresa M. Galligan (Pub.); Charles Kamins (Mng. Ed.); Heather N. Hayne (Prodn. Mgr.)
Main (survey) contact: Teresa M. Galligan

CANTON

FOR SALE BY OWNER CONNECTION

Street address 1: PO Box 602
Street address state: CT
Postal code: 06019-0602
County: Hartford
Country: USA
Mailing address: PO Box 602
Mailing city: Canton
Mailing state: CT
Mailing zip: 06019
Office phone: (860) 659-3726
Office fax: (860) 633-1850
General e-mail: info@cutthecommission.com
Website: www.cutthecommission.com
Zip Codes Served: 6019
Frequency: Mthly
Circulation Free: 60000
Audit By: Sworn/Estimate/Non-Audited

Audit Date: 12.07.2019
Personnel: Greg Castro (Circ. Mgr.)
Main (survey) contact: Greg Castro

CHARLOTTE

HOMES & LAND OF METRO CHARLOTTE

Street address 1: 4525 Park Rd
Street address 2: Ste B202
Street address state: NC
Postal code: 28209-3704
County: Mecklenburg
Country: USA
Mailing address: 4525 Park Rd Ste 202
Mailing city: Charlotte
Mailing state: NC
Mailing zip: 28209-3834
Office phone: (704) 527-6553
Office fax: (704) 527-6118
General e-mail: clthomes@attglobal.net
Website: www.homesandland.com
Frequency: Mthly
Circulation Free: 40000
Audit By: Sworn/Estimate/Non-Audited
Audit Date: 12.07.2019
Personnel: Carol York (Ed.)
Main (survey) contact: Carol York

CHATTANOOGA

BUY A HOME

Street address 1: 3407 Fleeta Ln
Street address state: TN
Postal code: 37416-2802
County: Hamilton
Country: USA
Mailing address: 3407 Fleeta Ln
Mailing city: Chattanooga
Mailing state: TN
Mailing zip: 37416-2802
Office phone: (423) 855-1831
Office fax: (423) 499-8543
Frequency: Mthly
Circulation Free: 18000
Audit By: Sworn/Estimate/Non-Audited
Audit Date: 12.07.2019
Personnel: Mike Connell (Pub.)
Main (survey) contact: Mike Connell

REAL ESTATE REVIEW

Street address 1: 3415 Fleeta Ln
Street address state: TN
Postal code: 37416-2802
County: Hamilton
Country: USA
Mailing address: PO Box 25218
Mailing city: Chattanooga
Mailing state: TN
Mailing zip: 37422-5218
Office phone: (423) 855-1831
Office fax: (423) 499-8543
General e-mail: r4rrpub@aol.com
Website: www.rivercountiesrealestatereview.com
Frequency: Mthly
Circulation Free: 15000
Audit By: Sworn/Estimate/Non-Audited
Audit Date: 12.07.2019
Personnel: Paula Stark (Pub.); Kathy Beckham (Circ. Mgr.); Marvin Cortner (Ed.); Rick Madewell (Asst. Ed.); Ellen Johnston (Prodn. Mgr.)
Main (survey) contact: Brian McBride

CHEYENNE

PREVIEW REAL ESTATE GUIDE

Street address 1: 2021 Warren Ave
Street address state: WY
Postal code: 82001-3725
County: Laramie
Country: USA
Mailing address: 2021 Warren Ave

Mailing city: Cheyenne
Mailing state: WY
Mailing zip: 82001-3725
Office phone: (307) 634-8895
Office fax: (307) 634-8530
General e-mail: publisher@wyopreview.com
Website: www.wyopreview.com
Year publication established: 1984
Mechanical specifications: Type page 7 x 9 3/4.
Frequency: Mthly
Circulation Free: 8000
Audit By: Sworn/Estimate/Non-Audited
Audit Date: 12.07.2019
Hardware: APP/Macs
Software: Multi-Ad/Creator.
Personnel: Michael Jones (Publisher); Stacey Fulgieri (Ed.)
Main (survey) contact: Michael Jones

COLTS NECK

HOME IMPROVEMENT GUIDE

Street address 1: 440 State Route 34
Street address state: NJ
Postal code: 07722-2525
County: Monmouth
Country: USA
Mailing address: 440 State Route 34
Mailing city: Colts Neck
Mailing state: NJ
Mailing zip: 07722-2513
Office phone: (732) 780-7474
Office fax: (732) 414-1736
General e-mail: info@homeimprovementguides.com
Website: www.homeimprovementguides.com
Year publication established: 2003
Advertising (open inch rate): see website
Delivery methods: Mail Racks
Mechanical specifications: see website
Frequency: Mthly
Circulation Free: 95000
Audit By: Sworn/Estimate/Non-Audited
Audit Date: 12.07.2019
Personnel: Larry Boerckel (Ed.)
Main (survey) contact: Larry Boerckel

CONYNGHAM

REAL ESTATE JOURNAL

Street address 1: PO Box 482
Street address state: PA
Postal code: 18219
County: Luzerne
Country: USA
Mailing address: PO Box 482
Mailing city: Conyngham
Mailing state: PA
Mailing zip: 18219
Office phone: (570) 233-5652
Office fax: (570) 371-4433
General e-mail: rej1@ptd.net
Website: www.therealestatejournal.com
Frequency: Mthly
Circulation Free: 15000
Audit By: Sworn/Estimate/Non-Audited
Audit Date: 12.07.2019
Hardware: APP/Mac
Presses: Software Ã‚Â– QPS/QuarkXPress.
Edition Names: 2 total Ã‚Â– Real Estate Journal Schuylkill County;
Personnel: Larry Boerckel (Ed.)
Main (survey) contact: Larry Boerckel

EL PASO

REAL ESTATE WEEKLY

Street address 1: 6006 N Mesa St
Street address 2: Ste 600
Street address state: TX
Postal code: 79912-4655
County: El Paso
Country: USA
Mailing address: 6006 N Mesa St Ste 600
Mailing city: El Paso
Mailing state: TX

Mailing zip: 79912-4655
Office phone: (915) 585-1000
Office fax: (915) 261-0234
General e-mail: sandy@mesapub.com
Website: www.mesapublishing.com
Year publication established: 1988
Zip Codes Served: 79901, 79999
Mechanical specifications: Type page 9 3/4 x 11 3/4.
Frequency: Thur
Circulation Free: 10000
Audit By: Sworn/Estimate/Non-Audited
Audit Date: 12.07.2019
Hardware: APP/Macs
Software: QPS/QuarkXPress
Personnel: Crystal The Realtor (Pub.)
Main (survey) contact: Crystal The Realtor

ELIZABETHTOWN

CENTRAL KENTUCKY HOMES REAL ESTATE

Street address 1: 408 W Dixie Ave
Street address state: KY
Postal code: 42701-2455
County: Hardin
Country: USA
Mailing address: 408 W Dixie Ave
Mailing city: Elizabethtown
Mailing state: KY
Mailing zip: 42701-2455
Office phone: (270) 769-1200
Office fax: (270) 765-7318
Advertising e-mail: Ljobe@thenewsenterprise.com
Website: www.newsenterpriseonline.com
Delivery methods: Racks
Zip Codes Served: 42701
Frequency: Mthly
Circulation Free: 10000
Audit By: Sworn/Estimate/Non-Audited
Audit Date: 12.07.2019
Personnel: Jim Stebens (Ed.); Nikki Stebens (Ed.)
Main (survey) contact: Jim Stebens

FALL RIVER

REAL ESTATE GUIDE

Street address 1: 207 Pocasset St
Street address state: MA
Postal code: 02721-1532
County: Bristol
Country: USA
Mailing address: 207 Pocasset St
Mailing city: Fall River
Mailing state: MA
Mailing zip: 02721-1532
Office phone: (508) 676-8211
Office fax: (508) 676-2588
General e-mail: news@heraldnews.com
Website: www.heraldnews.com
Advertising (open inch rate): Open inch rate $17.50
Mechanical specifications: Type page 10 1/2 x 12; E - 7 cols, 1 7/16, between; C - 7 cols, 1 7/16, between.
Frequency: Fri
Circulation Paid: 32173
Audit By: Sworn/Estimate/Non-Audited
Audit Date: 12.07.2019
Hardware: IBM, APP/Macs, MON
Presses: 9-G/Urbanite
Software: Dewar, Multi-Ad/Creator.
Personnel: Chris Ordway (Pub.); Ben Sheroan (Ed.); Portia Oldham (Circ. Mgr.); Larry Jobe (Advertising Director)
Main (survey) contact: Chris Ordway

GREEN BAY

GREEN BAY REAL ESTATE GUIDE

Street address 1: PO Box 2467
Street address state: WI
Postal code: 54306-2467

County: Brown
Country: USA
Mailing address: P.O. Box 23430
Mailing city: Green Bay
Mailing state: WI
Mailing zip: 54305-3430
Office phone: (920) 432-2941
Office fax: (920) 432-8581
General e-mail: chronicle@gogreenbay.com
Website: www.greenbaypressgazette.com
Year publication established: 1990
Advertising (open inch rate): Open inch rate $17.00
Zip Codes Served: 54301, 54302, 54303, 54304, 54311, 54115
Mechanical specifications: Type page 7 1/4 x 9 3/4.
Frequency: Mthly
Audit By: Sworn/Estimate/Non-Audited
Audit Date: 12.07.2019
Hardware: APP/Macs.
Personnel: Sean Burke (Pub.); Tom Booth (Adv. Dir.); Tom Amato (Circ. Dir.); Linda Murphy (Mng. Ed.); Jon Root (Mng. Ed.); Mike Niland (Prodn. Mgr.)
Main (survey) contact: Lisa Strattan

HOLMESVILLE

HOMESELLER MAGAZINE

Street address 1: 8068 Township Road 574
Street address state: OH
Postal code: 44633-9751
County: Holmes
Country: USA
Mailing address: PO Box 87
Mailing city: Millersburg
Mailing state: OH
Mailing zip: 44654-0087
Office phone: (330) 674-7653
Office fax: (330) 674-7653
Editorial e-mail: editor@homesellermagazine.com
Website: tdn.com/eedition/homeseller
Year publication established: 1988
Zip Codes Served: 44691, 44654, 44256
Frequency: Mthly
Circulation Free: 9000
Audit By: Sworn/Estimate/Non-Audited
Audit Date: 12.07.2019
Personnel: David Petruska (Pub.); Marilyn Jackson (Ed.)

KANSAS CITY

KANSAS HOMES

Street address 1: 1533 NE Rice Rd
Street address state: KS
Postal code: 66103
County: Wyandotte
Country: USA
Mailing address: 1533 NE Rice Rd
Mailing city: Kansas City
Mailing state: KS
Mailing zip: 66103
Office phone: (816) 738-3633
Website: www.kchomes.com
Zip Codes Served: 64103
Other Type of Frequency: Every other Thur
Circulation Free: 15000
Audit By: Sworn/Estimate/Non-Audited
Audit Date: 12.07.2019
Personnel: David Lovins (Pres./COO); Cassidy Murphy (Associate Publisher); Timothy Warren (Publisher/CEO)
Parent company: The Warren Group
Main (survey) contact: Timothy Warren; David Lovins; Cassidy Murphy

KISSIMMEE

OSCEOLA HOMEFINDER

Street address 1: 108 Church St
Street address state: FL
Postal code: 34741-5055
County: Osceola
Country: USA
Mailing address: 108 Church Street

Real Estate Publications in the U.S.

Mailing city: Kissimmee
Mailing state: FL
Mailing zip: 34741
Office phone: (407) 846-7600
Office fax: (321) 402-2946
Advertising phone: (321) 402-0413
Editorial phone: (321) 402-0436
Advertising e-mail: BBerry@osceolanewsgazette.com
Editorial e-mail: bmcbride@osceolanewsgazette.com
Website: www.aroundosceola.com
Advertising (open inch rate): Open inch rate $12.95
Zip Codes Served: 34741, 34743, 34744, 34746, 34747, 34758, 34759, 34769, 34771, 34772
Mechanical specifications: Type page 9 3/4 x 12 1/2; E - 6 cols, 1 3/8, 3/8 between; A - 6 cols, 1 3/8, 3/8 between; C - 6 cols, 1 3/8, 3/8 between.
Frequency: Mthly
Audit By: Sworn/Estimate/Non-Audited
Audit Date: 12.07.2019
Hardware: APP/Macs
Software: QPS/QuarkXPress 4.1, Adobe/Photoshop 6.0, Adobe/Illustrator 9.0.
Personnel: Tom Green (Pub.); Tom Savoy (Dir., Mktg.)
Main (survey) contact: Tom Savoy; Tom Green

LAS CRUCES
REAL ESTATE PRESS OF LAS CRUCES

Street address 1: 256 W Las Cruces Ave
Street address state: NM
Postal code: 88005-1804
County: Dona Ana
Country: USA
Mailing address: PO Box 1244
Mailing city: Las Cruces
Mailing state: NM
Mailing zip: 88004-1244
Office phone: (575) 541-5467
Office fax: (575) 541-5499
General e-mail: mderk@lcsun-news.com
Website: lcsun-news.com/marketplace/real-estate
Delivery methods: Racks
Zip Codes Served: 88001, 88005, 88007, 88011, 88012
Frequency: Mthly
Personnel: Al Frattura (Pub.); Don Negus (Adv. Dir.); Donna Pung (Adv. Mgr.); Rick Mills (Exec. Ed.)
Main (survey) contact: Jeannie Parent

MADISON
START RENTING MAGAZINE

Street address 1: 102 N Franklin St
Street address state: WI
Postal code: 53703-2376
County: Dane
Country: USA
Mailing address: 102 N Franklin St Frnt
Mailing city: Madison
Mailing state: WI
Mailing zip: 53703-4610
Office phone: (608) 257-4990
Office fax: (608) 257-6896
General e-mail: info@startrenting.com
Website: www.startrenting.com
Frequency: Mthly
Audit By: Sworn/Estimate/Non-Audited
Audit Date: 12.07.2019
Edition Names: 3 total Ã‚Â— Start Renting-Green Bay/Fox Cities (15,000); Start Renting Magazine-Madison (15,000);
Personnel: Christine Fox (Circ. Mgr.); Angel Norbury (Mktg. Cood.)
Main (survey) contact: Don Wyatt

MARTINEZ
HOME GUIDE

Street address 1: 109 Camilla Ave
Street address state: GA
Postal code: 30907-3406
County: Columbia
Country: USA
Mailing address: 109 Camilla Ave
Mailing city: Martinez
Mailing state: GA
Mailing zip: 30907-3406
Office phone: (706) 868-8544
Office fax: (706) 868-8381
General e-mail: handl@augustashomes.com
Website: www.augustashomes.com
Frequency: Mthly
Audit By: Sworn/Estimate/Non-Audited
Audit Date: 12.07.2019
Personnel: Jeannie Parent (Pub.)
Main (survey) contact: Teresa Goodrich

HOMES & LAND OF AUGUSTA

Street address 1: 109 Camilla Ave
Street address state: GA
Postal code: 30907-3406
County: Columbia
Country: USA
Mailing address: 109 Camilla Ave
Mailing city: Martinez
Mailing state: GA
Mailing zip: 30907-3406
Office phone: (706) 868-8544
Office fax: (706) 868-8381
General e-mail: handl@augustashomes.com
Website: www.augustashomes.com
Zip Codes Served: 30907
Frequency: Mthly
Circulation Free: 22000
Audit By: Sworn/Estimate/Non-Audited
Audit Date: 12.07.2019
Personnel: Jeff P. Cathey (Pub.)
Main (survey) contact: Jeff P. Cathey

MEDFORD
PROFESSIONAL IMAGE PUBLISHING

Street address 1: 3350 1/2 W Main St
Street address state: OR
Postal code: 97501-2132
County: Jackson
Country: USA
Mailing address: 3350 1/2 W Main St
Mailing city: Medford
Mailing state: OR
Mailing zip: 97501-2132
Office phone: (541) 773-5744
Office fax: (541) 776-0445
General e-mail: office@move2oregon.com
Website: www.move2oregon.com
Advertising (open inch rate): Open inch rate $12.50
Frequency: Mthly
Audit By: Sworn/Estimate/Non-Audited
Audit Date: 12.07.2019
Personnel: Nick Montalbano (Circ. Mgr.)
Main (survey) contact: Nick Montalbano

MORRISTOWN
HOMES & ESTATES MAGAZINE

Street address 1: 173 Morris St
Street address state: NJ
Postal code: 07960-4332
County: Morris
Country: USA
Mailing address: PO Box 525
Mailing city: Ridgewood
Mailing state: NJ
Mailing zip: 07451
Office phone: (201) 394-3084
Office fax: (973) 264-1153
Other phone: (973) 605-1877
General e-mail: gene@homesandestatesonline.com
Website: http://www.homesandestatesonline.com/skins/housemagazine/
Mechanical specifications: Type page 6 3/4 x 9 3/8.
Frequency: Wed
Circulation Free: 35000
Audit By: Sworn/Estimate/Non-Audited
Audit Date: 12.07.2019
Personnel: Peter Best (Pub.); Gene Petraglia (Pub.)
Main (survey) contact: Peter Best

MOUNT PLEASANT
NORTHERN MICHIGAN REAL ESTATE MARKETPLACE

Street address 1: 711 W Pickard St
Street address state: MI
Postal code: 48858-1585
County: Isabella
Country: USA
Mailing address: 311 1/2 E Mitchell St
Mailing city: Petoskey
Mailing state: MI
Mailing zip: 49770-2615
Office phone: (989) 779-6000
Office fax: (989) 779-6162
General e-mail: news@michigannewspapers.com
Website: www.themorningsun.com
Frequency: Mthly
Circulation Free: 25000
Audit By: Sworn/Estimate/Non-Audited
Audit Date: 12.07.2019
Personnel: Maria Derk
Main (survey) contact: Sylvia Soto

MOUNT PLEASANT
THE REAL ESTATE REVIEW

Street address 1: 711 W Pickard St
Street address state: MI
Postal code: 48858-1585
County: Isabella
Country: USA
Mailing address: 711 W Pickard St
Mailing city: Mount Pleasant
Mailing state: MI
Mailing zip: 48858-1585
Office phone: (800) 616-6397
Office fax: (989) 779-6009
Website: http://www.myhomemi.com/
Mechanical specifications: Type page 7 1/4 x 9 1/2; A - 4 cols, 1 5/8, 1/8 between.
Frequency: Mthly
Circulation Free: 15000
Audit By: Sworn/Estimate/Non-Audited
Audit Date: 12.07.2019
Personnel: Paul Weideman (Ed.); Wendy Ortega (Advertising AE)
Parent company: The New Mexican, Inc.
Main (survey) contact: Tom Cross

NAPA
NAPA VALLEY REGISTER

Street address 1: 1615 2nd St
Street address state: CA
Postal code: 94559-2818
County: Napa
Country: USA
Mailing address: 1615 Second St
Mailing city: Napa
Mailing state: CA
Mailing zip: 94559
Office phone: (707) 256-2244
Office fax: (707) 252-6047
Advertising phone: (707) 256-2244
Editorial phone: (707) 256-2244
Other phone: (707) 256-2244
General e-mail: jfawkes@napanews.com
Advertising e-mail: jfawkes@napanews.com
Editorial e-mail: jfawkes@napanews.com
Website: napavalleyregister.com
Advertising (open inch rate): Open inch rate $11.15
Delivery methods: Racks
Zip Codes Served: 94559 94558 94574 94515 94508 94503 94562 94567 94573 94576 94599
Mechanical specifications: Type page 7 1/2 x 9 3/4.
Frequency: Mthly
Circulation Free: 5000
Audit By: Sworn/Estimate/Non-Audited
Audit Date: 12.07.2019
Personnel: Kevin C. Wood (Pub.); Craig Martin (Adv. Mgr.); Renee Alborelli (Prodn. Mgr.)
Main (survey) contact: Kevin C. Wood

NAPA
WINE COUNTRY WEEKLY REAL ESTATE READER

Street address 1: 1436 2nd St
Street address 2: Unit 182
Street address state: CA
Postal code: 94559-5005
County: Napa
Country: USA
Mailing address: 1436 Second St.
Mailing city: Napa
Mailing state: CA
Mailing zip: 94558
Office phone: (707) 258-6150
Office fax: (707) 258-6152
Advertising phone: (707) 258-6150
General e-mail: publisher@rereader.com
Advertising e-mail: support@rereader.com
Website: www.rereader.com
Year publication established: 1987
Advertising (open inch rate): Open inch rate $30.00
Zip Codes Served: 94558
Mechanical specifications: Type page 10 1/4 x 13; E - 5 cols, 2, 1/8 between; C - 6 cols, 1 1/4, 1/8 between.
Frequency: Fri
Circulation Paid: 9500
Circulation Free: 57000
Audit By: Sworn/Estimate/Non-Audited
Audit Date: 12.07.2019
Hardware: APP/Mac.
Personnel: Mark Rigby (Pub.); Carol VanHise (Adv. Mgr.); John Bruno (Prodn. Mgr.)
Main (survey) contact: Mark Rigby

NEEDHAM
BOSTON HOMES

Street address 1: 254 2nd Ave
Street address state: MA
Postal code: 02494-2829
County: Norfolk
Country: USA
Office phone: (617) 262-0444
Office fax: (617) 266-7333
Advertising phone: (888) 828-1515
Editorial phone: (781) 433-8323
Website: http://www.linkbostonhomes.com
Personnel: Mark Rigby (Pub.); Carol VanHise (Adv. Mgr.); John Bruno (Prodn. Mgr.)
Main (survey) contact: Mark Rigby

NORTH PORT
FLORIDA MARINER/GULF MARINER

Street address 1: PO Box 8070
Street address state: FL
Postal code: 34290-8070
County: Sarasota
Country: USA
Mailing address: PO Box 8070
Mailing city: North Port
Mailing state: FL
Mailing zip: 34290
Office phone: (941) 488-9307
Office fax: (941) 488-9309
Other phone: (800)615-5089
General e-mail: flmariner@floridamariner.com
Editorial e-mail: cjones@floridamariner.com
Website: www.floridamariner.com
Advertising (open inch rate): Open inch rate $39.95
Other Type of Frequency: Every other Sun
Circulation Free: 23500
Audit By: Sworn/Estimate/Non-Audited
Audit Date: 12.07.2019
Personnel: Kevin Corrado (Pub.); Karen Alvord (Adv. Dir.)

NORWICH

HALLMARK HOMES

Street address 1: PO Box 626
Street address state: CT
Postal code: 06360-0626
County: New London
Country: USA
Mailing address: 193 Camp Moween Rd
Mailing city: Lebanon
Mailing state: CT
Mailing zip: 06249-2705
Office phone: (860) 886-5245
Office fax: (860) 886-5244
Advertising e-mail: hhhomesmag@aol.com
Website: http://www.hallmarkct.com/
Delivery methods: Carrier
Other Type of Frequency: Every other Wed
Circulation Free: 23000
Audit By: Sworn/Estimate/Non-Audited
Audit Date: 12.07.2019
Personnel: David Thornberry (Pub.)
Main (survey) contact: David Thornberry

PALM SPRINGS

HOMEFINDER

Street address 1: 750 N Gene Autry Trl
Street address state: CA
Postal code: 92262-5463
County: Riverside
Country: USA
Mailing address: PO Box 2734
Mailing city: Palm Springs
Mailing state: CA
Mailing zip: 92263-2734
Office phone: (760) 322-8889
Office fax: (760) 778-4560
Advertising fax: (760) 778-4528
Editorial fax: (760) 778-4654
General e-mail: mwinkler@gannet.com
Advertising e-mail: sbweaver@gannett.com
Editorial e-mail: grburton@gannett.com
Website: www.mydesert.com
Year publication established: 1927
Advertising (open inch rate): Open inch rate $46.00
Delivery methods: Carrier`Racks
Zip Codes Served: 92262, 92234, 92240, 92264, 92210, 92211, 92260, 92270, 92276, 92236, 92201, 92203, 92253
Frequency: Sat
Circulation Paid: 52213
Circulation Free: 50000
Audit By: Sworn/Estimate/Non-Audited
Audit Date: 12.07.2019
Presses: 6-G
Software: QPS/QuarkXPress 3.2, Adobe/Photoshop 6.0.
Personnel: Cynthia Rucklos (Pub.)
Main (survey) contact: Cynthia Rucklos

PEABODY

BANKER & TRADESMAN

Street address 1: 2 Corporation Way
Street address 2: Suite 250
Street address state: MA
Postal code: 01960
County: Suffolk
Country: USA
Mailing address: 280 Summer St Fl 8
Mailing city: Boston
Mailing state: MA
Mailing zip: 02210-1130
Office phone: (617) 428-5100
Advertising phone: (617) 896-5357
Editorial phone: (617) 896-5313
General e-mail: editorial@thewarrengroup.com
Advertising e-mail: advertising@thewarrengroup.com
Editorial e-mail: editorial@thewarrengroup.com
Website: www.bankerandtradesman.com

Main (survey) contact: Kevin Corrado

Year publication established: 1872
Delivery methods: Mail
Frequency: Mon
Circulation Free: 7000
Audit By: Sworn/Estimate/Non-Audited
Audit Date: 12.07.2019
Personnel: Nick Walser (Co-Pub.); Steve Walser (Co-Pub.); Craig Baker (Administrator)
Main (survey) contact: Craig Baker

PLATTSBURGH

ADIRONDACK PROPERTIES

Street address 1: 177 Margaret St
Street address state: NY
Postal code: 12901-1837
County: Clinton
Country: USA
Mailing address: 177 Margaret St
Mailing city: Plattsburgh
Mailing state: NY
Mailing zip: 12901-1837
Office phone: (518) 563-0100
Office fax: (518) 562-0303
General e-mail: pennysaver@westelcom.com
Website: www.adkpennysaver.com
Advertising (open inch rate): Open inch rate $15.00
Frequency: Mthly
Personnel: Shelly Meenan (Pub.); Andy Hachadorian (Ed.)
Main (survey) contact: Edward Condra

REAL ESTATE ADVERTISER

Street address 1: 177 Margaret St
Street address state: NY
Postal code: 12901-1837
County: Clinton
Country: USA
Mailing address: 177 Margaret St
Mailing city: Plattsburgh
Mailing state: NY
Mailing zip: 12901-1837
Office phone: (518) 563-0100
Office fax: (518) 562-0303
General e-mail: mail@adkpennysaver.com
Website: www.adkpennysaver.com
Advertising (open inch rate): Open inch rate $15.00
Other Type of Frequency: 4 x a year
Circulation Free: 18000
Audit By: Sworn/Estimate/Non-Audited
Audit Date: 12.07.2019
Personnel: Randy Harden (Pub.); Tammy Harden (Adv. Mgr.)
Main (survey) contact: Randy Harden

PONTIAC

HOMES FOR SALE

Street address 1: 48 W Huron St
Street address state: MI
Postal code: 48342-2101
County: Oakland
Country: USA
Mailing address: 48 W Huron St
Mailing city: Pontiac
Mailing state: MI
Mailing zip: 48342-2101
Office phone: (248) 745-4794
Office fax: (248) 332-3003
Website: www.theoaklandpress.com
Frequency: Thur
Circulation Free: 17000
Audit By: Sworn/Estimate/Non-Audited
Audit Date: 12.07.2019
Personnel: Tammy Harden (Adv. Mgr.); Randy Harden (Prodn. Mgr.)
Main (survey) contact: Tammy Harden

RUTLAND

PREFERRED PROPERTIES REAL ESTATE GUIDE

Street address 1: 27 Wales St

Street address state: VT
Postal code: 05701-4027
County: Rutland
Country: USA
Mailing address: PO Box 668
Mailing city: Rutland
Mailing state: VT
Mailing zip: 05702-0668
Office phone: (800) 776-5512
Office fax: (802) 775-2423
General e-mail: glenda.hawley@aol.com
Website: www.vermontclassifieds.com; www.rutlandherald.com
Advertising (open inch rate): Open inch rate $17.61
Zip Codes Served: 5701
Mechanical specifications: Type page 9 11/16 x 12; E - 5 cols, 1 13/16, 1/4 between; A - 5 cols, 1 13/16, 1/4 between.
Frequency: Mthly
Circulation Free: 22500
Audit By: Sworn/Estimate/Non-Audited
Audit Date: 12.07.2019
Personnel: Riley R. Stephens (Ed.); Ceci Marquez (Mng. Ed.); Nancy Wiseman (Prodn. Mgr.)
Parent company: Mesa Publishing Corp.
Main (survey) contact: Riley R. Stephens

SANTA FE

HOME|SANTA FE REAL ESTATE GUIDE

Street address 1: 202 E Marcy St
Street address state: NM
Postal code: 87501-2021
County: Santa Fe
Country: USA
Mailing address: PO Box 2048
Mailing city: Santa Fe
Mailing state: NM
Mailing zip: 87504-2048
Office phone: (505) 983-3303
Office fax: (505) 995-3875
Advertising phone: (505) 986-3007
Advertising fax: (505) 984-1785
Editorial phone: (505) 986-3043
Editorial fax: (505) 995-3875
General e-mail: reguide@sfnewmexican.com
Advertising e-mail: wortega@sfnewmexican.com
Editorial e-mail: pweideman@sfnewmexican.com
Website: www.santafenewmexican.com
Year publication established: 1997
Delivery methods: Mail`Newsstand`Carrier`Racks
Zip Codes Served: 87501, 87502, 87504, 87505, 87508, 87544, 87532, 87507, 87010
Mechanical specifications: Type page 9 3/4 x 11 1/2; E - 4 cols, 1 1/5, between; A - 4 cols, 1 1/5, between.
Digital Platform - Mobile: Apple`Android`Windows`Blackberry`Other
Digital Platform - Tablet: Apple iOS`Android`Windows 7`Blackberry Tablet OS`Kindle`Nook`Kindle Fire`Other
Frequency: Sun`Mthly
Circulation Paid: 18000
Audit By: Sworn/Estimate/Non-Audited
Audit Date: 12.07.2019
Hardware: APP/Macs, PCs
Presses: 9-G/Urbanite
Software: NewsEditPro/IQue 3.5.1, Adobe/InDesign 2.0.
Personnel: Pat Sager (OWNER/PUBLISHER); Tom Sager (Pub.)
Main (survey) contact: Pat Sager

SPRINGFIELD

APARTMENTS

Street address 1: 525 Belmont Ave
Street address state: MA
Postal code: 01108-1789
County: Hampden
Country: USA

Mailing address: 525 Belmont Ave
Mailing city: Springfield
Mailing state: MA
Mailing zip: 01108-1789
Office phone: (413) 734-3411
Office fax: (413) 734-0099
General e-mail: tomgreen@apt-4-rent.com, info@apt-4-rent.com
Website: www.apt-4-rent.com
Zip Codes Served: 1108
Frequency: Mthly
Circulation Free: 30000
Audit By: Sworn/Estimate/Non-Audited
Audit Date: 12.07.2019
Personnel: Donna McElligott (Marketing Mgr.)
Main (survey) contact: Donna McElligott

TROY

CAPITAL REGION REAL ESTATE GUIDE

Street address 1: 270 River Triangle
Street address 2: Ste 202B
Street address state: NY
Postal code: 12180
County: Rensselaer
Country: USA
Mailing address: 270 River Triangle, Ste. 202B
Mailing city: Troy
Mailing state: NY
Mailing zip: 12180
Office phone: (518) 270-1200
Office fax: (518) 270-1251
General e-mail: newsroom@troyrecord.com
Website: www.troyrecord.com
Mechanical specifications: Type page 5 1/4 x 9 1/2; E - 4 cols, 1 3/16, 1/8 between; A - 4 cols, 1 3/16, 1/8 between; C - 4 cols, 1 3/16, 1/8 between.
Other Type of Frequency: 2 x Mthly
Circulation Paid: 25946
Audit By: Sworn/Estimate/Non-Audited
Audit Date: 12.07.2019
Hardware: ACI
Presses: G
Software: Dewar.
Personnel: R. John Mitchell (Pub.); Catherine Nelson (Gen. Mgr.); Sean Bruke (Adv. Mgr.); Christina Mahoney (Adv. Design Mgr.)
Main (survey) contact: John Mitchell

TYLER

HOMES & LAND OF TYLER & EAST TEXAS

Street address 1: 5604 Old Bullard Rd
Street address 2: Ste 101
Street address state: TX
Postal code: 75703-4359
County: Smith
Country: USA
Mailing address: 5604 Old Bullard Rd Ste 101
Mailing city: Tyler
Mailing state: TX
Mailing zip: 75703-4359
Office phone: (903) 509-2339
Office fax: (903) 509-2326
Advertising phone: (903) 509-2339
Advertising fax: (903) 509-2326
Other phone: (903) 539-9782
Other fax: (903) 509-2343
General e-mail: psager@tyler.net
Advertising e-mail: psager@tyler.net
Editorial e-mail: psager&tyler.net
Website: www.tyleretex.com
Year publication established: 1977
Digital Platform - Mobile: Apple
Digital Platform - Tablet: Apple iOS
Frequency: Mthly
Circulation Free: 20000
Audit By: Sworn/Estimate/Non-Audited
Audit Date: 12.07.2019
Personnel: Al Rasmussen (Gen. Mgr.)
Main (survey) contact: Jim Fitzhenry

Real Estate Publications in the U.S.

WEST CHESTER

HOMES MAGAZINE

Street address 1: 250 N Bradford Ave
Street address state: PA
Postal code: 19382-1912
County: Chester
Country: USA
Mailing address: 250 N Bradford Ave
Mailing city: West Chester
Mailing state: PA
Mailing zip: 19382-1912
Office phone: (610) 430-6961
Office fax: (610) 430-1190
Editorial phone: (610) 430-1116
General e-mail: advertising@dailylocal.com
Website: www.dailylocal.com
Advertising (open inch rate): Open inch rate $2.75
Zip Codes Served: 19382
Mechanical specifications: Type page 6 x 10.
Frequency: Mthly
Audit By: Sworn/Estimate/Non-Audited
Audit Date: 12.07.2019
Hardware: Pentium/PC 200
Presses: G/Urbanite
Software: CNI.
Personnel: Dennis Barber (Adv.Mgr); Shawn Bacon (Acct. Exec.); Melissa Schwefel (Acct. Exec.)
Main (survey) contact: Dennis Barber

WICHITA

REAL ESTATE BOOK

Street address 1: PO Box 1897
Street address state: KS
Postal code: 67201-1897
County: Sedgwick
Country: USA
Mailing address: PO Box 1897
Mailing city: Wichita
Mailing state: KS
Mailing zip: 67201-1897
Office phone: (316) 788-0191
Office fax: (316) 794-8767
General e-mail: jstebens@aol.com
Frequency: Mthly
Audit By: Sworn/Estimate/Non-Audited
Audit Date: 12.07.2019
Personnel: Patrick Rice (Pub.); Bob Johnigan (Gen. Mgr.); Jeff Hite (Circ. Mgr.); Will Perrell (Ed.)
Main (survey) contact: Patrick Rice

RELIGIOUS NEWSPAPERS IN THE U.S.

ALBANY

THE EVANGELIST

Street address 1: 40 N Main Ave
Street address state: NY
Postal code: 12203-1481
County: Albany
Country: USA
Mailing address: 40 N Main Ave Ste 2
Mailing city: Albany
Mailing state: NY
Mailing zip: 12203-1483
Office phone: (518) 453-6688
Office fax: (518) 453-8448
Advertising phone: (518) 453-6696
Advertising fax: (518) 453-8448
Editorial phone: (518) 453-6688
Editorial fax: (518) 453-8448
General e-mail: christopher.ringwald@rcpa.org
Advertising e-mail: john.salvione@rcda.org
Website: www.evangelist.org
Year newspaper established: 1926
Advertising (open inch rate): Open inch rate $23.50
Mechanical specifications: Type page 9 3/4 x 13 1/2.
Frequency: Thur
Circulation Paid: 50000
Circulation Free: 280
Audit By: Sworn/Estimate/Non-Audited
Audit Date: 12.07.2019
Weeklies Equipment - Software: QPS/QuarkXPress 5.0.
Personnel: Kate Blain (Ed.); John Salvione (Adv. Rep.)
Main (survey) contact: Kate Blain

ALEXANDRIA

BAPTIST MESSAGE

Street address 1: PO Box 311
Street address state: LA
Postal code: 71309-0311
County: Rapides
Country: USA
Mailing address: PO Box 311
Mailing city: Alexandria
Mailing state: LA
Mailing zip: 71309-0311
Office phone: (318) 442-7728
Office fax: (318) 445-8328
General e-mail: info@baptistmessage.com
Advertising e-mail: advertising@baptistmessage.com
Editorial e-mail: editor@baptistmessage.com
Website: www.baptistmessage.com
Year newspaper established: 1886

ARLINGTON

ARLINGTON CATHOLIC HERALD

Street address 1: 200 N Glebe Rd
Street address 2: Ste 600
Street address state: VA
Postal code: 22203-3763
County: Arlington
Country: USA
Mailing address: 200 N Glebe Rd Ste 600
Mailing city: Arlington
Mailing state: VA
Mailing zip: 22203-3728
Office phone: (703) 841-2590
Office fax: (703) 524-2782
Advertising phone: (703) 841-2598
General e-mail: editorial@catholicherald.com
Advertising e-mail: csalinas@catholicherald.com
Website: www.catholicherald.com
Year newspaper established: 1976
Advertising (open inch rate): Open inch rate $42.00
Delivery methods: Mail`Racks
Digital Platform - Mobile: Windows
Frequency: Thur
Circulation Paid: 66500
Audit By: USPS
Audit Date: 12.12.2017
Personnel: Carlos Salinas (Adv. Mgr.); Joe Miller (Circ. Mgr.); Michael Flach (Ed.); Ann Augherton (Mng. Ed.); Stacy Rausch (Prodn. Coord.); Rev. Michael F. Burbidge
Main (survey) contact: Carlos Salinas

BALTIMORE

THE CATHOLIC REVIEW

Street address 1: 880 Park Ave
Street address state: MD
Postal code: 21201-4822
County: Baltimore City
Country: USA
Mailing address: PO Box 777
Mailing city: Baltimore
Mailing state: MD
Mailing zip: 21203-0777
Office phone: (443) 524-3150
Office fax: (443) 524-3155
Advertising phone: (443) 263-0247
Advertising fax: (443) 524-3155
Editorial phone: (443) 263-0259
Editorial fax: (443) 524-3160
General e-mail: mail@catholicreview.org
Advertising e-mail: mail@catholicreview.org
Editorial e-mail: mail@catholicreview.org
Website: www.catholicreview.org
Year newspaper established: 1914
Advertising (open inch rate): Open rate per column inch is $97.28 (based on a 1-time, 1/8-page ad). Per page is $2,950
Mechanical specifications: Type page 10 x 13; E - 4 cols x 11", 2.2475", .17" between; A - 4 cols x 11", 2.2475", .17" between; C - 4 cols x 11", 2.2475", .17" between.
Delivery methods: Mail`Racks
Zip Codes Served: 206XX-219XX
Digital Platform - Mobile: Blackberry
Frequency: Thur
Other Type of Frequency: Biweekly, alternate Thursdays
Circulation Paid: 47843
Circulation Free: 172
Audit By: USPS
Audit Date: 27.10.2011
Editions Count: 2
Edition Names: The Catholic Review, Review in the Pew
Personnel: Paul McMullen (Managing Ed.); Christopher Gunty (Assoc. Pub./Editor); Jeff Stintz (Advertising Mgr.)
Parent company: CR Media
Main (survey) contact: Christopher Gunty

BATON ROUGE

THE CATHOLIC COMMENTATOR

Street address 1: 1800 S Acadian Thruway
Street address state: LA
Postal code: 70808-1663
County: East Baton Rouge
Country: USA
Mailing address: PO Box 2028
Mailing city: Baton Rouge
Mailing state: LA
Mailing zip: 70821-2028
Office phone: (225) 387-0983
Office fax: (225) 336-8710
Website: www.diobr.org
Frequency: Mon
Personnel: Lisa Disney (Circulation)
Main (survey) contact: Laura Deavers; Richard Meek

BELLEVILLE

THE MESSENGER

Street address 1: 2620 Lebanon Ave
Street address state: IL
Postal code: 62221-3002
County: Saint Clair
Country: USA
Mailing address: 2620 Lebanon Ave Stop 2
Mailing city: Belleville
Mailing state: IL
Mailing zip: 62221-3001
Office phone: (618) 235-9601
Office fax: (618) 235-9605
General e-mail: cathnews@bellevillemessenger.org
Website: www.bellevillemessenger.org
Year newspaper established: 1808
Advertising (open inch rate): Open inch rate $8.54
Other Type of Frequency: 2 x Mthly
Circulation Paid: 10500
Audit By: Sworn/Estimate/Non-Audited
Audit Date: 19.10.2017
Personnel: Bernadette Middeke (Adv. Mgr.); Liz Quirin (Ed.)
Main (survey) contact: Liz Quirin

BILOXI

GULF PINE CATHOLIC

Street address 1: 1790 Popps Ferry Rd
Street address state: MS
Postal code: 39532-2118
County: Harrison
Country: USA
Mailing address: 1790 Popps Ferry Rd
Mailing city: Biloxi
Mailing state: MS
Mailing zip: 39532-2118
Office phone: (228) 702-2126
Office fax: (228) 702-2128
General e-mail: gulfpinecatholic&biloxidiocese.org
Advertising e-mail: gulfpinecatholic@biloxidiocese.org
Website: www.gulfpinecatholic.com
Year newspaper established: 1983
Advertising (open inch rate): Open inch rate $10.00
Mechanical specifications: Type page 10 1/4 x 11 1/4; E - 3 cols, 3 1/6, 1/12 between; A - 6 cols, 1/12 between.
Delivery methods: Mail
Other Type of Frequency: Everyother Fri
Circulation Paid: 17800
Audit By: Sworn/Estimate/Non-Audited
Audit Date: 12.07.2019
Weeklies Equipment - Software: QPS/QuarkXPress.
Personnel: Deborah Mowrey (Circ. Mgr.); Shirley M. Henderson (Ed.); Terrance Dickson (Reporter); Roger Morin (Bishop of Biloxi); Most Rev. Thomas J. Rodi (Pub.)
Main (survey) contact: Shirley M. Henderson

BIRMINGHAM

ONE VOICE

Street address 1: 2121 3rd Ave N
Street address state: AL
Postal code: 35203-3314
County: Jefferson
Country: USA
Mailing address: PO Box 10822

III-781

Mailing city: Birmingham
Mailing state: AL
Mailing zip: 35202-0822
Office phone: (205) 838-8305
Office fax: (205) 838-8319
General e-mail: onevoice@bhmdiocese.org
Website: www.bhmdiocese.org
Advertising (open inch rate): Open inch rate $9.00
Frequency: Fri
Circulation Paid: 19800
Circulation Free: 293
Audit By: Sworn/Estimate/Non-Audited
Audit Date: 12.07.2019
Personnel: Bishop Robert Baker (Pub.); Ann Lanzi (Circ. Mgr.); Mary Alice Crockett (Mng. Ed.)
Main (survey) contact: Bishop Robert Baker

BLOOMFIELD

THE CATHOLIC TRANSCRIPT

Street address 1: 467 Bloomfield Ave
Street address state: CT
Postal code: 06002-2903
County: Hartford
Country: USA
Mailing address: 467 Bloomfield Ave
Mailing city: Bloomfield
Mailing state: CT
Mailing zip: 06002-2903
Office phone: (860) 286-2828
Advertising phone:
Editorial phone:
General e-mail: info@catholictranscript.org
Editorial e-mail: swolf@catholictranscript.org
Website: www.catholictranscript.org
Year newspaper established: 1898
Mechanical specifications: Magazine
Delivery methods: Mail
Zip Codes Served: Hartford, Litchfield and New Haven County
Frequency: Other
Other Type of Frequency: 10 x year
Circulation Free: 174000
Audit By: Sworn/Estimate/Non-Audited
Audit Date: 12.07.2019
Personnel: Shelley Wolf (Ed.); Mary Chalupsky (Reporter); Leslie DiVinere (Design/Adv.); P. Blair (Archbishop/Pub.)
Main (survey) contact: Carole Cronsell; Shelley Wolf

BOISE

IDAHO CATHOLIC REGISTER

Street address 1: 1501 S Federal Way
Street address state: ID
Postal code: 83705-2588
County: Ada
Country: USA
Mailing address: 1501 S Federal Way Ste 450
Mailing city: Boise
Mailing state: ID
Mailing zip: 83705-2589
Office phone: (208) 342-1311
Office fax: (208) 342-0224
General e-mail: idcathreg@rcdb.org
Website: www.catholicidaho.org
Advertising (open inch rate): Open inch rate $9.95
Mechanical specifications: Type page 10 x 15; E - 5 cols, 1 7/8, 1/6 between; A - 5 cols, 1 7/8, 1/6 between; C - 5 cols, 1 7/8, 1/6 between.
Other Type of Frequency: Every other Fri
Circulation Paid: 16700
Audit By: Sworn/Estimate/Non-Audited
Audit Date: 12.07.2019
Personnel: Bishop Michael P. Driscoll (Pub.); Ann Bixby (Adv. Mgr.); Michael Brown (Ed.)
Main (survey) contact: Michael Brown

BRAINTREE

THE PILOT

Street address 1: 66 Brooks Dr
Street address state: MA
Postal code: 02184-3839
County: Norfolk
Country: USA
Mailing address: 66 Brooks Dr
Mailing city: Braintree
Mailing state: MA
Mailing zip: 02184-3839
Office phone: (617) 779-3780
Office fax: (617) 779-4562
Advertising phone: (617) 779-3788
Editorial phone: (617) 779-3782
General e-mail: editorial@TheBostonPilot.com
Advertising e-mail: advertising@TheBostonPilot.com
Editorial e-mail: editorial@TheBostonPilot.com
Website: www.TheBostonPilot.com.com
Year newspaper established: 1829
Advertising (open inch rate): Open inch rate $25.00
Delivery methods: Mail`Racks
Zip Codes Served: 01462-02494
Digital Platform - Mobile: Apple`Android
Digital Platform - Tablet: Apple iOS`Android`Kindle`Kindle Fire
Frequency: Fri
Circulation Paid: 21150
Circulation Free: 300
Audit By: USPS
Audit Date: 13.10.2012
Personnel: Larry Ricardo (Adv. Mgr.); Antonio Enrique (Ed.); Gregory Tracy (Mng. Ed.); Nan Wilkins (Prodn. Mgr.); Ernesto Cuevas (Bus. Mgr.); Jon Tan (Coord., Mktg./Circ.)
Parent company: iCatholic Media, Inc.
Main (survey) contact: Gregory Tracy

BROOKLYN

THE TABLET

Street address 1: 310 Prospect Park W
Street address state: NY
Postal code: 11215-6214
County: Kings
Country: USA
Office phone: (718) 965-7333
Office fax: (718) 965-7337
Advertising fax: (718) 965-7338
General e-mail: jcaragiulo@desalesmedia.org
Advertising e-mail: jdinapoli@desalesmedia.org
Website: www.thetablet.org
Year newspaper established: 1908
Advertising (open inch rate): Open inch rate $33.13
Mechanical specifications: Type page 10 1/4 x 14; E - 6 cols, 1 5/8, between; A - 6 cols, 1 5/8, between.
Frequency: Sat
Circulation Free: 67910
Audit By: AAM
Audit Date: 31.03.2019
Weeklies Equipment - Hardware: APP/Mac.
Personnel: Bishop Nicholas DiMarzio (Pub.); Father Kieran E. Harrington (Assoc. Pub.); Ed Wilkinson (Ed.); James Caragiulo (Circ. Mgr.); JoAnn DiNapoli (Dir. Sales)
Main (survey) contact: James Caragiulo; JoAnn DiNapoli

CAMDEN

CATHOLIC STAR HERALD

Street address 1: Pastoral Ctr 15 N Seventh St
Street address state: NJ
Postal code: 8102
County: Camden
Country: USA
Mailing address: Pastoral Ctr. 15 N. Seventh St.
Mailing city: Camden
Mailing state: NJ
Mailing zip: 08102
Office phone: (856) 583-6142
Office fax: (856) 756-7938
Advertising phone: (856) 583-6166
Advertising fax: (856) 756-7938
Editorial phone: (856) 583-6147
Advertising e-mail: pwothington@camdendiocese.org
Editorial e-mail: cpeters@camdendiocese.org
Website: www.catholicstarherald.org
Year newspaper established: 1951
Advertising (open inch rate): Open inch rate $25.90
Mechanical specifications: Type page 9 3/8 x 13 1/4; E - 4 cols, 2 1/4, between; A - 4 cols, 2 1/4, between; C - 4 cols, 2 1/4, between.
Delivery methods: Mail
Frequency: Bi-Mthly
Audit By: Sworn/Estimate/Non-Audited
Audit Date: 12.07.2019
Main (survey) contact: Carl Peters

CARY

BIBLICAL RECORDER

Street address 1: 205 Convention Dr
Street address state: NC
Postal code: 27511-4257
County: Wake
Country: USA
Mailing address: P.O. Box 1185
Mailing city: Cary
Mailing state: NC
Mailing zip: 27512-1185
Office phone: (919) 847-2127
Office fax: (919) 467-6180
General e-mail: editor@BRnow.org
Advertising e-mail: alison@BRnow.org
Editorial e-mail: editor@brnow.org
Website: www.BRnow.org
Year newspaper established: 1833
Advertising (open inch rate): Open inch rate $52.00
Mechanical specifications: Type page 10 x 15; E - 4 cols, 2 1/3, 1/3 between; A - 4 cols, 2 1/3, 1/3 between.
Delivery methods: Mail
Digital Platform - Mobile: Apple`Android`Windows
Digital Platform - Tablet: Apple iOS`Android`Windows 7
Frequency: Bi-Mthly
Other Type of Frequency: Every Other Sat
Circulation Paid: 12000
Circulation Free: 5000
Audit By: Sworn/Estimate/Non-Audited
Audit Date: 12.07.2019
Weeklies Equipment - Hardware: APP/Mac Aldus
Weeklies Equipment - Software: Adobe/PageMaker InDesign
Personnel: Alison McKinney (Bus. Mgr.); Allan Blume (Editor/President)
Parent company: Baptist State Convention of North Carolina
Main (survey) contact: Allan Blume

CHARLESTON

THE CATHOLIC MISCELLANY

Street address 1: 119 Broad St
Street address state: SC
Postal code: 29401-2435
County: Charleston
Country: USA
Mailing address: PO Box 818
Mailing city: Charleston
Mailing state: SC
Mailing zip: 29402-0818
Office phone: (843) 724-8375
Office fax: (843) 724-8368
Editorial e-mail: editor@catholic-doc.org
Website: www.catholic-doc.org
Advertising (open inch rate): Open inch rate $10.00
Mechanical specifications: Type page 10 x 14.
Frequency: Thur
Circulation Paid: 29000
Circulation Free: 247
Audit By: Sworn/Estimate/Non-Audited
Audit Date: 12.07.2019
Weeklies Equipment - Software: QPS/QuarkXPress 4.0.
Personnel: Deirdre C. Mays (Ed.); Karla Consroe (Circ./Adv. Coord.)
Main (survey) contact: Deirdre Mays

CHICAGO

CHICAGO CATÃ"LICO

Street address 1: 835 N. Rush St.
Street address state: IL
Postal code: 60611-2030
Country: USA
Mailing address: 835 N. Rush St.
Mailing city: Chicago
Mailing state: IL
Mailing zip: 60611-2030
Advertising e-mail: ccazares@archchicago.org
Editorial e-mail: editorial@catholicnewworld.com
Website: www.catolicoperiodico.com/publicidad
Year newspaper established: 1985
Zip Codes Served: Throughout Cook and Lake counties.
Frequency: Mthly
Personnel: Cesar Cazares (Adv. Mgr.)
Main (survey) contact: Cesar Cazares

THE CATHOLIC NEW WORLD

Street address 1: 835 N Rush St
Street address state: IL
Postal code: 60611-2030
County: Cook
Country: USA
Office phone: (312) 534-7777
Office fax: (312) 534-7350
General e-mail: editorial@catholicnewworld.com
Website: www.catholicnewworld.com
Year newspaper established: 1892
Mechanical specifications: Type page 10 1/4 x 14 5/8; A - 5 cols, 1 7/8, between; C - 5 cols, 1 7/8, between.
Delivery methods: Mail
Zip Codes Served: Cook and Lake counties
Other Type of Frequency: Every other Sat
Circulation Paid: 55000
Audit By: Sworn/Estimate/Non-Audited
Audit Date: 12.07.2019
Weeklies Equipment - Hardware: PC, APP/Mac
Weeklies Equipment - Software: QPS/QuarkXPress 4.0.
Personnel: Cardinal Francis E. George (Pub.); Dawn Vidmar (Adv. Mgr.); Joyce Duriga (Ed.); Tony Rodriguez (Prodn. Mgr.)
Main (survey) contact: Joyce Duriga

CINCINNATI

CHRISTIAN STANDARD

Street address 1: 8805 Governors Hill Dr
Street address 2: Ste 400
Street address state: OH
Postal code: 45249-3319
County: Hamilton
Country: USA
Mailing address: 8805 Governors Hill Dr Ste 400
Mailing city: Cincinnati
Mailing state: OH
Mailing zip: 45249-3319
Office phone: (513) 931-4050
Office fax: (877) 867-5751
General e-mail: christianstd@standardpub.com
Website: www.standardpub.com
Year newspaper established: 1866
Delivery methods: Mail
Audit By: Sworn/Estimate/Non-Audited
Audit Date: 12.07.2019
Personnel: Mark A. Taylor (Pub.); Jim Nieman (Mng. Ed.); Paul Williams (Ed.)
Main (survey) contact: Mark A. Taylor

THE CATHOLIC TELEGRAPH

Street address 1: 100 E 8th St
Street address state: OH
Postal code: 45202-2129
County: Hamilton
Country: USA
Mailing address: 100 E 8th St
Mailing city: Cincinnati
Mailing state: OH

Mailing zip: 45202-2129
Office phone: (513) 421-3131
Office fax: (513) 381-2242
General e-mail: thempel@catholiccincinnati.org
Website: www.catholiccincinnati.org/tct/curfeat1.htm
Advertising (open inch rate): Open inch rate $21.84
Frequency: Fri
Circulation Paid: 85000
Circulation Free: 400
Audit By: Sworn/Estimate/Non-Audited
Audit Date: 12.07.2019
Personnel: Daniel E. Pilarczyk (Pub.); Tim Mayer (Adv. Mgr.); Greg Hartman (Circ. Mgr.); Tricia Hempel (Ed.); Rick Barr (Prodn. Mgr.); Steve Trosley
Main (survey) contact: Greg Hartman

CLIFTON

THE BEACON

Street address 1: 775 Valley Rd
Street address state: NJ
Postal code: 07013-2205
County: Passaic
Country: USA
Mailing address: PO Box 1887
Mailing city: Clifton
Mailing state: NJ
Mailing zip: 07015-1887
Office phone: (973) 279-8845
Office fax: (973) 279-2265
General e-mail: catholicbeacon@patersondiocese.org; msbeacon@optonline.net
Website: www.patersondiocese.org
Year newspaper established: 1967
Advertising (open inch rate): Open inch rate $25.50
Mechanical specifications: Type page 10 x 14; E - 4 cols, 2 1/3, 1/6 between; A - 6 cols, 1 5/8, 1/6 between; C - 6 cols, 1 5/8, 1/6 between.
Delivery methods: Mail
Zip Codes Served: All of Passaic, Morris and Sussex Counties in Northern New Jersey
Frequency: Thur
Circulation Paid: 28750
Circulation Free: 200
Audit By: Sworn/Estimate/Non-Audited
Audit Date: 12.07.2019
Weeklies Equipment - Hardware: APP/Power Mac G3
Weeklies Equipment - Software: QPS/QuarkXPress 4.04, Adobe/Photoshop 5.0, Microsoft/Word.
Personnel: Arthur Serratelli (Pub.); Joyce DeCeglie (Circ. Mgr.); Richard Sokerka (Ed.)
Main (survey) contact: Arthur Serratelli

COLUMBIA

SOUTH CAROLINA UNITED METHODIST ADVOCATE

Street address 1: 4908 Colonial Dr
Street address 2: Ste 207
Street address state: SC
Postal code: 29203-6080
County: Richland
Country: USA
Mailing address: 4908 Colonial Dr Ste 207
Mailing city: Columbia
Mailing state: SC
Mailing zip: 29203-6080
Office phone: (803) 786-9486
Office fax: (803) 735-8168
General e-mail: advocate@umcsc.org
Website: www.advocatesc.org
Year newspaper established: 1836
Advertising (open inch rate): Open inch rate $19.00
Mechanical specifications: Type page 11 1/2 x 17 1/2; C - 3 cols, 3 1/4, 1/6 between.
Frequency: Mthly
Circulation Paid: 10000
Circulation Free: 1000
Audit By: Sworn/Estimate/Non-Audited
Audit Date: 12.07.2019

Weeklies Equipment - Hardware: Pentium, APP/Mac
Weeklies Equipment - Software: QPS/QuarkXPress 4.11.
Personnel: Allison Trussell (Circ. Mgr.); Jessica Connor (Editor); Emily Cooper (Ed.)
Main (survey) contact: Jessica Connor

UNITED METHODIST CONNECTION

Street address 1: 7178 Columbia Gateway Dr
Street address 2: Ste D
Street address state: MD
Postal code: 21046-2581
County: Howard
Country: USA
Mailing address: 7178 Columbia Gateway Dr Ste D
Mailing city: Columbia
Mailing state: MD
Mailing zip: 21046-2581
Office phone: (410) 309-3400
Office fax: (410) 309-9794
General e-mail: connection@bwcumc.org
Website: www.bwcumc.org
Advertising (open inch rate): Open inch rate $30.00
Other Type of Frequency: Every Other Wed
Circulation Paid: 10000
Audit By: Sworn/Estimate/Non-Audited
Audit Date: 12.07.2019
Personnel: Melissa Lauber (Ed.)
Main (survey) contact: Melissa Lauber

COLUMBUS

THE CATHOLIC TIMES

Street address 1: 197 E Gay St
Street address state: OH
Postal code: 43215-3229
County: Franklin
Country: USA
Mailing address: 197 E Gay St Ste 1
Mailing city: Columbus
Mailing state: OH
Mailing zip: 43215-3229
Office phone: (614) 224-5195
Office fax: (614) 241-2518
Website: www.colsdioc.org
Advertising (open inch rate): Open inch rate $16.50
Mechanical specifications: Type page 10 1/3 x 12 1/2; E - 3 cols, between; A - 6 cols, between.
Frequency: Sun
Circulation Paid: 18000
Audit By: Sworn/Estimate/Non-Audited
Audit Date: 19.10.2017
Weeklies Equipment - Software: QPS/QuarkXPress 3.32.
Personnel: Frederick Campbell (Pub.); Deacon Steve Demers (Adv. Mgr.); Jodie Shreddo (Circ. Mgr.); David Garick (Ed.)
Main (survey) contact: Frederick Campbell

CONKLIN

THE WINDSOR STANDARD

Street address 1: PO Box 208
Street address state: NY
Postal code: 13748-0208
County: Broome
Country: USA
Mailing address: PO Box 208
Mailing city: Conklin
Mailing state: NY
Mailing zip: 13748-0208
Office phone: (607) 775-0472
Office fax: (607) 775-5863
General e-mail: deinstein@stny.rr.com
Website: www.wecoverthetowns.com
Year newspaper established: 1880
Advertising (open inch rate): Open inch rate $4.50
Mechanical specifications: PDF
Delivery methods: Mail
Zip Codes Served: Eastern Broome County
Digital Platform - Mobile: Apple

Frequency: Wed
Circulation Paid: 1315
Circulation Free: 75
Audit By: Sworn/Estimate/Non-Audited
Audit Date: 12.07.2019
Weeklies Equipment - Hardware: Ma computers
Weeklies Equipment - Presses: none
Weeklies Equipment - Software: Adobe
Editions Count: 52
Personnel: Donald Einstein (Adv. Mgr.); Elizabeth Einstein (Ed.)
Parent company: Newspaper Publishers LLC
Main (survey) contact: Donald Einstein

CORPUS CHRISTI

SOUTH TEXAS CATHOLIC

Street address 1: 620 Lipan St
Street address state: TX
Postal code: 78401-2434
County: Nueces
Country: USA
Mailing address: 620 Lipan St
Mailing city: Corpus Christi
Mailing state: TX
Mailing zip: 78401-2434
Office phone: (361) 882-6191
Office fax: (361) 693-6701
Advertising phone: (361) 693-6605
Advertising fax: (361) 693-6701
Editorial phone: (361) 693-6609
Editorial fax: (361) 693-6701
General e-mail: stc@dicesecc.org
Website: www.southtexascatholic.com
Advertising (open inch rate): Varies
Delivery methods: Mail
Other Type of Frequency: 2 x Mthly
Circulation Paid: 43000
Audit By: Sworn/Estimate/Non-Audited
Audit Date: 12.07.2019
Personnel: Mary Cottingham (Mng. Ed.); Wm. Michael Mulvey (Bishop); Alfredo Cardenas (Editor); Adel Rivera (Office Mgr.); Father Joseph Lopez (Theological Consultant)
Main (survey) contact: Mary Cottingham

COVINGTON

THE MESSENGER

Street address 1: 402 E 21st St
Street address state: KY
Postal code: 41014-1588
County: Kenton
Country: USA
Mailing address: PO Box 15550
Mailing city: Covington
Mailing state: KY
Mailing zip: 41015-0550
Office phone: (859) 392-1500
General e-mail: mifcic@covingtondiocese.org
Website: www.covingtondiocese.org
Advertising (open inch rate): Open inch rate $19.00
Frequency: Fri
Circulation Paid: 27000
Circulation Free: 75
Audit By: Sworn/Estimate/Non-Audited
Audit Date: 12.07.2019
Weeklies Equipment - Hardware: APP/Macs
Weeklies Equipment - Software: Adobe/PageMaker 6.5, Microsoft/Word 6.0, Macromedia/Freehand 5.5, Adobe/Photoshop 3.01.
Personnel: Roger Foys (Pub.); Michael Ifcic (Adv. Mgr.); Judy Russo (Circ. Mgr.); Tim Fitzgerald (Ed.); Laura Keener (Asst. Ed.)
Main (survey) contact: Michael Ifcic

DALLAS

THE TEXAS CATHOLIC

Street address 1: 3725 Blackburn St
Street address state: TX
Postal code: 75219-4404
County: Dallas
Country: USA
Mailing address: PO Box 190347

Mailing city: Dallas
Mailing state: TX
Mailing zip: 75219-0347
Office phone: (214) 528-8792
Office fax: (214) 528-3411
General e-mail: texascatholic@msn.com
Website: www.texascatholic.com
Advertising (open inch rate): Open inch rate $37.00
Mechanical specifications: Type page 10 1/4 x 14; E - 4 cols, 2 3/8, between; A - 5 cols, 1 7/8, between; C - 5 cols, 1 7/8, between.
Other Type of Frequency: Every other Fri
Circulation Paid: 54000
Circulation Free: 857
Audit By: Sworn/Estimate/Non-Audited
Audit Date: 12.07.2019
Personnel: Kevin Farrell (Pub.); Tony Ramirez (Adv. Mgr.); Rosemary Allen (Circ. Mgr.); David Sedeno (Exec. Ed.)
Main (survey) contact: Tony Ramirez

DAVENPORT

THE CATHOLIC MESSENGER

Street address 1: 780 W Central Park Ave
Street address state: IA
Postal code: 52804-1901
County: Scott
Country: USA
Mailing address: 780 W. Central Park Ave.
Mailing city: Davenport
Mailing state: IA
Mailing zip: 52804
Office phone: (563) 323-9959
Office fax: (563) 323-6612
Advertising phone: (563) 323-9959
Editorial phone: (563) 888-4246
Other phone: (563) 320-0551
General e-mail: messenger@davenportdiocese.org
Advertising e-mail: hart@davenportdiocese.org
Editorial e-mail: arland-fye@davenportdiocese.org
Website: www.catholicmessenger.net
Year newspaper established: 1882
Advertising (open inch rate): Open inch rate $10.00
Delivery methods: Mail
Zip Codes Served: Multiple
Digital Platform - Mobile: Windows
Digital Platform - Tablet: Windows 7
Frequency: Thur
Circulation Paid: 17100
Circulation Free: 200
Audit By: Sworn/Estimate/Non-Audited
Audit Date: 12.07.2019
Weeklies Equipment - Software: QPS/QuarkXPress.
Editions Count: 50
Personnel: Barb Arland-Fye (Mng. Ed.); Anne Marie Amacher (Asst. Ed.); Jill Henderson (Circulation/Business Office Coordinator)
Main (survey) contact: Barb Arland-Fye

DENVER

DENVER CATHOLIC REGISTER

Street address 1: 1300 S Steele St
Street address state: CO
Postal code: 80210-2526
County: Denver
Country: USA
Mailing address: 1300 S Steele St
Mailing city: Denver
Mailing state: CO
Mailing zip: 80210-2526
Office phone: (303) 722-4687
Office fax: (303) 715-2045
Advertising phone: (303) 715-3212
General e-mail: dcrads@archden.org; info@archden.org
Website: www.archden.org
Year newspaper established: 1900
Advertising (open inch rate): Open inch rate $38.90
Mechanical specifications: Type page 10 1/4 x 13 3/4; E - 3 cols, between; A - 6 cols, between.

Frequency: Wed
Circulation Paid: 91165
Circulation Free: 379
Audit By: Sworn/Estimate/Non-Audited
Audit Date: 12.07.2019
Weeklies Equipment - Hardware: IBM
Weeklies Equipment - Software: Adobe/PageMaker 5.0, Archetype/Corel Draw.
Personnel: Charles J. Chaput (Pub.); Jeanette DeMelo (Gen. Mgr.); Chad Andrzejewski (Adv. Mgr.); Karen Mendoza (Circ. Mgr.); Roxanne King (Ed.)
Main (survey) contact: Chad Andrzejewski

EL PUEBLO CATOLICO

Street address 1: 1300 S Steele St
Street address state: CO
Postal code: 80210-2526
County: Denver
Country: USA
Mailing address: 1300 S Steele St
Mailing city: Denver
Mailing state: CO
Mailing zip: 80210-2526
Office phone: (303) 715-3219
Office fax: (303) 715-2045
General e-mail: elpueblo@archden.org
Website: www.archden.org
Advertising (open inch rate): Open inch rate $7.00
Mechanical specifications: Type page 10 1/4 x 12 1/2; E - 5 cols, 1 5/6, 1/8 between; A - 5 cols, 1 5/6, 1/8 between.
Audit By: Sworn/Estimate/Non-Audited
Audit Date: 12.07.2019
Weeklies Equipment - Hardware: IBM
Weeklies Equipment - Software: Adobe/PageMaker 5.0, QPS/QuarkXPress 6.0.
Personnel: Archbishop Charles J. Chaput (Pub.); Jeanette DeMelo (Gen. Mgr.); Ann Bush (Adv. Mgr.); Rosanna Goni (Ed.); Filippo Piccone (Prodn. Mgr.)
Main (survey) contact: Ann Bush

THE MICHIGAN CATHOLIC

Street address 1: 305 Michigan Ave
Street address state: MI
Postal code: 48226-2631
County: Wayne
Country: USA
Mailing address: 305 Michigan Ave Ste 400A
Mailing city: Detroit
Mailing state: MI
Mailing zip: 48226-2698
Office phone: (313) 224-8000
Office fax: (313) 224-8009
Website: www.themichigancatholic.com
Advertising (open inch rate): Open inch rate $21.00
Mechanical specifications: Type page 10 1/3 x 13; E - 5 cols, 2, between; A - 5 cols, 2, between.
Frequency: Fri
Other Type of Frequency: Bi-weekly
Circulation Paid: 25000
Audit By: Sworn/Estimate/Non-Audited
Audit Date: 19.10.2017
Weeklies Equipment - Hardware: PC
Weeklies Equipment - Software: Microsoft, Adobe/Photoshop, Adobe/Illustrator, Adobe/PageMaker.
Personnel: Michael Stechschulte (Managing Ed.)
Parent company: Archdiocese of Detroit
Main (survey) contact: Carlen Neely

DODGE CITY

THE SOUTHWEST KANSAS CATHOLIC

Street address 1: 910 Central Ave
Street address state: KS
Postal code: 67801-4905
County: Ford
Country: USA
Mailing address: PO Box 137
Mailing city: Dodge City
Mailing state: KS
Mailing zip: 67801-0137
Office phone: (620) 227-1519
Office fax: (620) 227-1545
Advertising phone: (620) 227-1556
Advertising fax: (620) 227-1545
Editorial phone: (620) 227-1519
Editorial fax: (620) 227-1545
General e-mail: skregister@dcdiocese.org
Advertising e-mail: twenzl@dcdiocese.org
Editorial e-mail: skregister@dcdiocese.org
Website: www.dcdiocese.org/swkscatholic
Year newspaper established: 1966
Advertising (open inch rate): Open inch rate $15.00
Mechanical specifications: 11x17 tabloid
Delivery methods: Mail Racks
Zip Codes Served: Southwest Quarter of Kansas
Digital Platform - Mobile: Windows
Frequency: Bi-Mthly Other
Other Type of Frequency: twice monthly
Circulation Free: 6000
Audit By: Sworn/Estimate/Non-Audited
Audit Date: 12.07.2019
Weeklies Equipment - Software: InDesign, Photoshop, Microsoft Word
Personnel: David Myers (Ed); Tim Wenzl (Adv Rep); Brungardt Bishop John (Pub)
Parent company: Catholic Diocese of Dodge City
Main (survey) contact: David Myers

DUBUQUE

THE WITNESS

Street address 1: 1229 Mount Loretta Ave
Street address 2: Box 917
Street address state: IA
Postal code: 52004-0917
County: Dubuque
Country: USA
Mailing address: PO Box 917
Mailing city: Dubuque
Mailing state: IA
Mailing zip: 52004-0917
Office phone: (563) 588-0556
Office fax: (563) 588-0557
General e-mail: dbqcwo@arch.pvt.k12.ia.us
Website: www.thewitnessonline.org
Advertising (open inch rate): Open inch rate $12.10
Mechanical specifications: Type page 13 1/4 x 21 1/2; E - 6 cols, 2, 3/16 between; A - 8 cols, 1 1/2, 3/16 between; C - 8 cols, 1 1/2, 3/16 between.
Frequency: Sun
Circulation Paid: 14000
Audit By: Sworn/Estimate/Non-Audited
Audit Date: 12.07.2019
Weeklies Equipment - Hardware: COM/MCS.
Personnel: Jerome Hanus (Pub.); Bret Fear (Adv. Mgr.); Catherine White (Circ. Mgr.); Sister Carol Hoverman (Ed.)
Main (survey) contact: Jerome Hanus

EDMOND

THE CHRISTIAN CHRONICLE

Street address 1: 2801 E Memorial Rd
Street address state: OK
Postal code: 73013-6474
County: Oklahoma
Country: USA
Mailing address: PO Box 11000
Mailing city: Oklahoma City
Mailing state: OK
Mailing zip: 73136-1100
Office phone: (405) 425-5070
Office fax: (405) 425-5076
Advertising phone: (405) 425-5071
Advertising fax: (405) 425-5076
Editorial phone: (405) 425-5070
General e-mail: lynn.mcmillon@christianchronicle.org
Advertising e-mail: tonya.patton@christianchronicle.org
Editorial e-mail: erik@christianchronicle.org
Website: www.christianchronicle.org.net
Year newspaper established: 1943
Delivery methods: Mail
Frequency: Mthly
Audit By: Sworn/Estimate/Non-Audited
Audit Date: 12.07.2019
Parent company: Oklahoma Christian University
Main (survey) contact: Erik Tryggested

EVANSVILLE

THE MESSAGE

Street address 1: 4200 N Kentucky Ave
Street address state: IN
Postal code: 47711-2752
County: Vanderburgh
Country: USA
Mailing address: PO Box 4169
Mailing city: Evansville
Mailing state: IN
Mailing zip: 47724-0169
Office phone: (812) 424-5536
Office fax: (812) 424-0972
General e-mail: message@evido.org
Advertising e-mail: messagead@evdio.org
Editorial e-mail: message@evdio.org
Website: www.themessageonline.org
Year newspaper established: 1970
Advertising (open inch rate): Open inch rate $8.00
Mechanical specifications: Type page 10 1/4 x 16; E - 5 cols, 1 11/12, 1/6 between; A - 5 cols, 1 11/12, 1/6 between.
Delivery methods: Mail
Digital Platform - Mobile: Apple
Digital Platform - Tablet: Apple iOS
Frequency: Fri
Circulation Paid: 5000
Audit By: Sworn/Estimate/Non-Audited
Audit Date: 12.07.2019
Weeklies Equipment - Hardware: APP/Mac
Weeklies Equipment - Software: QPS/QuarkXPress.
Personnel: Tim Lilley (Ed.); Sheila Barclay (Prod. Tech.); Trisha Smith (Assist. Ed.)
Main (survey) contact: Ruth Bandas

FALL RIVER

THE ANCHOR

Street address 1: 887 Highland Ave
Street address state: MA
Postal code: 02720-3820
County: Bristol
Country: USA
Mailing address: PO Box 7
Mailing city: Fall River
Mailing state: MA
Mailing zip: 02722-0007
Office phone: (508) 675-7151
Office fax: (508) 675-7048
General e-mail: theanchor@anchornews.org
Website: www.anchornews.org
Advertising (open inch rate): Open inch rate $13.75
Mechanical specifications: Type page 10 x 14; A - 5 cols, 2, between.
Audit By: Sworn/Estimate/Non-Audited
Audit Date: 12.07.2019
Weeklies Equipment - Hardware: 3-HP/486
Weeklies Equipment - Software: Microsoft/Windows 95, Adobe/PageMaker 6.0, Microsoft/Works 3.0.
Personnel: Most Rev. George W. Coleman (Pub.); Rev. Roger Landry (Exec. Ed.)
Main (survey) contact: Most Rev. George W. Coleman

FORT WAYNE

TODAYS CATHOLIC

Street address 1: 915 S Clinton St
Street address state: IN
Postal code: 46802-2601
County: Allen
Country: USA
Mailing address: PO Box 11169
Mailing city: Fort Wayne
Mailing state: IN
Mailing zip: 46856-1169
Office phone: (260) 456-2824
Office fax: (260) 744-1473
Advertising e-mail: jparker@diocesefwsb.org
Editorial e-mail: editor@diocesefwsb.org
Website: www.diocesefwsb.org; www.todayscatholicnews.org
Year newspaper established: 1926
Advertising (open inch rate): Open inch rate $15.85
Mechanical specifications: Type page 10 x 13; E - 5 cols, 1.875 inches, .167 between; A - 5 col, 2 inches.
Delivery methods: Mail Racks
Zip Codes Served: 14 counties in northeastern Indiana
Digital Platform - Mobile: Apple Android Windows Blackberry
Digital Platform - Tablet: Apple iOS Android Windows 7 Blackberry Tablet OS Kindle Nook Kindle Fire
Frequency: Sun
Other Type of Frequency: published 43 times per year
Circulation Paid: 207
Circulation Free: 10000
Audit By: Sworn/Estimate/Non-Audited
Audit Date: 12.07.2019
Personnel: Kevin Rhoades (Pub.); Stephanie Patka (Dir. of Comm.); Jodi Marlin (Ed.)
Main (survey) contact: Jodi Marlin

FORT WORTH

NORTH TEXAS CATHOLIC

Street address 1: 800 W Loop 820 S
Street address state: TX
Postal code: 76108-2936
County: Tarrant
Country: USA
Mailing address: 800 W Loop 820 S
Mailing city: Fort Worth
Mailing state: TX
Mailing zip: 76108-2936
Office phone: (817) 560-3300
Office fax: (817) 244-8839
General e-mail: jrusseau@fwdioc.org
Advertising e-mail: jrusseau@fwdioc.org
Editorial e-mail: jhensley@fwdioc.org
Website: www.fwdioc.org
Advertising (open inch rate): Open inch rate $48.00
Mechanical specifications: Type page 7.375 x 9.5; E - 4 cols, 1.625 1/6 between; A - 4 cols, 1.625, 1/6 between; C - 4 cols, 1.625, 1/6 between.
Delivery methods: Mail
Zip Codes Served: 76108
Other Type of Frequency: every other month
Circulation Paid: 27000
Circulation Free: 82000
Audit By: Sworn/Estimate/Non-Audited
Audit Date: 12.07.2019
Weeklies Equipment - Hardware: 4-APP/Mac G4
Weeklies Equipment - Software: Adobe/CS4 Indesign Adobe/Photoshop 6.0.
Personnel: Judy Russeau (Adv. Mgr.); Jeff Hensley (Ed)
Main (survey) contact: Judy Russeau

GARDEN GROVE

ORANGE COUNTY CATHOLIC

Street address 1: 13280 Chapman Ave
Street address state: CA
Postal code: 92840-4414
County: Orange
Country: USA
Office phone: (714) 282-3075
Advertising phone: (714) 881-1622
Other phone: (877) 627-7009
General e-mail: calmanza@rcbo.org
Advertising e-mail: ads@occatholic.com
Editorial e-mail: pmott@rcbo.org
Website: http://occatholic.com/
Delivery methods: Mail Newsstand
Zip Codes Served: Orange County
Frequency: Fri
Personnel: Hank Evers (Editor)
Parent company: Times Media Group

Religious Newspapers in the U.S.

GRAND ISLAND

WEST NEBRASKA REGISTER

Street address 1: 2708 Old Fair Rd
Street address state: NE
Postal code: 68803-5221
County: Hall
Country: USA
Mailing address: PO Box 608
Mailing city: Grand Island
Mailing state: NE
Mailing zip: 68802-0608
Office phone: (308) 382-4660
Office fax: (308) 382-6569
Website: www.gidiocese.org
Advertising (open inch rate): Open inch rate $8.56
Delivery methods: Mail
Zip Codes Served: 688, 689, 691, 692, 693, 686,
Digital Platform - Tablet: Apple iOS
Frequency: Fri
Other Type of Frequency: Twice monthly
Circulation Paid: 17153
Audit By: Sworn/Estimate/Non-Audited
Audit Date: 12.07.2019
Personnel: Mary Parlin (Ed.); Colleen Gallion (Assoc. Ed.)
Main (survey) contact: Mary Parlin

Main (survey) contact: Hank Evers

GRAND RAPIDS

THE BANNER

Street address 1: 1700 28th St SE
Street address state: MI
Postal code: 49508-1407
County: Kent
Country: USA
Mailing address: 1700 28th St. SE
Mailing city: Grand Rapids
Mailing state: MI
Mailing zip: 49508-1407
Office phone: (616) 224-0732
Office fax: (616) 224-0834
Advertising phone: (616) 224-5882
Editorial phone: (616) 224-0824
General e-mail: info@thebanner.org
Advertising e-mail: ads@thebanner.org
Website: www.thebanner.org
Mechanical specifications: Type page 7 1/3 x 10; A - 3 cols, 2 1/3, 1/6 between; C - 3 cols, 2 1/3, 1/6 between.
Delivery methods: Mail
Digital Platform - Mobile: Apple`Android
Digital Platform - Tablet: Apple iOS`Android
Frequency: Mthly
Circulation Free: 83500
Audit By: Sworn/Estimate/Non-Audited
Audit Date: 12.07.2019
Personnel: Shiao Chong (Editor in chief); Judy Hardy (Assoc. Ed.); Alissa Vernon (News Ed.); Gayla Postma (News Ed.); Kristy Quist (Mixed Media); Dean Heetderks (Art Dir.)
Main (survey) contact: Judith Hardy

GREENSBURG

THE CATHOLIC ACCENT

Street address 1: 725 E Pittsburgh St
Street address state: PA
Postal code: 15601-2660
County: Westmoreland
Country: USA
Mailing address: 725 E Pittsburgh St
Mailing city: Greensburg
Mailing state: PA
Mailing zip: 15601-2660
Office phone: (724) 834-4010
Office fax: (724) 836-5650
General e-mail: news@dioceseofgreensburg.org
Website: www.dioceseofgreensburg.org
Year newspaper established: 1961
Advertising (open inch rate): Open inch rate $16.50

Mechanical specifications: Type page 10 1/4 x 12 3/4; A - 5 cols, 1 7/8, 1/8 between.
Delivery methods: Mail
Zip Codes Served: 4 counties of the diocese (multiple)
Other Type of Frequency: Every Other Thur
Circulation Paid: 46500
Circulation Free: 924
Audit By: Sworn/Estimate/Non-Audited
Audit Date: 12.07.2019
Weeklies Equipment - Hardware: PC
Weeklies Equipment - Presses: G
Weeklies Equipment - Software: InDesign CS4
Personnel: Lawrence E. Brandt (Chief Executive Officer and Publisher); Rose Govi (Adv. Mgr.); Nancy Balfe (Circulation Coordinator); Jerome M. Zufelt (Editor, The Catholic Accent); Elizabeth Fazzini (Assistant Editor, The Catholic Accent); Valerie Rodell (Production Coordinator)
Main (survey) contact: Nancy Balfe

GREENVILLE

THE BAPTIST COURIER

Street address 1: 100 Manly St
Street address state: SC
Postal code: 29601-3025
County: Greenville
Country: USA
Mailing address: 100 Manly St
Mailing city: Greenville
Mailing state: SC
Mailing zip: 29601-3025
Office phone: (864) 232-8736
Office fax: (864) 232-8488
General e-mail: news@baptistcourier.com
Website: www.baptistcourier.com
Advertising (open inch rate): Open inch rate $75.00
Other Type of Frequency: Every Other Thur
Circulation Paid: 75000
Circulation Free: 2000
Audit By: Sworn/Estimate/Non-Audited
Audit Date: 12.07.2019
Personnel: Debbie Grooms (Bus. Mgr.); Butch Blame (Mng. Ed.); Don Kirkland (Ed.)
Main (survey) contact: Don Kirkland

HONOLULU

HAWAII CATHOLIC HERALD

Street address 1: 1184 Bishop St
Street address state: HI
Postal code: 96813-2859
County: Honolulu
Country: USA
Mailing address: 1184 Bishop St Ste A
Mailing city: Honolulu
Mailing state: HI
Mailing zip: 96813-2859
Office phone: (808) 585-3300
Office fax: (808) 585-3381
Editorial phone: (808) 585-3317
Editorial e-mail: herald@rcchawaii.org
Website: www.hawaiicatholicherald.org
Year newspaper established: 1936
Advertising (open inch rate): Open inch rate $48.00
Mechanical specifications: Type page 10 1/4 x 15; E - 5 cols, 1 11/12, 1/6 between; A - 5 cols, 1 11/12, 1/6 between; C - 5 cols, 1 11/12, 1/6 between.
Delivery methods: Mail
Audit By: Sworn/Estimate/Non-Audited
Audit Date: 12.07.2019
Personnel: Clarence Silva (Pub.); Donna Aquino (Circ. Mgr.); Patrick Downes (Ed.)
Parent company: Roman Catholic Church in the State of Hawaii
Main (survey) contact: Patrick Downes

HOUSTON

THE TEXAS CATHOLIC HERALD

Street address 1: 1700 San Jacinto St
Street address state: TX

Postal code: 77002-8216
County: Harris
Country: USA
Mailing address: 1700 San Jacinto St
Mailing city: Houston
Mailing state: TX
Mailing zip: 77002-8216
Office phone: (713) 659-5461
Office fax: (713) 659-3444
General e-mail: tch@archgh.org
Website: www.texascatholicherald.org
Advertising (open inch rate): Open inch rate $38.00
Mechanical specifications: Type page 9 3/4 x 12.
Zip Codes Served: 77002
Other Type of Frequency: 2 x Mthly
Circulation Paid: 72000
Circulation Free: 1680
Audit By: Sworn/Estimate/Non-Audited
Audit Date: 12.07.2019
Weeklies Equipment - Hardware: APP/Mac
Weeklies Equipment - Software: Adobe/PageMaker 6.0.
Personnel: Daniel DiNardo (Pub.)
Main (survey) contact: Daniel DiNardo

HUNTINGTON

OUR SUNDAY VISITOR

Street address 1: 200 Noll Plz
Street address state: IN
Postal code: 46750-4310
County: Huntington
Country: USA
Office phone: (260) 356-8400
Office fax: (260) 356-8472
Advertising phone: (260) 359-2578
Advertising fax: (260) 359-2578
Editorial phone: (260) 359-2546
Editorial fax: (260) 359-6446
General e-mail: oursunvis@osv.com
Advertising e-mail: tcalouette@osv.com
Editorial e-mail: gcrowe@osv.com
Website: www.osv.com
Year newspaper established: 1912
Advertising (open inch rate): Open inch rate $90.00
Mechanical specifications: Type page 10 1/8 x 13; E - 5 cols, 1 7/8, 1/8 between; A - 5 cols, 2, 1/8 between; C - 1 cols, 1 7/8, 1/8 between.
Delivery methods: Mail
Zip Codes Served: All/any
Frequency: Sun
Circulation Paid: 43000
Circulation Free: 4000
Audit By: Sworn/Estimate/Non-Audited
Audit Date: 12.07.2019
Weeklies Equipment - Hardware: 15-MAC
Weeklies Equipment - Software: QPS/QuarkXPress 4/5/6.
Edition Names: Volume 103 - Our Sunday Visitor
Personnel: Greg R. Erlandson (Pres./Pub.); Therese Calouette (Adv. Mgr.); John Christensen (Strategic Mktg. Dir.); Gretchen Crowe (Ed.); Chris Rice (Prodn. Mgr.)
Main (survey) contact: Greg R. Erlandson

HYATTSVILLE

EL PREGONERO

Street address 1: 5001 Eastern Ave
Street address state: MD
Postal code: 20782-3447
County: Prince Georges
Country: USA
Mailing address: PO Box 4464
Mailing city: Washington
Mailing state: DC
Mailing zip: 20017-0464
Office phone: (202) 281-2404
Office fax: (202) 281-2448
Advertising phone: (202) 281-2406
Editorial phone: (202) 281-2442
General e-mail: rafael@elpreg.org
Advertising e-mail: irieska@elpreg.org
Editorial e-mail: rafael@elpreg.org
Website: elpreg.org

Year newspaper established: 1977
Advertising (open inch rate): Open inch rate $19.00
Mechanical specifications: Type page 10 1/4 x 13 1/2; E - 5 cols, 1 5/6, 1/6 between; A - 5 cols, 1/6 between; C - 7 cols, 1 1/3, 1/6 between.
Delivery methods: Newsstand`Carrier
Frequency: Thur
Circulation Free: 24993
Audit By: AAM
Audit Date: 30.06.2018
Weeklies Equipment - Hardware: 5-APP/Mac, 3-APP/Mac LaserPrinters
Weeklies Equipment - Software: QPS/QuarkXPress, Adobe/Photoshop, Adobe/Illustrator, Multi-Ad/Creator, Baseview/NewsEdit Pro, Class Manager/Plus.
Personnel: Rafael Roncal (Ed.); Irieska D. Caetano (Circ. Mgr.)
Main (survey) contact: Rafael Roncal

INDIANAPOLIS

THE CRITERION

Street address 1: 1400 N Meridian St
Street address state: IN
Postal code: 46202-2305
County: Marion
Country: USA
Mailing address: PO Box 1717
Mailing city: Indianapolis
Mailing state: IN
Mailing zip: 46206-1717
Office phone: (317) 236-7325
Office fax: (317) 236-1593
General e-mail: criterion@archindy.org
Website: www.archindy.org
Audit By: Sworn/Estimate/Non-Audited
Audit Date: 12.07.2019
Personnel: Daniel Mark Buechlein (Pub.); Greg A. Otolski (Asst. Pub.); Ron Massey (Exec. Asst.); Mike Krokos (Ed.); John Shaughnessy (Asst. Ed.); Brandon A. Evans (Online Ed.)
Main (survey) contact: Daniel Mark Buechlein

JACKSON

MISSISSIPPI CATHOLIC

Street address 1: 237 E Amite St
Street address state: MS
Postal code: 39201-2405
County: Hinds
Country: USA
Mailing address: PO Box 2130
Mailing city: Jackson
Mailing state: MS
Mailing zip: 39225-2130
Office phone: (601) 969-3581
Office fax: (601) 960-8455
General e-mail: editor@mississippicathollic.com
Editorial e-mail: editor@mississippicatholic.com
Website: www.mississippicatholic.com
Year newspaper established: 1954
Advertising (open inch rate): Open inch rate $10.50
Delivery methods: Mail
Frequency: Fri
Circulation Paid: 13112
Audit By: Sworn/Estimate/Non-Audited
Audit Date: 12.07.2019
Personnel: Joseph N. Latino (Pub.); Elsa Baughman (Adv. Mgr.); Pamela Butler (Circ. Mgr.); Janna Avalon (Ed.); Tyna McNealy (Prodn. Mgr.)
Main (survey) contact: Janna Avalon

THE BAPTIST RECORD

Street address 1: 515 Mississippi Street
Street address state: MS
Postal code: 39205-0530
County: Hinds
Country: USA
Mailing address: PO Box 530

Mailing city: Jackson
Mailing state: MS
Mailing zip: 39205-0530
Office phone: (601) 968-3800
Office fax: (601) 292-3330
General e-mail: baptistrecord@mbcb.org
Website: www.mbcb.org
Year newspaper established: 1877
Delivery methods: Mail
Frequency: Thur
Circulation Paid: 57000
Circulation Free: 31
Audit By: Sworn/Estimate/Non-Audited
Audit Date: 12.07.2019
Personnel: Dana Richardson (Adv. Coord.); William H. Perkins (Ed.); Tony Martin (Assoc. Ed.); DeAnna Burgess (Circ. Mgr.)
Parent company: Mississippi Baptist Convention Board
Main (survey) contact: William H. Perkins

JEFFERSON CITY

THE CATHOLIC MISSOURIAN

Street address 1: PO Box 104900
Street address state: MO
Postal code: 65110-4900
County: Cole
Country: USA
Mailing address: PO Box 104900
Mailing city: Jefferson City
Mailing state: MO
Mailing zip: 65110-4900
Office phone: (573) 635-9127
Office fax: (573) 635-2286
General e-mail: cathmo@diojeffcity.org
Website: www.diojeffcity.org
Year newspaper established: 1957
Advertising (open inch rate): Open inch rate $8.03
Mechanical specifications: Type page 9 7/8 x 12 3/4.
Frequency: Fri
Circulation Paid: 20578
Circulation Free: 755
Audit By: Sworn/Estimate/Non-Audited
Audit Date: 12.07.2019
Personnel: Bishop John R. Gaydos (Pub.); Kelly Martin (Adv. Dir.); Jay Nies (Ed.)
Main (survey) contact: C Baker

THE PATHWAY

Street address 1: 400 E High St
Street address state: MO
Postal code: 65101-3215
County: Cole
Country: USA
Mailing address: 400 E High St
Mailing city: Jefferson City
Mailing state: MO
Mailing zip: 65101-3215
Office phone: (573) 636-0400
Office fax: (573) 635-5631
Advertising phone: (573) 636-0400
General e-mail: dhinkle@mobaptist.org
Advertising e-mail: bpeeper@mobaptist.org
Editorial e-mail: dhinkle@mobaptist.org
Website: www.mbcpathway.com
Year newspaper established: 2002
Advertising (open inch rate): Open inch rate $15.00
Delivery methods: Mail
Zip Codes Served: All
Digital Platform - Mobile: Apple
Digital Platform - Tablet: Apple iOS
Frequency: Other
Other Type of Frequency: 2 x Mthly
Circulation Paid: 25050
Audit By: Sworn/Estimate/Non-Audited
Audit Date: 12.07.2019
Weeklies Equipment - Hardware: APP/Mac
Weeklies Equipment - Software: indesign
Personnel: Don Hinkle (Editor); Brian Koonce (News Writer); Ben Hawkins
Parent company: Missouri Baptist Convention
Main (survey) contact: Don Hinkle

KANSAS CITY

NATIONAL CATHOLIC REPORTER

Street address 1: 115 E Armour Blvd
Street address state: MO
Postal code: 64111-1203
County: Jackson
Country: USA
Mailing address: 115 E Armour Blvd
Mailing city: Kansas City
Mailing state: MO
Mailing zip: 64111
Office phone: (816) 531-0538
Advertising phone: (816) 531-0538 opt 2
Editorial phone: (816) 531-0538 opt 5
Other phone: (800) 333-7373
General e-mail: mjudd@ncronline.org
Advertising e-mail: ncrad@ncronline.org
Editorial e-mail: mjudd@ncronline.org
Website: www.ncronline.org
Year newspaper established: 1964
Advertising (open inch rate): Open inch rate $65.00
Mechanical specifications: Type page 10 7/16 x 14 1/2; E - 4 cols, 2 7/16, 1/6 between; A - 4 cols, 2 7/16, 1/6 between; C - 4 cols, 2 7/16, 1/6 between.
Delivery methods: Mail
Zip Codes Served: National and International
Digital Platform - Mobile: Apple`Android`Windows`Blackberry
Digital Platform - Tablet: Apple iOS`Android`Windows 7`Blackberry Tablet OS`Kindle`Nook`Kindle Fire
Frequency: Other
Other Type of Frequency: Bi-Weekly
Circulation Paid: 25000
Circulation Free: 150
Audit By: Sworn/Estimate/Non-Audited
Audit Date: 12.07.2019
Personnel: Wally Reiter (CFO/Bus. Mgr.); Toni-Ann Ortiz (Art Dir.); Kim Rea (Adv Mgr); Sara Wiercinski (Aud Engagement Dir); Jo Schierhoff (Circ Mgr); Nancy Browne (Chief Advancement Officer); Tom Fox (President & CEO); Tom Roberts (Executive Editor)
Main (survey) contact: Megan Judd

KETTERING

CATHOLIC DIGEST MAGAZINE

Street address 1: PO Box 291826
Street address state: OH
Postal code: 45429
County: New Haven
Country: USA
Mailing address: PO Box 291826
Mailing city: Kettering
Mailing state: OH
Mailing zip: 45429
Office phone: (203) 985-4450
General e-mail: catholicdigest@sfsdayton.com
Advertising e-mail: michelle.kopfmann@bayard-inc.com
Editorial e-mail: pmckibben@bayard-inc.com
Website: http://www.catholicdigest.com/
Zip Codes Served: 6514
Audit By: Sworn/Estimate/Non-Audited
Audit Date: 12.07.2019
Weeklies Equipment - Hardware: APP/Mac
Weeklies Equipment - Software: Microsoft/Word 6.0.
Personnel: Paul Mckibben (Ed.); Michelle Kopfmann (Adv.)
Main (survey) contact: Paul Mckibben

LA CROSSE

THE CATHOLIC LIFE

Street address 1: 3710 East Ave S
Street address state: WI
Postal code: 54601-7215
County: La Crosse
Country: USA
Mailing address: PO Box 4004
Mailing city: La Crosse
Mailing state: WI
Mailing zip: 54602-4004
Office phone: (608) 788-1524
Office fax: (608) 788-0932
General e-mail: catholictimes@dioceseoflacrosse.com
Website: catholiclife.diolc.org
Mechanical specifications: Type page 10 x 13; E - 5 cols, 1 7/8, 1/6 between; A - 5 cols, 1 7/8, 1/6 between.
Other Type of Frequency: Every Other Thur
Circulation Paid: 31000
Circulation Free: 193
Audit By: Sworn/Estimate/Non-Audited
Audit Date: 12.07.2019
Weeklies Equipment - Hardware: APP/Mac
Weeklies Equipment - Software: Adobe/Photoshop 6.0, QPS/QuarkXPress 4.1, Adobe/Acrobat 4.0.
Personnel: Pamela Willer (Circ. Mgr.); Pam Willer (Subs./Adv.); Denis Downey (Associate Editor); Danelle Bjornson (Graphic Designer)
Main (survey) contact: Pam Willer

LAFAYETTE

THE CATHOLIC MOMENT

Street address 1: 610 Lingle Ave
Street address state: IN
Postal code: 47901-1740
County: Tippecanoe
Country: USA
Mailing address: PO Box 1603
Mailing city: Lafayette
Mailing state: IN
Mailing zip: 47902-1603
Office phone: (765) 742-2050
Office fax: (765) 269-4615
General e-mail: moment@dol-in.org
Website: dol-in.org/catholic-moment
Year newspaper established: 1945
Advertising (open inch rate): Open inch rate $13.00
Mechanical specifications: Type page 10 x 13; E - 5 cols, 1 7/8, 1/6 between; A - 5 cols, 1 7/8, 1/6 between.
Delivery methods: Mail
Zip Codes Served: Several
Frequency: Sun
Circulation Paid: 28500
Circulation Free: 264
Audit By: USPS
Audit Date: 01.10.2013
Weeklies Equipment - Hardware: 5-PC
Weeklies Equipment - Software: QPS/QuarkXPress 9.0, Adobe/Photoshop 7.0, Microsoft/Word, Adobe Acrobat Pro 9
Personnel: Most Rev. Timothy L. Doherty (Pub.); Carolyn McKinney (Circ. Mgr.); Laurie Cullen (Mng. Ed.); Kevin Cullen (Ed.)
Main (survey) contact: Carolyn McKinney

LINCOLN

SOUTHERN NEBRASKA REGISTER

Street address 1: 3700 Sheridan Blvd
Street address state: NE
Postal code: 68506-6100
County: Lancaster
Country: USA
Mailing address: PO Box 80329
Mailing city: Lincoln
Mailing state: NE
Mailing zip: 68501-0329
Office phone: (402) 488-0090
Office fax: (402) 488-3569
Advertising (open inch rate): Open inch rate $20.00
Mechanical specifications: Type page 11 1/2 x 17 3/4; E - 5 cols, 2, 1/8 between; A - 5 cols, 2, 1/8 between.
Frequency: Fri
Circulation Paid: 25000
Audit By: Sworn/Estimate/Non-Audited
Audit Date: 12.07.2019
Personnel: James Conley (Pub.); Kim Breitfelder (Circ. Mgr.); Nick Kipper (Editor)
Main (survey) contact: Nick Kipper

LITTLE ROCK

ARKANSAS CATHOLIC

Street address 1: 2500 N Tyler St
Street address state: AR
Postal code: 72207-3743
County: Pulaski
Country: USA
Mailing address: PO Box 7417
Mailing city: Little Rock
Mailing state: AR
Mailing zip: 72205
Office phone: (501)664-0125
Office fax: (501) 664-6572
Advertising phone: (501)664-0125
Editorial phone: (501)664-0125
General e-mail: mhargett@dolr.org
Advertising e-mail: pstabnick@dolr.org
Editorial e-mail: mhargett@dolr.org
Website: www.arkansas-catholic.org
Year newspaper established: 1911
Advertising (open inch rate): Open inch rate $17.00
Mechanical specifications: Type page 11 x 14; E - 4 cols, 2 2/5, 1/4 between; A - 4 cols, 2 2/5, 1/4 between.
Delivery methods: Mail
Zip Codes Served: All in Arkansas
Digital Platform - Mobile: Apple`Android`Windows`Blackberry
Digital Platform - Tablet: Apple iOS`Android`Windows 7`Blackberry Tablet OS`Kindle`Nook`Kindle Fire
Frequency: Sat
Circulation Paid: 4600
Circulation Free: 500
Audit By: Sworn/Estimate/Non-Audited
Audit Date: 12.07.2019
Personnel: Malea Hargett (Ed.); Emily Roberts (Prodn. Mgr.); Pete Stabnick (advertising manager); Aprille Hanson (associate editor)
Main (survey) contact: Malea Hargett

BAPTIST TRUMPET

Street address 1: 10712 Interstate 30
Street address state: AR
Postal code: 72209-5835
County: Pulaski
Country: USA
Mailing address: PO Box 192208
Mailing city: Little Rock
Mailing state: AR
Mailing zip: 72219-2208
Office phone: (501) 565-4601
Office fax: (501) 565-6397
Editorial e-mail: editor@baptisttrumpet.com
Website: www.baptisttrumpet.com
Year newspaper established: 1939
Advertising (open inch rate): Open inch rate $15
Mechanical specifications: Type page 10 1/4 x 12 1/4; E - 5 cols, 1 4/5, 1/4 between; A - 5 cols, 1 4/5, 1/4 between.
Frequency: Wed
Circulation Paid: 8300
Audit By: Sworn/Estimate/Non-Audited
Audit Date: 12.07.2019
Personnel: Diane Spriggs (Editor/Business Manager)
Main (survey) contact: Diane Spriggs

LOS ANGELES

THE TIDINGS

Street address 1: 3424 Wilshire Blvd
Street address 2: Fl 3
Street address state: CA
Postal code: 90010-2262
County: Los Angeles
Country: USA
Mailing address: 3424 Wilshire Blvd Fl 3
Mailing city: Los Angeles
Mailing state: CA
Mailing zip: 90010-2262
Office phone: (213) 637-7360
Office fax: (213) 637-6360
Advertising phone: (213) 637-7590
Editorial phone: (213) 637-7327

Religious Newspapers in the U.S.

General e-mail: info@the-tidings.com
Advertising e-mail: otorres@the-tidings.com
Editorial e-mail: pkay@the-tidings.com
Website: www.angelusnews.com
Year newspaper established: 1865
Advertising (open inch rate): Open inch rate $72.00
Delivery methods: Mail
Zip Codes Served: 90001£90899, 91001£93599,93001-9300993101-93109
Digital Platform - Mobile: Apple`Android`Windows
Digital Platform - Tablet: Apple iOS`Android`Kindle
Frequency: Fri
Circulation Paid: 50000
Circulation Free: 372
Audit By: Sworn/Estimate/Non-Audited
Audit Date: 12.07.2019
Weeklies Equipment - Hardware: Mac
Weeklies Equipment - Software: InDesign
Personnel: David Moore (Pub.); Chris Krause (Circulation)
Parent company: Archdiocese of Los Angeles
Main (survey) contact: David Moore

LOUISVILLE

SOUTHEAST OUTLOOK

Street address 1: 920 Blankenbaker Pkwy
Street address state: KY
Postal code: 40243-1845
County: Jefferson
Country: USA
Mailing address: 920 Blankenbaker Pkwy
Mailing city: Louisville
Mailing state: KY
Mailing zip: 40243-1845
Office phone: (502) 253-8650
Office fax: (502) 499-6968
General e-mail: badams@secc.org
Website: www.southeastoutlook.org
Delivery methods: Mail`Racks
Digital Platform - Mobile: Apple`Android`Windows
Digital Platform - Tablet: Apple iOS`Android`Windows 7`Blackberry Tablet OS`Kindle`Nook`Kindle Fire`Other
Frequency: Thur
Main (survey) contact: Brent Adams

THE RECORD

Street address 1: 1200 S Shelby St
Street address state: KY
Postal code: 40203-2627
County: Jefferson
Country: USA
Mailing address: 1200 S Shelby St
Mailing city: Louisville
Mailing state: KY
Mailing zip: 40203-2627
Office phone: (502) 471-2125
Office fax: (502) 636-2379
Advertising phone: (502) 471-2125
General e-mail: record@archlou.org
Advertising e-mail: record@archlou.org
Editorial e-mail: record@archlou.org
Website: www.therecordnewspaper.org
Year newspaper established: 1879
Advertising (open inch rate): Open inch rate starting at $25.00.
Mechanical specifications: Type page 10 x 21; E - 6 cols, 2 1/15, 1/10 between; A - 6 cols, 2 1/15, 1/10 between; C - 8 cols, 1 1/2, 1/6 between.
Delivery methods: Mail
Frequency: Thur
Circulation Paid: 59708
Audit By: Sworn/Estimate/Non-Audited
Audit Date: 12.07.2019
Note: Serving central Kentucky area.
Personnel: Marnie McAllister (Ed.); Jennifer Jenkins (Adv. Mgr.)
Parent company: Archdiocese of Louisville
Main (survey) contact: Marnie McAllister

WESTERN RECORDER

Street address 1: 13420 Eastpoint Centre Dr
Street address state: KY
Postal code: 40223-4160
County: Jefferson
Country: USA
Mailing address: PO Box 43969
Mailing city: Louisville
Mailing state: KY
Mailing zip: 40253-0969
Office phone: (502) 489-3535
Office fax: (502) 489-3565
Advertising phone: (502) 489-3428
Advertising fax: (502) 489-3228
Editorial phone: (502) 489-3442
Website: www.westernrecorder.org
Year newspaper established: 1826
Advertising (open inch rate): Open inch rate $30.00
Mechanical specifications: Type page 10 x 14.
Delivery methods: Mail
Zip Codes Served: Kentucky
Frequency: Tues
Circulation Paid: 24000
Circulation Free: 1384
Audit By: Sworn/Estimate/Non-Audited
Audit Date: 12.07.2019
Weeklies Equipment - Hardware: PC network
Weeklies Equipment - Software: Microsoft/Word, Adobe/PageMaker 6.0.
Personnel: Tom Townsend (Mktg. Mgr.)
Main (survey) contact: Tom Townsend

MADISON

CATHOLIC HERALD NEWSPAPER

Street address 1: 702 S High Point Rd
Street address state: WI
Postal code: 53719-4925
County: Dane
Country: USA
Mailing address: 702 S High Point Rd
Mailing city: Madison
Mailing state: WI
Mailing zip: 53719-3522
Office phone: (608) 821-3070
Office fax: (608) 821-3071
General e-mail: info@madisoncatholicherald.org
Website: www.madisoncatholicherald.org
Year newspaper established: 1948
Advertising (open inch rate): Open inch rate $18.50
Frequency: Thur
Circulation Paid: 26000
Audit By: Sworn/Estimate/Non-Audited
Audit Date: 12.07.2019
Weeklies Equipment - Hardware: APP/Mac
Weeklies Equipment - Software: QPS/QuarkXPress 4.0, Adobe/Acrobat 4.0.
Personnel: Robert Morlino (Pub.); Steve Hefty (Adv. Mgr.); Mary Uhler (Ed.); Pamela Payne (Assoc. Ed.)
Main (survey) contact: Pam Payne

MEMPHIS

THE WEST TENNESSEE CATHOLIC

Street address 1: 5825 Shelby Oaks Dr
Street address 2: Catholic Center
Street address state: TN
Postal code: 38134-7316
County: Shelby
Country: USA
Mailing address: PO Box 341669
Mailing city: Memphis
Mailing state: TN
Mailing zip: 38184-1669
Office phone: (901) 373-1231
Office fax: (901) 373-1269
Advertising phone: (901) 373-1209
General e-mail: fwt.editor@cc.cdom.org
Advertising e-mail: lorena.monge@cc.cdom.org
Editorial e-mail: fwt.editor@cc.cdom.org
Website: www.cdom.org
Year newspaper established: 1972
Digital Platform - Mobile: Apple`Android`Windows`Blackberry
Digital Platform - Tablet: Apple iOS`Android`Windows 7`Blackberry Tablet OS`Kindle`Nook`Kindle Fire
Frequency: Wed`Fri
Circulation Paid: 0
Circulation Free: 1000
Audit By: Sworn/Estimate/Non-Audited
Audit Date: 12.07.2019
Note: Electronic publication only
Personnel: Martin D. Bishop Holley (Pub.); Suzanne Aviles (Editor); Lorena Monge (Ads and subscriptions)
Parent company: Catholic Diocese of Memphis
Main (survey) contact: Suzanne Aviles

MERRILLVILLE

NORTHWEST INDIANA CATHOLIC

Street address 1: 9292 Broadway
Street address state: IN
Postal code: 46410-7047
County: Lake
Country: USA
Mailing address: 9292 Broadway
Mailing city: Merrillville
Mailing state: IN
Mailing zip: 46410-7088
Office phone: (219) 769-9292
Office fax: (219) 736-6577
General e-mail: nwic@dcgary.org
Website: www.nwicatholic.com
Year newspaper established: 1987
Advertising (open inch rate): Open inch rate $10.75
Mechanical specifications: Type page 10 1/2 x 16; E - 6 cols, 1 3/5, between; A - 6 cols, 1 3/5, between; C - 6 cols, 1 3/5, between.
Delivery methods: Mail
Frequency: Sun
Audit By: Sworn/Estimate/Non-Audited
Audit Date: 12.07.2019
Weeklies Equipment - Hardware: PC
Weeklies Equipment - Presses: Web Offset
Weeklies Equipment - Software: QPS/QuarkXPress, Microsoft/Word InDesign
Personnel: Carol Macinga (Circulation/Administrative Assistant/Accounts Receivable); Marlene Zloza (Staff writer); Doris LaFauci (Page and graphic designer); Anthony Alonzo (Photojournalist); Erin Ciszczon (Advertising Representative); ????
Parent company: Roman Catholic Diocese of Gary
Main (survey) contact: Debbie Bosak

MOBILE

THE CATHOLIC WEEK

Street address 1: 356 Government St
Street address state: AL
Postal code: 36602-2316
County: Mobile
Country: USA
Mailing address: PO Box 349
Mailing city: Mobile
Mailing state: AL
Mailing zip: 36601-0349
Office phone: (251) 434-1544
Office fax: (251) 434-1547
Advertising phone: (251) 434-1543
General e-mail: thecatholicweek@bellsouth.net
Advertising e-mail: cwadvertising@bellsouth.net
Website: www.mobilearchdiocese.org/catholicweek
Year newspaper established: 1934
Advertising (open inch rate): Open inch rate $11.00
Mechanical specifications: Type page 9 13/16 x 14 1/8.
Delivery methods: Mail
Frequency: Fri
Circulation Paid: 20000
Circulation Free: 362
Audit By: Sworn/Estimate/Non-Audited
Audit Date: 12.07.2019
Weeklies Equipment - Hardware: Software Ã‚Â— InDesign
Personnel: Thomas J. Rodi (Pub.); Mary Ann Stevens (Adv. Mgr.); Larry Wahl (Ed.); Pamela Wheeler (Production Manager)
Main (survey) contact: Larry Wahl

NASHVILLE

TENNESSEE REGISTER

Street address 1: 2400 21st Ave S
Street address state: TN
Postal code: 37212-5302
County: Davidson
Country: USA
Mailing address: 2400 21st Ave S
Mailing city: Nashville
Mailing state: TN
Mailing zip: 37212-5302
Office phone: (615)783-0750
Office fax: (615) 783-0285
General e-mail: tnregister@dioceseofnashville.com
Website: www.dioceseofnashville.com
Advertising (open inch rate): Open inch rate $8.75
Mechanical specifications: Type page 10 x 14; E - 5 cols, 1 11/12, 1/6 between; A - 4 cols, 2 1/3, 1/6 between; C - 4 cols, 2 1/3, 1/6 between.
Audit By: Sworn/Estimate/Non-Audited
Audit Date: 12.07.2019
Weeklies Equipment - Hardware: APP/Power Mac 7500/100, APP/Mac IIci, APP/Mac SE 30, APP/PowerBook 145B, LaserMaster 1200 dpi, Mk/Scanner 600zs, RasterOps/20
Weeklies Equipment - Software: QPS/QuarkXPress 4.04, Adobe/Photoshop 5.0.
Personnel: Byron Warner (Adv. Mgr.); Rick Musacchio (Ed. in Chief); Andy Telli (Mng. Ed.); Debbie Lane (Prodn. Mgr.)
Main (survey) contact: Rick Musacchio

THE UNITED METHODIST REPORTER

Street address 1: 1300 Old Hickory Blvd
Street address state: TN
Postal code: 37207-1417
County: Davidson
Country: USA
Mailing address: 1300 Old Hickory Blvd
Mailing city: Nashville
Mailing state: TN
Mailing zip: 37207-1417
Office phone: (615) 673-4236
General e-mail: news@circuitwritermedia.com
Advertising e-mail: cherrie@circuitwritermedia.com
Editorial e-mail: news@circuitwritermedia.com
Website: www.unitedmethodistreporter.org
Year newspaper established: 1847
Zip Codes Served: Nationwide
Digital Platform - Mobile: Apple`Android`Windows
Digital Platform - Tablet: Apple iOS`Android`Windows 7
Other Type of Frequency: Online only... perpetually updated
Audit By: Sworn/Estimate/Non-Audited
Audit Date: 12.07.2019
Personnel: Jay Vorhees (Executive Editor)
Parent company: UMR Communications; CircuitWriter Media LLC
Main (survey) contact: Jay Vorhees

NEW ORLEANS

CLARION HERALD

Street address 1: 1000 Howard Ave
Street address 2: Ste 400
Street address state: LA
Postal code: 70113-1926
County: Orleans
Country: USA
Mailing address: PO Box 53247
Mailing city: New Orleans
Mailing state: LA
Mailing zip: 70153-3247
Office phone: (504) 596-3035
Office fax: (504) 596-3020
Advertising phone: (504) 524-1618
Advertising fax: (504) 596-3039

Editorial phone: (504) 596-3030
Editorial fax: (504) 596-3020
General e-mail: clarionherald@clarionherald.org
Advertising e-mail: adsales@clarionherald.org
Editorial e-mail: clarionherald@clarionherald.org
Website: www.clarionherald.org
Year newspaper established: 1963

ADVERTISING (OPEN INCH RATE): OPEN INCH RATE $36.00 LESS 15 DISCOUNT

Mechanical specifications: Type page 9 1/4 x 11 1/8; E - 5 cols, 1 3/4, 1/6 between; A - 5 cols, 1 3/4, 1/6 between.
Delivery methods: Carrier Racks
Zip Codes Served: Southeast Louisiana
Frequency: Sat
Circulation Paid: 60000
Circulation Free: 400
Audit By: Sworn/Estimate/Non-Audited
Audit Date: 12.07.2019
Weeklies Equipment - Hardware: PCs, APP/Mac
Weeklies Equipment - Presses: The Advocate, Baton Rouge
Weeklies Equipment - Software: Adobe/Photoshop, Adobe/InDesign 2.0.
Edition Names: Bridal Wedding Guide, High School Information, Elder Outlook, Good Business Matters, Mommy & Me, Lenten Recipe Guide (Holy Smoke), SUmmer Activities, Graduation, Catholic Schools Week
Personnel: M.J. Cahill (Adv. Dir.); Peter Finney (Exec. Ed.)
Main (survey) contact: Peter Finney

NEW YORK

AMERICA

Street address 1: 106 W 56th St
Street address state: NY
Postal code: 10019-3866
County: New York
Country: USA
Mailing address: 106 W 56th St
Mailing city: New York
Mailing state: NY
Mailing zip: 10019-3893
Office phone: (212) 581-4640
Office fax: (212) 399-3596
General e-mail: america@americamagazine.org
Website: www.americamagazine.org
Advertising (open inch rate): Open inch rate $43.00
Mechanical specifications: Type page 8 1/8 x 10 1/2; E - 2 cols, 3 3/4, 1/4 between; A - 3 cols, 2 1/4, 1/4 between; C - 3 cols, 2 1/4, 1/4 between.
Frequency: Mon
Circulation Paid: 46000
Circulation Free: 283
Audit By: Sworn/Estimate/Non-Audited
Audit Date: 12.07.2019
Weeklies Equipment - Hardware: APP/Mac
Weeklies Equipment - Software: QPS/QuarkXPress 4.0.
Personnel: Rew Christiansen (Ed.); Robert C. Collins (Mng. Ed.)
Main (survey) contact: Rew Christiansen

CATHOLIC NEW YORK

Street address 1: 1011 1st Ave
Street address 2: Ste 1721
Street address state: NY
Postal code: 10022-4112
County: New York
Country: USA
Mailing address: 1011 1st Ave., Ste. 1721
Mailing city: New York
Mailing state: NY
Mailing zip: 10022
Office phone: (212) 688-2399
Office fax: (212) 688-2642
General e-mail: cny@cny.org
Advertising e-mail: ads@cny.org
Editorial e-mail: cny@cny.org
Website: www.cny.org
Year newspaper established: 1981
Advertising (open inch rate): Open inch rate $60.60
Mechanical specifications: Type page 10.25x11; E - 6 cols; A - modular; C - 7 cols, 1 1/3, 1/12 between.
Delivery methods: Mail
Zip Codes Served: 10001-10276
Digital Platform - Mobile: Apple`Android
Digital Platform - Tablet: Apple iOS`Android
Frequency: Bi-Mthly
Other Type of Frequency: Every Other Thursday, 26 issues per year.
Circulation Paid: 127000
Audit By: AAM
Audit Date: 31.12.2016
Weeklies Equipment - Hardware: Mac
Weeklies Equipment - Software: Adobe CS InDesign
Personnel: John Woods (Ed.)
Main (survey) contact: John Woods

THE FORWARD

Street address 1: 45 E 33rd St
Street address state: NY
Postal code: 10016-5336
County: New York
Country: USA
Mailing address: 45 E 33rd St
Mailing city: New York
Mailing state: NY
Mailing zip: 10016-5336
Office phone: (212) 889-8200
Office fax: (212) 689-4255
General e-mail: newsdesk@forward.com
Website: www.forward.com
Advertising (open inch rate): Open inch rate $48.00
Mechanical specifications: Type page 13 x 21; E - 6 cols, 2 1/16, between; A - 6 cols, 2 1/16, between; C - 6 cols, 2 1/16, between.
Audit By: Sworn/Estimate/Non-Audited
Audit Date: 12.07.2019
Personnel: Jerome Koenig (Adv. Mgr.); Lori Weinberg (Circ. Mgr.); J.J. Goldberg (Ed.); Wayne Hoffman (Mng. Ed.); Kurt Hoffman (Prodn. Mgr.)
Parent company: Joseph Jacobs Organization
Main (survey) contact: Jerome Koenig

NEWTON

MENNONITE WORLD REVIEW

Street address 1: 129 W 6th St
Street address state: KS
Postal code: 67114-2117
County: Harvey
Country: USA
Mailing address: PO Box 568
Mailing city: Newton
Mailing state: KS
Mailing zip: 67114-0568
Office phone: (316) 283-3670
Office fax: (316) 283-6502
Editorial e-mail: editor@mennoweekly.org
Website: mennoworld.org
Year newspaper established: 1923
Advertising (open inch rate): Open inch rate $22.00
Mechanical specifications: Type page 10 1/4 x 16; E - 5 cols, 1 11/12, 1/6 between; A - 5 cols, 1 11/12, 1/6 between; C - 5 cols, 1 11/12, 1/6 between.
Frequency: Mon
Circulation Paid: 10200
Circulation Free: 751
Audit By: Sworn/Estimate/Non-Audited
Audit Date: 12.07.2019
Weeklies Equipment - Hardware: APP/Mac G3
Weeklies Equipment - Software: QPS/QuarkXPress 3.1.
Personnel: Robert Schrag (Pub.); Paul Schrag (Ed.)
Main (survey) contact: Robert Schrag

OGDENSBURG

NORTH COUNTRY CATHOLIC

Street address 1: 622 Washington St
Street address state: NY
Postal code: 13669-1724
County: Saint Lawrence
Country: USA
Mailing address: PO Box 326
Mailing city: Ogdensburg
Mailing state: NY
Mailing zip: 13669-0326
Office phone: (315) 608-7556
Office fax: 866-314-7296
General e-mail: news@northcountrycatholic.org
Website: www.northcountrycatholic.org
Year newspaper established: 1946
Advertising (open inch rate): $40.00/M.
Mechanical specifications: Type page 9 3/4 x 13; E - 5 cols, 1 7/8, between; A - 5 cols, 1 7/8, between.
Delivery methods: Mail
Zip Codes Served: 12883 through 13690
Frequency: Sun
Circulation Paid: 4000
Circulation Free: 25
Audit By: Sworn/Estimate/Non-Audited
Audit Date: 12.07.2019
Editions Count: 11
Personnel: Mary Lou (Kilian)
Main (survey) contact: Darcy Fargo

OKLAHOMA CITY

BAPTIST MESSENGER

Street address 1: 3800 N May Ave
Street address state: OK
Postal code: 73112-6639
County: Oklahoma
Country: USA
Mailing address: PO Box 12130
Mailing city: Oklahoma City
Mailing state: OK
Mailing zip: 73157-2130
Office phone: (405) 942-3800
Office fax: (405) 942-3075
Advertising phone: (405) 942-3800 ext 4360
Advertising fax: 405-942-3075
Editorial phone: (405) 942-3800 ext 4361
Editorial fax: 405-942-3075
General e-mail: baptistmessenger@okbaptist.net
Advertising e-mail: baptistmessenger@okbaptist.net
Editorial e-mail: baptist messenger@okbaptist.net
Website: www.baptistmessenger.com
Year newspaper established: 1912
Advertising (open inch rate): Open inch rate $63.00
Mechanical specifications: Type page 11 x 17.
Delivery methods: Mail`Racks
Zip Codes Served: 730-749; various other US zip codes
Digital Platform - Mobile: Apple`Android
Digital Platform - Tablet: Apple iOS`Android
Frequency: Thur
Circulation Paid: 55670
Audit By: Sworn/Estimate/Non-Audited
Audit Date: 12.07.2019
Weeklies Equipment - Hardware: APP/Mac, ECR
Weeklies Equipment - Presses: G/Web, G
Weeklies Equipment - Software: Adobe/Indesign/
Editions Count: 50
Personnel: Dana Williamson (Assoc. Ed.); Karen Kinnaird (Account Manager); Ricardo Herrera (Art Director); Brian Hobbs (Editor); Bob Nigh (Managing Editor)
Main (survey) contact: Brian Hobbs

OMAHA

THE CATHOLIC VOICE

Street address 1: 6060 NW Radial Hwy
Street address state: NE
Postal code: 68104-3426
County: Douglas
Country: USA
Mailing address: PO Box 4010
Mailing city: Omaha
Mailing state: NE
Mailing zip: 68104-0010
Office phone: (402) 558-6611
Office fax: (402) 558-6614
General e-mail: tcvomaha@archomaha.org
Website: www.catholicvoiceomaha.com
Advertising (open inch rate): Open inch rate $29.95
Other Type of Frequency: Everyother Fri
Circulation Paid: 48000
Audit By: Sworn/Estimate/Non-Audited
Audit Date: 19.10.2017
Weeklies Equipment - Hardware: IBM
Weeklies Equipment - Software: Microsoft/Word '97, Adobe/PageMaker 6.5.
Personnel: Most Rev. Elden F. Curtiss (Pub.); Randy Grosse (Adv. Mgr.); Charlie Wieser (Exec. Ed.)
Main (survey) contact: Charlie Wieser

ORLANDO

THE FLORIDA CATHOLIC

Street address 1: 50 E Robinson St
Street address state: FL
Postal code: 32801-1619
County: Orange
Country: USA
Mailing address: PO Box 4993
Mailing city: Orlando
Mailing state: FL
Mailing zip: 32802-4993
Office phone: (407) 373-0075
Office fax: (407) 373-0087
General e-mail: info@thefloridacatholic.org
Website: www.thefloridacatholic.org
Advertising (open inch rate): Open inch rate $21.03
Other Type of Frequency: Every other Fri
Circulation Paid: 59000
Circulation Free: 60000
Audit By: Sworn/Estimate/Non-Audited
Audit Date: 12.07.2019
Personnel: Ann Borowski Slade (Pub.); Tim Shea (Adv. Sales Dir.); Tammy Osburne (Circ. Mgr.); Jean Gonzales (Ed. Dir.); Michael Jimenez (Adv. Graphic Des.)
Main (survey) contact: Ann Borowski Slade

PENSACOLA

THE FLORIDA CATHOLIC

Street address 1: 11 N B St
Street address state: FL
Postal code: 32502-4601
County: Escambia
Country: USA
Mailing address: 11 N B St
Mailing city: Pensacola
Mailing state: FL
Mailing zip: 32502-4601
Office phone: (850) 435-3500
Office fax: (850) 436-6414
Website: www.ptdiocese.org
Advertising (open inch rate): Open inch rate $11.75
Audit By: Sworn/Estimate/Non-Audited
Audit Date: 12.07.2019
Personnel: Christopher Gunty (Assoc. Pub.); David O'Leary (Adv. Sales Dir.); Maureen Neder (Circ. Mgr.)

PEORIA

THE CATHOLIC POST

Street address 1: 419 NE Madison Ave
Street address state: IL
Postal code: 61603-3719
County: Peoria
Country: USA
Mailing address: P.O. Box 1722
Mailing city: Peoria
Mailing state: IL
Mailing zip: 61656-1722
Office phone: (309) 671-1550

Religious Newspapers in the U.S.

Office fax: (309) 671-1579
General e-mail: cathpost@cdop.org
Advertising e-mail: sknelson@cdop.org
Website: www.thecatholicpost.com
Year newspaper established: 1934
Advertising (open inch rate): Open inch rate $14.50
Delivery methods: Mail
Zip Codes Served: Dozens throughout 26 counties in central Illinois
Frequency: Other
Other Type of Frequency: Bi-weekly
Circulation Paid: 12000
Audit By: Sworn/Estimate/Non-Audited
Audit Date: 12.07.2019
Personnel: Bishop Daniel R. Jenky (Pub.); Sonia Nelson (Adv. Mgr.); Tom Dermody (Ed.); Jennifer Willems; Theresa Lindley (Production assistant)
Main (survey) contact: Tom Dermody

PITTSBURGH

PITTSBURGH CATHOLIC

Street address 1: 135 1st Ave
Street address 2: Ste 200
Street address state: PA
Postal code: 15222-1529
County: Allegheny
Country: USA
Mailing address: 135 1st Ave Ste 200
Mailing city: Pittsburgh
Mailing state: PA
Mailing zip: 15222-1513
Office phone: (412) 471-1252
Office fax: (412) 471-4228
General e-mail: info@pittsburghcatholic.org
Advertising e-mail: jconnolly@pittsburghcatholic.org
Editorial e-mail: wcone@pittsburghcatholic.org
Website: www.pittsburghcatholic.com
Year newspaper established: 1844
Advertising (open inch rate): Open inch rate $38.05
Mechanical specifications: Type page 10.625 x 21; E - 5 cols, 2.025; A - 6 cols, 1.667; C -8 cols, 1.255.
Delivery methods: Mail
Frequency: Fri
Circulation Paid: 96000
Circulation Free: 7687
Audit By: Sworn/Estimate/Non-Audited
Audit Date: 12.07.2019
Weeklies Equipment - Hardware: APP/Mac
Weeklies Equipment - Software: Baseview.
Editions Count: 52
Personnel: John Connolly (Dir. of Adv.); Peggy Zezza (Circ. Mgr.); William Cone (Ed.); Carmella Weismantle (Prodn. Mgr.)
Main (survey) contact: Wililam Cone

PLANO

BAPTIST STANDARD

Street address 1: 7161 Bishop Rd
Street address 2: Ste 200
Street address state: TX
Postal code: 75024-3646
County: Collin
Country: USA
Mailing address: PO Box 259019
Mailing city: Plano
Mailing state: TX
Mailing zip: 75025-9019
Office phone: (214) 630-4571
Office fax: (214) 638-8535
General e-mail: bapstand@baptiststandard.com
Website: www.baptiststandard.com
Year newspaper established: 1888
Advertising (open inch rate): Open inch rate $65.00
Mechanical specifications: Type page 9 13/16 x 15; A - 5 cols, between; C - 2 cols, 1 7/8, 1/4 between.
Other Type of Frequency: Every other Mon
Circulation Paid: 90000
Circulation Free: 2104
Audit By: Sworn/Estimate/Non-Audited
Audit Date: 12.07.2019
Personnel: Kayla Andrews (Bus. Mgr.); Lance Freeman (Bus. Mgr.); Marv Knox (Ed.); Ken Camp (Mng. Ed.)
Main (survey) contact: Marv Knox

PORTLAND

CATHOLIC SENTINEL

Street address 1: 5536 NE Hassalo St
Street address state: OR
Postal code: 97213-3638
County: Multnomah
Country: USA
Mailing address: PO Box 18030
Mailing city: Portland
Mailing state: OR
Mailing zip: 97218-0030
Office phone: (503) 281-1191
Office fax: (503) 460-5496
General e-mail: sentinel@ocp.org
Website: www.sentinel.org
Advertising (open inch rate): Open inch rate $35.00
Mechanical specifications: Type page 10 5/16 x 15.
Digital Platform - Mobile: Apple`Android`Windows
Frequency: Tues`Other
Circulation Paid: 3000
Circulation Free: 25000
Audit By: Sworn/Estimate/Non-Audited
Audit Date: 12.07.2019
Weeklies Equipment - Hardware: Macbook Pro
Weeklies Equipment - Software: Indesign
Editions Count: 1
Edition Names: 1 total Ã‚Â— El Centinela (Spanish) (7,500);
Personnel: John Limb (Pub.); Ed Langlois (Managing editor)
Main (survey) contact: John Limb

CHURCH WORLD

Street address 1: 510 Ocean Ave
Street address state: ME
Postal code: 04103-4936
County: Cumberland
Country: USA
Mailing address: PO Box 11559
Mailing city: Portland
Mailing state: ME
Mailing zip: 04104-7559
Office phone: (207) 773-6471
Office fax: (207) 773-0182
General e-mail: churchworld@portlanddiocese.net
Website: www.portlanddiocese.org
Year newspaper established: 1930
Advertising (open inch rate): Open inch rate $8.00
Mechanical specifications: Type page 10 1/4 x 15 1/2; E - 5 cols, 1 7/8, 7/32 between; A - 5 cols, 1 7/8, 7/32 between.
Zip Codes Served: 04001, 04999
Audit By: Sworn/Estimate/Non-Audited
Audit Date: 12.07.2019
Weeklies Equipment - Hardware: APP/Mac
Weeklies Equipment - Software: QPS/QuarkXPress 4.1, Baseview/NewsEdit Pro, Adobe/Photoshop.
Personnel: Bishop Richard J. Malone (Pub.); Norman F. LeBlanc (Adv. Mgr.); Rita Coulombe (Circ. Mgr.); Thomas J. Kardos (Ed.)
Main (survey) contact: Thomas J. Kardos

PROVIDENCE

RHODE ISLAND CATHOLIC

Street address 1: 1 Cathedral Sq
Street address state: RI
Postal code: 02903-3601
County: Providence
Country: USA
Mailing address: 1 CATHEDRAL SQ
Mailing city: PROVIDENCE
Mailing state: RI
Mailing zip: 02903-3601
Office phone: (401) 272-1010
Office fax: (401) 421-8418
Advertising phone: (401) 272-1010
Advertising fax: (401) 421-8418
Editorial phone: (401) 272-1010
Editorial fax: (401) 421-8418
General e-mail: editor@thericatholic.com
Advertising e-mail: srichard@thericatholic.com
Editorial e-mail: rsnizek@thericatholic.com
Website: www.thericatholic.com
Year newspaper established: 1875
Advertising (open inch rate): Open inch rate $18.00
Mechanical specifications: Type page 10 x 13; E - 5 cols, 1 11/12, 1/6 between; A - 5 cols, 1 11/12, 1/6 between; C - 5 cols, 1 11/12, 1/6 between.
Delivery methods: Mail`Newsstand
Zip Codes Served: Providence County
Frequency: Thur
Circulation Paid: 27000
Circulation Free: 422
Audit By: Sworn/Estimate/Non-Audited
Audit Date: 12.07.2019
Weeklies Equipment - Hardware: APP/Mac
Weeklies Equipment - Software: Baseview/Ad Manager Pro.
Editions Count: 2
Edition Names: 2 total ÃƒÂ‚Ã‚Â— Rhode Island Catholic (English); Rhode Island Catholic en Espanol (4,500);
Personnel: Rev. Thomas J. Tobin (Pub.); Rick Snizek (Executive Editor); Richard Lafond (Display Advertising Manager); Laura Kilgus (Assistant Editor/Production Manager)
Main (survey) contact: Rick Snizek

RALEIGH

THE NORTH CAROLINA CATHOLIC

Street address 1: 715 Nazareth St
Street address state: NC
Postal code: 27606-2187
County: Wake
Country: USA
Mailing address: 715 Nazareth St
Mailing city: Raleigh
Mailing state: NC
Mailing zip: 27606-2187
Office phone: (919) 821-9730
Office fax: (919) 821-9705
Editorial e-mail: reece@raldioc.org
Website: www.nccatholics.org
Year newspaper established: 1946
Audit By: Sworn/Estimate/Non-Audited
Audit Date: 12.07.2019
Personnel: Michael F. Burbidge (Pub.); Holly Stringer (Adv. Mgr.); Richard Reece (Ed.)
Main (survey) contact: Holly Stringer

RICHMOND

THE PRESBYTERIAN OUTLOOK

Street address 1: 1 N 5th St
Street address 2: Ste 500
Street address state: VA
Postal code: 23219-2231
County: Richmond City
Country: USA
Mailing address: 1 N 5th St Ste 500
Mailing city: Richmond
Mailing state: VA
Mailing zip: 23219-2231
Office phone: (804) 359-8442
Office fax: (804) 353-6369
Advertising fax: (804) 353-6369
Advertising e-mail: gwhipple@pres-outlook.org
Editorial e-mail: jhaberer@pres-outlook.org
Website: www.pres-outlook.org
Year newspaper established: 1819
Advertising (open inch rate): Call for rates
Mechanical specifications: Type page 7 x 9 3/4; E - 3 cols, 2, 1/4 between; A - 3 cols, 2, 1/4 between; C - 3 cols, 2, 1/4 between.
Delivery methods: Mail
Zip Codes Served: We serve the entire U.S., Canada, and clergy,missionary, chaplains, serving in foreign countries.
Frequency: Mon
Other Type of Frequency: Published 26 times per year.
Circulation Paid: 7434
Circulation Free: 876
Audit By: USPS
Audit Date: 30.09.2012
Weeklies Equipment - Hardware: AG/Studio Scan Iisi, APP/Mac G3
Weeklies Equipment - Software: Adobe/Illustrator 8.0, Adobe/PageMaker 6.51, Adobe/Photoshop 5.5, QPS/QuarkXPress 4.1.
Edition Names: The Presbyterian Outlook
Personnel: Patricia Gresham (Bus. Mgr.); George Whipple (Adv. Mgr.); Stan Bailey (Prodn. Mgr.); Jack Haberer (Editor/CEO)
Main (survey) contact: Jack Haberer

THE RELIGIOUS HERALD

Street address 1: 2828 Emerywood Pkwy
Street address state: VA
Postal code: 23294-3718
County: Henrico
Country: USA
Mailing address: 2828 Emerywood Pkwy
Mailing city: Richmond
Mailing state: VA
Mailing zip: 23294-3718
Office phone: (804) 672-1973
Office fax: (804) 672-8323
General e-mail: rdilday@religiousherald.org
Website: www.religiousherald.org
Year newspaper established: 1808
Advertising (open inch rate): Open inch rate $25.00
Frequency: Thur
Circulation Paid: 21000
Audit By: Sworn/Estimate/Non-Audited
Audit Date: 12.07.2019
Personnel: Barbara Francis (Adv. Mgr.); James White (Ed.)
Main (survey) contact: David Wikinson

ROCHESTER

CATHOLIC COURIER

Street address 1: 1150 Buffalo Rd
Street address state: NY
Postal code: 14624-1823
County: Monroe
Country: USA
Mailing address: PO Box 24379
Mailing city: Rochester
Mailing state: NY
Mailing zip: 14624-0379
Office phone: (585) 529-9530
Office fax: (585)529-9532
Editorial fax: (585) 529-9509
Other phone: (800) 600-3628
General e-mail: info@catholiccourier.com
Advertising e-mail: ads@catholiccourier.com
Editorial e-mail: newsroom@catholiccourier.com
Website: www.catholiccourier.com
Year newspaper established: 1889
Advertising (open inch rate): Open inch rate $102.00
Mechanical specifications: Type page 9.4"x 10; E - 4 cols, 2.16, 1/4 between.
Delivery methods: Mail
Zip Codes Served: Generally 13021-14905 with some exceptions; specific circulation by zip code data available from circ. mgr.
Digital Platform - Tablet: Apple iOS`Kindle Fire
Frequency: Mthly
Other Type of Frequency: Weekly e-newsletter
Circulation Paid: 104812
Circulation Free: 0
Audit By: USPS
Audit Date: 07.10.2014
Weeklies Equipment - Hardware: Dell/Optiplex
Weeklies Equipment - Presses: MAN/Roland Geoman
Weeklies Equipment - Software: Adobe Creative Cloud, QuarkXPress 8-10, NewsEngin, AdWorks/AdForce, PICMan, MS Office
Editions Count: 5
Edition Names: Monroe East, West and Central, Finger Lakes; Southern Tier
Note: Issued in print first Wednesday of each

month, except July and January; issued in digital form (digital.catholiccourier.com) 12x/yr.
Personnel: Karen M. Franz (GM/Editor); Jennifer Ficcaglia (Asst. Ed.); Donna Stubbings (Circ. Mgr.); Bishop Salvatore. R Matano (President & Publisher); Matt Saxon (Graphics Mgr.); Angela Visconte (Advertising)
Parent company: Rochester Catholic Press Association, Inc
Main (survey) contact: Karen M. Franz

ROOSEVELT

THE LONG ISLAND CATHOLIC

Street address 1: 200 W Centennial Ave
Street address 2: Ste 201
Street address state: NY
Postal code: 11575-1937
County: Nassau
Country: USA
Mailing address: PO Box 9000
Mailing city: Roosevelt
Mailing state: NY
Mailing zip: 11575-9000
Office phone: (516) 594-1000
Office fax: (516) 594-1092
Editorial e-mail: editor@licatholic.org
Website: www.licatholic.org
Year newspaper established: 1962
Advertising (open inch rate): Open inch rate $69.00
Mechanical specifications: Type page 10 x 11 1/4; E - 5 cols, 2 3/8, 3/8 between; A - 5 cols, 2 3/8, 3/8 between; C - 8 cols, 1 1/8, between.
Frequency: Wed
Circulation Paid: 103000
Circulation Free: 899
Audit By: Sworn/Estimate/Non-Audited
Audit Date: 12.07.2019
Weeklies Equipment - Hardware: PCs
Weeklies Equipment - Presses: 3-G/486MFP
Weeklies Equipment - Software: Microsoft/Word, QPS/QuarkXPress 3.2, Novell.
Personnel: Art O'Brien (Adv. Mgr.); Mary Salegna (Opns. Mgr.)
Main (survey) contact: Art O'Brien

SAGINAW

THE CATHOLIC TIMES

Street address 1: PO Box 1405
Street address state: MI
Postal code: 48605-1405
County: Saginaw
Country: USA
Mailing address: PO Box 1405
Mailing city: Saginaw
Mailing state: MI
Mailing zip: 48605-1405
Office phone: (989) 793-7661
Office fax: (989) 793-7663
General e-mail: catholictimes@sbcglobal.net; catholicweekly@sbcglobal.net
Advertising (open inch rate): Open inch rate $7.25
Frequency: Fri
Circulation Paid: 8660
Circulation Free: 114
Audit By: Sworn/Estimate/Non-Audited
Audit Date: 12.07.2019
Personnel: Mark A. Myczkowiak (Pub.); Julie Root (Adv. Mgr.); Chris Brass (Circ. Mgr.); Mark Haney (Ed.)
Main (survey) contact: Mark Haney

SAGINAW

THE CATHOLIC WEEKLY

Street address 1: 1520 Court St
Street address state: MI
Postal code: 48602-4067
County: Saginaw
Country: USA
Mailing address: PO Box 1405
Mailing city: Saginaw

Mailing state: MI
Mailing zip: 48605-1405
Office phone: (989) 793-7661
Office fax: (989) 793-7663
General e-mail: catholicweekly@sbcglobal.net
Website: www.catholicweekly.org
Year newspaper established: 1942
Advertising (open inch rate): Open inch rate $7.75
Mechanical specifications: Type page 10.25 x 16; E - 6 cols, 1 5/8, 1/8 between; A - 8 cols, 1 1/2, 1/8 between; C - 6 cols, 1 5/8, 1/8 between.
Frequency: Fri
Circulation Paid: 13173
Circulation Free: 637
Audit By: Sworn/Estimate/Non-Audited
Audit Date: 12.07.2019
Weeklies Equipment - Hardware: APP/Mac G3
Weeklies Equipment - Software: Adobe/PageMaker 6.5, Adobe/Photoshop 5.5, Microsoft/Word.
Editions Count: 2
Edition Names: 2 total Ã‚Â— Catholic Weekly-Gaylord (4,150); Catholic Weekly-Saginaw (7,700);
Personnel: Mark A. Myczkowiak (Gen. Mgr./Adv. Mgr.); Chris Brass (Book Keeper); Mark Haney (Mng. Ed.); Julie Root
Parent company: G.L.S. Diocesan Reports, Inc.
Main (survey) contact: Mark A. Myczkowiak

SAINT CLOUD

ST. CLOUD VISITOR

Street address 1: 305 7th Ave N
Street address 2: Ste 206
Street address state: MN
Postal code: 56303-3633
County: Stearns
Country: USA
Mailing address: PO Box 1068
Mailing city: Saint Cloud
Mailing state: MN
Mailing zip: 56302-1068
Office phone: (320) 251-3022
Office fax: (320) 251-0424
General e-mail: news@stcloudvisitor.org
Website: www.stclouddiocese.org
Year newspaper established: 1938
Advertising (open inch rate): Open inch rate $17.00
Mechanical specifications: Type page 10 x 15; A - 5 cols, 2, between.
Other Type of Frequency: Every Other Thur
Circulation Paid: 45000
Circulation Free: 125
Audit By: Sworn/Estimate/Non-Audited
Audit Date: 12.07.2019
Weeklies Equipment - Hardware: QuarkXPress 4.1, Adobe/Photoshop 5.5.
Personnel: Bishop John Kinney (Pub.); Rose Kruger Fuchs (Adv. Mgr.); Paula Lemke (Circ. Mgr.); Joe Towalski (Ed.)
Main (survey) contact: Paula Lemke

SAINT FRANCIS

CATHOLIC HERALD

Street address 1: 3501 S Lake Dr
Street address state: WI
Postal code: 53235-0900
County: Milwaukee
Country: USA
Mailing address: PO Box 070913
Mailing city: Milwaukee
Mailing state: WI
Mailing zip: 53207-0913
Office phone: (414) 769-3500
Office fax: (414) 769-3468
General e-mail: catholicherald@archmil.org
Website: catholicherald.org
Advertising (open inch rate): Open inch rate $33.10
Mechanical specifications: Type page 10 1/4 x 12 1/2; E - 5 cols, 1 7/8, between; A - 5 cols, 1 7/8, between; C - 7 cols, 1 7/16, between.
Delivery methods: Mail
Frequency: Thur

Other Type of Frequency: Weekly, 44 times per year
Circulation Paid: 15000
Audit By: Sworn/Estimate/Non-Audited
Audit Date: 12.07.2019
Weeklies Equipment - Hardware: APP/Mac.
Personnel: Brian Olszewski (Gen. Mgr.); Maryangela Layman Roman
Parent company: Milwaukee Catholic Press Apstolate
Main (survey) contact: Maryangela Layman Roman

SAINT LOUIS

REPORTER

Street address 1: 1333 S Kirkwood Rd
Street address state: MO
Postal code: 63122-7226
County: Saint Louis
Country: USA
Mailing address: 1333 S Kirkwood Rd
Mailing city: Saint Louis
Mailing state: MO
Mailing zip: 63122-7226
Office phone: (314) 996-1231
Office fax: (314) 996-1126
General e-mail: adriane.dorr@lcms.org
Advertising e-mail: kathryn.gritts@lcms.org
Editorial e-mail: joe.isenhower@lcms.org
Website: www.reporter.lcms.org
Year newspaper established: 1974
Mechanical specifications: Type page 11 x 17; E - 4 cols, 2 1/3, 1/6 between; A - 4 cols, 2 1/3, 1/6 between.
Delivery methods: Mail
Frequency: Mthly
Circulation Free: 35000
Audit By: USPS
Audit Date: 01.10.2012
Weeklies Equipment - Hardware: APP/Mac
Weeklies Equipment - Software: Adobe/PageMaker 6.5.
Editions Count: 39
Personnel: David Strand (Executive Director); Joe Isenhower (Executive Editor, News & Information); Adriane Dorr (Executive Editor)
Parent company: The Lutheran Church–Missouri Synod
Main (survey) contact: David Strand

ST. LOUIS REVIEW

Street address 1: 20 Archbishop May Dr
Street address state: MO
Postal code: 63119-5738
County: Saint Louis
Country: USA
Mailing address: 20 Archbishop May Dr
Mailing city: Saint Louis
Mailing state: MO
Mailing zip: 63119-5738
Office phone: (314) 792-7500
Office fax: (314) 792-7534
General e-mail: slreview@stlouisreview.com
Website: www.stlouisreview.com
Advertising (open inch rate): Open inch rate $24.75
Mechanical specifications: Type page 11 5/8 x 20 15/16; E - 6 cols, 1 5/6, 1/12 between; A - 6 cols, 1 5/6, 1/12 between; C - 8 cols, 1 1/3, 1/30 between.
Frequency: Fri
Circulation Paid: 72000
Audit By: Sworn/Estimate/Non-Audited
Audit Date: 12.07.2019
Weeklies Equipment - Hardware: APP/Mac
Weeklies Equipment - Software: QPS/QuarkXPress.
Personnel: Teak Phillips (Ed.)
Main (survey) contact: Teak Phillips

SAINT PAUL

THE CATHOLIC SPIRIT

Street address 1: 244 Dayton Ave
Street address state: MN

Postal code: 55102-1802
County: Ramsey
Country: USA
Mailing address: 244 Dayton Ave
Mailing city: Saint Paul
Mailing state: MN
Mailing zip: 55102-1802
Office phone: (651) 291-4444
Office fax: (651) 291-4460
General e-mail: catholicspirit@archspm.org
Website: www.thecatholicspirit.com
Year newspaper established: 1911
Advertising (open inch rate): Open inch rate $43.00
Mechanical specifications: Type page 10 1/4 x 14; E - 4 cols, 2 1/3, 1/6 between; A - 4 cols, 2 1/3, 1/6 between; C - 5 cols, 1 5/6, 1/6 between.
Zip Codes Served: 55100, 55400, 55300, 56000
Frequency: Thur
Circulation Paid: 85000
Circulation Free: 106
Audit By: Sworn/Estimate/Non-Audited
Audit Date: 12.07.2019
Weeklies Equipment - Hardware: APP/Mac
Weeklies Equipment - Software: QPS/QuarkXPress 4.11.
Personnel: Archbishop John Nienstedt (Pub.); Bob Zyskowski (Assoc. Pub.); Martie McMahon (Acct. Suprv.); Joe Towalski (Ed.); Pat Norby (Mng. Ed.); John Wolszon (Prodn. Mgr.)
Main (survey) contact: Maria Wiering

SALT LAKE CITY

INTERMOUNTAIN CATHOLIC

Street address 1: 27 C St
Street address state: UT
Postal code: 84103-2302
County: Salt Lake
Country: USA
Mailing address: PO Box 2489
Mailing city: Salt Lake City
Mailing state: UT
Mailing zip: 84110-2489
Office phone: (801) 328-8641
Office fax: (801) 537-1667
General e-mail: icnews@icnp.com
Advertising e-mail: advertising@icatholic.org
Website: www.icatholic.org
Advertising (open inch rate): Open inch rate $20.00
Mechanical specifications: Type page 10 1/4 x 14; E - 6 cols, 2 1/3, 1/6 between; A - 6 cols, 1 3/4, between; C - 6 cols, 1 5/8, 1/6 between.
Zip Codes Served: All Utah Zip codes
Frequency: Fri
Circulation Paid: 14500
Circulation Free: 24
Audit By: Sworn/Estimate/Non-Audited
Audit Date: 12.07.2019
Weeklies Equipment - Hardware: 2-APP/Mac G4.
Personnel: Bishop John Charles Wester (Pub.); Arthur Heredia (Circ. Mgr.); Marie Mischel (Ed.); Christine Young (Assoc. Ed.)
Main (survey) contact: Arthur Heredia

SAN ANTONIO

TODAY'S CATHOLIC

Street address 1: 2718 W Woodlawn Ave
Street address state: TX
Postal code: 78228-5124
County: Bexar
Country: USA
Mailing address: PO Box 28410
Mailing city: San Antonio
Mailing state: TX
Mailing zip: 78228-0410
Office phone: (210) 734-2620
Office fax: (210) 734-2939
General e-mail: tcpaper@archdiosa.org
Website: www.satodayscatholic.org
Advertising (open inch rate): Open inch rate $15.00
Mechanical specifications: Type page 10 1/2 x 13; E - 5 cols, 2, 1/4 between; A - 5 cols, 2, 1/4 between.

Religious Newspapers in the U.S.

Other Type of Frequency: Every other Fri
Circulation Paid: 26000
Circulation Free: 467
Audit By: Sworn/Estimate/Non-Audited
Audit Date: 12.07.2019
Weeklies Equipment - Hardware: APP/Mac, Optiplex
Weeklies Equipment - Presses: 5-HI
Weeklies Equipment - Software: Micro Photoeditor, Adobe/Acrobat 4.1, Windows/98, Microsoft Office/2001, Microsoft Word/2000, Adobe/PageMaker 6.5, Adobe/Illustrator 7.0, Adobe/Photoshop 5.0.
Personnel: Kevin Rhoades (Publisher); Jodi Martin (Editor); Francis Hogan (Page Designer); Mark Weber (News Specialist); Emily Mae Schmid (Social Media Manager); Jackie Parker (Advertising Sales); Geoff Frank (Accounting/Circulation); Stephanie A. Patka (Business Mgr)
Main (survey) contact: Jason McMorrough

SAN DIEGO

THE SOUTHERN CROSS

Street address 1: 3888 Paducah Dr
Street address state: CA
Postal code: 92117-5349
County: San Diego
Country: USA
Mailing address: PO Box 81869
Mailing city: San Diego
Mailing state: CA
Mailing zip: 92138-1869
Office phone: (858) 490-8266
Office fax: (858) 490-8355
Advertising phone: (858) 490-8266
General e-mail: socross@sdcatholic.org
Advertising e-mail: dlightsey@sdcatholic.org
Editorial e-mail: cfuld@sdcatholic.org
Website: www.thesoutherncross.org
Year newspaper established: 1912
Advertising (open inch rate): Open inch rate $30.00
Mechanical specifications: Type page11.5 x 15; A - 4 cols, 2 1/3, between.
Delivery methods: Mail Racks
Zip Codes Served: 91901-92299 (MAINLY)
Digital Platform - Mobile: Windows
Frequency: Mthly
Circulation Paid: 34800
Circulation Free: 3200
Audit By: Sworn/Estimate/Non-Audited
Audit Date: 12.07.2019
Weeklies Equipment - Software: QPS/QuarkXPress 6.5
Personnel: Rev. Charles L. Fuld (Mng. Ed.); Denis Grasska (Asst. Ed.); Lucas Turnbloom (Art Dir.); Donna Lightsey (Advertising/Administrative Coordinator); Bishop Robert McElroy; Aida Bustos (Staff Writer (Spanish))
Main (survey) contact: Rev. Charles L. Fuld

SAVANNAH

SOUTHERN CROSS

Street address 1: 601 E Liberty St
Street address state: GA
Postal code: 31401-5118
County: Chatham
Country: USA
Mailing address: 601 E Liberty St
Mailing city: Savannah
Mailing state: GA
Mailing zip: 31401-5118
Office phone: (912) 201-4100
Office fax: (912) 201-4101
General e-mail: southerncross@diosav.org
Advertising e-mail: 2cents@diosav.org
Editorial e-mail: editor@diosav.org
Website: www.diosav.org
Year newspaper established: 1963
Advertising (open inch rate): Open inch rate $12.00
Mechanical specifications: Type page 10 x 14; E - 3 cols, 1/8 between; A - 2 cols, 5, between; C - 3 cols, 5, between.
Delivery methods: Mail
Frequency: Thur
Other Type of Frequency: Bi-weekly
Circulation Paid: 27600
Circulation Free: 100
Audit By: Sworn/Estimate/Non-Audited
Audit Date: 12.07.2019
Personnel: Gregory J. Hartmayer (Publisher); Michael J. Johnson (Editor)

SCHRIEVER

THE BAYOU CATHOLIC

Street address 1: 2779 Highway 311
Street address state: LA
Postal code: 70395-3273
County: Terrebonne
Country: USA
Mailing address: PO Box 505
Mailing city: Schriever
Mailing state: LA
Mailing zip: 70395-0505
Office phone: (985) 850-3132
Office fax: (985) 850-3232
General e-mail: bc@mobiletel.com
Website: www.htdiocese.org
Advertising (open inch rate): Open inch rate $15.34
Mechanical specifications: Type page 9 13/16 x 13; E - 5 cols, 1 13/16, between.
Frequency: Thur
Circulation Paid: 32000
Audit By: Sworn/Estimate/Non-Audited
Audit Date: 12.07.2019
Personnel: Pat Keese (Sec.); Peggy Adams (Adv. Mgr.); Louis G. Aguirre (Ed.)
Main (survey) contact: Pat Keese

SILVER SPRING

ADVENTIST REVIEW

Street address 1: 12501 Old Columbia Pike
Street address state: MD
Postal code: 20904-6601
County: Montgomery
Country: USA
Mailing address: 12501 Old Columbia Pike
Mailing city: Silver Spring
Mailing state: MD
Mailing zip: 20904-6601
Office phone: (301) 680-6560
Office fax: (301) 680-6638
Advertising phone: (301) 393-3054
General e-mail: letters@adventistreview.com
Website: www.adventistreview.org
Year newspaper established: 1849
Delivery methods: Mail
Zip Codes Served: all
Frequency: Mthly
Circulation Paid: 23500
Circulation Free: 700
Audit By: Sworn/Estimate/Non-Audited
Audit Date: 12.07.2019
Personnel: Bill Knott (Ed.); Stephen Chavez (Mng. Ed.); Merle Poirier (Tech. Pjcts. Coord.); Lael Caesar (associate editor); Gerald Klingbeil (associate editor); Wilona Karimabadi (assistant editor); Costin Jordache (Communication Director and News Editor)
Main (survey) contact: Stephen Chavez

SIOUX CITY

THE GLOBE

Street address 1: 1825 Jackson St
Street address state: IA
Postal code: 51105-1055
County: Woodbury
Country: USA
Mailing address: PO Box 5079
Mailing city: Sioux City
Mailing state: IA
Mailing zip: 51102-5079
Office phone: (712) 255-2550
Office fax: (712) 255-4901
General e-mail: rwebb@catholicglobe.org
Website: www.catholicglobe.org
Advertising (open inch rate): Open inch rate $12.50
Other Type of Frequency: Every Other Thur
Circulation Paid: 25268
Circulation Free: 500
Audit By: Sworn/Estimate/Non-Audited
Audit Date: 12.07.2019
Personnel: Bishop R. Walker Nickless (Pub.); Renee Webb (Ed.)
Main (survey) contact: Renee Webb

SMYRNA

THE GEORGIA BULLETIN

Street address 1: 2401 Lake Park Dr SE
Street address state: GA
Postal code: 30080-8862
County: Cobb
Country: USA
Mailing address: 2401 Lake Park Dr SE Ste 175
Mailing city: Smyrna
Mailing state: GA
Mailing zip: 30080-8815
Office phone: (404) 920-7430
Office fax: (404) 920-7431
Advertising phone: (404) 920-7441
Advertising fax: (404) 920-7431
Editorial phone: (404) 920-7430
Editorial fax: (404) 920-7431
General e-mail: editor@georgiabulletin.org
Advertising e-mail: ads@georgiabulletin.org
Editorial e-mail: editor@georgiabulletin.org
Website: www.georgiabulletin.org
Year newspaper established: 1963
Advertising (open inch rate): Open inch rate $14.00
Mechanical specifications: Type page 10 x 13 1/2; A - 5 cols, 2, between; C - 5 cols, 2, between.
Delivery methods: Mail
Zip Codes Served: 30002-33065
Frequency: Thur
Other Type of Frequency: Bi-weekly
Circulation Paid: 74000
Audit By: Sworn/Estimate/Non-Audited
Audit Date: 12.07.2019
Personnel: Archbishop Wilton Gregory (Pub.); Tom Aisthorpe (Adv. Mgr.); Mary Anne Castranio (Exec. Ed.); Gretchen R. Keiser (Ed.); Tom Schulte (Graphic Artist)
Main (survey) contact: Tom Aisthorpe

SPRINGFIELD

CATHOLIC TIMES

Street address 1: 1615 W Washington St
Street address state: IL
Postal code: 62702-4757
County: Sangamon
Country: USA
Mailing address: 1615 W Washington St
Mailing city: Springfield
Mailing state: IL
Mailing zip: 62702-4757
Office phone: (217) 698-8500
Office fax: (217) 698-0802
General e-mail: catholictimes@dio.org
Website: www.dio.org
Advertising (open inch rate): Open inch rate $18.73
Mechanical specifications: Type page 10 1/6 x 12 1/4; E - 4 cols, 2 1/3, 1/6 between; C - 4 cols, 2 1/3, 1/6 between.
Delivery methods: Mail
Frequency: Sun
Other Type of Frequency: bi-weekly
Circulation Paid: 44980
Circulation Free: 115
Audit By: USPS
Audit Date: 27.09.2012
Weeklies Equipment - Software: Adobe Creative Suites
Personnel: Paula Ruot (Adv. Mgr.); Laura Weakley (Circ. Mgr.); Kathie Sass (Ed.); Cathy Locher (Reporter); Diane Schlindwein (Reporter)
Main (survey) contact: Laura Weakley

THE MIRROR

Street address 1: 601 S Jefferson Ave
Street address state: MO
Postal code: 65806-3107
County: Greene
Country: USA
Mailing address: 601 S Jefferson Ave
Mailing city: Springfield
Mailing state: MO
Mailing zip: 65806-3107
Office phone: (417) 866-0841
Office fax: (417) 866-1140
Website: www.the-mirror.org
Year newspaper established: 1956
Advertising (open inch rate): Open inch rate $13.50
Mechanical specifications: Type page 10 3/8 x 13; A - 4 cols, 2 3/8, 1/8 between.
Delivery methods: Mail
Frequency: Fri
Circulation Paid: 17000
Audit By: Sworn/Estimate/Non-Audited
Audit Date: 12.07.2019
Weeklies Equipment - Hardware: APP/Power Mac G4
Weeklies Equipment - Software: QPS/QuarkXPress 4.1.
Personnel: Angie Toben (Administrative Assistant/Circulation Manager); Leslie Eidson (Ed.); Glenn Eckl (Production/Web)
Main (survey) contact: Angie Toben

STAFFORD

ALL NEWS

Street address 1: 1179 Courthouse Rd
Street address state: VA
Postal code: 22554-7106
County: Stafford
Country: USA
Mailing address: 1179 Courthouse Rd
Mailing city: Stafford
Mailing state: VA
Mailing zip: 22554-7106
Delivery methods: Mail
Zip Codes Served: all
Frequency: Bi-Mthly
Personnel: Robert Gasper (Editor); Michael Hichborn (Contributing Author)
Parent company: American Life League
Main (survey) contact: Robert Gasper

SUPERIOR

CATHOLIC HERALD

Street address 1: 1201 Hughitt Ave
Street address state: WI
Postal code: 54880-1631
County: Douglas
Country: USA
Mailing address: PO Box 969
Mailing city: Superior
Mailing state: WI
Mailing zip: 54880-0017
Office phone: (715) 392-8268
Office fax: (715) 392-8656
General e-mail: editor@catholicherald.org
Website: www.catholicherald.org
Mechanical specifications: Type page 10 1/4 x 12 1/2; E - 5 cols, 1 7/8, between; A - 5 cols, 1 7/8, between; C - 7 cols, 1 1/2, between.
Delivery methods: Mail
Frequency: Thur
Circulation Paid: 18000
Audit By: Sworn/Estimate/Non-Audited
Audit Date: 12.07.2019
Weeklies Equipment - Hardware: APP/Mac.
Personnel: Peter F. Christensen (Publisher)
Main (survey) contact: Julie Kelemen

SYRACUSE

CATHOLIC SUN

Street address 1: 420 Montgomery St
Street address state: NY
Postal code: 13202-2920
County: Onondaga
Country: USA
Mailing address: 420 Montgomery St
Mailing city: Syracuse
Mailing state: NY
Mailing zip: 13202-2920
Office phone: (315) 422-8153
Office fax: (315) 422-7549
General e-mail: catholicsun@yahoo.com
Website: www.thecatholicsun.com

Advertising (open inch rate): Open inch rate $25.00
Mechanical specifications: Type page 10 x 14; E - 4 cols, 2 2/5, 1/8 between; A - 4 cols, 2 2/5, 1/8 between; C - 6 cols, 2, 1/8 between.
Frequency: Thur
Circulation Paid: 28000
Circulation Free: 348
Audit By: Sworn/Estimate/Non-Audited
Audit Date: 12.07.2019
Weeklies Equipment - Hardware: APP/Mac
Weeklies Equipment - Software: QPS/QuarkXPress.
Personnel: James Moynihan (Pres.); Katherine Long (Ed. in Chief)
Main (survey) contact: Connie Berry

THE CATHOLIC SUN

Street address 1: 424 Montgomery St
Street address state: NY
Postal code: 13202-2920
County: Onondaga
Country: USA
Mailing address: 240 E ONONDAGA ST
Mailing city: SYRACUSE
Mailing state: NY
Mailing zip: 13202-2608
Office phone: (315) 422-8153
Office fax: (315) 422-7549
Advertising phone: (315) 579-0001
General e-mail: mklenz@syracusediocese.org
Editorial e-mail: info@thecatholicsun.com
Website: www.thecatholicsun.com
Year newspaper established: 1892
Mechanical specifications: Type page 10 x 12.5
Delivery methods: Mail
Zip Codes Served: Broome, Cortland, Chenango, Madison, Oneida, Onondaga, Oswego Counties
Frequency: Thur
Audit By: Sworn/Estimate/Non-Audited
Audit Date: 12.07.2019
Personnel: Katherine Long (Ed.); Mark Klenz (Ad. Director)
Main (survey) contact: Katherine Long

TOLEDO

CATHOLIC CHRONICLE

Street address 1: 1933 Spielbusch Ave
Street address state: OH
Postal code: 43604-5360
County: Lucas
Country: USA
Office phone: (419) 244-6711
Office fax: (419) 244-0468
General e-mail: ccnews@toledodiocese.org
Advertising e-mail: ncooke@toledodiocese.org
Website: www.catholicchronicle.org
Year newspaper established: 1934
Advertising (open inch rate): Open inch rate $64.00
Mechanical specifications: Type page 10 1/8 x 13 3/4; E - 4 cols, 2 7/16, 3/16 between; A - 6 cols, 1 9/16, 3/16 between; C - 6 cols, 1 9/16, 3/16 between.
Delivery methods: Mail'Racks
Zip Codes Served: 41017 13316 13402 43410 43420 43430 43431 43435 43440 43449 43445 43450 43452 43456 43460 43465 43502 43506 43511 43512 43516 43517 43521 43522 43524 43526 43527 43528 43537 43543 43545 43548 43551 43552 43558 43560 43566 43567 43571 43602 43604 43605 43606 43607 43608 43609 43610 43611 43612 43613 43614 43615 43616 43620 43623 43624 44089 44807 44809 44811 44820 44827 44830 44833 44839 44846 44847 44851 44853 44854 44857 44865 44874 44875 44882 44883 44889 44890 44902 44904 44905 45699 45801 15805 45817 45827 45830 45833 45840 45844 45848 45853 45856 45863 45872 45875 45876 45879 45887 45891 46225
Frequency: Mthly
Circulation Paid: 500
Circulation Free: 31000
Audit By: Sworn/Estimate/Non-Audited
Audit Date: 12.07.2019

Weeklies Equipment - Hardware: APP/Mac
Weeklies Equipment - Software: Adobe/PageMaker, Microsoft/Word, Microsoft/Excel, Adobe/Photoshop.
Personnel: Nancy Cooke (Adv. Sales Rep.); Sally Oberski (Commun. Dir.); Angela Kessler (Ed.); Rose Anne Conrad (Circ. Coord.); Keith Tarjanyi (Graphic Artist); Cherie Spino (Staff Writer); Bishop Daniel Thomas (Pub.)
Main (survey) contact: Angela Kessler

TRENTON

THE MONITOR

Street address 1: 701 Lawrence Rd
Street address state: NJ
Postal code: 08648-4209
County: Mercer
Country: USA
Mailing address: PO Box 5147
Mailing city: Trenton
Mailing state: NJ
Mailing zip: 08638-0147
Office phone: (609) 406-7404
Office fax: (609) 406-7423
Advertising phone: (609) 403-7117
General e-mail: monitor@dioceseoftrenton.org; info@dioceseoftrenton.org
Advertising e-mail: monitor-advertising@dioceseoftrenton.org
Editorial e-mail: monitor-news@dioceseoftrenton.org
Website: www.TrentonMonitor.com
Year newspaper established: 1953
Advertising (open inch rate): Open inch rate $32.00
Mechanical specifications: Type page 10 x 14; E - 4 cols, 2 1/4, between; A - 4 cols, 2 1/4, between; C - 6 cols, 1 1/2, between.
Delivery methods: Mail
Frequency: Thur'Other
Other Type of Frequency: Bi-weekly
Circulation Paid: 15000
Audit By: Sworn/Estimate/Non-Audited
Audit Date: 12.07.2019
Weeklies Equipment - Hardware: PCs
Weeklies Equipment - Software: InDesign
Personnel: Rayanne Bennett (Assoc. Pub.); George Stevenson (Bus. Dir.); Mary Stadnyk (Associate Ed); David M. O'Connell (Bishop); Mary Morrell (Mng Ed.)
Main (survey) contact: George W. Stevenson; Rayanne Bennett

TYLER

CATHOLIC EAST TEXAS

Street address 1: 1015 E Southeast Loop 323
Street address state: TX
Postal code: 75701-9656
County: Smith
Country: USA
Office phone: (903) 534-1077
Office fax: (903) 534-1370
Editorial phone: (903) 266-2144
General e-mail: editorcet3@excite.com
Editorial e-mail: editorcet3@excite.com
Website: www.dioceseoftyler.org
Year newspaper established: 1987
Advertising (open inch rate): Open inch rate $10.00
Mechanical specifications: Type page 10 x 14 1/4; E - 4 cols, 2 3/8, 1/6 between; A - 5 cols, 1 7/8, 1/6 between; C - 5 cols, 1 7/8, 1/6 between.
Delivery methods: Mail
Frequency: Mthly
Other Type of Frequency: online twice monthly
Circulation Paid: 17000
Circulation Free: 400
Audit By: Sworn/Estimate/Non-Audited
Audit Date: 12.07.2019
Weeklies Equipment - Software: Adobe Creative Suite â€" indesign, photoshop, illustrator.
Editions Count: 2
Personnel: Jim D'Avignon (Ed.)
Main (survey) contact: Jim D'Avignon

VENICE

THE FLORIDA CATHOLIC

Street address 1: 1000 Pinebrook Rd
Street address state: FL
Postal code: 34285-6426
County: Sarasota
Country: USA
Mailing address: 1000 Pinebrook Rd
Mailing city: Venice
Mailing state: FL
Mailing zip: 34285-6426
Office phone: (941) 484-9543
Office fax: (941) 486-4763
General e-mail: peace&justice@dioceseofvenice.org
Website: www.thefloridacatholic.org
Advertising (open inch rate): Open inch rate $14.25
Frequency: Fri
Circulation Paid: 16250
Audit By: Sworn/Estimate/Non-Audited
Audit Date: 19.10.2017
Personnel: Mark Caruso (Adv. Sales Mgr.); Kristie Nguyen (Ed.)

VISTA

GOOD NEWS, ETC.

Street address 1: PO Box 2660
Street address state: CA
Postal code: 92085-2660
County: San Diego
Country: USA
Mailing address: PO Box 2660
Mailing city: Vista
Mailing state: CA
Mailing zip: 92085-2660
Office phone: (760) 724-3075
General e-mail: goodnewseditor@cox.net
Advertising e-mail: goodnewseditor@cox.net
Editorial e-mail: goodnewseditor@cox.net
Website: www.goodnewsetc.com
Year newspaper established: 1984
Advertising (open inch rate): Open inch rate $42
Mechanical specifications: Type page 10x14 image area, 4 col.
Delivery methods: Racks
Frequency: Mthly
Circulation Paid: 32000
Circulation Free: 32000
Audit By: Sworn/Estimate/Non-Audited
Audit Date: 12.07.2019
Weeklies Equipment - Hardware: APP/Mac.
Editions Count: 2
Edition Names: 2 total ÃƒÂ£££ Good News Etc.-North County (20,000);
Personnel: Colleen Monroe (Adv. Mgr.); Rick Monroe (Ed.)
Main (survey) contact: Rick Monroe

WASHINGTON

CATHOLIC STANDARD

Street address 1: 145 Taylor St NE
Street address state: DC
Postal code: 20017-1008
County: District Of Columbia
Country: USA
Mailing address: PO Box 4464
Mailing city: Washington
Mailing state: DC
Mailing zip: 20017-0464
Office phone: (202) 281-2410
Office fax: (202) 281-2408
Website: www.cathstan.org; www.catholicstandard.com
Advertising (open inch rate): Open inch rate $27.75
Mechanical specifications: Type page 10 1/4 x 13 1/2; E - 4 cols, 1 5/6, between; A - 5 cols, 1 5/6, 1/6 between; C - 7 cols, 1 1/3, 1/6 between.
Frequency: Thur
Circulation Paid: 46000
Circulation Free: 368
Audit By: Sworn/Estimate/Non-Audited
Audit Date: 12.07.2019

Weeklies Equipment - Hardware: APP/Mac Workstations
Weeklies Equipment - Software: QPS/QuarkXPress 3.32, Baseview/News Edit Pro 2.1.3, Baseview/Admanger Pro 2.0.6, Baseview/Circulation Pro 1.10.3.
Personnel: Thomas H. Schmidt (Gen. Mgr.); Alan Hay (Dir., Sales/Mktg.); Irieska D. Caetano (Circ. Mgr.); Mark V. Zimmermann (Ed.)
Main (survey) contact: Thomas H. Schmidt

WICHITA

THE CATHOLIC ADVANCE

Street address 1: 424 N Broadway Ave
Street address state: KS
Postal code: 67202-2310
County: Sedgwick
Country: USA
Mailing address: 424 N Broadway St
Mailing city: Wichita
Mailing state: KS
Mailing zip: 67202-2310
Office phone: (316) 269-3965
Office fax: (316) 269-3902
General e-mail: advancenews@catholicdioceseofwichita.org
Advertising e-mail: advanceads@cdowk.org
Website: www.catholicadvance.org
Advertising (open inch rate): Open inch rate $12.75
Mechanical specifications: Type page 11 1/2 x 17; E - 5 cols, 1 7/8, between; A - 5 cols, 1 7/8, between; C - 5 cols, 1 7/8, between.
Delivery methods: Mail
Digital Platform - Mobile: Apple
Digital Platform - Tablet: Apple iOS
Frequency: Bi-Mthly
Circulation Paid: 37500
Circulation Free: 93
Audit By: Sworn/Estimate/Non-Audited
Audit Date: 12.07.2019
Personnel: Christopher M. Riggs (Ed.); Donald G. McClane (Prodn. Mgr.)
Main (survey) contact: Christopher M. Riggs

WORCESTER

THE CATHOLIC FREE PRESS

Street address 1: 49 Elm St
Street address state: MA
Postal code: 01609-2514
County: Worcester
Country: USA
Mailing address: 49 Elm St
Mailing city: Worcester
Mailing state: MA
Mailing zip: 01609-2598
Office phone: (508) 757-6387
Office fax: (508) 756-8315
General e-mail: cpfnews@catholicfreepress.org
Advertising e-mail: advertising@catholicfreepress.org
Editorial e-mail: editor@catholicfreepress.org
Website: www.catholicfreepress.org
Year newspaper established: 1951
Advertising (open inch rate): Open inch rate $19.50
Mechanical specifications: Type page 11 5/8 x 21; E - 6 cols, 1 4/5, 1/6 between; A - 6 cols, 1 4/5, 1/6 between.
Delivery methods: Mail
Zip Codes Served: 01401-01790
Digital Platform - Mobile: Apple
Digital Platform - Tablet: Apple iOS
Frequency: Fri
Circulation Paid: 11000
Circulation Free: 660
Audit By: Sworn/Estimate/Non-Audited
Audit Date: 12.07.2019
Weeklies Equipment - Hardware: APP/Mac
Weeklies Equipment - Software: Adobe Indesign
Personnel: Bishop Robert J. McManus (Pub.); Robert C. Ballantine (Adv. Mgr.); Margaret M. Russell (Ed.)
Parent company: The Roman Catholic Diocese of Worcester
Main (survey) contact: Margaret M. Russell

SCHOOLS AND DEPARTMENTS OF JOURNALISM

ALCORN STATE

ALCORN STATE UNIVERSITY

Street address 1: 1000 ASU Dr., #269
Street address state: MS
Postal code: 39096-7500
Mailing address: 1000 Alcorn Dr # 269
Mailing city: Lorman
Mailing state: MS
Mailing zip: 39096-7510
Office phone: (601) 877-6613
Office fax: (601) 877-2213
College Affiliation: ACA, BCCA, PBS-ALSS
College Degree: BA
College Departments: Department of Communications, 1990
College Facilities: FM, Video production editing facilities, satellite TVRO, electronic newsroom/layout design lab, public access cable channel, TV13
College Sequence: Print, Broadcast
Personnel: Sherlynn Byrd (Chair); Shafiquir Rahman (Prof./Title III Activity Dir./Gen. Mgr., ASU Cable-TV/WPRL-FM); Duanne Byrge (Asst. Prof.); Terrence Nimor (Instr./Newsletter Advisor); Robert Waller (Instr./Video Supvr./Internship Coord.); Angela Boykin (Instr./News Dir., WPRL-FM)

ALLENDALE

GRAND VALLEY STATE UNIVERSITY

Street address 1: 1 Campus Dr.
Street address state: MI
Postal code: 49401-9401
Mailing address: 1 Campus Dr
Mailing city: Allendale
Mailing state: MI
Mailing zip: 49401-9403
Office phone: (616) 331-3668
Office fax: (616) 331-2700
Web address: www.gvsu.edu
General e-mail: barkod@gvsu.edu
College Degree: BA, BS, MS
College Departments: School of Communications
College Facilities: WGVU-TV (PBS station) and WGVU-FM (NPR station)
College Sequence: Journalism Program: BA, BS degrees offered in Journalism, Advertising/PR, Photography, Broadcasting, Film/Video, Communication Studies, Theatre, and Health Communication. MS degree offered in Communication Management
Personnel: Alex Nesterenko (Dir.)

ALMA

ALMA COLLEGE

Street address 1: 614 W Superior St
Street address state: MI
Postal code: 48801-1504
Country: USA
Mailing address: 614 W Superior St
Mailing city: Alma
Mailing state: MI
Mailing zip: 48801-1599
Office phone: (989) 463-7161
Office fax: (989) 463-7161
Web address: students.alma.edu/organizations/almanian
General e-mail: almanian@alma.edu; almanianopinion@yahoo.com; almanian@hotmail.com
College Departments: Communication program
College Sequence: Communication program: Communication majors investigate the way messages and media influence individuals, groups, and societies through rigorous coursework and a required internship.

This investigation helps students better understand, analyze, and addres
Personnel: Robert Vivian (Advisor); Brendan Guilford (Ed. in Chief); Olga Wrobel (News Ed.)
Main (survey) contact: Anna Dysinger

AMES

IOWA STATE UNIVERSITY OF SCIENCE AND TECHNOLOGY

Street address 1: 101 Hamilton Hall
Street address state: IA
Postal code: 50011-1180
Mailing address: 101 Hamilton Hall
Mailing city: Ames
Mailing state: IA
Mailing zip: 50011-1180
Office phone: (515) 294-4342
Office fax: (515) 294-5108
General e-mail: greenlee@iastate.edu
College Affiliation: KTA, PBK, PKP, PRSA, PRSSA, SPJ, BEA, RTNDA, IBNA, NPPA, AAA, ACR, ICA, IABC
College Degree: BA, BS, MS
College Departments: Greenlee School of Journalism and Communication, 1905
College Facilities: AP, AdA, AM/FM, ETV-Channel 18 cable, CN, ComN, BTA, PRA, Integrated Multimedia Suite, Audio and Editing Bays, Focus Group Rooms, JM, VDT
College Sequence: Majors: Advertising, Journalism and Mass Communication
Personnel: Michael Bugeja (Dir.); Eric Abbott (Prof.); Thomas Beell (Prof.); Jane W. Peterson (Prof.); Kim Smith (Prof.); Lulu Rodriguez (Prof.); Joel Geske (Assoc. Prof.); Barbara Mack (Assoc. Prof.); Marcia Prior-Miller (Assoc. Prof.); Jeff Blevins (Asst. Prof.); David Bulla (Asst. Prof.); Dennis Chamberlin (Asst. Prof.); Michael Dahlstrom (Asst. Prof.); Daniela Dimitrova (Asst. Prof.); Jacob Groshek (Asst. Prof.); Chad Harms (Asst. Prof.); Suman Lee (Asst. Prof.); Jay Newell (Asst. Prof.); Sela Sar (Asst. Prof.); Erin Wilgenbusch (Sr. Lectr.)
Main (survey) contact: Eric Abbott

AMHERST

HAMPSHIRE COLLEGE

Street address 1: School of Communications & Cognitive Science
Street address state: MA
Postal code: 1002
Mailing address: School of Communications & Cognitive Science
Mailing city: Amherst
Mailing state: MA
Mailing zip: 1002
Office phone: (413) 549-4600
College Departments: School of Communications and Cognitive Science
College Sequence: Journalism Program: Interdisciplinary program in communication study; TV and print journalism; mass communication emphasis on liberal arts background
Personnel: Richard Muller (Dean)

UNIVERSITY OF MASSACHUSETTS

Street address 1: 108 Bartlett Hall
Street address state: MA
Postal code: 01003-0520
Mailing address: 108 Bartlett Hall
Mailing city: Amherst
Mailing state: MA
Mailing zip: 01003-0520
Office phone: (413) 545-1376
Office fax: (413) 545-3880

General e-mail: klist@journ.umass.edu
College Affiliation: KTA
College Degree: BA
College Departments: Journalism Department, 1971
College Facilities: FM, AP, CN, DR, VDT
College Sequence: News-Ed., Non-Fiction Writing
Personnel: Karen List (Dir.)

ANCHORAGE

UNIVERSITY OF ALASKA ANCHORAGE

Street address 1: 3211 Providence Dr.
Street address state: AK
Postal code: 99508
Mailing address: 3211 Providence Dr
Mailing city: Anchorage
Mailing state: AK
Mailing zip: 99508-4645
Office phone: (907) 786-4180
Office fax: (907) 786-4190
Web address: www.jpc.uaa.alaska.edu
General e-mail: journalism@jpc.alaska.edu
College Affiliation: AAF, PRSSA
College Degree: BA
College Departments: Department of Journalism and Public Communication, 1976
College Sequence: Journalism (convergent program includes print, broadcasting, magazine, web), Public Relations & Advertising, Telecommunications and Information Technology, Graphics and Design
Personnel: Fred Pearce (Chair)

ANDERSON

ANDERSON UNIVERSITY

Street address 1: 1100 E. Fifth St.
Street address state: IN
Postal code: 46012
Mailing address: 1100 E 5th St
Mailing city: Anderson
Mailing state: IN
Mailing zip: 46012-3495
Office phone: (765) 641-4340
College Affiliation: SCJ, ICVM
College Departments: Department of Communication, 1977
College Sequence: Journalism Program: Forty-five hour Mass Communication major with specializations in Journalism, Broadcast Journalism, Broadcast Production and Public Relations
Personnel: Donald G. Boggs (Chair)
Main (survey) contact: Donald G. Boggs

ANGWIN

PACIFIC UNION COLLEGE

Street address 1: Communication Dept.
Street address state: CA
Postal code: 94508
Mailing address: Communication Dept.
Mailing city: Angwin
Mailing state: CA
Mailing zip: 94508
Office phone: (707) 965-6437
Office fax: (707) 965-6624
Web address: www.puc.edu/Departments/Communication
College Departments: Communication Department, 1945
College Sequence: Journalism Program: Emphases in newspaper, magazine, broadcasting public relations for local, regional and national media. Includes internships, practicums. Majors in Journalism, Public Relations,

Communication, International Communication and Speech Pa
Personnel: Jennifer Wareham Best (Chair)

ANN ARBOR

UNIVERSITY OF MICHIGAN

Street address 1: Dept. of Communication Studies
Street address state: MI
Postal code: 48109-1285
Mailing address: Dept. of Communication Studies
Mailing city: Ann Arbor
Mailing state: MI
Mailing zip: 48109-1285
Office phone: (734) 764-0420
Office fax: (734) 764-3288
General e-mail: comm.studies.dept@umich.edu
College Affiliation: WICI, NABJ
College Degree: BA, PhD
College Departments: Department of Communication Studies, 1926
College Facilities: AM/FM, AP, CCTV, CN, VDT
College Sequence: BA- Communication Studies; PhD (interdepartmental)- Mass Communication
Personnel: Michael Traugott (Chair); Susan Douglas (Dir., Interdepartmental PhD Prog.)

ARCATA

HUMBOLDT STATE UNIVERSITY

Street address 1: 1 Harpst St.
Street address state: CA
Postal code: 95521
Mailing address: 1 Harpst St
Mailing city: Arcata
Mailing state: CA
Mailing zip: 95521-8299
Office phone: (707) 826-4775
Office fax: (707) 826-4770
General e-mail: mcmaster@humboldt.edu
College Degree: BA
College Departments: Department of Journalism and Mass Communication, 1960
College Facilities: FM, ComN, JM, JN, PRA, VDT, AM
College Sequence: News-Editorial, Public Relations, Broadcast News, Media Studies
Personnel: Mark Larson (Chair/Prof.); Craig Klein (Prof.); George Estrada (Assoc. Prof.); Marcy Burstiner (Asst. Prof.); Vicky Sama (Asst. Prof.)

ARKADELPHIA

HENDERSON STATE UNIVERSITY

Street address 1: 1100 Henderson St.
Street address state: AR
Postal code: 71999-0001
Mailing address: 1100 Henderson St
Mailing city: Arkadelphia
Mailing state: AR
Mailing zip: 71999-0001
Office phone: (870) 230-5182
Office fax: (870) 230-5144
General e-mail: taylorm@hsu.edu
College Degree: BA
College Departments: Communication and Theatre Arts Department, 1989
College Sequence: News-Editorial, Mass Media, PR, Communication, Theater
Personnel: Michael Miller (Chair); Michael Ray Taylor (Dir., Print Journalism)

ATHENS

UNIVERSITY OF GEORGIA

Street address 1: 120 Hooper St.

Street address state: GA
Postal code: 30602-3018
Mailing address: 120 Hooper St
Mailing city: Athens
Mailing state: GA
Mailing zip: 30602-5042
Office phone: (706) 542-1704
Office fax: (706) 542-2183
Web address: www.grady.uga.edu
College Affiliation: AD Club, NABJ, PRSSA, NPPA, UGAzine, Magazine Club, Di Gamma Kappa, Georgia Gameday, IABC
College Degree: ABJ (BA in Journalism and Mass Communication), MA, PhD
College Departments: Henry W. Grady College of Journalism and Mass Communication, 1915
College Facilities: AP, FM, CCTV, CN, ComN, DR, JM, PRA, VDT, Microwave uplink, Satellite downlink
College Sequence: Departments: Advertising & Public Relations, Journalism, Telecommunications
Personnel: E. Culpepper Clark (Dean/ Prof.); Alison Alexander (Prof./Sr. Assoc. Dean); Lee Becker (Prof./Dir., Cox Ctr.); Joseph R. Domnick (Prof./Interim Head, Telecomm. Dept.); Conrad C. Fink (Prof./Dir., Cox Inst.); Vicki S. Freimuth (Prof./Dir., Ctr. Health & Risk Commun.); John F. Greenman (Carter Prof.); Karen W. King (Prof./Head, Adv./PR Dept.); Bruce Klopfenstein (Prof.); Dean M. Krugman (Prof.); Jeffrey K. Springston (Prof./Assoc. Dean); Ruth Ann Lariscy (Prof.); William Lee (Prof.); Kent Middleton (Prof./Head, Journalism Dept.); Horace Newcomb (Prof./Peabody Awards Dir.); John Soloski (Prof.); Spencer F. Tinkham (Prof.); Leonard N. Reid (Prof.); Scott Shamp (Prof.); Patricia Thomas (Prof./Knight Chair)
Main (survey) contact: E. Culpepper Clark

ATHERTON

MENLO COLLEGE

Street address 1: 1000 El Camino Real
Street address state: CA
Postal code: 94027-4300
County: San Mateo County
Country: USA
Mailing address: 1000 El Camino Real
Mailing city: Atherton
Mailing state: CA
Mailing zip: 94027-4301
Telephone country code: 1
Office phone: (650) 543-3786
Web address: www.menlo.edu
General e-mail: pr@menlo.edu
College Affiliation: WSCUC
College Degree: B.A., B.S.
College Departments: Business marketing
College Facilities: Residential living, athletics facilities, student dining, classroom buildings, student union
College Sequence: 4-year program, with general Education classes focused primarily in first 2 years.
Personnel: Priscila de Souza (Dean of Enrollment Management)
Main (survey) contact: Priscila de Souza

ATLANTA

CLARK ATLANTA UNIVERSITY

Street address 1: 223 James P. Brawley Dr., SW
Street address state: GA
Postal code: 30314
Mailing address: 223 James P Brawley Dr SW
Mailing city: Atlanta
Mailing state: GA
Mailing zip: 30314-4385
Office phone: (440) 880-8304
General e-mail: olafjames@earthlink.net
College Degree: BA- Mass Media Arts
College Departments: Department of Mass Media Arts, 1977
College Sequence: Journalism, Public Relations, Radio/TV/Film
Personnel: James McJunkins (Chair)

GEORGIA STATE UNIVERSITY

Street address 1: 1027 One Park Pl. S
Street address state: GA
Postal code: 30303
Mailing address: 1027 One Park Pl. S
Mailing city: Atlanta
Mailing state: GA
Mailing zip: 30303
Office phone: (404) 651-3200
Office fax: (404) 651-1409
General e-mail: jouckw@langate.gsu.edu
College Affiliation: SPJ, PRSSA, WICI
College Degree: BA, MA
College Departments: Department of Communication, 1963
College Facilities: AP, FM, CCTV, CN
College Sequence: Print, Broadcast, Public Relations, Film/Video, Speech, Theatre
Personnel: Carol Winkler (Chair)

AUBURN

AUBURN UNIVERSITY

Street address 1: 217 Tichenor Hall
Street address state: AL
Postal code: 36849-5211
Mailing address: 217 Tichenor Hall
Mailing city: Auburn
Mailing state: AL
Mailing zip: 36849-0001
Office phone: (334) 844-2727
Office fax: (334) 844-4573
Web address: media.cla.auburn.edu/cmjn
College Affiliation: PRCA, SPJ
College Degree: BA, MA
College Departments: Department of Communication and Journalism, 1936 (Journalism Major offered before 1974 by English Dept.)
College Facilities: AM/FM, CN, ETV, JN, PRA, VDT
College Sequence: Journalism, Communication, Radio/Television/Film, Public Relations; Grad. Studies in Communication
Personnel: Mary Helen Brown (Chair/Assoc. Prof.); Susan Brinson (Prof.); George Plasketes (Prof.); Ed Williams (Prof.); J. Emmett Winn (Prof.); Brigitta Brunner (Assoc. Prof.); Nan Fairley (Assoc. Prof.); Margaret Fitch-Hauser (Assoc. Prof.); SeiHill Kim (Assoc. Prof.); Judy Sheppard (Assoc. Prof.); David Sutton (Assoc. Prof.); Debra Worthington (Assoc. Prof.); Robert Agne (Asst. Prof.); Jennifer Wood Adams (Asst. Prof.); John Carvalho (Asst. Prof.); Kristen Hoerl (Asst. Prof.); Hollie Lavenstein (Asst. Prof.); Chris Walker (Asst. Prof.); Kevin Smith (Asst. Prof.); Norman Youngblood (Asst. Prof.)

BALDWIN CITY

BAKER UNIVERSITY

Street address 1: PO Box 65
Street address state: KS
Postal code: 66006-0065
Country: USA
Mailing address: PO Box 65
Mailing city: Baldwin City
Mailing state: KS
Mailing zip: 66006-0065
Office phone: (913) 594-6451
Office fax: (913) 594-3570
Web address: www.thebakerorange.com
General e-mail: bayha@harvey.bakeru.edu
College Departments: Department of Communication and Theatre Arts, 1976
College Sequence: Journalism Program: Program is news-editorial oriented, emphasizing writing, editing, reporting and production skills. Mass Communication Program: Program is theory and production oriented, emphasizing radio and television production and post productio
Personnel: Gwyn Mellinger (Advisor); Ann Rosenthal (Chair); Dave Bostwick (Advisor); Chris Smith (Ed.)
Main (survey) contact: Chris

BALTIMORE

GOUCHER COLLEGE

Street address 1: 1021 Dulaney Valley Rd.
Street address state: MD
Postal code: 21204
Mailing address: 1021 Dulaney Valley Rd
Mailing city: Baltimore
Mailing state: MD
Mailing zip: 21204-2780
Office phone: (410) 337-6200
Office fax: (410) 337-6085
General e-mail: communications@goucher.edu
College Degree: MFA
College Departments: MFA in Creative Nonfiction, 1998
College Sequence: Program Offers: students are encouraged to pursue specific interests in television and film studies, radio and television production, print and radio and television journalism, photography, advertising and public relations, human communication and media r
Personnel: Patsy Sims (Dir.)

LOYOLA COLLEGE

Street address 1: 4501 N. Charles St.
Street address state: MD
Postal code: 21210-2601
Mailing address: 4501 N Charles St
Mailing city: Baltimore
Mailing state: MD
Mailing zip: 21210-2694
Office phone: (410) 617-2528
Office fax: (410) 617-2198
General e-mail: eking@loyola.edu
College Degree: BA
College Departments: Department of Communication
College Sequence: Communications Program: BA, professional program: Journalism, Advertising/Public Relations, TV-Radio, Digital Media, Creative Writing. Internships, international study, graphics, computer lab. Majors: 400.
Personnel: Russell Cook (Chair); Andrew Ciofalo (Journ.); Neil Alperstein (Adv./PR); Elliot King (Journ./PR); Michael Braden (TV-Radio); Diana Samet (Graphics)

BATON ROUGE

LOUISIANA STATE UNIVERSITY

Street address 1: 211 Journalism Bldg.
Street address state: LA
Postal code: 70803-7202
Mailing address: 211 Journalism
Mailing city: Baton Rouge
Mailing state: LA
Mailing zip: 70803-0001
Office phone: (225) 578-2336
Office fax: (225) 578-2125
Web address: www.manship.lsu.edu
College Affiliation: ABC, AAF, SPJ, KTA, PRSSA
College Degree: BMC, MMC, PhD
College Departments: Manship School of Mass Communication, 1925
College Facilities: AdA, CCTV, FM, CN, ComN, ComTV, DR, PRA
College Sequence: Advertising, Journalism, Political Communication, Public Relations
Personnel: John M. Hamilton (Prof./Dean); Timothy Cook (Prof.); Louis A. Day (Prof.); Ronald G. Garay (Prof.); Robert K. Goidel (Prof.); Ralph Izard (Prof.); Laura Lindsay (Prof.); Richard A. Nelson (Prof.); Jinx Brousssard (Assoc. Prof.); Margaret H. DeFleur (Assoc. Prof./Assoc. Dean); David D. Kurpius (Assoc. Prof./Assoc. Dean); Eileen Meehan (Assoc. Prof.); Anne Osborne (Assoc. Prof./Assoc. Dean); Jay L. Perkins (Assoc. Prof.); Judith Sylvester (Assoc. Prof.); Denis Wu (Assoc. Prof.); Lori Boyer (Asst. Prof.); Ketan Chitnis (Asst. Prof.); Emily Erickson (Asst. Prof.); Craig Freeman (Asst. Prof.)
Main (survey) contact: John M. Hamilton

BATON ROUGE

SOUTHERN UNIVERSITY AND A&M COLLEGE

Street address 1: 220 Stewart Hall
Street address state: LA
Postal code: 70813
Mailing address: 220 Stewart Hall
Mailing city: Baton Rouge
Mailing state: LA
Mailing zip: 70813-0001
Office phone: (225) 771-5790
Office fax: (225) 771-4943
General e-mail: mahmoud_braima@cxs.subr.edu
College Degree: BA, MA- Mass Communication
College Departments: Department of Mass Communications, 1978
College Facilities: AP, CCTV
College Sequence: Areas: Journalism, Broadcast, Public Relations
Personnel: Mahmoud Braima (Head)

BEMIDJI

BEMIDJI STATE UNIVERSITY

Street address 1: 1500 Birchmont Dr., NE
Street address state: MN
Postal code: 56601-2699
Mailing address: 1500 Birchmont Dr NE
Mailing city: Bemidji
Mailing state: MN
Mailing zip: 56601-2699
Office phone: (218) 755-3358
Office fax: (218) 755-4369
General e-mail: LMengelkock@bemidjistate.edu
College Degree: BS
College Departments: Department of Mass Communication
College Sequence: Mass Communication Program: Offers BS in Mass Communication, with concentrations in print, public relations and broadcast media
Personnel: Louise Mengelkoch (Chair)

BERKELEY

UNIVERSITY OF CALIFORNIA AT BERKELEY

Street address 1: North Gate Hall, UC
Street address state: CA
Postal code: 94720
Mailing address: N Gate Hall Uc
Mailing city: Berkeley
Mailing state: CA
Mailing zip: 94720-0001
Office phone: (510) 642-3383
Office fax: (501) 643-9136
College Degree: MJ
College Departments: Graduate School of Journalism, 1968 (as school)
College Sequence: News-Editorial, Radio News, Television News, Photography, Documentary Film, New Media, Magazine Writing

BIRMINGHAM

SAMFORD UNIVERSITY

Street address 1: Dept. of Journalism & Mass Communication
Street address state: AL
Postal code: 35229
Mailing address: Dept of Journalism & Mass Communication
Mailing city: Birmingham
Mailing state: AL
Mailing zip: 35229-0001
Office phone: (205) 726-2465
Office fax: (205) 726-2586
General e-mail: rnankney@samford.edu
College Affiliation: AAF, KTA, Nate. Broadcasting Society, PRSSA
College Degree: BA
College Departments: Department of Journalism

Schools and Departments of Journalism

and Mass Communication, 1985
College Facilities: AP, FM, CN, DR, VDT
College Sequence: Broadcast, News/Editorial, Public Relations, Advertising
Personnel: Bernie Ankney (Chair)

BLOOMINGTON

INDIANA UNIVERSITY

Street address 1: Bloomington Campus
Street address 2: Ernie Pyle Hall, Rm. 200, 940 E. Seventh St.
Street address state: IN
Postal code: 47405
Mailing address: Bloomington Campus
Mailing city: Bloomington
Mailing state: IN
Mailing zip: 47405
Office phone: (812) 855-9247
Office fax: (812) 855-0901
Web address: journalism.iupui.edu
College Affiliation: NPPA, PRSSA, SPJ, WICI
College Departments: School of Journalism, 1911
Personnel: Bradley Hamm (Dean/Prof.); John E. Dvorak (Prof.); Shannon Martin (Prof.); David P. Nord (Prof.); David H. Weaver (Prof./Roy W. Howard Research Prof.); David E. Boeyink (Assoc. Prof.); Bonnie J. Brownlee (Assoc. Prof./Assoc. Dean, Undergrad. Studies); Claude H. Cookman (Assoc. Prof.); Jon P. Dilts (Assoc. Prof.); Michael R. Evans (Assoc. Prof.); Tony Fargo (Assoc. Prof.); Owen V. Johnson (Assoc. Prof.); Jim Kelly (Assoc. Prof.); Radhika Parameswaran (Assoc. Prof.); Steven L. Raymer (Assoc. Prof.); Amy L. Reynolds (Assoc. Prof./Assoc. Dean, Grad. Studies); S. Holly Stocking (Assoc. Prof.); Mike Conway (Asst. Prof.); Lessa Hatley Major (Asst. Prof.); Emily Metzgar (Asst. Prof.)
Main (survey) contact: Bradley Hamm

BOISE

BOISE STATE UNIV.

Street address 1: 1910 University Dr
Street address state: ID
Postal code: 83725-0001
Country: USA
Mailing address: 1910 University Dr
Mailing city: Boise
Mailing state: ID
Mailing zip: 83725-0002
Office phone: (208) 426-6300
Office fax: (208) 426-3884
Web address: www.arbiteronline.com
General e-mail: mcox@boisestate.edu
College Degree: BA- Mass Communication/Journalism; MA- Communication
College Departments: Department of Communication
College Sequence: Mass Communication/Journalism Emphasis, Communication/English, Journalism Emphasis: The department offers courses in media studies, reporting and news writing, magazine writing, visual communication, audio and video production, new communication technolo
Personnel: Brad Arendt (Gen. Mgr.); V. Marvin Cox (Chrmn.); Steve Lyons (Advisor); Dwight Murphy (Avd. Mgr.); Shannon Morgan (Ed. in Chief)
Main (survey) contact: Brad Arendt; V. Marvin Cox

BOONE

APPALACHIAN STATE UNIVERSITY

Street address 1: PO Box 32039
Street address state: NC
Postal code: 28608
Mailing address: PO Box 32039
Mailing city: Boone
Mailing state: NC
Mailing zip: 28608-2039
Office phone: (828) 262-2405
Office fax: (828) 262-2543
General e-mail: townsws@appstate.edu
College Degree: BS
College Departments: Department of Communication
College Sequence: Journalism Program: Offered as major in the communication program, along with majors in electronic media/broadcasting, advertising, organizatonal/public communication, and public relations
Personnel: Stuart Towns (Chair)

BOSTON

BOSTON UNIVERSITY

Street address 1: 640 Commonwealth Ave.
Street address state: MA
Postal code: 2215
Mailing address: 640 Commonwealth Ave
Mailing city: Boston
Mailing state: MA
Mailing zip: 02215-2422
Office phone: (617) 353-3450
Office fax: (617) 353-3405
General e-mail: com@bu.edu
College Affiliation: PRSSA, SPJ, WICI, B/PAA, BEA
College Departments: College of Communication, 1947
College Sequence: Communication Programs: Undergraduate: Film and Television, Communication (Mass Communication, Advertising and Public Relations), Journalism (News Editorial, Magazine, Photojournalism, Broadcast Journalism). Graduate: Broadcast Journalism, Business and Ec
Personnel: Thomas E. Fiedler (Dean)

EMERSON COLLEGE

Street address 1: 120 Boylston St.
Street address state: MA
Postal code: 2116
Mailing address: 120 Boylston St Ste 414
Mailing city: Boston
Mailing state: MA
Mailing zip: 02116-4624
Office phone: (617) 824-8354
Office fax: (617) 824-8569
College Affiliation: SPJ, BEA, AER, NATAS, RTNDA
College Degree: BA, BFA, BS, MA
College Departments: School of Communication, 1997
College Facilities: FM, AP, UPI, TV Studios, VDT, CATV, CN, ComN, ComTV, DR
College Sequence: Video, Film, Audio, Print and Broadcast Journalism, Integrated Marketing Communication, Advertising, Public Relations
Personnel: Stuart J. Sigman (Dean)

NORTHEASTERN UNIVERSITY

Street address 1: 360 Huntington Ave.
Street address 2: 102 Lake Hall
Street address state: MA
Postal code: 02115-5000
Mailing address: 360 Huntington Ave # 315
Mailing city: Boston
Mailing state: MA
Mailing zip: 02115-5000
Office phone: (617) 373-3236
Office fax: (617) 373-8773
General e-mail: s.burgard@neu.edu
College Affiliation: PRSSA, KTA, New England Press Assn.
College Degree: BA, MA
College Departments: School of Journalism
College Facilities: CATV, CN, AdA, ComN, ComR, ComTV, DR, PRA, VDT, FM
Personnel: Stephen Burgard (Dir./Assoc. Prof); Nicholas Daniloff (Prof.); Belle Adler (Assoc. Prof.); Charles Fountain (Assoc. Prof.); William Kirtz (Assoc. Prof.); Laurel Leff (Assoc. Prof.); James Ross (Assoc. Prof.); Alan Schroeder (Assoc. Prof.); Elizabeth Matson (Asst. Prof.); Kellianne Murphy (Asst. Prof./Coord., Cooperative Educ. Placement); Carlene Hempel (Lectr.); Gladys McKie (Lectr.); Lincoln McKie (Lectr.); Daniel Kennedy (Vstg. Prof.); David Abel (Part-time Fac.); Dana Barbuto (Part-time Fac.); Michael Blanding (Part-time Fac.); James Chiavelli (Part-time Fac.); Allan Coukell (Part-time Fac.); Paul Della Valle (Part-time Fac.); Jonathan Kauffman (Dir.)

SIMMONS COLLEGE

Street address 1: Dept. of Communications
Street address state: MA
Postal code: 2115
Mailing address: Dept. of Communications
Mailing city: Boston
Mailing state: MA
Mailing zip: 2115
Office phone: (617) 521-2838
Office fax: (617) 521-3199
General e-mail: jcorcoran@bmsvax.simmons.edu
College Departments: Department of Communications
College Sequence: Journalism Program: Writing for news media. Reporting, features, interviews, editorials, reviews. Emphasis is on the practical, with students encouraged to supplement classroom experience and instruction through work on campus publications and supervise

SUFFOLK UNIVERSITY

Street address 1: 41 Temple St.
Street address state: MA
Postal code: 2114
Mailing address: 41 Temple St
Mailing city: Boston
Mailing state: MA
Mailing zip: 02114-4280
Office phone: (617) 573-8236
Office fax: (617) 742-6982
General e-mail: rrosenth@suffolk.edu
College Departments: Department of Communication and Journalism
College Facilities: HD Television Studio, Media Lab, Dark Room, Journalism Computer Lab
College Sequence: Journalism Programs: Print Journalism, Broadcast Journalism, Media Studies, Public Relations, Film, Communication Studies, Advertising, Organizational Communication.
Personnel: Dr. Robert Rosenthal (Chair)

BOULDER

UNIVERSITY OF COLORADO

Street address 1: Armory Bldg. 116, 1151 University Ave. 478 UCB
Street address state: CO
Postal code: 80309-0478
Mailing address: Armory Bldg. 116, 1151 University Ave. 478 UCB
Mailing city: Boulder
Mailing state: CO
Mailing zip: 80309-0478
Office phone: (303) 492-5007
Office fax: (303) 492-0969
General e-mail: sjmcdean@colorado.edu
College Affiliation: AAF, KTA, SPJ, WICI
College Degree: BS JR, MA, PhD
College Departments: School of Journalism and Mass Communication, 1922
College Facilities: AdA, AM, AP, CATV, ComN, ComR, ComTV, DR, JN, PRA, VDT
College Sequence: Advertising, Electronic Media (Broadcast News & Broadcast Production/Management), Media Studies, News-Editorial
Personnel: Paul S. Voakes (Prof./Dean); Andrew Calabrese (Prof./Assoc. Dean/Dir. Graduate Studies); Stewart M. Hoover (Prof./Dir., Ctr. for Media, Religion/Culture); Bella Mody (Prof./James E. de Castro Chair in Global Media Studies); Marguerite J. Moritz (Prof./UNESCO Chair in Int'l Journalism Educ.); Michael Tracey (Prof.); Robert Trager (Prof.); Len Ackland (Assoc. Prof./Co-Dir., Ctr. for Environmental Journalism); Shu-Ling Berggreen (Assoc. Prof./Head, Media Studies seq.); Michael McDevitt (Assoc. Prof.); Polly McLean (Assoc. Prof.); Janice Peck (Assoc. Prof.); Brett Robbs (Assoc. Prof.); David Slayden (Assoc. Prof./Head, Adv. Seq.); Jan Whitt (Assoc. Prof.); Tom Yulsman (Assoc. Prof./Co-Dir., Ctr. for Environmental Journalism/Head, News-Editorial seq.); Deserai Crow (Asst. Prof./Assoc. Dir., Ctr. for Environmental Journalism); Nabil Echchaibi (Asst. Prof.); Kendra Gale (Asst. Prof.); Lee Hood (Asst. Prof.)

BOWIE

BOWIE STATE UNIVERSITY

Street address 1: 14000 Jericho Park Rd.,
Street address state: MD
Postal code: 20715-9465
Mailing address: 14000 Jericho Park Rd
Mailing city: Bowie
Mailing state: MD
Mailing zip: 20715-9465
Office phone: (301) 860-3700
Office fax: (301) 860-3728
General e-mail: conwumechili@bowiestate.edu
College Departments: Department of Communications, 1978
College Sequence: Mass Communication Program: Prepares students for careers in News, Broadcasting, PR, Advertising and Telecommunications
Personnel: Dr. Chuka Onwumechili (Chair)

BOWLING GREEN

WESTERN KENTUCKY UNIVERSITY

Street address 1: 1660 Normal St
Street address 2: Western Kentucky University
Street address state: KY
Postal code: 42101-3536
Country: USA
Mailing address: 1906 College Heights Blvd # 11084
Mailing city: Bowling Green
Mailing state: KY
Mailing zip: 42101-1084
Office phone: (270) 745-2653
Web address: www.wkuherald.com
General e-mail: carrie.pratt@wku.edu
College Affiliation: CMA, ACP, KPA, KIPA
College Degree: BA
College Departments: School of Journalism & Broadcasting, 1999
College Facilities: AdA, AP, CCTV, CN, DR, ETV, FM, PRA, VDT
College Sequence: Programs: Advertising, Broadcasting, Mass Communication, News-Editorial, Photojournalism, PR, Film
Personnel: Sherry West (Operations Mgr); Carrie Pratt (Herald Adviser, Multiplatform News Adviser); Tracy Newton (Office Associate); Will Hoagland (Advt Adviser and Sales Mgr); Chuck Clark (Dir of Student Publications); Sam Oldenburg (Talisman adviser)
Main (survey) contact: Chuck Clark

BRIDGEPORT

UNIVERSITY OF BRIDGEPORT

Street address 1: Dept. of Mass Commun.
Street address state: CT
Postal code: 6601
Mailing address: Dept. of Mass Commun.
Mailing city: Bridgeport
Mailing state: CT
Mailing zip: 6601
Office phone: (203) 576-4705
General e-mail: carvethr@csusys.ctstateu.edu
College Affiliation: AAF, IABC, SPJ, WICI
College Departments: Department of Mass Communication, 1948
College Sequence: Journalism Program: The department offers sequences in news-editorial, advertising, and communication studies
Personnel: Rod Carveth (Chair)

BUIES CREEK

CAMPBELL UNIVERSITY

Street address 1: 180 Main St.
Street address state: NC
Postal code: 27506
Mailing address: 180 Main St.
Mailing city: Buies Creek
Mailing state: NC
Mailing zip: 27506
Office phone: (910) 893-1520
Office fax: (910) 893-1924
General e-mail: smithm@campbell.edu
College Degree: BA
College Departments: Department of Mass Communication, 1991
College Facilities: Mass Communication: Department offers BA degrees in Broadcast, Journalism, Public Relations and Advertising. Facilities include FM radio station, desktop publishing/graphic design computer labs, radio and television studios, photography labs, and ENG equi
College Sequence: Broadcast Journalism, Public Relations and Advertising
Personnel: Michael R. Smith (Chair); Archie K. Davis (Fellow Chair)

CANTON

CULVER-STOCKTON COLLEGE

Street address 1: 1 College Hl
Street address state: MO
Postal code: 63435-1257
Country: USA
Mailing address: 1 College Hl
Mailing city: Canton
Mailing state: MO
Mailing zip: 63435-1299
Office phone: (573) 231-6371
Office fax: (573) 231-6611
Web address: www.culver.edu
General e-mail: swiegenstein@culver.edu
College Departments: Communication Department
College Sequence: Communication Program: A general communication education in a liberal arts setting. Students may choose among three interdisciplinary tracks: interpersonal communication, journalism, and public relations
Personnel: Fred Berger (Asst. Prof Comm.); Tyler Tomlinson (Lecturer in Comm.)
Main (survey) contact: Tyler Tomlinson

CAPE GIRARDEAU

SOUTHEAST MISSOURI STATE UNIVERSITY

Street address 1: Dept. of Mass Communication
Street address state: MO
Postal code: 63701-2750
Mailing address: Dept. of Mass Communication
Mailing city: Cape Girardeau
Mailing state: MO
Mailing zip: 63701-2750
Office phone: (573) 651-2241
Office fax: (573) 651-5967
General e-mail: masscomm@semo.edu
College Affiliation: AAF, PRSSA, SPJ, MCA-I/ITVA, NBS, Missouri Broadcasters Assn., Missouri Press Assn
College Degree: BA, BS
College Departments: Department of Mass Communication, 1983
College Facilities: FM, CATV, CCTV, DR, JM, JN
College Sequence: Advertising, Communication Studies, Corporate Communication, Journalism, Media Studies, PR, Radio, Speech Education, Video Production
Personnel: Tamara Baldwin (Prof.); James Dufek (Prof.); Susan Gonders (Prof.); Bruce Mims (Prof.); Mike Weatherson (Prof.); Larry Underberg (Assoc. Prof.); Glen Williams (Assoc. Prof.); Karie Hollerbach (Asst. Prof.); Fred Jones (Asst. Prof.); Don Jung (Asst. Prof.); Roy Keller (Asst. Prof.); Karen Kight (Instr.); Cindie Jeter-Yanow (Instr.); Roger Stout (Instr.); Jennifer Summary (Instr.); Roseanna Whitlow (Instr.); Tamara Zellers-Buck (Instr.); Brooke Clubbs (Adj. Fac.); Kara Cracraft (Adj. Fac.); Ellen Dillon (Adj. Fac.)

CARBONDALE

SOUTHERN ILLINOIS UNIVERSITY CARBONDALE

Street address 1: 1100 Lincoln Dr.
Street address state: IL
Postal code: 62901-6606
Mailing address: 1100 Lincoln Dr
Mailing city: Carbondale
Mailing state: IL
Mailing zip: 62901-4306
Office phone: (618) 453-4308
Office fax: (618) 453-7714
General e-mail: mcma@siu.edu
College Affiliation: AAF, BEA, BICA, ITVA, KTA, NABJ, NAEB, NBS, SINBA, SCJ, SIRIS, SPE, UFVA, WICI
College Degree: BA- Cinema & Photography, Radio-Television; BS- Journalism; MA- Mass Communication and Media Arts with concentrations in Interactive Multimedia, Media Management, Media Theory and Research, Professional Media Practice, and Telecommunication; MFA- Mass Com
College Departments: College of Mass Communication and Media Arts, 1993
College Facilities: AdA, UPI, ComN, CCTV, ETV, JN, VDT
College Sequence: Cinema & Photography (cinema production, cinema studies, fine arts photography, professional photography), Journalism (advertising/IMC, news editorial, photojournalism), Radio-Television (management and sales, news, video/audio production)
Personnel: Gary P. Kolb (Prof./Dean); William Babcock (Prof.); John Downing (Prof./Dir. Global media Research Ctr.); John Hochheimer (Prof.); Phylis Johnson (Interim Chair, Radio- Television/Prof.); Dennis T. Lowry (Prof.); Eileen Meehan (Prof.); Lilly A. Boruszkowski (Assoc. Prof.); Lisa Brooten (Assoc. Prof.); Susan Felleman (Assoc. Prof.); William Freivogel (Assoc. Prof./Dir., Journ.); Katherine Frith (Assoc. Prof.); Walter B. Jaehnig (Assoc. Prof.); Jyotsna Kapur (Assoc. Prof.); Fern Logan (Assoc. Prof.); Daniel Overturf (Assoc. Prof.); Jake Podber (Assoc. Prof.); Jyotika Ramaprasad (Assoc. Prof.); Jan Peterson Roddy (Assoc. Prof./Interim Dir., Grad. Studies); R. William Rowley (Assoc. Prof.)
Main (survey) contact: Gary P. Kolb

CARSON

CALIFORNIA STATE UNIVERSITY, DOMINGUEZ HILLS

Street address 1: 1000 E. Victoria
Street address state: CA
Postal code: 90747
Mailing address: 1000 E Victoria
Mailing city: Carson
Mailing state: CA
Mailing zip: 90747-0001
Office phone: (310) 243-3313
Office fax: (310) 243-3779
General e-mail: ewhetmore@csudh.edu
College Affiliation: PRSSA, SPJ
College Degree: BA
College Departments: Communications Department, 1973
College Sequence: Communication Program: Offers BA degree in Communications, options in Mass Communications, Electronic Media Production, Public Relations; also minor in Advertising, certificate in Telecommunications
Personnel: Edward Whetmore (Chair)

CEDAR FALLS

UNIVERSITY OF NORTHERN IOWA

Street address 1: Communications Studies Dept., 326 Lang
Street address state: IA
Postal code: 50614-01397
Mailing address: Communications Studies Dept 326
Mailing city: Cedar Falls
Mailing state: IA
Mailing zip: 50614-0001
Office phone: (319) 273-2217
Office fax: (319) 273-7356
General e-mail: john.fritch@uni.edu
College Affiliation: BEA, PRSSA
College Departments: Communications Studies Department
College Sequence: Undergrad.: Communication Studies, Electronic Media, Public Relations. Grad.: Communication Education, Mass Communication, Organizational Communication/Human Resources, Performance Studies, Public Relations, General Communication Studies. Journalism Minor
Personnel: John Fritch (Dept. Chair)
Main (survey) contact: John Fritch

CHAPEL HILL

UNIVERSITY OF NORTH CAROLINA

Street address 1: School of Journalism & Mass Communication, Campus Box 3365
Street address 2: UNC-CH, 117 Carroll Hall
Street address state: NC
Postal code: 27514
Mailing address: School of Journalism & Mass Communication, Campus Box 3365
Mailing city: Chapel Hill
Mailing state: NC
Mailing zip: 27599-3365
Office phone: (919) 962-1204
Office fax: (919) 962-0620
Web address: www.jomc.unc.edu
General e-mail: jean_folkerts@unc.edu
College Affiliation: AAF, IABC, KTA, SPJ, NPPA, ENAC, SND, PRSSA
College Degree: BA, MA, PhD
College Departments: School of Journalism and Mass Communication, 1950
College Facilities: AP, CCTV, ComTV, CN, DR, ETV, JM, JN, VDT
College Sequence: Advertising, Electronic Communication, News-Editorial, Public Relations, Visual Communication
Personnel: Jean Folkerts (Dean/Alumni Distinguished Prof.); Penelope Muse Abernathy (Prof./Knight Chair in Journ. and Digital Media Economics); Jane Delano Brown (Prof./James L. Knight); Richard R. Cole (Dean Emer./John Thomas Kerr Distinguished Prof.); Anne Johnston (Prof./Assoc. Dean for Grad. Studies); Thomas R. Linden (Glaxo Wellcome Distinguished Prof. of Medical Journalism); Daniel Riffe (Prof./Richard Cole Eminent Prof.); Donald L. Shaw (Kenan Prof.); Richard Simpson (Prof.); Dulcie Straughan (Prof./Sr. Assoc. Dean); John Sweeney (Distinguished Prof. in Sports Commun.); Charles A. Tuggle (Prof.); Ruth Walden (James Howard & Hallie McLean Parker Distinguished Prof.); Jan Yopp (Walter Spearman Prof.); Xinshu Zhao (Prof.); Deb Aikat (Assoc. Prof.); Lois Boynton (Assoc. Prof.); George W. Cloud (Assoc. Prof.); Pat Davison (Assoc. Prof.); Frank Fee (Assoc. Prof.)

CHARLESTON

EASTERN ILLINOIS UNIVERSITY

Street address 1: 600 Lincoln Ave., 2521 Buzzard Hall
Street address state: IL
Postal code: 61920-3099
Mailing address: 600 Lincoln Ave # 2521
Mailing city: Charleston
Mailing state: IL
Mailing zip: 61920-3099
Office phone: (217) 581-6003
Office fax: (217) 581-7188
General e-mail: journal@eiu.edu
College Affiliation: KTA, NABJ, PRSSA, SCJ, WICI, SPJ, CMA
College Degree: BA
College Departments: Department of Journalism, 1975
College Facilities: AP, FM, CN, ComN, DR, ETV, JM , PRA, VDT, HS (sponsors high school press assn., hosts state high school journalism assn.), hosts state community college press assn., headquarters Mid-America Press Institute
College Sequence: Journalism Major. Journalism, Public Relations Minors. Concentrations: Writing and Reporting, Editing, Design, Photojournalism, Public Relations, New and Emerging Media, Broadcast News
Personnel: James Tidwell (Chair/Prof.); Brian Poulter (Prof.); L.R. Hyder (Prof.); John Ryan (Prof./Dir., Stud. Pubs.); Joe Gisondi (Assoc. Prof./Advisor, Minority Newspaper); Terry Johnson (Assoc. Prof./Advisor, PRSSA); Sally Turner (Assoc. Prof./Advisor, Yearbook); Janice Collins (Asst. Prof./Advisor, Broadcast); Eunseong Kim (Asst. Prof.); Lola McElwee (Asst. Prof./Advisor, Newspaper); Bryan Murley (Asst. Prof./Advisor, Online); Wanda Brandon (Instr.); Dan Hagen (Instr.); John Johnson (Instr.); Doug Lawhead (Instr.); Elizabeth Viall (Instr.)
Main (survey) contact: James Tidwell

CHARLOTTE

JOHNSON C. SMITH UNIVERSITY

Street address 1: 100 Beatties Ford Rd.
Street address state: NC
Postal code: 28216
Mailing address: 100 Beatties Ford Rd
Mailing city: Charlotte
Mailing state: NC
Mailing zip: 28216-5398
Office phone: (704) 378-1096
Office fax: (704) 378-3539
General e-mail: klharris@jcsu.edu
College Departments: Department of Communication Arts
College Facilities: Journalism, Graphic Design, and Audio/Video Production Labs
College Sequence: Communication Arts Program: Offers a B.A. degree to develop students who are trained in Media Production, Journalism, Public Relations or Marketing Communications.
Personnel: Kandace L. Harris (Interim Dept. Chair)

CHICAGO

COLUMBIA COLLEGE CHICAGO

Street address 1: 600 S. Michigan Ave.
Street address state: IL
Postal code: 60605-1996
Mailing address: 600 S Michigan Ave Fl 5
Mailing city: Chicago
Mailing state: IL
Mailing zip: 60605-1997
Office phone: (312) 369-7687
Office fax: (312) 369-8059
General e-mail: brice@colum.edu
College Departments: Department of Journalism
College Sequence: Undergraduate majors in News Reporting and Writing, Magazine, Broadcast Journalism (Radio & TV), Reporting on Health, Science & Environment. Undergraduate minor in Publication Production. Graduate program (MA) in Public Affairs Reporting
Personnel: Barry Rice (Acting Chair)
Main (survey) contact: Nancy Day

DEPAUL UNIVERSITY

Street address 1: 2320 N. Kenmore Ave.
Street address state: IL
Postal code: 60614
Mailing address: 2320 N Kenmore Ave

Schools and Departments of Journalism

Mailing city: Chicago
Mailing state: IL
Mailing zip: 60614-3210
Office phone: (773) 325-7585
Office fax: (773) 325-7584
General e-mail: bspeciche@depaul.edu
College Degree: BA, MA
College Departments: Department of Communication
College Sequence: Undergraduate course offerings in Public Relations and Advertising, Radio Television & Film, Journalism, Social & Political Discourse, Relational Group & Organizational Communication. Graduate coursework in Corporate Communication, Multicultural Communic
Personnel: Barbara L. Speicher (Chair)
Main (survey) contact: Barbara L. Speicher

LOYOLA UNIVERSITY OF CHICAGO

Street address 1: Lake Shore Campus, Loyola Hall, 1110 W. Loyola Ave.
Street address state: IL
Postal code: 60626
Mailing address: Lake Shore Campus, Loyola Hall, 1110 W. Loyola Ave.
Mailing city: Chicago
Mailing state: IL
Mailing zip: 60626
Office phone: (773) 508-3730
Office fax: (773) 508-8821
General e-mail: cmun@luc.edu
College Departments: Department of Communication, 1968
College Sequence: Journalism Program: Within an integrated communication curriculum, offers participatory learning in journalism as well as administrative and critical analyses of mass communication
Personnel: Bren A.O. Murphy (Chair)
Main (survey) contact: Bren A.O. Murphy

ROOSEVELT UNIVERSITY

Street address 1: 18 S. Michigan Ave.
Street address state: IL
Postal code: 60605
Mailing address: 430 S Michigan Ave
Mailing city: Chicago
Mailing state: IL
Mailing zip: 60605-1394
Office phone: (312) 281-3337
Office fax: (312) 281-3231
General e-mail: comm@roosevelt.edu
College Departments: Department of Communication
College Sequence: Journalism Program: Journalism, public relations, integrated communications (advertising). Grad. studies in journalism and integrated marketing communications. Campuses downtown and suburbs. All faculty professionals in their fields
Personnel: Linda Jones (Chair)
Main (survey) contact: Linda Jones

UNIVERSITY OF ILLINOIS-CHICAGO

Street address 1: 1007 W. Harrison St., MC132
Street address state: IL
Postal code: 60607-7137
Mailing address: 1140 Behavioral Sciences Bldg.,
Mailing city: Chicago
Mailing state: IL
Mailing zip: 60607-7137
Office phone: (312) 996-3187
Office fax: (312) 413-2125
General e-mail: comm@uic.edu
College Departments: Department of Communication
College Sequence: The Department of Communication provides undergraduate students with a broad liberal education that covers communication from the personal through the international levels and builds responsible citizenship. Students gain depth in understanding communicat
Personnel: Zizi Papacharissi (Head)

Main (survey) contact: Zizi Papacharissi

CHICO

CALIFORNIA STATE UNIVERSITY, CHICO

Street address 1: Tehama Hall
Street address state: CA
Postal code: 95929-0145
Mailing address: Tehama Hall
Mailing city: Chico
Mailing state: CA
Mailing zip: 95929-0001
Office phone: (530) 898-4015
Office fax: (530) 898-4345
College Affiliation: SPJ, IABC, Forensics, Designers in Progress, Digital Filmmakers Guild, Catapult Design, Graphic Arts Technical Organization, Instructional Technology Society
College Degree: BA, BS, MA, MS
College Departments: College of Communication and Education, 1969
College Facilities: AP, AdA, UPI, NPR-FM, CCTV, DR, EVT, JM, PRA, JN, VDT
College Sequence: Department of Communication Design: Media Arts, Graphic Design, Information and Communication Systems, Instructional Technology. Department of Communication Arts and Sciences: Human Communication, Organizational Communication. Department of Journalism
Personnel: Phyllis Fernlund (Dean)

COLLEGE PARK

UNIVERSITY OF MARYLAND

Street address 1: 1117 Journalism Bldg.
Street address state: MD
Postal code: 20742
Mailing address: 1117 Journalism Bldg
Mailing city: College Park
Mailing state: MD
Mailing zip: 20742-0001
Office phone: (301) 405-2383 (Dean's Office)
Office fax: (301) 314-9166
College Affiliation: KTA, SPJ, NABJ, RTNDA
College Degree: BA, MJ, MA, PhD
College Departments: Philip Merrill College of Journalism, 1947
College Facilities: AP, AMCFbA, AdA, CATV, CCTV, CN, ConiN, Comit, ComTV, DR, ETV, JM, PRA, VDT
College Sequence: The college has a core journalism curriculum, rather than sequences, with emphasis on print, broadcast, and online journalism and specializations in public affairs, business-finance and science environmental journalism
Personnel: Lee Thornton (Interim Dean/Prof./Richard Eaton Chair in Broadcast); Olive Reid (Assoc. Dean/Dir., Undergrad. Studies); Steve Crane (Acting Assoc. Dean); Marchelle Payne-Gassaway (Asst. Dean); Frank Quine (Asst. Dean); Linda Ringer (Asst. Dean/Dir., Bus. Administration); Sheila Young (Asst. Dean); David Broder (Prof.); Reese Cleghorn (Prof.); Jon Franklin (Prof./Merrill Chair in Journalism); Haynes Johnson (Prof./Knight Chair in Journalism); Eugene L. Roberts (Prof.); Linda Steiner (Prof.); Carl Sessions Stepp (Prof.); Ira Chinoy (Assoc. Prof.); Christopher Hanson (Assoc. Prof.); John Newhagen (Assoc. Prof.); Susan Moeller (Assoc. Prof.); Eric Zanot (Assoc. Prof.); Ron Yaros (Asst. Prof.)
Main (survey) contact: Tom Kunkel

UNIVERSITY OF MARYLAND

Street address 1: 2130A Skinner Hall
Street address state: MD
Postal code: 20742-7635
Mailing address: 2130A Skinner Hall
Mailing city: College Park
Mailing state: MD

Mailing zip: 20742-0001
Office phone: (301) 405-8077
Office fax: (301) 314-9471
College Departments: Department of Communication, 1998
Personnel: Elizabeth Toth (Chair/Prof., Pub. Rel./Feminist Scholarship); Edward L. Fink (Prof., Commun./Research Methods/Cognition/Persuasion); Robert N. Gaines (Prof., History of Rhetoric/Textual Criticism); James F. Klumpp (Prof., Contemporary Rhetorical Theory & Criticism/Social Change); Shawn J. Parry-Giles (Prof./Dir., Grad. Studies/Political Commun./Rhetorical, Feminist & Media Criticism); Andrew D. Wolvin (Prof., Listening/Commun. Mgmt./Commun. Educ.); Linda Aldoory (Assoc. Prof., Pub. Rel./Health Commun./Feminist Scholarship); Deborah A. Cai (Assoc. Prof., Intercultural Commun./Persuasion, Negotiation & Conflict); Dale Hample (Assoc. Prof., Argumentation/Interpersonal Commun.); Monique Mitchell Turner (Assoc. Prof., Social Influence/Persuasion/Compliance Gaining); Trevor Parry-Giles (Assoc. Prof., Rhetoric & Political Culture/Legal Commun.); Mari Boor Tonn (Assoc. Prof., Feminist & Rhetorical Criticism/Political Commun./Pub. Address); Kathleen E. Kendall (Research Prof., Political Campaign Commun.); Sahar Mohamed Khamis (Asst. Prof., Middle Eastern Media/Pub. Rel.); Meina Liu (Asst. Prof., Intercultural Commun./Organizational Commun., Negotiation & Conflict); Kristy Maddux (Asst. Prof., Rhetoric/Religion/Feminist Theory); Xiaoli Nan (Asst. Prof., Persuasion & Social Influence/Health Commun.); Nneka Ifeoma Ofulue (Asst. Prof., Feminist & Rhetorical Criticism/Religious Commun.); Torsten Reimer (Asst. Prof., Persuasion/Social Influence); Brecken Chinn Swartz (Vstg. Asst. Prof., Commun. Theory/Mass Media)
Main (survey) contact: Elizabeth Toth

COLUMBIA

STEPHENS COLLEGE

Street address 1: 1200 E. Broadway
Street address state: MO
Postal code: 65215
Mailing address: 1200 E Broadway
Mailing city: Columbia
Mailing state: MO
Mailing zip: 65215-0001
Office phone: (573) 876-7133
Office fax: (314) 876-7248
General e-mail: johnb@stephens.edu
College Affiliation: APR
College Departments: Mass Communication Department (TV-Radio-Journalism-Public Relations)
College Sequence: Journalism Program: Mass Communication major with choice of three emphases: Broadcast Media Production, Journalism or Public Relations. Mass Communication minors in Broadcast Media Production, Journalism, Public Relations
Personnel: John S. Blakemore (Chair)

UNIVERSITY OF MISSOURI

Street address 1: School of Journalism
Street address state: MO
Postal code: 65211
Mailing address: School of Journalism
Mailing city: Columbia
Mailing state: MO
Mailing zip: 65211-0001
Office phone: (573) 882-6686
Office fax: (573) 884-8989
College Affiliation: AAF, BEA, IABC, KAM, KTA, PRSSA, SPJ
College Degree: BJ, MA, PhD
College Departments: School of Journalism, 1908
College Facilities: AdA, AM/FM, AP, ComN, Corn TV, DR, ETV, JM, VDT
College Sequence: Advertising, Broadcast News, Magazine, News-Editorial, Photojournalism

Personnel: Dean Mills (Dean/Prof.); Jacqui Banaszynski (Prof./Knight Chair in Editing); Judy Bolch (Prof./Harte Chair in Innovation); Brian Brooks (Prof./Assoc. Dean, Undergrad. Studies and Admin.); Glen Cameron (Prof./Maxine Wilson Gregory Chair in Journ. Research); Brant Houston (Prof.); Stuart Loory (Prof.); Daryl Moen (Prof.); Geneva Overholser (Prof.); Byron Scott (Prof.); Zoe Smith (Prof.); Martha Steffens (Prof.); James Sterling (Prof.); Esther Thorson (Prof./Assoc. Dean, Grad. Studies/Research); Wayne Wanta (Prof.); Steve Weinberg (Prof.); Lee Wilkins (Prof.); Betty Winfield (Prof.); Clyde Bentley (Assoc. Prof.); Mary Kay Blakely (Assoc. Prof.)
Main (survey) contact: Dean Mills

COLUMBUS

MISSISSIPPI UNIVERSITY FOR WOMEN

Street address 1: 1100 College Street, MUW - 1619
Street address state: MS
Postal code: 39701-5800
Mailing address: 1100 College St Unit W1
Mailing city: Columbus
Mailing state: MS
Mailing zip: 39701-5802
Office phone: (662) 329-7354
Office fax: (662) 329-7250
General e-mail: mhatton@muw.edu
College Degree: BS/BA
College Departments: Department of Communication
College Sequence: Communication Division: Offers B.S./B.A. in new media convergence
Personnel: Martin L. Hatton (Chair/Assoc. Prof., Commun.)

CONWAY

UNIVERSITY OF CENTRAL ARKANSAS

Street address 1: Dept. of Speech, Theatre & Mass Commun.
Street address state: AR
Postal code: 72035
Mailing address: Dept of Speech Theatre & Mass Commun
Mailing city: Conway
Mailing state: AR
Mailing zip: 72035-0001
Office phone: (501) 450-3162
Office fax: (501) 450-3296
General e-mail: bobw@mail.uca.edu
College Affiliation: AER
College Degree: BA, BS
College Departments: Department of Speech, Theater and Mass Communication, 1943
College Sequence: Mass Communication Program: BA and BS degrees with emphasis in Telecommunications or Journalism. Courses offered in magazine/newspaper writing, photography, TV/radio production, desktop publishing/video, media theory/ethics/law
Personnel: Bob Willenbrink (Chair)

CORAL GABLES

UNIVERSITY OF MIAMI

Street address 1: 5202 University Dr.
Street address state: FL
Postal code: 33124
Mailing address: 5202 University Dr.
Mailing city: Coral Gables
Mailing state: FL
Mailing zip: 33124
Office phone: (305) 284-2265
Office fax: (305) 284-3648
General e-mail: sgrogg@miami.edu
College Affiliation: AAF, AER, BEA, NATAS, SPJ, PRSSA, 4-A Ad Club, WICI, RTNDA, Florida Assn. of Broadcasters

College Degree: BSC, BFA, MA, MFA, PhD
College Departments: School of Communication, 1985
College Facilities: AP, FM, CN, CATV, ComN, ComR, ComTV, DR, AdA, PRA, VDT
College Sequence: Majors: Advertising, Public Relations, Broadcasting, Broadcast Journalism, Media Management, Journalism, Visual Communication, Motion Pictures, Communication Studies
Personnel: Sam L. Grogg (Dean); Stanley Harrison (Prof.); Anthony Allegro (Prof.); Stephen Bowles (Prof.); Bruce Garrison (Prof.); Paul Lazarus (Prof.); Edward Pfister (Prof.); William Rothman (Prof.); Michael Salwen (Prof.); Mitchell Shapiro (Prof.); Don Stacks (Prof./Prog. Dir., PR); Thomas Steinfatt (Prof.); Grace Barnes (Assoc. Prof.); Marie-Helene Bourgoignie-Robert (Assoc. Prof./Prog. Dir., Vis Comm.); Sanjeev Chatterjee (Assoc. Prof./Vice Dean); Paul Driscoll (Assoc. Prof./Prog. Dir., Broadcast); Michel Dupagne (Assoc. Prof.); Leonardo Ferreira (Assoc. Prof.); Lisa Gottlieb (Assoc. Prof.); Robert Hosmon (Assoc. Prof./Vice Dean, External Affairs/Advancement)
Main (survey) contact: Sam L. Grogg

DEKALB

NORTHERN ILLINOIS UNIVERSITY

Street address 1: Dept. of Communication
Street address state: IL
Postal code: 60115
Mailing address: Dept. of Communication
Mailing city: Dekalb
Mailing state: IL
Mailing zip: 60115
Office phone: (815) 753-1563
Office fax: (815) 753-7109
Web address: www.niu.edu/comm
General e-mail: jchown@niu.edu
College Affiliation: KTA, PRSSA, NABJ, SPJ, WICI
College Degree: BA, BS, MA (Journalism area participates in the department's graduate program)
College Departments: Department of Communication, Journalism Area, 1959
College Facilities: AP, AM, CATV, CCTV, CN, DR, FM, PRA, VDT
College Sequence: Journalism: Students select courses in news-editorial, broadcast news, photojournalism and public relations
Personnel: Jeff Chown (Acting Chair); Orayb Najjar (Assoc. Prof.); Craig Seymour (Assoc. Prof.); Bill Cassidy (Asst. Prof./Journ. Area Coord.); Sabryna Cornish (Asst. Prof.); Induk Kim (Asst. Prof.); Thomas Oates (Asst. Prof.); Jason Akst (Instr.); Allen May (Supportive Professional Staff/Gen. Mgr., Broadcast News); Alex Wiertelak (Supportive Professional Staff/News Dir.)
Main (survey) contact: Jeff Chown

DENVER

METROPOLITAN STATE COLLEGE OF DENVER

Street address 1: PO Box 173362
Street address state: CO
Postal code: 80217-3362
Mailing address: PO Box 173362
Mailing city: Denver
Mailing state: CO
Mailing zip: 80217-3362
Office phone: (303) 556-3485
Office fax: (301) 556-3013
General e-mail: hurleyd@mscd.edu
College Departments: Department of Journalism, 1987
College Sequence: Journalism Program: The Journalism Dept. has three sequences: news/editorial, photojournalism and public relations. The department uses a hands-on approach to teach reporting and editing. All faculty are current or former reporters/editors. The depart
Personnel: Deborah C. Hurley (Chair)

UNIVERSITY OF DENVER

Street address 1: 2490 S. Gaylord St.
Street address state: CO
Postal code: 80208
Mailing address: 2490 S Gaylord St
Mailing city: Denver
Mailing state: CO
Mailing zip: 80210-5266
Office phone: (303) 871-3976
Office fax: (303) 871-4949
Web address: www.du.edu/mcom
General e-mail: mcom@du.edu
College Degree: BA, MA, MS
College Departments: Department of Mass Communications and Journalism Studies, 1956
College Facilities: AdA, CN, CCTV, PRA, VDT, ComN
College Sequence: Undergraduate: The department offers a BA in Communication with emphasis areas in General Communication, Communication Management, Culture and Communication, Film and Video Production, Interpersonal Communication; BA - Journalism Studies, Digital Media St
Personnel: Diane Waldman (Assoc. Prof./Chair); Renee Botta (Assoc. Prof./Dir., Mass Commun. Grad. Studies); Rodney Buxton (Assoc. Prof./Dir., Communication Undergrad. Studies); Lynn Clark (Assoc. Prof./Dir., Estlow Int'l. Ctr. Journalism/New Media); Tony Gault (Assoc. Prof.); Trace Reddell (Assoc. Prof./Dir., Digital Media Studies Grad. prog.); Margie Thompson (Assoc. Prof./Dir., Int'l & Intercultural Communication Grad. prog.); Christof Demont-Heinrich (Asst. Prof.); Catherine A. Grieve (Asst. Prof./Dir., Internships); Nadia Kaneva (Asst. Prof.); Sheila Schroeder (Asst. Prof.); Derigan Silver (Asst. Prof.); Bill Depper (Lectr.); Elizabeth Henry (Lectr.); Ania Savage (Lectr./Fac. Advisor to the Clarion); Steve Scully (Lectr.); Noel Jordan (Prof. Emer.); Harold Mendelsohn (Prof. Emer.)

DES MOINES

DRAKE UNIVERSITY

Street address 1: 2507 University Ave.
Street address state: IA
Postal code: 50311
Mailing address: 2507 University Ave
Mailing city: Des Moines
Mailing state: IA
Mailing zip: 50311-4505
Office phone: (515) 271-2838
Office fax: (515) 271-2798
Web address: www.drake.edu/journalism
General e-mail: charles.edwards@drake.edu
College Affiliation: AAF, KTA, PRSSA, SPJ
College Degree: BA
College Departments: School of Journalism and Mass Communication, 1920
College Facilities: AdA, CATV, CCTV, CN, ComN, ComR, ComTV, JM, PRA, VDT, WEBJ
College Sequence: Advertising (Creative Track and Management Track), Electronic Media (Radio and TV Production and Broadcast News), Magazines, News/Internet, Public Relations
Personnel: Charles Edwards (Dean); Todd Evans (Prof.); John Lytle (Prof.); Patricia Prijatel (Prof./Assoc. Dean); Janet Hill Keefer (Assoc. Prof.); Ronda Menke (Assoc. Prof.); Lee Jolliffe (Assoc. Prof.); Gary Wade (Assoc. Prof.); David Wright (Assoc. Prof./Asst. Dean); Koji Fuse (Asst. Prof.); Dorothy Pisarski (Asst. Prof.); Angela Renkoski (Asst. Prof.); Kathleen Richardson (Asst. Prof.); Jill Van Wyke (Asst. Prof.); William F. Francois (Prof. Emer.); Barry M. Foskit (Prof. Emer.); Henry Milam (Prof. Emer.); Joe R. Patrick (Prof. Emer.); Herbert Strentz (Prof. Emer.); Louis J. Wolter (Prof. Emer.)
Main (survey) contact: Charles Edwards

GRAND VIEW COLLEGE

Street address 1: 1331 Grandview Ave.
Street address state: IA
Postal code: 50316
Mailing address: 1331 Grandview Ave
Mailing city: Des Moines
Mailing state: IA
Mailing zip: 50316-1453
Office phone: (515) 263-2931
Office fax: (515) 263-2990
Web address: www.gvc.edu/academics/comm
General e-mail: wschaefer@gvc.edu
College Degree: BA
College Departments: Communication Department, 1974
College Sequence: Journalism Program: GVC has around 120 majors earning BA degrees in Mass Communication, Journalism, Broadcast and Graphic Journalism
Personnel: William Schaefer (Chair)

DETROIT

UNIVERSITY OF DETROIT MERCY

Street address 1: 4001 W. McNichols
Street address state: MI
Postal code: 48219-0900
Mailing address: PO Box 19900
Mailing city: Detroit
Mailing state: MI
Mailing zip: 48219-0900
Office phone: (313) 993-1698
Office fax: (313) 993-1166
General e-mail: bolzbj@udmercy.edu
College Departments: Communication Studies Department, 1956
College Sequence: Journalism Program: One of the most popular majors of the university, the department has opportunities in electronic broadcasting, communication, public relations/advertising and journalism
Personnel: Barbara J. Bolz (Chair)

WAYNE STATE UNIVERSITY

Street address 1: Dept. of Communication
Street address state: MI
Postal code: 48201
Mailing address: Dept. of Communication
Mailing city: Detroit
Mailing state: MI
Mailing zip: 48201
Office phone: (313) 577-2627
Office fax: (313) 577-6300
General e-mail: aa5200@wayne.edu
College Affiliation: SPJ
College Degree: BA- Major in Journalism
College Departments: Journalism Program, Department of Communication, 1948
Personnel: Benjamin Burns (Dir.)

DUBUQUE

CLARKE UNIVERSITY

Street address 1: 1550 Clarke Dr
Street address state: IA
Postal code: 52001-3117
Country: USA
Mailing address: 1550 Clarke Dr
Mailing city: Dubuque
Mailing state: IA
Mailing zip: 52001-3198
Office phone: (563) 588-6335
Office fax: (563) 588-6789
Web address: clarke.edu
General e-mail: abdul.sinno@clarke.edu
College Departments: Communication Department
College Sequence: Journalism Program: Communication Major: print journalism, advertising and PR multimedia
Personnel: Diana Russo (Advisor); Abdul Karim Sinno (Chair); Sarah Bradford (Ed.); David Deifell, Ph.D. (Assoc. Prof. Comm.)
Main (survey) contact: David Deifell

DURHAM

NORTH CAROLINA CENTRAL UNIV.

Street address 1: 1801 Fayetteville St
Street address state: NC
Postal code: 27707-3129
Country: USA
Mailing address: 1801 Fayetteville St
Mailing city: Durham
Mailing state: NC
Mailing zip: 27707-3129
Office phone: (919) 530-7116
Office fax: (919) 530-7991
Web address: www.campusecho.com
General e-mail: campusecho@nccu.edu
College Degree: BA
College Departments: Department of English & Mass Communication, 2003
College Facilities: CCTV, CN, VDT
College Sequence: Mass communication with concentrations in journalism, broadcast, or communication studies
Personnel: Dr. Bruce DePyssler (Advisor); Thomas Evans (Associate Professor); Carlton Koonce (Ed. in Chief)
Main (survey) contact: Thomas Evans; Dr. Bruce dePyssler

EAST LANSING

MICHIGAN STATE UNIVERSITY

Street address 1: College of Communication Arts & Sciences
Street address state: MI
Postal code: 48824-1212
Mailing address: College of Communication Arts & Sciences
Mailing city: East Lansing
Mailing state: MI
Mailing zip: 48824-1212
Office phone: (517) 355-3410
Office fax: (517) 432-1244
Web address: www.cas.msu.edu
College Affiliation: IABC, KTA, SND, SPJ, WICI, PRSSA
College Degree: BA- Advertising, Communication, Communicative Sciences and Disorders, Media Arts & Technology, Journalism, Telecommunication; Information Studies and Media; BS in Media & Communication Technology, Retailing; MA- Advertising, Communication, Communicative S
College Departments: College of Communication Arts and Sciences, 1955
College Facilities: AP, AM, FM, CCTV, ComN, CN, DR, ETV, VDT, Knight Center for Environmental Journalism, Quello Center for Telecommunication Management and Law, Health and Risk Communication Center, Games for Entertainment and Learning (GEL) Lab, Digital Media Arts and Tech
Personnel: Jane Briggs-Bunting (Prof./Dir., School of Journalism); Charles T. Salmon (Prof./Dean Brandt Chair, PR); Charles K. Atkin (Prof./Chair, Dept. of Commun.); Johannes M. Bauer (Prof./Co-Dir., Quello Ctr.); Frank Biocca (Prof./Dir., MIND Lab); Howard S. Bossen (Prof.); Franklin Boster (Prof.); Mary Bresnahan (Prof.); Sue Carter (Prof.); Richard Cole (Prof./Chair, Dept. of Adv., PR and Retailing); Lucinda D. Davenport (Prof./Dir., Media/Information Studies Doctoral Prog.); Jim Detjen (Prof./Dir., Knight Ctr.); William A. Donohue (Prof.); Frederick G. Fico (Prof.); Linda Good (Prof.); Carrie J. Heeter (Prof.); Patricia Huddleston (Prof.); Stephen R. Lacy (Prof.); Robert J. Larose (Prof.); Tim Levine (Prof.)
Main (survey) contact: Jane Briggs-Bunting

EASTON

STONEHILL COLLEGE

Street address 1: 320 Washington St.
Street address state: MA
Postal code: 2537
Mailing address: 320 Washington St.
Mailing city: Easton

Schools and Departments of Journalism

Mailing state: MA
Mailing zip: 2537
Office phone: (508) 565-1116
Office fax: (508) 565-1565
General e-mail: dwomack@stonehill.edu
College Degree: BA
College Departments: Department of Communication & Theatre Arts, 1983
College Sequence: BA in communication; minor in journalism. Emphasizes impact of media on society & theory and research. Required courses in media systems, media theory and electronic media industries.
Personnel: Israel Khyri Abraham (Chair)

EDWARDSVILLE

SOUTHERN ILLINOIS UNIVERSITY EDWARDSVILLE

Street address 1: Dept. of Mass Communications
Street address state: IL
Postal code: 62026-1775
Mailing address: Dept of Mass Communications
Mailing city: Edwardsville
Mailing state: IL
Mailing zip: 62026-0001
Office phone: (618) 650-2230
Office fax: (618) 650-3716
Web address: www.siue.edu/MASSCOMM
General e-mail: rdonald@siue.edu
College Affiliation: SPJ, AAF, MCAI
College Degree: BA, BS, MS
College Departments: Department of Mass Communications, 1969
College Facilities: FM, AdA, CCTV, CN, ComN, ComTV, DR, JM, VDT, ComR, CNN News Source, AP
College Sequence: Television and Radio, Corporate and Institutional Media, Media Advertising and Print and Electronic Journalism
Personnel: Patrick Murphy (Assoc. Prof./Chair); Ralph R. Donald (Prof.); Riley Maynard (Prof.); Gary Hicks (Assoc. Prof./Dir., Grad. Studies); Bala Baptiste (Asst. Prof.); Judy Landers (Asst. Prof.); Elza Ibroscheva (Instr.); Michael Montgomery (Instr.); Zixue Tai (Instr.); Kimberly Wilmot Voss (Instr.); John A. Regnell (Prof. Emer.); John R. Rider (Prof. Emer.); Jack Shaheen (Prof. Emer.); William G. Ward (Prof. Emer.); Nora Baker (Assoc. Prof. Emer.); Barbara Regnell (Assoc. Prof. Emer.)
Main (survey) contact: Stephen Woody

ELON

ELON UNIVERSITY

Street address 1: McEwen Communications Bldg., Campus Box 2850
Street address state: NC
Postal code: 27244
Mailing address: McEwen Communications Bldg., Campus Box 2850
Mailing city: Elon
Mailing state: NC
Mailing zip: 27244
Office phone: (336) 278-5724
Office fax: (336) 278-5734
Web address: www.elon.edu/communications
General e-mail: communications@elon.edu
College Affiliation: SPJ, RTNDA, PRSSA, Cinelon, E Pluribus Unum, Lambda Pi Eta
College Degree: BA, MA
College Departments: School of Communications, 2000
College Facilities: FM, AP, CCTV, CN, DR, ETV, VDT
College Sequence: Journalism, Strategic Communications, Media Arts & Entertainment, Communication Science
Personnel: Paul Parsons (Dean/Prof.); David Copeland (Prof./Fletcher Chair/Grad. Dir.); Janna Anderson (Assoc. Prof.); Brooke Barnett (Assoc. Prof.); Constance Book (Assoc. Dean/Assoc. Prof.); Vic Costello (Assoc. Prof.); Michael Frontani (Assoc. Prof.); Jessica Gisclair (Assoc. Prof.); Don Grady (Assoc. Prof./Dept. Chair); Anthony Hatcher (Assoc. Prof.); Byung Lee (Assoc. Prof.); Harlen Makemson (Assoc. Prof.); Tom Nelson (Assoc. Prof.); George Padgett (Assoc. Prof.); Michael Skube (Assoc. Prof./Pulitzer Prize winner); Frances Ward-Johnson (Assoc. Prof.); Lee Bush (Asst. Prof.); Ken Calhoun (Asst. Prof.); Ocek Eke (Asst. Prof.); Amanda Gallagher (Asst. Prof.)

EVANSTON

NORTHWESTERN UNIVERSITY

Street address 1: 1845 Sheridan Rd
Street address state: IL
Postal code: 60208-0815
Country: USA
Mailing address: 1845 Sheridan Rd
Mailing city: Evanston
Mailing state: IL
Mailing zip: 60208-0815
Office phone: (847) 467-1882
Office fax: (847) 491-5565
College Degree: BSJ, MSJ, MSIMC
College Facilities: JM, AP
Personnel: John Lavine (Dean); David Abrahamson (Prof.); Martin Block (Prof.); Jack Doppelt (Prof.); Loren Ghiglione (Prof.); Alec Klein (Prof.); Donna Leff (Prof.); Frank Mulhern (Prof.); Jon Petrovich (Prof.); David Protess (Prof.); Don Schultz (Prof.); Ellen Shearer (Prof.); Clarke Caywood (Assoc. Prof.); Mary Coffman (Assoc. Prof.); Tom Collinger (Assoc. Prof.); Doug Foster (Assoc. Prof.); Jeremy Gilbert (Assoc. Prof.); Rich Gordon (Assoc. Prof.); John Greening (Assoc. Prof.); Ava Greenwell (Assoc. Prof.)
Main (survey) contact: Loren Ghiglione

EVANSVILLE

UNIVERSITY OF EVANSVILLE

Street address 1: 1800 Lincoln Ave.
Street address state: IN
Postal code: 47722
Mailing address: 1800 Lincoln Ave
Mailing city: Evansville
Mailing state: IN
Mailing zip: 47714-1506
Office phone: (812) 488-2341
Office fax: (812) 488-2717
Web address: www.evansville.edu
General e-mail: dt4@evansville.edu
College Degree: BA, BS
College Departments: Department of Communication, 1955
College Facilities: FM, AP, CN, DR, VDT
College Sequence: Advertising, Public Relations/Media Writing, Video Production, Online Media Development
Personnel: Mark L. Shifflet (Prof./Chair); Hope Bock (Prof.); Michael J. Stankey (Prof.); T. Dean Thomlison (Prof.); Lori Smith (Instr.)
Main (survey) contact: T. Dean Thomlison

UNIVERSITY OF SOUTHERN INDIANA

Street address 1: 8600 University Blvd.
Street address state: IN
Postal code: 47712-3596
Mailing address: 8600 University Blvd
Mailing city: Evansville
Mailing state: IN
Mailing zip: 47712-3590
Office phone: (812) 461-5220
Office fax: (812) 465-7152
Web address: www.usi.edu/libarts/comm
General e-mail: wrinks@usi.edu
College Affiliation: SPJ, AAF, PRSSA
College Degree: BA, BS
College Departments: Department of Communications, 1985
College Facilities: AP, AdA, AM, CCTV, CN, ComN, ComTV, DR, JN, PRA, VDT
College Sequence: Majors: Public Relations and Advertising (sequence in each), Journalism (print journalism and online journalism), Communication Studies (speech), Radio and Television (R-TV production and broadcast journalism)
Personnel: J. Wayne Rinks (Chair/Assoc. Prof.); Karen H. Bonnell (Prof.); Gael L. Cooper (Prof.); Leigh Anne Howard (Assoc. Prof.); Chad R. Tew (Assoc. Prof.); David N. Black (Asst. Prof.); Wesley T. Durham (Asst. Prof.); Yoon-Joo Lee (Asst. Prof.); John K. Saliba (Asst. Prof.); Robert E. West (Asst. Prof.); Karen S. Braselton (Instr.); Erin Gibson (Instr.); Robert W. Jeffers (Instr.); John M. Morris (Instr.); Mary B. Reese (Instr.); Seymour Brodsky (Prof. Emer.); Dal M. Herring (Prof. Emer.); Helen R. Sands (Prof. Emer.); Mary A. Schroeder (Prof. Emer.); Kenneth G. Vance (Prof. Emer.)
Main (survey) contact: Dal M. Herring

FAIRBANKS

UNIVERSITY OF ALASKA AT FAIRBANKS

Street address 1: PO Box 756120
Street address state: AK
Postal code: 99775
Mailing address: PO Box 756120
Mailing city: Fairbanks
Mailing state: AK
Mailing zip: 99775-61
Office phone: (907) 474-7761
Office fax: (907) 474-6326
General e-mail: fyjnb@uaf.edu
College Affiliation: SPJ, KAM
College Departments: Department of Journalism, 1966
College Facilities: Two radio stations, a TV station, campus newspaper, computer writing lab, audio/video editing labs, online production lab, darkroom facilities, multimedia labs
College Sequence: Journalism Program: The ACEJMC-accredited department offers four sequences: News/editorial, broadcasting, photojournalism and multimedia
Personnel: Charles Mason (Chair)
Main (survey) contact: Charles Mason

FAIRFIELD

FAIRFIELD UNIVERSITY

Street address 1: English Dept., N. Benson Rd.
Street address state: CT
Postal code: 6824
Mailing address: English Dept., N. Benson Rd.
Mailing city: Fairfield
Mailing state: CT
Mailing zip: 6824
Office phone: (203) 254-4000
Office fax: (203) 254-4131
General e-mail: jsimon@mail.fairfield.edu
College Degree: BA
College Sequence: Journalism within English major; stand-alone minor
Personnel: James Simon (Chair/Fac.); Jack Cavanaugh (Fac.); Marcy Mangels (Fac.); Jean Santopatre (Fac.); Fran Silverman (Fac.)
Main (survey) contact: James Simon

FAYETTEVILLE

UNIVERSITY OF ARKANSAS

Street address 1: 116 Kimpel Hall
Street address state: AR
Postal code: 72701
Mailing address: 116 Kimpel Hall
Mailing city: Fayetteville
Mailing state: AR
Mailing zip: 72701
Office phone: (479) 575-3601
Office fax: (479) 575-4314
Web address: www.uark.edu/depts/jourinfo/public_html/
General e-mail: pwatkins@uark.edu
College Affiliation: AAF, PRSSA, SPJ, UAABJ
College Degree: BA, MA
College Departments: Walter J. Lemke Department of Journalism, 1930
College Facilities: AP, FM, CATV, CN, ComN, ComR, ComTV, JM, VDT
College Sequence: News/Magazine, Advertising/Public Relations, Broadcasting
Personnel: Patsy Watkins (Chair/Assoc. Prof.); Dale Carpenter (Prof.); Larry Foley (Prof.); Hoyt Purvis (Prof.); Jan LeBlanc Wicks (Prof.); Gerald Jordan (Assoc. Prof.); Phyllis Miller (Assoc. Prof.); Louise Montgomery (Assoc. Prof.); Rick Stockdell (Assoc. Prof.); Ignatius Fosu (Asst. Prof.); Eric Gorder (Instr.); Kim Martin (Instr.); Katherine Shurlds (Instr.); Roy Reed (Prof. Emer.)

FLAGSTAFF

NORTHERN ARIZONA UNIVERSITY

Street address 1: PO Box 5619
Street address state: AZ
Postal code: 86011-5619
Mailing address: PO Box 5619
Mailing city: Flagstaff
Mailing state: AZ
Mailing zip: 86011-0164
Office phone: (928) 523-2232
Office fax: (928) 523-1505
Web address: www.comm.nau.edu
General e-mail: school.communication@nau.edu
College Affiliation: AAF, AER, AZ Newspapers Assn., NPPA, PAD, PRSSA, RMCPA, SCA, SPJ, SWECJMC, WICI, WSCA, BEA
College Departments: School of Communnication, 1966
College Sequence: Communication Program: The School of Communication offers degrees in advertising, electronic media, journalism, merchandising, photography, public relations, speech communication and visual communication. Sequences offered within these disciplines includ
Personnel: Tom Knights (Dir.)
Main (survey) contact: Rory Faust

FORT COLLINS

COLORADO STATE UNIVERSITY

Street address 1: C-225 Clark Bldg. 1785 Campus Delivery
Street address 2: Colorado State University
Street address state: CO
Postal code: 80523
Mailing address: C225 Clark
Mailing city: Fort Collins
Mailing state: CO
Mailing zip: 80523-0001
Office phone: (970) 491-6310
Office fax: (970) 491-2908
Web address: www.colostate.edu/depts/tj
General e-mail: gluft@lamar.colostate.edu
College Affiliation: NPPA, PRSSA, SPJ, KTA
College Degree: BA, MS, PhD
College Departments: Department of Journalism and Technical Communication, 1968
College Facilities: FM, CATV, CCTV, CN, ComN, PRA, VDT
College Sequence: Computer-Mediated Communication, News-Editorial, Public Relations, Specialized/Technical Communication, Television News and Video Communication
Personnel: Gregory Luft (Prof./Chair); Kirk Hallahan (Prof.); Marilee Long (Prof.); Garrett O'Keefe (Prof.); Donna Rouner (Prof.); Donald Zimmerman (Prof./Dir., Center for Writing and Communication Technology); Cindy Christen (Assoc. Prof.); Kris Kodrich (Assoc. Prof.); James Landers (Assoc. Prof.); Patrick Plaisance (Assoc. Prof.); Peter Seel (Assoc. Prof./Adv., Information Science and Technology prog.); Jamie Switzer (Assoc. Prof.); Craig Trumbo (Assoc. Prof./Grad. Program Coord.); Joseph Champ (Asst. Prof.); Jangyul Kim (Asst. Prof.); Minjeong Kim (Asst. Prof.); Rosa Martey (Asst. Prof.); Jonna Pearson (Asst. Prof.); Jeff Browne (Instr.); Chryss Cada (Instr.)

FORT LAUDERDALE

KAPLAN UNIVERSITY

Street address 1: 6301 Kaplan University Ave.
Street address state: FL
Postal code: 33309
Mailing address: 6301 Kaplan University Ave
Mailing city: Fort Lauderdale
Mailing state: FL
Mailing zip: 33309-1905
Office phone: (954) 515-4015
Office fax: (888) 887-6494
Web address: www.kaplan.edu
General e-mail: Cstevenson@kaplan.edu
College Degree: AS, BS
College Departments: College of Arts and Sciences, Department of Communications
College Sequence: Communication Programs: The University offers an online BS in Communication degree with emphasis areas in technical writing and organizational communication. The degree program provides an interdisciplinary approach that combines both theory and applicati
Personnel: Carolyn N. Stephenson (Academic. Prog. Dir.)

FRANKLIN

FRANKLIN COLLEGE

Street address 1: 501 E. Monroe St.
Street address state: IN
Postal code: 46131
Mailing address: 101 Branigin Blvd
Mailing city: Franklin
Mailing state: IN
Mailing zip: 46131-2598
Office phone: (317) 738-8200
Office fax: (317) 738-8234
Web address: psj.franklincollege.edu
General e-mail: bbridges@franklincollege.edu
College Affiliation: SPJ
College Degree: BA
College Departments: Pulliam School of Journalism, 1940
College Facilities: AdA, AP, FM, DR, JM, JN, PRA, VDT
College Sequence: News/Editorial, Advertising/Public Relations, Broadcast Journalism, Secondary-School Teaching, Visual Communications
Personnel: Ray Begovich (Dir.)
Main (survey) contact: Ray Begovich

FREDERICK

HOOD COLLEGE

Street address 1: 401 Rosemont Ave
Street address state: MD
Postal code: 21701-8524
Country: USA
Mailing address: 401 Rosemont Ave
Mailing city: Frederick
Mailing state: MD
Mailing zip: 21701-8575
Office phone: (301) 696-3641
Office fax: (301) 696-3578
General e-mail: weinberg@hood.edu
College Degree: BA
College Departments: Communication Arts Program
College Sequence: Communication Program: BA in communication arts offered. Program requires a core of basic courses and then divides into the journalism track, emphasizing print or broadcast, and the public relations track
Personnel: Rita Davis (Ed.); Al Weinberg (Dir./Prof. of Journalism)
Main (survey) contact: Rita Davis

FRESNO

CALIFORNIA STATE UNIVERSITY,

FRESNO

Street address 1: 225 E. San Ramon Ave., M/S MF 10
Street address state: CA
Postal code: 93740-8029
Mailing address: 225 E San Ramon Ave MS MF10
Mailing city: Fresno
Mailing state: CA
Mailing zip: 93740-0001
Office phone: (559) 278-2087
Office fax: (559) 278-4995
General e-mail: sallyan@csufresno.edu
College Affiliation: ADS, NPPA, SPJ
College Degree: BA, MA
College Departments: Department of Mass Communication and Journalism, 1952
College Facilities: AP, AM, FM, AdA, CN, ComTV, DR, JN, PRA, VDT
Personnel: Donald M. Priest (Chair); Rich Marshall (General Manager)
Main (survey) contact: Rich Marshall

FT. GEORGE G. MEADE

DEFENSE INFORMATION SCHOOL

Street address 1: 6500 Mapes Rd.
Street address state: MD
Postal code: 20755-5620
Mailing address: 6500 Mapes Rd
Mailing city: Fort George G Meade
Mailing state: MD
Mailing zip: 20755-7082
Office phone: (301) 677-2173
Web address: www.dinfos.osd.mil
General e-mail: webmeisters@dinfos.osd.mil
College Sequence: The Defense Information School has a long-standing tradition of producing outstanding Public Affairs and Visual Information personnel for the Dept. of Defense
Personnel: Lt. Col. R. Steven Murray (Chief, Pub. Affairs Dept.)

FULLERTON

CALIFORNIA STATE UNIVERSITY, FULLERTON

Street address 1: PO Box 6846
Street address state: CA
Postal code: 92834-6846
Mailing address: PO Box 6846
Mailing city: Fullerton
Mailing state: CA
Mailing zip: 92834-6846
Office phone: (714) 278-3517
Office fax: (714) 278-2209
Web address: communications.fullerton.edu
College Affiliation: AAF, BEA, IABC, KTA, NPPA, PRSSA, SPJ
College Degree: BA, MA- Communications
College Departments: Department of Communications, 1961
College Facilities: AdA, CCTV, ComN, ComTV, DR, JM, JN, PRA, VDT, CATV
College Sequence: Concentrations: Advertising, Entertainment Studies, Journalism, Photo-Communications, Public Relations
Personnel: Anthony R. Fellow (Chair/Prof.); Jeff Brody (Prof.); David DeVries (Prof./Coord., Photocommunications); Cynthia King (Prof.); Paul Lester (Prof.); Coral Ohl (Prof.); Rick Pullen (Prof./Dean); Anthony Rimmer (Prof.); Shay Sayre (Prof./Early Ret. Prog.); Edgar Trotter (Prof.); Diane Witmer (Prof./Vice Chair, Grad. Coord.); Fred Zandpour (Prof./Assoc. Dean); Olan Farnall (Assoc. Prof.); Carolyn Johnson (Assoc. Prof./Early Ret. Prog.); Kuen-Hee Ju-Pak (Assoc. Prof./Coord., Advertising); Dean Kazoleas (Assoc. Prof.); Nancy Snow (Assoc. Prof.); Andi Stein (Assoc. Prof./Coord., Journalism); Carol Ames (Asst. Prof.); Assaf Avni (Asst. Prof.)

GAINESVILLE

BRENAU UNIVERSITY

Street address 1: One Centennial Cir.
Street address state: GA
Postal code: 30501
Mailing address: 1 Centennial Cir
Mailing city: Gainesville
Mailing state: GA
Mailing zip: 30501-3697
Office phone: (770) 538-4743
Office fax: (770) 538-4558
General e-mail: sblakley@lib.brenau.edu
College Departments: School of Business and Mass Communication, Department of Mass Communication
College Sequence: Mass Media Program: Two-year BA degree program in Journalism, Electronic Media, Public Relations and Corporate Communications follows the lower-division Liberal Arts core curriculum
Personnel: Stewart Blakley (Chair)

UNIVERSITY OF FLORIDA

Street address 1: 2096 Weimer
Street address state: FL
Postal code: 32611-8400
Mailing address: PO Box 118400
Mailing city: Gainesville
Mailing state: FL
Mailing zip: 32611-8400
Office phone: (352) 392-0466
Office fax: (352) 392-3919
Web address: www.jou.ufl.edu
College Affiliation: AAF, NBS/AER, BEA, KTA, PRSSA, SPJ, Florida Press Assn., Florida Public Relations Assn., Florida Assn. of Broadcasters, Florida Magazine Assn
College Degree: BS- Advertising, Journalism, Public Relations, Telecommunication; MA- Mass Communication, Advertising Management; PhD- Mass Communication; Joint MAMC-JD; Joint PhD-JD
College Departments: College of Journalism and Communications, 1925
College Facilities: AP, UPI, AM, FM, AdA, CATV, CCTV, CN, ComN, ComR, ETV, HDTV, PRA, VDT
Personnel: John Wright (Dean/Prof.); Laurence B. Alexander (Prof./Interim Assoc. Dean, UF Grad. School/UF Research Foundation Prof.); Bill F. Chamberlin (Prof./Joseph L. Brechner Eminent Scholar/Dir., Marion Brechner Citizen Access Proj.); Sylvia Chan-Olmsted (Prof./Assoc. Dean, Research/AI and Effie Flanagan Prof. in Journalism & Communications); Sandra Dickson (Prof./Co-Dir., Documentary Institute); Julie Dodd (Prof.); Mary Ann Ferguson (Prof.); Linda Childers Hon (Prof./Sr. Assoc. Dean/AI and Effie Flanagan Prof. in Journalism and Communications); Terry Hynes (Dean Emerita/Prof.); Lynda Lee Kaid (Prof.); John Kaplan (Prof./UF Res. Foundation Prof.); Kathleen Kelly (Prof.); Melinda (Mindy) McAdams (Prof./Knight Chair in Journalism Technologies and the Democratic Process); William McKeen (Prof./Chair, Dept. of Journalism); Jon D. Morris (Prof.); David Ostroff (Prof./Chair, Dept. of Telecommunication); Churchill Roberts (Prof./Co-Dir., Documentary Institute); Jon A. Roosenraad (Prof./Asst. Dean, Student Servs.); John C. Sutherland (Prof./Chair, Dept. of Adv.); Debbie Treise (Prof./Assoc. Dean, Grad. Studies/Research/AI and Effie Flanagan Prof. in Journalism & Communication)
Main (survey) contact: Terry Hynes

GOSHEN

GOSHEN COLLEGE

Street address 1: Dept. of Communication
Street address 2: 1700 South Main St.
Street address state: IN
Postal code: 46526-4798
Mailing address: Dept. of Communication
Mailing city: Goshen
Mailing state: IN
Mailing zip: 46526-4798
Office phone: (574) 535-7450
Office fax: (574) 535-7660
Web address: www.goshen.edu
General e-mail: dstoltzfus@goshen.edu
College Departments: Department of Communication
College Sequence: Majors in broadcasting, communication, journalism and public relations.
Personnel: Duane Stoltzfus (Prof.)
Main (survey) contact: Duane Stoltzfus

GRAMBLING

GRAMBLING STATE UNIVERSITY

Street address 1: PO Box 45
Street address state: LA
Postal code: 71245
Mailing address: PO Box 45
Mailing city: Grambling
Mailing state: LA
Mailing zip: 71245-0045
Office phone: (318) 274-2403
Office fax: (318) 274-3194
General e-mail: edum@gram.edu
College Affiliation: PRSSA, NABJ, NBS, SND, WICI
College Degree: BA, MA- Mass Communication
College Departments: Department of Mass Communication, 1988
College Facilities: FM, AP, CATV, DR, JN, VDT
College Sequence: News-Editorial, Public Relations, Visual Communication, Broadcasting
Personnel: Martin O. Edu (Acting Head)

GRAND JUNCTION

MESA STATE COLLEGE

Street address 1: PO Box 2647
Street address state: CO
Postal code: 81502
Mailing address: PO Box 2647
Mailing city: Grand Junction
Mailing state: CO
Mailing zip: 81502-2647
Office phone: (970) 248-1287
Office fax: (970) 248-1199
Web address: www.mesastate.edu/masscomm
General e-mail: bevers@mesastate.edu
College Degree: BA
College Departments: Mass Communications Department, 1981
College Sequence: Mass Communications Program: The department offers a Mass Communications bachelor's degree with concentrations in Media News-Editorial, Broadcast Production; Public Relations/Advertising; Print Media
Personnel: Byron Evers (Dir.)

GRAND RAPIDS

CALVIN COLLEGE

Street address 1: 3201 Burton SE
Street address state: MI
Postal code: 49546
Mailing address: 3201 Burton St SE
Mailing city: Grand Rapids
Mailing state: MI
Mailing zip: 49546-4388
Office phone: (616) 526-6283
Office fax: (616) 526-6601
General e-mail: bytw@calvin.edu
College Departments: Department of Communication Arts and Sciences; Department of English (Journalism minor)
College Sequence: Communication Programs: BA degree with liberal-arts emphases in mass media and film. Department of English (Journalism minor): Interdisciplinary liberal-arts program with strong writing component
Personnel: Randall Bytwerk (Chair, Dept. of Commun. Arts & Sciences); Don Hettinga (Prof., Dept. of English)
Main (survey) contact: Randall Bytwerk

Schools and Departments of Journalism

GREELEY

UNIVERSITY OF NORTHERN COLORADO

Street address 1: Dept. of Journalism
Street address state: CO
Postal code: 80639
Mailing address: Dept of Journalism
Mailing city: Greeley
Mailing state: CO
Mailing zip: 80639-0001
Office phone: (970) 351-2726
Office fax: (970) 351-2983
College Affiliation: SPJ
College Degree: BA
College Departments: Department of Journalism and Mass Communications, 1970
College Facilities: CN, CATV, 24 VDTs and 3 printers in news lab
College Sequence: Public Relations and Advertising Media, News-Editorial, Telecommunications
Personnel: Charles Ingold (Prof./Chair); Alice Klement (Endowed Prof.); Wayne Melanson (Assoc. Prof.); Lynn Klyde-Silverstein (Asst. Prof.); Lee Anne Peck (Asst. Prof.)

GREENCASTLE

DEPAUW UNIVERSITY

Street address 1: 609 S. Locust Street
Street address state: IN
Postal code: 46135-00037
Mailing address: PO Box 37
Mailing city: Greencastle
Mailing state: IN
Mailing zip: 46135-0037
Office phone: (765) 658-4495
Office fax: (765) 658-4499
General e-mail: jeffmccall@depauw.edu
College Departments: Department of English and Department of Communication Arts and Sciences
College Facilities: Pulliam Center for Contemporary Media
College Sequence: Mass Communication Program: Coursework offered in news writing and editing, magazine writing, broadcast journalism, media law, media criticism and organizational communication
Personnel: Jeffrey M. McCall (Professor of media studies)
Main (survey) contact: Jeffrey M. McCall

GREENSBORO

NORTH CAROLINA A&T STATE UNIVERSITY

Street address 1: 1601 E. Market St., A322 New General Classroom Bldg.
Street address state: NC
Postal code: 27411
Mailing address: 1601 E Market St
Mailing city: Greensboro
Mailing state: NC
Mailing zip: 27411-0001
Office phone: (336) 334-7900
Office fax: (336) 334-7770
College Degree: BS- Journalism and Mass Communication with a concentration in one of the above sequences
College Departments: Department of Journalism and Mass Communication, 1986
College Facilities: Journalism and Mass Communication Computer Lab, Journalism Newspaper Lab, Television Studio, Radio Station
College Sequence: Electronic Media and Journalism, Broadcast Production, Media Management, Print Journalism and Public Relations
Personnel: Humphrey A. Regis (Chair); Kevin Keenan (Prof.); Tamrat Mereba (Prof.); Linda Florence Callahan (Assoc. Prof.); Rita Lauria (Assoc. Prof.); Teresa Jo Styles (Assoc. Prof.); Nagatha Tonkins (Asst. Prof.); Anthony Welborne (Asst. Prof.); Sheila Whitley (Asst. Prof.); Gail Wiggins (Asst. Prof.); Kimberly Moore (Adj. Asst. Prof.); Emily Burch-Harris (Instr.); Bruce Clark (Instr.); Allen Johnson (Instr.); Jacqueline Jones (Instr.); Alexis Nyandwi (Instr.); Willis Smith (Instr.); Brian Tomlin (Instr.); Mary Vanderlinden (Instr.); Frances Ward Johnson (Instr.)

GREENVILLE

EAST CAROLINA UNIVERSITY

Street address 1: 102 Joyner E.
Street address state: NC
Postal code: 27858-4353
Mailing address: 102 Joyner E.
Mailing city: Greenville
Mailing state: NC
Mailing zip: 27858-4353
Office phone: (252) 328-4227
Office fax: (252) 328-1509
General e-mail: keyesa@mail.ecu.edu
College Degree: MA, BS
College Departments: School of Communication, Journalism Major, Public Relations Major, Media Production Major, Communication Studies Major, Media Studies Major
College Facilities: VDT, CN, non-linear editing, cable newscasts
College Sequence: Offers programs that lead to a BS in Communication with major concentration in journalism, public relations, media production, communication studies or media studies. MA in Communication studies
Personnel: Tim Hudson (Dir.)

HAMDEN

QUINNIPIAC UNIVERSITY

Street address 1: 275 Mount Carmel Ave
Street address state: CT
Postal code: 06518-1905
Country: USA
Mailing address: 275 Mount Carmel Ave
Mailing city: Hamden
Mailing state: CT
Mailing zip: 06518-1908
Office phone: 8608301017
Web address: www.quinnipiac.edu; quchronicle.com
General e-mail: editor@quchronicle.com
College Departments: School of Communications, Ed McMahon Center, 1993
Personnel: David Friedlander (Editor-in-Chief)
Main (survey) contact: David Friedlander

HAMMOND

SOUTHEASTERN LOUISIANA UNIVERSITY

Street address 1: 344 D. Vickers Hall, Sycamore St., SLU 10451
Street address state: LA
Postal code: 70402
Mailing address: 344 D Vickers Hall, Sycamore St, Slu 10451
Mailing city: Hammond
Mailing state: LA
Mailing zip: 70402-0001
Office phone: (504) 549-2105
Office fax: (504) 549-5014
General e-mail: fcom1157@selu.edu
College Degree: BA
College Departments: Department of Communication & Theatre, 2000
College Facilities: ComN, FM
College Sequence: Mass Communication and Journalism, Organizational Communication, Journalism Education
Personnel: Karen Fontenot (Head/Assoc. Prof.); Joe Mirando (Prof.); William Parrill (Prof.); T. Win Welford (Prof.); Jack Wellman (Prof.); Lynn Wellmann (Assoc. Prof.); Frances Brandau-Brown (Asst. Prof.); Joe Burns (Asst. Prof.); Mike Applin (Instr.); Terri Miller-Drufner (Instr.)

HATTIESBURG

UNIVERSITY OF SOUTHERM MISSISSIPPI

Street address 1: Box 5121
Street address state: MS
Postal code: 39406-5121
Mailing address: PO Box 5121
Mailing city: Hattiesburg
Mailing state: MS
Mailing zip: 39406-0001
Office phone: (601) 266-4258
Office fax: (601) 266-6473
Web address: www.usm.edu/mcj
General e-mail: journalism@usm.edu
College Affiliation: AAF, NABJ, NPPA, PRSSA, SPJ
College Degree: BA- Advertising, Journalism, Radio-Television-Film; MA, MS- Communication with Mass Communication Emphasis; MS- Public Relations; PhD- Communication with Mass Communication emphasis
College Departments: School of Mass Communication and Journalism, 2001
College Facilities: AdA, AP, CCTV, DR, FM, JN, PRA, VDT
College Sequence: Emphasis Areas: Advertising; Journalism (News/Editorial, News/Editorial with Photojournalism Concentration, Public Relations); Radio, Television, and Film (Broadcast Journalism, Film, Radio/Television Production)
Personnel: Christopher P. Campbell (Dir./Prof. School of Mass Commun. and Journ.); David R. Davies (Prof.); S.M. Mazharul Haque (Prof.); S. Dixon McDowell (Prof.); Phillip Gentile (Asst. Prof.); Cheryl Jenkins (Asst. Prof.); Keith F. Johnson (Asst. Prof.); Kim LeDuff (Asst. Prof.); Mary Lou Sheffer (Asst. Prof.); Jae-Hwa Shin (Asst. Prof.); Fei Xue (Asst. Prof.); Stephen Coleman (Professor of Practice); Gina Gayle (Professor of Practice); Joey Goodsell (Professor of Practice); Maggie Williams (Instr./Publication Mgr.); Ed Wheeler (Prof. Emer.); Gene Wiggins (Prof. Emer.); Clarence Williams (Photojournalist-in-Residence)
Main (survey) contact: Christopher P. Campbell

HAYS

FORT HAYS STATE UNIVERSITY

Street address 1: 600 Park St.
Street address state: KS
Postal code: 67601
County: Ellis
Country: U.S.A.
Mailing address: 600 Park St.
Mailing city: Hays
Mailing state: KS
Mailing zip: 67601-4099
Office phone: (785) 628-4018
Office fax: (785) 628-4075
Web address: www.fhsu.edu
General e-mail: lhunting@fhsu.edu
College Departments: Department of Communication Studies, Area of Journalism
College Sequence: Journalism Program: Coursework in journalism, mass communications, public relations, advertising, photography, desktop publishing and other journalism-related areas.
Personnel: Linn Ann Huntington (Dir.); Qing Jiang Yao (Dr.); Hsin-Yen Yang (Dr.)
Main (survey) contact: Linn Ann Huntington

HAYWARD

CALIFORNIA STATE UNIVERSITY, HAYWARD

Street address 1: 25800 Carlos Bee Blvd.
Street address state: CA
Postal code: 94542
Mailing address: 25800 Carlos Bee Blvd
Mailing city: Hayward
Mailing state: CA
Mailing zip: 94542-3000
Office phone: (510) 885-3292
Office fax: (510) 885-4099
General e-mail: jhammerb@csuhayward.edu
College Departments: Department of Mass Communication, 1973
College Sequence: Mass Communication, with options in Advertising, Broadcasting, Journalism, Photo-communication and Public Relations; Minor in Mass Communication, a Mass Communication Option in the Liberal Studies Major, and a Mass Communication emphasis in the waiver pro
Personnel: John Hammerback (Interim Chair)

HICKORY

LENOIR-RHYNE COLLEGE

Street address 1: School of Communication and Literature
Street address state: NC
Postal code: 28603
Mailing address: School of Communication and Literature
Mailing city: Hickory
Mailing state: NC
Mailing zip: 28603
Office phone: (828) 328-7164
Office fax: (828) 328-7163
General e-mail: Richter@lrc.edu
College Degree: BA
College Departments: School of Communication and Literature
College Facilities: FM, CCTV, CN, DR, VDT
College Sequence: Communication Program: Offers mass comm., journalism, television, speech, law, internship, PR and integrated liberal arts courses leading to an BA in Communication
Personnel: William Richter (Chair)

HIGH POINT

HIGH POINT UNIV.

Street address 1: 1 University Pkwy
Street address state: NC
Postal code: 27268-0002
Country: USA
Mailing address: 833 Montlieu Ave
Mailing city: High Point
Mailing state: NC
Mailing zip: 27262-4260
Office phone: (800) 345-6993
Office fax: (336) 841-4513
Web address: www.highpoint.edu
General e-mail: news@highpoint.edu
College Affiliation: Lambda Pi Eta
College Degree: BA
College Departments: The Nido R. Qubein School of Communication
College Facilities: Internet Radio, CCTV, Advertising/PR Agency, Game Design Studio, Student Newspaper, Television Production Studios, Multi-track Audio Recording Studio, Editing Suites, Computer Labs, Theatre-screening Room
College Sequence: Electronic Media Production, Games and Interactive Media Design, Journalism, Media and Popular Culture Studies, Strategic Communication.
Personnel: Bobby Hayes (Advisor); Wilfrid Tremblay (Dir./Prof.); Kate Fowkes (Prof.); Judy Isaksen (Assoc. Prof.); John Luecke (Assoc. Prof.); Nahed Eltantawy (Asst. Prof.); Jim Goodman (Asst. Prof.); Brad Lambert (Asst. Prof.); Jim Trammell (Asst. Prof.); Gerald Voorhees (Asst. Prof.); Kristina Bell (Lectr.); Don Moore (Opns. Mgr.); Martin Yount (Video Producer); Michelle Devlin (Admin. Asst.)
Main (survey) contact: Bobby Hayes; Dr. Ginny McDermott

HIGHLAND HEIGHTS

NORTHERN KENTUCKY UNIVERSITY

Street address 1: 134 Landrum Academic Center, Nunn Dr.
Street address state: KY
Postal code: 41099
Mailing address: 134 Landrum Academic Center Nunn Dr
Mailing city: Newport
Mailing state: KY
Mailing zip: 41099-0001
Office phone: (859) 572-5435
Office fax: (859) 572-6187
General e-mail: ragsdale@nku.edu
College Affiliation: AAF, BEA, PRSSA
College Degree: BA
College Departments: Communications Department, 1972
College Facilities: AM/FM, CATV, CCTV, CN, ComN, ComTV, DR, PRA, VDT
College Sequence: Journalism Sequences: Advertising, General Editorial, Public Relations, Photojournalism. Radio/Television Sequences: Business, Engineering, Programming. Speech Communication Sequences: Organizational Communication, Rhetorical Theory, Speech/Theatre A
Personnel: Gaut Ragsdale (Chair)

HOLLY SPRINGS

DEPARTMENT OF MASS COMMUNICATIONS, RUST COLLEGE

Street address 1: 150 Rust Avenue
Street address state: MS
Postal code: 38635
County: Marshall County
Mailing address: 150 Rust Avenue
Mailing city: Holly Springs
Mailing state: MS
Mailing zip: 38635-2328
Office phone: (662) 252-8000
Office fax: (662) 252-8869
General e-mail: dmoyo@rustcollege.edu
College Affiliation: Rust College
College Degree: B.A.
College Departments: Department of Mass Communications, 1981
College Facilities: WURC-FM 88.1; RC-TV2; The Rustorian
College Sequence: Journalism Programs: Broadcast Journalism (Television/Radio), Print Journalism (Newspaper/Magazine)
Personnel: Debayo R. Moyo (Department Chair)
Main (survey) contact: Debayo R. Moyo

HONOLULU

CHAMINADE, UNIVERSITY OF HONOLULU

Street address 1: Dept. of Communication
Street address state: HI
Postal code: 96816-1578
Mailing address: Dept. of Communication
Mailing city: Honolulu
Mailing state: HI
Mailing zip: 96816-1578
Office phone: (808) 735-4711
Office fax: (808) 739-8328
General e-mail: cbieberl@chaminade.edu
College Affiliation: NCA
College Degree: BA
College Departments: Department of Communication, 1985
College Sequence: Mass Communication, Marketing Communication
Personnel: Clifford Bieberly (Dir.)

HAWAII PACIFIC UNIVERSITY

Street address 1: 1136 Union Mall
Street address 2: Suite 208
Street address state: HI
Postal code: 96813
Mailing address: 1136 Union Mall
Mailing city: Honolulu
Mailing state: HI
Mailing zip: 96813
Office phone: (808) 544-0825
Office fax: (808) 544-0835
Web address: http://hpulamalama.com/wp/
General e-mail: editor@kalamalama.com
College Degree: BA, BS, MA/COM
College Departments: College of Communication
Personnel: Steven Combs (Dean/Prof.); John Hart (Prof.); John Barnum (Assoc. Prof.); Peter Britos (Assoc. Prof.); James Whitfield (Assoc. Prof.); Brian Cannon (Asst. Prof.); Matt George (Asst. Prof.); Serena Hashimoto (Asst. Prof.); Lowell Douglas Ing (Asst. Prof.); Anne Kennedy (Asst. Prof.); Laurence LeDoux (Asst. Prof.); Penny Smith (Asst. Prof.); Yanjun Zhao (Asst. Prof.); Dale Burke (Instr.); Katherine Clark (Instr.); Thomas Dowd (Instr.); Rose Helens-Hart (Instr.); Marianne Luken (Instr.); Malia Smith (Instr.); Lewis Trusty (Instr.)
Main (survey) contact: Mark Brians

UNIVERSITY OF HAWAII AT MANOA

Street address 1: 2550 Campus Rd.
Street address state: HI
Postal code: 96822
Mailing address: 2550 Campus Rd
Mailing city: Honolulu
Mailing state: HI
Mailing zip: 96822-2250
Office phone: (808) 956-8881
Office fax: (808) 956-5396
General e-mail: jour@hawaii.edu
College Affiliation: KTA, PRSSA, SPJ
College Degree: BA
College Departments: School of Communications, 1963
College Facilities: AP, FM, CN, ComN, ComR, ComTV, DR, PRS, VDT
College Sequence: Multiple Media Platforms: Print, Broadcast, Online & other new media formats.
Personnel: Gerald Kato (Chair/Assoc. Prof.); Thomas J. Brislin (Prof.); Beverly Deepe Keever (Prof.); Ann Auman (Assoc. Prof.); Jonathan Lillie (Asst. Prof.)

INDIANAPOLIS

BUTLER UNIV.

Street address 1: 4600 Sunset Ave
Street address state: IN
Postal code: 46208-3443
Country: USA
Mailing address: 4600 Sunset Ave # 112
Mailing city: Indianapolis
Mailing state: IN
Mailing zip: 46208-3487
Office phone: (317) 940-9358
Office fax: (317) 940-9713
Web address: dawgnet.butler.edu
General e-mail: mweiteka@butler.edu
College Departments: Eugene S. Pulliam School of Journalism
College Sequence: Journalism Program: The journalism major has course sequences in news-editorial, public relations, and integrated communication: public relations and advertising. The department also coordinates an interdisciplinary major in public and corporate commun
Personnel: Kwadwo Anokwa (Dir.); Charles St. Cyr (Advisor); Lauren Fisher (Adv. Mgr); Meg Shaw (Ed.)
Main (survey) contact: Kwadwo Anokwa; Charles St. Cyr

INDIANA UNIVERSITY

Street address 1: Indianapolis Campus
Street address 2: 535 W. Michigan St.
Street address state: IN
Postal code: 46202
Mailing address: Indianapolis Campus
Mailing city: Indianapolis
Mailing state: IN
Mailing zip: 46202
Office phone: (317) 278-5320
Office fax: (317) 278-5321
Web address: www.journalism.iupui.edu
General e-mail: dperkins@foi.iupui.edu
College Degree: BAJ, MA Prof., MA Res., PhD
College Facilities: AP, AM, FM, CATV, CCTV, CN, DR, ETV, JM, VDT
College Sequence: News-Editorial, Broadcast News, Photojournalism, Advertising, PR, Magazine, Media Management, Journalism Education
Personnel: James W. Brown (Prof./Exec. Assoc. Dean); Jonas Bjork (Prof.); Sherry Ricchiardi (Prof.); Pamela Laucella (Asst. Prof.); Robert Dittmer (Lectr.); Maggie Balough Hillery (Adj. Prof./Pub., The Sagamore); Patrick McKeand (Adj. Prof./Pub. Emer., The Sagamore); Shirley Quate (Prof. Emer.)
Main (survey) contact: James W. Brown

UNIVERSITY OF INDIANAPOLIS

Street address 1: 1400 E. Hanna Ave.
Street address state: IN
Postal code: 46227
Mailing address: 1400 E Hanna Ave
Mailing city: Indianapolis
Mailing state: IN
Mailing zip: 46227-3697
Office phone: (317) 788-3280
Office fax: (317) 788-3490
Web address: www.communication.uindy.edu
General e-mail: catchings@uindy.edu
College Departments: Department of Communication, 1993
College Sequence: Communication Program: Program includes skills and theory courses in journalism, electronic media, and public relations in a liberal arts Methodist-affiliated university, biweekly newspaper, radio station, television channel, and public relations agency.
Personnel: Billy Catchings (Chair)
Main (survey) contact: Billy Catchings

IOWA CITY

UNIVERSITY OF IOWA

Street address 1: 100 Adler Journalism Bldg., Rm. E305
Street address state: IA
Postal code: 52242-2004
Mailing address: 100 Adler Journalism Bldg Rm E305
Mailing city: Iowa City
Mailing state: IA
Mailing zip: 52242-2004
Office phone: (319) 335-3486
Office fax: (319) 335-3502
Web address: www.uiowa.edu/jmc
General e-mail: journalism-admin@uiowa.edu
College Affiliation: KTA, PRSSA, SPJ, NABJ, RTNDA, Ed On Campus
College Degree: BA, BS, MA, PhD
College Departments: School of Journalism and Mass Communication, 1924
College Facilities: AP, AM, FM, CATV, CCTV, CN, DR, JM, VDT
Personnel: Marc Armstrong (Interim Dir.); Kay Amert (Prof.); Dan Berkowitz (Prof.); Stephen Bloom (Prof.); Pamela J. Creedon (Prof./Dir.); Judy Polumbaum (Prof.); Carolyn Stewart Dyer (Prof.); Julie Andsager (Assoc. Prof.); Stephen Berry (Assoc. Prof.); Venise Berry (Assoc. Prof.); Meenakshi Gigi Durham (Assoc. Prof./Coord., Iowa Ctr. for Commun. Study/Advisor, Journal of Communication Inquiry); Lyombe(Leo) Eko (Assoc. Prof.); John Kimmich Javier (Assoc. Prof.); Donald McLeese (Assoc. Prof.); Jane Singer (Assoc. Prof.); John Bennett (Asst. Prof.); Stacey Cone (Asst. Prof.); Frank Durham (Asst. Prof.); Sujatha Sosale (Asst. Prof.); Ann Haugland (George H. Gallup Lectr.)
Main (survey) contact: Pamela J. Creedon

ITTA BENA

MISSISSIPPI VALLEY STATE UNIV.

Street address 1: 14000 Highway 82 W
Street address state: MS
Postal code: 38941-1400
County: Leflore
Country: USA
Mailing address: 14000 Highway 82 W
Mailing city: Itta Bena
Mailing state: MS
Mailing zip: 38941-1401
Office phone: (662) 254-3458
Office fax: (622) 254-6704
Web address: deltadevilsgazette.com
General e-mail: deltadevilsgazettefacad@gmail.com
College Degree: BA- Mass Communication, Speech Communication
College Departments: Department of Mass Communications, 1994
College Facilities: Macintosh computer lab; digital photo lab, performing arts theatre; FM radio station, television studio, radio studio(all state-of-the-art)
College Sequence: Broadcasting, Journalism, Public Relations, Speech Communication
Personnel: Esin C. Turk (Asst. Prof.); Samuel Osunde (Asst. Prof./Dir., Forensics); Carolyn Gordon; Zainul Abedin (Mr.)
Main (survey) contact: Esin Turk

JACKSON

JACKSON STATE UNIVERSITY

Street address 1: 1230 Raymond Rd.
Street address state: MS
Postal code: 39217-0990
Mailing address: PO Box 18590
Mailing city: Jackson
Mailing state: MS
Mailing zip: 39217-0001
Office phone: (601) 979-2151
Office fax: (601) 979-5800
Web address: www.jsums.edu/jsumasscom/
General e-mail: dwight.e.brooks@jsums.edu
College Departments: Department of Mass Communications
College Sequence: Mass Communications: seeks to educate student who can take their place in the leadership of mass communications industries and provide support for the mission of Jackson State University through a cooperative relationship with local media, businesses, in
Personnel: Dwight Brooks (Chair/Prof.); Olorundare E. Aworuwa (Assoc. Prof.); Joseph Clive Enos (Assoc. Prof.); Li-Jing Chang (Asst. Prof.); Andrea Dilworth (Asst. Prof./Coord., Adv.); Ayana Haaruun (Asst. Prof.); Teresa Taylor (Asst. Prof.); Sunny Smith (Instr./Dir., Programs); Gail H. M. Brown (Adj. Instr.); Riva Brown (Adj. Instr.); Elaina Jackson (Adj. Instr.); Dathan Thigpen (Adj. Instr.); Aly Ash (Admin. Asst.); Regina Clay (Sec.)

JACKSONVILLE

EDWARD WATERS COLLEGE

Street address 1: Mass Communications Program
Street address state: FL
Postal code: 32218
Mailing address: Mass Communications Program
Mailing city: Jacksonville
Mailing state: FL
Mailing zip: 32218
Office phone: (904) 366-2502
College Degree: BA
College Departments: Mass Communications Program, 1982/83
College Sequence: Radio/TV, Journalism
Personnel: Emmanuel C. Alozie (Coord.)

Schools and Departments of Journalism

ILLINOIS COLLEGE

Street address 1: 1101 West College Ave.
Street address state: IL
Postal code: 62650
Mailing address: 1101 W College Ave
Mailing city: Jacksonville
Mailing state: IL
Mailing zip: 62650-2299
Office phone: (217) 245-3000
College Departments: Journalism, 1970
College Sequence: Journalism Program: Students interested in a career in journalism may major in Communications or English. The college offers writing and communication courses and various internships. Local newspapers also employ students
Personnel: Jim Kerbaugh (Chair, English); Peter Verkruyse (Chair, Communications/Theatre)
Main (survey) contact: Jim Kerbaugh

JACKSONVILLE STATE UNIVERSITY

Street address 1: 700 Pelham Rd. N.
Street address state: AL
Postal code: 36265-1602
Mailing address: 700 Pelham Rd N
Mailing city: Jacksonville
Mailing state: AL
Mailing zip: 36265-1623
Office phone: (256) 782-5300
Office fax: (256) 782-8175
Web address: www.jsu.edu/depart/edprof/comm
General e-mail: kharbor@jsu.edu
College Affiliation: BEA, SPJ, PRSA, RTNDA, ASJMC, CMA
College Degree: BA- Communication; minor in Communication (ACEJMC - accredited communication program)
College Departments: Department of Communication
College Facilities: Macintosh computer lab, FM radio station, Two TV studios, Four Digital editing bays, Smart classrooms, affiliated TV station WJXS
College Sequence: Concentrations: Broadcasting, Print Journalism, Public Relations
Personnel: Kingsley O. Harbor (Chair/Prof.); Augustine Ihator (Prof.); Jerry Chandler (Asst. Prof./Internship Coord.); Jeffrey Hedrick (Asst. Prof.); Mike Stedham (Part-time Fac./Mgr., Stud. Media); Pamela Hill (Adj. Fac.); Laura Tutor (Adj. Fac.); Mickey Shadrix (Adj. Fac.); William Meehan

JACKSONVILLE UNIVERSITY

Street address 1: Dept. of Mass Communication Studies
Street address state: FL
Postal code: 32211
Mailing address: Dept. of Mass Communication Studies
Mailing city: Jacksonville
Mailing state: FL
Mailing zip: 32211
Office phone: (904) 744-3950
College Affiliation: SCJ, Florida Public Relations Assn.
College Departments: Department of Mass Communication Studies
College Facilities: Weekly newspaper, college magazine, yearbook, radio station, cable television access, national film studies journal
College Sequence: Journalism Program: JU's program blends the arts and sciences with a skills-oriented communications curriculum. Sequences available are Newspaper/Magazine, PR/Advertising, Radio/TV/Film. Many internship opportunities are available including a summer int
Personnel: Dennis Stouse (Dir.)

UNIVERSITY OF NORTH FLORIDA

Street address 1: 4567 St. Johns Bluff Rd. S.
Street address state: FL
Postal code: 32224-2645
Mailing address: 1 U N F Dr
Mailing city: Jacksonville
Mailing state: FL
Mailing zip: 32224-7699
Office phone: (904) 620-2651
Office fax: (904) 620-2652
Web address: www.unf.edu/coas/cva
General e-mail: opatters@unf.edu
College Affiliation: PRSSA, AdFed
College Degree: BA, BS, BFA
College Departments: Department of Communications and Visual Arts, 1987
College Facilities: CATV, CCTV, CN, ComN, DR, PRA, AdA
College Sequence: Mass Communications: Advertising, Broadcasting, Journalism, Public Relations; Visual Arts: Graphic Design (portfolio review required), Photography, Studio Arts, Art History
Personnel: Oscar Patterson (Chair)

JEFFERSON CITY

LINCOLN UNIVERSITY

Street address 1: Dept. of Humanities
Street address 2: MSC03 2240
Street address state: MO
Postal code: 65102
Mailing address: Dept. of Humanities
Mailing city: Jefferson City
Mailing state: MO
Mailing zip: 65102
Office phone: (573) 681-5280
Office fax: (573) 681-5438
General e-mail: govangd@lincolnu.edu
College Degree: BA, BS
College Departments: Department of Humanities, Fine Arts and Journalism Program, 1942
Personnel: Don Govang (Dept. Head/Assoc. Prof.); Ted Jacobs (Asst. Prof.); Art Fulcher (Asst. Prof.); Leslie Cross (Part-time Fac.); Tom Cwynar (Part-time Fac.)

JOLIET

UNIVERSITY OF ST. FRANCIS

Street address 1: 500 Wilcox St.
Street address state: IL
Postal code: 60435
Mailing address: 500 Wilcox St
Mailing city: Joliet
Mailing state: IL
Mailing zip: 60435-6188
Office phone: (815) 740-5064
Office fax: (815) 740-4285
General e-mail: trosner@stfrancis.edu
College Departments: Mass Communication Department, 1976
College Sequence: Mass Communication Program: Concentrations in Broadcasting, Public Relations/Advertising/Journalism, Media Arts. Internships in all areas
Personnel: Terre Layng Rosner (Chair)
Main (survey) contact: Terre Layng Rosner

JONESBORO

ARKANSAS STATE UNIVERSITY

Street address 1: 114 Cooley Dr., Rm. 331
Street address state: AR
Postal code: 72401
Mailing address: PO Box 540
Mailing city: State University
Mailing state: AR
Mailing zip: 72467-0540
Office phone: (870) 972-2468
Office fax: (870) 972-3856
Web address: comm.astate.edu
College Affiliation: AAF, NBS/AER, KTA, PRSSA, SPJ, AWC, ABC, BEA, NPPA, NABJ, Arkansas Press Association, Arkansas Broadcasters Association
College Degree: BS- Journalism, Radio-TV, Graphic Communications; BA- Communication Studies; BSE- Speech & Theatre; MSMC- Journalism, Radio-TV; MA- Speech & Theatre
College Departments: College of Communications, 1936
College Facilities: AP, FM, CATV, CN, DR, JR, VDT, NPR, AdA, JN, PRA
College Sequence: Radio-TV Dept.- Broadcast Journalism, Audio-Video Production, New Media, Electronic Media Sales & Promotion; Journalism Dept.- News-Editorial, Advertising, Public Relations, Photojournalism, Graphic Communications; Communications Studies Dept
Personnel: Russell E. Shain (Dean/Prof.); Osabuohien Amienyi (Chair, RTV/Prof.); Tom Baglan (Chair, Commun. Studies/Prof.); Gilbert L. Fowler (Prof.); Mary Jackson-Pitts (Prof.); Lillie Fears (Assoc. Prof.); Joel T. Gambill (Assoc. Prof./Chair, Journ.); Jack Zibluk (Assoc. Prof.); Carey Byars (Asst. Prof.); Holly Byars (Asst. Prof.); Linda Clark (Asst. Prof.); Sandra Combs (Asst. Prof.); Robert Franklin (Asst. Prof.); Myleea Hill (Asst. Prof.); Matt Ramsey (Asst. Prof.); Mathew Thatcher (Asst. Prof.); Marcilene Thompson-Hayes (Asst. Prof.); Lily Zeng (Asst. Prof.); Alex Brown (Instr.); Michael B. Doyle (Instr.)

JOPLIN

MISSOURI SOUTHERN UNIVERSITY

Street address 1: 3950 Newman Rd
Street address state: MO
Postal code: 64801-1512
Country: USA
Mailing address: 3950 Newman Rd
Mailing city: Joplin
Mailing state: MO
Mailing zip: 64801-1595
Office phone: (417) 625-9823
Office fax: (417) 625-9585
Web address: www.thechartonline.com
General e-mail: chart@mssu.edu
College Departments: Department of Communications, 1980
College Sequence: Communications Program: Offers majors with options in mass communications, public relations, speech communication, and international communication. The department publishes a weekly student newspaper and student magazine and operates a cable television s
Personnel: J.R. Moorman (Head); Chad Stebbins (Advisor); T.R. Hanrahan (Publications Mgr.); Alexandra Nicolas (Ed. in Chief)
Main (survey) contact: Chad Stebbins

KALAMAZOO

WESTERN MICHIGAN UNIVERSITY

Street address 1: 1903 W. Michigan St.
Street address state: MI
Postal code: 49008-3805
Mailing address: 1903 W Michigan Ave
Mailing city: Kalamazoo
Mailing state: MI
Mailing zip: 49008-5200
Office phone: (269) 387-3148
Office fax: (269) 387-3990
General e-mail: richard.junger@wmich.edu
College Degree: BA
College Departments: Department of Communication and Journalism, 1976
College Sequence: Broadcast, News-Editorial, Magazine
Personnel: Dr. Richard Junger (Prog. Dir.)

KANSAS CITY

UNIVERSITY OF MISSOURI-KANSAS CITY

Street address 1: 202 Haag Hall, 5120 Rockhill Rd.
Street address state: MO
Postal code: 64110
Mailing address: 5120 Rockhill Rd
Mailing city: Kansas City
Mailing state: MO
Mailing zip: 64110-2446
Office phone: (816) 235-1337
Office fax: (816) 235-5539
General e-mail: com-s@umkc.edu
College Affiliation: SCA, PRSA
College Degree: BA
College Departments: Department of Communication Studies, 1972
College Facilities: AM/FM, CN, DR, AdA, PRA
College Sequence: Communication Studies program offers emphasis in Journalism and Mass Communication, Interpersonal and Public Communication or Film and Media Arts
Personnel: Carol Koehler (Chair/Assoc. Prof.); Michael R. Neer (Prof.); Robert Unger (Prof.); G.Thomas Poe (Assoc. Prof.); Peter Morello (Assoc. Prof.); Greg Gutenko (Assoc. Prof.); Caitlin Horsmon (Asst. Prof.); Michael McDonald (Asst. Prof.); Angela Elam (Instr., Radio); Linda H. Kurz (Instr.); Judith K. McCoromick (Instr.); Gaylord Marr (Prof. Emer.); Gregory D. Black (Prof. Emer.); Joan E. Aitken (Prof. Emer.); Larry G. Ehrlich (Prof. Emer.); Robin League (Prof. Emer.)

KENNESAW

KENNESAW STATE UNIVERSITY

Street address 1: 1000 Chastain Rd., Box 2207
Street address state: GA
Postal code: 30144
Mailing address: 1000 Chastain Rd NW # 2207
Mailing city: Kennesaw
Mailing state: GA
Mailing zip: 30144-5591
Office phone: (770) 423-6298
Office fax: (770) 423-6740
General e-mail: bwassmut@kennesaw.edu
College Affiliation: ASJMC, NCA, PRSSA
College Degree: BS
College Departments: Department of Communication, 1991
College Facilities: AM/FM, CN, ComN, Digital Media Lab, JM, NYTS
College Sequence: Journalism and Citizen Media, Organizational Communication, Media Studies, Public Relations
Personnel: Birgit Wassmuth (Chair/Prof.); Deanna Womack (Prof.); Chuck Aust (Prof.); Charles Mayo (Assoc. Prof.); Leonard Witt (Assoc. Prof./Eminent Scholar/Robert D. Fowler Distinguished Chair); Audrey Allison (Asst. Prof.); Philip Aust (Asst. Prof.); Joshua Azriel (Asst. Prof.); Barbara Gainey (Asst. Prof.); May Gao (Asst. Prof.); Amber Hutchins (Asst. Prof.); Heeman Kim (Asst. Prof.); Georgios Triantis (Asst. Prof.); Emily Holler (Instr.); Jan Phillips (Instr.); Stephen J. McNeill (Lectr.); Jeffrey Anderson (Prof. Emer.)

KIRKSVILLE

TRUMAN STATE UNIVERSITY

Street address 1: Communication Dept.
Street address state: MO
Postal code: 63501
Mailing address: Communication Dept.
Mailing city: Kirksville
Mailing state: MO
Mailing zip: 63501
Office phone: (660) 785-4481
Office fax: (660) 785-7486
General e-mail: heinz@truman.edu
College Affiliation: IABC, SPJ
College Degree: BA
College Departments: Language and Literature Division, 1974
College Facilities: AP, CCTV, CN, ComN, ComR, ComTV, DR, PRA, VDT
College Sequence: Journalism, Speech Comm.
Personnel: Heinz D. Woehlk (Contact)

LA MIRADA

BIOLA UNIVERSITY

Street address 1: 13800 Biola Ave
Street address state: CA
Postal code: 90639-0002
Country: USA
Mailing address: 13800 Biola Ave
Mailing city: La Mirada
Mailing state: CA
Mailing zip: 90639-0001
Office phone: (562) 906-4569
Office fax: (562) 906-4515
Web address: chimes.biola.edu
General e-mail: lily.park@biola.edu
College Affiliation: PRSA, PRSSA
College Degree: BA
College Departments: Department of Journalism, 2007
College Facilities: AP, CN, JM, PRA, VDT
College Sequence: Print, Broadcast, Public Relations, Visual
Personnel: Michael A. Longinow (Chair/Prof.); Sarah Sjoberg (Advertising Manager); J. Douglas Tarpley (Prof.); Michael Bower (Assoc. Prof.); Tamara Welter (Asst. Prof.); James Hirsen (Instr.); Chi-Chung Keung (Instr.); Mark Landsbaum (Instr.); Greg Schneider (Instr.); Melissa Nunnally (Instr.)
Main (survey) contact: Michael A. Longinow

LAFAYETTE

CYPRESS LAKE WIRE

Street address 1: 231 Hebrard Blvd
Street address state: LA
Postal code: 70503
County: Lafayette
Country: United States
Office phone: 337-482-5221
Personnel: Stephenson Waters
Main (survey) contact: Stephenson Waters

UNIVERSITY OF LOUISIANA AT LAFAYETTE

Street address 1: Rm. 107, Burke-Hawthorne Hall, Hebrard Blvd.
Street address state: LA
Postal code: 70503
Mailing address: PO Box 43650
Mailing city: Lafayette
Mailing state: LA
Mailing zip: 70504-0001
Office phone: (337) 482-6103
Office fax: (337) 482-6104
Web address: comm.louisiana.edu
College Affiliation: AF, ACA, PRSSA, SPJ, SCM, SNPA, LPA, NCS, ICE, PIMS, LBEA, NAB, NAMJ, ASJMC, Hearst Awards program
College Degree: BA, MS
College Departments: Department of Communication, 1981
College Facilities: AM/FM, CATV, CCTV, ComN, DR, ETV, VDT
College Sequence: Interpersonal/Organizational Communication, Mass Communication (Advertising, Broadcasting or Journalism seq.) and Public Relations
Personnel: Bette J. Kauffman (Dept. Head/Assoc. Prof.); Jeffrey M. Gibson (Assoc. Prof.); Tae-hyun Kim (Asst. Prof.); Robert E. Lewis (Asst. Prof.); Joel R. Willer (Asst. Prof.); Jarrett Reeves (Instr.); Mark Simmons (Part-time Adj. Fac)

LAKE CHARLES

MCNEESE STATE UNIVERSITY

Street address 1: PO Box 90335
Street address state: LA
Postal code: 70609
Mailing address: PO Box 90335
Mailing city: Lake Charles
Mailing state: LA
Mailing zip: 70609-0001
Office phone: (337) 475-5290
Office fax: (337) 475-5291
General e-mail: hover@mcneese.edu
College Affiliation: PRSSA
College Degree: BS, BA
College Departments: Department of Mass Communication, 1990
College Facilities: Broadcast Studios (TV and Radio), and Control Room, two computer labs, including multi-media production, CD and DVD; five editing suites, cable radio station
College Sequence: Journalism, Radio/TV, Public Relations, General Communication, Speech Education, Professional Sales Communication
Personnel: Henry Overduin (Head/Prof.); Leonard Barchak (Prof.); Carrie Chrisco (Assoc. Prof.); Larry Vinson (Assoc. Prof., Speech Prog.); Patrick Roddy (Asst. Prof.); Tracy Standley (Asst. Prof.); Davey Stephens (Asst. Prof., Speech Prog.); Robert Markstrom (Instr., Speech Prog.); Amy Veuleman (Instr., Speech Prog.); Jim Beam (Editor Emer., American Press/Journalist-in-Residence)

LAKELAND

FLORIDA SOUTHERN COLLEGE

Street address 1: 111 Lake Hollingsworth Dr
Street address state: FL
Postal code: 33801-5607
Country: USA
Mailing address: 111 Lake Hollingsworth Dr
Mailing city: Lakeland
Mailing state: FL
Mailing zip: 33801-5698
Office phone: (863) 680-4155
Office fax: (863) 680-6244
Web address: www.fscsouthern.com
College Degree: BA, BS
College Departments: Department of Communication
College Sequence: Journalism Program: BA and BS in Communication with concentrations in Advertising, Journalism, and Public Relations
Personnel: Michael Trice (Advisor)
Main (survey) contact: Michael Trice

LAWRENCE

UNIVERSITY OF KANSAS

Street address 1: 1435 Jayhawk Blvd., 200 Stauffer-Flint Hall
Street address state: KS
Postal code: 66045-7575
Mailing address: 1435 Jayhawk Blvd # 200
Mailing city: Lawrence
Mailing state: KS
Mailing zip: 66045-7594
Office phone: (785) 864-4755
Office fax: (785) 864-4396
Web address: www.journalism.ku.edu
General e-mail: jschool@ku.edu
College Affiliation: AAF, PRSSA, KTA, Journalism Multicultural Scholars Program
College Degree: BS, MS
College Departments: William Allen White School of Journalism and Mass Communications, 1911 (Dept.), 1944 (School)
College Facilities: AdA, AP, CN, ETV, JM, PRA, VDT
College Sequence: News and Information (print, broadcast news, magazine, online); Strategic Communications (advertising, public relations, marketing, management)
Personnel: Ann M. Brill (Assoc. Prof./Dean); Pam Fine (Prof./Knight Chair on the News, Leadership/Community); Ted Frederickson (Prof.); James K. Gentry (Prof.); David D. Perlmutter (Prof.); Susanne Shaw (Prof./Accrediting Coun.); Robert Basow (Assoc. Prof.); Timothy Bengtson (Assoc. Prof./Chair, Strategic Commun.); John Broholm (Assoc. Prof.); David Guth (Assoc. Prof./Assoc. Dean); Carol Holstead (Assoc. Prof.); Linda Lee (Assoc. Prof.); Tien-Tsung Lee (Assoc. Prof.); Charles Marsh (Assoc. Prof.); Max Utsler (Assoc. Prof.); Tom Volek (Assoc. Prof./Interim Dir., Grad. Program); Mike Williams (Assoc. Prof./Chair, News Information); Barbara Barnett (Asst. Prof.); Mugur V. Geana (Asst. Prof.); Crystal Lumpkins (Asst. Prof.)

LEXINGTON

UNIVERSITY OF KENTUCKY

Street address 1: 107 Grehan Bldg.
Street address state: KY
Postal code: 40506-0042
Mailing address: 107 Grehan
Mailing city: Lexington
Mailing state: KY
Mailing zip: 40506-0001
Office phone: (859) 257-1730
Office fax: (859) 323-3168
General e-mail: amy.jarvis@uky.edu
College Affiliation: AAF, NABJ, PRSSA, SPJ
College Degree: BA, BS, College-wide MA, PhD- Communication
College Departments: School of Journalism and Telecommunications, 1914
College Facilities: AdA, AM/FM, AP, CN, DR, VDT
College Sequence: Integrated Strategic Communications, Journalism and Telecommunications
Personnel: Beth E. Barnes (Prof./Dir.); Richard Labunski (Prof.); Thomas Lindlof (Prof.); Chike Anyaegbunam (Assoc. Prof.); Dennis Altman (Assoc. Prof.); Jim Hertog (Assoc. Prof.); Elizabeth Scoobie Ryan (Assoc. Prof.); Leland Buck Ryan (Assoc. Prof.); Scott Whitlow (Assoc. Prof.); Deborah Chung (Asst. Prof.); John Clark (Asst. Prof.); Mel Coffee (Asst. Prof.); Al Cross (Asst. Prof.); Alyssa Eckman (Asst. Prof.); Michael Farrell (Asst. Prof.); Phillip Hutchison (Asst. Prof.); Bobi Ivanov (Asst. Prof.); Yung Soo Kim (Asst. Prof.); Zixue Tai (Asst. Prof.); Kathleen Kakie Urch (Asst. Prof.)
Main (survey) contact: Becca Clemons

LITTLE ROCK

UNIVERSITY OF ARKANSAS AT LITTLE ROCK

Street address 1: 2801 S. University
Street address state: AR
Postal code: 72204
Mailing address: 2801 S University Ave
Mailing city: Little Rock
Mailing state: AR
Mailing zip: 72204-1000
Office phone: (501) 569-3250
Office fax: (501) 569-8371
Web address: www.ualr.edu
College Affiliation: KTA, NABJ, NBS-AERho, PRSSA, SPJ
College Degree: BA, MA
College Departments: School of Mass Communication, 1971
College Facilities: AM/FM, AP, CATV, CN, ComN, ComR, ComTV, DR, JM, PRA, VDT, departmental statewide news service
College Sequence: Radio/TV/Film, News-Editorial, Broadcast Journalism, Professional and Technical Writing, Public Relations
Personnel: Jamie Byrne (Dir./Assoc. Prof.); David M. Guerra (Prof.); Bruce L. Plopper (Prof.); Jeanne Rollberg (Assoc. Prof.); Gregory Stefaniak (Assoc. Prof.); Tim Edwards (Asst. Prof.); Mark Giese (Asst. Prof.); Carlton Rhodes (Asst. Prof.); Kristie A. Swain (Asst. Prof.); David Weekley (Instr.); Ron Breeding (Part-time Lectr.); Frank Fellone (Part-time Lectr.); Ben Fry (Part-time Lectr.); John Paul Jones (Part-time Lectr.); Dixie Martin (Part-time Lectr.); Robert Pest (Part-time Lectr.); J.J. Thompson (Part-time Lectr.); Wally Tucker (Part-time Lectr.); Theresa Wallent (Part-time Lectr.); Edward Jay Friedlander (Fac. Emer.)

LIVONIA

MADONNA UNIVERSITY

Street address 1: 36600 Schoolcraft
Street address state: MI
Postal code: 48150
Mailing address: 36600 Schoolcraft Rd
Mailing city: Livonia
Mailing state: MI
Mailing zip: 48150-1176
Office phone: (734) 432-5559
Office fax: (734) 432-5393
Web address: www.madonna.edu
General e-mail: nhaldane@madonna.edu
College Departments: Journalism-Public Relations Program, 1947
College Sequence: Journalism Program: Program is broadly based to include aspects of newspaper, magazine, publicity, graphics, television, photography and advertising production. Video Communications: Aimed at those interested in writing, producing and directing for sing
Personnel: Neal Haldane (Dir.)

LONG BEACH

CALIFORNIA STATE UNIVERSITY, LONG BEACH

Street address 1: 1250 Bellflower Blvd.
Street address state: CA
Postal code: 90840-4601
Mailing address: 1250 Bellflower Blvd
Mailing city: Long Beach
Mailing state: CA
Mailing zip: 90840-0004
Office phone: (562) 985-4981
Office fax: (562) 985-5300
College Affiliation: KTA, PRSSA, SPJ
College Degree: BA- Journalism
College Departments: Department of Journalism, 1966
College Facilities: AP, CAW, FM, DR, JM, JN, VDT
College Sequence: Broadcast, Online, Print, Photojournalism, Public Relations
Personnel: Raul Reis (Interim Chair/Assoc. Prof.); William Babcock (Prof.); William Mulligan (Prof.); Emma Phillingane (Prof.); Christopher Burnett (Asst. Prof.); Jennifer Fleming (Asst. Prof.); Heloiza Herscovitz (Asst. Prof.); Christopher Karadjov (Asst. Prof.); Carla Yarbrough (Asst. Prof.); Judith Frutig (Lectr.); Barbara Kingsley (Lectr.); Amara Aguilar (Part-time Fac.); Lee Brown (Part-time Fac.); John Canalis (Part-time Fac.); Henrietta Charles (Part-time Fac.); Monica Edwards (Part-time Fac.); David Ferrell (Part-time Fac.); Daniel Garvey (Part-time Fac.); Greg Hardesty (Part-time Fac.); Cees Kendall (Part-time Fac.)

LOS ANGELES

CALIFORNIA STATE UNIVERSITY, LOS ANGELES

Street address 1: Music 104, 5151 State University Dr.
Street address state: CA
Postal code: 90032
Mailing address: 5151 State University Dr Music 104
Mailing city: Los Angeles
Mailing state: CA
Mailing zip: 90032-4226
Office phone: (323) 343-4200
Office fax: (323) 343-6467
College Departments: Department of Communication Studies, 1965
College Sequence: Communication Program: Sequences in Public Relations, Professional Communication and Broadcast Journalism

UNIVERSITY OF SOUTHERN

Schools and Departments of Journalism

CALIFORNIA

Street address 1: 3502 Watt Way, ASC 325
Street address state: CA
Postal code: 90089-0281
Mailing address: 3502 Watts Way Asc 325
Mailing city: Los Angeles
Mailing state: CA
Mailing zip: 90089-0054
Office phone: (213) 740-3914
Office fax: (213) 740-8624
Web address: www.annenberg.usc.edu
General e-mail: ascquery@usc.edu
College Affiliation: PRSSA, RTNDA
College Degree: BA, MA
College Departments: School of Journalism, USC Annenberg School for Communication, 1928
College Facilities: AP, AM, CATV, CN, ComN, ComTV, PRA
College Sequence: BA/MA- Journalism (emphases in Print Journalism, Broadcast Journalism, Online Journalism); MA - Strategic Public Relations, Specialized Journalism (emphases in The Arts)
Personnel: Geneva Overholser (Dir./Annenberg Family Chair in Commun. Leadership/ Univ. Prof.); Jay T. Harris (Wallis Annenberg Chair in Journalism and Democracy/ Prof.); Diane Winston (Knight Chair in Media and Religion/Assoc. Prof.); Geoffrey Cowan (Prof./Dean, Annenberg School for Communication); K.C. Cole (Prof.); Ed Cray (Prof.); Felix Gutierrez (Prof.); Bryce Nelson (Prof.); Michael Parks (Prof.); Joe Saltzman (Prof.); Philip Seib (Prof.); Roberto Suro (Prof.); Patricia Dean (Prof., Professional Practice/Assoc. Dir.); Gerald Swerling (Prof., Professional Practice); William Celis (Assoc. Prof.); Jonathan Kotler (Assoc. Prof.); Josh Kun (Assoc. Prof.); Judy Muller (Assoc. Prof.); Larry Pryor (Assoc. Prof.); Sandy Tolan (Assoc. Prof.)

LOUISVILLE

UNIVERSITY OF LOUISVILLE

Street address 1: Dept. of Communication
Street address 2: 310 Strickler Hall
Street address state: KY
Postal code: 40292
Mailing address: Dept. of Communication
Mailing city: Louisville
Mailing state: KY
Mailing zip: 40292-0001
Office phone: (502) 852-6976
Office fax: (502) 852-8166
Web address: comm.louisville.edu
General e-mail: al@Louisville.edu
College Degree: B.S. B.A. M.S.
College Departments: Department of Communication, 1971
College Facilities: Newspaper, studio, media labs, Nikon school locker
College Sequence: Communication Program: Bachelor's degree with major in Communication and concentrations in Communication Studies, Advertising and Public Relations, and Media (Print, Broadcast and Digital)
Personnel: Al Futrell (Chair)
Main (survey) contact: Ralph Merkel

MACOMB

WESTERN ILLINOIS UNIVERSITY

Street address 1: 1 University Cir.
Street address state: IL
Postal code: 61455
Mailing address: 1 University Cir
Mailing city: Macomb
Mailing state: IL
Mailing zip: 61455-1390
Office phone: (309) 298-1948
Web address: http://www.wiu.edu/cofac/bcj/
General e-mail: y-tang@wiu.edu
College Affiliation: College of Fine Arts and Communication
College Degree: BA- Journalism BA- Broadcasting
College Departments: Department of Broadcasting & Journalism
College Facilities: Computer and electronic class rooms, digital photography class room
College Sequence: Journalism Concentrations: News-Editorial, PR and Advertising. Opportunities: Internships in newspaper, public relations, and advertising firms Broadcasting Concentrations: Sports broadcasting, broadcasting production and broadcasting performance
Personnel: Yong Tang (Asst Prof Dir of Journalism); Teresa Simmons (Assoc. Prof./ Advisor, WAF)
Main (survey) contact: Jasmine Crighton

MACON

MERCER UNIVERSITY AT MACON

Street address 1: 1400 Coleman Ave.
Street address state: GA
Postal code: 31207-0001
Mailing address: 1400 Coleman Ave
Mailing city: Macon
Mailing state: GA
Mailing zip: 31207-0003
Office phone: (912) 752-2979
General e-mail: jottshall_cm@mercer.edu
College Departments: Communication and Theatre Arts Department, 1976
College Sequence: Communication Program: Administered by Communication and Theatre Arts Departments. Students may emphasize print journalism or broadcasting and film
Personnel: Cynthia Gottshall (Broadcast/Film)

MALIBU

PEPPERDINE UNIVERSITY

Street address 1: Communication Div.
Street address state: CA
Postal code: 90263
Mailing address: Communication Div.
Mailing city: Malibu
Mailing state: CA
Mailing zip: 90263
Office phone: (310) 456-4211
Office fax: (310) 456-3083
General e-mail: robert.chandler@pepperdine.edu
College Affiliation: AAF, AERho, PRSSA, SPJ, WICI
College Degree: BA, MA
College Departments: Communication Division, 1972
College Facilities: AdA, AP, FM, CCTV, CATV, ComN, ComTV, JN, JM, DR, PRA, VDT
College Sequence: Majors: Advertising, Journalism (News Editorial), Public Relations, Telecommunications
Personnel: Robert C. Chandler (Chair)

MANHATTAN

KANSAS STATE UNIVERSITY

Street address 1: 105 Kedzie Hall
Street address state: KS
Postal code: 66506-1501
Mailing address: 105 Kedzie Hall
Mailing city: Manhattan
Mailing state: KS
Mailing zip: 66506-1500
Office phone: (785) 532-6890
Office fax: (785) 532-5484
Web address: jmc.ksu.edu
General e-mail: journalism@ksu.edu
College Affiliation: AAF, ACT, NABJ, PRSSA, SCJ, SJEA, SND, SPJ
College Departments: A.Q. Miller School of Journalism and Mass Communications, 1910
College Facilities: AM/FM, AP, CATV, CN, JM, PRA, VDT
College Sequence: Advertising, Digital Media, Journalism, Public Relations
Personnel: Angela Powers (Prof./Dir.); William J. Adams (Prof.); Todd Simon (Prof./Head, PR seq.); Soontae An (Assoc. Prof.); Louise Benjamin (Assoc. Prof./Ross Beach Chair); Bonnie Bressers (Assoc. Prof./Head, Journalism Digital Media Sequence); Joye Gordon (Assoc. Prof.); Thomas Gould (Assoc. Prof.); Hyun-Seung Jin (Assoc. Prof./Assoc. Dir., Research/Grad. Studies); R. Charles Pearce (Assoc. Prof./Head, Adv. Seq.); J. Steven Smethers (Assoc. Prof./ Assoc. Dir., Undergrad. Studies); Kimetris Baltrip (Asst. Prof.); Fred Brock (Asst. Prof./R.M. Seaton Professional Chair); Gloria Freeland (Asst. Prof.); Ginger Loggins (Asst. Prof.); Sam Mwangi (Asst. Prof.); Nancy Muturi (Asst. Prof.); Linda Puntney (Asst. Prof./Dir., Student Publications Inc./Exec. Dir., Journalism Educ. Assn.); Seong-Hun Yun (Asst. Prof.); Stacy Neumann (Instr.)
Main (survey) contact: Angela Powers

MANKATO

MINNESOTA STATE UNIVERSITY MANKATO

Street address 1: 136 Nelson Hall
Street address state: MN
Postal code: 56001
Mailing address: 136 Nelson Hall
Mailing city: Mankato
Mailing state: MN
Mailing zip: 56001-6045
Office phone: (507) 389-6417
Office fax: (507) 389-5525
General e-mail: mass-communications@msus.edu
College Affiliation: SPJ
College Degree: BA, BS
College Departments: Mass Communications Department, 1968
College Facilities: CN, DR, FM, VDT
College Sequence: Journalism, Media Studies and Public Relations
Personnel: Charles Lewis (Chair/Prof.); Marshel Rossow (Prof.); Ellen M. Mrja (Assoc. Prof.); Jane McConnell (Assoc. Prof.); John Gaterud (Asst. Prof.); Scott Roemhildt (Adj. Fac.); Shelly Schultz (Adj. Fac.); Pete Steiner (Adj. Fac.); John Cross (Adj. Fac.); Dale Ericson (Adj. Fac.); Carlienne Frisch (Adj. Fac.); Rachael Hanel (Adj. Fac.); Bob McConnell (Adj. Fac.); Joe Tougas (Adj. Fac.); Tim Krohn (Adj. Fac.); Michael Larson (Adj. Fac.); Gladys B. Olson (Prof. Emer.)

MARION

INDIANA WESLEYAN UNIVERSITY

Street address 1: 4201 S Washington St
Street address state: IN
Postal code: 46953-4974
Country: USA
Mailing address: 4201 S Washington St
Mailing city: Marion
Mailing state: IN
Mailing zip: 46953-4974
Office phone: (765) 677-1818
Office fax: (765) 677-1755
Web address: https://www.indwes.edu/ undergraduate/majors/division-of-communication-and-theatre/
General e-mail: amy.smelser@indwes.edu
College Degree: BS in Journalism, BS in Media Communication
College Departments: Division of Communication and Theatre
College Facilities: Online university newspaper (The Sojourn), Online community newspaper (GrantCOnnected.net), television station, radio station and theatre guild
College Sequence: Communication Program: Majors in Communication Studies, Journalism, Media Communication, Public Relations and Theatre. Integrated theory and practical application program
Personnel: Amy Smelser (Ed.); Amy Smelser (Instructor)
Main (survey) contact: Randall King; Amy Shanks

MARYVILLE

NORTHWEST MISSOURI STATE UNIVERSITY

Street address 1: 800 University Dr., Wells Hall #237
Street address state: MO
Postal code: 64468-6001
Mailing address: 800 University Dr., Wells Hall #237
Mailing city: Maryville
Mailing state: MO
Mailing zip: 64468-6001
Office phone: (660) 562-1361
Office fax: (660) 562-1947
General e-mail: jerryd@mail.nwmissouri.edu
College Departments: Department of Mass Communication
College Sequence: Journalism Program: Programs in Mass Media, Broadcast Journalism, Media Advertising, Public Relations and Print Journalism
Personnel: Jerry Donnelly (Chair)

MILLEDGEVILLE

GEORGIA COLLEGE & STATE UNIVERSITY

Street address 1: Campus Box 32
Street address state: GA
Postal code: 31061
Mailing address: Campus Box 32
Mailing city: Milledgeville
Mailing state: GA
Mailing zip: 31061
Office phone: (478) 445-8260
Office fax: (478) 445-2364
General e-mail: maryjean.land@gcsu.edu
College Degree: BA- Mass Communication
College Departments: English Speech and Journalism, Mass Communication Program, 1984
College Facilities: Digital Media, Graphics Lab, Digital TV Studio, Student Operated Radio Station
College Sequence: Print Advertising, Public Relations, Telecommunications
Personnel: Mary Jean Land (Chair/Prof.); Ginger Carter Miller (Prof.); Macon McGinley (Asst. Prof.); Stephen Price (Asst. Prof.); Angela Criscoe (Instr.); Pate McMichael (Instr.); Hope Buchanan (Advisor)

MINNEAPOLIS

UNIVERSITY OF MINNESOTA

Street address 1: 111 Murphy Hall, 206 Church St. SE
Street address state: MN
Postal code: 55455-0418
Mailing address: 206 Church St SE
Mailing city: Minneapolis
Mailing state: MN
Mailing zip: 55455-0488
Office phone: (612) 625-1338
Office fax: (612) 626-8251
General e-mail: sjmc@umn.edu
College Affiliation: AAF, KTA, NABJ, PRISM, PRSSA, SPJ
College Degree: BA, MA, PhD
College Departments: School of Journalism and Mass Communication, 1924
College Facilities: AP, CCTV, CN, JM, AM/FM, AdA, VDT, ComN, PRA
Personnel: Albert R. Tims (Dir./Assoc. Prof.); Tsan-Kuo Chang (Prof.); John Eighmey (Prof./Mithun Land Grant Chair in Adv.); Ronald Faber (Prof.); Kathleen Hansen (Prof./Dir., Minnesota Journalism Ctr.); Jane Kirtley (Silha Prof./Dir., Silha Ctr.); Dan Sullivan (Prof./Cowles Chair); Daniel B. Wackman (Prof./Dir., Undergrad. Studies); Kenneth Doyle (Assoc. Prof.); Chris Ison (Assoc. Prof.); Mark Pedelty (Assoc. Prof.); Dona Schwartz (Assoc. Prof.); Gary Schwitzer (Assoc. Prof.); Brian Southwell

(Assoc. Prof./Dir., Grad. Studies); Catherine Squires (Assoc. Prof./John and Elizabeth Bates Cowles Prof., Journ., Diversity and Equality); Miranda Brady (Asst. Prof.); Giovanna Dell'Orto (Asst. Prof.); Jisu Huh (Asst. Prof.); Kathy Roberts Forde (Asst. Prof.); Amy Sanders (Asst. Prof.)
Main (survey) contact: Albert R. Tims

MISSISSIPPI STATE

MISSISSIPPI STATE UNIVERSITY

Street address 1: 130 McComas Hall
Street address state: MS
Postal code: 39762
Mailing address: PO Box Pf
Mailing city: Mississippi State
Mailing state: MS
Mailing zip: 39762-6006
Office phone: (662) 325-3320
Office fax: (662) 325-3210
Web address: www.comm.msstate.edu
General e-mail: jforde@comm.msstate.edu
College Departments: Department of Communication
College Sequence: Journalism Program: Offers major in Communication with concentrations in broadcasting, communication studies, journalism, public relations, theatre
Personnel: John Forde (Assoc. Prof./Head)

MISSOULA

THE UNIVERSITY OF MONTANA

Street address 1: 32 Campus Dr.
Street address state: MT
Postal code: 59812-0648
Mailing address: 32 Campus Dr
Mailing city: Missoula
Mailing state: MT
Mailing zip: 59812-0004
Office phone: (406) 243-4001
Web address: www.umt.edu/journalism
General e-mail: peggy.kuhr@umontana.edu
College Degree: BA, MA
College Departments: School of Journalism, 1914
College Facilities: AM/FM, AP, CCTV, CN, ComN, COMTV, DR, ETV, JM, VDT
College Sequence: Print, Photojournalism/Multi-media, Broadcast News, Broadcast Production
Personnel: Peggy Kuhr (Dean); Carol Van Valkenburg (Prof.); Dennis Swibold (Prof.); Clem Work (Prof.); Ray Ekness (Assoc. Prof.); Keith Graham (Assoc. Prof.); Denise Dowling (Assoc. Prof.); Ray Fanning (Asst. Prof.); Jeremy Lurgio (Asst. Prof.); Nadia White (Asst. Prof.); Nathaniel Blumberg (Prof. Emer.); Charles Hood (Prof. Emer.); Greg MacDonald (Prof. Emer.); Robert McGiffert (Prof. Emer.); Bill Knowles (Prof. Emer.); Jerry E. Brown (Prof. Emer.); Sharon Barrett (Prof. Emer.); Printer Bowler (Adj. Instr.); Gus Chambers (Adj. Instr.); Jeff Hull (Adj. Instr.)

MOBILE

SPRING HILL COLLEGE

Street address 1: 4000 Dauphin St
Street address state: AL
Postal code: 36608-1780
County: Mobile
Country: USA
Mailing address: 4000 Dauphin St
Mailing city: Mobile
Mailing state: AL
Mailing zip: 36608-1791
Office phone: (251) 380-3850
Office fax: (251) 460-2185
Web address: http://newswire.shc.edu/
General e-mail: shcmedia@shc.edu; sbabington@shc.edu
College Degree: BA
College Departments: Department of Communication Arts, 1971
College Sequence: BA with Concentrations: Integrated Communication (Advertising and Public Relations), Journalism and Electronic Media (Video/Audio Production in Digital Formats)
Personnel: Stuart Babington (Advisor); J.L. Stevens II (Integrated Multimedia Center (IMC) Operations Mgr and Student Media adviser)
Main (survey) contact: Stuart Babington

UNIVERSITY OF SOUTH ALABAMA

Street address 1: 1000 University Commons
Street address state: AL
Postal code: 36688
Mailing address: 1000 University Commons
Mailing city: Mobile
Mailing state: AL
Mailing zip: 36688
Office phone: (251) 380-2800
Office fax: (251) 380-2850
General e-mail: glwilson@usouthal.edu
College Degree: BA, MA
College Departments: Department of Communication, 1964
College Facilities: CATV, CCTV, CN, ComN, ComR, JN, PRA, VDT
College Sequence: Communication Technology, Interpersonal Communication and Rhetoric, Organizational Communication, Print and Broadcast Journalism, Public Relations and Advertising, Radio/TV/Film
Personnel: Gerald L. Wilson (Prof./Chair); Donald K. Wright (Prof.); James L. Aucoin (Assoc. Prof.); Steven C. Rockwell (Assoc. Prof.); Richard Ward (Assoc. Prof.); James F. Carstens (Asst. Prof.); Melva Kearney (Asst. Prof.); Patricia Mark (Asst. Prof.); Jeanne McPherson (Asst. Prof.); James M. Rosene (Asst. Prof.); Genevieve Dardeau (Instr.); April Dupree Taylor (Instr.); Heather Terry (Instr.); Jerold Aust (Lectr.); Carolyn Combs (Lectr.); Dre Comiskey (Lectr.); Jill Haynes (Lectr.); Kelly Kendall (Lectr.); Maureen Maclay (Lectr.); Jennifer Penry (Lectr.)

MONROE

UNIVERSITY OF LOUISIANA AT MONROE

Street address 1: Dept. of Communication
Street address state: LA
Postal code: 71209-0322
Mailing address: Dept of Communication
Mailing city: Monroe
Mailing state: LA
Mailing zip: 71209-0001
Office phone: (318) 342-1406
Office fax: (318) 342-1422
General e-mail: kauffman@ulm.edu
College Affiliation: KTA, PRAL, PRSSA, SPJ
College Degree: BA, MA
College Departments: Department of Communication, 1955
College Facilities: AP, CCTV, CN, ComN, ComR, ComTV, DR, FM (2), PRA, VDT
College Sequence: Journalism, Public Relations, Management and Marketing, Media Production
Personnel: Bette J. Kauffman (Dept. Head/Assoc. Prof.); Jeffrey M. Gibson (Assoc. Prof.); Tae-hyun Kim (Asst. Prof.); Robert E. Lewis (Asst. Prof.); Joel R. Willer (Asst. Prof.); Jarrett Reeves (Instr.); Mark Simmons (Part-time Adj. Fac.)

MONTGOMERY

ALABAMA STATE UNIV.

Street address 1: 915 S Jackson St
Street address state: AL
Postal code: 36104-5716
Country: USA
Mailing address: PO Box 271
Mailing city: Montgomery
Mailing state: AL
Mailing zip: 36101-0271
Office phone: (334) 229-4419
Office fax: (334) 229-4934
Web address: www.thehornettribune.com
General e-mail: ayoleke@aol.com
College Affiliation: ASJMC, SEJC, NCA, PRCA, NABJ, SSCA
College Degree: BA
College Departments: Department of Communications, 1984
College Facilities: TV Studio, Radio Lab, Radio Station, Computer Labs
College Sequence: Print Journalism, Radio/Television, Public Relations and Speech Communication
Personnel: David Okeowo (Prof./Chair); Bryan Weaver (Exec. Ed.); E.K. Daufin (Prof.); Julian K. Johnson (Mng. Ed.); Tracy Banks (Assoc. Prof./Dir., Forensics); James B. Lucy (News Ed.); Elizabeth Fitts (Assoc. Prof.); Richard Emmanuel (Asst. Prof.); James Adams (Instr.); Coke Ellington (Instr.); Valerie Heard (Instr.); Jonathan Himsel (Instr.); John Moore (Instr.); Walter Murphy (Instr.); Larry Owens (Instr.)
Main (survey) contact: James B. Lucy

MOORHEAD

MINNESOTA STATE UNIVERSITY, MOOREHEAD

Street address 1: Mass Communications Dept.
Street address state: MN
Postal code: 56563
Mailing address: Mass Communications Dept.
Mailing city: Moorhead
Mailing state: MN
Mailing zip: 56563
Office phone: (218) 477-2855
Office fax: (218) 477-4333
General e-mail: strandm@mnstate.edu
College Affiliation: AAF, PRSSA, SPJ
College Degree: BS, BA
College Departments: Mass Communications Department, 1967
College Facilities: AP, AM, AdA, CATV, CCTV, CN, ComN, ComR, ComTV, DR, PRA, VDT
College Sequence: Advertising, Broadcast Journalism, Photojournalism, Print Journalism, PR, dual major in English/Mass Communications, Integrated Advertising/PR, Online Journalism
Personnel: Mark Strand (Chair/Prof.); C.T. Hanson (Prof.); Martin Grindeland (Prof.); Wayne Gudmundson (Prof.); Shelton Gunaratne (Prof.); William B. Hall (Assoc. Prof.); Dan Johnson (Assoc. Prof.); Camilla Wilson (Assoc. Prof.); Jody Mattern (Asst. Prof.); Aaron Quanbeck (Asst. Prof.); Reggie Radnieck (Asst. Prof.); Mark Anthony (Instr.); David Arntson (Instr.); Marv Bossart (Instr.); David Christy (Instr.); Liz Conmy (Instr.); Nancy Edmonds Hanson (Instr.); David Howland (Instr.); Jason Hummel (Instr.); Kerstin Kealy (Instr.)
Main (survey) contact: C.T. Hanson

MORAGA

SAINT MARY'S COLLEGE OF CALIFORNIA

Street address 1: Dept. of Communications
Street address state: CA
Postal code: 94575
Mailing address: Dept. of Communications
Mailing city: Moraga
Mailing state: CA
Mailing zip: 94575
Office phone: (510) 631-4000
Office fax: (510) 631-0938
College Departments: Department of Communications, 1987
College Sequence: Journalism Program: A comprehensive Liberal Arts program including communications theory and practice in audio, video and print media
Personnel: Michael A. Russo (Chair)

MOREHEAD

MOREHEAD STATE UNIVERSITY

Street address 1: BR 115-A, Dept. of Communication & Theatre
Street address state: KY
Postal code: 40351
Mailing address: BR 115-A, Dept. of Communication & Theatre
Mailing city: Morehead
Mailing state: KY
Mailing zip: 40351
Office phone: (606) 783-5312
Office fax: (606) 783-2457
Web address: www.trailblazeronline.net
General e-mail: j.atkins@moreheadstate.edu
College Departments: Journalism Area, Department of Communication and Theatre
College Facilities: Wireless technology available in all labs and teaching facilities. Student practicum and work opportunities available via univerity-owned NPR affiliate radio station, student-produced cable TV news programs and a weekly student newspaper
College Sequence: Journalism Program: Undergraduate program in Journalism with both print and broadcast emphases. Other departmental majors include Advertising/Public Relations, Electronic Media Production, Organizational/Interpersonal Communication and Theatre. Master
Personnel: Robert Willenbrink (Chair); Joan Atkins (Journalism Coord.)
Main (survey) contact: Joan Atkins

MOSCOW

UNIVERSITY OF IDAHO

Street address 1: PO Box 443178
Street address state: ID
Postal code: 84844-3178
Mailing address: PO Box 443178
Mailing city: Moscow
Mailing state: ID
Mailing zip: 83844-3178
Office phone: (208) 885-6458
Office fax: (208) 885-6450
General e-mail: jamm@uidaho.edu
College Affiliation: SPJ, Ad Club, PR Club, NAJA
College Degree: BA, BS
College Departments: School of Journalism and Mass Media, 2003
College Facilities: FM, CN, ETV, ComN, VDT
College Sequence: Advertising, Journalism, Public Relations, Radio-TV-Digital Media Production
Personnel: Kenton Bird (Dir./Assoc. Prof.); Sandra Haarsager (Prof.); Mark Secrist (Assoc. Prof.); Patricia Hart (Asst. Prof.); Rebecca Tallent (Asst. Prof.); H. James Clark (Lectr.); Sue Hinz (Lectr.); Denise Bennett (Fac.); Glenn Mosley (Fac.); Vicki Rishling (Fac.); Bert Cross (Prof. Emer.); Peter Haggart (Prof. Emer.); Tom Jenness (Prof. Emer.); Paul Miles (Prof. Emer.); Jane Pritchett (Prof. Emer.)
Main (survey) contact: Kenton Bird

MOUNT BERRY

BERRY COLLEGE

Street address 1: 2277 Martha Berry Hwy.
Street address state: GA
Postal code: 30149-0299
Mailing address: PO Box 490299
Mailing city: Mount Berry
Mailing state: GA
Mailing zip: 30149-0299
Office phone: (706) 233-4089
Office fax: (706) 802-6738
General e-mail: bfrank@berry.edu
College Degree: BA
College Departments: Department of Communication, 1986
College Facilities: CATV, CCTV, ComN, DR, JM, PRA, VDT
College Sequence: Journalism, Public Relations, Visual Communication

Schools and Departments of Journalism

Personnel: Robert L. Frank (Chair)

MOUNT PLEASANT
CENTRAL MICHIGAN UNIVERSITY

Street address 1: 454 Moore Hall
Street address state: MI
Postal code: 48859
Mailing address: 454 Moore Hall
Mailing city: Mount Pleasant
Mailing state: MI
Mailing zip: 48859-0001
Office phone: (989) 774-3196
Office fax: (989) 774-7114
General e-mail: jrndept@cmich.edu
College Affiliation: AAF, PRSSA, SPJ, CPPA
College Degree: BA, BS
College Departments: Department of Journalism, 1959
College Facilities: AP, CATV, CN, DR, ETV, FM
College Sequence: Advertising, News-Editorial, Photojournalism, Public Relations
Personnel: Maria B. Marron (Chair/Prof.); John Hartman (Prof.); Dennis Jeffers (Prof.); John Palen (Prof.); Alice Tait (Prof.); Jiafei Yin (Prof.); Carole Eberly (Assoc. Prof.); Elliott Parker (Assoc. Prof.); Jim Wojcik (Full-time Assoc. Prof.); Tim Boudreau (Asst. Prof.); Yun Jung Choi (Asst. Prof.); Jong Hyuk Lee (Asst. Prof.); David London (Asst. Prof.); Ken McDonald (Full-time Asst. Prof.); Kent Miller (Full-time Asst. Prof.); Ed Hutchison (Part-time Asst. Prof.); Ron Marmarelli (Part-time Asst. Prof.); Tereza Dean (Instr.); Steve Jessmore (Instr.); Dawn Paine (Instr.); Cynthia Gall (Editor & Publisher)

MUNCIE
BALL STATE UNIVERSITY

Street address 1: Art and Journalism Bldg. 300
Street address state: IN
Postal code: 47306
Mailing address: Art & Journalism Bldg # 300
Mailing city: Muncie
Mailing state: IN
Mailing zip: 47306-0001
Office phone: (765) 285-6000
Office fax: (765) 285-6002
Web address: www.bsu.edu/journalism
General e-mail: bsujourn@bsu.edu
College Affiliation: AAF, JEA, NABJ, NPPA, PRSSA, SND, SPJ
College Degree: BA, BS, MA
College Departments: College of Communication, Information and Media, Department of Journalism
College Facilities: AdA, AP, AM/FM, CATV, CCTV, JM, JN, ComN, DR, ETC, PRA, VDT
College Sequence: Majors: Advertising, Journalism (Journalism Graphics, Magazine, News-Editorial, Photojournalism), Public Relations, Secondary Education
Personnel: Roger Lavery (Prof./Dean); Marilyn Weaver (Prof./Chair); Mark Masse (Prof.); David Sumner (Prof./Coord., Mag.); Robert Gustafson (Assoc. Prof.); Alfredo Marin-Carle (Assoc. Prof.); Robert Pritchard (Assoc. Prof./Coord., PR); Jennifer George-Palilonis (Asst. Prof./Coord., Journ. Graphics); Michael Hanley (Asst. Prof./Coord. Advertising); Kenneth Heinen (Asst. Prof.); Tendayi Kumbula (Asst. Prof.); Becky McDonald (Asst. Prof.); Thomas Price (Asst. Prof./Coord., Photojournalism); Mary Spillman (Asst. Prof./Coord., News-Editorial); Dustin Supa (Asst. Prof.); Daniel Waechter (Asst. Prof./Asst. Chair/Curricular Advising/Grad. Advisor); Pamela Farmen (Instr.); Brian Hayes (Instr./Coord. Secondary Education); Sy Jenkins (Instr./Mng. Ed., NewsLink); David Kitchell (Instr.); Pam Gard
Main (survey) contact: Marilyn Weaver

MURRAY
MURRAY STATE UNIVERSITY

Street address 1: 114 Wilson Hall
Street address state: KY
Postal code: 42071-3311
Mailing address: 114 Wilson Hall
Mailing city: Murray
Mailing state: KY
Mailing zip: 42071-3311
Office phone: (809) 762-2387
Office fax: (270) 809-2390
Web address: www.themurraystatenews.com
General e-mail: journalism@murraystate.edu
College Affiliation: SCJ, NBS-AERho, AAF, PRSSA
College Degree: BS, BA, MS, MA
College Departments: Department of Journalism and Mass Communications, 1975
College Facilities: AdA, AP, FM, CATV, DR, ETV, JN, PRA, VDT
College Sequence: Majors: Journalism, Advertising, Public Relations, Electronic Media
Personnel: Allen White (Prof./Interim Chair); John Dillon (Prof.); Roger Haney (Prof.); Bob Lochte (Prof./Grad. Coord.); Jeanne S. Scafella (Prof.); Ann Landini (Assoc. Prof.); Debbie Owens (Assoc. Prof.); Celia Wall (Assoc. Prof.); Bob Valentine (Sr. Lectr.); Gill Welsch (Sr. Lectr.); Joe Hedges (Lectr.); Jeremy McKeel (Lectr.); Robin B. Orvino-Proulx (Lectr.); Darryl Armstrong (Adj.); Janett Blythe (Adj.); Victoria Daughrity (Adj.); Kate Lochte (Adj.); Jeff Prater (Adj.); Ann Thrower (Adj.); Mark Welch (Adj.)
Main (survey) contact: Elizabeth Johnson

NATCHITOCHES
NORTHWESTERN STATE UNIVERSITY OF LOUISIANA

Street address 1: 103 John S. Kyser Hall
Street address state: LA
Postal code: 71497
Mailing address: PO Box 5273
Mailing city: Natchitoches
Mailing state: LA
Mailing zip: 71497-0001
Office phone: (318) 357-4425
Office fax: (318) 357-4434
Web address: www.liberalarts.nsula.edu/journalism
General e-mail: journalism@nsula.edu
College Degree: BA, major and minor available
College Departments: Department of Journalism, 1948
College Sequence: Public Relations, News Editorial, Broadcast
Personnel: Paula F. Furr (Dept. Head/Assoc. Prof.); Hesham Mesbah (Prof.); Mary Brocato (Assoc. Prof.); William Broussard (Asst. Prof.); Jung Lim (Asst. Prof.); Jerry Pierce (Asst. Prof.); Jarrett Reeves (Asst. Prof.); David Antilley (Dir./Producer NSU 22); Raymond Strother (Wise Endowed Chair); Thomas Whitehead (Prof. Emer.); Michael Lofton (Broadcast Technician); Marie Hall (Admin. Asst.)

NEW BRITAIN
CENTRAL CONNECTICUT STATE UNIV.

Street address 1: 1615 Stanley St
Street address state: CT
Postal code: 06050-2439
Country: USA
Mailing address: 1615 Stanley St
Mailing city: New Britain
Mailing state: CT
Mailing zip: 06050-2439
Office phone: (860) 832-3744
Office fax: (860) 832-3747
Web address: www.centralrecorder.com
General e-mail: ccsurecorder@gmail.com; ccsurecorder.ads@gmail.com

College Departments: Department of English, 1984 (minor), 2009 (major)
College Sequence: A 40-credit program in which students may focus on print or broadcast; all students receive multimedia training.
Personnel: Vivian B. Martin (Coord.); Melissa Traynor (Ed. in Chief); Michael Walsh (Mng. Ed.); Christopher Boulay (Sports Ed.); Christina LoBello (Opinion Ed.); Kelsey (Adv. Mgr.)
Main (survey) contact: Vivian B. Martin; Melissa Traynor

NEW HAVEN
SOUTHERN CONNECTICUT STATE UNIVERSITY

Street address 1: 501 Crescent St. Morrill 202
Street address state: CT
Postal code: 6515
Mailing address: 501 Crescent St Morrill 202
Mailing city: New Haven
Mailing state: CT
Mailing zip: 06515-1330
Office phone: (203) 392-5800
Office fax: (203) 392-5809
General e-mail: harrisf1@southernct.edu
College Affiliation: SPJ
College Degree: BA, BS
College Departments: Journalism Department, 1976
College Facilities: AM, AdA, AP, CATV, CCTV, CN, ComN, ComR, ComTV, DR, PRA, VDT
College Sequence: News-Editorial, Magazine, Broadcast, Public Relations
Personnel: Frank Harris (Chair)

NEW ORLEANS
LOYOLA UNIVERSITY NEW ORLEANS

Street address 1: 6363 St. Charles Ave., Box 201
Street address state: LA
Postal code: 70118
Mailing address: 6363 Saint Charles Ave # 201
Mailing city: New Orleans
Mailing state: LA
Mailing zip: 70118-6143
Office phone: (504) 865-3430
Office fax: (504) 865-2333
Web address: www.loyno.edu/communications
General e-mail: cfbolner@loyno.edu
College Affiliation: AAF, BEA, KTA, SPJ, PRSSA, RTNDA
College Degree: BA, MA
College Departments: Department of Communications, 1937
College Facilities: AdA, AP, CCTV, CN, ComN, ComTV, DR, JN, PRA, VDT
College Sequence: Advertising, Broadcast Journalism, Broadcast Production, Communications Studies, Film Studies, Photojournalism, Print Journalism, Public Relations
Personnel: Teri K. Henley (Chair/Assoc. Prof.); A.L. Lorenz (Prof.); S.L. Alexander (Assoc. Prof.); William M. Hammel (Assoc. Prof.); David M. Myers (Assoc. Prof./Dir., Grad. Prog.); Leslie G. Parr (Assoc. Prof.); J. Cathy Rogers (Assoc. Prof.); Debra A. Woodfork (Asst. Prof.); Lisa C. Martin (Instr.); Trish O'Kane (Instr.); Robert A. Thomas (Loyola University Chair for Environmental Communications)

UNIVERSITY OF NEW ORLEANS

Street address 1: 127 Liberal Arts Bldg.
Street address state: LA
Postal code: 70148
Mailing address: 127 Liberal Arts
Mailing city: New Orleans
Mailing state: LA
Mailing zip: 70148-0001
Office phone: (504) 286-6273
Office fax: (504) 286-6378 (student newspaper)
General e-mail: english@uno.edu
College Departments: Journalism Area, English Department

College Sequence: Journalism Program: Three-person journalism faculty offers coursework and minor in print journalism
Personnel: Peter Schock (Chair)

XAVIER UNIVERSITY OF LOUISIANA

Street address 1: 909 S. Jefferson Davis Pkwy.
Street address state: LA
Postal code: 70125
Mailing address: 1 Drexel Dr # 93
Mailing city: New Orleans
Mailing state: LA
Mailing zip: 70125-1056
Office phone: (504) 520-5092
Office fax: (504) 520-7919
General e-mail: jmelcher@xula.edu
College Departments: Department of Communications, 1982
College Sequence: Communications Program: Undergraduate liberal arts based program; Public Relations, Radio, TV or Print emphases available; houses student newspaper, Xavier Herald
Personnel: Joe Melcher (PD)

NEWARK
UNIVERSITY OF DELAWARE

Street address 1: Journalism Program
Street address state: DE
Postal code: 19716
Mailing address: Journalism Program
Mailing city: Newark
Mailing state: DE
Mailing zip: 19716
Office phone: (302) 451-2361
College Departments: Journalism Program
College Sequence: Journalism Program: Offers 21 hours of news writing, magazine writing and copy editing-layout courses, as well as extensive internship program with newspapers, magazines, electronic media and public relations offices

NORMAL
ILLINOIS STATE UNIVERSITY

Street address 1: Campus Box 4480
Street address state: IL
Postal code: 61790-4480
Mailing address: Campus # 4480
Mailing city: Normal
Mailing state: IL
Mailing zip: 61790-0001
Office phone: (309) 438-3671
Office fax: (309) 438-3048
General e-mail: communication@ilstu.edu
College Degree: BA, BS, MA, MS
College Departments: School of Communication
College Facilities: Television and two radio stations, daily newspaper, computer labs and digital photography facilities
College Sequence: Majors in Communication Studies and Communication Studies Education, Journalism, Mass Communication, and Public Relations. Concentrations in news editorial writing, broadcast journalism, visual communication, radio, television, interactive media, graphics
Personnel: Larry W. Long (Exec. Dir.)
Main (survey) contact: Larry W. Long

NORTH MIAMI
FLORIDA INTERNATIONAL UNIVERSITY

Street address 1: Biscayne Bay Campus, 3000 NE 151st St.
Street address state: FL
Postal code: 33181
County: Miami-Dade
Mailing address: 3000 NE 151st St
Mailing city: North Miami
Mailing state: FL

Mailing zip: 33181-3000
Office phone: (305) 919-5625
Office fax: (305) 919-5203
Web address: http://jmc.fiu.edu
General e-mail: kopenhav@fiu.edu
College Affiliation: PRSSA, AAF AWC, SPJ, KTA, AdFed
College Degree: BS, MS
College Departments: School of Journalism and Mass Communication, 1978
College Facilities: VDT, ComN, Graphics Lab, EDIT, ENG, TV Studio, CATV, 6 computer labs
College Sequence: Tracks: Undergraduate-Advertising, Journalism, Public Relations, Multimedia; Broadcasting; Graduate-Integrated Marketing Communications: Advertising and Public Relations, Spanish-language Journalism, Student Media Advising, Spanish/English-language Journalism
Personnel: Frederick Blevens (Prof.); Margo Berman (Assoc. Prof.); Mario Diament (Assoc. Prof.); Teresa Ponte (Assoc. Prof./Interim Chair, Dept. of Journ./Broadcasting); Neil Reisner (Assoc. Prof.); Allan Richards (Assoc. Prof./Interim Assoc. Dean); Lorna Veraldi (Assoc. Prof.); Mercedes Vigon (Assoc. Prof.); Lynn Farber (Asst. Prof.); Lilliam Martinez-Bustos (Asst. Prof./Coord., Spanish-language Journ. Master's Prog.); Elizabeth Marsh (Asst. Prof.); Michael Scott Sheerin (Asst. Prof.); Lillian Lodge Kopenhaver; David Park; Moses Shumow; Juliet Pinto; Ted Gutsche; Kathy Fitspatrick; Kurt Wise; Yu Liu; Weirui Wang; Maria Elena Villar; Sigal Segev
Main (survey) contact: Raul Reis

NORTHRIDGE

CALIFORNIA STATE UNIVERSITY, NORTHRIDGE

Street address 1: 18111 Nordhoff St
Street address state: CA
Postal code: 91330-0001
Country: USA
Mailing address: 18111 Nordhoff St
Mailing city: Northridge
Mailing state: CA
Mailing zip: 91330-8200
Office phone: (818) 677-3135
Office fax: (818) 677-3438
Web address: www.csun.edu
College Affiliation: KTA, PRSSA, SPJ, RTNDA, California Chicano News Media Assn
College Degree: BA, MA
College Departments: Department of Journalism, 1958
College Facilities: CNN, AP, UPI, FM, ComTV, ComN, ComR, DR, JM, JN, PRA, VDT
College Sequence: News Editorial
Personnel: Kent Kirkton (Chair/Prof.); Melissa Lalum (Pub.); Susan Henry (Prof.); Jody Holcomb (Gen. Mgr.); Maureen Rubin (Prof.); Rick Marks (Assoc. Prof.); Loren Townsley (Editor); Jose Luis Benavides (Asst. Prof.); David Blumenkrantz (Asst. Prof.); Linda Bowen (Asst. Prof.); Jim Hill (Asst. Prof.); Melissa Wall (Asst. Prof.); Lori Baker-Schena (Lectr.); Jerry Jacobs (Prof. Emer.); DeWayne Johnson (Prof. Emer.); Lawrence Schneider (Prof. Emer.); Joe Giampietro (Part-time Fac.); Henrietta Charles (Part-time Fac.); Jeffrey Duclos (Part-time Fac.); Barbara Eisenstock (Part-time Fac.); Mariel Garza (Part-time Fac.); Keith Goldstein (Part-time Fac.); Lincoln Harrison (Part-time Fac.)
Main (survey) contact: Melissa Lalum

NOTRE DAME

UNIVERSITY OF NOTRE DAME

Street address 1: Dept. of American Studies
Street address state: IN
Postal code: 46556
Mailing address: Dept. of American Studies
Mailing city: Notre Dame
Mailing state: IN
Mailing zip: 46556
Office phone: (219) 631-7316
Office fax: (219) 631-4268
General e-mail: al.astudiel.l@nd.edu
College Departments: Department of American Studies
College Sequence: Journalism Program: Students take courses on journalism and the media, as well as writing courses, within the context of American Studies, or they participate in the John W. Gallivan Program in Journalism, Ethics and Democracy, a five-course concentratio
Personnel: Robert Schmuhl (Dir., John W. Gallivan Program in Journalism, Ethics & Democracy)
Main (survey) contact: Robert Schmuhl

ORLANDO

UNIVERSITY OF CENTRAL FLORIDA

Street address 1: 4000 Central Florida Blvd.
Street address state: FL
Postal code: 32816-1344
Mailing address: PO Box 161344
Mailing city: Orlando
Mailing state: FL
Mailing zip: 32816-1344
Office phone: (407) 823-2681
Office fax: (407) 823-6360
Web address: communication.cos.ucf.edu
College Affiliation: AAF, BEA, FPRA, KTA, NPPA, NABJ, NAHJ, RTNDA, SPJ
College Departments: Nicholson School of Communication, 1964
College Sequence: Advertising/Public Relations, Interpersonal Communication, Journalism, Organizational Communication, Radio/Television; MA- track in Mass Communication, track in Interpersonal Communication
Personnel: Mary Alice Shaver (Prof.); Robert Davis (Prof./Head, Adv./PR); Fred Fedler (Prof./Head, Journalism); Burt Pryor (Prof./Grad. Dir.); Ron Smith (Prof.); George Bagley (Assoc. Prof./Head, Radio/TV); Jeff Butler (Assoc. Prof./Head, I/O); Denise DeLorme (Assoc. Prof.); W. Joe Hall (Assoc. Prof.); Jose Maunez (Assoc. Prof.); Maria Cristina Santana (Assoc. Prof.); Kimiko Akita (Asst. Prof.); Tim Brown (Asst. Prof.); Steve Collins (Asst. Prof.); Gene Costain (Asst. Prof.); Sally Hastings (Asst. Prof.); Jim Katt (Asst. Prof.); Rick Kenney (Asst. Prof.); Sam Lawrence (Asst. Prof.); John Malala (Asst. Prof.)
Main (survey) contact: Adrienne Cutway

ORONO

UNIVERSITY OF MAINE

Street address 1: Dept. of Communication & Journalism
Street address state: ME
Postal code: 04469-5724
Mailing address: Dept of Communication & Journalism
Mailing city: Orono
Mailing state: ME
Mailing zip: 04469-0001
Office phone: (207) 581-1283
Office fax: (207) 581-1286
General e-mail: john@maine.edu
College Affiliation: AAF, BEA, SPJ
College Degree: BA
College Departments: Department of Communication and Journalism, 1948
College Facilities: AP, CCTV, CN, ETV, FM, VDT
College Sequence: News-Editorial, Advertising, Mass Communication, Broadcast Journalism
Personnel: John C. Sherblom (Chair/Prof.); Kristin M. Langellier (Prof.); Paul Grosswiler (Assoc. Prof.); Kathryn Olmstead (Assoc. Prof.); Eric E. Peterson (Assoc. Prof.); Claire F. Sullivan (Assoc. Prof.); Lyombe Eko (Asst. Prof.); Shannon Martin (Asst. Prof.); Michael McCauley (Asst. Prof.); Nathan Stormer (Asst. Prof.); Natalia Tolstikova (Asst. Prof.); Katherine Heidinger (Instr.); Ann James Joles (Instr.); Margaret Nagle (Instr.); Marie Tessier (Instr.); Arthur Guesman (Prof. Emer.); Alan Miller (Prof. Emer.)

PEMBROKE

UNIVERSITY OF NORTH CAROLINA AT PEMBROKE

Street address 1: Box 1510
Street address state: NC
Postal code: 28372-1510
Mailing address: PO Box 1510
Mailing city: Pembroke
Mailing state: NC
Mailing zip: 28372-1510
Office phone: (910) 522-5723
Office fax: (910) 522-5795
General e-mail: masscomm@uncp.edu
College Departments: Department of Mass Communications, 1983
College Sequence: Department of Mass Communications: Join the most diverse student body in the UNC system, where we offer majors and minors in broadcasting, journalism, public relations, and media integration.
Personnel: Jamie Litty (Chair)

PENSACOLA

UNIVERSITY OF WEST FLORIDA

Street address 1: 11000 University Pkwy., Bldg. 36
Street address state: FL
Postal code: 32514
Mailing address: 11000 University Pkwy Bldg 36
Mailing city: Pensacola
Mailing state: FL
Mailing zip: 32514-5750
Office phone: (850) 474-2874
Office fax: (850) 474-3153
General e-mail: bswain@uwf.edu
College Affiliation: BEA, PRSSA, FPRA, AAF
College Degree: BA, MA
College Departments: Communication Arts, 1967
College Facilities: AdA, CCTV, ComN, ComTV, FM, JN, PRA, VDT
College Sequence: Journalism (broadcast and print), Advertising, Public Relations, Radio/Television/Film, Organizational Communication, Graduate Program in Health Communication Leadership
Personnel: Bruce Swain (Chair)

PEORIA

BRADLEY UNIVERSITY

Street address 1: Dept. of Communication
Street address state: IL
Postal code: 61625
Mailing address: Dept of Communication
Mailing city: Peoria
Mailing state: IL
Mailing zip: 61625-0001
Office phone: (309) 677-2354
Office fax: (309) 677-3446
General e-mail: pfg@bradley.edu
College Affiliation: AAF, PRSSA, SPJ, WICI
College Degree: BA, BS
College Departments: Department of Communication, 1947
College Facilities: CCTV, FM, CN, ETV, DR, VDT
College Sequence: Advertising, Electronic Media, Journalism, Organizational Communications, Public Relations
Personnel: Paul Gullifor (Chair/Prof.); Bob Jacobs (Prof.); Ali Zohoori (Prof.); Olatunji Dare (Assoc. Prof.); Chris Kasch (Assoc. Prof.); Ron Koperski (Assoc. Prof.); Ed Lamoureux (Assoc. Prof.); Gregory Pitts (Assoc. Prof.); Stephen Banning (Asst. Prof.); Maha Bashri (Asst. Prof.); Elena Gabor (Asst. Prof.); Sara Netzley (Asst. Prof.); Margaret Young (Asst. Prof.); Laura Garfinkel (Lectr.); B.J. Lawrence (Lectr.); Linda Strasma (Lectr.); Jan Frazier (Instr.); Tyler Billman (Instr./Asst. Dir., Forensics); Dan Smith (Dir., Forensics); E. Neal Claussen (Prof. Emer.)
Main (survey) contact: Paul Gullifor

PITTSBURG

PITTSBURG STATE UNIVERSITY

Street address 1: 1701 S. Broadway, 417 Grubbs Hall
Street address state: KS
Postal code: 66762
Mailing address: 1701 S Broadway St
Mailing city: Pittsburg
Mailing state: KS
Mailing zip: 66762-7500
Office phone: (620) 235-4716
Office fax: (620) 235-4686
General e-mail: jscott@pittstate.edu
College Departments: Department of Communication
College Sequence: Communication Program: A Communication major with tracks in Advertising, Broadcasting, Communication Education, News Editorial, Photojournalism, Public Relations, and Theatre (BA/BSEd degree). MA in Communication offered with specialized emphasis in app
Personnel: Peter K. Hamilton (Chair)

POCATELLO

IDAHO STATE UNIVERSITY

Street address 1: Campus Box 8009
Street address state: ID
Postal code: 83709
Mailing address: Campus Box 8009
Mailing city: Pocatello
Mailing state: ID
Mailing zip: 83709
Telephone country code: 1
Telephone city code: 208
Office phone: (208) 282-2247
Office fax: (208) 282-2258
Web address: isubengal.com
General e-mail: bgchief@isu.edu
Main (survey) contact: Jerry Miller

POINT LOOKOUT

COLLEGE OF THE OZARKS

Street address 1: Dept. of Mass Communication
Street address state: MO
Postal code: 65726
Mailing address: Dept. of Mass Communication
Mailing city: Point Lookout
Mailing state: MO
Mailing zip: 65726
Office phone: (417) 690-3458
General e-mail: schroeder@cofo.edu
College Degree: BA, BS
College Departments: Department of Mass Communication
College Sequence: Emphases in Journalism, Video Production and Radio/Sound Production.
Personnel: Jared Schroeder (Contact)
Main (survey) contact: Jared Schroeder

POMONA

CALIFORNIA STATE POLYTECHNIC UNIVERSITY, POMONA

Street address 1: 3801 W. Temple Ave.
Street address state: CA
Postal code: 91768-4007
Mailing address: 3801 W Temple Ave
Mailing city: Pomona
Mailing state: CA
Mailing zip: 91768-2557
Office phone: (909) 869-3520
Office fax: (909) 869-4823
General e-mail: rakallan@csupomona.edu

Schools and Departments of Journalism

College Affiliation: ASJSA, PRSSA, SPJ, WICI
College Degree: BS
College Departments: Communication Department, 1968
College Sequence: Journalism Program: BS program with options in Journalism, Public Relations, and Communication Studies
Personnel: Richard A. Kallan (Chair); Debra Shea

PUEBLO

COLORADO STATE UNIVERSITY, PUEBLO

Street address 1: 2200 Bonforte Blvd., AM-117
Street address state: CO
Postal code: 81001-4901
Mailing address: 2200 Bonforte Blvd # AM-117
Mailing city: Pueblo
Mailing state: CO
Mailing zip: 81001-4901
Office phone: (719) 549-2835
Office fax: (719) 549-2120
Web address: http://chass.colostate-pueblo.edu/mccnm/
General e-mail: jen.mullen@colostate-pueblo.edu
College Departments: Department of Mass Communications and Center for New Media
College Facilities: KTSC-FM, KTSC-RMPBS
College Sequence: Communications Program: Integrated umbrella program provides emphases in Integrated Communication, Electronic Media and Journalism
Personnel: Jennifer Mullen (Chair)

RICHMOND

EASTERN KENTUCKY UNIVERSITY

Street address 1: Combs Building, Room 326
Street address state: KY
Postal code: 40475-3102
Mailing address: Combs Building, Room 326
Mailing city: Richmond
Mailing state: KY
Mailing zip: 40475-3102
Office phone: (859) 622-1881
Office fax: (859) 622-2354
Web address: http://www.easternprogress.com/
General e-mail: reggie.beehner@eku.edu
Personnel: Reggie Beehner (Adviser, Eastern Progress)
Main (survey) contact: Wesley Robinson

ROCHESTER

OAKLAND UNIVERSITY

Street address 1: Journalism Program
Street address state: MI
Postal code: 48309-4401
Mailing address: Journalism Program
Mailing city: Rochester
Mailing state: MI
Mailing zip: 48309-4401
Office phone: (248) 370-4121
Office fax: (248) 370-4208
Web address: www.oakland.edu/rcj/jrn
General e-mail: shreve@oakland.edu
College Departments: Journalism Program, 1978
College Sequence: Journalism Program: Professional approach, designed to educate and train reporters, with emphases on print, new media, web, public relations, broadcast and advertising. Mandatory internship. Scholarships available
Personnel: Holly Shreve-Gilbert (Co-Dir.)

ROCK ISLAND

AUGUSTANA COLLEGE

Street address 1: 639 38th St
Street address state: IL
Postal code: 61201-2210
Country: USA
Mailing address: 639 38th St
Mailing city: Rock Island
Mailing state: IL
Mailing zip: 61201-2296
Office phone: (309) 794-3460
Office fax: (309) 794-3460
Web address: www.augustana.edu
General e-mail: observer@augustana.edu
College Degree: BA
College Departments: Department of Communication Studies
College Sequence: Majors: Communication Studies, Multimedia Journalism and Mass Communication
Personnel: Carolyn Yaschur (Advisor); David Schwartz (Advisor)
Main (survey) contact: David Schwartz

RUSSELLVILLE

ARKANSAS TECH UNIVERSITY

Street address 1: T-1, 1209 N. Fargo Ave.
Street address state: AR
Postal code: 72801
Mailing address: T-1, 1209 N. Fargo Ave.
Mailing city: Russellville
Mailing state: AR
Mailing zip: 72801
Office phone: (479) 964-0890
Office fax: (479) 964-0899
General e-mail: dvocate@atu.edu
College Degree: BA, MA
College Departments: Department of Speech, Theatre and Journalism
College Facilities: ETV, FM, CN, VDT, CCTV, DR
College Sequence: Print Journalism, Broadcast Journalism, Public Relations and Multimedia Journalism
Personnel: Donna R. Vocate (Head/Prof.); Seok Kang (Assoc. Prof.); Hanna Norton (Assoc. Prof.); Warren Byrd (Asst. Prof.); Anthony Caton (Asst. Prof.); Tommy Mumert (Asst. Prof.); Russ Hancock (Instr.)

RUSTON

LOUISIANA TECH UNIVERSITY

Street address 1: 152 Keeny
Street address state: LA
Postal code: 71272-0045
Mailing address: PO Box 10258
Mailing city: Ruston
Mailing state: LA
Mailing zip: 71272-0001
Office phone: (318) 257-4427
Office fax: (318) 257-4558
Web address: eb.journ.latech.edu
General e-mail: blick@latech.edu
College Degree: BA
College Departments: Journalism Department, 1928
College Facilities: FM, AdA, ComN, ComR, DR, JN, VDT
College Sequence: News-Editorial
Personnel: Thomas Edward Blick (Head)

SACRAMENTO

CALIFORNIA STATE UNIVERSITY, SACRAMENTO

Street address 1: 6000 J St.
Street address state: CA
Postal code: 95819-6070
Mailing address: 6000 J St
Mailing city: Sacramento
Mailing state: CA
Mailing zip: 95819-6000
Office phone: (916) 278-5340
General e-mail: valsmith@saclink.csus.edu
College Affiliation: SPJ
College Degree: BA- Journalism, Government/Journalism
College Departments: Communication Studies/Journalism, 1947
College Facilities: AdA, CATV, CN, ComN, ComR, ComTV, DR, JM, JN, PRA, VDT (IBM and Macintosh labs)
College Sequence: News-Editorial, Government Journalism
Personnel: Val Smith (Chair)

SAINT AUGUSTINE

FLAGLER COLLEGE

Street address 1: Communication Dept., 74 King St.
Street address state: FL
Postal code: 32085-1027
Mailing address: 74 King St
Mailing city: Saint Augustine
Mailing state: FL
Mailing zip: 32084-4342
Office phone: (904) 819-6247
Office fax: (904) 826-3471
General e-mail: halcombt@flagler.edu
College Degree: BA- Communication
College Departments: Communication Department, 1989
College Facilities: FM, CATV, CCTV, CN, DR, PRA, VDT
College Sequence: Journalism, Broadcasting, Public Relations
Personnel: Tracy Halcomb (Chair/Assoc. Prof.); Jim Gilmore (Assoc. Prof.); James Pickett (Asst. Prof.); Nadia Reardon (Asst. Prof.); Helena Sarkio (Asst. Prof.); Rosemary Tutt (Asst. Prof.); Rob Armstrong (Instr.); Dan McCook (Instr.); Victor Ostrowidzki (Instr.); Barry Sand (Instr.)

SAINT CHARLES

LINDENWOOD UNIVERSITY

Street address 1: 209 S. Kingshighway St.
Street address state: MO
Postal code: 63301
Mailing address: 209 S Kingshighway St
Mailing city: Saint Charles
Mailing state: MO
Mailing zip: 63301-1695
Office phone: (314) 949-4835
Office fax: (314) 949-4910
General e-mail: jwilson@lindenwood.edu
College Departments: Communications Division, 1948
College Sequence: Journalism Program: Majors offered in Corporate Communication and Mass Communication (emphases in Radio/TV, PR, Multimedia, Journalism, Industrial Communication, Sports Information, or Communication Management Sales)
Personnel: Jim Wilson (Dean)

SAINT CLOUD

ST. CLOUD STATE UNIVERSITY

Street address 1: 720 4th Ave. S
Street address state: MN
Postal code: 56301-4498
Mailing address: 720 4th Ave S
Mailing city: Saint Cloud
Mailing state: MN
Mailing zip: 56301-4498
Office phone: (320) 308-3293
Office fax: (320) 654-5337
Web address: www.stcloudstate.edu/comm/index.html
General e-mail: comm@stcloudstate.edu
College Affiliation: AAF, Minn. Newspaper Assoc., PRSSA, SPJ
College Degree: BS, MS
College Departments: Department of Mass Communications, 1972
College Facilities: AdA, AP, FM, CATV, CN, ComN, DR, PRA, VUT, JN
College Sequence: Advertising, Broadcast, News Editorial, Public Relations
Personnel: Roya Akhavan-Majid (Chair/Prof.); Niaz Ahmed (Prof./Grad. Prog. Dir.); Marjorie Fish (Prof.); Mark Mills (Prof.); Peter Przytula (Prof.); Michael Vadnie (Prof./Coord., News Editorial); Lisa Heinrich (Assoc. Prof.); Gregory Martin (Assoc. Prof./Coord., Broadcast); Gretchen Tiberghien (Assoc. Prof./Coord., PR); Marie Dick (Asst. Prof.); Mark Eden (Asst. Prof.); Bill Huntzicker (Asst. Prof.); Ilia Rodriguez (Asst. Prof.); Roger Rudolph (Asst. Prof./Coord., Adv.); Hon. Bernard Bolan (Adj. Prof.); Michael Larson (Adj. Prof.); Mike Knaak (Adj. Prof.); Paul Middlestaedt (Adj. Prof.); Michael Porter (Adj. Prof.); E. Scott Bryce (Prof. Emer.)
Main (survey) contact: Roya Akhavan-Majid

SAINT JOSEPH

MISSOURI WESTERN STATE COLLEGE

Street address 1: SS/C 208
Street address state: MO
Postal code: 64507
Mailing address: SS/C 208
Mailing city: Saint Joseph
Mailing state: MO
Mailing zip: 64507
Office phone: (816) 271-4310
Office fax: (816) 271-4543
General e-mail: klr9015@griffon.mwsc.edu
College Degree: BA
College Departments: Department of English, Foreign Languages, and Journalism, 1973
College Sequence: Journalism Program: Offers a journalism minor and three BAs in English, with emphases in public realations, writing, and technical communications. Produce a weekly newspaper, a yearbook and an annual literary publication.
Personnel: Ken Rosenauer (Chair)

SAINT LOUIS

MARYVILLE UNIVERSITY

Street address 1: 13550 Conway Rd.
Street address state: MO
Postal code: 63141
Mailing address: 650 Maryville University Dr
Mailing city: Saint Louis
Mailing state: MO
Mailing zip: 63141-5849
Office phone: (314) 529-9473
Office fax: (314) 542-9085
General e-mail: gboy@maryville.edu
College Departments: Communications Program
College Sequence: Communications Program: Students specialize in one of three areas offered through courses and/or internships: Public Communication, Business/Marketing Communication, or Broadcasting
Personnel: Gerald Boyer (PhD)

SAINT LOUIS UNIVERSITY

Street address 1: 3733 W. Pine Blvd.
Street address 2: Xavier Hall 300
Street address state: MO
Postal code: 63108
Mailing address: 3733 W Pine Blvd
Mailing city: Saint Louis
Mailing state: MO
Mailing zip: 63108
Office phone: (314) 977-3191
Office fax: (314) 977-3195
General e-mail: commdept@slu.edu
College Affiliation: AAF
College Degree: BA, MA, MA (Research)
College Departments: Department of Communication, 1976
College Facilities: AdA, CN, VDT
College Sequence: Communication Professions, Communication Technology
Personnel: Kathleen Farrell (Chair/Prof.); Rob Anderson (Prof.); Richard Burgin (Prof./Ed., Boulevard Magazine); Avis Meyer (Prof./Dir., Political Journ.); William Tyler (Prof.); Liese Hutchison (Assoc. Prof.); Robert Krizek (Assoc. Prof.); Karla Scott (Assoc. Prof.); Paaige Turner (Assoc. Prof.); Angela Beattie (Asst. Prof.); Matt Carlson (Asst. Prof.); Dan Kozlowski (Asst. Prof.); Jennifer Ohs (Asst. Prof.); Elizabeth Richard (Asst. Prof.); Gary Seibert (Asst. Prof.); Robert

Stahl (Asst. Prof.); April Trees (Asst. Prof.)

UNIVERSITY OF MISSOURI-ST. LOUIS

Street address 1: 1 University Blvd., 235 GSB
Street address state: MO
Postal code: 63121
Mailing address: 1 University Blvd # 235
Mailing city: Saint Louis
Mailing state: MO
Mailing zip: 63121-4400
Office phone: (314) 516-5496
Office fax: (314) 516-5816
General e-mail: murraymd@umsl.edu
College Departments: Mass Communication, 1982
College Sequence: Journalism Program: Undergraduate degree (BS in Media Studies). Minor in Public Affairs Reporting
Personnel: Michael D. Murray (UM Board of Curators' Distinguished Prof.)

WEBSTER UNIV.

Street address 1: 470 E Lockwood Ave
Street address state: MO
Postal code: 63119-3141
Country: USA
Mailing address: 470 E Lockwood Ave
Mailing city: Saint Louis
Mailing state: MO
Mailing zip: 63119-3194
Office phone: (314) 961-2660
Office fax: (314) 968-7059
Web address: www.webujournal.com
General e-mail: wujournal@gmail.com
College Departments: Department of Journalism/Media Communications Department, 1977
College Sequence: Journalism Program: Department is heavy on print/community newspaper orientation. Media program offers photojournalism, audio recording, video production, radio, and cable television access. Also offers media courses on Vienna and Leiden campuses. Grad
Personnel: Don Corrigan (Journ. Seq.); Kelly Kendall (Ed. in Chief)
Main (survey) contact: Don Corrigan

SAINT MARY-OF-THE-WOODS

SAINT MARY-OF-THE-WOODS COLLEGE

Street address 1: Hulman Hall, Rm. 011
Street address state: IN
Postal code: 47876
Mailing address: Hulman Hall, Rm. 011
Mailing city: Saint Mary-Of-The-Woods
Mailing state: IN
Mailing zip: 47876
Office phone: (812) 535-5132
Office fax: (812) 535-5228
General e-mail: nmayfield@smwc.edu
College Departments: Department of English, Journalism & Languages
College Sequence: Journalism Program: Stresses professional preparation of women in journalism in a liberal arts context. Classroom and External Degree formats. News/Editorial/Computer Layout and Design
Personnel: Nancy Pieters Mayfield (Chair)
Main (survey) contact: Nancy Pieters Mayfield

SAINT PAUL

UNIVERSITY OF ST. THOMAS

Street address 1: Dept. of Journalism & Mass Communication
Street address state: MN
Postal code: 55105

Mailing address: Dept. of Journalism & Mass Communication
Mailing city: Saint Paul
Mailing state: MN
Mailing zip: 55105
Office phone: (612) 962-5250
Office fax: (612) 962-6360
General e-mail: kebunton@stthomas.edu
College Affiliation: SPJ, PRSSA, Ad Fed
College Degree: BA
College Departments: Department of Communication & Journalism, 1958
College Facilities: AM, CATV, CCTV, CN, ComN, DR, PRA, VDT
College Sequence: Advertising, Broadcasting, News-Editorial, Communication Studies, Public Relations, Media Studies
Personnel: Kris Bunton (Chair/Prof.); Thomas B. Connery (Prof.); John Cragan (Prof.); Robert L. Craig (Prof.); Mark Neuzil (Prof.); Kevin Sauter (Prof.); Bernard Armada (Assoc. Prof.); Carol Bruess (Assoc. Prof.); Mike O'Donnell (Assoc. Prof.); Debra Petersen (Assoc. Prof.); Tim Scully (Assoc. Prof.); Betsy Anderson (Asst. Prof.); Craig Bryan (Asst. Prof.); Dina Gavrilos (Asst. Prof.); Stephanie Gelarneault (Asst. Prof.); John Purdy (Asst. Prof.); Ellen Riordan (Asst. Prof.); Wendy Wyatt (Asst. Prof.); Mark Anfinson (Part-time Instr.); Bruce Benidt (Part-time Instr.)

SAINT PETERSBURG

UNIVERSITY OF SOUTH FLORIDA ST. PETERSBURG

Street address 1: 140 7th Ave. S, FCT 204
Street address state: FL
Postal code: 33701-5016
Mailing address: 140 7th Ave S Fct 204
Mailing city: Saint Petersburg
Mailing state: FL
Mailing zip: 33701-5016
Office phone: (727) 873-4850
Office fax: (727) 873-4034
College Degree: BA, MA
College Departments: Dept. of Journalism and Media Studies, 1992
College Facilities: Apple computer lab
College Sequence: Journalism and Media Studies: Student chosen focuses include reporting, feature writing, editing, visualdDigital communication
Personnel: Robert Dardenne (Dir./Assoc. Prof.); Deni Elliott (Prof./Grad. Dir.); G. Michael Killenberg (Prof.); Tony Silvia (Prof.); Mark J. Walters (Assoc. Prof.); Xiaopeng (Paul) Wang (Asst. Prof.); Cheryl Koski (Adj. Fac.); Beth Reynolds (Adj. Fac.); Andrew Skerritt (Adj. Fac.); Deborah Wolfe (Adj. Fac.)
Main (survey) contact: Robert Dardenne

SAN DIEGO

POINT LOMA NAZARENE UNIV.

Street address 1: 3900 Lomaland Dr
Street address state: CA
Postal code: 92106-2810
Country: USA
Mailing address: 3900 Lomaland Dr
Mailing city: San Diego
Mailing state: CA
Mailing zip: 92106-2899
Office phone: (619) 849-2444
Office fax: (619) 849-7009
Web address: www.pointweekly.com
General e-mail: news@pointweekly.com; sports@pointweekly.com; advertising@pointweekly.com
College Affiliation: SPJ chapter, annual Writer's Symposium By The Sea
College Departments: Journalism and Mass Communications majors
College Sequence: Majors: Journalism, Broadcast Journalism, Media Communication
Personnel: Stephanie Gant (Adv. Mgr.); Dean Nelson (Journalism Dir.); Coco Jones (Ed. in Chief); Nathan Scharn (Features Ed.)

Main (survey) contact: Stephanie Gant

SAN DIEGO STATE UNIVERSITY

Street address 1: 5500 Campanile Dr.
Street address state: CA
Postal code: 92182-4561
Mailing address: 5500 Campanile Dr
Mailing city: San Diego
Mailing state: CA
Mailing zip: 92182-0003
Office phone: (619) 594-5450
Office fax: (619) 594-6246
General e-mail: jmsdesk@mail.sdsu.edu
College Affiliation: AAF, BEA, KTA, PRSSA, RTNDA, SPJ
College Degree: BA- Communication, Journalism; MA- Communication
College Departments: School of Journalism and Media Studies, 1951
College Facilities: AdA, CATV, ComN, ComR, ComTV, ETV, AM, FM, PRA, VDT
College Sequence: BA Journalism and Communication with emphasis in Advertising, Public Relations, Specialization in Media Studies; MA Communication with specialization in Mass Communication and Media Studies
Personnel: Diane Borden (Dir./Prof.); Joel Davis (Prof.); David Dozier (Prof.); Bill Eadie (Prof.); Barbara Mueller (Prof.); Tim Wulfemeyer (Prof.); Bey-Ling Sha (Assoc. Prof.); Mei Zhong (Assoc. Prof.); Noah Arceneaux (Asst. Prof.); Amy Schmitz Weiss (Asst. Prof.); Valerie Barker (Lectr.); Lora Cicalo (Man. Ed.); Rebecca Coates Nee (Lectr.); David Coddon (Lectr.); John Eger (Lectr./Van Deerlin Prof. of Commun. & Pub. Policy); David Feldman (Lectr.); Chad Harris (Lectr.); Martin Kruming (Lectr.); Lanie Lockwood (Lectr.); Jim McBride (Lectr.)

SAN FRANCISCO

SAN FRANCISCO STATE UNIVERSITY

Street address 1: 1600 Holloway Ave
Street address state: CA
Postal code: 94132-1722
Country: USA
Mailing address: 1600 Holloway Ave # 4200
Mailing city: San Francisco
Mailing state: CA
Mailing zip: 94132-1740
Office phone: (415) 338-1689
Office fax: (415) 338-2084
Web address: www.journalism.sfsu.edu
General e-mail: jour@sfsu.edu
College Degree: BA, Interdisciplinary master's degree
College Departments: Department of Journalism, 1961
College Facilities: Writing, Online, Digital Labs
College Sequence: Majors: Print and Online Journalism, Photojournalism. Minor: Journalism
Personnel: Venise Wagner (Dept. Chair/Assoc. Prof.); Jon Funabiki (Assoc. Dept. Chair/Prof.); Dottie Katzeff (Adv. Mgr.); John Burks (Prof.); Barbara Landes (Prodn. Mgr.); Nathan Codd (Ed. in Chief); Yvonne Daley (Prof.); Kenneth Kobre (Prof.); Erna R. Smith (Prof.); Rachele Kanigel (Assoc. Prof.); Austin Long-Scott (Assoc. Prof.); Cristina Azocar (Asst. Prof./Dir., Ctr. for Integration/Improvement of Journalism); Yumi Wilson (Asst. Prof.); John T. Johnson (Prof. Emer.); B.H. Liebes (Prof. Emer.); Betty Medsger (Prof. Emer.); Leonard Sellers (Prof. Emer.); Jerrold Werthimer (Prof. Emer.); Harriet Chiang (Lectr.); Roland DeWolk (Lectr.); Jesse Garnier (Lectr.); David Greene (Lectr.); Sibylla Herbrich (Lectr.)
Main (survey) contact: Barbara Landes

UNIVERSITY OF SAN FRANCISCO

Street address 1: 2130 Fulton St.
Street address state: CA

Postal code: 94117-1080
Mailing address: 2130 Fulton St
Mailing city: San Francisco
Mailing state: CA
Mailing zip: 94117-1050
Office phone: (415) 422-6680
Office fax: (415) 422-5680
General e-mail: goodwina@usfca.edu
College Departments: Department of Media Studies, Journalism emphasis, 1974
College Sequence: Journalism Program: Liberal arts media studies program with professional sequence in print journalism and in electronic media. Emphases: Media & Society, Journalism, Electronic Media
Personnel: Andrew Goodwin (Chair)

SAN JOSE

SAN JOSE STATE UNIVERSITY

Street address 1: One Washington Sq.
Street address state: CA
Postal code: 95192-0055
Mailing address: 1 Washington Sq
Mailing city: San Jose
Mailing state: CA
Mailing zip: 95192-0001
Office phone: (408) 924-3240
Office fax: (408) 924-3229
Web address: www.jmcweb.sjsu.edu
General e-mail: jmcinfo@casa.sjsu.edu
College Affiliation: AAF, KTA, NPPA, PRSSA, SPJ
College Degree: BS- Advertising, Journalism, Public Relations; MS- Mass Communications
College Departments: School of Journalism and Mass Communications, 1934
College Facilities: AP, FM, AdA, CCTV, ComTV, DR, JN, PRA, VDT
College Sequence: Broadcast News, Magazine, Photojournalism, Reporting/Editing
Personnel: William Briggs (Dir./Prof.); Cecelia Baldwin (Prof.); Harvey Gotliffe (Prof.); Clyde Lawrence (Prof.); Diana Stover (Prof.); William Tillinghast (Prof./Coord., Grad. Studies); Dennis Wilcox (Prof.); Richard Craig (Assoc. Prof.); Scott Fosdick (Assoc. Prof.); Tim Hendrick (Assoc. Prof.); Kathleen Martinelli (Assoc. Prof.); Robert Rucker (Assoc. Prof.); Lilly Buchwitz (Asst. Prof.); Michael Cheers (Asst. Prof.); George Coakley (Lectr.); Chris DiSalvo (Lectr.); Stephen Eckstone (Lectr.); Mack Lundstrom (Lectr.); Cynthia McCune (Lectr.); Dona Nichols (Lectr.)

SAN LUIS OBISPO

CALIFORNIA POLYTECHNIC STATE UNIVERSTIY

Street address 1: Journalism Dept.
Street address state: CA
Postal code: 93407
Mailing address: Journalism Dept.
Mailing city: San Luis Obispo
Mailing state: CA
Mailing zip: 93407
Office phone: (805) 756-2508
Office fax: (805) 756-5744
General e-mail: gmramos@calpoly.edu
College Affiliation: ACT, SPJ, PRSSA, California Newspaper Publishers Assn., Radio and Television News Directors Assn., California collegiate Media Assn.
College Degree: BS
College Departments: Journalism Department, 1953
College Facilities: AP, FM, ComN, ComR, ComTV, DR, JN, VDT
College Sequence: Specializations: Agricultural Journalism, Broadcast Journalism, News-Editorial, Public Relations
Personnel: George Ramos (Chair/Prof.); Nishan Havandjian (Prof.); Patrick Munroe (Prof.); Teresa Allen (Prof.); John Soares (Prof.); Douglas J. Swanson (Assoc. Prof.); Brady Teufel (Full-time Lectr.)

Schools and Departments of Journalism

SANTA CLARA
SANTA CLARA UNIVERSITY
Street address 1: 500 El Camino Real, Arts and Sciences Bldg., #229
Street address state: CA
Postal code: 95053
Mailing address: 500 El Camino Real Arts & Sciences Bldg # 229
Mailing city: Santa Clara
Mailing state: CA
Mailing zip: 95053-0001
Office phone: (408) 554-5498
Office fax: (408) 554-4913
College Degree: BA
College Departments: Department of Communication
College Sequence: Journalism Program: Department offers BA in Communication. Emphases in Mass Communication, Interpersonal Communication, Print, Online, Television Journalism, Video Production, New Technologies and Global Communication. Courses include newswriting, editin
Personnel: Stephen Lee (Head)

SEARCY
HARDING UNIVERSITY
Street address 1: Reynolds Center, 501 S. Burks Blvd.
Street address state: AR
Postal code: 72143
Mailing address: PO Box 10765
Mailing city: Searcy
Mailing state: AR
Mailing zip: 72149-0001
Office phone: (501) 279-4445
Office fax: (501) 279-4605
General e-mail: communication@harding.edu
College Affiliation: ABEA, AER, BEA, RTNDA
College Degree: BA, BS
College Departments: Department of Communication, 1983
College Facilities: TV studio, Cable TV Channel, FM Radio, 95.3Mhz KHVU, AM Radio 1660, KHCA
College Sequence: Advertising, Print Journalism, Public Relations, Interactive Media, Broadcast Journalism, Electronic Media Production
Personnel: Michael L. James (Dean/Prof.); Jack R. Shock (Prof.); Steven Frye (Prof.); Kelly Elander (Assoc. Prof.); Dutch Hoggatt (Assoc. Prof.); Jim Miller (Asst. Prof.); Steve Shaner (Asst. Prof.); Jeremy Beauchamp (Instr.); Bob Ritchie (Instr.); Mark Prior (Adj.)

SHREVEPORT
LOUISIANA STATE UNIVERSITY IN SHREVEPORT
Street address 1: Branson Hall, Rm. 330
Street address state: LA
Postal code: 71115
Mailing address: Branson Hall, Rm. 330
Mailing city: Shreveport
Mailing state: LA
Mailing zip: 71115
Office phone: (318) 797-5375
Office fax: (318) 797-5132
General e-mail: jnolan@lsus.edu
College Degree: BA
College Departments: Department of Communications
College Facilities: Writing, desktop publishing labs
College Sequence: Mass Communications (Journalism), Mass Communications (Public Relations), Speech, Speech Pathology
Personnel: Jack Nolan (Chair)

SILOAM SPRINGS
JOHN BROWN UNIV.
Street address 1: 2000 W University St
Street address state: AR
Postal code: 72761-2112
Country: USA
Mailing address: 2000 W University St
Mailing city: Siloam Springs
Mailing state: AR
Mailing zip: 72761-2121
Office phone: (479) 524-7255
Office fax: (479) 524-7394
Web address: advoacte.jbu.edu
General e-mail: advocate@jbu.edu
College Degree: BS
College Departments: Department of Communication, Division of Communication and Fine Arts, 1983
College Sequence: Journalism Program: A full program leading to a BS in Journalism, Broadcasting or PR
Personnel: Candy Gregor (Assistant Professor of Communication Faculty adviser for the Threefold Advocate); KJ Roh (Executive Editor of the Threefold Advocate)
Main (survey) contact: Marguita Smith

SPRINGFIELD
EVANGEL UNIVERSITY
Street address 1: 1111 N Glenstone Ave
Street address state: MO
Postal code: 65802-2125
Country: USA
Mailing address: 1111 N. Glenstone Ave.
Mailing city: Springfield
Mailing state: MO
Mailing zip: 65802-2125
Office phone: (417) 865-2815
Web address: http://www.evangellance.com
General e-mail: evangellance@gmail.com
College Departments: Department of Communication (with an emphasis in either journalism, communication studies, or electronic media)
College Sequence: Journalism Program: Includes a major, minor and concentration in the field; a secondary education major is also offered.
Personnel: Melinda Booze (Advisor)
Main (survey) contact: Melinda Booze

SPRINGFIELD
MISSOURI STATE UNIVERSITY
Street address 1: 901 S. National Ave.
Street address state: MO
Postal code: 65804
Mailing address: 901 S National Ave
Mailing city: Springfield
Mailing state: MO
Mailing zip: 65897-0001
Office phone: (417) 836-5218
Office fax: (417) 836-4637
General e-mail: mjf@missouristate.edu
College Affiliation: AER, AWC, IABC, PR Club
College Degree: BA, BS
College Departments: Department of Media, Journalism and Film, 1971
College Facilities: FM, CN, ComN, ComTV, DR, PRA, VDT
College Sequence: Journalism (Print and Broadcast); Film Studies, Media Operations, Media Production, Digital Film Production, Screenwriting and Electronic Arts.
Personnel: Karen Buzzard (Head/Prof.); Arlen Diamond (Prof.); Thomas Dickson (Prof.); Mark Paxton (Prof.); Joel Persky (Prof.); Mark Biggs (Assoc. Prof.); Jaime Bihlmeyer (Assoc. Prof.); Weiyan Wang (Assoc. Prof.); Timothy White (Assoc. Prof.); Andrew Cline (Asst. Prof.); Deborah Larson (Asst. Prof.); Mary Jane Pardue (Asst. Prof.); Cheryl Hellmann (Instr.); Jack Dimond (Lectr.)

STANFORD
STANFORD UNIVERSITY
Street address 1: McClatchy Hall
Street address state: CA
Postal code: 94305-2050
Mailing address: McClatchy Hall
Mailing city: Stanford
Mailing state: CA
Mailing zip: 94305-2050
Office phone: (650) 723-1941
Office fax: (650) 725-2472
Web address: communication.stanford.edu
General e-mail: comm-inforequest@lists.stanford.edu
College Degree: BA, MA, PhD
College Departments: Department of Communication
College Facilities: FM, RNA, CCTV, CN, ComN, ComTV, VDT
College Sequence: BA- Communication; MA- Journalism, Documentary Film/Video; PhD- Communication Research; John S. Knight Fellowship Program
Personnel: James Fishkin (Chair/Prof.); Theodore L. Glasser (Prof.); Shanto Iyengar (Chandler Prof.); Jon Krosnick (Frederic O. Glover Prof.); Clifford I. Nass (Prof.); Byron Reeves (Edwards Prof.); Jeremy Bailenson (Asst. Prof.); Fred Turner (Asst. Prof.); Joel Brinkley (Vstg. Prof.); Glenn Frankel (Vstg. Prof.); Ann Grimes (Vstg. Prof.); Beth Noveck (Vstg. Prof.); Robert Luskin (Vstg. Prof.); John Markoff (Lectr.); Howard Rheingold (Lectr.); James Wheaton (Lectr.); Gregg Zachary (Lectr.); Jan Krawitz (Courtesy Appointments); Lawrence Lessig (Courtesy Appointments); Walter Powell (Courtesy Appointments)

STATESBORO
GEORGIA SOUTHERN UNIVERSITY
Street address 1: Dept. of Communication Arts
Street address state: GA
Postal code: 30460
Mailing address: Dept of Communication Arts
Mailing city: Statesboro
Mailing state: GA
Mailing zip: 30460-0001
Office phone: (912) 681-5138
Office fax: (912) 681-0822
General e-mail: hfulmer@gasou.edu
College Degree: BS
College Departments: Journalism Program in Department of Communication Arts
College Sequence: Journalism Program: A BS degree program of practical news-editorial orientation. Curriculum emphasizes liberal arts. Internships optional. Journalism is one of five disciplines in Communication Arts. Others are Broadcasting (Radio-TV-Film), Public Re
Personnel: Ernest T. Wyatt (Program Head)

STOCKTON
UNIVERSITY OF THE PACIFIC
Street address 1: 3601 Pacific Ave.
Street address state: CA
Postal code: 95211
Mailing address: 3601 Pacific Ave
Mailing city: Stockton
Mailing state: CA
Mailing zip: 95211-0197
Office phone: (209) 946-2505
Office fax: (209) 946-2694
General e-mail: qdong@uop.edu
College Degree: BA, MA
College Departments: Department of Communication
College Sequence: Communication Program offers BA in Communication with an emphasis on one of three tracks: Communication Studies, Public Relations and Organizational Communication, and Media Studies. MA degree offered with concentration in Communication Theory, Interper
Personnel: Qingwen Dong (Chair)

STORRS
UNIVERSITY OF CONNECTICUT
Street address 1: Journalism Dept., 337 Mansfield Rd.
Street address state: CT
Postal code: 06269-1129
Mailing address: 337 Mansfield Rd
Mailing city: Storrs
Mailing state: CT
Mailing zip: 06269-9015
Office phone: (860) 486-4222
Office fax: (860) 486-3294
Web address: www.journalism.uconn.edu
General e-mail: jouadm01@unconnvm.uconn.edu
College Affiliation: New England Newspaper Assn.
College Degree: BA
College Departments: Journalism Department, 1948
College Facilities: AP, CN, ComN, ComTV, PRA, AM, FM, JN, VDT
College Sequence: News-Editorial
Personnel: Maureen Croteau (Prof./Head); Wayne Worcester (Prof.); Marcel Dufresne (Assoc. Prof.); Timothy Kenny (Assoc. Prof.); Robert Wyss (Asst. Prof.); Claire Bessette (Lectr.); Bob Hamilton (Lectr.); Douglas Hardy (Lectr.); Terese Karmel (Lectr.); Jonathan Lender (Lectr.); Gail MacDonald (Lectr.); Jon Sandberg (Lectr.); Julie Sprengelmeyer (Lectr.); Greg Stone (Lectr.)

TALLAHASSEE
FLORIDA A&M UNIVERSITY
Street address 1: 510 Orr Dr., Ste. 4003, School of Journalism & Graphic Communication Bldg.
Street address state: FL
Postal code: 32307-4800
Mailing address: 510 Orr Dr Ste 4003
Mailing city: Tallahassee
Mailing state: FL
Mailing zip: 32307-0001
Office phone: (850) 599-3379
Office fax: (850) 561-2399
General e-mail: james.hawkins@famu.edu
College Affiliation: BCCA, KTA, EPT, SPJ, PRSSA, NABJ, Florida Pubic Relations Assn., Graphic Arts Education Assn., American Assn. of University Printers, Graphic Arts Technical Foundation, ACEJMC, ACCGC
College Degree: BSJ, BS- Public Relations, Graphic Communication, Graphic Design; MS- Journalism
College Departments: School of Journalism and Graphic Communication, 1974
College Facilities: FM Radio, Educational Access Television, Student PR Agency, Eleven Computer Labs, Digital Photo Lab, B&W and Color Processing
College Sequence: Newspaper Journalism, Magazine Production, Broadcast Journalism, Public Relations, Printing Management, Photography, Graphic Design
Personnel: James E. Hawkins (Dean); Michael E. Abrams (Prof./Dir., Grad. Studies); F. Todd Bertolaet (Prof.); Dorothy Bland (Prof./Dir., Div. of Journalism); Vincent Blyden (Prof.); LaRae Donnellan (Prof.); Gerald O. Grow (Prof.); Arvid Mukes (Prof./Assoc. Dean./Dir., Div. of Graphic Communication); Joe Ritchie (Prof./Knight Chair); Kay Wilder (Prof.); Gale Workman (Prof.); Bettye Grable (Assoc. Prof.); Joseph Ippolito (Assoc. Prof.); Kenneth Jones (Assoc. Prof.); Yanela Gordon (Asst. Prof./Vstg. Dir., Career Devel. Servs.); M. Diane Hall (Asst. Prof./Dir., H.S./Community College Rel.); Gina Kinchlow (Asst. Prof.); Andrew Skerritt (Asst. Prof.); Valerie White (Asst. Prof.); Ernest Jones (Instr./Mgr., FAMU-TV 20)
Main (survey) contact: Leonard Horton

TAMPA

UNIVERSITY OF SOUTH FLORIDA

Street address 1: 4202 E. Fowler Ave., CIS 1040
Street address state: FL
Postal code: 33620-7800
Mailing address: 4202 E Fowler Ave Cis 1040
Mailing city: Tampa
Mailing state: FL
Mailing zip: 33620-9951
Office phone: (813) 974-2591
Office fax: (813) 974-2592
General e-mail: mcom@cas.usf.edu
College Affiliation: FBA, FPA, FSNE, AAF, KTA, PRSSA, RTNDA, SPJ
College Degree: BA, MA
College Departments: School of Mass Communications, 1970
College Facilities: AM/FM, AdA, CCTV, CN, ComN, DR, ETV, PRA, computer and graphics labs
College Sequence: Advertising, Journalism (magazine, news-editorial), Public Relations, Telecommunications (broadcast news, broadcast production)
Personnel: Edward Jay Friedlander (Prof./Dir.); Dan Bagley (Assoc. Prof.); Kim Golombisky (Assoc. Prof.); Kenneth Killebrew (Assoc. Prof./Grad. Dir.); Larry Leslie (Assoc. Prof.); Scott Liu (Assoc. Prof./Head, Adv. seq./Zimmerman Adv. Prog. Prof.); Randy Miller (Assoc. Prof./Head, Journalism seq.); Kelli Burns (Asst. Prof.); Roxanne Watson (Asst. Prof.); Kelly Page Werder (Asst. Prof./Head, PR seq.); Rick Wilber (Asst. Prof.); Bob Batchelor (Instr.); Marie Curkan-Flanagan (Instr./Head, Tele. seq.); Rebecca Hagen (Instr.); Charles O'Brien (Instr.); Kristin Arnold Ruyle (Instr.); Liisa Hyvarinen Temple (Vstg. Instr.); Kalah Mueller (Advisor); Denise Nicholas (Advisor); Neil Vicino (Adj. Fac.)
Main (survey) contact: Edward Jay Friedlander

TEMPE

ARIZONA STATE UNIVERSITY

Street address 1: 555 N. Central Ave.
Street address state: AZ
Postal code: 85004-1248
Mailing address: 555 N Central Ave
Mailing city: Phoenix
Mailing state: AZ
Mailing zip: 85004-1247
Office phone: (602) 496-3867
Office fax: (602) 496-7041
General e-mail: cronkiteinfol@asu.edu
College Affiliation: AMJ, NPPA, NATAS, PRSSA, RTNDA, SPJ, WICI
College Degree: BA, MMC
College Departments: Walter Cronkite School of Journalism and Mass Communication, 1957
College Facilities: AP, FM, CAT, CCTV, CN, ComN, ComTV, DR, ETV, PRA, VDT
College Sequence: Journalism, Media Management, Media Production, Strategic Media & Public Relations, Media Analysis & Criticism
Personnel: Christopher Callahan (Dean); John E. Craft (Prof.); Stephen K. Doig (Prof./Knight Chair in Journ.); Donald G. Godfrey (Prof.); Bruce D. Merrill (Prof./Dir., Media Research Program); Edward J. Sylvester (Prof.); George Watson (Prof.); Mike Pignataro (Assoc. Prof.); Marianne Barrett (Assoc. Prof.); Sharon Bramlett-Solomon (Class Manager); Mary-Lou Galician (Assoc. Prof.); Fran Matera (Assoc. Prof.); Joseph A. Russomanno (Assoc. Prof./Dir., Grad. Studies); Dennis Russell (Assoc. Prof.); Dina Gavrilos (Asst. Prof.); Carol Schwalbe (Asst. Prof.); William Silcock (Asst. Prof.); Xu Wu (Asst. Prof.); Bruce D. Itule (Clinical Prof.); Frederic A. Leigh (Clinical Prof./Assoc. Dir.)
Main (survey) contact: Jason Manning

TERRE HAUTE

INDIANA STATE UNIVERSITY

Street address 1: Dept. of Communication
Street address state: IN
Postal code: 47809
Mailing address: Dept of Communication
Mailing city: Terre Haute
Mailing state: IN
Mailing zip: 47809-0001
Office phone: (812) 237-3221
Office fax: (812) 237-3217
General e-mail: mbuchholz@isugw.indstate.edu
College Affiliation: SPJ
College Degree: BA, BS
College Departments: Department of Communication, 1952
College Facilities: AP, FM, CCTV, JN, DR, VDT
College Sequence: News/Editorial, Photojournalism and Magazine Writing
Personnel: Paul D. Hightower (Prof.); Michael O. Buchholz (Assoc. Prof.)
Main (survey) contact: Paul D. Hightower

THIBODAUX

NICHOLLS STATE UNIVERSITY

Street address 1: PO Box 2031
Street address state: LA
Postal code: 70310
Mailing address: PO Box 2031
Mailing city: Thibodaux
Mailing state: LA
Mailing zip: 70310-0001
Office phone: (985) 448-4586
Office fax: (985) 448-4577
Web address: www.nicholls.edu/maco
General e-mail: james.stewart@nicholls.edu
College Degree: BA
College Departments: Department of Mass Communication, 1957
College Facilities: AdA, FM, CATV, CN, ComN, ComTV, PRA, VDT
College Sequence: Broadcast Journalism, Print Journalism, Public Relations
Personnel: James L. Stewart (Head/Assoc. Prof.); Lloyd Chiasson (Prof.); Rickey Duet (Assoc. Prof.); Andy Simoncelli (Asst. Prof.); Lance Arnold (Instr.); Nicky Boudreaux (Instr.); Felicia Harry (Instr.); Alfred Delahaye (Prof. Emer.)

THOUSAND OAKS

CALIFORNIA LUTHERAN UNIVERSITY

Street address 1: 60 W Olsen Rd
Street address state: CA
Postal code: 91360-2700
Country: USA
Mailing address: 60 W Olsen Rd # 4200
Mailing city: Thousand Oaks
Mailing state: CA
Mailing zip: 91360-2787
Office phone: (805) 493-3366
Office fax: (805) 493-3479
General e-mail: kelley@robles.callutheran.edu
College Degree: BA
College Departments: Department of Communication Arts, 1981
College Sequence: Journalism Program: The Communication Arts Department offers a BA in Communication Arts along with concentrations in journalism, advertising/public relations and media production. The department also offers a BA in marketing communication in conjunction
Personnel: Colleen Cason (Advisor); Sharon Docter (Chair); Jonathan Culmer (Bus. Mgr.); Margaret Nolan (Ed. in Chief)
Main (survey) contact: Colleen Cason

TOCCOA FALLS

TOCCOA FALLS COLLEGE

Street address 1: School of Communication
Street address state: GA
Postal code: 30598
Mailing address: School of Communication
Mailing city: Toccoa Falls
Mailing state: GA
Mailing zip: 30598
Office phone: (706) 886-7299
Office fax: (706) 886-6412
General e-mail: comm@tfc.edu
College Degree: BA, BS
College Departments: School of Communication
College Sequence: Communication Program: Sequences in Broadcasting, Interpersonal/Organizational, Journalism
Personnel: Jerry Fliger (Dir.)

TOPEKA

WASHBURN UNIVERSITY

Street address 1: 316 Henderson Learning Resources Ctr.
Street address 2: 1700 SW College Ave.
Street address state: KS
Postal code: 66621
Mailing address: 316 Henderson Learning Resources Ctr.
Mailing city: Topeka
Mailing state: KS
Mailing zip: 66621
Office phone: (785) 670-1836
Office fax: (785) 670-1234
Web address: www.morforu.wikidot.com
General e-mail: massmedia@washburn.edu
College Departments: Mass Media Department
College Sequence: Mass Media: Major concentrations include broadcasting, film & video, media writing & publishing, advertising and public relations
Personnel: Dr. Barbara DeSanto (Chair/Fellow PRSA/Prof.); Frank Chorba (Prof.); Charles Cranston (Prof.); Kathy Menzie (Asst. Prof.); Maria Raicheva-Stover (Asst. Prof.); Regina Cassell (Lectr.)

TOUGALOO

TOUGALOO COLLEGE

Street address 1: 500 W County Line Rd
Street address state: MS
Postal code: 39174-9700
Country: USA
Mailing address: 500 W County Line Rd
Mailing city: Tougaloo
Mailing state: MS
Mailing zip: 39174-9700
Office phone: (601) 977-6159
Office fax: (601) 977-6160
General e-mail: cwhite@tougaloo.edu
College Sequence: Journalism Program: Course offerings represent a solid foundation in journalistic study in keeping with a liberal arts education. The college newspaper is The Harambee
Personnel: Teressa Fulgham (Mng. Ed.); Colleen White (Dir. Journ. Program)
Main (survey) contact: Arthur McLin

TOWSON

TOWSON UNIVERSITY

Street address 1: 8000 York Rd.
Street address state: MD
Postal code: 21252
Mailing address: 8000 York Rd
Mailing city: Towson
Mailing state: MD
Mailing zip: 21252-0002
Office phone: (410) 704-3431
Office fax: (410) 704-3656
General e-mail: cflippen@towson.edu
College Degree: BA, BS, MA
College Departments: Mass Communication and Communication Studies Department
College Sequence: Mass Communication Program: 1100 BA, BS and MA students (20 full-time and 50 part-time faculty). Tracks in Journalism and New Media, Advertising and Strategic Public Relations and Integrated Communication. Certificates in Broadcast Journalism and Interd
Personnel: Charles Flippen (Chair)

TROY

TROY STATE UNIVERSITY

Street address 1: 101 Wallace Hall
Street address state: AL
Postal code: 36082
Mailing address: 101 Wallace Hall
Mailing city: Troy
Mailing state: AL
Mailing zip: 36082-0001
Office phone: (334) 670-3289
Office fax: (334) 670-3707
General e-mail: info@jschool.troyst.edu
College Departments: Hall School of Journalism
College Sequence: Journalism Program: Professionally oriented programs to prepare students for entry-level positions in advertising, public relations, print and broadcast journalism
Personnel: Steven Padgett (Dir.)

TUCSON

UNIVERSITY OF ARIZONA

Street address 1: 845 N. Park Ave.
Street address state: AZ
Postal code: 85721-0158
Mailing address: 845 N Park Ave
Mailing city: Tucson
Mailing state: AZ
Mailing zip: 85719-4871
Office phone: (520) 621-7556
Office fax: (520) 621-7557
Web address: www.journalism.arizona.edu
General e-mail: journal@email.arizona.edu
College Affiliation: SPJ, AZ Newspaper Assn, KTA, Nat'l Assn of Hispanic Journalists, Native American Journalists Assn
College Degree: BA, MA
College Departments: Department of Journalism, 1951
College Facilities: CN, CATV, ETV, ComN, ComTV, JN (The Tombstone Epitaph, El Independiente, AZ Cat's Eye, Border Beat, The Cat Scan)
College Sequence: News-Editorial
Personnel: Jacqueline E. Sharkey (Head/Soldwedel Family Prof./Prof.); Terry Wimmer (Prof.); Bruce Itule (Prof.); Shahira Fahmy (Assoc. Prof.); William F. Greer (Assoc. Prof. Emer.); Alan Weisman (Assoc. Prof.); Maggy Zanger (Assoc. Prof.); David Cuillier (Asst. Prof.); Celeste GonzÃƒÂ‚Â‚Â lez de Bustamante (Asst. Prof.); Kevin R. Kemper (Asst. Prof.); Susan Knight (Asst. Prof.); Linda Lumsden (Asst. Prof.); Jeannine Relly (Asst. Prof.); Jay Rochlin (Asst. Prof.); Kim Newton (Asst. Prof.); Steve Auslander (Instr.); Rhonda Bodfield Bloom (Instr.); Mark Evans (Instr.); Tom Beal (Instr.); Cathalena Burch (Instr.)

TUSCALOOSA

UNIVERSITY OF ALABAMA

Street address 1: 490 Phifer Hall Ste. 490
Street address 2: Corner Colonial Dr., Univ. Blvd.
Street address state: AL
Postal code: 35487-0172
Mailing address: PO Box 870172
Mailing city: Tuscaloosa
Mailing state: AL
Mailing zip: 35487-0172
Office phone: (205) 348-5520
Office fax: (205) 348-3836
General e-mail: chammond@ua.edu
College Affiliation: ACES, NABJ, NPPA, SPJ
College Degree: BA, MA, MLIS, PhD
College Departments: College of Communication and Information Sciences, 1927
College Facilities: AP, CN, DR, ETV, JM, JN, FM, VDT
College Sequence: Advertising and Public

Schools and Departments of Journalism

Relations, Communication Studies, Journalism, School of Library and Information Studies, Telecommunication and Film

Personnel: Loy Singleton (Dean); Elizabeth Aversa (Prof./Dir., School of Library & Information Studies); Bruce Berger (Prof./Chair, Adv./PR); Rick Bragg (Prof.); Jennings Bryant (Prof./Reagan Chair, Assoc. Dean, Grad. Studies); Jeremy Butler (Prof.); Matthew Bunker (Phifer Prof.); Karen J. Cartee (Prof.); Gary Copeland (Prof./Chair, Telecommunication/Film); Margaret Dalton (Bristol-EBSCO Prof.); William Evans (Prof./Dir., Institute for Comm. & Information Research); William Gonzenbach (Prof.); Tom Harris (Prof.); Marsha Houston (Prof.); Steven Miller (Prof.); Yorgo Pasadeos (Prof.); Joseph Phelps (Prof./Phifer Prof.); David Sloan (Prof.); Beth Bennett (Assoc. Prof./Chair, Commun. Studies); Kimberly Bissell (Assoc. Prof.)

UNIVERSITY

UNIVERSITY OF MISSISSIPPI

Street address 1: 331 Farley Hall
Street address state: MS
Postal code: 38677-1848
Mailing address: PO Box 1848
Mailing city: University
Mailing state: MS
Mailing zip: 38677-1848
Office phone: (662) 915-7146
Office fax: (662) 915-7765
Web address: www.olemiss.edu/depts/Journalism
General e-mail: jebaker@olemiss.edu
College Affiliation: AAF, KTA, NABJ, RTNDA, SPJ
College Degree: BA, MA
College Departments: Department of Journalism, 1947
College Facilities: AP, CATV, CN, FM, VDT
College Sequence: Print, Radio/TV (PR, magazine emphases available)
Personnel: Samir A. Husni (Prof./Hederman Lectr.); Jeanni Atkins (Assoc. Prof.); Joe Atkins (Assoc. Prof./Head, Print seq.); Carmen Manning-Miller (Assoc. Prof./Grad. Coord.); Burnis Morris (Assoc. Prof./Talbert Lectr.); Ken Boutwell (Asst. Prof.); Ralph Braseth (Asst. Prof./Student Media Dir.); Flora Caldwell (Asst. Prof.); D. Michael Cheers (Asst. Prof.); Charles Raiteri (Asst. Prof.); Brad Schultz (Asst. Prof./Head, Broadcast seq.); Melanie Stone (Asst. Prof.); Kathleen Woodruff Wickham (Asst. Prof.); Robin Street (Instr./Dir., MS Scholastic Press); Jack Bass (Prof. Emer.); Jere Hoar (Prof. Emer.)
Main (survey) contact: Emily Roland

UNIVERSITY PARK

GOVERNORS STATE UNIV.

Street address 1: 1 University Pkwy
Street address 2: E2543
Street address state: IL
Postal code: 60484-3165
Country: USA
Mailing address: 1 University Pkwy.
Mailing city: University Park
Mailing state: IL
Mailing zip: 60484-3165
Office phone: (708) 534-4517
Office fax: (708) 534-7895
Web address: www.gsuphoenix.com
General e-mail: phoenix@govst.edu
College Affiliation: Arts and Sciences
College Degree: BA, MA
College Departments: Department of Communications
College Facilities: VDT
College Sequence: BA - Film/Video Production, Journalism, Multi Media Production, Public Relations, Speech; MA - Communication Studies, Human Performance and Training, Media Communications.
Personnel: Debbie James (Faculty Advisor); Michael Purdy (Emeritus Professor)
Main (survey) contact: Debbie James; Michael Purdy

UPLAND

TAYLOR UNIVERSITY

Street address 1: 236 West Reade Avenue
Street address state: IN
Postal code: 46989-1001
County: Grant
Country: USA
Mailing address: 236 West Reade Avenue
Mailing city: Upland
Mailing state: IN
Mailing zip: 46989-1001
Office phone: (765) 998-5590
Web address: www.taylor.edu
General e-mail: dnhensley@taylor.edu
College Affiliation: Taylor University
College Degree: Bachelor of Science in Communication
College Departments: Department of Communication
College Facilities: Second Floor, Nussbaum Hall, Taylor University
Personnel: Dennis E. Hensley (Director, Professional Writing major); Linda Taylor (Instructor in Professional Writing)
Main (survey) contact: Dennis E. Hensley

URBANA

UNIVERSITY OF ILLINOIS

Street address 1: 810 S. Wright St., 119 Gregory Hall/MC-462
Street address state: IL
Postal code: 61801
Mailing address: 810 S Wright St Gregory HALL/MC-462
Mailing city: Urbana
Mailing state: IL
Mailing zip: 61801-3644
Office phone: (217) 333-2350
Office fax: (217) 333-9882
Web address: www.comm.uiuc.edu
General e-mail: ccomm@uiuc.edu
College Affiliation: ACT, AAF, ADS, AHJ, KTA, NABJ, SPJ
College Degree: BS, MS, PhD
College Departments: College of Communications, 1927
College Facilities: AdA, AP, AM/FM, CATV, ComN, DR, CN, VDT, ETV
College Sequence: Advertising, Broadcast Journalism, News-Editorial Journalism, Media Studies
Personnel: Ronald E. Yates (Sleeman Prof./Dean); William F. Brewer (Prof.); Angharad N. Valdivia (Prof.); Clifford G. Christians (Prof./Dir., Institute for Comm. Research/Sandage); C.L. Cole (Prof.); Leon D. Dash (Prof./Swanlund Chair); Matthew C. Ehrlich (Prof.); Norman K. Denzin (Prof./College Scholar); Brant Houston (Knight Chair Prof.); Walter G. Harrington (Prof./Head, Journ.); Steve J. Helle (Prof.); Louis W. Liebovich (Prof.); John C. Nerone (Prof./Dir., Grad. Studies, Inst. of Comm. Research/College Scholar); Kent A. Ono (Prof.); Jan Slater (Prof./Head, Adv.); Amy J. Aidman (Assoc. Dean, Research/Assoc. Prof.); Christopher D. Benson (Assoc. Prof.); Nancy J. Benson (Assoc. Prof.); William E. Berry (Assoc. Prof.); Jay M. Rosenstein (Assoc. Prof.)
Main (survey) contact: Ronald E. Yates

VALDOSTA

VALDOSTA STATE UNIVERSITY

Street address 1: 1500 N. Patterson, Dept. Of Communication Arts
Street address state: GA
Postal code: 31698-0001
Mailing address: 1500 N Patterson Dept of
Mailing city: Valdosta
Mailing state: GA
Mailing zip: 31698-0001
Office phone: (229) 333-5820
Office fax: (229) 293-6182
General e-mail: ccates@valdosta.edu
College Departments: Department of Communication Arts
College Sequence: The Department of Communication Arts is a multidisciplinary department with the academic disciplines of Speech Communication, Intercultural Communication, Organizational Communication, Public Relations, Theatre, Dance, Mass Media, and Broadcast Journalis
Personnel: Carl Cates (Head)

VALPARAISO

VALPARAISO UNIVERSITY

Street address 1: 1809 Chapel Dr
Street address state: IN
Postal code: 46383-4517
Country: USA
Mailing address: 1809 Chapel Dr
Mailing city: Valparaiso
Mailing state: IN
Mailing zip: 46383-4517
Office phone: (219) 464-5271
Office fax: (219) 464-6742
Web address: www.valpo.edu/torch
General e-mail: douglas.kocher@valpo.edu
College Departments: Department of Communication
College Sequence: Communication Program: Five majors: Communication Law, New Media-Journalism, Public and Corporate Communication, Public Relations, Television-Radio. Practical experience stressed; internship required; co-op education available
Personnel: Douglas J. Kocher (Chair); Jason Paupore (Advisor); Andy Simmons (Bus. Mgr.); Luis Fifuentes (Adv.Mgr.); Kathryn Kattalia (Ed. in chief)
Main (survey) contact: Douglas J. Kocher; Andy Simmons

VINCENNES

JOURNALISM PROGRAM, VINCENNES UNIVERSITY

Street address 1: 1002 N 1st St
Street address state: IN
Postal code: 47591-1504
Country: USA
Mailing address: 1002 N 1st St
Mailing city: Vincennes
Mailing state: IN
Mailing zip: 47591-1500
Office phone: (812) 888-4551
Office fax: (812) 888-5531
Web address: www.vutrailblazernews.com
General e-mail: trailblazer@vinu.edu
College Departments: The Journalism Program
College Sequence: Journalism Program: Newspaper-oriented curriculum with two sequences, news-editorial and print media advertising. Five lecture courses, production laboratories for each sequence, and two inter-departmental photography courses.
Personnel: Emily Taylor (Journalism Asst. Professor, Department Chair of Media Production)
Main (survey) contact: Emily Taylor

WARRENSBURG

UNIVERSITY OF CENTRAL MISSOURI

Street address 1: Dept. of Communication
Street address state: MO
Postal code: 64093
Mailing address: Dept. of Communication
Mailing city: Warrensburg
Mailing state: MO
Mailing zip: 64093
Office phone: (660) 543-4840
Office fax: (660) 543-8006
General e-mail: fair@umco.edu
College Affiliation: BEA, PRSSA, SPJ, Missouri Broadcasters Assoc., Missouri Press Assoc., UFVA.
College Degree: BA, BS, BSE (teacher certification), MA
College Departments: Department of Communication
College Facilities: FM, CATV, ComN, ComR, ComTV, DR, ETV, JM, JN, PRA, VDT, Digital TV.
College Sequence: Mass Communication, Broadcasting and Film, Public Relations, Print Journalism (News Editorial)
Personnel: Charles Fair (Chair)

WASHINGTON

AMERICAN UNIVERSITY

Street address 1: 4400 Massachusetts Ave. NW
Street address state: DC
Postal code: 20016
Mailing address: 4400 Massachusetts Ave NW
Mailing city: Washington
Mailing state: DC
Mailing zip: 20016-8200
Office phone: (202) 885-2060
Office fax: (202) 885-2099
Web address: www.soc.american.edu
College Affiliation: KTA, NATAS, PRSSA, SPJ, WICI
College Degree: BA, BS, MA, MFA
College Departments: School of Communication, 1966
College Facilities: AP, AM, FM, CCTV, ComN, ComR, ComTV, DR, MM, PRA, VDT
College Sequence: Programs: Broadcast Journalism; Print Journalism; Public Communication; Film and Media Arts; Communication, Legal Institutions, Economics, and Government; Foreign Language and Communication Media; Multimedia Design and Development; Graduate Journalism and
Personnel: Larry Kirkman (Prof./Dean); Patricia Aufderheide (Prof.); Kathryn Montgomery (Prof.); Jack Orwant (Prof.); Chris Simpson (Prof.); Rodger Streitmatter (Prof.); Randall Blair (Assoc. Prof.); W. Joseph Campbell (Assoc. Prof.); Wendell Cochran (Assoc. Prof.); Barbara Diggs-Brown (Assoc. Prof.); John Doolittle (Assoc. Prof.); John Douglass (Assoc. Prof.); Charlene Gilbert (Assoc. Prof.); Jane Hall (Assoc. Prof.); Jill Olmsted (Assoc. Prof.); Rick Rockwell (Assoc. Prof.); Richard Stack (Assoc. Prof.); Leonard Steinhorn (Assoc. Prof.); Wendy Swallow (Assoc. Prof.); John Watson (Assoc. Prof.)

CATHOLIC UNIVERSITY SCHOOL OF LAW

Street address 1: Institute for Communications Law Studies
Street address state: DC
Postal code: 20064
Mailing address: Institute for Communications Law Studies
Mailing city: Washington
Mailing state: DC
Mailing zip: 20064-0001
Office phone: (202) 319-6295
Office fax: (202) 319-4459
College Departments: Institute for Communications Law Studies
College Sequence: Communications Program: Specialized legal training in communications law for JD degree candidates with journalism or telecommunications backgrounds
Personnel: Marin Scordato (Dir.)

GEORGE WASHINGTON UNIVERSITY

Street address 1: 805 21st St. NW, Ste. 400
Street address state: DC
Postal code: 20052

Mailing address: 805 21st St NW Ste 400
Mailing city: Washington
Mailing state: DC
Mailing zip: 20052-0029
Office phone: (202) 994-6227
Office fax: (202) 994-5806
Web address: www.gwu.edu/~smpa
General e-mail: smpa@gwu.edu
College Affiliation: Policomm Society, SPJ
College Degree: BA, MA
College Departments: Bachelor of Arts in Journalism, Political Communication, and Electronic Media; Master of Arts in Media and Public Affairs (School of Media and Public Affairs), 1947
College Facilities: AM/FM, CCTV, CN, VDT, ETV, ComN, Internet, Center for Survey Research

HOWARD UNIVERSITY

Street address 1: 525 Bryant St. NW
Street address state: DC
Postal code: 20059
Mailing address: 525 Bryant St NW
Mailing city: Washington
Mailing state: DC
Mailing zip: 20059-1005
Office phone: (202) 806-7690
Office fax: (202) 232-8305
Web address: www.soc.howard.edu
College Affiliation: SPJ, NABJ, PRSSA, AAF, BCCA, BEA
College Degree: BA- Communication and Culture, Journalism, R/TV/F; BS- Communication Sciences and Disorders; MA- Communication and Culture; MS- Communication Sciences and Disorders; MFA- Film; PhD- Communication and Culture, Communication Sciences and Disorders
College Departments: School of Communications, 1971
College Facilities: AM, AdA, RNA, FM, CN, ComN, ComR, CCTV, ETV, JN, PRA, VDT
College Sequence: Print/On-line Journalism, Broadcast News, Advertising/Public Relations, Film Audio Production, Television Production, Telecommunications Management, Legal Communication, Speech Communication, Speech-Language Pathology and Audiology
Personnel: Jannette L. Dates (Grad. Prof./Dean); Noma Anderson (Prof. (LWOP)); Anju Chaudhary (Prof.); Abraham Ford (Prof.); Haile Gerima (Prof.); Barbara Hines (Prof.); Lawrence Kaggwa (Prof.); Judi Moore Latta (Prof.); Abbas Malek (Prof.); Robert L. Nwanko (Prof.); Joan C. Payne (Prof.); Ronald C. Pearlman (Prof.); William H. Starosta (Grad. Prof. (LWOP)/Vice Provost); Orlando L. Taylor (Grad. Prof. (LWOP)/Vice Provost); Clint C. Wilson (Prof.); Richard Wright (Prof.); S. Torriano Berry (Assoc. Prof.); Debra A. Busacco (Assoc. Prof.); Alonzo Crawford (Assoc. Prof.); Melbourne S. Cummings (Assoc. Prof.)

WEST HARTFORD

UNIVERSITY OF HARTFORD

Street address 1: 200 Bloomfield Ave.
Street address state: CT
Postal code: 06117-1599
Mailing address: 200 Bloomfield Ave
Mailing city: West Hartford
Mailing state: CT
Mailing zip: 06117-1599
Office phone: (860) 768-4633
Office fax: (860) 768-4096
General e-mail: kelly@hartford.edu
College Degree: BA, MA
College Departments: School of Communication, 1956
College Sequence: Journalism Program: Offers BA and MA in Communication with emphasis in Journalism, Media, Advertising, Public Relations, Human Communication Studies, Integrated Communication
Personnel: Lynne Kelly (Dir.)

WEST LAFAYETTE

PURDUE UNIVERSITY/BRIAN LAMB SCHOOL OF COMMUNICATION

Street address 1: 100 N. University St.
Street address state: IN
Postal code: 47907-2098
County: Tippecanoe
Country: USA
Mailing address: BRNG 2114
Mailing city: West Lafayette
Mailing state: IN
Mailing zip: 47907-2098
Telephone country code: 01
Office phone: (765) 494-3429
Office fax: (765) 496-1394
Web address: www.cla.purdue.edu/communication
College Affiliation: College of Liberal Arts
College Sequence: Undergraduate majors Mass Communication and Public Relations. Courses in Journalism. MA and PhD programs in Public Relations and Mass Communication.
Main (survey) contact: Marifran Mattson

WHITING

CALUMET COLLEGE OF ST. JOSEPH

Street address 1: 2400 New York Ave
Street address state: IN
Postal code: 46394-2146
Country: USA
Mailing address: 2400 New York Ave
Mailing city: Whiting
Mailing state: IN
Mailing zip: 46394-2195
Office phone: (219) 473-4322
Office fax: (219) 473-4219
Web address: www.ccsj.edu
College Degree: BA- Communication Arts with journalism emphasis
College Departments: Division of Communication and Fine Arts
College Sequence: Journalism Program: News-Editorial sequence
Personnel: Dawn Muhammad (PD); Daren Jasieniecki (Mktg. Mgr.); Mark Cassello
Main (survey) contact: Mark Cassello; Dawn Muhammad

WICHITA

WICHITA STATE UNIVERSITY

Street address 1: Elliott School of Communication
Street address state: KS
Postal code: 67260-0031
Mailing address: Elliott School of Communication
Mailing city: Wichita
Mailing state: KS
Mailing zip: 67260-0001
Office phone: (316) 978-3185
Office fax: (316) 978-3006
General e-mail: susan.huxman@wichita.edu
College Affiliation: SPJ, AAF
College Degree: BA, MA
College Departments: Elliott School of Communication, 1927/1989
College Facilities: DR, CATV, CN, FM, ComN, ComTV, ADA, PRA, VDT
College Sequence: Strategic Communication, Broadcast Journalism, Electronic Media, Integrated Marketing Communications, Print Journalism
Personnel: Susan Huxman (Assoc. Prof./Dir.); Philip Gaunt (Prof.); Sharon Iorio (Prof.); Vernon Keel (Prof.); Les Anderson (Assoc. Prof.); Rick Armstrong (Assoc. Prof.); Dan Close (Assoc. Prof.); Patricia Dooley (Assoc. Prof.); Kevin Hager (Assoc. Prof.); Keith Williamson (Assoc. Prof.); Michael Boyle (Asst. Prof.); Jeff Jarman (Asst. Prof.); Amy Lauters (Asst. Prof.); Greg Stene (Asst. Prof.); Mike Wood (Asst. Prof.); Nancy Fisher (Instr.); Kevin Keplar (Instr.); Connie Morris (Instr.); Randy Brown (Sr. Fellow); Al Higdon (Professional-in-Residence)

WILMORE

ASBURY COLLEGE

Street address 1: 1 Macklem Dr
Street address state: KY
Postal code: 40390-1152
Country: USA
Mailing address: 1 Macklem Dr
Mailing city: Wilmore
Mailing state: KY
Mailing zip: 40390-1198
Office phone: (859) 858-3511
Office fax: (859) 858-3921
Web address: collegian.asbury.edu
General e-mail: mlonginow@asbury.edu
College Departments: Department of Communication Arts, 1983
College Facilities: Independent student newspaper with web edition, yearbook, literary magazine, campus-wide radio stations, cable TV covering surrounding county, Media 100, web page production, recording studio, special-interest magazines, internships in print and electroni
College Sequence: Journalism Program: Three sequences: News-Editorial, Public Relations, Magazine & Publishing; Literary Journalism. Media Communications Program: Five sequences: Performance, Production, Film Studies, Multimedia. Applied Communications Program: Five sequ
Personnel: Deanna Morono (Exec. Ed.); James R. Owens (Chair); Kayla Dubois (Mng. Ed.); Zack Klemme (News Ed.); Morgan Schutters (Web Design)
Main (survey) contact: Deanna Morono

WINONA

ST. MARY'S UNIVERSITY OF MINNESOTA

Street address 1: 700 Terrace Heights
Street address state: MN
Postal code: 55987
Mailing address: 700 Terrace Hts
Mailing city: Winona
Mailing state: MN
Mailing zip: 55987-1399
Office phone: (507) 457-1502
Office fax: (507) 457-1633
General e-mail: dbeckman@smumn.edu
College Departments: Media Communications Program, Department of Social Science.
College Sequence: Offers majors in Public Relations, Journalism and Electronic Publishing and minors in Public Relations, Journalism and Electronic Publishing
Personnel: Dean Beckman (Coord.)

WINONA STATE UNIVERSITY

Street address 1: Dept. of Mass Communication
Street address state: MN
Postal code: 55987
Mailing address: Dept. of Mass Communication
Mailing city: Winona
Mailing state: MN
Mailing zip: 55987
Office phone: (507) 457-5474
Office fax: (507) 457-5155
General e-mail: mscmdept@winona.edu
College Affiliation: AERO, IABC, SCJ, AAF
College Degree: BA
College Departments: Department of Mass Communication, 1981
College Facilities: AP, FM, CATV, CN, ComN, DR, ETV, JN, VDT
College Sequence: Advertising, Broadcast, Journalism, Photojournalism, Public Relations
Personnel: Cindy Killion (Chair)

YPSILANTI

EASTERN MICHIGAN UNIVERSITY

Street address 1: 612 Pray Harrold
Street address state: MI
Postal code: 48197-4210
Mailing address: 612 Pray Harrold
Mailing city: Ypsilanti
Mailing state: MI
Mailing zip: 48197-4210
Office phone: (734) 487-4220
Office fax: (734) 483-9744
General e-mail: carol.schlagheck@emich.edu
College Departments: Department of English Language and Literature
College Sequence: Journalism Program: Offers a major and minor in Journalism and an interdisciplinary major in Public Relations. Journalism courses cover news/feature writing, copyediting, editorial procedures of layout and design, history of journalism, law and Web journa
Personnel: Laura George (Head); Carol Schlagheck (Journ. Program Coord.)

SENIOR PUBLICATIONS IN THE U.S.

ALBUQUERQUE
PRIME TIME
Street address 1: 6300 Montano Rd NW
Street address 2: Ste G3
Street address state: NM
Postal code: 87120-1826
County: Bernalillo
Country: USA
Mailing Address: PO Box 67560
Mailing city: Albuquerque
Mailing state: NM
Mailing zip: 87193
Office phone: (505) 888-0470
General e-mail: primetime@swcp.com
Editorial e-mail: primeedit@swcp.com
Website: www.ptpubco.com
Year publication established: 1991
Advertising (open inch rate): Open inch rate $40.00
Mechanical specifications: Type page 10 1/4 x 15 3/4; E - 4 cols, 2 5/16, 3/8 between; A - 4 cols, 2 5/16, 3/8 between.
Zip Codes Served: 87191
Frequency: Mthly
Audit By: Sworn/Estimate/Non-Audited
Audit Date: 12.07.2019
Hardware: APP/Mac.
Personnel: Sydney Dickinson (Adv. Mgr.); David Rivord (Editor); Christine Carter (Prodn. Mgr.)
Main (survey) contact: David Rivord

ALLEGAN
SENIOR TIMES
Street address 1: 595 Jenner Dr
Street address state: MI
Postal code: 49010-1516
County: Allegan
Country: USA
Mailing Address: 595 Jenner Dr
Mailing city: Allegan
Mailing state: MI
Mailing zip: 49010-1516
Office phone: (269) 673-1720
Office fax: (269) 673-4761
General e-mail: debra.sloan@flashespublishers.com
Advertising e-mail: debra.sloan@flashespublishers.com
Website: flashpublishers.com
Advertising (open inch rate): full page = 1050; quarter page = $320
Mechanical specifications:
Frequency: Mthly
Circulation Paid: 18
Circulation Free: 16500
Audit By: Sworn/Estimate/Non-Audited
Audit Date: 12.07.2019
Personnel: Debbie Sloan (Mgr.)
Main (survey) contact: Debbie Sloan

ANCHORAGE
SENIOR VOICE
Street address 1: 3340 Arctic Blvd
Street address 2: Ste 106
Street address state: AK
Postal code: 99503-4550
County: Anchorage
Country: USA
Mailing Address: 3340 Artic Blvd.
Mailing city: Anchorage
Mailing state: AK
Mailing zip: 99503
Office phone: (907) 276-1059
Office fax: (907) 278-6724
Advertising phone: (907) 276-1059
Advertising fax: (907) 278-6724
Editorial phone: (907) 276-1059
Editorial fax: (907) 278-6724
General e-mail: info@seniorvoicealaska.com
Advertising e-mail: execdiropag@gci.net
Editorial e-mail: seniorvoice@gci.net
Website: www.seniorvoicealaska.com
Year publication established: 1969
Advertising (open inch rate): Open inch rate $22.00
Delivery methods: Mail`Newsstand`Carrier`Racks
Frequency: Mthly
Circulation Paid: 1300
Circulation Free: 11500
Audit By: Sworn/Estimate/Non-Audited
Audit Date: 12.07.2019
Personnel: David Washburn (Mng Ed); James Bailey (Execu Dir)
Main (survey) contact: David Washburn

BATTLE CREEK
SENIOR TIMES SOUTH CENTRAL MICHIGAN
Street address 1: 4642 Capital Ave SW
Street address state: MI
Postal code: 49015-9305
County: Calhoun
Country: USA
Mailing Address: 4642 Capital Ave SW
Mailing city: Battle Creek
Mailing state: MI
Mailing zip: 49015-9305
Office phone: (269) 979-1411
Office fax: (269) 979-3474
Advertising phone: (269) 979-1479 x106
Editorial phone: (269) 979-1412 x102
General e-mail: sherii@wwthayne.com
Advertising e-mail: sheriis@wwthayne.com
Editorial e-mail: sheriis@wwthayne.com
Website: www.scenepub.com/seniortimes
Year publication established: 1971
Mechanical specifications: Type page 10 1/4 x 16; E - 4 cols, 2 3/8, 1/4 between; A - 6 cols, 1 1/2, 1/4 between; C - 6 cols, 1 1/2, 1/4 between.
Zip Codes Served: 49017, 49015, 49016, 49068, 49245, 49092, 49224, 49021, 49011, 48813
Frequency: Mthly
Circulation Paid: 100
Circulation Free: 15850
Audit By: Sworn/Estimate/Non-Audited
Audit Date: 12.07.2019
Hardware: APP/Mac, Microsoft/WordPerfect
Software: QPS/QuarkXPress 4.0.
Personnel: Shirley DeRuiter (Asst. Pub.); Keith Sherban (Gen. Mgr.); Leslie Hole (Adv. Mgr.); Shelii Penny (Circ. Mgr.); Sherii Sherban (Publisher / Exec. Ed.)
Main (survey) contact: Sherii Sherban

BELLPORT
50+ LIFESTYLES
Street address 1: 146 S Country Rd
Street address 2: Ste 4
Street address state: NY
Postal code: 11713-2530
County: Suffolk
Country: USA
Mailing Address: 146 S Country Rd Ste 4
Mailing city: Bellport
Mailing state: NY
Mailing zip: 11713-2530
Office phone: (631) 286-0058
Office fax: (631) 286-6866
Advertising phone: (877) 677-6397
General e-mail: tim@50plusny.com
Editorial e-mail: editor@50plusny.com
Website: www.50plusny.com
Year publication established: 1975
Mechanical specifications: Type page 10 x 12 1/2.
Delivery methods: Mail`Newsstand`Racks
Zip Codes Served:
Digital Platform - Tablet: Other
Frequency: Mthly
Circulation Paid: 5000
Circulation Free: 100000
Audit By: Sworn/Estimate/Non-Audited
Audit Date: 12.07.2019
Editions Count: 2
Edition Names: Long Island and Metro NY
Personnel: Frank C. Trotta (Pres./Pub.); Gary P. Joyce (Ed.); Tim Edwards (Exec. Ed.); Suzanne DeLuca (Art Dir.)
Main (survey) contact: Tim Edwards

BOCA RATON
BOOMER TIMES AND SENIOR LIFE
Street address 1: 1515 N Federal Hwy
Street address 2: Ste 300
Street address state: FL
Postal code: 33432-1994
County: Palm Beach
Country: USA
Mailing Address: 1515 N Federal Hwy Ste 300
Mailing city: Boca Raton
Mailing state: FL
Mailing zip: 33432-1994
Office phone: (561) 736-8925
Office fax: (561) 369-1476
General e-mail: srlife@gate.net
Website: www.babyboomers-seniors.com
Year publication established: 1990
Mechanical specifications: 8-1/2 x 11
Delivery methods: Mail`Carrier`Racks
Digital Platform - Mobile: Windows
Digital Platform - Tablet: Windows 7
Frequency: Mthly
Circulation Paid: 19199
Circulation Free: 41000
Audit By: Sworn/Estimate/Non-Audited
Audit Date: 12.07.2019
Note: 19,000 of the 41,000 are inserted monthly in The Miami Herald for their subscribers.
Personnel: Marilyn Weiss (Vice Pres., Admin.); Anita R. Finley (Adv. Mgr.); Leoni Kendall (Mktg. Mgr.); Bill Finley (Mng. Ed./Travel Ed.); Connie Crimi (Prodn. Mgr.)
Main (survey) contact: Anita R. Finley

BUFFALO
FOREVER YOUNG
Street address 1: 1738 Elmwood Ave
Street address 2: Ste 103
Street address state: NY
Postal code: 14207-2465
County: Erie
Country: USA
Mailing Address: 1738 Elmwood Ave Suite 103
Mailing city: Buffalo
Mailing state: NY
Mailing zip: 14207-2465
Office phone: (716) 783-9119
Office fax: (716) 783-9983
General e-mail: calarlev@aol.com; circulation@buffalospree.com
Website: www.foreveryoungwny.com
Year publication established: 1988
Mechanical specifications: Type page 9.75 x 11.25.
Delivery methods: Newsstand`Racks
Zip Codes Served: 14043

Frequency: Mthly
Circulation Free: 36153
Audit By: CVC
Audit Date: 30.09.2013
Personnel: Laurence A. Levite (Pub.); Barbara E. Macks (Dir., Sales); Robin M. Lenhard (Dir., Circ.); Elizabeth Licata (Ed. in Chief.); Jade Z. Chen (Prod. Dir.); Jennifer Ellis (Prod. Mgr.)
Main (survey) contact: Larry Levite

DUNDEE
DENBAR PUBLISHING, INC
Street address 1: PO Box 478
Street address state: IL
Postal code: 60118-0478
County: Kane
Country: USA
Mailing Address: PO Box 478
Mailing city: Dundee
Mailing state: IL
Mailing zip: 60118-0478
Office phone: (847) 931-0234
Office fax: (847) 697-6817
Advertising phone: (847) 567-0234
Editorial phone: (630) 531-1670
General e-mail: sn50andbetter@yahoo.com; info@sn50andbetter.com
Advertising e-mail: chisrnews@aol.com
Editorial e-mail: chgoseniornews@yahoo.com
Website: www.sn50andbetter.com
Year publication established: 1986
Mechanical specifications: Type page 10 x 15 1/2; E - 4 cols, 2 1/2, between; A - 4 cols, 2 1/2, between.
Delivery methods: Mail`Racks
Zip Codes Served: chicaogland 5 counties
Frequency: Mthly
Audit By: Sworn/Estimate/Non-Audited
Audit Date: 12.07.2019
Hardware: HP
Presses: WPC
Software: Microsoft/Windows.
Editions Count: 10
Edition Names: 10 total; Senior News-City (Chicago) (15,000); Senior News-Cook North (20,000); Senior News-Cook South (15,000); Senior News-Cook West (15,000); Senior News-Dupage (20,000); Senior News-Kane (10,000); Senior News-Lake (8,000); Senior News-McHenry (4,000)
Personnel: Jim Thomas (Circ. Mgr.); Barbara Simonini (Ed.); Dennis Simonini (Mng. Ed.); Dawn Williams (Managing Editor); Jeff Busse (Prodn. Mgr.)
Main (survey) contact: Dennis Simonini

EAGLE
IDAHO SENIOR NEWS
Street address 1: 233 W State St
Street address 2: Ste E
Street address state: ID
Postal code: 83616-4982
County: Ada
Country: USA
Mailing Address: PO Box 937
Mailing city: Eagle
Mailing state: ID
Mailing zip: 83616-0937
Office phone: (208) 336-6707
Office fax: (208) 336-6752
Advertising phone: (800) 657-6470
General e-mail: editor@idahoseniornews.com
Advertising e-mail: advertising@idahoseniornews.com
Editorial e-mail: editor@idahoseniornews.com
Website: www.idahoseniornews.com
Year publication established: 1978
Mechanical specifications: Type page 10 3/8

x 15; E - 5 cols, 2, 1/16 between; A - 5 cols, 2, 1/16 between; C - 5 cols, 2, 1/16 between.
Delivery methods: Mail`Carrier`Racks
Frequency: Mthly
Circulation Paid: 3500
Circulation Free: 22000
Audit By: Sworn/Estimate/Non-Audited
Audit Date: 12.07.2019
Personnel: Jane Seil (Publisher/Owner)
Parent company: Graphic Arts Publishing, Inc.
Main (survey) contact: Jane Seil

EAST LONGMEADOW
PRIME TIMES

Street address 1: 280 N Main St
Street address state: MA
Postal code: 01028-1868
County: Hampden
Country: USA
Mailing Address: 280 N Main St
Mailing city: East Longmeadow
Mailing state: MA
Mailing zip: 01028-1868
Office phone: (413) 525-6661
Office fax: (413) 525-5882
General e-mail: news@thereminder.com
Website: www.thereminder.com
Advertising (open inch rate): Open inch rate $17.00
Mechanical specifications: Type page 10 x 16; E - 4 cols, 2 3/8, 1/8 between; A - 4 cols, 2 3/8, 1/8 between; C - 5 cols, 2, 1/8 between.
Zip Codes Served: 01001, 01002, 01013, 01020, 01027, 01028, 01033, 01036, 01038, 01040, 01056, 01060, 01075, 01089, 01095, 01101, 01105, 01106, 01108, 01109, 01118, 01119, 01128, 01129, 01301, 01337, 01338, 01342, 01375
Frequency: Mthly
Circulation Paid: 3
Circulation Free: 16826
Audit By: CVC
Audit Date: 30.06.2013
Hardware: APP/Mac
Software: QPS/QuarkXPress, Adobe/Photoshop.
Personnel: Daniel J. Buendo (Pub.); Christopher Buendo (Gen. Mgr.); Barbarra Terry (Adv. Mgr.); G.Michael Dobbs (Mng. Ed.)
Main (survey) contact: G. Michael Dobbs

FOND DU LAC
MATURITY TIMES

Street address 1: PO Box 1955
Street address state: WI
Postal code: 54936-1955
County: Fond Du Lac
Country: USA
Mailing Address: PO Box 1955
Mailing city: Fond Du Lac
Mailing state: WI
Mailing zip: 54936-1955
Office phone: (920) 922-8640
Office fax: (920) 922-0125
Advertising e-mail: classified@actionadvertiser.com
Editorial e-mail: scottw@actionprinting.com
Website: www.actiononline.net
Year publication established: 1987
Mechanical specifications: Type page 9 x 16; E - 4 cols, 2 1/2, between; A - 4 cols, 2 1/2, between.
Zip Codes Served: 54936
Frequency: Mthly
Circulation Free: 11000
Audit By: Sworn/Estimate/Non-Audited
Audit Date: 12.07.2019
Hardware: APP/Mac
Software: QPS/QuarkXPress, Adobe/Photoshop.
Personnel: Gloria Krueger (Adv. Mgr.); Scott Wittchow (Mng. Ed.)
Main (survey) contact: Gloria Krueger

FORT COLLINS
SENIOR VOICE

Street address 1: 1471 Front Nine Dr
Street address state: CO
Postal code: 80525-9459
County: Larimer
Country: USA
Mailing Address: 1471 Front Nine Dr
Mailing city: Fort Collins
Mailing state: CO
Mailing zip: 80525-9459
Office phone: (970) 223-9271
Office fax: (970) 223-9271
General e-mail: thevoice@frii.com
Website: www.theseniorvoice.net
Year publication established: 1980
Advertising (open inch rate): Open inch rate $36.80
Mechanical specifications: Type page 10 x 12 3/4; E - 4 cols, 2 1/3, 1/4 between; A - 4 cols, 2 1/3, 1/4 between.
Frequency: Mthly
Circulation Free: 42000
Audit By: Sworn/Estimate/Non-Audited
Audit Date: 12.07.2019
Personnel: William Lambdin (Pub.); Wolfgang Lambdin (Adv. Mgr.); Peggy Hunt (Prodn. Mgr.)
Main (survey) contact: William Lambdin

GRAND JUNCTION
BEACON SENIOR NEWSPAPER

Street address 1: 524 30 Rd
Street address 2: Ste 4
Street address state: CO
Postal code: 81504-4437
County: Mesa
Country: USA
Mailing Address: PO Box 3895
Mailing city: Grand Junction
Mailing state: CO
Mailing zip: 81502-3895
Office phone: (970) 243-8829
Office fax: (800) 536-7516
Advertising phone: (970) 243-8829
Advertising fax: (800) 536-7516
Editorial phone: (970) 243-8829
Editorial fax: (800) 536-7516
General e-mail: beacon@pendantpublishing.com
Advertising e-mail: kevin@pendantpublishing.com
Editorial e-mail: cloie@pendantpublishing.com
Website: www.beaconseniornews.com
Year publication established: 1987
Advertising (open inch rate): Open inch rate $28.44
Mechanical specifications: Type page 10.37" x 10.98"; 4 cols
Delivery methods: Mail`Newsstand`Carrier`Racks
Zip Codes Served: 81501, 81502, 81503, 81504, 81505, 81506, 81507, 81520, 81521, 81526, 81527, 81401, 81403, 81413, 81416, 81425, 81432
Digital Platform - Mobile: Apple`Android`Windows`Blackberry`Other
Digital Platform - Tablet: Apple iOS`Android`Windows 7`Blackberry Tablet OS`Kindle`Nook`Kindle Fire`Other
Frequency: Mthly
Circulation Paid: 1200
Circulation Free: 20000
Audit By: CVC
Audit Date: 30.06.2012
Hardware: APP/Macs Windows
Presses: The BIG kind.
Software: Adobe InDesign
Personnel: Kevin VanGundy (Pub.); Sue Bowen (Acct Exec); Karen Jones (Graphic Arts); Cloie Sandlin (Mgr Ed); Sidney Jayne (Acct Exec); Melissa Trottier (Graphic Artist)
Parent company: Pendant Publishing, Inc.
Main (survey) contact: Kevin VanGundy

HOLLAND
WEST MICHIGAN SENIOR TIMES

Street address 1: 54 W 8th St
Street address state: MI
Postal code: 49423-3104
County: Ottawa
Country: USA
Mailing Address: 54 W 8th St
Mailing city: Holland
Mailing state: MI
Mailing zip: 49423-3104
Office phone:
Office fax:
Advertising phone: (269) 673-1701
Editorial phone: (269) 673-1720
Advertising e-mail: tiffany.andrus@flashespublishers.com
Editorial e-mail: debra.sloan@flashespublishers.com
Website: flashespublishers.com
Year publication established: 1984
Advertising (open inch rate): Open inch rate $16.00
Mechanical specifications: Type page 9.375" x 14.5"; E - 4 cols, 1 col = 2.25", 1/8 between;
Delivery methods: Racks
Zip Codes Served: 49001 49002 49004 49006 49007 49008 49009 49010 49012 49013 49024 49048 49053 49055 49056 49062 49065 49067 49071 49073 49078 49079 49080 49083 49087 49090 49093 49097 49306 49315 49321
Frequency: Mthly
Other Type of Frequency: 2nd Friday of each month
Circulation Paid: 50
Circulation Free: 18000
Audit By: Sworn/Estimate/Non-Audited
Audit Date: 12.07.2019
Hardware: APP/Mac
Presses: G/Community
Software: QPS/QuarkXPress.
Personnel: Debbie Sloan (Editorial); Tiffany Andrus (Sales); Tricia Johnston (Publisher)
Parent company: The Hays Daily News
Main (survey) contact: Debbie Sloan

KENSINGTON
THE BEACON

Street address 1: 3720 Farragut Ave
Street address 2: Ste 105
Street address state: MD
Postal code: 20895-2110
County: Montgomery
Country: USA
Mailing Address: PO Box 2227
Mailing city: Silver Spring
Mailing state: MD
Mailing zip: 20915-2227
Office phone: (301) 949-9766
Office fax: (301) 949-8966
Advertising phone: 301-949-9766
Advertising fax: (301) 949-8966
Editorial phone: (301) 949-9766
Editorial fax: 301-949-8966
General e-mail: info@thebeaconnewspapers.com
Advertising e-mail: alan@thebeaconnewspapers.com
Editorial e-mail: barbara@thebeaconnewspapers.com
Website: www.thebeaconnewspapers.com
Year publication established: 1989
Advertising (open inch rate): Open inch rate $96.00
Mechanical specifications: Type page 10 x 13 1/2; E - 4 cols, 2 1/2, 1/6 between; A - 4 cols, 2 1/2, 1/6 between; C - 4 cols, 2 1/2, 1/6 between.
Delivery methods: Racks
Frequency: Mthly
Circulation Free: 230000
Audit By: CVC
Audit Date: 31.03.2017
Editions Count: 4
Edition Names: The Beacon - Baltimore (68,000); The Beacon - DC (110,000); The Beacon - Howard County (17,000); Fifty Plus Richmond, VA (35,000)
Personnel: Alan Spiegel (Vice President Sales & Marketing); Stuart Rosenthal (Ed.); Barbara Ruben (Mng. Ed.); Alan Spiegel (Sales Dir.)
Main (survey) contact: Alan Spiegel

LEBANON
MATURE LIFESTYLES OF TENNESSEE

Street address 1: PO Box 857
Street address state: TN
Postal code: 37088-0857
County: Wilson
Country: USA
Mailing Address: PO Box 857
Mailing city: Lebanon
Mailing state: TN
Mailing zip: 37088
Office phone: (615) 444-6008
Office fax: (615) 444-6818
Advertising phone: (615) 444-6008
Editorial phone: (615) 444-6008
Other phone: (615) 444-6008
General e-mail: bharville@mainstreetmediatn.com
Advertising e-mail: dgould@mainstreetmediatn.com
Editorial e-mail: bharville@mainstreetmediatn.com
Advertising (open inch rate): 15/inch
Mechanical specifications: 10" x 14"
Delivery methods: Racks
Zip Codes Served: Davidson, Williamson, Rutherford, Wilson and Sumner counties
Frequency: Mthly
Circulation Free: 13000
Audit By: Sworn/Estimate/Non-Audited
Audit Date: 12.07.2019
Personnel: Brian Harville (Ed)
Parent company: Main Street Media of Tennessee
Main (survey) contact: Dave Gould

MANITOU SPRINGS
LIFE AFTER 50

Street address 1: 329 Manitou Ave
Street address 2: Ste 103
Street address state: CO
Postal code: 80829-2590
County: El Paso
Country: USA
Mailing Address: 329 Manitou Ave Ste 103
Mailing city: Manitou Springs
Mailing state: CO
Mailing zip: 80829-2590
Office phone: (719) 685-9690
Office fax: (719) 685-9705
General e-mail: dennis@pikespeakpublishing.com
Advertising e-mail: sales@pikespeakpublishing.com
Website: www.pikespeakpublishing.com
Mechanical specifications: Type page 10 x 13 3/4; E - 4 cols, 2 5/16, 1/4 between; A - 4 cols, 2 5/16, 1/4 between; C - 4 cols, 2 5/16, 1/4 between.
Frequency: Mthly
Circulation Free: 20000
Audit By: Sworn/Estimate/Non-Audited
Audit Date: 12.07.2019
Hardware: Pentium/PC, 2-PC Celeron, PC 586, Pentium/PC II
Software: Adobe/PageMaker 6.5, Adobe/Photoshop 4.0.
Personnel: Dennis Ingmire (Pub.); Stephanie Stanford (Adv. Mgr.); Bruce Schlabough (Sales Mgr.); Jeanne Davant (Ed.); Don Bouchard (Prodn. Mgr.)
Main (survey) contact: Dennis Ingmire

Senior Publications in the U.S.

MEMPHIS

THE BEST TIMES

Street address 1: 4646 Poplar Avenue
Street address 2: Ste 344
Street address state: TN
Postal code: 38117
County: Shelby
Country: USA
Mailing Address: 4646 Poplar Avenue, Ste 344
Mailing city: Memphis
Mailing state: TN
Mailing zip: 38117
Office phone: (901) 458-2911
Office fax: (901) 207-2448
Advertising phone: (901) 505-0945
Editorial phone: (901) 505-0940
General e-mail: admin@thebesttimes.com
Advertising e-mail: jgrubbs@thebesttimes.com
Editorial e-mail: tjordan@thebesttimes.com
Website: thebesttimes.com
Year publication established: 1982
Advertising (open inch rate): modular
Mechanical specifications: modular tab
Delivery methods: Newsstand`Racks
Zip Codes Served: Shelby, Tipton, Fayette, Lauderdale, and Haywood Counties. TN - Desoto County, Marshall and Lafayette Counties MS and West Memphis, Arkansas
Digital Platform - Mobile: Windows
Digital Platform - Tablet: Windows 7`Other
Frequency: Mthly
Circulation Free: 25500
Audit By: Sworn/Estimate/Non-Audited
Audit Date: 12.07.2019
Hardware:
Presses: web offset
Software: Adobe In Design
Editions Count: 1
Edition Names: The Best Times
Note: Printing is contracted out
Personnel: Jimmy Grubbs (Publisher); Tom Jordan (managing editor); Sherry Greene (Assistant Publisher); Jeff Martin (Publisher's representative); William Mitchum (Social Media Specialist); Mindy Fulcher (Graphics Designer); Jeff Winstock (Account Executive); Jimmy Covington (Editor)
Parent company: The Best Times presented by Jimmy Grubbs
Main (survey) contact: Jimmy Grubbs

MINNEAPOLIS

GOOD AGE

Street address 1: 1115 Hennepin Ave
Street address state: MN
Postal code: 55403-1705
County: Hennepin
Country: USA
Mailing Address: 1115 Hennepin Ave
Mailing city: Minneapolis
Mailing state: MN
Mailing zip: 55403-1705
Office phone: (612) 825-9205
Office fax: (612) 825-0929
Website: www.mngoodage.com
Year publication established: 1981
Mechanical specifications: Type page 7 3/4 x 10 7/8; E - 4 cols, 2 1/4, 1/4 between; A - 6 cols, 1 5/12, between; C - 3 cols, 3 1/6, between.
Frequency: Mthly
Circulation Paid: 78
Circulation Free: 49892
Audit By: CVC
Audit Date: 24.03.2013
Hardware: APP/Power Mac G4
Software: Adobe/Photoshop 7.0, QPS/QuarkXPress 4.0.
Editions Count: 2
Edition Names: 2 total Ãƒâ€šÃ‚Â£Ãƒâ€šÃ‚Â£ Good Age-East Metro (29,000); Good Age-West Metro (43,500);
Personnel: Janis Hall (Pub.); Terry Gahan (Co-Pub.); Mellisa Ungerman Levy (Adv. Sales Mgr.); Tricia Cornell (Ed.); Jake Weyer (Asst. Ed.); Marlo Johnson (Dist. Mgr.)
Main (survey) contact: Janis Hall

NASHVILLE

FORWARD FOCUS

Street address 1: 174 Rains Ave
Street address state: TN
Postal code: 37203-5319
County: Davidson
Country: USA
Mailing Address: 174 Rains Ave
Mailing city: Nashville
Mailing state: TN
Mailing zip: 37203-5319
Office phone: (615) 743-3400
Office fax: (615) 743-3480
General e-mail: info@fiftyforward.org
Website: www.fiftyforward.org
Year publication established: 1956
Advertising (open inch rate): Open inch rate $20.00
Mechanical specifications: Type page 9 3/4 x 11 1/2; E - 4 cols, 2 3/8, between.
Frequency: Mthly
Circulation Free: 8000
Audit By: Sworn/Estimate/Non-Audited
Audit Date: 12.07.2019
Hardware: 3-APP/Mac Power Mac 6500/300, 5-APP/Mac 8.6
Software: QPS/QuarkXPress 5.0.
Personnel: Janet Jernigan (Pub.); Bob Newman (Adv. Mgr.); Paul Carlton (Ed.)
Main (survey) contact: Misa Acox

NEPTUNE

SENIOR SCOOP

Street address 1: 3600 Highway 66
Street address state: NJ
Postal code: 7754
County: Monmouth
Country: USA
Mailing Address: PO Box 1550
Mailing city: Neptune
Mailing state: NJ
Mailing zip: 07754
Office phone: 732-922-6000
Office fax: (732) 557-5659
General e-mail: senscoop@app.com
Website: www.app.com
Advertising (open inch rate): Open inch rate $40.23
Mechanical specifications: Type page 9 x 11 5/8; E - 5 cols, 1 4/5, between; A - 5 cols, 1 4/5, between.
Other Type of Frequency: 4x Yr
Circulation Free: 80000
Audit By: Sworn/Estimate/Non-Audited
Audit Date: 12.07.2019
Presses: G/Urbanite.
Editions Count: 2
Edition Names: 2 total Ã‚Â Monmouth County Senior Scoop (35,000); Ocean County Senior Scoop (45,000);
Personnel: Bonnie Russell (Adv. Mgr.)
Main (survey) contact: Hollis Towns

NEW ALBANY

SENIOR TIMES

Street address 1: PO Box 623
Street address state: OH
Postal code: 43054-0623
County: Franklin
Country: USA
Mailing Address: PO Box 623
Mailing city: New Albany
Mailing state: OH
Mailing zip: 43054
Office phone: (614) 337-2055
Office fax: (614) 337-7105
General e-mail: seniortimes@insight.rr.com
Year publication established: 1983

Mechanical specifications: Type page 10 1/4 x 14; E - 6 cols, 1 5/8, between.
Delivery methods: Mail`Racks
Frequency: Mthly
Circulation Free: 60000
Audit By: Sworn/Estimate/Non-Audited
Audit Date: 12.07.2019
Personnel: Stephen Pinsky (Pub.); Angela Miller (Adv. Mgr.); Lee Pinsky (Circ. Mgr.)
Main (survey) contact: Stephen Pinsky

NEW HOPE

ICON MAGAZINE

Street address 1: PO Box 120
Street address state: PA
Postal code: 18938-0120
County: Bucks
Country: USA
Mailing Address: PO Box 120
Mailing city: New Hope
Mailing state: PA
Mailing zip: 18938-0120
Office phone: (215) 862-9558
Office fax: (215) 862-9845
General e-mail: trobba@comcast.net
Website: www.icondv.com
Advertising (open inch rate): Open inch rate $38.00
Mechanical specifications: Type page 10 x 14; A - 6 cols, 1 1/2, 1/5 between; C - 6 cols, 1 1/2, 1/5 between.
Frequency: Mthly
Audit By: Sworn/Estimate/Non-Audited
Audit Date: 12.07.2019
Hardware: 3-APP/Mac 8500/150, 2-HP/Laserjet 4mv
Software: QPS/QuarkXPress 3.32.
Editions Count: 2
Edition Names: 2 total ÃƒÂ‚Ã‚Â Prime Time Monthly-Bucks County (PA) (26,500); Prime Time Monthly-S. Jersey (40,000);
Personnel: Trina McKenna (Ed.)
Main (survey) contact: Trina McKenna

OLATHE

THE BEST TIMES

Street address 1: 111 S Cherry St
Street address 2: Ste 3300
Street address state: KS
Postal code: 66061-3487
County: Johnson
Country: USA
Mailing Address: 111 South Cherry Street, Suite 3300
Mailing city: Olathe
Mailing state: KS
Mailing zip: 66061-7056
Office phone: (913) 715-8930
Office fax: (913) 715-0440
Advertising phone: (913) 715-8920
Advertising fax: (913) 715-0440
Editorial phone: (913) 715-0736
Editorial fax: (913) 715-0440
General e-mail: gerald.hay@jocogov.org
Advertising e-mail: cherell.bilquist@jocogov.org
Editorial e-mail: gerald.hay@jocogov.org
Website: www.jocogov.org/thebesttimes
Year publication established: 1982
Advertising (open inch rate): Variable; contact us for rate card.
Delivery methods: Mail`Racks
Zip Codes Served: Most, if not all, Zip Codes in Johnson County, KS
Frequency: Bi-Mthly
Other Type of Frequency: Bimonthly (first of month)
Circulation Paid: 300
Circulation Free: 68000
Audit By: Sworn/Estimate/Non-Audited
Audit Date: 12.07.2019
Personnel: Sharon Watson (Director of Public Affairs and Communications); Gerald Hay (Editor); Che'rell Bilquist (Advertising Manager)
Parent company: Johnson County (Kansas) Government
Main (survey) contact: Gerald Hay

PELHAM

WSN2DAY.COM

Street address 1: 629 Fifth Ave
Street address 2: Ste 213
Street address state: NY
Postal code: 10803-3708
County: Westchester
Country: USA
Mailing Address: 629 Fifth Ave Ste 213
Mailing city: Pelham
Mailing state: NY
Mailing zip: 10803-3708
Office phone: (914) 738-7869
Office fax: (914) 738-7876

General e-mail: shorelineproduction@gmail.com
Advertising e-mail: hp@shorelinepub.com
Editorial e-mail: hp@shorelinepub.com
Website: www.shorelinepub.com
Year publication established: 1992
Mechanical specifications: Type page 10 x 13; E - 4 cols, 2 1/4, between; A - 6 cols, 1 3/4, between.
Delivery methods: Carrier`Racks
Frequency: Mthly
Circulation Paid: 500
Circulation Free: 24000
Audit By: Sworn/Estimate/Non-Audited
Audit Date: 12.07.2019
Hardware: IBM
Software: Adobe/PageMaker 6.0.
Personnel: Edward Shapiro (CEO/Pub.); Helene Pollack (Ed. in Chief)
Parent company: Shoreline Publishing
Main (survey) contact: Edward Shapiro

PHILADELPHIA

MILESTONES

Street address 1: 642 N Broad St
Street address state: PA
Postal code: 19130-3424
County: Philadelphia
Country: USA
Mailing Address: 642 N Broad St
Mailing city: Philadelphia
Mailing state: PA
Mailing zip: 19130-3424
Office phone: (215) 765-9000
Office fax: (215) 765-9066
Advertising phone: (215) 765-9000 ext. 5051
Editorial phone: (215) 765-9000 ext 5080

General e-mail: milestonesnews@pcaphl.org
Advertising e-mail: milestones@pcaphl.org
Editorial e-mail: milestonesnews@pcaphl.org
Website: http://www.pcacares.org/default.aspx
Year publication established: 1987
Advertising (open inch rate): full page, one-time b&w inside page: $1980
Mechanical specifications: see website
Delivery methods: Mail`Racks
Zip Codes Served: All 191xxx
Frequency: Mthly
Circulation Paid: 25
Circulation Free: 67325
Audit By: CVC
Audit Date: 01.09.2012
Hardware: APP/Mac
Software: QPS/QuarkXPress 3.3.
Editions Count: 1
Note: Digital version, Milestones e-news is weekly, published on Wednesdays and has some identical, some different content. Available on web or via email subscription.
Personnel: Alicia Columbo (Editor); Joan Zaremba (Adv.); Emily Ozga (Dist.)
Parent company: Philadelphia Corporation for Aging
Main (survey) contact: Alicia Columbo

PITMAN

THE GOLDEN TIMES

Street address 1: PO Box 134
Street address state: NJ
Postal code: 08071-0134
County: Gloucester
Country: USA
Mailing Address: PO Box 134
Mailing city: Pitman
Mailing state: NJ
Mailing zip: 08071-0134
Office phone: (856) 582-3940
Office fax: (801) 720-9176
Website: www.thegoldentimes.com
Advertising (open inch rate): Open inch rate $35.00
Mechanical specifications: Type page 10 x 13; E - 5 cols, 1 9/10, 1/10 between.
Frequency: Mthly
Circulation Free: 47000
Audit By: Sworn/Estimate/Non-Audited
Audit Date: 12.07.2019
Hardware: IBM
Software: Microsoft/Windows 95, QPS/QuarkXPress.
Editions Count: 3
Edition Names: 3 total ÃƒÂ‚Â‚Â— The Golden Times-Camden County Edition (12,000); The Golden Times-Delaware Valley Edition (25,000); The Golden Times-Gloucester County Edition (10,000);
Personnel: Alex Augunas (Adv. Mgr.); Harry G. Armstrong (Ed.); Barbara Murphy (Mng. Ed.); Ryan Armstrong (Prodn. Mgr.)
Main (survey) contact: Harry G. Armstrong

RICHMOND

FIFTY PLUS

Street address 1: 1506 Staples Mill Rd
Street address 2: Ste 102
Street address state: VA
Postal code: 23230-3631
County: Richmond City
Country: USA
Mailing Address: 8010 Ridge Rd Ste F
Mailing city: Henrico
Mailing state: VA
Mailing zip: 23229-7288
Office phone: (804) 673-5203
Office fax: (804) 673-5308
Editorial phone: (804) 673-4966

General e-mail: mail@richmondpublishing.com
Website: www.fiftyplusrichmond.com
Frequency: Mthly
Circulation Free: 35000
Audit By: Sworn/Estimate/Non-Audited
Audit Date: 12.07.2019
Personnel: Mark Fetter (Pub.); Lisa Fracker (Office Mgr.); Lisa Crutchfield (Ed)
Main (survey) contact: Mark Fetter

SAN LUIS OBISPO

JOURNAL PLUS MAGAZINE

Street address 1: 654 Osos St
Street address state: CA
Postal code: 93401-2713
County: San Luis Obispo
Country: USA
Mailing Address: 654 Osos St
Mailing city: San Luis Obispo
Mailing state: CA
Mailing zip: 93401-2713
Office phone: (805) 546-0609
Office fax: (805) 546-8827

General e-mail: slojournal@fix.net
Website: www.slojournal.com
Mechanical specifications: Type page 7 1/2 x 10; E - 3 cols, 2 1/2, between; A - 3 cols, 2 1/2, between.
Delivery methods: Mail`Newsstand`Racks
Frequency: Mthly
Circulation Free: 25000
Audit By: Sworn/Estimate/Non-Audited

Audit Date: 12.07.2019
Personnel: Steve Owens (Pub.); Jan Owens (Adv. Mgr.); Erin Mott (Ed.)
Main (survey) contact: Steve Owens

SHREVEPORT

THE BEST OF TIMES

Street address 1: PO Box 19510
Street address state: LA
Postal code: 71149-0510
County: Caddo
Country: USA
Mailing Address: PO Box 19510
Mailing city: Shreveport
Mailing state: LA
Mailing zip: 71149-0510
Office phone: (318) 636-5510

General e-mail: gary.calligas@gmail.com
Advertising e-mail: gary.calligas@gmail.com
Editorial e-mail: gary.calligas@gmail.com
Website: www.thebestoftimesnews.com
Year publication established: 1993
Advertising (open inch rate): $71.79 per inch column (column width is 3.67 inches)
Mechanical specifications: Quarter page vertical ad = 3.6 inches by 4.75 inches height Half page horizontal ad = 7.5 inches by 4.75 inches Full page ad = 7.5 inches wide by 9.75 inches height.
Delivery methods: Mail`Racks
Zip Codes Served: Caddo Parish, Louisiana Bossier Parish, Louisiana Shreveport, Louisiana Bossier City, Louisiana
Digital Platform - Mobile: Apple`Android
Digital Platform - Tablet: Apple iOS`Android
Frequency: Mthly
Circulation Paid: 250
Circulation Free: 20000
Audit By: Sworn/Estimate/Non-Audited
Audit Date: 12.07.2019
Editions Count: 1
Edition Names: 1
Note: Monthly glossy magazine for readers who are 50 and older in age residing in Northwest Louisiana to help them celebrate age and maturity. Also, TBT Multimedia hosts a weekly one hour radio talk show at 9 am every Saturday morning on NEWSRADIO 710 KEEL in Shreveport, Louisiana and is also streaming live at www.710KEEL.COM and streaming via the RADIOPUP app on apple and android phones and tablets.
Personnel: Gary Calligas (Publisher)
Parent company: TBT Multimedia, LLC
Main (survey) contact: Gary Calligas

TACOMA

SENIOR SCENE

Street address 1: 223 N Yakima Ave
Street address state: WA
Postal code: 98403-2230
County: Pierce
Country: USA
Mailing Address: 223 N Yakima Ave
Mailing city: Tacoma
Mailing state: WA
Mailing zip: 98403-2230
Office phone: (253) 722-5687
Office fax: (253) 597-6456
Advertising phone: (253) 722-5687
Advertising fax: (253) 597-6456

General e-mail: seniormedia@lcsnw.org
Editorial e-mail: bdicskon@lcsnw.org
Website: www.seniorscene.org
Year publication established: 1975
Mechanical specifications: Type page 11 x 17; E - 3 cols, 3 1/8, 1/4 between; A - 3 cols, 3 1/8, 1/4 between; C - 3 cols, 3 1/8, 1/4 between.
Delivery methods: Mail`Racks
Frequency: Mthly
Audit By: Sworn/Estimate/Non-Audited
Audit Date: 12.07.2019
Hardware: PC
Software: Adobe Creative Suite, Microsoft Office
Personnel: Bonnie Dickson (Ed.); Christine Nagy (Adv. Mgr.); Jacky Lee (Circ. Mgr.); Judith Silva (Office Mgr.); George Kenworthy (Adv. Sales Suprv.)
Main (survey) contact: Bonnie Dickson

TEMPE

LOVIN' LIFE AFTER 50

Street address 1: 1620 W. Fountainhead Parkway
Street address 2: Ste. 219
Street address state: AZ
Postal code: 85282
County: Maricopa
Country: USA
Mailing Address: 1620 W. Fountainhead Parkway, Ste. 219
Mailing city: Tempe
Mailing state: AZ
Mailing zip: 85282
Office phone: (480) 898-5612
Office fax: (480) 898-5606

General e-mail: info@lovinlife.com
Advertising e-mail: mhiatt@timespublications.com
Editorial e-mail: ndandrea@timespublications.com
Website: lovinlife.com
Year publication established: 1979
Advertising (open inch rate): N/A
Mechanical specifications: Full page 10"X11"
Delivery methods: Carrier`Racks
Frequency: Mthly
Other Type of Frequency: Monthly
Circulation Free: 105283
Audit By: Sworn/Estimate/Non-Audited
Audit Date: 12.07.2019
Editions Count: 6
Edition Names: East Valley, Southeast Valley, West Valley, Scottsdale, Phoenix, Tucson
Personnel: Niki D'Andrea (Pub.)
Parent company: EOS Publishing, LLC
Main (survey) contact: Steve H. Fish

VANCOUVER

SENIOR MESSENGER

Street address 1: 400 E Evergreen Blvd
Street address 2: Ste 111
Street address state: WA
Postal code: 98660-3263
County: Clark
Country: USA
Mailing Address: 400 E Evergreen Blvd Ste 111
Mailing city: Vancouver
Mailing state: WA
Mailing zip: 98660-3263
Office phone: (360) 750-9900
Office fax: (360) 750-9907

General e-mail: circulation@seniormessenger.org
Advertising e-mail: ads@seniormessenger.org
Editorial e-mail: news@seniormessenger.org
Website: www.vanmessenger.org
Advertising (open inch rate): Open inch rate $14.00
Mechanical specifications: Type page 10 1/4 x 16; E - 4 cols, 2 5/12, 1/5 between; A - 4 cols, 2 5/12, 1/5 between.
Digital Platform - Mobile: Apple
Frequency: Mthly
Circulation Free: 15000
Audit By: Sworn/Estimate/Non-Audited
Audit Date: 12.07.2019
Hardware: PC ad MAC
Software: QuarkExpress, Photoshop, Acrobat
Personnel: Marita Sempio
Main (survey) contact: Greg Johnson

VERONA

JOURNEY OF AGING

Street address 1: PO Box 930156
Street address state: WI
Postal code: 53593-0156
County: Dane
Country: USA
Office phone: (608) 274-5200
Office fax: (608) 848-5474

General e-mail: mary@ogarapub.com
Advertising e-mail: mary@ogarapub.com
Editorial e-mail: mary@ogarapub.com
Website: www.JourneyofAging.com
Year publication established: 1994
Advertising (open inch rate): Call for rates
Mechanical specifications: Type page 10 x 16; E - 4 cols, 2 1/4, 3/16 between; A - 3 cols, 2 1/4, 3/16 between.
Delivery methods: Mail`Racks
Zip Codes Served: 53744, 53704, 53705, 53711, 53713, 53714, 53715, 53716, 53717, 53719
Other Type of Frequency: Annually
Circulation Free: 20000
Audit By: Sworn/Estimate/Non-Audited
Audit Date: 12.07.2019
Presses: Sheet-fed offset press, Heat-Set Web
Software: In Design Photoshop
Editions Count: 20000
Edition Names: Journey of Aging
Note: Since 1994, OGara Publishing has been producing niche publications for readers in the Greater Madison area. We are a locally owned and family-operated business focused exclusively on the community here in Dane County, WI. We currently produce the Journey of Aging Guide annually each September. This publicationÂ is a valuable and practical referenceÂ tool for information regarding aging resources, services and products in this area. Our target market is aging adults, disabled adults, adult children of parents,caregivers, social workers, case managers and discharge nurses. In September 2014, we will distribute 20,000 glossy, 4-color copies at over 150 locations throughout Dane County. We provide restocking throughout the year. We printed 17,500 copies in 2013 and our stock was depleted as of early May 2014.
Personnel: Mary O'Gara (Owner)
Parent company: O'Gara Publishing
Main (survey) contact: Mary O'Gara

WACO

SENIORIFIC NEWS

Street address 1: PO Box 23307
Street address state: TX
Postal code: 76702-3307
County: McLennan
Country: USA
Mailing Address: PO Box 23307
Mailing city: Waco
Mailing state: TX
Mailing zip: 76702-3307
Office phone: (800) 736-7350
Office fax: (877) 736-7350
Advertising phone: (800) 736-7350

General e-mail: ads@seniorific.com
Advertising e-mail: Ads@Seniorific.com
Editorial e-mail: editor@Seniorific.com
Website: seniorific.com
Year publication established: 1988
Advertising (open inch rate): N/A
Mechanical specifications: Type page 10 x 13; E - 4 cols, 2 3/8, 1/8 between; A - 4 cols, 2 3/8, between; C - 4 cols, 2 3/8, between.
Delivery methods: Racks
Zip Codes Served: Texas
Digital Platform - Mobile: Apple`Android`Windows
Digital Platform - Tablet: Apple iOS`Android`Windows 7
Frequency: Mthly
Other Type of Frequency: n/a
Circulation Paid: 4000
Circulation Free: 478000

Senior Publications in the U.S.

Audit By: CVC
Audit Date: 12.12.2017
Editions Count: 24
Edition Names: 24 total covering DFW, Houston, Austin, San Antonio and many mid-size Texas markets
Personnel: Dan McNeil (Pub.); Michael Fincher; Donovan McNeil (COO)
Main (survey) contact: Dan McNeil

WARNER ROBINS

SENIOR NEWS

Street address 1: 115 Bigham Dr
Street address state: GA
Postal code: 31088-3749
County: Houston
Country: USA
Mailing Address: PO Box 8389
Mailing city: Warner Robins
Mailing state: GA
Mailing zip: 31095-8389
Office phone: (478) 929-3636
Office fax: (478) 929-4258

General e-mail: seniornewsga@aol.com
Advertising e-mail: seniornewsga@cox.net
Editorial e-mail: seniornewsga@cox.net
Website: www.seniornewsgeorgia.com
Year publication established: 1987
Advertising (open inch rate): Open inch rate $26.00
Mechanical specifications: Type page 10 x 14; E - 4 cols, 2 5/16, 1/4 between; A - 4 cols, 2 5/16, 1/4 between.
Delivery methods:
Mail`Newsstand`Carrier`Racks
Zip Codes Served: 30001 30002 30004 30005 30012 30013 30014 30019 30024 30025 30030 30032 30033 30034 30035 30038 30040 30041 30042 30043 30044 30045 30047 30054 30057 30058 30059 30060 30062 30064 30067 30068 30071 30073 30075 30076 30078 30080 30082 30083 30084 30087 30088 30092 30093 30094 30096 30097 30101 30102 30106 30110 30114 30115 30116 30117 30120 30121 30122 30126 30127 30132 30134 30135 30136 30141 30144 30152 30168 30176 30188 30189 30201 30213 30214 30215 30224 30236 30252 30253 30260 30263 30265 30268 30269 30274 30281 30291 30297 30303 30305 30306 30307 30308 30309 30310 30311 30312 30314 30315 30316 30317 30318 30319 30324 30327 30328 30329 30331 30334 30337 30338 30339 30341 30342 30344 30345 30346 30349 30350 30354 30360 30501 30503 30506 30507 30518 30519 30566 30601 30605 30606 30622 30655 30656 30666 3068029801 29803 29841 29860 30809 30813 30814 30824 30901 30904 30906 30907 30909 31008 31030 31052 31069 31088 31093 31201 31204 31206 31210 31211 31216 31217 31220
Frequency: Mthly
Circulation Paid: 50
Circulation Free: 38000
Audit By: Sworn/Estimate/Non-Audited
Audit Date: 12.07.2019
Hardware: eMac
Software: QuarkXPress 4.1 Adobe Photoshop 5.0 Adobe Acrobat 5.0 AppleWorks6
Note: Senior News is delivered in the Atlanta, Augusta, and Macon, Georgia Metro Areas. Individual market information available.
Personnel: Billy R. Tucker (President/Publisher)
Parent company: Byron Publishing Corp., Inc.
Main (survey) contact: Billy R. Tucker

WICHITA

THE ACTIVE AGE

Street address 1: 125 S West St
Street address 2: Ste 105
Street address state: KS
Postal code: 67213-2114
County: Sedgwick
Country: USA
Mailing Address: 125 S West St Ste 105
Mailing city: Wichita
Mailing state: KS
Mailing zip: 67213-2114
Office phone: (316) 942-5385
Office fax: (316) 946-9180

General e-mail: editor@theactiveage.com
Advertising e-mail: teresa@theactiveage.com
Editorial e-mail: fran@theactiveage.com
Website: www.theactiveage.com
Year publication established: 1979
Advertising (open inch rate): Open inch rate $45.70
Mechanical specifications: Type page 10 x 14; E - 4 cols, 2 1/3, 4/15 between; A - 4 cols, 2 1/3, 4/15 between; C - 4 cols, 2 1/3, 4/15 between.
Delivery methods: Mail`Racks
Zip Codes Served: Three counties – Butler, Harvey and Sedgwick in Kansas
Digital Platform - Mobile: Apple
Digital Platform - Tablet: Apple iOS`Other
Frequency: Mthly
Circulation Free: 58000
Audit By: Sworn/Estimate/Non-Audited
Audit Date: 12.07.2019
Software: Adobe/InDesign, Adobe/Photoshop.
Note: 'Active aging' was re-named 'the active age' and was re-designed. Both debuted in May 2015. The editorial content, when possible, is now based on current events with an emphasis on news.
Personnel: Fran Kentling (Editor/Publisher); Teresa Schmeid (Advertising Manager); Tammara Fogel (Business and media manager)
Main (survey) contact: Fran Kentling

WILLISTON

VERMONT MATURITY MAGAZINE

Street address 1: PO Box 1158
Street address state: VT
Postal code: 05495-1158
County: Chittenden
Country: USA
Mailing Address: PO Box 1158
Mailing city: Williston
Mailing state: VT
Mailing zip: 05495-1158
Office phone: (802) 872-9000
Office fax: (802) 872-0151
Advertising phone: (802) 872-9000 x118

General e-mail: vermontmaturity@aol.com
Advertising e-mail: vermontmaturity@aol.com
Editorial e-mail: vermontmaturity@aol.com
Website: www.vermontmaturity.com
Year publication established: 1993
Mechanical specifications: Type page 7 1/4 x 9 3/4; E - 3 cols, 2 1/4, 1/4 between; A - 3 cols, 2 1/4, 1/4 between.
Delivery methods: Mail`Racks
Digital Platform - Mobile:
Apple`Android`Windows`Blackberry`Other
Digital Platform - Tablet: Apple iOS`Android`Windows 7`Blackberry Tablet OS`Kindle`Nook`Kindle Fire`Other
Frequency: Mthly`Other
Other Type of Frequency: Spring, Summer, Fall, Winter, EXPO Guide issue
Circulation Free: 10000
Audit By: Sworn/Estimate/Non-Audited
Audit Date: 12.07.2019
Software: InDesign
Personnel: Marianne Apfelbaum (Ed & Pub); Paul Apfelbaum (Pub.)
Parent company: Williston Publishing & Promotions
Main (survey) contact: Marianne Apfelbaum

WORCESTER

FIFTY PLUS ADVOCATE

Street address 1: 131 Lincoln St
Street address state: MA
Postal code: 01605-2408
County: Worcester
Country: USA
Mailing Address: 131 Lincoln St
Mailing city: Worcester
Mailing state: MA
Mailing zip: 01605-2408
Office phone: (508) 752-2512
Office fax: (508) 752-9057
Advertising phone: (508) 752-2512 x128

Advertising e-mail: rcapellari@fiftyplusadvocate.com
Website: www.fiftyplusadvocate.com
Year publication established: 1975
Advertising (open inch rate): B+W Full Page $1700.00; 4-Color Full Page $1900.00
Mechanical specifications: Type page 10 x 12.75; E - 4 cols, 2 1/2, between; A - 6 cols, 1 1/2, between.
Delivery methods: Mail`Racks
Zip Codes Served: Central or Eastern MA

Frequency: Mthly

Circulation Free: 50000
Audit By: CVC
Audit Date: 19.10.2017

Editions Count: 2
Edition Names: FiftyPlus Advocate Central MA, Fiftyplus Advocate Eastern MA
Personnel: Philip Davis (Pub.); Stacy Lemay (Circ. Mgr.); Bonnie Adams (Mng. Ed.); Barbara Clifford (Sales Coord.); Sue Clapham (Art Dir.)
Parent company: FiftyPlus Media
Main (survey) contact: Bonnie Adams

ALTERNATE DELIVERY SERVICES

ALBANY

DISTRIBUTION UNLIMITED, INC.

Street Address: PO Box 98, Guilderland Center
State: NY
ZIP Code: 12085
County: Clark
Country: USA
General Phone: 518-355-3112
General Fax: 518-355-3636
General/National Adv. E-mail: dahl@galesi.com
Primary Website: www.distributionunlimited.com
Year Established: 1969
Personnel: David Ahl (Sales Rep.); Steven Ribet (Sales Rep)

ALEXANDRIA

ALEXANDRIA DAILY TOWN TALK

Street Address: 1201 3rd St
State: LA
ZIP Code: 71301-8246
County: Rapides
Country: USA
General Phone: (318) 487-6409
General Fax: (318) 487-2952
Primary Website: www.thetowntalk.com
Year Established: 1883
Personnel: Melissa Gregory (Breaking News Reporter); Melinda Martinez (Photo.); Jeff Mathews (Storyteller); Patrick Denofrio (Reg. Sales Dir.); Jim Smilie (News Dir.)

ALLEGAN

MIDWEST INDEPENDENT POSTAL

Street Address: 595 Jenner Dr
State: MI
ZIP Code: 49010-1516
County: Allegan
Country: USA
General Phone: (269) 673-2141
General Fax: (269) 673-6768
General/National Adv. E-mail: gerald.raab@flashespublishers.com
Primary Website: www.flashespublishers.com
Year Established: 1988
Personnel: Gerald Raab (Prodn. Mgr.)

ALLENTOWN

DIRECT MARKETING DISTRIBUTION

Street Address: 101 N 6th St
State: PA
ZIP Code: 18101-1403
County: Lehigh
Country: USA
General Phone: 610-841-2301
General Fax: 610-841-2306
Primary Website: www.mcall.com
Year Established: 1988
Personnel: Todd Wendling (Sales Manager); James Feher (Vice Pres.)

ANTIOCH

ADS DELIVERY, INC.

Street Address: 236 W II Route 173
State: IL
ZIP Code: 60002-1834
County: Lake
Country: USA
General Phone: (847) 395-7500
General Fax: (847) 395-2814
General/National Adv. E-mail: advertising@advertisernetwork.com
Primary Website: www.advertisernetwork.com
Year Established: 1976
Personnel: Kris Shepard (Administrative Dir.)

ATHENS

MESSENGER CONSUMER SERVICES

Street Address: 9300 Johnson Hollow Rd
State: OH

ZIP Code: 45701-9028
County: Athens
Country: USA
General Phone: (740) 592-6612
General Fax: (740) 592-4647
General/National Adv. E-mail: sbossart@athensmessenger.com
Primary Website: www.athensmessenger.com
Year Established: 1992
Personnel: Sherrie Bossart (Adv. Mgr.); Monica Nieporte (Pub.).

ATLANTA

ATLANTA JOURNAL-CONSTITUTION

Street Address: 223 Perimeter Center Pkwy NE
State: GA
ZIP Code: 30346-1301
County: Dekalb
Country: USA
General Phone: (404) 526-7003
General Fax: (404) 526-5746
Advertising Phone: (404) 577-5775
Editorial Phone: (404) 526-2161
Editorial Fax: (404) 526-5746
General/National Adv. E-mail: allen.dunstan@coxinc.com
Display Adv. Email: eric.myers@ajc.com
Classified Adv. Email: ajcclass@ajc.com
Editorial Email: newstips@ajc.com
Primary Website: www.ajc.com
Year Established: 1868
News Services: Cox News Service, AP, DJ, LAT-WP, NYT, MCT, CNS, CQ, NNS, PNS, SHNS, TMS.
Special Editions: Breast Cancer Education (Annually); Golf/Masters (Apr); Back to School (Aug); Holiday Gift Guides (Dec); Brides (Feb); Safety Vehicles (Jan); Peachtree Road Race (Jul); Executive Homes (Jun); Braves Baseball Preview (Mar); Fun in the Sun (May); Pulse (Mon
Special Weekly Sections: Food & Drink (Thur); Go Guide, Cars (Fri); AJC Cars (Sat); Homefinder, Business, Jobs (Sun)
Syndicated Publications: Color Comics (S).
Delivery Methods:
Mail`Newsstand`Carrier`Racks
Areas Served - City/County or Portion Thereof, or Zip codes: 30002 30004 30005 30008 30009 30011 30012 30013 30014 30016 30017 30018 30019 30021 30022 30024 30025 30028 30030 30032 30033 30034 30035 30038 30039 30040 30041 30043 30044 30045 30046 30047 30052 30054 30055 30056 30058 30060 30062 30064 30066 30067 30068 30071 30075 30076 30078 30079 30080 30082 30083 30084 30087 30088 30092 30093 30094 30096 30097 30101 30102 30103 30104 30105 30106 30107 30108 30110 30113 30114 30115 30116 30117 30120 30121 30122 30124 30125 30126 30127 30132 30134 30135 30137 30141 30143 30144 30145 30147 30152 30153 30157 30161 30165 30168 30170 30171 30172 30173 30176 30178 30179 30180 30183 30184 30185 30187 30188 30189 30204 30213 30214 30215 30220 30223 30228 30229 30233 30236 30238 30248 30250 30252 30253 30259 30260 30263 30265 30268 30269 30272 30273 30274 30276 30277 30281 30288 30290 30291 30294 30295 30296 30297 30303 30305 30306 30307 30308 30309 30310 30311 30312 30313 30314 30315 30316 30317 30318 30319 30320 30322 30324 30326 30327 30328 30329 30331 30334 30336 30337 30338 30339 30340 30341 30342 30344 30345 30346 30349 30350 30354 30360 30361 30363 30501 30504 30506 30507 30510 30517 30518 30519 30523 30525 30527 30528 30529 30533 30534 30542 30548 30549 30554 30564 30566 30577 30601 30605 30606 30607 30620 30621 30622 30642 30655 30656 30666 30677 30680 30683 30701 30733 31024 31029 31030 31061 31088 31201
Own Printing Facility?: Y
Commercial printers?: N
Advertising (Open Inch Rate) Weekday/Saturday: Open inch rate $566.00 (Mon-Wed); $585.00 (Thur-Sat)
Advertising (Open inch rate) Sunday: Open inch rate $755.00
Market Information: ADS; Split run; TMC; Zoned editions.
Mechanical available: Offset; Black and 3 ROP colors; insert accepted - zoned areas; page cutoffs - 21 1/4.
Mechanical specifications: Type page 12 5/8 x 21 1/4; E - 6 cols, 1 13/16, 1/8 between; A - 6 cols, 1 13/16, 1/8 between; C - 10 cols, 1 1/16, 1/8 between.
Published: Mon`Tues`Wed`Thur`Fri`Sat`Sun
Weekday Frequency: m
Saturday Frequency: m
Avg Paid Circ: 139864
Sat. Circulation Paid: 127777
Sun. Circulation Paid: 207476
Audit By: AAM
Audit Date: 30.06.2018
Pressroom Software: Lines – 4-TKS/(20 half decks; 4 satellites) (Gwinnett); 2-TKS/7000CD tower units (Gwinnett); 4-TKS/(20 half decks; 4 satellites) (Fulton); Folders – 8-TKS/(Fulton), 8-TKS/(Gwinnett); Reels & Stands – 40, 40.;
Mailroom Equipment: Counter Stackers – 13-SH/257 (Fulton), 16-QWI/300-350 (Gwinnett); Inserters & Stuffers – 1-NP/1472, 3-QWI/201, 4-QWI/200 (Reach), 2-GMA/SLS 2000 30:2 (Gwinnett), 1-GMA/SLS 2000 36:2 (Gwinnett), 1-QWI/400 (Reach); Tying Machines – 11-Si/Fulton, 14;
Buisness Equipment: IBM/9672 RC4
Buisness Software: CA, Global
Classified Equipment: Hardware – 145-IBM/3192, 2-Ad Star;
Classified Software: In-house.
Display Equipment: Hardware – IBM 9672; Other Hardware – IBM/7060H75
Display Software: Ad Make-up Applications – NW/Admarc, NW/Discuss; Layout Software – DTI/Speed Planner.
Editorial Equipment: Hardware – 620-APP/Mac, 175-APP/Mac Powerbook/18-Sun/Server, 2-Dell/Gu55 Server; Printers – HP, Xante, Canon
Editorial Software: DTI.
Production Equipment: Hardware – 4-KFM/Bender single width, 2-Cx/Bidco, Glunz & Jensen/K2; Cameras – 4-C/Spartan; Scanners – 1-Howtek, 2-ECR/1800, 2-ECR/Autokon 1000, 2-Pixel Craft (tab size), 1-Scitex/Smartscan, 1-Tecsa/TS2470, 1-Tecsa/TS2570
Personnel: Amy Chown (VP, Marketing); Laura Inman (Dir., Mktg. Devel.); Chris Hood (Mktg. Mgr., Classified/Territory); Amy Glennon (Pub.); Kevin Riley (Ed.); Eric Myers (VP, Adv. Sales); Allen Dunstan (Sr. Dir., Nat'l Accts.); Brian Cooper (Sr. VP, Finance & Business Op.); Mark Medici (Sr. VP, Audience & Group Lead for CMG Newspapers); Joe McKinnon (VP, Fulfillment)
Parent company (for newspapers): Cox Media Group
footnotes: General/National Adv. E-mail: SRDS (11/5/2014); Display Adv. E-mail: SRDS (11/5/2014); Special Weekly Sections: SRDS (11/5/2014); Advertising (Open Inch Rate) Weekday/Saturday: SRDS (11/5/2014); Advertising (Open inch rate) Sunday: SRDS (11/5/2014)

BATON ROUGE

THE ADVOCATE NEWSPAPER

Street Address: 7290 Bluebonnet Blvd
State: LA
ZIP Code: 70810-1611
County: East Baton Rouge
Country: USA
General Phone: (225) 383-1111
General Fax: (225) 388-0348
General/National Adv. E-mail: lruth@theadvocate.com
Primary Website: www.theadvocate.com
Year Established: 1992
Published: Mon`Tues`Wed`Thur`Fri`Sat`Sun
Avg Paid Circ: 43475
Avg Free Circ: 44244
Audit By: AAM
Audit Date: 31.03.2019
Personnel: Larry Ruth (Mgr., Customer Sales); Paul Fugarino (Distr. Mgr.)

BOGALUSA

ROBERSON ADVERTISING SERVICE, INC.

Street Address: 315 Industrial Parkway Drive
State: LA
ZIP Code: 70427-4493
County: Jefferson
Country: USA
General Phone: (985) 520-6059
General/National Adv. E-mail: justin.schuver@bogalusadailynews.com
Primary Website: www.robersonadvertising.com
Year Established: 1939
Personnel: Michael Roberson (Pres.); Joe Chambers (Ed.)

BRIDGEPORT

CONNECTICUT POST

Street Address: 410 State St
State: CT
ZIP Code: 06604-4501
County: Fairfield
Country: USA
General Phone: (203) 842-2500
General Fax: (203) 738-1230
General/National Adv. E-mail: circulation@ctpost.com
Primary Website: www.connpost.com
Personnel: John Alcott (Mng. Ed.); Ralph Hohman (Asst. Mng. Ed.); Randi Weiner (Asst. Mng. Ed.)

CEDAR RAPIDS

THE GAZETTE COMPANY

Street Address: 501 2nd Ave SE
State: IA
ZIP Code: 52401-1303
County: Linn
Country: USA
General Phone: (319) 398-8422
General Fax: (319) 368-8505
General/National Adv. E-mail: customercare@thegazettecompany.com
Primary Website: www.thegazettecompany.com
Year Established: 1981
Product or Service: Multimedia/Interactive Products`Publisher/Media
Personnel: Joe Hadky (Chrmn.); Chuck Peters (President and CEO); Chris Edwards (VP Sales & Marketing)
Newspapers (for newspaper groups): The Gazette, Cedar Rapids

THE PENNY SAVER

Street Address: 100 E Cumberland St
State: IA
ZIP Code: 52401
County: Linn
Country: USA
General Phone: (319) 398-8222
General Fax: (319) 398-5846
Primary Website: pennysaverguide.com
Personnel: Ron Bode (Adv. Dir.)

CHEEKTOWAGA

METRO GROUP, INC.

Street Address: 75 Boxwood Ln
State: NY
ZIP Code: 14227-2707
County: Erie
Country: USA
General Phone: (716) 668-5223
General Fax: (716) 668-4526
General/National Adv. E-mail: edit@metrowny.com
Primary Website: www.metrowny.com
Year Established: 1968
Personnel: Lorne Marshall (Ed.)
Newspapers (for newspaper groups): Alden Metro Source, Buffalo; Amherst / Getzville Smart Shopper, Buffalo; Amherst / Tonawanda Metro Source (OOB), Buffalo; Clarence Metro Source, Buffalo; Depew Metro Source, Buffalo; Eggertsville / Snyder Smart Shopper, Buffalo; Gowanda News, Buffalo; Kenmore / Tonawanda Source, Buffalo; Lancaster Source, Buffalo; Lockport Retailer, Buffalo; North Buffalo Smart Shopper, Buffalo; North Cheektowaga Source, Buffalo; North Tonawanda Source, Buffalo; South Buffalo Metro Source, Buffalo; South Cheektowaga Source, Buffalo; Springville Journal, Buffalo; The Sun and Erie County Independent, Hamburg; Williamsville Smart Shopper, Buffalo

CHICO

CHICO NEWS & REVIEW

Street Address: 353 East Second St.
State: CA
ZIP Code: 95928
General Phone: (775) 324-4440
General Fax: (530) 892-1111
General/National Adv. E-mail: grege@newsreview.com
Display Adv. Email: jamied@newsreview.com
Editorial Email: jeffv@newsreview.com
Primary Website: www.newsreview.com
Year Established: 1977
Published: Thur
Avg Free Circ: 40070
Audit By: CVC
Audit Date: 30.06.2018
Personnel: Deborah Redmond; Jeff Vonkaenel (Pub.); Jamie DeGarmo (Adv.); Greg Erwin (Circ.); Valentina Flynn (Prod.)

CINCINNATI

THE CINCINNATI ENQUIRER

Street Address: 312 Elm St
State: OH
ZIP Code: 45202-2739
County: Hamilton
Country: USA
General Phone: (513) 721-2700
Advertising Phone: (513) 768-8404
Advertising Fax: (513) 242-4366
Editorial Phone: (513) 768-8600
Editorial Fax: (513) 768-8340
General/National Adv. E-mail: abaston@enquirer.com
Display Adv. Email: abaston@enquirer.com
Classified Adv. Email: abaston@enquirer.com
Editorial Email: ltrujillo@cincinnati.com
Primary Website: www.cincinnati.com; www.enquirermedia.com
Year Established: 1841
News Services: AP, NYT, MCT, GNS.
Special Editions: Summer Vacations-Travel (Apr); Tennis Championships (Aug); Holiday Home Gift Guides (Dec); National Cruise Month Celebration (Feb); Warm Weather Travel Destinations (Jan); Regional Adventures (Jul); Homearama (Jun); Family Vacations (May); Holiday Gift Gu
Special Weekly Sections: Weather, Sports (Daily); Business, Sunday Forum, Good News, (Sun); Food, Classifieds (Wed); Healthy Living, Hometown (Thur); Weekend, Business (Fri); Home, Style, Hometown (Sat)
Syndicated Publications: USA WEEKEND Magazine (S).
Advertising (Open Inch Rate) Weekday/Saturday: Awareness C $817.00; Awareness D $1633.00; 1/12 Pg V $3,901.00
Advertising (Open Inch rate) Sunday: Awareness C $851.00; Awareness D $1703.00; 1/12 Pg V $4,068.00
Market Information: Split run; Zoned editions.
Mechanical available: Offset; Black and 3 ROP colors; insert accepted - based on sample submitted; page cutoffs - 22 3/4.
Mechanical specifications: Type page 11 5/8 x

Alternate Delivery Services

21 1/2; E - 7 cols, 1 1/2, 1/8 between; A - 6 cols, 1 13/16, 1/8 between; C - 10 cols, 1 3/32, 1/8 between.
Published: Mon`Tues`Wed`Thur`Fri`Sat`Sun
Weekday Frequency: m
Saturday Frequency: m
Avg Paid Circ: 84723
Sat. Circulation Paid: 84430
Sun. Circulation Paid: 133477
Audit By: AAM
Audit Date: 31.03.2018
Pressroom Software: Lines – 10-G/Metro (6 half decks) 1978; 10-G/Metro (6 half decks) 1978; 10-G/Metro (6 half decks) 1980; 10-G/Metro (6 half decks) 1988; Folders – 4-G/double.;
Mailroom Equipment: Counter Stackers – 4-QWI/200, 5-QWI/400; Inserters & Stuffers – 1-HI/1472, 1-HI/1372, AM Graphics/NP 630, 1/Magnapack; Tying Machines – 8-/Dynaric; Address Machine – 1-/Ch, X;
Buisness Equipment: IBM/AS-400 520, PC Micro, HP/9000
Buisness Software: Genesys
Classified Equipment: Hardware – SII/Server Net; SII/Coyote QB, SII/Coyote 22, SII/Coyote 3; Printers – Centronics/351, Dataproducts/LZR-2600, Tetromix/Phaser 780, HP/8500, HP/4050;
Classified Software: SII/Sys 55, C Text/ALPS Classified Pagination.
Display Equipment: Hardware – 16-APP/Mac 7500, 1-APP/Mac WGS 80, 1763-350; Printers – APP/Mac LaserWriter NTX, Textronix/Phaser 780 I, GEI Color Proofer;
Display Software: Ad Make-up Applications – APP/Mac Appleshare 4.0, First class/BBS software; Layout Software – Multi-Ad/Creator II.
Editorial Equipment: Hardware – Tandem/CLX/SII/Coyote QB, SII/Dakota, APP/Mac, SII/CAT-ST, SII/Coyote 22, SII/Coyote 3; Printers – Centronics/351, Dataproducts/LZR 2600, APP/Mac LaserWriter NTX, Xante/8200, Textronix/Phaser 300 I
Editorial Software: SII/Sys 55, SII/Sys 7
Production Equipment: Hardware – Nova Publishing/Faxaction, 2-AU/APS 6108, 2-AU/APS 3850, 1-HQ-110PM; Cameras – 2-C/Newspager; Scanners – 1-ECR/Autokon 1000, Tecsa/3050.
Personnel: Michael McCarter (Interim Editor); Denette Pfaffenberger (Group Dir/Home Delivery); Kate McGinty (Dir of News Content); Joe Powell (Dir. of Print Prod); Chris Strong (VP of Sales); Peter Bhatia (Ed. & VP of Audience Engagement); Jeff Lawson (Market Sales & Distribution Director); Libby Korosec (Client Strategy Director); John Berry (Major Sales & Marketing Manager)
Parent company (for newspapers): Gannett
footnotes: General/National Adv. E-mail: SRDS (10/23/2014); Display Adv. E-mail: SRDS (10/23/2014)

COLUMBUS
THE COLUMBUS DISPATCH
Street Address: 62 E. Broad St.
State: OH
ZIP Code: 43215
County: Delaware
Country: USA
General Phone: (877) 734-7728
General/National Adv. E-mail: mcampbell@dispatch.com
Primary Website: www.dispatch.com
Personnel: Bradley Harmon (Pub.); Allan Miller (Ed.)

DALLAS
WILLOW BEND COMMUNICATIONS, INC.
Street Address: 18333 Preston Rd
State: TX
ZIP Code: 75252-5466
County: Collin
Country: USA
General Phone: (972) 553-3600
General Fax: (972) 732-8807
General/National Adv. E-mail: info@willowbend.com; support@willowbend.com
Primary Website: www.willowbend.com
Year Established: 1988
Personnel: Steve Thompson (Pres); Layton Kolb (Cust Sup Mgr); Diane Thompson (CFO); Steven Lerch (Chief Software Engineer); Jim Schell (VP Bus Development)

DAYTON
DAYTON CITY PAPER
Street Address: STE 240
State: OH
ZIP Code: 45402-1766
County: Montgomery
Country: USA
General Phone: (937) 222-8855
Advertising Phone: (937) 222-8855 x 603
Editorial Phone: (937) 222-8855 x 604
General/National Adv. E-mail: contactus@daytoncitypaper.com
Display Adv. Email: advertising@daytoncitypaper.com
Editorial Email: editor@daytoncitypaper.com
Primary Website: www.daytoncitypaper.com
Year Established: 2003
Delivery Methods: Carrier`Racks
Areas Served - City/County or Portion Thereof, or Zip codes: Entire metro Dayton Ohio region
Published: Tues
Avg Free Circ: 20120
Audit By: Sworn/Estimate/Non-Audited
Audit Date: 12.07.2019
Personnel: Paul Noah (CEO, Dayton City Media); Wanda Esken (Publisher)
Parent company (for newspapers): Dayton City Media

DENVER
ROAD RUNNER COURIER
Street Address: 1760 Ulster St
State: CO
ZIP Code: 80220-2053
County: Denver
Country: USA
General Phone: (833) 303-7874
Primary Website: rrcourier.com
Year Established: 1970
Personnel: Arnold Rundiks (Pres.)

DETROIT
STANLEY ADVERTISING & DISTRIBUTING CO.
Street Address: 1947 W Fort St
State: MI
ZIP Code: 48216-1817
County: Wayne
Country: USA
General Phone: (313) 961-7177
General Fax: (734) 525-2340
General/National Adv. E-mail: stanleysadvertising@gmail.com
Primary Website: www.stanleysadvertising.com
Year Established: 1964
Personnel: Stanley Wojtalik (Pres.)

ELMWOOD PARK
CBA INDUSTIRES
Street Address: 669 River Dr., Ste 404
State: NJ
ZIP Code: 07407-1361
County: Bergen
Country: USA
General Phone: (201) 414-5260
General Fax: (201) 414-5201
General/National Adv. E-mail: tjcastello@cbaol.com
Display Adv. Email: etkohn@cbaol.com
Primary Website: cbaol.com
Year Established: 1962
Published: Wed
Avg Free Circ: 997330
Audit By: AAM
Audit Date: 30.09.2018
Personnel: Harold Matzner (Chrmn.); Barry Schiro (Pres.); Tom Castello (Market Mapping Specialist); Eva Kohn (Adv. Dir.); Nikki Schultz (Midwest Regional Sales Representative); Nick Passariello (Senior VP, Marketing); John Durante (Senior VP, Sales); Tim Brahney (VP, Sales)

ENGLEWOOD
YANKEE PEDDLER POSTAL SERVICE
Street Address: 3375 S Bannock St
State: CO
ZIP Code: 80110-2404
County: Arapahoe
Country: USA
General Phone: (303) 761-4200
General Fax: (303) 761-4291
General/National Adv. E-mail: addenver@aol.com
Primary Website: http://www.yankeepeddlerpostal.com/
Personnel: John Minger (Treasurer)

FARMINGDALE
PUBLISHERS CIRCULATION FULFILLMENT INC.
Street Address: 303 Smith St, Ste. 1
State: NY
ZIP Code: 11735-1110
County: Suffolk
Country: USA
General Phone: (631) 2703133
General/National Adv. E-mail: sales@pcfcorp.com
Primary Website: www.pcfcorp.com
Industry: Newspaper Distribution Technology Services
Personnel: Jerry Giordana (Pres./CEO); Tom Dressler (VP of Growth and Development); James Cunningham

FORT WORTH
FORT WORTH WEEKLY
Street Address: 3311 Hamilton Ave
State: TX
ZIP Code: 76107-1877
County: Tarrant
Country: USA
General Phone: (817) 321-9700
General Fax: (817) 321-9733
Advertising Phone: (817) 321-9700
Advertising Fax: (817) 321-9733
Editorial Phone: (817) 321-9700
Editorial Fax: (817) 321-9575
General/National Adv. E-mail: Michael.Newquist@fwweekly.com
Display Adv. Email: Brian.Martin@fwweekly.com
Editorial Email: Gayle.Reaves@fwweekly.com
Primary Website: www.fwweekly.com
Year Established: 1994
Delivery Methods: Mail`Racks
Areas Served - City/County or Portion Thereof, or Zip codes: Tarrant County
Advertising (Open Inch Rate) Weekday/Saturday: Open inch rate $18.25
Published: Wed
Avg Free Circ: 23064
Audit By: VAC
Audit Date: 31.05.2017
Personnel: Gayle Reaves (Ed.); Michael Newquist (Adv. Dir.); Brian Martin (Classified Adv. Dir.); Eric Griffey

GREEN BAY
GREEN BAY COMMUNITY NEWS (EAST/WEST)
Street Address: 133 S Monroe Ave
State: WI
ZIP Code: 54301-4056
County: Brown
Country: USA
General Phone: (920) 432-2941
General Fax: (920) 432-8581
General/National Adv. E-mail: chronicle@itol.com
Primary Website: www.greenbaynewschronicle.com
Year Established: 1972
Personnel: Al Rasmussen (Vice Pres.); Keith Davis (Circ. Mgr.)

HAWKESBURY
CIE D'EDITION ANDRE PAQUETTE, INC.
Street Address: 1100 Aberdeen C.P.
State: ON
ZIP Code: K6A 1K7
County: Canada
General Phone: (613) 632-4155
General Fax: (613) 632-6383
General/National Adv. E-mail: francois.legault@eap.on.ca
Primary Website: editionap.ca
Year Established: 1947
Personnel: Bertrand Castonguay (Pres.); Francois Legault (Mng. Ed.)
Newspapers (for newspaper groups): L'argenteuil, Lachute; Le Carillon, Hawkesbury; Tribune Express, Hawkesbury; Vision; Le Reflet/News

HERMOSA BEACH
EASY READER
Street Address: PO Box 427
State: CA
ZIP Code: 90254-0427
County: Los Angeles
Country: USA
General Phone: (310) 372-4611
General Fax: (424) 212-6708
General/National Adv. E-mail: easyreader@easyreader.info
Display Adv. Email: classifiedads@easyreader.info; displayads@easyreader.info
Editorial Email: news@easyreader.info
Primary Website: http://www.easyreadernews.com/
Year Established: 1970
Delivery Methods: Mail`Newsstand`Carrier`Racks
Areas Served - City/County or Portion Thereof, or Zip codes: 90254, 90266, 90277, 90288, 90245. 90272, 90274
Advertising (Open Inch Rate) Weekday/Saturday: Open inch rate $20.00
Mechanical specifications: Type page 10 1/2 x 11 1/2; E - 4 cols, 2 1/4, 1/6 between; A - 4 cols, 2 1/4, 1/6 between; C - 7 cols, 1 1/4, 1/6 between.
Published: Thur
Avg Paid Circ: 27684
Audit By: AAM
Audit Date: 31.03.2015
Note: Easy Reader is the largest circulation, weekly newspaper serving the South Bay area of Los Angeles.
Personnel: Kevin Cody (Adv. Mgr.); Amy Berg (Dispaly Sales); Erin McCoy (Display Sales); Tami Quattrone (Classifieds); Bondo Wyszpolski (Arts/Entertainment Ed.); Mark McDermott (News Ed.); Graciela Huerta (Prodn. Dir.); Richard Budman
Parent company (for newspapers): C-VILLE Holdings LLC

HYDE PARK
CARRIGAN ADVERTISING

CARRIERS, INC.
Street Address: 40 Walnut St
State: MA
ZIP Code: 02136-2732
County: Suffolk
Country: USA
General Phone: (617) 361-1950
General Fax: (617) 361-1995
Year Established: 1932
Personnel: James Carrigan (Pres.)

LEBANON

KAPP ADVERTISING SERVICE, INC.
Street Address: 100 E Cumberland St
State: PA
ZIP Code: 17042-5400
County: Lebanon
Country: USA
General Phone: (717) 273-8127
General Fax: (717) 273-0420
General/National Adv. E-mail: sales@themerchandiser.com
Primary Website: www.themerchandiser.com
Year Established: 1950
Personnel: Valerie Stokes (Gen. Mgr.); Joanne Walkinshaw (Circ. Mgr.); Randy Miller (General Sales Manager)

LEXINGTON

COMMUNITY DELIVERY SERVICE
Street Address: 1010 E New Circle Rd
State: KY
ZIP Code: 40505-4117
County: Fayette
Country: USA
General Phone: (859) 231-3382
General Fax: (859) 231-3450
Year Established: 1989

LIVONIA

VALASSIS
Street Address: 19975 Victor Pkwy
State: MI
ZIP Code: 48152-7001
County: Wayne
Country: USA
General Phone: (734) 591-3000
Primary Website: www.valassis.com
Year Established: 1970
Personnel: Rob Mason (Pres. & CEO); Larry Berg (VP of ROP Sales); Ron Goolsby (Chief Operating Officer); Brian Husselbee (President and CEO, NCH Marketing Services, Inc.); Donna Schelby; Jeff Price (FSI Project Mgr.); Dave Safford (Sales Exec.); Laura Narbut (Senior Buyer); Bridget Rabel (Senior Buyer); Ruth Williams (Senior Buyer); Tracie Pollet (Senior Client Marketing Mgr.); Janene Graham (Senior Newspaper Specialist); Greg Bogich (Senior VP of Digital Media); Barry Haselden (VP Media Services); Tim Garvey (VP, Integrated Media Sales); Debbie Gauthier; Lisa Kershaw (Client Liason Manager); Lesa Kirkman (Sales Director); Kathy Trumbo (Manager, Media Services)

MEMPHIS

THE DAILY NEWS
Street Address: 193 Jefferson Ave
State: TN
ZIP Code: 38103-2322
County: Shelby
Country: USA
General Phone: (901) 523-1561
General Fax: (901) 526-5813
Advertising Phone: (901) 528-5283
Advertising Fax: (901) 526-5813
Editorial Phone: (901) 523-8501
Editorial Fax: (901) 526-5813
General/National Adv. E-mail: jjenkins@memphisdailynews.com
Display Adv. Email: jjenkins@memphisdailynews.com
Classified Adv. Email: jjenkins@memphisdailynews.com
Editorial Email: releases@memphisdailynews.com
Primary Website: www.memphisdailynews.com
Year Established: 1886
News Services: CNS
Delivery Methods: Mail
Areas Served - City/County or Portion Thereof, or Zip codes: Madison, Tipton, Fayette, Shelby
Advertising (Open Inch Rate) Weekday/Saturday: Open inch rate $13.50 (legal)
Online Advertising Rates - CPM (cost per thousand) by Size: Leaderboard (728x90): $550/month; Side Position (250x250): $400/month
Published: Mon`Tues`Wed`Thur`Fri
Weekday Frequency: m
Avg Paid Circ: 1000
Avg Free Circ: 2000
Audit By: Sworn/Estimate/Non-Audited
Audit Date: 12.07.2019
Personnel: Don Fancher (Public Notices); Janice Jenkins (Adv. Dir.); Terry Hollahan (Associate Publisher/Exec. Ed.)
Parent company (for newspapers): The Daily News Publishing Co.

MILWAUKEE

JOURNAL/SENTINEL, INC.
Street Address: 333 W State St
State: WI
ZIP Code: 53203-1305
County: Milwaukee
Country: USA
General Phone: (414) 224-2000
General Fax: (414) 224-2485
Primary Website: www.jsonline.com
Year Established: 1882
Personnel: George Stanley (Vice Pres., Ed.); John Diedrich (Investigative Reporter/Assistant Editor); Bob Dohr (Ed.); Chuck Melvin (Asst. Mng. Ed.)

MINNEAPOLIS

CITY PAGES
Street Address: 800 N 1st St, Ste 300
State: MN
ZIP Code: 55401-1387
County: Hennepin
Country: USA
General Phone: (612) 372-3700
General Fax: (612) 372-3737
General/National Adv. E-mail: adinfo@citypages.com
Primary Website: www.citypages.com
Advertising (Open Inch Rate) Weekday/Saturday: Open inch rate $61.00
Mechanical specifications: Type page 4 x 12.375; E - 4 cols, 2 2/5, 1/6 between; A - 6 cols, 1 9/16, 1/6 between; C - 8 cols, 1 3/16, 1/6 between.
Published: Wed
Avg Free Circ: 112025
Audit By: Sworn/Estimate/Non-Audited
Audit Date: 12.07.2019
Personnel: Tom Imberston (Circ. Mgr.); Kevin Hoffman (Ed. in Chief); Matt Smith (Mng. Ed.); Doug Snow (Prodn. Mgr.); Mary Erickson (Editor)

MOUNT VERNON

MARKETING INFORMATION DISTRIBUTION SERVICE
Street Address: 18 E Vine St
State: OH
ZIP Code: 43050-3226
County: Knox
Country: USA
General Phone: (740) 397-5333
General Fax: (740) 397-1321
General/National Adv. E-mail: csplain@mountvernonnews.com
Primary Website: www.mountvernonnews.com
Year Established: 1983
Personnel: Kay H. Culbertson (Pub.); Michael P. McNichols (MIDS Mgr.)

NASHUA

THE TELEGRAPH
Street Address: 110 Main St., Suite 1
State: NH
ZIP Code: 03060
County: Hillsborough
Country: USA
General Phone: (603) 594-1200
General Fax: (603) 882-5138
General/National Adv. E-mail: news@nashuatelegraph.com
Primary Website: www.nashuatelegraph.com
Year Established: 1832
Personnel: Heather Henline (Pub.); Matt Burdette (Ed-in-Cheif); Shawn Paulus (Circ. Dir.); Lynda Vallatini (Ad Director)

NEPTUNE

ADDRESSES UNLIMITED
Street Address: 3600 Hwy 66
State: NJ
ZIP Code: 7754
County: Monmouth
Country: USA
General Phone: (732) 922-6000
General Fax: (732) 643-3719
General/National Adv. E-mail: editors@app.com
Primary Website: www.app.com
Year Established: 1991
Personnel: Sam Sicliano (Vice Pres.)

NEWPORT NEWS

DAILY PRESS PORCH PLUS
Street Address: 7505 Warwick Blvd
State: VA
ZIP Code: 23607-1517
County: Newport News City
Country: USA
General Phone: (757) 247-4600
General Fax: (757) 245-7113
Primary Website: www.dailypress.com
Year Established: 1990
Personnel: Timothy Ryan (Pres./CEO/Pub.)

OKLAHOMA CITY

OKLAHOMA GAZETTE
Street Address: 3701 N Shartel Ave
State: OK
ZIP Code: 73118-7102
County: Oklahoma
Country: USA
General Phone: (405 605-6789
General Fax: (405) 528-4600
Display Adv. Email: advertising@tierramediagroup.com
Primary Website: www.okgazette.com
Year Established: 1979
Delivery Methods: Racks
Advertising (Open Inch Rate) Weekday/Saturday: Open inch rate $58
Mechanical specifications: Type page 10.25 x 12.25 Advertising - 4 columns, 2.2" wide with 1/8" between Classifeds - 6 columns, 1.5" wide with 1/16" between
Published: Wed
Avg Paid Circ: 0
Avg Free Circ: 36082
Audit By: VAC
Audit Date: 31.12.2016
Personnel: Peter Brzycki (Publisher)

OMAHA

R-J DELIVERY SYSTEMS, INC.
Street Address: 4535 Leavenworth Street , Ste 9
State: NE
ZIP Code: 68106
County: Washington
Country: USA
General Phone: (402) 345-2778
General/National Adv. E-mail: paul@rjdeliveryomaha.com
Primary Website: www.rjdeliveryomaha.com
Year Established: 1978
Personnel: Paul Green (Sales Rep.)

PLATTEVILLE

WOODWARD PRINTING SERVICES
Street Address: 11 Means Dr
State: WI
ZIP Code: 53818-3829
County: Grant
Country: USA
General Phone: (608) 348-2817
General Fax: (608) 348-2816
General/National Adv. E-mail: woodwardprint@wcinet.com
Primary Website: http://www.woodwardprinting.com/
Year Established: 1994
Personnel: Marty Tloessl (Gen. Mgr.)

RENO

RENO NEWS & REVIEW
Street Address: 760 Margrave Drive, Ste. 100
State: NV
ZIP Code: 89502
General Phone: (775) 324-4440
General Fax: (775) 324-2515
Primary Website: www.newsreview.com
Personnel: Deborah Redmond; Brad Bynum (Editor); Michael Gelbman (Sales Manager); Elisabeth Bayard-Arthur (Design Manager)

RICHMOND

RICHMOND DELIVERY SERVICE
Street Address: 7500 Ranco Rd
State: VA
ZIP Code: 23228-3750
County: Henrico
Country: USA
General Phone: (804) 775-2723
General Fax: (804) 775-2801
General/National Adv. E-mail: rneely@timesdispatch.com
Primary Website: www.timesdispatch.com
Year Established: 1992
Personnel: Richard Neeley (Sales Mgr.); Tom Smith (Metro Home Delivery Mgr.); Raymond Bruett (Circ. Dir.)

SACRAMENTO

ADCO MARKETING
Street Address: 5580 Power Inn Rd
State: CA
ZIP Code: 95820-6748
County: Sacramento
Country: USA
General Phone: (916) 388-1101
General Fax: (916) 388-1040
Personnel: Dick Avery (Pres.)

BEE NICHE PRODUCTS
Street Address: 2100 Q St
State: CA
ZIP Code: 95816-6816
County: Sacramento
Country: USA
General Phone: (916) 321-1000
General Fax: (916) 326-5578

Alternate Delivery Services

General/National Adv. E-mail: jpaquette@sacbee.com
Primary Website: www.sacbee.com
Year Established: 1983
Personnel: Linda Brooks (Vice-President, Human Resources)
Parent company (for newspapers): The McClatchy Company

SACRAMENTO NEWS & REVIEW

Street Address: 1124 Del Paso Blvd
State: CA
ZIP Code: 95815-3607
County: Sacramento
Country: USA
General Phone: (916) 498-1234
General Fax: (916) 498-7910
Advertising Phone: (916) 498-1234
Advertising Fax: (916) 498-7910
Editorial Phone: (916) 498-1234
Editorial Fax: (916) 498-7910
General/National Adv. E-mail: sacdofi@newsreview.com
Display Adv. Email: snradinfo@newsreview.com
Editorial Email: sactonewstips@newsreview.com
Primary Website: https://www.newsreview.com/sacramento
Year Established: 1989
Special Weekly Sections: medical cannabis
Delivery Methods: Mail`Newsstand`Racks
Areas Served - City/County or Portion Thereof, or Zip codes: 95602, 95603, 95605, 95608, 95610, 95616, 95618, 95619, 95621, 95624, 95626, 95628, 95630, 95648, 95650, 95652, 95655, 95658, 95660, 95661, 95662, 95663, 95667, 95670, 95673, 95677, 95678, 95682, 95691, 95693, 95695, 95742, 95746, 95747, 95757, 95758, 95762, 95765, 95776, 95811, 95814, 95815, 95816, 95817, 95818, 95819, 95820, 95821, 95822, 95823, 95824, 95825, 95826, 95827, 95828, 95829, 95831, 95832, 95833, 95834, 95835, 95837, 95838, 95841, 95842, 95843, 95864, 95945, 95949, 95959.
Commercial printers?: Y
Advertising (Open Inch Rate) Weekday/Saturday: Open inch rate $50.00
Mechanical specifications: Full page 10" x 10.5", 5 column and 8 column formats available
Published: Thur
Avg Free Circ: 68251
Audit By: CVC
Audit Date: 30.06.2018
Note: Chico Community Publishing, Inc is the parent company of Sacramento News & Review (SN&R), Chico News & Review (CN&R), Reno News & Review (RN&R) and N&R Publications
Personnel: Greg Erwin (Dist. Dir); Jeff von Kaenel (Pres.); Deborah Redmond (COO); Michael Gelbman (Sales Mgr.); Chris Terrazas (Design Mgr.)
Parent company (for newspapers): Chico Community Publishing, Inc.

SAINT LOUIS

THE RIVERFRONT TIMES

Street Address: 308 N 21st St
State: MO
ZIP Code: 63103-1642
County: Saint Louis City
Country: USA
General Phone: (314) 754-5966
General Fax: (314) 754-5955
Advertising Phone: (314) 754-5932
Advertising Fax: (314) 754-6449
Editorial Phone: (314) 754-6404
Editorial Fax: (314) 754-6416
General/National Adv. E-mail: Letters@riverfronttimes.com
Display Adv. Email: colin.bell@riverfronttimes.com
Editorial Email: tips@riverfronttimes.com
Primary Website: www.riverfronttimes.com
Year Established: 1977
Delivery Methods: Mail`Racks
Areas Served - City/County or Portion Thereof, or Zip codes: 63101, 63102, 63103, 63104, 63105, 63106, 63107, 63108, 63109, 63110, 63111, 63112, 63113, 63114, 63115, 63116, 63118, 63120
Advertising (Open Inch Rate) Weekday/Saturday: Open inch rate $57.62
Mechanical specifications: Type page 9.72 x 10.75
Published: Wed
Avg Paid Circ: 297
Avg Free Circ: 55000
Audit By: Sworn/Estimate/Non-Audited
Audit Date: 12.07.2019
Personnel: Kevin Powers (Circ. Mgr.); Sarah Fenske (Editor in Chief); Chris Keating (Publisher)
Parent company (for newspapers): Euclid Media Group

SAN ANTONIO

HARTE-HANKS

Street Address: 9601 McAllister Freeway, Ste. 610
State: TX
ZIP Code: 78216
Country: USA
General Phone: 210-829-9000
Primary Website: www.hartehanks.com
Year Established: 1978
Personnel: Tom Ugast (Gen. Mgr.)

SAN ANTONIO CURRENT

Street Address: 915 Dallas St
State: TX
ZIP Code: 78215-1433
County: Bexar
Country: USA
General Phone: (210) 227-0044
General Fax: (210) 227-7555
Primary Website: www.sacurrent.com
Year Established: 1986
Delivery Methods: Newsstand
Advertising (Open Inch Rate) Weekday/Saturday: Open inch rate $9.25
Mechanical specifications: Type page 10 x 12 1/2; E - 4 cols, 2 1/4, 1/20 between; A - 4 cols, 2 1/4, 1/20 between; C - 8 cols, 1 1/5, 1/20 between.
Published: Wed
Avg Free Circ: 19378
Audit By: VAC
Audit Date: 30.09.2015
Personnel: Michael Wagner (Publisher); Greg Harman (Advertising Director)

SAN JOSE

A & A DISTRIBUTION, INC.

Street Address: 1780 Rogers Ave
State: CA
ZIP Code: 95112-1109
County: Santa Clara
Country: USA
General Phone: (408) 436-2300
General Fax: (408) 436-0844
General/National Adv. E-mail: maustinjr2@gmail.com
Primary Website: www.aa-distribution.net
Year Established: 1970
Personnel: Manuel Austin (Pres.)

SANTA ANA

SPECIALIZED MARKETING SERVICES

Street Address: 3421 W Segerstrom Ave
State: CA
ZIP Code: 92704-6404
County: Orange
Country: USA
General Phone: (949) 553-0890
General Fax: (949) 553-0891
Primary Website: www.teamsms.com
Year Established: 1988

SPOKANE

NEW MEDIA VENTURE

Street Address: 999 W Riverside Ave
State: WA
ZIP Code: 99201-1005
County: Spokane
Country: USA
Personnel: Shaun Higgins (CEO)

STERLING

DHL SMART & GLOBAL MAIL

Street Address: 21240 Ridgetop Cir, Ste 160
State: VA
ZIP Code: 20166-6560
County: Loudoun
Country: USA
General Phone: (703) 463-2200
General Fax: (800) 455-6615
Primary Website: www.globalmail.com

TUCSON

TUCSON NEWSPAPERS/TMC

Street Address: 4850 S Park Ave
State: AZ
ZIP Code: 85714-1637
County: Pima
Country: USA
General Phone: (520) 573-4167
General Fax: (520) 807-8418
General/National Adv. E-mail: adserv@azstarnet.com
Primary Website: www.azstarnet.com
Personnel: Circ. Dept. (Circ.); Adv. Dept. (Adv.)

VANCOUVER

THE COLUMBIAN ALTERNATE DELIVERY SERVICE

Street Address: 701 W 8th St
State: WA
ZIP Code: 98660-3008
County: Clark
Country: USA
General Phone: (360) 694-3391
General Fax: (360) 735-4605
Primary Website: www.columbian.com
Year Established: 1890
Personnel: Marc Dailey (Circ. Dir.); Rachel Rose (Circ. Mgr., Promo./Sales)

VICTORVILLE

DAILY PRESS

Street Address: 13891 Park Ave
State: CA
ZIP Code: 92392-2435
County: San Bernardino
Country: USA
General Phone: (760) 241-7744
General Fax: (760) 241-7145
Advertising Phone: (760) 951-6288
Advertising Fax: (760) 241-7145
Editorial Phone: (760) 951-6270
Editorial Fax: (760) 241-7145
General/National Adv. E-mail: rlipscomb@vvdailypress.com
Display Adv. Email: acallahan@vvdailypress.com
Classified Adv. Email: acallahan@vvdailypress.com
Editorial Email: DKeck@vvdailypress.com
Primary Website: www.vvdailypress.com
Year Established: 1937
Advertising (Open Inch Rate) Weekday/Saturday: Open inch rate $40
Published: Mon`Tues`Wed`Thur`Fri`Sat`Sun
Weekday Frequency: m
Saturday Frequency: m
Avg Paid Circ: 8877
Avg Free Circ: 437
Sat. Circulation Paid: 8877
Sat. Circulation Free: 437
Sun. Circulation Paid: 10443
Sun. Circulation Free: 312
Audit By: AAM
Audit Date: 31.12.2018
Personnel: Steve Hunt (Pub.); Mario Mejia (Circ. Mgr.); Steve Nakutin (Interim Advertising Mgr.); Jason Vrtis (Ed.)
Parent company (for newspapers): Gatehouse Media, LLC

VIRGINIA BEACH

HOME EXPRESS

Street Address: 5457 Greenwich Rd
State: VA
ZIP Code: 23462-6539
County: Virginia Beach City
Country: USA
General Phone: (757) 446-2890
General Fax: (757) 499-1966
Year Established: 1984

WEST VALLEY CITY

MEDIA ONE OF UTAH

Street Address: 4770 S 5600 W
State: UT
ZIP Code: 84118-7400
County: Salt Lake
Country: USA
General Phone: (801) 204-6151
General Fax: 801-204-6399
Primary Website: www.mediaoneutah.com
Year Established: 2006

Personnel: Hal Mortensen (Vice President Circulation Operations)

NEWSPAPER BROKERS AND APPRAISERS

ADA

NATIONAL MEDIA ASSOCIATES

Street address 1: PO Box 849
State: OK
ZIP Code: 74821-0849
County: Pontotoc
Country: USA
Mailing address: PO Box 849
Mailing city: Ada
Mailing state: OK
Mailing zip: 74821-0849
General Phone: (580) 421-9600
General Fax: (580) 272-5070
Email: bolitho@nationalmediasales.com
Website: www.nationalmediasales.com
Year Established: 1995
Note:
Personnel: Thomas Bolitho (Pres.)
Personnel: Edward Anderson (Pres.)

ASSONET

FRENCH, BARRY

Street address 1: 3 Ashlawn Rd
State: MA
ZIP Code: 02702-1105
County: Bristol
Country: USA
Mailing address: 3 Ashlawn Rd
Mailing city: Assonet
Mailing state: MA
Mailing zip: 02702-1105
General Phone: (508) 644-5772
Email: barryfrench@yahoo.com
Year Established: 1986
Personnel: Barry French (Pres.)

ATLANTA

MEDIA AMERICA BROKERS

Street address 1: 1130 Piedmont Ave NE
Street address 2: Apt 912
State: GA
ZIP Code: 30309-3783
County: Fulton
Country: USA
General Phone: (404) 875-8787
Email: lonwwilliams@aol.com
Year Established: 1989
Personnel: Lon W Williams (Owner)

AUSTIN

ASSOCIATED TEXAS NEWSPAPERS, INC.

Street address 1: 4100 Jackson Ave
Street address 2: Apt 460
State: TX
ZIP Code: 78731-6067
County: Travis
Country: USA
Mailing address: 4100 Jackson Ave Apt 460
Mailing city: Austin
Mailing state: TX
Mailing zip: 78731-6067
General Phone: (512) 407-8283
General Fax: (512) 407-8289
Email: Billberger@austin.rr.com
Website: www.hondoanvilherald.com
Year Established: 1886
Personnel: Bill Berger (Pres.)
Personnel: Jeff Berger (Vice Pres.)

BRANSON

NATIONAL MEDIA ASSOCIATES

Street address 1: PO Box 2001
State: MO
ZIP Code: 65615-2001
County: Taney
Country: USA
Mailing address: PO Box 2001
Mailing city: Branson
Mailing state: MO
Mailing zip: 65615-2001
General Phone: (417) 338-6397
General Fax: (417) 338-6510
Email: Brokered1@gmail.com
Website: www.nationalmediasales.com
Year Established: 1997
Services: Brokers & Appraisers; Consulting Services: Financial;
Personnel: Edward M. Anderson (Owner)

CARROLL

KNOWLES MEDIA BROKERAGE SERVICES

Street address 1: PO Box 910
State: IA
ZIP Code: 51401-0910
County: Carroll
Country: USA
Mailing address: PO Box 910
Mailing city: Carroll
Mailing state: IA
Mailing zip: 51401-0910
General Phone: (712) 792-2179
General Fax: (712) 792-2309
Email: gregg.knowles@netzero.com
Website: www.media-broker.com
Year Established: 1987
Personnel: Gregg Knowles (Owner)

DALLAS

RICKENBACHER MEDIA

Street address 1: 6731 Desco Dr
State: TX
ZIP Code: 75225-2704
County: Dallas
Country: USA
Mailing address: 6731 Desco Dr
Mailing city: Dallas
Mailing state: TX
Mailing zip: 75225-2704
General Phone: (214) 384 2779
Email: rmedia@msn.com
Website: www.rickenbachermedia.com
Year Established: 1985
Services: Brokers & Appraisers
Personnel: Ted Rickenbacher (Pres./Exec. Dir.)
Personnel: Jim Afinowich (Western States Dir.)

DANVILLE

CBS ASSOCIATES

Street address 1: 423 Sutton Cir
State: CA
ZIP Code: 94506-1154
County: Contra Costa
Country: USA
Mailing address: 423 Sutton Cir
Mailing city: Danville
Mailing state: CA
Mailing zip: 94506-1154
General Phone: (925) 736-6350
General Fax: (925) 736-3034
Personnel: Carl B. Shaver (Contact)

FOLSOM

GOLD COUNTY ADVISORS, INC.

Street address 1: 604 Sutter St
Street address 2: Ste 394
State: CA
ZIP Code: 95630-2698
County: Sacramento
Country: USA
Mailing address: 604 Sutter St Ste 394
Mailing city: Folsom
Mailing state: CA
Mailing zip: 95630-2698
General Phone: (916) 673-9778
General Fax: (888) 933-0807
Email: jeff@goldcountryadvisors.com
Website: www.goldcountryadvisors.com
Year Established: 2003
Services: Brokers & Appraisers, Merger & Acquisition Advisors for the newspaper business.
Personnel: Jeffrey Potts (Principal)

HADDONFIELD

HEMPSTEAD & CO., INC.

Street address 1: 807 N Haddon Ave
State: NJ
ZIP Code: 08033-1749
County: Camden
Country: USA
Mailing address: 807 N Haddon Ave Ste 214
Mailing city: Haddonfield
Mailing state: NJ
Mailing zip: 08033-1749
General Phone: (856) 795-6026
General Fax: (856) 795-4911
Email: jeh@hempsteadco.com
Website: www.hempsteadco.com
Personnel: Mark Penny (Mng. Dir.)

HELENA

CRIBB, GREENE & COPE LLC

Street address 1: 825 Great Northern Blvd
Street address 2: Ste 202
State: MT
ZIP Code: 59601-3340
County: Lewis And Clark
Country: USA
Mailing address: 825 Great Northern Blvd
Mailing city: Helena
Mailing state: MT
Mailing zip: 59601
General Phone: (406) 579-2925
General Fax: (866) 776-8010
Email: jcribb@cribb.com
Website: www.cribb.com
Year Established: 1923
Personnel: John Cribb (Managing Dir.)
Personnel: Gary Greene (Managing Dir.)
Personnel: Randy Cope (Dir.)
Personnel: John Thomas Cribb (Assoc.)

LAWRENCEVILLE

CAPITAL ENDEAVORS, INC.

Street address 1: 232 W Crogan St
Street address 2: Ste C
State: GA
ZIP Code: 30046-4853
County: Gwinnett
Country: USA
Mailing address: PO Box 895
Mailing city: Lawrenceville
Mailing state: GA
Mailing zip: 30046-0895
General Phone: (770) 962-8399
General Fax: (770) 962-8640
Email: davidstill@capitalendeavors.com
Website: www.capitalendeavors.com
Personnel: David R. Still (Pres.)

MANAGEMENT PLANNING, INC.

Street address 1: 1000 Lenox Drive
State: NJ
ZIP Code: 08648
County: Mercer
Country: USA
Mailing address: 1000 Lenox Drive
Mailing city: Lawrenceville
Mailing state: NJ
Mailing zip: 08648
General Phone: (609) 924-4200
Email: jgitto@mpival.com
Website: www.mpival.com
Personnel: Mark E. Lingerfield (Senior Vice President)
Personnel: Joseph C. Hassan (Vice President)

LEBANON

HARVEY, FAYE

Street address 1: PO Box 1410
State: MO
ZIP Code: 65536-1410
County: Laclede
Country: USA
Mailing address: PO Box 1410
Mailing city: Lebanon
Mailing state: MO
Mailing zip: 65536-1410
General Phone: (417) 532-4809
Email: f_harvey@hotmail.com
Personnel: Faye Harvey (Broker)

NEW YORK

ADMEDIA PARTNERS, INC.

Street address 1: 3 Park Ave
Street address 2: Fl 31
State: NY
ZIP Code: 10016-5902
County: New York
Country: USA
General Phone: (212) 759-1870
General Fax: (212) 888-4960
Email: info@admediapartners.com
Website: www.admediapartners.com
Year Established: 1990
Personnel: Seth R. Alpert (Mgr. Dir.)
Personnel: Oliver Schweitzer (Principal)
Personnel: Greg Smith (Managing Dir.)
Personnel: Andy Schoder (Managing Dir.)
Personnel: Adam Birnbaum (Managing Dir.)
Personnel: Mike Mortell (Managing Dir.)

GRIMES, MCGOVERN & ASSOCIATES

Street address 1: 10 W 15th St
Street address 2: Ste 903
State: NY
ZIP Code: 10011-6823
County: New York
Country: USA
Mailing address: 10 West 15th Street
Mailing city: New York City
Mailing state: NY
Mailing zip: 10011
General Phone: (917) 881-6563
Email: lgrimes@mediamergers.com
Website: www.mediamergers.com
Year Established: 1959
Services: Brokers & Appraisers; Consulting Services: Advertising; Consulting Services: Financial; Consulting Services: Human Resources; Consulting Services: Marketing;
Note: Over 1,600 newspapers sold. Thousands Appraised. Regional Offices nationwide.
Personnel: Julie Bergman (V.P., Head of Newspaper Division)
Personnel: John Szefc (Senior Associate-Northeast/New England)
Personnel: David Slavin (Senior Associate-Southeast/South)
Personnel: John McGovern (Owner, CEO)

Newspaper Brokers and Appraisers

Personnel: Lewis Floyd (Senior Associate-Southern States)
Personnel: Gary Borders (Sr. Assoc.-SW/Plains)
Personnel: Gord Carley (Sr. Assoc.-CANADA-Mag. & Newspapers)
Personnel: Joe Bella (Sr. Advisor-Newspapers)
Personnel: Ken Amundson (Sr. Assoc.-Western/Mtn. States)
Personnel: Ken Blum (Senior Associate-Sales Nationwide)

JORDAN, EDMISTON GROUP, INC.

Street address 1: 150 E 52nd St
Street address 2: Fl 18
State: NY
ZIP Code: 10022-6260
County: New York
Country: USA
Mailing address: 150 E 52nd St Fl 18
Mailing city: New York
Mailing state: NY
Mailing zip: 10022-6260
General Phone: (212) 754-0710
General Fax: (212) 754-0337
Email: adamg@jegi.com
Website: www.jegi.com
Personnel: Wilma Jordan (CEO)
Personnel: Bill Hitzig (COO)
Personnel: Tolman Geffs (Mng. Dir.)
Personnel: Michael Marchesano (Mng. Dir.)
Personnel: Richard Mead (Mng. Dir.)
Personnel: Scott Peters (Mng. Dir.)
Personnel: Adam Gross (Vice Pres., Mktg.)

VERONIS SUHLER STEVENSON

Street address 1: 55 E 52nd St
Street address 2: Fl 33
State: NY
ZIP Code: 10055-0007
County: New York
Country: USA
Mailing address: 55 E 52nd St Fl 33
Mailing city: New York
Mailing state: NY
Mailing zip: 10055-0007
General Phone: (212) 935-4990
General Fax: (212) 381-8168
Email: stevensonj@vss.com
Website: www.vss.com
Personnel: John J. Veronis (Co-Founder/Mng. Partner/Chrmn./Co-CEO)
Personnel: John S. Suhler (Co-Founder/Mng. Partner)
Personnel: Jeffrey T. Stevenson (Mng. Partner/Co-CEO)

PONTE VEDRA

MEDIA SERVICES GROUP, INC.

Street address 1: 149 S Roscoe Blvd
State: FL
ZIP Code: 32082-4127
County: Saint Johns
Country: USA
Mailing address: 149 S Roscoe Blvd
Mailing city: Ponte Vedra
Mailing state: FL
Mailing zip: 32082-4127
General Phone: (904) 285-3239
General Fax: (904) 285-5618
Email: george@mediaservicesgroup.com
Website: www.mediaservicesgroup.com
Personnel: George R. Reed (Mng. Dir.)
Personnel: William H. Lytle (Dir.)
Personnel: Robert J. Maccini (Dir.)

Personnel: Thomas McKinley (Dir.)
Personnel: Gregory Merrill (Dir.)
Personnel: William L. Whitley (Dir.)
Personnel: Jody McCoy (Dir.)
Personnel: Eddie Esserman (Assoc.)
Personnel: Stephan Sloan (Assoc.)

PROSSER

FOURNIER MEDIA SERVICES, INC.

Street address 1: 613 7th St
State: WA
ZIP Code: 99350-1459
County: Benton
Country: USA
Mailing address: PO Box 750
Mailing city: Prosser
Mailing state: WA
Mailing zip: 99350-0750
General Phone: (206) 409-9216
General Fax: (509) 786-1779
Email: mutinybaydad@aol.com
Website: www.recordbulletin.com
Year Established: 1982
Personnel: John L. Fournier (Pres.)

RICHMOND

HARRIS WILLIAMS & CO.

Street address 1: 1001 Haxall Pt
Street address 2: Fl 9
State: VA
ZIP Code: 23219-3944
County: Richmond City
Country: USA
Mailing address: 1001 Haxall Pt Fl 9
Mailing city: Richmond
Mailing state: VA
Mailing zip: 23219-3944
General Phone: (804) 648-0072
General Fax: (804) 648-0073
Email: kbaker@harriswilliams.com
Website: www.harriswilliams.com
Year Established: 1999
Personnel: Kimberly Baker (Marketing Director)

SAN FRANCISCO

HARRIS WILLIAMS & CO.

Street address 1: 575 Market St
Street address 2: Fl 31
State: CA
ZIP Code: 94105-2854
County: San Francisco
Country: USA
Mailing address: 575 Market St Fl 31
Mailing city: San Francisco
Mailing state: CA
Mailing zip: 94105-2884
General Phone: (415) 288-4260
General Fax: (415) 288-4269
Email: tarmstrong@harriswilliams.com
Website: www.harriswilliams.com
Personnel: Tiff B. Armstrong (Mng. Dir.)

SANTA FE

DIRKS, VAN ESSEN, MURRAY & APRIL

Street address 1: 119 E Marcy St
Street address 2: Ste 100
State: NM
ZIP Code: 87501-2092

County: Santa Fe
Country: USA
Mailing address: 119 E Marcy St Ste 100
Mailing city: Santa Fe
Mailing state: NM
Mailing zip: 87501-2092
General Phone: (505) 820-2700
General Fax: (505) 820-2900
Website: www.dirksvanessen.com
Year Established: 1980
Services: Brokers & Appraisers; Consulting Services: Financial;
Personnel: Owen D. Van Essen (Pres.)
Personnel: Philip W. Murray (Exec. Vice Pres.)
Personnel: Sara April (Vice Pres.)
Personnel: Holly Myers (Analyst)

SAVANNAH

PHELPS, CUTLER & ASSOCIATES

Street address 1: 35 Barnard St
Street address 2: Ste 300
State: GA
ZIP Code: 31401-2515
County: Chatham
Country: USA
Mailing address: 35 Barnard St Ste 300
Mailing city: Savannah
Mailing state: GA
Mailing zip: 31401-2515
General Phone: (912) 351-9122
General Fax: (678) 826-4708
Email: phelpscutler@aol.com
Website: www.phelpscutler.com
Year Established: 1991
Personnel: Louise D. Phelps (Pres.)

SOUTH BEND

GAUGER MEDIA SERVICE, INC.

Street address 1: 900 Robert Bush Drive
State: WA
ZIP Code: 98586
County: Pacific
Country: USA
Mailing address: P.O. Box 627
Mailing city: Raymond
Mailing state: WA
Mailing zip: 98577
General Phone: (360) 942-3560
Email: dave@gaugermedia.com
Website: www.gaugermedia.com
Year Established: 1987
Personnel: Dave Gauger (Pres/Broker)

UNIONDALE

KAMEN & CO. GROUP SERVICES

Street address 1: 626 Rxr Plz
State: NY
ZIP Code: 11556-0626
County: Nassau
Country: USA
Mailing address: 626 RXR Plz
Mailing city: Uniondale
Mailing state: NY
Mailing zip: 11556-0626
General Phone: (516) 379-2797
General Fax: (516) 379-3812
Email: info@kamengroup.com
Website: www.kamengroup.com
Year Established: 1981
Services: Architects/Engineers (Includes Design/Construction Firms); Brokers & Appraisers; Circulation Equipment & Supplies; Consulting Services: Advertising; Consulting Services: Circulation; Consulting Services: Financial; Consulting Services: Human Resources; Consulting Services: Marketing; Training: Sales & Marketing; Tubes, Racks (Includes Racks: Motor Route Tubes);
Note: Media Appraisers, Accountants, Advisors & Brokers
Personnel: Kevin Brian Kamen (Pres./CEO)
Personnel: Celeste Myers (Vice Pres.)

KEVIN BRIAN KAMEN & CO. (KAMEN & CO. GROUP SERVICES)

Street address 1: 626 Rxr Plz
State: NY
ZIP Code: 11556-0626
County: Nassau
Country: USA
Mailing address: 626 Rxr Plz
Mailing city: Uniondale
Mailing state: NY
Mailing zip: 11556-0626
General Phone: (516) 379-2797
General Fax: (516) 379-3812
Email: info@KamenGroup.com
Website: www.KamenGroup.com
Year Established: 1981
Note: We provide financial media valuations and customized brokering services for newspapers, magazines, shoppers, directories, books, websites, digital components and broad channel publishing entities on a worldwide basis.
Personnel: Kevin Brian Kamen (Pres./CEO)
Personnel: Gary R. Kamen (Vice Pres., New York)
Personnel: Rosalyn Kamen (Vice Pres., Tampa)
Personnel: Mathew Kamen (Gen. Mgr., Los Angeles)
Personnel: Mary Hiscock (Office Mgr.)
Personnel: Tom Horowitz (Office Mgr.)

WEST HILLS

MAYO COMMUNICATIONS

Street address 1: 7248 Bernadine Ave
Street address 2: Fl 2
State: CA
ZIP Code: 91307-1410
County: Los Angeles
Country: USA
Mailing address: 7248 Bernadine Ave Fl 2
Mailing city: West Hills
Mailing state: CA
Mailing zip: 91307-1410
General Phone: (818) 340-5300
General Fax:
Email: Publicity@mayocommunications.com
Website: www.MAYOCommunications.com
Year Established: 1995
Note: Our services include, but are not limited to: Branding, public speaking, media training, crisis communications, governmental affairs, legal PR/lobbying, environmental affairs, social marketing, transportation, fundraising events and community outreach planning, special events, political campaigns, celebrity events and media relations. The MAYO niche: media coverage and placement in print, TV and radio. Social media.
Personnel: Aida Mayo (CEO & President)

NEWSPAPER DISTRIBUTED MAGAZINES AND TMC PUBLICATIONS

BENTON

THE SALINE COURIER TMC

Street address 1: 321 N Market St
Street address state: AR
ZIP Code: 72015-3734
County: Saline
Country: USA
Mailing address 1: PO Box 207
Mailing city: Benton
Mailing state: AR
Mailing ZIP Code: 72018-0207
Office phone: (501) 315-8228
Office fax: (501) 315-1230
General e-mail: news@bentoncourier.com
Web address: www.bentoncourier.com
Year established: 1876
Audited By: Sworn/Estimate/Non-Audited
Audit Date: 12.07.2019
Personnel: Vicki Dorsch (Bus. Mgr.); Lynda Hollenback (Assoc. Ed.); Patricia Stuckey (Prodn. Mgr.); Terri Leifeste (Publisher); David Wills (Addvertising Director); Megan Reynolds (Editor)
Parent company: Horizon Publications Inc.
Subsidiary: Steve Boggs

BLOOMFIELD HILLS

PARADE PUBLICATIONS, INC. - BLOOMFIELD HILLS, MI

Street address 1: 100 W Long Lake Rd
Street address state: MI
ZIP Code: 48304-2773
County: Oakland
Country: USA
Mailing address 1: 22824 Canterbury St
Mailing city: Saint Clair Shores
Mailing state: MI
Mailing ZIP Code: 48080-1920
Office phone: (248) 540-9820
Office fax: (248) 540-9891
General e-mail: det_sales@parade.com
Web address: www.parade.com
Audited By: Sworn/Estimate/Non-Audited
Audit Date: 12.07.2019
Personnel: Mike DeBartolo (Vice Pres., Adv.)
Subsidiary: Mike DeBartolo

CHICAGO

AMERICAN PROFILE - CHICAGO, IL

Street address 1: 500 N Michigan Ave
Street address 2: Ste 910
Street address state: IL
ZIP Code: 60611-3741
County: Cook
Country: USA
Mailing address 1: 500 N Michigan Ave Ste 910
Mailing city: Chicago
Mailing state: IL
Mailing ZIP Code: 60611-3741
Office phone: (312) 948-0333
Office fax: (312) 948-0555
Web address: www.americanprofile.com
Circ.: 10000000
Audited By: Sworn/Estimate/Non-Audited
Audit Date: 12.07.2019
Digital Edition Available: Y
Personnel: Nanci Davidson (Executive Director, Integrated Media)
Parent company: Publishing Group of America
Subsidiary: Joan Graff

PARADE PUBLICATIONS, INC. - CHICAGO, IL

Street address 1: 500 N Michigan Ave
Street address 2: Ste 910
Street address state: IL
ZIP Code: 60611-3741
County: Cook
Country: USA
Mailing address 1: 401 N Michigan Ave Ste 2900
Mailing city: Chicago
Mailing state: IL
Mailing ZIP Code: 60611-5517
Office phone: (312) 661-1620
Office fax: (312) 661-0776
General e-mail: chi_sales@parade.com
Web address: www.parade.com
Audited By: Sworn/Estimate/Non-Audited
Audit Date: 12.07.2019
Personnel: Eric Karaffa (Vice Pres./Mid-Western Mgr.)
Subsidiary: Eric Karaffa

RELISH - CHICAGO, IL

Street address 1: 500 N Michigan Ave
Street address 2: Ste 910
Street address state: IL
ZIP Code: 60611-3741
County: Cook
Country: USA
Mailing address 1: 500 N Michigan Ave Ste 910
Mailing city: Chicago
Mailing state: IL
Mailing ZIP Code: 60611-3741
Office phone: (312) 948-0333
Office fax: (312) 948-0555
Web address: www.pubgroup.com
Audited By: Sworn/Estimate/Non-Audited
Audit Date: 12.07.2019
Personnel: Andrea Blank (Adv. Coord.)
Subsidiary: Nanci Davidson

TMS SPECIALTY PRODUCTS

Street address 1: 435 N Michigan Ave
Street address 2: Ste 1400
Street address state: IL
ZIP Code: 60611-7551
County: Cook
Country: USA
Mailing address 1: 435 N Michigan Ave Ste 1400
Mailing city: Chicago
Mailing state: IL
Mailing ZIP Code: 60611-7551
Office phone: (800) 637-4082
Office fax: (312) 527-8256
General e-mail: ctrammell@tribune.com
Web address: www.tmsspecialtyproducts.com
Audited By: Sworn/Estimate/Non-Audited
Audit Date: 12.07.2019
Note: TMS Specialty Products provides articles and images suitable for use in advertorial sections, niche publications and other targeted media, as well as custom ordered content, including local and paginated products.
Personnel: Marco Buscaglia (Gen. Mgr.); Curtis Trammell (Sales manager); Mary Elson (Mng. Ed.); Todd Rector (Art Dir.)
Subsidiary: Marco Buscaglia

TRIBUNE MEDIA SERVICES TV LOG - CHICAGO, IL

Street address 1: 435 N Michigan Ave
Street address 2: Ste 1300
Street address state: IL
ZIP Code: 60611-4037
County: Cook
Country: USA
Mailing address 1: 435 N Michigan Ave Ste 1300
Mailing city: Chicago
Mailing state: IL
Mailing ZIP Code: 60611-4037
Office phone: (312) 222-3394
Web address: www.tribunemediaservices.com
Affiliated Newspapers: Allentown (PA) Morning Call; Arlington (IL) Daily Herald; Athens (GA) Daily News & Banner Herald; Atlanta (GA) Journal & Constitution; Atlantic City (NJ) Press; Bakersfield (CA) Californian; Baltimore (MD) Sun; Bangor (ME) News; Beaver (PA) County Times; Belleville (IL) News-Democrat; Bellevue (WA) Journal American; Boston (MA) Globe; Boston (MA) Herald; Boulder (CO) Daily Camera; Bridgeport (CT) Connecticut Post; Bridgewater (NJ) Courier News; Buffalo (NY) News; Canton (OH) Repository; Charlotte (NC) Observer; Chicago (IL) Sun-Times; Chicago (IL) Tribune; Cleveland (OH) Plain Dealer; Columbia (SC) State; Columbus (OH) Dispatch; Dallas (TX) News; Dayton (OH) News; Daytona Beach (FL) News-Journal; Denver (CO) Post; Denver (CO) Rocky Mountain News; Detroit (MI) Free Press; Detroit (MI) News; Durham (NC) Sun; Evansville (IN) Courier & Press; Everett (WA) Herald; Fort Lauderdale (FL) Sun-Sentinel; Fort Myers (FL) News Press; Fort Worth (TX) Star-Telegram; Fresno (CA) Bee; Galveston (TX) Daily News; Gary (IN) Post-Tribune; Glens Falls (NY) Post Star; Greensburg (PA) Tribune Review; Hackensack (NJ) Bergen County Record; Hartford (CT) Courant; Houston (TX) Chronicle; Indianapolis (IN) Star; Jacksonville (FL) Florida Times-Union; Jersey City (NJ) Jersey Journal; Kansas City (MO) Star; Kenosha (WI) News; Little Rock (AR) Democrat-Gazette; Long Beach (CA) Press Telegram; Long Island (NY) Newsday; Los Angeles (CA) Daily Breeze; Los Angeles (CA) Daily News; Lowell (MA) Sun; Los Angeles (CA) Times; Macomb (IL) Daily Journal; Mesa (AZ) Tribune; Miami (FL) Herald; Milwaukee (WI) Journal Sentinel; Minneapolis (MN) Star Tribune; Modesto (CA) Bee; Morristown (NJ) Daily Record; New Haven (CT) Register; New York (NY) Daily News; New York (NY) Post; Newport News (VA) Daily Press; Norfolk (VA) Virginian Pilot; Oakland (MI) Press; Oklahoma City (OK) Oklahoman & Times; Omaha (NE) World-Herald; Orange County (CA) Register; Orlando (FL) Sentinel; Palm Springs (CA) Desert Sun; Pasadena (CA) Star News; Philadelphia (PA) Daily News; Philadelphia (PA) Inquirer; Pittsburgh (PA) Post-Gazette; Port Huron (MI) Times Herald; Quincy (MA) Patriot Leader; Racine (WI) Journal Times; Raleigh (NC) News & Observer; Reading (PA) Eagle; Riverside (CA) Press; Rome (GA) News Tribune; Sacramento (CA) Bee; Salt Lake City (UT) Deseret News; Salt Lake City (UT) Tribune; San Antonio (TX) Express News; San Francisco (CA) Chronicle; San Francisco (CA) Examiner; San Jose (CA) Mercury News; Springfield (MO) News-Leader; St. Louis (MO) Post-Dispatch; St. Paul (MN) Pioneer Press; St. Petersburg (FL) Times; Trenton (NJ) Times; Tucson (AZ) Arizona Star; Vancouver (WA) Columbian; Washington (DC) Post; Washington (DC) Times; West Palm Beach (FL) Post; Wichita (KS) Eagle; Wilkes Barre (PA) Times-Leader; Wilmington (DE) News Journal; Worcester (MA) Telegram & Gazette; Youngstown (OH) Vindicator;
Circ.: 32853868
Audited By: Sworn/Estimate/Non-Audited
Audit Date: 12.07.2019
Personnel: David D.
Subsidiary: Cameron Yung

CULVER CITY

RELISH - LOS ANGELES, CA

Street address 1: 300 Corporate Pointe
Street address 2: Ste 340
Street address state: CA
ZIP Code: 90230-8713
County: Los Angeles
Country: USA
Mailing address 1: 300 Corporate Pointe Ste 340
Mailing city: Culver City
Mailing state: CA
Mailing ZIP Code: 90230-7614
Office phone: (310) 216-7270
Office fax: (310) 216-7212
Web address: www.relishmag.com
Audited By: Sworn/Estimate/Non-Audited
Audit Date: 12.07.2019
Personnel: Jamie Relis (Acct. Mgr.)
Subsidiary: Joy Lona

FRANKLIN

AMERICAN PROFILE - FRANKLIN, TN

Street address 1: 341 Cool Springs Blvd
Street address 2: Ste 400
Street address state: TN
ZIP Code: 37067-7224
County: Williamson
Country: USA
Mailing address 1: 131 3rd Ave N Ste 200
Mailing city: Franklin
Mailing state: TN
Mailing ZIP Code: 37064-2510
Office phone: (615) 468-6021
Web address: www.americanpub.com
Audited By: Sworn/Estimate/Non-Audited
Audit Date: 12.07.2019
Personnel: Frank Zier (Nashville/West Coast Assoc. Pub.)
Subsidiary: Frank Zier

RELISH - FRANKLIN, TN

Street address 1: 341 Cool Springs Blvd
Street address 2: Ste 400
Street address state: TN
ZIP Code: 37067-7224
County: Williamson
Country: USA
Mailing address 1: 131 3rd Ave N Ste 200
Mailing city: Franklin
Mailing state: TN
Mailing ZIP Code: 37064-2510
Office phone: (615) 468-6000
Office fax: (615) 468-6100
Web address: www.pubgroup.com
Audited By: Sworn/Estimate/Non-Audited
Audit Date: 12.07.2019
Personnel: Frank Zier (Nashville/West Coast Assoc. Pub.)
Subsidiary: Frank Zier

LOS ANGELES

AMERICAN PROFILE - LOS ANGELES, CA

Street address 1: 6255 W Sunset Blvd
Street address 2: Ste 705
Street address state: CA
ZIP Code: 90028-7408
County: Los Angeles
Country: USA
Mailing address 1: 6255 W Sunset Blvd Ste 705
Mailing city: Los Angeles
Mailing state: CA

Newspaper Distributed Magazines and TMC Publications

Mailing ZIP Code: 90028-7408
Office phone: (323) 467-5906
Office fax: (323) 467-7180
Web address: www.americanprofile.com
Audited By: Sworn/Estimate/Non-Audited
Audit Date: 12.07.2019
Personnel: Debbie Siegel (Adv Sales Rep.)
Subsidiary: Debbie Siegel

PARADE PUBLICATIONS, INC. - LOS ANGELES, CA

Street address 1: 6300 Wilshire Blvd
Street address state: CA
ZIP Code: 90048-5204
County: Los Angeles
Country: USA
Mailing address 1: 6300 Wilshire Blvd Fl 10
Mailing city: Los Angeles
Mailing state: CA
Mailing ZIP Code: 90048-5204
Office phone: (323) 965-3649
Office fax: (323) 965-4971
Web address: www.parade.com
Audited By: Sworn/Estimate/Non-Audited
Audit Date: 12.07.2019
Personnel: Greg Hancock (Acct. Dir.)
Subsidiary: Greg Hancock

TRIBUNE MEDIA SERVICES TV LOG - LOS ANGELES, CA

Street address 1: 5800 W Sunset Blvd
Street address state: CA
ZIP Code: 90028-6607
County: Los Angeles
Country: USA
Mailing address 1: 5800 W Sunset Blvd
Mailing city: Los Angeles
Mailing state: CA
Mailing ZIP Code: 90028-6607
Office phone: (310) 581-5011
Office fax: (310) 581-8025
Web address: www.tribunemediaservices.com
Audited By: Sworn/Estimate/Non-Audited
Audit Date: 12.07.2019
Subsidiary: Cameron Yung

MALVERN

MALVERN DAILY TMC

Street address 1: 219 Locust St
Street address state: AR
ZIP Code: 72104-3721
County: Hot Spring
Country: USA
Mailing address 1: PO Box 70
Mailing city: Malvern
Mailing state: AR
Mailing ZIP Code: 72104-0070
Office phone: (501) 337-7523
Office fax: (501) 337-1226
General e-mail: mdrecord@sbcglobal.net
Web address: www.malvern-online.com
Year established: 1914
Audited By: Sworn/Estimate/Non-Audited
Audit Date: 12.07.2019
Personnel: Kim Taber (Bus. Mgr.); Richard Folds (Adv. Dir.); Kathi Ledbetter (Circ. Mgr.); Mark Bivens (News Ed.); James Liegh (Online Ed.); LaJuan Monney (Sports Ed.); Jessica Mathis (Composing Mgr.)
Parent company: Horizon Publications Inc.
Subsidiary: Richard Folds

MARTINEZ

MARTINEZ NEWS-GAZETTE

Street address 1: 802 Alhambra Ave
Street address state: CA
ZIP Code: 94553-1604
County: Contra Costa
Country: USA
Mailing state: CA
Mailing ZIP Code: 94513

Office phone: (408) 603-5640
Office fax: (925) 228-1536
General e-mail: rickj64@gmail.com
Year established: 1858
Audited By: Sworn/Estimate/Non-Audited
Audit Date: 12.07.2019
Subsidiary: Rick Jones

MOLINE

MOLINE/ROCK ISLAND/QUAD CITY METRO UNIT

Street address 1: 1720 5th Ave
Street address state: IL
ZIP Code: 61265-7907
County: Rock Island
Country: USA
Office phone: (309) 764-4344
General e-mail: advertising@qconline.com
Web address: www.qconline.com
Affiliated Newspapers: Moline (IL) Dispatch; Rock Island (IL) Argus
Circ.: 39625
Audited By: CAC
Audit Date: 31.03.2015
Digital Edition Available: Y
Digital Platform - Mobile: Apple`Android`Blackberry
Personnel: Val Yazbec (CRO); Jerry Taylor (Ed.); Kelly Johannes (Adv. Dir.)
Subsidiary: Jerry Taylor

NEW YORK

AMERICAN PROFILE - NEW YORK, NY

Street address 1: 60 E 42nd St
Street address 2: Ste 1111
Street address state: NY
ZIP Code: 10165-1111
County: New York
Country: USA
Mailing address 1: 60 E 42nd St Ste 1111
Mailing city: New York
Mailing state: NY
Mailing ZIP Code: 10165-1111
Office phone: (212) 478-1900
Office fax: (646) 865-1921
Web address: www.americanprofile.com
Affiliated Newspapers: Aberdeen (SD) American News; Abilene (KS) Reflector-Chrnoicle; Alamogordo (NM) Daily News; Albuquerque (NM) Journal; Alexander City (AL) Outlook; Alice (TX) Echo-News Journal; Alliance (NE) Times-Herald; Alliance (OH) Review; Alton (IL) Telegraph; Altus (OK) Times; Andalusia (AL) Star-News; Ardmore (OK) Daily Ardmoreite; Arkadelphia (AR) Daily Siftings Herald; Ashland (WI) Daily Press; Ashtabula (OH) Star Beacon; Athens (AL) News-Courier; Athens (OH) Messenger; Athens (TX) Daily Review; Atlantic (IA) News-Telegraph; Attleboro (MA) Sun Chronicle; Augusta (KS) Daily Gazette; Baker City (OR) Herald; Baraboo (WI) News-Republic; Bartlesville (OK) Examiner-Enterprise; Bastrop (LA) Daily Enterprise; Batavia (NY) Daily News; Batesville (AR) Guard; Baytown (TX) Sun; Beatrice (NE) Daily Sun; Beaver Dam (WI) Daily Citizen; Bedford (PA) Gazette; Bennington (VT) Banner; Benton (AR) Courier; Benton (IL) Evening News; Big Rapids (MI) Pioneer; Big Spring (TX) Herald; Billings (MT) Gazette; Blackfoot (ID) Morning News; Bloomington (IL) Pantagraph; Bloomsburg (PA) Press Enterprise; Boone (IA) News-Republican; Boonville (MO) Daily News & Record; Borger (TX) News-Herald; Bowling Green (KY) Daily News; Brainerd (MN) Dispatch; Brattleboro (VT) Reformer; Brenham (TX) Banner-Press; Brookings (SD) Register; Brooksville (FL) Hernando Today; Brownwood (TX) Bulletin; Brunswick (GA) News; Bryan (OH) Times; Bryan (TX) Eagle; Bullhead City (AZ) Mohave Valley Daily News; Burley (ID) South Idaho Press; Burlington (NC) Times-News; Burlington (IA) Hawk Eye; Cadillac (MI) News; Camden

(AR) News; Camdenton (MO) Lake Sun Leader; Canon City (CO) Daily Record; Canton (IL) Daily Ledger; Carbondale (IL) Southern Illinoisan; Carlisle (PA) Sentinel; Carlsbad (NM) Current-Argus; Carroll (IA) Daily Times Herald; Carson City (NV) Nevada Appeal; Cartersville (GA) Daily Tribune News; Carthage (MO) Press; Casa Grande (AZ) Dispatch; Casper (WY) Star-Tribune; Catskill (NY) Daily Mail; Cedar Rapids (IA) Gazette; Centerville (IA) Ad Express & Daily Iowegian; Chanute (KS) Tribune; Charlotte Harbor (FL) Sun; Cheboygan (MI) Daily Tribune; Circleville (OH) Herald; Clanton (AL) Advertiser; Claremont (NH) Eagle Times; Claremore (OK) Daily Progress; Cleburne (TX) Times-Review; Cleveland (MS) Bolivar Commercial; Cleveland (TN) Daily Banner; Clinton (IA) Herald; Coeur d'Alene (ID) Press; Coffeyville (KS) Journal; Coldwater (MI) Daily Reporter; Columbia City (IN) Post & Mail; Columbus (NE) Telegram; Conway (AR) Log Cabin Democrat; Coos Bay (OR) World; Corry (PA) Journal; Council Bluffs (IA) Daily Nonpareil; Craig (CO) Daily Press; Creston (IA) News Advertiser; Crookston (MN) Daily Times; Crystal Lake (IL) Northwest Herald; Cullman (AL) Times; Cumming (GA) Forsyth County News; Cushing (OK) Daily Citizen; Danville (KY) Advocate-Messenger; Decatur (IN) Daily Democrat; Defiance (OH) Crescent-News; Delphos (OH) Daily Herald; Deming (NM) Headlight; Demopolis (AL) Times; Derby (KS) Reporter; Devils Lake (ND) Journal; Dover (NH) Foster's Daily Democrat; Du Quoin (IL) Evening Call; Duncan (OK) Banner; Dunn (NC) Daily Record; Durant (OK) Daily Democrat; Dyersburg (TN) State Gazette; Easton (MD) Star-Democrat; Edmond (OK) Sun; Effingham (IL) Daily News; El Centro (CA) Imperial Valley Press; El Dorado (AR) News-Times; El Dorado (KS) Times; Elizabethton (TN) Star; Elkton (MD) Cecil Whig; Ellensburg (WA) Daily Record; Elyria (OH) Chronicle-Telegram; Fairfield (CA) Daily Republic; Fairfield (IA) Ledger; Fallon (NV) Lahontan Valley News; Faribault (MN) Daily News; Farmington (NM) Daily Times; Fort Atkinson (WI) Daily Jeffersonian County Union; Fort Madison (IA) Daily Democrat; Fort Morgan (CO) Times; Fort Payne (AL) Times Journal; Frankfort (KY) State Journal; Frederick (MD) News-Post; Freeport (IL) Journal-Standard; Fremont (NE) Tribune; Gainesville (TX) Daily Register; Galion (OH) Inquirer; Gallup (NM) Independent; Gastonia (NC) Gaston Gazette; Geneva (IL) Kane County Chronicle; Gastonia (NC) Gaston Gaz
Circ.: 9801887
Audited By: BPA
Audit Date: 30.06.2008
Personnel: Amy Chernoff (Sr. Vice Pres./Grp. Pub.); Shannon Hay (Adv. Dir.); Linda Rich (Assoc. Ed., Direct Response)
Subsidiary: Amy Chernoff

PARADE

Street address 1: 60 E 42nd St
Street address 2: Ste 820
Street address state: NY
ZIP Code: 10165-0820
County: New York
Country: USA
Mailing address 1: 60 East 42nd Street, suite 820
Mailing address 2: Suite 820
Mailing city: New York
Mailing state: NY
Mailing ZIP Code: 10165
Office phone: (212) 478-1910
General e-mail: sales@amgparade.com
Web address: www.parade.com
Year established: 1941
Circ.: 22000000
Audited By: GfK MRI
Audit Date: 01.09.2017
Digital Edition Available: Y
Digital Platform - Mobile: Apple`Android`Other
Digital Platform - Tablet: Apple iOS`Android`Other
Personnel: David Barber (Sr. Vice Pres.,

Newspaper Rel.)
Parent company: AMG/Parade
Subsidiary: Alexis Collado

RELISH - NEW YORK, NY

Street address 1: 60 E 42nd St
Street address 2: Ste 1115
Street address state: NY
ZIP Code: 10165-1115
County: New York
Country: USA
Mailing address 1: 60 E 42nd St Ste 1115
Mailing city: New York
Mailing state: NY
Mailing ZIP Code: 10165-1115
Office phone: (212) 478-1900
Office fax: (646) 865-1921
Web address: www.relishmag.com
Affiliated Newspapers: Aberdeen (SD) American News; Alamogordo (NM) Daily News; Albany (OR) Democrat-Herald; Albert Lea (MN) Tribune; Albuquerque (NM) Journal; Amarillo (TX) Globe-News; Americus (GA) Times-Recorder; Ames (IA) Tribune; Annapolis (MD) Capital; Ardmore (OK) Daily Ardmoreite; Ashland (KY) Daily Independent; Ashland (WI) Daily Press; Ashtabula (OH) Star Beacon; Athens (AL) News-Courier; Athens (GA) Banner-Herald; Athens (TX) Daily Review; Attleboro (MA) Sun Chronicle; Augusta (GA) Chronicle; Austin (MN) Daily Herald; Baraboo (WI) News-Republic; Barre (VT) Times Argus; Baton Rouge (LA) Advocate; Beatrice (NE) Daily Sun; Beaver Dam (WI) Daily Citizen; Beckley (WV) Register-Herlad; Bellingham (WA) Herald; Bemidji (MN) Pioneer; Beverly (MA) Salem News; Billings (MT) Gazette; Bismarck (ND) Tribune; Bloomington (IL) Pantagraph; Blytheville (AR) Courier News; Borger (TX) News-Herald; Bowling Green (KY) Daily News; Brainerd (MN) Dispatch; Brazil (IN) Times; Brenham (TX) Banner-Press; Bridgeport (CT) Post; Brooksville (FL) Hernando Today; Bryan (OH) Times; Bryan (TX) Eagle; Burlington (IA) Hawk Eye; Camden (AR) News; Canon City (CO) Daily Record; Cape Girardeau (MO) Southeast Missourian; Carbondale (IL) Southern Illinoisan; Cartersville (GA) Daily Tribune News; Casper (WY) Star-Tribune; Cedar Rapids (IA) Gazette; Centerville (IA) Ad Express & Daily Iowegian; Chattanooga (TN) Times Free Press; Cherokee (IA) Chronicle Times; Chickasha (OK) Express-Star; Chico (CA) Enterprise-Record; Claremore (OK) Daily Progress; Coeur d'Alene (ID) Press; Cleburne (TX) Times-Review; Colorado Springs (CO) Gazette; Columbus (NE) Telegram; Cookeville (TN) Herald-Citizen; Coos Bay (OR) World; Corsicana (TX) Daily Sun; Corvallis (OR) Gazette-Times; Covina (CA) San Gabriel Valley Tribune; Creston (IA) News Advertiser; Crystal Lake (IL) Northwest Herald; Cullman (AL) Times; Cumberland (MD) Times-News; Dalton (GA) Daily Citizen; Danbury (CT) News-Times; Davenport (IA) Quad-City Times; Davis (CA) Enterprise; Dexter (MO) Daily Statesman; Dickinson (ND) Press; Dodge City (KS) Daily Globe; Dothan (AL) Eagle; Dubuque (IA) Telegraph Herald; Duncan (OK) Banner; Dyersburg (TN) State Gazette; Easton (MD) Star-Democrat; Easton (PA) Express-Times; Edmond (OK) Sun; El Centro (CA) Imperial Valley Press; El Dorado (AR) News-Times; Elizabethtown (KY) News Enterprise; Elko (NV) Daily Free Press; Elkton (MD) Cecil Whig; Ellensburg (WA) Daily Record; Eureka (CA) Times-Standard; Everett (WA) Daily Herald; Fargo (ND) Forum; Faribault (MN) Daily News; Fayetteville (NC) Observer; Flagstaff (AZ) Arizona Daily Sun; Fort Worth (TX) Star-Telegram; Frederick (MD) News-Post; Fremont (CA) Argus; Fremont (NE) Tribune; Gainesville (TX) Daily Register; Gallup (NM) Independent; Galveston (TX) County Daily News; Geneva (IL) Kane County Chronicle; Glasgow (KY) Daily Times; Glens Falls (NY) Post-Star; Gloucester (MA) Daily Times; Grand Forks (ND) Herald; Grand Island (NE) Independent; Greencastle (IN) Banner-Graphic; Greenfield (MA) Recorder;

Greensburg (IN) Daily News; Greenville (TX) Herald-Banner; Hackensack (NJ) Record; Hagerstown (MD) Herald Mail; Hanford (CA) Sentinel; Hannibal (MO) Courier-Post; Hayward (CA) Daily Review; Henderson (TX) Daily News; Hibbing (MN) Daily Tribune; Hillsdale (MI) Daily News; Hobbs (NM) News-Sun; Holland (MI) Sentinel; Hopkinsville (KY) New Era; Hot Springs (AR) Sentinel-Record; Huntsville (TX) Item; Independence (MO) Examiner; International Falls (MN) Daily Journal; Jacksonville (FL) Florida Times-Union; Jamestown (ND) Sun; Johnstown (PA) Tribune-Democrat; Jonesboro (GA) News Daily; Kankakee (IL) Daily Journal; Kearney (NE) Hub; Kellogg (ID) Shoshone News-Press; Kennett (MO) Daily Dunklin Democrat; Kerrville (TX) Daily Times; Kingman (AZ) Daily Miner; Klamath Falls (OR) Herald and News; Kokomo (IN) Tribune; La Crosse (WI) Tribune; Lakeport (CA) Lake County Record-Bee; Lancaster (PA) Intelligencer Journal & New Era; Las Vegas (NM) Optic; Laurel (MS) Leader-Call; Las Vegas (N

Circ.: 12005646
Audited By: BPA
Audit Date: 30.06.2008
Personnel: Amy Chernoff (Sr. Vice Pres./Grp. Pub.); Shannon Hay (Adv. Dir.); Linda Rich (Assoc. Ed., Direct Response)
Subsidiary: Amy Chernoff

NORTHVILLE

AMERICAN PROFILE - NORTHVILLE, MI

Street address 1: 22185 Heatheridge Ln
Street address state: MI
ZIP Code: 48167-9300
County: Oakland
Country: USA
Mailing address 1: 22185 Heatheridge Ln
Mailing city: Northville
Mailing state: MI
Mailing ZIP Code: 48167-9300
Office phone: (248) 991-1810
Web address: www.americanprofile.com
Audited By: Sworn/Estimate/Non-Audited
Audit Date: 12.07.2019
Personnel: Jim Main (Auto Adv. Mgr.)

Subsidiary: Amy Chernoff

QUEENSBURY

TRIBUNE MEDIA SERVICES TV LOG - QUEENSBURY, NY

Street address 1: 40 Media Dr
Street address state: NY
ZIP Code: 12804-4086
County: Warren
Country: USA
Mailing address 1: 40 Media Dr
Mailing city: Queensbury
Mailing state: NY
Mailing ZIP Code: 12804-4086
Office phone: (518) 792-9914
Office fax: (212) 210-2863
Web address: www.tribunemediaservices.com
Audited By: Sworn/Estimate/Non-Audited
Audit Date: 12.07.2019
Subsidiary: Cameron Yung

SAN FRANCISCO

PARADE PUBLICATIONS, INC. - SAN FRANCISCO, CA

Street address 1: 50 Francisco St
Street address 2: Ste 400
Street address state: CA
ZIP Code: 94133-2114
County: San Francisco
Country: USA
Mailing address 1: 50 Francisco St Ste 400
Mailing city: San Francisco
Mailing state: CA
Mailing ZIP Code: 94133-2114
Office phone: (415) 955-8222
Office fax: (415) 397-0562
General e-mail: sf_sales@parade.com
Web address: www.parade.com
Audited By: Sworn/Estimate/Non-Audited
Audit Date: 12.07.2019
Personnel: Bill Murray (Adv. Contact)
Subsidiary: Bill Murray

TORONTO

TVTIMES

Street address 1: 250 Yonge St.
Street address state: ON
ZIP Code: M5B 2L7
County: York
Country: Canada
Mailing address 1: 250 Yonge St.
Mailing city: Toronto
Mailing state: ON
Mailing ZIP Code: M5B 2L7
Office phone: (416) 593-6556
Office fax: (416) 593-7329
General e-mail: tvtimes3@canwest.com
Web address: www.canwest.com
Affiliated Newspapers: Windsor (ON) Star; Victoria (BC) Times-Colonist; Vancouver (BC) Sun; Saskatoon (SK) Star Phoenix; Regina (SK) Leader Post; Prince George (BC) Citizen; Ottawa (ON) Citizen; Montreal (QC) Gazette; Medicine Hat (AB) News; Kamloops (BC) Daily News; Edmonton (AB) Journal; Calgary (AB) Herald; Winnipeg (BC) Free Press
Circ.: 1124839
Audited By: ABC
Audit Date: 30.09.2007
Personnel: Quin Millar (Dir., Newspaper Sales)
Subsidiary: Quin Millar

WASHINGTON

ASSOCIATION OF ALTERNATIVE NEWSMEDIA

Street address 1: 1156 15th St NW
Street address 2: Ste 1005
Street address state: DC
ZIP Code: 20005-1722
County: District Of Columbia
Country: USA
Mailing address 1: 1156 15th St NW Ste 1005
Mailing city: Washington
Mailing state: DC
Mailing ZIP Code: 20005-1722
Office phone: 289-8484
Office fax: (202) 289-2004
General e-mail: web@aan.org
Web address: www.altweeklies.com

Year established: 1978
Audited By: Sworn/Estimate/Non-Audited
Audit Date: 12.07.2019
Note: Annual convention held in summer.
Personnel: Debra Silvestrin (Dir. of Meetings); Jason Zaragoza (Int. Exec. Dir.)
Subsidiary: Jason Zaragoza

WINSTON SALEM

SPOTLIGHT

Street address 1: 250 Yonge St
Street address state: NC
ZIP Code: 27101
County: Forsyth
Country: USA
Mailing address 1: PO Box 3159
Mailing city: Winston Salem
Mailing state: NC
Mailing ZIP Code: 27102-3159
Office phone: (800) 457-1156
Office fax: (336) 727-7156
Web address: www.starwatch.com
Audited By: Sworn/Estimate/Non-Audited
Audit Date: 12.07.2019
Personnel: Alan Cronk (Bus. Mgr.); Jody Stephenson Sarver (Sales Agent)
Subsidiary: Jody Stephenson Sarver; Jody Stephenson Sarver

STAR WATCH

Street address 1: 418 N Marshall St
Street address state: NC
ZIP Code: 27101-2815
County: Forsyth
Country: USA
Mailing address 1: PO Box 3159
Mailing city: Winston Salem
Mailing state: NC
Mailing ZIP Code: 27102-3159
Office phone: (336) 727-7406
Office fax: (800) 430-0532
Web address: www.starwatch.com
Audited By: Sworn/Estimate/Non-Audited
Audit Date: 12.07.2019
Personnel: Jody Stephenson Sarver (Sales Agent); Alan Cronk (Exec. Ed.)
Subsidiary: Jody Stephenson Sarver